W9-CBT-883

HARRAP'S
FRENCH
and ENGLISH
DICTIONARY

McGraw·Hill

New York   Chicago   San Francisco   Lisbon   London   Madrid   Mexico City
Milan   New Delhi   San Juan   Seoul   Singapore   Sydney   Toronto

The McGraw·Hill Companies

Copyright © 2004 by Chambers Harrap Publishers Ltd. All rights reserved. Printed in the United States of America. Except as permitted under the United States Copyright Act of 1976, no part of this publication may be reproduced or distributed in any form or by any means, or stored in a database or retrieval system, without the prior written permission of the publisher.

2 3 4 5 6 7 8 9 0   KGP/KGP   3 2 1 0 9 8 7 6 5 4

ISBN 0-07-144069-0

McGraw-Hill books are available at special quantity discounts to use as premiums and sales promotions, or for use in corporate training programs. For more information, please write to the Director of Special Sales, Professional Publishing, McGraw-Hill, Two Penn Plaza, New York, NY 10121-2298. Or contact your local bookstore.

This book is printed on acid-free paper.

Contents

Trademarks

Words considered to be trademarks have been designated in this dictionary by the symbol ®. However, no judgment is implied concerning the legal status of any trademark by virtue of the presence or absence of such a symbol.

Contributors

Editor-in-Chief
Patrick White

Editors

Stuart Fortey Isabelle Elkaim
Anna Stevenson Laurence Larroche
      Georges Pilard

Contributors

Ruth Blackmore Sophie Marin
Lynda Carey Martine Pierquin
Lesley Johnston Catherine Roux
Irene Lakhani Cécile Vanwalleghem
Ruth Noble

Computing terminology
Arnel Leyva Annick Morel

Canadianisms
Alain Garand

Data Management
Ilona Morison
Liam Rodger

Keyboarders
Sheena Cleland
Marian Shepherd

Preface

This dictionary is based on the the *Harrap Compact* English-French French-English dictionary, first published in 1997 and now updated and completely reset. It aims to provide as comprehensive coverage as possible of the basic vocabulary of both languages, covering a wide variety of idiomatic expressions, slang and colloquial language and literary terms. The result is an easy-to-use guide, with accurate, reliable translations.

The dictionary will find a place in school and workplace alike and therefore contains the broadest possible range of vocabulary, from fields as diverse as finance, education, the media, the sciences and the military. Encyclopedic information is also covered, with a wide selection of proper and geographical names featuring in the book.

Extra help is provided in the form of a useful supplement in the center of the book comprising an extensive French grammar and detailed French conjugation tables.

Structure of Entries

Field labels indicate senses belonging to a particular subject area

major ['meɪdʒə(r)] **1** *n* (**a**) *Mil* commandant *m*; **m. general** général *m* de division (**b**) *Am Univ (subject)* matière *f* principale **2** *adj* (**a**) *(important)* majeur(e); *(most important)* principal(e); *(accident, illness)* très grave; **of m. importance** de la plus haute importance (**b**) *Mus* majeur(e) **3** *vi Am Univ* **to m. in sth** se spécialiser en qch

American English senses indicated

Headword abbreviated to first letter only in phrases

IPA shown in full for all headwords

management ['mænɪdʒmənt] *n* (**a**) *(activity) (of company, project)* gestion *f*, direction *f*; *(of economy, resources, shop, hotel)* gestion; **m. consultant** conseiller(ère) *m,f* en gestion; **m. studies** études *fpl* de gestion (**b**) *(managers, employers)* direction *f*; **under new m.** *(sign)* changement de propriétaire; **m. buyout** = rachat d'une société par la direction; **m. team** équipe *f* dirigeante

Compounds placed under first element; listed in alphabetical order

managing director ['mænɪdʒɪŋdaɪ'rektə(r)] *n* directeur(trice) *m,f* général(e)

New grammatical category introduced by bold numeral, placed on new line

Phrasal verbs introduced by ▸

melt [melt] **1** *vt also Fig* faire fondre **2** *vi* fondre; **to m. into thin air** s'évaporer, disparaître; **to m. into the crowd** se fondre dans la foule
▸ **melt away** *vi (of snow)* fondre; *(of clouds, vapour)* se dissiper; *(of crowd)* se disperser; *(of objections, opposition)* s'évanouir
▸ **melt down** *vt sep (metal)* fondre

This label means that the translation also works in figurative contexts

Superscript number marks homographs

minute¹ ['mɪnɪt] **1** *n* (**a**) *(of time)* minute *f*; **ten minutes past/to three** trois heures dix/moins dix; **wait a m.!** attendez une minute!; **go downstairs this m.!** descends immédiatement!; **just a m.** une minute; **the m. my back was turned** dès que j'ai eu le dos tourné; **any m.** d'une minute à l'autre; **in a m.** dans une minute; **at the last m.** à la dernière minute; **m. hand** *(of watch)* grande aiguille *f*; **m. steak** steak *m* minute (**b**) *(note)* note *f*; **minutes** *(of meeting)* compte rendu *m* **2** *vt (make note of)* inscrire au procès-verbal
minute² [maɪ'njuːt] *adj* (**a**) *(small)* infime, minuscule (**b**) *(detailed)* minutieux(euse)

Gender of noun translations shown in italic

Sense indicators shown in italic in brackets

Feminine inflections shown consistently

Full form of abbreviation given consistently; all abbreviations have translations

mips [mɪps] *Comptr (abbr* **million instructions per second)** MIPS *m*

mollusc, *Am* **mollusk** ['mɒləsk] *n* mollusque *m*

American spelling variants shown

vi

Canadianisms, Belgian-French and Swiss-French words clearly labelled

abrier [abrije] *Can* **1** *vt* to wrap up (well) **2 s'abrier** *vpr* to wrap oneself up (well)

Explanations introduced by = when no translation possible

académie [akademi] *nf* (**a**) *(des lettres, des sciences, d'art)* academy; **l'A. française** ≡ learned society responsible for promoting the French language and imposing standards (**b**) *(école)* school, academy; **a. de musique/dessin** music/ art school (**c**) *(dans l'Éducation nationale) Br* ≈ local education authority, *Am* ≈ school district

Cultural equivalents introduced by ≈

acquiescer [16] [akjese] *vi* to acquiesce (**à** to); **a. d'un signe de tête** to nod in agreement

Typical prepositions indicated after translations

aider [ede] **1** *vt* to help; *(sujet: gouvernement)* to aid; **que puis-je faire pour vous à.** how may I help you; **je me suis fait a. par un ami** I got a friend to help me; **a. qn à faire qch** to help sb to do sth, **a. qn à monter/sortir** to help sb up/out; *Ironique* **tu veux que je t'aide** stop that!; **elle n'aide jamais** she never helps (out) **2 aider à** *vt ind* to contribute towards; **a. à faire qch** to help to do sth **3 s'aider** *vpr* (**a**) *(soi-même)* **s'a. de qch** to use sth; **marcher en s'aidant d'une canne/de béquilles** to walk with the aid of a stick/crutches; *Prov* **aide-toi et le ciel t'aidera** God helps those who help themselves (**b**) *(l'un l'autre)* to help each other

French reflexive verbs and verbs always taking a preposition given special status

Clear usage labels

New sense category introduced by bold letter in brackets

Number cross-refers user to verb tables

amnistier [66] [amnistje] *vt* to grant an amnesty to

Plural of all hyphenated French nouns shown

arrière-plan (*pl* **arrière-plans**) [arjerplɑ̃] *nm aussi Fig* background; **à l'a.** in the background

arrière-saison (*pl* **arrière-saisons**) [arjersɛzɔ̃] *nf Br* late autumn, *Am* late fall

Differences in British and American translations clearly labelled

arrière-train (*pl* **arrière-trains**) [arjertrɛ̃] *nm (d'un animal)* (hind)quarters; *Fam (d'une personne)* rump, rear

Level of language labels mark informal usages

artériosclérose [arterjoskleroz] *nf* hardening of the arteries, *Spéc* arteriosclerosis

Specialized translations not in everyday use clearly labelled

avril [avril] *nm* April; **le premier a.** *(jour des farces)* April Fools' Day; *Prov* **en a., ne te découvre pas d'un fil** ne'er cast a clout till May is out; *voir aussi* **janvier**

Cross-reference to an entry where more information is given

English Phonetic Symbols

Consonants

[b] but [bʌt]
[d] dab [dæb]
[dʒ] jam [dʒæm]; gem [dʒem]
[f] fat [fæt]
[g] go [gəʊ]
[h] hat [hæt]
[j] yet [jet]
[k] cat [kæt]
[l] lad [læd]
[m] mat [mæt]
[n] no [nəʊ]
[ŋ] bang [bæŋ]
[p] pat [pæt]
[r] rat [ræt]
[(r)] (*only pronounced when there is liaison with the following word*) far [fɑː(r)]
[s] sat [sæt]
[ʃ] sham [ʃæm]
[t] tap [tæp]
[tʃ] chat [tʃæt]
[θ] thatch [θætʃ]
[ð] that [ðæt]
[v] vat [væt]
[w] wall [wɔːl]
[z] zinc [zɪŋk]
[ʒ] pleasure ['pleʒə(r)]
[χ] loch [lɒχ]

Vowels

[æ] bat [bæt]
[ɑː] art [ɑːt]
[e] bet [bet]
[ɜː] curl [kɜːl]
[ə] amend [ə'mend]
[iː] bee [biː]
[ɪ] bit [bɪt]
[ɒ] wad [wɒd]
[ɔː] all [ɔːl]
[ʊ] put [pʊt]
[uː] shoe [ʃuː]
[ʌ] cut [kʌt]

Diphthongs

[aɪ] life [laɪf]
[aʊ] house [haʊs]
[eə] there [ðeə(r)]
[eɪ] date [deɪt]
[əʊ] low [ləʊ]
[ɪə] beer [bɪə(r)]
[ɔɪ] boil [bɔɪl]
[ʊə] poor [pʊə(r)]

French Phonetic Symbols

Consonants

- [b] beau [bo]
- [d] donner [dɔne]
- [f] feu [fø]
- [g] garde [gard]
- [ʒ] gilet [ʒilɛ]
- [k] camp [kã]
- [l] lait [lɛ]
- [m] mon [mɔ̃]
- [n] né [ne]
- [ŋ] parking [parkiŋ]
- [ɲ] campagne [kãpaɲ]
- [p] pain [pɛ̃]
- [r] rare [rar]
- [s] six [sis]
- [ʃ] chose [ʃoz]
- [t] table [tabl]
- [v] vie [vi]
- [z] zéro [zero]

Vowels

- [a] chat [ʃa]
- [ɑ] âge [ɑʒ]
- [e] été [ete]
- [ə] le [lə]; devin [dəvɛ̃]
- [ø] feu [fø]
- [œ] seul [sœl]
- [ɛ] père [pɛr]
- [i] vite [vit]
- [ɔ] donner [dɔne]
- [o] chaud [ʃo]
- [u] tout [tu]
- [y] cru [kry]
- [ã] enfant [ãfã]
- [ɛ̃] vin [vɛ̃]
- [ɔ̃] bon [bɔ̃]
- [œ̃] un [œ̃]

Semi-vowels

- [w] noir [nwar]
- [j] yoga [jɔga]; rail [raj]
- [ɥ] huit [ɥit]

Abbreviations

gloss	=	glose
[introduces an explanation]		[introduit une explication]
cultural equivalent	≃	équivalent culturel
[introduces a translation which		[introduit une traduction
has a roughly equivalent status		dont les connotations dans
in the target language]		la langue cible sont
		comparables]
abbreviation	*abbr, abrév*	abréviation
adjective	*adj*	adjectif
adverb	*adv*	adverbe
agriculture	*Agr*	agriculture
American English	*Am*	anglais d'Amérique du Nord
anatomy	*Anat*	anatomie
architecture	*Archit*	architecture
article	*art*	article
astrology	*Astrol*	astrologie
astronomy	*Astron*	astronomie
cars	*Aut*	automobile
auxiliary	*aux*	auxiliaire
aviation	*Av*	aviation
Belgian French	*Belg*	belgicisme
botany	*Bot*	botanique
British English	*Br*	anglais britannique
Canadian French	*Can*	canadianisme
chemistry	*Chem, Chim*	chimie
cinema	*Cin*	cinéma
commerce	*Com*	commerce
computing	*Comptr*	informatique
conjunction	*conj*	conjonction
construction	*Constr*	construction
cooking	*Culin*	cuisine
economics	*Econ, Écon*	économie
electricity, electronics	*Elec, Él*	électricité, électronique
euphemism	*Euph*	euphémisme
exclamation	*exclam*	exclamation
feminine	*f*	féminin
familiar	*Fam*	familier
figurative	*Fig*	figuré
finance	*Fin*	finance
geography	*Geog, Géog*	géographie
geology	*Geol, Géol*	géologie
grammar	*Gram*	grammaire
history	*Hist*	histoire
humorous	*Hum*	humoristique

industry	*Ind*	industrie
invariable	*inv*	invariable
journalism	*Journ*	journalisme
law	*Jur*	droit
linguistics	*Ling*	linguistique
literary	*Lit, Litt*	littéraire
masculine	*m*	masculin
mathematics	*Math*	mathématiques
medicine	*Med, Méd*	médecine
weather	*Met, Météo*	météorologie
military	*Mil*	militaire
music	*Mus*	musique
noun	*n*	nom
shipping	*Naut*	nautisme
feminine noun	*nf*	nom féminin
feminine plural noun	*nfpl*	nom féminin pluriel
masculine noun	*nm*	nom masculin
masculine and feminine noun [same form for both genders]	*nmf*	nom masculin et féminin [formes identiques]
masculine and feminine noun [different form in the feminine]	*nm,f*	nom masculin et féminin [formes différentes]
masculine plural noun	*nmpl*	nom masculin pluriel
plural noun	*npl*	nom pluriel
proper noun	*npr*	nom propre
computing	*Ordinat*	informatique
parliament	*Parl*	parlement
pejorative	*Pej, Péj*	péjoratif
photography	*Phot*	photographie
physics	*Phys*	physique
plural	*pl*	pluriel
politics	*Pol*	politique
past participle	*pp*	participe passé
prefix	*pref, préf*	préfixe
preposition	*prep, prép*	préposition
pronoun	*pron*	pronom
proverb	*Prov*	proverbe
psychology	*Psy*	psychologie, psychiatrie
past tense	*pt*	prétérit
something	*qch*	quelque chose
somebody	*qn*	quelqu'un
registered trademark	®	marque déposée
radio	*Rad*	radio
rail	*Rail*	chemins de fer
religion	*Rel*	religion
somebody	*sb*	quelqu'un
school	*Sch, Scol*	domaine scolaire
Scottish English	*Scot*	anglais d'Écosse
sports	*Sp*	sport

something	*sth*	quelque chose
suffix	*suff*	suffixe
technical term	*Tech*	terme technique
telecommunications	*Tel, Tél*	télécommunications
textiles	*Tex*	textile
theatre	*Th*	théâtre
television	*TV*	télévision
typography, printing	*Typ*	typographie, imprimerie
university	*Univ*	domaine universitaire
verb	*v*	verbe
intransitive verb	*vi*	verbe intransitif
reflexive verb	*vpr*	verbe pronominal
transitive verb	*vt*	verbe transitif
transitive verb used with a preposition [e.g. **parvenir à** (to reach); ils sont **parvenus à** un accord (they reached an agreement)]	*vt ind*	verbe transitif indirect [par exemple: **parvenir à**; ils sont **parvenus à** un accord]
inseparable transitive verb [phrasal verb where the verb and the adverb or preposition cannot be separated, e.g. **look after**; he **looked after** the children]	*vt insep*	verbe transitif à particule inséparable [par exemple: **look after**; he **looked after the** children]
separable transitive verb [phrasal verb where the verb and the adverb or preposition can be separated, e.g. **send back**; she **sent** the present **back** or she **sent back** the present]	*vt sep*	verbe transitif à particule séparable [par exemple **send back**; she **sent** the present **back** ou she **sent back** the present]
vulgar	*Vulg*	vulgaire
zoology	*Zool*	zoologie

All other labels are written in full.

A

A, a¹ [eɪ] *n* (**a**) *(letter)* A, a *m inv*, **to get from A to B** aller d'un point à un autre; **from A to Z** de A à Z; **A bomb** bombe *f* A; *Br Sch* **A level** = diplôme de fin d'études secondaires sanctionnant une matière déterminée; *Br Sch* **A levels** ≃ baccalauréat *m*; *Br* **A road** ≃ (route *f*) nationale *f*; **A side** *(of record)* face *f* A; **A-Z** *(street guide)* index *m* des rues; **an A-Z of gardening** le jardinage de A à Z (**b**) *Sch (grade)* **to get an A** *(in exam)* avoir mention bien ou très bien; *(in homework, essay)* ≃ avoir entre 14 et 20 (**c**) *Mus* la *m inv*

a² [ə, *stressed* eɪ]

> a devient **an** [ən, *stressed* æn] devant voyelle ou h muet

indefinite art (**a**) *(in general)* un (une); **a man** un homme; **a woman** une femme; **an hour** une heure; **he's got a red nose** il a le nez rouge; **I haven't got a car** je n'ai pas de voiture; **what a day!** quelle journée!
(**b**) *(with professions, nationalities)* **he's an Englishman/a father/a doctor** il est anglais/père/médecin
(**c**) *(with prices, rates)* **40 pence a kilo** 40 pence le kilo; **three times a week** trois fois par semaine; **50 kilometres an hour** 50 kilomètres (à l')heure
(**d**) *(a certain)* **a Mr Watkins phoned** un certain M Watkins a appelé

AA [eɪˈeɪ] *n* (**a**) *(abbr* **Alcoholics Anonymous**) AA *mpl* (**b**) *Br (abbr* **Automobile Association**) = club automobile britannique offrant notamment des services de dépannage

AAA *n* (**a**) [ˈθriːˈeɪz] *Br (abbr* **Amateur Athletics Association**) = fédération britannique d'athlétisme (**b**) [eɪeɪˈeɪ] *Am (abbr* **American Automobile Association**) = club automobile américain

AB [eɪˈbiː] *n Am (abbr* **Artium Baccalaureus**) *(diploma)* ≃ licence *f* de lettres; *(graduate)* ≃ licencié(e) *m,f* ès lettres

abaci [ˈæbəsaɪ] *pl of* **abacus**

aback [əˈbæk] *adv* **taken a. (by)** déconcerté(e) (par)

abacus [ˈæbəkəs] *(pl* **abaci** [ˈæbəsaɪ] *or* **abacuses** [ˈæbəkəsɪz])* *n* boulier *m*

abandon [əˈbændən] **1** *n* **with a.** avec abandon; **to drive with reckless a.** conduire avec insouciance
2 *vt* abandonner; *(match)* interrompre; **to a. ship** abandonner le navire

abase [əˈbeɪs] *vt* **to a. oneself** s'abaisser, s'humilier

abashed [əˈbæʃt] *adj* honteux(euse) (**at** de)

abate [əˈbeɪt] *vi (of storm, pain)* se calmer; *(of noise)* diminuer

abattoir [ˈæbətwɑː(r)] *n* abattoir *m*

abbess [ˈæbɪs] *n* abbesse *f*

abbey [ˈæbɪ] *(pl* **abbeys**) *n* abbaye *f*

abbot [ˈæbət] *n* abbé *m*

abbreviate [əˈbriːvɪeɪt] *vt* abréger

abbreviation [əbriːvɪˈeɪʃən] *n* abréviation *f*

ABC [eɪbiːˈsiː] *n* (**a**) *(alphabet)* alphabet *m*; **an ABC of gardening** un ABC du jardinage (**b**) *(abbr* **American Broadcasting Corporation**) = chaîne de télévision américaine (**c**) *(abbr* **Australian Broadcasting Corporation**) = chaîne de télévision australienne

abdicate [ˈæbdɪkeɪt] **1** *vt* **to a. the throne** abdiquer; **to a. responsibility** abdiquer devant ses responsabilités
2 *vi (of monarch)* abdiquer

abdication [æbdɪˈkeɪʃən] *n (of throne)* abdication *f*; *(of responsibilities)* abandon *m*

abdomen [ˈæbdəmən] *n Anat & Zool* abdomen *m*

abdominal [əbˈdɒmɪnəl] *adj Anat* abdominal(e)

abduct [əbˈdʌkt] *vt* enlever

abduction [əbˈdʌkʃən] *n* enlèvement *m*

aberration [æbəˈreɪʃən] *n* aberration *f*; **a mental a.** un moment de folie

abet [əˈbet] *(pt & pp* **abetted**) *vt Law* **to aid and a. sb** être le complice de qn

abetting [əˈbetɪŋ] *n Law* **aiding and a.** complicité *f*

abeyance [əˈbeɪəns] *n* **in a.** *(of law, custom)* en désuétude

abhor [əbˈhɔː(r)] *(pt & pp* **abhorred**) *vt* détester, avoir horreur de

abhorrence [əbˈhɒrəns] *n* horreur *f*

abhorrent [əbˈhɒrənt] *adj* odieux(euse)

abide [əˈbaɪd] *vt (tolerate)* **I can't a. him** je ne peux pas le supporter

▸ **abide by** *vt insep (promise)* tenir; *(rule, decision)* se plier à, se soumettre à; **I a. by what I said** je maintiens ce que j'ai dit

abiding [əˈbaɪdɪŋ] *adj (memory)* éternel(elle); *(impression)* durable

ability [əˈbɪlɪtɪ] *(pl* **abilities**) *n* (**a**) *(talent, skill)* capacités *fpl* (**in** en), compétence *f* (**in** en) (**b**) *(capability)* capacité *f* (**to** à); **to the best of one's a.** de son mieux

abject [ˈæbdʒekt] *adj (miserable)* malheureux(euse); *(contemptible)* abject(e); **to make an a. apology** s'excuser platement; **a. poverty** misère *f* noire

ablaze [əˈbleɪz] *adj* en feu, en flammes; **to set sth a.** embraser qch; *Fig* **her eyes were a. with anger** ses yeux brillaient de colère

able [ˈeɪbəl] *adj* (**a**) *(competent) (person, performance)* compétent(e) (**b**) **to be a. to do sth** *(be physically capable)* pouvoir faire qch; *(know how to)* savoir faire qch; **I won't be a. to come** je ne pourrai pas venir; **we waited all morning, but we weren't a. to see him** nous avons attendu toute la matinée mais nous n'avons pas réussi à le voir

able-bodied ['eɪbəl'bɒdɪd] *adj* robuste; *Naut* **a. seaman** matelot *m* de deuxième classe

abnormal [æb'nɔːməl] *adj* anormal(e)

abnormality [æbnɔː'mælɪtɪ] (*pl* **abnormalities**) *n (irregularity)* anomalie *f*; *(physical)* malformation *f*

aboard [ə'bɔːd] **1** *adv (on ship, aeroplane)* à bord; **to go a.** monter à bord **2** *prep (ship, aeroplane)* à bord de; *(bus, train)* dans

abode [ə'bəʊd] *n Lit* demeure *f*; *Law* **of no fixed a.** sans domicile fixe; *Law* **right of a.** droit *m* de séjour

abolish [ə'bɒlɪʃ] *vt* abolir; *(law)* abroger

abolition [æbə'lɪʃən] *n* abolition *f*; *(of law)* abrogation *f*

abominable [ə'bɒmɪnəbəl] *adj* abominable; **the a. snowman** l'abominable homme *m* des neiges

abomination [əbɒmɪ'neɪʃən] *n* abomination *f*

aborigine [æbə'rɪdʒɪnɪ] *n* aborigène *mf*

abort [ə'bɔːt] **1** *vt* **(a)** *Med (woman)* avorter; **the foetus was aborted** la grossesse a été interrompue **(b)** *(project)* & *Comptr* abandonner **2** *vi Med* avorter, faire une fausse couche

abortion [ə'bɔːʃən] *n* avortement *m*, IVG *f*; **to have an a.** se faire avorter

abortive [ə'bɔːtɪv] *adj (attempt, plan)* avorté(e)

abound [ə'baʊnd] *vi* abonder **(in** *or* **with** en)

about [ə'baʊt] **1** *prep* **(a)** *(regarding)* **a book a. France** un livre sur la France; **the good/bad thing a.…** ce qu'il y a de bien/de mauvais dans…; **what's it a.?** de quoi s'agit-il?; **to talk a. sth** parler de qch; **to argue a. sth** se disputer au sujet de qch; **we must do something a. this problem** il faut faire quelque chose à ce sujet **(b)** *(in various parts of)* **to walk a. the town** se promener dans la ville; **to look a. the room** parcourir la pièce du regard **2** *adv* **(a)** *(in different directions, places)* **to walk a.** se promener; **to run a.** courir à droite et à gauche; **to be lying a.** traîner **(b)** *(in the general area)* **is Jane a.?** est-ce que Jane est dans les environs *ou* parages?; **there was nobody a.** il n'y avait personne **(c)** *(approximately)* environ, à peu près; **a. thirty** environ trente, une trentaine; **a. ten years** environ dix ans, une dizaine d'années; **at a. five o'clock** vers cinq heures; **she's a. as tall as you** elle est grande à peu près comme toi; **I've just a. finished** j'ai pratiquement terminé; **a. time!** ce n'est pas trop tôt! **(d)** *(on the point of)* **to be a. to do sth** aller faire qch, être sur le point de faire qch; **I'm not a. to…** *(have no intention of)* je n'ai pas l'intention de…

about-face [ə'baʊt'feɪs], **about-turn** [ə'baʊt'tɜːn] *n (radical change)* revirement *m*

above [ə'bʌv] **1** *prep* **(a)** *(physically)* au-dessus de; **the Seine a. Paris** la Seine en amont de Paris **(b)** *(with numbers)* plus de; **the temperature didn't rise a. 10°C** la température n'a pas dépassé 10°C **(c)** *(in rank)* he is a. me il est mon supérieur **(d)** *(not subject to)* **to be a. suspicion** être au-dessus de tout soupçon; **her behaviour is a. criticism** il n'y a rien à redire à son attitude **(e)** *(superior to)* **he thinks he's a. all that** il se croit au-dessus de tout ça; **she's not a. telling lies** elle est capable de mentir; **to get a. oneself** se donner des airs **(f)** **a. all** surtout; **they value friendship a. all else** ils font passer l'amitié avant tout le reste **2** *adv* **(a)** *(in general)* au-dessus; **the tenants (of the flat) a.** les locataires du dessus; **from a.** *(from one's superiors)* d'en haut **(b)** *(in book, document)* ci-dessus

above-board [ə'bʌvbɔːd] *adj (honest)* franc (franche), honnête

above-mentioned [əbʌv'menʃənd], **above-named** [əbʌv'neɪmd] *adj* susdit(e), susnommé(e)

abrasion [ə'breɪʒən] *n (on skin)* écorchure *f*

abrasive [ə'breɪsɪv] **1** *n (substance)* abrasif *m* **2** *adj (surface, substance)* abrasif(ive); *(person, manner)* caustique

abreast [ə'brest] *adv* de front; **to come a. of** arriver à la hauteur de; **to keep a. of** *(events, progress)* se tenir au courant de

abridged [ə'brɪdʒd] *adj* abrégé(e)

abroad [ə'brɔːd] *adv* à l'étranger; **our colleagues from a.** nos collègues étrangers; **to get a.** *(of news)* se répandre

abrupt [ə'brʌpt] *adj* **(a)** *(sudden)* brusque, soudain(e); **the train came to an a. halt** le train s'est brusquement *ou* soudainement arrêté **(b)** *(curt)* abrupt(e), brusque

abruptly [ə'brʌptlɪ] *adv* **(a)** *(suddenly)* brusquement, soudainement **(b)** *(curtly)* de façon abrupte, avec brusquerie

abscess ['æbses] *n* abcès *m*

abscond [əb'skɒnd] *vi Formal* s'enfuir, prendre la fuite

abseil ['æbseɪl] *vi* descendre en rappel; **to a. down sth** descendre qch en rappel

abseiling ['æbseɪlɪŋ] *n* rappel *m*, descente *f* en rappel; **to go a.** faire du rappel

absence ['æbsəns] *n* absence *f*; **in the a. of** *(person)* en l'absence de; *(thing)* faute de; *Law* **sentenced in one's a.** condamné(e) par contumace; *Prov* **a. makes the heart grow fonder** l'éloignement renforce l'affection

absent 1 *adj* ['æbsənt] *(pupil, expression)* absent(e); *Mil* **a. without leave** porté(e) manquant(e) **2** *vt* [æb'sent] **to a. oneself (from)** s'absenter (de)

absentee [æbsən'tiː] *n* absent(e) *m,f*; **a. landlord** propriétaire *m* absentéiste

absenteeism [æbsən'tiːɪzm] *n* absentéisme *m*

absent-minded [æbsənt'maɪndɪd] *adj* distrait(e)

absent-mindedness [æbsənt'maɪndɪdnɪs] *n* distraction *f*

absolute ['æbsəluːt] *adj* **(a)** *(total)* absolu(e); **a. majority** majorité *f* absolue; **a. monarch** monarque *m* absolu **(b)** *(emphatic)* **he's an a. fool!** il est complètement idiot!; **a. rubbish!** n'importe quoi!; **an a. disgrace/disaster** un véritable scandale/désastre

absolutely [æbsə'luːtlɪ] *adv* absolument; **you're a. right** vous avez absolument *ou* tout à fait raison; **do you support him? – a./a. not** vous êtes de son avis? – absolument/absolument pas

absolution [æbsə'luːʃən] *n Rel* absolution *f*

absolve [əb'zɒlv] *vt Rel* absoudre **(from** *or* **of** de); *(from duty)* dispenser **(from** *or* **of** de); **to be absolved from blame** être innocenté(e)

absorb [əb'zɔːb] *vt (liquid)* absorber; *(losses)* essuyer; **to be absorbed in sth** être absorbé(e) par qch

absorbent [əb'zɔːbənt] *adj* absorbant(e)

absorbing [əb'zɔːbɪŋ] *adj (work)* absorbant(e); *(book, question)* passionnant(e)

abstain [əb'steɪn] *vi* s'abstenir **(from** de)

abstemious [əb'stiːmɪəs] *adj* sobre

abstention [əb'stenʃən] *n Pol* abstention *f*

abstinence ['æbstɪnəns] *n* abstinence *f*

abstract ['æbstrækt] **1** *n* **(a)** *(concept)* **the a.** l'abstrait *m* **(b)** *(of article)* résumé *m* **2** *adj* abstrait(e) **3** *vt* [æb'strækt] *Formal (remove)* extraire **(from** de)

abstraction [æb'strækʃən] *n* abstraction *f*

abstruse [əb'struːs] *adj* obscur(e)

absurd [əb'sɜːd] *adj* absurde

absurdity [əb'sɜːdɪtɪ] (*pl* **absurdities**) *n* absurdité *f*

abundance [ə'bʌndəns] *n* abondance *f*; **an a. of talent** un grand talent; **in a.** en abondance

abundant [ə'bʌndənt] *adj* abondant(e); **to be a. in sth** abonder en qch

abundantly [ə'bʌndəntlɪ] *adv* en abondance; **a. clear** tout à fait clair(e)

abuse 1 *n* [ə'bjuːs] (**a**) *(of power)* abus *m* (**b**) *(insults)* injures *fpl*, insultes *fpl*; **term of a.** injure *f*, insulte *f* (**c**) *(cruelty)* mauvais traitements *mpl*, maltraitance *f*; (**sexual**) *a.* sévices *mpl* sexuels
2 *vt* [ə'bjuːz] (**a**) *(misuse)* abuser de (**b**) *(insult)* injurier, insulter (**c**) *(ill-treat) (physically)* maltraiter; *(sexually)* faire subir des sevices sexuels à

abusive [ə'bjuːsɪv] *adj* (**a**) *(person, language)* grossier(ère) (**b**) *(behaviour, treatment)* brutal(e)

abysmal [ə'bɪzməl] *adj* *(ignorance)* sans bornes; *(performance, quality)* épouvantable

abyss [ə'bɪs] *n* *also Fig* abîme *m*, gouffre *m*

AC ['eɪ'siː] *n Elec (abbr* **alternating current**) courant *m* alternatif

a/c *n (abbr* **account**) compte *m*

academic [ækə'demɪk] **1** *n* *(university teacher)* universitaire *mf*; *(intellectual)* intellectuel(elle) *m,f*
2 *adj* (**a**) *(of school)* scolaire; *(of university)* universitaire; **her a. achievements are impressive** elle a fait de brillantes etudes (**b**) *(intellectual)* intellectuel(elle) (**c**) *(theoretical)* théorique; **it's entirely a. whether he did it or not** qu'il l'ait fait ou non n'a aucune importance

academy [ə'kædəmɪ] *(pl* **academies***) n* académie *f*; **a. of music** conservatoire *m* (de musique)

accede [æk'siːd] *vi Formal* (**a**) **to a.** *to (request, demand)* accéder à; *(agreement, changes)* accepter (**b**) *(of monarch)* **to a. to the throne** accéder au trône

accelerate [ək'seləreɪt] **1** *vt (progress)* accélérer; *(downfall)* précipiter
2 *vi (of car, driver)* accélérer; *(of pace)* s'accélérer

acceleration [əkselə'reɪʃən] *n* accélération *f*

accelerator [ək'seləreɪtə(r)] *n* accélérateur *m*

accent ['æksənt] *n* accent *m*; **to put the a. on sth** *(emphasize)* mettre l'accent sur qch

accentuate [æk'sentʃʊeɪt] *vt* accentuer

accept [ək'sept] *vt* (**a**) *(gift, apology, defeat)* accepter; *(responsibility)* assumer (**for** de); *(concede)* admettre; **to a. (that)...** admettre que... (**b**) *(into university)* admettre

acceptable [ək'septəbəl] *adj* *(place, explanation)* acceptable; **to be a. to sb** *(suit)* convenir à qn

acceptance [ək'septəns] *n* (**a**) *(of invitation, apology, defeat)* acceptation *f*; **to find a.** être reconnu(e) (**b**) *(to university)* admission *f*; **a. speech** = discours prononcé par le lauréat d'un prix

access ['ækses] **1** *n* accès *m* (**to** à), **to have a. to sth** avoir accès à qch; **to gain a. to** *(get inside)* s'introduire dans; *(reach)* accéder à; **a. road** route *f* d'accès; *(of motorway)* bretelle *f* d'accès; *Comptr* **a. code/time** code *m*/temps *m* d'accès
2 *vt Comptr* accéder à

accessible [ək'sesəbəl] *adj* *(place, explanation)* accessible; *(person)* joignable

accession [ək'seʃən] *n* *(to power, throne)* accession *f*; *(library book)* acquisition *f*

accessory [ək'sesərɪ] *(pl* **accessories***) n* (**a**) *(extra)* accessoire *m* (**b**) *Law* complice *mf* (**to** de)

accident ['æksɪdənt] *n* accident *m*; **by a.** par accident *ou* hasard; **to have an a.** avoir un accident; **a. insurance** assurance *f* accidents

accidental [æksɪ'dentəl] *adj* accidentel(elle); *Law* **a. death** mort *f* accidentelle

accidentally [æksɪ'dentəlɪ] *adv* accidentellement

accident-prone ['æksɪdəntprəʊn] *adj* prédisposé(e) aux accidents

acclaim [ə'kleɪm] **1** *n* louanges *fpl*; **to meet with great critical a.** être salué(e) par la critique
2 *vt (person)* acclamer; *(performance, film)* applaudir

acclamation [æklə'meɪʃən] *n* *(cheering)* acclamations *fpl*

acclimatize [ə'klaɪmətaɪz] *vi* s'acclimater (**to** à)

accolade ['ækəleɪd] *n* honneur *m*

accommodate [ə'kɒmədeɪt] *vt* (**a**) *(provide room for)* loger (**b**) *(satisfy)* satisfaire

accommodating [ə'kɒmədeɪtɪŋ] *adj* *(helpful)* obligeant(e); *(easy to please)* accommodant(e)

accommodation [əkɒmə'deɪʃən] *n* (**a**) *(lodging)* logement *m*; *(in hotel)* chambre *f* (d'hôtel) (**b**) *Formal (agreement)* compromis *m*

accompaniment [ə'kʌmpənɪmənt] *n Mus* accompagnement *m*; *Culin* garniture *f*

accompany [ə'kʌmpənɪ] *(pt & pp* **accompanied***) vt* accompagner; **to be accompanied by sth** s'accompagner de qch

accomplice [ə'kʌmplɪs] *n* complice *mf*

accomplish [ə'kʌmplɪʃ] *vt (task)* accomplir; *(aim)* atteindre

accomplished [ə'kʌmplɪʃt] *adj (performer)* accompli(e); *(performance)* très au point

accord [ə'kɔːd] **1** *n* accord *m*; **in a. with** en accord avec; **with one a.** d'un commun accord; **of one's own a.** de son plein gré
2 *vt* accorder (**to** à)
▸ **accord with** *vt insep* concorder avec

accordance [ə'kɔːdəns] *n* **in a. with** en accord avec; **his statement is not in a. with the facts** sa déclaration ne concorde pas avec les faits

according [ə'kɔːdɪŋ] **to** *prep* (**a**) *(depending on)* selon; **a. whether one is rich or poor** selon que l'on est riche ou pauvre; **a. which method you use** selon la méthode utilisée (**b**) *(in conformity with)* selon; **to go a. plan** se dérouler comme prévu (**c**) *(citing a source)* selon, d'après

accordingly [ə'kɔːdɪŋlɪ] *adv* (**a**) *(appropriately)* en conséquence (**b**) *(therefore)* par conséquent

accordion [ə'kɔːdɪən] *n* accordéon *m*

accost [ə'kɒst] *vt* accoster, aborder

account [ə'kaʊnt] *n* (**a**) *(at bank)* compte *m*; *Com* **accounts department** comptabilité *f* (**b**) *(reckoning)* **to keep (an) a. of sth** tenir un compte de qch; **to take sth into a.** *(of sth)* tenir compte de qch, prendre qch en compte; **taking everything into a.** *(after all)* au bout du compte; **to call sb to a.** demander des comptes à qn; **to be brought to a.** avoir des comptes à rendre (**c**) *(importance)* of no importance; **of little a.** de peu d'importance; **d'**aucun cas, surtout pas; **to set up in business on one's own a.** s'installer à son compte; **not on any a.! on my a.!** ne le faites surtout pas pour moi! (**e**) *(report)* description *f*; *Fig* **to give a good a. of oneself** *(in fight, contest)* bien se défendre; **by all accounts** au dire de tous
▸ **account for** *vt insep* (**a**) *(explain, justify)* expliquer; **five people have still not been accounted for** *(are still missing)* cinq personnes n'ont toujours pas été retrouvées;

there's no accounting for taste chacun ses goûts (**b**) *(constitute)* constituer

accountability [əkaʊntə'bɪlɪtɪ] *n* responsabilité *f* (**to** envers)

accountable [ə'kaʊntəbəl] *adj* responsable (**to sb** envers qn; **for sth** de qch); *(for sum of money)* redevable (**for** de); **to hold sb a.** tenir qn pour responsable

accountancy [ə'kaʊntənsɪ] *n* comptabilité *f*

accountant [ə'kaʊntənt] *n* comptable *mf*

accounting [ə'kaʊntɪŋ] *n* comptabilité *f*; **a. period** période *f* comptable

accrue [ə'kru:] *vi Fin (of interest)* s'accumuler; **to a. to sb** *(of interest, benefits)* revenir à qn

accumulate [ə'kju:mjʊleɪt] **1** *vt* accumuler
2 *vi* s'accumuler

accumulation [əkju:mjʊ'leɪʃən] *n* accumulation *f*

accuracy ['ækjʊrəsɪ] *n (of calculation, translation)* exactitude *f*, précision *f*; *(of firearm, shot)* précision; *(of portrayal)* fidélité *f*

accurate ['ækjʊrət] *adj (calculation, translation)* exact(e), précis(e); *(firearm, shot)* précis(e); *(portrayal)* fidèle

accurately ['ækjʊrətlɪ] *adv (calculate, translate)* avec exactitude *ou* précision; *(aim)* avec précision; *(portray)* fidèlement

accusation [ækjʊ'zeɪʃən] *n* accusation *f*; **to make an a. (against sb)** porter *ou* lancer une accusation (contre qn)

accuse [ə'kju:z] *vt* **to a. sb (of sth/of doing sth)** accuser qn (de qch/de faire qch)

accused [ə'kju:zd] *(pl* accused*) n Law* **the a.** l'inculpé(e) *m,f*

accuser [ə'kju:zə(r)] *n* accusateur(trice) *m,f*

accusing [ə'kju:zɪŋ] *adj (look, tone)* accusateur(trice)

accustom [ə'kʌstəm] *vt* accoutumer, habituer; **to be accustomed to sth/to doing sth** être habitué à qch/à faire qch; **to get** *or* **grow accustomed to sth/to doing sth** s'accoutumer *ou* s'habituer à qch/à faire qch

AC/DC ['eɪsi:'di:si:] *n Elec (abbr* **alternating current/ direct current)** courant alternatif/courant continu

ace [eɪs] **1** *n* (**a**) *(in cards)* as *m*; **a. of spades** as de pique; *Fig* **to have an a. up one's sleeve** avoir un atout en réserve; **to come within an a. of doing sth** être à deux doigts de faire qch (**b**) *(tennis)* ace *m* (**c**) *Fam (expert)* as *m*; **flying a.** as de l'aviation
2 *adj Br Fam (very good)* super *inv*

acerbic [ə'sɜ:bɪk] *adj* acerbe

acetate ['æsɪteɪt] *n Chem* acétate *m*

acetic acid [æ'si:tɪk'æsɪd] *n* acide *m* acétique

ache [eɪk] **1** *n* douleur *f*; **aches and pains** douleurs *fpl*
2 *vi (of person)* avoir mal; **my head aches** j'ai mal à la tête; **my leg aches** j'ai mal à la jambe, ma jambe me fait mal; *Fig* **to be aching to do sth** mourir d'envie de faire qch

achieve [ə'tʃi:v] *vt (aim)* atteindre, parvenir à; **to a. success** réussir; **to a. a lot** faire beaucoup de chemin

achievement [ə'tʃi:vmənt] *n (action)* réalisation *f*; *(thing achieved)* réussite *f*

acid ['æsɪd] **1** *n* (**a**) *(chemical)* acide *m* (**b**) *Fam (LSD)* acide *m*; **a. house** *(music)* acid house *m*
2 *adj* (**a**) *(chemical, taste)* acide; **a. rain** pluies *fpl* acides; *Fig* **a. test** test *m* décisif (**b**) *(tone, remark)* aigre

acidic [ə'sɪdɪk] *adj* acide; *(tone, remark)* aigre

acidity [ə'sɪdɪtɪ] *n (of chemical, taste)* acidité *f*; *(of tone, remark)* aigreur *f*

acknowledge [ək'nɒlɪdʒ] *vt (mistake, debt, truth)* admettre, reconnaître; **to a. (receipt of) a letter** accuser réception d'une lettre; **this restaurant is acknowledged**

to be the best in the city ce restaurant est considéré comme le meilleur de la ville; **she didn't a. me** *or* **my presence** elle m'a ignoré

acknowledg(e)ment [ək'nɒlɪdʒmənt] *n (of mistake, debt, truth)* reconnaissance *f*; **in a. of** *(service, achievement)* en reconnaissance de; *(letter)* en réponse à; **acknowledgements** *(in book)* remerciements *mpl*; **a. slip** *(for letter)* accusé *m* de réception

ACLU ['eɪsi:ɛlju:] *n (abbr* **American Civil Liberties Union)** = organisme américain qui milite pour les droits civiques

acne ['æknɪ] *n* acné *f*

acolyte ['ækəlaɪt] *n* disciple *mf*

acorn ['eɪkɔ:n] *n* gland *m*

acoustic [ə'ku:stɪk] *adj* acoustique; **a. guitar** guitare *f* acoustique

acoustics [ə'ku:stɪks] *npl* acoustique *f*

acquaint [ə'kweɪnt] *vt* (**a**) *(with person)* **to be acquainted with sb** connaître qn; **to become** *or* **get acquainted (with)** faire *ou* lier connaissance (avec) (**b**) *(with facts, situation)* **to be acquainted with sth** connaître qch; **to a. sb with sth** mettre qn au courant de qch; **to a. oneself with sth** se familiariser avec qch

acquaintance [ə'kweɪntəns] *n* (**a**) *(person)* connaissance *f* (**b**) *(familiarity) (with person, facts)* familiarité *f*; **to make sb's a.** faire la connaissance de qn

acquiesce [ækwɪ'es] *vi* consentir (**in** à)

acquiescence [ækwɪ'esəns] *n* consentement *m* (**in** à)

acquiescent [ækwɪ'esənt] *adj* consentant(e)

acquire [ə'kwaɪə(r)] *vt (knowledge, reputation, property)* acquérir; *(habit, accent, air)* prendre; **to a. a taste for sth** prendre goût à qch; **it's an acquired taste** c'est quelque chose que l'on apprend à aimer

acquisition [ækwɪ'zɪʃən] *n* acquisition *f*

acquisitive [ə'kwɪzɪtɪv] *adj* matérialiste

acquit [ə'kwɪt] *(pt & pp* acquitted*) vt* (**a**) *Law* acquitter (**b**) **to a. oneself well/badly** s'en sortir *ou* s'en tirer bien/mal

acquittal [ə'kwɪtəl] *n Law* acquittement *m*

acre ['eɪkə(r)] *n* = 4047 m², ≃ demi-hectare *m*; **acres of forest** des hectares de forêt; *Fam* **acres of space** plein de place

acrid ['ækrɪd] *adj* âcre

acrimonious [ækrɪ'məʊnɪəs] *adj (person, remark)* hargneux(euse); *(discussion)* virulent(e)

acrimony ['ækrɪmənɪ] *n* acrimonie *f*, hargne *f*

acrobat ['ækrəbæt] *n* acrobate *mf*

acrobatic [ækrə'bætɪk] *adj* acrobatique

acrobatics [ækrəʊ'bætɪks] **1** *n* acrobatie *f*
2 *npl Fig* **mental a.** gymnastique *f* intellectuelle

acronym ['ækrənɪm] *n* sigle *m*

across [ə'krɒs] **1** *prep* (**a**) *(from one side to the other of)* **to go a. sth** traverser qch; **to run a. the road** traverser la route en courant; **to swim a. a lake** traverser un lac à la nage; **the bridge a. the river** le pont sur la rivière; **she threw it a. the room** elle l'a lancé à l'autre bout de la pièce (**b**) *(on the other side of)* de l'autre côté de; **she lives a. the road** elle habite en face (**c**) *(throughout)* **a. the country** dans tout le pays; **a. the political spectrum** dans l'ensemble de la classe politique
2 *adv* (**a**) *(from one side to the other)* **to run/swim a.** traverser en courant/à la nage; **go a. and see her** traverse et va la voir (**b**) *(with distance)* **it's 10 cm/2 km a.** ça fait 10 cm/2 km de large (**c**) **a. from me/my house** en face de moi/de chez moi (**d**) *(in crosswords)* horizontalement

acrylic [ə'krılık] **1** n *(fabric)* acrylique m
2 adj *(paint, fibre)* acrylique; *(garment)* en acrylique
act [ækt] **1** n **(a)** *(thing done)* acte m; **to be in the a.** of
doing sth être en train de faire qch; **to catch sb in the a.** of
doing sth surprendre qn en train de faire qch; **to catch sb
in the a.** prendre qn sur le fait *ou* en flagrant délit; *Fam* **to
get in on the a.** *(get involved)* se mettre dans le coup; **a.** of
war acte m de guerre; *Law* **a. of God** catastrophe f
naturelle
   (b) *(of play)* acte m; *(in cabaret, circus)* numéro m; *Fig* **to put
on an a.** faire semblant; *Fig* **to get one's a. together** se
secouer; *Fig* **it's all an a.** c'est du cinéma
   (c) *Law & Pol* loi f; **a. of Parliament/Congress** loi du
Parlement/Congrès
   2 vt **(a)** *(character)* jouer (le rôle de), tenir le rôle de; *(play)*
jouer, *Fig* **to a. the part** se conduire comme il convient
   (b) *(behave like)* **to a. the fool** or **the goat** faire l'imbécile;
Fam **a. your age (not your shoe size)!** arrête de faire
l'enfant!
   3 vi **(a)** *(take action)* agir; **to a. for sb** *(of lawyer)*
représenter qn; **to a. as secretary/chairperson** remplir
les fonctions de secrétaire/président; **to a. as a warning**
servir d'avertissement; **to a. as an incentive** être une
motivation
   (b) *(behave)* agir, se comporter; **to a. stupid** faire l'idiot
   (c) *(of actor)* jouer; **I always wanted to a.** j'ai toujours
voulu être acteur
► **act out** vt sep *(fantasy)* vivre; *(scene)* jouer
► **act up** vi *(of car, child, injury)* faire des siennes
acting ['æktıŋ] **1** n *(performance)* jeu m; *(profession)*
métier m d'acteur
   2 adj *(temporary)* par intérim
action ['ækʃən] n **(a)** *(individual act)* acte m, action f; *Prov*
actions speak louder than words les actes en disent plus
long que les paroles **(b)** *(activity)* action f; **to take a.** prendre
des mesures; **to go into a.** passer à l'action; **to be out of a.**
(machine, car) être en panne; *(person)* être hors service;
Fam **where's the a. round here?** où est-ce que ça bouge
par ici?; **a. plan** objectifs mpl **(c)** *Mil* combats mpl; **to
see a.** combattre; **missing in a.** porté(e) disparu(e) **(d)** *(of
film, novel)* action f; *TV* **a. replay** = répétition d'une
séquence précédente **(e)** *Law* action f, procès m; **to bring
an a. against sb** intenter un procès à qn
activate ['æktıveıt] vt déclencher
active ['æktıv] adj **(a)** *(person, mind, imagination)*
actif(ive); *(interest, dislike)* vif (vive); *(volcano)* en activité;
to be a. in doing sth s'employer activement à faire qch; *Mil*
on a. service en service actif **(b)** *Gram* actif(ive)
actively ['æktıvlı] adv activement; **to a. dislike sb**
détester cordialement qn
activist ['æktıvıst] n *Pol* militant(e) m,f
activity [æk'tıvıtı] *(pl* **activities)** n activité f; *(in street)*
animation f
actor ['æktə(r)] n acteur m
actress ['æktrıs] n actrice f
actual ['æktʃʊəl] adj **(a)** *(real)* réel(elle); *(example)*
concret(ète); **in a. fact** en fait **(b)** *(specific)* **I can't
remember her a. words** je ne me rappelle pas ses paroles
exactes; **although the garden is big, the a. house is
small** le jardin est grand, mais la maison elle-même est
petite
actually ['æktʃʊəlı] adv **(a)** *(really)* réellement, vraiment;
what a. happened? qu'est-ce qui s'est passé au juste?;
what she a. means is... en réalité, ce qu'elle veut dire
c'est... **(b)** *(in fact)* en fait; **I'm not sure, a.** en fait, je ne suis
pas sûr
actuary ['æktʃʊərı] *(pl* **actuaries)** n actuaire mf

acumen ['ækjʊmən] n flair m; **business a.** sens m des
affaires
acupuncture ['ækjʊpʌŋktʃə(r)] n acupuncture f
acute [ə'kju:t] adj **(a)** *(pain)* aigu(ë); *(remorse, embarrassment)* vif (vive); *(problem, shortage)* grave **(b)** *(eye-sight)* per-
çant(e) **(c)** *(accent, angle)* aigu(ë)
acutely [ə'kju:tlı] adv *(painful, embarrassing)* extrêmement; *(aware)* profondément
AD [eı'di:] adv *(abbr* **Anno Domini)** apr. J.-C.
ad [æd] n *Fam (classified)* petite annonce f; *(on radio, TV)*
pub f
Adam ['ædəm] n *Fam* **I wouldn't know him from A.** je ne
le connais ni d'Ève ni d'Adam; **A.'s apple** pomme f d'Adam
adamant ['ædəmənt] adj formel(elle), catégorique
(about sur); **to be a. that...** soutenir que...
adapt [ə'dæpt] **1** vt adapter; **to a. oneself to sth** s'adapter
à qch
   2 vi s'adapter
adaptable [ə'dæptəbəl] adj *(instrument, tool)* adaptable;
(person) souple
adaptation [ædæp'teıʃən] n *(of book, play)* adaptation f;
(of machine, design) modification f
adapter [ə'dæptə(r)] n *(for several plugs)* prise f multiple;
(for foreign plugs) adaptateur m
ADC [eıdi:'si:] n *Mil (abbr* **aide-de-camp)** aide m de camp
add [æd] vt ajouter **(to** à); *(figures)* additionner; **this book
adds little to the debate** ce livre n'apporte pas grand-
chose au débat
► **add up** vt sep *(figures)* additionner
   2 vi *(give correct total)* être juste *ou* exact(e); *(make sense)*
tenir debout
► **add up to** vt insep *(amount to)* **it adds up to $95** ça fait
95 dollars au total *ou* en tout; **it all adds up to an
enjoyable day out** tout cela fera de cette excursion un
moment bien agréable; **it doesn't a. up to much** ça ne fait
pas grand-chose au bout du compte
adder ['ædə(r)] n *(snake)* vipère f
addict ['ædıkt] n *(drug)* a. toxicomane mf; **heroin a.**
héroïnomane mf; **to be a TV a.** être accro à la télé
addicted [ə'dıktıd] adj **to be a. to sth** *(drugs)* être
dépendant(e) de qch; *(TV programme)* être accro à qch
addiction [ə'dıkʃən] n *(to drugs)* dépendance f **(to** à),
accoutumance f **(to** à); *(to chocolate, films)* passion f **(to**
pour)
addictive [ə'dıktıv] adj *(substance)* qui crée une
dépendance *ou* accoutumance; **soap operas are very a.**
on devient vite accro aux feuilletons
Addis Ababa ['ædıs'æbəbə] n Addis-Abeba
addition [ə'dıʃən] n *(action)* addition f; *(thing added)*
ajout m **(to** à); *(person)* nouveau venu (nouvelle venue) m,f;
she's the latest a. to the team c'est la dernière arrivée
dans l'équipe; **in a. (to)** en plus (de)
additional [ə'dıʃənəl] adj supplémentaire
additive ['ædıtıv] n additif m
addled ['ædəld] adj *(egg)* pourri(e); *(brain)* confus(e)
add-on ['ædɒn] n *Comptr* produit m supplémentaire *ou*
complémentaire
address [ə'dres] **1** n **(a)** *(of person, letter)* adresse f; **a.
book** carnet m d'adresses **(b)** *(speech)* discours m,
allocution f
   2 vt **(a)** *(letter, remarks, criticism)* adresser **(to** à) **(b)** *(speak
to)* *(person, crowd)* s'adresser à; **he addressed her as "Your
Majesty"** il l'a appelée "Votre Majesté" **(c)** *(question,
problem)* aborder; **to a. oneself to sth** *(problem)* aborder
qch; *(task)* entreprendre qch

adenoids ['ædɪnɔɪdz] *npl Anat* végétations *fpl*

adept [ə'dept] *adj* habile (**at** à); **to be a.** at doing sth être habile à faire qch

adequate ['ædɪkwət] *adj (enough)* suffisant(e); *(satisfactory)* satisfaisant(e), adéquat(e); **you were given a. warning** on vous a prévenu suffisamment à l'avance

adhere [əd'hɪə(r)] *vi (stick)* adhérer (**to** à); **to a. to** *(rule)* observer; *(belief)* adhérer à; *(plan)* se conformer à

adherence [əd'hɪərəns] *n (to rule)* observation *f* (**to** de); *(to belief, plan)* adhésion *f* (**to** à)

adherent [əd'hɪərənt] *n* adhérent(e) *m,f*

adhesion [əd'hiːʒən] *n* (**a**) *(stickiness)* adhérence *f* (**b**) *(to belief, plan)* adhésion *f* (**to** à)

adhesive [əd'hiːsɪv] **1** *n* adhésif *m*, colle *f* **2** *adj* adhésif(ive), collant(e); **a. tape** ruban *m* adhésif

ad hoc ['æd'hɒk] *adj (measure)* ad hoc *inv*; *(arrangement)* temporaire; **a. committee** comité *m* spécial *ou* ad hoc; **on an a. basis** au coup par coup

ad infinitum ['ædɪnfɪ'naɪtəm] *adv* à l'infini; **and so on a.** et ainsi de suite à n'en plus finir

adjacent [ə'dʒeɪsənt] *adj* adjacent(e); *(street)* voisin(e); *(room)* contigu(ë)

adjective ['ædʒɪktɪv] *n* adjectif *m*

adjoin [ə'dʒɔɪn] *vt* être contigu(ë) *ou* attenant(e) à

adjoining [ə'dʒɔɪnɪŋ] *adj* attenant(e); **the a. room** la pièce voisine *ou* à côté

adjourn [ə'dʒɜːn] **1** *vt (meeting, trial)* ajourner, remettre à plus tard **2** *vi (of meeting, trial)* être ajourné(e); **to a. to another room** passer dans une autre pièce

adjournment [ə'dʒɜːnmənt] *n* ajournement *m*

adjudge [ə'dʒʌdʒ] *vt* **to a. sb** guilty/the winner déclarer qn coupable/vainqueur

adjudicate [ə'dʒuːdɪkeɪt] *vt* juger

adjudication [ədʒuːdɪ'keɪʃən] *n* jugement *m*, décision *f*

adjudicator [ə'dʒuːdɪkeɪtə(r)] *n (in dispute)* arbitre *m*; *(in competition)* juge *m*

adjunct ['ædʒʌŋkt] *n (thing)* accessoire *m*

adjust [ə'dʒʌst] **1** *vt (machine, mechanism)* régler, ajuster; *(pay, figures)* ajuster; *(clothes)* rajuster; **to a. oneself to sth** s'adapter à qch **2** *vi (of person)* s'adapter (**to** à)

adjustable [ə'dʒʌstəbəl] *adj* ajustable, réglable; **a. spanner** clé *f* à molette

adjustment [ə'dʒʌstmənt] *n (of machine, mechanism)* réglage *m*; *(to pay, figures)* réajustement *m*; **to make an a. to sth** régler qch; **a period of a.** une période d'adaptation

ad-lib ['æd'lɪb] **1** *adv* en improvisant, de manière improvisée **2** *vi (pt & pp* **ad-libbed)** improviser

ad-man ['ædmæn] *n Fam* publicitaire *m*

admin ['ædmɪn] *n Fam (work)* travail *m* administratif; *(department)* administration *f*

administer [əd'mɪnɪstə(r)] *vt* (**a**) *(estate, funds)* administrer, gérer; *(territory)* administrer (**b**) *(give)* *(punishment, medication)* administrer; *(blow)* donner

administration [ədmɪnɪ'streɪʃən] *n* (**a**) *(work)* administration *f* (**b**) *(government)* gouvernement *m*

administrative [əd'mɪnɪstrətɪv] *adj* administratif(ive)

administrator [əd'mɪnɪstreɪtə(r)] *n* administrateur(trice) *m,f*

admirable ['ædmərəbəl] *adj* admirable

admiral ['ædmərəl] *n* amiral *m*

Admiralty ['ædmərəltɪ] *n* **the A.** ≃ le ministère de la Marine

admiration [ædmə'reɪʃən] *n* admiration *f* (**for** pour)

admire [əd'maɪə(r)] *vt* admirer

admirer [əd'maɪərə(r)] *n* admirateur(trice) *m,f*

admiring [əd'maɪrɪŋ] *adj (look, glance)* admiratif(ive)

admissible [əd'mɪsɪbəl] *adj* (*behaviour, error*) admissible, acceptable; *Law* recevable

admission [əd'mɪʃən] *n* (**a**) *(entry) (to school, hospital)* admission *f*; *(to museum, exhibition)* entrée *f*; *(price)* (prix *m* d')entrée *f*; **no a.** *(sign)* entrée interdite (**b**) *(acknowledgement) (of guilt)* aveu *m*; *(of crime)* confession *f*; **by his own a.** de son propre aveu

admit [əd'mɪt] *(pt & pp* **admitted)** *vt* (**a**) *(allow to enter)* laisser entrer; *(to hospital, college)* admettre; **to be admitted to hospital** être admis(e) à l'hôpital; **children not admitted** *(sign)* les enfants ne sont pas admis; **a. one** *(on ticket)* entrée valable pour une personne (**b**) *(acknowledge) (fact, mistake, guilt)* admettre, reconnaître; *(crime)* avouer; **I must a. it's not easy** je dois reconnaître que ce n'est pas facile; **to a. defeat** s'avouer vaincu(e) **2** *vi* **to a.** *(mistake)* reconnaître; **I a. to being in a bad mood yesterday** je dois admettre que j'étais de mauvaise humeur hier

admittance [əd'mɪtəns] *n (entry)* accès *m*; **to gain a.** parvenir à entrer; **to refuse sb a.** refuser de laisser entrer qn; **no a.** *(sign)* entrée interdite

admittedly [əd'mɪtɪdlɪ] *adv* de l'aveu général; **a., it was dark when I saw him** je dois convenir qu'il faisait sombre quand je l'ai vu

admonish [əd'mɒnɪʃ] *vt (reprimand)* admonester, faire des remontrances à (**for** pour)

ad nauseam [æd'nɔːsɪæm] *adv* à n'en plus finir

adobe [ə'dəʊbɪ] *n (clay)* adobe *m*

adolescence [ædə'lesəns] *n* adolescence *f*

adolescent [ædə'lesənt] *n* adolescent(e) *m,f*

adopt [ə'dɒpt] *vt (child, custom, approach, measures)* adopter; *(career, candidate)* choisir; *(tone, attitude)* prendre

adopted [ə'dɒptɪd] *adj (child)* adopté(e); *(son, daughter)* adoptif(ive); **my a. country** mon pays d'adoption

adoption [ə'dɒpʃən] *n* adoption *f*

adorable [ə'dɔːrəbəl] *adj* adorable

adoration [ædə'reɪʃən] *n* adoration *f*

adore [ə'dɔː(ɪ)] *vt* adorer

adorn [ə'dɔːn] *vt* orner, parer (**with** de)

adornment [ə'dɔːnmənt] *n (decorations)* ornements *mpl*, parure *f*

ADP [eɪdiː'piː] *n Comptr (abbr* **automatic data processing)** traitement *m* automatique des données

adrenalin(e) [ə'drenəlɪn] *n* adrénaline *f*

Adriatic [eɪdrɪ'ætɪk] *n* **the A. (Sea)** la mer Adriatique, l'Adriatique *f*

adrift [ə'drɪft] *adv & adj* **to be a.** *(of boat)* aller à la dérive; **to go a.** *(of plan)* tomber à l'eau; **to come a.** *(come apart)* se défaire

adroit [ə'drɔɪt] *adj* habile (**at doing sth** à faire qch)

adulation [ædjʊ'leɪʃən] *n* adulation *f*

adult ['ædʌlt, ə'dʌlt] **1** *n* adulte *mf* **2** *adj* adulte; *(film)* pour adultes; **a. education** enseignement *m* pour adultes

adulterate [ə'dʌltəreɪt] *vt (food)* empoisonner; *(wine)* frelater; *(language)* corrompre

adulteration [ədʌltə'reɪʃən] *n (of food)* empoisonnement *m*; *(of wine)* frelatage *m*

adulterer [ə'dʌltərə(r)] n adultère mf
adulterous [ə'dʌltərəs] adj adultère
adultery [ə'dʌltəri] n adultère m; **to commit a.** commettre l'adultère
adulthood ['ædʌlthʊd] n âge m adulte
advance [əd'vɑːns] **1** n **(a)** (forward movement) avance f; (progress) progrès m; **to make advances to sb** faire des avances à qn; **in a.** (book, apply, inform) à l'avance; (pay) d'avance; **six weeks in a.** six semaines à l'avance; **a. booking** réservation f à l'avance; **a. notice** or **warning** préavis m **(b)** (loan) avance f
2 vt **(a)** (move forward) faire avancer; (chess piece) avancer; (science, knowledge) faire progresser, faire avancer **(b)** (idea, opinion) avancer, mettre en avant **(c)** (loan) avancer
3 vi (move forward) s'avancer **(towards** vers); (make progress) avancer
advanced [əd'vɑːnst] adj (child, country, technology) avancé(e); (course, education) supérieur(e); **she's very a. for her age** elle est très en avance pour son âge; **a. mathematics** mathématiques fpl supérieures
advantage [əd'vɑːntɪdʒ] n avantage m **(over** sur); **to take a. of** profiter de; **to turn a situation to one's a.** tourner une situation à son avantage; **it would be to your a. to...** il serait dans votre intérêt de...; **a. Ferrero** (in tennis) avantage Ferrero
advantageous [ædvən'teɪdʒəs] adj avantageux(euse) **(to** pour)
advent ['ædvənt] n (arrival) arrivée f; Rel **A.** l'Avent m
adventure [əd'ventʃə(r)] n aventure f; **a. playground** terrain m de jeux (spécialement aménagé); **a. story** récit m d'aventures; (novel) roman m d'aventure(s)
adventurer [əd'ventʃərə(r)] n aventurier(ère) m,f
adventurous [əd'ventʃərəs] adj (person) aventureux(euse); (plan) audacieux(euse)
adverb ['ædvɜːb] n adverbe m
adversary ['ædvəsəri] (pl **adversaries**) n adversaire mf
adverse ['ædvɜːs] adj défavorable
adversely ['ædvɜːsli] adv **to influence sb a.** exercer une influence défavorable sur qn; **a. affected** affecté(e)
adversity [əd'vɜːsɪti] n adversité f; **in a.** dans l'adversité
advert ['ædvɜːt] n (for product) pub f; (for job, event) annonce f
advertise ['ædvətaɪz] **1** vt **(a)** (product, service) faire de la réclame ou de la publicité pour; (job) mettre une annonce pour; **advertised on TV** vu(e) à la télé **(b)** (call attention to) **he didn't want to a. his presence** il ne voulait pas se faire remarquer
2 vi (for job) mettre une annonce; (to sell product) faire de la publicité ou de la réclame; **to a. for sb** passer une annonce pour trouver qn
advertisement [əd'vɜːtɪsmənt] n (for product, service) publicité f, réclame f; (for job, event) annonce f; Fig **you're not a good a. for your school** vous ne faites pas honneur à votre école
advertiser ['ædvətaɪzə(r)] n annonceur(euse) m,f
advertising ['ædvətaɪzɪŋ] n publicité f; **a. agency** agence f de publicité; **a. campaign** campagne f de publicité
advice [əd'vaɪs] n conseil(s) m(pl) **(on** sur); **a piece of a.** un conseil; **that's good a.** c'est un bon conseil; **to give sb a.** donner des conseils à qn; **to ask sb's a.** demander conseil à qn; **to take sb's a.** suivre le conseil ou les conseils de qn
advisable [əd'vaɪzəbəl] adj recommandé(e)
advise [əd'vaɪz] vt **(a)** (give advice to) conseiller; **to a. sb to do sth** conseiller à qn de faire qch; **to a. sb against doing sth** déconseiller à qn de faire qch; **I wouldn't a. it** je

ne le conseillerais ou recommanderais pas **(b)** (inform) **to a. sb that...** aviser qn que...
adviser, advisor [əd'vaɪzə(r)] n conseiller(ère) m,f
advisory [əd'vaɪzəri] adj consultatif(ive); **in an a. capacity** en tant que conseiller
advocate 1 n ['ædvəkət] **(a)** Scot Law avocat(e) m,f; **the Lord A.** ≃ le procureur général **(b)** (of cause, doctrine) partisan(e) m,f
2 vt ['ædvəkeɪt] (policy, plan) préconiser, conseiller
AEA [eɪiː'eɪ] n Br (abbr **Atomic Energy Authority**) ≃ Commissariat m à l'énergie atomique
AEC [eɪiː'siː] n Am (abbr **Atomic Energy Commission**) ≃ Commissariat m à l'énergie atomique
Aegean [ɪ'dʒiːən] n **the A.** (Sea) la mer Égée
aegis ['iːdʒɪs] n **under the a. of...** sous l'égide de
aeon, Am **eon** ['iːən] n Fig éternité f; **aeons ago** il y a une éternité
aerate ['eəreɪt] vt (water) gazéifier
aerial ['eərɪəl] **1** n (of radio, TV) antenne f
2 adj aérien(enne)
aerobics [eə'rəʊbɪks] n aérobic m
aerodrome ['eərədrəʊm] n aérodrome m
aerodynamic [eərəʊdaɪ'næmɪk] adj aérodynamique
aerogram(me) ['eərəgræm] n aérogramme m
aeronautic(al) [eərə'nɔːtɪk(əl)] adj aéronautique
aeroplane ['eərəpleɪn] n avion m
aerosol ['eərəsɒl] n aérosol m; **a. spray** atomiseur m
aesthetic, Am **esthetic** [ɪs'θetɪk] adj esthétique
afar [ə'fɑː(r)] adv Lit **from a.** de loin
affable ['æfəbəl] adj affable, courtois(e)
affair [ə'feə(r)] n **(a)** (matter, concern) affaire f; **that's my a.!** c'est mes affaires!; **to put one's affairs in order** mettre de l'ordre dans ses affaires; **current affairs** les questions fpl d'actualité; **foreign affairs** les affaires étrangères; **affairs of state** les affaires de l'État; **in the present state of affairs** dans l'état actuel des choses **(b)** (sexual) liaison f; **to have an a.** avoir une liaison avec qn **(c)** (event) affaire f; **the wedding was a quiet a.** le mariage fut célébré dans l'intimité; **what kind of a. was it?** c'était comment?
affect¹ [ə'fekt] vt **(a)** (have effect on) (person, organ, health) affecter; (decision) influencer; (of issue, law) concerner **(b)** (move emotionally) affecter, toucher; **to be deeply affected by sth** être très affecté(e) par qch
affect² vt (indifference, interest) affecter, feindre; **to a. an accent** prendre un accent
affectation [æfek'teɪʃən] n affectation f
affected [ə'fektɪd] adj (unnatural) affecté(e), maniéré(e)
affection [ə'fekʃən] n affection f
affectionate [ə'fekʃənət] adj affectueux(euse) **(towards** avec ou envers)
affidavit [æfɪ'deɪvɪt] n Law déclaration f par écrit et sous serment
affiliate 1 n [ə'fɪlɪət] (person) affilié(e) m,f
2 vt [ə'fɪlɪeɪt] affilier **(to** or **with** à); **affiliated company** filiale f
affiliation [əfɪlɪ'eɪʃən] n affiliation f
affinity [ə'fɪnɪti] (pl **affinities**) n **(a)** (liking, attraction) affinité f (for or with/between avec/entre); **to have an a. with sb/sth** avoir des affinités avec qn/qch **(b)** (relationship, connection) lien m (between/with entre/ avec)
affirm [ə'fɜːm] vt **(a)** (state) affirmer **(b)** (confirm) confirmer

affirmation [æfə'meɪ∫ən] n (**a**) *(statement)* affirmation f, assertion f (**b**) *(confirmation)* confirmation f

affirmative [ə'fɜːmətɪv] **1** n **to answer in the a.** répondre affirmativement *ou* par l'affirmative **2** adj affirmatif(ive)

affix 1 n ['æfɪks] *Ling* affixe m **2** vt [ə'fɪks] attacher (**to** à); *(notice, poster)* fixer (**to** à)

afflict [ə'flɪkt] vt affliger; **afflicted with rheumatism** affligé(e) de rhumatismes

affliction [ə'flɪk∫ən] n *(illness)* affection f; *(misfortune)* malheur m

affluent ['æfluənt] adj riche; **the a. society** la société d'abondance

afford [ə'fɔːd] vt (**a**) *(financially)* **to be able to a. sth** avoir les moyens d'acheter qch; **I can't a. it** mes moyens ne me le permettent pas; **we can't a. a new car** nous ne pouvons pas nous offrir une nouvelle voiture; **she can a. to go skiing twice a year** elle peut se permettre d'aller faire du ski deux fois par an (**b**) *(non-financial use)* **I can't a. to wait** je ne peux pas attendre; **can you a. the time?** est-ce que vous avez le temps?; **I can't a. not to** je n'ai pas le choix; **we can't a. another mistake** nous ne pouvons pas nous permettre une nouvelle erreur (**c**) *Formal (give)* offrir, procurer

affordable [ə'fɔːdəbəl] adj *(price, purchase)* abordable; *(house)* (d'un prix) abordable

affray [ə'freɪ] n rixe f

affront [ə'frʌnt] **1** n affront m, offense f **2** vt offenser, faire (un) affront à; **to be/feel affronted** être/se sentir offensé(e)

Afghan ['æfgæn] **1** n (**a**) *(person)* Afghan(e) m,f (**b**) *(dog)* lévrier m afghan **2** adj afghan(e); **A. hound** lévrier m afghan

Afghanistan [æf'gænɪstɑːn] n l'Afghanistan m

afield [ə'fiːld] adv **further a.** plus loin

AFL/CIO [eɪef'elsiːaɪˈəʊ] n *(abbr* **American Federation of Labor and Congress of Industrial Organizations)** = confédération syndicale américaine

afloat [ə'fləʊt] adv & adj à flot; **to stay a.** *(of boat, company)* se maintenir à flot

afoot [ə'fʊt] adv **there's something a.** il se prépare *ou* se trame quelque chose

aforementioned [ə'fɔːmen∫ənd] adj susmentionné(e)

afraid [ə'freɪd] adj (**a**) *(scared)* **to be a. (of)** avoir peur (de); **that's (exactly) what I was a. of!** c'est bien ce que je craignais!; **I was a. there would be an accident** je craignais un accident (**b**) *(sorry)* **I'm a. so/not** je crains que oui/que non; **I'm a. she's out** je regrette, mais elle est sortie; **I'm a. I can't help you** j'ai bien peur de ne pouvoir vous aider

afresh [ə'fre∫] adv de nouveau, à nouveau; **to start a.** recommencer

Africa ['æfrɪkə] n l'Afrique f

African ['æfrɪkən] **1** n Africain(e) m,f; **A. American** Noir(e) m,f américain(e) **2** adj africain(e)

Afrikaans [æfrɪ'kɑːnz] n afrikaans m

aft [ɑːft] adv *Naut* à l'arrière

after ['ɑːftə(r)] **1** prep (**a**) *(with time)* après; **a. dinner** après dîner; **a. three days** au bout de trois jours; **the day a. tomorrow** après-demain; **it's a. five** il est cinq heures passées; *Am* **it's twenty a. six** il est six heures vingt; **a. all** *(all things considered)* après tout; *(despite everything)* finalement (**b**) *(with motion)* après; **to run a. sb** courir après qn; **close**

the door a. you fermez la porte derrière vous; **a. you!** après vous! (**c**) *(in search of)* **to be a. sb/sth** chercher qn/qch (**d**) *(expressing sequence)* après; **a. her, he is the best** après elle, c'est lui le meilleur (**e**) *(expressing repetition)* après; **day a. day** jour après jour; **year a. year** d'une année sur l'autre, tous les ans; **time a. time** cent fois; **it's one thing a. another** j'ai/nous avons/ *etc* des problèmes à n'en plus finir (**f**) *(in honour of)* **to name sb/sth a. sb** donner le nom de qn à qn/qch **2** adv après; **soon/long a.** peu/longtemps après; **the week a.** la semaine d'après; **the day a.** le lendemain **3** conj *(when subject changes)* après que + *indicative or Fam subjunctive; (when subject stays the same)* après + *infinitive*; **I came a. he left** je suis arrivé après qu'il est *ou Fam* soit parti; **a. I saw him I went out** je suis sorti après l'avoir vu; **a. doing sth** après avoir fait qch

afterbirth ['ɑːftəbɜːθ] n placenta m

aftercare ['ɑːftəkeə(r)] n *(after operation)* soins mpl postopératoires; *(of convalescent, delinquent)* surveillance f

after-effect ['ɑːftərəfekt] n *(of event)* répercussion f, contrecoup m

after-life ['ɑːftəlaɪf] n vie f après la mort

aftermath ['ɑːftəmæθ] n suites fpl, conséquences fpl

afternoon [ɑːftə'nuːn] n après-midi m inv or f inv; **in the a.** *(pendant)* l'après-midi; **at four o'clock in the a.** à quatre heures de l'après-midi; **good a.!** bonjour!

aftersales service ['ɑːftə'seɪlz'sɜːvɪs] n *Com* service m après-vente

aftershave ['ɑːftə∫eɪv] n **a. (lotion)** (lotion f) après-rasage m

aftertaste ['ɑːfteteɪst] n *also Fig* arrière-goût m

afterthought ['ɑːftəθɔːt] n réflexion f après coup; **as an a.** après coup

afterwards ['ɑːftəwədz] adv après; **I regretted it a.** par la suite, je l'ai regretté

again [ə'gen] adv (**a**) *(in general)* de nouveau, encore; **to begin a.** recommencer; **he never came back a.** il n'est plus jamais revenu; **don't do it a.!** ne recommence pas!; **not you a.!** encore toi!; **once a.** encore une fois, une fois de plus; **a. and a.** à maintes reprises; **now and a.** de temps en temps, de temps à autre; **half as much a.** moitié plus; **I'd like half as much a.** je voudrais encore la moitié de ça; **what did you say a.?** qu'avez-vous dit déjà? (**b**) *(besides)* en outre; **(then) a.** *(on the other hand)* d'un autre côté; **a., I may have imagined it** cela dit, il se peut aussi que je l'aie imaginé

against [ə'genst] prep (**a**) *(in opposition to)* contre; **to be a. sb/sth** être contre qn/qch, être opposé(e) à qn/qch; **to have something/nothing a. sb/sth** avoir quelque chose/ne rien avoir contre qn/qch; **a. the law** contraire à la loi, illégal(e) (**b**) *(as protection from)* contre; **to warn sb a. sb/sth** mettre qn en garde contre qn/qch (**c**) *(in contact with)* contre; **to lean a. sth** s'appuyer contre qch (**d**) *(in comparison with)* contre; **three deaths this year (as) a. thirty in 2003** trois morts cette année contre trente en 2003; **the pound rose/fell a. the euro** la livre a augmenté/chuté par rapport à l'euro

age [eɪdʒ] **1** n (**a**) *(of person)* âge m; **to be twenty years of a.** avoir vingt ans, être âgé(e) de vingt ans; **what a. is she?, what's her a.?** quel âge a-t-elle?; **he doesn't look his a.** il ne fait pas son âge; **people of all ages** des gens de tout âge; **a. group** tranche f d'âge; **a. of consent** = âge légal où on peut avoir des rapports sexuels; **a. limit** limite f d'âge (**b**) **(old) a.** vieillesse f

(c) *(adulthood)* **to come of a.** atteindre sa majorité; **to be under a.** *Law* être mineur(e); *(not old enough to buy alcohol etc)* ne pas avoir l'âge **(d)** *(era)* âge *m*, époque *f* **(e)** *Fam (long time)* **it's ages since I saw him** il y a une éternité que je ne l'ai pas vu; **I've been waiting (for) ages** ça fait une éternité que j'attends **2** *vt & vi (continuous* **aging** *or* **ageing)** vieillir

aged *adj* **(a)** [eɪdʒd] *(of the age of)* **a. twenty** âgé(e) de vingt ans **(b)** ['eɪdʒɪd] *(old)* âgé(e), vieux (vieille)

ageing ['eɪdʒɪŋ] **1** *n (of person, wine)* vieillissement *m*; **a. process** processus *m* de vieillissement **2** *adj (becoming older)* vieillissant(e); *(old)* vieux (vieille)

ageism ['eɪdʒɪzəm] *n* âgisme *m*

agency ['eɪdʒənsɪ] *(pl* **agencies)** *n* **(a)** *Com* agence *f*; **advertising/travel a.** agence de publicité/de voyages **(b)**; **through the a. of** par l'entremise ou l'intermédiaire de

agenda [ə'dʒendə] *n (of meeting)* ordre *m* du jour; *Fig* programme *m*

agent ['eɪdʒənt] *n* **(a)** *(representative, spy)* agent *m* **(b)** *(instrument)* agent *m*; **to be the a. of sth** être l'instrument de qch

age-old ['eɪdʒəʊld] *adj* séculaire

aggravate ['ægrəveɪt] *vt* **(a)** *(worsen)* aggraver **(b)** *Fam (annoy)* agacer, exaspérer

aggravating ['ægrəveɪtɪŋ] *adj* **(a)** *Law* aggravant(e) **(b)** *Fam (annoying)* agaçant(e), exaspérant(e)

aggravation [ægrə'veɪʃən] *n* **(a)** *(worsening)* aggravation *f* **(b)** *Fam (annoyance)* embêtements *mpl*

aggregate ['ægrɪgət] **1** *n* total *m*, ensemble *m*; **on a.** au total **2** *adj* collectif(ive); **a. scores** résultats *mpl* globaux

aggression [ə'greʃən] *n* agressivité *f*; **an act of a.** une agression

aggressive [ə'gresɪv] *adj* agressif(ive)

aggressively [ə'gresɪvlɪ] *adv (violently)* d'une manière agressive; *(speak)* d'un ton agressif; *(vigorously)* énergiquement, avec dynamisme

aggressor [ə'gresə(r)] *n* agresseur *m*

aggrieved [ə'griːvd] *adj (expression, tone)* vexé(e); **to be** *or* **feel a.** se sentir lésé(e)

aggro ['ægrəʊ] *n Fam (violence)* grabuge *m*, bagarre(s) *f(pl)*; *(trouble)* enquiquinement *m*

aghast [ə'gɑːst] *adj* horrifié(e) **(at** par)

agile ['ædʒaɪl] *adj* agile

agility [ə'dʒɪlɪtɪ] *n* agilité *f*

agitate ['ædʒɪteɪt] **1** *vt (liquid, person)* agiter **2** *vi* **to a. for/against sth** mener une campagne en faveur de/contre qch

agitated ['ædʒɪteɪtɪd] *adj (person)* agité(e)

agitation [ædʒɪ'teɪʃən] *n* agitation *f*

agitator ['ædʒɪteɪtə(r)] *n Pol* agitateur(trice) *m,f*

aglow [ə'gləʊ] *adj (sky)* embrasé(e); **to be a. with** *(of person)* rayonner de

AGM [eɪdʒiː'em] *n Com (abbr* **annual general meeting)** AGA *f*

agnostic [æg'nɒstɪk] *n & adj* agnostique *mf*

ago [ə'gəʊ] *adv* **ten years a.** il y a dix ans; **long a.** il y a longtemps; **as long a. as 1840** déjà en 1840, dès 1840; **a short time a.** il y a peu de temps, tout à l'heure; **how long a. was that?** c'était il y a combien de temps?

agog [ə'gɒg] *adj* en émoi; **they were all a. to hear the end of the story** tout le monde brûlait d'apprendre la fin de l'histoire

agonize ['ægənaɪz] *vi* se ronger les sangs, se tourmenter **(over** à propos de)

agonizing ['ægənaɪzɪŋ] *adj (pain, death)* atroce; *(silence, wait)* angoissant(e); *(decision, dilemma)* pénible, déchirant(e)

agony ['ægənɪ] *(pl* **agonies)** *n (physical pain)* douleur *f* atroce; *(mental pain)* angoisse *f*; **to be in a.** être au supplice ou au martyre; **it's a. walking in these shoes!** c'est un véritable supplice de marcher avec ces chaussures!; **a. aunt** *(in newspaper)* = responsable de la rubrique courrier du cœur; **a. column** *(in newspaper)* courrier *m* du cœur

agoraphobia [ægərə'fəʊbɪə] *n* agoraphobie *f*

agrarian [ə'greərɪən] *adj* agraire

agree [ə'griː] **1** *vt* **(a)** *(reach agreement on) (price, time, conditions)* se mettre d'accord sur; **to a. to do sth** convenir de faire qch; **(are we) agreed?** (nous sommes) d'accord? **(b)** *(concur)* **to a. (that)...** s'accorder à dire que...; **I a. that's expensive, but...** c'est cher, j'en conviens, mais...; **everyone agrees (that) he's the best** tout le monde s'accorde à dire qu'il est le meilleur **(c)** *(consent)* **to a. to do sth** accepter de faire qch, consentir à faire qch; **we'll have to a. to differ on that** je crois qu'ici il va nous falloir accepter nos différences d'opinion; **it is generally agreed that...** il est généralement admis que...

2 *vi* **(a)** *(be of same opinion, concur)* être d'accord **(about/ with** sur/avec**)**; *(after discussion)* se mettre d'accord; **I quite** *or* **entirely a.** je suis entièrement d'accord; **I'm afraid I can't a.** j'ai bien peur de ne pas être du même avis; **I couldn't a. more!** ça c'est bien dit!; **I don't a. with all this violence on television** je n'approuve pas toute cette violence à la télévision **(b)** *(match) (of statements, facts, opinions)* concorder, coïncider **(with** avec**)**; *Gram* s'accorder **(with** avec**) (c)** *(accept)* consentir **(to** à**); to a. to a condition/ proposal** accepter une condition/une proposition ▸ **agree on** *vt insep* être d'accord sur, *(after discussion)* se mettre d'accord sur ▸ **agree with** *vt insep (of food)* réussir à

agreeable [ə'griːəbəl] *adj* **(a)** *(pleasant)* agréable; *(person)* aimable **(b)** *(acceptable)* **if that is a. to you** si cela vous convient

agreed [ə'griːd] *adj (price, time)* convenu(e)

agreement [ə'griːmənt] *n* **(a)** *(contract, assent) & Gram* accord *m* **(on** *or* **about** sur**); to come to an a.** tomber ou se mettre d'accord; **by mutual a.** d'un commun accord; **the proposal met with unanimous a.** la proposition a été reçue à l'unanimité; **to be in a. with sb** être d'accord avec qn; **to be in a. with a decision** approuver une décision **(b)** *(of facts, account)* **to be in a. with** concorder avec

agricultural [ægrɪ'kʌltʃərəl] *adj* agricole; **a. college** = école supérieure d'agriculture et d'agronomie

agriculture ['ægrɪkʌltʃə(r)] *n* agriculture *f*

agronomy [ə'grɒnəmɪ] *n* agronomie *f*

aground [ə'graʊnd] *adv* **to run a.** *(of ship)* s'échouer; *(of project, government)* échouer

ahead [ə'hed] *adv* **(a)** *(in space)* devant; **to go on a.** partir devant; **the road a. was clear** devant nous/moi/*etc* la route était libre; **a. of** devant **(b)** *(winning)* **to be a.** être en tête; **to get a.** *(in career)* avancer; **to get a. of sb** dépasser qn **(c)** *(in time)* **to plan a.** faire des projets; **in the years a.** dans les années à venir; **a. of** *(prior to)* avant; **a. of schedule** *(flight, train)* en avance sur l'horaire; *(project)* en avance sur les prévisions; **to be a. of one's time** être en avance sur son temps

ahoy [ə'hɔɪ] *exclam* **a. there!** oh(é)!

AI [eɪ'aɪ] *n (a) Comptr (abbr* **artificial intelligence)** IA *f* **(b)**

Biol (abbr **artificial insemination**) insémination *f* artificielle (**c**) *Pol (abbr* **Amnesty International**) Amnesty International *f*
aid [eɪd] **1** *n* (**a**) *(help, for disaster relief)* aide *f*, secours *m*; **with the a. of** sb avec l'aide de qn; **with the a. of** sth à l'aide de qch; **to go to** sb's **a.** aller *ou* se porter au secours de qn; **in a. of** *(fund-raising event)* au profit de; *Fam* **what's (all) this in a. of?** c'est en quel honneur? (**b**) *(device)* outil *m*; **teaching aids** matériel *m* pédagogique
2 *vt* aider; *Law* **to a. and abet** sb être le complice de qn

aide [eɪd] *n* assistant(e) *m,f*, conseiller(ère) *m,f*

aide-de-camp ['eɪd'dəkɒŋ] *(pl* **aides-de-camp**) *n Mil* aide *m* de camp

aiding ['eɪdɪŋ] *n Law* **a. and abetting** complicité *f*

AIDS [eɪdz] *n* sida *m*; **A. clinic** = clinique spécialisée dans le traitement du sida; **A. sufferer** sidéen(enne) *m,f*, malade *mf* du sida; **A. virus** virus *m* du sida

ailing ['eɪlɪŋ] *adj (person)* souffrant(e); *(company, economy)* qui bat de l'aile

ailment ['eɪlmənt] *n* mal *m*

aim [eɪm] **1** *n* (**a**) *(at target)* **to take a. (at)** viser; **her a. was good** elle visait bien (**b**) *(goal)* but *m*, dessein *m*; **with the a. of doing** sth dans le but *ou* dessein de faire qch
2 *vt (stone)* lancer (**at** à); *(camera)* braquer (**at** sur); **to a. a gun at** sb/sth mettre qn/qch en joue; **to a. a blow at** sb *(of remarks, TV programme)* être destiné(e) à qn
3 *vi* **to a. at** *(with gun)* viser; **to a. to do sth** *(intend)* avoir l'intention de faire qch

aimless ['eɪmlɪs] *adj (existence, remark)* sans but

ain't [eɪnt] *very Fam* (**a**) = is not, am not, are not (**b**) = has not, have not

air [eər] **1** *n* (**a**) *(in general)* air *m*; **by a.** par avion; **to be on the a.** *(of person)* être à l'antenne; *(of programme)* être diffusé(e); **to throw sth (up) in the a.** lancer qch en l'air; **our plans are up in the a.** *(undecided)* nos projets n'ont toujours pas de forme précise; **to be in the a.** *(of rumour)* circuler; *(of feeling, idea)* être dans l'air; **a. bag** sac *m* gonflable de sécurité; **a. bed** matelas *m* pneumatique; **a. filter** filtre *m* à air; **the A. Force** l'Armée *f* de l'air; **a. freight** fret *m* aérien; **a. freshener** désodorisant *m*; *Br* **a. hostess** hôtesse *f* de l'air; **a. raid** raid *m* aérien; **a. rifle** fusil *m* à air comprimé; **a. show** salon *m* de l'aéronautique; *Br* **a. steward** steward *m*; *Br* **a. stewardess** hôtesse *f* de l'air; **a. terminal** aérogare *f*; **a. traffic control** contrôle *m* aérien; **a. traffic controller** contrôleur *m* aérien, aiguilleur *m* du ciel (**b**) *(melody)* air *m* (**c**) *(look)* air *m*, apparence *f*; **he has a certain a. about him** c'est quelqu'un qui en impose; **to give oneself** *or* **to put on airs** se donner des airs
2 *vt* (**a**) *(room, clothing, bedding)* aérer (**b**) *(opinions, grievances)* exposer

airborne ['eəbɔ:n] *adj (seeds, particles)* en suspension dans l'air; *(troops)* aéroporté(e); **once we are a.** une fois que nous aurons décollé

air-conditioned ['eəkən'dɪʃənd] *adj* climatisé(e), à air conditionné

air-conditioning ['eəkən'dɪʃənɪŋ] *n* climatisation *f*

air-cooled ['eəku:ld] *adj* refroidi(e) par air

aircraft ['eəkrɑ:ft] *(pl* **aircraft**) *n* avion *m*; **a. carrier** porte-avions *m inv*

air-crew ['eəkru:] *n Av* équipage *m*

airfield ['eəfi:ld] *n* champ *m ou* terrain *m* d'aviation

airing ['eərɪŋ] *n* **to give sth an a.** *(room, clothes, bedding)* aérer qch; *(opinions, grievances)* exposer; *Br* **a. cupboard** = placard chauffé où l'on fait sécher le linge

airless ['eəlɪs] *adj (room)* qui sent le renfermé; *(evening, atmosphere)* lourd(e)

airlift ['eəlɪft] **1** *n* pont *m* aérien
2 *vt (supplies, troops)* transporter par avion; *(refugees)* évacuer par avion

airline ['eəlaɪn] *n* ligne *f ou* compagnie *f* aérienne; **a. pilot** pilote *m* de ligne

airlock ['eəlɒk] *n* (**a**) *(in submarine, spacecraft)* sas *m* (**b**) *(in pipe)* poche *f* d'air

airmail ['eəmeɪl] **1** *n (service)* poste *f* aérienne; **a. letter** aérogramme *m*
2 *adv* **to send sth a.** envoyer qch par avion
3 *vt (letter)* envoyer par avion

airplane ['eəpleɪn] *n Am* avion *m*

airport ['eəpɔ:t] *n* aéroport *m*

air-sea rescue ['eəsi:'reskju:] *n* sauvetage *m* aérien en mer

airship ['eəʃɪp] *n* dirigeable *m*

airsick ['eəsɪk] *adj* **to be a.** avoir le mal de l'air

airspace ['eəspeɪs] *n* espace *m* aérien

airstrip ['eəstrɪp] *n* piste *f* d'atterrissage

airtight ['eətaɪt] *adj* hermétique

airtime ['eətaɪm] *n Rad & TV* temps *m* d'antenne

airwaves ['eəweɪvz] *npl* ondes *fpl* (hertziennes)

airworthy ['eəwɜ:ðɪ] *adj (aircraft)* en état de voler

airy ['eərɪ] *adj (room, house)* bien aéré(e) (**b**) *(person, attitude)* insouciant(e), désinvolte

airy-fairy ['eərɪ'feərɪ] *adj Fam (idea, scheme)* farfelu(e)

aisle [aɪl] *n (in supermarket, cinema)* allée *f*; *(in church)* (at side) bas-côté *m*; *(central)* allée; *(in plane, bus)* couloir *m*; *Fam* **she had them rolling in the aisles** *(of comedian)* elle a fait mourir le public de rire; *Fig* **to walk down the a.** se marier; **a. seat** *(in plane)* place *f* côté couloir

ajar [ə'dʒɑ:(r)] *adv & adj* entrouvert(e)

aka [eɪkeɪ'eɪ] *adv (abbr* **also known as**) alias

akin [ə'kɪn] *adv & adj* **to be a. to** être apparenté(e) à

alabaster ['æləbæstə(r)] *n* albâtre *m*

alacrity [ə'lækrɪtɪ] *n* empressement *m*

alarm [ə'lɑ:m] **1** *n* (**a**) *(signal, device)* alarme *f*; **to raise** *or* **give the a.** donner l'alarme; **a. clock** réveil *m*, réveille-matin *m inv*; **a. signal** signal *m* d'alarme (**b**) *(fright, anxiety)* alarme *f*, frayeur *f*; **there's no cause for a.** il n'y a aucune raison de s'alarmer
2 *vt* effrayer, alarmer; **to be alarmed at sth** s'alarmer *ou* s'effrayer de qch

alarming [ə'lɑ:mɪŋ] *adj* alarmant(e), inquiétant(e)

alarmist [ə'lɑ:mɪst] *n & adj* alarmiste *mf*

alas [ə'læs] *exclam* hélas!

Albania [æl'beɪnɪə] *n* l'Albanie *f*

Albanian [æl'beɪnɪən] **1** *n* (**a**) *(person)* Albanais(e) *m,f* (**b**) *(language)* albanais *m*
2 *adj* albanais(e)

albatross ['ælbətrɒs] *n* albatros *m*

albeit [ɔ:l'bi:ɪt] *conj* quoique, bien que

albino [æl'bi:nəʊ] *(pl* **albinos**) *n* albinos *mf*

album ['ælbəm] *n (record, for photos, stamps)* album *m*

albumen ['ælbjʊmɪn] *n* (**a**) *(in egg)* albumen *m* (**b**) *(in blood)* albumine *f*

alchemy ['ælkəmɪ] *n* alchimie *f*

alcohol ['ælkəhɒl] *n* alcool *m*

alcoholic [ælkə'hɒlɪk] **1** *n (person)* alcoolique *mf*
2 *adj* alcoolique; *(drink)* alcoolisé(e)

alcoholism ['ælkəhɒlɪzəm] *n* alcoolisme *m*

alcove ['ælkəʊv] *n (in wall)* niche *f; (larger)* renfoncement *m*
alder ['ɔːldə(r)] *n* au(l)ne *m*
ale [eɪl] *n* = bière anglaise au malt
alert [ə'lɜːt] **1** *n* alerte *f;* **to be on the a.** être en état d'alerte, être sur le qui-vive **2** *adj (watchful)* éveillé(e); *(lively)* vif (vive); **to be a. to sth** *(aware of)* être conscient(e) de qch **3** *vt* alerter; **to a. sb to a danger** alerter *ou* avertir qn d'un danger
Aleutian Islands [æ'luːʃən'aɪləndz] *npl* **the A.** les îles *fpl* Aléoutiennes
Alexandria [ælɪg'zɑːndrɪə] *n* Alexandrie
alfalfa [æl'fælfə] *n* luzerne *f*
alfresco [æl'freskəʊ] *adv & adj* en plein air
algae ['ældʒiː] *npl* algues *fpl*
algebra ['ældʒɪbrə] *n* algèbre *f*
Algeria [æl'dʒɪərɪə] *n* l'Algérie *f*
Algerian [æl'dʒɪərɪən] **1** *n* Algérien(enne) *m,f* **2** *adj* algérien(enne)
Algiers [æl'dʒɪəz] *n* Alger
algorithm ['ælgərɪðəm] *n Comptr* algorithme *m*
alias ['eɪlɪəs] *(pl* **aliases)** **1** *n* nom *m* d'emprunt, faux nom **2** *adv* alias
alibi ['ælɪbaɪ] *n Law* alibi *m*
alien ['eɪlɪən] **1** *n* **(a)** *Formal (foreigner)* étranger(ère) *m,f* **(b)** *(from outer space)* extraterrestre *mf* **2** *adj* **(a)** *(strange)* étranger(ère) **(b)** *(from outer space)* extraterrestre
alienate ['eɪlɪəneɪt] *vt (supporters, readers)* s'aliéner; **they feel alienated from society** ils se sentent mis à l'écart de la société
alight[1] [ə'laɪt] *adj (burning)* en flammes, en feu; **to set sth a.** mettre le feu à qch
alight[2] *(pt & pp* alighted *or* alit [ə'lɪt]) *vi* **(a)** *Formal (from train, car)* descendre **(b)** *(of bird, eyes, glance)* se poser **(on** sur)
align [ə'laɪn] *vt* aligner; **to a. oneself with sb** s'aligner sur qn
alignment [ə'laɪnmənt] *n* alignement *m;* **out of a.** désaligné(e), **in a. (with)** aligné(e) (sur)
alike [ə'laɪk] **1** *adj* semblable, pareil(eille); **to look a.** se ressembler **2** *adv (dress, think)* de la même façon; **old and young a.** les vieux comme les jeunes
alimentary canal [ælɪ'mentərɪkə'næl] *n Anat* tube *m* digestif
alimony ['ælɪmənɪ] *n Law* pension *f* alimentaire
alit [ə'lɪt] *pt & pp of* alight
alive [ə'laɪv] *adj* **(a)** *(living)* **to be a.** être vivant(e); **to keep sb a.** maintenir qn en vie; **to keep a memory/ custom a.** entretenir un souvenir/une tradition; **to be a. and well** bien se porter; **the oldest woman a.** la doyenne du monde **(b)** *(aware)* **to be a. to sth** avoir parfaitement conscience de qch **(c)** *(full of vitality)* **I've never felt so a.** je ne me suis jamais senti aussi bien de ma vie; **to come a.** s'animer **(d)** *(teeming)* **to be a. with sth** grouiller de qch
alkali ['ælkəlaɪ] *n* alcali *m*
alkaline ['ælkəlaɪn] *adj* alcalin(e)
all [ɔːl] **1** *adj* **(a)** *(every one of)* tous (toutes); **a. men** tous les hommes; **a. the girls** toutes les filles; **a. the others** tous les autres; **a. four of them** tous les quatre; **at a. hours** à des heures impossibles **(b)** *(the whole of)* tout(e); **a. the bread** tout le pain; **a. day** toute la journée; **a. her life** toute sa vie; **a. the time** tout le temps

(c) *(for emphasis)* **a. sorts of things** toutes sortes de choses; **what's a. that noise?** c'est quoi, tout ce bruit?; **in a. honesty** en toute honnêteté; **for a. his wealth...** il a beau être riche...; **it's not a. that easy** ce n'est pas si facile (que ça); **you, of a. people, should understand** si quelqu'un doit comprendre ça, c'est bien toi; **of a. the stupid things to say!** ce n'est vraiment pas malin de dire un truc pareil!
2 *pron* **(a)** *(everyone)* tous (toutes) *mpl, fpl;* **a. of us** nous tous; **a. of them say that..., they a. say that...** ils disent tous que...; **a. together** tous ensemble **(b)** *(everything)* tout *m;* **that's a.** c'est tout; **he ate a. of it, he ate it a.** il a tout mangé; **a. I said was...** tout ce que j'ai dit, c'est...; **I did a. I could** j'ai fait tout ce que j'ai pu; **it was a. I could do not to laugh** j'ai bien failli rire; **best/worst of a., ...** le mieux/le pire, c'est que...; **I like this best of a.** c'est ça que je préfère; **most of a.** surtout, **when a. is said and done** au bout du compte; **it's a. the same to me** ça m'est égal; **thirty men in a.** trente hommes en tout *ou* au total; **a. in a.** dans l'ensemble; **it cost $260, a. in a.** ça a coûté 260 dollars tout compris; *Ironic* **it cost a. of $2** ça a coûté la coquette somme de 2 dollars
3 *adv* **(a)** *(entirely)* tout; **a. alone** tout(e) seul(e); **to be a. in black** être tout en noir; **to be a. for sth** être pour qch; **a. ears/smiles** tout ouïe/sourire; **I forgot a. about it** j'ai complètement oublié; **he's not a. bad** il n'a pas que de mauvais côtés; **a. over Spain/the world** dans toute l'Espagne/le monde entier; **a. over (the place)** partout; **a. too soon** trop tôt; **a. along** depuis le début; **a. but** *(almost)* presque, pratiquement; **it's/he's a. yours** il est à vous; *Fam* **a. in** *(exhausted)* crevé(e) **(b)** at a. *(in the slightest)* du tout; **do you know her at a.?** tu la connais?; **if it's at a. possible** si c'était possible; **not at a.** pas du tout; *(when thanked)* je t'en prie **(c)** *(with comparatives)* **a. the better/worse** d'autant mieux/plus mal; **a. the easier/faster** d'autant plus facile/ rapide **(d)** *(in games)* **2 a.** 2 partout; **4 (games) a.** *(in tennis)* 4 jeux partout; **15 a.** *(in tennis)* 15 partout **4** *n* **to give one's a.** se donner à fond
Allah ['ælə] *n* Allah
allay [ə'leɪ] *vt (doubts, suspicions)* dissiper; *(fear, pain)* soulager
all-clear ['ɔːl'klɪə(r)] *n (after air-raid)* (signal *m* de) fin *f* d'alerte; *Fig (for project)* feu *m* vert
allegation [ælɪ'geɪʃən] *n* allégation *f*
allege [ə'ledʒ] *vt* alléguer, prétendre, **it is alleged that...** on prétend que...
alleged [ə'ledʒd] *adj (thief, culprit)* présumé(e)
allegedly [ə'ledʒɪdlɪ] *adv* prétendument; **a. stole $500** il aurait volé 500 dollars
allegiance [ə'liːdʒəns] *n (to party, cause)* fidélité *f; (to king)* allégeance *f*
allegory ['ælɪgərɪ] *(pl* **allegories)** *n* allégorie *f*
all-embracing [ɔːlɪm'breɪsɪŋ] *adj (term, category)* large
allergic [ə'lɜːdʒɪk] *adj* allergique (to à)
allergy ['ælədʒɪ] *(pl* **allergies)** *n* allergie *f* (to à)
alleviate [ə'liːvɪeɪt] *vt* soulager, calmer
alley ['ælɪ] *(pl* **alleys)** *n (street)* ruelle *f;* **a. cat** chat *m* de gouttière
alleyway ['ælɪweɪ] *n (street)* ruelle *f*
alliance [ə'laɪəns] *n* alliance *f;* **to enter into an a. with sb** former une alliance avec qn
allied ['ælaɪd] *adj (countries)* allié(e); *(issues, phenomena)* lié(e)
alligator ['ælɪgeɪtə(r)] *n* alligator *m;* **a. shoes/handbag** chaussures *fpl*/sac *m* en crocodile

all-important ['ɔːlɪm'pɔːtənt] *adj* essentiel(elle), capital(e)

all-in ['ɔːlɪn] *adj (price)* tout compris; **a.** wrestling lutte *f* libre, catch *m*

alliteration [əlɪtə'reɪʃən] *n* allitération *f*

all-night ['ɔːlnaɪt] *adj (party, session)* qui dure toute la nuit

allocate ['æləkeɪt] *vt (resources, money)* affecter, attribuer (**to** à); *(duties)* assigner (**to** à); *(time)* prévoir (**to** pour)

allocation [ælə'keɪʃən] *n (distribution)* affectation *f*; *(share)* part *f*

allot [ə'lɒt] *(pt & pp* **allotted)** *vt (resources, money)* attribuer (**to** à); *(duties, job)* assigner (**to** à); **in the allotted time** dans le temps imparti

allotment [ə'lɒtmənt] *n* (**a**) *Br (land)* jardin *m* ouvrier (**b**) *(distribution) (of money)* affectation *f*; *(share)* part *f*

all-out ['ɔːl'laʊt] *adj (resistance, effort)* acharné(e); *(strike, war)* total(e)

allow [ə'laʊ] *vt* (**a**) *(permit)* permettre; **to a. sb to do sth** permettre à qn de faire qch; **a. me!** *(offering help)* permettez(-moi)!; **smoking is not allowed** il est interdit de fumer; **I'm not allowed to do it** je n'ai pas l'autorisation de le faire; **to a. oneself to be deceived/persuaded** se laisser abuser/convaincre (**b**) *(allocate, grant)* accorder; *(time)* compter, prévoir

▸ **allow for** *vt insep* tenir compte de; **add another hour to a. for delays** il faut prévoir une heure de plus au cas où il y aurait des retards

allowable [ə'laʊəbəl] *adj (error, delay)* admissible

allowance [ə'laʊəns] *n* (**a**) *(money given)* rente *f*, pension *f*; *(pocket money)* argent *m* de poche; **travel a.** indemnité *f* de transport (**b**) **to make a. for sth** tenir compte de qch; **I'm tired of making allowances for him** j'en ai assez de lui trouver des excuses

alloy ['ælɔɪ] *n* alliage *m*

all-powerful ['ɔːl'paʊəful] *adj* tout-puissant (toute-puissante)

all-purpose ['ɔːl'pɜːpəs] *adj* universel(elle); **a. cleaner/adhesive** détachant *m*/colle *f* tous usages

all right [ɔːl'raɪt] **1** *adj* **are you a.?** ça va?; **he was in a car crash but he's a.** il a eu un accident de voiture mais il n'a rien; **it's a.** *(acceptable)* ce n'est pas mal; *(not a problem)* ce n'est pas grave; **to be a. at math/French** se débrouiller en maths/français; *Br Fam* **she's a bit of a.!** elle est bien foutue!

2 *adv (yes)* oui; **is it a. if I smoke?** ça ne vous dérange pas si je fume?; **a., let's get started** bon, commençons

all-round ['ɔːl'raʊnd] *adj (education, improvement)* général(e); **an a. athlete** un athlète complet

all-rounder ['ɔːl'raʊndə(r)] *n* **she's a good a.** elle est bonne en tout

allspice ['ɔːlspaɪs] *n* poivre *m* de la Jamaïque

all-star ['ɔːl'stɑː(r)] *adj* **an a. cast** une distribution prestigieuse

all-time ['ɔːl'taɪm] *adj (record)* absolu(e); **unemployment has reached an a. high/low** le chômage n'a jamais été aussi élevé/bas

allude [ə'luːd] *vi* **to a.** to faire allusion à

allure [ə'lʊə(r)] *n* attrait *m*

allusion [ə'luːʒən] *n* allusion *f*; **to make an a. to sth** faire allusion à qch

ally 1 *n* ['ælaɪ] *(pl* **allies)** allié(e) *m,f*
2 *vt* [ə'laɪ] *(pt & pp* **allied) to a. oneself with** s'allier à *ou* avec

almanac ['ɔːlmənæk] *n* almanach *m*

almighty [ɔːl'maɪtɪ] **1** *n* **the A.** le Tout-Puissant
2 *adj Fam (fuss, row)* terrible

almond ['ɑːmənd] *n* amande *f*; **a. tree** amandier *m*

almost ['ɔːlməʊst] *adv* presque; **it's a. six o'clock** il est presque six heures; **we're a. there** *(in journey)* nous sommes presque arrivés; *(in task)* nous avons presque fini; **she a. missed the bus** elle a failli rater l'autobus

alms [ɑːmz] *npl* aumône *f*

aloft [ə'lɒft] *adv* en l'air

alone [ə'ləʊn] *adv & adj* seul(e); **to leave sb a.** laisser qn tranquille; **to leave sth a.** ne pas toucher à qch; **I did it a.** je l'ai fait tout seul; **to go it a.** faire cavalier seul; **we are not a. in thinking that...** nous ne sommes pas les seuls à penser que...; **you a. can help me** vous seul pouvez m'aider; **I can't afford a bicycle, let a. a car!** je n'ai pas assez d'argent pour m'acheter une bicyclette, encore moins une voiture!

along [ə'lɒŋ] **1** *prep* **le long de**; **to walk a. the shore** marcher le long de la côte; **to sail a. the coast** longer la côte; **I was walking a. the street** je marchais dans la rue; *Fig* **somewhere a. the way** à un moment donné
2 *adv* **to move a.** avancer; **she'll be a. in ten minutes** elle sera là dans dix minutes; **to bring sth a.** apporter qch; **to bring sb a.** amener qn; **he knew all a.** il le savait depuis le début; **a. with** *(as well as)* ainsi que

alongside [ə'lɒŋ'saɪd] *prep (next to)* à côté de; *(along)* le long de; *Naut* **to come a. a ship/quay** accoster un bateau/quai

aloof [ə'luːf] **1** *adj* distant(e)
2 *adv* **to remain a. (from sth)** rester à l'écart (de qch)

aloud [ə'laʊd] *adv* à haute voix; **I was thinking a.** je pensais tout haut

alpha ['ælfə] *n* alpha *m*; *Phys* **a. rays** rayons *mpl* alpha

alphabet ['ælfəbet] *n* alphabet *m*

alphabetical [ælfə'betɪkəl] *adj* alphabétique; **in a. order** dans l'ordre alphabétique

alphabetically [ælfə'betɪklɪ] *adv* alphabétiquement

Alpine ['ælpaɪn] *adj* alpin(e); **an A. village** un village des Alpes

Alps [ælps] *npl* **the A.** les Alpes *fpl*

already [ɔːl'redɪ] *adv* déjà; **have you finished a.?** vous avez déjà fini?

alright [ɔːl'raɪt] = **all right**

Alsatian [æl'seɪʃən] **1** *n (dog)* berger *m* allemand; *(person from Alsace)* Alsacien(enne) *m,f*
2 *adj* alsacien(enne)

also ['ɔːlsəʊ] *adv* aussi; **not only...but a....** non seulement... mais en plus...

also-ran ['ɔːlsəʊræn] *n (in horse race)* cheval *m* non classé; *Fig (person)* perdant(e) *m,f*

altar ['ɔːltə(r)] *n* autel *m*; **a. boy** enfant *m* de chœur

alter ['ɔːltə(r)] **1** *vt* changer; *(garment)* faire des retouches à; **he altered his opinion later** il a changé d'avis plus tard; **that doesn't a. the fact that...** cela ne change rien au fait que...
2 *vi* changer

alteration [ɔːltə'reɪʃən] *n (to design, plan)* modification *f*, changement *m*; *(to timetable)* changement; *(to garment)* retouche *f*

altercation [ɔːltə'keɪʃən] *n* altercation *f*

alter ego ['æltə'riːgəʊ] *n* alter ego *m*

alternate ['ɔːltəneɪt] **1** *adj* [ɔːl'tɜːnət] alterné(e); **on a. days** un jour sur deux
2 *vt* employer tour à tour
3 *vi* alterner (**with** avec)

alternately [ɔːl'tɜːnətlɪ] *adv* tour à tour, alternativement

alternating ['ɔ:ltəneɪtɪŋ] *adj* alterné(e); *Elec* **a. current** courant *m* alternatif

alternative [ɔ:l'tɜːnətɪv] **1** *n (choice)* choix *m*, solution *f*; **there is no a.** il n'y a pas le choix; **she had no a. but to obey** elle n'a pu faire autrement que d'obéir **2** *adj* **(a)** *(plan, route)* de remplacement; **an a. proposal** une contre-proposition **(b)** *(music, comedy)* alternatif(ive); **a. energy** énergies *fpl* de substitution; **a. medicine** médecine *f* douce

alternatively [ɔ:l'tɜːnətɪvlɪ] *adv (on the other hand)* ou bien

alternator ['ɔ:ltəneɪtə(r)] *n* alternateur *m*

although [ɔ:l'ðəʊ] *conj* bien que + *subjunctive*; **a. it's late** bien qu'il soit tard

altitude ['æltɪtjuːd] *n* altitude *f*

alto ['æltəʊ] *(pl* **altos)** *n (male voice)* haute-contre *f*; *(female voice)* contralto *m*; **a. clef** clef *f* d'ut; **a. saxophone** saxophone *m* ulto

altogether [ɔ:ltə'geðə(r)] **1** *adv* **(a)** *(entirely)* complètement; **I was not a. pleased** je n'étais pas ravi **(b)** *(in total)* en tout; **a. the bill came to $63** en tout l'addition s'élevait à 63 dollars **2** *n Br Fam* **in the a.** *(naked)* nu(e) comme un ver

altruism ['æltrʊɪzəm] *n* altruisme *m*

altruistic [æltrʊ'ɪstɪk] *adj* altruiste

aluminium [æljʊ'mɪnɪəm], *Am* **aluminum** [ə'luː-mɪnəm] *n* aluminium *m*; **a. foil** papier *m* d'aluminium

always ['ɔ:lweɪz] *adv* toujours; **I can a. try** je peux toujours essayer

AM ['eɪ'em] *n Rad (abbr* **amplitude modulation)** AM

am [æm] *1st pers singular of* **be**

a.m. ['eɪ'em] *adv (abbr* **ante meridiem)** du matin; **five a.m.** cinq heures du matin

amalgam [ə'mælgəm] *n* amalgame *m*

amalgamate [ə'mælgəmeɪt] **1** *vt (metals, ideas)* amalgamer; *(companies)* fusionner **2** *vi (of companies)* fusionner

amass [ə'mæs] *vt* amasser, accumuler

amateur ['æmətə(r)] **1** *n* amateur *m* **2** *adj (painter, musician)* amateur; *Pej (work, performance)* d'amateur

amateurish [æmə'tɜːrɪʃ] *adj Pej* d'amateur

amaze [ə'meɪz] *vt* stupéfier; **I was amazed by his courage** son courage m'a stupéfié

amazement [ə'meɪzmənt] *n* stupéfaction *f*, stupeur *f*; **in a.** avec stupéfaction ou stupeur; **to my a.** à ma stupéfaction

amazing [ə'meɪzɪŋ] *adj* **(a)** *(surprising)* stupéfiant(e); **it's a. that no one helped her** il est incroyable que personne ne lui soit venu en aide **(b)** *(excellent)* formidable

Amazon ['æməzən] *n* **(a) the A.** *(river)* l'Amazone *f*; *(region)* l'Amazonie *f* **(b)** *(female warrior)* Amazone *f*

ambassador [æm'bæsədə(r)] *n* ambassadeur(drice) *m,f*

amber ['æmbə(r)] **1** *n (colour, stone)* ambre *m*; *(of traffic light)* orange *m* **2** *adj (jewellery)* d'ambre; *(colour)* couleur d'ambre, ambré(e)

ambience, ambiance ['æmbɪəns] *n* ambiance *f*

ambiguity [æmbɪ'gjuːɪtɪ] *(pl* **ambiguities)** *n* ambiguïté *f*

ambiguous [æm'bɪgjʊəs] *adj* ambigu(ë)

ambition [æm'bɪʃən] *n* ambition *f*

ambitious [æm'bɪʃəs] *adj* ambitieux(euse)

ambivalent [æm'bɪvələnt] *adj* ambivalent(e)

amble ['æmbəl] *vi* marcher d'un pas tranquille

ambulance ['æmbjʊləns] *n* ambulance *f*; **a. man** ambulancier *m*; **a. woman** ambulancière *f*

ambush ['æmbʊʃ] **1** *n also Fig* embuscade *f* **2** *vt also Fig* tendre une embuscade à; **to be ambushed** tomber dans une embuscade

ameba *Am* = amoeba

amen ['ɑ:'men] *exclam* amen!, ainsi soit-il!

amenable [ə'miːnəbəl] *adj* souple; **to prove a. to a suggestion** approuver une proposition

amend [ə'mend] *vt (text, law)* modifier, amender; *(error)* corriger

amendment [ə'mendmənt] *n (to law, bill, constitution)* amendement *m*; **the Fifth A.** le cinquième amendement

amends [ə'mendz] *npl* **to make a. (for sth)** faire amende honorable (pour qch); **to make a. to sb for sth** dédommager qn de qch

amenities [ə'miːnɪtɪz] *npl (shops)* commerces *mpl*; *(facilities)* équipements *mpl* collectifs

America [ə'merɪkə] *n* l'Amérique *f*

American [ə'merɪkən] **1** *n* Américain(e) *m,f* **2** *adj* américain(e); **the A. Civil War** la guerre de Sécession; *Br* **A. football** football *m* américain; **A. Indian** Indien(enne) *m,f* d'Amérique

amethyst ['æmɪθɪst] *n* améthyste *f*

amiable ['eɪmɪəbəl] *adj* aimable

amicable ['æmɪkəbəl] *adj* amical(e); **an a. agreement** un arrangement à l'amiable

amid [ə'mɪd], **amidst** [ə'mɪdst] *prep* au milieu de

amino acid [æ'miːnəʊ'æsɪd] *n* acide *m* aminé

amiss [ə'mɪs] *adv* & *adj* **there's something a.** il y a quelque chose qui ne va pas; **to take sth a.** prendre qch de travers, mal prendre qch; **a cup of coffee wouldn't go a.** une tasse de café serait bienvenue

ammeter ['æmiːtə(r)] *n Elec* ampèremètre *m*

ammonia [ə'məʊnɪə] *n* ammoniac *m*

ammunition [æmjʊ'nɪʃən] *n (for guns)* munitions *fpl*; *Fig (in debate, argument)* arguments *mpl*

amnesia [æm'niːzɪə] *n* amnésie *f*

amnesty ['æmnɪstɪ] *(pl* **amnesties)** *n* amnistie *f*

amoeba, *Am* **ameba** [ə'miːbə] *n* amibe *f*

amok [ə'mɒk] *adv* **to run a.** être pris(e) de folie furieuse

among [ə'mʌŋ], **amongst** [ə'mʌŋst] *prep* parmi; **a. the crowd** au milieu de la foule; **we are a. friends** nous sommes entre amis; **they quarrel a. themselves** ils se disputent entre eux; **the money was divided a. them** l'argent a été divisé entre eux; **a. the best** parmi les meilleurs; **a. other things** entre autres choses

amoral [eɪ'mɒrəl] *adj* amoral(e)

amorphous [ə'mɔːfəs] *adj (mass, lump)* informe; *(ideas, beliefs)* confus(e)

amount [ə'maʊnt] **1** *n* **(a)** *(sum of money)* somme *f* **(b)** *(quantity)* quantité *f*; **a huge a. of time/effort** énormément de temps/d'énergie; **a certain a. of discomfort** un certain manque de confort; **in large amounts** en grande quantité; **in small amounts** en petites quantités

▸ **amount to** *vt insep* **(a)** *(add up to)* s'élever à; **her debts a. to $700** ses dettes s'élèvent à 700 dollars **(b)** *(mean)* it amounts to the same thing cela revient au même; *Fig* **he'll never a. to much** il n'arrivera jamais à rien

amp [æmp] *n* **(a)** *Elec (unit)* ampère *m*; **a 13-a. plug** une prise de 13 ampères **(b)** *Fam (amplifier)* ampli *m*

ampere ['æmpeə(r)] *n Elec* ampère *m*

ampersand ['æmpəsænd] *n* esperluette *f*

amphetamine [æm'fetəmɪn] *n* amphétamine *f*

amphibian [æm'fɪbɪən] **1** n amphibie m
2 adj amphibie
amphibious [æm'fɪbɪəs] adj amphibie
amphitheatre, Am **amphitheater** ['æmfɪθɪətə(r)]
n amphithéâtre m
ample ['æmpəl] adj **(a)** (large) (woman, bosom) fort(e) **(b)**
(plentiful) abondant(e); **to have a.** time **to do sth** avoir
largement le temps de faire qch; **to have a.** opportunity **to
do sth** avoir tout loisir de faire qch; **this will be a.** ce sera
largement suffisant
amplifier ['æmplɪfaɪə(r)] n amplificateur m
amplify ['æmplɪfaɪ] (pt & pp **amplified**) vt (essay,
remarks) développer; (current, volume) amplifier
amputate ['æmpjʊteɪt] vt amputer
amputation [æmpjʊ'teɪʃən] n amputation f
Amsterdam [æmstə'dæm] n Amsterdam
amuck [ə'mʌk] = **amok**
amulet ['æmjʊlet] n amulette f
amuse [ə'mjuːz] vt **(a)** (make laugh) amuser **(b)** (occupy)
occuper; **to a.** oneself by doing **sth** se distraire en faisant
qch; **to keep sb amused** distraire qn
amusement [ə'mjuːzmənt] n **(a)** (enjoyment) amusement
m; **much to everyone's a.** au grand amusement de tous **(b)**
(pastime) distraction f; **a.** arcade galerie f de jeux; **a. park**
parc m d'attractions
amusing [ə'mjuːzɪŋ] adj amusant(e)
an [ən, stressed æn] see **a²**
anabolic steroid [ænə'bɒlɪk'sterɔɪd] n stéroïde m
anabolisant
anachronism [ə'nækrənɪzəm] n anachronisme m
anaconda [ænə'kɒndə] n anaconda m
anaemia, Am **anemia** [ə'niːmɪə] n anémie f
anaemic, Am **anemic** [ə'niːmɪk] adj anémique
anaesthetic, Am **anesthetic** [ænəs'θetɪk] n
(substance) anesthésique m; (process) anesthésie f; **under
a.** sous anesthésie; **local/general a.** anesthésie locale/
générale
anaesthetist, Am **anesthetist** [ə'niːsθətɪst] n
anesthésiste mf
anaesthetize, Am **anesthetize** [ə'niːsθətaɪz] vt
anesthésier
anagram ['ænəgræm] n anagramme f
anal ['eɪnəl] adj anal(e)
analgesic [ænəl'dʒiːzɪk] **1** n analgésique m
2 adj analgésique
analog Am = **analogue**
analogous [ə'næləgəs] adj analogue (**to** à)
analogue, Am **analog** ['ænəlɒg] n analogue m; **a.
clock** horloge f à affichage analogique
analogy [ə'nælədʒɪ] (pl **analogies**) n analogie f
analyse, Am **analyze** ['ænəlaɪz] vt analyser; Psy
psychanalyser
analysis [ə'næləsɪs] (pl **analyses** [ə'næləsiːz]) n analyse f;
Psy psychanalyse f; Fig **in the final a.** en fin de compte, au
bout du compte
analyst ['ænəlɪst] n analyste mf; Psy (psych)analyste mf
analytic(al) [ænə'lɪtɪk(əl)] adj analytique
analyze Am = **analyse**
anarchist ['ænəkɪst] n anarchiste mf
anarchy ['ænəkɪ] n anarchie f
anathema [ə'næθəmə] n **(a)** Rel anathème m **(b)**
(repellent) **the very idea was a. to her** l'idée même lui
faisait horreur

anatomical [ænə'tɒmɪkəl] adj anatomique
anatomy [ə'nætəmɪ] n anatomie f
ANC [eɪen'siː] n (abbr **African National Congress**) ANC m
ancestor ['ænsestə(r)] n ancêtre mf
ancestral [æn'sestrəl] adj ancestral(e); **a. home** demeure
f ancestrale
ancestry ['ænsestrɪ] n (descent) ascendance f
anchor ['æŋkə(r)] **1** n Naut ancre f; Fig planche f de salut;
at a. au mouillage; **to drop a.** jeter l'ancre; **to weigh a.**
lever l'ancre
2 vt **(a)** Naut ancrer **(b)** (fix securely) ancrer (**to** à) **(c)** (radio,
TV programme) présenter
3 vi Naut jeter l'ancre
anchorman ['æŋkəmən] n (of radio, TV programme)
présentateur m principal
anchorwoman ['æŋkəwʊmən] n (of radio, TV programme) présentatrice f principale
anchovy ['æntʃəvɪ] (pl **anchovies**) n anchois m
ancient ['eɪnʃənt] **1** adj ancien(enne); Fig (person, car)
très vieux (vieille); **a. history** histoire f ancienne; **A. Rome**
la Rome antique
2 n **the ancients** les anciens mpl
ancillary [æn'sɪlərɪ] adj auxiliaire
and [ænd, unstressed ənd, ən] conj **(a)** (in general) et; **she
can read a. write** elle sait lire et écrire; **my brother a.
sister** mon frère et ma sœur; **a vodka a. orange** une vodka
orange; **do that again a. I'll hit you!** si tu recommences, je
te frappe!; **wait a. see** tu verras bien; **nice a. warm** bien
chaud(e)
(b) (to) go **a. look for it** va le chercher; **come a. see me**
viens me voir; **try a. help me** essaie de m'aider
(c) (in numbers) **two hundred a. two** deux cent deux;
four a. a half quatre et demi; **an hour a. twenty minutes**
une heure vingt; **four a. five make nine** quatre et ou plus
cinq font neuf
(d) (expressing repetition) **hours a. hours** pendant des
heures et des heures; **better a. better** de mieux en mieux;
smaller a. smaller de plus en plus petit(e); **she talked a.
talked** elle n'arrêtait pas de parler
(e) a. so on a. so forth et ainsi de suite
Andalusia [ændə'luːsɪə] n l'Andalousie f
Andes ['ændiːz] npl **the A.** les Andes fpl
Andorra [æn'dɔːrə] n l'Andorre f
Andorran [æn'dɔːrən] **1** n Andorran(e) m,f
2 adj andorran(e)
anecdotal [ænɪk'dəʊtəl] adj anecdotique
anecdote ['ænɪkdəʊt] n anecdote f
anemia, anemic Am = **anaemia, anaemic**
anemone [ə'nemənɪ] n (flower) anémone f; **sea a.**
anémone de mer
anesthetic, anesthetist etc Am = **anaesthetic,
anaesthetist** etc
anew [ə'njuː] adv encore, de nouveau; **to start a.**
recommencer
angel ['eɪndʒəl] n ange m; Fam **you're an a.!** tu es un
ange!
Angeleno [ændʒə'liːnəʊ] (pl **Angelenos**) n = personne
née à ou habitant Los Angeles
angelic [æn'dʒelɪk] adj angélique
anger ['æŋgə(r)] **1** n colère f; **a fit of a.** un accès de colère;
to speak in a. parler sous le coup de la colère
2 vt mettre en colère
3 vi **to be slow/quick to a.** ne pas se mettre facilement/se
mettre en colère
angina [æn'dʒaɪnə] n angine f de poitrine

angle ['æŋgəl] **1** n (a) Math angle m (b) (viewpoint) point m de vue; **seen from this a.** vu sous cet angle **2** vi (a) (fish) pêcher à la ligne (b) Br Fam **to a. for an invitation** chercher à se faire inviter
angler ['æŋglə(r)] n (person) pêcheur(euse) m,f à la ligne; **a. fish** baudroie f, lotte f de mer
Anglican ['æŋglɪkən] n & adj anglican(e) m,f
angling ['æŋglɪŋ] n (fishing) pêche f à la ligne
Anglo-American ['æŋgləʊə'merɪkən] adj anglo-américain(e)
Anglo-Saxon ['æŋgləʊ'sæksən] **1** n (a) (person) Anglo-Saxon(onne) m,f (b) (language) anglo-saxon m **2** adj anglo-saxon(onne)
Angola [æŋ'gəʊlə] n l'Angola m
Angolan [æŋ'gəʊlən] **1** n Angolais(e) m,f **2** adj angolais(e)
angora [æŋ'gɔːrə] n angora m; **a. sweater** pull m en angora
angrily ['æŋgrɪlɪ] adv avec colère
angry ['æŋgrɪ] adj (person) en colère, fâché(e); (voice, speech, letter) furieux(euse); **to get a. (at or with)** se fâcher (contre), se mettre en colère (contre); **to make sb a.** mettre qn en colère
anguish ['æŋgwɪʃ] n angoisse f
anguished ['æŋgwɪʃt] adj (look, cry) d'angoisse
angular ['æŋgjʊlə(r)] adj anguleux(euse)
animal ['ænɪməl] n animal m; **the a. kingdom** le règne animal; **a. rights** les droits mpl des animaux; **he's an a.** (uncivilized person) c'est une brute
animate 1 adj ['ænɪmɪt] animé(e) **2** vt ['ænɪmeɪt] animer
animated ['ænɪmeɪtɪd] adj (expression, discussion) animé(e); **to become a.** s'animer; **a. cartoon** dessin m animé
animation [ænɪ'meɪʃən] n animation f
animator ['ænɪmeɪtə(r)] n Cin animateur(trice) m,f
animism ['ænɪmɪzəm] n animisme m
animosity [ænɪ'mɒsɪtɪ] n animosité f
aniseed ['ænɪsiːd] n (flavour) anis m; (seed) graine f d'anis
Ankara ['æŋkərə] n Ankara
ankle ['æŋkəl] n cheville f; **a. boots** chaussures fpl montantes; **a. socks** socquettes fpl
anklet ['æŋklət] n (ankle bracelet) bracelet m de cheville
annals ['ænəlz] npl annales fpl
annex 1 vt [æ'neks] annexer **2** n ['æneks] Am = annexe
annexation [ænek'seɪʃən] n annexion f
annexe, Am annex ['æneks] n (of building, document) annexe f
annihilate [ə'naɪəleɪt] vt anéantir
annihilation [ənaɪə'leɪʃən] n anéantissement m
anniversary [ænɪ'vɜːsərɪ] (pl **anniversaries**) n anniversaire m; **wedding a.** anniversaire de mariage
anno Domini ['ænəʊ'dɒmɪnaɪ] adv en l'an de grâce
annotate ['ænəteɪt] vt annoter
announce [ə'naʊns] vt annoncer
announcement [ə'naʊnsmənt] n (of news) annonce f; (formal statement) avis m
announcer [ə'naʊnsə(r)] n (on radio, TV programme) annonceur(euse) m,f, speaker (speakerine) m,f
annoy [ə'nɔɪ] vt agacer; **to get annoyed** se mettre en colère, se fâcher; **to be annoyed with sb** être en colère contre qn

annoyance [ə'nɔɪəns] n (feeling) agacement m; (annoying thing) ennui m
annoying [ə'nɔɪɪŋ] adj agaçant(e), ennuyeux(euse); **how a.!** comme c'est ennuyeux!
annual ['ænjʊəl] **1** n (a) (plant) plante f annuelle (b) (book) publication f annuelle; (for children) album m (publié une fois par an) **2** adj annuel(elle); **a. general meeting** assemblée f générale annuelle
annually ['ænjʊəlɪ] adv (every year) tous les ans; (per year) par an
annul [ə'nʌl] (pt & pp **annulled**) vt Law (contract, marriage) annuler
anode ['ænəʊd] n anode f
anodyne ['ænədaɪn] adj (bland) anodin(e)
anoint [ə'nɔɪnt] vt oindre (with de)
anomalous [ə'nɒmələs] adj anormal(e)
anomaly [ə'nɒmələ] (pl **anomalies**) n anomalie f
anon¹ [ə'nɒn] adv Lit (soon) bientôt
anon² adj (abbr **anonymous**) anonyme
anonymity [ænə'nɪmɪtɪ] n anonymat m
anonymous [ə'nɒnɪməs] adj anonyme; **to remain a.** garder l'anonymat
anorak ['ænəræk] n anorak m
anorexia [ænə'reksɪə] n anorexie f; **a. nervosa** anorexie mentale
anorexic [ænə'reksɪk] adj anorexique
another [ə'nʌðə(r)] adj & pron (a) (additional) un (une) autre m,f; **a. cup of coffee** une autre tasse de café; **in a. ten years** dans dix ans; **don't say a. word** plus un mot; **a. Picasso/Vietnam** un nouveau Picasso/Viêt Nam (b) (different) un (une) autre m,f; **that's quite a. matter** c'est une tout autre affaire; **a. time, perhaps** (declining invitation) une autre fois, peut-être; **what with one thing and a., I forgot** c'est que s'est passé, j'ai oublié; **one way or a.** d'une façon ou d'une autre (c) (reciprocal) **they saw one a.** ils se sont vus
answer ['ɑːnsə(r)] **1** n (to question, letter) réponse f; (to problem) solution f; **I knocked but there was no a.** j'ai frappé mais personne n'a répondu; **there's no a.** (on telephone) ça ne répond pas; **he has an a. to everything** il a réponse à tout; Formal **in a. to your letter** en réponse à votre lettre **2** vt (person, question) répondre à; **"I'll do it tomorrow," he answered** "je le ferai demain", a-t-il répondu; **to a. the telephone** répondre au téléphone; **to a. the door** ouvrir (la porte) **3** vi (of person) répondre
▸ **answer back** vi (be impertinent) répondre
▸ **answer for** vt insep répondre de; **he has a lot to a.** il a beaucoup de comptes à rendre
▸ **answer to** vt insep (a) (be accountable to) **to a. to sb** être responsable devant qn; **she answers to no one** elle n'a de comptes à rendre à personne (b) (correspond to) (description) répondre à (c) **the dog answers to the name of Rover** le chien répond au nom de Rover
answerable ['ɑːnsərəbəl] adj **to be a. to sb** être responsable devant qn; **he is a. to nobody** il n'a de comptes à rendre à personne
answering machine ['ɑːnsərɪŋməʃiːn], **answerphone** ['ɑːnsəfəʊn] n (téléphonique)
ant [ænt] n fourmi f; **a. hill** fourmilière f
antagonism [æn'tægənɪzəm] n antagonisme m
antagonist [æn'tægənɪst] n antagoniste mf
antagonize [æn'tægənaɪz] vt rendre hostile
Antarctica [æn'tɑːktɪkə] n l'Antarctique m

ante ['æntɪ] *n Fam* **to up the a.** *(in gambling, conflict)* augmenter la mise

anteater ['ænti:tə(r)] *n* fourmilier *m*

antecedents [æntɪ'si:dəns] *npl* antécédents *mpl*

antelope ['æntɪləʊp] *n* antilope *f*

antenatal [æntɪ'neɪtəl] *adj* prénatal(e); **a. class** cours *m* de préparation à l'accouchement

antenna [æn'tenə] *n* (a) *(pl* **antennae** [æn'teni:]) *(of insect, snail)* antenne *f* (b) *(pl* **antennas**) *(of radio, TV)* antenne *f*

anteroom ['æntɪru:m] *n* antichambre *f*

anthem ['ænθəm] *n* hymne *m*; **national a.** hymne national

anthology [æn'θɒlədʒɪ] *(pl* **anthologies**) *n* anthologie *f*

anthracite ['ænθrəsaɪt] *n* anthracite *m*

anthrax ['ænθræks] *n (disease)* anthrax *m*

anthropologist [ænθrə'pɒlədʒɪst] *n* anthropologue *mf*

anthropology [ænθrə'pɒlədʒɪ] *n* anthropologie *f*

anti- ['æntɪ] *pref* anti-

anti-aircraft ['æntɪ'eəkrɑ:ft] *adj (gun, defences)* antiaérien(enne)

antibiotic [æntɪbaɪ'ɒtɪk] *n* antibiotique *m*

antibody ['æntɪbɒdɪ] *(pl* **antibodies**) *n Med* anticorps *m*

Antichrist ['æntɪkraɪst] *n* Antéchrist *m*

anticipate [æn'tɪsɪpeɪt] *vt* (a) *(expect)* prévoir, s'attendre à; *(foresee)* anticiper; **we hadn't anticipated such stiff resistance** nous ne nous attendions pas à une telle résistance; **as anticipated, there was trouble** comme on s'y attendait, il y eut des problèmes (b) *(foreshadow)* préfigurer, annoncer

anticipation [æntɪsɪ'peɪʃən] *n* (a) *(foresight)* prévoyance *f*; **in a. of trouble** en prévision de troubles; **thanking you in a.** en vous remerciant d'avance, avec mes remerciements anticipés (b) *(eagerness)* impatience *f*

anticlimax [æntɪ'klaɪmæks] *n* déception *f*

anti-clockwise [æntɪ'klɒkwaɪz] *Br* **1** *adj* **in an a. direction** dans le sens inverse des aiguilles d'une montre **2** *adv* dans le sens inverse des aiguilles d'une montre

antics [æntɪks] *npl* bouffonneries *fpl*; **he's been up to his usual a.** il a encore fait des siennes

anticyclone [æntɪ'saɪkləʊn] *n Met* anticyclone *m*

antidepressant [æntɪdɪ'presənt] *n* antidépresseur *m*

antidote ['æntɪdəʊt] *n also Fig* antidote *m* (**to** contre)

antifreeze ['æntɪfri:z] *n* antigel *m*

Antigua and Barbuda [æn'ti:gənbɑ:'bju:də] *n* Antigua-et-Barbuda

antipathy [æn'tɪpəθɪ] *n* antipathie *f* (**towards** pour)

antiperspirant [æntɪ'pɜ:spɪrənt] *n* déodorant *m*

Antipodes [æn'tɪpədi:z] *npl* **the A.** l'Australie *f* et la Nouvelle-Zélande

antiquarian [æntɪ'kweərɪən] **1** *n (dealer)* antiquaire *mf*; *(collector)* collectionneur(euse) *m,f* d'antiquités **2** *adj (book)* ancien(enne); **a. bookshop** = librairie spécialisée dans les livres anciens

antiquated ['æntɪkweɪtɪd] *adj* vieillot(otte)

antique [æn'ti:k] **1** *n* antiquité *f*; **a. dealer** antiquaire *mf*; **a. shop** magasin *m* d'antiquités **2** *adj* antique; **a. furniture** meubles *mpl* anciens

antiquity [æn'tɪkwɪtɪ] *(pl* **antiquities**) *n (historical period, ruin)* antiquité *f*

antiracist [æntɪ'reɪsɪst] *adj* antiraciste

anti-Semitic [æntɪsɪ'mɪtɪk] *adj* antisémite

antiseptic [æntɪ'septɪk] **1** *n* antiseptique *m* **2** *adj* (a) *(anti-bacterial)* antiseptique (b) *Fig (lacking character or warmth) (place)* aseptisé(e); *(person)* froid(e)

antisocial [æntɪ'səʊʃəl] *adj* (a) *(disruptive)* asocial(e) (b) *(unsociable)* peu sociable

antithesis [æn'tɪθɪsɪs] *(pl* **antitheses** [æn'tɪθɪsi:z]) *n (opposite)* opposé *m*

antlers ['æntləz] *npl* bois *mpl*

antonym ['æntənɪm] *n* antonyme *m*

Antwerp ['æntwɜ:p] *n* Anvers

anus ['eɪnəs] *n* anus *m*

anvil ['ænvɪl] *n* enclume *f*

anxiety [æŋ'zaɪətɪ] *(pl* **anxieties**) *n* (a) *(worry, concern)* inquiétude *f*; *(stronger)* anxiété *f*; **my main a. is...** mon principal souci est...; **there is no cause for a.** il n'y a pas de quoi s'inquiéter; **to feel a.** être anxieux(euse) (b) *(eagerness)* désir *m*, souci *m*; **in her a. to help** dans son désir ou souci de se rendre utile

anxious ['æŋkʃəs] *adj* (a) *(worried)* inquiet(ète); *(stronger)* anxieux(euse); **to be a. for sb** être inquiet ou s'inquiéter pour qn; **to be a. about sth** être inquiet ou s'inquiéter pour qch (b) *(worrying) (moment)* d'angoisse; *(period)* angoissant(e) (c) **to be a. to do sth** *(impatient)* être impatient(e) de faire qch; *(eager)* tenir à faire qch

anxiously ['æŋkʃəslɪ] *adv* (a) *(worriedly)* avec inquiétude; *(stronger)* anxieusement (b) *(with impatience)* impatiemment, avec impatience

any ['enɪ] **1** *pron* (a) *(some)* **have you got a.?** en avez-vous?; **is/are there a. left?** en reste-t-il?; **can a. of them speak English?** y en a-t-il parmi eux qui parlent anglais?
(b) *(in negatives)* **I haven't got a.** je n'en ai pas; **there was nothing in a. of the boxes** il n'y avait rien dans aucune des boîtes; **few, if a., can read** aucun, ou presque aucun, ne sait lire
(c) *(no particular one)* n'importe lequel (laquelle) *m,f*; **a. of them** n'importe lequel d'entre eux
(d) *(every one)* tous ceux (toutes celles) *mpl, fpl*; **keep a. you find** garde tous ceux que tu trouveras
2 *adj* (a) *(some) (singular)* du (de la); *(plural)* des; **have you a. milk/flour/apples?** avez-vous du lait/de la farine/des pommes?
(b) *(in negatives)* **he hasn't a. money** il n'a pas d'argent; **without a. doubt** sans aucun doute; **that won't do a. good** ça ne servira à rien
(c) *(no particular)* n'importe quel (quelle); **come a. day** venez n'importe quel jour; **a. minute now** d'une minute à l'autre
(d) *(every)* tout(e); **a. pupil who forgets his books will be punished** tout élève qui oubliera ses livres sera puni; **at a. rate, in a. case** en tout cas
3 *adv* (a) *(with comparative)* **does that make it a. easier?** est-ce que c'est plus facile comme ça?; **we don't see them a. longer or more** nous ne les voyons plus; **do you want a. more tea?** veux-tu encore du thé?; **I don't like her a. more than you do** je ne l'aime pas plus que toi
(b) *Fam* **a. old how** n'importe comment; **that didn't help us a.** ça ne nous a été d'aucun secours

anybody ['enɪbɒdɪ] *pron* (a) *(indeterminate)* quelqu'un; **would a. like some more cake?** quelqu'un veut-il encore du gâteau?; **she'll know if a. does** si quelqu'un doit le savoir, c'est bien elle
(b) *(in negatives)* **not a.** ne... personne; **there isn't a. here** il n'y a personne ici; **there was hardly a.** il n'y avait presque personne
(c) *(no matter who)* n'importe qui; **a. will tell you so** n'importe qui ou tout le monde vous le dira; **bring along a. you like** amenez qui vous voudrez; **a. else** ou but her would have refused tout autre qu'elle aurait refusé; **it's a.'s guess** Dieu seul le sait; **he's not just a.!** ce n'est pas n'importe qui!

(d) *(person with status)* **he'll never be a.** il ne fera jamais rien dans la vie

anyhow ['enɪhaʊ] *adv* (a) *(however)* de toute façon *ou* manière; **a., let's get back to what we were saying** bref, revenons à ce que nous disions; **I don't care, I'm going a.** ça m'est égal, j'y vais quand même (b) *Fam (carelessly)* n'importe comment

anyone ['enɪwʌn] = **anybody**

anyplace ['enɪpleɪs] *Am* = **anywhere**

anything ['enɪθɪŋ] **1** *pron* (a) *(indeterminate)* quelque chose; **is there a. I can do?** est-ce que je peux faire quelque chose?; **have you a. to write with?** as-tu de quoi écrire?; **will there be a. else?** *(in shop)* et avec ça?; **have you a. smaller?** avez-vous quelque chose de plus petit?; *(money)* vous n'avez pas plus petit?; **if a. should happen to me** s'il m'arrivait quelque chose *ou* quoi que ce soit; **is (there) a. wrong?** il y a quelque chose qui ne va pas? (b) *(in negatives)* **not a.** ne… rien; **he doesn't do a.** il ne fait rien; **hardly a.** presque rien

(c) *(no matter what)* n'importe quoi; **he eats a.** il mange de tout; **I love a. French** j'aime tout ce qui est français; **she would do a. for me** elle ferait n'importe quoi pour moi; **he was a. but friendly** il était tout sauf amical; **are you angry? – a. but** tu es fâché? – non, loin de là

2 *adv* **is it a. like the other one?** est-ce qu'il ressemble un peu à l'autre ou pas du tout?; **she doesn't look a. like her sister** elle ne ressemble pas du tout à sa sœur; **the food wasn't a. like as bad as they said** la nourriture était loin d'être aussi mauvaise que ce qu'on m'avait dit; *Fam* **as funny/strong as a.** drôle/fort(e) comme tout; *Fam* **it's not that you're wrong or a.** ce n'est pas que tu aies tort

anyway ['enɪweɪ] = **anyhow** (a)

anywhere ['enɪweə(r)] *adv* (a) *(in questions)* quelque part; **did you go a. yesterday?** êtes-vous allé quelque part hier?; **can you see it a.?** tu le vois? (b) *(in negatives)* **not a.** ne… nulle part; **I can't find it a.** je ne le trouve nulle part; **we're not getting a.** nous n'avançons pas; **he isn't a. near as clever as her** il est loin d'être aussi intelligent qu'elle (c) *(no matter where)* n'importe où; **put it a.** mets-le n'importe où; **I'd know her a.** je la reconnaîtrais entre mille; **it's miles from a.** c'est loin de tout; **a. else** n'importe où

AO(C)B [eɪəʊ(siː)'biː] *(abbr* any other (competent) business) *(in business meeting)* divers

aorta [eɪ'ɔːtə] *n* aorte *f*

apart [ə'pɑːt] *adv* (a) *(at a distance)* à l'écart **(from** de); **to stand a.** *(of person)* se tenir à l'écart; **the garage stands a. from the house** le garage est séparé de la maison (b) *(separated)* **they are far a.** ils sont éloignés l'un de l'autre; **the two towns are 10 kilometres a.** les deux villes sont à 10 kilomètres l'une de l'autre; **they're never a.** ils ne se séparent jamais; **with one's legs a.** les jambes écartées; **two years a.** à deux ans d'intervalle; **to set sth a. for sth** réserver qch à qch; **to live a.** vivre séparément; **it's difficult to tell them a.** il est difficile de les distinguer l'un de l'autre; **joking a., …** blague à part, … (c) *(to pieces)* **to take sth a.** *(machine)* démonter qch; **to come a.** *(of garment)* se découdre (d) *(excepting)* **a. from** à part; **a. from the fact that…** indépendamment du fait que…

apartheid [ə'pɑːtaɪt] *n* apartheid *m*

apartment [ə'pɑːtmənt] *n Am* appartement *m*; **a. building** immeuble *m* d'habitation

apathetic [æpə'θetɪk] *adj* qui manque d'enthousiasme; **to be a. about sth** être indifférent(e) à qch

apathy ['æpəθɪ] *n* manque *m* d'enthousiasme

ape [eɪp] **1** *n (animal)* grand singe *m*; *Fam* **to go a.** piquer une crise **2** *vt (imitate)* singer

aperitif [əperɪ'tiːf] *n* apéritif *m*

aperture ['æpətjʊə(r)] *n* ouverture *f*

apex ['eɪpeks] *n* sommet *m*

aphasia [ə'feɪzɪə] *n Med* aphasie *f*

aphid ['eɪfɪd] *n* puceron *m*

aphorism ['æfərɪzəm] *n* aphorisme *m*

aphrodisiac [æfrəʊ'dɪzɪæk] **1** *n* aphrodisiaque *m* **2** *adj* aphrodisiaque

apiece [ə'piːs] *adv* chacun(e); **they cost $3 a.** ils valent 3 dollars pièce *ou* chacun

aplenty [ə'plentɪ] *adv* en abondance

aplomb [ə'plɒm] *n* sang-froid *m*

apocalypse [ə'pɒkəlɪps] *n* apocalypse *f*

apocalyptic [əpɒkə'lɪptɪk] *adj* apocalyptique

apolitical [eɪpə'lɪtɪkəl] *adj* apolitique

apologetic [əpɒlə'dʒetɪk] *adj (tone, smile)* désolé(e); **to be a. about sth** s'excuser de qch; **she was quite a. about it** elle s'est répandue en excuses

apologize [ə'pɒlədʒaɪz] *vi* s'excuser; **to a. to sb for sth** s'excuser de qch auprès de qn, présenter ses excuses à qn pour qch; **she apologized for being late/for not telling him earlier** elle s'est excusée d'être en retard/de ne pas le lui avoir dit plus tôt

apology [ə'pɒlədʒɪ] *(pl* **apologies)** *n* excuses *fpl*; **to make/offer an a.** faire/présenter des excuses; **I owe you an a.** je vous dois des excuses; *Pej* **an a. for a dinner** un semblant de dîner

apoplectic [æpə'plektɪk] *adj Fig (angry)* furieux(euse); **to be a. with rage** s'étrangler de rage

apoplexy ['æpəpleksɪ] *n Med* apoplexie *f; Fig (anger)* rage *f*

apostle [ə'pɒsəl] *n* apôtre *m*

apostolic(al) [æpɒs'tɒlɪk(əl)] *adj* apostolique

apostrophe [ə'pɒstrəfɪ] *n* apostrophe *f*

appal, *Am* **appall** [ə'pɔːl] *(pt & pp* **appalled)** *vt (shock)* choquer, scandaliser; *(fill with horror)* horrifier; **to be appalled at *or* by sth** être choqué(e)/horrifié(e) par qch; **it appals me to think that…** je suis horrifié(e) à la pensée que…

appalling [ə'pɔːlɪŋ] *adj (behaviour)* scandaleux(euse); *(conditions, smell, weather, film)* épouvantable

apparatus [æpə'reɪtəs] *n (machine)* appareil *m*; *(set of machines, in laboratory)* équipement *m*; *(in gym)* agrès *mpl*; **a piece of a.** un appareil

apparel [ə'pærəl] *n Am (clothes)* vêtements *mpl*; *(industry)* confection *f*

apparent [ə'pærənt] *adj* (a) *(obvious)* clair(e), évident(e); **it soon became a. that…** il est vite devenu évident que… (b) *(seeming)* apparent(e)

apparently [ə'pærəntlɪ] *adv* apparemment; **a. he's going to Venice** il paraît qu'il va à Venise

apparition [æpə'rɪʃən] *n* apparition *f*

appeal [ə'piːl] **1** *n* (a) *(call)* appel *m* **(for** à); **to make an a. for help** lancer un appel à l'aide; **charity a.** = appel aux dons lancé par une organisation caritative (b) *Law* appel *m*; **on a.** en seconde instance; **A. Court, Court of A.** cour *f* d'appel (c) *(attraction)* attrait *m*; **to have great a.** *(of idea)* être très attrayant(e); *(of person)* avoir beaucoup de charme; **their music has a wide a.** leur musique attire un public très varié

2 *vt Law* **to a. a decision** faire appel d'une décision

3 *vi* (a) *(make a plea)* **to a. (to sb) for help/money**

demander de l'aide/de l'argent (à qn); **to a. to sb's generosity** faire appel à la générosité de qn (**b**) **to a. to sb** *(attract)* attirer qn (**c**) *Law* se pourvoir en appel; **to a. against a decision** faire appel d'une décision

appealing [ə'piːlɪŋ] *adj (idea)* séduisant(e); *(person, manner)* sympathique

appear [ə'pɪə(r)] *vi* (**a**) *(come into view)* apparaître; *(of publication)* paraître; **where did you a. from?** d'où sors-tu?; **to a. out of nowhere** sortir de nulle part; **to a. on TV** passer à la télé (**b**) *Law* comparaître (**c**) *(look, seem)* sembler; **to a. to be lost** avoir l'air d'être perdu(e); **there appears to be a mistake** il semble qu'il y ait une erreur; **so it would a.** c'est ce qu'on dirait

appearance [ə'pɪərəns] *n* (**a**) *(arrival)* apparition *f,* arrivée *f;* **to put in an a.** faire acte de présence (**b**) *(of actor)* **to make a television a.** passer à la télévision (**c**) *(of publication)* parution *f* (**d**) *Law (in court)* comparution *f* (**e**) *(looks, demeanour)* apparence *f;* **it's wrong to judge by appearances** il ne faut pas se fier aux apparences; **to keep up appearances** sauver les apparences

appease [ə'piːz] *vt (anger, person)* apaiser, calmer; *Pol* composer avec

appeasement [ə'piːzmənt] *n (of person, anger)* apaisement *m; Pol* conciliation *f*

append [ə'pend] *vt (list, document)* joindre (**to** à); *(one's signature)* apposer (**to** à)

appendage [ə'pendɪdʒ] *n* appendice *m;* **she was tired of being treated as her husband's a.** elle en avait assez de n'être traitée que comme la femme de son mari

appendicitis [əpendɪ'saɪtɪs] *n* appendicite *f*

appendix [ə'pendɪks] *(pl* **appendices** [ə'pendɪsiːz]) *n* (**a**) *Anat* appendice *m;* **to have one's a. (taken) out** se faire opérer de l'appendicite (**b**) *(of book)* appendice *m*

appetite ['æpɪtaɪt] *n* (**a**) *(for food)* appétit *m;* **to have a good a.** avoir bon appétit; **to spoil sb's a.** couper l'appétit à qn; **to give sb an a.** donner faim à qn; *(of fresh air, walk)* creuser qn (**b**) *(enthusiasm) (for knowledge, travel)* soif *f* (**for** de); *(for music, cinema)* goût *m* (**for** pour)

appetizer ['æpɪtaɪzə(r)] *n also Fig* amuse-gueule *m*

appetizing ['æpɪtaɪzɪŋ] *adj* appétissant(e)

applaud [ə'plɔːd] *vt & vi* applaudir

applause [ə'plɔːz] *n (clapping)* applaudissements *mpl; (approval)* approbation *f*

apple ['æpəl] *n (fruit)* pomme *f; (tree)* pommier *m;* **he was the a. of her eye** *(her favourite)* elle tenait à lui comme à la prunelle de ses yeux; **a. core** trognon *m* de pomme; **a. juice** jus *m* de pomme; **a. pie** *(covered)* tourte *f* aux pommes; **as American as a. pie** typiquement américain(e); **a. tart** *(uncovered)* tarte *f* aux pommes; **a. tree** pommier *m*

applecart ['æpəlkɑːt] *n* **to upset the a.** *(spoil plan)* tout chambouler

apple-pie ['æpəlpaɪ] *adj* **in a. order** parfaitement en ordre; *Br* **a. bed** lit *m* en portefeuille

appliance [ə'plaɪəns] *n* appareil *m;* **electrical/domestic a.** appareil électrique/ménager

applicable [ə'plɪkəbəl] *adj* applicable; **the rule is a. to everybody** la règle s'applique à tous; **delete where not a.** *(on form)* rayer les mentions inutiles

applicant ['æplɪkənt] *n (for job)* candidat(e) *m,f* (**for** à)

application [æplɪ'keɪʃən] *n* (**a**) *(for job)* candidature *f* (**for** à); *(for passport, patent)* demande *f* (**for** de); **a. form** *(for job)* formulaire *m* de candidature (**b**) *(of rule, theory, paint)* application *f* (**c**) *(effort)* application *f,* assiduité *f*

applied [ə'plaɪd] *adj (maths, physics)* appliqué(e)

apply [ə'plaɪ] *(pt & pp* **applied**) **1** *vt* (**a**) *(put on)* appliquer (**to** sur) (**b**) *(use) (system, theory)* appliquer (**to** à); **to a. one's**

mind to sth concentrer ses efforts sur qch; **to a. oneself (to one's work)** s'appliquer **2** *vi* (**a**) **to a. to sb for sth** s'adresser à qn pour obtenir qch; **to a. for a job** poser sa candidature pour un poste; **to a. for a grant** faire une demande de bourse (**b**) *(of law, rule)* s'appliquer (**to** à)

appoint [ə'pɔɪnt] *vt (person)* nommer; *(committee)* constituer; **to a. sb to a post** nommer qn à un poste; **to a. sb (as) manager** nommer qn directeur(trice)

appointed [ə'pɔɪntɪd] *adj Formal (agreed) (place, hour)* convenu(e), dit(e)

appointment [ə'pɔɪntmənt] *n* (**a**) *(meeting, with doctor)* rendez-vous *m;* **to make an a. with sb** prendre rendez-vous avec qn; *(with dentist, doctor)* prendre rendez-vous chez qn (**b**) *(to job)* nomination *f; (of committee)* constitution *f;* **to make an a.** pourvoir un poste; *Br Com* **by a. to His/Her Majesty** *(sign)* fournisseur de la Couronne; **appointments** *(in newspaper)* offres d'emploi

apportion [ə'pɔːʃən] *vt* répartir

appraisal [ə'preɪzəl] *n (of standards, personnel)* évaluation *f*

appraise [ə'preɪz] *vt (performance, situation)* évaluer; *(value)* estimer

appreciable [ə'priːʃɪəbəl] *adj (change, difference)* appréciable, sensible

appreciate [ə'priːʃɪeɪt] **1** *vt* (**a**) *(be grateful for) (help)* être reconnaissant(e) de; *(kindness)* être sensible à; **I a. your helping me** je vous suis reconnaissant de m'avoir aidé (**b**) *(grasp, understand)* être conscient(e) de; **he doesn't a. how lucky he is** il ne se rend pas compte de la chance qu'il a (**c**) *(acknowledge)* apprécier **2** *vi (of goods, investment)* prendre de la valeur; *(of value)* augmenter

appreciation [əpriːʃɪ'eɪʃən] *n* (**a**) *(gratitude)* gratitude *f,* reconnaissance *f;* **in a. of** en reconnaissance de (**b**) *(understanding)* conscience *f;* **she has no a. of what is involved** elle ne se rend pas compte de ce que cela implique (**c**) *(review, assessment)* critique *f;* **a musical/wine a. society** une société d'amateurs de musique/de vin (**d**) *Fin* **a. of assets** plus-value *f* d'actif

appreciative [ə'priːʃɪətɪv] *adj* (**a**) *(grateful)* reconnaissant(e); **to be a. of sb's help/efforts** être reconnaissant à qn de son aide ses efforts (**b**) *(review)* élogieux(euse); *(response)* favorable; **the audience were very a.** le public a beaucoup aimé; **to be a. of sth** apprécier qch

apprehend [æprɪ'hend] *vt (a) Law (arrest)* appréhender (**b**) *Formal (understand)* comprendre

apprehension [æprɪ'henʃən] *n* (**a**) *(fear)* appréhension *f* (**b**) *Law (arrest)* arrestation *f*

apprehensive [æprɪ'hensɪv] *adj* inquiet(ète); **to be a. about sth/doing sth** appréhender qch/de faire qch

apprentice [ə'prentɪs] **1** *n* apprenti(e) *m,f* **2** *vt* **to a. sb to sb** placer qn en apprentissage chez qn

apprenticeship [ə'prentɪʃɪp] *n also Fig* apprentissage *m;* **to serve one's a.** faire ses premières armes

approach [ə'prəʊtʃ] **1** *n* (**a**) *(coming) (of person, season)* approche *f;* **to make an a. to sb** *(proposal)* faire une proposition à qn (**b**) *(method)* approche *f* (**to** de); **let's try a different a.** essayons de traiter le problème différemment (**c**) *(route of access)* voie *f* d'accès; **the approaches to a town** les abords *mpl* d'une ville; **a. road** voie d'accès **2** *vt* (**a**) *(get nearer to)* approcher de; **I'm approaching thirty** je vais sur mes trente ans (**b**) *(go up to)* aborder; *(organization)* approcher; **to be easy/difficult to a.** être d'un abord facile/difficile (**c**) *(problem)* aborder **3** *vi* approcher

approachable [ə'prəʊtʃəbəl] adj (person) d'un abord facile

approaching [ə'prəʊtʃɪŋ] adj (holiday, season) qui approche; (car) qui vient en sens inverse

appropriate¹ [ə'prəʊprɪət] adj (suitable) approprié(e) (to à); (moment) opportun(e)

appropriate² [ə'prəʊprɪeɪt] vt (a) (take, steal) s'approprier (b) (set aside) (money, funds) affecter (to à)

appropriately [ə'prəʊprɪətlɪ] adv (suitably) de manière appropriée; (properly) convenablement

appropriation [əprəʊprɪ'eɪʃən] n (of funds) affectation f

approval [ə'pru:vəl] n approbation f; to meet with sb's a. obtenir l'approbation de qn; Com on a. à l'essai

approve [ə'pru:v] vt (action, proposal) approuver; (treaty) ratifier
▸ **approve of** vt insep approuver; I don't a. of your friends tes amis ne me plaisent pas; she doesn't a. of them smoking elle n'aime pas qu'ils fument

approving [ə'pru:vɪŋ] adj approbateur(trice)

approx (abbr approximately) env.

approximate 1 adj [ə'prɒksɪmɪt] approximatif(ive) **2** vi [ə'prɒksɪmeɪt] **to a. to sth** se rapprocher de qch

approximately [ə'prɒksɪmətlɪ] adv approximativement, environ

approximation [əprɒksɪ'meɪʃən] n approximation f

Apr (abbr April) avril

APR [eɪpi:'ɑ:(r)] n Fin (abbr annual percentage rate) TEG m

apricot ['eɪprɪkɒt] n (fruit) abricot m; a. tree abricotier m

April ['eɪprɪl] n avril m; A. showers ≃ giboulées fpl de mars; A. Fool's Day le premier avril; see also May

apron ['eɪprən] n (a) (clothing) tablier m; he's still tied to his mother's a. strings (dependent on her) il est toujours pendu aux jupes de sa mère (b) Av aire f de stationnement

apt [æpt] adj (a) (word, description) juste (b) (likely) to be a. to do sth avoir tendance à faire qch

aptitude ['æptɪtju:d] n aptitude f, don m; to have an a. for sth avoir une aptitude ou un don pour qch; a. test test m d'aptitude

aptly ['æptlɪ] adv (described) justement; (chosen) bien

aquamarine [ækwəmə'ri:n] **1** n (gem) aigue-marine f **2** adj (colour) bleu vert inv

aquarium [ə'kweərɪəm] n aquarium m

Aquarius [ə'kweərɪəs] n le Verseau; to be (an) A. être (du) Verseau

aquatic [ə'kwætɪk] adj aquatique

aqueduct ['ækwɪdʌkt] n aqueduc m

aquiline ['ækwɪlaɪn] adj aquilin(e)

Arab ['ærəb] **1** n Arabe mf **2** adj arabe

Arabia [ə'reɪbɪə] n l'Arabie f

Arabian [ə'reɪbɪən] adj arabe; the A. Sea la mer d'Oman

Arabic ['ærəbɪk] **1** n (language) arabe m **2** adj arabe, A. numerals chiffres mpl arabes

arable ['ærəbəl] adj arable

arachnid [ə'ræknɪd] n Zool arachnide m

arbiter ['ɑ:bɪtə(r)] n (in dispute) arbitre m; the a. of taste l'arbitre des élégances

arbitrary ['ɑ:bɪtrərɪ] adj arbitraire

arbitrate ['ɑ:bɪtreɪt] **1** vt arbitrer **2** vi servir d'arbitre (between entre)

arbitration [ɑ:bɪ'treɪʃən] n arbitrage m; to go to a. (of parties) avoir recours à l'arbitrage

arbitrator ['ɑ:bɪtreɪtə(r)] n médiateur(trice) m,f

arc [ɑ:k] n arc m; a. lamp lampe f à arc

arcade [ɑ:'keɪd] n (a) (for shopping) galerie f marchande (b) (for games) salle f de jeux électroniques; a. game jeu m électronique (c) Archit galerie f

arch¹ [ɑ:tʃ] **1** n (a) Archit arche f (b) (of foot) voûte f plantaire; to have fallen arches avoir les pieds plats **2** vt to a. one's back (inwards) se cambrer; (outwards) se voûter

arch² adj a. enemy ennemi(e) m,f juré(e)

arch³ adj (mischievous) espiègle

archaeological, Am archeological [ɑ:kɪə-'lɒdʒɪkəl] adj archéologique

archaeologist, Am archeologist [ɑ:kɪ'ɒlədʒɪst] n archéologue mf

archaeology, Am archeology [ɑ:kɪ'ɒlədʒɪ] adj archéologie f

archaic [ɑ:'keɪɪk] adj archaïque

archangel ['ɑ:keɪndʒəl] n archange m

archbishop [ɑ:tʃ'bɪʃəp] n archevêque m

archduke [ɑ:tʃ'dju:k] n archiduc m

archeological, archeologist etc Am = archaeological, archaeologist etc

archer ['ɑ:tʃə(r)] n archer m

archery ['ɑ:tʃərɪ] n tir m à l'arc

archetypal [ɑ:kɪ'taɪpəl] adj the a. English village l'archétype m du village anglais

archetype ['ɑ:kɪtaɪp] n archétype m

Archimedes [ɑ:kɪ'mi:di:z] n Archimède m

archipelago [ɑ:kɪ'peləgəʊ] (pl archipelagoes or archipelagos) n archipel m

architect ['ɑ:kɪtekt] n architecte mf; he was the a. of his own downfall il a été l'artisan de sa propre ruine

architecture ['ɑ:kɪtektʃə(r)] n architecture f

archives ['ɑ:kaɪvz] npl archives fpl

archway ['ɑ:tʃweɪ] n arche f

arctic ['ɑ:ktɪk] **1** n the A. l'Arctique m; the A. Circle le cercle (polaire) arctique; the A. Ocean l'océan m Arctique **2** adj (a) (climate) arctique (b) Fam (very cold) a spell of a. weather un froid polaire

ardent ['ɑ:dənt] adj (desire, love) ardent(e); (admirer, believer) fervent(e)

ardour ['ɑ:də(r)] n (of desire, love) ardeur f; (religious) ferveur f

arduous ['ɑ:djʊəs] adj ardu(e), pénible

are [ɑ:(r)] plural and 2nd pers singular of **be**

area ['eərɪə] n (a) (surface) superficie f, surface f; the room is 20 square feet in a. la pièce a une surface de 6 mètres carrés (b) (region) région f; (of countryside, forest) zone f; (in building) partie f; (of town, city) quartier m; (of knowledge) domaine m; the London a. la région de Londres; an a. of agreement un terrain d'entente; Tel a. code indicatif m; Com a. manager directeur(trice) m,f régional(e)

arena [ə'ri:nə] n (a) (Roman) arène f; (stadium) stade m (b) (area of activity) (economic, international) scène f

aren't [ɑ:nt] (a) = are not (b) a. I? = am I not?

Argentina [ɑ:dʒən'ti:nə] n l'Argentine f

Argentine [ɑ:dʒəntaɪn] **1** n (person) Argentin(e) m,f; Old-fashioned the A. (country) l'Argentine f **2** adj argentin(e)

Argentinian [ɑ:dʒən'tɪnɪən] **1** n Argentin(e) m,f **2** adj argentin(e)

arguable ['ɑːgjʊəbəl] *adj* **(a)** *(questionable)* discutable; **it is a.** whether it would have made any difference on peut se demander si ça aurait changé quoi que ce soit **(b)** *(conceivable)* défendable; **it is a. that...** on pourrait soutenir que...

arguably ['ɑːgjʊəblɪ] *adv* **it's a.** the city's best restaurant on peut dire que c'est le meilleur restaurant de la ville

argue ['ɑːgjuː] **1** *vt (position)* défendre; **to a.** the case for sth plaider en faveur de qch; **to a. that...** soutenir que... **2** *vi (quarrel)* se disputer **(about** à propos de**); to a.** for sth plaider en faveur de qch; **to a.** against sb/sth s'opposer à qn/qch; **don't a.!** ne discute pas!, pas de discussion!

argument ['ɑːgjʊmənt] *n* **(a)** *(quarrel)* dispute *f*, *(debate)* discussion *f*; **to have an a.** about sth *(quarrel)* se disputer à propos de qch; *(debate)* discuter de qch; **to get into an a.** se disputer; **and I don't want any arguments!** et pas de discussion! **(b)** *(reason)* **an a.** for/against doing sth une raison de faire/de ne pas faire qch **(c)** *(point)* argument *m* **(for/against** en faveur de/contre**); for a.'s** sake à titre d'exemple

argumentative [ɑːgjʊ'mentətɪv] *adj (person)* qui a l'esprit de contradiction; *(tone)* agressif(ive)

aria ['ɑːrɪə] *n* aria *f*

arid ['ærɪd] *adj* aride

Aries ['eəriːz] *n* le Bélier; **to be (an) A.** être (du) Bélier

arise [e'raɪz] *(pt* arose [ə'rəʊz], *pp* arisen [ə'rɪzən]) *vi (of problem, possibility)* surgir; *(of situation)* naître; *(of question)* se poser; *(of storm)* se lever; **if the need arises** si le besoin s'en fait sentir

aristocracy [ærɪs'tɒkrəsɪ] *n* aristocratie *f*

aristocrat ['ærɪstəkræt] *n* aristocrate *mf*

aristocratic [ærɪstə'krætɪk] *adj* aristocratique

Aristotle ['ærɪstɒtəl] *n* Aristote

arithmetic [ə'rɪθmətɪk] *n (calculations)* calculs *mpl*; *(subject)* calcul *m*, arithmétique *f*

arithmetical [ærɪθ'metɪkəl] *adj* arithmétique; **an a. error** une erreur de calcul

ark [ɑːk] *n* arche *f*; **Noah's A.** l'arche de Noé

arm [ɑːm] **1** *n* **(a)** *(of person, chair, garment)* bras *m*; **to carry sb/sth in one's arms** porter qn/qch dans ses bras; **to take sb's a.** prendre qn par le bras; **a. in a.** bras dessus bras dessous; **to receive sb with open arms** *(warmly welcome)* recevoir qn à bras ouverts; *Fig* **to keep sb at a.'s length** tenir qn à distance **(b)** arms *(weapons)* armement *m*; arms race course *f* aux armements **(c)** *(in heraldry)* **(coat of)** arms armoiries *fpl* **2** *vt (person, country)* armer; **to a.** oneself with the facts s'armer de faits

armadillo [ɑːmə'dɪləʊ] *(pl* armadillos) *n* tatou *m*

Armageddon [ɑːmə'gedən] *n* l'Apocalypse *f*; *Fig* apocalypse *f*

armaments ['ɑːməmənts] *npl* armement *m*, armes *fpl*

armband ['ɑːmbænd] *n (at funeral, for swimming)* brassard *m*

armchair ['ɑːmtʃeə(r)] *n* fauteuil *m*; **an a. sportsman** un sportif en chambre

armed [ɑːmd] *adj* armé(e) **(with** de**); a.** forces forces *fpl* armées; **a. robbery** vol *m* à main armée

Armenia [ɑː'miːnɪə] *n* l'Arménie *f*

Armenian [ɑː'miːnɪən] **1** *n* Arménien(enne) *m,f* **2** *adj* arménien(enne)

armhole ['ɑːmhəʊl] *n* emmanchure *f*

armistice ['ɑːmɪstɪs] *n* armistice *m*; **A. day** l'Armistice

armour, *Am* **armor** ['ɑːmə(r)] *n* **(a)** *(of knight)* armure *f*;

---

suit of a. armure complète **(b)** *Mil (of tank)* blindage *m*; *(tanks)* blindés *mpl*

armoured car, *Am* **armored car** ['ɑːməd'kɑː] *n* voiture *f* blindée

armoury, *Am* **armory** ['ɑːmərɪ] *(pl* armouries, *Am* armories*) n (store)* arsenal *m*

armpit ['ɑːmpɪt] *n* aisselle *f*

army ['ɑːmɪ] *(pl* armies*) n* armée *f*; *(land forces)* armée de terre; **to be in the a.** être dans l'armée, être militaire

aroma [ə'rəʊmə] *n* arôme *m*

aromatic [ærəʊ'mætɪk] *adj* aromatique

arose [ə'rəʊz] *pt of* arise

around [ə'raʊnd] **1** *prep* **(a)** *(position)* autour de; **a. the table** autour de la table; **there were hills all a. the town** il y avait des collines tout autour de la ville; **there were posters all a. the walls** il y avait des posters partout sur les murs; **a. here** par ici **(b)** *(motion)* autour de; **to look a. a room** jeter un coup d'œil à une pièce; **to travel a. the world** faire le tour du monde; **to walk a. the town** se promener en ville **2** *adv* **(a)** *(surrounding)* autour; **a garden with a fence a.** un jardin avec une clôture autour; **all a.** tout autour; **for miles a.** à des kilomètres à la ronde **(b)** *(in different directions)* **to walk a.** se promener; **there were books lying all a.** il y avait des livres qui traînaient partout **(c)** *(in the general area)* dans le coin; **is Jane a.?** est-ce que Jane est dans le coin?; **there was nobody a.** il n'y avait personne **(d)** *(approximately)* environ; **at a. five o'clock** vers cinq heures

arousal [ə'raʊzəl] *n (sexual)* excitation *f*; *(of interest, suspicion)* éveil *m*

arouse [ə'raʊz] *vt (sleeping person)* réveiller; *(emotion, desire, suspicion)* éveiller; *(enthusiasm, opposition)* soulever; *(sexually)* exciter

arraign [ə'reɪn] *vt Am Law* traduire en justice

arraignment [ə'reɪnmənt] *n Am Law* lecture *f* de l'acte d'accusation

arrange [ə'reɪndʒ] **1** *vt* **(a)** *(put in order)* arranger; *(classify)* ranger **(b)** *(organize) (wedding, meeting)* arranger; *(time, date)* fixer; *(accommodation)* s'occuper de; *(outing)* organiser; *(one's affairs)* mettre en ordre; **to a.** where to go/what to do prévoir où aller/quoi faire; **it was arranged that...** il a été prévu que...; **an arranged marriage** un mariage arrangé **2** *vi* **to a. to do sth** s'arranger pour faire qch; *(with someone else)* convenir ou prévoir de faire qch; **they arranged for a taxi to meet me** ils se sont arrangés pour qu'un taxi vienne me chercher

arrangement [ə'reɪndʒmənt] *n* **(a)** *(of objects, furniture)* disposition *f* **(b)** *(plan)* arrangement *m*; **to make arrangements** prendre des dispositions, faire le nécessaire; **I've made all the arrangements** j'ai tout arrangé **(c)** *(agreement)* arrangement *m*; **the a.** was that... il avait été convenu que...; **viewing by a.** *(sign)* visites sur rendez-vous; **to come to an a.** with sb parvenir à un arrangement avec qn **(d)** *Mus* arrangement *m*

array [ə'reɪ] *n (collection)* collection *f*, éventail *m*

arrears [ə'rɪəz] *npl* arriéré *m*; **to be two months in a. with the rent** devoir deux mois de loyer; **to be in a. with one's work** avoir du travail en retard; **to be paid monthly in a.** être payé(e) à la fin du mois

arrest [ə'rest] **1** *n* arrestation *f*; **to be under a.** être en état d'arrestation; **to make an a.** procéder à une arrestation **2** *vt (capture, stop)* arrêter; *(attention)* attirer

arresting [ə'restɪŋ] *adj (striking)* saisissant(e)

arrival [ə'raɪvəl] n arrivée f; **on a.** à l'arrivée; **a new a.** (at work, in club) un nouveau venu (une nouvelle venue); (baby) un nouveau-né (une nouvelle-née)

arrive [ə'raɪv] vi (**a**) (at place) arriver; **to a. at** (solution, decision) arriver à, parvenir à (**b**) Fam (attain success) réussir, arriver

arrogance ['ærəgəns] n arrogance f

arrogant ['ærəgənt] adj arrogant(e)

arrow ['ærəʊ] n flèche f

arrowhead ['ærəʊhed] n pointe f de flèche

arrowroot ['ærəʊruːt] n Culin arrow-root m

arse [ɑːs] n Br Vulg (**a**) (buttocks) cul m; **to make an a. of sth** saloper qch (**b**) (stupid person) connard (connasse) m,f; **to make an a. of oneself** se couvrir de ridicule
► **arse about, arse around** vi Br Vulg déconner

arsehole ['ɑːshəʊl] n Br Vulg (**a**) (anus) trou m du cul (**b**) (stupid person) connard (connasse) m,f; **don't be such an a.!** ne fais pas le salaud (la salope)!

arsenal ['ɑːsənəl] n arsenal m; (of devices, arguments) panoplie f

arsenic ['ɑːsənɪk] n arsenic m

arson ['ɑːsən] n incendie m criminel ou volontaire

arsonist ['ɑːsənɪst] n incendiaire mf

art [ɑːt] n (**a**) (in general) art m; (school subject) arts mpl plastiques; (college course) beaux-arts mpl; **the arts in Great Britain** la création artistique en Grande-Bretagne; **arts and crafts** artisanat m; **a. gallery** (museum) musée m d'art; (shop) galerie f d'art; **a. school** école f des beaux-arts, beaux-arts mpl (**b**) Univ arts lettres fpl (**c**) (technique) art m; **there's an a. to making pastry** la pâtisserie, c'est tout un art

artefact ['ɑːtɪfækt] n (manufactured object) objet m

arteriosclerosis [ɑːtɪərɪəʊskləˈrəʊsɪs] n Med artério sclérose f

artery ['ɑːtərɪ] (pl arteries) n artère f

artful ['ɑːtfʊl] adj (**a**) (skilful) (person) habile; (solution, reply) astucieux(euse) (**b**) (cunning) malin(igne)

arthritic [ɑː'θrɪtɪk] adj arthritique

arthritis [ɑː'θraɪtɪs] n arthrite f

arthropod ['ɑːθrəpɒd] n Zool arthropode m

arthrosis [ɑː'θrəʊsɪs] n Med arthrose f

artichoke ['ɑːtɪtʃəʊk] n (globe) a. artichaut m

article ['ɑːtɪkəl] **1** n article m; **a. of clothing** vêtement m; Gram **definite/indefinite a.** article défini/indéfini
2 vt Law mettre en apprentissage (**to** chez)

articulate[1] [ɑː'tɪkjʊlət] adj (person) qui s'exprime avec facilité; (account) clair(e)

articulate[2] [ɑː'tɪkjʊleɪt] vt (**a**) (word) articuler; **to a. one's words** articuler (**b**) (idea, feeling) exprimer

articulated lorry [ɑː'tɪkjʊleɪtɪd'lɒrɪ] n Br semi-remorque m

articulation [ɑːtɪkjʊ'leɪʃən] n articulation f

artificial [ɑːtɪ'fɪʃəl] adj artificiel(elle); **a. insemination** insémination f artificielle; Comptr **a. intelligence** intelli gence f artificielle; **a. respiration** respiration f artificielle

artificially [ɑːtɪ'fɪʃəlɪ] adv artificiellement

artillery [ɑː'tɪlərɪ] n artillerie f

artisan [ɑːtɪ'zæn] n artisan m

artist ['ɑːtɪst] n artiste mf

artistic [ɑː'tɪstɪk] adj artistique; (temperament, person) artiste

artistry ['ɑːtɪstrɪ] n (of painting, game) qualité f artistique; (of painter, footballer) art m

artless ['ɑːtlɪs] adj (simple) naturel(elle); (clumsy) maladroit(e)

artwork ['ɑːtwɜːk] n (in book, magazine) illustrations fpl

arty ['ɑːtɪ] adj Fam (person) prétentieux(euse) (et passionné d'art)

Aryan ['eərɪən] **1** n Aryen(enne) m,f
2 adj aryen(enne)

as [əz, stressed æz] **1** adv (**a**) (with manner) as promised/planned comme promis/prévu; **A as in Anne** A comme Anne
(**b**) (in comparisons) **as tall as me** aussi grand(e) que moi; **as white as a sheet** blanc (blanche) comme un linge; **twice as big as** deux fois plus grand que; **I came as fast as I could** je suis venu aussi vite que j'ai pu; **as much money/many people as** autant d'argent/de gens que; **as much/many as you want** autant que tu veux; **as soon as possible** dès que possible; **as recently as last week** pas plus tard que la semaine dernière
(**c**) **as if** comme si; **it isn't as if or though it's difficult** ce n'est pourtant pas compliqué; **she looked as if or though she wanted to leave** elle avait l'air de vouloir partir; **it looks as if or though he's already left** on dirait qu'il en déjà parti
(**d**) **as well** aussi, également; **he has two cats as well as a dog** il a un chien et aussi deux chats
(**e**) **as for** quant à
2 conj (**a**) (with time) **he went out as I came in** il sortit au moment où j'entrais; **as the day went on** à mesure que la journée passait; **we'll see as we go along** nous verrons au fur et à mesure; **as you get older** en vieillissant, avec l'âge; **as always** comme toujours
(**b**) (with manner) comme; **as I was saying** comme je le disais; **do as you're told** fais ce qu'on te dit; **as often happens,...** comme c'est souvent le cas,...; **it's hard/far enough as it is** c'est assez difficile/loin comme ça; **as it were** pour ainsi dire
(**c**) (concessive) **late as it was,...** bien qu'il fût tard,...; **try as she might,...** elle avait beau essayer,...; **strange as it may seem,...** aussi étrange que cela puisse paraître,...; **much as I like her,...** je l'aime bien, mais...
(**d**) (because) puisque, comme
(**e**) (in addition) **mother is well, as are the children** maman va bien, et les enfants aussi
3 prep comme; **to work as a team** travailler en équipe; **to regard sb as a friend** considérer qn comme un ami; **I meant it as a compliment** c'était un compliment; **she used it as a bandage** elle s'en est servi comme d'un bandage; **as a mother, I think that...** en tant que mère, je pense que...

asap [eɪeseɪ'piː] adv (abbr as soon as possible) dès que possible

asbestos [æs'bestəs] n amiante f

asbestosis [æsbes'təʊsɪs] n Med asbestose f

ascend [ə'send] **1** vt (mountain) gravir, faire l'ascension de; (throne) accéder à; (stairs) gravir
2 vi monter

ascendancy, ascendency [ə'sendənsɪ] n ascendant m

ascendant, ascendent [ə'sendənt] n to be in the a. prospérer

Ascension [ə'senʃən] n Rel l'Ascension f

ascent [ə'sent] n also Fig ascension f

ascertain [æsə'teɪn] vt établir

ascetic [ə'setɪk] **1** n ascète mf
2 adj ascétique

ASCII ['æskɪ] n (abbr American Standard Code for Information Interchange) ASCII m

ascribe [ə'skraɪb] vt attribuer (**to** à)

ASEAN ['æzɪæn] *n (abbr* Association of South-East Asian Nations) ANASE*f*

aseptic [eɪ'septɪk] *adj* aseptique

asexual [eɪ'seksjʊəl] *adj* asexué(e)

ash¹ [æʃ] *n (tree)* frêne *m*

ash² *n (from fire, cigarette)* cendre *f*; *Rel* A. Wednesday mercredi *m* des Cendres

ashamed [ə'ʃeɪmd] *adj* honteux(euse); **to feel a.** avoir honte; **to be a.** of avoir honte de; **I am a.** to say that... j'avoue à ma grande honte que...; **you ought to be a.** of yourself! tu devrais avoir honte!

ashen ['æʃən] *adj* blême

ashore [ə'ʃɔː(r)] *adv (on land)* à terre; **to go a.** débarquer

ashtray ['æʃtreɪ] *n* cendrier *m*

Asia ['eɪʒə] *n* l'Asie *f*; A. Minor l'Asie mineure

Asian ['eɪʒən] **1** *n* Asiatique *mf*; *Br (from Indian sub-continent)* = personne originaire du sous-continent indien; *Am* A. American Américain(e) *m,f* d'origine asiatique
2 *adj* asiatique; *Br (from Indian sub-continent)* du sous-continent indien; *Am* A. American américain(e) d'origine asiatique

Asiatic [eɪʒɪ'ætɪk] **1** *n* Asiatique *mf*
2 *adj* asiatique

aside [ə'saɪd] **1** *adv* to stand a. s'écarter; to take sb a. prendre qn à part; to put *or* set sth a. *(reserve)* mettre qch de côté; politics a.,... toute question de politique mise à part,...; a. from à part
2 *n* aparté *m*

asinine ['æsɪnaɪn] *adj* stupide

ask [ɑːsk] **1** *vt* (a) *(enquire about)* demander; to a. (sb) a question poser une question (à qn); to a. sb sth demander qch à qn; to a. sb the time demander l'heure à qn; to a. sb the way demander son chemin à qn; don't a. me! je n'en ai pas la moindre idée! (b) *(request)* demander; to a. sb for sth demander qch à qn; to a. to do sth demander à faire qch; to a. sb to do sth demander à qn de faire qch; to a. a favour of sb, to a. sb a favour demander un service à qn; if it isn't asking too much si ce n'est pas trop demander; to a. sb's permission to do sth demander à qn la permission de faire qch (c) *(invite)* inviter; to a. sb to dinner inviter qn à dîner
2 *vi* (a) *(enquire)* se renseigner (about sur) (b) *(request)* demander; you only have to a.! il n'y a qu'à demander!; to a. for sth demander qch; *Fam* he was asking for it il l'a cherché

▸ **ask after** *vt insep* demander des nouvelles de

askance [ə'skæns] *adv* to look a. at sb regarder qn de travers

askew [ə'skjuː] *adv* de travers

asking ['ɑːskɪŋ] *n* it's yours for the a. il suffit de le demander pour l'obtenir; a. price prix *m* demandé

ASL [eɪes'el] *n (abbr* American Sign Language) = langage par signes d'origine américaine

asleep [ə'sliːp] *adj* to be a. dormir; to fall a. s'endormir; to be fast *or* sound a. dormir profondément

asocial [eɪ'səʊʃəl] *adj* asocial(e)

asparagus [ə'spærəgəs] *n* asperge *f*

aspect ['æspekt] *n* (a) *(of problem, subject)* aspect *m* (b) *(of building)* exposition *f*

asperity [æ'sperɪtɪ] *n (of character, voice)* rudesse *f*

aspersions [ə'spɜːʃənz] *npl* to cast a. on sth mettre qch en doute; to cast a. on sb's honour porter atteinte à l'honneur de qn

asphalt ['æsfælt] *n* asphalte *m*

asphyxiate [æs'fɪksɪeɪt] *vt* asphyxier

asphyxiation [æsfɪksɪ'eɪʃən] *n* asphyxie *f*

aspic ['æspɪk] *n Culin* gelée *f*; it was as if the house had been preserved in a. la maison donnait l'impression de n'avoir pas subi le passage du temps

aspirate ['æspərət] *adj Ling* aspiré(e)

aspiration [æspɪ'reɪʃən] *n (ambition)* aspiration *f*

aspire [ə'spaɪə(r)] *vi* to a. to do sth aspirer à faire qch

aspirin ['æsprɪn] *n* aspirine *f*

aspiring [ə'spaɪərɪŋ] *adj* to be an a. actor/writer aspirer à devenir acteur/écrivain

ass¹ [æs] *n* (a) *(animal)* âne *m* (b) *Fam (idiot)* imbécile *mf*; to make an a. of oneself se ridiculiser

ass² *n Am very Fam* cul *m*

assail [ə'seɪl] *vt* (a) *(attack)* attaquer (b) to a. sb with questions assaillir qn de questions; assailed by doubts en proie au doute

assailant [ə'seɪlənt] *n* agresseur *m*

assassin [ə'sæsɪn] *n* assassin *m*

assassinate [ə'sæsɪneɪt] *vt* assassiner

assassination [əsæsɪ'neɪʃən] *n* assassinat *m*; a. attempt attentat *m*

assault [ə'sɔːlt] **1** *n Mil* assaut *m* (on de); *Law* agression *f* (on contre); *(criticism)* attaque *f* (on contre); *Mil* a. course parcours *m* du combattant
2 *vt Law* agresser; to be sexually assaulted être victime d'une agression sexuelle

assemble [ə'sembəl] **1** *vt (people)* rassembler, réunir; *(facts, objects)* rassembler; *(machine, furniture)* assembler, monter
2 *vi (of people)* se rassembler, se réunir

assembly [ə'semblɪ] *(pl* assemblies) *n* (a) *(gathering)* assemblée *f*; *Br Sch* = rassemblement des élèves d'une école avant d'entrer en classe; *Br Sch* a. hall = salle où se réunissent les élèves d'une école (b) *(of machine, furniture)* assemblage *m*, montage *m*; a. instructions instructions *fpl* de montage; *Ind* a. line chaîne *f* de montage

assent [ə'sent] **1** *n* assentiment *m*
2 *vi* donner son assentiment (to à)

assert [ə'sɜːt] *vt (one's rights, point of view)* faire valoir; to a. one's authority asseoir son autorité; to a. oneself s'imposer; to a. that... affirmer que...

assertion [ə'sɜːʃən] *n (statement)* déclaration *f*; *(of right)* revendication *f*

assertive [ə'sɜːtɪv] *adj* assuré(e)

assertiveness [ə'sɜːtɪvnɪs] *n* assurance *f*; a. training = cours pour adultes visant à améliorer la confiance en soi des participants

assess [ə'ses] *vt* (a) *(value, damage)* estimer; a. sb's income *(for tax purposes)* évaluer les revenus de qn (b) *(situation, impact)* étudier, analyser; *(performance, ability, quality)* évaluer

assessment [ə'sesmənt] *n* (a) *(of value)* estimation *f*; *(for insurance or tax purposes)* évaluation *f* (b) *(of situation)* étude *f*, analyse *f*; *(of performance, ability, quality)* évaluation *f*

assessor [ə'sesə(r)] *n Fin* contrôleur *m*

asset [æset] *n* atout *m*; she is a great a. to the firm c'est quelqu'un de très précieux pour l'entreprise; *Fin* assets avoir *m*; *Fin* a. stripper = personne qui rachète une société pour profiter de la réalisation de l'actif; *Fin* a. stripping démembrement *m (suite au rachat d'une société)*

asshole ['æshəʊl] *n Am Vulg* (a) *(anus)* trou *m* de cul (b) *(stupid person)* connard (connasse) *m,f*

assiduous [ə'sɪdjʊəs] *adj* assidu(e)

assign [ə'saɪn] *vt (task)* assigner (to à); *(funds)* affecter

(to à); *(importance)* attacher **(to à); to a.** sb **to do sth** charger qn de faire qch

assignation [æsɪg'neɪʃən] *n Formal or Hum (meeting)* rendez-vous *m*

assignment [ə'saɪnmənt] *n* **(a)** *(of funds)* affectation *f; (of tasks)* distribution *f;* **(b)** *(task) Sch* devoir *m; Journ* reportage *m; (of soldier, politician)* mission *f*

assimilate [ə'sɪmɪleɪt] **1** *vt* assimiler **2** *vi (of immigrants)* s'assimiler, s'intégrer

assimilation [əsɪmɪ'leɪʃən] *n* assimilation *f*

assist [ə'sɪst] **1** *vt (person)* aider, assister; *(process, development)* faciliter; **to a.** sb **in doing** *or* **to do sth** aider qn à faire qch **2** *vi* aider

assistance [ə'sɪstəns] *n* aide *f,* secours *m;* **to come to** **sb's a.** venir en aide à qn; **can I be of any a.?** puis-je être utile à quelque chose?

assistant [ə'sɪstənt] *n* assistant(e) *m,f; Br* **(shop) a.** vendeur(euse) *m,f;* **a. manager** sous-directeur(trice) *m,f*

assizes [ə'saɪzɪz] *npl Law* assises *fpl*

associate 1 *n* [ə'səʊsɪət] *(in business)* associé(e) *m,f; (in crime)* complice *mf* **2** *adj* [ə'səʊsɪət] *(company)* associé(e) **3** *vt* [ə'səʊsɪeɪt] **(a)** *(mentally)* associer **(with** à) **(b) to be** **associated with** avoir des liens avec **4** *vi* [ə'səʊsɪeɪt] **to a. with** sb fréquenter qn

associated [ə'səʊsɪeɪtɪd] *adj* associé(e); **a. company** société *f* affiliée

association [əsəʊsɪ'eɪʃən] *n* association *f;* **the name** **has unfortunate associations for her** ce nom lui évoque des souvenirs désagréables; **in a. with** en association avec

assorted [ə'sɔːtɪd] *adj (colours, flavours)* variés(ées); *(biscuits, sweets)* assortis(ies)

assortment [ə'sɔːtmənt] *n* assortiment *m*

assuage [ə'sweɪdʒ] *vt Lit* apaiser

assume [ə'sjuːm] *vt* **(a)** *(suppose)* supposer; **I a. he'll come** je suppose qu'il viendra; **he was assumed to be** **rich** on le supposait riche; **let us a. that...** supposons ou mettons que... **(b)** *(power, control)* prendre; *(name)* adopter; **to a. responsibility for sth** devenir responsable de qch; **an assumed name** un nom d'emprunt **(c)** *(appearance, shape)* prendre

assumption [ə'sʌmpʃən] *n* **(a)** *(supposition)* supposition *f;* **to work on the a. that...** se fonder sur l'hypothèse que... **(b)** *(of power)* prise *f;* **(c)** *Rel* **the A.** l'Assomption *f*

assurance [ə'ʃʊərəns] *n* **(a)** *(guarantee)* assurance *f;* **he** **gave me his a.** il me l'a assuré **(b)** *(confidence)* assurance *f* **(c)** *Br (insurance)* assurance *f*

assure [ə'ʃʊə(r)] *vt* assurer; **to a. sb of sth** assurer qn de qch

assured [ə'ʃʊəd] *adj (victory, success)* assuré(e), certain(e); *(person, performance)* plein(e) d'assurance

assuredly [ə'ʃʊərɪdlɪ] *adv* assurément

asterisk ['æstərɪsk] *n* astérisque *m*

asteroid ['æstərɔɪd] *n* astéroïde *m*

asthma ['æsmə] *n* asthme *m*

asthmatic [æs'mætɪk] *n & adj* asthmatique *mf*

astonish [ə'stɒnɪʃ] *vt* étonner; **to be astonished at** *or* **by** **sth** être étonné(e) par qch

astonishing [ə'stɒnɪʃɪŋ] *adj (amazing)* incroyable; *(performance)* extraordinaire; **I find it a. that...** je m'étonne que... + *subjunctive*

astonishment [ə'stɒnɪʃmənt] *n* étonnement *m;* **to my** **a.** à mon grand étonnement

astound [ə'staʊnd] *vt* stupéfier

astounding [ə'staʊndɪŋ] *adj* stupéfiant(e), incroyable

astral ['æstrəl] *adj* astral(e)

astray [ə'streɪ] *adv* **to go a.** *(become lost)* s'égarer; **to lead** **sb a.** *(morally)* détourner qn du droit chemin

astride [ə'straɪd] *prep* à cheval sur, à califourchon sur

astringent [ə'strɪndʒənt] **1** *n Med* astringent *m* **2** *adj Med* astringent(e); *Fig (person, voice)* caustique

astrologer [ə'strɒlədʒə(r)] *n* astrologue *mf*

astrological [æstrə'lɒdʒɪkəl] *adj* astrologique

astrology [ə'strɒlədʒɪ] *n* astrologie *f*

astronaut ['æstrənɔːt] *n* astronaute *mf*

astronomer [ə'strɒnəmə(r)] *n* astronome *mf*

astronomic(al) [æstrə'nɒmɪk(əl)] *adj* astronomique

astronomy [ə'strɒnəmɪ] *n* astronomie *f*

astrophysics [æstrəʊ'fɪzɪks] *n* astrophysique *f*

Astroturf® ['æstrəʊtɜːf] *n* gazon *m* artificiel

astute [ə'stjuːt] *adj* astucieux(euse)

astutely [ə'stjuːtlɪ] *adv* astucieusement

asunder [ə'sʌndə(r)] *adv Lit* **to tear** sth **a.** mettre qch en pièces

asylum [ə'saɪləm] *n* asile *m;* **(mental) a.** asile d'aliénés

asylum-seeker *n* demandeur(euse) *m,f* d'asile

asymmetric(al) [eɪsɪ'metrɪk(əl)] *adj* asymétrique

asymmetry [eɪ'sɪmɪtrɪ] *n* asymétrie *f*

at [æt, *unstressed* ət] *prep* **(a)** *(with place)* à; **at the office** au bureau; **at university** à l'université; **at the station** à la gare; **at the top/bottom (of)** en haut/bas (de), **at John's** **(house)** chez John; **at home** chez soi, à la maison **(b)** *(with time)* à; **at six o'clock** à six heures; **at night** la nuit; **at Christmas** à Noël; **at the beginning** au début; **at** **(the age of) twenty** à l'âge de) vingt ans **(c)** *(with price, speed)* à; **at 60 mph** ≃ à 90 km/h; **at 50** **cents a pound** à 50 cents la livre **(d)** *(with direction)* **to look at sb/sth** regarder qn/qch; **to** **shout at sb** crier après qn; **to throw sth at sb** jeter qch à qn **(e)** *(with cause)* **to be angry at sb** être fâché(e) contre qn; **to be surprised at sth** être surpris(e) de ou par qch; **to be** **shocked at sth** être choqué(e) par qch **(f)** *(with activity)* **to be at work/lunch** être en train de travailler/déjeuner; **she's been at it all weekend** elle n'a pas arrêté du week-end; **while you're at it** vas-y; **to be good/bad at sth** *(subject)* être bon (bonne)/ mauvais(e) en qch; **to be good/bad at doing sth** être/ne pas être doué(e) pour faire qch

atavistic [ætə'vɪstɪk] *adj* atavique

ate [eɪt] *pt of* eat

atheism ['eɪθɪɪzəm] *n* athéisme *m*

atheist ['eɪθɪɪst] *n* athée *mf*

Athens ['æθənz] *n* Athènes *f*

athlete ['æθliːt] *n* athlète *mf;* **a.'s foot** mycose *f*

athletic [æθ'letɪk] *adj (fit)* athlétique

athletics [æθ'letɪks] *npl* athlétisme *m*

Atlantic [ət'læntɪk] **1** *n* **the A.** l'Atlantique *m* **2** *adj (coast)* atlantique; *(island)* de l'Atlantique; **the A.** **Ocean** l'océan Atlantique

atlas ['ætləs] *n* atlas *m*

ATM [eɪtiː'em] *n (abbr* **automated teller machine)** DAB *m*

atmosphere ['ætməsfɪə(r)] *n* atmosphère *f; Fig* atmosphère, ambiance *f*

atmospheric [ætməs'ferɪk] *adj (pressure)* atmosphérique; *Fig (music, lighting)* d'ambiance

atoll ['ætɒl] *n Geog* atoll *m*

atom ['ætəm] *n* atome *m*; **a. bomb** bombe *f* atomique

atomic [ə'tɒmɪk] *adj* atomique; **a. bomb** bombe *f* atomique; **a. energy** énergie *f* atomique; **a. warfare** guerre *f* atomique *ou* nucléaire

▸ **atone for** [ə'təʊn] *vt insep (sin, crime)* expier; *(mistake)* racheter, réparer

atonement [ə'təʊnmənt] *n (for sin, crime)* expiation *f*; *(for mistake, behaviour)* réparation *f*

atrocious [ə'trəʊʃəs] *adj (crime)* atroce; *(behaviour)* ignoble; *(meal)* infect(e); *(decision, joke)* très mauvais(e); *(weather, conditions, journey)* épouvantable

atrocity [ə'trɒsɪtɪ] *(pl* **atrocities)** *n* atrocité *f*

atrophy ['ætrəfɪ] *(pt & pp* **atrophied)** *vi* s'atrophier

attach [ə'tætʃ] *vt (label, importance)* attacher **(to** à); *(blame, responsibility)* imputer **(to** à); *(document)* joindre **(to** à); *(employee)* détacher **(to** à); **to a.** oneself **to sb** ne pas lâcher qn d'une semelle; **to be attached to** *(like)* être attaché(e) à

attachment [ə'tætʃmənt] *n* **(a)** *(device)* accessoire *m* **(b)** *(secondment)* détachement *m* **(c)** *(fondness)* attachement *m*; **to form an a. to sb** s'attacher à qn

attack [ə'tæk] **1** *n* attaque *f*; **to be** *or* **come under a.** être attaqué(e); **to launch an a. on** attaquer; **an a. of fever** un accès de fièvre; **an a. of nerves** une crise de nerfs; **to have an a. of doubt** être assailli(e) par le doute **2** *vt* attaquer; *(rights)* porter atteinte à; *(problem, task)* s'attaquer à; **to be attacked** se faire attaquer

attacker [ə'tækə(r)] *n (assailant)* agresseur *m*; *(in sport)* attaquant(e) *m,f*

attain [ə'teɪn] *vt (goal, ambition)* réaliser; *(rank, age)* atteindre

attainable [ə'teɪnəbəl] *adj (goal, ambition)* réalisable

attainment [ə'teɪnmənt] *n (of goal, ambition)* réalisation *f*

attempt [ə'tempt] **1** *n* tentative *f*; **to make an a. at doing sth** *or* **to do sth** essayer *ou* tâcher de faire qch; **they made no a. to help** ils n'ont pas essayé d'aider; **to make an a. on sb's life** attenter à la vie de qn; **at the first a.** du premier coup **2** *vt* **to a. to do sth** essayer *ou* tenter de faire qch; **to a. a smile** essayer de sourire; *Law* **attempted murder** tentative *f* d'assassinat

attend [ə'tend] **1** *vt (meeting)* assister à; *(school)* aller à; *(of doctor)* suivre **2** *vi (be present)* être présent(e)

▸ **attend to** *vt insep (matter, problem, customer)* s'occuper de

attendance [ə'tendəns] *n (presence)* présence *f*; **to be in a. on sb** s'occuper de qn; **there was a good/poor a.** il y avait beaucoup de/peu de monde; **a. register** registre *m* des présences

attendant [ə'tendənt] *n (in museum, parking lot)* gardien(enne) *m,f*; *(in cloakroom)* préposé(e) *m,f*; *(at petrol pump)* pompiste *mf*

attention [ə'tenʃən] *n* **(a)** *(in general)* attention *f*; **to pay a. to** *(listen to)* écouter attentivement; *(watch)* regarder attentivement; **to pay a. to detail** faire attention aux détails; **to give sb/sth one's full a.** consacrer toute son attention à qn/qch; **to attract** *or* **catch sb's a.** attirer l'attention de qn; **to draw a. to oneself** se faire remarquer; **your a. please, ladies and gentlemen** mesdames et messieurs, votre attention s'il vous plaît; **for the a. of Mr Harvey** *(in letter)* à l'attention de M. Harvey **(b)** *(repairs)* **the engine needs some a.** le moteur a besoin d'être réparé **(c)** *Mil* **a.!** garde-à-vous!; **to stand at** *or* **to a.** être au garde-à-vous

attentive [ə'tentɪv] *adj (paying attention)* attentif(ive); *(considerate)* attentionné(e) **(to** pour)

attentively [ə'tentɪvlɪ] *adv* attentivement

attest [ə'test] **1** *vt* attester **2** *vi* **to a. to** témoigner de

attic ['ætɪk] *n* grenier *m*

attire [ə'taɪə(r)] *n* tenue *f*

attitude ['ætɪtjuːd] *n* **(a)** *(behaviour)* attitude *f* **(b)** *(opinion)* opinion *f*; **what's your a. to abortion?** quelle est votre position sur l'avortement?; **to take the a. that...** considérer que...; *Com* **a. survey** enquête *f* **(c)** *(pose)* pose *f*; **to strike an a.** prendre une pose affectée

attn *Com (abbr* **for the attention of)** à l'attention de

attorney [ə'tɜːnɪ] *(pl* **attorneys)** *n Am (lawyer)* avocat(e) *m,f*

attract [ə'trækt] *vt* attirer; **to a. attention/criticism** attirer l'attention/des critiques; **I'm extremely attracted to her** elle me plaît énormément; **the thought of working for him doesn't a. me** la perspective de travailler pour lui ne m'attire guère

attraction [ə'trækʃən] *n* **(a)** *(power)* attirance *f*; **the prospect holds little a. for me** cette perspective ne m'attire guère **(b)** *(attractive aspect)* attrait *m*

attractive [ə'træktɪv] *adj (person, offer)* séduisant(e); *(prospect)* attrayant(e); **do you find her a.?** est-ce qu'elle te plaît?

attribute **1** *n* ['ætrɪbjuːt] attribut *m* **2** *vt* [ə'trɪbjuːt] attribuer **(to** à)

attrition [ə'trɪʃən] *n* usure *f*; **war of a.** guerre *f* d'usure

attuned [ə'tjuːnd] *adj* **to be a. to sth** être accoutumé(e) à qch

atypical [eɪ'tɪpɪkəl] *adj* atypique

aubergine ['əʊbəʒiːn] *n Br* aubergine *f*

auburn ['ɔːbən] *adj (hair)* auburn *inv*

auction ['ɔːkʃən] **1** *n* vente *f* aux enchères; **to put sth up for a.** mettre qch aux enchères; **a. room** salle *f* des ventes **2** *vt* vendre aux enchères

▸ **auction off** *vt sep* vendre aux enchères

auctioneer [ɔːkʃə'nɪə(r)] *n* commissaire-priseur *m*

audacious [ɔː'deɪʃəs] *adj* audacieux(euse)

audacity [ɔː'dæsɪtɪ] *n* audace *f*

audible ['ɔːdɪbəl] *adj* audible

audience ['ɔːdɪəns] *n* **(a)** *(spectators, listeners)* public *m*; **a. participation** participation *f* du public **(b)** *(meeting with monarch, Pope)* audience *f*; **to grant sb an a.** accorder une audience à qn

audio ['ɔːdɪəʊ] *adj* **a. cassette** cassette *f* audio; **a. equipment** équipement *m* sonore

audiotypist [ɔːdɪəʊ'taɪpɪst] *n* audiotypiste *mf*

audiovisual [ɔːdɪəʊ'vɪzjʊəl] *adj* audiovisuel(elle)

audit ['ɔːdɪt] *Fin* **1** *n* audit *m* **2** *vt* vérifier

audition [ɔː'dɪʃən] **1** *n* audition *f* **2** *vt & vi* auditionner

auditor ['ɔːdɪtə(r)] *n Fin* commissaire *m* aux comptes

auditorium [ɔːdɪ'tɔːrɪəm] *n (of theatre, concert hall)* salle *f*; *(lecture theatre)* amphithéâtre *m*

auditory ['ɔːdɪtrɪ] *adj* auditif(ive)

Aug *(abbr* **August)** août

augment [ɔːg'ment] *vt* augmenter, accroître

augur ['ɔːgə(r)] *vi* **to a. well/badly** être de bon/mauvais augure

August ['ɔːgəst] *n* août *m*; *see also* **May**

august [ɔː'gʌst] adj Lit (distinguished) auguste

aunt [ɑːnt] n tante f

auntie, aunty ['ɑːntɪ] (pl aunties) n Fam tata f, tantine f

au pair [əʊ'peə(r)] n (jeune fille f) au pair f

aura ['ɔːrə] n aura f; (of place) atmosphère f

aural ['ɔːrəl] adj auditif(ive)

auspices ['ɔːspɪsɪz] npl under the a. of sous l'égide de

auspicious [ɔː'spɪʃəs] adj prometteur(euse)

Aussie ['ɒzɪ] Fam 1 n Australien(enne) m,f
2 adj australien(enne)

austere [ɒ'stɪə(r)] adj austère

austerity [ɒ'sterɪtɪ] n austérité f

Australasia [ɒstrə'leɪʒə] n l'Australasie f

Australasian [ɒstrə'leɪʒən] adj d'Australasie

Australia [ɒ'streɪlɪə] n l'Australie f

Australian [ɒ'streɪlɪən] 1 n Australien(enne) m,f
2 adj australien(enne)

Austria ['ɒstrɪə] n l'Autriche f

Austrian ['ɒstrɪən] 1 n Autrichien(enne) m,f
2 adj autrichien(enne)

autarchy ['ɔːtɑːkɪ] n autocratie f

authentic [ɔː'θentɪk] adj authentique

authenticate [ɔː'θentɪkeɪt] vt authentifier

authenticity [ɔːθen'tɪsɪtɪ] n authenticité f

author ['ɔːθə(r)] n auteur m

authoritarian [ɔːθɒrɪ'teərɪən] adj autoritaire

authoritative [ɔː'θɒrɪtətɪv] adj (a) (voice, manner) autoritaire (b) (work, document) qui fait autorité

authority [ɔː'θɒrɪtɪ] (pl authorities) n (a) (power) autorité f; the authorities les autorités fpl; I'd like to speak to someone in a. je voudrais parler à un responsable (b) (authorization) autorisation f; to give sb a. to do sth autoriser qn à faire qch; on one's own a. de son propre chef (c) (expert) to be an a. on sth faire autorité en matière de qch; to have sth on good a. tenir qch de source sûre

authorization [ɔːθəraɪ'zeɪʃən] n autorisation f

authorize ['ɔːθəraɪz] vt autoriser; to a. sb to do sth autoriser qn à faire qch

autism ['ɔːtɪzəm] n autisme m

autistic [ɔː'tɪstɪk] adj autiste

auto ['ɔːtəʊ] (pl autos) n Am auto(mobile) f, voiture f

auto- [ɔːtəʊ] pref auto-

autobiographical [ɔːtəʊbaɪə'græfɪkəl] adj autobiographique

autobiography [ɔːtəʊbaɪ'ɒgrəfɪ] (pl autobiographies) n autobiographie f

autocrat ['ɔːtəkræt] n autocrate m

autocratic [ɔːtə'krætɪk] adj autocratique

Autocue® ['ɔːtəkjuː] n Br téléprompteur m

autograph ['ɔːtəɡrɑːf] 1 n autographe m; a. album album m d'autographes
2 vt signer, dédicacer

automat ['ɔːtəmæt] n Am = cafétéria équipée de distributeurs automatiques

automate ['ɔːtəmeɪt] vt automatiser

automatic [ɔːtə'mætɪk] 1 n (car) (voiture f) automatique f; (pistol) (pistolet m) automatique m; (washing machine) machine f à laver automatique
2 adj automatique; Comptr a. data processing traitement m automatique des données; Av a. pilot pilote m automatique; Fig to be on a. pilot marcher au radar

automatically [ɔːtə'mætɪklɪ] adv automatiquement

automation [ɔːtə'meɪʃən] n automatisation f

automaton [ɔː'tɒmətən] n automate m

automobile ['ɔːtəməʊbiːl] n Am auto(mobile) f, voiture f

autonomous [ɔː'tɒnəməs] adj autonome

autonomy [ɔː'tɒnəmɪ] n autonomie f

autopsy ['ɔːtɒpsɪ] (pl autopsies) n autopsie f

autumn ['ɔːtəm] n automne m; in (the) a. en automne

autumnal [ɔː'tʌmnəl] adj automnal(e)

auxiliary [ɔːg'zɪlɪərɪ] 1 n (pl auxiliaries) (person) auxiliaire m,f; Ling auxiliaire m
2 adj auxiliaire

avail [ə'veɪl] 1 n of no a. (not effective) inutile; to no a. (in vain) en vain
2 vt to a. oneself of sth profiter de qch

availability [əveɪlə'bɪlɪtɪ] n disponibilité f

available [ə'veɪləbəl] adj disponible; tickets are still a. il reste des tickets; this model is a. in black and in red ce modèle existe en noir et en rouge

avalanche ['ævəlɑːntʃ] n also Fig avalanche f

avant-garde [ævɒŋ'gɑːd] adj d'avant-garde, avant-gardiste

avarice ['ævərɪs] n avarice f

Ave (abbr avenue) av.

avenge [ə'vendʒ] vt venger; to a. oneself on sb se venger sur qn

avenue ['ævɪnjuː] n avenue f; Fig possibilité f

aver [ə'vɜː(r)] vt (pt & pp averred) vt Lit déclarer, affirmer

average ['ævərɪdʒ] 1 n moyenne f; on a. en moyenne; above/below a. supérieur(e)/inférieur(e) à la moyenne
2 adj moyen(enne)
3 vt atteindre la moyenne de; to a. eight hours' work a day travailler en moyenne huit heures par jour
▸ **average out** vi it'll a. out over a month sur un mois ça s'équilibrera
▸ **average out at** vt insep my expenses. out at $800 per month mes dépenses s'élèvent en moyenne à 800 dollars par mois

averse [ə'vɜːs] adj opposé(e) (to à); he is not a. to a glass of wine il prend volontiers un verre de vin

aversion [ə'vɜːʃən] n aversion f; to have an a. to sb/sth avoir qn/qch en aversion

avert [ə'vɜːt] vt (a) (turn away) (eyes, thoughts) détourner (from de) (b) (prevent) (misfortune, accident) éviter, prévenir

aviary ['eɪvɪərɪ] (pl aviaries) n volière f

aviation [eɪvɪ'eɪʃən] n aviation f

avid ['ævɪd] adj avide (for de)

avidly ['ævɪdlɪ] adv avidement, avec avidité

avocado [ævə'kɑːdəʊ] (pl avocados) n a. (pear) avocat m

avoid [ə'vɔɪd] vt éviter; (question) esquiver; to a. doing sth éviter de faire qch; to a. sb/sth like the plague fuir qn/qch comme la peste

avoidable [ə'vɔɪdəbəl] adj évitable

avowed [ə'vaʊd] adj déclaré(e)

AWACS ['eɪwæks] n Mil (abbr Airborne Warning and Control System) AWACS m

await [ə'weɪt] vt attendre; Law to be awaiting trial être en instance de jugement

awake [ə'weɪk] 1 adj éveillé(e); he lay a. for hours worrying l'inquiétude l'a tenu éveillé pendant des heures; Fig he was a. to the danger il avait conscience du danger
2 vt (pt awoke [ə'wəʊk], pp awoken [ə'wəʊkən]) réveiller

3 vi s'éveiller, se réveiller; *Fig* to a. to a danger prendre conscience d'un danger

awaken [əˈweɪkən] *(pt* **awakened** [əˈweɪkənd], *pp* **awakened** *or* **awoken** [əˈwəʊkən]) **1** *vt* réveiller **2** *vi* s'éveiller, se réveiller

awakening [əˈweɪkənɪŋ] *n* réveil *m*; *Fig* **a rude a.** un réveil brutal

award [əˈwɔːd] **1** *n (prize)* prix *m*; *Law* dommages-intérêts *mpl* **2** *vt (prize, contract)* décerner; *(damages)* accorder; **to a. sb sth** décerner qch à qn

award-winning [əˈwɔːdwɪnɪŋ] *adj (film, book)* primé(e); *(writer, author)* lauréat(e)

aware [əˈweə(r)] *adj* **to be a.** of sth avoir conscience de qch; **to be a. that...** savoir que...; **not that I am a.** of pas que je sache; **as far as I'm a.** autant que je sache; **to become a.** of sth se rendre compte de qch; **politically a.** politisé(e)

awareness [əˈweənɪs] *n* conscience *f*

awash [əˈwɒʃ] *adj (flooded)* inondé(e)

away [əˈweɪ] *adv* **(a)** *(in space)* **a long way a.** très loin; **far a.** dans le lointain, au loin; **it's 10 miles a.** c'est à 16 kilomètres (d'ici); **to keep a.** from ne pas s'approcher de; **to go a.** partir, s'en aller; **go a.!** va-t'en!; **to put sth a.** ranger qch; **to take sth a.** from sb retirer qch à qn; **to stand a.** from sth se tenir à l'écart de qch; **to turn a.** se détourner **(b)** *(not at school, work)* **to be a.** être absent(e) **(c)** *(in time)* **Christmas is only two weeks a.** nous ne sommes qu'à deux semaines de Noël; **right a.** tout de suite

awe [ɔː] *n* crainte *f* mêlée de respect; **to be in a.** of sb/sth éprouver pour qn/qch une crainte mêlée de respect

awe-inspiring [ˈɔːɪnspaɪərɪŋ] *adj* imposant(e)

awesome [ˈɔːsəm] *adj* **(a)** *(incredible)* impressionnant(e) **(b)** *Am Fam (wonderful)* super *inv*

awful [ˈɔːfʊl] *adj* horrible, effroyable; **an a.** lot of people plein de monde; **it cost an a.** lot ça a coûté beaucoup d'argent

awfully [ˈɔːflɪ] *adv* **(a)** *(very badly)* terriblement mal **(b)**

(very) très; **I'm a. sorry** je regrette infiniment *ou* énormément; **I'm a. glad** je suis rudement content

awhile [əˈwaɪl] *adv* **wait a.** attendez un moment *ou* un peu

awkward [ˈɔːkwəd] *adj* **(a)** *(clumsy)* gauche, maladroit(e) **(b)** *(inconvenient) (situation, silence)* embarrassant(e); *(location)* peu pratique; **don't be so a.** arrête de nous moment; **the a. age** l'âge ingrat; *Fam* **he's an a. customer** il n'est pas commode

awl [ɔːl] *n* alène *f*, poinçon *m*

awning [ˈɔːnɪŋ] *n (of shop)* store *m*

awoke [əˈwəʊk] *pt of* awake

awoken [əˈwəʊkən] *pp of* awake, awaken

AWOL [ˈeɪwɒl] *adj (abbr* absent without leave) **to go A.** s'absenter sans permission; *Fig* disparaître

awry [əˈraɪ] *adv* **to go a.** aller de travers

axe, *Am* **ax** [æks] **1** *n* hache *f*; *Fig* **to have an a. to grind** avoir dans un but intéressé; *Fam* **two hospitals have been given the a.** on va fermer deux hôpitaux **2** *vt Fam (jobs)* supprimer; *(costs)* réduire

axes [ˈæksiːz] *pl of* axis

axiom [ˈæksɪəm] *n* axiome *m*

axiomatic [æksɪəˈmætɪk] *adj (evident)* évident(e)

axis [ˈæksɪs] *(pl* axes [ˈæksiːz]) *n Math* axe *m*; *Hist* the A. powers les puissances *fpl* de l'Axe

axle [ˈæksəl] *n (of vehicle)* essieu *m*

azalea [əˈzeɪlɪə] *n* azalée *f*

Azerbaijan [æzəbaɪˈdʒɑːn] *n* l'Azerbaïdjan *m*

Azerbaijani [æzəbaɪˈdʒɑːnɪ], **Azeri** [əˈzeərɪ] **1** Azerbaïdjanais(e) *m,f*, Azéri(e) *m,f* **2** *adj* azerbaïdjanais(e), azéri(e)

Azores [əˈzɔːz] *npl* the A. les Açores *fpl*

Aztec [ˈæztek] **1** *n* Aztèque *mf* **2** *adj* aztèque

azure [ˈæʒə(r)] **1** *n* azur *m* **2** *adj* d'azur, azuré(e)

B, b [biː] *n* **(a)** *(letter)* B, b *m inv*; **B-movie** série B *f*; *Br* **B road** route *f* secondaire **(b)** *Mus* si *m* **(c)** *Sch (grade)* **to get a B** *(in exam)* avoir mention assez bien; *(in homework, essay)* ≃ avoir 12 ou 13 sur 20

b *(abbr* **born)** né(e)

BA [biːˈeɪ] *n (abbr* **Bachelor of Arts) to have a BA in history** ≃ avoir une licence en histoire; **John Smith BA** ~ John Smith, licencié ès lettres/en histoire/*etc*

baa [baː] **1** *exclam* bêê!
2 *vi (pt & pp* **baaed** *or* **baa'd** [baːd]) bêler

babble [ˈbæbəl] **1** *vi* **(a)** *(of baby)* babiller; *(of adult)* bafouiller; **what are you babbling on about?** qu'est-ce que tu baragouines? **(b)** *(of water)* murmurer
2 *n* murmure *m*

babe [beɪb] *n* **(a)** *Lit (baby)* **b. (in arms)** bébé *m* **(b)** *Fam (woman)* belle nana *f*

baboon [bəˈbuːn] *n* babouin *m*

baby [ˈbeɪbɪ] **1** *n (pl* **babies) (a)** *(child)* bébé *m*; **b. brother** petit frère *m*; **b. sister** petite sœur *f*; **b. boom** baby-boom *m*; *Am* **b. carriage** landau *m*; **b. grand** *(piano)* demi-queue *m*; **b. talk** langage *m* enfantin **(b)** *(idioms)* **to throw the b. out with the bathwater** jeter le bébé avec l'eau du bain; **to leave sb holding the b.** refiler le bébé à qn
2 *vt (pt & pp* **babied)** materner

baby-faced [ˈbeɪbɪfeɪst] *adj* au visage poupin

babyhood [ˈbeɪbɪhʊd] *n* petite enfance *f*

babyish [ˈbeɪbɪɪʃ] *adj Pej* de bébé

baby-minder [ˈbeɪbɪmaɪndə(r)] *n* nourrice *f*

baby-sit [ˈbeɪbɪsɪt] *(pt & pp* **baby-sat** [ˈbeɪbɪsæt]) *vi* faire du baby-sitting; **to b. for sb** garder les enfants de qn

baby-sitter [ˈbeɪbɪsɪtə(r)] *n* baby-sitter *mf*

baby-walker [ˈbeɪbɪwɔːkə(r)] *n* trotteur *m*

bachelor [ˈbætʃələ(r)] *n* célibataire *m*; **b. flat** garçonnière *f*; *Univ* **B. of Arts** *(qualification)* ≃ licence *f* ès lettres/en histoire/*etc*; *(person)* ≃ licencié(e) *m,f* ès lettres/en histoire/ *etc*; *Univ* **B. of Science** *(qualification)* ≃ licence *f* ès sciences; *(person)* ≃ licencié(e) *m,f* ès sciences

bacillus [bəˈsɪləs] *(pl* **bacilli** [bəˈsɪlaɪ]) *n Biol* bacille *m*

back [bæk] **1** *n* **(a)** *(of person, animal)* dos *m*; *also Fig* **to turn one's b. on sb** tourner le dos à qn; **to sit/stand with one's b. to sb/sth** tourner le dos à qn/qch; **b. pain** mal *m* de dos; **to have b. problems** avoir des problèmes de dos; **b. slapping** *(self-congratulatory)* félicitations *fpl* excessives **(b)** *(of hand, page)* dos *m*; *(of chair)* dossier *m*; *(of car)* arrière *m*; *(of throat)* fond *m*; **at the b. (of),** *Am* **in b. (of)** *(behind)* derrière; *(at far end of)* au fond (de); **the dress fastens at the b.** cette robe s'attache dans le dos; **at the b. of the book** à la fin du livre; **the b. of the neck** la nuque; **he knows London like the b. of his hand**

il connaît Londres comme sa poche; *Fam* **in the b. of beyond** au diable; **b. to front** devant derrière, à l'envers **(c)** *(in sport)* arrière *mf*
(d) *(idioms)* **to do sth behind sb's b.** faire qch derrière le dos de qn; **I'll be glad to see the b. of him** je serai content d'en être débarrassé; **with one's b. to the wall** *(in desperate situation)* le dos au mur; **put your b. into it!** il faut t'y mettre!; **to break the b. of the work** faire le plus gros du travail; *Fam* **the boss was on my b. all day** j'ai eu le patron sur le dos toute la journée; *Fam* **get off my b.!** fiche-moi la paix!; *Fam* **to put** *or* **get sb's b. up** braquer qn
2 *adj* **(a)** *(in space) (part, wheel)* arrière *inv*; *Fig* **to put sth on the b. burner** remettre qch à plus tard; **b. door** porte *f* de derrière; *Fig* **he got it through the b. door** il a magouillé pour l'avoir; *Br* **b. garden** jardin *m* de derrière; **the b. page** la dernière page; *Euph* **b. passage** rectum *m*; **b. road** petite route *f*; **b. room** chambre *f* du fond; *Fig* **to take a b. seat** rester discret(ète); **b. yard** *Br (enclosed area)* arrière-cour *f*; *Am (garden)* jardin *m* de derrière
(b) *(in time)* **b. number** *(of magazine, newspaper)* vieux numéro *m*; **b. pay** rappel *m* de salaire; **b. rent** arriéré(s) *m(pl)* de loyer
3 *adv* **(a)** *(in space)* en arrière; **to stand** *or* **step b.** reculer; **to jump b.** faire un bond en arrière; **we passed it 3 kilometres b.** nous l'avons dépassé à 3 kilomètres d'ici **(b)** *(in return, retaliation)* **to hit sb b.** rendre son coup à qn; **to call sb b.** rappeler qn; **if you kick me I'll kick you b.** si tu me donnes un coup de pied, je te le rendrai; **to get one's own b. (on sb)** prendre sa revanche *(sur qn)*; **to get b. at sb** prendre sa revanche sur qn
(c) *(to original starting point)* **to come b.** revenir; **to go b.** retourner; **when will she be b.?** quand sera-t-elle de retour?; **b. in Britain** en Grande-Bretagne; **a few pages b.** quelques pages plus haut
(d) *(in time)* **a few years b.** il y a quelques années; **b. when...** à l'époque où...; **b. in the 70s** dans les années 70; **as far b. as 1914** dès 1914
4 *vt* **(a)** *(support)* soutenir, appuyer; *(financially)* financer **(b)** *(bet on)* parier *ou* miser sur **(c)** *(move backwards)* **to b. one's car into the garage** entrer au garage en marche arrière; **to b. one's car into a lamppost** rentrer dans un lampadaire en faisant marche arrière
5 *vi (move backwards)* reculer; *(in car)* faire marche arrière

▶ **back away** *vi* reculer **(from** devant)

▶ **back down** *vi (in argument)* céder; *(in conflict)* faire marche arrière

▶ **back off** *vi* reculer; *Fam* **b. off!** fiche-moi la paix!

▶ **back on to** *vt insep* donner sur

▶ **back out** *vi* **(a)** *(move backwards)* sortir à reculons; *(in car)* sortir en marche arrière **(b)** *(from agreement)* se dédire

▶ **back up 1** vt sep **(a)** (support) soutenir, appuyer; (story, account) étayer **(b)** Comptr (data, file) sauvegarder **2** vi **(a)** (move backwards) reculer; (in car) faire marche arrière **(b)** Comptr sauvegarder

backache ['bækeɪk] n mal m au dos

backbencher ['bæk'bentʃə(r)] n Br Parl député m de base

backbiting ['bækbaɪtɪŋ] n Fam médisance f

backbone ['bækbəʊn] n épine f dorsale, colonne f vertébrale; Fig **tourism is the b.** of the economy le tourisme est le pivot de l'économie; Fig **he's got no b.** il n'a rien dans le ventre

backbreaking ['bækbreɪkɪŋ] adj (work) éreintant(e)

backchat ['bæktʃæt], Am **backtalk** ['bæktɔːk] n Fam impertinence f

backcloth ['bækklɒθ] Br = **backdrop**

backdate ['bækdeɪt] vt antidater

backdrop ['bækdrɒp] n Th toile f de fond; Fig **against a b.** of continuing violence avec, comme toile de fond, un climat de violence permanente

backer ['bækə(r)] n (of political party) partisan m; (for project) commanditaire m

backfire [bæk'faɪə(r)] vi (of car) pétarader; Fig **the plan backfired on them** leur plan s'est retourné contre eux

backgammon ['bækgæmən] n backgammon m

background ['bækgraʊnd] n **(a)** (of scene) arrière-plan m, fond m; **in the b.** à l'arrière-plan, dans le fond; Fig **to stay in the b.** rester dans l'ombre; **b. music** (in restaurant) musique f d'ambiance; **she likes b. music when she's working** elle aime travailler avec un fond sonore; **b. noise** bruit m de fond **(b)** (social) origines fpl; (educational) formation f; (professional) expérience f; **from a disadvantaged b.** d'un milieu défavorisé; **we need someone with a b. in engineering** il nous faut quelqu'un qui s'y connaisse en ingénierie **(c)** (circumstances) contexte m; **against a b. of discord** dans un climat de mécontentement; **can you give me some b. information?** pouvez-vous me donner quelques renseignements?; **I need a bit more b.** il me faut plus de données

backhand ['bækhænd] n (in tennis) revers m

backhanded [bæk'hændɪd] adj (compliment) équivoque

backhander [bæk'hændə(r)] n Fam (bribe) pot-de-vin m

backing ['bækɪŋ] n (support) soutien m; **financial b.** financement m

backlash ['bæklæʃ] n (reaction) contrecoup m (against à); (political) réaction f (against à)

backlit ['bæklɪt] adj Comptr rétro-éclairé(e)

backlog ['bæklɒg] n retard m; **to have a b. of work** avoir du travail en retard

backpack ['bækpæk] **1** n sac m à dos **2** vi faire de la randonnée; **she backpacked around Europe** elle a fait toute l'Europe, sac à dos

backpacker ['bækpækə(r)] n routard(e) m,f

back-pedal ['bæk'pedəl] (pt & pp **back-pedalled**, Am **back-pedaled**) vi Fig faire marche arrière

backrest ['bækrest] n dossier m

back-seat ['bæksiːt] adj Fam **b. driver** = personne qui donne des conseils au conducteur

backside [bæk'saɪd] n Br Fam derrière m, postérieur m

backslash ['bækslæʃ] n Comptr barre f oblique inversée

backsliding ['bækslaɪdɪŋ] n Fam rechute f; **she was on the lookout for any signs of b.** elle nous surveillait pour voir si nous nous relâchions

backspace ['bækspeɪs] n Comptr retour m en arrière

backstage [bæk'steɪdʒ] adv also Fig dans les coulisses

backstairs [bæk'steəz] n escalier m de service

backstitch ['bækstɪtʃ] n (in sewing) point m de piqûre

backstreet ['bækstriːt] n petite rue f; **b. abortion** avortement m clandestin

backstroke ['bækstrəʊk] n (in swimming) dos m crawlé

backtalk ['bæktɔːk] Am = **backchat**

back-to-back [bæktə'bæk] **1** adj (victories, meetings) consécutifs(ives) **2** adv **(a)** (physically) dos à dos **(b)** (consecutively) de suite

backtrack ['bæktræk] vi **(a)** (retrace one's steps) revenir sur ses pas **(b)** (renege) faire marche arrière; **to b. on a promise/decision** revenir sur une promesse/une décision

backup ['bækʌp] n (support) soutien m, appui m; Mil renforts mpl; Comptr **b. copy/file** copie f/fichier m de sauvegarde; **b. system** système m de sauvegarde; **b. team** (providing support) équipe f technique; (on standby) équipe f de remplacement

backward ['bækwəd] adj **(a)** (direction) en arrière; **she left without a b. glance** elle est partie sans se retourner **(b)** (retarded) (child) arriéré(e); (country) en retard; Br Fam **he isn't b. in coming forward** il n'a pas peur de se mettre en avant **2** adv = **backwards**

backwardness ['bækwədnɪs] n (of child) arriération f mentale; (of country) retard m

backwards ['bækwədz] adv en arrière; (walk) à reculons; (fall) à la renverse; (read) à l'envers; **to walk b. and forwards** aller et venir; Fig **to know sth b.** connaître qch à fond

backwash ['bækwɒʃ] n (of boat) remous m; Fig conséquences fpl néfastes

backwater ['bækwɔːtə(r)] n (a) (of river) bras m mort (b) (isolated place) trou m perdu

bacon ['beɪkən] n **(a)** (food) bacon m **(b)** (idioms) Fam **to save sb's b.** sauver la peau de qn; Fam **to bring home the b.** (earn wages) faire bouillir la marmite; (succeed) réussir

bacteria [bæk'tɪərɪə] npl bactéries fpl

bacterial [bæk'tɪərɪəl] adj bactérien(enne)

bacteriological [bæktɪərɪə'lɒdʒɪkəl] adj bactériologique

bacteriology [bæktɪərɪ'ɒlədʒɪ] n bactériologie f

bad [bæd] (comparative **worse** [wɜːs], superlative **worst** [wɜːst]) adj **(a)** (of poor quality, unpleasant) mauvais(e); **it's not b.** (fair) ce n'est pas mal; (good) ce n'est pas mal du tout; **to be b. at maths** être mauvais en maths; **to be b. at cooking** être mauvais(e) cuisinier(ère); **things are going from b. to worse** c'est de pire en pire ou de mal en pis; **it was a b. time to arrive** ce n'était pas le moment d'arriver; **to have a b. time** passer un mauvais moment; **there's b. blood between them** il y a de la rancune entre eux; **to get into sb's b. books** se faire prendre en grippe par qn; **b. cheque** chèque m sans provision; Fin **b. debts** créances fpl douteuses; **in b. faith** de mauvaise foi; **b. feeling** animosité f; **I gave it up as a b. job** j'ai fini par laisser tomber; **to be a b. loser** être mauvais(e) perdant(e); **b. luck** malchance f; **b. manners** mauvaises manières fpl; **in a b. mood** de mauvaise humeur; Fig **she's b. news** elle ne t'/lui/etc apportera que des ennuis **(b)** (unfortunate) **it's (really) too b.!, that's too b.!** c'est vraiment dommage!; **to have a b. effect on sth** nuire à qch; **he'll come to a b. end** il finira mal **(c)** (not healthy) **to have a b. back/heart** avoir le dos/cœur fragile; **smoking is b. for you** fumer est mauvais pour la santé; **to be in a b. way** aller mal **(d)** (wicked) (person, behaviour) méchant(e); **to use b. language** dire des gros mots **(e)** (serious) (mistake, accident) grave; (pain) fort(e); **I've got**

a really **b.** headache j'ai vraiment très mal à la tête; **to have a b.** cold avoir un gros rhume **(f)** *(rotten)* mauvais(e); **to go b.** *(of fruit)* se gâter, pourrir; *(of milk)* tourner; *Fig* **a b.** **apple** une brebis galeuse **(g)** *(guilty)* **to feel b.** about sth s'en vouloir de qch

baddie, baddy ['bædɪ] *(pl* **baddies)** *n Fam* méchant(e) *m,f*

badge [bædʒ] *n (of company, organization)* badge *m*; *Br (fashion accessory)* pin's *m*; *Mil* insigne *m*

badger ['bædʒə(r)] **1** *n (animal)* blaireau *m* **2** *vt* harceler; **to b. sb into doing sth** harceler qn jusqu'à ce qu'il fasse qch

bad-looking [bæd'lʊkɪŋ] *adj* not **b.** pas mal

badly ['bædlɪ] *adv (comparative* **worse** [wɜːs], *superlative* **worst** [wɜːst]) **(a)** *(not well)* mal; **to do b.** *(in exam, competition)* avoir un mauvais résultat; **he didn't do b.** il ne s'en est pas mal tiré; **she took it very b.** elle a très mal pris la chose; **to be b. off for sth** *(lacking)* manquer de qch; **to be b. off for money** avoir des problèmes d'argent; **to get on b.** (with sb) ne pas s'entendre (avec qn) **(b)** *(seriously) (damaged, broken)* gravement; **to be b. beaten** *(physically)* être roué(e) de coups, *(in match, competition)* être battu(e) à plates coutures; **he b. injured** gravement ou grièvement blessé(e) **(c)** *(greatly)* **to want sth b.** avoir très envie de qch; **to be b. in need of sth** avoir grand besoin de qch

bad-mannered [bæd'mænəd] *adj* mal élevé(e)

badminton ['bædmɪntən] *n* badminton *m*

bad-mouth ['bædmaʊθ] *vt Am Fam* dire du mal de

badness ['bædnɪs] *n* **(a)** *(poor quality)* mauvaise qualité *f* **(b)** *(wickedness)* méchanceté *f*

bad-tempered [bæd'tempəd] *adj (person)* grincheux(euse); *(remark)* désagréable

BAF [biːeɪ'ef] *n (abbr* **British Athletics Federation)** = fédération britannique d'athlétisme

baffle ['bæfəl] *vt* **(a)** *(confuse)* laisser perplexe; **to be baffled** être perplexe; **I'm baffled as to why she did it** je ne comprends vraiment pas pourquoi elle a fait cela **(b)** *(foil) (plot, attempt)* déjouer

baffling ['bæfəlɪŋ] *adj* déconcertant(e)

BAFTA ['bæftə] *n (abbr* **British Academy of Film and Television Arts)** = organisation qui décerne chaque année des récompenses aux personnalités du cinéma et de la télévision britannique

bag [bæg] **1** *n* **(a)** *(of paper, plastic)* sac *m*; *(handbag)* sac à main; **to have bags under one's eyes** avoir des poches sous les yeux; *Fam* **to be a b. of bones** être un sac d'os; *Fig* **it's in the b.** *(of deal, victory)* c'est dans la poche **(b)** *Br Fam* **bags of** *(lots)* des masses de; **we've bags of time** nous avons tout le temps **(c)** *Br very Fam Pej (woman)* **old b.** vieille toupie *f* **2** *vt (pt & pp* **bagged) (a)** *(put in bag)* mettre en sac **(b)** *(in hunting)* abattre, tuer **(c)** *Fam (claim)* accaparer

bagel ['beɪgəl] *n* = petite couronne de pain

baggage ['bægɪdʒ] *n* bagages *mpl*; *Av* **b. allowance** franchise *f* de bagages; *Av* **b. handler** bagagiste *mf*; *Av* **b. reclaim** retrait *m* des bagages

baggy ['bægɪ] *adj (garment) (by design)* large; *(out of shape)* déformé(e)

Baghdad [bæg'dæd] *n* Bagdad

bagpipes ['bægpaɪps] *npl* cornemuse *f*

bah [bɑː] *exclam* bah!

Bahamas [bə'hɑːməz] *npl* **the B.** les Bahamas *fpl*

Bahrain [bɑː'reɪn] *n* Bahreïn

Bahraini [bɑː'reɪnɪ] **1** *n* Bahreïni(e) *m,f* **2** *adj* bahreïni(e)

bail [beɪl] *n Law (guarantee)* caution *f*; **on b.** sous caution; **to grant sb b.** libérer qn sous caution; **to stand b. for sb** se porter garant(e) de qn
▸ **bail out** *vt sep* **to b. sb out** *Law* se porter garant(e) de qn; *Fig* tirer qn d'affaire; *Fig* **to b. a company out** renflouer une entreprise

bailiff ['beɪlɪf] *n Br* **(a)** *Law* huissier *m* **(b)** *(on estate)* régisseur *m*

bait [beɪt] **1** *n also Fig* appât *m*; *Fig* **to rise to the b.** mordre à l'hameçon; *Fig* **to swallow** *or* **take the b.** mordre à l'hameçon **2** *vt (a) (torment)* harceler **(b)** *(attach bait to)* mettre l'appât à

baize [beɪz] *n* feutre *m*

bake [beɪk] **1** *vt (food)* (faire) cuire au four; *(clay)* cuire **2** *vi* **(a)** *(of food)* cuire au four; **(b)** *Fam* **I'm baking** je crève de chaleur

baked [beɪkt] *adj* **b. beans** haricots *mpl* blancs à la tomate; **b. potato** pomme *f* de terre au four

baker ['beɪkə(r)] *n* boulanger(ère) *m,f*; *Br* **b.'s (shop)** boulangerie *f*; **b.'s dozen** treize à la douzaine

bakery ['beɪkərɪ] *(pl* **bakeries)** *n* boulangerie *f*

baking ['beɪkɪŋ] **1** *n* **to do some b.** *(bread)* faire du pain; *(cakes)* faire de la pâtisserie; **b. powder** levure *f* chimique; **b. sheet** *or* **tray** plaque *f* (du four); **b. soda** bicarbonate *m* de soude; **b. tin** *(for meat)* plat *m* à rôtir; *(for cakes)* moule *m* à gâteau **2** *adj Fam* **it's b. (hot)** on crève de chaleur

balaclava [bælə'klɑːvə] *n* passe-montagne *m*

balance ['bæləns] **1** *n* **(a)** *(equilibrium)* équilibre *m*; **to keep/lose one's b.** garder/perdre son équilibre; **to throw sb off b.** faire perdre son équilibre à qn; *Fig* **to catch sb off b.** prendre qn au dépourvu; **the b. of power** l'équilibre *m* des pouvoirs; **on b.** tout compte fait; **to strike a b.** trouver le juste milieu **(b)** *(of bank account)* solde *m*; *(in accounting)* bilan *m*; *Fin* **b. of trade/payments** balance *f* commerciale/des paiements; **b. sheet** bilan **(c)** *(for weighing) balance f*, *Fig* **to hang** *or* **be in the b.** *(of decision, result)* être en jeu **2** *vt (object)* maintenir en équilibre; **he sought to b. the claims of the two parties** il a tenté de contenter les deux partis; **they b. each other well** *(of people)* ils sont complémentaires; *Fin* **to b. the books** arrêter les comptes **3** *vi* **(a)** *(physically)* tenir en équilibre **(b)** **she couldn't get the accounts to b.** elle n'arrivait pas à équilibrer les comptes

balanced ['bælənst] *adj (account, reporting)* objectif(ive); *(judgement)* pondéré(e); **b. diet** alimentation *f* équilibrée

balancing act ['bælənsɪŋækt] *n Fig* **to do a b.** faire des acrobaties

balcony ['bælkənɪ] *(pl* **balconies)** *n (in house, theatre)* balcon *m*

bald [bɔːld] *adj* **(a)** *(person)* chauve; *(tyre)* lisse; **to go b.** devenir chauve, perdre ses cheveux; *Br Fam* **as b. as a coot** chauve comme un œuf; **b. eagle** aigle *m* à tête blanche; **b. patch** tonsure *f* **(b)** *(plain)* **the b. truth** la vérité toute nue; **a b. statement of the facts** une simple exposition des faits

balding ['bɔːldɪŋ] *adj* qui commence à perdre ses cheveux; **a b. man** un homme à la calvitie naissante

baldly ['bɔːldlɪ] *adv (reply)* sèchement

baldness ['bɔːldnɪs] *n* **(a)** *(of person)* calvitie *f* **(b)** *(of statement, demand)* sécheresse *f*

bale [beɪl] *n (of cloth, paper)* balle *f*; *(of hay)* botte *f*
▸ **bale out** *vi (of pilot)* s'éjecter; *Fig (from difficult situation)* s'éclipser

Balearic [bælɪˈærɪk] n & adj the Balearics, the B. Islands les (îles fpl) Baléares fpl

baleful [ˈbeɪlfʊl] adj sinistre, maléfique; **she gave me a b. look** elle m'a lancé un regard noir

Bali [ˈbɑːlɪ] n Bali

Balinese [bælɪˈniːz] **1** n (a) (person) Balinais(e) m,f; the B. les Balinais mpl (**b**) (language) balinais m **2** adj balinais(e)

balk [bɔːlk] **1** vt (runner, racehorse) empêcher de passer **2** vi reculer (**at** devant)

Balkan [ˈbɔːlkən] **1** n the Balkans les Balkans fpl **2** adj balkanique

ball[1] [bɔːl] n (**a**) (in game) (for football, rugby, basketball) ballon m; (for cricket, tennis, golf) balle f; (for billiards) bille f; boule f; (of paper, of fire) boule; (of wool) pelote f; **to roll sth (up) into a b.** mettre qch en boule; **b. bearing** (ball) bille; (device) roulement m à billes; **b. boy/girl** (in tennis) ramasseur(euse) m,f de balles; **b. game** (in general) jeu m de balle; Am (baseball match) match m de baseball; Fig **that's a whole new b. game** (irrelevant) ça n'a rien à voir; (different situation) c'est une autre paire de manches (**b**) (of foot) plante f (**c**) Vulg **balls** (testicles) couilles fpl; (nonsense) conneries fpl; Fig **to have a lot of balls** avoir des couilles (**d**) (idioms) **to be on the b.** (alert) avoir de la présence d'esprit; (knowledgeable) connaître son affaire; **to start the b. rolling** faire démarrer les choses; **the b. is in your court** la balle est dans votre camp; **to play b.** (co-operate) jouer le jeu

ball[2] n (party) bal m; Fam **to have a b.** s'éclater; **b. dress** or **gown** robe f de bal

ballad [ˈbæləd] n ballade f

ball-and-socket joint [bɔːlənˈdʒsɒkɪtˈdʒɔɪnt] n Anat articulation f à emboîtement; Tech joint m à rotule

ballast [ˈbæləst] n (**a**) Naut lest m (**b**) Rail ballast m

ballcock [ˈbɔːlkɒk] n soupape f à flotteur

ballerina [bæləˈriːnə] n ballerine f; **prima b.** danseuse f étoile

ballet [ˈbæleɪ] n danse f classique; (work) ballet m; **b. dancer** danseur(euse) m,f classique; **b. shoe** chausson m de danse

ballistic [bəˈlɪstɪk] adj (missile) balistique; Br Fam Fig **to go b.** piquer une crise

ballistics [bəˈlɪstɪks] npl balistique f

balloon [bəˈluːn] n (**a**) (for party, travel) ballon m; Fam Fig **when the b. goes up** quand il va y avoir du grabuge (**b**) (in cartoon) bulle f **2** vi (swell) gonfler

ballooning [bəˈluːnɪŋ] n to go b. faire du ballon

balloonist [bəˈluːnɪst] n aérostier m

ballot [ˈbælət] **1** n (process) tour m de scrutin; (vote) scrutin m, vote m; **to hold a b.** organiser des élections; **to put sth to a b.** soumettre qch à un vote; **b. box** urne f; **this matter should be decided at the b. box** c'est aux urnes que doit se décider cette question; **b. paper** bulletin m de vote; **b. rigging** fraude f électorale **2** vt consulter

ballpark [ˈbɔːlpɑːk] **1** n Am terrain m de base-ball **2** adj **a b. figure** une estimation

ballpoint [ˈbɔːlpɔɪnt] n **b. (pen)** stylo m (à) bille

ballroom [ˈbɔːlruːm] n salle f de bal; **b. dancing** danses fpl de salon

► **balls up** vt sep Br very Fam foirer

balls-up [ˈbɔːlzʌp] n Br very Fam merdier m; **to make a b. of sth** foirer qch

ballyhoo [bælɪˈhuː] n Fam battage m publicitaire

balm [bɑːm] n baume m

balmy [ˈbɑːmɪ] adj (weather) doux (douce)

baloney [bəˈləʊnɪ] n (**a**) Am = saucisse à base de bœuf, veau et porc, mangée froide (**b**) Fam (nonsense) bêtises fpl

balsa [ˈbɔːlsə] n balsa m

balsam [ˈbɔːlsəm] n balsam m

Baltic [ˈbɔːltɪk] **1** n the B. la Baltique **2** adj (state) balte; **the B. Sea** la mer Baltique

balustrade [bæləˈstreɪd] n balustrade f

bamboo [bæmˈbuː] n bambou m; **b. shoots** pousses fpl de bambou

bamboozle [bæmˈbuːzəl] vt Fam embobiner

ban [bæn] **1** n interdiction f; **to impose a b. on sth** interdire qch **2** vt (pt & pp banned) interdire; **to b. sb from doing sth** interdire à qn de faire qch

banal [bəˈnæl] adj banal(e)

banality [bəˈnælɪtɪ] (pl banalities) n banalité f

banana [bəˈnɑːnə] n banane f; **b. tree** bananier m; Fam **to go bananas** (mad) devenir cinglé(e); (angry) piquer une crise; Fam **b. republic** république f bananière; also Fig **b. skin** peau f de banane; **b. split** banana split m inv

band[1] [bænd] n (**a**) (of metal) bande f, bague f; (around hat) ruban m; (around cigar) bague; (of colour) bande, raie f (**b**) Rad bande f de fréquence (**c**) (of ages, tax) tranche f; (of salaries) catégorie f

band[2] n (of friends) groupe m, cercle m; (of robbers) bande f; (of musicians) (rock) groupe; (jazz) orchestre m, groupe

► **band together** vi se liguer (**against** contre)

bandage [ˈbændɪdʒ] **1** n bandage m; (for support) bande f **2** vt bander; **to b. sb's arm** bander le bras à qn

► **bandage up** vt sep bander

Band-Aid® [ˈbændeɪd] n Am sparadrap m

B & B [biːənˈbiː] n (abbr bed and breakfast) (service) ≃ chambre f avec petit déjeuner; **to stay at a B & B** ≃ prendre une chambre d'hôte

bandit [ˈbændɪt] n bandit m

bandmaster [ˈbændmɑːstə(r)] n chef m de musique

bandsman [ˈbændzmən] n musicien m

bandstand [ˈbændstænd] n kiosque m à musique

b & w n Phot & Cin (abbr black and white) noir et blanc inv

bandwagon [ˈbændwægən] n Fam **to jump on the b.** prendre le train en marche

bandy[1] [ˈbændɪ] adj **to have b. legs** avoir les jambes arquées

bandy[2] (pt & pp bandied) vt (words, insults) échanger; **her name was being bandied about as a possible candidate** son nom est revenu plusieurs fois parmi ceux des candidats possibles

bandy-legged [bændɪˈleg(ɪ)d] adj aux jambes arquées

bane [beɪn] n plaie f; **he's the b. of my life** il m'empoisonne l'existence

bang [bæŋ] **1** n (**a**) (noise) claquement m; (explosion) détonation f; **the door shut with a b.** la porte s'est refermée en claquant; Fig **to go with a b.** (of party, event) être un grand succès (**b**) (blow) coup m violent; **to get a b. on the head** recevoir un coup sur la tête **2** adv Fam (**a**) **b. went my hopes of a quiet weekend** pour le week-end tranquille, c'était loupé (**b**) Br (exactly) **b. in the centre** en plein centre; **b. on time** pile à l'heure **3** exclam (sound of gun) pan!; (explosion) boum! **4** vt (hit) frapper (violemment); **to b. one's head** se cogner la tête

5 *vi (of door, window)* claquer, battre; **the door banged shut** la porte se ferma en claquant; **to b.** **at** *or* **on the door** frapper à la porte à coups violents; **to b.** **into sth** se cogner à qch

▸ **bang about, bang around** *vi (make noise)* faire du potin

▸ **bang on** *vi Br Fam* **he's always banging on about it** il n'arrête pas de bassiner tout le monde avec cela

▸ **bang up** *vt sep Br very Fam (imprison)* boucler

banger ['bæŋə(r)] *n Br* (**a**) *Fam (sausage)* saucisse *f* (**b**) *(firework)* pétard *m* (**c**) *Fam (car)* **old b.** vieille guimbarde *f*

Bangkok [bæŋ'kɒk] *n* Bangkok

Bangladesh [bæŋglə'deʃ] *n* le Bangladesh

Bangladeshi [bæŋglə'deʃɪ] **1** *n* Bangladeshi *mf*, Bangladais(e) *m,f* **2** *adj* bangladeshi, bangladais(e)

bangle ['bæŋgəl] *n* bracelet *m*

bangs [bæŋz] *npl Am* frange *f*

banish ['bænɪʃ] *vt (exile)* bannir (**from** de), *Fig (thought, fear)* chasser

banishment ['bænɪʃmənt] *n* bannissement *m*

banister ['bænɪstə(r)] *n* rampe *f* d'escalier

banjo ['bændʒəʊ] *(pl* **banjos** *or* **banjoes)** *n* banjo *m*

bank[1] [bæŋk] **1** *n* (**a**) *(of river)* berge *f*, bord *m*; *(of earth)* talus *m* (**b**) *(of clouds, fog)* banc *m* (**c**) *(of lights, switches)* rangée *f*
2 *vt* **the road is banked by trees** la route est bordée d'arbres
3 *vi* (**a**) *(of clouds, snow)* s'amonceler (**b**) *(of plane)* virer

bank[2] **1** *n* (**a**) *(financial institution)* banque *f*; **b. account** compte *m* en banque; **b. balance** solde *m*; **b. charges** frais *mpl* bancaires; **b. clerk** employé(e) *m,f* de banque; **b. draft** traite *f* bancaire; *Br* **b. holiday** jour *m* férié; **b. loan** prêt *m* bancaire; **b. manager** directeur(trice) *m,f* d'agence; *Fin* **b. rate** taux *m* de l'escompte; **b. statement** relevé *m* de banque (**b**) *(in gambling)* banque *f*; **to break the b.** faire sauter la banque; *Fig* **it won't break the b.** ça ne me/te/lc/ etc. ruinera pas (**c**) *(store)* **blood b.** banque *f* du sang; **data b.** banque de données
2 *vt (funds)* mettre ou déposer à la banque
3 *vi* **to b. with sb** avoir un compte chez qn; **who do you b. with?** à quelle banque êtes-vous?

▸ **bank on** *vt insep (outcome, success)* compter sur

bankbook ['bæŋkbʊk] *n* livret *m* ou carnet *m* de compte

banker ['bæŋkə(r)] *n Fin* banquier(ere) *m,f*; **b.'s draft** traite *f* bancaire

banking ['bæŋkɪŋ] *n (business)* opérations *fpl* bancaires; **she's in b.** elle travaille dans la banque

banknote ['bæŋknəʊt] *n* billet *m* de banque

bankroll ['bæŋkrəʊl] *vt Am (finance)* financer

bankrupt ['bæŋkrʌpt] **1** *n Fin* failli(e) *m,f*
2 *adj* failli(e); **to be b.** être en faillite; **to go b.** faire faillite; *Fig* **to be morally b.** avoir perdu toute crédibilité
3 *vt Law* mettre en faillite; *Fig (make poor)* ruiner

bankruptcy ['bæŋkrəptsɪ] *n Law* faillite *f*, *Fig (poverty)* ruine *f*

banner ['bænə(r)] *n* bannière *f*; **the Star-Spangled B.** la bannière étoilée; **b. headline** manchette *f*

bannister ['bænɪstə(r)] = **banister**

banns [bænz] *npl* bans *mpl*

banquet ['bæŋkwɪt] *n* banquet *m*

bantam ['bæntəm] *n* = poulet de petite taille

bantamweight ['bæntəmweɪt] *n (in boxing)* poids *m* coq

banter ['bæntə(r)] **1** *n* taquineries *fpl*
2 *vi* plaisanter

bap [bæp] *n* petit pain *m* rond

baptism ['bæptɪzəm] *n* baptême *m*; *Fig* **a b. of fire** un baptême du feu

baptismal [bæp'tɪzməl] *adj (certificate)* de baptême; **b. font** fonts *mpl* baptismaux

Baptist ['bæptɪst] *n* baptiste *mf*

baptize [bæp'taɪz] *vt* baptiser

bar [bɑː(r)] **1** *n* (**a**) *(of metal)* barre *f*; *(of gold)* lingot *m*; *(of chocolate, large)* tablette *f*, *(smaller)* barre; *(on window)* barreau *m*; *(of electric fire)* résistance *f*, **b. of soap** savonnette *f*, morceau *m* de savon; **to be behind bars** être derrière les barreaux; **b. chart** histogramme *m*; *Comptr* **b. code** code-barres *m*
(**b**) *(obstacle)* obstacle *m*; **to be a b.** **to sth** faire obstacle à qch; **to impose a b. on sth** interdire qch
(**c**) *Br Law* **the B.** ≈ l'Ordre *m* des avocats, le barreau; **to be called to the B.** s'inscrire au barreau; **to read for the B.** faire son droit; **the prisoner at the b.** l'accusé(e) *m,f*
(**d**) *(pub, in hotel)* bar *m*; *(pub counter)* comptoir *m*, bar
(**e**) *Mus* mesure *f*
2 *vt (pt & pp* **barred)** (**a**) *(door)* barrer; **to b. sb's way** barrer le passage à qn
(**b**) *(ban) (from club, pub)* exclure; **to b. sb from doing sth** interdire à qn de faire qch
3 *prep* sauf, à l'exception de; **the finest b.** **none** sans conteste le (la) meilleur(e)

barb [bɑːb] *n* (**a**) *(on hook, arrow)* barbillon *m* (**b**) *(remark)* pique *f*

Barbadian [bɑː'beɪdɪən] **1** *n* = personne née ou habitant la Barbade
2 *adj* de la Barbade

Barbados [bɑː'beɪdɒs] *n* la Barbade

barbarian [bɑː'beərɪən] *n & adj* barbare *mf*

barbaric [bɑː'bærɪk] *adj (barbare; (manners, behaviour)* de barbare

barbarism ['bɑːbərɪzəm] *n* barbarie *f*

barbarity [bɑː'bærɪtɪ] *(pl* **barbarities)** *n (cruelty)* barbarie *f*, *(act)* atrocité *f*

barbarous ['bɑːbərəs] *adj* barbare

barbecue ['bɑːbɪkjuː] **1** *n* barbecue *m*; **to have a b.** faire un barbecue; **b. sauce** sauce *f* barbecue
2 *vt* cuire au barbecue

barbed [bɑːbd] *adj* (**a**) *(hook)* barbelé(e); **b. wire** *(fil m* de fer) barbelé *m* (**b**) *(remark, comment)* acerbe

barber ['bɑːbə(r)] *n* coiffeur *m* pour hommes; *(old-fashioned)* barbier *m*; **to go to the b.'s** aller chez le coiffeur/barbier

barbershop ['bɑːbəʃɒp] *n Am* salon *m* de coiffure *(pour hommes)*; **b. quartet** = quatuor chantant en harmonie

barbiturate [bɑː'bɪtjərɪt] *n* barbiturique *m*

bard [bɑːd] *n Lit (poet)* barde *m*; **the B.** Shakespeare

bare [beə(r)] **1** *adj* (**a**) *(not covered)* nu(e); *(countryside)* dénudé(e); **in one's b. feet** (les) pieds nus; **to lay sth b.** mettre qch à nu, exposer qch (**b**) *(empty) (room, cupboard)* vide; **to strip a house b.** tout enlever dans une maison (**c**) *(just sufficient)* **the b. minimum** le strict minimum; **the b. bones of the case** les grandes lignes de l'affaire; **the b. necessities (of life)** le strict nécessaire; **a b. majority** une petite ou faible majorité
2 *vt* mettre à nu, découvrir; **to b. one's teeth** montrer les dents; **to b. one's heart** *or* **soul to sb** ouvrir son cœur à qn

bareback ['beəbæk] **1** *adj* (qui monte à cru
2 *adv* **to ride b.** monter à cru

barefaced ['beəfeɪst] *adj (impudence, lie, liar)* éhonté(e)

barefoot(ed) ['beəfʊt(ɪd)] **1** *adj* (aux) pieds nus **2** *adv* nu-pieds, (les) pieds nus

bareheaded [beə'hedɪd] **1** *adj* nu-tête *inv,* à la tête nue **2** *adv* nu-tête, (la) tête nue

bare-legged [beə'leg(ɪ)d] **1** *adj* aux jambes nues **2** *adv* (les) jambes nues

barely ['beəlɪ] *adv* **(a)** *(scarcely)* à peine; **b. enough** tout juste assez **(b)** *(sparsely)* **b. furnished** avec très peu de meubles

barf [bɑːf] *vi Fam* dégueuler

bargain ['bɑːgɪn] **1** *n* **(a)** *(agreement)* marché *m,* affaire *f;* **to make** *or* **strike a b. with sb** conclure un marché avec qn; **you haven't kept your side** *or* **part of the b.** vous n'avez pas tenu votre part du marché; **to drive a hard b.** ne pas faire de cadeaux; **into the b.** *(in addition)* par-dessus le marché, en plus **(b)** *(good buy)* affaire *f,* occasion *f;* **a good b.** une bonne affaire; **b. basement** rayon *m* des soldes, solderie *f;* **b. hunter** acheteur(euse) *m,f* à la recherche de bonnes affaires; **b. price** prix *m* exceptionnel **2** *vi* **to b. with sb** négocier avec qn

▸ **bargain away** *vt sep (rights, privileges)* brader

▸ **bargain for** *vt insep (reaction, question)* s'attendre à; **I didn't b. for that** je ne m'y attendais pas; **he got more than he bargained for** il ne s'attendait pas à cela

▸ **bargain on** *vt insep* **I didn't b. on that** je ne m'y attendais pas

barge [bɑːdʒ] *n* péniche *f*

▸ **barge in** *vi (enter)* faire irruption

bargepole ['bɑːdʒpəʊl] *n* gaffe *f; Br Fam* **I wouldn't touch it with a b.** *(it's disgusting)* ça me dégoûte d'y toucher; *(it's risky for you)* si j'étais vous, je ne m'en mêlerais pas

baritone ['bærɪtəʊn] *n* baryton *m*

barium ['beərɪəm] *n Chem* baryum *m; Med* **b. meal** (bouillie *f* de) sulfate *m* de baryum

bark¹ [bɑːk] **1** *n (of tree)* écorce *f* **2** *vt* **to b. one's shins** s'écorcher les jambes

bark² **1** *n (of dog)* aboiement *m; Fig* **his b. is worse than his bite** il n'est pas si méchant qu'il y paraît **2** *vt (order)* aboyer **3** *vi* aboyer **(at** après); *(of person)* crier **(at** sur); *Fam Fig* **you're barking up the wrong tree** tu fais fausse route

barkeeper ['bɑːkiːpə(r)] *n Am* barman *m*

barley ['bɑːlɪ] *n* orge *m;* **b. sugar** sucre *m* d'orge

barmaid ['bɑːmeɪd] *n Br* serveuse *f* (de bar)

barman ['bɑːmən] *n Br* serveur *m,* barman *m*

barmy ['bɑːmɪ] *adj Br Fam* toqué(e), cinglé(e)

barn [bɑːn] *n* grange *f; (for cows)* étable *f; (for horses)* écurie *f;* **b. dance** bal *m* folklorique; **b. owl** effraie *f*

barnacle ['bɑːnəkəl] *n* bernacle *f*

barnstorming ['bɑːnstɔːmɪŋ] *adj (speech, performance)* plein(e) de brio

barnyard ['bɑːnjɑːd] *n* cour *f* de ferme

barometer [bə'rɒmɪtə(r)] *n* baromètre *m*

baron ['bærən] *n* baron *m; Fig* **press/oil b.** magnat *m* de la presse/du pétrole

baroness ['bærənes] *n* baronne *f*

baronet ['bærənet] *n* baronet *m*

baroque [bə'rɒk] **1** *n* baroque *m* **2** *adj* baroque

barrack ['bærək] *vt (heckle)* chahuter

barracks ['bærəks] *npl* caserne *f;* **to be confined to b.** être consigné(e)

barracuda [bærə'kjuːdə] *n* barracuda *m*

barrage ['bærɑːʒ] **1** *n* **(a)** *(dam)* barrage *m* **(b)** *Mil* tir *m* de barrage; *Fig (of questions, abuse)* flot *m* **2** *vt* **to b. sb with** *(questions)* assaillir qn de; *(criticism)* accabler qn de

barrel ['bærəl] *n* **(a)** *(container)* tonneau *m,* fût *m;* *(of oil)* baril *m; Fam* **to have sb over a b.** tenir qn à sa merci; *Fam* **the play wasn't exactly a b. of laughs** cette pièce, ça n'a pas été une partie de rigolade; **b. organ** orgue *m* de Barbarie **(b)** *(of gun)* canon *m*

barren ['bærən] *adj (woman, land, discussion)* stérile; *(landscape)* désolé(e)

barrenness ['bærənnɪs] *n (of land, discussion)* stérilité *f*

barrette [bə'ret] *n Am* barrette *f*

barricade ['bærɪkeɪd] **1** *n* barricade *f* **2** *vt* barricader; **to b. oneself** se barricader

barrier ['bærɪə(r)] *n also Fig* barrière *f;* **the Great B. Reef** la Grande Barrière

barring ['bɑːrɪŋ] *prep* sauf; **b. accidents** sauf imprévu; **b. a miracle** à moins d'un miracle

barrister ['bærɪstə(r)] *n Br Law* ≃ avocat(e) *m,f*

barrow ['bærəʊ] *n (wheelbarrow)* brouette *f*

bartender ['bɑːtendə(r)] *n Am* serveur(euse) *m,f* (de bar)

barter ['bɑːtə(r)] **1** *n* troc *m* **2** *vt* troquer **(for** contre) **3** *vi* marchander

basalt ['bæsɔːlt] *n* basalte *m*

base [beɪs] **1** *n* **(a)** *(of cliff, column)* pied *m; (of lamp, statue)* socle *m; (of spine)* bas *m; (of jug)* cul *m; (of triangle, structure)* base *f; Fin* **b. rate** taux *m* de base **(b)** *(for expedition, campaign)* base *f; (for tourism)* point *m* de départ; **b. camp** camp *m* de base **(c)** *(in baseball)* base *f; Fig* **we didn't get past first b.** nous ne sommes pas arrivés à grand-chose; **to touch b. (with sb)** entrer en contact (avec qn) **2** *adj* **(a)** *Formal (motive, conduct)* bas (basse), vil(e) **(b)** **b. metals** métaux *mpl* vils **3** *vt (hopes, opinion)* fonder **(on** sur); **to be based on** *(of calculation, film)* être basé(e) sur; **to be based in** *(of job, troops, company)* être basé à

baseball ['beɪsbɔːl] *n* base-ball *m;* **b. bat** batte *f* de base-ball; **b. cap** casquette *f;* **b. mitt** gant *m* de base-ball

Basel ['bɑːzəl] *n* Bâle *f*

baseless ['beɪslɪs] *adj* sans fondement

baseline ['beɪslaɪn] *n (in tennis)* ligne *f* de fond

basement ['beɪsmənt] *n* sous-sol *m;* **b.** *Br* **flat** *or Am* **apartment** = appartement en partie en sous-sol

bases ['beɪsiːz] *pl of* basis

bash [bæʃ] *Fam* **1** *n* **(a)** *(blow)* coup *m; (with fist)* coup de poing; **to have a b. at sth/doing sth** essayer qch/de faire qch **(b)** *(party)* fête *f* **2** *vt* **to b. one's head** se cogner la tête

▸ **bash in** *vt sep Br Fam (door, headlight)* enfoncer; **I'll b. your face in!** je vais te défoncer la tête!

▸ **bash up** *vt sep Br Fam (person)* tabasser; *(car)* esquinter

bashful ['bæʃfʊl] *adj* timide; *(modest)* modeste

bashfulness ['bæʃfʊlnɪs] *n* timidité *f; (modesty)* modestie *f*

BASIC ['beɪsɪk] *n Comptr (abbr* **Beginners' All-purpose Symbolic Instruction Code)** basic *m*

basic ['beɪsɪk] **1** *n* **the basics** l'essentiel *m; (of language, science)* les rudiments *mpl;* **let's get down to basics** venons-en à l'essentiel; **to get back to basics** *(traditional values)* retrouver les vraies valeurs **2** *adj (principle, problem, vocabulary)* de base; *(accommodation, understanding)* rudimentaire; **I get the b.**

idea je vois en gros de quoi il s'agit; b. pay salaire m de base

basically ['beɪsɪklɪ] adv (a) (on the whole) en gros; (in fact) en fait (b) (fundamentally) fondamentalement

basil ['bæzəl] n basilic m

basilica [bə'zɪlɪkə] n basilique f

basin ['beɪsən] n (a) (for cooking) bol m; (for washing hands) lavabo m; (plastic, for washing up) bassine f, cuvette f (b) Geog bassin m

basis ['beɪsɪs] (pl bases ['beɪsiːz]) n (for discussion) base f; (for opinion, accusation) fondement m; to be paid on a weekly/monthly b. être payé à la semaine/au mois; on an informal b. à titre non officiel; to have a b. in fact être fondé(e); on the b. of what you've told me d'après ce que tu m'as dit

bask [baːsk] vi to b. in the sun se chauffer au soleil; he basked in her approval il se délectait à l'idée qu'il avait son approbation

basket ['baːskɪt] n (of fruit, for washing) corbeille f; (for shopping, in basketball) panier m; Fam he's a real b. case il est complètement cinglé

basketball ['baːskɪtbɔːl] n basket(-ball) m; b. player basketteur(euse) m,f

basketful ['baːskɪtfʊl] n (plein) panier m

Basle [baːl] n Bâle

Basque [buːsk] 1 n (a) (person) Basque mf (b) (language) basque m 2 adj basque; the B. Country le Pays basque

bas-relief [baːrɪ'liːf] n bas-relief m

bass¹ [bæs] n (seawater) bar m; (freshwater) perche f

bass² [beɪs] 1 n (voice, singer, guitar) basse f; (on amplifier) basses fpl; (double-bass) contrebasse f 2 adj (voice) de basse; (guitar, clarinet) bas (basse); b. clef clef f de fa; b. drum grosse caisse f

basset ['bæsɪt] n b. (hound) basset m

bassist ['beɪsɪst] n bassiste mf

bassoon [bə'nuːn] n basson m

bastard ['baːstəd] 1 n (a) (illegitimate child) bâtard(e) m,f (b) Vulg (unpleasant man) salaud m, you lucky b.! sacré veinard!; a b. of a job une vraie galère 2 adj (child) bâtard(e)

baste [beɪst] vt (meat) arroser de son jus

bastion ['bæstɪən] n also Fig bastion m

bat¹ [bæt] n (animal) chauve-souris f; Fam like a b. out of hell comme un fou (une folle)

bat² 1 n (for cricket, baseball) batte f; (for table tennis) raquette f; Fam to do sth off one's own b. faire qch de sa propre initiative 2 vt (pt & pp batted) she didn't b. an eyelid elle n'a pas sourcillé ou bronché 3 vi (in cricket, baseball) manier la batte

batch [bætʃ] n (of bread) fournée f; (of people) groupe m; (of goods) lot m; Comptr b. file fichier m séquentiel; Comptr b. processing traitement m par lots

bated ['beɪtɪd] adj with b. breath en retenant son souffle

bath [baːθ] 1 n (a) (action) bain m; to take or have a b. prendre un bain; to give sb a b. baigner qn; Br (swimming) baths piscine f; b. mat tapis m de bain; b. salts sels mpl de bain; b. towel drap m de bain f (object) baignoire f 2 vt baigner 3 vi se baigner

bathe [beɪð] 1 n Old-fashioned to go for a b. (aller) se baigner

2 vt (wound) laver; bathed in tears/sweat baigné(e) de larmes/de sueur 3 vi Old-fashioned (swim) se baigner

bather ['beɪðə(r)] n baigneur(euse) m,f

bathing ['beɪðɪŋ] n b. is prohibited (sign) la baignade est interdite; b. cap bonnet m de bain; b. costume maillot m de bain; b. suit maillot m de bain; b. trunks slip m de bain

bathos ['beɪθɒs] n chute f du sublime au ridicule

bathrobe ['baːθrəʊb] n peignoir m de bain

bathroom ['baːθruːm] n salle f de bains; Am (toilet) toilettes fpl; b. scales pèse-personne m

bathtub ['baːθtʌb] n baignoire f

batik [bə'tiːk] n batik m

batman ['bætmən] n Mil ordonnance f

baton ['bætən] n (in relay race) témoin m; (of conductor) baguette f; Br (of policeman) matraque f; b. charge f à la matraque

batsman ['bætsmən] n batteur m

battalion [bə'tæljən] n bataillon m

▶ **batten down** ['bætn] vt insep to b. down the hatches condamner les panneaux; Fig se tenir prêt(e)

batter¹ ['bætə(r)] n (in baseball) batteur m

batter² n (in cooking) pâte f à frire

batter³ vt (beat) cogner sur; (person) battre

battered ['bætəd] adj (a) b. women femmes fpl battues; b. child enfant m martyr (b) (hat, saucepan, car) cabossé(e); (furniture, house) délabré(e)

battering ram ['bætərɪŋræm] n bélier m

battery ['bætərɪ] (pl batteries) n (a) (of radio, clock) pile f; (of car) batterie f; to be b. operated or powered fonctionner sur piles; b. charger chargeur m de piles/batteries (b) Mil batterie f; Fig (of criticism, complaints) déluge m (c) a b. of tests une batterie de tests (d) b. farming élevage m en batterie; b. hen poule f de batterie

battle ['bætəl] 1 n bataille f; Fig combat m, lutte f; it was a b. of wits between them ils ont joué au plus fin; to do b. with sb être en conflit avec qn; that's half the b. la partie est à moitié gagnée; b. cry cri m de guerre; a b. royal violente empoignade 2 vi se battre, lutter

battleaxe ['bætəlæks] n hache f d'armes; Fam Pej (woman) virago f

battledress ['bætəldres] n tenue f de combat

battlefield ['bætəlfiːld], **battleground** ['bætəlgraʊnd] n also Fig champ m de bataille

battle-hardened ['bætəl'haːdənd] adj aguerri(e)

battlements ['bætəlmənts] npl remparts mpl

battle-scarred ['bætəl'skaːd] adj marqué(e) par la guerre

battleship ['bætəlʃɪp] n cuirassé m

bauble ['bɔːbəl] n (on Christmas tree) boule f; (worthless thing) babiole f

baud [bɔːd] n Comptr baud m; b. rate débit m en bauds

baulk [bɔːlk] = balk

bauxite ['bɔːksaɪt] n bauxite f

Bavaria [bə'veərɪə] n la Bavière

Bavarian [bə'veərɪən] 1 n Bavarois(e) m,f 2 adj bavarois(e)

bawdy ['bɔːdɪ] adj grivois(e), paillard(e)

bawl [bɔːl] 1 vt brailler 2 vi brailler; to b. at sb hurler après qn ▶ **bawl out** vt sep (a) (shout) hurler (b) (reprimand) passer un savon à

bay¹ [beɪ] *n (shrub)* laurier *m*; **b. leaf** feuille *f* de laurier

bay² **1** *n* **(a)** *(on coastline)* baie *f*; **the B. of Bengal** le golfe du Bengale; **the B. of Biscay** le golfe de Gascogne; **the B. of Pigs** la baie des Cochons **(b)** *Archit* travée *f*; **loading b.** aire *f* de chargement; **parking b.** place *f* de parking; **b. window** bow-window *m* **(c) to keep** *or* **hold sb at b.** tenir qn à distance; **to keep** *or* **hold sth at b.** se préserver de qch **2** *vi (of dog, wolf)* hurler

bayonet ['beɪənɪt] **1** *n* baïonnette *f* **2** *vt* **to b. sb** passer qn à la baïonnette

bazaar [bə'zɑː(r)] *n* **(a)** *(in Middle East)* bazar *m* **(b)** *(in aid of charity)* vente *f* de charité

bazooka [bə'zuːkə] *n* bazooka *m*

BBC [biːbiː'siː] *n (abbr* **British Broadcasting Corporation)** BBC *f*

BC [biː'siː] *adv (abbr* **before Christ)** av. J.-C.

be [biː]

> À l'oral et dans un style familier à l'écrit, le verbe **be** peut être contracté: **I am** devient **I'm**, **he/she/it is** deviennent **he's/she's/it's** et **you/we/they are** deviennent **you're/we're/they're**. Les formes négatives **is not/are not/was not** et **were not** se contractent respectivement en **isn't/aren't/wasn't** et **weren't**.

1 *vi (present* **I am, you/we/they are, he/she/it is;** *pt* **were** [wɜː(r)]; *1st and 3rd person singular* **was** [wɒz]; *pp* **been** [biːn]) **(a)** *(with state, condition)* être; **she's clever/pretty elle** est intelligente/jolie; **I'm a doctor/lawyer** je suis médecin/avocat; **they're English/French** ils sont anglais/français; **to be hungry/thirsty** avoir faim/soif; **to be cold/hot** *(of person)* avoir froid/chaud; *(of thing)* être froid(e)/chaud(e); **it's cold/hot** *(weather)* il fait froid/chaud; **to be 2 metres long/wide** faire 2 mètres de long/de large; **three and two are five** trois et deux font cinq **(b)** *(with location)* être; **where is the station?** où est *ou* se trouve la gare?; **here I am** me voici; **there you are!** te voilà!; **where was I?** *(after digression)* où en étais-je? **(c)** *(with time, date)* **it's six o'clock** il est six heures; **what day is it today?** quel jour sommes-nous?; **today's Friday/the tenth** c'est vendredi/le dix; **when is the concert?** quand a lieu le concert?; **it's two weeks since I saw him** je l'ai vu il y a quinze jours **(d)** *(with age)* **to be twenty (years old)** avoir vingt ans; **how old is he?** quel âge a-t-il? **(e)** *(with cost)* coûter, valoir; **how much is it?** combien ça coûte?; **the tickets are $10 each** les billets valent 10 dollars **(f)** *(with health)* aller; **how are you?** comment vas-tu?; **I'm fine** ça va; **he's better/worse** il va mieux/plus mal **(g)** *(with imperatives)* **be good!** sois sage!; **don't be stupid!** ne sois pas ridicule!; **let's be reasonable!** soyons raisonnables! **(h)** *(with question tags)* **she's beautiful, isn't she?** elle est belle, n'est-ce pas *ou* non?; **they're big, aren't they?** ils sont grands, n'est-ce pas *ou* non?; **he isn't English, is he?** il n'est pas anglais, si? **(i)** *(as past participle of* **go)** **I've been to New York/to the museum** je suis allé à New York/au musée; **where have you been?** où étais-tu passé?

2 *v aux* **(a)** *(in continuous tenses)* **to be doing sth** faire qch; **I was reading when the phone rang** j'étais en train de lire quand le téléphone a sonné; **she is/was crying** elle pleure/pleurait; **I'm leaving tomorrow** je pars demain; **it's raining** il pleut; **I've been waiting for hours** ça fait des heures que j'attends **(b)** *(with passives)* **he was killed** il a été tué; **he wasn't allowed to go on** on ne l'a pas autorisé à y aller **(c)** *(followed by infinitive)* **the house is to be sold** la maison doit être vendue; **there is to be an election** des

élections sont prévues; **she was never to see them again** elle ne devait jamais les revoir; **you are not to mention this to anyone** tu ne dois en parler à personne

beach [biːtʃ] **1** *n* plage *f*; **b. ball** gros ballon *m* en plastique; **b. hut** cabine *f* sur la plage **2** *vt (boat, ship)* échouer

beachcomber ['biːtʃkəʊmə(r)] *n* = personne qui ramasse des objets échoués ou abandonnés sur la plage

beachhead ['biːtʃhed] *n* tête *f* de pont

beacon ['biːkən] *n (signal, buoy)* balise *f*; *(lighthouse)* phare *m*; *(bonfire)* feu *m* d'alarme; *Fig* **a b. of hope** une source d'espoir

bead [biːd] *n* perle *f*; **a string of beads** un collier

beady ['biːdɪ] *adj* **to have one's b. eyes on sb/qch** surveiller qn/qch de près

beagle ['biːgəl] *n* beagle *m*

beak [biːk] *n* **(a)** *(of bird)* bec *m*; *Fam (nose)* nez *m* crochu **(b)** *Br Fam (magistrate)* juge *m*

beaker ['biːkə(r)] *n* gobelet *m*

be-all and end-all ['biːɔːləˈnendɔːl] *n Fam* **winning isn't the b.** gagner n'est pas tout

beam [biːm] **1** *n* **(a)** *(in building, in gymnastics)* poutre *f* **(b)** *(of sun, moon)* rayon *m*; *(of torch, headlamp)* faisceau *m* lumineux; *Phys* faisceau **(c)** *(idioms) Fam* **to be off b.** être à côté de la plaque; *Fam* **broad in the b.** *(of person)* large des hanches **2** *vt (programme, information)* transmettre **3** *vi (shine) (of sun, moon)* briller; **to b. with pride/pleasure** rayonner de fierté/de plaisir

bean [biːn] *n* **(a)** *(vegetable)* haricot *m*; *(of coffee)* grain *m*; **b. curd** pâte *f* de soja **(b)** *(idioms) Fam* **to be full of beans** être plein(e) d'énergie; *Fam* **it isn't worth a b.** ça ne vaut pas un radis; *Fam* **he hasn't a b.** il n'a pas un radis

beanbag ['biːnbæg] *n* **(a)** *(for juggling)* balle *f* lestée; *(for sitting on)* fauteuil *m* poire

beanfeast ['biːnfiːst] *n Br Hum* grande fête *f*

beanpole ['biːnpəʊl] *n* **(a)** *(stick)* rame *f* **(b)** *Fam (thin person)* asperge *f*

beansprout ['biːnspraʊt], **beanshoot** ['biːnʃuːt] *n* germe *m* de soja

beanstalk ['biːnstɔːk] *n* tige *f* de haricot

bear¹ [beə(r)] *n (animal)* ours *m*; *(female)* ourse *f*; **b. cub** ourson *m*; **to give sb a b. hug** serrer qn très fort dans ses bras; *Fin* **b. market** marché *m* à la baisse

bear² *(pt* **bore** [bɔː(r)], *pp* **borne** [bɔːn]) **1** *vt* **(a)** *(carry)* porter; *(weight, load)* supporter; *(bring)* apporter; **to b. sth away** emporter qch; **to b. sth in mind** *(remember)* se souvenir de qch; *(take into account)* tenir compte de qch; **it bears no relation to...** cela n'a aucun rapport avec...; **b. the responsibility for sth** assumer la responsabilité de qch **(b)** *(endure)* supporter; **I can't b. him** je ne peux pas le supporter; **I couldn't b. it any longer** je n'en pouvais plus; **he can't b. losing** il ne supporte pas de perdre; **it doesn't b. thinking about** l'idée même en est insupportable **(c)** *(produce) (child)* donner naissance à; *Fin (interest)* rapporter; **she bore him three children** elle lui a donné trois enfants; **to b. fruit** *(of tree)* porter des fruits; *(of effort, plan)* porter ses fruits **2** *vi (move)* **to b. (to the) right/left** tourner à droite/gauche

▸ **bear down (up)on** *vt insep* foncer sur

▸ **bear out** *vt sep* confirmer, corroborer

▸ **bear up** *vi* tenir le coup; **b. up!** courage!

▸ **bear with** *vt insep* supporter; **just b. with me a minute** patientez un instant

bearable ['beərəbəl] *adj* supportable

beard [bɪəd] *n* barbe *f*; **to have a b.** porter la barbe

bearded ['bɪədɪd] *adj* barbu(e)

bearer ['beərə(r)] *n* (*of news, cheque*) porteur(euse) *m,f*; (*of passport*) titulaire *mf*

bearing ['beərɪŋ] *n* (**a**) (*comportment*) port *m* (**b**) (*in mechanism, engine*) palier *m* (**c**) (*orientation*) **to find** *or* **get one's bearings** s'orienter; *Fig* **s'y retrouver; to lose one's bearings** être désorienté(e) (**d**) (*relevance*) rapport *m* (**on** avec)

beast [biːst] *n* (**a**) (*animal*) bête *f*; **b. of burden** bête de somme (**b**) *Fam* (*unpleasant person*) peau *f* de vache; (*cruel person*) brute *f*; **a b. of a job** un travail pénible

beastly ['biːstlɪ] *adj Fam* (*unpleasant*) horrible

beat [biːt] **1** *n* (**a**) (*of heart*) battement *m*; (*in bar, of music*) tempo *m*; (*rhythm*) rythme *m* (**b**) *Br* (*of policeman*) ronde *f*; **to be on the b.** faire sa ronde
2 *adj Fam* (*exhausted*) crevé(e); **dead b.** complètement crevé
3 *vt* (*pt* **beat,** *pp* **beaten** ['biːtən]) (**a**) (*person, eggs*) battre; **to b. a drum** battre du tambour; **to b. its wings** (*of bird*) battre des ailes; **to b. a path through the crowd** se frayer un chemin à travers la foule; *Fam* **b. it!** dégage! (**b**) (*defeat*) battre; **that will take some beating** c'est difficile de faire mieux; **I left early to b. the traffic** je suis parti tôt pour éviter les embouteillages; **he beat me to it** il a été plus rapide que moi; **you can't b. a good book** rien de tel qu'un bon livre; *Prov* **if you can't b. them, join them** il faut savoir hurler avec les loups; *Fam* **that beats everything!** ça c'est la meilleure!; *Fam* **it beats me why he did it** je ne pige vraiment pas pourquoi il a fait ça; *Fam* **it beats me!** ça me dépasse!
4 *vi* (**a**) (*of heart*) battre (**b**) **to b. about** *or* **around the bush** tourner autour du pot

▸ **beat back** *vt sep* repousser

▸ **beat down 1** *vt sep* (*price*) faire baisser; **I b. her down to $40** je lui ai fait baisser son prix à 40 dollars
2 *vi* (*of rain*) tomber à verse; (*of sun*) taper

▸ **beat off** *vt sep* repousser

▸ **beat out** *vt sep* (*fire, flames*) étouffer

▸ **beat up** *vt sep* (*assault*) tabasser

beaten ['biːtən] **1** *adj* **b. earth** terre *f* battue; *Fig* **off the b. track** à l'écart
2 *pp of* **beat**

beater ['biːtə(r)] *n* (**a**) (*in hunting*) rabatteur *m* (**b**) (*in cookery*) fouet *m*

beatification [biːætɪfɪ'keɪʃən] *n* béatification *f*

beating ['biːtɪŋ] *n* (*punishment*) correction *f*; (*in fight*) raclée *f*; (*defeat*) défaite *f*; **to give sb a b.** (*as punishment*) donner une correction à qn; (*beat up*) flanquer une raclée à qn

beat-up ['biːtʌp] *adj Fam* (*car*) tout(e) déglingué(e)

beaut [bjuːt] *n Fam* **what a b.!** quelle merveille!

beautician [bjuː'tɪʃən] *n* esthéticien(enne) *m,f*

beautiful ['bjuːtɪfʊl] *adj* (*person, weather, music*) (très) beau (belle); (*smell, taste*) très bon (bonne)

beautifully ['bjuːtɪfʊlɪ] *adv* merveilleusement bien

beautify ['bjuːtɪfaɪ] (*pt & pp* **beautified**) *vt* embellir

beauty ['bjuːtɪ] (*pl* **beauties**) *n* (*attribute, person*) beauté *f*; (*object*) bijou *m*; **that's the b. of it** c'est ça qui est bien; **b. contest** concours *m* de beauté; **b. parlour** *or* **salon** institut *m* de beauté; **b. queen** reine *f* de beauté; **b. spot** (*on face*) grain *m* de beauté; (*in country*) site *m* remarquable

beaver ['biːvə(r)] *n* castor *m*

▸ **beaver away** *vi* travailler d'arrache-pied (**at** à)

becalmed [bɪ'kɑːmd] *adj* encalminé(e)

became [bɪ'keɪm] *pt of* **become**

because [bɪ'kɒz] *conj* parce que; **why? – (just) b.** pourquoi? – parce que; **b. of** à cause de

beck [bek] *n* **to be at sb's b. and call** être aux ordres de qn

beckon ['bekən] **1** *vt* faire signe à; **to b. sb in** faire signe à qn d'entrer
2 *vi* (*of prospect*) être attirant(e); **to b. to sb** faire signe à qn; **fame beckons for him** la gloire l'attend

become [bɪ'kʌm] (*pt* **became** [bɪ'keɪm], *pp* **become**) **1** *vt Formal* (*of behaviour*) être digne de; (*of clothes, colour*) aller bien à
2 *vi* (**a**) (*come to be*) devenir; **to b. old** vieillir; **to b. thin** maigrir; **to b. known** (*of truth*) être révélé(e) (**b**) **what will b. of him?** que va-t-il devenir?

becoming [bɪ'kʌmɪŋ] *adj* (*behaviour*) convenable; (*clothes, colour*) seyant(e)

BEd [biː'ed] *n Univ* (*abbr* **Bachelor of Education**) (*qualification*) = diplôme universitaire d'aptitude à l'enseignement; (*person*) = titulaire d'un "BEd"

bed [bed] **1** *n* (**a**) (*for sleeping*) lit *m*; **to be in b.** être au lit; **to go to b.** aller au lit; **to put a child to b.** coucher un enfant; **to go to b. with sb** coucher avec qn; *Fam* **to get out of b. on the wrong side** se lever du pied gauche; **b. and breakfast** (*accommodation*) chambre *f* avec petit déjeuner; **to stay in a b. and breakfast** ≃ prendre une chambre d'hôte; **b. linen** draps *mpl* (*et taies d'oreiller etc*) (**b**) (*of river*) lit *m* (**c**) (*of flowers*) parterre *m*; (*of vegetables*) carré *m* (**d**) *Culin* lit *m*; **on a b. of rice** garni(e) de riz (**e**) *Geol* couche *f*
2 *vt* (*pt & pp* **bedded**) *Fam Old-fashioned* coucher avec

▸ **bed down** *vi* **to b. down (for the night)** s'installer (pour la nuit)

bedbug ['bedbʌg] *n* punaise *f*

bedclothes ['bedkləʊðz] *npl* draps *mpl* et couvertures *fpl*

bedding ['bedɪŋ] *n* draps *mpl* et couvertures *fpl*

bedevil [bɪ'devəl] (*pt & pp* **bedevilled,** *Am* **bedeviled**) *vt* **to be bedevilled by sth** (*complaints*) être assailli(e) de qch; (*problems*) (*of person*) être accablé(e) de qch; (*of project*) être sapé(c) par qch

bedfellow ['bedfeləʊ] *n Fig* **they make strange bedfellows** ils forment une drôle de paire

bedlam ['bedləm] *n* (*chaos*) bazar *m*

Bedouin ['beduɪn] **1** *n* Bédouin(e) *m,f*
2 *adj* bédouin(e)

bedpan ['bedpæn] *n* bassin *m*

bedpost ['bedpəʊst] *n* colonne *f* de lit

bedraggled [bɪ'drægəld] *adj* trempé(e) et crotté(e)

bedridden ['bedrɪdən] *adj* alité(e); (*permanently*) grabataire

bedrock ['bedrɒk] *n Geol* substrat *m* rocheux; *Fig* (*of beliefs, faith*) fondement *m*

bed-roll ['bedrəʊl] *n* matériel *m* de couchage

bedroom ['bedruːm] *n* chambre *f* (à coucher)

bedside ['bedsaɪd] *n* chevet *m*; **b. lamp** lampe *f* de chevet; **to have a good b. manner** (*of doctor*) savoir s'y prendre avec les malades; **b. table** table *f* de nuit *ou* de chevet

bedsit ['bedsɪt] *n Br* chambre *f* meublée

bedsock ['bedsɒk] *n* chaussette *f* pour le lit

bedsore ['bedsɔː(r)] *n* escarre *f*

bedspread ['bedspred] *n* dessus-de-lit *m inv*

bedstead ['bedsted] *n* châlit *m*

bedtime ['bedtaɪm] *n* **b.!** c'est l'heure d'aller au lit!; **it's**

past my b. je devrais déjà être couché; **b. story** histoire *f (pour endormir un enfant)*
bed-wetting ['bedwetɪŋ] *n* énurésie *f* nocturne
bee [biː] *n* abeille *f*; *Fam* **he's got a b.** in his bonnet about it c'est son idée fixe; *Br Fam* **she thinks she's the b.'s knees** elle ne se prend pas pour n'importe qui
beech [biːtʃ] *n* hêtre *m*
beechnut ['biːtʃnʌt] *n* faîne *f*
beef [biːf] **1** *n* (**a**) *(meat)* bœuf *m*; **b. stew** ragoût *m* de bœuf (**b**) *Fam (strength)* **to have plenty of b.** avoir du muscle; **give it some b.!** allez, du nerf! (**c**) *Fam (complaint)* **what's your b.?** c'est quoi ton problème?
2 *vi Fam (complain)* rouspéter (**about** contre)
▸ **beef up** *vt sep Fam (text, resources)* étoffer
beefburger ['biːfbɜːgə(r)] *n* hamburger *m*
beefeater ['biːfiːtə(r)] *n* = garde de la Tour de Londres
beefsteak ['biːfsteɪk] *n* bifteck *m*
beefy ['biːfɪ] *adj Fam (muscular)* costaud(e)
beehive ['biːhaɪv] *n (for bees)* ruche *f*
beekeeper ['biːkiːpə(r)] *n* apiculteur(trice) *m,f*
beeline ['biːlaɪn] *n Fam* **to make a b. for** foncer droit sur
been [biːn] *pp of* **be**
beep [biːp] **1** *n (of computer, alarm clock)* bip *m*; *(of car)* coup *m* de Klaxon®; *(device)* bip
2 *vt* biper
3 *vi (of computer, alarm clock)* faire bip; *(of car)* klaxonner
beer [bɪə(r)] *n* bière *f*; **b. garden** = jardin ou terrasse où les clients d'un pub peuvent consommer; **b. glass** verre *m* à bière
beery ['bɪərɪ] *adj (smell, taste)* de bière; *(breath)* qui sent la bière
beeswax ['biːzwæks] *n* cire *f* d'abeille
beet [biːt] *n* betterave *f*; *Am* = **beetroot**
beetle ['biːtəl] *n* scarabée *m*
beetroot ['biːtruːt] *n* betterave *f* (rouge); *Fam* **to go b.** devenir rouge comme une tomate
befall [bɪ'fɔːl] *(pt* befell [bɪ'fel]*, pp* befallen [bɪ'fɔːlən]) *vt Lit* arriver à
befit [bɪ'fɪt] *(pt & pp* befitted*) vt Formal* convenir à
befitting [bɪ'fɪtɪŋ] *adj* convenable
before [bɪ'fɔː(r)] **1** *prep* (**a**) *(with time)* avant; **I got here b. you** je suis arrivé avant toi; **the day b. the battle** la veille de la bataille; **b. that,...** avant,...
(**b**) *(with place)* devant; **b. my very eyes** sous mes propres yeux
(**c**) *(in importance)* avant; **she puts her family b. everything else** pour elle, la famille passe avant tout le reste
2 *adv* (**a**) *(with time)* avant; **two days b.** deux jours avant; **the day b.** le jour précédent, la veille; **the year b.** l'année précédente; **I've seen her b.** je l'ai déjà vue
(**b**) *(in space)* **this page and the one b.** cette page et celle d'avant ou et la précédente
3 *conj* **b. doing sth** avant de faire qch; **come and see me b. you leave** venez me voir avant de partir; **give it to her b. she cries** donne-le-lui avant qu'elle (ne) se mette à pleurer
beforehand [bɪ'fɔːhænd] *adv* à l'avance; **check b.** vérifiez au préalable
befriend [bɪ'frend] *vt* **to b. sb** se prendre d'amitié pour qn
befuddled [bɪ'fʌdəld] *adj (person)* perdu(e); *(mind)* embrouillé(e); **b. with drink** abruti(e) par l'alcool
beg [beg] *(pt & pp* begged*)* **1** *vt* **to b. sb to do sth** supplier qn de faire qch; **he begged a favour of me** il m'a supplié de lui rendre un service; **to b. sb's forgiveness** implorer le

pardon de qn; **I b. your pardon** *(I apologize)* (je vous demande) pardon; *(what did you say?)* pardon?; **I b. to differ** je me permets d'être d'un autre avis; **this begs the question why** on peut se demander pourquoi
2 *vi (for money)* mendier; **I b. of you!** je vous en supplie!; **to b. for sth** *(money)* mendier qch; *(help)* implorer qch; **to b. for mercy** demander grâce; **there are still a few tickets going begging** il reste encore quelques billets
began [bɪ'gæn] *pt of* **begin**
beggar ['begə(r)] **1** *n* mendiant(e) *m,f*; *Br Fam* **poor b.!** pauvre diable!; *Br Fam* **lucky b.!** veinard!; *Prov* **beggars can't be choosers** nécessité fait loi
2 *vt* **to b. belief** être incroyable; **to b. description** être indescriptible
begin [bɪ'gɪn] *(pt* began [bɪ'gæn]*, pp* begun [bɪ'gʌn]*)* **1** *vt* commencer; *(piece of work, new chapter)* commencer, entamer; **to b. to do sth, to b. doing sth** commencer à faire qch; **he began laughing** il s'est mis à rire; **I couldn't (even) b. to explain** je ne peux (vraiment) pas expliquer
2 *vi* commencer; **to b. by doing sth** commencer par faire qch; **to b. again** recommencer; **to b. with,...** pour commencer,...
beginner [bɪ'gɪnə(r)] *n* débutant(e) *m,f*
beginning [bɪ'gɪnɪŋ] *n* début *m*, commencement *m*; **in** *or* **at the b.** au début, au commencement; **at the b. of the year/month** au début de l'année/du mois; **I knew from the b. something was wrong** j'ai su dès le début que quelque chose n'allait pas; **to start from the b.** commencer au commencement; **from b. to end** *(read)* du début à la fin
begonia [bɪ'gəʊnɪə] *n* bégonia *m*
begrudge [bɪ'grʌdʒ] *vt* (**a**) *(resent)* **to b. doing sth** faire qch à contrecœur, rechigner à faire qch (**b**) *(envy)* **to b. sb sth** envier qch à qn
beguile [bɪ'gaɪl] *vt* (**a**) *(enchant)* envoûter (**b**) *(deceive)* enjôler; **to b. sb into doing sth** faire faire qch à qn en le séduisant
beguiling [bɪ'gaɪlɪŋ] *adj* enjôleur(euse)
begun [bɪ'gʌn] *pp of* **begin**
behalf [bɪ'hɑːf] *n* **on b. of sb, on sb's b.** au nom de qn, de la part de qn; **don't worry on my b.** ne vous inquiétez pas pour moi
behave [bɪ'heɪv] *vi (of person)* se conduire, se comporter; *(be good)* bien se tenir; *(of car, machine)* marcher, fonctionner; **b. yourself!** tiens-toi bien!; *(to child)* sois sage!
behavior, behavioral *etc Am* = **behaviour, behavioural** *etc*
behaviour, *Am* **behavior** [bɪ'heɪvjə(r)] *n* comportement *m*, conduite *f*; **to be on one's best b.** se tenir particulièrement bien
behavioural, *Am* **behavioral** [bɪ'heɪvjərəl] *adj* de comportement
behaviourism, *Am* **behaviorism** [bɪ'heɪvjərɪzəm] *n Psy* behaviorisme *m*
behead [bɪ'hed] *vt* décapiter
beheld [bɪ'held] *pt & pp of* **behold**
behest [bɪ'hest] *n* **at sb's b.**, **at the b. of sb** sur ordre de qn
behind [bɪ'haɪnd] **1** *prep* derrière; **he hid b.** it il s'est caché derrière; **to be b. sb** *(support)* être avec qn; **to be b. schedule** avoir du retard; **to be b.** *(forget)* ne plus penser à qch; **to be b.** *(time)* être en avance; **to be b. the times** *(old-fashioned)* retarder sur son temps; **these reasons b. sth** les raisons de qch; **what's b. all this?** qu'est-ce que ça cache?
2 *adv* derrière; **from b.** *(viewed)* de derrière; *(attacked)*

par-derrière; **to stay** *or* **remain b.** *(not leave)* rester; **to be b. with one's work** avoir du travail en retard; **to be b. with the rent** être en retard pour payer le loyer; **they are only three points b.** *(in contest)* ils ne sont qu'à trois points **3** *n Fam (buttocks)* derrière *m*

behindhand [bɪˈhaɪndhænd] *adv* en retard; **to be b. with the rent** être en retard pour payer le loyer; **to be b. with one's work** avoir du travail en retard

behold [bɪˈhəʊld] *(pt & pp* **beheld** [bɪˈheld]) *vt Lit* voir; **a sight to b.** un spectacle

beholden [bɪˈhəʊldən] *adj Formal* **to be b. to sb** être redevable à qn

beholder [bɪˈhəʊldə(r)] *n Prov* **beauty is in the eye of the b.** l'amour est aveugle

beige [beɪʒ] **1** *n* beige *m* **2** *adj* beige

Beijing [beɪˈʒɪŋ] *n* Pékin, Beijing

being [ˈbiːɪŋ] *n* **(a)** *(creature)* être *m* **(b)** *(existence)* **to come into b.** naître; **to be in b.** exister

Beirut [beɪˈruːt] *n* Beyrouth

Belarus [beləˈruːs] *n* la Biélorussie

belated [bɪˈleɪtɪd] *adj* tardif(ive); **wishing you a b. happy birthday** je te souhaite un bon anniversaire avec un peu de retard

belch [beltʃ] **1** *n (burp)* rot *m*; **to give a (loud) b.** roter (bruyamment) **2** *vt* **to b. smoke/flames** *(of fire, chimney)* cracher de la fumée/des flammes **3** *vi (of person)* roter

beleaguered [bɪˈliːɡəd] *adj (city, army)* assiégé(e); *(government)* assailli(e) de toutes parts; *(person)* accablé(e)

Belfast [belˈfɑːst] *n* Belfast

belfry [ˈbelfrɪ] *(pl* **belfries**) *n* beffroi *m*, clocher *m*

Belgian [ˈbeldʒən] **1** *n* Belge *mf* **2** *adj* belge

Belgium [ˈbeldʒəm] *n* la Belgique

Belgrade [belˈɡreɪd] *n* Belgrade

belie [bɪˈlaɪ] *vt (feelings, background)* ne pas refléter

belief [bɪˈliːf] *n* **(a)** *(conviction)* conviction *f*; *(religious)* croyance *f*; **in the b. that...** étant convaincu(e) que..., **it is my b. that...** je suis convaincu(e) que... **(b)** *(confidence)* foi *f* **(in** en)

believable [bɪˈliːvəbəl] *adj* crédible, plausible

believe [bɪˈliːv] **1** *vt* croire; **I b. (that) I'm right** je crois que j'ai raison; **I b. him to be innocent** je crois qu'il est innocent; **she is believed to be in hiding** on pense qu'elle se cache; **I don't b. a word of it** je n'en crois pas un mot; **I could scarcely b. my eyes** j'en croyais à peine mes yeux; **I don't b. it!** c'est pas vrai! **2** *vi* **(a) to b. in sth** *(have faith in)* croire à qch; **to b. in God** croire en Dieu; **to b. in sb** *(have confidence in)* avoir foi en qn; **to b. in oneself** avoir confiance en soi **(b) to believe in sth** *(be in favour of)* croire à qch; **I don't b. in making promises** je n'aime pas faire de promesses **(c)** *(think, suppose)* croire; **I b. not** je ne crois pas, je crois que non; **I b. so** je crois (que oui)

believer [bɪˈliːvə(r)] *n* **(a)** *(religious person)* croyant(e) *m,f*; **to be a b.** être croyant(e) **(b)** *(supporter)* **to be a b. in sth** croire à qch

belittle [bɪˈlɪtəl] *vt* rabaisser; **to b. oneself** se rabaisser

Belize [beˈliːz] *n* le Belize

bell [bel] *n (of church)* cloche *f*; *(handbell, on cat)* clochette *f*; *(on door, bicycle)* sonnette *f*; **to ring the b.** *(on door)* sonner; *Br Fam* **to give sb a b.** passer un coup de fil à qn; **b. jar** cloche; **b. tower** clocher *m*

belladonna [beləˈdɒnə] *n* belladone *f*

bell-bottoms [ˈbelbɒtəmz] *npl* pantalon *m* (à) pattes d'éléphant

bell-boy [ˈbelbɔɪ] *n Am Fam* groom *m*

belle [bel] *n* beauté *f*; **the b. of the ball** la reine du bal

bellhop [ˈbelhɒp] *n Am Fam* groom *m*

bellicose [ˈbelɪkəʊs] *adj* belliqueux(euse)

belligerence [beˈlɪdʒərəns] *n* agressivité *f*

belligerent [beˈlɪdʒərənt] **1** *n (in war)* belligérant(e) *m,f*; *(in dispute)* partie *f* **2** *adj (aggressive)* agressif(ive), belliqueux(euse); *(at war)* belligérant(e)

bellow [ˈbeləʊ] **1** *n (of bull)* beuglement *m*, mugissement *m*; *(of person)* braillement *m* **2** *vi (of bull)* beugler, mugir; *(of person)* brailler

bellows [ˈbeləʊz] *npl* **(pair of) b.** soufflet *m*

bell-ringer [ˈbelrɪŋə(r)] *n* carillonneur(euse) *m,f*

belly [ˈbelɪ] *(pl* **bellies**) *n* ventre *m*; **to have a full/an empty b.** avoir le ventre plein/vide; **b. dance** danse *f* du ventre; **b. laugh** gros rire *m*

bellyache [ˈbelɪeɪk] *Fam* **1** *n* mal *m* au ventre **2** *vi (complain)* rouspéter, râler **(about sb/about sth** après qn/au sujet de qch)

belly-button [ˈbelɪbʌtən] *n Fam* nombril *m*

belly-flop [ˈbelɪflɒp] **1** *n* plat *m* **2** *vi (pt & pp* **belly-flopped**) faire un plat

bellyful [ˈbelɪfʊl] *n Fam* **to have had a b. of sb/sth** en avoir marre ou ras le bol de qn/qch

belong [bɪˈlɒŋ] *vi* **(a) to b. to** *(be property of)* appartenir à; **that money belongs to me** cet argent m'appartient *ou* est à moi **(b) to b. to** *(club, party)* être membre de; *(category)* appartenir à **(c)** *(have a proper place)* aller; **to put sth back where it belongs** remettre qch à sa place; **the saucepans don't b. in that cupboard** les casseroles ne vont pas *ou* ne se rangent pas dans ce placard; **I feel I b. here** je me sens à ma place ici

belonging [bɪˈlɒŋɪŋ] *n* **to have a sense of b.** se sentir à sa place

belongings [bɪˈlɒŋɪŋz] *npl* affaires *fpl*

beloved 1 *n* [bɪˈlʌvɪd] *Lit* bien-aimé(e) *m,f* **2** *adj* [bɪˈlʌvd] bien-aimé(e)

below [bɪˈləʊ] **1** *prep* **(a)** *(line, age, temperature)* au-dessous de; *(bridge, ground)* sous **(b)** *(with numbers)* moins de **2** *adv* au-dessous, en bas; *(in text)* ci-dessous; **on the floor b.** à l'étage du dessous; **it's 10 degrees b.** il fait moins dix

belt [belt] **1** *n* **(a)** *(for trousers)* ceinture *f*; *Fig* **to tighten one's b.** se serrer la ceinture; *Fig* **to have sth under one's b.** *(driving licence, degree)* avoir qch en poche; *(experience)* avoir qch à son actif; *Fig* **that was a bit below the b.** *(of remark, criticism)* c'était un coup bas **(b)** *(of machine)* courroie *f* **(c)** *(of land)* région *f*, zone *f* **(d)** *Fam (blow)* coup *m*; **to give sb a b.** flanquer un gnon à qn **2** *vt (hit) (ball)* cogner dans; *(person)* flanquer un gnon à **3** *vi Fam (move quickly)* **to b. along** foncer; **she belted down the stairs** elle a descendu les escaliers quatre à quatre
> **belt out** *vt sep Fam (song)* brailler
> **belt up** *vi Br very Fam (be quiet)* la fermer; **b. up!** la ferme!

bemoan [bɪˈməʊn] *vt (loss, somebody's death)* pleurer; *(one's fate)* se lamenter sur

bemused [bɪˈmjuːzd] *adj* perplexe

bench [bentʃ] n *(seat)* & Pol banc m; *(worktable)* établi m; Br Law **the b.** *(magistrates)* la magistrature; *(court)* la cour; **to be on the b.** *(in football)* être remplaçant(e)

benchmark ['bentʃmɑːk] n *(for comparison)* référence f

bend [bend] **1** n **(a)** *(of road)* virage m, tournant m; *(of river)* méandre m; *(of pipe)* coude m; Br Fam **to drive sb round the b.** rendre qn dingue **(b)** **the bends** *(decompression sickness)* la maladie des caissons **2** vt *(pt & pp* bent [bent]) *(leg, arm, wire)* plier; *(head)* baisser; *(light)* réfracter; **do not b.** *(on envelope)* ne pas plier; **on bended knee** à genoux; **to b. the rules** faire une entorse au règlement; Br Fam **to b. sb's ear** tenir la jambe à qn **3** vi *(of road)* tourner; *(of river)* faire un coude; *(of branch)* plier

▸ **bend down** vi se pencher

▸ **bend over** vi se pencher; Fig **to b. over backwards to do sth** se décarcasser pour faire qch

bender ['bendə(r)] n Fam beuverie f; **to go on a b.** prendre une cuite

beneath [bɪ'niːθ] **1** prep **(a)** *(physically)* sous **(b)** *(unworthy of)* **to marry b. one** faire une mésalliance; **she thinks it's b. her to work** elle pense que travailler est indigne d'elle; **b. contempt** parfaitement méprisable **2** adv dessous, au-dessous; **from b.** de dessous

Benedictine [benɪ'dɪktɪn] adj Rel bénédictin(e)

benediction [benɪ'dɪkʃən] n Rel bénédiction f

benefactor ['benɪfæktə(r)] n bienfaiteur m

benefactress ['benɪfæktrɪs] n bienfaitrice f

beneficent [bɪ'nefɪsənt] adj *(system)* bienfaisant(e); *(person)* bon (bonne)

beneficial [benɪ'fɪʃəl] adj bénéfique **(to** pour)

beneficiary [benɪ'fɪʃərɪ] *(pl* **beneficiaries)** n bénéficiaire mf

benefit ['benɪfɪt] **1** n **(a)** *(advantage)* profit m; **to have the b. of sth** pouvoir profiter de qch; **for sb's b., for the b. of sb** à l'intention de qn; **that remark was for my b.** cette remarque m'était destinée; **to give sb the b. of the doubt** accorder à qn le bénéfice du doute **(b)** *(charity event)* spectacle m de bienfaisance; **b. match** match m de bienfaisance **(c)** *(state payment)* allocation f; **to be on b.** toucher une aide de l'État; **social security benefits** prestations fpl sociales **2** vt *(person, country)* profiter à; *(trade)* favoriser **3** vi **to b. from sth** tirer profit de qch; **you'll b. from a holiday** ça te fera du bien d'aller en vacances; **who stands to b. most?** à qui cela profitera-t-il le plus?

Benelux ['benɪlʌks] n Benelux m; **the B. countries** les pays du Benelux

benevolence [bɪ'nevələns] n bienveillance f

benevolent [bɪ'nevələnt] adj bienveillant(e); **b. society** association f de bienfaisance

Bengal [beŋ'gɔːl] n le Bengale

Bengali [beŋ'gɔːlɪ] **1** n **(a)** *(person)* Bengali mf **(b)** *(language)* bengali m **2** adj bengali

benign [bɪ'naɪn] adj *(attitude)* bienveillant(e); *(climate)* doux (douce); *(tumour)* bénin(igne)

Benin [be'niːn] n le Bénin

bent [bent] **1** n *(taste)* penchant m, inclination f; *(aptitude)* dispositions fpl; **to have a musical b.** avoir des dispositions pour la musique **2** adj **(a)** *(curved)* tordu(e); *(out of shape)* plié(e); *(person, back)* voûté(e) **(b)** Fam *(dishonest)* pourri(e); **b. cop** (flic m) ripou m **(c)** very Fam *(homosexual)* pédé, = terme injurieux qualifiant un homosexuel **(d)** **to be b. on doing sth**

(determined) être résolu(e) à faire qch; **to be b. on sth** vouloir à tout prix qch

3 pt & pp of **bend**

benzene ['benziːn] n Chem benzène m

benzine ['benziːn] n Chem benzine f

bequeath [bɪ'kwiːð] vt Formal léguer **(to** à)

bequest [bɪ'kwest] n Formal legs m

berate [bɪ'reɪt] vt réprimander

Berber ['bɜːbə(r)] **1** n Berbère mf **2** adj berbère

bereaved [bɪ'riːvd] **1** npl **the b.** la famille du défunt (de la défunte) **2** adj en deuil; **recently b.** qui vient de perdre un être cher

bereavement [bɪ'riːvmənt] n deuil m; **b. counselling** aide psychologique aux personnes en deuil

bereft [bɪ'reft] adj **to be b. of sth** être privé(e) de qch; **to feel b.** se sentir totalement seul(e)

beret ['bereɪ] n béret m

bergamot ['bɜːgəmɒt] n bergamote f

berk [bɜːk] n Br Fam andouille f; **to feel a right b.** se sentir idiot(e)

Berlin [bɜː'lɪn] n Berlin; **the B. Wall** le mur de Berlin

Berliner [bɜː'lɪnə(r)] n Berlinois(e) m,f

Bermuda [bə'mjuːdə] n les Bermudes fpl; **B. shorts** bermuda m; **the B. triangle** le triangle des Bermudes

Bern(e) [bɜːn] n Berne

berry ['berɪ] *(pl* **berries)** n baie f

berserk [bə'zɜːk] adj Fam **to go b.** devenir fou furieux (folle furieuse)

berth [bɜːθ] **1** n **(a)** *(on train, ship)* couchette f **(b)** *(in harbour)* poste m à quai; Fig **to give sb a wide b.** éviter qn **2** vt *(boat)* amarrer à quai **3** vi *(of boat)* aborder ou se ranger à quai

beseech [bɪ'siːtʃ] *(pt & pp* **besought** [bɪ'sɔːt]) vt Lit supplier

beseeching [bɪ'siːtʃɪŋ] adj suppliant(e)

beset [bɪ'set] *(pt & pp* **beset)** vt assaillir; **to be beset by doubts** être assailli(e) par le doute; **to be beset with dangers/difficulties** être en proie à toutes sortes de dangers/difficultés

beside [bɪ'saɪd] prep **(a)** *(next to)* à côté de; *(sea, lake)* au bord de; **that's b. the point** cela n'a rien à voir; **to be b. oneself with joy/anger** être fou (folle) de joie/de colère **(b)** *(compared to)* à côté de, par rapport à

besides [bɪ'saɪdz] **1** prep à part; **other people b. ourselves** d'autres gens que nous; **what else can you do b. type?** à part taper, que savez-vous faire?; **b. being an excellent singer, she also plays the violin** non seulement elle chante très bien, mais en plus elle joue du violon; **b. which she was unwell** sans compter qu'elle ne se sentait pas bien **2** adv *(in addition)* en plus; **many more b.** bien d'autres encore **(b)** *(furthermore)* **and b., it's too expensive** et d'ailleurs ou en plus, c'est trop cher

besiege [bɪ'siːdʒ] vt *(castle, town)* assiéger; Fig **to b. sb with complaints/requests** assaillir qn de plaintes/demandes

besmirch [bɪ'smɜːtʃ] vt Lit souiller

besotted [bɪ'sɒtɪd] adj **to be b. with** *(person, car)* s'être entiché(e) de; *(idea)* être obsédé(e) par

besought [bɪ'sɔːt] pt & pp of **beseech**

bespatter [bɪ'spætə(r)] vt éclabousser **(with** de)

bespectacled [bɪ'spektəkəld] adj qui porte des lunettes, à lunettes

bespoke [bɪ'spəʊk] adj (fait(e)) sur mesure; **b. tailor** tailleur m à façon

best [best] (superlative of **good, well**) **1** n the **b.** (the best thing) ce qu'il y a de mieux; **that's the b.** I could find c'est ce que j'ai trouvé de mieux; **at b.** au mieux; **the b. of it is...** le plus beau, c'est...; **at the b.** of times en temps normal; **to do one's b.** faire de son mieux (**to pour**); **to look one's b.** être à son avantage; **to be at one's b.** être au mieux de sa forme; **to bring out the b.** in sb révéler les qualités de qn; **to get the b. out of sth** tirer le meilleur parti de qch; **to make the b. of sth** s'accommoder de qch; **we are the b. of friends** nous sommes les meilleurs amis du monde; **to be in the b. of health** se porter à merveille; **to the b. of my knowledge** autant que je sache; **to the b. of one's ability** de son mieux; **he can sing with the b. of them** il chante aussi bien que n'importe qui; **to hope for the b.** avoir espoir; **to have or get the b. of both worlds** gagner sur les deux tableaux; Fam **all the b.!** bonne chance!; **my brother sends his b.** mon frère vous fait ses amitiés

2 adj meilleur(e); **my b. dress** ma plus belle robe; **she is b. at French** (of group of people) c'est la meilleure en français; **to put one's b. foot forward** faire de son mieux; **the b. part of a year** pratiquement un an; **I'm acting in your b. interests** j'agis au mieux de vos intérêts; **it is b. to...** le mieux, c'est de...; Com **b. before date** date f limite de consommation; **the b. case scenario** le scénario le plus optimiste; **b. man** (at wedding) garçon m d'honneur; **may the b. man win** (in contest) que le meilleur gagne

3 adv le mieux; **as b. I could** du mieux que j'ai pu, de mon mieux; **you know b.** c'est vous qui êtes le mieux placé pour savoir; **do as you think b.** fais comme bon te semblera; **the b. dressed man** l'homme le mieux habillé; **she came off b.** (in argument) elle a eu le dessus

4 vt (in contest, argument) l'emporter sur

bestial ['bestɪəl] adj bestial(e)

bestiality [bestɪ'ælɪtɪ] n bestialité f

bestow [bɪ'stəʊ] vt accorder (**on a**)

bestseller [best'selə(r)] n best-seller m

bestselling [best'selɪŋ] adj (book, author) à succès

bet [bet] **1** n pari m; **to make or place a b.** parier; Fig **my b. is that he'll come** je parie qu'il viendra; Fig **your best b. would be to...** ce que tu as de mieux à faire, c'est de...; Fig **it's a safe b.** il y a gros à parier

2 vt (pt & pp bet or betted) also Fig parier; Fam Fig **I b. you she'll win** je te parie qu'elle va gagner; Fam Fig **b. you I will!** chiche (que je le fais)!

3 vi parier (**on** sur); **to b. on a horse** miser sur un cheval; Fig **I wouldn't b. on it!** je n'y compterais pas trop!; Fam **you b.!** et comment!; Fam **John says he's sorry – I b. (he does)!** John dit qu'il regrette – tu parles!

betel ['biːtəl] n bétel m; **b. nut** noix f d'arec

Bethlehem ['beθlɪhem] n Bethléem

betide [bɪ'taɪd] vt Lit **woe b. him/you!** malheur à lui/à toi!

betray [bɪ'treɪ] vt also Fig trahir; **to b. sb to the enemy** livrer qn à l'ennemi

betrayal [bɪ'treɪəl] n (a) (of person, country) trahison f; **b. of trust** abus m de confiance (**b**) (of emotion) indice m

betrothal [bɪ'trəʊðəl] n Lit fiançailles fpl

betrothed [bɪ'trəʊðd] n & adj Lit fiancé(e) m,f

better ['betə(r)] (comparative of **good, well**) **1** n **I expected b. of you** j'attendais mieux de ta part; **you should respect your** (**elders and**) **betters** il faut respecter ses aînés; **to change for the b.** (of person) changer en bien; (of situation) s'améliorer; **to get the b. of sb** avoir le dessus sur qn; **her curiosity got the b. of her** sa curiosité a été trop forte; **the sooner/faster the b.** le plus tôt/vite possible sera le mieux

2 adj meilleur(e); **to be b.** (after illness) aller mieux; **to get b.** (of person, wound) aller mieux; (of situation, weather) s'arranger; **he's b. at maths/running than his brother** il est meilleur en maths/à la course que son frère; **it would be b. for you to go** il vaudrait mieux que vous y alliez; **that's b.!** voilà qui est mieux!; **b. luck next time!** tu feras mieux la prochaine fois!; **the b. part of a week** pratiquement une semaine; Br Fam **my b. half** ma moitié

3 adv mieux; **to look b.** (of ill person) avoir meilleure mine; **b. and b.** de mieux en mieux; **so much the b., all the b.** d'autant mieux; **for b. or for worse** pour le meilleur et pour le pire; **you had b. not stay** tu ferais mieux de ne pas rester; **to think b. of it** se raviser; **to be b. off** (financially) être plus à l'aise; (in situation) être mieux

4 vt (improve) améliorer; (surpass) faire mieux que; **to b. oneself** améliorer sa situation

betterment ['betəmənt] n amélioration f; (of mankind) progrès m

betting ['betɪŋ] n (bets) paris mpl; Fam Fig **the b. is that...** il y a fort à parier que...; **what's the b. that...?** combien tu paries que...?; **b. slip** bulletin m de pari; **b. shop** ≃ PMU m

between [bɪ'twiːn] **1** prep entre; (**in**) **b. now and Monday** d'ici lundi, **we bought it b. us** nous l'avons acheté à nous deux/trois/etc; **this is strictly b. you and me** que cela reste entre nous; **b. you, me and the gatepost** (soit dit) entre nous

2 adv (**in**) **b.** au milieu

bevel ['bevəl] **1** n biseau m

2 vt (pt & pp bevelled, Am beveled) biseauter

beverage ['bevərɪdʒ] n boisson f

bevvied ['bevɪd] adj Br Fam (drunk) bourré(e)

bevvy ['bevɪ] (pl bevvies) n Br Fam (drink) alcool m

bevy ['bevɪ] (pl bevies) n (group) nuée f

bewail [bɪ'weɪl] vt (loss) pleurer; (one's fate) se lamenter sur

beware [bɪ'weə(r)] vi se méfier (**of** de); **b.!** attention!; **b. of the dog** (sign) chien méchant

bewilder [bɪ'wɪldə(r)] vt dérouter, laisser perplexe

bewildered [bɪ'wɪldəd] adj dérouté(e), perplexe

bewildering [bɪ'wɪldərɪŋ] adj déroutant(e)

bewilderment [bɪ'wɪldəmənt] n perplexité f; **to his b.** à son grand étonnement

bewitch [bɪ'wɪtʃ] vt ensorceler

bewitching [bɪ'wɪtʃɪŋ] adj (smile, beauty) enchanteur(eresse)

beyond [bɪ'jɒnd] **1** prep (**a**) (in space, time) au-delà de; **the house is b. the church** la maison est après l'église (**b**) (surpassing) **to live b. one's means** vivre au-dessus de ses moyens; **it's b. me** (how they can do it) ça me dépasse (qu'ils puissent faire ça); **due to circumstances b. our control** en raison de circonstances indépendantes de notre volonté; **it's b. my power** ça ne dépend pas de moi pouvoir; **I'm b. caring** ça m'est complètement égal; **it's b. doubt** cela ne fait aucun doute; **it's b. a joke** ce n'est plus drôle; **b. belief** incroyable; **b. reach** hors de portée; **b. repair** irréparable (**c**) (except) à part

2 adv au-delà

3 n the b. l'au-delà m

Bhutan [buː'tɑːn] n le Bhoutan

bias ['baɪəs] **1** n (**a**) (inclination) préjugé m, parti m pris (**against/towards** contre/en faveur de) (**b**) (in sewing) biais m

2 vt (pt & pp bias(s)ed) influencer (**against/towards** contre/en faveur de)

bias(s)ed ['baɪəst] *adj (article, account)* partial(e); *(person) &* parti pris; *(opinion)* préconçu(e); **to be b.** in sb's favour avoir un préjugé en faveur de qn

bib [bɪb] *n (for baby)* bavoir *m*, bavette *f*; *(of apron, dungarees)* bavette

bible ['baɪbəl] *n also Fig* bible *f*; **the B.** la Bible; *Fam* **b. basher** grenouille *f* de bénitier; *Am* **the B. Belt** = ensemble des États du sud des États-Unis où le fondamentalisme chrétien est très répandu

biblical ['bɪblɪkəl] *adj* biblique; *Fam Hum* **to know sb in the b. sense** connaître qn au sens biblique du terme

bibliography [bɪblɪ'ɒgrəfɪ] *(pl* **bibliographies)** *n* bibliographie *f*

bibliophile ['bɪblɪəfaɪl] *n* bibliophile *mf*

bicameral [baɪ'kæmərəl] *adj Pol* bicaméral(e)

bicarbonate [baɪ'kɑːbəneɪt] *n* bicarbonate *m*; **b. of soda** bicarbonate de soude

bicentenary [baɪsen'tiːnərɪ], *Am* **bicentennial** [baɪsen'tenɪəl] **1** *n* bicentenaire *m*
2 *adj* bicentenaire

biceps ['baɪseps] *(pl* biceps) *n Anat* biceps *m*

bicker ['bɪkə(r)] *vi* se chamailler

bickering ['bɪkərɪŋ] *n* chamailleries *fpl*

bicycle ['baɪsɪkəl] *n* bicyclette *f*, vélo *m*; **to ride a b.** faire de la bicyclette *ou* du vélo; **b. clip** pince *f* à vélo; **b. kick** *(in football)* retourné *m* bicyclette

bid¹ [bɪd] **1** *n* **(a)** *(offer)* offre *f*; *(at auction)* enchère *f*; **to make a b. (for sth)** faire une offre (pour qch); *(at auction)* faire une enchère (sur qch) **(b)** *(attempt)* tentative *f* (**for sth /** **to do sth** de qch/pour faire qch); **a rescue/suicide b.** une tentative de sauvetage/de suicide; **to make a b. for power** *(legally)* viser le pouvoir; *(illegally)* faire une tentative de coup d'État
2 *vt (pt & pp* bid) *(offer)* offrir; *(at auction)* faire une enchère de; **what am I bid for this table?** que m'offrez-vous pour cette table?
3 *vi* **to b. for sth** faire une offre pour qch; *(at auction)* faire une enchère sur qch

bid² *(pt* bade [bæd, beɪd] *or* bid, *pp* bidden [bɪdən] *or* bid) *vt Lit* **to b. sb welcome** souhaiter la bienvenue à qn; **to b. sb goodbye** faire ses adieux à qn

bidder ['bɪdə(r)] *n (at auction)* enchérisseur(euse) *m,f*; **the highest b.** le plus offrant

bidding¹ ['bɪdɪŋ] *n (at auction)* enchères *fpl*

bidding² *n Lit (command)* **at sb's b.** sur l'ordre de qn

bide [baɪd] *vt* **to b. one's time** attendre le bon moment

bidet ['biːdeɪ] *n* bidet *m*

biennial [baɪ'enɪəl] **1** *n (plant)* plante *f* bisannuelle
2 *adj* bisannuel(elle)

bier [bɪə(r)] *n* brancards *mpl*

biff [bɪf] *Fam* **1** *n* gnon *m*
2 *vt* flanquer un gnon à

bifocal [baɪ'fəʊkəl] **1** *n* **bifocals** lunettes *fpl* à double foyer
2 *adj* à double foyer

big [bɪg] **1** *adj* **(a)** *(tall, large)* grand(e); *(fat)* gros (grosse); *(drop, increase)* fort(e); *(fashionable)* à la mode; **to get big(ger)** *(taller)* grandir; *(fatter)* grossir; **my b. sister** ma grande sœur; **a b. problem** un gros problème; **to be a b. eater** être un gros mangeur (une grosse mangeuse); **a b. hand for our guest!** on applaudit bien fort notre invité!; **the B. Apple** = surnom de New York; **b. business** les milieux d'affaires; *Aut* **b. end** tête *f* de bielle; **b. game** *(in hunting)* gros gibier *m*; **b. spender** panier *m* percé; **b. toe** gros orteil *m*; **b. top** *(of circus)* chapiteau *m*; **b. wheel** *(at fair)* grande roue *f*

(b) *(idioms)* **it's her b. day** tomorrow demain c'est son grand jour; **to have b. ideas** avoir de grands projets; **don't get any b. ideas!** ne t'excite pas trop!; *Fam* **what's the b. idea?** c'est quoi cette histoire?; **to earn b. money** gagner beaucoup d'argent; **to make it b.** réussir; **to go in for sth in a b. way** adorer qch; *Ironic* **that's b. of you!** tu es trop bon!; **to be too b. for one's boots** ne plus se sentir; **to be b. on sth** tenir à qch; **to have a b. mouth** *(be indiscreet)* parler trop; *Fam* **b. gun** gros bonnet *m*; *Fig* **a b. name** un grand nom; *Fam* **b. shot** *or* **noise** gros bonnet *m*; **the b. time** le succès
2 *adv* **to talk b.** faire l'important; **to think b.** voir grand

bigamist ['bɪgəmɪst] *n* bigame *mf*

bigamous ['bɪgəməs] *adj* bigame

bigamy ['bɪgəmɪ] *n* bigamie *f*

biggie, biggy ['bɪgɪ] *(pl* biggies) *n Fam* it's going to be a b. *(storm, new film)* ça va faire mal

bighead ['bɪghed] *n Fam* crâneur(euse) *m,f*

bigheaded [bɪg'hedɪd] *adj* crâneur(euse); **to get b.** commencer à avoir la grosse tête

big-hearted [bɪg'hɑːtɪd] *adj* **to be b.** avoir le cœur sur la main

bigot ['bɪgət] *n* sectaire *mf*

bigoted ['bɪgətɪd] *adj* sectaire (**against** à l'égard de)

bigotry ['bɪgətrɪ] *n* sectarisme *m*

bigwig ['bɪgwɪg] *n Fam* gros bonnet *m*

bike [baɪk] *n* vélo *m*; *(motorcycle)* moto *f*; *Br Fam* **on your b.!** *(go away)* dégage!; *(don't talk nonsense)* à d'autres!; **b. shed** remise *f* à vélos

biker ['baɪkə(r)] *n Fam* motard(e) *m,f*

bikini [bɪ'kiːnɪ] *n* bikini® *m*; **b. bottom** bas *m* de maillot; **b. top** haut *m* de maillot; **b. wax** épilation *f* maillot

bilateral [baɪ'lætərəl] *adj* bilatéral(e)

bilberry ['bɪlbərɪ] *(pl* bilberries) *n* myrtille *f*

bile [baɪl] *n* bile *f*; *Fig (bitterness)* hargne *f*

bilge [bɪldʒ] *n Fam (nonsense)* bêtises *fpl*

bilingual [baɪ'lɪŋgwəl] *adj* bilingue

bilious ['bɪlɪəs] *adj* **(a)** *(nauseous)* nauséeux(euse); **b. attack** crise *f* de foie; **b. yellow** jaunâtre **(b)** *(bad-tempered)* hargneux(euse)

Bill [bɪl] *n Br Fam* **the (Old) B.** *(the police)* les flics *mpl*

bill¹ [bɪl] **1** *n (of bird)* bec *m*
2 *vi Fam* **to b. and coo** roucouler

bill² **1** *n* **(a)** *(in restaurant)* addition *f*; *(for goods, services)* facture *f*; *(in hotel)* note *f*; *Fin* **b. of exchange** lettre *f* de change **(b)** *Am (banknote)* billet *m* **(c)** *(notice)* affiche *f*; **(stick) no bills** *(sign)* défense d'afficher; *Th* **to head** *or* **top the b.** être en tête d'affiche **(d)** *(list)* **b. of fare** menu *m*; **to give sb a clean b. of health** trouver qn en parfaite santé; *Fam* **to fit the b.** faire l'affaire **(e)** *Pol (proposed law)* projet *m* de loi; **B. of Rights** = les dix premiers amendements à la Constitution américaine
2 *vt* **(a)** *(give invoice to)* envoyer la facture à **(b)** *(publicize)* annoncer

billboard ['bɪlbɔːd] *n* panneau *m* d'affichage

billet ['bɪlɪt] *Mil* **1** *n* cantonnement *m*
2 *vt* cantonner

billfold ['bɪlfəʊld] *n Am* portefeuille *m*

billiard ['bɪlɪəd] *n* billiards billard *m*; **b. ball/table** boule *f*/table *f* de billard

billion ['bɪlɪən] *n (thousand million)* milliard *m*; *Fam* **I've got billions of things to do!** j'ai des tonnes de choses à faire!

billionaire [bɪlɪə'neə(r)] *n* milliardaire *mf*

billow ['bɪləʊ] **1** n (of smoke) nuage m
2 vi ondoyer
billowy ['bɪləʊɪ] adj ondoyant(e); (sea) houleux(euse)
billposter ['bɪlpəʊstə] n billposters will be prosecuted (sign) ≃ défense d'afficher
billy-can ['bɪlɪkæn] n gamelle f
billy-goat ['bɪlɪgəʊt] n bouc m
bimbo ['bɪmbəʊ] (pl bimbos) n Fam Pej minette f
bin [bɪn] **1** n poubelle f
2 vt (pt & pp binned) Fam mettre à la poubelle
binary ['baɪnərɪ] adj Math & Comptr binaire; **b. code/number** code m/nombre m binaire
bind [baɪnd] **1** n Fam plaie f; **to be in a b.** avoir un embêtement
2 vt (pt & pp bound [baʊnd]) (a) (tie) attacher; **to be bound hand and foot** être pieds et poings liés; **they are bound together by ties of friendship** ils sont unis par les liens de l'amitié
(**b**) (bandage) bander
(**c**) (book) relier
(**d**) (cause to stick) lier
(**e**) (oblige) **to be bound by sth** être lié(e) par qch; **she bound me to secrecy** elle m'a fait jurer de garder le secret; **you are bound to report any change in your income** vous êtes tenu de signaler tout changement dans vos revenus
▸ **bind over** vt sep Law sommer
▸ **bind up** vt sep (a) (cut, wound) bander (b) **to be bound up with sth** (involved) être lié(e) a qch
binder ['baɪndə(r)] n (a) (for papers) classeur m (b) (bookbinder) relieur(euse) m,f (c) (farm machinery) lieuse f
binding ['baɪndɪŋ] **1** n reliure f
2 adj (contract, promise) qui engage ou lie
binge [bɪndʒ] Fam **1** n (drinking spree) beuverie f; **to go on a b.** prendre une cuite; **to have a chocolate b.** faire une orgie de chocolat
2 vi **to b. on sth** (drink) s'enfiler des litres de qch; (food) s'empiffrer de qch
bingo ['bɪŋgəʊ] **1** n ≃ loto m; **b. hall** = salle où l'on joue au "bingo"
2 exclam et voilà!
binman ['bɪnmæn] n Br éboueur m
binoculars [bɪ'nɒkjʊləz] npl jumelles fpl
bint [bɪnt] n Br very Fam pétasse f
biochemical [baɪəʊ'kemɪkəl] adj biochimique
biochemist [baɪəʊ'kemɪst] n biochimiste mf
biochemistry [baɪəʊ'kemɪstrɪ] n biochimie f
biodegradable [baɪəʊdɪ'greɪdəbəl] adj biodégradable
biodiversity [baɪəʊdaɪ'vɜːsɪtɪ] n biodiversité f
biographer [baɪ'ɒɡrəfə(r)] n biographe mf
biographic(al) [baɪə'ɡræfɪk(əl)] adj biographique
biography [baɪ'ɒɡrəfɪ] (pl biographies) n biographie f
biological [baɪə'lɒdʒɪkəl] adj biologique; **b. warfare** guerre f bactériologique; **b. washing powder** lessive f aux enzymes
biologist [baɪ'ɒlədʒɪst] n biologiste mf
biology [baɪ'ɒlədʒɪ] n biologie f
biopsy ['baɪɒpsɪ] (pl biopsies) n Med biopsie f
biorhythm ['baɪəʊrɪðəm] n rythme m biologique
biosphere ['baɪəsfɪə(r)] n biosphère f
biotechnology [baɪəʊtek'nɒlədʒɪ] n biotechnologie f
bipartisan [baɪ'pɑːtɪzæn] adj Pol bipartite
biped ['baɪped] n bipède m

biplane ['baɪpleɪn] n biplan m
birch [bɜːtʃ] **1** n bouleau m; **to give sb the b.** fouetter qn
2 vt (beat) fouetter
bird [bɜːd] n (a) (in general) oiseau m; (poultry) volaille f; **b. of paradise** oiseau de paradis; **b. of prey** oiseau de proie, rapace m; **b. sanctuary** réserve f ornithologique; **b. table** mangeoire f pour oiseaux (b) Br Fam (woman) nana f (c) (idioms) Fam **a little b. told me** c'est mon petit doigt qui me l'a dit; **the b. has flown** l'oiseau s'est envolé; Prov **a b. in the hand is worth two in the bush** un tiens vaut mieux que deux tu l'auras; Prov **birds of a feather flock together** qui se ressemble s'assemble; **to kill two birds with one stone** faire d'une pierre deux coups; Euph **it's time you told him about the birds and the bees** il serait temps de lui expliquer que les bébés ne naissent pas dans les choux
birdbath ['bɜːdbɑːθ] n vasque f pour les oiseaux
bird-brained ['bɜːdbreɪnd] adj Fam (idea) extra vagant(e); **to be b.** (of person) avoir une cervelle d'oiseau
birdcage ['bɜːdkeɪdʒ] n cage f à oiseaux; (in zoo) volière f
birdie ['bɜːdɪ] n (a) Fam (bird) petit oiseau m; Fig **watch the b.!** (when taking photo) attention, le petit oiseau va sortir! (b) (in golf) birdie m
birdseed ['bɜːdsiːd] n graines fpl pour oiseaux
bird's-eye view ['bɜːdzaɪ'vjuː] n vue f d'ensemble
birdwatcher ['bɜːdwɒtʃə(r)] n ornithologue mf amateur
bird-watching ['bɜːdwɒtʃɪŋ] n **to go b.** aller observer les oiseaux
Birmingham ['bɜːmɪŋəm] n Birmingham
Biro® ['baɪrəʊ] (pl Biros) n Br stylo m (à) bille
birth [bɜːθ] n naissance f; **to give b. (to)** accoucher (de); **at b.** à la naissance; **by b.** de naissance; **from b.** (blind, deaf) de naissance; **b. certificate** acte m de naissance; **b. control** contrôle m des naissances; Fig **b. pangs** accouchement m douloureux; **b. rate** taux m de natalité
birthday ['bɜːθdeɪ] n anniversaire m; Fam **to be in one's b. suit** (of man) être en costume d'Adam; (of woman) être en costume d'Ève; **b. card/present** carte f/cadeau m d'anniversaire
birthmark ['bɜːθmɑːk] n tache f de naissance, envie f
birthplace ['bɜːθpleɪs] n lieu m de naissance
birthright ['bɜːθraɪt] n droit m acquis à la naissance; Fig droit élémentaire
Biscay ['bɪskeɪ] n see bay
biscuit ['bɪskɪt] n biscuit m; Fam **that really takes the b.!** ça, c'est le bouquet!
bisect [baɪ'sekt] vt couper en deux
bisexual [baɪ'seksjʊəl] n & adj bisexuel(elle) m,f
bishop ['bɪʃəp] n évêque m; (in chess) fou m
bishopric ['bɪʃəprɪk] n évêché m
bison ['baɪsən] n bison m
bistro ['biːstrəʊ] (pl bistros) n petit restaurant m
bit¹ [bɪt] n (a) (in horseriding) mors m; Fig **to get the b. between one's teeth** prendre le mors aux dents (b) (for drill) mèche f
bit² n (a) (piece) bout m; (of film, book) passage m, **a b. of news** une nouvelle; **to take sth to bits** démonter qch; **to tear sth to bits** déchirer qch en petits morceaux; **to smash sth to bits** réduire qch en mille morceaux; **he has eaten every b.** il a mangé jusqu'à la dernière miette; **to do one's b.** participer; Br Fam **she's a b.** of all right elle est pas mal; Br Fam **to have a b. on the side** (have male lover) avoir un amant; (have female lover) avoir une maîtresse; **bits and pieces** (personal belongings) affaires fpl; (small items) trucs mpl
(**b**) **a b. (of)** (expressing degree) un peu (de); **a b. late/**

heavy/tired un peu en retard/lourd(e)/fatigué(e); **we had a b.** of difficulty in finding him nous avons eu quelque difficulté à le trouver; **he's a b.** of a know-all il a un côté je-sais-tout; **b. by b.** petit à petit; **not a b.** of it! pas du tout!; **wait a b.!** attends une minute!; **it takes a b.** of getting used to il faut un moment pour s'y habituer; **a good b.** older nettement plus âgé(e); **a little b. (of)** un tout petit peu (de); **every b.** as good/interesting as tout aussi bon (bonne)/intéressant(e) que; *Fam* **that's a b. much!** ça c'est un peu fort!; **b. part** *(in play, film)* petit rôle *m*
  (c) *Comptr* bit *m*
  (d) *Fam (coin)* pièce *f*; *Am* **two bits** vingt-cinq cents *mpl*

bit³ *pt of* **bite**

bitch [bɪtʃ] **1** *n* **(a)** *(female dog)* chienne *f* **(b)** *very Fam Pej (woman)* garce *f*; **I've had a b.** of a day! j'ai eu une putain de journée!; **life's a b.!** chienne de vie!
  2 *vi Fam (complain)* râler, rouspéter **(about** après)

bitchy ['bɪtʃɪ] *adj Fam* vache

bite [baɪt] **1** *n* **(a)** *(of person)* coup *m* de dent; *(of dog)* morsure *f*; *(of insect)* piqûre *f*; *(of snake)* morsure, piqûre **(b)** *(mouthful)* bouchée *f*; **to take a b. out of sth** mordre dans qch; **let's stop for a b. to eat** arrêtons-nous pour manger un morceau
  (c) *Fig (of speech, article)* mordant *m*; *(of sauce)* piquant *m*
  2 *vt (pt* bit [bɪt], *pp* bitten ['bɪtən]) **(a)** *(of person, dog)* mordre; *(of insect)* piquer; *(of snake)* mordre, piquer; **the dog bit his hand** le chien l'a mordu à la main; **to b. one's nails** se ronger les ongles
  (b) *(idioms)* **to b. one's tongue** *(stay silent)* se mordre la langue; *Fam* **to b. the bullet** faire contre mauvaise fortune bon cœur; *Fam* **to b. the dust** *(of scheme, plan)* tomber à l'eau; **to b. the hand that feeds you** cracher dans la soupe; *Prov* **once bitten twice shy** chat échaudé craint l'eau froide
  3 *vi* **(a)** *(of person, dog)* mordre; *(of insect)* piquer; *(of snake)* mordre, piquer; **to b. into sth** mordre dans qch
  (b) *Fig (be felt)* se faire sentir
  ▸ **bite off** *vt sep* couper d'un coup de dent; *Fig* **to b. off more than one can chew** avoir les yeux plus gros que le ventre; *Fam Fig* **to b. sb's head off** rembarrer qn

biting ['baɪtɪŋ] *adj (wind, satire)* cinglant(e)

bit-mapped ['bɪtmæpt] *adj Comptr* pixélisé(e)

bitten ['bɪtən] *pp of* **bite**

bitter ['bɪtə(r)] **1** *n Br (beer)* = bière anglaise brune faite avec beaucoup de houblon
  2 *adj* **(a)** *(taste)* amer(ère); *Fig* **it was a b. pill to swallow** la pilule était amère, c'était dur à avaler **(b)** *(harsh) (wind, cold)* glacial(e); *(weather)* rigoureux(euse); *(opposition, resistance)* âpre; *(struggle)* implacable; *(tears, disappointment)* amer(ère); **to go on to the b. end** aller jusqu'au bout **(c)** *(resentful)* amer(ère); *(words)* acerbe; **to feel or be b. about sth** éprouver de l'amertume à propos de qch

bitterly ['bɪtəlɪ] *adv* **(a)** *(extremely)* extrêmement; *(opposed)* résolument, farouchement; **to b. regret doing sth** regretter amèrement d'avoir fait qch; **it was b. cold** il faisait un froid de canard **(b)** *(resentfully)* avec amertume

bitterness ['bɪtənɪs] *n* amertume *f*

bittersweet ['bɪtəswiːt] *adj also Fig* doux-amer (douce-amère)

bitty ['bɪtɪ] *adj Fam (patchy)* décousu(e)

bitumen ['bɪtjʊmɪn] *n* bitume *m*

bivouac ['bɪvʊæk] **1** *n* bivouac *m*
  2 *vi (pt & pp* bivouacked) bivouaquer

bi-weekly [baɪ'wiːklɪ] **1** *adj (fortnightly)* bimensuel(elle); *(twice weekly)* bihebdomadaire
  2 *adv (fortnightly)* deux fois par mois; *(twice weekly)* deux fois par semaine

bizarre [bɪ'zɑː(r)] *adj* bizarre

blab [blæb] *(pt & pp* blabbed) *Fam* **1** *vt* dire
  2 *vi (chatter)* bavarder; *(betray secret)* vendre la mèche; **don't go blabbing to everybody** ne va pas le dire à tout le monde

black [blæk] **1** *n* **(a)** *(colour)* noir *m*; **b. doesn't suit her** le noir ne lui va pas
  (b) *(person)* Noir(e) *m,f*
  (c) **in the b.** *(person)* solvable; *(account)* créditeur(trice)
  (d) *(idioms)* **it says here in b. and white** c'est écrit noir sur blanc; **he sees everything in b. and white** avec lui, c'est ou tout l'un ou tout l'autre
  2 *adj* **(a)** *(colour)* noir(e); **a b. man** un Noir; **a b. woman** une Noire; **to be b. and blue** *(bruised)* être couvert(e) de bleus; **b. belt** *(in martial arts)* ceinture *f* noire; **b. box** *(flight recorder)* boîte *f* noire; **b. coffee** café *m* noir; **b. eye** œil *m* poché; *Astron* **b. hole** trou *m* noir; **b. humour** humour *m* noir; **b. ice** verglas *m*; *Br* **b. pudding** boudin *m* noir; **b. sheep** brebis *f* galeuse
  (b) *(evil, unfavourable)* noir(e); **to give sb a b. look** jeter à qn un regard noir; **the future is looking b.** l'avenir est sombre; **b. magic** magie *f* noire; **it was a b. mark against him** c'était un mauvais point pour lui; **b. spot** *(for accidents)* point *m* noir
  (c) *(unofficial)* **b. economy** économie *f* souterraine; **b. market** marché *m* noir
  (d) *(in proper names)* **the B. Country** = la région de Birmingham *(qui est particulièrement industrielle)*; **the B. Death** la peste noire; **the B. Forest** la Forêt-Noire; *Br* **B. Maria** panier *m* à salade; **the B. Sea** la mer Noire
  3 *vt* **(a)** *(blacken)* noircir; **to b. one's face** se noircir le visage
  (b) *(boycott)* mettre à l'index, boycotter
  ▸ **black out 1** *vt sep* **(a)** *(censor)* rayer *(d'un gros trait noir)* **(b)** *(city)* plonger dans l'obscurité **(c)** *(TV programme)* interrompre
  2 *vi (faint)* perdre connaissance, s'évanouir

black-and-white [blækən'waɪt] *adj (film, photograph)* (en) noir et blanc *inv*; *(TV)* noir et blanc *inv*

blackball ['blækbɔːl] *vt* blackbouler

blackberry ['blækbərɪ] *(pl* blackberries) *n* mûre *f*

blackbird ['blækbɜːd] *n* merle *m* noir

blackboard ['blækbɔːd] *n* tableau *m* (noir)

blackcurrant ['blækkʌrənt] *n* cassis *m*

blacken ['blækən] *vt* noircir, *Fig* **to b. sb's character** calomnier qn

blackguard ['blægɑːd] *n Old-fashioned* fripouille *f*

blackhead ['blækhed] *n* point *m* noir

blackjack ['blækdʒæk] *n* **(a)** *Am (truncheon)* nerf *m* de bœuf **(b)** *(card game)* black jack *m*, ≃ vingt-et-un *m*

blackleg ['blækleg] *n Fam (strikebreaker)* jaune *m*

blacklist ['blæklɪst] **1** *n* liste *f* noire
  2 *vt* mettre sur la liste noire

blackmail ['blækmeɪl] **1** *n* chantage *m*; **emotional b.** chantage aux sentiments
  2 *vt* faire chanter

blackness ['blæknɪs] *n* noirceur *f*

blackout ['blækaʊt] *n* **(a)** *(during air-raid)* black-out *m inv*; *Fig* **to impose a news b.** empêcher la divulgation d'une information **(b)** *(fainting fit)* évanouissement *m*

blacksmith ['blæksmɪθ] *n* forgeron *m*; *(who shoes horses)* maréchal-ferrant *m*

bladder ['blædə(r)] *n* vessie *f*

blade [bleɪd] *n (of knife, sword)* lame *f*; *(of propeller, oar)* pale *f*; *(of grass)* brin *m*

blame [bleɪm] **1** *n* responsabilité *f,* faute *f;* **to put the b. (for sth) on sb** faire porter à qn la responsabilité (de qch); **to take the b. for sth** endosser la responsabilité de qch

2 *vt* rendre responsable, faire porter la responsabilité à **(for** de**); to b. sb for doing sth** reprocher à qn d'avoir fait qch; **I am to b.** je suis fautif, c'est de ma faute; **the bad weather was to b.** c'était à cause du mauvais temps; **I b. myself for what happened** je m'en veux pour ce qui est arrivé; **I don't b. you for wanting to leave** je ne te reproche pas de vouloir partir; **she has nobody to b. but herself** elle n'a de reproche à faire qu'à elle-même

blameless ['bleɪmlɪs] *adj* irréprochable

blameworthy ['bleɪmwɜːðɪ] *adj (person)* coupable, blâmable; *(conduct)* répréhensible

blanch [blɑːntʃ] **1** *vt Culin* blanchir

2 *vi (go pale)* blêmir, pâlir

blancmange [bləˈmɒnʒ] *n* blanc-manger *m*

bland [blænd] *adj (person, appearance)* terne; *(food)* insipide, fade; *(music)* sans intérêt; *(promise)* vain(e), **despite her b. assurances...** malgré ses protestations de politesse...

blandishments ['blændɪʃmənts] *npl* cajoleries *fpl;* **to resist sb's b.** ne pas se laisser amadouer par qn

blandly ['blændlɪ] *adv (speak, reply)* mielleusement

blank [blæŋk] **1** *n* **(a)** *(space)* blanc *m;* **my mind is a b.** j'ai un trou; *Fig* **to draw a b.** faire chou blanc **(b)** *(rifle cartridge)* cartouche *f* à blanc; **to fire blanks** tirer à blanc; *Fam Fig* être stérile

2 *adj (paper, screen)* blanc (blanche), vierge; *(face)* sans expression; **with a b. expression on his face** le visage sans expression; **to look b.** avoir l'air déconcerté *ou* ahuri; **my mind went b.** j'ai eu un trou; **b. cheque** chèque *m* en blanc; *Fig* **to give sb a b. cheque** donner carte blanche à qn; **b. tape** cassette *f* vierge; **b. verse** vers *mpl* blancs

▸ **blank out** *vt sep also Fig* effacer

blanket ['blæŋkɪt] **1** *n* couverture *f;* *Fig (of fog, cloud)* manteau *m*

2 *adj (general)* général(e), global(e); **the government imposed a b. ban on demonstrations** le gouvernement a interdit toutes les manifestations; **b. term** terme *m* général

blankly ['blæŋklɪ] *adv (without expression)* sans expression; *(without understanding)* l'air déconcerté; **she stared b. into space** elle avait le regard perdu dans le vide

blare ['bleə(r)] **1** *n* beuglements *mpl*

2 *vi (of TV, radio)* beugler

▸ **blare out 1** *vt sep* beugler

2 *vi* beugler; **the music was blaring out** la musique était à fond

blarney ['blɑːnɪ] *n Fam* boniments *mpl*

blasé ['blɑːzeɪ] *adj* blasé(e); **she was very b. about the accident** l'accident ne lui avait fait ni chaud ni froid

blaspheme [blæs'fiːm] *vi* blasphémer

blasphemous ['blæsfəməs] *adj* blasphématoire

blasphemy ['blæsfəmɪ] *n* blasphème *m*

blast [blɑːst] **1** *n* **(a)** *(of wind)* coup *m,* rafale *f;* *(of heat)* bouffée *f;* *(of steam)* jet *m;* *(of whistle, horn)* coup; **at full b.** *(radio, TV, heater)* à fond; **b. furnace** haut-fourneau *m* **(b)** *(explosion)* explosion *f;* *(shock wave)* souffle *m* d'une explosion; *Fam* **meeting/hearing that song was a real b. from the past!** la rencontre/cette chanson m'a ramené des années en arrière **(c)** *Am Fam (good time)* **it was a b.** c'était génial; **we had a b.** on s'est super marrés **2** *vt* **(a)** *(hole, tunnel)* creuser *(en dynamitant);* **the building had been blasted by a bomb** le bâtiment avait été détruit par une bombe; *Fam* **to b. sb's head off** faire sauter la tête

à qn **(b)** *Fam (criticize)* démolir **(c)** *Br Fam* **b. (it)!** zut alors!

▸ **blast off** *vi (of space rocket)* décoller

blast-off ['blɑːstɒf] *n (of space rocket)* lancement *m*

blatant ['bleɪtənt] *adj* flagrant(e), manifeste; *(lie)* éhonté(e)

blatantly ['bleɪtəntlɪ] *adv* de façon flagrante; **b. obvious** tout à fait évident(e)

blather ['blæðə(r)] *vi Fam* parler à tort et à travers

blaze [bleɪz] **1** *n* **(a)** *(fire)* feu *m;* **many people died in the b.** beaucoup de gens ont péri dans les flammes **(b)** *(of colour, light)* éclat *m;* **the film was released in a b. of publicity** ils ont fait une publicité monstre pour la sortie du film; **to go out in a b. of glory** s'en aller plein(e) de gloire **(c)** *Fam* **what the blazes does he want?** mais qu'est-ce qu'il veut, bon sang?

2 *vt Fig* **to b. a trail** ouvrir la voie

3 *vi (of fire, sun)* flamboyer; *(of light)* être éclatant(e); **to b. with anger** *(of person)* fulminer; *(of eyes)* lancer des éclairs de colère

blazer ['bleɪzə(r)] *n* blazer *m*

blazing ['bleɪzɪŋ] *adj (burning)* en feu, enflammé(e); *Fig* **a b. row** une violente dispute

bleach [bliːtʃ] **1** *n* (eau *f* de) Javel *f*

2 *vt (clothes)* passer à l'eau de Javel *ou* à la Javel; *(hair)* décolorer

bleak [bliːk] *adj (landscape, weather)* morne, triste; *(outlook)* lugubre; *(prospect)* peu encourageant(e)

bleary ['blɪərɪ] *adj (eyes)* rouge

bleary-eyed [blɪərɪ'aɪd] *adj* **to be b.** *(from lack of sleep)* avoir de petits yeux; *(from hay fever, crying)* avoir les yeux rouges

bleat [bliːt] **1** *n (of sheep)* bêlement *m*

2 *vi (of sheep)* bêler; *Fig (complain)* ronchonner **(about** à propos de)

bleed [bliːd] *(pt & pp* **bled** [bled]) **1** *vt Med* saigner; *(radiator)* purger; *Fig* **to b. sb dry** saigner qn à blanc

2 *vi* saigner; **her nose is bleeding** elle saigne du nez; **to b. to death** saigner à mort

bleeder ['bliːdə(r)] *n Br very Fam* salaud *m*

bleeding ['bliːdɪŋ] **1** *n* saignement *m;* **has the b. stopped?** est-ce que tu saignes/est-ce qu'il saigne/*etc* toujours?

2 *adj* **(a)** *(wound)* qui saigne **(b)** *Br very Fam (for emphasis)* **you b. liar!** sale menteur!; **you b. idiot!** espèce de con!

3 *adv Br very Fam (for emphasis)* foutrement; **that was b. stupid!** c'était vraiment con!

bleep [bliːp] **1** *n* bip *m*

2 *vi* faire bip

bleeper ['bliːpə(r)] *n (pager)* bip *m*

blemish ['blemɪʃ] **1** *n (mark)* marque *f;* *(on face)* bouton *m;* *Fig* **it left a b. on her reputation** cela a entaché sa réputation

2 *vt Fig (reputation)* entacher

blench [blentʃ] *vi* avoir un mouvement de recul

blend [blend] **1** *n* mélange *m*

2 *vt* mélanger *(***with** à *ou* avec)

3 *vi* se mélanger, se mêler; **the colours b. together well** ces couleurs se marient bien *ou* vont bien ensemble

▸ **blend in** *vi (with surroundings)* se fondre **(with** dans)

▸ **blend into** *vt insep (surroundings)* se fondre dans; **to b. into the background** se fondre dans le décor

blender ['blendə(r)] *n* mixer *m,* mixeur *m*

bless [bles] *(pt & pp* **blessed** *or* **blest** [blest]) *vt* **(a)** *(say blessing for)* bénir; **God b. you!** que Dieu te bénisse!; **b. you!** *(when somebody sneezes)* à tes souhaits! **(b)** **to be**

blessed with sth *(talent, beauty)* être doté(e) de qch; **they have been blessed with two fine children** ils ont deux beaux enfants

blessed ['blesɪd] *adj* (**a**) *(holy)* béni(e) (**b**) *Fam (for emphasis)* **the whole b.** day toute la sainte journée; **the whole b. lot** tout le bazar, tout le bataclan; **it's a b. nuisance having to…** quelle barbe d'avoir à…

blessing ['blesɪŋ] *n* (**a**) *(religious)* bénédiction *f*; *Fig* **to give sb/sth one's b.** donner à qn/qch sa bénédiction (**b**) *(benefit, advantage)* bienfait *m*; **it was a b. in disguise** finalement, ça a été une bonne chose; **it was a mixed b.** il y avait du bon et du mauvais; **to count one's blessings** s'estimer heureux de ce qu'on a

blest [blest] *pt & pp of* **bless**

blether ['bleðə(r)] *vi Fam* parler à tort et à travers; *Scot* papoter

blew [bluː] *pt of* **blow**

blight [blaɪt] **1** *n (on cereals)* rouille *f*; *(on potatoes)* brunissure *f*; *Fig* **to cast a b. over sth** jeter un froid sur qch **2** *vt Fig* assombrir; *(hopes)* anéantir

blighter ['blaɪtə(r)] *n Br Fam Old-fashioned* type *m*, gars *m*; **lucky b.** veinard *m*

blimey ['blaɪmɪ] *exclam Br Fam* zut alors!

blind¹ [blaɪnd] **1** *npl* **the b.** les aveugles *mpl*; **school for the b.** école *f* pour aveugles; **it's like the b. leading the b.** ils sont aussi nuls l'un que l'autre **2** *adj* (**a**) *also Fig* aveugle; **a b. man** un aveugle; **a b. woman** une aveugle; **b. in one eye** borgne, aveugle d'un œil; **as b. as a bat** myope comme une taupe; **to be b. to sth** ne pas voir qch; **to turn a b. eye to sth** fermer les yeux sur qch; **love is b.** l'amour est aveugle; **b. with rage** aveuglé(e) par la colère; *also Fig* **b. alley** impasse *f*; **b. date** = rencontre arrangée avec quelqu'un que l'on ne connaît pas; **b. man's buff** *(jeu m de)* colin-maillard *m*; **b. spot** *(for driver)* angle *m* mort; *Fig* **to have a b. spot for maths** être nul (nulle) en maths (**b**) *Fam (for emphasis)* **he didn't take a b. bit of notice** il n'y a pas prêté la moindre attention; **it didn't make a b. bit of difference** ça n'a pas fait la moindre différence **3** *adv* **b. drunk** ivre mort(e) **4** *vt* aveugler; *Fig* **love blinded her to his faults** aveuglée par l'amour, elle n'a pas vu ses défauts

blind² *n Br (for windows)* store *m*

blindfold ['blaɪndfəʊld] **1** *n* bandeau *m* **2** *vt* **to b.** sb mettre un bandeau à qn; **to be blindfolded** avoir les yeux bandés

blinding ['blaɪndɪŋ] *adj* (**a**) *(light)* aveuglant(e); *Fig (intensity, realization)* affolant(e) (**b**) *Br Fam (excellent)* génial(e)

blindly ['blaɪndlɪ] *adv Fig* aveuglément

blindness ['blaɪndnɪs] *n* cécité *f*; *Fig* aveuglement *m*

blink [blɪŋk] **1** *n* (**a**) *(of eyes)* clignement *m* de paupières (**b**) *Br Fam* **to be on the b.** *(of TV, machine)* faire des siennes **2** *vt* **to b. one's eyes** cligner des yeux **3** *vi (of person)* cligner des yeux; *(of light)* clignoter

blinkered ['blɪŋkəd] *adj (approach, attitude)* borné(e); **to be b.** *(of person)* avoir des œillères

blinkers ['blɪŋkəz] *npl* (**a**) *(for horse)* œillères *fpl*; *Fig* **to be wearing b.** avoir des œillères (**b**) *Fam (indicators)* clignotants *mpl*

blinking ['blɪŋkɪŋ] *adj* (**a**) *(light)* clignotant(e) (**b**) *Br Fam (for emphasis)* sacré(e); **what a b. nuisance!** quelle barbe!; **you b. idiot!** espèce d'imbécile!

blip [blɪp] *n (on radar screen)* spot *m*; *Fam (temporary problem)* hic *m inv*, os *m*

bliss [blɪs] *n* bonheur *m*, béatitude *f*; **breakfast in bed, what b.!** le petit déjeuner au lit, quel bonheur!

blissful ['blɪsfʊl] *adj (person)* (bien)heureux(euse); *(holiday)* plein(e) de bonheur; **I'd rather remain in b. ignorance** j'aime autant ne pas savoir

blissfully ['blɪsfʊlɪ] *adv* merveilleusement; **b. happy** au comble du bonheur; **to be b. unaware that…** ne pas se douter le moins du monde que…

blister ['blɪstə(r)] **1** *n (on skin)* ampoule *f*, cloque *f*; *(on paint)* cloque **2** *vt (skin)* provoquer des ampoules sur; *(paint)* faire des cloques sur **3** *vi (of skin)* se couvrir d'ampoules; *(of paint)* cloquer

blistering ['blɪstərɪŋ] *adj (sun, heat)* brûlant(e); *(criticism, attack)* virulent(e)

blithe ['blaɪð] *adj (attitude, disregard)* désinvolte; *Lit (person)* joyeux(euse), allègre

blithely ['blaɪðlɪ] *adv (ignore, disregard)* avec une complète désinvolture; *Lit (happily)* joyeusement, allègrement

blithering ['blɪðərɪŋ] *adj* **a b. idiot** un(e) sombre idiot(e)

blitz [blɪts] *n (air bombardment)* blitz *m*, bombardement *m* aérien; *Hist* **the B.** le Blitz; *Fam* **to have a b. on sth** s'attaquer à qch

blizzard ['blɪzəd] *n* tempête *f* de neige

bloated ['bləʊtɪd] *adj (stomach, face)* gonflé(e); *(ego)* énorme

blob [blɒb] *n* (**a**) *(of cream, jam, paint)* tache *f*; *(of ink)* pâté *m* (**b**) *(indistinct shape)* silhouette *f*

bloc [blɒk] *n Pol* bloc *m*

block [blɒk] **1** *n* (**a**) *(of wood, stone)* bloc *m*; *(for execution, of butcher)* billot *m*; *Br Fam* **I'll knock your b. off!** je vais te casser la gueule!; **b. and tackle** *(for lifting)* palan *m*; **b. capitals** majuscules *fpl* en caractères d'imprimerie; **b. diagram** *(flow chart)* schéma *m* fonctionnel (**b**) *Br (building)* immeuble *m*; *Am (group of buildings)* pâté *m* de maisons; *Am* **the school is five blocks away** l'école est à cinq rues d'ici; *Br* **b. of flats** immeuble (**c**) *(of shares)* paquet *m*; **b. of seats** bloc-sièges *m inv*; **b. booking** réservation *f* ou location *f* de groupe; **b. vote** vote *m* groupé **2** *vt* (**a**) *(pipe, road, progress)* bloquer; *(view)* cacher; **to b. sb's way** barrer *ou* bloquer le passage à qn; *Fin* **to b. a cheque** faire opposition à un chèque (**b**) *Comptr (text)* sélectionner

▸ **block off** *vt sep (road, exit)* barrer

▸ **block out** *vt sep (light)* empêcher d'entrer *ou* de passer; *(a memory)* refouler; *(music, noise)* faire abstraction de

▸ **block up** *vt sep (tunnel, passageway)* boucher; *(door, window)* murer; **to have a blocked-up nose** avoir le nez bouché

blockade [blɒ'keɪd] **1** *n* blocus *m* (**on** à) **2** *vt* bloquer, faire le blocus de

blockage ['blɒkɪdʒ] *n* obstruction *f*

blockbuster ['blɒkbʌstə(r)] *n (film)* film *m* à grand spectacle; *(novel)* best-seller *m*

blockhead ['blɒkhed] *n Fam* lourdaud *m*

bloke [bləʊk] *n Br Fam* type *m*

blonde [blɒnd] *n & adj* blond(e) *m,f*

blood [blʌd] **1** *n* (**a**) sang *m*; **to give b.** donner du sang; **b. bank** banque *f* du sang; **b. cell** globule *m* sanguin; **b. clot** caillot *m*; **b. count** numération *f* globulaire; **b. donor** donneur(euse) *m,f* de sang; **b. group** groupe *m* sanguin; **b. poisoning** septicémie *f*, toxémie *f*; **b. pressure** tension *f* (artérielle); **to have low/high b. pressure** avoir la tension basse/de la tension; **b. relation** parent(e) *m,f*; **b. sports** la chasse; **b. test** prise *f* de sang; **b. transfusion** transfusion *f* sanguine; **b. vessel** vaisseau *m* sanguin (**b**) *(idioms)* **to have b. on one's hands** avoir du sang sur les mains; **it makes my b. boil** ça me fait bouillir; **it makes my b. run**

cold ça me glace le sang; **in cold b.** de sang-froid; **he's after your b.** il en a après toi; **to have sth in one's b.** avoir qch dans le sang; **it's like trying to get b.** out of a stone c'est comme si on se heurtait à un mur; *Prov* **b. is thicker than water** la famille passe avant tout **2** *vt (initiate)* initier

bloodbath ['blʌdbɑːθ] *n* bain *m* de sang

bloodcurdling ['blʌdkɜːdlɪŋ] *adj* à vous tourner les sangs

bloodhound ['blʌdhaʊnd] *n* limier *m*

bloodless ['blʌdlɪs] *adj* **(a)** *(without bloodshed)* **it was a b. coup** le coup d'État s'est déroulé sans effusion de sang **(b)** *(pale)* exsangue

bloodletting ['blʌdletɪŋ] *n* **(a)** *Med* saignée *f* **(b)** *(slaughter, feud)* effusion *f* de sang

bloodshed ['blʌdʃed] *n* effusion *f* de sang; **without b.** sans verser le sang

bloodshot ['blʌdʃɒt] *adj (eyes)* injecté(e) de sang

bloodstain ['blʌdsteɪn] *n* tache *f* de sang

bloodstained ['blʌdsteɪnd] *adj* taché(e) de sang

bloodstream ['blʌdstriːm] *n* sang *m*

bloodsucker ['blʌdsʌkə(r)] *n also Fig* sangsue *f*

bloodthirsty ['blʌdθɜːstɪ] *adj (person)* sanguinaire; *(film)* sanglant(e)

bloody ['blʌdɪ] **1** *adj* **(a)** *(bleeding, bloodstained)* ensanglanté(e); *(battle, revolution)* sanglant(e); *Fig* **to give sb a b. nose** mettre une raclée à qn **(b)** *Br very Fam* foutu(e); **you b. fool!** espèce de connard!; **b. hell!** merde!
2 *adv Br very Fam* **it's b. hot!** il fait une putain de chaleur!; **I'm b. tired** putain, qu'est-ce que je suis crevé; **not b. likely!** putain, il n'y a pas de danger!; **he can b. well do it himself!** il peut parfaitement se démerder tout seul!

bloody-minded [blʌdɪ'maɪndɪd] *adj Br* **to be b.** être un(e) emmerdeur(euse); **don't be so b.!** arrête d'emmerder le monde!

bloom [bluːm] **1** *n* fleur *f*; **in (full) b.** *(tree)* en fleur(s); *(flower)* éclos(e); **in the b. of youth** à ou dans la fleur de l'âge
2 *vi (of garden, flower, talent)* fleurir; *Fig* **to be blooming with health** être resplendissant(e) *ou* éclatant(e) de santé

bloomer ['bluːmə(r)] *n* **(a)** *Fam (mistake)* bourde *f* **(b)** *(bread)* ≃ bâtard *m* court

bloomers ['bluːməz] *npl* culotte *f* bouffante

blooming ['bluːmɪŋ] *Br Fam (for emphasis)* **1** *adj* sacré(e); **you b. idiot!** espèce d'idiot!
2 *adv* **b. good** sacrément bon (bonne); **b. awful** carrément horrible; **he's b. useless!** il est totalement nul!

blossom ['blɒsəm] **1** *n* fleur *f*; **in b.** en fleur(s)
2 *vi* fleurir; *Fig* s'épanouir; *Fig* **she had blossomed into a charming young woman** elle était devenue une charmante jeune femme

blot [blɒt] **1** *n (of ink)* pâté *m*; *Fig* **a b. on sb's reputation** une tache faite à la réputation de qn; *Fig* **to be a b. on the landscape** gâcher le paysage
2 *vt (pt & pp blotted) (stain)* tacher; *(with ink)* faire un pâté/des pâtés sur; **to b. one's lipstick** fixer son rouge à lèvres *(en pressant les lèvres sur un mouchoir en papier)*; *Fig* **to b. one's copybook** ternir sa réputation
► **blot out** *vt sep (sun, light)* masquer; *(memory)* effacer

blotch [blɒtʃ] *n (on skin)* tache *f*

blotchy ['blɒtʃɪ] *adj (skin)* couvert(e) de taches

blotter ['blɒtə(r)] *n* buvard *m*

blotting paper ['blɒtɪŋpeɪpə(r)] *n* buvard *m*; **a sheet of b.** un buvard

blotto ['blɒtəʊ] *adj Br Fam (drunk)* bourré(e)

blouse [blaʊz] *n* chemisier *m*, corsage *m*

blow¹ [bləʊ] *n* **(a)** *(hit)* coup *m*; **to come to blows (over sth)** en venir aux mains (pour *ou* au sujet de qch); *Fig* **to strike a b.** atténuer le choc **(b)** *(setback)* coup *m*; **this news was a b. to us** cette nouvelle a été pour nous un coup rude; **it was a b. to her pride** son orgueil en a pris un coup

blow² *(pt blew* [bluː]*, pp blown* [bləʊn]*)* **1** *vt* **(a)** *(of wind, person)* **the wind blew down the fence** le vent a renversé la barrière; **to b. glass** souffler le verre; **to b. the horn** klaxonner; **to b. a whistle** donner un coup de sifflet; *Fig* **to b. the whistle on sb/sth** dénoncer qn/qch; **to b. the dust off sth** souffler sur qch pour en enlever la poussière; **to b. sb a kiss** envoyer un baiser à qn; **to b. bubbles** faire des bulles; **to b. one's nose** se moucher; *Fig* **to b. one's own trumpet** chanter ses propres louanges
(b) *Elec* **to b. a fuse** faire sauter un plomb; *Fig (of person)* disjoncter; *Fam* **to b. the Grand Canyon blew my mind!** quel pied, le Grand Canyon!
(c) *Fam (waste) (chance)* gâcher; **that's blown it!** ça a tout gâché!, ça a fait tout louper!
(d) *Fam (money)* claquer **(on sth** pour s'acheter qch)
2 *vi* **(a)** *(of wind, person)* souffler; **to b. down** *or* **over** *(of fence, tree)* se renverser; **the door blew open/shut** le vent a ouvert/fermé la porte; **to b. on one's fingers** se souffler sur les doigts; *Fig* **to b. hot and cold** souffler le chaud et le froid
(b) *Elec (of fuse)* sauter
► **blow away 1** *vt sep* **to b. sth away** *(of wind)* faire s'envoler qch; *Fam Fig* **to b. sb away** *(shoot dead)* descendre qn; *Fam Fig* **his latest film blew me away!** son dernier film, c'est le pied!
2 *vi (of paper, hat)* s'envoler
► **blow off 1** *vt sep (of wind)* emporter; *Fam Fig* **to b. sb's head off** faire sauter la cervelle à qn
2 *vi (of hat)* s'envoler
► **blow out** *vt sep (of wind)* éteindre; *(candle, match)* souffler
► **blow over** *vi (of storm, argument)* se calmer; **the scandal soon blew over** le scandale fut vite oublié
► **blow up 1** *vt sep* **(a)** *(balloon, tyre)* gonfler **(b)** *(explode)* faire sauter **(c)** *(enlarge) (photograph)* agrandir; *Fig* **the incident was blown up out of all proportion** on a fait une histoire incroyable autour de ce petit incident
2 *vi (of bomb)* exploser, sauter; *Fig (lose one's temper)* piquer une colère; **to b. up at sb/sth** se mettre en colère contre qn/qch

blow-by-blow [bləʊbaɪ'bləʊ] *adj (account)* minutieux(euse), détaillé(e)

blow-dry ['bləʊdraɪ] **1** *n* brushing *m*
2 *vt* **to b. sb's hair** faire un brushing à qn

blower ['bləʊə(r)] *n Br Fam (telephone)* bigophone *m*

blowhole ['bləʊhəʊl] *n (of whale)* évent *m*

blowjob ['bləʊdʒɒb] *n Vulg* pipe *f*; **to give sb a b.** tailler une pipe à qn

blowlamp ['bləʊlæmp] = **blowtorch**

blown [bləʊn] *pp of* **blow**

blow-out ['bləʊaʊt] *n* **(a)** *(of tyre)* éclatement *m* **(b)** *Fam (big meal)* gueuleton *m*

blowpipe ['bləʊpaɪp] *n* sarbacane *f*

blowtorch ['bləʊtɔːtʃ] *n (for welding)* chalumeau *m*, lampe *f* à souder; *(for removing paint)* brûloir *m*

blowzy ['blaʊzɪ] *adj* négligé(e)

blub [blʌb] *(pt & pp blubbed) vi Fam* pleurer comme une madeleine

blubber ['blʌbə(r)] **1** *n (fat)* graisse *f*
2 *vi Fam (cry)* pleurer comme une madeleine
bludgeon ['blʌdʒən] *vt* matraquer; *Fig* **to b. sb into** doing sth obliger brutalement qn à faire qch
blue [blu:] **1** *n* (**a**) *(colour)* bleu *m*; *Fig* **out of the b.** à l'improviste; **her resignation came out of the b.** sa démission nous a pris par surprise (**b**) **the blues** *(music)* le blues; *Fam* **to have the blues** *(be depressed)* avoir le cafard **2** *adj* (**a**) *(colour)* bleu(e); **b. with cold** bleu de froid; *Fam* **she can complain until she's b.** **in the face** elle peut se plaindre autant qu'elle veut; **once in a b. moon** tous les trente-six du mois; *Fam* **to scream b. murder** crier comme un putois; **b. blood** sang *m* bleu; **b. cheese** bleu *m*; **b. whale** baleine *f* bleue (**b**) *Fam (sad)* **to feel b.** avoir le cafard (**c**) *Fam (obscene) (joke)* grivois(e), paillard(e); *(film)* porno; **to tell b. stories** en raconter des vertes et de pas mûres
bluebell ['blu:bel] *n* jacinthe *f* des bois
blueberry ['blu:bərɪ] *(pl* **blueberries**) *n Am* airelle *f*, myrtille *f*
bluebird ['blu:bɜ:d] *n* rouge-gorge *m* bleu
bluebottle ['blu:bɒtəl] *n* mouche *f* de la viande
blue-chip ['blu:tʃɪp] *adj Fin* **b. shares** valeurs *fpl* de père de famille; **b. company** affaire *f* de premier ordre
blue-collar ['blu:'kɒlə(r)] *adj* **b. worker** col *m* bleu
blue-eyed ['blu:aɪd] *adj* aux yeux bleus; *Br Fam* **his mother's b. boy** le petit chéri de sa maman
blueprint ['blu:prɪnt] *n Archit & Ind* plan *m*; *Fig* projet *m*; **a b. for success** une garantie de succès
bluff¹ [blʌf] **1** *n (deception)* bluff *m*; **to call sb's b.** *(at cards)* inviter qn à mettre les cartes sur la table; *(in negotiation)* prendre qn au mot
2 *vt* **you're bluffing me** tu bluffes
3 *vi* bluffer
bluff² *n (cliff)* à-pic *m inv*
bluff³ *adj (manner)* direct(e)
blunder ['blʌndə(r)] **1** *n* gaffe *f*
2 *vi (make mistake)* faire une gaffe; **to b. along** *(move clumsily)* avancer d'un pas maladroit; **to b. into sb/sth** heurter qn/à qch
blunderbuss ['blʌndəbʌs] *n* tromblon *m*
blunt [blʌnt] **1** *adj* (**a**) *(blade)* émoussé(e); *(pencil)* mal taillé(e) (**b**) *(manner)* brutal(e); *(question, statement)* direct(e); *(refusal)* net (nette); *(person)* brusque; **to be b.,** ... pour parler franchement, ...
2 *vt (blade)* émousser; *(pencil)* épointer; *Fig (anger, enthusiasm)* émousser, atténuer
bluntly ['blʌntlɪ] *adv (frankly)* franchement; **I told him b. that...** je lui ai dit tout net que...
bluntness ['blʌntnɪs] *n* (**a**) *(of blade)* manque *m* de tranchant (**b**) *(of manner, statement)* rudesse *f*; *(of person)* franchise *f*
blur [blɜ:(r)] **1** *n (vague shape)* forme *f* vague; *(unclear memory)* vague souvenir *m*; **without my glasses, everything is a b.** sans mes lunettes, je suis complètement dans le brouillard; **to go by in a b.** *(of time)* passer à toute vitesse
2 *vt (t & pp* **blurred**) brouiller, troubler
3 *vi (of memories)* s'estomper
blurb [blɜ:b] *n (on book cover)* notice *f* publicitaire
blurred [blɜ:d] *adj (ink)* qui a bavé; *(writing, photo)* flou(e); *(vision)* trouble
▸ **blurt out** [blɜ:t] *vt sep* laisser échapper; **"I love you!"** **she blurted out** "je t'aime!" lâcha-t-elle
blush [blʌʃ] **1** *n* rougeur *f*; **to spare sb's blushes** éviter à qn un embarras

2 *vi* rougir; **to b. with shame** rougir de honte; **to b. at the thought of sth** rougir en pensant à qch; **I b. to admit it** j'ai honte de l'admettre
blusher ['blʌʃə(r)] *n* blush *m*, fard *m* à joues
bluster ['blʌstə(r)] **1** *n* protestations *fpl* véhémentes
2 *vi* protester avec véhémence
blustery ['blʌstərɪ] *adj (day)* venteux(euse), de grand vent; *(wind)* violent(e)
BMA [bi:e'meɪ] *n (abbr* **British Medical Association**) ≃ ordre *m* des médecins
BO [bi:'əʊ] *n Fam (abbr* **body odour**) odeur *f* corporelle; **to have BO** sentir mauvais
boa ['bəʊə] *n* **b. (constrictor)** boa *m* (constricteur); **(feather) b.** boa *m*
boar ['bɔ:(r)] *n (male pig)* verrat *m*; *(wild pig)* sanglier *m*
board [bɔ:d] **1** *n* (**a**) *(of wood)* planche *f*; *(for notices)* panneau *m*; *(for chess)* échiquier *m*; *(for draughts)* damier *m*; *(for Monopoly®* etc) tableau *m*; *(blackboard)* tableau; **to go by the b.** *(of plan, system)* être abandonné(e); **across the b.** globalement; **b. game** jeu *m* de société *(avec des pions etc)*
(**b**) *(of company)* conseil *m*, comité *m*; **b. (of directors)** conseil d'administration; **b. of enquiry** commission *f* d'enquête; **b. of examiners** jury *m* d'examen; *Br* **B. of Trade** ≃ ministère *m* du Commerce; **b. meeting** réunion *f* du conseil
(**c**) *(meals)* **half b.** demi-pension *f*; **full b.** pension *f* complète; **b. and lodging** *(in hotel)* pension complète
(**d**) **on b.** à bord; **to go on b.** monter à bord; *Fig* **to take sth on b.** *(idea, proposal)* prendre qch en considération; *(problem)* tenir compte de qch
2 *vt (ship, plane)* embarquer; *(train, bus)* monter dans
3 *vi* (**a**) *(lodge)* être en pension (**with** chez); *(at school)* aller en pension
(**b**) *Av* **flight 123 is now boarding** l'embarquement du vol 123 a commencé
▸ **board up** *vt sep (house, window)* condamner
boarder ['bɔ:də(r)] *n (lodger)* pensionnaire *mf*; *(at school)* interne *mf*, pensionnaire
boarding ['bɔ:dɪŋ] *n* (**a**) **b. card** *or* **pass** carte *f* d'embarquement (**b**) **b. house** pension *f* de famille; **b. school** internat *m*
boardroom ['bɔ:dru:m] *n* salle *f* de réunion *(du conseil d'administration)*
boardwalk ['bɔ:dwɔ:k] *n Am* = passage en bois sur la plage
boast [bəʊst] **1** *n* vantardise *f*
2 *vt* **the school boasts a fine library** l'école est fière de posséder une belle bibliothèque
3 *vi* se vanter **(about** de); **it's nothing to b. about!** il n'y a pas de quoi se vanter!
boastful ['bəʊstfʊl] *adj* vantard(e), fanfaron(onne)
boasting ['bəʊstɪŋ] *n* vantardise *f*, fanfaronnade *f*
boat [bəʊt] *n* bateau *m*; *(small)* canot *m*, embarcation *f*; **to come by b.** venir en bateau, prendre le bateau; *Fig* **we're all in the same b.** nous sommes tous dans le même cas; *Fig* **to push the b. out** *(celebrate lavishly)* faire des frais; **the B. Race** = traditionnelle course d'aviron qui oppose chaque année sur la Tamise une équipe d'Oxford à une équipe de Cambridge
boat-builder ['bəʊtbɪldə(r)] *n* constructeur *m* de bateaux
boater ['bəʊtə(r)] *n (hat)* canotier *m*
boathouse ['bəʊthaʊs] *n* hangar *m* pour bateaux
boating ['bəʊtɪŋ] *n* canotage *m*; **to go b.** faire du canotage

boat-load ['bəʊtləʊd] n cargaison f; Fig **by the b.** par bateaux entiers

boatswain ['bəʊsən] n Naut maître m d'équipage

boatyard ['bəʊtjɑːd] n chantier m de construction pour canots et bateaux de plaisance

Bob [bɒb] n Fam **and B.'s your uncle!** et voilà le travail!

bob¹ [bɒb] **1** n (**a**) (curtsey) petite révérence f (**b**) (hairstyle) (coupe f au) carré m (**c**) (bobsleigh) bobsleigh m
2 vt (pt & pp **bobbed**) (**a**) **to b. one's head** hocher la tête (**b**) **to have one's hair bobbed** se faire faire un carré **3** vi **to b. up and down** s'agiter; **to b. about** (on water) se balancer

bob² (pl **bob**) n Br Fam Old-fashioned (shilling) shilling m; **that must cost a few b.** à mon avis, ce n'est pas donné; **he's not short of a b. or two** il a de quoi

bobbin ['bɒbɪn] n bobine f

bobble ['bɒbəl] n (on hat) pompon m

bobby ['bɒbɪ] (pl **bobbies**) n Br Fam (policeman) flic m

bobsled ['bɒbsled], **bobsleigh** ['bɒbsleɪ] n bobsleigh m

bod [bɒd] n Fam (**a**) Br (man) type m; (woman) femme f (**b**) (body) corps m; **he's got a nice b.** il est bien foutu

bode [bəʊd] vi **to b. well/ill (for)** être de bon/mauvais augure (pour)

bodice ['bɒdɪs] n corsage m

bodily ['bɒdɪlɪ] **1** adj corporel(elle), physique; **b. functions** fonctions fpl corporelles; **b. needs** besoins mpl physiques
2 adv (grab) à bras le-corps; **he was carried b. to the door** on l'a saisi à bras-le-corps et puis on l'a transporté jusqu'à la porte

body ['bɒdɪ] (pl **bodies**) n (**a**) (of person, animal) corps m; (dead) cadavre m, corps; **to have enough to keep b. and soul together** avoir juste de quoi vivre; Fam **over my dead b.!** plutôt crever!; **b. bag** = sac servant au transport des dépouilles mortelles; Fig **to deliver a b. blow (to)** porter un coup terrible (à); **b. builder** culturiste mf; **b. building** culturisme m; **b. count** (of casualties) comptage m des morts; (of those present) comptage des présents; **b. language** langage m corporel; **b. odour** odeur f corporelle; **b. stocking** (without legs) body m; (with legs) combinaison f collante; **b. warmer** petit gilet m chaud (**b**) (of wine) corps m; (of hair) volume m (**c**) (group) corps m; **a large b. of people** une foule nombreuse; **b. of evidence** ensemble m de preuves; **b. of water** masse f d'eau; **public b.** organisme m public; **the b. politic** le corps politique (**d**) (main part) (of car) carrosserie f; (of letter) corps m; (of argument) essentiel m; **b. shop** atelier m de carrosserie (**e**) (garment) body m

bodyguard ['bɒdɪgɑːd] n (person) garde m du corps; (group) gardes mpl du corps

bodywork ['bɒdɪwɜːk] n (of car) carrosserie f

Boer ['bəʊə(r)] n Boer mf; **the B. War** la guerre des Boers

boffin ['bɒfɪn] n Br Fam Hum (scientist) savant m

bog [bɒg] n (**a**) (marsh) marécage m (**b**) Br very Fam (toilet) chiottes fpl; **b. roll** or **paper** PQ m

▶ **bog down** (pt & pp **bogged**) vt sep **to get bogged down (in)** (mud) s'enliser (dans), s'embourber (dans); (details) se perdre (dans)

bogey ['bəʊgɪ] (pl **bogeys**) n (**a**) (cause of fear) hantise f (**b**) Br Fam (from nose) crotte f de nez

bogeyman ['bəʊgɪmæn] n **the b.** le croque-mitaine, le Père fouettard

boggle ['bɒgəl] vi Fam **to b. at doing sth** rechigner à faire qch; **the mind boggles!** ça laisse rêveur!

Bogotá [bɒgə'tɑː] n Bogotá

bogus ['bəʊgəs] adj faux (fausse); Fam **he's completely b.** c'est vraiment un faux jeton

Bohemian [bəʊ'hiːmɪən] **1** n (native of Bohemia) Bohémien(enne) m,f; (artistic person) bohème mf
2 adj (person, lifestyle) bohème; (from Bohemia) bohémien(enne)

boil¹ [bɔɪl] n (on skin) furoncle m

boil² **1** n to come to the b. arriver à ébullition; **to bring sth to the b.** amener qch à ébullition; Fig **to go off the b.** ne plus marcher très fort
2 vt faire bouillir; **to b. the kettle** mettre de l'eau à chauffer
3 vi bouillir; **the kettle's boiling** la bouilloire siffle; **the saucepan has boiled dry** l'eau de la casserole s'est complètement évaporée; **to b. with rage** bouillir (de colère)

▶ **boil down to** vt insep Fam **it all boils down to...** ça revient à...

▶ **boil over** vi (of milk, soup) déborder; Fig (of situation) empirer, s'aggraver

▶ **boil up** vt sep (water, milk) faire bouillir

boiler ['bɔɪlə(r)] n chaudière f; **b. maker** chaudronnier m; **b. room** salle f des chaudières, chaufferie f; **b. suit** bleu m de chauffe

boiling ['bɔɪlɪŋ] **1** adj bouillant(e); Fam **I'm b.!** je crève de chaleur!; **b. point** point m d'ébullition; Fig **the situation has reached b. point** la situation est explosive
2 adv it's b. hot il fait une chaleur à crever

boisterous ['bɔɪstərəs] adj bruyant(e)

bold [bəʊld] adj (**a**) (brave) hardi(e), intrépide (**b**) (shameless) **as b. as brass** culotté(e) (**c**) (striking) (colour) vif (vive); (handwriting) vigoureux(euse); Typ **b. type** caractères mpl gras

boldly ['bəʊldlɪ] adv (bravely) hardiment

boldness ['bəʊldnɪs] n (bravery) hardiesse f

Bolivia [bə'lɪvɪə] n la Bolivie

Bolivian [bə'lɪvɪən] **1** n Bolivien(enne) m,f
2 adj bolivien(enne)

bollard ['bɒləd] n Naut bollard m; Br (traffic barrier) borne f

bollocking ['bɒləkɪŋ] n Br very Fam **to give sb a b.** engueuler qn

bollocks ['bɒləks] npl Br Vulg (testicles) couilles fpl; **b.!** (nonsense) c'est des conneries!

Bolshevik ['bɒlʃəvɪk] n & adj bolchevique mf

Bolshevism ['bɒlʃəvɪzəm] n bolchevisme m

bolshie, bolshy ['bɒlʃɪ] adj Fam râleur(euse)

bolster ['bəʊlstə(r)] **1** n (pillow) traversin m
2 vt (confidence, pride) renforcer, consolider

bolt [bəʊlt] **1** n (**a**) (on door) verrou m; (metal fastening) boulon m; Fam **he has shot his b.** il a échoué après avoir joué sa dernière carte (**b**) Fam (dash) **to make a b. for it** se sauver à toutes jambes; **she made a b. for the door** elle se précipita vers la porte; **b. hole** refuge m (**c**) **b. of lightning** foudre f; Fig **it came like a b. from the blue** ça a été comme un coup de tonnerre
2 adv **b. upright** droit(e) comme un i
3 vt (**a**) (lock) verrouiller; (fasten with bolts) boulonner (**b**) (food) engloutir
4 vi (of horse) s'emballer; (of person) décamper, déguerpir

▶ **bolt down** vt sep (food) engloutir

bomb [bɒm] **1** n bombe f; Br Fam **to go like a b.** foncer; Fam **to cost a b.** coûter les yeux de la tête; **this room looks like a b.'s hit** cette pièce est un véritable champ de

bataille; **b. disposal expert** démineur *m*; **b. scare** alerte *f* à la bombe
2 *vt* bombarder
3 *vi Am (fail)* faire un bide
▸ **bomb along** *vi Fam (go quickly)* foncer
bombard [bɒmˈbɑːd] *vt* bombarder; *Fig* **to b. sb with questions** bombarder *ou* assaillir qn de questions
bombardment [bɒmˈbɑːdmənt] *n* bombardement *m*
bombast [ˈbɒmbæst] *n* emphase *f*
bombastic [bɒmˈbæstɪk] *adj* ampoulé(e), emphatique
bomber [ˈbɒmə(r)] *n (aircraft)* bombardier *m*; *(person)* poseur(euse) *m,f* de bombe; **b. jacket** blouson *m* d'aviateur
bombing [ˈbɒmɪŋ] *n (aerial)* bombardement *m*; *(by terrorists)* attentat *m* à la bombe
bombshell [ˈbɒmʃel] *n* obus *m*; *Fig* **to drop a b.** faire une révélation fracassante; *Fam Fig* **a blonde b.** une magnifique blonde
bombsite [ˈbɒmsaɪt] *n* zone *f* bombardée; *Fig* **your bedroom is (like) a b.!** quel capharnaüm, ta chambre!
bona fide [ˈbəʊnəˈfaɪdɪ] *adj* véritable
bonanza [bəˈnænzə] *n* aubaine *f*; **a b. year** une année exceptionnelle
bonce [bɒns] *n Br Fam (head)* caboche *f*
bond [bɒnd] **1** *n* **(a)** *(attachment)* lien *m*; **to feel a b. with sb** se sentir lié(e) à qn **(b)** *Fin* obligation *f* **(c)** *Law* caution *f*; *Formal* **my word is my b.** je n'ai qu'une parole **(d)** *Com* **in b.** en dépôt
2 *vt* **(a)** *(stick)* coller **(b)** *Fig (unite)* **to b. together** créer des liens entre
3 *vi* **(a)** *(stick)* adhérer **(b)** *Fig (form attachment)* créer des liens affectifs **(with sb** avec qn**)**
bondage [ˈbɒndɪdʒ] *n* **(a)** *(slavery)* esclavage *m* **(b)** *(sexual)* = pratique sexuelle où l'un des partenaires est attaché
bonding [ˈbɒndɪŋ] *n (emotional attachment)* liens *mpl* affectifs; **male b.** activités *fpl* que l'on fait entre hommes; *Fam Hum* **they're doing some male b. in the pub** ils sont en train de célébrer leur amitié au pub
bone [bəʊn] **1** *n* **(a)** *(of person, animal)* os *m*; *(of fish)* arête *f*; **b. china** porcelaine *f* tendre; **b. meal** engrais *m (de cendre d'os)* **(b)** *(idioms)* **to work one's fingers to the b.** se tuer au travail; **b. idle** *or* **lazy** paresseux(euse) comme une couleuvre; **I feel it in my bones** je le sens; **b. of contention** sujet *m* de dispute; *Fam* **to have a b.** **to pick with sb** avoir un compte à régler avec qn; **she made no bones about it** elle ne l'a pas caché; **close to the b.** *(tactless, risqué)* limite
2 *vt (chicken, meat)* désosser; *(fish)* ôter les arêtes de
▸ **bone up on** *vt insep Fam* potasser
bone-dry [ˈbəʊnˈdraɪ] *adj* complètement sec (sèche)
bonfire [ˈbɒnfaɪə(r)] *n (for burning rubbish)* feu *m*; *(for celebration)* feu de joie
bong [bɒŋ] *n (sound)* bong *m*
bonhomie [ˈbɒnɒmiː] *n* bonhomie *f*
bonk¹ [bɒŋk] *vt Fam (hit)* frapper
bonk² *Br very Fam* **1** *n* **to have a b.** s'envoyer en l'air
2 *vt* s'envoyer en l'air avec
3 *vi* s'envoyer en l'air
bonkers [ˈbɒŋkəz] *adj Br Fam (mad)* dingue
Bonn [bɒn] *n* Bonn
bonnet [ˈbɒnɪt] *n* **(a)** *(hat)* bonnet *m* **(b)** *Br (of car)* capot *m*
bonny [ˈbɒnɪ] *adj Scot* joli(e)
bonsai [ˈbɒnzaɪ] *n* bonsaï *m*
bonus [ˈbəʊnəs] *(pl* **bonuses)** *n* **(a)** *(money)* prime *f*; **b.**

scheme système *m* de primes de rendement **(b)** *(advantage)* avantage *m*; **b. number** *(in lottery)* numéro *m* supplémentaire
bony [ˈbəʊnɪ] *adj (person, limb)* maigre, décharné(e); *(fish)* plein(e) d'arêtes
boo [buː] **1** *n (pl* **boos)** huée *f*
2 *vt (pt & pp* **booed)** huer; **he was booed off stage** il a quitté la scène sous les huées du public
3 *exclam* hou!; **he wouldn't say b. to a goose** c'est un grand timide
boob [buːb] *Fam* **1** *n* **(a)** *Br (mistake)* gaffe *f*; **to make a b.** faire une gaffe **(b)** *(breast)* nichon *m*; **to have a b. job** se faire refaire les nichons; **b. tube** *(garment)* bustier *m*
2 *vi (make mistake)* faire une gaffe
booby-prize [ˈbuːbɪpraɪz] *n* prix *m* décerné au dernier *(en guise de plaisanterie)*
booby-trap [ˈbuːbɪtræp] **1** *n (explosive device)* objet *m* piégé; *(practical joke)* piège *m*
2 *vt (pt & pp* **booby-trapped)** piéger *(en guise de farce)*
book [bʊk] *n* **1 (a)** *(in general)* livre *m*; *(of stamps)* carnet *m*; *(of matches)* pochette *f*; *Fin* **the books** *(of company)* les comptes *mpl*; **b. club** club *m* du livre; **b. end** serre-livres *m inv*; **b. token** chèque-cadeau *m* pour des livres **(b)** *(idioms)* **physics is a closed b. to me** je ne comprends absolument rien à la physique; **in my b.** à mon avis; **to be in sb's good books** être dans les petits papiers de qn, être bien vu(e) par qn; **to be in sb's bad books** être mal vu(e) par qn; **to bring sb to b.** forcer qn à rendre des comptes; **by the b.** selon la procédure; **to throw the b. at sb** infliger la peine maximale à qn
2 *vt* **(a)** *(seat, room, table, ticket)* réserver; *(performer)* engager; **to b. sb on a flight** réserver une place pour qn sur un vol; **fully booked** *(hotel, flight)* complet(ète) **(b)** *(for traffic offence)* dresser une contravention à; *(in football match)* donner un carton jaune à
▸ **book in 1** *vt sep* **to b. sb in** *(to hotel)* réserver une chambre à qn
2 *vi (take a room)* prendre une chambre; *(register)* inscrire son nom dans le registre d'un hôtel
▸ **book up 1** *vt sep* **the hotel is fully booked up** l'hôtel est complet; **I'm booked up for this evening** je suis pris toute la soirée
2 *vi (make reservation)* réserver
bookable [ˈbʊkəbəl] *adj (seat, flight)* qui peut être réservé(e)
bookbinder [ˈbʊkbaɪndə(r)] *n* relieur(euse) *m,f*
bookbinding [ˈbʊkbaɪndɪŋ] *n* reliure *f*
bookcase [ˈbʊkkeɪs] *n* bibliothèque *f*
bookie [ˈbʊkɪ] *n Fam (bookmaker)* bookmaker *m*
booking [ˈbʊkɪŋ] *n* **(a)** *(reservation)* réservation *f*; **to make a b.** effectuer une réservation; **b. office** bureau *m* de location **(b)** *(in football)* **to receive a b.** recevoir un carton jaune
bookish [ˈbʊkɪʃ] *adj (person)* studieux(euse); *Pej (approach, style)* livresque
bookkeeping [ˈbʊkiːpɪŋ] *n Fin* comptabilité *f*
booklet [ˈbʊklɪt] *n* brochure *f*
bookmaker [ˈbʊkmeɪkə(r)] *n (in betting)* bookmaker *m*
bookmark(er) [ˈbʊkmɑːk(ə(r))] *n* marque-page *m inv*
bookseller [ˈbʊkselə(r)] *n* libraire *mf*
bookshelf [ˈbʊkʃelf] *(pl* **bookshelves** [ˈbʊkʃelvz]**)** *n* étagère *f*; **bookshelves** *(furniture)* bibliothèque *f*
bookshop [ˈbʊkʃɒp] *n Br* librairie *f*
bookstall [ˈbʊkstɔːl] *n (in railway station, airport)* kiosque *m* à journaux; *(selling second-hand books)* étalage *m* de bouquiniste

bookstore ['bʊkstɔ:(r)] *n Am* librairie *f*
bookworm ['bʊkwɜ:m] *n Fig* passionné(e) *m,f* de lecture
boom¹ [bu:m] *n* (a) *Naut (barrier)* estacade *f; (for sail)* bôme *f* (b) *Cin & TV* perche *f*
boom² 1 *n (economic)* boom *m*; b. **town** ville *f* en plein essor économique
2 *vi (of business, trade)* être florissant(e)
boom³ 1 *n (sound)* détonation *f*
2 *vi (of thunder, gun)* gronder; *(of person)* tonitruer
boomerang ['bu:məræŋ] *n* boomerang *m*
booming ['bu:mɪŋ] *adj (voice)* tonitruant(e)
boon [bu:n] *n* bénédiction *f,* aubaine *f*
boor ['bʊə(r)] *n* rustaud(e) *m,f*
boorish ['bʊərɪʃ] *adj* rustre, grossier(ère)
boost [bu:st] 1 *n* to give sth a b. *(production, economy)* relancer qch; to give sb's confidence a b. redonner confiance à qn; to give sb's morale a b. remonter le moral à qn
2 *vt Tel (signal)* régénérer, *(production, economy)* relancer; to b. sb's hopes/confidence redonner espoir/confiance à qn
booster ['bu:stə(r)] *n* (a) b. **(rocket)** fusée *f* de démarrage (b) *Elec* survolteur *m* (c) *Med (injection)* rappel *m*
boot [bu:t] 1 *n* (a) *(footwear) (for walking)* brodequin *m; (for sport)* chaussure *f; (ankle-length)* bottine *f; (knee-length)* botte *f* (b) *Br (of car)* coffre *m* (c) *(idioms)* the b. is on the other foot les rôles sont inversés; *Fam* to give sb the b. mettre qn à la porte; *Fam* to get the b. se faire mettre à la porte; *Fam* they put *or* stuck the b. into him *(kicked)* ils l'ont roué de coups de pied; *(criticized)* ils lui ont passé un savon; he's a liar and a thief to b. c'est un menteur et par dessus le marché c'est un voleur
2 *vt* (a) *Fam (kick)* donner un coup de pied dans; to b. sb out mettre qn à la porte (b) *Comptr* amorcer
3 *vi Comptr* to b. (up) s'amorcer
bootee [bu:'ti:] *n* chausson *m (de bébé)*
booth [bu:ð] *n (at fair)* baraque *f,* stand *m; (for telephone)* cabine *f; (in voting)* isoloir *m; (in restaurant)* alcôve *f*
bootlace ['bu:tleɪs] *n* lacet *m (de botte)*
bootleg ['bu:tleg] *adj (alcohol)* de contrebande; *(recording)* pirate
bootstrap ['bu:tstræp] *n* (a) tirant *m* de botte; *Fig* to pull oneself up by one's bootstraps se faire tout(e) seul(e) (b) *Comptr* routine *f* d'amorçage
booty ['bu:tɪ] *n* (a) *(loot)* butin *m* (b) *Am Fam (buttocks)* cul *m*
booze [bu:z] *Fam* 1 *n* alcool *m*
2 *vi* picoler
boozer ['bu:zə(r)] *n Fam (person)* poivrot(e) *m,f; Br (pub)* pub *m*
booze-up ['bu:zʌp] *n Br Fam* beuverie *f;* to have a b. prendre une cuite
boozy ['bu:zɪ] *adj Fam (voice, breath)* aviné(e)
bop¹ [bɒp] *Fam* 1 *n (dance)* danse *f*
2 *vi (pt & pp* bopped) *(dance)* danser
bop² *Fam* 1 *n (blow)* léger coup *m*
2 *vt (pt & pp* bopped) *(hit)* donner un léger coup à
boracic [bə'ræsɪk] *adj Chem* borique
border ['bɔ:də(r)] 1 *n* (a) *(edge)* bord *m; (in garden)* plate-bande *f* (b) *(frontier)* frontière *f;* the Borders = région vallonnée du sud-est de l'Écosse; b. **guard** garde-frontière *m;* b. **town** ville *f* frontière *ou* frontalière
2 *vt (country)* avoir une frontière commune avec; *(road)* border
▸ **border on** *vt insep (of country)* avoir une frontière

commune avec; to b. **on insanity/the ridiculous** friser la folie/le ridicule
borderland ['bɔ:dəlænd] *n* zone *f* frontalière
borderline ['bɔ:dəlaɪn] *n* frontière *f,* ligne *f* de démarcation; a b. **case** un cas limite
bore¹ ['bɔ:(r)] 1 *n (person)* raseur(euse) *m,f; (thing)* chose *f* ennuyeuse; what a b.! quelle barbe!
2 *vt* ennuyer
bore² 1 *n (calibre)* calibre *m*
2 *vt (with drill)* forer; to b. a hole in sth percer un trou dans qch
bore³ *pt of* bear²
bored [bɔ:d] *adj (sigh, look)* d'ennui; to be b. s'ennuyer; *Fam* to be b. stiff *or* to tears s'ennuyer à mourir
boredom ['bɔ:dəm] *n* ennui *m*
boring ['bɔ:rɪŋ] *adj* ennuyeux(euse)
born [bɔ:n] 1 *adj* to be a b. writer/leader être un écrivain/leader né
2 *(pp of* bear) to be b. naître; I was b. in Chicago/in 1975 je suis né à Chicago/en 1975; *Fam* I wasn't b. yesterday je ne suis pas né de la dernière pluie
born-again ['bɔ:nəgen] *adj* b. Christian chrétien(enne) *m,f* régénéré(e)
borne [bɔ:n] *pp of* bear²
Borneo ['bɔ:nɪəʊ] *n* Bornéo
borough ['bʌrə] *n Br* circonscription *f* électorale urbaine
borrow ['bɒrəʊ] 1 *vt* emprunter **(from** sb à qn); can I b. this book? est-ce que je peux t'/vous emprunter ce livre?; to be living on borrowed time *(of ill person, government)* ne plus en avoir pour longtemps
2 *vi* emprunter **(from** sb à qn); to b. at interest emprunter à l'intérêt
borrower ['bɒrəʊə(r)] *n* emprunteur(euse) *m,f*
Bosnia(-Herzegovina) ['bɒznɪə('hɜ:tsəgə'vi:nə)] *n* la Bosnie-Herzégovine)
Bosnian ['bɒznɪən] 1 *n* Bosniaque *m,f*
2 *adj* bosniaque; B. **Croat/Muslim/Serb** Croate *m,f,/* Musulman(e) *m,f,/* Serbe *m,f* de Bosnie
bosom ['bʊzəm] 1 *n (of woman)* poitrine *f; Fig* in the b. of one's family au sein de sa famille
2 *adj* b. **friend** ami(e) *m,f* intime
Bosphorus ['bɒsfərəs] *n* the B. le Bosphore
boss¹ [bɒs] *n (on shield)* ombon *m,* ombo *m*
boss² *Fam* 1 *n (at work)* patron(onne) *m,f;* to be one's own b. être son propre patron; to show sb who's b. montrer à qn qui commande
2 *vt* to b. sb *(about or around)* donner des ordres à qn
bossy ['bɒsɪ] *adj* autoritaire; *Fam* a b. boots un petit chef, un tyran
bosun ['bəʊsən] *n Naut* maître *m* d'équipage
botanic(al) [bə'tænɪk(əl)] *adj* botanique; b. **garden(s)** jardin *m* botanique
botanist ['bɒtənɪst] *n* botaniste *m,f*
botany ['bɒtənɪ] *n* botanique *f*
botch [bɒtʃ] *Fam* 1 *n* travail *m* salopé; to make a b. of sth *(job)* saloper qch; *(interview, exam)* rater qch complètement
2 *vt* to b. sth (up) *(job)* saloper qch; *(interview, exam)* rater complètement
botched [bɒtʃt] *adj Fam* raté(e); *Fam* a b. job un travail de sagouin
both [bəʊθ] 1 *pron* les deux; b. **(of them)** are dead ils sont morts tous les deux; we b. saw it nous l'avons vu tous les deux
2 *adj* les deux; b. **(the) brothers** les deux frères; b. **my parents** mes deux parents; on b. **sides** des deux côtés;

you can't have it b. ways on ne peut pas tout avoir
3 *adv* **b. in Britain and in France** aussi bien en Grande-Bretagne qu'en France; **she is b.** intelligent and beautiful elle est à la fois intelligente et belle
bother ['bɒðə(r)] **1** *n (trouble)* ennui *m*; **if it's not too much b.** si cela ne vous dérange pas trop; **to go to the b. of doing sth** prendre la peine de faire qch
2 *vt* **(a)** *(annoy)* déranger; **my back's still bothering me** j'ai toujours des problèmes de dos; **I'm sorry to b. you but...** je suis désolé de vous déranger mais...; **don't b. him when he's resting** ne le dérange pas quand il se repose **(b)** *(care)* **to be bothered about sth** s'inquiéter de qch; *Fam* **I can't be bothered** ça ne me dit rien; *Fam* **I'm not bothered** ça m'est égal
3 *vi (care)* s'inquiéter **(about** de); **he didn't even b. to apologize** il n'a même pas pris la peine de s'excuser; **don't b.!** ce n'est pas la peine!
4 *exclam* zut!
bothersome ['bɒðəsəm] *adj* ennuyeux(euse), gênant(e)
Botswana [bɒt'swɑːnə] *n* le Botswana
bottle ['bɒtəl] **1** *n* **(a)** *(container)* bouteille *f*; *(for perfume)* flacon *m*; *(for baby)* biberon *m*; *Fam* **to take to** *or* **hit the b.** se mettre à picoler; **b. bank** conteneur *m* pour la récupération du verre usagé; **b. green** vert bouteille *inv*; **b. opener** ouvre-bouteilles *m inv*, décapsuleur *m*; **b. party** = soirée où chacun apporte une bouteille **(b)** *Br Fam (courage)* cran *m*
2 *vt* mettre en bouteille
▸ **bottle out** *vi Br very Fam* se dégonfler; **he bottled out of the fight** il a eu peur de se battre
▸ **bottle up** *vt sep (emotions, anger)* refouler, ravaler
bottled ['bɒtəld] *adj* en bouteille; **b. water** eau *f* minérale
bottle-feed ['bɒtəlfiːd] *(pt & pp* **bottle-fed** ['bɒtəlfed]) *vt* nourrir au biberon
bottleneck ['bɒtəlnek] *n (in road)* rétrécissement *m* de la chaussée; *(in traffic)* embouteillage *m (dû à un rétrécissement de la chaussée); (in production)* goulot *m* d'étranglement
bottom ['bɒtəm] **1** *n* **(a)** *(lowest part) (of well, box, sea)* fond *m*; *(of street)* bout *m*; *(of stairs, mountain, page)* bas *m*; *(of ship)* carène *f*, fond; **from the b. of one's heart** du fond du cœur; **to be at the b. of the class** être le (la) dernier(ère) de la classe; **to touch b.** *(of boat)* toucher le fond **(b)** *(buttocks)* derrière *m* **(c)** *(idioms)* **to be at the b. of sth** être à l'origine de qch; **to get to the b. of sth** aller au fond des choses; **at b.** au fond; **the b. has fallen out of the market** le marché s'est effondré; *Fam* **bottoms up!** cul sec!
2 *adj* du bas; **b. deck** *(on bus)* niveau *m* inférieur; **b. floor** rez-de-chaussée *m inv*; *Fam* **you can bet your b. dollar that...** vous pouvez être sûr que...; **in b. gear** en première; **the b. line** *(financially)* le solde final; *Fig* **the b. line is that he is unsuited to the job** le fait est qu'il n'est pas fait pour ce travail
▸ **bottom out** *vi (of recession, slump)* atteindre son maximum; *(of price)* atteindre son minimum
bottomless ['bɒtəmlɪs] *adj (abyss)* sans fond; *(reserve)* inépuisable; *Fig* **a b. pit** un gouffre
bottommost ['bɒtəmməʊst] *adj* le (la) plus bas (basse)
botulism ['bɒtjʊlɪzəm] *n* botulisme *m*
boudoir ['buːdwɑː(r)] *n* boudoir *m*
bouffant ['buːfɒn] *adj* gonflant(e)
bough [baʊ] *n* branche *f*
bought [bɔːt] *pt & pp of* buy
boulder ['bəʊldə(r)] *n* gros bloc *m* de roche
boulevard ['buːləvɑːd] *n* boulevard *m*
bounce [baʊns] **1** *n* **(a)** *(of ball)* rebond *m* **(b)** *Fig (energy)* entrain *m*

2 *vt* **(a)** *(ball)* faire rebondir; *Fig* **to b. an idea off sb** soumettre une idée à qn *(de manière informelle)* **(b)** *Fam (cheque)* refuser d'honorer
3 *vi* **(a)** *(of ball)* rebondir **(off** contre); **to b. into/out of a room** *(of person)* entrer/sortir d'une pièce en sautillant **(b)** *Fam* **the cheque bounced** le chèque a été refusé *(parce qu'il était sans provision)*
▸ **bounce back** *vi (after illness, disappointment)* se remettre rapidement
bouncer ['baʊnsə(r)] *n Fam (doorman)* videur *m*
bouncing ['baʊnsɪŋ] *adj* **a b. baby** un bébé en pleine santé
bouncy ['baʊnsɪ] *adj* **(a)** *(ball)* qui rebondit bien; *(mattress)* élastique **(b)** *Fig (person)* plein(e) d'entrain
bound¹ [baʊnd] **1** *n (leap)* bond *m*; **at one b.** d'un bond
2 *vi (leap)* bondir
bound² *adj* **(a)** *(destined)* **b. for** en route pour **(b)** *(in predictions)* **he's b. to come** il ne peut pas manquer de venir; **it was b. to happen** ça devait arriver
bound³ *pt & pp of* bind
boundary ['baʊndərɪ] *(pl* **boundaries)** *n* limite *f*
boundless ['baʊndlɪs] *adj* illimité(e), sans bornes
bounds [baʊndz] *npl (limit)* limites *fpl*; **out of b.** interdit(e); **it is not beyond the b. of possibility** c'est dans le domaine du possible; **to know no b.** *(of anger, ambition)* être sans bornes
bountiful ['baʊntɪfʊl] *adj* abondant(e)
bounty ['baʊntɪ] *(pl* **bounties)** *n* **(a)** *(reward)* récompense *f*; *Am* **b. hunter** chasseur *m* de primes **(b)** *(generosity)* générosité *f*
bouquet [bu:'keɪ] *n (of flowers, wine)* bouquet *m*
bourbon ['bɜːbən] *n (whisky)* bourbon *m*
bourgeois ['bʊəʒwɑː] *adj* bourgeois(e)
bourgeoisie [bʊəʒwɑː'ziː] *n* bourgeoisie *f*
bout [baʊt] *n* **(a)** *(of illness)* accès *m*; *(of work, activity)* période *f* **(b)** *(boxing match)* combat *m*
boutique [bu:'tiːk] *n* boutique *f*
bovine ['bəʊvaɪn] *adj* bovin(e)
bow¹ [bəʊ] *n* **(a)** *(weapon)* arc *m*; *(for violin)* archet *m* **(b)** *(in hair, on dress)* nœud *m*; **b. tie** nœud papillon
bow² [baʊ] *n (of ship)* proue *f*, avant *m*
bow³ [baʊ] **1** *n* salut *m*; **to take a b.** saluer
2 *vt* **to b. one's head** baisser la tête
3 *vi* **(a)** *(as greeting, sign of respect)* saluer; *Fig* **to b. down before sb** s'incliner devant qn **(b)** *(yield)* **to b. to sb/sth** s'incliner devant qn/qch
▸ **bow out** *vi (resign)* tirer sa révérence
bowdlerize ['baʊdləraɪz] *vt* expurger
bowed [baʊd] *adj (back)* voûté(e); *(head)* baissé(e); **b. with age** courbé(e) par le fardeau des ans
bowel ['baʊəl] *n* intestin *m*; *Lit* **the bowels of the earth** les entrailles *fpl* de la terre; **b. complaint** affection *f* intestinale
bower ['baʊə(r)] *n* tonnelle *f*
bowl¹ [bəʊl] *n* **(a)** *(small dish)* bol *m*; *(for salad)* saladier *m*; *(for soup)* assiette *f* creuse **(b)** *(of toilet)* cuvette *f*
bowl² **1** *n* bowls *(game)* boules *fpl*
2 *vi (in cricket)* lancer la balle
▸ **bowl along** *vi (of car, bicycle)* rouler à toute vitesse
▸ **bowl over** *vt sep (knock down)* renverser; *Fig (astound)* stupéfier; **to be bowled over by sth** être stupéfié(e) par qch
bow-legged [bəʊ'legɪd] *adj* aux jambes arquées
bowler ['bəʊlə(r)] *n* **(a)** *(hat)* chapeau *m* melon **(b)** *(in cricket)* lanceur *m*

bowling ['bəʊlɪŋ] *n (game)* jeu *m* de boules; **b. alley** piste *f* de bowling; *(building)* bowling *m*; **b. green** terrain *m* de boules *(gazonné)*

box [bɒks] **1** *n* (**a**) *(container)* boîte *f*; *(larger)* caisse *f*; *(postal)* boîte postale; **b. camera** appareil *m* photo rudimentaire (**b**) *(on form)* case *f*; *(containing text)* encadré *m*; **(penalty) b.** *(in football)* surface *f* de réparation (**c**) *Br Fam* **the b.** *(television)* la télé (**d**) *(in theatre)* loge *f*
2 *vt* (**a**) *(place in box)* mettre en boîte/en caisse (**b**) **to b. sb's ears** gifler qn **3** *vi (fight)* boxer
boxer ['bɒksə(r)] *n* (**a**) *(fighter)* boxeur *m*; **b. shorts, boxers** *(underwear)* caleçon *m* (**b**) *(dog)* boxer *m*
boxing ['bɒksɪŋ] *n* boxe *f*; **b. glove/match** gant *m*/match *m* de boxe; **b. ring** ring *m*
Boxing Day ['bɒksɪŋ'deɪ] *n* Br le lendemain de Noël
box-office ['bɒksɒfɪs] *n* bureau *m* de location; **a b. success** un succès au box-office
boxroom ['bɒksruːm] *n* petite chambre *f*
boy [bɔɪ] *n* garçon *m*; **a night out with the boys** une soirée avec les copains; *Fam* **oh b.!** ça alors!; *Fam* **boys will be boys** il faut bien que jeunesse se passe; **B. Scout** scout *m*
boycott ['bɔɪkɒt] **1** *n* boycott *m* **2** *vt* boycotter
boyfriend ['bɔɪfrend] *n* petit ami *m*
boyhood ['bɔɪhʊd] *n* enfance *f*
boyish ['bɔɪɪʃ] *adj (of man) (looks, behaviour)* de garçon; *(of woman) (looks)* de garçon, *(behaviour)* de garçon manqué
BR [biː'ɑː(r)] *n Br (abbr* **British Rail)** ≃ la SNCF
bra [brɑː] *n* soutien-gorge *m*
brace [breɪs] **1** *n* (**a**) *(on teeth)* appareil *m* dentaire *ou* orthodontique (**b**) *Br* **braces** *(for trousers)* bretelles *fpl* (**c**) *(pair) (of birds, pistols)* paire *f* (**d**) **b. and bit** *(tool)* vilebrequin *m (avec mèche)*
2 *vt* (**a**) **to b. oneself** *(for impact)* s'accrocher; *Fig* **to b. oneself (for sth)** se préparer (à qch) (**b**) *(reinforce)* consolider
bracelet ['breɪslɪt] *n* bracelet *m*
bracing ['breɪsɪŋ] *adj (wind, weather)* vivifiant(e)
bracken ['brækən] *n* fougère *f*
bracket ['brækɪt] **1** *n* (**a**) *(for shelves)* équerre *f* (**b**) *(in writing)* parenthèse *f*; **in brackets** entre parenthèses (**c**) *(category) (of tax)* tranche *f*; *(of salaries)* fourchette *f*; **the eighteen to thirty age b.** les dix-huit à trente ans
2 *vt* (**a**) *(word, phrase)* mettre entre parenthèses (**b**) *(classify)* associer; **to b. together** mettre dans la même catégorie
brackish ['brækɪʃ] *adj* saumâtre
brag [bræg] *(pt & pp* **bragged)** *vi* se vanter **(about** de)
braggart ['brægət] *n* vantard(e) *m,f*
braid [breɪd] **1** *n (of hair)* tresse *f*, natte *f*; *(of cloth)* galon *m* **2** *vt (hair, thread)* tresser
Braille [breɪl] *n* braille *m*
brain [breɪn] **1** *n* cerveau *m*; **brains** *(as food)* cervelle *f*; *Fam* **to have brains** être intelligent(e); *Fam* **she's the brains of the family** c'est elle le cerveau de la famille; *Fam* **to have money/sex on the b.** être obsédé(e) par l'argent/le sexe; **b. damage** lésions *fpl* cérébrales; **b. dead** dans un coma dépassé; **the b. drain** la fuite des cerveaux; **b. surgeon** neurochirurgien(enne) *m,f*; **b. tumour** tumeur *f* au cerveau; *Fam* **b. wave** *(brilliant idea)* idée *f* de génie **2** *vt Fam (hit)* assommer
brainbox ['breɪnbɒks] *n Fam* cerveau *m*

brainchild ['breɪntʃaɪld] *n (idea, project)* idée *f*, trouvaille *f*
brainless ['breɪnlɪs] *adj* stupide
brainpower ['breɪnpaʊə(r)] *n* intelligence *f*
brainstorm ['breɪnstɔːm] *n Fam* (**a**) *Br (mental confusion)* moment *m* d'égarement (**b**) *Am (brilliant idea)* idée *f* de génie
brainstorming ['breɪnstɔːmɪŋ] *n* brainstorming *m*, remue-méninges *m*
brainwash ['breɪnwɒʃ] *vt* faire un lavage de cerveau à; **to b. sb into doing sth** faire faire qch à qn à force d'endoctrinement
brainy ['breɪnɪ] *adj Fam* intelligent(e)
braise [breɪz] *vt* braiser
brake [breɪk] **1** *n* froin *m*; **to apply the brake(s)** freiner, *Fig* **to put the brakes on a project** ralentir l'exécution d'un projet; **b. fluid** liquide *m* de freins; **b. lights** feux *mpl* de stop; **b. pedal** pédale *f* de frein **2** *vi* freiner
braking distance ['breɪkɪŋ'dɪstəns] *n* distance *f* de freinage
bramble ['bræmbəl] *n* ronce *f*
bran [bræn] *n* son *m*
branch [brɑːntʃ] **1** *n* (**a**) *(of tree, family, subject)* branche *f*; *(of river)* bras *m*; *(of railway, road)* embranchement *m*; **b. line** *(of railway)* ligne *f* secondaire (**b**) *(of shop)* succursale *f*; *(of bank)* agence *f* **2** *vi* bifurquer
▸ **branch off** *vi (of discussion)* bifurquer **(into** vers)
▸ **branch out** *vi* se diversifier; **to b. out into** étendre ses activités à
brand [brænd] **1** *n* (**a**) *(of product)* marque *f*, *Fig* **she has her own b. of humour** elle a un sens de l'humour particulier; **b. image** image *f* de marque; **b. leader** marque la plus vendue; **b. name** marque; **b. recognition** identification *f* de la marque (**b**) *(on cattle)* marque *f (au fer rouge)*
2 *vt (cattle)* marquer au fer rouge; *Fig* **the image was branded on her memory** l'image était gravée dans sa mémoire; *Fig* **to b. sb (as) a liar/coward** coller à qn l'étiquette de menteur(euse)/lâche
brandish ['brændɪʃ] *vt* brandir
brand-new ['bræn(d)'njuː] *adj* flambant neuf (neuve)
brandy ['brændɪ] *(pl* **brandies)** *n (cognac)* cognac *m*; *(more generally)* eau-de-vie *f*; **b. cherry b.** cherry *m*
brash [bræʃ] *adj* exubérant(e)
brass [brɑːs] *n* (**a**) *(metal)* laiton *m*; *Br Fam* **it's not worth a b. farthing** ça ne vaut pas un clou; **to get down to b. tacks** en venir aux faits; *Br Fam* **it's b. monkey weather** il fait un froid de canard (**b**) *Mus (brass instruments)* cuivres *mpl*; **b. band** fanfare *f* (**c**) *Br Fam (money)* oseille *f*, pognon *m* (**d**) *Br Fam (cheek, nerve)* culot *m*; **to have a b. neck** avoir du culot, être culotté(e)
▸ **brass off** *vt sep Br Fam* **to be brassed off (with)** en avoir marre (de)
brassière ['bræzɪə(r)] *n* soutien-gorge *m*
brassy ['brɑːsɪ] *adj Fam (person, manner)* exubérant(e)
brat [bræt] *n Pej* morveux(euse) *m,f*
bravado [brə'vɑːdəʊ] *n* bravade *f*
brave [breɪv] **1** *n (native American)* brave *m*
2 *adj* courageux(euse); **a b. effort** un bel effort; **a b. new world** un paradis; *Pej & Ironic* un monde utopique; **to put a b. face on it** faire bonne contenance
3 *vt* braver
bravely ['breɪvlɪ] *adv* courageusement

bravery ['breɪvərɪ] *n* courage *m*

bravo [brɑːˈvəʊ] *exclam* bravo!

brawl [brɔːl] **1** *n* bagarre *f*; **a drunken b.** une querelle d'ivrognes **2** *vi* se bagarrer

brawn [brɔːn] *n Fam (strength)* muscle *m*; **he's all b. and no brain** il a du muscle mais rien dans la tête

brawny ['brɔːnɪ] *adj* musclé(e)

bray [breɪ] **1** *n (of donkey)* braiment *m*; *Fig (of person)* braillement *m* **2** *vi (of donkey)* braire; *Fig (of person)* brailler

brazen ['breɪzən] *adj* effronté(e), impudent(e); *(lie)* éhonté(e)

▸ **brazen out** *vt sep* **to b. it out** s'en tirer au culot

brazier ['breɪzɪə(r)] *n* brasero *m*

Brazil [brəˈzɪl] *n* le Brésil

brazil [brəˈzɪl] *n* **b. (nut)** noix *f* du Brésil

Brazilian [brəˈzɪlɪən] **1** *n* Brésilien(enne) *m,f* **2** *adj* brésilien(enne)

breach [briːtʃ] **1** *n* **(a)** *(in wall)* brèche *f*; *Fig* **to step into the b.** *(in emergency)* intervenir au pied levé **(b)** *(of agreement)* rupture *f* **(of** de); *(of trust)* abus *m* **(of** de); *(of discipline)* manquement *m* **(of** à); *(of rules)* infraction *f* **(of** à); *Law* **b. of the peace** atteinte *f* à l'ordre public **(c)** *(in relationship)* **it caused a b. in their relationship** cela les a conduits à se brouiller **2** *vt* **(a)** *(defences)* ouvrir une brèche dans **(b)** *(contract, agreement)* rompre; *(rules)* enfreindre

bread [bred] *n* **(a)** *(food)* pain *m*; **a loaf of b.** un pain; **b. and butter** du pain beurré; *Fig* gagne-pain *m*; *Fig* **he knows which side his b. is buttered on** il sait où est son intérêt; **b. bin** boîte *f* à pain; **b. knife** couteau *m* à pain **(b)** *very Fam (money)* blé *m*, pognon *m*

bread-and-butter [bredənˈbʌtə(r)] *adj Fam* **b. issues** questions *fpl* essentielles

breadbasket ['bredbɑːskɪt] *n* corbeille *f* à pain

breadboard ['bredbɔːd] *n* planche *f* à pain

breadcrumb ['bredkrʌm] *n* miette *f* de pain; **breadcrumbs** *(in recipe)* chapelure *f*; **fried in breadcrumbs** pané(e)

breadline ['bredlaɪn] *n* **on the b.** indigent(e), sans ressources

breadth [bredθ] *n* **(a)** *(width)* largeur *f* **(b)** *(of mind, opinions)* largeur *f*, *(of outlook, understanding)* ampleur *f*

breadwinner ['bredwɪnə(r)] *n* **to be the b.** faire bouillir la marmite

break [breɪk] **1** *n* **(a)** *(in bone)* fracture *f*; *(in wall, fence)* brèche *f*; *(in clouds)* trouée *f*; *(in electric circuit)* rupture *f*; **at b. of day** au point du jour; *Elec* **b. switch** disjoncteur *m* **(b)** *(interval, rest)* pause *f*; *(holidays)* vacances *fpl*; **(commercial) b.** *(on TV, radio)* page *f* de publicité; **without a b.** sans interruption; **a b. in the weather** un changement de temps; *Fam* **give me a b.!** fiche-moi la paix deux minutes! **(c)** *Fam (escape)* évasion *f*; **to make a b. for it** se faire la belle; **to make a b. for the exit** se précipiter vers la sortie **(d)** *Fam (chance)* chance *f*; **to have a lucky b.** avoir de la veine; **this could be your big b.** ça pourrait être la chance de ta vie **2** *vt (pt* **broke** [brəʊk], *pp* **broken** ['brəʊkən]) **(a)** *(in general)* casser; **to b. one's arm** se casser le bras; **to b. sth into pieces** mettre qch en morceaux; **to b. the sound barrier** franchir le mur du son; *Fig* **to b. the ice** briser la glace; **to b. one's journey** s'arrêter en route; *Fig* **a. a leg!** *(good luck!)* bonne chance! **(b)** *(cushion)* *(fall, force)* amortir

(c) *(destroy)* *(person, resistance, strike)* briser; *(health)* ruiner; **to b. sb's heart** briser le cœur à qn; **to b. sb's serve** *(in tennis)* prendre le service de qn **(d)** *(infringe)* *(agreement, promise)* rompre; *(rule, speed limit)* enfreindre **(e)** *(news, story)* annoncer **(to** à) **3** *vi* **(a)** *(of glass, machine, bone)* se casser; *(of weather)* changer; *(of day)* se lever; *(of waves)* se briser; *(of voice)* (with emotion) se briser; *(at puberty)* muer; **to b. in two** se casser en deux; **to b. loose** se détacher **(b)** *(of news, story)* éclater

▸ **break away** *vi* **(a)** *(escape)* s'évader; **to b. away from** *(person)* échapper à; *(place)* s'évader de **(b) to b. away from** *(cut ties with)* *(party, country)* quitter; *(family)* couper les ponts avec

▸ **break down 1** *vt sep* **(a)** *(destroy)* *(resistance)* briser **(b)** *(analyze)* *(argument, figures)* décomposer **(into** en) **2** *vi* **(a)** *(of car, machine)* tomber en panne; *(of talks)* échouer; *(of argument)* s'effondrer; *(of person under pressure)* craquer; **to b. down (in tears)** fondre en larmes **(b)** *(change chemically)* se décomposer **(into** en)

▸ **break even** *vi* rentrer dans ses frais

▸ **break in 1** *vt sep (horse)* dresser; *(new shoes)* faire; *(new recruit)* former; **to b. oneself in to sth** se faire à qch **2** *vi (of burglar)* entrer par effraction

▸ **break into** *vt insep* **(a)** *(of burglar)* entrer par effraction dans **(b)** *(begin suddenly)* **to b. into laughter** éclater de rire; **to b. into song/a run** se mettre à chanter/courir **(c)** *(showbusiness)* percer dans; *(market)* percer sur

▸ **break off 1** *vt sep* **(a)** *(detach)* *(twig, handle)* casser **(b)** *(terminate)* *(relations, engagement)* rompre **2** *vi* **(a)** *(become detached)* se casser **(b)** *(stop talking, working)* s'interrompre

▸ **break open 1** *vt sep (door)* enfoncer; *(lock, safe)* forcer **2** *vi* s'ouvrir

▸ **break out** *vi* **(a)** *(escape)* s'évader **(of** de) **(b)** *(of argument)* éclater; *(of disease)* se déclarer; **to b. out in a sweat** se mettre à transpirer; **to b. out in a rash** avoir une éruption de boutons

▸ **break through 1** *vt insep (wall)* faire une brèche dans; *(barrier)* forcer; *Fig (someone's reserve, shyness)* vaincre **2** *vi (of sun)* percer les nuages

▸ **break up 1** *vt sep* **(a)** *(reduce to pieces)* couper en morceaux **(b)** *(estate, company)* morceler; *(machine)* démonter **(c)** *(fight, quarrel)* faire cesser **2** *vi* **(a)** *(disintegrate)* se disloquer **(b)** *(end)* *(of talks)* cesser; *(of meeting, school term)* se terminer; *(of school)* fermer; *(of pupils)* être en vacances; *(of couple)* se séparer; **to b. up with sb** *(end relationship)* rompre avec qn

▸ **break with** *vt insep* rompre avec

breakable ['breɪkəbəl] **1** *n* **breakables** objets *mpl* fragiles **2** *adj* fragile

breakage ['breɪkɪdʒ] *n* **were there any breakages?** est-ce qu'il y a eu de la casse?; **all breakages must be paid for** *(sign)* tout article cassé doit être payé

breakaway ['breɪkəweɪ] *adj* dissident(e)

breakdown ['breɪkdaʊn] *n* **(a)** *(of car, machine, computer)* panne *f*; *(of talks, in communication)* rupture *f*; **(nervous) breakdown** dépression *f* (nerveuse); **to have a b.** *(of motorist)* tomber en panne; *(of person under pressure)* faire une dépression; **b. truck** dépanneuse *f*, camion *m* de dépannage **(b)** *(analysis)* *(of figures, costs)* détail *m*

breaker ['breɪkə(r)] *n (wave)* déferlante *f*

break-even point [breɪkˈiːvənpɔɪnt] *n Fin* seuil *m* de rentabilité

breakfast ['brekfəst] **1** *n* petit déjeuner *m*; **to have b.**

prendre son petit déjeuner, déjeuner; **b. cereal** céréales *fpl*; **b. television** émissions *fpl* (télévisées) du matin **2** *vi* prendre son petit déjeuner, déjeuner; **to b. on sth** manger qch au petit déjeuner

break-in ['breɪkɪn] *n* cambriolage *m*

breaking ['breɪkɪŋ] *n* (**a**) *Law* **b. and entering** entrée *f* par effraction (**b**) **b. point** *(of patience)* limite *f*; **to reach b. point** *(of person)* être à bout; *(of marriage)* être au bord de la rupture

breakneck ['breɪknek] *adj* **at b. speed** à toute allure

break-out ['breɪkaʊt] *n (from prison)* évasion *f*

breakthrough ['breɪkθruː] *n (discovery)* découverte *f* majeure; **there has been a b. in talks** un pas décisif a été franchi dans les négociations; **to make a b.** *(discovery)* faire une découverte majeure; *(in talks)* faire un pas décisif

breakwater ['breɪkwɔːtə(r)] *n* brise-lames *m inv*

bream [briːm] *(pl* **bream**) *n* brème *f*

breast [brest] *n (of woman)* & *Lit (of man)* sein *m*; *(of chicken)* blanc *m*; **to make a clean b. of it** tout avouer; **b. cancer** cancer *m* du sein; **b. pocket** poche *f* de poitrine

breastbone ['brestbəʊn] *n* sternum *m*

breast-feed ['brestfiːd] *(pt & pp* **breast-fed** ['brestfed]) *vt & vi* allaiter

breastplate ['brestpleɪt] *n* plastron *m (de cuirasse)*

breaststroke ['bres(t)strəʊk] *n* brasse *f*

breath [breθ] *n* souffle *m*; **to take a deep b.** inspirer profondément; **to pause for b.** s'arrêter pour reprendre sa respiration; **bad b.** mauvaise haleine *f*; **they are not to be mentioned in the same b.** on ne saurait les comparer; **in the next b.** aussitôt après; *also Fig* **to hold one's b.** retenir son souffle; *Fam* **don't hold your b.!** c'est pas demain la veille!; **to waste one's b.** gaspiller sa salive; **out of b.** à bout de souffle, hors d'haleine; **to get short of b.** s'essouffler; **to get one's b. back** reprendre haleine, reprendre son souffle; *under one's b.* à voix basse; *Fig* **to take sb's b. away** couper le souffle à qn; **a b. of wind/of air** un souffle de vent/d'air; **to go out for a b. of fresh air** sortir prendre l'air; *Fig* **she's a real b. of fresh air** elle apporte une bouffée d'air frais; **b. test** Alcotest® *m*

breathalyse, breathalyze ['breθəlaɪz] *vt* faire passer l'Alcotest® à

breathalyser, breathalyzer ['breθəlaɪzə(r)] *n* Alcotest® *m*

breathe [briːð] **1** *vt* (**a**) *(inhale)* respirer (**b**) *(idioms)* **to b. a sigh of relief** pousser un soupir de soulagement; *Lit* **to b. one's last** rendre son dernier soupir; **don't b. a word (of it)!** pas un mot!; **to b. fire** *(in anger)* jeter feu et flammes; **to b. new life into sth** *(project, scheme)* insuffler une force nouvelle à qch **2** *vi* respirer; *(exhale)* souffler; **to b. heavily** *(noisily)* respirer bruyamment; *(with difficulty)* respirer avec difficulté; *Fig* **to b. easily again** respirer; *Fig* **to b. down sb's neck** *(follow)* talonner qn; *(nag)* être tout le temps sur le dos de qn

▸ **breathe in 1** *vt* inhaler
2 *vi* inspirer

▸ **breathe out** *vi* expirer

breather ['briːðə(r)] *n Fam (rest)* pause *f*; **to take a b.** faire une pause

breathing ['briːðɪŋ] *n* respiration *f*; **b. apparatus** bouteille *f* d'oxygène et masque; *Fig* **to give sb some b. space** laisser respirer qn

breathless ['breθlɪs] *adj (person)* hors d'haleine; *(calm)* plat(e); *(silence)* profond(e)

breathtaking ['breθteɪkɪŋ] *adj (beauty, scenery)* à

couper le souffle; *(speed)* vertigineux(euse); *(audacity)* sidérant(e)

breathy ['breθɪ] *adj (voice)* haletant(e)

bred [bred] *pt & pp of* **breed**

breech [briːtʃ] *n* (**a**) *Med* **b. delivery** *or* **birth** (accouchement *m* par le) siège *m* (**b**) *(of gun)* culasse *f*

breed [briːd] **1** *n also Fig* race *f* **2** *vt (pt & pp* **bred** [bred]) *(animals)* élever; *Fig (discontent)* engendrer **3** *vi* se reproduire

breeder ['briːdə(r)] *n (of animals)* éleveur(euse) *m,f*; *Phys* **b. reactor** surgénérateur *m*

breeding ['briːdɪŋ] *n* (**a**) *(of animals)* élevage *m*; **b. ground** lieu *m* de reproduction; *Fig (of discontent, revolution)* foyer *m* (**b**) *(of person)* **(good) b.** éducation *f*, manières *fpl*

breeze [briːz] **1** *n* brise *f*; *Fam* **it was a b.** c'était du gâteau **2** *vi* **to b. in/out** *(quickly)* entrer/sortir en coup de vent; *(casually)* entrer/sortir avec désinvolture

breeze-block ['briːzblɒk] *n Br* parpaing *m*

breezy ['briːzɪ] *adj* (**a**) *(weather)* venteux(euse) (**b**) *(casual)* désinvolte

brethren ['breðrɪn] *npl Rel* frères *mpl*

Breton ['bretɒn] **1** *n* Breton(onne) *m,f* **2** *adj* breton(onne)

breviary ['briːvɪərɪ] *(pl* **breviaries**) *n Rel* bréviaire *m*

brevity ['brevɪtɪ] *n* brièveté *f*

brew [bruː] **1** *n (beer)* bière *f*; *(tea)* thé *m*; *Fig (mixture)* mélange *m* **2** *vt (beer)* brasser; *(tea)* faire infuser, préparer **3** *vi (of beer)* fermenter; *(of tea)* infuser; **there's a storm brewing** il y a de l'orage dans l'air; *Fig* **there's something brewing** il se trame quelque chose; **there's trouble brewing** il va y avoir du grabuge

▸ **brew up** *vi Br Fam* faire du thé

brewer ['bruːə(r)] *n* brasseur *m*

brewery ['bruːərɪ] *(pl* **breweries**) *n* brasserie *f (fabrique)*

briar ['braɪə(r)] *n (plant)* bruyère *f*; *(pipe)* pipe *f* de bruyère; **b. rose** églantine *f*

bribe [braɪb] **1** *n* pot-de-vin *m* **2** *vt* acheter; **to b. sb into doing sth** acheter qn pour qu'il fasse qch

bribery ['braɪbərɪ] *n* corruption *f*

bric-à-brac ['brɪkəbræk] *n* bric-à-brac *m*

brick [brɪk] *n (for building)* brique *f*; *Fig* **to drop a b.** faire une gaffe; **b. wall** mur *m* en briques; **you're banging your head against a b. wall** tu perds ton temps

▸ **brick up** *vt sep* murer

brickie ['brɪkɪ] *n Br Fam* maçon *m*

bricklayer ['brɪkleɪə(r)] *n* maçon *m*

brickwork ['brɪkwɜːk] *n* briquetage *m*

bridal ['braɪdəl] *adj* nuptial(e); **b. dress** *or* **gown** robe *f* de mariée; **b. suite** suite *f* nuptiale

bride [braɪd] *n* mariée *f*; **the b. and groom** les mariés *mpl*

bridegroom ['braɪdgruːm] *n* marié *m*

bridesmaid ['braɪdzmeɪd] *n* demoiselle *f* d'honneur

bridge[1] [brɪdʒ] **1** *n (over river)* pont *m*; *(on ship)* passerelle *f*; *(on teeth)* bridge *m*; *(of nose)* arête *f*; *Fig* **we'll cross that b. when we come to it** chaque chose en son temps; *Fig* **b. building** réconciliation *f* **2** *vt (river)* construire un pont sur; **to b. a gap** *(in knowledge)* combler une lacune; **to b. the gap between rich and poor** combler le fossé entre les riches et les pauvres

bridge² *n (card game)* bridge *m*
bridgehead ['brɪdʒhed] *n Mil* tête *f* de pont
bridging loan ['brɪdʒɪŋləʊn] *n Fin* prêt-relais *m*
bridle ['braɪdəl] **1** *n* bride *f*; **b. path** piste *f* cavalière
2 *vt (horse)* brider
3 *vi (with anger)* s'indigner **(at** de)
brief [briːf] **1** *n Law* dossier *m*; *(instructions)* consignes *fpl*
2 *adj* bref (brève); *(garment)* court(e); **in b.,…, to be b.,…**
en bref,…
3 *vt (inform)* mettre au courant **(on** de)
briefcase ['briːfkeɪs] *n* serviette *f*
briefing ['briːfɪŋ] *n (meeting)* briefing *m; (information)*
instructions *fpl*
briefly ['briːflɪ] *adv* brièvement; *(hesitate, smile)* pendant
un court instant; **(put) b.,…** en bref,…
briefs [briːfs] *npl (underwear)* slip *m*
brier ['braɪə(r)] = **briar**
brigade [brɪ'geɪd] *n* brigade *f*
brigadier [brɪɡə'dɪə(r)] *n* général *m* de brigade
brigand ['brɪɡənd] *n Lit* brigand *m*
bright [braɪt] **1** *adj* **(a)** *(sun, light)* brillant(e); *(day)* clair(e);
(colour) vif (vive); **to go b.** red *(blush)* devenir rouge
comme une tomate **(b)** *(hopeful)* **the future looks b.**
l'avenir s'annonce bien; **the situation is looking a bit**
brighter la situation commence à s'améliorer; *Fig* **the**
only b. spot is… la seule chose positive est…; **to look on**
the b. side (of things) prendre les choses du bon côté **(c)**
(cheerful) vif (vive) **(d)** *(clever) (person)* intelligent(e); *(idea)*
lumineux(euse)
2 *adv* **b. and early** de bon matin
brighten ['braɪtən] **1** *vt (room, mood)* égayer
2 *vi (of weather, sky)* s'éclaircir; *(of face, eyes)* s'éclairer; *(of*
prospects) s'améliorer
▸ **brighten up** *vt sep (room)* égayer
2 *vi (of person)* devenir plus gai(e); *(of weather, sky)*
s'éclaircir; *(of face)* s'éclairer; *(of prospects)* s'améliorer
bright-eyed ['braɪtaɪd] *adj* aux yeux brillants; *Fig*
(eager) enthousiaste; *Fam* **b. and bushy-tailed** frais
(fraîche) et dispos(e)
brightly ['braɪtlɪ] *adv (say)* gaiement; *(lit, coloured)*
vivement; **the sun was shining b.** il faisait un soleil
radieux; **to smile b.** faire un sourire radieux
brightness ['braɪtnɪs] *n (of light, sun, colour)* éclat *m*; *(of*
lighting) intensité *f*; *(on TV)* luminosité *f*
brilliance ['brɪljəns] *n* **(a)** *(of light, colour)* éclat *m* **(b)** *(of*
person) intelligence *f*; *(of idea)* ingéniosité *f*
brilliant ['brɪljənt] *adj* **(a)** *(light)* éclatant(e); *(sun, smile)*
radieux(euse) **(b)** *(scientist, career, pupil)* brillant(e) **(c)**
(excellent) formidable
brilliantly ['brɪljəntlɪ] *adv* **(a)** *(coloured, lit)* vivement **(b)**
(acted, played) brillamment
brim [brɪm] **1** *n (of cup, glass, hat)* bord *m*; **to be full to the**
b. (with) être plein(e) à ras bord (de)
2 *vi (pt & pp* **brimmed)** **to be brimming with sth** *(liquid)*
être rempli(e) à ras bord de qch; *(enthusiasm, ideas)*
déborder de qch; **eyes brimming with tears** yeux noyés
de larmes
▸ **brim over** *vi also Fig* déborder **(with** de)
brimful ['brɪmfʊl] *adj* plein(e) à ras bord; *Fig* **b. of**
health/life débordant(e) de santé/vie
brimstone ['brɪmstəʊn] *n Fig* **to preach fire and b.**
menacer les fidèles des feux de l'enfer
brine [braɪn] *n* saumure *f*
bring [brɪŋ] *(pt & pp* **brought** [brɔːt]) *vt* **(a)** *(cause to come)*
(object, letter, news) apporter; *(person, animal)* amener; **to b.**

sth to sb's attention signaler qch à l'attention de qn; **what**
brings you to Paris? qu'est-ce qui vous amène à Paris?; **to**
b. sth out of sth *(box, bag)* sortir qch de qch; **to b. a child**
into the world mettre un enfant au monde; *Law* **to b. an**
action against sb intenter un procès à qn
(b) *(cause)* provoquer; **it has brought me great**
happiness cela m'a procuré un grand bonheur; **to b.**
sb (good) luck/bad luck porter bonheur/malheur à qn;
to b. tears to sb's eyes faire venir les larmes aux yeux de qn
(c) *(to a particular condition)* **to b. sth into disrepute**
discréditer qch; **to b. sth into question** remettre en
question; **to b. sth to an end** mettre fin à qch; **to b. sth to**
light *(crime, secret)* révéler qch; **to b. sth to mind** faire
penser à qch; **I couldn't bring myself to do it** je n'ai pas pu
me décider *ou* me résoudre à le faire
(d) *(be sold for)* rapporter
▸ **bring about** *vt sep (cause)* entraîner, provoquer
▸ **bring along** *vt sep (person)* amener; *(object)* apporter
▸ **bring back** *vt sep* **(a)** *(person)* ramener; *(gift)* rapporter;
to b. sb back to life ramener qn à la vie; **to b. sb back to**
health rendre la santé à qn **(b)** *(memory)* rappeler; **that**
brings it all back to me ça me réveille tous mes souvenirs
(c) *(law, practice)* rétablir
▸ **bring down** *vt sep* **(a)** *(from shelf, attic)* descendre **(b)**
(soldier, plane) abattre; *(government)* faire tomber, renverser;
Fam **her performance brought the house down** son
interprétation lui a valu des applaudissements
enthousiastes **(c)** *(lower) (price, temperature)* faire baisser
(d) *Fam (depress)* déprimer
▸ **bring forward** *vt sep* **(a)** *(proposal)* émettre; *(plan)*
proposer; *(reasons, evidence)* avancer **(b)** *(advance time of)*
avancer **(c)** *Com (in bookkeeping)* reporter
▸ **bring in** *vt sep* **(a)** *(expert, consultant)* faire appel à; **the**
police brought him in for questioning la police l'a
emmené au poste pour l'interroger **(b)** *(earn) (of person)*
gagner; *(of investment, sale)* rapporter **(c)** *(law, act)*
introduire **(d)** *Law (verdict)* rendre
▸ **bring off** *vt sep (accomplish)* réussir
▸ **bring on** *vt sep (cause)* provoquer; **you've brought it**
on yourself tu l'as cherché
▸ **bring out** *vt sep* **(a)** *(publish)* sortir **(b)** *(cause to appear)*
to b. out the best/the worst in sb faire ressortir les
qualités/les défauts de qn; **strawberries b. her out in a**
rash les fraises lui donnent de l'urticaire; **to b. sb out of**
their shell faire sortir qn de sa coquille
▸ **bring round** *vt sep* **(a)** *(revive)* ranimer, faire revenir à
soi **(b)** *(persuade)* convaincre; **she brought him round to**
her point of view elle l'a rallié à son point de vue **(c)**
(conversation) amener **(to** sur)
▸ **bring to** *vt sep (revive)* ranimer, faire revenir à soi
▸ **bring together** *vt sep* réunir
▸ **bring up** *vt sep* **(a)** *(subject)* soulever **(b)** *(child)* élever; **I**
was brought up to be polite on m'a appris à être poli **(c)**
(vomit) vomir
bring-and-buy ['brɪŋən'baɪ] *n Br* **b. (sale)** vente *f* de
charité
brink [brɪŋk] *n also Fig* bord *m*; *Fig* **to be on the b. of sth**
(war, ruin, disaster) être au bord de qch; *(death, success)* être
à deux doigts de qch; **to be on the b. of doing sth** être à
deux doigts de faire qch
brinkmanship ['brɪŋkmənʃɪp] *n* politique *f* de la corde
raide
brisk [brɪsk] *adj* **(a)** *(weather)* frais (fraîche); *(wind)*
vivifiant(e) **(b)** *(person) (efficient)* énergique; *(dismissive)* vif
(vive) **(c)** *(rapid)* **at a b. pace** *(work)* rapidement; *(walk)*
d'un pas vif; **to go for a b. walk** se promener d'un pas vif;
business is b. les affaires marchent bien

briskly ['brɪsklɪ] adv (a) (efficiently) énergiquement; (dismissively) vivement (b) (rapidly) (walk) d'un pas vif

bristle ['brɪsəl] 1 n (of plant, brush, face) poil m; (of pig) soie f 2 vi (a) (of animal, animal's fur) se hérisser; to b. (with anger) (at) se hérisser (à) (b) to be bristling with (people) grouiller de; (difficulties) être hérissé(e) de

Brit [brɪt] n Fam Britannique mf

Britain ['brɪtən] n la Grande-Bretagne

British ['brɪtɪʃ] 1 npl the B. les Britanniques mpl 2 adj britannique; B. Columbia la Colombie-Britannique; the B. Isles les îles fpl Britanniques; B. SummerTime heure f d'été (en Grande-Bretagne)

Briton ['brɪtən] n Britannique mf; Hist ancient B. Breton(onne) m,f (de la Grande-Bretagne)

Brittany ['brɪtənɪ] n la Bretagne

brittle ['brɪtəl] adj (object, hair, voice) cassant(e); (bones) friable

broach [brəʊtʃ] vt (subject) aborder

broad[1] [brɔːd] adj (road, smile, sense, mind) large; (accent) fort(e), prononcé(e); (humour) grossier(ère); (hint) appuyé(e); in b. daylight en plein jour; Fig au grand jour; to be in b. agreement être d'accord sur l'essentiel; Fig to be a b. church admettre de nombreuses tendances; a b. outline les grandes lignes fpl; b. bean fève f

broad[2] n Am Fam (woman) gonzesse f

broadcast ['brɔːdkɑːst] 1 n émission f 2 vt (pt & pp broadcast) diffuser; Fam don't b. it! ne va pas le crier sur les toits! 3 vi (of station) émettre

broadcaster ['brɔːdkɑːstə(r)] n (person) (on TV, radio) présentateur(trice) m,f; (TV station) chaîne f de télévision; (radio station) station f de radio

broadcasting ['brɔːdkɑːstɪŋ] n (action) diffusion f; he works in b. (radio) il travaille à la radio; (TV) il travaille à la télé

broaden ['brɔːdən] 1 vt élargir; to b. one's horizons élargir son horizon 2 vi to b. (out) s'élargir

broadly ['brɔːdlɪ] adv (generally) en gros; to smile b. faire un large sourire; b. speaking en gros

broad-minded [brɔːd'maɪndɪd] adj (person) large d'esprit; (attitude) ouvert(e)

broadsheet ['brɔːdʃiːt] n journal m grand format (synonyme de qualité)

broad-shouldered [brɔːd'ʃəʊldəd] adj large d'épaules; Fig to be b. bien encaisser

broadside ['brɔːdsaɪd] n Naut to fire a b. tirer une bordée; Fig to fire a b. at sb/sth attaquer violemment qn/qch

brocade [brəʊ'keɪd] n brocart m

broccoli ['brɒkəlɪ] n brocolis mpl

brochure ['brəʊʃə(r)] n brochure f

brogue [brəʊg] n (accent) accent m

brogues [brəʊgz] npl (shoes) = chaussures solides souvent ornées de petits trous

broil [brɔɪl] vt & vi Am griller

broke [brəʊk] 1 adj Fam fauché(e); to be flat or Br stony b. être fauché comme les blés; to go for b. jouer le tout pour le tout 2 pt of **break**

broken ['brəʊkən] 1 adj (object, bone) cassé(e); (promise) rompu(e); (marriage, heart, person) brisé(e); (ground, surface) irrégulier(ère); to speak b. English parler un mauvais anglais; b. home famille f désunie 2 pp of **break**

brokenhearted [brəʊkən'hɑːtɪd] adj to be b. avoir le cœur brisé

broker ['brəʊkə(r)] n Fin (for shares, currency) agent m de change; Com (for goods, insurance) courtier m

brolly ['brɒlɪ] (pl brollies) n Br Fam pépin m, pébroc m

bromide ['brəʊmaɪd] n Chem bromure m; Fig banalité f

bronchial ['brɒŋkɪəl] adj Anat bronchique; b. pneumonia broncho-pneumonie f; b. tubes bronches fpl

bronchitic [brɒŋ'kɪtɪk] adj bronchitique

bronchitis [brɒŋ'kaɪtɪs] n bronchite f; to have b. avoir une bronchite

bronze [brɒnz] 1 n bronze m; to win a b. (medal) remporter une médaille de bronze; the B. Age l'âge m du bronze 2 adj (material) de ou en bronze; (colour) couleur bronze inv

bronzed [brɒnzd] adj bronzé(e)

brooch [brəʊtʃ] n broche f

brood [bruːd] 1 n (of birds) couvée f; Hum (of children) progéniture f 2 vi (of hen) couver; Fig to b. (over or about sth) ruminer (qch)

broody ['bruːdɪ] adj (hen) couveuse; Fig (woman) en mal d'enfant

brook[1] [brʊk] n (stream) ruisseau m

brook[2] vt Formal (tolerate) tolérer

broom [bruːm] n (a) (plant) genêt m (b) (for cleaning) balai m; Fig a new b. = un nouvel arrivant qui veut tout changer

broomstick ['bruːmstɪk] n manche m à balai

Bros npl Com (abbr Brothers) Carter B. Carter frères

broth [brɒθ] n (soup) (thin) bouillon m; (thick) potage m

brothel ['brɒθəl] n maison f close

brother ['brʌðə(r)] n frère m

brotherhood ['brʌðəhʊd] n fraternité f; Rel confrérie f; the b. of man la fraternité humaine

brother-in-law ['brʌðərɪnlɔː] (pl brothers-in-law) n beau-frère m

brought [brɔːt] pt & pp of **bring**

brow [braʊ] n (a) (forehead) front m; (eyebrow) sourcil m (b) (of hill) sommet m

browbeat ['braʊbiːt] (pt browbeat, pp browbeaten ['braʊbiːtən]) vt intimider; to b. sb into doing sth forcer qn à faire qch en usant d'intimidation

brown [braʊn] 1 n marron m 2 adj marron inv; (hair) brun(e); (skin) mat(e); (tanned) bronzé(e); (bread, flour, rice) complet(ète); b. paper papier m kraft; b. sugar sucre m roux, cassonade f 3 vt (in cooking) faire dorer 4 vi (in cooking) faire dorer

browned-off ['braʊnd'ɒf] adj Br Fam to be b. (with) en avoir marre (de); to be b. with doing sth en avoir marre de faire qch

Brownie ['braʊnɪ] n ≃ jeannette f; Fig to win or get b. points se faire bien voir

brownie ['braʊnɪ] n (cake) brownie m

brown-nose ['braʊnnəʊz] vi Vulg faire le lèche-cul

browse [braʊz] 1 n to have a b. (in shop) regarder; to have a b. through sth (collection, shelves) jeter un œil sur qch; (magazine) feuilleter qch 2 vt Comptr to b. the Web naviguer sur le Web 3 vi (a) (in shop) regarder; to b. through sth (collection, shelves) jeter un œil sur qch; (magazine) feuilleter qch (b) (of animal) brouter

browser ['braʊzə(r)] n Comptr logiciel m de navigation sur le Web

bruise [bru:z] **1** *n (on body)* bleu *m*; *(on fruit)* meurtrissure *f* **2** *vt (person)* faire un bleu à; *Fig (feelings, pride)* blesser; **to b. one's arm** se faire un bleu au bras **3** *vi (of person)* se faire des bleus; *(of fruit)* s'abîmer; **she bruises easily** elle se fait facilement des bleus

bruiser ['bru:zə(r)] *n Fam* grosse brute *f*

bruising ['bru:zɪŋ] **1** *n (bruises)* bleus *mpl* **2** *adj (encounter, experience)* douloureux(euse)

brunch [brʌntʃ] *n Fam* brunch *m*

Brunei [bru:'naɪ] *n* le Brunei

brunette [bru:'net] *n* brune *f*

brunt [brʌnt] *n* **to bear** *or* **take the b. of sth** *(attack)* essuyer le plus fort de qch; *(anger)* faire les frais de qch

brush [brʌʃ] **1** *n* **(a)** *(for clothes, hair, teeth)* brosse *f*; *(for sweeping)* balai *m*; *(for painting)* pinceau *m* **(b)** *(action)* **to give sth a b.** donner un coup de brosse à qch; **to give one's hair a b. floor a b.** donner un coup de balai; **to give one's hair a b.** se donner un coup de brosse **(c)** *(light touch)* effleurement *m*; *Fam* **to have a b. with the law** avoir des démêlés avec la justice **(d)** *(of fox)* queue *f* **(e)** *(undergrowth)* broussailles *fpl* **2** *vt* **(a)** *(clothes, shoes)* brosser; **to b. one's hair/teeth** se brosser les cheveux/les dents; **to b. the floor** balayer **(b)** *(touch lightly)* effleurer **3** *vi* **to b. against sb/sth** effleurer qn/qch; **to brush past sb/sth** effleurer qn/qch en passant

▸ **brush aside** *vt sep (objection, obstacle)* balayer; *(opponent)* écarter

▸ **brush off** *vt sep* **(a)** *(from clothes, shoes)* enlever d'un coup de brosse **(b)** *(person)* envoyer promener; *(insult, incident)* ignorer

▸ **brush up** *vt sep* **(a)** *(leaves, crumbs)* balayer **(b)** *Fam (subject, language)* **to b. up (on)** se remettre à

brushed [brʌʃt] *adj (cotton, nylon)* gratté(e)

brush-off ['brʌʃɒf] *n Fam* **to give sb the b.** envoyer promener qn

brush-up ['brʌʃʌp] *n Br* **to have a wash and b.** faire un brin de toilette

brushwood ['brʌʃwʊd] *n (as fuel)* petit bois *m*; *(undergrowth)* broussailles *fpl*

brushwork ['brʌʃwɜːk] *n Art* touche *f*

brusque [bru:sk] *adj* brusque

brusquely ['bru:sklɪ] *adv (behave)* avec brusquerie; *(say)* d'un ton brusque

Brussels ['brʌsəlz] *n* Bruxelles; **B. sprout** chou *m* de Bruxelles

brutal ['bru:təl] *adj* brutal(e); *(attack, crime)* sauvage

brutality [bru:'tælɪtɪ] *n* brutalité *f*; *(of attack, crime)* sauvagerie *f*

brutalize ['bru:təlaɪz] *vt (ill-treat)* brutaliser; *(make insensitive)* rendre insensible

brutally ['bru:təlɪ] *adv* avec brutalité; *(beat, attack)* sauvagement

brute [bru:t] **1** *n (animal)* bête *f*; *(person)* brute *f* **2** *adj* **b. force** *or* **strength** force *f* brutale

brutish ['bru:tɪʃ] *adj* bestial(e)

BSc [bi:es'si:] *n (abbr* **Bachelor of Science)** **to have a B. in computer science/biology** avoir une licence d'informatique/de biologie; **John Smith B.** John Smith, licencié en chimie/informatique/*etc*

BSE [bi:es'i:] *n (abbr* **bovine spongiform encephalopathy)** EBS *f*, maladie *f* de la vache folle

BSI [bi:es'aɪ] *n (abbr* **British Standards Institution)** = association britannique de normalisation

BST [bi:es'ti:] *n (abbr* **British Summer Time)** heure *f* d'été *(en Grande-Bretagne)*

bubble ['bʌbəl] **1** *n (of air, soap)* bulle *f*; *Fig* **the b. has burst** le rêve est terminé; **b. bath** bain *m* moussant; **b. gum** chewing-gum *m*; *Comptr* **b. jet printer** imprimante *f* à bulles **2** *vi (form bubbles)* bouillonner

▸ **bubble over** *vi (of liquid)* déborder; *Fig* **to b. over with joy** ne plus se tenir de joie

bubbly ['bʌblɪ] **1** *n Br Fam (champagne)* champ *m* **2** *adj* **(a)** *(liquid)* plein(e) de bulles **(b)** *(person)* débordant(e) de vitalité

bubonic [bju:'bɒnɪk] *adj* **b. plague** peste *f* bubonique

buccaneer [bʌkə'nɪə(r)] *n* boucanier *m*

Bucharest [bʊkə'rest] *n* Bucarest

buck [bʌk] **1** *n* **(a)** *Am Fam (dollar)* dollar *m*; **to make a fast** *or* **quick b.** faire du fric **(b)** *(of deer, rabbit)* mâle *m* **(c)** *Fam (responsibility)* **to pass the b.** refiler le bébé; **the b. stops here** en fin de compte c'est moi le responsable **2** *vt* **to b. the system/a trend** aller à l'encontre de l'ordre établi/d'une tendance **3** *vi (of horse)* faire le saut de mouton

▸ **buck up** *Br Fam* **1** *vt sep (encourage)* remonter le moral à; **to b. one's ideas up** se prendre en main **2** *vi Fam (cheer up)* reprendre courage; *(hurry)* se grouiller

bucket ['bʌkɪt] **1** *n* seau *m*; *Br Fam* **it's raining buckets** il tombe des cordes; *Fam* **to cry buckets** pleurer comme une madeleine; *Fam* **b. shop** *(for air tickets)* agence *f* de voyages à prix réduits **2** *vi Br Fam* **it's bucketing (down)** il tombe des cordes

buckle ['bʌkəl] **1** *n* boucle *f* **2** *vt* **(a)** *(fasten)* boucler **(b)** *(deform)* déformer; *(wheel)* voiler **3** *vi (deform)* se déformer; *(of wheel)* se voiler; *(of knees)* flancher; **she buckled at the knees** ses jambes ont cédé sous elle

▸ **buckle down** *vi* s'y mettre; **to b. down to a task** s'atteler à une tâche

buckshot ['bʌkʃɒt] *n* chevrotine *f*

buckskin ['bʌkskɪn] *n* daim *m (peau)*

buckteeth [bʌk'ti:θ] *npl* dents *fpl* de lapin

bucktoothed [bʌk'tu:θt] *adj* **to be b.** avoir des dents de lapin

buckwheat ['bʌkwi:t] *n* sarrasin *m*

bucolic [bju:'kɒlɪk] *adj Lit* bucolique

bud [bʌd] **1** *n (of leaf, branch)* bourgeon *m*; *(of flower)* bouton *m* **2** *vi (pt & pp* **budded)** *(of tree)* bourgeonner; *(of flowers)* être en boutons

Budapest ['bʊdəpest] *n* Budapest

Buddha ['bʊdə] *n* Bouddha

Buddhist ['bʊdɪst] **1** *n* bouddhiste *mf* **2** *adj (priest, doctrine)* bouddhiste; *(art, temple)* bouddhique

budding ['bʌdɪŋ] *adj (genius, actor)* en herbe; *(talent)* naissant(e)

buddy ['bʌdɪ] *(pl* **buddies)** *n Fam (friend)* pote *m*; **hey, b.!** dis donc, mec!

budge [bʌdʒ] **1** *vt (move)* bouger; *Fig (convince)* faire changer d'avis **2** *vi (move)* bouger; *Fig (yield)* céder

budgerigar ['bʌdʒərɪgɑ:(r)] *n* perruche *f*

budget ['bʌdʒɪt] **1** *n* budget *m*; *Br Pol* **the B.** le budget; **to go over b.** dépasser le budget; **to be within b.** être dans les limites du budget; **b. deficit/surplus** déficit *m*/ excédent *m* budgétaire **2** *vt (time, money)* gérer **3** *vi* **to b. for sth** prévoir qch

budgetary ['bʌdʒɪtərɪ] *adj Fin* budgétaire
budgie ['bʌdʒɪ] *n Fam* perruche *f*
Buenos Aires ['bwenɒ'saɪrɪz] *n* Buenos Aires
buff [bʌf] **1** *n* (**a**) *(colour)* couleur *f* chamois (**b**) *Fam* in the **b**. *(naked)* à poil (**c**) *(enthusiast)* mordu(e) *m,f*; **film b**. cinéphile *mf*
2 *adj* (couleur) chamois *inv*; *(envelope)* en papier kraft
3 *vt (polish)* lustrer
buffalo ['bʌfələʊ] (*pl* **buffalo** *or* **buffaloes**) *n* buffle *m*
buffer¹ ['bʌfə(r)] *n (on railway track)* butoir *m*; *Comptr* mémoire *f* tampon; **to act as a b**. faire tampon; **b. state** État *m* tampon; **b. zone** zone *f* tampon
buffer² *n Br Fam* old **b**. vieux schnock *m*
buffet¹ ['bʌfɪt] *vt (of wind)* secouer; *Fig* **to be buffeted by events** être ballotté(e) par les événements
buffet² ['bʊfeɪ] *n* (**a**) *(sideboard)* buffet *m* (**b**) *(meal)* buffet *m*; **b. lunch/dinner** buffet (**c**) *(in station)* buffet *m*; **b. (car)** wagon-restaurant *m*, voiture-restaurant *f*
buffeting ['bʌfɪtɪŋ] *n* **to take a b**. *(of ship)* être violemment ballotté(e); *Fig (of person)* être fortement ébranlé(e)
buffoon [bə'fuːn] *n* bouffon *m*; **to play the b**. faire le pitre
bug [bʌg] **1** *n* (**a**) *(insect)* insecte *m*; *(bed bug)* punaise *f* (**b**) *Fam (illness)* virus *m*, microbe *m*; **a stomach b**. un embarras gastrique; **there's a b. going round** il y a un virus qui traîne; *Fig* **the travel b**. le virus des voyages (**c**) *Comptr* bug *m*, bogue *m* (**d**) *(listening device)* micro *m*
2 *vt (pt & pp* **bugged**) (**a**) *(telephone)* mettre sur écoute; *(building, room)* cacher des micros dans (**b**) *Fam (annoy)* taper sur les nerfs à; *(nag)* embêter; **stop bugging me about it!** arrête de m'embêter avec ça!
bugbear ['bʌgbeə(r)] *n Fam* cauchemar *m*
bug-eyed [bʌg'aɪd] *adj* aux yeux exorbités
bug-free [bʌg'friː] *adj Comptr* sans bug
bugger ['bʌgə(r)] *Br* **1** *n very Fam (unpleasant person)* connard(asse) *m,f*; **you silly b**.! espèce d'andouille!; **the poor b**.! le pauvre!; **it's a b. of a job** c'est une vraie galère; **b. all** que dalle; **he knows b. all about it** il y connaît que dalle
2 *vt* (**a**) *(sodomize)* sodomiser (**b**) *very Fam* **b. (it)!** merde!; **I'll be buggered if I'm going to do it!** tu peux toujours courir pour que je le fasse!; **I'm buggered if I know** j'en sais foutre rien; **that's really buggered it!** ça a tout foutu en l'air!
▸ **bugger about, bugger around** *Br very Fam* **1** *vt sep* **to b. sb about** se foutre de la gueule de qn
2 *vi* glander
▸ **bugger off** *vi Br very Fam* se casser, foutre le camp
▸ **bugger up** *vt sep Br very Fam (plan)* foutre en l'air; *(TV, machine)* bousiller
buggered ['bʌgəd] *adj Br very Fam (broken)* foutu(e); *(exhausted)* nase
buggery ['bʌgərɪ] *n* (**a**) *Law* sodomie *f* (**b**) *Br very Fam* **to run like b**. prendre ses jambes à son cou
buggy ['bʌgɪ] (*pl* **buggies**) *n* (**a**) *Br (pushchair)* poussette *f*; *Am (pram)* landau *m* (**b**) *(carriage)* boghei *m*, buggy *m*
bugle ['bjuːgəl] *n* clairon *m*
bugler ['bjuːglə(r)] *n* (sonneur *m* de) clairon *m*
build [bɪld] **1** *n* carrure *f*
2 *vt (pt & pp* **built** [bɪlt]) construire; **to be built (out) of sth** être construit(e) en qch; **to b. sth into sth** *(include)* inclure qch dans qch; **to b. one's hopes on sth** fonder ses espoirs sur qch
▸ **build on 1** *vt sep (add)* ajouter
2 *vt insep (success)* tirer parti de

▸ **build up 1** *vt sep* (**a**) *(resources)* accumuler; **to b. up speed/one's strength** prendre de la vitesse/des forces; **don't b. your hopes up** ne te fais pas d'illusions (**b**) *(custom)* se constituer; *(reputation)* se faire; *(company)* développer; **to b. up an immunity (to sth)** s'immuniser (contre qch) (**c**) *(hype)* faire du battage autour de
2 *vi (of clouds)* s'amasser; *(of hurricane, storm)* se préparer; *(of tension, pressure)* s'accumuler
builder ['bɪldə(r)] *n* maçon *m*; *(business owner)* entrepreneur *m* (dans le bâtiment)
building ['bɪldɪŋ] *n* (**a**) *(structure)* bâtiment *m*; immeuble *m* (**b**) *(action)* construction *f*; **the b. trade** le bâtiment; **b. block** cube *m*; *Fig* élément *m* essentiel; **b. site** chantier *m* (de construction); *Br* **b. society** ≃ société *f* de crédit immobilier
build-up ['bɪldʌp] *n (of tension, forces)* accumulation *f*; *(hype)* battage *m*; **the b. to Christmas/the match** la période précédant Noël/le match
built [bɪlt] *pt & pp of* **build**
built-in ['bɪl'tɪn] *adj (cupboard)* encastré(e); *(included)* compris(e); **b. obsolescence** obsolescence *f* programmée
built-up ['bɪl'tʌp] *adj* **b. area** agglomération *f* urbaine
bulb [bʌlb] *n* (**a**) *(of plant)* bulbe *m* (**b**) *(light bulb)* ampoule *f*
bulbous ['bʌlbəs] *adj* bulbeux(euse); **a b. nose** un gros nez
Bulgaria [bʌl'geərɪə] *n* la Bulgarie
Bulgarian [bʌl'geərɪən] **1** *n* (**a**) *(person)* Bulgare *mf* (**b**) *(language)* bulgare *m*
2 *adj* bulgare
bulge [bʌldʒ] **1** *n* renflement *m*
2 *vi (of stomach)* être gonflé(e); *(of bag, pocket)* être bourré(e) (**with** de)
bulimia [bə'lɪmɪə] *n* boulimie *f*
bulk [bʌlk] **1** *n* (**a**) *(mass)* masse *f*; **the b. (of sth)** la majeure partie (de qch) (**b**) *Com* **in b**. en gros; **b. purchase** achat *m* en gros
2 *vt* **to b. sth out** étoffer qch
3 *vi* **to b. large** *(of problem)* occuper une place importante
bulkhead ['bʌlkhed] *n Naut* cloison *f*
bulky ['bʌlkɪ] *adj* volumineux(euse), encombrant(e)
bull¹ [bʊl] *n* (**a**) *(animal)* taureau *m*, **b. elephant** éléphant *m* mâle; *Fin* **b. market** marché *m* à la hausse (**b**) *very Fam (nonsense)* conneries *fpl* (**c**) *(idioms)* **to take the b. by the horns** prendre le taureau par les cornes; **like a b. in a china shop** comme un éléphant dans un magasin de porcelaine
bull² *n Rel* bulle *f*
bulldog ['bʊldɒg] *n* bouledogue *m*; **b. clip** pince *f* à dessin
bulldoze ['bʊldəʊz] *vt (land)* aplanir au bulldozer; *(building)* démolir au bulldozer; *Fig* **to b. sb into doing sth** forcer qn à faire qch
bulldozer ['bʊldəʊzə(r)] *n* bulldozer *m*
bullet ['bʊlɪt] *n* balle *f*; **b. hole** impact *m* de balle; **b. wound** blessure *f* par balle
bulletin ['bʊlɪtɪn] *n* bulletin *m*; **b. board** *Am (noticeboard)* panneau *m* d'affichage; *Comptr* serveur *m* télématique
bulletproof ['bʊlɪtpruːf] *adj (car, glass)* blindé(e); **b. vest** gilet *m* pare-balles
bullfight ['bʊlfaɪt] *n* corrida *f*, course *f* de taureaux; *(art)* tauromachie *f*
bullfighter ['bʊlfaɪtə(r)] *n* torero *m*
bullfighting ['bʊlfaɪtɪŋ] *n (bullfights)* courses *fpl* de taureaux; *(art)* tauromachie *f*
bullfinch ['bʊlfɪntʃ] *n* bouvreuil *m*
bullfrog ['bʊlfrɒg] *n* grenouille-taureau *f*

bullion ['bʊljən] n gold b. lingots mpl d'or

bullish ['bʊlɪʃ] adj Fin (market) à la hausse; Fig (optimistic) optimiste

bullock ['bʊlək] n bœuf m

bullring ['bʊlrɪŋ] n arène f

bull's-eye ['bʊlzaɪ] n mille m; also Fig **b.!** dans le mille!; **to hit the b.** mettre dans le mille

bullshit ['bʊlʃɪt] Vulg **1** n (nonsense) conneries fpl **2** exclam c'est des conneries tout ça! **3** vt (pt & pp **bullshitted**) **to b. sb** raconter des conneries à qn; **she bullshitted her way into the job** elle a bluffé pour avoir le poste **4** vi (talk nonsense) dire des conneries

bully ['bʊlɪ] **1** n (pl **bullies**) (child) terreur f; (adult) tyran m; **don't be such a b.** ne sois pas si tyrannique **2** vt (pt & pp **bullied**) maltraiter; **to b. sb into doing sth** forcer qn à faire qch; **he gets bullied at school** il se fait persécuter à l'école **3** exclam Ironic **b. for you!** bravo!

bully-boy ['bʊlɪbɔɪ] n voyou m; **b. tactics** manœuvres fpl d'intimidation

bullying ['bʊlɪɪŋ] **1** n brimades fpl **2** adj brutal(e)

bulrush ['bʊlrʌʃ] n jonc m

bulwark ['bʊlwɜːk] n also Fig rempart m (**against** contre)

bum [bʌm] Fam **1** n (a) Br (buttocks) derrière m (b) Am (tramp) clochard(e) m,f **2** adj (of poor quality) minable; **to get a b. deal** se faire avoir **3** vt (pt & pp **bummed**) **to b. a cigarette from** or **off sb** taxer une cigarette à qn; **to b. a ride** se faire prendre en stop

▸ **bum around** vi Fam (be idle) glander; (travel) vadrouiller

bumblebee ['bʌmbəlbiː] n bourdon m

bumbling ['bʌmbəlɪŋ] adj **b. fool** or **idiot** imbécile mf

bumf [bʌmf] n Fam paperasse f

bummer ['bʌmə(r)] n Fam **what a b.!** quelle poisse!

bump [bʌmp] **1** n (a) (jolt) secousse f; **to land with a b.** tomber violemment par terre; Fig **to come back down to earth with a b.** redescendre brusquement sur terre (b) (lump) bosse f **2** vt cogner; **to b. one's head** se cogner la tête

▸ **bump into** vt insep (collide with) rentrer dans; Fam (meet by chance) tomber sur

▸ **bump off** vt sep Fam (kill) liquider

▸ **bump up** vt sep Fam (price) gonfler, augmenter

bumper ['bʌmpə(r)] **1** n Br (of car) pare-chocs m inv; **b. car** (at fairground) auto f tamponneuse **2** adj **b. crop** récolte f exceptionnelle; **b. issue** numéro m exceptionnel

bumpkin ['bʌmpkɪn] n **(country) b.** péquenaud(e) m,f

bump-start ['bʌmpstɑːt] vt **to b. a car** pousser une voiture pour la faire démarrer

bumptious ['bʌmpʃəs] adj suffisant(e)

bumpy ['bʌmpɪ] adj (road) cahoteux(euse); (journey) agité(e); (landing) violent(e); Fam Fig **to give sb/sth a b. ride** malmener qn/qch

bun [bʌn] n (a) (sweet) petit gâteau m brioché; (for burger) petit pain m rond (b) (hairstyle) chignon m

bunch [bʌntʃ] n (of flowers) bouquet m; (of bananas) régime m; (of grapes) grappe f; (of keys) trousseau m; (of people) bande f; (of cyclists) peloton m; **bunches** (hairstyle) couettes fpl; **he's the best of a bad b.** c'est le moins mauvais du lot; **she's the best** or **the pick of the b.** c'est

la meilleure du lot; **a whole b. of stuff to do** tout un tas de trucs à faire

▸ **bunch together** vi (of people) se serrer

bundle ['bʌndəl] **1** n (of clothes) paquet m; (of banknotes, papers) liasse f; (of straw) botte f; Fam **I don't go a b. on horror films** je ne suis pas un fana de films d'horreur; Fam Ironic **you're a b. of laughs!** c'est fou ce que tu as l'air gai!; Fam **she's a b. of nerves** c'est un paquet de nerfs **2** vt **to b. sb out of the door** mettre qn dehors sans ménagement; **to b. sb into a car** embarquer qn dans une voiture

▸ **bundle off** vt sep (send) expédier

▸ **bundle up 1** vt sep (a) (tie up) mettre en paquet (b) (dress warmly) emmitoufler **2** vi s'emmitoufler

bung [bʌŋ] **1** n (a) (plug) bonde f (b) Br Fam (bribe) bakchich m **2** vt Br Fam (put) mettre; (throw) balancer; **b. it there** mets-le là; **b. me over an orange** balance-moi une orange

▸ **bung up** vt sep Fam boucher; **my nose is bunged up** j'ai le nez bouché

bungalow ['bʌŋɡələʊ] n pavillon m de plain-pied

bungee jumping ['bʌndʒiːdʒʌmpɪŋ] n saut m à l'élastique

bunghole ['bʌŋhəʊl] n bonde f

bungle ['bʌŋɡəl] **1** vt (attempt) rater; (job) gâcher **2** vi se tromper

bunion ['bʌnjən] n oignon m (au pied)

bunk¹ [bʌŋk] n (bed) lit m; (in train, ship) couchette f; **b. beds** lits superposés

bunk² n Br Fam **to do a b.** (run away) se faire la malle

▸ **bunk off** vi Br Fam (from school) sécher (les cours)

bunker ['bʌŋkə(r)] n (a) (for coal) coffre m à charbon (b) Mil (bunker) bunker m, blockhaus m; **nuclear b.** abri m antiatomique (c) Br (on golf course) bunker m

bunkum ['bʌŋkəm] n Fam âneries fpl

bunny ['bʌnɪ] n (pl **bunnies**) n Fam **b. (rabbit)** petit lapin m

Bunsen burner ['bʌnsən'bɜːnə(r)] n bec m Bunsen

bunting ['bʌntɪŋ] n (decorations) guirlandes fpl de fanions

buoy [bɔɪ] n bouée f

▸ **buoy up** vt sep (person, prices) soutenir

buoyancy ['bɔɪənsɪ] n (in water) flottabilité f; Fig (of market) stabilité f

buoyant ['bɔɪənt] adj (in water) qui flotte; Fig (economy, prices) stable; Fig (person, mood) plein(e) d'allant

burble ['bɜːbəl] vi (of stream) murmurer; (of person) marmonner

burden ['bɜːdən] **1** n also Fig fardeau m; **b. of taxation** pression f fiscale; Law **b. of proof** charge f de la preuve **2** vt Fig accabler (**with** de)

burdensome ['bɜːdənsəm] adj lourd(e)

bureau ['bjʊərəʊ] n (pl **bureaux** ['bjʊərəʊz]) n (a) (desk) bureau m, secrétaire m; Am (chest of drawers) commode f (b) (office) bureau m; Am (government department) service m

bureaucracy [bjʊə'rɒkrəsɪ] n bureaucratie f

bureaucrat ['bjʊərəkræt] n bureaucrate mf

bureaucratic [bjʊərə'krætɪk] adj bureaucratique

bureaux ['bjʊərəʊz] pl of **bureau**

burgeon ['bɜːdʒən] vi (of trade) se développer; (of crime) augmenter; (of relationship) s'épanouir; **a burgeoning talent** un talent qui s'affirme

burger ['bɜːɡə(r)] n hamburger m; **b. bar** fast-food m

burglar ['bɜːglə(r)] n cambrioleur(euse) m,f; **b. alarm** alarme f (de sécurité)

burglarize ['bɜːgləraɪz] vt Am cambrioler

burglar-proof ['bɜːgləpruːf] adj inviolable

burglary ['bɜːglərɪ] (pl **burglaries**) n cambriolage m

burgle ['bɜːgəl] vt cambrioler

Burgundy ['bɜːgəndɪ] n la Bourgogne

burgundy ['bɜːgəndɪ] adj (colour) bordeaux inv

burial ['berɪəl] n enterrement m; **b. ground** cimetière m

Burkina-Faso [bɜːˈkiːnəˈfæsəʊ] n le Burkina

burlesque [bɜːˈlesk] **1** n (caricature) parodie f; (style) burlesque m **2** adj burlesque

burly ['bɜːlɪ] adj bien bâti(e)

Burma ['bɜːmə] n Formerly la Birmanie

Burmese [bɜːˈmiːz] **1** npl **the B.** les Birmans mpl **2** n (a) (person) Birman(e) m,f (b) (language) birman m **3** adj birman(e)

burn¹ [bɜːn] **1** n brûlure f **2** vt (pt & pp **burnt** [bɜːnt] or **burned**) (a) (fuel, building) brûler; **to b. one's hand/one's mouth** se brûler la main/la bouche; **to b. a hole in sth** faire un trou dans qch (b) (idioms) **to have money to b.** avoir de l'argent à ne plus savoir quoi en faire; **to b. one's boats** or **one's bridges** brûler ses vaisseaux; **to b. the candle at both ends** brûler la chandelle par les deux bouts; **to b. the midnight oil** travailler tard

3 vi brûler; (of light) briller; **the fire is burning low** le feu baisse; Fig **to b. with desire** brûler de désir; **to b. with anger** bouillonner de colère; **to b. with enthusiasm** déborder d'enthousiasme

► **burn down 1** vt sep incendier **2** vi être détruit(e) par le feu

► **burn out 1** vt sep **to b. itself out** (of fire) s'éteindre; Fig **to b. oneself out** (become exhausted) s'épuiser **2** vi (of fire) s'éteindre

► **burn up 1** vt sep (energy) dépenser **2** vi (of rocket) se désintégrer

burn² n Scot (stream) ruisseau m

burner ['bɜːnə(r)] n brûleur m

burning ['bɜːnɪŋ] adj (on fire) en feu; (very hot) brûlant(e); (passion, ambition) dévorant(e); **a b. issue/question** une question brûlante

burnish ['bɜːnɪʃ] vt polir, brunir

burnt [bɜːnt] **1** adj brûlé(e) **2** pt & pp of **burn¹**

burnt-out ['bɜːntaʊt] adj (building, car) calciné(e); Fig (person) usé(e)

burp [bɜːp] **1** n rot m **2** vi roter

burr¹ [bɜː(r)] n (of plant) = petite boule renfermant des graines et pourvue de piquants qui, en se détachant, s'accroche aux vêtements

burr² n to speak with a **b.** grasseyer

burrow ['bʌrəʊ] **1** n (of animal) terrier m **2** vi (of animal) creuser la terre

bursar ['bɜːsə(r)] n Univ intendant(e) m,f

bursary ['bɜːsərɪ] (pl **bursaries**) n (grant) bourse f (d'études)

burst [bɜːst] **1** n (of laughter) éclat m; (of enthusiasm) élan m; **a b. of activity** une poussée d'activité; **a b. of applause** une salve d'applaudissements; **a b. of gunfire** une rafale; **a b. of speed** une pointe de vitesse **2** vt (pt & pp **burst**) (balloon, tyre) faire éclater; **to b. its banks** (of river) déborder, sortir de son lit

3 vi (of balloon, bubble, tyre, pipe) éclater; Fig **to be bursting with pride** déborder de fierté; **to be bursting with impatience** bouillir d'impatience; **to be bursting to do sth** mourir d'envie de faire qch; **to be bursting (for the toilet)** avoir un besoin pressant; Fig **to be bursting at the seams** (of room) être plein(e) à craquer

► **burst into** vt insep (a) (enter) faire irruption dans (b) (suddenly start) **to b. into flames** prendre feu; **to b. into song** se mettre à chanter; **to b. into laughter/tears** éclater de rire/en sanglots

► **burst open** vi (of door) s'ouvrir brusquement; (of packet) éclater

► **burst out** vi **to b. out laughing/crying** éclater de rire/en sanglots

Burundi [bəˈrʊndɪ] n le Burundi

bury ['berɪ] (pt & pp **buried**) vt (body, treasure) enterrer; (of avalanche, mudslide) & Fig (hide) ensevelir; **to b. oneself in one's work** se plonger dans son travail; **to b. one's face in one's hands** enfouir son visage dans ses mains; **to b. the hatchet** enterrer la hache de guerre

bus [bʌs] **1** (pl **buses** or **busses**) (a) (vehicle) bus m, autobus m; **by b.** en bus, b. **driver** chauffeur m de bus; **b. lane** couloir m de bus; **b. route** ligne f de bus; **b. shelter** Abribus® m; **b. station** gare f routière; **b. stop** arrêt m d'autobus (b) Comptr bus m **2** vt (pt & pp **bused** or **bussed**) transporter en autobus

bush [bʊʃ] n (plant) buisson m; **the b.** (in Africa, Australia) la brousse; Fam **b. telegraph** téléphone m arabe

bushed [bʊʃt] adj Fam (exhausted) vanné(e), claqué(e)

bushel [ˈbʊʃəl] n boisseau m; Fig **don't hide your light under a b.** ne cache pas ton talent

bushfire ['bʊʃfaɪə(r)] n feu m de brousse

bushy ['bʊʃɪ] adj touffu(e)

busily ['bɪzɪlɪ] adv **to be b. doing sth** être très occupé(e) à faire qch

business ['bɪznɪs] n (a) (task, concern) affaire f; **it's none of your b.** cela ne te regarde pas, ce ne sont pas tes affaires; **it's/it's not my b. to...** c'est/ce n'est pas à moi de...; **mind your own b.!** occupe-toi de tes affaires ou de ce qui te regarde!; **to make it one's b. to do sth** prendre sur soi de faire qch; **to go about one's b.** vaquer à ses occupations; **to get down to b.** se mettre au travail; **to mean b.** ne pas plaisanter; **I'm sick of the whole b.** j'en ai assez de toute cette histoire; **he was asking like nobody's b.** il travaillait très dur; Br Fam **it's the b.** (excellent) c'est génial (b) (individual company) affaire f, entreprise f; (commercial activity) affaires fpl; **in the entertainment b.** dans le spectacle; **I'm not in the b. of making compromises** ce n'est pas mon genre de faire des compromis; **to go into b.** se lancer dans les affaires; **to go into b. with sb** monter une affaire avec qn; **to go out of b.** fermer; **to go to London on b.** aller à Londres pour affaires; **how's b.?** comment vont les affaires?; **it's good/bad for b.** c'est bon/mauvais pour les affaires; **to talk b.** parler affaires; **to do b. with sb** traiter avec qn; Fin **b. account** compte m professionnel; **b. card** carte f de visite; **b. class** (on plane) classe f affaires; **b. hours** (of shop) heures fpl d'ouverture; (of office) heures de bureau; **b. lunch** déjeuner m d'affaires; **b. management** gestion f d'entreprise; **b. park** parc m d'activités; **b. school** école f de commerce; **b. studies** études fpl commerciales on de commerce; **b. trip** voyage m d'affaires

businesslike ['bɪznɪslaɪk] adj professionnel(le)

businessman ['bɪznɪsmæn] n homme m d'affaires

businesswoman ['bɪznɪswʊmən] n femme f d'affaires; **to be a good b.** avoir le sens des affaires

busk [bʌsk] *vi Br* jouer de la musique *(dans les rues ou le métro)*

busker ['bʌskə(r)] *n Br* musicien(enne) *m,f (dans les rues ou le métro)*

busman ['bʌsmən] *n Br Fam* **a b.'s holiday** = vacances pendant lesquelles on fait la même chose qu'à son travail

bust¹ [bʌst] *n* **(a)** *(of woman)* poitrine *f*; **b. measurement** tour *m* de poitrine **(b)** *(statue)* buste *m*

bust² *Fam* **1** *adj* **(a)** *(broken)* fichu(e) **(b) to go b.** *(bankrupt)* faire faillite

2 *vt (pt & pp* busted *or* bust) **(a)** *(break)* bousiller **(b)** *(arrest)* coffrer

▸ **bust out** *vi Fam (escape)* se tirer **(of** de)

▸ **bust up** *vt sep Fam (disrupt) (event)* interrompre; *(relationship)* ficher en l'air

bustle ['bʌsəl] **1** *n (commotion)* animation *f*
2 *vi* **to b. (about)** s'activer, s'affairer

bust-up ['bʌstʌp] *n Fam (dispute)* engueulade *f*; *(of relationship)* fin *f*; **to have a b.** *(argue)* s'engueuler

busy ['bɪzɪ] **1** *adj* **(a)** *(person)* occupé(e); *(day, week)* chargé(e); *(road)* à grande circulation; **to keep sb b.** occuper qn; **to keep oneself b.** s'occuper; **to be b.** doing sth être occupé à faire qch; **the train was very b.** il y avait beaucoup de monde dans le train **(b)** *Am (telephone line)* occupé(e); **I keep getting the b. signal** ça sonne toujours occupé
2 *vt (pt & pp* busied) **to b. oneself with sth** s'occuper à qch

busybody ['bɪzɪbɒdɪ] *(pl* busybodies) *n Fam* fouineur(euse) *m,f*

but [bʌt] **1** *prep (except)* sauf, à part; **any day b. today** n'importe quand sauf aujourd'hui; **it's nothing b. prejudice** ce ne sont rien que des préjugés; **she is anything b. stupid** elle est loin d'être bête; **b. for** sans; **the last b. one** l'avant-dernier(ère) *m,f*; **the next b. one** le (la) deuxième
2 *adv Formal* seulement; **he is b. a child** ce n'est qu'un enfant; **had I b. known!** si (seulement) j'avais su!; **one can b. try** on peut toujours essayer
3 *conj* mais; **not once b. twice** pas une fois, mais deux; **I told her to do it b. she refused** je lui ai dit de le faire mais elle a refusé; **b. I tell you I saw it!** mais puisque je te dis que je l'ai vu!; **I had no choice b. to tell the truth** je n'ai pas pu faire autrement que de dire la vérité; **what could I do b. invite him?** comment pouvais-je faire autrement que de l'inviter?
4 *n* **no buts!** il n'y a pas de "mais" qui tienne!

butane ['bjuːteɪn] *n* butane *m*

butch [bʊtʃ] *adj Fam* hommasse

butcher ['bʊtʃə(r)] **1** *n also Fig* boucher(ère) *m,f*; **b.'s** *(shop)* boucherie *f*; **to go to the b.'s** aller chez le boucher *ou* à la boucherie
2 *vt (animal)* abattre; *Fig (person, song)* massacrer

butchery ['bʊtʃərɪ] *n also Fig* boucherie *f*

butler ['bʌtlə(r)] *n* maître *m* d'hôtel

butt [bʌt] **1** *n* **(a)** *(of rifle)* crosse *f*; *(of cigarette)* mégot *m*; *Fig* **to be the b. of a joke** être la cible d'une plaisanterie **(b)** *Am Fam (buttocks)* fesses *fpl*
2 *vt (hit with head)* donner un coup de tête à

▸ **butt in** *vi (interrupt)* intervenir

butter ['bʌtə(r)] **1** *n* beurre *m*; **she looks as if b. wouldn't melt in her mouth** on lui donnerait le bon Dieu sans confession; **b. bean** = gros haricot blanc; **b. dish** beurrier *m*; **b. knife** couteau *m* à beurre
2 *vt* beurrer

▸ **butter up** *vt sep Fam (flatter)* passer de la pommade à

buttercup ['bʌtəkʌp] *n* bouton *m* d'or

butterfingers ['bʌtəfɪŋgəz] *n Fam* empoté(e) *m,f*

butterfly ['bʌtəflaɪ] *(pl* butterflies) *n* papillon *m*; *Fig* **to have butterflies (in one's stomach)** avoir l'estomac noué; **b. (stroke)** *(in swimming)* (brasse *f*) papillon *m*

buttermilk ['bʌtəmɪlk] *n* babeurre *m*

butterscotch ['bʌtəskɒtʃ] *n* caramel *m* dur au beurre

buttock ['bʌtək] *n* fesse *f*

button ['bʌtən] **1** *n* **(a)** *(on shirt, machine)* bouton *m*; **b. mushroom** petit champignon *m* de Paris **(b)** *Am (badge)* badge *m*
2 *vt (shirt, dress)* boutonner; *Fam* **b. it!** la ferme!

▸ **button up** *vt sep (shirt, dress)* boutonner

buttonhole ['bʌtənhəʊl] **1** *n* boutonnière *f*
2 *vt (detain)* coincer

buttress ['bʌtrɪs] **1** *n Archit* contrefort *m*; *Fig* pilier *m*
2 *vt Fig (support)* renforcer

buxom ['bʌksəm] *adj (plump)* plantureux(euse); *(full-bosomed)* à la poitrine généreuse

buy [baɪ] **1** *n* **a good/bad b.** une bonne/mauvaise affaire
2 *vt (pt & pp* bought [bɔːt]) **(a)** *(purchase)* acheter; **to b. sb sth, to b. sth for sb** acheter qch à qn; **to b. sth from sb** acheter qch à qn; *Fig* **to b. time** gagner du temps; **he's bought it** *(has died)* il a passé l'arme à gauche **(b)** *Fam (believe)* avaler; **I don't b. that** je ne le crois pas

▸ **buy in** *vt sep (supplies)* faire des stocks de

▸ **buy into** *vt insep (company, scheme)* acheter des parts de

▸ **buy off** *vt sep Fam* acheter

▸ **buy out** *vt sep Com* racheter la part de

▸ **buy up** *vt sep (land, shares)* acheter; *(supplies)* faire des stocks de

buyer ['baɪə(r)] *n* acheteur(euse) *m,f*; **b.'s market** marché *m* demandeur

buy-out ['baɪaʊt] *n Com* rachat *m*

buzz [bʌz] **1** *n* **(a)** *(noise)* bourdonnement *m*; *(of plane)* vrombissement *m*; *Fam* **b. word** mot *m* à la mode **(b)** *Fam (phone call)* **to give sb a b.** passer un coup de fil à qn **(c)** *Fam (thrill)* **to get a b. out of doing sth** prendre son pied à faire qch
2 *vt Fam (on intercom)* appeler à l'Interphone®; *(on pager)* biper
3 *vi (make noise)* bourdonner; *Fig* **to b. with excitement** *(of town)* bourdonner d'excitation; **my head was buzzing** j'avais la tête lourde; *Fam* **now we're buzzing!** maintenant on est lancés!

▸ **buzz off** *vi Br Fam* se tirer

buzzard ['bʌzəd] *n* buse *f*

buzzer ['bʌzə(r)] *n (on intercom)* bouton *m* de l'Interphone®; *(on clock, oven)* sonnerie *f*

buzzing ['bʌzɪŋ] *n* bourdonnement *m*

by [baɪ] *prep* **(a)** *(agent)* par; **he was arrested by the police** il a été arrêté par la police, la police l'a arrêté; **made by hand** fait(e) (à la) main; **a book by Dickens** un livre de Dickens
(b) *(with manner, means)* **by train/car/plane** en train/voiture/avion; **by doing sth** en faisant qch; **to pay by credit card** payer par carte de crédit; **to have a child by sb** avoir un enfant de qn; **to take sb by the hand/arm** prendre qn par la main/le bras; **to know sb by name/sight** connaître qn de nom/de vue; **to earn one's living by teaching** gagner sa vie en enseignant
(c) *(close to)* près de; **by the fire** près du feu; **by the sea** au bord de la mer; **by the side of the road** sur le bord de la route
(d) *(via)* par; **by land/sea** par terre/mer
(e) *(past)* **to walk by sb/sth** passer devant qn/qch; **to**

drive by sb/sth passer devant qn/qch (en voiture) **(f)** *(at or before)* **she should be here by now** elle devrait être ici à l'heure qu'il est; **it'll be ready by tomorrow** ce sera prêt pour demain; **by 1950 they were all dead** en 1950 ils étaient déjà tous morts; **by then it was too late** il était déjà trop tard **(g)** *(during)* **by day/night** de jour/nuit **(h)** *(with measurements, quantities, numbers)* **to divide/multiply by five** diviser/multiplier par cinq; **3 metres by 2** 3 mètres sur 2; **to sell sth by weight** vendre qch au poids; **one by one** un par un **(i)** *(according to)* **to go by appearances** se fier aux apparences; **to call sb by their first name** appeler qn par son prénom; **what do you mean by that?** qu'est-ce que tu entends par là?

(j) *(with reflexive pronouns)* **by oneself** tout(e) seul(e) **(k)** *(as a result of)* **by accident/chance/mistake** par accident/hasard/erreur

2 *adv* **(a) by and large** dans l'ensemble; **by the way,...** au fait,...

(b) *(past)* **to go/walk by** passer; **to drive by** passer (en voiture)

bye [baɪ] *exclam Fam* au revoir!, salut!; **b. for now!** à bientôt!

bye-bye ['baɪ'baɪ] *exclam Fam* au revoir!, salut!

by-election ['baɪɪlekʃən] *n Pol* élection *f* partielle

Byelorussia [bɪeləʊ'rʌʃə] = Belarus

Byelorussian [bɪeləʊ'rʌʃən] **1** *n* Biélorusse *mf* **2** *adj* biélorusse

bygone ['baɪɡɒn] **1** *n* **let bygones be bygones** oublions le passé **2** *adj* révolu(e); **in b. days** autrefois

by-line ['baɪlaɪn] *n (in newspaper)* signature *f*

bypass ['baɪpɑːs] **1** *n* **(a)** *(road)* rocade *f* **(b)** *(heart operation)* pontage *m* **2** *vt (of road)* also *Fig* contourner; *(middleman)* court-circuiter

by-product ['baɪprɒdʌkt] *n* sous-produit *m*, dérivé *m*; *Fig* conséquence *f* indirecte

bystander ['baɪstændə(r)] *n* passant(e) *m,f*

byte [baɪt] *n Comptr* octet *m*

byway ['baɪweɪ] *n (road)* petite route *f*

byword ['baɪwɜːd] *n* **to be a b. for** être synonyme de

Byzantine [bɪ'zæntaɪn] *adj also Fig* byzantin(e)

C, c [siː] n (**a**) (letter) C, c m inv (**b**) Mus do m, ut m (**c**) Sch (grade) **to get a C** (in exam) avoir mention passable; (in homework, essay) ≃ avoir 10 ou 11 sur 20

C (**a**) (abbr **centigrade**) C (**b**) (abbr **century**) s.; **C.19** XIXᵉ s.

c, ca (abbr **circa**) (approximately) env.; (with dates) vers

CAB [siːeɪ'biː] n (abbr **Citizens' Advice Bureau**) = organisme bénévole britannique de conseil, notamment en matière juridique et sociale

cab [kæb] n (**a**) (taxi) taxi m; **c. driver** chauffeur m de taxi (**b**) (of train, lorry) cabine f

cabaret ['kæbəreɪ] n cabaret m; **c. artist** artiste mf de cabaret

cabbage ['kæbɪdʒ] n chou m; **red c.** chou rouge; **c. white** (butterfly) piéride f du chou

cabbie, cabby ['kæbɪ] (pl **cabbies**) n Fam (chauffeur m de) taxi m

cabin ['kæbɪn] n (of ship, plane) cabine f; (hut) cabane f; **c. boy** (on ship) mousse m; **c. crew** (on plane) équipage m

cabinet ['kæbɪnɪt] n (**a**) (piece of furniture) meuble m (à tiroirs); (with glass front) vitrine f (**b**) Br Pol cabinet m; **c. meeting** ≃ Conseil m des ministres; **c. minister** ministre m, membre m du cabinet

cabinet-maker ['kæbɪnɪtmeɪkə(r)] n ébéniste mf

cable ['keɪbəl] **1** n (electrical) & Tel câble m; **c. car** téléphérique m; **c. (television)** (télévision f par) câble; **I watched it on c.** je l'ai vu sur le câble **2** vt (message) câbler; **to c. sb** envoyer un câble à qn

caboodle [kə'buːdəl] n Fam **the whole (kit and) c.** tout le bazar ou bataclan

cacao [kə'kɑːəʊ] n (plant) cacaotier m, cacaoyer m; **c. bean** fève f de cacao

cache [kæʃ] n (**a**) (of drugs, arms) cache f (**b**) Comptr mémoire-cache f

cack-handed [kæk'hændɪd] adj Fam maladroit(e)

cackle ['kækəl] **1** n (**a**) (of hen) caquet m (**b**) Fam (talking) caquetage m; (laugh) gloussement m; **cut the c.!** arrête de jacasser! **2** vi (**a**) (of hen) caqueter (**b**) Fam (laugh) glousser

cacophonous [kə'kɒfənəs] adj cacophonique

cactus ['kæktəs] (pl **cacti** ['kæktaɪ] or **cactuses**) n cactus m

CAD [siːeɪ'diː] n Comptr (abbr **computer-aided design**) CAO f

cad [kæd] n Br Fam Old-fashioned mufle m

cadaver [kə'dævə(r)] n cadavre m

cadaverous [kə'dævərəs] adj cadavérique

caddie ['kædɪ] n (in golf) caddie m

caddy ['kædɪ] (pl **caddies**) n (**tea**) **c.** boîte f à thé

cadence ['keɪdəns] n cadence f, rythme m

cadet [kə'det] n Mil élève m officier; **c. corps** peloton m de préparation militaire

cadge [kædʒ] vt Fam quémander (**from** or **off** sb); **to c. a meal off** or **from sb** se faire inviter à manger par qn; **can I c. a lift from you?** tu me déposes?

cadmium ['kædmɪəm] n Chem cadmium m

Caesarean, Caesarian [sɪ'zeərɪən] n **C. (section)** césarienne f

café, cafe ['kæfeɪ] n café m

cafeteria [kæfɪ'tɪərɪə] n cafétéria f

caffeine ['kæfiːn] n caféine f; **c. free** décaféiné(e)

cage [keɪdʒ] **1** n (for bird, animal) cage f; (of lift) cabine f **2** vt mettre en cage; **to feel caged in** se sentir prisonnier (ère)

cagey ['keɪdʒɪ] adj (evasive) évasif(ive) (**about** sur); (cautious) prudent(e)

cagoule [kə'guːl] n K-way® m inv

cahoots [kə'huːts] npl Fam **to be in c. (with sb)** être de mèche (avec qn)

CAI [siːeɪ'aɪ] n Comptr (abbr **computer-aided instruction**) EAO m

cairn ['keən] n cairn m

Cairo ['kaɪrəʊ] n Le Caire

cajole [kə'dʒəʊl] vt enjôler; **to c. sb into doing sth** persuader qn de faire qch

cake [keɪk] **1** n (**a**) (food) gâteau m; (pastry) petit gâteau; **c. shop** pâtisserie f; **c. tin** moule m à gâteau (**b**) (of soap) pain m (**c**) (idioms) **it's a piece of c.** c'est du gâteau; Prov **you can't have your c. and eat it** on ne peut pas avoir le beurre et l'argent du beurre **2** vt **her shoes were caked with mud** ses chaussures étaient couvertes de boue

CAL [kæl] n Comptr (abbr **computer-aided learning**) EAO m

calamity [kə'læmɪtɪ] (pl **calamities**) n calamité f

calcium ['kælsɪəm] n calcium m

calculate ['kælkjʊleɪt] **1** vt calculer; (consequences, risk) évaluer; **his remark was calculated to shock** sa remarque était destinée à choquer **2** vi **to c. on sth** compter sur qch; **to c. on doing sth** compter faire qch

calculated ['kælkjʊleɪtɪd] adj (risk) calculé(e); (crime) prémédité(e)

calculating ['kælkjʊleɪtɪŋ] adj calculateur(trice)

calculation [kælkjʊ'leɪʃən] n calcul m

calculator ['kælkjʊleɪtə(r)] n calculatrice f
calculus ['kælkjʊləs] n Math calcul m
calendar ['kælɪndə(r)] n calendrier m; **c. month** mois m
civil; **c. year** année f civile
calf¹ [kɑːf] (pl **calves** [kɑːvz]) n (animal) veau m; **the cow
is in** or **wlth c.** la vache est pleine; Fig **to kill the fatted c.**
tuer le veau gras
calf² (pl **calves** [kɑːvz]) n (of leg) mollet m
calfskin ['kɑːfskɪn] n veau m
caliber Am = **calibre**
calibrate ['kælɪbreɪt] vt étalonner, calibrer
calibre, Am **caliber** ['kælɪbə(r)] n also Fig calibre m
calico ['kælɪkəʊ] n calicot m
California [kælɪ'fɔːnɪə] n la Californie
call [kɔːl] **1** n (a) (shout) appel m, cri m
(b) (appeal) appel m (for à); **a c. to arms** un appel aux
armes
(c) (on phone) appel m, coup m de téléphone; **to give sb a c.**
passer un coup de téléphone à qn; **to make a c.** passer un
coup de téléphone ou de fil; **to return sb's c.** rappeler qn; **c.
girl** call-girl f
(d) (visit) visite f; **to pay a c. on sb** rendre visite à qn
(e) (demand) demande f; **there are a lot of calls on my
time** je suis très pris; **there's not much c. for it** il n'y a pas
beaucoup de demande; **there's no c. for that kind of
language!** inutile d'être impoli!; **to be on c.** (of doctor) être
de garde
2 vt (a) (shout to) appeler
(b) (summon) appeler; **he's been called away** il a dû
s'absenter; **he called me over to show me something** il
m'a appelé pour que je vienne voir quelque chose; **to c. a
meeting** décider d'organiser une réunion; **to c. a strike**
appeler à la grève; **to c. sb's attention to sth** attirer
l'attention de qn sur qch
(c) (on phone) appeler, téléphoner à, (taxi) appeler
(d) (name) appeler; **she's called Claire** elle s'appelle
Claire; **to c. sb names** injurier qn; **to c. sb a liar/a thief**
traiter qn de menteur/de voleur; **c. yourself a computer
expert!** et moi qui te croyais bon en informatique!; **let's c.
it $10** disons (que ce sera) 10 dollars; **do you c. that clean?**
tu trouves vraiment qça c'est propre?; **let's c. it a day** assez
pour aujourd'hui
3 vi (a) (shout) appeler; **to c. to sb** appeler qn; **to c. for
help** appeler au secours ou à l'aide
(b) (on phone) appeler, téléphoner; **to c. for an ambulance**
appeler une ambulance; **who's calling?** qui est à l'appareil?
(c) (visit) passer; **this train will c. at York and
Peterborough** ce train s'arrêtera à York et Peterborough
▸ **call back** vt sep & vi rappeler
▸ **call for** vt insep (a) (require) nécessiter; **this calls for a
celebration!** il faut fêter ça!; **that wasn't called for!** c'était
parfaitement déplacé! (b) (demand) réclamer
▸ **call in 1** vt sep (doctor, police) appeler, faire venir; (expert)
faire appel à
2 vi (visit) passer (**on sb** chez qn)
▸ **call off** vt sep (match, holiday) annuler; (search, strike)
mettre fin à; (engagement) rompre
▸ **call on** vt insep (a) (request) **to c. on sb to do sth**
(urgently) demander instamment à qn de faire qch; (politely)
inviter qn à faire qch (b) (visit) rendre visite à
▸ **call out 1** vt sep (a) (doctor, plumber, troops) appeler; **to c.
sb out on strike** donner l'ordre de grève à qn (b) (shout)
appeler
2 vi (shout) crier
▸ **call up** vt sep (a) (on phone) appeler, téléphoner à (b)
(memory, image) évoquer (c) Mil appeler (sous les drapeaux)
callbox ['kɔːlbɒks] n cabine f téléphonique

caller [kɔːlə(r)] n (visitor) visiteur(euse) m,f; (on phone)
correspondant(e) m,f; **next c.**, please appel suivant, s'il
vous plaît
calligraphy [kə'lɪgrəfɪ] n calligraphie f
calling ['kɔːlɪŋ] n (vocation) vocation f
callipers ['kælɪpəz] npl (a) (for legs) attelles fpl (b)
(measuring device) compas m
callisthenics [kælɪs'θenɪks] n gymnastique f rythmique
callous ['kæləs] adj dur(e)
call-up ['kɔːlʌp] n Mil appel m (sous les drapeaux); **c.
papers** ordre m d'incorporation
callus ['kæləs] n cal m
calm [kɑːm] **1** n calme m; also Fig **a dead c.** un calme plat;
also Fig **the c. before the storm** le calme qui précède la
tempête
2 adj calme, tranquille; (sea) calme; **to keep c.** rester
calme; **to grow calmer** se calmer
3 vt calmer, apaiser; **to c. one's nerves** se calmer
▸ **calm down 1** vt sep calmer
2 vi se calmer
calmly ['kɑːmlɪ] adv calmement
Calor Gas® [kælə'gæs] n butane m
calorie ['kælɒrɪ] n calorie f
calumny ['kæləmnɪ] (pl **calumnies**) n calomnie f
calve [kɑːv] vi (of cow) vêler
calves [kɑːvz] pl of **calf**
calypso [kə'lɪpsəʊ] (pl **calypsos**) n Mus calypso m
CAM [siːeɪ'em] n Comptr (abbr **computer-aided manufacture**) FAO f
cam [kæm] n Tech came f
Cambodia [kæm'bəʊdɪə] n le Cambodge
Cambodian [kæm'bəʊdɪən] **1** n Cambodgien(enne) m,f
2 adj cambodgien(enne)
camcorder ['kæmkɔːdə(r)] n Caméscope® m
came [keɪm] pt of **come**
camel ['kæməl] n chameau m; (female) chamelle f; **c. coat**
manteau m en poil de chameau; **c. driver** chamelier m
camelhair ['kæməlheə(r)] n poil m de chameau
camellia [kə'miːlɪə] n camélia m
cameo ['kæmɪəʊ] (pl **cameos**) n (a) (jewellery) camée m; (b)
(in film) **c. role** brève apparition f
(d'un acteur connu)
camera ['kæmərə] n (a) (photographic) appareil photo m;
TV & Cin caméra f; TV **off c.** hors champ; **on c.** à l'écran; **c.
crew** équipe f de prise de vue (b) Law **in c.** à huis clos
cameraman ['kæmərəmən] n cameraman m
Cameroon [kæmə'ruːn] n le Cameroun
camisole ['kæmɪsəʊl] n caraco m
camomile ['kæməmaɪl] n camomille f; **c. tea** camomille
camouflage ['kæməflɑːʒ] **1** n also Fig camouflage m
2 vt also Fig camoufler
camp¹ [kæmp] **1** n camp m, campement m; **c. bed** lit m de
camp; **c. site** (establishment) (terrain m de) camping m; (in
general) campement
2 vi **to c. (out)** camper
camp² adj Fam (effeminate) efféminé(e)
campaign [kæm'peɪn] **1** n campagne f
2 vi faire campagne (**for/against** pour/contre)
campaigner [kæm'peɪnə(r)] n militant(e) m,f; **to be a c.
for/against sth** faire campagne pour/contre qch
camper ['kæmpə(r)] n (person) campeur(euse) m,f;
(vehicle) camping-car m

campfire ['kæmfaɪə(r)] n feu m de camp
camphor ['kæmfə(r)] n camphre m
camping ['kæmpɪŋ] n camping m; **to go c.** faire du camping; **c.** site (terrain m de) camping
campus ['kæmpəs] n campus m
camshaft ['kæmʃɑːft] n Aut arbre m à cames
can¹ [kæn] **1** n (a) (of food) boîte f; (of drink) can(n)ette f; (for petrol) bidon m; (of paint) pot m; Fig **let's not open up that c.** of worms ne commençons pas avec cette série de problèmes; **c.** opener ouvre-boîte m **(b)** Am very Fam (toilet) chiottes fpl; (prison) taule f, tôle f
  2 vt (pt & pp **canned**) **(a)** (fruit, meat) mettre en boîte ou en conserve; Fig **canned laughter** (on radio, TV) rires mpl préenregistrés **(b)** Am Fam **c. it!** (keep quiet) la ferme!

can² [kən, stressed kæn]

Le verbe **can** n'a ni infinitif, ni gérondif, ni participe. Pour exprimer l'infinitif ou le participe on aura recours à la forme correspondante de **be able to** (he wanted to be able to speak English; she has always been able to swim). La forme négative est **can't**, qui s'écrit **cannot** dans la langue soutenue.

modal aux v **(a)** (be able to) pouvoir; **I c.** go je peux y aller; **I c.** see/hear them je les vois/entends; **we can't possibly do it** nous ne pouvons en aucun cas le faire; **he'll do what he c.** il fera ce qu'il pourra; **how c. you tell?** à quoi vis-tu ça?; **it can't be done** c'est impossible à faire
  (b) (know how to) savoir; **I c. swim** je sais nager; **c. you speak French?** parles-tu français?
  (c) (indicating possibility) pouvoir; **it c. get very hot here** il peut faire très chaud ici; **it can't have been easy for her** ça n'a pas dû être facile pour elle; **you CAN'T be serious!** tu n'es pas sérieux!; **what c. it be?** qu'est-ce que ça peut bien être?
  (d) (with requests, permission) pouvoir; **c. I ask you something?** je peux vous demander quelque chose?; **you can't smoke in here** on ne peut pas fumer ici
Canada ['kænədə] n le Canada
Canadian [kə'neɪdɪən] **1** n Canadien(enne) m,f
  2 adj canadien(enne)
canal [kə'næl] n canal m
Canary [kə'neərɪ] n **the C. Islands, the Canaries** les (îles fpl) Canaries fpl
canary [kə'neərɪ] (pl **canaries**) n canari m; **c. yellow** jaune canari inv
cancel ['kænsəl] (pt & pp **cancelled**, Am **canceled**) **1** vt annuler; (cheque) faire opposition à
  2 vi se décommander
  ▸**cancel out** vt sep annuler; **to c. each other out** s'annuler
cancellation [kænsə'leɪʃən] n annulation f; **c. fee** frais mpl d'annulation
Cancer ['kænsə(r)] n (sign of zodiac) le Cancer; **to be (a) C.** être (du) Cancer; Geog **the Tropic of C.** le tropique du Cancer
cancer ['kænsə(r)] n (disease) cancer m; **breast/skin c.** cancer du sein/de la peau; **c. research** cancérologie f
cancerous ['kænsərəs] adj Med cancéreux(euse)
candelabra [kændɪ'lɑːbrə] n candélabre m
candid ['kændɪd] adj franc (franche)
candidacy ['kændɪdəsɪ] n candidature f
candidate ['kændɪdeɪt] n candidat(e) m,f (**for** à); **to stand as a c.** poser sa candidature, se présenter
candidature ['kændɪdətʃə(r)] = **candidacy**
candidly ['kændɪdlɪ] adv franchement
candied ['kændɪd] adj glacé(e), confit(e); **c. peel** zeste m confit

candle ['kændəl] n bougie f; **he can't hold a c. to you** il ne t'arrive pas à la cheville; **it's not worth the c.** le jeu n'en vaut pas la chandelle
candlelight ['kændəllaɪt] n lumière f d'une bougie; **by c.** à la chandelle ou bougie
candlelit ['kændəllɪt] adj aux chandelles
candlestick ['kændəlstɪk] n bougeoir m; (taller) chandelier m
candour ['kændə(r)] n franchise f
candy ['kændɪ] (pl **candies**) n Am (sweet) bonbon m; (sweets) bonbons; **c. bar** barre f chocolatée; **c. store** confiserie f
candyfloss ['kændɪflɒs] n Br barbe f à papa
cane [keɪn] **1** n (of sugar, bamboo) canne f, tige f; (walking stick) canne; (for punishment) verge f, baguette f; **to get the c.** recevoir des coups de verge ou de baguette; **c. furniture** meubles mpl en rotin; **c. sugar** sucre m de canne
  2 vt (beat) frapper avec une verge ou une baguette
canine ['keɪnaɪn] **1** n (tooth) canine f
  2 adj canin(e)
canister ['kænɪstə(r)] n boîte f (en métal); (of gas) bonbonne f
canker ['kæŋkə(r)] n also Fig chancre m
cannabis ['kænəbɪs] n cannabis m
cannery ['kænərɪ] (pl **canneries**) n conserverie f
cannibal ['kænɪbəl] n cannibale mf
cannibalize ['kænɪbəlaɪz] vt cannibaliser
cannon ['kænən] (pl **cannons** or **cannon**) n canon m; **c. fodder** chair f à canon
cannonball ['kænənbɔːl] n boulet m de canon
cannot ['kænɒt] = **can not**
canny ['kænɪ] adj rusé(e)
canoe [kə'nuː] n canoë m
canoeing [kə'nuːɪŋ] n canoë-kayak m; **to go c.** faire du canoë-kayak
canoeist [kə'nuːɪst] n canoéiste mf
canon ['kænən] n **(a)** (religious decree) & Fig canon m; **c. law** droit m canon **(b)** (priest) chanoine m
canonize ['kænənaɪz] vt Rel canoniser
canoodle [kə'nuːdəl] vi Hum se faire des mamours
canopy ['kænəpɪ] (pl **canopies**) n (above bed) baldaquin m; (outside shop) auvent m; (parachute) parachute m; (of tree branches) canopée f
cant [kænt] n (hypocrisy) langage m hypocrite
can't [kɑːnt] = **can not**
cantaloup(e) ['kæntəluːp] n melon m (cantaloup)
cantankerous [kæn'tæŋkərəs] adj revêche, acariâtre
canteen [kæn'tiːn] n **(a)** (restaurant) cantine f **(b)** (water bottle) gourde f **(c)** (of cutlery) ménagère f
canter ['kæntə(r)] **1** n (on horse) petit galop m
  2 vi (of horse) aller au petit galop; Fig **to c. through a speech** expédier un discours; Fig **to c. through an exam** réussir un examen haut la main
cantilever ['kæntɪliːvə(r)] n Tech poutre f en porte-à-faux; **c. bridge** pont m cantilever
Cantonese [kæntə'niːz] **1** n (language) cantonais m
  2 adj cantonais(e)
canvas ['kænvəs] n **(a)** (cloth) (grosse) toile f; **under c.** (in tent) sous la tente; Naut sous voiles **(b)** Art toile f
canvass ['kænvəs] **1** vt **(a)** Pol **to c. sb** faire campagne auprès de qn **(b)** Com (consumers) sonder; Fig **to c. opinion** sonder l'opinion
  2 vi **(a)** Pol faire campagne, faire du porte-à-porte (dans le cadre d'une campagne électorale) **(b)** Com faire du démarchage

canvasser ['kænvəsə(r)] *n Pol* = personne qui fait du porte-à-porte dans le cadre d'une campagne électorale

canyon ['kænjən] *n* canyon *m*, cañon *m*

CAP [siːeɪ'piː] *n* (*abbr* **Common Agricultural Policy**) PAC *f*

cap [kæp] **1** *n* (**a**) (*hat*) (*without peak*) bonnet *m*; (*with peak*) casquette *f*; *Sp* **to win a c.** être sélectionné(e) dans l'équipe nationale; *Fig* **to go c.** **in hand to sb** se présenter chapeau bas devant qn; *Prov* **if the c. fits (wear it)** qui se sent morveux se mouche
(**b**) (*cover*) (*of bottle*) capsule *f*; (*of pen*) capuchon *m*
(**c**) (*for toy gun*) amorce *f*
(**d**) (*contraceptive*) diaphragme *m*
2 *vt* (*pt & pp* **capped**) (**a**) (*cover*) recouvrir (**with** de)
(**b**) **to have a tooth capped** se faire refaire l'émail d'une dent
(**c**) (*surpass, do better than*) surpasser; **that caps the lot!** c'est le bouquet!; **to c. it all,**… pour couronner le tout,…
(**d**) *Sp* **to be capped for England** être sélectionné(e) dans l'équipe d'Angleterre
(**e**) (*spending*) limiter

capability [keɪpə'bɪlɪtɪ] (*pl* **capabilities**) *n* capacité *f* (**to do** sth de faire qch); **it is beyond our capabilities** c'est au-dessus de nos moyens

capable ['keɪpəbəl] *adj* capable; **to be c. of doing sth** être capable de faire qch; **the matter is in c. hands** l'affaire est entre de bonnes mains

capably ['keɪpəblɪ] *adv* avec compétence

capacious [kə'peɪʃəs] *adj* vaste, spacieux(euse)

capacitor [kə'pæsɪtə(r)] *n Elec* condensateur *m*

capacity [kə'pæsɪtɪ] (*pl* **capacities**) *n* (**a**) (*of container, bus, theatre*) & *Elec* capacité *f*; **the stadium has a c. of 20,000** le stade peut accueillir 20000 spectateurs; **full to c.** plein(e); **there was a c. crowd at the match** le stade était bondé pour le match (**b**) (*aptitude*) **to have a c. for sth** être capable de qch; **to be beyond sb's c.** dépasser les compétences de qn; **to be within sb's c.** être dans les possibilités de qn; **c. for work** capacité *f* de travail (**c**) (*output*) capacité *f*; **at full c.** à plein (**d**) (*role*) **in my c. as…** en ma qualité de…

cape¹ [keɪp] *n* (*cloak*) pèlerine *f*, cape *f*

cape² *n Geog* cap *m*; **the C. of Good Hope** le cap de Bonne-Espérance; **C. Town** Le Cap

caper¹ ['keɪpə(r)] *n Culin* câpre *f*

caper² **1** *n* (*prank*) cabriole *f*; **what a c.!** (*fuss*) quel cirque! **2** *vi* **to c. (about)** faire des cabrioles

Cape Verde [keɪp'vɜːd] *n* le Cap-Vert

capillary [kə'pɪlərɪ] **1** (*pl* **capillaries**) *n* capillaire *m* **2** *adj* capillaire

capital ['kæpɪtəl] **1** *n* (**a**) (*letter*) majuscule *f*, capitale *f* (**b**) **c. (city)** capitale *f* (**c**) *Fin* capital *m*; *Fig* **to make c. out of sth** tirer parti de qch; **c. assets** actif *m* immobilisé; **c. expenditure** dépenses *fpl* en capital; **c. gains tax** impôt *m* sur les plus-values (*en capital*); **c. goods** biens *mpl* d'équipement; **c. investment** investissement *m* de capitaux
2 *adj* (**a**) (*letter*) majuscule; **c. T** T majuscule; **he's rich with a c. R** il est vraiment très riche (**b**) *Law* **c. crime** *or* **offence** crime *m* capital *ou* puni de mort; **c. punishment** peine *f* capitale (**c**) (*important*) capital(e); **of c. importance** d'une importance capitale (**d**) *Br Old-fashioned* (*splendid*) extra *inv*

capitalism ['kæpɪtəlɪzəm] *n* capitalisme *m*

capitalist ['kæpɪtəlɪst] *n & adj* capitaliste *mf*

capitalization [kæpɪtəlaɪ'zeɪʃən] *n Fin* capitalisation *f*

capitalize ['kæpɪtəlaɪz] *vt* (**a**) *Fin* capitaliser (**b**) (*initial*

letter*) écrire avec une majuscule; (*whole word*) écrire en majuscules
▸ **capitalize on** *vt insep* profiter de, tirer parti de

Capitol ['kæpɪtəl] *n Am Pol* **the C.** le Capitole; **C. Hill** = la colline du Capitole, à Washington, où se trouve le Congrès américain

capitulate [kə'pɪtjʊleɪt] *vi* capituler (**to** devant)

capon ['keɪpən] *n Culin* chapon *m*

caprice [kə'priːs] *n* caprice *m*

capricious [kə'prɪʃəs] *adj* capricieux(euse)

Capricorn ['kæprɪkɔːn] *n* (*sign of zodiac*) le Capricorne; **to be (a) C.** être (du) Capricorne; *Geog* **the Tropic of C.** le tropique du Capricorne

capsicum ['kæpsɪkəm] *n Culin* poivron *m*

capsize [kæp'saɪz] **1** *vt* faire chavirer **2** *vi* chavirer

capstan ['kæpstən] *n Naut* cabestan *m*

capsule ['kæpsjuːl] *n* (*of medicine*) gélule *f*; (*space*) **c. capsule** *f* spatiale

Capt (*abbr* **Captain**) Capt

captain ['kæptɪn] **1** *n* capitaine *m* **2** *vt* être le capitaine de; **he captained them to victory** il les a conduits à la victoire

captaincy ['kæptɪnsɪ] *n* (*in sport*) **during her c.** pendant qu'elle était capitaine

caption ['kæpʃən] *n* légende *f*

captivate ['kæptɪveɪt] *vt* fasciner

captivating ['kæptɪveɪtɪŋ] *adj* fascinant(e)

captive ['kæptɪv] *n & adj* captif(ive) *m,f*; **to be taken c.** être fait(e) prisonnier(ère); **to be held c.** être gardé(e) en captivité; **he had a c. audience** son auditoire était forcé de l'écouter

captivity [kæp'tɪvɪtɪ] *n* captivité *f*; **in c.** en captivité

captor ['kæptə(r)] *n* ravisseur(euse) *m,f*

capture ['kæptʃə(r)] **1** *n* capture *f*; (*of town, enemy, position*) prise *f* **2** *vt* (*person, animal*) capturer; (*town, enemy, position*) prendre (**from** à); (*in chess*) prendre; *Fig* (*mood*) rendre; **to c. sb's imagination** parler à l'imagination de qn; **to c. the moment** saisir l'instant

car [kɑː(r)] *n* (**a**) (*automobile*) voiture *f*, automobile *f*; **by c.** en voiture; **c. bomb** voiture piégée; *Br* **c. boot sale** = vente à la brocante où les vendeurs exposent leurs marchandises à l'arrière de leur voiture; **c. crash** accident *m* de voiture; **c. door** portière *f* de voiture; *Br* **c. hire, Am c. rental** location *f* de voitures; **c. industry** industrie *f* automobile; *Br* **c. park** parc *m* de stationnement, parking *m*; **c. phone** téléphone *m* de voiture; **c. pool** = groupe de personnes effectuant régulièrement un trajet dans la même voiture; **c. radio** autoradio *m* (**b**) *Am* (*rail wagon*) voiture *f*, wagon *m*

carafe [kə'ræf] *n* carafe *f*

caramel ['kærəməl] *n* caramel *m*

carat ['kærət] *n* carat *m*; **18-c. gold** or *m* (à) 18 carats

caravan ['kærəvæn] *n* caravane *f*; (*pulled by horse*) roulotte *f*; **c. holiday** vacances *fpl* en caravane; **c. site** camping *m* (pour caravanes)

caraway ['kærəweɪ] *n* carvi *m*, cumin *m* des prés; **c. seeds** graines *fpl* de carvi

carbohydrate [kɑːbəʊ'haɪdreɪt] *n* hydrate *m* de carbone; (*in food*) glucide *m*; **low-/high-c. diet** régime *m* hypoglucidique/hyperglucidique

carbolic [kɑː'bɒlɪk] *adj Chem* **c. acid** phénol *m*; **c. soap** ≃ savon *m* de Marseille

carbon ['kɑːbən] *n* carbone *m*; **c. copy** copie *f* (au carbone); *Fig* she is a c. copy of her mother c'est la copie conforme de sa mère; **c. dioxide** dioxyde *m* de carbone, gaz *m* carbonique; **c. fibre** fibre *f* de carbone; **c. monoxide** monoxyde *m* de carbone; **c. paper** (papier *m*) carbone

carbonated ['kɑːbəneɪtɪd] *adj* gazéifié(e); *(naturally)* gazeux(euse)

carbonize ['kɑːbənaɪz] *vt* carboniser

carbuncle ['kɑːbʌŋkəl] *n Med* furoncle *m*

carburettor, *Am* **carburetor** ['kɑːbjʊretə(r)] *n* carburateur *m*

carcase, carcass ['kɑːkəs] *n (of animal)* carcasse *f*

carcinogenic [kɑːsɪnə'dʒenɪk] *adj Med* carcinogène

card [kɑːd] *n* (a) *(for card game)* carte *f*; **to play cards** jouer aux cartes; **c. game** jeu *m* de cartes; **c. trick** tour *m* de cartes (b) *(with printed information)* carte *f*; *(postcard)* carte (postale); *Pol* **c. vote** = scrutin où chaque délégué muni d'une carte vote pour la totalité des membres qu'il représente; **c. index** *or* **file** fichier *m* (c) *(plastic)* carte *f* (d) *(cardboard)* carton *m* (fin) (e) *Comptr* carte *f* (f) *(idioms)* **if you play your cards right, you could get promoted** si tu mènes bien ton jeu, tu sera peut-être promu; **to lay one's cards on the table** jouer cartes sur table; **to have a c. up one's sleeve** avoir un atout dans son jeu; **it is Bron** *or* **Amin the cards that...** il est bien possible que...; *Br Fam* **to get one's cards** se faire virer

cardamom ['kɑːdəməm] *n* cardamome *f*

cardboard ['kɑːdbɔːd] *n* carton *m*; **c. box** (boîte *f* en) carton; **c. city** = campement où les sans-abri vivent dans des cartons; *Fig & Pej* **c. characters** personnages *mpl* sans aucune profondeur

card-carrying ['kɑːdkærɪɪŋ] *adj* **c. member** *(of group, party)* adhérent(e) *m,f*

cardiac ['kɑːdɪæk] *adj* cardiaque; **c. arrest** arrêt *m* cardiaque

cardigan ['kɑːdɪgən] *n* cardigan *m*

cardinal ['kɑːdɪnəl] **1** *n Rel* cardinal *m*
2 *adj* cardinal(e); *Fig* **it's a c. sin** c'est impardonnable

cardiograph ['kɑːdɪəgræf] *n* cardiographe *m*

cardiologist [kɑːdɪ'ɒlədʒɪst] *n* cardiologue *mf*

cardiology [kɑːdɪ'ɒlədʒɪ] *n* cardiologie *f*

cardiovascular [kɑːdɪəʊ'væskjʊlə(r)] *adj* cardiovasculaire

cardphone ['kɑːdfəʊn] *n* téléphone *m* à carte

cardsharp(er) ['kɑːdʃɑːp(ə(r))] *n* tricheur(euse) *m,f* professionnel(elle)

care [keə(r)] **1** *n* (a) *(worry)* souci *m*; **she doesn't have a c. in the world** elle n'a pas le moindre souci (b) *(attention)* soin *m*; *(medical treatment)* soins médicaux; **to do sth with great c.** faire qch avec beaucoup de soin; **to drive without due c.** conduire imprudemment; **to take c. of s'occuper de; to take c. of oneself** savoir se débrouiller tout(e) seul(e); *(healthwise)* prendre soin de sa santé; **to take c. to do sth** faire bien attention à faire qch; **take c.!** *(goodbye)* à bientôt!
(c) *(protection)* soins *mpl*; *(of clothes, machine)* entretien *m*; **to put a child in c.** mettre un enfant à l'Assistance publique; **to be in** *or* **under sb's c.** avoir été confié(e) à qn; **write to me c. of Mrs Jones** écrivez-moi chez Mme Jones *ou* aux bons soins de Mme Jones
2 *vi* (a) *(mind)* **I don't c. what he says** peu m'importe ce qu'il en dit; **I don't c. whether he likes it or not** peu m'importe que cela lui plaise ou non
(b) *(like)* **would you c. to join me?** aimeriez-vous me rejoindre?
3 *vi* (a) *(be concerned)* se préoccuper, se soucier (**about**

de); **that's all he cares about** c'est tout ce qui l'intéresse; **to c. about sb** *(be fond of)* aimer qn
(b) *(mind)* **I don't c.** ça m'est égal; **who cares?** qu'est-ce que ça peut faire?; **I could be dead for all they c.!** ils se moquent éperdument de ce qui peut m'arriver!; **I couldn't c. less** je m'en moque éperdument
▸ **care for** *vt insep* (a) *(look after)* soigner (b) *(like)* aimer; **I don't c. for chocolate** je n'aime pas beaucoup le chocolat

career [kə'rɪə(r)] **1** *n* carrière *f*; **it's a good/bad c. move** c'est bon/mauvais pour ma/ta/*etc* carrière; **careers officer** conseiller(ère) *m,f* d'orientation; **careers service** service *m* d'orientation professionnelle
2 *vi* **to c. (along)** aller à vive allure; **the car careered down the hill** la voiture a descendu la colline à toute vitesse

careerist [kə'rɪərɪst] *n Pej* carriériste *mf*

carefree ['keəfriː] *adj* insouciant(e)

careful ['keəfʊl] *adj* (a) *(cautious)* prudent(e); **be c. of that step** fais attention à la marche; (b) **c.!** fais attention!; **to be c. to do sth** faire bien attention à faire qch; **she was c. not to mention his name** elle a bien fait attention à ne pas mentionner son nom; **be c. what you say** fais attention à ce que tu dis; **you can't be too c. these days** on n'est jamais trop prudent de nos jours (b) *(thorough)* *(work, inspection)* minutieux(euse); **after c. consideration** après mûre réflexion

carefully ['keəfəlɪ] *adv* (a) *(cautiously)* prudemment (b) *(thoroughly)* soigneusement, avec soin; *(listen)* attentivement; **c. worded** aux termes choisis (avec soin)

careless ['keəlɪs] *adj* (a) *(negligent)* négligent(e); *(work)* négligé(e); **to be c. about one's appearance** être négligé; **a c. mistake** une faute d'inattention, une étourderie; **a c. remark** une remarque inconsidérée (b) *(unconcerned)* insouciant(e)

carelessly ['keəlɪslɪ] *adv (negligently)* négligemment

carelessness ['keəlɪsnɪs] *n (negligence)* négligence *f*

carer ['keərə(r)] *n (professional)* aide *mf* à domicile; *(relative)* = personne s'occupant d'un parent malade ou âgé

caress [kə'res] **1** *n* caresse *f*
2 *vt* caresser

caretaker ['keəteɪkə(r)] *n* concierge *mf*, gardien(enne) *m,f*; **c. government** gouvernement *m* intérimaire

careworn ['keəwɔːn] *adj* usé(e) par les soucis

cargo ['kɑːgəʊ] *(pl* **cargoes** *or* **cargos)** *n* cargaison *f*; **c. boat** *or* **ship** cargo *m*; **c. plane** avion-cargo *m*

Caribbean [kærɪ'biːən, *Am* kə'rɪbɪən] **1** *n* **the C. (Sea)** la mer des Caraïbes; **the C. (region)** la Caraïbe
2 *adj* caraïbe

caribou ['kærɪbuː] *n* caribou *m*

caricature ['kærɪkətjʊə(r)] **1** *n* caricature *f*
2 *vt* caricaturer

caricaturist [kærɪkə'tjʊərɪst] *n* caricaturiste *mf*

caries ['keərɪːz] *n Med* carie *f*

caring ['keərɪŋ] *adj (society, personality)* humain(e); *(parent)* aimant(e); *(atmosphere)* chaleureux(euse); **the c. professions** les professions *fpl* médicales et paramédicales

carnage ['kɑːnɪdʒ] *n* carnage *m*

carnal ['kɑːnəl] *adj* charnel(elle)

carnation [kɑː'neɪʃən] *n* œillet *m*

carnival ['kɑːnɪvəl] *n (celebration)* carnaval *m*; *(funfair)* fête *f* foraine

carnivore ['kɑːnɪvɔː(r)] *n* carnivore *m*

carnivorous [kɑː'nɪvərəs] *adj* carnivore

carob ['kærəb] *n (fruit)* caroube *f*; *(tree)* caroubier *m*

carol ['kærəl] *n* (Christmas) **c.** chant *m* de Noël

carouse [kə'raʊz] *vi* faire la fête

carousel [kærə'sel] *n* (**a**) *Am (at funfair)* chevaux *mpl* de bois, manège *m* (**b**) *(at airport)* carrousel *m* (pour bagages) (**c**) *(for slides)* magasin *m*

carp[1] [kɑːp] (*pl* **carp**) *n (fish)* carpe *f*

carp[2] *vi* se plaindre (**at** de)

Carpathians [kɑːˈpeɪθɪənz] *npl* **the C.** les Carpates *fpl*

carpenter ['kɑːpɪntə(r)] *n* menuisier *m*; *(on building site)* charpentier *m*

carpentry ['kɑːpɪntrɪ] *n* menuiserie *f*; *(on building site)* charpenterie *f*

carpet ['kɑːpɪt] **1** *n* (**a**) *(rug)* & *Fig (of flowers, snow)* tapis *m*; *(fitted)* moquette *f*; **c. bombing** bombardement *m* intensif; **c. slippers** pantoufles *fpl* (**b**) *(idioms)* **to pull the c. out from under sb** faire un tour de cochon à qn
2 *vt* (**a**) *(with rug)* recouvrir d'un tapis; *(with fitted carpet)* moquetter; *Fig* **to be carpeted with snow** être recouvert(e) de neige (**b**) *Fam (tell off)* sermonner

carpet-sweeper ['kɑːpɪtswiːpə(r)] *n* balai *m* mécanique

carport ['kɑːpɔːt] *n* abri *m* pour voiture

carriage ['kærɪdʒ] *n* (**a**) *(vehicle) (horse-drawn)* calèche *f*; *(together with horses and driver)* équipage *m* (**b**) *(of train)* voiture *f*, wagon *m* (**c**) *Br (of typewriter)* chariot *m*; **c. return** retour-chariot *m* (**d**) *Com (transport)* transport *m*; *(cost)* frais *mpl* de port; **c. forward** (en) port *m* dû; **c. free** franco de port; **c. paid** (en) port *m* payé (**e**) *(bearing) (of person)* port *m*

carriageway ['kærɪdʒweɪ] *n* chaussée *f*

carrier ['kærɪə(r)] *n* (**a**) *(of disease, germs)* porteur(euse) *m,f* (**b**) *Com (company, airline)* transporteur *m* (**c**) *(on bicycle)* porte-bagages *m inv* (**d**) **c. (bag)** sac *m* *(en papier ou en plastique)*

carrion ['kærɪən] *n* charogne *f*

carrot ['kærət] *n also Fig* carotte *f*; **a c. and stick approach** la carotte et le bâton

carry ['kærɪ] (*pt & pp* **carried**) **1** *vt* (**a**) *(transport, convey)* porter; *(goods, passengers)* transporter; *(electricity, fuel)* acheminer; *(gun, money)* avoir sur soi; *(a scar)* avoir; *(disease)* être porteur(euse) de; **the current carried the raft out to sea** le courant a emporté le radeau au large; **to c. an image in one's head** avoir une image en tête; **to be carrying sb's child** *(be pregnant)* porter l'enfant de qn; *Fig* **to c. the can** porter le chapeau; *Fig* **she refused to c. the can for their mistake** elle refusa qu'ils lui fassent porter la responsabilité de leur erreur
(**b**) *(involve) (risk)* comporter; **to c. a fine/penalty** être passible d'une amende/d'une peine; **to c. weight/authority** avoir du poids/de l'autorité
(**c**) *(develop)* **to c. sth too far** pousser qch trop loin; **to c. an argument to its logical conclusion** aller au bout d'un raisonnement
(**d**) *(capture, win)* **to c. all before one** *(be successful)* remporter tous les prix; *(win support, approval)* vaincre toutes les résistances; **his argument carried the day** son argument l'a emporté
(**e**) *(proposal, motion)* voter
(**f**) *(of newspaper, news programme) (story)* faire état de; *(advertisement)* contenir
(**g**) *Com (keep in stock)* vendre
(**h**) **to c. oneself** *(behave)* se conduire
(**i**) *Math* **c. two** et je retiens deux
(**j**) *(of sound)* porter; **her voice carries well** elle a une voix qui porte bien

▸ **carry away** *vt sep* (**a**) *(take away)* emporter (**b**) **to get carried away** *(excited)* s'emballer

▸ **carry forward** *vt sep Fin* reporter; **carried forward** report, à reporter

▸ **carry off** *vt sep* (**a**) *(take away)* emporter; *(prize)* remporter (**b**) *(do successfully)* **she carried it off (well)** elle s'en est bien sortie

▸ **carry on 1** *vt sep (tradition)* perpétuer; *(business, trade)* exercer; *(correspondence)* entretenir; *(conversation)* poursuivre
2 *vi* (**a**) *(continue)* continuer, poursuivre; **to c. on doing sth** continuer de *ou* à faire qch (**b**) *Fam (behave badly)* mal se conduire; **I don't like the way she carries on** je n'aime pas ses façons (**c**) *Fam (have an affair)* avoir une liaison (**with** avec) (**d**) *(talk)* parler sans cesse (**about** de)

▸ **carry out** *vt sep (plan, threat, decision)* mettre à exécution; *(experiment, test)* faire, effectuer; *(instructions)* exécuter

carrycot ['kærɪkɒt] *n* porte-bébé *m inv*

carry-on ['kærɪˈɒn] **1** *n Fam* ramdam *m*; **what a c.!** quel cirque!
2 *adj* **c. baggage** *(on plane)* bagages *mpl* à main

carry-out ['kærɪaʊt] *n Am & Scot (meal)* repas *m* à emporter; *(restaurant)* = boutique qui fait des plats à emporter

carsick ['kɑːsɪk] *adj* **to be c.** avoir mal au cœur en voiture

cart[1] [kɑːt] **1** *n (vehicle)* charrette *f*, *(trolley)* chariot *m*; *Fig* **to put the c. before the horse** mettre la charrue avant les bœufs
2 *vt Fam (carry)* trimballer

▸ **cart off** *vt sep Fam* **to c. sb off** emmener qn

cart[2] *n (abbr* **cartridge**) cassette *f*

carte blanche ['kɑːt'blɑːʃ] *n* **to give sb c.** (to do sth) donner carte blanche à qn (pour faire qch)

cartel [kɑːˈtel] *n Econ* cartel *m*

carthorse ['kɑːthɔːs] *n* cheval *m* de trait; *Fig* lourdaud *m*

cartilage ['kɑːtɪlɪdʒ] *n* cartilage *m*

cartographer [kɑːˈtɒgrəfə(r)] *n* cartographe *mf*

cartography [kɑːˈtɒgrəfɪ] *n* cartographie *f*

carton ['kɑːtən] *n (of yoghurt, cream)* pot *m*; *(of milk, fruit juice)* brique *f*; *(of cigarettes)* cartouche *f*

cartoon [kɑːˈtuːn] *n (drawing)* dessin *m* humoristique; *(film)* dessin animé; **c. (strip)** bande *f* dessinée

cartoonist [kɑːˈtuːnɪst] *n* dessinateur(trice) *m,f*

cartridge ['kɑːtrɪdʒ] *n* (**a**) *(for gun, pen, of film)* cartouche *f*; **c. belt** cartouchière *f* (**b**) **c. paper** papier *m* à cartouche

cartwheel ['kɑːtwiːl] *n* roue *f* de charrette; **to turn** *or* **do cartwheels** faire la roue

carve [kɑːv] *vt (wood, stone, statue)* sculpter; *(name)* graver; *(meat)* découper

▸ **carve out** *vt sep* **to c. out a career for oneself** faire carrière; **the company carved out a niche for itself** la société s'est taillé une place sur le marché

▸ **carve up** *vt sep Fig (territory)* découper

carving ['kɑːvɪŋ] *n* (**a**) *Art* sculpture *f* (**b**) **c. knife** *(for meat)* couteau *m* à découper

carwash ['kɑːwɒʃ] *n* = station de lavage automatique pour autos; *(sign)* lavage automatique

cascade [kæs'keɪd] **1** *n* cascade *f*
2 *vi* tomber en cascade

case[1] [keɪs] *n* (**a**) *(instance, situation)* & *Med* cas *m*; **a c. in point** un cas d'espèce; **in c. of emergency/accident** en cas d'urgence/d'accident; **in c. he isn't there** au cas où il ne serait pas là; **I'll take it just in c.** je vais le prendre au cas où; **in c. it rains** au cas où il pleuvrait; **in any c.** en tout cas; **in that c.** dans ce cas; **in such a c.** en pareil cas; **as the c. may be** suivant le cas; **if that's the c.** dans ce cas(-là), s'il en est ainsi; *Med* **c. history** antécédents *mpl*; **c. study** étude *f* de cas

(b) *Law* affaire *f*; **the c.** **will be heard on 5 March** l'audience aura lieu le 5 mars; **the c. for the defence** la défense; **the c. for the prosecution** l'accusation *f*; *Fig* **the c. for sb/sth** les arguments *mpl* en faveur de qn/qch; *Fig* **she has a good c.** elle a de bons arguments; **c. law** droit *m* jurisprudentiel

case² *n* **(a)** *(container) (for spectacles, cigarettes, musical instrument)* étui *m*; *(for jewellery)* écrin *m*; **(packing) c.** caisse *f*; **a c. of wine** une caisse de vin; **(display** *or* **glass) c.** vitrine *f* **(b)** *(suitcase)* valise *f*; *(briefcase)* porte-documents *m inv* **(c)** *Typ* **lower/upper c.** bas *m*/haut *m* de casse

casement ['keɪsmənt] *n* **c. (window)** fenêtre *f* à deux battants

cash [kæʃ] **1** *n (coins, banknotes)* liquide *m*; *Fam (money in general)* sous *mpl*; **to pay (in) c.** payer en liquide *ou* en espèces; **c. on delivery** paiement *m* à la livraison; **c. and carry** *(shop)* magasin *m* de demi-gros; **c. in hand** fonds *m ou* argent *m* en caisse; **c. box** caisse *f*; **c. card** carte *f* de retrait; **c. crop** culture *f* commerciale; **c. desk** caisse *f*; *Br* **c. dispenser** *or* **machine** distributeur *m* automatique de billets; *Fin* **c. flow** trésorerie *f*; **c. price** prix *m* au comptant; **c. register** caisse enregistreuse
2 *vt (cheque, postal order)* encaisser
▸ **cash in on** *vt insep Fam* profiter de, tirer profit de

cash-book ['kæʃbʊk] *n* livre *m ou* journal *m* de caisse

cashew ['kæʃuː] *n* **c. (nut)** noix *f* de cajou

cashier [kæ'ʃɪə(r)] *n* caissier(ère) *m,f*

cashmere ['kæʃmɪə(r)] *n* cachemire *m*

cashpoint ['kæʃpɔɪnt] *n Br* distributeur *m* automatique de billets

casing ['keɪsɪŋ] *n Tech* boîtier *m*; *(of sausage)* boyau *m*

casino [kə'siːnəʊ] *(pl* **casinos)** *n* casino *m*

cask [kɑːsk] *n* fût *m*, tonneau *m*

casket ['kɑːskɪt] *n* **(a)** *(for jewellery)* coffret *m* **(b)** *(coffin)* cercueil *m*

Caspian Sea ['kæspɪənsiː] *n* **the C.** la mer Caspienne

cassava [kə'sɑːvə] *n* manioc *m*

casserole ['kæsərəʊl] *n (pot)* cocotte *f*; *(food)* ragoût *m*

cassette [kæ'set] *n* cassette *f*; **c. player** lecteur *m* de cassettes; **c. recorder** magnétophone *m* à cassettes

cassock ['kæsək] *n* soutane *f*

cast [kɑːst] **1** *n* **(a)** *(of play, film)* (actors) acteurs *mpl*; *(list)* distribution *f* **(b)** *(moulded object)* moulage *m*, *Med* **(plaster) c.** plâtre *m*; *Fig* **c. of mind** tournure *f* d'esprit **(c)** **to have a c. in one's eye** *(squint)* avoir une coquetterie dans l'œil
2 *vt (pt & pp* **cast) (a)** *(throw) (stone)* jeter, lancer; *(shadow, net, line)* jeter; **to c. one's eyes over sth** parcourir qch des yeux; **to c. doubt on sth** jeter un doute sur qch, faire planer un doute sur qch; *Fig* **to c. light on sth** permettre de comprendre qch; **to c. one's mind back to sth** revenir sur qch, se rappeler qch; **to c. its skin** *(of reptile)* muer; **to c. a spell over sb** envoûter qn **(b)** **to c. one's vote (for)** voter (pour) **(c)** *(film, play)* faire la distribution de; **she was cast as** *or* **in the role of Desdemona** on l'a choisie pour le rôle de Desdémone **(d)** *(metal, statue)* couler; **c. iron** fonte *f*
▸ **cast about, cast around** *vi* **to c. about** *or* **around for sth** chercher qch
▸ **cast aside** *vt sep (idea, prejudice)* se défaire de
▸ **cast away** *vt sep* **to be cast away** faire naufrage
▸ **cast down** *vt sep* **to be cast down** être abattu(e) *ou* découragé(e)
▸ **cast off 1** *vt sep (clothes, chains)* rejeter, enlever; *(chains)* se libérer de
2 *vi* **(a)** *Naut* larguer les amarres **(b)** *(in knitting)* arrêter les mailles

▸ **cast on** *vi (in knitting)* monter les mailles

castanets [kæstə'nets] *npl* castagnettes *fpl*

castaway ['kɑːstəweɪ] *n* naufragé(e) *m,f*

caste [kɑːst] *n (social rank)* caste *f*

caster sugar ['kɑːstəʃʊgə(r)] *n* sucre *m* en poudre

castigate ['kæstɪgeɪt] *vt Formal* critiquer sévèrement

casting ['kɑːstɪŋ] **1** *n (of play, film)* distribution *f*, casting *m*
2 *adj* **c. vote** voix *f* prépondérante

cast-iron ['kɑːst'aɪən] *adj* en *ou* de fonte; *Fig (alibi, guarantee)* en béton

castle ['kɑːsəl] **1** *n* château *m*; *(in chess)* tour *f*; *Fig* **to build castles in the air** bâtir des châteaux en Espagne
2 *vi (in chess)* roquer

cast-off ['kɑːstɒf] **1** *n (garment)* vieux vêtement *m*; *(person)* laissé-pour-compte (laissée-pour-compte) *m,f*
2 *adj* **c. clothing** vieux vêtements *mpl*

castor ['kɑːstə(r)] *n (on furniture)* roulette *f*

castor oil [kɑːstə'rɔɪl] *n* huile *f* de ricin

castrate [kæs'treɪt] *vt* châtrer, castrer

castration [kæs'treɪʃən] *n* castration *f*

casual ['kæʒjʊəl] *adj* **(a)** *(offhand) (remark, glance)* en passant **(b)** *(relaxed, informal)* décontracté(e); *(conversation)* à bâtons rompus; *(clothes)* sport *inv* **(c)** *(careless)* désinvolte **(d)** *(superficial)* **to take a c. glance at sth** jeter un coup d'œil (rapide) à qch; **a c. relationship** une aventure **(e)** *(meeting)* fortuit(e) **(f)** *(employment, worker)* temporaire

casually ['kæʒjʊəlɪ] *adv* **(a)** *(remark, glance)* en passant **(b)** *(informally)* avec décontraction; *(dress)* sport **(c)** *(carelessly)* avec désinvolture **(d)** *(meet)* par hasard

casualty ['kæʒjʊəltɪ] *(pl* **casualties)** *n* victime *f*; *Br* **c. (department)** *(service m des)* urgences *fpl*

cat [kæt] *n* **(a)** *(animal)* chat *m*; *(female)* chatte *f*; **the big cats** les grands fauves *mpl*; **c. burglar** monte-en-l'air *m inv*; **c.'s eye®** *(on road)* catadioptre *m*; **c. flap** chatière *f*; **c. litter** litière *f* pour chats **(b)** *(idioms)* **to play a c.-and-mouse game with sb** jouer au chat et à la souris avec qn; *Fam* **to be like a c. on a hot tin roof** *or* **on hot bricks** ne pas tenir en place; **to let the c. out of the bag** vendre la mèche; **to fight like c. and dog** être comme chien et chat; **to set the c. among the pigeons** jeter un pavé dans la mare; *Fam* **there isn't enough room to swing a c.** il n'y a même pas la place de se retourner; *Fam* **he thinks he's the cat's whiskers** il se croit sorti de la cuisse de Jupiter; **has the c. got your tongue?** tu as perdu ta langue?

cataclysm ['kætəklɪzəm] *n* cataclysme *m*

Catalan ['kætəlæn] **1** *n* **(a)** *(person)* Catalan(e) *m,f* **(b)** *(language)* catalan *m*
2 *adj* catalan(e)

catalogue, *Am* **catalog** ['kætəlɒg] **1** *n* catalogue *m*
2 *vt* inventorier

Catalonia [kætə'ləʊnɪə] *n* la Catalogne

catalyst ['kætəlɪst] *n also Fig* catalyseur *m*

catamaran [kætəmə'ræn] *n* catamaran *m*

catapult ['kætəpʌlt] **1** *n (hand-held)* fronde *f*, lance-pierre *m*; *(on aircraft carrier)* & *Hist (weapon)* catapulte *f*
2 *vt* catapulter; **to c. sb to stardom** propulser qn vers la gloire

cataract ['kætərækt] *n (in river)* & *Med* cataracte *f*

catarrh [kə'tɑː(r)] *n* inflammation *f* des muqueuses respiratoires

catastrophe [kə'tæstrəfɪ] *n* catastrophe *f*

catastrophic [kætə'strɒfɪk] *adj* catastrophique

catatonic [kætə'tɒnɪk] *adj Med* catatonique

catcall ['kætkɔːl] *n* sifflet *m*
catch [kætʃ] **1** *n* (**a**) *(of ball)* prise *f* au vol; **good c.!** bien attrapé!
(**b**) *(in fishing)* prise *f*; *(of a whole day)* pêche *f*
(**c**) *(fastening) (of door)* loquet *m*; *(of window)* loqueteau *m*; *(of bracelet)* fermoir *m*
(**d**) *(disadvantage)* **where's the c.?** c'est quoi le truc *ou* le piège?; **it's a c.** -22 situation c'est un cercle vicieux
2 *vt (pt & pp* **caught** [kɔːt]) (**a**) *(ball, thief)* attraper; *(fish)* prendre; **c.!** attrape!; **caught you!** je t'y prends!; **to c. sb doing sth** surprendre qn en train de *ou* à faire qch; **you won't c. me doing that again** on ne m'y reprendra plus; **to be caught in a storm** être surpris(e) par un orage; **to c. the sun** *(of room, garden)* être ensoleillé(e); *(of person)* prendre des couleurs
(**b**) *(bus, train)* prendre; *(film)* voir
(**c**) *(hear)* saisir
(**d**) *(manage to find)* trouver; **you've caught me at a bad time** tu arrives/me téléphones au mauvais moment; **I'll c. you later!** on se voit plus tard!
(**e**) *(clothes)* accrocher (**on** à); **to c. one's fingers in the door** se prendre *ou* se coincer les doigts dans la porte
(**f**) *(attention)* attirer; **to c. sb's eye** attirer l'attention de qn
(**g**) *(illness)* attraper; **I caught this cold from you** c'est toi qui m'as passé ce rhume; **you'll c. your death out there!** tu vas attraper la mort!; **to c. fire** *or* **light** prendre feu
(**h**) *(of blow, missile)* atteindre; **the stone caught her on the arm** la pierre l'a atteinte au bras; **Fam you'll c. it!** *(get into trouble)* ça va être ta fête!
3 *vi* (**a**) *(of fire)* prendre
(**b**) *(in door)* se prendre, se coincer; *(on a nail)* s'accrocher
(**c**) *(of person)* **to c. at sth** s'accrocher à qch
▸ **catch on** *vi* (**a**) *(of fashion)* prendre (**b**) *Fam (understand)* piger
▸ **catch out** *vt sep (of difficult question)* piéger; *(of situation)* surprendre
▸ **catch up 1** *vt sep* (**a**) *(reach)* rattraper (**b**) **to get caught up in sth** *(discussion)* être entraîné(e) dans qch; *(book, film)* être absorbé(e) par qch; *(traffic jam)* être pris(e) dans qch
2 *vi (close gap, get closer)* **to c. up** rattraper qn; **to c. up with sb** rattraper qn; **to c. up with sth** *(news, gossip)* se mettre au courant de qch; **to c. up with one's work** se mettre à jour dans son travail; **his past caught up with him** son passé a resurgi
catch-all ['kætʃɔːl] *adj Fam* fourre-tout *inv*
catching ['kætʃɪŋ] *adj (disease, habit)* contagieux(euse)
catchment area ['kætʃməntɛərɪə] *n (of school)* = zone desservie par une école; *(of hospital)* = zone desservie par un hôpital
catchphrase ['kætʃfreɪz] *n (political)* slogan *m*; *(of comedian)* formule *f* favorite
catchy ['kætʃɪ] *adj (tune, slogan)* facile à retenir
catechism ['kætəkɪzəm] *n* catéchisme *m*
categorical [kætɪ'gɒrɪkəl] *adj (denial, refusal)* catégorique; *(evidence)* formel(elle)
categorize ['kætɪgəraɪz] *vt* étiqueter (**as** comme)
category ['kætɪgərɪ] *(pl* **categories**) *n* catégorie *f*
cater ['keɪtə(r)] *vi* (**a**) *(provide food)* s'occuper de la nourriture; **to c. for** *(guests)* fournir le repas pour; *(event)* fournir le(s) repas de (**b**) **to c. for** *(needs, tastes)* satisfaire; **parties catered for** *(sign in restaurant)* noces et banquets
caterer ['keɪtərə(r)] *n* traiteur *m*
catering ['keɪtərɪŋ] *n (trade)* restauration *f*; **to do the c.** fournir les repas; **c. school** école *f* hôtelière
caterpillar ['kætəpɪlə(r)] *n* chenille *f*; **c. track** *(on tank, tractor)* chenille
catfish ['kætfɪʃ] *n* poisson-chat *m*
cathartic [kə'θɑːtɪk] *adj* cathartique

cathedral [kə'θiːdrəl] *n* cathédrale *f*; **c. city** ville *f* épiscopale, évêché *m*
catheter ['kæθɪtə(r)] *n Med* cathéter *m*
cathode ['kæθəʊd] *n Elec* cathode *f*; **c. ray tube** tube *m* cathodique
Catholic ['kæθlɪk] *Rel* **1** *n* catholique *mf*; **to be a C.** être catholique
2 *adj* catholique
catholic ['kæθlɪk] *adj (wide-ranging)* éclectique
Catholicism [kə'θɒlɪsɪzəm] *n* catholicisme *m*
catkin ['kætkɪn] *n* chaton *m (d'arbre)*
catnap ['kætnæp] *n Fam* petit somme *m*
catsuit ['kætsuːt] *n* combinaison *f* collante
cattle ['kætəl] *npl* bétail *m*; **c. breeding** élevage *m* de bétail; **c. grid** = grille recouvrant une fosse et empêchant le passage du bétail; *also Fig* **c. market** marché *m ou* foire *f* aux bestiaux; **c. truck** bétaillère *f*
catty ['kætɪ] *adj Fam* vache; **c. remark** vacherie *f*
catwalk ['kætwɔːk] *n* podium *m*
Caucasian [kɔː'keɪʒən] **1** *n (white person)* Blanc (Blanche) *m,f (de type européen)*
2 *adj (in ethnology)* blanc (blanche) *(de type européen)*
Caucasus ['kɔːkəsəs] *n* **the C.** le Caucase
caucus ['kɔːkəs] *n Pol Br* = comité à l'intérieur d'un parti politique; *Am* caucus *m*
caught [kɔːt] *pt & pp of* catch
cauldron ['kɔːldrən] *n* chaudron *m*
cauliflower ['kɒlɪflaʊə(r)] *n* chou-fleur *m*; **c. cheese** chou-fleur au gratin; *Fam* **c. ear** oreille *f* en chou-fleur
cause [kɔːz] **1** *n* (**a**) *(origin)* cause *f*; **c. and effect** la cause et l'effet (**b**) *(reason)* raison *f*, motif *m*; **to have good c. for doing sth** avoir de bonnes raisons de faire qch; **and with good c.** et pour cause; **to give c. for complaint** donner lieu à des plaintes; **to give c. for concern** être inquiétant(e)
(**c**) *(purpose, mission)* cause *f*; **to make common c. (with sb)** faire cause commune (avec qn); **it's all in a good c.** *(for charity)* c'est pour une bonne cause; *Fig* c'est pour la bonne cause
2 *vt* provoquer; *(trouble)* causer; **to c. sb grief** faire de la peine à qn; **to c. sb to do sth** faire faire qch à qn; **he caused the plan to fail** il a fait échouer le plan
causeway ['kɔːzweɪ] *n* chaussée *f (sur un marécage)*
caustic ['kɔːstɪk] *adj also Fig* caustique; **c. soda** soude *f* caustique
cauterize ['kɔːtəraɪz] *vt Med* cautériser
caution ['kɔːʃən] **1** *n* (**a**) *(prudence)* prudence *f*; **c.!** *(sign)* attention!; **to exercise c.** être prudent(e); **to throw c. to the wind(s)** abandonner toute prudence (**b**) *(warning)* avertissement *m*
2 *vt* (**a**) *(warn)* mettre en garde (**against sth** contre qch); **to c. sb against doing sth** déconseiller à qn de faire qch
(**b**) *Sp* donner un avertissement à (**c**) *Law* **to c. sb** *(on arrest)* informer qn de ses droits; *(instead of prosecuting)* donner un avertissement à qn
cautionary ['kɔːʃənərɪ] *adj* **a c. tale** une histoire édifiante
cautious ['kɔːʃəs] *adj* prudent(e)
cautiously ['kɔːʃəslɪ] *adv* prudemment, avec prudence
cautiousness ['kɔːʃəsnɪs] *n* prudence *f*
cavalier [kævə'lɪə(r)] *adj* cavalier(ère)
cavalry ['kævəlrɪ] *n* cavalerie *f*
cave [keɪv] *n* grotte *f*; **c. dweller** *(contemporary)* troglodyte *m*; *(prehistoric)* homme *m* des cavernes; **c. paintings** peintures *fpl* rupestres

►**cave in** *vi (of ground, structure)* s'affaisser; *Fig (stop resisting)* céder (**to** à)

caveman ['keɪvmæn] *n* homme *m* des cavernes

cavern ['kævən] *n* caverne *f*

cavernous ['kævənəs] *adj* immense

caviar(e) ['kævɪɑː(r)] *n* caviar *m*

cavity ['kævɪtɪ] *(pl* **cavities)** *n* cavité *f*; **c. wall insulation** isolation *f* des murs creux

cavort [kə'vɔːt] *vi* faire des cabrioles; *Fig* batifoler

caw [kɔː] **1** *n* croassement *m*
2 *vi* croasser

cayenne [keɪ'en] *n* **c. (pepper)** (poivre *m* de) Cayenne *m*

CBI [siːbiː'aɪ] *n Br (abbr* **Confederation of British Industry)** = confédération du patronat britannique

cc [siː'siː] *n (abbr* **cubic centimetre(s))** cm³

CD [siː'diː] *n* (**a**) *(abbr* **compact disc)** CD *m*, compact *m*; **CD player** lecteur *m* laser *ou* de CD (**b**) *(abbr* **Corps Diplomatique)** CD

CDI [siːdiː'aɪ] *n Comptr (abbr* **compact disc interactive)** CD-I *m inv*

Cdr *n (abbr* **Commander)** commandant

Cdre *n (abbr* **Commodore)** contre-amiral

CD-ROM [siːdiː'rɒm] *n Comptr (abbr* **compact disc read-only memory)** CD-ROM *m inv*

cease [siːs] **1** *vt* cesser; **to c. doing sth** cesser de faire qch; **to c. fire** cesser le feu
2 *vi* cesser (**from doing sth** *or* **to do sth** de faire qch); **it never ceases to amaze me** ça ne laisse jamais de m'étonner

cease-fire ['siːsfaɪə(r)] *n* cessez-le-feu *m inv*

ceaseless ['siːslɪs] *adj* incessant(e), continuel(elle)

ceaselessly ['siːslɪslɪ] *adv* sans cesse, continuellement

cedar ['siːdə(r)] *n (tree, wood)* cèdre *m*

cede [siːd] *vt Law (territory, property)* céder; **to c. a point** concéder un point

cedilla [sɪ'dɪlə] *n* cédille *f*

Ceefax® ['siːfæks] *n Br =* télétexte de la BBC

ceilidh ['keɪlɪ] *n =* bal folklorique écossais ou irlandais

ceiling ['siːlɪŋ] *n (of room)* & *Fig (limit)* plafond *m*; *Fig* **to hit the c.** piquer une crise; **c. price** prix *m* plafond

celebrant ['selɪbrənt] *n Rel* officiant *m*

celebrate ['selɪbreɪt] **1** *vt (anniversary, win, occasion)* célébrer, fêter; *(mass)* célébrer
2 *vi* faire la fête

celebrated ['selɪbreɪtɪd] *adj* célèbre

celebration [selɪ'breɪʃən] *n* célébration *f*; **celebrations** *(festivities)* festivités *fpl*; **in c. of sth** pour célébrer *ou* fêter qch; **this calls for a c.!** il faut fêter *ou* arroser ça!

celebrity [sɪ'lebrɪtɪ] *(pl* **celebrities)** *n (person, fame)* célébrité *f*

celery ['selərɪ] *n* céleri *m*

celestial [sɪ'lestɪəl] *adj* céleste

celibacy ['selɪbəsɪ] *n (chastity)* absence *f* de rapports sexuels; *(by choice)* chasteté *f*; *Rel* célibat *m*

celibate ['selɪbət] *adj* **to be c.** ne pas avoir de rapports sexuels; *(by choice)* être chaste; *Rel* être célibataire

cell [sel] *n* cellule *f*; *Am* **c. phone** téléphone *m* cellulaire *ou* portable

cellar ['selə(r)] *n* cave *f*

cellist ['tʃelɪst] *n* violoncelliste *mf*

cello ['tʃeləʊ] *(pl* **cellos)** *n* violoncelle *m*

cellophane® ['seləfeɪn] *n Br* Cellophane® *f*

cellular ['seljʊlə(r)] *adj* cellulaire; *Am* **c. phone** téléphone *m* cellulaire *ou* portable

cellulite ['seljʊlaɪt] *n* cellulite *f*

celluloid® ['seljʊlɔɪd] *n* Celluloïd® *m*

cellulose ['seljʊləʊs] *n* cellulose *f*

Celsius ['selsɪəs] *adj* Celsius; **10 degrees C.** 10 degrés Celsius

Celt [kelt] *n* Celte *mf*

Celtic ['keltɪk] *adj* celte, celtique

cement [sɪ'ment] **1** *n* ciment *m*; **c. mixer** bétonnière *f*
2 *vt also Fig* cimenter

cemetery ['semətrɪ] *(pl* **cemeteries)** *n* cimetière *m*

cenotaph ['senətɑːf] *n* cénotaphe *m*

censor ['sensə(r)] **1** *n* censeur *m*; **the censors banned the film** la censure a interdit le film
2 *vt* censurer

censorious [sen'sɔːrɪəs] *adj* sévère (**of** vis-à-vis de)

censorship ['sensəʃɪp] *n* censure *f*

censure ['senʃə(r)] **1** *n* critique *f*; *Pol* **vote of c.** motion *f* de censure
2 *vt* blâmer; *(officially)* donner un blâme à

census ['sensəs] *n* recensement *m*

cent [sent] *n* cent *m*; *Am Fam* **I haven't got a c.** je n'ai pas un rond

centaur ['sentɔː(r)] *n* centaure *m*

centenarian [sentɪ'neərɪən] *n* centenaire *mf*

centenary [sen'tiːnərɪ], *Am* **centennial** [sen'tenɪəl] **1** *n* centenaire *m*
2 *adj* centenaire

center *Am =* **centre**

centigrade ['sentɪgreɪd] *adj* centigrade; **10 degrees c.** 10 degrés centigrades

centigram(me) ['sentɪgræm] *n* centigramme *m*

centilitre, *Am* **centiliter** ['sentɪliːtə(r)] *n* centilitre *m*

centime ['sɒntiːm] *n* centime *m*

centimetre, *Am* **centimeter** ['sentɪmiːtə(r)] *n* centimètre *m*

centipede ['sentɪpiːd] *n* mille-pattes *m inv*

central ['sentrəl] *adj* central(e); **C. London** le centre de Londres; **my office is quite c.** mon bureau est dans le centre; **of c. importance** d'une importance capitale; **C. America** l'Amérique *f* centrale; **C. American** d'Amérique centrale; **c. bank** banque *f* centrale; **C. Europe** l'Europe *f* centrale; **C. European** d'Europe centrale; **C. European Time** heure *f* de l'Europe centrale; **c. government** gouvernement *m* central; **c. heating** chauffage *m* central; *Aut* **c. locking** verrouillage *m* centralisé; **c. nervous system** système *m* nerveux central; *Comptr* **c. processing unit** unité *f* centrale; *Br* **c. reservation** *(on motorway)* terre-plein *m* central; *Am* **C. Standard Time** heure *f* du centre de l'Amérique du Nord

Central African Republic ['sentrəl'æfrɪkənrɪ-'pʌblɪk] *n* République *f* centrafricaine

centralize ['sentrəlaɪz] *vt* centraliser

centrally ['sentrəlɪ] *adv (funded, administered)* de façon centralisée; **c. located** central(e); **the apartment is c. heated** l'appartement a le chauffage central

centre, *Am* **center** ['sentə(r)] **1** *n* centre *m*; **in the c.** au centre; *Pol* **left/right of c.** du centre gauche/droit; **c. of gravity** centre de gravité; **c. of attention** centre d'attraction; **c. forward** *(in football)* avant-centre *m*
2 *vt (attention, interest)* concentrer (**on** sur)

centrefold, *Am* **centerfold** ['sentəfəʊld] *n (in*

magazine) double page *f* centrale détachable; *(nude photo)* photo *f* de pin-up

centrepiece, *Am* **centerpiece** ['sentəpi:s] *n (on table)* centre *m* de table; *(main attraction)* pièce *f* de résistance

centrifugal [sentrɪ'fju:gəl] *adj* centrifuge

century ['sentʃərɪ] *(pl* **centuries)** *n* siècle *m;* **the 18th c.** le XVIIIᵉ siècle

CEO [si:i:'əʊ] *n Com (abbr* **Chief Executive Officer)** D.G. *m;* **President and C.** président(e)-directeur(trice) *m,f* général(e), P.-D.G. *m,f*

ceramic [sə'ræmɪk] **1** *n (material)* céramique *f;* **ceramics** *(art)* céramique; *(objects)* céramiques *fpl*
2 *adj* en céramique

cereal ['sɪərɪəl] *n* céréale *f;* **(breakfast) c.** céréales

cerebellum [serɪ'beləm] *n Anat* cervelet *m*

cerebral ['serɪbrəl] *adj (intellectual)* & *Anat* cérébral(e); *Med* **c. palsy** paralysie *f* cérébrale

cerebrum ['serɪbrəm] *n Anat* cerveau *m*

ceremonial [serɪ'məʊnɪəl] **1** *n* cérémonial *m*
2 *adj* de cérémonie

ceremonious [serɪ'məʊnɪəs] *adj* cérémonieux(euse)

ceremony ['serɪmənɪ] *(pl* **ceremonies)** *n* cérémonie *f;* **without c.** sans cérémonies; **to stand on c.** faire des cérémonies

cert [sɜ:t] *n Fam* **it's a (dead) c.** c'est garanti

certain ['sɜ:tən] *adj* **(a)** *(sure) (failure, victory)* certain(e), assuré(e); *(cure, solution)* infaillible; **I can't say for c.** je ne peux pas l'affirmer; **I'll tell you next week for c.** je vous le dirai la semaine prochaine avec certitude; **to know sth for c.** être certain(e) de qch; **to be c. of sth** être sûr(e) ou certain(e) de qch; **they're c. of winning** ils sont assurés de gagner; **to make c. of sth** *(find out)* s'assurer de qch; *(be sure to get)* s'assurer qch; **he is c. to come** il viendra à coup sûr **(b)** *(particular)* certain(e); **a c. Martin Brown** un certain Martin Brown

certainly ['sɜ:tənlɪ] *adv* certainement; **c. not!** certainement pas!; **she's c. very clever, but...** certes elle est très intelligente, mais...

certainty ['sɜ:təntɪ] *(pl* **certainties)** *n (strong likelihood)* certitude *f; (conviction)* conviction *f;* **there is no c.** that **we will win** il n'est pas certain que nous gagnions; **to know sth for a c.** être certain(e) de qch

certifiable ['sɜ:tɪfaɪəbəl] *adj Fam (mad)* bon (bonne) pour l'asile

certificate [sə'tɪfɪkət] *n* certificat *m; (in education)* diplôme *m*

certify ['sɜ:tɪfaɪ] *(pt* & *pp* **certified)** *vt* **(a)** *(confirm)* certifier; **this is to c. that...** nous certifions par la présente que...; **to c. sb** *(insane)* déclarer que l'état de santé de qn nécessite l'internement psychiatrique **(b)** *(give certificate to)* délivrer un certificat à

certitude ['sɜ:tɪtju:d] *n* certitude *f*

cervical ['sɜ:vɪkəl, sə'vaɪkəl] *adj* **c. cancer** cancer *m* du col de l'utérus; **c. smear** frottis *m* vaginal

cervix ['sɜ:vɪks] *(pl* **cervices** ['sɜ:vɪsi:z]) *n Anat* col *m* de l'utérus

cessation [se'seɪʃən] *n* cessation *f*

cesspit ['sespɪt], **cesspool** ['sespu:l] *n* fosse *f* d'aisances; *Fig* cloaque *m*

Ceylon [sɪ'lɒn] *n Formerly* Ceylan *m*

cf [si:'ef] *(abbr* **confer, compare)** cf

CFC [si:ef'si:] *(pl* **CFCs)** *n (abbr* **chlorofluorocarbon)** CFC *m*

Chad [tʃæd] *n* leTchad

chafe [tʃeɪf] **1** *vt (skin)* irriter; *(of shoes)* blesser

2 *vi (of skin)* être irrité(e); *(of shoes)* frotter **(against** contre); *Fig* **to c. at** *or* **against sth** *(resent)* s'irriter de qch

chaff [tʃɑ:f] **1** *n* balle *f; Fig* **to separate the wheat from the c.** séparer le bon grain de l'ivraie
2 *vt (tease)* taquiner

chaffinch ['tʃæfɪntʃ] *n* pinson *m*

chagrin ['ʃægrɪn] *n* dépit *m*

chain [tʃeɪn] **1** *n* chaîne *f; (for medallion)* chaînette *f;* **in chains** enchaîné(e); **to pull the c.** *(in toilet)* tirer la chasse *(d'eau);* **c. gang** chaîne de forçats; **c. letter** = lettre faisant partie d'une chaîne; **c. mail** cotte *f* de mailles, **c. reaction** réaction *f* en chaîne; **c. saw** tronçonneuse *f;* **c. store** magasin *m* à succursales multiples
2 *vt (prisoner)* enchaîner; *(dog, bicycle)* attacher avec une chaîne **(to** à)
▶ **chain up** *vt sep (prisoner)* enchaîner; *(dog, bicycle)* attacher avec une chaîne **(to** à)

chain-smoke ['tʃeɪnsməʊk] *vi* fumer cigarette sur cigarette

chair [tʃeə(r)] **1** *n* **(a)** *(seat)* chaise *f; (armchair)* fauteuil *m* **(b)** *(chairperson)* président(e) *m,f;* **to be in the c.** présider **(c)** *Univ (of professor)* chaire *f*
2 *vt (meeting)* présider

chairlift ['tʃeəlɪft] *n* télésiège *m*

chairman ['tʃeəmən] *n (of meeting, political party)* président *m; (of company)* président-directeur *m* général, P.-D.G. *m*

chairmanship ['tʃeəmənʃɪp] *n* présidence *f*

chairperson ['tʃeəpɜ:sən] *n* président(e) *m,f*

chairwoman ['tʃeəwʊmən] *n* présidente *f*

chalet ['ʃæleɪ] *n* chalet *m*

chalice ['tʃælɪs] *n Rel* calice *m*

chalk [tʃɔ:k] **1** *n* craie *f;* **they are like c. and cheese** c'est le jour et la nuit; *Fam* **not by a long c.** loin s'en faut
▶ *vt (mark)* marquer à la craie; *(write)* écrire à la craie
▶ **chalk up** *vt sep (victory)* remporter

chalkboard ['tʃɔ:kbɔ:d] *n Am* tableau *m (noir)*

chalky ['tʃɔ:kɪ] *adj (soil, complexion)* crayeux(euse); *(taste, texture)* plâtreux(euse)

challenge ['tʃælɪndʒ] **1** *n* défi *m* **(to** à); **to launch a leadership c.** chercher à conquérir la direction du parti; **the job presents a real c.** ce travail est très stimulant
2 *vt* **(a)** *(of job)* être stimulant(e) pour; **to c. sb to do sth** défier qn de faire qch; **he challenged me to a fight** il m'a défié de me battre contre lui **(b)** *(statement, authority)* contester **(c)** *Mil* interpeller

challenger ['tʃælɪndʒə(r)] *n Sp* challenger *m*

challenging ['tʃælɪndʒɪŋ] *adj (job)* stimulant(e)

chamber ['tʃeɪmbə(r)] *n* **(a)** *(hall)* chambre *f; Pol* **Lower/Upper C.** Chambre basse/haute; **C. of Commerce** Chambre de commerce; **c. music** musique *f* de chambre; **c. pot** pot de chambre **(b)** *Law* **chambers** *(of barrister, judge)* cabinet *m (au tribunal)* **(c)** *(of heart)* cavité *f; (of revolver)* chambre *f*

chambermaid ['tʃeɪmbəmeɪd] *n* femme *f* de chambre

chameleon [kə'mi:lɪən] *n* caméléon *m*

chamois *n* **(a)** ['ʃæmɪ] **c. (leather)** peau *f* de chamois **(b)** ['ʃæmwɑ:] *(deer)* chamois *m*

champ¹ [tʃæmp] *n Fam* champion(onne) *m,f*

champ² *vi Fig* **to c. at the bit** ronger son frein

champagne [ʃæm'peɪn] *n* champagne *m*

champion ['tʃæmpɪən] **1** *n (in sport, of cause)* champion(onne) *m,f;* **world/Olympic c.** champion(onne) du monde/olympique
2 *vt* défendre

championship ['tʃæmpɪənʃɪp] *n* championnat *m*
chance [tʃɑːns] **1** *n* (**a**) *(luck)* hasard *m*; **by c.** par hasard; **to leave nothing to c.** ne rien laisser au hasard; **by any c.** par hasard; *Fam* **c. would be a fine thing!** ça ne risque pas! (**b**) *(opportunity)* occasion *f*; **to give sb a c.** donner une chance à qn; **she was trying to apologize but you didn't give her a c.** elle essayait de s'excuser mais tu ne lui en as pas laissé l'occasion; **now's your c.!** à toi de jouer!; **it's your last c.** c'est ta dernière chance; **to have an eye to the main c.** chercher à tirer profit de toutes les occasions (**c**) *(likelihood)* chance *f* (**of** de); **to have** *or* **stand a c. of doing sth** avoir des chances de faire qch; **there's no c. of that happening** il n'y a aucune chance que cela se produise; (**the**) **chances are (that)...** il y a fort à parier que... (**d**) *(risk)* risque *m*; **to take a c.** prendre un risque **2** *adj (discovery)* accidentel(elle); *(meeting)* fortuit(e) **3** *vt* **to c. doing sth** prendre le risque de faire qch; *Fam* **to c. one's arm** tenter le coup **4** *vi* **to c. to do sth** faire qch par hasard
▸ **chance on, chance upon** *vt insep* tomber (par hasard) sur

chancellor ['tʃɑːnsələ(r)] *n* (**a**) *Univ Br* président(e) *m,f* honoraire; *Am* président(e) *m,f* (**b**) *Pol (in Austria, Germany)* chancelier *m*; *Br Pol* **C. (of the Exchequer)** Chancelier de l'Échiquier, ≃ ministre *m* des Finances

chancy ['tʃɑːnsɪ] *adj Fam (risky)* risqué(e)

chandelier [ʃændə'lɪə(r)] *n* lustre *m*

change [tʃeɪndʒ] **1** *n* (**a**) *(alteration)* changement *m*; **a c. for the better/worse** une amélioration/détérioration; **a c. of address** un changement d'adresse; **a c. of clothes** des vêtements *mpl* de rechange; **to have a c. of heart** changer d'avis; **for a c.** pour une fois; *Ironic* pour changer; **that makes a c.** ça change un peu; **the c. (of life)** *(menopause)* le retour d'âge
(**b**) *(money)* monnaie *f*; **small** *or* **loose c.** petite *ou* menue monnaie; **have you got c. for a $10 bill?** avez-vous la monnaie de 10 dollars *ou* sur un billet de 10 dollars?
2 *vt* (**a**) *(alter)* changer; *(transform)* transformer (**into** en); **to c. one's mind** changer d'avis; **to c. the subject** changer de sujet
(**b**) *(exchange)* changer (**for** pour *ou* contre); **to c. hands** *(of money, car)* changer de mains; **to c. trains** changer de train; **to c. places with sb** changer de place avec qn; *Fig* **I wouldn't like to c. places with him** je ne voudrais pas être à sa place
(**c**) *(money)* changer; **to c. dollars into euros** changer des dollars en euros
(**d**) **to get changed** *(put on other clothes)* se changer
3 *vi* (**a**) *(alter)* changer; **to c. into sth** se transformer en qch (**b**) *(put on other clothes)* se changer (**c**) *(of passenger)* changer
▸ **change over** *vi* changer; **to c. over from sth to sth** passer de qch à qch; **to c. over to another channel** changer de chaîne

changeable ['tʃeɪndʒəbəl] *adj (person, mood)* changeant(e); *(weather)* variable

changeless ['tʃeɪndʒlɪs] *adj* immuable

changeover ['tʃeɪndʒəʊvə(r)] *n (to new system, currency)* passage *m* (**to** à); *(after election, appointment)* transition *f*

changing ['tʃeɪndʒɪŋ] *adj* changeant(e)

changing room ['tʃeɪndʒɪŋruːm] *n* vestiaire *m*; *(in shop)* cabine *f* d'essayage

channel ['tʃænəl] **1** *n* (**a**) *(waterway)* chenal *m*; *(of communication, distribution)* canal *m*; **to go through the proper channels** suivre la filière officielle (**b**) *TV* chaîne *f*; *Rad* bande *f* de fréquences (**c**) **the (English) C.** la Manche; **the C. Islands** les îles *fpl* Anglo-Normandes; **the C. Tunnel** le tunnel sous la Manche

2 *vt (pt & pp channelled, Am channeled)* canaliser (**to** vers)

chant [tʃɑːnt] **1** *n* (**a**) *(of demonstrators)* slogan *m* (**b**) *Rel* psalmodie *f*
2 *vt* scander
3 *vi (of demonstrators)* scander des slogans; *Rel* psalmodier

chaos ['keɪɒs] *n* chaos *m*; **our plans were thrown into c.** nos projets ont été bouleversés; **c. theory** théorie *f* du chaos

chaotic [keɪ'ɒtɪk] *adj* chaotique

chap [tʃæp] *n Br Fam (man)* bonhomme *m*, type *m*

chapel ['tʃæpəl] *n* chapelle *f*

chaperone ['ʃæpərəʊn] **1** *n* chaperon *m*
2 *vt* chaperonner

chaplain ['tʃæplɪn] *n Rel* aumônier *m*

chaplaincy ['tʃæplɪnsɪ] *n* aumônerie *f*

chapped [tʃæpt] *adj (lips, skin)* gercé(e)

chapter ['tʃæptə(r)] *n* chapitre *m*; **a c. of accidents** série noire; *Fig* **to quote c. and verse for sth** donner les références exactes de qch

char[1] [tʃɑː(r)] *(pt & pp charred) vt (burn)* carboniser

char[2] *n Br Fam (tea)* thé *m*

character ['kærɪktə(r)] *n* (**a**) *(in novel, film, play)* personnage *m*; **c. actor/actress** acteur(trice) *m,f* de composition (**b**) *(personality)* caractère *m*; **his remark was in/out of c.** ça lui ressemble bien/ça ne lui ressemble pas d'avoir fait une remarque pareille; **to have/lack c.** avoir du/manquer de caractère; **a person of good c.** une personne honorable; **c. assassination** diffamation *f*; **c. reference** *(when applying for job)* références *fpl*; *Law* **c. witness** témoin *m* de moralité (**c**) *(person)* individu *m*; **he's quite a c.!** c'est quelqu'un! (**d**) *(letter)* caractère *m*; *Comptr* **c. set** jeu *m* de caractères

characteristic [kærɪktə'rɪstɪk] **1** *n* caractéristique *f*
2 *adj* caractéristique; **it's c. of him** ça lui ressemble bien, c'est bien de lui

characterization [kærɪktəraɪ'zeɪʃən] *n (of problem, situation)* description *f*; *(in novel)* psychologie *f* des personnages

characterize ['kærɪktəraɪz] *vt (describe)* décrire; *(be characteristic of)* caractériser

charade [ʃə'rɑːd] *n (farce)* mascarade *f*; **charades** *(party game)* charades *fpl* mimées

charcoal ['tʃɑːkəʊl] *n* charbon *m* de bois; *Art* fusain *m*; **c. drawing** *(dessin m* au) fusain; **c. grey** anthracite *inv*

charge [tʃɑːdʒ] **1** *n* (**a**) *(cost)* frais *mpl*; **free of c.** gratuit; *(do something)* gratuitement; **c. account** compte *m* clients; **c. card** carte *f* de paiement *(de grand magasin)* (**b**) *Law* chef *m* d'accusation; **to be arrested on a c. of...** être arrêté(e) pour...; **to bring a c. against sb** accuser qn; **c. sheet** ≃ procès-verbal *m* (**c**) *(responsibility)* **to take c. of sth** prendre qch en charge; **to be in c.** être responsable de; **I'm in c. here!** c'est moi le chef ici! (**d**) *(of explosive)* charge *f*
2 *vt* (**a**) *(price)* faire payer, demander; **to c. sb $10** faire payer 10 dollars à qn; **c. it to my account** mettez ça sur mon compte (**b**) *Law* inculper (**with** de) (**c**) *(attack)* attaquer (**d**) *Elec* charger; *Fig* **a highly charged atmosphere** une atmosphère très tendue
3 *vi (rush)* charger; **to c. in/out** entrer/sortir en trombe

chariot ['tʃærɪət] *n* char *m*

charisma [kæ'rɪzmə] *n* charisme *m*

charismatic [kærɪz'mætɪk] *adj* charismatique

charitable ['tʃærɪtəbəl] *adj (person, action)* charitable; *(organization)* caritatif(ive); *(work)* pour une association caritative

charity ['tʃærɪtɪ] *(pl* **charities**) *n* (**a**) *(quality)* charité *f*;

Prov c. begins at home charité bien ordonnée commence par soi-même (**b**) *(organization)* association *f* caritative

charlatan ['ʃɑːlətən] *n* charlatan *m*

charm [tʃɑːm] **1** *n* (**a**) *(attractiveness)* charme *m*; **to turn on the c.** faire le charmeur/la charmeuse (**b**) *(spell)* charme *m*; **it worked like a c.** ça a marché comme sur des roulettes (**c**) **(lucky) c.** amulette *f*
2 *vt* charmer; **she charmed the money out of him** elle lui a extorqué son argent en lui faisant du charme; **to lead a charmed life** être né(e) sous une bonne étoile

charmer ['tʃɑːmə(r)] *n* charmeur(euse) *m,f*

charming ['tʃɑːmɪŋ] *adj also Ironic* charmant(e)

charred [tʃɑːd] *adj* carbonisé(e)

chart [tʃɑːt] **1** *n (graph)* diagramme *m*, graphique *m*; *(map)* carte *f*; **the charts** *(pop music)* le hit-parade
2 *vt* (**a**) *(on map)* porter sur une carte (**b**) *Fig (progress, rise)* retracer

charter ['tʃɑːtə(r)] **1** *n (of town)* charte *f*; *(of university)* statuts *mpl*; **c. flight** (vol *m*) charter *m*
2 *vt (plane, ship)* affréter

chartered accountant ['tʃɑːtədə'kaʊntənt] *n Br* expert-comptable *m*

charwoman ['tʃɑːwʊmən] *n Br* femme *f* de ménage

chary ['tʃeərɪ] *adj* circonspect(e); **to be c. of doing sth** hésiter à faire qch

chase [tʃeɪs] **1** *n (pursuit)* poursuite *f*; **to give c. to sb** donner la chasse à qn
2 *vt (pursue)* poursuivre, donner la chasse à; *(sexually)* courir après
3 *vi* **to c. after sb** *(pursue)* poursuivre qn, donner la chasse à qn; *(sexually)* courir après qn
► **chase up** *vt sep (person)* relancer; *(letter)* retrouver la trace de

chaser ['tʃeɪsə(r)] *n* = alcool bu après une bière ou vice versa; **a beer with a whisky c.** = une bière suivie d'un whisky

chasm ['kæzəm] *n also Fig* gouffre *m*, abîme *m*

chassis ['ʃæsɪ] *n (of car)* châssis *m*

chaste [tʃeɪst] *adj* chaste

chasten ['tʃeɪsən] *vt* rendre plus humble

chastise [tʃæs'taɪz] *vt* châtier; *(criticize)* fustiger

chastisement [tʃæs'taɪzmənt] *n* châtiment *m*; *(criticism)* fustigation *f*

chastity ['tʃæstɪtɪ] *n* chasteté *f*; **c. belt** ceinture *f* de chasteté

chat [tʃæt] **1** *n* discussion *f*; **to have a c. (with sb)** discuter *ou* bavarder (avec qn); **c. show** *(on TV)* talk-show *m*
2 *vi (pt & pp chatted)* bavarder; **to c. about sth** discuter de qch
► **chat up** *vt sep Br Fam* draguer

chattel ['tʃætəl] *n Law* bien *m* meuble

chatter ['tʃætər] **1** *n* bavardage *m*, papotage *m*
2 *vi (talk)* bavarder, papoter; **my teeth were chattering** je claquais des dents

chatterbox ['tʃætəbɒks] *n Fam* pie *f*

chatty ['tʃætɪ] *adj (person)* bavard(e); *(letter)* plein(e) de détails

chauffeur ['ʃəʊfə(r)] **1** *n* chauffeur *m*
2 *vt* conduire

chauvinism ['ʃəʊvɪnɪzəm] *n (patriotism)* chauvinisme *m*; **(male) c.** machisme *m*

chauvinist ['ʃəʊvɪnɪst] *n & adj (patriotic)* chauvin(e) *m,f*; **(male) c.** *(sexist)* macho *m*

chauvinistic [ʃəʊvɪ'nɪstɪk] *adj (patriotic)* chauvin(e); *(sexist)* macho

cheap [tʃiːp] **1** *n* **to do sth on the c.** faire qch à peu de frais *ou* pour pas cher
2 *adj* (**a**) *(inexpensive)* bon marché *inv*, pas cher (chère); **cheaper** meilleur marché *inv*, moins cher (chère); **c. rate** tarif *m* réduit (**b**) *(of little value)* de peu de valeur; *(vulgar)* de mauvais goût; **to feel c.** *(of person)* se sentir minable; **it's c. and nasty** c'est de la camelote
3 *adv Fam* **it was going c.** c'était bon marché

cheapen ['tʃiːpən] *vt (degrade)* gâcher; **to c. oneself** s'abaisser

cheaply ['tʃiːplɪ] *adv (buy)* (à) bon marché, à bas prix; *(live, travel)* à peu de frais, pour pas cher

cheapskate ['tʃiːpskeɪt] *n Fam* radin(e) *m,f*

cheat [tʃiːt] **1** *n (dishonest person)* escroc *m*; *(at games)* tricheur(euse) *m,f*; *(deception, trick)* tricherie *f*, triche *f*
2 *vt* duper, rouler; *(financially)* escroquer; **to c. sb out of sth** *(money)* escroquer qch à qn; *(chance)* priver qn de qch
3 *vi* tricher
► **cheat on** *vt insep (be unfaithful to)* tromper

cheating ['tʃiːtɪŋ] *n* tricherie *f*, triche *f*; **that's c.!** c'est de la triche!

check¹ [tʃek] **1** *n* (**a**) *(inspection)* vérification *f*, contrôle *m* (**on** de); **to run a c. on sb** enquêter sur qn (**b**) *(restraint)* **to keep sb in c.** tenir qn en échec; **to keep sth in c.** *(emotion, enemy advance)* contenir qch; *Pol* **checks and balances** équilibre *m* des pouvoirs (**c**) *(in chess)* échec *m*; **in c.** en échec (**d**) *Am (cheque)* chèque *m*; *(restaurant bill)* addition *f*
2 *vt* (**a**) *(verify, examine)* *(information, statement)* vérifier; *(passport, ticket)* contrôler; **to c. that...** vérifier *ou* s'assurer que... (**b**) *(restrain)* *(inflation)* enrayer; *(emotion, impulse, enemy advance)* contenir
3 *vi (verify)* **to c. on sth** vérifier qch; **to c. on sb** surveiller qn; **you'd better c. with her** vous feriez mieux de lui demander
► **check in** *vt sep (baggage)* enregistrer
2 *vi (at hotel)* remplir le registre; *(at airport)* se présenter à l'enregistrement
► **check out** *vt sep* (**a**) *(investigate)* *(person)* se renseigner sur; *(information)* vérifier (**b**) *Fam (look at)* viser
2 *vi (leave hotel)* quitter l'hôtel
► **check up** *vi* vérifier; **to c. up on sb** surveiller qn

check² *n (pattern)* carreaux *mpl*
2 *adj* à carreaux

checkbook ['tʃekbʊk] *n Am* carnet *m* de chèques, chéquier *m*

checkers ['tʃekəz] *npl Am* jeu *m* de dames

check-in ['tʃekɪn] *n Av* **c. (desk)** (comptoir *m* d')enregistrement *m*

checkmate ['tʃekmeɪt] **1** *n (in chess)* échec *m* et mat
2 *vt (in chess)* faire échec et mat à; *Fig (opponent)* mater

checkout ['tʃekaʊt] *n (in supermarket)* caisse *f*

checkpoint ['tʃekpɔɪnt] *n (poste m de)* contrôle *m*

checkup ['tʃekʌp] *n Med* bilan *m* complet

cheek [tʃiːk] **1** *n* (**a**) *(of face)* joue *f*; **to dance c. to cheek** danser joue contre joue; **c. by jowl (with sb)** coude à coude (avec qn); *Fig* **to turn the other c.** tendre l'autre joue (**b**) *(buttock)* fesse *f* (**c**) *Fam (impudence)* toupet *m*, culot *m*; **he's got a c.!** il est culotté *ou* gonflé!
2 *vt Fam (be impudent to)* être insolent(e) avec

cheekbone ['tʃiːkbəʊn] *n* pommette *f*

cheeky ['tʃiːkɪ] *adj Fam (remark)* effronté(e); *(behaviour)* impertinent(e)

cheep [tʃiːp] *vi (of bird)* piailler

cheer [tʃɪə(r)] **1** n (**a**) (shout) hourra m; **cheers** acclamations fpl, bravos mpl; **three cheers for Mike!** un ban pour Mike! (**b**) Fam **cheers!** (when drinking) (à votre) santé!; (goodbye) à bientôt!; (thanks) merci!
2 vt (**a**) (applaud) acclamer (**b**) (make happier) remonter le moral à
3 vi (shout) pousser des hourras ou des acclamations
▸ **cheer on** vt sep (support) encourager
▸ **cheer up 1** vt sep (person) remonter le moral à; (room) égayer
2 vi (of person) reprendre courage; **c. up!** courage!
cheerful ['tʃɪəfʊl] adj (person) gai(e), de bonne humeur; (room, music, mood) gai; (conversation) enjoué(e)
cheerfully ['tʃɪəfʊlɪ] adv gaiement, avec entrain; Fam **I could c. murder him!** je le tuerais volontiers!
cheerily ['tʃɪərɪlɪ] adv gaiement
cheerio [tʃɪərɪ'əʊ] exclam salut!
cheerleader ['tʃɪəliːdə(r)] n = majorette qui encourage les supporters d'une équipe sportive à manifester leur enthousiasme
cheerless ['tʃɪəlɪs] adj morne; (room) triste
cheery ['tʃɪərɪ] adj joyeux(euse), gai(e)
cheese [tʃiːz] n fromage m; Fam (say) **c.!** (for photograph) souriez!; **c. sandwich/omelette** sandwich m/omelette f au fromage
▸ **cheese off** vt sep Fam **to be cheesed off (with)** en avoir marre (de)
cheeseboard ['tʃiːzbɔːd] n (selection) plateau m de fromages
cheeseburger ['tʃiːzbɜːgə(r)] n cheeseburger m
cheesecake ['tʃiːzkeɪk] n gâteau m au fromage blanc
cheetah ['tʃiːtə] n guépard m
chef [ʃef] n chef m (cuisinier)
chemical ['kemɪkəl] **1** n produit m chimique
2 adj chimique; **c. warfare** guerre f chimique; **c. weapons** armes fpl chimiques
chemist ['kemɪst] n (**a**) Br (pharmacist) pharmacien(enne) m,f; **c.'s (shop)** pharmacie f (**b**) (scientist) chimiste mf
chemistry ['kemɪstrɪ] n chimie f; Fig **there was real c. between them** il y avait une grande affinité entre eux
chemotherapy [kiːməʊ'θerəpɪ] n Med chimiothérapie f
cheque, Am **check** [tʃek] n Fin chèque m; **to make out** or **write a c. (to sb)** faire un chèque (à l'ordre de qn); **a c. for £10** un chèque de 10 livres; **c. card** carte f bancaire (sans laquelle un chéquier n'est pas valable)
chequebook, Am **checkbook** ['tʃekbʊk] n carnet m de chèques, chéquier m
chequered ['tʃekəd] adj (patterned) à carreaux; Fig **she's had a c. career** elle a eu une carrière en dents de scie
cherish ['tʃerɪʃ] vt (memory, person) chérir; (hopes) caresser, nourrir
cherry ['tʃerɪ] (pl **cherries**) n (fruit) cerise f; **c. (tree)** cerisier m; **c. orchard** cerisaie f
cherub ['tʃerəb] (pl **cherubs** or **cherubim** ['tʃerəbɪm]) n chérubin m
chess [tʃes] n échecs mpl; **a game of c.** une partie d'échecs; **c. player** joueur(euse) m,f d'échecs
chessboard ['tʃesbɔːd] n échiquier m
chessman ['tʃesmæn], **chesspiece** ['tʃespiːs] n pièce f (de jeu d'échecs)
chest [tʃest] n (**a**) (of person) poitrine f; Fig **to get it off one's c.** dire ce qu'on a sur le cœur (**b**) (box) coffre m, caisse f; **c. of drawers** commode f

chestnut ['tʃesnʌt] **1** n (nut) châtaigne f; (tree, wood) châtaignier m; (horse) **c.** marron m d'Inde; Fam **an old c.** une plaisanterie usée
2 adj (hair) châtain; (horse) alezan(e)
chew [tʃuː] vt mâcher, mastiquer; (cigar, end of pen) mâchonner; **to c. one's nails** se ronger les ongles
▸ **chew over** vt sep Fam réfléchir à, cogiter sur
chewing gum ['tʃuːɪŋgʌm] n chewing-gum m
chewy ['tʃuːɪ] adj (meat) caoutchouteux(euse); (sweet) mou (molle)
chic [ʃiːk] adj élégant(e), chic
chick [tʃɪk] n (**a**) (young bird) oisillon m; (young chicken) poussin m (**b**) Fam (woman) nana f
chicken ['tʃɪkɪn] n (**a**) (bird) poulet m; Prov **don't count your chickens (before they are hatched)** il ne faut pas vendre la peau de l'ours avant de l'avoir tué; **c. feed** (food) nourriture f pour volaille; Fam Fig **that's c. feed!** c'est une misère! (**b**) (coward) lâche mf, froussard(e) m,f
2 adj Fam (cowardly) froussard(e)
▸ **chicken out** vi Fam se dégonfler
chickenpox ['tʃɪkɪnpɒks] n varicelle f
chickpea ['tʃɪkpiː] n pois m chiche
chicory ['tʃɪkərɪ] n endive f
chide [tʃaɪd] (pt **chided** or **chid** [tʃɪd], pp **chided** or **chidden** ['tʃɪdən]) vt Lit réprimander
chief [tʃiːf] **1** n (of tribe) chef m; Fam **the c.** (boss) le patron; Mil **c. of staff** chef d'état-major; (White House) **c. of staff** secrétaire m de la Maison-Blanche
2 adj (most important) principal(e); **c. assistant** principal(e) collaborateur(trice) m,f; Com **c. executive** directeur(trice) m,f général(e); Am **c. executive officer** directeur(trice) m,f général(e)
chiefly ['tʃiːflɪ] adv principalement, surtout
chieftain ['tʃiːftən] n (of clan) chef m
chiffon ['ʃɪfɒn] n mousseline f de soie
chilblain ['tʃɪlbleɪn] n engelure f
child [tʃaɪld] (pl **children** ['tʃɪldrən]) n enfant mf; **it's c.'s play** c'est un jeu d'enfant; **children's literature** littérature f enfantine ou pour enfants; **c. abuse** mauvais traitements mpl à enfant; (sexual) sévices mpl sexuels infligés à un enfant; **c. benefit** ≃ allocations fpl familiales; **c. labour** travail m des enfants; **c. minder** nourrice f
child-bearing ['tʃaɪldbeərɪŋ] n maternité f; **of c. age** en âge d'avoir des enfants
childbirth ['tʃaɪldbɜːθ] n accouchement m; **to die in c.** mourir en couches
childhood ['tʃaɪldhʊd] n enfance f
childish ['tʃaɪldɪʃ] adj Pej puéril(e); **don't be so c.!** ne faites pas l'enfant!
childless ['tʃaɪldlɪs] adj sans enfant(s)
childlike ['tʃaɪldlaɪk] adj enfantin(e)
childproof ['tʃaɪldpruːf] adj **c. lock** (in car) = serrure de sécurité pour enfants; **c. bottle** = bouteille f pourvue d'une capsule de sécurité
children ['tʃɪldrən] pl of **child**
Chile ['tʃɪlɪ] n le Chili
Chilean ['tʃɪlɪən] **1** n Chilien(enne) m,f
2 adj chilien(enne)
chill [tʃɪl] **1** n coup m de froid; **to catch a c.** prendre froid; **a c. of fear** un frisson de peur; **there's a c. in the air** le fond de l'air est frais
2 adj froid(e), glacé(e)
3 vt (wine, food) mettre au frais; (of wind) glacer; **serve chilled** (on product) servir frais

► **chill out** *vi Fam* se détendre; **c. out!** on se calme!

chilli ['tʃɪlɪ] (*pl* **chillis** *or* **chillies**) *n (dish)* chili *m* con carne; **c. (pepper)** piment *m* (rouge); **c. powder** piment en poudre

chilling ['tʃɪlɪŋ] *adj (frightening)* à vous donner le frisson

chilly ['tʃɪlɪ] *adj also Fig* froid(e)

chime [tʃaɪm] **1** *n (of bells)* carillon *m* **2** *vt* **the clock chimed nine** le carillon de l'horloge sonna neuf heures **3** *vi (of clock, bells)* carillonner

► **chime in** *vi Fam (in conversation)* intervenir

chimney ['tʃɪmnɪ] (*pl* **chimneys**) *n* cheminée *f; Fam* **to smoke like a c.** *(of person)* fumer comme un pompier; **c. sweep** ramoneur *m*

chimneypot ['tʃɪmnɪpɒt] *n* mitre *f*

chimpanzee [tʃɪmpæn'ziː], *Fam* **chimp** [tʃɪmp] *n* chimpanzé *m*

chin [tʃɪn] *n* menton *m*; *Fig* **to keep one's c.** up tenir bon, tenir le coup

China ['tʃaɪnə] *n* la Chine

china ['tʃaɪnə] *n* porcelaine *f*; **c. clay** kaolin *m*

Chinese [tʃaɪ'niːz] **1** *npl* **the C.** *(people)* les Chinois *mpl* **2** *n* (**a**) *(person)* Chinois(e) *m,f* (**b**) *(language)* chinois *m* **3** *adj* chinois(e)

chink¹ *n (gap)* fente *f*, lézarde *f; (of light)* rayon *m; Fig* **to find a c. in sb's armour** trouver le talon d'Achille de qn

chink² **1** *n (sound)* tintement *m* **2** *vt (coins, glasses)* faire tinter **3** *vi* tinter

chintz [tʃɪnts] *n* chintz *m*

chinwag ['tʃɪnwæg] *n Fam* **to have a c.** tailler une bavette

chip [tʃɪp] **1** *n* (**a**) *(of wood, glass)* éclat *m; (in plate, cup)* ébréchure *f*; **this cup has a c.** in it cette tasse est ébréchée (**b**) **chips** *Br (French fries)* frites *fpl; Am (crisps)* (pommes *fpl*) chips *mpl; Br* **c. shop** = petite boutique où l'on vend du poisson pané et frit, accompagné de frites (**c**) *(in gambling)* jeton *m* (**d**) *Comptr* puce *f* (**e**) *(idioms)* **he's a c.** off the old block c'est son père tout craché; **to have a c. on one's shoulder** en vouloir à tout le monde; *Fam* **when the chips are down** dans les moments critiques; *Fam* **he's had his chips** *(it's too late for him)* il est cuit *ou* fichu **2** *vt (pt & pp* **chipped**) (**a**) *(cut at) (stone, wood)* tailler; *(damage) (knife, cup)* ébrécher; *(furniture)* écorner; **to c. one's tooth** se casser un petit bout de dent (**b**) *(in sport)* **to c. the ball** frapper la balle par en dessous **3** *vi (of plate, cup)* s'ébrécher

► **chip in** *vi Fam (give money)* participer; **to c. in with a suggestion** intervenir pour faire une suggestion

chipboard ['tʃɪpbɔːd] *n* aggloméré *m*

chipmunk ['tʃɪpmʌŋk] *n* tamia *m* rayé

chiropodist [kɪ'rɒpədɪst] *n* pédicure *mf*

chiropody [kɪ'rɒpədɪ] *n* pédicurie *f*

chirp [tʃɜːp] **1** *n (of birds)* gazouillis *m*, pépiement *m; (of grasshopper)* chant *m* **2** *vt & vi (of bird)* gazouiller, pépier; *(of grasshopper)* chanter

chirpy ['tʃɜːpɪ] *adj* d'humeur joyeuse

chirrup ['tʃɪrəp] = **chirp**

chisel ['tʃɪzəl] **1** *n (tool)* ciseau *m; (for sculpture)* burin *m* **2** *vt (pt & pp* **chiselled**, *Am* **chiseled**) (**a**) *(in woodwork, sculpture)* ciseler (**b**) *very Fam (cheat)* rouler

chit [tʃɪt] *n* bon *m*

chitchat ['tʃɪttʃæt] *n Fam* bavardage *m*, papotage *m*

chivalrous ['ʃɪvəlrəs] *adj* chevaleresque; *(towards women)* galant(e)

chivalry ['ʃɪvəlrɪ] *n (courteous behaviour)* courtoisie *f*; *(towards women)* galanterie *f; Hist* chevalerie *f*

chives [tʃaɪvz] *npl* ciboulette *f*

chiv(v)y ['tʃɪvɪ] (*pt & pp* **chiv(v)ied**) *vt Br Fam* harceler; **to c. sb into doing sth** harceler qn jusqu'à ce qu'il fasse qch; **to c. sb along** faire se presser qn

chloride ['klɔːraɪd] *n Chem* chlorure *m*

chlorinate ['klɔːrɪneɪt] *vt* chlorer

chlorine ['klɔːriːn] *n Chem* chlore *m*

chloroform ['klɒrəfɔːm] *n Chem* chloroforme *m*

chlorophyl(l) ['klɒrəfɪl] *n Biol* chlorophylle *f*

choc-ice ['tʃɒkaɪs] *n Br* = glace individuelle rectangulaire enrobée de chocolat

chock [tʃɒk] *n (for wheel of car, plane)* cale *f*

chock-a-block ['tʃɒkə'blɒk] *adj Fam* plein(e) à craquer

chocolate ['tʃɒklət] **1** *n* chocolat *m*; **hot c.** chocolat chaud **2** *adj (made of chocolate)* en chocolat; *(chocolate-flavoured)* au chocolat; *Br* **c.(-coloured)**, *Am* **c.(-colored)** chocolat *inv*

choice [tʃɔɪs] **1** *n* choix *m*; **to make a c.** choisir, faire un choix; **you have no c.** vous n'avez pas le choix, **there isn't much c.** il n'y a pas grand choix; **available in a wide c. of colours** disponible dans une large gamme de coloris **2** *adj* (**a**) *(well chosen)* choisi(e); **she used some c. language** *(offensive)* elle a juré comme un charretier (**b**) *(food)* de choix; *(wine)* fin(e)

choir ['kwaɪə(r)] *n* chœur *m*

choirboy ['kwaɪəbɔɪ] *n* jeune choriste *m*

choke [tʃəʊk] **1** *n (of car)* starter *m* **2** *vt* (**a**) *(strangle)* étrangler (**b**) *(block) (sink, road)* boucher **3** *vi* s'étrangler; **to c. with anger** s'étrangler de colère; **she choked on a fishbone** elle a failli s'étouffer en avalant une arête

► **choke back** *vt sep (tears, words, anger)* ravaler

cholera ['kɒlərə] *n* choléra *m*

cholesterol [kə'lestərɒl] *n* cholestérol *m*

choose [tʃuːz] (*pt* **chose** [tʃəʊz], *pp* **chosen** ['tʃəʊzən]) **1** *vt* choisir; **to c. to do sth** choisir de faire qch; **there's not much to c. between them** ils se valent **2** *vi* choisir *(between* entre); **I'll do as I c.** je ferai comme il me plaît

choosy ['tʃuːzɪ] *adj Fam* difficile

chop [tʃɒp] **1** *n* (**a**) *(with axe)* coup *m; Fam* **to get the c.** *(get sacked)* se faire sacquer (**b**) *(of lamb, pork)* côtelette *f* **2** *vt (pt & pp* **chopped**) *(wood)* couper; *(meat, vegetables)* couper en morceaux; *(finely)* hacher **3** *vi* **to c.** and change changer sans cesse; **he's always chopping and changing** il change d'avis comme de chemise

► **chop down** *vt sep (tree)* abattre

► **chop off** *vt sep* trancher, couper; **to c. sb's head off** couper la tête à qn

chopper ['tʃɒpə(r)] *n* (**a**) *(cleaver)* couperet *m; (axe)* hachette *f* (**b**) *Fam (helicopter)* hélico *m*

chopping ['tʃɒpɪŋ] *n* **c. block** *(of butcher)* billot *m*; **c. board** planche *f* (à découper)

choppy ['tʃɒpɪ] *adj (sea, lake)* agité(e)

chopsticks ['tʃɒpstɪks] *npl* baguettes *fpl*

choral ['kɔːrəl] *adj* choral(e); **c. society** chorale *f*

chord [kɔːd] *n* (**a**) *Mus* accord *m; Fig* **her speech struck a c. with the audience** son discours a trouvé un écho auprès du public (**b**) *Math (of arc)* corde *f*

chore [tʃɔː(r)] n (a) **chores** (in household) travaux mpl ménagers (b) (unwelcome task) corvée f
choreograph ['kɒrɪəgrɑːf] vt faire la chorégraphie de; Fig orchestrer
choreography [kɒrɪ'ɒgrəfɪ] n chorégraphie f
chorister ['kɒrɪstə(r)] n choriste mf
chortle ['tʃɔːtəl] **1** n gloussement m (de joie) **2** vi glousser (de joie)
chorus ['kɔːrəs] **1** n (a) (of song) refrain m (b) (group of singers, actors) chœur m; Fig a **c. of protest** un concert de protestations; **c. girl** danseuse f de revue; **c. line** troupe f **2** vt dire en chœur
chose [tʃəʊz] pt of **choose**
chosen ['tʃəʊzən] **1** adj choisi(e); **the c. few** les heureux élus mpl **2** pp of **choose**
Christ [kraɪst] **1** n le Christ m, Jésus-Christ m **2** exclam very Fam bon Dieu!; **C. Almighty!** nom de Dieu!
christen ['krɪsən] vt (name) baptiser
christening ['krɪsənɪŋ] n baptême m
Christian ['krɪstʃən] **1** n chrétien(enne) m,f; **to be a C.** être chrétien **2** adj chrétien(enne); **C. name** prénom m
Christianity [krɪstɪ'ænɪtɪ] n christianisme m
Christmas ['krɪsməs] n Noël m; **at C.** à Noël; **Merry or Happy C.!** joyeux Noël!; **C. cake** gâteau m de Noël (fruits secs); **C. card** carte f de Noël; **C. carol** chant m de Noël; **C. Day** jour m de Noël; **C. Eve** veille f de Noël; **C. pudding** pudding m (de Noël); **C. tree** sapin m de Noël
chrome [krəʊm] adj chromé(e)
chromium ['krəʊmɪəm] n Chem chrome m
chromosome ['krəʊməsəʊm] n Biol chromosome m
chronic ['krɒnɪk] adj (a) (invalid, illness, unemployment) chronique (b) Fam (bad) atroce
chronicle ['krɒnɪkəl] **1** n chronique f; Fig (of disasters) suite f **2** vt faire la chronique de
chronological [krɒnə'lɒdʒɪkəl] adj chronologique
chronology [krə'nɒlədʒɪ] n chronologie f
chrysalis ['krɪsəlɪs] n Zool chrysalide f
chrysanthemum [krɪ'sænθəməm] n chrysanthème m
chubby ['tʃʌbɪ] adj potelé(e), dodu(e); (face) joufflu(e); **c.-cheeked** joufflu
chuck [tʃʌk] vt Fam (a) (throw) lancer, balancer (b) (boyfriend, girlfriend) plaquer
▸ **chuck away** vt sep Fam balancer; Fig (opportunity) foutre en l'air
▸ **chuck out** vt sep Fam (throw away) balancer; (from house, school, club) vider
chuckle ['tʃʌkəl] **1** n petit rire m **2** vi rire tout bas
chuffed [tʃʌft] adj Br Fam tout(e) content(e) (about de)
chug [tʃʌg] (pt & pp chugged) vi (train) haleter; Fam **he's still chugging along in the same job** il a toujours le même boulot pépère
chum [tʃʌm] n Fam copain (copine) m,f
chummy ['tʃʌmɪ] adj Fam copain (copine); **to be a bit too c.** être un peu trop familier(ère)
chump [tʃʌmp] n Fam (a) (foolish person) idiot(e) m,f (b) **to be off one's c.** être timbré(e)
chunk [tʃʌŋk] n gros morceau m; (of bread) quignon m; (of time) partie f
chunky ['tʃʌŋkɪ] adj Fam (well-built) bien bâti(e); (fat) grassouillet(ette); (pullover) gros (grosse)

church [tʃɜːtʃ] n (a) (building) église f; (French Protestant) temple m; **to go to c.** aller à l'église/au temple; **c. hall** salle f paroissiale; **c. service** office m (b) (institution) **the C. of England** l'Église f anglicane; **the C. of Scotland** l'Église d'Écosse
churchgoer ['tʃɜːtʃgəʊə(r)] n pratiquant(e) m,f
churchyard ['tʃɜːtʃjɑːd] n cimetière m
churlish ['tʃɜːlɪʃ] adj (rude) grossier(ère); (surly) revêche
churn [tʃɜːn] **1** n (for making butter) baratte f; (for milk) bidon m à lait **2** vt (butter) battre; **the propeller churned up the water** l'eau bouillonnait sous l'action des hélices **3** vi **my stomach's churning** (because of nervousness) j'ai l'estomac noué
▸ **churn out** vt sep Fam (books) pondre (en série); (goods) produire en série
chute [ʃuːt] n (a) (for parcels) glissière f; (rubbish) **c.** vide-ordures m inv (b) (in swimming pool, playground) toboggan m (c) Fam (parachute) parachute m
chutney ['tʃʌtnɪ] n chutney m
CIA [siːaɪ'eɪ] n Am (abbr **Central Intelligence Agency**) CIA f
cicada [sɪ'kɑːdə] n cigale f
CID [siːaɪ'diː] n Br (abbr **Criminal Investigation Department**) ≃ P.J.
cider ['saɪdə(r)] n cidre m; **c. apple** pomme f à cidre; **c. vinegar** vinaigre m de cidre
cigar [sɪ'gɑː(r)] n cigare m
cigarette [sɪgə'ret] n cigarette f; **c. ash** cendre f de cigarette; **c. butt or end** mégot m; **c. case** étui m à cigarettes; **c. holder** fume-cigarette m inv; **c. lighter** briquet m; (in car) allume-cigare m; **c. machine** distributeur m automatique de cigarettes; **c. packet** paquet m de cigarettes; **c. paper** papier m à cigarettes
C-in-C [siːɪn'siː] n Mil & Naut (abbr **Commander-in-Chief**) commandant m en chef
cinder ['sɪndə(r)] n **cinders** cendres fpl; **burnt to a c.** complètement carbonisé(e)
Cinderella [sɪndə'relə] n Cendrillon
cine ['sɪnɪ] adj **c. camera** caméra f; **c. film** pellicule f
cinema ['sɪnəmə] n cinéma m; Br **to go to the c.** aller au cinéma
cinnamon ['sɪnəmən] n cannelle f
cipher ['saɪfə(r)] n (code) chiffre m, code m; Fig **he's a mere c.** c'est un zéro
circa ['sɜːkə] prep (of time) aux alentours de, (of amount) environ
circle ['sɜːkəl] **1** n (a) (shape) cercle m; **to sit in a c.** s'asseoir en cercle; Fig **to go round in circles** tourner en rond (b) (movement) **to come full c.** revenir à son point de départ (c) (in theatre) balcon m; **lower/upper c.** premier/deuxième balcon (d) (group) cercle m, groupe m; **in certain circles** dans certains milieux **2** vt (a) (go round) tourner autour de (b) (surround) entourer (with de) **3** vi (of plane, birds) tourner en rond
circuit [sɜːkɪt] n (a) (electric) circuit m; **c. breaker** disjoncteur m (b) (in motor racing) (course) circuit m; (lap) tour m
circuitous [sə'kjuːɪtəs] adj (route) détourné(e); (reasoning) alambiqué(e)
circular ['sɜːkjʊlə(r)] **1** n (letter) circulaire f; (advertisement) prospectus m **2** adj (movement, argument) circulaire
circulate ['sɜːkjʊleɪt] **1** vt faire circuler **2** vi circuler

circulation [sɜːkjʊ'leɪʃən] *n (of air, blood, money)* circulation *f; (of newspaper)* tirage *m;* **for internal c.** only *(document)* à usage interne uniquement; *Fig* **to be out of c.** *(of person)* disparaître de la circulation

circumcise ['sɜːkəmsaɪz] *vt (boy)* circoncire; *(girl)* exciser

circumcision [sɜːkəm'sɪʒən] *n* circoncision *f;* **female c.** excision *f*

circumference [sə'kʌmfərəns] *n* circonférence *f*

circumflex ['sɜːkəmfleks] *n* accent *m* circonflexe

circumlocution [sɜːkəmlə'kjuːʃən] *n* circonlocution *f,* périphrase *f*

circumnavigate [sɜːkəm'nævɪgeɪt] *vt* **to c. sth** faire le tour de qch en bateau

circumscribe ['sɜːkəmskraɪb] *vt (limit)* limiter

circumspect ['sɜːkəmspekt] *adj* circonspect(e)

circumstances ['sɜːkəmstənsɪz] *npl* circonstances *fpl;* **in** *or* **under the c.** étant donné les circonstances; **in** *or* **under no c.** en aucun cas, sous aucun prétexte, **due to c. beyond our control** en raison de circonstances indépendantes de notre volonté

circumstantial [sɜːkəm'stænʃəl] *adj* **c. evidence** preuves *fpl* indirectes

circumvent [sɜːkəm'vent] *vt (law, rule)* contourner

circus ['sɜːkəs] *n* cirque *m*

cirrhosis [sɪ'rəʊsɪs] *n Med* cirrhose *f*

cissy ['sɪsɪ] *(pl* **cissies***) n Fam* poule *f* mouillée

cistern ['sɪstən] *n* citerne *f; (in lavatory)* réservoir *m* de chasse d'eau

citadel ['sɪtədel] *n* citadelle *f*

citation [saɪ'teɪʃən] *n* citation *f*

cite [saɪt] *vt* citer

citizen ['sɪtɪzən] *n* citoyen(enne) *m,f; (of city)* habitant(e) *m,f;* **c.'s arrest** = arrestation par un citoyen d'une personne soupçonnée d'avoir commis un délit

citizenship ['sɪtɪzənʃɪp] *n* citoyenneté *f*

citric acid ['sɪtrɪk'æsɪd] *n* acide *m* citrique

citrus fruit ['sɪtrəsfruːt] *n* agrumes *mpl;* **a c.** un agrume

city ['sɪtɪ] *(pl* **cities***) n* (grande) ville *f; Br* **the C.** la City *(quartier des affaires de Londres);* **c. centre** centre-ville *m*

civic ['sɪvɪk] *adj (duty, pride)* civique; *(building, authorities)* municipal(e); **c. centre** salle *f* municipale

civil ['sɪvəl] *adj* **(a)** *(of society)* civil(e); **c. aviation** aviation *f* civile; **c. defence** protection *f* civile; **c. disobedience** résistance *f* passive; **c. engineering** génie *m* civil; **c. law** *(subject)* droit *m* civil; *Law* **c. rights** droits civils; **c. servant** fonctionnaire *mf;* **the c. service** la fonction publique; **c. war** guerre *f* civile **(b)** *(polite)* poli(e)

civilian [sɪ'vɪljən] **1** *n* civil *m*
2 *adj* civil(e)

civility [sɪ'vɪlɪtɪ] *(pl* **civilities***) n* politesse *f*

civilization [sɪvɪlaɪ'zeɪʃən] *n* civilisation *f*

civilize ['sɪvɪlaɪz] *vt* civiliser

civilized ['sɪvɪlaɪzd] *adj* civilisé(e); **let's be c. about this** tâchons d'être conciliants

cl *(abbr* **centilitre***)* cl

clad [klæd] *adj* **c. in** vêtu(e) de

claim [kleɪm] **1** *n* **(a)** *(demand) (for damages, compensation)* demande *f* d'indemnisation; *(as a right)* revendication *f;* **to lay c. to sth** revendiquer qch; **I have many claims on my time** je suis très pris; **it's his only c. to fame** c'est la seule façon dont il se soit distingué **(b)** *(assertion)* déclaration *f;* **she makes no c. to originality** elle ne prétend pas être originale

2 *vt* **(a)** *(as a right)* revendiquer; **to c. damages (from sb)** réclamer des dommages et intérêts (à qn); **to c. responsibility for sth** revendiquer qch **(b)** *(assert)* **to c. that…** affirmer que…; **he claims to be an expert** il prétend être un expert **(c)** *(lost property)* réclamer **(d)** *(life)* **the earthquake claimed thousands of lives** le tremblement de terre a fait des milliers de victimes

claimant ['kleɪmənt] *n (to throne)* prétendant(e) *m,f; Law (for social security, insurance)* demandeur(eresse) *m,f*

clairvoyant [kleə'vɔɪənt] **1** *n* voyant(e) *m,f*
2 *adj* extralucide

clam [klæm] *n* palourde *f*
▶ **clam up** *(pt & pp* **clammed***) vi Fam* se fermer comme une huître

clamber ['klæmbə(r)] *vi* **to c. up sth** escalader qch

clammy ['klæmɪ] *adj* moite

clamorous ['klæmərəs] *adj* bruyant(e)

clamour, *Am* **clamor** ['klæmə(r)] **1** *n (noise)* clameur *f; (protest)* tollé *m*
2 *vi* **to c. for sth** réclamer qch à grands cris

clamp [klæmp] **1** *n (tool)* serre-joint *m; (fixed to bench)* étau *m; Med* clamp *m; Br* **(wheel) c.** sabot *m* (de Denver)
2 *vt (fasten)* fixer; *(car)* mettre un sabot à
▶ **clamp down** *vt insep* faire la chasse à

clampdown ['klæmpdaʊn] *n* répression *f* **(on** de)

clan [klæn] *n also Fig* clan *m*

clandestine [klæn'destɪn] *adj* clandestin(e)

clang [klæŋ] **1** *n* bruit *m* métallique
2 *vi (of bell)* retentir; **the gate clanged shut** le portail se ferma avec un bruit métallique

clanger ['klæŋə(r)] *n Fam* gaffe *f;* **to drop a c.** faire une gaffe

clank [klæŋk] **1** *n* bruit *m* métallique
2 *vi* cliqueter

clap [klæp] **1** *n* **(a)** *(with hands)* **to give sb a c.** applaudir qn; **a c. of thunder** un coup de tonnerre **(b)** *very Fam* **the c.** la chaude-pisse
2 *vt (pt & pp* **clapped***)* **(a)** *(applaud)* applaudir; **to c. one's hands** *(once)* frapper dans ses mains; **to c. sb on the back** donner une tape sur le dos à qn **(b)** *Fam* **to c. sb in prison** coller qn en prison; *Fam* **to c. eyes on sb/sth** voir qn/qch
3 *vi (applaud)* applaudir

clapped-out ['klæpt'aʊt] *adj Br Fam (car, machine)* déglingué(e)

clapper ['klæpə(r)] *n (of bell)* battant *m*

clapping ['klæpɪŋ] *n (applause)* applaudissements *mpl*

claptrap ['klæptræp] *n Fam* bêtises *fpl*

claret ['klærət] **1** *n (wine, colour)* bordeaux *m* (rouge)
2 *adj (colour)* bordeaux

clarification [klærɪfɪ'keɪʃən] *n* clarification *f,* éclaircissement *m*

clarify ['klærɪfaɪ] *(pt & pp* **clarified***) vt* clarifier, éclaircir

clarinet [klærɪ'net] *n* clarinette *f*

clarity ['klærɪtɪ] *n* clarté *f*

clash [klæʃ] **1** *n* **(a)** *(of opinions, interests)* conflit *m; (between people, armies)* affrontement *m* **(b)** *(of metal objects)* fracas *m*
2 *vi* **to c. with sb** s'affronter avec qn; **police clashed with protesters** il y a eu des heurts entre la police et les manifestants **(b)** *(of evidence, explanations)* ne pas correspondre; *(of colours)* jurer **(c)** *(of events)* **to c. with** tomber en même temps que **(d)** *(of metal objects)* s'entrechoquer

clasp [klɑːsp] **1** n (on necklace, purse) fermoir m; **c. knife** canif m
2 vt (grip) serrer; (embrace) étreindre; **to c. sb's hand** serrer la main à qn
class [klɑːs] **1** n (in school, category, social group) classe f; **to be in a c. of one's own** être insurpassable; **c. struggle** lutte f des classes
2 vt (classify) classer (**as** parmi)
classic ['klæsɪk] **1** n (**a**) (book) classique m (**b**) Sch & Univ **classics** lettres fpl classiques
2 adj classique
classical ['klæsɪkəl] adj classique; **c. music** musique f classique
classification [klæsɪfɪ'keɪʃən] n classification f; (of students) classement m
classified ['klæsɪfaɪd] **1** n the classifieds (in newspaper) les petites annonces fpl
2 adj (**a**) (secret) confidentiel(elle) (**b**) **c. advertisements** (in newspaper) petites annonces fpl
classify ['klæsɪfaɪ] (pt & pp classified) vt classer
classmate ['klɑːsmeɪt] n camarade mf de classe
classroom ['klɑːsruːm] n (salle f de) classe f
classy ['klɑːsɪ] adj Fam qui a de la classe; (bar) chic
clatter ['klætə(r)] **1** n (of shoes) claquement m; (of dishes) fracas m
2 vi (of falling object) faire du bruit; (of metallic object) faire un bruit de ferraille; (of dishes) s'entrechoquer bruyamment; **she was clattering around in the kitchen** elle s'activait bruyamment dans la cuisine
clause [klɔːz] n (of contract) clause f; Gram proposition f
claustrophobia [klɔːstrə'fəʊbɪə] n claustrophobie f
claustrophobic [klɔːstrə'fəʊbɪk] adj (person) claustrophobe
clavicle ['klævɪkəl] n clavicule f
claw [klɔː] **1** n (of animal) griffe f; (of bird of prey) serre f; (of crab, lobster) pince f; **c. hammer** arrache-clou m
2 vt (scratch) griffer; Fig **to c. one's way to the top** parvenir au sommet à force de travail
▸ **claw back** vt (money) récupérer
clay [kleɪ] n argile f, (terre f) glaise f; **c. court** (for tennis) court m en terre battue; **c. pigeon** pigeon m d'argile; **c. pigeon shooting** ball-trap m
clean [kliːn] **1** n **to give sth a good c.** bien nettoyer qch
2 adj (**a**) (not dirty) propre; (piece of paper) blanc (blanche); **a c. game/fight** un jeu/une bataille dans les règles; **c. living** vie f saine; **to have a c. driving licence** avoir tous ses points sur son permis de conduire (**b**) (not obscene) décent(e); **it's good c. fun** c'est innocent (**c**) (clear) (shape, outline) net (nette); **to make a c. break** (of couple) rompre une bonne fois pour toutes
3 adv (**a**) (completely) **to cut c. through sth** couper qch net; Fam **I c. forgot** j'ai complètement oublié (**b**) Fam **to come c.** dire la vérité
4 vt nettoyer; **to c. one's teeth/hands** se laver les dents/mains
▸ **clean out** vt sep (**a**) (cupboard, room) nettoyer à fond (**b**) Fam (leave without money) nettoyer, plumer
▸ **clean up 1** vt sep nettoyer
2 vi (**a**) (tidy up) nettoyer; (wash oneself) se laver (**b**) Fam (win money) toucher un gros paquet
clean-cut ['kliːn'kʌt] adj (features) net (nette), bien dessiné(e)
cleaner ['kliːnə(r)] n (person) agent m de service; (substance) produit m de nettoyage; **c.'s** (shop) pressing m; Fam **to take sb to the c.'s** (cheat) nettoyer ou plumer qn

cleaning ['kliːnɪŋ] n nettoyage m; (housework) ménage m; **c. lady** femme f de ménage
cleanliness ['klenlɪnɪs] n (of place, person) propreté f
cleanly ['kliːnlɪ] adv proprement; (fight) dans les règles
cleanse [klenz] vt nettoyer; (skin) démaquiller
cleanser ['klenzə(r)] n (for skin) démaquillant m
clean-shaven ['kliːn'ʃeɪvən] adj rasé(e) de près
cleansing lotion ['klenzɪŋləʊʃən] n lait m démaquillant
clear [klɪə(r)] **1** n **to be in the c.** (not under suspicion) être lavé(e) de tout soupçon; (out of danger) être hors de danger
2 adj (**a**) (liquid, image, directions) clair(e); (picture) net (nette); (glass) transparent(e); (skin) net; **on a c. day** par temps clair; **all c.!** la voie est libre!; **to have a c. conscience** avoir la conscience tranquille; **as c. as a bell** (of voice, sound) cristallin(e); **c. profit** bénéfice m net; **c. winner** vainqueur m incontesté (**b**) (obvious) clair(e), évident(e); **to make it c. to sb that...** bien faire comprendre à qn que...; **to make oneself c.** se faire comprendre; **I wasn't c. what she meant** je n'étais pas sûr d'avoir parfaitement compris ce qu'elle voulait dire (**c**) (space, road, passageway) libre (**d**) (authorize) (proposal, request) approuver; **I'll need to c. it with the boss** il faut que j'obtienne la permission du patron
5 vi (**a**) (of weather) s'éclaircir; (of sky) se dégager; (of fog) se lever (**b**) (of cheque) **the cheque hasn't cleared yet** le chèque n'a pas encore été viré
▸ **clear away** vt sep (dishes) ranger; (obstruction) enlever
▸ **clear off** vi Br Fam (leave) filer, se tirer; **c. off!** fiche le camp!
▸ **clear out 1** vt sep (cupboard) vider; (garage, shed) débarrasser
2 vi Fam (leave) filer, se tirer
▸ **clear up 1** vt sep (**a**) (room) ranger (**b**) (doubt, misunderstanding) dissiper; **to c. up a matter** tirer une affaire au clair
2 vi (of weather) s'éclaircir
clearance ['klɪərəns] n (**a**) Com **c. sale** liquidation f (**b**) (authorization) autorisation f (**c**) (space) espace m (libre)
clear-cut ['klɪə'kʌt] adj (division, outline, feature) net (nette); (opinion) tranché(e); **it's not as c. as that** ce n'est pas aussi simple que ça
clear-headed ['klɪə'hedɪd] adj lucide
clearing ['klɪərɪŋ] n (in forest) clairière f
clearing house ['klɪərɪŋhaʊs] n Fin chambre f de compensation
clearly ['klɪəlɪ] adv (**a**) (explain, write) clairement; (see) bien (**b**) (obviously) évidemment; **he is c. wrong** il est évident qu'il a tort
clearness ['klɪənɪs] n clarté f; (of image) netteté f
clearout ['klɪəraʊt] n to have a c. faire le nettoyage par le vide

(but she was clattering...)

3 adv **to steer c. of** éviter; **stand c. of the closing doors!** attention à la fermeture automatique des portières!
4 vt (**a**) (road, area) dégager; **the police cleared the square of demonstrators** la police a forcé les manifestants à évacuer la place; **to c. one's throat** se racler la gorge; **to c. the table** débarrasser la table; **to c. a debt** s'acquitter d'une dette; Fig **to c. the decks** déblayer le terrain; Fig **to c. the way for sth** ouvrir la voie à qch; Fig **to c. the air** mettre les choses au point (**b**) (exonerate) disculper, innocenter; **to c. sb of blame** disculper qn; **to c. sb's name** blanchir (le nom de) qn (**c**) (jump over) sauter, franchir

clear-sighted ['klɪə'saɪtɪd] *adj (perceptive)* clairvoyant(e)

cleavage ['kli:vɪdʒ] *n (of woman)* décolleté *m*

cleave [kli:v] *(pt* **cleaved** *or* **cleft** [kleft] *or* **clove** [kləʊv], *pp* **cleaved** *or* **cleft** *or* **cloven** ['kləʊvən]) *vt Lit* fendre
► **cleave to** *(pt & pp* **cleaved)** *vt insep Formal* être fidèle à

cleaver ['kli:və(r)] *n* hachoir *m*

clef [klef] *n Mus* clé *f,* clef *f*

cleft [kleft] **1** *n* fissure *f*
2 *adj* fendu(e); **c. palate** division *f* palatine; **to be caught in a c.** stick *(in awkward situation)* être entre le marteau et l'enclume
3 *pt & pp of* **cleave**

clemency ['klemənsɪ] *n* clémence *f*

clementine ['klemənti:n] *n* clémentine *f*

clench [klentʃ] *vt* **to c. one's fist/teeth** serrer le poing/les dents

Cleopatra ['kli:əʊ'pætrə] *n* Cléopâtre

clergy ['klɜ:dʒɪ] *n* clergé *m*

clergyman ['klɜ:dʒɪmən] *n* ecclésiastique *m; (Protestant)* pasteur *m; (Catholic)* prêtre *m*

cleric ['klerɪk] *n Rel* ecclésiastique *m*

clerical ['klerɪkəl] *adj* **(a)** *(administrative)* **c. assistant** employé(e) *m,f* de bureau, **c. work** travail *m* de bureau **(b)** *Rel* clérical(e)

clerk [klɑ:k, *Am* klɜ:rk] *n* **(a)** *(office worker)* employé(e) *m,f* de bureau **(b)** *Am (in shop)* vendeur(euse) *m,f*

clever ['klevə(r)] *adj (intelligent)* intelligent(e); *(plan, idea)* ingénieux(euse); **to be c. with one's hands** être adroit(e) de ses mains

cleverly ['klevəlɪ] *adv (intelligently)* intelligemment; *(planned)* ingénieusement

cleverness ['klevənɪs] *n (intelligence)* intelligence *f; (of plan)* ingéniosité *f; (skill)* adresse *f*

cliché ['kli:ʃeɪ] *n* cliché *m*

click [klɪk] **1** *n (sound)* petit bruit *m* sec
2 *vt (fingers, tongue)* faire claquer; **to c. one's heels** claquer les talons
3 *vi* **(a)** *(make a sound)* faire un petit bruit sec **(b)** *Fam (become obvious)* faire tilt **(c)** *Fam (of people)* **we clicked straight away** ça a accroché tout de suite entre nous

client ['klaɪənt] *n* client(e) *m,f*

clientele [kli:ən'tel] *n* clientèle *f*

cliff [klɪf] *n* falaise *f*

cliffhanger ['klɪfhæŋə(r)] *n (situation, story)* **it was a real c.** il y a eu du suspense jusqu'au bout

climactic [klaɪ'mæktɪk] *adj* qui constitue le point culminant

climate ['klaɪmət] *n* climat *m*

climatic [klaɪ'mætɪk] *adj* climatique

climax ['klaɪmæks] **1** *n (of series of events)* paroxysme *m; (of reign, career)* apogée *m; (of film, book)* point *m* culminant; *(sexual)* orgasme *m*
2 *vi (of series of events)* atteindre son paroxysme; *(of reign, career)* atteindre son apogée; *(of film, book)* atteindre son point culminant; *(sexually)* atteindre l'orgasme

climb [klaɪm] **1** *n* montée *f,* ascension *f*
2 *vt (tree)* grimper à; *(mountain)* faire l'ascension de; *(rock face)* escalader; *(stairs)* monter
3 *vi (of road, prices)* grimper; *(of plane)* prendre de l'altitude, monter; **to c. over sth** passer par-dessus qch
► **climb down 1** *vt insep (descend)* descendre
2 *vi* **(a)** *(descend)* descendre **(b)** *Fig (in argument)* revenir sur sa décision

climber ['klaɪmə(r)] *n* **(a)** *(mountaineer)* alpiniste *mf* **(b)** *(plant)* plante *f* grimpante

climbing ['klaɪmɪŋ] **1** *n (hill-walking)* randonnée *f* en montagne; *(of rockface)* escalade *f; (mountaineering)* alpinisme *m;* **c. frame** cage *f* à poules
2 *adj (plant)* grimpant(e)

clinch [klɪntʃ] **1** *n (of fighters)* corps à corps *m; (of lovers)* étreinte *f*
2 *vt (settle) (deal)* conclure; *(argument)* résoudre; **that clinches it!** voilà qui règle le problème une fois pour toutes!

cling [klɪŋ] *(pt & pp* **clung** [klʌŋ]) *vi* **to c. to** *(rope, person)* s'accrocher à; *Fig (opinion)* persister dans; *(faith)* se raccrocher à

clingfilm ['klɪŋfɪlm] *n Br* film *m* alimentaire

clinic ['klɪnɪk] *n (part of hospital)* service *m; Br (private hospital)* clinique *f*

clinical ['klɪnɪkəl] *adj* **(a)** *Med* clinique **(b)** *(unemotional)* froid(e)

clink[1] [klɪŋk] **1** *n (sound)* tintement *m*
2 *vt* faire tinter; **to c. glasses with sb** trinquer avec qn
3 *vi (of glasses)* tinter

clink[2] *n very Fam (prison)* taule *f*

clip[1] [klɪp] **1** *n (for paper)* trombone *m; (for hair)* barrette *f*
2 *vt (pt & pp* **clipped)** *(paper)* attacher *(avec un trombone)* (to à)

clip[2] **1** *n* **(a)** *Fam (blow)* **to give sb a c.** round the ear flanquer une taloche à qn **(b)** *(of film, programme)* extrait *m*
2 *(pt & pp* **clipped)** *vt* **(a)** *(hit)* **to c. sb round the ear** flanquer une taloche à qn **(b)** *(hedge)* tailler; *(ticket)* poinçonner; *(dog)* couper les poils à; *(hair, nails)* couper; *Fig* **to c. sb's wings** réduire la marge de manœuvre de qn

clipboard ['klɪpbɔ:d] *n* planchette *f* porte-papiers *(à pince)*

clip-on ['klɪpɒn] *adj* **c. earring** clip *m,* **c. microphone** micro-cravate *m;* **c. sunglasses** = verres teintés que l'on fixe à une autre paire de lunettes

clipped [klɪpt] *adj (speech, tone)* saccadé(e)

clipper ['klɪpə(r)] *n (ship)* clipper *m*

clippers ['klɪpəz] *npl (for hair)* tondeuse *f; (for nails)* coupe-ongles *m inv; (for hedge)* cisaille *f*

clipping ['klɪpɪŋ] *n (from newspaper)* coupure *f*

clique [kli:k] *n* clique *f*

clitoris ['klɪtərɪs] *n* clitoris *m*

cloak [kləʊk] **1** *n* cape *f; Fig* **under the c.** of darkness sous le couvert de la nuit
2 *vt Fig* **cloaked in secrecy** enveloppé(e) de mystère

cloak-and-dagger [kləʊkən'dægə(r)] *adj (film, book)* d'espionnage; *Fig (mysterious)* mystérieux(euse)

cloakroom ['kləʊkru:m] *n* vestiaire *m*

clobber[1] ['klɒbə(r)] *n Br Fam (clothes)* frusques *fpl,* fringues *fpl; (belongings)* barda *m*

clobber[2] *vt Fam (hit)* tabasser; *(defeat)* battre à plate couture

clock [klɒk] **1** *n* **(a)** *(large)* horloge *f; (small)* pendule *f;* **round the c.** vingt-quatre heures sur vingt-quatre; **a race against the c.** une course contre la montre; **to put the clocks forward/back** *(in spring, autumn)* avancer/retarder les pendules; *Fig* **to turn the c. back** revenir en arrière; **c. radio** radio-réveil *m; Fam (mileometer)* compteur *m* kilométrique
2 *vt (measure speed of)* chronométrer; *(reach speed of)* atteindre
► **clock in** *vi* pointer *(en arrivant sur son lieu de travail)*
► **clock off** *vi* pointer *(en quittant son lieu de travail)*

▸ **clock on** = clock in
▸ **clock out** = clock off
▸ **clock up** *vt sep (profits)* réaliser; *(votes)* totaliser; **this car has clocked up 12,000 miles** cette voiture a 12 000 miles au compteur
clockmaker ['klɒkmeɪkə(r)] *n* horloger(ère) *m,f*
clockwise ['klɒkwaɪz] *adv* dans le sens des aiguilles d'une montre
clockwork ['klɒkwɜːk] **1** *n* **to go like c.** *(of interview, ceremony)* marcher comme sur des roulettes; **to run like c.** *(of office, system)* être réglé(e) comme du papier à musique
2 *adj (toy)* mécanique
clod [klɒd] *n (of earth)* motte *f*
clog [klɒg] **1** *n (shoe)* sabot *m*
2 *vt (pt & pp* **clogged)** *(block)* boucher
3 *vi* se boucher
▸ **clog up 1** *vt sep* boucher
2 *vi* se boucher
cloister ['klɔɪstə(r)] *n* cloître *m*
cloistered ['klɔɪstəd] *adj* **to lead a c. life** mener une vie de reclus(e)
clone [kləʊn] **1** *n also Fig* clone *m*
2 *vt Biol* cloner
close¹ [kləʊs] **1** *adj* **(a)** *(in distance, time, relationship)* proche; **to be in c. contact with sb** être en contact étroit avec qn; **a c. friend** un ami intime; **a c. relative** un proche parent; **that was a c. call** *or* **shave** il s'en est fallu de peu; **at c. quarters** de près; **at c. range** de près; **c. combat** corps à corps *m* **(b)** *(inspection)* minutieux(euse); *(attention)* soutenu(e); **to keep a c. eye** *or* **watch on sb/sth** surveiller qn/qch de près **(c)** *(weather)* lourd(e); *(room)* qui sent le renfermé **(d)** *(contest, election)* serré(e)
2 *n (cul-de-sac)* impasse *f*
3 *adv (near)* près; **to hold sb c.** serrer qn; **c. to** près de; **c. to tears** au bord des larmes; **c. to victory** proche de la victoire; **to come c. to death** frôler la mort; **to be c. to sb** *(emotionally)* être proche de qn; **c. at hand** à proximité; **to follow c. behind sb** suivre qn de près; **to be c. on fifty** friser la cinquantaine; **c. up** de près
close² [kləʊz] **1** *n (end)* fin *f*; **to draw to a c.** tirer à sa fin; **to bring sth to a c.** clore qch
2 *vt* **(a)** *(door, eyes, book, road)* fermer; *Fig* **to c. ranks** around sb faire bloc autour de qn **(b)** *(meeting, debate)* clore; *(account)* fermer; *(deal)* conclure **(c)** *(business, shop)* fermer
3 *vi (of shop, business)* fermer; *(of door)* se fermer
▸ **close down 1** *vt (production, operations)* cesser; *(business, factory)* fermer
2 *vi (of business, factory)* fermer; **Channel 6 closes down at midnight** les émissions sur Channel 6 se terminent à minuit
▸ **close in** *vi (of night)* tomber; **to c. in on sb** se rapprocher de qn
▸ **close up 1** *vt sep (shop)* fermer
2 *vi* **(a)** *(of wound, hole)* se refermer **(b)** *(of shopkeeper)* fermer
close-cropped ['kləʊs'krɒpt] *adj (hair)* coupé(e) ras
closed [kləʊzd] *adj* fermé(e); **c. circuit television** télévision *f* en circuit fermé; **behind c. doors** à huis clos; *Ind* **c. shop** = usine ou société qui n'embauche que des travailleurs syndiqués
close-fitting ['kləʊs'fɪtɪŋ] *adj* bien ajusté(e)
close-knit ['kləʊs'nɪt] *adj (community, family)* très soudé(e)
closely ['kləʊslɪ] *adv* **(a)** *(examine, listen, watch)* attentivement; *(resemble)* beaucoup; **to be c. related** *(of*

concepts)* être étroitement liés(es); *(of people)* être proches parents; **c. contested** très serré(e) **(b)** *(populated)* densément; **c. packed** très serré(e)
closeness ['kləʊsnɪs] *n (physical proximity)* proximité *f*; *(of relationship, contact)* intimité *f*
close-run ['kləʊs'rʌn] *adj (election, race)* serré(e)
close-set ['kləʊs'set] *adj (eyes)* rapproché(e)
closet ['klɒzɪt] **1** *n* placard *m*; *Fig* **to come out of the c.** révéler son homosexualité
2 *adj* **c. homosexual** = personne qui cache son homosexualité; *Hum* **he's a c.** Cliff Richard fan il n'ose pas avouer qu'il aime Cliff Richard
3 *vt* enfermer; **to c. oneself away** s'enfermer, s'isoler
close-up ['kləʊsʌp] *n* gros plan *m*; **in c.** en gros plan
closing ['kləʊzɪŋ] *n* fermeture *f*; **c. date** date *f* limite; **c. prices** cours *mpl* de clôture; **c. speech** discours *m* de clôture; **c. time** heure *f* de fermeture
closure ['kləʊʒə(r)] *n* *(of company, shop)* fermeture *f* *(définitive)*
clot [klɒt] **1** *n* **(a)** *(of blood)* caillot *m* **(b)** *Fam (stupid person)* andouille *f*
2 *vi (pt & pp* **clotted)** *(of blood)* (se) coaguler
cloth [klɒθ] *n* **(a)** *(material)* tissu *m*; **a man of the c.** un membre du clergé **(b)** *(duster)* chiffon *m*
clothe [kləʊð] *(pt & pp* **clad** [klæd] *or* **clothed)** *vt* vêtir, habiller
clothes [kləʊðz] *npl* vêtements *mpl*; **to put one's c. on** s'habiller; **to take one's c. off** se déshabiller; **c. brush** brosse *f* à habits; **c. horse** séchoir *m (à linge)*; **c. line** corde *f* à linge; **c. peg** pince *f* à linge
clothing ['kləʊðɪŋ] *n (clothes)* vêtements *mpl*; **an article of c.** un vêtement; **the c. industry** l'industrie *f* du vêtement
clotted cream ['klɒtɪd'kriːm] *n* = crème fraîche très épaisse, typique du sud-ouest de l'Angleterre
cloud [klaʊd] **1** *n* **(a)** nuage *m*; *Fig (of insects)* nuée *f* **(b)** *(idioms)* **to leave under a c.** partir en disgrâce; **to have one's head in the clouds** être dans les nuages; *Fam* **to be on c.** nine être aux anges
2 *vt* **(a)** *(mirror)* embuer **(b)** *(happiness)* jeter une ombre sur; *(judgement)* affecter; **to c. the issue** embrouiller la question
▸ **cloud over** *vi (of sky)* se couvrir
cloudburst ['klaʊdbɜːst] *n* averse *f*
cloudless ['klaʊdlɪs] *adj* sans nuages
cloudy ['klaʊdɪ] *adj* **(a)** *(sky, day)* nuageux(euse) **(b)** *(liquid)* trouble
clout [klaʊt] *Fam* **1** *n* **(a)** *(blow)* coup *m*; **to give sb a c.** **(with sth)** frapper qn (avec qch) **(b)** *(power, influence)* influence *f*; **to have a lot of c.** avoir le bras long
2 *vt (hit)* flanquer une taloche à
clove¹ [kləʊv] *n (of garlic)* gousse *f*
clove² [kləʊv] *n (spice)* clou *m* de girofle
clove³ *pt of* cleave
cloven ['kləʊvən] **1** *adj* **c. hoof** sabot *m* fendu
2 *pp of* cleave
clover ['kləʊvə(r)] *n* trèfle *m*; *Fig* **to be in c.** être comme un coq en pâte
clown [klaʊn] **1** *n* clown *m*; **to act the c.** faire le clown
2 *vi* **to c. about** *or* **around** faire le clown
cloying ['klɔɪɪŋ] *adj (taste, smell)* écœurant(e)
club [klʌb] **1** *n* **(a)** *(society)* club *m*; *Fam Fig* **join the c.!** tu n'es pas le seul/la seule! **(b)** *(nightclub)* boîte *f* (de nuit) **(c)** *(weapon)* massue *f*, gourdin *m*; *(in golf)* club *m* **(d)** **clubs** *(in cards)* trèfle *m*; **ace of clubs** as *m* de trèfle

2 vt (pt & pp **clubbed**) (hit) frapper avec une massue
3 vi to go clubbing aller en boîte
▸ **club together** vi se cotiser (**to buy** pour acheter)
clubhouse ['klʌbhaʊs] n pavillon m
cluck [klʌk] **1** n gloussement m
2 vi glousser
clue [klu:] n (in crime, mystery) indice m; (in crossword) définition f; **to give sb a c.** donner un indice à qn, mettre qn sur la voie; Fam **where's John? – I haven't (got) a clue** ou est John? – je n'ai pas la moindre idée; Fam **he hasn't a c.** il est vraiment nul
▸ **clue up** vt sep Fam **to be clued up (on sth)** être très calé(e) (en qch)
clueless ['klu:lɪs] adj Fam nul (nulle)
clump [klʌmp] **1** n (a) (of bushes) massif m; (of people) groupe m (b) (sound) bruit m bref et sourd
2 vi to c. about marcher d'un pas lourd
clumsiness ['klʌmzɪnɪs] n (of person, movement) maladresse f
clumsy ['klʌmzɪ] adj (person, movement) maladroit(e)
clung [klʌŋ] pt & pp of **cling**
cluster ['klʌstə(r)] **1** n (of grapes) grappe f; (of people, islands, houses) groupe m
2 vi to c. round sb/sth se grouper autour de qn/qch
clutch¹ [klʌtʃ] **1** n (a) (in car) embrayage m; **to let the c. in/out** embrayer/débrayer; **c. pedal** pédale f d'embrayage (b) (grasp) **to fall into sb's clutches** tomber entre les griffes de qn
2 vt tenir fermement
3 vi **to c. at sth** s'agripper à qch; Fig **to c. at straws** se raccrocher à n'importe quoi
clutch² n (of eggs) couvée f
clutter ['klʌtə(r)] **1** n désordre m; **in a c.** en désordre
2 vt encombrer; **to be cluttered (up) with sth** être encombré(e) de qch
cluttered ['klʌtəd] adj encombré(e)
cm n (abbr **centimetre(s)**) cm
CNAA [si:ɛneɪ'eɪ] n Br (abbr **Council for National Academic Awards**) = organisme chargé de délivrer les diplômes dans les établissements d'enseignement supérieur non universitaires
CND [si:en'di:] n Br (abbr **Campaign for Nuclear Disarmament**) = mouvement prônant le désarmement nucléaire
CO [si:'əʊ] n Mil (abbr **Commanding Officer**) chef m de corps
Co, co [kəʊ] n (abbr **company**) Cie; Fig **Jane and co** Jane et compagnie
c/o [si:'əʊ] (abbr **care of**) chez, aux bons soins de
coach [kəʊtʃ] **1** n (a) Br (bus) car m; (horse-drawn carriage) carrosse m; (section of train) voiture f, wagon m; **c. party** excursionnistes mpl (voyageant en car); **c. trip** excursion f en car (b) (of athlete, team) entraîneur(euse) m,f
2 vt (athlete, team) entraîner; **to c. sb for an exam** donner des leçons particulières à qn en préparation à un examen
coachbuilder ['kəʊtʃbɪldə(r)] n Aut carrossier m
coagulant [kəʊ'ægjʊlənt] n Med coagulant m
coagulate [kəʊ'ægjʊleɪt] vi coaguler
coal [kəʊl] n (a) charbon m; **c. bunker** coffre m à charbon; **c. mine** mine f de charbon; **c. miner** mineur m; **c. mining** extraction f du charbon; **c. tar** goudron m de houille (b) (idioms) **to carry coals to Newcastle** porter de l'eau à la rivière; **to haul sb over the coals** réprimander qn vertement
coalesce [kəʊə'les] vi s'unir

coalfield ['kəʊlfi:ld] n bassin m houiller
coalition [kəʊə'lɪʃən] n coalition f
coalman ['kəʊlmæn] n charbonnier m
coarse [kɔ:s] adj (a) (person, language) grossier(ère), vulgaire (b) (surface, texture) grossier(ère); (hair) rêche
coarsely ['kɔ:slɪ] adv (a) (vulgarly) vulgairement (b) (roughly) **c. chopped/ground** haché(e)/moulu(e) grossièrement
coarseness ['kɔ:snɪs] n (a) (of person, language) grossièreté f, vulgarité f (b) (of surface, texture) grossièreté f
coast [kəʊst] **1** n côte f; Fig **the c. is clear** la voie est libre
2 vi (in car, on bicycle) avancer en roue libre; Fig **she coasted through her exams** elle a eu ses examens haut la main
coastal ['kəʊstəl] adj côtier(ère)
coaster ['kəʊstə(r)] n (a) (for glass) dessous m de verre (b) (ship) caboteur m
coastguard ['kəʊstgɑ:d] n garde-côte m
coastline ['kəʊstlaɪn] n littoral m
coat [kəʊt] **1** n (a) (garment) manteau m; **c. hanger** cintre m; **c. hook** patère f (b) (of horse) robe f; (of dog) pelage m (c) (of snow, paint) couche f (d) (in heraldry) **c. of arms** armoiries fpl
2 vt (with mud, paint) couvrir (**with** de); (with chocolate, sugar) enrober (**with** de)
coating ['kəʊtɪŋ] n (of paint, dust) couche f; (of chocolate) enrobage m
co-author [kəʊ'ɔ:θə(r)] n coauteur m
2 vt **to c. a book with sb** écrire un livre en collaboration avec qn
coax [kəʊks] vt enjôler; **to c. sb to do** or **into doing sth** amener qn à faire qch par des cajoleries; **to c. sth out of sb** obtenir qch de qn par des cajoleries
cob [kɒb] n (a) (horse) cob m (b) (of corn) épi m
cobalt ['kəʊbɔ:lt] n cobalt m; **c. blue** bleu m de cobalt
cobble ['kɒbəl] **1** n pavé m
2 vt paver
▸ **cobble together** vt sep bricoler
cobbled ['kɒbəld] adj (path, street) pavé(e)
cobbler ['kɒblə(r)] n cordonnier m
cobblers ['kɒbləz] npl Br (a) very Fam (nonsense) conneries fpl (b) Vulg (testicles) couilles fpl
COBOL ['kəʊbɒl] n Comptr (abbr **Common Business Oriented Language**) Cobol m
cobra ['kəʊbrə] n cobra m
cobweb ['kɒbweb] n toile f d'araignée; Fig **I'm going for a walk to blow away the cobwebs** je vais faire un tour pour me rafraîchir les idées; Fig **to brush the cobwebs off sth** ressortir qch
cocaine [kəʊ'keɪn] n cocaïne f
cock [kɒk] **1** n (a) (male fowl) coq m; **c. sparrow** moineau m mâle (b) Vulg (penis) bit(t)e f
2 vt (gun) armer; **to c. its ears** (of horse, dog) dresser les oreilles
▸ **cock up** vt sep Br very Fam (plan, arrangement) foirer; (exam) se planter à
cockade [kɒ'keɪd] n cocarde f
cock-a-doodle-doo ['kɒkədu:dəl'du:] exclam cocorico!
cock-a-hoop ['kɒkə'hu:p] adj enchanté(e)
cockatoo [kɒkə'tu:] n cacatoès m
cocked [kɒkt] adj **to knock sb into a c. hat** (outclass) surpasser qn
cockerel ['kɒkərəl] n jeune coq m

cocker spaniel [kɒkə'spænjəl] *n* cocker *m*

cockeyed ['kɒkaɪd] *adj Fam (decision, plan)* farfelu(e)

cockfight ['kɒkfaɪt] *n* combat *m* de coqs

cockle ['kɒkəl] *n* (**a**) *(shellfish)* coque *f* (**b**) *Fam* **it warms the cockles of your heart** ça réchauffe le cœur

Cockney ['kɒknɪ] **1** *n* (**a**) *(person)* cockney *mf* (**b**) *(dialect)* cockney *m* **2** *adj* cockney

cockpit ['kɒkpɪt] *n* cabine *f* de pilotage, cockpit *m*

cockroach ['kɒkrəʊtʃ] *n* cafard *m*

cocksure ['kɒk'ʃʊə(r)] *adj (person, manner)* présomptueux(euse)

cocktail ['kɒkteɪl] *n also Fig* cocktail *m*; **c. bar** bar *m (où l'on sert des cocktails)*; **c. dress** robe *f* de cocktail; **c. lounge** bar confortable *(dans un pub, un hôtel)*; **c. party** cocktail; **c. shaker** shaker *m*; **c. stick** pique *f*

cocky ['kɒkɪ] *adj Fam* culotté(e)

cocoa ['kəʊkəʊ] *n (powder, drink)* cacao *m*; **c. butter** beurre *m* de cacao

coconut ['kəʊkənʌt] *n* noix *f* de coco; **c. milk** lait *m* de coco; **c. palm** cocotier *m*

cocoon [kə'kuːn] **1** *n also Fig* cocon *m*
2 *vt Fig (protect)* couver

COD [siː'əʊ'diː] *n Com (abbr* **cash on delivery)** paiement *m* à la livraison

cod [kɒd] *n* morue *f*; **c. liver oil** huile *f* de foie de morue

coddle ['kɒdəl] *vt (child)* dorloter

code [kəʊd] **1** *n* (**a**) *(cipher)* code *m*; **in c.** codé(e); **c. book** code; **c. name** nom *m* de code; **c. number** numéro *m* de code (**b**) *(rules)* code *m*; **c. of conduct** code de conduite; **c. of ethics** déontologie *f*
2 *vt (message)* coder

codeine ['kəʊdiːn] *n* codéine *f*

codify ['kəʊdɪfaɪ] *(pt & pp* **codified)** *vt* codifier

codswallop ['kɒdzwɒləp] *n Fam* foutaises *fpl*

coeducational [kəʊedjʊ'keɪʃənəl] *adj (school)* mixte

coefficient [kəʊɪ'fɪʃənt] *n Math* coefficient *m*

coerce [kəʊ'ɜːs] *vt* forcer, contraindre; **to c. sb into doing sth** contraindre qn à faire qch

coercion [kəʊ'ɜːʃən] *n* coercition *f*

coexist [kəʊɪg'zɪst] *vi* coexister

coexistence [kəʊɪg'zɪstəns] *n* coexistence *f*

C of E [siː'əv'iː] *adj Rel (abbr* **Church of England)** anglican(e)

coffee ['kɒfɪ] *n* café *m*; **c. bar** café; **c. bean** grain *m* de café; **c. break** pause-café *f*; **c. cup** tasse *f* à café; **c. grinder** moulin *m* à café; **c. grounds** marc *m* de café; **c. machine** *(in café)* percolateur *m*; *(vending machine)* machine *f* à café; *(in home)* cafetière *f* électrique; **c. mill** moulin à café; **c. pot** cafetière; **c. spoon** cuillère *f* à café; **c. table** table *f* basse; **c. table book** grand livre *m* illustré

coffer ['kɒfə(r)] *n (chest)* coffre *m*; *Fig* **the coffers** *(of company, country)* les caisses *fpl*

coffin ['kɒfɪn] *n* cercueil *m*

cog [kɒg] *n (tooth on gearwheel)* dent *f*; *(gearwheel)* roue *f* dentée, rouage *m*; *Fig* **a c. in the machinery** un rouage dans la machine

cogent ['kəʊdʒənt] *adj* convaincant(e)

cogitate ['kɒdʒɪteɪt] *vi Formal* méditer, réfléchir

cognac ['kɒnjæk] *n* cognac *m*

cognition [kɒg'nɪʃən] *n* cognition *f*

cohabit [kəʊ'hæbɪt] *vi* vivre en concubinage (**with** avec)

cohabitation [kəʊhæbɪ'teɪʃən] *n* concubinage *m*

coherence [kəʊ'hɪərəns] *n* cohérence *f*

coherent [kəʊ'hɪərənt] *adj* cohérent(e)

cohesion [kəʊ'hiːʒən] *n* cohésion *f*

cohesive [kəʊ'hiːsɪv] *adj* cohésif(ive)

coiffure [kwɑː'fjʊə(r)] *n* coiffure *f*

coil [kɔɪl] **1** *n* (**a**) *(of rope, wire)* rouleau *m*; *(electrical)* bobine *f*; *(contraceptive device)* stérilet *m* (**b**) *(single loop)* anneau *m*
2 *vt* enrouler (**around** autour de)
▸ **coil up** *vi (of snake)* se lover

coin [kɔɪn] **1** *n* pièce *f* (de monnaie); *Fig* **the other side of the c.** le revers de la médaille
2 *vt (phrase, word)* inventer; **to c. money** battre monnaie; *Fam* **he's coining it** il se fait un fric fou; *Hum & Ironic* **..., to c. a phrase ...,** comme on dit

coinage ['kɔɪnɪdʒ] *n* (**a**) *(coins)* monnaie *f* (**b**) *(word)* mot *m* nouveau, néologisme *m*; *(phrase)* expression *f* nouvelle

coincide [kəʊɪn'saɪd] *vi* coïncider (**with** avec)

coincidence [kəʊ'ɪnsɪdəns] *n* coïncidence *f*

coincidental [kəʊɪnsɪ'dentəl] *adj* fortuit(e)

coin-operated ['kɔɪnɒpəreɪtɪd] *adj (machine)* à pièces

coitus ['kɔɪtəs] *n Formal* coït *m*; **c. interruptus** coït interrompu

coke [kəʊk] *n* (**a**) *(fuel)* coke *m* (**b**) *Fam (cocaine)* coke *f*

col [kɒl] *(abbr* **column)** col

colander ['kɒləndə(r)] *n* passoire *f*

cold [kəʊld] **1** *n* (**a**) *(low temperature)* froid *m*; **to feel the c.** être frileux(euse); *Fig* **to be left out in the c.** rester sur la touche (**b**) *(illness)* rhume *m*; **to have a c.** avoir un rhume; **to catch a c.** attraper un rhume
2 *adj also Fig* froid(e); **I'm c.** j'ai froid; **it's c.** *(weather)* il fait froid; **to get c.** *(of food)* refroidir; *(of weather)* se refroidir; *also Fig* **to be in a c. sweat** avoir des sueurs froides; *Fam* **that leaves me c.** ça me laisse froid; **that's c. comfort** c'est une maigre consolation; *Fig* **to get c. feet (about sth)** hésiter (à faire qch) à la dernière minute; **to give sb the c. shoulder** snober qn; **c. cream** cold-cream *m*; *Met* **c. front** front *m* froid; **c. meats** viandes *fpl* froides; **c. sore** bouton *m* de fièvre; **c. start** *(of car)* démarrage *m* à froid; **c. storage** conservation *f* par le froid; **c. war** guerre *f* froide
3 *adv Fam* **to be out c.** faire qch à froid; *Fam Fig* **to be out c.** être sans connaissance

cold-blooded ['kəʊld'blʌdɪd] *adj (animal)* à sang froid; *Fig (person)* froid(e), insensible; **c. murder** meurtre *m* commis de sang-froid

cold-hearted ['kəʊld'hɑːtɪd] *adj (person, decision)* impitoyable

coldly ['kəʊldlɪ] *adv* froidement

coldness ['kəʊldnɪs] *n* froideur *f*

cold-shoulder ['kəʊld'ʃəʊldə(r)] *vt* snober

coleslaw ['kəʊlslɔː] *n* = salade de chou blanc à la mayonnaise

colic ['kɒlɪk] *n* colique *f*

collaborate [kə'læbəreɪt] *vi also Pej* collaborer (**with** avec)

collaboration [kəlæbə'reɪʃən] *n also Pej* collaboration *f*

collaborator [kə'læbəreɪtə(r)] *n also Pej* collaborateur(trice) *m,f*

collage ['kɒlɑːʒ] *n* collage *m*

collapse [kə'læps] **1** *n (of building, prices)* effondrement *m*
2 *vi (of person, building, prices)* s'effondrer, s'écrouler

collapsible [kə'læpsəbəl] *adj (table, bed)* pliant(e)

collar ['kɒlə(r)] **1** *n (of shirt)* col *m*; *(for dog)* collier *m*
2 *vt Fam (seize)* pincer

collarbone ['kɒləbəʊn] n clavicule f
collate [kə'leɪt] vt rassembler
collateral [kə'lætərəl] **1** n Fin nantissement m
2 adj Mil **c. damage** victimes fpl civiles
colleague ['kɒliːg] n collègue mf
collect [kə'lekt] **1** adv Am **to call sb c.** appeler qn en PCV
2 vt (**a**) (stamps, paintings) collectionner, faire collection de (**b**) (gather) (belongings) rassembler; (information, news) recueillir; (rubbish) ramasser; (taxes) lever; **to c. sb** (pick up) passer prendre qn (**c**) (compose) **to c. one's thoughts** se concentrer; **to c. oneself** se calmer **3** vi (of people) se rassembler; (of things) s'amasser; (of dust) s'accumuler
collected [kə'lektɪd] adj (**a**) (calm) calme (**b**) **c. works** œuvres fpl complètes
collection [kə'lekʃən] n (**a**) (of stamps, paintings) collection f (**b**) (act of collecting) (of money) recouvrement m; (of rubbish) ramassage m; (of taxes) levée f; **to take a c.** (for charity) faire une collecte; **c. plate** (in church) plat m de quête
collective [kə'lektɪv] **1** n (group) collectif m; (farm) coopérative f agricole **2** adj collectif(ive); **c. bargaining** = négociations afin d'établir une convention collective; **c. noun** collectif m
collectively [kə'lektɪvlɪ] adv collectivement
collectivize [kə'lektɪvaɪz] vt collectiviser
collector [kə'lektə(r)] n (**a**) (of stamps, paintings) collectionneur(euse) m,f; **c.'s item** pièce f de collection (**b**) **c. of taxes** percepteur m
college ['kɒlɪdʒ] n Br (of further education) établissement m d'enseignement supérieur; Br (part of university) = association d'enseignants et d'étudiants au sein de certaines universités, disposant d'une semi-autonomie administrative; Am (university) université f; **to be at c.** être étudiant(e); **c. of education** ≃ école f normale
collide [kə'laɪd] vi entrer en collision (**with** avec)
collie ['kɒlɪ] n colley m
colliery ['kɒlɪərɪ] (pl collieries) n houillère f, mine f de charbon
collision [kə'lɪʒən] n collision f; Fig **to be on a c. course** aller droit au conflit
colloquial [kə'ləʊkwɪəl] adj familier(ère)
colloquialism [kə'ləʊkwɪəlɪzəm] n expression f familière
collude [kə'luːd] vi être de connivence (**with** avec)
collusion [kə'luːʒən] n collusion f; **to be in c. with sb** être de connivence avec qn
collywobbles ['kɒlɪwɒbəlz] npl Fam **to have the c.** avoir la trouille
cologne [kə'ləʊn] n eau f de Cologne
Colombia [kə'lʌmbɪə] n la Colombie
Colombian [kə'lʌmbɪən] **1** n Colombien(enne) m,f **2** adj colombien(enne)
colon ['kəʊlən] n (**a**) Anat côlon m (**b**) (punctuation mark) deux-points m
colonel ['kɜːnəl] n colonel m
colonial [kə'ləʊnɪəl] adj colonial(e)
colonialism [kə'ləʊnɪəlɪzəm] n colonialisme m
colonist ['kɒlənɪst] n colon m
colonize ['kɒlənaɪz] vt coloniser
colonnade [kɒlə'neɪd] n Archit colonnade f
colony ['kɒlənɪ] (pl colonies) n colonie f
color, colored etc Am = colour, coloured etc
colossal [kə'lɒsəl] adj colossal(e)

colour, Am **color** ['kʌlə(r)] **1** n (**a**) couleur f; **what c. is it?** de quelle couleur est-ce?; **c. bar** (racial discrimination) discrimination f raciale; **c. scheme** coloris mpl, couleurs fpl; **c. supplement** (of newspaper) supplément m en couleurs; **c. television** télévision f couleur (**b**) (idioms) **to be off c.** (of person) ne pas être dans son assiette; **to give c. to a story** rendre un récit plus vivant; **let's see the c. of your money** voyons la couleur de ton argent; **to pass with flying colours** être reçu(e) brillamment ou haut la main; **to show one's true colours** se montrer sous son vrai jour; **to nail one's colours to the mast** afficher ses opinions **2** vt (**a**) (of chemical, dye) colorer; (with felt-tips, crayons) colorier; **to c. one's hair** se faire une couleur (**b**) Fig (judgement, view) fausser **3** vi (blush) rougir
▸ **colour in,** Am **color in** vt sep colorier
colour-blind, Am **color-blind** ['kʌləblaɪnd] adj daltonien(enne)
colour-coded, Am **color-coded** ['kʌləkəʊdɪd] adj différencié(e) par des couleurs
coloured, Am **colored** ['kʌləd] adj (**a**) (illustration) en couleurs; (pen, ink) de couleur; **brightly c.** aux couleurs vives; Fig **a highly c. narrative** un récit haut en couleurs (**b**) (person) de couleur
colourful, Am **colorful** ['kʌləfʊl] adj coloré(e); (vivid) coloré, pittoresque; **a c. character** un personnage haut en couleurs
colouring, Am **coloring** ['kʌlərɪŋ] n (**a**) (in food) colorants mpl (**b**) (complexion) teint m; **to have dark/fair c.** avoir le teint mat/clair (**c**) **c. book** album m à colorier
colourless, Am **colorless** ['kʌlələs] adj (**a**) (clear) incolore (**b**) Fig (dull) insipide, fade
colt [kəʊlt] n poulain m
Columbus [kə'lʌmbəs] n **Christopher C.** Christophe Colomb
column ['kɒləm] n (of troops, text, in building) colonne f; (newspaper feature) rubrique f
columnist ['kɒləmɪst] n (for newspaper, magazine) chroniqueur(euse) m,f
coma ['kəʊmə] n coma m; **to be in/go into a c.** être/tomber dans le coma
comatose ['kəʊmətəʊs] adj also Fig comateux(euse)
comb [kəʊm] **1** n (**a**) (for hair) peigne m; **to give one's hair a c.** se donner un coup de peigne (**b**) (of cock) crête f **2** vt (**a**) (hair) peigner; **to c. one's hair** se peigner (**b**) (search) ratisser, passer au peigne fin
combat ['kɒmbæt] **1** n combat m; **c. jacket** veste f de treillis; **c. trousers** battledress m; **c. zone** zone f de combat **2** vt (disease, prejudice, crime) combattre
combatant ['kɒmbətənt] n & adj combattant(e) m,f
combination [kɒmbɪ'neɪʃən] n combinaison f; **a c. of circumstances** un concours de circonstances; **c. lock** serrure f à combinaison
combine 1 n ['kɒmbaɪn] (**a**) c. (**harvester**) moissonneuse-batteuse f (**b**) Econ cartel m **2** [kəm'baɪn] vt combiner, allier; **to c. business with pleasure** joindre l'utile à l'agréable **3** [kəm'baɪn] vi (of people) s'associer; (of companies) fusionner; (of chemical elements) se combiner
combustible [kəm'bʌstɪbəl] adj combustible
combustion [kəm'bʌstʃən] n combustion f; **c. chamber** chambre f de combustion
come [kʌm] (pt came [keɪm], pp come) vi (**a**) (move) venir (**from** de); (arrive) arriver; **to c. from France/Edinburgh** venir de France/d'Édimbourg; **to c. to the end of sth** arriver à la fin de qch; **here he comes!** le voilà!; **coming!**

j'arrive!; **c., c.!** allons, allons!; **she always comes to me for help** elle s'adresse toujours à moi quand elle a besoin d'aide; **she came running towards us** elle vint vers nous en courant, elle courut vers nous; **the rain came pouring down** il s'est mis à tomber des cordes; **nothing comes between her and her work** son travail passe avant tout; *Fig* **she has come a long way since then** elle a fait du chemin depuis; *Fam* **I don't know whether I'm coming or going!** je ne sais plus où j'en suis!

(**b**) *(in time)* **c.** **January** en janvier; **c.** **next summer** l'été prochain; **in the days/years to c.** dans les jours/années à venir; **it came as a shock/surprise to me** ça m'a fait un choc/une surprise; *Fam* **he had it coming (to him)** ça lui pendait au nez

(**c**) *(happen)* **to c. to do sth** finir par faire qch; **c. to think of it** maintenant que j'y pense; **to take things as they c.** prendre les choses comme elles viennent; **c. what may** quoi qu'il arrive; **how c....?** comment se fait-il que...? + *subjunctive*

(**d**) *(in sequence)* **to c.** **first/last** *(in race, competition)* finir premier/dernier; **Monday comes before Tuesday** lundi vient avant mardi; **what comes next?** qu'est-ce qui vient après?

(**e**) *(exist, be available)* **to c.** **in different sizes/colours** exister en différentes tailles/couleurs; **work of that quality doesn't c. cheap** du travail de cette qualité, ça se paie; **he's as tough as they c.** il n'y a pas plus dur que lui

(**f**) *(become)* **to c. loose** se défaire; **to c. true** se réaliser; **to c. open** s'ouvrir; **to c. of age** devenir majeur(e)

(**g**) *(reach)* **to c. up/down to** arriver (jusqu')à

(**h**) *very Fam (reach orgasm)* jouir

▸ **come about** *vi* se produire, arriver

▸ **come across 1** *vt insep (find)* tomber sur
2 *vi (make an impression)* **to c. across well/badly** bien/ mal passer; **he comes across as an intelligent man** il a l'air intelligent

▸ **come after** *vt insep (chase)* poursuivre

▸ **come along** *vi* (**a**) **c. along!** allons, pressons! (**b**) *(make progress) (of project, work)* avancer; **his French is coming along well** il fait des progrès en français (**c**) *(arrive)* venir

▸ **come at** *vt insep (attack)* attaquer

▸ **come away** *vi (become detached)* se détacher

▸ **come back** *vi* revenir; **it's all coming back to me** ça me revient; **to c. back to what I was saying...** pour revenir à ce que je disais...

▸ **come by 1** *vt insep (acquire)* obtenir, trouver
2 *vi (visit)* passer

▸ **come down** *vi* (**a**) *(descend)* descendre; *(of temperature, prices)* baisser; *Fig* **to c. down in the world** déchoir; **to c. down with the flu** attraper la grippe (**b**) *(decide)* **to c. down in favour of sb/sth** décider en faveur de qn/qch (**c**) **to c. down to** *(be a matter of)* se ramener à, se résumer à; **it comes down to the fact that...** le fait est que...

▸ **come down on** *vt insep (reprimand)* passer un savon à

▸ **come forward** *vi* se présenter; **no one has come forward with any suggestions** personne n'a fait de suggestions

▸ **come in** *vi* (**a**) *(of person)* entrer; *(of tide)* monter; **c. in!** entrez!; **to c. in first/second** arriver premier/deuxième (**b**) *(have a role)* intervenir; **and where do I c. in?** et moi, qu'est-ce que je fais?; **to c. in useful** être utile

▸ **come in for** *vt insep* **to c. in for criticism** faire l'objet de critiques

▸ **come into** *vt insep* (**a**) *(room, city)* entrer dans; **to c. into the world** venir au monde; **to c. into being** *or* **existence** être créé(e); **to c. into force** *or* **effect** *(of law, ruling)* entrer en vigueur; **to c. into power** arriver au

pouvoir; **luck didn't c. into it** la chance n'a rien à voir là-dedans (**b**) *(inherit)* hériter de

▸ **come of** *vi (result from)* **no good will c. of it** cela n'amènera rien de bon; **that's what comes of being too ambitious** c'est ce qui arrive lorsqu'on est trop ambitieux

▸ **come off 1** *vt insep* (**a**) *(fall from) (horse, bicycle)* tomber de (**b**) **c. off it!** arrête ton char!
2 *vi* (**a**) *(be removed) (of button)* se détacher; *(of paint)* s'écailler; *(of stain)* partir (**b**) *(succeed)* réussir; **to c. off well/badly** *(in contest)* bien/mal s'en tirer

▸ **come on** *vi* (**a**) **c. on!** allez! (**b**) *(make progress) (of project, work)* avancer; **his chess is coming on** il fait des progrès aux échecs; **I feel a headache coming on** je sens un mal de tête qui commence (**c**) *(of lights)* s'allumer; *(of heating)* se mettre en route

▸ **come on to** *vt insep* (**a**) *(proceed to consider)* aborder, passer à (**b**) *Fam (flirt with)* draguer

▸ **come out** *vi* (**a**) *(of person, magazine, film)* sortir; *(of sun)* paraître; *(of truth)* se faire jour; **to c. out on strike** se mettre en grève; **to c. out in a rash** se couvrir de boutons; **to c. out in favour of/against sth** se prononcer pour/contre qch; **he came out of the deal well/badly** il a fait une bonne/mauvaise affaire; **to c. out with** *(remark, opinion)* sortir (**b**) *(of tooth, hair)* tomber; *(of screw)* se dévisser; *(of stain)* partir (**c**) *(as gay or lesbian)* déclarer son homosexualité

▸ **come over 1** *vt insep (affect)* **a funny feeling came over me** j'ai eu une sensation bizarre; **what's come over you?** qu'est-ce qui te prend?
2 *vi* (**a**) *(visit)* passer (**b**) *(make impression)* **to c. over well/badly** bien/mal passer (**c**) *(feel)* **to c. over all funny** se sentir tout(e) drôle; **to c. over all dizzy** être pris(e) de vertiges

▸ **come round** *vi* (**a**) *(visit)* passer (**b**) *(regain consciousness)* reprendre connaissance (**c**) *(accept)* accepter; **to c. round to sb's way of thinking** se rallier à l'opinion de qn

▸ **come through 1** *vi (of message, news)* arriver
2 *vt insep (survive) (war, crisis, illness)* survivre à

▸ **come to 1** *vt insep* (**a**) *(amount to)* s'élever à; **the plans never came to anything** les projets n'ont jamais abouti (**b**) *(reach)* **to c. to the point** en venir au fait; **to c. to a conclusion** arriver à une conclusion; **what is the world coming to?** où va-t-on? (**c**) *(be a matter of)* **when it comes to...** pour ce qui est de...; **if it comes to that...** à ce compte-là...
2 *vi (regain consciousness)* reprendre connaissance

▸ **come together** *vi (gather)* se rassembler

▸ **come up 1** *vt insep (stairs, hill)* monter
2 *vi* (**a**) *(of sun)* se lever; *(of opportunity, question, problem)* se présenter; **to c. up against a problem** rencontrer un problème; **there are some interesting films coming up on television** il y a quelques films intéressants qui vont bientôt passer à la télévision; **I'll let you know if anything comes up** je te préviendrai si quelque chose se présente; **the case comes up (for trial) tomorrow** le procès commence demain (**b**) **to c. up with** *(funding, solution)* trouver; *(idea, theory)* proposer

▸ **come upon** *vt insep (find)* tomber sur

▸ **come up to** *vt insep* (**a**) *(approach)* s'approcher de (**b**) *(equal)* **the film didn't c. up to my expectations** le film n'était pas à la hauteur de mes espérances

comeback ['kʌmbæk] *n* **to make a c.** *(of fashion)* revenir; *(of actor, sportsperson)* faire un come-back

comedian [kə'miːdɪən] *n* comique *mf*; *Fig (practical joker)* farceur(euse) *m,f*

comedienne [kəmiːdɪ'en] *n* comique *f*

comedown ['kʌmdaʊn] *n Fam* régression *f*

comedy ['kɒmɪdɪ] (*pl* **comedies**) *n* (*play, film*) comédie *f*; *(of situation)* comique *m*; *(situation comedy)* sitcom *m*; **c. show** *(on TV)* spectacle *m* comique

come-on ['kʌmɒn] *n Fam (enticement)* appât *m*; **to give sb the c.** *(sexually)* faire du gringue à qn

comer ['kʌmə(r)] *n* **open to all comers** ouvert(e) à tous

comet ['kɒmɪt] *n* comète *f*

comeuppance [kʌm'ʌpəns] *n Fam* **to get one's c.** avoir ce qu'on mérite

comfort ['kʌmfət] **1** *n* (**a**) *(ease)* confort *m*; *(financial)* aisance *f*; **to do sth in the c. of one's own home** faire qch confortablement chez soi; **comforts** *(luxuries)* commodités *fpl*; **I like my home comforts** j'aime mon petit confort; **the animals were getting too close for c.** les animaux venaient un peu trop près à mon goût; *Am* **c. station** toilettes *fpl* publiques (**b**) *(consolation)* réconfort *m*, consolation *f*; **if it's any c.,...** si ça peut vous consoler,...; **to take c. from** *or* **in sth** trouver du réconfort dans qch **2** *vt (console)* réconforter, consoler

comfortable ['kʌmftəbəl] *adj* (**a**) *(place, bed, chair)* confortable; *(person)* bien *inv*, à l'aise; **to be c.** *(of patient)* ne pas souffrir; **to make oneself c.** se mettre à l'aise *ou* à son aise; **I wouldn't feel c. accepting that money** ça me mettrait mal à l'aise d'accepter cet argent (**b**) *(majority, income)* confortable; **to be in c. circumstances** mener une vie aisée

comfortably ['kʌmftəblɪ] *adv* (**a**) *(sit)* confortablement; **to be c. off** *(financially)* être à l'aise financièrement; **to live c.** mener une vie aisée (**b**) *(easily)* facilement; **to win c.** gagner avec une avance confortable

comforter ['kʌmfətə(r)] *n Am (quilt)* édredon *m*

comforting ['kʌmfətɪŋ] *adj* réconfortant(e)

comfy ['kʌmfɪ] *adj Fam (place, bed, chair)* confortable; *(person)* bien *inv*, à l'aise

comic ['kɒmɪk] **1** *n* (**a**) *(performer)* comique *mf* (**b**) *c.* (**book**) bande *f* dessinée, BD *f* **2** *adj* comique; **c. opera** opéra-comique *m*; **to provide some c. relief** détendre l'atmosphère; **c. strip** bande *f* dessinée, BD *f*

comical ['kɒmɪkəl] *adj* comique

coming ['kʌmɪŋ] **1** *n (of person)* venue *f*, arrivée *f*; *(of night)* approche *f*; **comings and goings** allées *fpl* et venues **2** *adj (year, week)* prochain(e); *(elections, difficulties)* à venir

comma ['kɒmə] *n* virgule *f*

command [kə'mɑːnd] **1** *n* (**a**) *(order)* ordre *m*; *Comptr* commande *f*; *Comptr* **c. language** langage *m* de commandes (**b**) *(authority, control)* commandement *m*; **to be in c. (of sth)** *(army, ship)* commander (qch); **to be in c. of the situation** maîtriser la situation; **to be at sb's c.** être aux ordres de qn; **to have sth at one's c.** avoir qch à sa disposition; **she has a good c. of English** elle a une bonne maîtrise de l'anglais; **c. economy** économie *f* planifiée **2** *vt* (**a**) *(give order to)* **to c. sb to do sth** ordonner *ou* commander à qn de faire qch (**b**) *(ship, regiment)* commander (**c**) *(have at one's disposal)* avoir à sa disposition (**d**) *(respect, admiration, attention)* forcer; **to c. a high price** se vendre cher

commandant [kɒmən'dænt] *n Mil* commandant *m*

commandeer [kɒmən'dɪə(r)] *vt* réquisitionner

commander [kə'mɑːndə(r)] *n Mil* commandant *m*; *Naut* capitaine *m* de frégate; **c.-in-chief** commandant en chef

commanding [kə'mɑːndɪŋ] *adj* (**a**) *Mil* **c. officer** chef *m* de corps (**b**) *(voice)* de commandement; *(appearance)* qui en impose; *(position)* dominant(e); *(lead)* considérable

commandment [kə'mɑːndmənt] *n Rel* commandement *m*

commando [kə'mɑːndəʊ] (*pl* **commandos** *or* **commandoes**) *n Mil (soldier, unit)* commando *m*

commemorate [kə'meməreɪt] *vt* commémorer

commemoration [kəmemə'reɪʃən] *n* commémoration *f*

commemorative [kə'memərətɪv] *adj* commémoratif(ive)

commence [kə'mens] *vt & vi Formal* commencer; **to c. doing sth** commencer à faire qch

commencement [kə'mensmənt] *n* (**a**) *Formal (beginning)* commencement *m*, début *m* (**b**) *Am Univ* remise *f* des diplômes

commend [kə'mend] *vt* (**a**) *(praise)* louer, féliciter; **to c. sb for bravery** louer qn pour sa bravoure (**b**) *(recommend)* recommander; **the town has little to c. it** je ne vous recommande pas la ville

commendable [kə'mendəbəl] *adj* louable

commendation [kɒmen'deɪʃən] *n (praise)* éloges *mpl*; *(in competition)* mention *f* spéciale, *Mil* citation *f*

commensurate [kə'menʃərət] *adj Formal* proportionnel(elle) (**with** à)

comment ['kɒment] **1** *n* commentaire *m*, observation *f* (**on** sur); **no c.!** sans commentaire! **2** *vi* **to c. that...** faire remarquer *ou* observer que...; **"how interesting," he commented** "comme c'est intéressant", remarqua-t-il *ou* observa-t-il **3** *vi* faire des commentaires (**on** sur)

commentary ['kɒməntərɪ] (*pl* **commentaries**) *n* commentaire *m*

commentate ['kɒmənteɪt] *vi* faire le commentaire; **to c. on sth** commenter qch

commentator ['kɒmənteɪtə(r)] *n* commentateur(trice) *m,f*

commerce ['kɒmɜːs] *n* commerce *m*

commercial [kə'mɜːʃəl] **1** *n (advertisement)* publicité *f*, pub *f* **2** *adj also Pej* commercial(e); **c. artist** graphiste *mf*; *Fin* **c. bank** banque *f* commerciale; **c. break** page *f* de publicité; **c. law** droit *m* commercial; **c. traveller** voyageur *m* de commerce; **c. value** valeur *f* marchande; **c. vehicle** véhicule *m* de commerce

commercialism [kə'mɜːʃəlɪzəm] *n Pej* mercantilisme *m*

commercialized [kə'mɜːʃəlaɪzd] *adj Pej* commercial(e)

commercially [kə'mɜːʃəlɪ] *adv* commercialement; **c. available** disponible dans le commerce

commie ['kɒmɪ] *n & adj Fam Pej* coco *mf*

commiserate [kə'mɪzəreɪt] *vi* **to c. with sb** être désolé(e) pour qn

commiseration [kəmɪzə'reɪʃən] *n* commisération *f*; **you have my commiserations** je suis désolé pour vous

commission [kə'mɪʃən] **1** *n* (**a**) *Com (payment)* commission *f* (**b**) *(of work, painting)* commande *f* (**c**) *(investigating body)* commission *f* (**d**) *Naut* **in c.** armé(e); **out of c.** désarmé(e); *Mil* brevet *m* d'officier **2** *vt* (**a**) *(order)* *(work, painting)* commander; **to c. sb to do sth** charger qn de faire qch (**b**) *Mil* **to be commissioned** être nommé(e) officier

commissionaire [kəmɪʃə'neə(r)] *n* portier *m*

commissioner [kə'mɪʃənə(r)] *n* membre *m* d'une commission; **c. of police** ≈ commissaire *m* de police; *Law* **c. for oaths** = homme de loi habilité à recevoir des déclarations sous serment

commit [kə'mɪt] *(pt & pp* **committed)** *vt* **(a)** *(error, crime)* commettre; **to c. suicide** se suicider **(b) to c. oneself** *(promise)* s'engager; **to c. oneself to (doing) sth** s'engager à (faire) qch; **to c. sth to sth** *(resources, troops)* engager qch dans qch **(c)** *(entrust)* confier **(to à)**; **to c. sth to writing** coucher qch par écrit; **to c. sth to memory** apprendre qch par cœur **(d)** *(confine)* **to c. sb (to prison)** incarcérer qn; **to c. sb** *(to mental institution)* interner qn **(e)** *Law* **to c. sb for trial** mettre qn en accusation

commitment [kə'mɪtmənt] *n* **(a)** *(obligation)* engagement *m*; **family/business commitments** obligations *fpl* familiales/professionnelles **(b)** *(dedication)* dévouement *m* **(to à)**; **to make a c.** s'engager; **she lacks c.** elle ne s'investit pas assez

committed [kə'mɪtɪd] *adj* dévoué(e) **(to à)**; *(Christian, socialist)* convaincu(e); **to be c. (to one's work)** beaucoup s'impliquer (dans son travail)

committee [kə'mɪtɪ] *n* comité *m*, commission *f*

commode [kə'məʊd] *n* **(a)** *(chest of drawers)* commode *f* **(b)** *(toilet)* chaise *f* percée

commodious [kə'məʊdɪəs] *adj* spacieux(euse)

commodity [kə'mɒdɪtɪ] *(pl* **commodities)** *n Econ* marchandise *f*, produit *m*; *Fin* matière *f* première; **to be a rare c.** être une denrée rare; **commodities market** marché *m* des matières premières

commodore ['kɒmədɔː(r)] *n Naut* ≃ contre-amiral *m*

common ['kɒmən] **1** *n* **(a) to have sth in c. (with)** avoir qch en commun (avec); **in c. with** *(similar to)* de même que **(b)** *(land)* terrain *m* communal **2** *adj* **(a)** *(frequent)* commun(e), courant(e); **in c. use** d'usage courant **(b)** *(shared)* commun(e); **it is by c. consent the best** de l'avis de tous, c'est le meilleur; **C. Agricultural Policy** politique *f* agricole commune; *also Fig* **c. denominator** dénominateur *m* commun; **the c. good** le bien commun; *Fig* **c. ground** terrain *m* d'entente; **it's c. knowledge (that)...** tout le monde sait que...; **the C. Market** le Marché commun; *Sch* **c. room** *(for pupils)* salle *f* commune; *(for teachers)* salle des professeurs **(c)** *(average)* **c. or garden** ordinaire, standard *inv*; **the c. cold** le rhume; **the c. man** l'homme *m* de la rue; **the c. people** les gens *mpl* ordinaires; **c. sense** bon sens *m* **(d)** *Pej (vulgar)* vulgaire

commoner ['kɒmənə(r)] *n* roturier(ère) *m,f*

common-law ['kɒmənlɔː] *adj* **c. husband** concubin *m*; **c. marriage** concubinage *m*; **c. wife** concubine *f*

commonly ['kɒmənlɪ] *adv* communément

commonplace ['kɒmənpleɪs] **1** *n* lieu *m* commun **2** *adj* courant(e)

Commons ['kɒmənz] *npl Br Pol* **the (House of) C.** la Chambre des communes

Commonwealth ['kɒmənwelθ] *n* **the C.** le Commonwealth

commotion [kə'məʊʃən] *n (noise)* vacarme *m*; *(disruption)* agitation *f*

communal ['kɒmjʊnəl] *adj* *(bathroom, resource)* commun(e); *(life)* communautaire

commune **1** *n* ['kɒmjuːn] *(collective)* communauté *f* **2** *vi* [kə'mjuːn] **to c. with nature** communier avec la nature

communicable [kə'mjuːnɪkəbəl] *adj* *(disease)* transmissible

communicant [kə'mjuːnɪkənt] *n Rel* communiant(e) *m,f*

communicate [kə'mjuːnɪkeɪt] **1** *vt* communiquer; *(illness)* transmettre
2 *vi* communiquer **(with** avec)

communication [kəmjuːnɪ'keɪʃən] *n* communication

f; **to be in c. with sb** être en contact avec qn; **c. cord** sonnette *f* d'alarme

communicative [kə'mjuːnɪkətɪv] *adj* communicatif(ive)

communion [kə'mjuːnjən] *n Rel* communion *f*; **to take C.** communier

communism ['kɒmjʊnɪzəm] *n* communisme *m*

communist ['kɒmjʊnɪst] *n & adj* communiste *mf*

community [kə'mjuːnɪtɪ] *(pl* **communities)** *n* communauté *f*; **the business c.** le milieu des affaires; **c. centre** foyer *m* municipal; **c. service** travail *m* d'intérêt général; **c. spirit** esprit *m* communautaire

commute [kə'mjuːt] **1** *vt Law* commuer **(to** en) **2** *vi* **to c. (to work)** faire la navette entre son domicile et son travail

commuter [kə'mjuːtə(r)] *n* banlieusard(e) *m,f (qui fait la navette entre son domicile et son travail)*; **c. train** train *m* de banlieue

Comoros ['kɒmərɒs] *n* **the C. (Islands)** les Comores *fpl*

compact [kəm'pækt] **1** *n* **(a)** *(for powder)* poudrier *m* **(b)** *(treaty)* accord *m* **(c)** *Am (car)* petite voiture *f* **2** *adj* compact(e); **c. disc** disque *m* compact; **c. disc player** lecteur *m* de disques compacts **3** *vt* compacter

companion [kəm'pænjən] *n* **(a)** *(friend)* compagnon (compagne) *m,f*; *(of elderly woman)* dame *f* de compagnie; **travelling c.** compagnon de voyage **(b)** *(guidebook)* guide *m*

companionable [kəm'pænjənəbəl] *adj (person)* sociable; *(manner)* amical(e)

companionship [kəm'pænjənʃɪp] *n* compagnie *f*

company ['kʌmpənɪ] *(pl* **companies)** *n* **(a)** *(companionship)* compagnie *f*; **in his c.** en sa compagnie; **to keep sb c.** tenir compagnie à qn; **to be good company** être de bonne compagnie; **to part c. with sb** *(split up)* se séparer de qn; *(disagree)* ne plus être d'accord avec qn; **to get into bad c.** avoir de mauvaises fréquentations; **to do sth in c.** *(in public)* faire qch en public; **to have c.** *(guests)* avoir de la visite **(b)** *(business)* société *f*; **publishing c.** maison *f* d'édition; **Hobbs and C.** Hobbs et Compagnie; **c. car** voiture *f* de fonction; **c. policy** politique *f* de la société; *Com* **c. secretary** secrétaire *mf* général(e) **(c)** *(army unit, theatre group)* compagnie *f*

comparable ['kɒmpərəbəl] *adj* comparable **(to** à)

comparative [kəm'pærətɪv] **1** *n Gram* comparatif *m*
2 *adj* **(a)** *(relative)* *(cost, comfort, wealth)* relatif(ive) **(b)** *(study, research)* *(psychology, literature)* comparé(e)

compare [kəm'peə(r)] **1** *vt* comparer **(with** *or* **to** avec *ou* à); **compared with** *or* **to** par rapport à, à côté de, à; *Fig* **to c. notes** échanger ses impressions
2 *vi* être comparable **(with** à); **to c. favourably with sth** ne le céder en rien à qch **3** *n Lit* **beyond c.** sans pareil(eille)

comparison [kəm'pærɪsən] *n* comparaison *f*; **in** *or* **by c. (with)** en comparaison (avec); **there is no c.** il n'y a pas de comparaison; **to draw** *or* **make a c. between sth and sth** faire la comparaison entre qch et qch

compartment [kəm'pɑːtmənt] *n* compartiment *m*

compass ['kʌmpəs] *n* **(a)** *(for finding direction)* boussole *f*; *(of boat)* compas *m* **(b)** *Math* **(pair of) compasses** compas *m* **(c)** *(scope)* *(of mind)* portée *f*; *(of powers)* étendue *f*

compassion [kəm'pæʃən] *n* compassion *f*

compassionate [kəm'pæʃənət] *adj* *(person, attitude)* compatissant(e); *(by nature)* humain(e); **to be c. towards sb** éprouver de la compassion pour qn; **on c. grounds** pour

raisons personnelles; **c. leave** congé *m* exceptionnel pour raisons personnelles
compatibility [kəmpætə'bılıtı] *n* compatibilité *f*
compatible [kəm'pætəbəl] *adj* compatible (**with** avec)
compatriot [kəm'pætrıət] *n* compatriote *mf*
compel [kəm'pel] (*pt & pp* **compelled**) *vt* forcer, obliger; **to c. sb to do sth** forcer *ou* obliger qn à faire qch; **to c. admiration/respect** forcer l'admiration/le respect
compelling [kəm'pelıŋ] *adj (film, performance)* captivant(e); *(argument)* convaincant(e); *(urge)* irrésistible
compendium [kəm'pendıəm] *n (book)* précis *m; (of games)* sélection *f*
compensate ['kɒmpenseıt] **1** *vt* dédommager (**for** de) **2** *vi* **to c. for sth** compenser qch
compensation [kɒmpen'seıʃən] *n* compensation *f; (money)* dédommagement *m*, indemnité *f*
compensatory [kɒmpen'seıtərı] *adj* compensatoire
compere ['kɒmpeə(r)] **1** *n* animateur(trice) *m,f*, présentateur(trice) *m,f* **2** *vt* animer, présenter
compete [kəm'piːt] *vi (contend)* rivaliser (**with** avec), *(of company)* être en concurrence (**with** avec); **to c. for sth** se disputer qch (**b**) *(in race, competition)* concourir (**for** pour)
competence ['kɒmpıtəns] *n* (**a**) *(ability)* compétence *f*, compétences *fpl* (**b**) *Law* compétence *f*
competent ['kɒmpıtənt] *adj (person)* compétent(e); **a c. piece of work** du bon travail
competition [kɒmpı'tıʃən] *n* (**a**) *(contest)* concours *m; (in sport)* compétition *f* (**b**) *(rivalry)* rivalité *f; (between companies, candidates)* concurrence *f;* **to be in c. with sb** être en concurrence avec qn; **the c.** *(opponents) (in sport)* les adversaires *mpl; (in business)* la concurrence; **there's no c.!** il n'y a aucune comparaison!
competitive [kəm'petıtıv] *adj (person)* qui a l'esprit de compétition; *(atmosphere)* de compétition; *(price, company)* compétitif(ive); **c. sports** sports *mpl* de compétition; *Com* **c. tendering** appel *m* d'offres
competitor [kəm'petıtə(r)] *n* concurrent(e) *m,f*
compilation [kɒmpı'leıʃən] *n* compilation *f*
compile [kəm'paıl] *vt (list)* dresser
complacency [kəm'pleısənsı] *n* autosatisfaction *f*
complacent [kəm'pleısənt] *adj* content(e) de soi; **to be c. about sth** faire de l'autosatisfaction à propos de qch
complain [kəm'pleın] *vi* se plaindre (**about** de); **to c. of** *(illness)* se plaindre de; **he complained about the food** il s'est plaigné de la cuisine; **how are things? – can't c.** comment ça va? – je n'ai pas à me plaindre
complaint [kəm'pleınt] *n* (**a**) *(grievance)* récrimination *f; (official)* plainte *f*, réclamation *f;* **to have cause** *or* **grounds for c.** avoir des raisons de se plaindre; **to lodge** *or* **make a c. against sb** porter plainte contre qn (**b**) *(illness)* maladie *f*
complement 1 *n* ['kɒmplımənt] (**a**) *Gram* complément *m* (**b**) *Naut & Fig* **the full c.** l'effectif *m* complet **2** *vt* ['kɒmplıment] compléter
complementary [kɒmplı'mentərı] *adj* complémentaire; **c. medicine** médecines *fpl* alternatives *ou* parallèles
complete [kəm'pliːt] **1** *adj* (**a**) *(whole)* complet(ète); *(utter)* total(e); **he is a c. fool** il est complètement idiot (**b**) *(finished)* achevé(e) **2** *vt* (**a**) *(finish)* achever; *(fill in) (form)* compléter (**b**) *(make whole)* compléter
completely [kəm'pliːtlı] *adv* complètement
completion [kəm'pliːʃən] *n* achèvement *m;* **on c.** *(of work)* à l'achèvement; **to near c.** toucher à sa fin

complex ['kɒmpleks] **1** *n (of buildings, psychological)* complexe *m;* **to have a c. about sth** être complexé(e) par qch **2** *adj* complexe
complexion [kəm'plekʃən] *n* teint *m;* **to have a good c.** avoir une belle peau; *Fig* **that puts a different c. on things** voilà qui change tout
complexity [kəm'pleksıtı] (*pl* **complexities**) *n* complexité *f*
compliance [kəm'plaıəns] *n* observation *f* (**with** de); **in c. with** conformément à
compliant [kəm'plaıənt] *adj* complaisant(e), accommodant(e)
complicate ['kɒmplıkeıt] *vt* compliquer
complicated ['kɒmplıkeıtıd] *adj* compliqué(e)
complication [kɒmplı'keıʃən] *n* complication *f*
complicity [kəm'plısıtı] *n* complicité *f* (**in** dans)
compliment 1 *n* ['kɒmplımənt] compliment *m;* **to pay sb a c.** faire un compliment à qn; **with compliments** avec nos compliments; **compliments of the season** meilleurs vœux; **compliments slip** papillon *m* à en-tête *(portant la mention "avec les compliments de...")* **2** *vt* ['kɒmplıment] **to c. sb on sth** *(bravery, command of language)* féliciter qn pour qch; *(dress, haircut)* faire des compliments à qn sur qch
complimentary [kɒmplı'mentərı] *adj* (**a**) *(praising)* élogieux(euse) (**about** à l'égard de) (**b**) *(free)* gratuit(e); **c. drink** boisson *f* offerte
comply [kəm'plaı] (*pt & pp* **complied**) *vi* **to c. with** *(rule)* se conformer à, se plier à; *(order)* obéir à; *(request)* accéder à
component [kəm'pəʊnənt] **1** *n (electrical, chemical)* composant *m; Fig* composante *f* **2** *adj* **c. part** pièce *f* détachée; *Fig* composante *f*
compose [kəm'pəʊz] *vt* (**a**) *(music, poetry)* composer (**b**) *(constitute)* **to be composed of** être composé(e) de, se composer de (**c**) *(calm)* **to c. oneself** se calmer
composed [kəm'pəʊzd] *adj* calme
composer [kəm'pəʊzə(r)] *n* compositeur(trice) *m,f*
composite ['kɒmpəzıt] *adj (photograph)* composite
composition [kɒmpə'zıʃən] *n* composition *f; (essay)* rédaction *f*
compositor [kəm'pɒzıtə(r)] *n Typ* compositeur(trice) *m,f*
compost ['kɒmpɒst] *n* compost *m;* **c. heap** tas *m* de compost
composure [kəm'pəʊʒə(r)] *n* sang-froid *m*
compound¹ ['kɒmpaʊnd] **1** *n Chem & Gram* composé *m* **2** *adj* composé(e); *Med* **c. fracture** fracture *f* compliquée; *Fin* **c. interest** intérêts *mpl* composés **3** *vt* [kəm'paʊnd] *(problem)* aggraver
compound² ['kɒmpaʊnd] *n (enclosure)* enceinte *f*
comprehend [kɒmprı'hend] *vt* comprendre
comprehensible [kɒmprı'hensəbəl] *adj* compréhensible
comprehension [kɒmprı'henʃən] *n* compréhension *f;* **it is beyond my c.** cela dépasse mon entendement
comprehensive [kɒmprı'hensıv] *adj (answer, programme)* complet(ète); *(study)* exhaustif(ive); *(view)* d'ensemble; *(defeat, victory)* écrasant(e); *Fin* **c. insurance** assurance *f* tous risques; *Br* **c. (school)** établissement *m* secondaire *(n'opérant pas de sélection à l'entrée)*
compress [kəm'pres] **1** *n* ['kɒmpres] *Med* compresse *f* **2** *vt* [kəm'pres] *(air, gas)* comprimer; *Fig (text)* condenser
compression [kəm'preʃən] *n (of air, gas)* compression *f; Fig* raccourcissement *m*
compressor [kəm'presə(r)] *n* compresseur *m*

comprise [kəm'praɪz] *vt* comprendre, se composer de; **to be comprised of** comprendre, se composer de

compromise ['kɒmprəmaɪz] **1** *n* compromis *m*; **c. solution** solution *f* de compromis **2** *vt (person, security)* compromettre; *(principles)* transiger sur; **to c. oneself** se compromettre **3** *vi* transiger **(on** sur**)**

compromising ['kɒmprəmaɪzɪŋ] *adj* compromettant(e)

compulsion [kəm'pʌlʃən] *n (urge)* besoin *m*; *(obligation)* contrainte *f*; **under c.** sous la contrainte; **to be under no c. to do sth** ne pas être obligé(e) de faire qch

compulsive [kəm'pʌlsɪv] *adj (smoker, gambler, liar)* invétéré(e); **c. eating** boulimie *f*; **it's c. viewing** c'est captivant

compulsory [kəm'pʌlsərɪ] *adj* obligatoire; **c. redundancy** ≃ licenciement *m* sec; **c. retirement** mise *f* à la retraite d'office

compunction [kəm'pʌŋkʃən] *n* remords *m*, scrupules *mpl*; **he has no c.** about cheating il n'hésite pas à tricher

computation [kɒmpjʊ'teɪʃən] *n* calcul *m*

compute [kəm'pju:t] *vt* calculer

computer [kəm'pju:tə(r)] *n* ordinateur *m*; **c. game** jeu *m* électronique; **to be c. literate** avoir des connaissances en informatique; **c. printout** impression *f*; **c. program** programme *m* informatique; **c. programmer** programmeur(euse) *m,f*; **c. programming** programmation *f*; **c. science** informatique *f*; **c. scientist** informaticien(enne) *m,f*; **c. simulation** simulation *f* par ordinateur

computerization [kəmpju:təraɪ'zeɪʃən] *n* informatisation *f*

computerize [kəm'pju:təraɪz] *vt* informatiser

computing [kəm'pju:tɪŋ] *n* informatique *f*

comrade ['kɒmreɪd] *n* camarade *mf*

comradeship ['kɒmreɪdʃɪp] *n* camaraderie *f*

con¹ [kɒn] *Fam* **1** *n (swindle)* arnaque *f*; **c. man** arnaqueur *m* **2** *vt (pt & pp* **conned)** *(swindle)* arnaquer; **to c. sth out of sb** arnaquer qn de qch; **to c. sb into doing sth** persuader qn de faire qch par la ruse

con² *n Fam (convict)* taulard(e) *m,f*

con³ *n (disadvantage) see* **pro**

concave [kɒn'keɪv] *adj* concave

conceal [kən'si:l] *vt* cacher, dissimuler **(from** à**)**

concealer [kən'si:lə(r)] *n (make-up)* camoufleur *m*

concede [kən'si:d] **1** *vt* concéder; **to c. defeat** s'avouer vaincu(e); **to c. that…** admettre que… **2** *vi* s'incliner

conceit [kən'si:t] *n (vanity)* vanité *f*, suffisance *f*

conceited [kən'si:tɪd] *adj* vaniteux(euse), suffisant(e)

conceivable [kən'si:vəbəl] *adj* concevable, imaginable; **it is c. that…** il est concevable que… + *subjunctive*

conceivably [kən'si:vəblɪ] *adv* **we might c. get there in time for dinner** il se peut que nous soyons arrivés pour l'heure du dîner; **she couldn't c. have done it** il est inconcevable qu'elle ait fait ça

conceive [kən'si:v] **1** *vt* **(a)** *(child, idea)* concevoir **(b)** *(understand)* concevoir **2** *vi* **to c. of sth** concevoir qch

concentrate ['kɒnsəntreɪt] **1** *n* concentré *m* **2** *vt* concentrer **(on** sur**) 3** *vi* se concentrer **(on** sur**); to c. on doing sth** s'appliquer à faire qch

concentration [kɒnsən'treɪʃən] *n* concentration *f*; **c. camp** camp *m* de concentration; **to have a short c. span** ne pas avoir une grande capacité de concentration

concentric [kɒn'sentrɪk] *adj Math* concentrique

concept ['kɒnsept] *n* concept *m*

conception [kən'sepʃən] *n* **(a)** *(of child, idea)* conception *f* **(b)** *(understanding)* **to have no c. of sth** n'avoir aucune idée ou notion de qch

conceptual [kən'septjʊəl] *adj* conceptuel(elle)

conceptualize [kən'septjʊəlaɪz] *vt* conceptualiser

concern [kən'sɜːn] **1** *n* **(a)** *(interest)* **it's no c. of mine/yours** cela ne me/vous regarde pas; **this is a matter of public c.** c'est une affaire qui nous concerne tous **(b)** *(worry, compassion)* inquiétude *f*, souci *m*; **to give cause for c.** être un sujet d'inquiétude; **there is no cause for c.** il n'y a pas de raison de s'inquiéter; **to show c.** se montrer inquiet(ète) **(c)** *(company)* entreprise *f* **2** *vt* **(a)** *(affect)* concerner; **to c. oneself with sth** se préoccuper ou se soucier de qch; **as far as I'm concerned,…** pour moi,…, en ce qui me concerne,…; **to whom it may c.** à qui de droit **(b)** *(worry)* inquiéter **(c)** *(be about) (of book)* traiter de; **it concerns your son** c'est au sujet de votre fils

concerned [kən'sɜːnd] *adj (worried)* inquiet(ète) **(about** au sujet de**)**

concerning [kən'sɜːnɪŋ] *prep* au sujet de

concert ['kɒnsət] *n* **(a)** *(musical)* concert *m*; **c. hall** salle *f* de concert; **c. pianist** concertiste *m,f* **(b)** *(cooperation)* **in c. (with)** de concert (avec)

concerted [kən'sɜːtɪd] *adj* concerté(e)

concertina [kɒnsə'ti:nə] *n* concertina *m*

concerto [kən'tʃɜːtəʊ] *(pl* **concertos)** *n* concerto *m*

concession [kən'seʃən] *n* **(a)** *(compromise, giving up)* concession *f* **(b)** *(discount)* tarif *m* réduit

concessionary [kən'seʃənərɪ] *adj (fare)* réduit(e)

conciliate [kən'sɪlɪeɪt] *vt* apaiser

conciliation [kənsɪlɪ'eɪʃən] *n* conciliation *f*; *(in dispute)* conciliation, arbitrage *m*; **the dispute went to c.** le conflit a été soumis à l'arbitrage

conciliatory [kən'sɪlɪətərɪ] *adj* conciliant(e)

concise [kən'saɪs] *adj* concis(e)

conclude [kən'klu:d] **1** *vt* **(a)** *(speech, book, treaty)* conclure; *(conference, festival)* clore **(b)** *(deduce)* **to c. that…** conclure que… **2** *vi* se conclure **(with** sur**)**; *(of speaker)* conclure **(with** sur**)**; *(of conference, festival)* se clore **(with** sur**)**

concluding [kən'klu:dɪŋ] *adj* final(e)

conclusion [kən'klu:ʒən] *n* **(a)** *(inference)* conclusion *f*; **to come to** *or* **reach a c.** arriver à une conclusion **(b)** *(end)* conclusion *f*; **in c.** pour conclure, en conclusion

conclusive [kən'klu:sɪv] *adj* concluant(e)

concoct [kən'kɒkt] *vt also Fig* concocter

concoction [kən'kɒkʃən] *n (drink, dish)* mixture *f*

concord ['kɒŋkɔːd] *n (harmony)* entente *f*

concordance [kən'kɔːdəns] *n (agreement)* accord *m*; **to be in c. with sth** être en accord avec qch

concourse ['kɒnkɔːs] *n (in airport, railway station)* hall *m*

concrete ['kɒnkri:t] **1** *n* béton *m*; **c. jungle** forêt *f* de béton; **c. mixer** bétonnière *f* **2** *adj* en béton; *Fig (definite)* concret(ète)

concubine ['kɒŋkjʊbaɪn] *n* concubine *f*

concur [kən'kɜː(r)] *(pt & pp* **concurred)** *vi (of person)* être d'accord **(with** avec**);** *(of findings, results)* concorder **(with** avec**)**

concurrent [kən'kʌrənt] *adj* simultané(e), concordant(e)

concurrently [kən'kʌrəntlɪ] *adv* simultanément

concussed [kən'kʌst] *adj* commotionné(e)
concussion [kən'kʌʃən] *n* commotion *f* cérébrale
condemn [kən'dem] *vt* (a) *(disapprove of)* condamner (b) *Law (sentence)* condamner (**to** à); **the condemned man** le condamné; **condemned cell** cellule de condamné à mort (c) *(building)* déclarer inhabitable
condemnation [kɒndem'neɪʃən] *n* condamnation *f*
condensation [kɒnden'seɪʃən] *n* (a) *(moisture) (on glass)* buée *f*, *(on walls)* condensation *f* (b) *(process)* condensation *f*
condense [kən'dens] **1** *vt* condenser; **condensed milk** lait *m* condensé
2 *vi* se condenser
condenser [kən'densə(r)] *n Tech* condensateur *m*
condescend [kɒndɪ'send] *vi* **to c. to do sth** condescendre à faire qch; **to c. towards sb** se montrer condescendant(e) envers qn
condescending [kɒndɪ'sendɪŋ] *adj* condescendant(e)
condescension [kɒndɪ'senʃən] *n* condescendance *f*
condiment ['kɒndɪmənt] *n* condiment *m*
condition [kən'dɪʃən] **1** *n* (a) *(state)* état *m*; *(of person)* forme *f*; **in good/bad c.** *(of machine, road)* en bon/mauvais état; **you're in no c. to drive** tu n'es pas en état de conduire; **to be in good c./out of c.** *(of person)* être/ne pas être en forme
(b) *(circumstances)* conditions *fpl*; **driving conditions** état *m* des routes; **working conditions** conditions de travail; *Law* **conditions of employment** contrat *m* de travail
(c) *(requirement)* condition *f*; **on the c. that...** à (la) condition que... + *subjunctive*; **on no c.** sous aucun prétexte, en aucun cas
(d) *(disease)* maladie *f*, **heart c.** maladie du cœur
2 *vt* (a) *(influence)* conditionner; **to be conditioned by** *(depend on)* dépendre de; **we have been conditioned to believe that...** on nous a appris que...; *Psy* **conditioned reflex** réflexe *m* conditionné
(b) *(hair)* mettre de l'après-shampo(o)ing sur
conditional [kən'dɪʃənəl] **1** *n Gram* the c. le conditionnel
2 *adj* conditionnel(elle); **to be c. on** dépendre de; *Law* **c. discharge** liberté *f* conditionnelle
conditionally [kən'dɪʃənəlɪ] *adv (accept, grant)* sous certaines conditions
conditioner [kən'dɪʃənə(r)] *n (for hair)* après-shampo(o)ing *m*
conditioning [kən'dɪʃənɪŋ] *n (psychological)* conditionnement *m*
condo ['kɒndəʊ] *(pl* **condos)** *n Am Fam (abbr* **condominium)** appartement *m* en copropriété
condolences [kən'dəʊlənsɪz] *npl* condoléances *fpl*
condom ['kɒndəm] *n* préservatif *m*
condominium [kɒndə'mɪnɪəm] *n Am (apartment)* appartement *m* en copropriété
condone [kən'dəʊn] *vt* excuser
condor ['kɒndɔː(r)] *n* condor *m*
conducive [kən'djuːsɪv] *adj* **to be c. to** être favorable *ou* propice à
conduct 1 *n* ['kɒndʌkt] *(behaviour)* conduite *f*
2 *vt* [kən'dʌkt] (a) *(business, orchestra)* diriger; *(campaign, inquiry, experiment)* mener; **to c. oneself** se conduire (b) *(guide)* guider; **we were conducted round the factory** on nous a fait visiter l'usine; **a conducted tour** une visite guidée (c) *(heat, electricity)* conduire
3 *vi* [kən'dʌkt] *Mus* diriger
conductivity [kɒndʌk'tɪvɪtɪ] *n Phys* conductivité *f*

conductor [kən'dʌktə(r)] *n* (a) *Br (on bus)* receveur(euse) *m,f* (b) *(of orchestra)* chef *m* d'orchestre (c) *Phys* conducteur *m*
conduit ['kɒndɪt] *n* conduit *m*
cone [kəʊn] *n* (a) *(shape)* cône *m* (b) *(of pine)* pomme *f* de pin (c) *(for ice cream)* cornet *m* (d) *(for traffic)* cône *m* de signalisation
cone-shaped ['kəʊnʃeɪpt] *adj* conique
confab ['kɒnfæb] *n Fam* **to have a c. about sth** discuter de qch
confectioner [kən'fekʃənə(r)] *n* confiseur(euse) *m,f*; **c.'s (shop)** confiserie *f*; *Am* **c.'s sugar** sucre *m* glace
confectionery [kən'fekʃənərɪ] *n (sweets)* confiserie *f*
confederacy [kən'fedərəsɪ] *n* confédération *f*
confederate [kən'fedərət] **1** *n (accomplice)* complice *mf*
2 *adj Pol* confédéré(e)
confederation [kənfedə'reɪʃən] *n* confédération *f*
confer [kən'fɜː(r)] *(pt & pp* **conferred)** **1** *vt (title, degree, powers)* octroyer *(on* à)
2 *vi (discuss) (of several people)* se consulter; **to c. with sb about sth** discuter de qch avec qn
conference ['kɒnfərəns] *n* conférence *f*, congrès *m*; *Com* **to be in c.** être en conférence
confess [kən'fes] **1** *vt (crime, mistake)* confesser, avouer; *(feeling)* avouer; *Rel* confesser; **to c. that...** confesser *ou* avouer que...
2 *vi* avouer; *Rel* se confesser; **to c. to sth** *(crime, mistake)* confesser *ou* avouer qch; *(feeling)* avouer qch
confession [kən'feʃən] *n* confession *f*, aveu *m*; *Rel* confession; **to go to c.** aller se confesser
confessional [kən'feʃənəl] *n Rel* confessionnal *m*
confessor [kən'fesə(r)] *n Rel* confesseur *m*
confetti [kən'fetɪ] *n* confettis *mpl*
confidante [kɒnfɪ'dænt] *n* confident(e) *m,f*
confide [kən'faɪd] **1** *vt* **to c. sth to sb** confier qch à qn
2 *vi* **to c. in sb** se confier à qn
confidence ['kɒnfɪdəns] *n* (a) *(trust)* confiance *f* (**in** en); **I have every c. that...** je ne doute pas un instant que...; **to take sb into one's c.** se confier à qn; **c. trick** escroquerie *f*, **c. trickster** escroc *m* (b) *(self-assurance)* confiance *f* en soi (c) *(secret)* confidence *f*; **in c.** en confidence
confident ['kɒnfɪdənt] *adj* (a) *(self-assured) (person)* sûr(e) de soi; *(smile, exterior)* confiant(e) (b) *(certain)* certain(e); **to be c. of doing sth** être certain de faire qch
confidential [kɒnfɪ'denʃəl] *adj* confidentiel(elle)
confidentiality [kɒnfɪdenʃɪ'ælɪtɪ] *n* confidentialité *f*
confidentially [kɒnfɪ'denʃəlɪ] *adv* confidentiellement, en confidence
confidently ['kɒnfɪdəntlɪ] *adv* (a) *(with self-assurance)* avec assurance (b) *(with certainty)* avec confiance
configuration [kənfɪgjʊ'reɪʃən] *n* configuration *f*
confine [kən'faɪn] *vt* (a) *(imprison)* enfermer; **to be confined to bed** être alité(e); **to be confined to barracks** être consigné(e); **confined space** espace *m* restreint (b) *(limit)* **to c. oneself to sth/doing sth** se limiter *ou* s'en tenir à qch/à faire qch
confinement [kən'faɪnmənt] *n* (a) *(in prison)* emprisonnement *m* (b) *Old-fashioned Med (labour)* couches *fpl*
confines ['kɒnfaɪnz] *npl (of town)* confins *mpl*; *Fig (limits)* limites *fpl*; **within the c. of** dans les limites de
confirm [kən'fɜːm] *vt* confirmer; *(power, position)* consolider, renforcer
confirmation [kɒnfə'meɪʃən] *n also Rel* confirmation *f*

confirmed [kən'fɜːmd] *adj (smoker, liar)* invétéré(e); *(bachelor)* endurci

confiscate ['kɒnfɪskeɪt] *vt* confisquer (**from** à)

confiscation [kɒnfɪs'keɪʃən] *n* confiscation *f*

conflict 1 *n* ['kɒnflɪkt] conflit *m*; **to come into c.** with entrer en conflit avec **2** *vi* [kən'flɪkt] être en contradiction (**with** avec)

conflicting [kən'flɪktɪŋ] *adj (opinions)* opposé(e); *(reports, evidence)* contradictoire

confluence ['kɒnfluəns] *n (of rivers)* confluent *m*

conform [kən'fɔːm] *vi* se plier aux règles; **to c. to** *(rules)* obéir à, se plier à; *(standards)* être en conformité avec; **to c. with** être conforme à

conformist [kən'fɔːmɪst] *n & adj* conformiste *mf*

conformity [kən'fɔːmɪtɪ] *n* conformité *f*; **in c. with** en conformité *ou* en accord avec

confound [kən'faʊnd] *vt* (**a**) *(puzzle)* laisser perplexe (**b**) *(frustrate) (plans)* faire échouer (**c**) *(surprise)* confondre

confront [kən'frʌnt] *vt* affronter, faire face à; **to be confronted by sth** être confronté(e) à qch; **to c. sb with sth** confronter qn à qch

confrontation [kɒnfrʌn'teɪʃən] *n* affrontement *m*

confuse [kən'fjuːz] *vt (bewilder)* embrouiller; *(mix up)* confondre (**with** avec)

confused [kən'fjuːzd] *adj (person)* perdu(e); *(instructions, account, mind)* confus(e); **I'm c.** je m'y perds; **to get c.** s'embrouiller

confusing [kən'fjuːzɪŋ] *adj (bewildering)* déroutant(e); *(muddled)* confus(e)

confusion [kən'fjuːʒən] *n (bewilderment)* perplexité *f*; *(disorder, lack of clarity)* confusion *f*; **to throw sth into c.** chambouler qch

congeal [kən'dʒiːl] *vi (of blood)* (se) coaguler

congenial [kən'dʒiːnɪəl] *adj* agréable

congenital [kən'dʒenɪtəl] *adj* congénital(e); *Fig* **he's a c. liar** il ment tout le temps, c'est congénital

conger ['kɒŋɡə(r)] *n* **c.** *(eel)* congre *m*

congested [kən'dʒestɪd] *adj (street, city, lungs)* congestionné(e); *(nose)* bouché(e)

congestion [kən'dʒestʃən] *n (of traffic)* encombrements *mpl*; *(of lungs, nose)* congestion *f*

conglomerate [kən'glɒmərət] *n* conglomérat *m*

Congo ['kɒŋɡəʊ] *n* **the C.** *(country)* le Congo

Congolese [kɒŋɡə'liːz] **1** *n* Congolais(e) *m,f* **2** *adj* congolais(e)

congratulate [kən'grætjʊleɪt] *vt* féliciter (**on** de); **to c. oneself on having done sth** se féliciter d'avoir fait qch

congratulations [kəngrætjʊ'leɪʃənz] *npl* félicitations *fpl*; **c. on your engagement/passing your exams** félicitations pour vos fiançailles/vos examens

congratulatory [kən'grætjʊleɪtərɪ] *adj* de félicitations

congregate ['kɒŋɡrɪɡeɪt] *vi* se rassembler, s'assembler

congregation [kɒŋɡrɪ'ɡeɪʃən] *n (of church)* assemblée *f* des fidèles

congress ['kɒŋɡres] *n (conference)* congrès *m*; *Am Pol* **C.** le Congrès *(assemblée législative américaine)*

Congressman ['kɒŋɡresmən] *n Am Pol* membre *m* du Congrès

Congresswoman ['kɒŋɡreswʊmən] *n Am Pol* membre *m* du Congrès

conical ['kɒnɪkəl] *adj* conique

conifer ['kɒnɪfə(r)] *n* conifère *m*

coniferous [kə'nɪfərəs] *adj (forest)* de conifères; **c. tree** conifère *m*

conjecture [kən'dʒektʃə(r)] **1** *n* conjecture *f*; **it's pure c.** ce ne sont que des suppositions **2** *vt* supposer **3** *vi* faire des conjectures

conjugal ['kɒndʒʊɡəl] *adj* conjugal(e)

conjugate ['kɒndʒʊɡeɪt] *Gram* **1** *vt* conjuguer **2** *vi* se conjuguer

conjugation [kɒndʒʊ'ɡeɪʃən] *n Gram* conjugaison *f*

conjunction [kən'dʒʌŋkʃən] *n* conjonction *f*; **in c. with** conjointement avec

conjunctivitis [kəndʒʌŋktɪ'vaɪtɪs] *n* conjonctivite *f*

conjure ['kʌndʒə(r)] *vi (do magic)* faire des tours de passe-passe; *Fig* **a name to c. with** un nom prestigieux
▶ **conjure up** *vt sep* (**a**) *(produce)* faire apparaître; **she conjured up a meal** elle a débrouillé pour préparer un repas en un rien de temps; **to c. sth up out of nowhere** faire apparaître qch comme par magie (**b**) *(call to mind)* évoquer

conjurer ['kʌndʒərə(r)] *n* prestidigitateur *m*, illusionniste *mf*

conjuring ['kʌndʒərɪŋ] *n* prestidigitation *f*; **c. trick** tour *m* de prestidigitation *ou* de passe-passe

conjuror ['kʌndʒərə(r)] *n* = **conjurer**

conk [kɒŋk] *n Br Fam (nose)* blair *m*, pif *m*
▶ **conk out** *vi Br Fam (stop working) (of machine, TV)* flancher; **the car conked out on me** la voiture m'a claqué entre les doigts (**b**) *(fall asleep)* se mettre à pioncer

conker ['kɒŋkə(r)] *n Fam (chestnut)* marron *m* d'Inde; *Br* **conkers** *(game)* = jeu qui consiste à faire éclater le marron que son adversaire tient au bout d'une ficelle

conman ['kɒnmæn] *n* escroc *m*

connect [kə'nekt] **1** *vt* (**a**) *(pipes, wires, circuits)* relier (**to** à); **to c. sth to the mains** brancher qch sur secteur (**b**) *(link, associate)* **to c. sb/sth to sb/sth** établir un lien entre qn/qch et qn/qch; **there is nothing to c. the two crimes** il n'y a aucun lien entre les deux crimes; **to be connected with** avoir un lien *ou* un rapport avec; **the two issues are not connected** les deux questions n'ont aucun rapport; **are they connected?** *(of people)* sont-ils parents?; **to be well connected** *(of person)* avoir des relations (**c**) *Tél* mettre en ligne *ou* en communication (**with** avec); **can you c. me with ticket sales?** pourriez-vous me passer la vente de billets? **2** *vi* (**a**) *(of pipes, wires, roads)* être relié(e) (**with** avec); *(of rooms)* communiquer (**with** avec) (**b**) *(of train, plane)* assurer la correspondance (**with** avec) (**c**) *(of blow)* atteindre son but; **the blow connected with his knee** le coup l'a atteint au genou
▶ **connect up** *vt sep (pipes, wires)* raccorder

connection [kə'nekʃən] *n* (**a**) *(link, association)* lien *m*, rapport *m*; **in c. with** à propos de; **in this c.** à ce propos (**b**) *(acquaintance)* relation *f*; **to have connections** avoir des relations en haut lieu (**c**) *(of pipes, wires)* raccordement *m* (**d**) *(train, plane)* correspondance *f*

connivance [kə'naɪvəns] *n* connivence *f*

connive [kə'naɪv] *vi* (**a**) *(conspire)* comploter; **to c. with sb** être de connivence avec qn (**b**) **to c. at sth** *(let happen)* laisser faire qch

conniving [kə'naɪvɪŋ] *adj* intrigant(e)

connoisseur [kɒnə'sɜː(r)] *n* connaisseur(euse) *m,f* (**of** en)

connotation [kɒnə'teɪʃən] *n* connotation *f*

conquer ['kɒŋkə(r)] *vt (country, someone's heart)* conquérir; *(difficulty, fears)* vaincre

conquering [ˈkɒŋkərɪŋ] *adj* victorieux(euse)

conqueror [ˈkɒŋkərə(r)] *n* vainqueur *m*

conquest [ˈkɒŋkwest] *n* conquête *f*; **to make a c.** of sb faire la conquête de qn

conscience [ˈkɒnʃəns] *n* conscience *f*; **to have a clear c.** avoir la conscience tranquille; **to have a guilty c.** avoir mauvaise conscience; **to have sth on one's c.** avoir qch sur la conscience; **to have no c.** about doing sth ne pas avoir de scrupules à faire qch; **in all c.** raisonnablement

conscientious [kɒnʃɪˈenʃəs] *adj* consciencieux(euse); **c. objector** objecteur *m* de conscience

conscious [ˈkɒnʃəs] *adj* **(a)** *(awake)* conscient(e) **(b)** *(aware)* **to be c. of sth/that...** être conscient(e) de qch/que...; **to become c. of sth** prendre conscience de qch, s'apercevoir de qch; *Psy* **the c. mind** la conscience **(c)** *(intentional)* conscient(e); **to make a c. effort to do sth** faire un effort particulier pour faire qch; **to make a c. decision to do sth** chercher délibérément à faire qch

consciousness [ˈkɒnʃəsnɪs] *n* **(a)** *(wakefulness)* conscience *f*; **to lose/regain c.** perdre/reprendre connaissance **(b)** *(awareness)* conscience *f* (of de); **to raise people's c.** of sth sensibiliser les gens à qch

conscript 1 *n* [ˈkɒnskrɪpt] conscrit *m*
2 *vt* [kənˈskrɪpt] enrôler; **to be conscripted** être appelé(e) (sous les drapeaux)

conscription [kənˈskrɪpʃən] *n* conscription *f*

consecrate [ˈkɒnsɪkreɪt] *vt Rel & Fig* consacrer

consecration [kɒnsɪˈkreɪʃən] *n* consécration *f*

consecutive [kənˈsekjʊtɪv] *adj* consécutif(ive); **on three c. days** trois jours consécutifs, trois jours de suite

consensus [kənˈsensəs] *n* consensus *m*

consent [kənˈsent] **1** *n* consentement *m*, assentiment *m*
2 *vi* **to c. to sth/to do sth** consentir à qch/à faire qch

consequence [ˈkɒnsɪkwəns] *n* **(a)** *(result)* conséquence *f*; **as a c., in c.** par conséquent; **to take the consequences** subir les conséquences **(b)** *(importance)* importance *f*; **of little c.** de peu d'importance; **of no c.** sans importance

consequent [ˈkɒnsɪkwənt] *adj* résultant(e); **c. upon sth** qui résulte de qch; **the war and its c. loss of life** la guerre et les pertes en vies humaines qui en résultent

consequently [ˈkɒnsɪkwəntlɪ] *adv* par conséquent

conservation [kɒnsəˈveɪʃən] *n* *(of environment)* protection *f*; *(of energy)* économies *fpl*; **c. area** *(of town, city)* quartier *m* préservé; *(nature reserve)* réserve *f* naturelle

conservationist [kɒnsəˈveɪʃənɪst] *n* défenseur *m* de l'environnement

Conservative [kənˈsɜːvətɪv] *Br Pol* **1** *n* conservateur(trice) *m,f*
2 *adj* conservateur(trice); **the C. Party** le Parti conservateur

conservative [kənˈsɜːvətɪv] **1** *n* conservateur(trice) *m,f*
2 *adj* conservateur(trice); *(conventional)* classique; **at a c. estimate** au bas mot

conservatory [kənˈsɜːvətərɪ] *(pl* **conservatories)** *n* **(a)** *(room)* véranda *f* **(b)** *Mus* conservatoire *m*

conserve 1 *n* [ˈkɒnsɜːv] *(jam)* confiture *f*
2 *vt* [kənˈsɜːv] *(monument, language, tradition)* préserver; *(water, energy)* faire des économies de

consider [kənˈsɪdə(r)] *vt* **(a)** *(think over)* considérer; *(offer, matter)* étudier; **he was considering whether to go out when...** il était en train de se demander s'il allait sortir lorsque...; **to c. doing sth** envisager de faire qch; **to c. sb for a job** envisager qn pour un poste **(b)** *(take into account)* penser, réfléchir à; *(possibility)* envisager; *(person's feelings)* tenir compte de; **all things considered** tout bien considéré **(c)** *(regard)* considérer; **I c. her a friend** je la considère

comme une amie; **c. it done** considère que c'est déjà fait; **c. yourself lucky** considère-toi comme heureux

considerable [kənˈsɪdərəbəl] *adj* considérable; **after c. difficulty** après bien des difficultés

considerate [kənˈsɪdərət] *adj* prévenant(e) **(towards** envers); **that wasn't very c. of you** ce n'était pas très aimable de ta part

consideration [kənsɪdəˈreɪʃən] *n* **(a)** *(deliberation)* **to be under c.** être à l'étude; **after due c.** après mûre réflexion; **to take sth into c.** prendre qch en considération **(b)** *(factor)* facteur *m* **(c)** *(respect)* considération *f*; **show some c.!** tu pourrais faire preuve d'un peu de considération!; **out of c. for** par égard pour **(d)** *(payment)* contribution *f*; **for a small c.** en échange d'une modique somme

considering [kənˈsɪdərɪŋ] **1** *prep* étant donné, vu
2 *conj* étant donné que; **c. (that) he is so young** étant donné son jeune âge
3 *adv* (after all) not bad **c.** pas mal après tout

consign [kənˈsaɪn] *vt* **(a)** *(dispose of)* reléguer **(to** à); **she was consigned to a life of loneliness** elle fut condamnée à une existence solitaire **(b)** *(entrust)* confier **(to** à) **(c)** *(send)* expédier **(to** à)

consignment [kənˈsaɪnmənt] *n* *(of goods)* envoi *m*, expédition *f*

▸ **consist of** [kənˈsɪst] *vt insep* consister en, se composer de

consistency [kənˈsɪstənsɪ] *n* **(a)** *(of substance, liquid)* consistance *f* **(b)** *(of arguments, ideas)* cohérence *f*; *(of behaviour, person)* logique *f*; *(of performer, results)* régularité *f*

consistent [kənˈsɪstənt] *adj* *(arguments, ideas)* cohérent(e); *(behaviour, person)* logique; *(quality, standard)* constant(e); *(performer, results)* régulier(ère); *(refusal, failure)* persistant(e); **to be c. with** concorder avec

consistently [kənˈsɪstəntlɪ] *adv* *(play, perform)* avec régularité; *(fail, deny, oppose)* toujours

consolation [kɒnsəˈleɪʃən] *n* consolation *f*; **if it's any c.** si ça peut te consoler; **c. prize** prix *m* de consolation

console¹ [ˈkɒnsəʊl] *n* *(control panel)* console *f*

console² [kənˈsəʊl] *vt* consoler; **to c.** (for de)

consolidate [kənˈsɒlɪdeɪt] **1** *vt also Fig* consolider; *(position)* renforcer; *(power)* asseoir
2 *vi* se consolider

consolidation [kənsɒlɪˈdeɪʃən] *n also Fig* consolidation *f*; *(of position, power)* renforcement *m*

consonant [ˈkɒnsənənt] **1** *n* consonne *f*
2 *adj Formal* **c. with** en accord avec

consort [ˈkɒnsɔːt] *n* *(spouse of monarch)* époux (épouse) *m,f*; **(prince) c.** prince *m* consort

▸ **consort with** [kənˈsɔːt] *vt insep* frayer avec, fréquenter

consortium [kənˈsɔːtɪəm] *(pl* **consortiums** *or* **consortia** [kənˈsɔːtɪə]) *n Com* consortium *m*

conspicuous [kənˈspɪkjʊəs] *adj* *(easily visible)* bien visible; *(bravery)* remarquable; **to look c.** ne pas passer inaperçu(e); **to make oneself c.** se faire remarquer; **in a c. position** bien en évidence; **to be c. by one's absence** briller par son absence; **c. consumption** consommation *f* ostentatoire

conspiracy [kənˈspɪrəsɪ] *(pl* **conspiracies)** *n* conspiration *f*, complot *m*; **c. theory** = théorie postulant l'existence d'un complot pour expliquer des événements demeurés mystérieux

conspirator [kənˈspɪrətə(r)] *n* conspirateur(trice) *m,f*

conspiratorial [kənspɪrəˈtɔːrɪəl] *adj* de conspirateur; **c. wink** un coup d'œil complice

conspire [kənˈspaɪə(r)] *vi* *(of person)* se liguer **(against** /

with contre/avec); *(for political reasons)* conspirer (against/with contre/avec); **circumstances conspired against me** les circonstances se sont liguées contre moi
constable ['kʌnstəbəl] *n Br* agent *m* de police; *(rural)* gendarme *m*; **chief c.** = commissaire *m* de police divisionnaire
constabulary [kən'stæbjʊlərɪ] *(pl* **constabularies)** *n Br* police *f*
constant ['kɒnstənt] **1** *n Math & Phys* constante *f* **2** *adj* **(a)** *(unchanging) (price, temperature)* constant(e); *(friend)* fidèle **(b)** *(continual) (attention, noise, care)* continuel(elle); *(questions, complaints)* incessant(e); **a c. stream of insults** un flot d'injures ininterrompu
constellation [kɒnstə'leɪʃən] *n* constellation *f*
consternation [kɒnstə'neɪʃən] *n* consternation *f*
constipated ['kɒnstɪpeɪtɪd] *adj also Fig* constipé(e)
constipation [kɒnstɪ'peɪʃən] *n* constipation *f*
constituency [kən'stɪtjʊənsɪ] *(pl* **constituencies)** *n* circonscription *f* (électorale)
constituent [kən'stɪtjʊənt] **1** *n* **(a)** *Pol* électeur(trice) *m,f* **(b)** *(part)* élément *m* constitutif **2** *adj* constitutif(ive); une **c. part** élément *m* constitutif
constitute ['kɒnstɪtjuːt] *vt* constituer
constitution [kɒnstɪ'tjuːʃən] *n* **(a)** *(of state, organization)* constitution *f* **(b)** *(of person)* constitution *f*; **to have an iron c.** avoir une santé de fer; **to have a weak c.** être de santé fragile
constitutional [kɒnstɪ'tjuːʃənəl] **1** *n (walk)* (courte) promenade *f* **2** *adj (reform, decision, monarchy)* constitutionnel(elle)
constrain [kən'streɪn] *vt* contraindre, obliger (**to do à** faire); **to feel constrained to do sth** se sentir obligé(e) de faire qch
constraint [kən'streɪnt] *n* contrainte *f*; **to place constraints upon** imposer des contraintes à; **under c.** sous la contrainte
constrict [kən'strɪkt] *vt (blood vessel)* resserrer; *(movement)* gêner; **to feel constricted** se sentir à l'étroit
constriction [kən'strɪkʃən] *n (of blood vessel)* constriction *f*; *(of person)* gêne *f*
construct 1 *n* ['kɒnstrʌkt] *(idea)* concept *m* **2** *vt* [kən'strʌkt] construire
construction [kən'strʌkʃən] *n* **(a)** *(building) & Gram* construction *f*; **under c.** en construction; **the c. industry** l'industrie *f* du bâtiment, le bâtiment; **c. site** chantier *m* (de construction); **c. worker** ouvrier *m* du bâtiment **(b)** *(interpretation)* **to put a favourable/an unfavourable c. on sth** bien/mal interpréter qch
constructive [kən'strʌktɪv] *adj* constructif(ive)
construe [kən'struː] *vt* interpréter
consul ['kɒnsəl] *n* consul *m*
consular ['kɒnsjʊlə(r)] *adj* consulaire
consulate ['kɒnsjʊlət] *n* consulat *m*
consult [kən'sʌlt] **1** *vt* consulter (**with sb/about sth** qn/à propos de qch) **2** *vi* consulter (**with sb/about sth** qn/à propos de qch)
consultancy [kən'sʌltənsɪ] *(pl* **consultancies)** *n* **(a)** *(of doctor)* poste *m* de spécialiste *(haut placé dans la hiérarchie hospitalière)* **(b)** *Com* conseil *m*; **to do c. work** être consultant(e)
consultant [kən'sʌltənt] *n* **(a)** *(doctor)* spécialiste *mf (pratiquant à l'hôpital)* **(b)** *(adviser)* consultant(e) *m,f*
consultation [kɒnsəl'teɪʃən] *n (reference)* consultation *f*; *(discussion)* délibération *f*; **to hold a c. with sb** s'entretenir avec qn; **in c. with sb** en consultation avec qn
consume [kən'sjuːm] *vt (food, fuel, power)* consommer;

to be consumed with jealousy/desire brûler de jalousie/ désir
consumer [kən'sjuːmə(r)] *n (of product)* consommateur(trice) *m,f*; **c. durables** biens *mpl* de consommation durables; **c. goods** biens de consommation; *Econ* **c. price index** indice *m* des prix de détails; **c. protection** la défense du consommateur; **c. society** société *f* de consommation
consumerism [kən'sjuːmərɪzəm] *n* consumérisme *m*
consummate 1 *adj* [kən'sʌmɪt] *(linguist, cook)* de premier ordre; *(snob, hypocrite)* parfait(e) **2** *vt* ['kɒnsəmeɪt] *(marriage, relationship)* consommer
consumption [kən'sʌmpʃən] *n* **(a)** *(of goods, resources)* consommation *f*; **unfit for human c.** impropre à la consommation **(b)** *Old-fashioned (tuberculosis)* consomption *f*
contact ['kɒntækt] **1** *n* **(a)** *(act of touching)* contact *m*; **to be in/come into c. with** être en/entrer en contact avec; **to make/lose c. with sb** prendre/perdre contact avec qn; **to lose c. with sb** perdre contact avec qn; **to get in c. with sb** contacter qn; **c. lenses**, *Fam* **contacts** lentilles *fpl* (de contact) **(b)** *(acquaintance)* relation *f*; **he has lots of contacts** il connaît beaucoup de monde **2** *vt* se mettre en rapport avec, contacter
contagious [kən'teɪdʒəs] *adj (disease)* contagieux(euse); *(laughter)* communicatif(ive)
contain [kən'teɪn] *vt* **(a)** *(hold)* contenir, renfermer; *(include)* contenir **(b)** *(control)* contenir; **to c. oneself** se contenir; **he was unable to c. his laughter** il ne put s'empêcher de rire
container [kən'teɪnə(r)] *n (for storage)* récipient *m*; *(for transport)* conteneur *m*; **c. lorry** camion *m* adapté au transport des conteneurs; **c. ship** (navire *m*) porte-conteneurs *m inv*; **c. terminal** terminal *m* à conteneurs
contaminate [kən'tæmɪneɪt] *vt also Fig* contaminer
contamination [kəntæmɪ'neɪʃən] *n* contamination *f*
contd *(abbr* **continued)** c. **on page 16** suite (à la) page 16
contemplate ['kɒntempleɪt] **1** *vt (look at)* contempler; *(consider)* réfléchir à; **to c. doing sth** envisager de ou songer à faire qch **2** *vi (consider)* méditer
contemplation [kɒntem'pleɪʃən] *n* contemplation *f*
contemplative [kən'templətɪv] *adj* contemplatif(ive)
contemporary *(pl* **contemporaries)** [kən'tempərərɪ] *& adj* contemporain(e) *m,f*
contempt [kən'tempt] *n* mépris *m*; **to hold sb/sth in c.** avoir du mépris pour qn/qch, mépriser qn/qch; **beneath c.** méprisable; *Law* **c. of court** outrage *m* au tribunal
contemptible [kən'temptəbəl] *adj* méprisable
contemptuous [kən'temptjʊəs] *adj* méprisant(e); **to be c. of sth** mépriser qch
contend [kən'tend] **1** *vt (maintain)* **to c.** prétendre *ou* soutenir que... **2** *vi* **(a)** *(struggle)* **to c. with sth** lutter contre qch; *(difficulties)* affronter qch; **they still had the chairman to c. with** il leur restait à régler le problème du P.D.-G. **(b)** *(compete)* **to c. for sth** se battre pour qch; *(for job, contract)* être en concurrence pour qch
contender [kən'tendə(r)] *n (in sport)* concurrent(e) *m,f*; *(in election, for job)* candidat(e) *m,f*
content¹ ['kɒntent] *n* **(a)** *(quantity)* teneur *f*; *(of book, speech, essay)* fond *m*; **protein/vitamin c.** teneur en protéines/vitamines **(b)** **contents** *(of pockets, drawer, house)* contenu *m*; **contents page** *(of book)* table *f* des matières

content² [kən'tent] **1** *adj (happy)* content(e), satisfait(e) (with de); **to be c.** with one's lot se contenter de son sort **2** *vt* contenter; **to c.** oneself with sth/with doing sth se contenter de qch/de faire qch

contented [kən'tentɪd] *adj (person)* content(e), satisfait(e) (with de); *(smile, sigh)* de satisfaction

contention [kən'tenʃən] *n* **(a)** *(dispute)* dispute *f* **(b)** *(competition)* **to be in c. (for sth)** être en compétition (pour qch) **(c)** *(opinion)* affirmation *f*; **it is my c. that...** j'affirme que...

contentious [kən'tenʃəs] *adj (issue, views)* controversé(e); *(person)* querelleur(euse)

contentment [kən'tentmənt] *n* contentement *m*

contest 1 *n* ['kɒntest] *(competition)* concours *m*; *(for job, presidency)* lutte *f*; *(in boxing)* combat *m* **2** *vt* [kən'test] *(right, ability, will)* contester; **to c. a seat** se porter candidat(e); **a fiercely contested election** une élection très disputée

contestant [kən'testənt] *n (in competition, game)* concurrent(e) *m,f*; *(in election)* candidat(e) *m,f*

context ['kɒntekst] *n* contexte *m*; **in/out of c.** en/hors contexte; **to put sth into c.** replacer qch dans son contexte

continent¹ ['kɒntɪnənt] *n (land mass)* continent *m*; *Br* **the C.** l'Europe *f* (continentale)

continent² *adj Med* continent(e)

continental [kɒntɪ'nentəl] *adj* **(a)** *(in geography)* continental(e); **c. drift** dérive *f* des continents; **c. shelf** plate-forme *f* continentale **(b)** *(European)* européen(enne); **c. breakfast** = petit déjeuner se composant de tartines et d'une boisson chaude; **c. quilt** couette *f*

contingency [kən'tɪndʒənsɪ] *(pl* **contingencies)** *n* éventualité *f*; **c. fund** caisse *f* ou fonds *m* de prévoyance; **c. plan** plan *m* d'urgence

continual [kən'tɪnjʊəl] *adj* continuel(elle), incessant(e)

continuation [kəntɪnjʊ'eɪʃən] *n (of story)* suite *f*; *(of action, work)* prolongation *f*; *(of road)* prolongement *m*

continue [kən'tɪnjuː] **1** *vt (activity, journey)* continuer, poursuivre, *(after interruption)* reprendre, continuer; *(tradition)* perpétuer; **to c.** to do *or* **doing sth** continuer à *ou* de faire qch; **to be continued** à suivre; **continued on page 30** suite (à la) page 30 **2** *vi* continuer; *(of situation)* se prolonger; **to c.** on one's way continuer *ou* poursuivre son chemin; **she will c.** as **manager until December** elle continuera d'assumer ses fonctions de directrice jusqu'en décembre; **the situation cannot c.** cette situation ne peut pas durer

continuity [kɒntɪ'njuːɪtɪ] *n* continuité *f*; **c.** announcer *(on TV, radio)* speaker(ine) *m,f*; **c. girl** scripte *f*

continuous [kən'tɪnjʊəs] *adj* continu(e); *Sch & Univ* **c.** assessment contrôle *m* continu; *Comptr* **c.** paper *or* **stationery** papier *m* (en) continu; *Cin* **c.** performance cinéma *m* permanent

contort [kən'tɔːt] **1** *vt* tordre **2** *vi* se tordre (with de)

contortion [kən'tɔːʃən] *n (of features)* crispation *f*; *(of body)* contorsion *f*

contour ['kɒntʊə(r)] *n* contour *m*; **c. (line)** courbe *f* de niveau; **c. map** carte *f* en courbes de niveau

contraband ['kɒntrəbænd] *n* contrebande *f*; **c. goods** marchandises *fpl* de contrebande

contraception [kɒntrə'sepʃən] *n* contraception *f*

contraceptive [kɒntrə'septɪv] **1** *n* contraceptif *m* **2** *adj* **c. pill** pilule *f* contraceptive

contract 1 *n* ['kɒntrækt] contrat *m*; **to be under c.** être sous contrat; **to enter into a c.** passer un contrat; **to take out a c. on sb** *(hire assassin)* engager un tueur à

gages pour assassiner qn; **c. killer** tueur *m* à gages **2** *vt* [kən'trækt] *(illness, debt)* contracter; **to c. to do sth** s'engager (par contrat) à faire qch **3** *vi* [kən'trækt] *(shrink)* se contracter

▸ **contract out 1** *vt sep (work)* sous-traiter **2** *vi Com (of insurance policy, pension plan)* arrêter de souscrire (**of** à)

contraction [kən'trækʃən] *n* contraction *f*

contractor [kən'træktə(r)] *n (businessperson)* entrepreneur *m* (en bâtiment); *(worker)* ouvrier *m* (en bâtiment)

contractual [kən'træktjʊəl] *adj* contractuel(elle)

contradict [kɒntrə'dɪkt] *vt (disagree with)* contredire; *(deny)* démentir; **to c.** oneself se contredire

contradiction [kɒntrə'dɪkʃən] *n* contradiction *f*; **it's a c. in terms** c'est parfaitement contradictoire

contradictory [kɒntrə'dɪktərɪ] *adj* contradictoire

contraflow ['kɒntrəfləʊ] *n* **c.** (system) *(on motorway)* = circulation sur une voie unique, lors de travaux routiers

contralto [kən'wæltəʊ] *(pl* **contraltos)** *n* contralto *m,f*

contraption [kən'træpʃən] *n Fam* machin *m*, truc *m*

contrary ['kɒntrərɪ] **1** *n* contraire *m*; **on the c.** au contraire; **unless you hear to the c.** sauf avis contraire; **there was no evidence to the c.** il n'y avait pas de preuve du contraire **2** *adj* **(a)** *(opposite)* contraire (**to** à), *(ideas, interests)* opposé(e) (**to** à); **c. to my expectations** contre mon attente; **c. to popular belief** contrairement à ce que croient la plupart des gens **(b)** [kən'treərɪ] *(awkward)* contrariant(e)

contrast 1 *n* ['kɒntrɑːst] contraste *m* (**between** entre); **in c. with** *or* **to** par opposition à; **by c.** par contraste **2** *vt* [kən'trɑːst] mettre en contraste (**with** avec) **3** *vi* [kən'trɑːst] faire contraste (**with** avec)

contravene [kɒntrə'viːn] *vt* enfreindre

contravention [kɒntrə'venʃən] *n (of law)* infraction *f* (**of** à); **in c. of** a treaty en violation d'un traité

contribute [kən'trɪbjuːt] **1** *vt (money)* verser; *(time, clothes)* donner; **to c. an article to a newspaper** écrire un article pour un journal; **he didn't c. anything to the discussion** il n'a pas pris part à la discussion **2** *vi* contribuer (**to** à); *(to charity)* donner (**to** à); *(to newspaper)* collaborer (**to** à); **to c. to a discussion** prendre part à une discussion

contribution [kɒntrɪ'bjuːʃən] *n* contribution *f* (**to** à); **the cake was David's c.** c'est David qu'il faut remercier pour le gâteau

contributor [kən'trɪbjʊtə(r)] *n (to charity)* donateur(trice) *m,f*; *(to newspaper)* collaborateur(trice) *m,f* (**to** de)

contributory [kən'trɪbjʊtərɪ] *adj (cause, factor)* concourant(e); **to be a c. factor in sth** concourir à qch; *Law* **c. negligence** manque *m* de précautions

contrite ['kɒntraɪt] *adj* contrit(e)

contrition [kən'trɪʃən] *n* contrition *f*

contrivance [kən'traɪvəns] *n (device)* appareil *m*; *(scheme, plan)* système *m*

contrive [kən'traɪv] *vt* inventer; **to c. to do sth** trouver le moyen de faire qch

contrived [kən'traɪvd] *adj* forcé(e), qui manque de naturel

control [kən'trəʊl] **1** *n* **(a)** *(power, restriction)* contrôle *m*; **to impose price controls** imposer le contrôle des prix; **to take c. (of the situation)** prendre les choses en main; **to have c. over** *(power)* contrôler; *(authority)* avoir le contrôle sur; **to be in c. of sth** contrôler qch; **to be back in c.** avoir repris le contrôle; **to get out of c.** devenir incontrôlable; **to**

let sth get out of c. perdre le contrôle de qch; **to bring a fire under c.** maîtriser un incendie; **to keep one's feelings under c.** maîtriser ses émotions; **everything is under c.** je domine/nous dominons/*etc* la situation; **to lose c.** *(of oneself)* ne plus être maître de soi; **to regain c.** *(of oneself)* se ressaisir; **c. group** groupe *m* témoin; **c. tower** *(at airport)* tour *f* de contrôle **(b)** *(device)* **the controls** les commandes *fpl*; **to be at the controls** être aux commandes; **c. panel** tableau *m* de bord

2 *vt (pt & pp* **controlled)** *(production, expenditure, prices)* contrôler; *(business)* diriger; *(child, pupils)* avoir de l'autorité sur; *(disease)* maintenir à un niveau raisonnable; *(vehicle)* garder le contrôle de; **to c. oneself** se maîtriser; **to c. one's anger** maîtriser sa colère

controlled [kən'trəʊld] *adj (person)* maître de soi, posé(e); *(experiment, explosion)* contrôlé(e)

controlling interest [kən'trəʊlɪŋ'ɪntrest] *n Fin* participation *f* majoritaire

controversial [kɒntrə'vɜːʃəl] *adj* **to be c.** *(of film, decision)* être controversé(e); *(of person)* être provocateur(trice)

controversy ['kɒntrəvɜːsɪ, kən'trɒvəsɪ] *(pl* **controversies)** *n* controverse *f*

conundrum [kə'nʌndrəm] *n (riddle)* devinette *f*; *(mystery)* énigme *f*

conurbation [kɒnɜː'beɪʃən] *n* conurbation *f*

convalesce [kɒnvə'les] *vi* être en convalescence

convalescence [kɒnvə'lesəns] *n* convalescence *f*

convalescent [kɒnvə'lesənt] *adj (patient)* convalescent(e); **c. home** maison *f* de repos

convection [kən'vekʃən] *n* convection *f*; **c. heater** convecteur *m*

convene [kən'viːn] *n* **1** *vt (meeting)* convoquer **2** *vi (of meeting, committee)* se réunir

convenience [kən'viːnɪəns] *n* commodité *f*; **at your c.** dès que possible; *Formal* **at your earliest c.** dans les meilleurs délais; **(public) c.** *(toilet)* toilettes *fpl* publiques; **c. food** aliments *mpl* tout prêts

convenient [kən'viːnɪənt] *adj (arrangement, method)* commode, pratique; **to be c. (for sb)** *(of arrangement)* être commode *ou* pratique (pour qn); *(of time)* convenir (à qn)

convent ['kɒnvənt] *n Rel* couvent *m*; **c. school** école *f* tenue par des sœurs

convention [kən'venʃən] *n* **(a)** *(conference)* convention *f*, congrès *m* **(b)** *(agreement)* convention *f* **(c)** *(established practice)* usage *m*; **the c. is that...** l'usage veut que...

conventional [kən'venʃənəl] *adj* conventionnel(elle); **c. warfare** guerre *f* conventionnelle; **c. weapon** arme *f* conventionnelle; **c. wisdom** sagesse *f* populaire

converge [kən'vɜːdʒ] *vi* converger **(on** sur)

conversant [kən'vɜːsənt] *adj* **to be c. with sth** s'y connaître en qch; *(with events, developments)* être au courant de qch

conversation [kɒnvə'seɪʃən] *n* conversation *f*; **to have a c. with sb** avoir une conversation avec qn; **to make c.** faire la conversation; **the vase is quite a c. piece** le vase alimente bien des conversations; *Fam* **to be a c. killer** arrêter net la conversation

conversational [kɒnvə'seɪʃənəl] *adj (style)* de la conversation; *Comptr (mode)* dialogue; **in a c. tone** sur le ton de la conversation

conversationalist [kɒnvə'seɪʃənəlɪst] *n* **to be a good c.** avoir de la conversation; **I'm not much of a c.** je ne suis pas brillant causeur

converse¹ [kən'vɜːs] *vi (talk)* converser **(about** sur), s'entretenir **(about** sur)

converse² ['kɒnvɜːs] *n (opposite)* **the c.** le contraire

conversion [kən'vɜːʃən] *n* **(a)** *(transformation)* conversion *f*; *(of building)* aménagement *m*; **c. table** *(for measurements)* table *f* de conversion **(b)** *(in rugby)* transformation *f*

convert [kən'vɜːt] **1** *n* ['kɒnvɜːt] *Rel & Fig* converti(e) *m,f* (to à) **2** *vt* (a) *Rel & Fig* convertir **(to** à); *(building)* aménager **(into** en) **(b)** *(in rugby)* **to c. a try** transformer un essai **3** *vi Rel & Fig* se convertir **(to** à)

convertible [kən'vɜːtəbəl] **1** *n (car)* décapotable *f* **2** *adj (sofa)* convertible; *(car)* décapotable; **c. currency** monnaie *f ou* devise *f* convertible

convex [kɒn'veks] *adj* convexe

convey [kən'veɪ] *vt* **(a)** *(communicate)* transmettre; **to c. one's meaning** communiquer sa pensée **(b)** *(transport)* transporter

conveyancing [kən'veɪənsɪŋ] *n Law* procédure *f* translative de propriété

conveyor belt [kən'veɪəbelt] *n* convoyeur *m*, tapis *m* roulant

convict 1 *n* ['kɒnvɪkt] détenu(e) *m,f* **2** *vt* [kən'vɪkt] **to c. sb (of)** déclarer qn coupable (de)

conviction [kən'vɪkʃən] *n* **(a)** *Law* condamnation *f*; **to have no previous convictions** n'avoir jamais été condamné(e) **(b)** *(belief)* conviction *f*; **to lack c.** manquer de conviction

convince [kən'vɪns] *vt* convaincre **(of/that** de/que); **I was convinced I was right** j'étais convaincu d'avoir raison

convincing [kən'vɪnsɪŋ] *adj* convaincant(e); *(defeat)* décisif(ive)

convivial [kən'vɪvɪəl] *adj (person)* chaleureux(euse); *(atmosphere)* joyeux(euse)

convoluted ['kɒnvəluːtɪd] *adj (argument, explanation)* compliqué(e)

convoy ['kɒnvɔɪ] *n* convoi *m*

convulse [kən'vʌls] *vt* secouer; **to be convulsed with laughter/pain** se tordre de rire/de douleur

convulsions [kən'vʌlʃənz] *npl Med* convulsions *fpl*; *Fig* **to be in c.** *(of laughter)* se tordre

coo [kuː] *(pt & pp* **cooed)** *vi (of dove)* roucouler; *Fam* **to c. over sb/sth** s'extasier devant qn/qch

cook [kʊk] **1** *n* cuisinier(ère) *m,f*; *Prov* **too many cooks spoil the broth** on n'arrive jamais à rien quand tout le monde met son grain de sel **2** *vt (meal)* préparer; *(food)* (faire) cuire; *Fig* **to c. the books** falsifier les comptes **3** *vi (of food)* cuire; *(of person)* faire la cuisine; *Fam* **what's cooking?** qu'est-ce qui se passe?

▸ **cook up** *vt sep (excuse, story)* inventer

cookbook ['kʊkbʊk] *n* livre *m* de cuisine

cooker ['kʊkə(r)] *n (stove)* cuisinière *f*

cookery ['kʊkərɪ] *n* cuisine *f*; **c. book** livre *m* de cuisine

cookie ['kʊkɪ] *n* **(a)** *Am (biscuit)* biscuit *m*; *Fam* **that's the way the c. crumbles!** c'est la vie(, que veux-tu)! **(b)** *(person)* **a tough c.** un(e) dur(e) à cuire; **a smart c.** un(e) malin(igne)

cooking ['kʊkɪŋ] *n (process)* cuisson *f*; *(activity)* cuisine *f*; **to do the c.** faire la cuisine; **c. apple** pomme *f* à cuire; **c. chocolate** chocolat *m* à cuire; **c. time** temps *m* de cuisson; **c. utensils** ustensiles *mpl* de cuisine

cool [kuːl] **1** *n* **(a)** *(coldness)* fraîcheur *f* **(b)** *(calm)* **to keep/lose one's c.** garder/perdre son sang-froid **2** *adj* **(a)** *(wind, weather, drink)* frais (fraîche); *(coffee, bathwater)* tiède; **it's c. outside** il fait frais dehors; *Fam* **I lost a c. thousand** j'ai bien perdu mille dollars/livres/*etc*

(b) *(calm)* calme; *(unfriendly)* froid(e); **c. as a cucumber** parfaitement calme; **keep c.!** ne t'angoisse pas!; **to keep a c. head** garder la tête froide; **to be a c. customer** être culotté(e) **(c)** *Fam (good)* cool *inv*; *(trendy)* branché(e) **3** *adv* *Fam* **to play it c.** rester calme **4** *vt* rafraîchir, refroidir; *Fam* **c. it!** on se calme!

5 *vi (of liquid)* refroidir; *(of anger)* passer; *(of passion, enthusiasm)* se refroidir

▸ **cool down 1** *vt sep* **(a)** *(of cold drink)* rafraîchir **(b)** *(make calm)* calmer **2** *vi* **(a)** *(of weather)* se rafraîchir; *(of liquid)* refroidir **(b)** *(become calm)* se calmer

▸ **cool off** *vi* **(a)** *(of person)* se rafraîchir **(b)** *(of passion, enthusiasm)* se refroidir; *(of angry person)* se calmer

coolant ['ku:lənt] *n* liquide *m* de refroidissement

cool-headed ['ku:l'hedɪd] *adj* calme; **to remain c.** garder la tête froide

cooling ['ku:lɪŋ] *adj (drink)* rafraîchissant(e); *(agent)* réfrigérant(e); *Ind & Com* **c. off period** période *f* de réflexion; **c. tower** tour *f* de réfrigération

coop [ku:p] *n (for chickens)* poulailler *m*

▸ **coop up** *vt sep* **to keep sb cooped up** tenir qn enfermé(e); **to feel cooped up** se sentir à l'étroit

co-op ['kəʊɒp] *n* cooperative *f*

cooperate [kəʊ'ɒpəreɪt] *vi* coopérer (**with** avec)

cooperation [kəʊɒpə'reɪʃən] *n* coopération *f*

cooperative [kəʊ'ɒpərətɪv] **1** *n* coopérative *f* **2** *adj* coopératif(ive)

coopt [kəʊ'ɒpt] *vt* coopter (**onto** à)

coordinate 1 *n* [kəʊ'ɔ:dɪnət] **(a)** *Math* coordonnée *f* **(b)** **coordinates** *(clothes)* coordonnés *mpl* **2** *vt* [kəʊ'ɔ:dɪneɪt] coordonner

coordination [kəʊɔ:dɪ'neɪʃən] *n* coordination *f*

coordinator [kəʊ'ɔ:dɪneɪtə(r)] *n* coordinateur(trice) *m,f*

co-owner ['kəʊ'əʊnə(r)] *n* copropriétaire *mf*

cop [kɒp] **1** *n Fam* **(a)** *(policeman)* flic *m*; **to play cops and robbers** jouer aux gendarmes et aux voleurs **(b)** **it's not much c.** ça ne vaut pas grand-chose **2** *vt (pt & pp* **copped)** **to c. it** *(be punished)* se faire pincer; *(die)* clamser

▸ **cop out** *vi Fam (avoid responsibility)* se détiler; *(choose easy solution)* choisir la solution de facilité; **to c. out of doing sth** ne pas avoir le cran de faire qch

cope [kəʊp] *vi* se débrouiller, s'en tirer; **to c. with** *(demand)* faire face à; **I just can't c.** je n'y arrive pas; **he can't c. with his job** il ne s'en sort pas dans son travail

Copenhagen [kəʊpən'heɪgən] *n* Copenhague

copier ['kɒpɪə(r)] *n (photocopier)* (photo)copieuse *f*

copilot ['kəʊpaɪlət] *n* copilote *m*

copious ['kəʊpɪəs] *adj* copieux(euse); *(tears, notes, amounts)* abondant(e)

cop-out ['kɒpaʊt] *n Fam* solution *f* de facilité

copper ['kɒpə(r)] **1** *n* **(a)** *(metal)* cuivre *m*; *Fam* **coppers** *(coins)* petite monnaie *f* **(b)** *Br Fam (policeman)* flic *m* **2** *adj Br* **c.(-coloured)**, *Am* **c.(-colored)** (couleur) cuivre *inv*, cuivré(e)

copperplate ['kɒpəpleɪt] *n* **c. (writing)** écriture *f* moulée

coppice ['kɒpɪs] *n* taillis *m*

coproduction [kəʊprə'dʌkʃən] *n Cin* coproduction *f*

copse [kɒps] *n* taillis *m*

copulate ['kɒpjʊleɪt] *vi* copuler

copulation [kɒpjʊ'leɪʃən] *n* copulation *f*

copy ['kɒpɪ] **1** *(pl* **copies)** *n* **(a)** *(reproduction)* copie *f* **(b)** *(of*

letter, document) copie *f*, double *m*; **c. typist** dactylo *mf* **(c)** *(of book)* exemplaire *m*; *(of newspaper)* numéro *m* **(d)** *Journ (written material)* copie *f*; **the story made good c.** ça a fait un bon sujet d'article; **c. editor** *(in journalism)* secrétaire *m* de rédaction; *(in publishing)* réviseur *m* **2** *vt (pt & pp* **copied)** *(painting, document, text)* copier **3** *vi (in exam)* copier

copybook ['kɒpɪbʊk] *n* cahier *m* d'écriture; **c. example** exemple *m* classique

copycat ['kɒpɪkæt] *Fam* **1** *n* copieur(euse) *m,f* **2** *adj* **c. crime/murder** délit *m*/meurtre *m* inspiré par un autre

copyright ['kɒpɪraɪt] **1** *n* droit *m* d'auteur, copyright *m*; **to be out of c.** être tombé(e) dans le domaine public **2** *adj* protégé(e) par le droit d'auteur

copywriter ['kɒpɪraɪtə(r)] *n* rédacteur(trice) *m,f* publicitaire

coquette [kɒ'ket] *n Lit* coquette *f*

coral ['kɒrəl] *n* corail *m*; **c. island** île *f* corallienne; **c. reef** récif *m* corallien; **the C. Sea** la mer de Corail

cord [kɔ:d] *n* **(a)** *(string)* grosse ficelle *f*; *(for curtains, pyjamas)* cordon *m* **(b)** *(corduroy)* velours *m* côtelé; **a c. jacket** une veste en velours côtelé; **cords** pantalon *m* en velours côtelé

cordial ['kɔ:dɪəl] **1** *n (drink)* sirop *m* **2** *adj (friendly)* cordial(e)

cordless ['kɔ:dlɪs] *adj* sans fil

cordon ['kɔ:dən] *n* cordon *m*

▸ **cordon off** *vt sep (road)* barrer; *(area)* boucler

corduroy ['kɔ:dərɔɪ] *n* velours *m* côtelé; **c. trousers** pantalon *m* en velours côtelé

core [kɔ:(r)] **1** *n* **(a)** *(of apple)* trognon *m*; *(of earth, magnet)* noyau *m*; *(of nuclear reactor)* cœur *m*; *(of argument, problem)* cœur *m*; **hard c.** noyau dur; **he's rotten to the c.** il est pourri jusqu'à la moelle; *Br Sch* **c. curriculum** tronc *m* commun **2** *vt (apple)* évider

Corfu [kɔ:'fu:] *n* Corfou

coriander [kɒrɪ'ændə(r)] *n* coriandre *f*

cork [kɔ:k] **1** *n (material)* liège *m*; *(stopper)* bouchon *m* (en liège) **2** *vt (bottle)* boucher

corked [kɔ:kt] *adj (wine)* bouchonné(e)

corkscrew ['kɔ:kskru:] *n* tire-bouchon *m*

cormorant ['kɔ:mərənt] *n* cormoran *m*

corn[1] [kɔ:n] *n* **(a)** *Br (wheat)* blé *m* **(b)** *Am (maize)* maïs *m*; **c. on the cob** maïs en épi; **c. bread** pain *m* à la farine de maïs; **c. meal** farine *f* de maïs; **c. oil** huile *f* de maïs

corn[2] [kɔ:n] *n (on foot)* cor *m*; **c. plaster** pansement *m* pour cors

cornea ['kɔ:nɪə] *n Anat* cornée *f*

corned beef [kɔ:nd'bi:f] *n* corned-beef *m*

corner ['kɔ:nə(r)] **1** *n* **(a)** *(of room, street, page, screen)* coin *m*; **out of the c. of one's eye** du coin de l'œil; **it's just round the c.** c'est juste au coin; *Fig* **Christmas is just round the c.** on est tout près de Noël; **to turn the c.** tourner au coin de la rue; *Fig (of economy, company)* passer la période critique; **c. shop** magasin *m* de quartier **(b)** *(bend in road)* tournant *m*; *Fig* **to cut corners** *(with time)* faire les choses à la va-vite; *(with materials, money)* faire les choses à l'économie **(c)** *(in football)* **c. (kick)** corner *m*; **to take a c.** tirer un corner

cornerstone ['kɔ:nəstəʊn] *n also Fig* pierre *f* angulaire

cornet ['kɔ:nɪt] n (a) (musical instrument) cornet m à pistons (b) (ice-cream) c. cornet m

cornfield ['kɔ:nfi:ld] n (of wheat) champ m de blé; (of maize) champ de maïs

cornflakes ['kɔ:nfleɪks] npl corn flakes mpl

cornflour ['kɔ:nflaʊə(r)] n Br farine f de maïs

cornflower ['kɔ:nflaʊə(r)] n (plant) bleuet m; c. blue bleu barbeau inv

cornice ['kɔ:nɪs] n corniche f

Cornish ['kɔ:nɪʃ] 1 npl the C. (people) les Cornouaillais mpl
2 n (language) cornique m
3 adj cornouaillais(e); Br C. pasty feuilleté m à la viande

Cornwall ['kɔ:nwəl] n Cornouailles f

corny ['kɔ:nɪ] adj Fam (joke) nul (nulle); (film, novel) tarte

corollary [kə'rɒlərɪ] (pl corollaries) n corollaire m

coronary ['kɒrənərɪ] Med 1 (pl coronaries) n infarctus m (du myocarde)
2 adj coronarien(enne); c. thrombosis infarctus m du myocarde

coronation [kɒrə'neɪʃən] n couronnement m; c. chicken = morceaux de poulet préparés avec de la mayonnaise au curry

coroner ['kɒrənə(r)] n Law coroner m

corporal[1] ['kɔ:pərəl] adj corporel(elle); c. punishment châtiment m corporel

corporal[2] n Mil (in infantry) caporal m; (in cavalry, artillery) brigadier m

corporate ['kɔ:pərət] adj Com d'entreprise; c. culture culture f d'entreprise; c. image image f de marque de l'entreprise

corporation [kɔ:pə'reɪʃən] n (a) Com société f; c. tax impôt m sur les sociétés (b) (council) conseil m municipal

corps [kɔ:(r)] (pl corps [kɔ:z]) n Mil corps m

corpse [kɔ:ps] n cadavre m

corpulent ['kɔ:pjʊlənt] adj corpulent(e)

corpuscle ['kɔ:pʌsəl] n Anat corpuscule m; red/white (blood) corpuscles globules mpl rouges/blancs

corral [kɒ'rɑ:l] n Am corral m

correct [kə'rekt] 1 adj (a) (accurate) exact(e); to prove c. se vérifier, s'avérer juste; if my memory is c. si j'ai bonne mémoire; he is c. (right) il a raison; that's c. c'est exact (b) (person, behaviour) correct(e), convenable; it wasn't the c. thing to say/do ce n'était pas la chose à dire/faire
2 vt (homework, error) corriger; (misunderstanding) dissiper; c. me if I'm wrong, but... reprenez-moi si je me trompe, mais...; I stand corrected j'avais tort

correction [kə'rekʃən] n correction f

correlate ['kɒrɪleɪt] 1 vt mettre en rapport ou en corrélation (with avec); they are closely correlated ils sont étroitement liés
2 vi être en rapport ou en corrélation (with avec)

correlation [kɒrɪ'leɪʃən] n corrélation f

correspond [kɒrɪs'pɒnd] vi (a) (be in accordance) correspondre (with or to à) (b) (be equivalent) correspondre (to à), être l'équivalent (to de) (c) (write letters) correspondre (with avec)

correspondence [kɒrɪs'pɒndəns] n (a) (relationship) rapport m (between entre) (b) (letter-writing) correspondance f; c. course cours m par correspondance

correspondent [kɒrɪs'pɒndənt] n correspondant(e) m,f

corresponding [kɒrɪ'spɒndɪŋ] adj correspondant(e)

corridor ['kɒrɪdɔ:(r)] n couloir m, corridor m; Fig the corridors of power les hautes sphères fpl du pouvoir

corroborate [kə'rɒbəreɪt] vt corroborer, confirmer

corroboration [kərɒbə'reɪʃən] n corroboration f, confirmation f

corrode [kə'rəʊd] 1 vt (metal) corroder, attaquer; Fig (society) miner; (optimism, friendship) entamer
2 vi (of metal) se corroder

corrosion [kə'rəʊʒən] n corrosion f

corrosive [kə'rəʊsɪv] 1 n corrosif m
2 adj corrosif(ive)

corrugated ['kɒrəgeɪtɪd] adj (cardboard) ondulé(e); c. iron tôle f ondulée

corrupt [kə'rʌpt] 1 adj (dishonest) corrompu(e)
2 vt corrompre; Comptr altérer; to c. sb's morals dépraver qn

corruption [kə'rʌpʃən] n corruption f

corset ['kɔ:sɪt] n corset m

Corsica ['kɔ:sɪkə] n la Corse

Corsican ['kɔ:sɪkən] 1 n Corse mf
2 adj corse

cortege [kɔ:'teʒ] n cortège m

cortex ['kɔ:teks] (pl cortices ['kɔ:tɪsi:z]) n cortex m

cortisone ['kɔ:tɪzəʊn] n cortisone f

cos[1] [kɒz] conj Br Fam parce que

cos[2] [kɒs] n c. (lettuce) romaine f

cosh [kɒʃ] Br 1 n matraque f
2 vt matraquer

cosmetic [kɒz'metɪk] 1 n cosmétique m, produit m de beauté
2 adj Fig (superficial) superficiel(elle); c. surgery chirurgie f esthétique

cosmic ['kɒzmɪk] adj cosmique; Fig prodigieux(euse)

cosmonaut ['kɒzmənɔ:t] n cosmonaute mf

cosmopolitan [kɒzmə'pɒlɪtən] adj cosmopolite

cosmos ['kɒzmɒs] n cosmos m

cosset ['kɒsɪt] vt couver, choyer

cost [kɒst] 1 n (a) (price) coût m; Law costs dépens mpl; also Fig at little/great c. à peu de/à grands frais; at great c. to his health au prix de sa santé; Econ c. of living coût de la vie; Com c. of production coût de production; Fin c. accounting comptabilité f analytique; Econ c. benefit analysis analyse f coûts-bénéfices; Com c. price prix m coûtant (b) (idioms) to count the c. of sth tirer la leçon de qch; at all costs à tout prix; as I found out to my c. comme je l'ai appris à mes dépens
2 vt (a) (pt & pp cost) also Fig coûter; how much does it c.? combien ça coûte?; it costs $25 ça coûte ou c'est 25 dollars; whatever it costs quel qu'en soit le prix; Fam to c. a fortune or the earth or an arm and a leg coûter les yeux de la tête; the attempt cost him his life cette tentative lui a coûté la vie (b) (pt & pp costed) Com (budget) évaluer le coût de

co-star ['kəʊstɑ:(r)] 1 n (in film) partenaire mf à l'écran
2 vt (pt & pp co-starred) the film co-stars Harvey Keitel Harvey Keitel joue aussi dans ce film; co-starring Ewan McGregor avec Ewan McGregor
3 vi jouer dans un des rôles principaux

Costa Rica ['kɒstə'ri:kə] n le Costa Rica

Costa Rican ['kɒstə'ri:kən] 1 n Costaricien(enne) m,f
2 adj costaricien(enne)

cost-effective [kɒstɪ'fektɪv] adj rentable

costing ['kɒstɪŋ] n Com (of job) évaluation f du coût; (of article) évaluation f du prix de revient

costly ['kɒstlɪ] adj cher (chère), coûteux(euse); it was a mistake c'est une erreur qui a coûté cher

costume ['kɒstjʊm] n costume m; **(swimming) c.** maillot m de bain; **c. drama** film m/pièce f en costumes d'époque; **c. jewellery** bijoux mpl fantaisie

cosy ['kəʊzɪ] adj (room, armchair, pub) confortable; **to feel c.** (in room) être confortablement installé(e); Fig & Pej **they have a c. relationship** ils sont un peu trop copain-copain

cot [kɒt] n Br (for child) lit m d'enfant, petit lit; Am (folding bed) lit pliant; **c. death** mort f subite du nourrisson

cottage ['kɒtɪdʒ] n = petite maison, généralement à la campagne; **c. cheese** fromage m blanc (égoutté); **c. hospital** = hôpital de médecine générale en zone rurale; **c. industry** industrie f artisanale; (at home) industrie familiale; **c. pie** hachis m Parmentier

cotton ['kɒtən] n coton m; **a c. shirt** une chemise en coton; **c. bud** Coton-Tige® m; Am **c. candy** barbe f à papa; **c. wool** ouate f, coton hydrophile
► **cotton on** vi Fam piger; **to c. on to sth** piger qch

couch [kaʊtʃ] **1** n divan m, canapé m; (at doctor's) lit m; Fam **c. potato** = personne qui passe sa vie devant la télé
2 vt (express) formuler

cougar ['kuːgə(r)] n couguar m, puma m

cough [kɒf] **1** n toux f; **to have a c.** tousser; **c. drop** pastille f pour la toux; **c. medicine** or **mixture** sirop m pour la toux
2 vi tousser
► **cough up 1** vt sep (phlegm, blood) cracher; Fam (money) allonger
2 vi Fam (pay) allonger

could [kʊd]

La forme négative est **couldn't**. Dans les contextes où il est nécessaire d'utiliser une langue plus soignée, on écrit **could not**.

modal aux v **(a)** (was able to) **we couldn't do it** nous n'avons pas pu le faire; **he did what he c.** il a fait ce qu'il pouvait; **I c. hear them talking** je les entendais parler; **I c. have tried harder** j'aurais pu faire plus d'efforts; **he couldn't have been kinder** il a été on ne peut plus aimable; **how COULD you!** comment as-tu pu faire ça?
(b) (knew how to) **I c. swim well at that age** à cet âge-là je savais déjà bien nager; **c. you speak French then?** tu parlais français à cette époque-là?
(c) (indicating possibility) **it c. be weeks before he's better** il pourrait se passer des semaines avant qu'il se rétablisse; **it c. have been worse** ça aurait pu être pire
(d) (with requests) **c. you get me some water?** est-ce que tu pourrais m'apporter de l'eau?
(e) (in conditional, suggestions) **(it) c. be** peut-être; **if I had more money I c. buy a new car** si j'avais plus d'argent je pourrais acheter une nouvelle voiture; **we c. always telephone** on pourrait toujours téléphoner

couldn't ['kʊdənt] = could not

couldn't-care-less ['kʊdəntkeə'les] adj **c. attitude** je-m'en-foutisme m

council ['kaʊnsəl] n **(a)** (assembly) conseil m; **C. of Europe** Conseil de l'Europe **(b)** (local government) municipalité f; **to be on the c.** être au conseil municipal; Br **c. house** ≃ habitation f à loyer modéré, H.L.M. f; Br **c. tax** = en Grande-Bretagne, impôt regroupant taxe d'habitation et impôts locaux

councillor ['kaʊnsɪlə(r)] n conseiller(ère) m,f, membre m du conseil

counsel ['kaʊnsəl] **1** n **(a)** (advice) conseil m, avis m; **to keep one's own c.** (about plans) garder ses projets pour soi; (about opinions) garder ses opinions pour soi **(b)** Br (lawyer) avocat(e) m,f; **c. for the defence** avocat m de la défense; **c. for the prosecution** procureur m; **King's/Queen's C.** = membre haut placé du barreau

2 vt (pt & pp **counselled**, Am **counseled**) (caution, patience) conseiller; **to c. sb** (advise) conseiller qn; (give psychological help to) apporter une aide psychologique à qn; **to c. sb to do sth** conseiller à qn de faire qch

counselling ['kaʊnsəlɪŋ] n assistance f psychosociale

counsellor ['kaʊnsələ(r)] n **(a)** (adviser, therapist) conseiller(ère) m,f **(b)** Am Law avocat(e) m,f

count¹ [kaʊnt] n (nobleman) comte m

count² [kaʊnt] **1** n **(a)** (calculation) compte m, comptage m; **at the last c.** au dernier comptage; **to keep c. of sth** tenir le compte de qch; **to lose c.** se perdre dans ses calculs; **I've lost c. of how many times I've asked you to...** je t'ai demandé je ne sais combien de fois de... **(b)** (in boxing) & Fig **to be out for the c.** être K.-O. **(c)** Law chef m d'accusation; Fig **on a number of counts** à plusieurs égards
2 vt **(a)** (enumerate) compter; **there were four of us counting/not counting the dog** nous étions quatre en comptant/sans compter le chien **(b)** (consider) considérer (as comme); **c. yourself lucky you weren't killed** estime-toi heureux de n'avoir pas été tué
3 vi **(a)** (add up) compter; **to c. (up) to ten** compter jusqu'à dix **(b)** (be important, valid) compter, that **doesn't c.** ça ne compte pas; **it counts as one of my worst experiences** ça a été la une de mes pires expériences
► **count against** vt insep jouer contre
► **count down** vi faire le compte à rebours
► **count in** vt sep (include) compter; **c. me in!** j'en suis!
► **count on** vt insep compter sur; **to c. on sb to do sth** compter sur qn pour faire qch
► **count out** vt sep **(a)** (money) compter **(b)** (exclude) **c. me out!** ne comptez pas sur moi! **(c)** (in boxing) **to be counted out** être (mis(e)) K.-O.
► **count up** vt sep compter

countable ['kaʊntəbəl] adj comptable

countdown ['kaʊntdaʊn] n compte m à rebours

countenance ['kaʊntɪnəns] Formal **1** n **(a)** (face) visage m **(b)** (support) **to give c. to** (rumours) accréditer; (plans) approuver
2 vt (support) approuver

counter¹ ['kaʊntə(r)] n **(a)** (in shop) comptoir m; (in supermarket) rayon m; (in bank) guichet m; **available over the c.** (medicine) en vente libre; **to buy/sell sth under the c.** acheter/vendre qch au noir **(b)** (token in game) jeton m **(c)** (counting device) compteur m

counter² ['kaʊntə(r)] **1** adv **c. to** contrairement à; **to run c. to** aller à l'encontre de
2 vt contrer; **to c. that...** riposter que...
3 vi riposter

counteract [kaʊntə'rækt] vt (influence) contrecarrer; (rumours, effects) neutraliser

counterattack ['kaʊntərətæk] **1** n contre-attaque f
2 vt & vi contre-attaquer

counter-clockwise [kaʊntə'klɒkwaɪz] Am **1** adj **in a c. direction** dans le sens inverse des aiguilles d'une montre
2 adv dans le sens inverse des aiguilles d'une montre

counterfeit ['kaʊntəfɪt] **1** n faux m
2 adj faux (fausse)
3 vt contrefaire

counterfoil ['kaʊntəfɔɪl] n talon m, souche f

counterintelligence [kaʊntərɪn'telɪdʒəns] n contre-espionnage m

countermand ['kaʊntəmɑːnd] vt annuler

countermeasure ['kaʊntəmeʒə(r)] n contre-mesure f

counteroffensive ['kaʊntərə'fensɪv] n contre-offensive f

counterpane ['kaʊntəpeɪn] n couvre-lit m

counterpart ['kaʊntəpɑːt] n (person) homologue mf; (system) équivalent m

counterpoint ['kaʊntəpɔɪnt] n Mus contrepoint m

counterproductive ['kaʊntəprə'dʌktɪv] adj contre-productif(ive)

counterproposal ['kaʊntəprə'pəʊzəl] n contre-proposition f

counter-revolution ['kaʊntərevə'luːʃən] n contre-révolution f

counter-revolutionary ['kaʊntərevə'luːʃənərɪ] n & adj contre-révolutionnaire mf

countersign ['kaʊntəsaɪn] vt contresigner, viser

counterweight ['kaʊntəweɪt] n contrepoids m

countess ['kaʊntɪs] n comtesse f

countless ['kaʊntlɪs] adj innombrable; **on c.** occasions à maintes occasions; **c. times** un nombre incalculable de fois

country ['kʌntrɪ] (pl countries) n (a) (political entity) pays m; **to go to the c.** (call elections) appeler le pays aux urnes (b) (as opposed to town) campagne f; **in the c.** à la campagne; **c. and western music** country m ou f

countryside ['kʌntrɪsaɪd] n campagne f

county ['kaʊntɪ] (pl counties) n comté m; **c. council** ≃ conseil m général; **c. town** chef-lieu m de comté

coup [kuː] n (surprising achievement) (beau) coup m; Pol **c. (d'état)** coup m d'État

couple ['kʌpəl] **1** n (a) (of things) **a c. of** (two) deux; (a few) quelques (b) (people) couple m; **the happy c.** les heureux époux mpl
2 vt (a) (associate) associer (**with** à) (b) (combine) allier (**with** à)

couplet ['kʌplɪt] n distique m

coupon ['kuːpɒn] n (form) coupon m; (money-off) **c.** (for discount) bon m de réduction

courage ['kʌrɪdʒ] n courage m; **to have the c. to do sth** avoir le courage de faire qch; **to have the c. of one's convictions** avoir le courage de ses opinions

courageous [kə'reɪdʒəs] adj courageux(euse)

courageously [kə'reɪdʒəslɪ] adv courageusement, avec courage

courgette [kʊə'ʒət] n Br courgette f

courier ['kʊrɪə(r)] n (messenger) messager m, coursier m; (in tourism) guide mf; (drug smuggler) passeur(euse) m,f

course [kɔːs] **1** n (a) (of river, time, events) cours m; **to be on c.** Naut suivre le cap; Fig être en bonne voie; Naut **to be off c.** dévier de son cap; **in the c. of time** (gradually) à la longue; (eventually) finalement; **in the c. of the evening** au cours de la soirée; **c. of action** ligne f de conduite; **to be in the c. of doing sth** être en train de faire qch; **in the normal c. of events** en temps normal; **to let things take** or **run their c.** laisser les choses suivre leur cours normal (b) **of c.** naturellement, bien sûr; **of c. not** bien sûr que non (c) (at college, university) cours m (**in** de); **c. of lectures** série f de conférences (d) Med **c. of treatment** traitement m (e) (of meal) plat m (f) (for race) parcours m; (for horseracing) champ m de courses; (for golf) terrain m
2 vi (of liquid) couler

court [kɔːt] **1** n (a) Law cour f, tribunal m; **to go to c.** aller en justice; **to take sb to c.** faire un procès à qn; **to settle a case out of c.** arranger une affaire à l'amiable; **c. of appeal** cour d'appel; **c. of inquiry** commission f d'enquête; **c. of law** cour, tribunal; **c. appearance** comparution f en justice; Mil **c. martial** cour martiale (b) (for tennis, squash) court m (c) (royal) cour f; **to hold c.** tenir des discours à un entourage admiratif; **c. shoe** escarpin m

2 vt (a) Old-fashioned (woo) courtiser (b) (seek) (friendship, favour) rechercher; (death) braver; (disaster, danger) aller au-devant de
3 vi Old-fashioned **to be courting** (of couple) se fréquenter

courteous ['kɜːtɪəs] adj courtois(e), poli(e)

courtesy ['kɜːtəsɪ] (pl courtesies) n courtoisie f, politesse f; **by c. of...** avec l'aimable autorisation de...; **to exchange courtesies** se faire des politesses; **c. call** visite f de politesse; **c. car** = voiture mise à la disposition d'un client par un hôtel ou un garage

courthouse ['kɔːthaʊs] n Am palais m de justice, tribunal m

courtier ['kɔːtɪə(r)] n (man) courtisan m; (woman) dame f de la cour

court-martial ['kɔːt'mɑːʃəl] (pt & pp court-martialled, Am court-martialed) vt faire passer en cour martiale; **to be court-martialled** passer en cour martiale

courtroom ['kɔːtruːm] n Law salle f d'audience

courtship ['kɔːtʃɪp] n (of people) cour f; (of animals) parade f nuptiale

courtyard ['kɔːtjɑːd] n cour f

cousin ['kʌzən] n cousin(e) m,f

cove [kəʊv] n crique f

covenant ['kʌvənənt] Law **1** n convention f, contrat m
2 vt promettre par contrat

Coventry ['kʌvəntrɪ, 'kɒvəntrɪ] n Fig **to send sb to C.** mettre qn en quarantaine

cover ['kʌvə(r)] **1** n (a) (lid) couvercle m (b) (soft covering) housse f; **covers** (blankets) couvertures fpl (c) (of book, magazine) couverture f; **from c. to c.** de la première à la dernière page; **c. price** prix m de vente (d) (shelter) **to take c.** s'abriter; **to break c.** sortir à découvert; Fig se manifester publiquement; **under c. of darkness** à la faveur de la nuit (e) Fin (in insurance) couverture f (f) (song) **c. (version)** reprise f
2 vt (a) (person, object) couvrir (**with/in** de); **to c. one's eyes** se couvrir les yeux; **to c. a wall with paint** recouvrir un mur de peinture; **to c. oneself with glory** se couvrir de gloire; **to c. one's costs** couvrir ses frais; **to c. a song** (of musician) reprendre une chanson (b) (hide) (one's embarrassment, confusion) dissimuler; **to c. one's tracks** brouiller les pistes (c) (travel over) parcourir; **we covered 100 km in one day** nous avons fait ou parcouru 100 km en un jour; Fig **to c. a lot of ground** traiter de nombreux problèmes (d) (include, deal with) (of book, lecture) traiter de; **to c. a story** (of journalist) couvrir un sujet (e) Fin (with insurance) couvrir (**for** or **against** contre); Fig **to c. oneself** (take precautions) se couvrir
▸ **cover for** vt insep (replace) remplacer; (provide excuses for) couvrir
▸ **cover up 1** vt sep (a) (corruption, mistakes) dissimuler; (scandal) étouffer (b) (put cover on) recouvrir
2 vi (conceal the truth) cacher la vérité (**for sb** pour protéger qn)

coverage ['kʌvərɪdʒ] n (on TV, in newspapers) couverture f médiatique

covering ['kʌvərɪŋ] n (on furniture) housse f; (of snow, dust) couche f; (of chocolate) nappage m

coverlet ['kʌvəlɪt] n dessus-de-lit m inv

covert ['kʌvət] adj (operation) secret(ète), clandestin(e); (look) furtif(ive)

cover-up ['kʌvərʌp] n **there was a c.** l'affaire a été étouffée

covet ['kʌvɪt] *vt* convoiter

covetous ['kʌvɪtəs] *adj* envieux(euse); **to be c.** of sth convoiter qch

cow¹ [kaʊ] *n* (a) *(animal)* vache *f*; *(female elephant, whale)* femelle *f*; **till the cows come home** *(wait)* jusqu'à la saint-glinglin; *(argue, talk)* à n'en plus finir (b) *very Fam Pej (woman)* peau *f* de vache

cow² *vt* intimider; **to look cowed** avoir un air de chien battu

coward ['kaʊəd] *n* lâche *mf*, poltron(onne) *m,f*

cowardice ['kaʊədɪs], **cowardliness** ['kaʊədlɪnəs] *n* lâcheté *f*, poltronnerie *f*

cowardly ['kaʊədlɪ] *adj* lâche

cowboy ['kaʊbɔɪ] *n* (a) *(cattle handler, in westerns)* cowboy *m* (b) *Br Fam Pej (workman)* filou *m*

cower ['kaʊə(r)] *vi* se tapir; **to c. before sb** trembler devant qn

cowhide ['kaʊhaɪd] *n* peau *f* de vache

cowl [kaʊl] *n* *(on monk's habit, on chimney)* capuchon *m*; **c. neck** col *m* boule

coworker ['kəʊwɜ:kə(r)] *n Am* collègue *mf*

cowshed ['kaʊʃed] *n* étable *f*

cox [kɒks] **1** *n (in rowing)* barreur(euse) *m,f*
2 *vt & vi* barrer

coy [kɔɪ] *adj (shy)* timide; *Pej (affectedly shy)* (faussement) timide *(about* à propos de)

coyote [kɔɪ'əʊtɪ] *n* coyote *m*

CPU [si:pi:'ju:] *n Comptr (abbr* **central processing unit)** unité *f* centrale

crab [kræb] *n* (a) *(crustacean)* crabe *m* (b) *Fam (pubic louse)* morpion *m* (c) **c. apple** pomme *f* sauvage

crabbed ['kræbɪd] *adj (writing)* en pattes de mouche

crabby ['kræbɪ] *adj Fam* maussade, grincheux(euse)

crack [kræk] **1** *n* (a) *(in glass, porcelain)* fêlure *f*; *(in wood)* fente *f*; *(in wall)* lézarde *f*; *(in ice, rock)* fissure *f*; **at the c. of dawn** à la pointe du jour
(b) *(sound)* *(of branches, ice)* craquement *m*; *(of whip)* claquement *m*; *(of gunfire)* détonation *f*; *Fig* **to give sb a fair c. of the whip** donner toutes ses chances à qn; *Fig* **to have a c. at sth** tenter sa chance à qch
(c) *(blow)* coup *m* (**on** sur)
(d) *Fam (joke, insult)* plaisanterie *f*
(e) *(drug)* crack *m*
2 *adj Fam (team, regiment)* d'élite; **c. shot** fin tireur *m*
3 *vt* (a) *(glass, porcelain)* fêler; *(wood)* fendre; *(wall)* lézarder; *(ice, rock)* fissurer
(b) *(make sound with)* *(whip)* faire claquer; *(fingers)* faire craquer
(c) *Fam (hit)* **to c. sb over the head** assommer qn; **she cracked her head against the wall** elle s'est cogné la tête contre le mur
(d) *(solve) (problem)* résoudre; *(code)* décrypter
(e) *(break into) (safe)* percer; *(nut)* casser
(f) *Fam (joke)* raconter
4 *vi* (a) *(of glass, porcelain)* se fêler; *(of wood)* se fendre; *(of wall)* se lézarder; *(of ice, rock)* se fissurer; *(of paint)* se craqueler
(b) *(of voice)* se casser
(c) *(of person under pressure)* craquer
(d) *(make sound) (of branches, ice)* craquer; *(of whip)* claquer; *(of gunfire)* retentir; *Fam Fig* **to get cracking** se grouiller
▸ **crack down** *vi* **to c. down (on)** prendre des mesures énergiques (en matière de)
▸ **crack up** *Fam* **1** *vt sep* **it's not all it's cracked up to be** ce n'est pas aussi bien qu'on le dit
2 *vi (go mad)* craquer

crackbrained ['krækbreɪnd] *adj Fam* dingue

crackdown ['krækdaʊn] *n* mesures *fpl* énergiques (**on** en matière de)

cracked [krækt] *adj Fam (mad)* dingue, cinglé(e)

cracker ['krækə(r)] *n* (a) *(biscuit)* biscuit *m* salé, cracker *m* (b) *(firework)* pétard *m*; *(at Christmas)* diablotin *m* (c) *Fam (excellent thing, person)* pure merveille *f*; **she's a c.** *(very attractive)* elle est canon

crackers ['krækəz] *adj Fam* dingue, cinglé(e)

crackle ['krækəl] **1** *n (of twigs)* craquement *m*; *(of shots, fire)* crépitement *m*; *(of frying)* grésillement *m*; *(of radio)* crachotement *m*
2 *vi (of twigs)* craquer; *(of shots, fire)* crépiter; *(of frying)* grésiller; *(of radio)* crachoter

crackling ['kræklɪŋ] *n* (a) *(of fire)* crépitement *m*; *(on radio)* crachotement *m* (b) *(pork skin)* couenne *f* grillée

crackpot ['krækpɒt] *Fam* **1** *n (person)* fêlé(e) *m,f*, cinglé(e) *m,f*
2 *adj (plan)* dingue

cradle ['kreɪdəl] **1** *n* (a) *(of child, civilization)* berceau *m*; **from the c. to the grave** du berceau à la tombe (b) *(for cleaning windows)* nacelle *f*
2 *vt (baby)* bercer *(dans ses bras)*; *(object)* tenir délicatement

craft¹ [krɑ:ft] *n* (a) *(skill)* habileté *f*; *(professional)* métier *m* (b) *(cunning)* ruse *f*

craft² *(pl* craft) *n (boat)* (petite) embarcation *f*

craftsman ['krɑ:ftsmən] *n* artisan *m*; **this is the work of a real c.** c'est l'œuvre d'un spécialiste

craftsmanship ['krɑ:ftsmənʃɪp] *n* habileté *f* (manuelle); **a wonderful piece of c.** un pur chef-d'œuvre; **the c. is magnificent** c'est vraiment du beau travail

crafty ['krɑ:ftɪ] *adj* malin(igne)

crag [kræg] *n* rocher *m* à pic

craggy ['krægɪ] *adj (rocky)* rocheux(euse); *(features)* anguleux(euse)

cram [kræm] *(pt & pp* crammed) **1** *vt* fourrer, entasser **(into** dans); **to c. food into one's mouth** se gaver, s'empiffrer; **to be crammed (with)** être bourré(e) (de)
2 *vi* (a) s'entasser **(into** dans) (b) *Fam (study)* bûcher

cramp [kræmp] **1** *n* crampe *f*
2 *vt (restrict)* gêner; *Fam* **to c. sb's style** priver qn de ses moyens

cramped [kræmpt] *adj (surroundings)* exigu(ë); **to be c. for space** être à l'étroit

cranberry ['krænbərɪ] *(pl* cranberries) *n* canneberge *f*; **c. sauce** sauce *f* à la canneberge

crane [kreɪn] **1** *n (lifting device, bird)* grue *f*; **c. fly** *(insect)* tipule *f*
2 *vt* **to c. one's neck** tendre le cou
3 *vi* **to c. forward** tendre le cou

cranium ['kreɪnɪəm] *(pl* crania ['kreɪnɪə]) *n Anat* boîte *f* crânienne

crank¹ [kræŋk] *n (gear mechanism)* manivelle *f*

crank² *n Fam (eccentric)* excentrique *mf*; **a religious c.** un fanatique religieux

crankshaft ['kræŋkʃɑ:ft] *n Aut* vilebrequin *m*

cranky ['kræŋkɪ] *adj Fam (eccentric)* excentrique

crap [kræp] **1** *n* (a) *Vulg (excrement)* merde *f*; **to have** *or* **take a c.** chier (b) *very Fam (junk)* saloperies *fpl*; *(nonsense)* conneries *fpl*; *(disgusting substance)* saloperie *f*; **don't talk c.!** ne dis pas de conneries!
2 *adj very Fam (bad)* nul (nulle)

crash [kræʃ] **1** *n* (a) *(noise)* fracas *m* (b) *(accident) (in car)* accident *m*; *(in train, plane)* catastrophe *f*; **c. barrier** glissière *f* de sécurité; **c. helmet** casque *m*; **c. landing**

atterrissage *m* en catastrophe (**c**) *(financial)* krach *m*
2 *adj* **c. course** cours *m* intensif; **c. diet** régime *m* amaigrissant intensif
3 *vt*(**a**) **to c. one's car** avoir un accident de voiture (**b**) *Fam* **to c. a party** = aller à une fête sans y être invité
4 *vi* (**a**) *(make noise)* s'écraser avec fracas; **to c. to the ground** s'écrouler avec fracas; **he was crashing around in the kitchen** il s'agitait bruyamment dans la cuisine (**b**) *(of cars)* se percuter; **to c. into** rentrer dans (**c**) *(of business)* faire faillite; *(of economy)* s'effondrer (**d**) *Comptr* tomber en panne (**e**) *Fam (go to sleep)* s'écrouler
▸ **crash out** *vi Fam (go to sleep)* s'écrouler, **he was crashed out on the sofa** il roupillait sur le divan
crashing ['kræʃɪŋ] *adj* **a c. bore** *(person)* une personne assommante; *(task)* une besogne assommante
crash-land ['kræʃ'lænd] *vi* atterrir en catastrophe
crass [kræs] *adj* grossier(ère); **c. ignorance** ignorance *f* crasse; **c. stupidity** immense bêtise *f*
crate [kreɪt] *n (box)* caisse *f; (for fruit)* cageot *m; (for bottles)* casier *m*
crater ['kreɪtə(r)] *n* cratère *m*
cravat [krə'væt] *n* foulard *m*
crave [kreɪv] **1** *vt (cigarette)* avoir très envie de; *(affection)* être en manque de; *(opportunity)* attendre avec impatience
2 *vi* **to be craving for sth** *(cigarette)* avoir très envie de qch; *(affection)* être en manque de qch; *(opportunity)* attendre qch avec impatience
craving ['kreɪvɪŋ] *n* envie *f;* **to have a c. for sth** *(cigarette)* avoir très envie de qch; *(affection)* être en manque de qch
crawl [krɔːl] **1** *n* (**a**) *(slow pace)* **to move at a c.** *(of car, driver)* rouler au pas; *(of person)* piétiner sur place (**b**) *(swimming stroke)* crawl *m*
2 *vi* (**a**) *(of person)* ramper; *(of baby)* marcher à quatre pattes; *(of car)* rouler au pas (**b**) *Fam (be infested)* **to be crawling with** grouiller de; **to make sb's skin c.** flanquer des boutons à qn (**c**) *Fam (be obsequious)* faire le lèche-bottes; **to c. to sb** lécher les bottes à qn
crawler ['krɔːlə(r)] *n Fam (obsequious person)* lèche-bottes *mf inv*
crayfish ['kreɪfɪʃ] *n* écrevisse *f*
crayon ['kreɪɒn] *n (wax)* crayon *m* gras; *(pencil)* crayon *m* de couleur
craze [kreɪz] *n* engouement *m* (**for** pour)
crazed [kreɪzd] *adj (look, person)* fou (folle)
crazy ['kreɪzɪ] *adj* fou (folle); **to go c.** devenir fou; **to drive sb c.** rendre qn fou; **to be c. about sb/sth** être fou de qn/qch; **like c.** *(run, work)* comme un fou (une folle); **c. paving** dallage *m* irrégulier en pierres plates
creak [kriːk] **1** *n (of hinge)* grincement *m; (of floor, shoes)* craquement *m*
2 *vi (of hinge)* grincer; *(of floor, shoes)* craquer
creaky ['kriːkɪ] *adj (hinge)* grinçant(e); *(floor)* qui craque; *Fig (plot, dialogue)* boiteux(euse)
cream [kriːm] **1** *n* (**a**) *(of milk)* crème *f;* **c. of tomato/chicken soup** crème de tomates/volaille; **c. cheese** fromage *m* frais à tartiner (**b**) *Fig* **the c.** *(best part)* la crème (de la crème) (**c**) *(lotion)* crème *f* (**d**) *(colour)* crème *m*
2 *adj* **c.(-coloured)** (de couleur) crème *inv*
3 *vt Culin (butter)* battre en crème
▸ **cream off** *vt sep Fig (money, profits)* écrémer; **the universities c. off the best students** les universités sélectionnent les meilleurs étudiants
creamy ['kriːmɪ] *adj (taste, consistency)* crémeux(euse); *(skin)* laiteux(euse)

crease [kriːs] **1** *n (in skin, fabric)* pli *m*
2 *vt (fabric)* froisser; **to c. one's brow** plisser le front
3 *vi (of fabric)* se froisser; *(of face, brow)* se plisser
▸ **crease up** *vi Fam (laugh)* se tordre (de rire)
create [kriː'eɪt] **1** *vt* créer; **to c. a sensation/a good impression** faire sensation/bonne impression
2 *vi Fam (get angry)* faire une scène
creation [kriː'eɪʃən] *n* création *f*
creative [kriː'eɪtɪv] *adj (person, activity)* créatif(ive); *(process, imagination)* créateur(trice); *Fin* **c. accounting** manipulations *fpl* comptables; **c. writing** techniques *fpl* de l'écriture
creator [kriː'eɪtə(r)] *n* créateur(trice) *m,f; Rel* **the C.** le Créateur
creature ['kriːtʃə(r)] *n (person)* créature *f,* être *m; (animal)* bête *f;* **to be a c. of habit** avoir ses petites habitudes; **c. comforts** confort *m* matériel; **to like one's c. comforts** aimer son confort
crèche [kreʃ] *n (nursery)* crèche *f; (in shopping centre)* halte-garderie *f*
credence ['kriːdəns] *n* **to give c. to sth** ajouter foi à qch
credentials [krɪ'denʃəlz] *npl* (**a**) *(proof of identity)* pièces *fpl* justificatives d'identité; *(of ambassador)* lettres *fpl* de créance (**b**) *(proof of ability)* références *fpl; Fig* **to establish one's c.** faire ses preuves
credibility [kredɪ'bɪlɪtɪ] *n* crédibilité *f*
credible ['kredɪbəl] *adj* crédible; **it is hardly c. that...** il est difficile de croire que...
credit ['kredɪt] **1** *n* (**a**) *(financial)* crédit *m;* **to be in c.** *(of person)* avoir un compte créditeur; *(of account)* être créditeur(trice); **to give sb c.** faire crédit à qn; **to buy/sell sth on c.** acheter/vendre qch à crédit; **c. card** carte *f* de crédit; *Econ* **c. control** encadrement *m* du crédit; **c. limit** plafond *m* de crédit; **c. note** avoir *m; Fin* **c. rating** degré *m* de solvabilité; *Econ* **c. squeeze** restrictions *fpl* de crédit; **c. transfer** transfert *m,* virement *m*
(**b**) *(belief)* **to give c. to sth** ajouter foi à qch; **to gain c.** *(of theory)* être accepté(e)
(**c**) *(recognition)* mérite *m;* **you have to give him c. for his honesty** tu es bien forcé de reconnaître qu'il est honnête; **to take the c. for sth** s'attribuer le mérite de qch; **to do sb c.** faire honneur à qn; **it does you c.** c'est tout à ton honneur; **c. where c.'s due** il faut rendre à César ce qui est à César; **to her c. she refused** c'est tout à son honneur d'avoir refusé; **she is a c. to the school** elle fait honneur à l'école
(**d**) **credits** *(of film)* générique *m*
2 *vt* (**a**) *(money)* virer (**to an account** sur un compte) (**b**) *(attribute)* **to c. sb with sth** attribuer qch à qn (**c**) *(believe)* croire; **would you c. it?** tu te rends compte?
creditable ['kredɪtəbəl] *adj (praiseworthy)* honorable; *(efforts, attempt)* louable
creditor ['kredɪtə(r)] *n Fin* créditeur(trice) *m,f*
credulity [krɪ'djuːlɪtɪ] *n* crédulité *f*
credulous ['kredjʊləs] *adj* crédule
creed [kriːd] *n also Fig* principes *mpl;* **political c.** credo *m* politique
creek [kriːk] *n (small bay)* crique *f; (stream)* ruisseau *m; Fam Fig* **to be up the c. (without a paddle)** être dans le pétrin
creep [kriːp] **1** *n Fam (unpleasant man)* type *m* répugnant; *(obsequious person)* lèche-bottes *mf inv* (**b**) **to give sb the creeps** faire froid dans le dos à qn
2 *vi (pt & pp* **crept** [krept]) *(of animal, person)* ramper; *(of plants)* ramper; *(vertically)* grimper; **to c. in/out** entrer/sortir à pas de loup; **to c. into bed** se glisser sous les draps; **old age has crept up on me** je me fais

vieux; *Fam* **it makes my flesh c.** ça me flanque des boutons

creeper ['kri:pə(r)] *n (plant)* plante *f* rampante; *(climbing)* plante grimpante

creeping ['kri:pɪŋ] *adj (gradual)* progressif(ive)

creepy ['kri:pɪ] *adj Fam* sinistre

creepy-crawly ['kri:pɪ'krɔ:lɪ] *(pl* **creepy-crawlies)** *n Fam* bestiole *f* rampante

cremate [krɪ'meɪt] *vt* incinérer

cremation [krɪ'meɪʃən] *n* incinération *f*

crematorium [kremə'tɔ:rɪəm] *(pl* **crematoria** [kremə-'tɔ:rɪə]) *n* crématorium *m*

creole ['kri:əʊl] **1** *n (a) (person)* Créole *mf* **(b)** *(language)* créole *m*
2 *adj* créole

creosote ['krɪəsəʊt] *n* créosote *f*

crêpe [kreɪp, krep] *n* **(a)** *(textile)* crêpe *m*; **c. bandage** bande *f* Velpeau®; **c. paper** papier *m* crépon; **c.** (-rubber) sole semelles *fpl* de crêpe **(b)** *(pancake)* crêpe *f*

crept [krept] *pt & pp of* **creep**

crescendo [krɪ'ʃendəʊ] *(pl* **crescendos)** *n Mus & Fig* crescendo *m inv*; **to rise to a c.** *(of music, complaints)* aller crescendo

crescent ['kresənt] **1** *n (shape)* croissant *m*; *(street)* rue *f* en croissant
2 *adj* **c.**(-shaped) en forme de croissant *ou* de demi-lune; **c. moon** croissant *m* de lune

cress [kres] *n* cresson *m*

crest [krest] *n (of bird, wave, helmet)* crête *f*; *(of hill)* sommet *m*; *(coat of arms)* armoiries *fpl*; *Fig* **to be on the c. of a wave** être dans une période faste

crestfallen ['krestfɔ:lən] *adj* abattu(e), découragé(e)

Cretan ['kri:tən] **1** *n* Crétois(e) *m,f*
2 *adj* crétois(e)

Crete [kri:t] *n* la Crète

cretin ['kretɪn] *n Fam* crétin(e) *m,f*

crevice ['krevɪs] *n (in rock)* crevasse *f*, fissure *f*; *(in wall)* lézarde *f*

crew [kru:] **1** *n (of ship, plane)* équipage *m*; *(of ambulance)* équipe *f*; *Fam (gang, group)* bande *f*; **c. cut** *(hairstyle)* brosse *f*, cheveux *mpl* (coupés) en brosse
2 *vt (ship)* **the ship was crewed by** le bateau avait un équipage de

crib [krɪb] **1** *n* **(a)** *(cradle)* berceau *m*; *(Nativity scene)* crèche *f* **(b)** *Fam* **c. (sheet)** *(in exam)* antisèche *f*
2 *vt (pt & pp* **cribbed)** *Fam (copy)* pomper

crick [krɪk] **1** *n* **to have a c. in one's neck** avoir un torticolis
2 *vt* **to c. one's neck** attraper un torticolis

cricket¹ ['krɪkɪt] *n (insect)* grillon *m*

cricket² *n (sport)* cricket *m*; *Fig* **that's not c.!** ce n'est pas du jeu!; **c. ball** balle *f* de cricket; **c. bat** batte *f* de cricket; **c. pitch** terrain *m* de cricket

crikey ['kraɪkɪ] *exclam Fam* mince alors!

crime [kraɪm] *n* crime *m*; *Law* délit *m*; **c. is on the increase** la criminalité augmente; *Fig* **it's a c. to waste money like that** c'est un crime de gaspiller de l'argent de cette façon; **c. wave** vague *f* de criminalité; **c. writer** auteur *m* de romans policiers

Crimea [kraɪ'mɪə] *n* la Crimée

Crimean [kraɪ'mɪən] *adj* de Crimée; **the C. War** la guerre de Crimée

criminal ['krɪmɪnəl] **1** *n* criminel(elle) *m,f*
2 *adj* criminel(elle); *Fig* **it's c. to knock down that**

building c'est un crime de démolir ce bâtiment; **to go to c. court** être jugé(e) au pénal; **c. law** droit *m* pénal; **c. lawyer** avocat *m* au pénal; **c. offence** délit *m*; *(more serious)* crime *m*; **c. record** casier *m* judiciaire

criminalize ['krɪmɪnəlaɪz] *vt* criminaliser

criminology [krɪmɪ'nɒlədʒɪ] *n* criminologie *f*

crimp [krɪmp] *vt (hair)* friser; *(pastry)* pincer

crimson ['krɪmzən] **1** *n* pourpre *m*
2 *adj* pourpre; **to go c. with rage** devenir rouge de colère

cringe [krɪndʒ] *vi* **(a)** *(show fear)* avoir un mouvement de recul **(b)** *(be embarrassed)* avoir envie de rentrer sous terre; **it makes me c.** ça me donne envie de rentrer sous terre

cringing ['krɪndʒɪŋ] *adj (afraid)* craintif(ive); *(servile)* servile

crinkle ['krɪŋkəl] **1** *n (in paper, fabric)* pli *m*
2 *vt (paper, fabric)* froisser; **to c. one's nose** froncer le nez
3 *vi (of brow, nose)* se froncer; *(of face)* se rider

crinkly ['krɪŋklɪ] *adj (skin)* ridé(e); *(paper, fabric)* froissé(e)

cripple ['krɪpəl] **1** *n* estropié(e) *m,f*
2 *vt* estropier; *Fig (industry, system)* paralyser

crippling ['krɪplɪŋ] *adj* **(a)** *(illness)* invalidant(e) **(b)** *(effort, strike)* paralysant(e); *(taxes)* écrasant(e)

crisis ['kraɪsɪs] *(pl* **crises** ['kraɪsi:z]) *n* crise *f*; **to be in c.** être en (pleine) crise; **c. management** habileté *f* à gérer les situations de crise; **c. point** point *m* critique

crisp [krɪsp] **1** *n Br* **(potato) crisps** (pommes *fpl)* chips *fpl*; **a c.** une chips
2 *adj (apple, lettuce)* croquant(e); *(pastry)* croustillant(e); *(bank note)* neuf (neuve); *(sheets)* frais (fraîche); *(snow)* qui crisse sous les pas; *(air, breeze)* vif (vive); *(style)* vif (vive) et précis(e); *(tone)* brusque, tranchant(e)

crispbread ['krɪspbred] *n* pain *m* suédois

crisply ['krɪsplɪ] *adv (say)* d'un ton brusque *ou* tranchant; *(write)* dans un style vif et précis

crispy ['krɪspɪ] *adj* croustillant(e)

criss-cross ['krɪskrɒs] **1** *vt* entrecroiser
2 *vi* s'entrecroiser

criterion [kraɪ'tɪərɪən] *(pl* **criteria** [kraɪ'tɪərɪə]) *n* critère *m*

critic ['krɪtɪk] *n (reviewer)* critique *mf*; *(opponent)* détracteur(trice) *m,f*

critical ['krɪtɪkəl] *adj* **(a)** *(judgemental)* critique **(of** à l'égard de); **to be c. of sb/sth** critiquer qn/qch **(b)** *(essay, study)* critique; **to be a c. success** être acclamé(e) par la critique; *(c)* *(decisive)* critique; **the next few days will be c.** les prochains jours seront décisifs; **in a c. condition** *(of patient)* dans un état critique

criticism ['krɪtɪsɪzəm] *n* critique *f*

criticize ['krɪtɪsaɪz] *vt* critiquer; **to c. sb for sth** reprocher qch à qn; **to c. sb for doing sth** reprocher à qn de faire/d'avoir fait qch

critique [krɪ'ti:k] *n* critique *f*

croak [krəʊk] **1** *n (of frog)* coassement *m*; *(of raven)* croassement *m*
2 *vi* **(a)** *(of frog)* coasser; *(of raven)* croasser; *(of person)* parler d'une voix rauque **(b)** *very Fam (die)* claquer

Croat ['krəʊæt] *n (person)* Croate *mf*
2 *adj* croate

Croatia [krəʊ'eɪʃə] *n* la Croatie

Croatian [krəʊ'eɪʃən] = **Croat**

crochet ['krəʊʃeɪ] **1** *n (travail m au)* crochet *m*; **c. hook** crochet *m*
2 *vt (shawl, blanket)* faire au crochet
3 *vi* faire du crochet

crock [krɒk] *n* **(a)** *(pot)* pot *m* de terre **(b)** *Fam* old c. *(person)* croulant(e) *m,f*

crockery ['krɒkərɪ] *n* vaisselle *f*

crocodile ['krɒkədaɪl] *n* **(a)** *(animal)* crocodile *m*; c. tears larmes *fpl* de crocodile **(b)** *(line of people)* to walk in a c. marcher en rangs par deux

crocus ['krəʊkəs] *n* crocus *m*

croft [krɒft] *n* petite ferme *f*

crone [krəʊn] *n Pej* old c.

crony ['krəʊnɪ] *(pl* cronies) *n* copain (copine) *m,f*

crook [krʊk] **1** *n* **(a)** *(criminal)* escroc *m* **(b)** *(of shepherd)* houlette *f*; *(of bishop)* crosse *f* **(c)** *(curve)* coude *m*; in the c. of one's arm au creux du bras **2** *vt (finger, arm)* plier

crooked ['krʊkɪd] *adj* **(a)** *(not straight)* de travers; *(nose)* tordu(e); a c. smile un sourire en coin **(b)** *(dishonest, illegal)* malhonnête

croon [kruːn] *vt & vi* chantonner, fredonner

crop [krɒp] **1** *n* **(a)** *(of fruit, vegetables)* récolte *f*; *(of cereals)* moisson *f*; *Fig* this year's c. of films la production cinématographique de cette année **(b)** *(handle of whip)* **(riding)** c. cravache *f* **(c)** *(of bird)* jabot *m* **(d)** *(short haircut)* coupe *f* très courte **2** *vt (pt & pp* cropped) **(a)** *(cut)* couper; *(hair)* couper ras **(b)** *(of cattle)* brouter

► **crop up** *vi (of issue, question)* surgir; *(of problem, opportunity)* se présenter; *(of name)* être mentionné(e)

cropper ['krɒpə(r)] *n Fam* to come a c. se prendre une gamelle

croquet ['krəʊkeɪ] *n* croquet *m*

croquette [krɒ'ket] *n Culin* croquette *f*

cross [krɒs] **1** *n* **(a)** *(sign, shape)* croix *f*; to make the sign of the c. faire le signe de croix **(b)** *(hybrid) & Fig* croisement *m* **(between** entre) **(c)** *(in boxing)* coup *m* croisé; *(in football)* centre *m* **2** *adj (annoyed)* fâché(e); to get c. (with sb) se fâcher (contre qn); to be c. with oneself s'en vouloir; we've never had a c. word nous n'avons jamais eu un mot plus haut que l'autre **3** *vt* **(a)** *(river, road)* traverser; to c. sb's path se trouver sur le chemin de qn; it crossed my mind that... il m'est venu à l'esprit que... **(b)** *(make into shape of cross)* croiser; to c. oneself se signer; to c. one's legs/arms croiser les jambes/bras; to keep one's fingers crossed croiser les doigts; to c. one's eyes loucher; *Fig* to c. swords (with sb) croiser le fer (avec qn); *Fig* we must have got our wires crossed nous avons dû mal nous comprendre; *Fam* my heart (and hope to die) croix de bois, croix de fer **(c)** *(oppose)* contrecarrer **(d)** *(animals, plants)* croiser (with avec) **(e)** *(in writing)* to c. a cheque barrer un chèque; to c. one's t's mettre une barre à ses t **4** *vi* **(a)** *(of roads, lines)* se croiser; our letters crossed in the post nos lettres se sont croisées **(b)** *(go across)* traverser; to c. from Dover to Calais faire la traversée de Douvres à Calais

► **cross off, cross out** *vt sep* barrer, rayer

crossbar ['krɒsbɑː(r)] *n (on bike)* barre *f*; *(of goalposts)* barre transversale

crossbow ['krɒsbəʊ] *n* arbalète *f*

crossbreed ['krɒsbriːd] *n (of animals)* croisement *m*; *(of plants)* hybride *m*

cross-Channel ['krɒs'tʃænəl] *adj* transmanche *inv*

crosscheck ['krɒs'tʃek] **1** *n* vérification *f* (par recoupement)

2 *vt* vérifier par recoupement

cross-country ['krɒs'kʌntrɪ] *adj* c. runner coureur(euse) *m,f* de fond; c. running cross *m*

cross-examination ['krɒsɪgzæmɪ'neɪʃən] *n Law* contre-interrogatoire *m*; *Fig* interrogatoire *m* serré

cross-examine ['krɒsɪg'zæmɪn] *vt Law* soumettre à un contre-interrogatoire; *Fig* soumettre à un interrogatoire serré; to c. sb about sth interroger qn en détail sur qch

cross-eyed ['krɒsaɪd] *adj* to be c. loucher

crossfire ['krɒsfaɪə(r)] *n* feu *m* croisé; *Fig* to be caught in the c. être pris(e) entre deux feux

crossing ['krɒsɪŋ] *n* **(a)** *(of sea, river)* traversée *f* **(b)** *(in street)* passage *m* (pour) piétons, passage clouté

cross-legged ['krɒs'leg(ɪ)d] *adv* to sit c. être assis(e) en tailleur

cross-platform [krɒs'plætfɔːm] *adj Comptr* multi-plateforme

cross-purposes ['krɒs'pɜːpəsɪz] *npl* to be at c. ne pas parler de la même chose

cross-reference ['krɒs'refərəns] *n* renvoi *m*

crossroads ['krɒsrəʊdz] *(pl* crossroads) *n* carrefour *m*, croisement *m*; *Fig (decisive moment)* point *m* crucial

cross-section ['krɒs'sekʃən] *n* coupe *f* ou section *f* transversale; *Fig (of population)* échantillon *m* représentatif

crosswind ['krɒswɪnd] *n* vent *m* de travers

crossword ['krɒswɜːd] *n* c. (puzzle) mots *mpl* croisés

crotch [krɒtʃ] *n* entrejambe *m*

crotchet ['krɒtʃɪt] *n Mus* noire *f*

crotchety ['krɒtʃətɪ] *adj Fam* grognon

crouch [kraʊtʃ] *vi (of animal)* se tapir; *(of person)* s'accroupir

croupier ['kruːpɪə(r)] *n* croupier *m*

crow [krəʊ] **1** *n (bird)* corbeau *m*; as the c. flies à vol d'oiseau; c.'s feet *(on face)* pattes *fpl* d'oie; c.'s nest *(on ship)* nid-de-pie *m* **2** *vi (of cock)* chanter **(b)** *(exult)* se vanter (about de)

crowbar ['krəʊbɑː(r)] *n* levier *m*

crowd [kraʊd] **1** *n* **(a)** *(large number of people)* foule *f*; *(at sporting event)* public *m*; there was a c. at the cinema il y avait beaucoup de monde au cinéma; *Fig* to stand out from the c. se distinguer de la masse; *Fig* to follow the c. suivre le mouvement; to be a c. puller attirer les foules **(b)** *Fam (group)* bande *f* **2** *vi (people, objects)* entasser; *(streets, square)* envahir; don't c. me! laisse-moi respirer! **3** *vi* to c. (together) s'entasser; to c. round sb se presser autour de qn

► **crowd out** *vt sep (of deal, market)* exclure (of de)

crowded ['kraʊdɪd] *adj (place)* bondé(e); *(day, schedule)* chargé(e)

crown [kraʊn] **1** *n* **(a)** *(of monarch)* couronne *f*; the C. (the monarchy) la Couronne; *Br Law* c. court ≃ assises *fpl*, Cour *f* d'assises; c. jewels joyaux *mpl* de la Couronne; c. prince prince *m* héritier **(b)** *(top)* c. (of head) sommet *m* de la tête; *(of hat)* haut *m*; *(of hill)* sommet; *(of tooth)* couronne *f* **2** *vt also Fig* couronner; *Fam* I'll c. you! (hit on the head) je vais te flanquer une calotte!; and to c. it all... et pour couronner le tout...

crowning ['kraʊnɪŋ] *adj (achievement)* suprême; c. glory couronnement *m*

crucial ['kruːʃəl] *adj (very important)* crucial(e)

crucible ['kruːsɪbəl] *n* creuset *m*; *Fig (test)* épreuve *f*

crucifix ['kruːsɪfɪks] *n* crucifix *m*

crucifixion [kru:sɪ'fɪkʃən] *n* crucifixion *f*

crucify ['kru:sɪfaɪ] (*pt & pp* **crucified**) *vt* crucifier; *Fig (criticize)* descendre en flammes; *(defeat)* écraser

crude [kru:d] *adj* **(a)** *(unsophisticated, unrefined)* grossier(ère); **c. (oil)** pétrole *m* brut **(b)** *(rude, vulgar)* vulgaire

cruel ['kruəl] *adj* cruel(elle); *(winter)* rude; **you have to be c. to be kind** qui aime bien châtie bien

cruelty ['kruəltɪ] *n* cruauté *f*

cruet ['kru:ɪt] *n* Culin **c. (stand** *or* **set)** service *m* à condiments

cruise [kru:z] **1** *n (on ship)* croisière *f*; **to go on a c.** faire une croisière; **c. missile** missile *m* de croisière
2 *vi (of passengers)* être en croisière; *(of taxi)* être en maraude; *(of car)* rouler; *Fam (look for sexual partner)* draguer; **cruising speed** *(of ship, plane)* vitesse *f* de croisière

cruiser ['kru:zə(r)] *n (ship)* **(battle) c.** croiseur *m*; **(cabin) c.** yacht *m* de croisière

crumb [krʌm] *n also Fig* miette *f*; **my only c. of comfort is…** mon seul petit réconfort est…

crumble ['krʌmbəl] **1** *n (dessert)* crumble *m*, – dessert aux fruits recouvert de pâte sablée
2 *vt (bread, cake)* émietter
3 *vi (of stone)* s'effriter; *(of bread)* s'émietter; *Fig (of empire, hopes)* s'effondrer

crumbly ['krʌmblɪ] *adj* friable

crumpet ['krʌmpɪt] *n* **(a)** *(teacake)* = petite crêpe épaisse mangée avec du beurre, de la confiture etc **(b)** *very Fam (women)* nanas *fpl*; **a nice bit of c.** une belle nana

crumple ['krʌmpəl] **1** *vt (material, dress)* froisser, chiffonner; **to c. sth into a ball** mettre qch en boule
2 *vi (of material, dress)* se froisser, se chiffonner; *Fig (of face)* se crisper

crunch [krʌntʃ] **1** *n (sound)* craquement *m*; *(of snow, gravel)* crissement *m*; *Fig* **when it comes to the c.** au moment crucial; *Fig* **if it comes to the c.** au pire
2 *vt (with teeth)* croquer (dans)
3 *vi (of snow, gravel)* crisser; **to c. on sth** *(with teeth)* croquer (dans) qch

crunchy ['krʌntʃɪ] *adj* croquant(e); *(snow, gravel)* qui crisse sous les pas

crusade [kru:'seɪd] *n also Fig* croisade *f*
2 *vi* **to c. for/against** se battre pour/contre qch

crusader [kru:'seɪdə(r)] *n Hist* croisé *m*; *Fig* militant(e) *m,f* **(for/against** pour/contre)

crush [krʌʃ] **1** *n* **(a)** *(crowd)* foule *f*; *(confusion)* bousculade *f*; **c. barrier** barrière *f* de sécurité **(b)** *(drink)* **orange/lemon c.** = boisson gazeuse à l'orange/au citron **(c)** *Fam (infatuation)* béguin *m*; **to have a c. on sb** avoir le béguin *ou* en pincer pour qn
2 *vt* écraser; *(grapes)* presser; *(ice)* piler; *(in a drawer, suitcase)* entasser; *Fig (opponent)* écraser; *(revolt)* étouffer; mater; *(hopes, person)* anéantir
3 *vi (be crammed)* s'entasser; *(crease)* se froisser

crushing ['krʌʃɪŋ] *adj (defeat)* écrasant(e); *(blow)* terrible; *(remark)* cinglant(e)

crust [krʌst] *n (of bread, pie, the earth)* croûte *f*; *Fam* **to earn a c.** gagner sa croûte

crustacean [krʌs'teɪʃən] *n* crustacé *m*

crusty ['krʌstɪ] *adj* **(a)** *(bread, roll)* croustillant(e) **(b)** *(person)* acariâtre

crutch [krʌtʃ] *n* **(a)** *(for walking)* béquille *f*; *Fig (support)* soutien *m*; **to be on crutches** marcher avec des béquilles **(b)** *(crotch)* entrejambe *m*

crux [krʌks] *n (of matter, problem)* cœur *m*

cruzado [cru:'zɑ:dəʊ] *(pl* **cruzados)** *n* cruzado *m*

cry [kraɪ] **1** *n (pl* **cries) (a)** *(call) (of person, animal)* cri *m*; *(in demonstration)* slogan *m*; **to give a c.** pousser un cri; **a c. for help** un appel au secours; **to be a far c. from sth** n'avoir rien à voir avec qch **(b)** *(weeping)* **to have a good c.** pleurer un bon coup
2 *vt (pt & pp* **cried** [kraɪd]) **(a)** *(exclaim)* crier **(b)** *(weep)* **to c. oneself to sleep** s'endormir en pleurant
3 *vi* **(a)** *(weep)* pleurer; **to c. over sth** se lamenter sur qch; *Prov* **it's no use crying over spilt milk** ce qui est fait est fait **(b)** *(shout, call)* crier; **to c. for help** appeler à l'aide *ou* au secours
▸ **cry off** *vi (from invitation)* se décommander
▸ **cry out 1** *vt sep* **(a)** *(shout)* crier **(b)** *(weep)* **to c. one's eyes** *or* **heart out** pleurer toutes les larmes de son corps
2 *vi (shout)* pousser un cri; *Fam* **for crying out loud!** mais bon sang!; *Fam* **that wall is crying out for a coat of paint** ce mur aurait grand besoin d'une couche de peinture

crybaby ['kraɪbeɪbɪ] *(pl* **crybabies)** *n Fam* pleurnicheur(euse) *m,f*

crying ['kraɪɪŋ] **1** *n (weeping)* pleurs *mpl*
2 *adj (need)* urgent(e); **it's a c. shame that…** il est scandaleux que… + *subjunctive*

crypt [krɪpt] *n* crypte *f*

cryptic ['krɪptɪk] *adj* énigmatique; **c. crossword** = mots croisés dont les définitions sont des énigmes

crystal ['krɪstəl] **1** *n* cristal *m*; **c. ball** boule *f* de cristal; **c. vase** vase *m* de *ou* en cristal
2 *adj (clear)* cristallin(e), limpide

crystal-clear ['krɪstəl'klɪə(r)] *adj (water)* limpide; *(explanation)* clair(e) comme de l'eau de roche

crystallize ['krɪstəlaɪz] **1** *vt Chem* cristalliser; **crystallized fruit** fruits *mpl* confits
2 *vi Chem & Fig* se cristalliser

CST [si:es'ti:] *n Am (abbr* **Central Standard Time)** = heure du centre de l'Amérique du Nord

cub [kʌb] *n (of fox)* renardeau *m*; *(of bear)* ourson *m*; *(of lion)* lionceau *m*; *(of wolf)* louveteau *m*; **C. (Scout)** louveteau *m*

Cuba ['kju:bə] *n* Cuba

Cuban ['kju:bən] **1** *n* Cubain(e) *m,f*
2 *adj* cubain(e)

cubbyhole ['kʌbɪhəʊl] *n* cagibi *m*

cube [kju:b] **1** *n (shape)* cube *m*; *(of sugar)* morceau *m*; *Math* **c. root** racine *f* cubique
2 *vt Math* élever au cube

cubic ['kju:bɪk] *adj* cubique; **c. capacity** volume *m*; **c. metre** mètre *m* cube

cubicle ['kju:bɪkəl] *n (in hospital, dormitory)* box *m*; *(in swimming pool)* cabine *f*; *(in public toilet)* W.-C. *m*

cubism ['kju:bɪzəm] *n Art* cubisme *m*

cuckold ['kʌkəld] **1** *n* cocu *m*
2 *vt* cocufier, faire cocu

cuckoo ['kʊku:] **1** *n (bird)* coucou *m*; **c. clock** coucou *m*
2 *adj Fam (mad)* dingue

cucumber ['kju:kʌmbə(r)] *n* concombre *m*

cud [kʌd] *n* **to chew the c.** ruminer

cuddle ['kʌdəl] **1** *n* câlin *m*; **to give sb a c.** faire un câlin à qn
2 *vt* câliner, faire des câlins à
3 *vi* se câliner, se faire des câlins; **to c. up to sb** se pelotonner *ou* se blottir contre qn

cuddly ['kʌdlɪ] *adj Fam (child, animal)* mignon(onne) à croquer; *Euph (plump)* rond(e); **c. toy** peluche *f*

cudgel ['kʌdʒəl] **1** *n* gourdin *m*, trique *f*; *Fig* **to take up the cudgels on sb's behalf** prendre fait et cause pour qn

2 vt (pt & pp **cudgelled**, Am **cudgeled**) donner des coups de gourdin ou de trique à; **to c. one's brains** se creuser la cervelle

cue¹ [kjuː] n (of actor) réplique f; Fig (signal) signal m; Fig **to take one's c. from sb** prendre exemple sur qn; **c. card** (for public speaker) aide-mémoire m inv

cue² n (in billiards, pool) queue f; **c. ball** boule f blanche

cuff¹ [kʌf] n (of shirt) poignet m; **cuffs** (handcuffs) menottes fpl; Fam **off the c.** au pied levé; **c. links** boutons mpl de manchette

cuff² **1** n (blow) calotte f

2 vt (hit) donner une calotte à

cuisine [kwɪˈziːn] n cuisine f

cul-de-sac ['kʌldəsæk] n also Fig impasse f

culinary ['kʌlɪnərɪ] adj culinaire

cull [kʌl] **1** n (of seals, deer) abattage m

2 vt (**a**) (herd) réduire la taille de; (animal) abattre (**b**) (select) sélectionner (**from** parmi)

culminate ['kʌlmɪneɪt] vi **to c. in sth** aboutir à qch

culmination [kʌlmɪˈneɪʃən] n point m culminant

culottes [kuːˈlɒts] npl jupe-culotte f

culpable ['kʌlpəbəl] adj coupable (**of** de); Scot Law **c. homicide** homicide m involontaire

culprit ['kʌlprɪt] n coupable mf

cult [kʌlt] n culte m; (sect) secte f; **c. figure** personnage m culte; **c. film** film m culte

cultivate ['kʌltɪveɪt] vt also Fig cultiver

cultivated ['kʌltɪveɪtɪd] adj cultivé(e)

cultivation [kʌltɪˈveɪʃən] n culture f

cultivator ['kʌltɪveɪtə(r)] n (for farm) cultivateur m; (for garden) motoculteur m; (person) cultivateur(trice) m,f

cultural ['kʌltʃərəl] adj culturel(elle)

culture ['kʌltʃə(r)] n (**a**) (artistic activity, refinement) culture f; Hum **c. vulture** fou (folle) m,f de culture (**b**) (society) culture f; **c. shock** choc m culturel (**c**) Biol culture f

cultured ['kʌltʃəd] adj (educated) cultivé(e); **c. pearl** perle f de culture

cumbersome ['kʌmbəsəm] adj (luggage, furniture) encombrant(e); (procedure, style) lourd(e)

cumin ['kʌmɪn] n cumin m

cumulative ['kjuːmjʊlətɪv] adj cumulatif(ive)

cunning ['kʌnɪŋ] **1** n (deviousness) ruse f; (ingenuity) astuce f, ingéniosité f

2 adj (devious) rusé(e); (ingenious) astucieux(euse), ingénieux(euse)

cunt [kʌnt] n Vulg (vagina) chatte f; (as insult) enculé(e) m,f

cup [kʌp] **1** n (**a**) (for drinking, measurement) tasse f; (plastic, paper) gobelet m; Fam Fig **it's not my c. of tea** ce n'est pas ma tasse de thé; **it's not everyone's c. of tea** tout le monde n'aime pas (**b**) (trophy) coupe f; **c. final** finale f de coupe; **c. tie** match m éliminatoire de coupe (**c**) (of bra) bonnet m

2 vt (pt & pp **cupped**) **to c. one's hands round one's mouth** mettre ses mains en porte-voix; **to c. one's hand behind one's ear** mettre sa main en cornet

cupboard ['kʌbəd] n placard m; Fam **c. love** amour m intéressé; **c. space** rangements mpl

cupcake ['kʌpkeɪk] n = sorte de madeleine

Cupid ['kjuːpɪd] n Cupidon m

cuppa ['kʌpə] n Br Fam tasse f de thé

curable ['kjʊərəbəl] adj guérissable

curate ['kjʊərət] n Rel vicaire m; **this book is a bit of a c.'s egg** il y a du bon et du mauvais dans ce livre

curator [kjʊəˈreɪtə(r)] n conservateur m

curb [kɜːb] **1** n (**a**) (limit) **to put a c. on sth** mettre un frein à qch (**b**) Am (of road) bordure f de trottoir

2 vt (spending) réduire; (emotions) refréner

curd [kɜːd] n **curd(s)** lait m caillé; **c. cheese** fromage m blanc battu

curdle ['kɜːdəl] **1** vt cailler

2 vi (se) cailler

cure ['kjʊə(r)] **1** n remède m (**for** contre); **there is no known c.** on n'a pas encore trouvé de remède; **beyond c.** (person) incurable; (situation) irrémédiable

2 vt (**a**) (person) guérir (**of** de) (**b**) (preserve) (by salting) saler; (by smoking) fumer; (by drying) sécher; (hides) traiter

cure-all ['kjʊərɔːl] n panacée f

curfew ['kɜːfjuː] n couvre-feu m

curio ['kjʊərɪəʊ] (pl **curios**) n curiosité f

curiosity [kjʊərɪˈɒsɪtɪ] (pl **curiosities**) n curiosité f; Prov **c. killed the cat** la curiosité est un vilain défaut

curious ['kjʊərɪəs] adj (inquisitive, strange) curieux(euse); **to be c. to see/know** vouloir voir/savoir par curiosité

curl [kɜːl] **1** n (of hair) boucle f; (of smoke) volute f

2 vt (hair) boucler; (tightly) friser; **to c. one's lip** faire une moue dédaigneuse; **to c. oneself into a ball** se rouler en boule

3 vi (of hair) boucler; (tightly) friser; (of paper, leaves) se recroqueviller; (of smoke) s'élever en volutes

▸ **curl up** vi (**a**) (make oneself comfortable) se pelotonner (**b**) (protect oneself) se rouler en boule (**c**) (of paper, leaves) se recroqueviller

curler ['kɜːlə(r)] n (for hair) bigoudi m

curlew ['kɜːljuː] n courlis m

curling ['kɜːlɪŋ] n (**a**) (sport) curling m (**b**) **c. tongs** fer m à friser

curly ['kɜːlɪ] adj (hair) bouclé(e); (tightly) frisé(e)

currant ['kʌrənt] n raisin m de Corinthe; Br **c. bun** petit pain m aux raisins

currency ['kʌrənsɪ] (pl **currencies**) n (**a**) (money) monnaie f; (foreign) devise f; **c. market** marché m monétaire (**b**) (acceptance) **to gain c.** (of theory) être accrédité(e); (of idea, belief) se répandre; **to give c. to a rumour** faire courir un bruit

current ['kʌrənt] **1** n (of river, electricity) & Fig (trend) courant m; Fig **to swim against the c.** aller à contre-courant

2 adj (**a**) (existing, present) actuel(elle); **c. affairs** actualité f; **c. issue** (of magazine) dernier numéro m (**b**) Br Fin **c. account** compte m courant; **c. assets** actif m de roulement; **c. expenditure** dépenses fpl courantes; **c. liabilities** passif m exigible (**c**) (common) courant(e)

currently ['kʌrəntlɪ] adv actuellement

curriculum [kəˈrɪkjʊləm] (pl **curricula** [kəˈrɪkjʊlə]) n Sch programme m; **c. vitae** curriculum vitae m inv

curry¹ ['kʌrɪ] **1** n (pl **curries**) curry m; **c. powder** curry

2 vt (pt & pp **curried**) **curried chicken/lamb** poulet m/agneau m au curry

curry² vt **to c. favour with sb** s'insinuer dans les bonnes grâces de qn

curse [kɜːs] **1** n (**a**) (jinx, affliction) malédiction f, mauvais sort m; (swearword) juron m; **to put a c. on sb** jeter un sort à qn (**b**) (scourge) fléau m

2 vt maudire; **to be cursed with sth** être affligé(e) de qch

3 vi jurer

cursor ['kɜːsə(r)] n Comptr curseur m; **c. key** touche f de déplacement

cursory ['kɜːsərɪ] adj superficiel(elle)

curt [kɜːt] adj sec (sèche)

curtail [kɜː'teɪl] *vt (shorten)* abréger, écourter; *(limit)* réduire

curtain ['kɜːtən] *n* rideau *m*; **to draw the curtains** *(open)* ouvrir les rideaux; *(close)* fermer *ou* tirer les rideaux; *Fam Fig* **it's curtains for her** elle est fichue; *Th* **c. call** rappel *m*; **c. raiser** *Th* lever *m* de rideau; *Fig* prélude *m* (**to** à); **c. rail** *or* **rod** tringle *f* à rideau; **c. ring** anneau *m* de rideau
► **curtain off** *vt sep* séparer par un rideau

curts(e)y ['kɜːtsɪ] **1** *n (pl* **curtsies** *or* **curtseys)** révérence *f*
2 *vi (pt & pp* **curtsied** *or* **curtseyed)** faire la révérence (**to** à)

curvaceous [kɜː'veɪʃəs] *adj* pulpeux(euse)

curvature ['kɜːvətʃə(r)] *n* courbure *f*; **c. of the spine** scoliose *f*

curve [kɜːv] **1** *n* courbe *f*; *(in road)* tournant *m*, virage *m*; *(in river)* méandre *m*
2 *vi (of spine)* se courber; *(of road)* faire une courbe; *(of river)* serpenter

curved [kɜːvd] *adj (line)* courbe; *(spine)* courbé(e)

cushion ['kʊʃən] **1** *n (on chair, of air)* coussin *m*, *(on billiard table)* bande *f*
2 *vt (blow, impact)* amortir; **to c. sb against sth** protéger qn contre qch

cushy ['kʊʃɪ] *adj Fam* pépère, peinard(e); **à c. number** une bonne planque

custard ['kʌstəd] *n Br* crème *f* anglaise; **c. pie** *(in slapstick comedy)* tarte *f* à la crème; **c. powder** préparation *f* instantanée pour crème anglaise

custodial [kʌs'təʊdɪəl] *adj Law* **c. sentence** peine *f* de prison

custodian [kʌs'təʊdɪən] *n* gardien(enne) *m,f*

custody ['kʌstədɪ] *n* (a) *(of children, important papers)* garde *f*; **to have c. of sb** avoir la garde de qn; **in safe c.** sous bonne garde (b) *Law* garde *f* à vue; **to take sb into c.** placer qn en garde a vue

custom ['kʌstəm] *n* (a) *(tradition, practice)* coutume *f*; **it was his c. to rise early** il avait l'habitude de se lever tôt (b) *Com* clientèle *f*; **to take one's c. elsewhere** aller se fournir ailleurs

customary ['kʌstəmərɪ] *adj (usual)* habituel(elle); *(traditional)* traditionnel(elle); **it is c. to…** il est d'usage de…

custom-built ['kʌstəmbɪlt] *adj (car, offices)* construit(e) sur mesure; *(kitchen units)* fabriqué(e) sur mesure

customer ['kʌstəmə(r)] *n* client(e) *m,f*; *Fam Fig* **he's an awkward c.** c'est un type pas commode; *Com* **c. services (department)** service *m* clientèle

customize ['kʌstəmaɪz] *vt (vehicle)* customiser; *(kitchen, computer)* personnaliser

custom-made ['kʌstəm'meɪd] *adj* (fait(e)) sur mesure

customs ['kʌstəmz] *npl* douane *f*; **to go through c.** passer la douane; **c. declaration** déclaration *f* en douane; **c. duty** droits *mpl* de douane; **c. officer** douanier(ère) *m,f*

cut [kʌt] **1** *n* (a) *(in flesh, text, film)* coupure *f*; *(in wood, cloth)* entaille *f*; **c. of meat** morceau *m* (de viande); *Fam* **to be a c. above sb/sth** être un cran au-dessus de qn/qch (b) *(in wages, prices)* réduction *f* (c) *(blow)* coup *m*; **the c. and thrust of debate** les joutes *fpl* oratoires (d) *Fam (share)* part *f* (e) *(style) (of clothes, hair)* coupe *f*
2 *adj Fig* **c. and dried** *(clear)* simple; *(decided)* décidé(e); **c. flowers** fleurs *fpl* coupées; **c. glass** cristal *m* taillé
3 *vt (pt & pp* **cut**) (a) *(in general)* couper; *(into slices)* trancher, découper; **to c. one's finger/nails** se couper le

doigt/les ongles; **to c. sb's hair** couper les cheveux à qn; **to have one's hair cut** se faire couper les cheveux; **to c. sth in two** *or* **in half** couper qch en deux; **to c. sth to pieces** couper qch en morceaux; **to c. oneself loose** *or* **free** se dégager, se libérer; **to c. a record** enregistrer un disque (b) *(wages, prices)* réduire
(c) *(idioms)* **to c. one's losses** limiter les dégâts; **to c. one's teeth on sth** se faire les dents sur qch; **to c. sb (dead)** faire semblant de ne pas voir qn; **it's cutting it** *or* **things (a bit) fine** ça fait (un peu) juste; **to c. sb short** couper la parole à qn; **to c. sth short** écourter qch; **to c. a long story short…** bref…
4 *vi* (a) *(of knife, scissors)* couper; *(of wind)* être cinglant(e); *Cin* **c.!** coupez!
(b) *(idioms)* **that's an argument that cuts both ways** c'est un argument à double tranchant; *Fam* **to c. and run** décamper
► **cut across** *vt insep* (a) *(field)* couper à travers (b) *(transcend)* transcender
► **cut back 1** *vt sep* (a) *(bush, tree)* tailler (b) *(costs, production)* réduire
2 *vi* **to c. back on sth** *(spending, time)* réduire qch; **to c. back on smoking/drinking** fumer/boire moins
► **cut down 1** *vt sep* (a) *(tree, soldier)* abattre; **to be c. down in one's prime** être fauché(e) à la fleur de l'âge (b) *(speech, text)* abréger, *(spending, time)* réduire; *Fig* **to c. sb down to size** rabattre son caquet à qn
2 *vi* = cut back
► **cut in** *vi* (a) *(interrupt conversation)* intervenir (b) *(in car)* **to c. in in front of sb** faire une queue de poisson à qn
► **cut into** *vt insep (with knife)* entamer; *(of rope, handle)* blesser
► **cut off** *vt sep* (a) *(remove)* couper; **to c. off sb's head** trancher la tête à qn, décapiter qn; *Fig* **that would be cutting off your nose to spite your face** ça va te retomber sur le nez (b) *(disconnect)* couper; **we've been cut off** *(had electricity disconnected)* on nous a coupé l'électricité; **I've been cut off** *(during phone conversation)* j'ai été coupé (c) *(isolate)* isoler; **to be cut off from** être coupé(e) de
► **cut out** *vt sep* (a) *(picture, article)* découper, *(tumour)* enlever, *Fam* **to have got one's work c. out** avoir du pain sur la planche; **to be cut out for sth** être fait(e) pour qch (b) *(stop)* supprimer; **to c. out smoking/desserts** arrêter de fumer/de manger des desserts; *Fam* **c. it out!** ça va maintenant! (c) *(exclude)* **to c. sb out of one's will** déshériter qn; **to c. sb out of a deal** évincer qn
2 *vi (of engine)* caler; *(of machine)* s'arrêter
► **cut up 1** *vt sep* (a) *(food, paper)* couper; *(into slices)* découper (b) *Fam (upset)* **to be c. up** *(about sth)* être complètement chamboulé(e) (par qch)
2 *vi Fam* **to c. up rough** *(of person)* devenir agressif(ive)

cutback ['kʌtbæk] *n* réduction *f*

cute [kjuːt] *adj* mignon(onne)

cuticle ['kjuːtɪkəl] *n* cuticule *f*

cutlery ['kʌtlərɪ] *n* couverts *mpl*; *Com* argenterie *f*

cutlet ['kʌtlɪt] *n* côtelette *f*

cutoff ['kʌtɒf] *n* **c. date** date *f* limite; **c. point** limite *f*; *(for tax)* seuil *m*

cutout ['kʌtaʊt] *n* (a) *(shape)* silhouette *f* (b) *Elec* disjoncteur *m*

cut-price ['kʌt'praɪs] *adj (goods)* à prix réduit; *(rate)* réduit(e)

cutthroat ['kʌtθrəʊt] **1** *n* assassin *m*
2 *adj (competition)* acharné(e); **c. razor** coupe-choux *m inv*

cutting ['kʌtɪŋ] **1** *n* (a) *(of plant)* bouture *f* (b)

(newspaper) c. coupure *f* de journal *ou* de presse **(c)** **(railway)** c. voie *f* en déblai

2 *adj (wind, remark)* cinglant(e); **c. edge** tranchant *m; Fig* **to be at the c. edge of technology** être à la pointe du progrès

cuttlefish ['kʌtəlfɪʃ] *n* seiche *f*

CV [siː'viː] *n Br (abbr* **curriculum vitae)** CV *m*

cyanide ['saɪənaɪd] *n Chem* cyanure *m*

cybercafé [saɪbə'kæfeɪ] *n* cybercafé *m*

cybernetics [saɪbə'netɪks] *n Comptr* cybernétique *f*

cyberspace ['saɪbəspeɪs] *n Comptr* cyberespace *m*

cyclamen ['sɪkləmən] *(pl* **cyclamen)** *n* cyclamen *m*

cycle ['saɪkəl] **1** *n* **(a)** *(pattern)* cycle *m* **(b)** *(bicycle)* bicyclette *f,* vélo *m*; **c. lane** voie *f* réservée aux vélos; **c. path** piste *f* cyclable; **c. racing** course *f* cycliste

2 *vi* aller à bicyclette *ou* à vélo

cyclic(al) ['saɪklɪk(əl)] *adj* cyclique

cycling ['saɪklɪŋ] *n* cyclisme *m*; **to go on a c. holiday** faire du cyclotourisme; **c. track** piste *f* cycliste

cyclist ['saɪklɪst] *n* cycliste *mf*

cyclone ['saɪkləʊn] *n Met* cyclone *m*

cygnet ['sɪgnɪt] *n* jeune cygne *m*

cylinder ['sɪlɪndə(r)] *n (shape)* cylindre *m; (gas container)* bouteille *f;* **four-/eight-c. engine** moteur *m* à quatre/huit cylindres; **c. block** bloc-cylindres *m*; **c. head** culasse *f*

cylindrical [sɪ'lɪndrɪkəl] *adj* cylindrique

cymbal ['sɪmbəl] *n* cymbale *f*

cynic ['sɪnɪk] *n* cynique *mf*

cynical ['sɪnɪkəl] *adj* cynique (**about** sur)

cypress ['saɪprəs] *n* cyprès *m*

Cypriot ['sɪprɪət] **1** *n* Chypriote *mf,* Cypriote *mf*

2 *adj* chypriote, cypriote

Cyprus ['saɪprəs] *n* Chypre

cyst [sɪst] *n Med* kyste *m*

cystitis [sɪs'taɪtɪs] *n Med* cystite *f*

czar [zɑː(r)] *n* tsar *m,* czar *m*

Czech [tʃek] **1** *n* **(a)** *(person)* Tchèque *mf* **(b)** *(language)* tchèque *m*

2 *adj* tchèque; **the C. Republic** la République tchèque

Czechoslovakia [tʃekəʊsləˈvækɪə] *n Formerly* la Tchécoslovaquie

D, d [diː] *n* (**a**) *(letter)* D, d *m inv* (**b**) *Mus* ré *m* (**c**) *Sch (grade)* to get a D avoir entre 8 et 10 sur 20
D *Am Pol (abbr* **Democrat)** démocrate
DA [diːˈeɪ] *n Am Law (abbr* **district attorney)** ≃ procureur *m* de la République
dab [dæb] **1** *n (of paint)* petit coup *m*; *(of glue)* point *m*; *(of perfume)* goutte *f*; *Br Fam* **dabs** *(fingerprints)* empreintes *fpl* (digitales)
  2 *adj* **to be a d.** hand at sth être doué(e) pour qch
  3 *vt (pt & pp* **dabbed)** *(paint)* passer; *(eyes, wound)* tamponner
dabble [ˈdæbəl] **1** *vt* **to d. one's feet in the water** balancer ses pieds dans l'eau
  2 *vi* **to d. in politics/journalism** faire vaguement de la politique/du journalisme
dabbler [ˈdæblə(r)] *n* amateur(trice) *m,f*
dachshund [ˈdækshʊnd] *n* teckel *m*
dad [dæd] *n Fam* papa *m*
daddy [ˈdædɪ] *(pl* **daddies)** *n Fam* papa *m*
daddy-longlegs [ˈdædɪˈlɒŋlegz] *(pl* **daddy-longlegs)** *n Fam* tipule *f*
daffodil [ˈdæfədɪl] *n* jonquille *f*
daft [dɑːft] *adj Br* idiot(e); **to be d.** about sb/sth être fou (folle) de qn/qch
dagger [ˈdægə(r)] *n* (**a**) *(weapon)* dague *f* (**b**) *(idioms)* **to be at daggers drawn (with sb)** être à couteaux tirés (avec qn); **to look daggers at sb** foudroyer qn du regard
dago [ˈdeɪgəʊ] *(pl* **dagoes** *or* **dagos)** *n very Fam* = terme injurieux désignant un Espagnol, un Portugais, un Italien ou un Latino-Américain
dahlia [ˈdeɪlɪə] *n* dahlia *m*
daily [ˈdeɪlɪ] **1** *n (pl* **dailies)** *(newspaper)* quotidien *m*
  2 *adj* quotidien(enne); **on a d.** basis *(paid, calculated)* à la journée; *(used)* quotidiennement; *Fam* **the d.** grind le train-train quotidien; **d. paper** quotidien *m*
  3 *adv* tous les jours, quotidiennement; **twice d.** deux fois par jour
dainty [ˈdeɪntɪ] *adj* délicat(e)
dairy [ˈdeərɪ] *(pl* **dairies)** *n (shop)* crémerie *f*; *(factory)* laiterie *f*; **d. cow** vache *f* laitière; **d. farm** = ferme spécialisée dans la production laitière; **d. farming** élevage *m* de vaches laitières; **d. produce** produits *mpl* laitiers
dais [ˈdeɪɪs] *n* estrade *f*
daisy [ˈdeɪzɪ] *(pl* **daisies)** *n* pâquerette *f*; *(bigger)* marguerite *f*; **to push up the daisies** manger les pissenlits par la racine; **d. chain** guirlande *f* de pâquerettes
daisywheel [ˈdeɪzɪwiːl] *n (on printer)* marguerite *f*
dale [deɪl] *n* vallée *f*

dalliance [ˈdælɪəns] *n Lit* badinage *m*
dally [ˈdælɪ] *(pt & pp* **dallied)** *vi (dawdle)* traîner, lambiner; **to d. over a decision** mettre du temps à se décider
Dalmatian [dælˈmeɪʃən] *n (dog)* dalmatien *m*
dam [dæm] **1** *n* barrage *m*
  2 *vt (pt & pp* **dammed)** *(river, lake)* construire un barrage sur
  ▸ **dam up** *vt sep (river, lake)* construire un barrage sur
damage [ˈdæmɪdʒ] **1** *n* (**a**) *(to machine, building)* dégâts *mpl*; *(to health, reputation)* mal *m*; **to do** *or* **cause d. to** *(building)* faire des dégâts dans; *(health, reputation)* nuire à; *Fig* **the d. is done** le mal est fait; *Br Fam* **what's the d.?** ça fait combien?; **we have to do some d. limitation** il faut limiter les dégâts (**b**) **damages** *(compensation)* dommages-intérêts *mpl*
  2 *vt (machine, building)* abîmer, endommager; *(health, reputation)* nuire à; *(chances)* compromettre; *(person)* faire du tort à
damaging [ˈdæmɪdʒɪŋ] *adj* préjudiciable (**to** à)
Damascus [dəˈmæskəs] *n* Damas
damask [ˈdæməsk] *n* damas *m*
dame [deɪm] *n* (**a**) *Am Fam (woman)* pépée *f* (**b**) *Br (title)* = titre donné à une femme ayant reçu une distinction honorifique
damn [dæm] **1** *n very Fam* **I don't give a d.** j'en ai rien à fiche; **it's not worth a d.** ça ne vaut pas un clou
  2 *adj very Fam* fichu(e); **you d. fool!** espèce d'idiot(e)!; **he's a d. nuisance!** qu'est-ce qu'il peut être casse-pieds!
  3 *adv very Fam* sacrément; **d. all** que dalle; **you know d. well what I mean!** tu sais fichtrement bien ce que je veux dire!
  4 *exclam very Fam* **d.!** zut!, mince!
  5 *vt* (**a**) *(criticize severely)* éreinter (**b**) *very Fam* **d. the expense!** au diable l'avarice!; **d. it!** zut!, mince!; **well I'll be damned!** ben mince alors!
damnation [dæmˈneɪʃən] **1** *n Rel* damnation *f*
  2 *exclam Fam* **d.!** bon sang!
damned [dæmd] **1** *npl Rel* **the d.** les damnés *mpl*
  2 *adj & adv very Fam* = **damn**
damning [ˈdæmɪŋ] *adj (admission, revelation)* accablant(e)
damp [dæmp] **1** *n* humidité *f*
  2 *adj* humide; *(skin)* moite; **d. course** isolant *m* contre l'humidité; *Fig* **d. squib** déception *f*
  3 *vt (make wet)* humecter; **to d. down a fire** couvrir un feu
dampen [ˈdæmpən] *vt (make wet)* humecter; *Fig* **to d. sb's spirits** décourager qn
damper [ˈdæmpə(r)] *n Mus* étouffoir *m*; *Fig* **to put a d. on sth** jeter un froid sur qch

damsel ['dæmzəl] *n Lit* damoiselle *f*; *Hum* **a d. in distress** une belle éplorée

damson ['dæmzən] *n (fruit)* prune *f* de Damas; *(tree)* prunier *m* de Damas

dance [dɑ:ns] **1** *n* danse *f*; *(event)* soirée *f* dansante; *(for young people)* boum *f*; *(formal)* bal *m*; *Fam* **to lead sb a (merry) d.** donner du fil à retordre à qn; **d. band** orchestre *m* de danse; **d. floor** piste *f* de danse; **d. hall** salle *f* de bal; **d. music** *(in clubs)* dance (music) *f*
2 *vt (waltz, tango)* danser
3 *vi* danser; **they danced down the street** ils ont descendu la rue en dansant

dancer ['dɑ:nsə(r)] *n* danseur(euse) *m,f*

dancing ['dɑ:nsɪŋ] *n* danse *f*; **d. shoes** chaussons *mpl* de danse

dandelion ['dændɪlaɪən] *n* pissenlit *m*

dander ['dændə(r)] *n Fam* **to get sb's d. up** hérisser qn

dandruff ['dændrəf] *n* pellicules *fpl*

dandy ['dændɪ] **1** *n (pl* **dandies)** dandy *m*
2 *adj Fam* génial(e); **everything's just (fine and) d.** tout marche comme sur des roulettes

Dane [deɪn] *n* Danois(e) *m,f*

danger ['deɪndʒə(r)] *n* danger *m*; **in d.** en danger; **out of d.** hors de danger; **to be in d. of doing sth** risquer de faire qch; **there's no d. that...** il n'y a pas de danger que... + *subjunctive*; **to be on the d. list** *(of patient)* être dans un état critique; **to be off the d. list** *(of patient)* être hors de danger; **d. money** prime *f* de risque; *Fig* **d. sign** signal *m* d'alarme

dangerous ['deɪndʒərəs] *adj* dangereux(euse)

dangerously ['deɪndʒərəslɪ] *adv* dangereusement; **they came d. close to losing** ils ont bien failli perdre

dangle ['dæŋgəl] **1** *vt* balancer; *Fig* **to d. sth in front of sb** faire miroiter qch à qn
2 *vi (of legs)* pendre; *(from rope, chain)* se balancer; *Fig* **to keep sb dangling** laisser qn dans l'incertitude

Danish ['deɪnɪʃ] **1** *n (language)* danois *m*
2 *adj* danois(e); **D. (pastry)** = sorte de chausson fourré aux fruits

dank [dæŋk] *adj* humide et froid(e)

Danube ['dænjuːb] *n* **the D.** le Danube

dapper ['dæpə(r)] *adj* soigné(e)

dappled ['dæpəld] *adj* tacheté(e); *(horse)* pommelé(e)

dare ['deə(r)] **1** *n* défi *m*; **to do sth for a d.** faire qch par défi
2 *vt* **to d. to do sth** oser faire qch; **to d. sb to do sth** défier qn de faire qch; **I d. you!** chiche!; **don't you d. (do that)!** ne t'avise pas de faire ça!; **how d. you!** comment oses-tu!; **I d. say** sans doute, c'est bien possible

daredevil ['deədevəl] **1** *n* casse-cou *mf inv*
2 *adj (person)* casse-cou *inv*; *(stunt, escape)* audacieux(euse)

daring ['deərɪŋ] **1** *n* audace *f*
2 *adj* audacieux(euse)

dark [dɑːk] **1** *n (a) (darkness)* obscurité *f*; **before/after d.** avant/après la tombée de la nuit; **in the d.** dans le noir **(b)** *(idioms)* **to be in the d. (about)** ne pas être au courant (de)
2 *adj (a) (not light)* sombre; *(skin, hair)* foncé(e); **it's d. by six o'clock** il fait nuit à six heures; **it's getting d.** il commence à faire nuit; **d. glasses** lunettes *fpl* noires; *Fig* **d. horse** *(competitor)* outsider *m*; *(in politics)* candidat(e) *m,f* surprise; *(secretive person)* personne *f* pleine de mystère **(b)** *Fig (thought)* sombre, morose; *(period)* sombre; *(look)* noir(e); *Hist* **the D. Ages** les le Haut Moyen Âge; *Fig* **to be in the D. Ages** être encore au Moyen Âge

darken ['dɑːkən] **1** *vt (sky, colour)* assombrir; **never d. my**

door again! ne remettez plus les pieds chez moi!
2 *vi (of sky, colour, thoughts)* s'assombrir

darkness ['dɑːknɪs] *n* obscurité *f*; **in d.** dans l'obscurité

darkroom ['dɑːkruːm] *n* chambre *f* noire

dark-skinned ['dɑːk'skɪnd] *adj* à la peau mate

darling ['dɑːlɪŋ] **1** *n (term of address) (to woman)* chérie *f*; *(to man)* chéri *m*; **she's the d. of the press** c'est la coqueluche des journaux
2 *adj (dear)* cher (chère); *(charming)* adorable

darn[1] [dɑːn] *vt (mend)* repriser

darn[2] *Fam* **1** *adj* sacré(e); **it's a d. nuisance!** c'est vachement embêtant!
2 *exclam* **d. (it)!** zut!

darning ['dɑːnɪŋ] *n* reprisage *m*; **d. needle** aiguille *f* à repriser

dart [dɑːt] **1** *n (a) (missile)* flèche *f*; **darts** *(game)* fléchettes *fpl* **(b)** *(movement)* **to make a d. for sth** se ruer vers qch
2 *vt* **to d. a glance at sb** jeter un regard à qn
3 *vi* **to d. in/out** entrer/sortir comme une flèche

dartboard ['dɑːtbɔːd] *n* cible *f (de jeu de fléchettes)*

dash [dæʃ] **1** *n (a) (of liquid)* goutte *f*; *(of humour, colour)* touche *f* **(b)** *(hyphen, in Morse code)* tiret *m* **(c)** *(run)* course *f* effrénée; **to make a d. for sth** se ruer vers qch; **to make a d. for it** s'enfuir **(d)** *(style)* panache *m*; **to cut a d.** avoir fière allure **(e)** *(of car)* tableau *m* de bord
2 *vt (a) (throw)* jeter; **to d. sth to the ground** jeter qch par terre **(b)** *(destroy) (hopes)* réduire à néant
3 *vi* **to d. in/out** entrer/sortir comme une flèche; **I dashed about** *or* **around all day** j'ai couru toute la journée; *Fam* **I must d.** il faut que je file
▸ **dash off 1** *vt sep (letter)* écrire en vitesse
2 *vi (leave)* filer

dashboard ['dæʃbɔːd] *n (of car)* tableau *m* de bord

dashing ['dæʃɪŋ] *adj (person)* fringant(e); *(appearance)* élégant(e)

DAT [diːeɪ'tiː] *n (abbr* **digital audio tape)** cassette *f* numérique

data ['deɪtə] *n* informations *fpl*; *Comptr* données *fpl*; **an item** *or* **piece of d.** une information/donnée; **d. bank** banque *f* de données; *Comptr* **d. processing** traitement *m* de l'information; **d. protection** protection *f* de l'information

database ['deɪtəbeɪs] *n Comptr* base *f* de données

date[1] [deɪt] *n (fruit)* datte *f*; **d. palm** palmier *m* dattier

date[2] **1** *n (a) (day)* date *f*; **d. of birth** date de naissance; **what's the d. (today)?** le combien sommes-nous (aujourd'hui)?; **to d.** à ce jour; **up to d.** *(with work)* à jour; *(with events, news)* au courant; *(in fashion)* à la mode; **out of d.** périmé(e); **d. stamp** tampon *m* ou timbre *m* à date **(b)** *(with girlfriend, boyfriend)* rendez-vous *m*; **d. rape** = viol commis par une connaissance de la victime **(c)** *Am (girlfriend, boyfriend)* ami(e) *m,f*
2 *vt (a) (letter, ticket)* dater **(b)** *(go out with)* sortir avec
3 *vi (a)* **to d. from** *or* **back to** *(of custom, practice)* remonter à; *(of building)* dater de **(b)** *(go out of fashion)* dater **(c)** *(go out on dates)* sortir avec des garçons/filles; **they've been dating for six months** ça fait six mois qu'ils sortent ensemble

dateline ['deɪtlaɪn] *n* date *f* et lieu de rédaction

dating agency ['deɪtɪŋeɪdʒənsɪ] *n* agence *f* matrimoniale

dative ['deɪtɪv] *n Gram* datif *m*

daub [dɔːb] *vt* barbouiller (**with** de)

daughter ['dɔːtə(r)] *n* fille *f*

daughter-in-law ['dɔːtərɪnlɔː] *(pl* **daughters-in-law)** *n* belle-fille *f*

daunt [dɔːnt] *vt* intimider; **nothing daunted** sans se décourager

daunting ['dɔːntɪŋ] *adj* intimidant(e)

dawdle ['dɔːdəl] *vi* traînasser, lambiner

dawn [dɔːn] **1** *n also Fig* aube *f*; **at d.** à l'aube; **from d.** **to dusk** du lever au coucher du soleil; **the d.** **chorus** le chant des oiseaux à l'aube

2 *vi (of day)* se lever; *Fig (of life, civilization)* naître
▸ **dawn on** *vt insep* **the truth finally dawned on her** la vérité a fini par lui apparaître; **it dawned on me that…** je me suis rendu compte que…

day [deɪ] *n* (**a**) *(period of daylight, twenty-four hours)* jour *m*; *(referring to duration)* journée *f*; **once/twice a d.** une fois/deux fois par jour; **the d.** **before yesterday** avant-hier; **the d.** **after tomorrow** après-demain; **all d.** toute la journée; **d. after d.** jour après jour; **to change from d. to d.** changer d'un jour sur l'autre; **to live from d. to d.** vivre au jour le jour; **one d.**, **one of these days** un de ces jours; **any d. now** d'un jour à l'autre; **the other d.** l'autre jour; **every other d.** tous les deux jours, un jour sur deux, **a year** **ago to the d.** il y a un an jour pour jour; **from d. one** dès le début; **to take a d. off** prendre un jour de congé; **to be** **paid by the d.** être payé(e) à la journée; **to work d. and** **night** travailler jour et nuit; *Fam* **he's sixty if he's a d.** il a soixante ans bien sonnés; **d. nursery** crèche *f*; **d. pupil** externe *mf*; **d. release** formation *f* continue en alternance; **d. return** *(train ticket)* aller et retour *m* valable pour la journée; **d. school** externat *m*; **d. shift** *(in factory)* équipe *f* de jour; **d. trip** excursion *f* d'une journée
(**b**) *(era)* in my d. de mon temps; in this d. and age à notre époque; this government/shirt has had its d. ce gouvernement/cette chemise a fait son temps; in the days of… du temps de…, these days de nos jours; in those days en ce temps-là; those were the days! c'était le bon temps!, in days to come à l'avenir
(**c**) *(idioms)* it's all in a d.'s work c'est la routine; to make sh's d. mettre qn de bonne humeur; *Fam* let's call it a d. ça suffit pour aujourd'hui; *Fam* that'll be the d.! c'est pas demain la veille!; to name the d. *(of wedding)* choisir la date de son mariage; to carry *or* win the d. l'emporter

daybreak ['deɪbreɪk] *n* lever *m* du jour; **at d.** au lever du jour

daydream ['deɪdriːm] **1** *n* rêverie *f*, *Pej* rêvasserie *f*
2 *vi* rêver (**about** à); *Pej* rêvasser

daylight ['deɪlaɪt] *n* jour *m*, lumière *f*; **it was still d.** il faisait encore jour; *Fig* **it's d. robbery!** c'est du vol pur et simple!

daytime ['deɪtaɪm] *n* jour *m*, journée *f*; **in the d.** pendant la journée; **d. TV** = émissions de télévision diffusées pendant la journée

day-to-day ['deɪtə'deɪ] *adj* courant(e), quotidien(enne); **on a d. basis** au jour le jour

daze [deɪz] **1** *n* **in a d.** *(from news)* abasourdi(e); *(from drug, blow)* étourdi(e)
2 *vt (of news)* abasourdir; *(of drug, blow)* étourdir

dazed [deɪzd] *adj (by news)* abasourdi(e); *(by drug, blow)* étourdi(e)

dazzle ['dæzəl] *vt also Fig* éblouir

dazzling ['dæzlɪŋ] *adj also Fig* éblouissant(e)

DC [diː'siː] *n* (*abbr* **direct current**) courant *m* continu (*Br*) *Elec*; (*abbr* **District of Columbia**) DC

deacon ['diːkən] *n Rel* diacre *m*

deaconess [diːkə'nes] *n Rel* diaconesse *f*

dead [ded] **1** *adj* (**a**) *(not alive)* mort(e); **a d. man** un mort; **a d. woman** une morte; *Fig* **to be d. to the world** dormir d'un sommeil profond; *Fam* **over my d. body!** moi vivant, jamais!; *Fam* **I wouldn't be seen d. in that hat!** je ne

porterais ce chapeau pour rien au monde!; *Fam* **as d. as a** **doornail** *or* **a dodo** mort et bien mort; *Fig* **d. and buried** mort et enterré; *Fam* **if Dad finds out, you're d.** si Papa l'apprend, il va te tuer; **the D. Sea** la mer Morte
(**b**) *(numb) (limb)* engourdi(e); **to go d.** s'engourdir
(**c**) *(voice, eyes)* éteint(e); *(phone)* sans tonalité; *(battery)* mort(e); **this place is d.** en hiver cet endroit est mort en hiver; **d. ball** *(in football)* ballon *m* mort; *also Fig* **d. end** cul-de-sac *m*; *Fig* **d. weight** poids *m* mort
(**d**) *(absolute)* **d. calm** calme *m* plat; **d. heat** *(in race)* arrivée *f* ex aequo; *Fam* **it was a d. loss** ça n'a servi à rien; **he's a d. loss** c'est un bon à rien; *Fam* **to be a d. ringer for** **sb** être le sosie de qn
2 *adv* (**a**) *(completely)* **to be d. set against sth** être totalement opposé(e) à qch; **to stop d.** s'arrêter net; *Fam* **d. beat** *or* **tired** crevé(e); **d. slow** *(sign)* roulez au pas
(**b**) *Fam (very)* vachement
(**c**) *(exactly)* **d. on six o'clock** à six heures précises; **d. on** **time** exactement à l'heure
3 *n* **at d. of night** au plus profond de la nuit; **in the d. of** **winter** au cœur de l'hiver
4 *npl* **the d.** les morts *mpl*; **to rise from the d.** ressusciter d'entre les morts

deadbeat ['dedbiːt] *n Fam* feignant(e) *m,f*

deaden ['dedən] *vt (blow, sound)* amortir; *(pain)* calmer; **to become deadened to sth** devenir insensible à qch

deadline ['dedlaɪn] *n (day)* date *f* limite; *(time)* heure *f* limite; **to work to a d.** avoir un délai à respecter

deadlock ['dedlɒk] **1** *n* impasse *f*
2 *vt* **to be deadlocked** *(of talks, negotiations)* être au point mort

deadly ['dedlɪ] **1** *adj* (**a**) *(poison, blow, enemy)* mortel(elle); *(weapon)* meurtrier(ère); *(silence)* de mort; **d.** **nightshade** belladone *f* (**b**) *Fam (boring)* mortel(elle)
2 *adv (very)* **d. accurate** extrêmement précis(e); **d. boring** d'un ennui mortel; **to be d. serious** être on ne peut plus sérieux(euse)

deadpan ['dedpæn] *adj (expression)* figé(e); *(humour)* pince-sans-rire *inv*

deadwood ['dedwʊd] *n Fig* personnes *fpl* inutiles

deaf [def] **1** *adj* sourd(e), **d. and dumb** sourd-muet, sourde-muette; **to go d.** devenir sourd; **as d. as a post** sourd comme un pot; **to turn a d. ear to sb/sth** faire la sourde oreille à qn/qch; **the appeal fell on d. ears** l'appel n'a pas été entendu
2 *npl* **the d.** les sourds *mpl*

deaf-aid ['defeɪd] *n* appareil *m* acoustique

deafen ['defən] *vt (make deaf)* rendre sourd(e); *(temporarily)* assourdir

deafening ['defənɪŋ] *adj* assourdissant(e)

deafness ['defnəs] *n* surdité *f*

deal¹ [diːl] *n (wood)* planche *f*

deal² **1** *n* (**a**) *(agreement)* affaire *f*, marché *m*; **to do a d.** conclure un marché; **it's a d.!** marché conclu!; **to get a** **good/bad d.** faire une bonne/mauvaise affaire; **he's had a** **raw d.** on ne lui a jamais fait de cadeaux; *Fam Ironic* **big d.!** la belle affaire! **it's no big d.** ce n'est pas bien grave (**b**) *(amount)* **a good** *or* **great d.** beaucoup; **not a great d.** peu; **to have a great d. to do** avoir beaucoup à faire; **a good** *or* **great d. of** mon temps; **a great partie de** mon temps; **good d. quicker/easier** beaucoup plus rapide/facile (**c**) *(in* *cards)* **whose d. is it?** c'est à qui de donner?; **your d.!** c'est à vous de donner!
2 *vt (pt & pp dealt [delt])* (**a**) *(cards)* donner, distribuer (**b**) **to d. sb/sth a blow** donner un coup à qn/qch (**c**) *(drugs)* vendre
3 *vi* (**a**) *(in card game)* donner, distribuer (**b**) *(trade)* **to d. in** **leather** faire le commerce des cuirs

▸**deal out** *vt sep (cards)* distribuer; **to d. out justice** rendre la justice

▸**deal with** *vt insep (subject)* traiter de; *(problem)* s'occuper de; **I know how to d.** with him je sais m'y prendre avec lui

dealer ['di:lə(r)] *n* (**a**) *(in card game)* donneur(euse) *m,f* (**b**) *Com* marchand(e) *m,f*; *(in cars)* concessionnaire *m*; *(in drugs)* dealer *m*, revendeur(euse) *m,f*

dealings ['di:liŋz] *npl* rapports *mpl*, relations *fpl*; **to have d. with sb** traiter avec qn

dealt [delt] *pt & pp of* deal

dean [di:n] *n Rel & Univ* doyen *m*

dear [diə(r)] **1** *n* (**my**) **d.** *(to man)* chéri; *(to woman)* chérie; **poor d.** mon pauvre/ma pauvre; **be a d. and...** sois un amour et...; *Fam* **an old d.** une grand-mère

2 *adj* (**a**) *(loved)* cher (chère); **to hold sb/sth d.** tenir à qn/qch; **a d. friend** un bon ami/une bonne amie; **a place d. to the hearts of...** un endroit cher à...; *Fam* **to run for d. life** se sauver à toutes jambes (**b**) *(in letter)* **D. Sir** Monsieur; **D. Madam** Madame; **D. Sir or Madam, D. Sir/Madam** Monsieur, Madame; **D. Mr Thomas** Cher M. Thomas; **D. Andrew** Cher Andrew; **My dearest Lucy** Ma chère Lucy (**c**) *(expensive)* cher (chère)

3 *adv (buy, sell)* cher; *Fig* **it cost me d.** ça m'a coûté cher **4** *exclam* **oh d.! mon** Dieu!

dearly ['diəli] *adv (very much)* **to love sb d.** aimer qn de tout son cœur; **I would d. love to know** j'aimerais vraiment savoir; *Fig* **she paid d. for her mistake** elle a payé très cher son erreur

dearth [dɜ:θ] *n* pénurie *f* (**of** de)

death [deθ] *n* (**a**) *(end of life)* mort *f*; **to put sb to d.** mettre qn à mort, exécuter qn; **a fight to the d.** une lutte à mort; **d. camp** camp *m* de la mort; **d. certificate** acte *m* de décès; **d. mask** masque *m* mortuaire; **d. penalty** peine *f* de mort; **d. rate** taux *m* de mortalité; *Am* **d. row** = quartier d'une prison où les condamnés attendent leur exécution; **d. sentence** condamnation *f* à mort; **d. squad** escadron *m* de la mort; **d. throes** agonie *f*; **d. toll** nombre *m* de morts; **D. Valley** la Vallée de la Mort; **d. warrant** ordre *m* d'exécution (**b**) *(idioms)* **to look like d. (warmed up)** avoir l'air d'un déterré/d'une déterrée; **to be sick to d. of sth** en avoir marre de qch; **to be scared to d.** être mort(e) de peur; **this job will be the d. of me!** ce travail finira par me tuer!; **you'll catch your d. (of cold)!** tu vas attraper la crève!; **to be at d.'s door** être à l'article de la mort; **to sound the d. knell for sth** sonner le glas de qch

deathbed ['deθbed] *n* lit *m* de mort

deathly ['deθli] *adj (pallor)* mortel(elle); *(silence)* de mort

deathtrap ['deθtræp] *n* **this house/car is a d.** cette maison/voiture est très dangereuse

deathwatch beetle ['deθwɒtʃ'bi:təl] *n* vrillette *f*

debacle [dei'bɑ:kəl] *n* débâcle *f*

debar [di:'bɑ:(r)] *(pt & pp* **debarred)** *vt (from club)* exclure; **to d. sb from doing sth** interdire à qn de faire qch

debase [di'beis] *vt (person)* rabaisser; *(reputation)* ternir; *(currency)* déprécier; **to d. oneself** se déprécier

debasement [di'beismənt] *n (of person)* rabaissement *m*; *(of currency)* dépréciation *f*

debatable [di'beitəbəl] *adj* discutable

debate [di'beit] **1** *n* discussion *f*; *(organized)* débat *m*; **after much d.** après bien des discussions

2 *vt (issue)* débattre de, discuter de; **I was debating whether to come or not** je me demandais si je viendrais ou non

3 *vi* participer à des débats

debating society [di'beitiŋsəsaiəti] *n* = société qui organise des débats

debauched [di'bɔ:tʃt] *adj* débauché(e)

debauchery [di'bɔ:tʃəri] *n* débauche *f*

debilitate [di'biliteit] *vt* débiliter

debilitating [di'biliteitiŋ] *adj* débilitant(e)

debility [di'biliti] *n* débilité *f*

debit ['debit] *Fin* **1** *n* débit *m*; *Fig* **on the d. side,...** l'inconvénient, c'est que...

2 *vt (person, account)* débiter (**with** de)

debonair [debə'neə(r)] *adj* élégant(e) et raffiné(e)

debrief [di:'bri:f] *vt* faire faire un compte rendu de fin de mission à

debriefing [di:'bri:fiŋ] *n* compte *m* rendu de fin de mission

debris ['debri:] *n (of building)* décombres *mpl*; *(of plane, car)* débris *mpl*

debt [det] *n* dette *f*; **to be in d.** avoir des dettes; *Fig* **I shall always be in your d.** je vous serai toujours redevable; **to owe sb a d. of gratitude** être redevable à qn; **d. collector** agent *m* de recouvrement

debtor ['detə(r)] *n* débiteur(trice) *m,f*

debug [di:'bʌg] *(pt & pp* **debugged)** *vt Comptr (program)* déboguer

debunk [di:'bʌŋk] *vt Fam (theory)* discréditer; *(myth)* détruire

debut ['deibju:] *n* début *m*; **to make one's d.** faire ses débuts; **d. album** premier album *m*; **d. performance** première apparition *f*

Dec *(abbr* **December)** décembre

decade ['dekeid] *n* décennie *f*

decadence ['dekədəns] *n* décadence *f*

decadent ['dekədənt] *adj* décadent(e)

decaffeinated [di:'kæfineitid] *adj* décaféiné(e)

decant [di'kænt] *vt* décanter

decanter [di'kæntə(r)] *n* carafe *f*

decapitate [di'kæpiteit] *vt* décapiter

decathlon [di'kæθlɒn] *n* décathlon *m*

decay [di'kei] **1** *n* (**a**) *(of wood)* pourriture *f*; *(of teeth)* carie *f* (**b**) *(of civilization)* déclin *m*; *(of building)* délabrement *m*

2 *vi* (**a**) *(of wood)* pourrir; *(of teeth)* se carier (**b**) *(of civilization)* péricliter; *(of building)* se délabrer

decease [di'si:s] *n Formal* décès *m*

deceased [di'si:st] *Formal* **1** *n* **the d.** le défunt/la défunte

2 *adj* décédé(e)

deceit [di'si:t] *n* tromperie *f*, supercherie *f*

deceitful [di'si:tfʊl] *adj (person)* fourbe; *(behaviour)* malhonnête

deceive [di'si:v] *vt* tromper, abuser; **to be deceived by appearances** se laisser abuser par les apparences; **to d. oneself** se mentir à soi-même; **to d. sb into doing sth** faire faire à qn en le manipulant; **I thought my eyes were deceiving me** je n'en croyais pas mes yeux

decelerate [di:'seləreit] *vi* ralentir

December [di'sembə(r)] *n* décembre *m*; *see also* **May**

decency ['di:sənsi] *n (respectability)* décence *f*; **to have the common d. to do sth** avoir la décence de faire qch; **he didn't even have the d. to tell us first** il n'a même pas eu la politesse de nous avertir avant

decent ['di:sənt] *adj* (**a**) *(respectable)* respectable; *Fam* **are you d.?** es-tu visible? (**b**) *(of acceptable quality, size)* convenable, correct(e) (**c**) *(kind)* gentil(ille)

decently ['di:səntlɪ] adv (a) (respectably) convenablement; to dress d. s'habiller décemment (b) (to an acceptable degree) convenablement, correctement (c) (kindly) gentiment

decentralization [di:sentrəlaɪ'zeɪʃən] n décentralisation f

decentralize [di:'sentrəlaɪz] vt décentraliser

deception [dɪ'sepʃən] n tromperie f, supercherie f

deceptive [dɪ'septɪv] adj trompeur(euse)

deceptively [dɪ'septɪvlɪ] adv it looks d. easy c'est moins facile que ça en a l'air; she looks d. shy c'est une fausse timide

decibel ['desɪbel] n décibel m

decide [dɪ'saɪd] 1 vt (outcome, match, future) décider de; to d. to do sth décider de faire qch; it was decided to wait for her reply il fut décidé d'attendre sa réponse; that was what decided me c'est ce qui m'a décidé; that decides the matter ça règle la question
2 vi décider; to d. on sth choisir qch; to d. against doing sth décider de ne pas faire qch; they decided against going out ils décidèrent de ne pas sortir; to d. in favour of doing sth décider de faire qch

decided [dɪ'saɪdɪd] adj (a) (person) décidé(c); (opinion) ferme (b) (difference, preference, improvement) net (nette)

decidedly [dɪ'saɪdɪdlɪ] adv (a) (answer, say) d'un ton résolu (b) (very) franchement; he was d. unfriendly il n'a pas été aimable du tout

decider [dɪ'saɪdə(r)] n (goal) but m décisif; (match) match m décisif

deciding [dɪ'saɪdɪŋ] adj décisif(ive)

deciduous [dɪ'sɪdjʊəs] adj à feuilles caduques

decimal ['desɪməl] 1 n décimale f
2 adj décimal(e); d. point virgule f; correct to five d. places exact(e) jusqu'à la cinquième décimale

decimalization [desɪməlaɪ'zeɪʃən] n décimalisation f

decimate ['desɪmeɪt] vt décimer

decipher [dɪ'saɪfə(r)] vt déchiffrer

decision [dɪ'sɪʒən] n (a) (of question) décision f (b) (resolve) fermeté f, résolution f

decision-making [dɪ'sɪʒənmeɪkɪŋ] n prise f de décision

decisive [dɪ'saɪsɪv] adj (a) (person, manner) résolu(e) (b) (action, event) décisif(ive)

deck [dek] 1 n (a) (of ship) pont m; (of bus) niveau m, étage m; on d. sur le pont; d. chair transat m (b) d. (of cards) jeu m (de cartes)
2 vt to d. oneself out in one's Sunday best se mettre sur son trente et un

declaim [dɪ'kleɪm] vt & vi déclamer

declamatory [dɪ'klæmətərɪ] adj déclamatoire

declaration [deklə'reɪʃən] n déclaration f; the D. of Independence la Déclaration d'indépendance

declare [dɪ'kleə(r)] 1 vt déclarer; to d. war (on) déclarer la guerre (à); have you anything to d.? (at customs) avez-vous quelque chose à déclarer?
2 vi to d. for/against sth se déclarer en faveur de/contre qch; Old-fashioned I do d.! ça alors!

declassify [di:'klæsɪfaɪ] (pt & pp declassified) vt (document) ne plus considérer comme confidentiel

declension [dɪ'klenʃən] n Gram déclinaison f

decline [dɪ'klaɪn] 1 n déclin m; to go into a d. (of person, company, industry) dépérir; (of economy) perdre de sa vigueur; (of health) se détériorer; to be on the d. (of inflation, crime) être en baisse
2 vt (a) (offer, invitation) décliner; to d. to do sth refuser de faire qch (b) Gram décliner

decline in importance perdre de son importance
baisser; to d. in importance perdre de son importance

declining [dɪ'klaɪnɪŋ] adj (decreasing) en baisse; (deteriorating) déclinant(e)

decode [di:'kəʊd] vt décoder

decompose [di:kəm'pəʊz] vi se décomposer

decomposition [di:kɒmpə'zɪʃən] n décomposition f

decompression [di:kəm'preʃən] n décompression f; d. chamber chambre f de décompression; d. sickness maladie f des caissons

decongestant [di:kən'dʒestənt] n Med décongestionnant m

decontaminate [di:kən'tæmɪneɪt] vt décontaminer

decor ['deɪkɔ:(r)] n décor m

decorate ['dekəreɪt] vt (a) (with decorations) décorer (with de) (b) (with paint) peindre; (with wallpaper) tapisser (c) (with medal) décorer

decoration [dekə'reɪʃən] n (a) (of room, cake) décoration f (b) (medal) décoration f; médaille f

decorative ['dekərətɪv] adj décoratif(ive)

decorator ['dekəreɪtə(r)] n (painter and) d. (peintre m) décorateur m

decorous ['dekərəs] adj Formal bienséant(e)

decorum [dɪ'kɔ:rəm] n convenances fpl, décorum m

decoy 1 ['di:kɔɪ] also Fig leurre m
2 vt [dɪ'kɔɪ] leurrer

decrease 1 n ['di:kri:s] diminution f, baisse f (in de); to be on the d. être en diminution
2 vt [dɪ'kri:s] réduire, baisser
3 vi [dɪ'kri:s] diminuer, baisser

decreasing [dɪ'kri:sɪŋ] adj décroissant(e), en baisse

decree [dɪ'kri:] 1 n décret m, Law d. absolute jugement irrévocable; d. nisi jugement m provisoire
2 vt décréter

decrepit [dɪ'krepɪt] adj (person) décrépit(e); (thing) délabré(e)

decriminalize [di:'krɪmɪnəlaɪz] vt dépénaliser

decry [dɪ'kraɪ] (pt & pp decried) vt décrier

dedicate ['dedɪkeɪt] vt (book, song) dédier (to à); to d. oneself to se consacrer à qch; she dedicated her life to helping the poor elle a consacré sa vie aux pauvres

dedicated ['dedɪkeɪtɪd] adj (a) (committed) consciencieux(euse); to be d. to sth se consacrer à qch; she is d. to helping the poor elle se consacre aux pauvres; he is d. to his family il est entièrement dévoué à sa famille (b) Comptr spécialisé(e); d. word processor machine f servant uniquement au traitement de texte

dedication [dedɪ'keɪʃən] n (a) (of book, song) dédicace f (b) (devotion) dévouement m

deduce [dɪ'dju:s] vt déduire (from de)

deduct [dɪ'dʌkt] vt déduire (from de)

deductible [dɪ'dʌktəbəl] adj déductible; Fin d. for tax purposes déductible des impôts

deduction [dɪ'dʌkʃən] n (a) (subtraction) déduction f; after deductions une fois les prélèvements effectués (b) (conclusion) déduction f; by a process of d. par déduction

deed [di:d] n (a) (action) acte m, action f; to do one's good d. the day faire sa bonne action de la journée (b) Law (document) acte m notarié; d. of covenant = document par lequel on s'engage à verser régulièrement une somme à un organisme; to change one's name by d. poll changer légalement son nom

deem [di:m] vt Formal juger, estimer

deep [di:p] 1 Lit the d. l'océan m

2 adj **(a)** (water, sleep, thinker, cut) profond(e); **to be 10 metres d.** faire 10 mètres de profondeur; **two/four d.** sur deux/quatre rangs; Fig **to be in d.** water être dans le pétrin; **d. in debt** criblé(e) de dettes; **d. in thought** plongé(e) dans ses pensées; **d.** end (of swimming pool) côté m le plus profond; Fig **to go off the d.** end **(at sb)** s'emporter (contre qn); Fig **to be thrown in at the d.** end être mis(e) dans le bain; **the D.** South (of United States) le Sud profond **(b)** (colour) foncé(e), sombre; (sound) grave **3** adv profondément; **to walk d.** into the forest pénétrer profondément dans la forêt; **to look d.** into sb's eyes pénétrer qn du regard; **to work d.** into the night travailler tard dans la nuit; **d.** down he's very kind au fond il est très gentil; **to run d.** (of emotions, prejudice, mistrust) être profond(e)

deepen ['di:pən] **1** vt (well, ditch) approfondir; (sorrow, interest) augmenter; **to d.** sb's understanding of sth permettre à qn de mieux comprendre qch **2** vi **(a)** (of river, silence) devenir plus profond(e); (of conviction, belief) augmenter; (of mystery) s'épaissir **(b)** (of sound, voice) devenir plus grave

deep-freeze ['di:p'fri:z] n congélateur m

deep-fry ['di:p'fraɪ] vt faire cuire dans la friture

deep-fryer ['di:p'fraɪə(r)] n friteuse f

deep-rooted [di:p'ru:tɪd] adj profondément enraciné(e)

deep-sea ['di:p'si:] adj **d.** diver plongeur m sous-marin; **d.** fishing pêche f hauturière

deep-seated ['di:p'si:tɪd] adj profond(e)

deer ['dɪə(r)] (pl deer) n (male) daim m; (female) biche f

deerstalker ['dɪəstɔ:kə(r)] n (hat) chapeau m de chasse (à la Sherlock Holmes)

deface [dɪ'feɪs] vt (monument, statue) dégrader; (poster, wall) barbouiller

de facto [deɪ'fæktəʊ] adj & adv de facto

defamation [defə'meɪʃən] n diffamation f

defamatory [dɪ'fæmətərɪ] adj diffamatoire

defame [dɪ'feɪm] vt diffamer

default [dɪ'fɔ:lt] **1** n **(a)** Law (failure to appear in court) défaut m; Fig **by d.** par défaut **(b)** Comptr **d.** drive lecteur m par défaut; **d.** font police f par défaut **2** vi Law **(a)** (fail to appear in court) ne pas comparaître **(b)** (fail to pay) **to d.** on alimony payments manquer au versement de la pension alimentaire

defaulter [dɪ'fɔ:ltə(r)] n Law contumace mf; (debtor) débiteur(trice) m, f défaillant(e)

defeat [dɪ'fi:t] **1** n défaite f **2** vt (army, opponent) vaincre; (government) mettre en minorité; **that defeats the object** or **purpose** ça va à l'encontre du but recherché

defeatism [dɪ'fi:tɪzəm] n défaitisme m

defeatist [dɪ'fi:tɪst] n & adj défaitiste mf

defecate ['defəkeɪt] vi déféquer

defect 1 n ['di:fekt] défaut m **2** vi [dɪ'fekt] **to d. to the enemy** passer à l'ennemi

defection [dɪ'fekʃən] n défection f

defective [dɪ'fektɪv] adj (machine, reasoning) défectueux(euse); (hearing) déficient(e)

defector [dɪ'fektə(r)] n transfuge mf

defence, Am **defense** [dɪ'fens] n défense f; **to come to sb's d.** venir à l'aide de qn; **she said in her d. that...** elle a dit à sa décharge que...; Law **d.** counsel avocat m de la défense; **d.** mechanism (psychological) mécanisme m de défense; Law **witness for the d.** témoin m à décharge

defenceless, Am **defenseless** [dɪ'fensləs] adj sans défense

defend [dɪ'fend] **1** vt défendre (**from** or **against** contre) **2** vi (in sport) défendre

defendant [dɪ'fendənt] n Law défendeur(eresse) m, f

defender [dɪ'fendə(r)] n défenseur m

defending [dɪ'fendɪŋ] adj **d.** champion champion(onne) m, f en titre

defense, defenseless Am = defence, defenceless

defensible [dɪ'fensəbəl] adj défendable

defensive [dɪ'fensɪv] **1** n on the **d.** sur la défensive **2** adj défensif(ive); **to be/get d.** être/se mettre sur la défensive

defer [dɪ'fɜ:(r)] (pt & pp deferred) **1** vt (postpone) différer, remettre **2** vi to **d.** to s'en remettre à

deference ['defərəns] n déférence f; out of or in **d.** to par déférence pour

deferential [defə'renʃəl] adj déférent(e)

deferment [dɪ'fɜ:mənt] n ajournement m, report m

defiance [dɪ'faɪəns] n défi m; in **d.** of au mépris de

defiant [dɪ'faɪənt] adj (gesture, look) de défi; (person) provocant(e)

deficiency [dɪ'fɪʃənsɪ] (pl deficiencies) n **(a)** (lack) (of resources) manque m; (of vitamins, minerals) carence f **(b)** (flaw) défaut m

deficient [dɪ'fɪʃənt] adj insuffisant(e); **to be d. in** manquer de

deficit ['defɪsɪt] n Fin déficit m

defile [dɪ'faɪl] vt (memory) salir; (sacred place, tomb) profaner

definable [dɪ'faɪnəbəl] adj définissable

define [dɪ'faɪn] vt définir

definite ['defɪnɪt] adj **(a)** (precise) (views, plan, date, answer) précis(e); (decision) définitif(ive) **(b)** (noticeable) (advantage, improvement) net (nette) **(c)** (certain) certain(e); (insistent) catégorique; **I can't be d.** je n'en suis pas sûr **(d)** Gram **d.** article article m défini

definitely ['defɪnɪtlɪ] adv **(a)** (certainly) sans aucun doute; **I'll d. be there** c'est sûr que j'y serai; **are you going? – d.!** est-ce que vous y allez? – absolument!; **d. not!** certainement pas! he told me very d. that he didn't want to go il m'a dit très clairement qu'il ne voulait pas y aller **(b)** (noticeably) (improved, superior) nettement

definition [defɪ'nɪʃən] n **(a)** (of word) définition f; **by d.** par définition **(b)** (of image) définition f; (of binoculars) netteté f

definitive [dɪ'fɪnɪtɪv] adj (book) qui fait autorité; (version) définitif(ive); **she was the D.** Juliet elle était la Juliette idéale

deflate [di:'fleɪt] **1** vt **(a)** (ball, tyre) dégonfler **(b)** Econ **to d. the economy** pratiquer une politique déflationniste **(c)** (person) démonter **2** vi (of tyre) se dégonfler

deflated [di:'fleɪtɪd] adj (person) déprimé(e)

deflation [di:'fleɪʃən] n Econ déflation f

deflationary [di:'fleɪʃənərɪ] adj Econ déflationniste

deflect [dɪ'flekt] **1** vt **(a)** (ball, bullet) (faire) dévier; (sound) renvoyer; (criticism) détourner; Fig (person) détourner (**from** de) **2** vi (of ball, bullet) dévier

deflection [dɪ'flekʃən] n (of ball, bullet) déviation f

deforestation [di:fɒrɪs'teɪʃən] n déboisement m

deform [dɪ'fɔ:m] vt déformer

deformation [diːfɔːˈmeɪʃən] n déformation f

deformity [dɪˈfɔːmɪtɪ] (pl **deformities**) n difformité f

defraud [dɪˈfrɔːd] vt (tax office) frauder; (employer) escroquer; **to d. sb of sth** escroquer qch à qn

defray [dɪˈfreɪ] vt Formal **to d. sb's expenses** défrayer qn; **to d. the cost of sth** rembourser les frais de qch

defrost [diːˈfrɒst] **1** vt (fridge) dégivrer; (food) décongeler **2** vi (of fridge) se dégivrer; (of food) se décongeler

deft [deft] adj adroit(e), habile

defunct [dɪˈfʌŋkt] adj (person) défunt(e); (organization) dissous(oute); (law) abandonné(e)

defuse [diːˈfjuːz] vt also Fig désamorcer

defy [dɪˈfaɪ] (pt & pp **defied**) vt (authority, law) braver; (logic, analysis) défier; **to d. description** défier toute description; **to d. sb to do sth** mettre qn au défi de faire qch

degenerate 1 n & adj [dɪˈdʒenərət] dégénéré(e) m,f **2** vi [dɪˈdʒenəreɪt] dégénérer (into en)

degeneration [dɪdʒenəˈreɪʃən] n dégénérescence f

degradation [degrəˈdeɪʃən] n avilissement m; (squalor) misère f

degrade [dɪˈgreɪd] vt avilir; **I won't d. myself by answering that** je ne m'abaisserai pas à répondre à cela

degrading [dɪˈgreɪdɪŋ] adj dégradant(e)

degree [dɪˈgriː] n (a) (extent) degré m, point m; **to a d., to some d.** jusqu'à un certain point; **to such a d. that...** à (un) tel point que...; **by degrees** petit à petit; **a d. of risk** un certain risque; **a d. of truth** une part de vérité (b) (of temperature, in geometry) degré m; **it's 30 degrees** (of temperature) il fait 30 degrés (c) (at university) diplôme m universitaire; (bachelor's) ≃ licence f; (master's) ≃ maîtrise f; (PhD) doctorat m; **to take or do a d.** préparer un diplôme

dehumanize [diːˈhjuːmənaɪz] vt déshumaniser

dehumidifier [diːhjuːˈmɪdɪfaɪə(r)] n déshumidificateur m

dehydrated [diːhaɪˈdreɪtɪd] adj déshydraté(e); **to get d.** se déshydrater

dehydration [diːhaɪˈdreɪʃən] n déshydratation f

de-icer [diːˈaɪsə(r)] n dégivreur m

deify [ˈdiːɪfaɪ] (pt & pp **deified**) vt déifier

deign [deɪn] vt **to d. to do sth** condescendre à ou daigner faire qch

deindustrialization [diːɪndʌstrɪəlaɪˈzeɪʃən] n désindustrialisation f

deity [ˈdiːɪtɪ] (pl **deities**) n divinité f, dieu (déesse) m,f

dejected [dɪˈdʒektɪd] adj abattu(e), découragé(e)

dejection [dɪˈdʒekʃən] n abattement m, découragement m

delay [dɪˈleɪ] **1** n retard m; **without d.** sans délai; **an hour's d.** une heure de retard; **all flights are subject to d.** tous les vols risquent d'avoir du retard **2** vt (a) (project, decision, act) retarder; (traffic) ralentir; **to be delayed** (of train, plane) avoir du retard; **delaying tactics** manœuvres fpl dilatoires (b) (put off) (decision, publication) différer; **we can't d. telling her any longer** on ne peut plus attendre davantage, nous devons le lui dire **3** vi tarder; **don't d.!** faites vite!

delayed-action [dɪleɪdˈækʃən] adj (drug, fuse, shutter) à retardement

delectable [dɪˈlektəbəl] adj délicieux(euse)

delegate 1 n [ˈdelɪgət] délégué(e) m,f **2** vt [ˈdelɪgeɪt] (power, responsibility) déléguer (**to** à); **to d. sb to do sth** déléguer qn pour faire qch **3** vi [ˈdelɪgeɪt] déléguer

delegation [delɪˈgeɪʃən] n délégation f

delete [dɪˈliːt] vt supprimer; **d. where inapplicable** rayer les mentions inutiles

deleterious [delɪˈtɪərɪəs] adj Formal délétère

deletion [dɪˈliːʃən] n suppression f

deli [ˈdelɪ] n (shop) épicerie f fine; (café) restaurant-traiteur m

deliberate 1 adj [dɪˈlɪbərət] (a) (intentional) délibéré(e); **it wasn't d.** ça n'était pas voulu (b) (unhurried) (movement) mesuré(e); (person) méticuleux(euse) **2** vi [dɪˈlɪbəreɪt] (think) réfléchir (**on** sur); (discuss) délibérer (**on** sur)

deliberately [dɪˈlɪbərətlɪ] adv (a) (intentionally) délibérément; **she did it d.** elle l'a fait exprès (b) (unhurriedly) de façon mesurée

deliberation [dɪlɪbəˈreɪʃən] n (a) (thought) réflexion f; (discussion) délibération f, débat m (b) (unhurriedness) mesure f; **with d.** posément

delicacy [ˈdelɪkənsɪ] (pl **delicacies**) n (a) (quality) délicatesse f (b) (food) mets m délicat

delicate [ˈdelɪkət] adj délicat(e)

delicately [ˈdelɪkətlɪ] adv (a) (finely) délicatement (b) (tactfully) avec délicatesse

delicatessen [delɪkəˈtesən] n (shop) épicerie f fine; (café) restaurant-traiteur m

delicious [dɪˈlɪʃəs] adj délicieux(euse)

delight [dɪˈlaɪt] **1** n plaisir m, joie f; **to my/her d.** à mon/son grand plaisir; **to take d. in sth** se réjouir de qch; **the car is a d. to drive** conduire cette voiture est un plaisir; **the delights of sailing** les joies de la voile; **the delights of Vermont** les charmes de Vermont **2** vt ravir, réjouir **3** vi **to d. in doing sth** prendre plaisir à faire qch; Hum **he delights in the name of Fergus Fotherington** il répond au joli nom de Fergus Fotherington

delighted [dɪˈlaɪtɪd] adj ravi(e), enchanté(e) (**with** de)

delightful [dɪˈlaɪtfəl] adj (person, smile) charmant(e); (meal, evening) délicieux(euse)

delightfully [dɪˈlaɪtfʊlɪ] adv (sing, write) merveilleusement

delimit [diːˈlɪmɪt] vt délimiter

delineate [dɪˈlɪnɪeɪt] vt (plan, proposal) définir

delinquency [dɪˈlɪŋkwənsɪ] n délinquance f

delinquent [dɪˈlɪŋkwənt] n & adj délinquant(e) m,f

delirious [dɪˈlɪrɪəs] adj also Fig délirant(e); **to be d.** délirer

deliriously [dɪˈlɪrɪəslɪ] adv follement; **d. happy** fou (folle) de joie

delirium [dɪˈlɪrɪəm] n also Fig délire m; Med **d. tremens** delirium tremens m

deliver [dɪˈlɪvə(r)] **1** vt (a) (letter, parcel) distribuer (**to** à); (water, electricity, gas) distribuer; (goods) livrer; **to have sth delivered** faire livrer qch; Fig **to d. the goods** tenir ses engagements (b) (blow) donner; Sp (puss) faire; (speech, verdict) prononcer; (ultimatum) poser; **to d. a service** proposer un service (c) (baby) mettre au monde **2** vi livrer; Fig (keep one's promise) tenir ses engagements; Com **we d.** nous livrons à domicile

deliverance [dɪˈlɪvərəns] n Formal délivrance f (**from** de)

delivery [dɪˈlɪvərɪ] (pl **deliveries**) n (a) (of letter, parcel) distribution f, remise f; (of goods) livraison f; **to take d. of sth** prendre livraison de qch; **d. date** date f de livraison; **d. man** livreur m; **d. van** camion m de livraison (b) (way of speaking) diction f (c) (of baby) accouchement m

delta ['deltə] *n (of river, Greek letter)* delta *m inv*; **d. wing** *(of plane)* aile *f* delta

delude [dɪ'luːd] *vt* tromper; **to d. oneself** se faire des illusions

deluge ['deljuːdʒ] **1** *n also Fig* déluge *m*
2 *vt* inonder (**with** de)

delusion [dɪ'luːʒən] *n* illusion *f*; **to be under a d.** se faire des illusions; **delusions of grandeur** mégalomanie *f*

de luxe [dɪ'lʌks] *adj* de luxe, haut de gamme *inv*

delve [delv] *vi also Fig* **to d. into** fouiller dans

demagogue ['deməgɒg] *n* démagogue *mf*

demand [dɪ'maːnd] **1** *n* (**a**) *(request)* demande *f*; exigence *f*; **to make demands on sb** exiger beaucoup de qn (**b**) *(for goods)* demande *f* (**for** de); **to be in d.** être demandé(e) *ou* recherché(e)
2 *vt* exiger, réclamer

demanding [dɪ'maːndɪŋ] *adj (person)* exigeant(e); *(job)* astreignant(e)

demarcation [diːmaː'keɪʃən] *n* démarcation *f*; *Ind* **d. dispute** conflit *m* d'attributions; **d. line** ligne *f* de démarcation

demean [dɪ'miːn] *vt* humilier; **to d. oneself** s'abaisser

demeanour, *Am* **demeanor** [dɪ'miːnə(r)] *n* comportement *m*

demented [dɪ'mentɪd] *adj* fou (folle)

dementia [dɪ'menʃɪə] *n* démence *f*

demerara sugar [deməˈreərəˈʃʊɡə(r)] *n* cassonade *f*

demigod ['demɪgɒd] *n* demi-dieu *m*

demilitarize [diːˈmɪlɪtəraɪz] *vt* démilitariser

demise [dɪ'maɪz] *n also Fig* disparition *f*

demister [diːˈmɪstə(r)] *n Br Aut* dispositif *m* antibuée

demo ['deməʊ] *(pl* demos) *n Fam* (**a**) *(protest)* manif *f* (**b**) **d. (tape)** maquette *f*

demob [diːˈmɒb] *(pt & pp* demobbed) *vt Br Fam* démobiliser

demobilize [diːˈməʊbɪlaɪz] *vt* démobiliser

democracy [dɪ'mɒkrəsɪ] *(pl* democracies) *n* démocratie *f*

Democrat ['deməkræt] *n Pol* démocrate *mf*

democrat ['deməkræt] *n* démocrate *mf*

democratic [deməˈkrætɪk] *adj* démocratique

democratically [deməˈkrætɪklɪ] *adv* démocratiquement

demographic [deməˈgræfɪk] *adj* démographique

demolish [dɪ'mɒlɪʃ] *vt (building, theory)* démolir; *Fam (eat)* engloutir; *(in game)* écraser

demolition [deməˈlɪʃən] *n* démolition *f*

demon ['diːmən] *n* démon *m*; *Fam* **he's a d. tennis player** c'est un as du tennis

demonic [dɪ'mɒnɪk] *adj* démoniaque

demonstrable [dɪ'mɒnstrəbəl] *adj* démontrable

demonstrate ['demənstreɪt] **1** *vt (fact, theory)* démontrer; **to d. how sth works** montrer comment qch fonctionne
2 *vi (protest)* manifester (**for/against** pour/contre)

demonstration [demənˈstreɪʃən] *n* (**a**) *(of fact, theory)* démonstration *f* (**b**) *(political)* manifestation *f*

demonstrative [dɪ'mɒnstrətɪv] *adj also Gram* démonstratif(ive)

demonstrator ['demənstreɪtə(r)] *n* (**a**) *(protester)* manifestant(e) *m,f* (**b**) *(of machine)* démonstrateur(trice) *m,f*

demoralize [dɪ'mɒrəlaɪz] *vt* démoraliser

demoralizing [dɪ'mɒrəlaɪzɪŋ] *adj* démoralisant(e)

demote [dɪ'məʊt] *vt* rétrograder

demotion [dɪ'məʊʃən] *n* rétrogradation *f*

demur [dɪ'mɜː(r)] *(pt & pp* demurred) *vi* soulever une objection

demure [dɪ'mjʊə(r)] *adj* réservé(e)

demystify [diːˈmɪstɪfaɪ] *(pt & pp* demystified) *vt* démystifier

den [den] *n* (**a**) *(of lion, fox, bear)* antre *m*, tanière *f*; *Fig (hideout)* repaire *m*, nid *m*; *Fig* **a d. of iniquity** un lieu de perdition; **a d. of thieves** un repaire de voleurs (**b**) *(room)* bureau *m*

denationalize [diːˈnæʃənəlaɪz] *vt* dénationaliser

denature [diːˈneɪtʃə(r)] *vt* dénaturer

denial [dɪ'naɪəl] *n* (**a**) *(of request)* refus *m*; *(of right)* atteinte *f*; **d. of justice** déni *m* de justice (**b**) *(of accusation, rumour, guilt)* démenti *m* (**c**) *(psychological)* dénégation *f*

denigrate ['denɪgreɪt] *vt* dénigrer

denim ['denɪm] *n* (toile *f* de) jean *m*, denim *m*; **denims** *(jeans)* un jean; **d. skirt/jacket** jupe *f*/veste *m* en jean

Denmark ['denmaːk] *n* le Danemark

denomination [dɪnɒmɪ'neɪʃən] *n* (**a**) *(religious)* confession *f* (**b**) *Fin* valeur *f*

denominator [dɪ'nɒmɪneɪtə(r)] *n Math* dénominateur *m*

denote [dɪ'nəʊt] *vt* indiquer

dénouement [deɪ'nuːmɒŋ] *n* dénouement *m*

denounce [dɪ'naʊns] *vt* dénoncer

dense [dens] *adj* (**a**) *(smoke, fog, jungle, crowd)* dense (**b**) *Fam (stupid)* bouché(e)

densely ['denslɪ] *adv* **d. populated** fortement peuplé(e); **d. wooded** très boisé(e)

density ['densɪtɪ] *n* densité *f*

dent [dent] **1** *n* bosse *f*; *Fig* **the new car put a d. in his savings** la voiture a fait un trou dans ses économies
2 *vt* cabosser; *Fig (confidence)* entamer

dental ['dentəl] *adj* dentaire; **d. appointment** rendez-vous *m* chez le dentiste; **d. floss** fil *m* dentaire; **d. hygiene** hygiène *f* dentaire; **d. nurse** assistant(e) *m,f* dentaire; **d. surgeon** chirurgien-dentiste *m*

dentist ['dentɪst] *n* dentiste *mf*; **to go to the d.'s** aller chez le dentiste

dentistry ['dentɪstrɪ] *n* dentisterie *f*

dentures ['dentʃəz] *npl* (**set of**) **d.** dentier *m*

denude [dɪ'njuːd] *vt* dénuder; **to be denuded of sth** être dépourvu(e) de qch

denunciation [dɪnʌnsɪ'eɪʃən] *n* dénonciation *f*

deny [dɪ'naɪ] *(pt & pp* denied) *vt* (**a**) *(request)* refuser; **to d. sb his rights** priver qn de ses droits; **to d. oneself sth** se priver de qch (**b**) *(fact)* nier; *(rumour)* démentir; **to d. responsibility for sth** nier être responsable de qch; **to d. doing sth** nier avoir fait qch; **there's no denying that...** il est indéniable que...; **to d. all knowledge of sth** nier avoir connaissance de qch

deodorant [diːˈəʊdərənt] *n* déodorant *m*; *(for room)* désodorisant *m*

depart [dɪ'paːt] *vi (leave)* partir (**from** de); **to d. from** *(tradition, subject, truth)* s'écarter de

department [dɪ'paːtmənt] *n (in company)* service *m*; *(in shop)* rayon *m*; *Univ* département *m*; *(of government)* ministère *m*; *Fig* **that's my d.** c'est mon rayon; **d. store** grand magasin *m*

departmental [diːpaːtˈmentəl] *adj (manager)* de service; *Univ* **d. head** chef *m* de département

departure [dɪ'paːtʃə(r)] *n (from place)* départ *m*; *(from* *tradition)* écart *m*; *(from plan)* modification *f*; **a new d.** un nouveau départ; **d. lounge** *(in airport)* salle *f* d'embarquement; **d. time** heure *f* de départ

depend [dɪ'pend] *vi* **to d.** on dépendre de; **that depends, it all depends** ça dépend; **to d. on sb** *(rely on)* compter sur qn; *(financially)* être à la charge de qn; **you can d. on it** tu peux compter là-dessus; **it depends on how much money I have** cela dépend de l'argent que j'ai; *Ironic* **you can d. on him to be late** tu peux compter sur lui pour être en retard

dependable [dɪ'pendəbəl] *adj (person, machine)* fiable; *(information)* sûr(e)

dependant [dɪ'pendənt] *n* personne *f* à charge

dependence [dɪ'pendəns] *n (reliance)* dépendance *f* (**on** à)

dependency [dɪ'pendənsɪ] *(pl* **dependencies)** *n* dépendance *f*

dependent [dɪ'pendənt] *adj (child)* à charge; **to be d. on** dépendre de; **to be d. on sb** *(financially)* être à la charge de qn

depict [dɪ'pɪkt] *vt (of painting)* représenter; *(of film, book)* décrire

depiction [dɪ'pɪkʃən] *n (in painting)* représentation *f*; *(in film, book)* description *f*

depilatory [dɪ'pɪlətərɪ] *adj* dépilatoire

deplete [dɪ'pliːt] *vt* réduire, diminuer

depletion [dɪ'pliːʃən] *n* réduction *f*, diminution *f*

deplorable [dɪ'plɔːrəbəl] *adj* déplorable

deplore [dɪ'plɔː(r)] *vt* déplorer

deploy [dɪ'plɔɪ] *vt* déployer

deployment [dɪ'plɔɪmənt] *n* déploiement *m*

depopulate [diː'pɒpjuleɪt] *vt* dépeupler

depopulation [diːpɒpju'leɪʃən] *n* dépeuplement *m*

deport [dɪ'pɔːt] *vt (criminal)* déporter; *(immigrant)* expulser

deportation [diːpɔː'teɪʃən] *n (of criminal)* déportation *f*; *(of immigrant)* expulsion *f*

deportment [dɪ'pɔːtmənt] *n (a) (posture)* maintien *m* (**b)** *(behaviour)* comportement *m*

depose [dɪ'pəʊz] *vt* déposer

deposit [dɪ'pɒzɪt] **1** *n* (**a)** *(in bank)* dépôt *m*; *Br* **d. account** compte *m* de dépôt (**b)** *(returnable)* caution *f*; *(first payment)* acompte *m*, arrhes *fpl*; **to put down a d. on sth** verser un acompte pour qch (**c)** *(of minerals)* gisement *m*; *(of wine)* dépôt *m* (**d)** *Br Pol* **to lose one's d.** perdre son cautionnement
2 *vt* déposer

deposition [diːpə'zɪʃən] *n Law* déposition *f*

depositor [dɪ'pɒzɪtə(r)] *n Fin* déposant(e) *m,f*

depot ['depəʊ] *n Mil & Com* dépôt *m*; *Am (bus station)* gare *f* routière

depravation [deprə'veɪʃən] *n* dépravation *f*

depraved [dɪ'preɪvd] *adj* dépravé(e)

depravity [dɪ'prævɪtɪ] *n* dépravation *f*

deprecate ['deprɪkeɪt] *vt* dévaloriser

deprecating ['deprɪkeɪtɪŋ], **deprecatory** ['deprɪkeɪtərɪ] *adj* désapprobateur(trice); **to be d. about sb/sth** dévaloriser qn/qch

depreciate [dɪ'priːʃɪeɪt] *vi (in value)* se déprécier

depreciation [dɪpriːʃɪ'eɪʃən] *n (in value)* dépréciation *f*

depress [dɪ'pres] *vt* (**a)** *(person)* déprimer; *Fig (prices)* faire baisser; *(economy, market)* affaiblir (**b)** *(press) (button, lever)* appuyer sur

depressed [dɪ'prest] *adj (person)* déprimé(e); *Fig*

(economy, market, region) touché(e) par la crise; **to make sb d.** déprimer qn

depressing [dɪ'presɪŋ] *adj* déprimant(e)

depression [dɪ'preʃən] *n* (**a)** *(of person, economy)* dépression *f* (**b)** *Met* dépression *f* (**c)** *(hollow)* creux *m*; *(in landscape)* dépression *f*

deprivation [deprɪ'veɪʃən] *n (hardship)* privations *fpl*; **emotional d.** carence *f* affective

deprive [dɪ'praɪv] *vt* **to d. sb of sth** priver qn de qch

deprived [dɪ'praɪvd] *adj* défavorisé(e); *(childhood)* malheureux(euse)

dept *(abbr* **department)** dép.

depth [depθ] *n* profondeur *f*; **in d.** *(investigate, discuss)* en profondeur; **to be out of one's d.** *(of swimmer)* ne plus avoir pied; *Fig* ne pas être à la hauteur; **in the depths of winter** au cœur de l'hiver; **in the depths of despair** au plus profond du désespoir; *Naut* **d. charge** grenade *f* sous-marine; *Phot* **d. of field** profondeur de champ

deputation [depjʊ'teɪʃən] *n* délégation *f*

depute [dɪ'pjuːt] *vt* **to d. sb to do sth** charger qn de faire qch

deputize ['depjʊtaɪz] *vi* **to d. for sb** remplacer qn

deputy ['depjʊtɪ] *(pl* **deputies)** *n (second-in-command)* adjoint(e) *m,f*; *(replacement)* remplaçant(e) *m,f*; *(political representative)* député *m*; *Am (policeman)* shérif *m* adjoint; **d. head** *(of school)* directeur(trice) *m,f* adjoint(e); **d. manager** directeur(trice) *m,f* adjoint(e); **d. prime minister** vice-Premier ministre *m*

derail [dɪ'reɪl] **1** *vt Fig (project, plan)* faire avorter; **to be derailed** *(of train)* dérailler
2 *vi (of train)* dérailler

derailment [dɪ'reɪlmənt] *n* déraillement *m*

deranged [dɪ'reɪndʒd] *adj* dérangé(e)

derby ['dɑːbɪ] *(pl* **derbies)** *n* (**a)** *(soccer match)* derby *m* (**b)** *Am (hat)* chapeau *m* melon

deregulate [diː'regjʊleɪt] *vt (economy, market)* déréguler; *(prices)* libérer; *(industry)* déréglementer

deregulation [diːregjʊ'leɪʃən] *n (of economy, market)* dérégulation *f*; *(of industry)* déréglementation *f*

derelict ['derəlɪkt] *adj* abandonné(e); *(ruined)* en ruines

dereliction [derɪ'lɪkʃən] *n* abandon *m*; **d. of duty** manquement *m* au devoir

deride [dɪ'raɪd] *vt* ridiculiser

derision [dɪ'rɪʒən] *n* dérision *f*

derisive [dɪ'raɪsɪv] *adj* moqueur(euse)

derisory [dɪ'raɪsərɪ] *adj* dérisoire

derivation [derɪ'veɪʃən] *n (source)* origine *f*

derivative [dɪ'rɪvətɪv] **1** *n Chem & Gram* dérivé *m*
2 *adj* banal(e), sans originalité

derive [dɪ'raɪv] **1** *vt* dériver, provenir (**from** de); **to d. pleasure from sth** prendre plaisir à qch; **to be derived from** provenir de
2 *vi* **to d. from** provenir de

dermatitis [dɜːmə'taɪtɪs] *n Med* dermite *f*, dermatite *f*

dermatology [dɜːmə'tɒlədʒɪ] *n Med* dermatologie *f*

derogatory [dɪ'rɒgətərɪ] *adj* désobligeant(e)

derrick ['derɪk] *n* derrick *m*

derv [dɜːv] *n Br (fuel)* gas-oil *m*, gazole *m*

desalination [diːsælɪ'neɪʃən] *n* dessalement *m*

descend [dɪ'send] **1** *vt (hill, stairs)* descendre
2 *vi* (**a)** *(go down)* descendre; *(of darkness, dusk)* tomber; **in descending order** en ordre décroissant; **every summer tourists d. on the town** chaque été les touristes débarquent en ville; *Fig* **to d. to sb's level** s'abaisser au

niveau de qn (**b**) **to d.** or **be descended from sb** (be related to) descendre de qn

descent [dɪ'sent] n (**a**) (of plane, from mountain) descente f (**b**) (ancestry) **to be of Irish d.** être d'origine irlandaise

describe [dɪs'kraɪb] vt décrire

description [dɪs'krɪpʃən] n description f; (issued by police) signalement m; **to answer** or **fit the d.** répondre au signalement; **beyond d.** indescriptible; **birds of all descriptions** des oiseaux de toutes sortes; **he's a journalist of some d.** il travaille dans le journalisme

descriptive [dɪs'krɪptɪv] adj descriptif(ive)

desecrate ['desɪkreɪt] vt profaner

desecration [desɪ'kreɪʃən] n profanation f

desegregation [diːsegrɪ'geɪʃən] n déségrégation f

desert¹ ['dezət] n désert m; **d. island** île f déserte

desert² [dɪ'zɜːt] **1** vt abandonner; **to d. one's post** (of soldier) déserter son poste
2 vi (from army) déserter

deserted [dɪ'zɜːtɪd] adj désert(e)

deserter [dɪ'zɜːtə(r)] n déserteur m

desertion [dɪ'zɜːʃən] n Law abandon m du domicile conjugal; Mil désertion f

deserts [dɪ'zɜːts] npl **he got his just d.** il a eu ce qu'il méritait

deserve [dɪ'zɜːv] vt mériter; **to d. to do sth** mériter de faire qch; **she deserves to be punished** elle mérite une punition

deserving [dɪ'zɜːvɪŋ] adj (person) méritant(e); (action, cause) méritoire; **to be d. of praise** être digne d'éloge

design [dɪ'zaɪn] **1** n (**a**) (pattern) (on fabric, wallpaper) motif m (**b**) (style) (of car, furniture) modèle m; (of clothes) coupe f (**c**) (drawing) (of building, machine) plan m (**d**) (subject) design m, stylisme m (**e**) (planning) (of product, machine) conception f (**f**) (intention) dessein m; **by d.** à dessein; **to have designs on** avoir des vues sur
2 vt (building, vehicle) concevoir; (clothes, furniture) créer; **to be designed for sth/to do sth** (intended) être destiné(e) à qch/à faire qch

designate ['dezɪgneɪt] **1** vt désigner; **to d. sb to do sth** désigner qn pour faire qch; **this restaurant has been designated a no-smoking area** ce restaurant est une zone non-fumeur; **designated driver** = personne qui s'engage à ne pas boire pour pouvoir reconduire les autres en voiture
2 adj désigné(e)

designation [dezɪg'neɪʃən] n (**a**) (appointment) nomination f; (of funds) affectation f (**b**) (title) désignation f

designer [dɪ'zaɪnə(r)] n concepteur(trice) m,f; (of building) architecte mf; (of clothes) styliste mf (de mode); (of theatre set) décorateur(trice) m,f; **d. clothes** vêtements mpl de marque; **d. drugs** drogues fpl de synthèse

desirable [dɪ'zaɪərəbəl] adj souhaitable; (job, location) attrayant(e); (sexually) désirable; **a d. residence** une belle résidence

desire [dɪ'zaɪə(r)] **1** n désir m, envie f; **I have no d. to go** je n'ai aucune envie d'y aller
2 vt désirer; **to d. to do sth** désirer faire qch, avoir envie de faire qch; **it leaves a lot to be desired** ça laisse beaucoup à désirer

desirous [dɪ'zaɪərəs] adj Formal désireux(euse) (**of** de)

desist [dɪ'zɪst] vi Formal cesser; **to d. from doing sth** cesser de faire qch

desk [desk] n (in school) table f; (with lid) pupitre m; (in office, home) bureau m; (hotel reception) réception f; **d. diary** agenda m; **a d. job** un travail de bureau; **d. lamp** lampe f de bureau

desktop ['desktɒp] n Comptr **d. computer** ordinateur m de bureau; **d. publishing** publication f assistée par ordinateur

desolate ['desələt] adj (place) désolé(e); (future, prospect) sombre; (person) abattu(e), affligé(e)

desolation [desə'leɪʃən] n désolation f; (of person) affliction f

despair [dɪs'peə(r)] **1** n désespoir m; **to be in d.** être désespéré(e); **to drive sb to d.** désespérer qn
2 vi désespérer; **I d. of** you tu me désespères

despairing [dɪ'speərɪŋ] adj désespéré(e)

despatch [dɪ'spætʃ] = dispatch

desperate ['despərət] adj désespéré(e); **to be in d. need of sth** avoir désespérément besoin de qch; **to be d. to do sth** vouloir à tout prix faire qch; **to be d. for sth** avoir désespérément besoin de qch

desperately ['despərətlɪ] adv désespérément; (ill) très gravement; **to be d. in love** être éperdument amoureux(euse); **to be d. sorry about sth** être affreusement désolé(e) de qch

desperation [despə'reɪʃən] n désespoir m; **in d.** par désespoir

despicable [dɪ'spɪkəbəl] adj méprisable

despise [dɪ'spaɪz] vt mépriser

despite [dɪs'paɪt] prep malgré

despondency [dɪs'pɒndənsɪ] n abattement m

despondent [dɪ'spɒndənt] adj abattu(e)

despot ['despɒt] n despote m

despotic [dɪs'pɒtɪk] adj despotique

despotism ['despətɪzəm] n despotisme m

dessert [dɪ'zɜːt] n dessert m; **d. wine** vin m doux

dessertspoon [dɪ'zɜːtspuːn] n cuillère f à dessert

destabilize [diː'steɪbəlaɪz] vt déstabiliser

destination [destɪ'neɪʃən] n destination f; **to reach one's d.** arriver à destination; Comptr **d. disk/drive** disquette f/lecteur m cible

destine ['destɪn] vt destiner

destined ['destɪnd] adj (**a**) (meant) destiné(e); **to be d. to do sth** être destiné à faire qch; **he was d. to become famous** (by fate) il était destiné à devenir célèbre; (reporting a fact) il devait plus tard devenir célèbre (**b**) (of plane, ship) **d. for** à destination de

destiny ['destɪnɪ] (pl **destinies**) n destin m, destinée f

destitute ['destɪtjuːt] adj sans ressources; **to be utterly d.** être dans la misère

destroy [dɪs'trɔɪ] vt (**a**) (damage, ruin) détruire (**b**) (animal) abattre; (vermin) éliminer

destroyer [dɪs'trɔɪə(r)] n (ship) contre-torpilleur m

destruction [dɪs'trʌkʃən] n destruction f; (damage) ravages mpl

destructive [dɪs'trʌktɪv] adj destructeur(trice)

desultory ['desəltərɪ] adj (conversation) décousu(e); (attempt) peu convaincant(e)

detach [dɪ'tætʃ] vt détacher (**from** de); **to d. oneself (from)** s'éloigner (de)

detachable [dɪ'tætʃəbəl] adj amovible

detached [dɪ'tætʃt] adj (**a**) (separate) détaché(e), séparé(e); **to become** or **get d. from sth** se détacher de qch; **d. house** maison f individuelle, pavillon m; Med **d. retina** décollement m de la rétine (**b**) (disinterested) (tone) détaché(e); **he's rather d.** il sait garder ses distances

detachment [dɪ'tætʃmənt] n (**a**) (military unit) détachement m (**b**) (objectivity) détachement m

detail ['diːteɪl] **1** n (**a**) (item of information) détail m; **to pay**

attention to d. être minutieux(euse); **to go into detail(s)** entrer dans les détails; **in d.** en détail; **details** *(information)* renseignements *mpl*; *(address and phone number)* coordonnées *fpl* (**b**) *Mil* détachement *m* **2** *vt* (**a**) *(describe)* détailler (**b**) *Mil* **to d. sb to do sth** donner l'ordre à qn de faire qch

detailed ['di:teɪld] *adj (account, description)* détaillé(e); *(work)* minutieux(euse)

detaln [dɪ'teɪn] *vt (in prison)* placer en détention; *(in hospital)* garder; *(delay)* retenir; **such details need not d. us** ne nous laissons pas arrêter par de tels détails

detainee [di:teɪ'ni:] *n* détenu(e) *m,f*

detect [dɪ'tekt] *vt* détecter

detection [dɪ'tekʃən] *n* travail *m* de détective; **to escape d.** *(of mistake, change)* passer inaperçu(e); *(of burglar)* ne pas être découvert(e)

detective [dɪ'tektɪv] *n (private)* détective *m*; *(police officer)* ≃ inspecteur(trice) *m,f* de police; **d. story** roman *m* policier; **d. work** enquêtes *fpl*

detector [dɪ'tektə(r)] *n* détecteur *m*

dótonte [doɪ'tɒnt] *n* détente *f*

detention [dɪ'tenʃən] *n* (**a**) *Law* détention *f*; **d. centre** – centre de détention pour mineurs (**b**) *Sch* retenue *f*

deter [dɪ'tɜ:(r)] *(pt & pp deterred)* *vt* dissuader; **to d. sb trom doing sth** dissuader qn de faire qch

detergent [dɪ'tɜ:dʒənt] *n (for cleaning)* produit *m* de nettoyage

deteriorate [dɪ'tɪərɪəreɪt] *vi* se détériorer

deterioration [dɪtɪərɪə'reɪʃən] *n* détérioration *f*

determination [dɪtɜ:mɪ'neɪʃən] *n* détermination *f*

determine [dɪ'tɜ:mɪn] *vt* (**a**) *(decide)* **to d. to do sth** décider de faire qch; **to d. that…** décider que… (**b**) *(cause, date)* déterminer

determined [dɪ'tɜ:mɪnd] *adj* déterminé(e), résolu(e); **to be d. to do sth** être déterminé ou résolu à faire qch, **I'm d. that we'll succeed** je suis déterminé à ce que nous réussissions

deterrent [dɪ'terənt] **1** *n* moyen *m* de dissuasion; **to act as a d.** avoir un effet dissuasif **2** *adj (effect)* dissuasif(ive)

detest [dɪ'test] *vt* détester

dethrone [dɪ'θrəʊn] *vt* détrôner

detonate ['detəneɪt] **1** *vt* faire exploser **2** *vi* exploser

detonation [detə'neɪʃən] *n* explosion *f*, détonation *f*

detonator ['detəneɪtə(r)] *n* détonateur *m*

detour ['di:tʊə(r)] *n* détour *m*

detoxification [di:tɒksɪfɪ'keɪʃən], *Fam* **detox** ['di:tɒks] *n* désintoxication *f*; **d. centre/programme** centre *m*/cure *f* de désintoxication

▸ **detract from** [dɪ'trækt] *vt insep* diminuer; **I don't want to d. from her achievement, but…** je ne veux pas minimiser ce qu'elle a accompli, mais…

detractor [dɪ'træktə(r)] *n* détracteur(trice) *m,f*

detriment ['detrɪmənt] *n* **to the d. of** au détriment de; **without d. to** sans porter préjudice à

detrimental [detrɪ'mentəl] *adj* préjudiciable (**to** à); **to have a d. effect on** nuire à

detritus [dɪ'traɪtəs] *n* détritus *mpl*

deuce [dju:s] *n (in tennis)* égalité *f*

Deutschmark ['dɔɪtʃmɑ:k] *n Formerly* (deutsche) mark *m*

devaluation [di:væljʊ'eɪʃən] *n* (**a**) *(of currency)* dévaluation *f* (**b**) *(of person, achievement)* dévalorisation *f*

devalue [di:'vælju:] *vt* (**a**) *(currency)* dévaluer (**b**) *(person, achievement)* dévaloriser

devastate ['devəsteɪt] *vt (crops, village)* dévaster; *(person)* anéantir; **I was devastated by the news** la nouvelle m'a anéanti

devastating ['devəsteɪtɪŋ] *adj (storm, bombardment)* dévastateur(trice); *(news, findings, argument)* accablant(e); *(criticism)* cinglant(e); *(charm, beauty)* irrésistible

devastation [devəs'teɪʃən] *n* dévastation *f*

develop [dɪ'veləp] **1** *vt* (**a**) *(skills, theory, argument)* développer; *(product)* mettre au point (**b**) *(region)* développer; *(site)* aménager; **developed countries** pays *mpl* développés (**c**) *(acquire) (infection, illness)* attraper; *(habit)* prendre; **to d. a liking** *or* **taste for sth** se mettre à aimer qch (**d**) *(film)* développer **2** *vi* (**a**) *(grow)* se développer; **to d. into** devenir (**b**) *(become apparent)* apparaître

developer [dɪ'veləpə(r)] *n* (**a**) *(of land)* promoteur *m* (**b**) *Phot* révélateur *m*

developing [dɪ'veləpɪŋ] *adj (region, country)* en (voie de) développement; *(crisis)* en évolution

development [dɪ'veləpmənt] *n* (**a**) *(growth)* développement *m*; *(of idea)* évolution *f*; **d. aid** aide *f* au développement; *Br* **d. area** = zone à fort taux de chômage où l'État incite les industries à venir s'installer (**b**) *(progress, change)* développement *m*; **there have been some interesting developments** il y a eu quelques faits nouveaux intéressants; **the latest developments in medical research** les dernières découvertes médicales (**c**) *(of film)* développement *m*

deviant ['di:vɪənt] *adj* déviant(e)

deviate ['di:vɪeɪt] *vi* dévier (**from** de); *Fig* s'écarter (**from** de)

devlation [di:vɪ'eɪʃən] *n* déviation *f* (**from** par rapport à); *Fig* écart *m* (**from** par rapport à)

device [dɪ'vaɪs] *n* (**a**) *(mechanism)* dispositif *m*; *(gadget)* appareil *m*; (**explosive**) **d.** engin *m* explosif (**b**) *(method, scheme)* stratagème *m*; **to leave sb to their own devices** laisser qn se débrouiller

devll ['devəl] *n* (**a**) *(evil spirit)* diable *m*; **the D.** le Diable (**b**) *Fam (person)* **poor d.!** pauvre diable!; **you little d.!** *(to child)* petit diable!; **you lucky d.!** veinard! (**c**) *Fam (for emphasis)* **what the d. are you doing?** mais qu'est-ce que tu fabriques?; **how the d.…?** comment diable…?; **we had a d. of a job finding it** nous avons eu un mal de chien à le trouver (**d**) *(idioms)* **he's a bit of a d.** il est un peu obsédé; **go on, be a d.!** allez, laisse-toi tenter!; **to work like the d.** travailler comme un(e) fou (folle); **to be (caught) between the d. and the deep blue sea** avoir à choisir entre la peste et le choléra; **talk of the d.!** quand on parle du loup!; *Prov* **better the d. you know (than the d. you don't)** on sait ce qu'on perd, on ne sait pas ce qu'on trouve; **to play d.'s advocate** se faire l'avocat du diable

devilish ['devəlɪʃ] *adj* diabolique

devil-may-care ['devəlmeɪ'keə(r)] *adj* insouciant(e)

devious ['di:vɪəs] *adj (person, mind)* retors(e); *(scheme, route)* tortueux(euse); *(means)* détourné(e)

devise [dɪ'vaɪz] *vt* imaginer, élaborer

devoid [dɪ'vɔɪd] *adj* dénué(e), dépourvu(e) (**of** de)

devolution [di:və'lu:ʃən] *n Pol* décentralisation *f*

devolve [dɪ'vɒlv] **1** *vt* déléguer **2** *vi* **to d. on** incomber à; **power devolves on the regional assembly** le pouvoir appartient à l'assemblée régionale

devote [dɪ'vəʊt] *vt* consacrer (**to** à); **to d. oneself to** se consacrer à

devoted [dɪ'vəʊtɪd] *adj (parent)* dévoué(e); *(admirer)* fervent(e); **years of d.** service des années de bons et loyaux services; **they are d.** to each other ils sont très attachés l'un à l'autre

devotee [devəʊ'tiː] *n (of writer, artist)* admirateur(trice) *m,f; (of idea)* partisan *m; (of sport, music)* passionné(e) *m,f*

devotion [dɪ'vəʊʃən] *n (to cause, friend, family)* dévouement *m; (to god, saint)* dévotion *f;* **devotions** *(prayers)* prières *fpl*

devour [dɪ'vaʊə(r)] *vt also Fig* dévorer

devout [dɪ'vaʊt] *adj (person)* dévot(e); *(wish)* fervent(e)

dew [djuː] *n* rosée *f*

dewy-eyed [djuːɪ'aɪd] *adj (loving)* ému(e); *(naive)* ingénu(e)

dexterity [deks'terɪtɪ] *n* dextérité *f*

dext(e)rous ['dekstrəs] *adj* adroit(e), habile

diabetes [daɪə'biːtiːz] *n* diabète *m*

diabetic [daɪə'betɪk] *n & adj* diabétique *mf;* **d. chocolate** chocolat *m* pour diabétiques

diabolical [daɪə'bɒlɪkəl] *adj (a) (evil)* diabolique **(b)** *Fam (very bad)* épouvantable

diadem ['daɪədem] *n* diadème *m*

diagnose ['daɪəgnəʊz] *vt also Fig* diagnostiquer

diagnosis [daɪəg'nəʊsɪs] *(pl* **diagnoses** [daɪəg'nəʊsiːz]) *n also Fig* diagnostic *m*

diagnostic [daɪəg'nɒstɪk] *adj* diagnostique

diagonal [daɪ'ægənəl] **1** *n* diagonale *f* **2** *adj* diagonal(e)

diagram ['daɪəgræm] *n* schéma *m*

dial ['daɪəl] **1** *n (of clock, phone)* cadran *m; (control knob)* bouton *m* **2** *vt (pt & pp* **dialled**, *Am* **dialed**) *(phone number)* composer; *(operator, country)* appeler

dialect ['daɪəlekt] *n* dialecte *m*

dialectic(al) [daɪə'lektɪk(əl)] *adj* dialectique

dialling ['daɪəlɪŋ] *n Br* **d. code** indicatif *m;* **d. tone** tonalité *f*

dialogue, *Am* **dialog** ['daɪəlɒg] *n* dialogue *m; Comptr* **d. box** boîte *f* de dialogue

dialysis [daɪ'ælɪsɪs] *n Med* dialyse *f*

diameter [daɪ'æmɪtə(r)] *n* diamètre *m;* **the wheel is 60 cm in d.** la roue a un diamètre de 60 cm

diametrically [daɪə'metrɪklɪ] *adv* diamétralement

diamond ['daɪəmənd] *n (gem)* diamant *m; (shape)* losange *m;* **diamonds** *(card suit)* carreau *m;* **d. jubilee** soixantième anniversaire *m;* **d. necklace/ring** collier *m/* bague *f* de *ou* en diamants; **d. wedding anniversary** noces *fpl* de diamant

diaper ['daɪəpə(r)] *n Am* couche *f*

diaphanous [daɪ'æfənəs] *adj* diaphane

diaphragm ['daɪəfræm] *n* diaphragme *m*

diarrhoea, *Am* **diarrhea** [daɪə'rɪə] *n* diarrhée *f*

diary ['daɪərɪ] *(pl* **diaries**) *n (personal)* journal *m* (intime); *(for appointments)* agenda *m*

diatribe ['daɪətraɪb] *n* diatribe *f* **(against** contre)

dice [daɪs] **1** *n (pl* **dice**) dé *m;* **to play d.** jouer aux dés **2** *vt (food)* couper en dés **3** *vi* **to d. with death** jouer avec sa vie

dicey ['daɪsɪ] *adj Fam* risqué(e)

dichotomy [daɪ'kɒtəmɪ] *(pl* **dichotomies**) *n* dichotomie *f*

dick [dɪk] *n* **(a)** *Vulg (penis)* bite *f* **(b)** *Am Fam (detective)* privé *m*

dickhead ['dɪkhed] *n Br Vulg (idiot)* tête *f* de nœud

dicky ['dɪkɪ] *adj Br Fam* **to have a d. heart** avoir le cœur fragile

dictate 1 *n* ['dɪkteɪt] ordre *m;* **she followed the dictates of her conscience** elle fit ce que lui dictait sa conscience **2** *vt* [dɪk'teɪt] **(a)** *(letter, passage, conditions)* dicter **(b)** *(determine)* imposer; *(choice)* dicter **3** *vi* [dɪk'teɪt] **(a)** *(dictate text)* dicter **(b)** *(give orders)* **to d. to sb** donner des ordres à qn; **I won't be dictated to!** je n'ai pas d'ordres à recevoir!

dictation [dɪk'teɪʃən] *n* dictée *f;* **to take d.** écrire sous la dictée

dictator [dɪk'teɪtə(r)] *n* dictateur *m*

dictatorial [dɪktə'tɔːrɪəl] *adj (power, regime)* dictatorial(e); *(manner, tone)* autoritaire

dictatorship [dɪk'teɪtəʃɪp] *n* dictature *f*

diction ['dɪkʃən] *n (pronunciation)* diction *f; (choice of words)* style *m*

dictionary ['dɪkʃənərɪ] *(pl* **dictionaries**) *n* dictionnaire *m*

did [dɪd] *pt of* **do**

didactic [dɪ'dæktɪk] *adj* didactique

diddle ['dɪdəl] *vt Fam* rouler; **he diddled me out of $500** il m'a escroqué 500 dollars

didn't ['dɪdənt] = **did not**

die¹ [daɪ] *n* **(a)** *(pl* **dice** [daɪs]) *(in games)* dé *m;* **the d. is cast** les dés sont jetés **(b)** *(pl* **dies** [daɪz]) *(mould)* matrice *f*

die² *(pt & pp* **died**, *continuous* **dying**) *vi* mourir **(from** *or* **of** sth); **she is dying** elle est mourante; **to d. hard** *(of habit, rumour)* avoir la vie dure; *Fam* **never say d.!** il ne faut jamais désespérer!; *Fam* **I nearly died (of shame)** j'ai cru mourir de honte; *Fam* **to be dying to do sth** mourir d'envie de faire qch; *Fam* **I'm dying for a cigarette** je meurs d'envie de fumer une cigarette; **the engine died on me/us** le moteur a calé **2** *vt* **to d. a natural/violent death** mourir de mort naturelle/violente; *Fig* **to a death** *(of proposal)* tomber à l'eau; *(of performer)* faire un bide

▸ **die away** *vi (of sound, voice)* s'affaiblir

▸ **die down** *vi (of fire)* baisser; *(of wind)* tomber; *(of sound)* s'affaiblir; *(of excitement, scandal)* se calmer

▸ **die off** *vi* mourir

▸ **die out** *vi (of family, species)* s'éteindre

die-hard ['daɪhɑːd] **1** *n* réactionnaire *mf* **2** *adj* pur(e) et dur(e)

diesel ['diːzəl] **1** *n (fuel)* gas-oil *m*, gazole *m; (car, railway engine)* diesel *m* **2** *adj (engine, train)* diesel; **d. oil** *or* **fuel** gas-oil *m*, gazole *m*

diet ['daɪət] **1** *n (usual food)* alimentation *f; (restricted food)* régime *m;* **to be/go on a d.** être/se mettre au régime **2** *vi* être au régime

dietary ['daɪətərɪ] *adj* alimentaire; **d. fibre** fibres *fpl* (alimentaires)

dietician [daɪə'tɪʃən] *n* diététicien(enne) *m,f*

differ ['dɪfə(r)] *vi* **(a)** *(be different)* différer **(from** de); **d. in size/colour** être de taille/couleur différente **(b)** *(disagree)* ne pas être d'accord; **I beg to d.** permettez-moi d'être d'un autre avis; **I beg to agree to d.** garder chacun son opinion

difference ['dɪfərəns] *n* **(a)** *(disparity)* différence *f* **(between/in** entre/de); **that doesn't make any d.** ça ne fait aucune différence; **it makes no d.** to me cela m'est égal; **that makes all the d.** voilà qui change tout; **a hotel with a d.** un hôtel pas comme les autres **(b)** *(disagreement)* désaccord *m;* **d. of opinion** divergence *f* d'opinion; **we have to settle our differences** il faut nous mettre d'accord

different ['dɪfərənt] *adj* **(a)** *(not the same)* différent(e) **(from** de**); that's quite a d.** matter ça, c'est une autre affaire; **she feels a d. person** elle ne se sent plus la même; **he just wants to be d.** il veut se singulariser **(b)** *(various)* différents(es), divers(es)

differential [dɪfə'renʃəl] **1** *n (in wages, prices)* écart *m*; *Math* **d.** calculus calcul *m* différentiel; *Aut* **d.** (gear) différentiel *m*
2 *adj* différentiel(elle)

differentiate [dɪfə'renʃɪəɪt] **1** *vt* différencier **(from** de) **2** *vi* faire la différence **(between** entre)

differently ['dɪfərəntlɪ] *adv* différemment

difficult ['dɪfɪkəlt] *adj* difficile; **to find it d. to do sth** avoir du mal à faire qch; **he's d. to get on with** il n'est pas commode; **you're just being d.** tu le fais exprès pour embêter le monde; **to make life d. for sb** compliquer la vie à qn

difficulty ['dɪfɪkəltɪ] *(pl* **difficulties)** *n* difficulté *f*; **to have d. in doing sth** avoir des difficultés *ou* du mal à faire qch; **with d.** avec difficulté *ou* peine; **to make difficulties for sb** créer des difficultés à qn

diffidence ['dɪfɪdəns] *n* manque *m* de confiance en soi

diffident ['dɪfɪdənt] *adj* peu sûr(e) de soi; **to be d. about doing sth** hésiter à faire qch

diffuse 1 *adj* [dɪ'fjuːs] diffus(e)
2 *vt* [dɪ'fjuːz] diffuser, répandre
3 *vi* [dɪ'fjuːz] se diffuser, se répandre

dig [dɪg] **1** *n* **(a)** *(in archaeology)* fouilles *fpl* **(b)** *(poke)* **a d. in the ribs** un coup de coude dans les côtes **(c)** *(remark)* pique *f*; **to have a d. at sb** lancer une pique à qn
2 *vt (pt & pp* **dug** [dʌg]) **(a)** *(hole, grave, ditch)* creuser; *(garden)* bêcher; *Fig* **she is digging her own grave** elle est en train de creuser sa propre tombe **(b)** *(thrust)* **to d. sth into sth** planter qch dans qch **(c)** *very Fam (understand)* piger; **you d.?** tu piges?
3 *vi (of person, animal)* creuser; *(in archaeology)* faire des fouilles; **to d. for sth** creuser pour trouver qch
▸ **dig in 1** *vt sep Fig* **to d. one's heels in** s'entêter
2 *vi* **(a)** *(of soldiers)* se retrancher **(b)** *Fam (eat)* **d. in!** allez-y!, attaquez!
▸ **dig out** *vt sep* **(a)** *(bullet, splinter)* extraire; *(person from ruins, snow drift)* dégager **(b)** *Fam (find) (information)* dénicher
▸ **dig up** *vt sep* **(a)** *(plant)* arracher; *(treasure, body)* déterrer; *(road)* excaver **(b)** *Fam (find) (information, person)* dénicher

digest 1 *n* ['daɪdʒest] *(summary)* condensé *m*
2 *vt* [dɪ'dʒest] *also Fig* digérer

digestible [dɪ'dʒestəbəl] *adj* digeste

digestion [dɪ'dʒestʃən] *n* digestion *f*

digestive [dɪ'dʒestɪv] *adj* digestif(ive); *Br* **d. (biscuit)** = sorte de sablé; **d. system/tract** système *m*/tube *m* digestif

digger ['dɪgə(r)] *n (machine)* excavateur *m*

digit ['dɪdʒɪt] *n* **(a)** *(finger)* doigt *m*; *(toe)* orteil *m* **(b)** *(number)* chiffre *m*

digital ['dɪdʒɪtəl] *adj* numérique; **d. recording** enregistrement *m* numérique

dignified ['dɪgnɪfaɪd] *adj* digne

dignify ['dɪgnɪfaɪ] *(pt & pp* **dignified)** *vt* donner de la dignité à; **I won't d. that remark with a response!** je ne m'abaisserai pas à répondre à cette remarque!

dignitary ['dɪgnɪtərɪ] *(pl* **dignitaries)** *n* dignitaire *m*

dignity ['dɪgnɪtɪ] *n* dignité *f*; **she considered it**

beneath her d. to respond elle estimait indigne d'elle de répondre

digress [daɪ'gres] *vi* faire une digression; **to d. from** s'écarter de; **..., but I d.** ..., mais je m'égare

digression [daɪ'greʃən] *n* digression *f*

digs [dɪgz] *npl Br Fam* chambre *f* meublée

dike [daɪk] = **dyke**

dilapidated [dɪ'læpɪdeɪtɪd] *adj* délabré(e)

dilapidation [dɪlæpɪ'deɪʃən] *n* délabrement *m*

dilate [daɪ'leɪt] **1** *vt* dilater
2 *vi* se dilater

dilation [daɪ'leɪʃən] *n* dilatation *f*

dilatory ['dɪlətərɪ] *adj Formal (reply)* dilatoire; **to be d. in doing sth** tarder à faire qch

dilemma [daɪ'lemə] *n* dilemme *m*; **to be in a d.** être placé(e) devant un dilemme

dilettante [dɪlɪ'tɑːntɪ] *n* dilettante *mf*

diligence ['dɪlɪdʒəns] *n* application *f*, zèle *m*

diligent ['dɪlɪdʒənt] *adj* consciencieux(euse)

dill [dɪl] *n* aneth *m*

dilly-dally ['dɪlɪ'dælɪ] *(pt & pp* **dilly-dallied)** *vi Fam (loiter)* traînasser; *(hesitate)* tergiverser

dilute [daɪ'luːt] **1** *adj* dilué(e)
2 *vt (liquid)* diluer; *Fig (policy, proposal)* édulcorer

dilution [daɪ'luːʃən] *n Fig (of policy, proposal)* édulcoration *f*

dim [dɪm] **1** *adj* **(a)** *(light, chance, hope)* faible; *(outline, memory)* vague; *(eyesight)* faible, trouble; *(future)* sombre; **to take a d. view of sth** avoir une piètre opinion de qch **(b)** *(stupid)* bête
2 *vt (pt & pp* **dimmed)** *(light)* baisser, atténuer
3 *vi (of light)* baisser

dime [daɪm] *n Am* (pièce *f* de) 10 cents *mpl*; *Fam* **it's not worth a d.** ça ne vaut pas un clou; *Fam* **they're a d. a dozen** il y en a à la pelle; **d. store** magasin *m* bon marché

dimension [daɪ'menʃən] *n also Fig* dimension *f*

diminish [dɪ'mɪnɪʃ] *vt & vi* diminuer; *Law* **diminished responsibility** responsabilité *f* atténuée

diminishing [dɪ'mɪnɪʃɪŋ] *adj* décroissant(e); **the law of d. returns** la loi des rendements décroissants

diminutive [dɪ'mɪnjʊtɪv] **1** *n Gram* diminutif *m*
2 *adj* minuscule

dimly ['dɪmlɪ] *adv (lit)* faiblement; *(remember, see)* vaguement

dimmer ['dɪmə(r)] *n* **d. (switch)** variateur *m*

dimple ['dɪmpəl] *n* fossette *f*

dimwit ['dɪmwɪt] *n Fam* andouille *f*

din [dɪn] *n* vacarme *m*

dine [daɪn] *vi* dîner
▸ **dine out** *vi* dîner dehors; **to d. out on a story** rabâcher une histoire

diner ['daɪnə(r)] *n* **(a)** *(person)* dîneur(euse) *m f* **(b)** *Am (restaurant)* petit restaurant *m*

ding-dong ['dɪŋdɒŋ] **1** *n* **(a)** *(sound)* ding dong *m* **(b)** *Fam (fight)* bagarre *f*
2 *adj Fam (argument, contest)* acharné(e)

dinghy ['dɪŋ(g)ɪ] *(pl* **dinghies)** *n* **(rubber) d.** canot *m* pneumatique; **(sailing) d.** dériveur *m*

dingo ['dɪŋgəʊ] *(pl* **dingoes)** *n* dingo *m*

dingy ['dɪndʒɪ] *adj (room, street)* miteux(euse); *(colour)* terne

dining ['daɪnɪŋ] *n* **d. car** *(on train)* wagon-restaurant *m*;

d. hall *(in school)* réfectoire *m*; **d. room** salle *f* à manger; **d. table** table *f* de salle à manger

dinner ['dɪnə(r)] *n (evening meal)* dîner *m*; *(lunch)* déjeuner *m*; **what's for d.?** qu'est-ce qu'on mange?; **to have d.** *(in evening)* dîner; *(at midday)* déjeuner; **d. hour** *(at school)* heure *f* du déjeuner; *Br* **d. jacket** smoking *m*; *Br* **d. lady** = femme de service dans une cantine scolaire; **d. party** dîner; **d. service** service *m* de table; **d. time** *(in evening)* heure du dîner; *(lunchtime)* heure du déjeuner

dinosaur ['daɪnəsɔː(r)] *n also Fig* dinosaure *m*

dint [dɪnt] *n Formal* **by d. of** à force de; **by d. of her efforts** grâce à ses efforts

diocese ['daɪəsɪs] *n Rel* diocèse *m*

diode ['daɪəʊd] *n Elec* diode *f*

dioxide [daɪ'ɒksaɪd] *n Chem* dioxyde *m*

dip [dɪp] **1** *n* **(a)** *(slope)* descente *f*; *(hollow)* dépression *f*; *(in prices, figures)* baisse *f* **(b)** *Fam (swim)* baignade *f*; **to go for a d.** faire trempette **(c)** *(sauce)* = sauce dans laquelle on trempe des crudités, des biscuits salés etc
2 *vt (pt & pp dipped)* **(a)** *(immerse)* plonger **(b)** *(lower)* baisser; *Br* **to d. one's headlights** se mettre en codes *(quand on est en pleins phares)*
3 *vi (of ground)* descendre; *(of prices, temperature)* baisser; **the sun dipped below the horizon** le soleil descendit derrière l'horizon
▸ **dip into** *vt insep (savings, capital)* puiser dans; *(book)* feuilleter

DipEd [dɪp'ed] *n Br (abbr Diploma in Education)* ≃ CAPES *m*

diphtheria [dɪf'θɪərɪə] *n Med* diphtérie *f*

diphthong ['dɪfθɒŋ] *n Ling* diphtongue *f*

diploma [dɪ'pləʊmə] *n* diplôme *m*

diplomacy [dɪ'pləʊməsɪ] *n also Fig* diplomatie *f*

diplomat ['dɪpləmæt] *n* diplomate *mf*

diplomatic [dɪplə'mætɪk] *adj* diplomatique; *Fig (person)* diplomate; **d. bag** valise *f* diplomatique; **d. corps** corps *m* diplomatique; **d. immunity** immunité *f* diplomatique

dipper ['dɪpə(r)] *n (ladle)* louche *f*; *Am* **the Big D.** *(constellation)* la Grande Ourse; *Br* **big d.** *(at fairground)* montagnes *fpl* russes

dipsomaniac [dɪpsə'meɪnɪæk] *n* dipsomane *mf*

dipstick ['dɪpstɪk] *n* **(a)** *Aut* jauge *f* de niveau d'huile **(b)** *Br Fam (idiot)* abruti(e) *m,f*

dire ['daɪə(r)] *adj (consequences)* tragique; *Fam (bad)* épouvantable; **to be in d. need of sth** avoir un besoin urgent de qch; **to be in d. straits** être dans une mauvaise passe

direct [dɪ'rekt, daɪ'rekt] **1** *adj* direct(e); *(refusal, denial)* catégorique; **the d. opposite** l'exact opposé; **to be a d. descendant of sb** descendre de qn en ligne directe; *Elec* **d. current** courant *m* continu; *Fin* **d. debit** prélèvement *m* automatique; **d. hit** coup *m* au but; **d. mail** publipostage *m*; *Gram* **d. object** complément *m* d'objet direct; *Pol* **d. rule** administration *f* centrale; *Com* **d. selling** vente *f* directe; *Gram* **d. speech** discours *m* direct; *Fin* **d. taxation** contributions *fpl* directes
2 *adv* directement; *(broadcast)* en direct **(from** de)
3 *vt* **(a)** *(remark)* adresser **(at** à); *(gaze, light)* diriger **(at** sur); *(funds, effort)* consacrer **(towards** à); **can you d. me to the post office?** pouvez-vous m'indiquer le chemin de la poste?
(b) *(company, actors)* diriger; *(traffic)* régler; *(play)* mettre en scène; *(film)* réaliser
(c) *(instruct)* **to d. sb to do sth** ordonner à qn de faire qch; **as directed** selon les instructions

direction [dɪ'rekʃən] *n* **(a)** *(way)* direction *f*, sens *m*; **in**

the d. of en direction de; **they ran off in all directions** ils sont partis en courant dans toutes les directions; **the town was surrounded by hills in all directions** la ville était entourée de tous côtés par des collines
(b) *(management) (of project)* direction *f*; *(of play)* mise *f* en scène; *(of film)* réalisation *f*; **under the d. of** *(orchestra)* sous la direction de
(c) **directions** *(to place)* indications *fpl*; *(for use)* instructions *fpl*; **to ask for directions** demander son chemin

directly [dɪ'rektlɪ, daɪ'rektlɪ] **1** *adv* **(a)** *(go, write)* directement; **to be d. descended from sb** descendre de qn en ligne directe **(b)** *(exactly)* juste; **d. opposite** juste en face de **(c)** *(frankly) (answer, speak)* ouvertement **(d)** *(soon)* immédiatement; **I'll be there d.** j'arrive tout de suite
2 *conj* aussitôt que, dès que; **I'll come d. I've finished** je viendrai dès que j'aurai fini

director [dɪ'rektə(r)] *n (manager)* directeur(trice) *m,f*; *(board member)* administrateur(trice) *m,f*; *(of film)* réalisateur(trice) *m,f*; *(of play)* metteur *m* en scène; *Br Law* **D. of Public Prosecutions** = magistrat dont le rôle recouvre à la fois celui du procureur général et celui du procureur de la République

directorate [dɪ'rektər(e)ɪt] *n (board)* conseil *m* d'administration

directorship [dɪ'rektəʃɪp] *n* direction *f*

directory [dɪ'rektərɪ] *n (pl directories) (of phone numbers)* annuaire *m*; *Comptr* répertoire *m*; **(street) d. index** *m* (des rues); *Br* **d. enquiries,** *Am* **d. assistance** renseignements *mpl* (téléphoniques)

dirge [dɜːdʒ] *n* chant *m* funèbre; *Fam Fig* chanson *f* lugubre

dirham [dɪ'ræm] *n* dirham *m*

dirt [dɜːt] *n* **(a)** *(on clothes, body)* saleté *f*; *(mud)* boue *f*; *(soil)* terre *f*; **to treat sb like d.** traiter qn comme un chien; *Fam* **dog d.** crotte *f* de chien; **d. road** *or* **track** chemin *m* de terre **(b)** *Fam (scandal)* cancans *mpl*, ragots *mpl*

dirt-cheap ['dɜːt'tʃiːp] *Fam* **1** *adj* donné(e)
2 *adv* pour trois fois rien

dirty ['dɜːtɪ] **1** *adj* **(a)** *(unclean) (person, hands, clothes)* sale; *(with mud)* crotté(e); **to get d.** se salir; *also Fig* **to get one's hands d.** se salir les mains; *Fig* **to wash one's d. linen in public** laver son linge sale en public **(b)** *Fig (unpleasant, unsavoury)* **it's a d. business** c'est une activité peu reluisante; **to give sb a d. look** regarder qn d'un sale œil; **d. work** sale boulot *m* **(c)** *(book, film, joke)* cochon(onne); *(language, word)* grossier(ère); **d. old man** vieux cochon *m*; **d. weekend** week-end *m* coquin; **"communism" is a d. word nowadays** "communisme" est un mot tabou de nos jours
2 *adv* **(a)** *(fight)* déloyalement **(b)** *(obscenely)* **to talk d.** dire des cochonneries **(c)** *Fam (for emphasis)* vachement; **a d. big hole** un sacré grand trou
3 *vt (pt & pp dirtied)* salir
4 *n Br Fam* **to do the d. on sb** jouer un sale tour à qn

disability [dɪsə'bɪlɪtɪ] *n (pl disabilities) n* handicap *m*, infirmité *f*; **d. allowance** pension *f* d'invalidité

disable [dɪs'eɪbəl] *vt (person)* rendre infirme; *(ship)* désemparer; *(alarm system)* désactiver

disabled [dɪs'eɪbəld] **1** *npl* **the d.** les handicapés *mpl*
2 *adj* handicapé(e); **d. toilet** toilettes *fpl* pour handicapés

disabuse [dɪsə'bjuːz] *vt Formal* **to d. sb (of an idea)** détromper qn

disadvantage [dɪsəd'vɑːntɪdʒ] **1** *n* désavantage *m*, inconvénient *m*; **to be at a d.** être désavantagé(e); **to put sb at a d.** désavantager qn
2 *vt* désavantager

disadvantaged [dɪsəd'vɑːntɪdʒd] *adj* défavorisé(e)

disaffected [dɪsə'fektɪd] adj mécontent(e); (stronger) révolté(e)

disaffection [dɪsə'fekʃən] n désaffection f

disagree [dɪsə'griː] vi (a) (quarrel) ne pas être d'accord; **to d.** with sb (about) ne pas être d'accord avec qn (sur) (b) (of reports, figures) ne pas concorder (c) (of climate, food) **to d.** with sb ne pas réussir à qn

disagreeable [dɪsə'griːəbəl] adj désagréable

disagreement [dɪsə'griːmənt] n (a) (failure to agree) désaccord m; **to be in d.** with sb être en désaccord avec qn (b) (quarrel) différend m (c) (discrepancy) différence f

disallow [dɪsə'laʊ] vt Formal (objection, claim) rejeter; (goal, try) refuser

disappear [dɪsə'pɪə(r)] vi disparaître

disappearance [dɪsə'pɪərəns] n disparition f

disappoint [dɪsə'pɔɪnt] vt décevoir

disappointed [dɪsə'pɔɪntɪd] adj déçu(e) (in or with par)

disappointing [dɪsə'pɔɪntɪŋ] adj décevant(e)

disappointment [dɪsə'pɔɪntmənt] n déception f; **to be a d.** être décevant(e)

disapproval [dɪsə'pruːvəl] n désapprobation f

disapprove [dɪsə'pruːv] vi désapprouver; **to d.** of sth désapprouver qch; **he disapproves of them** ils ne lui plaisent pas

disapproving [dɪsə'pruːvɪŋ] adj (tone, look) désapprobateur(trice); **to be d.** of sth désapprouver qch

disarm [dɪs'ɑːm] vt & vi désarmer

disarmament [dɪs'ɑːməmənt] n désarmement m; **d. talks** conférence f sur le désarmement

disarming [dɪs'ɑːmɪŋ] adj (smile, honesty) désarmant(e)

disarray [dɪsə'reɪ] n désordre m; **in d.** en désordre

disaster [dɪ'zɑːstə(r)] n désastre m; (earthquake, fire, crash) catastrophe f; **d. area** région f sinistrée; Fam Fig (person) maladroit(e) m,f; **d. movie** film m catastrophe

disastrous [dɪ'zɑːstrəs] adj désastreux(euse)

disband [dɪs'bænd] **1** vt (regiment) supprimer; (organization) dissoudre **2** vi (of organization) se dissoudre; (of regiment) être supprimé(e)

disbelief [dɪsbɪ'liːf] n incrédulité f; **in d.** (listen, watch) avec incrédulité

disbelieve [dɪsbɪ'liːv] vt ne pas croire

disburse [dɪs'bɜːs] vt Formal débourser

disc, Am disk [dɪsk] n disque m; Aut **d. brake** frein m à disque; **d. jockey** disc-jockey m

discard [dɪs'kɑːd] vt (person) laisser tomber; (plan, proposal) abandonner; (object) se débarrasser de

discern [dɪ'sɜːn] vt (shape, object) discerner; (sound, difference) percevoir

discernible [dɪ'sɜːnɪbəl] adj (shape, object) discernable; (sound, difference) perceptible

discerning [dɪ'sɜːnɪŋ] adj (person) perspicace, (taste) fin(e)

discharge 1 n ['dɪstʃɑːdʒ] (a) (of patient) sortie f; (authorization) autorisation f de sortie; (of prisoner) mise f en liberté, libération f; (of soldier) libération f; (for unfitness) réforme f (b) (of firearm) décharge f (c) (of gas, chemical) dégagement m; (of pus, fluid) écoulement m
2 vt [dɪs'tʃɑːdʒ] (a) (patient) laisser sortir; (prisoner) libérer; (employee) congédier, renvoyer; (soldier) libérer; (for unfitness) réformer (b) (firearm) décharger (c) (gas, chemical) dégager; (fluid) déverser; **to d. pus** suppurer (d) (duty, debt) s'acquitter de; (fine) payer

disciple [dɪ'saɪpəl] n disciple mf

disciplinary ['dɪsɪplɪnərɪ] adj disciplinaire

discipline ['dɪsɪplɪn] **1** n discipline f **2** vt (punish) punir; **to d.** oneself se discipliner

disclaim [dɪs'kleɪm] vt (renounce) renoncer à; (deny) démentir

disclaimer [dɪs'kleɪmə(r)] n démenti m

disclose [dɪs'kləʊz] vt révéler

disclosure [dɪs'kləʊʒə(r)] n révélation f

disco ['dɪskəʊ] (pl discos) n discothèque f, boîte f (de nuit)

discolour, Am discolor [dɪs'kʌlə(r)] vt (fade) décolorer; (stain) (with age) jaunir; (with smoke) noircir; **to become discoloured** se décolorer

discomfiture [dɪs'kʌmfɪtʃə(r)] n embarras m

discomfort [dɪs'kʌmfət] n (lack of comfort) inconfort m; (pain) légère douleur f; **to be in some d.** éprouver une légère douleur

disconcerting [dɪskən'sɜːtɪŋ] adj déconcertant(e)

disconnect [dɪskə'nekt] vt (gas, electricity, phone) couper; (machine, appliance) débrancher

disconsolate [dɪs'kɒnsələt] adj désespéré(e) (at par)

discontent [dɪskən'tent] n mécontentement m

discontented [dɪskən'tentɪd] adj mécontent(e) (with de)

discontinue [dɪskən'tɪnjuː] vt interrompre; Com **discontinued line** fin f de série

discord ['dɪskɔːd] n discorde f

discordant [dɪs'kɔːdənt] adj (opinions, sound) discordant(e)

discotheque ['dɪskətek] n discothèque f, boîte f (de nuit)

discount 1 n ['dɪskaʊnt] remise f; **at a d.** au rabais **2** vt (a) ['dɪskaʊnt] (price) baisser; (goods) solder (b) [dɪs'kaʊnt] (suggestion, rumours) ignorer, ne pas tenir compte de; (possibility, fact) écarter

discourage [dɪs'kʌrɪdʒ] vt (a) (dishearten) décourager (b) (dissuade) **to d.** sb from doing sth dissuader qn de faire qch

discouragement [dɪs'kʌrɪdʒmənt] n (a) (loss of enthusiasm) découragement m (b) (dissuasion) **to act as or be a d.** (to sth) avoir un effet dissuasif (sur qch)

discouraging [dɪs'kʌrɪdʒɪŋ] adj décourageant(e)

discourse Formal **1** n ['dɪskɔːs] (speech) discours m; (conversation) conversation f **2** vi [dɪs'kɔːs] **to d.** (up)on sth discourir sur qch

discourteous [dɪs'kɜːtɪəs] adj discourtois(e)

discourtesy [dɪs'kɜːtəsɪ] n impolitesse f

discover [dɪs'kʌvə(r)] vt découvrir

discovery [dɪs'kʌvərɪ] (pl discoveries) n découverte f

discredit [dɪs'kredɪt] n discrédit m; **to be a d. to sb/ sth** déshonorer qn/qch; **much to their d., they didn't even apologize** ils n'ont pas présenté mes excuses, ce qui ne leur fait pas honneur **2** vt (person, theory) discréditer

discreet [dɪs'kriːt] adj discret(ète)

discrepancy [dɪs'krepənsɪ] (pl discrepancies) n décalage m (between entre)

discretion [dɪs'kreʃən] n (a) (tact) discrétion f (b) (judgement) jugement m; **at the d. of the management** à la discrétion de la direction; **to use one's own d.** juger par soi-même

discretionary [dɪs'kreʃənərɪ] adj discrétionnaire

discriminate [dɪs'krɪmɪneɪt] **1** vt distinguer (from de) **2** vi **to d. between** faire la différence entre; **to d. against** faire de la discrimination envers; **to be discriminated**

against être victime de discrimination; **to d.** in favour of favoriser

discriminating [dɪsˈkrɪmɪneɪtɪŋ] *adj* perspicace

discrimination [dɪskrɪmɪˈneɪʃən] *n* (**a**) *(bias)* discrimination *f* (**b**) *(taste)* discernement *m* (**c**) *(differentiation)* différenciation *f*

discriminatory [dɪsˈkrɪmɪnətərɪ] *adj* discriminatoire

discursive [dɪsˈkɜːsɪv] *adj* discursif(ive)

discus [ˈdɪskəs] *n* disque *m*

discuss [dɪsˈkʌs] *vt* discuter de

discussion [dɪsˈkʌʃən] *n* discussion *f*; **under d.** en discussion

disdain [dɪsˈdeɪn] **1** *n* dédain *m*
2 *vt* dédaigner; **to d. to do sth** dédaigner de faire qch

disdainful [dɪsˈdeɪnfʊl] *adj* dédaigneux(euse)

disease [dɪˈziːz] *n* maladie *f*

diseased [dɪˈziːzd] *adj* malade

disembark [dɪsemˈbɑːk] *vt & vi* débarquer

disembodied [dɪsɪmˈbɒdɪd] *adj* désincarné(e)

disenchanted [dɪsɪnˈtʃɑːntɪd] *adj* désenchanté(e); **to be d. with** être déçu(e) par qch

disenchantment [dɪsɪnˈtʃɑːntmənt] *n* désenchantement *m*

disengage [dɪsɪnˈɡeɪdʒ] **1** *vt* dégager (**from** de); **to d. oneself from sth** se retirer de qch
2 *vi* se retirer (**from** de); *Mil* cesser le combat

disentangle [dɪsɪnˈtæŋɡəl] *vt* démêler

disfavour, *Am* **disfavor** [dɪsˈfeɪvə(r)] *n* **to be in d.** être en défaveur; **to fall into d. (with sb)** tomber en disgrâce (auprès de qn)

disfigure [dɪsˈfɪɡə(r)] *vt* défigurer

disfigurement [dɪsˈfɪɡəmənt] *n* défigurement *m*

disgrace [dɪsˈɡreɪs] **1** *n (shame)* honte *f*; **to be in d. (with sb)** être en disgrâce (auprès de qn); **to be a d. to one's family/country** déshonorer sa famille/son pays; **it's a d.!** c'est une honte!
2 *vt* déshonorer, couvrir de honte; **to d. oneself** se déshonorer

disgraceful [dɪsˈɡreɪsfʊl] *adj* honteux(euse); **it's d.!** c'est honteux *ou* scandaleux!

disgracefully [dɪsˈɡreɪsfʊlɪ] *adv* scandaleusement, honteusement

disgruntled [dɪsˈɡrʌntəld] *adj* mécontent(e)

disguise [dɪsˈɡaɪz] **1** *n (costume)* déguisement *m*; **in d.** déguisé(e)
2 *vt* déguiser; **to d. oneself as** se déguiser en; **there is no disguising the fact that...** on ne peut pas cacher le fait que...

disgust [dɪsˈɡʌst] **1** *n* dégoût *m*; **to fill sb with d.** remplir qn de dégoût, écœurer qn; **in d.** dégoûté(e), écœuré(e)
2 *vt* dégoûter; **to be disgusted with oneself** se dégoûter

disgusting [dɪsˈɡʌstɪŋ] *adj* répugnant(e)

dish [dɪʃ] **1** *n (bowl, food)* plat *m*; **d. of the day** plat du jour; **dishes** *(crockery)* vaisselle *f*; **to do the dishes** faire la vaisselle
2 *vt Fam* **to d. the dirt** tout raconter
► **dish out** *vt sep (food)* servir; *(money, advice)* distribuer
► **dish up** *vt sep (meal)* servir

disharmony [dɪsˈhɑːmənɪ] *n* désaccord *m*

dishcloth [ˈdɪʃklɒθ] *n (for washing)* lavette *f*; *(for drying)* torchon *m*

disheartening [dɪsˈhɑːtənɪŋ] *adj* décourageant(e)

dishevelled [dɪˈʃevəld] *adj (person, appearance)* débraillé(e); *(hair)* ébouriffé(e); *(clothes)* en désordre

dishonest [dɪsˈɒnɪst] *adj* malhonnête

dishonesty [dɪsˈɒnɪstɪ] *n* malhonnêteté *f*

dishonour, *Am* **dishonor** [dɪsˈɒnə(r)] **1** *n* déshonneur *m*
2 *vt* déshonorer

dishonourable, *Am* **dishonorable** [dɪsˈɒnərəbəl] *adj* déshonorant(e)

dishtowel [ˈdɪʃtaʊəl] *n* torchon *m*

dishwasher [ˈdɪʃwɒʃə(r)] *n (person)* plongeur(euse) *m,f*; *(machine)* lave-vaisselle *m inv*

dishwater [ˈdɪʃwɔːtə(r)] *n also Fig* eau *f* de vaisselle

disillusioned [dɪsɪˈluːʒənd] *adj* désillusionné(e); **to be d. with sb/sth** être déçu(e) par qn/qch; **to become d.** perdre ses illusions

disincentive [dɪsɪnˈsentɪv] *n* **to be a d. (to sth)** avoir un effet dissuasif (sur qch)

disinclination [dɪsɪŋklɪˈneɪʃən] *n* manque *m* d'enthousiasme *(***to do sth** à faire qch)

disinclined [dɪsɪnˈklaɪnd] *adj* **to be d. to do sth** être peu disposé(e) à faire qch

disinfect [dɪsɪnˈfekt] *vt* désinfecter

disinfectant [dɪsɪnˈfektənt] *n* désinfectant *m*

disinformation [dɪsɪnfəˈmeɪʃən] *n* désinformation *f*

disingenuous [dɪsɪnˈdʒenjʊəs] *adj (person, answer)* peu sincère; *(manner, smile)* faux (fausse)

disinherit [dɪsɪnˈherɪt] *vt* déshériter

disintegrate [dɪsˈɪntɪɡreɪt] *vi* se désintégrer; *(of confidence)* s'effriter; *(of marriage, relationship)* se désagréger

disintegration [dɪsɪntɪˈɡreɪʃən] *n* désintégration *f*; *(of marriage, relationship)* désagrégation *f*

disinterest [dɪsˈɪntərɪst] *n (impartiality)* impartialité *f*; *(lack of interest)* désintérêt *m*, indifférence *f*

disinterested [dɪsˈɪntərɪstɪd] *adj (unbiased)* impartial(e); *(uninterested)* indifférent(e)

disinvestment [dɪsɪnˈvestmənt] *n Fin* désinvestissement *m*

disjointed [dɪsˈdʒɔɪntɪd] *adj (style, speech)* décousu(e); *(movements)* saccadé(e)

disk [dɪsk] *n* (**a**) *Comptr* disque *m*; *(floppy)* disquette *f*; **d. drive** unité *f* de disques (**b**) *Am* = **disc**

diskette [dɪsˈket] *n Comptr* disquette *f*

dislike [dɪsˈlaɪk] **1** *n* aversion *f* (**of** or **for** pour); **we have the same likes and dislikes** nous avons les mêmes goûts; **to take a d. to sb/sth** prendre qn/qch en grippe
2 *vt* ne pas aimer; **I don't d. him** il ne me déplaît pas

dislocate [ˈdɪsləkeɪt] *vt* (**a**) *(shoulder, hip)* déboîter; **to d. one's shoulder** se déboîter l'épaule (**b**) *(plan, timetable)* perturber

dislocation [dɪsləˈkeɪʃən] *n* (**a**) *(of shoulder, hip)* déboîtement *m* (**b**) *(of plan, timetable)* perturbation *f*

dislodge [dɪsˈlɒdʒ] *vt (opponent, President)* déloger *(***from** de); *(brick, state)* arracher; *(obstacle)* déplacer; *(something stuck)* décoincer

disloyal [dɪsˈlɔɪəl] *adj* déloyal(e)

disloyalty [dɪsˈlɔɪəltɪ] *n* déloyauté *f*

dismal [ˈdɪzməl] *adj (face, countryside)* lugubre; *(failure, performance)* lamentable; *(future)* sombre

dismantle [dɪsˈmæntəl] *vt (empire, network)* démanteler; *(machine)* démonter

dismay [dɪsˈmeɪ] **1** *n* consternation *f*; **in d.** consterné(e); **(much) to my d.** à ma grande consternation
2 *vt* consterner

dismember [dɪsˈmembə(r)] *vt also Fig* démembrer

dismiss [dɪs'mɪs] vt (a) (from job) renvoyer (b) (send away) congédier; (pupils) libérer; Mil d.! rompez! (c) (thought, theory) rejeter; (proposal, suggestion) écarter; (danger, threat) ignorer; **she is dismissed as an airhead** elle est considérée comme une évaporée (d) Law (case) classer; (appeal, charge) rejeter

dismissal [dɪs'mɪsəl] n (a) (of employee) renvoi m, licenciement m (b) Law (of case) fin f de non-recevoir; (of appeal, charge) rejet m

dismissive [dɪs'mɪsɪv] adj dédaigneux(euse); **to be d. of sb/sth** faire peu de cas de qn/qch

dismount [dɪs'maʊnt] vi (from horse, bicycle) descendre, mettre pied à terre

disobedience [dɪsə'biːdɪəns] n désobéissance f

disobedient [dɪsə'biːdɪənt] adj désobéissant(e); **to be d. to sb** désobéir à qn

disobey [dɪsə'beɪ] vt (person, order) désobéir à; (law) enfreindre

disorder [dɪs'ɔːdə(r)] n (a) (confusion, unrest) désordre m; **in d.** en désordre (b) Med troubles mpl; **a nervous d.** des troubles nerveux

disordered [dɪs'ɔːdəd] adj désordonné(e)

disorderly [dɪs'ɔːdəlɪ] adj (untidy, unruly) désordonné(e); (crowd) agité(e); Law **d. conduct** atteinte f à l'ordre public

disorganization [dɪsɔːɡənaɪ'zeɪʃən] n désorganisation f

disorganized [dɪs'ɔːɡənaɪzd] adj désorganisé(e)

disorientate [dɪs'ɔːrɪənteɪt], **disorient** [dɪs'ɔːrɪənt] vt désorienter

disown [dɪs'əʊn] vt désavouer, renier

disparage [dɪs'pærɪdʒ] vt dénigrer

disparaging [dɪs'pærɪdʒɪŋ] adj méprisant(e)

disparate ['dɪspərɪt] adj disparate

disparity [dɪs'pærɪtɪ] (pl **disparities**) n disparité f

dispassionate [dɪs'pæʃənət] adj (calm) calme; (impartial) impartial(e)

dispatch [dɪs'pætʃ] 1 n (a) (of letter, parcel) expédition f, envoi m (b) (message) dépêche f; Mil **to be mentioned in dispatches** être cité(e) à l'ordre du jour; **d. rider** Mil estafette f; (courier) coursier(ère) m,f (c) Formal (promptness) promptitude f; **with d.** promptement
2 vt (a) (send) envoyer (b) (kill) liquider

dispel [dɪs'pel] (pt & pp **dispelled**) vt dissiper

dispensable [dɪs'pensəbəl] adj dont on peut se passer

dispensary [dɪs'pensərɪ] (pl **dispensaries**) n Med (in pharmacy) officine f; (in hospital) pharmacie f

dispensation [dɪspen'seɪʃən] n Law & Rel (exemption) dispense f (from de)

dispense [dɪs'pens] vt (justice) rendre; (advice) prodiguer; (medication) préparer; (of vending machine) distribuer

▸ **dispense with** vt insep se passer de; **to d. with the need for sth** rendre qch superflu(e)

dispensing chemist [dɪs'pensɪŋ'kemɪst] n Br pharmacien(enne) m,f

dispersal [dɪs'pɜːsəl] n dispersion f

disperse [dɪs'pɜːs] 1 vt (seeds, people) disperser; (knowledge, information) propager
2 vi (of crowd) se disperser; (of darkness, mist, clouds) se dissiper

dispirited [dɪs'pɪrɪtɪd] adj découragé(e), abattu(e)

displace [dɪs'pleɪs] vt (a) (shift) déplacer; **displaced persons** personnes fpl déplacées (b) (supplant) remplacer, supplanter

displacement [dɪs'pleɪsmənt] n (a) (of water, people) déplacement m (b) (substitution) remplacement m

display [dɪs'pleɪ] 1 n (a) (of goods) étalage m; (of handicrafts, paintings) exposition f; **on d.** à l'étalage; (sign, notice) affiché(e); **d. copy** (of book) exemplaire m de démonstration; **d. window** vitrine f (b) (demonstration) démonstration f (c) Comptr écran m
2 vt (a) (goods) exposer; (sign, notice) afficher (b) (emotion) manifester; (talent, concern, ignorance) faire preuve de

displease [dɪs'pliːz] vt mécontenter, contrarier; **to be displeased with sb/sth** ne pas être satisfait(e) de qn/qch

displeasure [dɪs'pleʒə(r)] n déplaisir m, mécontentement m

disposable [dɪs'pəʊzəbəl] adj (a) (nappy, lighter) jetable (b) (funds, income) disponible

disposal [dɪs'pəʊzəl] n (a) (getting rid) enlèvement m, élimination f (b) (of property) cession f, vente f (c) (availability) **to have sth at one's d.** avoir qch à sa disposition

dispose [dɪs'pəʊz] vt Formal (arrange) disposer

▸ **dispose of** vt insep (a) (rubbish) jeter, se débarrasser de; (problem) régler (b) (kill) se débarrasser de

disposed [dɪs'pəʊzd] adj (willing) **to be d. to do sth** être disposé(e) à faire qch

disposition [dɪspə'zɪʃən] n (a) (temperament) tempérament m, nature f (b) (inclination) tendance f; **to have a d. to do sth** avoir tendance à faire qch (c) Formal (arrangement) disposition f

dispossess [dɪspə'zes] vt déposséder (of de)

disproportionate [dɪsprə'pɔːʃənət] adj disproportionné(e) (to à)

disprove [dɪs'pruːv] (pp **disproved**, Law **disproven** [dɪs'prəʊvən]) vt réfuter

dispute [dɪs'pjuːt] 1 n (a) (debate) controverse f; (argument) dispute f; **the matter in d.** l'objet de la controverse; **it's beyond d.** c'est incontestable; **it's open to d.** c'est contestable; (industrial) conflit m social
2 vt (discuss) disputer; (call into question) contester
3 vi se quereller (with/about avec/à propos de)

disqualification [dɪskwɒlɪfɪ'keɪʃən] n (from competition) disqualification f; **d. from driving** retrait m de permis

disqualify [dɪs'kwɒlɪfaɪ] (pt & pp **disqualified**) vt (from competition) disqualifier; (from de); **to d. sb from driving** retirer le permis de conduire à qn

disquiet [dɪs'kwaɪət] n inquiétude f

disregard [dɪsrɪ'ɡɑːd] 1 n mépris m
2 vt ignorer, ne tenir aucun compte de

disrepair [dɪsrɪ'peə(r)] n délabrement m; **in (a state of) d.** délabré(e); **to fall into d.** se délabrer

disreputable [dɪs'repjʊtəbəl] adj (person) peu recommandable; (behaviour) peu honorable; (neighbourhood, pub) mal famé(e)

disrepute [dɪsrɪ'pjuːt] n discrédit m; **to bring sb/sth into d.** discréditer qn/qch; **to fall into d.** tomber en discrédit

disrespect [dɪsrɪ'spekt] n irrespect m; **to treat sb with d.** manquer de respect à qn; **I meant no d.** je ne voulais pas être irrespectueux

disrespectful [dɪsrɪ'spektfʊl] adj irrespectueux(euse); **to be d. to sb** manquer de respect à qn

disrupt [dɪs'rʌpt] vt perturber

disruption [dɪs'rʌpʃən] n (of traffic, life, routine) perturbation f; (of meeting) interruption f

disruptive [dɪs'rʌptɪv] adj perturbateur(trice); **to be d.** faire du chahut

dissatisfaction [dɪsætɪsˈfækʃən] n mécontentement m (**with** envers)

dissatisfied [dɪˈsætɪsfaɪd] adj mécontent(e) (**with** de)

dissect [dɪˈsekt] vt also Fig disséquer

dissemble [dɪˈsembəl] vt & vi dissimuler

disseminate [dɪˈsemɪneɪt] **1** vt propager, répandre **2** vi se propager, se répandre

dissension [dɪˈsenʃən] n dissension f

dissent [dɪˈsent] **1** n désaccord m **2** vi être en désaccord (**from** avec)

dissenter [dɪˈsentə(r)] n Pol dissident(e) m,f

dissenting [dɪˈsentɪŋ] adj dissident(e)

dissertation [dɪsəˈteɪʃən] n mémoire m

disservice [dɪˈsɜːvɪs] n to do sb/sth a d. rendre un mauvais service à qn/qch

dissident [ˈdɪsɪdənt] n & adj dissident(e) m,f

dissimilar [dɪˈsɪmɪlə(r)] adj différent(e) (**to** de)

dissipate [ˈdɪsɪpeɪt] **1** vt (fears, doubts) dissiper; (money, energy) gaspiller **2** vi (of mist, doubts) se dissiper

dissipation [dɪsɪˈpeɪʃən] n (debauchery) débauche f

dissociate [dɪˈsəʊsɪeɪt] vt dissocier (**from** de); **to d. oneself from sb/sth** se dissocier ou se désolidariser de qn/qch

dissolute [ˈdɪsəluːt] adj dissolu(e)

dissolve [dɪˈzɒlv] **1** vt dissoudre **2** vi se dissoudre; **to d. into tears** fondre en larmes

dissuade [dɪˈsweɪd] vt **to d. sb from doing sth** dissuader qn de faire qch

distance [ˈdɪstəns] **1** n distance f; **from a d.** de loin; **in the d.** au loin; **within five minutes' walking d.** à cinq minutes de marche; **a short d. away** tout près; **some d. away** assez loin; **to keep one's d.** garder ses distances; **to keep sb at a d.** tenir qn à distance; Sp & Fig **to go the d.** tenir la distance; **d. learning** enseignement m à distance **2** vt **to d. oneself from sb/sth** prendre ses distances vis-à-vis de qn/qch

distant [ˈdɪstənt] adj (**a**) (far-off) lointain(e); **in the d. past** il y a très longtemps; **in the d. future** dans un avenir lointain; **five kilometres d.** à cinq kilomètres de distance (**b**) (reserved) distant(e) (**c**) (distracted) distrait(e); **she had a d. look** son regard était perdu dans le vague

distantly [ˈdɪstəntlɪ] adv (**a**) **to be d. related to sb** être un parent éloigné de qn (**b**) (distractedly) distraitement

distaste [dɪsˈteɪst] n dégoût m (**for** pour)

distasteful [dɪsˈteɪstfʊl] adj déplaisant(e)

distemper¹ [dɪsˈtempə(r)] n (animal disease) maladie f de Carré

distemper² n (paint) détrempe f

distend [dɪsˈtend] **1** vt distendre **2** vi se distendre

distil, Am **distill** [dɪsˈtɪl] (pt & pp **distilled**) vt distiller

distillery [dɪsˈtɪlərɪ] (pl **distilleries**) n distillerie f

distinct [dɪsˈtɪŋkt] adj (**a**) (different) distinct(e) (**from** de); **as d. from** par opposition à (**b**) (clear) clair(e); (preference, improvement, difference) net (nette); **it's a d. possibility** c'est fort possible

distinction [dɪsˈtɪŋkʃən] n (**a**) (difference) distinction f; **to draw a d. between** faire une distinction entre (**b**) (honour, excellence) distinction f; Ironic **I had the d. of coming last** j'ai eu l'honneur de venir en dernier; **a writer/scientist of d.** un écrivain/scientifique réputé; **with d.** (perform, serve) brillamment (**c**) (in exam) mention f bien

distinctive [dɪsˈtɪŋktɪv] adj distinctif(ive)

distinctly [dɪsˈtɪŋktlɪ] adv (**a**) (clearly) (speak, hear) distinctement; (remember) très bien; **I d. told you not to do it** je t'ai clairement dit de ne pas le faire (**b**) (decidedly) (better, easier) nettement; (stupid, ill-mannered) vraiment

distinguish [dɪsˈtɪŋgwɪʃ] **1** vt (**a**) (recognize) distinguer (**b**) (characterize, differentiate) distinguer (**from** de); **distinguishing marks** (on passport) signes mpl particuliers (**c**) **to d. oneself (by sth/by doing sth)** se distinguer (par qch/en faisant qch) **2** vi **to d. between** faire la distinction entre

distinguished [dɪsˈtɪŋgwɪʃd] adj (performance, career) brillant(e); (person, air) distingué(e)

distort [dɪsˈtɔːt] vt also Fig déformer

distorted [dɪsˈtɔːtɪd] adj also Fig déformé(e)

distortion [dɪsˈtɔːʃən] n also Fig distorsion f, déformation f

distract [dɪsˈtrækt] vt distraire; **to d. sb's attention** détourner l'attention de qn; **to be easily distracted** se laisser facilement distraire

distracted [dɪsˈtræktɪd] adj préoccupé(e)

distracting [dɪsˈtræktɪŋ] adj gênant(e), qui distrait

distraction [dɪsˈtrækʃən] n (**a**) (interruption, amusement) distraction f (**b**) (madness) **to drive sb to d.** rendre qn fou (folle)

distraught [dɪsˈtrɔːt] adj angoissé(e); **d. with grief** fou (folle) de douleur

distress [dɪsˈtres] **1** n (mental) désarroi m; (physical) douleur f; **to be in d.** (mentally) être bouleversé(e); (physically) souffrir; (of ship) être en détresse; **d. signal** signal m de détresse **2** vt (upset) bouleverser

distressed [dɪsˈtrest] adj bouleversé(e)

distressing [dɪsˈtresɪŋ] adj bouleversant(e)

distribute [dɪsˈtrɪbjuːt] vt (give out) & Com (supply) distribuer; (spread out) répartir

distribution [dɪstrɪˈbjuːʃən] n (giving out) & Com (supplying) distribution f; (spreading out) répartition f; **d. of wealth** distribution des richesses; Com **d. cost** coût m de distribution; **d. rights** droits mpl de distribution

distributor [dɪsˈtrɪbjʊtə(r)] n (**a**) (person, company) distributeur(trice) m,f; (of cars) concessionnaire mf (**b**) Aut distributeur m

district [ˈdɪstrɪkt] n (of country) région f; (of town, city) quartier m; (administrative) district m; Am **d. attorney** ≃ procureur m de la République; Br **d. council** conseil m municipal; Br **d. nurse** infirmière f visiteuse

distrust [dɪsˈtrʌst] **1** n méfiance f (**of** à l'égard de) **2** vt se méfier de

distrustful [dɪsˈtrʌstfʊl] adj méfiant(e); **to be d. of** se méfier de

disturb [dɪsˈtɜːb] vt (**a**) (interrupt) déranger; (criminal) surprendre; (someone's sleep) troubler; Law **to d. the peace** troubler l'ordre public (**b**) (worry) perturber (**c**) (disarrange) (papers, room) déranger; (surface of water) agiter; (ground) remuer

disturbance [dɪsˈtɜːbəns] n (**a**) (nuisance) dérangement m (**b**) (atmospheric, emotional) perturbation f (**c**) (fight) bagarre f, (riot) émeute f; **to cause** ou **create a d.** semer le désordre; Law troubler l'ordre public

disturbed [dɪsˈtɜːbd] adj (night, sleep) agité(e); (mentally, emotionally) perturbé(e)

disturbing [dɪsˈtɜːbɪŋ] adj perturbant(e)

disunity [dɪsˈjuːnɪtɪ] n désunion f

disuse [dɪsˈjuːs] n **to fall into d.** tomber en désuétude

ditch [dɪtʃ] **1** n (at roadside) fossé m; (as defence) douve f; (for drainage) rigole f
2 vt Fam (get rid of) (thing) se débarrasser de; (plan, idea) abandonner; (boyfriend, girlfriend) plaquer

dither ['dɪðə(r)] Fam **1** n to be in a d. être dans tous ses états
2 vi hésiter, tergiverser; **stop dithering!** décide-toi!

ditto ['dɪtəʊ] adv idem; Fam I'm bored – d. je m'ennuie – itou ou moi aussi

ditty ['dɪtɪ] (pl ditties) n Fam chansonnette f

divan [dɪ'væn] n divan m; d. bed divan-lit m

dive [daɪv] **1** n (a) (of swimmer) plongeon m; (of submarine, diver) plongée f; to make a d. for sth (rush) se précipiter vers qch; to go into a d. (of plane) piquer du nez (b) Fam Pej (place) bouge m
2 vi (Am pt dove [dəʊv]) plonger; (of plane) piquer; to d. for cover plonger à couvert; to d. for the exit/into the bar se précipiter à la sortie/au bar

diver ['daɪvə(r)] n plongeur(euse) m,f; (deep sea) scaphandrier m

diverge [daɪ'vɜːdʒ] vi (of rays, opinions) diverger; (of roads) se séparer; (of people) avoir des opinions divergentes

divergence [daɪ'vɜːdʒəns] n divergence f

divergent [daɪ'vɜːdʒənt], **diverging** [daɪ'vɜːdʒɪŋ] adj divergent(e)

diverse [daɪ'vɜːs] adj divers(e)

diversification [daɪvɜːsɪfɪ'keɪʃən] n diversification f

diversify [daɪ'vɜːsɪfaɪ] (pt & pp diversified) **1** vt diversifier
2 vi se diversifier

diversion [daɪ'vɜːʃən] n (a) (of traffic) déviation f; (of plane, funds) détournement m; to create a d. faire diversion (b) (amusement) distraction f

diversity [daɪ'vɜːsɪtɪ] n diversité f

divert [daɪ'vɜːt, dɪ'vɜːt] vt (a) (traffic) dévier; (plane, funds, attention) détourner (b) (amuse) to d. oneself se distraire

divest [daɪ'vest] vt Formal to d. sb of sth (authority) priver qn de qch; (possession) débarrasser qn de qch

divide [dɪ'vaɪd] **1** vt (a) (money, food) partager (between/among entre); to d. sth in two/three diviser qch en deux/trois (by par) (c) (separate) séparer (from de)
2 vi (of road) bifurquer; (of group) se diviser; to d. and rule diviser pour régner
3 n fossé m

▸ **divide up** vt sep partager

divided [dɪ'vaɪdɪd] adj divisé(e)

dividend ['dɪvɪdend] n dividende m; Fig to pay dividends porter ses fruits

dividers [dɪ'vaɪdəz] npl (mathematical instrument) compas m à pointe sèche

dividing [dɪ'vaɪdɪŋ] adj d. line ligne f de démarcation; d. wall mur m de séparation

divine [dɪ'vaɪn] **1** adj also Fig divin(e)
2 vt deviner

diving ['daɪvɪŋ] n (in swimming pool) plongeon m; (subaqua) plongée f; d. bell cloche f à plongeur; d. board plongeoir m; d. suit scaphandre m

divinity [dɪ'vɪnɪtɪ] (pl divinities) n (a) (divine nature, god) divinité f (b) (subject) théologie f; (in school) instruction f religieuse

divisible [dɪ'vɪzɪbəl] adj divisible

division [dɪ'vɪʒən] n (a) (separation) partage m (b) (distribution) répartition f, partage m; d. of labour division

f du travail (c) (discord) division f (d) (unit) division f; first/second d. (in sporting league) première/deuxième division

divisive [dɪ'vaɪsɪv] adj qui crée des divisions

divorce [dɪ'vɔːs] **1** n divorce m; d. proceedings procédure f de divorce; to file for d. demander le divorce; to get a d. (from) divorcer (d'avec)
2 vt (a) (husband, wife) divorcer de; to get divorced (from sb) divorcer (de qn) (b) Fig séparer (from de)
3 vi divorcer

divorcee [dɪvɔː'siː] n divorcé(e) m,f

divulge [daɪ'vʌldʒ] vt divulguer

DIY [diːaɪ'waɪ] n (abbr do-it-yourself) bricolage m

dizzy ['dɪzɪ] adj (a) (unsteady) étourdi(e); to feel d. avoir le vertige; Fig to reach the d. heights of... atteindre les hauteurs vertigineuses de...; d. spell étourdissement m (b) Fam (frivolous) écervelé(e); a d. blonde une blonde évaporée

DJ ['diːdʒeɪ] n (a) (abbr disc jockey) DJ m (b) Fam (abbr dinner jacket) smoking m

Djibouti [dʒɪ'buːtɪ] n Djibouti

DNA [diːen'eɪ] n (abbr deoxyribonucleic acid) ADN m

do¹ [dəʊ] n Mus do m

do² [duː]

Les formes négatives sont **don't/doesn't** et **didn't**, qui deviennent **do not/does not** et **did** à l'écrit, dans un style plus soutenu.

1 v aux (3rd person singular does [dʌz], pt did [dɪd], pp done [dʌn]) (a) (in negatives) I don't speak Spanish je ne parle pas espagnol; I didn't see him je ne l'ai pas vu
(b) (in questions) do you speak French? (est-ce que) tu parles français?; did you see him? (est-ce que) tu l'as vu?; don't you speak French? tu ne parles pas français?; didn't you see him? tu ne l'as pas vu?
(c) (for emphasis) he does speak French! mais oui, il parle français!; I didn't see him! mais non, je ne l'ai pas vu!; it doesn't matter – it does matter! ce n'est pas grave – si, c'est grave!
(d) (as substitute for main verb) she sings better than I do elle chante mieux que moi; if you want to speak to her, do it now si tu veux lui parler, fais-le tout de suite; do you speak Spanish? – yes, I do/no, I don't parlez-vous espagnol? – oui/non; I like Paris – so do I j'aime Paris – moi aussi; you left the door unlocked – so I did tu as laissé la porte ouverte – effectivement; you said you'd call me – no, I didn't tu as dit que tu m'appelerais – non, ce n'est pas vrai
(e) (in tag questions) you speak French, don't you? vous parlez français, n'est-ce pas ou non?; Paul doesn't live there, does he? Paul n'habite pas là, si?; they said they'd come, didn't they? ils ont bien dit qu'ils viendraient, non?; you didn't see her, did you? est-ce que tu l'as vue ou pas?

2 vt (a) (in general) faire; what do you do? (what's your job?) que faites-vous dans la vie?; don't do that again! ne refais jamais ça!; what are you going to do about it? qu'est-ce que tu vas faire?
(b) (activity) faire; to do one's homework/the dishes faire ses devoirs/la vaisselle; to do one's hair se coiffer; to do one's teeth se brosser les dents; Fam to do drugs se droguer; Fam you do good food here ils font de la bonne cuisine ici; it just isn't done! ça ne se fait pas, c'est tout!; Fam let's do lunch! on se fait une bouffe?
(c) (have effect on) to do sb good faire du bien à qn; that hairstyle does nothing/does a lot for her cette coiffure ne la flatte pas/la flatte; this music does nothing for me cette musique ne me plaît pas tellement

(d) *(be enough for)* **will $10 do you?** est-ce que 10 dollars te suffiront?; **that'll do me** ça m'ira

(e) *(study)* faire; **to do French/physics** faire du français/de la physique

(f) *(with speed, distance)* **the car was doing 100 (miles per hour)** ≃ la voiture faisait du 160 (à l'heure); **we did 500 km on the first day** nous avons fait 500 km le premier jour

(g) *Br Fam (cheat)* avoir; **I've been done!** je me suis fait avoir!

(h) *Br Fam (prosecute)* pincer; **to get done for speeding** se faire pincer pour excès de vitesse

3 *vi* **(a)** *(act)* **to do well/badly** bien/mal se débrouiller; **do as you're told** fais ce qu'on te dit; **you would do well to accept** tu ferais bien d'accepter; **how do you do?** enchanté(e); **how are you doing?** (comment) ça va?

(b) *(be enough)* **two bottles of wine will do** deux bouteilles de vin suffiront; **that'll do** *(is satisfactory)* ça ira; *(stop it)* ça suffit maintenant!

4 *n* **(a)** **the do's and don'ts** les choses *fpl* à faire et à ne pas faire

(b) *(pl* **dos)** *Fam (party)* fête *f*

▸ **do away with** *vt insep* **(a)** *(abolish)* supprimer **(b)** *Fam (kill)* zigouiller

▸ **do down** *vt sep* rabaisser; **to do oneself down** se rabaisser

▸ **do for** *vt insep Fam* **to be done for** être fichu(e)

▸ **do in** *vt sep Br Fam* **(a)** *(murder)* zigouiller **(b)** *(exhaust)* **to be done in** être complètement crevé(e) **(c)** *(injure)* **to do one's back/knee in** se bousiller le dos/genou

▸ **do out of** *vt sep Br Fam* **to do sb out of sth** *(job)* priver qn de qch; *(money)* faire perdre qch à qn

▸ **do over** *vt sep Br Fam (beat up)* **to d. sb over** tabasser qn

▸ **do up** **1** *vt sep* **(a)** *(fasten)* fermer; *(shoelaces)* attacher **(b)** *(wrap)* envelopper **(c)** *Br (improve appearance of)* restaurer; *(room, house)* rénover; *Fam* **to do oneself up** *(dress smartly)* se faire beau (belle)

2 *vi (of clothes)* se fermer

▸ **do with** *vt insep* **(a)** *(benefit from)* **I could do with a cup of tea** je prendrais bien une tasse de thé; **you could do with a haircut** tu aurais bien besoin de te faire couper les cheveux **(b)** *(be connected with)* **to have nothing to do with sb/sth** *(be unconnected to)* n'avoir rien à voir avec qn/qch; *(not get involved with)* n'avoir rien à faire avec qn/qch; **I had nothing to do with it** je n'ai rien à voir là-dedans; **it's nothing to do with you** *(not your business)* ça ne te regarde pas **(c)** *(finish using)* **to have done with sth** avoir fini avec qch; **have you done with the scissors yet?** est-ce que tu as fini avec les ciseaux?; **it's all over and done with** c'est du passé

▸ **do without** **1** *vt insep* se passer de

2 *vi* se priver

doc [dɒk] *n Fam (doctor)* toubib *m*

docile ['dəʊsaɪl] *adj* docile

dock¹ [dɒk] **1** *n (for ships)* dock *m*; **d. workers** dockers *mpl*
2 *vi (of ship)* accoster; *(of two spacecraft)* s'arrimer

dock² *n Law* banc *m* des accusés

dock³ *vt* **(a)** *(tail)* couper **(b)** *(wages)* faire une retenue sur

docker ['dɒkə(r)] *n* docker *m*

dockyard ['dɒkjɑːd] *n* chantier *m* naval

doctor ['dɒktə(r)] **1** *n* **(a)** *(medical)* docteur *m*, médecin *m*; **to go to the d.('s)** aller chez le médecin; *Fam Fig* **just what the d. ordered** exactement ce qu'il me fallait **(b)** *Univ* docteur *m*; **D. of Science** docteur ès sciences
2 *vt* **(a)** *Fam (accounts, evidence)* falsifier **(b)** *(cat)* castrer

doctorate ['dɒktərɪt] *n Univ* doctorat *m* **(in** en)

doctrinaire [dɒktrɪ'neə(r)] *adj* doctrinaire

doctrinal [dɒk'traɪnəl] *adj* doctrinal(e)

doctrine ['dɒktrɪn] *n* doctrine *f*

document 1 *n* ['dɒkjʊmənt] document *m*; *Comptr* **d. reader** lecteur *m* de documents
2 *vt* ['dɒkjʊment] **(a)** *(show in detail)* présenter **(b)** *(support)* étayer; **the first documented case** le premier cas établi

documentary [dɒkjʊ'mentərɪ] **1** *n (pl* **documentaries)** *(TV programme)* documentaire *m*
2 *adj (film)* documentaire; *(proof)* littéral(e)

documentation [dɒkjʊmen'teɪʃən] *n* documentation *f*

dodder ['dɒdə(r)] *vi* marcher d'un pas hésitant

doddering ['dɒdərɪŋ] *adj (walk)* hésitant(e); **a d. old fool** un vieux gâteux (une vieille gâteuse)

doddle ['dɒdəl] *n Br Fam* **it's a d.** c'est simple comme bonjour

dodge [dɒdʒ] **1** *n* **(a)** *Fam (trick)* truc *m*, combine *f*; **tax d.** combine pour payer moins d'impôts **(b)** *(movement)* écart *m*
2 *vt (blow, responsibility, question)* esquiver; *(person)* éviter; *(police)* échapper à
3 *vi* **to d. (out of the way)** faire un bond de côté

dodgems ['dɒdʒəmz] *npl Br* autos *fpl* tamponneuses

dodgy ['dɒdʒɪ] *adj Br Fam (suspect)* louche; *(not working properly)* en mauvais état; *(risky)* risqué(e); *(milk, meat)* douteux(euse)

dodo ['dəʊdəʊ] *(pl* **dodoes** *or* **dodos)** *n* dodo *m*, dronte *m*; **(as) dead as a d.** mort(e) et enterré(e)

DOE [diːəʊ'iː] *n Br (abbr* **Department of the Environment)** ≃ ministère *m* de l'Environnement

doe [dəʊ] *n (deer)* biche *f*; *(rabbit)* lapine *f*

does [dʌz] *3rd person singular of* **do**

doesn't ['dʌzənt] = **does not**

doff [dɒf] *vt* **to d. one's cap to sb** se découvrir devant qn

dog [dɒg] **1** *n* **(a)** *(animal)* chien *m*; **d. biscuit** biscuit *m* pour chien; **d. collar** collier *m* de chien; *Fam (of cleric)* col *m* blanc *(d'un religieux)*; **d. food** nourriture *f* pour chien; **d. handler** maître-chien *m*; **to the d. paddle** nager comme un petit chien; **to the d. racing** courses *fpl* de lévriers; **d. tag** plaque *f* d'identité
(b) *Fam (person)* **you lucky d.!** sacré veinard!; **dirty d.** sale type *m*
(c) *Fam Pej (ugly woman)* laideron *m*
(d) *Am (hot dog)* hot dog *m*
(e) *(idioms) Fam* **to lead a d.'s life** avoir une vie de chien; *Fam* **to make a d.'s breakfast** *or* **dinner of sth** gâcher qch; *Fam* **it's a d.-eat-d. world** c'est un monde sans pitié; *Fam* **to go to the dogs** *(of place)* aller à vau-l'eau; *(of person)* filer un mauvais coton; *Fam* **to be a d. in the manger** être un empêcheur de tourner en rond; *Prov* **you can't teach an old d. new tricks** ce n'est pas aux vieilles habitudes qu'on la vie dure; *Prov* **every d. has its day** tout le monde a son heure de gloire
2 *vt (pt & pp* **dogged)** *(follow)* suivre de près; **to d. sb's footsteps** être sur les talons de qn; **to be dogged by misfortune** être poursuivi(e) par la malchance

dog-eared ['dɒgɪəd] *adj (page)* corné(e); *(book)* aux pages cornées

dogfight ['dɒgfaɪt] *n (between planes)* combat *m* aérien; *(between people)* bagarre *f*

dogfish ['dɒgfɪʃ] *n* roussette *f*

dogged ['dɒgɪd] *adj* tenace

doggerel ['dɒgərəl] *n (comical)* poésie *f* burlesque; *(bad)* vers *mpl* de mirliton

doggy ['dɒgɪ] *(pl* **doggies)** *n Fam* toutou *m*; **to the d. paddle** nager comme un petit chien; **d. bag** = petit sac fourni par certains restaurants pour que les clients puissent emporter les restes

doghouse [ˈdɒghaʊs] *n Fam* **to be in the d.** ne pas être en odeur de sainteté

dogma [ˈdɒgmə] *n* dogme *m*

dogmatic [dɒgˈmætɪk] *adj* dogmatique

do-gooder [ˈduːˈgʊdə(r)] *n Fam Pej* âme *f* charitable

dogsbody [ˈdɒgzbɒdɪ] (*pl* **dogsbodies**) *n Br Fam* factotum *m*

dog-tired [ˈdɒgˈtaɪəd] *adj Fam* claqué(e), crevé(e)

dogwood [ˈdɒgwʊd] *n* cornouiller *m*

doh [dəʊ] *n Mus* do *m*

doily [ˈdɔɪlɪ] (*pl* **doilies**) *n* napperon *m*

doing [ˈduːɪŋ] *n* (**a**) **this is his d.** c'est son œuvre; **it was none of my d.** je n'y étais pour rien; **that takes some d.** il faut le faire (**b**) **doings** faits *mpl* et gestes *mpl*

do-it-yourself [duːɪtjɔːˈself] *n* bricolage *m*; **a d. enthusiast** un(e) adepte du bricolage

doldrums [ˈdɒldrəmz] *npl* **to be in the d.** (*of person*) broyer du noir; (*of economy*) être en plein marasme

dole [dəʊl] *n Br Fam* (indemnités *fpl* de) chômage *m*; **to be on the d.** être au chômage; *Fig* **to join the d. queue** se retrouver au chômage

▸ **dole out** *vt sep Fam* distribuer

doleful [ˈdəʊlfʊl] *adj* triste

doll [dɒl] *n* poupée *f*; *Br* **d.'s** *or Am* **d. house** maison *f* de poupée

▸ **doll up** *vt sep Fam* **to d. oneself up** se pomponner

dollar [ˈdɒlə(r)] *n* dollar *m*; **d. bill** billet *m* de un dollar

dollop [ˈdɒləp] *n Fam* (*of cream, mashed potato*) bonne cuillerée *f*; (*of mud, clay*) tas *m*

dolly [ˈdɒlɪ] (*pl* **dollies**) *n* (**a**) *Fam (toy)* poupée *f* (**b**) *(for camera)* chariot *m*

dolphin [ˈdɒlfɪn] *n* dauphin *m*

dolt [dəʊlt] *n Fam* andouille *f*

domain [dəˈmeɪn] *n also Fig* domaine *m*

dome [dəʊm] *n* dôme *m*

domestic [dəˈmestɪk] *adj* (**a**) *(appliance, use, tasks)* ménager(ère); *(animal)* domestique; **d. bliss** bonheur *m* familial; **d. servant** domestique *mf* (**b**) *(policy, flight, affairs)* intérieur(e); *(economy, currency)* national(e)

domesticate [dəˈmestɪkeɪt] *vt (animal)* domestiquer; *Hum* **to be domesticated** *(of person)* se débrouiller plutôt bien avec les travaux ménagers

domicile [ˈdɒmɪsaɪl] *n Law* domicile *m*

dominance [ˈdɒmɪnəns] *n (of disease, gene)* dominance *f*; *(of race, political party)* prédominance *f*; *(of person)* supériorité *f*

dominant [ˈdɒmɪnənt] *adj* dominant(e); *(person, character)* dominateur(trice)

dominate [ˈdɒmɪneɪt] *vt & vi* dominer

domination [dɒmɪˈneɪʃən] *n* domination *f*

domineering [dɒmɪˈnɪərɪŋ] *adj* dominateur(trice)

Dominica [dəˈmɪnɪkə] *n* la Dominique

Dominican [dəˈmɪnɪkən] **1** *n* Dominicain(e) *m,f* **2** *adj* dominicain(e); **the D. Republic** la République Dominicaine

dominion [dəˈmɪnjən] *n* domination *f*

domino [ˈdɒmɪnəʊ] (*pl* **dominoes**) *n* domino *m*; *Pol & Fig* **d. effect** effet *m* d'entraînement

don¹ [dɒn] *n Br Univ* professeur *m* d'université *(surtout à Oxford et Cambridge)*

don² *(pt & pp* **donned**) *vt Formal (clothing)* mettre, revêtir

donate [dəˈneɪt] *vt* faire don de; **to d. blood** donner son sang

donation [dəˈneɪʃən] *n* donation *f*; don *m*

done [dʌn] *pp of* do

donkey [ˈdɒŋkɪ] (*pl* **donkeys**) *n (animal)* & *Fam (person)* âne *m*; *Fam* **I haven't seen her for d.'s years** je ne l'ai pas vue depuis une éternité; *Fam* **to talk the hind legs off a d.** avoir la langue bien pendue; **d. jacket** ≃ caban *m*; *Fam* **d. work** travail *m* pénible

donor [ˈdəʊnə(r)] *n* donneur(euse) *m,f*; **d. card** carte *f* de donneur d'organe

don't [dəʊnt] = do not

donut [ˈdəʊnʌt] *n Am* beignet *m*

doodle [ˈduːdəl] **1** *n* gribouillis *m*, gribouillage *m* **2** *vi* gribouiller

doom [duːm] *n* destin *m* (funeste); **to be all d. and gloom** voir tout en noir **2** *vt* **to be doomed** *(of person) (unlucky)* être marqué(e) par le destin; *(about to die)* être perdu(e); **to be doomed (to failure)** *(of project)* être voué(e) à l'échec; **to be doomed to do sth** être condamné(e) à faire qch

doom-laden [ˈduːmleɪdən] *adj* funeste, sinistre

doomsday [ˈduːmzdeɪ] *n* jour *m* du Jugement dernier; **till d.** indéfiniment

door [dɔː(r)] *n* porte *f*; *(of train, car)* portière *f*; **to answer the d.** aller ouvrir (la porte); **to see sb to the d.** raccompagner qn à la porte; **to shut the d. in sb's face** fermer la porte au nez de qn; **she lives two doors away** elle habite deux portes plus loin; *Fig* **to lay sth at sb's d.** imputer qch à qn; **out of doors** dehors, en plein air; **d. handle** poignée *f* de porte; *Am* **d. knocker** heurtoir *m*

doorbell [ˈdɔːbel] *n* sonnette *f*

doorkeeper [ˈdɔːkiːpə(r)] *n* portier *m*

doorknob [ˈdɔːnɒb] *n* bouton *m* de porte

doorman [ˈdɔːmən] *n (in hotel)* portier *m*; *(in block of flats)* concierge *m*

doormat [ˈdɔːmæt] *n* paillasson *m*; *Fig (person)* chiffe *f* molle; *Fig* **to treat sb like a d.** traiter qn comme un moins que rien

doorpost [ˈdɔːpəʊst] *n* montant *m* de porte

doorstep [ˈdɔːstep] *n* pas *m* de la porte, seuil *m*; *Fig* **on one's d.** à deux pas

doorstop [ˈdɔːstɒp] *n (fixed)* butoir *m*; *(wedge)* cale-porte *m*

door-to-door [ˈdɔːtəˈdɔː(r)] *adj* **d. canvassing** porte-à-porte *m* électoral; **d. salesman** démarcheur *m*

doorway [ˈdɔːweɪ] *n* porte *f*; **in the d.** dans l'embrasure de la porte

dope [dəʊp] **1** *n* (**a**) *very Fam (cannabis)* shit *m*; *Fam* **d. test** *(for athlete)* contrôle *m* antidopage (**b**) *Fam (idiot)* andouille *f* **2** *vt (person, horse) (to make faster)* doper; *(to make slower)* droguer; *(food, drink)* mettre une drogue dans

dopey [ˈdəʊpɪ] *adj Fam* idiot(e)

dorm [dɔːm] *n Fam (dormitory)* dortoir *m*

dormant [ˈdɔːmənt] *adj (volcano)* en sommeil; *(conflict, emotion)* latent(e); *(idea)* qui sommeille

dormitory [ˈdɔːmɪtərɪ] (*pl* **dormitories**) *n* (**a**) *(room)* dortoir *m*; **d. town** cité-dortoir *f* (**b**) *Am Univ* résidence *f* universitaire

dormouse [ˈdɔːmaʊs] (*pl* **dormice** [ˈdɔːmaɪs]) *n* loir *m*

dorsal [ˈdɔːsəl] *adj* dorsal(e)

DOS [dɒs] *n Comptr (abbr* **disk operating system**) DOS *m*

dose [dəʊs] **1** *n (amount)* dose *f*; **a bad d. of (the) flu** une bonne grippe; **to have a d. of measles** avoir la rougeole **2** *vt Fam* bourrer (**with** de); **to d. oneself (up) with vitamins** se bourrer de vitamines

doss [dɒs] *vi Br very Fam* **to d. (down)** crécher

dosser ['dɒsə(r)] *n Br very Fam (tramp)* clodo *mf*

doss-house ['dɒshaʊs] *n Br Fam* asile *m* de nuit

dossier ['dɒsɪeɪ] *n* dossier *m*

dot [dɒt] **1** *n* point *m*; **on the d.** à l'heure pile; **at six o'clock on the d.** à six heures pile; *Comptr* **d. matrix printer** imprimante *f* matricielle
2 *vt (pt & pp* **dotted)** parsemer (**with** de); **to d. an i/a j** mettre un point sur un i/un j; **dotted line** pointillé *m*; **to sign on the dotted line** ≃ signer à l'endroit indiqué; *Fig* donner son consentement; *Fig* **to d. the i's (and cross the t's)** peaufiner les détails

dotage ['dəʊtɪdʒ] *n* **to be in one's d.** être gâteux(euse)

▸ **dote on, dote upon** [dəʊt] *vt insep* adorer

dotty ['dɒtɪ] *adj Br Fam (person, idea)* toqué(e); **to be d. about sb** être fou (folle) de qn

double ['dʌbəl] **1** *n* (**a**) *(of person)* double *m*, sosie *m* (**b**) *(hotel room)* chambre *f* pour deux personnes (**c**) **doubles** *(in tennis)* double *m*; **a doubles match** un double (**d**) **at** *or* **on the d.** à l'instant (**e**) *(measure of drink)* double *m*
2 *adj* double; **d. m** *(when spelling)* deux m; **a d. vodka** un double vodka; **d. agent** agent *m* double; **d. bass** contrebasse *f*; **d. bed** grand lit *m*, lit à deux personnes; **d. bill** *(at cinema)* double programme *m*; **d. chin** double menton *m*; *Br* **d. cream** = crème *f* fraîche épaisse; *Br* **to talk d.** Dutch parler chinois; **d. fault** *(in tennis)* double faute *f*; **to be in d. figures** *(of statistic)* avoir atteint plus de dix; **inflation is now in d. figures** l'inflation a passé la barre des 10%; **to lead a d. life** mener une double vie; **d. meaning** double sens *m*; **d. room** chambre *f* pour deux personnes; **to have d. standards** faire deux poids, deux mesures; **to do a d. take** marquer un temps d'arrêt; *Br* **d. yellow line** = double ligne jaune indiquant une zone de stationnement interdit
3 *adv* **to see d.** voir double; **to fold sth d.** plier qch en deux; **to be bent d.** être plié(e) en deux
4 *vt* (**a**) *(multiply by two)* doubler (**b**) *(fold)* plier en deux
5 *vi* (**a**) *(increase twofold)* doubler (**b**) **to d. as sth** servir aussi de qch

▸ **double back** *vi* rebrousser chemin

▸ **double up** *vi (bend)* se plier en deux (**with** de)

double-barrelled ['dʌbəl'bærəld] *adj (shotgun)* à deux coups; *(surname)* à rallonge

double-breasted ['dʌbəl'brestɪd] *adj (jacket, suit)* croisé(e)

double-check ['dʌbəl'tʃek] *vt & vi* bien vérifier

double-cross ['dʌbəl'krɒs] *vt* trahir, doubler

double-dealing ['dʌbəl'diːlɪŋ] *n* fourberie *f*

double-decker ['dʌbəl'dekə(r)] *n Br (bus)* autobus *m* à impériale *ou* à étage

double-edged ['dʌbəl'edʒd] *adj also Fig* à double tranchant

double-glazing ['dʌbəl'gleɪzɪŋ] *n* double vitrage *m*

double-jointed [dʌbəl'dʒɔɪntəd] *adj* désarticulé(e)

double-lock ['dʌbəl'lɒk] *vt* fermer à double tour

double-park ['dʌbəl'pɑːk] *vi* se garer en double file

double-quick ['dʌbəl'kwɪk] *adv* en vitesse

doubly ['dʌbəlɪ] *adv* doublement; **to make d. sure** of sth bien vérifier qch; **d. difficult** deux fois plus difficile; **to be d. careful** redoubler de prudence

doubt [daʊt] **1** *n* doute *m*; **to have doubts about sth** avoir des doutes sur qch; **to be in d.** *(of person)* douter (**about** de); *(of outcome)* être incertain(e); **if in d.** en cas de doute, dans le doute; **beyond d.** sans le moindre doute; **no d.** sans doute; **there is no d. that...** il ne fait aucun doute que...; **there is no d. about her guilt** sa culpabilité ne fait

aucun doute; **there is some d. about...** il y a des doutes quant à...
2 *vt* douter de; **I d. it** j'en doute

doubtful ['daʊtfʊl] *adj* (**a**) *(uncertain)* *(person)* dubitatif(ive); *(outcome)* incertain(e); **to be d. about sth** avoir des doutes sur qch (**b**) *(questionable)* douteux(euse)

dough [dəʊ] *n* (**a**) *(for bread)* pâte *f* (**b**) *Fam (money)* fric *m*

doughnut ['dəʊnʌt] *n* beignet *m*

dour [dʊə(r)] *adj* austère

douse [daʊs] *vt* (**a**) *(soak)* arroser (**b**) *(extinguish)* éteindre

dove¹ [dʌv] *n* colombe *f*

dove² [dəʊv] *Am pt of* **dive**

dovecot(e) ['dʌvkɒt] *n* colombier *m*

Dover ['dəʊvər] *n* Douvres

dovetail ['dʌvteɪl] *vi (fit closely)* concorder, cadrer (**with** avec)

dowager ['daʊədʒə(r)] *n* douairière *f*

dowdy ['daʊdɪ] *adj (person)* inélégant(e); *(clothes, image)* démodé(e)

dowel ['daʊəl] *n* cheville *f*

down¹ [daʊn] *n (feathers)* duvet *m*

down² **1** *prep* **to go d. the stairs/the street** descendre les escaliers/la rue; **to run d. the stairs/the street** descendre les escaliers/la rue en courant; **to fall d. the stairs** dégringoler les escaliers; **the tears ran d. her cheeks** les larmes coulaient sur ses joues
2 *adv* (**a**) *(with motion)* **to come/go d.** descendre; **to fall d.** tomber; **to bend d.** se pencher; **petrol has come** *or* **gone d. in price** le prix de l'essence a baissé; **I'll be d. in a minute** je descends tout de suite; **d. with traitors!** à bas les traîtres!
(**b**) *(with position)* en bas; **d. here/there** ici/là en bas; **further d.** plus bas; **petrol is d. in price** le prix de l'essence a baissé; **one d., two to go!** et d'un! encore deux et c'est fini!; **everyone from the manager d.** tout le monde, même le directeur
(**c**) *(in crosswords)* verticalement
(**d**) *(idioms)* **to be d. on sb/sth** avoir une dent contre qn/ qch; **it's d. to her** *(her decision)* c'est à elle de décider; *(her achievement)* c'est grâce à elle; **I'm d. to my last dollar/ cigarette** il ne me reste plus qu'un dollar/une cigarette
3 *n Fam* **to have a d. on sb/sth** avoir une dent contre qn/ qch
4 *adj* (**a**) *(depressed)* déprimé(e) (**b**) **to be d.** *(of computer, telephones)* être en panne
5 *vt* (**a**) *(aircraft)* abattre (**b**) *(drink)* descendre; **to d. tools** *(of workers)* se mettre en grève

down-and-out ['daʊnən'aʊt] *Fam* **1** *n (tramp)* clochard(e) *m,f*
2 *adj* sans le sou

downbeat ['daʊnbiːt] *adj* (**a**) *(gloomy, pessimistic)* triste, pessimiste (**b**) *(restrained)* réservé(e) (**about** sur)

downcast ['daʊnkɑːst] *adj (eyes)* baissé(e); *(person)* abattu(e), découragé(e)

downer ['daʊnə(r)] *n Fam (drug)* tranquillisant *m* (**b**) *(depressing situation)* situation *f* déprimante (*depressing event)* événement *m* déprimant

downfall ['daʊnfɔːl] *n (of government)* chute *f*; *(of person)* ruine *f*

downgrade ['daʊngreɪd] *vt* rétrograder

downhearted [daʊn'hɑːtɪd] *adj* découragé(e)

downhill ['daʊn'hɪl] **1** *adj (slope)* en pente; **d. skiing** ski *m* alpin *ou* de descente
2 *adv* **to go d.** *(of road, car)* descendre; *Fig (of person, career)* être sur le déclin

download [daʊn'ləʊd] Comptr **1** n téléchargement m **2** vt télécharger

down-market [daʊn'mɑːkɪt] adj (product) bas de gamme inv; (area, place) populaire

down payment [daʊn'peɪmənt] n acompte m

downpour ['daʊnpɔː(r)] n averse f

downright ['daʊnraɪt] **1** adj (stupidity, dishonesty) véritable; it's a d. lie! c'est un mensonge flagrant! **2** adv (stupid, untrue) carrément

downsizing ['daʊnsaɪzɪŋ] n réduction f d'effectifs

Down's syndrome ['daʊnz'sɪndrəʊm] n trisomie f 21

downstairs 1 adj ['daʊnsteəz] (on a lower floor) de l'étage du dessous; (on ground floor) du rez-de-chaussée; the d. flat l'appartement du dessous; the d. bathroom la salle de bains du bas **2** adv [daʊn'steəz] en bas; to come/go d. descendre; he lives d. il habite à l'étage au-dessous

downstream [daʊn'striːm] adv en aval; (with movement) vers l'aval

downswing ['daʊnswɪŋ] n Econ tendance f à la baisse

down-to-earth ['daʊntə'ɜːθ] adj terre à terre inv

downtown ['daʊn'taʊn] Am **1** n (city centre) centre-ville m **2** adj du centre-ville; d. New York le centre de New York **3** adv au centre-ville

downtrodden ['daʊntrɒdən] adj opprimé(e)

downturn ['daʊntɜːn] n (economic) baisse f

down under [daʊn'ʌndə(r)] adv Br Fam (in Australia) en Australie; (in New Zealand) en Nouvelle-Zélande

downward ['daʊnwəd] adj vers le bas; a d. trend une tendance à la baisse

downwards ['daʊnwədz] adv vers le bas

dowry ['daʊrɪ] (pl dowries) n dot f

doze [dəʊz] **1** n somme m; to have a d. faire un somme **2** vi somnoler

▸ **doze off** vi s'assoupir

dozen ['dʌzən] n douzaine f; half a d./a d. eggs une demi-douzaine/une douzaine d'œufs; Fam dozens of times/people des dizaines de fois/gens

dozy ['dəʊzɪ] adj (a) (sleepy) to feel d. avoir envie de dormir (b) Fam (stupid) abruti(e)

Dr (abbr Doctor) Dr

drab [dræb] adj (person, colour) terne; (atmosphere, city) morne

drachma ['drækmə] n drachme f

draconian [drə'kəʊnɪən] adj draconien(enne)

draft¹ [drɑːft] **1** n (a) (of letter) brouillon m; (of law, proposal) avant-projet m; (of novel) jet m (b) Fin traite f (c) Am (conscription) conscription f; d. dodger insoumis m **2** vt (a) (letter) faire le brouillon de; (proposal) rédiger; (law, bill) préparer (b) (recruit) to d. sb in détacher qn

draft² Am = draught

draftsman Am = draughtsman

drafty Am = draughty

drag [dræg] **1** n (a) (air resistance) traînée f; d. racing courses fpl de dragsters (b) Fam (person) raseur(euse) m,f; (task) corvée f; the party was a real d. la soirée était vraiment rasante (c) Fam (on cigarette) taffe f; to take or have a d. on a cigarette tirer une taffe sur une cigarette (d) Fam (women's clothing worn by man) to be in d. être travesti; d. artist travesti m; d. queen travelo m **2** vt (pt & pp dragged) (a) (pull) traîner; Fig to d. one's feet traîner les pieds; Fig to d. oneself away from sth s'arracher à qch (b) (pond, canal) draguer

3 vi (of film, day) traîner en longueur; (of conversation) languir

▸ **drag on** vi (of meeting, film) traîner en longueur, s'éterniser

▸ **drag out** vt sep (meeting, speech) faire traîner

▸ **drag up** vt sep (refer to) ressortir

dragnet ['drægnet] n (in deep-sea fishing) seine f, senne f; Fig (to catch criminals) rafle f

dragon ['drægən] n also Fig dragon m

dragonfly ['drægənflaɪ] (pl dragonflies) n libellule f

dragoon [drə'guːn] **1** n (soldier) dragon m **2** vt to d. sb into doing sth forcer qn à faire qch

drain [dreɪn] **1** n (a) (for water, sewage) égout m; Fig to throw money down the d. jeter l'argent par les fenêtres; that's five years' work down the d. voilà cinq années de travail perdues; that's my holiday down the d. ce sont mes vacances qui tombent à l'eau (b) (on resources) ponction f (on sur); (on strength) perte (on de) **2** vt (liquid) vider; (vegetables) égoutter; to d. one's glass finir son verre; Fig to feel drained être épuisé(e) ou vidé(e) **3** vi (of liquid) s'écouler; (of dishes) égoutter; (of sink, washing machine) se vider; (of river) se jeter; the colour drained from her face elle est devenue blême

▸ **drain away** vi (of liquid) s'écouler; Fig (of strength, enthusiasm) s'épuiser; (of fear, tension) s'apaiser

drainage ['dreɪnɪdʒ] n drainage m

drainpipe ['dreɪnpaɪp] n tuyau m d'écoulement; d. trousers, drainpipes pantalon m cigarette

drake [dreɪk] n canard m (mâle)

dram [dræm] n (of whisky) goutte f

drama ['drɑːmə] n (a) (art form) théâtre m; (play) drame m; Fig to make a d. out of sth faire un drame de qch; d. queen comédien(enne) m,f; don't be such a d. queen! arrête ton cinéma!; d. school école f d'art dramatique (b) (excitement) action f

dramatic [drə'mætɪk] adj (a) (work) dramatique; (actor) de théâtre (b) (significant) spectaculaire (c) (theatrical) théâtral(e)

dramatist ['dræmətɪst] n auteur m dramatique, dramaturge mf

dramatize ['dræmətaɪz] vt (a) (adapt) adapter pour la scène; (for screen) adapter pour l'écran (b) (exaggerate) dramatiser

drank [dræŋk] pt of drink

drape [dreɪp] **1** npl Am drapes (curtains) rideaux mpl **2** vt (table, coffin) draper (with de); to d. sth over sth draper qch sur qch

drastic ['dræstɪk] adj (solution, change) radical(e); (improvement, decline) spectaculaire; (action) énergique; (shortage, difficulty) dramatique

drat [dræt] exclam Fam d. (it)! nom de nom!

draught, Am **draft** [drɑːft] n (a) (wind) courant m d'air; d. excluder bourrelet m (b) (of drink) gorgée f; (of air) bouffée f (c) on d. (beer) à la pression; d. beer bière f pression

draughtboard ['drɑːftbɔːd] n damier m

draughts ['drɑːfts] n (game) (jeu m de) dames fpl

draughtsman, Am **draftsman** ['drɑːftsmən] n dessinateur(trice) m,f

draughty, Am **drafty** ['drɑːftɪ] adj plein(e) de courants d'air

draw [drɔː] **1** n (a) (in match, argument) match m nul (b) (lottery) loterie f, tombola f; (for sporting competition) tirage m au sort (c) (attraction) attraction f

2 vt (pt **drew** [druː], pp **drawn** [drɔːn]) (**a**) (picture, diagram, map) dessiner; (circle, line) tracer; **to d. sb's picture** faire le portrait de qn (**b**) (pull) (cart) tirer; (person) attirer (**towards** vers); **to d. the curtains** (open or shut) tirer les rideaux; **to d. breath** souffler (**c**) (extract) retirer; (pistol, sword) dégainer; (water, wine) tirer; Fig (strength, comfort) retirer, puiser (**from** de); **to d. a knife on sb** menacer qn d'un couteau; **to d. a salary** toucher un salaire; **to d. blood** (of dog) mordre jusqu'au sang; (of cat) griffer jusqu'au sang; **to d. lots for sth** tirer qch au sort; **to d. a conclusion from sth** tirer une conclusion de qch; **she refused to be drawn on the subject** elle refusa de se laisser entraîner sur ce sujet; **they were drawn against the champions** (in competition) le tirage au sort a décidé qu'ils joueraient contre les champions (**d**) (attract) attirer; **to d. a crowd** (of incident) créer un attroupement; (of play) attirer le public; **to feel drawn to sb/sth** se sentir attiré(e) par qn/qch; Fig **to d. sb's fire** s'attirer les foudres de qn

3 vi (**a**) (make picture) dessiner (**b**) (in game) faire match nul (**with** avec) (**c**) (move) **to d. ahead of sb** devancer qn; **to d. level with sb** rattraper qn; **to d. to a close** tirer ou toucher à sa fin; **to d. near** (s')approcher; **to d. to a halt** s'arrêter

▸ **draw back 1** vt sep (sheet, veil) retirer
2 vi reculer; **to d. back from doing sth** hésiter à faire qch

▸ **draw in** vi (of night) raccourcir

▸ **draw on 1** vt insep (resources, savings) tirer sur; (experience) se servir de
2 vi (of evening) approcher

▸ **draw out** vt sep (**a**) (encourage to talk) faire parler (**b**) (prolong) faire durer

▸ **draw up 1** vt sep (**a**) (chair) approcher; **she drew herself up to her full height** elle s'est dressée de toute sa hauteur (**b**) (plan, document) dresser; (will) rédiger
2 vi (of vehicle) s'arrêter

drawback ['drɔːbæk] n inconvénient m

drawbridge ['drɔːbrɪdʒ] n pont-levis m

drawer [drɔː(r)] n tiroir m

drawers [drɔːz] npl Old-fashioned (for women) culotte f; (for men) caleçon m

drawing ['drɔːɪŋ] n dessin m; **d. board** planche f à dessin; Fig **it's back to the d. board!** retour à la case départ!; **d. paper** papier m à dessin; Br **d. pin** punaise f; **d. room** salon m

drawl [drɔːl] **1** n voix f traînante
2 vi parler d'une voix traînante

drawn [drɔːn] **1** adj (face) blême; (features) tiré(e); **to look d.** avoir les traits tirés
2 pp of **draw**

drawstring ['drɔːstrɪŋ] n cordon m

dread [dred] **1** n terreur f; **to have a d. of sth** avoir la hantise de qch
2 vt **to d. sth/doing sth** appréhender ou redouter qch/de faire qch; **I d. to think!** je n'ose pas imaginer!

dreaded ['dredɪd] adj redouté(e)

dreadful ['dredfʊl] adj (**a**) (terrible) épouvantable, affreux(euse); **to feel d.** se sentir vraiment mal; **I feel really d. about it!** quand j'y pense, je suis horriblement gêné! (**b**) Fam (for emphasis) terrible; **it's a d. shame!** c'est vraiment dommage!

dreadfully ['dredfʊlɪ] adv (**a**) (very badly) affreusement (**b**) Fam (extremely) terriblement, horriblement

dreadlocks ['dredlɒks] npl petites nattes fpl (des rastas)

dream [driːm] **1** n rêve m; **to have a d. (about)** rêver (de);

to have a bad d. faire un mauvais rêve; **a d. come true** un rêve devenu réalité; **it worked like a d.** ça a marché à merveille **2** adj de rêve; **my d. house** la maison de mes rêves; **d. world** monde m imaginaire; Fig **to live in a d. world** vivre en pleine utopie

3 vt (pt & pp **dreamt** [dremt] or **dreamed**) **to d. that...** rêver que...; Fig **I never dreamt you would take me seriously** je n'aurais jamais pensé que tu me prendrais au sérieux

4 vi rêver (**of** or **about** de); Fam **I wouldn't d. of it!** je n'y songerais même pas!

▸ **dream up** vt sep (scheme, excuse) imaginer, inventer

dreamer ['driːmə(r)] n rêveur(euse) m,f

dreamt [dremt] pt & pp of **dream**

dreamy ['driːmɪ] adj rêveur(euse)

dreary ['drɪərɪ] adj morne

dredge [dredʒ] vt (canal, harbour) draguer; Fig **to d. one's memory** fouiller dans ses souvenirs

▸ **dredge up** vt sep (body, object) repêcher; Fig (scandal, memory) déterrer

dredger ['dredʒə(r)] n (boat) dragueur m

dregs [dregz] npl (of wine) lie f; (of coffee) marc m; (in cup) fond m de tasse; Fig **the d. of society** les bas-fonds mpl de la société

drench [drentʃ] vt tremper (**with** or **in** de); **drenched to the skin** trempé(e) jusqu'aux os

dress [dres] **1** n (**a**) (for woman) robe f (**b**) (clothing) tenue f; **to have good d. sense/no d. sense** savoir/ne pas savoir s'habiller; **d. circle** premier balcon m; **d. rehearsal** (répétition f) générale f; **d. shirt** chemise f de soirée

2 vt (**a**) (person) habiller, vêtir; **to d. oneself, to get dressed** s'habiller; **to be dressed in white/in rags** être vêtu(e) de blanc/de haillons; **well/badly dressed** bien/mal habillé(e) (**b**) (wound) panser (**c**) (salad) assaisonner; **dressed crab** chair f de crabe

3 vi s'habiller

▸ **dress up** vi (elegantly) se faire beau (belle), s'habiller; (in fancy dress) se déguiser (**as** en)

dresser ['dresə(r)] n (**a**) (in kitchen) vaisselier m (**b**) Am (dressing table) coiffeuse f (**c**) Th (person) habilleur(euse) m,f

dressing ['dresɪŋ] n (**a**) **d. gown** robe f de chambre; **d. room** (in theatre) loge f; (in gym, sports centre) vestiaire m; (in home) cabinet m de toilette; Br **d. table** coiffeuse f (**b**) (for wound) pansement m (**c**) (for salad) assaisonnement m

dressing down ['dresɪŋ'daʊn] n Fam savon m; **to give sb a d.** passer un savon à qn

dressmaker ['dresmeɪkə(r)] n couturier(ère) m,f

dressmaking ['dresmeɪkɪŋ] n couture f

dressy ['dresɪ] adj (clothes, party) habillé(e)

drew [druː] pt of **draw**

drib [drɪb] n **in dribs and drabs** petit à petit

dribble ['drɪbəl] **1** n (of saliva) bave f; (of blood, oil) filet m
2 vi (**a**) (of person) baver (**b**) (of liquid) dégouliner; Fig **to d. in/out** (of people) entrer/sortir au compte-gouttes (**c**) (of footballer) dribbler

drier ['draɪə(r)] n (for clothes) séchoir m; (for hair) (on stand) casque m; (hand-held) sèche-cheveux m inv

drift [drɪft] **1** n (**a**) (of current) direction f, sens m; (of events) cours m; **the d. towards home ownership** la tendance actuelle à l'accession à la propriété; **d. net** (for fishing) filet m dérivant (**b**) (meaning) sens m général; Fam **I get the d.** j'ai compris; Fam **if you get my d.** si tu vois ce que je veux dire (**c**) (of snow) congère f; (of leaves) amoncellement m; (of fog, mist) traînée f
2 vi (**a**) (of boat) dériver, aller à la dérive; (of smoke) flotter;

(of events) tendre **(towards** vers); *(of person)* se laisser porter par les événements; **people drifted in and out** les gens entraient et sortaient nonchalamment; **to d. apart** *(of friends)* se perdre de vue; *(of couple)* devenir des étrangers l'un pour l'autre; **to d. into war/crime** être entraîné(e) vers la guerre/le crime **(b)** *(of sand, snow)* s'amonceler, s'entasser

drifter ['drɪftə(r)] *n (person)* **she's a bit of a d.** elle n'a pas vraiment de but dans la vie

driftwood ['drɪftwʊd] *n (in sea)* bois *m* flottant *ou* flotté; *(on shore)* bois rejeté par la mer

drill [drɪl] **1** *n* **(a)** *(tool)* foret *m*, mèche *f*; *(electric)* perceuse *f*; *(of dentist)* fraise *f*, roulette *f*; *(pneumatic)* marteau *m* piqueur; **d. bit** foret **(b)** *(training)* exercice *m*
2 *vt* **(a)** *(well)* forer; *(hole)* percer **(b)** *(train) (soldiers)* entraîner; *Fam* **to d. sth into sb** enfoncer qch dans la tête de qn
3 *vi* **(a)** *(for oil)* forer **(for** pour trouver); *(in wall, rock)* percer **(into** dans) **(b)** *(of troops)* faire l'exercice

drink [drɪŋk] **1** *n* boisson *f*; **to have a d.** prendre un verre, boire quelque chose; **to go for a d.** aller prendre un verre; **to pay for the drinks** payer les consommations; *Fam* **the d.** *(sea)* la baille; **to take to d.** se mettre à boire; **to have a d. problem** (trop) boire; **drinks machine** distributeur *m* automatique de boissons
2 *vt (pt* **drank** [dræŋk], *pp* **drunk** [drʌŋk]) boire; **she drank us all under the table** nous avions tous roulé sous la table depuis longtemps qu'elle était encore debout
3 *vi* boire; **to d. like a fish** boire comme un trou; **to d. to sb** *or* **to sb's health** boire à la santé de qn; *Fig* **to d. to sth** arroser qch; **to d. in the atmosphere** se pénétrer de l'atmosphère
▸ **drink up 1** *vt sep* finir (de boire)
2 *vi* vider son verre

drinkable ['drɪŋkəbəl] *adj (water)* potable; *(wine, beer)* buvable

drink-driving ['drɪŋk'draɪvɪŋ] *n* conduite *f* en état d'ivresse

drinker ['drɪŋkə(r)] *n* buveur(euse) *m,f*; **to be a heavy d.** boire beaucoup

drinking ['drɪŋkɪŋ] *n* **d. is bad for you** l'alcool est mauvais pour la santé; **d. chocolate** chocolat *m* en poudre; **d. fountain** fontaine *f* publique; **d. straw** paille *f*; **d. water** eau *f* potable

drip [drɪp] **1** *n* **(a)** *(drop)* goutte *f*; *(sound)* bruit *m* de l'eau qui goutte **(b)** *(in hospital)* goutte-à-goutte *m inv*; **to be on a d.** être sous perfusion **(c)** *Fam (weak person)* mou (molle) *m,f*
2 *vt (pt & pp* **dripped)** laisser tomber goutte à goutte; **you're dripping water everywhere!** tu mets de l'eau partout!; **to be dripping with sweat/blood** ruisseler de sueur/sang; *Fig* **to be dripping with diamonds** être couvert(e) de diamants
3 *vi (of liquid)* tomber goutte à goutte, goutter; *(of tap)* fuire

drip-dry ['drɪp'draɪ] *adj (shirt, fabric)* ne nécessitant aucun repassage

dripping ['drɪpɪŋ] **1** *n* graisse *f* de rôti
2 *adj (tap)* qui fuit
3 *adv* **d. wet** trempé(e)

drive [draɪv] **1** *n* **(a)** *(trip)* promenade *f* en voiture; **it's an hour's d. away** c'est à une heure en voiture; **to go for** *or* **take a d.** aller faire une promenade en voiture
(b) *(of car)* **left-hand d.** conduite *f* à gauche; **four-wheel d.** *(car)* quatre-quatre *m inv*; *(system)* propulsion *f* à quatre roues motrices; **front-wheel d.** *(car, system)* traction *f* avant; **rear-wheel d.** *(car, system)* traction *f* arrière
(c) *Comptr* lecteur *m*, unité *f*
(d) *(in golf, tennis)* drive *m*

(e) *(initiative)* énergie *f*, dynamisme *m*
(f) *(of house)* allée *f*
(g) *(campaign)* **sales/membership d.** campagne *f* pour attirer les acheteurs/de nouveaux membres
2 *vt (pt* **drove** [drəʊv], *pp* **driven** ['drɪvən]) **(a)** *(car, train)* conduire; **to d. sb somewhere** conduire qn en voiture quelque part
(b) *(direct, guide) (cattle)* mener, conduire; *(people)* chasser
(c) *(push)* **to d. sb to sth/to do sth** pousser qn à qch/à faire qch; **to d. sb mad** rendre qn fou (folle); **to d. oneself too hard** trop exiger de soi même; **to d. a hard bargain** ne pas faire de cadeau; **to d. prices up/down** faire monter/baisser les prix
(d) *(machine)* actionner, faire marcher; **to be driven by electricity** marcher à l'électricité
3 *vi (of car)* conduire; **can you d.?** savez-vous conduire?; **I don't d.** je n'ai pas mon permis; **to d. to work** aller au travail en voiture
▸ **drive at** *vt insep* **what are you driving at?** où voulez-vous en venir?
▸ **drive away 1** *vt sep (in car)* emmener en voiture **(b)** *(force to leave)* chasser
2 *vi (in car)* s'en aller en voiture
▸ **drive off** **1** *vt sep (repel) (attackers)* chasser
2 *vi (in car)* s'en aller en voiture
▸ **drive on** *vi (in car)* continuer (sa route)

drive-in ['draɪvɪn] *n (cinema)* drive-in *m*, ciné-parc *m*; *(restaurant)* = restaurant où on est servi dans sa voiture

drivel ['drɪvəl] *n Fam* bêtises *fpl*, balivernes *fpl*; **to talk (a load of) d.** dire n'importe quoi

driven ['drɪvən] *pp* **of drive**
2 *adj (person)* motivé(e), déterminé(e)

driver ['draɪvə(r)] *n* **(a)** *(of car, bus)* conducteur(trice) *m,f*; *(of lorry, taxi)* chauffeur(euse) *m,f*; *(of train)* mécanicien(enne) *m,f*; *Am* **d.'s license** permis *m* de conduire **(b)** *(golf club)* driver *m*

driveway ['draɪvweɪ] *n* allée *f*

driving ['draɪvɪŋ] **1** *n (in car)* conduite *f*; *Fig* **to be in the d. seat** commander; **d. instructor** moniteur(trice) *m,f* d'auto-école; **d. lessons** leçons *fpl* de conduite; *Br* **d. licence** permis *m* de conduire; **d. school** auto-école *f*; **d. test** *(examen m du)* permis de conduire
2 *adj (rain)* battant(e); *Fig* **d. force** moteur *m*

drizzle ['drɪzəl] **1** *n* crachin *m*
2 *vi* bruiner

droll [drəʊl] *adj* drôle, comique; *Ironic* **oh, very d.!** très drôle!

dromedary ['drɒmədərɪ] *(pl* **dromedaries)** *n* dromadaire *m*

drone [drəʊn] **1** *n* **(a)** *(bee)* faux-bourdon *m* **(b)** *(of conversation, traffic, plane)* bourdonnement *m*
2 *vi* **(a)** *(of bee)* bourdonner **(b)** *(of person)* parler d'un ton monotone
▸ **drone on** *vi* parler ad nauseam *(d'une voix monotone)* **(about** de)

drool [druːl] *vi (dribble)* baver; *Fig* **to d. over sb/sth** baver d'admiration devant qn/qch; *Fig* **she was drooling over the idea** elle en salivait d'avance

droop [druːp] *vi (of head)* pencher; *(of shoulders)* tomber; *(of flower)* pencher la tête; *Fig (of person)* perdre ses forces

drop [drɒp] **1** *n* **(a)** *(of liquid)* goutte *f*; **drops** *(for eyes, nose)* gouttes; **you've had a d. too much** *(to drink)* tu as bu un coup de trop; *Fig* **it's only a d. in the ocean** ce n'est qu'une goutte d'eau dans l'océan
(b) *(fall) (in prices, numbers)* chute *f*, baisse *f* **(in** de); *(by parachute)* parachutage *m*; **a d. of 10 metres** un à-pic *ou*

escarpement de 10 mètres; *Fig* **at the d.** of a hat sans la moindre hésitation

2 *vt* (*pt & pp* **dropped**) (**a**) *(allow to fall)* laisser tomber; *(bomb)* lâcher; **to d. sb a line** envoyer *ou* écrire un mot à qn; **I'll d. you at the station** *(in car)* je te déposerai à la gare (**b**) *(lower) (prices, one's eyes)* baisser (**c**) *(abandon) (subject, idea, plan)* abandonner; **to d. sb** *(as friend)* laisser tomber qn; *(from team)* écarter qn; **to d. maths/French** *(of student)* arrêter les maths/le français; *Law* **to d. the charges** abandonner les poursuites (**d**) *(omit) (letter, syllable)* omettre, supprimer; *(when speaking)* ne pas prononcer (**e**) *(lose) (points)* perdre

3 *vi* (**a**) *(of object)* tomber; *(of ground)* s'affaisser; **he dropped to sixth place** il est descendu à la sixième place; *Fam* **I'm ready to d.** *(with fatigue)* je tombe de fatigue; *Fam* **people are dropping like flies** les gens tombent comme des mouches; **to d. dead** tomber raide mort(e); *Fam* **d. dead!** va te faire voir!; *Fam* **let it d.!** laisse tomber!

(**b**) *(of prices, temperature, voice)* baisser; *(of wind)* tomber; *(of speed)* diminuer

▸ **drop by** *vi (visit)* passer

▸ **drop in** *vi* passer (**on sb** chez qn)

▸ **drop off 1** *vt sep (person from car)* déposer

2 *vi* (**a**) **to d. off (to sleep)** s'assoupir, s'endormir (**b**) *(of membership, attendance)* diminuer

▸ **drop out** *vi* (**a**) *(of object) (from pocket, bag)* tomber (**b**) *(of person) (from contest)* se retirer; *(from society)* devenir un(e) marginal(e); *(from university)* abandonner ses études

▸ **drop round 1** *vt sep (deliver)* déposer

2 *vi (visit)* passer

droplet ['drɒplɪt] *n* gouttelette *f*

dropout ['drɒpaʊt] *n Fam (from society)* marginal(e) *m,f*; *(from university)* étudiant(e) *m,f* qui abandonne ses études

dropper ['drɒpə(r)] *n (for medicine)* compte-gouttes *m inv*

droppings ['drɒpɪŋz] *npl (of birds)* fiente *f*; *(of animals)* crottes *fpl*

dross [drɒs] *n Br Fam (rubbish)* rebut *m*; **I've never heard such d. in all my life** j'ai rarement entendu de telles bêtises

drought [draʊt] *n* sécheresse *f*

drove [drəʊv] **1** **to arrive in droves** arriver en foule

2 *pt of* **drive**

drown [draʊn] **1** *vt* (**a**) *(in water)* noyer; **to d. oneself** se noyer; **to d. one's sorrows** noyer son chagrin dans l'alcool (**b**) *(sound)* couvrir

2 *vi (die)* se noyer

▸ **drown out** *vt sep (sound)* couvrir; *(person)* couvrir la voix de

drowse [draʊz] *vi* somnoler

drowsy ['draʊzɪ] *adj* **to be** *or* **feel d.** avoir envie de dormir

drudge [drʌdʒ] *n (man)* homme *m* de peine; *(woman)* bonne *f* à tout faire

drudgery ['drʌdʒərɪ] *n* travail *m* pénible *ou* ingrat

drug [drʌg] **1** *n* (**a**) *(medicine)* médicament *m*; *(narcotic)* drogue *f*; **hard/soft drugs** drogues dures/douces; **to take drugs** se droguer; *Fam* **to do drugs** se droguer; **d. abuse** usage *m* de stupéfiants; **d. addict** drogué(e) *m,f*; **d. dealer** *(large-scale)* trafiquant *m* de drogue; *(small-scale)* petit trafiquant de drogue, dealer *m*; **d. squad** brigade *f* des stupéfiants

2 *vt* (*pt & pp* **drugged**) droguer

druggist ['drʌgɪst] *n Am* pharmacien(enne) *m,f*

drugstore ['drʌgstɔː(r)] *n Am* drugstore *m*

druid ['druːɪd] *n* druide *m*

drum [drʌm] **1** *n* (**a**) *(musical instrument)* tambour *m*; **d.**

kit, drums batterie *f* (**b**) *(container)* fût *m*; *(for oil)* bidon *m*

2 *vt* (*pt & pp* **drummed**) **to d. one's fingers** tambouriner de ses doigts; **to d. sth into sb** enfoncer qch dans la tête de qn

3 *vi (play drums)* jouer de la batterie; **the rain was drumming on the window panes** la pluie tambourinait contre les vitres

▸ **drum up** *vt (support, enthusiasm)* rechercher

drummer ['drʌmə(r)] *n (in pop band)* batteur(euse) *m,f*; *(in military band)* tambour *m*

drumstick ['drʌmstɪk] *n* (**a**) *(for playing drums)* baguette *f* de tambour (**b**) *(chicken leg)* pilon *m*

drunk [drʌŋk] **1** *n (man)* homme *m* soûl; *(woman)* femme *f* soûle; *(habitual)* ivrogne *mf*

2 *adj* ivre, soûl(e); **to get d.** se soûler; *Law* **d. and disorderly** = en état d'ivresse sur la voie publique; *Fig* **d. with joy/power** ivre de joie/puissance

3 *pp of* **drink**

drunkard ['drʌŋkəd] *n* ivrogne *mf*

drunken ['drʌŋkən] *adj (person)* ivre; *(party)* bien arrosé(e); **in a d. stupor** hébété(e) par l'alcool; **d. brawl** querelle *f* d'ivrognes

dry [draɪ] **1** *adj* (**a**) *(weather, clothing, skin, hair, wine)* sec (sèche); *(day)* sans pluie; **to run** *or* **go d.** *(of river)* s'assécher; *(of spring)* (se) tarir, s'épuiser; **d. as a bone** complètement sec; *Naut* **d. dock** cale *f* sèche; **d. ice** neige *f* carbonique; **d. land** terre *f* ferme; **d. rot** pourriture *f* sèche; **d. run** coup *m* d'essai, test *m* (**b**) *(boring) (style, person)* ennuyeux(euse) (**c**) *(humour)* teinté(e) d'ironie

2 *vt* (*pt & pp* **dried**) sécher; *(clothes)* faire sécher; *(skin)* dessécher; *(dishes)* essuyer; **to d. oneself** se sécher; **to d. one's hair** se sécher les cheveux

3 *vi* sécher

▸ **dry out** *vi* (**a**) *(of alcoholic)* se faire désintoxiquer (**b**) *(of wood, ground)* sécher; *(of skin)* se dessécher

▸ **dry up** *vi* (**a**) *(of well, pool)* se dessécher, tarir (**b**) *(of funds, conversation)* tarir; *(of inspiration)* se tarir (**c**) *(forget one's lines)* oublier son texte; *(have nothing more to say)* ne plus rien avoir à dire

dry-clean ['draɪ'kliːn] *vt* nettoyer à sec

dry-cleaner's ['draɪ'kliːnəz] *n* teinturerie *f*, pressing *m*

dry-cleaning ['draɪ'kliːnɪŋ] *n* (**a**) *(process)* nettoyage *m* à sec (**b**) *(clothes)* vêtements *mpl* laissés chez le teinturier

dryer ['draɪə(r)] = **drier**

DSS [diːeˈses] *n Br (abbr* **Department of Social Security**) ≃ Sécurité *f* sociale

DTI [diːtiːˈaɪ] *n Br (abbr* **Department of Trade and Industry**) ≃ ministère *m* du Commerce et de l'Industrie

DTP [diːtiːˈpiː] *n Comptr (abbr* **desktop publishing**) PAO *f*

DTs [diːˈtiːz] *npl (abbr* **delirium tremens**) **the D.** le delirium tremens

dual ['djuːəl] *adj* double; *Br* **d. carriageway** *(road)* route *f* à deux chaussées; **d. nationality** double nationalité *f*; **d. ownership** copropriété *f*

dual-purpose ['djuːəl'pɜːpəs] *adj* à double emploi

dub [dʌb] (*pt & pp* **dubbed**) *vt* (**a**) *(film)* doubler (**into** en) (**b**) *(nickname)* surnommer

dubbing ['dʌbɪŋ] *n (of film)* doublage *m*

dubious ['djuːbɪəs] *adj* (**a**) *(uncertain)* incertain(e); **to be d. (about)** avoir quelques doutes (au sujet de) (**b**) *(questionable)* douteux(euse)

Dublin ['dʌblɪn] *n* Dublin

Dubliner ['dʌblɪnə(r)] *n* = personne née ou habitant à Dublin

duchess ['dʌtʃɪs] *n* duchesse *f*

duchy ['dʌtʃɪ] (pl **duchies**) n duché m
duck [dʌk] **1** n canard m; (female) cane f; **to take to sth
like a d.** to water faire qch comme si on l'avait fait toute sa
vie; **criticism runs off him like water off a d.**'s back les
critiques glissent sur lui; **d. pond** mare f aux canards
2 vt (a) (head) baisser subitement; **to d. sb** (under water)
faire faire le plongeon à qn (b) (avoid) (obligations) se
dérober à; **to d. the issue/question** se dérober
3 vi (lower head) baisser la tête, se baisser; (under water)
plonger sous l'eau; **to d. behind a tree** se cacher derrière
un arbre
▸ **duck out of** vt insep **to d. out of doing sth** éviter de
faire qch; **he ducked out of the meeting** il s'est débrouillé
pour ne pas assister à la réunion
duck-billed platypus ['dʌkbɪld'plætɪpəs] n ornithorynque m
duckling ['dʌklɪŋ] n (male) caneton m; (female) canette f
duct [dʌkt] n conduit m
dud [dʌd] Fam **1** n (person) incapable mf; (shell) obus m qui
n'a pas éclaté; (banknote) faux m
2 adj (shell) qui n'a pas éclaté; (banknote) faux (fausse);
(cheque) en bois
dude [du:d] n Am type m
due [dju:] **1** n (a) (what is owed) dû m; **to give her her d.**,
she did apologize pour lui rendre justice, il faut
reconnaître qu'elle s'est excusée
(b) **dues** (membership fees) cotisation f
2 adj (a) (owed) dû (due); **to fall d.** échoir, arriver à
échéance; **are you d. any money from her?** vous doit-
elle de l'argent?, **you're d. an apology** je vous dois/il vous
doit/etc une excuse; **d. to** par suite de, en raison de; **what
is it d. to?** c'est dû à quoi?; Fin **d. date** échéance f
(b) (merited, proper) dû (due), mérité(e); **to give sb d.
warning** avertir qn dans les formes; **after d.
consideration** après mûre réflexion; **with all d.
respect,...** avec tout le respect que je vous dois,...; **in d.
course** (when appropriate) en temps voulu; (eventually) le
moment venu
(c) (expected) **the train is d.** (in or to arrive) le train doit
arriver d'un moment à l'autre; **when is he due** (in or to
arrive)? quand doit-il arriver?; **when is the baby d.?** pour
quand la naissance est-elle prévue?; **she's d. back any
minute** elle doit revenir d'un moment à l'autre; **the film/
book is d. out soon** le film/livre va sortir sous peu
3 adv **d. north/south** plein nord/sud
duel ['dju:əl] **1** n duel m; **to fight a d.** se battre en duel
2 vi (pt & pp duelled, Am dueled) se battre en duel
duet [dju:'et] n duo m; (for piano) morceau m à quatre
mains
duff [dʌf] adj Fam nul (nulle)
▸ **duff up** vt sep Br Fam rosser, tabasser
duffel ['dʌfəl] = **duffle**
duffer ['dʌfə(r)] n Fam (incompetent person) nul (nulle) m,f
duffle ['dʌfəl] n **d. (coat)** duffle-coat m; **d. bag** sac m
(de) marin
dug [dʌg] pt & pp of **dig**
dugout ['dʌgaʊt] n (a) (canoe) pirogue f (b) (shelter) Mil
tranchée-abri f; Sp banc m de touche
duke [dju:k] n duc m
dull [dʌl] **1** adj (a) (boring) ennuyeux(euse), terne; **as d. as
ditchwater** ennuyeux comme la pluie; (unintelligent)
lent(e) (d) (not sharp) (pain, sound) sourd(e); (blade, senses)
émoussé(e) (d) (not bright) (colour, surface) terne; (eyes) sans
éclat; (weather, sky) sombre, maussade
2 vt (a) (pleasure) rendre moins vif (vive); (pain) endormir,
calmer; (sound) amortir, assourdir; (blade, senses) émousser
(b) (make less bright) ternir

duly ['dju:lɪ] adv (a) (properly) dûment (b) (as expected)
comme prévu
dumb [dʌm] adj (a) (unable to speak) muet(ette); **to be
struck d.** (with astonishment) en rester muet; **d. animal** bête
f; **d. insolence** silence m insolent (b) Fam (stupid) bête; **d.
blonde** blonde f évaporée
dumbbell ['dʌmbel] n haltère m
dumbfounded [dʌm'faʊndɪd], **dumbstruck** ['dʌm-
strʌk] adj abasourdi(e), ébahi(e)
dumbwaiter ['dʌmweɪtə(r)] n (lift) monte-plats m inv
dummy ['dʌmɪ] **1** n (pl **dummies**) (a) (in shop window)
mannequin m; (of ventriloquist) marionnette f; (model, fake)
objet m factice (b) (for baby) tétine f (c) Fam (idiot) abruti(e)
m,f
2 adj (fake) factice; **d. run** coup m d'essai
dump [dʌmp] **1** n (a) (for refuse) décharge f; Fam Pej (town)
bled m paumé; (house) dépotoir m; **d. truck** tombereau m,
dumper m (b) Mil (store) dépôt m (c) Comptr vidage m
2 vt (a) (put down) déposer (b) (dispose of) se débarrasser
de; (waste) déverser; Fam (boyfriend, girlfriend) plaquer (c)
Comptr (memory) vider
dumper ['dʌmpə(r)] n **d. (truck)** tombereau m, dumper m
dumping ['dʌmpɪŋ] n (a) **no d.** (sign) décharge interdite;
d. ground décharge f; Fig dépotoir m (b) Econ dumping m
dumpling ['dʌmplɪŋ] n (in stew) boulette f de pâte; Scot =
sorte de plum-pudding écossais
dumps [dʌmps] npl Fam **to be down in the d.** broyer du
noir, avoir le cafard
dumpy ['dʌmpɪ] adj Fam (person, appearance) bou-
lot(otte)
dunce [dʌns] n (at school) âne m, cancre m; **d.'s cap**
bonnet m d'âne
dune [dju:n] n dune f
dung [dʌŋ] n (of cow) bouse f; (of horse) crottin m; (of wild
animal) fumées fpl
dungarees [dʌŋgə'ri:z] npl Br (a pair of) **d.** une
salopette f; (of workman) un bleu de travail
dungeon ['dʌndʒən] n (underground) cachot m; Hist
(tower) donjon m
dunghill ['dʌŋhɪl] n tas m de fumier
dunk [dʌŋk] vt tremper
Dunkirk [dʌn'kɜːk] n Dunkerque f
duo ['dju:əʊ] (pl **duos**) n (in music) duo m; (two people)
couple m
duodenal [dju:əʊ'di:nəl] adj (ulcer) duodénal(e)
dupe [dju:p] **1** n dupe f
2 vt duper, tromper; **to d. sb into doing sth** faire faire qch
à qn en le dupant
duplicate ['dju:plɪkət] **1** n (of key) double m; (of letter,
receipt) double m, duplicata m; **in d.** en double, en deux
exemplaires
2 adj ['dju:plɪkət] **a d. key** un double de la clé; **a d. copy**
un duplicata
3 vt ['dju:plɪkeɪt] (a) (copy) faire un double/duplicata de;
(on photocopier) faire une photocopie de (b) (do again)
refaire
duplication [dju:plɪ'keɪʃən] n (a) (copying) reproduction f (b) (repetition) répétition f
duplicity [dju:'plɪsɪtɪ] n duplicité f
durability [djʊərə'bɪlɪtɪ] n (of material) résistance f; (of
friendship) durabilité f
durable ['djʊərəbəl] **1** n (consumer) **durables** biens mpl
durables
2 adj (material) résistant(e); (friendship) durable

duration [djʊ'reɪʃən] *n* durée *f*; **for the d.** pour longtemps

duress [djʊ'res] *n* **under d.** sous la contrainte

during ['djʊərɪŋ] *prep* pendant, durant; *(in the course of)* au cours de

dusk [dʌsk] *n* crépuscule *m*; **at d.** au crépuscule, à la tombée de la nuit

dust [dʌst] **1** *n* (**a**) *(dirt, powder)* poussière *f*; **d. cover** *(for furniture)* housse *f*; **d. cover** *or* **jacket** *(for book)* chemise *f*, jaquette *f* (**b**) *(action)* **to give sth a d.** passer un coup de chiffon sur qch (**c**) *(idioms)* **once the d. has settled** une fois que les choses se seront calmées; *Fam* **you won't see me for d.!** vous ne me reverrez pas de sitôt!
2 *vt* (**a**) *(clean)* dépoussiérer, épousseter (**b**) *(sprinkle)* (*with flour, sugar)* saupoudrer (**with** de)
3 *vi (clean)* épousseter
▸ **dust down, dust off** *vt sep (furniture)* épousseter; *Fig (legislation)* dépoussiérer; *(one's French)* se remettre à

dustbin ['dʌstbɪn] *n* *Br* poubelle *f*

dustcart ['dʌstkɑːt] *n* *Br* benne *f* à ordures

duster ['dʌstə(r)] *n* *(cloth)* chiffon *m* (à poussière); *(for blackboard)* brosse *f*

dustman ['dʌstmən] *n* *Br* éboueur *m*

dustpan ['dʌstpæn] *n* pelle *f* (à poussière)

dustsheet ['dʌstʃiːt] *n* housse *f*

dust-up ['dʌstʌp] *n* *Fam (brawl)* bagarre *f*; **to have a d. with sb** se bagarrer avec qn

dusty ['dʌstɪ] *adj* poussiéreux(euse), couvert(e) de poussière; **to get d.** se couvrir de poussière

Dutch [dʌtʃ] **1** *npl* **the D.** *(people)* les Hollandais *mpl*
2 *n (language)* hollandais *m*
3 *adj* hollandais(e); *Fam* **I need some D. courage** j'ai besoin d'un verre pour me donner du courage; **D. cap** *(contraceptive)* diaphragme *m*
4 *adv* *Fam* **to go D.** payer chacun sa part

Dutchman ['dʌtʃmən] *n* Hollandais *m*, Néerlandais *m*; *Br Fam* **if that's a real diamond, (then) I'm a D.** si ça c'est un vrai diamant, alors je mange mon chapeau

Dutchwoman ['dʌtʃwʊmən] *n* Hollandaise *f*, Néerlandaise *f*

dutiful ['djuːtɪfʊl] *adj (obedient)* obéissant(e)

duty ['djuːtɪ] *(pl* **duties)** *n* (**a**) *(obligation)* devoir *m* (**to** envers); **to do one's d.** faire son devoir; **to fail in one's d.** manquer à son devoir; **to make it one's d. to...** se faire un devoir de...; **it's your d. to...** il est de votre devoir de...
(**b**) *(task)* **duties** fonctions *fpl*; **to take up** *or* **assume one's duties** entrer en fonctions; **to carry out** *or* **perform one's duties** exercer ses fonctions
(**c**) *(of soldier, employee)* **to be on/off d.** être/ne pas être de service; **d. roster** tableau *m* de service

(**d**) *Fin (tax)* droit *m*; **to pay d. on sth** payer une taxe sur qch

duty-free ['djuːtɪ'friː] *adj (cigarettes, wine, perfume)* hors taxe; **d. shop** magasin *m* hors taxe

duvet ['duːveɪ] *n* couette *f*; **d. cover** housse *f* de couette

dwarf [dwɔːf] *(pl* **dwarfs** *or* **dwarves** [dwɔːvz]) **1** *n & adj* nain(e) *m,f*
2 *vt (be taller than)* écraser; *Fig (achievements, success)* éclipser

dwell [dwel] *(pt & pp* **dwelled** *or* **dwelt** [dwelt]) *vi Lit (live)* demeurer
▸ **dwell on, dwell upon** *vt insep* remâcher, ressasser; **let's not d. on it** n'y pensons plus

dwelling ['dwelɪŋ] *n Lit* **d. (place)** demeure *f*, résidence *f*; **d. house** maison *f* d'habitation

dwelt [dwelt] *pt & pp of* **dwell**

dwindle ['dwɪndəl] *vi* diminuer; **to d. (away) to nothing** se réduire à rien

dwindling ['dwɪndəlɪŋ] *adj (funds, membership)* en baisse; *(enthusiasm)* faiblissant(e)

dye [daɪ] **1** *n (for clothes, hair)* teinture *f*
2 *vt* teindre; **to d. sth black/red** teindre qch en noir/rouge; **to d. one's hair** se teindre les cheveux

dyed-in-the-wool ['daɪdɪnðə'wʊl] *adj (conservative, Englishman)* bon teint *inv*

dying ['daɪɪŋ] **1** *npl* **the d.** les mourants *mpl*, les moribonds *mpl*
2 *adj (person)* mourant(e), agonisant(e); *(industry, tradition)* moribond(e); **to my d. day** jusqu'à ma mort; **d. wish** dernières volontés *fpl*; **d. words** dernières paroles *fpl*

dyke [daɪk] *n (barrier)* digue *f* (**b**) *very Fam (lesbian)* gouine *f*, = terme injurieux désignant une lesbienne

dynamic [daɪ'næmɪk] **1** *n (driving force)* dynamique *f*
2 *adj also Fig* dynamique

dynamics [daɪ'næmɪks] *npl* dynamique *f*

dynamism ['daɪnəmɪzəm] *n (of person, society)* dynamisme *m*

dynamite ['daɪnəmaɪt] **1** *n also Fig* dynamite *f*; *Fam* **it's d.!** *(marvellous)* c'est du tonnerre!
2 *vt* dynamiter

dynamo ['daɪnəməʊ] *(pl* **dynamos)** *n* dynamo *f*

dynastic [dɪ'næstɪk] *adj* dynastique

dynasty ['dɪnəstɪ] *(pl* **dynasties)** *n* dynastie *f*

dysentery ['dɪsəntrɪ] *n* dysenterie *f*

dysfunctional [dɪs'fʌŋkʃənəl] *adj* **a d. family** une famille à problèmes

dyslexia [dɪs'leksɪə] *n* dyslexie *f*

dyslexic [dɪs'leksɪk] *adj* dyslexique

dystrophy ['dɪstrəfɪ] *n Med* dystrophie *f*

E

E, e [iː] *n* **(a)** *(letter)* E, e *m inv* **(b)** *Mus* mi *m* **(c)** *(abbr* **east)** E **(d)** *(abbr* **ecstasy)** X *m*, exta *m*

each [iːtʃ] **1** *adj* chaque; **e. one of us** chacun(e) de nous *ou* d'entre nous
2 *pron* **(a)** *(both, all)* chacun(e) *m,f*; **e. of us** chacun(e) de nous *ou* d'entre nous; **we e. earn $300** nous gagnons chacun 300 dollars; **peaches at 25 cents e.** pêches à 25 cents chacune *ou* 25 cents pièce; **a little of e.** un peu de chaque **(b)** *(reciprocal)* **e. other** *(two)* l'un l'autre (l'une l'autre); *(more than two)* les uns les autres (les unes les autres); **separated from e. other** séparé l'un de l'autre; **they hate e. other** ils se haïssent; **we write to e. other** nous nous écrivons

eager ['iːgə(r)] *adj (look, voice)* avide; *(supporter)* fervent(e); *(desire, hope)* ardent(e), vif (vive); **to be e. for sth/to do sth** désirer vivement qch/faire qch; **to be e. to please** être désireux(euse) de plaire

eagerly ['iːgəlɪ] *adv (listen)* avidement; *(work, talk)* avec enthousiasme; **e. awaited** attendu(e) avec impatience

eagerness ['iːgənɪs] *n* impatience *f*; *(to learn, please)* vif désir *m*; **to show e. in doing sth** montrer un intérêt très vif à faire qch

eagle ['iːgəl] *n* aigle *m*

eagle-eyed [iːgə'laɪd] *adj* aux yeux d'aigle

ear ['ɪə(r)] *n* **(a)** oreille *f*; **to have an e. for music** avoir l'oreille musicale; **to have an e. for languages** avoir une bonne oreille pour les langues; *Med* **e., nose and throat specialist** oto rhino(laryngologiste) *mf*; **e. lobe** lobe *m* de l'oreille **(b)** *(of wheat)* épi *m* **(c)** *(idioms)* **to play it by e.** *(improvise)* improviser; **to have sb's e.** avoir l'oreille de qn; **to keep one's e. to the ground** être sur le qui-vive; **to go in one e. and out the other** *(of words, information)* entrer par une oreille et sortir par l'autre; *Fam* **to be up to one's ears in debt** être endetté(e) jusqu'au cou; *Br Fam* **to be up to one's ears in work** être accablé(e) de travail; *Br Fam* **to be thrown out on one's e.** se faire jeter dehors *ou* sur le pavé; **I'm all ears** je suis tout ouïe; **my ears were burning** j'avais les oreilles qui sifflaient; **the house was crumbling around their ears** la maison s'écroulait tout autour d'eux

earache ['ɪəreɪk] *n* mal *m* d'oreille(s); **to have e.** avoir mal à l'oreille/aux oreilles

eardrum ['ɪədrʌm] *n* tympan *m*

earful ['ɪəfʊl] *n Fam* **to give sb an e.** passer un savon à qn; **to get an e.** se faire passer un savon

earl [ɜːl] *n* comte *m*

earlier ['ɜːlɪə(r)] **1** *adj (previous)* plus ancien(enne); **I caught an e. train** j'ai pris un train qui partait plus tôt; **her e. novels** ses romans précédents
2 *adv* **e. (on)** avant; **a few days e.** quelques jours plus tôt;

no e. than tomorrow pas avant demain; **as we saw e.** comme nous l'avons vu auparavant

earliest ['ɜːlɪəst] **1** *n* **at the e.** au plus tôt; **the e. I can be there is four o'clock** je pourrai être là à quatre heures au plus tôt
2 *adj (opportunity, memory)* premier(èrc); **from the e. times** depuis les temps les plus reculés; **at the e. possible moment** le plus tôt possible, dans les plus brefs délais

early ['ɜːlɪ] **1** *adj* **(a)** *(in the day)* matinal(e); **to have an e. night** se coucher tôt; **to be an e. riser** être matinal, se lever de bon matin; *Prov* **the e. bird catches the worm** l'avenir appartient à ceux qui se lèvent tôt **(b)** *(at beginning of period of time)* **in (the) e. summer** au début de l'été; **at an e. age** tout jeune; **in the e. 1950s** au début des années 50; **an e. example of...** un des premiers exemples de... **(c)** *(ahead of time)* en avance; **half an hour e.** en avance d'une demi-heure **(d)** *(premature) (death)* prématuré(e); **e. retirement** préretraite *f*; *Mil* **e. warning system** système *m* radar de préalerte **(e)** *(in future)* **at an e. date** prochainement
2 *adv* **(a)** *(in the day)* de bonne heure, tôt; **e. in the morning** le matin de bonne heure; **e. in the evening** tôt dans la soirée; **as e. as possible** le plus tôt possible **(b)** *(at beginning of period of time)* **e. in the year** au début de l'année; **e. on** dès l'abord; **e. in one's life** dans sa jeunesse; **e. in one's career** au début de sa carrière **(c)** *(ahead of time)* en avance; **too e.** trop tôt **(d)** *(prematurely) (die)* prématurément; **to retire e.** prendre une retraite anticipée

earmark ['ɪəmɑːk] *vt (funds)* assigner, affecter **(for** à); **the building is earmarked for closure** il est prévu que ce bâtiment soit fermé

earn [ɜːn] *vt (money)* gagner; *(rest, respect)* mériter; **to e. sb's love** gagner le cœur de qn; **to e. sb's respect** valoir le respect à qn; **to e. one's living** gagner sa vie

earner ['ɜːnə(r)] *n (wage)* **e.** salarié(e) *m,f*; **to be a big/small e.** gagner beaucoup/peu; *Br Fam* **a nice little e.** une bonne petite affaire

earnest ['ɜːnɪst] **1** *n* **in e.** sérieusement; **things have started in e.** les choses ont vraiment commencé
2 *adj (person, effort, discussion)* sérieux(euse); *(expression)* pénétré(e), grave; *(voice)* pressant(e); *(desire)* profond(e)

earnestly ['ɜːnɪstlɪ] *adv* sérieusement; *(desire)* profondément; *(hope, believe)* sincèrement

earning power ['ɜːnɪŋ'pauə(r)] *n* revenu *m* potentiel

earnings ['ɜːnɪŋz] *npl (of person)* salaire *m*; *(of company)* bénéfices *mpl*; **e. related** *(pensions, benefits)* proportionnel(elle) au salaire

earphones ['ɪəfəʊnz] *npl* écouteurs *mpl*

earpiece ['ɪəpiːs] *n (of telephone)* écouteur *m*

earplug ['ɪəplʌg] *n* boule *f* Quiès®

earring ['ɪərɪŋ] *n* boucle *f* d'oreille

earshot ['ɪəʃɒt] *n* within/out of e. à portée/hors de portée de voix

ear-splitting ['ɪəsplɪtɪŋ] *adj* à vous déchirer *ou* crever les tympans

earth [ɜːθ] **1** *n* (a) *(planet)* the E. la Terre; *Fam* where/ why on e....? où/pourquoi diable...?; to cost the e. coûter les yeux de la tête; to promise sb the e. promettre la lune à qn (b) *(ground)* sol *m*; *(soil)* terre *f*; *Fig* to come back to e. (with a bump) revenir (brutalement) sur terre; *Fig* to go to e. *(of fugitive)* se terrer (c) *Br Elec* terre *f*, masse *f*
   2 *vt Br Elec* mettre à la terre

earthenware ['ɜːθənweə(r)] **1** *n* poterie *f* (de terre)
   2 *adj* en *ou* de terre cuite

earthling ['ɜːθlɪŋ] *n* terrien(enne) *m,f*

earthly ['ɜːθlɪ] *adj* (a) *(life, existence)* terrestre (b) *Fam (for emphasis)* there's no e. reason why... il n'y a absolument aucune raison pour que...; she hasn't got an e. (chance) elle n'a pas la moindre chance

earthquake ['ɜːθkweɪk] *n* tremblement *m* de terre, séisme *m*

earth-shattering ['ɜːθʃætərɪŋ] *adj Fam* stupéfiant(e)

earthworks ['ɜːθwɜːks] *n* travaux *mpl* de terrassement; *Mil* fortifications *fpl* en terre

earthworm ['ɜːθwɜːm] *n* ver *m* de terre

earthy ['ɜːθɪ] *adj* (a) *(of or like earth)* terreux(euse); to have an e. smell sentir la terre (b) *(coarse)* truculent(e); *(uninhibited)* direct(e)

earwax ['ɪəwæks] *n* cérumen *m*, cire *f*

earwig ['ɪəwɪg] *n (insect)* perce-oreille *m*

ease [iːz] **1** *n* (a) *(facility)* facilité *f*, aisance *f*; with e. avec facilité *ou* aisance (b) *(comfort)* tranquillité *f*, bien-être *m*; at e. à l'aise; to put sb at (their) e. mettre qn à l'aise; to put *or* set sb's mind at e. rassurer qn; a life of e. une vie d'oisiveté
   2 *vt* (a) *(alleviate) (pain)* calmer, soulager; to e. sb's mind rassurer qn (b) *(relax) (pressure)* soulager; *(tension)* réduire; *(restrictions)* assouplir (c) *(move carefully, slowly)* déplacer doucement
   3 *vi (of pain, pressure)* s'atténuer; *(of wind, rain)* se calmer; *(of situation)* se détendre

▸ **ease off, ease up** *vi (of pain, rain)* se calmer

easel ['iːzəl] *n* chevalet *m*

easily ['iːzɪlɪ] *adv* (a) *(without difficulty)* facilement, sans difficulté; that's e. said c'est facile à dire (b) *(undoubtedly)* e. the best de loin le meilleur/la meilleure; he is e. forty il a au moins quarante ans (c) *(comfortably)* à son aise

easiness ['iːzɪnɪs] *n* (a) *(of task)* facilité *f* (b) *(of manner)* décontraction *f*

east [iːst] **1** *n* est *m*; to the e. (of) à l'est (de); the E. *(the Orient)* l'Orient *m*; *(Eastern Europe)* l'Est
   2 *adj (coast, side)* est *inv*; *(wind)* d'est; E. Africa l'Afrique *f* orientale; *Br* the E. End = les quartiers pauvres et populeux de l'est de Londres ou Glasgow; *Formerly* E. Germany l'Allemagne *f* de l'Est; *Old-fashioned* the E. Indies les Indes *fpl* orientales; the E. Side = les quartiers est de New York
   3 *adv* à l'est; *(travel)* vers l'est; e. of the Rhine à l'est du Rhin; to face e. être orienté(e) à l'est

eastbound ['iːstbaʊnd] *adj (train, traffic)* en direction de l'est

Easter ['iːstə(r)] *n* Pâques *fpl*; at E. à Pâques; E. egg œuf *m* de Pâques; E. Island l'île *f* de Pâques; E. Monday lundi *m* de

Pâques; E. Sunday dimanche *m* ou jour *m* de Pâques; E. week *(following Easter)* semaine *f* de Pâques; *(Holy Week)* semaine sainte

easterly ['iːstəlɪ] **1** *n (wind)* vent *m* d'est
   2 *adj (point)* à l'est; *(wind)* d'est, qui vient de l'est; in an e. direction vers l'est

eastern ['iːstən] *adj* est *inv*; *(of Far East)* oriental(e); e. France l'est *m* de la France; E. Europe l'Europe *f* de l'est; *Am* E. Standard Time heure *f* de la côte est de l'Amérique du Nord

eastward ['iːstwəd] **1** *adj (in the east)* à l'est, dans l'est
   2 *adv* = eastwards

eastwards ['iːstwədz] *adv (face, point)* à l'est; *(go, travel)* vers l'est

easy ['iːzɪ] **1** *adj* (a) *(not difficult)* facile; *(solution)* simple; to be e. to please ne pas être difficile; e. to get on with facile à vivre; *Fam* as e. as ABC *or* as pie facile comme tout, simple comme bonjour; the e. way out la solution de facilité; *Fam* e. money argent *m* facile; e. on the eye agréable à regarder; *Com* by e. payments, on e. terms avec facilités de paiement; *Br Fam* I'm e. (either way) *(I don't mind)* ça m'est égal (b) *(comfortable, relaxed) (pace, life)* tranquille; *(manners)* libre, dégagé(e); *(style)* facile, naturel(elle); *Fam* to be on e. street ne pas avoir de problèmes financiers; to have an e. time (of it) avoir la vie facile; e. chair fauteuil *m*
   2 *adv* to go e. on sb/sth y aller doucement avec qn/qch; to take things *or* it e. *(lead a life of ease)* mener une vie tranquille; *(not overdo things)* ralentir; take it e.! *(calm down)* t'en fais pas!; that's easier said than done c'est plus facile à dire qu'à faire; e. come, e. go ça va, ça vient

easy-going ['iːzɪ'gəʊɪŋ] *adj (tolerant)* coulant(e), accommodant(e); *(calm)* décontracté(e)

eat [iːt] *(pt* ate [et, eɪt], *pp* eaten ['iːtən]) **1** *vt* (a) manger; to e. one's breakfast prendre son petit déjeuner (b) *(idioms)* to e. sb out of house and home ruiner qn en nourriture; *Fam* I could e. a horse! j'ai une faim de loup!; *Fam* what's eating you? qu'est-ce qui te tracasse?; to e. one's words se rétracter; *Fam* if you're right, I'll e. my hat si tu as raison, je mange mon chapeau
   2 *vi* manger; *Fig* you'll have them eating out of your hand ils te mangeront dans la main

▸ **eat away at** *vt insep (erode) (rocks, self-confidence)* éroder, miner; *(foundations)* saper

▸ **eat into** *vt insep (erode)* ronger; *Fig (time, savings)* entamer

▸ **eat out** *vi* manger dehors, manger au restaurant

▸ **eat up 1** *vt sep* (a) *(food)* manger jusqu'à la dernière miette, finir (b) *(petrol, money)* consommer beaucoup par
   2 *vi* finir son assiette; e. up! mange!

eaten ['iːtən] *pp of* eat

eater ['iːtə(r)] *n* mangeur(euse) *m,f*

eatery ['iːtərɪ] *(pl* eateries) *n Am* (café-)restaurant *m*

eats [iːts] *npl Fam* bouffe *f*

eau de Cologne ['əʊdəkə'ləʊn] *n* eau *f* de Cologne

eaves ['iːvz] *npl* avant-toit *m*

eavesdrop ['iːvzdrɒp] *(pt & pp* eavesdropped) *vi* to e. (on sb/sth) écouter avec indiscrétion (qn/qch); she was eavesdropping outside the door elle écoutait à la porte

ebb [eb] **1** *n (of tide)* reflux *m*; e. tide marée *f* descendante; *Fig* the e. and flow *(of events)* les fluctuations *fpl*; *Fig* to be at a low e. *(of person, spirits)* être déprimé(e)
   2 *vi (of tide)* baisser

▸ **ebb away** *vi (of water)* s'écouler; *(of strength, enthusiasm)* faiblir, baisser

ebony ['ebənɪ] n ébène f
ebullience [ɪ'bʌlɪəns] n bouillonnement m, effervescence f
ebullient [ɪ'bʌlɪənt] adj bouillant(e), exubérant(e)
EC [iː'siː] n (abbr **European Community**) CE f
eccentric [ek'sentrɪk] n & adj excentrique mf
eccentricity [eksen'trɪsɪtɪ] n excentricité f
ecclesiastic [ɪkliːzɪ'æstɪk] **1** n ecclésiastique m **2** adj ecclésiastique
ECG [iːsiː'dʒiː] n Med (abbr **electrocardiograph**) électrocardiographe m
echelon ['eʃəlɒn] n échelon m
echo ['ekəʊ] **1** n (pl **echoes**) also Fig écho m **2** vt (pt & pp **echoed**) (words) répéter; (opinion) se faire l'écho de **3** vi résonner (**with** de)
eclair [eɪ'kleə(r)] n (pastry) éclair m; **chocolate e.** éclair au chocolat
eclectic [ə'klektɪk] adj (tastes, style) éclectique; (blend) hétérogène
eclipse [ɪ'klɪps] **1** n also Fig éclipse f **2** vt also Fig éclipser
eco-friendly ['iːkəʊfrendlɪ] adj (product) écologique, vert(e); (lifestyle, person) qui respecte l'environnement
ecological [iːkə'lɒdʒɪkəl] adj (damage, balance) écologique; (campaign, activist) écologiste
ecologist [ɪ'kɒlədʒɪst] n écologiste mf
ecology [ɪ'kɒlədʒɪ] n écologie f
e-commerce [iː'kɒmɜːs] n e-commerce m, commerce m électronique
economic [iːkə'nɒmɪk] adj (a) Econ économique (b) (profitable) rentable; **to make sth e.** rentabiliser qch
economical [iːkə'nɒmɪkəl] adj (cost-effective) économique; (style) concis(e); **to be e. with the truth** ne dire la vérité qu'à moitié
economically [iːkə'nɒmɪklɪ] adv économiquement; (written) dans un style concis
economics [iːkə'nɒmɪks] **1** n économie f **2** npl (financial aspects) aspects mpl financiers
economist [ɪ'kɒnəmɪst] n économiste mf
economize [ɪ'kɒnəmaɪz] vi économiser (**on** sur)
economy [ɪ'kɒnəmɪ] n (pl **economies**) n économie f; **economies of scale** économies d'échelle; Av **e. class** classe f économique; **e. drive** politique f de réduction des dépenses; **e. measure** mesure f d'économie; **e. size** (of packet) taille f économique
ecstasy ['ekstəsɪ] n (pl **ecstasies**) n (emotional state) extase f; (drug) ecstasy f; **to go into ecstasies over sth** s'extasier devant qch
ecstatic [ek'stætɪk] adj fou (folle) de joie; **he was e. about** or **over the news** la nouvelle l'a rendu fou de joie
ECT [iːsiː'tiː] n Med (abbr **electroconvulsive therapy**) traitement m par électrochocs
Ecuador ['ekwədɔː(r)] n l'Équateur m
ecumenical [iːkjʊ'menɪkəl] adj Rel œcuménique
eczema ['eksɪmə] n eczéma m; **to have e.** avoir de l'eczéma
ed [ed] (**a**) (abbr **edition**) éd(it) (**b**) (abbr **editor**) dir.
eddy ['edɪ] **1** n (pl **eddies**) tourbillon m **2** vi (pt & pp **eddied**) (of water) faire des remous; (of wind, snow) tourbillonner
Eden ['iːdən] n l'Éden m
edge [edʒ] **1** n (**a**) (of table, road, river) bord m; (of wood) lisière f; (of book) tranche f; **at the water's e.** au bord de

l'eau; **to be on the e. of** (new age) être au seuil de; (war) être au bord de; Fig **to be on the e. of one's seat** retenir son souffle (**b**) (of blade, tool) tranchant m; (of stone) arête f; **to take the e. off** (blade, appetite) émousser; (enjoyment) gâter; Fig **to be on e.** être énervé(e); Fig **to set sb on e.** énerver qn (**c**) (advantage) **to have the e.** (over sb) être avantagé(e) (par rapport à qn) **2** vt (in sewing) border (**with** de) **3** vi (move slowly) **to e.** past passer lentement devant qn; **to e.** towards avancer lentement vers
‣ **edge out** vt sep (supplant) évincer (**of** de)
edgeways ['edʒweɪz], **edgewise** ['edʒwaɪz] adv (on its edge) de chant; (from side) de côté; Fam **I can't get a word in e.** je ne peux pas en placer une
edgy ['edʒɪ] adj nerveux(euse); **to get e.** s'énerver
edible ['edɪbəl] adj (safe to eat) comestible; (fit to eat) mangeable
edict ['iːdɪkt] n Formal édit m
edification [edɪfɪ'keɪʃən] n édification f
edifice ['edɪfɪs] n also Fig édifice m
edify ['edɪfaɪ] (pt & pp **edified**) vt édifier
edifying ['edɪfaɪɪŋ] adj édifiant(e)
Edinburgh ['edɪnbrə] n Édimbourg
edit ['edɪt] vt (**a**) (correct) réviser; (prepare for publication) préparer pour la publication; **edited by** (coordinated by) sous la direction de (**b**) (film) monter (**c**) (manage) (newspaper, magazine) diriger (**d**) Comptr éditer
‣ **edit out** vt sep (scene) couper
editing ['edɪtɪŋ] n Cin montage m
edition [ɪ'dɪʃən] n (of book, newspaper) édition f; **in last night's e. of the programme** dans l'émission d'hier soir
editor ['edɪtə(r)] n (**a**) (of published work) (author) rédacteur(trice) m,f; (in charge) directeur(trice) m,f (**b**) (of film) monteur(euse) m,f (**c**) (of newspaper, magazine) rédacteur(trice) m,f en chef; (of section) rédacteur(trice) (**d**) Comptr (software) éditeur m
editorial [edɪ'tɔːrɪəl] **1** n éditorial m **2** adj de rédaction
EDP [iːdiː'piː] n Comptr (abbr **electronic data processing**) informatique f
educate ['edjʊkeɪt] vt éduquer, instruire; **he was educated at Harvard** il a fait ses études à Harvard
educated ['edjʊkeɪtɪd] adj instruit(e); **I made an e. guess** j'ai émis une hypothèse, mais je ne risquais guère de me tromper
education [edjʊ'keɪʃən] n (process of learning, knowledge) éducation f; (process of teaching) enseignement m; **to get (oneself) an e.** faire des études; **to complete one's e.** terminer ses études; Fig **it was an e. working over there** c'était instructif de travailler là-bas
educational [edjʊ'keɪʃənəl] adj (system) éducatif(ive); (establishment, publisher) scolaire; (qualification) d'enseignement; (experience, visit) instructif(ive)
Edwardian [ed'wɔːdɪən] adj (architecture, furniture) de l'époque d'Édouard VII
EEC [iːiː'siː] n Formerly (abbr **European Economic Community**) CEE f
eel [iːl] n anguille f
eerie ['ɪərɪ] adj (atmosphere, cry) sinistre; (silence) de mort; (feeling) étrange
eerily ['ɪərɪlɪ] adv étrangement
eff [ef] vi Br Fam Euph **to e. and blind** débiter des grossièretés
efface [ɪ'feɪs] vt effacer

effect [ɪ'fekt] **1** n (**a**) (result) effet m (**on** sur); **to take e.** (of drug, medicine) faire effet, agir; (of law) prendre effet; **to put sth into e.** mettre qch en application; **in e.** en fait; **or words to that e.** ou quelque chose d'approchant (**b**) (impression) effet m; **for e.** pour faire de l'effet (**c**) Formal **personal effects** effets mpl personnels **2** vt (cause) (change, rescue) effectuer; (saving, wish) réaliser; (solution) apporter (**to** à)

effective [ɪ'fektɪv] adj (**a**) (efficient, successful) efficace; (argument, speech) convaincant(e) (**b**) (actual, real) (profit, value) réel(elle); **she will assume e. control of the business** c'est elle qui dirigera concrètement l'entreprise (**c**) Law (in force) **to be e.** prendre effet

effectively [ɪ'fektɪvlɪ] adv (**a**) (efficiently) avec efficacité; (speak) de façon convaincante (**b**) (really) en fait, en réalité; **they are e. the same** en fait, ils sont identiques

effectiveness [ɪ'fektɪvnɪs] n efficacité f

effeminate [ɪ'femɪnət] adj efféminé(e)

effervescent [efə'vesənt] adj also Fig effervescent(e)

effete [ɪ'fiːt] adj (person) veule; (gesture) efféminé(e)

efficacious [efɪ'keɪʃəs] adj Formal efficace

efficacy [ɪ'fɪkəsɪ] n Formal efficacité f

efficiency [ɪ'fɪʃənsɪ] n efficacité f; (output, productivity) rendement m

efficient [ɪ'fɪʃənt] adj efficace; (productive) performant(e); **to be e. at sth** faire qch avec compétence

efficiently [ɪ'fɪʃəntlɪ] adv efficacement

effigy [ˈefɪdʒɪ] (pl **effigies**) n effigie f

effing [ˈefɪŋ] adj Br Fam Euph fichu(e)

effluent [ˈefluənt] n effluents mpl

effort [ˈefət] n (**a**) (exertion) effort m; **to make an e.** (to do sth) faire un effort (pour faire qch); **put some e. into it!** fais un effort!; **to be worth the e.** valoir la peine (**b**) (attempt) tentative f (**at doing sth** pour faire qch); **a good e.** un bel effort; **a poor e.** un effort insuffisant

effortless [ˈefətlɪs] adj (victory, success) facile; (skill, grace) naturel(elle)

effortlessly [ˈefətlɪslɪ] adv sans effort

effrontery [ɪ'frʌntərɪ] n effronterie f

effusive [ɪ'fjuːsɪv] adj (person) démonstratif(ive), expansif(ive); (welcome, speech) enthousiaste

effusively [ɪ'fjuːsɪvlɪ] adv (praise, welcome) avec un enthousiasme débordant; (thank) avec effusion

EFL [iːe'fel] n (abbr **English as a Foreign Language**) anglais m langue étrangère

EFT [iːef'tiː] n Comptr (abbr **electronic funds transfer**) transfert m de fonds électronique

EFTA [ˈeftə] n (abbr **European Free Trade Association**) AELE f

EFTPOS [ˈeftpɒs] n Comptr (abbr **electronic funds transfer at point of sale**) transfert m de fonds électronique sur point de vente

eg [iː'dʒiː] abbr p. ex.

egalitarian [ɪgælɪ'teərɪən] **1** n égalitariste mf **2** adj (society) égalitaire

egalitarianism [ɪgælɪ'teərɪənɪzəm] n égalitarisme m

egg [eg] n (**a**) œuf m; **e. cup** coquetier m; **e. timer** sablier m; **e. white** blanc m d'œuf; **e. yolk** jaune m d'œuf (**b**) (idioms) **to have e. on one's face** être ridicule; Prov **don't put all your eggs in one basket** il ne faut pas mettre tous ses œufs dans le même panier

▸ **egg on** vt sep encourager (**to do sth** à faire qch)

egghead [ˈeghed] n Hum or Pej intello mf

eggplant [ˈegplænt] n Am aubergine f

eggshell [ˈegʃel] n coquille f d'œuf

eggwhisk [ˈegwɪsk] n fouet m

egis [ˈiːdʒɪs] Am = **aegis**

ego [ˈiːgəʊ] (pl **egos**) n ego m; **to give sb's e. a boost** flatter l'ego de qn; Fam **he's on an e. trip** il fait ça uniquement parce que ça flatte son ego

egocentric [iːgəʊ'sentrɪk] adj égocentrique

egoist [ˈiːgəʊɪst] n égoïste mf

egotism [ˈiːgəʊtɪzəm] n égocentrisme m

egotist [ˈiːgəʊtɪst] n égocentrique mf

egotistic(al) [iːgəʊ'tɪstɪk(əl)] adj égocentrique

Egypt [ˈiːdʒɪpt] n l'Égypte f

Egyptian [ɪ'dʒɪpʃən] **1** n Égyptien(enne) m,f **2** adj égyptien(enne)

eiderdown [ˈaɪdədaʊn] n édredon m

eight [eɪt] **1** n huit m inv; **come at e.** venez à huit heures; **e. and e. are sixteen** huit et huit font seize; **there were e. of us** nous étions huit; **all e. of them left** tous les huit sont partis, ils sont partis tous les huit; **the e. of hearts** (in cards) le huit de cœur **2** adj huit; **e. cars** huit voitures; **e. dollars** huit dollars; on **page e.** (à la) page huit; **to be e. (years old)** avoir huit ans; **they live at number e.** ils habitent au numéro huit; **e. o'clock** huit heures; **it's e. minutes to five** il est cinq heures moins huit

eighteen [eɪ'tiːn] **1** n dix-huit m inv **2** adj dix-huit; see also **eight**

eighteenth [eɪ'tiːnθ] **1** n (**a**) (fraction) dix-huitième m; (in series) dix-huitième mf (**b**) (of month) dix-huit m inv **2** adj dix-huitième; see also **eighth**

eighth [eɪtθ] **1** n (**a**) (fraction) huitième m; (in series) huitième mf; **Edward the E.** Édouard Huit (**b**) (of month) huit m inv; **(on) the e. of May** le huit mai; **we're leaving on the e.** nous partons le huit **2** adj huitième

eightieth [ˈeɪtɪɪθ] **1** n (fraction) quatre-vingtième m; (in series) quatre-vingtième mf **2** adj quatre-vingtième

eighty [ˈeɪtɪ] **1** n quatre-vingts m inv; **he was doing e.** (in car) il faisait du quatre-vingt (à l'heure); **in the eighties** (decade) dans les années quatre-vingt; **to be in one's eighties** avoir quatre-vingts ans passés; **the temperature was in the eighties** il faisait dans les vingt-cinq degrés **2** adj quatre-vingts; **e. cars/people** quatre-vingts voitures/personnes; **e. percent** quatre-vingt pour cent; **she's about e. (years old)** elle a dans les quatre-vingts ans

Eire [ˈeərə] n l'Eire f

either [ˈaɪðə(r), ˈiːðə(r)] **1** adj (**a**) (one or the other) l'un (l'une) ou l'autre; **I didn't like e. book** je n'ai aimé ni l'un ni l'autre des deux livres; **e. candidate may win** les deux candidats ont des chances de gagner (**b**) (both) les deux; **on e. side** des deux côtés; **in e. case** dans les deux cas **2** pron (one or the other) l'un (l'une), l'autre; **either (of them) will do** l'un ou l'autre fera l'affaire; **I don't want e. (of them)** je n'en veux ni l'un ni l'autre; **I don't believe e. of you** je ne vous crois ni l'un ni l'autre **3** conj **e.... or...** ou... ou..., soit... soit...; **e. you or your sister** ou toi ou ta sœur, soit toi soit ta sœur; **she doesn't eat e. meat or fish** elle ne mange ni viande ni poisson; **e. come in or go out!** ou tu rentres ou tu sors! **4** adv **if you don't go, I won't go e.** si tu n'y vas pas, moi non plus; **I don't like him – I don't e.** je ne l'aime pas – moi non plus

either-or [ˈaɪðərɔː(r)] adj **it's an e. situation** c'est soit l'un soit l'autre

ejaculate [ı'dʒækjʊleıt] *vi* éjaculer

ejaculation [ıdʒækjʊ'leıʃən] *n* (a) *(of semen)* éjaculation *f* (b) *Old-fashioned (exclamation)* exclamation *f*

eject [ı'dʒekt] **1** *vt (cassette)* éjecter; *(troublemaker)* expulser
2 *vi (from plane)* s'éjecter

ejection [ı'dʒekʃən] *n (of cassette, from plane)* éjection *f*; *(of troublemaker)* expulsion *f*

ejector seat [ı'dʒektə(r)siːt] *n* siège *m* éjectable

▸ **eke out** [iːk] *vt sep (money)* dépenser avec parcimonie; *(rations, supplies)* consommer avec parcimonie; **to e. out a living** gagner péniblement sa vie

elaborate 1 *adj* [ı'læbərət] *(meal)* élaboré(e); *(drawing, description)* détaillé(e); *(excuse, scheme)* compliqué(e)
2 *vt* [ı'læbəreıt] *(formulate)* élaborer; *(flesh out)* développer
3 *vi* [ı'læbəreıt] être plus précis; **to e. on sth** donner plus de détails sur qch

elan [eı'lɑːn] *n Lit* impétuosité *f*

elapse [ı'læps] *vi* s'écouler

elastic [ı'læstık] **1** *n* élastique *m*
2 *adj also Fig* élastique; **e. band** élastique *m*, bracelet *m* en caoutchouc

elasticated [ı'læstıkeıtıd] *adj (garment, material)* extensible; *(waist)* élastique

elasticity [iːlæs'tısıtı] *n also Fig* élasticité *f*

Elastoplast® [ı'læstəplɑːst] *n Br* Élastoplast® *m*

elated [ı'leıtıd] *adj* transporté(e) (de joie)

elation [ı'leıʃən] *n* exaltation *f*

elbow ['elbəʊ] **1** *n* coude *m*; *Br Fig* **to give sb the e.** *(of employer)* se débarrasser de qn; *(of lover)* plaquer qn; *Fig* **to use some e. grease** mettre de l'huile de coude
2 *vt* **to e. sb (in the ribs)** donner un coup de coude (dans les côtes) à qn; **to e. sb aside** écarter qn d'un coup de coude; *Fig* jouer des coudes pour évincer qn; **to e. one's way through** se frayer un passage en jouant des coudes

elbowroom ['elbəʊrʊm] *n Fam Fig* **to have enough e.** avoir assez de liberté

elder¹ ['eldə(r)] **1** *n* (a) *(older person)* aîné(e) *m,f*; **young people should respect their elders** les jeunes doivent le respect à leurs aînés (b) *(of tribe)* ancien(enne) *m,f*; *(of church)* = membre d'une congrégation protestante chargé de seconder le ministre dans certaines tâches
2 *adj (brother, sister)* aîné(e); **e. statesman** grand homme *m* politique

elder² *n (tree)* sureau *m*

elderberry ['eldəberı] *(pl* **elderberries)** *n* baie *f* de sureau

elderly ['eldəlı] **1** *npl* **the e.** les personnes *fpl* âgées
2 *adj* âgé(e)

eldest ['eldıst] **1** *n* **the e.** l'aîné(e) *m,f*
2 *adj* aîné(e)

elect [ı'lekt] **1** *adj* élu(e)
2 *vt* (a) *(councillor, MP)* élire (b) *Formal (choose)* **to e. to do sth** choisir de faire qch

election [ı'lekʃən] *n* élection *f*; **to hold an e.** procéder à une élection; **to** *Br* **stand** *or Am* **run for e.** se présenter aux élections; **e. campaign** campagne *f* électorale

electioneering [ılekʃə'nıərıŋ] *n* propagande *f* électorale

elective [ı'lektıv] **1** *n Univ (course)* option *f*
2 *adj (assembly)* électif(ive); *Univ (course)* optionnel(elle)

elector [ı'lektə(r)] *n* électeur(trice) *m,f*

electoral [ı'lektərəl] *adj* électoral(e); *Am* **e. college** collège *m* électoral *(qui élit le Président des États-Unis)*; *Br* **e.**

reform réforme *f* du mode de scrutin; *Br* **e. register** *or* **roll** liste *f* électorale

electorate [ı'lektərət] *n* électorat *m*

electric [ı'lektrık] *adj* électrique; *Fig (atmosphere)* chargé(e) d'électricité; **e. blanket** couverture *f* chauffante; **e. chair** chaise *f* électrique; **e. cooker** cuisinière *f* électrique; **e. shock** décharge *f* électrique; *Med* électrochoc *m*

electrical [ı'lektrıkəl] *adj* électrique; **e. engineering** électrotechnique *f*

electrically [ı'lektrıkəlı] *adv* **e. powered/operated** qui fonctionne à l'électricité; **e. charged** chargé(e) d'électricité

electrician [ılek'trıʃən] *n* électricien(enne) *m,f*

electricity [ılek'trısıtı] *n* électricité *f*

electrification [ılektrıfı'keıʃən] *n* électrification *f*

electrify [ı'lektrıfaı] *(pt & pp* **electrified)** *vt* électrifier; *Fig (excite)* électriser

electrifying [ı'lektrıfaıŋ] *adj Fig* électrisant(e)

electrocardiogram [ılektrəʊ'kɑːdıəʊgræm] *n Med* électrocardiogramme *m*

electrocardiograph [ılektrəʊ'kɑːdıəʊgræf] *n Med* électrocardiographe *m*

electrocute [ı'lektrəkjuːt] *vt* électrocuter; **to e. oneself** s'électrocuter

electrocution [ılektrə'kjuːʃən] *n* électrocution *f*

electrode [ı'lektrəʊd] *n* électrode *f*

electrolysis [ılek'trɒlısıs] *n* électrolyse *f*

electromagnet *f*

electron [ı'lektrɒn] *n* électron *m*; **e. microscope** microscope *m* électronique

electronic [ılek'trɒnık] *adj* électronique; *Fin* **e. banking** bancatique *f*; *Comptr* **e. crime** crime *m* informatique; *Comptr* **e. mail** courrier *m* électronique; *Comptr* **e. money** argent *m* électronique; *Comptr* **e. office** bureau *m* informatisé; *Comptr* **e. payment** paiement *m* électronique

electronically [ılek'trɒnıklı] *adv* électroniquement

electronics [ılek'trɒnıks] **1** *n (subject)* électronique *f*; **e. company** société *f* d'électronique; **the e. industry** l'industrie *f* (de l')électronique
2 *npl* **the e.** *(of machine)* le système électronique

electroplated [ı'lektrəpleıtıd] *adj* plaqué(e) *(par électrodéposition)*

electroshock [ılektrəʊ'ʃɒk] *adj* **e. therapy** *or* **treatment** traitement *m* par électrochocs

elegance ['elıgəns] *n* élégance *f*

elegant ['elıgənt] *adj (appearance, movement)* élégant(e); *(reasoning)* clair(e) et simple

elegantly ['elıgəntlı] *adv* avec élégance; **e. proportioned** aux proportions élégantes

elegy ['elıdʒı] *(pl* **elegies)** *n* élégie *f*

element ['elımənt] *n* (a) *(constituent part)* part *f*; **an e. of danger/risk** une part de danger/risque; **this film has all the elements of a hit movie** ce film réunit tous les ingrédients d'un grand succès (b) *(factor)* facteur *m*; **e. of surprise** l'effet *m* de surprise; **the human/time e.** le facteur humain/temps (c) *(in society)* élément *m*; **the hooligan e.** la frange constituée par les hooligans (d) *(of kettle, electric fire)* résistance *f* (e) *(of nature)* **the four elements** les quatre éléments; *Fig* **to brave the elements** braver les éléments; **to be in one's e.** être dans son élément

elemental [elı'mentəl] *adj (basic)* fondamental(e)

elementary [elı'mentərı] *adj* élémentaire; *Am*

(education) primaire; **my Arabic is rather e.** je parle un arabe assez rudimentaire; *Am* **e.** school école *f* primaire

elephant ['elɪfənt] *n* éléphant *m*

elephantine [elɪ'fæntaɪn] *adj (movements)* lourd(e) et gauche; *(proportions)* éléphantesque

elevate ['elɪveɪt] *vt* élever **(to** à)

elevated ['elɪveɪtɪd] *adj (position, rank)* élevé(e); *(thoughts, discussion)* qui vole haut; *(language)* soutenu(e); **e. railway** métro *m* aérien

elevation [elɪ'veɪʃən] *n* **(a)** *(height)* altitude *f* **(b)** *(promotion)* élévation *f* **(to** à) **(c)** *Archit* élévation *f*

elevator ['elɪveɪtə(r)] *n* **(a)** *Am (lift)* ascenseur *m* **(b)** *(for goods)* élévateur *m* **(c)** *(on aeroplane wing)* gouvernail *m* de profondeur

eleven [ɪ'levən] **1** *n* onze *m inv*; **the French e.** *(football team)* le onze de France
2 *adj* onze; *see also* **eight**

elevenses [ɪ'levənzɪz] *npl Br Fam* casse-croûte *m inv (vers onze heures du matin)*

eleventh [ɪ'levənθ] **1** *n* **(a)** *(fraction)* onzième *m*; *(in series)* onzième *mf* **(b)** *(of month)* onze *m inv*
2 *adj* onzième; **at the e. hour** à la dernière minute; *see also* **eighth**

elf [elf] *(pl* **elves** [elvz]*)* *n* elfe *m*

elicit [ɪ'lɪsɪt] *vt (information, smile)* tirer **(from** de); *(reaction, response)* susciter **(from** de la part de)

eligibility [elɪdʒɪ'bɪlɪtɪ] *n (for grant, benefit)* droit *m* **(for** à)

eligible ['elɪdʒɪbəl] *adj* **to be e. for sth** avoir droit à qch; **e. bachelor** bon parti *m*

eliminate [ɪ'lɪmɪneɪt] *vt* éliminer

elimination [ɪlɪmɪ'neɪʃən] *n* élimination *f*; **by a process of e.** (en procédant) par élimination

elite [eɪ'liːt] **1** *n* élite *f*
2 *adj* d'élite

elitism [eɪ'liːtɪzəm] *n* élitisme *m*

elitist [eɪ'liːtɪst] *n & adj* élitiste *mf*

elixir [ɪ'lɪksə(r)] *n Lit* élixir *m*

Elizabethan [ɪlɪzə'biːθən] **1** *n* = Anglais vivant sous le règne d'Élisabeth 1ère
2 *adj* élisabéthain(e)

elk [elk] *n* élan *m*

ellipse [ɪ'lɪps] *n Math* ellipse *f*

ellipsis [ɪ'lɪpsɪs] *(pl* **ellipses** [ɪ'lɪpsiːz]*)* *n Gram* ellipse *f*

elm [elm] *n* orme *m*

elocution [elə'kjuːʃən] *n* élocution *f*, diction *f*

elongate ['iːlɒŋgeɪt] *vt* allonger

elope [ɪ'ləʊp] *vi* s'enfuir (pour se marier)

eloquence ['eləkwəns] *n* éloquence *f*

eloquent ['eləkwənt] *adj* éloquent(e)

else [els] *adv* **anyone e.** n'importe qui; *(in negative sentences)* personne d'autre; **is anyone e. interested?** quelqu'un d'autre est-il intéressé?; **someone e.** quelqu'un d'autre; **everyone e.** tous les autres; **no one e.** personne d'autre; **anything e.** n'importe quoi d'autre; *(in negative sentences)* rien d'autre; **have you anything e. to do?** as-tu autre chose à faire?; **something e.** autre chose, quelque chose d'autre; **everything e.** tout le reste; **nothing e.** rien d'autre; **somewhere e.** autre part, ailleurs; **anywhere e.** (n'importe où) ailleurs; *(in negative sentences)* nulle part ailleurs; **everywhere e.** partout ailleurs; **nowhere e.** nulle part ailleurs; **who e. was there?** qui d'autre était là?; **who broke it? – Neil, who e.?** qui l'a cassé? – Neil, qui d'autre veux-tu que ce soit!; **what e.?** quoi d'autre?; **when**

e.? à quel autre moment/quelle autre date?; **where e. did you go?** où êtes-vous allés encore?; **how e.?** de quelle autre manière?; **why e.?** pour quelle autre raison?; **little e.** pas grand-chose d'autre; **there isn't much e.** we can do nous ne pouvons pas faire grand-chose d'autre; **or e.** *(otherwise)* sinon; **do what I tell you or e.!** fais ce que je te dis ou sinon...!

elsewhere ['elsweə(r)] *adv* ailleurs, autre part

ELT [iːel'tiː] *n (abbr* **English Language Teaching***)* anglais *m* langue étrangère

elucidate [ɪ'luːsɪdeɪt] *vt (mystery)* élucider; *(reasons)* expliquer

elude [ɪ'luːd] *vt* échapper à

elusive [ɪ'luːsɪv] *adj (person)* insaisissable; *(concept)* difficile à saisir

elver ['elvə(r)] *n* civelle *f*

elves [elvz] *pl of* **elf**

emaciated [ɪ'meɪsɪeɪtɪd] *adj* émacié(e)

e-mail ['iːmeɪl] **1** *n* courrier *m* électronique; **to send an e.** to sb envoyer un courrier électronique à qn; **to send by e.** envoyer qch par courrier électronique; **to check one's e.** consulter sa boîte aux lettres électronique; **e. address** adresse *f* électronique
2 *vt* envoyer un courrier électronique à; **to e. sth to sb** envoyer qch à qn par courrier électronique

emanate ['eməneɪt] **1** *vt* dégager
2 *vi* émaner **(from** de)

emancipate [ɪ'mænsɪpeɪt] *vt* émanciper

emancipated [ɪ'mænsɪpeɪtɪd] *adj* émancipé(e)

emancipation [ɪmænsɪ'peɪʃən] *n* émancipation *f*

emasculate [ɪ'mæskjʊleɪt] *vt Fig* amputer

embalm [ɪm'baːm] *vt* embaumer

embankment [ɪm'bæŋkmənt] *n (beside railway)* talus *m*; *(beside river)* berge *f*, quai *m*

embargo [em'baːgəʊ] *(pl* **embargoes***)* **1** *n* embargo *m*; **to put an e. on** mettre un embargo sur
2 *vt* mettre un embargo sur

embark [ɪm'baːk] *vi* embarquer; *Fig* **to e. (up)on sth** s'embarquer dans qch

embarrass [ɪm'bærəs] *vt* embarrasser, gêner; *(make ashamed)* faire honte à

embarrassed [ɪm'bærəst] *adj (ashamed, uncomfortable)* embarrassé(e), gêné(e); *(financially)* gêné(e) (financièrement)

embarrassing [ɪm'bærəsɪŋ] *adj* embarrassant(e), gênant(e); **how e.!** comme ça a dû être/c'est embarrassant!

embarrassment [ɪm'bærəsmənt] *n* embarras *m*, gêne *f*; **much to my e.** à mon grand embarras; **to be an e. to sb** être une source d'embarras pour qn

embassy ['embəsɪ] *(pl* **embassies***)* *n* ambassade *f*; **the French E.** l'ambassade de France

embattled [ɪm'bætəld] *adj* assiégé(e) de toutes parts

embed [ɪm'bed] *(pt & pp* **embedded***)* *vt* **(a)** to be embedded in sth être fiché(e) dans qch; *(with cement)* être scellé(e) dans qch; *Fig* **to be embedded in sb's memory** être gravé(e) dans la mémoire de qn **(b)** *Comptr* intégrer

embellish [ɪm'belɪʃ] *vt (room)* embellir **(with** de); *(account)* enjoliver

embers ['embəz] *npl* braises *fpl*

embezzle [ɪm'bezəl] *vt* détourner **(from** de)

embezzlement [ɪm'bezəlmənt] *n* **e. (of funds)** détournement *m* de fonds

embezzler [ɪm'bezlə(r)] *n* escroc *m*

embitter [ɪm'bɪtə(r)] *vt (person)* aigrir, remplir d'amertume

embittered [ɪm'bɪtəd] *adj (person)* aigri(e)

emblazon [ɪm'bleɪzən] *vt (shield)* orner **(with** de); *Fig (name, headline)* étaler

emblem ['embləm] *n* emblème *m*

embodiment [ɪm'bɒdɪmənt] *n* incarnation *f*

embody [ɪm'bɒdɪ] *(pt & pp* **embodied)** *vt* incarner

embolden [ɪm'bəʊldən] *vt* enhardir; **to e. sb to do sth** donner à qn le courage de faire qch

embolism ['embəlɪzəm] *n Med* embolie *f*

embossed [ɪm'bɒst] *adj (metal, leather)* repoussé(e); *(letter, wallpaper, design)* en relief

embrace [ɪm'breɪs] **1** *n* étreinte *f*
2 *vt* **(a)** *(person)* étreindre; *Fig (belief, religion)* embrasser **(b)** *(include)* couvrir
3 *vi* s'étreindre

embroider [ɪm'brɔɪdə(r)] *vt (cloth)* broder; *Fig (account, report)* enjoliver

embroidery [ɪm'brɔɪdərɪ] *n* broderie *f*

embroil [ɪm'brɔɪl] *vt* entraîner (in dans), **to get embroiled in sth** se laisser entraîner dans qch

embryo ['embrɪəʊ] *(pl* **embryos)** *n* embryon *m*; *Fig* **in e.** *(plan, idea)* à l'état embryonnaire

embryonic [embrɪ'ɒnɪk] *adj Biol* embryonnaire; *(plan, idea)* à l'état embryonnaire

emend [ɪ'mend] *vt* corriger

emendation [iːmen'deɪʃən] *n* correction *f*

emerald ['emərəld] *n* émeraude *f*; **an e. necklace** un collier d'émeraudes; **e. (green)** (vert *m*) émeraude *m*; **the E. Isle** la verte Erin

emerge [ɪ'mɜːdʒ] *vi (of person, truth)* émerger **(from** de), **it later emerged that...** il est apparu par la suite que...

emergence [ɪ'mɜːdʒəns] *n (from hiding)* apparition *f*; *(of truth)* révélation *f*; *(of new state, new leader)* émergence *f*

emergency [ɪ'mɜːdʒənsɪ] *(pl* **emergencies)** *n* urgence *f*; **in an e., in case of e.** en cas d'urgence; **e. exit** sortie *f* de secours; **e. landing** atterrissage *m* forcé; **e. services** services *mpl* d'urgence; **e. stop** arrêt *m* d'urgence

emergent [ɪ'mɜːdʒənt] *adj (talent, ability)* naissant(e); *(nation)* en voie de développement

emery ['emərɪ] *n* émeri *m*; **e. board** lime *f* à ongles *(en papier émeri)*; **e. paper** papier *m* émeri

emetic [ɪ'metɪk] **1** *n* émétique *m*
2 *adj* émétique

emigrant ['emɪɡrənt] **1** *n* émigrant(e) *m,f*; *(when settled)* émigré(e) *m,f*
2 *adj* migrant(e); *(when settled)* émigré(e)

emigrate ['emɪɡreɪt] *vi* émigrer

emigration [emɪ'ɡreɪʃən] *n* émigration *f*

émigré ['emɪɡreɪ] *n* émigré(e) *m,f*

eminence ['emɪnəns] *n* **(a)** *(importance)* position *f* éminente; *(of post)* distinction *f* **(b)** *(title of cardinal)* **Your E.** Votre Éminence

eminent ['emɪnənt] *adj* éminent(e)

eminently ['emɪnəntlɪ] *adv* éminemment

emirate ['emɪreɪt] *n* émirat *m*

emissary ['emɪsərɪ] *(pl* **emissaries)** *n* émissaire *m*

emission [ɪ'mɪʃən] *n (of gas, light, bank notes)* émission *f*

emit [ɪ'mɪt] *(pt & pp* **emitted)** *vt (heat, signal, sound)* émettre; *(smell)* dégager; *(sigh, cry)* pousser

emotion [ɪ'məʊʃən] *n (strength of feeling)* émotion *f*; *(individual feeling)* sentiment *m*

emotional [ɪ'məʊʃənəl] *adj (person, reaction)* émotif(ive); *(problem, shock)* émotionnel(elle); *(film, farewell)* émouvant(e); **to get e.** être ému(e)

emotionally [ɪ'məʊʃənəlɪ] *adv (thank, welcome)* avec effusion; **to be e. involved with sb** avoir une relation intime avec qn; **to get e. involved (with sb)** s'attacher (à qn); **e. deprived** en manque d'affection

emotive [ɪ'məʊtɪv] *adj (issue)* sensible; *(argument, words)* qui fait vibrer la corde sensible

empathize ['empəθaɪz] *vi* **to e. with** *(person)* comprendre; *(plight, problems)* compatir à

empathy ['empəθɪ] *n* compassion *f*

emperor ['empərə(r)] *n* empereur *m*

emphasis ['emfəsɪs] *(pl* **emphases** ['emfəsiːz]) *n* accent *m*; **to lay** *or* **place e. on sth** *(point, fact)* mettre l'accent sur qch; *(word, syllable)* appuyer sur qch

emphasize ['emfəsaɪz] *vt (point, fact)* insister sur; *(word, syllable)* appuyer sur

emphatic [ɪm'fætɪk] *adj (denial, response, person)* catégorique; *(gesture, tone)* énergique

emphatically [ɪm'fætɪkəlɪ] *adv (say)* énergiquement; *(refuse, deny)* catégoriquement; **most e.!** absolument!

empire ['empaɪə(r)] *n also Fig* empire *m*

empirical [ɪm'pɪrɪkəl] *adj* empirique

empiricism [em'pɪrɪsɪzəm] *n* empirisme *m*

employ [ɪm'plɔɪ] **1** *Formal* **to be in sb's e.** être employé(e) par qn
2 *vt (workers, force, skills)* employer; *(tool, means)* utiliser

employee [em'plɔiː] *n* employé(e) *m,f*; **employees** *(staff)* personnel *m*, salariés *mpl*

employer [ɪm'plɔɪə(r)] *n* employeur(euse) *m,f*

employment [ɪm'plɔɪmənt] *n* **(a)** *(work)* emploi *m*; **to be in e.** avoir un emploi; **to be without e.** être sans emploi; **to give e. to sb** employer qn; **e. agency** *or* **bureau** bureau *m* ou agence *f* de placement **(b)** *(use) (of money, force)* emploi *m*; *(of tool)* utilisation *f*

empower [ɪm'paʊə(r)] *vt* **to e. sb to do sth** habiliter qn à faire qch

empress ['emprɪs] *n* impératrice *f*

emptiness ['emptɪnɪs] *n* vide *m*

empty ['emptɪ] **1** *n (bottle)* bouteille *f* vide
2 *adj (container, existence)* vide; *(promise, threat, words)* en l'air; **on an e. stomach** l'estomac vide, à jeun
3 *vt* vider
4 *vi* se vider
▸ **empty out** *vt sep (pockets)* vider

empty-handed ['emptɪ'hændɪd] *adv* les mains vides, bredouille

empty-headed ['emptɪ'hedɪd] *adj* sans cervelle; **to be e.** n'avoir rien dans la tête

EMS [iːem'es] *n (abbr* **European Monetary System)** SME *m*

EMU [iːem'juː] *n (abbr* **Economic and Monetary Union)** union *f* économique et monétaire

emu ['iːmjuː] *n* émeu *m*

emulate ['emjʊleɪt] *vt* imiter

emulsion [ɪ'mʌlʃən] *n* émulsion *f*

enable [ɪ'neɪbəl] *vt* **(a)** *(allow)* **to e. sb to do sth** permettre à qn de faire qch **(b)** *Comptr (function, device)* mettre en service

enact [ɪ'nækt] *vt (tragedy, play)* jouer; *(law)* promulguer

enamel [ɪ'næməl] **1** n émail m **2** vt (pt & pp **enamelled**, Am **enameled**) émailler

enamoured, Am **enamored** [ɪ'næməd] adj **to be e. of** être entiché(e) de; **I'm not exactly e. of the idea** je ne peux pas dire que cette idée me ravisse

encampment [ɪn'kæmpmənt] n Mil camp m, campement m

encapsulate [ɪn'kæpsjʊleɪt] vt résumer

encase [ɪn'keɪs] vt envelopper; (in concrete) noyer

enchant [ɪn'tʃɑːnt] vt (**a**) (charm) enchanter, ravir (**b**) (put under a spell) ensorceler

enchanting [ɪn'tʃɑːntɪŋ] adj (idea) très séduisant(e); (voice, person, smile) charmant(e), ravissant(e)

enchantment [ɪn'tʃɑːntmənt] n enchantement m

enchantress [ɪn'tʃɑːntrɪs] n enchanteresse f

encircle [ɪn'sɜːkəl] vt (of road, walls) entourer; (of army, police) encercler, cerner

enclave ['enkleɪv] n enclave f

enclose [ɪn'kləʊz] vt (**a**) (surround) entourer; **an enclosed space** un espace clos (**b**) (include in letter) joindre (**in** à); **please find enclosed...** veuillez trouver ci-joint ou ci-inclus...

enclosure [ɪn'kləʊʒə(r)] n (**a**) (area) enceinte f; (for animals) enclos m; (in horseracing) paddock m (**b**) (in letter) pièce f jointe

encode [en'kəʊd] vt coder, chiffrer; Comptr encoder

encompass [ɪn'kʌmpəs] vt englober, couvrir

encore ['ɒŋkɔː(r)] n = chanson, morceau etc exécutés à la suite d'un rappel; **to call for an e.** bisser; **e.!** bis!

encounter [ɪn'kaʊntə(r)] **1** n rencontre f **2** vt (person, difficulty) rencontrer; (enemy) affronter

encourage [ɪn'kʌrɪdʒ] vt encourager; **to e. sb to do sth** encourager qn à faire qch

encouragement [ɪn'kʌrɪdʒmənt] n encouragement m; **to give sb e.** encourager qn

encouraging [ɪn'kʌrɪdʒɪŋ] adj encourageant(e); (smile) d'encouragement

▸ **encroach on**, **encroach upon** [ɪn'krəʊtʃ] vt insep empiéter sur; **the sea is encroaching on the land** la mer gagne du terrain

encrusted [ɪn'krʌstɪd] adj **e. with** (jewels) incrusté(e) de; (mud) couvert(e) de

encumber [ɪn'kʌmbə(r)] vt **to be encumbered with** être encombré(e) par

encumbrance [ɪn'kʌmbrəns] n gêne f, embarras m (**to** pour)

encyclical [ɪn'sɪklɪkəl] n Rel encyclique f

encyclop(a)edia [ɪnsaɪklə'piːdɪə] n encyclopédie f

encyclop(a)edic [ɪnsaɪklə'piːdɪk] adj encyclopédique

end [end] **1** n (**a**) (extremity) bout m, extrémité f; **from one e. to the other** d'un bout à l'autre; **e. to e.** bout à bout; **to stand sth on e.** mettre qch debout; **his hair was standing on e.** ses cheveux se dressaient sur sa tête; Fig **to come to the e. of the road** or **line** être en fin de parcours (**b**) (of month, book, meeting) fin f; **for days on e.** pendant des jours entiers; **to put an e. to sth** mettre fin à qch; **to come to an e.** prendre fin; Fig **at the e. of the day** au bout du compte; **in the e.** à la longue; **she gave me the money back in the e.** elle a fini par me rembourser; **it's not the e. of the world** ce n'est pas la fin du monde; Fam **no e. of** énormément de; **e. product** produit m fini; Fig **result** m (**c**) (aim, purpose) fin f, but m; **an e. in itself** une fin en soi; **to what e.?** à quelle fin?, dans quel but?; **the e. justifies the means** la fin justifie les moyens (**d**) (idioms) Fam **to keep one's e. up** ne pas se laisser abattre; Fam **to make ends meet** joindre les deux bouts; Fam **this job will be the e. of me!** ce boulot, j'y laisserai ma peau!; Fam **to get the wrong e. of the stick** mal comprendre; **we shall never hear the e. of it!** on n'a pas fini d'en entendre parler!

2 vt finir, terminer; (argument, uncertainty) mettre fin à; Fam **to e. it all** (commit suicide) en finir

3 vi finir, se terminer; (of road, path) s'arrêter; **it ended in tears/a divorce** ça a fini en larmes/par un divorce

▸ **end up** vi finir; (in particular place) se retrouver; **to e. up doing sth** finir par faire qch

endanger [ɪn'deɪndʒə(r)] vt (person, life) mettre en danger; (chances, future, health) compromettre; **an endangered species** une espèce menacée

endear [ɪn'dɪə(r)] vt **to e. oneself to sb** se rendre sympathique aux yeux de qn

endearing [ɪn'dɪərɪŋ] adj (person, personality) attachant(e); (smile, habit) charmant(e)

endearment [ɪn'dɪəmənt] n **terms of e.** mots mpl tendres

endeavour, Am **endeavor** [ɪn'devə(r)] **1** n effort m **2** vi **to e. to do sth** s'efforcer de faire qch

endemic [en'demɪk] adj endémique; Fig **e. to** propre à

ending ['endɪŋ] n (of story) fin f; (of word) terminaison f

endive ['endaɪv] n (**a**) (curly) (chicorée f) frisée f (**b**) Am (chicory) endive f

endless ['endlɪs] adj (desert, number, possibilities) infini(e); (list, wait, task) interminable

endocrine ['endəʊkraɪn] adj Med **e. gland** glande f endocrine

endocrinology [endəʊkraɪ'nɒlədʒɪ] n endocrinologie f

endorse [ɪn'dɔːs] vt (**a**) (document, cheque) endosser; Br (driving licence) décompter des points sur (**b**) (approve) (action) approuver; (opinion) souscrire ou adhérer à; (candidature) appuyer (**c**) (product) faire de la publicité pour; **a drink endorsed by baseball stars** une boisson recommandée par de stars de base-ball

endorsement [ɪn'dɔːsmənt] n (**a**) (on document, cheque) endos m; Br (on driving licence) = mention portée sur le permis de conduire à la suite d'une infraction (**b**) (approval) (of action) approbation f (of de); (of opinion) adhésion f (of à); (of candidature) appui m (of à) (**c**) (of product) **the actress made a fortune from her e. of that make-up** l'actrice a fait une fortune en faisant de la publicité pour ce maquillage

endow [ɪn'daʊ] vt doter (**with** de)

endowment [ɪn'daʊmənt] n (**a**) Fin dotation f. **mortgage** = emprunt immobilier associé à une assurance-vie (**b**) (talent) don m, talent m

endurable [ɪn'djuːərəbəl] adj supportable

endurance [ɪn'djuːrəns] n endurance f; **beyond e.** au-delà des limites du supportable; **e. test** épreuve f d'endurance; Fig **this is a real e. test** ma patience est mise à rude épreuve

endure [ɪn'djuːə(r)] **1** vt (violence, hardship) endurer; (person, insults) supporter **2** vi (last) survivre

enduring [ɪn'djuːərɪŋ] adj durable

enema ['enəmə] n lavement m

enemy ['enəmɪ] **1** n (pl **enemies**) ennemi(e) m,f; **to be one's own worst e.** se desservir soi-même **2** adj (army, ship) ennemi(e)

energetic [enə'dʒetɪk] adj énergique

energetically [enə'dʒetɪklɪ] adv énergiquement

energy ['enədʒɪ] n énergie f; **to save e.** faire des économies d'énergie; **e. crisis** crise f de l'énergie

energy-saving ['enədʒɪseɪvɪŋ] adj qui économise l'énergie

enervating ['enəveɪtɪŋ] adj débilitant(e)

enfeeble [ɪn'fiːbəl] vt affaiblir

enfold [ɪn'fəʊld] vt envelopper (**in** dans); **to e. sb in one's arms** serrer qn dans ses bras

enforce [ɪn'fɔːs] vt (regulation) mettre en vigueur; (rights) faire valoir; **to e. the law** faire respecter la loi

enforcement [ɪn'fɔːsmənt] n (of a law) mise f en vigueur

enfranchise [ɪn'fræntʃaɪz] vt accorder le droit de vote à

engage [ɪn'geɪdʒ] **1** vt (**a**) (employ) engager; (workmen) embaucher (**b**) (occupy) (person) occuper; (attention) fixer; **to e. sb in conversation** engager la conversation avec qn; **to be engaged in doing sth** être occupé(e) à faire qch (**c**) Mil (enemy) attaquer (**d**) (cog, gear) mettre en prise; **to e. the clutch** embrayer
2 vi (**a**) **to e. in** (activity, sport) s'adonner à (**b**) (of cog wheel) (s')engager

engaged [ɪn'geɪdʒd] adj (**a**) (to be married) fiancé(e) (**b**) (busy) occupé(e) (**in** à); Br (phone, public toilet) occupé, **to be otherwise e.** avoir d'autres engagements

engagement [ɪn'geɪdʒmənt] n (**a**) (to be married) fiançailles fpl; **e. ring** bague f de fiançailles (**b**) (appointment) rendez-vous m (**c**) (military action) combat m, engagement m

engaging [ɪn'geɪdʒɪŋ] adj engageant(e), attrayant(e)

engender [ɪn'dʒendə(r)] vt faire naître, engendrer

engine ['endʒɪn] n (**a**) (of car, plane, ship) moteur m; **e. room** salle f des machines; **e. trouble** panne f de moteur (**b**) (of train) locomotive f; **e. driver** conducteur m, mécanicien m

engineer [endʒɪ'nɪə(r)] **1** n (technical specialist) ingénieur m; (mechanic) dépanneur m; (on ship) mécanicien m
2 vt (cause) (plan, downfall, defeat) machiner, manigancer; (situation) manigancer

engineering [endʒɪ'nɪərɪŋ] n ingénierie f

England ['ɪŋglənd] n l'Angleterre f

English ['ɪŋglɪʃ] **1** n (language) anglais m; **E. class/ teacher** cours m/professeur m d'anglais
2 npl **the E.** les Anglais mpl
3 adj anglais(e); **the E. Channel** la Manche

Englishman ['ɪŋglɪʃmən] n Anglais m

Englishwoman ['ɪŋglɪʃwʊmən] n Anglaise f

engrave [ɪn'greɪv] vt graver

engraver [ɪn'greɪvə(r)] n graveur m

engraving [ɪn'greɪvɪŋ] n gravure f

engrossed [ɪn'grəʊst] adj plongé(e) (**in** dans), absorbé(e) (**in** par)

engrossing [ɪn'grəʊsɪŋ] adj absorbant(e), captivant(e)

engulf [ɪn'gʌlf] vt (of waves, flames) engloutir; (of feeling) s'emparer de

enhance [ɪn'hɑːns] vt (quality of life, chances) améliorer; (beauty, colour) rehausser, mettre en valeur; (ability, effect) renforcer; (reputation, pleasure) accroître; (value) augmenter

enigma [ɪ'nɪgmə] n énigme f

enigmatic [enɪg'mætɪk] adj énigmatique

enjoy [ɪn'dʒɔɪ] vt (**a**) (take pleasure from) prendre plaisir à; (film, book, concert) aimer; (food, drink) savourer; **to e. doing sth** aimer faire qch; **to e. oneself** s'amuser (**b**) (benefit from) jouir de

enjoyable [ɪn'dʒɔɪəbəl] adj agréable

enjoyment [ɪn'dʒɔɪmənt] n plaisir m; **to get e. out of**

sth retirer du plaisir de qch; **to get e. out of doing sth** prendre plaisir à faire qch

enlarge [ɪn'lɑːdʒ] **1** vt agrandir; (hole) élargir
2 vi s'agrandir; **to e. (up)on sth** s'étendre sur qch

enlargement [ɪn'lɑːdʒmənt] n agrandissement m; (of hole) élargissement m

enlighten [ɪn'laɪtən] vt éclairer (**on** sur)

enlightened [ɪn'laɪtənd] adj éclairé(e)

enlightenment [ɪn'laɪtənmənt] n (clarification) éclaircissement m; **for your e.** pour votre édification; Hist **the E.** le Siècle des Lumières

enlist [ɪn'lɪst] **1** vt (support, help) s'assurer, (soldier) enrôler, engager
2 vi (of soldier) s'engager

enliven [ɪn'laɪvən] vt animer; (party) égayer, animer

en masse ['ɒn'mæs] adv en masse, tous ensemble

enmesh [ɪn'meʃ] vt **to be enmeshed in sth** être empêtré(e) dans qch

enmity ['enmɪtɪ] n inimitié f, hostilité f

enormity [ɪ'nɔːmɪtɪ] n énormité f

enormous [ɪ'nɔːməs] adj (in physical size) énorme; (patience, gratitude, power, intelligence) immense; (strength) colossal(e)

enormously [ɪ'nɔːməslɪ] adv énormément

enough [ɪ'nʌf] **1** adj assez de; **e. money/wine** assez d'argent/de vin; **more than e.** food plus de nourriture qu'il n'en faut
2 pron assez; **that's e.!** ça suffit!; **e. is e.** il ne faut pas exagérer; **to have e. to live on** avoir de quoi vivre; **e. said!** je vois!; **to have had e. of sb/sth** en avoir assez de qn/qch
3 adv (**a**) (sufficiently) assez; **good e.** assez bon (bonne); **he didn't try hard e.** il n'a pas vraiment essayé (**b**) (reasonably) assez; **she's a nice e. girl** c'est une fille assez sympa; **oddly or strangely e.,...** chose curieuse,...

enquire [ɪn'kwaɪə(r)] = **inquire**

enquiry [ɪn'kwaɪrɪ] = **inquiry**

enrage [ɪn'reɪdʒ] vt rendre furieux(euse)

enrapture [ɪn'ræptʃə(r)] vt éblouir, émerveiller

enraptured [ɪn'ræptʃəd] adj ébloui(e), émerveillé(e)

enrich [ɪn'rɪtʃ] vt enrichir

enrol, Am **enroll** [ɪn'rəʊl] (pt & pp enrolled) **1** vt (soldier) enrôler; (student) immatriculer; (worker) embaucher
2 vi (of soldier) s'enrôler; (of students) s'inscrire

enrolment, Am **enrollment** [ɪn'rəʊlmənt] n (of soldier) enrôlement m; (of student) immatriculation f; (of worker) embauche f

ensconce [ɪn'skɒns] vt **to e. oneself** s'installer confortablement (**in** dans)

ensemble [ɒn'sɒmbəl] n ensemble m

enshrine [ɪn'ʃraɪn] vt **to be enshrined in sth** (of belief, principle) être enraciné(e) dans qch

ensign ['ensaɪn] n (**a**) (flag) drapeau m; Naut pavillon m national (**b**) Am (naval officer) enseigne m (de vaisseau de deuxième classe)

enslave [ɪn'sleɪv] vt réduire à l'esclavage, asservir

ensnare [ɪn'sneə(r)] vt (animal, criminal) prendre au piège; Fig (lover) attirer dans ses filets

ensue [ɪn'sjuː] vi s'ensuivre

ensuing [ɪn'sjuːɪŋ] adj (in the past) qui a suivi; (in the future) qui suivra

en suite ['ɒn'swiːt] adj **e. bathroom** (in hotel) salle de bain f particulière; (in house) salle de bain f attenante

ensure [ɪnˈʃʊə(r)] *vt* assurer; **to e. that...** faire en sorte que... + *subjunctive*

ENT [iːenˈtiː] *n* (*abbr* **Ear, Nose and Throat**) ORL *f*; **E. specialist** ORL *mf*

entail [enˈteɪl] *vt* (**a**) (*involve*) entraîner, occasionner; (*difficulties*) comporter; **what does the job e.?** en quoi le travail consiste-t-il? (**b**) *Law* **to e. an estate** substituer un bien

entangle [ɪnˈtæŋɡəl] *vt* **to get** *or* **become entangled in sth** (*of person, animal*) s'empêtrer dans qch; (*of hair, string, wires*) s'emmêler dans qch; *Fig* **to be entangled with sb** (*emotionally*) avoir une histoire avec qn

entanglement [ɪnˈtæŋɡəlmənt] *n* enchevêtrement *m*; **emotional entanglements** complications *fpl* sentimentales

enter [ˈentə(r)] **1** *vt* (**a**) (*house, country, army*) entrer dans; (*university*) entrer à; (*race, exam, competition*) participer à; **to e. sb for an exam** inscrire qn à un examen; **to e. sb for a race** inscrire qn au nombre des participants d'une course; **it never entered my head that...** il ne m'est jamais venu à l'esprit que...; **to e. a protest** protester formellement (**b**) *Comptr* (*data*) entrer, introduire **2** *vi* (*go in*) entrer; **to e. for a race** se faire inscrire pour une course

► **enter into** *vt insep* (**a**) (*begin*) (*service, relationship*) entrer en; (*dispute*) entrer dans; (*negotiations*) entamer, engager; **to e. into partnership with sb** s'associer avec qn; **to e. into conversation with sb** engager une conversation avec qn (**b**) (*have a part in*) **money doesn't e. into it** l'argent n'entre pas en ligne de compte

enterprise [ˈentəpraɪz] *n* (**a**) (*undertaking, company*) entreprise *f* (**b**) (*initiative*) initiative *f*

enterprising [ˈentəpraɪzɪŋ] *adj* entreprenant(e); (*imaginative*) plein(e) d'imagination; (*solution*) ingénieux(euse)

entertain [entəˈteɪn] **1** *vt* (**a**) (*amuse*) divertir, amuser; **to e. guests** recevoir (des invités) (**b**) (*consider*) (*idea*) considérer; (*hope*) nourrir; (*fear, suspicion*) éprouver **2** *vi* (*receive guests*) recevoir

entertainer [entəˈteɪnə(r)] *n* fantaisiste *mf*; (*comedian*) comique *mf*

entertaining [entəˈteɪnɪŋ] **1** *n* (*of guests*) **to do a lot of e.** recevoir beaucoup **2** *adj* (*amusing*) divertissant(e), amusant(e)

entertainment [entəˈteɪnmənt] *n* (**a**) (*amusement*) divertissement *m*, amusement *m*; *Com* **e. allowance** indemnité *f* de représentation (**b**) (*performances*) spectacle *m*, divertissement *m*; **the e. business** l'industrie *f* du spectacle; **entertainments guide** guide *m* des spectacles

enthral, *Am* **enthrall** [ɪnˈθrɔːl] (*pt & pp* **enthralled**) *vt* captiver, passionner; (*of object, beauty*) fasciner; (*of prospect, idea*) enthousiasmer

enthralling [ɪnˈθrɔːlɪŋ] *adj* captivant(e), passionnant(e); (*object, beauty*) fascinant(e); (*prospect, idea*) enthousiasmant(e)

enthuse [ɪnˈθjuːz] **1** *vt* enthousiasmer **2** *vi* s'enthousiasmer (**about** *or* **over** pour)

enthusiasm [ɪnˈθjuːzɪæzəm] *n* enthousiasme *m*

enthusiast [ɪnˈθjuːzɪæst] *n* passionné(e) *m,f*; **a golf e.** un passionné de golf

enthusiastic [ɪnθjuːzɪˈæstɪk] *adj* enthousiaste

enthusiastically [ɪnθjuːzɪˈæstɪklɪ] *adv* avec enthousiasme

entice [ɪnˈtaɪs] *vt* attirer, séduire; **to e. sb to do sth** inciter qn à faire qch; **to e. sb away from sb/sth** appâter qn pour qu'il quitte qn/qch

enticing [ɪnˈtaɪsɪŋ] *adj* (*offer, idea*) séduisant(e), tentant(e); (*dish*) alléchant(e); (*smile*) charmeur(euse)

entire [ɪnˈtaɪə(r)] *adj* (**a**) (*whole*) entier(ère), tout(e); **the e. day** toute la journée, la journée entière (**b**) (*intact*) intact(e)

entirely [ɪnˈtaɪəlɪ] *adv* entièrement, complètement

entirety [ɪnˈtaɪərətɪ] *n* intégralité *f*; **in its e.** dans son intégralité, intégralement

entitle [ɪnˈtaɪtəl] *vt* (**a**) (*allow*) **to e. sb to sth** donner à qn droit à qch; **to e. sb to do sth** permettre à qn de faire qch; **to be entitled to sth** avoir droit à qch; **to be entitled to do sth** avoir le droit de faire qch (**b**) (*book, chapter, song*) intituler

entitlement [ɪnˈtaɪtəlmənt] *n* = ce qui revient de droit à quelqu'un

entity [ˈentɪtɪ] (*pl* **entities**) *n* entité *f*

entomologist [entəˈmɒlədʒɪst] *n* entomologiste *mf*

entomology [entəˈmɒlədʒɪ] *n* entomologie *f*

entourage [ˈɒntuːrɑːʒ] *n* entourage *m*

entrails [ˈentreɪlz] *npl* entrailles *fpl*

entrance¹ [ˈentrəns] *n* (**a**) (*way in, act of entering*) entrée *f*; **to make one's e.** faire son entrée; **to gain e. to** s'introduire *ou* pénétrer dans (**b**) (*admission*) (*to club*) admission *f*; (*to cinema*) entrée *f*; **e. examination** examen *m* d'entrée

entrance² [ɪnˈtrɑːns] *vt* (*charm*) ravir, transporter

entrancing [ɪnˈtrɑːnsɪŋ] *adj* ravissant(e), enchanteur(eresse)

entrant [ˈentrənt] *n* (*in race, competition*) inscrit(e) *m,f*; (*in examination*) candidat(e) *m,f*

entreat [ɪnˈtriːt] *vt* **to e. sb to do sth** implorer qn de faire qch

entreaty [ɪnˈtriːtɪ] (*pl* **entreaties**) *n* prière *f*, supplication *f*

entrée [ˈɒntreɪ] *n* (*dish before main course*) entrée *f*; *Am* (*main course*) plat *m* de résistance

entrenched [ɪnˈtrentʃd] *adj* (*views, ideas*) arrêté(e); (*customs*) enraciné(e)

entrepreneur [ɒntrəprəˈnɜː(r)] *n* entrepreneur *m*

entrepreneurial [ɒntrəprəˈnɜːrɪəl] *adj* (*person*) qui a l'esprit d'entreprise; (*skill, talents*) d'entrepreneur

entrust [ɪnˈtrʌst] *vt* **to e. sb with sth, to e. sth to sb** confier qch à qn

entry [ˈentrɪ] (*pl* **entries**) *n* (**a**) (*way in, act of entering*) entrée *f*; **to make one's e.** faire son entrée; **to gain e. to** s'introduire *ou* pénétrer dans (**b**) (*of competitor*) inscription *f*; **e. form** feuille *f* d'inscription (**c**) (*in encyclopedia*) article *m*; (*in dictionary*) entrée *f*; (*in diary*) note *f*

entryphone [ˈentrɪfəʊn] *n* Interphone*m*

entwine [ɪnˈtwaɪn] **1** *vt* entrelacer **2** *vi* s'entrelacer

enumerate [ɪˈnjuːməreɪt] *vt* énumérer, détailler

enunciate [ɪˈnʌnsɪeɪt] *vt* (*sound, word*) prononcer, articuler; (*opinion, view*) énoncer

envelop [ɪnˈveləp] *vt* envelopper (**in** dans)

envelope [ˈenvələʊp, ˈɒnvələʊp] *n* enveloppe *f*

enviable [ˈenvɪəbəl] *adj* enviable

envious [ˈenvɪəs] *adj* envieux(euse); **to be e. of sb** envier qn

enviously [ˈenvɪəslɪ] *adv* avec envie

environment [ɪnˈvaɪrənmənt] *n* (**a**) (*surroundings*) milieu *m* (**b**) (*nature*) **the e.** l'environnement *m*

environmental [ɪnvaɪrənˈmentəl] *adj* (**a**) **e. damage** dégâts *mpl* causés à l'environnement; **e. disaster** désastre *m* écologique; **e. policy** politique *f* de l'environnement

environmentalist [ɪnvaɪrən'mentəlɪst] n écologiste mf
environmentally [ɪnvaɪrən'mentəlɪ] adv écologiquement; **e. friendly** respectueux de l'environnement
environs [ɪn'vaɪrənz] npl environs mpl, alentours mpl
envisage [ɪn'vɪzɪdʒ], Am **envision** [en'vɪʒən] vt envisager
envoy ['envɔɪ] n envoyé(e) m,f
envy ['envɪ] **1** n envie f, jalousie f; **to be the e. of sb** être un objet d'envie pour qn
2 vt (pt & pp **envied**) envier; **to e. sb sth** envier qch à qn
enzyme ['enzaɪm] n enzyme f
EOC [iːəʊ'siː] n Br (abbr **Equal Opportunities Commission**) = organisme gouvernemental qui veille à l'égalité des chances sur le lieu de travail
eon Am = **aeon**
epaulette, Am **epaulet** ['epəlet] n épaulette f
ephemeral [ɪ'femərəl] adj éphémère
epic ['epɪk] **1** n (poem, novel) épopée f; (film) film m à grand spectacle
2 adj épique
epicentre, Am **epicenter** ['epɪsentə(r)] n épicentre m
epicurean [epɪkjʊ'rɪən] n & adj épicurien(enne) m,f
epidemic [epɪ'demɪk] also Fig**1** n épidémie f
2 adj épidémique
epidermis [epɪ'dɜːmɪs] n Anat épiderme m
epidural [epɪ'djuːrəl] n Med péridurale f
epigram ['epɪgræm] n épigramme f
epilepsy ['epɪlepsɪ] n épilepsie f
epileptic [epɪ'leptɪk] **1** n épileptique mf
2 adj épileptique; **e. fit** crise f d'épilepsie
epilogue ['epɪlɒg] n épilogue m
Epiphany [ɪ'pɪfənɪ] n Épiphanie f
episcopal [ɪ'pɪskəpəl] adj épiscopal(e); **e. palace** évêché m
episcopalian [ɪpɪskə'peɪlɪən] n & adj épiscopalien(enne) m,f
episode ['epɪsəʊd] n (part of story) épisode m, (incident) incident m
epistle [ɪ'pɪsəl] n also Hum épître f
epitaph ['epɪtɑːf] n épitaphe f
epithet ['epɪθet] n épithète f
epitome [ɪ'pɪtəmɪ] n **to be the e. of sth** être l'exemple même de qch
epitomize [ɪ'pɪtəmaɪz] vt incarner
epoch ['iːpɒk] n époque f
epoch-making ['iːpɒkmeɪkɪŋ] adj qui fait date
eponymous [ɪ'pɒnɪməs] adj éponyme
EPS [iːpiː'es] n (abbr **earnings per share**) BPA m
equable ['ekwəbəl] adj constant(e); (person) à l'humeur égale
equal ['iːkwəl] **1** n égal(e) m,f; **to treat sb as an e.** traiter qn d'égal à égal
2 adj **(a)** (identical) égal(e) (**to** à); **all things being e.** en principe; **in e. measure** en quantité égale; **on e. terms** sur un pied d'égalité; **e. opportunities** égalité f des chances; **e. pay** égalité des salaires; **e. rights** égalité des droits **(b)** (good enough) **to be e. to sth** être à la hauteur de qch
3 vt (pt & pp **equalled**, Am **equaled**) égaler
equality [ɪ'kwɒlɪtɪ] n égalité f
equalize ['iːkwəlaɪz] **1** vt égaliser; (chances, forces) équilibrer
2 vi (in sport) égaliser
equalizer ['iːkwəlaɪzə(r)] n **(a)** (in sport) but m égalisateur **(b)** Elec égaliseur m de potentiel

equally ['iːkwəlɪ] adv **(a)** (to an equal degree) tout aussi **(b)** (in equal amounts) (share, divide) en parts égales **(c)** (likewise) tout aussi bien
equanimity [ekwə'nɪmɪtɪ] n sérénité f
equate [ɪ'kweɪt] vt assimiler (**with** avec)
equation [ɪ'kweɪʒən] n équation f
equator [ɪ'kweɪtə(r)] n équateur m
equatorial [ekwə'tɔːrɪəl] adj équatorial(e); **E. Guinea** la Guinée équatoriale
equestrian [ɪ'kwestrɪən] **1** n cavalier(ère) m,f; (in circus) écuyer(ère) m,f
2 adj (sport, ability) équestre
equidistant [ekwɪ'dɪstənt] adj équidistant(e)
equilateral [ekwɪ'lætərəl] adj équilatéral(e)
equilibrium [ekwɪ'lɪbrɪəm] n équilibre m
equinox ['ekwɪnɒks] n équinoxe m
equip [ɪ'kwɪp] (pt & pp **equipped**) vt **(a)** (provide with equipment) équiper (**with** de) **(b)** (prepare) préparer (**for** pour)
equipment [ɪ'kwɪpmənt] n équipement m; (in factory) installations fpl, matériel m; **e. allowance** subvention f pour l'achat de matériel
equitable ['ekwɪtəbəl] adj équitable
Equity ['ekwɪtɪ] n = syndicat des artistes de théâtre et de télévision
equity ['ekwɪtɪ] (pl **equities**) n **(a)** (fairness) équité f **(b)** Fin (of shareholders) fonds mpl ou capitaux mpl propres; (of company) capital m actions; **equities** actions fpl ordinaires
equivalent [ɪ'kwɪvələnt] **1** n équivalent m
2 adj équivalent(e) (**to** à)
equivocal [ɪ'kwɪvəkəl] adj équivoque, ambigu(ë)
equivocate [ɪ'kwɪvəkeɪt] vi user d'équivoques ou de faux-fuyants
equivocation [ɪkwɪvə'keɪʃən] n paroles fpl équivoques, faux-fuyants mpl
ER [iː'ɑː(r)] n **(a)** Am (abbr **Emergency Room**) urgences fpl **(b)** Br (abbr **Elizabeth Regina**) la Reine Elizabeth
era ['ɪərə] n ère f
eradicate [ɪ'rædɪkeɪt] vt éradiquer
erase [ɪ'reɪz] vt effacer; (with eraser) gommer
eraser [ɪ'reɪzə(r)] n gomme f
erect [ɪ'rekt] **1** adj droit(e), debout; (penis, nipples) en érection
2 vt (building) ériger; (statue) élever, ériger; (scaffolding) dresser
erection [ɪ'rekʃən] n **(a)** (of building, statue) construction f, érection f **(b)** (erect penis) érection f
ergonomic [ɜːgə'nɒmɪk] adj ergonomique
ergonomics [ɜːgə'nɒmɪks] n ergonomie f
Eritrea [erɪ'treɪə] n l'Érythrée f
Eritrean [erɪ'treɪən] **1** n Érythréen(enne) m,f
2 adj érythréen(enne)
ERM [iːɑː'rem] n (abbr **Exchange Rate Mechanism**) mécanisme m de change
ermine ['ɜːmɪn] n hermine f
erode [ɪ'rəʊd] **1** vt (rock, soil) éroder; (metal) corroder, ronger; Fig (confidence, power) miner
2 vi (of rock, soil) s'éroder; (of metal) se corroder; Fig (of confidence, power) s'éroder peu à peu
erogenous [ɪ'rɒdʒɪnəs] adj érogène; **e. zone** zone f érogène
Eros ['ɪərɒs] n Éros

erosion [ɪ'rəʊʒən] *n (of rock, soil) & Fig (of confidence, power)* érosion *f; (of metal)* corrosion *f*

erotic [ɪ'rɒtɪk] *adj* érotique

eroticism [ɪ'rɒtɪsɪzəm] *n* érotisme *m*

err [ɜː(r)] *vi (make mistake)* faire erreur; **to e. on the side of caution** pécher par excès de prudence; *Prov* **to e. is human** l'erreur est humaine

errand [ɛrənd] *n* commission *f,* course *f;* **to run errands for sb** (aller) faire des commissions *ou* des courses pour qn; **e. boy** garçon *m* de courses

erratic [ɪ'rætɪk] *adj (service, results, pulse)* irrégulier(ère); *(playing, performance)* inégal(e); *(behaviour)* imprévisible; *(person)* lunatique; *(driving)* mal assuré(e)

erroneous [ɪ'rəʊnɪəs] *adj* erroné(e)

error ['erə(r)] *n (mistake)* erreur *f,* faute *f;* **to make an e.** faire une erreur; **in e.** par erreur; **an e. of judgement** une erreur de jugement; **to see the e. of one's ways** reconnaître ses erreurs

ersatz ['ɜːzæts] *adj* **e. coffee** un succédané de café

erstwhile ['ɜːstwaɪl] *adj Lit* ancien(enne)

erudite ['erʊdaɪt] *adj* érudit(e)

erudition [erʊ'dɪʃən] *n* érudition *f*

erupt [ɪ'rʌpt] *vi (of volcano)* entrer en éruption; *(of person)* exploser; *(of anger, violence)* éclater; *(of spot)* sortir

eruption [ɪ'rʌpʃən] *n* éruption *f*

escalate ['eskəleɪt] *vi (of prices)* monter en flèche; *(of conflict)* s'intensifier, s'aggraver

escalation [eskə'leɪʃən] *n (of prices)* montée *f* en flèche; *(of conflict)* escalade *f*

escalator ['eskəleɪtə(r)] *n* escalier *m* roulant, Escalator® *m*

escalope ['eskəlɒp] *n* escalope *f*

escapade ['eskəpeɪd] *n* fredaine *f,* frasque *f*

escape [ɪs'keɪp] **1** *n (of person)* évasion *f; (of gas, water)* fuite *f;* **to make one's e.** s'échapper; *Com* **e. clause** clause *f* échappatoire; **e. route** *(from fire)* itinéraire *m* de sortie de secours; *(of criminal)* itinéraire emprunté pour s'échapper
2 *vt (danger, punishment)* échapper à; **to e. sb's notice** échapper à l'attention de qn; **her name escapes me** son nom m'échappe
3 *vi (of person, gas, water)* s'échapper (**from** de); *(from prison)* s'évader (**from** de); **to e. unhurt** s'en tirer indemne; **to e. from reality** s'évader de la réalité

escapee [eskeɪ'piː] *n* évadé(e) *m,f*

escapism [ɪs'keɪpɪzəm] *n* évasion *f* (hors de la réalité)

escapist [ɪs'keɪpɪst] **1** *n* personne *f* qui cherche à s'évader de la réalité
2 *adj* d'évasion

escapologist [eskə'pɒlədʒɪst] *n* prestidigitateur *m* spécialiste de l'évasion

escarpment [ɪs'kɑːpmənt] *n* escarpement *m*

eschew [ɪs'tʃuː] *vt* éviter; **to e. sb's company** fuir *ou* éviter qn

escort 1 *n* ['eskɔːt] *(for convoy)* escorte *f; (for tourists)* guide *m; (from agency)* hôtesse *f; (ship)* bâtiment *m* d'escorte; **under e.** sous escorte; **e. agency** agence *f* d'hôtesses; *Mil* **e. duty** service *m* d'escorte
2 *vt* [ɪs'kɔːt] escorter; *(prisoner)* conduire sous escorte

escudo [e'skuːdəʊ] *(pl* **escudos**) *n Formerly* escudo *m*

Eskimo ['eskɪməʊ] **1** *n (pl* **Eskimos**) Esquimau(aude) *m,f*
2 *adj* esquimau(aude), eskimo *inv*

esophagus [iː'sɒfəgəs] *(pl* **esophagi** [iː'sɒfəgaɪ]) *Am* = oesophagus

esoteric [esəʊ'terɪk] *adj* ésotérique

ESP [iːes'piː] *n (abbr* **extrasensory perception**) perception *f* extra-sensorielle

especially [ɪs'peʃəlɪ] *adv* **(a)** *(in particular)* surtout **(b)** *(more than normally)* particulièrement; **we were e. lucky with the weather** le temps nous a été particulièrement favorable **(c)** *(expressly)* (tout) spécialement, exprès; **I did it e. for you** je l'ai fait spécialement *ou* exprès pour vous

Esperanto [espə'ræntəʊ] *n* l'Espéranto *m*

espionage ['espɪɒnɑːʒ] *n* espionnage *m*

esplanade [esplə'neɪd] *n* esplanade *f*

espouse [ɪs'paʊz] *vt* épouser

espresso [es'presəʊ] *(pl* **espressos**) *n* expresso *m*

Esq *Br (abbr* **Esquire**) **Derek Wilson, E.** = Monsieur Derek Wilson

essay ['eseɪ] *n (at school)* composition *f; (for younger pupils)* rédaction *f; (at university)* dissertation *f*

essayist ['eseɪɪst] *n* essayiste *mf*

essence ['esəns] *n* **(a)** *(most important part or quality)* essence *f; (of speech)* essentiel *m; (of question)* fond *m;* **in e.** essentiellement, surtout; **the very e. of bravery** le courage même; **time is of the e.** le temps est le facteur prioritaire **(b)** *Culin (extract)* extrait *m*

essential [ɪ'senʃəl] **1** *npl* **essentials** *(basic foodstuffs)* produits *mpl* de première nécessité; *(basic issues)* essentiel *m;* **just pack a few essentials** ne prends que l'essentiel
2 *adj* **(a)** *(basic)* essentiel(elle); **e. oil** huile *f* essentielle **(b)** *(indispensable)* essentiel(elle), indispensable (**to** *or* **for** à); **it is e. that...** il est essentiel que... + *subjunctive*

essentially [ɪ'senʃəlɪ] *adv* essentiellement

EST [iːes'tiː] *n Am (abbr* **Eastern Standard Time**) heure *f* de la côte est de l'Amérique du Nord

establish [ɪs'tæblɪʃ] *vt* **(a)** *(set up) (company)* fonder; *(custom)* instaurer; *(system, organization)* établir; **to e. oneself in business** s'établir dans les affaires; **to e. a reputation** se faire une réputation; **the film established her as an important director** avec ce film, elle s'est affirmée comme un metteur en scène important **(b)** *(prove)* établir

established [ɪs'tæblɪʃt] *adj* établi(e); *(fact)* acquis(e)

establishment [ɪs'tæblɪʃmənt] *n* **(a) the E.** *(dominant group)* l'establishment *m; (prevailing values)* l'ordre *m* établi **(b)** *(hotel, restaurant)* établissement *m* **(c)** *(of company, organization)* constitution *f; (of fact)* constatation *f*

estate [ɪs'teɪt] *n* **(a)** *Law (possessions)* biens *mpl* **(b)** *(land)* terre *f,* propriété *f; Br* **(housing) e.** lotissement *m; (with council houses)* cité *f* H.L.M.; *Br* **e. agency** agence *f* immobilière; *Br* **e. agent** agent *m* immobilier **(c)** *Br* **e. (car)** break *m*

esteem [ɪs'tiːm] **1** *n* estime *f,* considération *f;* **to hold sb in high e.** avoir qn en haute estime; **to hold sb in low e.** avoir peu d'estime pour qn
2 *vt* **(a)** *(person)* estimer; *(thing)* priser **(b)** *Formal (consider)* considérer; **she esteemed it a great honour to be invited** elle se sentit fort honorée d'avoir été invitée

esthetic *Am* = **aesthetic**

estimate 1 *n* ['estɪmət] *(calculation)* évaluation *f,* calcul *m; Com* devis *m;* **at a rough e.** à vue de nez
2 *vt* ['estɪmeɪt] estimer, évaluer; *(value)* estimer

estimation [estɪ'meɪʃən] *n* **(a)** *(calculation)* estimation *f,* évaluation *f* **(b)** *(judgement)* jugement *m,* opinion *f;* **in my e.** à mon avis; **to go up/down in sb's e.** monter/descendre dans l'estime de qn

Estonia [es'təʊnɪə] *n* l'Estonie *f*

Estonian [es'təʊnɪən] **1** *n* **(a)** *(person)* Estonien(enne) *m,f* **(b)** *(language)* estonien *m*
2 *adj* estonien(enne)

estranged [ɪs'treɪndʒd] *adj (couple)* séparé(e); **her e. husband** son mari, dont elle est séparée; **their e.** son leur fils, avec qui ils sont brouillés

estrogen ['iːstrədʒən] *Am* = oestrogen

estuary ['estjʊərɪ] *(pl* **estuaries)** *n* estuaire *m*

ETA [iːtiː'eɪ] *n (abbr* **estimated time of arrival)** heure *f* d'arrivée prévue

et al [et'æl] *(abbr* **et alii)** et autres

etc [et'setrə] *adv (abbr* **et cetera)** etc

etch [etʃ] *vt* graver à l'eau-forte; *Fig* **to be etched in sb's memory** être gravé(e) dans la mémoire de qn

etching ['etʃɪŋ] *n* (gravure *f* à l')eau forte *f*

eternal [ɪ'tɜːnəl] *adj* éternel(elle); *Fig (continual)* continuel(elle), sans fin

eternally [ɪ'tɜːnəlɪ] *adv* éternellement

eternity [ɪ'tɜːnɪtɪ] *n* éternité *f*; *Fam* **to wait/last an e.** attendre/durer une éternité; **e. ring** = bague entièrement sertie de pierres symbolisant l'éternité du mariage

ether ['iːθə(r)] *n* éther *m*

ethereal [ɪ'θɪərɪəl] *adj* éthéré(e); *(fragile)* léger(ère), impalpable

ethical ['eθɪkəl] *adj* éthique, moral(e)

ethically ['eθɪklɪ] *adv* sur le plan éthique; **to behave e.** suivre la déontologie

ethics ['eθɪks] *npl* éthique *f*, morale *f*; *(of profession)* déontologie *f*

Ethiopia [iːθɪ'əʊpɪə] *n* l'Éthiopie *f*

Ethiopian [iːθɪ'əʊpɪən] **1** *n (person)* Éthiopien(enne) *m,f* **2** *adj* éthiopien(enne)

ethnic ['eθnɪk] *adj* ethnique; **e. cleansing** purification *f* ethnique; **e. minority** minorité *f* ethnique

ethnically ['eθnɪklɪ] *adv* du point de vue ethnique

ethnocentric [eθnəʊ'sentrɪk] *adj* ethnocentrique

ethnography [eθ'nɒɡrəfɪ] *n* ethnographie *f*

ethnology [eθ'nɒlədʒɪ] *n* ethnologie *f*

ethos ['iːθɒs] *n (of people)* génie *m*; *(of class)* culture *f*

etiquette ['etɪket] *n* étiquette *f*; **professional e.** usages *mpl* professionnels

Etruscan [ɪ'trʌskən] **1** *n* **(a)** *(person)* Étrusque *mf* **(b)** *(language)* étrusque *m* **2** *adj* étrusque

etymological [etɪmə'lɒdʒɪkəl] *adj* étymologique

etymology [etɪ'mɒlədʒɪ] *n* étymologie *f*

EU [iː'juː] *n (abbr* **European Union)** UE *f*

eucalyptus [juːkə'lɪptəs] *n* eucalyptus *m*

Eucharist ['juːkərɪst] *n* **the E.** l'eucharistie *f*

eulogize ['juːlədʒaɪz] *vt* faire l'éloge de

eulogy ['juːlədʒɪ] *(pl* **eulogies)** *n* éloge *m*

eunuch ['juːnək] *n* eunuque *m*

euphemism ['juːfɪmɪzəm] *n* euphémisme *m*

euphemistic [juːfɪ'mɪstɪk] *adj* euphémique

euphoria [juː'fɔːrɪə] *n* euphorie *f*

euphoric [juː'fɒrɪk] *adj* euphorique

Eurasian [jʊə'reɪʒən] **1** *n* Eurasien(enne) *m,f* **2** *adj* eurasien(enne); *(continent)* eurasiatique

EURATOM [jʊə'rætəm] *n (abbr* **European Atomic Energy Community)** CEEA *f*, EURATOM *f*

eureka [jʊə'riːkə] *exclam* eureka!

euro ['jʊərəʊ] *(pl* **euros)** *n* euro *m*

Eurocheque ['jʊərəʊtʃek] *n* Eurocheque *m*

Eurodollar ['jʊərəʊdɒlə(r)] *n* eurodollar *m*

Euro-MP ['jʊərəʊempiː] *n* député(e) *m,f* européen(enne)

Europe ['jʊərəp] *n* l'Europe *f*

European [jʊərə'piːən] **1** *n* Européen(enne) *m,f* **2** *adj* européen(enne); **E. Commission** Commission *f* européenne; **E. Community** Communauté *f* européenne; **E. Court of Human Rights** Cour *f* européenne des droits de l'homme; **E. Court of Justice** Cour de justice européenne; **E. Economic Community** Communauté *f* économique européenne; **E. Free Trade Association** Association *f* européenne de libre-échange; **E. Monetary System** Système *m* monétaire européen; **E. Parliament** Parlement *m* européen; **E. Union** Union *f* européenne

Eurosceptic [jʊərəʊ'skeptɪk] *n* Br eurosceptique *mf*

Eustachian tube [juːs'teɪʃən'tjuːb] *n* Anat trompe *f* d'Eustache

euthanasia [juːθə'neɪzɪə] *n* euthanasie *f*

evacuate [ɪ'vækjʊeɪt] *vt* évacuer

evacuation [ɪvækjʊ'eɪʃən] *n* évacuation *f*

evacuee [ɪvækjʊ'iː] *n* évacué(e) *m,f*

evade [ɪ'veɪd] *vt (blow)* esquiver, éviter; *(question)* éluder; *(pursuer)* échapper à; *(responsibilities)* se soustraire à, se dérober à; **to e. tax** frauder le fisc

evaluate [ɪ'væljʊeɪt] *vt* évaluer

evaluation [ɪvæljʊ'eɪʃən] *n* évaluation *f*

evangelical [iːvæn'dʒelɪkəl] **1** *n* protestant(e) *m,f* évangélique **2** *adj* évangélique

evangelism [ɪ'vændʒɪlɪzəm] *n* évangélisme *m*

evangelist [ɪ'vændʒɪlɪst] *n* évangéliste *mf*

evangelize [ɪ'vændʒɪlaɪz] **1** *vt* évangéliser; *(person)* prêcher l'Évangile à **2** *vi* prêcher l'Évangile

evaporate [ɪ'væpəreɪt] **1** *vt* faire évaporer; **evaporated milk** lait *m* condensé **2** *vi (of liquid)* s'évaporer; *Fig (of enthusiasm, hope)* s'envoler

evaporation [ɪvæpə'reɪʃən] *n* évaporation *f*

evasion [ɪ'veɪʒən] *n (escape)* évasion *f*, fuite *f*; *(of pursuer, responsibilities, question)* dérobade *f*; **(tax) e.** fraude *f* fiscale

evasive [ɪ'veɪsɪv] *adj (person, reply)* évasif(ive); **to take e. action** faire une manœuvre d'évitement

eve [iːv] *n (day before)* veille *f*; **on the e. of** à la veille de

even [iːvən] **1** *adj* **(a)** *(flat)* égal(e); *(smooth)* uni(e) **(b)** *(regular)* *(breathing, pace)* régulier(ère), égal(e); *(temperature)* constant(e); **to have an e. temper** être d'humeur égale; **e. number** nombre *m* pair **(c)** *(equal)* **to have an e. chance (of doing sth)** avoir une chance sur deux (de faire qch); *Fig* **to get e. with sb** prendre sa revanche sur qn **2** *adv* **(a)** même; *(with comparatives)* encore; **without e. listening** sans même écouter; **I never e. saw it** je ne l'ai même pas vu; **e. older/more interesting** encore plus vieux (vieille)/intéressant(e); **e. as I speak** au moment même où je parle **(b)** *(in phrases)* **e. if** même si; **e. now** même maintenant, aujourd'hui encore; **e. so** cependant, quand même; **e. then** *(already)* déjà (à cette époque); *(all the same)* même dans ces conditions; **e. though** bien que + subjunctive **3** *vt (make equal)* rendre égal(e); **to e. the odds** égaliser les chances

▸ **even out** **1** *vt sep (differences)* niveler; *(workload)* répartir de façon équitable; *(inequalities)* réduire, aplanir **2** *vi (of differences)* se niveler; *(of workload)* être réparti(e) plus également; *(of inequalities)* se réduire

▸ **even up** *vt sep (differences)* niveler; *(chances)* égaliser les chances

even-handed ['iːvən'hændɪd] *adj* juste, équitable

evening ['i:vnɪŋ] *n* soir *m*; *(referring to duration)* soirée *f*; **tomorrow e.** demain soir; **yesterday e.** hier soir; **good e.!**, *Fam* **e.!** bonsoir!; **in the e.** le soir; **a musical/cultural e.** une soirée musicale/culturelle; **e. class** cours *m* du soir; **e. dress** *(for men)* tenue *f* de soirée; *(for women)* robe *f* du soir; **e. paper** journal *m* du soir; **e. performance** *(of play)* représentation *f* en soirée

evenly ['i:vənlɪ] *adv* **(a)** *(uniformly)* uniformément **(b)** *(regularly)* *(breathe)* régulièrement, de façon régulière; *(speak)* calmement **(c)** *(equally)* *(divide, distribute)* également, de façon égale; **e. matched** *(in size)* de grandeur égale; *(in strength)* de force égale

evensong ['i:vənsɒŋ] *n Rel* office *m* du soir

event [ɪ'vent] *n* **(a)** *(occurrence)* événement *m*; **in any e.** en tout cas; **in the e.** of an emergency en cas d'urgence; **in the e. of her refusing** au cas où elle refuserait; **after the e.** après coup **(b)** *(in athletics)* épreuve *f*

even-tempered ['i:vən'tempəd] *adj* d'humeur égale

eventful [ɪ'ventfʊl] *adj (day, life)* mouvementé(e), riche en événements

eventual [ɪ'ventʃʊəl] *adj* final(e), définitif(ive)

eventuality [ɪventʃʊ'ælɪtɪ] *(pl* **eventualities)** *n* éventualité *f*; **in that e.** dans cette éventualité

eventually [ɪ'ventʃʊəlɪ] *adv (in the end)* finalement, en fin de compte; *(at a future date)* par la suite; **they e. reached the castle** ils ont fini par arriver au château; **he'll do it e.** il le fera tôt ou tard

ever ['evə(r)] *adv* **(a)** *(at any time)* **have you e. been to Spain?** es-tu déjà allé en Espagne?; **do you e. see Laura these days?** ça t'arrive de voir Laura?; **the worst/best e.** le pire/meilleur qui soit; **more than e.** plus que jamais; **she's a liar/fool if e. there was one** c'est une menteuse/idiote de première **(b)** *(always)* **e. since (then)/1960** depuis (lors)/1960; **all she e. does is complain** elle ne fait que se plaindre; **she was as friendly as e.** elle était toujours aussi aimable; **the gentleman, he opened the door for her** toujours galant, il lui ouvrit la porte; **for e.** pour toujours **(c)** *(with negative sense)* **not e.** jamais; **hardly e.** jamais; **nothing e. happens** il ne se passe jamais rien; **I don't think I'll e. see him again** je ne pense pas que je le reverrai; **I seldom if e. see her** je la vois peu ou pas du tout **(d)** *(for emphasis)* **e. so kind** si gentil(ille); **e. so much** *or* **such a lot of money** tant d'argent; **e. so slightly** très légèrement; **e. such a nice girl** une fille si sympathique

evergreen ['evəgri:n] **1** *n (tree)* arbre *m* à feuilles persistantes; *(bush)* plante *m* à feuilles persistantes **2** *adj* à feuilles persistantes; *Fig* **e. topic** question *f* toujours d'actualité

everlasting [evə'lɑːstɪŋ] *adj (eternal)* éternel(elle); *(continual)* continuel(elle), sans fin

evermore [evə'mɔː(r)] *adv Formal* toujours; **for e.** à jamais

every ['evrɪ] *adj* **(a)** *(each)* chaque; **child tif of e. age** des enfants de tous âges; **at e. opportunity** à la moindre occasion; **from e. side** de tous côtés; **e. one of us** chacun(e) d'entre nous; **e. man for himself!** chacun pour soi! **(b)** *(indicating regular occurrence)* **e. week** chaque semaine, toutes les semaines; **e. ten years** tous les dix ans; **e. other** *or* **second day** tous les deux jours, un jour sur deux; **e. other line** une ligne sur deux; **e. so often, e. now and again** de temps en temps **(c)** *(for emphasis)* **you have e. right to be angry** vous avez tout lieu d'être mécontent; **e. bit as good/intelligent as...** tout aussi bon (bonne)/intelligent(e) que...; **she has e. chance of winning** elle a de très fortes chances de gagner

everybody ['evrɪbɒdɪ] *pron* tout le monde, chacun(e) *m,f*; **e. I know was there** tous ceux que je connais se trouvaient là; **e. else** tous les autres; **e. who is anybody** les gens qui comptent

everyday ['evrɪdeɪ] *adj* **(a)** *(daily)* journalier(ère), quotidien(enne); **it's an e.** occurrence ça se produit tous les jours **(b)** *(used every day)* de tous les jours; **for e. wear/use** à porter/utiliser tous les jours; **e. expression** expression *f* courante **(c)** *(ordinary)* usuel(elle), ordinaire

everyone ['evrɪwʌn] = everybody

everything ['evrɪθɪŋ] *pron* tout; **e. I did seemed to go wrong** tout ce que je faisais semblait voué à l'échec; **he did e. possible** il a fait tout son possible; **money isn't e.** l'argent n'est pas tout

everywhere ['evrɪweə(r)] *adv* partout; **to look e.** regarder partout; **e. you go** où que vous alliez, partout où vous allez; **e. you look there is poverty** de quelque côté que l'on se tourne, on voit la misère

evict [ɪ'vɪkt] *vt* expulser

eviction [ɪ'vɪkʃən] *n* expulsion *f*; **e. order** avis *m* d'expulsion

evidence ['evɪdəns] **1** *n* **(a)** *(reason for belief)* évidence *f*; *(indication)* marque *f*, signe *m*; **to be in e.** être en évidence; **to show e. of** donner des signes de; **there was no e. of his stay in the house** rien ne montrait qu'il eût séjourné dans la maison **(b)** *(in court case)* preuve *f*; *(testimony)* témoignage *m*; **to give e.** témoigner; **to call sb in e.** appeler qn à la barre des témoins; **to turn** *Br* **King's** *or Am* **State's e.** témoigner contre ses complices *(sous promesse de pardon)* **2** *vt Formal* **as evidenced by...** comme en témoigne...

evident ['evɪdənt] *adj* évident(e), manifeste

evidently ['evɪdəntlɪ] *adv* **(a)** *(clearly)* manifestement, à l'évidence; **there have e. been some problems** il est clair ou évident qu'il y a eu des problèmes **(b)** *(apparently)* apparemment; **so she won't be coming? – e. not** alors elle ne vient pas? – il semble bien que non

evil ['i:vəl] **1** *n* mal *m* **2** *adj (person, look)* mauvais(e), malveillant(e); *(influence, effect)* maléfique; *(spirit)* malfaisant(e), malin(igne); *(temper)* coléreux(euse)

evildoer ['i:vəlduː:ə(r)] *n Lit* homme (femme) *m,f* méchant(e)

evil-looking ['i:vəllʊkɪŋ] *adj* à l'aspect malfaisant

evil-minded ['i:vəl'maɪndɪd] *adj* malintentionné(e)

evil-smelling ['i:vəl'smelɪŋ] *adj* nauséabond(e)

evince [ɪ'vɪns] *vt Formal* faire montre de

evocation [evə'keɪʃən] *n* évocation *f*

evocative [ɪ'vɒkətɪv] *adj* évocateur(trice) **(of** de)

evoke [ɪ'vəʊk] *vt* **(a)** *(conjure up)* évoquer **(b)** *(provoke)* provoquer, susciter

evolution [i:və'luːʃən] *n* évolution *f*, développement *m*

evolutionary [i:və'luːʃənərɪ] *adj* évolutif(ive)

evolve [ɪ'vɒlv] **1** *vt (theory, plan)* élaborer, mettre au point **2** *vi (of species, situation)* évoluer, se développer

ewe [juː] *n* brebis *f*

ex [eks] *n Fam (former husband, wife, girlfriend, boyfriend)* ex *m,f*

ex- [eks] *pref (former)* ex-; **ex-minister/teacher** ancien ministre *m*/professeur *m*

exacerbate [eg'zæsəbeɪt] *vt* aggraver

exact [ɪg'zækt] **1** *adj* exact(e), précis(e); **the moment when...** juste au moment où..., au moment précis où...; **those were her e. words** c'est ce qu'elle a dit mot pour mot; **the e. opposite** exactement le contraire; **at five**

o'clock, to be e. à cinq heures, pour être précis **2** vt (obedience, tax) exiger (**from** de); (promise) extorquer (**from** à)

exacting [ɪg'zæktɪŋ] adj exigeant(e)

exactitude [ɪg'zæktɪtjuːd] n Formal exactitude f

exactly [ɪg'zæktlɪ] adv exactement; **not e.** pas tout à fait; Ironic pas vraiment

exaggerate [ɪg'zædʒəreɪt] vt & vi exagérer

exaggerated [ɪg'zædʒəreɪtɪd] adj exagéré(e)

exaggeration [ɪgzædʒə'reɪʃən] n exagération f

exalt [ɪg'zɔːlt] vt Formal exalter

exalted [ɪg'zɔːltɪd] adj (**a**) (high) (rank) élevé(e), (person) haut placé(e) (**b**) Formal (joyful) exalté(e)

exam [ɪg'zæm] n examen m; **to take** or **sit an e.** passer un examen; **e. result** résultat m d'examen

examination [ɪgzæmɪ'neɪʃən] n examen m; **to take** or **sit an e.** passer un examen; **to pass/to fail an e.** réussir à/ échouer à un examen; **e. board** ≃ académie f (division administrative de l'enseignement); **e. result** résultat m d'examen

examine [ɪg'zæmɪn] vt (evidence, patient, question) examiner; (student) faire passer un examen à; **to e. one's conscience** faire son examen de conscience

examinee [ɪgzæmɪ'niː] n candidat(e) m,f

examiner [ɪg'zæmɪnə(r)] n examinateur(trice) m,f

example [ɪg'zɑːmpəl] n exemple m; **for e.** par exemple; **to set an e. (to sb)** donner l'exemple (à qn); **to make an e. of sb** faire un exemple de qn; **to follow sb's e.** suivre l'exemple de qn; **to lead by e.** montrer l'exemple

exasperate [ɪg'zɑːspəreɪt] vt exaspérer; **to get exasperated** s'irriter

exasperating [ɪg'zɑːspəreɪtɪŋ] adj exaspérant(e)

exasperation [ɪgzɑːspə'reɪʃən] n exaspération f

excavate ['ekskəveɪt] vt (hole, tunnel) creuser; (remains) déterrer, exhumer; (site) faire des fouilles dans

excavation [ekskə'veɪʃən] n excavation f

excavator ['ekskəveɪtə(r)] n (machine) excavatrice f

exceed [ɪk'siːd] vt (a) (limits) excéder, dépasser; (hopes, fears) dépasser; (one's authority) outrepasser (**b**) (number, amount) dépasser

exceedingly [ɪk'siːdɪŋlɪ] adv extrêmement

excel [ɪk'sel] (pt & pp **excelled**) **1** vt also Ironic **to e. oneself** se surpasser **2** vi exceller (**at** or **in** à ou en)

excellence ['eksələns] n excellence f

excellency ['eksələnsɪ] n **Your/His E.** Votre/Son Excellence f

excellent ['eksələnt] adj excellent(e)

except [ɪk'sept] **1** prep sauf, à l'exception de; **nobody e. him** personne excepté ou sauf lui; **I would go, e. I'm busy** j'irais bien, mais je suis occupé; **e. for** à part; **e. that** excepté que, si ce n'est que; **e. when** sauf ou à part quand **2** vt excepter, exclure (**from** de); **present company excepted** les personnes présentes exceptées; **not excepting...** sans excepter...

exception [ɪk'sepʃən] n (**a**) (thing excepted) exception f; **to make an e. of sth/for sb** faire une exception pour qch/ qn; **with the e. of...** à l'exception de..., exception faite de...; **without e.** sans exception; **the e. proves the rule** c'est l'exception qui confirme la règle (**b**) **to take e. to sth** (be offended) se formaliser ou s'offenser de qch; (object) trouver à redire à qch

exceptionable [ɪk'sepʃənəbəl] adj Formal critiquable; (offensive) offensant(e)

exceptional [ɪk'sepʃənəl] adj exceptionnel(elle)

exceptionally [ɪk'sepʃənəlɪ] adv exceptionnellement; (in exceptional cases) à titre exceptionnel

excerpt ['eksɜːpt] n extrait m (**from** de)

excess [ɪk'ses] n excès m; **to do sth to e.** faire qch à l'excès; **to pay the e.** (on ticket) payer un supplément, **e. baggage** excédent m de bagages

excessive [ɪk'sesɪv] adj excessif(ive)

excessively [ɪk'sesɪvlɪ] adv extrêmement; (eat, drink) à l'excès

exchange [ɪks'tʃeɪndʒ] **1** n (**a**) (of prisoners, ideas) échange m; **in e. (for)** en échange (de); **a heated e.** un échange de paroles assez vives; **e. visit** échange (**b**) Fin (of currency) change m; **e. controls** contrôle m des changes; **e. rate** taux m de change; **e. rate mechanism** mécanisme m de change (**c**) (**Stock**) **E.** Bourse f (des valeurs) (**d**) (telephone) central m téléphonique **2** vt échanger; **to e. sth for sth** échanger qch contre qch

exchangeable [ɪks'tʃeɪndʒəbəl] adj échangeable (**for** contre)

exchequer [eks'tʃekə(r)] n Br **the E.** ≃ le Trésor Public; **the Chancellor of the E.** le Ministre des Finances

excise **1** n ['eksaɪz] **e.** (**duties**) (tax) droits mpl d'accise **2** vt [ɪk'saɪz] (remove) (tumour) exciser; (piece of text) couper

excitable [ɪk'saɪtəbəl] adj nerveux(euse)

excite [ɪk'saɪt] vt (**a**) (get worked up) énerver, surexciter; (arouse enthusiasm) enthousiasmer; (stimulate) exciter (**b**) (give rise to) (admiration, desire) provoquer; (envy, interest) susciter; (curiosity) piquer

excited [ɪk'saɪtɪd] adj (worked up) énervé(e), excité(e), (enthusiastic) enthousiaste; **to get e. (about)** s'exciter (pour); (angry) s'énerver (contre)

excitedly [ɪk'saɪtɪdlɪ] adv (speak, laugh) avec animation; (wait) avec une impatience fébrile

excitement [ɪk'saɪtmənt] n (agitation) agitation f; (enthusiasm) animation f, enthousiasme m; **to cause great e.** faire sensation

exciting [ɪk'saɪtɪŋ] adj passionnant(e); (idea, prospect) enthousiasmant(e)

exclaim [ɪks'kleɪm] **1** vt "leave me alone," he exclaimed "laissez-moi", s'est-il écrié **2** vi s'exclamer, s'écrier

exclamation [eksklə'meɪʃən] n exclamation f; Br **e. mark**, Am **e. point** point m d'exclamation

exclamatory [eks'klæmətərɪ] adj exclamatif(ive)

exclude [ɪks'kluːd] vt exclure (**from** de); (doubt, suspicion) écarter; **excluding...** à l'exclusion de...

exclusion [ɪks'kluːʒən] n exclusion f (**from** de); **to the e. of...** à l'exclusion de...

exclusive [ɪks'kluːsɪv] **1** n (in newspaper, on TV) exclusivité f **2** adj (**a**) (right, article, interview) exclusif(ive) (**b**) (chic) huppé(e); (club, social circle) très fermé(e); (clothing, jewellery) de grande marque (**c**) (only) seul(e), unique **3** adv **e. of delivery** frais de livraison non compris; **e. of tax** hors taxes

exclusively [ɪks'kluːsɪvlɪ] adv exclusivement; (in newspaper, on TV) en exclusivité

excommunicate [ekskə'mjuːnɪkeɪt] vt excommunier

excommunication [ekskəmjuːnɪ'keɪʃən] n excommunication f

excrement ['ekskrɪmənt] n excrément m

excrescence [eks'kresəns] n excroissance f

excrete [ɪks'kriːt] vt Formal excréter

excruciating [ɪksˈkruːʃɪeɪtɪŋ] *adj (pain, embarrassment)* atroce; **the whole evening was e.** *(embarrassing)* on a été gênés toute la soirée; *(boring)* on s'est horriblement ennuyés toute la soirée

excruciatingly [ɪksˈkruːʃɪeɪtɪŋlɪ] *adv (painful, embarrassing)* atrocement; *Fam* **e. funny** tordant(e)

excursion [ɪksˈkɜːʃən] *n* excursion *f*

excuse 1 *n* [ɪksˈkjuːs] excuse *f*; **to be a poor e. for** être nul (nulle) comme
2 *vt* [ɪksˈkjuːz] (**a**) *(forgive)* excuser, pardonner; **e. me!** pardon!, excusez-moi!; **e. me?** *(what did you say?)* pardon? (**b**) *(exempt)* exempter, dispenser (**from** de) (**c**) **to e. oneself** s'excuser

ex-directory [eksdɪˈrektərɪ] *adj Br* **to be e.** *(of person, number)* être sur la liste rouge

execrable [ˈeksɪkrəbəl] *adj* exécrable, abominable

execute [ˈeksɪkjuːt] *vt (prisoner, order)* exécuter; *(plan, operation)* mettre à exécution

execution [eksɪˈkjuːʃən] *n (of prisoner, order)* exécution *f*; **in the e.** of one's duty dans l'exercice de ses fonctions

executioner [eksɪˈkjuːʃənə(r)] *n* bourreau *m*

executive [ɪgˈzekjʊtɪv] **1** *n (businessperson)* cadre *m*; *(committee)* bureau *m*, comité *m* central
2 *adj (post)* de cadre; *(car, suite)* de luxe; *Br* **e. director** directeur *m* administratif

executor [ɪgˈzekjʊtə(r)] *n Law* exécuteur(trice) *m,f* testamentaire

exemplary [ɪgˈzemplərɪ] *adj* exemplaire

exemplify [ɪgˈzemplɪfaɪ] *(pt & pp* **exemplified)** *vt* illustrer

exempt [ɪgˈzempt] **1** *adj* exempté(e), dispensé(e) (**from** de)
2 *vt* exempter, dispenser (**from** de)

exemption [ɪgˈzem(p)ʃən] *n* exemption *f*, dispense *f* (**from** de)

exercise [ˈeksəsaɪz] **1** *n* exercice *m*; **to take** *or* **do e.** faire de l'exercice; **e. bike** vélo *m* d'appartement; **e. book** cahier *m*; **e. class** cours *m* de gymnastique
2 *vt* (**a**) *(body, mind)* exercer (**b**) *(right, influence)* exercer; *(caution, restraint)* user de
3 *vi* faire de l'exercice; *(train)* s'entraîner

exert [ɪgˈzɜːt] *vt (pressure, influence)* exercer; *(force)* faire usage de; **to e. oneself** se remuer, se donner du mal

exertion [ɪgˈzɜːʃən] *n (of force)* usage *m*, emploi *m*; *(effort)* effort *m*

exhale [eksˈheɪl] *vi* expirer

exhaust [ɪgˈzɔːst] **1** *n (on car)* échappement *m*; **e. (fumes)** gaz *mpl* d'échappement; **e. pipe** tuyau *m* d'échappement
2 *vt (person, resources)* épuiser

exhausted [ɪgˈzɔːstɪd] *adj* épuisé(e)

exhausting [ɪgˈzɔːstɪŋ] *adj* épuisant(e)

exhaustion [ɪgˈzɔːstʃən] *n* épuisement *m*

exhaustive [ɪgˈzɔːstɪv] *adj (list)* exhaustif(ive); *(analysis, description)* détaillé(e), minutieux(euse); *(enquiry, search)* approfondi(e)

exhibit [ɪgˈzɪbɪt] **1** *n (in art exhibition)* objet *m* exposé; *(in court case)* pièce *f* à conviction
2 *vt* (**a**) *(object, goods)* exhiber, montrer (**b**) *(painting in exhibition)* exposer (**c**) *(show) (courage, judgement)* faire preuve de; **to e. signs of stress/wear** donner des signes de tension/d'usure

exhibition [eksɪˈbɪʃən] *n* (**a**) *(of paintings)* exposition *f*; *Fam Fig* **to make an e. of oneself** se donner en spectacle (**b**) *(of courage, bad manners)* démonstration *f*; **it was a disgraceful e.** ce fut un spectacle honteux

exhibitionist [eksɪˈbɪʃənɪst] *n* (**a**) personne *f* qui aime se faire remarquer (**b**) *Psy* exhibitionniste *mf*

exhibitor [ɪgˈzɪbɪtə(r)] *n* exposant(e) *m,f*

exhilarated [ɪgˈzɪləreɪtɪd] *adj* grisé(e)

exhilarating [ɪgˈzɪləreɪtɪŋ] *adj (air, walk)* vivifiant(e); *(experience)* grisant(e); *(news)* enthousiasmant(e)

exhort [ɪgˈzɔːt] *vt* exhorter, encourager (**to do sth** à faire qch)

exhortation [ɪgzɔːˈteɪʃən] *n* exhortation *f*

exhume [eksˈhjuːm] *vt* exhumer, déterrer

exigent [ˈeksɪdʒənt] *adj* (**a**) *(urgent)* urgent(e), pressant(e) (**b**) *(demanding)* exigeant(e)

exile [ˈeksaɪl] **1** *n* (**a**) *(banishment)* exil *m*, bannissement *m*; **in e.** en exil (**b**) *(exiled person)* exilé(e) *m,f*
2 *vt* exiler

exist [ɪgˈzɪst] *vi* (**a**) *(be in existence)* exister; *(of conditions)* régner (**b**) *(survive)* se maintenir en vie, survivre (**on** avec)

existence [ɪgˈzɪstəns] *n* existence *f*; **in e.** existant(e), qui existe; **to come into e.** naître; **to go out of e.** disparaître, cesser d'exister

existential [egzɪsˈtenʃəl] *adj* existentiel(elle)

existentialism [egzɪsˈtenʃəlɪzəm] *n* existentialisme *m*

existentialist [egzɪsˈtenʃəlɪst] *n & adj* existentialiste *mf*

existing [ɪgˈzɪstɪŋ] *adj* existant(e), actuel(elle)

exit [ˈeksɪt] **1** *n* sortie *f*; **to make an e.** sortir; *Pol Br* **e. poll,** *Am* **e. survey** = sondage effectué auprès des électeurs immédiatement après qu'ils ont voté; **e. visa** visa *m* de sortie
2 *vi (leave)* & *Comptr* sortir

exodus [ˈeksədəs] *n* exode *m*

ex officio [eksəˈfɪʃɪəʊ] *adj (member)* de droit

exonerate [ɪgˈzɒnəreɪt] *vt (absolve)* disculper, innocenter (**from** *or* **of** de)

exorbitant [ɪgˈzɔːbɪtənt] *adj* exorbitant(e)

exorcism [ˈeksɔːsɪzəm] *n* exorcisme *m*

exorcist [ˈeksɔːsɪst] *n* exorciste *mf*

exorcize [ˈeksɔːsaɪz] *vt* exorciser

exotic [ɪgˈzɒtɪk] *adj* exotique

expand [ɪksˈpænd] **1** *vt (production, output)* accroître; *(empire)* agrandir; *(mind, circle of friends)* élargir; *(range, idea)* développer
2 *vi (of solid, gas)* se dilater; *(of company)* s'agrandir
▸ **expand on, expand upon** *vt insep* développer

expanded [ɪksˈpændɪd] *adj* étendu(e); *Comptr (memory)* expansé(e)

expanding [ɪksˈpændɪŋ] *adj (market, company)* en expansion, qui se développe; *(universe)* en expansion

expanse [eksˈpæns] *n* étendue *f*

expansion [eksˈpænʃən] *n* expansion *f*; *(of gas)* dilatation *f*; *Comptr* **e. card** carte *f* d'extension

expansive [ɪksˈpænsɪv] *adj (gas)* dilatable; *(person, mood)* expansif(ive)

expat [eksˈpæt] *n* & *adj Br Fam* expatrié(e) *m,f*

expatriate 1 *n* [eksˈpætrɪət] expatrié(e) *m,f*
2 *vt* [eksˈpætrɪeɪt] expatrier

expect [ɪksˈpekt] **1** *vt* (**a**) *(anticipate)* s'attendre à; **to e. to do sth** compter *ou* espérer faire qch; **to e. sb to do sth** s'attendre à ce que qn fasse qch; **I expected as much** je m'y attendais; **to e. the worst** s'attendre au pire; **to be expecting a baby** attendre un bébé
(**b**) *(require)* **to e. sb to do sth** attendre de qn qu'il/elle fasse qch; **to e. sth from sb** attendre qch de qn; **I know what is expected of me** je sais ce qu'on attend de moi; **to e. too much from sb/sth** trop attendre de qn/qch

(c) *(suppose)* **to e. (that)...** penser que...; **I e. so/not** je crois bien que oui/non
2 *vi (be pregnant)* **to be expecting** attendre un bébé
expectancy [ɪksˈpektənsɪ] *n* attente *f*; **an air of e. l'**air d'attendre quelque chose
expectant [ɪksˈpektənt] *adj* impatient(e); **e. mother** future maman *f*
expectation [ekspekˈteɪʃən] *n* espérance *f*; **in (the) e. of sth** dans l'attente de qch; **to have high expectations of sb/sth** attendre beaucoup de qn/qch; **to come up to expectations** se montrer à la hauteur; **to fall short of (sb's) expectations** décevoir (qn), **contrary to all expectations** contre toute attente
expected [ɪksˈpektɪd] *adj* attendu(e); *(hoped for)* espéré(e)
expectorant [ɪksˈpektərənt] **1** *n Med* expectorant *m*
2 *adj* expectorant(e)
expediency [ɪksˈpiːdɪənsɪ] *n* opportunité *f*; *Pej (opportunism)* opportunisme *m*
expedient [ɪksˈpiːdɪənt] **1** *n* expédient *m*
2 *adj* opportun(e), expédient(e)
expedite [ˈekspɪdaɪt] *vt Formal* activer, accélérer
expedition [ekspəˈdɪʃən] *n* expédition *f*; *Fam* **a shopping e.** une séance de shopping
expeditionary [ekspəˈdɪʃənərɪ] *adj Mil* **e. force/corps** force *f*/corps *m* expéditionnaire
expel [ɪksˈpel] *(pt & pp* **expelled)** *vt* expulser; *(from school)* renvoyer
expendable [ɪksˈpendəbəl] *adj (person)* qui n'est pas irremplaçable; *(troops)* que l'on peut sacrifier
expenditure [ɪksˈpendɪtʃə(r)] *n (of money, energy)* dépense *f*
expense [ɪksˈpens] *n* **(a)** *(cost)* dépense *f*, frais *mpl*; **to go to great e. (to do sth)** faire de grosses dépenses (pour faire qch); **no o. spared** sans regarder à la dépense, **at the e. of one's health/sanity** aux dépens de sa santé/santé mentale; **to make a joke at sb's e.** faire une plaisanterie aux dépens de qn **(b)** *Com* **expenses** frais *mpl*, dépenses *fpl*; **it's on expenses** ça va sur la note de frais; **all expenses paid** tous frais payés; **e. account** note *f* de frais
expensive [ɪksˈpensɪv] *adj (object, shop, restaurant)* cher (chère); *(procedure, habit)* couteux(euse); *(tastes)* de luxe; *(mistake)* qui coûte cher
experience [ɪksˈpɪərɪəns] **1** *n* expérience *f*; **to learn from e.** tirer les leçons d'une expérience; **in my e.** d'après mon expérience
2 *vt (emotions, pain)* ressentir; *(hunger, success)* connaître, faire l'expérience de; *(difficulties, problems)* avoir
experienced [ɪksˈpɪərɪənst] *adj* expérimenté(e); **to be e. in sth** avoir de l'expérience en qch; *(observer)* averti(e)
experiment [ɪksˈperɪmənt] **1** *n* expérience *f*; **as an e.** à titre d'essai
2 *vi* expérimenter **(on** sur); **to e. with** *(technique, drugs)* essayer
experimental [ɪkspeɪrɪˈmentəl] *adj* expérimental(e)
expert [ˈekspɜːt] **1** *n* expert *m*, spécialiste *mf*
2 *adj* expert(e), habile; *(advice, opinion)* d'un expert; **to be e. in** *or* **at sth** être expert en qch; *Comptr* **e. system** système *m* expert; *Law* **e. witness** expert *m* cité comme témoin
expertise [ekspɜːˈtiːz] *n (technical, financial)* compétence *f*, connaissances *fpl*; *(as cook, carpenter)* savoir-faire *m*
expertly [ˈekspɜːtlɪ] *adv* de manière experte
expiate [ˈekspɪeɪt] *vt Formal* expier
expire [ɪksˈpaɪə(r)] *vi* **(a)** *(of law, deadline, passport)* expirer **(b)** *Lit (die)* expirer

expiry [ɪksˈpaɪərɪ] *n* expiration *f*, fin *f*; **e. date** (date *f* d')échéance *f*, date d'expiration
explain [ɪksˈpleɪn] **1** *vt* expliquer; **to e. oneself** *(make oneself clear)* s'expliquer; *(justify oneself)* se justifier
2 *vi* donner des explications, expliquer; *(make oneself clear)* s'expliquer
▸ **explain away** *vt sep (give explanation for)* donner une explication satisfaisante à; *(justify)* justifier
explanation [ekspləˈneɪʃən] *n* explication *f*; **to give an e. of sth** *(make clear)* expliquer qch; *(justify)* justifier qch
explanatory [ɪksˈplænətərɪ] *adj* explicatif(ive)
expletive [ɪksˈpliːtɪv] *n* juron *m*
explicable [eksˈplɪkəbəl] *adj* explicable
explicit [eksˈplɪsɪt] *adj* explicite
explicitly [eksˈplɪsɪtlɪ] *adv* de manière explicite
explode [ɪksˈpləʊd] **1** *vt (bomb)* faire exploser; *Fig (idea, theory)* démontrer la fausseté de
2 *vi (of bomb) & Fig (with anger)* exploser; *(of mine)* sauter; **to e. with laughter** éclater de rire
exploit 1 *n* [ˈeksplɔɪt] exploit *m*
2 *vt* [eksˈplɔɪt] **(a)** *(take unfair advantage of)* exploiter **(b)** *(use)* *(resources, scandal)* exploiter; *(talents)* mettre à profit
exploitation [eksplɔɪˈteɪʃən] *n* exploitation *f*
exploration [eksplɔːˈreɪʃən] *n* exploration *f*
exploratory [ɪksˈplɒrətərɪ] *adj (trip)* d'exploration; *(surgery, discussions, talks)* exploratoire
explore [ɪksˈplɔː(r)] **1** *vt (area, countryside)* explorer; *(possibility, idea)* étudier
2 *vi* partir en exploration
explorer [ɪksˈplɔːrə(r)] *n* explorateur(trice) *m,f*
explosion [ɪksˈpləʊʒən] *n also Fig* explosion *f*
explosive [ɪksˈpləʊsɪv] **1** *n* explosif *m*
2 *adj also Fig* explosif(ive)
exponent [ɪksˈpəʊnənt] *n* **(a)** *(of theory, idea)* avocat(e) *m,f*; *(of piece of music)* interprète *mf* **(b)** *Math* exposant *m*
exponential [ekspəʊˈnenʃəl] *adj* exponentiel(elle)
export 1 *n* [ˈekspɔːt] **(a)** *(product)* article *m* d'exportation; **exports** *(of country)* exportations *fpl* **(b)** *(activity)* exportation *f*; **e. duty** droit(s) *m(pl)* de sortie; **e. licence** licence *f* d'exportation; **exports** exportations *fpl*
2 *vt* [eksˈpɔːt] *also Comptr* exporter
exportation [ekspɔːˈteɪʃən] *n* exportation *f*
exporter [eksˈpɔːtə(r)] *n* exportateur(trice) *m,f*
expose [ɪksˈpəʊz] *vt* **(a)** *(to air, cold, danger) & Phot* exposer **(b)** *(wire)* mettre à jour; **to e. oneself to danger** s'exposer au **(b)** *(reveal)* *(secret)* éventer; *(crime)* dévoiler; *(criminal)* démasquer; *(feelings)* afficher; **e. sb as a fraud/criminal** révéler que qn est un imposteur/criminel; **to e. oneself** *(of flasher)* s'exhiber
exposé [eksˈpəʊzeɪ] *n (article, book)* exposé *m*; *(of scandal, corruption)* révélations *fpl*
exposed [ɪksˈpəʊzd] *adj (place)* exposé(e) **(to** à)
exposition [ekspəˈzɪʃən] *n (explanation)* exposition *f*; exposé *m*
expostulate [ɪksˈpɒstjəleɪt] *vi Formal* vitupérer
exposure [ɪksˈpəʊʒə(r)] *n* **(a)** *(to air, cold, danger)* exposition *f*; **to die of e.** mourir de froid **(b)** *(publicity)* couverture *f*; **to get a lot of e.** faire l'objet d'une large couverture médiatique **(c)** *(of crime)* révélation *f*; *(of criminal, scandal)* dénonciation *f* **(d)** *Phot* pose *f*; **e. meter** posemètre *m*
expound [ɪksˈpaʊnd] *vt Formal* exposer
express [ɪksˈpres] **1** *n (train)* express *m*, rapide *m*
2 *adj* **(a)** *(clear)* *(purpose, instruction)* exprès(esse); *(order)*

formel(elle) (**b**) *(rapid) (letter, delivery)* exprès *inv*; *(train)* express *inv*
3 *adv* **to send sth e.** envoyer qch en exprès
4 *vt* exprimer; **to e.** oneself s'exprimer
expression [ɪks'preʃən] *n* expression *f*
expressionism [ɪks'preʃənɪzəm] *n* expressionnisme *m*
expressionist [ɪks'preʃənɪst] *n & adj* expressionniste *mf*
expressionless [ɪks'preʃənlɪs] *adj* sans expression
expressive [ɪks'presɪv] *adj* expressif(ive); *(gesture, silence)* éloquent(e)
expressly [ɪks'preslɪ] *adv* expressément
expropriate [eks'prəuprɪeɪt] *vt* exproprier
expropriation [eksprəuprɪ'eɪʃən] *n* expropriation *f*
expulsion [ɪks'pʌlʃən] *n* expulsion *f*; *(from school)* renvoi *m*
expunge [ɪks'pʌndʒ] *vt* effacer
expurgate ['ekspɜːgeɪt] *vt* expurger
exquisite ['ekskwɪzɪt] *adj* exquis(e); *(pleasure)* vif (vive)
exquisitely [eks'kwɪzɪtlɪ] *adv* d'une manière exquise
extant [eks'tænt] *adj* qui existe encore
extempore [ɪks'tempərɪ] **1** *adj (speech)* impromptu(e)
2 *adv* **to speak e.** improviser
extemporize [ɪks'tempəraɪz] *vi* improviser
extend [ɪks'tend] **1** *vt* (**a**) *(in space)* étendre, allonger; *(knowledge)* accroître; *(frontiers)* faire reculer; *(house)* agrandir (**b**) *(in time)* prolonger (**c**) *(give, offer) (one's hand)* tendre; *(thanks)* présenter; *(support)* offrir; *Fin* **to e. credit to sb** accorder un crédit à qn
2 *vi* (**a**) *(in space)* s'étendre (**b**) *(in time)* se prolonger, continuer
extended family [ɪks'tendɪd'fæmɪlɪ] *n* famille *f* au sens large
extension [ɪks'tenʃən] *n* (**a**) *(to building)* annexe *f* (**b**) *(in time)* prolongation *f*; *(for essay)* délai *m* supplémentaire (**c**) *(for telephone)* poste *m* (**d**) **e.** (**cable**) rallonge *f*
extensive [ɪks'tensɪv] *adj (area, knowledge)* vaste, étendu(e); *(damage, repairs)* important(e); **to make e. use of sth** faire un usage considérable de qch
extensively [ɪks'tensɪvlɪ] *adv (travel, read)* énormément; *(revised, rewritten)* entièrement; *(damaged)* gravement; **to use sth e.** se servir beaucoup de qch
extent [ɪks'tent] *n* (**a**) *(of land, damage, knowledge)* étendue *f* (**b**) *(degree)* **to an e., to a certain e., to some e.** jusqu'à un certain point, dans une certaine mesure; **to a large e.** en grande partie, dans une large mesure; **to such an e. that...** à tel point que...; **to what e.?** jusqu'à quel point?
extenuating circumstances [ɪks'tenjʊeɪtɪŋ'sɜːkəmstænsɪz] *npl* circonstances *fpl* atténuantes
exterior [ɪks'tɪərɪə(r)] **1** *n (of building, car)* extérieur *m*; *(of person)* extérieur, dehors *mpl*
2 *adj* extérieur(e)
exterminate [ɪks'tɜːmɪneɪt] *vt* exterminer; *(disease)* éradiquer
extermination [ɪkstɜːmɪ'neɪʃən] *n* extermination *f*; *(of disease)* éradication *f*
external [ɪks'tɜːnəl] *adj (events, trade, debt)* extérieur(e); *(angle, damage, wall)* externe; *Univ (examiner)* de l'extérieur; *Pol* **e. affairs** affaires *fpl* étrangères *ou* extérieures; **for e. use only** *(on medicine)* à usage externe
extinct [ɪks'tɪŋkt] *adj (animal, species)* disparu(e), qui n'existe plus; *(volcano)* éteint(e)
extinction [ɪks'tɪŋkʃən] *n* extinction *f*

extinguish [ɪks'tɪŋgwɪʃ] *vt (fire)* éteindre; *(hope)* anéantir
extinguisher [ɪks'tɪŋgwɪʃə(r)] *n* extincteur *m*
extirpate ['ekstɜːpeɪt] *vt Formal* extirper
extol, *Am* **extoll** [ɪks'təʊl] (*pt & pp* **extolled**) *vt (virtues, merits)* exalter, vanter; *(beauty)* célébrer, chanter
extort [ɪks'tɔːt] *vt (money)* extorquer (**from** à); *(promise)* arracher (**from** à)
extortion [ɪks'tɔːʃən] *n* extorsion *f*
extortionate [ɪks'tɔːʃənɪt] *adj* exorbitant(e)
extra ['ekstrə] **1** *n (in film)* figurant(e) *m,f*; *(on bill)* supplément *m*
2 *adj* (**a**) *(additional)* supplémentaire, de plus; **no e. charge** sans supplément de prix; **e. time** *(in sporting contest)* prolongation *f* (**b**) *(spare)* de réserve, de rechange
3 *adv* (**a**) *(more than usual)* extrêmement; **to be e. careful** faire particulièrement attention; **e. large** *(clothing)* grand patron; **e. special** très spécial(e) (**b**) *(charge, pay)* en plus, en sus
extract 1 *n* ['ekstrækt] (**a**) *(concentrate)* extrait *m*, concentré *m* (**b**) *(from book, film)* extrait *m*
2 *vt* [ɪks'trækt] *(tooth, raw material)* extraire (**from** de); *(confession, information)* soutirer (**from** à)
extraction [ɪks'trækʃən] *n* (**a**) *(removal)* extraction *f* (**b**) *(origin) (social)* extraction *f*; *(geographical)* origine *f*; **she is of Italian e.** elle est d'origine italienne
extractor fan [ɪks'træktə(r)] *n* aérateur *m*
extracurricular ['ekstrəkə'rɪkjələ(r)] *adj Sch* extrascolaire
extradite ['ekstrədaɪt] *vt* extrader
extradition [ekstrə'dɪʃən] *n* extradition *f*
extrajudicial ['ekstrədʒuː'dɪʃəl] *adj* extrajudiciaire
extramarital ['ekstrə'mærɪtəl] *adj* extraconjugal(e)
extramural ['ekstrə'mjʊərəl] *adj Univ* de formation continue
extraneous [ɪks'treɪnɪəs] *adj Formal (details)* sans rapport; *(considerations)* en dehors de la question
extraordinarily [ɪks'trɔːdənərɪlɪ] *adv* extraordinairement
extraordinary [ɪks'trɔːdənrɪ] *adj* extraordinaire; **e. powers** pouvoirs *mpl* extraordinaires; **e. general meeting** assemblée *f* générale extraordinaire
extrapolate [ɪk'stræpəleɪt] *vt & vi* extrapoler (**from** à partir de)
extrapolation [ɪkstræpə'leɪʃən] *n* extrapolation *f*
extrasensory perception ['ekstrə'sensərɪpə'sep-ʃən] *n* perception *f* extrasensorielle
extraterrestrial [ekstrətə'restrɪəl] *n & adj* extraterrestre *mf*
extravagance [ɪks'trævəgəns] *n* (**a**) *(excessive spending)* gaspillage *m* (**b**) *(extravagant purchase)* folie *f*
extravagant [ɪks'trævəgənt] *adj (person)* dépensier(ère); *(tastes)* dispendieux(euse); *(object)* hors de prix
extravaganza [ɪkstrævə'gænzə] *n* grand spectacle *m*
extreme [ɪks'triːm] **1** *n* extrême *m*; **in the e.** à l'extrême; **to go from one e. to the other** passer d'un extrême à l'autre; **to go to extremes** pousser les choses à l'extrême
2 *adj* extrême(s); *Pol* **the e. left/right** l'extrême gauche/droite
extremely [ɪks'triːmlɪ] *adv* extrêmement
extremism [ɪks'triːmɪzəm] *n* extrémisme *m*
extremist [ɪks'triːmɪst] *n & adj* extrémiste *mf*
extremity [ɪks'tremɪtɪ] (*pl* **extremities**) *n* (**a**) *(end)* extrémité *f* (**b**) **extremities** *(of body)* extrémités *fpl* (**c**)

(extreme situation) situation *f* extrême; *(extreme measure)* mesure *f* extrême

extricate ['ekstrɪkeɪt] *vt* dégager, tirer; **to e.** oneself from *(danger, difficulties)* se tirer de

extrovert ['ekstrəvɜːt] *n & adj* extraverti(e) *m,f*

exuberance [ɪg'zjuːbərəns] *n* exubérance *f*

exuberant [ɪg'zjuːbərənt] *adj* exubérant(e)

exude [ɪg'zjuːd] *vt (sweat, odour)* exsuder; *(health, confidence)* déborder de

exult [ɪg'zʌlt] *vi* exulter, se réjouir **(in** de)

exultant [ɪg'zʌltənt] *adj (mood)* joyeux(euse); *(cry)* de triomphe

eye [aɪ] **1** *n* **(a)** *(of person, storm)* œil *m*; *(of needle)* chas *m*; **to open/close one's eyes** ouvrir/fermer les yeux; **to look sb (straight) in the e.** regarder qn droit dans les yeux; **as far as the e. can see** à perte de vue; **to make e. contact with sb** regarder qn (droit) dans les yeux; **e. drops** *(medicine)* gouttes *fpl* pour les yeux; **at e. level** à la hauteur des yeux; **e. shadow** ombre *f* à paupières; **e. test** examen *m* de la vue

(b) *(idioms)* **in the eye(s) of the law** aux yeux de la loi; **to be in the public e.** occuper une position en vue; **to have an e. for a bargain** savoir reconnaître une bonne affaire; **to have an e. for detail/colour** avoir l'œil pour les détails/ les couleurs; **to look at sth with a critical e.** regarder qch d'un œil critique; **to see e. to e. with sb** voir les choses du même œil que qn; **for your eyes only** confidentiel(elle); **to keep one's eyes and ears open** rester en éveil; **to keep one's eyes peeled** ouvrir l'œil; **to open sb's eyes to sth** ouvrir *ou* dessiller les yeux à qn sur qch; **to shut** *or* **close one's eyes to sth** fermer les yeux sur qch; **to do sth with one's eyes open** faire qch en connaissance de cause; **to catch sb's e.** attirer l'attention de qn; **to have eyes in** *or* **at the back of one's head** avoir des yeux derrière la tête; **he only has eyes for her** il n'a d'yeux que pour elle; **to set** *or* **lay eyes on sth** poser les yeux sur qch; **I saw it with my own eyes** je l'ai vu de mes propres yeux; **to run** *or* **cast one's e. over sth** jeter un coup d'œil sur qch; **to keep an e. on sb/sth** surveiller qn/qch; **to keep an e. out for sth** être

à l'affût de qch; **to have one's e. on sb/sth** *(be watching)* avoir qn/qch à l'œil; *(have in mind)* avoir l'œil sur qn/qch; **with an e. to...** en vue de...; **to be up to one's eyes in work** avoir du travail par-dessus la tête; **to be up to one's eyes in debt** être endetté(e) jusqu'au cou; *Fam* **that's one in the e. for him!** ça lui fera les pieds!; **an e. for an e.(, a tooth for a tooth)** œil pour œil(, dent pour dent)

2 *vt* regarder, observer

▸ **eye up** *vt sep* reluquer

eyeball ['aɪbɔːl] *n* globe *m* oculaire

eyebrow ['aɪbraʊ] *n* sourcil *m*; *Fig* **to raise one's eyebrows** *(in surprise)* lever les sourcils

eye-catching ['aɪkætʃɪŋ] *adj* accrocheur(euse)

eyeful ['aɪfʊl] *n Fam* **to get an e. of sb/sth** *(look at)* reluquer qn/qch

eyeglass ['aɪglɑːs] *n* monocle *m*

eyeglasses ['aɪglɑːsɪz] *npl Am (spectacles)* lunettes *fpl*

eyelash ['aɪlæʃ] *n* cil *m*

eyelid ['aɪlɪd] *n* paupière *f*; *Fig* **she didn't bat an e.** elle n'a pas sourcillé

eyeliner ['aɪlaɪnə(r)] *n* eye-liner *m*

eye-opener ['aɪəʊpənə(r)] *n* révélation *f*; **it was an e. for him** ça lui a ouvert les yeux

eyepatch ['aɪpætʃ] *n* cache *m* (sur l'œil)

eyeshade ['aɪʃeɪd] *n* visière *f*

eyesight ['aɪsaɪt] *n* vue *f*

eyesore ['aɪsɔː(r)] *n* horreur *f*

eyestrain ['aɪstreɪn] *n* fatigue *f* oculaire

eyetooth ['aɪtuːθ] *(pl* **eyeteeth** ['aɪtiːθ]*) n* canine *f*; **I'd give my eyeteeth to go with them** je donnerais n'importe quoi pour aller avec eux

eyewash ['aɪwɒʃ] *n (for eye)* collyre *m*; *Fig (nonsense)* boniment *m*, poudre *f* aux yeux

eyewitness ['aɪwɪtnɪs] *n* témoin *m* oculaire

eyrie ['ɪərɪ] *n* aire *f*

F, f [ef] *n* (**a**) *(letter)* F, f *m inv; Br Euph* **the F word** = euphémisme désignant le mot "fuck" (**b**) *Mus* fa *m*

fa [fɑː] *n Mus* fa *m*

FA [eˈfeɪ] *n (abbr Football Association)* = fédération anglaise de football

fab [fæb] *adj Br Fam* sensass

fable [ˈfeɪbəl] *n* fable *f*

fabled [ˈfeɪbəld] *adj* légendaire; *Fig* fabuleux(euse)

fabric [ˈfæbrɪk] *n (cloth)* tissu *m*, étoffe *f*; *(of building)* structure *f*; *Fig* **the f. of society** le tissu social

fabricate [ˈfæbrɪkeɪt] *vt (news, story, alibi)* forger, fabriquer; *(make)* fabriquer

fabulous [ˈfæbjʊləs] *adj* fabuleux(euse)

fabulously [ˈfæbjʊləslɪ] *adv (rich)* fabuleusement

façade [fæˈsɑːd] *n also Fig* façade *f*

face [feɪs] **1** *n* (**a**) *(of person)* visage *m*, figure *f*; *very Fam* **shut your f.!** ferme-la!, la ferme!; **I told him to his f.** je le lui ai dit en face; **I shall never be able to look her in the f. again** je ne pourrai plus jamais la regarder en face; **to show one's f.** se montrer; **to set one's f. against sth** se braquer contre qch; **in the f. of** *(danger, threat, enemy)* devant, face à; *Fam* **in your f.** *(music, campaign)* percutant(e); **f. cloth** ≃ gant *m* de toilette; **f. cream** crème *f* pour le visage; **f. pack** masque *m*; **f. powder** poudre *f* (**b**) *(expression)* mine *f*; **to make** *or* **pull faces** faire des grimaces; **to keep a straight f.** garder son sérieux; **to put a good f. on it** garder le sourire (**c**) *(appearance)* **on the f. of it** à première vue; **to save f.** sauver la face; **to lose f.** perdre la face; **the changing f. of Britain** le visage changeant de la Grande-Bretagne; **to take sth at f. value** prendre qch au pied de la lettre (**d**) *(surface) (of the earth)* surface *f*; *(of clock)* cadran *m*; *(of coin, cliff)* face *f*; **to disappear off the f. of the earth** se volatiliser; **f. down** *(person)* sur le ventre; *(document)* face imprimée dessous; *(playing card)* à l'envers; **f. up** *(person)* sur le dos; *(document)* face imprimée dessus; *(playing card)* à l'endroit

2 *vt* (**a**) *(confront) (difficulty, danger)* affronter, faire face à; **to be faced with sth** être confronté(e) à qch; **to f. facts** regarder les choses en face; **he faces six months in prison** il risque six mois de prison; **I can't f. going to work today** je n'ai pas le courage d'aller travailler aujourd'hui; **let's f. it** soyons réalistes; *Fig* **to f. the music** *(deal with situation)* faire front; *(accept consequences)* assumer ses responsabilités (**b**) *(look towards)* faire face à; **to f. the front** regarder devant soi

3 *vi* **to f. north/south** *(of house)* être orienté(e) au nord/sud; **to f. towards** *(of person)* se tourner vers

▸ **face up to** *vt insep (person)* tenir tête à; *(reality, fears)* affronter

faceless [ˈfeɪslɪs] *adj* anonyme

facelift [ˈfeɪslɪft] *n (plastic surgery)* lifting *m*; *Fig (of building)* restauration *f*; **to have a f.** se faire faire un lifting

face-saving [ˈfeɪsseɪvɪŋ] *adj* qui permet de sauver la face

facet [ˈfæsɪt] *n (of gem, character)* facette *f*; *(of problem, situation)* dimension *f*

facetious [fəˈsiːʃəs] *adj* facétieux(euse); **don't be f.!** ne plaisante pas!

face-to-face [ˈfeɪstəˈfeɪs] **1** *adj* **a f. meeting** un face à face **2** *adv (meet)* face à face

facial [ˈfeɪʃəl] **1** *n* soin *m* du visage; **to have a f.** se faire faire un soin du visage **2** *adj* facial(e); *(expression, hair)* du visage

facile [ˈfæsaɪl] *adj Pej* facile

facilitate [fəˈsɪlɪteɪt] *vt* faciliter

facility [fəˈsɪlɪtɪ] *(pl* **facilities**) *n* (**a**) *(ease)* facilité *f* (**b**) *(skill)* **to have a f. for sth** avoir un don pour qch (**c**) **facilities** *(for cooking, washing)* équipement *m*; *(for sport)* installations *fpl*; **shopping facilities** magasins *mpl*; **transport facilities** moyens *mpl* de transport (**d**) *(building)* **a detention f.** un établissement pénitentiaire (**e**) *(feature) (of computer, stereo)* option *f*

facsimile [fækˈsɪmɪlɪ] *n (copy)* fac-similé *m*; *(fax)* télécopie *f*

fact [fækt] *n* fait *m*; **in f.** en fait; **to distinguish f. from fiction** discerner la fiction de la réalité; **the f. is (that)...** le fait est que...; **it's a f. that... c'est un fait que...; **for a f. (that)... savoir pertinemment que...; **it's a f. of life** c'est une réalité; **to tell sb the facts of life** expliquer à qn comment on fait les enfants

fact-finding [ˈfæktfaɪndɪŋ] *adj* d'enquête

faction [ˈfækʃən] *n* faction *f*

factor [ˈfæktə(r)] *n (aspect, in maths)* facteur *m*

factory [ˈfæktərɪ] *(pl* **factories**) *n* usine *f*; *(small)* fabrique *f*; **f. farming** élevage *m* industriel

factual [ˈfæktʃʊəl] *adj* basé(e) sur les faits

faculty [ˈfækəltɪ] *(pl* **faculties**) *n (of mind, in university)* faculté *f*; *Am* **the f.** *(teaching staff)* le personnel enseignant

fad [fæd] *n* mode *f* (**for** de)

fade [feɪd] **1** *vt* faner **2** *vi (of flower, material, colour)* se faner; *(of light)* baisser; *(of memory)* s'éteindre; *(of hope)* s'amenuiser; **to f. from memory** s'effacer de la mémoire

▸ **fade away** vi (of sound) s'éteindre; Fig (of person) s'éteindre peu à peu
▸ **fade out 1** vt sep Cin fermer en fondu; (music) terminer par un fondu
fade 2 vi se terminer en fondu
faded ['feɪdɪd] adj (flower, colour) fané(e); (photograph, garment) décoloré(e)
fading ['feɪdɪŋ] adj (light) pâlissant(e)
faeces ['fiːsiːz] npl fèces fpl
▸ **faff about, faff around** [fæf] vi Br Fam perdre son temps
fag [fæg] n (a) Br Fam (cigarette) clope m or f (b) Br Fam (unpleasant job) corvée f (c) Am very Fam (homosexual) pédé m, = terme injurieux désignant un homosexuel
faggot ['fægət] n (a) (firewood) fagot m (b) Br (meatball) boulette f de viande (c) Am very Fam (homosexual) pédé m, = terme injurieux désignant un homosexuel
Fahrenheit ['færənhaɪt] adj Fahrenheit inv
fail [feɪl] **1** n (a) (in exam) échec m (b) **without f. sans faute**
2 vt (exam, test) échouer à, rater; (candidate) recaler; **to f. a drugs test** être positif(ive) au contrôle anti-dopage; **words f. me** les mots me manquent; **his nerve failed him** le courage lui a fait défaut; **I won't f. you** vous pouvez compter sur moi
3 vi (of person, plan) échouer; (of business) faire faillite; (of engine) caler; (of memory, eyesight, light) baisser; (of brakes) lâcher; **to f. to do sth** (not succeed) ne pas arriver à faire qch; (forget) négliger de faire qch; **I f. to see how I can help** je ne vois pas comment je peux aider; **if all else fails** en désespoir de cause; **to f. in one's duty** manquer à son devoir; **it never fails** (of strategy, excuse) ça marche à tous les coups
failed [feɪld] adj (artist, politician) raté(e)
failing ['feɪlɪŋ] **1** n (fault) faiblesse f, défaut m
2 adj (sight, strength) qui baisse
3 prep à défaut de; **f. that** à défaut; **f. all else** en désespoir de cause
fail-safe ['feɪlseɪf] adj (mechanism) à sûreté intégrée
failure ['feɪljə(r)] n (of plan, attempt) échec m; (person) raté(e) m,f; (of machine) panne f; (of company) faillite f; **to be a f.** (of show, film) faire un bide; **f. to keep a promise** manquement à une promesse; **f. to pay a bill** défaut m de paiement d'une facture
faint [feɪnt] **1** n **to fall down in a f.** s'évanouir
2 adj (hope, light, sound) faible; (mark, writing) à peine visible; (colour) pâle; (idea) vague; **I haven't got the faintest idea** je n'en ai pas la moindre idée; **to feel** or **be f.** (of person) se sentir mal
3 vi (lose consciousness) s'évanouir
faint-hearted ['feɪnt'hɑːtɪd] adj timoré(e)
faintly ['feɪntlɪ] adv (a) (remember, hear, see) vaguement; (shine) faiblement (b) (slightly) (uneasy, ridiculous) légèrement
fair¹ ['feə(r)] n (a) Br (funfair) fête f foraine (b) (trade fair) foire f
fair² **1** adj (a) (just) juste, équitable; (price) raisonnable; (fight) loyal(e); **it's not f.** ce n'est pas juste; **fair's f.!** ce n'est que justice!; **f. enough!** (OK) d'accord!; (rightly so) ça se comprend!; **it is f. to say (that)…** on peut dire que…; **to be f.,…** pour être honnête,…; **by f. means or foul** par tous les moyens; Prov **all's f. in love and war** tous les moyens sont bons; Fam **to give sb a f. crack of the whip** donner sa chance à qn; **to be f. game** être une proie facile; **f. play** fair-play m; **to get one's f. share** recevoir son dû; **we've had our f. share of problems** nous avons eu notre lot de problèmes

(b) (quite good) assez bon (bonne); **a f. idea** une assez bonne idée; **at a f. pace** à une allure assez rapide; **a f. amount of** pas mal de; **f. to middling** comme ci comme ça
(c) (weather) beau (belle)
(d) (light-coloured) (hair) blond(c); (skin) pâle
(e) (attractive) beau (belle); Old-fashioned **the f. or fairer sex** le beau sexe
2 adv (act, fight) loyalement; (play) jouer franc jeu; **you can't say fairer than that** il n'y a pas plus équitable; **to beat sb f. and square** battre qn à plates coutures
fairground ['feəgraʊnd] n parc m d'attractions
fair-haired ['feə'heəd] adj blond(e)
fairly ['feəlɪ] adv (a) (quite) assez; **it is f. certain (that)…** il est à peu près certain que… (b) (justly) équitablement; (play, fight) loyalement; (describe) objectivement (c) (for emphasis) **we f. raced home** nous sommes rentrés ventre à terre
fair-minded ['feə'maɪndɪd] adj équitable
fairness ['feənɪs] n (a) (of person, decision) impartialité f; **in all f.** en toute justice (b) (of hair) blondeur f; (of skin) pâleur f
fair-sized ['feə'saɪzd] adj assez grand(e)
fairway ['feəweɪ] n fairway m
fair-weather friend ['feəweðə'frend] n ami(e) m,f des beaux jours
fairy ['feərɪ] (pl fairies) n (a) (magical being) fée f; **f. godmother** bonne fée f; **f. lights** guirlande f lumineuse (pour sapin de Noël) (b) very Fam (homosexual) tapette f, = terme injurieux désignant un homosexuel
fairytale ['feərɪteɪl] n conte m de fées; **a f. ending** une fin digne d'un conte de fées
faith [feɪθ] n foi f; **to have f. in sb** avoir foi en qn; **to be of the Catholic/Jewish f.** être de religion catholique/juive; **to keep f. with sb** tenir ses engagements envers qn; **in good f.** en toute bonne foi; **f. healer** guérisseur(euse) m,f
faithful ['feɪθfʊl] **1** npl **the f.** les fidèles mpl
2 adj fidèle
faithfully ['feɪθfʊlɪ] adv fidèlement; **yours f.** (in formal letter) recevez l'expression de mes/nos sentiments distingués
fake [feɪk] **1** n (object) faux m; (person) bluffeur m
2 adj faux (fausse)
3 vt (signature) contrefaire; (result) truquer; **to f. an illness** feindre d'être malade
falcon ['fɔːlkən] n faucon m
falconry ['fɔːlkənrɪ] n fauconnerie f
Falkland ['fɔːklənd] n **F. Islands, the Falklands** les Malouines fpl, les Falkland fpl
fall [fɔːl] **1** n (a) (of person, prices, besieged city, snow) chute f; **to have a f.** tomber, faire une chute; Fig **to be heading for a f.** courir à sa perte; Fam **f. guy** (scapegoat) bouc m émissaire
(b) Am (autumn) automne m
(c) **falls** (waterfall) chutes fpl
2 vi (pt fell [fel], pp fallen ['fɔːlən]) (a) (drop, fall over) tomber; **to f. down a hole** tomber dans un trou; **to f. off a bicycle/chair** tomber d'un vélo/d'une chaise; Fig **to f. into a trap** tomber dans un piège; also Fig **to f. flat** tomber à plat; **to f. to pieces** (of object) tomber en morceaux; Fig (of person) craquer; **to f. short of doing sth** ne pas réussir à faire qch
(b) (decrease) (of price, temperature, standards) chuter, baisser
(c) (of government, city, soldier) tomber
(d) (of silence, darkness, light) tomber; **the responsibility falls on you** c'est à vous qu'en incombe la responsabilité;

Formal **it falls to me to introduce…** j'ai l'honneur de vous présenter… (**e**) *(become)* **to f. asleep** s'endormir; **to f. ill** tomber malade; **to f. in love (with)** tomber amoureux(euse) (de); **to f. silent** se taire; **to f. victim to an epidemic** être victime d'une épidémie; **the baseball game fell victim to the weather** le match de base-ball a dû être annulé en raison du mauvais temps (**f**) *(be classified)* se classer; **to f. into two categories** se diviser en deux catégories; **suddenly everything fell into place** soudain tout est devenu clair (**g**) *(occur)* **Christmas Day falls on a Thursday this year** cette année Noël tombe un jeudi

▸ **fall away** *vi (of ground)* descendre; *(of attendance)* diminuer

▸ **fall back on** *vt insep (resort to)* se rabattre sur

▸ **fall behind** *vi (in race)* se faire distancer; **to f. behind with the rent** être en retard pour payer son loyer

▸ **fall down** *vi (of person)* tomber; *(of building)* s'écrouler, s'effondrer; **that's where your argument falls down** c'est par là que pèche ton raisonnement

▸ **fall for** *vt insep Fam* (**a**) *(fall in love with)* tomber amoureux(euse) de (**b**) *(trick)* se laisser prendre à; **to f. for it** s'y laisser prendre

▸ **fall in** *vi* (**a**) *(of roof)* s'écrouler, s'effondrer (**b**) *Mil (of troops)* former les rangs

▸ **fall off** *vi* (**a**) *(of object)* tomber (**b**) *(of profits, attendance)* diminuer

▸ **fall out** *vi* (**a**) *(quarrel)* se brouiller, se fâcher (**with** avec) (**b**) *Mil* rompre les rangs

▸ **fall over 1** *vi* tomber (par terre) **2** *vt insep (stumble on)* trébucher sur; *Fig* **to be falling over oneself to do sth** *(be very keen)* se mettre en quatre pour faire qch

▸ **fall through** *vi (of plan, deal)* tomber à l'eau

fallacious [fə'leɪʃəs] *adj* erroné(e)

fallacy ['fæləsɪ] *(pl* **fallacies**) *n* erreur *f*

fallen ['fɔ:lən] **1** *npl* **the f.** les soldats *mpl* tombés au combat **2** *adj (angel)* déchu(e); *(woman)* perdu(e) **3** *pp of* **fall**

fallible ['fælɪbəl] *adj* faillible

Fallopian tube [fə'ləʊpɪən'tju:b] *n Anat* trompe *f* de Fallope

fallout ['fɔ:laʊt] *n (nuclear)* retombées *fpl* radioactives; *Fig (from scandal)* retombées; **f. shelter** abri *m* antiatomique

fallow ['fæləʊ] *adj* en jachère; **to lie f.** être en jachère; *Fig* **a f. period** un passage à vide

false [fɔ:ls] *adj* faux (fausse); **f. alarm** fausse alerte *f*; *Fig* **f. dawn** faux espoir *m*; **f. economy** fausse économie *f*; **f. friend** *(in foreign language)* faux ami *m*; **f. modesty** fausse modestie *f*; *Fig* **to strike a f. note** *(in film)* sonner faux; *(of person)* faire une gaffe; **under f. pretences** *(illegally)* par des moyens frauduleux; *(by lying)* sous des prétextes fallacieux; **f. start** *(in race)* faux départ *m*; **f. teeth** dentier *m*; **to bear f. witness** faire un faux témoignage

falsehood ['fɔ:lshʊd] *n* mensonge *m*

falsely ['fɔ:lslɪ] *adv (described)* faussement; *(accused)* à tort; *(smile)* avec fausseté

falsetto [fɔ:l'setəʊ] *(pl* **falsettos**) *n Mus* voix *f* de fausset

falsify ['fɔ:lsɪfaɪ] *(pt & pp* **falsified**) *vt* (**a**) *(forge) (records, document)* falsifier (**b**) *(disprove) (theory)* prouver la fausseté de

falter ['fɔ:ltə(r)] *vi also Fig* vaciller; *(of voice)* hésiter

fame [feɪm] *n* renom *m*, renommée *f*; **to seek f. and fortune** rechercher la gloire et la fortune

famed [feɪmd] *adj* célèbre (**for** pour)

familiar [fə'mɪlɪə(r)] *adj* (**a**) *(well-known)* familier(ère) (**to** à) (**b**) *(intimate)* familier(ère), intime; **to be on f. terms with sb** avoir des rapports amicaux avec qn; **to get too f. with sb** se permettre trop de familiarités avec qn (**c**) *(acquainted)* **to be f. with sb/sth** bien connaître qn/qch

familiarity [fəmɪlɪ'ærɪtɪ] *n* (**a**) *(intimacy)* familiarité *f*; **f. breeds contempt** avec l'habitude vient la lassitude (**b**) *(acquaintance)* connaissance *f* (**with** de)

familiarize [fə'mɪlɪəraɪz] *vt* **to f. sb with sth** familiariser qn avec qch; **to f. oneself with sth** se familiariser avec qch

family ['fæmɪlɪ] *(pl* **families**) *n* famille *f*; **it runs in the f.** c'est de famille, ça tient de famille; **to start a f.** fonder une famille; **to treat sb as one of the f.** traiter qn comme un membre de la famille; *Fam Old-fashioned* **to be in the f. way** être enceinte; **f. allowance** allocations *fpl* familiales; **f. business** entreprise *f* familiale; **f. doctor/life** docteur *m*/ vie *f* de famille; **f. man** homme *m* attaché à sa famille; **f. planning** planning *m* familial; **f. planning clinic** (centre *m* de) planning familial; **f. resemblance** air *m* de famille; **f. tree** arbre *m* généalogique

famine ['fæmɪn] *n* famine *f*; **f. relief** aide *f* aux victimes d'une famine

famished ['fæmɪʃd] *adj* affamé(e)

famous ['feɪməs] *adj* célèbre (**for** pour)

famously ['feɪməslɪ] *adv Fam* **to get on f. (with sb)** s'entendre à merveille (avec qn)

fan¹ [fæn] **1** *n (cooling device) (hand-held)* éventail *m*; *(mechanical)* ventilateur *m*; **f. belt** *(of car)* courroie *f* de ventilateur; **f. heater** radiateur *m* soufflant **2** *vt (pt & pp* **fanned**) (**a**) *(face, person)* éventer; **to f. oneself** s'éventer (**b**) *(fire, passions)* attiser

▸ **fan out** *vi* se déployer en éventail

fan² *n (enthusiast)* fan *mf*; *(of sports team)* supporter *m*; *Fig* **I'm not a f. of digital cameras** je n'aime pas trop ces appareils photo numériques; **f. club** fan-club *m*; **f. mail** courrier *m* des admirateurs

fanatic [fə'nætɪk] *n & adj* fanatique *mf*

fanatical [fə'nætɪkəl] *adj* fanatique

fanciful ['fænsɪfʊl] *adj* (**a**) *(unrealistic) (idea, project)* chimérique; *(person)* qui se fait des idées (**b**) *(design, style)* plein(e) de fantaisie

fancy ['fænsɪ] **1** *(pl* **fancies**) *n* (**a**) *(imagination)* imagination *f* (**b**) *(whim)* fantaisie *f*, caprice *m* (**c**) *(liking)* **to take a f. to sb** prendre qn en affection; *(sexually)* s'enticher de qn; **to take a f. to sth** s'enticher de qch; **the house didn't take her f.** la maison ne lui a pas plu **2** *adj (jewels, gadget, hat)* fantaisie *inv*; *(party, hotel)* chic *inv*; *(food, decoration)* recherché(e); **f. dress** déguisement *m*; **f. dress party** soirée *f* déguisée **3** *vt (pt & pp* **fancied**) (**a**) *Fam (want)* **I didn't f. the idea** ça ne me tentait pas; **do you f. something to eat?** ça te dit de manger quelque chose? (**b**) *Br (be attracted to)* **he fancies her** elle lui plaît (**c**) *(imagine)* **to f. (that)…** croire *ou* penser que…; **I f. I've seen her before** j'ai l'impression de l'avoir déjà vue; *Fam* **f. that!** ça alors!; **f. meeting you here!** si je m'attendais à vous rencontrer ici! (**d**) *(have good opinion of)* **to f. sb to win** penser que qn va gagner; *Pej* **he fancies himself** il ne se prend pas pour n'importe qui; **to f. oneself as a writer/musician** se prendre pour un écrivain/musicien; **I don't f. his chances of getting the job** je crois qu'il a peu de chances d'obtenir le poste

fanfare ['fænfeə(r)] n fanfare f
fang [fæŋ] n (of dog) croc m; (of snake) crochet m
fanny ['fænɪ] (pl **fannies**) n (**a**) Br Vulg (vagina) chatte f (**b**) Am Fam (buttocks) derrière m, fesses fpl; f. **pack** banane f
fantasize ['fæntəsaɪz] vi fantasmer (**about** sur)
fantastic [fæn'tæstɪk] adj (**a**) Fam (excellent) formidable, fantastique (**b**) (enormous) (price) astronomique; (wealth, size) prodigieux(euse) (**c**) (unbelievable) (claim, story) grotesque, absurde (**d**) (strange) (creature) fantastique; (design) plein(e) de fantaisie
fantasy ['fæntəzɪ] (pl **fantasies**) n (**a**) (unrealistic idea) chimère f; (sexual) fantasme m (**b**) (imagination) fantaisie f (**c**) (literature) littérature f fantastique
FAO [efeɪˈəʊ] n (abbr **Food and Agriculture Organization**) FAO f
far [fɑː(r)] (comparative **farther** ['fɑːðə(r)] or **further** ['fɜːðə(r)], superlative **farthest** ['fɑːðɪst] or **furthest** ['fɜːðɪst]) **1** adj **in the f. distance** au loin, dans le lointain; **the f. end** l'autre bout; Pol **the f. left/right** l'extrême gauche f/droite f; **the F. East** l'Extrême-Orient m; **it's a f. cry from** ça n'a rien à voir avec
2 adv (**a**) (in distance) loin; **how f. is it to San Diego?** combien y a-t-il jusqu'à San Diego?; **f. away (from)** loin (de); **f. below/above** loin au-dessous/au-dessus, as **f.** as jusqu'à; also Fig **to go f.** aller loin; Fig **to go so f. as to do sth** aller jusqu'à faire qch; Fig **to go too f.** aller trop loin; also Fig **f. from...** loin de...; Fig **f. from it** loin de là; Fig **f. be it from me to...** loin de moi l'idée de...; **f. and wide** partout; Fig **as f. as I can see** pour autant que je puisse en juger; **as f. as I know** (pour) autant que je sache; **as f. as I'm concerned** en ce qui me concerne; Fig **as f. as possible** autant que possible
(**b**) (in time) so f. jusqu'ici, jusqu'à présent; so f. so good jusqu'ici tout va bien; **for as f. back as I can remember** d'aussi loin que je me souvienne; **to work f. into the night** travailler jusqu'à une heure avancée de la nuit
(**c**) (much) beaucoup; **f. better/bigger** beaucoup mieux/plus grand; **by f.** de loin; **f. and away the best** de loin le meilleur/la meilleure
faraway ['fɑːrəweɪ] adj lointain(e); (look) perdu(e) dans le vague
farce [fɑːs] n farce f; Fig **it's a f.!** c'est grotesque!
farcical ['fɑːsɪkəl] adj grotesque
fare [feə(r)] **1** n (**a**) (for journey) tarif m; **to pay one's f.** acheter son billet (**b**) (taxi passenger) client(e) m,f (**c**) Formal (food) chère f
2 vi se débrouiller
farewell [feəˈwel] n adieu m; **to say** or **make one's farewells** faire ses adieux; **f. dinner** dîner m d'adieu
far-fetched ['fɑːˈfetʃt] adj (idea, plan) tiré(e) par les cheveux
far-flung ['fɑːflʌŋ] adj lointain(e)
farm [fɑːm] **1** n ferme f; **f. animals** animaux mpl de ferme; **f. labourer** ouvrier m agricole
2 vt (land) cultiver, exploiter
3 vi être cultivateur(trice)
► **farm out** vt sep (work) confier en sous-traitance (**to** à); (child) confier (**to** à)
farmer ['fɑːmə(r)] n fermier(ère) m,f, agriculteur(trice) m,f
farmhouse ['fɑːmhaʊs] n (corps m de) ferme f
farming ['fɑːmɪŋ] n (business) agriculture f
farmland ['fɑːmlænd] n terres fpl arables
farmyard ['fɑːmjɑːd] n cour f de ferme
Faroe ['feərəʊ] n **the F. Islands, the Faroes** les îles fpl Féroé

far-off ['fɑːrɒf] adj (country, time) lointain(e); (place) éloigné(e)
far-out ['fɑːraʊt] adj Fam (strange) farfelu(e); (avant-garde) avant-gardiste; Old-fashioned **f.!** (fantastic) génial!
far-reaching ['fɑːˈriːtʃɪŋ] adj (decision, change) de grande envergure; (consequences) d'une grande portée
Farsi ['fɑːsiː] n farsi m
far-sighted ['fɑːˈsaɪtɪd] adj (**a**) (forward-looking) (person) prévoyant(e); (decision) avisé(e) (**b**) Am (long-sighted) presbyte
fart [fɑːt] Fam **1** n pet m
2 vi péter
► **fart about** vi Fam (waste time) glander
farther ['fɑːðə(r)] comparative of **far**
farthest ['fɑːðɪst] superlative of **far**
farthing ['fɑːðɪŋ] n Br Hist quart m de penny; Fam **he hasn't got a (brass) f.** il n'a pas le sou
fascinate ['fæsɪneɪt] vt fasciner
fascinating ['fæsɪneɪtɪŋ] adj fascinant(e)
fascination [fæsɪˈneɪʃən] n fascination f
fascism ['fæʃɪzəm] n fascisme m
fascist ['fæʃɪst] n & adj fasciste mf
fashion ['fæʃən] **1** n (**a**) (in clothes) mode f; **in f.** à la mode, **out of f.** démodé(e), passé(e) de mode; **f. designer** styliste mf; (big name) couturier m; **f. house** maison f de couture; **f. show** défilé m de mode; Pej **f. victim** esclave mf de la mode (**b**) (manner) manière f; **after a f.** tant bien que mal
2 vt (form) façonner; (make) confectionner
fashionable ['fæʃənəbəl] adj à la mode
fast¹ [fɑːst] **1** adj (**a**) (rapid) rapide; Fam **he pulled a f. one on me** il m'a joué un mauvais tour; **f. food** restauration f rapide; **f. food restaurant** fast-food m; **the f. lane** (of motorway) la voie rapide; Fig **to live life in the f. lane** vivre à cent à l'heure (**b**) (clock, watch) **my watch is (ten minutes) f.** ma montre avance (de dix minutes) (**c**) (secure) (grip) ferme, solide; (door, lid) bien fermé(e); (colour) résistant(e)
2 adv (**a**) (rapidly) vite, rapidement; **not so f.!** pas si vite!; **to play f. and loose with the facts** truquer les faits; **to play f. and loose with sb's emotions** jouer avec les sentiments de qn (**b**) (securely) solidement; **to hold f.** tenir bon; **f. asleep** profondément endormi(e)
fast² **1** n (lack of food) jeûne m; Rel **f. day** jour m de jeûne
2 vi jeûner; Med être à la diète
fasten ['fɑːsən] **1** vt (door, window) fermer; (belt, buttons) attacher; Fig **to f. one's eyes on sth** fixer son regard sur qch
2 vi (garment) s'attacher
fastener ['fɑːsnə(r)] n (of garment) (hook) agrafe f; (press stud) bouton-pression m; (of bag, jewellery) fermoir m
fast-forward [fɑːstˈfɔːwəd] **1** n avance f rapide
2 vt (cassette) mettre en avance rapide
fastidious [fæˈstɪdɪəs] adj difficile; (about manners, hygiene, dress) pointilleux(euse) (**about** sur)
fast-moving ['fɑːstˈmuːvɪŋ] adj rapide
fat [fæt] **1** n (**a**) (flesh) graisse f; (of cooked meat) gras m; (for cooking) matière grasse f; **f. content** teneur f en graisse ou en lipides (**b**) (idioms) Fam **the f.'s in the fire!** ça va chauffer!; **to live off the f. of the land** vivre comme un coq en pâte; **to chew the f. (with sb)** tailler le bout de gras (avec qn)
2 adj (person) gros (grosse), Fam (cheque, profit, salary) gros; **to get f.** grossir; Fig **to grow f. at the expense of others** (become rich) s'engraisser aux dépens des autres; Fam **a f. lot of good that did you!** ça te fera une belle

jambe!; *Fig* **f. cat** *(person)* gros salaire *m*; *Fam* **f. chance!** tu parles!

fatal ['feɪtəl] *adj* mortel(elle)

fatalistic [feɪtə'lɪstɪk] *adj* fataliste

fatality [fə'tælɪtɪ] *(pl* **fatalities)** *n* **(a)** *(person killed)* mort *m* **(b)** *(fate)* fatalité *f*

fatally ['feɪtəlɪ] *adv (wounded)* mortellement; **f. ill** condamné(e); **to be f. damaging to sth** causer un tort irréparable à qch

fate [feɪt] *n* destin *m*, sort *m*; **to suffer** *or* **share the same f.** avoir le même sort; **it's a f. worse than death** c'est ce qu'on peut imaginer de pire

fated ['feɪtɪd] *adj* **to be f. to do sth** être destiné(e) à faire qch

fateful ['feɪtfʊl] *adj (words, day)* fatidique

father ['fɑːðə(r)] **1** *n (parent, priest)* père *m*; **from f. to son** de père en fils; **he was like a f. to me** il était comme un père pour moi; **like f., like son** tel père, tel fils; **Our F.** *(God)* Notre Père; **F. Christmas** le Père Noël; **F.'s Day** la fête des pères; **to be a f. figure to sb** jouer le rôle du père pour qn

    2 *vt (child)* engendrer

fatherhood ['fɑːðəhʊd] *n* paternité *f*

father-in-law ['fɑːðərɪnlɔː] *n* beau-père *m*

fatherly ['fɑːðəlɪ] *adj* paternel(elle)

fathom ['fæðəm] **1** *n (unit of measurement)* = 1,8 m, brasse *f*

    2 *vt (understand)* comprendre

▸ **fathom out** *vt sep (understand)* comprendre

fatigue [fə'tiːg] **1** *n* **(a)** *(tiredness)* fatigue *f*; **metal f.** fatigue des métaux **(b)** *Mil* **f. (duty)** corvée *f*; **fatigues** *(clothes)* treillis *m*

    2 *vt (person)* fatiguer

fatso ['fætsəʊ] *(pl* **fatsos** *or* **fatsoes)** *n very Fam (man)* gros lard *m*; *(woman)* grosse vache *f*

▸ **fatten up** ['fætən] *vt sep* faire grossir, engraisser

fatty ['fætɪ] **1** *(pl* **fatties)** *n Fam* gros (grosse) *m,f*; **hey f.!** eh, bouboule!

    2 *adj (food, meat)* gras (grasse); *(tissue)* adipeux(euse); **f. acid** acide *m* gras

fatuous ['fætjʊəs] *adj* idiot(e)

faucet ['fɔːsɪt] *n Am* robinet *m*

fault [fɔːlt] **1** *n* **(a)** *(flaw)* défaut *m*; *(in mechanism, on phone line)* problème *m*; **to find f. with** trouver à redire à; **to be generous to a f.** être généreux(euse) à l'excès **(b)** *(guilt)* faute *f*; **to be at f.** être en faute; **whose f. is it?** à qui la faute?; **it's my f.** c'est (de) ma faute; **through no f. of mine** sans que ce soit de ma faute **(c)** *(in tennis, squash)* faute *f* **(d)** *(geological)* faille *f*

    2 *vt (person)* prendre en défaut; *(logic)* trouver une faille dans; **her attitude can't be faulted** il n'y a rien à redire à sa conduite

faultless ['fɔːltlɪs] *adj* impeccable

faulty ['fɔːltɪ] *adj* défectueux(euse)

faun [fɔːn] *n* faune *m*

fauna ['fɔːnə] *n* faune *f*

favor, favorable *etc Am* = **favour, favourable** *etc*

favour, *Am* **favor** ['feɪvə(r)] **1** *n* **(a)** *(approval)* **to be in/out of f.** *(of person)* être bien/mal vu(e); *(of method)* être/ne plus être en faveur; **to look on sth/sb with f.** être bien disposé(e) envers qch/qn; **to find f. with sb** trouver grâce aux yeux de qn **(b)** *(act of kindness)* service *m*; **to do sb a f.** rendre service à qn; *Br Fam* **do me a f. and shut up!** ferme-la, tu veux?; **to ask sb a f., to ask a f. of sb** demander un service à qn **(c)** *(advantage)* **that's a point in her f.** c'est un élément en sa faveur

(d) in f. of *(in preference to)* en faveur de; **to be in f. of sth** être partisan(e) de qch/être favorable à qch **2** *vt* **(a)** *(prefer)* être pour, être partisan(e) de; **to sb** *(be biased towards)* favoriser qn **(b)** *(honour)* **to f. sb with sth** gratifier qn de qch

favourable, *Am* **favorable** ['feɪvərəbəl] *adj* favorable; *(terms)* avantageux(euse); **in a f. light** sous un jour favorable

favourite, *Am* **favorite** ['feɪvərɪt] **1** *n* favori(ite) *m,f*; *(in betting)* favori

    2 *adj* favori(ite), préféré(e)

favouritism, *Am* **favoritism** ['feɪvərɪtɪzəm] *n* favoritisme *m*

fawn¹ [fɔːn] **1** *n* **(a)** *(deer)* faon *m* **(b)** *(colour)* fauve *m*

    2 *adj (colour)* fauve

fawn² *vi* **to f. on sb** ramper devant qn

fax [fæks] **1** *n (machine)* fax *m*, télécopieur *m*; *(message)* fax *m*, télécopie *f*; **f. number** numéro *m* de fax

    2 *vt (message, document)* faxer, envoyer par fax; *(person)* envoyer un fax à

faze [feɪz] *vt Fam* déconcerter

FBI [efbiː'aɪ] *n Am (abbr* **Federal Bureau of Investigation)** FBI *m*

fear [fɪə(r)] **1** *n* peur *f*; *(worry)* crainte *f*; **to be** *or* **go in f. of** avoir peur de, redouter; **to go in f. of one's life** craindre pour sa vie; *Fam* **to put the f. of God into sb** faire une peur bleue à qn; **he didn't tell her for f. of her reaction** il ne lui a rien dit par peur de sa réaction; **for f. of doing sth** de peur de faire qch; **I didn't tell him, for f. that he'd be angry** je ne lui ai rien dit, de peur qu'il ne se mette en colère; *Fam* **no f.!** pas de danger!

    2 *vt* craindre, redouter; **I f. there's been a misunderstanding** je crains qu'il (n')y ait eu un malentendu; **I f. so/not** je crains que oui/non; **to f. the worst** craindre le pire

    3 *vi* **to f. for** craindre pour; **never f.!** ne crains rien!

fearful ['fɪəfʊl] *adj* **(a)** *(pain, consequence, noise)* épouvantable **(b)** *(person)* apeuré(e); **to be f. of doing sth** avoir peur de faire qch

fearless ['fɪəlɪs] *adj* intrépide

fearlessly ['fɪəlɪslɪ] *adv* avec intrépidité

fearsome ['fɪəsəm] *adj* effrayant(e)

feasibility [fiːzə'bɪlɪtɪ] *n* possibilité *f*; *(of plan)* faisabilité *f*; **f. study** étude *f* de faisabilité

feasible ['fiːzəbəl] *adj* faisable

feast [fiːst] **1** *n* festin *m*, banquet *m*; *Rel* **f. day** (jour *m* de) fête *f*

    2 *vt* **to f. one's eyes on sth** repaître ses yeux de qch

    3 *vi* **to f. on se régaler de**

feat [fiːt] *n* exploit *m*; **a f. of skill** un tour de force

feather ['feðə(r)] **1** *n* plume *f*; **you could have knocked me down with a f.** je n'en revenais pas; *Fig* **that's a f. in her cap** elle peut en être fière; **f. bed** lit *m* de plumes

    2 *vt Fig* **to f. one's nest** faire son beurre

featherweight ['feðəweɪt] *n (in boxing)* poids *m* plume

feathery ['feðərɪ] *adj* doux (douce) et léger(ère) comme de la plume

feature ['fiːtʃə(r)] **1** *n* **(a)** *(of face)* trait *m* **(b)** *(characteristic)* caractéristique *f* **(c) f. (film)** long métrage *m* **(d)** *(in newspaper)* article *m* de fond; *(on television, radio)* reportage *m*; **f. writer** éditorialiste *mf*

    2 *vt (of magazine, exhibition)* présenter; **a film featuring** un film ayant pour vedette…

    3 *vi (appear)* figurer

featureless ['fiːtʃəlɪs] *adj* sans caractéristiques marquées

Feb *(abbr* **February)** février

febrile ['fiːbraɪl] adj fébrile

February ['febrʊərɪ] n février m; see also **May**

feckless ['feklɪs] adj (**a**) (irresponsible) irresponsable (**b**) (ineffectual) incapable

fed [fed] pt & pp of **feed**

federal ['fedərəl] adj fédéral(e)

federalism ['fedərəlɪzəm] n fédéralisme m

federalist ['fedərəlɪst] n & adj fédéraliste mf

federation [fedə'reɪʃən] n fédération f

fed up ['fedʌp] adj Fam **to be f. (with)** en avoir ras le bol (de), en avoir marre (de)

fee [fiː] n (of lawyer, doctor) honoraires mpl; (for entrance) droit m d'entrée; (for membership) cotisation f; **school fees** droits mpl d'inscription; **a f.-paying school** une école privée

feeble ['fiːbəl] adj faible; (attempt) peu convaincant(e)

feeble-minded ['fiːbəl'maɪndɪd] adj faible d'esprit

feebly ['fiːblɪ] adv faiblement; (protest, reprimand) mollement

feed [fiːd] **1** n (**a**) (animal food) nourriture f (**b**) (for baby) (from breast) tétée f; (from bottle) biberon m
2 vt (pt & pp **fed** [fed]) (**a**) (give food to) donner à manger à; (baby) (from breast) donner la tétée à; (from bottle) donner son biberon à; (plant) mettre de l'engrais à; **we were well fed** nous étions bien nourris; **to f. one's family** nourrir sa famille (**b**) (supply) **to f. a fire** alimenter un feu; **to f. coins into a machine** mettre des pièces dans une machine; **to f. sb with information** fournir des informations à qn
3 vi (survive) **to f. on** se nourrir de

feedback ['fiːdbæk] n Elec effet m Larsen; Fig (response) écho m, réactions fpl

feel [fiːl] **1** n (**a**) (sensation) toucher m; **the f. of silk against her skin** le contact de la soie contre sa peau; **his music has a Latin f. (to it)** il y a une influence latino-américaine dans sa musique
(**b**) (knack) **to have a f. for translation/music** avoir un sens inné de la traduction/musique; **to get the f. of sth** s'habituer à qch
2 vt (pt & pp **felt** [felt]) (**a**) (touch) toucher; (investigate) tâter; **to f. one's way** (in darkness) avancer à tâtons; Fig (in new situation) essayer de s'habituer
(**b**) (be physically aware of) sentir; **I felt the floor tremble** or **trembling** j'ai senti le sol trembler
(**c**) (experience) (relief, pain, despair) ressentir, éprouver; **I f. it in my bones** (have intuition) je le sens
(**d**) (believe) **to f. (that)…** penser que…
3 vi (**a**) (physically) **to f. tired** se sentir fatigué(e); **to f. ill** ne pas se sentir bien; **to f. hot/cold/hungry/thirsty** avoir chaud/froid/faim/soif; **my arm feels better** j'ai moins mal au bras; **how are you feeling?** comment ça va ou tu te sens-tu?; **I don't f. myself** je ne suis pas dans mon assiette; **to f. up to doing sth** (well enough) se sentir assez bien pour faire qch; (competent enough) se sentir de taille à faire qch; **to f. (like) a new man/woman** se sentir comme neuf/neuve
(**b**) (emotionally) se sentir; **to f. strongly about sth** avoir des idées très arrêtées sur qch; **I f. bad about leaving her** cela m'ennuie de la quitter; **how would you f. if…?** comment est-ce que tu te sentirais si…?; **it feels strange** c'est étrange; **I felt as if I'd seen him before** j'avais l'impression de l'avoir déjà vu; **to f. like doing sth** avoir envie de faire qch; **I f. like a beer** (would like) j'ai envie d'une bière
(**c**) (have sympathy) **to f. for sb** plaindre qn
(**d**) (of things) **to f. hard/hot** être dur(e)/chaud(e); **it feels like (it's going to) rain** on dirait qu'il va pleuvoir
(**e**) (search) **to f. in one's pockets for sth** chercher qch

dans ses poches; **he felt on the ground for the key** il cherchait sa clé à tâtons sur le sol

feeler ['fiːlə(r)] n (of insect) antenne f; (of snail) corne f; Fig **to put out feelers** tâter le terrain

feeling ['fiːlɪŋ] n (**a**) (sense of) f. toucher m; **to have no f. in one's leg** avoir la jambe morte (**b**) (sensation) (of cold, pain) sensation f (**c**) (emotion, impression) sentiment m; **a f. of joy/anger** de la joie/colère; **to speak with f.** (emotionally) parler avec émotion; (warmly) parler avec chaleur; **I know the f.!** je sais ce que c'est!; **I had a f. I might find you here** je pensais bien vous trouver ici; **to hurt sb's feelings** blesser qn; **to have no feelings** n'avoir aucun cœur; **feelings were running high** les esprits étaient très échauffés; **no hard feelings!** sans rancune! (**d**) (sensitivity) sensibilité f; **to have a f. for sth** (music, art) être sensible à qch

feet [fiːt] pl of **foot**

feign [feɪn] vt (anger, surprise) feindre; **to f. illness/sleep** feindre d'être malade/de dormir

feint [feɪnt] **1** n (in combat sports) feinte f
2 vi (in combat sports) faire une feinte

felicitous [fɪ'lɪsɪtəs] adj heureux(euse)

feline ['fiːlaɪn] **1** n félin m
2 adj félin(e)

fell¹ [fel] pt of **fall**

fell² vt (tree) abattre, couper; (opponent) terrasser

fell³ adj **at one f. swoop** d'un seul coup

fell⁴ n (hill) colline f

fellow ['feləʊ] n (**a**) (comrade) camarade mf; **f. citizen** concitoyen(enne) m,f; **f. countryman/countrywoman** compatriote mf; **f. passenger** compagnon m de voyage; **f. worker** collègue mf; **f. student** camarade d'études; **f. traveller** (in politics) compagnon de route (**b**) (teacher) professeur m titulaire; (student) boursier(ère) m,f; (of academy, society) membre m (**c**) Fam (man) gars m

fellowship ['feləʊʃɪp] n (**a**) (friendship) camaraderie f (**b**) (association) association f, corporation f (**c**) (at university) bourse f de recherche

felon ['felən] n Law criminel(elle) m,f

felony ['felənɪ] n (pl felonies) n Law crime m

felt¹ [felt] n (fabric) feutre m; (thinner) feutrine f

felt² pt & pp of **feel**

felt-tip ['felttɪp] n f. (**pen**) (crayon m) feutre m

female ['fiːmeɪl] **1** n (person) femme f; (animal, plant) femelle f
2 adj (person) féminin(e); (animal, plant) femelle

feminine ['femɪnɪn] **1** n Gram féminin m; **in the f.** au féminin
2 adj féminin(e)

femininity [femɪ'nɪnɪtɪ] n féminité f

feminism ['femɪnɪzəm] n féminisme m

feminist ['femɪnɪst] n & adj féministe mf

femur ['fiːmə(r)] n Anat fémur m

fen [fen] n (marshy land) marais m

fence [fens] **1** n (**a**) (barrier) clôture f; (more solid) barrière f; Fig **to sit on the f.** ménager la chèvre et le chou; Fig **to get off the f.** se prononcer (**b**) Fam (receiver of stolen property) receleur(euse) m,f
2 vi (as sport) faire de l'escrime

▸ **fence off** vt sep séparer par une clôture

fencing ['fensɪŋ] n (sport) escrime f

fend [fend] vi **to f. for oneself** se débrouiller (tout(e) seul(e))

▸ **fend off** vt sep (attack, blow) parer; (question) éluder

fender ['fendə(r)] *n* (a) *Am (of car)* aile *f* (b) *(for fireplace)* garde-feu *m inv*
fennel ['fenəl] *n* fenouil *m*
ferment 1 *n* ['fɜːment] *(commotion)* agitation *f*; **in a (state of) f.** en effervescence
2 *vi* [fə'ment] *(of alcoholic drink)* fermenter
fermentation [fɜːmen'teɪʃən] *n* fermentation *f*
fern [fɜːn] *n* fougère *f*
ferocious [fə'rəʊʃəs] *adj* féroce
ferocity [fə'rɒsɪtɪ] *n* férocité *f*
ferret ['ferɪt] **1** *n* furet *m*
2 *vi* **to f. (about) for sth** fouiller à la recherche de qch
▸ **ferret out** *vt sep (object, information)* dénicher
ferris wheel ['ferɪs'wiːl] *n* grande roue *f*
ferrous ['ferəs] *adj* ferreux(euse)
ferry ['ferɪ] **1** *n* (*pl* **ferries**) bac *m*; *(larger)* ferry *m*
2 *vt* (*pt & pp* **ferried**) transporter
3 *vi* **to f. back and forth** faire la navette
ferryman ['ferɪmən] *n* passeur *m*
fertile ['fɜːtaɪl] *adj also Fig* fertile
fertility [fə'tɪlɪtɪ] *n also Fig* fertilité *f*; **f. treatment** traitement *m* de la stérilité
fertilize ['fɜːtɪlaɪz] *vt (egg, plant)* féconder; *(soil)* fertiliser
fertilizer ['fɜːtɪlaɪzə(r)] *n* engrais *m*
fervent ['fɜːvənt] *adj (admirer, nationalist)* fervent(e); *(belief, desire)* ardent(e)
fervour, *Am* **fervor** ['fɜːvə(r)] *n* ferveur *f*
fester ['festə(r)] *vi (of wound)* s'infecter; *Fig (of situation)* s'envenimer; *(of dislike, resentment)* s'aviver
festival ['festɪvəl] *n* festival *m*; *(religious)* fête *f*
festive ['festɪv] *adj* de fête; **in f. mood** d'humeur festive; **the f. season** *(Christmas)* les fêtes (de fin d'année)
festivity [fes'tɪvɪtɪ] *(pl* **festivities**) *n (merriness)* gaieté *f*; **the festivities** *(celebrations)* les festivités *fpl*
festoon [fes'tuːn] *vt* orner **(with** de)
fetal ['fiːtəl] *Am* = **foetal**
fetch [fetʃ] *vt* (a) *(bring)* aller chercher (b) *(be sold for)* rapporter
▸ **fetch up** *vi (end up) (of people)* se retrouver
fetching ['fetʃɪŋ] *adj (person, hat, smile)* ravissant(e)
fête [feɪt] **1** *n* fête *f*
2 *vt* fêter
fetid ['fetɪd] *adj* fétide
fetish ['fetɪʃ] *n (object)* fétiche *m*; **to have a f. for sth** faire une fixation sur qch
fetter ['fetə(r)] **1** *n* **fetters** *(on slave, prisoner)* fers *mpl*; *Fig (on rights, freedom)* entraves *fpl*
2 *vt (slave, prisoner)* enchaîner; *Fig (union, women)* entraver la liberté de
fettle ['fetəl] *n* **in good** *or* **fine f.** en condition
fetus ['fiːtəs] *Am* = **foetus**
feud [fjuːd] **1** *n* querelle *f*
2 *vi* se quereller **(with** avec)
feudal ['fjuːdəl] *adj* féodal(e); *Fig (approach, attitude)* moyenâgeux(euse)
feudalism ['fjuːdəlɪzəm] *n* le système féodal
fever ['fiːvə(r)] *n also Fig* fièvre *f*; **to have a f.** avoir de la fièvre; **things are at f. pitch here** l'excitation ici est à son comble
feverish ['fiːvərɪʃ] *adj* fiévreux(euse); *Fig (atmosphere)* de fièvre
few [fjuː] **1** *adj* (a) *(not many)* peu de; **f. friends** peu d'amis; **too f.** trop peu de; **f. and far between** rarissime;

every f. minutes toutes les deux ou trois minutes; **as f. as a dozen finished the race** seuls une douzaine d'entre eux ont terminé la course (b) *(some)* **a f.** quelques; **a f. friends** quelques amis; **a good f., quite a f.** pas mal de; **in the next f. days** dans les jours qui suivent/suivirent
2 *pron* (a) *(not many)* peu; **there are too f. of us** nous sommes trop peu nombreux; **f. of them** peu d'entre eux; **f., if any children** aucun enfant ou presque (b) *(some)* **a f.** quelques-uns (quelques-unes) *mpl,fpl*; **a f. of the survivors** quelques-uns des survivants; **a f. of them** quelques-uns d'entre eux
3 *n* **the f. who came** les rares personnes *fpl* qui sont venues
fewer ['fjuːə(r)] *(comparative of* **few**) **1** *adj* moins de; **f. friends** moins d'amis; **no f. than thirty** pas moins de trente; **the houses became f.** les maisons devenaient plus rares; **f. and f. people** de moins en moins de gens
2 *pron* moins; **there are f. (of them) than I thought** il y en a moins que je ne pensais
fewest ['fjuːɪst] *(superlative of* **few**) **1** *adj* le moins de
2 *pron* le moins
fiasco [fɪ'æskəʊ] *(pl* **fiascos**) *n* fiasco *m*
fib [fɪb] *Fam* **1** *n* bobard *m*
2 *vi (pt & pp* **fibbed**) raconter des bobards
fibber ['fɪbə(r)] *n Fam* menteur(euse) *m,f*
fibre, *Am* **fiber** ['faɪbə(r)] *n* fibre *f*; *(in diet)* fibres *fpl*; **f. optics** fibres optiques
fibreglass, *Am* **fiberglass** ['faɪbəglɑːs] *n* fibre *f* de verre
fibrous ['faɪbrəs] *adj* fibreux(euse)
fickle ['fɪkəl] *adj (person)* lunatique; *(weather)* changeant(e)
fiction ['fɪkʃən] *n (genre)* fiction *f*; *(books)* livres *mpl* de fiction; *(lie)* invention *f*
fictional ['fɪkʃənəl] *adj* fictif(ive)
fictitious [fɪk'tɪʃəs] *adj* fictif(ive)
fiddle ['fɪdəl] **1** *n* (a) *(violin)* violon *m* (b) *Br Fam (swindle)* combine *f*; **to be on the f.** traficoter
2 *vt Br Fam (cheat)* combiner; **to f. the accounts** truquer les comptes
3 *vi* (a) *(play violin)* jouer du violon (b) *(fidget)* **to f. (about** *or* **around) with sth** tripoter qch
fiddler ['fɪdlə(r)] *n* violoniste *mf*
fiddlesticks ['fɪdəlstɪks] *exclam* *Old-fashioned (nonsense)* balivernes!; *(expressing annoyance)* zut de zut!
fiddly ['fɪdlɪ] *adj Fam* minutieux(euse)
fidelity [fɪ'delɪtɪ] *n* fidélité *f*
fidget ['fɪdʒɪt] **1** *n* **to be a f.** ne pas tenir en place
2 *vi* ne pas tenir en place; **stop fidgeting!** tiens-toi tranquille!
fidgety ['fɪdʒɪtɪ] *adj* agité(e)
field [fiːld] **1** *n* (a) *(of farm)* & *Comptr* champ *m*; *(for sport)* terrain *m*; *(of oil, coal)* gisement *m*; **to work in the f.** *(not in office)* travailler sur le terrain; **f. of vision** champ visuel; **f. events** *(in athletics)* le saut et le lancer; *Am* **f. hockey** hockey *m* sur gazon; **f. study** étude *f* sur le terrain; *Sch & Univ* **f. trip** voyage *m* d'étude; **f. work** *(scientific)* recherches *fpl* sur le terrain (b) *Mil* **in the f.** en campagne; *Fig* **to have a f. day** s'en donner à cœur joie; **f. glasses** jumelles *fpl*; **f. gun** canon *m* (de campagne); **f. hospital** antenne *f* chirurgicale; **f. marshal** maréchal *m* (c) *(of knowledge)* domaine *m* (**d)** *(in race, contest)* partants *mpl*; **to lead the f.** *Sp* mener le peloton; *Fig* occuper la première place
2 *vt* (a) *(team)* composer; *(candidates)* présenter (b) *(question)* répondre à

fieldmouse ['fi:ldmaʊs] *(pl* **fieldmice** ['fi:ldmaɪs]) *n* mulot *m*

fiend [fi:nd] *n (cruel person)* monstre *m; (demon)* démon *m;* **sex** *f.* obsédé(e) *m,f* sexuel(elle); **a health** *f.* un(e) maniaque de la santé

fiendish ['fi:ndɪʃ] *adj (scheme, question)* diabolique; *(weather, temper)* abominable

fiendishly ['fi:ndɪʃlɪ] *adv (difficult)* horriblement

fierce ['fɪəs] *adj (animal, look)* féroce; *(appearance, person)* redoutable; *(wind, storm, criticism)* violent(e); *(heat)* torride; *(contest)* acharné(e)

fiercely ['fɪəslɪ] *adv (look)* d'un œil féroce; *(fight)* avec acharnement; *(criticize)* violemment

fiery ['faɪərɪ] *adj (red)* ardent(e); *(sky)* enflammé(e); *(taste)* très épicé(e); *(person, character)* fougueux(euse)

FIFA ['fi:fə] *n (abbr* **Fédération Internationale de Football Association)** FIFA *f*

fifteen [fɪf'ti:n] **1** *n* (**a**) *(number)* quinze *m inv* (**b**) *Sp (rugby team)* quinze *m*
2 *adj* quinze; *see also* **eight**

fifteenth [fɪf'ti:nθ] **1** *n* (**a**) *(fraction)* quinzième *m* (**b**) *(in series)* quinzième *mf* (**c**) *(of month)* quinze *m inv*
2 *adj* quinzième; *see also* **eighth**

fifth [fɪfθ] **1** *n* (**a**) *(fraction)* cinquième *m* (**b**) *(in series)* cinquième *mf* (**c**) *(of month)* cinq *m inv*
2 *adj* cinquième; *Pol* **f. column** cinquième colonne *f; see also* **eighth**

fiftieth ['fɪftɪəθ] **1** *n* (**a**) *(fraction)* cinquantième *m* (**b**) *(in series)* cinquantième *mf*
2 *adj* cinquantième

fifty ['fɪftɪ] **1** *n* cinquante *m inv*
2 *adj* cinquante; *see also* **eighty**

fig[1] [fɪg] *n (fruit)* figue *f; Fam* **she doesn't give** *or* **care a f.** elle s'en fiche éperdument; **f. leaf** feuille *f* de figuier; *(in paintings)* feuille de vigne; **f. tree** figuier *m*

fig[2] *(abbr* **figure)** fig

fight [faɪt] **1** *n* (**a**) *(physical)* bagarre *f, (verbal)* dispute *f, (boxing match)* combat *m;* **to get into a f.** **with sb** *(physical)* se battre avec qn; *(verbal)* se disputer avec qn; **to start a f.** **(with sb)** provoquer une bagarre (avec qn); **to put up a good f.** bien se défendre (**b**) *(spirit)* **to show some f.** résister; **there was no f. left in him** il n'avait plus le cœur à se battre (**c**) *(struggle)* lutte *f* (**for/against** pour/contre)
2 *vt (pt & pp* **fought** [fɔ:t]) *(person)* se battre contre; *(decision, enemy)* combattre; *(disease, fire, temptation)* lutter contre; *(election)* participer à; **to f. a war** être en guerre; *Law* **to f. a case** *(of lawyer)* défendre une cause; *(of defendant)* être en procès; *Fig* **I'm not going to f. your battles for you** c'est à vous de vous débrouiller; **to f. one's way through a crowd** se frayer un chemin à travers une foule
3 *vi* (**a**) *(physically)* se battre (**against** contre); *(verbally)* se disputer; **to f. shy of doing sth** éviter à tout prix de faire qch (**b**) *(struggle)* lutter (**for/against** pour/contre); **to f. for breath** suffoquer

▸ **fight back 1** *vt sep (tears)* retenir; *(anger)* réprimer
2 *vi (retaliate)* se défendre

▸ **fight off** *vt sep (attacker)* repousser; *(illness)* combattre

▸ **fight out** *vt sep* **f. it out amongst yourselves** réglez ça entre vous

fighter ['faɪtə(r)] *n (in fight)* combattant(e) *m,f; (for cause)* lutteur(euse) *m,f;* **she's a real f.** *(determined)* c'est une battante(euse); **f. (plane)** avion *m* de chasse; **f. squadron/pilot** escadron *m*/pilote *m* de chasse

fighting ['faɪtɪŋ] **1** *n (scuffles)* bagarres *fpl; Mil* combat *m*
2 *adj* **to have a f. chance** avoir encore de bonnes chances; **to be f. fit** être dans une forme éblouissante

figment ['fɪgmənt] *n* **it's a f. of his imagination** c'est le fruit de son imagination

figurative ['fɪgərətɪv] *adj (sense)* figuré(e); *(art)* figuratif(ive)

figuratively ['fɪgərətɪvlɪ] *adv* **f. speaking** métaphoriquement parlant

figure ['fɪgə(r)] **1** *n* (**a**) *(number)* chiffre *m;* **to be good at figures** être bon (bonne) en calcul; **to reach double/three figures** atteindre la dizaine/centaine (**b**) *(body shape)* silhouette *f;* **to have a good f.** *(of woman)* avoir une jolie silhouette; **a fine f. of a man** un bel homme; **to cut a sorry f.** avoir l'air pitoyable (**c**) *(person, character)* personnage *m;* **a distinguished f.** une personnalité (**d**) *(illustration, geometric shape)* figure *f* (**e**) *(expression)* **f. of speech** figure *f* de rhétorique; **it's just a f. of speech** c'est une façon de parler
2 *vt* **to f. (that)…** *(think)* penser que…; *(estimate)* supposer que…
3 *vi* (**a**) *(appear)* figurer (**in** list, book) (**b**) *Fam (make sense)* **that figures!** ça se tient!

▸ **figure on** *vt insep* **to f. on doing sth** compter faire qch

▸ **figure out** *vt sep (amount)* calculer; *(solution)* trouver; *(problem, person)* arriver à comprendre

figurehead ['fɪgəhed] *n (on ship)* figure *f* de proue; *Fig & Pej (of country, party)* homme *m* de paille

Fiji ['fi:dʒi:] *n* les (îles *fpl)* Fidji *fpl*

Fijian [fi:'dʒi:ən] **1** *n* Fidjien(enne) *m,f*
2 *adj* fidjien(enne)

filament ['fɪləmənt] *n Elec* filament *m*

filch [fɪltʃ] *vt Fam* faucher (**from sb** à qn)

file[1] [faɪl] **1** *n (tool)* lime *f*
2 *vt (metal)* limer; **to f. one's nails** se limer les ongles

file[2] **1** *n* (**a**) *(folder)* chemise *f; (ring-bound)* classeur *m; (documents)* dossier *m* (**on** sujet); **to have sth on t.** avoir qch dans ses dossiers (**b**) *Comptr* fichier *m;* **f. manager** gestionnaire *m* de fichiers; **f. server** serveur *m* de fichiers
2 *vt* (**a**) *(documents, letters)* classer (**b**) *(complaint, claim, request)* déposer
3 *vi* **to f. for divorce** demander le divorce

file[3] **1** *n (line)* file *f;* **in single f.** en file indienne
2 *vi* **to f. past sb/sth** défiler devant qn/qch; **to f. in/out** entrer/sortir l'un(e) après l'autre

filial ['fɪlɪəl] *adj* filial(e)

filigree ['fɪlɪgri:] *n* filigrane *m*

Filipino [fɪlɪ'pi:nəʊ] **1** *n (pl* **Filipinos)** Philippin(e) *m,f*
2 *adj* philippin(e)

fill [fɪl] **1** *n* **to eat one's f.** manger à sa faim; *Fig* **to have had one's f. of sth** en avoir assez de qch
2 *vt* (**a**) *(container)* remplir (**with** de); **to be filled with admiration/hope** être plein(e) d'admiration/d'espoir; **to have a tooth filled** se faire plomber une dent (**b**) *(occupy)* *(time)* occuper; **to f. a vacancy** *(of employer)* pourvoir à un poste vacant
3 *vi* se remplir (**with** de)

▸ **fill in 1** *vt sep (hole)* combler, boucher; *(form)* remplir; **to f. in time** occuper son temps (**b**) *Fam (inform)* **to f. sb in** **(on sth)** mettre qn au courant (de qch)
2 *vi* **to f. in for sb** remplacer qn

▸ **fill out 1** *vt sep (form, application)* remplir
2 *vi (get fatter)* grossir

▸ **fill up 1** *vt sep (glass)* remplir jusqu'au bord
2 *vi* (**a**) *(of tank, container)* se remplir (**b**) *(buy petrol)* faire le plein

fillet ['fɪlɪt] **1** *n (of fish, beef)* filet *m;* **f. steak** filet de bœuf
2 *vt (fish)* découper en filets

filling ['fɪlɪŋ] **1** n (**a**) *(in tooth)* plombage m; *(in sandwich, pie)* garniture f(**b**) **f. station** station-service f **2** adj *(food, meal)* nourrissant(e)

filly ['fɪlɪ] *(pl* **fillies)** n *(horse)* pouliche f

film [fɪlm] **1** n *(movie)* film m; *(layer, for camera)* pellicule f; **a (roll of) f.** une pellicule, un rouleau de pellicule; **f. actor/ actress** acteur m/actrice f de cinéma; **f. critic** critique m f de cinéma; **f. director** réalisateur(trice) m,f; **the f. industry** l'industrie f cinématographique; **f. library** cinémathèque f; **f. maker** cinéaste m f; **f. script** scénario m, script m; **f. star** vedette f de cinéma, star f; **f. studio** studio m de cinéma **2** vt & vi filmer

filter ['fɪltə(r)] **1** n filtre m; **f. coffee** café m filtre; **f. paper** papier m filtre; *Br Aut* **f. lane** = voie réservée aux véhicules qui tournent; *Br Aut* **f. signal** *(on traffic light)* flèche f de dégagement **2** vt filtrer **3** vi (**a**) *(move slowly)* **to f. in/out** entrer/sortir lentement (**b**) *Br Aut (of traffic)* **to f. to the right/left** dégager à droite/ gauche pour tourner

▸ **filter out** vt sep *also Fig* éliminer

▸ **filter through 1** vt insep *(of liquid, light)* passer à travers **2** vi *(of information)* filtrer

filth [fɪlθ] n *(dirt)* crasse f; *(in street)* immondices fpl; *(obscene words)* obscénités fpl; **it's f.** *(of book, film)* c'est dégoûtant

filthy ['fɪlθɪ] **1** adj (**a**) *(very dirty)* dégoûtant(e) (**b**) *(very bad)* **in a f. temper** d'une humeur massacrante; **to give sb a f. look** regarder qn d'un sale œil; *Br* **f. weather** temps m de chien (**c**) *(obscene)* obscène **2** adv *Fam* **f. rich** pourri(e) de fric

fin [fɪn] n *(of fish)* nageoire f; *(of aeroplane)* empennage m; *Am (of swimmer)* palme f

final ['faɪnəl] **1** n (**a**) *(of competition)* **the f.** la finale (**b**) *Univ* **finals** *Br* examens mpl de dernière année; *Am* examens mpl finaux **2** adj (**a**) *(last)* dernier(ère); **f. demand** dernier avis m; **f. warning** dernier avertissement m (**b**) *(definitive)* final(e); **the referee's decision is f.** la décision de l'arbitre est sans appel; **and that's f.!** un point, c'est tout!

finale [fɪ'nɑːlɪ] n finale m

finalist ['faɪnəlɪst] n finaliste mf

finalize ['faɪnəlaɪz] vt *(details, plans)* mettre au point; *(deal)* conclure

finally ['faɪnəlɪ] adv (**a**) *(lastly)* finalement (**b**) *(at last)* enfin; **she f. agreed to come** elle a fini par accepter de venir (**c**) *(irrevocably)* définitivement; **it hasn't been f. decided yet** aucune décision définitive n'a encore été prise

finance [faɪ'næns, fɪ'næns] **1** n (**a**) *(subject)* finance f; **f. company** or **house** société f financière (**b**) **finances** *(funds)* finances fpl **2** vt financer

financial [faɪ'nænʃəl, fɪ'nænʃəl] adj financier(ère); **it was not a f. success** cela n'a pas rapporté beaucoup d'argent; **f. adviser** conseiller(ère) m,f financier(ère); **f. market** marché m financier; **f. statement** bilan m financier; *Br* **f. year** exercice m comptable

financially [faɪ'nænʃəlɪ, fɪ'nænʃəlɪ] adv financièrement

financier [faɪ'nænsɪə(r)] n financier m

finch [fɪntʃ] n fringillidé m

find [faɪnd] **1** n découverte f; **it's quite a f.** c'est une fameuse trouvaille **2** vt *(pt & pp* **found** [faʊnd]) (**a**) *(discover)* trouver; **to try to f. sth** chercher qch; **she was nowhere to be found** elle était introuvable; **I found her waiting in the hall** je l'ai

trouvée qui attendait dans le vestibule; **this flower is commonly found in Europe** on trouve couramment cette fleur en Europe; **I found myself back where I'd started** je me suis retrouvé à mon point de départ; **you will f. that I'm right** tu verras que j'ai raison; **I was surprised to f. that...** j'ai découvert avec surprise que...; **he couldn't f. it in his heart to tell her** il n'avait pas le cœur à le lui dire; **to f. one's way** trouver son chemin; **to f. a way to do sth** trouver moyen de faire qch; **to f. oneself** *(spiritually)* se trouver (**b**) *(experience)* trouver; **they will f. it easy/difficult** cela leur sera facile/difficile; **to f. it necessary to do sth** se trouver dans la nécessité de faire qch; **she found it impossible to understand him** elle avait beaucoup de mal à le comprendre; **how did you f. the hotel?** l'hôtel vous a-t-il plu?; **I found myself agreeing with her** il s'est trouvé que j'étais d'accord avec elle (**c**) *Law* **to f. sb guilty/not guilty** déclarer qn coupable/ non coupable **3** vi *Law* **to f. for/against sb** rendre un verdict en faveur de/contre qn

▸ **find out 1** vt sep (**a**) *(discover)* découvrir (**b**) *(person)* prendre en défaut **2** vi **to f. out about sth** apprendre qch

finder ['faɪndə(r)] n **the f. of the money** la personne qui trouva/trouvera l'argent; *Fam* **finders keepers (losers weepers)** celui qui le trouve le garde

findings ['faɪndɪŋz] npl conclusions fpl; *Law (of jury, court)* verdict m

fine¹ [faɪn] **1** n *(penalty)* amende f **2** vt condamner à une amende; **to f. sb \$10** infliger une amende de 10 dollars à qn

fine² **1** adj (**a**) *(excellent)* excellent(e); *(foods, wine)* fin(e); *(weather)* beau; **to appeal to sb's finer feelings** faire appel aux bons sentiments de qn; **she's a f. woman** c'est une femme admirable; **f. art, the f. arts** les beaux-arts mpl; **she's got it down to a f. art** elle fait ça à la perfection (**b**) *(satisfactory)* bien inv; **she's/everything's f.** elle/tout va bien; **that's f. by me** je n'y vois aucune objection (**c**) *Ironic* **you're a f. one to talk!** tu peux bien parler! (**d**) *(thin)* *(hair, rain, line)* fin(e) (**e**) *(subtle)* *(distinction)* subtil(e); **not to put too f. a point on it** pour parler carrément; **there's a f. line between eccentricity and madness** il n'y a qu'un pas de l'excentricité à la folie **2** adv très bien, **they get on f.** ils s'entendent (très) bien

finely ['faɪnlɪ] adv (**a**) *(judged)* soigneusement; *(written, painted)* admirablement; *Fig* **f. balanced** équilibré(e) (**b**) *(chopped, ground, grated)* finement

finery ['faɪnərɪ] n parure f; **she was dressed in all her f.** elle était habillée avec élégance

finesse [fɪ'nes] n finesse f

finger ['fɪŋgə(r)] **1** n (**a**) *(of hand, glove)* doigt m; **to keep one's fingers crossed** croiser les doigts; **f. bowl** rince-doigts m inv; **f. food** *(snacks)* amuse-gueule mpl (**b**) *(measure)* **a f. of Scotch** un doigt de whisky (**c**) *Av* passerelle f (**d**) *(idioms)* **he's got them (wrapped) round his little f.** il fait d'eux ce qu'il veut; **to have a f. in every pie** être mêlé(e) à tout; **don't you dare lay a f. on him** je vous défends de le toucher; **she never lifts a f. to help me** elle ne lève jamais le petit doigt pour m'aider; **I can't quite put my f. on it** je n'arrive pas à mettre le doigt dessus; **to get one's fingers burnt** se brûler les doigts; *Br very Fam* **get** or **pull your f. out!** remue-toi! **2** vt (**a**) *(feel)* tâter (**b**) *very Fam (inform on)* balancer

fingernail ['fɪŋgəneɪl] n ongle m

fingerprint ['fɪŋgəprɪnt] n empreinte f digitale

fingertip ['fɪŋgətɪp] *n* bout *m* du doigt; **to have sth at one's fingertips** savoir qch sur le bout des doigts

finicky ['fɪnɪkɪ] *adj (person)* tatillon(onne); *(job, device)* compliqué(e)

finish ['fɪnɪʃ] **1** *n* (a) *(end) (of day, meeting)* fin *f*; *(of race)* arrivée *f* (b) *(surface) (of fabric, leather)* apprêt *m*; **paint with a gloss/matt f.** peinture *f* vernie/mate (c) *(workmanship)* finition *f*
2 *vt* (a) *(end)* finir, terminer; **to f. doing sth** finir *ou* terminer de faire qch (b) *(kill) (person)* achever; *Fam* **he's finished!** il est fini!
3 *vi* finir, se terminer; **to f. fourth** *(in race, contest)* finir *ou* terminer quatrième
▸ **finish off 1** *vt sep* (a) *(complete, use up)* finir, terminer (b) *(kill)* achever; *(ruin) (chances, hopes)* anéantir
2 *vi* finir, terminer
▸ **finish up 1** *vt sep (use up)* finir
2 *vi (end up)* se retrouver; **to f. up doing sth** finir par faire qch
▸ **finish with** *vt insep* (a) *(stop using)* to f. **with sth** finir de se servir de qch (b) *(boyfriend, girlfriend)* laisser tomber

finished ['fɪnɪʃt] *adj* (a) *(completed)* fini(e); *(supplies)* épuisé(e) (b) *(performance)* soigné(e)

finishing ['fɪnɪʃɪŋ] *adj* **to put the f. touches to sth** mettre la dernière main à qch; **f. line** ligne *f* d'arrivée; **f. school** = école d'arts d'agrément pour les jeunes filles

finite ['faɪnaɪt] *adj* limité(e); *Gram (verb)* conjugué(e)

Finland ['fɪnlənd] *n* la Finlande

Finn [fɪn] *n (person)* Finlandais(e) *m,f*, Finnois(e) *m,f*

Finnish ['fɪnɪʃ] **1** *n (language)* finnois *m*
2 *adj* finlandais(e), finnois(e)

fir [fɜː(r)] *n* **f.** *(tree)* sapin *m*; **f. cone** pomme *f* de pin

fire ['faɪə(r)] **1** *n* (a) *(in hearth)* feu *m*; *(large, destructive)* incendie *m*; *(heater)* appareil *m* de chauffage; **electric/gas f.** radiateur *m* électrique/au gaz; **on f.** en feu; **to catch f.** prendre feu; **to set f. to sth, to set sth on f.** mettre le feu à qch; **f.!** au feu!; *Fig* **to play with f.** jouer avec le feu; *Fig* **to fight f. with f.** combattre le feu par le feu; **f. alarm** sirène *f* d'incendie; *Br* **f. brigade,** *Am* **f. department** sapeurs-pompiers *mpl*, pompiers *mpl*; **f. door** porte *f* coupe-feu; **f. drill** exercice *m* d'évacuation en cas d'incendie; **f. engine** voiture *f* de pompiers; **f. escape** escalier *m* de secours; **f. extinguisher** extincteur *m*; **f. fighter** pompier *m*; **to be a f. hazard** constituer un risque d'incendie; **f. hydrant** bouche *f* d'incendie; **f. insurance** assurance *f* contre l'incendie; **f. regulations** *(plans)* normes *fpl* de protection contre les incendies; *(instructions)* consignes *fpl* en cas d'incendie; **f. sale** = vente au rabais de marchandises ayant subi de légers dégâts à la suite d'un incendie; **f. station** caserne *f* de pompiers (b) *(of artillery)* tirs *mpl*; **to open f.** ouvrir le feu; **to hold one's f.** ne pas tirer; **to come under f.** être exposé(e) aux tirs; *Fig (be criticized)* être exposé à de sévères critiques; **f. power** puissance *f* de tir (c) *Fig (enthusiasm)* fougue *f*, ardeur *f*
2 *vt* (a) *(shoot) (missile, flare)* lancer; **to f. a gun (at)** tirer un coup de fusil (sur); *Fig* **to f. a question at sb** poser une question à qn à brûle-pourpoint (b) *(dismiss)* virer (c) **oil-/gas-fired central heating** chauffage *m* central au mazout/au gaz; *Fig* **to f. sb's imagination** enflammer l'imagination de qn (d) *(pottery)* cuire
3 *vi* (a) *(with gun)* tirer (**at** sur); *Fam Fig* **f. away!** *(to questioner)* allez-y! (b) *(of engine)* tourner

firearm ['faɪərɑːm] *n* arme *f* à feu

firebrand ['faɪəbrænd] *n (torch)* tison *m*, brandon *m*; *Fig (person)* brandon de discorde

firecracker ['faɪəkrækə(r)] *n* pétard *m*

firefly ['faɪəflaɪ] *(pl* **fireflies)** *n* luciole *f*

fireguard ['faɪəgɑːd] *n* garde-feu *m inv*

firelight ['faɪəlaɪt] *n* lumière *f* du feu

firelighter ['faɪəlaɪtə(r)] *n* allume-feu *m inv*

fireman ['faɪəmən] *n* pompier *m*

fireplace ['faɪəpleɪs] *n* cheminée *f*

fireproof ['faɪəpruːf] *adj* ignifugé(e)

fireside ['faɪəsaɪd] *n* **by the f.** au coin du feu

firewall ['faɪəwɔːl] *n Comptr* firewall *m*, contrôle *m* d'accès

firewood ['faɪəwʊd] *n* bois *m* de chauffage

firework ['faɪəwɜːk] *n* pièce *f* d'artifice; **fireworks** *(display)* feu *m* d'artifice; *Fig* **there'll be fireworks** il va y avoir du grabuge; **f. display** feu d'artifice

firing ['faɪərɪŋ] *n* tir *m*; *Fig* **to be in the f. line** être l'objet de violentes critiques; **f. squad** peloton *m* d'exécution

firm¹ [fɜːm] *n (company)* entreprise *f*, firme *f*

firm² **1** *adj* (a) *(fruit, body, mattress, handshake)* ferme; *Fig (foundations, friendship)* solide; **the f. favourite** le/la grand(e) favori(ite); **it's my f. belief (that)...** j'ai la ferme conviction... (b) *(strict)* ferme (c) *(definite) (decision)* ferme; *(date)* précis(e); *(evidence)* sérieux(euse)
2 *adv* **to stand f.** tenir bon *ou* ferme; **to hold f. to one's principles/beliefs** être fidèle à ses principes/croyances

firmly ['fɜːmlɪ] *adv* (a) *(securely)* solidement; **I f. believe (that)...** j'ai la ferme conviction que... (b) *(strictly)* fermement

first [fɜːst] **1** *n* (a) *(in series)* premier(ère) *m,f*; **we were the f. to arrive** nous étions les premiers arrivés; **it's the f. I've heard of it** c'est la première fois que j'en entends parler, première nouvelle!; **Louis the F.** Louis Premier (b) *(of month)* premier *m*; **we're leaving on the f.** nous partons le premier
(c) *(beginning)* **from f. to last** du début jusqu'à la fin; **from the f.** dès le début; **at f.** d'abord
(d) *Br Univ* **to get a f.** *(in degree)* ≃ avoir sa licence avec mention bien ou très bien
(e) *(first gear)* première *f*
(f) *(unique event)* première *f*
2 *adj* premier(ère); **for the f. time** pour la première fois; **at f. hand** de première main; **f. things f.!** commençons par le commencement!; **I don't know the f. thing about motorbikes** je ne connais absolument rien aux motos; **f. thing (in the morning)** dès le matin; **at f. light** aux premières lueurs du jour; **at f. sight** à première vue; **in the f. place** d'abord; **the F. World War** la Première Guerre mondiale; **f. aid** *(skill)* secourisme *m*; *(treatment)* premiers soins *mpl*; **f. cousin** cousin(e) *m,f* germain(e); **f. edition** édition *f* originale; **f. gear** première *f* (vitesse *f*); *Am* **the f. lady** première dame des États-Unis *(épouse du président)*; *Naut* **f. mate** second *m*; **f. name** prénom *m*; **f. night** *(of play)* première *f*; *Law* **f. offender** = personne qui commet un délit pour la première fois
3 *adv* (a) *(firstly)* d'abord; **f. and foremost** avant toute chose; **f. of all** en premier lieu, d'abord
(b) *(for the first time)* **I f. met her in Toronto** je l'ai rencontrée pour la première fois à Toronto
(c) *(before others)* premier(ère); **you go f.!** *(in queue)* passez devant!; **to come f.** *(in race)* arriver premier(ère); *(in exam)* être reçu(e) premier(ère); **my family comes f.** ma famille passe avant le reste; **f. come, f. served** les premiers arrivés sont les premiers servis; **ladies f.!** les femmes d'abord!; **I won't do it, I'd resign f.** plutôt démissionner que de faire ça

first-aid [fɜːst'eɪd] *adj* **f. certificate** brevet *m* de secourisme; **f. kit** trousse *f* de secours

first-born ['fɜːstbɔːn] *n Lit (boy)* premier-né *m*; *(girl)* première-née *f*

first-class ['fɜːstklɑːs] **1** *adj* **(a)** *(compartment, ticket)* de première classe **(b)** f. **stamp** timbre *m* au tarif normal **(c)** *Univ* f. **honours (degree)** ≃ licence *f* avec mention bien ou très bien **(d)** *(excellent)* excellent(e) **2** *adv* **(a)** *(travel)* en première classe **(b)** *(post)* au tarif normal

first-degree ['fɜːstdɪ'griː] *adj* **(a)** *Med (burns)* au premier degré **(b)** *Am Law* f. **murder** assassinat *m*

first-hand ['fɜːsthænd] *adj & adv* de première main

firstly ['fɜːstlɪ] *adv* premièrement, en premier lieu

first-past-the-post ['fɜːstpɑːstðə'pəʊst] *adj Pol* f. **system** scrutin *m* à un tour

first-rate ['fɜːstreɪt] *adj* excellent(e)

first-time buyer ['fɜːst'taɪm'baɪə(r)] *n* = personne achetant une propriété pour la première fois

fiscal ['fɪskəl] *adj* fiscal(e); f. **policy** politique *f* budgétaire; f. **year** exercice *m* comptable

fish [fɪʃ] **1** *n (pl* **fish** *or* **fishes)** **(a)** poisson *m*; *Br* f. **and chips** poisson frit avec des frites; f.**-and-chip shop** = magasin où l'on vend du poisson frit et des frites ainsi que d'autres produits cuits dans la friture; f. **cake** croquette *f* de poisson; f. **farm** établissement *m* piscicole; *Br* f. **fingers**, *Am* f. **sticks** bâtonnets *mpl* de poisson; f. **knife** couteau *m* à poisson; *Am* f. **merchant** poissonnier(ère) *m,f*; f. **slice** pelle *f* à poisson; f. **tank** aquarium *m* **(b)** *(idioms)* **there are plenty more f. in the sea** un de perdu, dix de retrouvés; **to have other f. to fry** avoir d'autres chats à fouetter; **to feel like a f. out of water** ne pas se sentir dans son élément; **to be neither f. nor fowl** n'être ni chair ni poisson **2** *vt* **(a)** *(river)* pêcher **(b)** *(remove)* **to f. sth/sth from somewhere** sortir qn/qch de quelque part **3** *vi* pêcher; *Fig* **to f. for compliments** rechercher les compliments; **she fished around in her pocket for some change** elle a fouillé dans sa poche pour trouver de la monnaie

fisherman ['fɪʃəmən] *n* pêcheur *m*

fish-hook ['fɪʃhʊk] *n* hameçon *m*

fishing ['fɪʃɪŋ] *n* pêche *f*; **to go f.** aller à la pêche; f. **boat** bateau *m* de pêche; f. **grounds** lieux *mpl* de pêche; f. **line** ligne *f*; f. **net** filet *m* de pêche; f. **port** port *m* de pêche; f. **rod** canne *f* à pêche

fishmonger ['fɪʃmʌŋgə(r)] *n Br* poissonnier(ère) *m,f*; f.'**s** *(shop)* poissonnerie *f*

fishnet ['fɪʃnet] *adj (stockings, tights)* résille *inv*

fishy ['fɪʃɪ] *adj* **(a)** *(smell, taste)* de poisson **(b)** *Fam (suspicious)* louche

fission ['fɪʃən] *n* fission *f*

fissure ['fɪʃə(r)] *n (in mountain, rock)* fissure *f*; *Med* scissure *f*

fist [fɪst] *n* poing *m*; *Fig* **she made a good f. of it** elle s'en est plutôt bien sortie

fistful ['fɪstfʊl] *n* poignée *f*

fisticuffs ['fɪstɪkʌfs] *npl Hum* coups *mpl* de poing

fit¹ [fɪt] *n (seizure)* attaque *f*; **to have a f.** avoir une attaque; *Fam Fig* **to have** *or* **throw a f.** piquer une crise; **in a f. of temper** dans un accès de colère; **a f. of coughing** une quinte de toux; **a f. of crying** une crise de larmes; **to be in fits (of laughter)** se tordre de rire; **in fits and starts** par à-coups

fit² **1** *n* **the jacket is a good f.** cette veste me/te/*etc* va bien; **comfortable/tight f.** coupe *f* confortable/ajustée **2** *adj* **(a)** *(appropriate)* f. **to eat** mangeable; f. **to drink** buvable; f. **for the bin** bon (bonne) à jeter; f. **for human consumption** propre à la consommation; **a meal f. for a king** un repas digne d'un *ou* de roi; **do as you see** *or* **think f.** faites comme bon vous semblera; **to be f. to do sth**

juger bon de faire qch; **that's all he's f. for** il n'est bon qu'à cela; **to be f. to do sth** *(worthy of)* être digne de faire qch; **to be f. to drop** tomber de fatigue **(b)** *(healthy)* en forme; **to get f.** retrouver la forme; **to keep f.** se maintenir en forme; **to be f. to do sth** *(healthy enough)* être en état de faire qch; *Fam* **to be as f. as a fiddle** péter la forme **(c)** *Fam (attractive)* canon *inv* **3** *vt (pt & pp* **fitted)** **(a)** *(match)* correspondre à; **to make the punishment f. the crime** proportionner la peine au délit **(b)** *(be the right size for)* **to f. sb** aller à qn; **this key fits the lock** cette clé rentre dans la serrure **(c)** *(install)* adapter **(to/on** à/sur); **to f. a carpet** poser de la moquette; **to f. sth with sth** équiper *ou* pourvoir qch de qch **(d)** *(insert)* **to f. sth into/onto sth** faire rentrer qch dans/ sur qch; **f. another two people inside** il y a encore de la place pour deux personnes **4** *vi* **(a)** *(be the right size) (of lid, key, plug)* aller; **to f. together** s'adapter; **to f. into sth** rentrer dans qch **(b)** *(of clothes)* **it fits perfectly** ça me/te/*etc* va parfaitement

▸ **fit in 1** *vt sep (in timetable)* caser **2** *vi* **(a)** *(go into place)* aller **(b)** *(of person)* être à sa place

▸ **fit up** *vt sep very Fam (frame)* **to be fitted up** être victime d'un coup monté

fitful ['fɪtfʊl] *adj (sleep)* agité(e); **to make f. progress** progresser par à-coups

fitness ['fɪtnɪs] *n* **(a)** *(health)* forme *f* **(b)** *(suitability)* aptitude *f* **(for** à)

fitted ['fɪtɪd] *adj* **(a)** *(jacket, dress)* ajusté(e); f. **carpet** moquette *f*; f. **sheet** drap-housse *m* **(b)** *(kitchen)* intégré(e); *(wardrobe)* encastré(e)

fitting ['fɪtɪŋ] **1** *n* **(a)** *(of clothes)* essayage *m*; f. **room** cabine *f* d'essayage **(b)** **fittings** *(in office)* installations *fpl*; *(in house)* accessoires *mpl* **2** *adj* approprié(e) **(to** à)

five [faɪv] **1** *n* cinq *m inv* **2** *adj* cinq; f. **o'clock shadow** barbe *f* d'un jour; *see also* **eight**

fiver ['faɪvə(r)] *n Br Fam (sum)* cinq livres *fpl*; *(note)* billet de cinq livres

fix [fɪks] **1** *n* **(a)** *Fam (difficulty)* **to be in a f.** être dans le pétrin; **to get into a f.** se fourrer dans le pétrin **(b)** *very Fam (of drug)* dose *f*; *Fig* **she needs her daily f. of coffee** il lui faut sa dose quotidienne de café **(c)** *Fam* **to be a f.** *(of election, contest)* être truqué(e) **2** *vt* **(a)** *(attach securely)* fixer **(to** à); **to f. sth in one's memory** graver qch dans sa mémoire; **to f. one's attention on sth** fixer son attention sur qch; **to f. one's eyes on sb/sth** fixer qn/qch **(b)** *(decide) (limit, price)* fixer **(c)** *(repair)* arranger, réparer **(d)** *(arrange) (meeting)* arranger; **to f. one's hair** se coiffer; *Fam* **I'll f. him!** je vais lui faire son affaire! **(e)** *Fam (election, contest)* truquer

▸ **fix up** *vt sep* **(a)** *(arrange)* arranger **(b)** *(provide)* **to f. sb up with a job** trouver un emploi à qn; **I've fixed you up with a date** je t'ai arrangé un rendez-vous

fixation [fɪk'seɪʃən] *n* fixation *f*; **to have a f. about sth** faire une fixation sur qch

fixed [fɪkst] *adj* **(a)** *(price, costs, income)* fixe; f. **assets** immobilisations *fpl* **(b)** *(definite) (ideas)* bien arrêté(e); *(plans)* précis(e) **(c)** *Fam* **how are you f. for money/time?** tu as de l'argent/le temps? **(d)** *Fam (election, contest)* truqué(e)

fixer ['fɪksə(r)] *n Fam* combinard(e) *m,f*

fixture ['fɪkstʃə(r)] *n* **(a)** **fixtures** *(in house, office)* éléments *mpl* fixes; **bathroom fixtures** sanitaires *mpl*;

Fam **to be a f.** *(of person)* faire partie des meubles (**b**) *Br (in sport)* rencontre *f*

fizz [fɪz] **1** *n* (**a**) *(sound)* pétillement *m*; *(bubbles)* gaz *m* (**b**) *Fam (soft drink)* boisson *f* gazeuse; *(champagne)* champ *m* **2** *vi (of champagne)* pétiller

▸ **fizzle out** ['fɪzəl] *vi Fam (of plan)* tomber à l'eau; *(of enthusiasm, interest)* retomber; *(of relationship)* partir en eau de boudin

fizzy ['fɪzɪ] *adj (wine)* mousseux(euse); *(soft drink)* gazeux(euse)

fjord [fjɔːd] *n* fjord *m*

flab [flæb] *n Fam (fat)* graisse *f*

flabbergasted ['flæbəgɑːstɪd] *adj Fam* abasourdi(e)

flabby ['flæbɪ] *adj (person, features)* bouffi(e); *(limbs)* mou (molle); *Fig (argument, reasoning)* qui manque de rigueur

flaccid ['flæsɪd] *adj* flasque

flag [flæg] **1** *n* drapeau *m*; *Naut* pavillon *m*; **F. Day** *(in United States)* = le 14 juin, fête commémorant l'adoption du drapeau américain **2** *vt (pt & pp* **flagged**) marquer; *(mark)* signaler; **to f. (down) a taxi** héler un taxi **3** *vi (of person, conversation, interest)* faiblir; *(of strength, spirits)* baisser

flagellate ['flædʒəleɪt] *vt* flageller

flagpole ['flægpəʊl] *n* mât *m (de drapeau)*

flagrant ['fleɪgrənt] *adj* flagrant(e)

flagrantly ['fleɪgrəntlɪ] *adv* de façon flagrante; **f. dishonest** d'une malhonnêteté flagrante

flagship ['flægʃɪp] *n (of fleet)* navire *m* amiral; *Fig (of range of products, party)* fleuron *m*

flagstone ['flægstəʊn] *n* dalle *f*

flail [fleɪl] **1** *n (tool)* fléau *m* **2** *vt* agiter **3** *vi (of rope, cable)* se balancer; *(of arms, legs)* s'agiter dans tous les sens

▸ **flail about, flail around** *vi (of arms, legs)* s'agiter dans tous les sens; *(of person)* se débattre

flair ['fleə(r)] *n* don *m* (**for** pour); **to do sth with f.** faire qch avec style; **to have a f. for business** avoir le sens des affaires; **to have a f. for doing sth** avoir le don de faire qch

flak [flæk] *n* tir *m* antiaérien *ou* de DCA; *Fig* critiques *fpl*; **she got a lot of f. for her decision** sa décision a été très critiquée; **f. jacket** gilet *m* pare-balles

flake [fleɪk] **1** *n (of snow, cereal)* flocon *m*; *(of paint)* écaille *f*; *(of soap)* paillette *f*; **a f. of skin** un bout de peau morte **2** *vi (of paint)* s'écailler; **my skin is flaking** je pèle

▸ **flake out** *vi Fam* s'effondrer de fatigue

flaky ['fleɪkɪ] *adj* (**a**) *(paint)* écaillé(e); *(pastry)* feuilleté(e) (**b**) *Am (eccentric)* loufoque

flamboyant [flæm'bɔɪənt] *adj (person)* extraverti(e); *(gesture)* théâtral(e); *(clothes, colours)* voyant(e)

flame [fleɪm] **1** *n* flamme *f*; **to go up in flames** prendre feu; *Fig (of hopes, chances)* partir en fumée; **to burst into flames** s'enflammer; *Fam* **an old f.** *(man)* un ancien amoureux; *(woman)* une ancienne amoureuse **2** *vi (of fire)* flamber

flameproof ['fleɪmpruːf] *adj* ignifugé(e); *(dish)* qui va sur le feu

flamethrower ['fleɪmθrəʊə(r)] *n* lance-flammes *m inv*

flaming ['fleɪmɪŋ] **1** *adj* (**a**) *(burning)* enflammé(e); *Fig (sunset)* flamboyant(e); **a f. temper** une colère noire (**b**) *Br Fam (for emphasis)* sacré(e); *don't Br Fam* vachement; **don't be so stupid!** ne sois pas si bête, merde!

flamingo [flə'mɪŋgəʊ] *(pl* **flamingos**) *n* flamant *m*

flammable ['flæməbəl] *adj* inflammable

flan [flæn] *n* tarte *f*

Flanders ['flɑːndəz] *n* les Flandres *fpl*, la Flandre

flank [flæŋk] **1** *n* flanc *m*; *(of beef, mutton)* flanchet *m* **2** *vt* flanquer (**with** *or* **by** de)

flannel ['flænəl] *n* (**a**) *(fabric)* flanelle *f*; (**pair of**) **flannels** pantalon *m* en flanelle (**b**) *Br (face-cloth)* ≃ gant *m* de toilette (**c**) *Br Fam (evasive words, flattery)* blabla *m*

flap [flæp] **1** *n* (**a**) *(of envelope, book cover, tent)* rabat *m*; *(of aeroplane)* volet *m* (**b**) *Fam (panic)* **to be in a f.** être affolé(e), paniquer **2** *vt (pt & pp* **flapped**) **to f. its wings** *(of bird)* battre des ailes; **to f. one's arms** agiter les bras **3** *vi* (**a**) *(of wings, flag)* battre (**b**) *Fam (panic)* s'affoler, paniquer

flapjack ['flæpdʒæk] *n* (**a**) *Br (biscuit)* = biscuit épais à l'avoine (**b**) *Am (pancake)* = petite crêpe épaisse

flare [fleə(r)] **1** *n* (**a**) *(signal)* signal *m* lumineux; *(rocket)* fusée *f* éclairante (**b**) **(pair of) flares** pantalon *m* (à) pattes d'éléphant **2** *vt (nostrils)* dilater **3** *vi (of fire)* flamboyer; **tempers flared** les esprits se sont échauffés

▸ **flare up** *vi (of fire)* s'embraser; *(of medical condition)* se déclencher; *(of anger, trouble)* éclater

flash [flæʃ] **1** *n* (**a**) *(of light)* éclair *m*; **f. of lightning** éclair *m*; **f. of wit** trait *m* d'esprit; **f. of inspiration** éclair de génie; **in a f.** *(very quickly)* en un clin d'œil; *Fig* **a f. in the pan** un feu de paille; **f. flood** crue *f* subite; **f. point** *(of situation)* point *m* de rupture; *(region)* point chaud (**b**) *(in photography)* flash *m*; **f. photography** photographie *f au* flash **2** *adj Br Fam (showy) (clothes, car, jewellery)* tape-à-l'œil *inv*; *(person)* aux goûts tapageurs **3** *vt (smile, look)* lancer (**at** à); *(card, badge)* montrer rapidement (**at** à); **to f. one's headlights** faire un appel de phares à qn **4** *vi* (**a**) *(of diamond)* briller; *(of light)* clignoter (**b**) *(move quickly)* **to f. past** passer comme un éclair; **my life flashed before me** ma vie a défilé devant mes yeux (**c**) *Fam (expose oneself)* s'exhiber (**at** devant)

flashback ['flæʃbæk] *n (in novel, film)* flash-back *m inv*, retour *m* en arrière

flasher ['flæʃə(r)] *n Br Fam* (**a**) *(man exposing himself)* exhibitionniste *m* (**b**) *(car indicator)* clignotant *m*

flashing ['flæʃɪŋ] *adj (light)* clignotant(e)

flashlight ['flæʃlaɪt] *n* torche *f* électrique

flashy ['flæʃɪ] *adj Fam (clothes, car, jewellery)* tape-à-l'œil *inv*; *(person)* aux goûts tapageurs

flask [flɑːsk] *n (for alcohol)* flasque *f*; *(in chemistry)* fiole *f*; (**Thermos®**) **f.** (bouteille *f*) Thermos® *f*

flat [flæt] **1** *n* (**a**) *Br (apartment)* appartement *m* (**b**) *Fam (flat tyre)* pneu *m* à plat; *(punctured)* pneu crevé **2** *adj* (**a**) *(surface)* plat(e); *(nose)* camus; **as f. as a pancake** plat comme une galette; *Fam (flat-chested)* plate comme une limande; **f. cap** casquette *f*; **f. racing** plat *m*; **f. rate** tarif *m* unique; **f. tyre** pneu *m* à plat; *(punctured)* pneu crevé (**b**) *(refusal)* net (**c**) *(existence)* monotone; *(voice)* terne; *(battery)* à plat; *(drink)* éventé(e) (**d**) *(in music) (a semitone lower)* bémol; *(out of tune)* en dessous du ton; **B f.** si *m inv* bémol **3** *adv* (**a**) *(level)* à plat; **to fall f. on one's face** tomber à plat ventre; *Fig* se casser le nez; *Fig* **to fall f.** *(of joke)* tomber à plat; **he pressed himself f. against the wall** il s'est plaqué contre le mur (**b**) *(completely)* **to turn sb down f.** opposer un refus catégorique à qn; **ten seconds f.** en dix secondes pile; **to work f. out** travailler d'arrache-pied; *Fam* **to be f. broke** être complètement fauché(e)

flat-chested ['flæt'tʃestɪd] *adj* to be f. avoir peu de poitrine

flatfish ['flætfɪʃ] *n* poisson *m* plat

flat-footed ['flæt'fʊtɪd] *adj* to be f. avoir les pieds plats

flatly ['flætlɪ] *adv (refuse, deny)* catégoriquement

flatmate ['flætmeɪt] *n Br* colocataire *mf*; we used to be flatmates nous partagions un appartement

flatten ['flætən] *vt* aplatir; to f. oneself against a wall s'aplatir contre un mur; *Fam* to f. sb casser la tête à qn

flatter ['flætə(r)] *vt (of person, clothes)* flatter; *Fam* don't f. yourself! ne te fais pas trop d'illusions!

flattering ['flætərɪŋ] *adj (words, photo)* flatteur(euse) *(clothes, colour)* qui avantage

flattery ['flætərɪ] *n* flatterie *f*

flatulence ['flætjʊləns] *n Med* flatulence *f*

flaunt [flɔ:nt] *vt (knowledge, wealth)* étaler; *(jewels)* exhiber; *Fig (ignorance, bad manners)* étaler sans complexes

flavour, *Am* **flavor** ['fleɪvə(r)] **1** *n* **(a)** *(of food)* goût *m*; *(of ice cream, yoghurt)* parfum *m* **(b)** *(characteristic)* note *f*; her stories have a Provençal f. ses histoires fleurent bon la Provence
2 *vt (savoury food)* relever (with de); *(sweet food)* parfumer (with à); **vanilla flavoured** parfumé(e) à la vanille

flavouring, *Am* **flavoring** ['fleɪvərɪŋ] *n* parfum *m*; artificial f. arôme *m* artificiel

flavourless, *Am* **flavorless** ['fleɪvəlɪs] *adj Br* sans saveur, insipide

flaw [flɔ:] *n* défaut *m*; *(in plan, argument)* faille *f*

flawed [flɔ:d] *adj* qui a un défaut/des défauts; *(plan, argument)* bancal(e)

flawless ['flɔ:lɪs] *adj* parfait(e)

flax [flæks] *n* lin *m*

flay [fleɪ] *vt (flog)* fouetter; *Fig (criticize)* éreinter

flea [fli:] *n* puce *f*; *Fam* to send sb away with a f. in his ear envoyer promener qn; f. market (marché *m* aux) puces *fpl*

fleabite ['fli:baɪt] *n* piqûre *f* de puce

flea-bitten ['fli:bɪtən] *adj (person, animal)* plein(e) de puces; *Fam (shabby)* miteux(euse)

fleck [flek] **1** *n (of colour, light)* petite tache *f*; *(of dust)* grain *m*
2 *vt* tacheter (with de); hair flecked with grey cheveux *mpl* grisonnants

fled [fled] *pt & pp of* flee

fledgling ['fledʒlɪŋ] **1** *n (young bird)* oisillon *m*
2 *adj Fig (person)* novice, débutant(e); *(company, state)* naissant(e)

flee [fli:] *(pt & pp* fled [fled]) *vi* fuir, s'enfuir; to f. from persecution fuir la persécution

fleece [fli:s] **1** *n* **(a)** *(of sheep)* toison *f* **(b)** *(garment)* fourrure *f* polaire
2 *vt Fam (cheat)* estamper

fleecy ['fli:sɪ] *adj* duveteux(euse)

fleet [fli:t] *n (of ships)* flotte *f*; *(of taxis, buses)* parc *m*; *Fig (convoy)* file *f*

fleet-footed ['fli:t'fʊtɪd] *adj Lit* au pied léger

fleeting ['fli:tɪŋ] *adj (moment, happiness, glance)* fugace; *(beauty)* éphémère; *(visit)* court(e), rapide; to catch a f. glimpse of sb/sth entrevoir qn/qch

Flemish ['flemɪʃ] **1** *n (language)* flamand *m*
2 *adj* flamand(e)

flesh [fleʃ] *n* chair *f*; in the f. en chair et en os; to make sb's f. creep *or* crawl donner la chair de poule à qn; his

own f. and blood *(children)* la chair de sa chair; *(close family)* les siens *mpl*; f. wound blessure *f* superficielle
▸ **flesh out** *vt sep (plan, remarks)* étoffer

fleshy ['fleʃɪ] *adj* charnu(e)

flew [flu:] *pt of* fly

flex [fleks] **1** *n Br (cable)* cordon *m*
2 *vt (arms, knees)* fléchir; *(muscles)* faire jouer; *Fig* they're just flexing their muscles ce n'est qu'une démonstration d'autorité de leur part

flexible ['fleksɪbəl] *adj* flexible

flexitime ['fleksɪtaɪm], *Am* **flextime** ['flekstaɪm] *n* horaires *mpl* flexibles *ou* à la carte

flick [flɪk] **1** *n* **(a)** *(with finger)* pichenette *f*; *(of whip, tail)* petit coup *m*; at the f. of a switch en appuyant juste sur un bouton; f. knife couteau *m* à cran d'arrêt **(b)** *Br Fam Old-fashioned* the flicks *(cinema)* le ciné, le cinoche
2 *vt (with finger)* donner une chiquenaude à; he flicked the cigarette ash onto the carpet il fit tomber la cendre de sa cigarette sur le tapis; to f. the hair out of one's eyes écarter les cheveux de ses yeux
▸ **flick through** *vt insep (book, magazine)* feuilleter; *(photographs)* passer rapidement en revue

flicker ['flɪkə(r)] **1** *n (of flame)* vacillement *m*; *Fig (of hope)* lueur *f*; *(of interest, annoyance)* pointe *f*; a f. of light une lueur vacillante
2 *vi (of flame, light)* vaciller

flier ['flaɪə(r)] *n* **(a)** *(passenger)* = personne qui voyage en avion **(b)** *(leaflet)* prospectus *m*

flight [flaɪt] *n* **(a)** *(act of flying, specific trip)* vol *m*; it's five hours' f. from Boston c'est à cinq heures de vol de Boston; *Fig* f. of fancy lubie *f*; f. attendant *(male)* steward *m*; *(female)* hôtesse *f* de l'air; f. deck *(of aircraft)* poste *m ou* cabine *f* de pilotage; f. path trajectoire *f* de vol; f. recorder enregistreur *m* de vol; f. simulator simulateur *m* de vol **(b)** *(group of birds)* vol *m*, volée *f*; *Fig* in the top f. parmi les tout premiers **(c)** f. (of stairs) escalier *m*; two flights up from me deux étages au-dessus de chez moi **(d)** *(escape)* fuite *f*; to put sb to f. mettre qn en fuite

flightless ['flaɪtlɪs] *adj* coureur(euse)

flighty ['flaɪtɪ] *adj (fickle)* volage

flimsy ['flɪmzɪ] *adj (structure, fence)* peu solide; *(dress, excuse, plot)* léger(ère); *(evidence)* ténu(e)

flinch [flɪntʃ] *vi (with pain)* tressaillir; *(at an idea)* frémir; to do sth without flinching faire qch sans broncher; to f. from doing sth hésiter à faire qch

fling [flɪŋ] **1** *n Fam (affair)* aventure *f*
2 *vt (pt & pp* flung [flʌŋ]) *(ball)* lancer; he flung himself into the armchair il s'est jeté dans le fauteuil; to f. one's arms around sb prendre qn dans ses bras; *Fig* to f. oneself into a task se lancer dans une tâche
▸ **fling out** *vt sep (object)* jeter; *(person)* mettre à la porte; *(proposal, case)* rejeter

flint [flɪnt] *n (stone)* silex *m*; *(of lighter)* pierre *f* (à briquet)

flip [flɪp] **1** *n Fam* the f. side *(of record)* la face B; *Fig (of situation)* le revers de la médaille
2 *vt (pt & pp* flipped) *(record, pancake, card)* retourner; to f. the switch appuyer sur l'interrupteur; to f. a coin jouer à pile ou face; *Fam* to f. one's lid *(get angry)* piquer une crise; *(go mad)* perdre la boule
3 *vi Fam (get angry)* piquer une crise; *(go mad)* perdre la boule
▸ **flip through** *vt insep (book, magazine)* feuilleter; *(photos, samples)* jeter un coup d'œil à

flip-flops ['flɪpflɒps] *npl Br* (a pair of) f. des tongs *fpl*

flippant ['flɪpənt] *adj* désinvolte, cavalier(ère)

flipper ['flɪpə(r)] *n (of animal)* nageoire *f*; *(of diver)* palme *f*

flirt [flɜ:t] **1** n charmeur(euse) m,f
2 vi flirter (**with** avec); Fig **to f. with an idea** caresser une
idée
flirtatious [flɜ:'teɪʃəs] adj (look, smile) charmeur(euse);
to be f. aimer flirter; **to be f. with sb** flirter avec qn
flit [flɪt] **1** n Br Fam **to do a moonlight f.** déménager à la
cloche de bois
2 vi (pt & pp **flitted**) **to f. about** (of bird) voleter; Fig **to f.
from one thing to another** (of person) s'éparpiller
float [fləʊt] **1** n (**a**) (on fishing line) bouchon m; (for
swimming, on net) flotteur m (**b**) (in procession) char m (**c**)
(money) fonds m de caisse
2 vt (**a**) (ship) mettre à flot (**b**) (idea, proposal) émettre;
(company) introduire en Bourse
3 vi flotter; **to f. to the surface** remonter à la surface;
Fam Fig **he's floating around somewhere** il traîne par là
floating ['fləʊtɪŋ] adj flottant(e); (population)
fluctuant(e); **f. voter** électeur(trice) m,f indécis(e)
flock [flɒk] **1** n (of sheep) troupeau m; (of birds) vol m, volée
f; Rel (congregation) ouailles fpl; Fig (of people) foule f
2 vi (gather) **to f. around sb** s'attrouper autour de qn;
people are flocking to the exhibition les gens vont en
masse ou en foule voir l'exposition
flog [flɒg] (pt & pp **flogged**) vt (**a**) (beat) fouetter; Fam **to
be flogging a dead horse** se dépenser en pure perte; Fam
to f. a subject to death s'étendre indéfiniment sur un sujet
(**b**) Br Fam (sell) vendre
flood [flʌd] **1** n inondation f; (of light) flot m; **the F.** (in the
Bible) le Déluge; **to be in floods (of tears)** verser des
torrents de larmes
2 vt (land, bathroom) inonder; **to be flooded with light**
être inondé(e) de lumière; **the river flooded its banks** la
rivière a débordé ou est sortie de son lit; **to f. the market
(with sth)** inonder le marché (de qch); **to be flooded with
applications/letters** être submergé(e) de demandes/
lettres
3 vi (of river) déborder; **the sun's rays came flooding
through the window** les rayons du soleil entraient à flots
par la fenêtre; **letters came flooding in** nous avons/ils
ont/etc été submergés de lettres; **it all came flooding back**
tout m'/lui/etc est revenu d'un coup
floodgate ['flʌdgeɪt] n Fig **to open the floodgates to
sth** laisser la porte ouverte à qch
flooding ['flʌdɪŋ] n inondation(s) f(pl)
floodlight ['flʌdlaɪt] n projecteur m; **by f.** à la lumière
des projecteurs
floodlit ['flʌdlɪt] adj (stadium, match) éclairé(e) aux
projecteurs; (building) illuminé(e)
floor [flɔ:(r)] **1** n (**a**) (of room, forest) sol m; (of Stock
Exchange) parquet m (**b**) (of ocean) fond m; **f. show** spectacle
m de cabaret (**b**) (at meeting, debate) **to give sb the f.**
donner la parole à qn; **to take the f.** prendre la parole;
questions from the f. questions fpl du public (**c**) (storey)
étage m; **to live ten floors up** habiter au dixième étage
2 vt (knock down) envoyer au tapis; Fig (of question,
criticism) désarçonner
floorboard ['flɔ:bɔ:d] n latte f de plancher
floozie, floozy ['flu:zɪ] (pl **floozies**) n very Fam
pouffiasse f
flop [flɒp] **1** n (failure) fiasco m, bide m; **to be a f.** (of film)
faire un bide; (of party) être un bide
2 vi (pt & pp **flopped**) (**a**) (fall) (into water) tomber; (onto
seat) s'affaler (**b**) (fail) échouer; (of film) faire un bide; (of
party) être un bide
floppy ['flɒpɪ] **1** n (pl **floppies**) Comptr disquette f
2 adj (ears) pendant(e); (garment) flottant(e); (hat) mou
(molle); Comptr **f. disk** disquette f

flora ['flɔ:rə] n (plant life) flore f
floral ['flɔ:rəl] adj floral(e); **f. tribute** (at funeral)
couronne f de fleurs
Florence ['flɒrəns] n Florence
florid ['flɒrɪd] adj (style) fleuri(e); (complexion) rubicond(e)
Florida ['flɒrɪdə] n la Floride
florist ['flɒrɪst] n fleuriste mf; **f.'s (shop)** fleuriste m
floss [flɒs] **1** n (dental) **f.** fil m dentaire
2 vt nettoyer avec du fil dentaire
flotation [fləʊ'teɪʃən] n Com (of company) lancement m
flotsam ['flɒtsəm] n **f. (and jetsam)** débris mpl refoulés
par la mer; Fig **the f. of society** les laissés-pour-compte
mpl de la société
flounce [flaʊns] **1** n (in sewing) volant m
2 vi **to f. in/out** entrer/sortir de façon théâtrale
flounder ['flaʊndə(r)] **1** n (fish) flet m
2 vi (in water, mud) patauger; (in job, course, speech) perdre
pied
flour ['flaʊə(r)] **1** n farine f
2 vt fariner
flourish ['flʌrɪʃ] **1** n (gesture) grand geste m théâtral;
(musical, in writing) fioriture f
2 vt (brandish) brandir
3 vi (of plant, person) prospérer; (of business, arts) être
florissant(e)
flourishing ['flʌrɪʃɪŋ] adj (plant) qui prospère;
(business) florissant(e)
flout [flaʊt] vt (rule, instruction) faire fi de, (person) défier
l'autorité de; (authority) défier
flow [fləʊ] **1** n (of liquid) écoulement m; (of electrical
current, information) circulation f; (of tide, capital) flux m; **f.
of traffic** circulation; Fig **in full f.** en plein discours; Fig **to
follow the f. of an argument** suivre (le fil d')un
raisonnement; Fig **to go with the f.** suivre le
mouvement; **f. chart** organigramme m
2 vi (**a**) (of liquid) couler; (of electrical current) circuler; (of
traffic) s'écouler; Fig (of writing) couler bien; (of ideas)
affluer; **to f. into the sea** (of river) se jeter dans la mer (**b**)
to f. from (result from) découler de
flower ['flaʊə(r)] **1** n fleur f; **to be in f.** être en fleur(s); Fig
in the first f. of youth dans la fleur de l'âge; **f. arranging**
art m floral; **f. garden** jardin m d'agrément; **f. girl** = jeune
demoiselle d'honneur; **f. show** exposition f florale
2 vi fleurir
flowerbed ['flaʊəbed] n parterre m de fleurs
flowerpot ['flaʊəpɒt] n pot m de fleurs
flowing ['fləʊɪŋ] adj (hair) flottant(e); (movement, style)
fluide
flown [fləʊn] pp of **fly**
flu [flu:] n (influenza) grippe f; **a dose or bout of (the) f.** une grippe;
to have (the) f. avoir la grippe
fluctuate ['flʌktjʊeɪt] vi (of prices) fluctuer; (of pulse,
temperature) varier
fluctuation [flʌktjʊ'eɪʃən] n (of prices) fluctuation f; (of
pulse, temperature) variation f
flue [flu:] n (of heater, chimney) tuyau m
fluency ['flu:ənsɪ] n aisance f (**of/in** de/en)
fluent ['flu:ənt] adj (speech, style) fluide; **he is f. in
Spanish, he speaks f. Spanish** il parle couramment
espagnol
fluently ['flu:əntlɪ] adv (express oneself) avec facilité ou
aisance; (speak language) couramment
fluff [flʌf] **1** n peluche f; **a bit of f.** une peluche
2 vt (**a**) **to f. sth (up)** (pillow, duvet) remettre qch en forme
(en le secouant) (**b**) Fam (botch) rater

fluffy ['flʌfɪ] *adj* duveteux(euse); *(clouds)* cotonneux(euse)

fluid ['fluːɪd] **1** *n* fluide *m*, liquide *m*; **bodily fluids** sécrétions *fpl* **2** *adj (substance)* fluide, liquide; *(style, movement)* fluide; *(situation, plans)* mal défini(e); **f. ounce** = 0,03 l

fluidity [fluːˈɪdɪtɪ] *n (of style, movement)* fluidité *f*; *(of situation, plans)* imprécision *f*

fluke [fluːk] *n Fam (stroke of luck)* coup *m* de veine *ou* de bol; **by a f.** par hasard; **his success was a pure f.** c'est un hasard qu'il ait réussi

fluk(e)y ['fluːkɪ] *adj Fam (person)* veinard(e)

flummox ['flʌməks] *vt Fam* scier

flung [flʌŋ] *pt & pp of* fling

flunk [flʌŋk] *Fam* **1** *vt (exam)* rater; *(student)* recaler, coller **2** *vi (in exam)* être recalé(e) *ou* collé(e)

flunkey ['flʌŋkɪ] *(pl* **flunkeys)** *n Fam Pej* larbin *m*

fluorescent [fluəˈresənt] *adj* fluorescent(e)

fluoride ['fluəraɪd] *n* fluorure *m*; **f. toothpaste** dentifrice *m* au fluor

flurry ['flʌrɪ] *(pl* **flurries)** *n (of snow)* bourrasque *f*; **a f. of activity/excitement** une soudaine activité/excitation

flush [flʌʃ] **1** *n* **(a)** *(beginning)* **in the first f.** of youth dans tout l'éclat de sa jeunesse **(b)** *(in cards)* flush *m* **(c)** *(in toilet)* chasse *f* (d'eau) **2** *adj* **(a)** *(even)* de niveau **(with** avec) **(b)** *Fam (rich)* plein(e) aux as **3** *vt* **to f. the toilet** tirer la chasse (d'eau) **4** *vi* **(a)** *(of person)* rougir **(with** de) **(b)** *(of toilet)* **the toilet isn't flushing properly** la chasse d'eau ne fonctionne pas bien
► **flush out** *vt sep (force to emerge)* déloger

flushed [flʌʃd] *adj (person, face)* rouge **(with** de)

fluster ['flʌstə(r)] *vt* démonter; **to get flustered** se démonter

flute [fluːt] *n* flûte *f* traversière

flutter ['flʌtə(r)] **1** *n* **(a)** *(of wings, eyelashes, heart)* battement *m*; *Fig* **to be in a f.** *(of excitement)* être en émoi **(b)** *Br Fam (bet)* petit pari *m*; **to have a f.** parier *ou* jouer une petite somme **(on** sur) **2** *vt* **to f. its wings** *(of bird)* battre des ailes; **to f. one's eyelashes at sb** regarder qn en battant des cils **3** *vi (of birds, insects)* voleter; *(of heart)* battre; *(of flag)* flotter

flux [flʌks] *n* **to be in a state of f.** changer perpétuellement

fly¹ [flaɪ] *n* **(a)** **f., flies** *(of trousers)* braguette *f* **(b)** **f. sheet** *(of tent)* auvent *m*

fly² *Br Fam* **1** *n* **to do sth on the f.** *(spontaneously)* faire qch sur le coup **2** *adj (cunning)* malin(igne)

fly³ *(pl* **flies)** *n (insect)* mouche *f*; **he wouldn't hurt a f.** il ne ferait pas de mal à une mouche; **they were dropping like flies** ils tombaient comme des mouches; *Fig* **a f. in the ointment** un os; *Fam Fig* **there are no flies on her** elle est loin d'être bête; **I wish I could be a f. on the wall** *(at interview, meeting)* si je pouvais être une petite souris

fly⁴ *(pt* **flew** [fluː], *pp* **flown** [fləʊn]) **1** *vt* **(a)** *(plane)* piloter; *(goods)* transporter en avion; *(route)* emprunter; **to f. Air India** voyager avec Air India **(b)** *(kite)* faire voler; **to f. a flag** *(of ship)* arborer un pavillon; *Fig* **to f. the flag** *(for one's country)* défendre les couleurs de son pays **(c)** *(flee)* s'enfuir de; *Fig* **to f. the nest** *(of child)* quitter le nid **2** *vi* **(a)** *(of bird, plane)* voler; *(of passenger)* voyager en avion, prendre l'avion; **to f. over Berlin** survoler Berlin; **to f. across the Atlantic** traverser l'Atlantique en avion **(b)** *(of

flag, hair) flotter **(c)** *(move quickly)* **I must f.** il faut que je file; **to f. to sb's help** voler au secours de qn; **how time flies!** comme le temps passe! **the door flew open** la porte s'est ouverte brusquement; **to f. into a rage** sortir de ses gonds; *Fam* **to send sb/sth flying** envoyer rouler qn/qch; **to f. in the face of reason/logic** défier la raison/toute logique
► **fly away** *vi (of bird, papers)* s'envoler
► **fly in 1** *vt sep (troops, rescuers)* transporter en avion **2** *vi (of passenger)* arriver en avion
► **fly out 1** *vt sep (survivors)* transporter en avion **2** *vi (of passenger)* partir en avion

fly-by-night ['flaɪbaɪnaɪt] *adj Fam Pej (company)* véreux(euse)

flyer ['flaɪə(r)] = flier

flying ['flaɪɪŋ] **1** *n (as pilot)* pilotage *m*; *(as passenger)* voyages *mpl* en avion; **she loves f.** *(as pilot)* elle adore piloter; *(as passenger)* elle adore prendre l'avion; **f. club** aéro-club *m*; **f. lessons** leçons *fpl* de pilotage; **f. hours** heures *fpl* de vol **2** *adj* **(a)** *(bird, fish)* volant(e); **they were hurt by f. glass** ils ont été blessés par des éclats de verre; **to pass with f. colours** réussir haut la main; **f. boat** hydravion *m*; **f. doctor** médecin *m* volant; **f. saucer** soucoupe *f* volante **(b)** *(rapid)* **a f. visit** une visite éclair; **to get off to a f. start** très bien démarrer

flyleaf ['flaɪliːf] *(pl* **flyleaves** ['flaɪliːvz]) *n* page *f* de garde

flyover ['flaɪəʊvə(r)] *n Br Aut* pont *m* routier

flypaper ['flaɪpeɪpə(r)] *n* papier *m* tue-mouches

fly-past ['flaɪpaːst] *n Av* défilé *m* aérien

flyweight ['flaɪweɪt] *n (in boxing)* poids *m* mouche

FM [eˈfem] *n (abbr* **frequency modulation)** FM *f*

FO [eˈfəʊ] *n Br (abbr* **Foreign Office)** (ministère *m* des) Affaires *fpl* étrangères

foal [fəʊl] **1** *n (horse)* poulain *m*; *(female)* pouliche *f* **2** *vi* pouliner

foam [fəʊm] **1** *n (on sea)* écume *f*; *(on beer, bath)* mousse *f*; **f. rubber** caoutchouc *m* Mousse® **2** *vi (of sea)* écumer; *(of beer, bath)* mousser; **to f. at the mouth** baver; *Fig* écumer de rage

foamy ['fəʊmɪ] *adj (sea)* écumeux(euse); *(beer)* moussant(e)

fob [fɒb] *n* chaîne *f* (de montre); **f. watch** montre *f* de gousset
► **fob off** *(pt & pp* **fobbed)** *vt sep Fam* **to f. sb off with an excuse** se débarrasser de qn en lui racontant des salades; **to f. sth off on sb** refiler *ou* fourguer qch à qn

focal ['fəʊkəl] *adj* focal(e); **f. point** foyer *m*; *Fig (of discussion)* point *m* central

focus ['fəʊkəs] **1** *n (pl* **focuses** *or* **foci** ['fəʊkaɪ]) *(of lens)* foyer *m*; *Fig (of discontent)* cible *f*; *(of interest, attention)* centre *m*; **f. group** *(of customers)* groupe *m* témoin; **to be in f.** être au point; **to be out of f.** ne pas être au point **2** *vt (lens, camera)* mettre au point; *(rays, attention, energy)* concentrer **(on** sur); **all eyes were focused on him** tous les regards étaient tournés vers lui **3** *vi* **to f. on sth** *(with camera)* faire la mise au point sur qch; *(with eyes)* fixer qch; *Fig (of debate, speaker)* se concentrer sur qch

fodder ['fɒdə(r)] *n* fourrage *m*

foe [fəʊ] *n* ennemi *m*

foetal, *Am* **fetal** ['fiːtəl] *adj* fœtal(e); **in the f. position** en position fœtale

foetus, *Am* **fetus** ['fiːtəs] *n* fœtus *m*

fog [fɒg] *n* brouillard *m*; *Fig* **to be in a f.** *(confused)* être dans le brouillard; **f. lamp** *or* **light** *(on car)* (phare *m*) antibrouillard *m*

▸ **fog up** *(pt & pp* **fogged)** *vi (of windows, glasses)* s'embuer

fogbound ['fɒgbaʊnd] *adj (port, airport)* bloqué(e) en raison du brouillard

fogey ['fəʊgɪ] *(pl* **fogeys)** *n Fam* old **f.** vieux (vieille) schnock *m,f*

foggy ['fɒgɪ] *adj* brumeux(euse); **it's f.** il y a du brouillard; *Fam* **I haven't (got) the foggiest (idea)!** je n'en ai pas la moindre idée!

foghorn ['fɒghɔːn] *n (on ship)* corne *f* de brume; *Fam* **a voice like a f.** une voix de stentor

fogy ['fəʊgɪ] *(pl* **fogies)** = **fogey**

foible ['fɔɪbəl] *n (habit)* manie *f; (weakness)* point *m* faible

foil [fɔɪl] **1** *n* **(a)** *(metal sheet)* feuille *f*; **(cooking** *or* **kitchen) f.** papier *m* alu(minium) **(b)** *(complement)* **to act as a f. (to** *or* **for)** servir de repoussoir (à) **(c)** *(sword)* fleuret *m*
2 *vt (plan, ambitions)* contrecarrer; *(attempt, coup)* faire échouer

foist [fɔɪst] *vt* refiler **(on à)**; *(ideas)* imposer **(on à)**

fold¹ [fəʊld] *n (sheep)* **f.** parc *m* à moutons

fold² **1** *n* pli *m*; *(of fat)* bourrelet *m*
2 *vt* **(a)** plier; **to f. sth in two** *or* **in half** plier qch en deux; **to f. one's arms** croiser les bras **(b)** *(in cooking)* mélanger délicatement
3 *vi* **(a)** *(of chair, table)* se plier, se replier **(b)** *Fam (of business)* plier boutique

▸ **fold up 1** *vt sep* plier, replier
2 *vi (of map, chair)* se plier, se replier

foldaway ['fəʊldəweɪ] *adj (table, bed)* pliant(e)

folder ['fəʊldə(r)] *n (file, document wallet)* chemise *f*; *(ring binder)* classeur *m*; *Comptr* répertoire *m*

folding ['fəʊldɪŋ] *adj (chair, table)* pliant(e); **f. doors** porte *f* en accordéon

foliage ['fəʊlɪɪdʒ] *n* feuillage *m*

folio ['fəʊlɪəʊ] *(pl* **folios)** *n* folio *m*

folk [fəʊk] **1** *npl Fam (people)* gens *mpl*; **my/your folks** *(family)* ma/ta famille
2 *adj (traditional)* folklorique; **f. (music)** *(musique f)* folk *m*; **f. singer** chanteur(euse) *m,f* folk; **f. song** chanson *f* folk

folklore ['fəʊklɔː(r)] *n* folklore *m*

follow ['fɒləʊ] **1** *vt* suivre; *(act, performance)* passer après; *(career)* poursuivre; **the road follows the coast** la route longe la côte; **to f. one's nose** *(go straight ahead)* aller tout droit; *(act instinctively)* y aller à l'instinct
2 *vi* **(a)** *(come after)* suivre; **proceed as follows** procéder comme suit **(b)** *(result)* s'ensuivre; **it follows that…** il s'ensuit que… **(c)** *(understand)* suivre

▸ **follow on** *vi* **(a)** *(go after)* **you go ahead, we'll f. on** pars devant, nous te suivons **(b)** *(continue)* **to f. on from sth** découler de qch

▸ **follow through 1** *vt sep (project, plan)* mener à son terme
2 *vi* **he's full of ideas but he seldom follows through** il a beaucoup d'idées, mais il les met rarement à exécution

▸ **follow up** *vt sep (advantage, success)* exploiter; *(opportunity)* saisir; *(contact)* garder; *(clue)* suivre

follower ['fɒləʊə(r)] *n (of team)* supporter *m*; *(of ideas, politician)* partisan(e) *m,f*; *(of philosopher)* disciple *m*

following ['fɒləʊɪŋ] **1** *n (supporters) (of team)* supporters *mpl*; *(of ideas, politician)* partisans *mpl*; *(of programme)* public *m*
2 *pron* **the f.** *(things, points)* ce qui suit; *(people)* les personnes *fpl* suivantes

3 *adj* suivant(e); **(on) the f. day** le jour suivant, le lendemain
4 *prep* après

follow-up ['fɒləʊʌp] *n Com (of orders)* suivi *m*

folly ['fɒlɪ] *n* folie *f*; **an act of f.** une folie

foment [fə'ment] *vt Lit* fomenter

fond [fɒnd] *adj* **(a)** **to be f. of sb/sth** aimer bien qn/qch; **to become f. of sb** s'attacher à qn; **to become f. of sth** prendre goût à qch; **to be f. of doing sth** aimer bien faire qch **(b)** *(loving)* tendre, affectueux(euse); **f. memories (of)** de bons souvenirs (de) **(c)** *(hope)* naïf(ïve)

fondle ['fɒndəl] *vt* caresser

fondly ['fɒndlɪ] *adv* **(a)** *(lovingly)* tendrement, affectueusement **(b)** *(naively)* naïvement

fondness ['fɒndnɪs] *n* **(a)** *(affection)* tendresse *f*, affection *f* **(for** pour) **(b)** *(liking)* penchant *m* **(for** pour)

font [fɒnt] *n* **(a)** *Rel* fonts *mpl* baptismaux **(b)** *Typ & Comptr* police *f* de caractères, fonte *f*

food [fuːd] *n* nourriture *f*; **Mexican f.** la cuisine mexicaine; **to be off one's f.** ne pas avoir d'appétit; **to give sb f. for thought** donner à penser *ou* à réfléchir à qn; *Biol* **f. chain** chaîne *f* alimentaire; **f. industry** industrie *f* alimentaire; **f. poisoning** intoxication *f* alimentaire; **f. processor** robot *m* de cuisine

foodstuffs ['fuːdstʌfs] *npl* produits *mpl* alimentaires

fool [fuːl] **1** *n (stupid person)* imbécile *mf*, idiot(e) *m,f*; *(jester)* fou *m*; **you'd be a f. to agree** tu serais bien bête d'accepter; **any f. knows that** le premier imbécile venu sait ça; **a f. of a politician** un imbécile de politicien; **to play** *or* **act the f.** faire l'idiot; **to make a f. of sb** *(make look ridiculous)* ridiculiser qn; *(tease)* se moquer de qn; **to make a f. of oneself** se couvrir de ridicule; **the more f. you!** tu es vraiment bête!; **I felt such a f.** je me suis senti vraiment bête; **she's no** *or* **nobody's f.** on ne la lui fait pas, elle est maligne; **to live in a f.'s paradise** se bercer d'illusions; *Fam* **there's no f. like an old f.** il n'y a pire fou qu'un vieux fou
2 *vt (deceive)* avoir, duper; **you can't f. me** on ne m'a pas comme ça; **to let oneself be fooled by sth** se laisser avoir par qch; **you could have fooled me!** je ne l'aurais pas cru!

▸ **fool about, fool around** *vi* **(a)** *(act foolishly)* faire l'imbécile; **to f. about** *or* **around with sth** *(clumsily, for fun)* jouer avec qch; *(fiddle)* tripoter qch **(b)** *(waste time)* perdre son temps **(c)** *(have affair(s))* avoir une aventure/des aventures

foolhardy ['fuːlhɑːdɪ] *adj* téméraire, imprudent(e)

foolish ['fuːlɪʃ] *adj (stupid)* idiot(e); *(imprudent)* insensé(e); **to make sb look f.** ridiculiser qn

foolishly ['fuːlɪʃlɪ] *adv (stupidly)* bêtement; *(imprudently)* imprudemment

foolproof ['fuːlpruːf] *adj (method, plan)* infaillible; *(device)* indétraquable

foot [fʊt] *(pl* **feet** [fiːt]) **1** *n* **(a)** *(of person, horse, chair)* pied *m*; *(of other animal)* patte *f*; **to put one's feet up** *(have a rest)* se reposer; **to set f. on** poser le pied sur; **I shall never set f. in his house again** je ne remettrai jamais plus les pieds chez lui; **to be on one's feet all day** être debout du matin au soir; **to be on one's feet again** *(after illness)* être de nouveau sur pied; **on f.** à pied; **under f.** sous les pieds; *Mil* **f. patrol** patrouille *f* à pied; **f. pump** pompe *f* à pied; **f. soldier** fantassin *m*, soldat *m* d'infanterie
(b) *(of mountain, stairs)* pied *m*; *(of page)* bas *m*; *(of bed, table)* bout *m*
(c) *(in poetry)* pied *m*
(d) *(unit of measurement)* = 0,3048 m, pied *m* (anglais); **three f.** *or* **feet six (inches)** trois pieds six pouces
(e) *(idioms)* **to have one's feet firmly on the ground** avoir les pieds sur terre; **to have one f. in the grave** avoir

un pied dans la tombe; **she hasn't put a f. wrong** elle n'a pas commis la moindre erreur; **to put one's f. down** *(be firm)* faire preuve de fermeté; *(refuse)* mettre le holà; *Fam* **to put one's f. in it** faire une gaffe; **to find one's feet** s'adapter; **to get a f. in the door** avoir un pied dans la place; *Fam* **my f.!** mon œil! **2** *vt* **to f. the bill** payer la note

footage ['fʊtɪdʒ] *n Cin* séquences *fpl*, images *fpl*

foot-and-mouth disease [fʊtən'maʊθdɪ'ziːz] *n* fièvre *f* aphteuse

football ['fʊtbɔːl] *n (soccer)* football *m*; *(American)* football américain; *(ball)* ballon *m* (de football); **f. club** club *m* de foot(ball); **f. fan** supporter *m* d'une équipe de football; **f. ground** terrain *m* de football; **f. hooligan** hooligan *m*; **f. pitch** terrain de football; **f. player** *Br* footballeur(euse) *m,f*; *Am* joueur(euse) *m,f* de football américain; **f. supporter** supporter d'une équipe de football

footballer ['fʊtbɔːlə(r)] *n* footballeur(euse) *m,f*

footbridge ['fʊtbrɪdʒ] *n* passerelle *f*

foothills ['fʊthɪlz] *npl* contreforts *mpl*

foothold ['fʊthəʊld] *n* prise *f* (pour le pied); *Fig* **to gain a f.** *(of theory, feeling)* se propager

footing ['fʊtɪŋ] *n* **(a)** *(balance)* **to lose one's f.** perdre l'équilibre **(b)** *(level)* **on an equal f.** sur un pied d'égalité; **to be on a friendly f. with sb** avoir des rapports amicaux avec qn

footlights ['fʊtlaɪts] *npl Th* rampe *f*

footloose ['fʊtluːs] *adj* libre; **to be f. and fancy-free** être libre comme l'air

footman ['fʊtmən] *n* valet *m* de pied

footnote ['fʊtnəʊt] *n* note *f* de bas de page; *Fig* détail *m*

footpath ['fʊtpɑːθ] *n* sentier *m*

footprint ['fʊtprɪnt] *n* trace *f* de pas; *(of bare foot)* empreinte *f* de pied

footrest ['fʊtrest] *n* repose-pieds *m inv*

footsie ['fʊtsɪ] *n Fam* **to play f. with sb** faire du pied à qn

footsore ['fʊtsɔː(r)] *adj* **to be f.** avoir mal aux pieds

footstep ['fʊtstep] *n* pas *m*; *Fig* **to follow in sb's footsteps** suivre les traces de qn

footwear ['fʊtweə(r)] *n* chaussures *fpl*

footwork ['fʊtwɜːk] *n* jeu *m* de jambes; *Fig* **it required some rather fancy f.** il a fallu faire des pieds et des mains

fop [fɒp] *n* dandy *m*

foppish ['fɒpɪʃ] *adj* de dandy

for [fɔː(r), *unstressed* fə(r)] **1** *prep* **(a)** *(expressing purpose, destination)* pour; **to leave f. England** partir pour l'Angleterre; **there's no time f. that** il n'y a pas de temps pour ça; **what's it f.?** c'est pour quoi faire?; **can you give me something f. the pain?** pouvez-vous me donner quelque chose contre la douleur?
(b) *(because of)* pour, en raison de; **she couldn't sleep f. the pain** elle ne pouvait pas dormir à cause de la douleur **(c)** *(expressing cost, amount)* **I bought it f. $10** je l'ai acheté 10 dollars; **a cheque f. £50** un chèque de 50 livres **(d)** *(considering)* pour; **he is big f. his age** il est grand pour son âge; **f. all the good it will do** pour ce que ça changera; **f. all his wealth, he was still unhappy** en dépit de toutes ses richesses, il était toujours malheureux
(e) *(representing)* **A f. Anne** A comme Anne; **what's the French f. "book"?** comment dit-on "book" en français? **(f)** *(duration)* **I was there f. a month** je suis resté là-bas (pendant) un mois; **I've been here f. a month** il y a un mois que je suis ici, je suis ici depuis un mois; **I will be here f. a month** je serai ici pendant un mois; **I haven't been there f. a month** je n'y suis pas allé depuis un mois; **I'm**

going away f. two weeks je pars pour quinze jours; **we have enough food f. two days** nous avons suffisamment à manger pour deux jours **(g)** *(with point in time)* **f. the first/last time** pour la première/dernière fois; **I need it f. Friday** j'en ai besoin pour vendredi **(h)** *(as compared to)* pour; **there's one female applicant f. every five males** sur six postulants il y a une femme et cinq hommes **(i)** *(in favour of)* **to be f. sth** être pour qch, être favorable à qch; *Fam* **I'm all f. it!** je suis tout à fait pour! **(j)** *(introducing an infinitive clause)* **it is too early f. me to decide** il est trop tôt pour que je prenne une décision; **it will be difficult f. her to come** il lui sera difficile de venir; **it took an hour f. us to get there** il nous a fallu une heure pour arriver là-bas **(k)** *(idioms)* **f. all I know** pour ce que j'en sais; **that's men f. you!** c'est bien les hommes!; *Fam* **he's f. it!** qu'est-ce qu'il va prendre!
2 *conj Lit (because)* car

forage ['fɒrɪdʒ] **1** *n (animal food)* fourrage *m*; *Mil* **f. cap** calot *m*
2 *vi* **to f. for sth** fouiller pour trouver qch

foray ['fɒreɪ] *n* incursion *f* (**into** dans)

forbear [fɔː'beə(r)] *(pt* forbore [fɔː'bɔː(r)], *pp* forborne [fɔː'bɔːn]) *vi Formal* **to f. to do sth** s'abstenir de faire qch

forbearance [fɔː'beərəns] *n Formal* patience *f*

forbid [fə'bɪd] *(pt* forbade [fə'bæd, fə'beɪd], *pp* forbidden [fə'bɪdən]) *vt* interdire; **to f. sb to do sth** interdire à qn de faire qch; **smoking is forbidden** il est interdit de fumer; **God f.!** Dieu m'en/nous en préserve!

forbidding [fə'bɪdɪŋ] *adj (appearance, look, landscape)* sinistre; *(task)* rébarbatif(ive)

force [fɔːs] **1** *n* **(a)** *(strength, power, influence)* force *f*; **by sheer** *or* **brute f.** par la force; **by f. of circumstance(s)** par la force des circonstances; **f. of habit** la force de l'habitude; **several forces conspired to bring about his downfall** plusieurs facteurs ont contribué à provoquer sa chute **(b)** *Mil* **the (armed) forces** les forces *fpl* armées; **to join forces (to do sth)** joindre ses efforts (pour faire qch); **they turned out in (full) f.** ils sont venus en masse **(c)** *(effect)* **to come into f.** entrer en vigueur
2 *vt* **(a)** *(compel)* **to f. sb to do sth** *or* **into doing sth** forcer *ou* obliger à faire qch; **to f. sth on sb** imposer qch à qn; **they forced the enemy back** ils ont repoussé l'ennemi **(b)** *(obtain by effort)* **to f. the issue** précipiter les choses; **to f. sb's hand** forcer la main à qn; **to f. one's way through a crowd** se frayer un passage à travers la foule; **to f. oneself on sb** *(sexually)* essayer d'abuser de qn physiquement
▸ **force down** *vt sep* **(a)** *(aircraft)* obliger à atterrir **(b)** *(food)* se forcer à avaler
▸ **force open** *vt sep (door, window, lock)* forcer

forced [fɔːst] *adj (manner, laugh)* forcé(e), artificiel(elle); **f. labour** travail *m* forcé; *Av* **f. landing** atterrissage *m* forcé; *Mil* **f. march** marche *f* forcée

force-feed ['fɔːsfiːd] *(pt & pp* force-fed ['fɔːsˈfed]) *vt (person)* nourrir de force; *(livestock)* gaver

forceful ['fɔːsfʊl] *adj (person, language)* énergique; *(argument)* puissant(e)

forceps ['fɔːseps] *npl* forceps *mpl*; **f. delivery** accouchement *m* aux forceps

forcible ['fɔːsɪbəl] *adj* **(a)** *Law* **f. entry** entrée *f* par effraction **(b)** *(argument)* puissant(e); *(reminder)* brutal(e)

forcibly ['fɔːsɪblɪ] *adv* **(a)** *(by force)* de force **(b)** *(argue)* vigoureusement

ford [fɔːd] **1** *n* gué *m*
2 *vt* traverser à gué

fore [fɔː(r)] **1** *n* **to come to the f.** *(of person)* commencer à être connu(e); *(of issue)* être mis(e) en évidence **2** *adj Naut* à l'avant

forearm ['fɔːrɑːm] *n* avant-bras *m inv*

forebear ['fɔːbeə(r)] *n* ancêtre *mf*

foreboding [fɔːˈbəʊdɪŋ] *n* (mauvais) pressentiment *m*

forecast ['fɔːkɑːst] **1** *n* prévisions *fpl*; *(in horseracing)* pronostics *mpl* (des courses); **(weather) f.** prévisions météorologiques, météo *f* **2** *vt* *(pt & pp* **forecast(ed))** prévoir; *(in horseracing)* pronostiquer

foreclose [fɔːˈkləʊz] *vt Fin* **to f. a mortgage** saisir un immeuble hypothéqué

forecourt ['fɔːkɔːt] *n (of petrol station)* devant *m*

forefathers ['fɔːfɑːðəz] *npl* aïeux *mpl*

forefinger ['fɔːfɪŋgə(r)] *n* index *m*

forefront ['fɔːfrʌnt] *n* **to be in the f. of** être au premier plan de

forego [fɔːˈgəʊ] *(pt* **forewent** [fɔːˈwent], *pp* **foregone** [fɔːˈgɒn]) *vt* renoncer à

foregone ['fɔːgɒn] **to be a f. conclusion** être couru(e) d'avance

foreground ['fɔːgraʊnd] **1** *n* premier plan *m*; **in the f.** au premier plan **2** *vt* mettre au premier plan

forehand ['fɔːhænd] *n (in tennis)* coup *m* droit; **f. volley** volée *f* de face

forehead ['fɒrɪd, 'fɔːhed] *n* front *m*

foreign [ˈfɒrɪn] *adj* étranger(ère); **f. affairs** les affaires *fpl* étrangères; **f. aid** aide *f* aux pays étrangers; *(from point of view of recipient)* aide de l'étranger; *Med* **f. body** corps *m* étranger; *Journ* **f. correspondent** correspondant(e) *m,f* à l'étranger; **f. currency** devises *fpl* étrangères; **f. legion** légion *f* étrangère; *Pol* **F. Minister,** *Br* **F. Secretary** ministre *m* des Affaires étrangères; *Br* *Pol* **F. Office** ministère *m* des Affaires étrangères; **f. trade** commerce *m* extérieur

foreigner ['fɒrɪnə(r)] *n* étranger(ère) *m,f*

foreleg ['fɔːleg] *n* patte *f* de devant; *(of horse)* membre *m* antérieur

foreman ['fɔːmən] *n (of workers)* contremaître *m*; *(of jury)* président *m*

foremost ['fɔːməʊst] *adj* le (la) plus important(e)

forename ['fɔːneɪm] *n* prénom *m*

forensic [fəˈrensɪk] *adj Law* légal(e); **f. evidence** preuves relevées lors d'une expertise criminalistique; **f. medicine** médecine *f* légale; **f. scientist** médecin *m* légiste

foreplay ['fɔːpleɪ] *n* préliminaires *mpl* amoureux

forerunner ['fɔːrʌnə(r)] *n* **(a)** *(person)* précurseur *m* **(of** de) **(b)** *(sign)* signe *m* précurseur **(of** de)

foresee [fɔːˈsiː] *(pt* **foresaw** [fɔːˈsɔː], *pp* **foreseen** [fɔːˈsiːn]) *vt* prévoir

foreseeable [fɔːˈsiːəbəl] *adj* prévisible; **in the f. future** dans un avenir proche; **for the f. future** dans l'immédiat

foreshadow [fɔːˈʃædəʊ] *vt* annoncer

foresight ['fɔːsaɪt] *n* prévoyance *f*

foreskin ['fɔːskɪn] *n Anat* prépuce *m*

forest ['fɒrɪst] *n* forêt *f*; **f. fire** incendie *m* de forêt

forestall [fɔːˈstɔːl] *vt* devancer

forester ['fɒrɪstə(r)] *n* (garde *m*) forestier *m*

forestry ['fɒrɪstrɪ] *n* sylviculture *f*; *Br* **the F. Commission** ≃ Les Eaux et Forêts *fpl*; **f. worker** *(forester)* forestier *m*; *(lumberjack)* bûcheron *m*

foretaste ['fɔːteɪst] *n* avant-goût *m* **(of** de)

foretell [fɔːˈtel] *(pt & pp* **foretold** [fɔːˈtəʊld]) *vt* prédire

forethought ['fɔːθɔːt] *n* prévoyance *f*

forever [fəˈrevə(r)] *adv* **(a)** *(eternally)* pour toujours; **nothing lasts f.** tout a une fin; **the journey seemed to last f.** il semblait que le voyage ne finirait jamais **(b)** *(repeatedly)* sans cesse; **he's f. finding fault** il trouve toujours à redire **(c)** *Fam (a long time)* une éternité; **to take f. (to do sth)** mettre un temps infini (à faire qch)

forewarn [fɔːˈwɔːn] *vt* prévenir, avertir; *Prov* **forewarned is forearmed** un homme averti en vaut deux

forewent [fɔːˈwent] *pt of* **forego**

foreword ['fɔːwɜːd] *n* avant-propos *m inv*, préface *f*

forfeit ['fɔːfɪt] *n* **1** *(in game)* gage *m*; *Law* amende *f* **2** *vt (rights)* être déchu(e) de; *(property)* se faire confisquer; *(someone's respect)* perdre

forgave [fəˈgeɪv] *pt of* **forgive**

forge [fɔːdʒ] **1** *n* forge *f* **2** *vt* **(a)** *(metal, alliance)* forger **(b)** *(cheque, signature, banknote)* contrefaire; **to f. a document/passport** faire un faux document/passeport

▸ **forge ahead** *vi* **(a)** *(make progress)* faire des progrès; *(of company)* aller de l'avant **(b)** *(outstrip competitors)* prendre de l'avance **(of** sur)

forged [fɔːdʒd] *adj* faux (fausse)

forgery ['fɔːdʒərɪ] *(pl* **forgeries)** *n* **(a)** *(activity)* contrefaçon *f*; *(of document, banknote)* falsification *f* **(b)** *(thing forged)* faux (fausse) *m,f*

forget [fəˈget] *(pt* **forgot** [fəˈgɒt], *pp* **forgotten** [fəˈgɒtən]) **1** *vt* oublier; **to f. to do sth** oublier de faire qch; **to f. how to do sth** oublier comment on fait qch, ne plus savoir faire qch; **to be forgotten** tomber dans l'oubli; **f. it!** *(in reply to apology, thanks)* il n'y a pas de quoi!; *(stop talking about it)* laisse tomber! **2** *vi* oublier; **to f. about sb/sth** oublier qn/qch, **you can f. about going to London!** tu peux faire une croix sur ton voyage à Londres! **let's f. about it** n'y pensons plus

forgetful [fəˈgetfʊl] *adj* **to be f.** avoir mauvaise mémoire

forget-me-not [fəˈgetmiːnɒt] *n* myosotis *m*

forgivable [fəˈgɪvəbəl] *adj* excusable, pardonnable

forgive [fəˈgɪv] *(pt* **forgave** [fəˈgeɪv], *pp* **forgiven** [fəˈgɪvən]) **1** *vt* pardonner; **to f. sb for sth** pardonner qch à qn; **if you'll f. the pun** pardonnez-moi ce jeu de mots; **f. me for interrupting** pardonnez-moi de vous interrompre **2** *vi* pardonner; **to f. and forget** oublier sa rancune

forgiveness [fəˈgɪvnɪs] *n* pardon *m*

forgiving [fəˈgɪvɪŋ] *adj* indulgent(e)

forgo [fɔːˈgəʊ] = **forego**

forgot [fəˈgɒt] *pt of* **forget**

forgotten [fəˈgɒtən] *pp of* **forget**

fork [fɔːk] **1** *n* **(a)** *(for food)* fourchette *f* **(b)** *(for gardening)* fourche *f* **(c)** *(in road, path)* bifurcation *f* **2** *vi (of road, path)* bifurquer

▸ **fork out** *Fam* **1** *vt sep* allonger **2** *vi* casquer **(for** pour)

forked [fɔːkt] *adj (stick, tongue)* fourchu(e); **f. lightning** éclairs *mpl*

fork-lift truck ['fɔːklɪftʌk] *n* chariot *m* (élévateur) à fourche

forlorn [fəˈlɔːn] *adj (person, look)* triste, malheureux(euse); *(hope, attempt)* désespéré(e)

form [fɔːm] **1** *n* **(a)** *(shape)* *(of object, animal)* forme *f*; *(of person)* silhouette *f*; **to take the f. of sth** prendre la forme de qch **(b)** *(type)* forme *f*; **in the f. of** sous forme de; **f. of address** titre *m* de politesse **(c)** *(politeness)* **as a matter of f., for f.'s sake** pour la forme, par pure formalité; **it's good/**

bad f. to... cela se fait/ne se fait pas de... **(d)** *(for applications, orders)* formulaire *m* **(e)** *(condition, performance)* forme *f; (in horseracing)* performances *fpl;* **to be in** *or* **on good f.** être en forme; **on present f.** si l'on en juge par la situation actuelle **(f)** *Br Sch (class, year)* classe *f*
2 *vt (government, character)* former; *(idea)* avoir; *(opinion)* se faire, se former; *(relationship, friendship)* nouer; *(organization, obstacle)* constituer; **to f. a plan to do sth** projeter de faire qch; **to f. part of sth** faire partie de qch
3 *vi* se former

formal ['fɔːməl] *adj (manner)* cérémonieux(euse); *(offer, occasion, invitation)* officiel(elle); *(language)* soutenu(e); **f. dress** tenue *f* de soirée

formality [fɔː'mælɪtɪ] *(pl* **formalities)** *n (procedure)* formalité *f*

formalize ['fɔːməlaɪz] *vt* officialiser

formally ['fɔːməlɪ] *adv (behave)* de façon cérémonieuse; *(invite, announce)* officiellement; **to dress f.** porter une tenue de soirée

format ['fɔːmæt] **1** *n* format *m*
2 *vt (pt & pp* **formatted)** *Comptr* formater

formation [fɔː'meɪʃən] *n (act, arrangement)* formation *f; (of idea, plan)* élaboration *f;* **f. flying** vol *m* de groupe

formative ['fɔːmətɪv] *adj* formateur(trice); **the f. years** les années *fpl* de formation

former ['fɔːmə(r)] **1** *pron* **the f.** celui-là (celle-là); *(plural)* ceux-là (celles-là)
2 *adj (pupil, colleague, job)* ancien(enne) *(before noun);* **in f. times** autrefois; **in a f. life** dans une vie antérieure

formerly ['fɔːməlɪ] *adv* autrefois; **Mrs Walker, f. Miss Cox** Mme Walker, née Cox; **Zambia, f. Northern Rhodesia** la Zambie, ancienne Rhodésie du Nord

formidable ['fɔːmɪdəbəl] *adj (opponent, difficulty)* redoutable; *(performance, talent)* formidable

formula ['fɔːmjʊlə] *(pl* **formulas** *or* **formulae** ['fɔːmjʊliː]) *n* **(a)** *(scheme, in maths, chemistry)* formule *f;* **the f. for success** la clé de la réussite; **a peace f.** une solution en faveur de la paix; *Aut* **F. 1** formule 1 **(b)** *Am (baby food)* lait *m* en poudre

formulate ['fɔːmjʊleɪt] *vt (plan, proposal)* élaborer; *(thought, opinion)* formuler

fornication [fɔːnɪ'keɪʃən] *n Formal* fornication *f*

forsake [fə'seɪk] *(pt* **forsook** [fə'sʊk], *pp* **forsaken** [fə'seɪkən]) *vt Lit* **(a)** *(abandon)* abandonner **(b)** *(renounce)* renoncer à

forswear [fɔː'sweə(r)] *(pt* **forswore** [fɔː'swɔː(r)], *pp* **forsworn** [fɔː'swɔːn]) *vt Lit* renoncer à

fort [fɔːt] *n* fort *m*, forteresse *f; Fig* **to hold the f.** monter la garde

forte ['fɔːtɪ] *n* fort *m*

forth [fɔːθ] *adv* en avant; **to go f.** avancer; **to walk back and f.** marcher de long en large, faire les cent pas; **from that day f.** à dater de ce jour; **and so f.** et cetera, et ainsi de suite

forthcoming [fɔːθ'kʌmɪŋ] *adj* **(a)** *(election)* prochain(e); *(book, film)* qui sortira bientôt **(b)** *(available)* **no money was f.** l'argent n'est pas arrivé **(c)** *(informative)* expansif(ive) **(about** sur)

forthright ['fɔːθraɪt] *adj* franc (franche)

forthwith [fɔːθ'wɪθ] *adv Formal* immédiatement, sur-le-champ

fortieth ['fɔːtɪəθ] **1** *n* **(a)** *(fraction)* quarantième *m* **(b)** *(in series)* quarantième *mf*
2 *adj* quarantième

fortification [fɔːtɪfɪ'keɪʃən] *n* fortification *f*

fortified ['fɔːtɪfaɪd] *adj* **(a)** *(town)* fortifié(e) **(b)** **f. wine** vin *m* viné

fortify ['fɔːtɪfaɪ] *(pt & pp* **fortified)** *vt Mil* fortifier; **to f. oneself** se prémunir

fortitude ['fɔːtɪtjuːd] *n* force *f* morale

fortnight ['fɔːtnaɪt] *n Br* quinzaine *f,* quinze jours *mpl;* **a f. today** aujourd'hui en quinze

fortnightly ['fɔːtnaɪtlɪ] *Br* **1** *adj* bimensuel(elle)
2 *adv* tous les quinze jours, bimensuellement

fortress ['fɔːtrɪs] *n* forteresse *f*

fortuitous [fɔː'tjuːɪtəs] *adj* fortuit(e)

fortunate ['fɔːtʃənət] *adj* heureux(euse); **to be f.** avoir de la chance; **to be f. enough to do sth** avoir la chance de faire qch

fortunately ['fɔːtʃənətlɪ] *adv* heureusement, par bonheur

fortune ['fɔːtʃən] *n* **(a)** *(riches)* fortune *f;* **to make a** *or* **one's f.** faire fortune; *Fam* **to cost a (small) f.** coûter une fortune *ou* les yeux de la tête **(b)** *(luck)* chance *f;* **good f.** chance; **bad f.** malchance *f;* **to tell sb's f.** dire la bonne aventure à qn

fortune-teller ['fɔːtʃəntelə(r)] *n* diseur(euse) *m,f* de bonne aventure

forty ['fɔːtɪ] **1** *n* quarante *m inv*
2 *adj* quarante; *Fam* **to have f. winks** piquer *ou* faire un petit somme; *see also* **eighty**

forum ['fɔːrəm] *n* forum *m; Comptr (on Internet)* groupe *m* de discussions; **a f. for debate** un lieu de débat

forward ['fɔːwəd] **1** *n (in sport)* avant *m*
2 *adj* **(a)** *(position)* avant *inv; (movement)* en avant, vers l'avant; **f. planning** planification *f; Fin* **f. market** marché *m* à terme **(b)** *(impudent, bold)* effronté(e), hardi(e)
3 *adv* **(a)** *(of time)* from this/that day **f.** à partir d'aujourd'hui/de ce jour-là; **to put the clocks f.** avancer les pendules **(b)** *(of direction)* en avant; **to walk f.** avancer **(c)** *(of position)* à l'avant; **we're sitting too far f.** *(in cinema, theatre)* nous sommes assis trop près; **the seat is too far f.** le siège est trop avancé
4 *vt* **(a)** *(letter)* faire suivre; *(complaint, query)* faire passer **(to** à) **(b)** *(one's career, interests)* favoriser

forwarding agent ['fɔːwədɪŋ'eɪdʒənt] *n Com* (agent *m*) transitaire *m*

forward-looking ['fɔːwədlʊkɪŋ] *adj* progressiste

forwards ['fɔːwədz] *adv* = **forward**

fossil ['fɒsəl] *n* fossile *m; Fam* **an old f.** *(man)* un vieux croûton; *(woman)* une vieille bique; **f. fuel** combustible *m* fossile

fossilized ['fɒsɪlaɪzd] *adj* fossilisé(e); *Fig* sclérosé(e)

foster ['fɒstə(r)] **1** *adj* **f. child** = enfant placé dans une famille d'accueil; **f. parents** famille *f* d'accueil, parents *mpl* nourriciers
2 *vt* **(a)** *(child)* prendre en famille d'accueil **(b)** *(idea, hope)* nourrir, entretenir; *(friendship)* stimuler

fought [fɔːt] *pt & pp of* **fight**

foul [faʊl] **1** *n (in sport)* faute *f*
2 *adj* **(a)** *(disgusting)* *(smell, taste)* infect(e), nauséabond(e); *(weather)* sale; *(air)* vicié(e); *(language)* ordurier(ère); **to be in a f. mood** être d'une humeur massacrante **(b)** *(illegal)* **f. play** *Sp* jeu *m* irrégulier; *Law* acte *m* criminel
3 *adv* **(a)** **to smell f.** puer; **to taste f.** avoir un goût infect **(b)** **to fall f. of the law** avoir des démêlés avec la justice
4 *vt* **(a)** *(pollute)* salir **(b)** *(entangle)* s'enchevêtrer autour de **(c)** *(in sport)* commettre une faute contre
▸ **foul up** *vt sep Fam (ruin)* gâcher

foul-mouthed [faʊl'maʊðd] *adj* au langage ordurier *ou* grossier

found¹ [faʊnd] *vt*(**a**) *(city, organization)* fonder; *(company)* créer; *(empire)* établir (**b**) *(base)* baser, fonder (**on** sur)

found² *pt & pp of* **find**

foundation [faʊn'deɪʃən] *n* (**a**) *(of city, organization)* fondation *f*; *(of company)* création *f* (**b**) *(basis)* fondement *m*, base *f*; **to be without f.** être dénué(e) de fondement (**c**) **foundations** *(of building, society)* fondations *fpl* (**d**) *(make-up)* **f. (cream)** fond *m* de teint

founder¹ ['faʊndə(r)] *n (of hospital, school)* fondateur(trice) *m,f*; **f. member** membre *m* fondateur

founder² *vi (of ship)* s'échouer; *Fig (of project, talks)* avorter

founding father ['faʊndɪŋ'fɑːðə(r)] *n* père *m* fondateur

foundling ['faʊndlɪŋ] *n Old-fashioned* enfant *mf* trouvé(e)

foundry ['faʊndrɪ] *(pl* **foundries**) *n* fonderie *f*

fount [faʊnt] *n Lit & Fig* source *f*

fountain ['faʊntɪn] *n* fontaine *f*; **f. pen** stylo *m* (à) plume

four [fɔː(r)] **1** *n* quatre *m inv*; **on all fours** à quatre pattes
2 *adj* quatre; **to the f. corners of the earth** aux quatre coins du monde; *see also* **eight**

four-eyes ['fɔːraɪz] *n Fam* binoclard(e) *m,f*

four-figure [fɔː'fɪgə(r)] *adj* **a f. sum** un montant de quatre chiffres

fourfold ['fɔːfəʊld] **1** *adj* **a f. increase** une augmentation au quadruple
2 *adv* **to increase f.** quadrupler

four-legged [fɔː'legɪd] *adj* quadrupède; *Hum* **f. friend** ami *m* à quatre pattes

four-letter word ['fɔːletə'wɜːd] *n* gros mot *m*

four-poster ['fɔː'pəʊstə(r)] *n* **f. (bed)** lit *m* à baldaquin

foursome ['fɔːsəm] *n* groupe *m* de quatre personnes

fourteen ['fɔːtiːn] **1** *n* quatorze *m inv*
2 *adj* quatorze; *see also* **eight**

fourteenth [fɔː'tiːnθ] **1** *n* (**a**) *(fraction)* quatorzième *m* (**b**) *(in series)* quatorzième *mf* (*of month)* quatorze *m inv*
2 *adj* quatorzième; *see also* **eighth**

fourth [fɔːθ] **1** *n* (**a**) *(fraction)* quatrième *m* (**b**) *(in series)* quatrième *mf* (*of month)* quatre *m inv*
2 *adj* quatrième; *see also* **eighth**

fourthly ['fɔːθlɪ] *adv* quatrièmement

fowl [faʊl] *(pl* **fowl**) *n* volaille *f*

fox [fɒks] **1** *n* renard *m*; *Fig* **a sly old f.** *(cunning person)* un vieux renard; **f. cub** renardeau *m*; **f. hunt** chasse *f* au renard
2 *vt (perplex)* laisser perplexe; *(deceive)* duper

foxglove ['fɒksglʌv] *n* digitale *f* (pourprée)

fox-hunting ['fɒkshʌntɪŋ] *n* chasse *f* au renard

foxtrot ['fɒkstrɒt] *n* fox-trot *m inv*

foxy ['fɒksɪ] *adj* (**a**) *Fam (sly)* rusé(e) (**b**) *Am Fam* sexy *inv*

foyer ['fɔɪeɪ] *n (in theatre)* foyer *m*; *(in cinema, hotel)* hall *m*

fraction ['frækʃən] *n (in maths)* fraction *f*; *Fig (small part)* petite partie *f*; **a f. too small/large** un tout petit peu trop petit(e)/grand(e)

fractional ['frækʃənəl] *adj (very small)* infime

fractious ['frækʃəs] *adj (adult)* de mauvaise humeur; *(baby)* pleurnicheur(euse); *(tone, expression)* irrité(e)

fracture ['fræktʃə(r)] **1** *n* fracture *f*
2 *vt (bone)* fracturer; *(pipe)* fendre
3 *vi (of bone)* se fracturer; *(of pipe)* se fendre

fragile ['frædʒaɪl] *adj* fragile; *Fam* **I'm feeling a bit f. this morning** *(after drinking)* j'ai un peu la gueule de bois ce matin

fragility [frə'dʒɪlɪtɪ] *n* fragilité *f*

fragment 1 ['frægmənt] fragment *m*; **I only heard a f. of what was said** je n'ai entendu que des bribes de la conversation
2 *vi* [fræg'ment] *(of object)* se fragmenter; *(of organization)* éclater

fragrance ['freɪgrəns] *n* parfum *m*

fragrant ['freɪgrənt] *adj* odorant(e), parfumé(e)

frail [freɪl] *adj (person)* frêle; *(object)* fragile

frailty ['freɪltɪ] *n* faiblesse *f*

frame [freɪm] **1** *n* (**a**) *(of picture)* cadre *m*, encadrement *m*; *(of door, window)* encadrement (**b**) *(of person, animal)* ossature *f*; *(of building, bridge)* charpente *f*; *(of bicycle)* cadre *m*; *(of spectacles)* monture *f* (**c**) **f. of mind** état *m* d'esprit; **f. of reference** système *m* de référence
2 *vt* (**a**) *(surround)* encadrer (**b**) *(compose)* (*answer)* formuler; *(law)* rédiger (**c**) *Fam (falsely incriminate)* monter un coup contre

franc [fræŋk] *n (currency)* franc *m*; *Formerly* **Belgian/French f.** franc belge/français; **Swiss f.** franc suisse

France [frɑːns] *n* la France

franchise ['fræntʃaɪz] **1** *n* (**a**) *Com* franchise *f* (**b**) *Pol* droit *m* de vote
2 *vt Com* franchiser

francophile ['fræŋkəʊfaɪl] *n & adj* francophile *mf*

francophone ['fræŋkəʊfəʊn] *n & adj* francophone *mf*

frank [fræŋk] **1** *adj* franc (franche); **to be f. ...** pour être franc...
2 *vt (letter)* affranchir

Frankfurt [fræŋkfɜːt] *n* Francfort

frankfurter ['fræŋkfɜːtə(r)] *n* saucisse *f* de Francfort

frankincense ['fræŋkɪnsens] *n* encens *m*

frankly ['fræŋklɪ] *adv* franchement

frantic ['fræntɪk] *adj (rush, pace)* frénétique; *(attempt, effort)* désespéré(e); **f. with worry** fou (folle) d'inquiétude

frantically ['fræntɪklɪ] *adv* frénétiquement; *(work, write)* avec frénésie; *(try)* désespérément

fraternal [frə'tɜːnəl] *adj* fraternel(elle)

fraternity [frə'tɜːnɪtɪ] *(pl* **fraternities**) *n* (**a**) *(brotherliness)* fraternité *f* (**b**) *(group)* confrérie *f*; **the banking/medical f.** la confrérie des banquiers/médecins (**c**) *Am Univ* = confrérie d'étudiants; **f. house** = maison communautaire (d'étudiants d'une même confrérie)

fraternize ['frætənaɪz] *vi* fraterniser (**with** avec)

fraud [frɔːd] *n* (**a**) *(person)* imposteur *m* (**b**) *(deception)* supercherie *f*; *(crime)* fraude *f*; *Br* **the F. Squad** ≃ (le service de) la Répression des Fraudes

fraudulent ['frɔːdjʊlənt] *adj (charge, accusation, feelings)* faux (fausse); *(claim, transaction)* frauduleux(euse)

fraught [frɔːt] *adj (person, situation)* tendu(e); *(day)* éprouvant(e); **f. with danger** rempli(e) d'embûches; **f. with emotion** chargé(e) d'émotion

fray¹ [freɪ] *n (brawl)* bagarre *f*; **to enter the f.** entrer dans l'arène

fray² **1** *vt (material)* user
2 *vi (of material)* s'user; *(of tempers)* s'échauffer; *(of nerves)* craquer

frazzle ['fræzəl] *n* **to be burnt to a f.** *(of food)* être carbonisé(e); *Fam (of person)* être brûlé(e) par le soleil

frazzled ['fræzəld] *adj Fam (person)* lessivé(e), épuisé(e); *(nerves)* à plat

freak [friːk] **1** *n* (**a**) *(strange being)* monstre *m*, phénomène *m*; **f. show** exhibition *f* de monstres (**b**) *(strange event)* **by a f. of fortune** par un coup de chance; **f. accident** accident

m imprévisible; **f. storm** orage *m* inattendu (**c**) *(enthusiast)* fana *mf*; **a fitness f.** un(e) fana de la forme
2 *vi* = **freak out**
▸ **freak out** *Fam* **1** *vt sep (shock, scare)* faire flipper
2 *vi (panic)* paniquer; *(become angry)* piquer une crise

freckle ['frekəl] *n* tache *f* de rousseur

free [fri:] **1** *adj* (**a**) *(unrestricted)* libre (**from** *or* **of** de); *(movement)* dégagé(e); **to be f.** of sb être débarrassé(e) de qn; **f. from worry** sans souci; **to be f. to do sth** être libre de faire qch; **to set sb f.** rendre sa liberté à qn; **f. and easy** décontracté(e); *Fam* **feel f. to borrow my cellphone** n'hésitez pas à emprunter mon portable; (**as**) **f. as a bird** libre comme l'air; **to be a f. agent** être libre (de ses mouvements); *Fig* **to have a f. hand** avoir pleine liberté d'action; *Econ* **f. enterprise** libre entreprise *f*; **f. fall** *(of parachutist, economy)* chute *f* libre; **f. kick** *(in football)* coup *m* franc; *Econ* **f. market** économie *f* de marché; **f. speech** liberté *f* d'expression; **f. throw** *(in basketball)* lancer *m* franc; **f. trade** libre-échange *m*; **f. verse** vers *mpl* libres; **f. will** libre arbitre *m*; **to do sth of one's own f. will** faire qch de son plein gré
(**b**) *(unoccupied) (person, seat, table, time)* libre
(**c**) *(without charge)* gratuit(e); **f. gift** cadeau *m*
(**d**) *(generous)* **to be f. with one's advice** être prodigue en conseils
2 *adv (without charge)* gratuitement; **to do sth for f.** faire qch gratuitement
3 *vt (pt & pp freed* [fri:d]) *(prisoner, time, place)* libérer (**from** de); *(something stuck)* dégager (**from** de); **to f. oneself from** *or* **of sth** se libérer de qch

freedom ['fri:dəm] *n* liberté *f*; **to have the f. to do sth** être libre de faire qch; **f. of information** libre accès *m* à l'information; **f. of speech/worship** liberté d'expression/ de culte; **to give sb the f. of the city** nommer qn citoyen(enne) d'honneur de la ville; **f. fighter** guérillero *m*, révolutionnaire *mf*

free-for-all ['fri:fərɔ:l] *n Fam* bagarre *f*

freehold ['fri:həʊld] *n Law* propriété *f* foncière perpétuelle et libre

freeholder ['fri:həʊldə(r)] *n* propriétaire *m* foncier (à perpétuité)

freelance ['fri:lɑ:ns] **1** *n* travailleur(euse) *m,f* indépendant(e)
2 *adj* indépendant(e), free-lance *inv*
3 *adv* **to work f.** travailler en indépendant(e) *ou* en free-lance
4 *vi* travailler en indépendant(e) *ou* en free-lance

freeloader ['fri:ləʊdə(r)] *n Fam* pique-assiette *mf inv*, parasite *m*

freely ['fri:lɪ] *adv (give)* sans compter; *(speak)* en toute liberté; *(spend)* libéralement; **f. available** *(for sale)* en vente libre; *(easy to get hold of)* qu'on peut se procurer facilement

freemason ['fri:meɪsən] *n* franc-maçon *m*

freemasonry ['fri:meɪsənrɪ] *n* franc-maçonnerie *f*

Freepost® ['fri:pəʊst] *n Br* ≃ correspondance-réponse *f*

free-range ['fri:'reɪndʒ] *adj* de ferme

freestyle ['fri:staɪl] *n (in swimming)* nage *f* libre

freethinker ['fri:θɪŋkə(r)] *n* libre-penseur(euse) *m,f*

freeway ['fri:weɪ] *n Am* autoroute *f*

freewheel ['fri:'wi:l] *vi (on bicycle)* être en roue libre; *(in car)* rouler au point mort

freeze [fri:z] **1** *n (in weather)* gel *m*, gelée *f*; **price/wage f.** gel des prix/salaires
2 *vt (pt froze* [frəʊz], *pp frozen* ['frəʊzən]) *(food)* congeler; *(prices, assets)* geler; **to be frozen to death** être mort(e) de froid

3 *vi* (**a**) *(of weather)* **it's freezing** *(below zero)* il gèle; *Fig (very cold)* on gèle (**b**) *(of liquid, food)* geler; **to f. to death** mourir de froid; *Fam* **I'm freezing** je suis gelé (**c**) *(stand still)* s'arrêter net, se figer; **f.!** ne bougez plus!
▸ **freeze out** *vt sep Fam* **to f. sb out** *(of conversation, deal)* exclure qn; *Com* **to f. out the competition** évincer les concurrents
▸ **freeze over** *vi (of pond, river)* geler
▸ **freeze up** *vi (of pond, mechanism)* geler

freeze-dried ['fri:z'draɪd] *adj (coffee, herbs)* lyophilisé(e)

freeze-frame ['fri:z'freɪm] *n Cin* arrêt *m* sur image

freezer ['fri:zə(r)] *n* congélateur *m*; *(ice-box)* freezer *m*

freezing ['fri:zɪŋ] *adj* **f.** (**cold**) *(room, weather, temperature)* glacial(e); *(water)* glacé(e); **it's f. cold in here** on meurt de froid ici

freight [freɪt] *Com* **1** *n (transport)* fret *m*, transport *m* de marchandises; *(goods)* cargaison *f*; *(price)* prix *m* de transport; **f. train** train *m* de marchandises
2 *vt (goods)* transporter

freighter ['freɪtə(r)] *n (ship)* cargo *m*

French [frentʃ] **1** *n (language)* français *m*; *Hum* **pardon my F.** *(after swearing)* excusez mon langage; **F. class/ teacher** classe *f*/professeur *m* de français
2 *npl* **the F.** *(people)* les Français *mpl*
3 *adj* français(e); **F. fries** frites *fpl*; **F. horn** cor *m* d'harmonie; **F. kiss** baiser *m* avec la langue; *Br Old-fashioned* **F. letter** capote *f* anglaise; **F. loaf** *or* **stick** baguette *f*; **F. Polynesia** la Polynésie Française; **F. window** porte-fenêtre *f*

Frenchman ['frentʃmən] *n* Français *m*

French-speaking ['frentʃ'spi:kɪŋ] *adj* francophone

Frenchwoman ['frentʃwʊmən] *n* Française *f*

frenetic [frə'netɪk] *adj* frénétique

frenzied ['frenzɪd] *adj (person)* affolé(e); *(attack)* déchaîné(e); *(activity)* frénétique; **f. with rage/worry** fou (folle) de rage/d'inquiétude

frenzy ['frenzɪ] *(pl frenzies) n* frénésie *f*, folie *f*; **to work oneself into a f.** se mettre dans tous ses états

frequency ['fri:kwənsɪ] *(pl frequencies) n* fréquence *f*; **f. band** bande *f* de fréquences

frequent 1 *adj* ['fri:kwənt] fréquent(e); **it's a f. occurrence** cela se produit souvent
2 *vt* [frɪ'kwent] fréquenter

frequently ['fri:kwəntlɪ] *adv* fréquemment, souvent

fresco ['freskəʊ] *(pl frescos or frescoes) n* fresque *f*

fresh [freʃ] **1** *adj* (**a**) *(food, news)* frais (fraîche); **to smell f.** sentir bon le frais; **to get some f. air** s'aérer; **f. water** *(not salty)* eau *f* douce; **it's still f. in my mind** c'est encore frais dans ma mémoire; **as f. as a daisy** frais et dispos *inv* (**b**) *(page, attempt, drink)* nouveau(elle) *(before noun)*; **to make a f. start** recommencer à zéro (**c**) *(original) (approach, writing)* nouveau(elle), original(e) (**d**) *Am Fam (cheeky)* insolent(e); **to get f. with sb** *(sexually)* faire des avances à qn
2 *adv* **f. from** *(school, university)* frais émoulu(e) de; **we're f. out of olives** nous n'avons plus d'olives

freshen ['freʃən] *vi (of wind, weather)* rafraîchir
▸ **freshen up** *vi (wash)* faire un brin de toilette

fresher ['freʃər] *n Br Univ* étudiant(e) *m,f* de première année; **freshers' week** = semaine d'orientation précédant la rentrée universitaire pour les nouveaux étudiants

freshly ['freʃlɪ] *adv* fraîchement; **f. baked** sortant du four; **f. made** qui vient d'être fait

freshman ['freʃmən] *n Am Univ* étudiant(e) *m,f* de première année

freshness ['freʃnɪs] n (**a**) (of food) fraîcheur f (**b**) (originality) nouveauté f, originalité f
freshwater ['freʃwɔːtə(r)] adj (fish) d'eau douce
fret [fret] (pt & pp **fretted**) vi (worry) s'inquiéter, se tourmenter
fretful ['fretfʊl] adj inquiet(ète)
Freudian ['frɔɪdɪən] adj freudien(enne); F. **slip** lapsus m
FRG [efɑːˈdʒiː] n Formerly (abbr **Federal Republic of Germany**) RFA f
Fri (abbr **Friday**) vendredi
friar ['fraɪə(r)] n religieux m, moine m
fricassee [frɪkəˈsiː] n fricassée f
friction ['frɪkʃən] n also Fig friction f
Friday ['fraɪdɪ] n vendredi m; see also **Saturday**
fridge [frɪdʒ] n frigo m
fridge-freezer ['frɪdʒˈfriːzə(r)] n frigo m avec congélateur
fried [fraɪd] adj frit(e)
friend [frend] n ami(e) m,f; **to be friends with sb** être ami avec qn; **to make friends with sb** devenir ami avec qn, **that's what friends are for** c'est à ça que servent les amis; **we're just good friends** nous sommes bons amis, c'est tout; **he's no f.** of mine ce n'est pas un ami; **to have friends in high places** avoir des amis bien placés; **to be a f.** of the arts être un défenseur des beaux-arts; Prov a f. in need is a f. indeed c'est dans le besoin que l'on connaît ses amis
friendless ['frendlɪs] adj (person) sans amis; (childhood) solitaire
friendly ['frendlɪ] **1** n Sp match m amical
2 adj amical(e); **f. advice** conseils mpl d'ami; **a f. nation** un pays ami; **to be f. with sb** être ami(e) avec qn; **to be on f. terms with sb** être en bons termes avec qn; Mil f. **fire** tirs mpl provenant de son propre camp
friendship ['frendʃɪp] n amitié f
fries [fraɪz] npl (**French**) f. frites fpl
frieze [friːz] n Art & Archit frise f
fright [fraɪt] n peur f, effroi m; **to take f.** prendre peur; **to get a f.** avoir peur; **to give sb a f.** faire peur à qn; Fam **to look a f.** être à faire peur
frighten ['fraɪtən] **1** vt effrayer, faire peur à; **to f. sb into doing sth** faire peur à qn jusqu'à ce qu'il fasse qch; Fam **to f. the life** or **the wits out of sb** rendre qn fou (folle) de peur
2 vi I **don't f. easily** je ne me laisse pas effrayer facilement
frightened ['fraɪtənd] adj apeuré(e); **to be f. (of)** avoir peur (de); **to be f.** to do sth avoir peur de faire qch
frightening ['fraɪtənɪŋ] adj effrayant(e)
frightful ['fraɪtfʊl] adj épouvantable, affreux(euse)
frightfully ['fraɪtfʊlɪ] adv terriblement
frigid ['frɪdʒɪd] adj (sexually) frigide; (smile, atmosphere) glacial(e)
frill [frɪl] n volant m; Fig with **no frills** (ceremony) sans chichis; (holiday) rudimentaire
frilly ['frɪlɪ] adj à volants
fringe [frɪndʒ] n (**a**) (of hair, on clothes, lampshade) frange f (**b**) (edge) (of forest) lisière f; (of town) abords mpl; **on the fringes of society** en marge de la société; **f. benefits** avantages mpl divers; Pol f. **group** groupuscule m; **f. theatre** théâtre m alternatif
frisk [frɪsk] **1** vt (search) fouiller
2 vi to f. **about** gambader
frisky ['frɪskɪ] adj (person) plein(e) d'entrain; (horse) nerveux(euse)

fritter ['frɪtə(r)] n Culin beignet m
▸ **fritter away** vt sep gaspiller
frivolity [frɪˈvɒlɪtɪ] (pl **frivolities**) n frivolité f
frivolous ['frɪvələs] adj frivole; (remark) futile
frizzy ['frɪzɪ] adj crépu(e)
fro [frəʊ] adv **to go to and f.** aller et venir
frock [frɒk] n (dress) robe f; f. **coat** redingote f
frog [frɒg] n (**a**) (animal) grenouille f; Fam **to have a f. in one's throat** avoir un chat dans la gorge (**b**) Br Fam (French person) = terme xénophobe, souvent humoristique, désignant un Français
frogman ['frɒgmən] n homme-grenouille m
frogmarch ['frɒgmɑːtʃ] vt emmener de force
frogspawn ['frɒgspɔːn] n œufs mpl de grenouille
frolic ['frɒlɪk] (pt & pp **frolicked**) vi s'ébattre
from [frɒm, unstressed frəm] prep (**a**) (expressing place of origin) de; **where are you f.?, where do you come f.?** d'où êtes-vous?, d'où venez-vous?; **she's f. Portugal** elle vient du Portugal; f. **New York to Los Angeles** de New York à Los Angeles; **the train f. Saratoga** le train de Saratoga; **10 km f. Nice** à 10 km de Nice
(**b**) (expressing time) à partir de; **f. tomorrow** à partir de demain; **f. then (on)** depuis ce jour-là; **f. the beginning** dès le début; **f. six to seven o'clock** de six heures à sept heures; **f. morning to** or **till night** du matin au soir; **five years f. now** dans cinq ans; **blind f. birth** aveugle de naissance
(**c**) (expressing range, change) f. … to… de… à…; **children f. seven to nine years** les enfants de sept à neuf ans; **wine f. $10 a bottle** du vin à partir de 10 dollars la bouteille
(**d**) (expressing source) de; **to buy sth f. sb** acheter qch à qn; **to drink f. a cup** boire dans une tasse; **a quotation f. the Bible** une citation tirée de la Bible; **made f. rubber** en caoutchouc
(**e**) (expressing removal) de; **to take sth f. sb** prendre qch à qn; **he was banned f. the club** il a été exclu du club
(**f**) (on the basis of) f. **what I heard/saw…** d'après ce que j'ai entendu/vu…

frond [frɒnd] n (of fern) fronde f; (of palm) feuille f
front [frʌnt] **1** n (**a**) (not back) devant m; (of car, plane, boat) avant m; (of building) façade f; **on the f. of the book** sur la couverture du livre; **at the f. of the book** au début du livre; **I sat in (the) f.** (of car) j'étais assis devant; Br **the f.** (at seaside) le front de mer, la promenade
(**b**) (outward appearance) **his kindness is only a f.** sa gentillesse n'est que une façade; **the company is a f. for their arms dealing** l'entreprise sert de couverture à leur trafic d'armes; **f. man** (of TV, radio programme) présentateur m; (of pop group, organization) leader m
(**c**) Mil, Pol & Met front m; Fig **on all fronts** sur tous les fronts; **f. warm/cold f.** front chaud/froid
(**d**) **in f.** devant; (in race, contest) en tête; **in f. of** devant
(**e**) Fam **to pay up f.** payer d'avance; **to be up f. about sth** être franc (franche) au sujet de qch
2 adj de devant; Br Pol f. **bench** = le banc des ministres et celui du cabinet fantôme; f. **door** porte f d'entrée; Mil f. **line** front m; f. **cover** couverture f; f. **page** (of newspaper) première page f; f. **room** (lounge) salon m; f. **row** premier rang m; **to have a f.-row seat** (in theatre) être (assis(e)) au premier rang; Fig être aux premières loges; f. **seat** (in car) siège m avant; f. **teeth** dents fpl de devant; f. **view** vue f de face
3 vt (organization, pop group) être à la tête de; (government) diriger; (TV programme) présenter
4 vi (of building) **the house fronts onto the river** la maison donne sur le fleuve

frontage ['frʌntɪdʒ] *n (of building)* façade *f*; *(of shop)* devanture *f*

frontal ['frʌntəl] *adj Anat* frontal(e); *Mil (attack)* de front

frontier ['frʌntɪə(r)] *n* frontière *f*; **the frontiers** *(of knowledge, science)* les limites *fpl*; **f. guard** garde-frontière *m*; **f. town** ville *f* frontalière

frontispiece ['frʌntɪspiːs] *n* frontispice *m*

frontrunner ['frʌntrʌnə(r)] *n* favori(ite) *m,f*

frost [frɒst] *n* gel *m*; **there was a f.** il a gelé

▸ **frost over, frost up** *vi (of window)* se couvrir de givre

frostbite ['frɒstbaɪt] *n* gelure *f*

frostbitten ['frɒstbɪtən] *adj* gelé(e)

frosted ['frɒstɪd] *adj (glass)* dépoli(e)

frosting ['frɒstɪŋ] *n Am (on cake)* glaçage *m*

frosty ['frɒstɪ] *adj (night, air)* glacé(e); *Fig (welcome, smile)* glacial(e)

froth [frɒθ] **1** *n (on beer, cappuccino)* mousse *f*; *(on waves)* écume *f*
2 *vi (of liquid)* mousser; **he was frothing at the mouth** il bavait; *(with anger)* il écumait de rage

frothy ['frɒθɪ] *adj (beer, cappuccino)* mousseux(euse)

frown [fraʊn] **1** *n* froncement *m* de sourcils
2 *vi* froncer les sourcils; **to f. at sb** regarder qn en fronçant les sourcils

▸ **frown on, frown upon** *vt insep (disapprove of)* désapprouver

froze [frəʊz] *pt of* freeze

frozen ['frəʊzən] **1** *adj (food)* congelé(e), surgelé(e); *(lake, hands)* gelé(e)
2 *pp of* freeze

fructose ['frʌktəʊs] *n* fructose *f*

frugal ['fruːɡəl] *adj* frugal(e)

fruit [fruːt] *n* fruit *m*; **some f.** *(several pieces)* des fruits; *(one piece)* un fruit; *Fig* **to bear f.** *(of plan, investment)* porter ses fruits; **fruits of the forest** fruits des bois; **f. bowl** coupe *f* à fruits; **f. juice** jus *m* de fruit; *Br* **f. machine** machine *f* à sous; **f. salad** salade *f* de fruits; **f. tree** arbre *m* fruitier

fruitcake ['fruːtkeɪk] *n* cake *m*; *Fam (mad person)* fou (folle) *m,f*

fruitful ['fruːtfʊl] *adj (discussion)* fructueux(euse)

fruition [fruːˈɪʃən] *n* to come to f. *(of plan, effort)* porter ses fruits

fruitless ['fruːtlɪs] *adj (attempt, search, trip)* infructueux(euse)

fruity ['fruːtɪ] *adj (taste)* fruité(e); *Fam (voice)* étoffé(e)

frump [frʌmp] *n Fam* **she's a f.** elle fait mémère

frumpish ['frʌmpɪʃ], **frumpy** ['frʌmpɪ] *adj Fam* **to be f.** faire mémère

frustrate [frʌsˈtreɪt] *vt (person)* décevoir, frustrer; *(plan)* contrarier

frustrated [frʌsˈtreɪtɪd] *adj* frustré(e)

frustrating [frʌsˈtreɪtɪŋ] *adj* frustrant(e)

frustration [frʌsˈtreɪʃən] *n* frustration *f*

fry [fraɪ] *(pt & pp* fried*)* **1** *vt* faire frire
2 *vi* frire

frying pan ['fraɪɪŋpæn] *n* poêle *f* (à frire); **to jump out of the f. into the fire** tomber de Charybde en Scylla

ft *(abbr* foot *or* feet*)* p., pd.

FTP [eftiːˈpiː] *n Comptr (abbr* File Transfer Protocol*)* FTP

fuchsia ['fjuːʃə] *n* fuchsia *m*

fuck [fʌk] *Vulg* **1** *n (intercourse)* baise *f*; **to have a f.** baiser; **I don't give a f.** j'en ai rien à foutre; **what the f. do you** think you're doing? putain, mais qu'est-ce que tu fous?; **f. knows why he came!** mais pourquoi il est venu, bordel!; **f.! bordel!, merde!**
2 *vt* baiser; **f. it!** et merde!; **f. you!** va te faire foutre!
3 *vi* baiser

▸ **fuck about, fuck around** *vi Vulg (play the fool)* déconner; *(waste time)* glander

▸ **fuck off** *vi Vulg (go away)* se casser; **f. off!** va te faire foutre!

fuck-all ['fʌkˈɔːl] *n Vulg* **he's done f. this week** il a fait que dalle cette semaine; **she knows f. about it** elle en sait que dalle

fucked ['fʌkt] *adj Vulg (broken)* foutu(e)

fucking ['fʌkɪŋ] *Vulg* **1** *adj* **he's a f. idiot!** c'est un connard!; **where's the f. car?** où est cette putain de voiture?
2 *adv (cold, brilliant, stupid)* foutrement

fuddy-duddy ['fʌdɪdʌdɪ] *(pl* fuddy-duddies*)* *n* an old f. *(man)* un vieux schnock; *(woman)* une vieille mémère

fudge [fʌdʒ] **1** *n (sweet)* caramel *m* mou
2 *vt* **f. an issue** éluder une question

fuel ['fjʊəl] **1** *n* combustible *m*; *(for engine)* carburant *m*; *Fig* **to add f. to the flames** jeter de l'huile sur le feu; **f. consumption** *(of car)* consommation *f* (d'essence); **f. gauge** jauge *f* de carburant; **f. injection** injection *f* de carburant; **f. pump** pompe *f* d'alimentation; **f. tank** réservoir *m*
2 *vt (pt & pp* fuelled, *Am* fueled*)* *Fig (hatred)* attiser; *(speculation)* nourrir

fug [fʌɡ] *n Br Fam* odeur *f* de renfermé; *(in smoke-filled room)* atmosphère *f* enfumée

fugitive ['fjuːdʒɪtɪv] *n* fugitif(ive) *m,f*

fugue [fjuːɡ] *n Mus* fugue *f*

fulcrum ['fʌlkrəm] *n* pivot *m*

fulfil, *Am* **fulfill** [fʊlˈfɪl] *(pt & pp* fulfilled*)* *vt (plan, ambition)* réaliser; *(condition, duty)* remplir; *(need)* répondre à; **to feel fulfilled** *(of person)* se sentir épanoui(e)

fulfilment, *Am* **fulfillment** [fʊlˈfɪlmənt] *n (of plan, condition)* réalisation *f*; *(satisfaction)* épanouissement *m*; **to find** *or* **achieve f.** s'épanouir

full [fʊl] **1** *adj* **(a)** *(container)* plein(e) *(of* de); *(hotel, bus, car park)* complet(ète); *(day)* chargé(e); **to be f. of praise for sb** ne pas tarir d'éloges sur qn; **to be f. of oneself** être imbu(e) de soi-même; **f. to the brim** plein à ras bords; **don't speak with your mouth f.!** ne parle pas la bouche pleine!; **to be f. (up)** *(of person)* être rassasié(e); **on a f. stomach** le ventre plein
(b) *(complete) (amount)* intégral(e); *(explanation, recovery)* complet(ète); *(support)* total(e); **to take f. responsibility for sth** assumer l'entière responsabilité de qch; **she gave me the f. story** elle m'a raconté toute l'histoire; **the f. horror** toute l'horreur; **to lead a f. life** avoir une vie bien remplie; **I waited two f. hours** *or* **a f. two hours** j'ai attendu deux bonnes heures; **in f. flow** *(speaker)* en plein discours; **to be in f. swing** *(of party, sales)* battre son plein; **in f. view** de vos yeux de; **f. board** pension *f* complète; *Phot* **in f. colour** en couleur; **f. fare** plein tarif *m*; **f. house** *(in theatre)* salle *f* comble; *(in cards)* main *f* pleine; **f. moon** pleine lune *f*; **f. name** nom *m* et prénom *m*; **f. price** plein tarif; **f. stop** *(punctuation)* point *m* final; **f. time** *(in sport)* fin *f* de match
(c) *(maximum)* **at f. speed** à toute vitesse; **at f. stretch** *(work)* à plein rendement; **to get f. marks** *(in exam)* obtenir le maximum de points
(d) *(skirt, sleeve)* bouffant(e); **a f. figure** *(of woman)* un corps épanoui; **f. lips** lèvres *fpl* pleines
2 *adv* **you know f. well that...** tu sais parfaitement que...; **it hit him f. in the face** il a reçu le coup en pleine figure

3 *n* **to pay in f.** payer intégralement; **name in f.** nom et prénoms; **to live life to the f.** vivre pleinement

fullback ['fʊlbæk] *n (in football, rugby)* arrière *m*

full-blown ['fʊl'bləʊn] *adj (row)* vrai(e); *(crisis)* de grande envergure; **to have f. AIDS** avoir le sida

full-bodied ['fʊl'bɒdɪd] *adj (wine)* corsé(e)

full-grown ['fʊl'grəʊn] *adj* adulte

full-length ['fʊl'leŋθ] *adj (portrait, mirror)* en pied; *(dress)* long (longue); **f. film** long métrage *m*

fullness ['fʊlnɪs] *n* **in the f. of time** avec le temps

full-page ['fʊl'peɪdʒ] *adj (advert, illustration)* pleine page

full-scale ['fʊl'skeɪl] *adj* **(a)** *(model)* grandeur nature *inv* **(b)** *(search)* de grande envergure; **f. war** guerre *f* généralisée

full-time ['fʊl'taɪm] *adj & adv* à temps complet, à plein temps; *Fig* **looking after the baby is a f. job** s'occuper du bébé ne laisse pas une minute de libre; **to be in f. employment** travailler à plein temps

full-timer ['fʊl'taɪmər] *n* travailleur(euse) *m,f* à temps complet *ou* à plein temps

fully ['fʊlɪ] *adv* **(a)** *(completely)* complètement, entièrement; *(understand, be aware)* parfaitement, tout à fait, **f. booked** complet(ète); **f. grown** adulte **(b)** *(at least)* **it takes f. two hours** cela prend au moins deux heures

fully-fledged ['fʊlɪ'fledʒd] *adj Br Fig* qualifié(e)

fulminate ['fʌlmɪneɪt] *vi* fulminer **(against** contre)

fulness [fʌlnɪs] = **fullness**

fulsome ['fʊlsəm] *adj* enthousiaste; **to be f. in one's praise or sb/sth** porter qn/qch aux nues

fumble ['fʌmbəl] **1** *vt (ball)* mal attraper **2** *vi* fouiller; **to f. for sth** fouiller pour trouver qch; *(in dark)* tâtonner pour trouver qch; **to f. for words** chercher ses mots, **he fumbled with the switch** il a essayé maladroitement de faire fonctionner l'interrupteur

fume [fjuːm] **1** *npl* **fumes** émanations *fpl*; *(from car exhaust)* gaz *mpl* d'échappement; **petrol fumes** vapeurs *fpl* d'essence
2 *vi* **(a)** *(give off fumes)* fumer **(b)** *(be angry)* **to be fuming** rager

fumigate ['fjuːmɪgeɪt] *vt* désinfecter par fumigation

fun [fʌn] *n* plaisir *m*; **to have f.** s'amuser; **it's/he's great f.** c'est/il est très amusant; **there'll be f. and games** *(trouble)* il va y avoir du grabuge; **it's no f. having to walk home in the rain** ce n'est pas drôle de devoir rentrer à pied sous la pluie; **to make f. of** se moquer de; **to say sth in f.** dire qch pour rire ou en plaisantant; **to do sth for f. or for the f. of it** faire qch pour s'amuser; *Ironic* **what f.!** c'est drôle!

function ['fʌŋkʃən] **1** *n* **(a)** *(role)* & *Math* fonction *f*; *Comptr* **f. key** touche *f* de fonction **(b)** *(party)* réception *f*; *(public)* cérémonie *f*
2 *vi* fonctionner; **to f. as** jouer le rôle de, faire fonction de

functional ['fʌŋkʃənəl] *adj* **(a)** *(practical)* fonctionnel(elle) **(b)** *(operational)* opérationnel(elle)

functionary ['fʌŋkʃənərɪ] *(pl* **functionaries)** *n* fonctionnaire *mf*

fund [fʌnd] **1** *n* **(a)** *(of money)* fonds *m*; **funds** fonds *mpl*, capitaux *mpl*; **to be in funds** être en fonds; *Fin* **f. manager** gestionnaire *mf* de fonds **(b)** *(of information)* mine *f*
2 *vt* financer

fundamental [fʌndə'mentəl] **1** *n* **fundamentals** principes *mpl*, fondements *mpl*
2 *adj* fondamental(e), essentiel(elle); **her f. honesty** sa profonde honnêteté

fundamentalist [fʌndə'mentəlɪst] *n & adj (religious)* intégriste *mf*, fondamentaliste *mf*

fundamentally [fʌndə'mentəlɪ] *adv* fondamentalement

funding ['fʌndɪŋ] *n* financement *m*

fundraiser ['fʌndreɪzə(r)] *n (person)* collecteur(trice) *m,f* de fonds; *(event)* = projet organisé pour collecter des fonds

funeral ['fjuːnərəl] *n* enterrement *m*; *(formal)* funérailles *fpl*, obsèques *fpl*; *Fam* **that's your f.!** c'est ton problème!; **f. director** entrepreneur *m* de pompes funèbres; **f. home** établissement *m* de pompes funèbres; *Mus* **f. march** marche *f* funèbre; *Br* **f. parlour** établissement *m* de pompes funèbres; **f. procession** cortège *m* funèbre; **f. service** service *m* funèbre

funfair ['fʌnfeə(r)] *n* fête *f* foraine

fungal ['fʌŋgəl] *adj* **f. infection** mycose *f*

fungus ['fʌŋgəs] *(pl* **fungi** ['fʌŋgaɪ]) *n (mushroom, toadstool)* champignon *m*; *(on walls)* moisissure *f*; *Med* fongus *m*

funk [fʌŋk] *n* **(a)** *Fam Old-fashioned (fright)* **to be in a f.** avoir une peur bleue **(b)** *(music)* funk *m*

funky ['fʌŋkɪ] *adj very Fam (clothing, suggestion, music)* cool *inv*

funnel ['fʌnəl] **1** *n* **(a)** *(of locomotive, steamship)* cheminée *f* **(b)** *(for filling)* entonnoir *m*
2 *vt (pt & pp* **funnelled,** *Am* **funneled)** *(direct) (funds)* acheminer **(to** vers); **to f. liquid into sth** verser un liquide dans qch

funnily ['fʌnɪlɪ] *adv (strangely)* bizarrement; **f. enough,...** bizarrement,...

funny ['fʌnɪ] *adj* **(a)** *(amusing)* drôle, amusant(e); **are you trying to be f.?** tu te crois drôle?, *Ironic* **v. funny!** très drôle!; *Br Fam* **f. bone** petit juif *m* **(b)** *(strange)* bizarre, drôle; **I feel a bit f.** *(ill)* je me sens un peu bizarre; **to taste/smell f.** avoir un drôle de goût/une drôle d'odeur; **f.. I thought I'd locked the door** c'est curieux, je croyais avoir fermé la porte à clé; **(it's) f. you should say that** c'est drôle que tu dises ça, *Fam* **he's a bit f. in the head** il est un peu bizarre; *Fam* **I don't want any f. business!** et pas de blagues!; *Fam* **f. farm** maison *f* de fous

fur [fɜː(r)] *n* **(a)** *(hair)* poils *mpl*; *(animal skin)* fourrure *f*; *Fig* **the f. was flying** ça chauffait; **f. coat** manteau *m* de fourrure; **f. trade** commerce *m* de fourrures **(b)** *(in kettle, boiler)* tartre *m*

furious ['fjʊərɪəs] *adj (person)* furieux(euse) **(with** contre); *(quarrel, storm)* violent(e); **to be f. with oneself** être en colère contre soi-même; **at a f. speed** à une vitesse folle

furiously ['fjʊərɪəslɪ] *adv* furieusement; *(work, write)* frénétiquement

furlong ['fɜːlɒŋ] *n* = 201 m, furlong *m*

furnace ['fɜːnɪs] *n* fourneau *m*; *Fig* **it's like a f. in here!** quelle fournaise!

furnish ['fɜːnɪʃ] *vt* **(a)** *(house, flat)* meubler **(b)** *Formal (provide)* fournir; **to f. sb with sth** fournir qch à qn

furnished ['fɜːnɪʃd] *adj (flat, room)* meublé(e); **f. accommodation** *(uncountable)* logements *mpl* meublés

furnishings ['fɜːnɪʃɪŋz] *npl* ameublement *m*

furniture ['fɜːnɪtʃə(r)] *n* meubles *mpl*, mobilier *m*; **a piece of f.** un meuble; **f. polish** encaustique *f* pour les meubles; **f. remover** déménageur *m*; **f. shop** magasin *m* de meubles *ou* d'ameublement; **f. van** camion *m* de déménagement

furore, *Am* **furor** ['fjʊərɔː(r)] *n (uproar)* scandale *m*

furrow ['fʌrəʊ] **1** *n (in field)* sillon *m*; *(on face)* ride *f* profonde
2 *vt Lit* **his brow was furrowed with worry** son front était plissé par l'inquiétude

furry ['fɜːrɪ] *adj (animal)* à poil; **f. toy** peluche *f*; **to have a f. tongue** avoir la langue chargée

further ['fɜːðə(r)] *(comparative of* **far)** **1** *adj* **(a)** *(more distant)* plus loin **(b)** *(additional)* supplémentaire; **upon f. consideration** après plus ample réflexion; **until f. notice** jusqu'à nouvel ordre; **without f. delay** sans plus attendre; *Br* **f. education** = enseignement supérieur dispensé par un établissement autre qu'une université **2** *adv* **(a)** *(in general)* plus loin; **this mustn't go any f.** *(don't tell anyone else)* il faut que cela reste entre nous; **I didn't question him any f.** je ne l'ai pas interrogé davantage; **that doesn't get us much f.** ça ne nous avance pas beaucoup; **f. back** *(in space)* plus loin en arrière; *(in time)* plus loin dans le temps; **f. on** *(in space)* plus loin; *(in time)* plus tard **(b)** *Formal (moreover)* de plus; **f. to your letter…** suite à votre lettre… **3** *vt (cause, career)* faire avancer

furthermore [fɜːðə'mɔː(r)] *adv Formal* en outre, de plus

furthermost ['fɜːðəmaʊst] *adj Lit* le (la) plus reculé(e)

furthest ['fɜːðɪst] *(superlative of* **far)** **1** *adj* le (la) plus éloigné(e) **2** *adv* le plus loin

furtive ['fɜːtɪv] *adj* sournois(e)

fury ['fjʊərɪ] *n (of person, storm)* fureur *f*; **to be in a f.** *(of person)* être furieux(euse); *Fam* **to work like f.** travailler avec acharnement

fuse, *Am* **fuze** [fjuːz] **1** *n* **(a)** *(for plug)* fusible *f*; **f. box** boîte *f* à fusibles; **f. wire** fusible *m* **(b)** *(for dynamite)* détonateur *m*; *(in bomb)* amorce *f*; *Fam Fig* **to have a short f.** *(be short-tempered)* se mettre facilement en colère **2** *vt (melt)* fondre; *(join)* fusionner **3** *vi* **(a)** *(of metals)* fondre; **to f. together** fusionner **(b)** *(of organizations, parties)* fusionner **(c)** *Br Elec* **the lights have fused** les plombs ont sauté

fused, *Am* **fuzed** [fjuːzd] *adj Elec (plug, appliance)* muni(e) d'un fusible

fuselage ['fjuːzəlɑːʒ] *n* fuselage *m*

fusillade [fjuːzɪ'leɪd] *n (of bullets)* fusillade *f*; *Fig (of criticism, questions)* avalanche *f*

fusion ['fjuːʒən] *n* fusion *f*

fuss [fʌs] **1** *n* histoires *fpl*; **what's all the f. about?** qu'est-ce que c'est que toutes ces histoires?; **I don't want any f.** pas de cérémonie; **a lot of f. about** *or* **over nothing** beaucoup d'histoires pour pas grand-chose; **I don't see what all the f. is about** je ne vois pas pourquoi on en fait un tel cas; **to kick up** *or* **make a f.** faire des histoires; **to make a f. of sb** être aux petits soins pour qn **3** *vi* faire des histoires; **to f. about** s'activer

fusspot ['fʌspɒt] *n Fam* chichiteux(euse) *m,f*

fussy ['fʌsɪ] *adj* **(a)** *(person)* difficile, exigeant(e); **I'm not f.** *(I don't mind)* ça m'est égal **(b)** *(dress, décor)* surchargé(e) *f* futile

futile ['fjuːtaɪl] *adj (attempt, protest)* vain(e); *(remark, suggestion)* futile

futility [fjuː'tɪlɪtɪ] *n* futilité *f*

futon ['fuːtɒn] *n* futon *m*

future ['fjuːtʃə(r)] **1** *n* **(a)** *(in time)* avenir *m*; **in (the) f.** à l'avenir; **in the near/distant f.** dans un avenir proche/lointain; **she's got a job with a (good) f.** elle a une situation pleine d'avenir **(b)** *Fin* **futures** opérations *fpl* à terme **(c)** *Gram* futur *m*; **the f. perfect** le futur antérieur **2** *adj* futur(e); **at some f. date** à une date ultérieure; **for f. reference** à titre d'information

futuristic ['fjuːtʃə'rɪstɪk] *adj* futuriste

fuze, fuzed *Am* = fuse, fused

fuzz [fʌz] *n* **(a)** *(on fabric)* peluches *fpl*; *(on peach, skin)* duvet *m* **(b)** *Fam* **the f.** *(police)* les flics *mpl*

fuzzy ['fʌzɪ] *adj (outline, photo)* flou(e); *(idea)* vague; *(hair)* crépu(e); **f. logic** logique *f* floue

G

G, g [dʒiː] n **(a)** (letter) G, g m inv **(b)** Mus sol m

g (abbr **gramme**) gr

gab [gæb] (pt & pp **gabbed**) vi Fam (talk) papoter; (gossip) jaser

gabardine [gæbə'diːn] n gabardine f

gabble ['gæbəl] **1** n a **g. of conversation** un bruit de conversation **2** vi (incoherently) bredouiller; **to g. on** papoter

gable ['geɪbəl] n pignon m; **g. end** (wall) pignon

Gabon ['gæbən] n le Gabon

Gabonese [gæbə'niːz] **1** n Gabonais(e) m,f **2** adj gabonais(e)

► gad about [gæd] (pt & pp **gadded**) vi Fam être en vadrouille

gadfly ['gædflaɪ] (pl **gadflies**) n (insect) taon m; Fig (person) casse-pieds mf inv

gadget ['gædʒɪt] n gadget m

Gaelic ['geɪlɪk, Scot 'gælɪk] **1** n gaélique m **2** adj gaélique

Gaels [geɪlz] npl **the G.** les Gaëls mpl

gaff [gæf] n **(a)** (in fishing) gaffe f **(b)** Br Fam (home) piaule f **(c)** Fam **to blow the g.** (on) vendre la mèche (à propos de)

gaffe [gæf] n (blunder) gaffe f

gaffer ['gæfə(r)] n Br Fam (boss) chef m

gag [gæg] **1** n **(a)** (on mouth) bâillon m **(b)** Fam (joke) blague f **2** vt (pt & pp **gagged**) (person) bâillonner; Fig (media, opposition) museler **3** vi (retch) avoir des haut-le-cœur

gaga ['gɑːgɑː] adj Fam gâteux(euse), gaga inv

gage Am = **gauge**

gaggle ['gægəl] n also Fig troupeau m

gaiety ['geɪətɪ] n gaieté f

gaily ['geɪlɪ] adv (happily) joyeusement; (laugh) de bon cœur; **g. coloured** aux couleurs gaies

gain [geɪn] **1** n **(a)** (profit) gain m, profit m; **for personal g.** par intérêt personnel **(b)** (increase) augmentation f (**in** de); Fin (on stock market) hausse f **2** vt **(a)** (advantage, degree) obtenir; (victory, prize) remporter; (reputation, experience) acquérir; (sympathy, respect) gagner; **to g. entrance (to)** entrer (dans); (of burglar) s'introduire (dans) **(b)** (increase) **to g. weight/ speed** prendre du poids/de la vitesse; also Fig **to g. ground on** gagner du terrain sur; **to g. time** gagner du temps **3** vi **(a)** (benefit) **to g. by sth** bénéficier de qch **(b)** (increase) **to g. in confidence** gagner de l'assurance; **to g. in popularity** devenir populaire **(c)** (of clock) avancer

► gain on vt insep also Fig gagner du terrain sur

gainful ['geɪnfʊl] adj **g. employment** un emploi rémunéré

gainfully ['geɪnfʊlɪ] adv **to be g. employed** avoir un emploi rémunéré

gainsay [geɪn'seɪ] (pt & pp **gainsaid** [geɪn'sed]) vt Formal contredire; **there's no gainsaying her ability** son talent est indéniable

gait [geɪt] n démarche f

gal [gæl] n Fam Old-fashioned fille f

gala ['gɑːlə] n gala m; **swimming g.** compétition f de natation; **g. evening/performance** soirée f/représentation f de gala

galactic [gə'læktɪk] adj galactique

Galapagos [gə'læpəgəs] npl **the G. (Islands)** les (îles f)pl) Galapagos fpl

galaxy ['gæləksɪ] (pl **galaxies**) n galaxie f; Fig **a g. of stars** une pléiade de vedettes

gale [geɪl] n (strong wind) vent m violent; Fig **a g. of laughter** un éclat de rire

gall [gɔːl] **1** n **(a)** Med bile f; **g. bladder** vésicule f biliaire **(b)** (impudence) culot m **2** vt (annoy) irriter, exaspérer

gallant ['gælənt] adj (brave) brave, vaillant(e); (polite) galant(e)

gallantry ['gæləntrɪ] n (bravery) bravoure f; (politeness) galanterie f

galleon ['gælɪən] n galion m

gallery ['gælərɪ] (pl **galleries**) n **(a)** (art) **g.** (for sale) galerie f (d'art); (for exhibition) musée m **(b)** (in theatre) galerie f; **to play to the g.** (of politician) chercher à épater la galerie

galley ['gælɪ] (pl **galleys**) n **(a)** (ship) galère f; **g. slave** galérien m **(b)** (ship's kitchen) cuisine f **(c)** Typ **g. (proof)** placard m

Gallic ['gælɪk] adj (French) français(e); Hist (of Gaul) gaulois(e)

galling ['gɔːlɪŋ] adj humiliant(e)

► gallivant about, gallivant around ['gælɪvænt] vi être en vadrouille

gallon ['gælən] n (in UK) = 4,54 l, gallon m; (in US) = 3,78 l, gallon

gallop ['gæləp] **1** n galop m; **at a g.** au galop **2** vi galoper; Fig **to g. through one's work** expédier son travail

gallows ['gæləʊz] n potence f, gibet m; **g. humour** humour m noir

gallstone ['gɔːlstəʊn] n calcul m biliaire

galore [gə'lɔː(r)] adv Fam à profusion, à gogo

galvanize ['gælvənaɪz] vt also Fig galvaniser; **to g. sb into action** pousser qn à agir

galvanized ['gælvənaɪzd] adj galvanisé(e)

Gambia ['gæmbɪə] n **the G.** la Gambie

Gambian ['gæmbɪən] **1** n Gambien(enne) m,f **2** adj gambien(enne)

gambit ['gæmbɪt] n (in chess) gambit m; (in negotiation, diplomacy) tactique f; **opening g.** (in negotiation, diplomacy) manœuvre f d'approche

gamble ['gæmbəl] **1** n (risk) risque m; **to take a g.** prendre un risque **2** vt (money) jouer, parier **3** vi jouer (de l'argent); **to g. on the horses** jouer aux courses; **she gambled on nobody noticing** elle comptait sur le fait que personne ne s'en apercevrait

gambler ['gæmblə(r)] n joueur(euse) m,f

gambling ['gæmblɪŋ] n jeux mpl d'argent; **g. debts** dettes fpl de jeu; **g. den** tripot m

gambol ['gæmbəl] (pt & pp **gambolled,** Am **gamboled**) vi gambader

game [geɪm] **1** n (a) (activity, sport) jeu m; (of cards, pool, chess) partie f; (match) match m; **to have a g. of tennis/squash** faire une partie de tennis/squash; **g., set and match** (in tennis) jeu, set et match; **games** Br (school subject) sports mpl de plein air; (sporting event) jeux mpl; **politics is just a g. to them** pour eux, la politique n'est qu'un jeu; **g. show** jeu m télévisé (**b**) (skill) jeu m (**c**) (animals, food) gibier m; **g. reserve** réserve f de gibier (**d**) (idioms) **to play the g.** jouer le jeu; **two can play at that g.** on peut jouer à deux à ce petit jeu-là; **to beat sb at his own g.** battre qn à sa propre jeu; **to play games with sb** jouer avec qn; **to give the g. away** vendre la mèche; **what's his g.?** où veut-il en venir?; **I know what your g. is!** je sais bien où vous voulez en venir!; **the g.'s up for him** c'est fichu pour lui; **I've been in this g. a long time** ça fait longtemps que je suis de la partie; Br Fam **to be on the g.** (of prostitute) faire le trottoir **2** adj (**a**) (brave) courageux(euse); **to be g. (to do sth)** (willing) être partant(e) (pour faire qch) (**b**) Fam **a g. leg** une patte folle

gamekeeper ['geɪmkiːpə(r)] n garde-chasse m

gamely ['geɪmlɪ] adv courageusement

gamma ['gæmə] n gamma m; Phys **g. rays** rayons mpl gamma

gammon ['gæmən] n jambon m; **g. steak** = tranche épaisse de jambon (à servir grillée)

gammy ['gæmɪ] adj Br Fam **a g. leg** une patte folle

gamut ['gæmət] n gamme f; **to run the g. of** (emotions) passer par toute la gamme de

gamy ['geɪmɪ] adj (flavour) faisandé(e)

gander ['gændə(r)] n (**a**) (male goose) jars m (**b**) Br very Fam **to take a g. (at)** (look) jeter un coup d'œil (à)

gang [gæŋ] n (of criminals, children, friends) bande f; (of workers) équipe f

▸ **gang up** vi **to g. up on sb** se liguer contre qn; **to g. up with sb** s'allier avec qn

gangbang ['gæŋbæŋ] n very Fam (group rape) viol m collectif

Ganges ['gændʒiːz] n **the G.** le Gange

gangland ['gæŋlænd] n (underworld) milieu m, pègre f; **g. boss/killer** caïd m/tueur m du milieu; **g. killing** règlement m de compte (entre gangsters)

gangling ['gæŋglɪŋ] adj dégingandé(e)

ganglion ['gæŋglɪən] (pl **ganglia** ['gæŋglɪə]) n ganglion m

gangplank ['gæŋplæŋk] n passerelle f

gangrene ['gæŋgriːn] n gangrène f; **to have g.** avoir la gangrène

gangrenous ['gæŋgrɪnəs] adj gangreneux(euse)

gangster ['gæŋstə(r)] n gangster m

gangway ['gæŋweɪ] n (in theatre) allée f; (in plane, train) couloir m; (on ship) passerelle f; **g.!** dégagez, s'il vous plaît!

gannet ['gænɪt] n (bird) fou m de Bassan; Fig (greedy person) goinfre m,f

gantry ['gæntrɪ] (pl **gantries**) n (for crane, over railway) portique m; (for rocket) tour f de lancement

gaol [dʒeɪl] Br = **jail**

gap [gæp] n (**a**) (space) espace m; (narrower) interstice m; (in wall) brèche f; (in text) blanc m (**b**) (difference) (in age, ability) écart m; **the g. between rich and poor** le fossé entre les riches et les pauvres (**c**) (in knowledge) lacune f; **his death leaves a g. in all our lives** sa mort nous laisse un vide; Com **a g. in the market** un créneau (**d**) (in time) intervalle m (**e**) (mountain pass) col m

gape [geɪp] vi (**a**) (stare) rester bouche bée; **to g. at sb/sth** regarder qn/qch bouche bée (**b**) **to g. (open)** (of door, blouse) s'ouvrir tout(e) grand(e); (of wound, hole) être béant(e)

gaping ['geɪpɪŋ] adj béant(e)

garage ['gærɑːʒ, 'gærɪdʒ] n (for storing or repairing car) garage m; (petrol station) station-service f

garb [gɑːb] n Lit costume m

garbage ['gɑːbɪdʒ] n (**a**) Am (rubbish) ordures fpl; **g. can** poubelle f; **g. heap** tas m d'ordures; **g. man** éboueur m (**b**) (nonsense) âneries fpl; **to talk g.** dire n'importe quoi

garbled ['gɑːbəld] adj confus(e)

garden ['gɑːdən] **1** n jardin m; Fig **to lead sb up the garden path** faire marcher qn; **g. centre** jardinerie f; Br **g. flat** appartement m en rez-de-chaussée avec jardin; **g. furniture** meubles mpl de jardin; **g. party** réception f en plein air, garden-party f **2** vi jardiner, faire du jardinage

gardener ['gɑːdnə(r)] n jardinier(ère) m,f

gardening ['gɑːdnɪŋ] n jardinage m; **to do the g.** s'occuper du jardin

gargantuan [gɑː'gæntjʊən] adj gargantuesque

gargle ['gɑːgəl] vi se gargariser (**with** avec)

gargoyle ['gɑːgɔɪl] n gargouille f

garish ['geərɪʃ] adj (clothes) voyant(e); (taste) vulgaire; (colours) criard(e); (light) cru(e)

garland ['gɑːlənd] **1** n guirlande f **2** vt enguirlander (**with** de)

garlic ['gɑːlɪk] n ail m; **g. bread** = pain chaud au beurre d'ail; **g. butter** beurre m d'ail; **g. sausage** saucisson m à l'ail

garment ['gɑːmənt] n vêtement m

garnet ['gɑːnɪt] n grenat m

garnish ['gɑːnɪʃ] **1** n garniture f **2** vt garnir (**with** avec)

garret ['gærət] n mansarde f

garrison ['gærɪsən] **1** n garnison f; **g. duty** service m de garnison; **g. town** ville f de garnison **2** vt (troops) mettre en garnison

garrotte [gə'rɒt] **1** n garrot m **2** vt exécuter au garrot

garrulous ['gærʊləs] adj (person) loquace, bavard(e); (account, letter) verbeux(euse)

garter ['gɑːtə(r)] n jarretière f; Am g. belt porte-jarretelles m inv; g. snake couleuvre f

gas [gæs] **1** n (a) gaz m inv; Med (gaz) anesthétique m; g. bill note f de gaz; g. chamber chambre f à gaz; g. cooker cuisinière f à gaz; g. cylinder bouteille f de gaz; g. fire radiateur m à gaz; g. lamp lampe f à gaz; g. mask masque m à gaz (b) Am (gasoline) essence f; Fam to step on the g. appuyer sur le champignon; g. station station-service f; g. tank réservoir m (c) Fam (amusing situation) to have a g. rigoler; what a g.! quelle rigolade!
2 vt (pt & pp gassed) (person) asphyxier; (deliberately) gazer; to g. oneself se suicider au gaz
3 vi Fam (chat) jacasser

gasbag ['gæsbæg] n Fam (chatterbox) bavard(e) m,f; (boaster) vantard(e) m,f

gaseous ['gæsɪəs, 'geɪsɪəs] adj gazeux(euse)

gash [gæʃ] **1** n (in skin, wood) entaille f; (in metal) fente f
2 vt entailler

gasket ['gæskɪt] n (in engine) joint m de culasse; Fam to blow a g. piquer une colère

gasoline ['gæsəliːn] n Am essence f

gasometer [gæ'sɒmɪtə(r)] n gazomètre m

gasp [gɑːsp] **1** n (of surprise) sursaut m; to be at one's last g. être sur le point de rendre son dernier soupir
2 vi avoir le souffle coupé (with or in de); to make sb g. couper le souffle à qn; to g. for breath or for air haleter, suffoquer; Fam to be gasping for a cigarette/a drink mourir d'envie de fumer une cigarette/de boire un verre

gassy ['gæsɪ] adj gazeux(euse)

gastric ['gæstrɪk] adj gastrique; g. flu grippe f gastro-intestinale; g. juices sucs mpl gastriques; g. ulcer ulcère m à l'estomac

gastritis [gæs'traɪtɪs] n gastrite f; to have g. avoir une gastrite

gastro-enteritis [gæstrəʊentə'raɪtɪs] n gastro-entérite f; to have g. avoir une gastro-entérite

gastronomic [gæstrə'nɒmɪk] adj gastronomique

gastronomy [gæs'trɒnəmɪ] n gastronomie f

gasworks ['gæswɜːks] n usine f à gaz

gate [geɪt] n (a) (in garden, field) barrière f; (of city, in airport) porte f (b) Sp (spectators) nombre m de spectateurs; (takings) recette f

gâteau ['gætəʊ] (pl gâteaux ['gætəʊz]) n gros gâteau m à la crème

gatecrash ['geɪtkræʃ] vt Fam to g. a party aller à une fête sans y être invité(e)

gatecrasher ['geɪtkræʃə(r)] n Fam intrus(e) m,f

gatehouse ['geɪthaʊs] n loge f

gatekeeper ['geɪtkiːpə(r)] n gardien(enne) m,f

gatepost ['geɪtpəʊst] n montant m (de porte); Fam between you, me and the g. entre nous

gateway ['geɪtweɪ] n entrée f; Fig the g. to the East la porte de l'Orient; the g. to success la voie de la réussite

gather ['gæðə(r)] **1** vt (a) (collect) (people, belongings) rassembler; (information) recueillir; (wood, papers) ramasser; (fruit, flowers) cueillir; (harvest) rentrer; to g. one's thoughts rassembler ses idées; to g. sb in one's arms serrer qn dans ses bras (b) (accumulate) to g. dirt s'encrasser; also Fig to g. dust ramasser de la poussière; to g. speed prendre de la vitesse (c) (conclude, understand) to g. that... croire comprendre que...; as you may already have gathered,... comme vous avez déjà dû le deviner,...
2 vi (of people) se rassembler; (of things) s'accumuler; (of storm) se préparer

▸ **gather round 1** vt insep se rassembler autour de
2 vi se rassembler

▸ **gather together 1** vt sep (belongings) rassembler; (evidence) recueillir
2 vi (of people) se rassembler

▸ **gather up** vt sep ramasser

gathering ['gæðərɪŋ] **1** n (group) attroupement m; (meeting) réunion f
2 adj (darkness, speed) croissant(e); also Fig the g. storm l'orage qui se prépare

GATT [gæt] n (abbr General Agreement on Tariffs and Trade) GATT m

gauche [gəʊʃ] adj gauche, maladroit(e)

gaudily ['gɔːdɪlɪ] adv de façon criarde

gaudy ['gɔːdɪ] adj tape-à-l'œil inv; (colours) criard(e)

gauge [geɪdʒ] **1** n (a) (size) (of screw, wire, gun) calibre m; (of railway track) écartement m (b) (measuring device) jauge f (c) Fig (indicator) signe m, indicateur m (of de)
2 vt évaluer

Gaul [gɔːl] n Hist (region) la Gaule; (inhabitant) Gaulois(oise) m,f

gaunt [gɔːnt] adj décharné(e)

gauntlet ['gɔːntlɪt] n (glove) gant m à manchette; Hist gantelet m; Fig to throw or fling down the g. (to sb) jeter le gant (à qn); Fig to take up the g. relever le gant; Fig to run the g. of sth s'exposer à qch

gauze [gɔːz] n gaze f

gave [geɪv] pt of give

gavel ['gævəl] n marteau m

gawk [gɔːk] vi Fam rester bouche bée; to g. at sb/sth rester bouche bée à regarder qn/qch

gawky ['gɔːkɪ] adj Fam gauche, empoté(e)

gawp [gɔːp] vi Fam rester bouche bée; to g. at sb/sth rester bouche bée à regarder qn/qch

gay [geɪ] **1** n (homosexual) homosexuel(elle) m,f
2 adj (a) (homosexual) homosexuel(elle), gay inv; g. rights les droits mpl des homosexuels (b) Old-fashioned (happy) gai(e); what a g. abandon avec insouciance

Gaza ['gɑːzə] n Gaza; the G. Strip la Bande de Gaza

gaze [geɪz] **1** n regard m; to meet or return sb's g. regarder qn dans les yeux
2 vi to g. at sb/sth regarder fixement qn/qch; to g. into space regarder dans le vague

gazelle [gə'zel] n gazelle f

gazette [gə'zet] n journal m officiel

gazetteer [gæzɪ'tɪə(r)] n index m géographique

gazump [gə'zʌmp] vt Br Fam = revenir sur une promesse de vente de maison pour accepter l'offre plus élevée d'une tierce personne

GB ['dʒiː'biː] n (abbr Great Britain) GB

GBH [dʒiːbiː'eɪtʃ] n Law (abbr grievous bodily harm) coups mpl et blessures fpl

GCHQ [dʒiːsiːeɪtʃ'kjuː] n Br (abbr Government Communications Headquarters) = service de renseignement et d'écoute du gouvernement britannique

GCSE [dʒiːsiːes'iː] n Br (abbr General Certificate of Secondary Education) = diplôme de fin de premier cycle de l'enseignement secondaire, sanctionnant une matière déterminée

GDP [dʒiːdiː'piː] n Econ (abbr gross domestic product) PIB m

GDR [dʒiːdiː'ɑː(r)] n Formerly (abbr German Democratic Republic) the G. la RDA

gear [gɪə(r)] n (a) (on car, bicycle) vitesse f; Fig to put sb's

plans out of g. perturber les projets de qn; **first/second g.** première *f*/seconde *f* (vitesse); *Br* **g. lever** changement *m* de vitesse (**b**) *Fam (equipment)* attirail *m*; *(belongings)* affaires *fpl* (**c**) *Fam (clothes)* fringues *fpl*

▸ **gear to** *vt sep* to g. sth to sth adapter qch à qch

▸ **gear towards** *vt sep* to be geared towards sb/sth s'adresser à qn/qch

gearbox ['gɪəbɒks] *n* boîte *f* (de changement) de vitesses

gearstick ['gɪəstɪk] *n* changement *m* de vitesses

gee [dʒiː] *exclam* (**a**) *(to horse)* **g. up!** hue! (**b**) *Am* **g. (whizz)!** mince alors!

gee-gee ['dʒiːdʒiː] *n Fam (in children's language)* dada *m*

geese [giːs] *pl of* **goose**

geezer ['giːzə(r)] *n Fam* (**a**) *Br (man)* type *m*; **old g.** vieux bonhomme *m* (**b**) *Am (old person)* vioc (vioque) *m,f*

Geiger counter ['gaɪgə'kaʊntə(r)] *n* compteur *m* Geiger

gel [dʒel] **1** *n* gel *m*
2 *vi (of liquid)* se gélifier; *Fig (of ideas, plans)* prendre forme; *(of team)* se souder

gelatine ['dʒelətiːn] *n* gélatine *f*

gelatinous [dʒɪ'lætɪnəs] *adj* gélatineux(euse)

gelding ['geldɪŋ] *n* hongre *m*

gelignite ['dʒelɪgnaɪt] *n* gélignite *f*

gem [dʒem] *n (precious stone)* pierre *f* précieuse; *Fig (person)* perle *f*; *(film, joke, goal)* pure merveille *f*

Gemini ['dʒemɪnaɪ] *n (sign of zodiac)* les Gémeaux *mpl*; **to be (a) G.** être (des) Gémeaux

gemstone ['dʒemstəʊn] *n* pierre *f* gemme

gen [dʒen] *n Br Fam (information)* tuyaux *mpl*

gender ['dʒendə(r)] *n* (**a**) *Gram* genre *m* (**b**) *(sex)* sexe *m*

gene [dʒiːn] *n Biol* gène *m*; *Fig* **it's in his genes** *(of talent, characteristic)* c'est héréditaire

genealogy [dʒiːnɪ'ælədʒɪ] *n* généalogie *f*

genera ['dʒenərə] *pl of* **genus**

general ['dʒenərəl] **1** *n* (**a**) **in g.** en général (**b**) *Mil* général *m*
2 *adj* général(e); **as a g. rule** en règle générale; **in g. terms** en termes généraux; **g. anaesthetic** anesthésie *f* générale; **G. Assembly** *(of United Nations)* Assemblée *f* générale; **g. election** élections *fpl* générales; **g. knowledge** culture *f* générale; **g. manager** directeur(trice) *m,f* général(e); **g. meeting** assemblée *f* générale; **g. practice** *(in medicine)* médecine *f* générale, **g. practitioner** *(doctor)* médecin *m* généraliste; **the g. public** le grand public; **g. store** bazar *m*; **g. strike** grève *f* générale

generality [dʒenə'rælɪtɪ] *(pl* **generalities**) *n* généralité *f*

generalization [dʒenərəlaɪ'zeɪʃən] *n* généralisation *f*

generalize ['dʒenərəlaɪz] **1** *vt* **to become generalized** *(of practice, belief)* se généraliser
2 *vi* généraliser

generally ['dʒenərəlɪ] *adv (taken overall)* dans l'ensemble; *(as a general rule)* généralement, en général; **g. speaking** d'une manière générale

generate ['dʒenəreɪt] *vt (electricity, heat)* produire; *(income)* créer; *(reaction, response)* provoquer; *(interest, ideas)* faire naître

generation [dʒenə'reɪʃən] *n* (**a**) *(of people, products)* génération *f*; **from g. to g.** de génération en génération; **the younger/older g.** la jeune/l'ancienne génération; **the g. gap** le fossé entre les générations (**b**) *(of electricity)* production *f*

generator ['dʒenəreɪtə(r)] *n Elec* générateur *m*

generic [dʒɪ'nerɪk] *adj* générique

generosity [dʒenə'rɒsɪtɪ] *n* générosité *f*

generous ['dʒenərəs] *adj* généreux(euse)

generously ['dʒenərəslɪ] *adv* généreusement

genesis ['dʒenɪsɪs] *n* genèse *f*; **(the Book of) G.** la Genèse

genetic [dʒɪ'netɪk] *adj* génétique; **g. code** code *m* génétique; **g. engineering** génie *m* génétique; **g. fingerprinting** empreinte *f* génétique

genetically [dʒɪ'netɪklɪ] *adv* génétiquement

genetics [dʒɪ'netɪks] *n* génétique *f*

Geneva [dʒɪ'niːvə] *n* Genève; **Lake G.** le Lac de Genève, le Lac Léman; **the G. Convention** la Convention de Genève

genial ['dʒiːnɪəl] *adj* cordial(e)

geniality [dʒiːnɪ'ælɪtɪ] *n* cordialité *f*

genially ['dʒiːnɪəlɪ] *adv* cordialement

genie ['dʒiːnɪ] *(pl* **genii** ['dʒiːnɪaɪ]) *n* génie *m*

genital ['dʒenɪtəl] **1** *npl* **genitals** organes *mpl* génitaux
2 *adj* génital(e)

genitive ['dʒenɪtɪv] *Gram* **1** *n* génitif *m*; **in the g.** au génitif
2 *adj* génitif(ive)

genius ['dʒiːnɪəs] *n* génie *m*; *Ironic* **to have a g. for sth/doing sth** avoir le génie de qch/de faire qch; **man/work of g.** homme *m*/œuvre *f* de génie

Genoa ['dʒenəʊə] *n* Gênes

genocide ['dʒenəsaɪd] *n* génocide *m*

genre ['ʒɒnrə] *n (of film, novel)* genre *m*

gent [dʒent] *n Br Fam* (**a**) *(well-bred man)* gentleman *m* (**b**) *(man)* homme *m*; **gents' footwear** chaussures *fpl* pour hommes; **gents** *(toilets)* toilettes *fpl* des hommes; *(sign)* messieurs

genteel [dʒen'tiːl] *adj (refined)* distingué(e); *(respectable)* comme il faut; *Pej (affected)* maniéré(e)

Gentile ['dʒentaɪl] *n* gentil *m*

gentle ['dʒentəl] *adj (person, manner)* doux (douce); *(push, breeze, rise, slope)* léger(ère); *(hint)* discret(ète); *(exercise)* modéré(e); **to be g. with sb** être doux avec qn; **to be g. with sth** faire attention à qch; *Fam* **a g. giant** un agneau sous des airs de brute

gentleman ['dʒentəlmən] *n* (**a**) *(well-bred man)* gentleman *m*; **g.'s agreement** gentleman's agreement *m* (**b**) *(man)* homme *m*; **ladies and gentlemen!** mesdames et messieurs!

gentlemanly ['dʒentəlmənlɪ] *adj* bien élevé(e)

gentleness ['dʒentəlnɪs] *n* douceur *f*

gently ['dʒentlɪ] *adv (speak, remind)* gentiment; *(slope)* en pente douce; **g. (does it)!** allez-y doucement!

gentrification [dʒentrɪfɪ'keɪʃən] *n Br* embourgeoisement *m*

gentry ['dʒentrɪ] *n* petite noblesse *f*

genuflect ['dʒenjʊflekt] *vi Formal* faire une génuflexion

genuine ['dʒenjʊɪn] *adj* (**a**) *(manuscript, painting)* authentique; *(gold, leather)* véritable; *(excuse)* valable; *(offer)* sérieux(euse) (**b**) *(sincere)* sincère; **it was a g. mistake** ce n'était pas intentionnel

genuinely ['dʒenjʊɪnlɪ] *adv (sincerely)* sincèrement, vraiment

genus ['dʒiːnəs] *(pl* **genera** ['dʒenərə]) *n Biol* genre *m*

geo- ['dʒiːəʊ] *pref* géo-

geographer [dʒɪ'ɒgrəfə(r)] *n* géographe *mf*

geographic(al) [dʒɪə'græfɪk(əl)] *adj* géographique

geography [dʒɪ'ɒgrəfɪ] *n* géographie *f*

geologic(al) [dʒɪə'lɒdʒɪk(əl)] *adj* géologique

geologist [dʒɪ'ɒlədʒɪst] *n* géologue *mf*
geology [dʒɪ'ɒlədʒɪ] *n* géologie *f*
geometric(al) [dʒɪə'metrɪk(əl)] *adj* géométrique
geometry [dʒɪ'ɒmɪtrɪ] *n* géométrie *f*
geophysics [dʒɪəʊ'fɪzɪks] *n* géophysique *f*
geopolitics [dʒɪəʊ'pɒlɪtɪks] *n* géopolitique *f*
Georgia ['dʒɔːdʒɪə] *n (country, US state)* la Géorgie
Georgian ['dʒɔːdʒɪən] **1** *n* (**a**) *(person)* Géorgien(enne) *m,f* (**b**) *(language)* géorgien *m*
 2 *adj* géorgien(enne)
geothermal [dʒiːəʊ'θɜːməl] *adj* géothermique
geranium [dʒə'reɪnɪəm] *n* géranium *m*
gerbil ['dʒɜːbɪl] *n* gerbille *f*
geriatric [dʒerɪ'ætrɪk] **1** *n* malade *mf* gériatrique; *Fam Pej (old person)* gâteux(euse) *m,f*
 2 *adj (hospital)* gériatrique; *(care)* aux vieillards; **g. medicine** gériatrie *f*
geriatrics [dʒerɪ'ætrɪks] *n* gériatrie *f*
germ [dʒɜːm] *n* (**a**) *(causing disease)* microbe *m*; **g. warfare** guerre *f* bactériologique (**b**) *(of seed)* & *Fig (of idea)* germe *m*
German ['dʒɜːmən] **1** *n* (**a**) *(person)* Allemand(e) *m,f* (**b**) *(language)* allemand *m*; **G. class/teacher** cours *m*/professeur *m* d'allemand
 2 *adj* allemand(e); **G. measles** rubéole *f*; **G. shepherd** berger *m* allemand
germane [dʒɜː'meɪn] *adj Formal* approprié(e); **to be g. to sth** avoir rapport à qch
Germanic [dʒɜː'mænɪk] *adj* germanique
Germany ['dʒɜːmənɪ] *n* l'Allemagne *f*
germinate ['dʒɜːmɪneɪt] *vi* germer
germination [dʒɜːmɪ'neɪʃən] *n* germination *f*
gerrymandering ['dʒerɪmændərɪŋ] *n Pol* charcutage *m* electoral
gerund ['dʒerənd] *n Gram* gérondif *m*
gestation [dʒes'teɪʃən] *n also Fig* gestation *f*; **g. period** période *f* de gestation
gesticulate [dʒes'tɪkjʊleɪt] *vi* gesticuler
gesture ['dʒestʃə(r)] **1** *n also Fig* geste *m*; *Fig* **as a g. of friendship** en témoignage d'amitié
 2 *vi (single action)* faire un geste; *(repeatedly)* faire des gestes; **to g. to sb** faire signe à qn; **to g. towards sb/sth** désigner qn/qch d'un geste
get [get] *(pt & pp got* [gɒt], *Am pp gotten* ['gɒtən]) **1** *vt* (**a**) *(obtain)* obtenir; *(job)* trouver; **to g. sth for sb** obtenir qch pour qn; **I got the idea from a book** j'ai trouvé l'idée dans un livre; **to g. the right answer** trouver la solution; **to g. the wrong answer** se tromper
 (**b**) *(buy)* acheter; **to g. sth for sb** acheter qch à qn
 (**c**) *(receive) (present, reply)* recevoir; *(surprise, shock)* avoir; **we can't g. Radio 4 here** on ne reçoit pas Radio 4 ici; **to g. $15,000 a year** gagner 15 000 dollars par an; **we don't g. many visitors here** nous ne recevons pas beaucoup de visites ici
 (**d**) *(catch) (person, disease)* attraper; *(train, bus)* prendre; *Fam* **I'll g. you for that** je t'aurai
 (**e**) *(fetch)* aller chercher; **to g. sth for sb** aller chercher qch pour qn; **can I g. you anything?** je te rapporte quelque chose?
 (**f**) *Fam (annoy)* énerver
 (**g**) *Fam (understand)* piger; **do you g. my meaning?** tu vois ce que je veux dire?; **to g. the point** piger; **to g. a joke** saisir une blague
 (**h**) *(send)* **to g. sth to sb** faire parvenir qch à qn
 (**i**) *(cause to be in a certain state)* **to g. sth dry/wet** sécher/

mouiller qch; **to g. sth clean/dirty** nettoyer/salir qch; **you've got him worried** tu l'as fait s'inquiéter; **to g. sb pregnant** mettre qn enceinte; **to g. the children to bed** envoyer les enfants au lit
 (**j**) *(cause to be done)* **to g. sth done** faire faire qch; **to g. the house painted** faire peindre la maison; **she got her work finished** elle a terminé son travail
 (**k**) *(cause to do)* **to g. sb to do sth** faire faire qch à qn; **she got me to help her** elle m'a persuadé de l'aider; **you can g. them to wrap it for you** tu peux leur demander de te l'emballer
 (**l**) *(do gradually)* **to g. to know sb** apprendre à connaître qn; **you'll g. to like him** tu finiras par l'apprécier; **she soon got to thinking that…** elle se mit bientôt à penser que…
 (**m**) *(have opportunity)* **to g. to do sth** avoir l'occasion de faire qch
 (**n**) *(possess) (with have)* **she hasn't got a car** elle n'a pas de voiture; **she's got measles/AIDS** elle a la rougeole/le sida; **what's that got to do with it?** qu'est-ce que ça a à voir?
 (**o**) *(must) (with have)* **I've got to go** il faut que j'y aille; **it's got to be done** il faut que ce soit fait
 2 *vi* (**a**) *(arrive)* arriver; **to g. home** arriver chez soi; **to g. back** arriver; **how do you g. there?** comment fait-on pour y aller?; **he got as far as chapter five** il est allé jusqu'au chapitre cinq; **it got to the point where…** ça en est arrivé à un point où…
 (**b**) *(move) also Fig* **to g. in sb's way** se mettre sur le chemin de qn; **where has he got to?** où est-il passé?; **we're getting nowhere** on n'avance pas
 (**c**) *(become)* **to g. angry** se mettre en colère; **to g. better** s'améliorer; **to g. drunk** se soûler; **to g. old** vieillir
 (**d**) *(with past participle)* **to g. broken** être cassé(e); **to g. stolen** être volé(e); **to g. killed** se faire tuer; **to g. dressed** s'habiller; **to g. married** se marier
 (**e**) *(start)* **to g. going** *(leave)* se mettre en route; *(start working)* se mettre au travail; **to g. talking with sb** entrer en conversation avec qn
 ▶ **get about** *vi (of person)* se déplacer; *(of news, rumour)* circuler
 ▶ **get across** *vt sep (ideas, message)* faire passer
 ▶ **get ahead** *vi* avancer
 ▶ **get along** *vi* (**a**) *(leave)* s'en aller, partir (**b**) *(progress)* **how are you getting along in your new job?** comment ça va, votre nouveau travail?; **we can g. along without them** nous pouvons très bien nous passer d'eux (**c**) *(have good relationship)* s'entendre
 ▶ **get around 1** *vt insep (problem, difficulty)* contourner; **there's no getting around it, we'll have to** on n'a pas le choix, il va falloir lui faire
 2 *vi* = **get about**
 ▶ **get around to** *vt insep* **to g. around to doing sth** trouver le temps de faire qch
 ▶ **get at** *vt insep* (**a**) *(have access to)* accéder à; *(reach)* atteindre; **to g. at the truth** découvrir la vérité (**b**) *(imply)* **what are you getting at?** où veux-tu en venir? (**c**) *Fam (criticize)* s'en prendre à
 ▶ **get away** *vi (escape, leave)* se sauver; *(have a holiday)* s'échapper; *Fam* **g. away!** *(expressing disbelief)* sans blague!
 ▶ **get away with** *vt insep* (**a**) *(fine, warning)* s'en tirer avec (**b**) *(crime)* **he stole the money and got away with it** il a volé l'argent et il ne s'est pas fait prendre; *Fig* **that child gets away with murder** on lui passe tout à cet enfant
 ▶ **get back 1** *vt sep (recover)* récupérer; *(strength)* reprendre
 vi (return) revenir
 ▶ **get back at** *vt insep* **to g. back at sb (for sth)** se venger de qn (pour qch)

▸ **get behind 1** *vt insep (support)* soutenir
2 *vi (become delayed)* prendre du retard (**with** *or* **in** dans)
▸ **get by** *vi (manage)* se débrouiller, s'en tirer (**on/in** avec/en)
▸ **get down 1** *vt sep* (**a**) *(reduce) (weight)* perdre; *(costs, temperature)* faire baisser (**b**) *(depress)* déprimer (**c**) *(fetch)* descendre
2 *vi (descend)* descendre (**from** de)
▸ **get down to** *vt insep* se mettre à; **to g. down to the facts** en venir aux faits
▸ **get in 1** *vt sep* (**a**) *(bring inside)* rentrer (**b**) *(insert)* **I couldn't g. a word in** je n'ai pas pu en placer une (**c**) *(stock up with)* faire provision de
2 *vi* (**a**) *(gain entrance)* entrer (**b**) *(arrive)* arriver (**c**) *(be elected)* être élu(e)
▸ **get into** *vt insep* (**a**) *(house)* entrer dans; *(car)* monter dans; **to g. into Harvard** admis(e) à Harvard; **to g. into trouble** s'attirer des ennuis; *Fam* **I don't know what's got into her** je ne sais pas ce qui lui prend (**b**) *(clothes, boots)* enfiler; **I can't g. into my dress any more** je n'entre plus dans ma robe (**c**) *Fam (become interested in) (activity)* commencer à s'intéresser à; *(book)* rentrer dans
▸ **get in with** *vt insep (group of people)* se mettre bien avec
▸ **get off 1** *vt sep* (**a**) **to g. sb off** *(save from punishment)* tirer qn de là (**b**) *(send)* **to g. the children off to school** envoyer les enfants à l'école
2 *vt insep (train, bus)* descendre de
3 *vi* (**a**) *(from train, bus)* descendre; *Fig* **I told him where to g. off** je l'ai envoyé promener (**b**) *(go unpunished)* s'en tirer (**c**) *(begin)* **to g. off to sleep** s'endormir; **to g. off to a good/bad start** commencer bien/mal
▸ **get off on** *vt insep very Fam* **to g. off on sth** être excité(e) par qch; **to g. off on doing sth** prendre son pied à faire qch
▸ **get off with** *vt insep Br Fam* lever
▸ **get on 1** *vt sep (clothes)* mettre, enfiler
2 *vt insep (train, bus, plane)* monter dans
3 *vi* (**a**) *(enter train, bus)* monter (**b**) *(progress)* réussir; **to g. on in life** *or* **in the world** réussir dans la vie; **how are you getting on?** *(how are you?)* comment ça va?; **how did you g. on?** *(in exam, at meeting)* comment ça s'est passé? (**c**) *(have good relationship)* s'entendre; **to g. on well/badly with sb** s'entendre bien/mal avec qn (**d**) *(age)* **to be getting on (in years)** se faire vieux (vieille)
▸ **get on for** *vt insep (approach)* **he must be getting on for sixty now** il doit approcher la soixantaine; **it was getting on for midnight** il était presque minuit; **there were getting on for 200 people there** on approchait les 200 personnes
▸ **get onto** *vt insep* (**a**) *(contact)* se mettre en rapport avec (**b**) *(move onto subject of)* en arriver à; **they eventually got onto (the subject of) money** ils en vinrent finalement à parler d'argent
▸ **get out 1** *vt sep* (**a**) *(bring out)* sortir (**b**) *(remove) (nail, splinter)* retirer; *(stain)* faire partir
2 *vi* (**a**) *(leave)* sortir (**b**) *(of secret, news)* transpirer
▸ **get out of** *vt insep (vehicle)* sortir de; **to g. out of the way** s'écarter; **g. out of here!** *(go away)* va-t-en!; *Fam (I don't believe you)* arrête de dire des bêtises!; **to g. out of doing sth** s'arranger pour ne pas faire qch
▸ **get over 1** *vt sep (idea, information)* faire passer; *(facts)* expliquer
2 *vt insep* (**a**) *(road, river)* traverser, franchir; *(wall, fence)* passer par-dessus (**b**) *(illness, trauma)* se remettre de
▸ **get over with** *vt sep* **to g. sth over with** en finir avec qch

▸ **get round 1** *vt insep* = **get around**
2 *vi* = **get about**
▸ **get round to** *vt insep* = **get around to**
▸ **get through 1** *vt sep (communicate)* **to g. sth through to sb** faire comprendre qch à qn
2 *vt insep* (**a**) *(pass through) (hole, roof)* passer à travers (**b**) *(survive) (test, interview)* survivre à; *(period of time)* tenir (**c**) *(finish)* achever (**d**) *(consume) (food, drink)* consommer; *(money)* dépenser
3 *vi* (**a**) *(arrive) (of news)* parvenir; *(of messenger)* arriver (**b**) **to g. through to sb** *(on telephone)* obtenir la communication avec qn; *Fig (make understand)* se faire comprendre par qn
▸ **get together 1** *vt sep (money)* réunir; *(belongings, ideas)* rassembler
2 *vi (of people)* se réunir
▸ **get up 1** *vt sep* (**a**) *(out of bed)* faire lever (**b**) *(dress up)* **he got himself up in his best clothes** il a mis ses plus beaux vêtements (**c**) *very Fam (achieve erection)* **he couldn't g. it up** il n'a pas réussi à bander
2 *vt insep Fig* **to g. up sb's nose** taper sur les nerfs à qn
3 *vi (rise)* se lever
▸ **get up to** *vt insep (do)* **what have you been getting up to recently?** qu'est-ce que tu as fait ces derniers temps?; **to g. up to mischief** faire des bêtises; **he's been getting up to his old tricks** il a encore fait des siennes

getaway ['getəweɪ] *n (take) f*; **to make one's g.** prendre la fuite; **g. car** = voiture utilisée pour prendre la fuite
get-rich-quick ['get'rɪtʃ'kwɪk] *adj Fam* **a g. scheme** un moyen de devenir riche rapidement
get-together ['gettəgeðə(r)] *n Fam* réunion *f* (entre amis)
get-up ['getʌp] *n Fam (clothes)* accoutrement *m*; *(fancy dress)* déguisement *m*
get-up-and-go ['getʌpənd'gəʊ] *n Fam* énergie *f*
get-well card ['get'wel'kɑːd] *n* carte *f* de prompt rétablissement
geyser ['giːzə(r)] *n* (**a**) *(spring)* geyser *m* (**b**) *Br (water heater)* chauffe-eau *m inv*
Ghana ['gɑːnə] *n* le Ghana
Ghanaian [gɑːˈneɪən] **1** *n* Ghanéen(enne) *m,f*
2 *adj* ghanéen(enne)
ghastly ['gɑːstlɪ] *adj (terrible)* horrible, épouvantable; *(mistake)* monstrueux(euse)
Ghent [gent] *n* Gand
gherkin ['gɜːkɪn] *n* cornichon *m*
ghetto ['getəʊ] (*pl* **ghettoes** *or* **ghettos**) *n* ghetto *m*; *Fam* **g. blaster** radiocassette *m*
ghost [gəʊst] **1** *n* fantôme *m*; **you look as though you've seen a g.** on dirait que tu as vu un revenant; **not the g. of a chance** pas la moindre chance; **to give up the g.** *(of person, machine)* rendre l'âme; **g. story** histoire *f* de fantôme; **g. town** ville *f* fantôme
2 *vt* **to g. a book** servir de nègre pour un livre
ghostly ['gəʊstlɪ] *adj* spectral(e)
ghostwrite ['gəʊstraɪt] *vt* **to g. a book** servir de nègre pour un livre
ghostwriter ['gəʊstraɪtə(r)] *n* nègre *m*
ghoul [guːl] *n (evil spirit)* goule *f*; *Fig (morbid person)* personne *f* morbide
ghoulish ['guːlɪʃ] *adj (humour, remark)* morbide; *(scene)* macabre
GHQ [dʒiːeɪtʃ'kjuː] *n Mil (abbr* **General Headquarters)** QG *m inv*
GI [dʒiːˈaɪ] *n Am Fam* GI *m inv*

giant ['dʒaɪənt] **1** n géant(e) m,f; **g. killer** (in sport) vainqueur m surprise
2 adj géant(e)
gibber ['dʒɪbə(r)] vi baragouiner
gibbering ['dʒɪbərɪŋ] adj au discours incohérent; Fam a
g. idiot un(e) pauvre idiot(e)
gibberish ['dʒɪbərɪʃ] n charabia m; **to talk g.** dire n'importe quoi
gibbet ['dʒɪbɪt] n gibet m, potence f
gibbon ['gɪbən] n gibbon m
gibe [dʒaɪb] **1** n moquerie f
2 vi **to g. at sb** se moquer de qn
giblets ['dʒɪblɪts] npl abats mpl
Gibraltar [dʒɪ'brɔːltə(r)] n Gibraltar
giddiness ['gɪdɪnɪs] n étourdissement m, vertige m
giddy ['gɪdɪ] adj **to be** or **feel g.** avoir le vertige; **it makes me (feel) g.** ça me donne le vertige; Fig **the g. heights of success** les hautes cimes de la réussite
GIF [dʒɪf] n Comptr (abbr Graphic Information Format) GIF m
gift [gɪft] n (**a**) (present) cadeau m; Prov **never look a g. horse in the mouth** à cheval donné on ne regarde pas la bouche; **g. shop** boutique f de cadeaux; **g. token** chèquecadeau m (**b**) (talent) don m; **to have a g. for sth** être doué(e) pour qch; **to have the g. of the gab** (be talkative) avoir la langue bien pendue; (speak persuasively) avoir du bagout
gifted ['gɪftɪd] adj doué(e); (artist, musician) de talent
gift-wrapped ['gɪftræpt] adj sous paquet-cadeau
gig [gɪg] n (**a**) (carriage) cabriolet m (**b**) Fam (pop concert) concert m
gigabyte ['dʒɪgəbaɪt] n Comptr gigaoctet m
gigantic [dʒaɪ'gæntɪk] adj colossal(e), gigantesque
giggle ['gɪgəl] **1** n (laugh) petit rire m idiot; **to have (a fit of) the giggles** avoir le fou rire (**b**) Fam (amusement) **what a g.!** quelle rigolade!; **to do sth for a g.** faire qch pour rigoler
2 vi rire (nerveusement)
giggly ['gɪgəlɪ] adj **to be g.** pouffer de rire
gigolo ['dʒɪgələʊ] n (pl gigolos) n gigolo m
gild [gɪld] (pt & pp gilded or gilt [gɪlt]) vt dorer; Fig **to g. the lily** surcharger
gill [dʒɪl] n (liquid measure) = 0,142 l, quart m de pinte
gills [gɪlz] npl (of fish) ouïes fpl, branchies fpl; Fig **to be green about the g.** avoir le teint verdâtre
gilt [gɪlt] **1** n dorure f; Fin **gilts** titres mpl ou fonds mpl d'État
2 adj doré(e)
3 pt & pp of **gild**
gilt-edged ['gɪltedʒd] adj Fin **g. securities** or **stocks** titres mpl ou fonds mpl d'État
gimlet ['gɪmlɪt] n (tool) vrille f; Fig **g. eyes** yeux mpl perçants
gimme ['gɪmiː] very Fam = give me
gimmick ['gɪmɪk] n truc m, astuce f
gimmicky ['gɪmɪkɪ] adj artificiel(elle)
gin [dʒɪn] n gin m; **a g. and tonic** un gin tonic
ginger ['dʒɪndʒə(r)] **1** n gingembre m; **g. ale** = boisson gazeuse au gingembre pouvant servir à couper un alcool; **g. beer** limonade f au gingembre
2 adj (hair) roux (rousse)
► **ginger up** vt sep Fam (person, group) stimuler; (film, story) donner du punch à
gingerbread ['dʒɪndʒəbred] n pain m d'épice; **g. man** bonhomme m en biscuit parfumé au gingembre

gingerly ['dʒɪndʒəlɪ] adv avec précaution
gingham ['gɪŋəm] n vichy m
gingivitis [dʒɪndʒɪ'vaɪtɪs] n Med gingivite f
ginormous [dʒaɪ'nɔːməs] adj Fam gigantesque, énorme
ginseng ['dʒɪnseŋ] n ginseng m
gipsy ['dʒɪpsɪ] (pl gipsies) n (Eastern European) tzigane mf; (Spanish) gitan(e) m,f; **g. caravan** roulotte f
giraffe [dʒɪ'rɑːf] n girafe f
gird [gɜːd] (pt & pp girded or girt [gɜːt]) vt Lit **to g. one's loins** se ceindre les reins
girder ['gɜːdə(r)] n poutre f (métallique)
girdle ['gɜːdəl] **1** n (corset) gaine f
2 vt Lit (surround) ceindre, entourer
girl [gɜːl] n fille f; **a French g.** une (jeune) Française; Br **G. Guide** éclaireuse f
girlfriend ['gɜːlfrend] n (lover) petite amie f; (friend) amie f
girlhood ['gɜːlhʊd] n enfance f, jeunesse f
girlie ['gɜːlɪ] n Fam **g. mag** magazine m érotique
girlish ['gɜːlɪʃ] adj (of girl) de fille; (of woman, effeminate man) de jeune fille; **g. laughter** rire m de jeune fille
giro ['dʒaɪrəʊ] (pl giros) n Br (**a**) Fin **g. account** compte m chèque postal, CCP m (**b**) Fam (unemployment cheque) allocation f (de) chômage
girt [gɜːt] pt & pp of **gird**
girth [gɜːθ] n (of tree) circonférence f; (of person) corpulence f
gist [dʒɪst] n essentiel m; **to get the g.** saisir l'essentiel
git [gɪt] n Br very Fam con (conne) m,f
give [gɪv] **1** vt (pt gave [geɪv], pp given ['gɪvən]) (**a**) (in general) donner; (as present) offrir; **to g. sth to sb, to g. sb sth** donner qch à qn; (as present) offrir qch à qn; **to g. sb a dirty look** lancer un regard noir à qn; **he was given ten years/a fine** il a été condamné à dix ans de prison/à une amende; **g. her my love** embrasse-la pour moi; **she gave me to understand that...** elle m'a fait comprendre que...; **g. or take a few minutes/pence** à quelques minutes/pence près
(**b**) (with reference to verbal expressions) **to g. a laugh** partir d'un éclat de rire; **to g. a sigh** pousser un soupir; **to g. sb a smile** sourire à qn; **to g. sb a fright** faire peur à qn; **to g. sb a kiss** embrasser qn; **he gave his face a wash** il s'est lavé le visage; **she gave the sauce a stir** elle a remué la sauce
2 vi (**a**) (donate) donner; **please g. generously** soyez généreux, s'il vous plaît; **to g. of one's time** donner de son temps
(**b**) (yield, break) (of cloth, shoes) se faire; (of rope) lâcher; (of support, door) céder
(**c**) Am Fam **what gives?** quoi de neuf?
3 n (of fabric) élasticité f
► **give away** vt sep (**a**) (give for nothing) donner (**b**) (prize) distribuer; **to g. the bride away** conduire la mariée à l'autel (**c**) (reveal) trahir
► **give back** vt sep rendre
► **give in 1** vt sep (hand over) remettre
2 vi (surrender) céder (**to** à); (admit defeat) abandonner
► **give off** vt sep (smell, heat) dégager
► **give onto** vt insep **the house gives directly onto the street** la maison donne directement sur la rue
► **give out 1** vt sep (**a**) (money, food) distribuer; (information) donner (**b**) (noise) émettre; (heat) répandre
2 vi (of supplies, patience) s'épuiser; (of luck) tourner
► **give over 1** vt sep (money, objects) remettre; (devote) consacrer (**to** à)

2 *vi Br Fam (stop)* **g. over, will you?** arrête, d'accord?
► **give up 1** *vt sep (possessions)* renoncer à; *(activity, hope)* abandonner; **to g.** up smoking arrêter de fumer; **to g.** up **one's job** quitter son emploi; **to g. sb up for dead** considérer qn comme mort(e) **2** *vi* abandonner; **to g. up on sb** perdre tout espoir en qn; *(of doctors)* perdre tout espoir en ce qui concerne qn; **to g.** up on sth laisser tomber qch
► **give way** *vi* **(a)** *(collapse) (of support)* céder; *(of floor, ceiling)* s'effondrer; *(of rope, legs)* lâcher; *(of ground)* se dérober **(b)** *(yield) (in argument)* céder **(to à);** *(in car)* céder le passage **(to à); her tears gave way to laughter** ses larmes ont cédé la place au rire

give-and-take ['gɪvən'teɪk] *n* concessions *fpl* (mutuelles); **there has to be some g.** il faut que chacun y mette du sien

giveaway ['gɪvəweɪ] *n Fam* **(a)** *(revelation)* **what she said about the night before was the g.** ce qu'elle a dit sur la soirée précédente l'a trahie; **it was a dead g.** cela en disait long **(b)** *(free gift)* cadeau *m*; **g. price** prix *m* imbattable

given ['gɪvən] **1** *adj* **(a)** *(specific) (time, place)* donné(e); **at a g. point** à un moment donné; **g. name** prénom *m* **(b)** *(apt, likely)* **to be g. to doing sth** avoir tendance à faire qch **2** *conj* **(a)** *(considering)* étant donné; **g. that...** étant donné que...; **g. the nature of the case** étant donné la nature de l'affaire **(b) g. the chance again** si l'occasion se représentait **3** *pp of* **give**

gizmo ['gɪzməʊ] *(pl* **gizmos)** *n Fam* truc *m*, machin *m*

gizzard ['gɪzəd] *n* gésier *m*

glacé cherry ['glæseɪ'tʃerɪ] *n* cerise *f* confite

glacial ['gleɪsɪəl] *adj* glaciaire; *Fig* glacial(e)

glacier ['glæsɪə(r)] *n* glacier *m*

glad [glæd] *adj* heureux(euse), content(e) **(about** de); **I would be g. to assist you** je serais ravi de pouvoir vous aider; **to be g. of sth** *(grateful for)* être heureux d'avoir qch; *Fam* **to put on one's g. rags** se mettre sur son trente et un

gladden ['glædən] *vt* réjouir

glade [gleɪd] *n Lit* clairière *f*

gladiator ['glædɪeɪtə(r)] *n* gladiateur *m*

gladiolus [glædɪ'əʊləs] *(pl* **gladioli** [glædɪ'əʊlaɪ]) *n* glaïeul *m*

gladly ['glædlɪ] *adv* avec plaisir, volontiers

glamorize ['glæməraɪz] *vt* rendre séduisant(e) *ou* attrayant(e)

glamorous ['glæmərəs] *adj (person)* élégant(e); *(place, job, image)* prestigieux(euse); *(dress)* magnifique

glamour, *Am* **glamor** ['glæmə(r)] *n (of person)* séduction *f*; *(of job, lifestyle)* prestige *m*; *Fam* **g. girl** belle fille *f*, pin-up *f*

glance [glɑːns] **1** *n* coup *m* d'œil; **to have a g. at sth** jeter un coup d'œil à qch; **at a g.** d'un coup d'œil; **at first g.** au premier coup d'œil **2** *vi* **to g. at** regarder brièvement, jeter un coup d'œil à; **to g. through** sth parcourir qch rapidement
► **glance off** *vt insep (of blow, missile)* ricocher sur

glancing ['glɑːnsɪŋ] *adj (blow)* oblique

gland [glænd] *n* glande *f*

glandular ['glændjʊlə(r)] *adj* glandulaire; **g. fever** mononucléose *f* infectieuse

glare [gleə(r)] **1** *n* **(a)** *(angry stare)* regard *m* furieux **(b)** *(bright light)* éclat *m*, lumière *f* éblouissante; *Fig* **in the full g. of publicity** sous les feux des médias **2** *vi (stare angrily)* **to g. at sb/sth** fixer qn/qch d'un air furieux

glaringly ['gleərɪŋlɪ] *adv* **it's g. obvious** ça saute aux yeux

glass [glɑːs] *n* verre *m*; *(glassware)* verrerie *f*; **a g. of wine** un verre de vin; **g. bottle** bouteille *f* en verre; **g. case** vitrine *f*; **g. door** porte *f* vitrée; **g. eye** œil *m* de verre; **g. wool** laine *f* de verre

glass-blowing ['glɑːsbləʊɪŋ] *n* soufflage *m* du verre

glasses ['glɑːsɪz] *npl (spectacles)* lunettes *fpl*

glassful ['glɑːsfʊl] *n* verre *m*

glasshouse ['glɑːshaʊs] *n Br* serre *f*; *Prov* **people who live in glasshouses shouldn't throw stones** il faut être sans défauts pour critiquer autrui

glasspaper ['glɑːspeɪpə(r)] *n* papier *m* de verre

glassware ['glɑːsweə(r)] *n* verrerie *f*

glassworks ['glɑːswɜːks] *n* verrerie *f*; *(for crystal)* cristallerie *f*

glassy ['glɑːsɪ] *adj (eyes, look)* vitreux(euse); *(water)* immobile

glaucoma [glɔː'kəʊmə] *n* glaucome *m*; **to have g.** avoir un glaucome

glaze [gleɪz] **1** *n (on pottery)* vernis *m*; *(on pastry)* glaçage *m* **2** *vt* **(a)** *(window)* vitrer **(b)** *(pottery)* vernisser; *(pastry)* glacer
► **glaze over** *vi (of eyes)* devenir vitreux(euse)

glazed [gleɪzd] *adj* **(a)** *(roof, door)* vitré(e) **(b)** *(pottery)* vernissé(e)

glazier ['gleɪzɪə(r)] *n* vitrier *m*

gleam [gliːm] **1** *n (of light)* rayon *m*; *Fig* **a g. of hope** une lueur d'espoir **2** *vi* luire, briller; *(of water)* miroiter

gleaming ['gliːmɪŋ] *adj* étincelant(e)

glean [gliːn] *vt* glaner

glee [gliː] *n (delight)* joie *f*; *(malicious pleasure)* jubilation *f*

gleeful ['gliːfʊl] *adj (happy)* joyeux(euse); **to be g.** *(maliciously happy)* jubiler

glen [glen] *n Scot* vallée *f*

glib [glɪb] *adj (person, excuse)* désinvolte; *(reply)* spécieux(euse)

glibly ['glɪblɪ] *adv (reply)* de façon désinvolte; *(speak)* avec aisance

glide [glaɪd] *vi (move smoothly)* glisser; *(of aircraft, bird)* planer

glider ['glaɪdə(r)] *n (aircraft)* planeur *m*

gliding ['glaɪdɪŋ] *n (sport)* vol *m* à voile

glimmer ['glɪmə(r)] **1** *n* faible lueur *f*; *(of water)* reflet *m*; *Fig* **a g. of hope** une lueur d'espoir **2** *vi (of light)* luire; *(of water)* miroiter; *(of metal)* étinceler

glimpse [glɪmps] **1** *n* **to catch a g. of** entrevoir; **a g. of the future** un aperçu de (ce que sera) l'avenir **2** *vt* entrevoir

glint [glɪnt] **1** *n (of light) (flash)* éclat *m*; *(continuous)* scintillement *m*; *(of water)* reflet *m*; **with a g. in her eye** avec une lueur dans le regard **2** *vi (of light, eye)* briller; *(of water, metal)* scintiller

glisten ['glɪsən] *vi (of water, metal)* scintiller; **his forehead glistened with sweat** la sueur perlait sur son front

glitter ['glɪtə(r)] **1** *n (sparkle)* scintillement *m*; *Fig (occasion)* éclat *m*, faste *m* **2** *vi* scintiller; *Prov* **all that glitters is not gold** ce qui brille n'est pas d'or

glittering ['glɪtərɪŋ] *adj (jewels)* scintillant(e); *Fig (occasion, career)* brillant(e)

glitz [glɪts] *n* clinquant *m*, tape-à-l'œil *m*

glitzy ['glɪtsɪ] *adj Fam* tape-à-l'œil *inv*
gloat [gləʊt] *vi (at one's own success)* jubiler (**at** à l'idée de); *(about somebody else's misfortune)* se réjouir (**about** *or* **over** de); **I don't like to g., but...** ce n'est pas que ça me réjouisse, mais...
global ['gləʊbəl] *adj (comprehensive)* global(e); *(worldwide)* mondial(e); **g. village** village *m* planétaire; **g. warming** réchauffement *m* de la planète
globally ['gləʊbəlɪ] *adv (comprehensively)* globalement; *(worldwide)* mondialement
globe [gləʊb] *n (sphere)* globe *m*; *(with map)* globe terrestre; **the g.** *(the earth)* le globe terrestre; **to travel the g.** voyager dans le monde entier
globetrotter ['gləʊbtrɒtə(r)] *n Fam* globe-trotter *mf*
globule ['glɒbjuːl] *n* gouttelette *f*
gloom [gluːm] *n* (**a**) *(darkness)* obscurité *f* (**b**) *(sadness)* morosité *f*
gloomily ['gluːmɪlɪ] *adv (sadly)* sombrement
gloomy ['gluːmɪ] *adj* (**a**) *(dark)* sombre; *(weather)* morose (**b**) *(sad)* triste (**c**) *(pessimistic)* pessimiste; **g. thoughts** idées *fpl* noires
glorified ['glɔːrɪfaɪd] *adj* **she's just a g. secretary** elle n'est rien de plus qu'une secrétaire
glorify ['glɔːrɪfaɪ] *(pt & pp* **glorified***) vt* (**a**) *(extol)* célébrer; *Rel* **to g. God** rendre gloire à Dieu (**b**) *(war, violence)* glorifier
glorious ['glɔːrɪəs] *adj* (**a**) *(reign, victory)* glorieux(euse) (**b**) *(view, sunshine)* magnifique
gloriously ['glɔːrɪəslɪ] *adv* (**a**) *(die, reign)* avec gloire (**b**) *(beautifully)* superbement; **it was g. sunny** il faisait un soleil splendide
glory ['glɔːrɪ] *n* (**a**) *(honour)* gloire *f* (**b**) *(splendour)* splendeur *f*
▸ **glory in** *vt insep* se glorifier de
gloss¹ [glɒs] *n (in text)* glose *f*
gloss² *n (shine)* lustre *m*; *Fig* vernis *m*; *Fig* **to take the g. off sth** gâcher qch; **g. paint** peinture *f* brillante
▸ **gloss over** *vt insep* passer sur
glossary ['glɒsərɪ] *(pl* **glossaries***) n* glossaire *m*
glossy ['glɒsɪ] *adj* brillant(e); **g. brochure** brochure *f* luxueuse; **g. magazine** magazine *m* de luxe; **g. paper** papier *m* glacé
glottal stop ['glɒtəl'stɒp] *n* coup *m* de glotte
glove [glʌv] *n* gant *m*; *Fig* **the gloves are off** tous les coups sont permis; **g. compartment** *(in car)* boîte *f* à gants; **g. puppet** marionnette *f* à gaine
glow [gləʊ] **1** *n (light)* lueur *f*; *(on cheeks)* couleurs *fpl*; **the g. of the setting sun** l'embrasement du couchant; *Fig* **a g. of pride/satisfaction** un vif sentiment de fierté/satisfaction
2 *vi (of light, fire)* rougeoyer; *Fig* **to be glowing with health** être resplendissant(e) de santé; *Fig* **to g. with pride/pleasure** rayonner de fierté/plaisir
glower ['glaʊə(r)] *vi* **to g. at sb** lancer des regards noirs à qn
glowing ['gləʊɪŋ] *adj (cigarette, coal)* incandescent(e); *(metal)* chauffé(e) au rouge; *Fig (praise, words)* chaleureux(euse); *(description, report)* enthousiaste; *Fig* **to paint sth in g. colours** présenter qch sous un jour très favorable
glow-worm ['gləʊwɜːm] *n* ver *m* luisant
glucose ['gluːkəʊs] *n* glucose *m*
glue [gluː] **1** *n* colle *f*
2 *vt* coller (**to** à); *Fig* **to be glued to the television** être cloué(e) devant la télévision

glue-sniffing ['gluːsnɪfɪŋ] *n* inhalation *f* de colle
glum [glʌm] *adj* maussade
glut [glʌt] **1** *n (of goods)* encombrement *m*
2 *vt (pt & pp* **glutted***)* (**a**) *(market, economy)* encombrer, inonder (**b**) **to g. oneself (on)** se gaver (de)
glutinous ['gluːtɪnəs] *adj* gluant(e)
glutton ['glʌtən] *n (greedy person)* goinfre *mf*, glouton(onne) *m,f*; *Fig* **to be a g. for punishment** être masochiste
gluttony ['glʌtənɪ] *n* goinfrerie *f*, gloutonnerie *f*
glycerin ['glɪsərɪn], **glycerine** ['glɪsəriːn], **glycerol** ['glɪsərɒl] *n* glycérine *f*
GMT [dʒiːem'tiː] *n (abbr* **Greenwich Mean Time***)* GMT *m*
gnarled [nɑːld] *adj* noueux(euse)
gnash [næʃ] *vt* **to g. one's teeth** grincer des dents
gnat [næt] *n* moucheron *m*
gnaw [nɔː] **1** *vt (of rodent)* ronger
2 *vi (of rodent)* **to g. through sth** ronger qch (**b**) *Fig (of doubt, guilt)* **to g. away at sb** ronger qn
gnome [nəʊm] *n* gnome *m*
GNP [dʒiːen'piː] *n Econ (abbr* **Gross National Product***)* PNB *m*
gnu [nuː] *n* gnou *m*
go [gəʊ] **1** *vi (3rd person singular* **goes** [gəʊz], *pt* **went** [went], *pp* **gone** [gɒn])* (**a**) *(move)* aller; **to go to Belgium** aller en Belgique; **to go to the doctor** aller chez le docteur; **to go home** rentrer chez soi; **to go swimming, to go skiing** (aller) nager/skier; **the proceeds will go to charity** l'argent recueilli sera versé à des œuvres de charité; *Fig* **where do we go from here?** et maintenant, qu'est-ce qu'on fait?
(**b**) *(leave)* partir, s'en aller; **I've got to go** il faut que j'y aille; **let's go!** allons-y!
(**c**) *(function)* marcher; *(of bell)* sonner; **to keep the conversation going** entretenir la conversation
(**d**) *(progress)* aller; **to go well/badly** bien/mal se passer; *Fam* **how's it going?** comment ça va?; **how does the tune/story go?** c'est quoi, l'air/l'histoire, déjà?
(**e**) *(of time)* passer; **the time went quickly/slowly** le temps a passé vite/lentement; **it has just gone eight** il est huit heures à peine passées; **there are only five minutes to go** il ne reste que cinq minutes
(**f**) *(disappear, deteriorate)* disparaître; *(of light bulb)* griller; *(of fuse)* sauter; *(of batteries)* s'user; **her sight/voice is going** elle est en train de perdre la vue/la voix; **most of my income goes on food** l'essentiel de mon argent passe dans la nourriture
(**g**) *(forming future)* **to be going to do sth** aller faire qch; **I was going to walk** j'allais y aller à pied; **it's going to rain** il va pleuvoir
(**h**) *(match)* **(with** avec); **these colours go/don't go** ces couleurs vont bien/ne vont pas ensemble
(**i**) *(be available)* **there's a job going at the factory** il y a une place à l'usine; **is there any wine going?** est-ce qu'il y a du vin?; **it went for $12** on l'a vendu 12 dollars
(**j**) *(fit)* entrer; **the piano won't go through the door** le piano ne passera pas par la porte; **four into three won't go** trois n'est pas divisible par quatre
(**k**) *(belong)* aller; **the cups go on that shelf** les tasses vont sur cette étagère
(**l**) *(become)* devenir; **to go crazy** devenir fou (folle); **to go red** rougir; **to go cold** refroidir
(**m**) *(be the rule)* **what she says goes** c'est elle qui commande
(**n**) *Fam (urinate)* aller aux toilettes
(**o**) *Am* **two burgers to go** *(to take away)* deux hamburgers à emporter

2 *vt* **(a)** *(make sound)* & *Fam (say)* faire; **cows go moo** la vache fait meuh; **to go bang/plop** faire paf/plouf **(b)** *(idioms)* **to go it alone** se lancer en solo; **to go one better than sb** faire mieux que qn, surenchérir sur qn; *Fam* **I could really go a beer!** je me ferais bien une bière!

3 *n* (*pl* **goes**) **(a)** *(expressing activity)* **to be on the go** ne pas arrêter; **she had three boyfriends on the go at the same time** elle avait trois copains en même temps; **it's all go** ça n'arrête pas; **from the word go** dès le début **(b)** *(energy)* **to be full of go** être dynamique **(c)** *(success)* **to make a go of sth** réussir qch **(d)** *(turn)* tour *m*; **(it's) your go!** *(in game)* c'est ton tour!, c'est à toi!; **to have a g. at doing sth** essayer de faire qch; *Fam* **let's have a go!** allons-y!; *(let me try)* laisse-moi essayer!; **at one go** d'un coup; **£1 a go** *(at fair)* 1 livre le tour **(e)** *(idioms)* **to have a go at sb** incendier qn

▸ **go about 1** *vi (circulate) (of person)* se promener; *(of rumour)* circuler; **you can't go about saying things like that!** il ne faut pas raconter des choses pareilles!; **there's a bug going about** il y a un microbe qui se promène **2** *vt insep* **(a)** *(travel) (country)* parcourir **(b)** *(tackle) (task)* vaquer à; **to go about doing sth** s'y prendre pour faire qch; **how do I go about getting a licence?** que dois-je faire pour obtenir un permis?

▸ **go across** *vt insep* & *vi* traverser

▸ **go after** *vt insep (pursue)* **to go after sb** courir après qn; **to go after sth** essayer d'obtenir qch

▸ **go against** *vt insep* **(a)** *(contradict) (principles, instincts)* aller à l'encontre de **(b)** *(be unfavourable to)* **the decision went against him** la décision lui a été défavorable

▸ **go ahead** *vi* **(a)** *(take place)* avoir lieu; **to go ahead with sth** commencer *ou* entreprendre qch; **may I say something?** – **go ahead** puis-je dire quelque chose? – allez-y **(b)** *(go in front)* passer devant; **to go ahead of sb** devancer qn

▸ **go along** *vi (proceed)* se dérouler; **as we go along** en chemin; **to do sth as one goes along** faire qch au fur et à mesure

▸ **go along with** *vt insep (suggestion, plan)* approuver, être d'accord avec

▸ **go at** *vt insep (person, task)* s'attaquer à

▸ **go away** *vi (leave)* partir; *(disappear)* disparaître; **go away!** allez-vous-en!; **to go away on business/for the weekend** partir en voyage d'affaires/en week-end

▸ **go back** *vi* **(a)** *(return)* revenir; **to go back to doing sth** se remettre à faire qch; **to go back to sleep** se rendormir; **to go back to one's old ways** reprendre ses anciennes habitudes **(b)** *(in time)* **to go back to** remonter à; *Fam* **we go back a long way** ça fait longtemps qu'on se connaît

▸ **go back on** *vt insep (promise)* revenir sur

▸ **go before 1** *vi (precede)* précéder **2** *vt insep* **to go before the court** *(of defendant, case)* passer au tribunal

▸ **go by 1** *vi* **(a)** *(pass)* passer; **to watch the world go by** regarder passer les gens **(b)** *(of time)* s'écouler **2** *vt insep* **(a)** *(be guided by)* **to go by appearances** juger d'après les apparences; **to go by the rules** respecter les règles **(b)** *(be known by)* **to go by the name of** être connu(e) sous le nom de

▸ **go down 1** *vt insep (descend)* descendre **2** *vi* **(a)** *(descend)* descendre; *(of sun)* se coucher; *(of ship)* sombrer; **to go down on one's knees** s'agenouiller; *Fig* se mettre à genoux; **to go down with an illness** tomber malade **(b)** *(be defeated)* être vaincu(e); **I'm not going to go down without a fight** je me battrai jusqu'au bout **(c)** *(of level, temperature, prices)* baisser; *(of tyre, balloon)* se dégonfler **(d)** *(be received)* **to go down well/badly** être bien/mal reçu(e); **he has gone down in history as a**

tyrant l'histoire a retenu de lui l'image d'un tyran

▸ **go for** *vt insep* **(a)** *(attack)* attaquer; **if you really want the job, go for it!** si tu veux vraiment le poste, bats-toi!; *Fam* **go for it!** vas-y! **(b)** *(like)* avoir un faible pour **(c)** *(choose)* prendre **(d)** **he has got a lot going for him** il a bien des atouts **(e)** *(apply to)* s'appliquer à; **the same goes for you** ça vaut aussi pour toi

▸ **go in** *vi (enter)* entrer; *(fit)* rentrer; *(of sun)* se cacher

▸ **go in for** *vt insep* **(a)** *(competition)* s'inscrire à **(b)** *(like)* **she doesn't go in for opera** elle n'est pas très portée sur l'opéra

▸ **go into** *vt insep* **(a)** *(enter)* entrer dans **(b)** *(examine)* examiner

▸ **go off 1** *vi* **(a)** *(leave)* partir **(with** avec) **(b)** *(of meat, fish)* s'avarier; *(of milk)* tourner **(c)** *(of bomb)* exploser; *(of alarm)* se déclencher; **the gun went off** le coup est parti **(d)** *(of event)* **to go off well** *or* **smoothly** se dérouler bien **(e)** *(stop working)* **the power went off** l'électricité a été coupée; **the light went off** la lumière s'est éteinte **2** *vt insep (lose liking for)* ne plus aimer, se lasser de; **I've gone off the idea** l'idée ne me séduit plus

▸ **go on** *vi* **(a)** *(continue)* continuer; **to go on doing sth** continuer à faire qch; **as time went on** avec le temps **(b)** *(proceed)* **to go on to sth** passer à qch; **to go on to do sth** poursuivre en faisant qch **(c)** *(talk excessively)* **don't go on about it!** arrête de parler de ça!; **he does go on a bit** il est un peu soûlant; **to go on at sb** s'en prendre à qn **(d)** *(happen)* se passer; **what's going on here?** qu'est-ce qui se passe ici? **(e)** *(of electricity, light, heating)* s'allumer **2** *vt insep (be guided by)* se fonder sur; **the police have nothing to go on** la police n'a rien sur quoi se fonder **(b)** *(approach)* **she's two going on three** elle va sur ses trois ans

▸ **go out** *vi* **(a)** *(leave)* sortir; **to go out for a meal** aller au restaurant; **to go out on strike** se mettre en grève **(b)** *(date)* sortir ensemble; **to go out with sb** sortir avec qn **(c)** *(of fire, light)* s'éteindre **(d)** *(become unfashionable)* passer de mode **(e)** *(be eliminated)* être éliminé(e) **(f)** *(of TV, radio programme)* être diffusé(e)

▸ **go over** *vi* **(a)** *(cross)* **to go over to sb** aller vers qn **(b)** *(switch)* **to go over to sth** passer à qch **(c)** *(of suggestion, joke)* **to go over well/badly** être bien/mal reçu(e) **2** *vt insep* **(a)** *(bridge)* passer; *(road)* traverser; **the ball went over the wall** la balle est passée par-dessus le mur **(b)** *(examine)* passer en revue; *(figures, accounts)* vérifier; **to go over sth in one's mind** repasser qch dans son esprit

▸ **go round 1** *vt insep* **to go round town** faire un tour en ville; **to go round the shops** faire les magasins **2** *vi* **(a)** *(visit)* **I said I'd go round (and see her)** j'ai dit que j'irai la voir; **she's gone round to a friend's** elle est allée voir un ami **(b)** *(circulate) (of rumour)* circuler; *(of cold, flu)* se promener **(c)** *(be enough)* **there was enough food/drink to go round** il y avait assez à manger/boire pour tout le monde

▸ **go through 1** *vt insep* **(a)** *(penetrate)* traverser **(b)** *(suffer)* subir **(c)** *(complete) (formalities)* accomplir **(d)** *(examine)* passer en revue; *(one's notes, speech)* revoir; *(suitcase, house)* fouiller; **to go through sb's pockets** fouiller les poches de qn **(e)** *(use up) (money)* dépenser; **we've gone through six bottles of wine** nous avons bu six bouteilles de vin **2** *vi (be completed) (of deal)* être conclu(e); *(of bill)* passer; *(of divorce)* être prononcé(e)

▸ **go through with** *vt insep* aller jusqu'au bout de; **I can't go through with the wedding** finalement, je ne me marie plus; **I can't go through with it** je ne peux pas le faire

▸ **go under** *vi (of ship)* couler; *Fig (of firm)* faire faillite

▸**go up 1** *vt insep* monter
2 *vi* **(a)** *(climb, rise)* monter; *(of theatre curtain)* se lever; to go up to bed monter se coucher; **a shout went up from the crowd** un cri s'éleva de la foule; *Fig* to go up in the world *(socially)* faire son chemin **(b)** *(of prices, temperature)* monter, grimper; **to go up in sb's estimation** monter dans l'estime de qn **(c)** *(explode)* sauter

▸**go up to** *vt insep* **(a)** *(approach)* se diriger vers **(b)** *(reach)* aller jusqu'à

▸**go with** *vt insep* **(a)** *(accompany)* aller (de pair) avec; **a company car goes with the job** le poste donne droit à une voiture de fonction **(b)** *(harmonize with)* aller avec

▸**go without 1** *vi* se priver; **I'd rather go without** je préfère m'en passer
2 *vt insep* se passer de

goad [gəʊd] **1** *n Fig (remark, criticism)* aiguillon *m*
2 *vt Fig (person)* provoquer; to g. sb into doing sth harceler qn jusqu'à ce qu'il fasse qch

▸**goad on** *vt sep* aiguillonner

go-ahead ['gəʊəhed] **1** *n* to give sb/sth the g. donner le feu vert à qn/qch
2 *adj (enterprising)* entreprenant(e), dynamique

goal [gəʊl] *n* **(a)** *(aim)* but *m*, objectif *m* **(b)** *(in football, hockey)* but *m*, g. kick coup *m* de pied de but; g. line ligne *f* de but; g. scorer buteur(euse) *m,f*

goalkeeper ['gəʊlkiːpə(r)], *Fam* **goalie** ['gəʊlɪ] *n* gardien *m* de but, goal *m*

goalless ['gəʊlɪs] *adj* g. draw match *m* nul

goalmouth ['gəʊlmaʊθ] *n (in football)* (entrée *f* du) but *m*

goalpost ['gəʊlpəʊst] *n* poteau *m* de but; the goalposts les buts *mpl; Fig* to move *or* shift the goalposts changer les règles du jeu

goat [gəʊt] *n* chèvre *f*; g.'s cheese (fromage *m* de) chèvre *m*; g.'s milk lait *m* de chèvre; *Fam* it really gets my g.! ça me tape vraiment sur les nerfs!; *Fam* to act *or* play the g. faire l'idiot(e)

goatherd ['gəʊthɜːd] *n* chevrier(ère) *m,f*

goatskin ['gəʊtskɪn] *n* peau *f* de chèvre

gob [gɒb] *Br very Fam* **1** *n (mouth)* gueule *f*; shut your g.! (ferme) ta gueule!
2 *vi (pt & pp gobbed) (spit)* mollarder

gobble ['gɒbəl] **1** *vt (eat)* engloutir
2 *vi (of turkey)* glouglouter

▸**gobble up** *vt sep also Fig* engloutir

gobbledygook ['gɒbəldɪguːk] *n Fam* charabia *m*

go-between ['gəʊbɪtwiːn] *n* intermédiaire *mf*

goblet ['gɒblɪt] *n* verre *m* à pied; *(in medieval times)* coupe *f*

goblin ['gɒblɪn] *n* lutin *m*

gobsmacked ['gɒbsmækt] *adj Br very Fam* to be g. en rester estomaqué(e)

go-cart ['gəʊkaːt] *n* = go-kart

god [gɒd] *n* **(a)** *(divine being)* dieu *m*; G. Dieu *m*; G. forbid! Dieu m'en garde!; G. willing si Dieu le veut; I wish to G. I hadn't accepted si seulement je n'avais pas accepté; in G.'s name au nom du Ciel; *Fam* (oh) my G.! mon Dieu!; *Fam* for G.'s sake! pour l'amour du ciel!; *Fam* G. knows Dieu seul le sait; *Fam* he thinks he's G.'s gift to women il s'imagine que toutes les femmes sont folles de lui **(b)** *Fam* the gods *(in theatre)* le poulailler

godchild ['gɒdtʃaɪld] *n* filleul(e) *m,f*

goddaughter ['gɒdɔːtə(r)] *n* filleule *f*

goddess ['gɒdɪs] *n* déesse *f*

godfather ['gɒdfɑːðə(r)] *n* parrain *m*

god-fearing ['gɒdfɪərɪŋ] *adj* pieux(euse)

godforsaken ['gɒdfəseɪkən] *adj* perdu(e)

godless ['gɒdlɪs] *adj* impie

godmother ['gɒdmʌðə(r)] *n* marraine *f*

godparent ['gɒdpeərənt] *n (godfather)* parrain *m*; *(godmother)* marraine *f*; my godparents mon parrain et ma marraine

godsend ['gɒdsend] *n* aubaine *f*

godson ['gɒdsʌn] *n* filleul *m*

go-getter ['gəʊgetə(r)] *n Fam* battant(e) *m,f*

goggle ['gɒgəl] *vi* ouvrir des yeux ronds; to g. at sb/sth regarder qn/qch avec des yeux ronds

goggle-eyed ['gɒgəlaɪd] *adv Fam* avec des yeux ronds

goggles ['gɒgəlz] *npl (for swimming)* lunettes *fpl* de plongée; *(for skiing)* lunettes de ski; *(for worker)* lunettes protectrices

go-go dancer ['gəʊgəʊ'dɑːnsə(r)] *n* danseuse *f* de boîte de nuit

going ['gəʊɪŋ] **1** *n* **(a)** *(progress)* that's very good g.! voilà qui n'est pas mal du tout!; it's slow g. *(at work)* ça n'avance pas vite **(b)** *(condition of ground)* terrain *m, Fig* the book/film was pretty heavy g. le livre/film était plutôt indigeste; *Fig* to get out while the g. is good se retirer tant que la chance nous/leur/etc est favorable
2 *adj* **(a)** *(successful)* a g. concern une affaire qui tourne **(b)** *(current) (price, rate)* courant(e), actuel(elle)

going-away ['gəʊɪŋə'weɪ] *adj* g. outfit = tenue de voyage de noces; g. party/present fête *f*/cadeau *m* d'adieu

going-over ['gəʊɪŋ'əʊvə(r)] *n Fam* to give sb a g. *(beating)* tabasser qn; *(criticism)* sonner les cloches à qn

goings-on ['gəʊɪŋzɒn] *npl Fam (activities)* activités *fpl; (events)* événements *mpl*

goitre, *Am* **goiter** ['gɔɪtə(r)] *n* goitre *m*

go-kart ['gəʊkɑːt] *n (child's toy)* petit chariot *m; (with engine)* kart *m*; g. racing karting *m*

gold [gəʊld] **1** *n or m;* g. bullion or en barre; g. dust poussière *f* d'or; tickets are like g. dust les billets valent de l'or; g. leaf *or* foil feuille *f* d'or; g. medal médaille *f* d'or; also *Fig* g. mine mine *f* d'or; g. plate orfèvrerie *f; Fin* g. reserves réserves *fpl* d'or

2 *adj (made of gold)* en or; *(gold-coloured)* doré(e)

gold-digger ['gəʊld'dɪgə(r)] *n Fam Pej (woman)* croqueuse *f* de diamants

golden ['gəʊldən] *adj (made of gold)* en or; *(gold-coloured)* doré(e); a g. opportunity une occasion en or; the g. age l'âge *m* d'or; g. boy enfant *m* chéri; g. eagle aigle *m* royal; g. girl enfant *f* chérie; g. handshake *(retirement bonus)* indemnité *f* de départ; g. jubilee jubilé *m*; g. rule règle *f* d'or; *Fin* g. share action *f* privilégiée; g. wedding noces *fpl* d'or

goldfinch ['gəʊldfɪntʃ] *n* chardonneret *m*

goldfish ['gəʊldfɪʃ] *(pl* goldfish*)* *n* poisson *m* rouge; g. bowl bocal *m* à poissons rouges; it's like living in a g. bowl c'est comme vivre en vitrine

gold-plated [gəʊld'pleɪtɪd] *adj* plaqué(e) or

goldsmith ['gəʊldsmɪθ] *n* orfèvre *m*

golf [gɒlf] *n* golf *m*; g. ball balle *f* de golf; g. club *(stick, association)* club *m* de golf; g. course terrain *m* de golf

golfer ['gɒlfə(r)] *n* joueur(euse) *m,f* de golf

golfing ['gɒlfɪŋ] *n* golf *m*; g. umbrella grand parapluie (de golf)

golly ['gɒlɪ] *exclam Fam Old-fashioned* fichtre!

gondola ['gɒndələ] *n (a) (boat)* gondole *f* **(b)** *(cable car)* cabine *f* de téléphérique

gondolier [gɒndə'lɪə(r)] *n* gondolier *m*

gone [gɒn] **1** *adj* **(a)** *(past)* **it's g. nine o'clock** il est neuf heures passées **(b)** *Fam* **to be six months g.** *(pregnant)* être enceinte de six mois; *Fam* **to be pretty far g.** *(drunk)* être complètement bourré(e); *Fam* **to be g. on sb** *(infatuated)* avoir le béguin pour qn **2** *pp of* **go**

goner ['gɒnə(r)] *n Fam* **I thought she was a g.** *(would die)* j'ai cru qu'elle allait y passer; **I'm a g.** *if she finds out* si elle l'apprend, je suis mort

gong [gɒŋ] *n* gong *m*; *Br Fam (medal)* breloque *f*

gonna ['gənə] *Fam* = going to

gonorrhoea, *Am* **gonorrhea** [gɒnə'rɪə] *n* blennorragie *f*; **to have g.** avoir une blennorragie

goo [gu:] *n Fam* **(a)** *(sticky substance)* substance *f* visqueuse **(b)** *(sentimentality)* guimauve *f*

good [gʊd] **1** *n* **(a)** bien *m*; **to do g.** faire le bien; **he's up to no g.** il prépare un mauvais coup; **to see the g. in sb/sth** voir les bons côtés de qn/qch **(b)** *(benefit)* **I did it for your own g.** je l'ai fait pour ton bien; **it was all to the g.** c'était tout bénéfice; **we were $100 to the g.** nous avons fait 100 dollars de bénéfice; **for the g. of one's health** pour sa santé; **for the common g.** dans l'intérêt général; **it will do you g.** cela te fera du bien; **it won't do any g.** cela ne servira à rien; **what's the g. of that?** à quoi bon?; **it's no g.** ça ne sert à rien; **it's no g. complaining** cela ne sert à rien de se plaindre; **he's no g.** *(incompetent)* il est nul; *(morally bad)* il ne vaut pas grand-chose **(c)** *for* **g.** *(permanently)* pour toujours; **she is gone for g.** elle est partie pour de bon

2 *adj* (*comparative* **better** ['betə(r)], *superlative* **best** [best]) **(a)** *(quality)* bon (bonne); *(weather, handwriting)* beau (belle); **she looks g.** in that hat ce chapeau lui va bien, elle est bien avec ce chapeau; **to taste g.** avoir bon goût; **(that) sounds g.!** bonne idée!; **g. to eat** comestible; **it's g. to see you** ça fait plaisir de vous voir; *Fam* **that's a g. one!** *(of story, joke)* elle est bien bonne!; **he thinks he's too g. for us** il se croit trop bien pour nous; **to earn g. money** bien gagner sa vie; **you've got a g. chance** tu as tes chances; **to be on to a g. thing** être sur un bon filon; **to have a g. time** s'amuser; **to show sb a g. time** faire passer un bon moment à qn; **all in g. time** chaque chose en son temps; **too g. to be true** trop beau pour être vrai; **as g. as new** comme neuf (neuve); **he as g. as called me a liar** pour un peu, il m'aurait traité de menteur; **the g. old days** le bon vieux temps; **g. afternoon!** bonjour!; **the G. Book** la sainte Bible; **he's a g. friend** c'est un ami; **G. Friday** le Vendredi Saint; *Fam* **g. grief!** fichtre!; **the g. life** la belle vie; *Fam* **g. Lord!, g. heavens!, g. gracious!** bon sang!; **g. morning!** bonjour!; **g. night!** bonne nuit!; **the G. Samaritan** le bon Samaritain **(b)** *(advantageous)* **a g. opportunity** une bonne occasion; **to be in a g. position to do sth** être bien placé(e) pour faire qch; **it's looking g.** ça se présente bien **(c)** *(beneficial)* bon (bonne); **he doesn't know what's g. for him** il n'a pas un sou de bon sens; **to be g. for business** être bon pour les affaires; **it's a g. thing we stayed at home** heureusement que nous sommes restés à la maison; **g. riddance!** bon débarras! **(d)** *(skilful)* bon (bonne) (**at** en); **to be g. with one's hands** être habile de ses mains; **to be g. with children** savoir y faire avec les enfants; **to be g. in bed** bien faire l'amour **(e)** *(well-behaved)* sage; **be g.!** *(to child)* sois sage!; **to be as g. as gold** être sage comme une image; **to lead a g. life** mener une vie respectable; **g. conduct** *or* **behaviour** bonne conduite *f* **(f)** *(kind)* gentil(ille); **that's very g. of you** c'est bien aimable *ou* très gentil de votre part; **he was very g. about** it il s'est montré très compréhensif; **to do sb a g. turn** rendre un service à qn **(g)** *(valid)* **a g. reason** une bonne raison, une raison valable; **he's g. for $25,000** *(has in credit)* il dispose de 25 000 dollars **(h)** *(for emphasis)* bon (bonne); **a g. two hours** deux bonnes heures; **a g. deal of, a g. many** beaucoup de; **to have a g. look at sb/sth** bien regarder qn/qch; **to have a g. cry** pleurer un bon coup; **a g. long time** un bien long moment **(i)** **to make g.** *(of person)* faire son chemin; **to make g. one's losses** compenser ses pertes; **to make g. one's promise** tenir sa promesse; **he made g. his escape** il a réussi son évasion

3 *adv* **(a)** **I'll do it when I'm g. and ready** je le ferai quand ça me chantera **(b)** *(as comment, answer)* bien; **I feel better today – g.** je me sens mieux aujourd'hui – tant mieux

goodbye [gʊd'baɪ] *n* au revoir *m*; **g.!** au revoir!; **to say g. to sb** dire au revoir à qn; **he can say g. to a career as a doctor** il peut dire adieu à sa carrière de médecin

good-for-nothing ['gʊdfənʌθɪŋ] *n* bon (bonne) à rien *m,f*

good-humoured, *Am* **good-humored** [gʊd-'hju:məd] *adj* *(debate, meeting)* détendu(e); **to be g.** *(of person)* avoir un caractère enjoué

good-looking ['gʊdlʊkɪŋ] *adj* beau (belle)

good-natured [gʊd'neɪtʃəd] *adj* *(person)* d'un caractère agréable; *(remarks, laugh)* bon enfant *inv*

goodness ['gʊdnɪs] *n* **(a)** *(of person)* bonté *f* **(b)** *(of food)* qualités *fpl* nutritives **(c)** *(in exclamations)* **g. (me)!** mon Dieu!; **thank g.!** Dieu merci!; **for g. sake!** pour l'amour de Dieu!

goods [gʊdz] *npl* **(a)** *Law* biens *mpl* **(b)** *(articles)* articles *mpl*, marchandises *fpl*; *Fig* **to deliver the g.** remplir ses engagements; *Fig* **to come up with the g.** faire le nécessaire; **g. train/depot** train *m*/dépôt *m* de marchandises

good-tempered [gʊd'tempəd] *adj* *(person)* d'un caractère facile; *(discussion)* aimable

goodwill [gʊd'wɪl] *n* **(a)** *(benevolence)* bienveillance *f*; *(willingness)* bonne volonté *f* **(b)** *Com* fonds *m* de commerce

goody ['gʊdɪ] **1** *n* *(pl* **goodies***)* *Fam* **(a)** *(person)* bon *m*; **the goodies and the baddies** les bons *mpl* et les méchants *mpl* **(b)** **goodies** *(nice food)* bonnes choses *fpl*; *(nice things)* petits cadeaux *mpl* **2** *exclam* chouette!

goody-goody ['gʊdɪgʊdɪ] *Fam Pej* **1** *n* *(pl* **goody-goodies***)* fayot *m* **2** *adj* fayot

gooey ['gu:ɪ] *adj* *Fam* **(a)** *(sticky)* gluant(e) **(b)** *(sentimental)* à la guimauve

goof [gu:f] *Am Fam* **1** *n* **(a)** *(blunder)* gaffe *f*, bourde *f* **(b)** *(idiot)* cave *m* **2** *vi* faire une gaffe *ou* une bourde

▶ **goof about, goof around** *vi Am Fam* faire l'idiot(e)

▶ **goof off** *Am Fam* **1** *vt insep* **to g. off work** ne pas aller bosser **2** *vi* flemmarder, glandouiller

goofy ['gu:fɪ] *adj Fam* **(a)** *(stupid)* loufoque **(b)** *Br (buck-toothed)* qui a les dents en avant

goolies ['gu:lɪz] *npl Br very Fam (testicles)* couilles *fpl*

goon [gu:n] *n Fam* **(a)** *Br (stupid person)* imbécile *mf* **(b)** *Am (thug)* gorille *m*

goose [gu:s] *(pl* **geese** [gi:s]*)* *n* oie *f*; *Fig* **his g. is cooked** il est fichu; **to kill the g. that lays the golden egg** tuer la poule aux œufs d'or; *Br* g. pimples, *Am* g. bumps chair *f* de poule

gooseberry ['gʊzbərɪ] (*pl* **gooseberries**) *n* groseille *f* à maquereau; *Br Fam* **to play g.** tenir la chandelle; g. **bush** groseillier *m*

gooseflesh ['gu:sfleʃ] *n* chair *f* de poule

goose-step ['gu:sstep] **1** *n* pas *m* de l'oie **2** *vi* (*pt & pp* **goose-stepped**) marcher au pas de l'oie

gopher ['gəʊfə(r)] *n* (*animal*) spermophile *m*

gore [gɔ:(r)] **1** *n* (*blood*) sang *m* (versé) **2** *vt* (*of bull*) encorner; **to be gored to death** être tué(e) à coups de corne

gorge [gɔ:dʒ] **1** *n* (*valley*) gorge *f*, défilé *m* **2** *vt* **to g. oneself** se gorger, se gaver (**on** de) **3** *vi* se gorger, se gaver (**on** de)

gorgeous ['gɔ:dʒəs] *adj* magnifique; (*meal, food*) excellent(e)

gorilla [gə'rɪlə] *n* gorille *m*

gormless ['gɔ:mlɪs] *adj Br Fam* balourd(e)

gorse [gɔ:s] *n* ajoncs *mpl*

gory ['gɔ:rɪ] *adj* (*film, crime, war*) sanglant(e); (*covered in blood*) ensanglanté(e); *Fig & Hum* **in g. detail** avec tous les détails

gosh [gɒʃ] *exclam Fam* ça alors!

goshawk ['gɒshɔ:k] *n* autour *m*

gosling ['gɒzlɪŋ] *n* oison *m*

go-slow [gəʊ'sləʊ] *n Br* grève *f* du zèle

gospel ['gɒspəl] *n* évangile *m*; **to take sth as g.** accepter qch comme parole d'évangile; g. (**music**) gospel *m*; g. **singer** chanteur(euse) *m,f* de gospel

gossamer ['gɒsəmə(r)] *n* (**a**) (*spider's web*) fils *mpl* de la Vierge (**b**) (*fabric*) gaze *f* légère

gossip ['gɒsɪp] **1** *n* (**a**) (*person*) bavard(e) *m,f*; (*ill-natured*) commère *f* (**b**) (*talk*) bavardages *mpl*; (*ill-natured*) commérage(s) *m(pl)*; **have you heard the latest g.?** tu sais la nouvelle?; **to have a g. (about)** bavarder (à propos de), g. **column** (*in newspaper*) chronique *f* mondaine **2** *vi* bavarder; (*ill-naturedly*) colporter des commérages

gossipy ['gɒsɪpɪ] *adj* (*person*) bavard(e); (*ill-natured*) cancanier(ère); (*letter, conversation*) plein(e) de petits potins

got [gɒt] *pt & pp of* **get**

Gothic ['gɒθɪk] **1** *n* (*artistic style, language*) gothique *m* **2** *adj* gothique

gotta ['gɒtə] *very Fam* = **got to**

gotten ['gɒtən] *Am pp of* **get**

▸ **gouge out** [gaʊdʒ] *vt sep* (*hole, path*) creuser; **to g. sb's eye out** arracher l'œil à qn

goulash ['gu:læʃ] *n* goulasch *m*

gourd ['gʊəd] *n* gourde *f*

gourmet ['gʊəmeɪ] *n* gourmet *m*, gastronome *mf*; g. **restaurant** restaurant *m* gastronomique

gout [gaʊt] *n* (*disease*) goutte *f*

Gov (**a**) (*abbr* **government**) gouvernement *m* (**b**) (*abbr* **governor**) gouverneur *m*

govern ['gʌvən] *vt* (**a**) (*state, country*) gouverner (**b**) (*of scientific law*) régir (**c**) (*emotions*) maîtriser, contenir

governess ['gʌvənɪs] *n* gouvernante *f*

governing ['gʌvənɪŋ] *adj* (*party, coalition*) au pouvoir; (*concept, principle*) directeur(trice); g. **body** conseil *m* d'administration

government ['gʌvənmənt] *n* gouvernement *m*; g. **intervention** intervention *f* du gouvernement

governmental [gʌvən'mentəl] *adj* gouvernemental(e)

governor ['gʌvənə(r)] *n* (*of colony, bank, US state*) gouverneur *m*; (*of prison*) directeur *m*; (*of school*) = fonctionnaire gestionnaire d'une école; *Br Fam* **the g.** (*boss*) le patron; g. **general** gouverneur *m* général

governorship ['gʌvənəʃɪp] *n* (*post*) poste *m* de gouverneur; (*function*) fonctions *fpl* de gouverneur

Govt (*abbr* **government**) gouvernement *m*

gown [gaʊn] *n* (*of woman*) robe *f*; (*of magistrate, academic*) robe, toge *f*; (*of surgeon*) blouse *f*

GP [dʒi:'pi:] *n Br* (*abbr* **general practitioner**) (médecin *m*) généraliste *mf*

gr (*abbr* **gramme(s)**) g

grab [græb] **1** *n* **to make a g. at** *or* **for sth** essayer d'attraper qch; *Fam* **to be up for grabs** être à qui veut le prendre; (*be for sale*) être à qui veut l'acheter **2** *vt* (*pt & pp* **grabbed**) (**a**) (*seize*) **to g. (hold of) sb/sth** saisir qn/qch; (*more tightly*) empoigner qn/qch; **I'll g. a sandwich later** j'avalerai un sandwich plus tard (**b**) *Fam* (*attract*) **the idea doesn't g. me** ça ne me dit rien; **how does that g. you?** ça te dit? **3** *vi* **to g. at sb** essayer de s'agripper à qn; **to g. at sth** essayer d'attraper qch

grace [greɪs] **1** *n* (**a**) (*of movement, dancer, manners*) grâce *f*; **to do sth with (a) good/bad g.** faire qch de bonne/mauvaise grâce; **to have the (good) g. to do sth** avoir la grâce de faire qch (**b**) (*favour*) to be in sb's good graces être dans les bonnes grâces de qn (**c**) *Rel* **in a state of g.** en état de grâce; **to fall from g.** perdre la grâce; *Fig* tomber en disgrâce; **there, but for the g. of God, go I** je remercie le ciel de m'avoir épargné (**d**) (*for payment of a bill*) **seven days'** etc. **g.** sept jours de délai ou de grâce (**e**) (*prayer before meal*) bénédicité *m* (**f**) (*form of address*) **Your G.** (*to bishop*) Monseigneur *m*; (*to duke*) Monsieur le duc; (*to duchess*) Madame la duchesse **2** *vt* (**a**) (*honour*) honorer (**with** de) (**b**) (*decorate*) embellir, enjoliver

graceful ['greɪsfʊl] *adj* (*person, movement*) gracieux(euse); (*speech, style*) élégant(e)

gracefully ['greɪsfʊlɪ] *adv* avec grâce, gracieusement

graceless ['greɪslɪs] *adj* (**a**) (*inelegant*) disgracieux(euse) (**b**) (*rude*) effronté(e)

gracious ['greɪʃəs] **1** *adj* (**a**) (*kind, polite*) poli(e), affable; (*in victory*) courtois(e) (**b**) (*elegant*) pleine(e) de raffinement **2** *exclam* **g. (me)!, goodness g.!** mon Dieu!

graciously ['greɪʃəslɪ] *adv* avec grâce; (*accept, invite*) de bonne grâce

gradation [grə'deɪʃən] *n* (*of colours*) gradation *f*; (*on thermometer*) degré *m*; (*of meaning*) nuance *f*

grade [greɪd] **1** *n* (**a**) (*rank*) grade *m*, rang *m*; (*in profession*) échelon *m*; (**b**) (*quality*) qualité *f*; (*of vegetable, fruit*) calibre *m*; *Fig* **to make the g.** se montrer à la hauteur (**c**) *Am Sch* (*mark*) note *f* (**d**) *Am* (*year at school*) classe *f*; g. **school** ≃ école *f* primaire **2** *vt* (**a**) (*classify*) classer; (*fruit, vegetables*) calibrer (**b**) *Am* (*essay, exercise*) noter

gradient ['greɪdɪənt] *n* (**a**) (*of slope*) dénivellation *f* (**b**) (*of temperature*) gradient *m*

gradual ['grædjʊəl] *adj* graduel(elle), progressif(ive)

gradualism ['grædjʊəlɪzm] *n* gradualisme *m*

gradually ['grædjʊəlɪ] *adv* graduellement, progressivement

graduate 1 *n* ['grædjʊət] *Br* (*from university*) ≃ licencié(e) *m,f*; *Am* (*from high school*) bachelier(ère) *m,f* **2** *adj* ['grædjʊət] *Am* (*postgraduate*) g. **studies** études *fpl* de troisième cycle **3** *vi* ['grædjʊeɪt] (**a**) *Br* (*from university*) obtenir sa licence; *Am* (*from high school*) avoir son bac (**b**) (*progress*) **to g. from sth to sth** passer de qch à qch

graduated ['grædjʊeɪtɪd] *adj (thermometer)* gradué(e); *(pay rise)* progressif(ive)

graduation [grædjʊ'eɪʃən] *n (from school, university)* remise *f* des diplômes; **g. ceremony** cérémonie *f* de remise des diplômes

graffiti [græ'fiːtiː] *n* graffiti *mpl*; **a piece of g.** un graffiti

graft¹ [grɑːft] **1** *n (technique)* greffe *f*; *(thing grafted)* greffon *m*
  2 *vt* greffer **(onto** sur)

graft² *Fam* **1** *n* **(a)** *Am (bribe)* pot-de-vin *m* **(b)** *Br (work)* **(hard)** *g.* boulot *m*
  2 *vi Br (work hard)* bosser dur

grafter ['grɑːftə(r)] *n Br Fam* bosseur(euse) *m,f*

grain [greɪn] *n* **(a)** *(of wheat, salt, sand)* grain *m*; **a g. of truth** une once de vérité **(b)** *(in photo, wood)* grain *m*; *(in meat, material)* fil *m*; *Fig* **it goes against the g. for me to do it** ce n'est pas dans ma nature de le faire **(c)** *(cereals)* céréales *fpl*

grainy ['greɪnɪ] *adj* granuleux(euse)

gram [græm] *n* gramme *m*

grammar ['græmə(r)] *n* grammaire *f*; **g. (book)** (livre *m* de) grammaire; *Br* **g. school** ≃ lycée *m*

grammarian [grə'meərɪən] *n* grammarien(enne) *m,f*

grammatical [grə'mætɪkəl] *adj* grammatical(e)

grammatically [grə'mætɪklɪ] *adv* grammaticalement

gramme [græm] *n* gramme *m*

gramophone ['græməfəʊn] *n Br Old-fashioned* gramophone *m*

gran [græn] *n Br Fam (grandmother)* grand-mère *f*; *(term of address)* mamie *f*, mémé *f*

granary ['grænərɪ] *(pl* **granaries)** *n* grenier *m*; *Br* **g. bread** = sorte de pain complet

grand [grænd] **1** *adj* **(a)** *(imposing)* grandiose, imposant(e); **to do things on a g. scale** faire les choses en grand; *Mus & Fig* **g. finale** apothéose *f*; *Am* **g. jury** = jury qui décide si une affaire doit être portée ou non devant les tribunaux; **g. master** *(in chess)* grand maître *m*; **the G. National** = steeple-chase le plus célèbre d'Angleterre; **g. piano** piano *m* à queue; **g. slam** grand chelem *m*; **g. total** somme *f* totale **(b)** *Fam (excellent)* excellent(e)
  2 *n (pl* **grand)** *Fam (thousand pounds)* mille livres *fpl*; *(thousand dollars)* mille dollars *mpl*

grandchild ['græntʃaɪld] *(pl* **grandchildren** ['græntʃɪldrən])* *n (boy)* petit-fils *m*; *(girl)* petite fille *f*; **grandchildren** petits-enfants *mpl*

gran(d)dad ['grændæd] *n Fam* **(a)** *(grandfather)* grand-père *m*; *(term of address)* papi *m*, pépé *m* **(b)** *Pej (old man)* pépé *m*

grandaddy ['grændædɪ] *(pl* **grandaddies)** *n Fam* grand-père *m*; *(term of address)* papi *m*, pépé *m*

granddaughter ['grændɔːtə(r)] *n* petite fille *f*

grandeur ['grændjə(r)] *n (of person)* grandeur *f*, noblesse *f*; *(of building, surroundings)* splendeur *f*, magnificence *f*

grandfather ['grænfɑːðə(r)] *n* grand-père *m*; **g. clock** horloge *f* comtoise

grandiloquent [græn'dɪləkwənt] *adj* grandiloquent(e)

grandiose ['grændɪəʊs] *adj (building)* monumental(e); *(term, title)* pompeux(euse); *(idea, scheme)* démesuré(e)

grandly ['grændlɪ] *adv (impressively)* de façon grandiose; *(pompously)* de façon pompeuse

grandma ['grænmɑː] *n Fam* grand-mère *f*; *(term of address)* mamie *f*, mémé *f*

grandmother ['grænmʌðə(r)] *n* grand-mère *f*

grandpa ['grænpɑː] *n Fam* grand-père *m*; *(term of address)* papi *m*, pépé *m*

grandparent ['grænpeərənt] *n* grand-parent *m*

grandson ['grænsʌn] *n* petit-fils *m*

grandstand ['grænstænd] *n* tribune *f* d'honneur; *Fig* **to have a g. view of sth** être bien placé(e) pour voir qch

granite ['grænɪt] *n* granit *m*

granny ['grænɪ] *(pl* **grannies)** *n Fam* grand-mère *f*; *(term of address)* mamie *f*, mémé *f*; *Br* **g. flat** = partie d'une maison aménagée indépendamment pour héberger un parent âgé; **g. knot** double nœud *m*

grant [grɑːnt] **1** *n (financial aid)* subvention *f*; *(for student)* bourse *f* (d'études)
  2 *vt* **(a)** *(allow) (permission)* donner; *(interview, request)* accorder; **to take sth for granted** considérer qch comme allant de soi ou comme étant dû; **to take sb for granted** croire que qn sera toujours là **(b)** *(award) (money, subsidy)* accorder, allouer **(c)** *(admit)* admettre; **granted, he's not very intelligent, but...** d'accord, il n'est pas très intelligent, · mais...

granular ['grænjʊlə(r)] *adj* granuleux(euse)

granulated sugar ['grænjʊleɪtɪd'ʃʊgə(r)] *n* sucre *m* semoule

granule ['grænjʊl] *n (of salt, sand)* grain *m*; *(of coffee)* granule *m*

grape [greɪp] *n* grain *m* de raisin; **some grapes** du raisin; **g. harvest** vendange(s) *f(pl)*; **g. juice** jus *m* de raisin; **g. picker** vendangeur(euse) *m,f*

grapefruit ['greɪpfruːt] *n* pamplemousse *m*; **g. juice** jus *m* de pamplemousse

grapevine ['greɪpvaɪn] *n* vigne *f*; *(climbing)* treille *f*; *Fam* **I heard on the g. that...** j'ai entendu par le téléphone arabe que...

graph [grɑːf] *n* graphique *m*, diagramme *m*; **g. paper** papier *m* millimétré

graphic ['græfɪk] *adj* **(a)** *(vivid)* très détaillé(e); *(language)* cru(e); **in g. detail** de façon très détaillée **(b)** **g. artist** graphiste *mf*; **g. arts** arts *mpl* graphiques; **g. designer** graphiste *m*; **g. equalizer** égaliseur *m* graphique; **g. novel** bande *f* dessinée (pour adultes)

graphically ['græfɪklɪ] *adv (describe)* de façon très détaillée

graphics ['græfɪks] **1** *n (art)* arts *mpl* graphiques
  2 *npl Comptr* graphismes *mpl*, graphiques *mpl*

graphite ['græfaɪt] *n* graphite *m*, mine *f* de plomb

graphology [græ'fɒlədʒɪ] *n* graphologie *f*

grapnel ['græpnəl] *n Naut* grappin *m*

grapple ['græpəl] *vi (fight)* lutter corps à corps (**with** avec); *Fig (with problem)* se débattre (**with** avec)

grappling hook ['græplɪŋ'hʊk], **grappling iron** ['græplɪŋ'aɪən] *n Naut* grappin *m*

grasp [grɑːsp] **1** *n* **(a)** *(hold)* prise *f*; *Fig* **to have sth within one's g.** avoir qch à sa portée **(b)** *(understanding)* compréhension *f* (**of** de)
  2 *vt* **(a)** *(hold firmly)* saisir; *(more tightly)* empoigner; **to g. sb's arm** saisir qn par le bras; *Fig* **to g. the opportunity** saisir l'occasion **(b)** *(understand)* saisir, comprendre

grasping ['grɑːspɪŋ] *adj (mean)* avide, cupide

grass [grɑːs] **1** *n* **(a)** *(plant)* herbe *f*; *Fig* **she doesn't let the g. grow under her feet** elle ne perd pas de temps; *Fig* **g. roots** *(of organization)* base *f*; **g. roots support/opposition** soutien *m*/opposition *f* de la base; **g. snake** couleuvre *f* (à collier); **g. widow** = femme dont le mari est souvent en déplacement **(b)** *(lawn)* pelouse *f*, gazon *m*; **keep off the g.** *(sign)* pelouse interdite; **g. court** *(in tennis)* court *m* en gazon **(c)** *(pasture)* herbe *m*; *Fig* **to put sb out to g.** mettre qn à la retraite **(d)** *Fam (marijuana)* herbe *f* (**e)** *Br very Fam (informer)* balance *f*, indic *m*

2 *vi Br very Fam (inform)* moucharder; **to g.** on sb balancer qn

grasshopper ['grɑːshɒpə(r)] *n* sauterelle *f*

grassland ['grɑːslænd] *n* prairie *f*, pré *m*

grassy ['grɑːsɪ] *adj* herbu(e), herbeux(euse)

grate¹ [greɪt] *n (of hearth)* grille *f*; *(fireplace)* foyer *m*

grate² **1** *vt (cheese, nutmeg)* râper
2 *vi (of machinery)* grincer; **to g. on the ear** *(of voice)* écorcher les oreilles; *(of sound)* faire mal aux oreilles; **it really grates on me** *or* **on my nerves** ça me tape vraiment sur les nerfs

grateful ['greɪtfʊl] *adj* reconnaissant(e) **(for** dc); **I would be g. if you could let me know** je vous serais reconnaissant de m'en informer

gratefully ['greɪtfʊlɪ] *adv* avec reconnaissance

grater ['greɪtə(r)] *n* râpe *f*

gratification [grætɪfɪ'keɪʃən] *n* satisfaction *f*

gratified ['grætɪfaɪd] *adj* satisfait(e), content(e)

gratify ['grætɪfaɪ] *(pt & pp* **gratified)** *vt (person)* faire plaisir à; *(wish, desire)* satisfaire

gratifying ['grætɪfaɪɪŋ] *adj* satisfaisant(e)

grating¹ ['greɪtɪŋ] *adj (noise)* grinçant(e); *(voice)* éraillé(e)

grating² *n (grille)* grille *f*

gratis ['grɑːtɪs] *adv* gratis

gratitude ['grætɪtjuːd] *n* gratitude *f*, reconnaissance *f*

gratuitous [grə'tjuːɪtəs] *adj* gratuit(e)

gratuitously [grə'tjuːɪtəslɪ] *adv* gratuitement, sans raison

gratuity [grə'tjuːɪtɪ] *(pl* **gratuities)** *n* Formal *(tip)* pourboire *m*

grave [greɪv] **1** *n* tombe *f*; Fig **it would make him turn in his g.** ça le ferait se retourner dans sa tombe
2 *adj (manner, voice)* solennel(elle); *(situation)* grave; **to make a g. mistake** se tromper lourdement

gravedigger ['greɪvdɪgə(r)] *n* fossoyeur *m*

gravel ['grævəl] *n* gravier *m*; **g. path** allée *f* de gravier; **g. pit** carrière *f* de gravier

gravelly ['grævəlɪ] *adj (sand, soil)* graveleux(euse); *(voice)* râpeux(euse)

gravely ['greɪvlɪ] *adv* gravement

graven ['greɪvən] *adj* **g. image** idole *f*

graveside ['greɪvsaɪd] *n* **at the g.** près de la tombe

gravestone ['greɪvstəʊn] *n* pierre *f* tombale

graveyard ['greɪvjɑːd] *n* cimetière *m*

gravitate ['grævɪteɪt] *vi* **to g. towards sth** *(of person)* être attiré(e) par qch; **most of the guests had gravitated towards the kitchen** la plupart des invités s'étaient rassemblés dans la cuisine

gravitational [grævɪ'teɪʃənəl] *adj* gravitationnel(elle); **g. pull** gravitation *f*

gravity ['grævɪtɪ] *n* **(a)** *(physical force)* gravité *f*, pesanteur *f* **(b)** *(seriousness)* gravité *f*

gravy ['greɪvɪ] *n* = sauce à base de jus de viande; **g. boat** saucière *f*; Fam **to get on the g. train** trouver un filon

gray *Am* = **grey**

graze¹ [greɪz] **1** *vt (of farmer) (cattle)* faire paître
2 *vi (of cattle)* paître

graze² **1** *n* écorchure *f*; *(less serious)* égratignure *f*
2 *vt* écorcher; *(less seriously)* égratigner

grease [griːs] **1** *n* graisse *f*; **g. gun** pistolet *m* graisseur
2 *vt (machine)* graisser, lubrifier; *(cake tin)* beurrer; **to g. back one's hair** se gominer les cheveux; Fam Fig **to g. sb's**

palm graisser la patte à qn; Fam **like greased lightning** en quatrième vitesse

greasepaint ['griːspeɪnt] *n* maquillage *m* de théâtre

greaseproof paper ['griːspruːf'peɪpə(r)] *n* papier *m* sulfurisé

greasy ['griːsɪ] *adj* **(a)** *(covered in grease)* graisseux(euse); *(hair, skin, food)* gras (grasse) **(b)** Fam *(manner)* mielleux(euse)

great [greɪt] **1** *n* grand nom *m*
2 *adj* **(a)** *(large, important)* grand(e); **a g. many people** beaucoup de monde; **to reach a g. age** parvenir à un âge avancé; **to take g. care (of)** prendre grand soin (de); **they are g. friends** ce sont de grands amis
(b) *(in proper names)* **G. Britain** la Grande-Bretagne; **G. Lakes** les Grands Lacs *mpl*; **Greater London** Londres et son agglomération; *I list* **the G. War** la Grande Guerre
(c) Fam *(very good)* formidable, génial(e); **to have a g. time** bien s'amuser
(d) *(enthusiastic)* **to be a g. knitter/reader** adorer tricoter/la lecture; **to be a g. believer in doing sth** être partisan(e) de faire qch; Fam **she's a g. one for having everything planned in advance** avec elle, on peut être sûr que tout sera préparé à l'avance
3 *adv* Fam **(a)** *(well)* très bien; **to feel g.** se sentir en super forme
(b) *(for emphasis)* **a g. big dog** un chien énorme; **you g. fat slob!** espèce de gros tas!

great-aunt ['greɪtɑːnt] *n* grand-tante *f*

greatcoat ['greɪtkəʊt] *n* pardessus *m*

great-grandchild ['greɪt'græntʃaɪld] *(pl* **great-grandchildren** ['greɪt'græntʃɪldrən]) *n (boy)* arrière-petit fils *m*; *(girl)* arrière-petite-fille *f*; **great-grandchildren** arrière-petits-enfants *mpl*

great-granddaughter ['greɪt'grændɔːtə(r)] *n* arrière-petite-fille *f*

great-grandfather ['greɪt'grænfɑːðə(r)] *n* arrière-grand-père *m*

great-grandmother ['greɪt'grænmʌðə(r)] *n* arrière-grand-mère *f*

great-grandparents ['greɪt'grænpeərənts] *npl* arrière-grands-parents *mpl*

great-grandson ['greɪt'grænsʌn] *n* arrière-petit-fils *m*

greatly ['greɪtlɪ] *adv* très

greatness ['greɪtnɪs] *n* **(a)** *(of person, action)* grandeur *f*; **to achieve g.** rejoindre les plus grands **(b)** *(of thing, problem)* importance *f*

great-uncle ['greɪtʌŋkəl] *n* grand-oncle *m*

grebe [griːb] *n* grèbe *m*

Grecian ['griːʃən] *adj* grec (grecque)

Greece [griːs] *n* la Grèce

greed [griːd] *n (for food)* gourmandise *f*; *(for money)* avidité *f*, cupidité *f*; *(for fame, power)* recherche *f* avide **(for** de)

greedily ['griːdɪlɪ] *adv (eat)* goulûment; *(look, say)* avec gourmandise

greediness ['griːdɪnɪs] = **greed**

greedy ['griːdɪ] *adj (for food)* gourmand(e); *(for money, fame, power)* avide; Fam **g. guts** goinfre *mf*

Greek [griːk] **1** *n* **(a)** *(person)* Grec (Grecque) *m,f* **(b)** *(language)* grec *m*; **modern G.** le grec moderne; Fam **it's all G. to me** c'est de l'hébreu pour moi
2 *adj* grec (grecque)

green [griːn] **1** *n* **(a)** *(colour)* vert *m* **(b)** **greens** *(vegetables)* légumes *mpl* verts **(c)** *(grassy area)* pelouse *f*; gazon *m*; *(in golf)* green *m* **(d)** *(environmentalist)* écologiste *mf*

2 adj **(a)** *(colour)* vert(e); **to go** *or* **turn g.** *(of traffic lights)* passer au vert; *(of person, fields)* verdir; **to be g.** with envy être vert de jalousie; *Fig* **to give sb the g. light (to do sth)** donner le feu vert à qn (pour faire qch); **to have g. fingers** avoir la main verte; **g. beans** haricots *mpl* verts; **g. belt** zone *f* verte; *Am* **g. card** ≃ permis *m* de travail; **g. salad** salade *f* verte **(b)** *(young, inexperienced)* jeune, inexpérimenté(e); *(naive)* naïf (naïve) **(c)** *(environmentalist)* écologiste; **the G. Party** le parti écologiste

greenback ['griːnbæk] *n Am Fam* billet *m* vert

greenery ['griːnərɪ] *n* verdure *f*

green-eyed ['griːnaɪd] *adj* aux yeux verts; **the g. monster** la jalousie

greenfield ['griːnfiːld] *n* **g. site** *(for factory)* terrain *m* non-bâti

greenfly ['griːnflaɪ] *(pl* **greenflies)** *n* puceron *m*

greengage ['griːngeɪdʒ] *n* reine-claude *f*

greengrocer ['griːnɡrəʊsə(r)] *n Br* marchand(e) *m,f* de fruits et légumes; **g.'s (shop)** magasin *m* de fruits et légumes

greenhouse ['griːnhaʊs] *n* serre *f*; **g. effect** effet *m* de serre

Greenland ['griːnlənd] *n* le Groenland

Greenlander ['griːnləndə(r)] *n* Groenlandais(e) *m,f*

Greenwich Mean Time ['grenɪtʃ'miːntaɪm] *n* temps *m* universel

greet [griːt] *vt (say hello to)* saluer; *(welcome) (person, idea)* accueillir

greeting ['griːtɪŋ] *n* salut *m*; *(more formal)* salutation *f*; **New Year greetings** vœux *mpl* de bonne année; **greetings card** carte *f* de vœux

gregarious [grɪ'geərɪəs] *adj* sociable

gremlin ['gremlɪn] *n Fam* diablotin *m*

Grenada [grə'neɪdə] *n* la Grenade

grenade [grə'neɪd] *n* grenade *f*

grenadier [grenə'dɪə(r)] *n* grenadier *m*

grenadine ['grenədiːn] *n* grenadine *f*

grew [gruː] *pt of* **grow**

grey, *Am* **gray** [greɪ] **1** *n (colour)* gris *m*
2 *adj* gris(e); *Fig (dull)* morne; **to go g.** *(grey-haired)* grisonner; *Fig* **a g. area** une zone d'ombre; **g. matter** *(brain)* matière *f* grise
3 *vi (of hair)* grisonner

grey-haired, *Am* **gray-haired** ['greɪheəd] *adj* aux cheveux gris

greyhound ['greɪhaʊnd] *n* lévrier *m*; **g. stadium** cynodrome *m*

greying, *Am* **graying** ['greɪɪŋ] *adj (hair)* grisonnant(e)

grid [grɪd] *n* **(a)** *(bars)* grille *f*, grillage *m* **(b)** *(on map)* quadrillage *m*; **g. layout** *(of town)* quadrillage, damier *m*; **g. reference** coordonnées *fpl* **(c)** *(for electricity)* réseau *m* électrique

griddle ['grɪdəl] *n (for cooking)* tôle *f*

gridiron ['grɪdaɪən] *n* **(a)** *(for cooking)* gril *m* **(b)** *Am (American football)* football *m* américain; *(playing field)* terrain *m* de football

gridlock ['grɪdlɒk] *n* embouteillage *m* monstre

grief [griːf] *n (a) (pain)* chagrin *m*; **to come to g.** échouer; *Fam* **good g.!** mon Dieu! **(b)** *Fam (hassle)* **to give sb g.** embêter qn

grief-stricken ['griːfstrɪkən] *adj* accablé(e) de douleur *ou* de chagrin

grievance ['griːvəns] *n* **(a)** *(resentment)* grief *m* **(b)** *(complaint)* doléance *f*; **to air one's grievances** exprimer ses doléances; *Ind* **g. procedure** procédure *f* pour porter plainte

grieve [griːv] **1** *vt* chagriner, affliger
2 *vi* **to g. for sb/over sth** pleurer qn/qch

grieving ['griːvɪŋ] *adj* éploré(e)

grievous ['griːvəs] *adj Formal* grave; *Law* **g. bodily harm** coups *mpl* et blessures *fpl*

grievously ['griːvəslɪ] *adv (seriously)* gravement; **you are g. mistaken** vous commettez une grave erreur

griffin ['grɪfɪn] *n* griffon *m*

grill [grɪl] **1** *n Br (for cooking)* gril *m*; *(food)* grillade *f*; **a mixed g.** un assortiment de grillades
2 *vt* **(a)** *Br (cook)* griller **(b)** *Fam (interrogate)* cuisiner

grille [grɪl] *n (bars)* grille *f*; **(radiator) g.** *(on car)* calandre *f*

grilling ['grɪlɪŋ] *n Fam (interrogation)* **to give sb a g.** cuisiner qn

grim [grɪm] *adj* **(a)** *(stern)* sinistre; **to hang on like g. death** se cramponner; **to look g.** *(of person) (serious)* avoir un air sinistre; *(ill)* avoir très mauvaise mine **(b)** *Fam (bad)* lamentable; **how do you feel? – pretty g.!** comment te sens-tu? – pas terrible!

grimace ['grɪməs] **1** *n* grimace *f*
2 *vi* grimacer, faire la grimace

grime [graɪm] *n* saleté *f*

grimly ['grɪmlɪ] *adv (fight, hold on)* avec acharnement

grimy ['graɪmɪ] *adj* encrassé(e)

grin [grɪn] *n* grand sourire *m*
2 *vi (pt & pp* grinned) faire un grand sourire **(at** à); *Fig* **to g. and bear it** tâcher de garder le sourire

grind [graɪnd] **1** *n Fam (work)* corvée *f*; **the daily g.** le train-train quotidien
2 *vt (pt & pp* ground [graʊnd]) **(a)** *(grain, coffee)* moudre; **to g. one's teeth** grincer des dents **(b)** *(glass, gems)* dépolir
3 *vi (of wheels, gears)* grisser; **to g. to a halt** *(of car, machine)* s'immobiliser; *(of project, economy)* s'arrêter

▸ **grind down** *vt sep Fig* venir à bout de

▸ **grind on** *vi (proceed relentlessly)* ne pas en finir

▸ **grind out** *vt sep (article, novel)* pondre

grinder ['graɪndə(r)] *n (for coffee, pepper)* moulin *m*; *(for polishing)* polissoire *f*; *(for sharpening)* meule *f*

grinding ['graɪndɪŋ] *adj (poverty)* extrême; **to come to a g. halt** *(of car, machine)* s'immobiliser; *(of project, economy)* s'arrêter

grindstone ['graɪndstəʊn] *n* meule *f*; *Fig* **to keep one's nose to the g.** travailler dur

gringo ['grɪŋɡəʊ] *(pl* gringos) *n Am Fam* gringo *m*

grip [grɪp] **1** *n (a) (hold, grasp)* prise *f*; **to have a strong g.** avoir une bonne poigne; **to get a g. on sth** avoir prise sur qch; *Fig* **to get to grips with sth** s'attaquer à qch; *Fig* **to get a g. on oneself** se ressaisir; *Fam* **get a g.!** reprends-toi!, ressaisis-toi!; *Fig* **to have a firm g. on a situation** avoir la situation bien en main; **to lose one's g.** lâcher prise; **to lose one's g.** on sth lâcher qch; *Fig* **to lose one's g. on reality** perdre pied avec la réalité; *Fig* **to be in the g. of a disease/a crisis** être en proie à une maladie/une crise **(b)** *(handle)* poignée *f* **(c)** *(hair)* **g.** pince *f* (à cheveux) **(d)** *Am (bag)* mallette *f*
2 *vt (pt & pp* gripped) *(seize)* saisir, prendre; *(hold)* empoigner, agripper; *(of tyres)* adhérer à; *Fig* **to be gripped by panic** être pris(e) de panique; *Fig* **the audience was gripped by the play** la pièce a captivé les spectateurs
3 *vi (of tyre)* adhérer

gripe [graɪp] **1** *n (a) Fam (complaint)* **to have a g. about sth** avoir à se plaindre de qch; **what's your g.?** de quoi te

plains-tu? **(b)** *(pain)* **gripes** coliques *fpl*; **g.** water =
médicament pour coliques infantiles
  2 *vi Fam (complain)* ronchonner, râler **(about** à propos de)
gripping ['grɪpɪŋ] *adj* passionnant(e)
grisly ['grɪzlɪ] *adj* macabre, sinistre
grist [grɪst] *n* **it's all g. to the mill** cela apporte de l'eau à
mon/ton/etc moulin
gristle ['grɪsəl] *n* nerfs *mpl*
gristly ['grɪslɪ] *adj* nerveux(euse)
grit [grɪt] **1** *n* **(a)** *(gravel)* gravillons *mpl*; *(in eye)* poussière
f; *(for icy roads)* sable *m* **(b)** *(courage, determination)* cran *m*
  2 *vt (pt & pp* **gritted) (a)** *(road)* sabler **(b)** *(clench)* **to g.
one's teeth** grincer des dents; *Fig* serrer les dents
gritter ['grɪtə(r)] *n Br* camion *m* de sablage
gritty ['grɪtɪ] *adj* **(a)** *(soil, road)* plein(e) de gravillons **(b)**
(determined) qui a du cran, résolu(e) **(c) g. realism** réalisme
m cru
grizzle ['grɪzəl] *vi (complain)* ronchonner, râler **(about** à
propos de)
grizzled ['grɪzəld] *adj (hair, person)* grisonnant(e)
grizzly ['grɪzlɪ] **1** *n (pl* **grizzlies) g. (bear)** grizzly *m*
  2 *adj (hair, person)* grisonnant(e)
groan [grəʊn] **1** *n (of pain)* gémissement *m*; *(of
disappointment, dismay)* grognement *m*; *(of chair, floor)*
grincement *m*
  2 *vi (in pain)* gémir, pousser un gémissement; *(in
disappointment, dismay)* grogner, pousser un grognement;
to g. under the weight of sth *(of shelf, chair)* se creuser
sous le poids de qch
grocer ['grəʊsə(r)] *n* épicier(ère) *m,f*; **g.'s (shop)** épicerie *f*
groceries ['grəʊsərɪz] *npl (provisions)* provisions *fpl*
grocery ['grəʊsərɪ] *(pl* **groceries)** *n (shop)* épicerie *f*
grog [grɒg] *n Fam* grog *m*
groggy ['grɒgɪ] *adj Fam* groggy *inv*
groin [grɔɪn] *n* aine *f*
groom [gruːm] **1** *n* **(a)** *(of horse)* palefrenier *m* **(b)** *(at
wedding)* marié *m*
  2 *vt (horse)* panser; *(dog)* toiletter; *Fig (candidate)* préparer
groove [gruːv] *n (in wood, metal)* rainure *f*; *(in record)*
sillon *m*; *Fig* **to get stuck in a g.** s'encroûter
groovy ['gruːvɪ] *adj Fam* chouette
grope [grəʊp] **1** *vt* **(a)** **to g. one's way forward** avancer à
tâtons **(b)** *Fam (sexually)* peloter, tripoter
  2 *vi* **to g. (about) for sth** chercher qch à tâtons
gross [grəʊs] **1** *n (pl* **gross)** *(quantity)* grosse *f*, douze
douzaines *fpl*
  2 *adj* **(a)** *(fat)* obèse **(b)** *(blatant) (error)* grossier(ère);
(ignorance) crasse; *(abuse)* choquant(e); *(injustice)* fla-
grant(e); *Law* **g. negligence** négligence *f* coupable **(c)**
(vulgar) grossier(ère) **(d)** *(profit, income, weight)* brut(e);
Econ **g. domestic product** produit *m* intérieur brut; **g.
national product** produit national brut **(e)** *Fam (disgusting)*
répugnant(e)
  3 *vt (profit)* gagner brut; **to g. $40,000 a year** gagner brut
40 000 dollars par an
grossly ['grəʊslɪ] *adv (exaggerated)* grossièrement;
(negligent) extrêmement; *(unfair)* vraiment; **g. overweight** obèse
grotesque [grəʊ'tesk] *adj* grotesque
grotto ['grɒtəʊ] *(pl* **grottoes** *or* **grottos)** *n* grotte *f*
grotty ['grɒtɪ] *adj Br Fam* minable; **to feel g.** se sentir
vaseux(euse)
grouch [graʊtʃ] *Fam* **1** *n* **(a)** *(person)* râleur(euse) *m,f* **(b)**
(complaint) plainte *f*
  2 *vi* râler, ronchonner **(about** à propos de)

grouchy ['graʊtʃɪ] *adj Fam* râleur(euse), ronchon(onne)
ground [graʊnd] **1** *n* **(a)** *(earth)* sol *m*, terre *f*; **to sit on the
g.** s'asseoir par terre; **above g.** en surface; **below g.** sous
terre; **burnt to the g.** entièrement brûlé(e); *Fig* **to get off
the g.** *(of project)* démarrer; *Fig* **to work oneself into the
g.** se tuer au travail; **to go to g.** se cacher; **to run sb to g.**
traquer qn; **g. control** contrôle *m* au sol; **g. crew** personnel
m au sol; *Br* **g. floor** rez-de-chaussée *m*; *Mil* **g. forces** forces
fpl au sol; **g. frost** gelée *f* blanche; **at g. level** au rez-de-
chaussée; **g. rules** règles *fpl* de base; **g. staff** = personnel
responsable de l'entretien d'un terrain de sport
  (b) *(land)* terrain *m*; *Fig* **to find common g. for
negotiations** trouver un terrain d'entente en vue de
négociations; **to be sure of one's g.** être sûr(e) de son
fait; *Fig* **to be on shaky g.** être en terrain miné; *Fig* **to
change** *or* **shift one's g.** changer de tactique; *Fig* **to break
new g.** faire œuvre de pionnier; *Fig* **to cover a lot of g.** *(of
book, lecture)* couvrir de très nombreux domaines; *Fig* **to
gain g. on sb** gagner du terrain sur qn; *Fig* **to lose g. to sb**
perdre du terrain sur qn; *Fig* **to stand** *or* **hold one's g.** tenir
bon
  (c) grounds *(of school, hospital, country house)* parc *m*
  (d) grounds *(reasons)* raisons *fpl*, motifs *mpl*; **to have
(good) grounds for doing sth** avoir de bonnes raisons de
faire qch; **on grounds of ill-health** pour raisons de santé;
Law **grounds for divorce** motif *m* de divorce
  2 *adj (coffee, pepper)* moulu(e); *Am* **g. meat** viande *f*
hachée
  3 *vt* **(a)** *(base)* baser, appuyer **(on** sur)
  (b) *(educate)* **to g. sb in sth** former qn à qch
  (c) *Am (electrical current)* mettre à la masse
  (d) *(aeroplane)* interdire de vol
  (e) *(prevent from going out)* priver de sortie
  4 *pt & pp of* **grind**
groundhog ['graʊndhɒg] *n* marmotte *f* d'Amérique
grounding ['graʊndɪŋ] *n* **(a)** *(basis)* fondement *m* **(b)**
(basic knowledge) bases *fpl* **(in** de *ou* en)
groundless ['graʊndlɪs] *adj* sans fondement
groundnut ['graʊndnʌt] *n Br* arachide *f*; **g. oil** huile *f*
d'arachide
groundsheet ['graʊndʃiːt] *n* tapis *m* de sol
groundsman ['graʊndzmən] *n* = responsable de
l'entretien d'un terrain de sport
groundswell ['graʊndswel] *n* **a. of support** un raz-
de-marée
groundwork ['graʊndwɜːk] *n* travail *m* préparatoire; **to
do** *or* **lay the g. (for sth)** préparer le terrain (pour qch)
group [gruːp] **1** *n* groupe *m*; **g. decision** décision *f*
collective; **g. dynamics** dynamique *f* de groupe; **g.
photograph** photographie *f* de groupe; **g. therapy**
thérapie *f* de groupe
  2 *vt* grouper
  3 *vi* se grouper
groupie ['gruːpɪ] *n Fam* groupie *f*
grouping ['gruːpɪŋ] *n (of people)* groupe *m*
grouse[1] [graʊs] *(pl* **grouse)** *n (bird)* tétras *m*, grouse *f*
grouse[2] *Fam* **1** *n (complaint)* **to have a g. (about sth)**
avoir des raisons de se plaindre (de qch)
  2 *vi* ronchonner, grogner **(about** au sujet de)
grout [graʊt] *n* mastic *m*
grove [grəʊv] *n* bosquet *m*
grovel ['grɒvəl] *(pt & pp* **grovelled**, *Am* **groveled)** *vi (on
ground)* être à quatre pattes; **to g. to sb** ramper *ou* s'aplatir
devant qn
grovelling *Am* **groveling** ['grɒvəlɪŋ] *adj* obsé-
quieux(euse)
grow [grəʊ] *(pt* **grew** [gruː], *pp* **grown** [grəʊn]) **1** *vt* **(a)**

(vegetables) cultiver; *(flowers)* faire pousser; **to g. a beard** se laisser pousser la barbe; **to g. one's hair** se laisser pousser les cheveux **(b)** *Com (company)* développer **2** *vi* **(a)** *(increase in size) (plant)* pousser; *(person, animal)* grandir; *(problem)* s'aggraver; *(economy, feeling)* croître; *Fam* **it'll g. on you** *(of music, book)* tu finiras par t'y intéresser **(b)** *(become)* devenir; **to g. old** vieillir; **to g. angry** se fâcher **(c)** *(come eventually)* **to g. to like sth** finir par aimer qch
▸ **grow apart** *vi (of people)* s'éloigner
▸ **grow out of** *vt insep* **(a)** *(become too big for)* **he's grown out of all his clothes** tous ses vêtements sont maintenant trop petits pour lui **(b)** *(become too old for)* **she grew out of her dolls** elle a passé l'âge de jouer à la poupée; **most children g. out of such behaviour** la plupart des enfants cessent de se conduire ainsi en grandissant
▸ **grow up** *vi (become adult)* grandir; **when I g. up** quand je serai grand; **when I was growing up** quand j'étais petit; *Fam* **g. up!** ne fais pas l'enfant!

grower ['grəʊə(r)] *n (person)* cultivateur(trice) *m,f*; *(of trees, flowers)* horticulteur(trice) *m,f*

growing ['grəʊɪŋ] *adj (child)* en pleine croissance; *(town, population)* en pleine expansion; *(debt)* qui augmente, qui va croissant; *(discontent)* croissant(e); **there was a g. fear that...** on craignait de plus en plus que...; **g. pains** *(of child)* douleurs *fpl* de croissance; *Fig (of firm, country)* difficultés *fpl* de croissance

growl [graʊl] **1** *n (of dog)* grondement *m* **2** *vi (of dog)* gronder; *(of person)* grogner, grommeler (**at** contre)

growling ['graʊlɪŋ] *n (of dog)* grondement *m*

grown [grəʊn] **1** *adj* grand(e); **a g. woman** une adulte; **to be fully g.** avoir atteint sa taille adulte
2 *pp of* **grow**

grown-up 1 *n* ['grəʊnʌp] grand(e) *m,f*, grande personne *f*; **the grown-ups** les grands, les grandes personnes
2 *adj* [grəʊn'ʌp] *(person, topic)* adulte; **he was very g. about it** il a fait preuve de beaucoup de maturité

growth [grəʊθ] *n* **(a)** *(of person, plant, economy)* croissance *f*; *(of population, demand)* augmentation *f*; **a week's g. of beard** une barbe d'une semaine; **g. area** secteur *m* en expansion; **g. industry** industrie *f* en expansion **(b)** *(tumour)* grosseur *f*

grub [grʌb] *n* **(a)** *(larva)* larve *f* **(b)** *Fam (food)* bouffe *f*; **g.'s up!** à la bouffe!
▸ **grub about, grub around** *(pt & pp* **grubbed***)* *vi Fam* farfouiller (**for sth** pour trouver qch)

grubby ['grʌbɪ] *adj* crasseux(euse)

grudge [grʌdʒ] **1** *n* rancune *f*; **to bear sb a g.** en vouloir à qn
2 *vt* **(a)** *(give unwillingly)* **to g. sb sth** donner qch à qn à contrecœur **(b)** *(resent)* **to g. doing sth** faire qch à contrecœur; **she grudges him his success** elle lui en veut parce qu'il a réussi

grudging ['grʌdʒɪŋ] *adj* accordé(e) à contrecœur; **to be g. in one's praise** être avare de compliments

grudgingly ['grʌdʒɪŋlɪ] *adv* à contrecœur, à regret

gruel ['gruːəl] *n* gruau *m*

gruelling, *Am* **grueling** ['gruːəlɪŋ] *adj (journey, experience)* épuisant(e)

gruesome ['gruːsəm] *adj* abominable, horrible; **to relate sth in g. detail** raconter qch jusqu'aux détails les plus horribles

gruesomely ['gruːsəmlɪ] *adv* abominablement

gruff [grʌf] *adj (tone, manner)* bourru(e); *(voice)* gros (grosse)

gruffly ['grʌflɪ] *adv* d'un ton bourru

grumble ['grʌmbəl] **1** *n* grommellement *m*, grognement *m*; **she obeyed without so much as a g.** elle a obéi sans la moindre protestation
2 *vi (of person)* grommeler; *(of stomach)* gargouiller; **to g. about sth** rouspéter contre qch; **(I) mustn't g.** il ne faut pas se plaindre

grumbler ['grʌmblə(r)] *n* grincheux(euse) *m,f*

grumbling ['grʌmblɪŋ] **1** *n* ronchonnements *mpl*
2 *adj* grognon(onne); **g. appendix** appendicite *f* chronique

grump [grʌmp] *n Fam* grincheux(euse) *m,f*

grumpily ['grʌmpɪlɪ] *adv* en ronchonnant

grumpy ['grʌmpɪ] *adj* grognon(onne)

grunge [grʌndʒ] *n (music, fashion)* grunge *m*

grunt [grʌnt] **1** *n (of pig, person)* grognement *m*; **to give a g.** pousser un grognement
2 *vi (of pig, person)* grogner

Guadeloupe [gwɑːdə'luːp] *n* la Guadeloupe

guarantee [gærən'tiː] **1** *n (spoken, written)* garantie *f*; **there's no g. that she'll come** ce n'est pas sûr qu'elle vienne; *Com* **under g.** sous garantie
2 *vt* garantir; **I can't g. that she'll come** je ne garantis pas qu'elle viendra; **the watch is guaranteed for two years** cette montre est garantie deux ans; *Fin* **to g. sb against loss** garantir qn contre les pertes

guaranteed [gærən'tiːd] *adj* garanti(e)

guarantor [gærən'tɔː(r)] *n* garant(e) *m,f*

guard [gɑːd] **1** *n* **(a)** *(defences)* **to be on one's g.** être sur ses gardes; **to put sb on his g.** mettre qn en garde; **to put sb off his g.** déjouer la vigilance de qn; **to catch sb off his g.** prendre qn au dépourvu; **his g. was down** il ne se méfiait pas **(b)** *(supervision)* garde *f*; **to keep sb under g.** garder qn sous surveillance; **to be on g. duty** être de garde; **g. dog** chien *m* de garde **(c)** *(sentry)* garde *m*; *(on train)* chef *m* de train; *Am (in prison)* gardien *m*; *Mil (group of sentries)* garde *f*; **g. of honour** garde *f* d'honneur; *Br* **g.'s van** *(on train)* fourgon *m* du chef de train **(d)** *(device) (on machine)* protection *f* **(e)** *(in basketball)* défenseur *m*
2 *vt* garder; **to g. sb from danger** protéger qn d'un danger
▸ **guard against** *vt insep* se prémunir contre; **how can we g. against such accidents (happening)?** comment éviter que de tels accidents arrivent?

guarded ['gɑːdɪd] *adj* prudent(e)

guardedly ['gɑːdɪdlɪ] *adv* avec circonspection, avec prudence

guardhouse ['gɑːdhaʊs] *n Mil* poste *m* de garde; *(prison)* prison *f*

guardian ['gɑːdɪən] *n (of standards)* gardien(enne) *m,f*; *Law (of minor)* tuteur(trice) *m,f*; **g. angel** ange *m* gardien

guardianship ['gɑːdɪənʃɪp] *n Law (of minor)* tutelle *f*

guardrail ['gɑːdreɪl] *n* garde-fou *m*, parapet *m*; *(on ship)* bastingage *m*

guardroom ['gɑːdruːm] *n* corps *m* de garde

guardsman ['gɑːdzmən] *n* garde *m (de la garde royale)*

Guatemala [gwætɪ'mɑːlə] *n* le Guatemala

Guatemalan [gwætɪ'mɑːlən] **1** *n* Guatémaltèque *mf*
2 *adj* guatémaltèque

guava ['gwɑːvə] *n* goyave *f*; **g. tree** goyavier *m*

guerrilla [gə'rɪlə] *n* guérillero *m*; **g. warfare** guérilla *f*

guess [ges] **1** *n* estimation *f*; **to have** *or* **make a g.** deviner; *Fam* **I'll give you three guesses!** devine!; **at a g., (I'd say) 300** je dirais environ 300; **your g. is as good as mine** j'en ai pas la moindre idée; **it's anybody's g.** qui sait?

2 *vt* (**a**) *(attempt to answer)* deviner; **g. who I saw!** devine qui j'ai vu!; **g. what!** tu sais quoi?; **you've guessed it!** tu as deviné! (**b**) *(suppose)* supposer, croire; **I g. you're right** tu dois avoir raison
3 *vi* deviner; **to g. right** deviner juste; **to g. wrong** se tromper; **to keep sb guessing** laisser qn dans l'ignorance; **to g. at sth** essayer de deviner qch

guessing game ['gesɪŋ'geɪm] *n* jeu *m* de devinettes; *Fig* **it's a bit of a g.** on ne peut que spéculer

guesstimate ['gestɪmɪt] *n Fam* calcul *m* au pif

guesswork ['geswɜːk] *n* conjecture *f*; **it's pure** *or* **sheer g.** c'est de la pure conjecture

guest [gest] *n* (*at home, party, on TV programme*) invité(e) *m,f*; *(at hotel)* client(e) *m,f*; **be my g.!** je t'en prie!; **to make a g. appearance** *(on TV programme)* passer en invité vedette; *(in film)* participer à titre exceptionnel; **g. artist** invité vedette; **g. room** chambre *f* d'amis; **g. speaker** conférencier(ère) *m,f*

guesthouse ['gesthaʊs] *n* pension *f* de famille

guff [gʌf] *n Fam* âneries *fpl*

guffaw [gʌ'fɔː] **1** *n* gros rire *m*
2 *vi* s'esclaffer

GUI ['guːɪ] *n Comptr (abbr* **Graphical User Interface)** interface *f* utilisateur graphique

Guiana [gaɪ'ɑːnə] *n* la Guyane

guidance ['gaɪdəns] *n* direction *f*; **under the g. of** sous la direction de; **for your g.** à titre d'information

guide [gaɪd] **1** *n* (**a**) *(person)* guide *m*; (**Girl**) **G.** éclaireuse *f*; **g. dog** chien *m* d'aveugle (**b**) *(book)* guide *m* (**to** de) (**c**) *(indication)* indication *f* (**to** sur); **as a g.** à titre indicatif
2 *vt* guider; **to be guided by sth** suivre qch

guidebook ['gaɪdbʊk] *n* guide *m*

guided ['gaɪdɪd] *adj* **g. missile** missile *m* guidé; **g. tour** visite *f* guidée

guideline ['gaɪdlaɪn] *n (indication)* indication *f*; **guidelines** directives *fpl*; **as a general g.** en règle générale

guiding ['gaɪdɪŋ] *adj (principle, concept)* directeur(trice)

guild [gɪld] *n (association)* association *f*

guilder ['gɪldə] *n* florin *m*

guile [gaɪl] *n* ruse *f*

guileless ['gaɪllɪs] *adj* candide

guillemot ['gɪlɪmɒt] *n* guillemot *m*

guillotine ['gɪlətiːn] **1** *n (for execution)* guillotine *f*; *(for cutting paper)* massicot *m*; *Br Pol* **to put a g. on a bill** = imposer une limite de temps aux débats précédant un vote
2 *vt (execute)* guillotiner

guilt [gɪlt] *n* culpabilité *f*; **to feel g.** se sentir coupable; **g. complex** complexe *m* de culpabilité

guiltily ['gɪltɪlɪ] *adv* d'un air coupable

guiltless ['gɪltlɪs] *adj* innocent(e)

guilty ['gɪltɪ] *adj* coupable; **to find sb g./not g.** déclarer qn coupable/non coupable; **to feel g.** se sentir coupable; **to have a g. conscience** avoir mauvaise conscience; **g. secret** secret *m* inavouable

Guinea ['gɪnɪ] *n* la Guinée

guinea ['gɪnɪ] *n* (**a**) *Br (coin)* guinée *f* (**b**) **g. fowl** pintade *f*; **g. pig** cobaye *m*, cochon *m* d'Inde; *Fig* **to be a g. pig** servir de cobaye

Guinea-Bissau ['gɪnɪbɪ'saʊ] *n* la Guinée-Bissau

Guinean [gɪ'neɪən] **1** *n* Guinéen(enne) *m,f*
2 *adj* guinéen(enne)

guise [gaɪz] *n* apparence *f*; **in** *or* **under the g. of** sous l'apparence de; **in a different g.** sous une autre forme

guitar [gɪ'tɑː(r)] *n* guitare *f*

guitarist [gɪ'tɑːrɪst] *n* guitariste *mf*

gulch [gʌltʃ] *n Am* ravin *m*

gulf [gʌlf] *n* (**a**) *(bay)* golfe *m*; **the (Persian) G.** le golfe Persique; **the G. of Mexico** le golfe du Mexique; **the G. Stream** le Gulf Stream; **the G. War** la guerre du Golfe (**b**) *(between people, ideas)* abîme *m*, gouffre *m* (**between** entre)

gull [gʌl] *n* mouette *f*, goéland *m*

gullet ['gʌlɪt] *n* gosier *m*

gullibility [gʌlɪ'bɪlɪtɪ] *n* crédulité *f*

gullible ['gʌlɪbəl] *adj* crédule

gully ['gʌlɪ] *(pl* **gullies)** *n* petit ravin *m*

gulp [gʌlp] **1** *n* (**a**) *(of food)* bouchée *f*; *(of drink)* gorgée *f*; **in** *or* **at one g.** d'un coup (**b**) *(of surprise)* serrement *m* de gorge
2 *vt (food, drink)* engloutir
3 *vi (with surprise)* avoir un serrement de gorge
▸ **gulp down** *vt sep (food, drink)* engloutir

gum [gʌm] **1** *n* (**a**) *(in mouth)* gencive *f*; **g. disease** gingivite *f* (**b**) *(adhesive)* colle *f* (**c**) **(chewing) g.** chewing gum *m* (**d**) *(resin)* **g. arabic** gomme *f* arabique; **g. tree** gommier *m*; *Fig* **to be up a g. tree** être dans le pétrin
2 *vt (pt & pp* **gummed)** *(stick)* coller
▸ **gum up** *vt sep (mechanism)* enrayer; *(eyes)* coller

gumboot ['gʌmbuːt] *n* botte *f* de caoutchouc

gummed [gʌmd] *adj* gommé(e)

gummy ['gʌmɪ] *adj* collant(e)

gumption ['gʌmʃən] *n Fam (common sense)* jugeote *f*; *(courage)* cran *m*

gumshield ['gʌmʃiːld] *n* protège-dents *m inv*

gun [gʌn] **1** *n* (**a**) *(pistol)* pistolet *m*; *(rifle)* fusil *m*; *(artillery piece)* canon *m*; **g. carriage** affût *m* de canon; **g. dog** chien *m* d'arrêt; **g. laws** législation *f* sur les armes à feu; **g. licence** permis *m* de port d'armes (**b**) *(idioms)* *Fam* **big g.** huile *f*; *Fam* **to be going great guns** marcher très fort; **to stick to one's guns** tenir bon; **to jump the g.** s'emballer
2 *vt (pt & pp* **gunned)** *(engine)* accélérer
▸ **gun down** *vt sep* abattre
▸ **gun for** *vt insep* **to be gunning for sb** en avoir après qn; **she's gunning for his job** elle fait tout ce qu'elle peut pour lui prendre son poste

gunboat ['gʌnbəʊt] *n* cannonière *f*; **g. diplomacy** politique *f* de la cannonière

gunfight ['gʌnfaɪt] *n* fusillade *f*

gunfire ['gʌnfaɪə(r)] *n (of artillery)* tirs *mpl* d'artillerie; *(of smaller guns)* coups *mpl* de feu

gunge [gʌndʒ] *n Fam* matière *f* gluante

gung-ho [gʌŋ'həʊ] *adj* (**a**) *(overly enthusiastic)* d'un enthousiasme irritant (**b**) *(keen for war)* va-t-en-guerre *inv*

gunk [gʌŋk] *n Fam* matière *f* gluante

gunman ['gʌnmən] *n* homme *m* armé

gunner ['gʌnə(r)] *n* artilleur *m*

gunpoint ['gʌnpɔɪnt] *n* **at g.** sous la menace d'une arme à feu

gunpowder ['gʌnpaʊdə(r)] *n* poudre *f* (à canon)

gunrunner ['gʌnrʌnə(r)] *n* trafiquant(e) *m,f* d'armes

gunrunning ['gʌnrʌnɪŋ] *n* trafic *m* d'armes

gunship ['gʌnʃɪp] *n* **(helicopter) g.** hélicoptère *m* de combat

gunshot ['gʌnʃɒt] *n* coup *m* de feu; **g. wound** blessure *f* par balle

gunsmith ['gʌnsmɪθ] *n* armurier *m*

gunwale ['gʌnəl] *n Naut* plat-bord *m*

gurgle ['gɜːgəl] **1** n (of liquid) gargouillement m; (of baby) gazouillis m
2 vi (of liquid) gargouiller; (of baby) gazouiller

guru ['gʊruː] n gourou m

gush [gʌʃ] **1** n (of water) jaillissement m; Fig (of words) flot m
2 vi (a) (of water) jaillir; **tears gushed from her eyes** elle pleurait à chaudes larmes (b) Pej (talk effusively) s'extasier (**over** or **about** devant)

gushing ['gʌʃɪŋ] adj Pej (person, praise) exubérant(e)

gusset ['gʌsɪt] n soufflet m

gust [gʌst] **1** n (of wind) rafale f; (of hot air) bouffée f
2 vi (of wind) souffler par rafales

gusto ['gʌstəʊ] n enthousiasme m

gusty ['gʌstɪ] adj (wind) qui souffle par rafales; (day, weather) de grand vent

gut [gʌt] **1** n (a) (intestine) intestin m; Fam **guts** (of person, machine) entrailles fpl; Fam **to sweat** or **work one's guts out** se tuer à la tâche; Fam **to hate sb's guts** ne pas pouvoir sentir qn; Fam **I'll have his guts for garters** je vais le massacrer; **a g. feeling** une intuition; **g. reaction** réaction f viscérale (b) Fam **guts** (courage) cran m; **I didn't have the guts to tell them** je n'ai pas eu le courage de le leur dire
2 vt (pt & pp **gutted**) (a) (fish) vider (b) (building) (of fire) ravager; (of builder) vider entièrement

gutless ['gʌtlɪs] adj Fam lâche

gutsy ['gʌtsɪ] adj Fam courageux(euse)

gutted ['gʌtɪd] adj Br Fam (disappointed) effondré(e)

gutter ['gʌtə(r)] **1** n (in street) caniveau m; (on roof) gouttière f; Fig **to end up in the g.** finir sous les ponts; Fig **to drag oneself out of the g.** se sortir de la misère; Fam Pej **g. press** presse f à scandales
2 vi (of candle) vaciller

guttural ['gʌtərəl] adj guttural(e)

guy¹ [gaɪ] n Fam (a) (man) type m, mec m; **a tough g.** un dur (b) (person) **hi guys!** salut la compagnie!

guy² n g. (rope) (for tent) tendeur m

Guyana [gaɪ'ænə] n le Guyana

Guyanese [gaɪə'niːz] **1** n Guyanais(e) m,f
2 adj guyanais(e)

guzzle ['gʌzəl] vt Fam (food) engloutir; (drink) siffler

gym [dʒɪm] n (gymnasium) gymnase m; (gymnastics) gym f; **g. shoes** chaussures fpl de gym

gymkhana [dʒɪm'kɑːnə] n concours m hippique

gymnasium [dʒɪm'neɪzɪəm] n gymnase m

gymnast ['dʒɪmnæst] n gymnaste mf

gymnastic [dʒɪm'næstɪk] adj gymnastique

gymnastics [dʒɪm'næstɪks] **1** n gymnastique f
2 npl Fig **mental/verbal g.** gymnastique f intellectuelle/verbale

gynaecological, Am **gynecological** [gaɪnɪkə'lɒdʒɪkəl] adj gynécologique

gynaecologist, Am **gynecologist** [gaɪnɪ'kɒlədʒɪst] n gynécologue mf

gynaecology, Am **gynecology** [gaɪnɪ'kɒlədʒɪ] n gynécologie f

gyp [dʒɪp] n Br Fam **to give sb g.** faire souffrir qn

gypsum ['dʒɪpsəm] n gypse m

gypsy ['dʒɪpsɪ] = gipsy

gyrate [dʒaɪ'reɪt] vi (of planet, sphere) tourner; (of dancer) tournoyer

gyration [dʒaɪ'reɪʃən] n giration f

gyroscope ['dʒaɪrəskəʊp] n gyroscope m

H, h [eɪtʃ] *n (letter)* H, h *m inv*; **H bomb** bombe *f* H
haberdashery ['hæbədæʃərɪ] *(pl* **haberdasheries)** *n* **(a)** *Br (sewing items, shop)* mercerie *f* **(b)** *Am (men's clothes, shop)* chemiserie *f*
habit ['hæbɪt] *n* **(a)** *(custom, practice)* habitude *f*; **to be in the h.** of doing sth avoir l'habitude de faire qch; **to get into the h.** of doing sth prendre l'habitude de faire qch; **to get out of the h.** of doing sth perdre l'habitude de faire qch; **don't make a h.** of it! que cela ne devienne pas une habitude!; **from force of h.** par habitude **(b)** *Fam (addiction to drugs)* accoutumance *f*; **to kick the h.** décrocher **(c)** *(of monk, nun)* habit *m*
habitable ['hæbɪtəbəl] *adj* habitable
habitat ['hæbɪtæt] *n* habitat *m*
habitation [hæbɪ'teɪʃən] *n* habitation *f*; **there were no signs of h.** l'endroit semblait inhabité; **fit for h.** habitable; **unfit for h.** inhabitable
habitual [hə'bɪtjʊəl] *adj (generosity, rudeness)* habituel(elle); *(liar, drunk)* invétéré(e)
habitually [hə'bɪtjʊəlɪ] *adv* habituellement
habituate [hə'bɪtjʊeɪt] *vt* habituer **(to** à); **to become habituated to sth** s'habituer à qch
hack¹ [hæk] **1** *vt* **(a)** *(cut)* tailler, taillader; **to h. sb/sth to pieces** tailler qn/qch en pièces; **to h. one's way through the jungle** se frayer un chemin dans la jungle à la machette **(b)** *very Fam (cope with)* **he can't h. it** il ne s'en sort pas **2** *vi* **(a)** *(cut)* **to h. at sth** taillader qch **(b)** *(cough)* tousser d'une toux sèche **(c)** *Comptr* **to h. into sth** entrer dans qch par effraction
▸ **hack down** *vt sep* abattre
▸ **hack off** *vt sep* **(a)** *(branch, limb)* couper **(b)** *Fam* **to be hacked off (with sb/sth)** en avoir marre (de qn/qch)
hack² *n* **(a)** *Fam Pej (journalist)* journaliste *mf* besogneux(euse); *(political activist)* militant(e) *m,f* **(b)** *(horserider)* **to go for a h.** aller faire une promenade à cheval **(c)** *Am Fam (taxi)* taxi *m*
hacker ['hækə(r)] *n Comptr* pirate *m* informatique
hacking jacket ['hækɪŋ'dʒækɪt] *n* veste *f* d'équitation
hackles ['hækəlz] *npl (of dog)* poils *mpl* du cou; *(of bird)* plumes *fpl* du cou; *Fig* **to make sb's h. rise** hérisser qn
hackney cab ['hæknɪkæb], **hackney carriage** ['hæknɪ'kærɪdʒ] *n Formal (taxi)* fiacre *m*
hackneyed ['hæknɪd] *adj (argument)* rebattu(e); *(language)* banal(e); **h. expression** lieu *m* commun
hacksaw ['hæksɔː] *n* scie *f* à métaux
had [hæd] *pt & pp of* **have**
haddock ['hædək] *(pl* **haddock** *or* **haddocks)** *n* églefin *m*

hadn't ['hædənt] = had not
haemoglobin, *Am* **hemoglobin** [hiːməʊ'gləʊbɪn] *n* hémoglobine *f*
haemophilia, *Am* **hemophilia** [hiːmən'fɪlɪə] *n* hémophilie *f*
haemophiliac, *Am* **hemophiliac** [hiːməʊ'fɪlɪæk] *n* hémophile *mf*
haemorrhage, *Am* **hemorrhage** ['hemərɪdʒ] **1** *n also Fig* hémorragie *f* **2** *vi Med* faire une hémorragie; *Fig (of support, funds)* diminuer
haemorrhoids, *Am* **hemorrhoids** ['hemərɔɪdz] *npl Med* hémorroïdes *fpl*
hag [hæg] *n Pej* vieille taupe *f*
haggard ['hægəd] *adj* hâve
haggle ['hægəl] *vi* marchander **(with sb** avec qn), **to h. over sth** marchander qch; **to h. about** *or* **over the price of sth** chicaner sur le prix de qch
hagiography [hægɪ'ɒgrəfɪ] *n* hagiographie *f*
Hague [heɪg] *n* **the H.** La Haye
hail¹ [heɪl] **1** *n* grêle *f*; *Fig* **a h. of bullets/insults** une pluie de balles/d'injures; **a h. of blows** une volée de coups **2** *vi* **it's hailing** il grêle
hail² *vt* **(a)** *(attract attention of)* héler **(b)** *(acclaim)* saluer **(as** comme)
▸ **hail from** *vt insep* être originaire de
hailstone ['heɪlstəʊn] *n* grêlon *m*
hailstorm ['heɪlstɔːm] *n* averse *f* de grêle
hair [heə(r)] *n (on head)* cheveux *mpl*; *(on body, animal)* poils *mpl*; *(single hair) (on head)* cheveu *m*; *(on body, animal)* poil *m*; **to have fair/long h.** avoir les cheveux clairs/longs; **to do one's h.** se coiffer; **to comb one's h.** se peigner; **to brush one's h.** se brosser les cheveux; **to have** *or* **get one's h. cut** se faire couper les cheveux; **if you harm** *or* **touch a h. on that child's head...** si tu touches à un cheveu de la tête de cet enfant...; **to make sb's h. stand on end** faire dresser les cheveux sur la tête à qn; *Fam* **keep your h. on!** calmez-vous!; *Fam* **to get in sb's h.** enquiquiner qn; *Fig* **to let one's h. down** se laisser aller; *Fam* **h. of the dog** *(for hangover)* = verre d'alcool pris pour calmer la gueule de bois; **h. gel** gel *m* pour les cheveux; *Br* **h. slide** barrette *f*
hairband ['heəbænd] *n* bandeau *m*
hairbrush ['heəbrʌʃ] *n* brosse *f* à cheveux
haircut ['heəkʌt] *n* coupe *f* de cheveux; **to have a h.** se faire couper les cheveux
hairdo ['heəduː] *(pl* **hairdos)** *n Fam* coiffure *f*
hairdresser ['heədresə(r)] *n* coiffeur(euse) *m,f*; **to go to the h.'s** aller chez le coiffeur

hairdressing ['heədresɪŋ] n coiffure f; h. salon salon m de coiffure

hairdryer ['heədraɪə(r)] n sèche-cheveux m inv

hairgrip ['heəgrɪp] n pince f à cheveux

hairless ['heəlɪs] adj (face) glabre; (puppy) sans poils

hairline ['heəlaɪn] n (a) (of person) naissance f des cheveux; to have a receding h. avoir le front qui se dégarnit (b) h. crack (in pipe, wall) légère fêlure f; h. fracture (of bone) fêlure f

hairnet ['heənet] n résille f, filet m à cheveux

hairpiece ['heəpi:s] n postiche m

hairpin ['heəpɪn] n épingle f à cheveux; h. bend (on road) virage m en épingle à cheveux

hair-raising ['heəreɪzɪŋ] adj à faire dresser les cheveux sur la tête

hair's-breadth ['heəzbredθ] n by a h. (win, lose) de justesse; the car missed him by a h. la voiture l'a frôlé; to be within a h. of être à deux doigts de

hairspray ['heəspreɪ] n laque f

hairstyle ['heəstaɪl] n coiffure f

hairy ['heərɪ] adj (a) (covered in hair) velu(e), poilu(e) (b) Fam (scary) effrayant(e)

Haiti ['heɪtɪ] n Haïti

Haitian ['heɪʃən] 1 n Haïtien(enne) m,f 2 adj haïtien(enne)

hake [heɪk] (pl hake or hakes) n merlu m, colin m

halcyon days ['hælsɪən'deɪz] npl Lit jours mpl heureux

hale [heɪl] adj vigoureux(euse); to be h. and hearty être en pleine forme

half [hɑ:f] 1 n (pl halves [hɑ:vz]) (a) (in general) moitié f; h. an hour une demi-heure; h. past ten dix heures et demie; it's h. past il est la demie; to fold/cut sth in h. plier/couper qch en deux; h. a dozen une demi-douzaine; h. of them la moitié d'entre eux; to have h. a mind to do sth avoir bien envie de faire qch; Hum my better or other h. ma moitié; she is too clever by h. elle est beaucoup trop maligne; she doesn't do things by halves elle ne fait pas les choses à moitié; to go halves with sb partager avec qn; Fam you don't know the h. of it! tu ne sais pas tout! (b) (fraction) demie f, moitié f; three and a h. trois et demi (c) first/second h. (in match) première/deuxième mi-temps f (d) (ticket) billet m demi-tarif (e) Br (half-pint of beer) demi m 2 adj demi(e); h. board demi-pension f; h. day demi-journée f; h. hour demi-heure f; every h. hour toutes les demi-heures; h. price demi-tarif m; at h. price à moitié prix 3 adv à moitié; to h. do sth faire qch à moitié; h. full/empty à moitié plein(e)/vide; you're h. right tu n'as pas tout à fait tort

half- [hɑ:f] pref h.-asleep à moitié endormi(e); h.-dead à moitié mort(e); h.-naked à moitié nu(e)

half-baked [hɑ:f'beɪkt] adj Fam bancal(e)

halfbreed ['hɑ:fbri:d] n métis(isse) m,f

half-brother ['hɑ:fbrʌðə(r)] n demi-frère m

half-caste ['hɑ:fkɑ:st] n métis(isse) m,f

half-cock ['hɑ:f'kɒk] n Fam Fig to go off at h. (of plan, event) avorter, échouer

half-hearted [hɑ:f'hɑ:tɪd] adj (effort, performance) timide, hésitant(e); (belief, support) peu enthousiaste

half-heartedly [hɑ:f'hɑ:tɪdlɪ] adv sans grand enthousiasme, sans conviction

half-hourly [hɑ:f'aʊəlɪ] adv toutes les demi-heures

half-life ['hɑ:flaɪf] n Phys demi-vie f

half-mast [hɑ:f'mɑ:st] n Br at h. (flag) en berne; Fam (socks) en accordéon

half-sister ['hɑ:f'sɪstə(r)] n demi-sœur f

half-size ['hɑ:f'saɪz] n (in shoes) demi-pointure f

half-time ['hɑ:f'taɪm] n (in match) mi-temps f

half-truth ['hɑ:f'tru:θ] n demi-vérité f

halfway [hɑ:f'weɪ] 1 adj at the h. point (in space) à mi-chemin; (in time) à la moitié; h. line (on sports pitch) ligne f médiane 2 adv à mi-chemin; Fig to meet sb h. faire un compromis avec qn

halfwit ['hɑ:fwɪt] n simple m f d'esprit

halfwitted [hɑ:f'wɪtɪd] adj stupide

half-yearly ['hɑ:f'jɪəlɪ] adj semestriel(elle)

halibut ['hælɪbət] (pl halibut or halibuts) n flétan m

halitosis [hælɪ'təʊsɪs] n mauvaise haleine f

hall [hɔ:l] n (a) (entrance room) entrée f; (corridor) couloir m (b) (for concerts, meetings) salle f (c) Br Univ h. of residence résidence f universitaire

hallmark ['hɔ:lmɑ:k] n (on metal) poinçon m; Fig (typical quality) signe m

hallo [hə'ləʊ] = hello

hallowed ['hæləʊd] adj saint(e), béni(e)

Hallowe'en [hæləʊ'i:n] n = veille de la Toussaint durant laquelle les enfants se déguisent en fantôme ou en sorcière

hallucinate [hə'lu:sɪneɪt] vi avoir des hallucinations

hallucination [həlu:sɪ'neɪʃən] n hallucination f

hallucinatory [hə'lu:sɪnətərɪ] adj hallucinatoire

hallucinogenic [həlu:sɪnəʊ'dʒenɪk] adj hallucinogène

hallway ['hɔ:lweɪ] n (entrance room) entrée f; (corridor) couloir m

halo ['heɪləʊ] (pl haloes or halos) n auréole f

halt [hɒlt] 1 n halte f, arrêt m; to come to a h. s'arrêter; to bring sth to a h. interrompre ou faire cesser qch; to call a h. to sth mettre fin à qch 2 vt interrompre 3 vi s'arrêter

halter ['hɔ:ltə(r)] n (for horse) licou m

halterneck ['hɔ:ltənek] adj (dress, top) dos-nu inv

halting ['hɔ:ltɪŋ] adj (voice, progress) hésitant(e)

halve [hɑ:v] vt (a) (divide in two) diviser en deux; (cake, fruit) couper en deux (b) (reduce by half) réduire de moitié

halves [hɑ:vz] pl of half

ham [hæm] 1 n (a) (meat) jambon m (b) Fam (actor) cabotin(e) m,f; h. acting cabotinage m 2 vt (pt & pp hammed) Fam (of actor) to h. it up en faire trop

Hamburg ['hæmbɜ:g] n Hambourg

hamburger ['hæmbɜ:gə(r)] n hamburger m

ham-fisted ['hæm'fɪstɪd] adj Fam maladroit(e)

hamlet ['hæmlɪt] n hameau m

hammer ['hæmə(r)] 1 n marteau m; to come under the h. (be auctioned) être mis(e) aux enchères; Fam to go at it h. and tongs mettre le paquet; the h. and sickle la faucille et le marteau 2 vt (a) (hit with hammer) (nail) enfoncer (into dans); (wall) taper à coups de marteau; Fig to h. one's point home insister lourdement (b) (hit with fist) (object) frapper du poing; (person) frapper à coups de poing (c) Fam (defeat) écraser

▸ **hammer away** vt insep Fig (problem) travailler avec acharnement sur

▸ **hammer out** vt sep Fig (plan, compromise) mettre au point

hammering ['hæmərɪŋ] n (a) (noise) martèlement m (b) Fam (defeat) raclée f; **they gave us a real h.** ils nous ont mis une vraie raclée

hammock ['hæmək] n hamac m

hamper ['hæmpə(r)] **1** n (for food) panier m; (Christmas) **h.** = panier garni de gourmandises offert à Noël **2** vt (hinder) gêner, entraver

hamster ['hæmstə(r)] n hamster m

hamstring ['hæmstrɪŋ] **1** n tendon m du jarret **2** vt (pt & pp **hamstrung** ['hæmstrʌŋ]) (incapacitate) paralyser

hand [hænd] **1** n (a) (part of body) main f; (of clock, watch) aiguille f; **to hold hands** se tenir par la main; **h. in h.** la main dans la main; **to hold sth in one's h.** tenir qch à la main; **to take sb by the h.** prendre qn par la main; **on one's hands and knees** à quatre pattes; **by h.** (make, wash) à la main; **hands off!** pas touche!; **hands up!** haut les mains!; **h. basin** lavabo m; **h. cream** crème f pour les mains; **h. grenade** grenade f; **h. luggage** bagages mpl à main (b) (worker) ouvrier(ère) m,f; (sailor) matelot m; **to be an old h. at** sth avoir une expérience considérable de qch (c) (handwriting) **in his own h.** de sa main (d) (in cards) main f, jeu m; Fig **to show one's h.** dévoiler son jeu (e) (idioms) **at or on h.** disponible; **to have sth to h.** avoir qch sous la main; **to ask for sb's h. (in marriage)** demander la main de qn; **to be in good hands** être en de bonnes mains; **to fall into the wrong hands** tomber en de mauvaises mains; **it's out of my hands** ça ne dépend plus de moi; **to change hands** (of money, car) changer de mains; **to have a h. in sth** être impliqué(e) dans qch; **to go h. in h. with sth** aller de pair avec qch; **to try one's h. at sth** s'essayer à qch; **to turn one's h. to sth** s'essayer à qch; **to give sb a big h.** (applaud) applaudir qn bien fort; **to suffer at sb's hands** souffrir aux mains de qn; **on (the) one h.** d'une part; **on the other h.** d'autre part; **to have time on one's hands** avoir du temps à soi; **to have a situation in h.** contrôler une situation; **to take sb in h.** prendre qn en main; **to get out of h.** devenir incontrôlable; **to dismiss a suggestion out of h.** rejeter une proposition sur-le-champ; **to have one's hands full** être débordé(e); **to have one's hands tied** avoir les mains liées; **to be h. in glove with sb** être de mèche avec qn; **to live from h. to mouth** mener une existence précaire; **to lose money h. over fist** perdre des sommes considérables; **to make money h. over fist** gagner une fortune; **to win hands down** gagner haut la main **2** vt donner, passer; **he handed her the letter to read** il lui a passé la lettre pour qu'elle la lise; Fig **to h. sth to sb on a plate** apporter qch à qn sur un plateau; Fig **you've got to h. it to him** c'est une qualité qu'il faut lui reconnaître

▸ **hand back** vt sep rendre, repasser

▸ **hand down** vt sep (a) (jewellery, tradition, skill) transmettre (b) (give) passer

▸ **hand in** vt sep remettre; **to h. in one's resignation** donner sa démission

▸ **hand on** vt sep transmettre

▸ **hand out** vt sep distribuer

▸ **hand over** vt sep donner

▸ **hand round** vt sep faire circuler

handbag ['hændbæg] n sac m à main

handball ['hændbɔːl] n (a) (game) handball m (b) (offence) main f

handbook ['hændbʊk] n guide m, manuel m

handbrake ['hændbreɪk] n frein m à main

handclap ['hændklæp] n **to give sb the slow h.** = applaudir qn très lentement pour signifier son dédain

handcuff ['hændkʌf] vt passer les menottes à

handcuffs ['hændkʌfs] npl menottes fpl

handful ['hændfʊl] n (of sand, rice, people) poignée f; Fig **that child is a real h.** cet enfant n'est pas facile

handgun ['hændɡʌn] n revolver m, pistolet m

hand-held ['hænd'held] adj (appliance) à main; (camera) portatif(ive); **h. computer** ordinateur m de poche

handicap ['hændɪkæp] **1** n handicap m **2** vt (pt & pp **handicapped**) handicaper

handicapped ['hændɪkæpt] **1** npl **the h.** les handicapés mpl **2** adj handicapé(e)

handicraft ['hændɪkrɑːft] n (skill) artisanat m; (object) objet m artisanal

handiwork ['hændɪwɜːk] n travail m manuel; Hum **this looks like Jane's h.!** ça, c'est signé Jane!

handkerchief ['hæŋkətʃɪf] n mouchoir m

handle ['hændəl] **1** n (of broom, knife, saucepan) manche m; (of suitcase, door) poignée f; (of cup) anse f; Fig **to fly off the h.** piquer une colère; Fig **to get a h. on sth** piger qch **2** vt (a) (touch, hold) manipuler, toucher à; **h. with care** (on parcel) ≃ fragile (b) Fam (cope with) (situation, crisis) faire face à; **you handled that very well** tu as très bien réglé les choses (c) Com (business, contract, client) s'occuper de **3** vi (of car, boat) **to h. well** être maniable

handlebars ['hændəlbɑː(r)z] npl guidon m

handmade ['hænd'meɪd] adj fait(e) à la main

hand-me-downs ['hændmɪdaʊnz] npl Fam **I wear my brother's h.** je mets les vieilles frusques de mon frère

handout ['hændaʊt] n (a) (donation) don m (b) (leaflet) prospectus m

hand-picked ['hænd'pɪkd] adj (person, team) trié(e) sur le volet

handrail ['hændreɪl] n rampe f

handset ['hændset] n (of telephone) combiné m

handshake ['hændʃeɪk] n poignée f de main

hands-off ['hænd'zɒf] adj (approach, style) non-interventionniste

handsome ['hænsəm] adj (a) (physically attractive) beau (belle) (b) (praise) sincère; (price, profit) considérable; (reward) beau (belle)

handsomely ['hænsəmlɪ] adv (a) (dressed, furnished) élégamment (b) (rewarded, paid) généreusement

hands-on ['hænd'zɒn] adj **the director has a h. style of management** le directeur n'a pas peur de mettre la main à la pâte; **h. training** formation f pratique

handstand ['hændstænd] n **to do a h.** faire un équilibre sur les mains

hand-to-hand ['hæntə'hænd] adj (combat) au corps à corps

hand-to-mouth ['hæntə'maʊθ] **1** adj (existence) précaire **2** adv **to live h.** tirer le diable par la queue

handwriting ['hændraɪtɪŋ] n écriture f

handwritten ['hændrɪtən] adj manuscrit(e)

handy ['hændɪ] adj (a) (useful) pratique; **to come in h.** être utile (b) (convenient) commode; **the apartment is very h. for the mall** l'appartement est tout près du centre commercial (c) (within reach) à portée de la main; **have you got a pen h.?** est-ce que tu as un stylo à portée de la main?

(d) *(skilful)* bricoleur(euse); **he's very h. in the kitchen** il est bon cuisinier

handyman ['hændɪmæn] *n* homme *m* à tout faire; *Am* **h.'s special** = maison qui a besoin de beaucoup de travaux

hang [hæŋ] **1** *n Fam* **to get the h. of sth** piger qch **2** *vt* (*pt & pp* **hung** [hʌŋ]) (**a**) *(suspend) (from ceiling)* pendre, suspendre; *(on wall)* accrocher (**b**) **to h. one's head** baisser la tête; **he hung his head in shame** il baissa la tête sous l'effet de la honte (**c**) (*pt & pp* **hanged**) *(criminal)* pendre **3** *vi* (**a**) *(be suspended) (from ceiling)* être suspendu(e); *(on wall)* être accroché(e); *Fig* **she hung on his every word** elle était pendue à ses lèvres (**b**) *(be executed)* être pendu(e) (**c**) *(of clothes)* tomber

▸ **hang about, hang around** *vi Fam (wait)* poireauter; **to keep sb hanging about** *or* **around** faire poireauter qn

▸ **hang back** *vi* hésiter

▸ **hang in** *vi Fam* **h. in there!** accroche-toi!, tiens bon!

▸ **hang on 1** *vi* (**a**) *Fam (wait)* patienter, attendre (**b**) *(survive)* tenir le coup **2** *vt insep (depend on)* dépendre de

▸ **hang on to** *vt insep* garder

▸ **hang out 1** *vt sep (washing)* étendre **2** *vi* (**a**) *(from pocket, box)* dépasser (**b**) *Fam (spend time)* traîner

▸ **hang together** *vi (of argument, statements)* se tenir

▸ **hang up 1** *vt sep (hat, picture)* accrocher **2** *vi (on telephone)* raccrocher; **to h. up on sb** raccrocher au nez de qn

hangar ['hæŋə(r)] *n* hangar *m*

hangdog ['hæŋdɒg] *adj (look, expression)* de chien battu

hanger ['hæŋə(r)] *n (for clothes)* cintre *m*

hanger-on [hæŋə'rɒn] (*pl* **hangers-on**) *n* parasite *m*, pique-assiette *m inv*

hang-glider ['hæŋglaɪdə(r)] *n* deltaplane *m*

hang-gliding ['hæŋglaɪdɪŋ] *n* deltaplane *m*; **to go h.** faire du deltaplane

hanging ['hæŋɪŋ] *n (execution)* pendaison *f*

hangman ['hæŋmən] *n* bourreau *m*

hangnail ['hæŋneɪl] *n* envie *f*

hang-out ['hæŋaʊt] *n Fam* repaire *m*

hangover ['hæŋəʊvə(r)] *n* (**a**) *(from drinking)* gueule *f* de bois (**b**) *(practice, belief)* reste *m*, vestige *m*

hang-up ['hæŋʌp] *n Fam* complexe *m*; **to have a h. about sth** être complexé(e) à propos de qch

hanker ['hæŋkə(r)] *vi* **to h. after** *or* **for sth** avoir très envie de qch

hankering ['hæŋkərɪŋ] *n* **to have a h. for sth** avoir très envie de qch

hankie, hanky ['hæŋkɪ] (*pl* **hankies**) *n Fam* mouchoir *m*

hanky-panky ['hæŋkɪ'pæŋkɪ] *n Fam* (**a**) *(sexual activity)* galipettes *fpl* (**b**) *(underhand behaviour)* entourloupettes *fpl*

Hanover ['hænəʊvə(r)] *n* Hanovre

haphazard [hæp'hæzəd] *adj (choice, decision)* pris(e) au hasard; *(attempt)* mal organisé(e)

haphazardly [hæp'hæzədlɪ] *adv* n'importe comment

hapless ['hæplɪs] *adj* infortuné(e)

happen ['hæpən] *vi* arriver, se produire; **it happened two years ago** c'est arrivé il y a deux ans; **what happened?** que s'est-il passé?; **to h. again** se reproduire; **it so happens (that)...** il se trouve justement que...; **as if nothing had happened** comme si de rien n'était; **as it happens,...** justement...; **what has happened to him?** que lui est-il arrivé?; **to h. to meet sb** rencontrer qn par

hasard; **I h. to know (that)...** il se trouve que je sais que...; **do you h. to know whether...?** savez-vous par hasard si...?

▸ **happen on, happen upon** *vt insep* tomber sur

happening ['hæpənɪŋ] **1** *n* événement *m* **2** *adj Fam (town)* dynamique

happily ['hæpɪlɪ] *adv* (**a**) *(play)* gentiment; *(chat)* tranquillement; **a h. married couple** un ménage heureux; **they lived h. ever after** ≃ ils vécurent heureux et eurent beaucoup d'enfants (**b**) *(fortunately)* heureusement, par bonheur (**c**) *(willingly)* volontiers

happiness ['hæpɪnɪs] *n* bonheur *m*

happy ['hæpɪ] *adj* (**a**) *(content, cheerful)* heureux(euse); **to be h. with sth** être satisfait(e) de qch; **to make sb h.** rendre qn heureux; **to keep sb h.** satisfaire qn; **a story with a h. ending** une histoire qui finit bien; **a h. medium** le juste milieu; **h. birthday/Christmas!** joyeux anniversaire/Noël!; **h. New Year!** bonne année! (**b**) *(fortunate) (choice, phrase)* heureux(euse) (**c**) *(willing)* **to be h. to do sth** être heureux(euse) de faire qch

happy-go-lucky ['hæpɪgəʊ'lʌkɪ] *adj* insouciant(e)

harangue [hə'ræŋ] **1** *n* harangue *f* **2** *vt* haranguer (**about** au sujet de)

harass [hə'ræs, 'hærəs] *vt* harceler

harassed [hə'ræst, 'hærəst] *adj* stressé(e)

harassment ['hærəsmənt, hə'ræsmənt] *n* harcèlement *m*; **police h.** harcèlement policier

harbour, *Am* **harbor** ['hɑːbə(r)] **1** *n* port *m* **2** *vt (fugitive)* cacher; *(hope, suspicion)* nourrir; **to h. a grudge against sb** garder rancune à qn

hard [hɑːd] **1** *adj* (**a**) *(substance)* dur(e); *(fact, evidence)* tangible; *Fig* **to be as h. as nails** être dur; **in h. cash** en liquide; *Comptr* **h. copy** copie *f* sur papier; **h. core** *(of group)* noyau *m* dur; **h. court** *(for tennis)* court *m* en dur; *Comptr* **h. disk** disque *m* dur; **h. drugs** drogues *fpl* dures; **h. hat** casque *m*; *Pol* **h. left/right** extrême gauche *f*/droite *f*; *Comptr* **h. return** retour *m* chariot obligatoire; *Br* **h. shoulder** *(on motorway)* bande *f* d'arrêt d'urgence (**b**) *(difficult)* difficile; *(strenuous)* pénible; **it was h. work persuading him to come** ça n'a pas été facile de le convaincre de venir; **it's h. to say...** il est difficile de dire...; **to be h. to please** être difficile (à satisfaire); **to learn sth the h. way** apprendre qch à ses dépens; **to do things the h. way** se compliquer la vie; **h. of hearing** dur(e) d'oreille (**c**) *(harsh) (person, conditions, life)* dur(e); **to have a h. time (of it)** en baver; **to be h. on sb** être dur avec qn; **to give sb a h. time** mener la vie dure à qn; **a h. winter** un hiver rigoureux; **no h. feelings?** sans rancune?; **to take a h. line on sth** prendre une position très ferme sur qch; **h. luck!**, *Fam* **h. cheese!** pas de chance! (**d**) *(intense)* **to be a h. worker** travailler dur; *Law* **labour** travaux *mpl* forcés; *Com* **to give sb the h. sell** essayer de convaincre qn d'acheter à toute force (**e**) *(water)* calcaire **2** *adv* (**a**) *(work)* dur; *(push, hit)* fort; **to try h.** faire de son mieux; **to look h. at sb/sth** regarder qn/qch fixement; **to think h.** bien réfléchir; **to be h. at work** être en plein travail; **it's raining h.** il pleut à verse; **to feel h. done by** se sentir brimé(e); *Fam* **h. up** *(broke)* fauché(e) (**b**) *(near)* **h. by** tout près de; **to follow h. upon sb/sth** suivre qn/qch de près

hard-and-fast ['hɑːdən'fɑːst] *adj (rule)* absolu(e)

hardback ['hɑːdbæk] *n* livre *m* relié

hardball ['hɑːdbɔːl] *n Am (game)* base-ball *m*; *(ball)* balle *f* de base-ball; *Fam Fig* **to play h.** employer les grands moyens

hard-bitten ['hɑːd'bɪtən] adj endurci(e)
hardboard ['hɑːdbɔːd] n aggloméré m
hard-boiled [hɑːd'bɔɪld] adj (egg) dur(e); Fig (person) dur à cuire
hard-core ['hɑːdkɔː(r)] adj (supporter) inconditionnel(elle); (pornography) hard inv; (punk) hard-core inv
hard-earned [hɑːd'ɜːnd] adj durement gagné(e)
harden ['hɑːdən] 1 vt endurcir; **to h. oneself to sth** s'endurcir à qch 2 vi (of substance, attitude) durcir
hardened ['hɑːdənd] adj (steel) trempé(e); (drinker) invétéré(e); (criminal) endurci(e)
hard-fought ['hɑːd'fɔːt] adj (election, contest) âprement disputé(e)
hard-headed ['hɑːd'hedɪd] adj (attitude, person) réaliste
hard-hearted ['hɑːd'hɑːtɪd] adj dur(e)
hard-hitting [hɑːd'hɪtɪŋ] adj (criticism, report) sans indulgence
hardliner [hɑːd'laɪnə(r)] n (politician, activist) jusqu'au-boutiste mf
hardly ['hɑːdlɪ] adv (scarcely) à peine; **h. had I arrived when...** j'étais à peine arrivé que...; **you can h. expect me to do that** vous ne vous attendez tout de même pas à ce que je fasse ça; **I can h. believe it** j'ai du mal à y croire; also Ironic **I can h. wait** j'ai hâte d'y être; **h. ever** presque jamais; **h. anyone/anything** presque personne/rien
hardness ['hɑːdnɪs] n (a) (of substance) dureté f (b) (of problem) difficulté f
hard-on ['hɑːdɒn] n Vulg **to have/get a h.** bander
hard-pressed [hɑːd'prest], **hard-pushed** [hɑːd-'pʊʃt] adj en difficulté; **to be h. for time/money** manquer de temps/d'argent; **to be h. to do sth** avoir du mal à faire qch
hardship ['hɑːdʃɪp] n épreuve f; **to live in h.** vivre dans la misère
hardware ['hɑːdweə(r)] n (a) (tools) matériel m; (military) h. (weapons) matériel militaire, armement m; h. store quincaillerie f (b) Comptr matériel m, hardware m
hard-wearing [hɑːd'weərɪŋ] adj résistant(e)
hard-won [hɑːd'wʌn] adj durement acquis(e)
hard-working ['hɑːd'wɜːkɪŋ] adj travailleur(euse)
hardy ['hɑːdɪ] adj résistant(e), robuste
hare [heə(r)] 1 n lièvre m 2 vi **to h. off** partir en trombe
harebrained ['heəbreɪnd] adj écervelé(e)
harelip ['heəlɪp] n bec-de-lièvre m
harem [hɑː'riːm] n harem m
haricot ['hærɪkəʊ] n **h. (bean)** haricot m blanc
hark [hɑːk] exclam Lit écoutez!
▸ **hark back** vi **to h. back to sth** évoquer qch; **he's always harking back to that mistake I made** il revient toujours sur l'erreur que j'ai faite
harlot ['hɑːlət] n Lit prostituée f
harm [hɑːm] 1 n mal m; (to reputation) tort m; **to do sb h. faire du mal à qn; to do oneself h. se faire du tort; it will do more h. than good** cela va faire plus de mal que de bien; **I can't see any h. in it** je ne vois pas de mal à ça; **there's no h. in trying** ça ne coûte rien d'essayer; **you will come to no h.** il ne t'arrivera rien (de mal); **out of h.'s way** en sûreté, en lieu sûr 2 vt (physically) faire du mal à; (health, reputation, cause) nuire à; (skin, fabric) abîmer
harmful ['hɑːmfʊl] adj (influence, activity) néfaste; (substance, ray) nocif(ive)

harmless ['hɑːmlɪs] adj (person, animal) inoffensif(ive); (joke) innocent(e); **it's just a bit of h. fun** ça ne fait de mal à personne
harmonica [hɑː'mɒnɪkə] n harmonica m
harmonious [hɑː'məʊnɪəs] adj harmonieux(euse)
harmonization [hɑːmənaɪ'zeɪʃən] n harmonisation f
harmonize ['hɑːmənaɪz] 1 vt harmoniser 2 vi s'harmoniser (with avec)
harmony ['hɑːmənɪ] (pl harmonies) n also Fig harmonie f; **in h. with** en harmonie ou en accord avec; **to live in h. (with)** vivre en harmonie (avec)
harness ['hɑːnɪs] 1 n (a) (for horse, baby, of parachute) harnais m; (for climber) baudrier m (b) (idioms) **to work in h. (with)** travailler en équipe (avec); **to die in h.** mourir à la tâche 2 vt (horse) harnacher; (to a cart) atteler; (resources) exploiter
harp [hɑːp] n harpe f
▸ **harp on** vi **to h. on about sth** revenir sans arrêt sur qch
harpist ['hɑːpɪst] n harpiste mf
harpoon [hɑː'puːn] 1 n harpon m 2 vt harponner
harpsichord ['hɑːpsɪkɔːd] n clavecin m
harpy ['hɑːpɪ] (pl harpies) n harpie f
harrow ['hærəʊ] n herse f
harrowing ['hærəʊɪŋ] adj (experience, sight) pénible; (account, image) déchirant(e)
harry ['hærɪ] (pt & pp harried) vt harceler
harsh [hɑːʃ] adj (voice, sound) strident(e); (climate) rude; (treatment, person) dur(e)
harshly ['hɑːʃlɪ] adv (answer, speak, treat) durement
harvest ['hɑːvɪst] 1 n (of fruit) récolte f; (of crops) moisson f; (of grapes) vendange f; **h. festival** = fête religieuse pour célébrer la fin de la moisson 2 vt (fruit) récolter; (crops) moissonner; (grapes) vendanger; Fig (information) récolter
has [hæz] 3rd pers singular of **have**
has-been ['hæzbiːn] n Fam Pej **has been** mf inv
hash [hæʃ] n (a) (stew) hachis m; **h. browns** = pommes de terre râpées et sautées présentées parfois sous forme de galette (b) very Fam (hashish) hasch m (c) (idioms) Fam **to make a h. of sth** faire un beau gâchis de qch
hashish ['hæʃiːʃ] n haschich m
hasn't ['hæznt] = **has not**
hassle ['hæsəl] Fam 1 n embêtements mpl; **it's too much h.** c'est trop de tintouin; **it's a real h.** buying a house l'achat d'une maison est un vrai casse-tête; **to give sb h.** faire des histoires à qn 2 vt embêter; **don't h. me!** arrête de m'embêter!
haste [heɪst] n hâte f; **in h.** en hâte, à la hâte; **to make h.** se dépêcher, se hâter; Prov **more h. less speed** hâtez-vous lentement
hasten ['heɪsən] 1 vt (accelerate) précipiter; **to h. sb's departure** avancer ou hâter le départ de qn 2 vi se presser; **I h. to add...** je m'empresse d'ajouter...
hastily ['heɪstɪlɪ] adv (write, prepare) hâtivement; (say, eat) précipitamment; **too h.** trop vite
hasty ['heɪstɪ] adj (departure, removal) précipité(e); (meal) rapide; (reply, decision) irréfléchi(e); **to jump to a h. conclusion** conclure à la légère
hat [hæt] n chapeau m; also Fig **to take one's h. off to sb** tirer son chapeau à qn; Fig **to pass the h. round** (collect money) faire la quête; Fig **to throw one's h. in the ring** (enter contest) se porter candidat(e); Fam Fig **to keep sth**

under one's h. garder qch pour soi; *Fig* **I'm speaking with my lawyer's h.** on je parle en ma qualité de juriste; **h. stand** portemanteau *m*; **h. trick** *(of goals)* = trois buts marqués par le même joueur; *(of victories)* triplé *m*

hatch¹ [hætʃ] *n (of ship)* écoutille *f*; *Fam* **down the h.!** cul sec!; **(serving) h.** passe-plat *m*

hatch² **1** *vt (egg)* faire éclore; *Fig (scheme, plot)* tramer
2 *vi (of egg)* éclore

hatchback ['hætʃbæk] *n (car) (three-door)* voiture *f* à trois portes, trois-portes *f inv*; *(five-door)* voiture *f* à cinq portes, cinq-portes *f inv*

hatchet ['hætʃɪt] *n* hachette *f*; *Fam* **to do a h. job on sb/ sth** *(of critic, reviewer)* démolir qn/qch; *Fam* **h. man** homme *m* de main

hate [heɪt] **1** *n* haine *f*; **h. mail** lettres *fpl* d'injures
2 *vt* détester, haïr; **to h. doing sth** détester faire qch, avoir horreur de faire qch; **she hates to be contradicted** elle a horreur qu'on la contredise; **I h. it when he's in a bad mood** je déteste quand il est de mauvaise humeur; *Fam* **I h. to tell you, but I think you've missed your train** ça m'ennuie de te le dire, mais je pense que tu as raté ton train

hateful ['heɪtfʊl] *adj* odieux(euse)

hatpin ['hætpɪn] *n* épingle *f* à chapeau

hatred ['heɪtrɪd] *n* haine *f* **(of/for** de/pour)

haughty ['hɔːtɪ] *adj* hautain(e)

haul [hɔːl] **1** *n* **(a)** *(fish caught)* prise *f*; *(loot)* butin *m*; *(of drugs, stolen goods)* saisie *f* **(b)** *Fam (journey)* parcours *m*, trajet *m*; **it's a long h.** la route est longue; *Fig* c'est un travail de longue haleine
2 *vt* **(a)** *(pull)* tirer; *(tow)* remorquer; *Fam* **he was hauled in for questioning** on l'a emmené pour l'interroger; *Fam Fig* **to h. sb over the coals** *(reprimand)* passer un savon à qn; **she was hauled up before the principal** elle a été convoquée chez le proviseur **(b)** *(transport)* transporter par camion

haulage ['hɔːlɪdʒ] *n (transportation)* transport *m* (routier); *(costs)* (frais *mpl* de) transport; **h. firm** entreprise *f* de transports routiers

haulier ['hɔːlɪə(r)], *Am* **hauler** ['hɔːlə(r)] *n (company)* entreprise *f* de transports routiers

haunch [hɔːntʃ] *n (of person)* hanche *f*; *(of venison)* cuissot *m*; **to sit** *or* **squat on one's haunches** être accroupi(e)

haunt [hɔːnt] **1** *n (of criminals)* repaire *m*; *(of group of people)* (lieu *m* de) rendez-vous *m*; **it's one of his usual haunts** *(bar, restaurant etc)* c'est un des endroits qu'il fréquente habituellement
2 *vt also Fig* hanter

haunted ['hɔːntɪd] *adj (castle, room)* hanté(e); *Fig* **he has a h. look** il a l'air égaré

haunting ['hɔːntɪŋ] *adj* obsédant(e)

Havana [hə'vænə] *n* la Havane; **H. (cigar)** havane *m*

have [hæv]

> Les formes négatives, **haven't** et **hasn't**, s'écrivent **have not** et **has not** dans un style plus soutenu.

1 *vt (pt & pp* **had)** **(a)** *(own)* avoir; **they've (got) a big house** ils ont une grande maison; **she doesn't h.** *or* **hasn't got a car** elle n'a pas de voiture; **I've (got) things to do** j'ai des choses à faire; **you can h. it back tomorrow** je te le rendrai demain; **to h. sb in one's power** tenir qn à sa merci; **to h. it on good authority that...** tenir de source sûre que...
(b) *(with noun to denote activity)* **to h. a swim** se baigner; **to h. a shave** se raser; **to h. lunch** déjeuner; **to h. a cigarette** fumer une cigarette; **to h. a drink** prendre un verre; **to h. a good/bad time** passer un bon/mauvais moment

(c) *(with illnesses)* **to h. a cold** être enrhumé(e); **to h. flu/ cancer** avoir la grippe/un cancer
(d) *(cause to do, to be done)* **to h. sb do sth** faire faire qch à qn; **to h. sth done** faire faire qch; **to h. one's hair cut** se faire couper les cheveux; **h. him call me** dis-lui de m'appeler; **I'll h. you know that...!** je vous signale que...!
(e) *(in passive constructions)* **I had my watch stolen** on m'a volé ma montre; **three houses had their windows broken** il y a des fenêtres brisées dans trois maisons
(f) *(allow)* **I won't h. it!** je n'accepte pas ça!; **I won't h. you causing trouble!** pas question que tu fasses des histoires!
(g) *(be compelled)* **to h. (got) to do sth** devoir faire qch; **I h.** *or* **I've got to go** je dois y aller; **you don't h. to come with me** tu n'es pas obligé de venir avec moi; **do you h.** *or* **h. you got to work?** est-ce qu'il faut vraiment que tu travailles?; **it has** *or* **it's got to be done** il faut que ce soit fait
(h) *Fam (idioms)* **to be had** *(cheated)* se faire avoir; **to h. had it** être fichu(e); **to h. had it with sb/sth** en avoir marre de qn/qch; **he had it coming** ça lui pendait au nez
2 *v aux* avoir/être

> Most French verbs will conjugate with **avoir** to form the perfect tense. However, all reflexive verbs and many intransitive verbs – mainly of motion – will conjugate with **être**.

to h. seen avoir vu; **to h. left** être parti(e); **to h. hurt oneself** s'être blessé(e); **I've worked here for three years** je travaille ici depuis trois ans; **we've seen this film before – no we haven't!** nous avons déjà vu ce film – mais non!; **you haven't done the dishes – yes, I h.!** tu n'as pas fait la vaisselle – si, je l'ai faite!; **you h. told him, haven't you?** tu le lui as dit, n'est-ce pas *ou* non?; **you haven't forgotten, h. you?** tu n'as pas oublié, n'est-ce pas *ou* hein?
3 *n* the haves and the have-nots les riches *mpl* et les pauvres

▸ **have in** *vt sep Fam* **to h. it in for sb** en avoir après qn
▸ **have off** *vt sep Br very Fam* **to h. it off (with sb)** *(have sexual intercourse)* s'envoyer en l'air (avec qn)
▸ **have on** *vt sep* **(a)** *(be wearing)* porter; **to h. nothing on** être nu(e) **(b)** *Fam* **to h. sb on** faire marcher qn **(c)** *(have arranged)* **to h. a lot on** avoir beaucoup à faire; **to h. nothing on** n'avoir rien de prévu **(d)** *Fam* **to h. sth on sb** disposer d'informations compromettantes pour qn
▸ **have out** *vt sep* **(a)** *(have removed)* **to h. a tooth out** faire arracher une dent; **to h. one's appendix out** se faire opérer de l'appendicite **(b)** *(resolve)* **to h. it out with sb** s'expliquer avec qn

haven ['heɪvən] *n* refuge *m*

haven't ['hævnt] = have not

haversack ['hævəsæk] *n* sac *m* à dos

havoc ['hævək] *n* **(a)** *(damage)* ravages *mpl*, dégâts *mpl*; **to cause** *or* **wreak h.** faire des ravages **(b)** *(confusion)* pagaille *f*; **to play h. with sth** *(plans)* chambouler qch

Hawaii [hə'waɪiː] *n* Hawaii

Hawaiian [hə'waɪən] **1** *n* Hawaiien(enne) *m,f*
2 *adj* hawaiien(enne)

hawk¹ [hɔːk] *n also Pol* faucon *m*; **to watch sb/sth like a h.** regarder qn/qch d'un œil perçant

hawk² *vt* **to h. one's wares** *(in market, street)* vendre ses marchandises à la criée; *(from door to door)* faire du porte-à-porte

hawk-eyed ['hɔːkaɪd] *adj* **to be h.** avoir les yeux de lynx

hawkish ['hɔːkɪʃ] *adj Pol* belliciste

hawser ['hɔːzə(r)] *n* aussière *f*

hawthorn ['hɔːθɔːn] *n* aubépine *f*

hay [heɪ] *n* foin *m*; **to make h.** faire les foins; *Fig* **to make h.** while the sun shines en profiter tant que ça dure

hayfever ['heɪfiːvə(r)] *n* rhume *m* des foins

hayloft ['heɪlɒft] *n* fenil *m*

haystack ['heɪstæk] *n* meule *f* de foin

haywire ['heɪwaɪə(r)] *adv Fam* **to go h.** *(of plan)* mal tourner; *(of mechanism)* se détraquer

hazard ['hæzəd] **1** *n (danger)* danger *m*, risque *m*; **a fire h.** un risque d'incendie; **a health h.** un danger pour la santé; **h. lights** feux *mpl* de détresse
2 *vt (one's life, fortune)* risquer; *(opinion)* hasarder; **to h. a guess** essayer de deviner

hazardous ['hæzədəs] *adj* dangereux(euse); *(financial venture)* hasardeux(euse)

haze [heɪz] **1** *n (mist)* brume *f*; *(of doubt, confusion)* atmosphère *f*; **my mind was in a h.** j'avais l'esprit embrouillé
2 *vt Am (at university)* brimer, bizuter

hazel ['heɪzəl] *n (colour)* (couleur *f*) noisette *f*; **h. (tree)** noisetier *m*

hazelnut ['heɪzəlnʌt] *n* noisette *f*

hazily ['heɪzɪlɪ] *adv* vaguement

hazing ['heɪzɪŋ] *n Am (at university)* bizutage *m*

hazy ['heɪzɪ] *adj (weather)* brumeux(euse); *(image, memory)* flou(e), vague; **to be h. about sth** *(remember vaguely)* n'avoir qu'un vague souvenir de qch

he [hiː] **1** *pron* il; **he's Scottish** il est écossais; **HE hasn't got it!** ce n'est pas lui qui l'a!
2 *n* **it's a he** *(of animal)* c'est un mâle

head [hed] **1** *n* **(a)** *(of person)* tête *f*; **a fine h. of hair** une belle chevelure; **from h. to foot** *or* **toe** de la tête aux pieds; **to stand on one's h.** faire le poirier; *Fig* **to stand sth on its h.** retourner qch; **to win by a h.** *(of horse)* gagner d'une tête; *Fig* **she's h. and shoulders above the other candidates** les autres candidats ne lui arrivent pas à la cheville; **h. cold** rhume *m* de cerveau; **h. start** *(advantage)* avantage *m*, *(in race)* avance *f*
(b) *(intellect, mind)* tête *f*; **to do sums in one's h.** calculer de tête; **to have a good h. on one's shoulders** avoir la tête sur les épaules; **to have a good h. for business** avoir le sens des affaires, **to have a good h. for figures** être à l'aise avec les chiffres, **to have a (good) h. for heights** ne pas avoir le vertige; **to take it into one's h. to do sth** se mettre en tête de faire qch; **to have a good h. that...** se mettre dans la tête que...; **it never entered my h. that...** il ne m'est jamais venu à l'esprit que...; **to put ideas into sb's h.** donner des idées à qn; *Fam* **he's not right in the h.** il a un grain
(c) *(of pin, hammer, list, bed)* tête *f*; *(of arrow)* pointe *f*; *(of page, stairs)* haut *m*; *(of table)* bout *m*; *(on beer)* mousse *f*; *(on tape recorder)* tête; **a h. of lettuce/cabbage** un pied de laitue/chou; **heads or tails?** *(when tossing coin)* pile ou face?; **to build up a h. of steam** *(of campaign)* s'intensifier; *(of person)* progresser rapidement; **to come to a h.** *(of conflict, crisis)* atteindre un paroxysme
(d) *(person in charge)* *(of family, the Church, business)* chef *m*; **h. of state** chef d'État; *Br Sch* **h. (teacher)** directeur(trice) *m,f*; **h. office** siège *m (social)*; **h. waiter** maître *m* d'hôtel
(e) *(unit)* $30 per h. *or* a h. 30 dollars par personne; **six h. of cattle** six têtes de bétail
(f) *(idioms)* **to keep our heads together** nous nous y sommes tous mis; **they'll have your h. (on a plate) for this** cela te coûtera ta tête; **to bury** *or* **have one's h. in the sand** se mettre la tête dans le sable; **to give sb his h.** lâcher la bride à qn; **on your own h. be it** à tes risques et périls; **to go over sb's h.** *(appeal to higher authority)* ne pas consulter qn *(en suivant la voie hiérarchique)*; *Fam* **to shout one's h. off** crier à tue-tête; **the wine/praise went to his**

h. le vin/compliment lui est monté à la tête; *Prov* **two heads are better than one** deux avis valent mieux qu'un; **off the top of one's h.** au hasard; **it was** *or* **went over my h.** ça m'a dépassé; **I can't make h. nor tail of this** ça n'a ni queue ni tête; *Fam* **to lose one's h.** *(panic)* perdre la tête; *(get angry)* perdre son calme; *Fam* **to keep one's h.** garder son calme; *Fam* **to be off one's h.** avoir perdu la boule
2 *vt* **(a)** *(lead) (organization, campaign)* diriger; *(list)* venir en tête de
(b) *(steer)* diriger; **one of the locals headed me in the right direction** un des habitants m'a indiqué la bonne direction
(c) *(put a title on) (page, chapter)* intituler
(d) *(in football)* **to h. the ball** faire une tête
3 *vi (move)* se diriger; **they were heading out of town** ils sortaient de la ville
▸ **head for** *vt insep* se diriger vers; **you're heading for disaster** vous avez droit au désastre; **you're heading for trouble** tu vas avoir des ennuis
▸ **head off 1** *vt sep (divert)* éviter
2 *vi (depart)* partir

headache ['hedeɪk] *n* mal *m* de tête; *Fig (problem)* casse-tête *m inv*; **to have a h.** avoir mal à la tête

headband ['hedbænd] *n* bandeau *m*

headboard ['hedbɔːd] *n* tête *f* de lit

headbutt ['hedbʌt] *vt* donner un coup de tête à

headcase ['hedkeɪs] *n Fam* cinglé(e) *m,f*

headdress ['heddres] *n* coiffure *f*

headed ['hedɪd] *adj* **h. (note)paper** papier *m* à en-tête

header ['hedə(r)] *n* **(a)** *Typ* en-tête *m* **(b)** *(in football)* (coup *m* de) tête *f*

headfirst ['hed'fɜːst] *adv* la tête la première

headgear ['hedgɪə(r)] *n* couvre-chef *m*

headhunt ['hedhʌnt] *vt Com* **to be headhunted** être recruté(e) par un chasseur de têtes

headhunter ['hedhʌntə(r)] *n Com* chasseur *m* de têtes

heading ['hedɪŋ] *n (of chapter, article)* titre *m*; *(of letter)* en-tête *m*; **it comes** *or* **falls under the h. of...** c'est à mettre sous la rubrique de...

headlamp ['hedlæmp] *n (on car)* phare *m*

headland ['hedlənd] *n* cap *m*, pointe *f*

headlight ['hedlaɪt] *n (on car)* phare *m*

headline ['hedlaɪn] **1** *n (of TV news)* titre *m*; *(of newspaper)* (gros) titre; **to hit the headlines** faire la une des journaux; **to be h. news** faire la une des journaux
2 *vt (article, story)* intituler

headlong ['hedlɒŋ] **1** *adj* **there was a h. rush for the bar** tout le monde s'est rué vers le bar
2 *adv (fall)* la tête la première; *(rush)* tête baissée

headmaster [hed'mɑːstə(r)] *n Br Sch* directeur *m*

headmistress [hed'mɪstrɪs] *n Br Sch* directrice *f*

head-on ['hed'dɒn] *adj & adv* de front; **to meet sb's h.** aborder qn de front; **a h. collision** une collision frontale

headphones ['hedfəʊnz] *npl* écouteurs *mpl*

headquarters [hed'kwɔːtəz] *npl (of organization)* siège *m (social)*, *Mil* quartier *m* général

headrest ['hedrest] *n* appui-tête *m inv*

headroom ['hedruːm] *n (under bridge, inside car)* hauteur *f*

headscarf ['hedskɑːf] *(pl* **headscarves** ['hedskɑːvz]*) n* foulard *m*

headset ['hedset] *n* écouteurs *mpl*

headstone ['hedstəʊn] *n (on grave)* pierre *f* tombale

headstrong ['hedstrɒŋ] *adj* têtu(e), entêté(e)

headway ['hedweɪ] *n* **to make h.** avancer, faire des progrès

headwind ['hedwɪnd] *n* vent *m* contraire; *Naut* vent debout

heady ['hedɪ] *adj (atmosphere)* enivrant(e); *(wine, perfume)* capiteux(euse); *(heights, days)* grisant(e)

heal [hiːl] **1** *vt (wound, person)* guérir; *(disagreement)* régler; *Fig* **time heals all wounds** le temps guérit toutes les blessures **2** *vi (of wound)* **to h.** **(up** *or* **over)** cicatriser

health [helθ] *n* santé *f*; **to be in good/poor h.** être en bonne/mauvaise santé; *Fig* **the economy is in good h.** l'économie se porte bien; **the Department of H.** ≃ le ministère de la Santé; **to drink (to) sb's h.** boire à la santé de qn; **h. care** soins *mpl* médicaux; *Br* **h. centre** centre *m* médico-social; **h. cover** *(insurance)* assurance *f* médicale; **h. farm** centre *m* de remise en forme; **h. food** produits *mpl* biologiques; **h. hazard** *or* **risk** risque *m* pour la santé; **h. insurance** assurance maladie; **h. resort** station *f* climatique; *(by sea)* station balnéaire; *Br* **the H. Service** ≃ la Sécurité *f* sociale; **h. visitor** = infirmière effectuant des visites de contrôle à domicile

healthy ['helθɪ] *adj (person)* en bonne santé; *(climate)* salubre; *(food, habit, economy)* sain(e); **a h. appetite** un bon appétit; **it is a h. sign that...** c'est bon signe que...; **he has a h. respect for his opponents** il apprécie ses adversaires à leur juste valeur

heap [hiːp] **1** *n* tas *m*; *Fig* **people at the top/bottom of the h.** ceux qui sont en haut/bas de l'échelle sociale; *Br Fam* **we've got heaps of time** on a largement le temps **2** *vt* entasser; **his plate was heaped with food** son assiette était remplie de nourriture; **to h. sth with** remplir qch de; **a heaped spoonful** *(in recipe)* une cuillerée bien pleine; **to h. riches/praise on sb** couvrir qn de richesses/d'éloges; **to h. insults on sb** abreuver qn d'injures

hear [hɪə(r)] *(pt & pp* **heard** [hɜːd]) **1** *vt* **(a)** *(perceive)* entendre; **to h. sb speak** entendre qn parler; **I can hardly h. myself think!** on ne s'entend plus ici!; **to make oneself heard** se faire entendre; **let's h. it for...** applaudissons bien fort...; **have you heard the one about...?** est-ce que tu connais celle de...? **(b)** *(listen to)* écouter; **h., h.!** *(at meeting)* bravo!; *Law* **to h. a case** juger une affaire **(c)** *(find out)* entendre (dire), apprendre; **have you heard the news?** tu connais la nouvelle?; **I h. you're getting married** j'ai entendu dire que tu te mariais **2** *vi* entendre; **I can't h. properly** je n'entends pas bien; **to h. from sb** avoir des nouvelles de qn; **you'll be hearing from my lawyer!** vous allez entendre parler de mon avocat!; **to h. of** *or* **about sth** entendre parler de qch; **I won't h. of it!** je ne veux pas en entendre parler!
▸ **hear out** *vt sep* **to h. sb out** écouter qn jusqu'au bout

hearing ['hɪərɪŋ] *n* **(a)** *(sense)* ouïe *f*, audition *f*; **h. aid** audiophone *m* **(b)** *(earshot)* **to be within/out of h.** être à portée/hors de portée de voix **(c)** *(chance to explain)* **to give sb a fair h.** laisser parler qn, laisser qn s'expliquer **(d)** *Law (inquiry)* audition *f*

hearsay ['hɪəseɪ] *n* ouï-dire *m inv*, on-dit *m inv*; *Law* **h. evidence** déposition *f* sur la foi d'autrui

hearse [hɜːs] *n* corbillard *m*

heart [hɑːt] *n* **(a)** *(organ)* cœur *m*; **to have h. trouble, to have a weak** *or* **bad h.** être cardiaque; **h. attack** crise *f* cardiaque; **h. disease** maladie *f* cardiaque; **h. failure** arrêt *m* cardiaque; **h. surgery** chirurgie *f* cardiaque; **h. transplant** transplantation *f* cardiaque **(b)** *(seat of the emotions)* cœur *m*; **to have a big h.** avoir bon cœur; **a h. of gold** un cœur d'or; **a h. of stone** un cœur de pierre; **have a h.!** ayez un peu de cœur!; **her h.'s in the right place** elle a bon cœur; **with a heavy h.** le cœur gros;

my h. sank j'ai été très déçu; **to have one's h. in one's mouth** être terrorisé(e); **to break sb's h.** briser le cœur à qn; **to wear one's h. on one's sleeve** ne pas cacher ses sentiments; **affairs** *or* **matters of the h.** affaires *fpl* de cœur; *Ironic* **my h. bleeds for you** ça me fait de la peine pour toi; **in my h. of hearts** au fond de mon cœur; **from the bottom of one's h.** du fond du cœur; **he loved her with all his h.** il l'aimait de toute son âme; **at h.** au fond; **to have sb's welfare/interests at h.** avoir le bien-être/les intérêts de qn à cœur; **to take sth to h.** prendre qch à cœur; **to set one's h. on sth** vouloir qch à tout prix; **he's a man after my own h.** il est comme moi; **to one's h.'s content** tout son soûl **(c)** *(enthusiasm, courage)* **to take h.** reprendre courage; **to lose h.** se décourager; **he tried to convince them but his h. wasn't in it** il a essayé de les convaincre mais le cœur n'y était pas; **I didn't have the h. to tell him** je n'ai pas eu le cœur de lui dire **(d)** *(shape)* cœur *m*; **a pattern of red hearts** un motif de cœurs rouges **(e)** **by h.** *(know)* par cœur **(f)** *(centre)* *(of city, forest)* cœur *m*; **the h. of the matter** le fond du problème **(g)** *(in cards)* **hearts** cœur *m*

heartache ['hɑːteɪk] *n* chagrin *m*, peine *f*

heartbeat ['hɑːtbiːt] *n (rhythm)* pouls *m*; *(single beat)* battement *m* de cœur; **an irregular h.** un battement irrégulier

heartbreaking ['hɑːtbreɪkɪŋ] *adj* déchirant(e), navrant(e)

heartbroken ['hɑːtbrəʊkən] *adj* **to be h.** avoir le cœur brisé

heartburn ['hɑːtbɜːn] *n (indigestion)* brûlures *fpl* d'estomac

hearten ['hɑːtən] *vt* encourager

heartening ['hɑːtənɪŋ] *adj* encourageant(e)

heartfelt ['hɑːtfelt] *adj* sincère, qui vient du cœur

hearth [hɑːθ] *n (fireplace, home)* foyer *m*

heartily ['hɑːtɪlɪ] *adv (welcome, applaud)* chaleureusement; *(agree)* de tout cœur; *(eat)* avec appétit; **to be h. sick of sth** être profondément dégoûté(e) de qch

heartlands ['hɑːtlændz] *npl* centre *m*, cœur *m*

heartless ['hɑːtlɪs] *adj* sans cœur, cruel(elle)

heart-rending ['hɑːtrendɪŋ] *adj* déchirant(e), navrant(e)

heart-searching ['hɑːtsɜːtʃɪŋ] *n* **after much h.** après avoir longuement réfléchi

heartstrings ['hɑːtstrɪŋz] *npl* **to tug at sb's h.** jouer sur la corde sensible de qn

heart-throb ['hɑːtθrɒb] *n Fam* idole *f*

heart-to-heart ['hɑːtəˈhɑːt] *n* **to have a h. (with sb)** avoir une conversation à cœur ouvert (avec qn)

heart-warming ['hɑːtwɔːmɪŋ] *adj* réconfortant(e), qui réchauffe le cœur

hearty ['hɑːtɪ] *adj* **(a)** *(person, laugh)* jovial(e); *(approval, welcome)* chaleureux(euse); **to have a h. dislike of sth** avoir une sainte horreur de qch; **my heartiest congratulations** mes plus sincères félicitations **(b)** *(substantial) (meal, appetite)* solide

heat [hiːt] **1** *n* **(a)** *(high temperature)* chaleur *f*; **to give out h.** dégager de la chaleur; **to cook at a moderate/low h.** faire cuire à feu moyen/doux; **you shouldn't go out in this h.** tu ne devrais pas sortir par cette chaleur; **h. exhaustion** coup *m* de chaleur; **h. haze** brume *f* de chaleur; **h. loss** déperdition *f* de chaleur; **h. rash** boutons *mpl* de chaleur; *Med* **h. treatment** thermothérapie *f* **(b)** *(passion)* feu *m*; in

the h. of the moment/argument dans le feu de l'action/
de la discussion (**c**) *Fam (pressure)* to turn up the h. mettre
la pression; the h. is on la tension est à son comble (**d**) *(of
female animal)* in *or* on h. en chaleur (**e**) *(in sport)*
éliminatoire *f*
2 *vt (food, water)* faire chauffer; *(room, building)* chauffer
▸ **heat up 1** *vt sep* réchauffer
2 *vi (of water)* chauffer; *(of room)* se réchauffer; *Fig (of
argument, contest)* s'animer
heated ['hi:tɪd] *adj* (**a**) *(room, building, swimming pool)*
chauffé(e) (**b**) *(argument)* animé(e); to become h. *(of person)*
s'échauffer
heater ['hi:tə(r)] *n* radiateur *m*
heath [hi:θ] *n (land)* lande *f*
heathen ['hi:ðən] *n Rel* païen(enne) *m,f; Hum* barbare *mf*
heather ['heðə(r)] *n* bruyère *f*
heating ['hi:tɪŋ] *n* chauffage *m*
heatproof ['hi:tpru:f] *adj* résistant(e) à la chaleur;
(clothing) isolant(e)
heatstroke ['hi:tstrəʊk] *n* coup *m* de chaleur
heatwave ['hi:tweɪv] *n* vague *f* de chaleur
heave [hi:v] **1** *n* effort *m*
2 *vt* (**a**) *(pull)* tirer fort; *(push)* pousser fortement; *(lift)*
soulever avec effort; she heaved herself out of her chair
elle s'extirpa de sa chaise; to h. a sigh of relief pousser un
soupir de soulagement (**b**) *Fam (throw)* balancer
3 *vi* (**a**) *(pull)* they heaved on the rope ils tirèrent sur la
corde fortement (**b**) *(of deck, ground)* tanguer, se soulever;
(of bosom) se soulever (**c**) *(retch)* avoir des haut-le-cœur;
(vomit) vomir (**d**) *(pt & pp* hove [həʊv]) *also Fig* to h. into
view paraître à l'horizon
▸ **heave to** *(pt & pp* hove [həʊv]) *vi Naut* se mettre en
panne
heaven ['hevən] *n* paradis *m*, ciel *m*; in h. au paradis, au
ciel; *Fig (overjoyed)* aux anges; this is h.! c'est le paradis!; to
move h. and earth to do sth remuer ciel et terre pour faire
qch; the heavens opened il s'est mis à pleuvoir à torrents;
Fam it stinks to high h. ça pue; (good) heavens!,
heavens above! juste ciel!, mon Dieu!; thank h. (for
that)! Dieu merci!; h. knows why... Dieu seul sait
pourquoi...; for h.'s sake! pour l'amour du ciel!; h. forbid!
que le ciel nous en préserve!
heavenly ['hevənlɪ] *adj* (**a**) h. body corps *m* céleste
(**b**) *Fam (weather, food)* divin(e)
heaven-sent ['hevənsent] *adj* providentiel(elle)
heavily ['hevɪlɪ] *adv (fall, walk, tax)* lourdement; *(sleep)*
profondément; *(breathe)* bruyamment; to drink/smoke h.
boire/fumer beaucoup; it was raining h. il pleuvait à
torrents; to rely *or* depend h. on dépendre beaucoup de;
h. built solidement charpenté(e); to be h. defeated subir
une lourde défaite
heavy ['hevɪ] **1** *n (pl* heavies) *Fam (tough guy)* dur *m*
2 *adj* (**a**) *(in weight, food)* lourd(e); how h. is it? combien
est-ce que ça pèse?; a h. blow un coup violent; *Fig* un coup
rude; h. goods vehicle poids *m* lourd; h. industry
industrie *f* lourde; h. metal *Chem* métal *m* lourd; *(music)*
heavy metal *m*
(**b**) *(large, thick) (coat, shoes)* gros (grosse); h. losses
lourdes pertes *fpl*
(**c**) *(intense) (fighting)* violent(e); *(rain, showers)* fort(e);
(drinker, smoker) gros (grosse); a h. cold un gros rhume;
there was h. traffic il y avait beaucoup de circulation; to
be a h. sleeper avoir le sommeil lourd; to come under h.
fire essuyer un feu nourri
(**d**) *(oppressive) (smell)* fort(e); *(sky, fine, sentence)* lourd(e); h.
responsibility lourde responsabilité *f*
(**e**) *(hard) (work, day, breathing)* pénible; it was h. going

c'était difficile *ou* ardu; h. seas grosse mer *f*
(**f**) *Fam (threatening) (situation)* difficile, pénible; to get h.
with sb être agressif(ive) avec qn
(**g**) *Fam (serious) (book, article)* intello
heavy-duty [hevɪ'dju:tɪ] *adj (machine)* à usage
industriel, *(clothing, boots)* résistant(e)
heavy-handed [hevɪ'hændɪd] *adj (clumsy)* mala-
droit(e); *(government, policy)* autoritaire; the police res-
ponded in a h. way la police est intervenue de façon très
agressive
heavyweight ['hevɪweɪt] *n (in boxing)* poids *m* lourd;
Fig a political h. un grand ponte de la politique; an
intellectual h. un grand intellectuel
Hebrew ['hi:bru:] **1** *n (language)* hébreu *m*
2 *adj* hébraïque
Hebrides ['hebrɪdi:z] *npl* the H. les (îles *fpl*) Hébrides *fpl*
heck [hek] *n Fam* h.! zut!; what the h. are you doing
here? qu'est-ce que tu fiches là?; what the h.! et puis
flûte!; a h. of a lot des masses
heckle ['hekəl] **1** *vt* interpeller, interrompre
2 *vi* chahuter
heckler ['heklə(r)] *n* chahuteur(euse) *m,f*
heckling ['hekəlɪŋ] *n* chahut *m*
hectare ['hekta:(r)] *n* hectare *m*
hectic ['hektɪk] *adj (busy)* agité(e); *(eventful)*
mouvementé(e); a h. life une vie trépidante
hector ['hektə(r)] *vt* rudoyer
hectoring ['hektərɪŋ] *adj* autoritaire
he'd [hi:d] = he had, he would
hedge [hedʒ] **1** *n* (**a**) *(in field, garden)* haie *f* (**b**) *(barrier)* a
h. against inflation une protection contre l'inflation
2 *vt* (**a**) *(field)* entourer d'une haie (**b**) to h. one's bets se
couvrir
3 *vi (in discussion)* ne pas se mouiller
hedgehog ['hedʒhɒg] *n* hérisson *m*
hedgerow ['hedʒrəʊ] *n* haie *f*
hedonism ['hedənɪzəm] *n* hédonisme *m*
heed [hi:d] **1** *n* to pay (no) h. to, to take (no) h. of *(ne*
pas) tenir compte de
2 *vt (warning, advice)* tenir compte de
heedless ['hi:dlɪs] *adj* to be h. of ne pas tenir compte de
heel [hi:l] **1** *n (of foot, shoe, sock)* talon *m*; high heels talons
hauts; he had the police at his heels il avait la police sur
les talons *ou* à ses trousses; to take to one's heels prendre
ses jambes à son cou; to turn on one's heels tourner les
talons; *Fam* to cool *or* kick one's heels *(wait)* poireauter;
Fig to bring sb to h. *(bring under control)* mettre qn au pas
2 *vt (shoe)* réparer le talon de
hefty ['heftɪ] *adj Fam (person)* costaud(e); *(suitcase, box)*
lourd(e); *(blow)* puissant(e); *(bill, fine)* gros (grosse)
heifer ['hefə(r)] *n* génisse *f*
height [haɪt] *n (of building, tree)* hauteur *f*; *(of mountain)*
altitude *f*; *(of person)* taille *f*; of average h. de taille
moyenne; what h. are you? combien mesurez-vous?; to
gain/lose h. *(of plane)* prendre/perdre de l'altitude; to be
afraid of heights avoir le vertige; she's at the h. of her
powers elle est au maximum de ses capacités; she's at the
h. of her career elle est à l'apogée de sa carrière; the h. of
fashion la dernière mode; it's the h. of madness! c'est de
la folie pure!; at the h. of the storm au plus fort de l'orage
heighten ['haɪtən] *vt (sensation)* intensifier; *(tension)*
augmenter; to h. public awareness sensibiliser l'opinion
heinous ['heɪnəs] *adj Formal (crime)* abominable, atroce
heir [eə(r)] *n* héritier(ère) *m,f*; to be h. to sth être l'héritier
de qch; h. apparent héritier présomptif

heiress ['eərɪs] *n* héritière *f*
heirloom ['eəluːm] *n* a family h. un objet de famille
held [held] *pt & pp of* **hold**
helicopter ['helɪkɒptə(r)] *n* hélicoptère *m*
heliport ['helɪpɔːt] *n* héliport *m*
helium ['hiːlɪəm] *n* hélium *m*
hell [hel] *n* (**a**) *Rel* enfer *m*; *Fam* **h.!** bon Dieu!
(**b**) *Fam (for emphasis)* a h. of a price un prix salé; what the h. do you think you're doing? qu'est-ce que tu fous?; who the h. are you? qui diable êtes-vous?; she put up a h. of a fight elle s'est bien défendue; to have a h. of a time *(good)* s'éclater; *(bad)* en baver; a h. of a lot of... énormément de...; he's one *or* a h. of a guy c'est un brave type
(**c**) *Fam (idioms)* it was h. c'était l'enfer; to feel like h. se sentir horriblement mal; to make sb's life h. faire de la vie de qn un enfer; these shoes are giving me h. ces chaussures me font un mal de chien; all h. was let *or* broke loose ce fut le chaos; there'll be h. to pay if... ça va barder si...; go to h.! va te faire voir!; to run like h. courir comme un dératé; like h. (I will)! certainement pas!; until h. freezes over jusqu'à la saint-glinglin; come h. or high water quoi qu'il arrive; to run h. for leather courir ventre à terre; to do sth for the h. of it faire qch sans raison particulière
he'll [hiːl] = he will, he shall
hellbent ['helbent] *adj Fam* to be h. on doing sth vouloir à tout prix faire qch
hellhole ['helhəʊl] *n Fam (bar, club)* bouge *m*; *(prison)* enfer *m*
hellish ['helɪʃ] *adj Fam* infernal(e)
hello [he'ləʊ] *exclam* bonjour!; *(on phone)* allô!; to say h. to sb dire bonjour à qn; h., what's this? *(indicating surprise)* tiens, qu'est-ce que c'est que ça?
hellraiser ['helreɪzə(r)] *n Fam* perturbateur(trice) *m,f*
helm [helm] *n (of ship)* barre *f*; *also Fig* to be at the h. être à la barre
helmet ['helmɪt] *n* casque *m*
helmsman ['helmzmən] *n* timonier *m*
help [help] **1** *n* (**a**) *(aid)* aide *f*; to shout for h. crier à l'aide; h.! à l'aide!, au secours!; to be of h. to sb aider qn; thank you, you've been a great h. merci beaucoup de votre aide; there was no h. for it il n'y avait rien à faire; with the h. of sb avec l'aide de qn; with the h. of sth *(implement)* à l'aide de qch (**b**) *(cleaning woman)* femme *f* de ménage
2 *vt* (**a**) *(aid)* aider; to h. sb (to) do sth aider qn à faire qch; to h. sb to their feet aider qn à se mettre debout; to h. sb on/off with his coat aider qn à mettre/enlever son manteau; to h. one another s'entraider; to h. oneself to sth se servir en *ou* de qch; h. yourself! servez-vous! (**b**) *(prevent)* I can't h. it je ne peux pas m'en empêcher; it can't be helped on n'y peut rien; I couldn't h. laughing/overhearing je ne pouvais pas m'empêcher de rire/d'écouter; he can't h. being bald ce n'est pas de sa faute s'il est chauve; not if I can h. it! pas si je peux l'éviter!
3 *vi* aider; can I h.? puis-je vous aider?; that doesn't h. very much cela ne nous avance pas beaucoup
▸ **help out** *vt sep & vi* aider
helper ['helpə(r)] *n* aide *mf*, assistant(e) *m,f*
helpful ['helpfʊl] *adj (person)* serviable; *(advice, device, book)* utile; to be h. *(of person)* se rendre utile, aider
helpfully ['helpfʊlɪ] *adv* obligeamment
helping ['helpɪŋ] **1** *n (portion)* part *f*, portion *f*; I had a second h. of pasta je me suis resservi des pâtes
2 *adj* to lend a h. hand donner un coup de main
helpless ['helplɪs] *adj (powerless)* impuissant(e); *(invalid)*

impotent(e); I feel so h. je ne sais vraiment pas quoi faire; to be h. with laughter être plié(e) de rire
helplessly ['helplɪslɪ] *adv (watch)* sans pouvoir agir; *(struggle)* en vain
helpline [helplaɪn] *n* service *m* d'assistance téléphonique
Helsinki [hel'sɪŋkɪ] *n* Helsinki
helter-skelter ['heltə'skeltə(r)] **1** *n (at fairground)* toboggan *m*
2 *adv* to run h. courir comme un(e) fou (folle); to fall h. faire une chute spectaculaire
hem [hem] **1** *n* ourlet *m*
2 *vt (pt & pp* **hemmed**) ourler
▸ **hem in** *vt sep (surround)* cerner
he-man ['hiːmæn] *n Fam* homme *m* viril
hemisphere ['hemɪsfɪə(r)] *n* hémisphère *m*
hemline ['hemlaɪn] *n* ourlet *m*
hemlock ['hemlɒk] *n* ciguë *f*
hemoglobin, hemophilia *etc Am* = haemoglobin, haemophilia *etc*
hemorrhage, hemorrhoids *Am* = haemorrhage, haemorrhoids
hemp [hemp] *n* chanvre *m*
hen [hen] *n* poule *f*; *Br Fam* h. party = soirée organisée entre amies avant le mariage de l'une d'entre elles
hence [hens] *adv* (**a**) *(thus)* d'où; h. his anger d'où sa colère (**b**) *(from now)* d'ici; seven years h. d'ici sept ans
henceforth [hens'fɔːθ] *adv Formal* dès lors, désormais
henchman ['henʃmən] *n Pej* acolyte *m*
hencoop ['henkuːp] *n* cage *f* à poules
henhouse ['henhaʊs] *n* poulailler *m*
henna ['henə] *n* henné *m*
henpecked ['henpekt] *adj* mené(e) par le bout du nez
hepatitis [hepə'taɪtɪs] *n* hépatite *f*
her [unstressed hə(r), stressed hɜː(r)] **1** *pron* (**a**) *(direct object)* la; I hate h. je la déteste; I love h. je l'aime; I can understand her son but not HER je comprends son fils, mais elle, je ne la comprends pas (**b**) *(indirect object)* lui; I gave h. the book je lui ai donné le livre; I gave it to h. je le lui ai donné (**c**) *(after preposition)* elle; I'm thinking of h. je pense à elle (**d**) *(as complement of verb to be)* it's h.! c'est elle!; it was h. who did it c'est elle qui l'a fait
2 *possessive adj* (**a**) *(singular)* son (sa); *(plural)* ses; h. husband son mari; h. family sa famille; h. parents ses parents; it wasn't HER idea! ce n'est pas elle qui en a eu l'idée! (**b**) *(for parts of body)* she hit h. head elle s'est cogné la tête
herald ['herəld] **1** *n (messenger)* héraut *m*; *Fig (sign)* signe *m* avant-coureur
2 *vt* annoncer
heraldry ['herəldrɪ] *n* héraldique *f*
herb [hɜːb] *n* herbe *f* aromatique
herbal ['hɜːbəl] *adj* à base de plantes; h. tea tisane *f*
herbalist ['hɜːbəlɪst] *n* herboriste *mf*
herbicide ['hɜːbɪsaɪd] *n* herbicide *m*
herbivorous [hɜː'bɪvərəs] *adj* herbivore
herd [hɜːd] **1** *n (of cattle, sheep, elephants)* troupeau *m*; *(of horses)* troupe *f*; *(of people)* groupe *m*; *Pej* troupeau *m*; the h. instinct l'instinct grégaire
2 *vt (cattle, people)* rassembler
herdsman ['hɜːdzmən] *n* gardien *m* de troupeau
here [hɪə(r)] **1** *adv* ici; over h. par ici; h. it/he is le voilà; h.! *(at roll call)* présent!; come h.! viens ici!; h., come and look at this! eh! viens voir çal; she's not h. elle n'est pas là; h. she comes la voilà; h. and now immédiatement; h. and

there çà et là; *Fig* that's neither h. nor there ça n'a aucun rapport; what have we h.? qu'est-ce que c'est que ça?; h.'s what you have to do voilà ce que tu as à faire; h. goes! allons-y!; h.'s to the future! à l'avenir!
2 *n* the h. and now le présent

hereafter [hɪər'ɑːftə(r)] **1** *n Lit* the h. l'au-delà *m* **2** *adv Formal (below)* ci-après; *(in the future)* dorénavant

hereby [hɪə'baɪ] *adv Formal (in writing)* par la présente; *(in speech)* solennellement

hereditary [hɪ'redɪtərɪ] *adj* héréditaire

heredity [hɪ'redɪtɪ] *n* hérédité *f*

heresy ['herəsɪ] *(pl* heresies) *n* hérésie *f*

heretic ['herətɪk] *n* hérétique *mf*

heretical [hɪ'retɪkəl] *adj* hérétique

heritage ['herɪtɪdʒ] *n* patrimoine *m*

hermaphrodite [hɜː'mæfrədaɪt] *n & adj* hermaphrodite *mf*

hermetic [hɜː'metɪk] *adj* hermétique

hermetically [hɜː'metɪklɪ] *adv* hermétiquement

hermit ['hɜːmɪt] *n* ermite *m*; **h. crab** bernard-l'ermite *m inv*

hernia ['hɜːnɪə] *n* hernie *f*

hero ['hɪərəʊ] *(pl* heroes) *n* (a) *(person)* héros *m*; h. worship adulation *f*, idolâtrie *f* (b) *Am (sandwich)* = sorte de gros sandwich

heroic [hɪ'rəʊɪk] *adj* héroïque

heroically [hɪ'rəʊɪklɪ] *adv* héroïquement

heroics [hɪ'rəʊɪks] *npl* coup *m* d'éclat

heroin [ˈherəʊɪn] *n (drug)* héroïne *f*; h. addict héroïnomane *mf*

heroine ['herəʊɪn] *n (female hero)* héroïne *f*

heroism ['herəʊɪzəm] *n* héroïsme *m*

heron ['herən] *n* héron *m*

hero-worship ['hɪərəʊwɜːʃɪp] *(pt & pp* **-worshipped**) *vt* idolâtrer

herpes ['hɜːpiːz] *n* herpès *m*

herring ['herɪŋ] *(pl* herring *or* herrings) *n* hareng *m*

hers [hɜːz] *possessive pron* (a) *(singular)* le sien (la sienne) *m,f*; *(plural)* les siens (les siennes) *mpl, fpl*; my car is big, but h. is bigger j'ai une grande voiture, mais la sienne est plus grande encore (b) *(used attributively)* this book is h. ce livre est à elle; a friend of h. un de ses amis; where's that brother of h.? où son frère a-t-il bien pu passer?

herself [hɜː'self] *pron* (a) *(reflexive)* she spoils h. elle se gâte; she hurt h. elle s'est blessée (b) *(emphatic)* elle-même; she h. has never... elle-même n'a jamais...; she told me h. elle me l'a dit elle-même; she's not h. today elle n'est pas dans son état normal aujourd'hui (c) *(after preposition)* she lives by h. elle vit seule; she bought it for h. elle se l'est acheté; she talks to h. elle parle toute seule

he's [hiːz] = he is, he has

hesitancy ['hezɪtənsɪ] *n* hésitation *f*

hesitant ['hezɪtənt] *adj* hésitant(e), to be h. about doing sth hésiter à faire qch

hesitate ['hezɪteɪt] *vi* hésiter

hesitation [hezɪ'teɪʃən] *n* hésitation *f*; without h. sans hésitation, sans hésiter

heterogeneous [hetərə'dʒiːnɪəs] *adj* hétérogène

heterosexual [hetərəʊ'seksjʊəl] *n & adj* hétérosexuel(elle) *m,f*

heuristics [hjuː'rɪstɪks] *npl* heuristique *f*

hew [hjuː] *(pp* hewn [hjuːn] *or* hewed [hjuːd]) *vt (wood)* couper; *(rock)* tailler

hexagon ['heksəgən] *n* hexagone *m*

hexagonal [hek'sægənəl] *adj* hexagonal(e)

hey [heɪ] *exclam* eh!; h. presto! le tour est joué!

heyday ['heɪdeɪ] *n* apogée *m*; in its h. à son apogée; in his h. au sommet de sa gloire

HGV [eɪtʃdʒiː'viː] *n Br (abbr* heavy goods vehicle) PL *m*; H. licence permis *m* PL

hi [haɪ] *exclam Fam* salut!

hiatus [haɪ'eɪtəs] *n (interruption)* interruption *f*; *(in conversation)* silence *m*; *(in manuscript, records)* lacune *f*

hibernate ['haɪbəneɪt] *vi* hiberner

hibernation [haɪbə'neɪʃən] *n* hibernation *f*; to go into h. entrer en hibernation

hiccup ['hɪkʌp] **1** *n* hoquet *m*; *Fig (in plan)* accroc *m*; to have (the) hiccups avoir le hoquet **2** *vi* avoir le hoquet; *(once)* avoir un hoquet

hick [hɪk] *n Am Fam* péquenaud(e) *m,f*

hickory ['hɪkərɪ] *(pl* hickories) *n (tree, wood)* hickory *m*, noyer *m* blanc d'Amérique; h. chips *(for barbecue)* copeaux *mpl* de hickory

hid [hɪd] *pt of* hide

hidden ['hɪdən] **1** *adj* caché(e); h. agenda programme *m* secret **2** *pp of* hide

hide¹ [haɪd] **1** *(for birdwatching)* affût *m* **2** *vt (pt* hid [hɪd], *pp* hidden ['hɪdən]) cacher (from à); to have nothing to h. n'avoir rien à cacher; to be hidden from sight être caché(e); to h. oneself se cacher **3** *vi* se cacher (from de)

hide² *n (skin)* peau *f*; *Fig* to save one's h. sauver sa peau; I haven't seen h. nor hair of her je ne l'ai pas vue du tout

hide-and-go-seek [haɪdəngəʊ'siːk] *n Am* cache-cache *m*; to play h. jouer à cache-cache

hidebound ['haɪdbaʊnd] *adj* rigide

hideous ['hɪdɪəs] *adj (ugly)* hideux(euse); *(horrific)* horrible

hideously ['hɪdɪəslɪ] *adv* horriblement, affreusement

hide-out ['haɪdaʊt] *n* cachette *f*

hiding¹ ['haɪdɪŋ] *n (concealment)* to be in h. se cacher; to go into h. se cacher; to come out of h. sortir de sa cachette; *(after war)* sortir de la clandestinité; h. place cachette *f*

hiding² *n Fam (beating)* raclée *f*; to give sb a h. donner une raclée à qn; *Fig* to be on a h. to nothing n'avoir aucune chance

hierarchical [haɪə'rɑːkɪkəl] *adj* hiérarchique

hierarchy ['haɪərɑːkɪ] *(pl* hierarchies) *n* hiérarchie *f*

hieroglyphics [haɪərə'glɪfɪks] *npl* hiéroglyphes *mpl*

hi-fi ['haɪfaɪ] *n* hi-fi *f inv*; *(stereo system)* chaîne *f* (hi-fi)

higgledy-piggledy ['hɪgəldɪ'pɪgəldɪ] *Fam* **1** *adj* en désordre **2** *adv* pêle-mêle

high [haɪ] **1** *n* (a) *(peak) (in career, performance)* sommet *m*; *(in quantity, degree)* maximum *m*; prices have reached a new h. les prix ont atteint leur maximum; to be on a h. *(from drugs)* planer; *(from success)* être sur un petit nuage; the highs and lows les hauts *mpl* et les bas *mpl* (b) *(weather front)* anticyclone *m* **2** *adj* (a) *(mountain, building)* haut(e), élevé(e); how h. is that building? quelle est la hauteur de ce bâtiment?; to be 2 metres h. faire 2 mètres de haut; *Fam* to be left h. and dry être laissé(e) en plan; h. jump saut *m* en hauteur; *Fam Fig* you'll be for the h. jump tu vas te faire engueuler; h. jumper sauteur(euse) *m,f* en hauteur; h. tide marée *f* haute; h. wire corde *f* raide (**b**) *(price, speed, standards)* élevé(e); *(quality)* premier(ère); **to have a h.** opinion of sb avoir une haute opinion de qn; **h.** explosif *m* puissant; **h. point** point *m* culminant; **in h.** spirits plein(e) d'entrain; *Law* **h. treason** haute trahison *f*; **h. winds** vents *mpl* forts (**c**) *(rank, position)* haut(e); **to act all h.** and mighty agir avec beaucoup d'arrogance; *Mil* **h. command** haut commandement *m*; **H. Commission** haut-commissariat *m*; **H. Court** ≃ tribunal *m* de grande instance; **H. Mass** grand-messe *f*; **h. school** = école secondaire qui accueille les élèves de 11 à 18 ans; **h. society** haute société *f* (**d**) *(in tone, pitch)* aigu(ë); *Fig* **h. note** *(of career, performance)* point *m* culminant (**e**) *(with time)* **it's h. time you got yourself a job** il est grand temps que tu trouves un travail; **h. noon** plein midi; **h. summer** plein été; *Br* **h. tea** = dîner pris assez tôt dans la soirée (**f**) *(meat)* avancé(e) (**g**) *Fam* **to be h.** *(on drugs)* planer; *Fig (on success, excitement)* être euphorique **3** *adv (aim, jump)* haut; **to hunt h. and low for sth** remuer ciel et terre pour trouver qch; **feelings were running h.** la tension montait

highbrow ['haɪbraʊ] *adj* intellectuel(elle)

highchair ['haɪtʃeə(r)] *n* chaise *f* haute

higher education ['haɪəredjʊ'keɪʃən] *n* enseignement *m* supérieur

high-flier, high-flyer ['haɪ'flaɪə(r)] *n (person)* battant(e) *m,f*; *(company)* société *f* qui va de l'avant

high-flying ['haɪ'flaɪɪŋ] *adj* ambitieux(euse)

high-frequency [haɪ'fri:kwənsɪ] *adj* (à) haute fréquence *inv*

high-handed [haɪ'hændɪd] *adj* autoritaire, despotique

high-heeled ['haɪ'hi:ld] *adj* à talons hauts

Highland ['haɪlənd] *adj (from Scottish Highlands)* des Highlands; **H. cattle** vaches *fpl* des Highlands

Highlander ['haɪləndə(r)] *n (of Scotland)* habitant(e) *m,f* des Highlands

Highlands ['haɪləndz] *npl* **the H.** *(of Scotland)* les Highlands *fpl*

high-level ['haɪlevəl] *adj (talks)* à haut niveau; *(delegation)* de haut niveau

highlight ['haɪlaɪt] **1** *n* (**a**) *(of performance, career)* point *m* culminant; **highlights** *(of match, event)* moments *mpl* forts (**b**) **highlights** *(in hair) (artificial)* mèches *fpl*; *(natural)* reflets *mpl* **2** *vt* (**a**) *(problem, difference)* mettre en évidence, souligner (**b**) *(with highlighter)* surligner; *Comptr (block of text)* sélectionner

highlighter ['haɪlaɪtə(r)] *n (pen)* surligneur *m*

highly ['haɪlɪ] *adv* (**a**) *(very)* très, extrêmement; **h. paid** très bien payé(e); **h. seasoned** fortement assaisonné(e); **h. strung** hypersensible (**b**) *(favourably)* **to think h. of sb** avoir une haute opinion de qn; **to speak h. of sb** parler de qn en termes élogieux

high-minded ['haɪ'maɪndɪd] *adj (sentiments, behaviour)* noble; *(person)* qui a des principes

Highness ['haɪnɪs] *n* **His/Her Royal H.** Son Altesse *f*

high-pitched ['haɪpɪtʃt] *adj* aigu(ë)

high-powered ['haɪ'paʊəd] *adj (engine, car, telescope)* très puissant(e); *(job)* à hautes responsabilités; *(person)* qui occupe un poste à hautes responsabilités

high-pressure ['haɪ'preʃə(r)] *adj* (**a**) *(cylinder, gas, machine)* à haute pression (**b**) *(job, profession)* stressant(e); *(salesman)* agressif(ive)

high-profile ['haɪ'prəʊfaɪl] *adj (person)* très en vue; *(campaign)* de grande envergure

high-rise ['haɪ'raɪz] **1** *n (block of flats)* tour *f* **2** *adj* **h. building** tour *f*

high-risk ['haɪrɪsk] *adj (strategy, investment)* à haut risque

highroad ['haɪrəʊd] *n Old-fashioned* grand-route *f*; *Fig* **the h. to success** la voie du succès

high-speed ['haɪ'spi:d] *adj* ultrarapide; *(train)* à grande vitesse

high-spirited [haɪ'spɪrɪtɪd] *adj* plein(e) d'entrain

high-tech ['haɪ'tek] *adj (appliance)* perfectionné(e); *(industry)* de pointe; *(approach, solution)* qui a recours à une technologie de pointe

high-up ['haɪʌp] *adj Fam (important)* haut placé(e)

highway ['haɪweɪ] *n (main road)* (route *f*) nationale *f*; *(motorway)* autoroute *f*; *Br* **H. Code** code *m* de la route

highwayman ['haɪweɪmən] *n* bandit *m* de grand chemin

hijack ['haɪdʒæk] *vt (plane)* détourner; *(car, lorry)* s'emparer de force de; *(idea)* s'approprier

hijacker ['haɪdʒækə(r)] *n (of plane)* pirate *m* de l'air

hike [haɪk] **1** *n* (**a**) *(walk)* randonnée *f*; **to go on** *or* **for a h.** faire une randonnée; *Fam Fig* **go take a h.!** lâche-moi les baskets! (**b**) *(in prices)* hausse *f* **2** *vt (prices)* augmenter **3** *vi (walk)* faire de la randonnée

hiker ['haɪkə(r)] *n* randonneur(euse) *m,f*

hiking ['haɪkɪŋ] *n* randonnée *f*; **to go h.** faire de la randonnée; **h. boots** chaussures *fpl* de marche

hilarious [hɪ'leərɪəs] *adj* hilarant(e)

hilariously [hɪ'leərɪəslɪ] *adv* **h. funny** à se tordre de rire; **to laugh h.** se tordre de rire

hilarity [hɪ'lærɪtɪ] *n* hilarité *f*; **his suggestion was greeted with much h.** sa suggestion déclencha l'hilarité générale

hill [hɪl] *n* (**a**) *(small mountain)* colline *f*; *Fig* **to be over the h.** commencer à se faire vieux (vieille) (**b**) *(slope)* côte *f*, pente *f*; **to go down/up the h.** descendre/monter la côte

hillbilly ['hɪlbɪlɪ] *(pl* **hillbillies***)* n Am* péquenaud(e) *m,f*

hillock ['hɪlək] *n* butte *f*

hillside ['hɪlsaɪd] *n* coteau *m*

hilltop ['hɪltɒp] *n* sommet *m* de la colline

hillwalker ['hɪlwɔ:kə(r)] *n* randonneur(euse) *m,f*

hillwalking ['hɪlwɔ:kɪŋ] *n* randonnée *f* en basse montagne

hilly ['hɪlɪ] *adj* vallonné(e)

hilt [hɪlt] *n (of sword)* poignée *f*; *(of knife, dagger)* manche *m*; *Fig* **to back sb to the h.** soutenir qn sans réserve

him [hɪm] *pron* (**a**) *(direct object)* le; **I hate h.** je le déteste; **I love h.** je l'aime; **I can understand his son but not HIM** je comprends son fils, mais lui, je ne le comprends pas (**b**) *(indirect object)* lui; **I gave h. the book** je lui ai donné le livre; **I gave it to h.** je le lui ai donné (**c**) *(after preposition)* lui; **I'm thinking of h.** je pense à lui (**d**) *(as complement of verb to be)* lui; **it's h.!** c'est lui!; **it was h. who did it** c'est lui qui l'a fait

Himalayan [hɪmə'leɪən] *adj* himalayen(enne)

Himalayas [hɪmə'leɪəz] *npl* **the H.** l'Himalaya *m*

himself [hɪm'self] *pron* (**a**) *(reflexive)* **he spoils h.** il se gâte; **he hurt h.** il s'est blessé (**b**) *(emphatic)* lui-même; **he h. has never...** lui-même n'a jamais...; **he told me h.** il me l'a dit lui-même; **he's not h. today** il n'est pas dans son état normal aujourd'hui (**c**) *(after preposition)* **he lives by h.** il vit seul; **he bought it for h.** il se l'est acheté; **he talks to h.** il parle tout seul

hind¹ [haɪnd] *adj (back)* de derrière; **h. legs** pattes *fpl* de derrière

hind² *n (female deer)* daim *m* femelle

hinder ['hɪndə(r)] *vt (impede)* gêner; *(delay)* retarder; **to h. sb from doing sth** empêcher qn de faire qch

Hindi ['hɪndɪ] *n (language)* hindi *m*

hindquarters ['haɪndkwɔːtəz] *npl* arrière-train *m*

hindrance ['hɪndrəns] *n* entrave *f*, obstacle *m*

hindsight ['haɪndsaɪt] *n* recul *m*; **with (the benefit of) h.** avec le recul

Hindu ['hɪndu:] **1** *n* Hindou(e) *m,f*
2 *adj* hindou(e)

Hinduism ['hɪndu:ɪzəm] *n* hindouisme *m*

hinge [hɪndʒ] *n* charnière *f*, gond *m*; **to come off its hinges** sortir de ses gonds
▸ **hinge on, hinge upon** *vt insep (depend on)* dépendre de

hint [hɪnt] **1** *n* **(a)** *(allusion)* allusion *f*; *(clue)* indice *m*; **to drop (sb) a h.** faire une allusion (à l'intention de qn); **to take the h.** comprendre l'allusion, he **can't take a h.** il faut lui mettre les points sur les i **(b)** *(sign)* signe *m* **(c)** *(small amount)* soupçon *m* **(d)** *(piece of advice)* truc *m*, conseil *m*
2 *vt* **to h. that…** insinuer *ou* laisser entendre que…
▸ **hint at** *vt insep* faire allusion à

hinterland ['hɪntəlænd] *n* arrière-pays *m inv*

hip¹ [hɪp] *n (part of body)* hanche *f*; **h. flask** flasque *f*; **h. joint** articulation *f* de la hanche; **h. pocket** poche *f* revolver

hip² *adj Fam (trendy)* branché(e)

hippo ['hɪpəʊ] *(pl hippos) n Fam* hippopotame *m*

hippopotamus [hɪpə'pɒtəməs] *(pl* **hippopotami** [hɪpə'pɒtəmaɪ]) *n* hippopotame *m*

hippy ['hɪpɪ] *(pl hippies) n* hippie *mf*

hire [haɪə(r)] **1** *n Br (of car, equipment)* location *f*; **for h.** à louer; *(taxi)* libre; **h. car** voiture *f* de location; *Com* **h. purchase** achat *m* à crédit; **h. purchase agreement** contrat *m* de vente à tempérament
2 *vt* **(a)** *(car, equipment)* louer **(b)** *(lawyer, worker)* engager
▸ **hire out** *vt sep Br (boat, bicycle)* louer; *(one's services)* offrir

hired ['haɪəd] *adj (car, suit)* de location; **h. hand** *(on farm)* ouvrier(ère) *m,f* agricole

hirsute ['hɜːsjuːt] *adj Lit* velu(e)

his [hɪz] **1** *possessive adj* **(a)** *(singular)* son (sa); *(plural)* ses; **h. job** son travail; **h. wife** sa femme; **h. parents** ses parents; **it wasn't HIS idea!** ce n'est pas lui qui en a eu l'idée! **(b)** *(for parts of body)* **he hit h. head** il s'est cogné la tête
2 *possessive pron* **(a)** *(singular)* le sien (la sienne) *m,f*; *(plural)* les siens (les siennes) *mpl, fpl*; **my house is big, but h. is bigger** j'ai une grande maison, mais la sienne est plus grande encore **(b)** *(used attributively)* **this book is h.** ce livre est à lui; **a friend of h.** un de ses amis; **where's that brother of h.?** où son frère a-t-il bien pu passer?

Hispanic [hɪs'pænɪk] **1** *n Am* Latino-Américain(e) *m,f*
2 *adj* hispanique

hiss [hɪs] **1** *n (sound)* sifflement *m*; *(to express disapproval)* sifflet *m*
2 *vt & vi* siffler

histogram ['hɪstəgræm] *n* histogramme *m*

historian [hɪs'tɔːrɪən] *n* historien(enne) *m,f*

historic [hɪs'tɒrɪk] *adj* historique

historical [hɪs'tɒrɪkəl] *adj* historique

historically [hɪs'tɒrɪklɪ] *adv* historiquement

history ['hɪstərɪ] *(pl histories) n* **(a)** histoire *f*; **to go down in h., to make h.** *(of event)* faire date; *(of person)* entrer dans l'histoire; *Fig* **that's (ancient) h.** c'est de l'histoire ancienne; **h. book/teacher** livre *m* / professeur *m* d'histoire **(b)** *(medical record)* antécédents *mpl*; **there is a h. of heart disease in my family** il y a des antécédents de maladie cardiaque dans ma famille

histrionic [hɪstrɪ'ɒnɪk] *adj Pej* théâtral(e)

histrionics [hɪstrɪ'ɒnɪks] *npl Pej* scène *f*; **to have h.** faire une scène

hit [hɪt] **1** *n* **(a)** *(blow)* coup *m*; *(in shooting)* tir *m* réussi; **to score a direct h.** taper dans le mille; **h. list** *(of targets)* liste *f* noire; **h. man** tueur *m* à gages **(b)** *(success)* succès *m*; **to be a h. with sb** avoir beaucoup de succès auprès de qn; **h. (record)** hit *m*, tube *m* **(c)** *Comptr (visit to website)* hit *m*, accès *m*; *(in search)* occurrence *f*
2 *adj (film, play)* à succès
3 *vt (pt & pp* **hit)** **(a)** *(of person)* frapper; *(of bullet)* atteindre; *(of car)* percuter; *Comptr (key)* frapper, appuyer sur; **to h. one's head (on sth)** se cogner la tête (contre qch); *Fig* **it suddenly hit me that…** j'ai réalisé tout d'un coup que…, *Fig* **he didn't know what had hit him** il n'a pas eu le temps de se rendre compte de ce qui lui arrivait **(b)** *(reach)* *(barrier, difficulty)* se heurter à; **to h. a note** atteindre une note; **to h. 90 (miles an hour)** ≃ faire du 140 (à l'heure); **to h. an all-time low** *(of investment, relationship)* être au plus bas; **the circus hits town tomorrow** le cirque arrive en ville demain; **it hits the stores next week** c'est en vente la semaine prochaine; *Fam* **to h. the road** *(leave)* se mettre en route **(c)** *(affect)* toucher; **to be hard hit by sth** être durement touché(e) par qch
4 *vi* frapper
▸ **hit back** *vt sep* **to h. sb back** rendre un coup à qn
2 *vi also Fig* riposter **(at** à)
▸ **hit off** *vt sep Fam* **to h. it off** accrocher
▸ **hit on, hit upon** *vt insep (idea, solution)* trouver
▸ **hit out** *vi* **to h. out at sb** *(physically)* frapper qn; *(verbally)* s'en prendre à qn

hit-and-run ['hɪtən'rʌn] *adj* **h. accident** = accident à la suite duquel l'automobiliste prend la fuite

hitch [hɪtʃ] **1** *n* **(a)** *(difficulty)* problème *m*; **without a h.** sans anicroche **(b)** *(knot)* nœud *m*
2 *vt* **(a)** *(attach)* attacher **(to** à); *Fam Fig* **to get hitched** *(married)* passer devant Monsieur le Maire **(b)** *Fam* **to h. a ride** faire du stop
3 *vi Fam* faire du stop; **to h. to Paris** aller à Paris en stop
▸ **hitch up** *vt sep (trousers, skirt)* remonter

hitchhike ['hɪtʃhaɪk] *vi* faire de l'auto-stop; **to h. to Paris** aller à Paris en auto-stop

hitchhiker ['hɪtʃhaɪkə(r)] *n* auto-stoppeur(euse) *m,f*

hi-tech ['haɪ'tek] = **high-tech**

hither ['hɪðə(r)] *adv Lit* ici; **h. and thither** çà et là

hitherto ['hɪðə'tuː] *adv* jusqu'ici, jusqu'à présent

hit-or-miss ['hɪtɔː'mɪs] *adj* aléatoire, approximatif(ive)

HIV [eɪtʃaɪ'viː] *n (abbr* **human immunodeficiency virus)** VIH *m*; **to be H. positive/negative** être séropositif(ive)/séronégatif(ive)

hive [haɪv] *n* ruche *f*; *Fig* **a h. of activity** une véritable ruche
▸ **hive off** *vt sep (money, profits)* séparer

HMG [eɪtʃem'dʒiː] *n Br (abbr* **Her/His Majesty's Government)** = le gouvernement de sa majesté *(expression utilisée sur les documents officiels)*

HMS [eɪtʃem'es] *n (abbr* **Her/His Majesty's Ship)** =

abréviation précédant le nom des navires de la marine britannique

HMSO [eɪtʃemes'əʊ] *n (abbr* **Her/His Majesty's Stationery Office)** ≃ Imprimerie *f* nationale

hoard [hɔːd] **1** *n (of food)* réserve *f,* provisions *fpl; (of money)* trésor *m*
2 *vt (food)* amasser, stocker; *(money)* amasser, thésauriser

hoarder ['hɔːdə(r)] *n* personne *f* qui fait des réserves; **she's a real h.** elle ne jette rien

hoarding ['hɔːdɪŋ] *n* (**a**) *(of food)* stockage *m* (**b**) *(for poster)* panneau *m* d'affichage

hoarfrost ['hɔːfrɒst] *n* givre *m,* gelée *f* blanche

hoarse [hɔːs] *adj* enroué(e); **to shout oneself h.** s'enrouer à force de crier

hoary ['hɔːrɪ] *adj (story)* vieux (vieille); *(joke)* éculé(e)

hoax [həʊks] **1** *n* canular *m*; **to play a h. on sb** faire un canular à qn; **h. caller** auteur *m* de canular(s) téléphonique(s) **2** *vt* faire un canular à

hob [hɒb] *n (on electric cooker)* table *f* de cuisson; *(on hearth)* plaque *f*

hobble ['hɒbəl] *vi* boitiller

hobby ['hɒbɪ] *(pl* **hobbies)** *n* passe-temps *m inv,* hobby *m*

hobbyhorse ['hɒbɪhɔːs] *n (toy)* cheval *m* de bois *(tête emmanchée sur un bâton); Fig (favourite subject)* dada *m*

hobnail boot ['hɒbneɪl'buːt] *n* chaussure *f* ferrée

hobnob ['hɒbnɒb] *(pt & pp* **hobnobbed)** *vi* Fam **to h. with sb** frayer avec qn

hock¹ [hɒk] *n (wine)* vin *m* du Rhin

hock² [hɒk] *Fam* **1** *n* **to be in h.** *(of object)* être au clou; *(of person)* être endetté(e) **2** *vt* mettre au clou

hockey ['hɒkɪ] *n Br (on grass)* hockey *m* (sur gazon); *Am (on ice)* hockey (sur glace); **h. stick** *Br* crosse *f* de hockey; *Am* crosse de hockey sur glace

hocus-pocus ['həʊkəs'pəʊkəs] *n (trickery)* tromperie *f,* supercherie *f, (talk)* paroles *fpl* trompeuses

hoe [həʊ] **1** *n* houe *f,* binette *f* **2** *vt (pt & pp* **hoed)** biner, sarcler

hog [hɒg] **1** *n* (**a**) *(pig)* porc *m* châtré; *Fam* **to go the whole h.** aller jusqu'au bout (**b**) *(glutton)* glouton(onne) *m,f,* goinfre *mf*
2 *vt (pt & pp* **hogged)** *Fam (monopolize)* monopoliser; **to h. the limelight** monopoliser l'attention

Hogmanay [hɒgmə'neɪ] *n Scot* la Saint-Sylvestre

hogwash ['hɒgwɒʃ] *n Fam* âneries *fpl*

hoist [hɔɪst] **1** *n (device)* appareil *m* de levage **2** *vt* hisser; *Fig* **to be hoist with one's own petard** se faire prendre à son propre piège

hoity-toity ['hɔɪtɪ'tɔɪtɪ] *adj* **to be h.** se donner de grands airs

hold [həʊld] **1** *n* (**a**) *(grip)* prise *f;* **to have h. of sb/sth** tenir qn/qch; **to catch** *or* **take h. of sth** saisir qch; *Fig* **to get h. of sb** *(find)* trouver qn; *(on phone)* joindre qn; *Fig* **to get h. of sth** se procurer qch; **to let go one's h.** relâcher son étreinte, lâcher prise; **to lose one's h. on reality** perdre le sens des réalités; *Fig* **to have a h. on** *or* **over sb** avoir de l'emprise sur qn
(**b**) *(in wrestling)* prise *f, Fig* **no holds barred** tous les coups sont permis
(**c**) **to be on h.** *(of project)* être en suspens; *(of telephone caller)* être en attente; **to put sth on h.** mettre qch en suspens; **to put sb on h.** *(on telephone)* mettre qn en attente (**d**) *(of ship)* cale *f; (of plane)* soute *f*
2 *vt (pt & pp* **held** [held]) (**a**) *(grip)* tenir; **to h. sb/sth tight**

tenir qn/qch serré(e), serrer qn/qch; **to h. hands** se tenir (par) la main; **to h. sth in position** maintenir qch en place; **to h. sb prisoner** retenir qn prisonnier(ère); **the police are holding him for questioning** il a été placé en garde à vue; **to h. sb's interest/attention** retenir l'intérêt/l'attention de qn; **to h. sb to his promise** obliger qn à tenir sa promesse; **to h. one's breath** retenir sa respiration *ou* son souffle; *Fig* **don't h. your breath!** ce n'est pas pour demain! **there's no holding her** il n'y a pas moyen de l'arrêter; **h. your tongue!** tais-toi!; *Fam* **h. it!, h. your horses!** attendez!, minute!; **to h. a note** *(of singer)* tenir une note; **h. the line!** *(on telephone)* ne quittez pas!
(**b**) *(keep) (town, position)* tenir; *(ticket, room)* réserver; **to h. one's ground** tenir bon; **to h. one's own** se défendre (**c**) *(carry)* **to h. one's head high** garder la tête haute; **to h. oneself well** se tenir bien
(**d**) *(contain)* contenir; *Fig* **to h. water** *(of theory, story)* tenir la route; **nobody knows what the future holds** personne ne sait ce que l'avenir nous réserve; **it holds no interest for me** ça ne présente aucun intérêt pour moi
(**e**) *(conduct) (negotiations)* mener; *(meeting)* organiser; *(conversation)* avoir
(**f**) *(possess) (title, rank, opinion)* avoir; *(job, position)* occuper; *(record)* détenir; **to h. office** être en fonction
(**g**) *(consider)* **to h. sb responsible** tenir qn pour responsable; **to h. sb in respect** respecter qn; **to h. that...** soutenir que...
3 *vi* (**a**) *(of rope)* tenir; **h. tight!** tiens bon!
(**b**) *(of agreement, weather)* durer; *(of luck)* persister; **the same holds (true) for you** cela vaut aussi pour toi

▸ **hold against** *vt sep* **to h. sth against sb** reprocher qch à qn

▸ **hold back 1** *vt sep* (**a**) *(restrain) (person, emotion)* retenir; *(progress, project)* ralentir, freiner (**b**) *(conceal)* cacher
2 *vi (refrain)* se retenir **(from doing** de faire)

▸ **hold down** *vt sep* (**a**) *(restrain) (person)* immobiliser; *(taxes, prices)* bloquer (**b**) *(job) (occupy)* avoir; *(keep)* garder

▸ **hold forth** *vi* disserter, pérorer *(about or on* sur)

▸ **hold off 1** *vt sep* (**a**) *(keep at bay)* tenir à distance (**b**) *(delay)* remettre à plus tard, repousser; **to h. off making a decision** remettre une décision à plus tard
2 *vi (delay)* attendre

▸ **hold on** *vi* (**a**) *(last)* tenir (**b**) *(wait)* patienter; **h. on!** attendez!; *(on telephone)* ne quittez pas! (**c**) *(not let go)* s'accrocher

▸ **hold on to** *vt insep* (**a**) *(rope, handle)* s'agripper à; *Fig (idea, hope)* s'accrocher à (**b**) *(keep)* garder

▸ **hold out 1** *vt sep* (**a**) *(one's hand)* tendre; *(hope, opportunity)* offrir
2 *vi* (**a**) *(resist)* tenir (le coup) (**b**) *(wait)* **to h. out for a better offer** attendre une meilleure offre (**c**) *(last)* durer

▸ **hold over** *vt sep* remettre, reporter

▸ **hold together** *vt sep* **to h. sth together** faire tenir qch; **to be held together with sth** tenir avec qch
2 *vi (of party, group of people)* rester uni(e); *(of marriage, relationship)* tenir

▸ **hold up 1** *vt sep* (**a**) *(support)* soutenir (**b**) *(raise)* lever; *Fig* **to h. sb/sth up as an example** montrer *ou* citer qn/qch en exemple; *Fig* **to h. sb/sth up to ridicule** tourner qn/qch en ridicule (**c**) *(delay)* retarder (**d**) *(rob)* attaquer
2 *vi* (**a**) *(of theory, alibi)* tenir; *(of good weather)* se maintenir; **she's holding up well under the pressure** elle tient bien le coup

▸ **hold with** *vt insep (agree with)* être d'accord avec; *(approve of)* approuver

holdall ['həʊldɔːl] *n Br* fourre-tout *m inv*

holder ['həʊldə(r)] *n* (**a**) *(of licence, ticket, record, trophy)* détenteur(trice) *m,f*; *(of passport, degree)* titulaire *mf*; *(of belief, opinion)* tenant *m* **(b)** *(device)* support *m*

holding ['həʊldɪŋ] *n* **(a)** *(property)* propriété *f* **(b)** *(of shares)* participation *f*; *Com* **h. company** holding *m* **(c)** *Fig* **h. operation** opération *f* destinée à gagner du temps

hold-up ['həʊldʌp] *n* **(a)** *(delay) (in plan)* retard *m*; *(of traffic)* ralentissement *m* **(b)** *(armed robbery)* hold-up *m inv*, attaque *f* à main armée **(c) hold-ups** *(stockings)* bas *mpl* jarretière

hole [həʊl] **1** *n* **(a)** *(opening)* trou *m*; *(of rabbit, fox)* terrier *m*; *also Fig* **to make a h. in** sth faire un trou dans qch; *Fig* **to pick holes in sth** relever les failles de qch; *Fig* **a h. in the law** un vide juridique; **to get a h. in one** *(in golf)* faire un trou en un; *Fam Fig* **to be in a h.** *(in difficulty)* être dans le pétrin **(b)** *Fam Pej (room, house)* taudis *m*; *(town)* trou *m*
2 *vt (ship)* faire une brèche dans; *(in golf)* **to h. a putt** faire le trou
▸ **hole up** *vi Fam (hide)* se terrer

holiday ['hɒlɪdeɪ] **1** *n* **(a)** *Br (vacation)* vacances *fpl*; **a month's h.** un mois de vacances; **to be on h.** être en vacances; **to go on h.** aller *ou* partir en vacances; **h. camp** camp *m* de vacances; *Fig* **it was no h. camp** ce n'était pas une partie de plaisir; **h. home** résidence *f* secondaire; **h. season** saison *f* touristique **(b)** *(day off)* (jour *m* de) congé *m* **(c)** *(public)* jour *m* férié
2 *vi Br* passer les vacances; *(in summer)* passer les vacances d'été

holidaymaker ['hɒlɪdeɪˌmeɪkə(r)] *n Br* vacancier(ère) *m,f*; *(in summer)* estivant(e) *m,f*

holiness ['həʊlɪnɪs] *n* sainteté *f*; **Your H.** Votre Sainteté

holistic [həʊ'lɪstɪk] *adj* holistique

Holland ['hɒlənd] *n* la Hollande

holler ['hɒlə(r)] *vi Fam* brailler

hollow ['hɒləʊ] **1** *n* creux *m*
2 *adj* **(a)** *(container, cheeks)* creux(euse); *(eyes)* cave **(b)** *(sound)* creux(euse); *(voice)* blanc (blanche); *(laugh)* forcé(e) **(c)** *(promise, guarantee)* vain(e); *(victory)* sans signification
3 *adv* **(a) to sound h.** sonner creux **(b)** *Fam* **to beat sb h.** battre qn à plate(s) couture(s)
▸ **hollow out** *vt sep* évider

holly ['hɒlɪ] *n* houx *m*

hollyhock ['hɒlɪhɒk] *n* rose *f* trémière

holocaust ['hɒləkɔːst] *n* holocauste *m*

hologram ['hɒləgræm] *n* hologramme *m*

holster ['həʊlstə(r)] *n* étui *m* de revolver

holy ['həʊlɪ] *adj* saint(e); *Fam* **h. cow** *or* **smoke** *or* **mackerel!** ça alors!; **the H. Bible** la Sainte Bible; **H. Communion** communion *f*; **the H. Father** le saint-père; **the H. Ghost** *or* **Spirit** le Saint-Esprit; *Fam Pej* **H. Joe** grenouille *f* de bénitier; **the H. Land** la Terre Sainte; **h. orders** ordres *mpl*; **h. war** guerre *f* sainte; **h. water** eau *f* bénite; **H. Week** la semaine sainte

homage ['hɒmɪdʒ] *n* hommage *m*; **to pay h. to sb** rendre hommage à qn

home [həʊm] **1** *n* **(a)** *(house)* maison *f*; *(of animal, plant)* habitat *m*; **at h.** à la maison, chez soi; **to feel at h.** se sentir chez soi; **make yourself at h.** faites comme chez vous; **to leave h.** *(in the morning)* partir de chez soi; *(one's parents' home)* partir de chez ses parents; **to be away from h.** être en déplacement; **to be a h. from h.** être un second chez-soi; **to make one's h. in France** s'établir en France; **children's h.** foyer *m* pour enfants; **h. address** adresse *f* personnelle, domicile *m*; **h. banking** banque *f* à domicile; **h. brew** bière *f* maison; **h. cooking** cuisine *f* familiale; *Br* **the H. Counties** = les comtés limitrophes de Londres; **h. economics** *(school subject)* arts *mpl* ménagers; **h. help** aide

f ménagère; **h. life** vie *f* de famille; *Fin* **h. loan** prêt *m* immobilier; **h. movie** film *m* amateur; **h. owner** propriétaire *mf*; *Am Sch* **h. room** salle *f* où l'on fait l'appel; **h. run** *(in baseball)* tour *m* complet; **the h. straight** *(in athletics)* la dernière ligne droite; **h. town** ville *f* natale; **to tell sb a few h. truths** dire ses quatre vérités à qn **(b)** *(country, region)* patrie *f*; **at h. and abroad** dans notre pays et à l'étranger; **an example nearer h.** un exemple qui nous concerne plus; **Milan, the h. of fashion** Milan, capitale de la mode; **h. front** arrière *m*; **h. news** nouvelles *fpl* nationales; *Br Pol* **H. Office** ≃ ministère *m* de l'Intérieur; *Pol* **h.** rule régime *m* d'autonomie politique; *Br Pol* **the H. Secretary** ≃ le ministre de l'Intérieur
2 *adv* **(a)** *(to or at one's house)* à la maison, chez soi; *Fig* **to bring sth h. to sb** faire comprendre qch à qn; **to send sb h.** *(to have)* renvoyer qn chez soi; *(to home country)* rapatrier qn **(b)** *(all the way)* **he hammered the nail h.** il enfonça complètement le clou; **the bolt slid h.** le verrou se ferma
▸ **home in on** *vt insep (target)* se diriger vers; *(mistake, evidence)* relever

homecoming ['həʊmˌkʌmɪŋ] *n (to one's house)* retour *m* (au foyer); *(to one's country)* retour au pays

home-grown ['həʊm'grəʊn] *adj (vegetables)* du jardin; *Fig (not imported)* national(e)

homeland ['həʊmlænd] *n* patrie *f*, pays *m* (d'origine)

homeless ['həʊmlɪs] **1** *npl* **the h.** les sans-abri *mpl*
2 *adj* sans abri

homely ['həʊmlɪ] *adj* **(a)** *Br (person, atmosphere, decor)* agréable et sans prétention **(b)** *Am (plain)* sans charme

home-made ['həʊm'meɪd] *adj* fait(e) maison

homeopath ['həʊmɪəʊpæθ] *n* homéopathe *mf*

homeopathic [həʊmɪəʊ'pæθɪk] *adj* homéopathique

homeopathy [həʊmɪ'ɒpəθɪ] *n* homéopathie *f*

homesick ['həʊmsɪk] *adj* **to be** *or* **feel h.** avoir le mal du pays; *(of child)* s'ennuyer de ses parents; **to be h. for sth** avoir la nostalgie de qch

homesickness ['həʊmsɪknɪs] *n* mal *m* du pays

homespun ['həʊmspʌn] *adj Fig (wisdom, advice)* simple

homestead ['həʊmsted] *n* propriété *f*; *(farm)* ferme *f*

homeward ['həʊmwəd] **1** *adj* de retour
2 *adv (to one's house)* vers sa maison; *(to one's country)* vers son pays; **to be h.-bound** être sur le chemin du retour

homewards ['həʊmwədz] *adv* = **homeward**

homework ['həʊmwɜːk] *n Sch* devoirs *mpl*; **to do one's h.** faire ses devoirs; *Fig* faire des recherches

homicidal [hɒmɪ'saɪdəl] *adj* meurtrier(ère)

homicide ['hɒmɪsaɪd] *n* homicide *m*

homily ['hɒmɪlɪ] *n (pl* **homilies**) homélie *f*, sermon *m*

homing ['həʊmɪŋ] *adj* **h. device** mécanisme *m* d'autoguidage; **h. pigeon** pigeon *m* voyageur

homogeneous [hɒmə'dʒiːnɪəs, həʊ'mɒdʒɪnəs] *adj* homogène

homogenize [hə'mɒdʒənaɪz] *vt* homogénéiser

homonym ['hɒmənɪm] *n* homonyme *m*

homophobia [hɒmə'fəʊbɪə] *n* homophobie *f*

homosexual [hɒmə'seksjʊəl] *n & adj* homosexuel(elle) *m,f*

homosexuality [hɒməseksjʊ'ælɪtɪ] *n* homosexualité *f*

Hon *adj Br Parl (abbr* **Honourable**) **the H. member for** Monsieur/Madame le député de

honcho ['hɒntʃəʊ] *n (pl* **honchos**) *n Fam* **the head h.** le boss

Honduras [hɒn'djʊərəs] *n* le Honduras

hone [həʊn] *vt (skill)* peaufiner

honest ['ɒnɪst] adj honnête (**with** avec); **she has an h. face** elle a une visage franc; **the h. truth** la vérité vraie; **to be h., I don't know** honnêtement ou à dire vrai, je ne sais pas; **to earn an h. living** gagner honnêtement sa vie; *Hum* **to make an h. woman of sb** *(marry)* faire de qn une honnête femme

honestly ['ɒnɪstlɪ] adv (**a**) *(legitimately, sincerely)* honnêtement; **to obtain sth h.** obtenir qch par des moyens honnêtes; **I can h. say that...** honnêtement, je peux dire que... (**b**) *(expressing indignation)* **well h.!** franchement!; **h.! some people!** il y a des gens, je te jure!

honesty ['ɒnɪstɪ] n honnêteté f; **in all h.** en toute honnêteté; *Prov* **h. is the best policy** l'honnêteté est toujours récompensée

honey ['hʌnɪ] n (**a**) *(food)* miel m (**b**) *Fam (term of endearment)* chéri(e) m,f

honeycomb ['hʌnɪkəʊm] **1** n rayon m de miel **2** vt **the mountain is honeycombed with tunnels** la montagne est truffée de tunnels

honeymoon ['hʌnɪmuːn] **1** n *(period)* lune f de miel; *(trip)* voyage m de noces; *Fig* **the h. is over** l'état de grâce est terminé **2** vi partir en voyage de noces

honeysuckle ['hʌnɪsʌkəl] n chèvrefeuille m

Hong Kong ['hɒŋ'kɒŋ] n Hongkong

honk [hɒŋk] **1** n *(of goose)* cri m; *(of car horn)* coup m de Klaxon® **2** vi *(of goose)* cacarder; *(of car driver)* klaxonner

honky ['hɒŋkɪ] *(pl* **honkies**) n *Am very Fam* sale Blanc (Blanche) m,f, = terme injurieux désignant un Blanc

honor, honorable *etc Am* = honour, honourable *etc*

honorary ['ɒnərərɪ] adj *(member)* honoraire; *(title)* honorifique; *Univ* **h. degree** grade m honoris causa

honour, *Am* **honor** ['ɒnə(r)] **1** n (**a**) *(respect)* honneur m; **in h. of** en l'honneur de; **in h. of the occasion** pour l'occasion; **to have the h. of doing sth** avoir l'honneur de faire qch; *Hum* **to what do I owe this h.?** qu'est-ce qui me vaut cet honneur?; **Your H.** *(judge)* Votre Honneur (**b**) *(good name)* honneur m; **to feel h. bound to do sth** se sentir tenu(e) par l'honneur de faire qch; **on my (word of) h.!** parole d'honneur!; *Prov* **(there is) h. among thieves** les loups ne se mangent pas entre eux (**c**) *(award, distinction)* **honours list** = liste de distinctions honorifiques accordées par le souverain britannique; *Br* **honours degree** diplôme m universitaire; **he was buried with full military honours** il a été enterré avec tous les honneurs militaires; *Hum* **to do the honours** *(serve food or drink)* faire les honneurs; *(make introductions)* faire les présentations **2** vt honorer; **I felt honoured that they had invited me** je me suis senti honoré par leur invitation

honourable, *Am* **honorable** ['ɒnərəbəl] adj honorable; *Br Parl* **the H. member for** Monsieur/Madame le député de **m; h. mention** mention f spéciale

honourably, *Am* **honorably** ['ɒnərəblɪ] adv honorablement

hooch [huːtʃ] n *Am Fam (liquor)* gnôle f

hood [hʊd] n (**a**) *(of coat, cloak)* capuche f; *(with eye-holes)* cagoule f; *Br (of car, pram)* capote f; *Am (car bonnet)* capot m; *(over cooker, fireplace)* hotte f (**b**) *Am Fam (gangster)* truand m

hoodlum ['huːdləm] n *Fam* voyou m

hoodwink ['hʊdwɪŋk] vt *Fam* embobiner; **to h. sb into doing sth** embobiner qn pour qu'il fasse qch

hoof [huːf] **1** n *(pl* **hooves** [huːvz]*)* sabot m; **I had lunch on the h.** à midi j'ai mangé sur le pouce **2** vt *Fam* **to h. it** aller à pinces

hoo-ha ['huːhɑː] n *Fam (fuss)* tintouin m

hook [hʊk] **1** n (**a**) *(for hanging) (in general)* crochet m; *(for coats)* patère f; *(for meat)* croc m; *(on clothes)* agrafe f; *(for fishing)* hameçon m; **to leave the phone off the h.** *(on purpose)* laisser le téléphone décroché; *(accidentally)* mal raccrocher son téléphone; *Fam Fig* **to get** or **let sb off the h.** tirer qn d'affaire; *Fam* **he swallowed it h., line and sinker** *(believed it)* il a tout gobé; *Fam* **by h. or by crook** coûte que coûte (**b**) *(in boxing)* crochet m **2** vt accrocher; **to h. a fish** attraper un poisson

▸ **hook up 1** vt sep *Comptr* connecter (**to** à) **2** vi (**a**) *(of dress)* s'agrafer (**b**) *Comptr* se connecter; *TV* **to h. up with** faire une émission en duplex avec

hooked [hʊkt] adj (**a**) **h. nose** nez m crochu (**b**) *Fam (addicted)* **to be h. (on)** *(drugs)* être accro (à); *(on TV, chocolate)* être mordu(e) (de)

hooker [hʊkər] n (**a**) *Br (in rugby)* talonneur m (**b**) *Fam (prostitute)* pute f

hooky ['hʊkɪ] n *Am Fam* **to play h.** sécher les cours

hooligan ['huːlɪgən] n hooligan m, vandale m

hooliganism ['huːlɪgənɪzəm] n hooliganisme m, vandalisme m

hoop [huːp] n cerceau m; *(in croquet)* arceau m; *Fig* **to put sb through the hoops** mettre qn à l'épreuve

hooray [hʊ'reɪ] exclam hourra!

hoosegow ['huːsgaʊ] n *Am Fam (prison)* taule f

hoot [huːt] **1** n (**a**) *(of owl)* hululement m; *(of horn)* coup m de Klaxon®; *(of ship, factory whistle)* mugissement m; **hoots of laughter** éclats mpl de rire; *Fam Fig* **I don't give a h.** or **two hoots** je m'en fiche comme de l'an quarante (**b**) *Fam* **she's a h.!** elle est tordante!; **it was a h.!** c'était tordant! **2** vt *(person)* huer; **he was hooted off the stage** il a quitté la scène sous les huées **3** vi *(of owl)* hululer; *(of train)* siffler; *(of car)* klaxonner; **to h. with laughter** hurler de rire

hooter ['huːtə(r)] n *Br (of ship, factory)* sirène f; *(of car)* Klaxon® m (**b**) *Fam (nose)* pif m

hoover® ['huːvə(r)] *Br* **1** n aspirateur m **2** vt *(room)* passer l'aspirateur dans; *(carpet)* passer l'aspirateur sur

hooves [huːvz] pl of **hoof**

hop [hɒp] **1** n *(jump)* saut m; *Fam (dance)* bal m; **a short h.** *(journey)* un petit voyage; *Fam Fig* **to catch sb on the h.** prendre qn de court ou au dépourvu **2** vt *(pt & pp* **hopped**) *Fam* **h. it!** fiche le camp! **3** vi *(jump)* sautiller; *(on one leg)* sauter à cloche-pied; *Fam* **h. in!** *(to car)* allez, grimpe!; **he hopped onto the first train** il a sauté dans le premier train

▸ **hop off** vi *Fam* ficher le camp

hope [həʊp] **1** n espoir m; **in the h. of doing sth** dans l'espoir de faire qch; **in the h. that...** dans l'espoir que...; **to have little h. of doing sth** avoir peu de chances de faire qch; **to live in h.** vivre dans l'espoir de faire qch; **don't get your hopes up** n'espère pas trop; **to raise hopes of sth** faire naître l'espoir de qch; **she hasn't got a h. of winning** elle n'a aucun espoir de gagner; *Ironic* **some h.!** tu peux toujours rêver!; *Fam* **we live in h.** l'espoir fait vivre! **2** vt **to h. to do sth** espérer faire qch; **to h. (that)...** espérer que...; **I h. you're right** j'espère que tu as raison; **I h. and pray that...** je prie le ciel que...; **I h. so** j'espère (bien); **I h. not** j'espère que non **3** vi espérer; **to h. for sth** espérer qch; **don't h. for too much** n'en attends pas trop; **we'll just have to h. for the best** espérons pour le mieux; **to h. against all h.** espérer malgré tout

hopeful ['həʊpfʊl] **1** n *Fam* **a young h.** un jeune espoir

2 adj (situation) encourageant(e); (person) optimiste; **to be h. that...** avoir bon espoir que...

hopefully ['həʊpfʊlɪ] adv **(a)** (with luck) avec un peu de chance; **h.** not espérons que non **(b)** (in a hopeful manner) **to do sth h.** faire qch plein(e) d'espoir

hopeless ['həʊplɪs] adj **(a)** (without hope) (person, cause, situation) désespéré(e); **it's h.!** ça ne sert à rien! **(b)** Fam (very bad) nul (nulle) (**at** en)

hopelessly ['həʊplɪslɪ] adv **(a)** (inconsolably) avec désespoir **(b)** (completely) complètement; **he was h. in love with her** il était éperdument amoureux d'elle

hopping ['hɒpɪŋ] adv Fam **to be h. mad** être fou (folle) de rage

hops [hɒps] npl (for making beer) houblon m

hopscotch ['hɒpskɒtʃ] n marelle f

horde [hɔːd] n horde f

horizon [hə'raɪzən] n horizon m; **on the h.** à l'horizon; Fig en vue

horizontal [hɒrɪ'zɒntəl] **1** n horizontale f **2** adj horizontal(e)

horizontally [hɒrɪ'zɒntəlɪ] adv horizontalement

hormonal [hɔː'məʊnəl] adj hormonal(e)

hormone ['hɔːməʊn] n hormone f; **h. replacement therapy** traitement m hormonal

horn [hɔːn] n **(a)** (of animal) corne f; (of insect) antenne f **(b)** (musical instrument) cor m; (on car) Klaxon® m; **to sound one's h.** klaxonner **(c)** (idioms) **to be on the horns of a dilemma** être en proie à un dilemme

horned [hɔːnd] adj à cornes

hornet ['hɔːnɪt] n frelon m; Fig **to stir up a h.'s nest** mettre le feu aux poudres

hornpipe ['hɔːnpaɪp] n matelote f

horn-rimmed ['hɔːnrɪmd] adj **h. spectacles** or **glasses** lunettes fpl à monture d'écaille

horny ['hɔːnɪ] adj **(a)** (hands) calleux(euse) **(b)** very Fam (sexually aroused) excité(e); (sexually attractive) bandant(e)

horoscope ['hɒrəskəʊp] n horoscope m

horrendous [hɒ'rendəs] adj horrible, affreux(euse)

horrendously [hɒ'rendəslɪ] adv horriblement, affreusement

horrible ['hɒrəbəl] adj **(a)** (unpleasant) horrible, affreux(euse); **how h.!** quelle horreur! **(b)** (unkind) méchant(e) (**to** avec)

horribly ['hɒrɪblɪ] adv horriblement; **to behave h.** se conduire horriblement mal

horrid ['hɒrɪd] adj **(a)** (unpleasant) affreux(euse) **(b)** (unkind) méchant(e) (**to** avec)

horrific [hɒ'rɪfɪk] adj horrible

horrify ['hɒrɪfaɪ] (pt & pp horrified) vt horrifier

horrifying ['hɒrɪfaɪɪŋ] adj horrifiant(e)

horror ['hɒrə(r)] n horreur f; **to my h.,...** à ma grande horreur,...; **to have a h. of sth** avoir horreur de qch; **it gives me the horrors** ça me donne le frisson; Fam **that child's a little h.** cet enfant est un petit monstre; **h. film** film m d'horreur; Fig **h. story** histoire f épouvantable

horror-stricken ['hɒrəstrɪkən], **horror-struck** ['hɒrəstrʌk] adj frappé(e) d'horreur

horse [hɔːs] n **(a)** (animal) cheval m; **to ride a h.** monter à cheval; **h. chestnut** (tree) marronnier m; (fruit) marron m; **h. racing** courses fpl de chevaux; **h. riding** équitation f; **h. trading** (in negotiation) maquignonnage m **(b)** (in gymnastics) cheval m d'arçons **(c)** (idioms) **to get on one's high h.** monter sur ses grands chevaux; **to eat like a h.**

manger comme quatre; **to hear sth from the h.'s mouth** entendre qch de la bouche de l'intéressé

▸ **horse about, horse around** vi chahuter

horseback ['hɔːsbæk] n **on h.** à cheval

horsebox ['hɔːsbɒks] n van m

horse-drawn ['hɔːsdrɔːn] adj tiré(e) par des chevaux

horsefly ['hɔːsflaɪ] (pl horseflies) n taon m

horsehair ['hɔːsheə(r)] n crin m (de cheval)

horseman ['hɔːsmən] n cavalier m

horsemanship ['hɔːsmənʃɪp] n (skill) talent m de cavalier

horseplay ['hɔːspleɪ] n chahut m

horsepower ['hɔːspaʊə(r)] n puissance f (en chevaux); (unit) cheval-vapeur m

horseradish ['hɔːsrædɪʃ] n raifort m

horseshoe ['hɔːsʃuː] n fer m à cheval

horsewhip ['hɔːswɪp] **1** n cravache f **2** vt (pt & pp horsewhipped) cravacher

horsewoman ['hɔːswʊmən] n cavalière f

hors(e)y ['hɔːsɪ] adj **(a)** (horse-like) chevalin(e) **(b)** (keen on horses) passionné(e) de chevaux

horticultural [hɔːtɪ'kʌltʃərəl] adj horticole

horticulture ['hɔːtɪkʌltʃə(r)] n horticulture f

hose [həʊz] **1** n (pipe) tuyau m **2** vt arroser (au jet d'eau)

▸ **hose down** vt sep laver au jet

hosepipe ['həʊzpaɪp] n tuyau m d'arrosage

hosiery ['həʊzɪərɪ] n bonneterie f

hospice ['hɒspɪs] n (hospital) = établissement pour malades en phase terminale

hospitable [hɒs'pɪtəbəl] adj hospitalier(ère)

hospitably [hɒs'pɪtəblɪ] adv avec hospitalité

hospital ['hɒspɪtəl] n hôpital m; Br **in h.**, Am **in the h.** à l'hôpital; **h. bed/food** lit m/nourriture f d'hôpital; **h. care** soins mpl hospitaliers

hospitality [hɒspɪ'tælɪtɪ] n hospitalité f

hospitalize ['hɒspɪtəlaɪz] vt **to be hospitalized** être hospitalisé(e)

host¹ [həʊst] **1** n **(a)** (at home, party) hôte m; (on TV, radio) animateur(trice) m,f; **h. city/country** ville f/pays m d'accueil **(b)** Biol (of parasite) hôte m **2** vt (party) donner, organiser; (TV, radio show) animer

host² n (great number) **a (whole) h. of** (toute) une foule de

host³ n Rel hostie f

hostage ['hɒstɪdʒ] n otage m; **to take/hold sb h.** prendre/garder qn en otage; **to offer a h. to fortune** hypothéquer l'avenir

hostel ['hɒstəl] n (for homeless people, students) foyer m; (youth hostel) auberge f de jeunesse

hostess ['həʊstɪs] n (at home, party) hôtesse f; (on TV, radio) animatrice f; (on plane) hôtesse (de l'air)

hostile ['hɒstaɪl, Am 'hɒstəl] adj hostile (**to** à)

hostility [hɒs'tɪlɪtɪ] (pl hostilities) n hostilité f (**towards** envers); **hostilities** (fighting) hostilités

hot [hɒt] adj **(a)** (having high temperature) chaud(e); **to get h.** (of person) commencer à avoir chaud; **to be h.** (of person) avoir chaud; (of thing) être chaud; **it's h.** (of weather) il fait chaud; Med Br **h. flush**, Am **h. flash** bouffée f de chaleur; **h. tub** Jacuzzi® m
(b) (spicy) (food) épicé(e); (pepper, mustard) fort(e)
(c) (close) **you're getting h.** (in guessing game) tu brûles; **to be h. on sb's trail** être aux trousses de qn
(d) Fam (good) **to be h. on sth** (be knowledgeable about)

être calé(e) en qch; *(attach importance to)* être très à cheval sur qch; **it wasn't such a h.** idea l'idée n'était pas si géniale; **how are you? – not so h.** comment ça va? – pas terrible; **to be h. stuff (at)** être un as (en) **(e)** *Fam (sexy)* sexy *inv* **(f)** *Fam (stolen)* chouré(e) **(g)** *(idioms)* **h. off the press** *(of news)* de dernière minute; *(of book)* qui vient juste de paraître; **too h. to handle** *(issue)* brûlant(e); **to have a h. temper** s'emporter facilement; **to get h. under the collar** se mettre en colère; **a h. favourite** *(in race)* un grand favori; *Fam* **it's all just h. air** tout ça, c'est du vent; **they're selling like h. cakes** ils se vendent comme des petits pains; **the h. gossip** les derniers potins; **h. line** *(telephone number)* permanence *f* téléphonique; **h. news** les toutes dernières nouvelles; *Fam* **h. potato** *(controversial issue)* sujet *m* brûlant; **to be in the h. seat** *(of politician, manager)* avoir toutes les responsabilités; **h. spot** *(trouble spot)* point *m* chaud; *Fam* **to get into h. water** *(in difficult situation)* s'attirer des ennuis

▸ **hot up** *(pt & pp hotted)* *vi Fam (of situation, conflict)* s'envenimer; *(of race, debate, contest)* s'animer

hot-air balloon ['hɒteəbə'luːn] *n* montgolfière *f*

hotbed ['hɒtbed] *n* **a h. of rebellion/intrigue** un foyer de rébellion/d'intrigue

hot-blooded ['hɒt'blʌdɪd] *adj* au sang chaud, passionné(e)

hotchpotch ['hɒtʃpɒtʃ] *n Fam* mélange *m*

hotdog ['hɒtdɒg] *n* hot dog *m*

hotel [həʊ'tel] *n* hôtel *m*; **h. room/manager** chambre *f*/gérant(e) *m,f* d'hôtel; **the h. trade** l'industrie *f* hôtelière

hotelier [həʊ'teljeɪ] *n* hôtelier(ère) *m,f*

hotfoot ['hɒt'fʊt] *Fam* **1** *adv* en vitesse **2** *vt* **to h. it** aller à toute vitesse

hothead ['hɒthed] *n* tête *f* brûlée

hotheaded ['hɒt'hedɪd] *adj* exalté(e)

hothouse ['hɒthaʊs] *n* serre *f* (chaude)

hotly ['hɒtlɪ] *adv (reply, protest)* vivement; **h. contested** âprement disputé(e)

hotplate ['hɒtpleɪt] *n (on cooker)* plaque *f* (chauffante); *(for keeping food warm)* chauffe-plat *m*

hotpot ['hɒtpɒt] *n (stew)* ragoût *m*

hots ['hɒts] *npl very Fam* **to have the h. for sb** *(of man)* bander pour qn; *(of woman)* mouiller pour qn

hotshot ['hɒtʃɒt] *n Fam (expert)* as *m*, crack *m*

hot-tempered ['hɒt'tempəd] *adj* colérique, coléreux(euse)

hot-water [hɒt'wɔːtə(r)] *adj* d'eau chaude; **h. bottle** bouillotte *f*

hound [haʊnd] **1** *n (dog)* chien *m* de chasse **2** *vt (persecute)* traquer, pourchasser

hour ['aʊə(r)] *n* heure *f*; **an h. and a half** une heure et demie; **half an h.** une demi-heure; **to pay sb by the h.** payer qn à l'heure; **to take hours over sth** mettre des heures à faire qch; **we've been waiting for hours** ça fait des heures que nous attendons; **to work long hours** faire de longues journées *(de travail)*; **to keep late hours** *(of person)* se coucher tard; **till all hours** jusqu'à très tard; **h. hand** *(of watch, clock)* petite aiguille *f*

hourglass ['aʊəglɑːs] *n* sablier *m*; **an h. figure** une taille de guêpe

hourly ['aʊəlɪ] **1** *adj* **at h. intervals** toutes les heures; **h. rate** taux *m* horaire **2** *adv (every hour)* toutes les heures; *(at any time)* d'un moment à l'autre

house 1 *n* [haʊs] **(a)** *(dwelling)* maison *f*; **to stay at sb's h.** loger chez qn; **from h. to h.** de porte à porte; **they keep**

open h. leur maison est toujours ouverte; *Fig* **to put one's h. in order** balayer devant sa porte; **to get on like a h. on fire** *(very well)* s'entendre comme larrons en foire; **the H. of Commons/Lords** la Chambre des communes/lords; **the Houses of Parliament** le Parlement; **the H. of Representatives** la Chambre des représentants; *Law* **to be under h. arrest** être assigné(e) à résidence; **h. guest** invité(e) *m,f*; **h. martin** hirondelle *f* de fenêtre; **h. painter** peintre *m* en bâtiment; **h. party** partie *f* de campagne; **h. plant** plante *f* d'intérieur *ou* d'appartement; **h. spider** araignée *f* commune

(b) *Com (company)* maison *f*; **h. style** style *m* de la maison **(c)** *(restaurant)* **on the h.** aux frais de la maison; **h. wine** vin *m* de la maison

(d) *Th* **an empty/good h.** une salle vide/pleine **(e)** **h.** *(music)* house music *f* **(f)** *Br Sch* = groupe d'élèves d'une école qui disputent ensemble des compétitions sportives etc

2 *vt* [haʊz] *(person)* loger; *(collection, mechanism)* contenir, recevoir

houseboat ['haʊsbəʊt] *n* péniche *f* aménagée

housebound ['haʊsbaʊnd] *adj* confiné(e) chez soi

housebreaker ['haʊsbreɪkə(r)] *n* cambrioleur(euse) *m,f*

housebreaking ['haʊsbreɪkɪŋ] *n* cambriolage *m*

housecoat ['haʊskəʊt] *n* robe *f* d'intérieur

housefly ['haʊsflaɪ] *(pl* **houseflies)** *n* mouche *f* domestique

household ['haʊshəʊld] *n* ménage *m*; **h. appliance** appareil *m* électroménager; **h. chores** tâches *fpl* ménagères; **he's a h. name** tout le monde connaît son nom

householder ['haʊshəʊldə(r)] *n (owner)* propriétaire *mf*; *(tenant)* locataire *mf*

househusband ['haʊs'hʌzbənd] *n* homme *m* au foyer

housekeeper ['haʊskiːpə(r)] *n (private)* gouvernante *f*; *(in institution)* intendante *f*

housekeeping ['haʊskiːpɪŋ] *n* **h. (money)** argent *m* du ménage

housemaid ['haʊsmeɪd] *n* femme *f* de chambre; **h.'s knee** *(inflammation)* inflammation *f* du genou

houseman ['haʊsmən] *n Br Med* interne *m*

housemaster ['haʊsmɑːstə(r)] *n Br Sch* = dans une école privée, professeur chargé d'un "house"

housemistress ['haʊsmɪstrɪs] *n Br Sch* = dans une école privée, professeur chargée d'un "house"

houseproud ['haʊspraʊd] *adj* **she's very h.** elle prend grand soin de son intérieur

house-to-house ['haʊstə'haʊs] *adj* **to make a h. search** fouiller chaque maison

house-trained ['haʊstreɪnd] *adj (dog)* propre; *Hum (husband, partner)* bien dressé(e)

housewarming ['haʊswɔːmɪŋ] *n* **h. (party)** pendaison *f* de crémaillère; **to have a h. party** pendre la crémaillère

housewife ['haʊswaɪf] *(pl* **housewives** ['haʊswaɪvz]) *n* femme *f* au foyer

housework ['haʊswɜːk] *n* ménage *m*

housing ['haʊzɪŋ] *n* logement *m*; *Br* **h. association** = organisme chargé du logement; *Br* **h. benefit** ≃ allocation *f* logement; *Br* **h. estate** *(council-owned)* cité *f* HLM; *(private)* lotissement *m*; **the h. market** le marché de l'immobilier; *Am* **h. project** cité HLM

hove [həʊv] *pt & pp of* **heave**

hovel ['hɒvəl] *n* taudis *m*

hover ['hɒvə(r)] *vi* **(a)** *(of bird)* planer; *(of helicopter)* effectuer un vol stationnaire **(b)** *(of person)* **to h. near sb** être derrière le dos de qn

hovercraft ['hɒvəkrɑːft] *n* hovercraft *m*, aéroglisseur *m*
how [haʊ] *adv* (**a**) *(in what way, by what means)* comment; **h. did they find out?** comment l'ont-ils appris?; **h. do you spell this word?** comment s'écrit ce mot?; *Fam* **h. come?** comment ça se fait?; *Fam* **and h.! et comment!**
(**b**) *(to what extent)* **h. much money?** combien d'argent?; **h. many people?** combien de gens?; **h. old are you?** quel âge as-tu?; **h. big is it?** c'est grand comment?; **h. long have you been here?** depuis combien de temps êtes-vous ici?; **h. often do you see him?** tu le vois tous les combien?; **you know h. difficult it is** tu sais à quel point c'est difficile; **h. useful will it be?** est-ce que ce sera très utile?
(**c**) *(greetings, enquiries after health)* **h. are you?** comment vas-tu?; *Fam* **h. are things?** ça va?; **h.'s business?** comment vont les affaires?
(**d**) *(in exclamations)* que, comme; **h. pretty she is!** qu'elle est jolie!, comme elle est jolie!; **h. disgusting!** c'est vraiment dégoûtant!; **h. true!** c'est bien vrai!; **h. she's changed!** comme elle a changé!
(**e**) *(in suggestions)* **h. about a game of cards?** et si on faisait une partie de cartes?; **h. about going out for a meal?** et si on allait manger quelque part?; **h. about it?** ça te dirait?; **h. about you?** et toi?

however [haʊ'evə(r)] **1** *adv* (**a**) *(in whatever degree)* si... que + *subjunctive;* **h. clever she is** si intelligente qu'elle soit; **h. hard she tried, she couldn't do it** elle avait beau essayer, elle n'y arrivait pas (**b**) *(in whatever way)* **h. you look at it...** de quelque façon qu'on envisage la chose... (**c**) *(in what way)* comment; **h. did she find out?** comment a-t-elle bien pu l'apprendre?
2 *conj* pourtant, cependant; **h., this does not explain why she...** ceci n'explique pourquoi pas pourquoi elle...

howl [haʊl] **1** *n (of animal, person)* hurlement *m*; **howls of derision** des huées *fpl*
2 *vi (of animal, person)* hurler; **to h. with laughter** hurler de rire
▸ **howl down** *vt sep* huer

howler ['haʊlə(r)] *n Fam (mistake)* bourde *f*

howling ['haʊlɪŋ] **1** *n (of wind, wolf)* hurlement *m; (of baby)* hurlements
2 *adj (wolf)* qui hurle; *(gale, wind)* furieux(euse); *Fam* **it wasn't exactly a h. success** ça n'a pas vraiment eu un succès fou

HP, hp [eɪtʃ'piː] *n* (**a**) *(abbr* **horsepower**) CV *m* (**b**) *(abbr* **hire purchase**) achat *m* à crédit

HQ [eɪtʃ'kjuː] *n (abbr* **headquarters**) QG *m*

hr *(abbr* **hour**) h

HRH [eɪtʃɑːr'eɪtʃ] *n Br (abbr* **Her/His Royal Highness**) SAR

HRT [eɪtʃɑːr'tiː] *n Med (abbr* **hormone replacement therapy**) traitement *m* hormonal

HTML [eɪtʃtiːem'el] *n Comptr (abbr* **Hyper Text Markup Language**) HTML

HTTP [eɪtʃtiːtiː'piː] *n Comptr (abbr* **Hyper Text Transfer Protocol**) HTTP

hub [hʌb] *n* (**a**) *(of wheel)* moyeu *m* (**b**) *(of community)* centre *m*

hubbub ['hʌbʌb] *n* brouhaha *m*

hubby ['hʌbɪ] *(pl* **hubbies**) *n Fam* petit mari *m*

hubcap ['hʌbkæp] *n (of wheel)* enjoliveur *m*

huddle ['hʌdəl] **1** *(of people)* petit groupe *m; (of things)* tas *m*
2 *vi* se blottir
▸ **huddle together** *vi* se blottir les uns contre les autres
▸ **huddle up** *vi* se blottir les uns contre les autres

Hudson Bay [hʌdsən'beɪ] *n* la baie d'Hudson

hue¹ [hjuː] *n (colour)* teinte *f*

hue² *n* **h. and cry** tollé *m;* **to raise a h. and cry about sth** crier haro sur qch

huff [hʌf] **1** *n Fam* **to be in a h.** faire la tête
2 *vi* **to h. and puff** *(blow)* souffler; *Fig (show annoyance)* maugréer

huffy ['hʌfɪ] *adj Fam (sulky)* susceptible

hug [hʌg] **1** *n* étreinte *f;* **to give sb a h.** serrer qn (dans ses bras)
2 *vt (pt & pp* **hugged**) (**a**) *(embrace)* serrer (dans ses bras) (**b**) *Fig (shore, kerb)* serrer; *(ground)* raser

huge [hjuːdʒ] *adj (very big)* énorme; *(very tall, long)* immense

hugely ['hjuːdʒlɪ] *adv* énormément, extrêmement; **the project has been h. successful** le projet a été un succès complet

hulk [hʌlk] *n* (**a**) *(of ship)* épave *f* (**b**) *(person)* mastodonte *m*

hulking ['hʌlkɪŋ] *adj Fam* **a h. great man** une armoire à glace

hull [hʌl] **1** *n* (**a**) *(of ship)* coque *f* (**b**) *(of pea)* cosse *f*
2 *vt (peas)* écosser

hullabaloo [hʌləbə'luː] *(pl* **hullabaloos**) *n Fam* raffut *m*

hullo [hʌ'ləʊ] = hello

hum [hʌm] **1** *n* bourdonnement *m*
2 *vt (pt & pp* **hummed**) *(tune)* fredonner
3 *vi* (**a**) *(of person)* fredonner; *(of insect, computer)* bourdonner; *(of engine, fridge)* ronronner; **to h. and haw** hésiter; **to h. with activity** bourdonner d'activité (**b**) *Fam (smell)* chlinguer

human ['hjuːmən] **1** *n* (être *m*) humain *m*
2 *adj* humain(e); **h. being** être *m* humain; **h. error** erreur *f* humaine; **h. nature** la nature humaine; **h. resources** ressources *fpl* humaines; **h. rights** droits *mpl* de l'homme

humane [hjuː'meɪn] *adj* humain(e)

humanely [hjuː'meɪnlɪ] *adv* humainement

humanism ['hjuːmənɪzəm] *n* humanisme *m*

humanistic [hjuːmə'nɪstɪk] *adj* humaniste

humanitarian [hjuːmænɪ'teərɪən] **1** *n* philanthrope *mf*
2 *adj* humanitaire

humanity [hjuː'mænɪtɪ] *n* humanité *f; Univ* **humanities** lettres *fpl*

humanize ['hjuːmənaɪz] *vt* humaniser

humankind [hjuːmən'kaɪnd] *n* humanité *f*

humanly ['hjuːmənlɪ] *adv* **to do everything h. possible** faire tout ce qui est humainement possible

humble ['hʌmbəl] **1** *adj (meek)* humble; *(unpretentious)* modeste; **in my h. opinion** à mon humble avis; *Fig* **to eat h. pie** reconnaître qu'on a tort
2 *vt* humilier

humbling ['hʌmblɪŋ] *adj* humiliant(e)

humbly ['hʌmblɪ] *adv (meekly)* humblement; *(modestly)* modestement

humbug ['hʌmbʌg] *n* (**a**) *(nonsense)* balivernes *fpl* (**b**) *(hypocrite)* charlatan *m* (**c**) *Br (sweet)* berlingot *m*

humdinger ['hʌmdɪŋə(r)] *n Fam* **a h. of a film/book** un film/livre extra

humdrum ['hʌmdrʌm] *adj* monotone

humerus ['hjuːmərəs] *(pl* **humeri** ['hjuːməraɪ]) *n Anat* humérus *m*

humid ['hjuːmɪd] *adj* humide

humidifier [hjuː'mɪdɪfaɪə(r)] *n* humidificateur *m*

humidity [hjuː'mɪdɪtɪ] *n* humidité *f*

humiliate [hjuː'mɪlɪeɪt] *vt* humilier

humiliating [hjuː'mɪlɪeɪtɪŋ] *adj* humiliant(e)

humiliation [hjʊmɪlɪˈeɪʃən] *n* humiliation *f*

humility [hjʊˈmɪlɪtɪ] *n* humilité *f*

hummingbird [ˈhʌmɪŋbɜːd] *n* oiseau-mouche *m*, colibri *m*

humor, humorless *Am* = humour, humourless

humorous [ˈhjuːmərəs] *adj (situation)* drôle, comique; *(writer, drawing, remark)* humoristique

humorously [ˈhjuːmərəslɪ] *adv* avec humour

humour, *Am* **humor** [ˈhjuːmə(r)] **1** *n* (**a**) *(fun)* humour *m* (**b**) *Formal (mood)* humeur *f*
2 *vt (indulge)* faire plaisir à

humourless, *Am* **humorless** [ˈhjuːməlɪs] *adj* dépourvu(e) d'humour

hump [hʌmp] **1** *n (on back, road)* bosse *f*
2 *vt* (**a**) *Fam (carry)* trimbaler (**b**) *Vulg (have sex with)* sauter

humpback [ˈhʌmpbæk] *n* **h. bridge** pont *m* en dos d'âne; **h. whale** baleine *f* à bosse

humus [ˈhjuːməs] *n* humus *m*

hunch [hʌntʃ] **1** *n (intuition)* intuition *f*; **I have a h. we'll meet again** j'ai comme un pressentiment que nous nous reverrons
2 *vt* **to h. one's shoulders** rentrer les épaules

hunchback [ˈhʌntʃbæk] *n* bossu(e) *m,f*

hundred [ˈhʌndrəd] **1** *n* cent *m*; **one** *or* **a h. and twenty-five pages** cent vingt-cinq pages; **two h. pages** deux cents pages; **I've told you hundreds of times** je te l'ai dit des centaines de fois; **to live to be a h.** vivre jusqu'à cent ans
2 *adj* cent; **a h. kilometres an hour** cent kilomètres à l'heure; **one** *or* **a h. per cent** cent pour cent; **to be a h. per cent certain** être sûr(e) à cent pour cent; **I'm not feeling a h. per cent** je ne me sens pas au mieux de ma forme; **the h. metres** *(in athletics)* le cent mètres

hundredfold [ˈhʌndrədfəʊld] *adv* **to increase a h.** centupler

hundredth [ˈhʌndrədθ] **1** *n* (**a**) *(fraction)* centième *m* (**b**) *(in series)* centième *mf*
2 *adj* centième; *Fam* **for the h. time, no!** pour la centième fois, non!; *see also* **eighth**

hundredweight [ˈhʌndrədweɪt] *n Br* = 50,8 kg, (poids *m* de) 112 livres *fpl*; *Am* = 45,36 kg, (poids de) 100 livres

hung [hʌŋ] **1** *adj* **h. jury/parliament** jury *m*/parlement *m* sans majorité
2 *pt & pp of* **hang**

Hungarian [hʌŋˈgeərɪən] **1** *n* (**a**) *(person)* Hongrois(e) *m,f* (**b**) *(language)* hongrois *m*
2 *adj* hongrois(e)

Hungary [ˈhʌŋgərɪ] *n* la Hongrie

hunger [ˈhʌŋgə(r)] *n* faim *f*; *Fig (for power)* soif *f* (**for** de); **h. strike** grève *f* de la faim

▸ **hunger after, hunger for** *vt insep Fig* avoir soif de

hungrily [ˈhʌŋgrɪlɪ] *adv also Fig* avidement

hungry [ˈhʌŋgrɪ] *adj* **to be h.** avoir faim; **to be h. for knowledge** être avide de connaissances

hunk [hʌŋk] *n* (**a**) *(of bread, meat)* gros morceau *m* (**b**) *Fam (attractive man)* beau mec *m*

hunky [ˈhʌŋkɪ] *adj Fam (man)* bien foutu

hunt [hʌnt] **1** *n (for animals)* chasse *f*; *(for person, work)* recherche *f*
2 *vt (animal)* chasser; *(criminal)* pourchasser
3 *vi* (**a**) *(search)* **to h. for** rechercher; *Fig* **I've hunted high and low for it** j'ai remué ciel et terre pour le retrouver (**b**) *(kill animals)* chasser

▸ **hunt down** *vt sep (animal, person)* traquer; *(information)* dénicher

▸ **hunt out** *vt sep (find) (person)* retrouver; *(thing)* dénicher

hunted [ˈhʌntɪd] *adj (look)* hagard(e)

hunter [ˈhʌntə(r)] *n* chasseur *m*

hunting [ˈhʌntɪŋ] *n* chasse *f*; **to go h.** aller à la chasse; **h. dog** chien *m* de chasse; **h. ground** terrain *m* de chasse; **h. lodge** pavillon *m* de chasse

huntsman [ˈhʌntsmən] *n* chasseur *m*

hurdle [ˈhɜːdəl] **1** *n (in race)* haie *f*; *Fig (obstacle)* obstacle *m*
2 *vt (jump over)* sauter, franchir

hurdler [ˈhɜːdlə(r)] *n Sp* coureur(euse) *m,f* de haies

hurdling [ˈhɜːdəlɪŋ] *n Sp* course *f* de haies

hurl [hɜːl] **1** *vt* jeter, lancer (**at** sur); *(insults)* lancer (**at** à); **to h. oneself at sb** se jeter *ou* se ruer sur qn
2 *vi Fam (vomit)* dégobiller

hurly-burly [ˈhɜːlɪˈbɜːlɪ] *n Fam* tohu-bohu *m inv*

hurrah [hʊˈrɑː], **hurray** [hʊˈreɪ] *exclam* hourra!

hurricane [ˈhʌrɪkən, *Am* ˈhʌrɪkeɪn] *n* ouragan *m*; **h. lamp** lampe *f* tempête

hurried [ˈhʌrɪd] *adj (gesture, conversation, meal)* rapide; *(departure)* précipité(e); *(work)* fait(e) à la hâte; *(decision, choice)* pris(e) à la hâte

hurriedly [ˈhʌrɪdlɪ] *adv* précipitamment

hurry [ˈhʌrɪ] **1** *n* hâte *f*; **to be in a h. (to do sth)** être pressé(e) (de faire qch); **to do sth in a h.** faire qch à la hâte; **to leave in a h.** partir à la hâte; **I won't do that again in a h.** je ne suis pas prêt de recommencer; **there's no h.** rien ne presse; **what's the h.?** qu'est-ce qui presse?
2 *vt (pt & pp* **hurried**) *(person)* presser; *(work)* hâter; **he was hurried into making a choice** on l'a pressé de faire un choix
3 *vi* se dépêcher, se presser; **to h. to do sth** se dépêcher *ou* se presser de faire qch; **to h. into/out of a room** se précipiter dans une/hors d'une pièce

▸ **hurry along 1** *vt sep (person)* faire se dépêcher; *(work)* accélérer
2 *vi* se presser

▸ **hurry back** *vi* se dépêcher de revenir

▸ **hurry on 1** *vt sep (person)* faire circuler; *(work)* faire accélérer
2 *vi (leave)* partir en hâte

▸ **hurry up 1** *vt sep* faire accélérer
2 *vi* se dépêcher; **h. up!** vite!, dépêche-toi!

hurt [hɜːt] **1** *n (emotional)* blessure *f*
2 *adj* blessé(e)
3 *vt (pt & pp* **hurt**) (**a**) *(physically)* faire mal à; *(reputation, chances)* nuire à; **to h. oneself** se faire mal; **to h. one's foot** se faire mal au pied; **to get h.** se blesser; *Fig* **it won't h. him to have to wait** ça ne lui fera pas de mal d'attendre un peu (**b**) *(emotionally)* faire du mal ou de la peine à; **to h. sb's feelings** blesser qn
4 *vi* (**a**) *(cause pain)* faire mal; **where does it h.?** où est-ce que ça fait mal?; **my arm hurts** j'ai mal au bras, mon bras me fait mal (**b**) *(emotionally)* faire mal

hurtful [ˈhɜːtfʊl] *adj* blessant(e)

hurtle [ˈhɜːtəl] *vi* **to h. along** avancer à toute vitesse; **to h. down the street** dévaler la rue; **to h. towards** foncer sur

husband [ˈhʌzbənd] **1** *n* mari *m*
2 *vt Formal (one's resources)* ménager

husbandry [ˈhʌzbəndrɪ] *n* agriculture *f*; **animal h.** élevage *m*

hush [hʌʃ] **1** *n (quiet)* silence *m*; **h.!** chut!
2 *vt* calmer

▸ **hush up** *vt sep (scandal)* étouffer

hushed [hʌʃt] *adj (conversation)* étouffé(e); *(silence)* profond(e); **to talk in h.** tones parler à voix basse
hush-hush [hʌʃ'hʌʃ] *adj Fam* top secret *inv*
husk [hʌsk] **1** *n (of seed)* enveloppe *f; (of pea)* cosse *f; (of nut)* brou *m*
2 *vt (grain)* décortiquer
husky¹ ['hʌskɪ] *adj (voice)* rauque
husky² *(pl* huskies) *n (dog)* husky *m*
hussar [hʊ'zɑː(r)] *n Mil* hussard *m*
hussy ['hʌsɪ] *(pl* hussies) *n Old-fashioned or Hum* gourgandine *f*
hustings ['hʌstɪŋz] *npl* on the h. en campagne
hustle ['hʌsəl] **1** *n* h. (and bustle) effervescence *f*
2 *vt (shove, push)* to h. sb away emmener qn de force; I was hustled into a small room on m'a poussé dans une petite pièce
hustler ['hʌslə(r)] *n Am Fam (swindler)* arnaqueur(euse) *m,f*
hut [hʌt] *n (shed)* cabane *f; (dwelling)* hutte *f*
hutch [hʌtʃ] *n (for rabbit)* clapier *m*
hyacinth ['haɪəsɪnθ] *n* jacinthe *f*
hybrid ['haɪbrɪd] **1** *n* hybride *m*
2 *adj* hybride
hydrangea [haɪ'dreɪndʒə] *n* hortensia *m*
hydrant ['haɪdrənt] *n* prise *f* d'eau; **fire h.** bouche *f* d'incendie
hydraulic [haɪ'drɔːlɪk] *adj* hydraulique; **h. engineering** hydraulique *f*
hydraulics [haɪ'drɔːlɪks] *n* hydraulique *f*
hydrocarbon [haɪdrəʊ'kɑːbən] *n* hydrocarbure *m*
hydrochloric acid [haɪdrəʊ'klɒrɪk'æsɪd] *n* acide *m* chlorhydrique
hydroelectric [haɪdrəʊɪ'lektrɪk] *adj* hydroélectrique
hydroelectricity [haɪdrəʊɪlek'trɪsɪtɪ] *n* hydroélectricité *f*
hydrofoil ['haɪdrəfɔɪl] *n* hydrofoil *m*, hydroptère *m*
hydrogen ['haɪdrədʒən] *n* hydrogène *m*; **h. bomb** bombe *f* à hydrogène
hydrolysis [haɪ'drɒlɪsɪs] *n* hydrolyse *f*
hydrophobia [haɪdrə'fəʊbɪə] *n Med (rabies)* rage *f*
hydroplane ['haɪdrəpleɪn] *n (boat)* hydroglisseur *m; (seaplane)* hydravion *m*
hydroxide [haɪ'drɒksaɪd] *n* hydroxyde *m*
hyena [haɪ'iːnə] *n* hyène *f*
hygiene ['haɪdʒiːn] *n* hygiène *f*
hygienic [haɪ'dʒiːnɪk] *adj* hygiénique
hymen ['haɪmen] *n* hymen *m*
hymn [hɪm] *n* cantique *m*; **h. book** livre *m* de cantiques
hymnal ['hɪmnəl] *n* livre *m* de cantiques
hype [haɪp] *Fam* **1** *n (publicity)* battage *m* publicitaire
2 *vt (publicize)* faire du battage publicitaire pour
▸ **hype up** *vt sep Fam* **(a)** *(publicize)* faire du battage publicitaire pour **(b)** **to be hyped up** *(excited)* être surexcité(e)

hyper ['haɪpə(r)] *adj Fam (overexcited)* surexcité(e)
hyperactive [haɪpə'ræktɪv] *adj* hyperactif(ive)
hyperbola [haɪ'pɜːbələ] *n Math* hyperbole *f*
hyperbole [haɪ'pɜːbəlɪ] *n* hyperbole *f*
hypercritical [haɪpə'krɪtɪkəl] *adj* hypercritique
hypermarket ['haɪpəmɑːkɪt] *n* hypermarché *m*
hypersensitive [haɪpə'sensɪtɪv] *adj* hypersensible
hypertension [haɪpə'tenʃən] *n Med* hypertension *f*
hypertext ['haɪpətekst] *n Comptr* hypertexte *m*; **h. link** lien *m* hypertexte
hyphen ['haɪfən] *n* trait *m* d'union
hyphenate ['haɪfəneɪt] *vt (word)* mettre un trait d'union à; **a hyphenated word** un mot à trait d'union
hypnosis [hɪp'nəʊsɪs] *n* hypnose *f*
hypnotic [hɪp'nɒtɪk] *adj* hypnotique
hypnotism ['hɪpnətɪzəm] *n* hypnotisme *m*
hypnotist ['hɪpnətɪst] *n* hypnotiseur(euse) *m,f*
hypnotize ['hɪpnətaɪz] *vt* hypnotiser
hypoallergenic [haɪpəʊælə'dʒenɪk] *adj* hypoallergénique
hypochondria [haɪpə'kɒndrɪə] *n* hypocondrie *f*
hypochondriac [haɪpə'kɒndrɪæk] *n* hypocondriaque *mf*
hypocrisy [hɪ'pɒkrɪsɪ] *n* hypocrisie *f*
hypocrite ['hɪpəkrɪt] *n* hypocrite *mf*
hypocritical [hɪpə'krɪtɪkəl] *adj* hypocrite
hypodermic [haɪpə'dɜːmɪk] **1** *n* seringue *f* hypodermique
2 *adj* hypodermique
hypotenuse [haɪ'pɒtənjuːz] *n Math* hypoténuse *f*
hypothermia [haɪpəʊ'θɜːmɪə] *n* hypothermie *f*; **to have h.** faire de l'hypothermie
hypothesis [haɪ'pɒθəsɪs] *(pl* hypotheses [haɪ'pɒθə-siːz]) *n* hypothèse *f*
hypothesize [haɪ'pɒθəsaɪz] **1** *vt* to h. that... émettre l'hypothèse que…
2 *vi* faire des hypothèses
hypothetical [haɪpə'θetɪkəl] *adj* hypothétique
hysterectomy [hɪstə'rektəmɪ] *(pl* hysterectomies) *n* hystérectomie *f*; **to have a h.** subir une hystérectomie
hysteria [hɪs'tɪərɪə] *n* **(a)** *(panic)* hystérie *f* **(b)** *(laughter)* fou rire *m*
hysterical [hɪs'terɪkəl] *adj* **(a)** *(uncontrolled)* hystérique; **to be h.** faire une crise de nerfs; **h. laughter** fou rire *m* **(b)** *(very funny)* tordant(e)
hysterically [hɪs'terɪklɪ] *adv* **(a)** *(uncontrolledly)* sans pouvoir se contrôler; **to laugh h.** avoir le fou rire **(b)** **h. funny** tordant(e)
hysterics [hɪs'terɪks] *npl* **(a)** *(panic)* crise *f* de nerfs; **to go into** *or* **have h.** avoir une crise de nerfs **(b)** *(laughter)* fou rire *m*; **to be in h.** avoir le fou rire

I¹, i [aɪ] *n (letter)* I, i *m inv*

I² *pron* je; **I'm American** je suis américain; **I haven't got it!** ce n'est pas moi qui l'ai!

IAEA [aɪeɪiː'eɪ] *n (abbr* International Atomic Energy Agency) AIEA *f*

IBA [aɪbiː'eɪ] *n (abbr* Independent Broadcasting Authority) ≃ CSA *m (organisme qui contrôle les chaînes de télévision et de stations de radio privées britanniques)*

Iberian [aɪ'biːrɪən] *adj* ibérique; **the I. Peninsula** la péninsule Ibérique

ibex ['aɪbeks] *n* bouquetin *m*

ibid ['ɪbɪd] *adv (abbr* ibidem) ibid

IBM [aɪbiː'em] *n (abbr* intercontinental ballistic missile) MBI *m*

IBRD [aɪbiːɑː'diː] *n (abbr* International Bank for Reconstruction and Development) BIRD *f*

IBS [aɪbiː'es] *n (abbr* irritable bowel syndrome) colopathie *f* fonctionnelle

ice [aɪs] **1** *n* **(a)** *(frozen water, ice-cream)* glace *f; (on road)* verglas *m;* **i. age** période *f* glaciaire; **i. cube** glaçon *m;* **i. floe** banquise *f;* **i. hockey** hockey *m* sur glace; **i. pack** sachet *m* de glace; **i. pick** pic *m* à glace; **i. rink** patinoire *f* **(b)** *(idioms)* **to put a project on i.** geler un projet; **to break the i.** rompre la glace; **to be skating on thin i.** avancer sur un terrain glissant; **that cuts no i. with me** ça ne marche pas avec moi

2 *vt (cake)* glacer

▸ **ice over** *vi* geler

▸ **ice up** *vi* se givrer

iceberg ['aɪsbɜːg] *n* iceberg *m; Fig* **that's just the tip of the i.** ce n'est que la partie visible de l'iceberg; **i. lettuce** = variété de laitue aux feuilles serrées et croquantes

icebound ['aɪsbaʊnd] *adj* bloqué(e) par les glaces

icebox ['aɪsbɒks] *n Br (in fridge)* freezer *m; Am (fridge)* réfrigérateur *m*

icebreaker ['aɪsbreɪkə(r)] *n (ship)* brise-glace *m inv; Fig (at party, in conversation)* **it's a good i.** c'est un bon moyen de briser la glace

icecap ['aɪskæp] *n* calotte *f* glaciaire

ice-cold ['aɪs'kəʊld] *adj* glacé(e); *(wind)* glacial(e)

iced [aɪst] *adj* **(a)** *(water)* avec des glaçons **(b)** *Br (cake)* glacé(e)

Iceland ['aɪslənd] *n* l'Islande *f*

Icelander ['aɪsləndə(r)] *n* Islandais(e) *m,f*

Icelandic [aɪs'lændɪk] **1** *n (language)* islandais *m*

2 *adj* islandais(e)

ice-skate ['aɪs'skeɪt] **1** *n* patin *m* à glace

2 *vi* faire du patin à glace

ice-skating ['aɪs'skeɪtɪŋ] *n* patinage *m* (sur glace)

icicle ['aɪsɪkəl] *n* glaçon *m (qui pend d'une gouttière etc)*

icing ['aɪsɪŋ] *n Br (on cake)* glaçage *m; Fig* **the i. on the cake** la cerise sur le gâteau; **i. sugar** sucre *m* glace

icon ['aɪkɒn] *n also Fig* icône *f*

iconoclastic [aɪkɒnəʊ'klæstɪk] *adj* iconoclaste

icy ['aɪsɪ] *adj* **(a)** *(road)* verglacé(e); *(ground)* gelé(e); *(water, hands)* glacé(e); *(wind)* glacial(e) **(b)** *Fig (expression, reply)* glacial(e)

ID [aɪ'diː] *n (abbr* identification) papiers *mpl* (d'identité); **ID card** carte *f* d'identité

I'd [aɪd] = **I had, I would**

idea [aɪ'dɪə] *n* **(a)** *(individual notion)* idée *f;* **to put an i. into sb's head** mettre une idée dans la tête de qn; **the very i.!** quelle idée!; *Fam* **what's the big i.?** qu'est-ce qui te prend? **(b)** *(concept)* conception *f;* **to have an i. that...** avoir l'impression que...; **that's not my i. of fun** ce n'est pas vraiment comme ça que je m'amuserais; **it's her i. of a joke** elle trouve ça drôle; **I have no i.** je n'ai aucune idée; **I had no i. that...** je ne savais pas que...; **I thought the i. was for them to come here** je croyais qu'il était prévu qu'ils viennent ici; **the general i. is to...** l'idée est de...

ideal [aɪ'diːəl] **1** *n* idéal *m*

2 *adj* idéal(e) **(for** pour)

idealism [aɪ'dɪəlɪzəm] *n* idéalisme *m*

idealist [aɪ'dɪəlɪst] *n* idéaliste *mf*

idealistic [aɪdɪə'lɪstɪk] *adj* idéaliste

idealize [aɪ'dɪəlaɪz] *vt* idéaliser

ideally [aɪ'diːəlɪ] *adv* **(a)** *(extremely well)* idéalement; **they're i. matched** ils vont très bien ensemble **(b)** *(in an ideal situation)* dans l'idéal

identical [aɪ'dentɪkəl] *adj* identique; **i. twins** *(boys)* vrais jumeaux *mpl; (girls)* vraies jumelles *fpl*

identification [aɪdentɪfɪ'keɪʃən] *n* **(a)** *(of body, criminal)* identification *f* **(b)** *(documents)* papiers *mpl* (d'identité)

identify [aɪ'dentɪfaɪ] *(pt & pp* identified) **1** *vt* **(a)** *(recognize)* identifier **(b)** *(associate)* **to i. sth with sth** identifier qch à qch

2 *vi* s'identifier **(with** sb à qn); **I can't i. with his problems** j'ai du mal à comprendre ses problèmes

identifying mark [aɪ'dentɪfaɪɪŋ'mɑːk] *n* signe *m* particulier

Identikit® [aɪ'dentɪkɪt] *n* **I. (picture)** portrait-robot *m*

identity [aɪ'dentɪtɪ] *(pl* identities) *n* identité *f;* **it was a case of mistaken i.** il y a eu erreur sur la personne; **i. card**

carte *f* d'identité; **i. crisis** crise *f* d'identité; **i.
parade** séance *f* d'identification

ideological [aɪdɪə'lɒdʒɪkəl] *adj* idéologique
ideology [aɪdɪ'ɒlədʒɪ] *(pl* **ideologies)** *n* idéologie *f*
idiocy ['ɪdɪəsɪ] *n* idiotie *f*
idiom ['ɪdɪəm] *n (expression)* expression *f*, locution *f*;
(dialect) idiome *m*
idiomatic [ɪdɪə'mætɪk] *adj* idiomatique
idiosyncrasy [ɪdɪəʊ'sɪŋkrəsɪ] *(pl* **ideosyncrasies)** *n*
particularité *f*; *(foible)* petite manie *f*
idiosyncratic [ɪdɪəʊsɪŋ'krætɪk] *adj* particulier(ère)
idiot ['ɪdɪət] *n* idiot(e) *m,f*
idiotic [ɪdɪ'ɒtɪk] *adj* idiot(e)
idle ['aɪdəl] **1** *adj* **(a)** *(unoccupied) (factory, machine)*
arrêté(e); *(person)* désœuvré(e); **an i. moment** un moment
libre **(b)** *(lazy)* oisif(ive) **(c)** *(futile) (threat, boast)* vain(e);
(gossip, rumour) pour passer le temps; *(curiosity)* simple
2 *vi (of engine)* tourner au ralenti
▸ **idle away** *vt sep (time)* passer à ne rien faire; **we idled
the afternoon away chatting** nous avons passé l'après-
midi à bavarder
idleness ['aɪdəlnɪs] *n* **(a)** *(inaction)* inactivité *f* **(b)**
(laziness) oisiveté *f*
idler ['aɪdlə(r)] *n (lazy person)* paresseux(euse) *m,f*
idly ['aɪdlɪ] *adv* **(a)** *(inactively)* sans rien faire **(b)**
(casually) négligemment
idol ['aɪdəl] *n* idole *f*
idolatry [aɪ'dɒlətrɪ] *n* idolâtrie *f*
idolize ['aɪdəlaɪz] *vt* idolâtrer
idyll ['ɪdɪl] *n (situation)* situation *f* idyllique; *(place)*
endroit *m* idyllique
idyllic [ɪ'dɪlɪk] *adj* idyllique
ie ['aɪ'iː] *(abbr* **id est)** c.-à-d.
if [ɪf] **1** *conj* **(a)** *(conditional)* si; **if I were rich...** si j'étais
riche...; **if I were you...** si j'étais toi..., à ta place
(b) *(conceding)* **the movie was good, if rather long** le
film était un peu long, mais bien; **if anything it's better**
c'est presque mieux
(c) *(whether)* si; **I asked if it was true** j'ai demandé si c'était
vrai
(d) *(in phrases)* **if not** sinon; **there were hundreds, if not
thousands, of people** il y avait des centaines de gens,
voire des milliers; **if so** si c'est le cas; **if only I had more
money...** si seulement j'avais plus d'argent...; **if and when
they arrive...** quand ils arriveront, s'ils arrivent...; **she
sees them rarely, if at all** *or* **if ever** elle ne les voit jamais,
ou alors très rarement
2 *n* **ifs and buts** restrictions *fpl*; **it's a big if** c'est un grand
point d'interrogation
iffy ['ɪfɪ] *adj Fam (doubtful)* incertain(e); *(suspect)* louche
igloo ['ɪgluː] *(pl* **igloos)** *n* igloo *m*
ignite [ɪg'naɪt] **1** *vt (fire)* allumer; *(paper)* enflammer; *Fig
(conflict)* déclencher
2 *vi (of fire)* prendre; *(of paper)* s'enflammer; *Fig (of conflict)*
se déclencher
ignition [ɪg'nɪʃən] *n (of car)* allumage *m*; **to switch on/
off the i.** mettre/couper le contact; **i. key** clé *f* de contact
ignoble [ɪg'nəʊbəl] *adj* ignoble
ignominious [ɪgnə'mɪnɪəs] *adj* ignominieux(euse)
ignoramus [ɪgnə'reɪməs] *n* ignorant(e) *m,f*, ignare *mf*
ignorance ['ɪgnərəns] *n* **(a)** *(lack of knowledge)* ignorance
f; **out of** *or* **through i.** par ignorance **(b)** *(ill manners)*
manque *m* d'éducation
ignorant ['ɪgnərənt] *adj* **(a)** *(lacking knowledge) (person)*

ignorant(e); *(remark)* d'ignorant; **to be i. of sth** ignorer qch
(b) *(ill-mannered)* mal élevé(e)
ignore [ɪg'nɔː(r)] *vt* ignorer; **just i. him!** ne fais pas
attention à lui!
iguana [ɪg'wɑːnə] *n* iguane *m*
ilk [ɪlk] *n* **of that i.** de ce genre
ill¹ [ɪl] **1** *npl* **ills** maux *mpl*
2 *adj* **(a)** *(unwell)* malade; **to feel i.** ne pas se sentir bien;
to fall *or* **be taken i.** tomber malade **(b)** *(bad, poor)* i.
effects effets *mpl* néfastes; **i. feeling** animosité *f*; **i.
fortune** malchance *f*; **to be in i. health** être en mauvaise
santé; **i. at ease** mal à l'aise; **of i. repute** mal famé(e); **i. will**
malveillance *f*; **I bear them no i. will** je ne leur en veux
pas
3 *adv* mal; **I can i. afford it** je peux difficilement me le
permettre; **to speak/think i. of sb** dire/penser du mal de
qn
ill² *(abbr* **illustration)** ill
I'll [aɪl] = **I will, I shall**
ill-advised ['ɪləd'vaɪzd] *adj (person)* malavisé(e),
(decision, comment) peu judicieux(euse); **to be i. to do sth**
être malavisé de faire qch
ill-bred ['ɪl'bred] *adj* mal élevé(e)
ill-concealed ['ɪlkən'siːld] *adj* mal dissimulé(e)
ill-considered ['ɪlkən'sɪdəd] *adj* irréfléchi(e)
ill-disposed ['ɪldɪs'pəʊzd] *adj* **to be i. towards sb/sth**
être mal disposé(e) envers qn/qch
illegal [ɪ'liːgəl] *adj* illégal(e); *(immigrant)* clandestin(e)
illegality [ɪlɪ'gælɪtɪ] *n* illégalité *f*
illegible [ɪ'ledʒɪbəl] *adj* illisible
illegitimate [ɪlɪ'dʒɪtɪmət] *adj* illégitime
ill-equipped ['ɪlɪ'kwɪpd] *adj* mal équipé(e); *Fig* **to be i.
to do sth** ne pas être apte à faire qch
ill-fated ['ɪl'feɪtɪd] *adj (day, occasion)* fatal(e); *(person,
enterprise)* malheureux(euse)
ill-founded ['ɪl'faʊndɪd] *adj* sans fondement
ill-gotten gains ['ɪlgɒtn'gaɪnz] *npl* biens *mpl* mal
acquis
illiberal [ɪ'lɪbərəl] *adj (person)* intolérant(e); *(measure)*
restrictif(ive)
illicit [ɪ'lɪsɪt] *adj* illicite
ill-informed [ɪlɪn'fɔːmd] *adj* mal informé(e); *(idea)*
inexact(e)
ill-intentioned ['ɪlɪn'tenʃənd] *adj* malintentionné(e)
illiteracy [ɪ'lɪtərəsɪ] *n* analphabétisme *m*
illiterate [ɪ'lɪtərət] **1** *n* analphabète *mf*
2 *adj* analphabète
ill-mannered ['ɪl'mænəd] *adj* grossier(ère)
ill-natured ['ɪl'neɪtʃəd] *adj* désagréable
illness ['ɪlnɪs] *n* maladie *f*
illogical [ɪ'lɒdʒɪkəl] *adj* illogique
ill-suited ['ɪl'suːtɪd] *adj* inapproprié(e) *(to* à); *(person)*
inapte **(to** à)
ill-tempered ['ɪl'tempəd] *adj (person)* qui a mauvais
caractère; *(remark)* désagréable
ill-timed ['ɪl'taɪmd] *adj* inopportun(e)
ill-treat ['ɪl'triːt] *vt* maltraiter
illuminate [ɪ'luːmɪneɪt] *vt* **(a)** *(light up) (room)* éclairer;
(building) illuminer **(b)** *(clarify)* éclairer
illuminating [ɪ'luːmɪneɪtɪŋ] *adj* éclairant(e)
illumination [ɪluːmɪ'neɪʃən] *n* **(a)** *(lighting)* éclairage *m*;
illuminations *(decorative lights)* illuminations *fpl* **(b)**
(clarification) éclaircissements *mpl*

ill-use 1 *n* ['ɪl'juːs] mauvais traitement *m*
2 *vt* ['il'juːz] maltraiter
illusion [ɪ'luːʒən] *n* illusion *f*; **to be under the i. that**...
s'imaginer que...; **to be under** or **have no illusions about sb/sth** ne se faire aucune illusion sur qn/qch
illusory [ɪ'luːsərɪ] *adj* illusoire
illustrate ['ɪləstreɪt] *vt* illustrer
illustration [ɪləs'treɪʃən] *n* illustration *f*
illustrator ['ɪləstreɪtə(r)] *n* illustrateur(trice) *m,f*
illustrious [ɪ'lʌstrɪəs] *adj* illustre
ILO [aɪe'ləʊ] *n* (*abbr* International Labour Organization) OIT *f*
I'm [aɪm] = I am
image ['ɪmɪdʒ] *n* image *f*; **to be the i. of sb** être le portrait de qn; **many people have the wrong i. of life in New York** beaucoup de gens se font une fausse idée de la vie à New York; **the company has an i. problem** l'entreprise a un problème d'image
imagery ['ɪmɪdʒərɪ] *n* imagerie *f*, images *fpl*
imaginary [ɪ'mædʒɪnərɪ] *adj* imaginaire
imagination [ɪmædʒɪ'neɪʃən] *n* imagination *f*; **it's (all in) your i.** tu te fais des idées
imaginative [ɪ'mædʒɪnətɪv] *adj* (*person*) imaginatif(ive); (*excuse, solution*) original(e)
imagine [ɪ'mædʒɪn] *vt* imaginer; **to i. doing sth** s'imaginer faire qch; **to i. sb doing sth** imaginer qn faisant qch; **I can't i. why**... je n'arrive pas à comprendre pourquoi...; **you're imagining things** tu te fais des idées; **you must have imagined it** tu as dû rêver
imbalance [ɪm'bæləns] *n* déséquilibre *m*
imbecile ['ɪmbɪsiːl] *n* imbécile *mf*
imbibe [ɪm'baɪb] *vt Formal* (*drink*) absorber; *Fig* (*knowledge, ideas*) absorber, assimiler
imbue [ɪm'bjuː] *vt Formal* **to i. sb with sth** imprégner qn de qch; **his words were imbued with resentment** ses paroles étaient pleines de ressentiment
IMF [aɪe'mef] *n* (*abbr* International Monetary Fund) FMI *m*
imitate ['ɪmɪteɪt] *vt* imiter
imitation [ɪmɪ'teɪʃən] *n* (*action, copy*) imitation *f*; **in i. of** à l'imitation de; **i. jewellery** faux bijoux *mpl*; **i. leather** similicuir *m*, imitation cuir
imitative ['ɪmɪtətɪv] *adj* imitatif(ive)
imitator ['ɪmɪteɪtə(r)] *n* imitateur(trice) *m,f*
immaculate [ɪ'mækjʊlət] *adj* impeccable; *Rel* **the I. Conception** l'Immaculée Conception *f*
immaterial [ɪmə'tɪərɪəl] *adj* sans importance
immature [ɪmə'tjʊə(r)] *adj* immature
immaturity [ɪmə'tjʊərɪtɪ] *n* immaturité *f*
immeasurable [ɪ'meʒərəbəl] *adj* incommensurable
immediacy [ɪ'miːdɪəsɪ] *n* immédiateté *f*; (*of danger, disaster*) imminence *f*
immediate [ɪ'miːdɪət] *adj* (**a**) (*instant*) immédiat(e); (*danger*) imminent(e) (**b**) (*nearest*) (*vicinity*) proche; (*future*) immédiat(e); **the i. family** les proches parents *mpl*
immediately [ɪ'miːdɪətlɪ] **1** *adv* immédiatement, tout de suite
2 *conj* dès que
immemorial [ɪmɪ'mɔːrɪəl] *adj* **from time i.** depuis des temps immémoriaux
immense [ɪ'mens] *adj* immense
immensely [ɪ'menslɪ] *adv* (*interesting, painful*) extrêmement; (*rich*) immensément; (*enjoy oneself*) énormément

immensity [ɪ'mensɪtɪ] *n* immensité *f*; (*of problem, task*) énormité *f*
immerse [ɪ'mɜːs] *vt also Fig* plonger (**in** dans); **to i. oneself in sth** se plonger dans qch
immigrant ['ɪmɪgrənt] *n & adj* immigré(e) *m,f*
immigrate ['ɪmɪgreɪt] *vi* immigrer
immigration [ɪmɪ'greɪʃən] *n* immigration *f*; **to go through i.** passer (à) l'immigration; **i. control** contrôle *m* de l'immigration; **i. officer** agent *m* des services de l'immigration
imminent ['ɪmɪnənt] *adj* imminent(e)
immobile [ɪ'məʊbaɪl] *adj* immobile
immobilize [ɪ'məʊbɪlaɪz] *vt* immobiliser
immoderate [ɪ'mɒdərət] *adj* immodéré(e)
immodest [ɪ'mɒdɪst] *adj* (*vain*) présomptueux(euse); (*indecent*) impudique
immoral [ɪ'mɒrəl] *adj* immoral(e); **i. earnings** gains *mpl* du proxénétisme
immorality [ɪmə'rælɪtɪ] *n* immoralité *f*
immortal [ɪ'mɔːtəl] **1** *n* immortel(elle) *m,f*
2 *adj* immortel(elle); (*memory*) impérissable
immortality [ɪmɔː'tælɪtɪ] *n* immortalité *f*
immovable [ɪ'muːvəbəl] *adj* (*object*) fixe; *Fig* (*person, opposition*) inébranlable
immune [ɪ'mjuːn] *adj* (*to disease*) immunisé(e) (**to** contre); *Fig* (*to criticism*) imperméable (**to** à); **i. from taxation** exonéré(e) d'impôts; *Med* **i. system** système *m* immunitaire
immunity [ɪ'mjuːnɪtɪ] *n* (*to disease*) immunité *f*; (*from taxation*) exonération *f*; *Law* **i. (from prosecution)** immunité
immunization [ɪmjʊnaɪ'zeɪʃən] *n* immunisation *f*
immunize ['ɪmjʊnaɪz] *vt* immuniser (**against** contre)
immutable [ɪ'mjuːtəbəl] *adj* immuable
imp [ɪmp] *n* (*sprite*) lutin *m*; *Fig* (*mischievous child*) garnement *m*
impact 1 *n* ['ɪmpækt] impact *m*; **to make an i. on sb/sth** avoir un impact sur qn/qch; **on i.** au moment de l'impact
2 *vt* [ɪm'pækt] (*collide with*) heurter; (*influence*) avoir un impact sur
impacted [ɪm'pæktɪd] *adj* (*tooth*) inclus(e)
impair [ɪm'peə(r)] *vt* (*sight, hearing*) affaiblir; (*relations, chances*) compromettre
impale [ɪm'peɪl] *vt* empaler (**on** sur)
impart [ɪm'pɑːt] *vt Formal* (*heat, quality*) donner; (*knowledge, news*) transmettre
impartial [ɪm'pɑːʃəl] *adj* impartial(e)
impartiality [ɪmpɑːʃɪ'ælɪtɪ] *n* impartialité *f*
impassable [ɪm'pɑːsəbəl] *adj* (*river, barrier*) infranchissable; (*road*) impraticable
impasse ['æmpɑːs] *n* impasse *f*; **to have reached an i.** être dans une impasse
impassioned [ɪm'pæʃənd] *adj* passionné(e)
impassive [ɪm'pæsɪv] *adj* impassible
impassively [ɪm'pæsɪvlɪ] *adv* impassiblement
impatience [ɪm'peɪʃəns] *n* impatience *f*
impatient [ɪm'peɪʃənt] *adj* impatient(e); **to be i. to do sth** être impatient de faire qch; **to be i. for sth** avoir soif de qch; **to get i. (with sb)** s'impatienter (contre qn)
impatiently [ɪm'peɪʃəntlɪ] *adv* avec impatience
impeach [ɪm'piːtʃ] *vt Am Law* mettre en accusation (*selon la procédure qui vise les hauts fonctionnaires américains*)
impeccable [ɪm'pekəbəl] *adj* impeccable

impede [ɪm'piːd] *vt* gêner

impediment [ɪm'pedɪmənt] *n* (a) *(obstacle)* obstacle *m* (b) *(disability)* handicap *m*

impel [ɪm'pel] *(pt & pp* **impelled***) vt* (a) *(oblige)* obliger; *(incite)* pousser (b) *(push)* propulser

impending [ɪm'pendɪŋ] *adj* imminent(e)

impenetrable [ɪm'penɪtrəbəl] *adj (defences, mystery)* impénétrable; *(jargon)* incompréhensible

imperative [ɪm'perətɪv] **1** *n Gram* impératif *m*; **in the i.** à l'impératif **2** *adj* impératif(ive); **it is i. that he should come** il faut impérativement qu'il vienne

imperceptible [ɪmpə'septɪbəl] *adj* imperceptible

imperfect [ɪm'pɜːfɪkt] **1** *n Gram* **the i.** l'imparfait *m*; **in the i.** à l'imparfait **2** *adj (not perfect)* imparfait(e); *Gram* de l'imparfait; **i. tense** imparfait *m*

imperfection [ɪmpə'fekʃən] *n* imperfection *f*

Imperial [ɪm'pɪərɪəl] *adj* (a) *(of empire)* impérial(e) (b) *(weights and measures)* = relatif au système de mesure anglo-saxon utilisant les miles, les pints etc

imperialism [ɪm'pɪərɪəlɪzəm] *n* impérialisme *m*

imperialist [ɪm'pɪərɪəlɪst] *n & adj* impérialiste *mf*

imperil [ɪm'perɪl] *(pt & pp* **imperilled***, Am* **imperiled***) vt* mettre en péril

imperious [ɪm'pɪərɪəs] *adj* impérieux(euse)

impermanent [ɪm'pɜːmənənt] *adj* temporaire

impersonal [ɪm'pɜːsənəl] *adj* impersonnel(elle)

impersonate [ɪm'pɜːsəneɪt] *vt (pretend to be)* se faire passer pour; *(imitate)* imiter

impersonation [ɪmpɜːsə'neɪʃən] *n (pretence of being)* usurpation *f* d'identité; *(imitation)* imitation *f*

impersonator [ɪm'pɜːsəneɪtə(r)] *n (impostor)* imposteur *m*; *(mimic)* imitateur(trice) *m,f*

impertinence [ɪm'pɜːtɪnəns] *n* impertinence *f*

impertinent [ɪm'pɜːtɪnənt] *adj* impertinent(e)

imperturbable [ɪmpə'tɜːbəbəl] *adj* imperturbable

impervious [ɪm'pɜːvɪəs] *adj also Fig* imperméable **(to** à)

impetuous [ɪm'petjʊəs] *adj* impétueux(euse)

impetus ['ɪmpɪtəs] *n* élan *m*

▸ **impinge on** [ɪm'pɪndʒ] *vt insep* affecter, avoir un effet sur

impious ['ɪmpɪəs] *adj* impie

impish ['ɪmpɪʃ] *adj* espiègle

implacable [ɪm'plækəbəl] *adj* implacable

implant 1 *n* ['ɪmplɑːnt] *Med* implant *m* **2** *vt* [ɪm'plɑːnt] (a) *Med* implanter (b) *(opinion, belief)* inculquer

implausible [ɪm'plɔːzɪbəl] *adj* peu plausible, invraisemblable

implement 1 *n* ['ɪmplɪmənt] instrument *m*; *(for cooking)* ustensile *m*; *(for gardening, home improvements)* outil *m* **2** *vt* ['ɪmplɪment] *(plan, agreement)* mettre en application

implementation [ɪmplɪmen'teɪʃən] *n (of plan, agreement)* mise *f* en œuvre, application *f*

implicate ['ɪmplɪkeɪt] *vt* impliquer

implication [ɪmplɪ'keɪʃən] *n* implication *f*; **by i.** implicitement

implicit [ɪm'plɪsɪt] *adj* (a) *(implied)* implicite; **it was i. in her remarks** c'était implicite dans ses remarques (b) *(absolute)* absolu(e); **i. faith** confiance *f* aveugle

implied [ɪm'plaɪd] *adj* implicite

implore [ɪm'plɔː(r)] *vt* implorer; **to i. sb to do sth** implorer qn de faire qch

imploring [ɪm'plɔːrɪŋ] *adj* implorant(e)

imply [ɪm'plaɪ] *(pt & pp* **implied***) vt* (a) *(insinuate)* insinuer, sous-entendre (b) *(involve)* impliquer; *(presuppose)* supposer

impolite [ɪmpə'laɪt] *adj* impoli(e)

impoliteness [ɪmpə'laɪtnɪs] *n* impolitesse *f*

imponderable [ɪm'pɒndərəbəl] **1** *n* impondérable *m* **2** *adj* impondérable

import 1 *n* ['ɪmpɔːt] (a) *(item, activity)* importation *f*; **i. duty** droit *m* de douane à l'importation (b) *Formal (importance)* importance *f* **2** *vt* [ɪm'pɔːt] *also Comptr* importer

importance [ɪm'pɔːtəns] *n* importance *f*; **of the utmost i.** de la plus haute importance; **it is of no great i.** ça n'a pas grande importance; **to attach i. to sth** attacher de l'importance à qch; **to be full of one's own i.** être important pour qn; **to become more i.** prendre de l'importance; **it's not i.** c'est sans importance

important [ɪm'pɔːtənt] *adj* important(e); **to be i. to sb** être important pour qn; **to become more i.** prendre de l'importance; **it's not i.** c'est sans importance

importantly [ɪm'pɔːtəntlɪ] *adv (speak)* d'un air important; **but, more i....** mais, plus important...

importation [ɪmpɔː'teɪʃən] *n* importation *f*

importer [ɪm'pɔːtə(r)] *n* importateur(trice) *m,f*

import-export ['ɪmpɔːt'ekspɔːt] *n* **i.** (trade) import-export *m*

importune [ɪm'pɔːtjuːn] *vt Formal* importuner

impose [ɪm'pəʊz] **1** *vt (silence, one's will, restrictions)* imposer **(on** à); **to i.** a **tax on sth** taxer qch; **to i.** a **fine on sb** condamner qn à (payer) une amende **2** *vi (take advantage)* s'imposer

▸ **impose on, impose upon** *vt insep (take advantage of)* abuser de; **to i. on** *or* **upon sb** abuser de la gentillesse de qn

imposing [ɪm'pəʊzɪŋ] *adj* imposant(e)

imposition [ɪmpə'zɪʃən] *n* (a) *(of tax, fine)* imposition *f* (b) *(unfair demand)* **it was a bit of an i.** il y avait de l'abus

impossibility [ɪmpɒsɪ'bɪlɪtɪ] *(pl* **impossibilities***) n* impossibilité *f*; **it's a physical i.** c'est matériellement impossible

impossible [ɪm'pɒsɪbəl] **1** *n* **the i.** l'impossible *m*; **to do/achieve the i.** faire/réussir l'impossible **2** *adj* impossible; **to make it i. for sb to do sth** mettre qn dans l'impossibilité de faire qch

impossibly [ɪm'pɒsɪblɪ] *adv (extremely)* incroyablement

impostor [ɪm'pɒstə(r)] *n* imposteur *m*

impotence ['ɪmpətəns] *n* impuissance *f*

impotent ['ɪmpətənt] *adj* impuissant(e)

impound [ɪm'paʊnd] *vt Law* saisir; *(car)* mettre à la fourrière

impoverish [ɪm'pɒvərɪʃ] *vt* appauvrir

impoverished [ɪm'pɒvərɪʃd] *adj* appauvri(e)

impracticable [ɪm'præktɪkəbəl] *adj* impraticable, irréalisable

impractical [ɪm'præktɪkəl] *adj (suggestion)* irréaliste; *(person)* qui manque de sens pratique

imprecise [ɪmprɪ'saɪs] *adj* imprécis(e)

imprecision [ɪmprɪ'sɪʒən] *n* imprécision *f*

impregnable [ɪm'pregnəbəl] *adj (fortress)* imprenable; *Fig (argument)* irréfutable, inattaquable

impregnate ['ɪmpregneɪt] *vt* (a) *(fertilize)* féconder (b) *(soak)* imprégner **(with** de)

impresario [ˌɪmpreˈsɑːrɪəʊ] (pl **impresarios** or **impresari** [ˌɪmpreˈsɑːriː]) n imprésario m

impress [ɪmˈpres] vt (a) (make an impression on) impressionner; **to be impressed with** or **by sb/sth** être impressionné(e) par qn/qch; **I'm not in the least impressed** ça ne m'impressione pas du tout (b) (emphasize) **to i. sth on sb** faire comprendre qch à qn (c) (imprint) **to i. sth on sth** imprimer qch sur qch

impression [ɪmˈpreʃən] n (a) (effect) impression f; **to make an i. on sb** marquer qn; **to make an i. on sth** avoir un impact sur qch; **to make a good/bad i. (on sb)** faire bonne/mauvaise impression (à qn); **to create a false i.** donner une fausse impression; **to be under the i. that...** avoir l'impression que...; **to give the i. that...** donner l'impression que... (b) (imprint) (in wax, snow) empreinte f (c) (of book) réimpression f (d) (imitation) imitation f; **to do impressions** faire des imitations; **to do an i. of sb** imiter qn

impressionable [ɪmˈpreʃənəbəl] adj impressionnable

impressionism [ɪmˈpreʃənɪzəm] n Art impressionnisme m

impressionist [ɪmˈpreʃənɪst] **1** n (a) Art impressionniste mf (b) (mimic) imitateur(trice) m,f **2** adj Art impressionniste

impressionistic [ˌɪmpreʃəˈnɪstɪk] adj vague

impressive [ɪmˈpresɪv] adj impressionnant(e)

imprint 1 n [ˈɪmprɪnt] empreinte f **2** vt [ɪmˈprɪnt] imprimer (**on** sur); **her words are imprinted on my memory** ses mots restent gravés dans ma mémoire

imprison [ɪmˈprɪzən] vt emprisonner

imprisonment [ɪmˈprɪzənmənt] n emprisonnement m; **sentenced to six months' i.** condamné à six mois de prison

improbability [ɪmˌprɒbəˈbɪlɪtɪ] (pl **improbabilities**) n improbabilité f

improbable [ɪmˈprɒbəbəl] adj (unlikely) improbable; (unbelievable) invraisemblable

impromptu [ɪmˈprɒmptjuː] **1** adj (speech, party) improvisé(e) **2** adv (unexpectedly) à l'improviste; (ad lib) au pied levé

improper [ɪmˈprɒpə(r)] adj (a) (use, purpose) mauvais(e); (behaviour) déplacé(e); Law **i. practices** pratiques fpl malhonnêtes (b) (lewd) indécent(e)

impropriety [ˌɪmprəˈpraɪətɪ] n inconvenance f; (of language) impropriété f

improve [ɪmˈpruːv] **1** vt améliorer; (invention, technique) perfectionner; **to i. one's mind** se cultiver **2** vi s'améliorer; (of business) reprendre
▸ **improve on, improve upon** vt insep améliorer; **to i. on a bid** surenchérir

improved [ɪmˈpruːvd] adj (system, design) perfectionné(e)

improvement [ɪmˈpruːvmənt] n amélioration f (**in** de); (of invention, technique) perfectionnement m; **to be an i. on** être meilleur(e) que; **there's room for i.** on peut faire mieux; **to make improvements (to a house)** faire des travaux d'aménagement (dans une maison)

improvident [ɪmˈprɒvɪdənt] adj Formal (person) imprévoyant(e)

improvisation [ˌɪmprəvaɪˈzeɪʃən] n improvisation f

improvise [ˈɪmprəvaɪz] vt & vi improviser

imprudent [ɪmˈpruːdənt] adj imprudent(e)

impudence [ˈɪmpjʊdəns] n impudence f, insolence f

impudent [ˈɪmpjʊdənt] adj impudent(e), insolent(e)

impugn [ɪmˈpjuːn] vt Formal mettre en doute

impulse [ˈɪmpʌls] n impulsion f; **to feel an i. to do sth** avoir une soudaine envie de faire qch; **on i.** sur un coup de tête; **I bought it on i.** je l'ai acheté sur un coup de tête; **i. buying** achat m d'impulsion

impulsive [ɪmˈpʌlsɪv] adj impulsif(ive)

impunity [ɪmˈpjuːnɪtɪ] n impunité f; **with i.** en toute impunité

impure [ɪmˈpjʊə(r)] adj impur(e)

impurity [ɪmˈpjʊərɪtɪ] (pl **impurities**) n impureté f

impute [ɪmˈpjuːt] vt Formal **to i. sth to sb** imputer ou attribuer qch à qn

in [ɪn] **1** prep (a) (with place) dans; **in the garden** dans le jardin; **in France** en France; **in Japan** au Japon; **in the USA** aux États-Unis; **in Paris** à Paris; **in hospital** à l'hôpital; **in town** en ville; **in bed** au lit; **in here** ici; **in there** là (b) (with expressions of time) **in 1927/April** en 1927/avril; **in (the) spring** au printemps; **in (the) summer** en été; **in the afternoon** l'après-midi; **in the 70s** dans les années 70 (c) (expressing manner) **in French** en français; **to write in pen** écrire au stylo; **in a loud voice** d'une voix forte; **in this way** ainsi, de cette façon (d) (within, during) **she did it in three hours** elle l'a fait en trois heures; **he'll be here in three hours** il sera ici dans trois heures; **I haven't seen him in years** ça fait des années que je ne l'ai pas vu (e) (with situation, arrangement) **in the rain** sous la pluie; **in the sun** au soleil; **dressed in white** habillé(e) en blanc; **in danger** en danger; **in twos** deux par deux; **in a circle/line** en rond/rang (f) (with numbers, quantities, ratios) **one in ten** un sur dix; **in small/large quantities** en petite/grande quantité; **2 metres in length/height/width** 2 mètres de long/de haut/de large; **she's in her sixties** elle a la soixantaine; **the temperature was in the nineties** ≃ il faisait dans les trente degrés (g) (with gerund) **to have no difficulty in doing sth** ne pas avoir de mal à faire qch; **in saying this...** en disant cela... (h) (with field of activity) **to be in insurance/publishing** être dans les assurances/l'édition (i) (idioms) **I didn't think she had it in her to...** je n'aurais pas cru capable de... **2** adv (a) (inside) dedans; **to go in** entrer, rentrer (b) (not out) là; **is your mother in?** est-ce que ta mère est là?; **to stay in** (at home) rester à la maison (c) **to be in** (of plane, train) être arrivé(e) (d) (fashionable) à la mode (e) **in that...** puisque..., vu que... (f) (idioms) **to be in for it** en vouloir à qn; **she's in for a shock/surprise** elle va avoir un choc/une surprise; **to be in on a plan/secret** être dans le coup; **he's in for it** ça va être la guerre **3** adj **the in crowd** les branchés mpl **4** n **the ins and outs** (of question) les tenants mpl et les aboutissants; (of plot) les subtilités fpl

inability [ˌɪnəˈbɪlɪtɪ] n incapacité f (**to do sth** à faire qch)

inaccessibility [ˌɪnəksesɪˈbɪlɪtɪ] n inaccessibilité f

inaccessible [ˌɪnækˈsesɪbəl] adj inaccessible (**to** à)

inaccuracy [ɪnˈækjʊrəsɪ] (pl **inaccuracies**) n (of estimate, translation, report) inexactitude f; (of rifle, instrument) manque m de précision

inaccurate [ɪnˈækjʊrət] adj (estimate, translation, report) inexact(e); (rifle, instrument) qui manque de précision

inaction [ɪnˈækʃən] n inaction f

inactive [ɪnˈæktɪv] adj inactif(ive)

inactivity [ɪnæk'tɪvɪtɪ] n inactivité f
inadequacy [ɪn'ædɪkwəsɪ] (pl **inadequacies**) n insuffisance f; **a feeling of i.** un complexe d'infériorité
inadequate [ɪn'ædɪkwət] adj insuffisant(e); **to feel i.** ne pas se sentir à la hauteur
inadmissible [ɪnəd'mɪsɪbəl] adj Law (evidence) irrecevable
inadvertent [ɪnəd'vɜːtənt] adj involontaire
inadvertently [ɪnəd'vɜːtəntlɪ] adv par inadvertance
inadvisable [ɪnəd'vaɪzəbəl] adj déconseillé(e)
inalienable [ɪn'eɪlɪənəbəl] adj Formal inaliénable
inane [ɪ'neɪn] adj idiot(e), stupide
inanimate [ɪn'ænɪmət] adj inanimé(e)
inanity [ɪ'nænɪtɪ] n ineptie f
inapplicable [ɪn'æplɪkəbəl] adj inapplicable (**to** à); **delete where i.** (sign) rayer la mention inutile
inappropriate [ɪnə'prəʊprɪət] adj (behaviour, remark) déplacé(e); (dress) peu approprié(e) (**to** à); (time) inopportun(e)
inapt [ɪn'æpt] adj peu approprié(e)
inarticulate [ɪnɑː'tɪkjʊlɪt] adj (sound) inarticulé(e); **to be i.** (of person) avoir du mal à s'exprimer; **to be i. with rage** bégayer de rage
inasmuch as [ɪnəz'mʌtʃəz] conj Formal dans la mesure où
inattention [ɪnə'tenʃən] n inattention f
inattentive [ɪnə'tentɪv] adj inattentif(ive) (**to** à)
inaudible [ɪn'ɔːdɪbəl] adj inaudible
inaugural [ɪ'nɔːgjʊrəl] adj inaugural(e)
inaugurate [ɪ'nɔːgjʊreɪt] vt (building, exhibition) inaugurer; (president) investir
inauguration [ɪnɔːgjʊ'reɪʃən] n (of building, exhibition) inauguration f; (of president) investiture f
inauspicious [ɪnɔːs'pɪʃəs] adj peu propice; **to get off to an i. start** mal commencer
inauthentic [ɪnɔː'θentɪk] adj inauthentique
in-between [ɪnbɪ'twiːn] adj intermédiaire
inborn ['ɪnbɔːn] adj inné(e)
inbred ['ɪnbred] adj (person) de parents consanguins; (distrust, confidence) inné(e)
in-built ['ɪnbɪlt] adj (trait) inhérent(e); **his height gives him an i. advantage** sa taille lui donne un avantage dès le départ
Inc [ɪŋk] adj (abbr **Incorporated**) ≃ SARL
Inca ['ɪŋkə] **1** n Inca mf
2 adj inca
incalculable [ɪn'kælkjʊləbəl] adj (consequences, damage) incalculable; (help, value) inestimable
incandescent [ɪnkæn'desənt] adj incandescent(e); Fig **i. with rage** fou (folle) de rage
incantation [ɪnkæn'teɪʃən] n incantation f
incapable [ɪn'keɪpəbəl] adj incapable (**of** de); (through illness) impotent(e); (through drink) ivre mort(e); **to be i. of doing sth** être incapable de faire qch
incapacitate [ɪnkə'pæsɪteɪt] vt rendre impotent(e); **to be incapacitated for work** être inapte au travail
incapacity [ɪnkə'pæsɪtɪ] n incapacité f; **i. to do sth** incapacité à faire qch
incarcerate [ɪn'kɑːsəreɪt] vt Formal incarcérer
incarceration [ɪnkɑːsə'reɪʃən] n Formal incarcération f
incarnate [ɪn'kɑːneɪt] adj incarné(e)
incarnation [ɪnkɑː'neɪʃən] n incarnation f; **in a previous i.** dans une vie antérieure

incautious [ɪn'kɔːʃəs] adj imprudent(e)
incendiary [ɪn'sendɪərɪ] **1** n (pl **incendiaries**) (arsonist) incendiaire mf; (bomb) bombe f incendiaire
2 adj also Fig incendiaire
incense¹ ['ɪnsens] n encens m
incense² [ɪn'sens] vt (anger) rendre furieux(euse)
incentive [ɪn'sentɪv] n (stimulus) motivation f; (payment) prime f; **he has no i. to work harder** rien ne le motive à travailler plus dur; **i. scheme** (for workers) système m de primes
inception [ɪn'sepʃən] n début m
incessant [ɪn'sesənt] adj incessant(e)
incest ['ɪnsest] n inceste m
incestuous [ɪn'sestjʊəs] adj incestueux(euse); Fig (environment, group) très fermé(e)
inch [ɪntʃ] n (a) (unit of measurement) = 2,54 cm, pouce m; **i. by i.** petit à petit, peu à peu (b) (idioms) **I know every i. of this town** je connais cette ville comme ma poche; **he's every i. the gentleman** c'est le parfait gentleman; **to miss sth by inches** manquer qch d'un cheveu; **to be within an i. of doing sth** être à deux doigts de faire qch; **she won't give an i.** elle ne cédera pas d'un pouce; **give her an i. and she'll take a mile** tu lui en donnes jusqu'au coude, elle en demande long comme le bras
▸ **inch along, inch forward** vi avancer tout doucement
incidence ['ɪnsɪdəns] n (frequency) taux m; (of disease) incidence f
incident ['ɪnsɪdənt] n incident m; (in book, film) scène f; **the meeting went off without i.** la réunion s'est déroulée sans incident
incidental [ɪnsɪ'dentəl] adj (minor) accessoire (**to** par rapport à); **i. expenses** faux frais mpl; **i. music** (in film) musique f
incidentally [ɪnsɪ'dentəlɪ] adv (by the way) au fait
incinerate [ɪn'sɪnəreɪt] vt incinérer, Fig carboniser
incineration [ɪnsɪnə'reɪʃən] n incinération f
incinerator [ɪn'sɪnəreɪtə(r)] n incinérateur m
incipient [ɪn'sɪpɪənt] adj Formal naissant(e)
incision [ɪn'sɪʒən] n incision f
incisive [ɪn'saɪsɪv] adj incisif(ive)
incisor [ɪn'saɪzə(r)] n incisive f
incite [ɪn'saɪt] vt (violence, unrest) inciter à; **to i. sb to do sth** inciter qn à faire qch
incitement [ɪn'saɪtmənt] n incitation f (**to** à)
inclement [ɪn'klemənt] adj Formal (weather) inclément(e)
inclination [ɪnklɪ'neɪʃən] n (a) (liking) inclination f, penchant m (**for** pour); (desire) envie f; **to have an i. to do sth** avoir envie de faire qch (b) (tendency) tendance f (**towards** à); **to have an i. to do sth** avoir tendance à faire qch; **by i.** de ou par nature (c) (angle) inclinaison f
incline 1 n ['ɪnklaɪn] (slope) pente f
2 vt [ɪn'klaɪn] (**a**) (cause) to **i. sb to do sth** inciter qn à faire qch (**b**) (lean) **to i. one's head** incliner la tête (c) **to be inclined to do sth** (tend) avoir tendance à faire qch; **I'm inclined to agree** j'aurais tendance à être d'accord
3 vi [ɪn'klaɪn] (lean) s'incliner; (tend) **to i.** to ou **towards** pencher pour; **to i. to the belief that...** être porté(e) à croire que…
include [ɪn'kluːd] vt inclure, comprendre; (in letter) joindre; **the price does not i. sales tax** la TVA n'est pas comprise dans le prix; **my duties i. sorting the mail** trier le courrier entre dans mes attributions
including [ɪn'kluːdɪŋ] prep y compris; **seven not i. the children** sept sans compter les enfants

inclusion [ɪn'kluːʒən] *n* inclusion *f*

inclusive [ɪn'kluːsɪv] *adj (price, sum)* net, nette; **to be i.** of comprendre; **i. of sales tax** TVA comprise; **from February 4 to 12 i.** du 4 au 12 février inclus

incognito [ɪnkɒg'niːtəʊ] *adv* incognito

incoherence [ɪnkəʊ'hɪərəns] *n* incohérence *f*

incoherent [ɪnkəʊ'hɪərənt] *adj* incohérent(e)

income ['ɪnkəm] *n* revenu *m*; **i. tax** impôt *m* sur le revenu

incoming ['ɪnkʌmɪŋ] *adj (government, president)* nouveau(elle); *(plane, train, mail)* à l'arrivée; montant(e); *(phone call)* de l'extérieur; *(tide)* montant(e)

incommensurate [ɪnkə'menʃərɪt] *adj* **to be i. with** ne pas être proportionné(e) à

incommunicado [ɪnkəmjuːnɪ'kɑːdəʊ] *adj (uncontactable)* injoignable

in-company ['ɪnkʌmpənɪ] *adj* **i. training** formation *f* sur le lieu de travail

incomparable [ɪn'kɒmpərəbəl] *adj* incomparable

incompatible [ɪnkəm'pætɪbəl] *adj* incompatible (**with** avec)

incompetence [ɪn'kɒmpɪtəns] *n* incompétence *f*

incompetent [ɪn'kɒmpɪtənt] *adj* incompétent(e)

incomplete [ɪnkəm'pliːt] *adj* **(a)** *(not whole)* incomplet(ète) **(b)** *(not finished)* inachevé(e)

incomprehensible [ɪnkɒmprɪ'hensɪbəl] *adj* incompréhensible

incomprehension [ɪnkɒmprɪ'henʃən] *n* incompréhension *f*

inconceivable [ɪnkən'siːvəbəl] *adj* inconcevable

inconclusive [ɪnkən'kluːsɪv] *adj (evidence, results)* peu concluant(e); **the results are i.** les résultats sont peu concluants

incongruity [ɪnkɒŋ'gruːɪtɪ] *(pl* **incongruities)** *n* incongruité *f*

incongruous [ɪn'kɒŋgrʊəs] *adj* incongru(e)

inconsequential [ɪnkɒnsɪ'kwenʃəl] *adj* insignifiant(e), sans importance

inconsiderate [ɪnkən'sɪdərɪt] *adj (person)* sans égards pour les autres; *(remark)* déplacé(e); **it was i.** of you not to invite them ce n'est pas gentil de ta part de ne pas l'avoir invitée

inconsistency [ɪnkən'sɪstənsɪ] *(pl* **inconsistencies)** *n (in argument)* incohérence *f*; *(between reports, descriptions)* contradiction *f*; *(uneven quality)* irrégularité *f*

inconsistent [ɪnkən'sɪstənt] *adj (person)* incohérent(e); *(uneven)* irrégulier(ère); **to be i. with** ne pas concorder *ou* cadrer avec

inconsolable [ɪnkən'səʊləbəl] *adj* inconsolable

inconspicuous [ɪnkən'spɪkjʊəs] *adj* qui passe inaperçu(e)

incontestable [ɪnkən'testəbəl] *adj* incontestable

incontinence [ɪn'kɒntɪnəns] *n* incontinence *f*

incontinent [ɪn'kɒntɪnənt] *adj* incontinent(e)

incontrovertible [ɪnkɒntrə'vɜːtɪbəl] *adj Formal* incontestable

inconvenience [ɪnkən'viːnjəns] **1** *n* désagrément *m*; **to be an i. to sb** déranger qn; **we apologize for any i.** nous vous prions de nous excuser pour tout désagrément éventuel

2 *vt* déranger

inconvenient [ɪnkən'viːnjənt] *adj (time)* mauvais(e); *(place, arrangement)* peu commode; **it's a bit i. just now** ça ne tombe pas très bien en ce moment

incorporate [ɪn'kɔːpəreɪt] *vt* incorporer; *(have as quality)* comprendre

incorrect [ɪnkə'rekt] *adj* incorrect(e)

incorrigible [ɪn'kɒrɪdʒɪbəl] *adj* incorrigible

incorruptible [ɪnkə'rʌptɪbəl] *adj* incorruptible

increase 1 *n* ['ɪnkriːs] *(in price, rate, sales)* augmentation *f*, hausse *f* (**in** de); *(in salary)* augmentation (de salaire); *(in pain, population)* accroissement *m* (**in** de); **to be on the i.** être en hausse

2 *vt* [ɪn'kriːs] augmenter; **to i. one's efforts** redoubler d'efforts; **to i. one's speed** accélérer

3 *vi* [ɪn'kriːs] augmenter; **to i. in price** augmenter; **to i. in value** prendre de la valeur

increasing [ɪn'kriːsɪŋ] *adj* croissant(e)

increasingly [ɪn'kriːsɪŋlɪ] *adv* de plus en plus

incredible [ɪn'kredɪbəl] *adj* **(a)** *(unbelievable)* incroyable **(b)** *Fam (excellent)* génial(e)

incredibly [ɪn'kredɪblɪ] *adv* **(a)** *(extremely)* incroyablement; *Fam* **i. good** génial(e) **(b)** *(unbelievably)* **i.**, no one was hurt aussi incroyable que cela puisse paraître, personne n'a été blessé

incredulous [ɪn'kredjʊləs] *adj* incrédule

increment ['ɪnkrɪmənt] *n* augmentation *f*

incriminate [ɪn'krɪmɪneɪt] *vt* incriminer, mettre en cause

incriminating [ɪn'krɪmɪneɪtɪŋ] *adj* compromettant(e); **i. evidence** pièces *fpl* à conviction

incubate ['ɪnkjʊbeɪt] *vt (of bird)* couver; *(baby)* mettre en couveuse

incubation [ɪnkjʊ'beɪʃən] *n* incubation *f*; *Med* **i. period** *(of infection)* durée *f* d'incubation

incubator ['ɪnkjʊbeɪtə(r)] *n (for babies)* couveuse *f*; *(for eggs)* incubateur *m*

inculcate ['ɪnkʌlkeɪt] *vt Formal* **to i. sth in sb, to i. sb with sth** inculquer qch à qn

incumbent [ɪn'kʌmbənt] **1** *n* **the present i. (of the presidency)** le président en exercice

2 *adj* **it is i. on sb to do sth** il incombe *ou* appartient à qn de faire qch

incur [ɪn'kɜː(r)] *(pt & pp* **incurred)** *vt (blame, expense)* encourir; *(loss)* subir; *(risk)* courir; *(person's anger)* s'attirer; *(debt)* contracter

incurable [ɪn'kjʊərəbəl] *adj also Fig* incurable

incursion [ɪn'kɜːʃən] *n Formal* incursion *f*

indebted [ɪn'detɪd] *adj (financially)* endetté(e); *(for help, advice)* redevable (**to** à); **I am i. to my family for all their support** je suis reconnaissant à ma famille pour son soutien

indebtedness [ɪn'detɪdnɪs] *n (financial)* endettement *m*; *(for help, advice)* dette *f* (**to** envers)

indecency [ɪn'diːsənsɪ] *n* indécence *f*; *Law* attentat *m* à la pudeur

indecent [ɪn'diːsənt] *adj* indécent(e); **to do sth with i. haste** mettre un empressement déplacé à faire qch; *Law* **i. assault** attentat *m* à la pudeur; *Law* **i. exposure** outrage *m* public à la pudeur

indecipherable [ɪndɪ'saɪfərəbəl] *adj* indéchiffrable

indecision [ɪndɪ'sɪʒən] *n* indécision *f*

indecisive [ɪndɪ'saɪsɪv] *adj (person)* indécis(e); *(battle, election)* à l'issue peu claire

indecorous [ɪn'dekərəs] *adj Formal* peu digne

indeed [ɪn'diːd] *adv* **(a)** *(used with 'very')* vraiment; **very big i.** vraiment très grand; **thank you very much i.** merci mille fois

(b) *(in confirmation)* en effet, effectivement; *(certainly)* certainement; **there was i. a problem** il y avait effectivement un problème **(c)** *(what's more)* en fait, et même; **I think so, I. I'm sure of it** je pense que oui, en fait j'en suis sûr **(d)** *(expressing ironic surprise)* **have you i.?** vraiment?

indefatigable [ˌɪndɪˈfætɪgəbəl] *adj Formal* infatigable

indefensible [ˌɪndɪˈfensɪbəl] *adj (behaviour, attitude)* injustifiable, impardonnable; *(theory)* indéfendable

indefinable [ˌɪndɪˈfaɪnəbəl] *adj* indéfinissable

indefinite [ɪnˈdefɪnɪt] *adj* **(a)** *(period of time, number)* indéterminé(e) **(b)** *(idea, plan)* mal défini(e) **(c)** *Gram* indéfini(e)

indefinitely [ɪnˈdefɪnɪtlɪ] *adv* indéfiniment

indelible [ɪnˈdelɪbəl] *adj also Fig* indélébile

indelicate [ɪnˈdelɪkət] *adj* indélicat(e)

indemnify [ɪnˈdemnɪfaɪ] *(pt & pp* **indemnified)** *vt* **i. sb for sth** *(compensate)* indemniser *ou* dédommager qn de qch; **to i. sb against sth** *(give security)* assurer qn contre qch

indemnity [ɪnˈdemnɪtɪ] *(pl* **indemnities)** *n (guarantee)* garantie *f*, assurance *f*; *(money)* indemnité *f*, dédommagement *m*

Indent *Typ* **1** *n* [ˈɪndent] alinéa *m* **2** *vt* [ɪnˈdent] mettre en retrait

indentation [ˌɪndenˈteɪʃən] *n (mark)* trace *f*, empreinte *f*; *(in coastline)* découpure *f*; *Typ* alinéa *m*

independence [ˌɪndɪˈpendəns] *n* indépendance *f* **(from** par rapport à); **I. Day** fête *f* nationale de l'Indépendance *(aux États-Unis)*

independent [ˌɪndɪˈpendənt] *adj* indépendant(e) **(of** de); *Br* **i. school** école *f* privée

independently [ˌɪndɪˈpendəntlɪ] *adv* indépendamment; **i. of** indépendamment de; **to live i.** être indépendant(e)

In-depth [ˈɪndepθ] *adj* approfondi(e), en profondeur

indescribable [ˌɪndɪsˈkraɪbəbəl] *adj* indescriptible

indestructible [ˌɪndɪsˈtrʌktəbəl] *adj* indestructible

indeterminate [ˌɪndɪˈtɜːmɪnət] *adj* indéterminé(e)

index [ˈɪndeks] **1** *n (of book)* index *m*; *(in library)* fichier *m*; **i. finger** index **2** *vt* **(a)** *(book)* dresser l'index de **(b)** *Fin (wages)* indexer *(to* sur)

index-linked [ˈɪndeksˈlɪŋkt] *adj Fin* indexé(e)

India [ˈɪndɪə] *n* l'Inde *f*

Indian [ˈɪndɪən] **1** *n* Indien(enne) *m,f* **2** *adj* indien(enne); **I. elephant** éléphant *m* d'Asie; **in I. file** en file indienne; **the I. Ocean** l'océan *m* Indien; **I. summer** été *m* indien

indicate [ˈɪndɪkeɪt] **1** *vt* **(a)** *(point to, show)* indiquer **(b)** *(intention, opposition, willingness)* signaler **2** *vi (of car driver)* mettre son clignotant

indication [ˌɪndɪˈkeɪʃən] *n (sign)* signe *m*; *(information)* indication *f*; **she gave no i. of her feelings** elle n'a rien laissé voir de ses sentiments; **there is every i. that…, all the indications are that…** tout porte à croire que…

indicative [ɪnˈdɪkətɪv] **1** *n Gram* indicatif *m*; **in the i.** à l'indicatif **2** *adj* **to be i. of** être symptomatique de

indicator [ˈɪndɪkeɪtə(r)] *n* **(a)** *(sign)* indice *m*; **economic indicators** indicateurs *mpl* économiques **(b)** *Br (of car)* clignotant *m*

indict [ɪnˈdaɪt] *vt Law* inculper **(for** de)

indictable [ɪnˈdaɪtəbəl] *adj Law* **i. offence** délit *m*

indictment [ɪnˈdaɪtmənt] *n Law* inculpation *f*; *Fig* **it is an i. of our society** c'est une preuve accablante de l'état de notre société

indie [ˈɪndɪ] *adj Br (music, band)* indépendant(e)

indifference [ɪnˈdɪfərəns] *n* indifférence *f* **(to** pour)

indifferent [ɪnˈdɪfərənt] *adj* **(a)** *(not interested)* indifférent(e) **(to** à); **I am or feel i.** about him il m'est indifférent **(b)** *(mediocre)* médiocre

indigenous [ɪnˈdɪdʒɪnəs] *adj* indigène

indigestible [ˌɪndɪˈdʒestɪbəl] *adj also Fig* indigeste

indigestion [ˌɪndɪˈdʒestʃən] *n* troubles *mpl* digestifs; **to have an attack of i.** avoir des troubles digestifs

indignant [ɪnˈdɪgnənt] *adj* indigné(e); **to get i. about sth** s'indigner de qch

indignation [ˌɪndɪgˈneɪʃən] *n* indignation *f*

indignity [ɪnˈdɪgnɪtɪ] *n* indignité *f*

indigo [ˈɪndɪgəʊ] **1** *n* indigo *m* **2** *adj* indigo *inv*

indirect [ˌɪndɪˈrekt] *adj* indirect(e); *(person)* pas direct(e); *Com* **i. costs** frais *mpl* indirects; *Gram* **i. object** complément *m* d'objet indirect; *Gram* **i. speech** discours *m* indirect

indirectly [ˌɪndɪˈrektlɪ] *adv* indirectement

indiscernible [ˌɪndɪˈsɜːnɪbəl] *adj (reason)* obscur(e); *(difference)* imperceptible

indiscipline [ɪnˈdɪsɪplɪn] *n* indiscipline *f*

indiscreet [ˌɪndɪsˈkriːt] *adj* indiscret(ète)

indiscretion [ˌɪndɪsˈkreʃən] *n* indiscrétion *f*

indiscriminate [ˌɪndɪsˈkrɪmɪnɪt] *adj* **i. killing** tuerie *f* générale; **to be i. in one's praise** distribuer les compliments à tort et à travers

indispensable [ˌɪndɪsˈpensəbəl] *adj* indispensable

indisposed [ˌɪndɪsˈpəʊzd] *adj Formal (ill)* indisposé(e)

indisputable [ˌɪndɪsˈpjuːtəbəl] *adj (evidence, argument)* incontestable; *(leader)* incontesté(e)

indissoluble [ˌɪndɪˈsɒljəbəl] *adj Formal* indissoluble

indistinct [ˌɪndɪsˈtɪŋkt] *adj* indistinct(e)

indistinguishable [ˌɪndɪsˈtɪŋgwɪʃəbəl] *adj* impossible à distinguer **(from** de)

individual [ˌɪndɪˈvɪdjʊəl] **1** *n (person)* individu *m*; **a private i.** un particulier **2** *adj* **(a)** *(of or for one person)* individuel(elle); *(bathroom)* privé(e); *Am* **i. retirement account** plan *m* d'épargne retraite personnel **(b)** *(characteristic)* personnel(elle)

individualist [ˌɪndɪˈvɪdjʊəlɪst] *n* individualiste *mf*

individuality [ˌɪndɪvɪdjʊˈælɪtɪ] *n* individualité *f*

individually [ˌɪndɪˈvɪdjʊəlɪ] *adv* individuellement

indivisible [ˌɪndɪˈvɪzɪbəl] *adj* indivisible

Indochina [ˌɪndəʊˈtʃaɪnə] *n* l'Indochine *f*

indoctrinate [ɪnˈdɒktrɪneɪt] *vt* endoctriner; **to i. sb with an idea** inculquer une idée à qn

indoctrination [ˌɪndɒktrɪˈneɪʃən] *n* endoctrinement *m*

indolent [ˈɪndələnt] *adj Formal* paresseux(euse)

indomitable [ɪnˈdɒmɪtəbəl] *adj* indomptable

Indonesia [ˌɪndəʊˈniːzɪə] *n* l'Indonésie *f*

Indonesian [ˌɪndəʊˈniːʒən] **1** *n* **(a)** *(person)* Indonésien(enne) *m,f* **(b)** *(language)* indonésien *m* **2** *adj* indonésien(enne)

indoor [ˈɪndɔː(r)] *adj (swimming pool, tennis court)* couvert(e); *(plant)* d'appartement; *(photography)* d'intérieur; **i. athletics** athlétisme *m* en salle

indoors [ˌɪnˈdɔːz] *adv* à l'intérieur; **to go i.** rentrer; **I've been i. all day** je suis resté enfermé toute la journée

induce [ɪnˈdjuːs] *vt* **(a)** *(persuade)* **to i. sb to do sth** persuader qn de faire qch **(b)** *(cause)* provoquer **(c)** *Med* **to i. labour** provoquer l'accouchement; **she's had to be induced** il a fallu provoquer l'accouchement

inducement [ɪn'dju:smənt] *n (incentive)* incitation *f*; *(financial)* avantage *m* financier

induction [ɪn'dʌkʃən] *n* (a) *(into job)* période *f* d'introduction; **i. course** stage *m* de formation (b) *Med (of labour)* déclenchement *m* (c) *Elec* induction *f*

inductive [ɪn'dʌktɪv] *adj (reasoning)* inductif(ive)

indulge [ɪn'dʌldʒ] **1** *vt (child)* gâter; *(passion)* donner libre cours à; **they indulged his every whim** ils lui passaient tous ses caprices; **to i. oneself** se faire plaisir; **go on, i. me!** allez, fais-moi plaisir! **2** *vi* **to i. in sth** *(as a habit)* se livrer à qch; *(as a treat)* s'offrir qch

indulgence [ɪn'dʌldʒəns] *n* (a) *(leniency)* indulgence *f* (b) *(treat)* gâterie *f*

indulgent [ɪn'dʌldʒənt] *adj* indulgent(e) (**to** avec)

industrial [ɪn'dʌstrɪəl] *adj* industriel(elle); **i. accident** accident *m* du travail; **i. action** grève *f*; **to take i. action** faire grève; **i. disease** maladie *f* professionnelle; **i. dispute** conflit *m* entre la direction et les travailleurs; **i. espionage** espionnage *m* industriel; *Br* **i. estate** zone *f* industrielle; **i. injury** accident *m* du travail; *Am* **i. park** zone *f* industrielle; **i. relations** relations *fpl* entre les travailleurs et le patronat; **the I. Revolution** la révolution industrielle; *Br* **i. tribunal** ≃ conseil *m* de prud'hommes; **i. unrest** conflits *mpl* sociaux; **i. waste** déchets *mpl* industriels

industrialist [ɪn'dʌstrɪəlɪst] *n* industriel *m*

industrialize [ɪn'dʌstrɪəlaɪz] *vt* industrialiser

industrious [ɪn'dʌstrɪəs] *adj* travailleur(euse)

industry ['ɪndəstrɪ] *(pl* **industries)** *n* (a) *(economic sector)* industrie *f*; **heavy/light i.** l'industrie lourde/légère; **the oil/movie i.** l'industrie pétrolière/cinématographique; **the tourist/entertainment i.** l'industrie du tourisme/du spectacle (b) *(hard work)* assiduité *f*

inebriated [ɪn'i:brɪeɪtɪd] *adj Formal or Hum* ivre

inedible [ɪn'edɪbəl] *adj (plant, mushroom)* non comestible; *(food)* immangeable

ineffable [ɪn'efəbəl] *adj Formal* ineffable

ineffective [ɪnɪ'fektɪv] *adj* inefficace

ineffectual [ɪnɪ'fektjʊəl] *adj* inefficace

inefficiency [ɪnɪ'fɪʃənsɪ] *n* inefficacité *f*, manque *m* d'efficacité

inefficient [ɪnɪ'fɪʃənt] *adj* inefficace

inelegant [ɪn'elɪgənt] *adj* inélégant(e)

ineligible [ɪn'elɪdʒɪbəl] *adj* **to be i. for sth** ne pas avoir droit à qch; **to be i. to do sth** ne pas avoir le droit de faire qch

inept [ɪn'ept] *adj (person)* incompétent(e); *(remark)* inepte

ineptitude [ɪn'eptɪtju:d] *n* incompétence *f*

inequality [ɪnɪ'kwɒlɪtɪ] *(pl* **inequalities)** *n* inégalité *f*

inequitable [ɪn'ekwɪtəbəl] *adj Formal* inéquitable

inert [ɪ'nɜ:t] *adj* inerte

inertia [ɪ'nɜ:ʃɪə] *n* inertie *f*

inescapable [ɪnɪ'skeɪpəbəl] *adj (conclusion)* incontournable; *(resemblance)* indéniable; **it's an i. fact that...** il est indéniable que...

inessential [ɪnɪ'senʃəl] *adj* non essentiel(elle)

inestimable [ɪn'estɪməbəl] *adj* inestimable

inevitability [ɪnevɪtə'bɪlɪtɪ] *n* caractère *m* inévitable

inevitable [ɪn'evɪtəbəl] **1** *n* **the i.** l'inévitable *m* **2** *adj* inévitable; *(conclusion)* incontournable

inevitably [ɪn'evɪtəblɪ] *adv* inévitablement

inexact [ɪnɪg'zækt] *adj (memory, estimate)* imprécis(e)

inexcusable [ɪnɪks'kju:zəbəl] *adj* inexcusable

inexhaustible [ɪnɪg'zɔ:stɪbəl] *adj* inépuisable

inexorable [ɪn'eksərəbəl] *adj* inexorable

inexpensive [ɪnɪks'pensɪv] *adj* pas cher (chère), bon marché *inv*

inexperience [ɪnɪks'pɪərɪəns] *n* inexpérience *f*

inexperienced [ɪnɪks'pɪərɪənst] *adj* inexpérimenté(e); **to be i. in doing sth** ne pas avoir l'habitude de faire qch

inexplicable [ɪnɪks'plɪkəbəl] *adj* inexplicable

inexpressible [ɪnɪks'presɪbəl] *adj* inexprimable

inexpressive [ɪnɪks'presɪv] *adj* inexpressif(ive)

inextricably [ɪneks'trɪkəblɪ] *adv* inextricablement

infallibility [ɪnfælɪ'bɪlɪtɪ] *n* infaillibilité *f*

infallible [ɪn'fælɪbəl] *adj* infaillible

infamous ['ɪnfəməs] *adj (well-known)* tristement célèbre; *(crime, rumour)* infâme

infamy ['ɪnfəmɪ] *n Formal* infamie *f*

infancy ['ɪnfənsɪ] *n (childhood)* petite enfance *f*; *Fig* **when medicine was still in its i.** alors que la médecine en était encore à ses balbutiements

infant ['ɪnfənt] *n* bébé *m*; **i. mortality** mortalité *f* infantile

infanticide [ɪn'fæntɪsaɪd] *n* infanticide *m*

infantile ['ɪnfəntaɪl] *adj Pej* infantile, puéril(e)

infantry ['ɪnfəntrɪ] *n* infanterie *f*

infantryman ['ɪnfəntrɪmən] *n* soldat *m* d'infanterie, fantassin *m*

infatuated [ɪn'fætjʊeɪtɪd] *adj* **to be i. with sb** être entiché(e) de qn

infatuation [ɪnfætjʊ'eɪʃən] *n (with person)* tocade *f*, passade *f* (**with** pour)

infect [ɪn'fekt] *vt (water, food)* contaminer; *(with prejudice)* corrompre; **to become infected** *(of wound)* s'infecter; **to i. sb with sth** transmettre qch à qn; **her enthusiasm infected us all** elle nous a communiqué son enthousiasme

infection [ɪn'fekʃən] *n* infection *f*

infectious [ɪn'fekʃəs] *adj* (a) *(disease)* infectieux(euse); *(person)* contagieux(euse) (b) *(laughter, enthusiasm)* communicatif(ive)

infer [ɪn'fɜ:(r)] *(pt & pp* **inferred)** *vt* déduire (**from** de)

inference ['ɪnfərəns] *n* conclusion *f*; **by i.** par déduction

inferior [ɪn'fɪərɪə(r)] **1** *n* inférieur(e) *m,f*; **to be sb's i.** être inférieur à qn **2** *adj* inférieur(e) (**to** à)

inferiority [ɪnfɪərɪ'ɒrɪtɪ] *n* infériorité *f*; **i. complex** complexe *m* d'infériorité

infernal [ɪn'fɜ:nəl] *adj* (a) *(diabolical)* infernal(e), diabolique (b) *Fam (for emphasis)* **it's an i. nuisance** c'est diablement embêtant; **that i. idiot!** cette espèce d'idiot!

inferno [ɪn'fɜ:nəʊ] *(pl* **infernos)** *n (hell)* enfer *m*; *(blaze)* brasier *m*

infertile [ɪn'fɜ:taɪl] *adj* stérile

infertility [ɪnfə'tɪlɪtɪ] *n* stérilité *f*

infest [ɪn'fest] *vt* **to be infested with** *or* **by sth** être infesté(e) de qch

infidelity [ɪnfɪ'delɪtɪ] *n* infidélité *f*

infighting ['ɪnfaɪtɪŋ] *n* querelles *fpl* intestines

infiltrate ['ɪnfɪltreɪt] **1** *vt* infiltrer **2** *vi* s'infiltrer

infiltration [ɪnfɪl'treɪʃən] *n* infiltration *f*

infinite ['ɪnfɪnɪt] **1** *n* **the i.** l'infini *m* **2** *adj* infini(e); *Rel & Hum* **in her i. wisdom** dans son infinie sagesse

infinitely ['ɪnfɪnɪtlɪ] *adv* infiniment

infinitesimal [ɪnfɪnɪ'tesɪməl] *adj* infinitésimal(e)
infinitive [ɪn'fɪnɪtɪv] *n Gram* infinitif *m*; **in the i.** à l'infinitif
infinity [ɪn'fɪnɪtɪ] *n* infinité *f*; *Math* infini *m*
infirm [ɪn'fɜːm] *adj* infirme
infirmary [ɪn'fɜːmərɪ] *(pl* **infirmaries)** *n (hospital)* hôpital *m; (in school, prison)* infirmerie *f*
infirmity [ɪn'fɜːmɪtɪ] *(pl* **infirmities)** *n (weakness)* infirmité *f*
inflame [ɪn'fleɪm] *vt* **(a)** *(desire)* allumer; *(curiosity)* attiser; *(crowd)* enflammer **(b) to become inflamed** *(of wound)* s'enflammer
inflammable [ɪn'flæməbəl] *adj (substance)* inflammable; *Fig (situation)* explosif(ive)
inflammation [ɪnflə'meɪʃən] *n* inflammation *f*
inflammatory [ɪn'flæmətrɪ] *adj* incendiaire
inflatable [ɪn'fleɪtəbəl] **1** *n (rubber dinghy)* canot *m* pneumatique
2 *adj* gonflable
inflate [ɪn'fleɪt] **1** *vt* **(a)** *(tyre, lifejacket)* gonfler **(b)** *(prices)* faire monter
2 *vi* se gonfler
inflated [ɪn'fleɪtɪd] *adj (tyre, lifejacket)* gonflé(e); **to have an i. opinion of oneself** avoir une opinion trop flatteuse de soi-même
inflation [ɪn'fleɪʃən] *n Econ* inflation *f*
inflationary [ɪn'fleɪʃənrɪ] *adj Econ* inflationniste
inflect [ɪn'flekt] **1** *vt* **(a)** *(voice)* moduler **(b)** *Gram* ajouter la désinence de
2 *vi Gram* prendre une désinence
inflexibility [ɪnfleksɪ'bɪlɪtɪ] *n* rigidité *f*
inflexible [ɪn'fleksɪbəl] *adj* rigide
inflict [ɪn'flɪkt] *vt (suffering, punishment, defeat)* infliger **(on** à); *(damage)* causer **(on** à); **to i. oneself on sb** infliger sa présence à qn
in-flight ['ɪnflaɪt] *adj* **i. entertainment** distractions *fpl* en vol; **i. meal** repas *m* servi pendant le vol
influence ['ɪnflʊəns] **1** *n* influence *f* **(on** sur); **to be a good/bad i. (on sb)** avoir une bonne/mauvaise influence (sur qn); **to have i. over sb** avoir de l'influence sur qn; **under the i. of drink** sous l'empire de la boisson
2 *vt* influencer; **to be easily influenced** être influençable
influential [ɪnflʊ'enʃəl] *adj* influent(e)
influenza [ɪnflʊ'enzə] *n* grippe *f*
influx ['ɪnflʌks] *n* afflux *m*
info ['ɪnfəʊ] *n Fam* renseignements *mpl; (leaflets, brochures)* documentation *f*
infomercial [ɪnfəʊ'mɜːʃəl] *n* infomercial *m*
inform [ɪn'fɔːm] **1** *vt* informer **(of** *or* **about** de); **to keep sb informed of sth** tenir qn au courant de qch
2 *vi* **to i. on sb** dénoncer qn
informal [ɪn'fɔːməl] *adj* **(a)** *(unaffected)* simple **(b)** *(casual)* décontracté(e); *(word, language)* familier(ère) **(c)** *(unofficial) (meeting, talks)* officieux(euse)
informality [ɪnfɔː'mælɪtɪ] *n* **(a)** *(unaffectedness)* simplicité *f* **(b)** *(casualness)* décontraction *f* **(c)** *(of talks)* caractère *m* officieux
informally [ɪn'fɔːməlɪ] *adv* **(a)** *(unaffectedly)* avec simplicité **(b)** *(casually)* avec décontraction **(c)** *(hold talks)* officieusement
informant [ɪn'fɔːmənt] *n* informateur(trice) *m,f*

information [ɪnfə'meɪʃən] *n* **(a)** *(news, facts)* renseignements *mpl*; **a piece of i.** un renseignement; **for further i.** pour de plus amples renseignements; **i. bureau** bureau *m* des renseignements **(b)** *Comptr* **i. processing** traitement *m* de l'information; **i. retrieval** recherche *f* documentaire; **i. science** informatique *f*; **the i. superhighway** l'autoroute *f* de l'information; **i. technology** informatique
informative [ɪn'fɔːmətɪv] *adj* instructif(ive); **she was very i.** elle nous a appris beaucoup de choses
informed [ɪn'fɔːmd] *adj (person)* bien renseigné(e), bien informé(e); **my i. guess is that...** en me basant sur ce que je sais, je dirais que...; **an i. decision** une décision prise en connaissance de cause
informer [ɪn'fɔːmə(r)] *n* indicateur *m*
infra dig ['ɪnfrə'dɪg] *adj Fam* rabaissant(e), dégradant(e)
infrared [ɪnfrə'red] *adj* infrarouge
infrastructure ['ɪnfrəstrʌktʃə(r)] *n* infrastructure *f*
infrequent [ɪn'friːkwənt] *adj* rare, peu fréquent(e)
infringe [ɪn'frɪndʒ] *vt (rule, law)* enfreindre; *(right)* empiéter sur
▸ **infringe on** *vt insep* empiéter sur
infringement [ɪn'frɪndʒmənt] *n (of rule, law)* infraction *f* **(of** à); *(of right)* atteinte *f* (of à)
infuriate [ɪn'fjuːrɪeɪt] *vt* exaspérer
infuriating [ɪn'fjuːrɪeɪtɪŋ] *adj* exaspérant(e)
infuse [ɪn'fjuːz] **1** *vt* **(a)** *(energy, hope)* insuffler **(into** à) **(b)** *(tea)* faire infuser
2 *vi (of tea)* infuser
infusion [ɪn'fjuːʒən] *n (drink)* infusion *f*
ingenious [ɪn'dʒiːnɪəs] *adj* ingénieux(euse)
ingenuity [ɪndʒɪ'njuːɪtɪ] *n* ingéniosité *f*
ingenuous [ɪn'dʒenʊəs] *adj (native)* ingénu(e); *(frank)* franc (franche)
inglorious [ɪn'glɔːrɪəs] *adj* déshonorant(e), honteux(euse)
ingot ['ɪŋgət] *n* lingot *m*
ingrained [ɪn'greɪnd] *adj (prejudice, habit)* enraciné(e); **i. dirt** crasse *f*
ingratiate [ɪn'greɪʃɪeɪt] *vt* **to i. oneself (with sb)** se faire bien voir (de qn ou par qn)
ingratiating [ɪn'greɪʃɪeɪtɪŋ] *adj* doucereux(euse)
ingratitude [ɪn'grætɪtjuːd] *n* ingratitude *f*
ingredient [ɪn'griːdɪənt] *n also Fig* ingrédient *m; Fig* **the missing i.** l'élément *m* manquant
ingrowing ['ɪngrəʊɪŋ], **ingrown** ['ɪngrəʊn] *adj* **i.** toenail ongle *m* incarné
inhabit [ɪn'hæbɪt] *vt* habiter
inhabitable [ɪn'hæbɪtəbəl] *adj* habitable
inhabitant [ɪn'hæbɪtənt] *n* habitant(e) *m,f*
inhabited [ɪn'hæbɪtɪd] *adj* habité(e) **(by** par)
inhale [ɪn'heɪl] **1** *vt (gas, fumes)* inhaler; *(cigarette smoke)* avaler
2 *vi* inspirer; *(in smoking)* avaler la fumée
inhaler [ɪn'heɪlə(r)] *n (for asthmatics)* inhalateur *m*
inherent [ɪn'herənt] *adj* inhérent(e) **(in** à)
inherit [ɪn'herɪt] *vt* hériter **(from** de)
inheritance [ɪn'herɪtəns] *n* héritage *m*; **i. tax** droits *mpl* de succession
inhibit [ɪn'hɪbɪt] *vt (progress, growth)* entraver; *(person)* inhiber
inhibited [ɪn'hɪbɪtɪd] *adj (person)* inhibé(e)
inhibition [ɪnɪ'bɪʃən] *n* inhibition *f*; **to have no inhibitions about doing sth** n'avoir aucune honte à faire qch
inhospitable [ɪnhɒ'spɪtəbəl] *adj* inhospitalier(ère)

in-house [ˈɪnˈhaʊs] **1** *adj (training)* interne; *(staff)* qui travaille sur place
2 *adv* sur place
inhuman [ɪnˈhjuːmən] *adj* inhumain(e)
inhumane [ɪnhjuːˈmeɪn] *adj* inhumain(e)
inhumanity [ɪnhjuːˈmænɪtɪ] *n* inhumanité *f*, cruauté *f*
inimical [ɪˈnɪmɪkəl] *adj (people)* ennemi(e), hostile; *(conditions)* contraire **(to** à)
inimitable [ɪˈnɪmɪtəbəl] *adj* inimitable
iniquitous [ɪˈnɪkwɪtəs] *adj* inique
iniquity [ɪˈnɪkwɪtɪ] *(pl* **iniquities)** *n* iniquité *f*
initial [ɪˈnɪʃəl] **1** *n* initiale *f*; **initials** *(signature)* paraphe *m*
2 *adj* initial(e), premier(ère); **in the i. stages of sth** au stade initial de qch; *Am* **i. public offering** introduction *f* en Bourse
3 *vt (pt & pp* **initialled,** *Am* **initialed)** parapher
initially [ɪˈnɪʃəlɪ] *adv* au début
initiate [ɪˈnɪʃɪeɪt] *vt* **(a)** *(negotiations)* amorcer; *(rumour, project)* lancer; *Law* **to i. proceedings (against sb)** entamer des poursuites (contre qn) **(b) to i. sb into a secret society/gang** faire subir à qn les épreuves initiatiques d'une société secrète/d'un gang
initiation [ɪnɪʃɪˈeɪʃən] *n* **(a)** *(beginning)* commencement *m*, début(s) *m(pl)* **(b)** *(induction)* initiation *f*; **i. ceremony** rite *m* d'initiation
initiative [ɪˈnɪʃətɪv] *n* initiative *f*; **to take the i. (in doing sth)** prendre l'initiative (de faire qch); **to use one's i.** faire preuve d'initiative; **on one's own i.** de sa propre initiative
inject [ɪnˈdʒekt] *vt (drug, money)* injecter; *(enthusiasm)* communiquer; **to i. new life into sth** donner un nouvel essor à qch
injection [ɪnˈdʒekʃən] *n* injection *f*, piqûre *f*; *Fig* injection; **rabies i.** vaccin *m* contre la rage; **to give sb an i.** faire une piqûre à qn
injudicious [ɪndʒuːˈdɪʃəs] *adj* peu judicieux(euse), malavisé(e)
injunction [ɪnˈdʒʌŋkʃən] *n Law* arrêt *m*, jugement *m*; **to take out an i. against sb** mettre qn en demeure
injure [ˈɪndʒə(r)] *vt (person)* blesser; *(reputation, interests)* nuire à; **to i. oneself** se blesser; **to i. one's knee** se blesser au genou; **her pride is injured** elle est blessée dans son orgueil
injured [ˈɪndʒəd] **1** **the i.** les blessés *mpl*
2 *adj* blessé(e); *(look, voice)* offensé(e); *Law* **the i. party** la partie lésée
injurious [ɪnˈdʒʊrɪəs] *adj* nuisible, préjudiciable **(to** à)
injury [ˈɪndʒərɪ] *(pl* **injuries)** *n (physical)* blessure *f*; **to do oneself an i.** se blesser; **i. time** *(in football match)* arrêts *mpl* de jeu
injustice [ɪnˈdʒʌstɪs] *n* injustice *f*; **to do sb an i.** être injuste envers qn
ink [ɪŋk] *n* encre *f*; **i. pad** tampon *m* (encreur)
ink-jet [ˈɪŋkdʒet] *adj Comptr* **i. (printer)** imprimante *f* à jet d'encre
inkling [ˈɪŋklɪŋ] *n* soupçon *m*; **to have an i. of sth** se douter de qch
inkwell [ˈɪŋkwel] *n* encrier *m (de pupitre)*
inky [ˈɪŋkɪ] *adj* **(a)** *(stained with ink)* taché(e) d'encre **(b) i. (black)** noir(e) comme (de) l'encre
inlaid [ɪnˈleɪd] *adj (with wood)* marqueté(e); *(with jewels)* incrusté(e) **(with** de)
inland 1 *adj* [ˈɪnlənd] intérieur(e); *Br* **the I. Revenue** ≃ le fisc
2 *adv* [ɪnˈlænd] *(travel)* vers l'intérieur; *(live)* dans les terres

in-laws [ˈɪnlɔːz] *npl (spouse's parents)* beaux-parents *mpl*; *(spouse's family)* belle-famille *f*
inlet [ˈɪnlet] *n* **(a)** *(of sea)* petit bras *m* de mer **(b)** *(of pipe, machine)* (orifice *m* d')entrée *f*
inmate [ˈɪnmeɪt] *n (in prison)* détenu(e) *m,f*; *(in mental hospital)* interné(e) *m,f*
inn [ɪn] *n* auberge *f*
innards [ˈɪnədz] *npl* entrailles *fpl*
innate [ɪˈneɪt] *adj* inné(e)
inner [ˈɪnə(r)] *adj* **(a)** *(chamber, lining)* intérieur(e); **i. circle** *(of party, association)* initiés *mpl*; **i. city** quartiers *mpl* déshérités du centre-ville; **i. ear** oreille *f* interne; **i. tube** chambre *f* à air **(b)** *(thought, feeling)* intime; *(peace)* intérieur(e)
innermost [ˈɪnəməʊst] *adj (part)* le (la) plus profond(e); *(thoughts, feelings)* le (la) plus secret(ète)
innings [ˈɪnɪŋz] *n (in cricket)* tournée *f*, tour *m* de batte
innkeeper [ˈɪnkiːpə(r)] *n* aubergiste *mf*
innocence [ˈɪnəsəns] *n* innocence *f*
innocent [ˈɪnəsənt] **1** *n* innocent(e) *m,f*; **to act the i.** faire l'innocent
2 *adj* innocent(e)
innocuous [ɪˈnɒkjʊəs] *adj* inoffensif(ive); *(remark)* anodin(e)
innovate [ˈɪnəveɪt] *vi* innover
innovation [ɪnəˈveɪʃən] *n* innovation *f*
innovative [ˈɪnəveɪtɪv] *adj* (in)novateur(trice)
innovator [ˈɪnəveɪtə(r)] *n* (in)novateur(trice) *m,f*
innuendo [ɪnjʊˈendəʊ] *(pl* **innuendos** *or* **innuendoes)** *n (insinuation)* insinuation *f*; *(in jokes)* allusion *f* grivoise
innumerable [ɪˈnjuːmərəbəl] *adj* innombrable
inoculate [ɪˈnɒkjʊleɪt] *vt* vacciner; **to i. sb with sth** inoculer qch à qn; **to i. sb against sth** vacciner qn contre qch
inoculation [ɪnɒkjʊˈleɪʃən] *n* inoculation *f*
inoffensive [ɪnəˈfensɪv] *adj (animal, person)* inoffensif(ive); *(remark, humour)* qui n'a rien d'offensant; *(odour)* qui n'a rien de désagréable
inoperable [ɪnˈɒpərəbəl] *adj* inopérable
inoperative [ɪnˈɒpərətɪv] *adj (rule)* inopérant(e); *(machine)* arrêté(e)
inopportune [ɪnˈɒpətjuːn] *adj* inopportun(e)
inordinate [ɪnˈɔːdɪnət] *adj* démesuré(e)
inorganic [ɪnɔːˈgænɪk] *adj* inorganique
in-patient [ˈɪnpeɪʃənt] *n* patient(e) *m,f* hospitalisé(e)
input [ˈɪnpʊt] **1** *n* **(a)** *Elec* puissance *f* d'alimentation; *(terminal)* entrée *f*; *Comptr* entrée *f*, introduction *f* **(b)** *(contribution)* contribution *f*; **we'd like some i. from marketing** Elec nous aimerions consulter le service marketing d'abord
2 *vt (pt & pp* **input)** *Comptr (data)* entrer
inquest [ˈɪnkwest] *n Law* enquête *f*; *Fig (in politics, business)* analyse *f*; **to hold an i.** *Law (of coroner)* mener une enquête **(into** sur); *(in politics, business)* faire une analyse **(into** de)
inquire [ɪnˈkwaɪə(r)] **1** *vt* demander
2 *vi* se renseigner **(about** sur); **i. within** *(sign)* s'adresser ici
▸ **inquire after** *vt insep* demander des nouvelles de
▸ **inquire into** *vt insep* faire des recherches sur
inquiring [ɪnˈkwaɪrɪŋ] *adj (mind)* curieux(euse); *(look, voice)* interrogateur(trice)
inquiry [ɪnˈkwaɪrɪ] *(pl* **inquiries)** *n* **(a)** *(official investigation)* enquête *f*; **to hold an i. (into sth)** faire une

enquête (sur qch) (**b**) *(request for information)* demande *f* de renseignements; **to make inquiries (about sth)** se renseigner (sur qch); **i. desk** bureau *m* de(s) renseignements

Inquisition [ɪnkwɪ'zɪʃən] *n* the **l**. l'Inquisition *f*

inquisitive [ɪn'kwɪzɪtɪv] *adj (person, mind)* curieux(euse); *(look)* interrogateur(trice)

inroads ['ɪnrəʊdz] *npl* **to make i.** *into (capital, savings)* entamer; *(market)* pénétrer

INS [aɪen'es] *n Am (abbr* **Immigration and Naturalization Service)** = services américains de contrôle de l'immigration

insane [ɪn'seɪn] *adj (person)* dément(e); *Fam (desire, scheme)* fou (folle); **to go i.** devenir fou, perdre la raison; **to be i. with grief/jealousy** être fou de douleur/jalousie

insanely [ɪn'seɪnlɪ] *adv* comme un fou (une folle); **i. jealous** d'une jalousie maladive

insanitary [ɪn'sænɪtrɪ] *adj* insalubre, malsain(e)

insanity [ɪn'sænɪtɪ] *n (of person)* démence *f*; *Fam (of desire, scheme)* folie *f*

insatiable [ɪn'seɪʃəbəl] *adj* insatiable

inscribe [ɪn'skraɪb] *vt (write)* écrire; *(engrave)* inscrire, graver

inscription [ɪn'skrɪpʃən] *n (on stone, coin)* inscription *f*; *(in book)* dédicace *f*

inscrutable [ɪn'skru:təbəl] *adj (look, face)* impénétrable; *(remark)* énigmatique

insect ['ɪnsekt] *n* insecte *m*; **i. bite** piqûre *f* d'insecte; **i. repellent** anti-moustiques *m inv*

insecticide [ɪn'sektɪsaɪd] *n* insecticide *m*

insecure [ɪnsɪ'kjʊə(r)] *adj* (**a**) *(person)* angoissé(e) (**b**) *(government)* fragile; *(job, future)* précaire; **to be financially i.** être dans une situation financière précaire

insecurity [ɪnsɪ'kjʊərɪtɪ] *n* (**a**) *(of person)* angoisse *f* (**b**) *(of job, future)* précarité *f*

insemination [ɪnsemɪ'neɪʃən] *n* insémination *f*

insensible [ɪn'sensɪbəl] *adj (unaware, unconscious)* inconscient(e) (**to** de)

insensitive [ɪn'sensɪtɪv] *adj (person)* insensible (**to** à); *(remark)* indélicat(e)

insensitivity [ɪnsensɪ'tɪvɪtɪ] *n* insensibilité *f*

inseparable [ɪn'separəbəl] *adj* inséparable

insert 1 *n* ['ɪnsɜ:t] *(in magazine)* encart *m*
2 *vt* [ɪn'sɜ:t] *(key, finger)* introduire (**into** dans); *(clause)* insérer (**in** dans); *(advertisement)* mettre (**in** dans)

insertion [ɪn'sɜ:ʃən] *n* insertion *f*

inset ['ɪnset] *n (in map, picture)* médaillon *m*

inshore [ɪn'ʃɔ:(r)] **1** *adj (navigation, fishing)* côtier(ère)
2 *adv (be situated)* sur la côte; *(travel)* vers la côte, vers les terres

inside 1 ['ɪn'saɪd] (**a**) *(of house)* intérieur *m*; **on/from the i.** à/de l'intérieur; **to overtake on the i.** *(in Britain)* doubler par la gauche; *(in Europe, USA)* doubler par la droite (**b**) *Fam* **insides** *(internal organs)* entrailles *fpl* (**c**) *(in phrases)* **i. out** *(clothes)* à l'envers; *Fig* **to know sth i. out** connaître qch comme sa poche
2 *adj* ['ɪnsaɪd] intérieur(e); **to have i. information** avoir des informations de première main; *Fam* **it's an i. job** c'est quelqu'un de la maison qui a fait ça; **i. lane** *(in Britain)* voie *f* de gauche; *(in Europe, USA)* voie de droite; **i. left** *(in football)* intérieur *m* gauche; **to know the i. story** connaître les dessous de l'affaire
3 *adv* ['ɪnsaɪd] (**a**) *(indoors)* à l'intérieur; **come i.!** entrez!
(**b**) *(within oneself)* en son for intérieur (**c**) *Fam (in prison)* en taule

4 *prep* [ɪn'saɪd] (**a**) *(place)* à l'intérieur de, dans (**b**) *(with time)* **i. (of) a week/an hour** en moins d'une semaine/heure

insider [ɪn'saɪdə(r)] *n* initié(e) *m,f*; *Fin* **i. dealing, i. trading** délit *m* d'initié

insidious [ɪn'sɪdɪəs] *adj* insidieux(euse)

insight ['ɪnsaɪt] *n* (**a**) *(perspicacity)* perspicacité *f* (**b**) *(understanding)* aperçu *m*; **to get an i. into sth** avoir un aperçu de qch

insignia [ɪn'sɪgnɪə] *n* insigne *m*

insignificance [ɪnsɪg'nɪfɪkəns] *n* insignifiance *f*; **to pale into i. (beside sth)** sembler totalement insignifiant(e) (à côté de qch)

insignificant [ɪnsɪg'nɪfɪkənt] *adj* insignifiant(e)

insincere [ɪnsɪn'sɪə(r)] *adj* peu sincère, faux (fausse)

insincerity [ɪnsɪn'serɪtɪ] *n* manque *m* de sincérité, fausseté *f*

insinuate [ɪn'sɪnjʊeɪt] *vt* insinuer; **to i. oneself into sb's favour** s'insinuer dans les bonnes grâces de qn

insinuation [ɪnsɪnjʊ'eɪʃən] *n* insinuation *f*

insipid [ɪn'sɪpɪd] *adj* insipide

insist [ɪn'sɪst] **1** *vt* (**a**) *(maintain)* **to i. that...** soutenir *ou* maintenir que... (**b**) *(demand)* **to i. (that) sb does sth** insister pour que qn fasse qch
2 *vi* insister; **to i. on sth** exiger qch; **to i. on doing sth** tenir à faire qch

insistence [ɪn'sɪstəns] *n* insistance *f* (**on** à); **I stayed at her i.** elle insista, et je restai

insistent [ɪn'sɪstənt] *adj (person, demand)* pressant(e); **to be i.** se montrer pressant; **to be i. about sth** insister sur qch

insofar as ['ɪnsəʊ'fɑ:rəz] *adv* dans la mesure où

insole ['ɪnsəʊl] *n* semelle *f* intérieure

insolence ['ɪnsələns] *n* insolence *f* (**to** envers)

insolent ['ɪnsələnt] *adj* insolent(e) (**to** envers)

insoluble [ɪn'sɒljʊbəl] *adj* insoluble

insolvency [ɪn'sɒlvənsɪ] *n Fin (of person)* insolvabilité *f*; *(of company)* faillite *f*

insolvent [ɪn'sɒlvənt] *adj Fin (person)* insolvable; *(company)* en faillite

insomnia [ɪn'sɒmnɪə] *n* insomnie *f*

insomniac [ɪn'sɒmnɪæk] *n* insomniaque *mf*

inspect [ɪn'spekt] *vt (passport, luggage, picture)* (school, factory) inspecter; *(troops)* passer en revue

inspection [ɪn'spekʃən] *n (of passport, luggage, picture)* examen *m*; *(of school, factory)* (visite *f* d')inspection *f*; *(of troops)* revue *f*; **on closer i.** en y regardant de plus près

inspector [ɪn'spektə(r)] *n (of schools, factories)* inspecteur(trice) *m,f*; *Br (on train, bus)* contrôleur(euse) *m,f*; *Br* (**police**) **i.** inspecteur *m* de police

inspiration [ɪnspɪ'reɪʃən] *n* inspiration *f*; **to be an i. to sb** inspirer qn

inspire [ɪn'spaɪə(r)] *vt* inspirer; **to i. sb to do sth** pousser qn à faire qch; **to i. sth in sb, to i. sb with sth** inspirer qch à qn

inspired [ɪn'spaɪəd] *adj* inspiré(e)

inspiring [ɪn'spaɪərɪŋ] *adj* exaltant(e)

instability [ɪnstə'bɪlɪtɪ] *n* instabilité *f*

install, *Am* **instal** [ɪn'stɔ:l] *vt* installer; **to i. sb in a post** mettre qn à un poste; **to i. oneself in an armchair** s'installer dans un fauteuil

installation [ɪnstə'leɪʃən] *n* installation *f*

instalment, *Am* **installment** [ɪn'stɔ:lmənt] *n* (**a**) *(part payment)* versement *m*; **to pay by instalments** payer par versements échelonnés (**b**) *(of radio, TV programme)* épisode *m*

instance ['ɪnstəns] *n (example)* cas *m*; **for i.** par exemple; **in the first i.** en (tout) premier lieu

instant ['ɪnstənt] **1** *n (moment)* instant *m*, moment *m*; **this i.** immédiatement; **not an i.** too soon juste à temps; **the i. I** saw her dès que je l'ai vue **2** *adj* (**a**) *(reply, success, dislike)* immédiat(e); *(solution)* instantané(e); *TV* **i. replay** reprise *f* de l'action (**b**) *(coffee, soup)* instantané(e)

instantaneous [ɪnstən'teɪnɪəs] *adj* instantané(e)

instantly ['ɪnstəntlɪ] *adv* instantanément; **he was killed i.** il a été tué sur le coup

instead [ɪn'sted] *adv (in place of sth)* à la place; *(in place of sb)* à ma/sa/*etc* place; **i. of** *(thing)* au lieu de; *(person)* à la place de; **i. of doing sth** au lieu de faire qch; **her son came i. of her** son fils est venu à sa place

instep ['ɪnstep] *n (of foot)* cou-de-pied *m*; *(of shoe)* cambrure *f*

instigate ['ɪnstɪgeɪt] *vt* être à l'origine de

instigation [ɪnstɪgeɪʃən] *n* instigation *f*; **at sb's i.** à l'instigation de qn

instigator ['ɪnstɪgeɪtə(r)] *n* instigateur(trice) *m,f*

instil, *Am* **instill** [ɪn'stɪl] *(pt & pp* **instilled**) *vt (courage, pride)* inspirer (**in** à); *(doubt, jealousy)* instiller (**in** à); *(idea)* inculquer (**into** à)

instinct ['ɪnstɪŋkt] *n* instinct *m*; **she has an i. for business** elle a le sens des affaires

instinctive [ɪn'stɪŋktɪv] *adj* instinctif(ive)

institute ['ɪnstɪtjuːt] **1** *n* institut *m* **2** *vt (system, procedure)* établir, instituer; *(search)* lancer; *Law (enquiry)* ordonner; **to i. proceedings (against sb)** entamer *ou* engager des poursuites (contre qn)

institution [ɪnstɪ'tjuːʃən] *n (organization)* institution *f*; *(public, financial)* établissement *m*; *(for old people)* hospice *m*; *(for mental patients)* asile *m*; *Fig* **to become a national i.** *(of event, TV programme)* devenir une institution nationale

institutional [ɪnstɪ'tjuːʃənəl] *adj* institutionnel(elle)

institutionalize [ɪnstɪ'tjuːʃənəlaɪz] *vt* (**a**) *(put in a home)* placer dans un établissement spécialisé; **to become institutionalized** *(of prisoner, patient)* devenir complètement dépendant(e) (**b**) *(turn into an institution)* institutionnaliser

instruct [ɪn'strʌkt] *vt* (**a**) *(teach)* enseigner; **to i. sb in sth** enseigner qch à qn (**b**) *(command)* ordonner; **to i. sb to do sth** ordonner à qn de faire qch

instruction [ɪn'strʌkʃən] *n* (**a**) *(training)* instruction *f*, enseignement *m* (**b**) **instructions** *(orders)* instructions *fpl*, directives *fpl* (**c**) **instructions (for use)** notice *f* (d'emploi); **i. manual** manuel *m* d'entretien

instructive [ɪn'strʌktɪv] *adj* instructif(ive)

instructor [ɪn'strʌktə(r)] *n* (**a**) *(of sporting activity, driving)* moniteur(trice) *m,f* (**b**) *Am (university lecturer)* professeur *m*

instrument ['ɪnstrəmənt] *n* instrument *m*; **i. board** *or* **panel** *(in plane, car)* tableau *m* de bord

instrumental [ɪnstrʊ'mentəl] **1** *n (music without words)* instrumental *m* **2** *adj* (**a**) *(contributory)* **to be i. in sth** jouer un rôle décisif dans qch (**b**) *(in music)* instrumental(e)

instrumentalist [ɪnstrʊ'mentəlɪst] *n* instrumentiste *mf*

instrumentation [ɪnstrʊmen'teɪʃən] *n* instrumentation *f*

insubordinate [ɪnsə'bɔːdɪnət] *adj* insubordonné(e)

insubordination [ɪnsəbɔːdɪ'neɪʃən] *n* insubordination *f*

insubstantial [ɪnsəb'stænʃəl] *adj (structure, argument)* peu solide; *(meal)* frugal(e); *(book)* creux(euse), qui manque de substance

insufferable [ɪn'sʌfrəbəl] *adj* insupportable, intolérable

insufficient ['ɪnsəfɪʃənt] *adj* insuffisant(e)

insular ['ɪnsjʊlə(r)] *adj* borné(e); *(climate)* insulaire

insulate ['ɪnsjʊleɪt] *vt* isoler; *Fig* **to be insulated from sth** être protégé(e) de qch

insulating tape ['ɪnsjʊleɪtɪŋ'teɪp] *n* chatterton *m*

insulation [ɪnsjʊ'leɪʃən] *n* isolation *f*

insulin [ɪnsjʊlɪn] *n* insuline *f*

insult 1 *n* ['ɪnsʌlt] *(words, action)* insulte *f*; **to add i. to injury** aggraver les choses **2** *vt* [ɪn'sʌlt] insulter

insulting [ɪn'sʌltɪŋ] *adj* insultant(e)

insuperable [ɪn'suːpərəbəl] *adj* insurmontable

insurance [ɪn'ʃʊərəns] *n* assurance *f*; *Fig (protection)* garantie *f*; **to take out i.** prendre une assurance; **i. broker** courtier *m* en assurances; **i. claim** demande *f* d'indemnité; *(for more serious damage)* déclaration *f* de sinistre; **i. company** companie *f* d'assurances; **i. policy** police *f* d'assurance; **i. premium** prime *f* d'assurance

insure [ɪn'ʃʊə(r)] *vt* assurer (**against** contre); **to i. one's life** s'assurer sur la vie

insured [ɪn'ʃʊəd] *adj* assuré(e) (**against** contre); **i. value** valeur *f* assurée

insurer [ɪn'ʃʊərə(r)] *n* assureur *m*

insurgent [ɪn'sɔːdʒənt] *n* insurgé(e) *m,f*

insurmountable [ɪnsə'maʊntəbəl] *adj* insurmontable

insurrection [ɪnsə'rekʃən] *n* insurrection *f*

intact [ɪn'tækt] *adj* intact(e)

intake ['ɪnteɪk] *n* (**a**) *(of alcohol, food)* consommation *f*; *(of calories)* absorption *f* (**b**) *(pupils)* élèves *mpl*; *(recruits)* contingent *m* (**c**) *Tech* admission *f*

intangible [ɪn'tændʒɪbəl] *adj* impalpable

integer ['ɪntɪdʒə(r)] *n Math* nombre *m* entier

integral ['ɪntɪgrəl] *adj (essential)* indispensable; **to be an i. part of sth** faire partie intégrante de qch; *Math* **i. calculus** calcul *m* intégral

integrate ['ɪntɪgreɪt] **1** *vt* intégrer (**into** à) **2** *vi* s'intégrer (**into** à)

integrated ['ɪntɪgreɪtɪd] *adj* intégré(e); *(school)* qui pratique la déségrégation raciale

integration [ɪntɪ'greɪʃən] *n* intégration *f*

integrity [ɪn'tegrɪtɪ] *n* intégrité *f*

intellect ['ɪntɪlekt] *n* intellect *m*, intelligence *f*

intellectual [ɪntɪ'lektjʊəl] **1** *n* intellectuel(elle) *m,f* **2** *adj* intellectuel(elle)

intelligence [ɪn'telɪdʒəns] *n* (**a**) *(faculty)* intelligence *f*; *Psy* **i. quotient** quotient *m* intellectuel; **i. test** test *m* d'intelligence (**b**) *(secret service)* services *mpl* secrets; **i. officer** agent *m* de renseignements; **i. service** services secrets

intelligent [ɪn'telɪdʒənt] *adj* intelligent(e)

intelligible [ɪn'telɪdʒɪbəl] *adj* intelligible

intemperate [ɪn'tempərət] *adj (climate)* rude; *(person, behaviour)* intempérant(e)

intend [ɪn'tend] *vt* **to i. to do sth** avoir l'intention de faire qch; **to i. sth for sb** destiner qch à qn; **was that intended?** était-ce intentionnel?; **it was intended as a compliment/a joke** c'était un compliment/pour plaisanter

intended [ɪn'tendɪd] **1** *n Old-fashioned or Hum (future spouse)* futur(e) *m,f*
2 *adj (consequence, outcome)* prévu(e); *(effect)* escompté(e); *(insult, mistake)* voulu(e)

intense [ɪn'tens] *adj* intense; *(interest, anger)* vif (vive); *(person)* passionné(e)

intensely [ɪn'tenslɪ] *adv* **(a)** *(amusing, boring)* extrêmement **(b)** *(look at, speak)* intensément, avec intensité

intensify [ɪn'tensɪfaɪ] *(pt & pp* **intensified)** **1** *vt (search, effort)* intensifier; *(pressure)* augmenter
2 *vi* s'intensifier

intensity [ɪn'tensɪtɪ] *n* intensité *f*

intensive [ɪn'tensɪv] *adj* intensif(ive); *Med* **i. care** soins *mpl* intensifs

intent [ɪn'tent] **1** *n* intention *f*; **to all intents and purposes** quasiment
2 *adj (look)* intense; **to be i. on doing sth** être résolu(e) *ou* déterminé(e) à faire qch

intention [ɪn'tenʃən] *n* intention *f*; **to have every i. of doing sth** avoir la ferme intention de faire qch; **to have no i. of doing sth** n'avoir nullement l'intention de faire qch

intentional [ɪn'tenʃənəl] *adj* intentionnel(elle), voulu(e)

intentionally [ɪn'tenʃənəlɪ] *adv* intentionnellement; **I didn't do it I.** je ne l'ai pas fait exprès

intently [ɪn'tentlɪ] *adv (listen, look at)* attentivement

inter [ɪn'tɜ:(r)] *(pt & pp* **interred)** *vt* inhumer, enterrer

interact [ɪntə'rækt] *vi* **(a)** *(of person)* communiquer **(with** avec); *(of two or more people)* communiquer entre eux (elles) **(b)** *(of chemical)* réagir **(with** avec); *(of two or more chemicals)* réagir entre eux (elles)

interaction [ɪntə'rækʃən] *n* interaction *f*

interactive [ɪntə'ræktɪv] *adj* interactif(ive)

intercede [ɪntə'si:d] *vi* intercéder **(with/for** auprès de/ en faveur de)

intercept [ɪntə'sept] *vt* intercepter

interception [ɪntə'sepʃən] *n* interception *f*

intercession [ɪntə'seʃən] *n* intercession *f*

interchange 1 *n* ['ɪntətʃeɪndʒ] *(exchange)* échange *m*; *(on motorway)* échangeur *m*
2 *vt* [ɪntə'tʃeɪndʒ] *(exchange)* échanger; *(transpose)* intervertir

interchangeable [ɪntə'tʃeɪndʒəbəl] *adj* interchangeable

intercom ['ɪntəkɒm] *n* Interphone *m*

interconnect [ɪntəkə'nekt] *vt* interconnecter

intercontinental [ɪntəkɒntɪ'nentəl] *adj* intercontinental(e); **i. ballistic missile** missile *m* balistique intercontinental

intercourse ['ɪntəkɔ:s] *n* **(a)** *(sexual)* **i.** rapports *mpl* (sexuels) **(b)** *Formal (dealings)* commerce *m*, relations *fpl*

interdependent ['ɪntədɪ'pendənt] *adj* interdépendant(e)

interest ['ɪntrest] **1** *n* **(a)** *(curiosity)* intérêt *m*; *(hobby)* centre *m* d'intérêt; **of i.** intéressant(e); **of historical i.** intéressant du point de vue historique; **to be of i. to sb** intéresser qn; **to take an i. in sth** s'intéresser à qch; **to lose i. (in sth)** se désintéresser (de qch)
(b) *(stake)* intérêt *m*; **to have a financial i. in sth** avoir investi financièrement dans qch
(c) *(benefit)* intérêt *m*; **to act in sb's interests** agir dans l'intérêt de qn; **the public i.** l'intérêt public; **it's in my i. to do it** j'ai tout intérêt à le faire; **in the interests of…** dans l'intérêt de…
(d) *(on loan, investment)* intérêt(s) *m(pl)*

2 *vt* intéresser; **to i. sb in sth** intéresser qn à qch; **can I i. you in a drink?** je peux vous offrir un verre?

interested ['ɪntrestɪd] *adj* intéressé(e); **to be i. in sth** s'intéresser à qch; **he seemed i. in the proposal** il a semblé intéressé par cette proposition

interest-free ['ɪntrest'fri:] *adj (loan)* sans intérêt; *(credit)* gratuit(e)

interesting ['ɪntrestɪŋ] *adj* intéressant(e)

interface ['ɪntəfeɪs] *n Comptr* interface *f*

interfere [ɪntə'fɪə(r)] *vi* **(a)** *(meddle)* se mêler **(in** de); **he's always interfering** il est toujours à se mêler de ce qui ne le regarde pas; **don't i. with my papers** ne touche pas à mes papiers; *Euph* **to i. with sb** *(sexually)* abuser de qn **(b) to i. with sth** *(hinder)* gêner qch

interference [ɪntə'fɪərəns] *n* **(a)** *(meddling)* ingérence *f* **(b)** *Rad & TV* interférences *fpl*

interfering [ɪntə'fɪərɪŋ] *adj* importun(e)

interim ['ɪntərɪm] **1** *n* **in the i.** entre-temps
2 *adj (agreement, report)* provisoire

interior [ɪn'tɪərɪə(r)] **1** *n* intérieur *m*
2 *adj* intérieur(e); **i. decorator** décorateur(trice) *m,f* (d'intérieurs); **i. designer** architecte *mf* d'intérieur

interject [ɪntə'dʒekt] *vt (remark)* lancer; *(protest)* émettre

interjection [ɪntə'dʒekʃən] *n* interjection *f*

interlocking [ɪntə'lɒkɪŋ] *adj (parts)* emboîtable; *(gears)* qui s'enclenchent

interlocutor [ɪntə'lɒkjutə(r)] *n Formal* interlocuteur (trice) *m,f*

interloper ['ɪntələupə(r)] *n* intrus(e) *m,f*

interlude ['ɪntəlu:d] *n also Fig* intermède *m*

intermarriage [ɪntə'mærɪdʒ] *n (within a family)* mariage *m* consanguin; *(with member of another group)* mariage

intermarry [ɪntə'mærɪ] *(pt & pp* **intermarried)** *vi* se marier *(au sein de la même famille)*

intermediary [ɪntə'mi:dɪərɪ] *(pl* **intermediaries)** *n* intermédiaire *mf*

intermediate [ɪntə'mi:dɪət] *adj* intermédiaire; *(student)* de niveau moyen

interminable [ɪn'tɜ:mɪnəbəl] *adj* interminable

intermingle [ɪntə'mɪŋgəl] **1** *vt* mélanger **(with** avec)
2 *vi* se mêler **(with** à), se mélanger **(with** avec)

intermission [ɪntə'mɪʃən] *n* entracte *m*

intermittent [ɪntə'mɪtənt] *adj* intermittent(e)

intern 1 *n* ['ɪntɜ:n] *Am Med* interne *mf*
2 *vt* [ɪn'tɜ:n] interner

internal [ɪn'tɜ:nəl] *adj* interne; *(flight)* intérieur(e); **i. combustion engine** moteur *m* à combustion interne

internalize [ɪn'tɜ:nəlaɪz] *vt* intérioriser

internally [ɪn'tɜ:nəlɪ] *adv* intérieurement; **not to be taken i.** *(on medicine container)* à usage externe

international [ɪntə'næʃənəl] **1** *n (in sport) (player)* international(e) *m,f*; *(match)* match *m* international
2 *adj* international(e); **I. Date Line** ligne *f* de changement de date; *Fin* **I. Monetary Fund** Fonds *m* monétaire international

internee [ɪntɜ:'ni:] *n* interné(e) *m,f*

Internet ['ɪntənet] *n Comptr* **the I.** (l')Internet *m*; **to surf the I.** naviguer sur (l')Internet; **I. café** cybercafé *m*

internment [ɪn'tɜ:nmənt] *n* internement *m*

interpersonal [ɪntə'pɜ:sənəl] *adj* interpersonnel(elle)

interplay ['ɪntəpleɪ] *n* interaction *f* **(of** or **between** entre)

Interpol ['ɪntəpɒl] *n* Interpol *m*

interpolate [ɪn'tɜ:pəleɪt] *vt (remark, question)* glisser; *(word, passage)* intercaler

interpose [ɪntə'pəʊz] *vt* interposer **(between** entre)

interpret [ɪn'tɜ:prɪt] **1** *vt* interpréter **2** *vi* faire l'interprète

interpretation [ɪntɜ:prɪ'teɪʃən] *n* interprétation *f*

interpreter [ɪn'tɜ:prɪtə(r)] *n* interprète *mf*

interracial [ɪntə'reɪʃəl] *adj* interracial(e)

interrelated [ɪntərɪ'leɪtɪd] *adj* lié(e)

interrogate [ɪn'terəgeɪt] *vt* interroger

interrogation [ɪntərə'geɪʃən] *n* interrogatoire *m*

interrogative [ɪntə'rɒgətɪv] **1** *n Gram* interrogatif *m*; *(question mark)* point *m* d'interrogation **2** *adj (look, tone)* interrogateur(trice); *Gram* interrogatif(ive)

interrogator [ɪn'terəgeɪtə(r)] *n* interrogateur(trice) *m,f*

interrupt [ɪntə'rʌpt] **1** *vt* interrompre **2** *vi* it's rude to i. ce n'est pas poli d'interrompre les gens; **I'm sorry to i.** je suis désolé de vous interrompre

interruption [ɪntə'rʌpʃən] *n* interruption *f*

intersect [ɪntə'sekt] **1** *vt* couper **2** *vi* se couper

intersection [ɪntə'sekʃən] *n (of roads)* carrefour *m*

intersperse [ɪntə'spɜ:s] *vt* **to be interspersed with sth** être parsemé(e) de qch; **sunshine interspersed with showers** temps ensoleillé entrecoupé d'averses

intertwine [ɪntə'twaɪn] **1** *vt* entremêler **(with** de); **to be intertwined** *(of two things)* être entrelacés(ées) **2** *vi* s'entrelacer

interval ['ɪntəvəl] *n* intervalle *m*; *(at theatre)* entracte *m*; **at regular intervals** à intervalles réguliers; **at weekly intervals** toutes les semaines; **sunny intervals** éclaircies *fpl*

intervene [ɪntə'vi:n] *vi (of person)* intervenir **(in** dans)*; (of event)* survenir

intervening [ɪntə'vi:nɪŋ] *adj* intermédiaire; **in the i. period** entre-temps, dans l'intervalle

intervention [ɪntə'venʃən] *n* intervention *f*

interview ['ɪntəvju:] **1** *n (for job)* entretien *m*; *TV & Journ* interview *f* **2** *vt (for job)* faire passer un entretien à; *TV & Journ* interviewer

interviewee [ɪntəvju:'i:] *n (for job)* candidat(e) *m,f (à qui l'on fait passer un entretien)*; *TV & Journ* personne *f* interviewée

interviewer ['ɪntəvju:ə(r)] *n (for job)* = personne qui fait passer un entretien; *TV & Journ* interviewer(euse) *m,f*

intestate [ɪn'testeɪt] *adj Law* **to die i.** mourir intestat

intestinal [ɪntes'taɪnəl] *adj* intestinal(e)

intestine [ɪn'testɪn] *n* intestin *m*; **large i.** gros intestin; **small i.** intestin grêle

intimacy ['ɪntɪməsɪ] *n (of relationship, atmosphere)* intimité *f*; *Euph (sexual)* relations *fpl* intimes

intimate 1 *n* ['ɪntɪmət] intime *mf* **2** *adj* ['ɪntɪmət] *(friend, restaurant)* intime; *(knowledge)* approfondi(e); *Euph* **to be i. with sb** *(sexually)* avoir des relations intimes avec qn **3** *vt* ['ɪntɪmeɪt] *Formal (hint at)* faire comprendre; *(make known)* signifier

intimately ['ɪntɪmətlɪ] *adv* intimement

intimidate [ɪn'tɪmɪdeɪt] *vt* intimider; **to i. sb into doing sth** forcer qn à faire qch en usant d'intimidation

intimidation [ɪntɪmɪ'deɪʃən] *n* intimidation *f*

into ['ɪntʊ] *prep* **(a)** *(with motion, direction)* dans; **to go i. a**

room entrer dans une pièce; **come i. my office** venez dans mon bureau; **to get i. bed** se mettre au lit; **to crash i. sth** rentrer dans qch **(b)** *(expressing change)* en; **to change i. sth** se changer en qch; **to translate sth i. English** traduire qch en anglais; **to break sth i. pieces** mettre qch en morceaux **(c)** *(in division)* **three i. six goes twice** six divisé par trois donne deux **(d)** *Fam (keen on)* **I was never really i. pop music** je n'ai jamais été un fana de musique pop; **is he i. drugs?** est-ce qu'il se drogue?; **he's really i. my sister** il en pince vraiment pour ma sœur

intolerable [ɪn'tɒlərəbəl] *adj* intolérable

intolerance [ɪn'tɒlərəns] *n* intolérance *f*

intolerant [ɪn'tɒlərənt] *adj* **to be i. of sb** être intolérant(e) à l'égard de qn; **to be i. of sth** ne pas tolérer qch

intonation [ɪntə'neɪʃən] *n* intonation *f*

intone [ɪn'təʊn] *vt (speak)* débiter; *(of preacher)* psalmodier

intoxicated [ɪn'tɒksɪkeɪtɪd] *adj (drunk)* ivre; *Fig* **i. with power/fame** ivre de puissance/gloire

intoxication [ɪntɒksɪ'keɪʃən] *n also Fig* ivresse *f*

intractable [ɪn'træktəbəl] *adj (person)* intraitable; *(problem)* très délicat(e)

intransigence [ɪn'trænzɪdʒəns] *n Formal* intransigeance *f* **(over** sur)

intransigent [ɪn'trænzɪdʒənt] *adj Formal* intransigeant(e) **(over** sur)

intransitive [ɪn'trænzɪtɪv] *adj Gram* intransitif(ive)

intrauterine device ['ɪntrə'ju:təraɪndɪ'vaɪs] *n Med* stérilet *m*

intravenous ['ɪntrə'vi:nəs] *adj Med (drip)* veineux(euse); **i. injection** intraveineuse *f*

in-tray ['ɪntreɪ] *n* bac *m* du courrier à traiter

intrepid [ɪn'trepɪd] *adj* intrépide

intricacy ['ɪntrɪkəsɪ] *n (pl intricacies)* complexité *f*; **the intricacies of the law** les subtilités du droit

intricate ['ɪntrɪkət] *adj* compliqué(e)

intrigue 1 *n* ['ɪntri:g] intrigue *f* **2** *vt* [ɪn'tri:g] *(interest)* intriguer

intrinsic [ɪn'trɪnsɪk] *adj* intrinsèque

introduce [ɪntrə'dju:s] *vt* **(a)** *(person)* présenter **(to** à); **to i. oneself** se présenter; **to i. sb to sth** initier qn à qch **(b)** *(reform, practice)* introduire

introduction [ɪntrə'dʌkʃən] *n* **(a)** *(of person)* présentation *f*; **to make the introductions** faire les présentations; **(b)** *(to book)* avant-propos *m inv*, introduction *f* **(c)** *(of reform, practice)* introduction *f* **(d)** *(first experience)* initiation *f* **(to** à)

introductory [ɪntrə'dʌktərɪ] *adj* d'introduction; *(price, offer)* de lancement

introspection [ɪntrə'spekʃən] *n* introspection *f*

introspective [ɪntrə'spektɪv] *adj (person)* introverti(e); *(mood)* introspectif(ive)

introvert ['ɪntrəvɜ:t] *n* introverti(e) *m,f*

introverted ['ɪntrəvɜ:tɪd] *adj* introverti(e)

intrude [ɪn'tru:d] *vi* **(a)** *(impose oneself)* déranger **(b)** *(interfere)* **her work intrudes on her family life** son travail empiète sur sa vie de famille; **to i. on sb's privacy** s'immiscer dans la vie privée de qn

intruder [ɪn'tru:də(r)] *n* intrus(e) *m,f*

intrusion [ɪn'tru:ʒən] *n* intrusion *f*

intrusive [ɪn'tru:sɪv] *adj* importun(e)

intuition [ɪntjuː'ɪʃən] *n* intuition *f*
intuitive [ɪn'tjuːɪtɪv] *adj* intuitif(ive)
Inuit ['ɪnʊɪt] **1** *n* Inuit *mf*
  2 *adj* inuit
inundate ['ɪnʌndeɪt] *vt* inonder (**with** de); *Fig (with phone calls, letters)* submerger (**with** de)
invade [ɪn'veɪd] *vt* envahir; **to i. sb's privacy** s'immiscer dans la vie privée de qn
invader [ɪn'veɪdə(r)] *n* envahisseur(euse) *m,f*
invalid¹ [ɪn'vælɪd] *adj (document, argument)* non valable; *(marriage)* non valide
invalid² ['ɪnvəlɪd] *n (disabled person)* invalide *mf,* infirme *mf; (ill person)* malade *mf*
invalidate [ɪn'vælɪdeɪt] *vt (theory)* infirmer; *(document, contract)* invalider
invaluable [ɪn'væljʊəbəl] *adj* précieux(euse)
invariable [ɪn'veərɪəbəl] *adj* invariable
invariably [ɪn'veərɪəblɪ] *adv* invariablement
invasion [ɪn'veɪʒən] *n* invasion *f*
invective [ɪn'vektɪv] *n* invectives *fpl*
inveigh [ɪn'veɪ] *vi Formal* **to i. against** invectiver contre
inveigle [ɪn'veɪgəl] *vt* **to i. sb into doing sth** entortiller qn pour qu'il fasse qch
invent [ɪn'vent] *vt* inventer
invention [ɪn'venʃən] *n* (**a**) *(action, thing invented)* invention *f* (**b**) *(creativity)* inventivité *f*
inventive [ɪn'ventɪv] *adj* inventif(ive)
inventiveness [ɪn'ventɪvnəs] *n* inventivité *f*
inventor [ɪn'ventə(r)] *n* inventeur(trice) *m,f*
inventory ['ɪnventərɪ] *(pl* **inventories)** *n (list)* inventaire *m; (stock)* stock(s) *m(pl)*
inverse ['ɪnvɜːs] *adj* inverse
invert [ɪn'vɜːt] *vt (turn upside down)* renverser; *(reverse)* inverser, intervertir
invertebrate [ɪn'vɜːtɪbrɪt] **1** *n* invertébré *m*
  2 *adj* invertébré(e)
inverted [ɪn'vɜːtɪd] *adj (upside down)* renversé(e); *(reversed)* inversé(e); **i. commas** guillemets *mpl;* **to be an i. snob** faire du snobisme à l'envers
invest [ɪn'vest] **1** *vt* (**a**) *(money, time)* investir (**in** dans) (**b**) *(right, power)* investir (**with** de)
  2 *vi* investir (**in** dans)
investigate [ɪn'vestɪgeɪt] *vt (crime)* enquêter sur; *(question)* examiner
investigation [ɪnvestɪ'geɪʃən] *n* enquête *f*
investigative [ɪn'vestɪgətɪv] *adj (journalism)* d'investigation
investigator [ɪn'vestɪgeɪtə(r)] *n* enquêteur(euse) *m,f*
investment [ɪn'vestmənt] *n* investissement *m;* **i. account** compte *m* d'investissement; **i. analyst** analyste *mf* en placements; **i. bank** banque *f* d'affaires; **i. income** revenu *m* provenant d'investissements; **i. trust** société *f* de placement
investor [ɪn'vestə(r)] *n* investisseur *m*
inveterate [ɪn'vetərɪt] *adj (gambler, drunkard, liar)* invétéré(e); *(critic)* acharné(e)
invidious [ɪn'vɪdɪəs] *adj (choice, comparison)* inéquitable; *(position, task)* peu enviable
invigilate [ɪn'vɪdʒɪleɪt] *Br* **1** *vt (exam)* surveiller
  2 *vi* surveiller les candidats *(à un examen)*
invigilator [ɪn'vɪdʒɪleɪtə(r)] *n Br (in exam)* surveillant(e) *m,f (des candidats à un examen)*
invigorating [ɪn'vɪgəreɪtɪŋ] *adj* vivifiant(e)

invincible [ɪn'vɪnsɪbəl] *adj* invincible
inviolable [ɪn'vaɪələbəl] *adj Formal* inviolable
inviolate [ɪn'vaɪələt] *adj Formal* inviolé(e)
invisible [ɪn'vɪzɪbəl] *adj* invisible (**to** à); **i. earnings** invisibles *mpl;* **i. ink** encre *f* sympathique
invitation [ɪnvɪ'teɪʃən] *n* invitation *f*
invite **1** *n* ['ɪnvaɪt] *Fam* invit' *f*
  2 *vt* [ɪn'vaɪt] (**a**) *(guest)* inviter; **to i. sb in/up** inviter qn à entrer/monter; **to i. sb to do sth** inviter qn à faire qch; **applications are invited for the post of...** ≃ nous recrutons un...; (**b**) *(trouble, criticism) (of person)* aller au-devant de
inviting [ɪn'vaɪtɪŋ] *adj* attrayant(e); *(food)* appétissant(e)
in vitro fertilization [ɪn'viːtrəʊfɜːtɪlaɪ'zeɪʃən] *n* fécondation *f* in vitro
invoice ['ɪnvɔɪs] *Com* **1** *n* facture *f;* **to make out an i.** établir une facture
  2 *vt (goods)* facturer; *(person, company)* envoyer la facture à
invoke [ɪn'vəʊk] *vt Formal (God, law)* invoquer; *(spirit, feeling)* évoquer; **to i. sb's aid** appeler qn à son secours
involuntary [ɪn'vɒlʌntərɪ] *adj* involontaire
involve [ɪn'vɒlv] *vt* (**a**) *(implicate)* **to i. sb in sth** impliquer qn dans qch; **this doesn't i. you** ça ne te concerne pas (**b**) *(entail) (work, expense)* impliquer, entraîner; **my job involves a lot of travel** je suis amené à voyager pour mon travail
involved [ɪn'vɒlvd] *adj* (**a**) *(implicated)* **to be/get i. in sth** *(crime, affair)* être impliqué(e) dans qch; **to be i. in an accident** avoir un accident; **to be i. in teaching/banking** être dans l'enseignement/la banque; **50 people were i. in the project** 50 personnes ont pris part au projet; **the police became i.** la police est intervenue; **don't get i.!** ne te mêle pas de ça!; **how much money is i.?** de combien d'argent s'agit-il?
  (**b**) *(emotionally)* **to be/get i. with sb** sortir avec qn; **I don't want to get i.** je ne veux pas m'engager
  (**c**) *(engrossed)* **to get i. in a book/movie** s'absorber dans un livre/film
  (**d**) *(complicated)* compliqué(e)
involvement [ɪn'vɒlvmənt] *n* (**a**) *(participation)* participation *f* (**in** à) (**b**) *(commitment)* engagement *m* (**in** dans)
invulnerable [ɪn'vʌlnərəbəl] *adj* invulnérable (**to** à)
inward ['ɪnwəd] *adj* (**a**) *(thoughts, feelings)* intime (**b**) *(movement)* vers l'intérieur; *Econ* **i. investment** investissements *mpl* étrangers
inward-looking ['ɪnwədlʊkɪŋ] *adj* replié(e) sur soi-même
inwards ['ɪnwədz] *adv* vers l'intérieur
iodine ['aɪədiːn, *Am* 'aɪədaɪn] *n Chem* iode *m; (antiseptic)* teinture *f* d'iode
ion ['aɪən] *n* ion *m*
Ionian [aɪ'əʊnɪən] *n* **the I. (Sea)** la mer Ionienne
ionize ['aɪənaɪz] *vt* ioniser
iota [aɪ'əʊtə] *n* iota *m;* **she hadn't changed one i.** elle n'avait pas du tout changé; **not an i. of truth** pas une once de vérité
IOU [aɪəʊ'juː] *n (abbr* **I owe you)** reconnaissance *f* de dette
IP [aɪ'piː] *n Comptr (abbr* **Internet Protocol) IP address** adresse *f* IP
IPA [aɪpiː'eɪ] *n (abbr* **International Phonetic Alphabet)** API *m*
IQ [aɪ'kjuː] *n (abbr* **intelligence quotient)** QI *m*
IRA [aɪ'ɑː'reɪ] *n* (**a**) *(abbr* **Irish Republican Army)** IRA *f* (**b**)

Am (abbr **individual retirement account**) plan *m* d'épargne retraite personnel

Iran [ɪ'rɑːn] *n* l'Iran *m*

Iranian [ɪ'reɪnɪən] **1** *n* **(a)** *(person)* Iranien(enne) *m,f* **(b)** *(language)* iranien *m* **2** *adj* iranien(enne)

Iraq [ɪ'rɑːk] *n* l'Irak *m*

Iraqi [ɪ'rɑːkɪ] **1** *n* Irakien(enne) *m,f,* Iraquien(enne) *m,f* **2** *adj* irakien(enne), iraquien(enne)

irascible [ɪ'ræsɪbəl] *adj (person)* irascible; *(temperament)* colérique

irate [aɪ'reɪt] *adj* furieux(euse)

ire ['aɪə(r)] *n Lit* courroux *m*

Ireland ['aɪələnd] *n* l'Irlande *f*

iris ['aɪrɪs] *n* iris *m*

Irish ['aɪrɪʃ] **1** *npl (people)* **the I.** les Irlandais *mpl* **2** *n (language)* irlandais *m* **3** *adj* irlandais(e); **I. coffee** Irish coffee *m*; **the I. Sea** la mer d'Irlande; **I. stew** = ragoût de mouton, aux pommes de terre et aux oignons

Irishman ['aɪrɪʃmən] *n* Irlandais *m*

Irishwoman ['aɪrɪʃwʊmən] *n* Irlandaise *f*

irk [ɜːk] *vt* agacer

irksome ['ɜːksəm] *adj* agaçant(e)

iron ['aɪən] **1** *n* **(a)** *(metal, golf club)* fer *m*; **made of i.** en fer; **to have an i. constitution** avoir une santé de fer; **an i. will** une volonté de fer; **i. discipline** discipline *f* de fer; **the I. Age** l'âge *m* de fer; **the I. Curtain** le rideau de fer; **i. lung** poumon *m* d'acier; **i. ore** minerai *m* de fer **(b)** *(for clothes)* fer *m* (à repasser); *Fig* **to have several irons in the fire** avoir plusieurs fers au feu **(c)** *(in diet)* fer *m*; **i. deficiency** carence *f* en fer **2** *vt & vi (clothes)* repasser

▸ **iron out** *vt sep (difficulty)* aplanir; *(problem)* résoudre

ironic(al) [aɪ'rɒnɪk(əl)] *adj* ironique

ironing ['aɪənɪŋ] *n* repassage *m*; **to do the i.** repasser, faire le repassage; **i. board** planche *f* ou table *f* à repasser

ironmonger ['aɪənmʌŋgə(r)] *n Br* quincaillier(ère) *m,f*; **i.'s (shop)** quincaillerie *f*

irony ['aɪrənɪ] *(pl* **ironies)** *n* ironie *f*; **the i. is that...** ce qu'il y a d'ironique, c'est que...

irrational [ɪ'ræʃənəl] *adj* irrationnel(elle)

irreconcilable [ɪrekən'saɪləbəl] *adj (enemy)* irréconciliable; *(hatred)* implacable; *(belief, idea)* incompatible, inconciliable

irredeemable [ɪrɪ'diːməbəl] *adj (fault)* irréparable; *(situation)* irrémédiable

irrefutable [ɪrɪ'fjuːtəbəl] *adj* irréfutable

irregular [ɪ'regjʊlə(r)] *adj* irrégulier(ère)

irregularity [ɪregjʊ'lærɪtɪ] *(pl* **irregularities)** *n* irrégularité *f*

irrelevance [ɪ'reləvəns], **irrelevancy** [ɪ'reləvənsɪ] *n (of remark, advice)* manque *m* d'à-propos

irrelevant [ɪ'reləvənt] *adj (remark, advice)* hors de propos; **that's i.** cela n'a rien à voir (avec la question)

irreligious [ɪrɪ'lɪdʒəs] *adj* irréligieux(euse)

irremediable [ɪrɪ'miːdɪəbəl] *adj Formal (situation, loss)* irrémédiable; *(mistake)* irréparable

irreparable [ɪ'repərəbəl] *adj* irréparable

irreplaceable [ɪrɪ'pleɪsəbəl] *adj* irremplaçable

irrepressible [ɪrɪ'presɪbəl] *adj (urge)* irrépressible; *(good humour)* à toute épreuve; **he's i.** rien n'entame sa bonne humeur

irreproachable [ɪrɪ'prəʊtʃəbəl] *adj* irréprochable

irresistible [ɪrɪ'zɪstɪbəl] *adj* irrésistible

irresolute [ɪ'rezəluːt] *adj* irrésolu(e), indécis(e)

irrespective of [ɪrɪ'spektɪvəv] *prep* indépendamment de, sans tenir compte de

irresponsible [ɪrɪ'spɒnsɪbəl] *adj* irresponsable

irretrievable [ɪrɪ'triːvəbəl] *adj (loss)* irrémédiable; *(money)* irrécupérable; *(mistake, situation)* irréparable

irreverent [ɪ'revərənt] *adj* irrévérencieux(euse)

irreversible [ɪrɪ'vɜːsɪbəl] *adj (decision, process)* irréversible

irrevocable [ɪ'revəkəbəl] *adj* irrévocable

irrigate ['ɪrɪgeɪt] *vt* irriguer

irrigation [ɪrɪ'geɪʃən] *n* irrigation *f*; **i. canal** *or* **ditch** canal *m* d'irrigation

irritable ['ɪrɪtəbəl] *adj* irritable; **i. bowel syndrome** colopathie *f* fonctionnelle

irritant ['ɪrɪtənt] *n (to eyes, skin)* irritant *m*; *(to person, government)* empêcheur(euse) *m,f* de tourner en rond

irritate ['ɪrɪteɪt] *vt (annoy)* agacer, irriter; *Med* irriter

irritating ['ɪrɪteɪtɪŋ] *adj* agaçant(e), irritant(e)

irritation [ɪrɪ'teɪʃən] *n* agacement *m*, irritation *f*; *Med* irritation *f*

IRS [aɪɑː'res] *n Am (abbr* **Internal Revenue Service)** **the I.** ≃ le fisc

is [ɪz] *3rd pers singular of* **be**

ISBN [aɪesbiː'en] *n (abbr* **International Standard Book Number)** ISBN *m*

Islam ['ɪzlɑːm] *n* l'Islam *m*

Islamic [ɪz'læmɪk] *adj* islamique

island ['aɪlənd] *n* île *f*; *(small)* îlot *m*; *(in road)* refuge *m*

islander ['aɪləndə(r)] *n (in general)* insulaire *mf*; *(of specific island)* habitant(e) *m,f* de l'île

isle [aɪl] *n* île *f*; **the I. of Man** l'île de Man; **the I. of Wight** l'île de Wight

isn't ['ɪzənt] = **is not**

ISO [aɪes'əʊ] *n (abbr* **International Standards Organization)** ISO *f*

isobar ['aɪsəʊbɑː(r)] *n* isobare *f*

isolate ['aɪsəleɪt] *vt* isoler (**from** de)

isolated ['aɪsəleɪtɪd] *adj* isolé(e)

isolation [aɪsə'leɪʃən] *n* isolement *m*; **in i. (from)** isolément (de); **i. ward** salle *f* des contagieux

isotope ['aɪsəʊtəʊp] *n Phys* isotope *m*

ISP [aɪes'piː] *n (abbr* **Internet Service Provider)** fournisseur *m* d'accès à l'Internet

Israel ['ɪzreɪəl] *n* Israël *m*

Israeli [ɪz'reɪlɪ] **1** *n* Israélien(enne) *m,f* **2** *adj* israélien(enne)

Israelite ['ɪzrəlaɪt] *n Hist* Israélite *mf*

issue ['ɪʃuː, 'ɪʃuː] **1** *n* **(a)** *(topic)* problème *m*, question *f*; **the issues of the day** les questions du jour; **that's not the i.** ce n'est pas (là) le problème; **to avoid the i.** esquiver le problème; **to confuse the i.** compliquer les choses; **to make an i. of sth** faire toute une affaire de qch; **at i.** en cause; **to take i. with sb** exprimer son désaccord avec qn **(b)** *(of banknotes, stamps)* émission *f* **(c)** *(of magazine)* numéro *m* **2** *vt (banknote, stamp)* émettre; *(order)* donner; **to i. sb with sth** délivrer qch à qn; **to i. a statement** faire une déclaration; *Law* **to i. a summons** notifier une citation **3** *vi Formal (of blood, smoke, water)* s'échapper *(* **from** *de); (of noise)* provenir *(* **from** *de)*

Istanbul [ɪstæn'bʊl] *n* Istanbul

isthmus ['ɪsməs] *n* isthme *m*

IT [aɪ'tiː] *n* Comptr (abbr **information technology**) l'informatique *f*

it [ɪt] *pron* (**a**) *(subject)* il (elle) *m,f;* **where's the book? – it's on the shelf** où est le livre? – il est sur l'étagère; **put the TV on – it's not working** allume la télé – elle est en panne; **it's a big car** c'est une grande voiture; **it's the best movie I've ever seen** c'est le meilleur film que j'aie jamais vu (**b**) *(direct object)* le (la) *m,f;* **I can do it** je peux le/la faire; **I saw it** je l'ai vu (**c**) *(indirect object)* lui; **give it something to eat** donne-lui à manger (**d**) *(prepositional object)* **on it** dessus; **under it** dessous; **beside it** à côté; **I forgot about it** j'ai oublié (**e**) *(as impersonal subject)* **it's snowing** il neige; **it's ten o'clock** il est dix heures; **it's cold today** il fait froid aujourd'hui; **it's impossible to work in this heat** il est impossible de travailler avec cette chaleur; **it's me** c'est moi (**f**) *(as complement of verb* **to be)** **that's it** *(that's all)* c'est tout

Italian [ɪ'tæljən] **1** *n* (**a**) *(person)* Italien(enne) *m,f* (**b**) *(language)* italien *m;* **I. class/teacher** classe *f*/professeur *m* d'italien **2** *adj* italien(enne)

italic [ɪ'tælɪk] *Typ* **1** *n* **italic(s)** italique *m* **2** *adj* italique

Italy ['ɪtəlɪ] *n* l'Italie *f*

itch [ɪtʃ] **1** *n* démangeaison *f; Fig* **to have an i. to do sth** brûler d'envie de faire qch **2** *vi (of person)* éprouver des démangeaisons; **my foot itches** j'ai le pied qui me démange; *Fig* **to be itching to do sth** brûler d'envie de faire qch

itchy ['ɪtʃɪ] *adj* **I've got an i. foot, my foot's i.** j'ai le pied qui me démange; *Fig* **to have i. feet** avoir la bougeotte

it'd ['ɪtəd] = **it would, it had**

item ['aɪtəm] *n (in collection, list)* article *m; (in news)* entrefilet *m; (longer)* article; **an i. of clothing** un vêtement; **personal items** objets *mpl* personnels; *Fam* **they're an i.** ils sortent ensemble

itemize ['aɪtəmaɪz] *vt* détailler

iterative ['ɪtərətɪv] *adj Comptr* itératif(ive)

itinerant [ɪ'tɪnərənt] *adj (preacher)* itinérant(e), *(salesman, musician)* ambulant(e)

itinerary [aɪ'tɪnərərɪ] *(pl* **itineraries)** *n* itinéraire *m*

it'll ['ɪtəl] = **it will**

its [ɪts] *possessive adj* (**a**) *(singular)* son (sa); *(plural)* ses; **i. bone** son os; **i. litter** sa litière; **i. kittens** ses châtons (**b**) *(for parts of body)* **the bear hurt i. paw** l'ours s'est blessé à la patte

it's [ɪts] = **it is, it has**

itself [ɪt'self] *pron* (**a**) *(reflexive)* **the cat's hurt i.** le chat s'est blessé (**b**) *(emphatic)* **this method is simplicity i.** cette méthode est la simplicité même; **the town i. isn't very interesting** la ville (elle-)même n'est pas d'un grand intérêt (**c**) *(after preposition)* **by i.** tout(e) seul(e); **in i.** en soi

ITV [aɪtiː'viː] *n Dr (abbr* **Independent Television)** – chaîne de télévision privée britannique

IUD [aɪjuː'diː] *n Med (abbr* **intrauterine device)** stérilet *m*

I've [aɪv] = **I have**

IVF [aɪviː'ef] *n Med (abbr* **in vitro fertilization)** FIV *f*

ivory ['aɪvərɪ] *n* ivoire *m;* **the I. Coast** la Côte d'Ivoire; *Fig* **i. tower** tour *f* d'ivoire

ivy ['aɪvɪ] *n (plant)* lierre *m; Am* **I. League** = ensemble des huit universités les plus prestigieuses du nord-est des États-Unis

J, j [dʒeɪ] *n (letter)* J, j *m inv*

jab [dʒæb] **1** *n* (**a**) *(with elbow, finger)* coup *m; (in boxing)* direct *m* (**b**) *Br Fam (injection)* piqûre *f*
2 *vt (pt & pp* **jabbed**) **he jabbed her in the arm with a pen** il lui a enfoncé un stylo dans le bras; **to j. a finger at sb** agiter son doigt sous le nez de qn

jabber ['dʒæbə(r)] *vi Fam (talk unclearly)* marmonner; *(chatter)* jacasser

Jack [dʒæk] *n* **J. Frost** le Bonhomme Hiver; *Br Fam* **I'm all right, J.** moi, ça va, merci

jack [dʒæk] *n* (**a**) *(person)* **every man j.** of them absolument tout le monde; **j. of all trades** touche-à-tout *mf* (**b**) *(for car)* cric *m* (**c**) *(in cards)* valet *m* (**d**) *(electric plug)* prise *f* ou fiche *f* mâle
▸ **jack in** *vt sep Br Fam* plaquer
▸ **jack up** *vt sep Fam (price, salaries)* augmenter

jackal ['dʒækəl] *n* chacal *m*

jackass ['dʒækæs] *n also Fig* âne *m*

jackboot ['dʒækbuːt] *n* botte *f* de cavalier; *Fig* **under the j. of** sous la botte de

jackdaw ['dʒækdɔː] *n* choucas *m*

jacket ['dʒækɪt] *n (coat)* veste *f; (of book)* jaquette *f; (of boiler)* chemise *f,* enveloppe *f;* **j. potatoes** pommes de terre *fpl* en robe des champs *ou* en robe de chambre

jackhammer ['dʒækhæmə(r)] *n* marteau-piqueur *m*

jack-in-the-box ['dʒækɪnðəbɒks] *n* diable *m* à ressort

jackknife ['dʒæknaɪf] **1** *n (pl* **jackknives**) couteau *m* de poche
2 *vi (of articulated lorry)* **the lorry jackknifed** la remorque du camion s'est soudain mise en travers de la route

jack-o'-lantern ['dʒækəˈlæntən] *n Am* = lanterne faite dans une citrouille sur laquelle on a creusé un visage

jackpot ['dʒækpɒt] *n (in lottery)* gros lot *m;* **to hit** *or* **win the j.** gagner le gros lot

jack rabbit *n* = gros lièvre commun en Amérique du Nord

Jacobean [dʒækəˈbɪən] *adj* = de l'époque de Jacques 1er (1603-1625)

Jacobite ['dʒækəbaɪt] *n & adj* Jacobite *mf*

Jacuzzi® [dʒəˈkuːzɪ] *n* Jacuzzi® *m*

jade [dʒeɪd] **1** *n (stone, colour)* jade *m*
2 *adj (colour)* **j.(-green)** vert jade

jaded ['dʒeɪdɪd] *adj (tired)* las (lasse); *(bored)* blasé(e); **to be j. with sth** être las de qch; **to have a j. palate** avoir le palais blasé

jag [dʒæg] *n Fam* **to go on a (drinking) j.** prendre une cuite; **to have a crying j.** avoir une crise de larmes

jagged ['dʒægɪd] *adj (coastline, mountain top)* déchiqueté(e), découpé(e); *(blade)* ébréché(e)

jaguar [*Br* 'dʒægjʊə(r), *Am* 'dʒægwɑː(r)] *n* jaguar *m*

jail [dʒeɪl] **1** *n* prison *f;* **to be in j.** être en prison; **to go to j.** aller en prison
2 *vt* emprisonner, mettre en prison

jailbird ['dʒeɪlbɜːd] *n Fam (in prison)* taulard(e) *m,f; (recidivist)* cheval *m* de retour

jailbreak ['dʒeɪlbreɪk] *n* évasion *f*

jailer ['dʒeɪlə(r)] *n* geôlier(ère) *m,f*

jailhouse ['dʒeɪlhaʊs] *n Am* prison *f*

jailor ['dʒeɪlə(r)] = **jailer**

Jakarta [dʒəˈkɑːtə] *n* Djakarta

jalop(p)y [dʒəˈlɒpɪ] *(pl* **jalop(p)ies**) *n Fam* vieille guimbarde *f,* vieux tacot *m*

jam¹ [dʒæm] **1** *n* (**a**) *(crowd) (of people)* foule *f; (of traffic)* encombrement *m* (**b**) *Fam (difficult situation)* **to be in/ get into a (bit of a) j.** être/se fourrer dans le pétrin (**c**) *(improvised performance)* **j. (session)** jam-session *f,* bœuf *m*
2 *vt (pt & pp* **jammed**) (**a**) *(pack tightly) (objects)* entasser (**into** dans); *(container)* bourrer (**with** de); **all my clothes are jammed into one drawer** tous mes vêtements sont entassés dans un seul tiroir; **people/cars jammed the street** la rue était noire de monde/embouteillée (**b**) *(immobilize) (drawer, mechanism)* coincer, bloquer; *(radio broadcast, station)* brouiller; *(switchboard)* saturer
3 *vi* (**a**) *(of drawer, mechanism)* se coincer, se bloquer (**b**) *(of crowd)* s'entasser (**into** dans) (**c**) *(of musicians)* improviser
▸ **jam on** *vt sep* **to j. on the brakes** écraser la pédale de frein

jam² *n (fruit preserve)* confiture *f;* **j. tart** tarte *f* à la confiture

Jamaica [dʒəˈmeɪkə] *n* la Jamaïque

Jamaican [dʒəˈmeɪkən] **1** *n* Jamaïcain(e) *m,f*
2 *adj* jamaïcain(e)

jamb [dʒæm] *n* montant *m*

jamboree [dʒæmbəˈriː] *n (scouts' meeting)* jamboree *m; Fam (celebration)* fête *f*

jamming ['dʒæmɪŋ] *n (of radio broadcast, station)* brouillage *m*

jammy ['dʒæmɪ] *adj* (**a**) *(covered with jam)* plein(e) de confiture (**b**) *Br Fam (lucky)* verni(e)

jam-packed ['dʒæm'pækd] *adj* plein(e) à craquer; *(street)* noir(e) de monde, bondé(e)

Jan *(abbr* **January**) janvier

jangle ['dʒæŋgəl] **1** *n* cliquetis *m*
2 *vt* faire cliqueter

3 *vt* cliqueter; *Fig* her voice made his nerves **j.** sa voix lui mettait les nerfs en pelote

janitor ['dʒænɪtə(r)] *n Am & Scot (caretaker)* concierge *mf*

January ['dʒænjʊərɪ] *n* janvier *m*; *see also* **May**

Jap [dʒæp] *n very Fam* Jap *mf,* = terme raciste désignant un Japonais

Japan [dʒə'pæn] *n* le Japon

Japanese [dʒæpə'niːz] **1** *npl (people)* **the J.** les Japonais *mpl*
2 *n* (**a**) *(person)* Japonais(e) *m,f* (**b**) *(language)* japonais *m*; **J. class/teacher** classe *f*/professeur *m* de japonais
3 *adj* japonais(e)

jape [dʒeɪp] *n* blague *f*

jar¹ [dʒɑː(r)] **1** *n (jolt)* choc *m*, secousse *f*
2 *vt (pt & pp* jarred*) also Fig* secouer; **someone jarred my elbow** quelqu'un m'a cogné le coude
3 *vi* (**a**) *(make unpleasant sound)* rendre un son discordant; **to j. on the ears** écorcher les oreilles; **to j. on the nerves** taper sur les nerfs (**b**) *(of colours)* jurer; *(of ideas)* être en contradiction

jar² *n (container)* pot *m*; *(earthenware)* jarre *f, Br Fam* **to have a j.** prendre un pot

jargon ['dʒɑːgən] *n Pej* jargon *m*

jarring ['dʒɑːrɪŋ] *adj (noise, voice)* discordant(e); *(blow)* qui ébranle tout le corps

jasmine ['dʒæzmɪn] *n* jasmin *m*

jaundice ['dʒɔːndɪs] *n* jaunisse *f*

jaundiced ['dʒɔːndɪst] *adj Fig (attitude, view)* aigu(ë), amer(ère)

jaunt [dʒɔːnt] *n* excursion *f,* sortie *f*

jauntiness ['dʒɔːntɪnɪs] *n (cheerfulness)* enjouement *m*; *(carefreeness)* insouciance *f*

jaunty ['dʒɔːntɪ] *adj (cheerful)* enjoué(e); *(carefree)* insouciant(e)

Java ['dʒɑːvə] *n* Java

javelin ['dʒævlɪn] *n* javelot *m*

jaw [dʒɔː] **1** *n* mâchoire *f*; **jaws** *(of animal)* gueule *f*; **the jaws of death** les griffes *fpl* de la mort
2 *vi Fam (chat)* papoter

jawbone ['dʒɔːbəʊn] *n* maxillaire *m*

jay [dʒeɪ] *n* geai *m*

jaywalker ['dʒeɪwɔːkə(r)] *n* = piéton qui traverse en dehors des passages cloutés

jaywalking ['dʒeɪwɔːkɪŋ] *n* = fait de traverser en dehors des passages cloutés

jazz [dʒæz] *n* jazz *m*; *Fam* **and all that j.** et tout le tremblement ou le bazar

▸ **jazz up** *vt sep Fam (enliven) (clothes, room, style)* égayer; *(party)* animer; *(taste)* relever

jazzy ['dʒæzɪ] *adj (tune)* jazzy *inv*; *(clothes, pattern)* aux couleurs vives

JCS [dʒeɪsiː'es] *npl Am (abbr* **Joint Chiefs of Staff**) = organe consultatif du ministère américain de la Défense, composé des chefs d'état-major des trois armées

jealous ['dʒeləs] *adj* jaloux(ouse); **to be j. of sb** être jaloux de qn

jealously ['dʒeləslɪ] *adv* jalousement; **to guard sth j.** veiller jalousement sur qch

jealousy ['dʒeləsɪ] *n* jalousie *f*

jeans [dʒiːnz] *npl* jeans *m*

Jeep® [dʒiːp] *n* Jeep® *f*

jeer [dʒɪə(r)] **1** *n (mocking)* moquerie *f*; **the jeers of the crowd** *(booing)* les huées *fpl* de la foule
2 *vt (boo)* huer; *(mock)* se moquer de

3 *vi* **to j. at sb/sth** *(boo)* huer qn/qch; *(mock)* se moquer de qn/qch

jeering ['dʒɪərɪŋ] **1** *n (booing)* huées *fpl*; *(mocking)* moqueries *fpl*
2 *adj* railleur(euse), moqueur(euse)

jeez [dʒiːz] *exclam Fam* mince alors!

Jehovah [dʒɪ'həʊvə] *n* Jéhovah; **J.'s Witness** témoin *m* de Jéhovah

jell [dʒel] *vi (of liquid)* se gélifier; *Fig (of ideas, plans)* prendre forme; *Fig (of team)* constituer un ensemble cohérent

Jell-o® ['dʒeləʊ] *n Am (dessert)* gelée *f*

jelly ['dʒelɪ] *(pl* jellies*) n (dessert, jam)* gelée *f; Am* **j. roll** *(gâteau, m)* roulé *m*

jellybean ['dʒelɪbiːn] *n* = bonbon couvert de sucre, en forme de haricot

jellyfish ['dʒelɪfɪʃ] *n* méduse *f*

jemmy ['dʒemɪ] *(pl* jemmies*) n Br* pince-monseigneur *f*

jeopardize ['dʒepədaɪz] *vt* compromettre; *(life)* mettre en danger

jeopardy ['dʒepədɪ] *n* in **j.** en danger, en péril; **to put sb/ sth in j.** mettre qn/qch en danger *ou* en péril

jerk¹ [dʒɜːk] **1** *n (sudden pull)* secousse *f*, coup *m* sec; **to give sth a j.** tirer sur qch d'un coup sec
2 *vt (pull)* tirer brusquement; *(in order to move)* déplacer par à-coups
3 *vi* **to j. forward** *(of car)* faire un bond en avant; *(of head)* partir en avant; **to j. to a halt** s'arrêter avec des soubresauts

jerk² *n Fam (person)* abruti(e) *m,f*

▸ **jerk off** *vi Vulg (masturbate)* se branler

jerkily ['dʒɜːkɪlɪ] *adv* de manière saccadée

jerky ['dʒɜːkɪ] *adj (movement)* saccadé(e); *(style)* hâché(e)

jerrican ['dʒerɪkæn] *n* jerrican *m*

jerry-built ['dʒerɪbɪlt] *adj* construit(e) à la va-vite

Jersey ['dʒɜːzɪ] *n (island)* Jersey. **J. (cow)** jersiaise *f*

jersey ['dʒɜːzɪ] *(pl* jerseys*) n (garment)* pull(-over) *m*, tricot *m*

Jerusalem [dʒə'ruːsələm] *n* Jérusalem; **J. artichoke** topinambour *m*

jest [dʒest] **1** *n* plaisanterie *f*; **to say sth in j.** dire qch pour plaisanter
2 *vi* plaisanter

jester ['dʒestə(r)] *n* farceur(euse) *m,f; Hist* (**court**) **j.** fou *m* (du roi)

jesting ['dʒestɪŋ] *adj (remark)* pour rire; *(tone)* de la plaisanterie

Jesuit ['dʒezjʊɪt] *n* jésuite *m*

Jesus ['dʒiːzəs] **1** *n* Jésus *m*; **J. Christ** Jésus-Christ
2 *exclam Fam* **J. (Christ)!** nom de Dieu!

jet¹ [dʒet] **1** *n* (**a**) *(plane)* jet *m*, avion *m* à réaction; **j. engine** réacteur *m*, moteur *m* à réaction; **j. fighter** chasseur *m* à réaction; **j. lag** fatigue *f* due au décalage horaire; **j. propulsion** propulsion *f* par réaction; **the j. set** la jet-set (**b**) *(nozzle, of liquid)* jet *m*
2 *vi (pt & pp* jetted*) Fam (travel by plane)* **to j. in** venir en avion; **to j. off** s'envoler; **to j. around the world** passer son temps dans les avions

jet² **1** *n (stone)* jais *m*
2 *adj* **j. (black)** de jais

jet-lagged ['dʒetlægd] *adj* fatigué(e) par le décalage horaire

jet-powered [dʒet'paʊəd], **jet-propelled** [dʒetprə-'peld] *adj* à réaction

jettison ['dʒetɪsən] *vt (cargo)* jeter à la mer *ou* par-dessus bord; *(plan, tradition)* abandonner

jetty ['dʒetɪ] *(pl* **jetties)** *n* jetée *f*; *(for landing)* embarcadère *m*

Jew [dʒuː] *n* Juif (Juive) *m,f*

jewel ['dʒuːəl] *n (gem, piece of jewellery)* bijou *m*; *Fig (person)* perle *f*

jeweller, *Am* **jeweler** ['dʒuːələ(r)] *n* bijoutier(ère) *m,f*; **j.'s (shop)** bijouterie *f*

jewellery, *Am* **jewelry** ['dʒuːəlrɪ] *n* bijoux *mpl*; **a piece of j.** un bijou

Jewess ['dʒuːɪs] *n Old-fashioned* Juive *f*

Jewish ['dʒuːɪʃ] *adj* juif (juive)

Jewry ['dʒuːərɪ] *n* the **J.** la communauté juive

jib¹ [dʒɪb] *n* **(a)** *(sail)* foc *m* **(b)** *(of crane)* flèche *f*

jib² *(pt & pp* **jibbed)** *vi* **to j. at sth/at doing sth** rechigner à qch/à faire qch

jibe [dʒaɪb] **1** *n* moquerie *f*
2 *vi* **to j. at sb** se moquer de qn

jiffy ['dʒɪfɪ] *n Fam* **in a j.** dans un instant, tout de suite

jig [dʒɪg] **1** *n (dance, music)* gigue *f*
2 *vi (pt & pp* **jigged)** *(dance)* danser la gigue

jigger ['dʒɪgə(r)] *vt Fam (TV, microwave)* bousiller; **to j. one's back/knee** s'esquinter le dos/genou

jiggered ['dʒɪgəd] *adj Fam (TV, microwave)* bousillé(e); *(back, knee)* esquinté(e)

jiggery-pokery ['dʒɪgərɪ'pəʊkərɪ] *n Br Fam* micmac *m*

jiggle ['dʒɪgəl] **1** *vt* secouer rapidement
2 *vi* remuer dans tous les sens
▸ **jiggle about, jiggle around** = jiggle

jigsaw ['dʒɪgsɔː] *n* **(a)** *(saw)* scie *f* sauteuse **(b)** *(game)* **j. (puzzle)** puzzle *m*

jihad [dʒɪ'hæd] *n* djihad *m*

jilt [dʒɪlt] *vt (lover)* plaquer

jingle ['dʒɪŋgəl] **1** *n* **(a)** *(of bells, coins)* tintement *m*; *(of keys)* cliquetis *m* **(b)** *(catchy tune)* jingle *m*
2 *vt (bells, coins)* faire tinter; *(keys)* faire cliqueter
3 *vi (of bells, coins)* tinter; *(of keys)* cliqueter

jingoism ['dʒɪŋgəʊɪzəm] *n Pej* chauvinisme *m*

jingoistic ['dʒɪŋgəʊ'ɪstɪk] *adj Pej* chauvin(e)

jinx [dʒɪŋks] *Fam* **1** *n (spell, curse)* (mauvais) sort *m*; **to put a j. on sb/sth** jeter un sort à qn/qch
2 *vt* **to be jinxed** avoir la poisse

JIT [dʒɪt] *adj Com (abbr* **just in time)** juste à temps

jitters ['dʒɪtəz] *npl Fam* **to have** *or* **get the j.** être à cran

jittery ['dʒɪtərɪ] *adj Fam* à cran

jive [dʒaɪv] **1** *n (music, dance)* swing *m*
2 *vi (dance)* danser le swing

Jnr *(abbr* **Junior) John Green, J.** John Green fils

job [dʒɒb] *n* **(a)** *(employment, post)* travail *m*, emploi *m*; **to be out of a j.** être sans travail *ou* emploi; **j. creation** création *f* d'emploi; **j. description** description *f* de poste; **to go j. hunting** chercher du travail; **j. losses** suppressions *fpl* d'emplois; **j. offer** offre *f* d'emploi; **j. opportunities** débouchés *mpl*; **j. satisfaction** satisfaction *f* dans le travail; **j. security** sécurité *f* de l'emploi; **j. sharing** partage *m* de poste; **j. title** fonction *f*
(b) *(piece of work, task)* tâche *f*; **to do a good j.** faire du beau travail; *Fig* **to do the j.** *(serve purpose)* convenir, faire l'affaire; **it was quite a j. getting her to come** la convaincre de venir n'a pas été une mince affaire; *Com* **j. lot** lot *m*
(c) *(responsibility, duty)* travail *m*; **to have the j. of doing sth** être chargé(e) de faire qch
(d) *Fam (crime)* coup *m*

(e) *(idioms) Br* **it's a good j. (that)…!** heureusement que…!; **that's just the j.!** c'est juste ce qu'il faut!

jobbing ['dʒɒbɪŋ] *adj Br (carpenter, electrician)* à la tâche *ou* pièce

Jobcentre ['dʒɒbsentə(r)] *n Br* ≃ agence *f* nationale pour l'emploi, ANPE *f*

jobless ['dʒɒblɪs] **1** *npl* **the j.** les sans-emploi *mpl*
2 *adj* sans emploi

job-share ['dʒɒbʃeə(r)] **1** *n* poste *m* partagé
2 *vi* partager un poste

jockey ['dʒɒkɪ] **1** *n (pl* **jockeys)** jockey *m*
2 *vi* **to j. for position** jouer des coudes

jockstrap ['dʒɒkstræp] *n* suspensoir *m*

jocular ['dʒɒkjʊlə(r)] *adj* enjoué(e)

jodhpurs ['dʒɒdpəz] *npl* jodhpurs *mpl*

Joe [dʒəʊ] *n Am Fam* **he's an ordinary J.** c'est un mec ordinaire; *Br* **J. Bloggs,** *Am* **J. Blow** Monsieur Tout-le-monde

jog [dʒɒg] **1** *n* **(a)** *(push)* secousse *f*; *(with elbow)* coup *m* de coude; **to give sb's memory a j.** rafraîchir la mémoire de qn **(b)** *(run)* course *f* (à petites foulées); **to break into a j.** se mettre à courir (à petites foulées); **to go for a j.** aller faire un jogging
2 *vt (pt & pp* **jogged)** *(push)* pousser; **to j. sb's elbow** donner un coup de coude à qn; **to j. sb's memory** rafraîchir la mémoire à qn
3 *vi (run)* faire du jogging; **to go jogging** aller faire un jogging
▸ **jog along** *vi (run)* courir à petites foulées; *Fig (in job, life)* aller son petit bonhomme de chemin

jogger ['dʒɒgə(r)] *n* joggeur(euse) *m,f*

jogging ['dʒɒgɪŋ] *n* jogging *m*; **j. bottoms** pantalon *m* de jogging; **j. suit** tenue *f* de jogging

joggle ['dʒɒgəl] *vt* secouer légèrement

Johannesburg [dʒəʊ'hænɪzbɑːg] *n* Johannesburg *m*

john [dʒɒn] *n Am Fam (lavatory)* petit coin *m*

John Bull [dʒɒn'bʊl] *n (Englishman)* l'Anglais *m* moyen; *(England)* l'Angleterre *f*

join [dʒɔɪn] **1** *n* raccord *m*; *(in fabric)* couture *f*
2 *vt* **(a)** *(unite, connect)* relier; *(planks)* joindre; **to j. two things together** relier une chose à une autre; **to j. battle** engager le combat; **to j. forces (with sb)** s'unir (à qn) **(b)** *(club, political party)* adhérer à; *(army)* s'engager dans; *(discussion, game)* se joindre à; **to j. a union** se syndiquer; **to j. the queue** se mettre dans la queue; *Fam Fig* **j. the queue!** tu n'es pas le seul (la seule)!
(c) *(meet with)* rejoindre; **may I j. you?** *(to someone at table)* puis-je me joindre à vous?; **will you j. me for a drink?** vous prendrez bien un verre avec moi?
(d) *(of river, road)* rejoindre; **where the river joins the sea** où le fleuve se jette dans la mer
3 *vi* **(a)** *(of pipes, roads, rivers)* se rejoindre **(b)** *(in club, political party)* adhérer; *(in union)* devenir membre
▸ **join in 1** *vt insep* participer à, prendre part à
2 *vi* participer
▸ **join up** *vi Mil* s'engager

joiner ['dʒɔɪnə(r)] *n Br (carpenter)* menuisier *m*

joint [dʒɔɪnt] **1** *n* **(a)** *(in body)* articulation *f*; **out of j.** déboîté(e); *Br Fig* **to put sb's nose out of j.** dépiter qn **(b)** *(in woodwork)* assemblage *m*; *(in metalwork)* joint *m* **(c)** *(of beef)* rôti *m*; *(of lamb)* gigot *m* **(d)** *Fam (nightclub)* boîte *f*; *(restaurant)* resto *m* **(e)** *Fam (cannabis cigarette)* joint *m*
2 *adj* commun(e); *(effort)* conjugué(e); **j. account** compte *m* joint; **j. custody** garde *f* jointe; **j. ownership** copropriété

f; **j. stock company** société *f* par actions; **j. venture** entreprise *f* commune
3 *vt (chicken)* découper
jointly ['dʒɔɪntlɪ] *adv* conjointement
joist [dʒɔɪst] *n* solive *f*
joke [dʒəʊk] **1** *n* **(a)** *(remark)* plaisanterie *f*, blague *f*; *(prank, trick)* tour *m*, farce *f*; **to tell** *or* **crack a j.** *(about* **sth)** raconter une blague (sur qch); **to make a j.** *(about* **sth)** faire une plaisanterie (sur qch); **to make a j. of sth** rire de qch; **to say/do sth for a j.** dire/faire qch pour rire; **the j. was on him** la plaisanterie s'est retournée contre lui; **she can't take a j.** elle n'aime pas la plaisanterie; **it's no j.!** ce n'est pas une mince affaire!; **it's no j. waiting for hours** ce n'est pas drôle d'attendre pendant des heures; **it's getting beyond a j.** ça n'est plus drôle, la plaisanterie a assez duré; **to play a j. on sb** jouer un tour à qn **(b)** *Fam* **to be a j.** *(ridiculous)* être lamentable
2 *vi* plaisanter; **to j. about sth** plaisanter sur qch; **I was only joking** je plaisantais; **you're joking!, you must be joking!** tu plaisantes!, tu veux rire!; **joking apart...** blague à part...
joker ['dʒəʊkə(r)] *n* **(a)** *(clown)* farceur(euse) *m,f*, *(incompetent person)* plaisantin *m* **(b)** *(in cards)* joker *m*; *Fig* **the j. in the pack** la grande inconnue
jokily ['dʒəʊkɪlɪ] *adv* en plaisantant
jokingly ['dʒəʊkɪŋlɪ] *adv* en plaisantant
joky ['dʒəʊkɪ] *adj (person)* blagueur(euse); *(mood, conversation)* jovial(e); *(remark, comment)* moqueur(euse)
jolly ['dʒɒlɪ] **1** *adj (cheerful)* joyeux(euse), gai(e)
2 *adv Br Fam (very)* rudement, drôlement; **j. good!** super!; **it serves him j. well right!** c'est vraiment bien fait pour lui!
3 *vt (pt & pp jollied)* **to j. sb into doing sth** amadouer qn pour qu'il fasse qch; **to j. sb along** amadouer qn
jolt [dʒəʊlt] **1** *n* **(a)** *(shake)* secousse *f* **(b)** *(shock, surprise)* choc *m*, coup *m*; **to give sb a j.** faire un choc *ou* un coup à qn
2 *vt (shake)* secouer; *(shock, surprise)* ébranler; **to j. sb into action** secouer les puces à qn; **to j. sb out of a depression** faire sortir qn de son état dépressif
3 *vi (shake)* secouer; **to j. along** *(of vehicle)* cahoter; **to j. to a stop** *(of vehicle)* s'arrêter avec des à-coups; **his head jolted forward/back** sa tête est partie en avant/en arrière
Jordan ['dʒɔːdən] *n (country)* la Jordanie; **the (River) J.** le Jourdain
Jordanian [dʒɔːˈdeɪnɪən] **1** *n* Jordanien(enne) *m,f*
2 *adj* jordanien(enne)
josh [dʒɒʃ] *vt Fam* mettre en boîte
joss stick ['dʒɒsstɪk] *n* bâton *m* d'encens
jostle ['dʒɒsəl] **1** *vt* bousculer; **to j. sb out of the way** écarter qn en jouant des coudes
2 *vi (push)* se bousculer; **to j. for position** *(in contest, job)* jouer des coudes
jot [dʒɒt] *n* **he doesn't care a j.** il s'en fiche complètement; **there isn't a j. of truth in what you say** il n'y a pas une once de vérité dans ce que vous dites; **it doesn't make a j. of difference** ça ne fait pas la moindre différence
▸ **jot down** *(pt & pp jotted) vt sep* noter
jotter ['dʒɒtə(r)] *n Br* cahier *m*
jottings ['dʒɒtɪŋz] *npl* notes *fpl*
joule [dʒuːl] *n Phys* joule *m*
journal ['dʒɜːnəl] *n (publication)* revue *f*; *(diary)* journal *m*; **to keep a j.** tenir un journal
journalese [dʒɜːnəˈliːz] *n Fam Pej* jargon *m* journalistique
journalism ['dʒɜːnəlɪzəm] *n* journalisme *m*
journalist ['dʒɜːnəlɪst] *n* journaliste *mf*

journalistic [dʒɜːnəˈlɪstɪk] *adj* journalistique
journey ['dʒɜːnɪ] **1** *n (pl* **journeys)** voyage *m*; *(short)* trajet *m*; **a train j.** un voyage en train; **to make a j.** faire un voyage; **to go (away) on a j.** partir en voyage; **to get to** *or* **reach the end of one's j.** arriver à destination; **the j. home** *or* **back** le (voyage de) retour
2 *vi* voyager
joust [dʒaʊst] *vi Hist* jouter; *Fig (compete)* se chamailler
jovial ['dʒəʊvɪəl] *adj* jovial(e), enjoué(e)
jovially ['dʒəʊvɪəlɪ] *adv* jovialement
jowl [dʒaʊl] *n (jaw)* mâchoire *f*; *(cheek)* bajoue *f*
joy [dʒɔɪ] *n* **(a)** *(happiness)* joie *f* **(b)** *(pleasure)* plaisir *m*; **she's a j. to be with** c'est un plaisir d'être avec elle **(c)** *Br Fam (success)* **(did you have** *or* **get) any j.?** ça a marché?
joyful ['dʒɔɪfʊl] *adj (occasion, news)* heureux(euse); *(person, party)* joyeux(euse)
joyfully ['dʒɔɪfəlɪ] *adv* joyeusement
joyless ['dʒɔɪlɪs] *adj* triste
joyous ['dʒɔɪəs] *adj (occasion, news)* heureux(euse); *(person, party)* joyeux(euse)
joyride ['dʒɔɪraɪd] *n (in stolen car)* = virée dans une voiture volée; **to go for a j.** = faire une virée dans une voiture volée
joyrider ['dʒɔɪraɪdə(r)] *n* = chauffard qui conduit une voiture volée
joystick ['dʒɔɪstɪk] *n (in aircraft)* manche *m* à balai; *(for computer)* manette *f*
JP [dʒeɪˈpiː] *n Br Law (abbr* **Justice of the Peace)** juge *m* de paix
Jr *(abbr* **Junior) John Green, Jr** John Green fils
jubilant ['dʒuːbɪlənt] *adj (shouts)* de joie; *(expression)* réjoui(e); *(person)* exultant(e); *(celebration)* joyeux(euse); **to be j. (at** *or* **about sth)** être transporté(e) de joie (par qch)
jubilation [dʒuːbɪˈleɪʃən] *n (grande)* joie *f*, jubilation *f*
jubilee ['dʒuːbɪliː] *n (golden)* j. cinquantième anniversaire *m*; jubilé *m*; **silver/diamond j.** vingt-cinquième/ soixantième anniversaire
Judaic [dʒuːˈdeɪɪk] *adj* judaïque
Judaism ['dʒuːdeɪɪzəm] *n* judaïsme *m*
Judas ['dʒuːdəs] *n (traitor)* Judas *m*
judder ['dʒʌdə(r)] *vi Br* être agité(e) de secousses; **to j. to a halt** s'arrêter avec des secousses
judge [dʒʌdʒ] **1** *n* **(a)** *(in law, sport)* juge *m*; *(in competition)* membre *m* du jury **(b)** *(expert)* **to be a good/poor j. of sth** s'y connaître/ne pas s'y connaître en qch; **I will be the j. of that** c'est moi qui (en) jugerai
2 *vt* **(a)** *(in law, sport)* juger **(b)** *(assess critically)* juger; **to j. sb** *or* **sth** juger qn sur *ou* d'après qch; **to j. sb/sth a success/failure** considérer qch *ou* qn comme réussi/échoué; **to j. it necessary to do sth** estimer *ou* juger nécessaire de faire qch; **don't j. a book by its cover** l'habit ne fait pas le moine **(c)** *(estimate)* estimer, évaluer
3 *vi* juger; **to j. by appearances** juger d'après les apparences; **to j. for oneself** juger par soi-même; **judging by...** à en juger par...
judg(e)ment, *Am* **judgment** ['dʒʌdʒmənt] *n* **(a)** *(decision)* jugement *m*; **to sit in j.** *(of judge, court)* siéger; **to pass j.** *(of judge, court)* rendre un jugement; *Fig* **to sit in** *or* **pass j.** se poser en juge des jugements sur qn; *Rel* **J. Day** le jour du Jugement; **Jugement dernier (b)** *(opinion)* avis *m*, opinion *f*; **to form a j.** se faire un avis *ou* se former une opinion **(c)** *(discernment)* jugement *m*; **to have good j.** faire preuve de jugement; **to have poor j.** manquer de jugement; **to trust sb's j.** s'en remettre au jugement de qn; **in my j.** à mon sens; **against my better j.** en sachant que c'est/c'était une erreur

judg(e)mental [dʒʌdʒ'mentəl] *adj* critique
judicial [dʒu:'dɪʃəl] *adj* judiciaire
judiciary [dʒu:'dɪʃɪərɪ] *n (judges)* magistrature *f; (branch of government)* pouvoir *m* judiciaire
judicious [dʒu:'dɪʃəs] *adj* judicieux(euse)
judiciously [dʒu:'dɪʃəslɪ] *adv* judicieusement
judiciousness [dʒu:'dɪʃəsnɪs] *n* bon sens *m*
judo ['dʒu:dəʊ] *n* judo *m*
jug [dʒʌg] *n* (**a**) *(for wine, water)* pichet *m*; *(for cream, milk)* pot *m* (**b**) *very Fam (prison)* **in the j.** en taule
juggernaut ['dʒʌgənɔ:t] *n Br* poids *m* lourd
juggle ['dʒʌgəl] *also Fig* **1** *vt* jongler avec
  2 *vi* jongler (**with** avec)
juggler ['dʒʌglə(r)] *n* jongleur(euse) *m,f*
jugular ['dʒʌgjʊlə(r)] **1** *n* jugulaire *f; Fig* **to go for the j.** frapper au point sensible
  2 *adj* jugulaire
juice [dʒu:s] *n* (**a**) *(of fruit, meat)* jus *m*; *(of plant)* suc *m* (**b**) *Fam (petrol)* jus *m*
juicy ['dʒu:sɪ] *adj* (**a**) *(fruit)* juteux(euse); *(meat)* qui rend du jus (**b**) *Fig (contract, deal)* juteux(euse); *(story)* croustillant(e)
jukebox ['dʒu:kbɒks] *n* juke-box *m*
Jul *(abbr* **July)** juillet
July [dʒu:'laɪ] *n* juillet *m*; *see also* **May**
jumble ['dʒʌmbəl] **1** *n* (**a**) *(of things)* tas *m*; *(of ideas, words)* fatras *m*; **in a j.** *(things)* en désordre, en pagaïe; *(ideas, words)* embrouillé(e); *Br* **j. sale** vente *f* de charité (**b**) *Am (cake)* = petit gâteau en forme d'anneau
  2 *vt (things)* mélanger; *(ideas, words)* embrouiller
jumbo ['dʒʌmbəʊ] *adj* **(sized)** énorme, géant(e); **j. jet** jumbo jet *m*, gros-porteur *m*
jump [dʒʌmp] **1** *n* (**a**) *(leap)* saut *m*; *Fig* **go take a j.!** va te faire voir ailleurs!; *Fig* **to be one j. ahead** avoir une longueur d'avance; **j. jet** ADAV *m*; *Br* **j. leads** câbles *mpl* de démarrage; **j. suit** combinaison *f*
  (**b**) *(rise)* hausse *f* soudaine (**in** de)
  (**c**) *(on racecourse)* obstacle *m*
  2 *vt (hedge, ditch)* sauter; *Fam* **to j. sb** attaquer qn; **to j. bail** se dérober à la justice *(alors qu'on est en liberté provisoire)*; **to j. the gun** *(in race)* faire un faux départ; *Fig* anticiper, agir prématurément; **to j. the lights** *(in car)* brûler un feu rouge; *Br* **to j. the queue** passer avant son tour; **to j. ship** déserter le navire
  3 *vi* (**a**) *(leap)* sauter; **to j. to one's feet** se lever d'un bond; **to j. for joy** sauter de joie; **to j. onto a train** sauter dans un train; **to j. out of the window** sauter par la fenêtre; **to j. to conclusions** tirer des conclusions hâtives; *Fig* **let's wait and see which way she jumps** attendons de voir ce qu'elle va faire; *Fam* **to j. down sb's throat** rabrouer qn; *Fig* **to j. out at sb** *(of mistake, opportunity)* sauter aux yeux de qn (**b**) *(go directly)* **to j. from one subject to another** or **to the next** sauter d'un sujet à l'autre; **the film then jumps to the present** le film passe d'un seul coup au présent
  (**c**) *(of unemployment, inflation)* faire un bond
  (**d**) *(make a sudden movement) (of person)* sursauter; *(of heart)* faire un bond; *(of record player needle)* sauter; **we nearly jumped out of our skins** ça nous a fichu un coup
  ► **jump at** *vt insep (offer, chance)* sauter sur
  ► **jump on** *vt insep Fam (reprimand)* sauter sur (**for doing** d'avoir fait)
jumped-up [dʒʌmp'tʌp] *adj Br Fam Pej* prétentieux(euse)
jumper ['dʒʌmpə(r)] *n Br (sweater)* pull(-over) *m*; *Am (sleeveless dress)* robe-chasuble *f*
jumping-off place ['dʒʌmpɪŋ'ɒf'pleɪs], **jumping-**

off point ['dʒʌmpɪŋ'ɒf'pɔɪnt] *n* point *m* de départ; *Fig* tremplin *m*
jump-start ['dʒʌmpstɑ:t] *vt (car)* faire démarrer avec des câbles de démarrage; *Fig (economy)* relancer
jumpy ['dʒʌmpɪ] *adj* nerveux(euse)
Jun *(abbr* **June)** juin
junction ['dʒʌŋkʃən] *n (of roads, railway lines)* embranchement *m*; *Elec* **j. box** boîte *f* de dérivation
juncture ['dʒʌŋktʃə(r)] *n Formal* **at this j.** à ce moment(-là)
June [dʒu:n] *n* juin *m*; *see also* **May**
jungle ['dʒʌŋgəl] *n also Fig* jungle *f*
junior ['dʒu:nɪə(r)] **1** *n* (**a**) *(in age)* **to be sb's j.** être plus jeune que qn; **he's three years my j.** il a trois ans de moins que moi (**b**) *(in rank)* subalterne *mf*
  2 *adj* (**a**) *(in age)* **to be j. to sb** être plus jeune que qn; **John Green, J.** John Green fils; *Am* **j. high (school)** *(between 11 and 15)* ≃ collège *m* d'enseignement secondaire; *Br* **j. school** *(between 7 and 11)* = classes primaires du cours élémentaire au cours moyen (**b**) *(in rank)* subalterne; **to be j. to sb** être au-dessous de qn; **j. teacher/executive** jeune professeur *m*/cadre *m*; *Br Parl* **j. minister** secrétaire *mf* d'État
juniper ['dʒu:nɪpə(r)] *n* **j. (tree)** genévrier *m*, genièvre *m*; **j. berry** baie *f* de genièvre
junk¹ [dʒʌŋk] **1** *n (unwanted objects)* bric-à-brac *m*; *(inferior goods)* camelote *f; Fin* **j. bond** obligation *f; j.* **food** cochonneries *fpl*; **j. mail** prospectus *mpl*; **j. shop** brocante *f*
  2 *vt Fam (discard) (objects)* bazarder; *(plan)* laisser tomber
junk² *n (boat)* jonque *f*
junket ['dʒʌŋkɪt] *n* (**a**) *(food)* lait *m* caillé (**b**) *Pej (trip by public official)* voyage *m* aux frais du contribuable
junkie, junky ['dʒʌŋkɪ] *(pl* **junkies)** *n Fam (drug addict)* drogué(e) *m,f*; **a fast-food/game-show j.** un accro des fast-food/jeux télévisés
junkyard ['dʒʌŋkjɑ:d] *n (for metal)* ferraille *f*
junta ['dʒʌntə] *n* junte *f*
Jupiter ['dʒu:pɪtə(r)] *n (planet)* Jupiter
jurisdiction [dʒʊərɪs'dɪkʃən] *n* juridiction *f*; **to have j. over sb** avoir autorité sur qn; **to come within** or **under the j. of...** être sous la juridiction de...
jurisprudence [dʒʊərɪs'pru:dəns] *n* philosophie *f* du droit
jurist ['dʒʊərɪst] *n Br (legal expert)* juriste *mf*; *Am (judge)* juge *m*
juror ['dʒʊərə(r)] *n Law* juré(e) *m,f*
jury ['dʒʊərɪ] *(pl* **juries)** *n Law* jury *m*; **to be** or **serve on the j.** être membre *ou* faire partie du jury; **to be on j. duty** or **service** être convoqué(e) pour faire partie d'un jury; *Fig* **the j. is still out on that one** ça reste à voir; **j. box** banc *m* des jurés
just [dʒʌst] **1** *adj (fair)* juste; **it's only j. that...** c'est normal que... + *subjunctive*; **to get one's j. deserts** n'avoir que ce que l'on mérite
  2 *adv* (**a**) *(exactly)* exactement; **that's j. what I told her** c'est exactement ce que je lui ai dit; **j. how many are there?** combien y en a-t-il au juste?; **that's j. the point!** justement!, précisément!; **j. my luck!** c'est bien ma chance!; **it's j. as good/difficult as...** c'est tout aussi bon/difficile que...; **j. then** juste à ce moment-là; **j. now** en ce moment; **j. as I was leaving...** juste au moment où je partais...; **I can j. see her as a doctor** je la vois très bien médecin
  (**b**) *(only)* juste; **she's j. a baby** ce n'est qu'un bébé; **it costs $10** ça coûte juste 10 dollars
  (**c**) *(barely)* juste; **j. before/after** juste avant/après; **j. over/under $50** à peine plus/moins de 50 dollars; **j. in**

time juste à temps; **it's only j. big enough** c'est tout juste assez grand; **they j. caught the train** ils ont eu le train de justesse; **they j. missed the train** ils ont raté le train d'un cheveu (**d**) *(recently)* **to have j. done sth** venir de faire qch; **j. yesterday/last year** pas plus tard qu'hier/que l'année dernière (**e**) *(simply)* **it was j. wonderful/dreadful!** c'était tout simplement merveilleux/affreux!; **he j. refuses to listen!** il refuse carrément d'écouter!; **j. ask if you need money** si tu as besoin d'argent, tu n'as qu'à demander (**f**) *(in threats, exhortations)* **j. (you) try/wait!** essaie/ attends un peu pour voir!; **(that's) j. as well!** heureusement! (**g**) **j. about** *(almost)* à peu près; **they're j. about the same** ils se valent; **I can j. about manage** j'y arrive tout juste; **to be j. about to do sth** être sur le point de faire qch

justice ['dʒʌstɪs] *n* (**a**) *(power of law)* justice *f*; **to bring sb to j.** traduire qn en justice (**b**) *(fairness)* légitimité *f*; **this photograph doesn't do him j.** cette photo ne le met pas en valeur; **to do j. to a meal** faire honneur à un repas; **to do oneself j.** se montrer sous son meilleur jour (**c**) *(judge)* juge *m*; Br **J. of the Peace** juge de paix

justifiable ['dʒʌstɪfaɪəbəl] *adj* justifié(e), légitime; **j. homicide** légitime défense *f*

justifiably ['dʒʌstɪfaɪəblɪ] *adv* à juste titre

justification [dʒʌstɪfɪ'keɪʃən] *n* justification *f*; **in j. of sth** pour justifier qch

justify ['dʒʌstɪfaɪ] *(pt & pp* **justified**) *vt* justifier; **to be justified in doing sth** avoir de bonnes raisons de faire qch

justly ['dʒʌstlɪ] *adv (fairly)* avec justice; *(deservedly)* à juste titre

▸ **jut out** [dʒʌt] *(pt & pp* **jutted**) **1** *vt sep (chin)* avancer **2** *vi (of balcony, rock)* faire saillie; **to j. out over sth** surplomber qch; **to j. out into the sea** s'avancer dans la mer

jute [dʒuːt] *n* jute *m*

juvenile ['dʒuːvɪnaɪl] **1** *n Law* mineur(e) *m,f* **2** *adj* (**a**) *Law (crime, delinquency)* juvénile; **j. court** tribunal *m* pour enfants; **j. delinquent** jeune délinquant(e) *m,f* (**b**) *Pej (childish)* puéril(e)

juxtapose [dʒʌkstə'pəʊz] *vt* mettre en juxtaposition (**with** avec)

juxtaposition [dʒʌkstəpə'zɪʃən] *n* juxtaposition *f*

K

K, k [keɪ] *n* **(a)** *(letter)* K, k *m inv* **(b)** *(abbr* **thousand,
thousand pounds)** he earns 30**K** il gagne 30000 livres
sterling **(c)** *Comptr (abbr* **kilobyte)** KO
Kabul ['kɑːbʊl] *n* Kaboul
Kaffir ['kæfə(r)] *n very Fam* nègre (négresse) *m,f,* = terme
raciste désignant un(e) Noir(e) d'Afrique du Sud
kaftan ['kæftæn] *n* caf(e)tan *m*
kale [keɪl] *n* chou *m* frisé
kaleidoscope [kə'laɪdəskəʊp] *n* kaléidoscope *m*
kamikaze [kæmɪ'kɑːzɪ] **1** *n also Fig* kamikaze *m*
2 *adj* kamikaze
Kampuchea [kæmpʊ'tʃɪə] *n Formerly* le Kampuchéa
kangaroo [kæŋgə'ruː] *n* kangourou *m*; **k. court** tribunal
m irrégulier
kaput [kə'pʊt] *adj Fam* kaput *inv*
karate [kə'rɑːtɪ] *n* karaté *m*; **k. chop** coup *m* de karaté
Kashmir [kæʃ'mɪə(r)] *n* Cachemire
Kashmiri [kæʃ'mɪərɪ] **1** *n* **(a)** *(person)* Cachemirien
(enne) *m,f* **(b)** *(language)* cachemirien *m*
2 *adj* cachemirien(enne)
Katmandu [kætmæn'duː] *n* Katmandou
kayak ['kaɪæk] *n* kayak *m*
Kazak(h)stan [kæzæk'stɑːn] *n* Kazakhstan *m*
kebab [kə'bæb] *n* brochette *f*; **shish k.** chiche-kébab *m*;
doner k. sandwich *m* grec
kedgeree [kedʒə'riː] *n* = riz pilaf au poisson fumé et aux
œufs durs
keel [kiːl] *n (of ship)* quille *f*; *Fig* **to be on an even k.** être
stable
► **keel over** *vi (of boat)* chavirer; *Fam (of person)*
s'écrouler
keen [kiːn] *adj* **(a)** *(enthusiastic)* enthousiaste; *(student)*
assidu(e); **to be k. on sb** avoir un faible pour qn; **to be k.
on doing sth** *(habitually)* adorer faire qch; *(want to do)* avoir
très envie de faire qch; **to be k. to do sth** avoir très envie de
faire qch; **to be k. for sth to happen** tenir beaucoup à ce
que qch arrive; *Fam* **to be as k. as mustard** déborder
d'enthousiasme; **to take a k. interest in sth** s'intéresser de
très près à qch
(b) *(eye, mind, look)* vif (vive); *(price)* compétitif(ive); **to
have a k. eye for detail** remarquer jusqu'au moindre
détail
(c) *(intense)* vif (vive); *(remorse)* cuisant(e); *(competition)*
intense
keenly ['kiːnlɪ] *adv* **(a)** *(enthusiastically)* avec
enthousiasme **(b)** *(intensely)* profondément; **to be k.
aware of sth** avoir une conscience aiguë de qch; **k.
contested** âprement disputé(e)

keep [kiːp] **1** *n* **(a) to pay for one's k.** payer sa pension; **to
earn one's k.** *(make a living)* gagner sa vie; *(pay one's way)*
payer sa pension
(b) *(of castle)* donjon *m*
(c) *Fam* **for keeps** pour de bon
2 *vt (pt & pp* **kept** [kept]**) (a)** *(retain)* garder; *(store)* ranger;
to k. sth from sb dissimuler qch à qn; **to k. its shape/
colour** *(of garment)* ne pas se déformer/déteindre; **to k. sb's
attention** retenir l'attention de qn; **k. the change** gardez la
monnaie
(b) *(maintain)* **to k. a journal** tenir un journal; **to k. order**
maintenir l'ordre; **to k. a record of sth** garder une trace
écrite de qch; **to k. a secret** garder un secret
(c) *(maintain in a certain condition)* **to k. sth secret** garder
qch secret; **to k. sb awake** empêcher qn de (s'en)dormir;
to k. sb waiting faire attendre qn; **she keeps her flat
clean** son appartement est toujours bien tenu
(d) *(look after) (poultry, cows)* élever; *(shop)* tenir; *(family,
mistress)* entretenir; **a kept woman** une femme entretenue
(e) *(detain)* retenir; **what kept you?** pourquoi ce retard?
(f) *(observe)* respecter; *(promise)* tenir; **to k. late hours** se
coucher tard; **to k. one's word** tenir parole
3 *vi* **(a)** *(remain)* rester; **to k. well** rester en bonne santé; **to
k. quiet** se tenir tranquille; **how are you keeping?**
comment allez-vous?
(b) *(continue)* **to k. straight on** continuer tout droit; **k. (to
the) left/right** serrez à gauche/à droite; **to k. doing sth**
ne pas arrêter de faire qch; **to k. smiling** garder le sourire;
to k. going tenir le coup
(c) *(of food)* se conserver; *Fig* **it will k.** *(of problem)* ça peut
attendre
► **keep away 1** *vt sep* **to k. sb away (from sb/sth)**
empêcher qn de s'approcher (de qn/qch)
2 *vi* **to k. away from sb/sth** ne pas s'approcher de qn/qch
► **keep back 1** *vt sep* **(a)** *(crowd, tears)* retenir; **to k. sth
back from sb** cacher qch à qn **(b)** *(delay)* retarder
2 *vi (not approach)* ne pas s'approcher
► **keep down 1** *vt sep* **(a)** *(head)* baisser; **to k. one's voice
down** parler moins fort; **to k. the noise down** faire moins
de bruit; *Fig* **to k. one's head down** ne pas se faire
remarquer; **I can't k. my food down** je vomis tout ce que
je mange **(b)** *(repress) (people)* opprimer; *(prices)* empêcher
d'augmenter
2 *vi (not stand up)* se tapir
► **keep from** *vt sep* **to k. sb from doing sth** empêcher
qn de faire qch; **to k. sb from his work** empêcher qn de
travailler
► **keep in** *vt sep (pupil)* garder en retenue; **to k. sb in
overnight** *(in hospital)* garder qn pour la nuit
► **keep in with** *vt insep Fam* **to k. in with sb** rester en
bons termes avec qn

▸ **keep off** 1 *vt sep* to k. one's hands off sb/sth ne pas toucher à qn/qch
2 *vt insep* k. off the grass *(sign)* Pelouse interdite
3 *vi (stay away)* ne pas intervenir
▸ **keep on** 1 *vt sep (clothing, employee)* garder; *(lights, TV)* laisser allumé(e); *Fam* k. your hair on! on se calme!
2 *vi* continuer; to k. on doing sth continuer de faire qch; to keep on about sth insister constamment sur qch
▸ **keep on at** *vt insep Fam* to k. on at sb (to do sth) être toujours sur le dos de qn (pour qu'il fasse qch)
▸ **keep out** 1 *vt sep (not allow to enter)* empêcher d'entrer
2 *vi (stay away from)* to keep out of sth éviter qch; to k. out of sb's way éviter qn; to k. out of danger rester à l'abri du danger; to k. out of trouble ne pas s'attirer d'ennuis; to k. out of an argument rester en dehors d'une dispute; k. out *(sign)* défense d'entrer
▸ **keep to** 1 *vt sep* (a) *(hold)* to k. sb to a promise faire tenir une promesse à qn; to k. sth to a minimum minimiser qch (b) *(not reveal)* to k. sth to oneself garder qch pour soi; to k. oneself to oneself rester à l'écart
2 *vt insep (promise)* tenir; *(contract, agreement)* respecter; *(subject)* s'en tenir à; to k. to one's bed garder le lit
▸ **keep up** 1 *vt sep* (a) *(custom)* conserver; to k. up the payments continuer à payer; to k. it up *(continue to do well)* continuer comme ça; k. up the good work! continuez à bien travailler!; to k. up appearances sauver les apparences (b) *(keep awake)* empêcher de dormir
2 *vi* (a) *(of rain, snow)* continuer (b) *(remain level)* tenir le rythme; to k. up with sb aller à la même allure que qn; to k. up with the Joneses rivaliser de standing avec ses voisins; to k. up with events se tenir informé(e) de l'actualité; to k. up with the times être à la page

keeper ['ki:pə(r)] *n (in zoo, park, museum)* gardien(enne) *m,f; (gamekeeper)* garde-chasse *m*

keep-fit ['ki:p'fɪt] *n* gymnastique *f*; to do k. faire de la gymnastique; k. class cours *m* de gymnastique

keeping ['ki:pɪŋ] *n* (a) *(care)* garde *f*; to have sb/sth in one's k. avoir qn/qch sous sa garde (b) *(conformity)* in k. with conformément à; out of k. with en désaccord avec

keepsake ['ki:pseɪk] *n* souvenir *m*

keg [keg] *n* baril *m*

ken [ken] *n* to be beyond sb's k. être en dehors des compétences de qn

kennel ['kenəl] *n Br (doghouse)* niche *f; Am (for boarding or breeding)* chenil *m*

Kenya ['kenjə, 'ki:njə] *n* Kenya *m*

Kenyan ['kenjən] 1 *n* Kenyan(e) *m,f*
2 *adj* kenyan(e)

kept [kept] *pt & pp of* keep

kerb [kɜ:b] *n Br* bordure *f* de trottoir

kerbcrawler ['kɜ:bkrɔ:lə(r)] *n* = personne qui longe le trottoir en voiture à la recherche d'une prostituée

kerbcrawling ['kɜ:bkrɔ:lɪŋ] *n* = recherche d'une prostituée en voiture

kerbstone ['kɜ:bstəʊn] *n Br* bordure *f* de trottoir

kerfuffle [kə'fʌfəl] *n Fam (fuss)* histoires *fpl; (noise, excitement)* remue-ménage *m*

kernel ['kɜ:nəl] *n (of nut)* amande *f; (of grain)* grain *m; Fig (of problem)* fond *m*, essentiel *m*

kerosene ['kerəsi:n] *n* (a) *Am* pétrole *m* (lampant); k. lamp lampe *f* à pétrole (b) *(aircraft fuel)* kérosène *m*

kestrel ['kestrəl] *n* faucon *m* crécerelle

ketchup ['ketʃəp] *n* (tomato) k. ketchup *m*

kettle ['ketəl] *n* bouilloire *f*; to put the k. on mettre l'eau à chauffer; *Fam* a different k. of fish une autre affaire

kettledrum ['ketəldrʌm] *n* timbale *f*

key [ki:] 1 *n* (a) *(of door, clock, toy)* clé *f; (of piano, computer)* touche *f; Fig* the k. to happiness/success la clé du bonheur/de la réussite (b) *(to map)* légende *f; (to exercise)* solutions *fpl* (c) *(in music)* ton *m*; in the k. of C en ut; to be off k. *(of singer)* chanter faux; *(of musician)* jouer faux
2 *adj (role, factor, figure)* clé; *(influence, consideration)* capital(e); k. person pivot *m*
▸ **key in** *vt sep (data)* saisir
keyboard ['ki:bɔ:d] *n (of piano, computer)* clavier *m*
keyhole ['ki:həʊl] *n* trou *m* de serrure; k. surgery chirurgie *f* à incision minimale
keynote ['ki:nəʊt] 1 *n* tonique *f; Fig (of speech, approach)* point *m* essentiel
2 *adj (speech)* programme; *(speaker)* principal(e)
keypad ['ki:pæd] *n Comptr* pavé *m*
keyring ['ki:rɪŋ] *n* porte-clés *m inv*
keystone ['ki:stəʊn] *n also Fig* clé *f* de voûte
keystroke ['ki:strəʊk] *n Comptr* touche *f*
kg *(abbr kilogram)* kg
KGB [keɪdʒi:'bi:] *n Formerly* KGB *m*
khaki ['kɑ:kɪ] 1 *n* kaki *m*
2 *adj* kaki *inv*
Khartoum [kɑ:'tu:m] *n* Khartoum
kHz *(abbr kilohertz)* kHz
kibbutz [kɪ'bʊts] *(pl kibbutzim* [kɪbʊt'si:m]) *n* kibboutz *m*
kibosh ['kaɪbɒʃ] *n Fam* to put the k. on sth faire tomber qch à l'eau

kick [kɪk] 1 *n* (a) *(with foot)* coup *m* de pied; *(of horse)* ruade *f; (of gun)* recul *m*; to give sb/sth a k. donner un coup de pied à qn/dans qch; *Fam Fig* she needs a k. in the pants a besoin d'un bon coup de pied au derrière; *Fig* that was a k. in the teeth for him ça a été une gifle pour lui; that drink has a real k. to it! cette boisson est vraiment traître! (b) *Fam (thrill)* to get a k. out of doing sth prendre son pied à faire qch; to do sth for kicks faire qch pour s'amuser
2 *vt* donner un coup/des coups de pied à; *(football)* taper dans; to get kicked recevoir un coup/des coups de pied; *Fam* to k. the bucket casser sa pipe; *Fig* you shouldn't k. a man when he's down il ne faut pas s'acharner sur quelqu'un qui a déjà été fortement éprouvé; I could have kicked myself je me serais donné des gifles; to k. the habit *(stop taking drugs)* arrêter (la drogue)
3 *vi* donner un coup/des coups de pied; *(of horse)* ruer; *(of gun)* reculer; *Fam Fig* to k. against sth regimber contre qch
▸ **kick about, kick around** 1 *vt sep (ball)* taper dans; *Fam (idea)* tester; don't let them k. you around on ne devrais pas les laisser te traiter comme ça
2 *vi Fam (hang around)* traîner; there are plenty of people like that kicking around des gens comme ça, ce n'est pas ce qui manque
▸ **kick in** *vt sep (door)* enfoncer à coups de pied; *Fam* to k. sb's head in casser la tête à qn
▸ **kick off** *vi (in football)* donner le coup d'envoi; *Fam Fig (in meeting, debate)* démarrer
▸ **kick out** *vt sep Fam* mettre à la porte
▸ **kick up** *vt sep Fam* to k. up a fuss faire tout un plat *ou* toute une histoire; to k. up a row *or* a racket faire du boucan

kickback ['kɪkbæk] *n Fam (payment)* pot-de-vin *m*

kickoff ['kɪkɒf] *n (in football)* coup *m* d'envoi; *Fam Fig* for a k. *(to start with)* pour commencer

kick-start ['kɪkstɑ:t] 1 *n (on motorbike)* kick *m*

2 *vt (motorbike)* démarrer au kick; *Fig (economy)* donner un sérieux coup de pouce à

kid [kɪd] **1** (**a**) *Fam (child)* gamin(e) *m,f,* gosse *mf;* **my k. brother** mon petit frère; **it's k.'s stuff** *(easy)* c'est un jeu d'enfant; *(childish)* c'est bon pour les gosses (**b**) *(young goat)* chevreau *m; (female)* chevrette *f; (skin)* chevreau; **k. gloves** gants *mpl* en chevreau; *Fig* **to handle sb with k. gloves** prendre des gants avec qn
2 *vt (pt & pp* **kidded**) *Fam (fool)* faire marcher; **to k. oneself** se faire des illusions
3 *vi* **to be kidding** plaisanter; **no kidding!** sans blague!

kidnap ['kɪdnæp] *(pt & pp* **kidnapped,** *Am* **kidnaped**) *vt* kidnapper, enlever

kidnapper ['kɪdnæpə(r)] *n* ravisseur(euse) *m,f,* kidnappeur(euse) *m,f*

kidnapping ['kɪdnæpɪŋ] *n* enlèvement *m,* kidnapping *m*

kidney ['kɪdnɪ] *(pl* **kidneys**) *n (of person)* rein *m; (offal)* rognon *m;* **k. bean** haricot *m* rouge; **k. donor** donneur(euse) *m,f* de rein; **k. machine** rein artificiel

kill [kɪl] **1** *n (in hunting) (action)* mise *f* à mort; *(animals killed)* tableau *m* de chasse; **to be in at the k.** assister à la mise à mort; *Fig* assister au dénouement
2 *vt* (**a**) *(person, animal)* tuer; **to k. oneself** se tuer; *Fam* **to k. oneself laughing** mourir de rire; *Ironic* **don't k. yourself!** surtout, ne te surmène pas!; *Fam* **this one'll k. you** *(of joke)* ça va te faire mourir de rire; **to k. two birds with one stone** faire d'une pierre deux coups; *Fam* **my feet/these shoes are killing me** mes pieds/ces chaussures me font un mal de chien (**b**) *Fig (friendship)* détruire; *(sound)* amortir; *(pain)* calmer; *(chances)* anéantir; *Journ* **to k. a story** retirer une information; **to k. time** tuer le temps
► **kill off** *vt sep (people)* tuer; *(character in film, novel)* faire mourir; *Fig (hope)* anéantir

killer ['kɪlə(r)] *n* tueur(euse) *m,f;* **he knew his k.** il connaissait son meurtrier; *Fam Fig* **those steps were a k.!** ces escaliers m'ont tué!; *Fam Fig* **this one's a k.** *(joke)* celle-ci est à mourir de rire; **k. (disease)** maladie *f* meurtrière; *Fig* **to have the k. instinct** être impitoyable; **k. whale** épaulard *m*

killing ['kɪlɪŋ] **1** *n (of person)* meurtre *m; (of animals)* destruction *f; Fam* **to make a k.** faire un bénéfice énorme
2 *adj Fam (exhausting)* tuant(e); *(very amusing)* tordant(e)

killjoy ['kɪldʒɔɪ] *n* rabat-joie *m inv*

kiln [kɪln] *n* four *m*

kilo ['kiːləʊ] *(pl* **kilos**) *n* kilo *m*

kilobyte ['kɪləbaɪt] *n Comptr* kilo-octet *m*

kilogram(me) ['kɪləgræm] *n* kilogramme *m*

kilohertz ['kɪləʊhɜːts] *(pl* **kilohertz**) *n* kilohertz *m*

kilometre, *Am* **kilometer** ['kɪləmiːtə(r), kɪ'lɒmɪtə(r)] *n* kilomètre *m*

kilowatt ['kɪləwɒt] *n* kilowatt *m;* **k.-hour** kilowatt-heure *m*

kilt [kɪlt] *n* kilt *m*

kilter ['kɪltə(r)] *n Fam* **out of k.** *(of machine part)* déréglé(e) *(with* par rapport à); *(of budget)* déséquilibré(e)

kimono [kɪ'məʊnəʊ] *(pl* **kimonos**) *n* kimono *m*

kin [kɪn] *n Formal* parents *mpl*

kind¹ [kaɪnd] *n* (**a**) *(sort)* genre *m,* espèce *f;* **all kinds of...** toutes sortes de…; **something of the k.** quelque chose comme ça, quelque chose de ce genre; **I said nothing of the k.** je n'ai jamais dit ça!; **she's really boring – she's nothing of the k.!** elle est vraiment ennuyeuse – mais pas du tout!; **in a k. of way** d'une certaine manière; **well, it's coffee of a k.** je suppose qu'on peut appeler ça du café; **we're two of a k.** nous sommes pareils; **it's the**

only one of its k. c'est le seul de ce genre; **he's that k. of person** il est comme ça; **this is my k. of party!** voilà le genre de soirée que j'aime!; **this k. of thing** ce genre de chose (**b**) **in k.** *(payment)* en nature (**c**) *Fam* **you look k. of tired** tu as l'air un peu fatigué; **I k. of expected this** je m'y attendais un peu; **do you like it? – k. of ça te plaît?** – oui, plus ou moins; **it was a k. of saucershaped thing** c'était quelque chose qui ressemblait à une soucoupe

kind² *adj* gentil(ille); **to be k. to sb** être gentil avec qn; *Formal* **would you be k. enough to or so k. as to...?** auriez-vous la bonté de…?; **k. to the skin** *(of detergent, soap)* qui n'irrite pas la peau; **by k. permission of...** avec l'aimable autorisation de…

kinda ['kaɪndə] *very Fam* = **kind of**

kindergarten ['kɪndəgɑːtən] *n* jardin *m* d'enfants

kind-hearted ['kaɪnd'hɑːtɪd] *adj (person)* qui a bon cœur; *(action)* généreux(euse)

kindle ['kɪndəl] *vt (flame)* allumer; *Fig (emotions)* éveiller

kindling ['kɪndlɪŋ] *n* petit bois *m*

kindly ['kaɪndlɪ] **1** *adv* gentiment; **to speak k. of sb** dire du bien de qn; *Formal* **(would you). k. be quiet!** voudriez-vous avoir la bonté de vous taire!; **she didn't take k. to being criticized** elle n'a pas apprécié qu'on la critique
2 *adj (person)* gentil(ille); *(tone, advice)* bienveillant(e)

kindness ['kaɪndnɪs] *n* gentillesse *f;* **to do sth out of the k. of one's heart** faire qch par bonté d'âme; **to do sb a k. rendre service à qn**

kindred ['kɪndrɪd] *adj* du même genre, de la même nature; **we are k. spirits** c'est mon alter ego

kinetic [kɪ'netɪk] *adj* cinétique

king [kɪŋ] *n* roi *m;* **the three kings** *(in the Bible)* les Rois mages; **the k. of the beasts** le roi des animaux

kingdom ['kɪŋdəm] *n* royaume *m;* **the k. of heaven** le royaume des cieux; **the animal/plant k.** le règne animal/végétal; **Fam until or till k. come** jusqu'à la saint-glinglin; *Fam* **to send sb to k. come** envoyer qn ad patres

kingfisher ['kɪŋfɪʃə(r)] *n* martin-pêcheur *m*

kingpin ['kɪŋpɪn] *n Fig (of organization, company)* cheville f ouvrière

king-size(d) ['kɪŋ'saɪz(d)] *adj* (**a**) *(cigarette)* long (longue) (**b**) *(bed, mattress)* (très) grand format *(de 2 m sur 1 m 95)*

kink [kɪŋk] *n (in wire, rope)* boucle *f; (in hair)* frisette *f (in character)* bizarrerie *f*

kinky ['kɪŋkɪ] *adj* (**a**) *(hair)* frisotté(e) (**b**) *Fam (person) (sexually)* qui a des goûts sexuels bizarres; *(eccentric)* extravagant(e); *(garment)* sexy *inv; (behaviour, practice)* pervers(e)

kinship ['kɪnʃɪp] *n* parenté *f*

kinsman ['kɪnzmən] *n Lit* parent *m*

kinswoman ['kɪnzwʊmən] *n Lit* parente *f*

kiosk ['kiːɒsk] *n* kiosque *m*

kip [kɪp] *Br Fam* **1** *n (sleep)* **to have a k.** piquer un roupillon; **to get some k.** roupiller
2 *vi (pt & pp* **kipped**) *(sleep)* roupiller

kipper ['kɪpə(r)] *n* hareng *m* salé et fumé

Kirg(h)izia [kɜː'giːzɪə], **Kirg(h)izstan** [kɜːgɪz'stæn] *n* le Kirghizistan

kirk [kɜːk] *n Scot* église *f;* **the K.** l'Église (presbytérienne) d'Écosse

kiss [kɪs] **1** *n* baiser *m;* **to give sb a k.** donner un baiser à qn; **to give sb the k. of life** faire du bouche-à-bouche à qn; *Fig* **to be the k. of death for sth** porter fatal à qch; *Fig* **k. curl** accroche-cœur *m*

2 *vt* embrasser; **to k. sb goodbye** dire au revoir à qn en l'embrassant; *Fig* **you can k. your money goodbye** tu peux faire une croix sur ton fric **3** *vi* s'embrasser; **to k. and make up** se réconcilier; **to k. and tell** dévoiler à la presse ses secrets d'alcôve *(impliquant généralement une personne célèbre)*

kissogram ['kɪsəgræm] *n* = service permettant de faire délivrer un message, un poème, une chanson etc, souvent grivois, accompagnés d'un baiser, pour une occasion particulière

kit [kɪt] *n* **(a)** *(equipment)* équipement *m*, matériel *m* **(b)** *(sports clothes)* tenue *f*; **(c)** *(for assembly)* **(model) k.** maquette *f*; **to make sth from a k.** faire qch à partir de pièces détachées; **in k. form** en kit

▸ **kit out** *(pt & pp kitted) vt sep* équiper **(with** de)

kitbag ['kɪtbæg] *n* sac *m* de marin; *Mil* sac à paquetage

kitchen ['kɪtʃɪn] *n* cuisine *f*; **k. knife** couteau *m* de cuisine; **k. roll** essuie-tout *m inv*, Sopalin® *m*; **k. sink** évier *m*; *Fam* **to take everything but the k. sink** emporter des tonnes de choses; *(of thief)* ne laisser que les murs; **k. unit** élément *m* de cuisine

kitchenette [kɪtʃɪ'net] *n* coin-cuisine *m*, kitchenette *f*

kitchenware ['kɪtʃɪnweə(r)] *n* vaisselle *f* et ustensiles *mpl* de cuisine

kite [kaɪt] *n* **(a)** *(toy)* cerf-volant *m*; **to fly a k.** faire voler un cerf-volant; *Fig* lancer un ballon d'essai; *Fam* **go fly a k.!** va voir là-bas si j'y suis!; *Fam* **as high as a k.** excité(e) comme une puce **(b)** *(bird)* milan *m*

kith [kɪθ] *n Lit* **k. and kin** parents *mpl* et amis *mpl*

kitsch [kɪtʃ] *n* kitsch *m*

kitten ['kɪtən] *n* chaton *m*; *Fig* **to have kittens** être dans tous ses états

kitty ['kɪtɪ] *(pl* **kitties)** *n* **(a)** *Fam (cat)* minou *m* **(b)** *(for bills, in cards)* cagnotte *f*

kiwi ['kiːwiː] *n* **(a)** *(bird)* kiwi *m*; **k. fruit** kiwi **(b)** *Fam* **K.** *(New Zealander)* Néo-Zélandais(e) *m,f*

kleptomania [kleptə'meɪnɪə] *n* kleptomanie *f*

kleptomaniac [kleptə'meɪnɪæk] *n* kleptomane *mf*

km *(abbr* **kilometre)** km

kmph *(abbr* **kilometres per hour)** km/h

knack [næk] *n* talent *m*; *(for manual activity)* tour *m* de main; **to have the k. of** *or* **a k. for doing sth** avoir un don pour faire qch; *Ironic* avoir le don de faire qch; **to get the k. (of doing sth)** attraper le tour de main (pour faire qch)

knacker ['nækə(r)] *n* équarrisseur *m*; **k.'s yard** chantier *m* d'équarrissage

knackered ['nækəd] *adj Br very Fam (tired)* crevé(e); *(broken, damaged)* foutu(e)

knapsack ['næpsæk] *n* sac *m* à dos

knave [neɪv] *n* **(a)** *(in cards)* valet *m* **(b)** *Lit (scoundrel)* coquin *m*, fripon *m*

knead [niːd] *vt (dough)* pétrir; *(muscles)* masser

knee [niː] **1** *n* genou *m*; **to go down on one's knees** s'agenouiller; *Fig* **to bring sb to his knees** obliger qn à capituler

2 *vt (hit with knee)* donner un coup de genou à

kneecap ['niːkæp] **1** *n* rotule *f*

2 *vt (pt & pp* **kneecapped)** tirer dans les rotules à

knee-deep ['niː'diːp] *adj* **to be k. in sth** *(in water, snow)* être enfoncé(e) jusqu'aux genoux dans qch; *Fig (in problems)* avoir qch jusqu'au cou; *(in work)* être débordé(e) de qch

knee-high ['niː'haɪ] *adj* **to be k.** *(of water, snow)* arriver à hauteur du genou; *Fam* **when I was k. to a grasshopper** quand j'étais haut comme trois pommes

kneejerk ['niːdʒɜːk] *adj (reaction, response)* instinctif(ive)

kneel [niːl] *(pt & pp* **knelt** [nelt]) *vi* s'agenouiller, se mettre à genoux **(before/to** devant)

knee-length ['niːleŋθ] *adj (skirt)* qui descend jusqu'aux genoux; *(boots, socks)* qui monte jusqu'aux genoux

knell [nel] *n Lit* glas *m*, to toll the **k. for sb** signer l'arrêt de mort de qn; **to toll the k. for sth** sonner le glas de qch

knelt [nelt] *pt & pp of* **kneel**

knew [njuː] *pt of* **know**

knickerbockers ['nɪkəbɒkəz] *npl* knickers *mpl*

knickers ['nɪkəz] *npl* **(a)** *(underwear)* culotte *f*, slip *m*; *Br Fam* **to get one's k. in a twist** perdre les pédales **(b)** *Am (breeches)* knickers *mpl*

knick-knack ['nɪknæk] *n Fam* babiole *f*

knife [naɪf] **1** *n (pl* **knives** [naɪvz]) couteau *m*; **k. and fork** couvert *m*; *Fig* **to get** *or* **have one's k. into sb** en vouloir à qn; **k. sharpener** aiguisoir *m*

2 *vt (stab)* donner un coup de couteau à, poignarder

knife-edge ['naɪfedʒ] *n Fig* **to be on a k.** *(of person)* être sur les nerfs; **to be balanced on a k.** *(of situation, game)* ne tenir qu'à un fil

knife-point ['naɪfpɔɪnt] *n* **at k.** sous la menace d'un couteau

knifing ['naɪfɪŋ] *n* agression *f* au couteau

knight [naɪt] **1** *n* chevalier *m*; *(in chess)* cavalier *m*

2 *vt* faire chevalier

knighthood ['naɪthʊd] *n (title)* **to be given a k.** être fait chevalier

knit [nɪt] *(pt & pp* **knitted** *or* **knit) 1** *vt (sweater)* tricoter; **to k. one's brows** froncer les sourcils

2 *vi* tricoter, faire du tricot

▸ **knit together** *vi (of broken bones)* se ressouder

knitted ['nɪtɪd] *adj* tricoté(e)

knitting ['nɪtɪŋ] *n (item produced)* tricot *m*; **to do sth k.** tricoter; **k. machine** machine *f* à tricoter; **k. needle** aiguille *f* à tricoter

knitwear ['nɪtweə(r)] *n* lainages *mpl*

knives [naɪvz] *pl of* **knife**

knob [nɒb] *n (on cane)* pommeau *m*; *(on banisters)* pomme *f*, *(on drawer, door)* poignée *f*; *(on radio)* bouton *m*; **a k. of butter** une noix de beurre

knobbly ['nɒblɪ] *adj* couvert(e) de bosses; *(tree)* noueux(euse); **k. knees** genoux *mpl* cagneux

knock [nɒk] **1** *n (blow)* coup *m*; **there was a k. at the door** on frappa à la porte

2 *vt* **(a)** *(hit)* frapper, heurter; **to k. sb to the ground** faire tomber qn en le frappant; **to k. sb unconscious** assommer qn; **to k. one's head against sth** se cogner la tête contre qch; **to k. a hole in sth** faire un trou dans qch; **to k. holes in an argument** démolir un argument; **to k. some sense into sb** apprendre à vivre à qn; *Fig* **to k. sth into shape** mettre qn au pas **(b)** *Fam (criticize)* débiner; **don't k. it until you've tried it** il faut essayer avant de critiquer

3 *vt (hit)* frapper; **to k. at the door** frapper à la porte; **to k. against sth** heurter qch; **his knees were knocking** ses genoux s'entrechoquaient **(b)** *(of engine)* cogner

▸ **knock about, knock around 1** *vt sep (a)* malmener; *(beat up)* battre **(b)** *Fam (idea, suggestion)* discuter de

2 *vi Fam (hang around)* traîner; **to k. about with sb** fréquenter qn

3 *vt insep Fam (spend time in)* **to k. about the world** rouler sa bosse; **she spent a year knocking about Europe** elle a passé une année à voyager en Europe

▸ **knock back** *vt sep Fam* (a) *(drink)* s'envoyer (b) *(reject)* envoyer bouler

▸ **knock down** *vt sep* (a) *(pedestrian)* renverser (b) *(building)* abattre (c) *(price)* baisser

▸ **knock off** *1 vt sep* (a) *(cause to fall off)* faire tomber; **he was knocked off his bike by a car** une voiture a heurté son vélo et il est tombé; *Fam* **to k. sb's head** *or* **block off** casser la figure à qn; *Fam* **to k. something off the price** baisser un peu le prix (b) *very Fam (steal)* piquer, faucher (c) *Fam (kill)* zigouiller (d) *Fam* **k. it off!** *(stop it)* ça suffit!, arrête! (e) *Fam (produce quickly)* expédier
2 vi (finish work) finir

▸ **knock out** *vt sep* (a) *(make unconscious)* mettre K.-O.; *Fam* **to k. sb's brains** *or* **teeth out** arranger le portrait à qn (b) *(eliminate from competition)* éliminer

▸ **knock over** *vt sep* faire tomber

▸ **knock up** *vt sep* (a) *(make hastily)* construire en vitesse; *(meal)* préparer en vitesse (b) *very Fam (make pregnant)* mettre en cloque

knockdown price ['nɒkdaʊn'praɪs] *n Fam* **at a k.** à très bas prix

knocker ['nɒkə(r)] *n* (a) *(on door)* heurtoir *m* (b) *very Fam* **knockers** *(breasts)* nichons *mpl*

knocking ['nɒkɪŋ] *n (at door)* coups *mpl*; *(of engine)* cognement *m*

knock-kneed ['nɒk'niːd] *adj* **to be k.** avoir les genoux en dedans

knock-on effect ['nɒkɒnɪ'fekt] *n* **to have a k.** déclencher une réaction en chaîne

knockout ['nɒkaʊt] *1 n* (a) *(in boxing)* knock-out *m inv*; *Fig* coup *m* de grâce (b) *Fam* **he's/she's a k.** *(attractive)* il/ elle est canon
2 adj (a) **k. blow** *(in boxing)* coup *m* qui provoque un K.-O.; *Fig* coup de grâce; *Fig* **to deliver the k. blow** donner le coup de grâce (b) **k. competition** compétition *f* avec épreuves éliminatoires

knot [nɒt] *1 n* (a) *(in general)* nœud *m*; **to tie/untie a k.** faire/défaire un nœud; *Fam Fig* **to tie the k.** *(get married)* se marier (b) *Naut (unit of speed)* nœud *m*; *Fam Fig* **at a rate of knots** à toute allure (c) *(group of people)* petit groupe *m*
2 vt (pt & pp knotted) (rope, string) nouer; *very Fam* **get knotted!** va te faire voir!

knotty ['nɒtɪ] *adj (problem)* épineux(euse)

know [nəʊ] *1 n Fam* **to be in the k.** être au courant
2 vt (pt knew [njuː], *pp known* [nəʊn]) (a) *(be acquainted with)* connaître; **to get to k. sb** apprendre à connaître qn; **when I first knew her** quand j'ai fait sa connaissance; **I k. her to say hello to** nous nous saluons, c'est tout; **knowing him, he'll still be in bed** tel que je le connais, il sera toujours au lit
(b) *(have knowledge of)* savoir; **she thinks she knows all the answers** elle croit avoir réponse à tout; **to k. French** connaître le français; **to k. a lot/a little about sth** bien s'y connaître/s'y connaître un peu en qch; **she knows what she is talking about** elle sait de quoi elle parle; **to k. how to do sth** savoir faire qch; *Fam* **to k. a thing or two** être malin(igne); **to k. one's own mind** savoir ce que l'on veut; **heaven** *or* **God knows!** Dieu seul le sait!
(c) *(recognize)* reconnaître (**by** à); *(distinguish)* distinguer (**from** de); **to k. right from wrong** savoir faire la distinction entre le bien et le mal
3 vi savoir; **to k. about sth** être au courant de qch; **to get to k. of sth** apprendre qch; **as far as I k.** (pour) autant que je sache; **how should I k.?** comment le saurais-je?; **you**

---

never k. on ne sait jamais; not that I k. of pas que je sache; **to k. better than to do sth** savoir qu'il ne faut pas faire qch; **you k.... tu sais...**

know-all ['nəʊɔːl] *n Br Fam* monsieur *m*/madame *f* je-sais-tout

know-how ['nəʊhaʊ] *n Fam* savoir-faire *m*; *(technical)* know-how *m*

knowing ['nəʊɪŋ] *1 n* **there's no k.** c'est impossible à savoir
2 adj (look, smile) entendu(e)

know-it-all ['nəʊɪtɔːl] *n Am Fam* monsieur *m*/madame *f* je-sais-tout

knowledge ['nɒlɪdʒ] *n* (a) *(of fact)* connaissance *f*; **(not) to my k.** (pas) à ma connaissance; **to have no k. of sth** ignorer qch; **to have full k. of sth** avoir pleine connaissance de qch; **it is common k. that...** c'est un fait notoire que...; *Formal* **it has recently come to our k. that...** il a été récemment porté à notre connaissance que... (b) *(learning)* savoir *m*, connaissances *fpl*; *Prov* **k. is power** savoir c'est pouvoir; *Comptr* **k.-based system** *m* basé sur les connaissances

knowledgeable ['nɒlɪdʒəbəl] *adj* savant(e); **to be k. about sth** bien s'y connaître en qch

known [nəʊn] *1 adj* connu(e); *(notorious)* notoire
2 pp of **know**

knuckle ['nʌkəl] *n* articulation *f* ou jointure *f* (du doigt)

▸ **knuckle down** *vi Fam* se mettre au boulot; **to k. down to sth** se mettre à qch

▸ **knuckle under** *vi Fam* mettre les pouces

knuckle-duster ['nʌkəldʌstə(r)] *n* coup-de-poing *m* américain

KO ['keɪ'əʊ] *Fam 1 n (pl* **KO's** ['keɪ'əʊz]) *(in boxing)* K.-O. *m*
2 vt (pt & pp **KO'd** ['keɪ'əʊd]) *(in boxing)* mettre K.-O.

koala [kəʊ'ɑːlə] *n* **k. (bear)** koala *m*

kopeck ['kəʊpek] *n* kopeck *m*

Koran [kə'rɑːn] *n* **the K.** le Coran

Koranic [kə'rænɪk] *adj* coranique

Korea [kə'rɪə] *n* la Corée; **North/South K.** la Corée du Nord/du Sud

Korean [kə'rɪən] *1 n* (a) *(person)* Coréen(enne) *m,f* (b) *(language)* coréen *m*
2 adj coréen(enne); **the K. War** la guerre de Corée

kosher ['kəʊʃə(r)] *adj* (a) *(in Judaism)* casher *inv*, kasher *inv* (b) *Fam (legitimate)* réglo *inv*

kowtow ['kaʊ'taʊ] *vi* **to k. to sb** faire des courbettes devant qn

Kraut [kraʊt] *n very Fam* Boche *mf*, = terme injurieux désignant un Allemand

krona ['krəʊnə] *(pl* **kronor** ['krəʊnɔː(r)]) *n* couronne *f*

krone ['krəʊnə] *(pl* **kroner** ['krəʊnə(r)]) *n* couronne *f*

kudos ['kjuːdɒs] *n (prestige)* prestige *m*; *(fame)* célébrité *f*

Kurd [kɜːd] *1 n* Kurde *mf*
2 adj kurde

Kurdish ['kɜːdɪʃ] *1 n (language)* kurde *m*
2 adj kurde

Kurdistan [kɜːdɪ'stæn] *n* le Kurdistan

Kuwait [kʊ'weɪt] *n* le Koweït

Kuwaiti [kʊ'weɪtɪ] *1 n* Koweïtien(enne) *m,f*
2 adj koweïtien(enne)

kW *(abbr* **kilowatt)** kW

L, l [el] *n* **(a)** *(letter)* L, l *m inv* **(b)** *Br* **L-plate** = plaque apposée sur une voiture pour signaler que le conducteur est en conduite accompagnée

LA [el'eɪ] *n (abbr* **Los Angeles**) Los Angeles

Lab *Br Pol (abbr* **Labour**) les travaillistes *mpl*

lab [læb] *n Fam (abbr* **laboratory**) labo *m*

label ['leɪbəl] **1** *n* **(a)** *also Fig* étiquette *f* **(b)** *(of record company)* label *m*
2 *vt (pt & pp* **labelled,** *Am* **labeled**) *also Fig* étiqueter; *Fig* **to l. sb a troublemaker** qualifier qn de fauteur de troubles

labor, labored *etc Am* = **labour, laboured** *etc*

laboratory [lə'bɒrətrɪ] *(pl* **laboratories**) *n* laboratoire *m*; **l. assistant** laborantin(e) *m,f*

laborious [lə'bɔːrɪəs] *adj (work)* pénible, fatigant(e); *(explanation)* laborieux(euse)

laboriously [lə'bɔːrɪəslɪ] *adv* laborieusement

labour, *Am* **labor** ['leɪbə(r)] **1** *n* **(a)** *(work)* labeur *m*; **l. camp** camp *m* de travail
(b) *(workers)* main-d'œuvre *f*; **l. costs** coût *m* de la main-d'œuvre; **l. dispute** conflit *m* du travail; **l. force** effectifs *mpl*; **l. market** marché *m* du travail; **l. shortage** pénurie *f* de main-d'œuvre
(c) *Br Pol* **L., the L. Party** le parti travailliste, les travaillistes *mpl*
(d) *(task)* effort *m*; **to do sth as a l. of love** faire qch pour le plaisir
(e) *(childbirth)* travail *m*; **to be in l.** être en travail; **l. pains** douleurs *fpl* de l'accouchement
2 *vt* **to l. a point** s'étendre sur un sujet
3 *vi* **(a)** *(of person)* peiner *(over* sur); **to l. in vain** s'échiner en vain
(b) *(of engine)* peiner

laboured, *Am* **labored** ['leɪbəd] *adj* laborieux(euse)

labourer, *Am* **laborer** ['leɪbərə(r)] *n* manœuvre *m*; *(on farm)* ouvrier(ère) *m,f* agricole

labouring, *Am* **laboring** ['leɪbərɪŋ] *adj* **a l. job** du travail *m* de manœuvre

labour-intensive, *Am* **labor-intensive** [leɪbərɪn'tensɪv] *adj* qui demande une main-d'œuvre importante

labour-saving, *Am* **labor-saving** ['leɪbəseɪvɪŋ] *adj* qui simplifie la tâche

labrador ['læbrədɔː(r)] *n* labrador *m*

laburnum [lə'bɜːnəm] *n* cytise *m*

labyrinth ['læbərɪnθ] *n* labyrinthe *m*

labyrinthine [læbə'rɪnθaɪn] *adj Archit* en labyrinthe; *Fig* labyrinthique

lace [leɪs] **1** *n* **(a)** *(cloth)* dentelle *f*; **l. curtain** rideau *m* en *ou* de dentelle **(b)** *(of shoe)* lacet *m*
2 *vt* **(a)** *(shoes)* **to l. (up)** lacer **(b)** *(drink)* ajouter de l'alcool à; *Fig (story)* entremêler **(with** de); **to l. a drink with sth** ajouter qch dans une boisson

lacerate ['læsəreɪt] *vt* lacérer

laceration [læsə'reɪʃən] *n* lacération *f*

lace-up ['leɪsʌp] **1** *n (shoe)* chaussure *f* à lacets
2 *adj (shoe)* à lacets

lachrymose ['lækrɪməʊs] *adj Lit* larmoyant(e)

lack [læk] **1** *n* manque *m* **(of** de); **for l. of...** faute de...
2 *vt* manquer de
3 *vi* **to be lacking in sth** manquer de qch

lackadaisical [lækə'deɪzɪkəl] *adj* désinvolte

lackey ['lækɪ] *(pl* **lackeys**) *n Pej* larbin *m*

lacklustre, *Am* **lackluster** ['læklʌstə(r)] *adj* terne

laconic [lə'kɒnɪk] *adj* laconique

lacquer ['lækə(r)] **1** *n* laque *f*
2 *vt* laquer

lacrosse [lə'krɒs] *n Sp* crosse *f*

lacuna [lə'kjuːnə] *(pl* **lacunae** [lə'kjuːniː] *or* **lacunas**) *n* lacune *f*

lad [læd] *n Fam* **(a)** *(young man)* jeune gars *m*; *(boy)* garçon *m*; **he's a big l.** c'est un grand gaillard; **he's a bit of a l.** *or* **quite a l.** c'est un sacré fêtard **(b)** *(pl* **lads**) *(friends)* **he's gone out with the lads** il est sorti avec les copains; **come on, lads!** allez les mecs!

ladder ['lædə(r)] **1** *n (for climbing)* échelle *f*; *Br (in tights)* maille *f* filée; **the social l.** l'échelle sociale; *Fig* **to get one's foot on the l.** mettre un pied à l'étrier; *Fig* **to reach the top of the l.** atteindre le sommet de l'échelle
2 *vt Br (tights)* filer
3 *vi Br (of tights)* filer

laden ['leɪdən] *adj* chargé(e) **(with** de)

ladle ['leɪdəl] **1** *n* louche *f*
2 *vt (soup)* servir (à la louche)
▸ **ladle out** *vt sep (soup)* servir (à la louche); *Fig* **to l. out advice/praise** distribuer les conseils/les compliments

lady ['leɪdɪ] *(pl* **ladies**) *n* **(a)** dame *f*; **a young l.** *(unmarried)* une jeune fille; *(married)* une jeune dame; **ladies and gentlemen!** mesdames et messieurs!; **ladies' man** homme *m* à femmes; **ladies' (room)** toilettes *fpl* (des dames); **l. friend** amie *f* **(c)** *Br (title)* **L. Browne** lady Browne *(titre de noblesse féminin)*; **L. Luck** la chance; *Fam* **to act like L. Muck** jouer à la grande dame

ladybird ['leɪdɪbɜːd], *Am* **ladybug** ['leɪdɪbʌg] *n* coccinelle *f*

lady-in-waiting ['leɪdɪɪn'weɪtɪŋ] *(pl* **ladies-in-waiting**) *n* dame *f* d'honneur

lady-killer ['leɪdɪkɪlə(r)] *n Fam* bourreau *m* des cœurs

ladylike [ˈleɪdɪlaɪk] *adj (woman)* comme il faut; *(air, behaviour)* distingué(e)

ladyship [ˈleɪdɪʃɪp] *n also Ironic* **Her/Your L.** madame

lag [læg] **1** *n* (**a**) *(gap)* décalage *m* (**b**) *very Fam (prisoner)* **old l.** repris *m* de justice
2 *vt (pt & pp* **lagged**) *(pipes, boiler)* isoler
3 *vi (of person, economy)* **to l. behind** être à la traîne; **to l. behind sb/sth** être à la traîne derrière qn/qch

lager [ˈlɑːgə(r)] *n Br* bière *f* blonde

laggard [ˈlægəd] *n* traînard(e) *m,f*

lagoon [ləˈguːn] *n* lagune *f; (of atoll)* lagon *m*

laid [leɪd] *pt & pp of* **lay**

laid-back [leɪdˈbæk] *adj Fam* cool *inv,* relax *inv*

lain [leɪn] *pp of* **lie²**

lair [leə(r)] *n* repaire *m*

laird [leəd] *n Scot* propriétaire *m* foncier

laisser-faire [leseɪˈfeə(r)] **1** *n* laisser-faire *m*
2 *adj* de laisser-faire

laity [ˈleɪɪtɪ] *n* **the l.** les laïques *mpl*

lake [leɪk] *n* lac *m;* **L. Geneva** le lac de Genève, le lac Léman; **the L. District, the Lakes** la région des lacs *(dans le nord-ouest de l'Angleterre)*

lamb [læm] *n* agneau *m;* **poor l.!** pauvre biquet!; **like lambs to the slaughter** comme des veaux que l'on mène à l'abattoir; **l. chop** côtelette *f* d'agneau

lambast [læmˈbæst] *vt* fustiger

lambing [ˈlæmɪŋ] *n* agnelage *m*

lambskin [ˈlæmskɪn] *n* peau *f* d'agneau

lambswool [ˈlæmswʊl] **1** *n* lambswool *m*
2 *adj* en lambswool

lame [leɪm] **1** *adj also Fig* boiteux(euse); **to be l.** boiter; **to go l.** se mettre à boiter; *Fig* **l. duck** canard *m* boiteux
2 *vt* rendre boiteux(euse)

lamé [ˈlɑːmeɪ] *n* lamé *m;* **a l. dress** une robe en lamé

lamely [ˈleɪmlɪ] *adv* maladroitement

lament [ləˈment] **1** *n* lamentation *f; Mus* complainte *f*
2 *vt* se lamenter sur; **the late lamented Mr Shaw** le regretté M. Shaw
3 *vi* se lamenter (**over** sur)

lamentable [ˈlæməntəbəl] *adj* lamentable; *(decision, loss)* déplorable

lamentably [ˈlæməntəblɪ] *adv* lamentablement

lamentation [læmənˈteɪʃən] *n* lamentation *f*

laminate [ˈlæmɪnət] *n* stratifié *m*

laminated [ˈlæmɪneɪtəd] *adj* (**a**) *(glass)* feuilleté(e); *(wood, plastic)* stratifié(e) (**b**) *(paper, identity card)* plastifié(e)

lamp [læmp] *n* lampe *f*

lamplight [ˈlæmplaɪt] *n* **by l.** à la lumière d'une lampe

lampoon [læmˈpuːn] **1** *n* pamphlet *m*
2 *vt* brocarder

lamppost [ˈlæmppəʊst] *n* réverbère *m*

lamprey [ˈlæmprɪ] *(pl* **lampreys**) *n* lamproie *f*

lampshade [ˈlæmpʃeɪd] *n* abat-jour *m inv*

lampstand [ˈlæmpstænd] *n* pied *m* de lampe

LAN [eleɪˈen] *n Comptr (abbr* **local area network**) réseau *m* local

lance [lɑːns] **1** *n (weapon)* lance *f*
2 *vt (abscess)* percer, inciser

lance corporal [ˈlɑːnsˈkɔːpərəl] *n* ≃ caporal *m*

lancer [ˈlɑːnsə(r)] *n (soldier)* lancier *m*

lancet [ˈlɑːnsɪt] *n* lancette *f*

land [lænd] **1** *n* (**a**) *(ground, nation)* terre *f;* **on l.** sur terre; **to live off the l.** vivre du produit de la terre; **to be in the l. of the living** être toujours de ce monde; *Mil* **l. forces** armée *f* de terre; **l. reclamation** mise *f* en valeur des sols; **l. reform** réforme *f* agraire
(**b**) *(property)* terres *fpl*
2 *vt* (**a**) *(passengers, cargo)* débarquer
(**b**) *(plane)* poser
(**c**) *(fish)* sortir de l'eau
(**d**) *Fam (job, prize)* décrocher
(**e**) *Fam (put)* **to l. sb in prison/court** mener qn en prison/au tribunal; **to l. sb in trouble** attirer des ennuis à qn
(**f**) *Fam* **to be landed with sth** rester avec qch sur les bras; **I got landed with organizing the party** c'est moi qui ai dû me taper l'organisation de la fête
(**g**) *Fam (hit)* **to l. sb one** en coller une à qn
3 *vi* atterrir; *(of gymnast)* se réceptionner; *Fig* **to l. on one's feet** retomber sur ses pieds
► **land up** *vi* atterrir

landed [ˈlændəd] *adj* **l. gentry** noblesse *f* terrienne; **l. proprietor** propriétaire *mf* terrien(enne)

landfall [ˈlændfɔːl] *n Naut* **to make l.** arriver en vue des côtes

landfill site [ˈlændfɪlˈsaɪt] *n* décharge *f* publique

landing [ˈlændɪŋ] *n* (**a**) *(of cargo, troops)* débarquement *m;* **l. card** carte *f* de débarquement; **l. craft** navire *m* de débarquement; **l. stage** débarcadère *m* (**b**) *(of aircraft)* atterrissage *m;* **l. gear** train *m* d'atterrissage; **l. lights** phares *mpl* d'atterrissage; **l. strip** piste *f* d'atterrissage (**c**) *(of staircase)* palier *m*

landlady [ˈlændleɪdɪ] *(pl* **landladies**) *n* (**a**) *(of rented accommodation)* propriétaire *f* (**b**) *(of small hotel)* logeuse *f; (of pub)* patronne *f*

landlocked [ˈlændlɒkt] *adj* sans accès à la mer

landlord [ˈlændlɔːd] *n* (**a**) *(of rented accommodation)* propriétaire *m* (**b**) *(of pub)* patron *m*

landmark [ˈlændmɑːk] *n (distinctive feature)* point *m* de repère; *Fig (important event)* événement *m* marquant

landmass [ˈlændmæs] *n* masse *f* continentale

landmine [ˈlændmaɪn] *n* mine *f* terrestre

landowner [ˈlændəʊnə(r)] *n* propriétaire *mf* foncier(ère)

landowning [ˈlændəʊnɪŋ] *adj* **the l. classes** la classe des propriétaires fonciers

landscape [ˈlændskeɪp] **1** *n* paysage *m;* **l. design** aménagement *m* d'espaces verts; **l. gardener** jardinier(ère) *m,f* paysagiste; *Comptr* **l. (orientation)** format *m* paysage; **l. painter** paysagiste *mf*
2 *vt* aménager en espaces verts

landslide [ˈlændslaɪd] *n* (**a**) *(of earth, rocks)* glissement *m* de terrain (**b**) *(election victory)* raz *m inv* de marée électoral; **to win by a l.** gagner avec une majorité écrasante

landslip [ˈlændslɪp] *n* glissement *m* de terrain

landward [ˈlændwəd] **1** *adj (wind)* marin(e); **on the l. side** du côté des terres
2 *adv* vers la terre

lane [leɪn] *n* (**a**) *(in country)* chemin *m; (in town)* ruelle *f,* passage *m* (**b**) *(on road)* voie *f,* file *f;* **get in l.** *(sign)* = panneau indiquant aux automobilistes de se placer dans la file appropriée (**c**) *(for runner, swimmer)* couloir *m*

language [ˈlæŋgwɪdʒ] *n* (**a**) *(of a people)* langue *f; Fam Fig* **we don't talk the same l.** nous ne parlons pas la même langue; **l. laboratory** laboratoire *m* de langues; **l. learning/teaching** apprentissage *m*/enseignement *m* des langues (**b**) *(style of speech or writing)* langage *m*

languid [ˈlæŋgwɪd] *adj* alangui(e)

languidly ['læŋgwɪdlɪ] *adv* paresseusement
languish ['læŋgwɪʃ] *vi* languir **(for** après**); to l.** in prison moisir en prison
languor ['læŋgə(r)] *n* langueur *f*
languorous ['læŋgərəs] *adj* alangui(e)
lank [læŋk] *adj (hair)* terne
lanky ['læŋkɪ] *adj* dégingandé(e)
lanolin(e) ['lænəlɪn] *n* lanoline *f*
lantern ['læntən] *n* lanterne *f*
Laos [laʊs] *n* le Laos
Laotian ['laʊʃɪən] **1** *n* Laotien(enne) *m,f*
2 *adj* laotien(enne)
lap¹ [læp] *n* **(a)** *(knees)* genoux *mpl*; **to sit on sb's l.** s'asseoir sur les genoux de qn; **l. dancing** = type de danse exécutée par une entraîneuse nue pour un client **(b)** *(idioms)* **it's in the l. of the gods** on ne peut que s'en remettre au sort; **she expects everything to fall into her l.** elle s'attend à ce que tout lui tombe tout cuit dans le bec; **to live in the l. of luxury** vivre dans le luxe
lap² **1** *n (in race)* tour *m*; **l. of honour** tour d'honneur
2 *vt (pt & pp lapped) (overtake)* prendre un tour d'avance sur
lap³ *vi (pt & pp lapped) (of animal)* laper; **to l. against sth** *(of waves)* clapoter contre qch
▸ **lap up** *vt sep (drink)* laper; *Fam Fig (enjoy indiscriminately)* se délecter de; *(believe)* gober, avaler
lapdog ['læpdɒg] *n* chien *m* d'appartement; *Fig* toutou *m*
lapel [lə'pel] *n* revers *m*
Lapland ['læplænd] *n* la Laponie
Laplander ['læplændə(r)] *n* Lapon(one) *m,f*
Lapp [læp] **1** *n* **(a)** *(person)* Lapon(one) *m,f* **(b)** *(language)* lapon *m*
2 *adj* lapon(one)
lapse [læps] **1** *n* **(a)** *(of time)* laps *m* de temps **(b)** *(in standards, concentration)* baisse *f* **(in** de**)**; *(in behaviour)* écart *m* **(in** de**)**
2 *vi* **(a)** *(of concentration, standards)* baisser; *(of person)* retomber dans un travers; **to l. into silence** se taire **(b)** *(of permit, membership)* expirer
lapsed [læpst] *adj (Catholic)* qui ne pratique plus
laptop ['læptɒp] *n Comptr* portable *m*
lapwing ['læpwɪŋ] *n* vanneau *m*
larceny ['lɑːsənɪ] *n Law* vol *m*
larch [lɑːtʃ] *n* mélèze *m*
lard [lɑːd] **1** *n (fat)* saindoux *m*
2 *vt Fam Fig* **an essay larded with quotations** une rédaction truffée de citations
larder ['lɑːdə(r)] *n* garde-manger *m inv*
large [lɑːdʒ] **1** *n* **to be at l.** être en liberté; **people at l., the public at l.** le grand public
2 *adj* **(a)** *(big)* grand(e); *(fat, bulky)* gros (grosse); *(audience)* nombreux(euse); **to grow** *or* **get larger** s'agrandir; *(of person)* grossir; **to make sth larger** agrandir qch; **as l. as life** en chair et en os; **larger than life** haut(e) en couleur **(b)** *(extensive, significant)* **to a l. extent** en grande partie; **a l. part of** une grande partie de
3 *adv* **by and l.** dans l'ensemble
largely ['lɑːdʒlɪ] *adv* en grande partie
large-scale ['lɑːdʒ'skeɪl] *adj (map)* à grande échelle; *(undertaking)* ambitieux(euse); *(disaster)* immense
largesse [lɑː'ʒes] *n* largesse *f*
lark¹ [lɑːk] *n (bird)* alouette *f*; **to rise with the l.** se lever au chant du coq
lark² *n (joke)* rigolade *f*; **to do sth for a l.** faire qch

pour rire; **I don't like this fancy dress l.** je n'aime pas du tout cette histoire de bal masqué
▸ **lark about, lark around** *vi* faire le fou (la folle)
larva ['lɑːvə] *(pl* **larvae** ['lɑːviː]*) n* larve *f*
laryngitis [lærɪn'dʒaɪtɪs] *n* laryngite *f*; **to have l.** avoir une laryngite
larynx ['lærɪŋks] *n* larynx *m*
lasagne [lə'sænjə] *n* lasagnes *fpl*
lascivious [lə'sɪvɪəs] *adj* lascif(ive)
laser ['leɪzə(r)] *n* laser *m*; **l. beam** rayon *m* laser; **l. printer** imprimante *f* laser; **l. surgery** chirurgie *f* au laser
lash [læʃ] **1** *n* **(a)** *(eyelash)* cil *m* **(b)** *(of whip)* coup *m* de fouet
2 *vt* **(a)** *(with whip)* cingler; *(of rain, waves)* fouetter **(b)** *(tie)* lier, attacher
3 *vi* **the rain** *or* **it was lashing down** il pleuvait dru
▸ **lash out** *vi* **(a)** **to l. out at sb** *(physically)* donner un coup/des coups à qn; *(verbally)* s'en prendre violemment à qn **(b)** *Fam (spend extravagantly)* claquer un fric fou **(on** pour**)**
lashings ['læʃɪŋz] *npl Br Fam (lots)* des tas; **l. of cream** une tonne de crème
lass [læs] *n* jeune fille *f*
lassitude ['læsɪtjuːd] *n (weariness)* lassitude *f*; *(laziness)* paresse *f*
lasso [læ'suː] **1** *n (pl* **lassoes** *or* **lassos)** lasso *m*
2 *vt (pt & pp lassoed)* attraper au lasso
last¹ [lɑːst] **1** *n* **the l.** le dernier (la dernière) *m,f*; **the l. but one** l'avant-dernier(ère) *m,f*; **we'll never hear the l. of it** on n'a pas fini d'en entendre parler; **I don't think we've heard the l. of him** je crois que nous n'en sommes pas encore débarrassés; **that's the l. I saw of her** je ne l'ai pas revue depuis; **that's the l. of the wine** on a fini le vin, **to or till the l.** jusqu'à la fin; **at (long) l.** enfin
2 *adj* **(a)** *(final)* dernier(ère), **you are my l. hope** vous êtes mon dernier espoir; **to have the l. word** avoir le dernier mot, **the l. word in comfort/style** le summum du confort/de l'élégance; **l. moment** *or* **minute** au dernier moment, à la dernière minute; **l. thing at night** avant de se coucher; **to be on one's l. legs** être au bout du rouleau; **he's the l. person I'd ask to help me** c'est (bien) la dernière personne à qui je demanderais de m'aider; **that's the l. thing I'd do** c'est (bien) la dernière chose que je ferais; **as a l. resort** en dernier recours; **the L. Judgement** le Jugement dernier; **l. name** nom *m* de famille; **l. rites** derniers sacrements *mpl*; *Fig* **the l. straw** la goutte d'eau qui a fait déborder le vase
(b) *(most recent)* dernier(ère); **the l. time I saw him** la dernière fois que je l'ai vu; **l. January** en janvier (dernier); **l. night** *(during the night)* la nuit dernière; *(in the evening)* hier (au) soir; **l. Sunday** dimanche dernier; **l. week** la semaine dernière
3 *adv* **to arrive/finish l.** arriver/finir dernier; **when I l. saw him** la dernière fois que je l'ai vu; **l. but not least** enfin
last² *n (for shoe)* forme *f* (à chaussure)
last³ **1** *vi* **it will l. me a lifetime** j'en ai pour la vie; **it has lasted him well** ça lui a fait de l'usage
2 *vi (be too good to l.)* c'est trop beau pour durer; **the supplies won't l. a week** ces provisions ne seront pas suffisantes pour une semaine; **he won't l. long in that job** il ne tiendra pas très longtemps à ce poste; **she won't l. the night** elle ne passera pas la nuit
▸ **last out** *vt sep* **to l. the year out** *(of person)* survivre jusqu'à la fin de l'année; *(of supplies)* suffire pour l'année
2 *vt (supplies)* tenir le coup; *(of supplies)* suffire
last-ditch [lɑːst'dɪtʃ] *adj* ultime
lasting ['lɑːstɪŋ] *adj* durable

lastly ['lɑːstlɪ] *adv* pour finir, en dernier lieu

last-minute [lɑːst'mɪnɪt] *adj* de dernière minute

latch [lætʃ] *n* loquet *m*
► **latch onto** *vt insep Fam* **(a)** *(attach oneself to)* to l. onto sb/sth s'accrocher à qn/qch **(b)** *(understand)* to l. onto sth piger qch

latchkey ['lætʃkiː] *(pl* **latchkeys**) *n* clé *f* de la porte d'entrée; l. **child** = enfant dont les parents travaillent et qui doit rentrer seul après l'école

late [leɪt] **1** *adj* **(a)** *(not on time)* en retard; to be l. (for sth) être en retard (pour qch); **to be an hour l.** avoir une heure de retard **(b)** *(far on in time)* tard; **it's getting l.** il se fait tard; **to keep l. hours** se coucher tard; **in the l. afternoon** en fin d'après-midi; **in l. summer** vers la fin de l'été; **to be in one's l. thirties** approcher de la quarantaine; **in the l. nineties** vers la fin des années 90; *Fig* **it's a bit l. in the day to...** il est un peu tard pour... **(c)** *(dead)* feu(e); **my l. husband** feu mon mari
2 *adv* **(a)** *(in general)* tard; **to work l.** travailler tard; **l. into the night** jusqu'à une heure avancée de la nuit; **l. in the year** vers la fin de l'année; **l. in life** sur le tard; *Prov* **better l. than never** mieux vaut tard que jamais **(b)** *(recently)* **as l. as last week** pas plus tard que la semaine dernière; **of l.** récemment

latecomer ['leɪtkʌmə(r)] *n* retardataire *mf*

lately ['leɪtlɪ] *adv* dernièrement, récemment; **until l.** jusqu'à ces derniers temps

lateness ['leɪtnɪs] *n (of person, train)* retard *m*; **the l. of the hour** l'heure *f* tardive

latent ['leɪtənt] *adj (disease, tendency)* latent(e); *(period)* de latence

later ['leɪtə(r)] **1** *adj* ultérieur(e); **l caught a l. train** j'ai pris un train qui partait plus tard; **l. events proved that...** la suite des événements a prouvé que...; **her l. novels** ses derniers romans; **in l. life** avec l'âge
2 *adv* **l. (on)** plus tard; **a few days l.** quelques jours plus tard; **no l. than tomorrow** demain au plus tard; **as we shall see l.** comme nous le verrons par la suite; *Fam* **see you l.!** à plus tard!

lateral ['lætərəl] *adj* latéral(e); **l. thinking** approche *f* originale

latest ['leɪtɪst] **1** *n* **at the l.** au plus tard; **the l. I can stay is seven o'clock** je peux rester jusqu'à sept heures au plus tard; **have you heard the l.?** vous savez la dernière?
2 *adj (most recent)* dernier(ère)

latex ['leɪteks] *n* latex *m*

lathe [leɪð] *n* tour *m*

lather ['læðə(r)] **1** *n* mousse *f*; *Fam* **to work oneself** *or* **get into a l. (about sth)** se mettre dans tous ses états (à propos de qch)
2 *vt* savonner

Latin ['lætɪn] **1** *n* **(a)** *(person) (European)* Latin(e) *m,f*; *(Latin American)* Latino-Américain(e) *m,f* **(b)** *(language)* latin *m*
2 *adj* latin(e); **L. America** l'Amérique *f* latine; **L. American** latino-américain(e)

Latino [læ'tiːnəʊ] *(pl* **Latinos**) *n* latino *mf*

latitude ['lætɪtjuːd] *n also Fig* latitude *f*

latrine [lə'triːn] *n* latrines *fpl*

latte ['læteɪ] *n (café m)* crème *m*

latter ['lætə(r)] **1** *n (of two)* the l. *(of two)* le second (la seconde)
2 *adj* **(a)** *(of two)* second(e) **(b)** *(last)* dernier(ère); **the l. half** *or* **part of June** la deuxième moitié de juin

latter-day ['lætə'deɪ] *adj* moderne; *Rel* **the L. Saints** les mormons *mpl*

latterly ['lætəlɪ] *adv (recently)* dernièrement, récemment; *(towards the end of a period)* vers la fin

lattice ['lætɪs] *n* treillis *m*; **l. window** fenêtre *f* à croisillons de plomb

latticework ['lætɪswɜːk] *n* treillis *m*

Latvia ['lætvɪə] *n* la Lettonie

Latvian ['lætvɪən] **1** *n* **(a)** *(person)* Letton(onne) *m,f* **(b)** *(language)* letton *m*
2 *adj* letton(onne)

laudable ['lɔːdəbəl] *adj* louable, digne de louanges

laudanum ['lɔːdənəm] *n* laudanum *m*

laugh [lɑːf] **1** *n* rire *m*; *Fam* **to have a good l.** bien se marrer; *Fam* **to do sth for a l.** faire qch pour rire; *Ironic* **that's a l.!** la bonne blague!; *Fam* **he's a good l.** on se marre avec lui; **to have the last l.** être bien vengé(e)
2 *vi* rire (at de); *Fam* **don't make me l.!** laisse-moi rire!; *Fam* **to l. one's head off** être mort(e) de rire; *Fam* **if you get that job, you'll be laughing** si tu obtiens le poste, ça sera super; **he'll be laughing on the other side of his face when...** il rira jaune quand...; *Fam* **to l. all the way to the bank** s'en mettre plein les poches; *Prov* **he who laughs last laughs longest** rira bien qui rira le dernier
3 *vt* **to l. oneself silly** se tordre de rire; **you'll be laughed out of court** vous vous couvrirez de ridicule
► **laugh off** *vt sep* tourner en plaisanterie

laughable ['lɑːfəbəl] *adj* ridicule

laughing ['lɑːfɪŋ] **1** *n* rires *mpl*
2 *adj* rieur(euse); **it's no l. matter** ce n'est pas à prendre à la légère; **she was in no l. mood** elle n'était pas d'humeur à rire; **l. gas** gaz *m* hilarant; **l. stock** risée *f*; **to make sb a l. stock** faire de qn un sujet de plaisanterie

laughter ['lɑːftə(r)] *n* rires *mpl*

launch [lɔːntʃ] **1** *n* **(a)** *(boat)* chaloupe *f*; **(motor) l.** vedette *f* **(b)** *(of ship, rocket, product)* lancement *m*; **l. pad** plate-forme *f* de lancement
2 *vt (ship, rocket, product)* lancer; *(enquiry)* ouvrir; **to l. sb on a career** *(of event)* marquer le début de la carrière de qn
► **launch into** *vt insep (attack, story, complaint)* se lancer dans

launching ['lɔːntʃɪŋ] *n (of ship, rocket, product)* lancement *m*; *(of enquiry)* ouverture *f*; **l. pad** plate-forme *f* de lancement

launder ['lɔːndə(r)] *vt also Fig* blanchir

laundrette [lɔːn'dret] *n Br* laverie *f* automatique

laundry ['lɔːndrɪ] *n* linge *m*; **to do the l.** faire la lessive; **l. basket** panier *m* à linge

laurel ['lɒrəl] *n* laurier *m*; *Fig* **to rest on one's laurels** se reposer sur ses lauriers; **l. wreath** couronne *f* de lauriers

lava ['lɑːvə] *n* lave *f*

lavatory ['lævətrɪ] *(pl* **lavatories**) *n* toilettes *fpl*; **to go to the l.** aller aux toilettes; **l. paper** papier *m* hygiénique

lavender ['lævɪndə(r)] **1** *n (shrub)* lavande *f*; **l. water** (eau *f* de Cologne à la) lavande
2 *adj (colour)* bleu lavande *inv*

lavish ['lævɪʃ] **1** *adj* **(a)** *(person)* prodigue **(with/in** de) **(b)** *(gift, meal, décor)* somptueux(euse); *(spending)* extravagant(e); *(portion)* généreux(euse)
2 *vt* **to l. sth on sb** couvrir qn de qch

lavishly ['lævɪʃlɪ] *adv* somptueusement; **to spend l.** dépenser sans compter; **to praise sb l.** couvrir qn d'éloges

law [lɔː] *n* **(a)** *(rule)* loi *f*; **there's no l. against it** aucune loi ne l'interdit; **the laws of gravity** les lois de la pesanteur; **to be a l. unto oneself** n'en faire qu'à sa tête **(b)** *(set of rules)* loi *f*; **to break the l.** enfreindre la loi; **to be above the l.** être au-dessus des lois; **to take the l. into one's own hands** se faire justice soi-même; **l. and order**

l'ordre *m* public; **l. enforcement** le respect de la loi; **l. firm** cabinet *m* d'avocats **(c)** *(system of justice, subject)* droit *m*; **to practise l.** exercer une profession juridique **(d)** *Fam* **the l.** *(police)* les flics *mpl*

law-abiding ['lɔːəbaɪdɪŋ] *adj* respectueux(euse) des lois

lawbreaker ['lɔːbreɪkə(r)] *n* personne *f* qui transgresse la loi

lawcourt ['lɔːkɔːt] *n* cour *f* de justice

lawful ['lɔːfʊl] *adj (legal)* légal(e); *(rightful)* légitime

lawless ['lɔːlɪs] *adj (country, society)* livré(e) à l'anarchie; *(mob)* sans foi ni loi

lawlessness ['lɔːlɪsnɪs] *n* anarchie *f*

lawmaker ['lɔːmeɪkə(r)] *n* législateur(trice) *m,f*

lawn [lɔːn] *n* pelouse *f*, gazon *m*; **l. tennis** tennis *m*

lawnmower ['lɔːnməʊə(r)] *n* tondeuse *f* (à gazon)

lawsuit ['lɔːsuːt] *n* action *f* en justice; **to bring a l. against sb** intenter une action en justice contre qn

lawyer ['lɔːjə(r)] *n* avocat(e) *m,f*; *(for wills, conveyancing)* notaire *m*; *(in company)* conseiller(ère) *m,f* juridique

lax [læks] *adj (discipline, principles, conduct)* relâché(e); *(person)* laxiste

laxative ['læksətɪv] **1** *n* laxatif *m* **2** *adj* laxatif(ive)

laxity ['læksɪtɪ], **laxness** ['læksnɪs] *n (of discipline, principles, conduct)* relâchement *m*; *(of person)* laxisme *m*

lay¹ [leɪ] *adj Rel* laïque; **l. preacher** prédicateur *m* laïque

lay² **1** *vt (pt & pp laid* [leɪd]) **(a)** *(place)* mettre, poser; **to l. sb flat** coucher *ou* étendre qn; **to l. sth flat** poser *ou* coucher qch à plat; **to l. sb to rest** inhumer qn; **to l. one's hands on sth** mettre la main sur qch; **she reads everything she can l. her hands on** elle lit tout ce qu'elle tombe sous la main; **if you l. a finger on her...** si tu touches à un seul cheveu de sa tête..., **to have nowhere to l. one's head** n'avoir nulle part où dormir; **to l. eyes on sb/sth** poser les yeux sur qn/qch; **to l. emphasis on sth** insister sur qch; **to l. the facts before sb** exposer les faits à qn; **to l. claim to sth** prétendre à qch; **to l. the blame on sb** faire porter la responsabilité à qn; **to l. sth bare** mettre qch à nu; **to l. oneself open to criticism** s'exposer à la critique; **to l. sb's fears to rest** apaiser les craintes de qn **(b)** *(foundations, carpet, trap, cable)* poser; *Br* **to l. the table** mettre la table **(c)** *(egg)* pondre **(d)** **to l. a bet** parier **(on** sur) **(e)** *very Fam* **to get laid** s'envoyer en l'air **2** *vi (of bird)* pondre **3** *pt of* **lie²**

▸ **lay aside** *vt sep* **(a)** *(money)* mettre de côté **(b)** *(prejudices, doubt)* oublier

▸ **lay by** *vt sep (money)* mettre de côté

▸ **lay down** *vt sep* **(a)** **to l. down one's arms** rendre *ou* déposer les armes; **to l. down one's life** sacrifier sa vie **(b)** *(principle, rule)* établir, poser; **to l. down the law** dicter sa loi

▸ **lay in** *vt sep (supplies, food)* stocker

▸ **lay into** *vt insep Fam (physically)* rosser; *(verbally)* voler dans les plumes à

▸ **lay off** **1** *vt sep (make redundant)* licencier; *(temporarily)* mettre en chômage technique **2** *vt insep Fam* **(a)** *(abstain from)* arrêter; **to l. off drink** arrêter de boire **(b)** *(leave alone)* ficher la paix à **3** *vi Fam (desist)* arrêter

▸ **lay on** *vt sep (food, drink)* fournir; *(party, entertainment)* organiser

▸ **lay out** *vt sep* **(a)** *(arrange, display)* arranger, disposer; *(dead body)* faire la toilette de **(b)** *(house, town)* concevoir

layabout ['leɪəbaʊt] *n Fam* bon (bonne) *m,f* à rien

lay-by ['leɪbaɪ] *(pl* **lay-bys)** *n* aire *f* de stationnement

layer ['leɪə(r)] **1** *n* couche *f* **2** *vt (hair)* dégrader; **to have one's hair layered** se faire faire un dégradé

layman ['leɪmən] *n Rel* laïque *m*; *(non-specialist)* profane *m*

lay-off ['leɪɒf] *n* licenciement *m*; *(temporary)* mise *f* en chômage technique

layout ['leɪaʊt] *n (of town)* plan *m*; *(of building)* agencement *m*; *(of text)* mise *f* en page

laywoman ['leɪwʊmən] *n Rel* laïque *f*; *(non-specialist)* profane *f*

laze [leɪz] *vi* **to l. (about** *or* **around)** paresser, fainéanter

laziness ['leɪzɪnɪs] *n* paresse *f*, fainéantise *f*

lazy ['leɪzɪ] *adj (person)* paresseux(euse), fainéant(e); *(afternoon)* passé(e) à ne rien faire

lazybones ['leɪzɪbəʊnz] *(pl* **lazybones)** *n Fam* flemmard(e) *m,f*

lb *(abbr* **pound)** livre *f*

LCD [elsiː'diː] *n (abbr* **liquid crystal display)** affichage *m* à cristaux liquides

LDC [eldiː'siː] *n Econ (abbr* **less developed country)** PVD *m*

lead¹ [led] *n* **(a)** *(metal)* plomb *m*; **l. poisoning** saturnisme *m* **(b)** *(for pencil)* mine *f* **(c)** *(idioms)* **to go down like a l. balloon** tomber à plat, *Fam* to fill sb full of l. truffer qn de plomb; *Fam* **to swing the l.** tirer au flanc

lead² [liːd] *n* **(a)** *(advantage)* avance *f*; **to be in the l.** être en tête; **to take** *or* **go into the l.** prendre la tête; *Ind* **l. time** *(for production)* délai *m* de production; *(for delivery)* délai de livraison **(b)** *(example)* exemple *m*; **to give sb the l.** donner l'exemple à qn; **to follow sb's l.** suivre l'exemple de qn **(d)** *(in card game)* **it's your l.** à vous de jouer **(e)** *(in film, play)* premier rôle *m*, rôle principal **(f)** *(for dog)* laisse *f* **(g)** *(cable)* câble *m ou* fil *m* (électrique) **2** *vt (pt & pp* **led** [led]) **(a)** *(guide)* mener, conduire; **you l. the way** montre-nous le chemin; **l. the conversation away from a subject** détourner la conversation; **to be easily led** être très influençable; **that leads me to believe that...** cela m'amène à penser que... **(b)** *(life)* mener une vie heureuse/triste **(c)** *(be leader of)* mener **(d)** *(be ahead of)* **to l. the field** mener; *Fig* **to l. the field in sth** être en tête du domaine de qch; **to l. sb by 8 points** mener une avance de 8 points sur qn **3** *vi* **(a)** *(of road)* mener, conduire (**to** à) **(b)** **to l. to sth** *(cause)* mener à qch **(c)** *(in competition, race)* mener; *(in card game)* jouer le premier; **you l. and I'll follow** vas-y, je te suis

▸ **lead away** *vt sep* emmener

▸ **lead off** *vi* **(a)** *(road, corridor)* partir *(from* de) **(b)** *(in discussion)* commencer

▸ **lead on** *vt sep (deceive)* tromper, duper

▸ **lead up to** *vt insep (of person)* en venir à; *(of event)* précéder; **what are you leading up to?** où veux-tu en venir?

leaded ['ledɪd] *adj* **l. window** fenêtre *f* à croisillons de plomb; **l. petrol** essence *f* au plomb

leaden ['ledən] *adj (heavy)* lourd(e)

leader ['liːdə(r)] *n* **(a)** *(of group)* chef *m*; *(of riot)*

meneur(euse) *m,f; (in race)* premier(ère) *m,f;* **to be a born l.**
être fait(e) pour commander **(b)** *(in newspaper)* éditorial *m*
leadership ['li:dəʃɪp] *n (people in charge)* dirigeants *mpl; (position)* direction *f; (quality)* qualités *fpl* d'encadrement

lead-free [led'fri:] *adj (petrol, paint)* sans plomb
lead-in ['li:dɪn] *n TV & Rad* introduction *f*
leading ['li:dɪŋ] *adj* **(a)** *(best, most important)* principal(e); **l. article** *(in newspaper)* éditorial *m;* **l. lady** *(in film, play)* premier rôle *m* féminin; *Fig* **l. light** personnalité *f* de premier plan; **l. man** *(in film, play)* premier rôle masculin; **l. role** *(in film, play)* premier rôle **(b)** *(team, runner)* de tête **(c)** **l. question** question *f* tendancieuse

leaf [li:f] *(pl leaves* [li:vz]) *n* **(a)** *(of plant)* feuille *f; (of book)* feuillet *m; Fig* **to turn over a new l.** s'acheter une conduite; *Fig* **to take a l. out of sb's book** prendre exemple sur qn **(b)** *(of table) (inserted)* rallonge *f; (hinged)* battant *m*
▸ **leaf through** *vt insep (book, magazine)* feuilleter
leaflet ['li:flɪt] **1** *n* prospectus *m; (political)* tract *m; (folded)* dépliant *m*
2 *vt (area)* distribuer des prospectus dans
leafy ['li:fɪ] *adj (tree)* feuillu(e); *(street)* ombragé(e); **a l. suburb** une banlieue verte

league [li:g] *n* ligue *f; (in sport)* championnat *m;* **to be in l. with sb** être de mèche avec qn; *Fig* **to be in a different l.** être hors classe; **l. champions** vainqueurs *mpl* du championnat

leak [li:k] **1** *n also Fig* fuite *f; (in boat)* voie *f* d'eau; *Fam* **to take** *or* **have a l.** pisser un coup
2 *vt (information)* divulguer **(to** à); **the pipe was leaking gas/water** du gaz/de l'eau fuyait du tuyau
3 *vi* fuir; *(of shoe)* prendre l'eau; *(of boat)* faire eau; **the roof is leaking** il y a une fuite dans le toit
leakage ['li:kɪdʒ] *n* fuite *f*
leaky ['li:kɪ] *adj (bucket, pipe, tap)* qui fuit; *(roof)* qui a une fuite; *(shoe)* qui prend l'eau; *(boat)* qui fait eau
lean¹ [li:n] *adj* **(a)** *(person, face)* mince; *(meat)* maigre **(b)** *(harvest)* maigre; *(year)* de vaches maigres
lean² *(pt & pp* **leant** [lent] *or* **leaned)** **1** *vt* **to l. sth on/ against sth** appuyer qch sur/contre qch
2 *vi (of building)* pencher; **to l. on/against sth** s'appuyer sur/contre qch; *Fig* **to l. on sb** *(rely on)* s'appuyer sur qn; *(pressurize)* faire pression sur qn; **the Leaning Tower of Pisa** la tour de Pise; **to l. out of the window** se pencher à la fenêtre
▸ **lean back** *vi* se pencher en arrière
▸ **lean over** **1** *vt insep* **to l. over sb/sth** se pencher par-dessus qn/qch
2 *vi* se pencher
leaning ['li:nɪŋ] *n (tendency)* inclination *f,* penchant *m* **(towards** pour); **to have artistic leanings** avoir des dispositions artistiques
leant [lent] *pt & pp of* **lean**
lean-to ['li:ntu:] *(pl* **lean-tos)** *n* appentis *m*
leap [li:p] **1** *n* saut *m,* bond *m; Fig* **to take a l. in the dark** faire un saut dans l'inconnu; *Fig* **to advance by leaps and bounds** avancer à pas de géant; **l. year** année *f* bissextile
2 *vt (pt & pp* **leapt** [lept] *or* **leaped)** franchir d'un bond *ou* d'un saut
3 *vi* sauter, bondir; **to l. to one's feet** se lever d'un bond; **to l. at the chance** sauter sur l'occasion; **to l. for joy** sauter de joie
leapfrog ['li:pfrɒg] **1** *n* saute-mouton *m;* **to play l.** jouer à saute-mouton
2 *vt (pt & pp* **leapfrogged)** *Fig* passer avant
leapt [lept] *pt & pp of* **leap**

learn [lɜ:n] *(pt & pp* **learnt** [lɜ:nt] *or* **learned)** **1** *vt* apprendre
2 *vi* apprendre; **to l. of** *or* **about sth** apprendre qch; **to l. from one's mistakes** tirer un enseignement de ses erreurs
learned ['lɜ:nɪd] *adj* savant(e), érudit(e)
learner ['lɜ:nə(r)] *n (beginner)* débutant(e) *m,f; (student)* étudiant(e) *m,f;* **to be a quick/slow l.** apprendre vite/ lentement; **l. (driver)** apprenti(e) *m,f* conducteur(trice)
learning ['lɜ:nɪŋ] *n (act of learning)* apprentissage *m; (knowledge)* savoir *m,* connaissances *fpl;* **l. curve** courbe *f* d'assimilation
learnt [lɜ:nt] *pt & pp of* **learn**
lease [li:s] **1** *n* bail *m; Fig* **to give sb a new l. of life** redonner à qn goût à la vie
2 *vt* louer **(from/to** à)
leasehold ['li:shəʊld] *n (contract)* bail *m; (property)* location *f* à bail
leaseholder ['li:shəʊldə(r)] *n* locataire *mf*
leash [li:ʃ] *n (for dog)* laisse *f; Fig* **to keep sb on a tight l.** tenir la bride haute à qn
leasing ['li:sɪŋ] *n Com* location-vente *f*
least [li:st] **1** *n* **the l.** le moins; **…, to say the l.** le moins qu'on puisse dire, c'est que…; **it's the l. I can do** c'est le moindre des choses; **that's the l. of my worries** c'est le cadet de mes soucis; **at l.** au moins; **he's leaving, at l. that's what I've heard** il part, du moins c'est ce que j'ai entendu dire; **at l. as old as…** au moins aussi vieux que…; **at the very l. they should pay your expenses** ce serait vraiment la moindre des choses qu'ils te remboursent tes frais; **not in the l.** pas du tout; **it doesn't matter in the l.** cela n'a pas la moindre importance
2 *adj (superlative of* **little)** *(smallest)* moindre; **the l. thing annoys her** un rien l'agace
3 *adv* **the l. difficult** le (la) moins difficile; **l. of all her** elle encore moins que les autres; **when I was l. expecting it** au moment où je m'y attendais le moins
leather ['leðə(r)] **1** *n* cuir *m*
2 *vt Fam (beat)* tanner le cuir à
leather-bound ['leðəbaʊnd] *adj (book)* relié(e) en cuir
leathery ['leðərɪ] *adj (face, skin)* tanné(e); *(meat)* coriace
leave [li:v] **1** *n* **(a)** *(permission)* permission *f,* autorisation *f;* **to ask l. to do sth** demander la permission *ou* l'autorisation de faire qch; **to grant** *or* **give sb l. to do sth** accorder *ou* donner à qn l'autorisation de faire qch **(b)** *(holiday)* congé *m;* **to be on l.** *(from work)* être en congé; *(from army)* être en permission; **l. of absence** *(from work)* congé exceptionnel; *(from army)* permission *f* exceptionnelle **(c)** *(farewell)* **to take one's l. (of sb)** prendre congé (de qn); **to take l. of one's senses** perdre l'esprit
2 *vt (pt & pp* **left** [left]) **(a)** *(depart from)* quitter; **to l. the table** se lever de table; **the car left the road** la voiture a quitté la route
(b) *(put, deposit)* **to l. sth somewhere** *(on purpose)* laisser qch quelque part; *(accidentally)* oublier qch quelque part; **take it or l. it** *(of offer)* c'est à prendre ou à laisser; **to l. sth unfinished** laisser qch inachevé(e); **to l. sb to do sth** laisser qn faire qch; **l. it to me** laisse-moi faire; **to l. much** *or* **a lot to be desired** laisser beaucoup à désirer; **to l. that** restons-en là; **to l. well alone** ne pas s'en mêler; **l. me alone!** fiche-moi la paix!
(d) *(bequeath)* laisser **(to** à); **he leaves a wife and three children** *(after dying)* il laisse une femme et trois enfants
(e) **to be left** *(remain)* rester; **there are a few candies**

left il reste quelques bonbons; **three from seven leaves four** sept moins trois égale quatre
  3 *vi (depart)* partir
▸ **leave behind** *vt sep* **to l. sth behind** *(on purpose)* laisser qch; *(accidentally)* oublier qch; **to l. sb behind** partir sans qn
▸ **leave off 1** *vt insep Fam* **to l. off doing sth** arrêter de faire qch; **to l. off work** cesser le travail
  2 *vi* s'arrêter
▸ **leave on** *vt sep (light, TV)* laisser allumé(e)
▸ **leave out** *vt sep* **(a)** *(omit)* omettre **(b)** *(not involve)* **to l. sb out of sth** laisser qn en dehors de qch; **to feel left out** se sentir exclu(e) **(c)** *(leave ready, available)* **I'll l. your dinner out on the table for you** je laisserai ton dîner sur la table; **l. the disks out where I can see them** laisse les disquettes en évidence **(d)** *(leave outside)* laisser dehors; **who left the milk out?** qui a oublié de mettre le lait au frigo? **(e)** *Br Fam* **l. it out!** *(stop it)* arrête!
▸ **leave over** *vt sep* **to be left over** *(of food, money)* rester; **there's some lasagne left over** il reste des lasagnes

leaven ['levən] *n* levain *m*
leaves [li:vz] *pl of* **leaf**
leave-taking ['li:veɪkɪŋ] *n* adieux *mpl*
Lebanese [lebə'ni:z] **1** *npl (people)* **the L.** les Libanais *mpl*
  2 *n (pl* **Lebanese)** *(person)* Libanais(e) *m,f*
  3 *adj* libanais(e)
Lebanon ['lebənən] *n* le Liban
lecher ['letʃə(r)] *n* obsédé *m*
lecherous ['letʃərəs] *adj* lubrique
lechery ['letʃərɪ] *n* lubricité *f*
lectern ['lektən] *n* lutrin *m*
lecture ['lektʃə(r)] **1** *n* **(a)** *(talk)* conférence *f; (at university)* cours *m* magistral; **l. theatre** amphithéâtre *m* **(b)** *Fam (reprimand)* sermon *m*; **to give sb a l.** faire la morale à qn
  2 *vt Fam (reprimand)* faire la morale à
  3 *vi (give public lectures)* donner une conférence/des conférences; *(at university)* donner un cours magistral/des cours magistraux
lecturer ['lektʃərə(r)] *n Univ* enseignant(e) *m,f (d'université)*
LED [eli:'di:] *n Elec (abbr* **light-emitting diode)** LED *f*
led [led] *pt & pp of* **lead**
ledge [ledʒ] *n (on cliff)* corniche *f; (of window, on building)* rebord *m*
ledger ['ledʒə(r)] *n* grand livre *m*
leech [li:tʃ] *n also Fig* sangsue *f*; **to cling to sb like a l.** se cramponner à qn comme une sangsue
leek [li:k] *n* poireau *m*
leer ['lɪə(r)] **1** *n (lustful)* regard *m* lubrique; *(cruel)* regard *m* sadique
  2 *vi* **to l. at sb** *(lustfully)* regarder qn d'un air lubrique; *(cruelly)* regarder qn d'un air sadique
lees [li:z] *npl (of wine)* lie *f*
leeward ['li:wəd] **1** *n* côté *m* sous le vent
  2 *adj* sous le vent; **the L. Islands** les îles *fpl* Sous-le-Vent
leeway ['li:weɪ] *n* marge *f* de manœuvre
left¹ [left] **1** *n* gauche *f*; **on** *or* **to the l.** à gauche; **on my l.** à ma gauche
  2 *adj* gauche; **the l. wing** *(of party)* l'aile *f* gauche
  3 *adv* à gauche
left² *pt & pp of* **leave**
left-field ['left'fi:ld] *adj Am Fam (bizarre)* bizarroïde
left-hand ['left'hænd] *adj* de gauche; *(corner, side)*

gauche; **l. drive** conduite *f* à gauche; **on the l. side** à gauche
left-handed [left'hændɪd] **1** *adj* gaucher(ère)
  2 *adv* de la main gauche
left-hander [left'hændə(r)] *n (person)* gaucher(ère) *m,f*
left luggage (office) ['left'lʌgɪdʒ('ɒfɪs)] *n Br* consigne *f*
leftover ['leftəʊvə(r)] **1** *adj* **l. food/paint** un reste de nourriture/de peinture
  2 **leftovers** restes *mpl*
left-wing [left'wɪŋ] *adj* de gauche
left-winger ['left'wɪŋə(r)] *n* homme (femme) *m,f* de gauche
leg [leg] **1** *n* **(a)** *(of person, trousers)* jambe *f; (of animal)* patte *f; (of table, chair)* pied *m* **(b)** *Culin (of lamb)* gigot *m; (of chicken)* cuisse *f; (of pork)* rôti *m* **(c)** *(of journey, race)* étape *f* **(d)** *(idioms)* **to pull sb's l.** faire marcher qn; **to show a l.** se lever; **to shake a l.** se remuer; **you don't have a l. to stand on** tu n'as rien sur quoi t'appuyer; **to give sb a l. up** donner un coup de pouce à qn; *very Fam* **to get one's l. over** baiser
  2 *vt (pt & pp* **legged)** *Fam* **to l. it** jouer des gambettes
legacy ['legəsɪ] *(pl* **legacies)** *n also Fig* legs *m; to* **come into a l.** faire un héritage
legal ['li:gəl] *adj* légal(e); **to take l. action (against sb)** intenter une action (contre qn); **to take l. advice** consulter un avocat; **l. aid** aide *f* juridique; **the l. profession** les professions *fpl* juridiques; **to be l. tender** avoir cours (légal)
legality [lɪ'gælɪtɪ] *n* légalité *f*
legalization [li:gəlaɪ'zeɪʃən] *n* légalisation *f*
legalize ['li:gəlaɪz] *vt* légaliser
legally ['li:gəlɪ] *adv* légalement
legate ['legɪt] *n Rel* légat *m*
legation [lɪ'geɪʃən] *n* légation *f*
legend ['ledʒənd] *n* légende *f*; **to be a l. in one's own lifetime** être une légende vivante
legendary ['ledʒəndərɪ] *adj* légendaire
leggings ['legɪŋz] *npl (of woman)* caleçon *m; (of cowboy)* jambières *fpl*
leggy ['legɪ] *adj (person)* tout en jambes
legible ['ledʒɪbəl] *adj* lisible
legion ['li:dʒən] *n* légion *f*
legionary ['li:dʒənərɪ] *(pl* **legionaries)** *n* légionnaire *m*
legionnaire [li:dʒə'neə(r)] *n* légionnaire *m*; **l.'s disease** maladie *f* du légionnaire
legislate ['ledʒɪsleɪt] *vi* légiférer **(against** contre)
legislation [ledʒɪs'leɪʃən] *n (laws)* législation *f; (action)* élaboration *f* des lois
legislative ['ledʒɪslətɪv] *adj* législatif(ive)
legislator ['ledʒɪsleɪtə(r)] *n* législateur(trice) *m,f*
legislature ['ledʒɪslətjə(r)] *n* corps *m* législatif
legitimacy [lɪ'dʒɪtɪməsɪ] *n* légitimité *f*
legitimate 1 *adj* [lɪ'dʒɪtɪmət] légitime
  2 *vt* [lɪ'dʒɪtɪmeɪt] légitimer
legitimately [lɪ'dʒɪtɪmətlɪ] *adv* légitimement
legless ['leglɪs] *adj Fam (drunk)* complètement bourré(e)
legroom ['legrʊm] *n* place *f* pour les jambes
legume ['legju:m] *n Bot* légumineuse *f*
legwarmers ['legwɔ:məz] *npl* jambières *fpl*
leisure ['leʒə(r), *Am* 'li:ʒər] *n* loisirs *mpl*; **to do sth at one's l.** faire qch à son rythme; **a life of l.** une vie de loisirs; **l. activities** activités *fpl* de loisirs; **l. centre** centre *m* de loisirs

leisurely ['leʒəlɪ, *Am* 'liːʒərlɪ] *adj (weekend)* relax *inv; at a* **l. pace** sans se presser; **to make l.** progress avancer à son rythme; **to go for a l.** stroll se promener tranquillement

lemming ['lemɪŋ] *n* lemming *m;* **to follow sb like lemmings** suivre qn comme des moutons

lemon ['lemən] **1** *n* **(a)** *(fruit, colour)* citron *m; Fam* **l felt like a real l.** j'ai vraiment eu l'air malin; **l. curd** = pâte à tartiner au citron; **l. sole** limande-sole *f;* **l. squeezer** presse-citron *m;* **l. tea** thé *m* au citron; **l. tree** citronnier *m* **(b)** *(useless car)* voiture *f* de mauvaise qualité **2** *adj* **l. (coloured)** jaune citron *inv*

lemonade [lemə'neɪd] *n (carbonated)* limonade *f; (freshly squeezed)* citronnade *f*

lemur ['liːmə(r)] *n* maki *m*

lend [lend] *(pt & pp* **lent** [lent]) *vt (money, book, pen)* prêter; *(support)* apporter **(to à);** **to l.** credibility to sth rendre qch crédible; **to l. sb a (helping) hand** donner un coup de main à qn; **to l. an ear** *or* **one's ear to...** prêter l'oreille à...; **her work doesn't l.** itself **to being filmed** son œuvre ne se prête pas à une adaptation cinématographique

lender ['lendə(r)] *n* prêteur(euse) *m,f*

lending ['lendɪŋ] *n* prêt *m;* **l. library** bibliothèque *f* de prêt; **l. rate** taux *m (d'un prêt)*

length [leŋθ] *n* **(a)** *(in space)* longueur *f;* **it's 4.50 m in l.** ça fait 4,50 m de long; **the l. and breadth of the country** dans tout le pays **(b)** *(in time)* durée *f;* **at (great) l.** longuement; **a great l. of time** longtemps; **l. of service** ancienneté *f* **(c)** **to go to the l. of doing sth** aller jusqu'à faire qch; **to go to great lengths to do sth** se donner beaucoup de mal pour faire qch; **he would go to any lengths to meet her** il ferait n'importe quoi pour la rencontrer **(d)** *(of wood, string)* morceau *m*

lengthen ['leŋθən] **1** *vt* allonger, rallonger **2** *vi (of days)* allonger, rallonger; *(of shadows)* s'allonger

lengthily ['leŋθɪlɪ] *adv* longuement

lengthways ['leŋθweɪz], **lengthwise** ['leŋθwaɪz] *adv* dans le sens de la longueur

lengthy ['leŋθɪ] *adj* long (longue)

lenient ['liːnɪənt] *adj* indulgent(e)

Leningrad ['lenɪŋgræd] *n Formerly* Leningrad

lens [lenz] *(pl* **lenses** *n (of spectacles)* verre *m; (of camera)* objectif *m; (of eye)* cristallin *m;* **(contact) l.** lentille *f* (de contact); **l. cap** capuchon *m* d'objectif

Lent [lent] *n Rel* carême *m;* **to keep L.** faire carême

lent [lent] *pt & pp of* **lend**

lentil ['lentɪl] *n* lentille *f*

Leo ['liːəʊ] *(pl* **Leos** *n (sign of zodiac)* le Lion; **to be (a) L.** être (du) Lion

leopard ['lepəd] *n* léopard *m*

leotard ['liːətɑːd] *n* justaucorps *m*

leper ['lepə(r)] *n* lépreux(euse) *m,f;* **l. colony** léproserie *f*

leprechaun ['leprəkɔːn] *n* lutin *m*, farfadet *m*

leprosy ['leprəsɪ] *n* lèpre *f;* **to have l.** avoir la lèpre

lesbian ['lezbɪən] **1** *n* lesbienne *f* **2** *adj* lesbien(enne)

lesion ['liːʒən] *n* lésion *f*

Lesotho [lɪ'suːtəʊ] *n* le Lesotho

less [les] **1** *adj (comparative of* **little)** moins de; **it's l. than a week's work** cela représente moins d'une semaine de travail; **the distance is l. than I thought** c'est moins loin que je ne pensais **2** *prep* moins; **a year l. two days** un an moins deux jours; **I've got $50, l. what I spent on the train ticket** j'ai 50

dollars, moins ce que j'ai dépensé pour le billet de train **3** *pron* moins; **I don't think any (the) l. of you** tu n'as pas baissé dans mon estime; **I see l. of them nowadays** je les vois moins ces temps-ci; **in l. than an hour** en moins d'une heure; **the l.** said about it **the better** moins on en parle mieux c'est; *Fam* **l. of that!** ça suffit! **4** *adv* moins; **l. and l.** de moins en moins; **no more, no l.** ni plus ni moins; **still l., even l.** encore moins; **nothing l. than total obedience** rien moins qu'une obéissance totale; **she was driving a Rolls, no l.!** elle conduisait une Rolls, rien que ça!; **I expected no l.** from you je n'en attendais pas moins de vous; **they haven't got a fridge, much l. a freezer** ils n'ont pas de réfrigérateur et encore moins de congélateur

lessen ['lesən] **1** *vt (importance, cost)* diminuer, réduire; *(noise)* atténuer; *(enthusiasm, pain)* calmer **2** *vi (of pain, anger)* se calmer; *(of noise)* s'atténuer

lesser ['lesə(r)] *adj (in size)* plus petit(e); *(in importance)* moindre; **l. of two evils** le moindre mal; **to a l. extent** *or* **degree** dans une moindre mesure

lesson ['lesən] *n* leçon *f; Fig* **he has learnt his l.** ça lui a servi de leçon; *Fig* **to teach sb a l.** *(of person)* donner une bonne leçon à qn; *(of event, experience)* servir de leçon à qn

lest [lest] *conj Formal* de peur *ou* de crainte que + subjunctive; **l. we forget** *(on war memorial)* pour ne pas oublier

let¹ [let] *n (in tennis)* let *m*

let² *n (of property)* location *f;* **short/long l.** location *f* de courte/longue durée **2** *vt (pt & pp* **let)** *(rent out)* louer; **(house) to l.** (maison) à louer

let³ *vt (pt & pp* **let)** **(a)** *(allow)* **to l. sb do sth** laisser qn faire qch, permettre à qn de faire qch; **l. me see** voyons un peu; *(show me)* fais(-moi) voir; **to l. sb know sth** faire savoir qch à qn; **to l. sb pass** laisser passer qch; **to l. sb go** laisser qch; **to l. oneself go** se laisser aller; **to l. sb go** laisser partir qn; *(make redundant)* se séparer de qn; **don't l. it get you down/get you to** ne te laisse pas abattre/affecter par ça; **don't l. me see you here again!** que je ne vous retrouve plus ici!; **can you l. me have it back tomorrow?** pouvez-vous me le rendre demain?; *Math* **l. AB be equal to CD** soit AB égal à CD **(b)** *(with suggestions)* **l.'s go!** allons-y!; **l.'s hurry!** dépêchons-nous!; **l.'s not have an argument about it!** on ne va pas se disputer pour ça!; **now, don't l.'s have any nonsense!** allons, pas de bêtises!

▸ **let by** *vt sep (allow to pass)* laisser passer

▸ **let down** *vt sep* **(a)** *(hem)* rallonger; *(tyre)* dégonfler; *Fig* **to l. one's hair down** se défouler **(b)** *Fam (disappoint, fail)* laisser tomber; **the car l. us down again** la voiture nous a encore lâchés

▸ **let in** *vt sep* **(a)** *(allow to enter)* laisser entrer; **to l. oneself in** *(to house)* entrer; **to l. in the light** laisser entrer *ou* passer la lumière; **to l. in water** *(of shoes)* prendre l'eau **(b)** **to l. sb in on a plan** mettre qn au courant d'un projet; **to l. sb in on a secret** mettre qn dans le secret **(c)** *Fam* **to l. oneself in for a hard time** aller au-devant de grandes difficultés; **what are you letting yourself in for?** est-ce que tu sais à quoi tu t'exposes?

▸ **let into** *vt sep* **to l. sb into the house** faire entrer qn; **to l. sb into a secret** mettre qn dans le secret

▸ **let off** *vt sep* **(a)** *(bomb)* lâcher; *(firework)* tirer; **to l. off steam** se défouler **(b)** *(excuse)* ne pas sanctionner; **I'll l. you off this time** ça va pour cette fois; **they l. him off with a fine** il s'en est tiré avec une amende

▸ **let on** *vt sep Fam* **(a)** *(tell)* dire; **don't l. on** on that I was there n'allez pas dire que j'y étais **(b)** *(claim)* prétendre; **he** wasn't as ill as he I. on il n'était pas aussi malade qu'il le prétendait

▸ **let out** *vt sep* (**a**) *(release) (person)* laisser sortir; *(prisoner)* libérer; *(air, yell)* laisser échapper; *(secret)* divulguer (**b**) *(jacket, trousers)* élargir (**c**) *(rent out)* louer

▸ **let up** *vi (lessen)* diminuer; *(stop)* cesser; **once he's started, he never lets up** une fois lancé, il ne s'arrête plus

let-down ['letdaʊn] *n Fam* déception *f*

lethal ['liːθəl] *adj* mortel(elle); *Fam* **that vodka's l.!** elle est mortelle, cette vodka!; **l. dose** dose *f* létale *ou* mortelle; **l. weapon** arme *f* meurtrière

lethargic [lɪ'θɑːdʒɪk] *adj* mou (molle)

lethargy ['leθədʒɪ] *n* mollesse *f*

let-out ['letaʊt] *n Fam (from obligation)* excuse *f*, prétexte *m*

letter [letə(r)] *n* lettre *f*; **the l. of the law** la lettre de la loi; **to do sth to the l.** faire qch à la lettre; *Com* **l. of credit / exchange** lettre de crédit/de change; **l. of acknowledgement** accusé *m* de réception; **l. bomb** lettre piégée; **l. box** boîte *f* aux lettres; **l. opener** coupe-papier *m inv*

letterhead ['letəhed] *n* en-tête *m*, *(paper)* papier *m* à en-tête

lettuce ['letɪs] *n* salade *f* (verte)

let-up ['letʌp] *n Fam (in conflict)* trêve *f*; *(in weather)* accalmie *f*; *(in pressure)* relâchement *m*; **it's been raining for days without (a) l.** ça fait des jours qu'il n'arrête pas de pleuvoir

leukaemia, *Am* **leukemia** [luː'kiːmɪə] *n* leucémie *f*

level ['levəl] **1** *n* niveau *m*; **at eye l.** à (la) hauteur des yeux; **to be on a l. with sb** être sur un pied d'égalité avec qn; *Fam* **on the l.** régulier(ère); **to come down to sb's l.** se mettre à la portée de qn; **to sink to sb's l.** tomber au niveau de qn; **at ministerial/international l.** à l'échelon ministériel/international

2 *adj* (**a**) *(not sloping)* plat(e); *Fig* **a l. playing field** une situation qui ne défavorise personne

(**b**) **to be l. with sb/sth** *(physically)* être au niveau de qn/qch; *(in race, ability, progress)* être au même niveau que qn/qch; **to draw l. with** *(in race, match)* rattraper; **to do one's l. best** faire tout son possible; **l. crossing** passage *m* à niveau; **l. pegging** à égalité; **l. spoonful** cuillerée *f* rase

(**c**) *(voice, tone)* égal(e); **to keep a l. head** garder son sang-froid

3 *vt (pt & pp* **levelled,** *Am* **leveled**) (**a**) *(make level)* niveler, égaliser; *(building)* raser

(**b**) *(aim) (blow)* porter (**at** à); *(criticism)* adresser (**at** à); *(accusation)* porter (**at** contre)

4 *vi Fam* **to l. with sb** parler franchement à qn

▸ **level off, level out** *vi (of ground)* s'aplanir; *(of prices, demand)* se stabiliser; *(of aircraft)* se redresser

level-headed ['levəl'hedɪd] *adj* pondéré(e)

lever ['liːvə(r), *Am* 'levə(r)] **1** *n also Fig* levier *m*

2 *vt* **to l. sth open** ouvrir qch au moyen d'un levier

leverage ['liːvərɪdʒ, *Am* 'levərɪdʒ] *n (power)* effet *m* de levier; *Fig (influence)* pression *f*

leveraged buyout ['liːvərɪdʒd'baɪaʊt, *Am* 'levərɪdʒd-'baɪaʊt] *n Fin* OPA *f* à crédit

levitate ['levɪteɪt] *vi* léviter

levitation [levɪ'teɪʃən] *n* lévitation *f*

levity ['levɪtɪ] *n* légèreté *f*

levy ['levɪ] **1** *n (pl* **levies**) taxe *f* (**on** sur)

2 *vt (pt & pp* **levied**) lever, percevoir (**on** sur)

lewd [luːd] *adj* obscène

lexical ['leksɪkəl] *adj* lexical(e)

lexicographer [leksɪ'kɒgrəfə(r)] *n* lexicographe *mf*

liability [laɪə'bɪlɪtɪ] *n (pl* **liabilities**) (**a**) *Law (responsibility)* responsabilité *f* (**for** de); *Fin* **liabilities** passif *m* (**b**) *(disadvantage)* handicap *m* (**to** pour)

liable ['laɪəbəl] *adj* (**a**) *Law (responsible)* responsable (**for** de) (**b**) *(to tax)* assujetti(e) (**to** à); *(to fine)* passible (**to** de) (**c**) *(likely)* **to be l. to do sth** risquer de faire qch

liaise [lɪ'eɪz] *vi* **to l. with sb** *(be in contact with)* assurer la liaison avec qn; *(work together with)* collaborer avec qn

liaison [lɪ'eɪzɒn] *n* (**a**) *(contact)* liaison *f*; *(co-operation)* collaboration *f*; *Mil* **l. officer** officier *m* de liaison (**b**) *(love affair)* liaison *f*

liar ['laɪə(r)] *n* menteur(euse) *m,f*

libel ['laɪbəl] *Law* **1** *n* diffamation *f*; **l. action** procès *m* en diffamation; **l. suit** procès *m* en diffamation

2 *vt (pt & pp* **libelled,** *Am* **libeled**) diffamer (par écrit)

libellous, *Am* **libelous** ['laɪbələs] *adj* diffamatoire

liberal ['lɪbərəl] **1** *Pol* **L.** libéral(e) *m,f*

2 *adj* (**a**) *(tolerant)* libéral(e) (**b**) *(generous, abundant)* généreux(euse); **to be l. with one's praise/advice** ne pas être avare de compliments/de conseils (**c**) *Pol* **L.** libéral(e)

liberalism ['lɪbərəlɪzəm] *n* libéralisme *m*

liberalize ['lɪbərəlaɪz] *vt* libéraliser; *(law)* assouplir

liberally ['lɪbərəlɪ] *adv* libéralement, généreusement

liberate ['lɪbəreɪt] *vt* libérer

liberated ['lɪbəreɪtɪd] *adj (person)* libéré(e); *(views, ideas)* progressiste

liberation [lɪbə'reɪʃən] *n* libération *f*; **l. movement** mouvement *m* de libération

liberator ['lɪbəreɪtə(r)] *n* libérateur(trice) *m,f*

Liberia [laɪ'bɪərɪə] *n* le Libéria

Liberian [laɪ'bɪərɪən] **1** *n* Libérien(enne) *m,f*

2 *adj* libérien(enne)

libertarian [lɪbə'teərɪən] *n & adj* libertaire *mf*

liberty ['lɪbətɪ] *n (pl* **liberties**) liberté *f*; **at l.** en liberté; **to be at l. to do sth** être libre de faire qch; **to take the l. of doing sth** prendre la liberté de faire qch; **to take liberties with sb/sth** prendre des libertés avec qn/qch; *Fam* **what a l.!** quel culot!

libido [lɪ'biːdəʊ] *n* libido *f*

Libra ['liːbrə] *n (sign of zodiac)* la Balance; **to be (a) L.** être (de la) Balance

librarian [laɪ'breərɪən] *n* bibliothécaire *mf*

library ['laɪbrərɪ] *n (pl* **libraries**) bibliothèque *f*; **l. book** livre *m* de bibliothèque; **l. card** carte *f* de bibliothèque

libretto [lɪ'bretəʊ] *n (pl* **librettos** *or* **libretti** [lɪ'bretiː]) *n Mus* livret *m*

Libya ['lɪbɪə] *n* la Libye

Libyan ['lɪbɪən] **1** *n* Libyen(enne) *m,f*

2 *adj* libyen(enne)

lice [laɪs] *pl of* **louse**

licence, *Am* **license[1]** ['laɪsəns] *n* (**a**) *(permit)* permis *m*; *Com* **under l.** sous licence; *Br (driving)* **l.,** *Am* **driver's l.** permis de conduire; *(TV)* **l.** redevance *f* (télé); **l. number** *(of car)* numéro *m* d'immatriculation; **l. plate** plaque *f* d'immatriculation (**b**) *(freedom)* liberté *f*; *(excessive freedom)* licence *f*

license[2] *vt Com* accorder une licence à; **to be licensed to carry a gun** avoir un permis de port d'armes

licensed ['laɪsənst] *adj* **l. premises** débit *m* de boissons; **l. restaurant** = restaurant possédant une licence de débit de boissons

licensing ['laɪsənsɪŋ] *n* **l. hours** *(of pub)* heures *fpl* d'ouverture; **l. laws** lois *fpl* relatives aux débits de boissons

licentious [laɪ'senʃəs] *adj* licencieux(euse)

lichen ['laɪkən] *n* lichen *m*

lick [lɪk] **1** *n* **(a)** *(with tongue)* coup *m* de langue; **a l. of paint** un petit coup de peinture **(b)** *Fam* **at a great l.**, **at full l.** à toute allure **2** *vt* **(a)** *(with tongue)* lécher; **to l. one's lips** se lécher les lèvres; *Fig* se (pour)lécher les babines; *Fig* **to l. one's wounds** panser ses blessures; *Fam Fig* **to l. sb's boots** lécher les bottes à qn; *Br Vulg* **to l. sb's arse** faire du lèche-cul à qn; *Fam* **to l. sb into shape** dresser qn **(b)** *Fam (defeat)* mettre une raclée à

licorice ['lɪkərɪs] = **liquorice**

lid [lɪd] *n* **(a)** *(of pot, jar)* couvercle *m* **(b)** *(idioms)* **to take the l. off sth** exposer qch au grand jour; **to keep the l. on sth** étouffer qch

lie¹ [laɪ] **1** *n* mensonge *m*; **to tell a l.** dire un mensonge; **to give the l. to sth** démentir qch; **l. detector** détecteur *m* de mensonges **2** *vi* mentir; **to l. through one's teeth** mentir effrontément

lie² **1** *n* **to find out the l. of the land** *(in politics, business)* tâter le terrain **2** *vi* *(pt* **lay** [leɪ], *pp* **lain** [leɪn]) **(a)** *(of person, animal) (be in a lying position)* être couché(e) *ou* allongé(e); *(get down)* se coucher, s'allonger; **here lies...** *(on gravestone)* ci-gît…; **to l. in bed** rester au lit; **I lay awake all night** je n'ai pas dormi de la nuit; *Fig* **to l. low** garder un profil bas; *Fig* **to l. in wait for sb** guetter l'arrivée de qn **(b)** *(of object)* être, se trouver; **snow lay on the hills** il y avait de la neige sur les collines; **to l. in ruins** *(of building)* être en ruines; *(of career, hopes)* être détruit(e) **(c)** *(of abstract thing)* **the responsibility lies with the management** la responsabilité incombe à la direction; **to know where one's interests lie** savoir où se trouve son intérêt; **the difference lies in that...** la différence réside dans le fait que…; **a brilliant future lies before her** un brillant avenir s'ouvre devant elle; **what lies behind this unexpected decision?** que cache cette décision soudaine?

▸ **lie about** *vi* traîner

▸ **lie back** *vi* s'allonger

▸ **lie down** *vi* se coucher, s'étendre; *Fig* **to take criticism/ an insult lying down** se laisser critiquer/insulter sans réagir; **I'm not going to take this lying down** je ne vais pas me laisser faire

▸ **lie in** *vi* faire la grasse matinée

Liechtenstein ['lɪktənstaɪn] *n* le Liechtenstein

lie-down ['laɪ'daʊn] *n* **to have a l.** faire une sieste

lie-in ['laɪ'ɪn] *n* **to have a l.** faire la grasse matinée

lieu [ljuː, luː] *n* **in l.** à la place; **in l. of** au lieu de

lieutenant [*Br* lef'tenənt, *Am* luː'tenənt] *n Mil* lieutenant *m*; *Naut* lieutenant de vaisseau; *Am (police officer)* inspecteur *m* de police; *Fig (helper)* lieutenant; **l. colonel** lieutenant-colonel *m*

life [laɪf] *(pl* **lives** [laɪvz]) *n* **(a)** *(existence)* vie *f*; **to take sb's l.** tuer qn; **to take one's own l.** se suicider; **to bring sb back to l.** ramener qn à la vie; **a matter of l. and death** une question de vie ou de mort; **l. after death** la vie après la mort; **to risk one's l.**, **to risk l. and limb** risquer sa vie *ou* sa peau; **to escape with one's l.** avoir la vie sauve; **to lose one's l.** perdre la vie; **no lives were lost** on ne déplore aucune victime; **he held on to the rope for dear l.** il s'accrochait au cordage avec l'énergie du désespoir; **run for your lives!** sauve qui peut!; *Fam* **not on your l.!** jamais de la vie!; *Fam* **I couldn't for the l. of me remember** je n'arrivais absolument pas à me rappeler; **from l.** *(to draw, paint)* d'après nature; **bird l.** oiseaux *mpl*; **plant l.** végétaux *mpl*; **l. belt** ceinture *f* de sauvetage; **l. cycle** cycle *m* de vie; **l.**

force force *f* vitale; **l. form** forme *f* de vie; **l. jacket** gilet *m* de sauvetage; **l. sciences** sciences *fpl* de la vie **(b)** *(period of existence)* vie *f*; **she had worked all her l.** elle avait travaillé toute sa vie; **never in (all) my l.** jamais de ma vie; **a l. of Tolstoy** une biographie de Tolstoï; *Fam* **to get l.** en prendre pour perpète; **l. annuity** rente *f* viagère; **l. expectancy** espérance *f* de vie; **l. imprisonment** emprisonnement *m* à vie; **l. insurance** assurance-vie *f*; **l. member** membre *m* à vie; *Br* **l. peer** pair *m* à vie; **l. pension** pension *f* à vie; **l. sentence** condamnation *f* à perpétuité; **l. span** *(of person, animal)* espérance *f* de vie; *(of machine)* durée *f* de vie; **to write one's l. story** écrire son autobiographie **(c)** *(mode of existence)* vie *f*; *Fam* **to live** *or* **lead the l. of Riley** se la couler douce; **to make a new l. for oneself** refaire sa vie; **way of l.** style *m* de vie; **he makes her l. a misery** il lui rend la vie insupportable; **to make l. worth living** donner un sens à l'existence; *Fam* **how's l.?** comment ça va?; **what a l.!** quelle vie!; **such is** *or* **that's l.!** c'est la vie!; **this is the l.!** voilà ce que j'appelle vivre!; *Fam* **get a l.!** t'es vraiment nul! **(d)** *(liveliness)* **to come to l.** s'animer; **to bring sb to l.** *(of book, author)* donner vie à qn; **the l. and soul of the party** le boute-en-train de la soirée; **there's l. in the old dog yet** il n'a pas encore dit son dernier mot, le vieux

lifeblood ['laɪfblʌd] *n (of person)* souffle *m* vital; *Fig (of economy, society)* moteur *m*

lifeboat ['laɪfbəʊt] *n* canot *m* de sauvetage

life-giving ['laɪfgɪvɪŋ] *adj (sun, water)* nourricier(ère); *(aid)* vital(e)

lifeguard ['laɪfgɑːd] *n (at the seaside)* surveillant(e) *m,f* de baignade; *(at swimming pool)* maître *m* nageur

lifeless ['laɪflɪs] *adj* sans vie; *(performance, style)* qui manque de vie

lifelessly ['laɪflɪslɪ] *adv* sans vie

lifelike ['laɪflaɪk] *adj (portrait)* très ressemblant(e)

lifeline ['laɪflaɪn] *n Fig* planche *f* (de salut); **to throw sb a l.** offrir *ou* tendre à qn une planche (de salut)

lifelong ['laɪflɒŋ] *adj* de toujours

lifer ['laɪfə(r)] *n Fam (prisoner)* condamné(e) *m,f* à perpète

life-saver ['laɪfseɪvə(r)] *n Fam* **seatbelts can be life-savers** le port de la ceinture de sécurité peut sauver des vies; *Fig* **you're a l.!** tu me sauves la vie!

life-saving ['laɪfseɪvɪŋ] *adj* salvateur(trice); *(equipment)* de réanimation; **she needed a l. operation** elle devait se faire opérer, c'était une question de vie ou de mort

life-size(d) ['laɪfsaɪz(d)] *adj* grandeur nature *inv*

lifestyle ['laɪfstaɪl] *n* style *m ou* mode *m* de vie

life-support ['laɪfsəpɔːt] *adj* **l. system** *or* **machine** respirateur *m* artificiel

life-threatening ['laɪfθretnɪŋ] *adj (disease)* potentiellement mortel(le); **to be in a l. situation** être en danger de mort

lifetime ['laɪftaɪm] *n (of person)* vie *f*; **in my l.** de mon vivant; **it's the chance of a l.** une telle chance ne se présente qu'une fois dans la vie; **the holiday of a l.** des vacances exceptionnelles

lift [lɪft] **1** *n* **(a)** *Br (elevator)* ascenseur *m*; **(goods) l.** monte-charge *m*; **l. attendant** garçon *m* d'ascenseur; **l. shaft** cage *f* d'ascenseur **(b)** *Br (car ride)* **to give sb a l.** prendre *ou* emmener qn en voiture; **could you give me a l. to the station?** est-ce que tu peux m'emmener à la gare? **(c)** *Fam* **to give sb a l.** *(cheer up)* remonter le moral à qn **2** *vt* **(a)** *(one's head, eyes, arm)* lever; **he won't l. a finger to help** il ne lèvera pas le petit doigt; **to l. sb (up)** *(after fall)*

aider qn à se relever; **to l.** a child up prendre un enfant dans ses bras
(**b**) *Fam (take, steal)* piquer; *(arrest)* choper
(**c**) *(restrictions, siege)* lever
3 *vi (of mist, fog)* se lever, se dissiper
▸ **lift off** *vi (of rocket)* décoller
lift-off ['lɪftɒf] *n (of rocket)* décollage *m*
ligament ['lɪgəmənt] *n* ligament *m*
light¹ [laɪt] **1** *n* (**a**) *(illumination)* lumière *f*; by the **l.** of the moon à la clarté de la lune; **things will look different in the cold l.** of day demain vous verrez les choses sous un autre jour; **to be in sb's l.** faire de l'ombre à qn; *Comptr* **l. pen** crayon *m* lumineux; **l. year** année-lumière *f*
(**b**) *(lamp)* lumière *f*; *Fam* **to go out like a l.** s'endormir aussitôt couché(e); **(traffic) lights** feux *mpl* de circulation; **l. bulb** ampoule *f*
(**c**) *(fire)* **to set l. to sth** mettre le feu à qch; **have you got a l.?** vous avez du feu?
(**d**) *(idioms)* **the l.** at the end of the tunnel le bout du tunnel; **to throw** *or* **cast l. on sth** faire la lumière sur qch; **to bring sth to l.** mettre qch en lumière; **to come to l.** être découvert(e); **to see sb/sth in a new/different l.** voir qn/ qch sous un jour nouveau/différent; **in (the) l. of…** *(considering)* à la lumière de…
2 *adj (not dark)* clair(e); **it will soon be l.** il fera bientôt jour
3 *vt (pt & pp* lit [lɪt]) (**a**) *(fire, cigarette)* allumer (**b**) *(room, street)* éclairer, illuminer
light² **1** *adj* (**a**) *(not heavy)* léger(ère); **to be l.** on one's feet avoir le pas léger; **to be a l. sleeper** avoir le sommeil léger; **to have a l. touch** avoir la main légère; **l. aircraft** avion *m* petit porteur; **l. artillery** artillerie *f* légère; **l. infantry** infanterie *f* légère
(**b**) *(not severe)* *(job, exercise)* facile, peu fatigant(e); *(rain)* fin(e); *(prison sentence)* léger(ère)
(**c**) *(not serious)* léger(ère); **to make l. of sth** prendre qch à la légère; **l. entertainment** variétés *fpl*; **l. reading** lectures *fpl* récréatives; **l. verse** poésie *f* facile
2 *adv* **to travel l.** voyager léger
▸ **light on** *(pt & pp* **lighted)** *vt insep* tomber sur
▸ **light up 1** *vt sep (house, room)* éclairer; *(cigarette)* allumer
2 *vi* s'éclairer; *Fam (of smoker)* allumer une cigarette
lighten¹ ['laɪtən] **1** *vt (make less dark)* éclaircir
2 *vi (of sky)* s'éclaircir
lighten² *vt (make less heavy)* alléger; *Fig* **to l. sb's load** soulager qn
▸ **lighten up** *vi Fam* se détendre
lighter ['laɪtə(r)] *n* briquet *m*; **l. fluid** *or* **fuel** essence *f* à briquet
light-fingered [laɪt'fɪŋgəd] *adj Fam* **to be l.** être chapardeur(euse)
light-headed [laɪt'hedɪd] *adj* étourdi(e)
light-hearted [laɪt'hɑːtɪd] *adj (person, discussion)* enjoué(e); *(remark)* badin(e); **to take a l.** look at sth poser un regard amusé sur qch
lighthouse ['laɪthaʊs] *n* phare *m*; **l. keeper** gardien *m* de phare
lighting ['laɪtɪŋ] *n (act, system)* éclairage *m*
lightly ['laɪtlɪ] *adv* légèrement; **to sleep l.** avoir le sommeil léger; **to get off l.** s'en tirer à bon compte; **to speak l.** of sth parler de qch à la légère; **to speak l.** of sb parler de qn sur un ton léger; **to take a decision l.** prendre une décision à la légère
lightness ['laɪtnɪs] *n* (**a**) *(brightness)* clarté *f* (**b**) *(in weight)* légèreté *f*
lightning ['laɪtnɪŋ] *n* (**a**) *(bolt)* éclairs *mpl*, foudre *f*; **l. conductor** paratonnerre *m* (**b**) *(idioms)* **as quick as l., with**

l. speed rapide comme l'éclair; **l. attack** attaque *f* éclair; **l. strike** grève *f* surprise; **l. visit** visite *f* éclair
lightweight ['laɪtweɪt] **1** *n (in boxing)* poids *m* léger; *Fig & Pej (in character, intellect)* personne *f* qui manque d'envergure
2 *adj (garment, fabric)* léger(ère)
lignite ['lɪgnaɪt] *n* lignite *m*
like¹ [laɪk] **1** *n* he and his **l.** lui et ses semblables; **it's not for the likes of me** ce n'est pas pour des gens comme moi; **Pilates, yoga and the l.** le Pilates, le yoga et autres choses du même genre; **I've never seen the l. of it** je n'ai jamais vu une chose pareille
2 *adj* semblable, pareil(eille); **they are as l. as two peas (in a pod)** ils se ressemblent comme deux gouttes d'eau
3 *prep* (**a**) *(similar to)* **to be l. sb/sth** être semblable à qn/ qch, ressembler à qn/qch; **to taste l. sth** avoir le même goût que qch; **to look l. sb/sth** ressembler à qn/qch; **what's the weather l.?** comment est le temps?; **people l. you** des gens comme vous; **you know what she's l.** tu sais comme elle est; **it costs something l. $10** cela coûte dans les 10 dollars, that's more l. it voilà qui est mieux; **we don't have anything l. as many as that** on est loin d'en avoir autant; **there's nothing l. it!** il n'y a rien de tel!; **she is nothing l. as intelligent as you** elle est loin d'être aussi intelligente que vous; **that's not l. her** cela ne lui ressemble pas; **that's just l. him!** c'est bien de lui!; *Prov* **l. father, l. son** tel père, tel fils
(**b**) *(in the manner of)* comme; **just l. anybody else** comme tout le monde; *Fam* **don't be l. that!** ne fais pas l'idiot!
(**c**) *(such as)* tel (telle) que; **take more exercise, l. jogging** fais plus d'exercice, du jogging par exemple
4 *adv* **as l. as not** à coup sûr
5 *conj Fam* **do it l. I said** fais comme je t'ai dit; **he looked l. he'd seen a ghost** on aurait dit qu'il avait vu un fantôme; **it's not l. he's ill or anything** ce n'est pas comme si il était malade ou quoi que ce soit
like² *n* likes goûts *mpl*, préférences *fpl*; **likes and dislikes** préférences *fpl*
2 *vt* (**a**) *(person)* bien aimer; **she is well liked** elle est très appréciée
(**b**) *(enjoy)* aimer; **whether she likes it or not,…** que ça lui plaise ou non,…; **l l. to think my father would have agreed** j'aime à penser que mon père aurait approuvé; *Fam Ironic* **well, l l. that!** elle est bien bonne, celle-là!
(**c**) *(want)* **would you l. a coffee?** aimerais-tu un café?; **l would very much l. to go** j'aimerais beaucoup y aller; **l would l. nothing better than…** rien ne me ferait plus plaisir que…; **he doesn't l. people to talk about it** il n'aime pas que l'on en parle; **he thinks he can do anything he likes** il se croit tout permis; **if/when you l.** si/quand vous voulez; **as much as you l.** tant que vous voulez; **as often as you l.** aussi souvent que vous voulez; **l didn't l. to mention it** je n'ai préféré ne pas le mentionner
likeable ['laɪkəbəl] *adj* sympathique
likelihood ['laɪklɪhʊd] *n* probabilité *f*; **in all l.** selon toute vraisemblance *ou* probabilité; **there is little l. of finding it** il y a peu de chance pour qu'on le trouve; **the l. is that…** il est probable que… **+ subjunctive**
likely ['laɪklɪ] **1** *adj* (**a**) *(probable)* probable; **it's more than l.** c'est plus que probable; **it's l. to rain** il est probable qu'il pleuve, il pleuvra probablement; *Ironic* **a l. story!** à d'autres! (**b**) *(suitable)* approprié(e)
2 *adv* **very l.** très probablement; **as l. as not** sûrement; *Fam* **not l.!** tu plaisantes!
like-minded [laɪk'maɪndɪd] *adj* des mêmes avis; *(having same tastes)* qui ont les mêmes goûts
liken ['laɪkən] *vt* comparer (**to** à)
likeness ['laɪknɪs] *n* (**a**) *(similarity)* ressemblance *f*; **family l.** air *m* de famille (**b**) *(portrait)* portrait *m*

likewise ['laɪkwaɪz] *adv (similarly)* de même, aussi; **to do l.** en faire autant

liking ['laɪkɪŋ] *n* goût *m*, penchant *m*; **is it to your l.?** cela est-il à votre goût?; **to have a l.** for sth avoir du goût pour qch, aimer qch; **to take a l.** to sth prendre goût à qch; **to take a l.** to sb se prendre d'amitié pour qn

lilac ['laɪlək] **1** *n* lilas *m*
  2 *adj* lilas *inv*

Lilo® ['laɪləʊ] *(pl* **Lilos)** *n* matelas *m* pneumatique

lilt [lɪlt] *n (of voice)* inflexions *fpl*

lilting ['lɪltɪŋ] *adj* chantant(e)

lily ['lɪlɪ] *(pl* **lilies)** *n* lis *m*; **l. of the valley** muguet *m*

lily-livered ['lɪlɪlɪvəd] *adj Fam* froussard(e)

lima bean ['liːmə'biːn] *n* haricot *m* de Lima

limb [lɪm] *n* **(a)** *(of body)* membre *m*; **to tear sb l. from l.** déchiqueter qn, mettre qn en pièces **(b)** *(of tree)* grosse branche *f*; *Fig* **to be out on a l.** être dans une situation délicate

limber ['lɪmbə(r)] *adj* souple
  ▸ **limber up** *vi* s'échauffer

limbo ['lɪmbəʊ] *(pl* **limbos)** *n* **(a)** *Rel* les limbes *mpl*; *Fig* **to be in l.** être dans les limbes **(b)** *(dance)* limbo *m*

lime¹ [laɪm] *n (fruit)* citron *m* vert; *(citrus tree)* limettier *m*; *(linden tree)* tilleul *m*; **l. green** vert *m* anis; **l. juice** jus *m* de citron vert

lime² *n Chem* chaux *f*

limelight ['laɪmlaɪt] *n* **to be in the l.** être sous les projecteurs

limerick ['lɪmərɪk] *n* = poème burlesque en cinq vers

limestone ['laɪmstəʊn] *n* calcaire *m*

limey ['laɪmɪ] *(pl* **limeys)** *n Am Fam (British person)* Rosbif *m*

limit ['lɪmɪt] **1** *n* limite *f*; **within limits** jusqu'à un certain point; **off limits (to)** inaccessible (à); *(forbidden)* interdit(e) (à); **to know no limits** être sans limites; **that's the l.!** ce n'est plus possible!; **he's the l.!** il est impossible!
  2 *vt* limiter; **to l. oneself to sth/to doing sth** se limiter à qch/à faire qch

limitation [lɪmɪ'teɪʃən] *n* limitation *f*; **to know one's limitations** connaître ses limites

limited ['lɪmɪtəd] *adj* limité(e); **l. company** société *f* à responsabilité limitée; **l. edition** édition *f* à tirage limité; *Law* **l. liability** responsabilité *f* limitée

limitless ['lɪmɪtlɪs] *adj (wealth, amount, supply)* illimité(e); *(generosity)* sans bornes

limo ['lɪməʊ] *(pl* **limos)** *n Fam* limousine *f*

limousine [lɪmə'ziːn] *n* limousine *f*

limp¹ [lɪmp] **1** *n* boitement *m*; **to have a l.** boiter
  2 *vi* boiter

limp² *adj* mou (molle); **to go l.** s'affaisser

limpet ['lɪmpɪt] *n* bernique *f*, patelle *f*; *Fig* **to stick to sb like a l.** ne pas lâcher qn; *Mil* **l. mine** mine *f* magnétique

limpid ['lɪmpɪd] *adj* limpide

limply ['lɪmplɪ] *adv* mollement

linchpin ['lɪntʃpɪn] *n Fig (person)* cheville *f* ouvrière; *(thing)* clé *f* de voûte

linctus ['lɪŋktəs] *n* sirop *m*

linden ['lɪndən] *n* **l. (tree)** tilleul *m*

line¹ [laɪn] **1** *n* **(a)** *(mark)* ligne *f*; *(drawn)* trait *m*; *(on face)* ride *f*; *Fig* **to draw the l. at doing sth** se refuser à faire qch; **l. drawing** dessin *m* au trait
  (b) *(row)* ligne *f*, rangée *f*; *(one behind the other)* file *f*; *Am (queue)* queue *f*; **to stand in a l.** être en rang; *(one behind the other)* être en file; *Am* **to stand in l.** *(queue)* faire la queue;

Fig **to be out of l.** dépasser les bornes; **to be in l. with sth** être conforme à qch; *Fig* **to be in l. for promotion** être sur la liste des promotions; *Fig* **to be on the l.** *(of one's job, reputation)* être en jeu; *Com & Ind* **l. manager** chef *m* d'équipe
  (c) *(rope)* ligne *f*; *(for clothes)* fil *m* à linge
  (d) *(railway track)* voie *f*; *(railway route)* ligne *f*
  (e) *(direction)* **l. of argument** raisonnement *m*; **l. of attack** plan *m* d'attaque; **to be in the l. of fire** être dans la ligne de tir; *Fig* être en butte aux critiques; **to be on the right/wrong lines** être sur la bonne/mauvaise voie; **something along the lines of...** quelque chose dans le genre de...
  (f) *(policy)* ligne *f*; **the party l.** la ligne du parti; **to take a firm l. with sb** se montrer ferme avec qn
  (g) *(of text)* ligne *f*; *(of poem)* vers *m*; **to drop sb a l.** écrire un mot à qn; **to learn one's lines** apprendre son rôle; *Fig* **to read between the lines** lire entre les lignes
  (h) *(family)* lignée *f*; **in a direct l.** en ligne directe
  (i) *(telephone connection)* ligne *f*
  (j) *Fam (job)* **what l. (of business) are you in?** vous travaillez dans quelle branche?
  (k) *Com (of goods)* ligne *f*
  2 *vt (road, river)* border; **the crowd lined the street** la foule s'alignait le long du trottoir
  ▸ **line up 1** *vt sep* **(a)** *(form into a line)* mettre en ligne, aligner **(b)** *(prepare)* **to have sb lined up for sth** avoir qn en vue pour qch; **have you got anything lined up for the weekend?** avez-vous quelque chose de prévu pour le week-end?
  2 *vi (form a line)* se mettre en rang

line² *vt (coat, curtain)* doubler **(with** de); *(box, drawer)* tapisser **(with** de); *Fig* **to l. one's pockets** se remplir les poches

lineage ['lɪnɪɪdʒ] *n* lignée *f*

linear ['lɪnɪə(r)] *adj* linéaire; *Math* **l. equation** équation *f* linéaire; *Comptr* **l. programming** programmation *f* linéaire

lined¹ [laɪnd] *adj (paper)* réglé(e); *(face)* ridé(e)

lined² *adj (coat, curtain)* doublé(e) **(with** de)

linen ['lɪnɪn] *n* **(a)** *(fabric)* lin *m*; **a l. dress** une robe en lin **(b)** *(clothes)* linge *m*; *Fig* **don't wash your dirty l. in public** il faut laver son linge sale en famille; **l. basket** panier *m* à linge

liner ['laɪnə(r)] *n (ship)* (paquebot *m*) transatlantique *m*

linesman ['laɪnzmən] *n (in tennis)* juge *m* de ligne; *(in football)* juge de touche

line-up ['laɪnʌp] *n* **(a)** *(of team)* composition *f*; *(on TV show)* plateau *m* **(b)** *Am (identity parade)* séance *f* d'identification

linger ['lɪŋgə(r)] *vi (of person)* s'attarder; *(of smell, custom)* subsister, persister; **to l. behind** rester en arrière; **to l. over doing sth** prendre son temps pour faire qch

lingerie ['lɔːnʒərɪ] *n* lingerie *f*

lingo ['lɪŋgəʊ] *(pl* **lingoes)** *n Fam (language)* langue *f*; *(jargon)* charabia *m*

lingua franca ['lɪŋgwə'fræŋkə] *n* langue *f* véhiculaire

linguist ['lɪŋgwɪst] *n* **(a)** *(specialist in linguistics)* linguiste *mf* **(b)** *(polyglot)* **to be a good l.** être doué(e) pour les langues

linguistic [lɪŋ'gwɪstɪk] *adj* linguistique

linguistics [lɪŋ'gwɪstɪks] *n* linguistique *f*

lining ['laɪnɪŋ] *n (of coat, curtain)* doublure *f*; *(of brakes)* garniture *f*; *(of stomach)* paroi *f*

link [lɪŋk] *n* **(a)** *(of chain)* chaînon *m*, maillon *m*; *Fig* **the weak l.** *(in argument)* le point faible; *(in team)* l'élément *m* faible **(b)** *(connection)* lien *m* **(between** entre)

2 vt (physically) relier; (by association) lier; **to l. hands** se donner la main

▶ **link up 1** vt relier

2 vi (of roads, travellers) se rejoindre

lino ['laɪnəʊ] n Fam lino m

linoleum [lɪ'nəʊlɪəm] n linoléum m

linseed ['lɪnsiːd] n graine f de lin; **l. oil** huile f de lin

lintel ['lɪntəl] n linteau m

lion ['laɪən] n lion m; Fig **the l.'s share** la part du lion; **l. cub** lionceau m; **l. tamer** dresseur m de lions

lioness ['laɪənes] n lionne f

lion-hearted ['laɪən'hɑːtɪd] adj courageux(euse) comme un lion

lip [lɪp] n (a) (of person) lèvre f; (of animal) babine f; **to read sb's lips** lire sur les lèvres de qn; **to pay l. service to sth** faire semblant de s'intéresser à qch (b) (of jug) bec m (c) Fam (impudence) insolence f; **less of your l.!** sois un peu moins insolent(e)!

lip-read ['lɪpriːd] (pt & pp **lip-read** ['lɪpred]) **1** vt lire sur les lèvres de

2 vi lire sur les lèvres

lipstick ['lɪpstɪk] n rouge m à lèvres

liquefy ['lɪkwɪfaɪ] (pt & pp **liquefied**) **1** vt liquéfier

2 vi se liquéfier

liqueur [lɪ'kjʊə(r)] n liqueur f

liquid ['lɪkwɪd] **1** n liquide m

2 adj liquide; Fin **l. assets** liquidités fpl; **l. crystal display** affichage m à cristaux liquides

liquidate ['lɪkwɪdeɪt] vt (a) Fin (company, debt) liquider; (capital) mobiliser (b) Fam (kill) liquider

liquidation [lɪkwɪ'deɪʃən] n Fin (of company, debt) liquidation f; (of capital) mobilisation f; **to go into l.** entrer en liquidation

liquidity [lɪ'kwɪdɪtɪ] n Fin liquidité f; **l. ratio** ratio m de liquidité

liquidize ['lɪkwɪdaɪz] vt (a) (gas, solid) liquéfier (b) (food) passer au mixeur

liquidizer ['lɪkwɪdaɪzə(r)] n mixeur m

liquor ['lɪkə(r)] n Am alcool m; **l. store** magasin m de vins et spiritueux

liquorice ['lɪkərɪs] n réglisse f

lira ['lɪərə] (pl **lire** ['lɪərə]) n lire f

Lisbon ['lɪzbən] n Lisbonne

lisp [lɪsp] **1** n zézaiement m; **to have a l.** avoir un cheveu sur la langue

2 vi avoir un cheveu sur la langue

list¹ [lɪst] **1** n liste f

2 vt (enter in list) faire une liste de; **her phone number isn't listed in the directory** son numéro de téléphone ne figure pas dans l'annuaire; **to be listed on the Stock Exchange** être coté(e) en Bourse; Br **listed building** bâtiment m classé

list² **1** n (of ship) bande f, gîte f

2 vi (of ship) donner de la bande ou de la gîte

listen ['lɪsən] vi écouter; **to l. to sb/sth** écouter qn/qch; **to l. for sth** tendre l'oreille afin d'entendre qch; **to l. (out) for the phone** guetter la sonnerie du téléphone; **to l. to reason** entendre raison; **he wouldn't l.** il n'a rien voulu savoir

▶ **listen in** vi to l. in (on sth) écouter (qch)

listener ['lɪsnə(r)] n (a) **to be a good l.** savoir écouter (b) (to radio programme) auditeur(trice) m,f

listing ['lɪstɪŋ] n (list) liste f; **listings** (in newspaper) rubrique f des spectacles; **listings magazine** programme m de spectacles

listless ['lɪstlɪs] adj apathique

lit [lɪt] pt & pp of **light**

litany ['lɪtənɪ] (pl **litanies**) n litanie f

liter Am = **litre**

literacy ['lɪtərəsɪ] n alphabétisation f; **l. rate** taux m d'alphabétisation

literal ['lɪtərəl] adj littéral(e)

literally ['lɪtərəlɪ] adv littéralement; **to take sth l.** prendre qch au pied de la lettre

literary ['lɪtərərɪ] adj littéraire

literate ['lɪtərɪt] adj to be l. (able to read and write) savoir lire et écrire; (educated) être cultivé(e)

literature ['lɪtrɪtʃə(r)] n (a) (fiction, poetry) littérature f (b) (information) documentation f

lithe [laɪð] adj agile

lithium ['lɪθɪəm] n lithium m

lithograph ['lɪθəgræf] n lithographie f

Lithuania [lɪθjʊ'eɪnɪə] n la Lituanie

Lithuanian [lɪθjʊ'eɪnɪən] **1** n (a) (person) Lituanien(enne) m,f (b) (language) lituanien m

2 adj lituanien(enne)

litigant ['lɪtɪgənt] n Law partie f

litigate ['lɪtɪgeɪt] vi Law intenter une action en justice

litigation [lɪtɪ'geɪʃən] n Law action f en justice

litmus ['lɪtməs] n **l. paper** papier m (de) tournesol; Fig **l. test** test m décisif

litre, Am liter ['liːtə(r)] n litre m

litter ['lɪtə(r)] n (a) (rubbish) détritus mpl, ordures fpl; **l. bin** poubelle f; **l. lout** = personne qui jette des détritus n'importe où (b) (of animal) portée f (c) (for cat) litière f

2 vt to be littered with être couvert(e) ou jonché(e) de

litterbug ['lɪtəbʌg] n Fam = personne qui jette des détritus n'importe où

little ['lɪtəl] **1** n peu m; **to eat l. or nothing** manger peu ou pas du tout; **he knows very l.** il ne sait pas grand-chose; **a l. more** un peu plus; **a l. hot/slow** un peu chaud(e)/lent(e); **every l. helps** les petits ruisseaux font les grandes rivières

2 adj (a) (small) petit(e); **a l. while** un petit moment; **l. finger** petit doigt m (b) (comparative less, superlative least) (not much) peu; **l. money** peu d'argent; **a l. money** un peu d'argent; **it makes l. sense** ça n'a pas beaucoup de sens

3 adv (comparative less, superlative least) peu; **l. by l.** peu à peu; **l. more than an hour ago** il y a à peine une heure; **that's l. short of bribery** ça frise la corruption; **l. did I think that...** j'étais loin de penser que...

littoral ['lɪtərəl] **1** n littoral m

2 adj littoral(e)

liturgy ['lɪtədʒɪ] (pl **liturgies**) n liturgie f

live¹ [laɪv] **1** adj (a) (person, animal) vivant(e), en vie; Fam **a real l. cowboy** un cow-boy, un vrai de vrai; **a l. issue** un sujet brûlant (b) (performance, broadcast) en direct (c) (bomb) non explosé(e); **l. ammunition** balles fpl réelles; **l. wire** fil m sous tension; Fig **to be a l. wire** déborder de vie

2 adv (broadcast) en direct; **to perform l.** (of comedian, dancer) être sur scène; (of band) jouer en concert

live² [lɪv] vt vivre; **to l. a long life** vivre longtemps; **to l. a happy life** mener une vie heureuse; **to l. a lie** vivre dans le mensonge; **it makes life worth living** cela donne un sens à la vie

2 vi vivre; (reside) habiter, vivre; **to l. with sb** vivre avec qn; **as long as I l.** tant que je vivrai; **to l. a little** profiter un peu de la vie; **l. and let l.!** un peu de tolérance!; **you l. and learn** on en apprend tous les jours

▶ **live down** vt sep (mistake, one's past) faire oublier; **I'll**

never l. it down! je n'ai pas fini d'en entendre parler!
▸ **live off** vt insep **to l.** off sth vivre de qch; **to l. off sb** vivre aux crochets de qn
▸ **live on 1** vt insep (food) se nourrir de; (capital) vivre sur; **it's not enough to l. on** ce n'est pas suffisant pour vivre **2** vi (of person) continuer à vivre; (of memory) survivre
▸ **live out** vt sep **to l. out one's life** or **days** passer ses jours; **to l. out a fantasy** réaliser un fantasme
▸ **live through** vt insep connaître, vivre
▸ **live together** vi vivre ensemble
▸ **live up** vt sep Fam **to l. it up** faire la fête
▸ **live up to** vt insep **to l. up to sb's expectations** répondre aux attentes de qn; **to fail to l. up to expectations** ne pas tenir ses promesses; **to l. up to one's reputation** être à la hauteur de sa réputation

live-in ['lɪvɪn] adj (chauffeur, nanny) logé(e) et nourri(e); **l. lover** compagnon (compagne) m,f

livelihood ['laɪvlɪhʊd] n gagne-pain m inv; **to earn one's l.** gagner sa vie

liveliness ['laɪvlɪnɪs] n vivacité f

lively ['laɪvlɪ] adj (person) plein(e) de vie; (place, party, conversation) animé(e); (music) entraînant(e); (imagination) fertile; **to take a l. interest in sth** s'intéresser vivement à qch; Fam **look l.!** grouillez-vous!
▸ **liven up** ['laɪvən] **1** vt sep (person) égayer; (place, party, conversation) animer; (proceedings) activer **2** vi (of person) s'égayer; (of place, party, conversation) s'animer

liver ['lɪvə(r)] n foie m

livery ['lɪvərɪ] n livrée f

lives [laɪvz] pl of **life**

livestock ['laɪvstɒk] n bétail m

livid ['lɪvɪd] adj (a) (angry) furieux(euse) (b) (bluish-grey) livide, blême

living ['lɪvɪŋ] **1** n vie f; **to earn one's l.** gagner sa vie; **what does she do for a l.?** qu'est-ce qu'elle fait dans la vie?; **l. conditions** conditions fpl de vie; **l. expenses** faux frais mpl; **l. room** (salle f de) séjour m, salon m **2** adj vivant(e); **there is not a l. soul to be seen** il n'y a pas âme qui vive; **within l. memory** de mémoire d'homme

lizard ['lɪzəd] n lézard m

llama ['lɑːmə] n lama m

lo [ləʊ] exclam Lit or Hum **lo and behold…** ô surprise…

load [ləʊd] **1** n (a) (burden) fardeau m, charge f; **to share** or **spread the l.** répartir le travail; **that's a l. off my mind!** cela m'enlève un poids! (b) Fam (lot) **a l. of, loads of** plein de; **it's just a l. of nonsense!** c'est n'importe quoi!; **we've got loads of time** on a largement le temps **2** vt (lorry, gun, camera) charger; (software) installer; (washing machine) remplir **3** vi (of lorry) prendre un chargement
▸ **load up 1** vt sep charger **2** vi prendre un chargement

loaded ['ləʊdɪd] adj (a) (lorry, gun, camera) chargé(e) (b) (dice) pipé(e); (question) insidieux(euse) (c) Fam (rich) plein(e) aux as

loading ['ləʊdɪŋ] n chargement m; **l. bay** aire f de chargement

loaf [ləʊf] n (pl **loaves** [ləʊvz]) **a l. (of bread)** un pain; Br Fig **to use one's l.** faire marcher son ciboulot
▸ **loaf about, loaf around** vi traîner

loafer ['ləʊfə(r)] n (a) (person) fainéant(e) m,f (b) (shoe) mocassin m

loam [ləʊm] n terreau m

loan [ləʊn] **1** n (from lender's point of view) prêt m; (from borrower's point of view) emprunt m; **to give sb a l. of sth** prêter qch à qn; **to take out a l.** faire un emprunt; Fam **l. shark** usurier(ère) m,f **2** vt (money) prêter

loath [ləʊθ] adj **to be l. to do sth** répugner à faire qch

loathe [ləʊð] vt détester; **to l. doing sth** détester faire qch

loathing ['ləʊðɪŋ] n dégoût m, répugnance f

loathsome ['ləʊðsəm] adj répugnant(e)

loaves [ləʊvz] pl of **loaf**

lob [lɒb] **1** n (in tennis) lob m **2** vt (pt & pp **lobbed**) (a) (in tennis) lober (b) Fam (throw) balancer

lobby ['lɒbɪ] **1** n (pl **lobbies**) (a) (of hotel) hall m; (of theatre) foyer m (b) (pressure group) groupe m de pression, lobby m **2** vt (pt & pp **lobbied**) faire pression sur **3** vi **to l. for/against sth** faire pression en faveur de/ contre qch

lobbyist ['lɒbɪɪst] n membre m d'un groupe de pression

lobe [ləʊb] n lobe m

lobotomy [lə'bɒtəmɪ] n (pl **lobotomies**) n lobotomie f

lobster ['lɒbstə(r)] n homard m; **as red as a l.** (sunburnt) rouge comme une écrevisse; **l. pot** casier m à homards

local ['ləʊkəl] **1** n (a) (person) **the locals** les gens mpl du coin (b) Br Fam (pub) = pub du voisinage **2** adj local(e); **l. anaesthetic** anesthésie f locale; Br **l. government** ≃ administration f communale

locale [ləʊ'kɑːl] n (of events) lieu m; (for a film) lieu m de tournage

locality [ləʊ'kælɪtɪ] (pl **localities**) n voisinage m, environs mpl

locally ['ləʊkəlɪ] adv dans le quartier

locate [ləʊ'keɪt] **1** vt (find) localiser; (situate) situer **2** vi (of company) s'installer

location [ləʊ'keɪʃən] n (a) (place) emplacement m; Cin **on l.** en extérieur; Cin **l. shot** plan m en extérieur (b) (act of finding) localisation f

loch [lɒχ] n Scot (lake) loch m, lac m

lock¹ [lɒk] **1** n (a) (on door) serrure f; **under l. and key** (object) sous clef; (person) sous les verrous; Fig **l., stock and barrel** en entier (b) (in wrestling) clef f (c) (on canal) écluse f **2** vt (door, padlock) fermer à clef; **to be locked in each other's arms** être étroitement enlacés(ées); Fig **to l. horns with sb** livrer bataille à qn **3** vi (of door) se fermer; (of car wheels) se bloquer
▸ **lock in** vt sep enfermer à clef
▸ **lock out** vt sep enfermer dehors; **I locked myself out of my flat** je me suis enfermé dehors
▸ **lock up 1** vt sep (person, valuables) enfermer; (house) fermer à clef **2** vi fermer

lock² n (of hair) mèche f

locker ['lɒkə(r)] n casier m; Am **l. room** vestiaire m

locket ['lɒkɪt] n médaillon m

lockjaw ['lɒkdʒɔː] n Old-fashioned tétanos m

lock-out ['lɒkaʊt] n lock-out m inv

locksmith ['lɒksmɪθ] n serrurier m

lockup ['lɒkʌp] n (a) Br (for storage) garage m (b) Fam (police cells) violon m, bloc m

locomotion [ləʊkə'məʊʃən] n locomotion f

locomotive [ləʊkə'məʊtɪv] **1** n (train) locomotive f **2** adj locomotif(ive)

locum ['ləʊkəm] n Br remplaçant(e) m,f

locust ['ləʊkəst] *n* sauterelle *f*

locution [ləʊ'kjuːʃən] *n* locution *f*

lodge [lɒdʒ] **1** *n (of porter, caretaker, masons)* loge *f*; *(small house)* pavillon *m*
2 *vt* **(a)** *(accommodate)* loger, héberger **(b)** *Law* to **l. an appeal** faire appel; **to l. a complaint** porter plainte
3 *vi* **(a)** *(live)* loger **(b)** *(become fixed)* se loger; **to be lodged in sb's memory** être gravé(e) dans la mémoire de qn

lodger ['lɒdʒə(r)] *n* locataire *mf* (en meublé); *(who has meals provided)* pensionnaire *mf*

lodging ['lɒdʒɪŋ] *n* logement *m*; **lodgings** chambre *f* meublée; **l. house** (hôtel *m*) garni *m*

loft [lɒft] *n* grenier *m*

lofty ['lɒftɪ] *adj (aim, desire)* noble **(b)** *Lit (high)* haut(e)

log [lɒg] **1** *n* **(a)** *(of wood)* bûche *f*; **to sleep like a l.** dormir comme une souche; **l. cabin** hutte *f* en rondins; **l. fire** feu *m* de bois **(b)** *(record)* registre *m*; *(of ship, traveller)* journal *m* de bord; *(of plane)* carnet *m* de vol
2 *vt (pt & pp* **logged)** *(record)* enregistrer; *(in ship's, traveller's log)* noter dans le journal de bord; *(in plane's log)* noter dans le carnet de vol
▸ **log in** *vi Comptr* entrer
▸ **log off** *vi Comptr* sortir
▸ **log on** *vi Comptr* entrer
▸ **log out** *vi Comptr* sortir

logarithm ['lɒgərɪθəm] *n* logarithme *m*

logbook ['lɒgbʊk] *n* **(a)** *(of ship, traveller)* journal *m* de bord; *(of plane)* carnet *m* de vol **(b)** *Br (for car)* ≃ carte *f* grise

loggerheads ['lɒgəhedz] *n Fam* **to be at l. with sb** être en conflit avec qn

logic ['lɒdʒɪk] *n* logique *f*

logical ['lɒdʒɪkəl] *adj* logique

logically ['lɒdʒɪklɪ] *adv* logiquement

logistic(al) [lə'dʒɪstɪk(əl)] *adj* logistique

logistics [lə'dʒɪstɪks] *npl* logistique *f*

logjam ['lɒgdʒæm] *n* impasse *f*

logo ['ləʊgəʊ] *(pl* **logos)** *n* sigle *m*, logo *m*

loin [lɔɪn] *n* **(a)** *(of beef)* aloyau *m*; *(of mutton, pork)* filet *m*; *(of veal)* longe *f*; **l. chop** côtes *fpl* premières **(b)** **loins** *(of person)* reins *mpl*

loincloth ['lɔɪnklɒθ] *n* pagne *m*

loiter ['lɔɪtə(r)] *vi* traîner; *(suspiciously)* rôder; *Law* **to l. with intent** = rôder d'une manière suspecte

lollipop ['lɒlɪpɒp] *n* sucette *f*; *Br Fam* **l. man/lady** = contractuel qui aide les écoliers à traverser la rue

lollop ['lɒləp] *vi Fam* **to l. along** courir lourdement

lolly ['lɒlɪ] *n* **(a)** *(pl* **lollies)** *n Br Fam* **(l.** **(ice)** **l.** glace *f* à l'eau **(b)** *(lollipop)* sucette *f* **(c)** *(money)* fric *m*, flouze *m*

London ['lʌndən] *n* Londres

Londoner ['lʌndənə(r)] *n* Londonien(enne) *m,f*

lone [ləʊn] *adj (single, solitary)* solitaire; *Fig* **a l. wolf** un(e) solitaire

loneliness ['ləʊnlɪnɪs] *n (feeling)* solitude *f*; *(of place)* isolement *m*

lonely ['ləʊnlɪ] *adj (person)* seul(e); *(life, job)* solitaire; *(place)* isolé(e); **to feel l.** se sentir seul; **l. hearts club** club *m* de rencontres; **l. hearts column** rubrique *f* rencontres

loner ['ləʊnə(r)] *n* solitaire *mf*

lonesome ['ləʊnsəm] **1** *n Fam* **to be on one's l.** être abandonné(e) à son triste sort
2 *adj Am* solitaire, seul(e)

long¹ [lɒŋ] **1** *n* **the l. and the short of it is that...** bref,...

2 *adj* **(a)** *(in size)* long (longue); **how l. is the table?** quelle est la longueur de la table?; **to be three metres l.** faire trois mètres de long; **to go the l. way (round)** prendre le chemin le plus long; *Fig* **the best by a l.** way de loin le meilleur (la meilleure); *Fig* **she'll go a l.** way elle ira loin; *Fig* **to go a l.** way towards doing sth beaucoup contribuer à faire qch; *Fam* **to be l.** on charm/good ideas être plein(e) de charme/de bonnes idées; **the l.** arm of the law (le bras de) la justice; *Fig* **to have a l.** face faire une tête de six pieds de long; **it's a l.** shot ça n'a pas beaucoup de chances de réussir; **not by a l.** shot or chalk loin s'en faut; **l.** johns caleçon *m* long; **l.** jump saut *m* en longueur **(b)** *(in time)* long (longue); **a l.** time ago il y a longtemps; **it's been a l.** day ça a été une longue journée; **the days are getting longer** les jours rallongent; **to take a l.** look at sth regarder longuement qch; **in the l.** term or run à long terme, à longue échéance; **to have a l.** memory avoir bonne mémoire; **l.** weekend long week-end *m*, week-end prolongé
3 *adv* **(a)** *(for a long period)* longtemps; **l. live the King/Queen!** vive le roi/la reine!; **as l.** as *(providing)* du moment que, tant que; *(while)* tant que; **to think l.** and hard (about sth) réfléchir longuement (à qch); **she won't be l.** elle ne tardera pas; *(will soon have finished)* elle n'en a pas pour longtemps; **I have l.** been convinced of it j'en suis convaincu depuis longtemps; **how l.** have you known her? depuis combien de temps la connais-tu?; *Fam* **so l.!** au revoir!, à bientôt!; **l.** before/after longtemps avant/après; **l.** ago il y a longtemps **(b)** *(for the duration of)* **all day l.** toute la journée **(c)** **I could no longer hear him** je ne l'entendais plus; **I couldn't wait any longer** je ne pouvais plus attendre; **five minutes longer** cinq minutes de plus

long² *vi* **to l. to do sth** rêver de faire qch; **to l. for sth** rêver de qch; *(look forward to)* attendre qch avec impatience; **we're longing for them to leave** il nous tarde qu'ils partent; **a longed-for holiday** des vacances *fpl* très attendues

long³ *(abbr* **longitude)** long

longboat ['lɒŋbəʊt] *n* chaloupe *f*

longbow ['lɒŋbəʊ] *n* arc *m*

long-distance ['lɒŋ'dɪstəns] **1** *adj (runner, race)* de fond; *(telephone call)* longue distance; *Br* **l.** lorry driver conducteur(trice) *m,f* de poids lourd
2 *adv* **to telephone l.** faire un appel longue distance

longevity [lɒn'dʒevɪtɪ] *n* longévité *f*

long-forgotten ['lɒŋfə'gɒtən] *adj* depuis longtemps oublié(e)

longhaired ['lɒŋ'heəd] *adj (cat, dog)* à poil(s) long(s); *(person)* aux cheveux longs

long-haul ['lɒŋ'hɔːl] *adj* long-courrier

longing ['lɒŋɪŋ] *n* profond désir *m*, grande envie *f* (**for** de)

longingly ['lɒŋɪŋlɪ] *adv* avec envie

longitude ['lɒndʒɪtjuːd] *n* longitude *f*

longitudinal [lɒndʒɪ'tjuːdɪnəl] *adj* longitudinal(e)

long-life ['lɒŋ'laɪf] *adj (juice, milk)* longue conservation *inv*; *(battery)* longue durée *inv*

long-lost ['lɒŋ'lɒst] *adj* perdu(e) depuis longtemps; *(relative)* perdu de vue depuis longtemps

long-range ['lɒŋ'reɪndʒ] *adj (missile)* longue portée; *(forecast)* à long terme; *(plane)* à long rayon d'action

longshoreman [lɒŋ'ʃɔːmən] *n Am* docker *m*

long-sighted [lɒŋ'saɪtɪd] *adj (from birth)* hypermétrope; *(from adulthood)* presbyte

long-sleeved [lɒŋ'sliːvd] *adj* à manches longues

long-standing [lɒŋ'stændɪŋ] *adj (arrangement, friendship)* de longue date

long-suffering [lɒŋ'sʌfərɪŋ] *adj* patient(e)

long-term ['lɒŋtɜ:m] *adj (prisoner)* condamné(e) à une longue peine; *(loan, planning)* à long terme; **the l. unemployed** les chômeurs *mpl* de longue durée

long-winded [lɒŋ'wɪndɪd] *adj* verbeux(euse)

loo [lu:] *(pl* **loos***) n Br Fam* cabinets *mpl*; **l. paper** papier *m* toilette

loofah ['lu:fə] *n* loofa *m*, luffa *m*

look [lʊk] **1** *n* **(a)** *(act of looking)* **to have** *or* **take a l. at sth** regarder qch; *(quickly)* jeter un coup d'œil à *ou* sur qch; **to have a l. for sth** chercher qch; **let me have a l.** fais(-moi) voir; **to have a l. round the town** faire un tour dans la ville; **to have a l. through some magazines** jeter un coup d'œil à des magazines

(b) *(glance)* regard *m*; **to give sb. a dirty l.** jeter un regard noir à qn; **if looks could kill** il y a des regards qui tuent

(c) *(appearance)* air *m*; **I don't like the l. of this** cela ne me dit rien qui vaille; **I don't like the l. of him** sa tête ne me revient pas; **by the l. of it,…** on dirait bien que…

(d) (good) looks beauté *f*; **to have lost one's looks** être moins beau (belle); **looks don't matter** le physique n'a pas d'importance

2 *vt* **to l. sb in the face** regarder qn en face *ou* dans les yeux; **to l. sb up and down** toiser qn; **l. what you've done!** regarde ce que tu as fait!; **l. where you're going!** vous ne pouvez pas faire attention, non?

3 *vi* **(a)** *(in general)* regarder; **to l. at sb/sth** regarder qn/ qch; **he's not much to l. at** il n'est pas très beau; *Fig* **to l. the other way** fermer les yeux; **I'm just looking, thank you** *(in shop)* je ne fais que regarder, merci; **to l. on the bright side** voir les choses du bon côté; **l. here!** dites donc!; **I don't l. at it that way** je ne vois pas les choses comme ça; *Prov* **l. before you leap** il faut réfléchir avant d'agir

(b) *(search)* **to l. for sb/sth** chercher qn/qch; **we've looked everywhere** nous avons cherché partout

(c) *(seem, appear)* avoir l'air, paraître; **to l. old** avoir l'air vieux (vieille); **things are looking bad** les choses prennent une mauvaise tournure; **things are looking good** ça a l'air de bien se passer; **to l. one's age** faire son âge; **to l. the part** avoir l'allure qui convient; **what does she l. like?** comment est-elle?; **to l. like sb** ressembler à qn; **it looks like** *or* **as if…** on dirait que…; **it looks like rain** on dirait qu'il va pleuvoir; **you l. as if you've slept badly** vous avez l'air d'avoir mal dormi

▸ **look after** *vt insep (take care of)* s'occuper de; **to l. after oneself** se débrouiller tout(e) seul(e); **to l. after sb's house/bag** surveiller la maison/le sac de qn; **can you l. after the children tomorrow?** tu peux t'occuper des enfants demain?

▸ **look around 1** *vt insep (town, shops)* faire un tour dans **2** *vi (in town)* faire un tour; *(in shop)* jeter un coup d'œil; **to l. around for sth** essayer de trouver qch

▸ **look back** *vi* **(a)** *(in space)* regarder en arrière *ou* derrière soi **(b)** *(in time)* **to l. back on sth** revenir sur qch; **she has never looked back since that day** depuis ce jour sa situation n'a cessé de s'améliorer

▸ **look down** *vi (from above)* regarder en bas *ou* vers le bas; *(lower one's eyes)* baisser les yeux; *Fig* **to l. down on sb** regarder qn de haut

▸ **look forward to** *vt insep* **to l. forward to sth** attendre qch avec impatience; **I'm looking forward to seeing her again** il me tarde de la revoir; **I l. forward to hearing from you** *(in letter)* dans l'attente de vous lire

▸ **look in** *vi* **to l. in (on sb)** passer (voir qn)

▸ **look into** *vt insep* examiner

▸ **look on 1** *vt insep (consider)* **to l. on sb/sth as** considérer qn/qch comme **2** *vi (watch)* regarder

▸ **look out 1** *vt sep (find)* trouver, dénicher **2** *vi* **(a)** *(from indoors)* regarder dehors; **to l. out of the window** regarder par la fenêtre **(b)** *(be careful)* faire attention; **l. out!** attention!

▸ **look out for** *vt insep* **(a)** *(look for) (person)* guetter; *(thing)* chercher **(b)** *(be on guard for)* faire attention à

▸ **look over** *vt insep* jeter un coup d'œil sur

▸ **look round** = **look around**

▸ **look through** *vt insep* **(a)** *(inspect) (written material)* parcourir; *(clothes, CDs)* passer en revue **(b)** *(not see)* **to l. straight through sb** regarder qn sans le voir; *(deliberately)* ignorer qn

▸ **look to** *vt insep* **(a)** *(rely on)* **to l. to sb (for sth)** compter sur qn (pour qch) **(b)** **to l. to the future** se tourner vers l'avenir

▸ **look up 1** *vt sep (word, address)* chercher; *(person)* passer voir **2** *vi (from below)* regarder vers le haut; *(raise one's eyes)* lever les yeux; *Fig* **things are looking up** la situation s'améliore

▸ **look upon** *vt insep (consider)* **to l. upon sb/sth as** considérer qn/qch comme

▸ **look up to** *vt insep* respecter, estimer

lookalike ['lʊkəlaɪk] *n* sosie *m*

look-in ['lʊkɪn] *n Fam (chance)* **he won't have** *or* **get a l.** il n'a pas la moindre chance; *(in conversation)* il ne pourra pas en placer une

looking-glass ['lʊkɪŋglɑ:s] *n Old-fashioned* miroir *m*

lookout ['lʊkaʊt] *n (person)* guetteur *m*; *(on ship)* vigie *f*; **to keep a l. for sb/sth** guetter qn/qch; **to be on the l. for sb/sth** être à la recherche de qn/qch; *Fam* **that's your l.!** ça c'est ton affaire!; **l. post/tower** poste *m*/tour *f* de guet

loom¹ [lu:m] *n (for making cloth)* métier *m* à tisser

loom² *vi (of person, building)* se dresser; *(of danger, event)* être imminent(e); **to l. large** être très présent(e)

loony ['lu:nɪ] *Fam* **1** *n (pl* **loonies***)* dingue *mf*; **l. bin** maison *f* de fous **2** *adj* dingue

loop [lu:p] **1** *n* boucle *f* **2** *vt* faire une boucle/des boucles à; **to l. sth around sth** enrouler qch autour de qch; **to l. the loop** *(in plane)* faire un looping

loophole ['lu:phəʊl] *n (in law)* vide *m* juridique

loopy ['lu:pɪ] *adj Fam* barjo(t)

loose [lu:s] **1** *n* **to be on the l.** *(of prisoner)* être en cavale; *(of animal)* être en liberté **2** *adj (animal)* qui s'est échappé(e); *(tooth, plank)* qui bouge; *(piece of clothing)* large, ample; *(skin)* flasque; *(alliance, network)* peu structuré(e); *(translation)* approximatif(ive); *(morals, lifestyle)* dissolu(e); **to come l.** *(of knot)* se défaire; *(of screw)* se desserrer; **to let sb l.** relâcher qn; **to let sb l. on sth** laisser qn toucher à qch; **don't let him l. in the kitchen!** ne le laisse pas faire la cuisine tout seul!; **to let l. a torrent of abuse** lâcher des torrents d'injures; **to buy sth l.** acheter qch en vrac; **l. change** petite *ou* menue monnaie *f*; **l. connection** *(in appliance)* faux contact *m*; **to be at a l. end** ne pas savoir quoi faire; *Fig* **to tie up the l. ends** régler les derniers détails; **l. talk** propos *mpl* irréfléchis; **a l. woman** une femme de mauvaise vie **3** *vt Lit (arrow)* décocher; *(bullet)* tirer

▸ **loose off** *vt sep (arrow)* décocher; *(bullet)* tirer

loose-fitting ['lu:sfɪtɪŋ] *adj* ample, large

loose-leaf ['lu:sli:f] *adj* à feuilles mobiles; **l. binder** classeur *m*

loose-limbed ['lu:s'lɪmd] *adj* souple

loosely ['lu:slɪ] *adv* **(a)** *(attached)* de façon lâche; **l. packed** *(snow)* poudreux(euse) **(b)** *(roughly)* de façon approximative; **to be l.** connected avoir un lointain rapport; **l. speaking** en gros

loosen ['lu:sən] **1** *vt (screw, knot, belt)* desserrer; *(restrictions)* assouplir; **to l. one's grip** relâcher son étreinte; **to l. sb's tongue** délier la langue à qn **2** *vi* se desserrer

▸ **loosen up** *vi (relax)* se détendre

loot [lu:t] **1** *n (booty)* butin *m*; *Fam (money)* oseille *f* **2** *vt* piller

looter ['lu:tə(r)] *n* pillard(e) *m,f*

looting ['lu:tɪŋ] *n* pillage *m*

lopsided [lɒp'saɪdɪd] *adj (face)* asymétrique; *(picture)* de guingois, de travers; *(grin)* en coin

loquacious [lɒ'kweɪʃəs] *adj* loquace

lord [lɔ:d] **1** *n* **(a)** *(aristocrat)* noble *m*; *(feudal)* seigneur *m*; **L.** Browne lord Browne *(titre de noblesse masculin)*; *Br* **the (House of) Lords** la Chambre des Lords; **the L. Mayor** le lord-maire **(b)** *Rel* **the L.** le Seigneur; **the L.'s Prayer** le Notre Père; *Fam* **good L.!** mon Dieu!; *Fam* **L. knows** Dieu seul le sait **2** *vt* **to l. it over sb** traiter qn de haut

lordly ['lɔ:dlɪ] *adj (noble)* altier(ère); *Pej (arrogant)* hautain(e)

lordship ['lɔ:dʃɪp] *n* autorité *f*; *also Ironic* **His/Your L.** monsieur; *(to judge)* son/votre l lonneur

lore [lɔ:(r)] *n* tradition *f* orale

lorry ['lɒrɪ] *(pl lorries) n Br* camion *m*; *Fam Euph* **it fell off the back of a l.** *(was stolen)* c'est de la marchandise volée; **l. driver** chauffeur *m* de poids lourd

Los Angeles [lɒs'ændʒəli:z] *n* Los Angeles

lose [lu:z] *(pt & pp* **lost** [lɒst]) **1** *vt* perdre; **to have nothing to l.** n'avoir rien à perdre; **he had lost interest in his wife** sa femme ne l'intéressait plus; **it loses something in translation** ça perd à la traduction; **to be lost at sea** périr en mer; **the joke was lost on him** il n'a pas saisi la plaisanterie; **that clock loses five minutes a day** cette pendule retarde de cinq minutes par jour; **that mistake lost her the match** cette erreur lui a coûté le match; **to l. one's way, to get lost** se perdre; *Fam* **get lost!** va te faire voir!; **to l. one's balance** perdre l'équilibre; **to l. sight of sb/sth** perdre qn/qch de vue; *Fam* **Fig you've lost me!** je ne vous suis plus!; **to l. weight** perdre du poids; **we lost him in the crowd** nous avons été séparés dans la cohue; **to l. oneself in a book/one's work** se plonger dans un livre/son travail **2** *vi (in contest)* perdre

▸ **lose out** *vi* être perdant(e) **(to sb** par rapport à qn); **to l. out on sth** laisser échapper qch

loser ['lu:zə(r)] *n* **(a)** *(in contest)* perdant(e) *m,f*; **to be a bad l.** être mauvais(e) perdant(e) **(b)** *Fam (unsuccessful person)* minable *mf*; **a born l.** un(e) perdant(e)

losing ['lu:zɪŋ] *adj* **to fight a l. battle** être battu(e) d'avance; **the l. side** *(in war)* les vaincus *mpl*; *(in contest)* l'équipe *f* perdante

loss [lɒs] *n* **(a)** *(in contest, war)* perte *f*; **there was a great l. of life** il y a eu de grosses pertes en vies humaines; **to suffer heavy losses** subir de grosses pertes; **it's no great l.** ce n'est pas une grosse perte; *Fam* **it's your l.!** tu ne sais pas ce que tu perds!; **without l. of face** sans perdre la face; **to be at a l.** être incapable de faire qch; **she's never at a l. for an answer** elle a toujours réponse à tout

(b) *(financial)* **to make a l.** perdre de l'argent, être déficitaire; **to sell at a l.** vendre à perte; *Fig* **to cut one's losses** sauver les meubles; **l. leader** article *m ou* produit *m* d'appel

loss-making ['lɒsmeɪkɪŋ] *adj* déficitaire

lost [lɒst] **1** *adj* perdu(e); **to give sb/sth up for l.** abandonner tout espoir de retrouver qn/qch; **l. cause** cause *f* perdue; **l. property (office)** *(bureau m des)* objets *mpl* trouvés; **l. soul** âme *f* en peine **2** *pt & pp of* **lose**

lot [lɒt] **1** *n* **(a)** *(large quantity)* **a l., lots** beaucoup; **the l.** tout; **I bought the l.** j'ai tout acheté; **a l.** *or* **lots of people** beaucoup de monde; **I see quite a l. of her** je la vois assez souvent; **we had a l. of** *or* **lots of fun** nous nous sommes bien amusés; *Fam* **listen, you l.!** écoutez, vous tous!; *Fam* **that l. next door** la bande d'à côté; *Fam* **he's a bad l.** c'est un bon à rien **(b)** *(destiny)* sort *m*, destin *m*; **to draw** *or* **cast lots for sth** tirer qch au sort; **to throw in one's l. with sb** partager le sort de qn **(c)** *(piece of land)* (lot *m* de) terrain *m*; *(at auction)* lot *m* **2** *adv* **a l.** beaucoup; **a l. bigger** beaucoup *ou* bien plus grand(e); **thanks a l.** merci beaucoup

lotion ['ləʊʃən] *n* lotion *f*

lottery ['lɒtərɪ] *(pl lotteries) n also Fig* loterie *f*

lotto ['lɒtəʊ] *n* loto *m*

lotus ['ləʊtəs] *n* lotus *m*; **l. position** (position *f* du) lotus

loud [laʊd] **1** *adj* **(a)** *(noise)* bruyant(e); *(voice, music)* fort(e); *Pej (person)* fort(e) en gueule; **to be l. in one's support/condemnation of sth** soutenir/condamner qch avec force **(b)** *(colour, clothes)* voyant(e) **2** *adv* fort; **to think out l.** penser tout haut, **l. and clear** parfaitement

loudhailer [laʊd'heɪlə(r)] *n* porte-voix *m inv*

loudly ['laʊdlɪ] *adv* fort; *(complain)* bruyamment

loudmouth ['laʊdmaʊθ] *n Fam* **to be a l.** être *ou* avoir une grande gueule

loudmouthed ['laʊdmaʊðd] *adj Fam* fort(e) en gueule

loudness ['laʊdnɪs] *n (of noise, voice)* volume *m*

loudspeaker [laʊd'spi:kə(r)] *n* haut-parleur *m*

Louisiana [lu:ɪzɪ'ænə] *n* la Louisiane

lounge [laʊndʒ] **1** *n (in house, hotel)* salon *m*; **l. suit** complet-veston *m* **2** *vi* fainéanter

▸ **lounge about, lounge around** *vi* traîner

louse [laʊs] *n* **(a)** *(pl* **lice** [laɪs]) *(insect)* pou *m* **(b)** *Fam (pl* **louses)** *(person)* salaud *m*

lousy ['laʊzɪ] *adj Fam* nul (nulle); *(weather)* dégueulasse; *(trick)* sale; **to feel l.** se sentir vraiment mal; **we had a l. holiday** nous avons passé des vacances nulles

lout [laʊt] *n* voyou *m*

loutish ['laʊtɪʃ] *adj* de voyou

louvre door ['lu:və'dɔ:(r)] *adj* porte *f* à persiennes

lovable ['lʌvəbəl] *adj* attachant(e)

love [lʌv] **1** *n* **(a)** *(for family, country)* amour *m* **(of** *or* **for** de *ou* pour); **give my l. to your parents** embrasse tes parents pour moi; **with l. from...** *(at end of letter)* affectueusement,...; **Tania sends her l.** Tania vous fait ses amitiés; **there's no l. lost between them** ils ne peuvent pas se sentir; **I wouldn't do it for l. or money** je ne le ferais pour rien au monde; **to do sth for the l. of it** faire qch pour le plaisir

(b) *(between lovers)* amour *m*; **to be/fall in l. with sb** être/tomber amoureux(euse) de qn; **to make l. with** *or* **to sb** faire l'amour avec qn; **the l. of my life** l'homme (la femme) de ma vie; **it was l. at first sight** ce fut le coup de foudre;

(my) l. *(term of endearment)* mon amour; **a l.-hate relationship** une relation faite à la fois d'amour et de haine; **l. affair** aventure *f*; *Euph* **l. child** enfant *mf* de l'amour; **l. letter** lettre *f* d'amour; **l. life** vie *f* amoureuse; **l. match** mariage *m* d'amour; **l. nest** nid *m* d'amour **(c)** *(in tennis)* **15 l.**15 à rien; **l. game** jeu *m* blanc **2** *vt (person)* aimer; *(thing)* adorer; **l l. Japanese food** j'adore manger japonais; **to l. to do** *or* **doing sth** adorer faire qch; **I'd l. to come** j'aimerais beaucoup venir

lovebird ['lʌvbɜːd] *n Fam Fig* **a pair of lovebirds** un couple de tourtereaux

lovebite ['lʌvbaɪt] *n Br* suçon *m*

loveless ['lʌvlɪs] *adj* sans amour

lovely ['lʌvlɪ] *adj (idea, smell)* très bon (bonne); *(weather)* beau (belle); *(person)* charmant(e); **to have a l. time** passer un bon moment; *Fam* **it's l. and warm** il fait bon

lovemaking ['lʌvmeɪkɪŋ] *n (sexual intercourse)* ébats *mpl* amoureux

lover ['lʌvə(r)] *n (of person) (man)* amant *m*; *(woman)* maîtresse *f*; *(of nature, good food)* amoureux(euse) *m,f*

lovesick ['lʌvsɪk] *adj* qui languit d'amour

lovey-dovey ['lʌvɪ'dʌvɪ] *adj Fam (talk)* mièvre, à la guimauve; *(person)* roucoulant(e)

loving ['lʌvɪŋ] *adj* affectueux(euse), tendre

low¹ [ləʊ] **1** *n* **(a) to reach a new** *or* **an all-time l.** atteindre son niveau le plus bas **(b)** *(weather front)* zone *f* de basse pression **2** *adj* **(a)** *(not high, not loud)* bas (basse); *(neckline)* profond(e); **fuel is getting l.** on n'a plus beaucoup d'essence; **to cook sth over a l. heat** cuire qch à feu doux; **of l. birth** de basse extraction; **the lower classes** les classes les moins aisées; **lower ranks** *(in army)* rangs *mpl* inférieurs; **to have a l. opinion of sb** avoir une mauvaise opinion de qn; *Fig* **a l. blow** un coup bas; **the L. Countries** les Pays-Bas *mpl*; **l. tide** marée *f* basse **(b)** *(depressed)* déprimé(e) **(c)** *(ignoble)* **the lowest of the l.** le dernier des derniers (la dernière des dernières); **that's a l. trick!** c'est vraiment un coup vache! **3** *adv* bas; **the l. paid** les petits salaires *mpl*; **turn the music/the lights down l.** baisse la musique/la lumière; **to be running l. on sth** être presque à court de qch

low² *vi (of cattle)* meugler

lowbrow ['ləʊbraʊ] *adj (tastes, interests)* peu intellectuel(elle)

low-budget [ləʊ'bʌdʒɪt] *adj (film)* à petit budget; *(holiday)* bon marché *inv*

low-calorie [ləʊ'kælərɪ] *adj* basses calories, hypocalorique

low-cost [ləʊ'kɒst] *adj* économique; *(housing)* à loyer modéré

low-cut [ləʊ'kʌt] *adj* décolleté(e)

low-down ['ləʊdaʊn] *n Fam* **to give sb the l. on sth** tuyauter qn sur qch; **what's the l. on Jane's resignation?** tu as des tuyaux sur la démission de Jane?

lower¹ ['ləʊə(r)] *vt* baisser; *(sail)* amener; *also Fig* **to l. one's guard** baisser sa garde; **to l. one's voice** baisser la voix; **to l. oneself into/onto sth** se laisser glisser dans/sur qch; **to l. oneself (to do sth)** s'abaisser (à faire qch)

lower² ['laʊə(r)] *vi (of sky)* se couvrir; **to l. at sb** *(of person)* lancer des regards noirs à qn

low-flying ['ləʊ'flaɪɪŋ] *adj* volant à basse altitude

low-grade ['ləʊ'greɪd] *adj* de qualité inférieure

low-key [ləʊ'kiː] *adj (approach, debate)* modéré(e); *(film, style)* sobre, dépouillé(e); *(person)* réservé(e)

lowlands ['ləʊləndz] *npl* basses terres *fpl*; **the L.** *(of Scotland)* les Basses Terres de l'Écosse

low-level ['ləʊ'levəl] *adj* **(a)** *(discussion)* à bas niveau **(b)** *(radiation)* de faible intensité

lowly ['ləʊlɪ] *adj* humble, modeste

low-lying ['ləʊ'laɪɪŋ] *adj* de basse altitude

low-spirited ['ləʊ'spɪrɪtɪd] *adj* abattu(e)

low-tech ['ləʊtek] *adj* rudimentaire

loyal ['lɔɪəl] *adj (friend)* loyal(e), dévoué(e); **to be l. to sb/ sth** être fidèle à qn/qch

loyalist ['lɔɪəlɪst] *n & adj* loyaliste *mf*

loyally ['lɔɪəlɪ] *adv* loyalement

loyalty ['lɔɪəltɪ] *(pl* **loyalties)** *n* loyauté *f*; **you'll have to decide where your loyalties lie** il faudra que vous décidiez de quel côté vous êtes; **to have divided loyalties** être partagé(e)

lozenge ['lɒzɪndʒ] *n (shape)* losange *m*; *(cough sweet)* pastille *f*

LP [el'piː] *n (abbr* **long player)** 33 tours *m*

LSD [eles'diː] *n (abbr* **lysergic acid diethylamide)** LSD *m*

Lt *(abbr* **Lieutenant)** lt

Ltd *Br (abbr* **limited)** ≃ SARL

lubricant ['luːbrɪkənt] *n* lubrifiant *m*

lubricate ['luːbrɪkeɪt] *vt* lubrifier

lubrication [luːbrɪ'keɪʃən] *n* lubrification *f*

lucid ['luːsɪd] *adj* lucide; *(explanation)* clair(e)

luck [lʌk] *n* chance *f*; **(good) l.** bonheur *m*, chance; **good l.!** bonne chance!; **bad l.** malchance *f*; **bad l.!** pas de chance!; **to wish sb l.** souhaiter bonne chance à qn; **to be in l.** avoir de la chance; **to be out of l.** ne pas avoir de chance; **to be down on one's l.** être sur la paille; **to try one's l.** tenter sa chance; **don't push your l.!** ne pousse pas le bouchon trop loin!; **some people have all the l.** il y a vraiment des gens qui ont de la veine; **just my l.!** c'est bien ma chance!; **no such l.!** je n'ai pas (eu) cette chance!; **with any l.** avec un peu de chance

luckily ['lʌkɪlɪ] *adv* par bonheur, heureusement

lucky ['lʌkɪ] *adj (person)* **to be l.** avoir de la chance; **to make a l. guess** tomber juste; **to have a l. escape** l'échapper belle; *Fam* **l. devil, l. beggar** sacré(e) veinard(e) *m,f*; *Ironic* **you'll be l.!** tu peux toujours courir!; **it's l. you came when you did** c'est une chance que tu sois arrivé à ce moment-là; **she's l. to be alive** elle a de la chance d'être encore en vie; **my l. number** mon chiffre porte-bonheur; **it's not my l. day** ce n'est pas mon jour de chance; **that was l.** ça a été un coup de chance; **to strike it l.** décrocher le gros lot; **l. charm** porte-bonheur *m inv*; *Br* **l. dip** = baquet rempli de sciure etc où l'on plonge la main pour en retirer une surprise; **you can thank your l. stars she didn't see you!** tu peux t'estimer heureux qu'elle ne t'ait pas vu!

lucrative ['luːkrətɪv] *adj* lucratif(ive)

lucre ['luːkə(r)] *n Pej or Hum* lucre *m*

ludicrous ['luːdɪkrəs] *adj* risible, ridicule

lug [lʌg] *(pt & pp* **lugged)** *vt Fam* trimbaler

luggage ['lʌgɪdʒ] *n* bagages *mpl*; **l. label** étiquette *f* à bagages; **l. locker** consigne *f* automatique; **l. rack** *(in train)* porte-bagages *m inv*; *(on car)* galerie *f*; *Br* **l. van** *(on train)* fourgon *m*

lughole ['lʌghəʊl] *n Br Fam* esgourde *f*

lugubrious [luː'guːbrɪəs] *adj* lugubre

lukewarm ['luːkwɔːm] *adj also Fig* tiède; **a l. reception** *(of person)* un accueil peu chaleureux; *(of book, movie)* un accueil mitigé

lull [lʌl] **1** *n (in fighting)* accalmie *f*; *(in conversation)* pause *f*; *Fig* **the l. before the storm** le calme avant la tempête **2** *vt* **to l. sb to sleep** endormir qn en le berçant; **to l. sb into a false sense of security** endormir la méfiance de qch

lullaby ['lʌləbaɪ] (pl **lullabies**) n berceuse f
lumbago [lʌm'beɪɡəʊ] n lumbago m
lumbar ['lʌmbə(r)] adj Anat lombaire
lumber ['lʌmbə(r)] **1** n (a) Br (junk) bric-à-brac m; **l. room** débarras m (b) Am (wood) bois m de charpente ou de construction **2** vt to **get lumbered with sth** se taper ou se coltiner qch; **I got lumbered with him for the whole evening** je l'ai eu sur le dos pendant toute la soirée **3** vi to **l. about** or **around** avancer d'un pas lourd
lumbering ['lʌmbərɪŋ] adj (walk) lourd(e), pesant(e)
lumberjack ['lʌmbədʒæk] n bûcheron m
luminary ['luːmɪnərɪ] (pl **luminaries**) n Lit sommité f
luminescent [luːmɪ'nesənt] adj luminescent(e)
luminous ['luːmɪnəs] adj (paint, road sign, colour) fluorescent(e)
lump [lʌmp] **1** n (a) (of earth) motte f; (of stone, coal) morceau m; (in sauce) grumeau m; (on body) grosseur f; **a l. of sugar** un sucre; Fig **it brought a l. to my throat** (made me sad) ma gorge se serra; Fin **l. sum** somme f forfaitaire; **to pay in a l. sum** payer en une seule fois (b) Fam (person) empoté(e) m,f **2** vt (a) (group) to **l. (together)** regrouper; Pej mettre dans le même sac (b) Fam (endure) **you'll just have to (like it or) l. it!** il faudra que tu fasses avec!
lumpy ['lʌmpɪ] adj (sauce) grumeleux(euse); (mattress) bosselé(e)
lunacy ['luːnəsɪ] n folie f
lunar ['luːnə(r)] adj lunaire; **l. eclipse** éclipse f de lune; **l. landing** alunissage m
lunatic ['luːnətɪk] **1** n fou (folle) m,f; **l. asylum** asile m d'aliénés **2** adj (idea, behaviour) dément(e); **the l. fringe** la frange extrémiste
lunch [lʌntʃ] **1** n déjeuner m; **to have l.** prendre son déjeuner, déjeuner; Fam Fig **to be out to l.** (be crazy) débloquer; **l. hour** heure f du déjeuner **2** vi déjeuner (on de)
luncheon ['lʌntʃən] n (a) Formal déjeuner m (b) **l. meat** = viande à base de porc présentée en tranches; Br **l. voucher** chèque-restaurant m
lunchtime ['lʌntʃtaɪm] n heure f du déjeuner
lung [lʌŋ] n poumon m; **l. cancer** cancer m des poumons
lunge [lʌndʒ] **1** n mouvement m brusque en avant; **to make a l. for** se ruer vers **2** vi se ruer (at vers)
lupin ['luːpɪn] n lupin m
lurch [lɜːtʃ] **1** n (of ship, car) embardée f; **a l. to the left/right** (of politician, party) un virage à gauche/droite; Fam **to leave sb in the l.** laisser qn dans le pétrin **2** vi (of ship, car) faire une embardée; (of person) tituber; **to**

l. to the left/right (of politician, party) virer à gauche/droite
lure ['lʊə(r)] **1** n (attraction) attrait m **2** vt (into trap, ambush) attirer; **nothing could l. her away from the TV** rien ne pouvait l'éloigner de la télé
lurid ['lʊərɪd] adj (a) (story, description) cru(e); **she described it in l. detail** elle en a fait une description qui ne laissait rien à l'imagination (b) (gaudy) criard(e)
lurk [lɜːk] vi être tapi(e); (of doubt, fear) subsister
luscious ['lʌʃəs] adj (woman) appétissant(e); (fruit) succulent(e)
lush [lʌʃ] adj (plant, vegetation) luxuriant(e); Fig (surroundings) luxueux(euse)
lust [lʌst] n (sexual) désir m (charnel); Fig (for power, knowledge) soif f (for de)
▸ **lust after** vt insep convoiter
luster Am = lustre
lustful ['lʌstfʊl] adj lubrique
lustre, Am **luster** ['lʌstə(r)] n lustre m, éclat m
lustrous ['lʌstrəs] adj brillant(e)
lusty ['lʌstɪ] adj (person) vigoureux(euse); (cry, blow) puissant(e)
lute [luːt] n luth m
Luxemb(o)urg ['lʌksəmbɜːɡ] n le Luxembourg
Luxemb(o)urger ['lʌksəmbɜːɡə(r)] n Luxembourgeois(e) m,f
luxuriant [lʌɡ'zjʊərɪənt] adj luxuriant(e)
luxuriate [lʌɡ'zjʊərɪeɪt] vi se prélasser (in dans)
luxurious [lʌɡ'zjʊərɪəs] adj somptueux(euse)
luxury ['lʌkʃərɪ] n (pl **luxuries**) luxe m; **to lead a life of l.** vivre dans le luxe **2** adj de luxe
lychee [laɪ'tʃiː] n litchi m
lying ['laɪɪŋ] **1** n mensonges mpl **2** adj (person) menteur(euse)
lymph [lɪmf] n Anat lymphe f; **l. node** ganglion m lymphatique
lymphatic [lɪm'fætɪk] adj lymphatique
lynch [lɪntʃ] vt lyncher
lynching ['lɪntʃɪŋ] n lynchage m
lynx [lɪŋks] n lynx m
Lyons [liːɒn] n Lyon m
lyre ['laɪə(r)] n lyre f
lyric ['lɪrɪk] adj lyrique
lyrical ['lɪrɪkəl] adj lyrique
lyricism ['lɪrɪsɪzəm] n lyrisme m
lyricist ['lɪrɪsɪst] n parolier(ère) m,f
lyrics ['lɪrɪks] npl (of song) paroles fpl

M¹, m [em] *n (letter)* M, m m *inv*
M² *Br Aut (abbr* **motorway)** autoroute *f*
m **(a)** *(abbr* **metre(s))** m **(b)** *(abbr* **mile(s))** mile(s)
MA [em'eɪ] *n Univ (abbr* **Master of Arts)** to have an MA in linguistics avoir une maîtrise de linguistique; John Smith MA John Smith, titulaire d'une maîtrise de lettres/droit/*etc*
ma [mɑː] *n Fam* maman *f*
ma'am [mɑːm] *n Old-fashioned* madame *f*
mac [mæk] *n Br Fam (raincoat)* imper *m*
macabre [mə'kɑːbə(r)] *adj* macabre
macaroni [mækə'rəʊnɪ] *n* macaronis *mpl; Br* m. **cheese,** *Am* m. **and cheese** gratin *m* de macaronis
macaroon [mækə'ruːn] *n* macaron *m*
macaw [mə'kɔː] *n* ara *m*
Mace® [meɪs] *n (spray)* gaz *m* lacrymogène
mace¹ [meɪs] *n (weapon, symbol of office)* masse *f*
mace² *n (spice)* macis *m*
Macedonia [mæsə'dəʊnɪə] *n* la Macédoine
Macedonian [mæsə'dəʊnɪən] **1** *n* **(a)** *(person)* Macédonien(enne) *m,f* **(b)** *(language)* macédonien *m* **2** *adj* macédonien(enne)
Mach [mæk] *n Phys* **M. (number)** (nombre *m* de) Mach; **to fly at M. 2** voler à Mach 2
machete [mə'ʃetɪ] *n* machette *f*
Machiavellian [mækɪə'velɪən] *adj* machiavélique
machinations [mæʃɪ'neɪʃənz] *npl* machinations *fpl*, manœuvres *fpl*
machine [mə'ʃiːn] **1** *n* machine *f; Fig (person)* robot *m*; **party/propaganda m.** appareil *m* du parti/de la propagande; *Comptr* **m. code** code *m* machine; **m. gun** mitrailleuse *f; Comptr* **m. language** langage *m* machine; **m. shop** atelier *m* d'usinage; **m. tool** machine-outil *f* **2** *vt* **(a)** *Ind* usiner **(b)** *(with sewing machine)* coudre *ou* piquer à la machine
machine-gun [mə'ʃiːngʌn] *vt* mitrailler
machine-readable [mə'ʃiːn'riːdəbəl] *adj Comptr* lisible par ordinateur
machinery [mə'ʃiːnərɪ] *n (machines)* machines *fpl*, machinerie *f; Fig (of organization)* rouages *mpl*
machinist [mə'ʃiːnɪst] *n (on sewing machine)* mécanicienne *f; (on machine tool)* ouvrier(ère) *m,f*
machismo [mæ'tʃɪzməʊ] *n* machisme *m*
macho [mætʃəʊ] *adj* macho *inv*
macintosh [mækɪntɒʃ] = **mackintosh**
mackerel [mækrəl] *n* maquereau *m*

mackintosh [mækɪntɒʃ] *n* imperméable *m*
macro [mækrəʊ] *(pl* macros) *n Comptr* macro *f*, macrocommande *f*
macrobiotics [mækrəʊbaɪ'ɒtɪks] *n* macrobiotique *f*
macroeconomics [mækrəʊiːkə'nɒmɪks] *n* macroéconomie *f*
mad [mæd] *adj* **(a)** *(insane) (person)* fou (folle); *(idea, plan)* insensé(e); *(dog)* enragé(e); **to go m.** devenir fou; **to drive sb m.** rendre qn fou; **as m. as a hatter** fou à lier; **m. with fear** mort(e) de peur; **there was a m.** rush for the door les gens se ruèrent vers la porte; *Fam* **to run/work like m.** courir/travailler comme un(e) fou (folle); *Fam* **m. cow disease** maladie *f* de la vache folle **(b)** *Fam (enthusiastic)* **to be m. about sth** être fou (folle) de qch; **the crowd went m.** ce fut le délire parmi les spectateurs **(c)** *Fam (angry)* furieux(euse) **(with** *or* **at** contre); **to go m.** piquer une colère
Madagascan [mædə'gæskən] **1** *n* Malgache *mf* **2** *adj* malgache
Madagascar [mædə'gæskə(r)] *n* Madagascar
madam [mædəm] *n (as form of address)* madame *f; Br Fam* **she's a little m.** c'est une vraie petite pimbêche
madcap [mædkæp] *adj* insensé(e)
madden [mædən] *vt* exaspérer
maddening [mædənɪŋ] *adj* exaspérant(e)
made [meɪd] *pt & pp of* **make**
Madeira [mə'dɪərə] *n (island)* Madère *f; (wine)* madère *m*
made-up [meɪ'dʌp] *adj* **(a)** *(story, excuse)* inventé(e) de toutes pièces **(b)** *(wearing make-up)* maquillé(e)
madhouse [mædhaʊs] *n Fam* maison *f* de fous
madly [mædlɪ] *adv* **(a)** *(insanely, desperately)* comme un(e) fou (folle) **(b)** *Fam (exciting, interested, jealous)* follement; **m. in love** follement *ou* éperdument amoureux(euse)
madman [mædmən] *n* fou *m*, dément *m*
madness [mædnɪs] *n* folie *f*, démence *f*; **it's absolute m.!** c'est de la folie pure!
madonna [mə'dɒnə] *n* madone *f*
Madrid [mə'drɪd] *n* Madrid
madwoman [mædwʊmən] *n* folle *f*, démente *f*
maelstrom [meɪlstrəm] *n (confusion)* tourbillon *m*
maestro [maɪstrəʊ] *(pl* maestros) *n* maestro *m*
Mafia [mæfɪə] *n* the M. la Mafia
mag [mæg] *n Fam* magazine *m*, revue *f*
magazine [mægə'ziːn] *n* **(a)** *(publication)* magazine *m*, revue *f* **(b)** *(on radio, TV)* **m. (show)** magazine *m* **(c)** *(for gun)* magasin *m; (ammunition store)* dépôt *m* de munitions

magenta [mə'dʒentə] **1** n magenta m
2 adj magenta inv
maggot ['mægət] n asticot m
Maghreb [mæ'greb] n the M. le Maghreb
Maghrebi [mæ'grebɪ] **1** n Maghrébin(e) m,f
2 adj maghrébin(e)
Magi ['meɪdʒaɪ] npl the M. les Rois mpl mages
magic ['mædʒɪk] **1** n magie f; **as if by m.** comme par enchantement; **black/white m.** magie noire/blanche
2 adj (**a**) (supernatural) magique; **m. wand** baguette f magique (**b**) Br Fam (excellent) génial(e)
▸ **magic away** (pt & pp **magicked**) vt sep faire disparaître comme par enchantement
magical ['mædʒɪkəl] adj magique
magician [mə'dʒɪʃən] n magicien(enne) m,f
magisterial [mædʒɪs'tɪərɪəl] adj magistral(e); Br Law de magistrat
magistrate ['mædʒɪstreɪt] n Br Law magistrat m, magistrates' court ≃ tribunal m d'instance
magnanimity [mægnə'nɪmɪtɪ] n magnanimité f
magnanimous [mæg'nænɪməs] adj magnanime
magnate ['mægneɪt] n magnat m
magnesium [mæg'niːzɪəm] n Chem magnésium m
magnet ['mægnɪt] n aimant m; Fig (for tourists, investors) pôle m d'attraction
magnetic [mæg'netɪk] adj also Fig magnétique; **m. compass** boussole f; **m. tape** bande f magnétique
magnetism ['mægnɪtɪzəm] n also Fig magnétisme m
magnification [mægnɪfɪ'keɪʃən] n grossissement m, (of sound) amplification f
magnificence [mæg'nɪfɪsəns] n magnificence f
magnificent [mæg'nɪfɪsənt] adj magnifique, (meal, wine) excellent(e)
magnify ['mægnɪfaɪ] (pt & pp **magnified**) vt (image) grossir, agrandir; (sound) amplifier; Fig (importance, problem) exagérer
magnifying glass ['mægnɪfaɪɪŋ'glɑːs] n loupe f
magnitude ['mægnɪtjuːd] n ampleur f; **a problem of the first m.** un problème majeur
magnolia [mæg'nəʊlɪə] n (tree) magnolia m; (colour) rose m pâle
magnum ['mægnəm] n (of champagne) magnum m
magpie ['mægpaɪ] n pie f; Fig **he's a bit of a m.** il a quelque chose du collectionneur fou
mahogany [mə'hɒgənɪ] **1** n (wood, colour) acajou m
2 adj en acajou
maid [meɪd] n (servant) bonne f, domestique f; **m. of honour** or Am **honor** (to queen) demoiselle f d'honneur; Am (at wedding) première demoiselle d'honneur
maiden ['meɪdən] **1** n Lit (girl) jeune fille f
2 adj **m. aunt** tante f célibataire; **m. flight** vol m inaugural; **m. name** nom m de jeune fille; Parl **m. speech** premier discours m
mail¹ [meɪl] **1** n (**a**) (letters, parcels) courrier m; **it came in the m.** c'est arrivé au courrier (**b**) (system) poste f; **by m.** par la poste; Comptr **m. merge** publipostage m; Com **m. order** vente f par correspondance; **m. order catalogue/company** catalogue m/entreprise f de vente par correspondance; **by m. order** par correspondance; **m. train** train m postal
2 vt poster
mail² n (armour) mailles fpl
mailbag ['meɪlbæg] n sac m postal; **she gets a huge m.** (of celebrity, politician) elle reçoit énormément de courrier

mailbox ['meɪlbɒks] n Am & Comptr boîte f aux lettres
mailing ['meɪlɪŋ] n (mailshot) publipostage m, mailing m; **m. list** fichier m d'adresses
mailshot ['meɪlʃɒt] n publipostage m, mailing m
maim [meɪm] vt mutiler, estropier
main [meɪn] **1** n (**a**) (pipe) conduite f (principale); the **mains** (electricity) le secteur; **to turn the water off at the mains** couper l'arrivée d'eau; **gas from the mains** gaz de ville (**b**) in the m. (generally) en général, en gros
2 adj principal(e); the **m. thing is to…** l'essentiel est de…; Gram **m. clause** proposition f principale; **m. course** plat m de résistance; **m. entrance** entrée f principale; Rail **m. line** grande ligne f; **m. road** grande route f; Fam **m. squeeze** petit(e) ami(e) m,f; **m. street** rue f principale
mainframe ['meɪnfreɪm] n Comptr ordinateur m central
mainland ['meɪnlænd] n continent m; **m. Europe** l'Europe continentale
mainline ['meɪnlaɪn] vi Fam (inject drugs) se piquer
mainly ['meɪnlɪ] adv principalement; **the passengers were m. old men** la plupart des passagers étaient des vieux messieurs
mainspring ['meɪnsprɪŋ] n Fig (of change, revolution) moteur m
mainstay ['meɪnsteɪ] n (of economy, philosophy) pilier m, base f
mainstream ['meɪnstriːm] **1** n courant m principal
2 adj ordinaire
maintain [meɪn'teɪn] vt (**a**) (preserve) (order, reputation) maintenir; (silence, attitude) garder; **to m. one's enthusiasm** rester enthousiaste (**b**) (building, machine, road) entretenir (**c**) (family) subvenir aux besoins de (**d**) (state) to m. that… soutenir que…
maintenance ['meɪntɪnəns] n (**a**) (of car, building, roads) entretien m; **m. costs** frais mpl d'entretien (**b**) Law (alimony) pension f alimentaire
maisonette [meɪzə'net] n (appartement m) duplex m
maize [meɪz] n maïs m
Maj (**a**) Mil (abbr **Major**) Cdt (**b**) Mus (abbr **Major**) M
majestic [mə'dʒestɪk] adj majestueux(euse)
majesty ['mædʒəstɪ] n majesté f; His/Her M. Sa Majesté le Roi/la Reine
major ['meɪdʒə(r)] **1** n (**a**) Mil commandant m; **m. general** général m de division (**b**) Am Univ (subject) matière f principale
2 adj (**a**) (important) majeur(e), (most important) principal(e); (accident, illness) très grave; **of m. importance** de la plus haute importance (**b**) Mus majeur(e)
3 vi Am Univ **to m. in sth** se spécialiser en qch
Majorca [mə'jɔːkə] n Majorque f
Majorcan [mə'jɔːkən] **1** n Majorquin(e) m,f
2 adj majorquin(e)
majority [mə'dʒɒrɪtɪ] (pl **majorities**) n (**a**) (in vote) majorité f; **to be in a** or **the m.** être majoritaire; **m. decision** décision f prise à la majorité; Pol **m. rule** système m majoritaire; Law **m. verdict** verdict m de la majorité; Pol **there was a m. vote in favour of…** on a voté à la majorité pour… (**b**) Law (age) majorité f
make [meɪk] **1** vt (pt & pp **made** [meɪd]) (**a**) (produce, perform) faire; (payment) effectuer; (decision) prendre; **made in Spain** fabriqué(e) en Espagne; **made from** or **of stone/wood** en pierre/bois; **I'll show them what I'm made of!** je vais leur montrer de quel bois je me chauffe!; **I'm not made of money!** je ne suis pas millionnaire!; **to m. something of oneself** faire quelque chose de sa vie; **two and two m. four** deux et deux font quatre; **to m. a choice** prendre une décision; **it doesn't m. any difference** cela ne

change rien; **to m. a noise** faire du bruit **(b)** *(earn)* gagner; **to m. a living** gagner sa vie; **to m. a name for oneself** se faire un nom **(c)** *(make successful)* **this is the book that made her** ce livre l'a rendue célèbre; *Fam* **to m. it** *(be successful)* réussir; **you've got it made** tu as la belle vie; **it's m.** or **break** ça passe ou ça casse; **it made my day** il m'a fait très plaisir **(d)** *(cause to be)* **to m. sb happy/sad** rendre qn heureux(euse)/triste; **to m. sb hungry** donner faim à qn; **to m. sb tired** fatiguer qn **(e)** *(compel)* **to m. sb do sth** faire faire qch à qn; **don't m. me laugh!** tu me fais rire! **(f)** *(estimate, calculate)* **what time do you m. it?** quelle heure avez-vous?; **I m. it $100 in total** j'arrive à 100 dollars en tout **(g)** *(reach)* **to m. it** *(arrive in time)* arriver à temps; *(finish in time)* finir à temps; **to m. the final** *(of team, competitor)* arriver en finale; **to m. the first team** être sélectionné(e) pour jouer dans la première équipe **(h)** *(become, be)* **she'll m. a good doctor/singer** elle fera un bon médecin/une bonne chanteuse; **the report makes interesting reading** le rapport est intéressant à lire **(i)** *(manage to attend) (show, meeting)* assister à; **I can m. two o'clock** je peux être là à deux heures

2 *vi* **(a) to m. as if** *or* **as though to do sth** *(get ready to)* s'apprêter à faire qch; *(pretend)* faire semblant de faire qch **(b) to m. do** *(cope)* se débrouiller; **to m. do with** se contenter de; **to m. believe (that)…** imaginer que…

(c) to m. sure *or* **certain of** s'assurer de

3 *n* **(a)** *(brand)* marque *f*

(b) *Fam* **to be on the m.** *(financially)* chercher à s'en mettre plein les poches; *(sexually)* draguer

▸ **make after** *vt insep (chase)* se lancer à la poursuite de

▸ **make for** *vt insep* **(a)** *(head towards)* se diriger vers **(b)** *(contribute to)* contribuer à

▸ **make of** *vt sep* **what do you m. of the new manager?** que pensez-vous du nouveau directeur?; **I don't know what to m. of that remark** je ne sais pas comment interpréter cette remarque; **you're making too much of it** tu y attaches trop d'importance

▸ **make off** *vi Fam (leave)* filer, décamper

▸ **make off with** *vt insep Fam (steal)* filer avec

▸ **make out 1** *vt sep* **(a)** *(understand, decipher)* comprendre; *(see, hear)* distinguer; *(handwriting)* déchiffrer **(b)** *(write) (list, cheque)* faire **(c)** *Fam (claim)* **to m. out (that)…** prétendre que…

2 *vi Am Fam (sexually)* se peloter

▸ **make over** *vt sep (transfer)* céder **(to** à)

▸ **make up 1** *vt sep* **(a)** *(story, excuses)* inventer **(b)** *(deficit, loss)* combler; **I'll m. it up to you later, I promise** je te le revaudrai, je te le promets **(c)** *(complete) (team, amount)* compléter **(d)** *(form)* constituer, composer; **to m. up one's mind** se décider **(e)** *(put together) (list)* faire; *(parcel, bed)* faire; **to m. up a prescription** préparer les médicaments prescrits sur une ordonnance **(f)** *(apply make-up to)* maquiller; **to m. oneself up** se maquiller

2 *vi (end quarrel)* se réconcilier

▸ **make up for** *vt insep* compenser; *(lost time)* rattraper

make-believe ['meɪkbɪliːv] **1** *n* fantaisie *f*; **to live in a land of m.** ne pas avoir le sens des réalités

2 *adj* imaginaire

makeover ['meɪkəʊvə(r)] *n (of appearance)* séance *f* de maquillage; *Fig* transformation *f*

maker ['meɪkə(r)] *n* **(a)** *(manufacturer)* fabricant *m*; *(of planes, cars)* constructeur *m* **(b) to meet one's M.** monter au ciel

makeshift ['meɪkʃɪft] *adj* de fortune

make-up ['meɪkʌp] *n* **(a)** *(cosmetics)* maquillage *m*; **m. artist** maquilleur(euse) *m,f*; **m. bag** trousse *f* à maquillage; **m. remover** démaquillant *m* **(b)** *(composition) (of team, group)* composition *f*; *(of person)* caractère *m*

making ['meɪkɪŋ] *n (of goods)* fabrication *f*; **the movie was four years in the m.** le tournage du film a duré quatre ans; **history in the m.** l'histoire en train de se faire; **a poet in the m.** un poète en herbe; **the problem is of her own m.** c'est un problème qu'elle s'est elle-même créé; **he has the makings of an actor** il a tout ce qu'il faut pour devenir acteur

maladjusted [mælə'dʒʌstɪd] *adj* inadapté(e)

maladroit [mælə'drɔɪt] *adj* maladroit(e)

malady ['mælədɪ] *(pl* **maladies)** *n Fig* mal *m*

Malagasy ['mæləgæsɪ] **1** *n (language)* malgache *m* **2** *adj* malgache

malaise [mæ'leɪz] *n* malaise *m*

malaria [mə'leərɪə] *n* malaria *f*, paludisme *m*

Malawi [mə'lɑːwɪ] *n* le Malawi

Malawian [mə'lɑːwɪən] **1** *n* Malawien(enne) *m,f* **2** *adj* malawien(enne)

Malay [mə'leɪ] **1** *n* **(a)** *(person)* Malais(e) *m,f* **(b)** *(language)* malais *m* **2** *adj* malais(e)

Malaysia [mə'leɪzɪə] *n* la Malaisie

Malaysian [mə'leɪzɪən] **1** *n* Malais(e) *m,f* **2** *adj* malais(e)

Maldives ['mɔːldiːvz] *npl* **the M.** (îles *fpl*) Maldives *fpl*

male [meɪl] **1** *n (person)* homme *m*; *(animal)* mâle *m* **2** *adj* mâle; *(sex, attitude, public)* masculin(e); **m. chauvinist pig** phallocrate *m*; **m. nurse** infirmier *m*

malefactor ['mælɪfæktə(r)] *n Lit* malfaiteur(trice) *m,f*

malevolence [mə'levələns] *n* malveillance *f*

malevolent [mə'levələnt] *adj* malveillant(e)

malformed [mæl'fɔːmd] *adj* difforme

malfunction [mæl'fʌŋkʃən] **1** *n* mauvais fonctionnement *m* **2** *vi* mal fonctionner

Mali ['mɑːlɪ] *n* le Mali

malice ['mælɪs] *n* méchanceté *f*; *Law* **with m. aforethought** avec préméditation

malicious [mə'lɪʃəs] *adj* méchant(e), malveillant(e)

maliciously [mə'lɪʃəslɪ] *adv* méchamment, avec malveillance

malign [mə'laɪn] **1** *adj* pernicieux(euse) **2** *vt* calomnier, diffamer

malignant [mə'lɪgnənt] *adj (person)* malveillant(e), méchant(e); *(tumour)* malin(igne)

malinger [mə'lɪŋgə(r)] *vi* faire semblant d'être malade

malingerer [mə'lɪŋgərə(r)] *n* simulateur(trice) *m,f*

mall [mɔːl] *n Am (shopping)* **m.** centre *m* commercial

mallard ['mælɑːd] *n* colvert *m*

malleable ['mælɪəbəl] *adj also Fig* malléable

mallet ['mælɪt] *n* maillet *m*

malnutrition [mælnjuː'trɪʃən] *n* malnutrition *f*

malpractice [mæl'præktɪs] *n* faute *f* professionnelle

malt [mɔːlt] *n* malt *m*; **m. vinegar** vinaigre *m* de malt; **m. whisky** whisky *m* de malt

Malta ['mɔːltə] *n* Malte *f*

Maltese [mɔːl'tiːz] **1** *n* **(a)** *(person)* Maltais(e) *m,f*; **the M.** les Maltais *mpl* **(b)** *(language)* maltais *m* **2** *adj* maltais(e); **the M. cross** la croix de Malte

maltreat [mæl'triːt] *vt* maltraiter

maltreatment [mæl'tri:tmənt] *n* mauvais traitements *mpl*

mammal ['mæməl] *n* mammifère *m*

mammary ['mæmərı] *adj Anat* mammaire; **m. gland** glande *f* mammaire

mammography [mæ'mɒgrəfı] *n Med* mammographie *f*

mammoth ['mæməθ] **1** *n (animal)* mammouth *m* **2** *adj (huge)* gigantesque

mammy ['mæmı] *(pl* **mammies)** *n Fam* maman *f*

man [mæn] **1** *n (pl* **men** [men]) **(a)** *(adult male)* homme *m; Fam* hey, **m.!** eh toi!; *Fam* how are you doing, **m.?** comment ça va, vieux?; **a m.'s jacket/bicycle** une veste/bicyclette d'homme; **the army will make a m.** of him l'armée en fera un homme; **he took it like a m.** il a pris ça courageusement; **this will separate the men from the boys** ceci distinguera les hommes des gamins; **to be m.** **enough to do sth** être assez courageux pour faire qch; **to talk to sb m. to m.** parler à qn d'homme à homme; **he's just the m.** for the job c'est l'homme qu'il nous faut; **to be one's own m.** être son *(propre)* maître, être à **m.'s m.** o'est un homme à vrai; **the m.** in the street l'homme de la rue; **a m.** of God un homme d'église **(b)** *(individual, person)* homme *m;* **any m.** n'importe qui; **few men** peu d'hommes; **to reply as one m.** répondre d'une seule voix; **they were patriots to a m.** ils étaient tous patriotes **(c)** *(husband, partner)* **my m.** mon homme **(d)** *(humanity)* l'homme *m* **(e)** *(employee) (in factory)* homme *m,* ouvrier *m; (servant)* valet *m,* domestique *m; (soldier)* homme, soldat *m;* **our m. in Rome** *(diplomat)* notre envoyé à Rome; *(spy)* notre agent à Rome; *(reporter)* notre correspondant à Rome **(f)** *(in chess)* pièce *f; (in draughts)* pion *m* **2** *vt (pt & pp* **manned)** *(machine)* assurer le fonctionnement de; *(plane, boat)* être membre de l'équipage de; **to m. the phone** répondre au téléphone; **à manned flight** un vol habité

manacles ['mænəkəlz] *npl* menottes *fpl*

manage ['mænıdʒ] **1** *vt* **(a)** *(company, project)* diriger; *(shop, hotel)* être le gérant de; *(economy, resources, money, time)* gérer **(b)** *(deal with) (situation)* gérer; **to know how to m. sb** savoir *(comment)* prendre qn; **to m. to do sth** *(succeed)* réussir *ou* arriver à faire qch; **I can't m.** three **suitcases** je ne peux pas porter trois valises; **£500 is the most that I can m.** *(to pay)* je ne peux pas aller au-delà de 500 livres; **can you m. dinner tomorrow?** est-ce que vous pouvez venir dîner demain? **2** *vi (cope)* se débrouiller **(with** avec); **to m. without sb/ sth** pouvoir se passer de qn/qch; **he'll never m. on his own** il n'y arrivera pas tout seul

manageable ['mænıdʒəbəl] *adj (object, size, vehicle)* maniable; *(hair)* facile à coiffer

management ['mænıdʒmənt] *n* **(a)** *(activity) (of company, project)* gestion *f,* direction *f; (of economy, resources, shop, hotel)* gestion; **m. consultant** conseiller(ère) *m,f* en gestion; **m. studies** *fpl* de gestion **(b)** *(managers, employers)* direction *f;* **under new m.** *(sign)* changement de propriétaire; **m. team** équipe *f* dirigeante d'une société par la direction; **m. buyout** = rachat

manager ['mænıdʒə(r)] *n (of bank, company)* directeur(trice) *m,f; (of shop, hotel, bar)* gérant(e) *m,f; (of boxer, singer, football team)* manager *m*

managerial [mænı'dʒıərıəl] *adj* directorial(e); **m. staff** cadres *mpl;* **m. skills** qualités *fpl* de gestionnaire

managing director ['mænıdʒıŋdaı'rektə(r)] *n* directeur(trice) *m,f* général(e)

Manchester ['mæntʃestə(r)] *n* Manchester

Mandarin ['mændərın] *n (language)* mandarin *m*

mandarin ['mændərın] *n* **(a)** *(fruit)* mandarine *f* **(b)** *(official)* mandarin *m*

mandate ['mændeıt] *n* mandat *m*

mandatory ['mændətərı] *adj* obligatoire

mandible ['mændıbəl] *n (of insect)* mandibule *f, (of vertebrate)* mâchoire *f* inférieure

mandolin ['mændəlın] *n* mandoline *f*

mane [meın] *n* crinière *f*

man-eater ['mæni:tə(r)] *n* **(a)** *(animal)* mangeur *m* d'hommes **(b)** *Hum (woman)* mangeuse *f* d'hommes

man-eating ['mæni:tıŋ] *adj* mangeur(euse) d'hommes

maneuver *Am* = manoeuvre

manfully ['mænfʊlı] *adv* courageusement, vaillamment

manganese [mæŋgə'ni:z] *n Chem* manganèse *m*

mange [meındʒ] *n* gale *f*

manger ['meındʒə(r)] *n* mangeoire *f*

mangle ['mæŋgəl] **1** *n (for clothes)* essoreuse *f* (à rouleaux) **2** *vt (body)* mutiler; *(car)* broyer; *(text)* massacrer

mango ['mæŋgəʊ] *(pl* **mangoes)** *n (fruit)* mangue *f; (tree)* manguier *m*

mangrove ['mæŋgrəʊv] *n* palétuvier *m;* **m. swamp** mangrove *f*

mangy ['meındʒı] *adj (animal)* galeux(euse); *(carpet, coat)* minable, miteux(euse)

manhandle ['mænhændəl] *vt (person)* malmener; *(large object)* transporter à la force des bras

manhole ['mænhəʊl] *n (in road)* bouche *f* d'égout; **m. cover** plaque *f* d'égout

manhood ['mænhʊd] *n* **(a)** *(maturity)* âge *m* d'homme; **to reach m.** devenir un homme **(b)** *(masculinity)* virilité *f* **(c)** *(men collectively)* American *m.* les hommes américains

man-hour ['mænaʊə(r)] *n Econ* heure *f* de travail

manhunt ['mænhʌnt] *n* chasse *f* à l'homme

mania ['meınıə] *n* **(a)** *(liking)* passion *f* **(for** pour); *(psychological)* manie *f;* **to have a m. for doing sth** avoir la manie de faire qch

maniac ['meınıæk] *n* fou (folle) *m,f;* **to drive like a m.** conduire comme un fou

manic ['mænık] *adj Fig (person)* stressé(e); *(activity)* frénétique

manic-depressive ['mænıkdı'presıv] *n & adj Psy* maniaco-dépressif(ive) *m,f*

manicure ['mænıkjʊə(r)] **1** *n* manucure *f;* **to have a m.** se faire faire les ongles **2** *vt* **to m. one's nails** se faire les ongles

manifest ['mænıfest] **1** *n (of ship, aircraft)* manifeste *m* **2** *adj* manifeste, évident(e) **3** *vt* manifester

manifestation [mænıfes'teıʃən] *n* manifestation *f*

manifestly ['mænıfestlı] *adv* manifestement

manifesto [mænı'festəʊ] *(pl* **manifestos)** *n Pol* manifeste *m*

manifold ['mænıfəʊld] **1** *n Aut* collecteur *m* **2** *adj Lit (numerous)* multiple, nombreux(euse)

Manila [mə'nılə] *n* Manille

mani(l)la envelope [mə'nılə'envələʊp] *n* enveloppe *f* en papier kraft

manipulate [mə'nıpjʊleıt] *vt also Fig* manipuler

manipulation [mənıpjʊ'leıʃən] *n also Fig* manipulation *f*

manipulative [mə'nıpjʊlətıv] *adj Pej* manipulateur(trice)

mankind [mæn'kaɪnd] n l'humanité f

manliness ['mænlɪnɪs] n virilité f

manly ['mænlɪ] adj viril(e)

man-made ['mænmeɪd] adj (fabric, product) synthétique; (lake, beach) artificiel(elle); **a m. disaster** un désastre provoqué par l'homme

mannequin ['mænɪkɪn] n (person) mannequin m

manner ['mænə(r)] n (a) (way, method, style) manière f, façon f; **the m. in which...** la manière ou façon dont...; **in a m. of speaking** pour ainsi dire, en quelque sorte (b) **manners** (etiquette) manières fpl; **it's bad manners to stare** il est mal élevé de dévisager les gens; **he's got no manners** il ne sait pas se tenir (c) (type) **all m. of people/things** toutes sortes de gens/choses; **by no m. of means, not by any m. of means** absolument pas (d) (attitude, behaviour) **I don't like his m.** je n'aime pas sa façon d'être; **she's got a very abrasive m.** elle est très acerbe (e) **manners** (social usages) mœurs fpl

mannered ['mænəd] adj maniéré(e)

mannerism ['mænərɪzəm] n manie f, tic m

manoeuvrable, Am **maneuverable** [mə'nu:vrəbəl] adj maniable

manoeuvre, Am **maneuver** [mə'nu:və(r)] **1** n also Fig manœuvre f; Fig **there wasn't much room for m.** la marge de manœuvre était assez limitée; **to be on manoeuvres** (of soldiers) être en manœuvre(s) **2** vt manœuvrer; **she manoeuvred the car into the space** elle a garé la voiture dans l'emplacement **3** vi manœuvrer

manor ['mænə(r)] n m. (house) manoir m

manpower ['mænpaʊə(r)] n main-d'œuvre f

mansion ['mænʃən] n (in country) château m; (in town) hôtel m particulier

manslaughter ['mænslɔ:tə(r)] n Law homicide m involontaire

mantelpiece ['mæntəlpi:s] n dessus m de cheminée; **on the m.** sur la cheminée

mantis ['mæntɪs] n Am mante f religieuse

mantle ['mæntəl] n (a) Lit (of snow) manteau m; Fig **to take on the m. of office** assumer les responsabilités qui incombent au poste (b) (of gas lamp) manchon m (c) Geol manteau m

man-to-man [mæntʊ'mæn] adj & adv d'homme à homme

manual ['mænjʊəl] **1** n (handbook) manuel m **2** adj (work, worker) manuel(elle); **m. dexterity** dextérité f

manually ['mænjʊəlɪ] adv manuellement

manufacture [mænjʊ'fæktʃə(r)] **1** n fabrication f; (of vehicles) construction f **2** vt fabriquer; (vehicles) construire; (clothes) confectionner; Fig (evidence) fabriquer (de toutes pièces)

manufacturer [mænjʊ'fæktʃərə(r)] n Ind fabricant m; (of vehicles) constructeur m

manufacturing [mænjʊ'fæktʃərɪŋ] **1** n Ind l'industrie f (manufacturière) **2** adj (centre, sector) industriel(elle); **m. capacity** capacité f de production; **m. industries** industries fpl manufacturières

manure [mə'njʊə(r)] **1** n fumier m; **liquid m.** purin m **2** vt engraisser

manuscript ['mænjʊskrɪpt] n manuscrit m

many ['menɪ] (comparative **more** [mɔ:(r)], superlative **most** [məʊst]) **1** pron beaucoup; **m. of us/them** beaucoup d'entre nous/eux; **not m.** pas beaucoup; **too m.** trop; **as m. as you like** autant que vous voulez; **as m. as 500 people**

were there il y avait bien jusqu'à 500 personnes; Fam **to have had one too m.** avoir bu un coup de trop **2** adj beaucoup de; **m. people** beaucoup de gens; **m. times** souvent, bien des fois; **not m.** pas beaucoup de; **in m. ways** de bien des façons; **not in so m. words** pas aussi explicitement; **there were so m. people that...** il y avait tant de gens que...; **a good m. people** un bon nombre de gens; **too m.** trop de; **as m.... as** autant de... que; **m.'s the time I've done that** j'ai fait ça bien des fois; Prov **m. hands make light work** à plusieurs, l'ouvrage avance vite

many-coloured, Am **many-colored** ['menɪ'kʌləd] adj multicolore

Maori ['maʊrɪ] **1** n Maori(e) m,f **2** adj maori(e)

map [mæp] **1** n carte f; (of underground, town) plan m; Fig **this will put Schenectady on the m.** cela va faire parler de Schenectady; **m. reference** coordonnées fpl **2** vt (pt & pp mapped) (region) dresser une carte de ▸ **map out** vt sep (route) tracer; (plan, programme) élaborer; **she had her career all mapped out** sa carrière était toute tracée

maple ['meɪpəl] n érable m; **m. leaf** feuille f d'érable; **m. syrup** sirop m d'érable

mar [mɑ:(r)] (pt & pp marred) vt gâcher

Mar (abbr **March**) mars

maracas [mə'rækəz] npl Mus maracas fpl

marathon ['mærəθən] n also Fig marathon m; **a m. speech** un discours-marathon; **m. runner** marathonien(enne) m,f

marauder [mə'rɔ:də(r)] n maraudeur(euse) m,f

marauding [mə'rɔ:dɪŋ] adj en maraude

marble ['mɑ:bəl] n (a) (stone) marbre m (b) (glass ball) bille f; **to play marbles** jouer aux billes; Fam Fig **to lose one's marbles** (go mad) perdre la boule

marbled ['mɑ:bəld] adj marbré(e)

March [mɑ:tʃ] n mars m; see also **May**

march [mɑ:tʃ] **1** n marche f; Fig **the m. of time** la marche du temps; **on the m.** en marche; **m. past** défilé m (of soldiers) faire défiler les gens; **he was marched off to prison** il a été emmené en prison **3** vi (of soldiers) marcher au pas; (of soldiers on parade, demonstrators) défiler; **to m. off** partir; **to m. by** or **past** (sb/sth) défiler (devant qn/qch)

marcher ['mɑ:tʃə(r)] n (demonstrator) manifestant(e) m,f

marching orders ['mɑ:tʃɪŋ'ɔ:dəz] npl Fam **to give sb his m.** mettre qn à la porte

mare [meə(r)] n jument f

margarine [mɑ:dʒə'ri:n] n margarine f

margin ['mɑ:dʒɪn] n (a) (on page) marge f; **in the m.** dans la marge (b) (edge) (of forest) orée f; **on the margin(s) of society** en marge de la société (c) (gap) **to win by a narrow m.** gagner de justesse; **to win by an enormous m.** gagner haut la main; **a m. of error** une marge d'erreur (d) Com **marge f bénéficiaire**

marginal ['mɑ:dʒɪnəl] **1** n Br Pol siège m à majorité précaire **2** adj (a) (improvement, increase) léger(ère) (b) (note) en marge (c) Br Pol (seat) à majorité précaire

marginalize ['mɑ:dʒɪnəlaɪz] vt marginaliser

marginally ['mɑ:dʒɪnəlɪ] adv légèrement

marigold ['mærɪɡəʊld] n souci m

marihuana, marijuana [mærɪ'wɑ:nə] n marijuana f

marina [mə'ri:nə] n port m de plaisance

marinade ['mærɪneɪd] Culin **1** n marinade f **2** vt (faire) mariner

marinate ['mærɪneɪt] *vt Culin* (faire) mariner

marine [mə'riːn] **1** *n (soldier)* fusilier *m* marin; *Am Fam* **(go) tell it to the marines!** (allez dire ça) à d'autres! **2** *adj (life, biology)* marin(e); **m. engineering** génie *m* maritime

mariner ['mærɪnə(r)] *n Lit* marin *m*

marionette [mærɪə'net] *n* marionnette *f* à fils

marital ['mærɪtəl] *adj* conjugal(e); **m. status** situation *f* de famille

maritime ['mærɪtaɪm] *adj* maritime

marjoram ['maːdʒərəm] *n* marjolaine *f*

mark¹ [maːk] *n Formerly (German currency)* mark *m*

mark² **1** *n* **(a)** *(scratch, stain)* tache *f*, marque *f* **(b)** *(symbol)* marque *f* **(c)** *(sign, proof)* signe *m*; **as a m. of respect** en signe de respect; **years of imprisonment had left their m.** on him ses années de captivité l'avaient marqué; **to make one's m.** *(succeed)* faire ses preuves **(d)** *(target)* **his comments hit the m.** ses remarques ont touché en plein dans le mille; **unemployment has passed the nine million m.** le nombre des chômeurs a dépassé la barre des neuf millions; **her accusation was wide of the m.** son accusation était complètement à côté de la plaque; **he's not up to the m.** il n'est pas à la hauteur **(e)** *(in test, exam)* note *f*; **full marks** la note maximale **(f)** *(in race)* **on your marks! get set! go!** à vos marques! prêts! partez!; **to be quick off the m.** démarrer vite; *Fig* avoir l'esprit vif; **to be slow off the m.** prendre un mauvais départ; *Fig* être long à la détente **(g)** *(model, of machine)* **m. II/III** série II/III **(h)** *Br (on cooker)* **(gas) m. 4** thermostat *m* 4 **2** *vt* **(a)** *(put mark on)* marquer **(b)** *(homework, exam)* noter; **to m. sth right/wrong** compter qch comme juste/faux **(c)** *(indicate)* indiquer; *(anniversary, end, occasion)* marquer; **this decision marks a change in policy** cette décision est le signe d'un changement de politique; *Fig* **to m. time** *(wait)* piétiner **(d)** *(characterize)* caractériser; **his comments were marked by their sarcasm** ses commentaires étaient empreints de sarcasme **(e)** *(in sport) (opponent)* marquer **(f)** *(pay attention to)* **m. my words** notez bien ce que je vais dire

▸ **mark down** *vt sep* **(a)** *(make note of)* noter; **they had him marked down as a troublemaker** ils l'avaient étiqueté comme fauteur de troubles **(b)** *Com (price)* baisser; *(goods)* démarquer

▸ **mark off** *vt sep* **(a)** *(area)* délimiter **(b)** *(tick off)* cocher

▸ **mark out** *vt sep* **to m. sb out** distinguer

▸ **mark up** *vt sep (price)* augmenter, majorer; **to be marked up** *(of goods)* avoir augmenté

marked [maːkt] *adj* **(a)** *(difference, improvement)* marqué(e), sensible **(b)** **m. cards** cartes truquées *ou* marquées; **to be a m. man** être surveillé

markedly ['maːkɪdlɪ] *adv* nettement

marker ['maːkə(r)] *n* **(a)** *(of essay, exam)* correcteur(trice) *m,f*; **he's a hard m.** il note sévèrement **(b)** **m. (pen)** marqueur *m* **(c)** *(flag, post)* balise *f*; **m. buoy** bouée *f* de balisage

market ['maːkɪt] **1** *n* marché *m*; **to put sth on the m.** mettre qch en vente; *Fin* **m. analyst** analyste *mf* du marché; **m. day** jour *m* de marché; *Econ* **(free) m. economy** économie *f* de marché; *Econ* **m. forces** tendances *fpl* du marché; **m. garden** jardin *m* maraîcher; *Com* **m. leader** leader *m* du marché; *Econ* **m. price** prix *m* du marché; *Com* **m. research** étude *f* de marché; *Com* **m. share** part *f* de

marché; *Com* **m. survey** étude *f* de marché; **m. town** ville *f* de marché **2** *vt* commercialiser

marketable ['maːkɪtəbəl] *adj* commercialisable

marketing ['maːkɪtɪŋ] *n Com (study, theory)* marketing *m*, mercatique *f*; *(of product)* commercialisation *f*; **m. campaign** campagne *f* de marketing; **m. department** service *m* de marketing; **m. manager** responsable *mf ou* directeur(trice) *m,f* du marketing; **m. strategy** stratégie *f* marketing

marketplace ['maːkɪtpleɪs] *n* **(a)** *(in village, town)* place *f* du marché **(b)** *Econ* marché *m*; **in the m.** sur le marché

marking ['maːkɪŋ] *n* **(a)** **markings** *(on animal) (spots)* taches *fpl*; *(stripes)* rayures *fpl*; *(on plane)* insignes *mpl* **(b)** *(of essay, exam)* correction *f*; **I've got a lot of m. to do** j'ai beaucoup de copies à corriger

markka ['maːkə] *n Formerly* mark *m* finlandais

marksman ['maːksmən] *n* tireur *m* d'élite

mark-up ['maːkʌp] *n (on price)* majoration *f*

marmalade ['maːməleɪd] *n* confiture *f* d'oranges

maroon¹ [mə'ruːn] *n* **(a)** *(colour)* bordeaux *m* **(b)** *(firework)* fusée *f* de détresse

maroon² *vt* abandonner; **we were marooned by the floods** nous étions isolés à cause des inondations

marquee [maː'kiː] *n* grande tente *f*; *(at circus)* chapiteau *m*

marquis ['maːkwɪs] *n* marquis *m*

Marrakech, Marrakesh ['mærəkeʃ] *n* Marrakech

marriage ['mærɪdʒ] *n also Fig (wedding)* mariage *m*; **a happy m.** un ménage heureux; **she's my aunt by m.** c'est ma tante par alliance; **m. of convenience** mariage de convenance; *Fig* **it was a m. of minds** c'était la rencontre de deux esprits; **m. certificate** certificat *m* de mariage; **m. guidance** *Br* **counsellor** *or Am* **counselor** conseiller(ère) *m,f* conjugal(e); **m. vows** vœux *mpl* du mariage

marriageable ['mærɪdʒəbəl] *adj* **a girl of m. age** une fille en âge de se marier

married ['mærɪd] *adj* marié(e); **to get m. (to)** se marier (avec); **they're happily m.** ils sont heureux en ménage; **m. life** la vie maritale; **m. name** nom *m* de femme mariée; *Mil* **m. quarters** logements *mpl* pour familles

marrow ['mærəʊ] *n* **(a)** *(of bone)* moelle *f* **(b)** *(vegetable)* courge *f*

marrowbone ['mærəʊbəʊn] *n* os *m* à moelle

marrowfat pea ['mærəʊfætpiː] *n* pois *m* carré

marry ['mærɪ] *(pt & pp* **married)** **1** *vt* **(a)** *(get married to)* épouser, se marier avec; *(of priest, parent)* marier; **will you m. me?** veux-tu m'épouser?; *Fig* **he's married to his job** il n'y a que son travail qui compte **(b)** *(combine)* marier **2** *vi* se marier

▸ **marry off** *vt sep* marier

Mars [maːz] *n (planet)* Mars *f*

Marseilles [maː'seɪ] *n* Marseille

marsh [maːʃ] *n* marais *m*, marécage *m*

marshal ['maːʃəl] **1** *n* **(a)** *(army officer)* maréchal *m* **(b)** *(at race, demonstration)* membre *m* du service d'ordre **2** *vt (pt & pp* **marshalled,** *Am* **marshaled)** *(vehicles, troops)* rassembler; *(crowd)* canaliser; *(arguments, thoughts)* mettre en ordre

marshland ['maːʃlænd] *n* région *f* marécageuse

marshmallow [maːʃ'mæləʊ] *n* guimauve *f*

marshy ['maːʃɪ] *adj* marécageux(euse)

marsupial [maː'suːpɪəl] *n* marsupial *m*

martial ['maːʃəl] *adj* martial(e); **m. arts** arts *mpl* martiaux; **to declare m. law** proclamer la loi martiale

Martian ['mɑːʃən] *n* Martien(enne) *m,f*

martyr ['mɑːtə(r)] **1** *n* martyr(e) *m,f; Fig* **to be a m.** to rheumatism souffrir le martyre à cause de rhumatismes **2** *vt* martyriser

martyrdom ['mɑːtədəm] *n* martyre *m*

marvel ['mɑːvəl] **1** *n* merveille *f;* **to work marvels** faire des merveilles; *Fam* **you're a m.!** tu es un as! **2** *vi (pt & pp* **marvelled**, *Am* **marveled**) s'émerveiller (**at** de)

marvellous, *Am* **marvelous** ['mɑːvələs] *adj* merveilleux(euse); *Ironic* (**isn't it**) **m.!** ça, c'est le bouquet *ou* le comble!

Marxism ['mɑːksɪzəm] *n* marxisme *m*

Marxist ['mɑːksɪst] *n & adj* marxiste *mf*

marzipan ['mɑːzɪpæn] *n* pâte *f* d'amandes

mascara [mæs'kɑːrə] *n* mascara *m*

mascot ['mæskət] *n* mascotte *f*

masculine ['mæskjʊlɪn] **1** *n Gram* masculin *m;* **in the m.** au masculin **2** *adj* masculin(e)

masculinity [mæskjʊ'lɪnɪtɪ] *n* masculinité *f*

mash [mæʃ] **1** *n* (**a**) *Br Fam (mashed potato)* purée *f* (**b**) *(for pigs, poultry)* pâtée *f* **2** *vt* **to m. (up)** broyer; *(vegetables)* écraser

mashed potato [mæʃtpə'teɪtəʊ] *n* purée *f* (de pommes de terre)

mask [mɑːsk] **1** *n* masque *m; (for eyes only)* loup *m* **2** *vt (conceal)* dissimuler

masked [mɑːskt] *adj* masqué(e)

masking tape ['mɑːskɪŋteɪp] *n* ruban *m* de papier adhésif

masochism ['mæsəkɪzəm] *n* masochisme *m*

masochist ['mæsəkɪst] *n* masochiste *mf*

masochistic [mæsə'kɪstɪk] *adj* masochiste

mason ['meɪsən] *n (builder)* maçon *m; (freemason)* franc-maçon *m*

masonry ['meɪsənrɪ] *n (stonework)* maçonnerie *f*

masquerade [mæskə'reɪd] **1** *n* (**a**) *Fig (disguise)* mascarade *f* (**b**) *(dance)* bal *m* masqué **2** *vi* **to m. as sb** se faire passer pour qn

mass¹ [mæs] **1** *n* (**a**) *(large number)* foule *f,* multitude *f; Fam* **I've got masses (of things) to do** j'ai des tas de choses à faire; *Fam* **there's masses of room** il y a plein de place; **m. grave** charnier *m;* **m. hysteria** hystérie *f* collective; **m. media** (mass) médias *mpl;* **m. meeting** grand rassemblement *m;* **m. murderer** tueur *m* fou; **m. production** fabrication *f* en série; **m. protest** protestation *f* en masse (**b**) *(shapeless substance)* masse *f* (**c**) *Pol* **the masses** le peuple *m* (**d**) *Phys* masse *f* **2** *vi (of troops, people, clouds)* se masser

mass² [mæs] *n Rel* messe *f;* **to go to m.** aller à la messe

massacre ['mæsəkə(r)] **1** *n* massacre *m; Fam Fig* **it was a m.** *(in sport, election)* ça a été le massacre **2** *vt also Fig* massacrer

massage ['mæsɑːʒ] **1** *n* massage *m;* **m.** *Br* **parlour** *or Am* **parlor** salon *m* de massage **2** *vt (body)* masser; *Fig* **to m. the figures** manipuler les chiffres

masseur [mæ'sɜː(r)] *n* masseur *m*

masseuse [mæ'sɜːz] *n* masseuse *f*

massive ['mæsɪv] *adj (increase, scale, dose)* massif(ive); *(amount, building, obstacle)* énorme; *(room)* immense; *(heart attack, stroke)* foudroyant(e)

mass-produce [mæsprə'djuːs] *vt* fabriquer en série

mast [mɑːst] *n (of ship)* mât *m; (of radio, TV transmitter)* pylône *m*

mastectomy [mæs'tektəmɪ] *(pl* **mastectomies**) *n Med* mastectomie *f*

master ['mɑːstə(r)] **1** *n* (**a**) *(man in charge)* maître *m; (of ship)* capitaine *m;* **the m.** of the house le maître de maison; **to be one's own m.** être son propre maître; **to be m.** of the situation être maître de la situation; **m. of ceremonies** maître des cérémonies; *(for TV programme)* présentateur *m;* **m. bedroom** chambre *f* principale; **m. copy** original *m;* **m. key** passe-partout *m;* **m. plan** plan *m* d'ensemble; **m. race** race *f* supérieure (**b**) *(skilled person)* maître *m,* expert(e) *m,f; Univ* **M. of Arts** *(qualification)* ≃ maîtrise *f* ès lettres; *(person)* ≃ maître ès lettres; *Univ* **M. of Science** *(qualification)* ≃ maîtrise *f* ès sciences; *(person)* ≃ maître ès sciences; **m. mason/builder** maître maçon/d'œuvre; *Mus* **m. class** cours *m* de maître; *Univ* **m.'s (degree)** maîtrise *f* (**in** de) (**c**) *(teacher)* professeur *m;* **fencing/dancing m.** maître d'escrime/de ballet (**d**) *(young boy)* **M. William Thornton** Monsieur William Thornton (**e**) *Art* **an old m.** une œuvre de maître **2** *vt* maîtriser; *(situation)* dominer

masterful ['mɑːstəfʊl] *adj* autoritaire

masterly ['mɑːstəlɪ] *adj* magistral(e)

mastermind ['mɑːstəmaɪnd] **1** *n* cerveau *m* **2** *vt (project)* diriger, organiser; *(plot, crime)* échafauder

masterpiece ['mɑːstəpiːs] *n* chef-d'œuvre *m*

masterstroke ['mɑːstəstrəʊk] *n* coup *m* de maître

mastery ['mɑːstərɪ] *n* maîtrise *f*

mastiff ['mæstɪf] *n* mastiff *m*

mastitis [mæs'taɪtəs] *n Med* mastite *f*

masturbate ['mæstəbeɪt] *vi* se masturber

masturbation [mæstə'beɪʃən] *n* masturbation *f*

mat [mæt] *n (on floor)* tapis *m; (of straw)* natte *f; (at door)* paillasson *m; (for plates)* set *m* de table; *(for dishes)* dessous-de-plat *m inv*

match¹ [mætʃ] *n (for lighting fire, cigarette)* allumette *f*

match² [mætʃ] *n* (**a**) *(in sport)* match *m;* **m. point** *(in tennis)* balle *f* de match (**b**) **they're a good m.** *(of clothes)* ils vont bien ensemble; **to meet one's m.** trouver son maître; **to be no m. for sb** ne pas être à la hauteur par rapport à qn (**c**) *(marriage)* **to make a good m.** faire un bon mariage **2** *vt* (**a**) *(equal)* égaler (**b**) *(of colours, clothes)* être assorti(e) à; *(description, account)* concorder avec (**c**) **we can't m. their prices** nous ne pouvons pas rivaliser avec leurs prix; **to m. sb against sb** opposer qn à qn; **to be well matched** *(of teams, players)* être de même niveau; *(of couple)* un couple bien assorti **3** *vi (of colours, clothes)* être assorti(e)s(ties); *(of descriptions, accounts)* concorder

▸ **match up 1** *vt sep (colours, clothes)* assortir **2** *vi (of clothes, colours)* être assorti(e)s(ties); *(of explanations)* concorder; **to m. up to sb's expectations** répondre à l'attente de qn

matchbox ['mætʃbɒks] *n* boîte *f* d'allumettes

matching ['mætʃɪŋ] *adj* assorti(e)

matchless ['mætʃlɪs] *adj* sans pareil

matchmaker ['mætʃmeɪkə(r)] *n* marieur(euse) *m,f*

matchstick ['mætʃstɪk] *n* allumette *f;* **m. man** *or* **figure** bonhomme *m* dessiné de simples traits

mate¹ [meɪt] **1** *n* (**a**) *(sexual partner) (male animal)* mâle *m; (female animal)* femelle *f; (person)* partenaire *mf* (**b**) *Br Fam (friend)* copain (copine) *m,f;* **thanks, m.** merci mon vieux (**c**)

(assistant) assistant(e) *m,f* **(d)** *(on ship)* officier *m*; **(first) m.**
second *m*
2 *vt (animals)* accoupler
3 *vi (of animals)* s'accoupler
mate² *(in chess)* **1** *n* mat *m*
2 *vt* mettre mat
material [mə'tɪərɪəl] **1** *n* **(a)** *(substance)* matériau *m*, matière *f*; *Fig* **he isn't management m.** il n'a pas l'étoffe d'un directeur **(b)** *(for book, article)* matériaux *mpl*; **reading m.** de quoi lire; **she writes all her own m.** *(of singer)* elle écrit ses chansons elle-même **(c)** *(cloth)* tissu *m* **(d)** **materials** *(equipment)* matériel *m*
2 *adj* **(a)** *(needs, possessions)* matériel(elle) **(b)** *(important, relevant)* essentiel(elle); *(fact)* pertinent(e); **the point is m. to my argument** c'est un point essentiel de mon argumentation
materialism [mə'tɪərɪəlɪzəm] *n* matérialisme *m*
materialistic [mətɪərɪə'lɪstɪk] *adj* matérialiste
materialize [mə'tɪərɪəlaɪz] *vi (of hope, threat)* se réaliser; *(of event)* avoir lieu; *(of spirit)* apparaître
materially [mə'tɪərɪəlɪ] *adv* **(a)** *(in money, goods)* matériellement **(b)** *(appreciably)* sensiblement
maternal [mə'tɜːnəl] *adj* maternel(elle)
maternity [mə'tɜːnɪtɪ] *n* maternité *f*; **m. dress** robe *f* de grossesse; **m. hospital** maternité; **m. leave** congé *m* de maternité; **m. ward** maternité
matey ['meɪtɪ] *Br Fam* **1** *n* **listen, m.** écoute, mon pote
2 *adj* pote **(with** avec**)**
math [mæθ] *n Am* maths *fpl*
mathematical [mæθə'mætɪkəl] *adj* mathématique
mathematician [mæθəmə'tɪʃən] *n* mathématicien-(enne) *m,f*
mathematics [mæθə'mætɪks] *n (subject)* mathématiques *fpl*; *(calculations)* calculs *mpl*
maths [mæθs] *n Br* maths *fpl*
matinée ['mætɪneɪ] *n (of play, film)* matinée *f*
mating ['meɪtɪŋ] *n* accouplement *m*; **m. call** appel *m* du mâle; **m. season** saison *f* des amours
matriarch ['meɪtrɪɑːk] *n* = femme ayant le statut de chef de famille
matriarchal ['meɪtrɪɑːkəl] *adj* matriarcal(e)
matriculate [mə'trɪkjʊleɪt] *vi* s'inscrire
matriculation [mətrɪkjʊ'leɪʃən] *n* inscription *f*
matrimonial [mætrɪ'məʊnɪəl] *adj* matrimonial(e)
matrimony ['mætrɪmənɪ] *n* mariage *m*
matrix ['meɪtrɪks] *(pl* **matrixes** ['meɪtrɪksɪz] *or* **matrices** ['meɪtrɪsiːz]*) n Math & Tech* matrice *f*
matron ['meɪtrən] *n* **(a)** *Br (in hospital)* infirmière *f* en chef; *(in school)* = intendante et infirmière **(b)** *(older woman)* matrone *f* **(c) m. of** *Br* **honour** *or Am* **honor** *(at wedding)* première demoiselle *f* d'honneur
matt [mæt] *adj* mat(e)
matted ['mætɪd] *adj (hair)* emmêlé(e)
matter ['mætə(r)] **1** *n* **(a)** *(affair, issue)* question *f*, problème *m*; **that's a m. of opinion/taste** c'est une question d'opinion/de goût; **it's no easy m.** ce n'est pas simple; **that's quite another m.** ce n'est pas du tout la même chose; **within a m. of hours** en quelques heures; **for that m.** d'ailleurs; **as a m. of course** bien évidemment; **as a m. of fact** en fait; **as matters stand** au point où en sont les choses; **and to make matters worse…** et pour aggraver les choses…; **military matters** questions *fpl* militaires; **business matters** affaires *fpl*
(b) *(problem)* **what's the m.?** qu'est-ce que c'est?; **what's the m. with you?** qu'est-ce que tu as?; **there's something**

---

the m. with the car/my foot j'ai un problème avec la voiture/mon pied
(c) *(substance)* matière *f*
(d) *(with no)* **no m.!** peu importe!; **no m. who/where** qui/où que ce soit; **no m. how hard I try…** j'ai beau essayer; **no m. what I do** quoi que je fasse
2 *vi* avoir de l'importance **(to** pour**)**; **it doesn't m.** cela n'a pas d'importance, ça ne fait rien; **nothing else matters** le reste est sans importance; **it doesn't m. to me** ça m'est égal
Matterhorn ['mætəhɔːn] *n* **the M.** le mont Cervin
matter-of-fact ['mætərə'fækt] *adj (person, statement)* terre à terre; *(tone, voice)* neutre; **he was very m. about it** il avait l'air très détaché
matting ['mætɪŋ] *n* tapis *m* de sol tressé
mattress ['mætrɪs] *n* matelas *m*
mature [mə'tjʊə(r)] **1** *adj (person, fruit)* mûr(e); *(hard cheese)* fort(e); *Br Univ* **m. student** = adulte qui reprend des études
2 *vt (wine)* faire vieillir
3 *vi (of person, fruit)* mûrir; *(of wine)* vieillir; *Fin (of investment)* arriver à échéance
maturity [mə'tjʊərɪtɪ] *n* maturité *f*; *Fin* **on m. à** l'échéance
maudlin ['mɔːdlɪn] *adj* larmoyant(e)
maul [mɔːl] *vt (of lion, tiger)* mutiler; *Fig (criticize)* tailler en pièces
Mauritania [mɒrɪ'teɪnɪə] *n* la Mauritanie
Mauritanian [mɒrɪ'teɪnɪən] **1** *n* Mauritanien(enne) *m,f*
2 *adj* mauritanien(enne)
Mauritian [mə'rɪʃən] **1** *n* Mauricien(enne) *m,f*
2 *adj* mauricien(enne)
Mauritius [mə'rɪʃəs] *n* l'île *f* Maurice
mausoleum [mɔːsə'liːəm] *n* mausolée *m*
mauve [məʊv] **1** *n* mauve *m*
2 *adj* mauve
maverick ['mævərɪk] *n* franc-tireur *m*, non-conformiste *mf*
mawkish ['mɔːkɪʃ] *adj Pej* mièvre
max [mæks] *(abbr* **maximum)** max
maxim ['mæksɪm] *n* maxime *f*
maximize ['mæksɪmaɪz] *vt* maximaliser
maximum ['mæksɪməm] **1** *n (pl* **maximums** *or* **maxima** ['mæksɪmə]*)* maximum *m*; **to the m.** au maximum
2 *adj* maximum *inv*, maximal(e)
May [meɪ] *n* mai *m*; **In M.** en mai, au mois de mai; **at the beginning/end of M.** début/fin mai; **during M.** en mai; **each** *or* **every M.** chaque année en mai; **in the middle of M.** mi-mai; **last/next M.** mai dernier/prochain; **on the sixteenth of M.,** *Am* **on M. sixteenth** le seize mai; **she was born on 22 M.** *or Am* **M. 22** 1953 elle est née le 22 mai 1953; **M. Day** le Premier Mai
may [meɪ] *v aux (3rd person singular* **may,** *pt* **might** [maɪt]*)*

May et might peuvent s'utiliser indifféremment dans la plupart des expressions de la catégorie **(a)**.

(a) *(expressing possibility)* **he m. return at any moment** il pourrait rentrer à tout moment; **he m. have lost it** il se peut *ou* se pourrait qu'il l'ait perdu; **he m. be that…** il se peut *ou* se pourrait que… + *subjunctive*; **you m. be wondering why…** vous vous demandez peut-être pourquoi…; **you m. well ask!** bonne question!; **we m. as well go** autant y aller; **you m. as well tell them the truth** autant que tu leur dises la vérité
(b) *Formal (asking for or giving permission)* **m. I come in?** puis-je entrer?; **if I m. say so** si je peux me permettre; **m. I?** *(when borrowing)* vous permettez?

(c) *Formal (expressing wish, purpose)* **m. she rest in peace!**
paix à son âme!; **m. the best man win!** que le meilleur
gagne!
(d) *(with concessions)* **he m.** be very rich but I still don't
like him il est peut-être très riche, mais il me déplaît
quand même; **be that as it m., that's as m.** be quoi qu'il
en soit

Mayan ['maɪən] **1** *n* Maya *mf* **2** *adj* maya

maybe ['meɪbiː] *adv* peut-être; **m. she won't accept** elle
n'acceptera peut-être pas

Mayday ['meɪdeɪ] *n (distress signal)* signal *m* de détresse,
S.O.S. *m*; **M.!** mayday!

mayhem ['meɪhem] *n* it was m. c'était la pagaille

mayonnaise [meɪə'neɪz] *n* mayonnaise *f*

mayor ['meə(r)] *n* maire *m*

mayoress ['meəres] *n* mairesse *f*; *(mayor's wife)* femme *f*
du maire

maypole ['meɪpəʊl] *n Br* ≃ arbre *m* de mai, = mât autour
duquel les gens dansent pour célébrer le Premier mai

maze [meɪz] *n* labyrinthe *m*; *Fig* dédale *m*

MBA [embiː'eɪ] *n Univ (abbr* **Master of Business
Administration)** MBA *m*

MBO [embiː'əʊ] *n Com (abbr* **management buyout)** =
rachat d'une entreprise par ses cadres

MC [em'siː] *n (abbr* **Master of Ceremonies)** maître *m* des
cérémonies; *(forTV programme)* présentateur *m*

MD [em'diː] *n* **(a)** *Med (abbr* **Doctor of Medicine)** docteur
m en médecine **(b)** *Com (abbr* **Managing Director)**
directeur(trice) *m,f* général(e)

ME [eˈmiː] *n Med (abbr* **myalgic encephalomyelitis)**
encéphalomyélite *f* myalgique

me¹ [*unstressed* mɪ, *stressed* miː] *pron* **(a)** *(direct object)* me;
she hates me elle me déteste; **she loves me** elle m'aime;
she can understand my son but not ME elle comprend
mon fils, mais moi, elle ne me comprend pas
(b) *(indirect object)* **she gave me the book** elle m'a donné
le livre; **she gave it to me** elle me l'a donné
(c) *(after preposition)* moi; **she's thinking of me** elle pense
à moi
(d) *(as complement of verb* **to be***)* moi; **it's me!** c'est moi!; **it
was me who did it** c'est moi qui l'ai fait
(e) *(with interjections)* **silly me!** que je suis bête!; **poor me!**
pauvre de moi!

me² [miː] *n Mus* mi *m*

meadow ['medəʊ] *n* prairie *f*, pré *m*

meagre, *Am* **meager** ['miːgə(r)] *adj* maigre

meal¹ [miːl] *n* repas *m*; *Fig* **to make a m. of sth** faire tout
un plat de qch

meal² *n (flour)* farine *f*

mealtime ['miːltaɪm] *n* heure *f* du repas

mealy ['miːlɪ] *adj* farineux(euse)

mealy-mouthed [miːlɪ'maʊðd] *adj Pej* mielleux(euse)

mean¹ [miːn] **1** *n (average)* moyenne *f*
2 *adj (average)* moyen(enne)

mean² *adj* **(a)** *(miserly)* avare **(b)** *(nasty)* méchant(e); **she
has a m. streak** elle peut être méchante quand elle veut;
that was a m. thing to do/say ce n'est pas chic d'avoir dit
ça/fait ça **(c)** *(poor)* **she's no m. photographer** c'est une
sacrée photographe; **it was no m. feat** ce n'est pas un
mince exploit **(d)** *Fam (good)* **he plays a m. game of soccer**
c'est un as du foot

mean³ *(pt & pp* **meant** [ment]*) vt* **(a)** *(signify)* **(of word,
event)** signifier; *(of person)* vouloir dire; **what does the
word "tacky" m.?** que signifie le mot "tacky"?; **this is Bill, I**

m. Will je vous présente Bill, je veux dire Will; **I know what
you m.** je comprends; **what do you m.?** qu'est-ce que tu
veux dire?; **it doesn't m. anything** ça ne veut rien dire
(b) *(be serious about)* **do you think he meant what he
said?** pensez-vous qu'il l'ait dit sérieusement?; **I didn't m.
that** ce n'est pas ce que je voulais dire; **I m. it** je parle
sérieusement; **you don't m. it!** tu plaisantes!
(c) *(be of importance)* **the price means nothing to him** le
prix importe peu pour lui; **it means a lot to me** c'est très
important pour moi
(d) *(intend)* **to m. to do sth** avoir l'intention de faire qch; **I
didn't m. to do it** je ne l'ai pas fait exprès; **I m. him no
harm** je ne lui veux pas de mal; **she means well** ses
intentions sont bonnes; **I m. to succeed** je veux réussir;
she meant you to have this ring elle voulait que tu aies
cette bague; **it was meant as a joke/compliment** c'était
une blague/un compliment; **this portrait is meant to be
of the duke** ce portrait est censé représenter le duc; **you
were meant to be here at eight** vous étiez censé arriver à
huit heures; **it's meant to be a good film** il paraît que c'est
un bon film; **they were meant for each other** ils sont faits
l'un pour l'autre

meander [mɪ'ændə(r)] **1** *n* méandre *m*
2 *vi (of river, road)* serpenter; *(of person)* flâner

meaning ['miːnɪŋ] *n* sens *m*, signification *f*; *Fam* **if you
get my m.** si tu vois ce que je veux dire; **what's the m. of
this?** *(expressing indignation)* qu'est-ce que ça signifie?; **the
m. of life** le sens de la vie

meaningful ['miːnɪŋfʊl] *adj* significatif(ive); *(relationship)* sérieux(euse)

meaningless ['miːnɪŋlɪs] *adj* vide de sens, sans
signification

meanness ['miːnnɪs] *n* **(a)** *(miserliness)* avarice *f* **(b)**
(nastiness) mesquinerie *f*

means [miːnz] *n (pl* **means)** *(method)* moyen *m*; **by m.
of…** au moyen de…, à l'aide de…; **there is no m. of
escape** il n'y a aucun moyen de s'échapper; **by some m. or
other** d'une manière ou d'une autre; **a m. to an end** un
moyen d'arriver à ses fins; **by all m.** *(certainly)* je vous en
prie; **by no m.** du tout, nullement; **she is by no m.
stupid** elle est loin d'être bête; **m. of communication**
moyen de communication; **m. of production** moyens de
production; **m. of transport** moyen de transport
2 *npl (income, wealth)* moyens *mpl*, ressources *fpl*; **a man
of m.** un homme fortuné; **to live beyond/within one's m.**
vivre au-dessus de/selon ses moyens; **m. test** *(for state
benefit)* enquête *f* sur les revenus

meant [ment] *pt & pp of* **mean**

meantime ['miːntaɪm], **meanwhile** ['miːnwaɪl] **1** *n*
in the m. *(at the same time)* pendant ce temps; *(between two
events)* entre-temps
2 *adv (at the same time)* pendant ce temps; *(between two
events)* entre-temps

measles ['miːzəlz] *n* rougeole *f*; **to have (the) m.** avoir la
rougeole

measly ['miːzlɪ] *adj Fam* minable

measurable ['meʒərəbəl] *adj* mesurable; *Fig (difference,
improvement)* notable, sensible

measure ['meʒə(r)] **1** *n* **(a)** *(measurement, quantity)*
mesure *f*; **this was a m. of how serious the situation
was** cela montrait à quel point la situation était sérieuse;
they allowed her a m. of freedom on lui accordait une
certaine liberté; **m. of sb** jauger qn; **then he was
called me a liar for good m.** par-dessus le marché, il m'a
traité de menteur **(b)** *(degree)* **in some m.** dans une certaine
mesure **(c)** *(action, step)* mesure *f*; **to take measures to do
sth** prendre des mesures pour faire qch
2 *vt & vi* mesurer

▸ **measure up** vi être à la hauteur (**to** de)

measured ['meʒəd] adj mesuré(e)

measurement ['meʒəmənt] n mesure f

measuring ['meʒərɪŋ] n m. **cup** gobelet m doseur; m. **jug** verre m gradué; m. **spoon** cuillère-mesure f; m. **tape** mètre m ruban

meat [miːt] n (**a**) (food) viande f; Fig **to be m. and drink to sb** être une aubaine pour qn (**b**) Fig (substantial content) substance f

meatball ['miːtbɔːl] n boulette f de viande

meaty ['miːtɪ] adj (taste, smell) de viande; Fig (book, film) riche

Mecca ['mekə] n La Mecque; Fig paradis m

mechanic [mɪ'kænɪk] n mécanicien(enne) m,f

mechanical [mɪ'kænɪkəl] adj also Fig mécanique; m. **engineer** ingénieur m mécanicien; m. **engineering** construction f mécanique

mechanics [mɪ'kænɪks] **1** n (**a**) (science) mécanique f (**b**) (working parts) mécanisme m **2** npl Fig (processes) mécanisme m

mechanism ['mekənɪzəm] n mécanisme m

mechanize ['mekənaɪz] vt mécaniser

mechanized ['mekənaɪzd] adj m. **industry** industrie f mécanisée; m. **troops** troupes fpl motorisées

MEd [e'med] n Univ (abbr **Master of Education**) maîtrise f en sciences de l'éducation

medal ['medəl] n médaille f

medalist Am = **medallist**

medallion [mɪ'dæljən] n médaillon m

medallist, Am **medalist** ['medəlɪst] n médaillé(e) m,f

meddle ['medəl] vi (interfere) se mêler (in de); (tamper) toucher (**with** à)

meddler ['medlə(r)] n indiscret(ète) m,f

meddlesome ['medəlsəm] adj indiscret(ète)

media ['miːdɪə] n (a) (TV, press) médias mpl; m. **coverage** couverture f médiatique; m. **studies** études fpl de communication (**b**) pl of **medium**

mediaeval [medɪ'iːvəl] adj médiéval(e)

median ['miːdɪən] Math **1** n médiane f **2** adj médian(e)

mediate ['miːdɪeɪt] vi servir de médiateur (**for/ between** pour/entre)

mediation [miːdɪ'eɪʃən] n médiation f; **to go to m.** recourir à une médiation

mediator ['miːdɪeɪtə(r)] n médiateur(trice) m,f

medic ['medɪk] n Fam (student) étudiant(e) m,f en médecine; (doctor) médecin m

medical ['medɪkəl] **1** adj (record, treatment, profession) médical(e); (book) de médecine; (student) en médecine; **to seek m. advice** consulter un médecin; m. **examiner** médecin m légiste; m. **insurance** assurance f maladie; m. **practitioner** médecin m; m. **records** dossier m médical **2** n (physical examination) visite f médicale; **to pass/fail a m.** être déclaré(e) apte/inapte à la visite médicale

medicated ['medɪkeɪtɪd] adj (soap) médical(e); (shampoo) traitant(e)

medication [medɪ'keɪʃən] n médicaments mpl; **to be on m.** être sous traitement

medicinal [me'dɪsɪnəl] adj médicinal(e)

medicine ['medsɪn] n (**a**) (science) médecine f; **to practise m.** exercer la médecine; **to study m.** faire des études de médecine (**b**) (drugs) médicament m; Fig **to give sb a taste of his own m.** rendre à qn la monnaie

de sa pièce; m. **chest** or **cabinet** (armoire f à) pharmacie f; m. **man** (traditional healer) sorcier m, guérisseur m

medieval [medɪ'iːvəl] adj médiéval(e)

mediocre [miːdɪ'əʊkə(r)] adj médiocre

mediocrity [miːdɪ'ɒkrɪtɪ] n médiocrité f

meditate ['medɪteɪt] vi méditer (**on** sur)

meditation [medɪ'teɪʃən] n méditation f

Mediterranean [medɪtə'reɪnɪən] **1** n the M. la (mer) Méditerranée **2** adj méditerranéen(enne); the M. **Sea** la mer Méditerranée

medium ['miːdɪəm] **1** n (**a**) (pl media ['miːdɪə] or mediums) (means of communication) moyen m de communication; (means of expression) moyen d'expression; **through the m. of the press** par voie de presse (**b**) (in spiritualism) médium m,f **2** adj moyen(enne); of m. **height** de taille moyenne; in the m. **term** à moyen terme; m. **dry** demi-sec; m. **rare** à point; m. **wave** ondes fpl moyennes

medley ['medlɪ] n (pl medleys) n (mixture) mélange m; (in music) pot-pourri m; the **400 metres m.** (in swimming) le 400 mètres quatre nages

meek [miːk] adj docile; m. **and mild** doux (douce) comme un agneau

meekly [miːklɪ] adv docilement

meet [miːt] (pt & pp met [met]) **1** vt (**a**) (encounter) (by accident) rencontrer; (by arrangement) rejoindre, retrouver; (collect) attendre, aller chercher; **his eyes met mine** nos regards se sont croisés; **a remarkable sight met our eyes** un spectacle extraordinaire s'offrait à nos yeux; **there's more to this than meets the eye** on ne connaît pas les dessous de cette affaire; **there's more to her than meets the eye** elle cache bien son jeu (**b**) (become acquainted with) rencontrer, faire la connaissance de; **have you met my husband?** connaissez-vous mon mari?; m. **Mr Campbell** je vous présente M. Campbell (**c**) (join with) (river) se jeter dans; (road) rejoindre (**d**) (satisfy) (demand, order) satisfaire; (condition, requirement) satisfaire à; (objection, criticism) répondre à; (cost, expense) prendre en charge, payer (**e**) (danger) affronter; (difficulties) rencontrer; **to m. one's death** trouver la mort; **to m. one's match** trouver son maître **2** vi (**a**) (encounter) (by accident) se rencontrer; (by arrangement) se retrouver; **our eyes met** nos regards se sont croisés (**b**) (become acquainted) se rencontrer (**c**) (of society, assembly) se réunir (**d**) (join) (of rivers, roads) se rejoindre

▸ **meet up** vi (by accident) se rencontrer; (by arrangement) se retrouver; **to m. up with sb** (by accident) rencontrer qn; (by arrangement) retrouver qn

▸ **meet with** vt insep (difficulty, refusal) se heurter à; (danger) affronter; **to m. with disaster** se solder par un désastre; **to m. with failure** échouer; **to m. with an accident** avoir un accident; **to m. with sb's approval** recevoir l'accord de qn

meeting ['miːtɪŋ] n (**a**) (encounter) (by accident) rencontre f; (by arrangement) rendez-vous m; m. **place** (lieu m de) rendez-vous (**b**) (for business, discussion) réunion f; (of shareholders) assemblée f; **to be in a m.** être en réunion; **to hold a m.** se réunir

megabyte ['megəbaɪt] n Comptr mégaoctet m

megahertz ['megəhɜːts] (pl megahertz) n Elec mégahertz m

megalomania [megələʊ'meɪnɪə] n mégalomanie f

megalomaniac [megələʊ'meɪnɪæk] n mégalomane mf
megaphone ['megəfəʊn] n mégaphone m, porte-voix m
inv
megaton ['megətʌn] n mégatonne f
megawatt ['megəwɒt] n Elec mégawatt m
melancholy ['melənkəlɪ] **1** n mélancolie f
2 adj (person) mélancolique; (atmosphere, news) triste
melee ['meleɪ] n mêlée f
mellifluous [mə'lɪflʊəs] adj mélodieux(euse)
mellow ['meləʊ] **1** adj (flavour) suave; (voice, colour)
chaud(e); (wine) moelleux(euse); (light) doux (douce);
(person) détendu(e), serein(e)
2 vi s'adoucir
melodic [mɪ'lɒdɪk] adj mélodique
melodious [mɪ'ləʊdɪəs] adj mélodieux(euse)
melodrama ['melədrɑːmə] n mélodrame m
melodramatic [melədrə'mætɪk] adj mélodramatique
melody ['melədɪ] (pl melodies) n mélodie f
melon ['melən] n melon m
melt [melt] **1** vt also Fig faire fondre
2 vi fondre; **to m.** into thin air s'évaporer, disparaître; **to
m.** into the crowd se fondre dans la foule
▸ **melt away** vi (of snow) fondre; (of clouds, vapour) se
dissiper; (of crowd) se disperser; (of objections, opposition)
s'évanouir
▸ **melt down** vt sep (metal) fondre
meltdown ['meltdaʊn] n Phys fusion f
melting ['meltɪŋ] n m. point point m de fusion; Fig m.
pot melting-pot m
member ['membə(r)] **1** n membre m; Br Pol **M.** of
Parliament député m
2 adj m. country/state pays m/État m membre
membership ['membəʃɪp] n (a) (state) adhésion f; m.
card carte f de membre ou d'adhérent; m. fee cotisation f
(b) (members) membres mpl, adhérents mpl; a large/small
m. une forte/faible adhésion
membrane ['membreɪn] n membrane f
memento [mɪ'mentəʊ] (pl mementos or mementoes) n
souvenir m
memo ['meməʊ] (pl memos) n note f de service; m. pad
bloc-notes m
memoir ['memwɑː(r)] n (essay) mémoire m; (biography)
biographie f; memoirs (autobiography) mémoires
memorable ['memərəbəl] adj mémorable
memorandum [memə'rændəm] (pl memoranda
[memə'rændə] or memorandums) n note f de service
memorial [mɪ'mɔːrɪəl] **1** n (monument) mémorial m
2 adj commémoratif(ive)
memorize ['meməraɪz] vt mémoriser
memory ['memərɪ] (pl memories) n (a) (faculty) &
Comptr mémoire f; to have a good/bad m. avoir (une)
bonne/mauvaise mémoire; if my m. serves me right si ma
mémoire est bonne; from m. de mémoire; to lose one's m.
perdre la mémoire; to commit sth to m. apprendre qch
par cœur; within living m. de mémoire d'homme (b) (thing
remembered) souvenir m; in m. of... en souvenir de…, à la
mémoire de…; to take a trip down m. lane se remémorer
le passé
men [men] pl of **man**
menace ['menɪs] **1** n (threat) menace f; (danger) danger
m; Fam Fig (pest) plaie f
2 vt menacer
menacing ['menəsɪŋ] adj menaçant(e)
menagerie [mɪ'nædʒərɪ] n ménagerie f

mend [mend] **1** vt (repair) réparer; (clothing) raccommoder; **to m.** one's ways s'amender
2 vi (of broken bone) se ressouder
3 n Fam to be on the m. aller mieux
menfolk ['menfəʊk] npl the m. les hommes mpl
menial ['miːnɪəl] **1** n Pej laquais m
2 adj (job) subalterne
meningitis [menɪn'dʒaɪtɪs] n méningite f; to have m.
avoir la méningite
menopause ['menəpɔːz] n ménopause f
menstrual ['menstrʊəl] adj menstruel(elle)
menstruate ['menstrʊeɪt] vi avoir ses règles
menstruation [menstrʊ'eɪʃən] n menstruation f
menswear ['menzweə(r)] n vêtements mpl pour
hommes
mental ['mentəl] adj (a) (state, age) mental(e); to make a
m. note of sth/to do sth essayer de se souvenir de qch/de
faire qch; m. arithmetic calcul m mental; m. breakdown
dépression f (nerveuse); m. health santé f mentale; m.
hospital hôpital m psychiatrique; m. illness maladie f
mentale (b) very Fam (mad) malade, dingue; to go m. (lose
one's temper) devenir dingue
mentality [men'tælɪtɪ] (pl mentalities) n mentalité f
mentally ['mentəlɪ] adv mentalement; to be m.
handicapped être handicapé(e) mental(e); to be m. ill
avoir une maladie mentale
menthol ['menθɒl] n menthol m; m. cigarettes
cigarettes fpl mentholées
mention ['menʃən] **1** n mention f; he gets a brief m. in
her autobiography elle le mentionne brièvement dans
son autobiographie; to make no m. of sth ne pas faire
référence à qch
2 vt parler de; (allude to) mentionner; to m. that... dire
que…; to m. sb in one's will coucher qn sur son testament;
to be mentioned in dispatches être cité(e) à l'ordre du
jour; not to m.... sans parler de…; now (that) you m. it
maintenant que tu le dis; don't m. it! il n'y a pas de quoi!
menu ['menjuː] n (a) (in restaurant) (set) menu m; (à la
carte) carte f (b) Comptr menu m
MEP [emiː'piː] n Pol (abbr Member of the European
Parliament) député m au Parlement européen
mercantile ['mɜːkəntaɪl] adj commercial(e)
mercenary ['mɜːsɪnərɪ] **1** n (pl mercenaries) mercenaire m
2 adj Pej intéressé(e)
merchandise ['mɜːtʃəndaɪz] **1** n marchandises fpl
2 n vt marchander
merchandising ['mɜːtʃəndaɪzɪŋ] n merchandising m,
marchandisage m
merchant ['mɜːtʃənt] n (retail) marchand(e) m,f;
(wholesale) négociant(e) m,f; m. bank banque f d'affaires;
m. navy marine f marchande; m. seaman marin m de la
marine marchande; m. ship navire m marchand
merchantman ['mɜːtʃəntmən] n (ship) navire m marchand
merciful ['mɜːsɪfʊl] adj (person) clément(e); (act)
charitable
mercifully ['mɜːsɪfʊlɪ] adv (a) (showing mercy) avec
clémence (b) (fortunately) heureusement
merciless ['mɜːsɪlɪs] adj sans pitié, impitoyable
mercurial [mɜː'kjʊərɪəl] adj (lively) vif (vive);
(changeable) changeant(e), lunatique
Mercury ['mɜːkjʊrɪ] n (planet) Mercure f
mercury ['mɜːkjʊrɪ] n (metal) mercure m

mercy ['mɜːsɪ] (*pl* **mercies**) *n* (**a**) *(clemency)* pitié *f*, clémence *f*; **to have m. on sb** avoir pitié de qn; **to beg for m.** demander grâce; **at the m. of** à la merci de; **m. killing** acte *m* d'euthanasie (**b**) *(blessing)* bonheur *m*, chance *f*; **it's a m. that...** c'est une chance que...; **to be thankful** *or* **grateful for small mercies** apprécier ce dont on dispose

mere [mɪə(r)] *adj* simple; **he's a m. child** ce n'est qu'un enfant

merely ['mɪəlɪ] *adv* simplement, seulement

merge [mɜːdʒ] **1** *vt (of companies)* & *Comptr* fusionner **2** *vi (of colours, sounds)* se fondre, se confondre; *(of companies)* fusionner; **to m. into the background** se fondre dans le décor

merger ['mɜːdʒə(r)] *n* fusion *f*

meridian [mə'rɪdɪən] *n* méridien *m*

meringue [mə'ræŋ] *n* meringue *f*

merit ['merɪt] **1** *n (advantage, worth)* mérite *m*; **of little/ great m.** de peu de/grande valeur; **to judge sth on its merits** juger qch pour ce qu'il vaut; **in order of m.** par ordre de mérite **2** *vt* mériter

meritocracy [merɪ'tɒkrəsɪ] *(pl* **meritocracies**) *n* méritocratie *f*

meritorious [merɪ'tɔːrɪəs] *adj Formal* méritoire, louable

mermaid ['mɜːmeɪd] *n* sirène *f*

merrily ['merɪlɪ] *adv* joyeusement, gaiement

merriment ['merɪmənt] *n* gaieté *f*

merry ['merɪ] *adj* (**a**) *(happy)* joyeux(euse), gai(e); **to make m.** s'amuser; **M. Christmas!** Joyeux Noël!; **the more the merrier** plus on est de fous, plus on rit (**b**) *(slightly drunk)* gai(e)

merry-go-round ['merɪɡəʊraʊnd] *n* manège *m*

mesh [meʃ] **1** *n (of net, sieve)* mailles *fpl* **2** *vi (of gears)* s'engrener

mesmerize ['mezməraɪz] *vt* hypnotiser

mess [mes] **1** *n* (**a**) *(disorder)* désordre *m*; **you look a m.!** tu es dans un triste état!; **to be (in) a m.** *(of room)* être en désordre; *Fig (of person)* être dans le pétrin; *(of one's life)* être un désastre; *Fig* **to make a m. of sth** *(essay, job)* saloper qch; **he's a m.** il est dans un triste état (**b**) *(dirt)* saletés *fpl*; **to make a m. of sth** salir qch; **the dog's done a m. on the carpet** le chien a fait ses besoins sur le tapis (**c**) *Mil (for officers)* mess *m*; *(for soldiers)* réfectoire *m*; **m. tin** gamelle *f* **2** *vi Fam (of dog, cat)* faire ses besoins

▸ **mess about**, **mess around 1** *vt sep (treat badly)* se moquer de **2** *vi* (**a**) *(fool about)* faire l'imbécile; *(waste time)* traîner (**b**) *(tinker)* **to m. about** *or* **around with sth** tripoter qch

▸ **mess up** *vt sep (hair, room, papers)* mettre en désordre; *(plans)* ficher en l'air

message ['mesɪdʒ] *n* message *m*; **to leave a m. for sb** laisser un message pour qn; **to get one's m. across** se faire comprendre; *Fam Fig* **to get the m.** piger

messenger ['mesɪndʒə(r)] *n* messager(ère) *m,f*; **m. boy** garçon *m* de courses, coursier *m*

Messiah [mɪ'saɪə] *n Rel* Messie *m*

messianic [mesɪ'ænɪk] *adj* messianique

messily ['mesɪlɪ] *adv* salement; *Fig* **to end m.** *(of relationship)* mal terminer

Messrs ['mesəz] *(abbr* **Messieurs**) MM

messy ['mesɪ] *adj* (**a**) *(dirty)* sale; *(job)* salissant(e); **to be a m. eater** manger salement (**b**) *(untidy) (room, hair)* en désordre; *(handwriting)* peu soigné(e); *(appearance)* négligé(e) (**c**) *(unpleasantly complex) (affair, situation)* embrouillé(e); *(private life)* troublé(e)

met [met] *pt & pp of* **meet**

metabolic [metə'bɒlɪk] *adj* métabolique

metabolism [mɪ'tæbəlɪzəm] *n* métabolisme *m*

metal ['metəl] **1** *n* métal *m*; **m. detector** détecteur *m* de métaux **2** *adj* en métal

metalled road, *Am* **metaled road** ['metəld'rəʊd] *n* route *f* empierrée

metallic [mɪ'tælɪk] *adj (sound, voice)* métallique; *(paint)* métallisé(e); *(taste)* de métal

metallurgy [me'tælədʒɪ] *n* métallurgie *f*

metalwork ['metəlwɜːk] *n* ferronnerie *f*

metamorphosis [metə'mɔːfəsɪs] *(pl* **metamorphoses** [metə'mɔːfəsiːz]) *n* métamorphose *f*

metaphor ['metəfə(r)] *n* métaphore *f*

metaphoric(al) [metə'fɒrɪk(əl)] *adj* métaphorique

metaphysical [metə'fɪzɪkəl] *adj* métaphysique

metaphysics [metə'fɪzɪks] *n* métaphysique *f*

▸ **mete out** [miːt] *vt sep (punishment)* infliger (**to** à); *(justice)* rendre

meteor ['miːtɪə(r)] *n* météore *m*

meteoric [miːtɪ'ɒrɪk] *adj* météorique; *Fig* **a m. rise** une ascension fulgurante

meteorite ['miːtɪəraɪt] *n* météorite *f*

meteorological [miːtɪərə'lɒdʒɪkəl] *adj* météorologique

meteorology [miːtɪə'rɒlədʒɪ] *n* météorologie *f*

meter¹ ['miːtə(r)] *n* compteur *m*; **to read the m.** relever le compteur; **(parking) m.** parcmètre *m*

meter² *Am* = **metre**

methane ['miːθeɪn] *n* méthane *m*

method ['meθəd] *n* méthode *f*; **there's m. in his madness** il n'est pas aussi fou qu'il en a l'air; **m. acting** méthode de Stanislavski

methodical [mɪ'θɒdɪkəl] *adj* méthodique

Methodism ['meθədɪzəm] *n Rel* méthodisme *m*

Methodist ['meθədɪst] *n Rel* méthodiste *mf*

methodology [meθə'dɒlədʒɪ] *n* méthodologie *f*

meths [meθs] *n Br Fam (methylated spirits)* alcool *m* à brûler

methylated spirits ['meθɪleɪtɪd'spɪrɪts] *n Br* alcool *m* à brûler

meticulous [mɪ'tɪkjʊləs] *adj* méticuleux(euse)

metre¹, *Am* **meter** ['miːtə(r)] *n (measurement)* mètre *m*

metre², *Am* **meter** *n (of poetry)* mètre *m*

metric ['metrɪk] *adj* métrique

metronome ['metrənəʊm] *n* métronome *m*

metropolis [mɪ'trɒpəlɪs] *n* métropole *f*

metropolitan [metrə'pɒlɪtən] *adj* urbain(e); **M. France** la France métropolitaine; **the M. Police** la police de Londres

mettle ['metəl] *n (courage)* courage *m*; **to be on one's m.** être fin prêt(e); **to show one's m.** montrer de quoi on est capable

mew [mjuː] **1** *n* miaulement *m* **2** *vi* miauler

mews [mjuːz] *(pl* **mews**) *n Br* ruelle *f*

Mexican ['meksɪkən] **1** *n* Mexicain(e) *m,f* **2** *adj* mexicain(e); **M. wave** *(at match)* vague *f*

Mexico ['meksɪkəʊ] *n* le Mexique; **M. City** Mexico

mezzanine ['metsəniːn] *n* **m. (floor)** mezzanine *f*

mg [em'dʒiː] *n (abbr* **milligram(s)**) mg

Mgr *(abbr* **Monsignor**) Mgr

MHz (*abbr* megahertz) MHz

mi [miː] *n Mus* mi *m*

MI5 [emaɪˈfaɪv] *n Br* (*abbr* **Military Intelligence Section 5**) ≃ DST *f*

MI6 [emaɪˈsɪks] *n Br* (*abbr* **Military Intelligence Section 6**) ≃ DGSE *f*

miaow [mɪˈaʊ] **1** *n* miaulement *m*; **m.!** miaou! **2** *vi* miauler

mica [ˈmaɪkə] *n* mica *m*

mice [maɪs] *pl of* **mouse**

Michelangelo [ˈmaɪkəlˈændʒələʊ] *n* Michel-Ange

mickey [ˈmɪkɪ] *n Br Fam* **to take the m.** (out of sb) se moquer (de qn)

Mickey Mouse [ˈmɪkɪˈmaʊs] *adj Fam Pej* (*job, qualification*) à la noix

micro [ˈmaɪkrəʊ] (*pl* **micros**) *n* micro *m*

microbe [ˈmaɪkrəʊb] *n* microbe *m*

microbiology [maɪkrəʊbaɪˈɒlədʒɪ] *n* microbiologie *f*

microchip [ˈmaɪkrəʊtʃɪp] *n* microprocesseur *m*

microcomputer [ˈmaɪkrəʊkəmˈpjuːtə(r)] *n* micro-ordinateur *m*

microcosm [ˈmaɪkrəʊkɒzəm] *n* microcosme *m*

microfiche [ˈmaɪkrəʊfiːʃ] *n* microfiche *f*

microfilm [ˈmaɪkrəʊfɪlm] **1** *n* microfilm *m* **2** *vt* microfilmer

micrometer [maɪˈkrɒmɪtə(r)] *n* micromètre *m*

microphone [ˈmaɪkrəfəʊn] *n* microphone *m*

microprocessor [ˈmaɪkrəʊˈprəʊsesə(r)] *n* microprocesseur *m*

microscope [ˈmaɪkrəskəʊp] *n* microscope *m*

microscopic [maɪkrəˈskɒpɪk] *adj* microscopique

microsurgery [maɪkrəʊˈsɜːdʒərɪ] *n* microchirurgie *f*

microwave [ˈmaɪkrəʊweɪv] **1** *n Phys* micro-onde *f*; **m.** (oven) (four *m* à) micro-ondes *m inv* **2** *vt* faire cuire au micro-ondes

mid [mɪd] *adj* **in m. ocean** au milieu de l'océan; **m. June** mi-juin; **he stopped in m. sentence** il s'est arrêté au milieu d'une phrase

midair [mɪdˈeə(r)] **1** *n* **in m.** en plein ciel **2** *adj* (*collision*) en plein ciel

mid-Atlantic accent [mɪdətˈlæntɪkˈæksent] *n* accent *m* mi-américain mi-britannique

midday [ˈmɪdˈdeɪ] *n* midi *m*; **m. meal** déjeuner *m*

middle [ˈmɪdəl] **1** *n* (a) (*centre*) milieu *m*; **to be in the m. of doing sth** être en train de faire qch; **in the m. of the night** en pleine nuit; **in the m. of nowhere** dans un coin perdu; *Fig* **to split sth down the m.** partager qch en deux (**b**) (*waist*) taille *f* **2** *adj* du milieu; **m. age** l'âge *m* mûr; *Hist* **the M. Ages** le Moyen Âge; *Mus* **C do** *m* du milieu du clavier; **the m. class** la classe moyenne; *Fig* **to steer a m. course** adopter une solution intermédiaire; **in the m. distance** au second plan; **the M. East** le Moyen-Orient; **M. Eastern** du Moyen-Orient; *Pol* **the m. ground** le centre; **m. management** cadres *mpl* moyens; **m. name** deuxième prénom *m*; *Fam* **"generosity" isn't exactly his m. name!** on ne peut pas dire qu'il soit particulièrement généreux!

middle-aged [mɪdəlˈeɪdʒd] *adj* d'âge mûr

middlebrow [ˈmɪdəlbraʊ] *adj* moyen(enne); **a m.** novelist un romancier sans prétentions

middle-class [mɪdəlˈklɑːs] *adj* bourgeois(e)

middleman [ˈmɪdəlmæn] *n* intermédiaire *mf*

middle-of-the-road [ˈmɪdləvðəˈrəʊd] *adj* (*policy*) modéré(e); (*music*) grand public *inv*

middle-sized [ˈmɪdəlˈsaɪzd] *adj* de taille moyenne

middleweight [ˈmɪdəlweɪt] *n* (*in boxing*) poids *m* moyen

middling [ˈmɪdlɪŋ] *adj* (*fairly good*) moyen(enne); (*mediocre*) médiocre

midfield [mɪdˈfiːld] *n* (*in football*) milieu *m* de terrain; **m. player** milieu de terrain

midfielder [mɪdˈfiːldə(r)] *n* (*in football*) milieu *m* de terrain

midge [mɪdʒ] *n* moucheron *m*

midget [ˈmɪdʒɪt] **1** *n* (*small person*) nain(e) *m,f* **2** *adj* (*miniature*) miniature

midi system [ˈmɪdɪsɪstəm] *n* (*stereo*) chaîne *f* midi

midlife crisis [ˈmɪdlaɪfˈkraɪsɪs] *n* crise *f* aux alentours de la cinquantaine

midmorning [mɪdˈmɔːnɪŋ] *n* milieu *m* de matinée

midnight [ˈmɪdnaɪt] *n* minuit *m*; **to burn the m. oil** travailler tard dans la nuit; *Am Hist* **the m. ride** = épisode héroïque de la guerre d'Indépendance américaine

midriff [ˈmɪdrɪf] *n* ventre *m*

midshipman [ˈmɪdʃɪpmən] *n* aspirant *m* de marine

midst [mɪdst] *n* milieu *m*, cœur *m*; **in the m. of** au milieu de; **in our/their m.** parmi nous/eux

midstream [mɪdˈstriːm] *n* **in m.** au milieu du courant; *Fig* (*when speaking*) en plein milieu d'une phrase

midsummer [ˈmɪdsʌmə(r)] *n* milieu *m* de l'été; **M.'s Day** la Saint-Jean

midterm [ˈmɪdtɜːm] *n* (a) *Pol Br* **m. by-election** = élection législative en milieu de mandat; *Am* **m. elections** = élections qui ont lieu au milieu du mandat présidentiel (**b**) *Sch & Univ* milieu *m* du trimestre; **m. break** vacances *fpl* de milieu de trimestre

midtown [ˈmɪdtaʊn] *n Am* = partie d'une ville située à mi-chemin entre le centre et les quartiers périphériques

midway [ˈmɪdweɪ] **1** *adj* **at the m. point** (*in space*) à la mi-chemin; (*in time*) à la moitié **2** *adv* à mi-chemin

midweek [mɪdˈwiːk] *adv* en milieu de semaine

Mid-West [mɪdˈwest] *n* Midwest *m*

Mid-Western [mɪdˈwestən] *adj* du Midwest

midwife [ˈmɪdwaɪf] (*pl* **midwives** [mɪdwaɪvz]) *n* sage-femme *f*

midwifery [mɪdˈwɪfərɪ] *n* profession *f* de sage-femme

midwinter [mɪdˈwɪntə(r)] *n* milieu *m* de l'hiver

might[1] [maɪt] *n* (*strength*) force *f*; **with all one's m.** de toutes ses forces; *Prov* **m. is right** la raison du plus fort est toujours la meilleure

might[2] *v aux*

La forme négative **mightn't** s'écrit **might not** dans un style plus soutenu. **Might** et **may** peuvent s'utiliser indifféremment ou presque dans les expressions de la catégorie (**a**).

(**a**) (*expressing possibility*) **it m. be difficult** il se peut ou se pourrait que ce soit difficile; **it m. be better to phone first** il vaudrait peut-être mieux téléphoner d'abord; **I m. be that...** il se peut ou se pourrait que... + *subjunctive*; **you m. want to...** tu pourrais peut-être...; **we m. as well go home** autant rentrer; **you m. as well stay here** autant que vous restiez ici; **I m. as well be talking to myself!** autant parler à un mur!

(**b**) (*as past form of* **may**) **I knew he m. be angry** je me doutais qu'il pourrait se fâcher; **he said he m. be late** il a dit qu'il se pourrait qu'il soit en retard

(**c**) *Formal* (*asking for permission*) **m. I have a word with you?** pourrais-je vous parler un instant?

(d) *(with concessions)* it might not be the fastest car in the world, but... ce n'est peut-être pas la voiture la plus rapide du monde, mais...

mightily ['maɪtɪlɪ] *adv* **(a)** *(powerfully)* avec force, vigoureusement **(b)** *Am Fam (for emphasis)* drôlement

mightn't ['maɪtənt] = might not

might've ['maɪtəv] = might have

mighty ['maɪtɪ] **1** *adj* **(a)** *(powerful) (nation, army)* puissant(e); *(blow)* grand(e) **(b)** *(large, imposing)* majestueux(euse) **2** *adv Am Fam (for emphasis)* drôlement

migraine ['miːgreɪn] *n* migraine *f*; **to have a m.** avoir la migraine

migrant ['maɪgrənt] **1** *n (person)* migrant(e) *m,f*; *(bird)* (oiseau *m*) migrateur *m* **2** *adj (bird)* migrateur(trice); **m. worker** travailleur *m* immigré

migrate [maɪ'greɪt] *vi (of bird)* migrer; *(of person)* émigrer

migration [maɪ'greɪʃən] *n (of birds)* migration *f*; *(of people)* émigration *f*

migratory ['maɪgrətrɪ] *adj* migratoire; *(bird)* migrateur(trice)

mike [maɪk] *n Fam (microphone)* micro *m*

mild [maɪld] *adj (person, climate, soap, cheese)* doux (douce); *(curry)* peu épicé(e); *(punishment, annoyance, amusement, criticism)* léger(ère); *(illness)* bénin(igne)

mildew ['mɪldjuː] *n* moisissure *f*

mildly ['maɪldlɪ] *adv* **(a)** *(say)* doucement, ... **to put it m.** ... pour ne pas dire plus **(b)** *(moderately)* légèrement

mildness ['maɪldnɪs] *n (of person, weather, punishment)* douceur *f*; *(of criticism)* modération *f*

mile [maɪl] *n (distance)* = 1609 m, mille *m*; **à 200-m. journey** ≃ un voyage de 320 km; **to see for miles** voir à des kilomètres; **it's miles from anywhere** c'est loin de tout; **miles per hour** ≃ kilomètres à l'heure; **he lives miles away** il habite très loin d'ici; *Fam Fig* **to be miles away** être dans la lune; *Fam* **miles better** cent fois mieux; *Fam* **it sticks out** *or* **stands out a m.** ça crève les yeux

mileage ['maɪlɪdʒ] *n* **(a)** *(distance travelled)* ≃ kilométrage *m*, **m. allowance** ≃ indemnité *f* kilométrique **(b)** *(rate of fuel consumption)* consommation *f*; *Fig* **to get a lot of m. out of sth** tirer le maximum de qch

milestone ['maɪlstəʊn] *n (on road)* ≃ borne *f* kilométrique; *Fig (in career, history)* étape *f* importante

milieu ['miːljɜː] *n* milieu *m*

militant ['mɪlɪtənt] *adj & n* militant(e) *m,f*

militarism ['mɪlɪtərɪzəm] *n* militarisme *m*

military ['mɪlɪtərɪ] **1** *adj* militaire; **m. academy** école *f* militaire; **m. man** militaire *m*; **m. police** police *f* militaire; **m. service** service *m* militaire **2** *npl* **the m.** les militaires *mpl*, l'armée *f*

militate ['mɪlɪteɪt] *vi* **to m. against sth** compromettre qch

militia [mɪ'lɪʃə] *n* milice *f*

milk [mɪlk] **1** *n* lait *m*; **m. of magnesia** lait *m* de magnésie; **m. bottle** bouteille *f* de lait; **m. chocolate** chocolat *m* au lait; **m. churn** bidon *m* à lait; **m. jug** pot *m* à lait; **m. round** tournée *f* du laitier; **m. shake** milk-shake *m*; **m. tooth** dent *f* de lait; *Am* **m. truck** camionnette *f* de laitier **2** *vt (cow)* traire; *Fam Fig* **to m. sb dry** dépouiller qn; *Fig* **they milked the story for all it was worth** ils ont tiré tout ce qu'ils ont pu de l'histoire

milking ['mɪlkɪŋ] *n* traite *f*; **m. machine** trayeuse *f*

milkman ['mɪlkmən] *n* = homme qui livre le lait à domicile

milky ['mɪlkɪ] *adj (drink)* avec du lait; *(taste)* de lait; *(colour)* laiteux(euse); **the M. Way** la Voie lactée

mill [mɪl] **1** *n* **(a)** *(grinder)* moulin *m*; *Fam* **to put sb through the m.** en faire baver à qn **(b)** *(textile factory)* filature *f* **2** *vt (grain)* moudre ► **mill about, mill around** *vi (of crowd)* grouiller; *(of thoughts, ideas)* se bousculer

millennium [mɪ'lenɪəm] *n* millénaire *m*

miller ['mɪlə(r)] *n* meunier(ère) *m,f*

millet ['mɪlɪt] *n* millet *m*

milligram(me) ['mɪlɪgræm] *n* milligramme *m*

millilitre, *Am* **milliliter** ['mɪlɪliːtə(r)] *n* millilitre *m*

millimetre, *Am* **millimeter** ['mɪlɪmiːtə(r)] *n* millimètre *m*

milliner ['mɪlɪnə(r)] *n* modiste *mf*

million ['mɪljən] *n* million *m*; **two m. dollars** deux millions de dollars; *Fam* **I've told him a m. times** je le lui ai dit mille fois; *Fam* **thanks a m.!** merci mille fois!; *Fam* **she's one in a m.** elle est unique

millionaire [mɪljə'neə(r)] *n* millionnaire *m*

millionairess [mɪljə'neərɪs] *n* millionnaire *f*

millionth ['mɪljənθ] **1** *n* **(a)** *(fraction)* millionième *m* **(b)** *(in series)* millionième *mf* **2** *adj* millionième; *see also* **eighth**

millipede ['mɪlɪpiːd] *n* mille-pattes *m inv*

millpond ['mɪlpɒnd] *n* **as calm as a m.** *(of sea)* d'huile

millstone ['mɪlstəʊn] *n* meule *f*; *Fig* **it's a m. round my neck** c'est un boulet que je traîne

milometer [maɪ'lɒmɪtə(r)] *n (in car)* ≃ compteur *m* (kilométrique)

mime [maɪm] **1** *n* mime *mf* **2** *vt* mimer **3** *vi* mimer; *(of singer)* chanter en play-back

mimic ['mɪmɪk] **1** *n* imitateur(trice) *m,f* **2** *vt (pt & pp* **mimicked***)* imiter

mimicry ['mɪmɪkrɪ] *n* imitation *f*

Min *Mus (abbr* **Minor***)*

min **(a)** *(abbr* **minute(s)***)* min **(b)** *(abbr* **minimum***)* min

minaret [mɪnə'ret] *n* minaret *m*

mince [mɪns] **1** *n Br* viande *f* hachée; **m. pie** *(containing meat)* tourte *f* à la viande hachée; *(containing fruit)* = tartelette fourrée aux fruits secs et aux épices **2** *vt (chop up)* hacher; *Fig* **she doesn't m. her words** elle ne mâche pas ses mots **3** *vi (walk)* marcher à petits pas

mincemeat ['mɪnsmiːt] *n* = mélange de fruits secs et d'épices utilisé en pâtisserie; *Fam Fig* **to make m. of sb** faire de la chair à pâté de qn

mincer ['mɪnsə(r)] *n* hachoir *m*

mincing ['mɪnsɪŋ] *adj (walk, voice)* affecté(e)

mind [maɪnd] **1** *n* **(a)** *(thoughts)* esprit *m*; in one's m.'s eye en imagination; **to put** *or* **set sb's m. at rest** rassurer qn; **to bear** *or* **keep sth in m.** garder qch à l'esprit *ou* en tête; **it went completely** *or* **clean out of my m.** ça m'est complètement sorti de l'esprit *ou* de la tête; **to have sth on one's m.** être préoccupé(e) par qch; **to take sb's m. off sth** distraire qn de qch; **I couldn't get it off my m.** je ne pouvais pas m'empêcher d'y penser; **it puts me in m. of sb/sth** ça me rappelle qn/qch **(b)** *(opinion)* **to my m.** à mon avis; **to speak one's m.** dire ce qu'on pense; **to change one's m.** changer d'avis *(about sth)*; *Fam* **to give sb a piece of one's m.** dire à qn sa façon de penser; **to be of one m.,** **to be of the same m.** être du même avis

(c) *(will)* to know one's own m. savoir ce qu'on veut; **to have a** m. of one's own savoir penser par soi-même; **to make up one's** m. se décider; **to be in two minds (about sth/about doing sth)** hésiter (sur qch/à faire qch); **to have a good** m./half a m. avoir bien envie/presque envie de faire qch; **this shopping trolley has a** m. of its own ce caddie n'en fait qu'à sa tête; **to have sb in** m. avoir qn en vue; **to have sth in** m. avoir qch en tête **(d)** *(attention)* to keep one's m. on sth se concentrer sur qch; **my** m. isn't on the job je n'ai pas la tête à ce que je fais; **if you put your** m. to it you could do it si tu t'y mettais, tu pourrais le faire **(e)** *(reason)* raison *f*; her m. is going elle perd la raison; *Fam* to be out of one's m. avoir perdu la tête; **to be bored out of one's** m. s'ennuyer à mourir; **to be out of one's** m. **with worry** être fou (folle) d'inquiétude; **no one in his right** m. would do that aucune personne saine d'esprit ne ferait ça **(f)** *(person)* esprit *m*; *Prov* great minds think alike les grands esprits se rencontrent

2 *vt*(**a**) *(pay attention to)* faire attention à; m. you don't fall fais attention à ne pas tomber; m. you're not late! fais en sorte de ne pas être en retard!; **m. the step!** attention à la marche!; **to** m. one's language/manners surveiller son langage/ses manières **(b)** *(concern oneself with)* never m. the car/money ne t'inquiète pas pour la voiture/l'argent; **m. you,...** remarque,... **(c)** *(object to)* what I m. is... ce qui me gêne, c'est...; I don't m. the cold le froid ne me gêne pas; I don't m. trying je veux bien essayer; **if you don't** m. my asking,... si je peux me permettre,...; **would you** m. not doing that? pourrais-tu arrêter ça?; **I wouldn't** m. a cup of tea je prendrais bien une tasse de thé **(d)** *(look after)* s'occuper de, garder

3 *vi*(**a**) *(object)* I don't m. ça m'est égal; **do you** m.! dites donc!; **do you** m. if I smoke? ça vous dérange si je fume?; **I don't** m. if I do! *(accepting offer)* ce n'est pas de refus! **(b)** *(concern oneself)* never m.! ça ne fait rien!; **never** m. about that now ne t'inquiète pas de ça maintenant; *Fam* never you m.! occupe-toi de tes oignons!

mind-blowing ['maɪndbləʊɪŋ], **mind-boggling** ['maɪndbɒglɪŋ] *adj Fam* époustouflant(e)

minded ['maɪndɪd] *adj* to be m. to do sth vouloir faire qch; to be mechanically m. avoir le sens de la mécanique; to be scientifically m. avoir l'esprit scientifique

minder ['maɪndə(r)] *n Fam (bodyguard)* gorille *m*

mindful ['maɪndfʊl] *adj* to be m. of sth être soucieux(euse) de qch

mindless ['maɪndlɪs] *adj (destruction, violence)* gratuit(e); *(task, job)* abrutissant(e)

mind-reader ['maɪndriːdə(r)] *n Fam Hum* I'm not a m.! je ne suis pas devin!

mine¹ [maɪn] **1** *n* (**a**) *(for coal, tin, diamonds)* mine *f*; *Fig* a m. of information une mine d'informations; m. shaft puits *m* de mine (**b**) *(bomb)* (land) m. mine *f*; m. detector détecteur *m* de mines

2 *vt* (**a**) *(coal, gold)* extraire; *(seam)* exploiter (**b**) *(place mines in)* miner

3 *vi* to m. for coal/gold extraire du charbon/de l'or

mine² *possessive pron* (**a**) *(singular)* le mien (la mienne) *m,f*; *(plural)* les miens (les miennes) *mpl, fpl*; her car is big but m. is bigger elle a une grande voiture, mais la mienne est plus grande encore (**b**) *(used attributively)* this book is m. ce livre est à moi; a friend of m. un de mes amis; where's that brother of m.? où mon frère a-t-il bien pu passer?

minefield ['maɪnfiːld] *n* champ *m* de mines; *Fig* terrain *m* miné

miner ['maɪnə(r)] *n* mineur *m*

mineral ['mɪnərəl] *n* minéral *m*; *(extracted)* minerai *m*; m. water eau *m* minérale

minesweeper ['maɪnswiːpə(r)] *n* dragueur *m* de mines

mingle ['mɪŋgəl] **1** *vt* mélanger, mêler

2 *vi (of things)* se mélanger, se mêler; *(of person)* parler un peu à tout le monde; **to** m. with the crowd se mêler à la foule

mini ['mɪnɪ] *n (miniskirt)* minijupe *f*

miniature ['mɪnɪtʃə(r)] **1** *n* miniature *f*

2 *adj* miniature

miniaturize ['mɪnɪtʃəraɪz] *vt* miniaturiser

minibus ['mɪnɪbʌs] *n* minibus *m*

minicab ['mɪnɪkæb] *n* radio-taxi *m*

minim ['mɪnɪm] *n Mus* blanche *f*

minimal ['mɪnɪməl] *adj* minime

minimize ['mɪnɪmaɪz] *vt (importance)* minimiser; *(noise, risk)* réduire au minimum

minimum ['mɪnɪməm] **1** *n* minimum *m*; **to keep sth to a** m. réduire qch au minimum

2 *adj* minimum *inv*, minimal(e); m. wage salaire *m* minimum

mining ['maɪnɪŋ] *n* exploitation *f* minière; m. engineer ingénieur *m* des mines; m. industry industrie *f* minière

minion ['mɪnjən] *n* esclave *mf*

miniskirt ['mɪnɪskɜːt] *n* minijupe *f*

minister ['mɪnɪstə(r)] **1** *n* (**a**) *Pol* ministre *m*; *Br* M. of Defence/Health ministre de la Défense/de la Santé (**b**) *Rel* pasteur *m*

2 *vi* to m. to sb s'occuper de qn; **to** m. to sb's needs pourvoir aux besoins de qn

ministerial [mɪnɪ'stɪərɪəl] *adj Pol* ministériel(elle)

ministry ['mɪnɪstrɪ] *(pl* ministries) *n* (**a**) *Pol* ministère *m*; *Br* the M. of Defence le ministère de la Défense (**b**) *Rel* the m. le sacerdoce

mink [mɪŋk] *n* vison *m*; m. (coat) (manteau *m* de) vison

minnow ['mɪnəʊ] *n (fish)* vairon *m*; *Fig* second couteau *m*

minor ['maɪnə(r)] **1** *adj* (**a**) *(unimportant)* mineur(e); *(operation)* bénin(igne); *(road)* secondaire (**b**) *Mus* mineur(e)

2 *n Law* mineur(e) *m,f*

Minorca [mɪ'nɔːkə] *n* Minorque *f*

Minorcan [mɪ'nɔːkən] **1** *n* Minorquin(e) *m,f*

2 *adj* minorquin(e)

minority [maɪ'nɒrɪtɪ] *(pl* minorities) *n* minorité *f*; to be in a *or* the m. être en minorité; m. party/government parti *m*/gouvernement *m* minoritaire

minstrel ['mɪnstrəl] *n* ménestrel *m*

mint¹ [mɪnt] *n (plant)* menthe *f*; *(sweet)* bonbon *m* à la menthe; m. sauce sauce *f* à la menthe; m. tea infusion *f* de menthe

mint² **1** *n* the (Royal) M. ≃ (l'hôtel *m* de) la Monnaie; *Fam* to make a m. gagner une fortune; **in** m. condition à l'état neuf

2 *vt (coins)* frapper

minuet [mɪnjʊ'et] *n Mus* menuet *m*

minus ['maɪnəs] **1** *n (sign)* moins *m*; *(negative aspect)* inconvénient *m*

2 *adj (quantity, number)* négatif(ive); B m. *(grade)* B moins; **on the** m. side quant aux inconvénients; m. sign signe *m* moins

3 *prep* moins; **ten** m. eight leaves two dix moins huit égale deux; **it's** m. 12 (degrees) il fait moins 12; **he managed to escape, but** m. his luggage il a réussi à s'enfuir, mais sans ses bagages

minuscule ['mɪnəskjuːl] *adj* minuscule

minute¹ ['mɪnɪt] **1** *n* (**a**) *(of time)* minute *f*; **ten minutes past/to three** trois heures dix/moins dix; **wait a m.!** attendez une minute!; **go downstairs this m.!** descends immédiatement!; **just a m.** une minute; **the m.** my back was turned dès que j'ai eu le dos tourné; **any m.** d'une minute à l'autre; **in a m.** dans une minute; **at the last m.** à la dernière minute; **m.** hand *(of watch)* grande aiguille *f*; **m.** steak steak *m* minute (**b**) *(note)* note *f*; **minutes** *(of meeting)* compte rendu *m*
2 *vt (make note of)* inscrire au procès verbal

minute² [maɪ'njuːt] *adj* (**a**) *(small)* infime, minuscule (**b**) *(detailed)* minutieux(euse)

minutely [maɪ'njuːtlɪ] *adv* minutieusement

mips [mɪps] *Comptr (abbr* million instructions per second) MIPS *m*

miracle ['mɪrəkəl] *n also Fig* miracle *m*; **to perform** *or* **work miracles** faire des miracles; **by a** *or* **some m.** par miracle; **m. worker** faiseur(euse) *m,f* de miracles

miraculous [mɪ'rækjʊləs] *adj also Fig* miraculeux(euse)

mirage [mɪ'rɑːʒ] *n* mirage *m*

Miranda rights [mɪ'rændaɔɪts] *npl Am Law* = droit accordé à tout prévenu d'être défendu par un avocat et de garder le silence

mire [maɪə(r)] *n (mud)* boue *f*; *Fig* bourbier *m*

mirror ['mɪrə(r)] **1** *n* miroir *m*, glace *f*; *Fig* **to hold a m. to sth** refléter qch; **m. image** *(reversed image)* image *f* inversée; *(exact copy)* copie *f* conforme
2 *vt also Fig* refléter

mirth [mɜːθ] *n* gaieté *f*, joie *f*

misadventure [mɪsəd'ventʃə(r)] *n* mésaventure *f*; *Law* **death by m.** mort *f* accidentelle

misanthropic [mɪsən'θrɒpɪk] *adj* misanthrope

misanthropist [mɪ'sænθrəpɪst] *n* misanthrope *mf*

misapprehension [mɪsæprɪ'henʃən] *n* malentendu *m*; **to be** *(Br* labouring *or Am* laboring) **under a m.** se méprendre

misappropriation ['mɪsəprəʊprɪ'eɪʃən] *n* détournement *m*

misbehave [mɪsbɪ'heɪv] *vi* se conduire mal

misbehaviour, *Am* **misbehavior** [mɪsbɪ'heɪvjə(r)] *n* mauvaise conduite *f*

misc *(abbr* miscellaneous) divers

miscalculate [mɪs'kælkjʊleɪt] **1** *vt* mal calculer; *Fig* mal évaluer
2 *vi* faire une erreur de calcul; *Fig* faire un mauvais calcul

miscalculation [mɪskælkjʊ'leɪʃən] *n* erreur *f* de calcul; *Fig* mauvais calcul *m*

miscarriage ['mɪskærɪdʒ] *n* (**a**) *Med* fausse couche *f*; **to have a m.** faire une fausse couche (**b**) *Law* **m. of justice** erreur *f* judiciaire

miscarry [mɪs'kærɪ] *(pt & pp* miscarried) *vi* (**a**) *(of woman)* faire une fausse couche (**b**) *Fig (of plan)* avorter

miscast [mɪs'kɑːst] *(pt & pp* miscast) *vt* **he was m. in the part** ce n'était pas un rôle qui lui convenait

miscellaneous [mɪsə'leɪnɪəs] *adj* divers(es)

miscellany [mɪ'selənɪ] *(pl* miscellanies) *n* mélange *m*

mischief ['mɪstʃɪf] *n* (**a**) *(naughtiness)* espièglerie *f*; **to get up to m.** faire des bêtises; *Hum* **to keep sb out of m.** occuper qn (**b**) *(trouble)* problèmes *mpl*; **to make m.** (**for sb**) créer des problèmes (à qn) (**c**) *Fam (injury)* **to do oneself a m.** se faire mal

mischievous ['mɪstʃɪvəs] *adj (naughty)* espiègle; *(malicious)* malveillant(e)

misconception [mɪskən'sepʃən] *n* idée *f* fausse

misconduct [mɪs'kɒndʌkt] *n* inconduite *f*

misconstrue [mɪskən'struː] *vt* mal interpréter

misdemeanour, *Am* **misdemeanor** [mɪsdɪ'miːnə(r)] *n Law* délit *m*

misdiagnose [mɪsdaɪəg'nəʊz] *vt* mal diagnostiquer

misdirect [mɪsdɪ'rekt] *vt* (**a**) *(person)* mal orienter (**b**) *(letter)* mal adresser

miser ['maɪzə(r)] *n* avare *mf*

miserable ['mɪzərəbəl] *adj* (**a**) *(unhappy)* malheureux(euse), triste; **to make sb's life m.** faire de la vie de qn un enfer (**b**) *(unpleasant)* déplorable; *(weather)* épouvantable (**c**) *(wretched)* misérable; **I only got a m. five dollars** je n'ai eu que cinq malheureux dollars

miserably ['mɪzərəblɪ] *adv* (**a**) *(unhappily)* tristement (**b**) *(wretchedly)* misérablement (**c**) *(very badly)* lamentablement

miserly ['maɪzəlɪ] *adj* avare

misery ['mɪzərɪ] *(pt* miseries) *n* (**a**) *(unhappiness)* détresse *f*; *(suffering)* malheur *m*; **to make sb's life a m.** faire de la vie de qn un enfer; **to put an animal out of its m.** achever un animal; *Hum* **to put sb out of his m.** *(tell secret)* mettre fin au supplice de qn (**b**) *Br Fam (person)* grincheux(euse) *m,f*

misery-guts ['mɪzərɪgʌts] *n Fam* grincheux(euse) *m,f*

misfire [mɪs'faɪə(r)] *vi (of gun)* faire long feu; *Fig (of plan)* rater

misfit ['mɪsfɪt] *n* inadapté(e) *m,f*

misfortune [mɪs'fɔːtʃən] *n* malheur *m*, malchance *f*

misgiving [mɪs'gɪvɪŋ] *n* doute *m*; **to have misgivings (about sth)** avoir des doutes (sur qch)

misgovern [mɪs'gʌvən] *vt* mal gouverner

misguided [mɪs'gaɪdɪd] *adj (person, decision)* mal inspiré(e); *(attempt)* malencontreux(euse); *(energy, idealism)* mal placé(e)

mishandle [mɪs'hændəl] *vt (device)* mal utiliser *(situation)* mal gérer; *(person)* malmener

mishap ['mɪshæp] *n* incident *m*; **without m.** sans encombre

mishear [mɪs'hɪə(r)] *(pt & pp* misheard [mɪs'hɜːd]) *vt & vi* mal comprendre

mishmash ['mɪʃmæʃ] *n Fam* méli-mélo *m*

misinterpret [mɪsɪn'tɜːprɪt] *vt (words)* mal interpréter; *(person)* mal interpréter les paroles de

misjudge [mɪs'dʒʌdʒ] *vt (person)* mal juger; *(distance, situation)* mal évaluer

misjudg(e)ment [mɪs'dʒʌdʒmənt] *n* erreur *f* de jugement

mislay [mɪs'leɪ] *(pt & pp* mislaid [mɪs'leɪd]) *vt* égarer

mislead [mɪs'liːd] *(pt & pp* misled [mɪs'led]) *vt* induire en erreur, tromper

misleading [mɪs'liːdɪŋ] *adj* trompeur(euse)

mismanage [mɪs'mænɪdʒ] *vt* mal gérer

mismanagement [mɪs'mænɪdʒmənt] *n* mauvaise gestion *f*

misnomer [mɪs'nəʊmə(r)] *n* terme *m* mal approprié

miso ['miːsəʊ] *n Culin* miso *m*

misogynist [mɪ'sɒdʒɪnɪst] *n* misogyne *mf*

misplace [mɪs'pleɪs] *vt* (**a**) *(mislay)* égarer (**b**) *(trust, confidence)* mal placer

misprint ['mɪsprɪnt] *n* faute *f* d'impression, coquille *f*

mispronounce [mɪsprə'naʊns] *vt* mal prononcer

mispronunciation [mɪsprənʌnsɪ'eɪʃən] *n* mauvaise prononciation *f*

misquote [mɪs'kwəʊt] *vt* citer incorrectement

misread [mɪs'riːd] *(pt & pp* **misread** [mɪs'red]) *vt* **(a)** *(notice, timetable)* mal lire **(b)** *(misinterpret)* mal interpréter

misrepresent [mɪsreprɪ'zent] *vt (facts, theory)* dénaturer, déformer; *(person)* présenter sous un faux jour

misrepresentation [mɪsreprɪzen'teɪʃən] *n* déformation *f*

misrule [mɪs'ruːl] *n* mauvais gouvernement *m*

Miss [mɪs] *n* Mademoiselle *f*; **M. World** Miss Monde

miss [mɪs] **1** *n* coup *m* manqué; *Fam* **to give sth a m.** *(event)* s'abstenir d'aller à **2** *vt* **(a)** *(target, bus, chance)* manquer, rater; *Fig* **to m. the boat** louper le coche; **you're missing the point** ce n'est pas le problème; **you've just missed him** tu l'as loupé de peu **(b)** *(not hear)* ne pas entendre; **she doesn't m. a thing** rien ne lui échappe **(c)** *(feel lack of)* **I m. you** tu me manques; **do you m. me?** est-ce que je te manque? **(d)** *(avoid)* **the car just missed me** la voiture m'a évité de peu; **she just missed being killed** elle a failli *ou* manqué être tuée **(e)** *(word, line)* sauter **(f)** *(lack)* **the table is missing one of its legs** il manque un pied à la table **3** *vi (miss target)* rater *ou* manquer son coup
▸ **miss out 1** *vt sep (accidentally)* oublier; *(intentionally)* omettre **2** *vi (not benefit)* **to m. out on sth** rater qch; **you missed out there** tu as raté quelque chose

missal ['mɪsəl] *n Rel* missel *m*

misshapen [mɪs'ʃeɪpən] *adj* difforme

missile ['mɪsaɪl, *Am* 'mɪsəl] *n (rocket)* missile *m*; *(object thrown)* projectile *m*; **m. launcher** lance-missiles *m inv*

missing ['mɪsɪŋ] *adj (person) (lost)* disparu(e); *(absent)* absent(e); *(object)* manquant(e); **nothing is m.** il ne manque rien; **m. link** chaînon *m* manquant; **m. person** personne *f* disparue

mission ['mɪʃən] *n* mission *f*

missionary ['mɪʃənərɪ] *(pl* **missionaries)** *n Rel* missionnaire *mf*; **the m. position** la position du missionnaire

missive ['mɪsɪv] *n Formal* missive *f*

misspell ['mɪs'spel] *(pt & pp* **misspelt** ['mɪs'spelt]) *vt* mal écrire

misspent ['mɪs'spent] *adj (time, money)* gaspillé(e); **m. youth** jeunesse *f* dissipée

mist [mɪst] *n (fog)* brume *f*; *(condensation)* buée *f*
▸ **mist over, mist up** *vi (of mirror, glasses)* s'embuer

mistakable [mɪs'teɪkəbəl] *adj* facile à confondre **(for** avec)

mistake [mɪs'teɪk] **1** *n* erreur *f*; *(in grammar, spelling)* faute *f*; **to make a m.** faire *ou* commettre une erreur; **by m.** par erreur; *Fam* **this is hard work and no m.!** pas de doute, c'est vraiment très dur! **2** *vt (pt* **mistook** [mɪs'tʊk], *pp* **mistaken** [mɪs'teɪkən]) **(a)** *(misunderstand)* se tromper sur **(b)** *(confuse)* **to m. sb for** prendre qn pour; **there's no mistaking a voice like that!** avec une voix pareille, on ne peut pas se tromper!

mistakeable [mɪs'teɪkəbəl] = **mistakable**

mistaken [mɪs'teɪkən] *adj (belief, impression)* erroné(e), faux (fausse); **to be m.** se tromper

Mister ['mɪstə(r)] *n* Monsieur *m*

mistime [mɪs'taɪm] *vt* mal calculer

mistletoe ['mɪsəltəʊ] *n* gui *m*

mistranslation [mɪstræns'leɪʃən] *n* erreur *f* de traduction

mistreat [mɪs'triːt] *vt* maltraiter

mistress ['mɪstrɪs] *n* maîtresse *f*; *(in secondary school)* professeur *m*

mistrial [mɪs'traɪəl] *n Law Br* jugement *m* entaché d'un vice de procédure; *Am* = procès dans lequel le jury ne parvient pas à prendre de décision

mistrust [mɪs'trʌst] **1** *n* méfiance *f* **(of** à l'égard de) **2** *vt* se méfier de, ne pas avoir confiance en

mistrustful [mɪs'trʌstfʊl] *adj* méfiant(e); **to be m. of** se méfier de

misty ['mɪstɪ] *adj (place, weather)* brumeux(euse); *(outline, shape)* flou(e)

misunderstand [mɪsʌndə'stænd] *(pt & pp* **misunderstood** [mɪsʌndə'stʊd]) *vt & vi* mal comprendre

misunderstanding [mɪsʌndə'stændɪŋ] *n* **(a)** *(misconception)* malentendu *m* **(about** sur) **(b)** *(disagreement)* mésentente *f*

misuse 1 *n* [mɪs'juːs] *(of equipment, resources)* mauvais emploi *m*; *(of authority)* abus *m*; *(of funds)* détournement *m* **2** *vt* [mɪs'juːz] *(equipment, resources)* mal employer; *(authority)* abuser de; *(funds)* détourner

mite [maɪt] *n* **(a)** *(bug)* acarien *m* **(b)** *Fam (child)* **poor little m.!** pauvre petit! **(c)** *Fam (little bit)* **a m. expensive/tired** un tantinet cher (chère)/fatigué(e)

miter *Am* = **mitre**

mitigate ['mɪtɪgeɪt] *vt* atténuer; *Law* **mitigating circumstances** circonstances *fpl* atténuantes

mitigation [mɪtɪ'geɪʃən] *n* atténuation *f*; *Law* **to say sth in m.** dire qch pour sa défense

mitre, *Am* **miter** ['maɪtə(r)] *n Rel* mitre *f*

mitt [mɪt] *n* **(a)** *(mitten)* moufle *f*; **baseball m.** gant *m* de base-ball **(b)** *Fam (hand)* patte *f*

mitten ['mɪtən] *n (glove)* moufle *f*

mix [mɪks] **1** *vt* mélanger; *(drink)* préparer; **to m. business with pleasure** mélanger les affaires et le plaisir **2** *vi* **(a)** *(blend)* se mélanger **(with** avec) **(b)** *(socially)* **to m. with** fréquenter **3** *n* mélange *m*; *(in music)* remix *m*
▸ **mix up** *vt sep* **(a)** *(ingredients, papers)* mélanger **(b)** *(people, dates)* confondre **(c)** *Fam* **to be mixed up in sth** *(involved)* être mêlé(e) à qch, être impliqué(e) dans qch; **to get mixed up with sb** se mettre à fréquenter qn

mixed ['mɪkst] *adj* mélangé(e); *Fam* **it was a m. bag** il y avait de tout; **to have m. feelings (about sth)** avoir des sentiments mitigés (envers qch); **m. doubles** *(in tennis)* double *m* mixte; **m. grill** assortiment *m* de grillades; **m. marriage** mariage *m* mixte; **m. school** école *f* mixte

mixed-up [mɪks'tʌp] *adj Fam (person)* déboussolé(e)

mixer ['mɪksə(r)] *n* **(a)** *(for cooking)* mixe(u)r *m*; *Br* **m. tap** *(robinet m)* mélangeur *m* **(b)** *(socially)* **to be a good m.** être très sociable **(c)** *(drink)* = boisson servant à allonger un alcool **(d)** *Am Fam (party)* = soirée pour permettre aux étudiants de faire connaissance

mixing bowl ['mɪksɪŋ'bəʊl] *n* saladier *m*

mixture ['mɪkstʃə(r)] *n* mélange *m*

mix-up ['mɪksʌp] *n* confusion *f* **(over** *or* **with** dans)

ml *(abbr* **millilitre(s))** ml

mm *(abbr* **millimetre(s))** mm

mnemonic [nɪ'mɒnɪk] *n* moyen *m* mnémotechnique

moan [məʊn] **1** *n* **(a)** *(sound)* gémissement *m* **(b)** *(complaint)* plainte *f* **2** *vi* **(a)** *(make sound)* gémir **(b)** *(complain)* ronchonner; **to m. about sth** se plaindre de qch

moat [məʊt] *n* douve *f*

mob [mɒb] **1** *n (crowd)* foule *f*; *Fam* **the M.** la Mafia; **m. rule** loi *f* de la rue **2** *vt (pt & pp* **mobbed)** prendre d'assaut

mobile [maɪl] **1** *adj* mobile; **m. home** mobile home *m*; *Br* **m. phone** téléphone *m* portable

2 n **(a)** *(hanging ornament)* mobile m **(b)** *Br Fam (mobile phone)* (téléphone m) portable m

mobility [məʊˈbɪlɪtɪ] n mobilité f

mobilize [ˈməʊbɪlaɪz] vt mobiliser

mobster [ˈmɒbstə(r)] n Am Fam gangster m

moccasin [ˈmɒkəsɪn] n mocassin m

mock [mɒk] **1** adj faux (fausse), factice; Br Sch m. exam examen m blanc **2** vt *(ridicule)* se moquer de

mockery [ˈmɒkərɪ] n **(a)** *(ridicule)* moqueries fpl **(b)** *(travesty)* parodie f; to make a m. of sb ridiculiser qn; to make a m. of sth faire perdre toute crédibilité à qch

mockingbird [ˈmɒkɪŋbɜːd] n moqueur m

mock-up [ˈmɒkʌp] n maquette f

mod cons [ˈmɒdˈkɒnz] npl Fam with all m. *(house)* tout confort; *(car)* avec toutes les options

mode [məʊd] n mode m

model [ˈmɒdəl] **1** n **(a)** *(small version)* maquette f, modèle m réduit; **m. aircraft** maquette d'avion **(b)** *(example, paragon)* modèle m; **m. pupil** élève m f modèle **(c)** *(fashion model)* mannequin m; *(for artist)* modèle m **2** vt *(pt & pp modelled, Am modeled)* **(a)** to m. oneself on sb prendre exemple sur qn **(b)** to m. clothes être mannequin **(c)** Comptr modéliser **3** vi *(on catwalk, for photographer)* travailler comme mannequin; *(for artist)* poser

modem [ˈməʊdem] n Comptr modem m

moderate 1 n [ˈmɒdərɪt] Pol modéré(e) m f **2** adj [ˈmɒdərɪt] modéré(e) **3** vt [ˈmɒdəreɪt] modérer **4** vi [ˈmɒdəreɪt] Formal présider

moderately [ˈmɒdərɪtlɪ] adv **(a)** *(in moderation)* modérément **(b)** *(quite)* assez

moderation [mɒdəˈreɪʃən] n modération f; in m. avec modération

modern [ˈmɒdən] adj moderne; m. languages langues fpl vivantes

modernism [ˈmɒdənɪzəm] n modernisme m

modernization [mɒdənaɪˈzeɪʃən] n modernisation f

modernize [ˈmɒdənaɪz] **1** vt moderniser **2** vi se moderniser

modest [ˈmɒdɪst] adj **(a)** *(unassuming, moderate)* modeste **(b)** *(chaste)* pudique

modestly [ˈmɒdɪstlɪ] adv **(a)** *(unassumingly)* modestement **(b)** *(moderately)* assez, moyennement

modesty [ˈmɒdɪstɪ] n modestie f

modicum [ˈmɒdɪkəm] n a m. of un minimum de

modification [mɒdɪfɪˈkeɪʃən] n modification f; to make modifications to sth apporter des modifications à qch

modify [ˈmɒdɪfaɪ] *(pt & pp modified)* vt modifier

modular [ˈmɒdjʊlə(r)] adj modulaire

modulate [ˈmɒdjʊleɪt] vt moduler

modulation [mɒdjʊˈleɪʃən] n modulation f

module [ˈmɒdjuːl] n module m

mogul [ˈməʊgəl] n Fig magnat m; a movie m. un grand manitou du cinéma

mohair [ˈməʊheə(r)] n mohair m; m. sweater pull m en mohair

Mohammed [məʊˈhæmɪd] n Mahomet m

moist [mɔɪst] adj humide; *(skin, hand)* moite; *(cake)* moelleux(euse)

moisten [ˈmɔɪsən] vt humecter

moisture [ˈmɔɪstʃə(r)] n humidité f

moisturize [ˈmɔɪstʃəraɪz] vt hydrater

moisturizer [ˈmɔɪstʃəraɪzə(r)] n crème f hydratante

molar [ˈməʊlə(r)] n molaire f

molasses [məˈlæsɪz] n mélasse f

mold, molder etc Am = mould, moulder etc

Moldavia [mɒlˈdeɪvɪə], **Moldova** [mɒlˈdəʊvə] n la Moldavie

Moldavian [mɒlˈdeɪvɪən], **Moldovan** [mɒlˈdəʊvən] **1** n Moldave m f **2** adj moldave

mole¹ [məʊl] n *(birthmark)* grain m de beauté

mole² [məʊl] n *(animal, spy)* taupe f

molecular [məˈlekjʊlə(r)] adj moléculaire

molecule [ˈmɒlɪkjuːl] n molécule f

molehill [ˈməʊlhɪl] n taupinière f

molest [məˈlest] vt *(pester)* importuner; *(sexually)* agresser (sexuellement)

mollify [ˈmɒlɪfaɪ] *(pt & pp mollified)* vt calmer, apaiser

mollusc, Am **mollusk** [ˈmɒləsk] n mollusque m

mollycoddle [ˈmɒlɪkɒdəl] vt Fam dorloter

molten [ˈməʊltən] adj en fusion

mom [mɒm] n Am Fam maman f

moment [ˈməʊmənt] n moment m, instant m; at the m. en ce moment; at the last m. au dernier moment; for the m. pour le moment ou l'instant; in a m. dans un instant; any m. d'un instant à l'autre; wait a m.!, one m.! un moment!, un instant! the m. he arrives dès qu'il arrive; without a m.'s hesitation sans une seconde d'hésitation; to live for the m. profiter du moment présent, the man of the m., l'homme du moment; the m. of truth le moment de vérité; the movie has its moments le film est parfois intéressant ou a de bons passages

momentary [ˈməʊməntərɪ] adj momentané(e)

momentous [məʊˈmentəs] adj capital(e)

momentum [məʊˈmentəm] n Phys moment m, to gather m. *(of campaign)* prendre de l'ampleur; to lose m. *(of campaign)* s'essouffler

mommy [ˈmɒmɪ] n Am Fam maman f

Mon *(abbr* Monday) lundi

Monaco [ˈmɒnəkəʊ] n Monaco m

monarch [ˈmɒnək] n monarque m

monarchist [ˈmɒnəkɪst] n monarchiste m f

monarchy [ˈmɒnəkɪ] *(pl* monarchies) n monarchie f

monastery [ˈmɒnəstrɪ] *(pl* monasteries) n monastère m

monastic [məˈnæstɪk] adj monastique, monacal(e)

Monday [ˈmʌndɪ] n lundi m; see also Saturday

monetarism [ˈmʌnɪtərɪzm] n monétarisme m

monetarist [ˈmʌnɪtərɪst] n & adj monétariste m f

monetary [ˈmʌnɪtərɪ] adj monétaire

money [ˈmʌnɪ] n argent m; to do sth for the m. faire qch pour l'argent; to make m. *(of person)* gagner de l'argent; *(of business)* rapporter de l'argent; to be worth a lot of m. *(of thing)* valoir cher; *(of person)* être très riche; there's no m. in it ça ne paie pas; Fam to be in the m. être plein(e) aux as; to get one's m.'s worth en avoir pour son argent; Fam it was m. for old rope c'était de l'argent facilement gagné; to put one's m. where one's mouth is joindre le geste à la parole; Fam on the m. *(correct)* correct(e), exact(e); *(on time)* à l'heure; Fam to spend m. like water dépenser sans compter; Fam m. doesn't grow on trees! l'argent ne se trouve pas sous le sabot d'un cheval; Fin m. market marché m monétaire; Econ m. supply masse f monétaire

moneybags ['mʌnɪbægz] *n Fam (person)* richard(e) *m,f*

moneybox ['mʌnɪbɒks] *n* tirelire *f*

moneyed ['mʌnɪd] *adj* fortuné(e)

moneylender ['mʌnɪlendə(r)] *n* prêteur(euse) *m,f*

moneymaker ['mʌnɪmeɪkə(r)] *n* to be a m. *(of shop, business, product)* rapporter

moneymaking ['mʌnɪmeɪkɪŋ] *adj* qui rapporte

Mongol ['mɒŋgəl] *Hist* **1** *n* Mongol(e) *m,f*
2 *adj* mongol(e)

mongol ['mɒŋgəl] *n Old-fashioned* mongolien(enne) *m,f,* = terme injurieux désignant un trisomique

Mongolia [mɒŋ'gəʊlɪə] *n* la Mongolie

Mongolian [mɒŋ'gəʊlɪən] **1** *n* Mongol(e) *m,f*
2 *adj* mongol(e)

mongoose ['mɒŋguːs] *n* mangouste *f*

mongrel ['mʌŋgrəl] *n* bâtard *m*

monitor ['mɒnɪtə(r)] **1** *n* **(a)** *(supervisor)* superviseur *m*
(b) *TV & Comptr (screen)* moniteur *m*
2 *vt (broadcast, conversation)* écouter; *(patient's condition, operation, results)* surveiller; *(performance)* suivre

monk [mʌŋk] *n* moine *m*

monkey ['mʌŋkɪ] *(pl* **monkeys***) n (animal)* singe *m*; *Fam Fig (naughty child)* petit(e) diable(esse) *m,f; Fam* **to make a m.** out of sb se payer la tête de qn; *very Fam* **I don't give a m.'s** je m'en fous complètement; *Fam* **m. business** *(dishonest behaviour)* magouilles *fpl*; *(mischief)* bêtises *fpl*; **m. nut** cacah(o)uète *f*; **m. puzzle** *(tree)* désespoir *m* des singes; **m. wrench** clef *f* anglaise *ou* à molette

▸ **monkey about, monkey around** *vi Fam (fool around)* faire l'imbécile

monkfish ['mʌŋkfɪʃ] *n* lotte *f*

mono ['mɒnəʊ] *n* mono *f*

monochrome ['mɒnəkrəʊm] *adj* monochrome; *(photo)* en noir et blanc

monocle ['mɒnəkəl] *n* monocle *m*

monogamous [mɒ'nɒgəməs] *adj* monogame

monogamy [mɒ'nɒgəmɪ] *n* monogamie *f*

monogram ['mɒnəgræm] *n* monogramme *m*

monograph ['mɒnəgræf] *n* monographie *f*

monolingual [mɒnəʊ'lɪŋwəl] *adj* monolingue

monolithic [mɒnə'lɪθɪk] *adj* monolithique

monologue ['mɒnəlɒg] *n* monologue *m*

monopolize [mə'nɒpəlaɪz] *vt also Fig* monopoliser

monopoly [mə'nɒpəlɪ] *(pl* **monopolies***) n also Fig* monopole *m*; **to have a m. on sth** avoir le monopole de qch

monorail ['mɒnəʊreɪl] *n* monorail *m*

monosyllabic [mɒnəʊsɪ'læbɪk] *adj (word)* monosyllabique; *(reply)* laconique

monosyllable [mɒnəʊ'sɪləb(ə)l] *n* monosyllabe *m*

monotone ['mɒnətəʊn] *n* ton *m* monotone; **to speak in a m.** parler d'une voix monotone

monotonous [mə'nɒtənəs] *adj* monotone

monotony [mə'nɒtənɪ] *n* monotonie *f*

Monsignor [mɒn'siːnjə(r)] *n* Monseigneur *m*

monsoon [mɒn'suːn] *n* mousson *f*

monster ['mɒnstə(r)] **1** *n* monstre *m*
2 *adj Fam (enormous)* monstre, colossal(e)

monstrosity [mɒn'strɒsɪtɪ] *(pl* **monstrosities***) n* monstruosité *f*

monstrous ['mɒnstrəs] *adj* monstrueux(euse)

montage [mɒn'tɑːʒ] *n* montage *m*

month [mʌnθ] *n* mois *m*; **in the m. of August** au mois

d'août; *Fam* **never in a m. of Sundays** jamais de la vie

monthly ['mʌnθlɪ] **1** *n (pl* **monthlies***) (magazine)* mensuel *m*
2 *adj* mensuel(elle); **m. payment, m.** *Br* **instalment** *or Am* **installment** mensualité *f*
3 *adv* tous les mois

monument ['mɒnjʊmənt] *n also Fig* monument *m* **(to** à**)**

monumental [mɒnjʊ'mentəl] *adj* monumental(e); *(importance)* capital(e)

moo [muː] **1** *n (pl* **moos***)* meuglement *m*, beuglement *m*; **m.!** meuh!
2 *vi (pt & pp* **mooed***)* meugler, beugler

▸ **mooch about, mooch around** [muːtʃ] *vi Fam* traîner

mood [muːd] *n* **(a)** *(state of mind)* humeur *f*; **to be in a good/bad m.** être de bonne/mauvaise humeur; **she's in one of her moods** elle est de mauvaise humeur; **to be in the m. for sth** avoir envie de qch; **to be in the m. for doing sth** être d'humeur à faire qch **(b)** *Gram* mode *m*

moodily ['muːdɪlɪ] *adv (answer, speak)* d'un ton maussade

moody ['muːdɪ] *adj* **(a)** *(sulky)* maussade **(b)** *(changeable)* lunatique

moon [muːn] **1** *n* lune *f*; **the M.** la Lune; *Fam* **to ask for the m.** demander la lune; *Fam* **to promise sb the m.** promettre la lune à qn; *Fam* **to be over the m.** être aux anges; **m. landing** alunissage *m*
2 *vi Fam (expose one's buttocks)* montrer ses fesses

▸ **moon about, moon around** *vi* musarder, flâner

moonbeam ['muːnbiːm] *n* rayon *m* de lune

moonlight ['muːnlaɪt] **1** *n* clair *m* de lune; **in the m., by m.** au clair de lune
2 *vi Fam (work illegally)* travailler au noir

moonlighting ['muːnlaɪtɪŋ] *n Fam* travail *m* au noir

moonlit ['muːnlɪt] *adj* éclairé(e) par la lune

moonshine ['muːnʃaɪn] *n Fam* **(a)** *(nonsense)* balivernes *fpl*, bêtises *fpl* **(b)** *Am (illegally made alcohol)* alcool *m* de contrebande

Moor [mʊə(r)] *n* Maure *mf*

moor[1] [mʊə(r)] *n (heath)* lande *f*

moor[2] [mʊə(r)] *vt (ship)* amarrer

mooring ['mʊərɪŋ] *n* **(a)** *(place)* mouillage *m* **(b)** **moorings** *(chains, ropes)* amarres *fpl*

Moorish ['mʊərɪʃ] *adj* maure, mauresque

moorland ['mʊələnd] *n* lande *f*

moose [muːs] *(pl* **moose***) n* orignal *m*

moot [muːt] *adj* **it's a m. point** c'est difficile à dire

mop [mɒp] **1** *n* **(a)** *(for floor)* balai *m* à franges; *(with sponge)* balai-éponge *m*; *Fam* **m. (of hair)** tignasse *f*
2 *vt (pt & pp* **mopped***)* **to m. the floor** laver par terre; **m. one's brow** s'éponger le front

▸ **mop up** *vt sep (liquid)* éponger; *Fig (enemy forces)* liquider

▸ **mope about, mope around** [məʊp] *vi* broyer du noir

moped ['məʊped] *n (motorbike)* Mobylette® *f*

moral ['mɒrəl] **1** *n* **(a)** *(of story)* morale *f* **(b)** **morals** *(principles)* moralité *f*
2 *adj* moral(e); **m. fibre** force *f* de caractère; **m. support** soutien *m* moral; **m. victory** victoire *f* morale

morale [mɒ'rɑːl] *n* moral *m*; **to be good/bad for m.** être bon (bonne)/mauvais(e) pour le moral

moralistic [mɒrə'lɪstɪk] *adj* moraliste

morality [mə'rælɪtɪ] n moralité f
moralize ['mɒrəlaɪz] vi faire la morale, moraliser
morally ['mɒrəlɪ] adv moralement; **m. right** moralement correct(e); **m. wrong** contraire à la morale
morass [mə'ræs] n (marsh) marais m; Fig (of detail, despair) bourbier m
moratorium [mɒrə'tɔ:rɪəm] (pl **moratoria** [mɒrə'tɔ:rɪə] or **moratoriums**) n moratoire m (**on** sur)
morbid ['mɔ:bɪd] adj morbide
morbidly ['mɔ:bɪdlɪ] adv de façon morbide
mordant ['mɔ:dənt] adj Formal (sarcasm, wit) mordant(e)
more [mɔ:(r)] (comparative of **many, much**) **1** pron plus; **there are m. of us** nous sommes plus nombreux; **have (some) m.** reprenez-en; **there's no m.** il n'y en a plus; **let's say no m. about it** n'en parlons plus; **she knows m. than you** elle en sait plus long que toi; **we should see m. of each other** nous devrions nous voir plus souvent; **it's just m. of the same** c'est encore et toujours la même chose; **the m. I see her, the m. I like her** plus je la vois, plus elle me plaît; **what's m.,...** qui plus est, ; **what m. can I say?** que puis-je dire de plus?
2 adj (**a**) (larger quantity or number of) plus de; **m. wine/ cars** plus de vin/de voitures; **m. than a hundred people were there** il y avait plus de cent personnes; **he has m. patience than I have** il a plus de patience que moi; **there are m. and m. accidents every year** chaque année, il y a de plus en plus d'accidents
(**b**) (additional quantity or number of) **one m. month** un mois de plus; **is there any m. milk?** est-ce qu'il y a encore du lait?; **I've no m. money** je n'ai plus d'argent; **I need m. time** il me faut plus de temps
3 adv (**a**) (to form comparative of adjectives and adverbs) plus (**than** que); **m. interesting** plus intéressant(e); **m. easily** plus facilement; **things are getting m. and m. difficult** les choses deviennent de plus en plus difficiles
(**b**) (to a greater extent) plus; **you should eat m.** tu devrais manger plus; **I'm m. than satisfied** je suis plus que satisfait; **he was m. surprised than annoyed** il était plus surpris que fâché; **I like her m. than I used to** je l'aime plus qu'avant; **that's m. like it!** voilà qui est mieux!; **m. or less** plus ou moins
(**c**) (with time) **once/twice m.** une/deux fois de plus; **he doesn't drink any m.** il ne boit plus; **I can't see you any m.** nous ne pouvons plus nous voir
moreover [mɔ:'rəʊvə(r)] adv de plus
mores ['mɔ:reɪz] npl Formal mœurs fpl
morgue [mɔ:g] n morgue f; Fig **this place is like a m.** c'est complètement mort ici
moribund ['mɒrɪbʌnd] adj moribond(e)
Mormon ['mɔ:mən] n Rel mormon(e) m,f
morning ['mɔ:nɪŋ] n matin m; (referring to duration) matinée f; **tomorrow m.** demain matin; **yesterday m.** hier matin; **the next m., the m. after** le lendemain matin; **the m. before** la veille au matin; Fam **it's the m. after (the night before)** c'est un lendemain de cuite; **m., noon and night** du matin au soir; **in the m.** le matin; **on Sunday m.** dimanche matin; **good m.!**, Fam **m.!** bonjour!; **m. dress** habit m; **m. sickness** nausées fpl matinales; **m. star** étoile f du matin
morning-after pill ['mɔ:nɪŋ'ɑ:ftəpɪl] n pilule f du lendemain
Moroccan [mə'rɒkən] **1** n Marocain(e) m,f
2 adj marocain(e)
Morocco [mə'rɒkəʊ] n le Maroc
moron ['mɔ:rɒn] n crétin(e) m,f
moronic [mə'rɒnɪk] adj débile

morose [mə'rəʊs] adj morose
Morse [mɔ:s] n **M. (code)** morse m
morsel ['mɔ:səl] n morceau m
mortal ['mɔ:təl] **1** n mortel(elle) m,f
2 adj mortel(elle); **m. enemy** ennemi m mortel; **m. remains** dépouille f mortelle; **m. sin** péché m mortel; **m. wound** blessure f mortelle
mortality [mɔ:'tælɪtɪ] n mortalité f
mortally ['mɔ:təlɪ] adv mortellement
mortar ['mɔ:tə(r)] n mortier m
mortgage ['mɔ:gɪdʒ] **1** n (from lender's point of view) prêt m immobilier; (from borrower's point of view) emprunt m immobilier; **m. (re)payments** remboursements mpl d'emprunt; **m. rate** taux m de crédit immobilier
2 vt (property, one's future) hypothéquer
mortician [mɔ:'tɪʃən] n Am entrepreneur m de pompes funèbres
mortification [mɔ:tɪfɪ'keɪʃən] n Rel mortification f; Fig (embarrassment) honte f
mortify ['mɔ:tɪfaɪ] (pt & pp **mortified**) vt Rel mortifier; Fig **to be mortified** être mort(e) de honte
mortise ['mɔ:tɪs] n mortaise f; **m. lock** serrure f encastrée
mortuary ['mɔ:tjʊərɪ] (pl **mortuaries**) n morgue f
mosaic [məʊ'zeɪɪk] n also Fig mosaïque f
Moscow ['mɒskəʊ] n Moscou
Moses ['məʊzɪz] n Moïse
Moslem ['mɒzləm] n & adj musulman(e) m,f
mosque [mɒsk] n mosquée f
mosquito [məs'ki:təʊ] (pl **mosquitos** or **mosquitoes**) n moustique m; **m. bite** piqûre f de moustique; **m. net** moustiquaire f
moss [mɒs] n mousse f
most [məʊst] (superlative of **many, much**) **1** pron (**a**) (the majority) la plupart; **m. of the people/time** la plupart des gens/du temps; **m. of us/them** la plupart d'entre nous/ eux; **he is more interesting than m.** il est plus intéressant que la plupart des gens
(**b**) (greatest amount) **the m.** le plus; **he earns the m.** c'est lui qui gagne le plus; **at the (very) m.** au maximum; **to make the m. of sth** (situation, talents) tirer le meilleur parti de qch; (time, holiday) profiter au maximum de qch
2 adj (**a**) (the majority of) la plupart de; **m. women** la plupart des femmes
(**b**) (greatest amount of) **the m.** le plus de; **he has the m. money** c'est lui qui a le plus d'argent; **for the m. part** dans l'ensemble
3 adv (**a**) (to form superlative of adjectives and adverbs) plus; **the m. interesting movie** le film le plus intéressant; **the m. beautiful woman** la plus belle femme; **these are the m. expensive** ce sont les plus chers; **those who answered m. honestly** ceux qui ont répondu le plus franchement
(**b**) (to the greatest extent) le plus; **the one who works (the) m. is...** celui qui travaille le plus est...; **that's what worries me (the) m.** c'est ce qui m'inquiète le plus; **who do you like m.?** qui préfères-tu?; **what I want m.** ce que je veux par-dessus tout
(**c**) (very) extrêmement; **m. unhappy** extrêmement malheureux/euse f
mostly ['məʊstlɪ] adv (**a**) (in the main) principalement, surtout (**b**) (most often) le plus souvent, la plupart du temps
motel [məʊ'tel] n motel m
moth [mɒθ] n papillon m de nuit; (in clothes) mite f
mothball ['mɒθbɔ:l] n boule f de naphtaline; Fig **to put a project in mothballs** mettre un projet au placard

moth-eaten ['mɒθiːtən] *adj* mité(e); *Fam (in poor condition)* miteux(euse)

mother ['mʌðə(r)] **1** *n* mère *f*; **M.'s Day** la fête des Mères; **m. country** patrie *f*; **M. Nature** Dame Nature *f*; *Rel* **M. Superior** Mère supérieure; **m. tongue** langue *f* maternelle **2** *vt* materner

motherboard ['mʌðəbɔːd] *n Comptr* carte *f* mère

motherhood ['mʌðəhʊd] *n* maternité *f*

mother-in-law ['mʌðərɪnlɔː] *(pl* **mothers-in-law)** *n* belle-mère *f*

motherland ['mʌðəlænd] *n* patrie *f*

mother-of-pearl ['mʌðərəv'pɜːl] *n* nacre *f*

mother-to-be ['mʌðətə'biː] *(pl* **mothers-to-be)** *n* future mère *f*

motif [məʊ'tiːf] *n* motif *m*

motion ['məʊʃən] **1** *n* **(a)** *(movement)* mouvement *m*; **to set sth in m.** *(machine)* mettre qch en marche; *(process)* déclencher qch; *Fig* **to go through the motions** agir machinalement; *Am* **m. picture** film *m* **(b)** *(in meeting, debate)* motion *f*; **to propose/second a m.** présenter/ appuyer une motion **(c)** *(faeces)* selles *fpl* **2** *vt* **to m. sb to do sth** faire signe à qn de faire qch **3** *vi* **to m. to sb to do sth** faire signe à qn de faire qch

motionless ['məʊʃənlɪs] *adj* immobile

motivate ['məʊtɪveɪt] *vt* motiver

motivation [məʊtɪ'veɪʃən] *n* motivation *f*

motive ['məʊtɪv] **1** *n* *(reason)* motif *m*; *Law (for crime)* mobile *m* **2** *adj* **m. force** *or* **power** force *f* motrice

motley ['mɒtlɪ] *adj* hétéroclite; **m. crew** groupe *m* hétéroclite

motor ['məʊtə(r)] **1** *n* *(engine)* moteur *m*; **m. industry** industrie *f* automobile; **m. insurance** assurance *f* automobile; **m. racing** courses *fpl* automobiles; **m. show** salon *m* de l'automobile; **m. vehicle** véhicule *m* automobile **2** *vi* voyager en voiture

motorbike ['məʊtəbaɪk] *n* moto *f*

motorboat ['məʊtəbəʊt] *n* canot *m* à moteur

motorcade ['məʊtəkeɪd] *n* cortège *m* de voitures

motorcycle ['məʊtəsaɪkəl] *n* moto *f*, motocyclette *f*

motorcyclist ['məʊtəsaɪklɪst] *n* motocycliste *mf*

motoring ['məʊtərɪŋ] *n* conduite *f*; **school of m.** auto-école *f*

motorist ['məʊtərɪst] *n* automobiliste *mf*

motorize ['məʊtəraɪz] *vt* motoriser

motorized ['məʊtəraɪzd] *adj* motorisé(e)

motorway ['məʊtəweɪ] *n Br* autoroute *f*; **m. services** services *mpl* autoroutiers

mottled ['mɒtld] *adj (skin)* marbré(e); *(coat, surface)* tacheté(e), moucheté(e)

motto ['mɒtəʊ] *(pl* **mottoes)** *n* devise *f*

mould¹, *Am* **mold** [məʊld] *n (fungus)* moisissure *f*

mould², *Am* **mold 1** *n (in art, cooking)* moule *m*; *Fig* **cast in the same m.** fait(e) dans le même moule; *Fig* **a star in the Cary Grant m.** une star dans le style Cary Grant; *Fig* **to break the m.** rompre avec la tradition **2** *vt (plastic, person's character)* modeler, façonner

moulder, *Am* **molder** ['məʊldə(r)] *vi (of food)* moisir; *(of building)* se délabrer

moulding, *Am* **molding** ['məʊldɪŋ] *n Archit* moulure *f*

mouldy, *Am* **moldy** ['məʊldɪ] *adj* moisi(e)

moult [məʊlt] *vi (of bird)* muer; *(of cat, dog)* perdre ses poils

mound [maʊnd] *n (hill)* butte *f*; *(of earth, sand)* tas *m*

mount¹ [maʊnt] *n (mountain)* mont *m*; **M. Vesuvius** le Vésuve

mount² **1** *n* **(a)** *(for painting)* carton *m* de montage; *(for slide)* cadre *m* **(b)** *(horse)* monture *f* **2** *vt* **(a)** *(bicycle, horse)* monter sur, enfourcher; *(stairs)* monter; *(ladder)* monter à **(b)** *(photograph, exhibition)* monter; *(machine gun)* installer; *(offensive)* lancer; **to m. guard** monter la garde **3** *vi* **(a)** *(get onto horse)* se mettre en selle **(b)** *(increase)* monter, augmenter

▸ **mount up** *vi (of cost, debts)* monter, augmenter

mountain ['maʊntɪn] *n also Fig* montagne *f*; **a m. of papers** une énorme pile de papiers; **to make a m. out of a molehill** faire une montagne d'un rien; **m. bike** vélo *m* tout terrain; **m. climbing** alpinisme *m*; **m. lion** puma *m*; **m. range** chaîne *f* de montagnes; **m. rescue team** équipe *f* de secours en montagne; *Am* **M. Standard Time** heure *f* des montagnes Rocheuses

mountaineer [maʊntɪ'nɪə(r)] *n* alpiniste *mf*

mountaineering [maʊntɪ'nɪərɪŋ] *n* alpinisme *m*

mountainous ['maʊntɪnəs] *adj* montagneux(euse)

mounted ['maʊntɪd] *adj* monté(e), à cheval; **the m. police** la police montée

mounting ['maʊntɪŋ] **1** *n (for engine, gun)* support *m* **2** *adj (increasing)* croissant(e)

mourn [mɔːn] **1** *vt* pleurer **2** *vi* **to m. for sb/sth** pleurer qn/qch

mourner ['mɔːnə(r)] *n* = personne assistant aux obsèques; **the streets were lined with mourners** la foule en deuil s'était massée sur les trottoirs

mournful ['mɔːnfʊl] *adj* triste

mourning ['mɔːnɪŋ] *n* deuil *m*; **to be in m. (for sb)** être en deuil (de qn); **to go into m.** prendre le deuil

mouse [maʊs] *(pl* **mice** [maɪs]) *n also Comptr* souris *f*

mousetrap ['maʊstræp] *n* tapette *f*, souricière *f*

mousse [muːs] *n* mousse *f*; **chocolate m.** mousse au chocolat

moustache [mə'stɑːʃ], *Am* **mustache** ['mʌstæʃ] *n* moustache *f*

mousy ['maʊsɪ] *adj* **(a)** *(hair)* châtain terne *inv* **(b)** *(person, manner)* timide, effacé(e)

mouth 1 *n* [maʊθ] *(of person, horse)* bouche *f*; *(of other animal)* gueule *f*; *(of tunnel)* entrée *f*; *(of river)* embouchure *f*; **we have seven mouths to feed** nous avons sept bouches à nourrir; *Fam* **keep your m. shut about this** garde ça pour toi; *Fam Fig* **to have a big m.** avoir une grande gueule; *Fam* **he's all m.** c'est une grande gueule; **don't put words into my m.** ne me fais pas dire ce que je n'ai pas dit; **m. organ** harmonica *m* **2** *vt* [maʊð] *(insincerely)* débiter; *(silently)* articuler silencieusement

mouthful ['maʊθfʊl] *n (of food)* bouchée *f*; *(of drink)* gorgée *f*; *Fam Fig (long word)* = mot long et difficile à prononcer; *(long name)* nom *m* à coucher dehors; *Fam* **to give sb a m.** engueulander qn

mouthpiece ['maʊθpiːs] *n* **(a)** *(of musical instrument)* embouchure *f*; *(of telephone)* microphone *m* **(b)** *(of government, political party)* porte-parole *m inv*

mouth-to-mouth resuscitation ['maʊθtə'maʊθrɪsʌsɪ'teɪʃən] *n* bouche-à-bouche *m inv*

mouthwash ['maʊθwɒʃ] *n* bain *m* de bouche

mouthwatering ['maʊθwɔːtərɪŋ] *adj (smell)* appétissant(e); *(prospect)* alléchant(e)

movable ['muːvəbəl] *adj* mobile; *Rel* **m. feast** fête *f* mobile

move [muːv] **1** *n* **(a)** *(motion)* mouvement *m*; **to make a m.**
(leave) partir; **to make a m. towards sb/sth** se diriger vers
qn/qch; **on the m.** en mouvement; *Fam* **to get a m. on** se
grouiller, se magner
(b) *(action, step)* pas *m*, démarche *f*; **to make the first m.**
faire le premier pas
(c) *(from home)* déménagement *m*; *(from job)* changement
m de poste
(d) *(in games)* coup *m*; **(it's) your m.** (c'est) à toi de jouer
2 *vt* **(a)** *(change position of)* déplacer; *(set in motion)* remuer;
(employee) muter; **to m. house/premises** déménager; **to
m. jobs** *(within company, sector)* changer de poste; *Fam* **to
m. oneself** se remuer
(b) *Fig (sway)* faire changer d'avis; **to feel moved to do
sth** se sentir obligé(e) de faire qch
(c) *(affect emotionally)* émouvoir; **to m. sb to anger**
provoquer la colère de qn; **to m. sb to tears** émouvoir qn
jusqu'aux larmes
(d) *(in debate)* proposer
3 *vi* **(a)** *(change position)* se déplacer; *(stir)* bouger;
(progress, advance) avancer; *(leave)* partir; **to get things
moving** faire avancer les choses; **could you m., please?**
pourriez-vous vous pousser, s'il vous plaît?; *Fam* **come on,
m.!** allez, remue-toi!
(b) *(act)* agir
(c) *(to new home, office)* emménager; **to m. to another job**
changer de travail; **to m. to the country** s'installer à la
campagne
(d) *Fig (be swayed)* céder
(e) *(in games) (of player)* jouer; *(of piece)* avancer
▸ **move about, move around 1** *vt sep (furniture)*
déplacer; *(employee)* muter, transférer
2 *vi (change position)* se déplacer; *(stir)* bouger; **he moves
around a lot** *(in job)* il est souvent en déplacement
▸ **move along** = move on
▸ **move away 1** *vt sep* éloigner, écarter **(from** de)
2 *vi (from window, person)* s'éloigner, s'écarter **(from** de);
(move house) déménager
▸ **move back 1** *vt sep (further away)* reculer; *(to former
position)* remettre en place
2 *vi (retreat)* s'écarter, (se) reculer; *(to former position)*
retourner **(to** à)
▸ **move forward 1** *vt sep (object, date, meeting)* avancer;
(troops) faire avancer
2 *vi (of person, car)* (s')avancer
▸ **move in** *vi (take up residence)* emménager
▸ **move off** *vi (go away)* partir, s'éloigner; *(start journey)* se
mettre en marche; *(of car)* démarrer
▸ **move on 1** *vt sep (crowd)* faire circuler
2 *vi* **(a)** time's moving on il se fait tard; **it's time we were
moving on** il est temps de partir **(b)** *(change subject)* passer
à autre chose; **to m. on to sth** passer à qch **(c)** *(progress,
develop)* changer
▸ **move out** *vi (leave home)* déménager
▸ **move over** *vi (make room)* se pousser
▸ **move up** *vi* **(a)** *(make room)* se pousser **(b)** *(be promoted)*
avoir de l'avancement
moveable ['muːvəbəl] = movable
movement ['muːvmənt] *n* mouvement *m*; **to watch sb's
movements** surveiller les faits et gestes de qn; **(bowel) m.**
selles *fpl*
mover ['muːvə(r)] *n* **(a)** *(in debate)* motionnaire *mf* **(b)**
(physical) **sloths are slow movers** les paresseux sont des
animaux à mouvements lents; **the movers and shakers** les
grands pontes *mpl* **(c)** *Am (removal company)* déménageur *m*
movie ['muːvɪ] *n Am* film *m*; **to go to the movies** aller au

cinéma; **to be in the movies** faire du cinéma; **m. actor/
actress** acteur *m*/actrice *f* de cinéma; **m. camera** caméra *f*;
m. industry industrie *f* cinématographique; **m. star**
vedette *f* de cinéma; **m. theater** cinéma *m*
moviegoer ['muːvɪɡəʊə(r)] *n Am* spectateur(trice) *m,f*
de cinéma
moving ['muːvɪŋ] *adj* **(a)** *(in motion)* en mouvement;
(train, vehicle) en marche; *(parts)* mobile; **m. staircase**
escalier *m* mécanique **(b)** *(touching)* émouvant(e)
mow [məʊ] *(pp* **mown** [məʊn]*) vt (lawn)* tondre; *(hay)*
faucher
▸ **mow down** *vt sep (slaughter)* faucher
Mozambican [məʊzæm'biːkən] **1** *n* Mozambicain(e) *m,f*
2 *adj* mozambicain(e)
Mozambique [məʊzæm'biːk] *n* le Mozambique
MP [em'piː] *n* **(a)** *Br Pol (abbr* **Member of Parliament)**
député *m* **(b)** *Mil (abbr* **Military Police)** police *f* militaire
mpg [empiː'dʒiː] *n (abbr* **miles per gallon)** ≃ litre *m* aux
cent (kilomètres)
mph [empiː'eɪtʃ] *n (abbr* **miles per hour)** ≃ km/h
Mr ['mɪstə(r)] *(abbr* **Mister) Mr McLean** M. McLean; **Mr
Right** *(ideal husband)* l'homme *m* idéal
Mrs ['mɪsɪz] *(abbr* **Mistress) Mrs Sole** Mme Sole
Ms [mɪz] ≃ Mme *(ne donne pas d'indications sur le statut de
famille)*
MS *n* **(a)** *(abbr* **multiple sclerosis)** sclérose *f* en plaques **(b)**
(abbr **manuscript)** manuscrit *m*
ms *(abbr* **millisecond)** millième *m* de seconde
MSc [emes'siː] *n Univ (abbr* **Master of Science) to have an
M. in chemistry** avoir une maîtrise de chimie; **Colin
Morris M.** Colin Morris, titulaire d'une maîtrise de sciences
MSG [emes'dʒiː] *n Culin (abbr* **monosodium glutamate)**
glutamate *m* de sodium
MST [emes'tiː] *n Am (abbr* **Mountain Standard Time)**
heure *f* d'hiver des montagnes Rocheuses
Mt *(abbr* **Mount)** Mt.
much [mʌtʃ] *(comparative* **more** [mɔː(r)]*, superlative* **most**
[məʊst]*)* **1** *pron* beaucoup; **there isn't m. left** il n'en reste
pas beaucoup; **it's not worth m.** ça ne vaut pas grand-
chose; *Formal* **m. has happened since you left** il s'est
passé beaucoup de choses depuis ton départ; **I'll say this
m. for him, he's very polite** je dois reconnaître une chose,
c'est qu'il est très poli; **I don't think m. of him** je n'ai pas
grande estime pour lui; **it didn't come as m. of a surprise**
ça n'a pas été une grande surprise; **she isn't m. of a
translator** comme traductrice, elle n'est pas très bonne;
twice as m. deux fois plus; **I thought as m.** c'est ce que je
pensais; **as m. as possible** autant que possible; **it was as
m. as we could do to stay upright** nous avions déjà assez
de mal à rester debout; **he left without so m. as saying
goodbye** il est parti sans même dire au revoir; **he has
drunk so m. that...** il a tellement bu que...; **so m.** tant
better tant mieux; **so m. so that...** à tel point que...; **so m.
for her promises of help!** c'était bien la peine de
promettre qu'elle m'/nous/*etc* aiderait!; *Fam* **that's a bit
m.!** c'est un peu fort!
2 *adj*

> Hormis dans la langue soutenue et dans certaines
> expressions, ne s'utilise que dans des structures
> négatives ou interrogatives.

how m. money? combien d'argent?; **there isn't m. traffic**
il n'y a pas beaucoup de circulation; **too m. work** trop de
travail; **so m. time** tant de temps; **as m. food** as autant de
nourriture que; *Formal* **m. work still needs to be done** il
reste encore beaucoup de travail à faire
3 *adv* beaucoup; **I don't like it m.** ça ne me plaît pas

beaucoup; **m. better** bien meilleur(e); **m. more difficult** beaucoup plus difficile; **m. the best** de loin le meilleur (la meilleure); **m. the most interesting** de loin le (la) plus intéressant(e); **thank you very m.** merci beaucoup; **m. the same** presque pareil(eille); **m. to my astonishment** à mon grand étonnement; **m. as I like him, I don't really trust him** j'ai beau l'apprécier, je ne lui fais pas vraiment confiance; **the result was m. as I expected** le résultat correspondait assez à mes attentes; **so m.** autant; **I love him so m.** je l'aime tellement; **too m.** trop; **$10 too m.** 10 dollars de trop; **this is (really) too m.!** trop c'est trop!

muchness ['mʌtʃnɪs] *n Fam* **they're much of a m.** ils se valent

muck [mʌk] *n Fam (dirt)* saleté *f*; *(manure)* fumier *m*; *(bad food)* cochonneries *fpl*; *(bad quality book, TV programme)* idioties *fpl*
▸ **muck about, muck around** *Br Fam* = **mess about, mess around**
▸ **muck in** *vi Br Fam (help)* s'y mettre
▸ **muck out** *vt sep (stables)* nettoyer
▸ **muck up** *vt sep Fam* **(a)** *(make dirty)* cochonner **(b)** *(task)* bâcler; *(plans)* chambouler; *(interview, exam)* rater

muckraking ['mʌkreɪkɪŋ] *n Fam (in journalism)* = pratique consistant à révéler et exploiter à fond des scandales

mucky ['mʌkɪ] *adj Br Fam* sale

mucous ['mjuːkəs] *adj* muqueux(euse)

mucus ['mjuːkəs] *n* mucus *m*, mucosités *fpl*

mud [mʌd] *n* boue *f*; *Fig* **to throw m. at sb** couvrir qn de boue; *Fam* **his name is m.** il n'a pas la cote; **m. hut** hutte *f* en terre

mudbank ['mʌdbæŋk] *n* banc *m* de vase

mudflat ['mʌdflæt] *n* banc *m* de boue

muddle ['mʌdəl] **1** *n* confusion *f*; **to be in a m.** *(of things)* être en désordre; *(of person)* ne plus s'y retrouver; **to get into a m.** *(of things)* se mélanger; *(of person)* s'embrouiller **2** *vt* **(a)** *(put in disorder)* mélanger **(b)** *(bewilder)* embrouiller; **to get muddled** s'embrouiller
▸ **muddle along** *vi* se débrouiller tant bien que mal
▸ **muddle through** *vi* se débrouiller
▸ **muddle up** *vt sep* **(a)** *(put in disorder)* mélanger **(b)** *(confuse)* embrouiller; **to get muddled up** s'embrouiller

muddleheaded [mʌdəl'hedɪd] *adj (person)* brouillon(onne); *(thinking)* confus(e)

muddy ['mʌdɪ] **1** *adj (path, water)* boueux(euse); *(clothing, hands)* couvert(e) de boue; *(complexion)* terreux(euse); *(colour)* sale **2** *vt (pt & pp muddied)* salir; *Fig* **to m. the waters** brouiller les pistes

mudguard ['mʌdgɑːd] *n* garde-boue *m inv*

mudpack ['mʌdpæk] *n* masque *m* à l'argile

mudslinging ['mʌdslɪŋɪŋ] *n Fam* = fait de dénigrer systématiquement ses adversaires

muesli ['mjuːzlɪ] *n* muesli *m*

muff¹ [mʌf] *vt Br Fam (bungle)* rater, louper

muff² *n (for hands)* manchon *m*

muffin ['mʌfɪn] *n (cake)* muffin *m*

muffle ['mʌfəl] *vt* **(a)** *(sound)* assourdir, étouffer **(b)** **to m. oneself up** s'emmitoufler

muffled ['mʌfəld] *adj (sound, footstep)* assourdi(e), étouffé(e)

muffler ['mʌflə(r)] *n* **(a)** *(scarf)* cache-nez *m inv* **(b)** *Am (of car)* silencieux *m*

mufti ['mʌftɪ] *n Fam* **in m.** *(soldier)* en civil

mug [mʌg] **1** *n* **(a)** *(cup)* grande tasse *f* **(b)** *Fam (face)* gueule *f*; **m. shot** photo *f* d'identité judiciaire **(c)** *Br Fam (gullible person)* poire *f*; **it's a m.'s game** on est toujours perdant à ce jeu-là **2** *vt (pt & pp mugged) (attack)* agresser
▸ **mug up** *vi Br Fam (study)* bûcher; **to m. up on sth** potasser qch

mugger ['mʌgə(r)] *n* agresseur *m*

mugging ['mʌgɪŋ] *n* agression *f*

muggins ['mʌgɪnz] *n Br Fam* mézigue

muggy ['mʌgɪ] *adj* lourd(e), étouffant(e)

mulatto [mjuː'lætəʊ] *(pl* mulattos *or* mulattoes) *n* mulâtre *mf*

mulberry ['mʌlbərɪ] *(pl* mulberries) *n (fruit)* mûre *f*; *(tree)* mûrier *m*

mule [mjuːl] *n* mulet *m*; *(female)* mule *f*

▸ **mull over** [mʌl] *vt sep (consider)* **to m. sth over** retourner qch dans sa tête

mulled wine ['mʌld'waɪn] *n* vin *m* chaud épicé

mullet ['mʌlɪt] *n* **grey m.** mulet *m* gris; **red m.** rouget *m*

multi-access ['mʌltɪ'ækses] *adj Comptr* à accès multiple

multicoloured, *Am* **multi-colored** ['mʌltɪkʌləd] *adj* multicolore

multicultural [mʌltɪ'kʌltʃərəl] *adj* multiculturel(elle)

multifarious [mʌltɪ'feərɪəs] *adj* varié(e), divers(e)

multi-functional [mʌltɪ'fʌŋkʃənəl] *adj* multifonctions *inv*

multilateral [mʌltɪ'lætərəl] *adj* multilatéral(e)

multimedia [mʌltɪ'miːdɪə] *adj* multimédia

multimillionaire [mʌltɪmɪlɪə'neə(r)] *n* multimillionnaire *mf*

multinational [mʌltɪ'næʃənəl] **1** *n* multinationale *f* **2** *adj* multinational(e)

multiparty [mʌltɪ'pɑːtɪ] *adj* **m. system** pluripartisme *m*

multiple ['mʌltɪpəl] **1** *n* **(a)** *Math* multiple *m* **(b)** *Com (chain store)* chaîne *f* de magasins **2** *adj* multiple; **m. sclerosis** sclérose *f* en plaques

multiple-choice ['mʌltɪpl'tʃɔɪs] *adj* à choix multiple

multiplex ['mʌltɪpleks] *n Cin* complexe *m* multisalles, cinéma *m* multisalle

multiplication [mʌltɪplɪ'keɪʃən] *n* multiplication *f*; **m. table** table *f* de multiplication

multiplicity [mʌltɪ'plɪsɪtɪ] *n* multiplicité *f*

multiply ['mʌltɪplaɪ] *(pt & pp multiplied)* **1** *vt* multiplier **(by** par) **2** *vi (reproduce)* se multiplier

multipurpose [mʌltɪ'pɜːpəs] *adj* polyvalent(e)

multiracial [mʌltɪ'reɪʃəl] *adj* multiracial(e)

multistorey, *Am* **multistory** [mʌltɪ'stɔːrɪ] *adj* à étages; **m. (car park)** parking *m* à plusieurs niveaux

multitude ['mʌltɪtjuːd] *n* multitude *f*

mum [mʌm] *Fam* **1** *n Br (mother)* maman *f*; **m.'s the word!** motus et bouche cousue! **2** *adv* **to keep m. (about sth)** ne pas souffler mot (de qch)

mumble ['mʌmbəl] **1** *n* marmonnement *m* **2** *vt & vi* marmonner

mumbo jumbo ['mʌmbəʊ'dʒʌmbəʊ] *n (nonsense)* âneries *fpl*; *(jargon)* charabia *m*

mummify ['mʌmɪfaɪ] *(pt & pp mummified)* *vt* momifier

mummy¹ ['mʌmɪ] *(pl* mummies) *n (embalmed body)* momie *f*

mummy² *n Br Fam (mother)* maman *f*; **a m.'s boy** un petit garçon à sa maman

mumps [mʌmps] *n* *(illness)* oreillons *mpl*; **to have m.**
avoir les oreillons
munch [mʌntʃ] *vt* mâcher
munchies ['mʌntʃɪz] *npl Fam* **(a)** *(snacks)* amuse-gueule
mpl **(b)** *(desire to eat)* **to have the m.** avoir la fringale
mundane [mʌn'deɪn] *adj* banal(e), ordinaire
municipal [mju:'nɪsɪpəl] *adj* municipal(e)
municipality [mju:nɪsɪ'pælɪtɪ] *(pl* **municipalities)** *n*
municipalité *f*
munitions [mju:'nɪʃənz] *npl* munitions *fpl*
mural ['mjʊərəl] *n* peinture *f* murale
murder ['mɜːdə(r)] **1** *n* **(a)** *(killing)* meurtre *m*; *Fig* **she
gets away with m.** elle peut tout se permettre; **m. case**
affaire *f* de meurtre; **m. inquiry** enquête *f* sur une affaire de
meurtre **(b)** *Fam Fig (difficult task)* cauchemar *m*, enfer *m*;
finding a parking place on a Saturday is m. c'est l'enfer
pour trouver à se garer le samedi
2 *vt* **(a)** *(kill)* assassiner; *Fam Fig* **I'll m. you!** je vais te tuer!;
Br Fam **I could m. a beer/pizza** je me taperais bien une
bière/une pizza **(b)** *Fig (song, tune)* massacrer
murderer ['mɜːdərə(r)] *n* meurtrier(ère) *m,f*, assassin *m*
murky ['mɜːkɪ] *adj (weather, sky)* sombre; *(details, past)*
trouble
murmur ['mɜːmə(r)] **1** *n* murmure *m*, **to do sth without
a m.** faire qch sans broncher
2 *vi also Fig* murmurer
muscle ['mʌsəl] *n* muscle *m*; *Fig (power)* poids *m*; **not to
move a m.** rester immobile
▸ **muscle in** *vi* inter venir **(on** dans)
muscleman ['mʌsəlmæn] *n* Monsieur *m* muscle
Muscovite ['mʌskəvaɪt] **1** *n* Moscovite *mf*
2 *adj* moscovite
muscular ['mʌskjʊlə(r)] *adj (tissue, pain)* musculaire;
(person) musclé(e); **m. dystrophy** myopathie *f*
Muse [mju:z] *n (in mythology)* Muse *f*; *(of poet)* muse *f*
muse [mju:z] *vi* rêvasser, songer **(on** or **about** à)
museum [mju:'zɪəm] *n* musée *m*
mush [mʌʃ] *n* **(a)** *(pulp)* bouillie *f* **(b)** *Fig (sentimentality)*
mièvrerie *f*
mushroom ['mʌʃrʊm] **1** *n* champignon *m*; **m. cloud**
champignon atomique
2 *vi (of costs, prices)* grimper (en flèche); *(of town)* se
développer; *(of houses, factories)* pousser comme des
champignons
mushy ['mʌʃɪ] *adj* **(a)** *(food)* en bouillie; *(ground)*
détrempé(e) **(b)** *Fam Fig (sentimental)* à l'eau de rose, mièvre
music ['mju:zɪk] *n* musique *f*; *Fig* **those words were m.
to her ears** elle était ravie d'entendre ces mots; **m. box**
boîte *f* à musique; **m. hall** music-hall *m*; **m. stand** pupitre *m*
(à musique); **m. teacher** professeur *m* de musique
musical ['mju:zɪkəl] **1** *n (show, film)* comédie *f* musicale
2 *adj (tuneful)* musical(e); *(musically gifted)* musi-
cien(enne); **m. box** boîte *f* à musique; **m. chairs** (jeu *m*
des) chaises *fpl* musicales; *also Fig* **to play m. chairs** jouer
aux chaises musicales; **m. instrument** instrument *m* de
musique
musician [mju:'zɪʃən] *n* musicien(enne) *m,f*
musicologist [mju:zɪ'kɒlədʒɪst] *n* musicologue *mf*
musings ['mju:zɪŋz] *npl* rêverie(s) *f(pl)*
musk [mʌsk] *n* musc *m*
musket ['mʌskɪt] *n* mousquet *m*
musketeer [mʌskə'tɪə(r)] *n* mousquetaire *m*
muskrat ['mʌskræt] *n* rat *m* musqué
Muslim ['mʊzlɪm] *n & adj* musulman(e) *m,f*

muslin ['mʌzlɪn] *n* mousseline *f*
mussel ['mʌsəl] *n* moule *f*; **m. bed** parc *m* à moules
must [mʌst] **1** *modal aux v* **(a)** *(expressing obligation)*
devoir; **you m. do it** tu dois le faire, il faut que tu le fasses;
they mustn't find out il ne faut pas qu'ils l'apprennent;
you mustn't tell anyone surtout, n'en parle à personne;
this plant m. be watered daily cette plante doit être
arrosée chaque jour; **I m. say I thought it was rather
good** je dois avouer que j'ai trouvé ça plutôt bon; **will you
come with me?** – **if I m.** tu viens avec moi? – s'il le faut;
take it if you m. prends-le, si tu le veux vraiment; **m. you
be so silly?** tu te sens obligé d'être aussi bête? **(b)**
(suggesting, inviting) **you m. come and visit us** il faut
vraiment que vous nous rendiez visite; **we m. go out for
a drink sometime** il faudrait que nous allions prendre un
verre, un de ces jours **(c)** *(expressing probability)* devoir; **you
m. be hungry** vous devez avoir faim; **I m. have made a
mistake** j'ai dû faire une erreur; **you m. be joking!** tu veux
rire!
2 *n Fam* **(a)** *(necessity)* **to be a m.** être une nécessité;
sunglasses/hiking boots are a m. il faut absolument
emporter des lunettes de soleil/des chaussures de marche
(b) *(thing not to be missed)* **this film's a m.** ce film est un must
mustache ['mʌstæʃ] *Am* = **moustache**
mustard ['mʌstəd] *n* moutarde *f*; *Am Fam Fig* **he couldn't
cut the m.** il n'a pas été à la hauteur; **m. gas** gaz *m* moutarde
muster ['mʌstə(r)] **1** *n Fig* **to pass m.** être acceptable
2 *vt (gather)* rassembler; **to m. one's strength/courage**
rassembler ses forces/son courage
musty ['mʌstɪ] *adj (smell)* de moisi, **to have a m. smell** *(of
room)* sentir le renfermé
mutant ['mju:tənt] *n & adj* mutant(e) *m,f*
mutate [mju:'teɪt] *vi* muter
mutation [mju:'teɪʃən] *n* mutation *f*
mute [mju:t] **1** *n* **(a)** *(dumb person)* muet(ette) *m,f* **(b)** *Mus*
sourdine *f*
2 *adj* muet(ette)
muted ['mju:tɪd] *adj (sound)* assourdi(e); *(applause)*
faible; *(protest, criticism)* voilé(e); *(colour)* sourd(e)
mutilate ['mju:tɪleɪt] *vt also Fig* mutiler
mutilation [mju:tɪ'leɪʃən] *n* mutilation *f*
mutineer [mju:tɪ'nɪə(r)] *n* mutiné(e) *m,f*
mutinous ['mju:tɪnəs] *adj* rebelle
mutiny ['mju:tɪnɪ] **1** *n (pl* **mutinies)** *(on ship)* mutinerie *f*;
(of workers) révolte *f*
2 *vi (pt & pp* **mutinied)** *(of crew, soldiers)* se mutiner; *(of
workers)* se révolter
mutt [mʌt] *n Fam (dog)* clébard *m*
mutter ['mʌtə(r)] **1** *n* murmure *m*
2 *vt & vi* marmonner
mutton ['mʌtən] *n* mouton *m*; *Fam* **to look like m.
dressed as lamb** être habillé(e) trop jeune pour son âge
mutual ['mju:tʃʊəl] *adj (reciprocal)* mutuel(elle), réciproque; *(shared)* commun(e); **the feeling is m.** c'est réciproque
mutually ['mju:tʃʊəlɪ] *adv* mutuellement, réciproquement; **to be m. exclusive** s'exclure mutuellement
Muzak® ['mju:zæk] *n* musique *f* de fond, fond *m* sonore
muzzle ['mʌzəl] **1** *n* **(a)** *(dog's nose)* museau *m*; *(guard)*
muselière *f* **(b)** *(of gun)* canon *m*
2 *vt also Fig* museler
MW *(a) (abbr* **Medium Wave)** OM **(b)** *Elec (abbr* **Mega-
watts)** MW
my [maɪ] **1** *possessive adj* **(a)** *(singular)* mon (ma); *(plural)*
mes; **my job** mon travail; **my wife** ma femme; **my parents**

mes parents; **it wasn't MY idea!** ce n'est pas moi qui en ai eu l'idée! **(b)** *(with parts of body)* **I hit my head** je me suis cogné la tête **2** *exclam* oh là là!

Myanmar [maɪæn'mɑ:(r)] *n* le Myanmar

mynah ['maɪnə] *n* **m. (bird)** mainate *m*

myopia [maɪ'əʊpɪə] *n* myopie *f*; *Fig* manque *m* de perspicacité

myopic [maɪ'ɒpɪk] *adj* myope; *Fig* à courte vue

myriad ['mɪrɪəd] *adj Lit* innombrable

myrrh [mɜ:(r)] *n* myrrhe *f*

myrtle ['mɜ:təl] *n* myrte *m*

myself [maɪ'self] *pron* **(a)** *(reflexive)* **I hurt m.** je me suis blessé **(b)** *(emphatic)* moi-même; **I m. have never...** moi-même n'ai jamais...; **I told her m.** je lui ai dit moi-même; **I'm not m.** today je ne suis pas dans mon état normal aujourd'hui **(c)** *(after preposition)* moi; **I live by m.** je vis seul; **I bought it for m.** je me le suis acheté; **I talk to m.** je parle tout seul

mysterious [mɪs'tɪərɪəs] *adj* mystérieux(euse)

mysteriously [mɪs'tɪərɪəslɪ] *adv* mystérieusement

mystery ['mɪstərɪ] **1** *n (pl* **mysteries)** mystère *m*; **m. tour** voyage *m* surprise **2** *adj (guest, prize)* surprise *inv*; *(benefactor, witness)* mystérieux(euse)

mystic ['mɪstɪk] *n & adj* mystique *mf*

mystical ['mɪstɪkəl] *adj (person)* mystique; *(power, ceremony)* occulte

mysticism ['mɪstɪsɪzəm] *n* mysticisme *m*

mystify ['mɪstɪfaɪ] *(pt & pp* **mystified)** *vt* déconcerter

mystique [mɪs'ti:k] *n* mystère *m*

myth [mɪθ] *n* mythe *m*

mythical ['mɪθɪkəl] *adj* mythique

mythological [mɪθə'lɒdʒɪkəl] *adj* mythologique

mythology [mɪ'θɒlədʒɪ] *(pl* **mythologies)** *n* mythologie *f*

myxomatosis [mɪksəmə'təʊsɪs] *n* myxomatose *f*

N, n [en] *n* **(a)** *(letter)* N, n *m inv* **(b)** *(abbr* **north**) N

NAACP [enɪeɪsiːˈpiː] *n Am Pol (abbr* **National Association for the Advancement of Colored People)** = association pour la défense des droits des personnes de couleur

naan [nɑːn] *n* **n. (bread)** = sorte de pain indien servi
comme accompagnement

nab [næb] *(pt & pp* **nabbed)** *vt Fam* **(a)** *(catch, arrest)*
choper **(b)** *(steal)* piquer, faucher

nadir ['neɪdɪə(r)] *n Astron* nadir *m*; *Fig* **to reach a n.**
atteindre son niveau le plus bas

naff [næf] *adj Br Fam (of poor quality)* nul (nulle); *(of poor
taste)* ringard(e)
► **naff off** *vi Br Fam* **n. off!** dégage!

nag[1] [næg] *n Fam (horse)* carne *f*

nag[2] **1** *n (person)* emp
uiquineur(euse) *m,f*
2 *vt (pt & pp* **nagged)** *(of person)* être sur le dos de; *(of
doubt, conscience)* tourmenter; **to n. sb into doing sth**
harceler qn pour qu'il fasse qch
3 *vi* **he's always nagging** il est tout le temps sur mon
dos

nagging ['nægɪŋ] **1** *n* harcèlement *m*; **I've had enough
of your n.** arrête de me harceler
2 *adj (pain, doubt, worry)* tenace

nail [neɪl] **1** *n* **(a)** *(in carpentry)* clou *m*; *Fig* **it was another
n. in his coffin** c'était un pas de plus vers la fin; *Fig* **the
final n. in the coffin** la goutte d'eau qui fait déborder le
vase; *Fig* **to hit the n. on the head** mettre le doigt dessus
(b) *(of person)* ongle *m*; **n. file** lime *f* à ongles; **n. scissors**
ciseaux *mpl* à ongles; **n. polish** vernis *m* à ongles; **n. polish
remover** dissolvant *m*
2 *vt* **(a)** *(attach)* clouer; **to n. sth shut** clouer qch; *Fig* **to
stand nailed to the spot** rester cloué(e) sur place **(b)**
(idioms) Fam **to n. sb** *(for crime)* coincer qn; *Fam* **to n. a lie**
dénoncer un mensonge
► **nail down** *vt sep (fasten)* clouer, fixer avec des clous;
Fam Fig **to n. sb down to a date/price** obtenir de qn qu'il
fixe une date/un prix

nail-biting ['neɪlbaɪtɪŋ] *adj Fam (contest, finish)*
palpitant(e); *(wait)* angoissant(e)

nailbrush ['neɪlbrʌʃ] *n* brosse *f* à ongles

naive [naɪˈiːv] *adj* naïf(ïve)

naively [naɪˈiːvlɪ] *adv* naïvement

naivety [naɪˈiːvətɪ] *n* naïveté *f*

naked ['neɪkɪd] *adj (body, flame)* nu(e); *Fig (aggression,
exploitation)* délibéré(e); **visible to the n. eye** visible à l'œil nu

namby-pamby ['næmbɪˈpæmbɪ] **1** *n (pl* **namby-
pambies)** mollasson(onne) *m,f*
2 *adj* gnangnan *inv*

name [neɪm] **1** *n* **(a)** *(in general)* nom *m*; **my n. is…** je
m'appelle…; **what's your n.?** comment t'appelles-tu?; **to
mention sb by n.** désigner nommément qn; **a big n. in the
movies** un grand nom du cinéma; **to put one's n. down
(for sth)** s'inscrire (pour qch); **to go by** *or* **under the n.
of…** être connu(e) sous le nom de…; **in the n. of…** au nom
de…; **in the n. of God** *or* **Heaven!** au nom du Ciel!; **he was
President in all but n.** c'était lui le président, même s'il n'en
avait pas le titre; **to call sb names** insulter qn; **he hasn't
got a penny to his n.** il n'a pas un sou **(b)** *(reputation)*
réputation *f*; **to have a good/bad n.** avoir (une) bonne/
mauvaise réputation; **to have a n. for** être réputé(e) pour;
to make a n. for oneself se faire un nom
2 *vt* **(a)** *(give name to, appoint)* nommer; **to n. sb** *Br* **after** *or*
Am **for sb** donner à qn le nom de qn **(b)** *(designate, identify)*
citer; **to n. names** donner des noms; **n. your price** dites
votre prix

name-calling ['neɪmkɔːlɪŋ] *n* insultes *fpl*

name-dropper ['neɪmdrɒpə(r)] *n Fam* = personne qui
se vante de connaître des gens célèbres

name-dropping ['neɪmdrɒpɪŋ] *n Fam* = fait de se
vanter de connaître des gens célèbres

nameless ['neɪmlɪs] *adj (person)* anonyme; **someone
who shall remain n.** quelqu'un que je ne nommerai pas

namely ['neɪmlɪ] *adv* c'est-à-dire, à savoir

nameplate ['neɪmpleɪt] *n* plaque *f*

namesake ['neɪmseɪk] *n* homonyme *mf*

Namibia [nəˈmɪbɪə] *n* la Namibie

Namibian [nəˈmɪbɪən] **1** *n* Namibien(enne) *m,f*
2 *adj* namibien(enne)

nancy ['nænsɪ] *(pl* **nancies)** *n very Fam* **n. (boy)**
(homosexual) tapette *f*, pédale *f*; *(effeminate man)* chochotte *f*

nanny ['nænɪ] *(pl* **nannies)** *n* **(a)** *(for children)* jeune fille *f*
au pair **(b)** **n. goat** chèvre *f*

nanosecond ['nænəʊsekənd] *n Phys* nanoseconde *f*

nap[1] [næp] **1** *n (sleep)* (petit) somme *m*; **to take** *or* **have a
n.** faire un (petit) somme
2 *vi (pt & pp* **napped)** faire un (petit) somme; *Fig* **to be
caught napping** être pris(e) au dépourvu

nap[2] *n (of cloth)* poil *m*

napalm ['neɪpɑːm] *n* napalm *m*

nape [neɪp] *n* **n. (of the neck)** nuque *f*

naphthalene ['næfθəliːn] *n* naphtaline *f*

napkin ['næpkɪn] *n* **(a)** *(table)* **n.** serviette *f* (de table); **n.
ring** rond *m* de serviette **(b)** *Am (sanitary towel)* serviette *f*
hygiénique

Naples ['neɪpəlz] *n* Naples

Napoleonic [nəpəʊlɪˈɒnɪk] *adj* napoléonien(enne)

nappy ['næpɪ] (pl **nappies**) n Br couche f; n. rash érythème m fessier

narc [nɑːk] n Am Fam agent m de la brigade des stups

narcissus [nɑːˈsɪsəs] (pl **narcissi** [nɑːˈsɪsaɪ]) n narcisse m

narcosis [nɑːˈkəʊsɪs] n narcose f

narcotic [nɑːˈkɒtɪk] **1** n (medicine) narcotique m; (illegal drug) stupéfiant m; Am **narcotics agent** agent m de la brigade des stupéfiants
2 adj narcotique

nark [nɑːk] n Br Fam (a) (informer) indic m (b) (irritable person) râleur(euse) m,f

narky ['nɑːkɪ] adj Br Fam grognon

narrate [nəˈreɪt] vt raconter

narrative ['nærətɪv] **1** n récit m
2 adj narratif(ive)

narrator [nəˈreɪtə(r)] n narrateur(trice) m,f

narrow ['nærəʊ] **1** adj étroit(e); (majority) faible; **to grow** or **become n.** se rétrécir; **to have a n. mind** avoir l'esprit étroit; **to have a n. escape** l'échapper belle; **to win/lose by a n. margin** gagner/perdre de justesse; **to take a n. view of sth** adopter un point de vue étroit sur qch
2 vt to n. one's eyes (in suspicion, anger) froncer les sourcils
3 vi (of road) se rétrécir, se resserrer
▸ **narrow down** vt sep limiter, réduire

narrowly ['nærəʊlɪ] adv (only just) de peu; **she n. missed being run over** elle a failli se faire écraser

narrow-minded [nærəʊˈmaɪndɪd] adj étroit(e) d'esprit, borné(e)

NASA ['næsə] n (abbr **National Aeronautics and Space Administration**) NASA f

nasal ['neɪzəl] adj nasal(e); **to have a n. voice** parler du nez

nastily ['nɑːstɪlɪ] adv méchamment

nastiness ['nɑːstɪnɪs] n (of person, remark) méchanceté f

nasturtium [nəˈstɜːʃəm] n capucine f

nasty ['nɑːstɪ] adj mauvais(e); (crime) ignoble; (shock, business) sale; (accident) grave; **to be n. to sb** être méchant(e) avec qn; **to have a n. mind** penser toujours à mal; **to turn n.** (of situation, weather) se dégrader, se gâter; **that was a really n. thing to do** c'était vraiment ignoble de sa/ta/etc part; Fig **it left a n. taste in my mouth** ça m'a laissé un arrière-goût désagréable; **a n. piece of work** (man) un sale type; (woman) une vraie peste

nation ['neɪʃən] n nation f

national ['næʃənəl] **1** n (a) (person) ressortissant(e) m,f (b) (newspaper) journal m national
2 adj national(e); **n. anthem** hymne m national; **n. curriculum** programme m scolaire; **n. debt** dette f publique; **N. Front** = parti britannique d'extrême droite; **n. grid** réseau m national (d'électricité); Br **N. Health Service** = système de santé britannique; Br **N. Insurance** contributions fpl sociales; **n. park** parc m national; **n. service** service m militaire; Br **N. Trust** = organisme britannique de conservation du patrimoine historique et naturel

nationalism ['næʃənəlɪzəm] n nationalisme m

nationalist ['næʃənəlɪst] n & adj nationaliste mf

nationalistic [næʃənəˈlɪstɪk] adj nationaliste

nationality [næʃəˈnælɪtɪ] (pl **nationalities**) n nationalité f

nationalization [næʃənəlaɪˈzeɪʃən] n nationalisation f

nationalize ['næʃənəlaɪz] vt nationaliser

nationally ['næʃənəlɪ] adv nationalement

nationwide ['neɪʃənwaɪd] **1** adj national(e)
2 adv dans tout le pays

native ['neɪtɪv] **1** n (person) natif(ive) m,f; (plant) plante f indigène; (animal) animal m indigène; **to be a n. of** être originaire de; **she speaks English like a n.** elle parle anglais comme si c'était sa langue maternelle
2 adj natal(e); **he returned to his n.** Detroit il est retourné à Detroit, sa ville natale; **n. American** Indien(enne) m,f d'Amérique; **n. land** pays m natal; **n. language** langue f maternelle; **I'm not a n. speaker of Spanish** ma langue maternelle n'est pas l'espagnol

Nativity [nəˈtɪvɪtɪ] n Rel **the N.** la Nativité f; **N. play** mystère m de la Nativité

NATO ['neɪtəʊ] n Mil (abbr **North Atlantic Treaty Organization**) l'OTAN f

natter ['nætə(r)] Br Fam **1** n **to have a n.** bavarder, papoter (about sur)
2 vi bavarder, papoter (**about** sur)

natty ['nætɪ] adj Fam chic inv

natural ['nætʃərəl] **1** adj (a) (colour, taste) naturel(elle); (gift, talent) inné(e); **to die from n. causes** mourir de mort naturelle; **n. childbirth** accouchement m naturel; **n. disaster** catastrophe f naturelle; **n. gas** gaz m naturel; **n. history** histoire f naturelle; **n. mother** mère f naturelle; **n. resources** ressources fpl naturelles; **n. sciences** sciences fpl naturelles; **n. yoghurt** yaourt m nature (**b**) (normal) naturel(elle); **it's only n.** c'est tout à fait naturel; Ind **n. wastage** = réduction des effectifs due aux départs d'employés non remplacés (**c**) (unaffected) naturel(elle)
2 n **he's a n. as an actor** c'est un acteur né

naturalism ['nætʃərəlɪzəm] n naturalisme m

naturalist ['nætʃərəlɪst] n naturaliste mf

naturalistic ['nætʃərəlɪstɪk] adj naturaliste

naturalization [nætʃərəlaɪˈzeɪʃən] n naturalisation f

naturalize ['nætʃərəlaɪz] vt naturaliser

naturally ['nætʃərəlɪ] adv (a) (unaffectedly) naturellement; (by nature) de nature; **to come n. to sb** être un don chez qn (b) (of course) naturellement

nature ['neɪtʃə(r)] n (a) (the natural world) nature f; **to let n. take its course** laisser faire la nature; **n. reserve** réserve f naturelle; **n. trail** = sentier aménagé doté d'explications concernant la faune et la flore (b) (character) nature f; **to have a jealous n.** être d'une nature jalouse; **it's not in her n.** ça n'est pas dans sa nature; **to be lazy by n.** être paresseux de nature (c) (sort) nature f, genre m; **problems of this n.** des problèmes de cette nature; Formal **what is the n. of your complaint?** quelle est la nature de votre réclamation?

naught [nɔːt] n (a) Lit (nothing) néant m; **to come to n.** se réduire à néant (b) Am = **nought**

naughtily ['nɔːtɪlɪ] adv **to behave n.** être vilain(e)

naughty ['nɔːtɪ] adj (child) méchant(e), vilain(e); (book, picture) coquin(e)

nausea ['nɔːzɪə] n nausée f

nauseate ['nɔːzɪeɪt] vt donner la nausée à; Fig écœurer

nauseating ['nɔːzɪeɪtɪŋ] adj also Fig écœurant(e)

nauseous ['nɔːzɪəs] adj (disgusting) écœurant(e); **to feel n.** avoir envie de vomir

nautical ['nɔːtɪkəl] adj nautique; **n. mile** m marin ou nautique

naval ['neɪvəl] adj naval(e); **n. battle** bataille f navale; **the N. College** ≃ l'École f navale; **n. officer** officier m de marine

nave [neɪv] n (of church) nef f

navel ['neɪvəl] n nombril m

navigable ['nævɪgəbəl] adj navigable

navigate ['nævɪgeɪt] **1** vt (seas) naviguer sur; (ship, plane) piloter

2 vi (in ship, plane) naviguer; (in car) faire le pilote

navigation [nævɪ'geɪʃən] n navigation f

navigational [nævɪ'geɪʃənəl] adj de navigation

navigator ['nævɪgeɪtə(r)] n (in ship, plane) navigateur(trice) m,f; (in car) copilote mf

navvy ['nævɪ] (pl **navvies**) n Br terrassier m

navy ['neɪvɪ] (pl **navies**) n marine f; **n. (blue)** bleu marine m inv

Nazi ['nɑːtsɪ] **1** n Nazi(e) m,f
2 adj nazi(e)

Nazism ['nɑːtsɪzəm] n nazisme m

NB [en'biː] (abbr **nota bene**) NB

NBA [enbiː'eɪ] n Am (abbr **National Basketball Association**) = fédération américaine de basket-ball

NCO [ensiː'əʊ] n Mil (abbr **non-commissioned officer**) sous-officier m

NE (abbr **northeast**) N-E

Neanderthal [nɪ'ændətɑːl] **1** n (a) (during Stone Age) homme m de Neandertal (b) Fig (uncivilized man) homme m des cavernes
2 adj (a) (during Stone Age) **N. man** homme m de Neandertal (b) Fig (attitude, behaviour) d'homme des cavernes

Neapolitan [nɪə'pɒlɪtən] **1** n Napolitain(e) m,f
2 adj napolitain(e)

near [nɪə(r)] **1** adj proche; **to the nearest metre** au mètre près; **in the n. future** dans un avenir proche; **it was a n. thing** il s'en est fallu de peu; **the N. East** le Proche-Orient
2 adv près; **to be n. to sth** (in space) être près de qch; (in time) être proche de qch; **n. at hand** (of thing) tout près; (of event) tout proche; **to be n. to doing sth** être sur le point de faire qch; **n. to tears/despair** au bord des larmes/du désespoir; **she's nowhere n. finished** elle est loin d'avoir fini; **she's a n. total failure** un échec presque total
3 prep près de; **he came n. to being run over** il a failli se faire écraser; **nobody comes anywhere n. her** (in skill, performance) il n'y a personne à son niveau
4 n Fam **my nearest and dearest** mes plus proches parents
5 vt (s')approcher de; **to be nearing completion** être presque terminé(e)

nearby 1 adj ['nɪəbaɪ] proche
2 adv [nɪə'baɪ] tout près

nearly ['nɪəlɪ] adv presque; **we're n. there** (finished) nous y sommes presque; (at destination) nous sommes presque arrivés; **he n. died** il a failli mourir; **not n. enough money/time** vraiment pas assez d'argent/de temps; **not n. so beautiful** bien moins beau (belle)

nearly-new ['nɪəlɪ'njuː] adj = d'occasion mais en parfait état

nearside ['nɪəsaɪd] **1** n (on right) côté m droit; (on left) côté m gauche
2 adj (on right) droit(e); (on left) gauche

near-sighted [nɪə'saɪtɪd] adj Am myope

neat [niːt] adj (a) (in habits) ordonné(e); (in appearance) soigné(e); (work, handwriting) soigné; (room, house) bien rangé(e); **she made a n. job of it** elle a fait du bon travail (b) (undiluted) pur(e) (c) Am Fam (good) super inv

▸ **neaten up** ['niːtən] vt sep (hair, garden) arranger; (piece of work) peaufiner

neatly ['niːtlɪ] adv (a) (carefully) soigneusement (b) (skilfully) habilement, adroitement

neatness ['niːtnɪs] n (of appearance) aspect m soigné; (of

work) soin m; (of handwriting) netteté f; (of room, house) ordre m

nebula ['nebjʊlə] (pl **nebulas** or **nebulae** ['nebjʊlaɪ]) n Astron nébuleuse f

nebulous ['nebjʊləs] adj (vague) nébuleux(euse)

necessarily [nesɪ'serəlɪ] adv nécessairement, forcément

necessary ['nesɪsərɪ] **1** adj nécessaire; **it is n. to remind them** il faut le leur rappeler; **to do what is n.** faire le nécessaire; **when(ever) n.** si nécessaire, si besoin est; **a n. evil** un mal nécessaire
2 n Fam **the n.** (thing, action) le nécessaire; (money) l'argent

necessitate [nɪ'sesɪteɪt] vt nécessiter, rendre nécessaire

necessity [nɪ'sesɪtɪ] (pl **necessities**) n nécessité f; **out of n.** par nécessité; **the necessities** (things needed) le nécessaire; Prov **n. is the mother of invention** en cas de besoin, on trouve toujours une solution

neck [nek] **1** n (a) (of person, animal) cou m; (of dress) encolure f; col m; (of bottle) goulot m; (of guitar, violin) manche m; (of land) langue f; (of lamb, beef) collier m (b) (idioms) Fam **to risk one's n.** risquer sa peau; Fam **he got it in the n.** il s'est pris un savon; Fam **he's in it up to his n.** il est impliqué là-dedans jusqu'au cou; Fam **to stick one's n. out** se lancer; Fam **in this n. of the woods** dans le coin
2 vi Fam (of couple) se peloter

necklace ['neklɪs] n collier m

neckline ['neklaɪn] n encolure f

necromancy ['nekrəʊmænsɪ] n Formal necromancie f

nectar ['nektə(r)] n nectar m

nectarine ['nektəriːn] n nectarine f, brugnon m

née [neɪ] adj née; **Mrs Richardson, n. Johnston** Mme Richardson, née Johnston

need [niːd] **1** n besoin m (for de); **there is no n. to shout/worry** inutile de crier/de t'inquiéter; **if n. be** en cas de besoin; **to be in n.** (poor) être dans le besoin; **to be in n. of sth** avoir besoin de qch; **in time of n.** dans les moments difficiles; **their n. is greater than mine** ils en ont plus besoin que moi
2 vt **to n. sth/to do sth** avoir besoin de qch/de faire qch; **I n. more time** il me faut plus de temps; **you'll n. to take more money** il te faudra prendre plus d'argent, il faudra que tu prennes plus d'argent; **I didn't n. to be reminded of it** je n'avais pas besoin qu'on me le rappelle, il était inutile de me le rappeler; **his hair needs cutting** il a besoin d'une coupe de cheveux; **the flashlight needs a new battery** la lampe a besoin d'une nouvelle pile; **this work needs a lot of patience** ce travail demande beaucoup de patience; Ironic **that's all I n.!** il ne (me) manquait plus que ça!
3 modal aux v

La forme modale de **need** est la même à toutes les personnes, et s'utilise sans **do/does** (**he need only worry about himself**; **need she go?**; **it needn't matter**).

you needn't worry inutile de t'inquiéter; **you needn't wait** tu n'as pas besoin d'attendre; **n. I say more?** ai-je besoin d'en dire plus?

needful ['niːdfʊl] n Fam **to do the n.** faire le nécessaire

needle ['niːdəl] **1** n aiguille f; **it's like looking for a n. in a haystack** c'est comme chercher une aiguille dans une botte de foin; Fam **to give sb the n.** taper sur les nerfs de qn; Fam **n. match** (in football) match m acharné
2 vt Fam asticoter

needlecraft ['niːdəlkrɑːft] n travaux mpl d'aiguille

needless ['niːdlɪs] adj (waste, suffering, worry) inutile; (remark) déplacé(e); **n. to say...** il va de soi que...

needlessly ['niːdlɪslɪ] *adv* inutilement

needlework ['niːdəlwɜːk] *n (sewing)* couture *f*; *(embroidery)* broderie *f*

need-to-know [niːdtə'nəʊ] *adj* **information is given on a n. basis** les renseignements ne sont donnés qu'aux personnes concernées

needy ['niːdɪ] **1** *npl* **the n.** les nécessiteux *mpl* **2** *adj (person)* nécessiteux(euse), dans le besoin

nefarious [nɪ'feərɪəs] *adj* infâme, ignoble

negate [nɪ'geɪt] *vt (effect)* annuler; *(work, efforts)* anéantir

negation [nɪ'geɪʃən] *n (of work, efforts)* anéantissement *m*

negative ['negətɪv] **1** *n* **(a)** *Gram* **the n.** la forme négative; **to answer in the n.** répondre par la négative **(b)** *(of photo)* négatif *m* **2** *adj* négatif(ive); **don't be so n.** ne sois pas si négatif; *Fin* **n. equity** plus-value *f* immobilière négative; **n. feedback** réaction *f* négative

negatively ['negətɪvlɪ] *adv* négativement

negativity [negə'tɪvɪtɪ] *n* négativité *f*

neglect [nɪ'glekt] **1** *n (of person)* négligence *f*; *(of machine, garden)* manque *m* d'entretien; *(of duties, responsibilities)* manquement *m*; **from** *or* **through n.** par négligence **2** *vt* **(a)** *(not care for)* négliger; **to n. oneself** se négliger **(b)** *(ignore) (duties, responsibilities)* manquer à; *(post)* abandonner; **to n. to do sth** négliger de faire qch

neglectful [nɪ'glektfʊl] *adj* négligent(e); **to be n. of sb/sth** négliger qn/qch

négligée ['neglɪʒeɪ] *n* négligé *m*, déshabillé *m*

negligence ['neglɪdʒəns] *n* négligence *f*; *(of duties, responsibilities)* manquement *m* **(of** à)

negligent ['neglɪdʒənt] *adj* négligent(e)

negligently ['neglɪdʒəntlɪ] *adv* négligemment

negligible ['neglɪdʒɪbəl] *adj* négligeable

negotiable [nɪ'gəʊʃəbəl] *adj (demand, salary)* négociable; *(price)* à débattre; *(obstacle)* franchissable; *(road)* praticable

negotiate [nɪ'gəʊʃɪeɪt] **1** *vt* **(a)** *(price, treaty, salary, contract)* négocier **(b)** *(obstacle)* franchir; *(difficulty)* surmonter; *(bend)* négocier **2** *vi* négocier

negotiation [nɪgəʊʃɪ'eɪʃən] *n* négociation *f*; **under n.** en négociation

negotiator [nɪ'gəʊʃɪeɪtə(r)] *n* négociateur(trice) *m,f*

Negress ['niːgrɪs] *n Old-fashioned* négresse *f*

Negro ['niːgrəʊ] *Old-fashioned* **1** *n (pl* **Negroes)** nègre *m* **2** *adj* nègre; **N. spiritual** *(song)* Negro spiritual *m*

neigh [neɪ] **1** *n* hennissement *m* **2** *vi* hennir

neighbor, neighborhood *etc Am* = **neighbour, neighbourhood** *etc*

neighbour, *Am* **neighbor** ['neɪbə(r)] *n* voisin(e) *m,f*; **to be a good n.** être bon voisin

neighbourhood, *Am* **neighborhood** ['neɪbəhʊd] *n* **(a)** *(district)* quartier *m*; *(people)* voisinage *m*; *Br* **n. watch** = système de surveillance mis en œuvre par les habitants d'un quartier **(b)** *(vicinity)* voisinage *m*, environs *mpl*; **in the n.** dans les environs; **a figure in the n. of $2,000** un chiffre avoisinant les 2000 dollars

neighbouring, *Am* **neighboring** ['neɪbərɪŋ] *adj* voisin(e)

neighbourliness, *Am* **neighborliness** ['neɪbəlɪnɪs] *n* (relations *fpl* de) bon voisinage *m*

neighbourly, *Am* **neighborly** ['neɪbəlɪ] *adj* **they're very n.** ce sont de très bons voisins

neither ['naɪðə(r), 'niːðə(r)] **1** *conj* **n.... nor...** ni... ni...; **n. you nor your brother** ni toi ni ton frère; **he n. drinks nor smokes** il ne boit pas et ne fume pas non plus; *Fig* **that's n. here nor there** là n'est pas la question **2** *adv* **n. do I** moi non plus; **if you don't go n. shall I** si tu n'y vas pas, moi non plus; **the workers aren't happy and n. is the management** les ouvriers ne sont pas contents et la direction non plus **3** *adj* **n. driver was injured** aucun des deux conducteurs n'a été blessé **4** *pron* **n. (of them) will do** aucun (des deux) ne fera l'affaire; **n. of my two brothers can come** aucun de mes deux frères ne peut venir

neo- ['niːəʊ] *pref* néo-

neoclassical [niːəʊ'klæsɪkəl] *adj* néoclassique

neofascist [nɪəʊ'fæʃɪst] *n & adj* néofasciste *mf*

neolithic [niːəʊ'lɪθɪk] *adj* néolithique

neon ['niːɒn] *n* néon *m*; **n. light** lumière *f* au néon; **n. sign** enseigne *f* au néon

Nepal [nɪ'pɔːl] *n* le Népal

Nepalese [nepə'liːz], **Nepali** [ne'pɔːlɪ] **1** *n (pl* **Nepalese** *or* **Nepalis)** **(a)** *(person)* Népalais(e) *m,f* **(b)** *(language)* népalais *m* **2** *adj* népalais(e)

nephew ['nefjuː] *n* neveu *m*

nepotism ['nepətɪzəm] *n* népotisme *m*

Neptune ['neptjuːn] *n (planet)* Neptune *f*

nerd [nɜːd] *n Fam* crétin(e) *m,f*

nerve [nɜːv] **1** *n* **(a)** *(in body)* nerf *m*; *Fam* **to get on sb's nerves** taper sur les nerfs à qn; **her nerves were in a terrible state** elle était à bout de nerfs; *Anat* **n. cell** cellule *f* nerveuse; *Fig* **n. centre** *(of organization)* centre *m* nerveux; **n. gas** gaz *m* neurotoxique **(b)** *(courage)* courage *m*; **to have nerves of steel** avoir des nerfs d'acier; **to keep/lose one's n.** garder/perdre son sang-froid **(c)** *Fam (cheek)* culot *m*; **to have the n. to do sth** avoir le culot de faire qch **2** *vt* **to n. oneself to do sth** s'armer de courage pour faire qch

nerve-(w)racking ['nɜːvrækɪŋ] *adj* éprouvant(e)

nervous ['nɜːvəs] *adj* **(a)** *(apprehensive)* nerveux(euse), anxieux(euse); **to be n. about sth/doing sth** être nerveux *ou* anxieux à l'idée de qch/de faire qch **(b)** *(energy, exhaustion)* nerveux(euse); **n. breakdown** dépression *f* nerveuse; *Fig* **n. system** système *m* nerveux

nervously ['nɜːvəslɪ] *adv* nerveusement

nervousness ['nɜːvəsnɪs] *n* nervosité *f*

nervy ['nɜːvɪ] *adj Fam (tense)* nerveux(euse)

nest [nest] **1** *n (of bird, insects)* nid *m*; *Fig (of criminals)* repaire *m*; *Fig* **to fly the n.** quitter le nid; **n. of tables** tables *fpl* gigognes; *Fig* **n. egg** pécule *m* **2** *vi (of bird)* faire son nid

nestle ['nesəl] *vi* se pelotonner, se blottir; **to n. up to sb** se blottir contre qn

nestling ['neslɪŋ] *n* oisillon *m*

Net [net] *n Fam Comptr* **the N.** le Net

net¹ [net] **1** *n* filet *m*; *Fig* **to slip through the n.** passer à travers les mailles du filet; **n. curtain** voilage *m* **2** *vt (pt & pp* **netted)** *(animals, fish)* prendre au filet; *Fig (drugs, criminals)* mettre la main sur; *(donations, contracts)* récolter

net² **1** *adj (weight, price, profit)* net (nette) **2** *vt (earn)* **to n. $2,000** gagner 2000 dollars net

netball ['netbɔːl] *n* = sport féminin proche du basketball

Netherlands ['neðələndz] *npl* **the N.** les Pays-Bas *mpl*

netting ['netɪŋ] *n* filet *m*

nettle ['netəl] **1** *n (plant)* ortie *f*
2 *vt (irritate)* irriter, énerver

network ['netwɜːk] **1** *n* réseau *m*
2 *vi (make contacts)* établir un réseau de contacts
networking ['netwɜːkɪŋ] *n (making contacts)* établissement *m* d'un réseau de contacts

neural ['njʊərəl] *adj Anat* neural(e)

neuralgia [njʊ'ræ1dʒə] *n* névralgie *f*

neurologist [njʊə'rɒlədʒɪst] *n* neurologue *mf*

neurology [njʊə'rɒlədʒɪ] *n* neurologie *f*

neuron ['njʊərɒn] *n Anat* neurone *m*

neurosis [njʊ'rəʊsɪs] *(pl* **neuroses** [njʊ'rəʊsiːz]) *n* névrose *f*

neurosurgery ['njʊərəʊ'sɜːdʒərɪ] *n* neurochirurgie *f*

neurotic [njʊ'rɒtɪk] **1** *n* névrosé(e) *m,f*
2 *adj* névrosé(e), to be n. about sth être obsédé(e) par qch

neuter ['njuːtə(r)] **1** *n Gram* neutre *m*
2 *adj Gram* neutre
3 *vt (animal)* castrer, châtrer

neutral ['njuːtrəl] **1** *n* **(a)** *(country)* pays *m* neutre; *(person)* personne *f* neutre **(b)** *(of car)* point *m* mort; **in n.** au point mort
2 *adj (country, colour)* neutre

neutrality [njuː'trælɪtɪ] *n* neutralité *f*

neutralize ['njuːtrəlaɪz] *vt* neutraliser

neutrino [njuː'triːnəʊ] *(pl* **neutrinos***) n Phys* neutrino *m*

neutron ['njuːtrɒn] *n Phys* neutron *m*; **n. bomb** bombe *f* à neutrons

never ['nevə(r)] *adv* **(a)** *(not once)* jamais; **I've n. met him** je ne l'ai jamais rencontré; **n. again!** plus jamais!; **he's n. yet been beaten** il n'a encore jamais été battu, **I've n. yet understood why** je n'ai jamais compris pourquoi **(b)** *(emphatic negative)* **she n. said a word** elle n'a pas dit un mot; **I n. expected this** je ne m'attendais vraiment pas à ça; **he n. even congratulated me** il ne m'a même pas félicité; *Fam* **well I n.!** ça alors!

never-ending [nevər'endɪŋ] *adj* interminable

never-never ['nevə'nevə(r)] *n Br Fam* **to buy sth on the n.** acheter qch à crédit

nevertheless [nevəðə'les] *adv* néanmoins, cependant

new [njuː] *adj* nouveau(elle); *(not used)* neuf (neuve); **what's n.?** quoi de neuf?; **that's nothing n.!** ça n'est pas nouveau!; **she's n. to this work** elle débute dans ce travail; **to be n. to a town** être nouveau dans une ville; **N. Age** *(music, thinking)* new age *inv*; **N. Brunswick** le Nouveau-Brunswick; **N. Caledonia** la Nouvelle-Calédonie; **N. Delhi** New Delhi; **N. England** la Nouvelle-Angleterre; **N. Guinea** la Nouvelle-Guinée; **N. Man** homme *m* de la nouvelle génération; **N. Mexico** le Nouveau-Mexique; **n. moon** nouvelle lune *f*; **N. Orleans** la Nouvelle-Orléans; **N. South Wales** la Nouvelle-Galles du Sud; **the N. Testament** le Nouveau Testament; **n. town** ville *f* nouvelle; **n. wave** *(trend)* Nouvelle Vague *f*; **the N. World** le Nouveau Monde; **N. Year** Nouvel An *m*; **N. Year's Day** le jour de l'an; **N. Year's Eve** la Saint-Sylvestre; **N. Year's resolution** résolution *f* du jour de l'an; **N. York** New York; **N. Yorker** New-Yorkais(e) *m,f*

newborn ['njuːbɔːn] *adj* nouveau-né(e); **n. baby** nouveau-né(e) *m,f*

newcomer ['njuːkʌmə(r)] *n* nouveau(elle) venu(e) *m,f* (**to** dans)

newfangled [njuː'fæŋgəld] *adj Pej (idea)* nouveau(elle); *(gadget)* dernier cri *inv*

Newfoundland ['njuːfəndlænd] *n* Terre-Neuve

newly ['njuːlɪ] *adv* nouvellement, récemment

newlyweds ['njuːlɪwedz] *npl* jeunes mariés *mpl*

newness ['njuːnɪs] *n (of design)* nouveauté *f*; *(of clothing)* état *m* neuf

news [njuːz] *n* nouvelles *fpl*; *(on TV, radio)* informations *fpl*; **a piece of n.** une nouvelle; **in the n.** sous les feux de l'actualité; *Fam* **he's bad n.** il n'est pas fréquentable; *Fam* **that's n. to me!** première nouvelle!; *Prov* **no n. is good n.** pas de nouvelles, bonnes nouvelles; **n. agency** agence *f* de presse; **n. bulletin** bulletin *m* d'informations; **n. conference** conférence *f* de presse; **n. item** information *f*, nouvelle *f*; **n. summary** rappel *m* des titres

newsagent ['njuːzeɪdʒənt] *n Br* marchand(e) *m,f* de journaux; **n.'s (shop)** marchand *m* de journaux

newscaster ['njuːzkɑːstə(r)] *n* présentateur(trice) *m,f* du journal

newsdealer ['njuːzdiːlə(r)] *n Am* marchand(e) *m,f* de journaux

newsflash ['njuːzflæʃ] *n* flash *m* d'informations

newsgroup ['njuːzgruːp] *n Comptr* newsgroup *m*, forum *m* de discussion

newsletter ['njuːzletə(r)] *n* bulletin *m*

newspaper ['njuːzpeɪpə(r)] *n* journal *m*; **n. report** reportage *m*

newspaperman ['njuːzpeɪpəmæn] *n (reporter)* journaliste *m*; *(proprietor)* propriétaire *m* d'un journal

newsprint ['njuːzprɪnt] *n* papier *m* journal

newsreader ['njuːzriːdə(r)] *n* présentateur(trice) *m,f* du journal

newsreel ['njuːzriːl] *n* actualités *fpl*

newsroom ['njuːzruːm] *n (salle f de)* rédaction *f*

newsstand ['njuːzstænd] *n* kiosque *m* à journaux

newsworthy ['njuːzwɜːðɪ] *adj* d'un intérêt médiatique

newt [njuːt] *n* triton *m*

New Zealand [njuː'ziːlənd] *n* la Nouvelle-Zélande

New Zealander [njuː'ziːləndə(r)] *n* Néo-Zélandais(e) *m,f*

next [nekst] **1** *adj* **(a)** *(in space)* d'à côté; **n. door** à côté (**b**) *(in time, order)* prochain(e); *(subsequent)* suivant(e), d'après; **n. week** la semaine prochaine; **the n. week** la semaine suivante *ou* d'après; **the year after n.** pas l'année prochaine, celle d'après; **the n. time** la prochaine fois; **your name is n. on the list** votre nom est le suivant sur la liste; **the n. but one** le prochain, mais celui d'après; **(the) n. to arrive was Carmen** Carmen fut arrivée ensuite; **who's n.?** c'est à qui?; **n. please!** au suivant!; **the n. size up/down** la taille au-dessus/au-dessous
2 *adv* **(a)** *(in space)* **n. to** à côté de **(b)** *(in time, order)* ensuite, après; *Fam* **what will they think of n.?** qu'est-ce qu'ils vont encore inventer?; **n. to Paris I like Madrid best** après Paris, la ville que je préfère, c'est Madrid; **when shall we meet n.?** quand nous reverrons-nous?; **the n. best thing would be to...** à défaut, le mieux serait de...; **the n. fastest after the Ferrari was...** la voiture la plus rapide après la Ferrari était...; **who is the n. oldest/youngest** after Angus? qui est le plus âgé/le plus jeune après Angus?; **n. to nothing** quasiment rien; **there is n. to no evidence** il n'y a pratiquement aucune preuve; **in n. to no time** en rien de temps

next-door [neks'dɔː(r)] *n* à côté; **n. neighbour** voisin(e) *m,f* d'à côté

next-of-kin [nekstəv'kɪn] *n* plus proche parent *m*

NFL [enef'el] *n Am (abbr* **National Football League)** = fédération nationale de football américain

NGO [endʒiː'əʊ] *n (abbr* **non-governmental organization)** ONG *f*

NHS [eneɪtʃ'es] *n Br (abbr* **National Health Service)** = système de santé britannique

NI [en'aɪ] *n Br (abbr* **National Insurance)** contributions *fpl* sociales

nib [nɪb] *n* plume *f*

nibble ['nɪbəl] **1** *n* to have a n. at sth grignoter qch; **nibbles** *(snacks)* amuse-gueule *mpl*
2 *vt* grignoter

Nicaragua [nɪkə'rægjʊə] *n* le Nicaragua

Nicaraguan [nɪkə'rægjʊən] **1** *n* Nicaraguayen(enne) *m,f*
2 *adj* nicaraguayen(enne)

nice [naɪs] *adj* **(a)** *(pleasant)* agréable; *(physically attractive)* beau (belle); *(tasty)* bon (bonne); **a n.** idea une bonne idée; **to be n. to sb** se montrer aimable avec qn; **to have a n. time** bien s'amuser; **have a n. day!** bonne journée!; **it was n. of her to...** c'était gentil de sa part de...; *Ironic* **that's a n. way to talk!** en voilà une façon de parler! **(b)** *(intensive)* **n. and easy** très facile; **n. and handy** bien commode; **a n. warm bath** un bain bien chaud

nice-looking ['naɪslʊkɪŋ] *adj* beau (belle)

nicely ['naɪslɪ] *adv (ask)* gentiment; *(behave, sit)* bien; **to be doing n.** aller bien; **to do n. for oneself** bien se débrouiller

niceties ['naɪsɪtɪz] *npl* subtilités *fpl*

niche [niːʃ] *n (in wall)* niche *f; (in market)* créneau *m*; **to find one's (in life)** trouver sa voie

nick [nɪk] **1** *n* **(a)** *(in wood, on face)* entaille *f* **(b) in the n. of time** juste à temps **(c)** *Fam (condition)* **in good/bad n.** en bon/mauvais état **(d)** *Br Fam (prison)* taule *f; (police station)* poste *m*
2 *vt* **(a)** *(cut)* entailler **(b)** *Br Fam (arrest)* pincer, épingler **(c)** *Br Fam (steal)* piquer, faucher

nickel ['nɪkəl] *n* **(a)** *(metal)* nickel *m* **(b)** *Am (coin)* pièce *f* de cinq cents

nickname ['nɪkneɪm] **1** *n* surnom *m*
2 *vt* surnommer

nicotine ['nɪkətiːn] *n* nicotine *f*

niece [niːs] *n* nièce *f*

niff [nɪf] *Br Fam* **1** *n (bad smell)* puanteur *f*
2 *vi (smell bad)* puer

nifty ['nɪftɪ] *adj Fam* **(a)** *(idea, device)* génial(e) **(b)** *(agile)* vif (vive)

Niger ['naɪdʒə] *n* le Niger

Nigeria [naɪ'dʒɪərɪə] *n* le Nigéria

Nigerian [naɪ'dʒɪərɪən] **1** *n* Nigérian(e) *m,f*
2 *adj* nigérian(e)

niggardly ['nɪgədlɪ] *adj (person)* avare, pingre; *(sum, portion)* maigre

nigger ['nɪgə(r)] *n* nègre (négresse) *m,f,* = terme raciste désignant un Noir

niggle ['nɪg(ə)l] **1** *vt (worry)* tracasser
2 *vi (be overfussy)* couper les cheveux en quatre; **to n. (away) at sb** *(worry)* tracasser qn; *(hassle)* enquiquiner qn

niggling ['nɪgəlɪŋ] *adj (detail)* insignifiant(e); *(pain, doubt)* persistant(e); **I have a n. feeling that...** je ne peux pas m'empêcher de penser que...

nigh [naɪ] *adv* **(a)** *Lit (near)* près, proche; **the end is n.!** la fin est proche! **(b) well n.** *(almost)* presque

night [naɪt] *n* nuit *f; (evening)* soir *m*; **at n.** la nuit; *(in the evening)* le soir; **late at n.** tard dans la nuit; **all n.** toute la nuit; **last n.** la nuit dernière; *(evening)* hier soir; **tomorrow n.** demain soir; **on Thursday n.** jeudi soir; **good n.!** *(when going to bed)* bonne nuit!, bonsoir!; *(when leaving)* bonsoir!; **to work nights** travailler la nuit; **to have a n. out** sortir; **let's make a n. of it** et si on continuait la soirée?; **n. flight**

vol *m* de nuit; **n. owl** oiseau *m* de nuit; **n. school** cours *m* du soir; **n. watchman** veilleur *m* de nuit

nightcap ['naɪtkæp] *n* **(a)** *(hat)* bonnet *m* de nuit **(b)** *(drink)* petit verre *m (avant d'aller se coucher)*

nightclub ['naɪtklʌb] *n* boîte *f* de nuit

nightdress ['naɪtdres] *n* chemise *f* de nuit

nightfall ['naɪtfɔːl] *n* tombée *f* de la nuit; **at n.** à la nuit tombante

nightgown ['naɪtgaʊn] *n* chemise *f* de nuit

nightie ['naɪtɪ] *n Fam* chemise *f* de nuit

nightingale ['naɪtɪŋgeɪl] *n* rossignol *m*

nightjar ['naɪtdʒɑː(r)] *n* engoulevent *m* (d'Europe)

nightlife ['naɪtlaɪf] *n* vie *f* nocturne; **there's not much n.** il n'y a pas grand-chose à faire le soir

nightlong ['naɪtlɒŋ] *adj* qui dure toute la nuit

nightly ['naɪtlɪ] **1** *adj* de toutes les nuits; *(in the evening)* du soir
2 *adv* toutes les nuits; *(in the evening)* tous les soirs

nightmare ['naɪtmeə(r)] *n also Fig* cauchemar *m*

nightmarish ['naɪtmeərɪʃ] *adj* cauchemardesque

nightshirt ['naɪtʃɜːt] *n* chemise *f* de nuit

night-time ['naɪttaɪm] **1** *n* nuit *f;* **at n.** la nuit
2 *adj* nocturne

nihilistic [naɪ(h)ɪ'lɪstɪk] *adj* nihiliste

nil [nɪl] *n* néant *m; (in sport)* zéro *m*; **two n.** deux à zéro

Nile [naɪl] *n* **the N.** le Nil

nimble ['nɪmbəl] *adj (person)* souple; *(leap, movement)* leste; *(fingers)* preste; *(mind)* vif (vive)

nimbly ['nɪmbəlɪ] *adv* avec souplesse

nine [naɪn] **1** *n* neuf *m inv; Fam* **dressed up to the nines** sur son trente et un
2 *adj* neuf; **n. times out of ten** neuf fois sur dix; **a n.-to-five job** un travail de bureau; **to have n. lives** *(of person)* avoir l'âme chevillée au corps; *see also* **eight**

nineteen [naɪn'tiːn] **1** *n* dix-neuf *m inv; Br Fam* **to talk n. to the dozen** bavarder comme une pie
2 *adj* dix-neuf; *see also* **eight**

nineteenth [naɪn'tiːnθ] **1** *n* **(a)** *(fraction)* dix-neuvième *m* **(b)** *(in series)* dix-neuvième *mf* **(c)** *(of month)* dix-neuf *m inv*
2 *adj* dix-neuvième; *Fam Hum* **the n. hole** *(of golf course)* le bar du golf; *see also* **eighth**

ninetieth ['naɪntɪɪθ] **1** *n* **(a)** *(fraction)* quatre-vingt-dixième *m* **(b)** *(in series)* quatre-vingt-dixième *mf*
2 *adj* quatre-vingt-dixième; *see also* **eighth**

ninety ['naɪntɪ] **1** *n* quatre-vingt-dix *m inv*
2 *adj* quatre-vingt-dix; **n. nine times out of a hundred** quatre-vingt-dix-neuf fois sur cent; *see also* **eighty**

ninth [naɪnθ] **1** *n* **(a)** *(fraction)* neuvième *m* **(b)** *(in series)* neuvième *mf* **(c)** *(of month)* neuf *m inv*
2 *adj* neuvième; *see also* **eighth**

nip [nɪp] **1** *n* **(a)** *(pinch)* pincement *m; (bite)* morsure *f* légère **(b)** *(of cold, frost)* **there's a n. in the air** il fait frisquet **(c)** *Fam (of drink)* petit verre *m*
2 *(pt & pp* **nipped)** *vt* **(a)** *(pinch)* pincer; *(bite)* mordre légèrement; *Fam Fig* **to n. sth in the bud** étouffer qch dans l'œuf **(b)** *(of cold, frost)* pincer, piquer
3 *vi (sting)* piquer
▸ **nip out** *vi Br Fam* sortir quelques instants; **to n. out to the shop/pub** faire un saut au magasin/au pub

nipper ['nɪpə(r)] *n Br Fam (child)* gamin(e) *m,f*

nipple ['nɪp(ə)l] *n* mamelon *m; (on baby's bottle)* tétine *f*

nippy ['nɪpɪ] *adj Fam* **(a)** *(person, car)* rapide **(b)** *Br (cold)* vif (vive); **it's a bit n. today** il fait plutôt frisquet aujourd'hui

nit [nɪt] *n (in hair)* lente *f*; **to have nits** avoir des poux

nit-picker ['nɪtpɪkə(r)] *n Fam* chipoteur(euse) *m,f*

nit-picking ['nɪtpɪkɪŋ] *Fam* **1** *n* chipotage *m* **2** *adj* chipoteur(euse)

nitrate ['naɪtreɪt] *n* nitrate *m*

nitric ['naɪtrɪk] *adj* nitrique

nitrogen ['naɪtrədʒən] *n* azote *m*

nitroglycerine ['naɪtrəʊ'glɪsəri:n] *n* nitroglycérine *f*

nitrous ['naɪtrəs] *adj* nitreux(euse)

nitty-gritty ['nɪtɪ'grɪtɪ] *n Fam* **to get down to the n.** entrer dans le vif du sujet

nitwit ['nɪtwɪt] *n Fam* crétin(e) *m,f*

NNE *(abbr north-northeast)* NNE

NNW *(abbr north-northwest)* NNO

No, no *(abbr number)* n°

no [nəʊ] **1** *n (pl* **noes** *or* **nos)** non *m*; **she won't take no for an answer** elle n'accepte pas qu'on lui dise non **2** *adj* **(a)** *(not any)* pas de; **there's no bread** il n'y a pas de pain; **of no importance** sans importance; **I am in no way surprised** je ne suis pas du tout surpris; **he's no friend of mine** je ne le compte certainement pas au nombre de mes amis; *Fam* **no way!** pas question!

(b) *(with gerund)* **there's no denying it** on ne peut pas le nier; **there's no pleasing him** il n'est jamais satisfait; **no smoking** *(sign)* interdiction de fumer **3** *adv* **(a)** *(interjection)* non **(b)** *(not any)* **no richer/poorer** pas plus riche/pauvre; **no more/less than £100** pas plus/moins de 100 dollars; **he no longer lives there** il n'habite plus là

Noah ['nəʊə] *n* Noé; **N.'s ark** l'arche *f* de Noé

nobble ['nɒbəl] *vt Br Fam* **(a)** *(bribe)* payer **(b)** *(waylay)* coincer

Nobel Prize [nəʊ'bel'praɪz] *n* prix *m* Nobel

nobility [nəʊ'bɪlɪtɪ] *n* noblesse *f*

noble ['nəʊbəl] **1** *n* noble *mf* **2** *adj* noble; *Fig (building)* majestueux(euse)

nobleman ['nəʊbəlmən] *n* noble *m*

nobleminded [nəʊbəl'maɪndɪd] *adj (person)* au cœur noble, magnanime; *(sentiment, action)* noble

noblewoman ['nəʊbəlwʊmən] *n* noble *f*

nobly ['nəʊbəlɪ] *adv* avec noblesse

nobody ['nəʊbədɪ] **1** *pron* personne; **n. spoke to me** personne ne m'a parlé; **n. else** personne d'autre; **she's n.'s fool** elle n'est pas née de la dernière pluie; **if you don't have money, you're n.** si on n'a pas d'argent on est un moins que rien **2** *n (pl* **nobodies)** **a n.** un(e) moins que rien

no-claims bonus ['nəʊ'kleɪmz'bəʊnəs] *n* bonus *m*

nocturnal [nɒk'tɜ:nəl] *adj* nocturne

nod [nɒd] **1** *n (in greeting, as signal)* signe *m* de tête; *(in agreement)* signe de tête affirmatif; *Fig* **to give sb/sth the n.** donner le feu vert à qn/qch; **2** *vt (pt & pp* **nodded)** **to n. one's head** *(in greeting, as signal)* faire un signe de tête; *(in agreement)* faire oui de la tête; **to n. one's agreement/approval** consentir/approuver d'un signe de tête **3** *vi* **to n. in agreement/approval** consentir/approuver d'un signe de tête

▸ **nod off** *vi Fam* s'assoupir

node [nəʊd] *n (of curve, plant)* nœud *m*; *Med* ganglion *m*; *Comptr* noyau *m*

nodule ['nɒdju:l] *n* nodule *m*

no-frills [nəʊ'frɪlz] *adj* tout(e) simple

no-go area ['nəʊ'gəʊeərɪə] *n* zone *f* interdite

no-good ['nəʊgʊd] *adj Fam* **a n.** idiot un imbécile propre à rien; **that n. husband of hers** son bon à rien de mari

no-hoper [nəʊ'həʊpə(r)] *n* tocard(e) *m,f*

noise [nɔɪz] *n* bruit *m*; *Fig* **to make noises about doing sth** parler de faire qch; *Fig* **a big n.** une huile

noiselessly ['nɔɪzlɪslɪ] *adv* sans bruit, silencieusement

noisily ['nɔɪzɪlɪ] *adv* bruyamment

noisy ['nɔɪzɪ] *adj* bruyant(e)

nomad ['nəʊmæd] *n & adj* nomade *mf*

nomadic [nəʊ'mædɪk] *adj* nomade

no man's land ['nəʊmænz'lænd] *n Fig* no man's land *m*

nomenclature [nəʊ'menklətʃə(r)] *n* nomenclature *f*

nominal ['nɒmɪnəl] *adj* nominal(e); *(damages)* symbolique; *(rent)* insignifiant(e)

nominally ['nɒmɪnəlɪ] *adv* nominalement

nominate ['nɒmɪneɪt] *vt (propose)* proposer **(for/as** *pour/comme)*; *(appoint)* nommer **(to/as** à/comme)

nomination [nɒmɪ'neɪʃən] *n* **(a)** *(proposal)* candidature *f*; *(for film, TV awards)* nomination *f* **(b)** *(appointment)* nomination *f*

nominee [nɒmɪ'ni:] *n (proposed)* candidat(e) *m,f*, *(appointed)* personne *f* nommée

non- [nɒn] *pref* non(-)

non-aggression pact [nɒnə'greʃən'pækt] *n Pol* pacte *m* de non-agression

nonalcoholic [nɒnælkə'hɒlɪk] *adj* sans alcool

nonaligned [nɒnə'laɪnd] *adj* *(of non-alliance)*

nonattendance [nɒnə'tendəns] *n* absence *f*

nonchalance ['nɒnʃələns] *n* désinvolture *f*

nonchalant ['nɒnʃələnt] *adj* désinvolte

nonchalantly ['nɒnʃələntlɪ] *adv* avec désinvolture

noncombatant ['nɒn'kɒmbətənt] *n & adj Mil* non-combattant(e) *m,f*

noncommissioned officer ['nɒnkə'mɪʃənd'ɒfɪsə(r)] *n Mil* sous-officier *m*

noncommittal [nɒnkə'mɪtəl] *adj (answer)* de Normand; **to be n.** ne pas s'engager

nonconformist [nɒnkən'fɔ:mɪst] *n & adj* nonconformiste *mf*

nondescript ['nɒndɪskrɪpt] *adj* banal(e); *(colour)* fade

none [nʌn] **1** *pron* aucun(e) *m,f*; **n. of you** aucun d'entre vous/nous; **n. of my friends** aucun de mes amis; **n. of this interests me** rien de tout cela ne m'intéresse; **it was n. other than the President** c'était le Président, rien de moins; **there was/were n. left** il n'en restait plus; *Fam* **we'll have n. of that!** pas de ça! **2** *adv* **his answer left me n. the wiser** sa réponse ne m'a pas avancé; **n. too pleased** pas très satisfait(e); **n. too soon** pas trop tôt

nonentity [nɒ'nentɪtɪ] *(pl* **nonentities)** *n* personne *f* sans intérêt

nonessential [nɒnɪ'senʃəl] *adj* qui n'est pas essentiel(elle)

nonetheless [nʌnðə'les] *adv* néanmoins, cependant

nonevent [nɒnɪ'vent] *n* **to be a n.** être décevant(e)

nonexecutive director [nɒnɪg'zekjʊtɪvdaɪ'rektə(r)] *n* = administrateur à titre consultatif

nonexistent [nɒnɪg'zɪstənt] *adj* inexistant(e)

non-fiction [nɒn'fɪkʃən] *n* ouvrages *mpl* généraux

nonflammable [nɒn'flæməbəl] *adj* ininflammable

non-linear [nɒn'lɪnɪə(r)] *adj Comptr* non linéaire

non-negotiable [nɒnnɪ'gəʊʃəbəl] *adj* non négociable

non-nuclear [nɒn'nju:klɪə(r)] *adj (country)* non nucléarisé(e); *(war, defence)* non nucléaire

no-no ['nəʊnəʊ] *(pl* **no-nos** *or* **no-noes**) *n Fam* **that's a n.** c'est à ne pas faire

no-nonsense [nəʊ'nɒnsəns] *adj* direct(e)

non-partisan [nɒn'pɑːtɪzæn] *adj* impartial(e)

non-payment [nɒn'peɪmənt] *n* non-paiement *m*

non-person ['nɒn'pɜːsən] *n* proscrit(e) *m,f*

nonplussed [nɒn'plʌst] *adj* interloqué(e)

non-profit-making [nɒn'prɒfɪtmeɪkɪŋ] *adj* à but non lucratif

non-racist [nɒn'reɪsɪst] *adj* non raciste

nonresident [nɒn'rezɪdənt] *n (of country)* nonrésident(e) *m,f; (of hotel)* client(e) *m,f*

nonreturnable [nɒnrɪ'tɜːnəbəl] *adj (bottle)* non consigné(e); *(deposit)* non remboursable

nonsense ['nɒnsəns] *n* bêtises *fpl,* idioties *fpl;* **n.!** n'importe quoi!; **to talk (a lot of) n.** dire des bêtises; **to make a n. of sth** ôter tout sens à qch

nonsensical [nɒn'sensɪkəl] *adj* absurde, qui n'a pas de sens

non sequitur [nɒn'sekwɪtə(r)] *n* absurdité *f*

non-sexist [nɒn'seksɪst] *adj* non sexiste

non-smoker [nɒn'sməʊkə(r)] *n* non-fumeur(euse) *m,f; (train compartment)* compartiment *m* non-fumeurs

non-specialist [nɒn'speʃəlɪst] **1** *n* non-spécialiste *mf* **2** *adj* non spécialisé(e)

nonstarter [nɒn'stɑːtə(r)] *n* **to be a n.** *(of plan)* être fichu(e) d'avance

nonstick ['nɒn'stɪk] *adj (surface)* anti-adhésif(ive); *(frying pan)* qui n'attache pas

non-stop ['nɒn'stɒp] **1** *adj (journey)* sans arrêt; *(flight)* sans escale **2** *adv* sans arrêt; *(fly)* sans escale

non-tariff barrier ['nɒn'tærɪf'bærɪə(r)] *n Econ* barrière *f* non tarifaire

nontransferable ['nɒntræns'fɜːrəbəl] *adj (ticket, membership)* nominatif(ive); *(property, right)* incessible

nonverbal [nɒn'vɜːbəl] *adj* non-verbal(e)

nonviolent [nɒn'vaɪələnt] *adj* non-violent(e)

noodles ['nuːdəlz] *npl* nouilles *fpl*

nook [nʊk] *n (corner)* recoin *m; (retreat)* coin *m;* **every n. and cranny** le moindre recoin

nookie, nooky ['nʊkɪ] *n Br very Fam* crac-crac *m*

noon [nuːn] *n* midi; **at n.** à midi

noonday ['nuːndeɪ] *n Lit* midi *m;* **the n. sun** le soleil de midi

no-one ['nəʊwʌn] = **nobody**

noose [nuːs] *n* nœud *m* coulant; *Fig* **to put one's head in a n.** signer son arrêt de mort

nope [nəʊp] *adv Fam* non

nor [nɔː(r)] **1** *conj* **neither you n. your brother** ni toi ni ton frère; **neither... n.** ni... ni; **he neither drinks n. smokes** il ne boit pas et ne fume pas non plus **2** *adv* **n. do I** moi non plus; **if you don't go n. shall I** si tu n'y vas pas, moi non plus

Nordic ['nɔːdɪk] *adj* nordique

norm [nɔːm] *n* norme *f*

normal ['nɔːməl] **1** *n* **above/below n.** *(temperature, rate)* au-dessus/au-dessous de la normale; **to get back to n.** redevenir normal(e) **2** *adj* normal(e)

normality [nɔː'mælɪtɪ], *Am* **normalcy** ['nɔːməlsɪ] *n* normalité *f;* **a return to n.** un retour à la normale

normalization [nɔːməlaɪ'zeɪʃən] *n* normalisation *f*

normalize ['nɔːməlaɪz] **1** *vt* normaliser **2** *vi* redevenir normal(e)

normally ['nɔːməlɪ] *adv* normalement

Norman ['nɔːmən] **1** *n* Normand(e) *m,f* **2** *adj* normand(e)

Normandy ['nɔːməndɪ] *n* la Normandie

north [nɔːθ] **1** *n* nord *m;* **to the n. (of)** au nord (de) **2** *adj (coast, side)* nord; *(wind)* du nord; **N.** Africa Afrique *f* du Nord; **N.** African nord-africain(e); *(person)* Nord-Africain(e) *m,f;* **N.** America Amérique *f* du Nord; **N.** American nord-américain(e); *(person)* Nord-Américain(e) *m,f;* **N.** Carolina la Caroline du Nord; **N.** Dakota le Dakota du Nord; **N.** Korea Corée *f* du Nord; **N.** Korean nord-coréen(enne); *(person)* Nord-Coréen(enne) *m,f;* **the N.** Pole le Pôle Nord; **the N.** Sea la mer du Nord **3** *adv* au nord; *(travel)* vers le nord; **to face n.** *(of house)* être exposé(e) au nord

northbound ['nɔːθbaʊnd] *adj (train, traffic)* en direction du nord; **n. carriageway** voie *f* nord

northeast [nɔːθ'iːst] **1** *n* nord-est *m* **2** *adj (side)* nord-est; *(wind)* du nord-est **3** *adv* au nord-est; *(travel)* vers le nord-est

northeasterly [nɔːθ'iːstəlɪ] **1** *n (wind)* vent *m* du nord-est **2** *adj (direction)* vers le nord-est; *(wind)* du nord-est

northeastern [nɔːθ'iːstən] *adj (region)* (du) nord-est

northerly ['nɔːðəlɪ] **1** *n (pl* **northerlies)** *(wind)* vent *m* du nord **2** *adj (direction)* vers le nord; *(wind)* du nord; **the most n. point** le point le plus au nord

northern ['nɔːðən] *adj (region, accent)* du nord; **n.** France le nord de la France; **n.** hemisphere hémisphère *m* nord; **N.** Ireland l'Irlande *f* du Nord; **N.** Irish de l'Irlande du Nord; **the N.** Irish les Irlandais *mpl* du Nord; **N.** Lights aurore *f* boréale

northerner ['nɔːðənə(r)] *n Br* habitant(e) *m,f* du Nord *(de l'Angleterre)*

north-facing ['nɔːθ'feɪsɪŋ] *adj* exposé(e) au nord

north-northeast [nɔːθnɔːθ'iːst] *adv* au nord-nord-est; *(travel)* vers le nord-nord-est

north-northwest [nɔːθnɔːθ'west] *adv* au nord-nord-ouest; *(travel)* vers le nord-nord-ouest

northward ['nɔːθwəd] **1** *adj* au nord **2** *adv* vers le nord

northwards ['nɔːθwədz] *adv* vers le nord

northwest [nɔːθ'west] **1** *n* nord-ouest *m* **2** *adj (side)* nord-ouest; *(wind)* du nord-ouest **3** *adv* au nord-ouest; *(travel)* vers le nord-ouest

northwesterly [nɔːθ'westəlɪ] **1** *n (pl* **north-westerlies)** *(wind)* vent *m* du nord-ouest **2** *adj (direction)* vers le nord-ouest; *(wind)* du nord-ouest

northwestern [nɔːθ'westən] *adj (region)* (du) nord-ouest

North-West Territories ['nɔːθ'west'terɪtriːz] *npl* les Territoires *mpl* du Nord-Ouest

Norway ['nɔːweɪ] *n* la Norvège

Norwegian [nɔː'wiːdʒən] *n* **(a)** *(person)* Norvégien(enne) *m,f* **(b)** *(language)* norvégien *m* **2** *adj* norvégien(enne)

nose [nəʊz] *n* **(a)** *(of person, animal, aeroplane)* nez *m;* **her n. is bleeding** elle saigne du nez; **to blow one's n.** se moucher (le nez); **to hold one's n.** se boucher le nez; *Fam* **to have a n. job** se faire refaire le nez; **the traffic was n. to tail** les voitures se suivaient pare-chocs contre pare-chocs **(b)** *(idioms)* **it's under your n.** vous l'avez sous le nez;

turn one's n. up at sth dédaigner qch; **she walked by with her n.** in the air elle passa, l'air dédaigneux; **to look down one's n.** at sb prendre qn de haut; **to pay through the n.** for sth payer qch une fortune; **to get up sb's n.** taper sur les nerfs à qn; **to lead sb by the n.** mener qn par le bout du nez; **to keep one's n. clean** se tenir à carreau; **to have a n.** for sth savoir flairer qch; **to poke one's n. into other people's business** fourrer son nez dans les affaires des autres
‣ **nose about, nose around** vi Fam fouiner

nosebleed ['nəʊzbliːd] n **to have a n.** saigner du nez

nose-dive ['nəʊzdaɪv] **1** n (of plane) (vol m en) piqué m; Fig (of prices) chute f rapide
2 vi (of plane) piquer du nez; Fig (of prices) chuter fortement

nosey ['nəʊzɪ] adj Fam fouineur(euse); (questions) indiscret(ète)

nosh [nɒʃ] Br Fam **1** n (food) bouffe f
2 vi (eat) bouffer

no-show [nəʊ'ʃəʊ] n (for flight) = passager qui ne se présente pas à l'embarquement; (for show) = personne qui a réservé une place mais n'assiste pas au spectacle

nosiness ['nəʊzɪnəs] n curiosité f

no-smoking [nəʊ'sməʊkɪŋ] adj (carriage, area) non-fumeurs; (seat) non-fumeur

nostalgia [nɒs'tældʒɪə] n nostalgie f

nostalgic [nɒs'tældʒɪk] adj nostalgique

nostalgically [nɒs'tældʒɪklɪ] adv avec nostalgie

nostril ['nɒstrɪl] n narine f

nosy ['nəʊzɪ] = nosey

not [nɒt] adv

> À l'oral, et à l'écrit dans un style familier, on utilise généralement not à la forme contractée lorsqu'il suit un modal ou un auxiliaire (don't go!; she wasn't there; he couldn't see me).

n. me/him pas moi/lui; **I don't know** je ne sais pas; **don't move!** ne bouge pas!; **whether she likes it or n.** que ça lui plaise ou non; **I think/hope n.** je pense/j'espère que non; **she asked me n. to tell him** elle m'a demandé de ne pas le lui dire; **n. wishing to cause an argument, he said nothing** ne voulant pas provoquer de dispute, il s'est tu; **you understand, don't you?** tu comprends, n'est-ce pas?; **n. at all** pas du tout; (you're welcome) je vous en prie; **n. any more** plus maintenant; **n. even** pas même, même pas; **n. only..., but also...** non seulement..., mais encore...; **n. yet** pas encore; **n. that I minded** non pas que ça me dérangeait; **n. that it matters** non pas que ça ait de l'importance; **n. that I know of** pas que je sache

notable ['nəʊtəbəl] adj (person, thing) notable; (achievement, success) remarquable; **with a few n. exceptions** à quelques exceptions près, et non des moindres

notably ['nəʊtəblɪ] adv notamment

notary ['nəʊtərɪ] (pl notaries) n Law **n. (public)** notaire m

notation [nəʊ'teɪʃən] n notation f

notch [nɒtʃ] **1** n (a) (in stick) encoche f; (in belt) cran m (b) (grade, level) cran m
2 vt encocher
‣ **notch up** vt sep (victory, sale) remporter; (points) marquer

note [nəʊt] **1** n (a) (information, reminder) note f; (short letter) mot m; (lecture) notes notes (de cours); **to take or make a n. of sth** prendre note de qch; **to take n. of sb/sth** remarquer qn/qch (b) (musical) note f; Fig (of impatience, anger) pointe f; **on a lighter/more serious n.** pour en venir

à un sujet moins/plus sérieux (c) (banknote) billet m (d) (significance) **of n.** remarquable
2 vt noter, remarquer; (error) relever; (fact) constater
‣ **note down** vt sep prendre note de, noter

notebook ['nəʊtbʊk] n carnet m; (larger) cahier m; Comptr agenda m

noted ['nəʊtɪd] adj éminent(e); **to be n. for sth** être réputé(e) pour qch

notepad ['nəʊtpæd] n bloc-notes m

notepaper ['nəʊtpeɪpə(r)] n papier m à lettres

noteworthy ['nəʊtwɜːðɪ] adj remarquable

nothing ['nʌθɪŋ] **1** pron rien; **n. happened** il ne s'est rien passé; **I have n. to do** je n'ai rien à faire; **to have n. to do with sb/sth** (be unconnected to) n'avoir rien à voir avec qn/qch; (not get involved with) n'avoir rien à faire avec qn/qch; **to say n. of...** sans parler de...; **she was n. if not discreet** elle a été très discrète; **n. new/remarkable** rien de nouveau/d'exceptionnel; **n. but** rien que; **n. else** rien d'autre; **n. much** pas grand-chose; **there is n. more to be said** il n'y a plus rien à dire; **there's n. like a nice steak!** rien de tel qu'un bon steak!; **as a singer, he has n. on his brother** en tant que chanteur, son frère n'a rien à lui envier; **there's n. in it** (it's untrue) il n'y a rien de vrai dans tout ça; **to think n. of doing sth** trouver normal de faire qch; Fam **there's n. to it** ce n'est pas sorcier; **$1,000 is n. to her** 1000 dollars, ce n'est pour elle; **to get angry/worried for n.** se fâcher/s'inquiéter pour un rien; **to do sth for n.** (in vain, free of charge) faire qch pour rien
2 n to come to n. être anéanti(e); **a hundred pounds? – a mere n.!** cent livres? – une bagatelle!
3 adv **she looks n. like her mother** elle ne ressemble pas du tout à sa mère; **it was n. like as they said** c'était loin d'être aussi difficile qu'on le disait

notice ['nəʊtɪs] **1** n (a) (warning) avertissement m; (of resignation, redundancy) préavis m; **to give sb n.** (of sth) avertir qn (de qch); (of resignation, redundancy) donner un préavis à qn (pour qch); **until further n.** jusqu'à nouvel ordre; **at short n.** au pied levé; **at a moment's n.** sur-le-champ; **to give in one's n.** (resign) donner sa démission, démissionner; **to give sb n.** (of employer) licencier qn (b) (attention) **to take n. of sb/sth** faire ou prêter attention à qn/qch; **to take no n. of sb/sth** ne pas prêter la moindre attention à qn/qch; **the fact escaped everyone's n.** ce fait a échappé à tout le monde; **it has come to my n. that...** (I was told) on m'a signalé que...; (I read it) je me suis rendu compte que... (c) (sign) écriteau m, pancarte f; (poster) affiche f (d) (criticism of play, film) critique f
2 vt remarquer, s'apercevoir de; **to be noticed, to get oneself noticed** se faire remarquer
3 vi remarquer

noticeable ['nəʊtɪsəbəl] adj (change, difference) sensible, perceptible; **it was n. that...** il était évident que...

noticeably ['nəʊtɪsəblɪ] adv sensiblement

noticeboard ['nəʊtɪsbɔːd] n Br panneau m d'affichage

notification [nəʊtɪfɪ'keɪʃən] n avis m, notification f; **to give sb n. of sth** avertir qn de qch

notify ['nəʊtɪfaɪ] (pt & pp notified) vt annoncer, notifier; **to n. sb of sth** avertir qn de qch

notion ['nəʊʃən] n notion f; **to have a n. that...** avoir dans l'idée que...; **to have a n. to do sth** avoir envie de faire qch

notoriety [nəʊtə'raɪətɪ] n notoriété f; **to achieve or gain n.** se rendre tristement célèbre

notorious [nəʊ'tɔːrɪəs] adj tristement célèbre; (criminal) notoire; (place) mal famé(e); (liar) fieffé(e)

notoriously [nəʊ'tɔːrɪəslɪ] adv **to be n. tactless/rude** être bien connu(e) pour son manque de tact/son impolitesse; **Scottish weather is n.** unpredictable il est bien connu qu'en Écosse, le temps est très changeant

notwithstanding [nɒtwɪθ'stændɪŋ] *Formal* **1** *prep* en dépit de, malgré **2** *adv* néanmoins; **difficulties n.,**... ces difficultés mises à part,...

nougat ['nuːgaː] *n* nougat *m*

nought [nɔːt] *n* zéro *m*; *Br* **noughts and crosses** ≃ morpion *m (jeu)*

noun [naʊn] *n* nom *m*

nourish ['nʌrɪʃ] *vt* nourrir

nourishing ['nʌrɪʃɪŋ] *adj* nourrissant(e)

nourishment ['nʌrɪʃmənt] *n* nourriture *f*; *(nourishing quality)* richesse *f* nutritive

Nov *(abbr* **November)** novembre

Nova Scotia ['nəʊvə'skəʊʃə] *n* la Nouvelle-Écosse

novel ['nɒvəl] **1** *n* roman *m* **2** *adj (original)* nouveau(elle), original(e)

novelist ['nɒvəlɪst] *n* romancier(ère) *m,f*

novelty ['nɒvəltɪ] *(pl* **novelties)** *n (newness)* nouveauté *f*; *(cheap object)* bricole *f*; **the n. will soon wear off** l'attrait de la nouveauté ne tardera pas à s'estomper; **n. value** attrait *m* de la nouveauté

November [nəʊ'vembə(r)] *n* novembre *m*; *see also* **May**

novice ['nɒvɪs] *n (beginner)* débutant(e) *m,f* **(at** en); *Rel* novice *mf*

now [naʊ] **1** *adv* **(a)** *(at this moment, these days)* maintenant; **it's n. or never** c'est maintenant ou jamais; **that'll do for n.** ça suffit pour le moment; **it's two years n.** since his mother died ça fait maintenant deux ans que sa mère est morte; **she won't be long n.** elle ne va plus tarder; **any minute/day n.** d'une minute/d'un jour à l'autre; **n. is the time to...** c'est le moment de...; **right n.** *(immediately)* tout de suite; *(at the moment)* pour le moment; **(every) n. and then, (every) n. and again** de temps en temps, de temps à autre; **up to** *or* **until n.** jusqu'à présent *ou* maintenant; **from n. on** dorénavant; **a week from n.** dans une semaine; **she ought to be here by n.** elle devrait déjà être ici; **and n. for some music** et maintenant, un peu de musique **(b)** *(before statement, argument)* bon; **n., there are two ways of interpreting this** bon, il y a deux interprétations possibles; **come n.!** allons!; **n., n.! stop quarrelling!** allons, allons! arrêtez de vous disputer!
2 *conj* **n. (that)...** maintenant que...; **n. (that) you mention it,...** maintenant que tu le dis,...

nowadays ['naʊədeɪz] *adv* de nos jours

nowhere ['nəʊweə(r)] **1** *adv* nulle part; **n. else** nulle part ailleurs; **she was n. to be found** elle était introuvable; **qualifications alone will get you n.** les diplômes seuls ne servent à rien; **to be n. near as nice/stupid (as)** être loin d'être aussi agréable/stupide (que); **it's n. near the city centre** c'est à des kilomètres du centre-ville; **to finish n.** *(in contest)* finir loin derrière les autres; *Fam* **we're getting n. fast** on perd notre temps
2 *n* **in the middle of n.** dans un coin paumé; **he came from n. to win the race** il a gagné la course après une remontée spectaculaire

noxious ['nɒkʃəs] *adj* nocif(ive)

nozzle ['nɒzəl] *n (of petrol pump)* pistolet *m*; *(of vacuum cleaner)* suceur *m*; *(of pipe)* jet *m*; *(for icing)* douille *f*

nr *(abbr* **near)** près de

NRA [enɑː'reɪ] *n Am (abbr* **National Rifle Association)** = association américaine favorable à la généralisation des armes à feu

NSPCC [enespiːsiː'siː] *n Br (abbr* **National Society for the**

Prevention of Cruelty to Children) = comité britannique pour la protection des enfants maltraités

nth [enθ] *adj Fam* énième

nuance ['njuːɒns] *n* nuance *f*

nub [nʌb] *n (of question, argument)* cœur *m*

nubile ['njuːbaɪl] *adj* désirable

nuclear ['njuːklɪə(r)] *adj* nucléaire; **n. disarmament** désarmement *m* nucléaire; **n. energy** énergie *f* nucléaire *ou* atomique; **n. family** famille *f* nucléaire; **n. physics** physique *f* nucléaire; **n. power** énergie *f* nucléaire; **n. power station** centrale *f* atomique *ou* nucléaire; **n. war** guerre *f* atomique *ou* nucléaire; **n. waste** déchets *mpl* nucléaires; **n. weapon** arme *f* atomique *ou* nucléaire; **n. winter** hiver *m* nucléaire

nuclear-free zone ['njuːklɪə'friː'zəʊn] *n* zone *f* dénucléarisée

nucleus ['njuːklɪəs] *(pl* **nuclei** ['njuːklɪaɪ]) *n also Fig* noyau *m*

nude [njuːd] **1** *n* nu *m*; **in the n.** tout(e) nu(e) **2** *adj* nu(e)

nudge [nʌdʒ] **1** *n* coup *m* de coude **2** *vt* donner un coup de coude à

nudist ['njuːdɪst] *n* nudiste *mf*; **n. camp** *or* **colony** camp *m* de nudistes

nudity ['njuːdɪtɪ] *n* nudité *f*

nugatory ['njuːgətɒrɪ] *adj* sans valeur

nugget ['nʌgɪt] *n* **(a)** *(of gold)* pépite *f*; *Fig* **a n. of information** un renseignement précieux **(b) chicken nuggets** morceaux *mpl* de poulet frit

nuisance ['njuːsəns] *n* **to be a n.** *(of person, situation)* être embêtant(e); **to make a n. of oneself** embêter le monde; **n. call** *(on telephone)* appel *m* anonyme

nuke [njuːk] *vt Fam* lâcher la bombe sur

null [nʌl] *adj* nul (nulle); **n. and void** nul et non avenu

nullify ['nʌlɪfaɪ] *(pt & pp* **nullified)** *vt* annuler; *(decree)* invalider

numb [nʌm] **1** *adj* engourdi(e); **to go n.** s'engourdir; **n. with cold** engourdi par le froid; **n. with fear** paralysé(e) par la peur **2** *vt (of cold)* engourdir; *(of fear)* paralyser

number ['nʌmbə(r)] **1** *n* **(a)** *(numeral)* nombre *m*; *(when written)* chiffre *m*; *Comptr* **n. crunching** calculs *mpl* (rapides) **(b)** *(of house, page, telephone)* numéro *m*; **I live at n. 25** j'habite au (numéro) 25; **(telephone) n.** numéro de téléphone; *Fam* **to look after n. one** s'occuper de sa petite personne; *Br* **N. Ten** le dix Downing Street *(résidence du premier ministre britannique)* **(c)** *(quantity)* nombre *m*; **a large n. of** un grand nombre de; **in small/great numbers** en petit/grand nombre **(d)** *(song)* chanson *f* **(e)** *(idioms)* **he's my n. two** *(subordinate)* c'est mon adjoint; *Fam* **his n.'s up** son compte est bon; *Fam* **that car/dress is a nice little n.** c'est une jolie petite voiture/robe; *Fam* **she's got a nice little n. there** *(situation)* elle s'est dégoté un bon plan
2 *vt* **(a)** *(assign number to)* numéroter **(b)** *(count)* compter; **his days are numbered** ses jours sont comptés; **to n. sb among one's friends** compter qn parmi ou au nombre de ses amis

numberplate ['nʌmbəpleɪt] *n Br* plaque *f* d'immatriculation *ou* minéralogique

numbly ['nʌmlɪ] *adv* (say, react) mollement; *(stare)* d'un air hébété

numbness ['nʌmnɪs] *n (in body)* engourdissement *m*; *(of emotions)* torpeur *f*

numbskull ['nʌmskʌl] n Br Fam bêta(asse) m,f
numeracy ['nju:mərəsɪ] n degré m d'aptitude en calcul
numeral ['nju:mərəl] n chiffre m
numerate ['nju:mərət] adj to be n. savoir compter
numerator ['nju:məreɪtə(r)] n Math numérateur m
numerical [nju:'merɪkəl] adj numérique
numerically [nju:'merɪklɪ] adv numériquement
numerous ['nju:mərəs] adj nombreux(euse); **on n. occasions** en de nombreuses occasions
nun [nʌn] n religieuse f, nonne f; **to become a n.** prendre la voile
nunnery ['nʌnərɪ] (pl **nunneries**) n couvent m
nuptial ['nʌpʃəl] **1** npl Hum or Lit **nuptials** noces fpl **2** adj Lit nuptial(e)
nurse [nɜ:s] **1** n (a) (medical) infirmière f; **(male) n.** infirmier m (b) (looking after children) nurse f **2** vt (look after) soigner; (suckle) allaiter; Fig (feeling, hope) nourrir; (grievance) entretenir; **to n. sb back to health** faire recouvrer la santé à qn
nursery ['nɜ:sərɪ] (pl **nurseries**) n (a) (for children) (establishment) garderie f; (room in house) chambre f d'enfants; Br **n. education** enseignement m en maternelle; **n. rhyme** comptine f; Br **n. (school)** maternelle f; Br **n. slopes** (in skiing) pistes fpl pour débutants (b) (for plants) pépinière f
nursing ['nɜ:sɪŋ] n (profession) profession f d'infirmière; (care) soins mpl; **n. home** (for old people) maison f de retraite; **n. staff** personnel m soignant
nurture ['nɜ:tʃə(r)] vt (a) (feed) (children, plants) nourrir; (plan, idea) élaborer (b) (bring up) faire l'éducation de
NUS [enju:'es] n Br (abbr **National Union of Students**) = syndicat britannique d'étudiants
NUT [enju:'ti:] n Br (abbr **National Union of Teachers**) = syndicat britannique d'enseignants
nut [nʌt] n (a) (food) = noix, noisette, cacahuète, pistache ou autre fruit sec de cette nature; Fig **he's a hard** or **tough**

n. c'est un dur; Fig **a tough** or **hard n. to crack** (problem) un problème difficile à résoudre (b) Br Fam (head) caboche f; **to do one's n.** piquer une crise (c) Fam (mad person) dingue mf; **a sci-fi n.** un dingue de SF (d) (for fastening bolt) écrou m; Fig **the nuts and bolts** les notions de base (e) very Fam **nuts** (testicles) couilles fpl
nutcase ['nʌtkeɪs] n Fam cinglé(e) m,f
nutcrackers ['nʌtkrækəz] npl (pair of) n. casse-noisettes m inv, casse-noix m inv
nuthouse ['nʌthaʊs] n Fam maison f de fous
nutmeg ['nʌtmeg] n (noix f de) muscade f
nutrient ['nju:trɪənt] **1** n élément m nutritif **2** adj nutritif(ive)
nutrition [nju:'trɪʃən] n nutrition f
nutritional [nju:'trɪʃənəl] adj nutritionnel(elle); (value) nutritif(ive)
nutritious [nju:'trɪʃəs] adj nutritif(ive)
nuts [nʌts] adj Fam (mad) dingue; **to be n. about sb/sth** être dingue de qn/qch
nutshell ['nʌtʃel] n coquille f de noix/noisette/etc; Fig **in a n.,...** bref,...
nutter ['nʌtə(r)] n Br Fam (mad person) dingue mf
nutty ['nʌtɪ] adj (a) (in taste) au goût de noisette/noix/etc; (containing nuts) aux noisettes/noix/etc (b) Fam (mad) dingue
nuzzle ['nʌzəl] **1** vt renifler **2** vi **to n.** against sb renifler qn
NW (abbr northwest) N-O
NY [en'waɪ] n Am (abbr **New York**) New York
nylon ['naɪlɒn] n Nylon®m; **nylons** (stockings) bas mpl Nylon®
nymph [nɪmf] n nymphe f
nymphomania [nɪmfəʊ'meɪnɪə] n nymphomanie f
nymphomaniac [nɪmfəʊ'meɪnɪæk] n nymphomane f
NZ (abbr **New Zealand**) la Nouvelle-Zélande

O, o [əʊ] *n* **(a)** *(letter)* O, o *m* *inv* **(b)** *(zero)* zéro *m*

oaf [əʊf] *n* lourdaud *m*

oak [əʊk] *n* chêne *m*; **o. apple** noix *f* de galle

OAP [əʊeɪ'piː] *n Br (abbr* **old age pensioner***)* retraité(e) *m,f*

oar [ɔː(r)] *n* aviron *m*, rame *f*; *Fig* **to put** *or* **stick one's o. in** mettre son grain de sel

oarsman ['ɔːzmən] *n* rameur *m*

oarswoman ['ɔːzwʊmən] *n* rameuse *f*

OAS [əʊeɪ'es] *n (abbr* **Organization of American States)** OEA *f*

oasis [əʊ'eɪsɪs] *(pl* **oases** [əʊ'eɪsiːz]*) n also Fig* oasis *f*

oatcake ['əʊtkeɪk] *n* galette *f* d'avoine

oath [əʊθ] *n* **(a)** *(pledge)* serment *m*; **o. of allegiance** serment d'allégeance; **to take** *or* **swear an o.** prêter serment; **on** *or* **under o.** sous serment **(b)** *(swear word)* juron *m*

oatmeal ['əʊtmiːl] *n* farine *f* d'avoine; *(colour)* beige *m*

oats [əʊts] *npl (plant)* avoine *f*; **(porridge) o.** *(food)* flocons *mpl* d'avoine; *Br very Fam* **to get one's o.** s'envoyer en l'air

OAU [əʊeɪ'juː] *n (abbr* **Organization of African Unity)** OUA *f*

obdurate ['ɒbdjʊrɪt] *adj* obstiné(e)

obedience [ə'biːdɪəns] *n* obéissance *f*

obedient [ə'biːdɪənt] *adj* obéissant(e)

obelisk ['ɒbəlɪsk] *n* obélisque *m*

obese [əʊ'biːs] *adj* obèse

obesity [əʊ'biːsɪtɪ] *n* obésité *f*

obey [ə'beɪ] **1** *vt* obéir à **2** *vi* obéir

obfuscation [ɒbfʌ'skeɪʃən] *n* obscurcissement *m*

obituary [ə'bɪtjʊərɪ] *(pl* **obituaries)** *n* nécrologie *f*; **o. column** rubrique *f* nécrologique; **o. notice** nécrologie

object 1 *n* ['ɒbdʒɪkt] **(a)** *(thing, recipient)* objet *m*; **an o. of contempt/desire** un objet de mépris/de désir; **an o. lesson in** un parfait exemple de **(b)** *(aim)* objet *m*, but *m*; **the o. of the exercise is to...** cet exercice a pour objet *ou* but de... **(c)** *(obstacle)* **money/distance is no o.** le prix/la distance importe peu **(d)** *Gram* complément *m* d'objet **2** *vi* [ə'bdʒekt] émettre une objection; **to o. to sth/to doing sth** ne pas être d'accord avec qch/pour faire qch

objection [ə'bdʒekʃən] *n* **(a)** *(protest)* objection *f*; **to have no o.** ne voir aucune objection à qch; **I have no o. to going** ça ne me dérange pas d'y aller **(b)** *(reason for objecting)* inconvénient *m* **(to** de)

objectionable [ə'bdʒekʃənəbəl] *adj (unpleasant)* déplaisant(e)

objective [əb'dʒektɪv] **1** *n (aim, goal)* objectif *m* **2** *adj (impartial)* objectif(ive)

objectively [əb'dʒektɪvlɪ] *adv* objectivement

objectivity [ɒbdʒek'tɪvɪtɪ] *n* objectivité *f*

obligation [ɒblɪ'geɪʃən] *n* obligation *f*; **to be under an o. to sb** avoir une dette envers qn; **to be under an o. to do sth** être dans l'obligation de faire qch

obligatory [ɒ'blɪgətərɪ] *adj* obligatoire

oblige [ə'blaɪdʒ] *vt* **(a)** *(compel)* obliger; **to be obliged to do sth** être obligé(e) de faire qch **(b)** *(do a favour for)* rendre service à **(c)** *(be grateful)* **to be obliged to sb** être reconnaissant(e) à qn; **I'd be obliged if you'd...** ça me rendrait service si vous pouviez...; **much obliged** merci infiniment

obliging [ə'blaɪdʒɪŋ] *adj* serviable; **it was very o. of her** c'était très aimable de sa part

oblique [ə'bliːk] *adj (line, angle)* oblique; *(reference, hint)* indirect(e)

obliterate [ə'blɪtəreɪt] *vt* **(a)** *also Fig (erase)* effacer **(b)** *(destroy)* détruire; *(town)* rayer de la carte

oblivion [ə'blɪvɪən] *n* oubli *m*; **to sink into o.** sombrer dans l'oubli

oblivious [ə'blɪvɪəs] *adj* **to be o. to sth** ne pas avoir conscience de qch

oblong ['ɒblɒŋ] **1** *n* rectangle *m* **2** *adj* rectangulaire

obnoxious [əb'nɒkʃəs] *adj (person, action)* odieux(euse); *(smell)* repoussant(e)

oboe ['əʊbəʊ] *n* hautbois *m*

oboist ['əʊbəʊɪst] *n* hautboïste *mf*

obscene [əb'siːn] *adj* obscène; *Fig (profits, prices)* scandaleux(euse)

obscenely [əb'siːnlɪ] *adv* d'une manière obscène; *Fig (rich)* scandaleusement

obscenity [əb'senɪtɪ] *(pl* **obscenities)** *n* obscénité *f*

obscure [əb'skjʊə(r)] **1** *adj* obscur(e) **2** *vt* **(a)** *(hide from view)* cacher **(b)** *(make unclear)* obscurcir

obscurity [əb'skjʊərɪtɪ] *n* obscurité *f*; **to fall into o.** tomber dans l'oubli

obsequious [əb'siːkwɪəs] *adj* obséquieux(euse)

observable [əb'zɜːvəbəl] *adj* observable; *(change, difference)* perceptible

observance [əb'zɜːvəns] *n (of law, custom)* observation *f*

observant [əb'zɜːvənt] *adj* observateur(trice)

observation [ɒbzə'veɪʃən] *n* observation *f*; *(by police)* surveillance *f*; **to keep sb under o.** surveiller qn; *(in hospital)* garder qn en observation; **to escape o.** passer inaperçu(e); **to make an o.** faire une observation; *Mil* **o. post** poste *m* d'observation

observatory [əb'zɜːvətərɪ] *(pl* **observatories)** *n* observatoire *m*

observe [əb'zɜːv] *vt* observer

observer [əb'zɜːvə(r)] *n* observateur(trice) *m,f*

obsess [əb'ses] *vt* obséder; **to be obsessed with** *or* **by sb** faire une fixation sur qn; **to be obsessed with** *or* **by sth** être obsédé(e) par qch

obsession [əb'seʃən] *n* obsession *f*; **to become an o.** tourner à l'obsession

obsessive [əb'sesɪv] *adj (person)* à tendances obsessionnelles; *(fear, hatred, behaviour)* obsessionnel(elle)

obsolescence [ɒbsə'lesəns] *n* obsolescence *f*

obsolete ['ɒbsəliːt] *adj* obsolète; *(design, model)* dépassé(e), démodé(e)

obstacle ['ɒbstəkəl] *n* obstacle *m*; **to put obstacles in sb's way** mettre des bâtons dans les roues à qn; *also Fig* **o. course** course *f* d'obstacles

obstetrician [ɒbstə'trɪʃən] *n* obstétricien(enne) *m,f*

obstetrics [ɒb'stetrɪks] *n* obstétrique *f*

obstinacy ['ɒbstɪnəsɪ] *n* obstination *f*

obstinate ['ɒbstɪnɪt] *adj* obstiné(e); **to be o. about doing sth** s'obstiner à vouloir faire qch

obstreperous [əb'strepərəs] *adj* tapageur(euse); **to get o. (about sth)** faire un scandale (à propos de qch)

obstruct [əb'strʌkt] *vt* **(a)** *(block) (road, pipe)* obstruer; *(view)* boucher, cacher **(b)** *(hinder)* gêner; *(in sport)* faire obstruction à; *Pol* **to o. a bill** faire de l'obstruction; *Law* **to o. the course of justice** entraver le cours de la justice

obstruction [əb'strʌkʃən] *n* **(a)** *(action) (of street, in sport)* obstruction *f* **(b)** *(blockage) (in road)* encombrement *m*; *(in pipe)* engorgement *m*; **to cause an o.** *(on road)* entraver la circulation

obstructive [əb'strʌktɪv] *adj* **to be o.** faire de l'obstruction

obtain [əb'teɪn] **1** *vt* obtenir
2 *vi Formal (of practice)* avoir cours; *(of rule)* être en vigueur

obtainable [əb'teɪnəbəl] *adj* que l'on peut se procurer; **easily o.** facile à obtenir

obtrusive [əb'truːsɪv] *adj (person, behaviour)* importun(e); *(smell)* pénétrant(e)

obtuse [əb'tjuːs] *adj* obtus(e)

obverse ['ɒbvɜːs] **1** *n* **(a)** *(of medal)* avers *m* **(b)** *(opposite)* contraire *m*
2 *adj* **o. side** *(of medal)* avers *m*

obviate ['ɒbvɪeɪt] *vt Formal (difficulty, danger)* parer à

obvious ['ɒbvɪəs] **1** *n* **to state the o.** enfoncer une porte ouverte
2 *adj* évident(e)

obviously ['ɒbvɪəslɪ] *adv* **(a)** *(in an obvious way)* manifestement **(b)** *(of course)* évidemment; **o. not** certainement pas

occasion [ə'keɪʒən] **1** *n* **(a)** *(time)* occasion *f*; **on one o.** une fois; **on several occasions** plusieurs fois, à plusieurs reprises; **on o.** parfois, de temps en temps **(b)** *(event)* occasion *f*, événement *m*; **on the o. of...** à l'occasion de...; **a sense of o.** une atmosphère de fête **(c)** *(opportunity)* occasion *f*; **I'd like to take this o. to...** j'aimerais profiter de cette occasion pour... **(d)** *Formal (cause)* sujet *m*, cause *f*; **to have o. for complaint** avoir des raisons de se plaindre; **to have o. to do sth** avoir lieu de faire qch
2 *vt Formal (cause)* occasionner, causer

occasional [ə'keɪʒənəl] *adj* occasionnel(elle); *(showers)*

intermittent(e); **I have the o. cigarette** il m'arrive de fumer une cigarette de temps en temps; **o. table** table *f* d'appoint

occasionally [ə'keɪʒənəlɪ] *adv* occasionnellement, de temps en temps

occidental [ɒksɪ'dentəl] *adj* occidental(e)

occult [ɒ'kʌlt] **1** *n* **the o.** l'occulte *m*
2 *adj* occulte

occupant ['ɒkjʊpənt] *n (of house, car)* occupant(e) *m,f*; *(of bus, plane)* passager(ère) *m,f*

occupation [ɒkjʊ'peɪʃən] *n* **(a)** *(profession)* métier *m*, profession *f*; *(pastime)* occupation *f* **(b)** *(of house, land)* occupation *f*

occupational [ɒkjʊ'peɪʃənəl] *adj* **o. disease** maladie *f* professionnelle; **o. hazard** risque *m* du métier; **o. therapist** ergothérapeute *mf*; **o. therapy** ergothérapie *f*

occupied ['ɒkjʊpaɪd] *adj* occupé(e); **to be o. with sth** être occupé à qch; **to keep sb o.** occuper qn

occupier ['ɒkjʊpaɪə(r)] *n (of house)* occupant(e) *m,f*

occupy ['ɒkjʊpaɪ] *(pt & pp* occupied) *vt (house, attention)* occuper; **to o. one's time (in doing sth)** occuper son temps (à faire qch)

occur [ə'kɜː(r)] *(pt & pp* occurred) *vi* **(a)** *(happen) (of event)* avoir lieu; *(of opportunity)* se présenter; *(of problem)* surgir **(b)** *(be present)* apparaître **(c)** *(of idea)* **to o. to sb** venir à l'esprit de qn

occurrence [ə'kʌrəns] *n* **(a)** *(event)* événement *m* **(b)** *(of disease)* incidence *f*; **to be a regular o.** se produire régulièrement

ocean ['əʊʃən] *n* océan *m*; *Am* **the o.** *(the sea)* la mer

ocean-going ['əʊʃəngəʊɪŋ] *adj* de haute mer

Oceania [əʊʃɪ'eɪnɪə] *n* l'Océanie *f*

oceanic [əʊʃɪ'ænɪk] *adj* océanique

ocelot ['ɒsəlɒt] *n* ocelot *m*

ochre, *Am* **ocher** ['əʊkə(r)] **1** *n* ocre *m*
2 *adj* ocre *inv*

o'clock [ə'klɒk] *adv* **(it's) one o.** (il est) une heure; **two o.** deux heures

OCR [əʊsiː'ɑː(r)] *n Comptr* **(a)** *(abbr* **optical character reader)** lecteur *m* optique **(b)** *(abbr* **optical character recognition)** ROC *f*

Oct *(abbr* **October)** octobre

octagon ['ɒktəgən] *n* octogone *m*

octagonal [ɒk'tægənəl] *adj* octogonal(e)

octane ['ɒkteɪn] *n Chem* octane *m*; **o. number** indice *m* d'octane

octave ['ɒktɪv] *n* octave *f*

October [ɒk'təʊbə(r)] *n* octobre *m*; *see also* **May**

octogenarian [ɒktədʒɪ'neərɪən] *n & adj* octogénaire *mf*

octopus ['ɒktəpəs] *n* pieuvre *f*, poulpe *m*

OD [əʊ'diː] *(pt & pp* OD'd, OD'ed) *vi Fam (abbr* **overdose)** faire une overdose **(on** de); *Fig* **I've rather OD'd on chocolate** j'y suis allé un peu fort sur le chocolat

odd [ɒd] **1** *adj* **(a)** *(strange)* bizarre, curieux(euse) **(b)** *(number)* impair(e); **to be the o. man out** être à part **(c)** *(one of a pair)* dépareillé(e) **(d)** *(occasional)* **I smoke the o. cigarette** il m'arrive de fumer une cigarette de temps en temps; **you've made the o. mistake** tu as fait deux ou trois fautes; **o. jobs** petits travaux *mpl*
2 *adv* **a hundred o. sheep** cent et quelques moutons; **she must be thirty o.** elle doit avoir trente ans ou plus

oddball ['ɒdbɔːl] *n & adj Fam* excentrique *mf*

oddity ['ɒdɪtɪ] *(pl* **oddities)** *n* **(a)** *(strangeness)* bizarrerie *f* **(b)** *(person) (strange)* excentrique *mf*; *(exceptional)* cas *m* à part; *(thing)* curiosité *f*

oddly [ˈɒdlɪ] *adv* bizarrement, curieusement; **o. enough,...** chose curieuse,...

oddness [ˈɒdnɪs] *n* bizarrerie *f*

odds [ɒdz] *npl* (**a**) *(probability)* chances *fpl*; *(in betting)* cote *f*; **the o. are that...** il y a de grandes chances pour que... **+** *subjunctive*; **the o. are against her/in her favour** il y a peu de chance(s)/de grosses chances qu'elle réussisse; **against the o.** contre toute attente; **to pay over the o.** *(for sth)* payer (qch) plus cher que le tarif normal; *Fam* **it makes no o.** ça n'a pas d'importance (**b**) **to be at o.** *(with sb)* *(of person)* être en désaccord (avec qn); **to be at o. with sth** *(of thing)* contredire qch (**c**) *Fam* **o. and ends, o. and sods** bricoles *fpl*

odds-on [ɒdˈzɒn] *adj (horse)* **o. favourite** grand favori *m*; *Fam* **it's o. that...** il y a gros à parier que...

ode [əʊd] *n* ode *f*

odious [ˈəʊdɪəs] *adj* odieux(euse)

odour, *Am* **odor** [ˈəʊdə(r)] *n* odeur *f*

odourless, *Am* **odorless** [ˈəʊdəlɪs] *adj* inodore

odyssey [ˈɒdɪsɪ] *(pl* **odysseys)** *n* odyssée *f*

OECD [əʊiːsiːˈdiː] *n (abbr* **Organization for Economic Co-operation and Development)** OCDE *f*

Oedipal [ˈiːdɪpəl] *adj* oedipien(enne)

oesophagus, *Am* **esophagus** [iːˈsɒfəgəs] *(pl* **oesophagi,** *Am* **esophagi** [iːˈsɒfəgaɪ]) *n* œsophage *m*

oestrogen, *Am* **estrogen** [ˈiːstrədʒən] *n* œstrogène *m*

of [ɒv, *unstressed* əv] *prep* (**a**) *(belonging to)* de; **a friend of mine** un de mes amis; **a car of her own** une voiture à elle; **the University of Manchester** l'université de Manchester (**b**) *(with amount, quantity)* **a pint of milk** ≃ un demi-litre de lait; **a bottle of wine** une bouteille de vin; **a year of her life** un an de sa vie; **many of us** beaucoup d'entre nous; **there are six of us** nous sommes six; **hundreds of people** des centaines de gens; **a girl of ten** une fille de dix ans; **you of all people should know that** si quelqu'un doit le savoir, c'est bien toi (**c**) *(indicating agency)* **it was nice/clever of you to...** c'était gentil/intelligent de ta part de... (**d**) *(with material)* **made of wood/glass** en bois/verre (**e**) *(with dates, time)* **the 4th of October** le 4 octobre; *Am* **a quarter of one** une heure moins le quart

off [ɒf] **1** *adj* (**a**) *(not functioning)* *(light, TV)* éteint(e); *(water, electricity)* coupé(e); **the rain is o.** il ne pleut plus; **o. and on, on and o.** *(intermittently)* par intermittence (**b**) *(cancelled)* annulé(e); **the deal is o.** l'affaire ne se fera pas (**c**) *(absent from work, school)* absent(e) (**d**) *(food)* abîmé(e); *(milk)* tourné(e) (**e**) *(unsuccessful)* **I'm having an o. day** c'est un jour sans; **the o. season** *(in tourism)* la morte-saison (**f**) **to be well/badly o.** être aisé(e)/pauvre; **you'd be better o. staying where you are** tu ferais mieux de rester où tu es

2 *adv* (**a**) *(away)* **two weeks o.** dans deux semaines; **5 miles o.** ≃ à 8 kilomètres; **to be o.** *(leave)* s'en aller; **I'm o. to Chicago** je pars pour Chicago; **o. you go!** allez, file maintenant!

(**b**) *(indicating removal)* **to take o. one's coat** enlever son manteau; **the handle has come o.** la poignée est partie (**c**) *(with prices)* **20 percent/$5 o.** 20 pour cent/5 dollars de réduction (**d**) *(away from work, school)* **to have a day/week o.** avoir un jour/une semaine de congé; **to take some time o.** prendre des vacances

3 *prep* (**a**) *(away from)* **o. the coast** au large de la côte; **o. the main road** qui donne dans la rue principale; **o. the record** officieusement

(**b**) *(indicating removal from)* **to fall/jump o. sth** tomber/

sauter de qch; **the handle has come o. the saucepan** la poignée s'est détachée de la casserole

(**c**) *(with prices)* **20 percent/$5 o. the price** 20 pour cent/5 dollars de réduction sur le prix

(**d**) *(absent from)* **to be o. work/school** être absent(e) de son travail/de l'école

(**e**) *(not liking)* **to be o. one's food** ne pas avoir d'appétit; **to go o. sb/sth** ne plus aimer qn/qch

(**f**) *Fam* *(from)* **to buy/borrow sth o. sb** acheter/emprunter qch à qn; **to get a cold o. sb** attraper le rhume de qn

offal [ˈɒfəl] *n* abats *mpl*

offbeat [ˈɒfbiːt] *adj Fam* original(e)

off-chance [ˈɒftʃɑːns] *n* **on the o.** à tout hasard; **on the o. that...** en espérant que...

off-colour, *Am* **off-color** [ɒfˈkʌlə(r)] *adj* (**a**) *Br* *(unwell)* **to be o.** ne pas se sentir dans son assiette (**b**) *(joke)* d'un goût douteux

offcut [ˈɒfkʌt] *n* chute *f*

off-duty [ˈɒfˈdjuːtɪ] *adj* qui n'est pas de service

offence, *Am* **offense** [əˈfens] *n* (**a**) *Law* infraction *f*; *(more serious)* délit *m* (**b**) *(displeasure)* **to cause sb o.** *(of person, remark)* vexer qn; *(of film, book)* choquer qn; **to take o.** se vexer; **to take o. at sth** mal prendre qch; **no o., but...** ne le prends pas mal, mais...

offend [əˈfend] **1** *vt* *(of person, remark)* vexer; *(of book, film)* choquer; **to be offended at** *or* **by sth** mal prendre qch

2 *vi Law* commettre une infraction; *(more serious)* commettre un délit; **to o. against good taste** être une insulte au bon goût

offended [əˈfendɪd] *adj* vexé(e)

offender [əˈfendə(r)] *n Law* délinquant(e) *m,f*

offending [əˈfendɪŋ] *adj* fautif(ive)

offense *Am* = **offence**

offensive [əˈfensɪv] **1** *n also Fig* offensive *f*; **to be on/take the o.** être passé(e)/passer à l'attaque

2 *adj* choquant(e); *(smell)* repoussant(e); **to be o. to sb** se montrer blessant(e) envers qn; **o. weapon** arme *f* offensive

offer [ˈɒfə(r)] **1** *n* offre *f*, proposition *f*; **to make sb an o.** faire une offre *ou* une proposition à qn; **on special o.** en promotion; **o. of marriage** demande *f* en mariage

2 *vt* offrir; *(explanation)* donner; *(apologies)* présenter; **to o. sb sth, to o. sth to sb** offrir qch à qn; **to o. to do sth** offrir *ou* proposer de faire qch

▸ **offer up** *vt sep* offrir

offering [ˈɒfərɪŋ] *n* offre *f*; *(in church)* offrande *f*

offhand [ɒfˈhænd] **1** *adj* désinvolte

2 *adv* *(immediately)* au pied levé; *(at a rough guess)* à première vue

office [ˈɒfɪs] *n* (**a**) *(place)* bureau *m*; **o. building** immeuble *m* de bureaux; **o. hours** heures *fpl* de bureau; **o. junior** *=* employé de bureau chargé de tâches mineures; **o. manager** chef *m* de bureau; **o. worker** employé(e) *m,f* de bureau (**b**) *(position)* charge *f*, fonctions *fpl*; **to hold o.** être au pouvoir; **to be out of o.** ne plus être au pouvoir

officeholder [ˈɒfɪshəʊldə(r)] *n* responsable *mf*

officer [ˈɒfɪsə(r)] *n (in army)* officier *m*; *(in police)* agent *m* de police; *(in local government)* fonctionnaire *mf* municipal(e)

official [əˈfɪʃəl] **1** *n (in public sector)* fonctionnaire *mf*; *(of political party)* responsable *mf*

2 *adj* officiel(elle); *Br* **O. Secrets Act** *=* document relatif au secret-défense, signé par tous les fonctionnaires

officialdom [əˈfɪʃəldəm] *n Pej* bureaucratie *f*

officialese [əfɪʃəˈliːz] *n Pej* jargon *m* administratif

officially [ə'fɪʃəlɪ] *adv* officiellement

officiate [ə'fɪʃɪeɪt] *vi Rel* officier

officious [ə'fɪʃəs] *adj* trop zélé(e)

officiously [ə'fɪʃəslɪ] *adv* avec trop de zèle

offing ['ɒfɪŋ] *n* in the **o.** en perspective, en vue

off-key ['ɒf'kiː] **1** *adj* faux (fausse); *Fig (remark)* déplacé(e)
2 *adv* faux

off-licence ['ɒflaɪsəns] *n Br* ≃ magasin *m* de vins et spiritueux

off-line ['ɒflaɪn] *adj Comptr (processing)* en différé; *(printer)* déconnecté(e)

off-load [ɒf'ləʊd] *vt (surplus goods)* écouler; to **o.** sth onto sb *(task)* se décharger de qch sur qn; *(blame, responsibility)* rejeter qch sur qn; to **o.** sb on sb refiler qn à qn

off-peak ['ɒf'piːk] *adj (electricity)* consommé(e) pendant les heures creuses; *(holidays)* en basse saison; *(telephone call, travel)* en dehors des heures de pointe

offprint ['ɒfprɪnt] *n Typ* tirage *m* à part

off-putting ['ɒfpʊtɪŋ] *adj* peu engageant(e)

off-sales ['ɒfseɪlz] *n Br =* vente de boissons alcoolisées à emporter

off-season ['ɒfsiːzən] *adj* hors saison, en basse saison

offset ['ɒfset] **1** *n Typ* offset *m*
2 *vt (pt & pp offset)* compenser

offshoot ['ɒfʃʊt] *n (of tree)* rejeton *m*; *(of family)* branche *f*; *(of political party, artistic movement)* ramification *f*

offshore **1** *adj* ['ɒfʃɔː(r)] *(island)* proche de la côte, *(oil rig)* offshore *inv*; *Fin* **o.** investment placement *m* off-shore
2 *adv* [ɒf'ʃɔː(r)] au large, en mer

offside ['ɒfsaɪd] **1** *n* côté *m* du conducteur
2 *adj* **(a)** *(of car)* côté conducteur **(b)** [ɒf'saɪd] *(in sport)* hors jeu

offspring ['ɒfsprɪŋ] *n* progéniture *f*

offstage [ɒf'steɪdʒ] *adj & adv* dans les coulisses

off-the-cuff [ɒfðə'kʌf] **1** *adj* impromptu(e)
2 *adv* au pied levé

off-the-record [ɒfðə'rekɔːd] *adj* officieux(euse)

off-the-wall [ɒfðə'wɔːl] *adj Fam* loufoque

off-white ['ɒf'waɪt] **1** *n* blanc *m* cassé
2 *adj* blanc cassé *inv*

often ['ɒfən, 'ɒftən] *adv* souvent; how **o.?** *(how many times?)* combien de fois?; *(how frequently?)* tous les combien?; **as o.** as not très souvent; more **o.** than not le plus souvent; **every so o.** de temps en temps, de temps à autre

ogle ['əʊgəl] *vt* lorgner, reluquer

ogre ['əʊgə(r)] *n* ogre *m*

ogress ['əʊgrɪs] *n* ogresse *f*

oh [əʊ] *exclam* oh!

ohm [əʊm] *n* ohm *m*

OHMS [əʊeɪtʃem'es] *Br (abbr* On Her/His Majesty's Service) = formule apposée sur le courrier émis par les services gouvernementaux

oho [əʊ'həʊ] *exclam* ah ah!

oil [ɔɪl] **1** *n (for cooking, lubricating)* huile *f*; *(petroleum)* pétrole *m*; *(for heating)* mazout *m*; *Fig* to pour **o.** on troubled waters apaiser les esprits; **o.** company compagnie *f* pétrolière; **o.** drum bidon *m* à pétrole; **o.** lamp lampe *f* à pétrole; **o.** painting peinture *f* à l'huile; *Fig Hum* she's no **o.** painting ce n'est pas une beauté; **o.** refinery raffinerie *f* de pétrole; *(offshore)* plate-forme *f* pétrolière *ou* de forage; **o.** slick

nappe *f* de pétrole; **o. tanker** pétrolier *m*; **o. well** puits *m* de pétrole
2 *vt* huiler, lubrifier; *Fig* to **o. the wheels** faciliter les choses

oilcan ['ɔɪlkæn] *n (for applying oil)* burette *f*; *(large container)* bidon *m* à huile

oilfield ['ɔɪlfiːld] *n* gisement *m* de pétrole

oil-fired ['ɔɪlfaɪəd] *adj (heating)* au mazout

oilskin ['ɔɪlskɪn] *n (fabric)* toile *f* cirée; **oilskins** *(garment)* ciré *m*

oily ['ɔɪlɪ] *adj* **(a)** *(hands, rag)* graisseux(euse); *(skin, hair)* gras (grasse); *(food)* huileux(euse) **(b)** *Pej (manner)* onctueux(euse)

oink [ɔɪŋk] *vi* grogner

ointment ['ɔɪntmənt] *n* pommade *f*

OK, okay ['əʊ'keɪ] *Fam* **1** *adj (in order)* correct(e), exact(e); *(acceptable)* pas mal; that's OK by *or* with me ça me va; is it OK to wear jeans? ça va si on vient en jean?; no, it is NOT OK (il n'en est) pas question; she was OK about it elle n'a pas fait d'histoires; he's an OK sort of guy c'est un type plutôt bien; are we OK for time? est-ce qu'on a assez de temps?
2 *exclam* OK!; OK, OK! I'll do it now OK, ça va, je vais le faire
3 *n* to give (sb) the OK donner le feu vert (à qn)
4 *vt (pt & pp* OK'd *or* okayed) donner le feu vert à

okra ['ɒkrə] *n* gombo *m*, okra *m*

old [əʊld] **1** *adj* **(a)** *(aged) (person)* vieux (vieille), âgé(e); *(car)* vieux; to grow *or* get older vieillir; **o. age** vieillesse *f*; *Br* **o. age pension** (pension *f* de) retraite *f*; *Br* **o. age pensioner** retraité(e) *m,f*; to go over **o. ground** revenir sur des choses qui ont déjà été dites; to be an **o.** hand at sth être rompu(e) à qch; to be an **o.** hat être démodé(e); *Fig* to be one of the **o.** school être de la vieille école; the O. Testament l'Ancien Testament *m*; **o. wives' tale** conte *m* de bonne femme
(b) *(with specific age)* how **o.** are you? quel âge avez-vous?; to be five years **o.** avoir cinq ans; when you're older *(to child)* quand tu seras plus grand; at ten years **o.** à (l'âge de) dix ans; a two-year-o. (child) un enfant (âgé) de deux ans; you're **o.** enough to do that yourself tu es assez grand pour le faire toi-même
(c) *(former)* ancien(enne); in the **o. days** autrefois; **o. boy/girl** *(of school)* ancien(enne) élève *mf*; the **o. boy network** = la franc-maçonnerie des écoles privées et des universités; an **o. flame** un(e) ancien(enne) amoureux(euse)
(d) *(longstanding)* an **o. friend** un(e) vieil (vieille) ami(e); **o. habits die hard** il n'est pas facile de se défaire de ses habitudes
(e) *Fam (intensifier)* any **o.** how n'importe comment; any **o. thing** n'importe quoi
(f) *Fam (affectionate)* **o.** Fred ce vieux Fred; the poor **o. thing** le (la) pauvre vieux (vieille); my *or* old **o.** man *(father)* le (mon) père; *(husband)* mon homme; my *or* the **o. lady** *(mother)* la mater; *(wife)* la bourgeoise
2 *npl* the **o.** les personnes *fpl* âgées

old-fashioned [əʊld'fæʃənd] *adj* **(a)** *(outdated)* démodé(e); *(person)* vieux jeu *inv* **(b)** *(traditional)* à l'ancienne

old-timer [əʊld'taɪmə(r)] *n Fam* **(a)** *(experienced person)* ancien(enne) *m,f*; *(b) Am (form of address)* vieux *m*

old-world ['əʊld'wɜːld] *adj (atmosphere, elegance)* suranné(e); *(furnishings)* à l'ancienne

oleander [əʊlɪ'ændə(r)] *n* laurier-rose *m*

olfactory [ɒl'fæktərɪ] *adj* olfactif(ive)

oligarchy ['ɒlɪgɑːkɪ] *(pl* **oligarchies)** *n* oligarchie *f*

olive [ˈɒlɪv] **1** *n* olive *f*; *Fig* **to hold out the o. branch** proposer la paix; **o. grove** oliveraie *f*; **o. oil** huile *f* d'olive; **o. tree** olivier *m* **2** *adj (skin)* olivâtre; **o. (green)** (vert) olive *inv*

Olympic [əˈlɪmpɪk] **1** *n* **the Olympics** les Jeux *mpl* olympiques **2** *adj* olympique; **the O. Games** les Jeux *mpl* olympiques

Oman [əʊˈmæn] *n* Oman

Omani [əʊˈmænɪ] **1** *n* Omanais(e) *m,f* **2** *adj* omanais(e)

ombudsman [ˈɒmbʊdzmən] *n Br* ≃ médiateur *m* de la République

omelette, Am omelet [ˈɒmlɪt] *n* omelette *f*; **cheese o.** omelette au fromage

omen [ˈəʊmən] *n* présage *m*, augure *m*

ominous [ˈɒmɪnəs] *adj* inquiétant(e); *(event)* de mauvais augure; **an o.-looking sky** un ciel menaçant; **an emergency meeting? – that sounds o.** une réunion d'urgence? – ça ne présage rien de bon

ominously [ˈɒmɪnəslɪ] *adv* **she spoke o.** ce qu'elle a dit ne présage rien de bon; **it was o. quiet** il régnait un silence inquiétant

omission [əʊˈmɪʃən] *n* omission *f*

omit [əʊˈmɪt] *(pt & pp* **omitted)** *vt* omettre; **to o. to do sth** omettre de faire qch

omnibus [ˈɒmnɪbəs] **1** *n (book)* recueil *m*; *(TV programme)* rediffusion *f* de plusieurs épisodes en continu **2** *adj* **o. edition** *(of stories, poems)* recueil *m*; *(on TV, radio)* rediffusion *f* de plusieurs épisodes en continu

omnipotence [ɒmˈnɪpətəns] *n* omnipotence *f*, toute-puissance *f*

omnipotent [ɒmˈnɪpətənt] *adj* omnipotent(e), tout-puissant (toute-puissante)

omnipresent [ɒmnɪˈprezənt] *adj* omniprésent(e)

omniscient [ɒmˈnɪsɪənt] *adj* omniscient(e)

omnivorous [ɒmˈnɪvərəs] *adj* omnivore; *Fig (reader)* qui lit de tout

on [ɒn] **1** *adv* **(a)** *(in operation) (light, television)* allumé(e); *(engine)* en marche; **the "on" position** la position marche **(b)** *(taking place)* **what's on?** *(on TV)* qu'est-ce qu'il y a à la télé?; *(at cinema)* qu'est-ce qui passe au cinéma?; **is the meeting still on?** la réunion doit-elle toujours avoir lieu?; **I've got a lot on** j'ai beaucoup de choses à faire; **on and off, off and on** *(intermittently)* par intermittence **(c)** *(on duty)* (in hospital, surgery) de garde; *(in shop)* de service **(d)** *(with clothing)* **to have sth on** porter qch; **to put sth on** mettre qch; **to have nothing on** être nu(e) **(e)** *(in time)* **earlier on** plus tôt; **later on** plus tard; **from that day on** à dater *ou* à partir de ce jour **(f)** *(expressing continuation)* **to read/talk/work on** continuer à lire/bavarder/travailler; **to carry on** *(doing sth)* continuer (à faire qch); **he went on and on about it** il n'en finissait pas **(g)** *(in phrases) Fam* **it's not on** c'est inadmissible **2** *prep* **(a)** *(expressing position)* sur; **on the table** sur la table; **on the second floor** au deuxième étage; **on the wall** le mur; *(hanging)* au mur; **on page 4** à la page 4; **on the right/left** à droite/gauche; **on foot** à pied; **on horseback** à cheval; **on (the) television** à la télévision; **to be on a committee** faire partie d'un comité; **I haven't got any money on me** je n'ai pas d'argent sur moi **(b)** *(with time)* **on the 15th** le 15; **on Sunday** dimanche; **on the hour** à l'heure pile; **on that occasion** à cette occasion **(c)** *(about)* sur; **a book on plants** un livre sur les plantes **(d)** *(introducing a gerund)* **on completing the test, you should...** une fois l'examen terminé, les candidats

devront...; **on discovering the corpse, she screamed** elle hurla lorsqu'elle découvrit le corps **(e)** *(expressing use, support)* **to live on $300 a week** vivre avec 300 dollars par semaine; **the drinks are on me** c'est ma tournée; **to be on antibiotics/the pill** prendre des antibiotiques/la pilule; **to be on drugs** se droguer

once [wʌns] **1** *adv* **(a)** *(on one occasion)* une fois; **not o.** jamais; **o. a week** une fois par semaine; **o. or twice** une ou deux fois, une fois ou deux; **o. in a while** une fois de temps en temps; **o. more, o. again** encore une fois; **o. too often** une fois de trop; **o. and for all** une fois pour toutes; **a o.-in-a-lifetime opportunity** une occasion qui ne se présente qu'une fois **(b)** *(formerly)* autrefois; **o. upon a time there was a princess** il était une fois une princesse **(c)** **at o.** *(immediately)* immédiatement, tout de suite; *(at the same time)* à la fois, en même temps **2** *conj* **o. he reached home, he collapsed** une fois arrivé chez lui, il s'effondra; **o. he finishes, we can leave** une fois qu'il aura terminé, nous pourrons partir

once-over [ˈwʌnsəʊvə(r)] *n Fam* **to give sb/sth the o.** jeter un coup d'œil à qn/qch

oncoming [ˈɒnkʌmɪŋ] *adj (traffic)* venant en sens inverse

one [wʌn] **1** *n (number)* un (une) *m,f*; **in ones and twos** par petits groupes; *Fam* **to get o. up on sb** prendre l'avantage sur qn **2** *pron* **(a)** *(identifying)* **this o.** celui-ci (celle-ci); **that o.** celui-là (celle-là); **these ones** ceux-ci (celles-ci); **those ones** ceux-là (celles-là); **which o. do you want?** lequel veux-tu?; **the o. I told you about** celui dont je t'ai parlé; **the big o.** le (la) grand(e); **the ones with the long sleeves** ceux qui ont les manches longues; **that's a difficult o.!** *(question)* c'est une question difficile! **(b)** *(indefinite)* un (une); **have you got o.?** tu en as un?; **any of us** n'importe lequel d'entre nous; **she's o. of the family** elle fait partie de la famille; **o. of these days** un de ces jours; **it was just o. of those things** on n'y peut rien; **o. after the other** l'un après l'autre; **o. at a time** un à la fois; **o. by o.** un par un; **to have had o. too many** *(drinks)* avoir bu un coup de trop **(c)** *(particular person)* **to act like o. possessed** se conduire comme un (une) possédé(e); **I, for o., do not believe it** quant à moi, je n'y crois pas; **I'm not o. to complain** je ne suis pas du genre à me plaindre; *Br* **she's not a great o. for parties** les soirées, ce n'est pas son fort **(d)** *(people in general) (subject)* on; *(object)* vous; **o. never knows** on ne sait jamais; **to do o.'s best** faire de son mieux **3** *adj* **(a)** *(number)* un (une); **page/number o.** page/numéro un; **o. o'clock** une heure; **to be o. (year old)** avoir un an; **o. day/evening** un jour/soir; **o. or two people** une ou deux personnes; **for o. thing...** d'abord... **(b)** *(single)* un (une) seul(e); **I have just o. thing to say** je n'ai qu'une seule chose à dire; **my o. regret** mon seul regret; **the o. person who...** la seule personne qui...; **my o. and only suit** mon seul et unique costume **(c)** *(same)* le même (la même); **they all live in o. house** ils habitent dans la même maison; **they are o. and the same thing/person** ne font qu'un; *Fam* **it's all o. to me** ça m'est égal

one-armed [ˈwʌnɑːmd] *adj (person)* manchot(e); *Br Fam* **o. bandit** machine *f* à sous

one-eyed [ˈwʌnaɪd] *adj* borgne

one-horse town [ˈwʌnhɔːstaʊn] *n Fam* trou *m* perdu

one-legged [wʌnˈlegɪd] *adj* unijambiste

one-liner [wʌnˈlaɪnə(r)] *n Fam* bon mot *m*

one-man [ˈwʌnmæn] *adj (job)* pour un seul homme; **o. band** homme-orchestre *m*; **o. show** one-man-show *m inv*; *Fig (company, team)* entreprise *f* individuelle

one-night stand ['wʌn'naɪt'stænd] n Fam (sexual encounter) rencontre f sans lendemain ou d'un soir

one-off ['wʌnɒf] Br Fam **1** n (object) objet m unique; (event) événement m unique; **it was a o.** (mistake, success) ça ne se reproduira pas **2** adj unique

one-parent family ['wʌnpeərənt'fæmɪlɪ] n famille f monoparentale

one-party ['wʌn'pɑːtɪ] adj à parti unique

one-piece swimsuit ['wʌn'piːs'swɪmsuːt] n maillot m de bain une pièce

onerous ['əʊnərəs] adj lourd(e)

oneself [wʌn'self] pron (**a**) (reflexive) se; **to look after o.** (when ill) se soigner; (generally) s'occuper de soi; **to feel o. again** se sentir complètement rétabli(e) (**b**) (emphatic) soi-même; **to do sth all by o.** faire qch tout(e) seul(e); **to see for o.** regarder soi-même

one-sided [wʌn'saɪdɪd] adj (**a**) (unequal) (contest) inégal(e); (relationship) à sens unique (**b**) (biased) partial(e)

one-time ['wʌntaɪm] adj ancien(enne)

one-to-one ['wʌntə'wʌn] adj (talk, meeting) seul à seul, en tête à tête; **o. tuition** cours mpl particuliers

one-track ['wʌntræk] adj **to have a o. mind** (be obsessed with one thing) avoir une idée fixe; (be obsessed with sex) être obsédé(e), ne penser qu'à ça

one-upmanship [wʌn'ʌpmənʃɪp] n Fam = tendance à s'affirmer supérieur aux autres

one-way ['wʌnweɪ] adj (street, traffic) à sens unique; **o. ticket** aller m (simple)

ongoing ['ɒngəʊɪŋ] adj en cours; (situation, problem) qui dure

onion ['ʌnjən] n oignon m; Br Fam **to know one's onions** connaître son affaire

on-line [ɒn'laɪn] adj & adv Comptr en ligne

onlooker ['ɒnlʊkə(r)] n spectateur(trice) m,f; (at accident) badaud m

only ['əʊnlɪ] **1** adj seul(e), unique; **o. child** (boy) fils m unique; (girl) fille f unique; **you're the o. one** tu n'es pas le seul **2** adv seulement, ne...que; **I was o. joking** c'était (uniquement) pour rire; **permit holders o.** (sign) stationnement réservé; **o. an expert could advise us** seul un expert pourrait nous conseiller; **I o. touched it** je n'ai fait que le toucher; **I shall be o. too pleased to come** je serais ravi de venir; **if o. they knew!, if they o. knew!** s'ils savaient!; **not o..., but also...** non seulement..., mais encore...; **I saw her o. yesterday** je l'ai vue pas plus tard qu'hier; **o. just** de justesse; **it's o. me** ce n'est que moi **3** conj mais

ono [əʊen'əʊ] adv Com (abbr **or nearest offer**) à débattre

on-off switch ['ɒn'ɒf'swɪtʃ] n interrupteur m marche-arrêt

onomatopoeic [ɒnəmætə'piːɪk] adj onomatopéique

onrush ['ɒnrʌʃ] n (of emotions) vague f; (of people) ruée f

onset ['ɒnset] n début m, commencement m

on-site ['ɒnsaɪt] adj & adv sur place

onslaught ['ɒnslɔːt] n assaut m, attaque f (**on** contre)

onto ['ɒntʊ, unstressed 'ɒntə] prep (**a**) (with direction) sur (**b**) (idioms) **to be o. sb** être sur la piste de qn; **to get o. sb** contacter qn; Br Fam **to be o. a good thing** avoir tiré le gros lot

onus ['əʊnəs] n responsabilité f, obligation f; **the o. is on the government to resolve the problem** il incombe au

gouvernement de résoudre ce problème; Law **o. of proof** charge f de la preuve

onward ['ɒnwəd] **1** adj en avant **2** adv = onwards

onwards ['ɒnwədz] adv **from tomorrow o.** à partir de demain; **from now o.** désormais, dorénavant; **from then o.** à partir de ce moment-là

onyx ['ɒnɪks] n onyx m

oodles ['uːdəlz] npl Fam **o. of** des tonnes de

oomph [ʊmf] n Fam (energy) punch m; **to have plenty of o.** avoir du punch

oops [uːps] exclam houp là!

ooze [uːz] **1** n (a) (mud) vase f (b) (flow) suintement m **2** vt (liquid) laisser suinter; Fig (confidence) déborder de; **to o. charm** avoir un charme fou **3** vi (of liquid) suinter (**from** de); Fig **to o. with confidence** déborder d'assurance

op [ɒp] n Fam (medical operation) opération f

opal ['əʊpəl] n opale f

opaque [əʊ'peɪk] adj opaque; Fig (difficult to understand) obscur(e)

op cit [ɒp'sɪt] n (abbr **opere citato**) op. cit.

OPEC ['əʊpek] n (abbr **Organization of Petroleum-Exporting Countries**) OPEP f

open ['əʊpən] **1** n **in the o.** (outside) dehors; (not hidden) sur la place publique; **to bring sth out into the o.** étaler qch au grand jour; **to come out into the o. about sth** révéler qch (**b**) (sporting competition) open m **2** adj (**a**) (not shut) ouvert(e); **o. to the public** ouvert au public; **o. late** ouvert en nocturne; **to be o. to sb/sth** (irreversible n) être ouvert à qn/qch; **to be o. to doubt** être sujet(ette) à caution; **to be o. to ridicule** s'exposer à être ridiculisé(e); **to be o. to suggestions** être ouvert à toute suggestion; **in the o. air** au grand air; **to welcome sb with o. arms** accueillir qn à bras ouverts; **o. country** rase campagne f; Law **in o. court** en audience publique; Br **o. day**, Am **o. house** journée f portes ouvertes; **o. invitation** invitation f permanente; Fig (to thieves) invitation; Econ **o. market** marché m libre; **to keep an o. mind** (on sth) réserver son jugement (sur qch); **o. prison** prison f ouverte; **o. sandwich** canapé m; **the o. sea** le large, la haute mer; **o. season** (for hunting) saison f de la chasse; Fig **to declare o. season on sb/sth** partir en guerre contre qn/qch; **o. spaces** (parks) espaces mpl verts; **o. ticket** billet m open; Br **o. University** = organisme d'enseignement universitaire par correspondance doublé d'émissions de télévision et de radio; Law **o. verdict** verdict m de décès sans cause déterminée; **o. wound** plaie f béante (**b**) (person, manner) **o. letter** (in newspaper) lettre f ouverte; **o. secret** secret m de Polichinelle **3** adv **to cut/break sth o.** couper/casser qch; **the door flew o.** la porte s'ouvrit brusquement **4** vt ouvrir; (legs, arms) écarter; (negotiations, conversation) entamer; **to o. the door to sth** (make possible) ouvrir la porte à qch; Fig **to o. one's heart to sb** ouvrir son cœur à qn, s'ouvrir à qn **5** vi (of door, window, flower) s'ouvrir; (of shop, bank) ouvrir; (of film) sortir; (of meeting, negotiations) commencer; **to o. o. late** (of shop) ouvrir en nocturne; **to o. onto sth** donner sur qch; **the play opens with a love scene** la pièce s'ouvre sur une scène d'amour

▸ **open out** **1** vt (paper, map) ouvrir, déplier **2** vi (of flower) s'ouvrir; (of wings) se déployer; (of view) s'étendre; (of road, valley) s'élargir

▸ **open up** **1** vt sep (shop, business, area) ouvrir (à); (possibility, opportunity) offrir

2 *vi (of shopkeeper, new shop)* ouvrir; *(of flower)* s'ouvrir; *Fig (of person)* s'ouvrir, s'épancher

open-air [əʊpə'neə(r)] *adj (restaurant, market)* en plein air; *(swimming pool)* découvert(e)

open-and-shut case [əʊpənən'ʃʌt'keɪs] *n* to be an o. ne pas faire l'ombre d'un doute

opencast ['əʊpənkɑːst] *adj* à ciel ouvert

open-door policy ['əʊpən'dɔːpɒlɪsɪ] *n (for immigrants)* politique *f* d'ouverture des frontières; *(for university)* politique non sélective

open-ended ['əʊpən'endɪd] *adj (contract)* à durée indéterminée; *(question)* ouvert(e); *(discussion)* sans cadre strict

open-heart surgery ['əʊpən'hɑːt'sɜːdʒərɪ] *n* opération *f* à cœur ouvert

opening ['əʊpənɪŋ] **1** *n* **(a)** *(of play, new era)* commencement *m; (of negotiations, Parliament)* ouverture *f* **(b)** *(gap)* ouverture *f,* trou *m* **(c)** *(of cave, tunnel)* entrée *f* **(d)** *(opportunity)* occasion *f* favorable; *(job)* débouché *m* **2** *adj* **o. address** *or* **speech** *(in court case)* déclaration *f* préliminaire; **o. ceremony** cérémonie *f* d'ouverture, inauguration *f;* **o. gambit** *(in chess)* gambit *m; (in conversation, negotiation)* manœuvre *f* d'approche; **o. hours** heures *fpl* d'ouverture; *Br* **o. time** *(of pub)* heure d'ouverture

openly ['əʊpənlɪ] *adv* ouvertement

open-minded [əʊpən'maɪndɪd] *adj* **to be o.** avoir l'esprit ouvert

open-mouthed [əʊpən'maʊðd] *adj & adv* bouche bée *inv*

openness ['əʊpənnɪs] *n* franchise *f*

open-plan ['əʊpənplæn] *adj (office)* paysager(ère); *(house)* sans cloisons; **o. kitchen** coin-cuisine *m*

opera ['ɒpərə] *n* opéra *m;* **o. glasses** jumelles *fpl* de théâtre; **o. house** opéra; **o. singer** chanteur(euse) *m,f* d'opéra

operable ['ɒpərəbəl] *adj* opérable

operate ['ɒpəreɪt] **1** *vt (machine)* faire fonctionner; *(bus service)* assurer; **to be operated by electricity** fonctionner à l'électricité **2** *vi* **(a)** *(of machine)* fonctionner; *(of company)* opérer, travailler **(b)** *(of surgeon)* opérer; **to o. on sb (for)** opérer qn (de); **to be operated on** se faire opérer

operatic [ɒpə'rætɪk] *adj* d'opéra

operating ['ɒpəreɪtɪŋ] *adj* **o. costs** coûts *mpl ou* frais *mpl* d'exploitation; *Comptr* **o. system** système *m* d'exploitation; **o. table** table *f* d'opération; *Br* **o. theatre**, *Am* **o. room** salle *f* d'opération

operation [ɒpə'reɪʃən] *n* **(a)** *(of machine)* fonctionnement *m;* **to be in o.** *(of machine)* être en service; *(of law)* être en vigueur; **to come into o.** *(of law)* entrer en vigueur **(b)** *(process)* opération *f* **(c)** *(of company)* activité *f* **(d)** *(military, surgical)* opération *f;* **to have an o. (for/on sth)** se faire opérer (de qch); *Mil* **operations room** salle *f* d'opérations *(d'un état-major)*

operational [ɒpə'reɪʃənəl] *adj (system, factory)* opérationnel(elle)

operative ['ɒpərətɪv] **1** *n (manual worker)* ouvrier(ère) *m,f; (of machine)* opérateur(trice) *m,f; Am (spy)* agent *m* **2** *adj (law, rule)* en vigueur; **to become o.** entrer en vigueur; **the o. word** le mot-clé

operator ['ɒpəreɪtə(r)] *n* **(a)** *(of machine)* opérateur(trice) *m,f* **(b)** *Tél* opérateur(trice) *m,f;* **(switchboard) o.** standardiste *mf* **(c)** *Fam* **a smooth o.** un petit finaud

operetta [ɒpə'retə] *n* opérette *f*

ophthalmology [ɒfθæl'mɒlədʒɪ] *n* ophtalmologie *f*

opinion [ə'pɪnjən] *n* opinion *f;* **in my o.** à mon avis; **to be**

of the o. that... être d'avis *ou* estimer que...; **to ask sb's o.** demander l'avis *ou* l'opinion de qn; **to form an o.** of sb/sth se faire une opinion sur qn/qch; **to have a high/low o.** of sb avoir une haute/mauvaise opinion de qn; **o. poll** sondage *m* (d'opinion)

opinionated [ə'pɪnjəneɪtɪd] *adj* dogmatique

opium ['əʊpɪəm] *n* opium *m;* **o. addict** opiomane *mf;* **o. den** fumerie *f* d'opium

opossum [ɒ'pɒsəm] *n* opossum *m*

opp *(abbr* **opposite)** ci-contre

opponent [ə'pəʊnənt] *n* adversaire *mf; (of government)* opposant(e) *m,f* (of à)

opportune ['ɒpətjuːn] *adj* opportun(e)

opportunism [ɒpə'tjuːnɪzəm] *n* opportunisme *m*

opportunist [ɒpə'tjuːnɪst] *n & adj* opportuniste *mf*

opportunity [ɒpə'tjuːnɪtɪ] *(pl* **opportunities)** *n* occasion *f;* **to have the o.** of doing *or* to do sth avoir l'occasion de faire qch; **at every o.** à la moindre occasion; **at the first** *or* **earliest o.** à la première occasion; **if you get an/the o.** si tu en as l'occasion; **the o. of a lifetime** la chance de sa/ta/etc vie; **a job with opportunities** un emploi qui offre des perspectives

oppose [ə'pəʊz] *vt* s'opposer à; **to be opposed to sth** être opposé(e) à qch; **as opposed to...** par opposition à...

opposing [ə'pəʊzɪŋ] *adj (characters, viewpoints)* opposé(e); *(armies)* ennemi(e); *(team)* adverse

opposite ['ɒpəzɪt] **1** *n* **the o.** le contraire **2** *adj* **(a)** *(side, shore)* opposé(e); *(page)* d'en face; **on the o. side of the street** de l'autre côté de la rue **(b)** *(opinion)* contraire; **in the o. direction** en sens inverse, dans le sens opposé; **the o. sex** l'autre sexe **3** *adv* en face; **the house o.** la maison d'en face **4** *prep* en face de

opposition [ɒpə'zɪʃən] *n* **(a)** *(resistance)* opposition *f* (to à); **to meet with o.** *(of idea, plan)* être contesté(e) **(b)** *(contrast)* **in o. to** contre **(c)** *(opponents)* **the o.** le camp adverse; *Br Pol* **the O.** l'opposition *f; Br Pol* **to be in o.** être dans l'opposition

oppress [ə'pres] *vt* opprimer

oppressed [ə'prest] **1** *npl* **the o.** les opprimés *mpl* **2** *adj* opprimé(e)

oppression [ə'preʃən] *n* oppression *f*

oppressive [ə'presɪv] *adj* **(a)** *(law, regime)* oppressif(ive) **(b)** *(atmosphere, heat)* oppressant(e), étouffant(e)

opt [ɒpt] **1** *vt* **to o. to do sth** choisir de faire qch **2** *vi* **to o. for sth** opter pour qch

► **opt out** *vi (of local authority control)* devenir autonome; *(of project, responsibilities)* se désengager

optic ['ɒptɪk] *adj* optique; **o. nerve** nerf *m* optique

optical ['ɒptɪkəl] *adj* optique; *(instrument)* d'optique; *Comptr* **o. character reader** lecteur *m* optique de caractères; *Comptr* **o. character recognition** reconnaissance *f* optique de caractères; *Comptr* **o. disk** disque *m* optique; **o. fibre** fibre *f* optique; **o. illusion** illusion *f* d'optique

optician [ɒp'tɪʃən] *n (prescribing)* ophtalmologue *mf; (dispensing)* opticien(enne) *m,f*

optics ['ɒptɪks] *n* optique *f*

optimism ['ɒptɪmɪzəm] *n* optimisme *m*

optimist ['ɒptɪmɪst] *n* optimiste *mf*

optimistic [ɒptɪ'mɪstɪk] *adj* optimiste **(about** quant à)

optimize ['ɒptɪmaɪz] *vt* optimiser

optimum ['ɒptɪməm] **1** *n* optimum *m* **2** *adj* optimum *inv,* optimal(e)

option ['ɒpʃən] *n* **(a)** *(choice)* option *f,* choix *m;* **to have**

the o. of doing sth avoir la possibilité de faire qch; **to have no o. (but to do sth)** ne pas pouvoir faire autrement (que de faire qch); **a soft** *or* **easy o.** une solution de facilité; **to leave** *or* **keep one's options open** ne pas prendre de décision tout de suite **(b)** *Fin* option *f* **(c)** *(school or university subject)* option *f*

optional ['ɒpʃənəl] *adj* facultatif(ive); **o. extra** *(accessoire m* en) option *f;* **o. subject** *(at school, university)* matière *f* à option

opt-out ['ɒptaʊt] **1** *n* désengagement *m* **2** *adj* de désengagement

opulent ['ɒpjʊlənt] *adj* opulent(e)

OR [əʊ'ɑ:(r)] *n Am* *(abbr* **operating room)** salle *f* d'opération

or [ɔ:(r), *unstressed* ə(r)] *conj* **(a)** *(in general)* ou; **an hour or so** une heure environ; **in a day or two** dans un jour ou deux; **did she do it or not?** est-ce qu'elle l'a fait ou pas?; **rain or no rain, I'm going!** qu'il pleuve ou pas, j'y vais! **(b)** *(otherwise)* sinon; **stop it or I'll tell mom!** arrête, sinon je vais le dire à maman! **(c)** *(with negative)* ni; **she didn't write or phone** elle n'a ni écrit ni téléphoné

oracle ['ɒrəkəl] *n* oracle *m*

oral ['ɔːrəl] **1** *n (exam)* oral *m* **2** *adj (tradition, contraception)* oral(e); *(medication)* par voie orale; *(hygiene)* buccal(e); **o. examination** examen *m* oral *m;* **o. sex** rapports *mpl* bucco-génitaux

orally ['ɔːrəlɪ] *adv* oralement, de vive voix; *(take medicine)* par voie orale

orange ['ɒrɪndʒ] **1** *n (fruit)* orange *f; (colour)* orange *m;* **o. blossom** fleurs *fpl* d'oranger; **o. grove** orangeraie *f;* **o. juice** jus *m* d'orange; **o. peel** peau *f* ou écorce *f* d'orange, *Br* **o. squash** ~ orangeade *f;* **o. tree** oranger *m* **2** *adj (colour)* orange *inv*

orang-outan(g) [ɔ:'ræŋu:tæŋ] *n* orang-outan(g) *m*

oration [ɔ:'reɪʃən] *n* allocution *f*

orator ['ɒrətə(r)] *n* orateur(trice) *m,f*

oratory ['ɒrətərɪ] *(pl* **oratories)** *n* **(a)** *(art of speaking)* art *m* oratoire, éloquence *f* **(b)** *Rel (chapel)* oratoire *m*

orb [ɔ:b] *n (of regalia)* globe *m; Lit (sphere)* orbe *m*

orbit ['ɔ:bɪt] **1** *n* **(a)** *(of planet)* orbite *f;* **in o.** en orbite; **to go into o.** se mettre en orbite **(b)** *(scope)* domaine *m* **2** *vi* être en orbite *ou* décrire une orbite autour de **3** *vi* être en orbite, décrire une orbite

orchard ['ɔ:tʃəd] *n* verger *m*

orchestra ['ɔ:kɪstrə] *n* orchestre *m;* **o. pit** fosse *f* d'orchestre

orchestral [ɔ:'kestrəl] *adj* orchestral(e)

orchestrate ['ɔ:kɪstreɪt] *vt also Fig* orchestrer

orchid ['ɔ:kɪd] *n* orchidée *f*

ordain [ɔ:'deɪn] *vt* **(a)** *Formal (decree)* ordonner; *(measure)* décréter; *Fig* **fate ordained that we should meet** il était écrit que nous devions nous rencontrer **(b)** *(priest)* ordonner

ordeal [ɔ:'di:l] *n* épreuve *f;* **it was a bit of an o.** ça a été éprouvant

order ['ɔ:də(r)] **1** *n* **(a)** *(instruction)* ordre *m;* **to give sb an o.** donner un ordre à qn; **to be under orders (to do sth)** avoir reçu des ordres (pour faire qch); **to take orders from sb** recevoir des ordres de qn; *Fin* **pay to the o. of S. Fraser** payer à l'ordre de S. Fraser **(b)** *Com* commande *f;* **to place an o. (with sb)** passer (une) commande (à qn); **to make sth to o.** faire qch sur commande; **o. book** carnet *m* de commandes; **o. form** bon *m* de commande **(c)** *(peace, tidiness)* ordre *m; Fig* **to put one's own house in o.** faire le ménage chez soi

(d) *(condition)* **out of o.** *(lift, toilets, machine)* hors service; *(telephone)* en dérangement; **in (good) working** *or* **running o.** en (bon) état de fonctionnement **(e)** *(in meeting)* **o. of the day** ordre *m* du jour; **to call sb to o.** rappeler qn à l'ordre; *Fig* **I think a celebration is in o.** je pense que ça mérite d'être fêté; *Br Fam* **that's out of o.!** ça ne se fait vraiment pas!; *Rel* **o. of service** office *m; Pol* **o. paper** (copie *f* de l')ordre du jour **(f)** *(system)* ordre *m;* **the new world o.** le nouvel ordre mondial **(g)** *(sequence)* ordre *m;* **in the right/wrong o.** dans le bon ordre/le désordre; **in o.** en ordre; **out of o.** en désordre; **in o. of age/size** par ordre d'âge/de taille **(h)** *(degree)* ordre *m;* **of the highest o.** de premier ordre; **the higher/lower orders** *(social classes)* les classes *fpl* supérieures/inférieures **(i)** *Rel* ordre *m;* **to take holy orders** entrer dans les ordres **(j)** **in o. to do sth** afin de *ou* pour faire qch; **in o. that...** afin *ou* pour que... + *subjunctive*

2 *vt* **(a)** *(instruct)* **to o. sb to do sth** ordonner à qn de faire qch; **to be ordered to do sth** recevoir l'ordre de faire qch; *Law* **to be ordered to pay costs** être condamné(e) aux dépens **(b)** *Com & (in restaurant)* commander **(c)** *(arrange) (papers, books)* classer, ranger; *(one's thoughts)* mettre de l'ordre dans; **to o. sth according to size** classer *ou* ranger qch par taille **3** *vi (in restaurant)* commander; **are you ready to o.?** vous avez choisi?

▸ **order about, order around** *vt sep (person)* commander

▸ **order in** *vt sep (supplies)* commander; *(troops)* faire venir

ordered ['ɔ:dəd] *adj (organized)* ordonné(e); *(life)* régulier(ère)

orderly ['ɔ:dəlɪ] **1** *n (pl* **orderlies)** *(in army)* planton *m; (in hospital)* aide-soignant(e) *m,f* **2** *adj* **(a)** *(tidy)* méthodique; *(life, room)* rangé(e) **(b)** *(well-behaved)* discipliné(e); **in an o. fashion** avec calme

ordinal ['ɔ:dɪnəl] **1** *n (nombre m)* ordinal *m* **2** *adj* ordinal(e)

ordinance ['ɔ:dɪnəns] *n Formal (decree)* ordonnance *f*

ordinarily ['ɔ:dɪnərɪlɪ] *adv* normalement

ordinary ['ɔ:dɪnərɪ] **1** *n* **out of the o.** qui sort de l'ordinaire, exceptionnel(elle) **2** *adj* ordinaire; **she was just an o. tourist** c'était une autre; *Br Fin* **o. share** action *f* ordinaire

ordination [ɔ:dɪ'neɪʃən] *n Rel* ordination *f*

ordnance ['ɔ:dnəns] *n Mil (supplies)* matériel *m; (guns)* artillerie *f;* **o. factory** manufacture *f* d'artillerie; *Br* **O. Survey** ≃ Institut *m* Géographique National

ore [ɔ:(r)] *n* minerai *m*

oregano [ɒrɪ'gɑ:nəʊ] *n* origan *m*

organ ['ɔ:gən] *n* **(a)** *(part of body, newspaper)* organe *m;* **o. donor** donneur(euse) *m,f* d'organe; **o. transplant** greffe *f* d'organe **(b)** *(musical instrument)* orgue *m*

organ-grinder ['ɔ:gəngraɪndə(r)] *n* joueur(euse) *m,f* d'orgue de Barbarie

organic [ɔ:'gænɪk] *adj (disease, chemistry)* organique; *(food, farming)* biologique; **an o. whole** un tout

organism ['ɔ:gənɪzəm] *n* organisme *m*

organist ['ɔ:gənɪst] *n* organiste *mf*

organization [ɔ:gənaɪ'zeɪʃən] *n* organisation *f*

organize ['ɔ:gənaɪz] **1** *vt* **(a)** *(put into order)* organiser; **to o. one's time** s'organiser **(b)** *(take care of)* s'occuper de **2** *vi (of workers)* se syndiquer

organizer ['ɔːgənaɪzə(r)] *n (person)* organisateur(trice) *m,f; (diary)* agenda *m*

orgasm ['ɔːgæzəm] *n* orgasme *m;* **to have an o.** avoir un orgasme

orgy ['ɔːdʒɪ] *(pl* **orgies)** *n* orgie *f; Fig* **an o. of violence** un déchaînement de violence

orient ['ɔːrɪənt] **1** *n* **the O.** l'Orient *m*
2 *vt* = **orientate**

oriental [ɔːrɪ'entəl] **1** *n Old-fashioned* **O.** Oriental(e) *m,f*
2 *adj* oriental(e)

orientate ['ɔːrɪənteɪt] *vt* orienter (**to** *or* **towards** vers); **to o. oneself** s'orienter; **to be orientated towards sb/sth** *(aimed at)* être destiné(e) à qn/qch

orientation [ɔːrɪən'teɪʃən] *n* orientation *f;* **o. course** stage *m* d'initiation

orienteering [ɔːrɪən'tɪərɪŋ] *n* course *f* d'orientation

orifice ['ɒrɪfɪs] *n* orifice *m*

origin ['ɒrɪdʒɪn] *n* origine *f;* **country of o.** pays *m* d'origine; **of Greek o.** d'origine grecque

original [ə'rɪdʒɪnəl] **1** *n (painting, document)* original *m*
2 *adj* **(a)** *(not copied, innovative)* original(e) **(b)** *(first)* d'origine; *Rel* **o. sin** péché *m* originel

originality [ərɪdʒɪ'nælɪtɪ] *n* originalité *f*

originally [ə'rɪdʒɪnəlɪ] *adv* **(a)** *(initially)* à l'origine, au départ; **where are you from o.?** d'où êtes-vous originaire? **(b)** *(in an innovative way)* d'une façon originale

originate [ə'rɪdʒɪneɪt] **1** *vt* être à l'origine de
2 *vi (of fire)* prendre naissance; **to o. from** *(of person)* être originaire de; **to o. in** *(of custom)* être originaire de

Orkney ['ɔːknɪ] *n* **the O. Islands, the Orkneys** les Orcades *fpl*

ornament 1 *n* ['ɔːnəmənt] ornement *m*
2 *vt* ['ɔːnəment] orner

ornamental [ɔːnə'mentəl] *adj* ornemental(e), décoratif(ive); **o. lake** pièce *f* d'eau

ornate [ɔː'neɪt] *adj (building, surroundings)* orné(e), ornementé(e); *(style)* fleuri(e)

ornithology [ɔːnɪ'θɒlədʒɪ] *n* ornithologie *f*

orphan ['ɔːfən] **1** *n* orphelin(e) *m,f;* **to be left an o.** devenir orphelin
2 *adj* **an o. child** un (une) orphelin(e)
3 *vt* **to be orphaned** devenir orphelin(e)

orphanage ['ɔːfənɪdʒ] *n* orphelinat *m*

orthodontist [ɔːθəʊ'dɒntɪst] *n* orthodontiste *mf*

orthodox ['ɔːθədɒks] *adj* orthodoxe

orthodoxy ['ɔːθədɒksɪ] *n* orthodoxie *f*

orthopaedic, *Am* **orthopedic** [ɔːθə'piːdɪk] *adj* orthopédique; **o. surgeon** (chirurgien *m*) orthopédiste *mf*

orthopaedics, *Am* **orthopedics** [ɔːθə'piːdɪks] *n* orthopédie *f*

oscillate ['ɒsɪleɪt] *vi* osciller

osmosis [ɒz'məʊsɪs] *n also Fig* osmose *f*

osprey ['ɒspreɪ] *(pl* **ospreys)** *n* balbuzard *m*

ossify ['ɒsɪfaɪ] *(pt & pp* **ossified)** *vi Anat* s'ossifier; *Fig (of person)* se fossiliser; *(of system, organization)* se scléroser

ostensible [ɒs'tensɪbəl] *adj* soi-disant *inv*

ostensibly [ɒs'tensɪblɪ] *adv* soi-disant

ostentation [ɒsten'teɪʃən] *n* ostentation *f*

ostentatious [ɒsten'teɪʃəs] *adj (person)* m'as-tu-vu *inv; (thing)* prétentieux(euse)

osteoarthritis [ɒstɪəʊɑː'θraɪtɪs] *n* ostéoarthrite *f*

osteopath ['ɒstɪəpæθ] *n* ostéopathe *mf*

ostracism ['ɒstrəsɪzəm] *n* ostracisme *m*

ostracize ['ɒstrəsaɪz] *vt* mettre en quarantaine

ostrich ['ɒstrɪtʃ] *n* autruche *f*

OTC [əʊtiː'siː] *n Br Mil (abbr* **Officers' Training Corps)** = centre de formation pour ceux qui envisagent de devenir officier dans l'armée

other ['ʌðə(r)] **1** *adj* autre; **the o. one** l'autre; **every o. day/week** un jour/une semaine sur deux; **the o. day/ week** l'autre jour/semaine; **the o. four** les quatre autres; **o. people seem to like it** d'autres ont l'air de bien aimer ça; **any o. man** n'importe quel autre homme; **somebody o. than me** quelqu'un d'autre que moi
2 *pron* autre; **others** d'autres; **the others** les autres; **one after the o.** l'un(e) après l'autre; **one or o. of us** l'un d'entre nous; **somewhere or o.** quelque part; **somebody or o.** quelqu'un; **some woman or o.** une femme
3 *adv* **it's a bit old, but o. than that, it's perfect** il est un peu vieux mais à part cela, il est très bien; **she never speaks of him o. than admiringly** elle ne parle jamais de lui autrement qu'avec admiration

otherwise ['ʌðəwaɪz] **1** *adv* autrement; **to be o. engaged** avoir d'autres engagements; **except where o. stated** sauf indication contraire
2 *conj* autrement, sinon

other-worldly [ʌðə'wɜːldlɪ] *adj (person)* détaché(e) de ce monde

OTT [əʊtiː'tiː] *adj Br Fam (abbr* **over the top)** trop *inv*

Ottawa ['ɒtəwə] *n* Ottawa

otter ['ɒtə(r)] *n* loutre *f*

Ottoman ['ɒtəmən] *Hist* **1** *n* Ottoman(e) *m,f*
2 *adj* ottoman(e)

ottoman ['ɒtəmən] *n (furniture)* ottomane *f*

OU [əʊ'juː] *n Br (abbr* **Open University)** = organisme d'enseignement universitaire par correspondance doublé d'émissions de télévision et de radio

ouch [aʊtʃ] *exclam (expressing pain)* aïe!, ouïe!

ought [ɔːt] *v aux*

> La forme négative **ought not** s'écrit **oughtn't** en forme contractée.

(a) *(expressing obligation, desirability)* **I o. to be going** je devrais m'en aller; **you oughtn't to worry so much** vous ne devriez pas vous inquiéter autant; **he had drunk more than he o. to** il n'aurait pas dû boire autant; **this o. to have been done before** on aurait dû le faire avant; **they o. not to have waited** ils n'auraient pas dû attendre **(b)** *(expressing probability)* **they o. to be in Paris by now** ils ont dû arriver à Paris maintenant; **you o. to be able to get $2000 for the painting** vous devriez pouvoir tirer 2000 dollars de ce tableau

oughtn't ['ɔːtənt] = **ought not**

ounce [aʊns] *n (unit of weight)* = 28,35 g, once *f; Fig* **an o. of** une once de

our ['aʊə(r)] *possessive adj* **(a)** *(singular)* notre; *(plural)* nos; **o. job** notre travail; **o. wives** nos femmes; **it wasn't OUR idea!** ce n'est pas nous qui en avons eu l'idée! **(b)** *(for parts of body)* **we hit o. heads** nous nous sommes cogné la tête

ours ['aʊəz] *possessive pron* **(a)** *(singular)* le nôtre (la nôtre) *m,f; (plural)* les nôtres; **their house is big but o. is bigger** leur maison est grande, mais la nôtre est plus grande encore **(b)** *(used attributively)* **this CD is o.** ce CD est à nous; **a friend of o.** un de nos amis; **where's that brother of o.?** où notre frère a-t-il bien pu passer?

ourselves [aʊə'selvz] *pron* **(a)** *(reflexive)* **we hurt o.** nous nous sommes blessés **(b)** *(emphatic)* nous-mêmes; **we o. have never…** nous-mêmes n'avons jamais…; **we told you o.** nous vous l'avons dit nous-mêmes; **we're not o. today**

nous ne sommes pas dans notre état normal aujourd'hui (**c**) *(after preposition)* **we live by o.** nous vivons seuls; **we bought it for o.** nous nous le sommes acheté; **we talk to o.** nous parlons tout seuls

oust [aʊst] *vt* évincer (**from** de)

out [aʊt] **1** *adv* (**a**) *(outside)* dehors; **to go o.** sortir; **o. here** ici; **o. there** dehors; **o.!** *(in tennis)* faute! (**b**) *(not at home, not in)* **to be o.** être sorti(e); **to stay o. late** rentrer tard (**c**) *(not concealed)* **the secret is o.** on a révélé le secret; **he's o.** *(openly gay)* il a révélé son homosexualité; **the sun is o.** il y a du soleil; **the moon is o.** la lune est levée (**d**) *(published)* sorti(e) (**e**) *(not in fashion)* passé(e) de mode (**f**) *(indicating aim)* **to be o. to do sth** chercher à faire qch; **to be o. for money** vouloir à tout prix de l'argent; *Fam* **to be o. to get sb** chercher la perte de qn (**g**) *(unconscious, asleep)* **to be o. cold** or **for the count** être K-O; *Fam* **to go o. like a light** s'endormir comme une masse (**h**) *(extinguished)* éteint(e) (**i**) **to be o. (on strike)** faire grève (**j**) *(inaccurate)* faux (fausse); **I was £25 o.** *(over)* j'avais 25 livres de trop; *(under)* il me manquait 25 livres (**k**) *(indicating completion)* **before the week is o.** avant la fin de la semaine (**l**) *(in phrases with of)* **o. of** *(outside)* hors de; **to go o. of the office** sortir du bureau; **to look o. of the window** regarder par la fenêtre; **to be o. of the country** être en voyage à l'étranger; **o. of reach/danger** hors de portée/ danger; **to be o. of cash/ideas** ne plus avoir de liquide/ d'idées; **to be o. of sth o. of friendship/curiosity** faire qch par amitié/curiosité; **she paid for it o.** of her own money elle l'a payé de ses propres deniers; **10 o. of 10** 10 sur 10; **three days o. of four** trois jours sur quatre; *Fam* **to be o. of it** *(excluded)* ne pas être dans le coup; *(drunk, on drugs)* être raide; **to feel o. of it** *(excluded)* ne pas se sentir dans le coup **2** *prep (through)* **to look o. the window** regarder par la fenêtre

out-and-out [aʊtə'naʊt] *adj (villain, liar)* fieffé(e); *(failure)* total(e); *(disgrace, scandal)* véritable

outback ['aʊtbæk] *n* **the o.** l'intérieur *m*

outbid [aʊt'bɪd] *(pt & pp* **outbid**) *vt* enchérir avec succès sur

outboard ['aʊtbɔːd] **1** *n (motor)* moteur *m* hors-bord **2** *adj* **o. motor** moteur *m* hors-bord

outbreak ['aʊtbreɪk] *n (of hostilities, war)* déclenchement *m*; *(of rioting, violence)* flambée *f*; *(of disease)* épidémie *f*

outbuilding ['aʊtbɪldɪŋ] *n* dépendance *f*

outburst ['aʊtbɜːst] *n* éclat *m*; *(of activity, temper)* accès *m*; *(of hatred, violence)* explosion *f*; *(of enthusiasm)* élan *m*

outcast ['aʊtkɑːst] *n* paria *m*

outclass [aʊt'klɑːs] *vt* surclasser

outcome ['aʊtkʌm] *n* résultat *m*, issue *f*

outcrop ['aʊtkrɒp] *n* affleurement *m*

outcry ['aʊtkraɪ] *(pl* **outcries**) *n (protest)* tollé *m*; **public o.** tollé général

outdated [aʊt'deɪtɪd] *adj* démodé(e)

outdid [aʊt'dɪd] *pt of* **outdo**

outdistance [aʊt'dɪstəns] *vt* distancer, dépasser

outdo [aʊt'duː] *(pt* **outdid** [aʊt'dɪd], *pp* **outdone** [aʊt'dʌn]) *vt* surpasser; **not to be outdone,...** pour ne pas être en reste,...

outdoor ['aʊtdɔː(r)] *adj (life)* au grand air; *(activities,*

games) de plein air; *(swimming pool)* découvert(e); **she's an o. person** elle aime le grand air

outdoors [aʊt'dɔːz] **1** *n* **the great o.** les grands espaces *mpl* **2** *adv* dehors

outer ['aʊtə(r)] *adj* extérieur(e); *Br* **O. London** la grande banlieue de Londres; **o. space** espace *m* intersidéral

outermost ['aʊtəmaʊst] *adj (nearest the outside)* le (la) plus à l'extérieur; *(most remote)* le (la) plus reculé(e)

outfit ['aʊtfɪt] *n* (**a**) *(clothes)* ensemble *m* (**b**) *Fam (organization)* boîte *f*

outflank [aʊt'flæŋk] *vt Mil* déborder; *Fig* prendre par surprise

outflow ['aʊtfləʊ] *n (of liquid)* écoulement *m*; *(of capital)* fuite *f*

outgoing ['aʊtgəʊɪŋ] *adj* (**a**) *(departing)* sortant(e) (**b**) *(sociable)* communicatif(ive)

outgoings ['aʊtgəʊɪŋz] *npl* dépenses *fpl*

outgrow [aʊt'grəʊ] *(pt* **outgrew** [aʊt'gruː], *pp* **outgrown** [aʊt'grəʊn]) *vt (habit, behaviour, toys)* passer l'âge de; **she's outgrown her jacket** son blouson est devenu trop petit pour elle

outhouse ['aʊthaʊs] *n* dépendance *f*

outing ['aʊtɪŋ] *n* (**a**) *(excursion)* excursion *f*, sortie *f* (**b**) *(of homosexual)* = fait, principalement pour une organisation militante, de rendre publique l'homosexualité d'une personne connue

outlandish [aʊt'lændɪʃ] *adj* incongru(e), bizarre

outlast [aʊt'lɑːst] *vt (object)* durer plus longtemps que; *(person)* survivre à

outlaw ['aʊtlɔː] **1** *n* hors-la-loi *m inv* **2** *vt (practice)* rendre illégal(e); *(person)* mettre hors la loi

outlay ['aʊtleɪ] *n (expense)* frais *mpl*, dépenses *fpl*

outlet ['aʊtlet] *n* (**a**) *(for water, steam)* orifice *m* de sortie; *(for emotions, energy)* exutoire *m* (**b**) *(shop)* point *m* de vente

outline ['aʊtlaɪn] **1** *n* (**a**) *(shape)* silhouette *f*; *(drawing)* tracé *m* (**b**) *(summary) (of play, novel)* résumé *m*; *(of plan, policy)* grandes lignes *fpl*; **in o.** en gros, dans les grandes lignes **2** *vt* (**a**) *(shape)* repasser les contours de; **her figure was outlined against the sky** sa silhouette se découpait sur le ciel (**b**) *(plot of novel)* résumer; *(plan, policy)* donner les grandes lignes de

outlive [aʊt'lɪv] *vt* survivre à; **she will o. us all** elle nous enterrera tous; **to have outlived its usefulness** *(of machine, theory)* ne plus servir (à rien)

outlook ['aʊtlʊk] *n* (**a**) *(prospect)* perspectives *fpl*; *(of weather)* prévisions *fpl* (**b**) *(attitude)* façon *f* de voir les choses; **o. on life** conception *f* de la vie (**c**) *(view)* vue *f* (**over** sur)

outlying ['aʊtlaɪɪŋ] *adj* éloigné(e), isolé(e)

outmanoeuvre, *Am* **outmaneuver** [aʊtmə'nuː-və(r)] *vt Mil* l'emporter tactiquement sur; *(in politics, sport)* déjouer les tactiques de

outmoded [aʊt'məʊdɪd] *adj* démodé(e)

outnumber [aʊt'nʌmbə(r)] *vt* l'emporter en nombre sur; **we were outnumbered** ils étaient plus nombreux (que nous)

out-of-doors [aʊtəv'dɔːz] *adv* = **outdoors**

out-of-pocket expenses [aʊtəv'pɒkɪtɪk'spensɪz] *npl* menues dépenses *fpl*

out-of-the-way [aʊtəvðə'weɪ] *adj (remote)* écarté(e), loin de tout; *(unusual)* insolite, qui sort de l'ordinaire

outpatient ['aʊtpeɪʃənt] *n* malade *mf* en consultation externe; **outpatients (department)** service *m* des consultations externes

outplacement ['aʊtpleɪsmənt] *n* = aide à la recherche

d'un nouvel emploi, fournie par l'employeur lors d'un licenciement

outpost ['aʊtpəʊst] *n Mil* poste *m* avancé; *Fig* bastion *m*

output ['aʊtpʊt] **1** *n (of goods)* production *f; (of data, information)* sortie *f; (of generator, machine)* débit *m* **2** *vt (pt & pp* **output)** produire; *(data, information)* sortir

outrage ['aʊtreɪdʒ] **1** *n* (**a**) *(act)* atrocité *f;* **it's an o.!** c'est un scandale! (**b**) *(indignation)* indignation *f* (**at** face à) **2** *vt (make indignant)* scandaliser, outrer

outrageous [aʊt'reɪdʒəs] *adj (shocking)* scandaleux(euse); *(clothes, haircut)* extravagant(e)

outrageously [aʊt'reɪdʒəslɪ] *adv (expensive)* scandaleusement; *(behave)* de façon scandaleuse; *(dressed)* de façon extravagante

outreach worker ['aʊtriːtʃwɜːkə(r)] *n* = employé d'une association travaillant sur le terrain

outright 1 *adv* [aʊt'raɪt] (**a**) *(completely)* **to buy sth o.** acheter qch au comptant; **he was killed o.** il fut tué sur le coup (**b**) *(ask, tell)* franchement; *(refuse)* catégoriquement **2** *adj* ['aʊtraɪt] *(refusal)* catégorique; *(failure)* total(e); *(winner)* incontesté(e)

outrun [aʊt'rʌn] *(pt* **outran** [aʊt'ræn]*, pp* **outrun)** *vt* courir plus vite que

outsell [aʊt'sel] *(pt & pp* **outsold** [aʊt'səʊld])* vt* se vendre mieux que

outset ['aʊtset] *n* **at the o.** au départ; **from the o.** dès le départ

outshine [aʊt'ʃaɪn] *(pt & pp* **outshone** [aʊt'ʃɒn]) *vt (surpass)* éclipser

outside 1 ['aʊtskɜːts, aʊt'saɪd] **1** *n* extérieur *m*, dehors *m*; **on the o.** à l'extérieur; *Fig* extérieurement; **from the o.** du dehors, de l'extérieur; **at the o.** *(of estimate)* tout au plus **2** *adj (influence)* extérieur(e); *Rad & TV* **o. broadcast** reportage *m*; **o. lane** *(when driving on left)* file *f* de droite; *(when driving on right)* file de gauche; **the o. world** le monde extérieur; **an o. chance** une petite chance **3** *adv* dehors, à l'extérieur; **to go o.** sortir **4** *prep* (**a**) *(physically)* en dehors de, à l'extérieur de; *(in front of)* devant; **o. office hours** en dehors des heures de bureau (**b**) *(apart from)* en dehors de; **o. (of) a few friends** en dehors de quelques amis

outsider [aʊt'saɪdə(r)] *n* (**a**) *(socially)* étranger(ère) *m,f* (**b**) *(in race, election)* outsider *m*

outsize ['aʊtsaɪz] *adj (clothes)* très grande taille; *(appetite, ego)* démesuré(e)

outskirts ['aʊtskɜːts] *npl* **the o.** la banlieue

outsmart [aʊt'smɑːt] *vt* se montrer plus fin(e) que

outsourcing ['aʊtsɔːsɪŋ] *n Com* sous-traitance *f*

outspoken [aʊt'spəʊkən] *adj* franc (franche)

outstanding [aʊt'stændɪŋ] *adj* (**a**) *(remarkable)* exceptionnel(elle) (**b**) *(unresolved) (business)* en suspens (**c**) *(unpaid) (amount, debt)* impayé(e); *(payment)* en retard; *(interest)* échu(e)

outstay [aʊt'steɪ] *vt* **I hope I haven't outstayed my welcome** j'espère ne pas avoir abusé de votre hospitalité

outstretched ['aʊtstretʃt] *adj (leg, arm)* tendu(e)

outstrip [aʊt'strɪp] *(pt & pp* **outstripped)** *vt* dépasser

out-tray ['aʊttreɪ] *n* courrier *m* à expédier

outward ['aʊtwəd] **1** *adj* (**a**) *(external)* extérieur(e) (**b**) **o. voyage** *or* **journey** voyage *m* aller **2** *adv* = **outwards**

outwardly ['aʊtwədlɪ] *adv* en apparence

outwards ['aʊtwədz] *adv* vers l'extérieur

outweigh [aʊt'weɪ] *vt (be more important than)* l'emporter sur

outwit [aʊt'wɪt] *(pt & pp* **outwitted)** *vt* se montrer plus malin(igne) que

outworker ['aʊtwɜːkə(r)] *n* travailleur(euse) *m,f* à domicile

outworn [aʊt'wɔːn] *adj (theory, idea)* périmé(e)

ova ['əʊvə] *pl of* **ovum**

oval ['əʊvəl] **1** *n* ovale *m* **2** *adj* ovale

ovarian [əʊ'veərɪən] *adj Anat* ovarien(enne)

ovary ['əʊvərɪ] *(pl* **ovaries)** *n Anat* ovaire *m*

ovation [əʊ'veɪʃən] *n* ovation *f;* **to give sb a standing o.** se lever pour applaudir qn

oven ['ʌvən] *n* four *m; Br* **o. glove,** *Am* **o. mitt** gant *m* isolant

oven-proof ['ʌvənpruːf] *adj* qui va au four

oven-ready ['ʌvənredɪ] *adj* prêt(e) à rôtir

ovenware ['ʌvənweə(r)] *n* vaisselle *f* allant au four

over ['əʊvə(r)] **1** *prep* (**a**) *(above)* au-dessus de; **the plane flew o. our heads** l'avion est passé au-dessus de nos têtes; **I couldn't hear her o. the noise** impossible de l'entendre avec tout ce bruit; *Fig* **her talk was way o. my head** son exposé m'est passé complètement au-dessus de la tête (**b**) *(on top of)* sur; **to put a blanket o. sb** mettre une couverture sur qn (**c**) *(from one side to the other of)* par-dessus; **to throw sth o. the wall** jeter qch par-dessus le mur; **to read o. sb's shoulder** lire par-dessus l'épaule de qn (**d**) *(across)* **to go o. the road** traverser la rue; **to live o. the road** habiter en face; **o. the border** de l'autre côté de la frontière; **the bridge o. the river** le pont qui traverse la rivière (**e**) *(about)* **to laugh o. sth** rire de qch; **to fight o. sth** se battre pour qch (**f**) *(more than)* plus de; **he's o. fifty** il a plus de cinquante ans; **children o. five** les enfants de plus de cinq ans; **o. and above** en plus de (**g**) *(during)* pendant; **o. the last three years** les trois dernières années; **o. lunch** en déjeunant (**h**) *(recovered from)* **to get/be o. sth** *(illness, disappointment)* se remettre/s'être remis(e) de qch; *Fam* **to get/be o. sb** *(ex)* ne plus penser à qn (**i**) *Fam Fig* **o. the top** *(excessive)* excessif(ive) **2** *adv* (**a**) *(across)* **o. here** ici; **o. there** là-bas; **to cross o.** *(the street)* traverser; **to ask** *or* **invite sb o. (to one's house)** inviter qn (chez soi) (**b**) *(down)* **to fall o.** tomber; **to bend o.** se pencher; **to push sb/sth o.** faire tomber qn/qch (**c**) *(everywhere)* **famous the world o.** célèbre dans le monde entier (**d**) *(expressing repetition)* **three times o.** trois fois de suite; **o. and o. again** encore et encore; **to do sth all o. again** refaire qch (**e**) *(in excess)* **children of five and o.** les enfants de cinq ans et plus; **there was £5 left o.** il restait 5 livres (**f**) *(on radio)* **o.!** à vous!; **o. and out!** terminé! **3** *adj* **to be (all) o.** être fini(e); **to get sth o. (and done) with** en finir avec qch **4** *n (in cricket)* = série de six balles

overabundant [əʊvərə'bʌndənt] *adj* surabondant(e)

overactive [əʊvər'æktɪv] *adj (imagination)* débridé(e)

overall 1 *adj* [əʊvər'ɔːl] **1** *adj* global(e); *(size, area)* total(e); **she has o. responsibility for sales** elle est responsable de l'ensemble du service des ventes **2** *adv* dans l'ensemble; **$10 o.** 10 dollars en tout; **third o.** troisième au classement général

overalls ['əʊvərɔːlz] *npl* (**a**) *(work garment)* bleu *m* de travail (**b**) *Am (dungarees)* salopette *f*

overanxious [əʊvər'æŋkʃəs] *adj* trop inquiet(ète)

overawe [əʊvəˈrɔː] *vt* to be overawed by sb/sth se laisser impressionner par qn/qch

overbalance [əʊvəˈbæləns] *vi (of person)* perdre l'équilibre; *(of pile, load)* se renverser

overbearing [əʊvəˈbeərɪŋ] *adj* autoritaire

overblown [əʊvəˈbləʊn] *adj (style)* ampoulé(e)

overboard [ˈəʊvəbɔːd] *adv* par-dessus bord; **man o.!** un homme à la mer!; *Fig* **to go o.** (about) s'emballer (pour)

overbook [ˈəʊvəbʊk] *vt* faire du surbooking sur

overcapacity [ˈəʊvəkəˈpæsɪtɪ] *n Ind* surcapacité *f*

overcast [ˈəʊvəkɑːst] *adj (sky, day)* nuageux(euse)

overcautious [əʊvəˈkɔːʃəs] *adj* trop prudent(e)

overcharge [əʊvəˈtʃɑːdʒ] *vt* **to o. sb for sth** faire payer qch trop cher à qn; **he overcharged me by a dollar** il m'a fait payer une dollar en trop

overcoat [ˈəʊvəkəʊt] *n* pardessus *m*

overcome [əʊvəˈkʌm] *(pt* **overcame** [əʊvəˈkeɪm]*, pp* **overcome)** *vt (opponent, one's fears)* vaincre; *(problem, obstacle)* surmonter; **to be overcome with** *or* **by grief** être accablé(e) de chagrin; **I was quite overcome** j'ai été bouleversé

overcompensate [əʊvəˈkɒmpenseɪt] *vi* **to o. for sth** surcompenser qch

overconfident [əʊvəˈkɒnfɪdənt] *adj* trop confiant(e)

overcook [əʊvəˈkʊk] *vt* (faire) trop cuire

overcrowded [əʊvəˈkraʊdəd] *adj* bondé(e)

overcrowding [əʊvəˈkraʊdɪŋ] *n* surpeuplement *m*

overdeveloped [əʊvədɪˈveləpt] *adj* trop développé(e)

overdo [əʊvəˈduː] *(pt* **overdid** [əʊvəˈdɪd]*, pp* **overdone** [əʊvəˈdʌn]) *vt* exagérer; **to o. it** *(work too hard)* se surmener; **to o. the salt/make-up** forcer sur le sel/le maquillage

overdose [ˈəʊvədəʊs] **1** *n* overdose *f* **2** *vi* faire une overdose (**on** de); *Fig* **to o. on chocolate** exagérer avec le chocolat

overdraft [ˈəʊvədrɑːft] *n Fin* découvert *m*

overdrawn [əʊvəˈdrɔːn] *adj* à découvert

overdressed [əʊvəˈdrest] *adj* trop habillé(e)

overdrive [ˈəʊvədraɪv] *n Fig* **to go into o.** passer à la vitesse supérieure

overdue [əʊvəˈdjuː] *adj (person, train)* en retard; *(bill)* impayé(e); *(library book)* qui n'a pas été rendu(e); **this measure is long o.** cette mesure aurait dû être prise il y a longtemps

overeat [əʊvəˈriːt] *(pt* **overate** [əʊvəˈret]*, pp* **overeaten** [əʊvəˈriːtən]) *vi* trop manger

overemphasize [əʊvərˈemfəsaɪz] *vt* trop mettre l'accent sur

overenthusiastic [ˈəʊvərɪnθjuːzɪˈæstɪk] *adj* trop enthousiaste

overestimate [əʊvəˈrestɪmeɪt] *vt* surestimer; *(danger)* exagérer

overexcited [əʊvərɪkˈsaɪtɪd] *adj* surexcité(e)

overexpose [əʊvərɪksˈpəʊz] *vt Phot* surexposer

overextended [əʊvərɪkˈstendɪd] *adj Fin* incapable de faire face à ses engagements

overflow 1 *n* [ˈəʊvəfləʊ] *(liquid)* trop-plein *m*; **o. (pipe)** trop-plein **2** *vi* [əʊvəˈfləʊ] déborder; **his desk was overflowing with papers** son bureau disparaissait sous la paperasse

overgrown [əʊvəˈɡrəʊn] *adj (garden)* envahi(e) par les

mauvaises herbes; **he's like an o. schoolboy** il se conduit comme un collégien

overhang 1 *n* [ˈəʊvəhæŋ] *(of roof, cliff)* surplomb *m* **2** *vt* [əʊvəˈhæŋ] *(pt & pp* **overhung** [əʊvəˈhʌŋ]) surplomber

overhaul 1 *n* [ˈəʊvəhɔːl] *also Fig* révision *f* **2** *vt* [əʊvəˈhɔːl] **(a)** *(machine, policy)* réviser **(b)** *(overtake)* dépasser

overhead 1 *n* [əʊvəhed] *Am Com* = **overheads** **2** *adj* [ˈəʊvəhed] *(cable)* aérien(enne); **o. projector** rétroprojecteur *m* **3** *adv* [əʊvəˈhed] au-dessus; **a plane flew o.** un avion passa au-dessus de nos têtes

overheads [ˈəʊvəhedz] *npl Br Com* frais *mpl* généraux

overhear [əʊvəˈhɪə(r)] *(pt & pp* **overheard** [əʊvəˈhɜːd]) *vt (person)* entendre (par hasard); *(words)* surprendre

overheat [əʊvəˈhiːt] *vi (of engine)* chauffer; *(of economy)* être en surchauffe

overindulge [əʊvərɪnˈdʌldʒ] **1** *vt (child)* trop gâter; **to o. oneself** *(drink, eat to excess)* faire des excès **2** *vi* faire des excès

overjoyed [əʊvəˈdʒɔɪd] *adj* absolument ravi(e) **(at** de)

overkill [ˈəʊvəkɪl] *n* it's **o.** c'est exagéré, c'est trop; **media o.** matraquage *m*

overland [ˈəʊvəlænd] *adv & adj* par voie de terre

overlap 1 *n* [ˈəʊvəlæp] *(between planks, tiles)* chevauchement *m* **2** *vi* [əʊvəˈlæp] *(pt & pp* **overlapped)** *(of planks, tiles, periods)* se chevaucher; *(of theories)* avoir des points communs (**with** avec); **to o. with** *(in time)* empiéter sur

overleaf [əʊvəˈliːf] *adv* au verso; **see o.** voir au verso

overload 1 *n* [ˈəʊvələʊd] *Elec* surcharge *f* **2** *vt* [əʊvəˈləʊd] *also Fig* surcharger (**with** de)

overlong [əʊvəˈlɒŋ] *adj* trop long (longue)

overlook [əʊvəˈlʊk] *vt* **(a)** *(of building, window)* donner sur; **the town is overlooked by the castle** le château surplombe la ville **(b)** *(fail to notice)* oublier **(c)** *(disregard)* fermer les yeux sur

overly [ˈəʊvəlɪ] *adv* excessivement, trop

overmanning [əʊvəˈmænɪŋ] *n* sureffectifs *mpl*

overmuch [əʊvəˈmʌtʃ] *adv* outre mesure, trop

overnight 1 *adv* [əʊvəˈnaɪt] **(a)** *(during the night)* (pendant) la nuit; **to stay o.** passer la nuit; **leave to soak o.** laisser tremper toute la nuit **(b)** *(suddenly)* du jour au lendemain **2** *adj* [ˈəʊvənaɪt] **(a)** *(for one night)* **o. train/flight** train *m*/vol *m* de nuit; **o. bag** petit sac *m* de voyage; **o. stay** séjour *m* d'une nuit; *(in hotel)* nuit *f* **(b)** *(sudden)* soudain(e)

overoptimistic [əʊvərɒptɪˈmɪstɪk] *adj* trop optimiste **(about** quant à)

overpaid [əʊvəˈpeɪd] *adj* trop payé(e)

overpass [ˈəʊvəpɑːs] *n (road)* pont *m*; *(for pedestrians)* passerelle *f*

overpayment [əʊvəˈpeɪmənt] *n (of taxes)* trop-perçu *m*; *(of employee)* rémunération *f* excessive

overpopulation [əʊvəpɒpjʊˈleɪʃən] *n* surpopulation *f*, surpeuplement *m*

overpower [əʊvəˈpaʊə(r)] *vt* maîtriser

overpowering [əʊvəˈpaʊərɪŋ] *adj (heat, smell)* suffocant(e); *(taste)* qui prend à la gorge; *(desire)* irrépressible

overpriced [əʊvəˈpraɪst] *adj* trop cher(ère)

overproduction [əʊvəprəˈdʌkʃən] *n Econ* surproduction *f*

overrated [əʊvəˈreɪtɪd] *adj* surfait(e)

overreach [əʊvə'riːtʃ] *vt* to o.
oneself trop présumer de
ses forces
overreact [əʊvərɪ'ækt] *vi* réagir de façon excessive
override [əʊvə'raɪd] *vt* (*pt* **overrode** [əʊvə'rəʊd], *pp*
overridden [əʊvə'rɪdən]) **(a)** *(objections, wishes,
regulations)* passer outre à; *(decision)* annuler **(b)** *(take
precedence over)* avoir la priorité sur; *Tech (device)* annuler
overriding [əʊvə'raɪdɪŋ] *adj (importance)* capital(e);
(factor) prépondérant(e)
overrule [əʊvə'ruːl] *vt (opinion)* rejeter; *(decision)*
annuler; **she was overruled by her boss** son patron a
rejeté sa proposition
overrun 1 *vt* [əʊvə'rʌn] (*pt* **overran** [əʊvə'ræn], *pp*
overrun) **(a)** *(country)* envahir; **the house was overrun
with mice** la maison était infestée de souris **(b)** *(allotted
time)* dépasser
  2 *vi* [əʊvə'rʌn] *(of TV, radio programme)* déborder sur
l'horaire
  3 *n* ['əʊvərʌn] *Com* **(cost)** o. dépassement *m* du budget
overseas 1 *adj* ['əʊvəsiːz] d'outre-mer; *(trade, debt)*
extérieur(e)
  2 *adv* [əʊvə'siːz] à l'étranger
oversee [əʊvə'siː] (*pt* **oversaw** [əʊvə'sɔː], *pp* **overseen**
[əʊvə'siːn]) *vt* superviser
overseer ['əʊvəsɪə(r)] *n Old-fashioned* contremaître *m*
oversensitive [əʊvə'sensɪtɪv] *adj* hypersensible
oversexed [əʊvə'sekst] *adj* qui a une libido démesurée
overshadow [əʊvə'ʃædəʊ] *vt Fig (of atmosphere, threat)*
planer sur; *(of person)* éclipser
overshoe ['əʊvəʃuː] *n Am* caoutchouc *m*
overshoot [əʊvə'ʃuːt] (*pt & pp* **overshot** [əʊvə'ʃɒt]) *vt*
dépasser
oversight ['əʊvəsaɪt] *n* oubli *m*, omission *f*
oversimplify [əʊvə'sɪmplɪfaɪ] (*pt & pp* **oversimplified**) *vt* simplifier à outrance
oversized ['əʊvəsaɪzd] *adj (very big)* énorme; *(clothes)*
trop grand(e)
oversleep [əʊvə'sliːp] (*pt & pp* **overslept** [əʊvə'slept]) *vi*
ne pas se réveiller à temps
overspend [əʊvə'spend] (*pt & pp* **overspent** [əʊvə-
'spent]) **1** *vt* to o. **one's budget** dépasser son budget
  2 *vi* trop dépenser
overspill ['əʊvəspɪl] *n (of population)* excédent *m*; *(from
meeting, party)* trop-plein *m*
overstaffing [əʊvə'stɑːfɪŋ] *n* sureffectifs *mpl*
overstate [əʊvə'steɪt] *vt* exagérer
overstay [əʊvə'steɪ] = **outstay**
overstep [əʊvə'step] (*pt & pp* **overstepped**) *vt* outrepasser; *Fig* to o. **the mark** dépasser les bornes
oversubscribed [əʊvəsəb'skraɪbd] *adj Fin* sursous-crit(e)
overt [əʊ'vɜːt] *adj* manifeste
overtake [əʊvə'teɪk] (*pt* **overtook** [əʊvə'tʊk], *pp*
overtaken [əʊvə'teɪkən]) *vt & vi* dépasser, doubler; **to
be overtaken by events** être dépassé(e) par les événements
overthrow 1 *n* ['əʊvəθrəʊ] renversement *m*
  2 *vt* [əʊvə'θrəʊ] (*pt* **overthrew** [əʊvə'θruː], *pp* **over-
thrown** [əʊvə'θrəʊn]) renverser
overtime ['əʊvətaɪm] **1** *n* heures *fpl* supplémentaires
  2 *adv* **to work o.** faire des heures supplémentaires; *Fig (of
imagination)* s'emballer
overtly [əʊ'vɜːtlɪ] *adv* ouvertement
overtone ['əʊvətəʊn] *n (of sadness, bitterness)* pointe *f*; *(of
violence, racism)* relent *m*

overture ['əʊvətjʊə(r)] *n Mus* ouverture *f*; *Fig* **to make
overtures to sb** faire des avances à qn
overturn [əʊvə'tɜːn] **1** *vt (table, government)* renverser;
(boat) faire chavirer; *(decision)* annuler
  2 *vi* se renverser; *(of boat)* chavirer
overuse 1 *n* [əʊvə'juːs] emploi *m* excessif
  2 *vt* [əʊvə'juːz] abuser de
overvalue [əʊvə'væljuː] *vt (currency)* surévaluer; *(ability)*
surestimer
overview ['əʊvəvjuː] *n* vue f d'ensemble
overweight [əʊvə'weɪt] *adj* trop gros (grosse); **to be 20
pounds o.** ≃ avoir 10 kilos de trop
overwhelm [əʊvə'welm] *vt (enemy, opponent)* écraser;
overwhelmed with joy au comble de la joie; **overwhelmed by grief/with work** accablé(e) de chagrin/de
travail
overwhelming [əʊvə'welmɪŋ] *adj (need, desire)*
irrépressible; *(pressure, defeat, majority)* écrasant(e)
overwhelmingly [əʊvə'welmɪŋlɪ] *adv* massivement
overwork [əʊvə'wɜːk] **1** *n* surmenage *m*
  2 *vt (person)* surcharger de travail
  3 *vi* se surmener
overwrite [əʊvə'raɪt] (*pt* **overwrote** [əʊvə'rəʊt], *pp*
overwritten [əʊvə'rɪtən]) *vt Comptr (file)* écraser
overwrought [əʊvə'rɔːt] *adj* à bout; **to get o.**
beaucoup s'énerver
ovulate ['ɒvjʊleɪt] *vi Biol* ovuler
ovulation [ɒvjʊ'leɪʃən] *n Biol* ovulation *f*
ovum ['əʊvəm] (*pl* **ova** ['əʊvə]) *n Biol* ovule *m*
ow [aʊ] *exclam* aïe!, ouïe!
owe [əʊ] *vt also Fig* devoir; **to o. sb sth, to o. sth to sb**
devoir qch à qn; **to o. sb an apology** devoir des excuses à
qn; **to o. it to oneself to do sth** se devoir de faire qch
owing ['əʊɪŋ] *adj* **(a)** **the money o. to me** l'argent qui
m'est dû **(b)** **o. to** *(because of)* en raison de, à cause de
owl [aʊl] *n* hibou *m*, chouette *f*
own [əʊn] **1** *adj* propre; **her o. money** son propre argent; **I
saw it with my o.** eyes je l'ai vu de mes propres yeux; **I
make my o. clothes** je fais mes vêtements moi-même;
she's famous in her o. right elle est célèbre aussi; **o.
goal** *(in soccer)* = but marqué contre son propre camp; *Fig*
to score an o. goal apporter de l'eau au moulin de
l'adversaire
  2 *pron* **(a)** **my o.** le mien (la mienne); **the house is my o.**
la maison est à moi; **I have money of my o.** j'ai de l'argent à
moi; **to make sth one's o.** s'approprier qch; **for reasons of
her o.** pour des raisons qui ne regardent qu'elle **(b)** **to do
sth on one's o.** *(without company)* faire qch tout(e) seul(e); **I
am (all) on my o.** je suis seul; **you're on your o.!** *(I won't
support you)* débrouille-toi tout seul! **(c)** *(idioms)* **to come
into one's o.** montrer ce dont on est capable; **to get one's
o. back** *(be se venger (de qn); **to hold one's o.** se
maintenir
  3 *vt* **(a)** *(property)* posséder, être propriétaire de; **who
owns this dog?** à qui est ce chien?; **he behaves as if he
owns the place** il se conduit comme en pays conquis **(b)**
Old-fashioned (admit) avouer
  ▸ **own up** *vi (confess)* avouer; **to o. up to sth** avouer qch
own-brand ['əʊnbrænd] *adj Com* vendu(e) sous la
marque du distributeur
owner ['əʊnə(r)] *n* propriétaire *mf*
owner-occupier ['əʊnər'ɒkjəpaɪə(r)] *n* propriétaire *mf*
occupant(e)
ownership ['əʊnəʃɪp] *n* propriété *f*; **under new o.** *(sign)*
changement de propriétaire; **to be in private/public o.**
appartenir au secteur privé/public

ox [ɒks] (*pl* **oxen** ['ɒksən]) *n* bœuf *m*
Oxbridge ['ɒksbrɪdʒ] *n Br* les universités *fpl* d'Oxford et de Cambridge
oxide ['ɒksaɪd] *n Chem* oxyde *m*
oxidize ['ɒksɪdaɪz] *Chem* **1** *vt* oxyder
2 *vi* s'oxyder
oxtail ['ɒksteɪl] *n* queue *f* de bœuf
oxyacetylene [ɒksɪə'setɪliːn] *n Chem* **o. torch** chalumeau *m* oxyacétylénique
oxygen ['ɒksɪdʒən] *n* oxygène *m*; **o. bottle** *or* **cylinder**

bouteille *f* d'oxygène; **o. mask** masque *m* à oxygène
oyster ['ɔɪstə(r)] *n* huître *f*; *Fig* **the world's your o.** le monde t'appartient; **o. bed** parc *m* à huîtres
oystercatcher ['ɔɪstəkætʃə(r)] *n* huîtrier *m*
Oz [ɒz] *n Fam* l'Australie *f*
oz (*abbr* **ounce(s)**) once *f*
ozone ['əʊzəʊn] *n Chem* ozone *m*; **the o. layer** la couche d'ozone
ozone-friendly ['əʊzəʊn'frendlɪ] *adj* qui préserve la couche d'ozone

P, p [piː] *n (letter)* P, p *m inv; Fam* **to mind one's P's and Q's** bien se tenir

p [piː] *Br (abbr* **penny)** penny *m; (abbr* **pence)** pence *mpl*

PA ['piː'eɪ] *n* (**a**) *(abbr* **public address) PA (system)** (système *m* de) sonorisation *f* (**b**) *Com (abbr* **personal assistant)** secrétaire *mf* de direction

pa [pɑː] *n Am Fam (dad)* papa *m*

p.a. *(abbr* **per annum)** par an

pace [peɪs] **1** *n* (**a**) *(step)* pas *m; Fig* **to put sb through his paces** mettre qn à l'épreuve (**b**) *(speed)* vitesse *f*, allure *f;* **at a slow/fast p.** à petite/vive allure; **to set the p.** donner l'allure; *Fig* montrer la voie; **to keep p. with sb** suivre qn; *Fig (in activity)* suivre le rythme de qn **2** *vt (room, street)* arpenter; **to p. oneself** *(in race, work)* trouver son rythme **3** *vi* **to p.** up and down faire les cent pas

pacemaker ['peɪsmeɪkə(r)] *n* (**a**) *(in race)* meneur(euse) *m,f* de train (**b**) *(for heart)* stimulateur *m* cardiaque

Pacific [pə'sɪfɪk] *adj* **the P. (Ocean)** le Pacifique, l'océan *m* Pacifique; **the P. Rim** les pays *mpl* de l'Asie-Pacifique; *Am* **P. Standard Time** heure *f* de la côte ouest de l'Amérique du Nord

pacifier ['pæsɪfaɪə(r)] *n Am* tétine *f*

pacifism ['pæsɪfɪzəm] *n* pacifisme *m*

pacifist ['pæsɪfɪst] *n & adj* pacifiste *mf*

pacify ['pæsɪfaɪ] *(pt & pp* **pacified)** *vt (country)* pacifier; *(person)* apaiser, calmer

pack [pæk] **1** *n* (**a**) *(rucksack)* sac *m* à dos (**b**) *(of cigarettes, washing powder)* paquet *m; (of beer)* pack *m; (of playing cards)* jeu *m* (**c**) *(of thieves, photographers)* bande *f; (of runners, cyclists)* peloton *m; (in rugby)* pack *m; (of wolves)* meute *f;* **a p. of lies** un tissu de mensonges; **p. animal** animal *m* de bât; **p. ice** banquise *f* **2** *vt* (**a**) *(in box, suitcase)* mettre (**b**) *(cram) (earth into hole)* tasser; *(passengers into bus, train)* entasser (**c**) *(fill) (hole, box)* bourrer **(with** de); *also Fig* **to p. one's bags** faire ses valises (**d**) **to p. a punch** *(of fighter)* cogner dur; *(of drink)* être costaud **3** *vi* (**a**) *(prepare luggage)* faire ses valises *ou* bagages; *Fam Fig* **to send sb packing** envoyer promener qn (**b**) *(cram)* **to p. into a room/bus** s'entasser dans une pièce/un bus

▸ **pack in** *Fam* **1** *vt (job, course)* laisser tomber; **p. it in!** arrête!, ça suffit!
2 *vi (of car, machine)* tomber en rade

▸ **pack off** *vt sep Fam (send away)* expédier

▸ **pack up 1** *vt sep (tidy away)* ranger
2 *vi Fam* (**a**) *(of car, machine)* tomber en rade (**b**) *(finish work)* arrêter

package ['pækɪdʒ] **1** *n (parcel)* paquet *m*, colis *m; (of measures, laws)* ensemble *m; (contract)* contrat *m* global; **p.**

deal *or* **holiday** forfait *m (comprenant au moins transport et logement)* **2** *vt* emballer, conditionner; *Fig* **to p. sb** *(pop star, politician)* créer l'image de marque de qn

packaging ['pækɪdʒɪŋ] *n* emballage *m*

packed [pækt] *adj* (**a**) *(crowded)* bondé(e) (**b**) **p. lunch =** déjeuner qu'on emporte à l'école ou au bureau

packer ['pækə(r)] *n (person)* emballeur(euse) *m,f*

packet ['pækɪt] *n* (**a**) *(of food, washing powder, cigarettes)* paquet *m; (of soup, seeds)* sachet *m* (**b**) *Fam (lot of money)* **to make** *or* **earn a p.** se faire un fric fou; **that'll cost a p.** ça va coûter bonbon

packhorse ['pækhɔːs] *n* cheval *m* de bât

packing ['pækɪŋ] *n* (**a**) *(packing material)* emballage *m*; **p. case** caisse *f* d'emballage (**b**) *(for trip)* **to do one's p.** faire ses valises *ou* bagages

pact [pækt] *n* pacte *m*

pad [pæd] *n* (**a**) *(for protection)* protection *f; (of dog's, cat's paw)* coussinet *m; (of cotton wool)* tampon *m; (for helicopters)* aire *f* d'atterrissage; **(writing) p.** bloc *m* (**b**) *Fam (home)* piaule *f*
2 *vt (pt & pp* **padded)** *(furniture)* capitonner **(with** avec)
3 *vi* **to p. about** aller et venir à pas feutrés

▸ **pad out** *vt sep (speech, essay)* étoffer

padded ['pædɪd] *adj (furniture, wall, cell)* capitonné(e); *(jacket)* matelassé(e)

padding ['pædɪŋ] *n (for clothes)* ouate *f; Fig (in speech, essay)* remplissage *m*

paddle ['pædəl] **1** *n* (**a**) *(for canoe)* pagaie *f; (of paddle boat)* aube *f;* **p. boat** bateau *m* à aubes (**b**) *(walk in water)* **to have a p.** patauger
2 *vt* **to p. a canoe** pagayer
3 *vi* (**a**) *(in canoe)* pagayer; *(of duck)* nager (**b**) *(walk in water)* patauger

paddling pool ['pædlɪŋ'puːl] *n* (**a**) *(inflatable)* piscine *f* gonflable (**b**) *(in park)* pataugeoire *f*

paddock ['pædək] *n* paddock *m*

Paddy ['pædɪ] *(pl* **Paddies)** *n Fam (Irish man)* Irlandais *m*

paddy ['pædɪ] *(pl* **paddies)** *n* **p. (field)** rizière *f*

padlock ['pædlɒk] **1** *n* cadenas *m*
2 *vt* cadenasser

padre ['pɑːdreɪ] *n* aumônier *m* (militaire)

paediatric, *Am* **pediatric** [piːdɪ'ætrɪk] *adj Med (ward)* de pédiatrie; *(specialist, nurse)* en pédiatrie

paediatrician, *Am* **pediatrician** [piːdɪə'trɪʃən] *n Med* pédiatre *mf*

paediatrics, *Am* **pediatrics** [piːdɪ'ætrɪks] *n Med* pédiatrie *f*

paedophile, Am **pedophile** ['piːdəʊfaɪl] n pédophile mf

pagan ['peɪgən] n & adj païen(enne) m,f

paganism ['peɪgənɪzəm] n paganisme m

page¹ [peɪdʒ] n (of book) page f; **on p. 6** (à la) page 6

page² 1 n (servant, at wedding) page m 2 vt (call) (by loudspeaker) appeler par haut-parleur; (by electronic device) biper

pageant ['pædʒənt] n (procession) spectacle m grandiose; (historical) spectacle m historique

pageantry ['pædʒəntrɪ] n pompe f

pageboy ['peɪdʒbɔɪ] n page m; **p. (haircut)** coiffure f à la Jeanne d'Arc

pager ['peɪdʒə(r)] n récepteur m d'appel

pagination [pædʒɪ'neɪʃən] n Typ pagination f

pagoda [pə'gəʊdə] n pagode f

paid [peɪd] 1 adj (a) (person, work) rémunéré(e), payé(e) (b) to put p. to sb's chances/hopes réduire les chances/espoirs de qn à néant 2 pt & pp of pay

paid-up ['peɪdʌp] adj (member) qui a payé sa cotisation

pail [peɪl] n seau m

pain [peɪn] 1 n (a) (physical) douleur f; (emotional) peine f; **to cause sb p.** (physical) faire souffrir qn; (emotional) faire de la peine à qn; **to be in p.** souffrir; **I have a p. in my side** j'ai une douleur au côté (b) (trouble) **to take pains** or **be at great pains to do sth** se donner du mal pour faire qch; **for my pains** pour ma peine (c) Formal **under p. of death** sous peine de mort (d) (idioms) Fam **he's a p. (in the neck)** il est casse-pieds; Vulg **it's a p. in the** Br **arse** or Am **ass** c'est chiant; Fam **housework is such a p.!** c'est tellement casse-pieds de faire le ménage! 2 vt peiner

pained [peɪnd] adj (look, expression) peiné(e), affligé(e)

painful ['peɪnfʊl] adj (physically) douloureux(euse), (emotionally) pénible; **it's p. to watch** c'est un spectacle pénible

painfully ['peɪnfʊlɪ] adv (walk) avec difficulté; **she fell p.** elle s'est fait mal en tombant; Fig **p. shy** d'une timidité maladive

painkiller ['peɪnkɪlə(r)] n analgésique m

painless ['peɪnlɪs] adj (not painful) indolore; Fig (easy) facile

painstaking ['peɪnzteɪkɪŋ] adj minutieux(euse)

paint [peɪnt] 1 n peinture f; **wet p.** (sign) peinture fraîche; **p. gun** pistolet m à peinture; **p. remover** décapant m 2 vt peindre; **to p. one's nails** se faire les ongles; Fig **to p. a favourable picture of a situation** brosser un tableau favorable d'une situation; Fig **to p. the town red** faire la noce 3 vi peindre

paintbox ['peɪntbɒks] n boîte f de couleurs

paintbrush ['peɪntbrʌʃ] n pinceau m

painter ['peɪntə(r)] n peintre m; **p. and decorator** peintre-tapissier m

painting ['peɪntɪŋ] n (picture) tableau m, peinture f; (activity) la peinture

paintwork ['peɪntwɜːk] n peinture f

pair [peə(r)] 1 n paire f; **in pairs** deux par deux; **a p. of glasses** une paire de lunettes; **a p. of scissors** une paire de ciseaux; **a p. of trousers** un pantalon 2 vt **to p. sb with sb** mettre qn avec qn

▸ **pair off** 1 vt sep (people) mettre deux par deux 2 vi (of people) se mettre deux par deux

▸ **pair up** vi se mettre ensemble

pajamas Am = **pyjamas**

Pakistan [pɑːkɪ'stɑːn] n le Pakistan

Pakistani [pɑːkɪ'stɑːnɪ] 1 n Pakistanais(e) m,f 2 adj pakistanais(e)

PAL [pæl] n TV (abbr phase alternation line) PAL

pal [pæl] n Fam copain (copine) m,f; **listen, p.!** fais gaffe, mon vieux!

palace ['pælɪs] n palais m

palatable ['pælətəbəl] adj (food) agréable au palais; Fig (suggestion) acceptable

palate ['pælɪt] n (in mouth) palais m

palatial [pə'leɪʃəl] adj (impressive) grandiose; (luxurious) luxueux(euse)

palaver [pə'lɑːvə(r)] n Fam (fuss) histoire f

pale¹ [peɪl] 1 adj pâle; **to turn p. (with fright)** pâlir 2 vi (of person) pâlir; **to p. into insignificance** être insignifiant(e)

pale² n **beyond the p.** (behaviour) inacceptable; (person) infréquentable

paleness ['peɪlnɪs] n pâleur f

Palestine ['pælɪstaɪn] n la Palestine

Palestinian [pælɪ'stɪnɪən] 1 n Palestinien(enne) m,f 2 adj palestinien(enne)

palette ['pælɪt] n Art palette f; **p. knife** couteau m à palette

palings ['peɪlɪŋz] npl (fence) palissade f

palisade [pælɪ'seɪd] n palissade f

pall¹ [pɔːl] n (of smoke) voile m

pall² vi (become uninteresting) perdre son attrait

pallbearer ['pɔːlbeərə(r)] n porteur m (du cercueil)

pallet ['pælɪt] n palette f

palliative ['pælɪətɪv] n palliatif m

pallid ['pælɪd] adj blême, blafard(e)

pally ['pælɪ] adj Fam **to be p. with sb** être copain (copine) avec qn

palm¹ [pɑːm] n **p. (tree)** palmier m; **p. (leaf)** palme f; **P. Sunday** Dimanche m des Rameaux

palm² n (of hand) paume f; Fig **to have sb in the p. of one's hand** avoir qn dans sa poche

▸ **palm off** vt sep **to p. sth off on sb** refiler qch à qn

palmistry ['pɑːmɪstrɪ] n chiromancie f

palomino [pælə'miːnəʊ] (pl **palominos**) n (horse) palomino m

palpable ['pælpəbəl] adj (atmosphere) palpable; (lie) manifeste; (difference) sensible

palpate ['pælpeɪt] vt Med palper

palpitate ['pælpɪteɪt] vi also Fig palpiter

palpitations [pælpɪ'teɪʃənz] npl palpitations fpl

paltry ['pɔːltrɪ] adj (amount, sum) dérisoire; (excuse) piètre

pamper ['pæmpə(r)] vt (person) dorloter; **to p. oneself** se faire plaisir

pamphlet ['pæmflɪt] n (informative) brochure f; (political) pamphlet m

pan¹ [pæn] 1 n (saucepan) casserole f; (frying pan) poêle f; (of scales) plateau m; (of lavatory) cuvette f; Fam Fig **to go down the p.** s'en aller en fumée 2 vi (pt & pp **panned**) **to p. for gold** faire de l'orpaillage

pan² (pt & pp **panned**) vt Fam (criticize) descendre en flammes

▸ **pan out** vi Fam (turn out) marcher; **if things p. out as planned** si tout marche comme prévu

panacea [pænə'sɪə] n panacée f

panache [pə'næʃ] *n* panache *m*
Pan-African [pæn'æfrɪkən] *adj* panafricain(e)
Panama ['pænəmɑ:] *n* le Panama; **the P. Canal** le canal de Panama; **P. (hat)** panama *m*
Panamanian [pænə'meɪnɪən] **1** *n* Panaméen(enne) *m,f* **2** *adj* panaméen(enne)
Pan-American [pænə'merɪkən] *adj* panaméricain(e)
pancake ['pænkeɪk] *n* crêpe *f*; **P. Day** *or* **Tuesday** mardi *m* gras
pancreas ['pæŋkrɪəs] *n Anat* pancréas *m*
panda ['pændə] *n* panda *m*; *Br* **p. car** voiture *f* de police
pandemonium [pændɪ'məʊnɪəm] *n (confusion)* chaos *m*; *(uproar)* vacarme *m* assourdissant
pander ['pændə(r)] *vi* **to p. to sb/sth** flatter qn/qch
p & p [pi:ən'pi:] *n Br (abbr* **postage and packing**) frais *mpl* de port et d'emballage
pane [peɪn] *n* **p. (of glass)** vitre *f*
panel ['pænəl] *n* **(a)** *(of wood, metal)* panneau *m* **(b)** *(of switches, lights)* tableau *m* de bord; **p. beater** carrossier *m* **(c)** *(of experts)* comité *m*; **p. discussion** table *f* ronde; *(on radio, TV programme)* invités *mpl*
panelling, *Am* **paneling** ['pænəlɪŋ] *n* lambris *m*
panellist, *Am* **panelist** ['pænəlɪst] *n (on radio, TV programme)* invité(e) *m,f*
pang [pæŋ] *n (of guilt, jealousy)* accès *m*; **pangs of hunger** tiraillements *mpl* d'estomac
panic ['pænɪk] **1** *n* panique *f*, affolement *m*; **in a p.** paniqué(e), affolé(e); **to get into a p.** paniquer, s'affoler; **p. attack** crise *f* d'angoisse; **p. button** bouton *m* déclencheur du signal d'alarme; *Fin* **p. buying/selling** achat *m*/vente *f* sous le coup de la panique; *Fam* **it was p. stations** c'était l'affolement général **2** *vt (pt & pp* **panicked**) affoler **3** *vi* paniquer, s'affoler
panicky ['pænɪkɪ] *adj Fam* **to be/get p.** paniquer, s'affoler
panic-stricken ['pænɪkstrɪkən] *adj* pris(e) de panique, affolé(e)
pannier ['pænɪə(r)] *n (on bicycle)* sacoche *f*; *(on animal)* panier *m* de bât
panoply ['pænəplɪ] *n* panoplie *f*
panorama [pænə'rɑ:mə] *n* panorama *m*
panoramic [pænə'ræmɪk] *adj* panoramique
panpipes ['pænpaɪps] *npl Mus* flûte *f* de Pan
pansy ['pænzɪ] *(pl* **pansies**) *n* **(a)** *(flower)* pensée *f* **(b)** *Fam (effeminate man)* tante *f*
pant [pænt] *vi* haleter; **to p. for breath** chercher son souffle
panther ['pænθə(r)] *n* panthère *f*
panties ['pæntɪz] *npl* (petite) culotte *f*, slip *m*
pantomime ['pæntəmaɪm] *n* **(a)** *Br (show)* = spectacle de Noël inspiré d'un conte de fée **(b)** *(mime)* mime *m*
pantry ['pæntrɪ] *(pl* **pantries**) *n* garde-manger *m inv*
pants [pænts] *npl* **(a)** *Br (underwear)* slip *m* **(b)** *Am (trousers)* pantalon *m*; *Fam* **to scare the p. off sb** flanquer la trouille à qn
pantyhose, pantihose ['pæntɪhəʊz] *n Am* collant *m*
pap [pæp] *n Fam Pej (nonsense)* idioties *fpl*
papa [pə'pɑ:] *n Old-fashioned* papa *m*
papacy ['peɪpəsɪ] *n* papauté *f*
papal ['peɪpəl] *adj* papal(e)
paper ['peɪpə(r)] **1** *n* **(a)** *(material)* papier *m*; **a piece of p.** un bout *ou* un morceau de papier; *Fig* **on p.** *(in theory)* sur le

papier; **p. aeroplane** avion *m* en papier; **p. bag** sac *m* en papier; **p. cup** gobelet *m* en carton; *Comptr* **p. feed** alimentation *f* en papier; **p. mill** papeterie *f*; **p. money** papier-monnaie *m*; **p. towel** essuie-tout *m inv*; *Comptr* **p. tray** chariot *m* d'alimentation en papier **(b)** **papers** *(documents)* papiers *mpl* **(c)** *(examination)* épreuve *f* écrite **(d)** *(scholarly study, report)* article *m*; **to read** *or* **give a p.** faire un exposé **(e)** *(newspaper)* journal *m*; *Br* **p. boy/girl** livreur *m*/livreuse *f* de journaux; *Br* **p. round** tournée *f* de distribution des journaux; *Br* **p. shop** marchand *m* de journaux **2** *vt (wall, room)* tapisser
▸ **paper over** *vt sep (with wallpaper)* recouvrir de papier peint; *Fig* **to p. over the cracks** masquer les problèmes
paperback ['peɪpəbæk] *n* livre *m* de poche
paperclip ['peɪpəklɪp] *n* trombone *m*
paperknife ['peɪpənaɪf] *(pl* **paperknives**) *n* coupe-papier *m*
paperweight ['peɪpəweɪt] *n* presse-papiers *m inv*
paperwork ['peɪpəwɜ:k] *n* travail *m* administratif, paperasserie *f*; *(documentation)* documents *mpl*
papery ['peɪpərɪ] *adj (skin)* parcheminé(e)
papier-mâché ['pæpjeɪ'mæʃeɪ] *n* papier *m* mâché
paprika ['pæprɪkə] *n* paprika *m*
Papuan ['pæpjʊən] **1** *n* Papou(e) *m,f* **2** *adj* papou(e)
Papua New Guinea ['pæpjʊənju:'gɪni:] *n* Papouasie-Nouvelle-Guinée *f*
papyrus [pə'paɪrəs] *n* papyrus *m*
par [pɑ:(r)] *n* **(a)** *(equality)* égalité *f*, pair *m*; **to be on a p. with sb/sth** être au même niveau que qn/qch **(b)** *(in golf)* par *m*; **a p.-three (hole)** un par trois; *Fig* **to be up to p. for the course** n'avoir rien de surprenant **(c)** *Fin (of bills, shares)* pair *m*; **above/below p.** au-dessus/au-dessous du pair; *Fig* **to feel below p.** ne pas être dans son assiette
parable ['pærəbəl] *n* parabole *f*
parabolic [pærə'bɒlɪk] *adj* parabolique
paracetamol [pærə'si:təmɒl] *n* paracétamol *m*
parachute ['pærəʃu:t] **1** *n* parachute *m*; **p. jump** saut *m* en parachute; **to make a p. jump** sauter en parachute **2** *vt* parachuter **3** *vi* sauter en parachute
parachuting ['pærəʃu:tɪŋ] *n* parachutisme *m*; **to go p.** faire du parachutisme
parachutist ['pærəʃu:tɪst] *n* parachutiste *mf*
parade [pə'reɪd] *n* **1** *(procession)* défilé *m*; **on p.** *(troops)* à l'exercice; **p. of shops** une rangée de magasins; **p. ground** terrain *m* de manœuvres **2** *vt (troops)* faire étalage de; *Fig (wealth, knowledge)* faire étalage de **3** *vi (of troops)* défiler; **to p. about** *or* **around** *(of person)* se pavaner
paradigm ['pærədaɪm] *n* paradigme *m*
paradise ['pærədaɪs] *n* paradis *m*; **bird of p.** oiseau *m* de paradis
paradox ['pærədɒks] *n* paradoxe *m*
paradoxical [pærə'dɒksɪkəl] *adj* paradoxal(e)
paraffin ['pærəfɪn] *n* paraffine *f*; **p. heater** chauffage *m* à pétrole; **p. lamp** lampe *f* à pétrole; **p. wax** paraffine
paragliding ['pærəglaɪdɪŋ] *n* parapente *m*; **to go p.** faire du parapente
paragon ['pærəgən] *n* modèle *m*; **a p. of virtue** un modèle de vertu
paragraph ['pærəgræf] *n* paragraphe *m*
Paraguay ['pærəgwaɪ] *n* Paraguay *m*

Paraguayan [pærə'gwaɪən] **1** n Paraguayen(enne) m,f
2 adj paraguayen(enne)
parakeet ['pærəki:t] n perruche f
parallel ['pærəlel] **1** n Math parallèle f; Fig (analogy) parallèle m; **to draw a p.** between two things établir un parallèle entre deux choses; **without p.** sans égal, sans pareil
2 adj Math parallèle; Fig (analogous) pareil(eille), semblable; **to be** or **run p.** to sth être parallèle à qch; **p. bars** barres fpl parallèles; **p. lines** lignes fpl parallèles; Comptr **p. processing** traitement m en simultanéité
3 vt (be similar to) être analogue à; (be equal to) égaler
parallelogram [pærə'leləgræm] n parallélogramme m
paralyse, Am **paralyze** ['pærəlaɪz] vt also Fig paralyser
paralysis [pə'ræləsɪs] (pl **paralyses**) n paralysie f
paralytic [pærə'lɪtɪk] **1** n paralytique mf
2 adj paralytique; Fam (very drunk) complètement bourré(e)
paralyze Am = **paralyse**
paramedic [pærə'medɪk] n auxiliaire mf médical(e)
parameter [pə'ræmɪtə(r)] n paramètre m
paramilitary [pærə'mɪlɪtrɪ] adj paramilitaire
paramount ['pærəmaʊnt] adj primordial(e); **of p. importance** d'une importance capitale
paranoia [pærə'nɔɪə] n paranoïa f
paranoid ['pærənɔɪd] adj paranoïaque; **to be p. about** sth être obsédé(e) par qch
paranormal [pærə'nɔ:məl] **1** n the **p.** le paranormal
2 adj paranormal(e)
parapet ['pærəpet] n parapet m
paraphernalia [pærəfə'neɪlɪə] n (equipment) attirail m; (things) affaires fpl; (clutter) bazar m
paraphrase ['pærəfreɪz] **1** n paraphrase f
2 vt paraphraser
paraplegic [pærə'pli:dʒɪk] n & adj paraplégique mf
parascending ['pærəsendɪŋ] n parachute m ascensionnel
parasite ['pærəsaɪt] n also Fig parasite m
parasitic [pærə'sɪtɪk] adj also Fig parasite; (existence) de parasite
parasol ['pærəsɒl] n ombrelle f
paratrooper ['pærətru:pə(r)] n parachutiste m
parboil ['pa:bɔɪl] vt faire cuire à demi
parcel ['pa:səl] n (a) (package) colis m, paquet m; **p. bomb** colis piégé; **p. post** service m de colis postaux (b) (of land) parcelle f
▸ **parcel out** (pt & pp **parcelled**, Am **parceled**) vt sep répartir
▸ **parcel up** vt sep empaqueter, emballer
parchment ['pa:tʃmənt] n parchemin m; **p. paper** papier m parchemin
pardon ['pa:dən] **1** n (forgiveness) pardon m; Law grâce f; **(I beg your) p.?** (what did you say?) pardon?, comment?; **I beg your p.!** (in apology) je vous demande pardon!
2 vt (action, person) pardonner; Law gracier; **to p. sb for** sth pardonner qch à qn; **p. me?** (what did you say?) (je vous demande) pardon?; **p. me!** (in apology) pardonnez-moi!
pardonable ['pa:dənəbəl] adj pardonnable, excusable
pare [peə(r)] vt (vegetable) éplucher; (apple) peler; (nails) rogner; (expenses) réduire
▸ **pare down** vt sep (expenses) réduire
parent ['peərənt] n (father) père m; (mother) mère f; **parents** parents mpl; **p. company** société f ou maison f mère; **p.-teacher association** = association des parents d'élèves et des professeurs

parentage ['peərəntɪdʒ] n origine f
parental [pə'rentəl] adj parental(e)
parenthesis [pə'renθəsɪs] (pl **parentheses** [pə'renθəsi:z]) n parenthèse f; **in parentheses** entre parenthèses
parenthood ['peərənthʊd] n (fatherhood) paternité f; (motherhood) maternité f; **the responsibilities of p.** les responsabilités parentales
parenting ['peərəntɪŋ] n art m d'être parent; **p. skills** capacité f à élever des enfants
pariah [pə'raɪə] n paria m
Paris ['pærɪs] n Paris
parish ['pærɪʃ] n paroisse f; **p. church** église f paroissiale; **p. council** conseil m municipal
parishioner [pə'rɪʃənə(r)] n paroissien(enne) m,f
Parisian [pə'rɪzɪən] **1** n Parisien(enne) m,f
2 adj parisien(enne)
parity ['pærɪtɪ] n égalité f; **to achieve p.** (of pay) obtenir l'égalité
park [pa:k] **1** n jardin m public, parc m; **p. keeper** gardien(enne) m,f de parc
2 vt (car) garer; Fam **to p. oneself in a chair/in front of the TV** s'installer dans un fauteuil/devant la télé
parka ['pa:kə] n parka f
parking ['pa:kɪŋ] n stationnement m; **no p.** (sign) défense de stationner; **p. attendant** gardien(enne) m,f de parking; **p. bay** place f de stationnement; **p. lights** (on car) feux mpl de position; Am **p. lot** parking m; **p. meter** parcmètre m; **p. space** place f (de parking); **p. ticket** contravention f
Parkinson's disease ['pa:kɪnsənz'dɪzi:z] n la maladie de Parkinson
parkland ['pa:klænd] n espace m vert
parkway ['pa:kweɪ] n Am route f bordée d'arbres et de verdure
parlance ['pa:ləns] n langage m; **in legal/political p.** en termes juridiques/politiques; **in common p.** en langage ordinaire
parley ['pa:lɪ] vi parlementer (**with** avec); (more officially) être en pourparlers (**with** avec)
parliament ['pa:ləmənt] n parlement m
parliamentarian [pa:ləmen'teərɪən] n parlementaire mf
parliamentary [pa:lə'mentərɪ] adj parlementaire; **p. privilege** immunité f parlementaire
parlour, Am **parlor** ['pa:lə(r)] n salon m
Parmesan [pa:mɪ'zæn] n **P. (cheese)** parmesan m
parochial [pə'rəʊkɪəl] adj Rel paroissial(e); Fig & Pej de clocher; **to be p.** (of person) avoir l'esprit de clocher
parody ['pærədɪ] **1** n (pl **parodies**) parodie f (**of** de)
2 vt (pt & pp **parodied**) parodier
parole [pə'rəʊl] **1** n liberté f conditionnelle; **to be (out) on p.** être en liberté conditionnelle; **p. officer** contrôleur m judiciaire
2 vt mettre en liberté conditionnelle
paroxysm ['pærəksɪzəm] n (of anger, guilt, jealousy) crise f; **to be in paroxysms of laughter** avoir le fou rire
parquet ['pa:keɪ] n **p. (floor)** parquet m
parrot ['pærət] **1** n as **p.** perroquet m
2 vt répéter comme un perroquet
parrot-fashion ['pærətfæʃən] adv comme un perroquet
parry ['pærɪ] (pt & pp **parried**) vt (blow) parer; (question) éluder
parsimonious [pa:sɪ'məʊnɪəs] adj parcimonieux-(euse)

parsley ['pɑːslɪ] *n* persil *m*

parsnip ['pɑːsnɪp] *n* panais *m*

parson ['pɑːsən] *n* pasteur *m*

parsonage ['pɑːsənɪdʒ] *n* presbytère *m*

part [pɑːt] **1** *n* (**a**) *(portion, component)* partie *f*; **p. of the body** partie du corps; **p. of speech** partie du discours; **(spare) parts** pièces *fpl* détachées; **p. two** *(of TV series, story)* deuxième partie; **in that p.** of the world dans cette région du monde; **in these parts** dans ces régions; **good in parts** bon (bonne) en partie; **the best/worst p.** was when he started laughing le meilleur/le pire ça a été quand il s'est mis à rire; **the difficult p.** is remembering ce qui est difficile, c'est de se souvenir; **for the best** *or* greater **p. of six years** pendant presque six ans; **the greater p. of the population** la plus grande partie de la population; **to be p. of sth** faire partie de qch; **it's all p. of growing up** c'est ce qui arrive quand on grandit; **it is p. and parcel of…** c'est partie intégrante de…; **in p.** en partie; **for the most p.** pour la plupart; **p. exchange** reprise *f* (en compte); **p. owner** copropriétaire *mf*
(**b**) *(role)* rôle *m*; **to take p. (in sth)** prendre part (à qch); **to have** *or* **play a p. in sth** jouer un rôle dans qch; **I want no p. in it** je ne veux rien avoir à faire là-dedans
(**c**) *(side)* **to take sb's p.** prendre le parti de qn; **on the p. of…** de la part de…; **for my p.** pour ma part
(**d**) *Am (in hair)* raie *f*
2 *adv* **she's p. Spanish** elle est en partie espagnole; **p. silk p. cotton** soie et coton
3 *vt (fighters, lovers)* séparer; **to p. one's hair** se faire une raie; **to p. company** se séparer
4 *vi (separate)* se rompre; **to p. (as) friends** se séparer (en) bons amis; **to p. with sth** se défaire de qch

partake [pɑːˈteɪk] (*pt* **partook** [pɑːˈtʊk], *pp* **partaken** [pɑːˈteɪkən]) *vi Formal* (**a**) **to p. of** *(eat, drink)* prendre (**b**) *(have quality)* **to p. of** relever de

partial ['pɑːʃəl] *adj* (**a**) *(incomplete)* partiel(elle) (**b**) *(biased)* partial(e) (**c**) *(fond)* **to be p. to sb/sth** avoir un faible pour qn/qch

partially ['pɑːʃəlɪ] *adv* (**a**) *(in part)* en partie, partiellement (**b**) *(with bias)* avec partialité

participant [pɑːˈtɪsɪpənt] *n* participant(e) *m,f*

participate [pɑːˈtɪsɪpeɪt] *vi* participer (**in** à)

participation [pɑːtɪsɪˈpeɪʃən] *n* participation (**in** à)

participle ['pɑːtɪsɪpəl] *n Gram* participe *m*

particle ['pɑːtɪkəl] *n (of matter)* particule *f*; *(of dust, sand)* grain *m*; *Fig (of truth)* once *f*

particular [pəˈtɪkjʊlə(r)] **1** *n* détail *m*; **in p.** en particulier; **I didn't see anything in p.** je n'ai rien vu de particulier; **to go into particulars** entrer dans les détails; **to take down sb's particulars** noter les coordonnées de qn
2 *adj* (**a**) *(specific)* particulier(ère); *(reason, case, example)* précis(e); **which p. thing/person did you have in mind?** à quoi/à qui pensiez-vous en particulier?; **on that p. day** ce jour-là (**b**) *(special)* particulier(ère); **a p. favourite of mine** un (une) de mes favoris (favorites); **she is a p. friend of mine** c'est une de mes meilleures amies; **to take p. care over sth** mettre un soin particulier à qch (**c**) *(exacting)* méticuleux(euse); **to be p. about sth** être exigeant(e) pour qch; **I'm not p.** ça m'est égal

particularly [pəˈtɪkjʊləlɪ] *adv (especially)* particulièrement, spécialement

parting ['pɑːtɪŋ] *n* (**a**) *(separation)* séparation *f*; **the p. of the ways** la croisée des chemins; **p. shot** pique *f (lancée en partant)*; **p. words** mots *mpl* d'adieu (**b**) *Br (in hair)* raie *f*

partisan [pɑːtɪˈzæn] *n & adj* partisan(e) *m,f*

partition [pɑːˈtɪʃən] **1** *n (in room)* cloison *f*
2 *vt (country)* partager
‣ **partition off** *vt sep (room)* cloisonner

partly ['pɑːtlɪ] *adv* partiellement, en partie

partner ['pɑːtnə(r)] **1** *n (in games)* partenaire *mf*; *(in business)* associé(e) *m,f*; *(in dancing)* cavalier(ère) *m,f*; *(in relationship)* compagnon (compagne) *m,f*; **p. in crime** complice *mf*
2 *vt (in games)* faire équipe avec; *(in dancing)* être le (la) cavalier(ère) de

partnership ['pɑːtnəʃɪp] *n* association *f*; **to enter** *or* **go into p. (with sb)** s'associer (avec qn)

partridge ['pɑːtrɪdʒ] *n* perdrix *f*

part-time [pɑːtˈtaɪm] *adj & adv* à temps partiel

part-timer [pɑːtˈtaɪmə(r)] *n* travailleur(euse) *m,f* à temps partiel

partway ['pɑːtweɪ] *adv* **I'm only p. through the book** je n'ai pas fini le livre; **this will go p. towards covering the costs** cela couvrira en partie les dépenses

party ['pɑːtɪ] **1** *n (pl parties)* (**a**) *(political)* parti *m*; **to follow** *or* **toe the p. line** suivre la ligne du parti; **p. member** membre *m* du parti; *Br* **p. political broadcast** émission *f* réservée à un parti politique (**b**) *(celebration)* fête *f*; **to have** *or* **give** *or* **throw a p.** organiser *ou* faire une fête; *Fig* **the p.'s over** la fête est finie; *Fam* **p. animal** fêtard(e) *m,f* (**c**) *(group)* groupe *m*; *(of workers)* équipe *f*; *Tel* **p. line** ligne *f* commune (à plusieurs abonnés); **p. wall** mur *m* mitoyen (**d**) *Law (participant)* partie *f*; **to be (a) p. to sth** être complice de qch
2 *vi (pt & pp partied)* *Fam (celebrate)* faire la fête

pass¹ [pɑːs] *n (over mountains)* col *m*

pass² **1** *n* (**a**) *(permit)* laissez-passer *m inv*; *Mil* sauf-conduit *m*; *(for travel)* carte *f* d'abonnement
(**b**) *(in examination)* **to get a p.** avoir la moyenne; **p. mark** moyenne *f*
(**c**) *(in sport)* passe *f*
(**d**) *Fam* **to make a p. at sb** faire des avances à qn
2 *vt* (**a**) *(go past) (person)* croiser; *(destination)* dépasser; *(frontier)* traverser; *(car, runner)* dépasser, doubler
(**b**) *(exam, test)* réussir
(**c**) *(bill, resolution)* voter
(**d**) *(give)* passer; **p. (me) the wine, please** passe-moi le vin, s'il te plaît
(**e**) **to p. the time** *(of person)* passer le temps; **it passes the time** ça fait passer le temps
(**f**) *Law* **to p. sentence** prononcer le verdict; **to p. judgment on sb** porter un jugement sur qn
(**g**) **to p. water** uriner; **to p. wind** avoir des vents
3 *vi* (**a**) *(go past)* passer; *(overtake)* dépasser, doubler; **to p. unobserved** passer inaperçu(e); **to let sth p.** laisser tomber qch; *also Fig* **p.!** je passe!; **I think I'll p. on the onions** je crois que je ne prendrai pas d'oignons
(**b**) *(of time)* s'écouler
(**c**) *(go away)* passer
(**d**) *(in exam)* avoir la moyenne
(**e**) *Lit (take place)* **it came to p. that…** c'est alors qu'il arriva que…
‣ **pass away** *vi Euph* décéder
‣ **pass down** *vt sep (knowledge, tradition)* transmettre
‣ **pass for** *vt insep* passer pour; **she'd p. for 45** on pourrait lui donner 45 ans
‣ **pass off 1** *vt sep* **to p. oneself off as sb** se faire passer pour qn; **to p. sth off as sth** faire passer qch pour qch; **she passed it off as a joke** elle a prétendu que c'était une plaisanterie
2 *vi (take place)* se passer
‣ **pass on 1** *vt sep (object)* faire passer; *(news, information)*

faire circuler; *(disease)* passer
2 *vi Euph* décéder
▸**pass out** *vi* (**a**) *(faint)* perdre connaissance (**b**) *(of military cadet)* sortir avec ses diplômes
▸**pass over** *vt sep* to p.
sb over (for promotion) ignorer qn au moment d'une promotion
▸**pass through 1** *vt insep* traverser
2 *vi* passer
▸**pass up** *vt sep (opportunity)* laisser passer
passable ['pɑːsəbəl] *adj* (**a**) *(of acceptable quality)* passable (**b**) *(road, bridge)* praticable; *(river)* franchissable
passage ['pæsɪdʒ] *n* (**a**) *(journey)* passage *m*; **with the p. of time** avec le temps; **to work one's p.** *(on ship)* travailler pour payer sa traversée (**b**) *(corridor)* couloir *m*, corridor *m*; *(alley)* passage *m* (**c**) *(extract)* passage *m*
passageway ['pæsɪdʒweɪ] *n* *(corridor)* couloir *m*, corridor *m*; *(alley)* passage *m*
passé [pæ'seɪ] *adj* dépassé(e)
passenger ['pæsəndʒə(r)] *n* passager(ère) *m,f*; **p. seat** place *f* du passager
passer-by ['pɑːsə'baɪ] *(pl* **passers-by**) *n* passant(e) *m,f*
passing ['pɑːsɪŋ] **1** *n* (**a**) *(going past)* passage *m*; **to say sth in p.** dire qch en passant; **p. place** *(on road)* aire *f* de croisement (**b**) *(of time)* écoulement *m* (**c**) *(death)* décès *m*
2 *adj* *(car, motorist)* qui passe; *(remark)* en passant; *(whim, attraction)* passager(ère)
passion ['pæʃən] *n* *(desire)* passion *f*; *(anger, vehemence)* emportement *m*, colère *f*; **to have a p. for sth** adorer qch; **in a fit of p.** sous le coup de la passion; **she hates him with a p.** elle le hait de toute son âme; **crime of p.** crime *m* passionnel; *Rel* **the P. (of Christ)** la Passion (du Christ); **p. fruit** fruit *m* de la passion
passionate ['pæʃənɪt] *adj* *(lover, embrace)* passionné(e); *(plea, speech)* véhément(e); *(believer, defender)* fervent(e); **to make p. love** faire l'amour avec passion
passive ['pæsɪv] **1** *n* *Gram* **the p.** le passif; **in the p.** au passif
2 *adj* passif(ive); **p. resistance** résistance *f* passive; **p. smoking** tabagisme *m* passif
passively ['pæsɪvlɪ] *adv* passivement, avec passivité
passkey ['pɑːskiː] *n* *(pl* **passkeys**) *n* passe-partout *m*
Passover ['pɑːsəʊvə(r)] *n* *Rel* la Pâque (Juive)
passport ['pɑːspɔːt] *n* passeport *m*; **p. photo** photo *f* d'identité
password ['pɑːswɜːd] *n* mot *m* de passe
past [pɑːst] **1** *n* passé *m*; **in the p.** autrefois; **a thing of the p.** une chose qui appartient au passé; **to live in the p.** vivre dans le passé
2 *adj* passé(e); **those days are p.** ces jours sont révolus; **in times p.** autrefois; **to be a p. master at sth** être passé(e) maître dans l'art de qch; **the p. week** la semaine dernière; **the p. few days** ces derniers jours; *Gram* **p. participle** participe *m* passé; **the p. tense** au passé
3 *prep (beyond)* au-delà de; **to walk p. the house** passer devant la maison; **it's p. four (o'clock)** il est quatre heures passées; **ten p. four** quatre heures dix; **I'm p. caring** je n'en ai plus rien à faire; *Fam* **to be p. it** avoir fait son temps; *Fam* **I wouldn't put it p. her** elle en est bien capable
4 *adv* **to walk** *or* **go p.** passer; **to run p.** passer en courant
pasta ['pæstə] *n* pâtes *fpl*
paste [peɪst] **1** *n* (**a**) *(substance)* pâte *f* (**b**) *(pâté)* mousse *f* (**c**) *(glue)* colle *f*
2 *vt (glue)* coller
pastel ['pæstəl] **1** *n* pastel *m*
2 *adj* pastel *inv*; **p. shades** tons *mpl* pastel

pasteurize ['pæstjʊraɪz] *vt* pasteuriser; **pasteurized milk** lait *m* pasteurisé
pastiche [pæ'stiːʃ] *n* pastiche *m*
pastille ['pæstɪl] *n* pastille *f*
pastime ['pɑːstaɪm] *n* passe-temps *m inv*
pasting ['peɪstɪŋ] *n Fam (beating)* raclée *f*; **to give sb a p.** flanquer une raclée à qn
pastor ['pɑːstə(r)] *n Rel* pasteur *m*
pastoral ['pɑːstərəl] *adj* (**a**) *(rural)* pastoral(e) (**b**) *(work, activities)* de conseiller(ère)
pastry ['peɪstrɪ] *(pl* **pastries**) *n* *(dough)* pâte *f*; *(cake)* pâtisserie *f*; **p. chef** pâtissier(ère) *m,f*
pasture ['pɑːstʃə(r)] *n* pâture *f*, pré *m*; **to be put out to p.** *(of animals)* être mis(e) au pré; *Fig (of person)* être mis au vert; *Fig* **to move on to pastures new** aller vers de nouveaux horizons
pasty[1] ['pæstɪ] *(pl* **pasties**) *n (savoury)* ≃ feuilleté *m*
pasty[2] ['peɪstɪ] *adj (face, complexion)* terreux(euse); **p.-faced** au teint terreux
pat [pæt] **1** *n* (**a**) *(tap)* petite tape *f*; *(on animal)* caresse *f*; *Fig* **to give sb a p. on the back** féliciter qn (**b**) *(of butter)* médaillon *m*
2 *adj (answer, explanation)* tout(e) prêt(e)
3 *adv* **to know** *or* **have sth off p.** savoir qch par cœur
4 *vt (pt & pp* **patted**) *(tap)* tapoter; *(animal)* caresser; **to p. sb on the head/shoulder** donner une tape sur la tête/l'épaule de qn; *Fig* **to p. sb on the back** féliciter qn
Patagonia [pætə'gəʊnɪə] *n* la Patagonie
patch [pætʃ] **1** *n* (**a**) *(of cloth)* pièce *f*; (**eye**) **p.** bandeau *m*; *Fam* **his last movie isn't a p. on the others** son dernier film est loin de valoir les autres (**b**) *(of colour, light)* tache *f*; *(of fog, mist)* nappe *f*, *(of ice)* plaque *f*; **a p. of blue sky** un coin de ciel bleu; *Fam* **to be going through a bad p.** traverser une mauvaise passe (**c**) *(of land)* lopin *m*; *(of prostitute, salesperson)* secteur *m*; *Fam* **keep off my p.!** hors de mon territoire!
2 *vt (hole, garment)* rapiécer
▸**patch up** *vt sep Fam (wounded person)* donner les premiers soins à; *(marriage, friendship)* raccommoder; **to p. things up** *(after argument)* se raccommoder
patchwork ['pætʃwɜːk] *n also Fig* patchwork *m*; **p. quilt** couvre-lit *m* en patchwork
patchy ['pætʃɪ] *adj* inégal(e)
pâté ['pæteɪ] *n* pâté *m*
patent ['peɪtɒnt] **1** *n* *(licence)* brevet *m* d'invention; **to take out a p. on sth** faire breveter qch; *Com* **p. applied for, p. pending** demande de brevet déposée
2 *adj* (**a**) *(patented)* breveté(e); **p. medicine** spécialité *f* pharmaceutique (**b**) *(evident)* manifeste (**c**) **p. leather** cuir *m* verni
3 *vt (of authorities)* breveter; *(of inventor)* faire breveter
patently ['peɪtəntlɪ] *adv* manifestement
paternal [pə'tɜːnəl] *adj (feelings)* paternel(elle); *(duty, responsibilities)* de père
paternally [pə'tɜːnəlɪ] *adv* paternellement
paternity [pə'tɜːnɪtɪ] *n* paternité *f*; *Law* **p. suit** action *f* en recherche de paternité
path [pɑːθ] **1** *n* (**a**) *(track)* chemin *m*; *(narrow)* sentier *m*; *(in garden)* allée *f*; **their paths had crossed before** leurs chemins s'étaient croisés auparavant (**b**) *(of rocket, planet)* trajectoire *f*; *(of inquiry, to success)* voie *f*; **the storm destroyed everything in its p.** la tempête a tout détruit sur son passage (**c**) *Comptr* chemin *m*
pathetic [pə'θetɪk] *adj (useless)* lamentable; *(touching)* attendrissant(e)

pathetically [pə'θetɪklɪ] *adv (uselessly)* lamentablement; *(touchingly)* de manière attendrissante

pathological [pæθə'lɒdʒɪkəl] *adj* pathologique

pathologist [pə'θɒlədʒɪst] *n* pathologiste *mf*

pathology [pə'θɒlədʒɪ] *n* pathologie *f*

pathos ['peɪθɒs] *n* pathétique *m*

pathway ['pɑːθweɪ] *n* sentier *m*

patience ['peɪʃəns] *n* (**a**) *(quality)* patience *f*; **to try** *or* **tax sb's p.** mettre la patience de qn à l'épreuve; **to exhaust sb's p.** abuser de la patience de qn; **to lose one's p.** (with sb) perdre patience (avec qn); **I've no p. with him** il m'énerve (**b**) *(card game)* réussite *f*; **to play p.** faire une réussite

patient ['peɪʃənt] **1** *n* patient(e) *m,f*
2 *adj* patient(e)

patiently ['peɪʃəntlɪ] *adv* patiemment

patio ['pætɪəʊ] *(pl* **patios***) n* patio *m*

patriarch ['peɪtrɪɑːk] *n* patriarche *m*

patriarchal [peɪtrɪ'ɑːkəl] *adj* patriarcal(e)

patriarchy ['peɪtrɪɑːkɪ] *(pl* **patriarchies***) n* patriarcat *m*

patrimony ['pætrɪmənɪ] *n* patrimoine *m*, héritage *m*

patriot ['pætrɪət, 'peɪtrɪət] *n* patriote *mf*

patriotic [pætrɪ'ɒtɪk, peɪtrɪ'ɒtɪk] *adj* patriotique

patriotism ['pætrɪətɪzəm, 'peɪtrɪətɪzəm] *n* patriotisme *m*

patrol [pə'trəʊl] **1** *n* patrouille *f*; **to be on p.** être de patrouille; **p. car** voiture *f* de police
2 *vt (pt & pp* **patrolled***)* patrouiller dans
3 *vi* patrouiller; **to p. up and down** faire les cent pas

patrolman [pə'trəʊlmæn] *n Am* agent *m* de police

patron ['peɪtrən] *n* (**a**) *(of arts)* protecteur(trice) *m,f*, mécène *m*; *(of charity)* patron(onne) *m,f*; **p. saint** (saint(e)) patron(onne) *m,f* (**b**) *(of shop)* client(e) *m,f*

patronage ['pætrənɪdʒ] *n* (**a**) *(of arts, charity)* patronage *m*; **under the p. of** sous la patronage de (**b**) *Pej (in politics)* copinage *m*

patronize ['pætrənaɪz] *vt* (**a**) *(arts)* protéger; *(shop, restaurant)* fréquenter (**b**) *(treat condescendingly)* traiter avec condescendance

patronizing ['pætrənaɪzɪŋ] *adj* condescendant(e)

patter[1] ['pætə(r)] **1** *n (of footsteps)* petit bruit *m*; *(of rain)* crépitement *m*
2 *vi (of rain)* crépiter; **she pattered down the corridor** elle trottinait le long du couloir

patter[2] *n Fam (talk)* boniment *m*, baratin *m*

pattern ['pætən] **1** *n* (**a**) *(design)* dessin *m*, motif *m*; **p. book** catalogue *m* d'échantillons (**b**) *(of behaviour* comportement *m* type; **a normal p.** of events une suite typique d'événements; **the weekend followed the usual p.** le week-end s'est déroulé comme d'habitude (**c**) *(in sewing)* patron *m*; *(in knitting)* modèle *m* (**d**) *(norm)* modèle *m*; **to set a p.** créer un modèle
2 *vt (model)* **to p. sth on sth** modeler qch sur qch

patterned ['pætənd] *adj* à motifs

paunch [pɔːntʃ] *n* ventre *m*; **to have a p.** avoir du ventre

pauper ['pɔːpə(r)] *n* indigent(e) *m,f*; **p.'s grave** fosse *f* commune

pause [pɔːz] **1** *n (in conversation)* silence *m*; *(rest)* pause *f*; *(in music)* point *m* d'orgue
2 *vi* faire une pause; **to p. for breath** reprendre son souffle

pave [peɪv] *vt (road)* paver (**with** de); *Fig* **to p. the way for sth** ouvrir la voie à qch

pavement ['peɪvmənt] *n Br (beside road)* trottoir *m*; *Am (roadway)* chaussée *f*; **p. artist** artiste *mf* qui dessine sur les trottoirs; **p. café** café *m* avec terrasse

pavilion [pə'vɪlɪən] *n* pavillon *m*

paving ['peɪvɪŋ] *n (with tiles)* carrelage *m*; *(with slabs)* dallage *m*; **p. stone** pavé *m*

paw [pɔː] **1** *n* patte *f*; *Fam* **paws off!** bas les pattes!
2 *vt (of animal)* donner un coup/des coups de patte à; **to p. the ground** frapper le sol du sabot

pawn[1] [pɔːn] *vt* mettre au mont-de-piété *ou* en gage

pawn[2] *n also Fig* pion *m*

pawnbroker ['pɔːnbrəʊkə(r)] *n* prêteur(euse) *m,f* sur gage

pawnshop ['pɔːnʃɒp] *n* mont-de-piété *m*, bureau *m* de prêt sur gage

pay [peɪ] **1** *n* paie *f*, salaire *m*; **the p.'s good/bad** ça paie bien/mal; **to be in sb's p.** être à la solde de qn; *Br* **p. cheque,** *Am* **pay check** chèque *m* de paie; **p. packet** enveloppe *f* de paie; **p. rise** augmentation *f* de salaire; **p. slip** bulletin *m* de salaire; **p. talks** négociations *fpl* salariales
2 *vt (pt & pp* **paid** [peɪd]) (**a**) *(person, money, bill)* payer; **I paid £5 for it** je l'ai payé 5 livres; **to be well/badly paid** être bien/mal payé(e); **I wouldn't do it if you paid me** je ne le ferais pas même si on me payait; **to p. one's way** payer son écot; **to p. cash** payer (argent) comptant; **to p. money into sb's account** verser de l'argent sur le compte de qn (**b**) *(give)* **to p. sb a compliment** faire un compliment à qn; **to p. sb a visit** rendre visite à qn; **to p. tribute to sb** rendre hommage à qn; **to p. one's respects to sb** présenter ses respects à qn (**c**) *(profit)* **it will p. you to do it** c'est dans votre intérêt de le faire
3 *vi* (**a**) *(give payment)* payer; **to p. through the nose** payer le prix fort; **to p. by cheque** payer par chèque (**b**) *(be profitable)* être rentable; **crime doesn't p.** le crime ne paie pas; **it pays to be honest** l'honnêteté est toujours récompensée

▸ **pay back** *vt sep (loan, person)* rembourser; *Fig* **I'll p. you back for this!** tu me le paieras!

▸ **pay in** *vt (cheque, money)* verser sur un compte

▸ **pay off 1** *vt sep* (**a**) *(debt)* régler; *(mortgage)* purger; *Fam* **to p. sb off** *(bribe)* soudoyer qn (**b**) *(make redundant)* licencier
2 *vi (of work, efforts)* porter ses fruits

▸ **pay out 1** *vt sep* (**a**) *(money)* débourser, dépenser (**b**) *(pt* **payed***) (rope)* laisser filer
2 *vi* payer

▸ **pay up** *vi* payer

payable ['peɪəbəl] *adj* payable; **to make a cheque p. to sb** libeller un chèque à l'ordre de qn

pay-as-you-earn [peɪæzjuː'ɜːn] *n Br* prélèvement *m* de l'impôt à la source

payday ['peɪdeɪ] *n* jour *m* de paie

PAYE [piːeɪwaɪ'iː] *n Br (abbr* **pay-as-you-earn***)* prélèvement *m* de l'impôt à la source

payee [peɪ'iː] *n* bénéficiaire *mf*

paying ['peɪɪŋ] *adj* payant(e); **p. guest** hôte *m* payant

payload ['peɪləʊd] *n* charge *f* utile

paymaster ['peɪmɑːstə(r)] *n* caissier *m*

payment ['peɪmənt] *n* paiement *m*; **to make a p.** effectuer un versement; **to stop p. (on a cheque)** faire opposition sur un chèque; **on p. of $500** contre paiement de 500 dollars; **p. by instalments** paiement par acomptes; **p. in full** paiement intégral

payoff ['peɪɒf] *n Fam* (**a**) *(bribe)* pot-de-vin *m* (**b**) *(reward)* récompense *f*

payphone ['peɪfəʊn] *n* téléphone *m* public

payroll ['peɪrəʊl] *n Com* liste *f* du personnel; **to be on the p.** faire partie du personnel

PBS [piːbiːˈes] *n* (*abbr* **Public Broadcasting Service**) = société américaine de production télévisuelle

PC [ˈpiːˈsiː] **1** *n* (**a**) *Br* (*abbr* **Police Constable**) = agent de police (**b**) (*abbr* **personal computer**) PC *m* **2** *adj* (*abbr* **politically correct**) politiquement correct(e)

pc (*abbr* **postcard**) carte *f* postale

PDQ *adv Fam* (*abbr* **pretty damn quick**) illico

PE [ˈpiːˈiː] *n Br* (*abbr* **physical education**) EPS *f*

pea [piː] *n* pois *m*; **like two peas in a pod** comme deux gouttes d'eau

peace [piːs] *n* paix *f*; **at p.** en paix; **to make (one's) p. with sb** faire la paix avec qn; **p. of mind** tranquillité *f* d'esprit; *Law* **to disturb the p.** troubler l'ordre public; **p. campaigner** militant(e) *m,f* pour la paix; **P. Corps** = organisation américaine d'aide aux pays du tiers-monde, composée de bénévoles intervenant sur le terrain; **p. movement** mouvement *m* pour la paix; **p. offering** cadeau *m* de réconciliation; **p. talks** pourparlers *mpl* de paix; **p. treaty** traité *m* de paix

peaceable [ˈpiːsəbəl] *adj* pacifique

peaceful [ˈpiːsfʊl] *adj* (*calm*) paisible; (*non-violent*) pacifique

peacekeeping [ˈpiːskiːpɪŋ] *n* maintien *m* de la paix; **p. force** force *f* de maintien de la paix

peace-loving [ˈpiːslʌvɪŋ] *adj* pacifique

peacetime [ˈpiːstaɪm] *n* temps *m* de paix

peach [piːtʃ] *n* (*fruit*) pêche *f*; *Fam* **she's a p.** elle est canon; *Fam* **a p. of a goal** un but de toute beauté; **p. Melba** pêche Melba; **p. tree** pêcher *m*

peacock [ˈpiːkɒk] *n* paon *m*

peak [piːk] **1** *n* (**a**) (*summit of mountain*) sommet *m*; (*mountain*) pic *m*, *Fig* (*of success, career*) apogée *m* (**b**) (*of price, inflation, fitness*) maximum *m*; **in p. condition** dans une forme excellente; **p. period** (*for traffic*) heures *fpl* de pointe; (*in shop*) heures d'affluence; **p. season** haute saison *f* (**c**) (*of cap*) visière *f* **2** *vi* culminer (**at à**)

peaky [ˈpiːkɪ] *adj Fam* patraque

peal [piːl] *n* (*of bells*) sonnerie *f*; (*of thunder*) coup *m*; **peals of laughter** éclats *mpl* de rire
▸ **peal out** *vi* (*of bells*) sonner à toute volée

peanut [ˈpiːnʌt] *n* cacah(o)uète *f*; *Fam Fig* **peanuts** (*small sum of money*) clopinettes *fpl*; **p. butter** beurre *m* de cacah(o)uètes; **p. oil** huile *f* d'arachide

pear [peə(r)] *n* poire *f*; **p. tree** poirier *m*

pearl [pɜːl] *n* (**a**) (*jewel*) perle *f*; **p. diver** pêcheur(euse) *m,f* de perles; **p. necklace** collier *m* de perles (**b**) (*idioms*) **pearls of wisdom** paroles *fpl* pleines de sagesse; **to cast pearls before swine** jeter des perles aux cochons

pearly [ˈpɜːlɪ] *adj* nacré(e); **the P. Gates** les portes *fpl* du paradis

peasant [ˈpezənt] *n* paysan(anne) *m,f*; *Pej* (*ignorant person*) péquenaud(e) *m,f*

peashooter [ˈpiːʃuːtə(r)] *n* petite sarbacane *f*

peat [piːt] *n* tourbe *f*; **p. bog** tourbière *f*

pebble [ˈpebəl] *n* caillou *m*; (*on beach*) galet *m*; **p. beach** plage *f* de galets

pebbledash [ˈpebəldæʃ] *n* crépi *m*

pebbly [ˈpeblɪ] *adj* caillouteux(euse); (*beach*) de galets

pecan [ˈpiːkən] *n* p. (**nut**) noix *f* de pecan; **p. pie** tarte *f* à la noix de pecan

peccary [ˈpekərɪ] (*pl* **peccaries**) *n* pécari *m*

peck [pek] **1** *n* (**a**) (*of bird*) coup *m* de bec (**b**) (*kiss*) bise *f*; **to give sb a p. on the cheek** faire une bise à qn

2 *vt* (**a**) (*of bird*) (*grain*) picorer; (*person*) donner un coup/des coups de bec à (**b**) (*kiss*) **to p. sb on the cheek** faire une bise à qn

peckish [ˈpekɪʃ] *adj Fam* **to be p.** avoir un creux

pecs [peks] *npl Fam* (*pectoral muscles*) pectoraux *mpl*

pectin [ˈpektɪn] *n Chem* pectine *f*

pectoral [ˈpektərəl] **1** *n* **pectorals** pectoraux *mpl* **2** *adj* pectoral(e)

peculiar [pɪˈkjuːlɪə(r)] *adj* (**a**) (*strange*) curieux(euse), bizarre (**b**) (*particular*) à, propre à; **this species is p. to Australia** cette espèce n'existe qu'en Australie

peculiarity [pɪkjuːlɪˈærɪtɪ] (*pl* **peculiarities**) *n* (*strangeness*) singularité *f*, bizarrerie *f*; (*unusual characteristic*) particularité *f*

peculiarly [pɪˈkjuːlɪəlɪ] *adv* (**a**) (*strangely*) singulièrement (**b**) (*especially*) particulièrement

pecuniary [pɪˈkjuːnɪərɪ] *adj Formal* pécuniaire

pedagogic(al) [pedəˈgɒdʒɪk(əl)] *adj* pédagogique

pedagogy [ˈpedəgɒdʒɪ] *n* pédagogie *f*

pedal [ˈpedəl] **1** *n* pédale *f*; **p. bin** poubelle *f* à pédale **2** *vt* (*pt & pp* **pedalled**, *Am* **pedaled**) **to p. a bicycle** être à bicyclette **3** *vi* pédaler

pedalo [ˈpedələʊ] (*pl* **pedaloes** *or* **pedalos**) *n* Pédalo® *m*

pedant [ˈpedənt] *n* pédant(e) *m,f*

pedantic [pɪˈdæntɪk] *adj* pédant(e)

pedantry [ˈpedəntrɪ] *n* pédantisme *m*, pédanterie *f*

peddle [ˈpedəl] *vt* (*goods, ideas, theories*) colporter; (*drugs*) faire du trafic de

peddler [ˈpedlə(r)] *n* (*of goods, ideas, theories*) colporteur (euse) *m,f*; (*of drugs*) trafiquant(e) *m,f*

pederast [ˈpedəræst] *n Formal* pédéraste *m*

pedestal [ˈpedɪstəl] *n* piédestal *m*; *Fig* **to put sb on a p.** mettre qn sur un piédestal; **p. lamp** lampe *f* sur piédestal

pedestrian [pɪˈdestrɪən] **1** *n* piéton(onne) *m,f*; **p. crossing** passage *m* pour piétons, passage clouté; **p. precinct** zone *f* piétonnière

2 *adj* (*unimaginative*) banal(e)

pedestrianize [pɪˈdestrɪənaɪz] *vt* transformer en zone piétonnière

pediatric, pediatrician *Am* = **paediatric, paediatrician**

pedicure [ˈpedɪkjʊə(r)] *n* **to have a p.** se faire soigner les pieds

pedigree [ˈpedɪgriː] **1** *n* (**a**) (*of animal*) pedigree *m* (**b**) (*of person*) ascendance *f*, généalogie *f*; *Fig* (*background*) passé *m*, antécédents *mpl*

2 *adj* (*animal*) de race

pedlar [ˈpedlə(r)] *n* colporteur(euse) *m,f*

pedophile *Am* = **paedophile**

pee [piː] *Fam* **1** *n* pipi *m*; **to have a p.** faire pipi

2 *vi* faire pipi

peek [piːk] **1** *n* coup *m* d'œil furtif; **to take** *or* **have a p. (at)** jeter un coup d'œil furtif (à)

2 *vi* jeter un coup d'œil furtif (**at** à)

peel [piːl] **1** *n* (*of apple, vegetable*) peau *f*; (*of orange, lemon*) écorce *f*

2 *vt* (*fruit*) éplucher; (*vegetable*) éplucher; *Fam* **to keep one's eyes peeled** ouvrir l'œil

3 *vi* (*of paint*) s'écailler; (*of skin, person*) peler
▸ **peel off 1** *vt sep* enlever

2 *vt sep* (*of skin*) peler; (*of label*) s'enlever

peelings [ˈpiːlɪŋz] *npl* (*of potato, carrot*) épluchures *fpl*

peep¹ [pi:p] **1** *n (furtive glance)* coup *m* d'œil furtif; **to have** *or* **take a p. (at)** jeter un coup d'œil furtif (à) **2** *vi* **to p. at sb/sth** jeter un coup d'œil furtif à qn/qch; **to p. through the keyhole** regarder par le trou de la serrure

peep² *n (sound) (of bird)* pépiement *m*; *(of mouse)* cri *m*; *Fam* **I don't want to hear another p. out of you** je ne veux plus entendre un mot

peephole ['pi:phəʊl] *n* judas *m*

Peeping Tom ['pi:pɪŋ'tɒm] *n Fam* voyeur *m*

peer¹ [pɪə(r)] *n* **(a)** *(equal)* pair *m*; **p. group** pairs *mpl*; **p. pressure** influence *f* du groupe **(b)** *Br (nobleman)* pair *m*

peer² *vi* **to p. at sb/sth** scruter qn/qch du regard; **to p. over sth** jeter un coup d'œil par-dessus qch

peerage ['pɪərɪdʒ] *n Br (rank)* pairie *f*; **the p.** les pairs *mpl*

peeress [pɪə'res] *n Br* pairesse *f*

peerless ['pɪəlɪs] *adj* sans pareil(eille), hors pair

peeve [pi:v] *vt Fam* mettre en rogne; **to be peeved (at)** être en rogne (à cause de)

peevish ['pi:vɪʃ] *adj* irritable, maussade

peewit ['pi:wɪt] *n* vanneau *m* (huppé)

peg [peg] **1** *n (wooden)* cheville *f*; *(metal)* fiche *f*; *(for coat, hat)* patère *f*; **(clothes) p.** pince *f* à linge; **(tent) p.** piquet *m* de tente; **to buy clothes off the p.** acheter du prêt-à-porter; *Fig* **to take sb down a p. (or two)** remettre qn à sa place **2** *vt (pt & pp pegged)* **(a)** **to p. sth in place** fixer qch avec des piquets; **to p. the washing on the line** étendre le linge *(en utilisant des pinces à linge)* **(b)** *(prices)* stabiliser

▸ **peg out** *vi Fam (die)* casser sa pipe

pejorative [pɪ'dʒɒrətɪv] *adj* péjoratif(ive)

Pekinese [pi:kɪ'ni:z] *n (dog)* pékinois *m*

Peking [pi:'kɪŋ] *n* Pékin *m*

pelican ['pelɪkən] *n* pélican *m*; *Br* **p. crossing** feux *mpl (à commande manuelle)*

pellet ['pelɪt] *n (of paper, bread, clay)* boulette *f*; *(for gun)* plomb *m*

pell-mell ['pel'mel] *adv (run)* de façon désordonnée

pelmet ['pelmɪt] *n* cantonnière *f*

pelt¹ [pelt] *n (animal skin)* peau *f*, fourrure *f*

pelt² **1** *vt* bombarder **(with** de) **2** *vi Fam* **(a)** *(rain)* **it was pelting down** il pleuvait à verse **(b)** *(go fast)* aller à toute allure; **to p. upstairs** grimper l'escalier quatre à quatre; **she came pelting along the corridor** elle a déboulé du fond du couloir

pelvic ['pelvɪk] *adj* pelvien(enne)

pelvis ['pelvɪs] *n* pelvis *m*

pen¹ [pen] **1** *n (for writing)* stylo *m*; **to put p. to paper** prendre la plume; **p. friend** *or* **pal** correspondant(e) *m,f*; **p. name** nom *m* de plume **2** *vt (pt & pp penned)* écrire, rédiger

pen² *n (for sheep, cattle)* enclos *m*

pen³ *n Am Fam (prison)* taule *f*

▸ **pen in** *vt sep (animals, people)* parquer

penal ['pi:nəl] *adj* pénal(e); **p. code** code *m* pénal; **p. colony** colonie *f* pénitentiaire; **p. servitude** travaux *mpl* forcés

penalize ['pi:nəlaɪz] *vt* pénaliser

penalty ['penəltɪ] *(pl* **penalties)** *n* **(a)** *(punishment)* peine *f*; **to impose a p. (on sb)** prendre une sanction (contre qn); **on** *or* **under p. of death** sous peine de mort; *Fig* **to pay the p. for sth** subir les conséquences de qch; *Com* **p. clause** clause *f* pénale **(b)** *(in soccer)* penalty *m*; *(in rugby)* pénalité *f*; **p. area** surface *f* de réparation; **p. kick** penalty

penance ['penəns] *n also Fig* pénitence *f*; **to do p. (for sth)** faire pénitence (pour qch)

pence [pens] *pl of* **penny**

pencil ['pensəl] **1** *n* crayon *m*; **p. case** trousse *f*; **p. drawing** dessin *m* au crayon; **p. sharpener** taille-crayon *m* **2** *vt (pt & pp* **pencilled,** *Am* **penciled)** *(draw)* dessiner au crayon; *(write)* écrire au crayon

▸ **pencil in** *vt sep (date)* fixer provisoirement; **to p. sb in** fixer provisoirement un rendez-vous à qn

pendant ['pendənt] *n* pendentif *m*

pending ['pendɪŋ] **1** *adj (trial)* en instance; *(negotiations)* en cours; *(documents)* en souffrance, en attente **2** *prep* en attendant

pendulum ['pendjʊləm] *n* pendule *m*

penetrate ['penɪtreɪt] *vt & vi* pénétrer

penetrating ['penɪtreɪtɪŋ] *adj (sound, wind, cold)* pénétrant(e); *(voice, scream, stare)* perçant(e)

penetration [penɪ'treɪʃən] *n* pénétration *f*

penguin ['peŋgwɪn] *n* manchot *m*

penicillin [penɪ'sɪlɪn] *n* pénicilline *f*

peninsula [pɪ'nɪnsjʊlə] *n* péninsule *f*; *(smaller)* presqu'île *f*

peninsular [pɪ'nɪnsjʊlə(r)] *adj* péninsulaire

penis ['pi:nɪs] *n* pénis *m*

penitence ['penɪtəns] *n* pénitence *f*, repentir *m*

penitent ['penɪtənt] *n & adj* pénitent(e) *m,f*

penitentiary [penɪ'tenʃərɪ] *(pl* **penitentiaries)** *n Am* pénitencier *m*

penknife ['pennaɪf] *(pl* **penknives** ['pennaɪvz]) *n* canif *m*

pennant ['penənt] *n* flamme *f*

penniless ['penɪlɪs] *adj* sans le sou

Pennsylvania [pensɪl'veɪnɪə] *n* la Pennsylvanie

penny ['penɪ] *n* **(a)** *Br (coin) (pl* **pence** [pens]) penny *m*; **a 50 pence piece** une pièce de 50 pence; **it was worth every p.** ça valait le coup; **it didn't cost them a p.** cela ne leur a pas coûté un sou; **p. farthing** vélocipède *m*; **p. pinching** économies *fpl* de bouts de chandelle; **p. whistle** flûtiau *m* **(b)** *Am (cent)* cent *m* **(c)** *(idioms)* **they haven't a p. to their name** il n'ont pas un sou vaillant; **the p.'s dropped** ça a fait tilt; **they're ten a p.** il y en a à la pelle; **a bad p.** un(e) bon (bonne) à rien

penny-pinching ['penɪpɪntʃɪŋ] *adj (person)* pingre; *(ways, habits)* de radin

pension ['penʃən] *n* pension *f*; *(after retirement)* (pension de) retraite *f*; **to be on a p.** recevoir une pension; *(after retirement)* recevoir une retraite; **p. fund** caisse *f* de retraite; **p. scheme** plan *m* de retraite

▸ **pension off** *vt sep* mettre à la retraite

pensionable ['penʃənəbəl] *adj* **p. age** âge *m* de départ en retraite

pensioner ['penʃənə(r)] *n* **(old-age) p.** retraité(e) *m,f*

pensive ['pensɪv] *adj* pensif(ive), songeur(euse)

pensively ['pensɪvlɪ] *adv* pensivement

pentagon ['pentəgən] *n* pentagone *m*; **the P.** *(building)* le Pentagone

pentathlon [pen'tæθlən] *n* pentathlon *m*

Pentecost ['pentɪkɒst] *n* la Pentecôte

penthouse ['penthaʊs] *n* = appartement de standing au dernier étage d'un immeuble

pent-up [pen'tʌp] *adj (desire)* refoulé(e); *(rage, energy)* contenu(e)

penultimate [pe'nʌltɪmɪt] *adj* pénultième, avant-dernier(ère)

penury ['penjʊrɪ] *n* indigence *f*

peony ['piːənɪ] (*pl* **peonies**) *n* pivoine *f*

people ['piːpəl] **1** *npl* (**a**) *(as group)* gens *mpl*; *(as individuals)* personnes *fpl*; **most p.** la plupart des gens; **old p.** les personnes âgées; **he's one of those p.** who think (that)... c'est le genre de type qui pense que...; **p. say (that)...** les gens disent que... (**b**) *(citizens)* peuple *m*; **the common p.** le peuple; **a man of the p.** un homme du peuple; **p. power** pouvoir *m* populaire; **P.'s Republic** République *f* populaire (**c**) *Fam (family)* **my/his p.** ma/sa famille
2 *n (nation)* peuple *m*; **the Irish p.** les Irlandais *mpl*
3 *vt* peupler

pep [pep] *n Fam* entrain *m*, allant *m*; **p. pill** excitant *m*; **p. talk** petit discours *m* d'encouragement
▸ **pep up** *(pt & pp* **pepped**) *vt sep Fam (person)* ragaillardir, revigorer; *(event)* animer; *(dish)* relever

pepper ['pepə(r)] **1** *n (spice)* poivre *m*; *(vegetable)* poivron *m*; **p. mill** moulin *m* à poivre; **p. pot** poivrière *f*
2 *vt* (**a**) *(in cooking)* poivrer (**b**) *Fig (speech, essay)* parsemer (**with** de); **to p. sb with bullets** cribler qn de balles

peppercorn ['pepəkɔːn] *n* grain *m* de poivre

peppermint ['pepəmɪnt] *n (plant)* menthe *f* poivrée; *(sweet)* bonbon *m* à la menthe; **p. tea** thé *m* à la menthe

peppery ['pepərɪ] *adj* (**a**) *(dish)* poivré(e) (**b**) *(irritable)* irascible, colérique

peptic ulcer ['peptɪk'ʌlsə(r)] *n* ulcère *m* gastroduodénal

per [pɜː(r)] *prep* par; **p. day** par jour, $15 **p. hour** 15 dollars de l'heure; *Formal* **as p. your instructions** conformément à vos instructions; **as p. usual** comme d'habitude; **p. annum** par an; **p. capita** par habitant; **p. se** en soi

perceive [pə'siːv] *vt* percevoir

percent [pə'sent] **1** *n* pourcentage *m*
2 *adv* pour cent

percentage [pə'sentɪdʒ] *n* pourcentage *m*

perceptible [pə'septɪbəl] *adj* perceptible

perceptibly [pə'septɪblɪ] *adv* sensiblement

perception [pə'sepʃən] *n* perception *f*

perceptive [pə'septɪv] *adj (person, remark)* perspicace; *(analysis, article)* pertinent(e)

perch¹ [pɜːtʃ] **1** *n (for bird) & Fig* perchoir *m*; *Fam Fig* **to knock sb off his p.** détrôner qn
2 *vi* se percher

perch² *n (fish)* perche *f*

percolate ['pɜːkəleɪt] **1** *vt (coffee)* passer; **percolated coffee** = café préparé dans une cafetière à pression
2 *vi (of liquid)* passer; *Fig (of information)* filtrer

percolator ['pɜːkəleɪtə(r)] *n* cafetière *f* à pression

percussion [pə'kʌʃən] *n* percussion *f*; **p. instrument** instrument *m* à percussion

percussionist [pə'kʌʃənɪst] *n* percussionniste *mf*

peregrine falcon ['perɪɡrɪn'fɔːlkən] *n* faucon *m* pèlerin

peremptory [pə'remptərɪ] *adj* péremptoire; *(refusal)* absolu(e)

perennial [pə'renɪəl] **1** *n (plant)* plante *f* vivace
2 *adj (plant)* vivace; *(problem, beauty)* éternel(elle); *(worry)* perpétuel(elle)

perfect 1 *adj* ['pɜːfɪkt] (**a**) *(ideal)* parfait(e); **nobody's p.** personne n'est parfait; **tomorrow would be p.** demain me conviendrait parfaitement; **to have p. pitch** avoir l'oreille absolue (**b**) *(complete)* **it makes p. sense** c'est parfaitement logique; **she's a p. stranger** je ne la connais pas du tout; **he's a p. idiot** c'est un parfait imbécile (**c**) *Gram* **the p. (tense)** le passé composé
2 *vt* [pə'fekt] parfaire

perfection [pə'fekʃən] *n* perfection *f*

perfectionist [pə'fekʃənɪst] *n* perfectionniste *mf*

perfectly ['pɜːfɪktlɪ] *adv (faultlessly)* à la perfection; *(completely)* parfaitement

perfidious [pə'fɪdɪəs] *adj Lit* perfide

perforate ['pɜːfəreɪt] *vt* perforer

perforated ['pɜːfəreɪtɪd] *adj* perforé(e); **p. ulcer** perforation *f* ulcéreuse

perforation [pɜːfə'reɪʃən] *n (hole)* perforation *f*; *(on stamp)* dentelure *f*

perform [pə'fɔːm] **1** *vt (play, role, piece of music)* jouer; *(miracle)* faire; *(one's duty)* remplir; **to p. an operation on sb** opérer qn
2 *vi (of machine, car)* marcher; *(of actor)* jouer; *(of singer)* chanter

performance [pə'fɔːməns] *n* (**a**) *(of task, duty)* accomplissement *m*; **p. appraisal** appréciation *f*, évaluation *f* (**b**) *(of sportsperson)* performance *f*; *(of actor)* interprétation *f*; *(of pupil, economy)* résultats *mpl*, performance; *(of machine, car)* performances *fpl* (**c**) *(of play)* représentation *f*; *Fig* **to make a p.** faire toute une histoire

performer [pə'fɔːmə(r)] *n* artiste *mf (des arts du spectacle)*

performing [pə'fɔːmɪŋ] *adj (dog, seal)* savant(e); **p. arts** arts *mpl* du spectacle

perfume 1 ['pɜːfjuːm] *n* parfum *m*; **p. counter** rayon *m* parfumerie
2 *vt* [pə'fjuːm] parfumer

perfumed ['pɜːfjuːmd] *adj* parfumé(e)

perfunctory [pə'fʌŋktərɪ] *adj (examination, glance)* rapide; *(smile)* mécanique; *(letter, instructions)* sommaire

perhaps [pə'hæps] *adv* peut-être; **p. so/not** peut-être que oui/non; **p. she'll come** elle viendra peut-être, peut-être qu'elle viendra

peril ['perəl] *n* péril *m*, danger *m*; **at one's p.** à ses risques et périls

perilous ['perɪləs] *adj* dangereux(euse)

perilously ['perɪləslɪ] *adv* dangereusement

perimeter [pə'rɪmɪtə(r)] *n* périmètre *m*; **p. fence** clôture *f*

period ['pɪərɪəd] *n* (**a**) *(stretch of time)* période *f*; **within the agreed p.** dans les délais convenus; **sunny periods** intervalles *mpl* ensoleillés (**b**) *(in school)* heure *f* de cours; **during the Latin p.** pendant le cours de latin (**c**) *(menstruation)* règles *fpl*; **to have one's p.** avoir ses règles; **p. pains** règles douloureuses (**d**) *(historical age)* époque *f*; **p. drama** *(on TV)* drame *m* historique; **p. dress** costume(s) *m(pl)* d'époque; **p. furniture** meubles *mpl* d'époque (**e**) *Am (full stop)* point *m*

periodic [pɪərɪ'ɒdɪk] *adj* périodique; *Chem* **p. table** classification *f* périodique

periodical [pɪərɪ'ɒdɪkəl] *n* périodique *m*

periodically [pɪərɪ'ɒdɪklɪ] *adv* périodiquement

peripheral [pə'rɪfərəl] **1** *n Comptr* périphérique *m*
2 *adj (area, vision)* périphérique; *(issue, importance)* accessoire

periphery [pə'rɪfərɪ] (*pl* **peripheries**) *n* périphérie *f*

periscope ['perɪskəʊp] *n* périscope *m*

perish ['perɪʃ] *vi* (**a**) *(of person)* périr; **p. the thought!** loin de moi cette pensée! (**b**) *(of rubber, leather)* se détériorer; *(of food)* s'avarier

perishable ['perɪʃəbəl] **1** *n* perishables denrées *fpl* périssables
2 *adj* périssable
perishing ['perɪʃɪŋ] *adj Fam (very cold)* it's p. il fait un froid de canard
peritonitis [perɪtə'naɪtɪs] *n* péritonite *f*
perjure ['pɜːdʒə(r)] *vt Law* **to p. oneself** faire un faux témoignage
perjury ['pɜːdʒərɪ] *n Law* faux témoignage *m*; **to commit p.** faire un faux témoignage
perk [pɜːk] *n Br Fam* avantage *m*, à-côté *m*
▸**perk up** *Fam* **1** *vt sep (revive)* requinquer, ragaillardir; *(cheer up)* remonter le moral à
2 *vi (revive)* se requinquer, se ragaillardir; *(cheer up)* retrouver sa bonne humeur
perky ['pɜːkɪ] *adj Fam (lively)* plein(e) d'entrain; *(cheerful)* guilleret(ette)
perm [pɜːm] **1** *n* permanente *f*; **to have a p.** se faire faire une permanente
2 *vt* **to have one's hair permed** se faire faire une permanente
permanence ['pɜːmənəns] *n* permanence *f*
permanent ['pɜːmənənt] *adj* permanent(e); *(ink, stain)* indélébile; *(residence, address)* fixe; **p. wave** permanente *f*
permeate ['pɜːmɪeɪt] **1** *vt* **to be permeated with sth** *(liquid)* être saturé(e) de qch; *(smell)* être rempli(e) de qch; *Fig (feeling)* être imprégné(e) de qch
2 *vi* **to p. through sth** *(of liquid)* passer à travers qch; *(of smell)* se répandre dans qch; *Fig (of feeling)* imprégner qch
permissible [pə'mɪsɪbəl] *adj* admissible, acceptable
permission [pə'mɪʃən] *n* permission *f*, autorisation *f*; **to ask for p. to do sth** demander la permission de faire qch; **to give sb p. to do sth** donner à qn la permission de faire qch, autoriser qn à faire qch
permissive [pə'mɪsɪv] *adj* permissif(ive)
permit 1 *n* ['pɜːmɪt] permis *m*; **p. holders only** *(sign)* réservé aux personnes autorisées
2 *vt* [pə'mɪt] *(pt & pp* **permitted)** permettre; **to p. sb to do sth** permettre à qn de faire qch, autoriser qn à faire qch
3 *vi* **weather permitting** si le temps le permet
permutation [pɜːmjʊ'teɪʃən] *n* permutation *f*
pernicious [pə'nɪʃəs] *adj* pernicieux(euse)
pernickety [pə'nɪkɪtɪ] *adj Fam (person)* tatillon(onne), pointilleux(euse); *(task)* délicat(e), minutieux(euse)
peroxide [pə'rɒksaɪd] *n Chem* peroxyde *m*; **p. blonde** blonde *f* décolorée
perpendicular [pɜːpən'dɪkjʊlə(r)] **1** *n* perpendiculaire *f*
2 *adj* perpendiculaire
perpetrate ['pɜːpɪtreɪt] *vt (crime)* perpétrer; *(fraud, error)* commettre
perpetrator ['pɜːpɪtreɪtə(r)] *n* auteur *m*
perpetual [pə'petjʊəl] *adj (eternal)* perpétuel(elle), éternel(elle); *(constant)* incessant(e), continuel(elle); *Phys* **p. motion** mouvement *m* perpétuel
perpetually [pə'petjʊəlɪ] *adv* perpétuellement
perpetuate [pə'petjʊeɪt] *vt* perpétuer
perpetuity [pɜːpɪ'tjuːɪtɪ] *n Formal* perpétuité *f*; **in p.** à perpétuité
perplex [pə'pleks] *vt* rendre *ou* laisser perplexe
perplexing [pə'pleksɪŋ] *adj* difficile; *(person)* déconcertant(e)
perplexity [pə'pleksɪtɪ] *n* perplexité *f*
persecute ['pɜːsɪkjuːt] *vt* persécuter

persecution [pɜːsɪ'kjuːʃən] *n* persécution *f*; *Psy* **p. complex** délire *m* de persécution
persecutor ['pɜːsɪkjuːtə(r)] *n* persécuteur(trice) *m,f*
perseverance [pɜːsɪ'vɪərəns] *n* persévérance *f*
persevere [pɜːsɪ'vɪə(r)] *vi* persévérer (**with** dans); **to p. in doing sth** persister à faire qch
Persia ['pɜːʒə] *n Hist* la Perse
Persian ['pɜːʒən] **1** *n* (**a**) *(person)* Hist Perse *mf*; *(after 7th century)* Persan(e) *m,f*(**b**) *(language)* persan *m*
2 *adj Hist* perse; *(after 7th century)* persan(e); **the P. Gulf** le golfe Persique
persimmon [pɜː'sɪmən] *n (tree)* plaqueminier *m*; *(fruit)* kaki *m*
persist [pə'sɪst] *vi* persister; **to p. in doing sth** s'obstiner à faire qch; **to p. in one's belief that...** persister à croire que...
persistence [pə'sɪstəns] *n (of person)* ténacité *f*, obstination *f*; *(of fog, belief)* persistance *f*
persistent [pə'sɪstənt] *adj (person)* tenace; *(problems, pain)* incessant(e), continuel(elle); *(rumours)* persistant(e); **p. offender** récidiviste *mf*
persistently [pə'sɪstəntlɪ] *adv* continuellement
person ['pɜːsən] *(pl* **people** ['piːpəl], *Formal* **persons**) *n* personne *f*; **in p.** en personne; **on one's p.** sur soi; *Gram* **in the first/second/third p.** à la première/deuxième/troisième personne; *Law* **by a p. or persons unknown** par un ou plusieurs inconnus
personable ['pɜːsənəbəl] *adj* charmant(e)
personage ['pɜːsənɪdʒ] *n* personnage *m*
personal ['pɜːsənəl] *adj* personnel(elle); **to make a p. appearance** venir *ou* apparaître en personne; **for p. reasons** pour des raisons personnelles; **don't be p.** ne parle pas de choses aussi personnelles; **it's nothing p., but...** ça n'a rien de personnel, mais...; **p. friend** ami(e) *m,f* personnel(elle); **p. ad** petite annonce *f*; **p. assistant** secrétaire *mf* particulier(ère); **p. best** *(in sport)* record *m* personnel; **p. column** petites annonces; **p. computer** ordinateur *m* individuel, PC *m*; **p. effects** effets *mpl* personnels; **p. growth** développement *m* personnel; **p. hygiene** hygiène *f*; **p. loan** prêt *m* personnel; **p. organizer** *(book)* agenda *m*; *(electronic)* agenda électronique; *Gram* **p. pronoun** pronom *m* personnel; **p. stereo** baladeur *m*
personality [pɜːsə'nælɪtɪ] *(pl* **personalities**) *n* personnalité *f*; **p. cult** culte *m* de la personnalité; *Psy* **p. disorder** trouble *m* de la personnalité
personally ['pɜːsənəlɪ] *adv* personnellement; **don't take it p.** n'en faites pas une affaire personnelle
personification [pɜːsɒnɪfɪ'keɪʃən] *n* incarnation *f*; **to be the p. of meanness** être l'avarice incarnée
personify [pɜː'sɒnɪfaɪ] *(pt & pp* **personified)** *vt* personnifier
personnel [pɜːsə'nel] *n* personnel *m*; **p. department** service *m* du personnel; **p. manager** directeur(trice) *m,f* du personnel
perspective [pə'spektɪv] *n* perspective *f*; **to see things in p.** relativiser les choses; **to put sth in(to) p.** relativiser qch
perspicacious [pɜːspɪ'keɪʃəs] *adj Formal* perspicace
perspiration [pɜːspə'reɪʃən] *n* transpiration *f*
perspire [pə'spaɪə(r)] *vi* transpirer
persuade [pə'sweɪd] *vt* persuader, convaincre; **to p. sb to do sth** persuader *ou* convaincre qn de faire qch; **to p. sb not to do sth** dissuader qn de faire qch
persuasion [pə'sweɪʒən] *n* (**a**) *(act, ability)* persuasion *f*; **powers of p.** pouvoir *m* de persuasion (**b**) *(beliefs)* **political**

p. opinions *fpl* politiques; **religious p.** religion *f*, confession *f*

persuasive [pə'sweɪzɪv] *adj (person)* persuasif(ive); *(argument)* convaincant(e)

persuasively [pə'sweɪzɪvlɪ] *adv (say)* d'un ton persuasif; *(argue)* de façon convaincante

pert [pɜːt] *adj* **(a)** *(cheeky)* espiègle; *(reply)* direct(e) **(b)** *(nose, breasts)* pointu(e); *(bottom)* petit(e) et ferme

pertain [pə'teɪn] *vi Formal* **to p. to** *(belong to)* appartenir à; *(be relevant to)* se rapporter à

pertinent ['pɜːtɪnənt] *adj* pertinent(e); **to be p. to** avoir rapport à

perturb [pə'tɜːb] *vt* inquiéter, troubler

Peru [pə'ruː] *n* le Pérou

perusal [pə'ruːzəl] *n Formal* lecture *f*

peruse [pə'ruːz] *vt Formal (read carefully)* lire attentivement; *(read quickly)* feuilleter; *(article)* survoler

Peruvian [pə'ruːvɪən] **1** *n* Péruvien(enne) *m,f* **2** *adj* péruvien(enne)

pervade [pə'veɪd] *vt* imprégner

pervasive [pə'veɪsɪv] *adj (feeling)* général(e); *(smell)* envahissant(e)

perverse [pə'vɜːs] *adj* **(a)** *(contrary)* contrariant(e); **he's just being p.** il fait ça pour contrarier; **to take a p. pleasure in doing sth** prendre un malin plaisir à faire qch **(b)** *(sexually deviant)* pervers(e)

perversely [pə'vɜːslɪ] *adv (contrarily)* par pur esprit de contradiction

perversion [pə'vɜːʃən] *n (sexual)* perversion *f*; *(of truth, justice)* travestissement *m*

pervert 1 *n* ['pɜːvɜːt] *(sexual deviant)* pervers(e) *m,f* **2** *vt* [pə'vɜːt] *(corrupt)* pervertir; *(distort)* altérer, dénaturer; *Law* **to p. the course of justice** entraver le cours de la justice

peseta [pə'seɪtə] *n Formerly* peseta *f*

pesky ['peskɪ] *adj Am Fam* embêtant(e), empoisonnant(e)

peso ['peɪsəʊ] *(pl* **pesos**) *n* peso *m*

pessary ['pesərɪ] *(pl* **pessaries**) *n* ovule *m*

pessimism ['pesɪmɪzəm] *n* pessimisme *m*

pessimist ['pesɪmɪst] *n* pessimiste *mf*

pessimistic [pesɪ'mɪstɪk] *adj* pessimiste

pest [pest] *n* **(a)** *(animal)* animal *m* nuisible; *(insect)* insecte *m* nuisible **(b)** *Fam (nuisance)* poison *m*, plaie *f*

pester ['pestə(r)] *vt* tourmenter, importuner; **to p. sb to do sth** harceler qn pour qu'il fasse qch; **to p. sb into doing sth** harceler qn jusqu'à ce qu'il fasse qch

pesticide ['pestɪsaɪd] *n* pesticide *m*

pestilence ['pestɪləns] *n Lit* peste *f*

pestle ['pesəl] *n* pilon *m*; **p. and mortar** pilon et mortier

pet [pet] **1** *n* **(a)** *(animal)* animal *m* familier *ou* domestique; **p. food** nourriture *f* pour animaux familiers; **p. shop** animalerie *f* **(b)** *(favourite)* **the teacher's p.** le chouchou du professeur; **p.** *(term of address)* mon petit chou **2** *adj* **p. hate** bête *f* noire; **p. name** surnom *m*; **p. subject** dada *m* **3** *vt (pt & pp* **petted**) *(person, dog)* caresser, câliner **4** *vi Fam (sexually)* se peloter

petal ['petəl] *n* pétale *m*

▸ **peter out** ['piːtə(r)] *vi (of conversation, enthusiasm)* tarir; *(of scheme)* n'aboutir à rien; *(of path, stream)* disparaître

petite [pə'tiːt] *adj* menu(e)

petition [pɪ'tɪʃən] **1** *n* pétition *f* **2** *vt (court, sovereign)* adresser *ou* présenter une pétition à

3 *vi* **to p. for sth** faire une pétition pour qch; *Law* **to p. for divorce** faire une demande de divorce

petitioner [pɪ'tɪʃənə(r)] *n Law (for divorce)* pétitionnaire *mf*; requérant(e) *m,f*

petrify ['petrɪfaɪ] *(pt & pp* **petrified**) *vt* pétrifier

petrochemical [petrəʊ'kemɪkəl] **1** *n* produit *m* pétrochimique **2** *adj* pétrochimique

petrol ['petrəl] *n Br* essence *f*; **p. bomb** cocktail *m* Molotov; **p. can** bidon *m* d'essence; **p. pump** pompe *f* à essence, **p. station** station *f* d'essence, station-service *f*; **p. tank** réservoir *m* d'essence

petroleum [pə'trəʊlɪəm] *n* pétrole *m*; **p. jelly** vaseline *f*

petticoat ['petɪkəʊt] *n (from waist)* jupon *m*; *(full-length)* combinaison *f*

petty ['petɪ] *adj* **(a)** *(insignificant)* insignifiant(e); **p. cash** petite caisse *f*; **p. crime** petite délinquance *f*; *Naut* **p. officer** second maître *m* **(b)** *(small-minded)* mesquin(e)

petulance ['petjʊləns] *n* irascibilité *f*

petulant ['petjʊlənt] *adj* irascible

petunia [pɪ'tjuːnɪə] *n* pétunia *m*

pew [pjuː] *n* banc *m* d'église

pewter ['pjuːtə(r)] *n* étain *m*

PG [piː'dʒiː] *adj Br Cin (abbr* **Parental Guidance**) = désigne un film dont certaines scènes peuvent choquer, ≃ tous publics *(l'accord des parents étant souhaitable)*

pH [piː'eɪtʃ] *n Chem* pH *m*

phalanx ['fælæŋks] *n Mil Hist* phalange *f*, *Fig (of officials, journalists)* armée *f*

phallic ['fælɪk] *adj* phallique; **p. symbol** symbole *m* phallique

phallus ['fæləs] *n* phallus *m*

phantom ['fæntəm] *n* fantôme *m*, spectre *m*; **p. pregnancy** grossesse *f* nerveuse

Pharaoh ['feərəʊ] *n* pharaon *m*

pharmaceutical [fɑːmə'sjuːtɪkəl] **1** *n* pharmaceutical produits *mpl* pharmaceutiques **2** *adj* pharmaceutique

pharmacist ['fɑːməsɪst] *n* pharmacien(enne) *m,f*

pharmacology [fɑːmə'kɒlədʒɪ] *n* pharmacologie *f*

pharmacy ['fɑːməsɪ] *(pl* **pharmacies**) *n* pharmacie *f*

phase [feɪz] *n* phase *f*; **it's just a p. (he's going through)** ça lui passera; *Fig* **out of p.** déphasé(e)

▸ **phase in** *vt sep* mettre en place progressivement

▸ **phase out** *vt sep* éliminer progressivement

phased [feɪzd] *adj* progressif(ive)

PhD [piːeɪtʃ'diː] *n Univ (abbr* **Doctor of Philosophy**) *(person)* docteur *m*; *(degree)* doctorat *m (in* de)

pheasant ['fezənt] *n* faisan *m*

phenomenal [fɪ'nɒmɪnəl] *adj* phénoménal(e)

phenomenally [fɪ'nɒmɪnəlɪ] *adv* prodigieusement

phenomenon [fɪ'nɒmɪnən] *(pl* **phenomena** [fɪ-'nɒmɪnə]) *n* phénomène *m*

phew [fjuː] *exclam (when hot)* pfff!; *(in relief)* ouf!

phial ['faɪəl] *n* fiole *f*

Philadelphia [fɪlə'delfɪə] *n* Philadelphie

philanderer [fɪ'lændərə(r)] *n Pej* coureur *m* de jupons

philanthropic [fɪlən'θrɒpɪk] *adj* philanthropique; *(person)* philanthrope

philanthropist [fɪ'lænθrəpɪst] *n* philanthrope *mf*

philanthropy [fɪ'lænθrəpɪ] *n* philanthropie *f*

philately [fɪ'lætəlɪ] *n* philatélie *f*

philharmonic [fɪləˈmɒnɪk] *Mus* **1** *n* (orchestre *m*) philharmonique *m*
2 *adj* philharmonique
Philippines [ˈfɪlɪpiːnz] *npl* the **P.** les Philippines *fpl*
philology [fɪˈlɒlədʒɪ] *n* philologie *f*
philosopher [fɪˈlɒsəfə(r)] *n* philosophe *mf*
philosophic(al) [fɪləˈsɒfɪk(əl)] *adj* philosophique; *(person, attitude)* philosophe
philosophize [fɪˈlɒsəfaɪz] *vi* philosopher
philosophy [fɪˈlɒsəfɪ] *(pl* **philosophies***) n* philosophie *f*
phlegm [flem] *n* flegme *m*
phlegmatic [flegˈmætɪk] *adj* flegmatique
phobia [ˈfəʊbɪə] *n* phobie *f;* **to have a p. about sth** avoir la phobie de qch
phoenix [ˈfiːnɪks] *n* phénix *m;* **to rise like a p.** renaître tel un phénix
phone [fəʊn] **1** *n* téléphone *m;* **to be on the p.** *(talking)* être au téléphone; *(have a telephone)* avoir le téléphone; **to give sb a p.** donner un coup de téléphone à qn; **p. bill** facture *f* de téléphone; **p. book** annuaire *m* (du téléphone); **p. box/booth** cabine *f* téléphonique; **p. call** coup *m* de téléphone; **p. number** numéro *m* de téléphone
2 *vt* téléphoner à
3 *vi* téléphoner
phonecard [ˈfəʊnkɑːd] *n* carte *f* de téléphone
phone-in [ˈfəʊnɪn] *n* **p.** **(programme)** = émission au cours de laquelle les téléspectateurs ou les auditeurs peuvent intervenir par téléphone
phoneme [ˈfəʊniːm] *n* phonème *m*
phonetic [fəˈnetɪk] *adj* phonétique
phonetics [fəˈnetɪks] **1** *n (science)* phonétique *f*
2 *npl (symbols)* symboles *mpl* phonétiques
phoney, *Am* **phony** [ˈfəʊnɪ] *(pl* **phonies***) Fam* **1** *n (impostor)* imposteur *m;* *(insincere person)* faux jeton *m;* *(thing)* faux *m*
2 *adj* bidon
phosphate [ˈfɒsfeɪt] *n* phosphate *m*
phosphorescent [fɒsfəˈresənt] *adj* phosphorescent(e)
phosphorus [ˈfɒsfərəs] *n* phosphore *m*
photo [ˈfəʊtəʊ] *(pl* **photos***) n* photo *f;* **to take sb's p.** prendre qn en photo; **p. album** album *m* (de) photos; **p. finish** photo-finish *f;* **it's just another p. opportunity** ce n'est qu'un nouveau prétexte pour se faire photographier
photocopier [ˈfəʊtəʊkɒpɪə(r)] *n* photocopieuse *f*
photocopy [ˈfəʊtəʊkɒpɪ] **1** *n (pl* **photocopies***)* photocopie *f*
2 *vt (pt & pp* **photocopied***)* photocopier
photoelectric [fəʊtəʊɪˈlektrɪk] *adj* photoélectrique; **p. cell** cellule *f* photoélectrique
photogenic [fəʊtəˈdʒenɪk] *adj* photogénique
photograph [ˈfəʊtəgrɑːf] **1** *n* photographie *f;* **to take sb's p.** prendre qn en photo; **p. album** album *m* de photographies
2 *vt* photographier, prendre en photo
photographer [fəˈtɒgrəfə(r)] *n* photographe *mf*
photographic [fəʊtəˈgræfɪk] *adj* photographique; **to have a p. memory** avoir une mémoire photographique
photography [fəˈtɒgrəfɪ] *n* photographie *f*
photosensitive [fəʊtəʊˈsensɪtɪv] *adj* photosensible
Photostat® [ˈfəʊtəʊstæt] *n* photostat *m*
photosynthesize [fəʊtəʊˈsɪnθɪsaɪz] *vt Bot* fabriquer par photosynthèse
phrasal verb [ˈfreɪzəlˈvɜːb] *n Gram* verbe *m* à particule

phrase [freɪz] **1** *n* phrase *f;* **p. book** manuel *m* *ou* guide *m* de conversation
2 *vt* **(a)** *(verbally)* exprimer; *(in writing)* tourner **(b)** *Mus* phraser
phraseology [freɪzɪˈɒlədʒɪ] *n* phraséologie *f*
physical [ˈfɪzɪkəl] **1** *n (examination)* visite *f* médicale
2 *adj* physique; **p. education** éducation *f* physique; **p. exercise** *or* **training** (exercices *mpl* de) gymnastique *f;* **p. fitness** forme *f* physique; **p. geography** géographie *f* physique; **it's a p. impossibility** c'est physiquement impossible; **p. sciences** sciences *fpl* physiques
physically [ˈfɪzɪklɪ] *adv* physiquement; **p. fit** en bonne forme physique; **p. handicapped** handicapé(e) physique
physician [fɪˈzɪʃən] *n* médecin *m*
physicist [ˈfɪzɪsɪst] *n* physicien(enne) *m,f*
physics [ˈfɪzɪks] *n* physique *f*
physiognomy [fɪzɪˈɒnəmɪ] *n Formal* physionomie *f*
physiological [fɪzɪəˈlɒdʒɪkəl] *adj* physiologique
physiology [fɪzɪˈɒlədʒɪ] *n* physiologie *f*
physiotherapist [fɪzɪəʊˈθerəpɪst] *n* kinésithérapeute *mf*
physiotherapy [fɪzɪəʊˈθerəpɪ] *n* kinésithérapie *f*
physique [fɪˈziːk] *n* physique *m*
pianist [ˈpɪənɪst] *n* pianiste *mf*
piano [pɪˈænəʊ] *(pl* **pianos***) n* piano *m;* **p. concerto** concerto *m* pour piano; **p. stool** tabouret *m* de piano; **p. tuner** accordeur *m* de pianos
piccolo [ˈpɪkələʊ] *(pl* **piccolos***) n* piccolo *m*
pick [pɪk] **1** *n* **(a)** *(tool)* pic *m*, pioche *f* **(b)** *(choice)* **to take one's p.** choisir; **the p. of the bunch** le (la) meilleur(e) du lot
2 *vt* **(a)** *(choose)* choisir; **to p. a fight (with sb)** chercher la bagarre (avec qn) **(b)** *(flowers, fruit)* cueillir **(c)** *(other uses)* **to p. a lock** crocheter une serrure; **to p. a guitar** pincer la guitare; **to p. one's nose** mettre les doigts dans le nez; **to p. one's teeth** se curer les dents; **to p. a spot** tripoter un bouton; **to p. sb's pocket** voler dans les poches de qn; **to p. a hole in sth** faire un trou à qch en tirant dessus; *Fig* **to p. holes in sth** trouver des failles dans qch; **to p. sb's brains** soumettre quelque chose à la sagacité de qn
3 *vi* **to p. and choose** se permettre de choisir
▸ **pick off** *vt sep (remove)* enlever, ôter; *(of gunman, sniper)* éliminer
▸ **pick on** *vt insep* utiliser comme souffre-douleur
▸ **pick out** *vt sep* **(a)** *(remove)* retirer **(b)** *(select)* choisir **(c)** *(recognize)* repérer
▸ **pick up** **1** *vt sep* **(a)** *(lift up)* ramasser; *(to upright position)* relever; **to p. up the phone** décrocher (le téléphone); *Fig* **to p. oneself up** se remettre, se reprendre; *Fig* **to p. up the pieces** ramasser les morceaux; *Fig* **to p. up the bill** payer l'addition **(b)** *(collect)* prendre; *(arrest)* arrêter; **to p. up survivors** recueillir des survivants **(c)** *Fam (sexually)* ramasser **(d)** *(learn)* apprendre; *(acquire)* acquérir; **to p. up speed** prendre de la vitesse **(e)** *(radio station, message)* capter **(f)** *(notice)* relever **(g)** *(discussion)* reprendre **(h)** *(make better)* remonter
2 *vi* **(a)** *(improve)* s'améliorer; *(after illness)* se remettre; *(of match, party)* s'animer; **the market is picking up** le marché commence à prendre **(b)** *(continue)* **let's p. up where we left off** reprenons (là où nous en étions restés)
pickaxe [ˈpɪkæks] *n* pioche *f,* pic *m*
picket [ˈpɪkɪt] **1** *n* **(a)** *(in strike)* piquet *m* de grève; **p. line** piquet de grève **(b)** *(stake)* piquet *m*, pieu *m;* **p. fence** palissade *f*
2 *vt (during strike)* former un piquet de grève aux portes de
pickings [ˈpɪkɪŋz] *npl* bénéfices *mpl;* **rich p.** gros bénéfices

pickle ['pɪkəl] **1** n Br (condiment) = condiment à base de légumes conservés dans du vinaigre; Am (gherkin) cornichon m; **pickles** conserves fpl au vinaigre; Fam Fig **to be in a p.** être dans le pétrin

2 vt conserver dans du vinaigre; **pickled cabbage/ onions** chou m rouge/oignons mpl au vinaigre

pick-me-up ['pɪkmɪʌp] n Fam remontant m

pickpocket ['pɪkpɒkɪt] n pickpocket m, voleur(euse) m,f à la tire

pick-up ['pɪkʌp] n (a) p. (arm) (on record player) lecteur m (phonographique); **p. (truck)** pick-up m inv (petite camionnette à plateau); **p. point** (for goods, passengers) point m de ramassage (b) Fam (improvement) amélioration f; (of business) reprise f

picky ['pɪkɪ] adj Fam difficile (about sur)

picnic ['pɪknɪk] **1** n pique-nique m; **to go on a p.** aller faire un pique-nique, aller pique-niquer; Fam Fig **it was no p.** ça n'a pas été une partie de plaisir; **p. basket** or **hamper** panier m à pique-nique

2 vi (pt & pp **picnicked**) pique-niquer, faire un pique-nique

picnicker ['pɪknɪkə(r)] n pique-niqueur(euse) m,f

Pict [pɪkt] n Hist Picte mf

pictorial [pɪk'tɔːrɪəl] adj (magazine) illustré(e); (representation) en images

picture ['pɪktʃə(r)] **1** n (a) (painting) tableau m; (drawing) dessin m; (in book, on TV) image f; (photograph) photo f; Fig (situation) situation f; **to be the p. of health** respirer la santé; **her face was a p.** elle a fait une de ces têtes; Fig **to put sb in the p.** mettre qn au courant; Fam Fig **I get the p.** je pige; **p. book** livre m d'images; **p. frame** cadre m; **p. gallery** galerie f de peintures; **p. postcard** carte f postale illustrée; **p. window** baie f vitrée (b) Br Fam (movie) film m; **the pictures** le cinéma

2 vt (a) (imagine) **to p. sth (to oneself)** s'imaginer qch; **to p. sb/sth as sth** s'imaginer qn/qch en qch; **to p. sb doing sth** s'imaginer qn en train de faire qch (b) (in photo, painting) représenter; Fig (in words) dépeindre, décrire

picturesque [pɪktʃə'resk] adj pittoresque

pidgin ['pɪdʒɪn] n pidgin m; **p. English** pidgin, pidgin-English m

pie [paɪ] n tourte f; Fam **p. in the sky** des châteaux en Espagne; **p. chart** camembert m

piece [piːs] n (a) (in general) morceau m; (smaller) bout m; (of cake) part f; (newspaper article) article m; **p. of land** (parcelle f de) terrain m; **a p. of furniture** un meuble; **a p. of luggage** (suitcase) une valise; (bag) un sac; **a p. of advice** un conseil; **a p. of luck** un coup de chance; **a p. of news** une nouvelle; **p. rate** (pay) salaire m à la pièce (b) (in chess, of jigsaw puzzle) pièce f; (in dominoes) domino m; (in draughts) pion m (c) (coin) pièce f (d) (of music) morceau m (e) (of artillery) pièce f; (firearm) arme f (f) (idioms) **to be still in one p.** être encore entier(ère); **to give sb a p. of one's mind** dire ses quatre vérités à qn; **to say one's p.** dire ce qu'on a à dire; **p. by p.** par morceaux; Fig **to go to pieces** s'effondrer (complètement); **to fall to pieces** tomber en morceaux; (of house) se délabrer, crouler; (of garment) partir en morceaux; **to take sth to pieces** démonter qch; **to be a p. of cake** être facile comme tout; Fam **he's a nasty p. of work** c'est un sale type

▸ **piece together** vt sep (parts) assembler les morceaux de; (something broken) recoller les morceaux de; (facts) reconstituer

piecemeal ['piːsmiːl] **1** adj fragmentaire, parcellaire; (work) fait(e) petit à petit **2** adv petit à petit

piecework ['piːswɜːk] n travail m à la tâche ou à la pièce

Piedmont ['piːdmɒnt] n le Piémont

pier [pɪə(r)] n (landing stage) embarcadère m; (at seaside resort) jetée f; (of bridge) pilier m

pierce [pɪəs] vt percer, transpercer; **to have pierced ears** avoir les oreilles percées

piercing ['pɪəsɪŋ] adj (cry, look) perçant(e); (cold) vif (vive)

piety ['paɪətɪ] n piété f

pig [pɪg] **1** n (a) (animal) cochon m, porc m (b) Fam (greedy person) goinfre m, glouton(onne) m,f; (unpleasant man) salaud m; (unpleasant woman) salope f (c) Fam (policeman) poulet m (d) Fam (idioms) **to buy a p. in a poke** acheter chat en poche; **pigs might fly!** on peut toujours rêver!; **to make a p.'s ear of sth** bousiller qch, saloper qch; **to make a p. of oneself** s'en mettre plein la lampe

2 vt (pt & pp **pigged**) Fam **to p. oneself** s'en mettre plein la lampe

▸ **pig out** vi Fam s'en mettre plein la lampe

pigeon ['pɪdʒɪn] n pigeon m

pigeonhole ['pɪdʒɪnhəʊl] **1** n casier m **2** vt (person) étiqueter, mettre une étiquette à

piggy ['pɪgɪ] Fam **1** n (pl **piggies**) petit cochon m; **p. bank** tirelire f **2** adj (eyes) de cochon

piggyback ['pɪgɪbæk] n **to give sb a p.** porter qn sur son dos

pig-headed [pɪg'hedɪd] adj entêté(e), têtu(e)

piglet ['pɪglɪt] n porcelet m

pigment ['pɪgmənt] n pigment m

pigmentation [pɪgmən'teɪʃən] n pigmentation f

pigmy ['pɪgmɪ] (pl **pigmies**) n Pigmée mf

pigsty ['pɪgstaɪ] (pl **pigsties**) n also Fig porcherie f

pigtail ['pɪgteɪl] n natte f

pike[1] [paɪk] n (weapon) pique f

pike[2] n (fish) brochet m

pilchard ['pɪltʃəd] n pilchard m

pile[1] [paɪl] **1** n (a) (heap) tas m; (stack) pile f; **to put things in(to) a p.** (heap) mettre des choses en tas; (stack) empiler des choses; Fam **he made his p. in the fur trade** il a fait fortune dans le commerce de la fourrure; Fam **to have piles of** or **a p. of things/work to do** avoir un tas de choses/des tonnes de travail à faire; Fam Fig **to be at the top/bottom of the p.** être favorisé(e)/défavorisé(e) (b) (of carpet) poils mpl (c) Phys (atomic) **p.** pile f atomique (d) (building) édifice m, (column, pillar) pieu m

2 vt entasser; (stack) empiler; **to p. food onto one's plate** bien remplir son assiette

3 vi Fam **to p. into a car** s'entasser dans une voiture

▸ **pile in** vi s'entasser

▸ **pile on** vt sep **to p. on the pressure** faire monter la pression; **to be on the agony** dramatiser; Fam **to p. it on** (exaggerate) en rajouter

▸ **pile out** vi sortir en masse

▸ **pile up** vi s'accumuler

pile-driver ['paɪldraɪvə(r)] n sonnette f

piles [paɪlz] npl (haemorrhoids) hémorroïdes fpl; **to have p.** avoir des hémorroïdes

pile-up ['paɪlʌp] n Fam carambolage m

pilfer ['pɪlfə(r)] vt & vi chaparder

pilgrim ['pɪlgrɪm] n pèlerin(e) m,f

pilgrimage ['pɪlgrɪmɪdʒ] n pèlerinage m; **to go on** or **make a p.** aller en pèlerinage, faire un pèlerinage

pill [pɪl] **1** n pilule f; **the p.** (contraceptive) la pilule; **to be on the p.** prendre la pilule

pillage ['pɪlɪdʒ] **1** n pillage m
2 vt & vi piller
pillar ['pɪlə(r)] n also Fig pilier m; **to go from p.**
to post courir à droite et à gauche; **to be a p.** of strength être d'un
grand soutien; **p. box** bôite f aux lettres
pillion ['pɪljən] **1** n p. (seat) siège m arrière
2 adv **to ride p.** monter derrière
pillory ['pɪlərɪ] **1** n (pl **pillories**) pilori m
2 vt (pt & pp **pilloried**) mettre au pilori
pillow ['pɪləʊ] n oreiller m
pillowcase ['pɪləʊkeɪs], **pillowslip** ['pɪləʊslɪp] n taie
f d'oreiller
pilot ['paɪlət] **1** n (of plane, ship) pilote m; **p. (programme)**
(on TV) émission f pilote; **p. light** veilleuse f; **p. scheme**
projet-pilote m; **p. study** étude-pilote f
2 vt (plane, ship) piloter
pimp [pɪmp] n souteneur m, proxénète m
pimple ['pɪmpəl] n bouton m
pimply ['pɪmplɪ] adj boutonneux(euse)
PIN [pɪn] n (abbr **personal identification number**) code
m confidentiel
pin [pɪn] **1** n (for sewing) épingle f; (for surgery) broche f; (in
grenade) goupille f; **three-p.** plug prise f à trois broches;
(firing) **p.** percuteur m; (safety) **p.** épingle à nourrice;
Fam **to have pins and needles** avoir des fourmis; **you
could have heard a p. drop** on aurait entendu une
mouche voler; **p. money** argent m de poche
2 vt (pt & pp **pinned**) (fasten with pin) épingler; (with
drawing pin, safety pin) attacher; **to p. sb against** or **to a
wall** plaquer qn contre un mur; **to p. the blame on sb**
rejeter la responsabilité sur qn; **to p. one's hopes on sb/
sth** mettre tous ses espoirs en qn/qch
▸ **pin down** vt sep (a) (trap) coincer (b) (identify) mettre le
doigt sur (c) (force to be definite) **to p. sb down** obliger qn à
s'engager; **to p. sb down to a date** obliger qn à donner une
date
▸ **pin up** vt sep (notice) fixer ou accrocher au mur; (hair)
relever; (hem) rabattre avec des épingles
pinafore ['pɪnəfɔː(r)] n (apron) tablier m; **p. (dress)** robe
chasuble f
pinball ['pɪnbɔːl] n flipper m
pincer ['pɪnsə(r)] n (of crab, insect) pince f; Mil **p.
movement** mouvement m en tenailles
pincers ['pɪnsəz] npl (tool) tenailles fpl, pince f
pinch [pɪntʃ] **1** n (a) (action) pincement m; **to give sb a p.**
pincer qn; Fam Fig **to feel the p.** être gêné(e); **at a p.** à la
rigueur (b) (of salt, herbs) pincée f; Fig **to take sth with a p.
of salt** ne pas prendre qch pour argent comptant
2 vt (a) (nip) pincer; **these shoes p. my feet** ces
chaussures me serrent (b) Br Fam (steal) piquer, faucher
3 vi (of shoes) serrer
pincushion ['pɪnkʊʃən] n pelote f à épingles
pine¹ [paɪn] n (tree, wood) pin m; **p. cone** pomme f de pin;
p. forest pinède f; **p. needle** aiguille f de pin; **p. nut** pignon m
pine² vi **to p. for sb/sth** se languir de qn/qch
▸ **pine away** vi languir
pineapple ['paɪnæpəl] n ananas m
ping [pɪŋ] **1** n tintement m
2 vi tinter
ping-pong ['pɪŋpɒŋ] n ping-pong m
pinion ['pɪnjən] **1** n pignon m
2 vt (restrain) **to p. sb (to/against)** clouer ou plaquer qn
(à/contre)
pink [pɪŋk] **1** n (a) (colour) rose m; Fam **to be in the p.** être
en parfaite santé (b) (flower) œillet m

2 adj rose; **to turn p.** rosir; **p. gin** = cocktail à base de gin
et d'angusture
pinkeye ['pɪŋkaɪ] n Am conjonctivite f infectieuse
pinkie ['pɪŋkɪ] n Am & Scot petit doigt m
pinnacle ['pɪnəkəl] n sommet m; Fig (of fame, career)
apogée m
pinpoint ['pɪnpɔɪnt] vt déterminer, identifier; (place)
localiser exactement
pinprick ['pɪnprɪk] n piqûre f d'aiguille
pinstripe ['pɪnstraɪp] n rayures fpl fines; **p. suit** costume
m rayé
pint [paɪnt] n (unit of measurement) Br = 0,568 l, pinte f; Am
= 0,473 l, pinte; Br **a p.** (of beer) ≃ un demi-litre de bière;
I'm going for a p. je vais prendre une bière
pinto bean ['pɪntəʊ'biːn] n haricot m pinto
pint-size(d) ['paɪntsaɪz(d)] adj Fam minuscule
pin-up ['pɪnʌp] n Fam pin-up f inv
pioneer [paɪə'nɪə(r)] **1** n also Fig pionnier(ère) m,f
2 vt **to p. sth** être le (la) premier(ère) à mettre au point qch
pioneering [paɪə'nɪərɪŋ] adj (work) innovateur(trice),
(person) qui fait œuvre de pionnier
pious ['paɪəs] adj pieux(euse)
piously ['paɪəslɪ] adv pieusement, avec piété
pip [pɪp] **1** n (a) (of fruit) pépin m (b) (on card, die) point m
(c) Br (sound) **the pips** (on radio) les bips mpl sonores
2 vt (pt & pp **pipped**) Fam **to be pipped at the post** être
coiffé(e) sur le poteau
pipe [paɪp] **1** n (a) (tube) tuyau m, canalisation f; (musical
instrument) chalumeau m; **the pipes** la cornemuse; **p. band**
orchestre m de cornemuses (b) (for smoking) pipe f; **to
smoke a p.** fumer la pipe; Fam Fig **put that in your p. and
smoke it!** mettez ça dans votre poche et votre mouchoir
par-dessus!; **p. cleaner** cure-pipe m; **p. dream** chimère f
2 vt (water, oil) canaliser; Fam **piped music** musiquette f
▸ **pipe down** vi Fam (make less noise) faire moins de bruit;
(not talk so much) se taire
▸ **pipe up** vi (of person) risquer un commentaire; (of voice)
se faire entendre
pipeline ['paɪplaɪn] n (for oil) pipeline m, oléoduc m (for
gas) gazoduc m; Fig **to be in the p.** être en préparation
piper ['paɪpə(r)] n (bagpipe player) joueur(euse) m,f de
cornemuse; Prov **he who pays the p. calls the tune** il est
normal que celui qui paie ait le droit de choisir
pipette [pɪ'pet] n pipette f
piping ['paɪpɪŋ] **1** n (a) (pipes) tuyauterie f, canalisations
fpl (b) (sound of bagpipes) son m de la cornemuse (c) (on
uniform) passepoil m
2 adj (sound, voice) flûté(e)
3 adv **p. hot** tout(e) chaud(e)
pipsqueak ['pɪpskwiːk] n Fam minus m
piquant ['piːkənt] adj piquant(e)
pique [piːk] **1** n dépit m; **in a fit of p.** dans un accès de
dépit
2 vt piquer
piracy ['paɪrəsɪ] n (a) (of ships) piraterie f (b) (of videos,
software) piratage m
piranha [pɪ'rɑːnə] n piranha m
pirate ['paɪrət] n pirate m; **p. edition** édition f pirate; **p.
radio** radio f pirate
pirouette [pɪrʊ'et] **1** n pirouette f
2 vi pirouetter
Pisa ['piːzə] n Pise
Pisces ['paɪsiːz] n les Poissons mpl; **to be (a) P.** être
Poissons

piss [pɪs] *very Fam* **1** *n (urine)* pisse *f*; **to have a p.** pisser; *Fig* **to take the p. out of sb/sth** se foutre de qn/qch; **p. artist** soûlard(e) *m,f*
2 *vt* **to p. oneself, to p. one's pants** pisser dans son froc
3 *vi* pisser
▸ **piss about, piss around** *vi very Fam (behave foolishly)* déconner; *(waste time)* glandouiller
▸ **piss off** *very Fam* **1** *vt sep (annoy)* faire chier; **to be pissed off** en avoir plein le cul
2 *vi (go away)* foutre le camp

pissed [pɪst] *adj very Fam* **(a)** *Br (drunk)* bourré(e); **to get p.** se soûler la gueule **(b)** *Am (angry)* en rogne

piss-up ['pɪsʌp] *n very Fam* beuverie *f*

pistachio [pɪ'stɑːʃɪəʊ] *(pl* **pistachios)** *n (nut)* pistache *f; (tree)* pistachier *m*

pistol ['pɪstəl] *n* pistolet *m*; **p. shot** coup *m* de pistolet

piston ['pɪstən] *n* piston *m*

pit¹ [pɪt] *n* **(a)** *(hole in ground)* fosse *f; (coal mine)* mine *f;* **in the p. of one's stomach** au creux de l'estomac; *Fam* **to be the pits** être nul (nulle) **(b)** *(in theatre)* parterre *m;* **the pits** *(in motor racing)* les stands *mpl* de ravitaillement **(c)** *(on metal, glass)* piqûre *f; (on skin)* marque *f,* cicatrice *f*

pit² *n (of cherry, olive)* noyau *m*

pit³ *(pt & pp* **pitted)** *vt* **to p. sb against sb** mettre qn aux prises avec qn, opposer qn à qn; **to p. oneself against sb** se mesurer à qn; **to p. one's wits against sb** se mesurer à qn intellectuellement à qn

pit-a-pat ['pɪtə'pæt] **1** *n (of rain)* crépitement *m; (of feet)* trottinement *m; (of heart)* battement *m*
2 *adv* **to go p.** *(of rain)* crépiter; *(of feet)* trottiner; *(of heart)* palpiter

pitch¹ [pɪtʃ] **1** *n* **(a)** *Br (for market stall)* place *f,* emplacement *m* **(b)** *(for sport)* terrain *m* **(c)** *(in music)* hauteur *f; Fig* **how did their relationship reach such a p.?** comment leurs relations ont-elles pu se détériorer à ce point? **(d)** *(talk) (sales)* **p.** baratin *m* publicitaire **(e)** *(slope)* inclinaison *f*
2 *vt* **(a)** *(throw)* lancer **(b)** *(aim)* adapter **(at** à) **(c)** *(tent)* monter, dresser
3 *vi (of ship, plane)* tanguer
▸ **pitch in** *vi* mettre du sien

pitch² *n (tar)* poix *f*

pitch-black [pɪtʃ'blæk] *adj* noir(e) comme dans un four; **it's p. outside** il fait nuit noire

pitched [pɪtʃt] *adj* **(a)** *(sloping)* en pente **(b)** **p. battle** bataille *f* rangée

pitcher¹ ['pɪtʃə(r)] *n Am (jug)* cruche *f,* pichet *m*

pitcher² *n Am (in baseball)* lanceur *m*

pitchfork ['pɪtʃfɔːk] *n* fourche *f*

piteous ['pɪtɪəs] *adj* pitoyable

pitfall ['pɪtfɔːl] *n* piège *m*

pith [pɪθ] *n (of orange)* peau *f* blanche; *(of argument, idea)* essence *f;* **p. helmet** casque *m* colonial (en sola)

pithy ['pɪθɪ] *adj* concis(e)

pitiable ['pɪtɪəbəl] *adj* pitoyable

pitiful ['pɪtɪfʊl] *adj* pitoyable

pitifully ['pɪtɪfʊlɪ] *adv* pitoyablement

pitiless ['pɪtɪlɪs] *adj* impitoyable

pitta bread ['pɪtəbred] *n* pita *m*

pittance ['pɪtəns] *n* salaire *m* de misère

pituitary gland [pɪ'tjuːɪtərɪ'glænd] *n* hypophyse *f*

pity ['pɪtɪ] **1** *n* **(a)** *(compassion)* pitié *f;* **to take** *or* **have p. on sb** prendre qn en pitié; **for p.'s sake!** par pitié! **(b)** *(misfortune)* **it's a p. (that...)** c'est dommage (que... +

subjunctive); **what a p.!** quel dommage!; **more's the p.** c'est bien dommage
2 *vt (pt & pp* **pitied)** plaindre, avoir pitié de

pitying ['pɪtɪɪŋ] *adj* compatissant(e)

pivot ['pɪvət] **1** *n also Fig* pivot *m*
2 *vi* pivoter **(on** sur); *Fig (of plan)* reposer **(on** *or* **around** sur)

pivotal ['pɪvətəl] *adj (position)* clef; *(importance)* capital(e)

pixel ['pɪksəl] *n Comptr* pixel *m*

pixie ['pɪksɪ] *n* lutin *m*

pizza ['piːtsə] *n* pizza *f;* **p.** *Br* **parlour** *or Am* **parlor** pizzeria *f*

Pk *abbr* **Park**

pkt *(abbr* **packet)** paquet

Pl *abbr* **Place**

placard ['plækɑːd] *n* pancarte *f*

placate [plə'keɪt] *vt* apaiser, calmer

place [pleɪs] **1** *n* **(a)** *(location)* endroit *m,* lieu *m; (in street names)* rue *f;* **a p. to live/eat** un logement/un restaurant; **I can't be in two places at once** je ne peux pas être à deux endroits à la fois; *Fam* **all over the p.** *(everywhere)* un peu partout; **my hair was all over the p.** j'étais coiffé n'importe comment; **at the interview he was all over the p.** à l'entretien, il a raconté n'importe quoi; *Fam Fig* **to go places** réussir (dans la vie); **p. of birth/death/business** lieu de naissance/décès/travail; **p. of residence** domicile *m;* **p. of worship** lieu *m* de culte; **p. name** nom *m* de lieu
(b) *(assigned to person, thing)* place *f;* **to find a p. for sb** *(job)* trouver une place pour qn; **to get a p. at university** être admis(e) à l'université; **there's a time and a p. for everything** il y a un temps pour tout; **to hold sth in p.** tenir qch en place; **to lose one's p.** *(in a book)* perdre sa page; **to take p.** avoir lieu; **to take sb's p.** remplacer qn; *(oust)* prendre la place de qn; *Fig* **out of p.** *(remark)* déplacé(e); **to feel out of p.** ne pas se sentir à sa place
(c) *Fam (residence)* chez soi; **my mother's p.** chez ma mère; **your p. or mine?** on va chez toi ou chez moi?
(d) *(seat, position in queue)* place *f;* **to set** *or* **lay an extra p. at the table** mettre un couvert de plus; **to change places with sb** changer de place avec qn; *Fig* être à la place de qn; *Fig* **put yourself in my p.** mettez-vous à ma place; **p. mat** set *m* de table
(e) *(in competition, society)* place *f,* rang *m;* **in first/second p.** à la première/seconde place; **in the first p....,** en second lieu...; **you shouldn't have said it in the first p.** d'abord, tu n'aurais pas dû le dire; **to know one's p.** savoir où est sa place; **to put sb in his p.** remettre qn à sa place
(f) *Math* **to three decimal places** à trois décimales
2 *vt* **(a)** *(put)* placer, mettre; **the house is well placed** la maison est bien située; **to be well placed to do sth** être bien placé(e) pour faire qch; **I never had her face but I can't p. her** je l'ai déjà vue mais je ne sais pas où
(b) *Com & Fin (order)* passer **(with** à); *(contract)* adjuger **(with** à); **to p. a bet (on sth)** parier (sur qch)
(c) *(find a job for)* placer
(d) *(classify)* classer; **to be placed third** se classer troisième

placebo [plæ'siːbəʊ] *(pl* **placebos)** *n also Fig* placebo *m*

placement ['pleɪsmənt] *n* stage *m*

placenta [plə'sentə] *n* placenta *m*

placid ['plæsɪd] *adj* placide, calme

plagiarism ['pleɪdʒərɪzəm] *n* plagiat *m*

plagiarize ['pleɪdʒəraɪz] *vt* plagier

plague [pleɪg] **1** *n (disease)* peste *f; (of insects, frogs)* invasion *f;* **to avoid sb/sth like the p.** éviter qn/qch comme la peste

2 vt *(of person)* harceler; *(of problem)* tourmenter; **to p. sb with questions** harceler qn de questions

plaice [pleɪs] n carrelet m

plaid [plæd] n *(fabric)* tissu m écossais; *(garment)* plaid m

plain [pleɪn] **1** n plaine f
2 adj **(a)** *(clear, unambiguous)* clair(e), évident(e); **to make sth p. to sb** faire comprendre qch à qn; **I'll be quite p. with you** je vais être franc avec vous; *Fam* **it's as p. as the nose on your face** ça se voit comme le nez au milieu de la figure; **in p. English** clairement; *Fig* **to be p. sailing** aller tout seul; **p. speaking** franc-parler m **(b)** *(simple)* simple; *Fam* **that's just p. foolishness/ignorance** c'est de la pure bêtise/ignorance; **one p., one purl** *(in knitting)* une maille à l'endroit, une maille à l'envers; *Br* **p. chocolate** chocolat m noir; **a p. clothes policeman** un agent en civil; **p. flour** farine f *(sans levure)* **(c)** *(not beautiful)* quelconque; **a p. Jane** une jeune fille plutôt quelconque

plainly ['pleɪnlɪ] adv **(a)** *(clearly)* clairement, nettement; **to speak p.** parler franchement *ou* sans détours **(b)** *(simply)* simplement

plain-spoken [pleɪn'spəʊkən] adj franc (franche)

plaintiff ['pleɪntɪf] n Law plaignant(e) m,f

plaintive ['pleɪntɪv] adj plaintif(ive)

plaintively ['pleɪntɪvlɪ] adv d'un ton plaintif

plait [plæt] Br **1** n natte f, tresse f
2 vt natter, tresser

plan [plæn] **1** n **(a)** *(proposal, intention)* projet m; **to go according to p.** marcher comme prévu; **the best p. would be to...** le mieux serait de... **(b)** *(of building, town, essay)* plan m
2 vt *(pt & pp* **planned)** **(a)** *(arrange)* projeter; *(crime)* comploter, tramer; **to p. to do sth** projeter de faire qch; **to go as planned** marcher comme prévu **(b)** *(building, town)* faire le plan de; *(economy)* planifier
3 vi faire des projets; **to p. for the future** faire des projets d'avenir

▸ **plan out** vt sep prévoir (en détail)

plane¹ [pleɪn] n *(surface)* plan m

plane² n *(aeroplane)* avion m; **by p.** en avion; **p. ticket** billet m d'avion

plane³ **1** n *(tool)* rabot m
2 vt raboter, aplanir

plane⁴ n p. *(tree)* platane m

planet ['plænɪt] n planète f

planetarium [plænɪ'teərɪəm] *(pl* **planetariums** *or* **planetaria** [plænɪ'teərɪə])* n planétarium m

planetary ['plænɪtərɪ] adj planétaire

plank [plæŋk] n *(of wood)* planche f; *Fig (policy)* point m

plankton ['plæŋktən] n plancton m

planner ['plænə(r)] n planificateur(trice) m,f; *(for towns)* urbaniste mf

planning ['plænɪŋ] n conception f, élaboration f; **it's still at the p. stage** c'est encore à l'état de projet; **p. permission** permis m de construire

plant [plɑːnt] **1** n **(a)** *(living thing)* plante f; **p. life** flore f **(b)** *Ind (equipment)* matériel m; *(factory)* usine f; **p. hire** location f de matériel industriel; **p. maintenance** entretien m du matériel
2 vt *(tree, flower)* planter; *(crops, field)* semer; *(bomb)* poser; **to p. an idea in sb's mind** mettre une idée dans l'esprit de qn; *Fam* **to p. sth on sb** cacher qch dans les affaires de qn *(pour le/la compromettre en cas de découverte)*

plantain ['plæntɪn] n **(a)** *(wild plant)* plantain m **(b)** *(fruit)* banane f des Antilles; *(tree)* bananier m du paradis

plantation [plæn'teɪʃən] n plantation f

planter ['plɑːntə(r)] n *(person)* planteur(euse) m,f; *(machine)* planteuse

plaque [plɑːk] n **(a)** *(sign)* plaque f (commémorative) **(b)** *(on teeth)* plaque f dentaire

plasma ['plæzmə] n plasma m

plaster ['plɑːstə(r)] **1** n **(a)** *(on wall)* plâtre m; **p. of Paris** plâtre de Paris; **to put sb's leg in p.** mettre la jambe de qn dans le plâtre; **p. cast** *(for broken bone)* plâtre; *(in art)* moulage m en plâtre **(b)** *Br* **(sticking) p.** pansement m adhésif
2 vt **(a)** *(wall)* plâtrer **(b)** *(cover)* tapisser **(with** de); **plastered with mud** couvert(e) de boue; **her name was plastered over the front pages** son nom s'étalait en première page

plasterboard ['plɑːstəbɔːd] n placoplâtre® m

plastered ['plɑːstəd] adj Fam *(drunk)* beurré(e)

plasterer ['plɑːstərə(r)] n plâtrier m

plastic ['plæstɪk] **1** n **(a)** *(material)* plastique m **(b)** *Fam (credit cards)* cartes fpl de crédit; **do they take p.?** est-ce qu'ils acceptent les cartes de crédit?
2 adj *(cup, bag)* en plastique; *(bullet)* de plastique; **p. explosive** plastic m; **p. surgeon** chirurgien(enne) m,f esthétique; **p. surgery** *(cosmetic)* chirurgie f esthétique; *(after accident)* chirurgie réparatrice

plate [pleɪt] **1** n **(a)** *(for food)* assiette f; *(for church offering)* plateau m de quête; *Fam Fig* **to have a lot on one's p.** avoir du pain sur la planche; *Fam Fig* **to hand sth to sb on a p.** apporter qch à qn sur un plateau; **p. rack** égouttoir m **(b)** *(sheet of glass)* lamelle f; *(sheet of metal)* plaque f; **p. glass** vitrage m très épais
2 vt *(with gold)* plaquer en or; *(with silver)* plaquer en argent

plateau ['plætəʊ] *(pl* **plateaux** ['plætəʊz] *or* **plateaus)** n Geog plateau m; *Fig* **to reach a p.** *(of career, economy)* atteindre un palier

platform ['plætfɔːm] n **(a)** *(raised flat surface)* plate-forme f; *(in train station)* quai m; *(where passengers stand)* quai m; *(where train stops)* voie f; Rail **p. 4** quai n° 4; **p. shoes** chaussures fpl à semelles compensées *(à la façon des années 70)* **(b)** *(at meeting)* estrade f, tribune f; *(political programme)* programme m

platform-independent ['plætfɔːmɪndɪ'pendənt] adj Comptr indépendant(e) de la plate-forme

platinum ['plætɪnəm] n Chem platine m; **p. blond hair** cheveux blond platine

platitude ['plætɪtjuːd] n platitude f

platonic [plə'tɒnɪk] adj platonique

platoon [plə'tuːn] n Mil section f, peloton m

platter ['plætə(r)] n *(serving plate)* plat m

platypus ['plætɪpəs] n ornithorynque m

plausible ['plɔːzəbəl] adj *(excuse, argument)* plausible; *(person)* convaincant(e)

play [pleɪ] **1** n **(a)** *(drama)* pièce f (de théâtre) **(b)** *(of children)* **at p.** en train de jouer; **to make great p. of sth** beaucoup insister sur qch; **p. on words** jeu m de mots **(c)** *(in sport)* jeu m; **in p.** en jeu; **out of p.** hors jeu; *Fig* **to come into p.** entrer en jeu; *Fig* **to make a p. for sth** tenter sa chance à qch **(d)** *Tech* jeu m
2 vt **(a)** *(game, sport)* jouer à; *(opponent)* affronter; *(shot, card, position)* jouer; **to p. tennis/chess** jouer au tennis/aux échecs; *Fig* **stop playing games!** arrête de te moquer de moi!; *Fig* **to p. ball** *(co-operate)* coopérer; *Fig* **to p. the Stock Exchange** jouer à la Bourse; **to p. a joke** *ou* **a trick on sb** jouer un tour à qn
(b) *(in play, film)* jouer; **to p. Macbeth** jouer le rôle de Macbeth; *Fig* **to p. an important part in sth** jouer un rôle

important dans qch; *Fig* **to p. no part in sth** ne pas intervenir dans qch; *Fig* **to p. the fool** faire l'idiot **(c)** *(musical instrument)* jouer de; *(piece, tune)* jouer; *(CD, tape, record)* mettre; **to p. the violin/the flute** jouer du violon/de la flûte **3** *vi* **(a)** *(of children)* jouer; *(of animals)* folâtrer; **to p. with sth** *(pen, hair)* tripoter qch; *Fig* **to p. with fire** jouer avec le feu; *Fam Fig* **what's she playing at?** à quoi elle joue? **(b)** *(of sportsperson)* jouer; **to p. fair/dirty** jouer franc jeu/ en traître; *Fig* **to p. for time** essayer de gagner du temps; *Fig* **to p. into sb's hands** faire le jeu de qn; *Fig* **to p. safe** ne pas prendre de risques **(c)** *(of musician)* jouer **(d)** *(of actor)* jouer; *(of film, play)* être à l'affiche
▸ **play about, play around** *vi* jouer, s'amuser
▸ **play along** *vi* coopérer
▸ **play back** *vt sep (tape, recording) (for first time)* écouter; *(replay)* réécouter
▸ **play down** *vt sep* minimiser
▸ **play off** *vt sep* **to p. sb off against sb** monter qn contre qn
▸ **play on 1** *vt insep (feelings, fears)* jouer sur **2** *vi (of musician, sportsperson)* continuer à jouer
▸ **play out** *vt sep* **the events being played out on the world's stage** les événements qui se déroulent dans le monde
▸ **play up** *vi Br Fam (of car, child, injury)* faire des siennes
play-acting ['pleɪæktɪŋ] *n* comédie *f*
playboy ['pleɪbɔɪ] *n* play-boy *m*
player ['pleɪə(r)] *n (of game, instrument)* joueur(euse) *m,f; (actor)* acteur(trice) *m,f*
playful ['pleɪfʊl] *adj (person, animal)* joueur(euse); *(mood, tone)* enjoué(e); *(remark)* espiègle
playground ['pleɪgraʊnd] *n (at school)* cour *f* de récréation; *(in park)* aire *f* de jeu
playgroup ['pleɪgruːp] *n* garderie *f*
playhouse ['pleɪhaʊs] *n (theatre)* théâtre *m*
playing ['pleɪɪŋ] *n* **p. card** carte *f* à jouer; **p. field** terrain *m* de jeu
playmate ['pleɪmeɪt] *n* camarade *mf* de jeu
play-off ['pleɪɒf] *n Sp* match *m* de barrage
playpen ['pleɪpen] *n* parc *m (pour bébé)*
playroom ['pleɪruːm] *n* salle *f* de jeu
playschool ['pleɪskuːl] *n* garderie *f*
plaything ['pleɪθɪŋ] *n* jouet *m*
playtime ['pleɪtaɪm] *n (at school)* récréation *f*
playwright ['pleɪraɪt] *n* auteur *m* dramatique
plaza ['plɑːzə] *n Am (shopping centre)* centre *m* commercial
PLC, plc [piːel'siː] *n Br Com (abbr* **public limited company)** ≃ SA *f*
plea [pliː] *n (a) (appeal)* appel *m (for à) (b) (excuse)* excuse *f (c) Law* **to enter a p. of guilty/not guilty** plaider coupable/non coupable; *Am* **p. bargaining** = possibilité donnée à l'accusé de voir ses charges réduites s'il plaide coupable
plead [pliːd] **1** *vt Law* **to p. sb's case** *(of lawyer)* plaider la cause de qn; *Law* **to p. insanity** plaider la démence; **to p. ignorance** faire l'ignorant(e) **2** *vi* **to p. with sb (to do sth)** supplier qn (de faire qch); *Law* **to p. guilty/not guilty** plaider coupable/non coupable
pleasant ['plezənt] *adj* agréable
pleasantly ['plezəntlɪ] *adv (smile, behave)* aimablement; *(surprised)* agréablement

pleasantry ['plezəntrɪ] *(pl* **pleasantries)** *n (joke)* plaisanterie *f;* **to exchange pleasantries** *(polite remarks)* échanger des politesses
please [pliːz] **1** *adv* s'il vous/te plaît; **could you pass the salt, p.** peux-tu me passer le sel, s'il te plaît?; **come in, p.** entrez, je vous prie; **p. don't cry** s'il te plaît, ne pleure pas, **may I? – p. do** puis-je? – je vous en prie; **p. sit down** asseyez-vous, je vous en prie; **yes, p.** oui, s'il te plaît **2** *vt* faire plaisir à; **you can't p. everybody** on ne peut pas contenter tout le monde; **p. yourself!** fais comme tu voudras!; **p. God!** plaise à Dieu! **3** *vi* **(a)** *(like)* **to do as one pleases** faire ce que l'on veut; **this way, if you p.** par ici, s'il vous plaît; **and then, if you p., he blamed me for it!** et le comble, c'est qu'il a dit que c'était de ma faute! **(b)** *(give pleasure)* **to be eager to p.** vouloir plaire
pleased [pliːzd] *adj* content(e) **(with** de); **to be p. to do sth** faire qch avec plaisir; **to be p. for sb** être content pour qn; **to be as p. as Punch** être content comme tout; **he's very p. with himself** il est très content de lui; **p. to meet you!** enchanté!; **I'm p. to say that...** je suis heureux de vous dire que...
pleasurable ['pleʒərəbəl] *adj* agréable
pleasure ['pleʒə(r)] *n (a) (contentment, enjoyment)* plaisir *m;* **to take p. in doing sth** prendre plaisir à faire qch; **with p.** avec plaisir; **my p.!** ot t'en prie!; *Formal* **I have p. in informing you that...** j'ai le plaisir de vous informer que...; **p. boat** bateau *m* de plaisance; **p. trip** excursion *f* **(b)** *(will)* **at your p.** à votre gré; *Br Law* **to be detained at or during Her Majesty's p.** être emprisonné(e)
pleat [pliːt] *n* pli *m*
pleated ['pliːtɪd] *adj* plissé(e)
plebeian [plə'biːən] *n & adj* plébéien(enne) *m,f*
plebiscite ['plebɪsɪt] *n* plébiscite *m*
plectrum ['plektrəm] *n Mus* médiator *m*
pledge [pledʒ] **1** *n (a) (promise)* promesse *f* **(b)** *(object)* gage *m* **2** *vt (promise)* **to p. to do sth** s'engager à faire qch; **to p. one's loyalty/support** accorder sa loyauté/son soutien; **to p. money** *(in radio, television appeal)* faire une promesse de don
plenary ['pliːnərɪ] *adj* plénier(ère); **p. session** séance *f* plénière
plentiful ['plentɪfʊl] *adj* abondant(e)
plenty ['plentɪ] **1** *n* abondance *f;* **a land of p.** un pays d'abondance **2** *pron* **$50 should be p.** 50 dollars devraient suffire (amplement); **p. of beaucoup de; you've got p. of time** tu as largement le temps; **that's p.** *(of food)* merci, j'en ai assez **3** *adv Fam* **it's p. big enough** c'est bien assez grand
plethora ['pleθərə] *n* pléthore *f*
pleurisy ['plʊərɪsɪ] *n* pleurésie *f*
pliable ['plaɪəbəl] *adj (wood, plastic)* souple; *(person)* malléable
pliers ['plaɪəz] *npl* pince *f,* tenaille *f;* **a pair of p.** une pince, une tenaille
plight [plaɪt] *n* situation *f* critique; *(of refugees)* détresse *f*
plimsolls ['plɪmsəlz] *npl* tennis *mpl*
plinth [plɪnθ] *n* socle *m*
PLO [piːel'əʊ] *n (abbr* **Palestine Liberation Organization)** OLP *f*
plod [plɒd] *(pt & pp* **plodded)** *vi (a) (walk)* marcher péniblement **(b)** *(work)* **to p. (away)** trimer
plonk¹ [plɒŋk] **1** *n (sound)* bruit *m* sourd

2 vt Fam just **p.** it down there tu n'as qu'à le poser là; **she plonked herself down in an armchair** elle s'est affalée dans un fauteuil

plonk² n Br Fam (wine) vin m ordinaire

plop [plɒp] **1** n plouf m **2** vi (pt & pp **plopped**) faire plouf

plot [plɒt] **1** n (**a**) (conspiracy) complot m (**b**) (of play, novel) intrigue f; Fig **the p. thickens** l'affaire se corse (**c**) (land) parcelle f; (**vegetable**) **p.** potager m **2** vt (pt & pp **plotted**) (**a**) (plan) comploter; **to p. to do sth** comploter de faire qch (**b**) (position, course) déterminer; (progress, development) suivre de près (**c**) Math tracer

plotter ['plɒtə(r)] n (conspirator) conspirateur(trice) m,f

plough, Am **plow** [plaʊ] **1** n charrue f; **the P.** (constellation) le Grand Chariot **2** vt (field) labourer; Fig (profits) réinvestir **3** vi labourer; Fig **to p. through sth** (work, reading) avancer péniblement dans qch; Fig **to p. into sth** (of vehicle) rentrer dans qch
► **plough on with** vt insep poursuivre laborieusement
► **plough up** vt sep (field) labourer

ploughman ['plaʊmən] n laboureur m; Br **p.'s lunch** = assiette de fromage ou jambon avec de la salade et des condiments

plover ['plʌvə(r)] n pluvier m

plow Am = **plough**

ploy [plɔɪ] n stratagème m, ruse f

pluck [plʌk] **1** n (courage) courage m **2** vt (hair, feathers) arracher; (flower) cueillir; (chicken, turkey) plumer; (string of guitar) pincer; **to p. one's eyebrows** s'épiler les sourcils; **they were plucked from danger by a helicopter** un hélicoptère les a sauvés du danger **3** vt **to p. at sb's sleeve** tirer qn par la manche
► **pluck up** vt sep **to p. up the courage to do sth** trouver le courage de faire qch

plucky ['plʌkɪ] adj courageux(euse)

plug [plʌg] **1** n (**a**) (for sink) bonde f (**b**) (electrical) (on device) fiche f; (socket) prise f (de courant); Fam Fig **to pull the p. on sth** arrêter de financer qch (**c**) Aut (**spark**) **p.** bougie f (**d**) Fam (publicity) pub f **2** vt (pt & pp **plugged**) (**a**) (gap, hole) boucher; (leak) colmater (**b**) Fam (promote) faire de la pub pour
► **plug away** vi Fam s'acharner (**at** sur)
► **plug in** vt sep brancher

plughole ['plʌghəʊl] n trou m d'écoulement; Fam Fig **that's £300 down the p.!** c'est 300 livres foutues en l'air!

plug-in ['plʌgɪn] n Comptr module m externe

plum [plʌm] **1** n (fruit) prune f; **p. pudding** plum-pudding m; **p. tree** prunier m **2** adj (**a**) (colour) prune inv (**b**) Fam (very good) **a p. job** un boulot en or

plumage ['plu:mɪdʒ] n plumage m

plumb [plʌm] **1** n **p. (line)** fil m à plomb; **to be out of p.** ne pas être d'aplomb **2** adv (exactly) **p. in the centre** en plein centre **3** vt Fig **to p. the depths** toucher le fond; **his movies p. the depths of bad taste** ses films sont d'un mauvais goût inimaginable
► **plumb in** vt sep (washing machine) brancher

plumber ['plʌmə(r)] n plombier m

plumbing ['plʌmɪŋ] n (job, system) plomberie f

plume [plu:m] n (on hat) aigrette f; (of smoke) volute f

plummet ['plʌmɪt] vi (of morale, standards) chuter; (of

prices) s'effondrer; **the plane plummeted to the ground** l'avion a piqué et s'est écrasé au sol

plummy ['plʌmɪ] adj Fam (voice, accent) snob inv

plump [plʌmp] adj dodu(e); (cheeks, face) rond(e)
► **plump down** vt sep Fam laisser tomber lourdement
► **plump for** vt insep Fam (choose) se décider pour

plunder ['plʌndə(r)] **1** n (action) pillage m; (loot) butin m **2** vt piller

plunge [plʌndʒ] **1** n (dive) plongeon m; Fig (decrease) chute f; Fam Fig **to take the p.** (dare) se jeter à l'eau; (get married) se mettre la corde au cou **2** vt plonger (**into** dans) **3** vi (fall) plonger; Fig (decrease) chuter; **she plunged to her death** elle a fait une chute mortelle

plunger ['plʌndʒə(r)] n (of cafetière, syringe) piston m; (for clearing sink) ventouse f

plunging ['plʌndʒɪŋ] adj (prices) en chute libre; **p. neckline** décolleté m plongeant

pluperfect ['plu:'pɜ:fɪkt] n Gram **the p.** le plus-que-parfait

plural ['plʊərəl] Gram **1** adj pluriel(elle) **2** n pluriel m

pluralism ['plʊərəlɪzəm] n pluralisme m

plurality [plʊə'rælɪtɪ] n pluralité f

plus [plʌs] **1** n (pl plusses ['plʌsɪz]) (**a**) **p. (sign)** (signe m) plus m (**b**) (advantage) plus m **2** adj but **on the p. side…** mais d'un autre côté…; **fifteen p.** plus de quinze **3** prep plus; **seven p. nine** sept plus neuf

plush [plʌʃ] **1** n Tex peluche f **2** adj Fam luxueux(euse)

Pluto ['plu:təʊ] n (planet) Pluton f

plutonium [plu:'təʊnɪəm] n Chem plutonium m

ply¹ [plaɪ] n **three-p.** (wood, paper handkerchief) triple épaisseur; (wool) à trois fils

ply² (pt & pp **plied**) **1** vt (trade) exercer; **to p. sb with questions** assaillir qn de questions; **to p. sb with drink** ne pas arrêter de verser à boire à qn **2** vi (of ship, bus) **to p. between** faire la navette entre

plywood ['plaɪwʊd] n contreplaqué m

PM [pi:'em] n (abbr **Prime Minister**) Premier ministre m

p.m. ['pi:em] adv (abbr **post meridiem**) **6 p.m.** 18 h

PMS [pi:em'es] n Am (abbr **premenstrual syndrome**) syndrome m prémenstruel

PMT [pi:em'ti:] n Br (abbr **premenstrual tension**) syndrome m prémenstruel

pneumatic [nju:'mætɪk] adj pneumatique; **p. drill** marteau m piqueur

pneumonia [nju:'məʊnɪə] n pneumonie f

PO [pi:'əʊ] n (**a**) (abbr **Post Office**) poste f; **PO Box** BP (**b**) (abbr **postal order**) mandat m postal

poach¹ [pəʊtʃ] vt Culin (eggs, fish) pocher

poach² vt (**a**) (catch illegally) (fish) pêcher sans permis; (game) chasser sans permis (**b**) (employee) débaucher

poacher ['pəʊtʃə(r)] n (of fish, game) braconnier m

pocket ['pɒkɪt] **1** n (**a**) (of clothes, bag) poche f; **to go through sb's pockets** faire les poches à qn; **prices to suit every p.** des prix pour toutes les bourses; **to be out of p.** en être de sa poche; **how much are you out of p.?** tu en as eu pour combien?; **to pay for sth out of one's own p.** payer qch de sa poche; Fig **to line one's pockets** se remplir les poches; Fig **to have sb in one's p.** avoir qn dans sa poche; **p. calculator** calculette f; **p. money** argent m de

poche (**b**) *(in snooker, pool)* poche *f*, blouse *f* (**c**) *(of gas, air, resistance)* poche *f*
2 *vt (put in pocket)* empocher; *Fam (steal)* rafler
pocketbook ['pɒkɪtbʊk] *n Am (wallet)* portefeuille *m*; *(handbag)* sac *m* à main
pocketknife ['pɒkɪtnaɪf] *(pl* **pocketknives** ['pɒkɪtnaɪvz]) *n* couteau *m* de poche
pockmarked ['pɒkmɑːkt] *adj* grêlé(e)
pod [pɒd] *n (of plant)* gousse *f*
podgy ['pɒdʒɪ] *adj* grassouillet(ette)
podiatrist [pə'daɪətrɪst] *n Am* pédicure *mf*
podium ['pəʊdɪəm] *n (for speaker, conductor)* estrade *f*; *(for winner)* podium *m*
poem ['pəʊɪm] *n* poème *m*
poet ['pəʊɪt] *n* poète *m*
poetic [pəʊ'etɪk] *adj* poétique; **it's p. justice that...**, ça n'est que justice que...; **p. licence** licence *f* poétique
poetical [pəʊ'etɪkəl] *adj* poétique
poetry ['pəʊɪtrɪ] *n* poésie *f*; **p. in motion** un véritable plaisir; **p. reading** lecture *f* de textes poétiques
poignancy ['pɔɪnjənsɪ] *n* caractère *m* poignant
poignant ['pɔɪnjənt] *adj* poignant(e)
point [pɔɪnt] **1** *n* (**a**) *(location)* endroit *m*; **the highest p.** le point le plus haut; **p. of sale** point *m* de vente; **p. of view** point *m* de vue
(**b**) *(in time)* moment *m*; **at this p. in time** actuellement; **at this p. the phone rang** à ce moment le téléphone a sonné; **to be on the p. of doing sth** être sur le point de faire qch; **to reach the p. of no return** arriver au point de non-retour; **outspoken to the p. of rudeness** d'une franchise qui frise l'impolitesse
(**c**) *(of argument, discussion)* point *m*; **the p. is,...** c'est que...; **I take your p.** je vois ce que tu veux dire; **she has a p.** elle a raison; **to make a p.** faire une remarque; **to get to the p.** on arrive au fait; **that's beside the p.** ça n'a rien à voir; **that's not the p.** il ne s'agit pas de cela; **what's the p.?** à quoi bon?; **to make a p. of doing sth** mettre un point d'honneur à faire qch; **there is no p. in waiting any longer** cela ne sert à rien d'attendre plus longtemps; **in p. of fact** en fait; **to the p.** *(relevant)* pertinent(e); **it has its good points** ça a ses avantages; **up to a p.** jusqu'à un certain point; **not to put too fine a p. on it...** pour parler franchement...; **p. of grammar/of law** question *f* de grammaire/de droit; **p. of order** question *f* de procédure
(**d**) *(punctuation mark)* point *m*; *Math* (**decimal**) **p.** virgule *f* (décimale); **three p. five** trois virgule cinq
(**e**) *(in game, exam, on scale)* point *m*; **to win on points** gagner aux points
(**f**) *(on compass)* point *m*
(**g**) *(of needle, pencil, sword)* pointe *f*; **to end in a p.** avoir un bout pointu
(**h**) *(plug socket)* prise *f* (de courant)
(**i**) *(of land)* pointe *f*
(**j**) *Rail* **points** aiguillage *m*
2 *vt (camera, gun)* braquer (**at** sur); *Fig* **to p. the finger at sb** montrer qn du doigt; **can you p. me in the right direction?** pouvez-vous me dire quelle direction je dois prendre?; **to p. the way (to)** montrer le chemin (à); *Fig* montrer la voie (à)
3 *vi* **to p. at** *or* **to sb/sth** *(with finger)* montrer qn/qch du doigt; **to p. north** *(of arrow, compass needle)* indiquer le nord; **to be pointing towards sth** *(of car, chair)* être face à qch; **this points to the fact that...** ceci montre *ou* indique que...; **all the evidence points to suicide** tout laisse penser à un suicide
▸ **point out** *vt sep (with finger)* montrer; *(error, fact)* signaler

▸ **point up** *vt sep (highlight)* mettre en évidence
point-blank ['pɔɪnt'blæŋk] **1** *adj (refusal, denial)* catégorique; **at p. range** à bout portant
2 *adv (fire)* à bout portant; *(ask)* de but en blanc; *(refuse, deny)* catégoriquement
pointed ['pɔɪntɪd] *adj* (**a**) *(sharp)* pointu(e) (**b**) *(remark)* mordant(e)
pointedly ['pɔɪntɪdlɪ] *adv* ostensiblement
pointer ['pɔɪntə(r)] *n* (**a**) *(indicator)* aiguille *f*; *(stick)* baguette *f* (**b**) *Fam (advice)* tuyau *m* (**c**) *(dog)* pointer *m*
pointless ['pɔɪntlɪs] *adj* inutile, *(life)* absurde; **It's p. trying to convince him** ça ne sert à rien d'essayer de le convaincre
poise [pɔɪz] *n (composure)* assurance *f*; *(balance)* équilibre *m*
poised [pɔɪzd] *adj* (**a**) *(composed)* posé(e) (**b**) *(ready)* **to be p. to do sth** être prêt(e) à faire qch (**c**) *(suspended)* suspendu(e)
poison ['pɔɪzən] **1** *n* poison *m*, *Fam* **what's your p.?** qu'est-ce que tu veux boire?; **p. gas** gaz *m* toxique; **p. ivy** sumac *m* vénéneux, *Am* **pen letter** lettre *f* anonyme
2 *vt* (**a**) *(person, food)* empoisonner; **to p. sb's mind against sb** monter qn contre qn (**b**) *(pollute)* contaminer
poisoning ['pɔɪzənɪŋ] *n* (**a**) *(of person, food)* empoisonnement *m*; **to die of p.** mourir empoisonné(e) (**b**) *(pollution)* contamination *f*
poisonous ['pɔɪzənəs] *adj (snake, remark)* venimeux(euse); *(chemical, fumes)* toxique; *(plant, mushroom)* vénéneux(euse); *Fig (rumour, doctrine)* pernicieux(euse)
poke [pəʊk] **1** *n* coup *m* léger
2 *vt (person)* donner un coup à; *(object)* tâter; *(fire)* attiser; **to p. sb in the eye** mettre le doigt dans l'œil à qn; **to p. sb in the ribs** *(with elbow)* donner un coup de coude à qn; **to p. a hole in sth** faire un trou dans qch; **to p. one's nose into other people's business** mettre son nez dans les affaires des autres; **to p. one's head out of the window** passer la tête par la fenêtre; **to p. fun at** se moquer de
3 *vi* **to p. at sth (with one's finger/a stick)** tâter qch (du doigt/avec bout d'un bâton)
▸ **poke about, poke around** *vi (search) (of person)* fouiller; *(be nosy)* fourrer son nez partout
▸ **poke out 1** *vt sep* **you nearly poked my eye out!** un peu plus et tu me crevais l'œil!
2 *vi (protrude)* sortir, dépasser
poker[1] ['pəʊkə(r)] *n (for fire)* tisonnier *m*
poker[2] *n (card game)* poker *m*
poker-faced ['pəʊkəfeɪst] *adj* au visage impassible
poky ['pəʊkɪ] *adj Fam* (**a**) *Br (cramped)* exigu(uë); **a p. little flat** un appartement riquiqui (**b**) *Am (slow)* lambin(e)
Poland ['pəʊlənd] *n* la Pologne
polar ['pəʊlə(r)] *adj* polaire; **p. bear** ours *m* polaire *ou* blanc
polarity [pəʊ'lærɪtɪ] *n* polarité *f*
polarization [pəʊləraɪ'zeɪʃən] *n (of opinion, country)* division *f*
polarize ['pəʊləraɪz] *vt (opinion, country)* diviser
Polaroid® ['pəʊlərɔɪd] *n (camera, photo)* polaroïd® *m*
Pole [pəʊl] *n* Polonais(e) *m,f*
pole[1] [pəʊl] *n (post, stick)* perche *f*; *(for flag)* hampe *f*; **the p. vault** le saut à la perche
pole[2] *n Elec & Geog* pôle *m*; *Fig* **to be poles apart** être diamétralement opposé; **the P. Star** l'étoile *f* polaire
poleax(e) ['pəʊlæks] *vt (physically)* assommer; *(emotionally)* abasourdir
polecat ['pəʊlkæt] *n* putois *m*

polemic [pə'lemɪk] *n* polémique *f*

polemical [pə'lemɪkəl] *adj* polémique

police [pə'liːs] **1** *npl* the p. la police; **two hundred p.** deux cents policiers; **p. car** voiture *f* de police; **p. constable** agent *m* de police; *Am* **p. department** service *m* de police; **p. dog** chien *m* policier; **p. force** police; **p. officer** policier *m*; **p. record** casier *m* judiciaire; **p. state** État *m* policier; **p. station** poste *m* de police

2 *vt (area, city)* maintenir l'ordre dans; *Fig* réglementer

policeman [pə'liːsmən] *n* agent *m* de police

policewoman [pə'liːswʊmən] *n* femme *f* policier

policy ['pɒlɪsɪ] *(pl* **policies)** *n* **(a)** *(of government, personal)* politique *f*; **it's a matter of p.** c'est une question de principe; **a good/bad p.** une bonne/mauvaise idée **(b)** *Fin* **(insurance) p.** police *f* (d'assurance); *Fin* **p. holder** assuré(e) *m,f*

polio ['pəʊlɪəʊ] *n* polio *f*

Polish ['pəʊlɪʃ] **1** *n (language)* polonais *m*
2 *adj* polonais(e)

polish ['pɒlɪʃ] **1** *n* **(a)** *(for shoes)* cirage *m*; *(for furniture, floors)* cire *f*; *(for metal)* pâte *f* à polir; *(for nails)* vernis *m* à ongles **(b)** *(finish, shine)* éclat *m*, brillant *m*; **to give sth a p.** faire briller qch **(c)** *(refinement)* raffinement *m*
2 *vt (silver, brass)* astiquer; *(shoes, furniture, floor)* cirer; *(stone, metal)* polir

▸ **polish off** *vt sep Fam (food)* avaler; *(drink)* descendre; *(work)* expédier; *(opponent)* liquider

▸ **polish up** *vt sep (improve)* perfectionner

polished ['pɒlɪʃt] *adj (shoes, furniture, floor)* ciré(e); *(metal, stone, glass)* poli(e); *Fig (manners, style)* raffiné(e)

polite [pə'laɪt] *adj* poli(e) **(to** avec); **in p. society** chez les gens bien

politely [pə'laɪtlɪ] *adv* poliment

politeness [pə'laɪtnɪs] *n* politesse *f*

politic ['pɒlɪtɪk] *adj Formal* sage

political [pə'lɪtɪkəl] *adj* politique; **she isn't very p.** elle ne s'intéresse pas beaucoup à la politique; **p. asylum** asile *m* politique; **p. prisoner** prisonnier(ère) *m,f* politique; **p. science** sciences *fpl* politiques

politically [pə'lɪtɪklɪ] *adv* politiquement; **p. correct** politiquement correct(e)

politician [pɒlɪ'tɪʃən] *n* homme *m*/femme *f* politique

politicize [pə'lɪtɪsaɪz] *vt* politiser

politics ['pɒlɪtɪks] **1** *n* politique *f*
2 *npl* **(a)** *(views)* opinions *fpl* politiques **(b)** **office p.** intrigues *fpl* de bureau

polka ['pɒlkə] *n* polka *f*; **a p. dot tie** une cravate à pois

poll [pəʊl] **1** *n (votes cast)* scrutin *m*; **(opinion) p.** *(survey)* sondage *m*; **to go to the polls** aller aux urnes
2 *vt (votes)* obtenir; *(people)* sonder

pollen ['pɒlən] *n* pollen *m*; **p. count** taux *m* de pollen dans l'atmosphère

pollinate ['pɒlɪneɪt] *vt* polliniser

polling ['pəʊlɪŋ] *n* élections *fpl*, scrutin *m*; **p. booth** isoloir *m*; **p. day** jour *m* du scrutin; **p. station** bureau *m* de vote

pollutant [pə'luːtənt] *n* polluant *m*

pollute [pə'luːt] *vt* polluer

polluter [pə'luːtə(r)] *n* pollueur(euse) *m,f*

pollution [pə'luːʃən] *n* pollution *f*

polo ['pəʊləʊ] *n (sport)* polo *m*; **p. neck (sweater)** (pull *m* à) col *m* roulé; **p. shirt** polo *m (chemise)*

poltergeist ['pɒltəɡaɪst] *n* esprit *m* frappeur

poly bag ['pɒlɪ'bæɡ] *n Br Fam* sac *m* en plastique

polyester [pɒlɪ'estə(r)] *n* polyester *m*

polygamy [pə'lɪɡəmɪ] *n* polygamie *f*

polyglot ['pɒlɪɡlɒt] *n & adj* polyglotte *mf*

polygon ['pɒlɪɡɒn] *n* polygone *m*

polymer ['pɒlɪmə(r)] *n Chem* polymère *m*

Polynesia [pɒlɪ'niːzɪə] *n* la Polynésie

Polynesian [pɒlɪ'niːzɪən] **1** *n* Polynésien(enne) *m,f*
2 *adj* polynésien(enne)

polyp ['pɒlɪp] *n Med* polype *m*

polyphonic [pɒlɪ'fɒnɪk] *adj Mus* polyphonique

polystyrene [pɒlɪ'staɪriːn] *n* polystyrène *m*

polythene ['pɒlɪθiːn] *n* polyéthylène *m*; **p. bag** sac *m* en plastique

polyunsaturated [pɒlɪʌn'sætjʊreɪtɪd] *adj* polyinsaturé(e)

polyurethane [pɒlɪ'jʊərɪθeɪn] *n* polyuréthane *m*

pomegranate ['pɒmɪɡrænɪt] *n (fruit)* grenade *f*; **p. (tree)** grenadier *m*

pomp [pɒmp] *n* pompe *f*; **p. and circumstance** grand apparat *m*

pompom ['pɒmpɒm] *n* pompon *m*

pomposity [pɒm'pɒsɪtɪ] *n* suffisance *f*

pompous ['pɒmpəs] *adj* pompeux(euse)

ponce [pɒns] *n Br very Fam* **(a)** *(effeminate man)* tapette *f* **(b)** *(pimp)* maquereau *m*

▸ **ponce about, ponce around** *vi Br Fam* **(a)** *(waste time)* traîner **(b)** *(act effeminate man)* se pavaner

poncho ['pɒntʃəʊ] *(pl* **ponchos)** *n* poncho *m*

pond [pɒnd] *n* étang *m*; *(smaller)* mare *f*

ponder ['pɒndə(r)] **1** *vt* réfléchir à, considérer
2 *vi* réfléchir **(on** *or* **over** à)

ponderous ['pɒndərəs] *adj (movement, person)* lourd(e); *(progress, piece of writing)* laborieux(euse)

pong [pɒŋ] *Fam* **1** *n (smell)* puanteur *f*
2 *vi* puer

pontiff ['pɒntɪf] *n* pontife *m*

pontificate [pɒn'tɪfɪkeɪt] *vi* pontifier **(about** sur)

pontoon[1] [pɒn'tuːn] *n (float)* ponton *m*; **p. bridge** pont *m* flottant

pontoon[2] *n (card game)* vingt-et-un *m*

pony ['pəʊnɪ] *(pl* **ponies)** *n* poney *m*; **p. trekking** randonnée *f* à dos de poney

ponytail ['pəʊnɪteɪl] *n* queue *f* de cheval

poo [puː] *n Fam* caca *m*; **to do** *or* **have a p.** faire caca

poodle ['puːdəl] *n* caniche *m*

poof [pʊf], **poofter** ['pʊftə(r)] *n Br very Fam* pédé *m*, = terme injurieux désignant un homosexuel

pooh[1] [puː] *exclam* bah!

pooh[2] = poo

pooh-pooh ['puː'puː] *vt* rejeter

pool[1] [puːl] *n (pond, of blood)* mare *f*; *(puddle)* flaque *f*; **(swimming) p.** piscine *f*

pool[2] **1** *n (of money, helpers)* réserve *f*; *(of knowledge)* mine *f*; **car p.** parc *m* de voitures
2 *vt (ideas, resources)* mettre en commun, grouper

pool[3] *n (game)* billard *m* américain; **p. table** (table *f* de) billard

pooped [puːpt] *adj Fam* vanné(e)

poor [pʊə(r)] **1** *adj* **(a)** *(not rich)* pauvre; **the p. man's champagne** le champagne du pauvre **(b)** *(bad)* mauvais(e); *(chances)* faible; *(harvest, reward)* maigre; **to be in p. health** ne pas bien se porter; **to have a p. memory** ne pas avoir une bonne mémoire; **to be p. at maths** être faible en maths; **p. loser** mauvais(e) perdant(e) *m,f*; **in p. taste** de mauvais goût **(c)** *(expressing sympathy)* **you p. thing!** pauvre petit(e)!; **p. (old) Simon** le pauvre Simon **2** *npl* **the p.** les pauvres *mpl*

poorly ['puəlɪ] **1** *adv* mal; *(dressed)* pauvrement; **to be p. off** être pauvre **2** *adj Fam* patraque

pop¹ [pɒp] **1** *n (music)* pop *f* **2** *adj* **p. art** pop art *m*; **p. group** groupe *m* de pop; **p. music** musique *f* pop; **p. singer** chanteur(euse) *m,f* pop; **p. song** chanson *f* pop

pop² *n Am (father)* papa *m*

pop³ 1 *n* **(a)** *(sound)* bruit *m* sec **(b)** *Fam (fizzy drink)* soda *m* **2** *vt (pt & pp* **popped)** **(a)** *(burst)* faire éclater **(b)** *Fam (put quickly)* mettre, **to p. one's head out of the window** passer la tête par la fenêtre; *Fam* **to p. the question** faire sa demande en mariage; **to p. pills** se bourrer de comprimés **3** *vi* **(a)** *(burst)* éclater; *(of cork)* sauter; *(of ears)* se déboucher **(b)** *Fam (go quickly)* **I'm just popping next door** je fais juste un saut chez les voisins; **they popped round to see us** ils sont passés nous voir

▸ **pop in** *vi Fam* passer
▸ **pop off** *vi very Fam (die)* claquer
▸ **pop out** *vi Fam (go out)* sortir

pop. *(abbr* **population)** population *f*

popcorn ['pɒpkɔːn] *n* pop-corn *m*

pope [pəʊp] *n* pape *m*

popgun ['pɒpgʌn] *n* pistolet *m* à bouchon

poplar ['pɒplə(r)] *n* peuplier *m*

poplin ['pɒplɪn] *n* popeline *f*

popper ['pɒpə(r)] *n Br Fam (fastener)* bouton-pression *m*

poppet ['pɒpɪt] *n Fam Old-fashioned* **she's a p.** elle est charmante; **my p.!** ma puce!

poppy ['pɒpɪ] *(pl* **poppies)** *n* coquelicot *m*; **p. seed** graine *f* de pavot

poppycock ['pɒpɪkɒk] *n Fam (nonsense)* bêtises *fpl*

populace ['pɒpjʊləs] *n Formal* **the p.** la population

popular ['pɒpjʊlə(r)] *adj* populaire; *(fashionable)* à la mode; *(restaurant, film)* qui a beaucoup de succès; **to make oneself p.** se faire bien voir; **she is p. with her colleagues** elle est appréciée par ses collègues; **by p. demand** à la demande générale; **contrary to p. belief** contrairement à ce que les gens croient

popularity [pɒpjʊ'lærɪtɪ] *n* popularité *f*; **p. rating** cote *f* de popularité

popularize ['pɒpjʊləraɪz] *vt* populariser

popularly ['pɒpjʊləlɪ] *adv* communément; **it is p. believed that...** les gens croient généralement que...

populate ['pɒpjʊleɪt] *vt* peupler

population [pɒpjʊ'leɪʃən] *n* population *f*; **p. explosion** explosion *f* démographique

populous ['pɒpjʊləs] *adj* populeux(euse)

porcelain ['pɔːslɪn] *n* porcelaine *f*; **p. ware** porcelaine

porch [pɔːtʃ] *n Br (entrance)* porche *m*; *Am (veranda)* véranda *f*

porcupine ['pɔːkjʊpaɪn] *n* porc-épic *m*

pore [pɔːr] *n* pore *m*
▸ **pore over** *vt insep (examine closely)* étudier soigneusement

pork [pɔːk] *n* porc *m*; **p. chop** côte *f* de porc

porn [pɔːn] *n Fam* porno *m*

pornographic [pɔːnə'græfɪk] *adj* pornographique

pornography [pɔː'nɒgrəfɪ] *n* pornographie *f*

porous ['pɔːrəs] *adj* poreux(euse)

porpoise ['pɔːpəs] *n* marsouin *m*

porridge ['pɒrɪdʒ] *n* porridge *m*; **p. oats** flocons *mpl* d'avoine

port¹ [pɔːt] *n (harbour, town)* port *m*; **in p.** au port; *also Fig* **p. of call** escale *f*; *Prov* **any p. in a storm** nécessité fait loi

port² *n Naut (left-hand side)* bâbord *m*

port³ *n (drink)* porto *m*

portable ['pɔːtəbəl] *adj* portable

Port-au-Prince [pɔːtəʊ'prɛs] *n* Port-au-Prince

portcullis [pɔːt'kʌlɪs] *n* sarrasine *f*

portend [pɔː'tend] *vt Formal* présager

portent ['pɔːtent] *n Formal* présage *m*

portentous [pɔː'tentəs] *adj Formal* majeur(e)

porter ['pɔːtə(r)] *n (for carrying luggage)* porteur *m*; *(door attendant)* chasseur *m*; *(in hospital)* brancardier *m*

portfolio [pɔːt'fəʊlɪəʊ] *(pl* **portfolios)** *n (for documents)* porte-documents *m*; *(for drawings)* carton *m*; *(of shares, government minister)* portefeuille *m*; *(of model, artist)* book *m*

porthole ['pɔːthəʊl] *n* hublot *m*

portion ['pɔːʃən] *n* part *f*, partie *f*; *(of food)* portion *f*
▸ **portion out** *vt sep* partager

portly ['pɔːtlɪ] *adj* corpulent(e)

portrait ['pɔːtrət] *n also Fig* portrait *m*; **to have one's p. painted** faire faire son portrait; **p. gallery** galerie *f* de portraits; *Comptr* **p. (orientation)** (orientation *f*) portrait; **p. painter** portraitiste *mf*

portray [pɔː'treɪ] *vt (describe)* dépeindre; *(of actor)* interpréter

portrayal [pɔː'treɪəl] *n (description)* tableau *m*; *(by actor)* interprétation *f*

Portugal ['pɔːtjʊgəl] *n* le Portugal

Portuguese [pɔːtjʊ'giːz] **1** *npl* **the P.** *(people)* les Portugais *mpl* **2** *n* **(a)** *(person)* Portugais(e) *m,f* **(b)** *(language)* portugais *m* **3** *adj* portugais(e)

POS [piːəʊ'es] *n Com (abbr* **point of sale)** PDV *m*

pose [pəʊz] **1** *n* **(a)** *(position)* pose *f* **(b)** *Pej (affectation)* **it's just a p.** c'est pour épater la galerie **2** *vt (problem, question)* poser; *(danger, threat)* représenter **3** *vi also Pej* poser; **a man posing as a police officer** un homme se faisant passer pour un policier

poser ['pəʊzə(r)] *n Fam* **(a)** *Pej (affected person)* poseur(euse) *m,f* **(b)** *(difficult question)* colle *f*

posh [pɒʃ] *Br* **1** *adj (person)* huppé(e); *(accent)* snob *inv*; *(restaurant, area, clothes)* chic *inv* **2** *adv* **to talk p.** parler d'une manière snob

position [pə'zɪʃən] **1** *n* **(a)** *(of person) (posture, opinion)* position *f* **(b)** *(of object)* emplacement *m*; *(of enemy, plane, in team sport)* position *f*; **in the on/off p.** *(of switch, lever)* en position marche/arrêt; **in p.** en place; **out of p.** déplacé(e) **(c)** *(situation)* situation *f*; **to be in a strong p.** être dans une position forte; **put yourself in my p.** mets-toi à ma place; **to be in a p. to do sth** être en mesure de faire qch; **to be in no p. to do sth** être mal placé(e) pour faire qch **(d)** *(job)* poste *m*; **p. of responsibility** un poste à responsabilité **2** *vt (object)* placer; *(town)* situer; *(troops)* poster; **to p. oneself** se placer; **to be well/poorly positioned to do sth** être bien/mal placé(e) pour faire qch

positioning [pə'zɪʃənɪŋ] *n Com* positionnement *m*

positive ['pɒzɪtɪv] *adj* **(a)** *(person, answer, test)* positif(ive); *(evidence, proof)* formel(elle); **to be p. about sth** être optimiste à propos de qch; **on the p. side,...** le bon côté des choses, c'est que…; p. **discrimination** = mesures antidiscriminatoires favorisant les groupes minoritaires **(b)** *(certain)* certain(e), sûr(e) **(about** de) **(c)** *Fam (for emphasis)* véritable **(d)** *Math & Elec* positif(ive)

positively ['pɒzɪtɪvlɪ] *adv* **(a)** *(identify)* formellement **(b)** *(think, react)* de façon positive **(c)** *(for emphasis)* absolument

posse ['pɒsɪ] *n (to catch criminal)* = dans le Far West, groupe d'hommes commandé par un shérif, lancé à la poursuite d'un criminel; *(of reporters)* troupe *f; Fam (of friends)* bande *f*

possess [pə'zes] *vt* **(a)** *(property)* posséder; *(quality, faculty)* avoir **(b)** *(of evil spirit)* posséder; **possessed by fear** pris(e) de terreur; **what possessed you to buy that?** qu'est-ce qui t'a pris d'acheter ça?

possession [pə'zeʃən] *n (ownership)* possession *f; (thing possessed)* bien *m*; **to be in p. of sth** être en possession de qch; **in full p. of one's faculties** en pleine possession de ses facultés

possessive [pə'zesɪv] **1** *n Gram* **the p.** le possessif **2** *adj* possessif(ive); **she's very p.** about *or* of her children c'est une mère possessive

possessor [pə'zesə(r)] *n* possesseur *m*

possibility [pɒsɪ'bɪlɪtɪ] *(pl* possibilities) *n* possibilité *f*; **to be within/outside the bounds of p.** être dans la limite du possible/au-delà des limites du possible; **it's a distinct p.** c'est bien possible

possible ['pɒsɪbəl] **1** *adj* possible; **it's p. that…** il est possible que… + *subjunctive*; **as soon as p.** dès que possible; **as much as p.** autant que possible; **anything's p.** tout est possible
2 *n (person)* candidat(e) possible *m,f; (thing)* option *f*

possibly ['pɒsɪblɪ] *adv* **(a)** *(perhaps)* peut-être; **p. not** peut-être pas **(b)** *(for emphasis)* **I can't p. accept it** je ne peux vraiment pas l'accepter; **I'll do all I p. can** je ferai tout mon possible

post¹ [pəʊst] **1** *n* **(a)** *(wooden stake)* piquet *m; (of goal)* poteau *m* **(b)** *(job, military position)* poste *m*
2 *vt (assign)* affecter

post² *vt (affix)* afficher; **p. no bills** *(sign)* défense d'afficher

post³ *Br* **1** *n (mail)* courrier *m*; **the first p.** la première distribution; **to miss the p.** manquer la levée; **it's in the p.** c'est parti au courrier; **p. office** poste *f*; **the P. Office** *(government department)* ≃ la Poste
2 *vt (letter)* poster; *Fam Fig* **to keep sb posted** tenir qn au courant

postage ['pəʊstɪdʒ] *n* affranchissement *m*; **p. and packing** frais *mpl* de port et d'emballage; **p. paid** port *m* payé; **p. stamp** timbre-poste *m*

postal ['pəʊstəl] *adj* postal(e); **p. order** mandat *m* postal; **p. vote** *n* par correspondance

postbag ['pəʊstbæg] *n Br* sac *m* postal

postbox ['pəʊstbɒks] *n Br* boîte *f* aux lettres

postcard ['pəʊstkɑːd] *n* carte *f* postale

postcode ['pəʊstkəʊd] *n Br* code *m* postal

postdate ['pəʊst'deɪt] *vt* postdater

poster ['pəʊstə(r)] *n (for advertising)* affiche *f; (for decoration)* poster *m*; **p. paint** gouache *f*

posterior [pɒs'tɪərɪə(r)] *n Hum (buttocks)* postérieur *m*

posterity [pɒs'terɪtɪ] *n* postérité *f*

postgraduate [pəʊst'grædjʊɪt] **1** *n* étudiant(e) *m,f* de troisième cycle
2 *adj* de troisième cycle

posthaste ['pəʊst'heɪst] *adv* en toute hâte

posthumous ['pɒstjʊməs] *adj* posthume

posthumously ['pɒstjʊməslɪ] *adv* à titre posthume

posting ['pəʊstɪŋ] *n (assignment)* affectation *f*

postman ['pəʊstmən] *n Br* facteur *m*

postmark ['pəʊstmɑːk] *n* cachet *m* de la poste

postmaster ['pəʊstmɑːstə(r)] *n* receveur *m* des postes

postmistress ['pəʊstmɪstrɪs] *n* receveuse *f* des postes

postmortem [pəʊst'mɔːtəm] *n* autopsie *f*

postnatal [pəʊst'neɪtəl] *adj* postnatal(e)

postoperative [pəʊst'ɒpərətɪv] *adj* postopératoire

postpone [pəʊst'pəʊn] *vt* reporter

postponement [pəʊst'pəʊnmənt] *n* report *m*

postscript ['pəʊsskrɪpt] *n* post-scriptum *m*

postulate ['pɒstjʊleɪt] *vt* poser comme hypothèse

posture ['pɒstʃə(r)] **1** *n* **(a)** *(physical)* posture *f*; **to have good/bad p.** se tenir bien/mal **(b)** *Fig (attitude)* position *f*
2 *vi* prendre des poses

postwar ['pəʊst'wɔː(r)] *adj* d'après-guerre; **the p. period** l'après-guerre *m*

posy ['pəʊzɪ] *(pl* posies) *n* petit bouquet *m*

pot [pɒt] **1** *n* **(a)** *(container)* pot *m; (saucepan)* casserole *f; (for tea)* théière *f; (for coffee)* cafetière *f*; **pots and pans** casseroles *fpl*; **a p. of tea** un thé; *Fam* **to have pots of money** avoir plein de fric; *Fam* **to go to p.** aller à la ruine; **to take a p. shot at sth** tirer à vue sur qch; **p. plant** plante *f* en pot **(b)** *Fam (marijuana)* hasch *m*
2 *vt (pt & pp* potted**)** **(a)** *(butter, meat)* mettre en pot; *(plant)* empoter **(b)** *(in snooker, pool)* blouser

potash ['pɒtæʃ] *n* potasse *f*

potassium [pə'tæsɪəm] *n* potassium *m*

potato [pə'teɪtəʊ] *(pl* potatoes) *n* pomme *f* de terre; *Br* **p. crisps**, *Am* **p. chips** chips *mpl*; **p. peeler** épluche-légumes *m*; **p. salad** salade *f* de pommes de terre

potbellied [pɒt'belɪd] *adj (from over-eating)* bedonnant(e); *(from malnourishment)* au ventre ballonné; **p. stove** poêle *m*

potency ['pəʊtənsɪ] *n* puissance *f; (virility)* virilité *f*

potent ['pəʊtənt] *adj* puissant(e); *(drink)* fort(e)

potentate ['pəʊtənteɪt] *n* potentat *m*

potential [pə'tenʃəl] **1** *n* potentiel *m*; **to have p.** avoir du potentiel; **to fulfil one's p.** aller au maximum de ses capacités
2 *adj* potentiel(elle)

potentially [pə'tenʃəlɪ] *adv* potentiellement

pothole ['pɒthəʊl] *n (cave)* marmite *f* torrentielle; *(in road)* nid *m* de poule

potholer ['pɒthəʊlə(r)] *n* spéléologue *mf*

potholing ['pɒthəʊlɪŋ] *n* spéléologie *f*; **to go p.** faire de la spéléologie

potion ['pəʊʃən] *n* potion *f*

potluck [pɒt'lʌk] *n Fam* **to take p.** prendre ce que l'on trouve

potpourri [pəʊ'pʊərɪ] *n (of flowers, music)* pot-pourri *m*

potted ['pɒtɪd] *adj* **(a)** *(food)* en terrine **(b)** *(description, history)* condensé(e)

potter ['pɒtə(r)] *n* potier(ère) *m,f*; **p.'s wheel** tour *m* de potier
▸ **potter about, potter around** *vi Br (do odd jobs)* bricoler; *(spend time leisurely)* traîner

pottery ['pɒtərɪ] *(pl* potteries) *n* poterie *f*

potty¹ ['pɒtɪ] *(pl* potties) *n* pot *m*; **p. training** apprentissage *m* de la propreté

potty² *adj Br Fam (crazy)* dingue **(about** de)

potty-trained ['pɒtɪtreɪnd] *adj* propre

pouch [paʊtʃ] *n* **(a)** *(for money)* bourse *f; (for tobacco)* blague *f*; *(for ammunition)* étui *m* **(b)** *(of marsupial)* poche *f*

pouf(fe) [puːf] *n* pouf *m*

poulterer ['pəʊltərə(r)] *n* volailler(ère) *m,f*

poultice ['pəʊltɪs] *n* cataplasme *m*

poultry ['pəʊltrɪ] *n* volaille *f*; **p.** **farm** élevage *m* de volaille; **p.** **farmer** éleveur(cuse) *m,f* de volaille

pounce [paʊns] *vi* **to p.** **on** *(of animal)* bondir sur; *(of person)* se précipiter sur

pound¹ [paʊnd] *n* **(a)** *(unit of weight)* = 453,6 g, livre *f* **(b)** *(British currency)* livre *f*; **p.** **sign** symbole *m* de la livre sterling; **p.** **sterling** livre sterling

pound² *n* *(for dogs, cars)* fourrière *f*

pound³ **1** *vt* *(crush)* *(spices, garlic)* piler; *(meat)* attendrir; *(with artillery)* pilonner; **to p.** **sth to pieces** réduire qch en miettes
  2 *vi* *(of heart)* battre à tout rompre; **to p.** **on the door** cogner à la porte; **my head is pounding** j'ai des élancements dans la tête

pour [pɔː(r)] **1** *vt* verser *(into/down* dans*)*; **to p.** **sb a drink** verser à boire à qn; **to p.** **money into sth** investir beaucoup d'argent dans qch
  2 *vi* couler; **it's pouring (with rain)** il pleut à verse; **sweat was pouring off him** il ruisselait de sueur; **tourists were pouring into the museum** les touristes entraient en masse dans le musée
▸ **pour in 1** *vt sep (liquid)* verser
  2 *vi (of liquid)* couler; *Fig (of people, letters)* affluer
▸ **pour out 1** *vt sep (tea, coffee)* verser; *Fig (anger, grief)* déverser; *(emotions)* déballer
  2 *vi (of liquid)* se déverser; *Fig (of people)* sortir en masse

pouring ['pɔːrɪŋ] *adj (rain)* torrenticl(cllc)

pout [paʊt] **1** *n* moue *f*
  2 *vi* faire la moue

poverty ['pɒvətɪ] *n* pauvreté *f*; *Fig (of ideas, resources)* pénurie *f*; **to live in p.** vivre dans la misère; **p. line** seuil *m* de pauvreté

poverty-stricken ['pɒvətɪstrɪkən] *adj* très pauvre

POW [piːəʊˈdʌbəljuː] *n (abbr* **prisoner of war)** prisonnier(ère) *m,f* de guerre

powder ['paʊdə(r)] **1** *n* poudre *f*; *Fig* **p.** **keg** poudrière *f*; **p.** **puff** houppe *f*; **p.** **room** toilettes *fpl* pour dames
  2 *vt* saupoudrer *(with* de*)*; **to p.** **one's face** se poudrer le visage; *Euph* **to p.** **one's nose** aller se laver les mains

powdered ['paʊdəd] *adj (milk, eggs)* en poudre

powdery ['paʊdərɪ] *adj* poudreux(euse)

power ['paʊə(r)] **1** *n* **(a)** *(authority, capacity)* pouvoir *m*; **to come to/be in p.** arriver/être au pouvoir; **to have sb in one's p.** tenir qn à sa merci; **to have the p. to do sth** avoir le pouvoir de faire qch; **to do everything in one's p. (to do sth)** faire tout ce qui est en son pouvoir (pour faire qch); **to be at the height** *or* **peak of one's powers** être au sommet de ses capacités; **it is beyond my p. to help you** je ne peux pas t'aider, cela dépasse mes capacités; *Fam* **to do sb a p.** **of good** faire énormément de bien à qn; **powers of concentration/persuasion** force *f* de concentration/persuasion; **p.** **of speech** usage *m* de la parole; **p.** **base** base *f* politique; **p.** **struggle** lutte *f* de pouvoir
  (b) *(physical strength)* force *f*, puissance *f*; **p.** **steering** *(in car)* direction *f* assistée
  (c) *(powerful person, group, nation)* puissance *f*; *Fig* **the p.** **behind the throne** l'éminence *f* grise; **the powers that be** les autorités *fpl*
  (d) *Law* pouvoir *m*; **p.** **of attorney** procuration *f*
  (e) *(electricity)* courant *m*; **p.** **cut** coupure *f* de courant; **p.** **pack** bloc *m* d'alimentation; **p.** **plant** centrale *f* électrique; **p.** **point** prise *f* de courant; **p.** **station** centrale *f* électrique

(f) *Math* puissance *f*; **three to the p.** **of ten** trois (à la) puissance dix
  2 *vt (provide with power)* actionner; **powered by two engines** propulsé(e) par deux moteurs

power-assisted steering ['paʊərəsɪstɪd'stɪərɪŋ] *n Aut* direction *f* assistée

powerful ['paʊəfʊl] *adj (muscles, engine, voice, country)* puissant(e); *(politician)* influent(e); *(drug, smell)* fort(e); *(speech, image)* impressionnant(e)

powerhouse ['paʊəhaʊs] *n Fam (person)* moteur *m*

powerless ['paʊələs] *adj* impuissant(e); **to be p.** **to do sth** être impuissant(e) à faire qch

PR [piːˈɑː(r)] *n* **(a)** *(abbr* **public relations)** RP **(b)** *Pol (abbr* **proportional representation)** représentation *f* proportionnelle

practicable ['præktɪkəbəl] *adj* réalisable

practical ['præktɪkəl] **1** *n (lesson)* travaux *mpl* pratiques; *(exam)* épreuve *f* pratique
  2 *adj* **(a)** *(mind, solution)* pratique; **she's very p.** elle a l'esprit pratique; **for all p. purposes** dans la pratique; **p.** **joke** farce *f* **(b)** *(virtual)* **it's a p. certainty** c'est pratiquement certain

practicality [præktɪˈkælɪtɪ] *(pl* **practicalities)** *n (of suggestion, plan)* aspect *m* pratique; **practicalities** détails *mpl* pratiques

practically ['præktɪklɪ] *adv* **(a)** *(in a practical manner)* de façon pratique **(b)** *(almost)* pratiquement, presque

practice ['præktɪs] **1** *n* **(a)** *(action, exercise)* pratique *f*; *(in sport)* entraînement *m*; **in p.** dans la *ou* en pratique; **to put sth into p.** mettre qch en pratique; **to be out of p.** avoir perdu l'habitude; *Prov* **p.** **makes perfect** c'est en forgeant qu'on devient forgeron; **p.** **match** *(in football, rugby)* match *m* d'entraînement **(b)** *(of medicine, law)* exercice *m* **(c)** *(surgery)* centre *m* médical; *(lawyer's office)* cabinet *m* d'avocat **(d)** *(custom)* pratique *f*; **to make a p. of doing sth** se faire une règle de faire qch; **to be good/bad p.** être conseillé(e)/déconseillé(e)
  2 *vt & vi Am* = **practise**

practiced, practicing *Am* = **practised, practising**

practise, *Am* **practice** ['præktɪs] **1** *vt* **(a)** *(musical instrument)* travailler; *(language, sport)* pratiquer; **(b)** *(medicine, law)* exercer **(c)** *(religion, custom)* pratiquer; **to p. what one preaches** mettre en pratique ce que l'on prêche
  2 *vi* **(a)** *(of musician)* s'exercer; *(of sportsperson)* s'entraîner **(b)** *(of doctor, lawyer)* exercer

practised, *Am* **practiced** ['præktɪst] *adj (teacher, nurse, speaker)* expérimenté(e); *(liar)* professionnel(elle); *(eye, ear)* exercé(e); *(charm)* étudié(e)

practising, *Am* **practicing** ['præktɪsɪŋ] *adj (doctor, lawyer)* en exercice; *(Christian)* pratiquant(e)

pragmatic [prægˈmætɪk] *adj* pragmatique

pragmatism ['prægmətɪzəm] *n* pragmatisme *m*

pragmatist ['prægmətɪst] *n* pragmatiste *mf*

Prague [prɑːg] *n* Prague

prairie ['preərɪ] *n* prairie *f*; **p.** **dog** chien *m* de prairie; *Am* **p.** **schooner** chariot *m* bâché

praise [preɪz] **1** *n* éloges *mpl*; **to sing the praises of** faire l'éloge de
  2 *vt* faire l'éloge de; *(God)* louer; **to p.** **sb to the skies** porter qn aux nues

praiseworthy ['preɪzwɜːðɪ] *adj* digne d'éloges

pram [præm] *n Br* landau *m*

prance [prɑːns] *vi (of horse)* caracoler; *(of person)* sautiller; **to p.** **in/out** entrer/sortir en sautillant

prank [præŋk] *n* farce *f*; **to play a p.** **on sb** faire une farce à qn

prat [præt] *n Br Fam* andouille *f*

prattle ['prætəl] **1** *n* papotage *m*
2 *vi* papoter (**about** de)

prawn [prɔːn] *n* crevette *f* rose; **p. cocktail** crevettes à la mayonnaise; **p. cracker** beignet *m* de crevette

pray [preɪ] *vi* prier (**for** pour); **to p. to God** prier Dieu; *Fig* **to p. for good weather/rain** prier pour qu'il fasse beau/qu'il pleuve

prayer [preə(r)] *n* prière *f;* **to say one's prayers** dire ses prières; *Fam Fig* **he doesn't have a p.** il n'a aucune chance; **p. beads** chapelet *m;* **p. book** livre *m* de prières; **p. mat** tapis *m* de prière; **p. meeting** réunion *f* de prière

preach [priːtʃ] **1** *vt* prêcher
2 *vi* prêcher; *Fig (moralize)* faire la morale; *Fig* **that's preaching to the converted** c'est essayer de prêcher un converti

preacher ['priːtʃə(r)] *n* prédicateur(trice) *m,f*

preamble [priː'æmbəl] *n Formal* préambule *m*

prearranged [priːə'reɪndʒd] *adj* convenu(e)

precarious [prɪ'keərɪəs] *adj* précaire

precariously [prɪ'keərɪəslɪ] *adv* de façon précaire; **p. balanced** en équilibre précaire

precaution [prɪ'kɔːʃən] *n* précaution *f;* **to take precautions** prendre des précautions; **as a p.** par précaution

precautionary [prɪ'kɔːʃənərɪ] *adj* préventif(ive)

precede [prɪ'siːd] *vt* précéder

precedence ['presɪdəns] *n* priorité *f;* **in order of p.** par ordre de préséance; **to take p. over sb** avoir la préséance sur qn; **to take p. over sth** passer avant qch

precedent ['presɪdənt] *n* précédent *m*

preceding [prɪ'siːdɪŋ] *adj* précédent(e)

precept ['priːsept] *n* précepte *m*

precinct ['priːsɪŋkt] *n* (**a**) *Br (area)* (**shopping**) **p.** quartier *m* commerçant piétonnier; **within the precincts of** dans l'enceinte de (**b**) *Am (administrative district)* circonscription *f;* (police division) quartier *m*

precious ['preʃəs] **1** *n (term of endearment)* **my p.** mon trésor **2** *adj also Pej* précieux(euse); **that letter is very p. to me** cette lettre m'est très chère; *Ironic* **you and your p. books!** toi et tes sacrés bouquins!
3 *adv Fam (for emphasis)* **p. little** très peu; **p. little money** très peu d'argent

precipice ['presɪpɪs] *n* précipice *m*

precipitate 1 *n* [prɪ'sɪpɪtɪt] *Chem* précipité *m*
2 *adj* [prɪ'sɪpɪtɪt] *Formal* précipité(e)
3 *vt* [prɪ'sɪpɪteɪt] *Formal* précipiter

precipitately [prɪ'sɪpɪtətlɪ] *adv* précipitamment

precipitation [prɪsɪpɪ'teɪʃən] *n* précipitation *f;* **annual p.** précipitations annuelles

precipitous [prɪ'sɪpɪtəs] *adj (descent)* à pic; *(steps)* raide

précis ['preɪsiː] *(pl* **précis** ['preɪsiːz]) *n* résumé *m*

precise [prɪ'saɪs] *adj* (**a**) *(exact)* précis(e); **..., to be p. ...,** pour être précis (**b**) *(meticulous)* méticuleux(euse)

precisely [prɪ'saɪslɪ] *adv* exactement, précisément; **at ten (o'clock) p.** à dix heures précises; **p.!** exactement!

precision [prɪ'sɪʒən] *n* précision *f; Mil* **p. bombing** bombardement *m* de précision; **p. instrument** instrument *m* de précision

preclude [prɪ'kluːd] *vt* empêcher; **to p. sb from doing sth** empêcher qn de faire qch

precocious [prɪ'kəʊʃəs] *adj* précoce

precociousness [prɪ'kəʊʃəsnɪs], **precocity** [prɪ'kɒsɪtɪ] *n* précocité *f*

preconceived [priːkən'siːvd] *adj* préconçu(e)

preconception [priːkən'sepʃən] *n* idée *f* préconçue; *(prejudice)* préjugé *m*

precondition [priːkɒn'dɪʃən] *n* condition *f* préalable

precooked [priː'kʊkt] *adj* précuit(e)

precursor [prɪ'kɜːsə(r)] *n* précurseur *m*

predate [priː'deɪt] *vt* (**a**) *(precede)* précéder (**b**) *(put earlier date on)* antidater

predator ['predətə(r)] *n* prédateur *m*

predatory ['predətərɪ] *adj* prédateur(trice); *Fig* avide

predecessor ['priːdɪsesə(r)] *n (person)* prédécesseur *m;* *(object)* précédent(e) *m,f*

predestination [priːdestɪ'neɪʃən] *n* prédestination *f*

predestine [priː'destɪn] *vt* **to be predestined to do sth** être prédestiné(e) à faire qch

predetermine [priːdɪ'tɜːmɪn] *vt* prédéterminer

predicament [prɪ'dɪkəmənt] *n* situation *f* difficile; **to be in a p.** être dans le pétrin

predicate 1 *n* ['predɪkət] *Gram* prédicat *m*
2 *vt* ['predɪkeɪt] **to be predicated on sth** être fondé(e) sur qch

predict [prɪ'dɪkt] *vt (from instinct)* prédire; *(from information)* prévoir

predictable [prɪ'dɪktəbəl] *adj* prévisible; **the movie was very p.** le film était sans surprise; *Fam* **you're so p.!** j'aurais pu le deviner!

predictably [prɪ'dɪktəblɪ] *adv* de manière prévisible; **p., she forgot to tell him** comme on pouvait s'y attendre, elle a oublié de le lui dire

prediction [prɪ'dɪkʃən] *n (from instinct)* prédiction *f;* *(from information)* prévision *f*

predispose [priːdɪs'pəʊz] *vt* prédisposer; **to be predisposed to do sth** être prédisposé(e) à faire qch

predisposition [priːdɪspə'zɪʃən] *n* prédisposition *f* (**to** or **towards** envers)

predominance [prɪ'dɒmɪnəns] *n* prédominance *f*

predominant [prɪ'dɒmɪnənt] *adj* prédominant(e)

predominantly [prɪ'dɒmɪnəntlɪ] *adv* en majorité, principalement

predominate [prɪ'dɒmɪneɪt] *vi* prédominer

pre-eminence [priː'emɪnəns] *n* prééminence *f*

pre-eminent [priː'emɪnənt] *adj* prééminent(e)

pre-empt [priː'empt] *vt* devancer

pre-emptive [priː'emptɪv] *adj* préventif(ive)

preen [priːn] *vt* **to p. itself** *(of bird)* se lisser les plumes; **to p. oneself** *(of person)* se faire beau (belle)

pre-established [priːɪs'tæblɪʃt] *adj* préétabli(e)

prefab ['priːfæb] *n Fam (house)* préfabriqué *m*

prefabricated [priː'fæbrɪkeɪtɪd] *adj* préfabriqué(e)

preface ['prefɪs] **1** *n (of book)* préface *f;* *(to speech)* préambule *m*
2 *vt* commencer (**with** par)

prefect ['priːfekt] *n Br Sch* = élève des grandes classes chargé de la surveillance

prefer [prɪ'fɜː(r)] *(pt & pp* **preferred**) *vt* (**a**) *(favour)* préférer (**to** à); **to p. to do sth** préférer faire qch (**b**) *Law* **to p. charges** porter plainte

preferable ['prefərəbəl] *adj* préférable

preferably ['prefərəblɪ] *adv* de préférence

preference ['prefərəns] *n* préférence *f;* **to give sb p., to give p. to sth** donner la préférence à qch; **in p. to** plutôt que; **in order of p.** par ordre de préférence

preferential [prefə'renʃəl] *adj (treatment)* de faveur; *(tariff)* préférentiel(elle)

preferred [prɪ'fɜːd] adj préféré(e)
prefigure [priː'fɪɡə(r)] vt préfigurer
prefix ['priːfɪks] n préfixe m
pregnancy ['prɛɡnənsɪ] (pl **pregnancies**) n grossesse f; **p. test** test m de grossesse
pregnant ['prɛɡnənt] adj (**a**) (woman) enceinte; (animal) pleine; **to be three months p.** être enceinte de trois mois (**b**) Fig (pause, silence) éloquent(e)
preheat [priː'hiːt] vt préchauffer
prehensile [prɪ'hɛnsaɪl] adj préhensile
prehistoric [priːhɪs'tɒrɪk] adj préhistorique
prehistory [priː'hɪstərɪ] n préhistoire f
prejudge [priː'dʒʌdʒ] vt (actions, motives) préjuger de; (person) juger sans connaître
prejudice ['prɛdʒʊdɪs] **1** n (a) (bias) préjugé m (**against/ in favour of** contre/en faveur de) (**b**) Law **without p.** to sans préjudice de
2 vt (**a**) (bias) prévenir (**against/in favour of** contre/en faveur de) (**b**) (harm) nuire à, faire du tort à
prejudiced ['prɛdʒʊdɪst] adj **to be p.** avoir des préjuges (**against/in favour of** contre/en faveur de)
prejudicial [prɛdʒʊ'dɪʃəl] adj préjudiciable (**to** à)
preliminary [prɪ'lɪmɪnərɪ] **1** (pl **preliminaries**) n préliminaire m; **preliminaries** (to investigation, meeting) préliminaires
2 adj préliminaire
prelude ['prɛljuːd] n prélude m
premarital [priː'mærɪtəl] adj avant le mariage
premature ['prɛmətjʊə(r)] adj (baby, action, comment) prématuré(e); (baldness, senility, ejaculation) précoce; Fam **you're being a bit p.!** tu vas un peu vite!
prematurely ['prɛmətjʊəlɪ] adv prématurément
premeditated [priː'mɛdɪteɪtɪd] adj prémédité(e)
premenstrual [priː'mɛnstrʊəl] adj prémenstruel(elle); **p.** Am **syndrome** or Br **tension** syndrome m prémenstruel
premier ['prɛmɪə(r)] **1** n (prime minister) Premier ministre m
2 adj premier(ère)
premiere ['prɛmɪeə(r)] n (of play, film) première f
premise ['prɛmɪs] **1** n (of argument, theory) prémisse f
2 vt **to be premised on sth** être fondé(e) sur qch
premises ['prɛmɪsɪz] npl locaux mpl; **business p.** locaux commerciaux; **on the p.** sur place; **off the p.** en dehors de l'établissement; **to see sb off the p.** accompagner qn jusqu'au dehors
premium ['priːmɪəm] n (**a**) Fin (for insurance) prime f; (additional sum) supplément m; **at a p.** au prix fort; Br **p. bonds** ≃ obligations fpl à lots (**b**) (idioms) **to be at a p.** être très recherché(e); **to put a p. on sth** accorder de l'importance à qch
premonition [prɛmə'nɪʃən] n prémonition f; **to have a p. that...** avoir le préssentiment que...
prenatal [priː'neɪtəl] adj prénatal(e)
preoccupation [priːɒkjʊ'peɪʃən] n préoccupation f (**with** pour); **to have a p. with sth** être préoccupé(e) par qch
preoccupied [priː'ɒkjʊpaɪd] adj préoccupé(e) (**with** par)
preoccupy [priː'ɒkjʊpaɪ] (pt & pp **preoccupied**) vt préoccuper au plus haut point
prep [prɛp] n Br Fam (homework) devoirs mpl; **p. school** école f primaire privée
prepaid [priː'peɪd] adj prépayé(e)
preparation [prɛpə'reɪʃən] n préparation f; pre-

parations (for ceremony, party) préparatifs mpl
preparatory [prɪ'pærətərɪ] adj préparatoire; **p. school** Br école f primaire privée; Am école préparatoire
prepare [prɪ'peə(r)] **1** vt préparer
2 vi se préparer (**for** à); **to p. to do sth** se préparer à faire qch
prepared [prɪ'peəd] adj (**a**) (willing) **to be p. to do sth** être prêt(e) à faire qch (**b**) (ready) **to be p. for sth** s'attendre à qch (**c**) (made in advance) préparé(e) à l'avance; (excuse, explanation) tout(e) prêt(e)
prepayment [priː'peɪmənt] n paiement m d'avance
preponderance [prɪ'pɒndərəns] n prépondérance f
preposition [prɛpə'zɪʃən] n préposition f
prepositional [prɛpə'zɪʃənəl] adj prépositif(ive)
prepossessing [priːpə'zesɪŋ] adj avenant(e), engageant(e)
preposterous [prɪ'pɒstərəs] adj ridicule
preppy ['prɛpɪ] adj Am Fam ≃ BCBG inv
preprogrammed [priː'prəʊɡræmd] adj Comptr préprogrammé(e)
prerecorded [priːrɪ'kɔːdɪd] adj préenregistré(e)
prerequisite [priː'rɛkwɪzɪt] n condition f
prerogative [prɪ'rɒɡətɪv] n prérogative f
presage ['prɛsɪdʒ] Lit **1** n présage m
2 vt présager
Presbyterian [prɛzbɪ'tɪərɪən] n & adj presbytérien(enne) m,f
preschool [priː'skuːl] adj préscolaire
prescribe [prɪ'skraɪb] vt (medicine, punishment) prescrire; (solution) préconiser; (task, rule) exiger
prescription [prɪ'skrɪpʃən] n ordonnance f; **available only on p.** délivré(e) seulement sur ordonnance; Dr **p. charge** = prix fixe payé sur chaque médicament prescrit sur ordonnance; **p. drug** = médicament délivré uniquement sur ordonnance
presence ['prɛzəns] n présence f; **in the p. of** en présence de; **to have p.** avoir de la présence; **to make one's p. felt** ne pas passer inaperçu(e); **p. of mind** présence d'esprit
present¹ ['prɛzənt] **1** n **the p.** le présent; **at p.** en ce moment; **for the p.** pour l'instant
2 adj (**a**) (in attendance) présent(e) (**at** à) (**b**) (current) actuel(elle); **at the p. time** or **moment** actuellement; Gram **p. tense** le présent; Gram **p. participle** participe m présent
present² **1** n ['prɛzənt] (gift) cadeau m; **to give sb a p.** offrir un cadeau à qn
2 vt [prɪ'zent] (**a**) (introduce, put forward) présenter; **if the opportunity presents itself** si l'occasion se présente (**b**) (give) (gift) donner; (award, certificate) remettre; **to p. sth to sb, to p. sb with sth** (gift) donner qch à qn; (award, certificate) remettre qch à qn (**c**) Mil **arms!** présentez armes!
presentable [prɪ'zentəbəl] adj présentable; **to make oneself p.** s'arranger
presentation [prɛzən'teɪʃən] n (**a**) (of person) présentation f (**b**) (of gift, award) remise f; **to make a p. to sb** (give present) offrir un cadeau à qn; (give award) remettre un prix à qn (**c**) (formal talk) présentation f; (by student) exposé m (**d**) (of passport, coupon) sur présentation de
present-day [prɛzənt'deɪ] adj actuel(elle)
presenter [prɪ'zentə(r)] n (on radio, TV) présentateur(trice) m,f
presentiment [prɪ'zentɪmənt] n pressentiment m

presently ['prezəntlɪ] adv (a) (soon) bientôt; (soon afterwards) peu de temps après (b) Am (now) actuellement

preservation [prezə'veɪʃən] n (a) (maintenance) maintien m (b) (protection) (of species) protection f; (of building) conservation f; **to put a p. order on a building** classer un bâtiment monument historique

preservative [prɪ'zɜːvətɪv] n conservateur m

preserve [prɪ'zɜːv] **1** n (a) (jam) confiture f (b) (in hunting) réserve f (c) (area of dominance) domaine m; **medecine is no longer a male p.** le métier de médecin n'est plus réservé aux hommes **2** vt (a) (custom, belief) préserver; (calm, sense of humour) garder; (dignity, self-respect) conserver (b) (leather, wood) entretenir (c) (fruit) mettre en conserve (d) (protect) préserver (**from** de); **saints p. us!** le ciel nous préserve!

preshrunk [priː'ʃrʌŋk] adj lavé(e)

preside [prɪ'zaɪd] vi présider; **to p. over a meeting** présider une réunion

presidency ['prezɪdənsɪ] (pl **presidencies**) n présidence f

president ['prezɪdənt] n (of country) président m; Am (of company) P-DG m

presidential [prezɪ'denʃəl] adj présidentiel(elle)

press [pres] **1** n (a) (act of pushing) pression f; **at the p. of a button** en appuyant sur le bouton; **p. stud** bouton-pression m
(**b**) (newspapers) **the p.** la presse; **to get a good/bad p.** avoir bonne/mauvaise presse; **p. agency** agence f de presse; **p. box** tribune f de la presse; **p. conference** conférence f de presse; **p. cutting** coupure f de presse; **p. photographer** photographe mf de presse; **p. release** communiqué m de presse
(**c**) (machine) (**printing**) **p.** presse f (typographique); **to go to p.** (of newspaper) partir à l'impression
2 vt (a) (button, switch) appuyer sur; (into clay, cement) enfoncer; **she pressed the note into my hand** elle m'a glissé le billet dans la main
(**b**) (squeeze) serrer
(**c**) (grapes, olives, flowers) presser
(**d**) (iron) repasser
(**e**) (pressurize) faire pression sur; **to p. sb to do sth** presser qn de faire qch; **to be pressed for time/money** être pressé(e) par le temps/l'argent
(**f**) (force) **to p. sth on sb** forcer qn à accepter qch; **to p. home one's advantage** profiter de son avantage; **to p. one's attentions on sb** faire des avances à qn
(**g**) (insist on) Law **to p. charges (against sb)** porter plainte (contre qn); **I didn't p. the point** je n'ai pas insisté
3 vi (push) se presser
▸ **press ahead** = press on
▸ **press for** vt insep (demand) exiger
▸ **press on** vi continuer; **to p. on with one's work** continuer de travailler

press-gang ['presgæŋ] vt **to p. sb into doing sth** forcer qn à faire qch

pressing ['presɪŋ] adj (urgent) pressant(e)

pressman ['presmən] n Br journaliste m

press-up ['presʌp] n (exercise) pompe f

pressure ['preʃə(r)] **1** n pression f; **to put p. on sb (to do sth)** faire pression sur qn (pour qu'il/elle fasse qch); **to be under p.** être stressé(e); **p. of work** stress m lié au travail; **p. cooker** Cocotte-Minute® f, autocuiseur m; **p. gauge** manomètre m; **p. group** groupe m de pression; Med **p. point** point m de compression
2 vt **to p. sb to do sth** or **into doing sth** faire pression sur qn pour qu'il/elle fasse qch

pressurize ['preʃəraɪz] vt (a) Tech (container) pressuriser

(b) (person) **to p. sb (into doing sth)** faire pression sur qn (pour qu'il/elle fasse qch)

prestige [pres'tiːʒ] n prestige m

prestigious [pres'tɪdʒəs] adj prestigieux(euse)

presumably [prɪ'zjuːməblɪ] adv sans doute; **p. she'll call you** je suppose qu'elle t'appelera

presume [prɪ'zjuːm] **1** vt présumer, supposer; **to p. to do sth** se permettre de faire qch; **I p. so** je suppose que oui **2** vi abuser; **I don't want to p. on you** je ne voudrais pas abuser

presumption [prɪ'zʌmpʃən] n présomption f

presumptuous [prɪ'zʌmptjʊəs] adj présomptueux(euse)

presuppose [priːsə'pəʊz] vt présupposer, supposer

presupposition [priːsʌpə'zɪʃən] n présupposition f

pretence [prɪ'tens] n simulation f; **he says he's ill but it's all a p.** il dit qu'il est malade mais il fait semblant; **to make a p. of doing sth** faire semblant de faire qch

pretend [prɪ'tend] **1** vt (a) (feign) feindre, simuler; **to p. to do sth** faire semblant de faire qch; **they pretended that nothing had happened** ils ont fait comme si de rien n'était
(**b**) (claim) prétendre
2 vi (put on an act) faire semblant
3 adj Fam **p. money** de l'argent pour faire semblant; **a. p. slap** une gifle pour rire

pretension [prɪ'tenʃən] n prétention f

pretentious [prɪ'tenʃəs] adj prétentieux(euse)

pretentiousness [prɪ'tenʃəsnəs] n prétention f

preterite ['pretərɪt] n Gram **the p.** le prétérit

pretext ['priːtekst] n prétexte m; **under** or **on the p. of doing sth** sous prétexte de faire qch

Pretoria [prɪ'tɔːrɪə] n Prétoria

pretty ['prɪtɪ] **1** adj joli(e); **it's not a p. sight** ce n'est pas beau à voir; **to cost a p. penny** coûter la peau des fesses
2 adv (a) (fairly) plutôt; **p. certain** pratiquement sûr(e); **they're p. much the same** ils sont pratiquement pareils (**b**) Fam **to be sitting p.** ne pas avoir à s'en faire

pretzel ['pretzəl] n bretzel m

prevail [prɪ'veɪl] vi (a) (be successful) l'emporter (**over** sur) (**b**) (persuade) **to p. (up)on sb to do sth** amener qn à faire qch (**c**) (predominate) prédominer

prevailing [prɪ'veɪlɪŋ] adj prédominant(e); (wind) dominant(e)

prevalent ['prevələnt] adj très répandu(e)

prevaricate [prɪ'værɪkeɪt] vi tergiverser

prevarication [prɪværɪ'keɪʃən] n tergiversation f

prevent [prɪ'vent] vt empêcher, éviter; **to p. sb from doing sth** empêcher qn de faire qch; **to p. sth from happening** empêcher que qch n'arrive

preventable [prɪ'ventəbəl] adj évitable

preventative [prɪ'ventətɪv] = preventive

prevention [prɪ'venʃən] n prévention f; Prov **p. is better than cure** mieux vaut prévenir que guérir

preventive [prɪ'ventɪv] adj préventif(ive)

preview ['priːvjuː] **1** n (of play, movie) avant-première f; (of new product) aperçu m
2 vt **to be previewed** (of film) sortir en avant-première

previous ['priːvɪəs] **1** adj précédent(e); **to have a p. engagement** être déjà pris(e); Law **p. conviction** condamnation f antérieure
2 adv **p. to** avant

previously ['priːvɪəslɪ] adv auparavant

prewar ['priːwɔː(r)] adj d'avant-guerre

prey [preɪ] *n* proie *f*; *Fig* **to be a p. to** être la proie de; **to fall p. to** devenir la proie de
▸ **prey on, prey upon** *vt insep (person)* prendre pour cible; *(fears, doubts)* exploiter; **to p. on sb's mind** tourmenter qn

price [praɪs] **1** *n* prix *m*; **to rise** *or* **increase in p.** augmenter; **at any p.** à tout prix; **not at any p.** à aucun prix; *Fig* **to pay the p.** (for sth) faire les frais (de qch); *Fig* **it's too high a p.** (to pay) c'est trop cher payé; **to put** *or* **set a p. on sb's head** mettre la tête de qn à prix; *Fig* **everyone has his p.** il n'y a pas d'homme qu'on ne puisse acheter; *Fam* **what p. patriotism now?** que vaut le patriotisme maintenant?; **p. cut** baisse *f* des prix; **p. freeze** gel *m* des prix; **p. increase** hausse *f* des prix; **p. index** indice *m* des prix; **p. list** liste *f* de prix; **p. range** gamme *f* de prix; *(budget)* budget *m*; **p. tag** étiquette *f* de prix; **p. war** guerre *f* des prix
2 *vt (decide cost of)* fixer le prix de; *(indicate cost of)* mettre le prix sur; **the book is priced at $17** le prix du livre est 17 dollars; **to p. oneself out of the market** perdre ses clients en pratiquant des prix trop élevés

price-cutting ['praɪs'kʌtɪŋ] *n Com* baisse *f* des prix

price-fixing ['praɪs'fɪksɪŋ] *n Com* alignement *m* des prix

priceless ['praɪslɪs] *adj* **(a)** *(invaluable)* qui n'a pas de prix **(b)** *Fam (funny)* impayable

pricey ['praɪsɪ] *adj Fam* cher(ère)

prick [prɪk] **1** *n* **(a)** *(of needle)* piqûre *f*; *Fig (of conscience)* remords *m* **(b)** *Vulg (penis)* bite *f*; *(person)* con (conne) *m,f*
2 *vt (sausage, potato)* piquer; *(balloon)* percer; **to p. one's finger** se piquer le doigt; **to p. a hole in sth** percer qch
▸ **prick up** *vt sep* **to p. up one's ears** *(of animal)* dresser les oreilles; *(of person)* tendre l'oreille

prickle ['prɪkəl] **1** *n* **(a)** *(of hedgehog)* piquant *m*; *(of plant)* épine *f* **(b)** *(sensation)* picotement *m*
2 *vi (of skin)* picoter

prickly ['prɪklɪ] *adj* **(a)** *(animal)* couvert(e) de piquants; *(plant)* à épines; *Fig (person)* susceptible; **p. pear** *(tree)* figuier *m* de Barbarie; *(fruit)* figue *f* de Barbarie **(b)** *(sensation)* de picotement; **p. heat** miliaire *f*

pride [praɪd] **1** *n* **(a)** *(satisfaction)* fierté *f*; *(self-esteem)* amour-propre *m*; *Pej (vanity)* orgueil *m*; **to take p. in sth** mettre sa fierté dans qch **(b)** *(person, thing)* **she is the p. of the family** elle fait la fierté de la famille; **the p. of my collection** le clou de ma collection; **she's his p. and joy** elle fait son bonheur; **to have p. of place** trôner **(c)** *(of lions)* troupe *f*
2 *vt* **to p. oneself on sth** être fier(ère) de qch

priest [priːst] *n* prêtre *m*

priestess ['priːstɪs] *n* prêtresse *f*

priesthood ['priːsthʊd] *n* prêtrise *f*; **to enter the p.** entrer dans les ordres

prig [prɪg] *n* prêcheur(euse) *m,f*

priggish ['prɪgɪʃ] *adj* prêcheur(euse)

prim [prɪm] *adj* **p. (and proper)** *(person, expression)* collet monté *inv*; *(manner)* guindé(e)

primacy ['praɪməsɪ] *n* primauté *f*

prima facie ['praɪmə'feɪʃɪ] **1** *adj Law* **p. case** = affaire qui, au premier abord, paraît légitime
2 *adv* de prime abord

primarily ['praɪmərɪlɪ] *adv* principalement

primary ['praɪmərɪ] **1** *n (pl* **primaries)** *(election)* primaire *f*
2 *adj* **(a)** *(main)* principal(e); **p. colours** couleurs *fpl* fondamentales *ou* primaires **(b)** *(initial)* primaire; **p. education** enseignement *m* primaire; **p. school** école *f* primaire

primate ['praɪmeɪt] *n* **(a)** *(animal)* primate *m* **(b)** *Rel* primat *m*

prime [praɪm] **1** *n (best time)* **the p. of life** la fleur de l'âge; **to be in one's p.** être à la fleur de l'âge; **to be past one's p.** ne plus être de première jeunesse
2 *adj* **(a)** *(principal)* principal(e); *(importance)* capital(e); **p. minister** premier ministre *m*; *Math* **p. number** nombre *m* premier; **p. time** *(on TV)* prime time *m* **(b)** *(excellent)* excellent(e); **a p. example (of)** un exemple typique (de); **p. quality** de premier choix
3 *vt* **(a)** *(engine, pump)* amorcer; *(surface)* apprêter **(b)** *(provide with information)* **to p. sb for an interview/an exam** préparer qn à un entretien/un examen

primer[1] ['praɪmə(r)] *n (paint)* apprêt *m*

primer[2] *n (textbook)* manuel *m* élémentaire

primeval [praɪ'miːvəl] *adj* primitif(ive)

primitive ['prɪmɪtɪv] *adj (original)* primitif(ive); *(basic)* de base

primly ['prɪmlɪ] *adv* d'une manière guindée

primordial [praɪ'mɔːdɪəl] *adj* primordial(e); **p. soup** soupe *f* primitive

primrose ['prɪmrəʊz] *n (plant)* primevère *f*; **p. yellow** jaune pâle *inv*

primula ['prɪmjʊlə] *n* primula *f*

primus (stove)® ['praɪməs('stəʊv)] *n* réchaud *m* portatif

prince [prɪns] *n* prince *m*; **the P. of Wales** le prince de Galles; **P. Charming** le prince charmant

princely ['prɪnslɪ] *adj also Fig* princier(ère)

princess [prɪn'ses] *n* princesse *f*; **the P. Royal** la princesse royale *(fille aînée du souverain)*

principal ['prɪnsɪpəl] **1** *n (of school)* proviseur *m*; *(of university)* ≃ président *m*
2 *adj* principal(e)

principality [prɪnsɪ'pælɪtɪ] *(pl* **principalities)** *n* principauté *f*

principle ['prɪnsɪpəl] *n* principe *m*; **in p.** en principe; **on p.** par principe

principled ['prɪnsɪpəld] *adj (person)* de principes; *(behaviour)* dicté(e) par des principes; **to be p.** avoir des principes

print [prɪnt] **1** *n* **(a)** *(of fingers)* empreinte *f* **(b)** *(printed matter)* texte *m*; **in p.** disponible en librairie; **out of p.** épuisé(e); **to appear in p.** être publié(e) **(c)** *(characters)* caractères *mpl*; *Fig* **to read the small p.** *(in contract)* lire ce qu'il y a d'écrit en petits caractères **(d)** *(engraving)* estampe *f*; *(photograph)* épreuve *f*; *(textile)* imprimé *m*
2 *vt* **(a)** *(book, newspaper)* imprimer **(b)** *(write clearly)* écrire en script **(c)** *(in photography)* **to p. a negative** tirer une épreuve d'un négatif
3 *vi (write clearly)* écrire en script
▸ **print out** *vt sep Comptr* imprimer

printed ['prɪntɪd] *adj* imprimé(e); **p. circuit** circuit *m* imprimé; **p. matter** imprimés *mpl*

printer ['prɪntə(r)] *n (person)* imprimeur *m*; *(machine)* imprimante *f*

printing ['prɪntɪŋ] *n (process, industry)* imprimerie *f*; *(action)* tirage *m*; **p. error** faute *f* d'impression; **p. press** presse *f*

printout ['prɪntaʊt] *n Comptr* sortie *f* papier

prior[1] ['praɪə(r)] **1** *adj* antérieur(e); **to have p. knowledge (of sth)** avoir une connaissance préalable (de qch)
2 *adv* **p. to** avant

prior[2] *n Rel* prieur *m*

prioritize [praɪ'ɒrɪtaɪz] **1** vt donner la priorité à **2** vi établir ses priorités

priority [praɪ'ɒrɪtɪ] (pl **priorities**) n priorité f; **to have** or **take p.** over sb/sth avoir la priorité sur qn/qch; **to get one's priorities right/wrong** savoir/ne pas savoir ce qui est important

priory ['praɪərɪ] (pl **priories**) n Rel prieuré m

prise [praɪz] vt to p. **sth off/open** retirer/ouvrir qch en forçant; Fig to p. **sth out of sb** (secret, truth) soutirer qch à qn

prism ['prɪzəm] n prisme m

prison ['prɪzən] n prison f; p. **camp** camp m de prisonniers; p. **officer** gardien(enne) m,f de prison

prisoner ['prɪzənə(r)] n prisonnier(ère) m,f; **to take/ hold sb p.** faire/retenir qn prisonnier; Fig **to take no prisoners** être impitoyable; p. **of war** prisonnier de guerre

prissy ['prɪsɪ] adj Fam collet monté inv

pristine ['prɪstiːn] adj impeccable

privacy ['prɪvəsɪ, 'praɪvəsɪ] n intimité f; **in the p. of one's own home** dans l'intimité de son foyer

private ['praɪvɪt] **1** adj (a) (personal) personnel(elle); **can we go somewhere p.?** est-ce qu'on peut se voir en privé?; p. **life** vie f privée; Parl p. **member** simple député m; Fam p. **parts** parties fpl (secret) confidentiel(elle); p. **and confidential** (on letter) confidentiel (c) (for personal use) privé(e); p. **house** maison f particulière; p. **lessons** leçons fpl particulières; p. **line** ligne f privée; p. **office** bureau m personnel; p. **secretary** secrétaire mf particulier(ère) (d) (not state-run) privé(e); p. **detective** or **investigator** détective m privé; p. **education** enseignement m privé; p. **enterprise** entreprise f privée; p. **school** école f privée (e) (not for the public) privé(e); p. **party** soirée f privée; p. **property** propriété f privée; p. **road** voie f privée **2** n (a) **in p.** en privé (b) (soldier) simple soldat m

privately ['praɪvɪtlɪ] adv (in private) en privé; **to be p. educated** faire sa scolarité dans le privé; p. **owned** (company) privé(e); (hotel) familial(e)

privation [praɪ'veɪʃən] n privation f

privatization [praɪvɪtaɪ'zeɪʃən] n privatisation f

privatize ['praɪvɪtaɪz] vt privatiser

privet ['prɪvɪt] n troène m

privilege ['prɪvɪlɪdʒ] n privilège m; **to have the p. of doing sth** avoir le privilège de faire qch **2** vt **to be privileged to do sth** avoir le privilège de faire qch

privy ['prɪvɪ] **1** n (pl **privies**) Old-fashioned (toilet) cabinets mpl **2** adj (a) Formal **to be p. to sth** avoir connaissance de qch (b) Br Pol P. **Council** le Conseil privé du souverain

prize¹ [praɪz] **1** n (award) prix m; **to win a p.** remporter un prix; Fig **no prizes for guessing** ce n'est pas difficile de deviner; p. **day** jour m de distribution des prix; p. **draw** tombola f; p. **money** argent m du prix **2** vt (value) attacher de la valeur à

prize² = **prise**

prizefight ['praɪzfaɪt] n combat m professionnel

prizefighter ['praɪzfaɪtə(r)] n boxeur m professionnel

prizegiving ['praɪzgɪvɪŋ] n distribution f des prix

prizewinner ['praɪzwɪnə(r)] n gagnant(e) m,f

pro¹ [prəʊ] (pl **pros**) n Fam (professional) pro mf

pro² **1** n (advantage) **the pros and cons** le pour et le contre **2** prep (in favour of) pour

proactive [prəʊ'æktɪv] adj qui fait preuve d'initiative

pro-am ['prəʊ'æm] n Sp tournoi m professionnel-amateur

probability [prɒbə'bɪlɪtɪ] (pl **probabilities**) n probabilité f; **in all p.**... il y a de fortes chances que...

probable ['prɒbəbəl] adj probable

probably ['prɒbəblɪ] adv probablement

probation [prə'beɪʃən] n (in job) période f d'essai; Law mise f en liberté surveillée; **on p.** (in job) à l'essai; Law en liberté surveillée; p. **officer** agent m de probation

probationary [prə'beɪʃənərɪ] adj d'essai

probationer [prə'beɪʃənə(r)] n (in job) personne f à l'essai

probe [prəʊb] **1** n (a) (instrument) sonde f; (space) p. sonde spatiale (b) Fam (enquiry) enquête f **2** vt (a) (prod) sonder (b) (enquire into) enquêter sur **3** vi **to p. into sth** (past, private life) fouiller dans qch

probity ['prəʊbɪtɪ] n Formal probité f

problem ['prɒbləm] n problème m; Fam **no p.!** pas de problème!; p. **area** (in town) quartier m à problèmes; (in project) source f de problèmes; p. **child** enfant mf à problèmes; p. **page** courrier m du cœur

problematic(al) [prɒblɪ'mætɪk(əl)] adj problématique

procedure [prə'siːdʒə(r)] n procédure f

proceed [prə'siːd] **1** vt **to p. to do sth** se mettre à faire qch **2** vi (a) (go on) se poursuivre; **to p. to sth** passer à qch; **to p. with sth** poursuivre qch; **how shall we p.?** comment allons-nous procéder? (b) (result) **to p. from** provenir de

proceedings [prə'siːdɪŋz] npl (a) (events) opérations fpl (b) Law poursuites fpl; **to take p.** (against sb) engager des poursuites (contre qn)

proceeds ['prəʊsiːdz] npl recette f

process¹ ['prəʊses] **1** n processus m; **by a p. of elimination** en procédant par élimination; **she fell down the stairs, breaking her arm in the p.** elle est tombée dans les escaliers, et s'est cassée les bras; **to be in the p. of doing sth** être en train de faire qch **2** vt (raw material, information, application) traiter; (film) développer; **processed food** aliments mpl conditionnés

process² [prə'ses] vi (walk in procession) défiler

processing ['prəʊsesɪŋ] n (of raw material, information) traitement m; (of photographs) développement m; Comptr p. **language** langage m de traitement; Comptr p. **speed** vitesse f de traitement

procession [prə'seʃən] n défilé m; **in p.** en cortège

processor ['prəʊsesə(r)] n Comptr processeur m

pro-choice [prəʊt'ʃɔɪs] adj partisan(e) de l'avortement

proclaim [prə'kleɪm] vt proclamer

proclamation [prɒklə'meɪʃən] n proclamation f

proclivity [prəʊ'klɪvɪtɪ] (pl **proclivities**) n Formal tendance f (for à)

procrastinate [prəʊ'kræstɪneɪt] vi atermoyer

procrastination [prəʊkræstɪ'neɪʃən] n atermoiements mpl

procreate ['prəʊkrɪeɪt] vi procréer

procreation [prəʊkrɪ'eɪʃən] n procréation f

procure [prə'kjʊə(r)] vt procurer (for sb à qn); **to p. sth (for oneself)** se procurer qch

procurement [prə'kjʊəmənt] n acquisition f

prod [prɒd] **1** n **to give sb a p.** donner un petit coup à qn; Fig pousser qn; **to give sth a p.** donner un petit coup à qch **2** vt (pt & pp **prodded**) (poke) donner un petit coup dans; Fig **to p. sb (into doing sth)** pousser qn (à faire qch)

prodigal ['prɒdɪgəl] adj prodigue

prodigious [prə'dɪdʒəs] adj prodigieux(euse)

prodigy ['prɒdɪdʒɪ] (pl **prodigies**) n prodige m

produce 1 n ['prɒdjuːs] *(products)* produits *mpl*
2 *vt* [prə'djuːs] **(a)** *(create)* produire; *(machine, car)* fabriquer; *(reaction, feeling)* entraîner **(b)** *(present)* *(ticket, passport)* présenter; *(documents, alibi)* fournir; *(from pocket, bag)* sortir **(c)** *(movie, play, radio, TV programme)* produire
producer [prə'djuːsə(r)] n **(a)** *(of crops, goods)* producteur(trice) *m,f* **(b)** *(of movie, play, radio, TV programme)* producteur(trice) *m,f*
product ['prɒdʌkt] n produit *m*; *Com* **p.** development mise *f* au point de produit
production [prə'dʌkʃən] n **(a)** *(manufacture)* production *f*; fabrication *f*; **to go into/out of p.** être/ne plus être fabriqué(e); **p. costs** coûts *mpl* de production; **p. line** chaîne *f* de fabrication; **p. manager** directeur(trice) *m,f* de production; **p. process** procédé *m* de fabrication; **p. target** cible *f* de production **(b)** *(of document, ticket)* présentation *f*; **on p. of** sur présentation de **(c)** *(play)* mise *f* en scène; *(movie, radio, TV programme)* production *f*
productive [prə'dʌktɪv] *adj* productif(ive)
productivity [prɒdʌk'tɪvɪtɪ] n *Ind* productivité *f*; **p. agreement** accord *m* de productivité; **p. bonus** prime *f* de rendement
Prof *(abbr* **Professor)** **(a)** *(title)* Professeur **(b)** *Fam* prof *mf*
profane [prə'feɪn] **1** *adj* **(a)** *(language)* grossier(ère) **(b)** *Rel (secular)* profane
2 *vt* profaner
profanity [prə'fænɪtɪ] *(pl* **profanities)** n grossièreté *f*
profess [prə'fes] *vt* **(a)** *(declare)* professer **(b)** *(claim)* prétendre
professed [prə'fest] *adj* **(a)** *(self-declared)* avoué(e) **(b)** *(pretended)* prétendu(e)
profession [prə'feʃən] n **(a)** *(occupation)* profession *f*; **the medical/teaching p.** le corps médical/enseignant; **by p.** de profession **(b)** *(declaration)* déclaration *f*
professional [prə'teʃənəl] **1** n professionnel(elle) *m,f*
2 *adj* *(paid, competent)* professionnel(elle); *(soldier, army)* de carrière; **he made a very p. job of it** il a fait du bon travail; **to turn** *or* **go p.** *(of sportsperson)* passer en catégorie professionnelle; **to take p. advice about sth** demander l'avis d'un professionnel sur qch; **p. misconduct** faute *f* professionnelle; **p. training** formation *f* professionnelle
professionalism [prə'feʃənəlɪzəm] n professionnalisme *m*
professor [prə'fesə(r)] n *Univ Br* ≃ professeur *m*; *Am* enseignant(e) *m,f* d'université
proffer ['prɒfə(r)] *vt* *Formal (advice)* offrir; *(opinion)* avancer; *(thanks)* présenter; *(hand, object)* tendre
proficiency [prə'fɪʃənsɪ] n compétence *f* (**in** *or* **at** en *ou* dans); *(in language)* maîtrise *f* (**in** en)
proficient [prə'fɪʃənt] *adj* compétent(e) (**in** *or* **at** en *ou* dans)
profile ['prəʊfaɪl] **1** n **(a)** *(side view, outline)* profil *m*; **to keep a low p.** garder un profil bas **(b)** *(description)* portrait *m*
2 *vt* *(describe)* faire le portrait de
profit ['prɒfɪt] **1** n **(a)** *(of company, on deal)* bénéfice *m*, profit *m*; **at a p.** à profit; **to make a p.** réaliser un bénéfice; **p. and loss account** compte *m* de pertes et profits; **p. margin** marge *f* bénéficiaire **(b)** *(advantage)* avantage *m*
2 *vi* **to p. by** *or* **from** tirer profit de
profitability [prɒfɪtə'bɪlɪtɪ] n rentabilité *f*
profitable ['prɒfɪtəbəl] *adj* *(company, deal)* rentable; *(experience)* profitable
profitably ['prɒfɪtəblɪ] *adv* *(trade, operate)* à profit; *(use one's time)* profitablement
profiteer [prɒfɪ'tɪə(r)] *Pej* **1** n profiteur(euse) *m,f*

2 *vi* profiter d'une situation pour faire des bénéfices
profit-making ['prɒfɪtmeɪkɪŋ] *adj* rentable
profit-sharing ['prɒfɪt'ʃeərɪŋ] n *Com* intéressement *m*
profligate ['prɒflɪgət] *adj* *Formal* prodigue
profound [prə'faʊnd] *adj* profond(e)
profundity [prə'fʌndɪtɪ] *(pl* **profundities)** n profondeur *f*
profuse [prə'fjuːs] *adj* abondant(e)
profusely [prə'fjuːslɪ] *adv* *(sweat, bleed)* abondamment; **to apologize p.** se confondre en excuses; **to thank sb p.** remercier qn avec effusion
profusion [prə'fjuːʒən] n profusion *f*
progeny ['prɒdʒɪnɪ] *(pl* **progenies)** n *Formal* progéniture *f*
prognosis [prɒg'nəʊsɪs] *(pl* **prognoses** [prɒg'nəʊsiːz]) n *Med* pronostic *m*; *Fig* pronostics
program¹ ['prəʊgræm] *Comptr* **1** n programme *m*
2 *vt & vi* programmer
program² *Am* = **programme**
programmable [prəʊ'græməbəl] *adj* programmable
programme, *Am* **program** ['prəʊgræm] **1** n *(for play, of political party)* programme *m*; *(on TV, radio)* émission *f*; **p. seller** vendeur(euse) *m,f* de programmes
2 *vt* *(machine)* programmer; **to p. sth to do sth** programmer qch pour faire qch
programmed ['prəʊgræmd] *adj* **p. instruction** *or* **learning** enseignement *m* programmé
programmer ['prəʊgræmə(r)] n *Comptr* programmeur(euse) *m,f*
progress n ['prəʊgrɪs] **(a)** *(improvement)* progrès *m*; **to make p.** faire des progrès **(b)** *(movement)* marche *f*; **in p.** en cours; **to make p.** *(in sth)* progresser *(dans qch)*; **p. report** rapport *m*
2 *vi* [prə'gres] **(a)** *(improve)* progresser **(b)** *(advance)* avancer; *(of meeting)* progresser
progression [prə'greʃən] n progression *f*
progressive [prə'gresɪv] **1** *adj* **(a)** *(increasing)* progressif(ive); **p. disease** maladie *f* évolutive **(b)** *(radical)* progressiste
2 n *(radical)* progressiste *mf*
progressively [prə'gresɪvlɪ] *adv* progressivement
prohibit [prə'hɪbɪt] *vt* interdire; **to p. sb from doing sth** interdire à qn de faire qch
prohibition [prəʊɪ'bɪʃən] n interdiction *f*; *Am Hist* **la Prohibition**
prohibitive [prə'hɪbɪtɪv] *adj* prohibitif(ive)
prohibitively [prə'hɪbɪtɪvlɪ] *adv* **p. expensive** à un prix prohibitif
project 1 n ['prɒdʒekt] *(undertaking, plan)* projet *m*; *(at school)* dossier *m*; *(at university)* mémoire *m*; *Com* **p. manager** directeur(trice) *m,f* de projet
2 *vt* [prə'dʒekt] **(a)** *(plan)* projeter **(b)** *(propel)* projeter; **to p. one's voice** projeter sa voix
3 *vi* [prə'dʒekt] *(protrude)* dépasser
projectile [prə'dʒektaɪl] n projectile *m*
projection [prə'dʒekʃən] n **(a)** *(in general)* projection *f*; *(in cinema)* salle *f* de projection **(b)** *(protruding part)* saillie *f*
projectionist [prə'dʒekʃənɪst] n projectionniste *mf*
projector [prə'dʒektə(r)] n projecteur *m*
prolapse ['prəʊlæps] n *Med* prolapsus *m*
proletarian [prəʊlɪ'teərɪən] **1** n prolétaire *mf*
2 *adj* prolétarien(enne)
proletariat [prəʊlɪ'teərɪət] n prolétariat *m*

pro-life ['prəʊlaɪf] *adj* contre l'avortement

proliferate [prə'lɪfəreɪt] *vi* proliférer

proliferation [prəlɪfə'reɪʃən] *n* prolifération *f*

prolific [prə'lɪfɪk] *adj* prolifique

prolix ['prəʊlɪks] *adj Formal* prolixe

prologue ['prəʊlɒg] *n* prologue *m*

prolong [prə'lɒŋ] *vt* prolonger

prom [prɒm] *n* (**a**) *Br Fam (at seaside)* front *m* de mer (**b**) *Br Fam (concert)* concert *m* (**c**) *Am (school dance)* bal *m (de lycéens ou d'étudiants)*; **p. queen** reine *f* du bal

promenade ['prɒmənɑːd] **1** *n Br (at seaside)* front *m* de mer; **p. deck** *(on ship)* pont *m* promenade
2 *vi* se promener

prominence ['prɒmɪnəns] *n* (**a**) *(of land)* saillie *f*; *(of physical feature)* proéminence *f* (**b**) *(importance)* importance *f*; **to give sth p.** donner de l'importance à qch; **to come to p.** devenir célèbre

prominent ['prɒmɪnənt] *adj* (**a**) *(peak, landscape)* en saillie; *(physical feature)* proéminent(e); **to be in a p. position** être en évidence (**b**) *(important)* important(e)

prominently ['prɒmɪnəntlɪ] *adv* bien en vue; **to figure p. in sth** figurer en bonne place dans qch

promiscuity [prɒmɪs'kjuːɪtɪ] *n* promiscuité *f*

promiscuous [prə'mɪskjʊəs] *adj* qui a des partenaires multiples

promise ['prɒmɪs] **1** *n* (**a**) *(pledge)* promesse *f*; **to make a p.** faire une promesse; **to keep/break one's p.** tenir sa promesse (**b**) *(potential)* to show **p.** promettre; **she never fulfilled her early p.** *(as a writer, musician)* elle n'a jamais eu le succès qu'elle promettait d'avoir
2 *vt* promettre (**to do** de faire); **to p. sth to sb, to p. sb sth** promettre qch à qn; **it promises to be hot** le temps promet d'être chaud

promising ['prɒmɪsɪŋ] *adj* prometteur(euse)

promontory ['prɒməntərɪ] *(pl* **promontories**) *n* promontoire *m*

promote [prə'məʊt] *vt* (**a**) *(raise in rank, encourage)* promouvoir; **to be promoted** *(of officer, employee)* être promu(e); *(of soccer team)* passer dans la division supérieure; **to p. sb's interests** servir les intérêts de qn (**b**) *Com* faire la publicité de

promoter [prə'məʊtə(r)] *n (of theory, cause)* défenseur(euse) *m,f*; *(of boxing match)* organisateur(trice) *m,f*; *(of show)* imprésario *m*

promotion [prə'məʊʃən] *n* promotion *f*

promotional [prə'məʊʃənəl] *adj* promotionnel(elle)

prompt [prɒmpt] **1** *adj* (**a**) *(swift)* rapide; **p. payment** paiement *m* dans les plus brefs délais (**b**) *(punctual)* ponctuel(elle)
2 *adv* **at three o'clock p.** à trois heures précises
3 *vt* (**a**) *(cause)* provoquer; **to p. sb to do sth** pousser qn à faire qch (**b**) **to p. sb** *(encourage to speak)* aider qn à répondre en lui suggérant quelque chose; **"was he wearing glasses?" the policeman prompted** "est-ce qu'il portait des lunettes?" suggéra le policier (**c**) *(in theatre)* souffler à
4 *n* (**a**) **to give an actor a p.** souffler sa réplique à un acteur (**b**) *Comptr* invite *f*

prompter ['prɒmptə(r)] *n Th* souffleur(euse) *m,f*

promptly ['prɒmptlɪ] *adv (rapidly, punctually)* rapidement; *(immediately)* immédiatement

prone [prəʊn] *adj* (**a**) *(inclined)* **to be p. to sth** être sujet(ette) à qch; **to be p. to do sth** avoir tendance à faire qch (**b**) *Formal (lying face down)* couché(e) sur le ventre

prong [prɒŋ] *n (of fork)* dent *f*

pronoun ['prəʊnaʊn] *n Gram* pronom *m*

pronounce [prə'naʊns] **1** *vt* (**a**) *(word)* prononcer (**b**) *(declare) (opinion)* émettre; **to p. that...** déclarer que...; **to p. oneself for/against sth** se prononcer en faveur de/contre qch; **he was pronounced dead/innocent** il a été déclaré mort/innocent; *Law* **to p. sentence** rendre le verdict
2 *vi* **to p. on** se prononcer sur

pronounced [prə'naʊnst] *adj* prononcé(e)

pronouncement [prə'naʊnsmənt] *n Formal* déclaration *f*

pronto ['prɒntəʊ] *adv Fam* illico

pronunciation [prənʌnsɪ'eɪʃən] *n* prononciation *f*

proof [pruːf] **1** *n* (**a**) *(evidence)* preuve *f*; **to give p. of sth** prouver qch; **p. of identity** pièce *f* d'identité; **p. of purchase** preuve *f* d'achat; **to put sth to the p.** mettre qch à l'épreuve; *Prov* **the p. of the pudding is in the eating** il faut juger les choses à l'usage (**b**) *Typ* épreuve *f* (**c**) *(of alcohol)* teneur *f* (en alcool); **to be 40% p.** faire 40 degrés
2 *adj (resistant)* **to be p. against sth** être résistant(e) à qch

proofread ['pruːfriːd] *(pt & pp* **proofread** ['pruːfred]) *vt Typ* relire, corriger

proofreader ['pruːfriːdə(r)] *n Typ* correcteur(trice) *m,f*

pro rata ['prəʊ'rɑːtə] *adj & adv* au prorata

prop [prɒp] **1** *n* (**a**) *(physical support)* support *m*; *(emotional support)* soutien *m* (**b**) *(in theatre)* accessoire *m*
2 *vt (pt & pp* **propped**) **to p. sth against sth** appuyer qch contre qch
▸ **prop up** *vt sep (building, tunnel)* étayer; *Fig (economy, regime)* soutenir; **to p. sth up against sth** appuyer qch contre qch

propaganda [prɒpə'gændə] *n* propagande *f*

propagate ['prɒpəgeɪt] **1** *vt* propager
2 *vi* se propager

propagation [prɒpə'geɪʃən] *n* propagation *f*

propane ['prəʊpeɪn] *n Chem* propane *m*

propel [prə'pel] *(pt & pp* **propelled**) *vt* propulser; *Fig* pousser

propellant, propellent [prə'pelənt] *n (for rocket)* propergol *m*; *(for aerosol)* gaz *m* propulseur

propeller [prə'pelə(r)] *n* hélice *f*

propelling pencil [prə'pelɪŋ'pensəl] *n* porte-mine *m inv*

propensity [prə'pensɪtɪ] *(pl* **propensities**) *n* propension *f* (**for** à)

proper ['prɒpə(r)] *adj* (**a**) *(correct, real)* vrai(e); *(word)* correct(e); *Gram* **p. noun** nom *m* propre (**b**) *(appropriate)* bon (bonne); *(equipment, clothing)* adéquat(e); *(behaviour)* convenable (**c**) *(characteristic)* **p. to** propre à

properly ['prɒpəlɪ] *adv* (**a**) *(correctly)* correctement (**b**) *(suitably)* convenablement

property ['prɒpətɪ] *(pl* **properties**) *n* (**a**) *(possessions)* biens *mpl*; *(land, house)* propriété *f*; **p. developer** promoteur(trice) *m,f* (immobilier(ère)); **p. market** marché *m* immobilier; **p. tax** impôt *m* foncier (**b**) *(quality)* propriété *f*

prophecy ['prɒfɪsɪ] *(pl* **prophecies**) *n* prophétie *f*

prophesy ['prɒfɪsaɪ] *(pt & pp* **prophesied**) *vt* prédire

prophet ['prɒfɪt] *n* prophète *m*

prophetic [prə'fetɪk] *adj* prophétique

prophylactic [prɒfɪ'læktɪk] *Med* **1** *n* prophylactique *m*; *(condom)* préservatif *m*
2 *adj* prophylactique

propitiate [prə'pɪʃɪeɪt] *vt Formal* gagner les faveurs de

propitious [prə'pɪʃəs] *adj Formal* favorable

proportion [prə'pɔːʃən] **1** *n* (**a**) *(relationship)* proportion *f*; **in p.** proportionné(e); **out of p.** disproportionné(e); **the payment is out of all p.** to the work involved la rétribution n'est pas du tout proportionnelle au travail requis (**b**) *(part, amount)* proportion *f*; **to get sth out of p.** exagérer qch; **try to keep things in p.** essaie de ne pas dramatiser (**c**) **proportions** *(dimensions)* proportions *fpl* **2** *vt* proportionner

proportional [prə'pɔːʃənəl] *adj* proportionnel(elle) (**to** à); *Pol* **p. representation** (représentation *f*) proportionnelle *f*

proportionate [prə'pɔːʃənɪt] *adj* proportionnel(elle) (**to** à)

proposal [prə'pəʊzəl] *n (offer)* proposition *f*; *(plan)* projet *m*; **p. (of marriage)** demande *f* en mariage

propose [prə'pəʊz] **1** *vt* proposer; **to p. a toast** porter un toast; **to p. to do sth, to p. doing sth** *(suggest)* suggérer de faire qch; *(intend)* avoir l'intention de faire qch **2** *vi* **to p. to sb** demander qn en mariage

proposition [prɒpə'zɪʃən] **1** *n* proposition *f* **2** *vt* faire des avances à

propound [prə'paʊnd] *vt Formal* exposer

proprietary [prə'praɪɪtərɪ] *adj (air, attitude)* possessif(ive); *Com* **p. brand** marque *f* déposée

proprietor [prə'praɪətə(r)] *n* propriétaire *mf*

propriety [prə'praɪətɪ] *n* bienséance *f*

propulsion [prə'pʌlʃən] *n* propulsion *f*

prosaic [prəʊ'zeɪɪk] *adj* prosaïque

proscribe [prəʊ'skraɪb] *vt* proscrire

prose [prəʊz] *n Br* prose *f*; *(translation in exam)* thème *m*

prosecute ['prɒsɪkjuːt] *Law* **1** *vt* poursuivre en justice **2** *vi (of lawyer)* représenter le ministère public

prosecution [prɒsɪ'kjuːʃən] *n Law (proceedings)* poursuites *fpl* judiciaires; **the p.** *(in trial)* les plaignants *mpl*; *(in crown case)* ≃ le ministère public

prosecutor ['prɒsɪkjuːtə(r)] *n Law* procureur *m*

prospect 1 *n* ['prɒspekt] (**a**) *(expectation, thought)* perspective *f* (**b**) *(chance, likelihood)* perspectives *fpl*; **there is no p. of success** il n'y a aucune chance de réussite; **future prospects** perspectives d'avenir; **a job with prospects** un travail qui offre des perspectives d'avenir (**c**) *(view)* vue *f* **2** *vi* [prə'spekt] **to p. for gold** chercher de l'or

prospective [prə'spektɪv] *adj (future)* futur(e); *(potential)* potentiel(elle)

prospector [prə'spektə(r)] *n* prospecteur(trice) *m,f*; *(for gold)* chercheur(euse) *m,f*

prospectus [prə'spektəs] *n* prospectus *m*

prosper ['prɒspə(r)] *vi* prospérer

prosperity [prɒs'perɪtɪ] *n* prospérité *f*

prosperous ['prɒspərəs] *adj* prospère

prostate ['prɒsteɪt] *n Anat* **p. (gland)** prostate *f*

prosthesis [prɒs'θiːsɪs] *(pl* **prostheses** [prɒs'θiːsiːz]*) n* prothèse *f*

prostitute ['prɒstɪtjuːt] **1** *n* prostituée *f*; **male p.** prostitué *m* **2** *vt also Fig* **to p. oneself** se prostituer

prostitution [prɒstɪ'tjuːʃən] *n* prostitution *f*

prostrate 1 *adj* ['prɒstreɪt] *(lying down)* couché(e); *Fig* **p. with grief** terrassé(e) par le chagrin **2** *vt* [prə'streɪt] **to p. oneself** se prosterner

protagonist [prə'tægənɪst] *n* protagoniste *mf*; *(of idea, theory)* partisan(e) *m,f*

protect [prə'tekt] *vt* protéger (**from** *or* **against** de)

protection [prə'tekʃən] *n* protection *f*; **p. money** = argent versé à un racketteur; **p. racket** racket *m*

protectionism [prə'tekʃənɪzəm] *n Econ* protectionnisme *m*

protective [prə'tektɪv] *adj* protecteur(trice); **to put sb in p. custody** mettre qn en lieu sûr

protector [prə'tektə(r)] *n (device)* protecteur *m*; *(person)* protecteur(trice) *m,f*

protégé ['prɒtəʒeɪ] *n* protégé(e) *m,f*

protein ['prəʊtiːn] *n* protéine *f*

protest 1 *n* ['prəʊtest] protestation *f*; **to do sth under p.** faire qch contre son gré; **to do sth in p.** faire qch en signe de protestation; **p. song** chanson *f* engagée; **p. vote** vote *m* de protestation **2** *vt* [prə'test] (**a**) *(protest against)* protester contre (**b**) *(one's innocence, love)* protester de; **to p. that...** protester en disant que... **3** *vi* [prə'test] protester (**about/against** à propos de/ contre)

Protestant ['prɒtɪstənt] *n & adj* protestant(e) *m,f*

Protestantism ['prɒtɪstəntɪzəm] *n* protestantisme *m*

protestation [prɒtes'teɪʃən] *n* protestation *f*

protester [prə'testə(r)] *n* protestataire *mf*

protocol ['prəʊtəkɒl] *n* protocole *m*

proton ['prəʊtɒn] *n Phys* proton *m*

prototype ['prəʊtətaɪp] *n* prototype *m*

protracted [prə'træktɪd] *adj* prolongé(e)

protractor [prə'træktə(r)] *n* rapporteur *m*

protrude [prə'truːd] *vi* dépasser (**from** de); *(of jaw, teeth)* avancer

protruding [prə'truːdɪŋ] *adj* en saillie; *(jaw, teeth)* qui avance

protuberance [prə'tjuːbərəns] *n* protubérance *f*

proud [praʊd] **1** *adj (person)* fier(ère) (**of** de); *(moment)* grand(e), **as p. as a peacock** fier comme un paon **2** *adv* **to do sb p.** faire honneur à qn; **to do oneself p.** se distinguer

proudly ['praʊdlɪ] *adv* fièrement

prove [pruːv] (*pp* **proven** ['pruːvən, 'prəʊvən] *or* **proved**) **1** *vt (demonstrate)* prouver; **to p. sb wrong/guilty** prouver que qn a tort/est coupable; **to p. oneself** se prouver quelque chose **2** *vi* **to (be) correct** se révéler correct(e)

proverb ['prɒvɜːb] *n* proverbe *m*

proverbial [prə'vɜːbɪəl] *adj* proverbial(e)

provide [prə'vaɪd] *vt* (**a**) *(supply)* fournir; *(service, support)* offrir; **to p. sb with sth** fournir qch à qn (**b**) *(stipulate)* stipuler

▸ **provide against** *vt insep (danger, possibility)* parer à

▸ **provide for** *vt insep* (**a**) *(support)* pourvoir aux besoins de; **he left his wife well provided for** il a laissé sa femme à l'abri du besoin (**b**) *Formal (allow for)* parer à

provided [prə'vaɪdɪd] *conj* **p. (that)** à condition que *+ subjunctive*

providence ['prɒvɪdəns] *n* providence *f*

providential [prɒvɪ'denʃəl] *adj* providentiel(elle)

provider [prə'vaɪdə(r)] *n* pourvoyeur(euse) *m,f*

providing [prə'vaɪdɪŋ] *conj* **p. (that)** à condition que *+ subjunctive*

province ['prɒvɪns] *n* (**a**) *(of country)* province *f*; **in the provinces** en province (**b**) *Fig (domain)* domaine *m*

provincial [prə'vɪnʃəl] *adj* de province; *Pej (parochial)* provincial(e)

provision [prə'vɪʒən] *n* **(a)** **provisions** *(supplies)* provisions *fpl* **(b)** *(supplying)* approvisionnement *m* **(of** en); *(of services)* prestation *f* **(of** de) **(c)** *(allowance)* **to make p.** for sth prévoir qch **(d)** *(in treaty)* disposition *f; (in contract)* clause *f*

provisional [prə'vɪʒənəl] *adj* provisoire

provisionally [prə'vɪʒənəlɪ] *adv* provisoirement

proviso [prə'vaɪzəʊ] *(pl* **provisos** *or* **provisoes)** *n* condition *f;* **with the p.** that à condition que + *subjunctive*

provocation [prɒvə'keɪʃən] *n* provocation *f;* **at the slightest p.** pour un rien

provocative [prə'vɒkətɪv] *adj* provocateur(trice)

provoke [prə'vəʊk] *vt* provoquer; **to p. sb into doing sth** pousser qn à faire qch

provoking [prə'vəʊkɪŋ] *adj (irritating)* agaçant(e)

provost ['prɒvəst] *n* **(a)** *Br Univ (head of college)* doyen *m* **(b)** *Scot (mayor)* maire *m*

prow [praʊ] *n (of ship)* proue *f*

prowess ['praʊɪs] *n (skill)* prouesses *fpl*

prowl [praʊl] **1** *n* **to be on the p.** *(of person, animal)* être en chasse; **to be on the p. for sth** être à l'affût de qch **2** *vt (streets, area)* rôder dans **3** *vi* rôder

prowler ['praʊlə(r)] *n* rôdeur(euse) *m,f*

proximity [prɒk'sɪmɪtɪ] *n* proximité *f;* **in p. to** à proximité de

proxy ['prɒksɪ] *(pl* **proxies)** *n (power)* procuration *f; (person)* mandataire *mf;* **by p.** par procuration

prude [pruːd] *n* prude *f*

prudence ['pruːdəns] *n* prudence *f*

prudent ['pruːdənt] *adj* prudent(e)

prudish ['pruːdɪʃ] *adj* pudibond(e)

prune¹ [pruːn] *n (fruit)* pruneau *m*

prune² *vt (bush, tree)* tailler; *Fig (article)* élaguer

prurient ['prʊərɪənt] *adj* malsain(e)

Prussia ['prʌʃə] *n* la Prusse

Prussian ['prʌʃən] **1** *n* Prussien(enne) *m,f* **2** *adj* prussien(enne)

pry [praɪ] *(pt & pp* **pried)** *vi* être indiscret(ète); **to p. into sth** mettre son nez dans qch

prying ['praɪɪŋ] *adj* indiscret(ète)

PS ['piːes] *n (abbr* **postscript)** PS *m*

psalm [sɑːm] *n* psaume *m*

pseud [sjuːd] *n Fam* prétentieux(euse) *m,f*

pseudo- ['sjuːdəʊ] *pref Fam* pseudo-

pseudonym ['sjuːdənɪm] *n* pseudonyme *m*

PST [piːes'tiː] *n Am (abbr* **Pacific Standard Time)** PST *m*

psyche ['saɪkɪ] *n* psychisme *m*

▸ **psyche out** [saɪk] *vt sep Fam (unnerve)* déstabiliser

▸ **psyche up** [saɪk] *vt sep Fam* **to p. sb up (for sth)** préparer qn psychologiquement (à qch); **to p. oneself up (for sth)** se préparer psychologiquement (à qch)

psychedelic [saɪkə'delɪk] *adj* psychédélique

psychiatric [saɪkɪ'ætrɪk] *adj* psychiatrique

psychiatrist [saɪ'kaɪətrɪst] *n* psychiatre *mf*

psychiatry [saɪ'kaɪətrɪ] *n* psychiatrie *f*

psychic ['saɪkɪk] **1** *n* médium *m* **2** *adj* **(a)** *(paranormal)* paranormal(e) **(b)** *(clairvoyant)* **to be p., to have p. powers** être médium; *Fam* **I'm not p.!** je ne suis pas devin!

psycho ['saɪkəʊ] *(pl* **psychos)** *n Fam* dingue *mf*

psychoanalysis [saɪkəʊə'nælɪsɪs] *n* psychanalyse *f*

psychoanalyst [saɪkəʊ'ænəlɪst] *n* psychanalyste *mf*

psychoanalyze [saɪkəʊ'ænəlaɪz] *vt* psychanalyser

psychological [saɪkə'lɒdʒɪkəl] *adj* psychologique; **p. warfare** guerre *f* psychologique

psychologist [saɪ'kɒlədʒɪst] *n* psychologue *mf*

psychology [saɪ'kɒlədʒɪ] *n* psychologie *f*

psychometric [saɪkə'metrɪk] *adj* psychométrique

psychopath ['saɪkəʊpæθ] *n* psychopathe *mf*

psychosis [saɪ'kəʊsɪs] *(pl* **psychoses** [saɪ'kəʊsiːz]) *n* psychose *f*

psychosomatic [saɪkəʊsə'mætɪk] *adj* psychosomatique

psychotherapist [saɪkəʊ'θerəpɪst] *n* psychothérapeute *mf*

psychotherapy [saɪkəʊ'θerəpɪ] *n* psychothérapie *f*

psychotic [saɪ'kɒtɪk] *n & adj* psychotique *mf*

PT [piː'tiː] *n (abbr* **physical training)** EPS *f*

PTA [piːtiː'eɪ] *n Sch (abbr* **Parent-Teacher Association)** ≃ APE *f*

ptarmigan ['tɑːmɪgən] *n* lagopède *m*

Pte *Mil (abbr* **private)** P. **Robbie McLean** = Soldat Robbie McLean

PTO [piːtiː'əʊ] *(abbr* **please turn over)** TSVP

pub [pʌb] *n Br* pub *m*

pub-crawl ['pʌbkrɔːl] *n Br Fam* **to go on a p.** faire la tournée des bars

puberty ['pjuːbətɪ] *n* puberté *f*

pubic ['pjuːbɪk] *adj* pubien(enne), du pubis

public ['pʌblɪk] **1** *n* **the (general) p.** le grand public; **in p.** en public **2** *adj* public(ique); *(library, swimming pool)* municipal(e); **to go p. with sth** *(reveal information)* révéler qch *(à la presse)*; **the company's going p.** la compagnie va être cotée en Bourse; **to make sth p.** rendre qch public; **to be in the p. domain** être dans le domaine public; **at p. expense** aux frais du contribuable; **to be in the p. eye** être très en vue; **a p. figure** une personnalité en vue; **in the p. interest** dans l'intérêt du public; **p. address system** sonorisation *f;* **p. convenience** toilettes *fpl* publiques; *Com* **p. enterprise** entreprise *f* publique; **p. holiday** jour *m* férié; **p. house** pub *m;* **p. limited company** ≃ société *f* anonyme; **p. opinion** l'opinion *f* publique, *Law* **p. prosecutor** procureur *m;* **p. relations** relations *fpl* publiques; **p. school** *Br* école *f* privée, *Am* école publique; **p. sector** secteur *m* public; **p. spending** dépenses *fpl* publiques; **p. transport** transports *mpl* en commun; *Com* **p. utility** service *m* public

publican ['pʌblɪkən] *n* patron(onne) *m,f* d'un pub

publication [pʌblɪ'keɪʃən] *n* publication *f*

publicity [pʌb'lɪsɪtɪ] *n* publicité *f;* **p. campaign** campagne *f* publicitaire; **p. stunt** coup *m* de pub

publicize ['pʌblɪsaɪz] *vt* faire connaître au public

publicly ['pʌblɪklɪ] *adv* publiquement; **p. owned** à capitaux publics

public-spirited ['pʌblɪk'spɪrɪtɪd] *adj (person)* qui a le sens civique; *(gesture, response)* dicté(e) par le sens civique

publish ['pʌblɪʃ] *vt* publier

publisher ['pʌblɪʃə(r)] *n (person)* éditeur(trice) *m,f; (company)* maison *f* d'édition

publishing ['pʌblɪʃɪŋ] *n* édition *f;* **p. house** maison *f* d'édition

pucker ['pʌkə(r)] **1** *vt (brow)* froncer; *(lips)* pincer **2** *vi (of face)* se rider; *(lips)* se plisser

pudding ['pʊdɪŋ] *n* (a) *(dessert)* dessert *m* (b) *(dish)* pudding *m*; **p. basin** *or* **bowl** jatte *f*
puddle ['pʌdəl] *n* flaque *f*
pudgy ['pʌdʒɪ] *adj* rondelet(ette)
puerile ['pjʊəraɪl] *adj Pej* puéril(e)
Puerto Rican [pweətəʊ'ri:kən] **1** *n* Portoricain(e) *m,f* **2** *adj* portoricain(e)
Puerto Rico [pweətəʊ'ri:kəʊ] *n* Porto Rico
puff [pʌf] **1** *n* (of breath, air) souffle *m*; (of smoke, cigarette) bouffée *f*; *Fam* **to be out of p.** être essoufflé(e); *Am* **p. paste,** *Br* **p. pastry** pâte *f* feuilletée
2 *vt* **to p. smoke into sb's face** envoyer de la fumée à la figure de qn
3 *vi* (of person) souffler; (of steam engine) lancer des bouffées de vapeur; **to p. on a cigarette** fumer une cigarette
▸ **puff out** *vt sep* (cheeks, chest) gonfler
▸ **puff up** *vt sep* (cheeks) gonfler; **to be puffed up with pride** être gonflé(e) d'orgueil
puffin ['pʌfɪn] *n* macareux *m*
puffy ['pʌfɪ] *adj* gonflé(e)
pug [pʌg] *n* (dog) carlin *m*; **p.-nosed** au nez camus
pugnacious [pʌg'neɪʃəs] *adj* pugnace
puke [pju:k] *Fam* **1** *n* dégueulis *m*
2 *vt & vi* dégueuler
pull [pʊl] **1** *n* (a) (act of pulling) traction *f*; (of water current) force *f*; **to give sth a p.** tirer qch
(b) *Fam* (influence) influence *f*; **to have a lot of p.** avoir le bras long
2 *vt* (a) (tug) tirer; **to p. sth open/shut** ouvrir/fermer qch; **to p. a muscle** se froisser un muscle; **to p. the trigger** appuyer sur la gâchette; *Fig* **to p. sth to pieces** démolir qch; *Fam Fig* **to p. sb's leg** faire marcher qn; *Fam Fig* **p. the other one! (it's got bells on)** à d'autres!
(b) (attract) attirer
(c) (extract) (cork) retirer, enlever; (tooth) arracher; **to p. a gun on sb** braquer un pistolet sur qn; *Fam Fig* **it's like pulling teeth** il faut t'/lui/etc arracher les vers du nez
(d) *Br Fam* (sexually) **to p. sb** se faire qn
(e) (idioms) **to p. a face** faire la grimace; *Fam* **to p. a bank job** se faire une banque; *Fam* **to p. a fast one on sb** rouler qn
3 *vi* tirer (**on** sur); **to p. clear of sth** s'éloigner de qch
▸ **pull about** *vt sep* (handle roughly) malmener
▸ **pull ahead** *vi* (in race, election) prendre la tête (**of** de)
▸ **pull apart** *vt sep* (break up) séparer; *Fig* (criticize) massacrer
▸ **pull away** *vi* (of car, train) partir; (from embrace) s'écarter
▸ **pull back 1** *vt sep* (curtains) ouvrir
2 *vi* (of person) se retirer
▸ **pull down** *vt sep* (demolish) démolir
▸ **pull in 1** *vt sep* (a) (rope, fishing line) ramener (b) (money) gagner; (of deal) rapporter; **to p. sb in for questioning** arrêter qn pour l'interroger (c) (attract) attirer
2 *vi* (of car) s'arrêter; (of train, bus) arriver
▸ **pull off** *vt sep* (a) (clothes) retirer (b) (task, deal) réaliser; (bank raid, burglary) réussir; **to p. it off** réussir
▸ **pull on** *vt sep* (clothes) mettre
▸ **pull out 1** *vt sep* (tooth) arracher; *Fam Fig* **to p. out all the stops** faire tout son possible
2 *vi* (a) (of car) déboîter; (of train) partir (b) (from race, agreement, deal) se retirer
▸ **pull over** *vi* (of driver) s'arrêter
▸ **pull through** *vi* (recover) s'en sortir

▸ **pull together 1** *vt sep* **to p. oneself together** se ressaisir
2 *vi* s'entendre
▸ **pull up 1** *vt sep Fig* **to p. one's socks up** se ressaisir; **to p. sb up (short)** couper qn dans son élan
2 *vi* (of car) s'arrêter
pull-down menu ['pʊldaʊn'menju:] *n Comptr* menu *m* déroulant
pullet ['pʊlɪt] *n* poulette *f*
pulley ['pʊlɪ] (pl **pulleys**) *n* poulie *f*
pull-out ['pʊlaʊt] *n* (in newspaper, magazine) supplément *m* détachable
pullover ['pʊləʊvə(r)] *n* pull-over *m*
pulmonary ['pʌlmənərɪ] *adj* pulmonaire
pulp [pʌlp] *n* (of fruit) pulpe *f*; **to reduce sth to a p.** écraser qch; *Fam* **to beat sb to a p.** mettre qn en bouillie; **p. fiction** romans *mpl* de gare
2 *vt* écraser
pulpit ['pʊlpɪt] *n* chaire *f*
pulsate [pʌl'seɪt] *vi* (of vein) palpiter; (of room, music) vibrer; (of heart) battre
pulse¹ [pʌls] *n* (of blood) pouls *m*; (of light, sound) vibration *f*; **to feel** *or* **take sb's p.** prendre le pouls de qn
pulse² *n* (seed) légumineuse *f*
pulverize ['pʌlvəraɪz] *vt* pulvériser; *Fam Fig* (beat up) démolir; (defeat heavily) pulvériser
puma ['pju:mə] *n* puma *m*
pumice ['pʌmɪs] *n* **p. (stone)** pierre *f* ponce
pummel ['pʌməl] (*pt & pp* pummelled, *Am* pummeled) *vt* marteler
pump¹ [pʌmp] *n* (flat shoe) escarpin *m*; (ballet shoe) ballerine *f*; (plimsoll) tennis *m* ou *f*
pump² **1** *n* (machine) pompe *f*
2 *vt* pomper; **to p. sb's stomach** faire un lavage d'estomac à qn; *Fig* **to p. money into sth** injecter des capitaux dans qch; *Fam* **to p. sb for information** tirer les vers du nez à qn; **to p. sb's hand** (shake vigorously) donner une poignée de main vigoureuse à qn; *Fam* **to p. iron** (do weightlifting) faire de la gonflette
3 *vi* (of heart) battre; (of machine) pomper
▸ **pump out** *vt sep* pomper
▸ **pump up** *vt sep* gonfler
pumpkin ['pʌmpkɪn] *n* potiron *m*; (smaller) citrouille *f*
pun [pʌn] *n* jeu *m* de mots
punch¹ [pʌntʃ] **1** *n* (tool) poinçon *m*; (for tickets) poinçonneuse *f*
2 *vt* (metal) percer; (ticket) poinçonner
punch² **1** *n* (a) (blow) coup *m* (de poing); *Fig* **she didn't pull her punches** elle n'y est pas allée de main morte (b) (energy) punch *m*; **p. line** (of joke, story) chute *f*
2 *vt* (hit) donner un coup de poing à; **to p. sb in the face/ on the nose** donner un coup de poing à qn dans la figure/ dans le nez
punch³ *n* (drink) punch *m*
Punch and Judy show ['pʌntʃən'dʒu:dɪ'ʃəʊ] *n* ≃ spectacle *m* de Guignol
punchbag ['pʌntʃbæg] *n* sac *m* de sable
punchball ['pʌntʃbɔ:l] *n* punching-ball *m*
punch-drunk ['pʌntʃdrʌŋk] *adj* assommé(e)
punch-up ['pʌntʃʌp] *n Fam* bagarre *f*
punchy ['pʌntʃɪ] *adj Fam* plein(e) de punch
punctilious [pʌŋk'tɪlɪəs] *adj* pointilleux(euse)
punctual ['pʌŋktjʊəl] *adj* ponctuel(elle)
punctuality [pʌŋktjʊ'ælɪtɪ] *n* ponctualité *f*

punctually ['pʌŋktjʊəlɪ] *adv* à l'heure
punctuate ['pʌŋktjʊeɪt] *vt* ponctuer (**with** de)
punctuation [pʌŋktjʊ'eɪʃən] *n* ponctuation *f*; **p. mark** signe *m* de ponctuation
puncture ['pʌŋktʃə(r)] **1** *n (in tyre)* crevaison *f*; *(in skin, metal)* perforation *f*; **to have a p.** *(of cyclist, driver)* crever; *(of bicycle, car)* avoir un pneu crevé
2 *vt (tyre)* crever; *(metal, lung)* perforer; *(blister, abscess)* percer
pundit ['pʌndɪt] *n* expert(e) *m,f*
pungent ['pʌndʒənt] *adj (smell, taste)* âcre; *(style, wit)* mordant(e)
punish ['pʌnɪʃ] *vt* punir; **to p. sb for doing sth** punir qn pour avoir fait qch
punishment ['pʌnɪʃmənt] *n* punition *f*; *Law* peine *f*; **to make the p. fit the crime** adapter la punition à la faute; **to take a lot of p.** être mis(e) à rude épreuve
punitive ['pju:nɪtɪv] *adj* punitif(ive)
punk [pʌŋk] *n* punk *mf*; **p. (rock)** punk *m*
punnet ['pʌnɪt] *n* barquette *f*
punt¹ [pʌnt] **1** *n (boat)* barque *f* à fond plat
2 *vi* **to go punting** faire de la barque
punt² [pʊnt] *n (Irish currency)* livre *f* irlandaise
punter ['pʌntə(r)] *n (gambler)* parieur(euse) *m,f*; *Fam (customer)* client(e) *m,f*
puny ['pju:nɪ] *adj* chétif(ive)
pup [pʌp] *n (of dog)* chiot *m*; *(of seal)* bébé-phoque *m*
pupil¹ ['pju:pəl] *n (student)* élève *mf*
pupil² *n (of eye)* pupille *f*
puppet ['pʌpɪt] *n also Fig* marionnette *f*; *Fig* **p. government** gouvernement *m* fantoche; **p. show** (spectacle *m* de) marionnettes *fpl*
puppy ['pʌpɪ] *(pl* **puppies**) *n* chiot *m*; **p. fat** rondeurs *fpl* préadolescentes; **p. love** amour *m* d'adolescence
purchase ['pɜ:tʃɪs] **1** *n* (**a**) *(action, thing bought)* achat *m*; **p. price** prix *m* d'achat (**b**) *(grip)* prise *f*; **to get a p. on sth** trouver une prise sur qch
2 *vt* acheter
purchaser ['pɜ:tʃəsə(r)] *n* acheteur(euse) *m,f*
purchasing ['pɜ:tʃəsɪŋ] *n* **p. manager** directeur(trice) *m,f* des achats; **p. power** pouvoir *m* d'achat
pure [pjʊə(r)] *adj* pur(e); **by p. chance** par pur hasard; **p. mathematics** mathématiques *fpl* pures
purebred ['pjʊəbred] *adj (dog)* de race pure; *(horse)* pur-sang *inv*
purée ['pjʊəreɪ] **1** *n* purée *f*
2 *vt* réduire en purée
purely ['pjʊəlɪ] *adv* purement; **p. and simply** purement et simplement
purgatory ['pɜ:gətərɪ] *n Rel* purgatoire *m*; *Fig* enfer *m*
purge [pɜ:dʒ] **1** *n* purge *f*
2 *vt* purger
purification [pjʊərɪfɪ'keɪʃən] *n* purification *f*
purify ['pjʊərɪfaɪ] *(pt & pp* **purified**) *vt* purifier
purist ['pjʊərɪst] *n* puriste *mf*
puritan ['pjʊərɪtən] *n* puritain(e) *m,f*
puritanical [pjʊərɪ'tænɪkəl] *adj* puritain(e)
purity ['pjʊərɪtɪ] *n* pureté *f*
purl [pɜ:l] **1** *n* maille *f* à l'envers
2 *vt* tricoter à l'envers
purloin [pɜ:'lɔɪn] *vt* dérober
purple ['pɜ:pəl] **1** *n* violet *m*
2 *adj* violet(ette); **to turn** *or* **go p.** *(of person)* devenir cramoisi(e); **pages of p. prose** des pages d'un style ampoulé

purport *Formal* **1** *n* ['pɜ:pɔ:t] teneur *f*
2 *vt* [pɜ:'pɔ:t] **to p. to be sth** prétendre être qch
purpose ['pɜ:pəs] *n* (**a**) *(object, aim)* but *m*, objectif *m*; **on p.** exprès; **what is the p. of your visit?** quel est l'objet de votre visite?; **to have a sense of p.** savoir ce que l'on veut; **to be to no p.** ne servir à rien (**b**) *(use)* utilité *f*; **to serve a p.** servir à quelque chose; **to serve no p.** ne servir à rien; **to serve sb's purpose(s)** faire l'affaire de qn; **for all practical purposes** à toutes fins utiles; **for the purposes of** pour les besoins de
purpose-built ['pɜ:pəs'bɪlt] *adj* spécialement construit(e)
purposeful ['pɜ:pəsfʊl] *adj* résolu(e)
purposely ['pɜ:pəslɪ] *adv* délibérément; **to be p. rude** faire exprès d'être grossier(ère)
purr [pɜ:(r)] **1** *n* ronron *m*, ronronnement *m*
2 *vi* ronronner
purse [pɜ:s] **1** *n Br (wallet)* porte-monnaie *m inv*; *Am (handbag)* sac *m* à main; **the public p.** le Trésor public; *Fig* **to hold the p. strings** tenir les cordons de la bourse
2 *vt* **to p. one's lips** pincer les lèvres
pursue [pə'sju:] *vt* poursuivre; *(pleasure, happiness)* rechercher; *(profession)* exercer
pursuer [pə'sju:ə(r)] *n* poursuivant(e) *m,f*
pursuit [pə'sju:t] *n* (**a**) *(of person, animal)* poursuite *f*; *(of pleasure, knowledge, happiness)* quête *f*; **to be in p. of** être à la poursuite de; **in hot p.** à ses trousses (**b**) *(activity)* activité *f*
purveyor [pə'veɪə(r)] *n Formal* fournisseur(euse) *m,f*
pus [pʌs] *n* pus *m*
push [pʊʃ] **1** *n* (**a**) *(act of pushing)* poussée *f*; **to give sb/sth a p.** pousser qn/qch; *Fam* **to give sb the p.** *(of employer)* virer qn; *(of lover)* plaquer qn; **at a p.** à la rigueur; **when p. comes to shove, if it comes to the p.** dans le pire des cas (**b**) *(attack)* poussée *f*; **sales p.** campagne *f* de vente; **to make a p. for sth** lutter pour qch
2 *vt* (**a**) *(in general)* pousser; *(button)* appuyer sur; **to p. the door shut/open** fermer/ouvrir la porte; **p.** *(sign)* poussez; **to p. sb out of the way** écarter qn; **to p. one's way through the crowd** se frayer un chemin à travers la foule; *Fig* **don't p. yourself too hard** ne force pas trop; *Fig* **to p. sb into doing sth** pousser qn à faire qch; **to p. one's luck** y aller un peu fort; **to be pushed for time** être très pressé(e) (**b**) *(promote)* faire la promotion de; *(theory)* promouvoir (**c**) *Fam (drugs)* vendre (**d**) *Fam* **to be pushing sixty** approcher de la soixantaine
3 *vi (in general)* pousser; *(move forward)* avancer; **to p. past sb** passer devant qn en le bousculant; **to p. forward** pousser en avant
▸ **push about, push around** *vt sep Fam Fig (bully)* **to p. sb about** faire de qn ce que l'on veut
▸ **push ahead** *vi* continuer; **to p. ahead with sth** continuer qch
▸ **push aside** *vt sep also Fig* écarter
▸ **push in** *vi (in queue)* resquiller
▸ **push off** *vi Fam* ficher le camp
▸ **push on** *vi (continue)* continuer; **to p. on with sth** continuer qch
▸ **push over** *vt sep* faire tomber
▸ **push through** *vt sep (reform, law)* faire passer
push-bike ['pʊʃbaɪk] *n Fam* vélo *m*
push-button ['pʊʃ'bʌtən] *adj* à touches
pushchair ['pʊʃtʃeə(r)] *n (for baby)* poussette *f*

pusher ['pʊʃə(r)] *n Fam* **(drug) p.** dealer *m*
pushover ['pʊʃəʊvə(r)] *n Fam* **the exam was a p.** l'examen était un jeu d'enfant; **she's no p.** ce n'est pas facile de la faire changer d'avis
push-up ['pʊʃʌp] *n* pompe *f*
pushy ['pʊʃɪ] *adj Fam* batailleur(euse)
puss [pʊs] *n Fam (cat)* minou *m*
pussy ['pʊsɪ] *(pl* pussies) *n Fam* **p. (cat)** minou *m*; **p. willow** saule *m* blanc
pussyfoot ['pʊsɪfʊt] *vi Fam* **to p. (around** *or* **about)** *(when speaking)* tourner autour du pot; *(in one's actions)* toujours remettre les choses à plus tard
pustule ['pʌstjuːl] *n* pustule *f*
put [pʊt] *(pt & pp* put**) 1** *vt* **(a)** *(place)* mettre; **(on flat surface)** poser; **to p. one's arms around sb** prendre qn dans ses bras; **to p. a man on the moon** envoyer un homme sur la lune; **to p. a limit on sth** mettre une limite à qch; *Fam* **p. it there!** *(shake hands)* tope là!; *Fig* **to p. oneself in sb's hands** s'en remettre à qn; *Fig* **to p. sb in his place** remettre qn à sa place; *Fig* **to p. yourself in my position** mets-toi à ma place; **to p. a matter right** mettre les choses au point; **to p. money on a horse** parier sur un cheval; **to p. a lot of work into sth** beaucoup travailler à qch; **to p. a stop to sth** mettre fin à qch; **to p. a child to bed** mettre un enfant au lit; **to p. sb to the test** mettre qn à l'épreuve; *Fam Fig* **I didn't know where to p. myself** je ne savais pas où me mettre
(b) *(present)* **to p. a question to sb** poser une question à qn; **to p. a proposal to sb** soumettre une proposition à qn; **I p. it to you that…** *(in court)* n'est-il pas vrai que…?
(c) *(express)* **to p. sth well** bien tourner qch; **I couldn't have put it better myself** je n'aurais pas mieux dit; **to p. it bluntly** pour parler franchement; **how shall I p. it…?** comment dire…?
(d) *(estimate)* estimer **(at** à); **I would p. her age at forty** je dirais qu'elle a quarante ans
2 *vi* **to p. to sea** prendre la mer
▸ **put about** *vt sep (rumour)* faire courir; **to p. it about that…** faire courir le bruit que…
▸ **put across** *vt sep (message, idea)* faire comprendre **(to** à); **to p. oneself across well/badly** *(at interview)* se mettre/ne pas se mettre en valeur
▸ **put aside** *vt sep* **(a)** *(goods, money)* mettre de côté **(b)** *(problem, fact)* laisser de côté
▸ **put away** *vt sep* **(a)** *(tidy away)* ranger **(b)** *Fam (prisoner)* enfermer **(c)** *Fam (eat, drink)* s'enfiler, ingurgiter
▸ **put back** *vt sep* **(a)** *(replace)* remettre **(b)** *(postpone)* reporter; *(clock, schedule)* retarder; *Fig* **that puts the clock back ten years** cela nous ramène dix ans en arrière
▸ **put by** *vt sep (save)* mettre de côté
▸ **put down** *vt sep* **(a)** *(set down)* poser; **I couldn't put it down** *(book)* je ne pouvais pas m'arrêter de (le) lire **(b)** *(revolt, opposition)* réprimer **(c)** *(write)* écrire, mettre par écrit; **to p. sth down in writing** mettre qch par écrit; **to p. one's name down for** s'inscrire à qch **(d)** *(attribute)* **to p. sth down to sb/sth** attribuer qch à qn/qch **(e)** *(animal)* piquer; **to have a cat/dog put down** faire piquer un chat/un chien **(f)** *(criticize)* rabaisser; **to p. oneself down** se rabaisser
▸ **put forward** *vt sep* **(a)** *(plan, theory, candidate)* proposer; *(proposal)* faire **(b)** *(clock, time of meeting)* avancer
▸ **put in 1** *vt sep* **(a)** *(install)* installer **(b)** *(claim, application)* soumettre; **to p. in a (good) word for sb** dire un mot en faveur de qn **(c)** *(time)* passer; **they've p. in a lot of work** ils ont énormément travaillé
2 *vi (of ship)* faire escale

▸ **put off** *vt sep* **(a)** *(postpone)* remettre à plus tard; **to p. off doing sth** retarder le moment de faire qch **(b)** *(cause to dislike)* **to p. sb off sth** dégoûter qn de qch **(c)** *(disturb)* gêner **(d)** *(discourage)* **to p. sb off doing sth** enlever à qn l'envie de faire qch **(e)** *(make wait)* faire patienter
▸ **put on** *vt sep* **(a)** *(clothes)* mettre; **to p. on one's make-up** se maquiller; **to p. on an act** jouer la comédie; **to p. on an accent** prendre un accent; *Fam* **she's just putting it on!** elle fait semblant!; **to p. on weight** grossir, prendre du poids **(b)** *(light, TV, heating)* allumer; *(music, video)* mettre; **to p. the kettle on** mettre l'eau à chauffer **(c)** *(play, show)* monter
▸ **put out** *vt sep* **(a)** *(fire, light)* éteindre **(b)** *(place outside)* mettre dehors **(c)** *(extend)* **to p. out one's hand** tendre la main **(d)** *(arrange for use)* sortir **(e)** *(report, statement)* publier **(f)** *(annoy)* **to be put out** être contrarié(c) **(g)** *(inconvenience)* déranger; **to p. oneself out (for sb)** se donner du mal (pour qn) **(h)** *(dislocate)* **to p. one's shoulder/knee out** se démettre l'épaule/le genou
▸ **put through** *vt sep (on phone)* **to p. sb through to sb** passer qn à qn **(b)** *(subject to)* **to p. sb through sth** faire subir qch à qn; **to p. sb through hell** faire souffrir le martyre à qn
▸ **put together** *vt sep (assemble)* assembler; *(file, report)* préparer; *(meal, team)* composer; **she's more intelligent than the rest of them put together** elle est cent fois plus intelligente qu'eux; *Fig* **to p. two and two together** tirer ses conclusions
▸ **put up** *vt sep* **(a)** *(tent, fence)* monter; *(ladder)* dresser; *(building)* construire; *(statue)* ériger; *(notice)* afficher; *(painting)* accrocher; *(umbrella)* ouvrir; **to p. up one's hand** lever la main; **to p. one's hair up** relever ses cheveux **(b)** *(increase)* augmenter **(c)** *(provide accommodation for)* loger, héberger **(d)** *(provide (money)* verser, fournir; *(candidate)* présenter; **to p. sth up for sale** mettre qch en vente; **to p. up a fight** *or* **a struggle** se défendre
▸ **put upon** *vt insep* **to feel put upon** se sentir exploité(e)
▸ **put up to** *vt sep* **to p. sb up to doing sth** pousser qn à faire qch; **he put me up to it** c'est lui qui m'a poussé à le faire
▸ **put up with** *vt insep* supporter
putative ['pjuːtətɪv] *adj Formal* putatif(ive)
put-down ['pʊtdaʊn] *n Fam* remarque *f* humiliante
putrefy ['pjuːtrɪfaɪ] *(pt & pp* putrefied) *vi* se putréfier
putrid ['pjuːtrɪd] *adj* putride
putsch [pʊtʃ] *n* putsch *m*
putt [pʌt] **1** *n (in golf)* putt *m* **2** *vi (in golf)* putter
putter ['pʌtə(r)] *n (golf club)* putter *m*
putty ['pʌtɪ] *n* mastic *m*; *Fig* **he's p. in her hands** elle en fait ce qu'elle veut
put-up job ['pʊtʌp'dʒɒb] *n Br Fam* coup *m* monté
puzzle ['pʌzl] **1** *n* **(a)** *(game)* casse-tête *m*; *(mental)* devinette *f*; *(jigsaw)* puzzle *m*; **p. book** livre *m* de devinettes et de jeux *(b)* *(mystery)* énigme *f*
2 *vt (person)* rendre perplexe
▸ **puzzle out** *vt sep (solution, meaning)* trouver; *(action, motive)* essayer de comprendre
▸ **puzzle over** *vt insep* essayer de comprendre
puzzled ['pʌzld] *adj* perplexe
puzzling ['pʌzlɪŋ] *adj* bizarre
PVC [piːviː'siː] *n (abbr* polyvinyl chloride) PVC *m*
pygmy ['pɪgmɪ] *(pl* pygmies) *n* pygmée *m*

pyjamas, *Am* **pajamas** [pə'dʒɑːməz] *npl* pyjama *m*; **a pair of p.** un pyjama

pylon ['paɪlən] *n* pylône *m*

pyramid ['pɪrəmɪd] *n* pyramide *f*

pyre ['paɪə(r)] *n* bûcher *m* (funéraire)

Pyrenean [pɪrə'nɪən] *adj* pyrénéen(enne)

Pyrenees [pɪrə'niːz] *npl* **the P.** les Pyrénées *fpl*

Pyrex® ['paɪreks] *n* pyrex® *m*; **P. dish** plat *m* en pyrex®

pyromaniac [paɪrəʊ'meɪnɪæk] *n* pyromane *mf*

pyrotechnics [paɪrəʊ'tekniks] **1** *n (science)* pyrotechnie *f*
2 *npl (fireworks display)* feu *m* d'artifice; *Fig (in speech, writing)* prouesses *fpl*

python ['paɪθən] *n* python *m*

Q, q [kjuː] *n (letter)* Q, q *m inv*
Qatar [kæˈtɑː(r)] *n* le Qatar
Qatari [kæˈtɑːrɪ] **1** *n* habitant(e) *m,f* du Qatar
 2 *adj* du Qatar
QC [kjuːˈsiː] *n Br Law (abbr* **Queen's Counsel**) = membre haut placé du barreau
QED [kjuːiːˈdiː] *(abbr* **quod erat demonstrandum**) CQFD
qty *Com (abbr* **quantity**) qté
quack¹ [kwæk] **1** *n (of duck)* coin-coin *m*
 2 *vi (of duck)* faire coin-coin
quack² *n (doctor) Pej* charlatan *m*; *Hum* toubib *m*
quad [kwɒd] *n Fam (of school, college)* cour *f*
quadrangle [ˈkwɒdræŋgəl] *n* **(a)** *(shape)* quadrilatère *m* **(b)** *(of school, college)* cour *f*
quadrant [ˈkwɒdrənt] *n* quart *m* de cercle
quadraphonic [kwɒdrəˈfɒnɪk] *adj* quadriphonique
quadratic equation [kwɒˈdrætɪkɪˈkweɪʒən] *n Math* équation *f* du second degré
quadrilateral [kwɒdrɪˈlætərəl] **1** *n* quadrilatère *m*
 2 *adj* quadrilatéral(e)
quadriplegic [kwɒdrɪˈpliːdʒɪk] *n & adj* tétraplégique *mf*
quadruped [ˈkwɒdrʊped] *n* quadrupède *m*
quadruple [kwɒˈdrʊpəl] **1** *adj* quadruple
 2 *vt & vi* quadrupler
quadruplet [ˈkwɒdrʊplet] *n* quadruplé(e) *m,f*
quaff [kwɒf] *vt Lit* boire
quagmire [ˈkwæɡmaɪə(r)] *n also Fig* bourbier *m*
quail¹ [kweɪl] *(pl* quail) *n (bird)* caille *f*
quail² *vi (of person)* avoir un mouvement de recul
quaint [kweɪnt] *adj (picturesque)* pittoresque; *(old-fashioned)* vieillot(otte)
quake [kweɪk] **1** *n Fam (earthquake)* tremblement *m* de terre
 2 *vi* trembler; **to q. in one's boots** trembler de peur
Quaker [ˈkweɪkə(r)] *n Rel* quaker(eresse) *m,f*
qualification [kwɒlɪfɪˈkeɪʃən] *n* **(a)** *(diploma)* diplôme *m*; *(skill)* compétence *f* **(b)** *(completion of studies)* **on/after q.** une fois le diplôme obtenu **(c)** *(modification)* précision *f* **(d)** *(for competition)* qualification *f*
qualified [ˈkwɒlɪfaɪd] *adj* **(a)** *(having diploma)* diplômé(e); *(competent)* compétent(e); **to be q. to do sth** *(have diploma)* avoir les diplômes requis pour faire qch; *(be competent)* avoir les compétences requises pour faire qch **(b)** *(modified)* mitigé(e); **a q. success** un demi-succès
qualifier [ˈkwɒlɪfaɪə(r)] *n* **(a)** *(person, team)* qualifié(e) *m,f*; *(match)* match *m* de qualification **(b)** *Gram* qualificatif *m*

qualify [ˈkwɒlɪfaɪ] *(pt & pp* **qualified**) **1** *vt* **(a)** *(make competent)* **to q. sb to do sth** donner les compétences nécessaires à qn pour faire qch **(b)** *(modify)* nuancer
 2 *vi* **(a)** *(in competition)* se qualifier; **to q. as a doctor/teacher** obtenir son diplôme de médecin/professeur **(b)** *(be eligible)* **to q. for sth** avoir droit à qch
qualifying [ˈkwɒlɪfaɪɪŋ] *adj* **(a)** *(round, match)* éliminatoire **(b)** *(exam)* d'entrée
qualitative [ˈkwɒlɪtətɪv] *adj* qualitatif(ive)
quality [ˈkwɒlɪtɪ] *(pl* **qualities**) *n* qualité *f*; **of good/poor q.** de bonne/mauvaise qualité; **q. of life** qualité de la vie; **q. circle** cercle *m* de qualité; **q. control** contrôle *m* (de) qualité; **q. goods** marchandises *fpl* de qualité
qualm [kwɑːm] *n* doute *m*; **to have no qualms about doing sth** *(doubts)* ne pas hésiter une seconde avant de faire qch; *(scruples)* n'avoir aucun scrupule à faire qch
quandary [ˈkwɒndərɪ] *(pl* **quandaries**) *n* dilemme *m*; **to be in a q. (about sth)** être face à un dilemme (à propos de qch)
quango [ˈkwæŋɡəʊ] *(pl* **quangoes**) *n Br Pol (abbr* **quasi-autonomous non-governmental organization**) = organisme créé par le gouvernement et doté de pouvoirs quasi autonomes
quantifier [ˈkwɒntɪfaɪə(r)] *n Math* quantificateur *m*
quantify [ˈkwɒntɪfaɪ] *(pt & pp* **quantified**) *vt* évaluer
quantitative [ˈkwɒntɪtətɪv] *adj* quantitatif(ive)
quantity [ˈkwɒntɪtɪ] *(pl* **quantities**) *n* quantité *f*; **q. surveyor** métreur vérificateur *m*
quantum [ˈkwɒntəm] *n Phys* quantum *m*; *Fig* **q. leap** bond *m* en avant; **q. mechanics** mécanique *f* quantique; **q. theory** théorie *f* des quanta
quarantine [ˈkwɒrəntiːn] **1** *n* quarantaine *f*; **to be in q.** être en quarantaine
 2 *vt* mettre en quarantaine
quark [kwɑːk] *n Phys* quark *m*
quarrel [ˈkwɒrəl] **1** *n* **(a)** *(argument)* dispute *f*, querelle *f*; **to have a q.** se disputer; **to pick a q. with sb** chercher querelle à qn **(b)** *(disagreement)* désaccord *m*; **to have no q. with sb** n'avoir rien à reprocher à qn
 2 *vi (pt & pp* **quarrelled**, *Am* **quarreled**) **(a)** *(argue)* se disputer (with avec); **(b)** *(disagree)* **to q. with sth** ne pas être d'accord avec qch
quarrelling, *Am* **quarreling** [ˈkwɒrəlɪŋ] *n* disputes *fpl*
quarrelsome [ˈkwɒrəlsəm] *adj* querelleur(euse)
quarry¹ [ˈkwɒrɪ] *(pl* **quarries**) *n (prey) & Fig* proie *f*
quarry² **1** *(pl* **quarries**) *n (for stone)* carrière *f*
 2 *vt (pt & pp* **quarried**) *(hill)* exploiter; *(stone)* extraire

quart [kwɔːt] *n (liquid measurement) Br* = 1,136 l; *Am* = 0,946 l

quarter ['kwɔːtə(r)] **1** *n* (**a**) *(fraction)* quart *m*; *(of orange, moon)* quartier *m*; **a q.** of a century un quart de siècle; **a q. of an hour** un quart d'heure; **a q.** (of a pound) = 113,4 g, un quart de livre; **three quarters** trois quarts; **three and a q.** trois un quart; **three and a q.** litres trois litres un quart; **a q.** full au quart plein(e) (**b**) *(in telling time) Br* **a q. to six,** *Am* **a q. of six** six heures moins le quart; **it's a q. to** il est moins le quart; *Br* **a q. past six,** *Am* **a q. after six** six heures un *ou* et quart; **it's a q. past** il est le quart (**c**) *(three-month period)* trimestre *m* (**d**) *(area)* quartier *m* (**e**) *(group)* milieu *m*; **help came from an unexpected q.** nous avons reçu une aide inespérée (**f**) *Mil* **quarters** *(lodgings)* quartiers *mpl* (**g**) *Am (coin)* pièce *f* de 25 cents

2 *vt* (**a**) *(divide into four)* partager en quatre (**b**) *Mil (troops)* loger

quarterback ['kwɔːtəbæk] *n Am* arrière *m*

quarterdeck ['kwɔːtədek] *n (of ship)* plage *f* arrière

quarterfinal [kwɔːtə'faɪnəl] *n* quart *m* de finale

quarterly ['kwɔːtəlɪ] **1** *n* (*pl* **quarterlies**) publication *f* trimestrielle
2 *adj* trimestriel(elle)
3 *adv* tous les trimestres

quartermaster ['kwɔːtəmɑːstə(r)] *n Mil* intendant *m*

quartet [kwɔː'tet] *n* quatuor *m*

quarto ['kwɔːtəʊ] (*pl* **quartos**) *n* in-quarto *m*

quartz [kwɔːts] *n* quartz *m*; **q. watch** montre *f* à quartz

quasar ['kweɪzɑː(r)] *n Astron* quasar *m*

quash [kwɒʃ] *vt (objection, plan)* rejeter; *(revolt, feeling)* réprimer; *Law (sentence)* annuler

quaver ['kweɪvə(r)] **1** *n* (**a**) *Mus* croche *f* (**b**) *(in voice)* tremblement *m*
2 *vi (of voice)* trembler

quay [kiː] *n* quai *m*

quayside ['kiːsaɪd] *n* quai *m*

queasy ['kwiːzɪ] *adj* **to feel q.** avoir mal au cœur

Quebec [kwɪ'bek] *n* le Québec; **Q. City** Québec

queen [kwiːn] *n* (**a**) *(of country, in cards, chess)* reine *f*; *Br* **Q.'s Counsel** = membre haut placé du barreau; **the Q.'s English** l'anglais *m* correct; **the Q. Mother** la reine mère (**b**) *very Fam (homosexual)* tante *f*, folle *f*, = terme injurieux désignant un homosexuel

queer ['kwɪə(r)] **1** *adj* (**a**) *(strange)* bizarre (**b**) *very Fam (homosexual)* homo, pédé
2 *n very Fam (male homosexual)* homo *m*, pédé *m*, = terme injurieux désignant un homosexuel
3 *vt Fam* **to q. the pitch for sb,** to q. sb's pitch boulverser les plans de qn

quell [kwel] *vt (revolt)* réprimer; *(doubt, worry)* dissiper

quench [kwentʃ] *vt (thirst)* étancher

querulous ['kwerʊləs] *adj (person)* grincheux(euse); *(tone)* maussade, plaintif(ive)

query ['kwiːərɪ] **1** *n* (*pl* **queries**) question *f*
2 *vt* (*pt & pp* **queried**) mettre en question; **to q. if** *or* **whether...** mettre en question le fait que...

quest [kwest] *n Lit* **in q.** quête *f*, poursuite *f* (**for** de); **to go** *or* **be in q. of sth** être en quête *ou* à la poursuite de qch
2 *vi* **to q. after** *or* **for sth** être en quête *ou* à la poursuite de qch

question ['kwestʃən] **1** *n* (**a**) *(query)* question *f*; **to ask (sb) a q.** poser une question (à qn); **q. mark** point *m* d'interrogation; *Fig* **a q. mark hangs over the future of the project** l'avenir du projet reste en suspens; *Br Pol* **q. time** ≃ session *f* des questions orales à *l'Assemblée nationale* (**b**) *(doubt)* doute *m*; **to call sth into q.** mettre

qch en doute; **beyond q.** indiscutable; **it's open to q. whether...** reste à savoir si...; **without q.** indiscutable (**c**) *(matter)* question *f*, problème *m*; **it is a q. of...** il s'agit de...; **there is no q. of our agreeing to** that il n'est pas question que nous acceptions cela; **to be out of the q.** être hors de question; **it's only a q. of time** ce n'est qu'une question de temps; **the matter/person in q.** l'affaire/la personne en question
2 *vt* (**a**) *(put questions to)* interroger (**on** sur) (**b**) *(cast doubt on)* mettre en doute

questionable ['kwestʃənəbəl] *adj* discutable

questioning ['kwestʃənɪŋ] **1** *n* *(interrogation)* interrogation *f*; **to be held for q.** *(by police)* être interrogé(e)
2 *adj (look)* interrogateur(trice); *(mind)* curieux(euse)

questionnaire [kwestʃə'neə(r)] *n* questionnaire *m*

queue [kjuː] *Br* **1** *n* queue *f*, file *f* (d'attente); **to jump the q.** resquiller
2 *vi* faire la queue

queue-jump ['kjuːdʒʌmp] *vi Br* resquiller

quibble ['kwɪbəl] **1** *n* petite question *f*
2 *vi* chipoter (**about** *or* **over** à propos de)

quiche [kiːʃ] *n* quiche *f*

quick [kwɪk] **1** *adj* (**a**) *(rapid)* rapide; **to have a q. shower/drink** prendre une douche/un verre en vitesse; **to be q.** *(hurry)* faire vite; **that was q.!** tu as fait vite!; **(as) q. as a flash** rapide comme l'éclair; **to be q. to do sth** faire qch vite *ou* rapidement; **to be q. off the mark** *(to act)* réagir vite; *(to understand)* avoir l'esprit vif; **to be q.** *(to understand)* avoir l'esprit vif; **temper** s'emporter facilement (**b**) *(clever)* vif (vive)
2 *adv Fam (run, take, think)* vite
3 *n* **to bite one's nails to the q.** se ronger les ongles jusqu'au sang; *Fig* **to cut sb to the q.** piquer qn au vif

quicken ['kwɪkən] **1** *vt* (**a**) *(make faster)* accélérer; **to q. one's pace** presser le pas (**b**) *(imagination)* stimuler; *(interest)* éveiller, exciter
2 *vi (of pace, pulse)* s'accélérer

quickfire ['kwɪkfaɪə(r)] *adj* rapide

quickie ['kwɪkɪ] *Fam* **1** *n* **to have a q.** *(drink)* prendre un verre en vitesse; *(sex)* faire l'amour en vitesse
2 *adj* **q. divorce** divorce *m* rapide

quicklime ['kwɪklaɪm] *n* chaux *f* vive

quickly ['kwɪklɪ] *adv* vite, rapidement

quickness ['kwɪknɪs] *n (speed)* rapidité *f*; *(of mind)* vivacité *f*

quicksand ['kwɪksænd] *n* sables *mpl* mouvants

quicksilver ['kwɪksɪlvə(r)] *n Old-fashioned (mercury)* vif-argent *m*

quick-tempered ['kwɪk'tempəd] *adj* emporté(e)

quick-witted ['kwɪk'wɪtɪd] *adj* vif (vive)

quid [kwɪd] (*pl* **quid**) *n Br Fam (pound)* livre *f*

quiescent [kwaɪ'esənt] *adj Formal* passif(ive)

quiet ['kwaɪət] **1** *n* silence *m*; *Fam* **to do sth on the q.** faire qch en douce
2 *adj* (**a**) *(not loud)* silencieux(euse); *(voice)* petit(e); *(music)* doux (douce); **to keep sb q.** faire tenir qn tranquille; **to keep q.** *(make no noise)* ne pas faire de bruit; *(say nothing)* se taire; **to keep q. about sth** ne rien dire au sujet de qch; **to keep sth q.** cacher qch; **be q.!** tais-toi!; **as q. as a mouse** *(person)* silencieux (**b**) *(discreet)* discret(ète); **to have a q. laugh at sb/sth** se moquer discrètement de qn/qch (**c**) *(peaceful)* tranquille (**d**) *(business, market)* calme

▸ **quiet down** = **quieten down**

quieten ['kwaɪətən] *vt* calmer
▸ **quieten down 1** *vt sep* calmer
     2 *vi* se calmer

quietly ['kwaɪətlɪ] *adv* **(a)** *(silently)* tranquillement, silencieusement **(b)** *(discreetly)* discrètement; **to be q.** confident être optimiste sans excès

quietness ['kwaɪətnɪs] *n (of person, place)* tranquillité *f*; *(of manner)* douceur *f*

quiff [kwɪf] *n (of hair)* toupet *m*

quill [kwɪl] *n (feather)* penne *f*; *(pen)* plume *f* d'oie; *(of porcupine)* piquant *m*

quilt [kwɪlt] **1** *n* édredon *m*; *(duvet)* couette *f* **2** *vt (garment)* matelasser; **quilted jacket** veste *f* matelassée

quince [kwɪns] *n* coing *m*; **q. jelly** gelée *f* de coing

quinine [kwɪ'niːn] *n* quinine *f*

quintessentIal [kwɪntɪ'senʃəl] *adj Formal* quintessentiel(elle)

quintessentially [kwɪntɪ'senʃəlɪ] *adv Formal* fondamentalement

quintet [kwɪn'tet] *n* quintette *m*

quintuplet [kwɪn'tʊplɪt] *n* quintuplé(e) *m,f*

quip [kwɪp] **1** *n* boutade *f* **2** *vi (pt & pp* **quipped)** plaisanter

quirk [kwɜːk] *n* **(a)** *(of character)* particularité *f* **(b)** *(of fate, nature)* caprice *m*; **by a q. of fate** par un caprice du destin

quirky ['kwɜːkɪ] *adj* bizarre, insolite

quisling ['kwɪzlɪŋ] *n* collaborateur(trice) *m,f*

quit [kwɪt] **1** *vt (pt & pp* **quit)** *(person, place)* quitter; *Comptr (programme)* sortir de; **to q. one's job** démissionner; **to q. doing sth** arrêter de faire qch; **q. it!** arrête!
2 *vi (give up)* abandonner; *(resign)* démissionner; *Comptr* sortir; **I quit!** j'abandonne!
3 *adj* **to be q. of** être débarrassé(e) de

quite [kwaɪt] *adv* **(a)** *(entirely)* tout à fait; **q. enough** bien assez, that's **q. enough of that!** ça suffit comme ça!; **q. apart from the fact that...** mis à part le fait que...; **q.!**

tout à fait!; **that's q. all right** *(it doesn't matter)* ça n'a pas d'importance du tout; *(you're welcome)* mais pas du tout!; **you know q. well what I mean!** vous savez parfaitement ce que je veux dire!; **I q. understand** je comprends parfaitement **(b)** *(fairly)* assez, plutôt; **I q. like him** il me plaît bien; **q. a lot of people** pas mal de monde **(c)** *(for emphasis)* **it was q. a surprise** ça a été une véritable surprise; **it's been q. a day!** quelle journée!; **that film is q. something** ce film, c'est vraiment quelque chose!

quits [kwɪts] *adj* **to be q. (with sb)** être quitte (envers qn); **let's call it q.** restons-en là

quiver[1] ['kwɪvə(r)] *n (for arrows)* carquois *m*

quiver[2] **1** *n (tremble)* tremblement *m* **2** *vi (tremble)* trembler **(with** de); *(of flame)* vaciller

quivering ['kwɪvərɪŋ] *adj* tremblant(e)

quixotic [kwɪk'sɒtɪk] *adj* chimérique

quiz [kwɪz] **1** *n (pl* **quizzes) (a)** *(on TV)* jeu *m* télévisé; *(on radio)* jeu radiophonique; *(in magazine)* questionnaire *m*; **q. show** jeu télévisé/radiophonique **(b)** *(at school)* interrogation *f* écrite **2** *vt (pt & pp* **quizzed)** interroger

quizzical ['kwɪzɪkəl] *adj (look, air)* interrogateur(trice)

quorum ['kwɔːrəm] *n* quorum *m*

quota ['kwəʊtə] *n (share)* quota *m*

quotation [kwəʊ'teɪʃən] *n* **(a)** *(from author)* citation *f*; **q. marks** guillemets *mpl* **(b)** *Com (for work)* devis *m*

quote [kwəʊt] **1** *n Fam* **(a)** *(from author)* citation *f*; **in quotes** *(in quotation marks)* entre guillemets **(b)** *Com (for work)* devis *m* **2** *vt (author, passage)* citer; **she was quoted as saying that...** elle aurait dit que... **(b)** *Com (price)* indiquer; *Fin* **quoted company** société *f* cotée en Bourse

quotient ['kwəʊʃənt] *n Math* quotient *m*

R, r [ɑ:(r)] *n (letter)* R, r *m inv*; *Fam* **the three R's** = la lecture, l'écriture et l'arithmétique, fondements de l'enseignement primaire

R *Am Pol (abbr* **Republican)** républicain(e)

RA [ɑ:'reɪ] *n Br (abbr* **Royal Academy)** = académie royale des beaux-arts

rabbi ['ræbaɪ] *n* rabbin *m*

rabbit ['ræbɪt] *n* lapin *m*; **r. hole** terrier *m*; **r. hutch** clapier *m*

▸ **rabbit on** *vi Br Fam* ne pas cesser de parler

rabble ['ræbəl] *n* foule *f* bruyante; **r. rouser** agitateur(trice) *m,f*

rabid ['ræbɪd] *adj (animal)* & *Fig (person)* enragé(e); *(prejudice)* profondément enraciné(e)

rabies ['reɪbi:z] *n* rage *f*

RAC [ɑ:reɪ'si:] *n Aut (abbr* **Royal Automobile Club)** = club automobile britannique offrant notamment des services de dépannage

raccoon [rə'ku:n] *n* raton *m* laveur

race¹ [reɪs] **1** *n (contest)* course *f*; *Fig* **a r. against time** une course contre la montre; **the races** *(horseraces)* les courses; **r. meeting** *(for horseraces)* courses *fpl* de chevaux

2 *vt* **(a)** *(person)* faire la course avec; **I'll r. you home!** on fait la course jusqu'à la maison! **(b)** *(horse)* faire courir

3 *vi* **(a)** *(of athlete, horse)* courir **(b)** *(move quickly)* aller à toute vitesse; **to r. in/out** entrer/sortir à toute vitesse; **to r. down the street** dévaler la rue à toute vitesse; **to r. by** *(of time)* passer vite, filer **(c)** *(of engine)* s'emballer; *(of pulse, heart)* battre la chamade

race² *n (of people, animals)* race *f*; **the human r.** la race humaine; **r. relations** relations *fpl* interraciales

racecourse ['reɪskɔ:s] *n* champ *m* de courses

racehorse ['reɪshɔ:s] *n* cheval *m* de course

racer ['reɪsə(r)] *n (person)* coureur(euse) *m,f*; *(bicycle)* vélo *m* de course

racetrack ['reɪstræk] *n (for athletes, cars)* piste *f*; *Am (for horses)* champ *m* de courses

racial ['reɪʃəl] *adj* racial(e); **r. discrimination** discrimination *f* raciale

racing ['reɪsɪŋ] **1** *n* les courses *fpl*
2 *adj* **r. bike/car** vélo *m*/voiture *f* de course

racism ['reɪsɪzəm] *n* racisme *m*

racist ['reɪsɪst] *n & adj* raciste *mf*

rack [ræk] **1** *n* **(a)** *(for bottles)* casier *m*; *(for plates)* égouttoir *m*; *(for goods in shop)* présentoir *m*; *(for luggage)* porte-bagages *m inv* **(b)** *(for torture)* chevalet *m*; *Fig* **to be on the r.** avoir des ennuis **(c)** *(idioms)* **to go to r. and ruin** aller de mal en pis

2 *vt (torment)* tourmenter; **to be racked with guilt** être rongé(e) par le remords; **to be racked with pain** être tenaillé(e) par la douleur; **to r. one's brains** se creuser la tête

racket¹ ['rækɪt] *n (for tennis)* raquette *f*

racket² *n Fam* **(a)** *(noise)* vacarme *m*, tapage *m*; **to make a r.** faire du vacarme *ou* tapage **(b)** *(criminal activity)* racket *m*

racketeer [rækɪ'tɪə(r)] *n* racketteur *m*

racketeering [rækɪ'tɪərɪŋ] *n* racket *m*

racquet ['rækɪt] *n (for tennis)* raquette *f*

racy ['reɪsɪ] *adj (risqué)* osé(e); *(lively)* savoureux(euse), piquant(e)

RADA ['rɑ:də] *n Br (abbr* **Royal Academy of Dramatic Art)** ≃ le Conservatoire national d'art dramatique

radar ['reɪdɑ:(r)] *n* radar *m*; **r. operator** radariste *mf*; **r. screen** écran *m* radar

radial ['reɪdɪəl] **1** *n (tyre)* pneu *m* radial
2 *adj* radial(e)

radiance ['reɪdɪəns] *n* éclat *m*, rayonnement *m*

radiant ['reɪdɪənt] *adj (light)* éclatant(e); *(person)* resplendissant(e)

radiate ['reɪdɪeɪt] **1** *vt (heat, light)* émettre; *Fig (happiness, health)* être rayonnant(e) de; *Fig (optimism, enthusiasm)* être débordant(e) de
2 *vi* rayonner **(from** à partir de)

radiation [reɪdɪ'eɪʃən] *n* radiation *f*

radiator ['reɪdɪeɪtə(r)] *n (heater)* radiateur *m*

radical ['rædɪkəl] *n & adj* radical(e) *m,f*

radicalism ['rædɪkəlɪzəm] *n* radicalisme *m*

radio ['reɪdɪəʊ] **1** *n (pl* **radios)** radio *f*; **r. cassette (recorder** *or* **player)** radiocassette *m*; **r. station** station *f* de radio
2 *vt (pt & pp* **radioed)** *(information)* communiquer par radio; *(person)* contacter par radio
3 *vi* **to r. for help** demander de l'aide par radio

radioactive [reɪdɪəʊ'æktɪv] *adj* radioactif(ive); **r. waste** déchets *mpl* radioactifs

radioactivity [reɪdɪəʊæk'tɪvɪtɪ] *n* radioactivité *f*

radio-controlled [reɪdɪəʊkən'trəʊld] *adj* télécommandé(e)

radiographer [reɪdɪ'ɒgrəfə(r)] *n* radiologue *mf*

radiography [reɪdɪ'ɒgrəfɪ] *n* radiographie *f*

radiologist [reɪdɪ'ɒlədʒɪst] *n* radiologue *mf*

radiology [reɪdɪ'ɒlədʒɪ] *n* radiologie *f*

radiotherapy [reɪdɪəʊ'θerəpɪ] *n* radiothérapie *f*

radish ['rædɪʃ] *n* radis *m*

radium ['reɪdɪəm] *n Chem* radium *m*

radius ['reɪdɪəs] (*pl* **radii** ['reɪdɪaɪ]) *n* rayon *m*; **within a r.** of dans un rayon de

radon ['reɪdɒn] *n Chem* radon *m*

RAF [ɑːreɪ'ef] *n Mil* (*abbr* **Royal Air Force**) = armée de l'air britannique

raffia ['ræfɪə] *n* raphia *m*

raffish ['ræfɪʃ] *adj* canaille

raffle ['ræfəl] **1** *n* tombola *f*; **r. ticket** billet *m* de tombola **2** *vt* donner comme lot à une tombola

raft [rɑːft] *n* radeau *m*

rafter ['rɑːftə(r)] *n* chevron *m*

rag[1] [ræg] *n* (**a**) (*piece of cloth*) chiffon *m*; **rags** (*clothes*) haillons *mpl*, guenilles *fpl*; **hers is a rags to riches story** elle est partie de rien; **r. doll** poupée *f* de chiffon; *Fam* **the r. trade** la confection (**b**) *Fam Pej* (*newspaper*) torchon *m*

rag[2] **1** *n Old-fashioned* (*prank*) farce *f*, canular *m*; *Br Univ* **r. week** = semaine de divertissements organisés par les étudiants au profit d'œuvres de charité **2** *vt* (*pt & pp* **ragged**) *Old-fashioned* (*tease*) taquiner

ragamuffin ['rægəmʌfɪn] *n* polisson(onne) *m,f*

rag-and-bone man [rægən'bəʊnmæn] *n* chiffonnier *m*

ragbag ['rægbæg] *n* ramassis *m*

rage [reɪdʒ] **1** *n* (**a**) (*fury*) rage *f*, fureur *f*; **to be in a r.** être furieux(euse) (**b**) *Fam* (*fashion*) **to be all the r.** faire fureur **2** *vi* (**a**) (*of person*) être furieux(euse) (**against** *or* **at** contre) (**b**) (*of sea*) être démonté(e); (*of epidemic, war*) faire rage

ragged ['rægɪd] *adj* (*clothes*) en haillons, en lambeaux; (*edge*) irrégulier(ère); (*person*) en haillons; *Fam* **to run oneself r.** s'épuiser

raging ['reɪdʒɪŋ] *adj* (**a**) (*person*) furieux(euse); **to be in a r. temper** être furieux (**b**) (*sea*) démonté(e), (*fever, headache*) violent(e); (*thirst*) terrible

ragwort ['rægwɔːt] *n* séneçon *m*

raid [reɪd] **1** *n* (*on bank*) hold-up *m inv*; (*by army*) raid *m*; (*by police*) descente *f* **2** *vt* (*of robbers*) attaquer; (*of army*) faire un raid sur, (*of police*) faire une descente dans; *Fig & Hum* **to r. the fridge** faire la razzia dans le frigo

raider ['reɪdə(r)] *n* (*criminal*) voleur(euse) *m,f*

rail[1] [reɪl] *n* (**a**) (*of stairway*) rampe *f*; (*of balcony*) balustrade *f* (**b**) (*train system*) chemin *m* de fer; (*track*) rail *m*; **by r.** par le ou en chemin de fer; *Fig* **to go off the rails** (*of person*) s'écarter du droit chemin; **r. network** réseau *m* ferroviaire; **r. strike** grève *f* des chemins de fer *ou* des cheminots

rail[2] *vi* **to r. at** *or* **against sth** s'insurger contre qch

railcar ['reɪlkɑː(r)] *n Am* wagon *m*

railcard ['reɪlkɑːd] *n* carte *f* d'abonnement de train; *Br* **young person's r.** ≃ carte Jeunes

railings ['reɪlɪŋz] *npl* grille *f*

railroad ['reɪlrəʊd] **1** *n Am* (*system*) chemin *m* de fer; (*track*) voie *f* ferrée **2** *vt Fam* **to r. sb into doing sth** forcer qn à faire qch

railway ['reɪlweɪ] *n Br* (*system*) chemin *m* de fer; (*track*) voie *f* ferrée; **r. carriage** voiture *f*; **r. line** ligne *f* de chemin de fer; **r. station** gare *f*

railwayman ['reɪlweɪmən] *n* cheminot *m*

rain [reɪn] **1** *n* pluie *f*; **in the r.** sous la pluie; **it looks like r.** on dirait qu'il va pleuvoir; **the rains** la saison des pluies; **come r. or shine** (*whatever the weather*) qu'il pleuve ou qu'il vente; (*whatever the circumstances*) quoi qu'il arrive; **r. cloud** nuage *m* de pluie; **r. dance** danse *f* de la pluie **2** *vt* **to r. gifts on sb** couvrir qn de cadeaux; **to r. blows** **3** *vi* pleuvoir; **it's raining** il pleut; *Br Fam* **it's raining cats**

and dogs il pleut des cordes; *Prov* **it never rains but it pours** un malheur n'arrive jamais seul

rainbow ['reɪnbəʊ] *n* arc-en-ciel *m*; **r. coalition** coalition *f* des minorités; **r. trout** truite *f* arc-en-ciel

raincoat ['reɪnkəʊt] *n* imperméable *m*

raindrop ['reɪndrɒp] *n* goutte *f* de pluie

rainfall ['reɪnfɔːl] *n* précipitations *fpl*

rainforest ['reɪnfɒrɪst] *n* forêt *f* tropicale humide

rainproof ['reɪnpruːf] *adj* imperméable

rainstorm ['reɪnstɔːm] *n* pluie *f* torrentielle

rainwater ['reɪnwɔːtə(r)] *n* eau *f* de pluie

rainy ['reɪnɪ] *adj* pluvieux(euse); (*day*) de pluie; *Fig* **to save sth for a r. day** mettre qch de côté; **the r. season** la saison des pluies

raise [reɪz] **1** *vt* (**a**) (*lift*) lever; **to r. one's voice** élever la voix; **to r. one's glass to sb** porter son verre à ses lèvres; *Fig* **to r. one's hat to sb** tirer son chapeau à qn; *Fam Fig* **to r. the roof** faire du raffut (**b**) (*price, salary*) augmenter; (*standard*) élever; *Fig* **to r. the stakes** faire monter la mise (**c**) (*problem, subject*) soulever (**d**) (*fears, doubts*) faire naître; **to r. a smile/laugh** faire sourire/rire; **to r. sb's hopes** donner trop d'espoir à qn; **to r. the alarm** donner l'alarme; *Fam* **to r. hell** *or* **Cain** faire un foin d'enfer (**e**) (*money*) rassembler; (*for charity*) collecter (**f**) (*children, cattle*) élever, (*crops*) cultiver (**g**) (*statue*) dresser **2** *n Am* (*pay increase*) augmentation *f* (de salaire)

raisin ['reɪzən] *n* raisin *m* sec

rake [reɪk] **1** *n* (**a**) (*garden tool*) râteau *m*; **to be as thin as a r.** être maigre comme un clou (**b**) (*dissolute man*) libertin *m* **2** *vt* (*leaves, soil*) ratisser, **to r. one's memory** fouiller dans sa mémoire

▸ **rake about, rake around** *vi* (*search*) fouiller (**for** pour trouver)

▸ **rake in** *vt sep Fam* (*money*) rapporter; **she's raking it in!** elle s'en met plein les poches!

▸ **rake off** *vt sep Fam* (*money*) empocher

▸ **rake over** *vt sep* (*subject, the past*) ressasser

rakish ['reɪkɪʃ] *adj* (*dissolute*) libertin(e); (*jaunty*) désinvolte

rally ['rælɪ] **1** *n* (*pl* **rallies**) (**a**) (*protest gathering*) manifestation *f* (**b**) (*in tennis*) échange *m* (**c**) (*car race*) rallye *m*; **r. driver** pilote *m* de rallye **2** *vt* (*pt & pp* **rallied**) (*troops*) rallier; **to r. support for sb/ sth** gagner des appuis à la cause de qn/qch; **to r. sb's spirits** redonner courage à qn; **rallying cry** cri *m* de ralliement **3** *vi* (*of prices*) se redresser; (*of patient*) aller mieux; **to r. to sb's defence** se porter au secours de qn

▸ **rally round 1** *vt insep* soutenir **2** *vi* apporter son soutien

RAM [ræm] *n Comptr* (*abbr* **random access memory**) mémoire *f* vive

ram [ræm] **1** *n* (**a**) (*animal*) bélier *m* (**b**) (*implement*) (*battering*) **r.** bélier *m* **2** *vt* (*pt & pp* **rammed**) (**a**) (*crash into*) percuter; (*of ship*) aborder (**b**) (*force into place*) tasser; *Fam* **to r. one's views down sb's throat** bassiner qn avec ses opinions

Ramadan ['ræmədæn] *n Rel* le ramadan

ramble ['ræmbəl] **1** *n* (*walk*) randonnée *f* (pédestre) **2** *vi* (**a**) (*walk*) faire une randonnée (**b**) (*digress*) divaguer

▸ **ramble on** *vi* divaguer; **to r. on about sth** radoter à propos de qch

rambler ['ræmblə(r)] *n* (*walker*) randonneur(euse) *m,f*

rambling ['ræmblɪŋ] **1** *n* (**a**) (*walking*) **to go r.** aller en randonnée (**b**) **ramblings** (*words*) divagations *fpl*

2 *adj* (**a**) *(letter, speech)* décousu(e) (**b**) *(house)* plein(e) de coins et de recoins; **r. rose** rosier *m* grimpant

ramification [ræmɪfɪˈkeɪʃən] *n (consequence)* conséquence *f*

ramp [ræmp] *n* rampe *f*; *(to plane)* passerelle *f*; *(on road)* petit dos *m* d'âne

rampage 1 *n* [ˈræmpeɪdʒ] **to go on the r.** *(lose control)* se déchaîner; *(cause damage)* tout saccager **2** *vi* [ræmˈpeɪdʒ] **to r. about** se déchaîner

rampant [ˈræmpənt] *adj* endémique

rampart [ˈræmpɑːt] *n* rempart *m*

ramrod [ˈræmrɒd] *n (for rifle)* écouvillon *m*; *Fig* **r. straight** raide comme un piquet

ramshackle [ˈræmʃækəl] *adj (building)* délabré(e); *(economy, organization)* qui s'effondre

ran [ræn] *pt of* **run**

ranch [rɑːntʃ] *n* ranch *m*

rancher [ˈrɑːntʃə(r)] *n* propriétaire *mf* de ranch

rancid [ˈrænsɪd] *adj* rance; **to go r.** rancir

rancour [ˈræŋkə(r)] *n* rancœur *f*

rand [rænd] *n* rand *m*

random [ˈrændəm] **1** *n* **at r.** au hasard **2** *adj (choice, sample)* (fait(e)) au hasard; *Comptr* **r. access memory** mémoire *f* vive; **r. sampling** prélèvement *m* d'échantillons au hasard

randy [ˈrændɪ] *adj Br Fam* excité(e)

rang [ræŋ] *pt of* **ring²**

range [reɪndʒ] **1** *n* (**a**) *(of weapon, telescope)* portée *f*; **within r.** *(of fire)* à portée de tir; *(of hearing)* à portée de la voix; **out of r.** hors de portée (**b**) *(of prices, colours, products)* gamme *f*; *(of instrument, voice)* registre *m*; *(of mountains, research)* étendue *f* (**c**) *(of hills, mountains)* chaîne *f* (**d**) *(practice area)* **(shooting) r.** champ *m* de tir (**e**) *(cooker)* fourneau *m* **2** *vt* (**a**) *(arrange in row)* ranger; **to r. oneself with sb** se ranger du côté de qn; **to r. oneself against sb** s'opposer à qn (**b**) *(travel)* parcourir **3** *vi* (**a**) *(extend)* **to r. from...to** aller de...à (**b**) **to r. over** *(include)* porter sur

rangefinder [ˈreɪndʒfaɪndə(r)] *n* télémètre *m*

ranger [ˈreɪndʒə(r)] *n (in forest)* garde *m* forestier; *Am Mil* commando *m*

rangy [ˈreɪndʒɪ] *adj* élancé(e)

rank¹ [ræŋk] **1** *n* (**a**) *(status)* grade *m*; *Fig* **to pull r.** abuser de son rang (**b**) *(row)* rangée *f*; *Mil* **the ranks** les hommes *mpl* du rang; *Fig* **to rise from the ranks** sortir du rang; *Fig* **the ranks of the unemployed** les rangs des chômeurs; *Fig* **to break ranks (with)** se désolidariser (de); *Fig* **to close ranks** se montrer solidaire; **(taxi) r.** station *f* de taxis **2** *vt* placer (**among** parmi); **to r. sb/sth as** considérer qn/qch comme **3** *vi* compter (**among** parmi); **to r. as** être considéré(e) comme; **to r. above/below sb** être supérieur(e)/inférieur(e) à qn; **this ranks as a major disaster** on peut qualifier ceci de catastrophe majeure

rank² *adj* (**a**) *(foul-smelling)* fétide; *Br Fam (disgusting)* dégueulasse (**b**) *(absolute)* total(e); **she's a r. outsider** elle n'est vraiment pas dans la course

rank-and-file [ræŋkənˈfaɪl] *n* **the r.** *(in army)* les hommes *mpl* du rang; *(of political party)* la base

ranking [ˈræŋkɪŋ] *n (classification)* classement *m*

rankle [ˈræŋkəl] *vi* **it still rankles with me** cela m'est resté sur l'estomac

ransack [ˈrænsæk] *vt (house, desk)* mettre sens dessus dessous; *(shop, town)* piller

ransom [ˈrænsəm] **1** *n* rançon *f*; **to hold sb to r.** rançonner qn; *Fig* retenir qn en otage **2** *vt* rançonner

rant [rænt] *vi Fam* déblatérer (**about/at** au sujet de/ contre); **to r. and rave** tempêter (**about/at** au sujet de/ contre)

rap [ræp] **1** *n* (**a**) *(sharp blow)* coup *m* sec; *Fig* **to take the r. for sth** écoper *ou* trinquer pour qch (**b**) *(music)* rap *m* **2** *vt (pt & pp* **rapped**) *(window, door)* frapper à; *(table)* frapper sur; *Fig* **to r. sb's knuckles, to r. sb over the knuckles** taper sur les doigts de qn **3** *vi* (**a**) *(hit)* frapper (**on** à) (**b**) *(sing)* rapper

rapacious [rəˈpeɪʃəs] *adj* rapace

rape¹ [reɪp] **1** *n (crime)* viol *m*; *Fig (of countryside, environment)* destruction *f* **2** *vt* violer

rape² *n (crop)* colza *m*

rapid [ˈræpɪd] *adj* rapide; **r. reaction force** force *f* d'intervention rapide

rapidity [rəˈpɪdɪtɪ] *n* rapidité *f*

rapidly [ˈræpɪdlɪ] *adv* rapidement

rapids [ˈræpɪdz] *npl (in river)* rapides *mpl*

rapier [ˈreɪpɪə(r)] *n* rapière *f*

rapist [ˈreɪpɪst] *n* violeur *m*

rapper [ˈræpə(r)] *n (singer)* rappeur(euse) *m,f*

rapport [ræˈpɔː(r)] *n* **to have a good r. (with sb)** avoir de bons rapports (avec qn)

rapt [ræpt] *adj (attention)* profond(e); *(look)* absorbé(e); *(smile)* d'extase

rapture [ˈræptʃə(r)] *n* extase *f*; **to be in raptures** être ravi(e); **to go into raptures over sb/sth** s'extasier devant qn/sur qch

rapturous [ˈræptʃərəs] *adj (cries)* d'extase; *(applause)* frénétique; *(reception, welcome)* enthousiaste

rare [reə(r)] *adj* (**a**) *(animal, stamp)* rare; **to have a r. gift (for sth)** être exceptionnellement doué(e) (pour qch) (**b**) *(steak)* saignant(e)

rarefied [ˈreərɪfaɪd] *adj (air, gas)* raréfié(e); *Fig (atmosphere, ideas)* fermé(e)

rarely [ˈreəlɪ] *adv* rarement

raring [ˈreərɪŋ] *adj* **to be r. to do sth** être impatient(e) de faire qch; **to be r. to go** piaffer d'impatience

rarity [ˈreərɪtɪ] *n (pl* **rarities**) *n* rareté *f*; **to be/become a r.** être/devenir rare; **r. value** rareté

rascal [ˈrɑːskəl] *n (child)* coquin(e) *m,f*; *Old-fashioned or Hum (scoundrel)* vaurien(enne) *m,f*

rash¹ [ræʃ] *n* (**a**) *(on skin) (spots)* éruption *f*; *(red area)* rougeurs *fpl* (**b**) *(series)* série *f*

rash² *adj (imprudent)* irréfléchi(e)

rasher [ˈræʃə(r)] *n Br (of bacon)* tranche *f*

rashly [ˈræʃlɪ] *adv* sans réfléchir

rasp [rɑːsp] **1** *n* (**a**) *(tool)* râpe *f* (**b**) *(sound)* grincement *m* **2** *vt (say hoarsely)* grogner

raspberry [ˈrɑːzbərɪ] *n (pl* **raspberries**) *n (fruit)* framboise *f*; *(plant)* framboisier *m*; *Fam Fig* **to blow a r.** souffler en signe de dérision

rat [ræt] **1** *n* (**a**) *(animal)* rat *m*; **r. poison** mort-aux-rats *f inv*; **r. trap** piège *m* à rats, ratière *f* (**b**) *Fam (scoundrel)* dégueulasse *mf* (**c**) *(idioms)* **to smell a r.** flairer quelque chose de louche; **r. race** foire *f* d'empoigne **2** *vi (pt & pp* **ratted**) *Fam (inform)* **to r. on sb** dénoncer qn

ratchet [ˈrætʃɪt] *n* rochet *m*; **r. (wheel)** roue *f* à rochet

rate [reɪt] **1** *n* (**a**) *(of inflation, interest)* taux *m*; *Fin* **r. of return** taux de rendement (**b**) *(speed)* rythme *m*; **at this r.** à ce rythme (**c**) **at any r.** en tout cas (**d**) *(price, charge)* tarif *m* (**e**) *Br Formerly* **rates** *(local tax)* impôts *mpl* locaux **2** *vt* (**a**) *(classify)* placer (**among** parmi); **to r. sb/sth as** considérer qn/qch comme; **to r. sb/sth highly** tenir qn/qch en haute estime (**b**) *(deserve)* mériter; **to r. a mention** mériter d'être mentionné(e) **3** *vi* **to r. as** être considéré(e) comme

rateable value ['reɪtəbəl'væljuː] *n Br Formerly* valeur *f* locative nette

ratepayer ['reɪtpeɪə(r)] *n Br Formerly* contribuable *mf (pour les impôts locaux)*

rather ['rɑːðə(r)] *adv* (**a**) *(preferably)* **I'd r. stay** j'aimerais mieux rester; **I'd r. not go** j'aimerais mieux ne pas y aller; **I'd r. not** je n'y tiens pas; **r. you than me!** je n'aimerais pas être à ta place (**b**) *(more exactly)* plutôt; **he sounded surprised or, r.,** annoyed il semblait surpris, ou plutôt, fâché (**c**) *(fairly)* assez; **I r.** liked it j'ai bien aimé (**d**) **r. than him** plutôt que lui; **r. than staying** plutôt que de rester

ratification [rætɪfɪ'keɪʃən] *n* ratification *f*

ratify ['rætɪfaɪ] *(pt & pp* **ratified***)* *vt* ratifier

rating ['reɪtɪŋ] *n (of popularity)* classement *m*; **the ratings** *(for TV, radio)* l'indice *m* d'écoute, l'audimat® *m*

ratio ['reɪʃɪəʊ] *(pl* **ratios***) n* rapport *m*

ration ['ræʃən, *Am* 'reɪʃən] **1** *n* ration *f*; *Fig (dose)* dose *f*; **rations** *(supplies)* provisions *fpl*; **r. book** carte *f* de rationnement **2** *vt* rationner

rational ['ræʃənəl] *adj (sensible)* raisonnable, sensé(e); *(sane)* rationnel(elle)

rationalism ['ræʃənəlɪzəm] *n* rationalisme *m*

rationalist ['ræʃənəlɪst] *n* rationaliste *mf*

rationalization [ræʃənəlaɪ'zeɪʃən] *n (of company)* rationalisation *f*

rationalize ['ræʃənəlaɪz] *vt* (**a**) *(action, dislike)* justifier (**b**) *(company)* rationaliser

rationally ['ræʃənəlɪ] *adv (sensibly)* raisonnablement; *(sanely)* rationnellement

rationing ['ræʃənɪŋ] *n* rationnement *m*

rattle ['rætəl] **1** *n* (**a**) *(for baby)* hochet *m* (**b**) *(noise) (of train, chains, keys)* cliquetis *m*; *(of gunfire)* crépitement *m*; *(of door, window)* frottement *m* **2** *vt* (**a**) *(chains, keys)* faire cliqueter; *(door, window)* faire vibrer (**b**) *Fam (make nervous)* démonter **3** *vi (of chains, keys)* cliqueter; *(of door, window)* vibrer

▸ **rattle off** *vt sep Fam (list, facts)* débiter

▸ **rattle on** *vi Fam* parler sans cesse

▸ **rattle through** *vt insep Fam (work, book)* expédier

rattlesnake ['rætəlsneɪk] *n* serpent *m* à sonnette

ratty ['rætɪ] *adj Br Fam (annoyed)* irrité(e); *(irritable)* irritable

raucous ['rɔːkəs] *adj (hoarse)* rauque; *(rowdy)* bruyant(e)

raunchy ['rɔːntʃɪ] *adj Fam (film, scene, lyrics)* osé(e); *(dress)* provocant(e)

ravage ['rævɪdʒ] **1** *npl* **ravages** ravages *mpl* **2** *vt* ravager

rave [reɪv] **1** *n* rave *f* **2** *adj (review)* dithyrambique **3** *vi (deliriously)* délirer; **to r. about sb/sth** *(enthusiastically)* être dithyrambique à propos de qn/qch

raven ['reɪvən] **1** *n (bird)* grand corbeau *m* **2** *adj (colour)* noir de jais *inv*

ravenous ['rævənəs] *adj (animal)* vorace; *(person)* affamé(e)

raver ['reɪvə(r)] *n Br Fam (socially active person)* noceur(euse) *m, f*; *(who goes to raves)* raver *mf*

rave-up ['reɪvʌp] *n Br Fam* fiesta *f*, nouba *f*

ravine [rə'viːn] *n* ravin *m*

raving ['reɪvɪŋ] *adj* (**a**) *(delirious)* **r. mad** complètement fou (folle); **a r. lunatic** un fou furieux (une folle furieuse) (**b**) *(success)* éclatant(e)

ravish ['rævɪʃ] *vt* (**a**) *Lit (delight)* enchanter, ravir (**b**) *Old-fashioned (rape)* violenter

ravishing ['rævɪʃɪŋ] *adj* magnifique

raw [rɔː] *adj* (**a**) *(food)* cru(e); *(silk, sugar, statistics)* brut(e); **r. materials** *fpl* premières; **r. recruit** bleu *m* (**b**) *(skin)* écorché(e); *Fig* **to get a r. deal** être mal traité(e); *Fig* **to touch a r. nerve** toucher un point sensible (**c**) *(weather, wind)* glacial(e)

ray[1] [reɪ] *n (of light, sun)* rayon *m*; *Fig (of hope)* lueur *f*

ray[2] *n (fish)* raie *f*

rayon ['reɪɒn] *n (fabric)* rayonne *f*

raze [reɪz] *vt* **to r. sth to the ground** raser qch

razor ['reɪzə(r)] *n* rasoir *m*; **r. blade** lame *f* de rasoir

razor-sharp ['reɪzəʃɑːp] *adj (knife)* effilé(e); *Fig (intelligence, wit)* vif (vive)

razor-shell ['reɪzəʃel] *n* couteau *m*

razzmatazz ['ræzmətæz] *n Fam* tape-à-l'œil *m inv*

RC [ɑː'siː] *n & adj (abbr* **Roman Catholic***)* catholique *mf*

R & D [ɑːrən'diː] *n Com (abbr* **research and development***)* recherche et développement

Rd *(abbr* **Road***)* rue

RDA [ɑːdiː'eɪ] *n (abbr* **recommended daily allowance***)* recommandation *f* quotidienne officielle *(en vitamines, sels minéraux etc)*

RE [ɑː'riː] *n Br (abbr* **Religious Education***)* instruction *f* religieuse

re[1] [riː] *prep* concernant; **re your letter** suite à votre lettre; **re: 2003 sales figures** Réf: les ventes de 2003

re[2] [reɪ] *n Mus* ré *m*

reach [riːtʃ] **1** *n* (**a**) *(accessibility)* portée *f*; **within r.** *(thing)* à portée de main; *(location)* tout(e) proche; **out of r.** hors de portée (**b**) *(of river)* **the upper reaches** l'amont *m* **2** *vt* (**a**) *(destination, conclusion)* atteindre, arriver à; *(agreement)* aboutir à; *(decision)* prendre; **the news didn't r. her** les nouvelles ne lui sont pas parvenues (**b**) *(contact)* joindre; **to r. a wider audience** toucher un public plus important (**c**) *(stretch as far as) (one's shoulder, waist)* atteindre, arriver jusqu'à **3** *vi (extend) (of forest, property)* s'étendre (**to** jusqu'à); *(of noise, voice)* porter (**to** jusqu'à); **to r. for sth** tendre le bras pour prendre qch; *Fig* **to r. for the sky** *or* **the stars** viser très haut

▸ **reach out** *vi* tendre le bras

reachable ['riːtʃəbəl] *adj* accessible

react [rɪ'ækt] *vi* réagir (**against/to** contre/à)

reaction [rɪ'ækʃən] *n* réaction *f*

reactionary [rɪ'ækʃənərɪ] *(pl* **reactionaries***) n & adj* réactionnaire *mf*

reactivate [rɪ'æktɪveɪt] *vt* réactiver

reactor [rɪ'æktə(r)] *n* réacteur *m*

read [riːd] **1** *n* **to have a r. (of sth)** lire (qch); **to be a good r.** être agréable à lire **2** *vt (pt & pp* **read** [red]*)* (**a**) *(book, newspaper, letter)* lire; **do you r. me?** *(on radio)* est-ce que vous me recevez?; *Fig* **to take it as read that...** considérer comme acquis que... (**b**) *(interpret)* interpréter; **to r. sb's mind** lire dans les pensées de qn; **to r. the future** prédire l'avenir (**c**) *Br Univ (study)* étudier (**d**) *(of dial, thermometer)* indiquer; *(of inscription)* être; **the sign read...** sur l'écriteau, on pouvait lire... **3** *vi* (**a**) *(of person)* lire; **to r. aloud** lire à haute voix; *Fig* **to r.**

between the lines lire entre les lignes **(b)** *(of text)* **to r. well/badly** se lire facilement/difficilement
▸ **read out** *vt sep* lire (à haute voix)
▸ **read up on** *vt sep* étudier
readable ['ri:dəbəl] *adj (book)* facile à lire ; *(handwriting)* lisible
reader ['ri:də(r)] *n* **(a)** *(person)* lecteur(trice) *m,f* **(b)** *(reading book)* livre *m* de lecture **(c)** *(device)* lecteur *m*
readily ['redɪlɪ] *adv (willingly)* volontiers ; *(easily)* facilement
reading ['ri:dɪŋ] *n* **(a)** *(action, interpretation, pastime)* lecture *f* ; **r. glasses** lunettes *fpl* de lecture ; **r. list** *(syllabus)* liste *f* des ouvrages au programme ; *(for further study)* liste des ouvrages recommandés ; **r. room** salle *f* de lecture **(b)** *(measurement)* relevé *m*
readjust [ri:ə'dʒʌst] **1** *vt (figures, salaries)* réajuster ; *(instrument)* remettre au point ; *(clothing)* rajuster
2 *vi* se réadapter **(to** à)
readjustment [ri:ə'dʒʌstmənt] *n (of figures, salaries)* réajustement *m* ; *(of person)* réadaptation *f*
readmit [ri:əd'mɪt] *(pt & pp* **readmitted)** *vt (to club, party)* réintégrer **(to** à) ; **to r. sb (to hospital)** réhospitaliser qn
read-only memory ['ri:d'əʊnlɪ'memərɪ] *n* Comptr mémoire *f* morte
readvertise [ri:'ædvətaɪz] *vt* repasser une annonce pour
ready ['redɪ] **1** *adj* **(a)** *(prepared)* prêt(e) **(for** pour) ; **to be r. to do sth** être prêt à faire qch ; **to get r.** se préparer ; **to get sth r.** préparer qch ; **to be r. for bed** être prêt à se coucher ; Br **r.!, steady!, go!,** Am **r.!, set!, go!** à vos marques, prêts, partez! ; **r. cash** argent *m* liquide ; **r. meal** plat *m* préparé **(b)** Br *(willing)* **to be r. to do sth** être prêt(e) ou disposé(e) à faire qch **(c)** *(quick)* **to have a r. wit** avoir l'esprit vif
2 *vt (pt & pp* **readied)** *(prepare)* préparer
3 *n* **(a)** **at the r.** prêt(e) **(b)** Br Fam **readies** *(cash)* ronds *mpl*
ready-made [redɪ'meɪd] *adj (food)* tout(e) préparé(e) ; *(excuse, phrase)* tout(e) fait(e)
reaffirm [ri:ə'fɜ:m] *vt* réaffirmer
reafforestation [ri:əfɒrɪ'steɪʃən] *n* reboisement *m*
real [rɪəl] **1** *adj* **(a)** *(authentic)* vrai(e) ; *(gold, leather)* véritable ; *(danger, fear, effort)* réel(elle) ; **r. ale** *(o* bière brune de fabrication traditionnelle **(b)** *(actual)* réel(elle) ; **the r. world** la réalité ; **what does that mean in r. terms?** qu'est-ce que cela signifie en clair? ; Com **r. estate** *(property)* biens *mpl* immobiliers ; *(profession)* l'immobilier *m* **(c)** *(for emphasis)* **a r. idiot** un véritable idiot
2 *adv* Am Fam *(very)* très
realism ['rɪəlɪzəm] *n* réalisme *m*
realist ['rɪəlɪst] *n* réaliste *mf*
realistic [rɪə'lɪstɪk] *adj* réaliste
reality [rɪ'ælɪtɪ] *(pl* **realities)** *n* réalité *f* ; **in r.** en réalité ; **r. TV** télé *f* réalité
realize ['rɪəlaɪz] *vt* **(a)** *(become aware of)* se rendre compte de ; **I r. he's busy, but...** j'ai bien conscience qu'il est occupé mais... **(b)** *(ambition, dream)* réaliser
really ['rɪəlɪ] *adv* vraiment ; *(in actual fact)* en réalité
realm [relm] *n* **(a)** *(kingdom)* royaume *m* **(b)** *(field)* domaine *m*
realtor ['rɪəltə(r)] *n* Am agent *m* immobilier
ream [ri:m] *n (of paper)* rame *f* ; Fig **reams of** des quantités de
reanimate [ri:'ænɪmeɪt] *vt* r(é)animer
reap [ri:p] *vt* moissonner ; **to r. the benefits (of)** récolter les bénéfices (de)
reaper ['ri:pə(r)] *n (machine)* moissonneuse *f*

reappear [ri:ə'pɪə(r)] *vi* réapparaître
reappearance [ri:ə'pɪərəns] *n* réapparition *f*
reapply [ri:ə'plaɪ] *(pt & pp* **reapplied)** *vi (for job)* poser à nouveau sa candidature **(for** à)
reappraise [ri:ə'preɪz] *vt* réévaluer ; *(policy)* réexaminer
rear¹ [rɪə(r)] *n* **(a)** *(back part)* arrière *m* ; **at the r. of** *(inside)* à l'arrière de ; *(behind)* derrière ; **in the r.** à l'arrière ; **to bring up the r.** être en queue ; **r. admiral** contre-amiral *m* ; **r. entrance** entrée *f* de derrière ; **r. legs** pattes *fpl* de derrière ; **r. lights** feux *mpl* arrière ; **r. window** vitre *f* arrière **(b)** Fam *(buttocks)* derrière *m*
rear² *vt* **(a)** *(child, livestock)* élever **(b)** *(one's head)* relever ; Fig **to r. its ugly head** faire son apparition
▸ **rear up** *vi (of horse)* se cabrer
rearguard ['rɪəgɑ:d] *n* Mil arrière-garde *f* ; also Fig **r. action** combat *m* d'arrière-garde
rearm [ri:'ɑ:m] *vt & vi* réarmer
rearmament [ri:'ɑ:məmənt] *n* réarmement *m*
rearrange [ri:ə'reɪndʒ] *vt (books, furniture)* changer la disposition de ; *(appointment)* changer
reason ['ri:zən] *n* **(a)** *(cause, motive)* raison *f* **(for** de) ; **for no particular r.** sans raison précise ; **I don't know the r. why** je ne sais pas pourquoi ; Ironic **for reasons best known to himself** pour une raison connue de lui seul ; **give me one good r. why I should!** donne-moi une raison valable de le faire! **(b)** *(sanity, common sense)* raison *f* ; **to listen to** or **see r.** entendre raison ; **it stands to r.** il va de soi ou sans dire ; **within r.** dans des limites raisonnables
2 *vt* **to r. that** estimer que
3 *vi* raisonner **(about/with** sur/avec)
reasonable ['ri:zənəbəl] *adj* **(a)** *(fair)* raisonnable ; *(excuse)* valable **(b)** *(quite good)* passable
reasonably ['ri:zənəblɪ] *adv* **(a)** *(behave, act)* raisonnablement **(b)** *(quite)* plutôt
reasoning ['ri:zənɪŋ] *n (thinking)* raisonnement *m*
reassemble [ri:ə'sembəl] **1** *vt (people)* rassembler ; *(machine)* remonter
2 *vi (of people)* se rassembler
reassess [ri:ə'ses] *vt* **(a)** *(policy, situation)* reconsidérer **(b)** Fin *(tax, property)* réévaluer
reassurance [ri:ə'ʃʊərəns] *n (comfort)* réconfort *m* ; *(guarantee)* assurance *f*
reassure [ri:ə'ʃʊə(r)] *vt* rassurer
reassuring [ri:ə'ʃʊərɪŋ] *adj* rassurant(e)
reawaken [ri:ə'weɪkən] **1** *vt (interest, feeling)* faire renaître
2 *vi (of person)* se réveiller à nouveau
rebate ['ri:beɪt] *n (refund)* remboursement *m* ; *(discount)* rabais *m*
rebel 1 *n* ['rebəl] rebelle *mf*
2 *vi* [rɪ'bel] *(pt & pp* **rebelled)** se rebeller **(against** contre)
rebellion [rɪ'beljən] *n* rébellion *f*
rebellious [rɪ'beljəs] *adj* rebelle
rebirth [ri:'bɜ:θ] *n* renaissance *f*
reborn [ri:'bɔ:n] *adj* **to be r.** renaître
rebound 1 *n* ['ri:baʊnd] *(of ball)* rebond *m* ; Fig **she's dating him on the r.** elle sort avec lui à la suite d'une déception sentimentale
2 *vi* [rɪ'baʊnd] *(of ball)* rebondir ; Fig *(of joke, lie)* se retourner (on contre)
rebuff [rɪ'bʌf] **1** *n (of person)* rebuffade *f* ; *(of suggestion)* refus *m* ; **to meet with a r.** *(of person)* essuyer une rebuffade ; *(of suggestion)* être repoussé(e)
2 *vt* repousser
rebuild [ri:'bɪld] *(pt & pp* **rebuilt** [ri:'bɪlt]*)* *vt* reconstruire

rebuke [rɪ'bjuːk] **1** *n* réprimande *f*
2 *vt* réprimander
rebut [rɪ'bʌt] *(pt & pp* **rebutted)** *vt* réfuter
rebuttal [rɪ'bʌtəl] *n* réfutation *f*
recalcitrant [rɪ'kælsɪtrənt] *adj* récalcitrant(e)
recall 1 *n* [rɪ'kɔːl] *(memory)* mémoire *f*; **lost beyond r.** irrévocablement perdu(e)
2 *vt* [rɪ'kɔːl] **(a)** *(remember)* se souvenir de, se rappeler; **to r. doing sth** se souvenir d'avoir fait qch, se rappeler avoir fait qch **(b)** *(defective goods)* rappeler; *(library book)* demander le retour de; *Br Pol* **to r. Parliament** rappeler le Parlement en session extraordinaire
recant [rɪ'kænt] **1** *vt (opinion)* rétracter
2 *vi* se rétracter
recap ['riːkæp] **1** *n (summary)* récapitulation *f*
2 *vi (pt & pp* **recapped)** récapituler
recapitulate [riːkə'pɪtjʊleɪt] *vt & vi* récapituler
recapture [riː'kæptʃə(r)] **1** *n (of criminal)* capture *f*; *(of town, territory)* reprise *f*
2 *vt* **(a)** *(criminal)* capturer; *(town, territory)* reprendre **(b)** *Fig (memory, atmosphere)* faire revivre; *(one's youth)* retrouver
recede [rɪ'siːd] *vi (of tide)* se retirer; *(of coastline)* reculer; **to have a receding chin** avoir le menton fuyant; **to have a receding hairline** avoir le front qui se dégarnit
receipt [rɪ'siːt] *n* **(a)** *(act of receiving)* réception *f*; **to be in r. of sth** avoir reçu qch **(b)** *(proof of payment)* reçu *m*; **receipts** *(at box office)* recette *f*, entrées *fpl*
receive [rɪ'siːv] *vt* recevoir; *(stolen goods)* receler; **to be well/badly received** *(of film, proposal)* être bien/mal reçu(e); **to r. sb into the Church** admettre qn au sein de l'Église
received [rɪ'siːvd] *adj (idea)* reçu(e); *(opinion)* admis(e); **r. pronunciation** la prononciation standard de l'anglais *(celle du sud-est de l'Angleterre)*
receiver [rɪ'siːvə(r)] *n* **(a)** *(of stolen goods)* receleur(euse) *m,f* **(b)** *(of telephone, radio set)* récepteur *m*; **to pick up the r.** décrocher; **to replace the r.** raccrocher **(c)** *Fin* administrateur *m* judiciaire
receivership [rɪ'siːvəʃɪp] *n Fin* **to go into r.** être placé(e) sous règlement judiciaire
receiving [rɪ'siːvɪŋ] **1** *n (of stolen goods)* recel *m*
2 *adj Fam* **to be on the r. end (of sth)** faire les frais (de qch)
recent ['riːsənt] *adj* récent(e); *(acquaintance)* nouveau(elle); *(development)* dernier(ère); **in r. months** au cours des derniers mois; **in r. times** récemment
recently ['riːsəntlɪ] *adv* récemment; **as r. as yesterday** pas plus tard qu'hier; **until quite r.** jusqu'à ces derniers temps
receptacle [rɪ'septəkəl] *n* récipient *m*
reception [rɪ'sepʃən] *n* **(a)** *(of guests, announcement, book)* accueil *m*; **to get a warm r.** être accueilli(e) chaleureusement; **r. centre** *(for refugees)* centre *m* d'accueil **(b)** *(party)* réception *f*; **(wedding) r.** réception **(c)** *(in hotel)* **r. (desk)** réception *f* **(d)** *(of radio, TV programme)* réception *f*
receptionist [rɪ'sepʃənɪst] *n* réceptionniste *mf*
receptive [rɪ'septɪv] *adj* réceptif(ive)
recess ['riːses] *n* **(a)** *(of law courts, Parliament)* vacances *fpl* **(b)** *(in wall)* renfoncement *m*; *(smaller)* niche *f*; *(of mind, past)* recoins *mpl* **(c)** *Am Sch (between classes)* récréation *f*
recession [rɪ'seʃən] *n* récession *f*
recharge [riː'tʃɑːdʒ] *vt (battery)* recharger; *Fig* **to r. one's batteries** recharger ses batteries

rechargeable [riː'tʃɑːdʒəbəl] *adj* rechargeable
recidivism [rɪ'sɪdɪvɪzəm] *n Law* récidivisme *m*
recipe ['resɪpɪ] *n also Fig* recette *f*; **a r. for success** le secret de la réussite; **to be a r. for disaster** mener à la catastrophe; **r. book** livre *m* de recettes
recipient [rɪ'sɪpɪənt] *n (of gift, letter)* destinataire *mf*; *(of cheque, money)* bénéficiaire *mf*; *(of award, honour)* lauréat(e) *m,f*
reciprocal [rɪ'sɪprəkəl] *adj* réciproque
reciprocate [rɪ'sɪprəkeɪt] *vt* **1** retourner
2 *vi* rendre la pareille
recital [rɪ'saɪtəl] *n (of poetry, music)* récital *m*
recitation [resɪ'teɪʃən] *n (of poem)* récitation *f*
recite [rɪ'saɪt] **1** *vt (poem)* réciter; *(complaints, details)* énumérer
2 *vi* réciter
reckless ['reklɪs] *adj* imprudent(e); **r. driver** chauffard *m*
reckon ['rekən] **1** *vt* **(a)** *(consider)* considérer; **she is reckoned to be...** on la considère comme... **(b)** *(calculate)* calculer **(c)** *Fam (think)* penser
2 *vi* compter, calculer
▸ **reckon on** *vt insep* compter sur
▸ **reckon up** *vt sep* calculer
▸ **reckon with** *vt insep* compter avec
reckoning ['rekənɪŋ] *n* estimation *f*; **by my r.** d'après mes calculs; **day of r.** moment *m* de vérité
reclaim [rɪ'kleɪm] *vt (lost property, waste materials)* récupérer; *(expenses)* se faire rembourser; **to r. land from the sea/the desert** gagner du terrain sur la mer/le désert
reclamation [reklə'meɪʃən] *n (of waste materials)* récupération *f*
recline [rɪ'klaɪn] *vi* s'allonger
reclining [rɪ'klaɪnɪŋ] *adj* **in a r. position** *(person)* en position allongée; **r. seat** siège *m* à dossier inclinable
recluse [rɪ'kluːs] *n* reclus(e) *m,f*
recognition [rekəg'nɪʃən] *n (act) also Fig* to have changed beyond or out of all r. être devenu(e) méconnaissable; **in r. of** en reconnaissance de
recognizable [rekəg'naɪzəbəl] *adj* reconnaissable
recognize ['rekəgnaɪz] *vt* reconnaître
recognized ['rekəgnaɪzd] *adj* reconnu(e); **to be a r. authority (on sth)** faire autorité (en matière de qch)
recoil 1 *n* ['riːkɔɪl] *(of gun)* recul *m*
2 *vi* [rɪ'kɔɪl] *(of gun)* reculer; *(of person)* avoir un mouvement de recul
recollect [rekə'lekt] *vt* se souvenir de
recollection [rekə'lekʃən] *n* souvenir *m*; **to the best of my r.** autant que je m'en souvienne
recommend [rekə'mend] *vt* **(a)** *(praise)* recommander; **to r. sth to sb** recommander qch à qn; **the proposal has a lot to r. it** cette proposition présente de nombreux avantages **(b)** *(advise)* recommander, conseiller; **to r. sb to do sth** conseiller à qn de faire qch; *Com* **recommended retail price** prix *m* conseillé
recommendation [rekəmen'deɪʃən] *n* recommandation *f*
recompense ['rekəmpens] **1** *n* dédommagement *m*; **in r. for** en dédommagement de
2 *vt* dédommager
reconcile ['rekənsaɪl] *vt* **(a)** *(person)* réconcilier; **to be reconciled with sb** s'être réconcilié(e) avec qn; **to become reconciled to sth** se résigner à qch **(b)** *(facts, differences, opinions)* concilier
reconciliation [rekənsɪlɪ'eɪʃən] *n* réconciliation *f*

reconditioned [riːkən'dɪʃənd] *adj (TV, washing machine)* remis(e) à neuf

reconnaissance [rɪ'kɒnɪsəns] *n Mil* reconnaissance *f; r.* flight/mission vol *m*/mission *f* de reconnaissance

reconquer [riː'kɒŋkə(r)] *vt* reconquérir

reconquest [riː'kɒŋkwest] *n* reconquête *f*

reconsider [riːkən'sɪdə(r)] **1** *vt* réexaminer **2** *vi* réfléchir

reconstitute [riː'kɒnstɪtjuːt] *vt* reconstituer

reconstruct [riːkən'strʌkt] *vt* reconstruire; *(crime, event)* reconstituer

reconstruction [riːkən'strʌkʃən] *n* reconstruction *f; (of crime, event)* reconstitution *f*

record 1 *n* ['rekɔːd] **(a)** *(account)* rapport *m; (file)* dossier *m;* **we have no r.** of this nous n'en avons aucune trace; **to keep a r.** of sth garder une trace écrite de qch; **the hottest summer on r.** l'été le plus chaud qu'on ait jamais enregistré; **she's on r.** as saying that... elle a déclaré officiellement que...; **(just) for the r.** au passage; **to put** *or* **set the r. straight** mettre les choses au point; **r.** office archives *fpl* **(b)** *(personal history)* passé *m; (achievements)* résultats *mpl; (of criminal)* casier *m* judiciaire; **to have a good/bad safety r.** avoir bonne/mauvaise réputation en matière de sécurité **(c)** *(musical)* disque *m;* **r. company** maison *f* de disques; **r. player** tourne-disques *m inv* **(d)** *(best performance)* record *m* **(e)** *Comptr* enregistrement *m* **2** *adj* ['rekɔːd] record *inv;* **in r. time** en un temps record; **unemployment is at a r. high/low** le chômage a atteint son taux le plus haut/bas **3** *vt* [rɪ'kɔːd] **(a)** *(on video, cassette)* enregistrer **(b)** *(write down)* noter; *Br* **to send sth recorded delivery** envoyer qch en recommandé

record-breaking ['rekɔːdbreɪkɪŋ] *adj* record *inv*

recorder [rɪ'kɔːdə(r)] *n (musical instrument)* flûte *f* à bec

record-holder ['rekɔːdhəʊldə(r)] *n* détenteur(trice) *m,f* du record

recording [rɪ'kɔːdɪŋ] *n (on tape)* enregistrement *m;* **r. studio** studio *m* d'enregistrement

recount [rɪ'kaʊnt] *vt (relate)* raconter

re-count ['riːkaʊnt] *n (in election)* deuxième décompte *m*

recoup [rɪ'kuːp] *vt* récupérer

recourse [rɪ'kɔːs] *n* recours *m;* **to have r. to** avoir recours à

recover [rɪ'kʌvə(r)] **1** *vt (territory, customers)* & *Comptr* récupérer; *(one's appetite, balance)* retrouver **2** *vi (from illness, setback)* se remettre; *(after running, travelling)* récupérer; *Fig (of economy)* se redresser; *(of sales)* reprendre

recoverable [rɪ'kʌvərəbəl] *adj (money)* recouvrable

recovery [rɪ'kʌvərɪ] *(pl recoveries) n* **(a)** *(of lost or stolen item)* récupération *f;* **r. vehicle** dépanneuse *f* **(b)** *(from illness)* rétablissement *m; Fig (of economy)* redressement *m; (of sales)* reprise *f;* **to make a r.** se rétablir

re-create [riːkrɪ'eɪt] *vt* recréer

recreation [rekrɪ'eɪʃən] *n (leisure)* divertissement *m; Sch (break)* récréation *f;* **r. ground** terrain *m* de jeux; **r. room** salle *f* de jeux

recreational [rekrɪ'eɪʃənəl] *adj* de loisirs; **r. drug** = drogue prise occasionnellement, dans un but récréatif

recrimination [rɪkrɪmɪ'neɪʃən] *n* récrimination *f*

recruit [rɪ'kruːt] *also Mil* **1** *n* recrue *f* **2** *vt* recruter

recruitment [rɪ'kruːtmənt] *n also Mil* recrutement *m*

rectangle ['rektæŋgəl] *n* rectangle *m*

rectangular [rek'tæŋgjʊlə(r)] *adj* rectangulaire

rectify ['rektɪfaɪ] *(pt & pp* **rectified)** *vt* rectifier

rectitude ['rektɪtjuːd] *n Formal* rectitude *f*

rector ['rektə(r)] *n* **(a)** *Rel* pasteur *m* anglican **(b)** *Scot Univ* = personnalité élue par les étudiants pour les représenter; *Scot Sch* ≃ proviseur *m*

rectory ['rektərɪ] *(pl* **rectories)** *n Rel* presbytère *m*

rectum ['rektəm] *n* rectum *m*

recumbent [rɪ'kʌmbənt] *adj Formal* allongé(e)

recuperate [rɪ'kuːpəreɪt] *vi (from illness)* se rétablir

recuperation [rɪkuːpə'reɪʃən] *n (from illness)* rétablissement *m*

recur [rɪ'kɜː(r)] *(pt & pp* **recurred)** *vi (of event, problem)* se reproduire; *(of theme, illness)* revenir, réapparaître

recurrence [rɪ'kʌrəns] *n* récurrence *f*

recurring [rɪ'kɜːrɪŋ] *adj (problem)* récurrent(e); *(nightmare)* qui revient souvent; **six point six r.** six virgule six à l'infini

recycle [riː'saɪkəl] *vt* recycler

recycling [riː'saɪklɪŋ] *n* recyclage *m;* **r. facility, r. point** installation *f* de recyclage; **r. plant** usine *f* de recyclage

red [red] **1** *n (colour)* rouge *m; Fam Fig* **to see r.** *(get angry)* voir rouge; **to be in the r.** *(in debt)* être à découvert *ou* dans le rouge **2** *adj* rouge; *(hair)* roux (rousse); **to turn** *or* **go r.** rougir; **to be as r. as a beetroot** être rouge comme une pivoine; **r. alert** alerte *f* rouge; **the R. Army** l'Armée *f* rouge; **r. card** *(in soccer)* carton *m* rouge; *Fig* **to roll out the r. carpet** dérouler le tapis rouge; **the R. Cross** la Croix-Rouge; *Fig* **r. herring** diversion *f; (in film, book)* fausse piste *f; Old-fashioned* **R. Indian** Peau-Rouge *mf;* **r. light** feu *m* rouge; **r. light district** quartier *m* chaud; **r. meat** viande *f* rouge; *Br* **r. pepper** poivron *m* rouge; **mentioning her name to him is like a r. rag to a bull** le simple fait d'entendre son nom le met dans une colère noire; **(Little) R. Riding Hood** le Petit Chaperon rouge; **the R. Sea** la mer Rouge; **r. tape** paperasserie *f;* **r. wine** vin *m* rouge

red-blooded [red'blʌdɪd] *adj* **a r. male** un homme viril

redbrick ['redbrɪk] *adj (building)* en brique rouge; *Br* **r. university** = université construite à la fin du XIXᵉ siècle

redcurrant ['redkʌrənt] *n* groseille *f*

redden ['redən] **1** *vt* rougir **2** *vi (of sky)* rougeoyer; *(of person)* rougir

reddish ['redɪʃ] *adj (light, colour)* rougeâtre; *(hair)* légèrement roux (rousse)

redecorate [riː'dekəreɪt] *vt (repaint)* refaire la peinture de; *(re-wallpaper)* retapisser

redeem [rɪ'diːm] *vt* **(a)** *(pawned item)* racheter; *(promise)* tenir; *(gift token, coupon)* échanger; *(mortgage, loan)* rembourser **(b)** *(rescue)* racheter; **to r. oneself** se racheter

Redeemer [rɪ'diːmə(r)] *n Rel* **the R.** le Rédempteur

redeeming [rɪ'diːmɪŋ] *adj* **he has no r. features** il n'a rien pour le racheter; **his one r. feature is...** la seule chose qui le rachète, c'est...

redemption [rɪ'dem(p)ʃən] *n Rel* rédemption *f; also Fig* **to be beyond** *or* **past r.** être irrécupérable

redeploy [riːdɪ'plɔɪ] *vt (troops)* redéployer; *(staff)* réaffecter

redeployment [riːdɪ'plɔɪmənt] *n (of troops)* redéploiement *m; (of staff)* réaffectation *f*

redevelop [riːdɪ'veləp] *vt* réaménager

red-faced ['red'feɪst] *adj (naturally)* rougeaud(e); *(with anger, embarrassment)* rouge

red-handed ['red'hændɪd] *adj* **to be caught r.** être pris(e) la main dans le sac

redhead ['redhed] *n* roux (rousse) *m,f*

red-hot [red'hɒt] *adj* **(a)** *(very hot)* brûlant(e) **(b)** *Fam (very good)* super bon (bonne); **r. news** des nouvelles de dernière minute

redial 1 *n* ['ri:daɪəl] **r. button** *(on phone)* touche *f* bis
2 *vt* [ri:'daɪəl] *(pt & pp* **redialled**, *Am* **redialed)** *(phone number)* recomposer

redirect [ri:dɪ'rekt, ri:daɪ'rekt] *vt (letter)* faire suivre; *(plane, traffic)* dévier; *(energy)* canaliser

rediscover [ri:dɪs'kʌvə(r)] *vt* redécouvrir

redistribute [ri:dɪs'trɪbju:t] *vt* redistribuer

red-letter day ['red'letə(r)deɪ] *n* journée *f* mémorable

redo [ri:'du:] *(pt* **redid** [ri:'dɪd], *pp* **redone** [ri:'dʌn]) *vt* refaire

redolent ['redələnt] *adj* **to be r. of** *(smell of)* sentir; *(suggest)* avoir un parfum de

redraft [ri:'drɑːft] *vt* rédiger de nouveau

redress [rɪ'dres] **1** *n (of injustice, grievance)* réparation *f*
2 *vt (injustice, grievance)* réparer; **to r. the balance** rétablir l'équilibre

redskin ['redskɪn] *n Old-fashioned* Peau-Rouge *mf*

reduce [rɪ'dju:s] *vt* **(a)** *(cost, amount, tax)* réduire; *(importance)* minimiser; *(price)* baisser; *(number of people)* faire baisser; *(sauce)* faire réduire; **to r. speed** ralentir **(b)** *(bring to a certain state)* **to r. sth to ashes/dust** réduire qch en cendres/poussière; **to r. sb to silence** réduire qn au silence; **to r. sb to tears** faire fondre qn en larmes; **to be reduced to doing sth** être réduit(e) à faire qch

reduced [rɪ'dju:st] *adj* réduit(e); **to live in r. circumstances** vivre dans la gêne

reduction [rɪ'dʌkʃən] *n (of price, temperature)* baisse *f* (**in** de); *(of spending, on item)* réduction *f* (**in/on** de/sur)

redundancy [rɪ'dʌndənsɪ] *(pl* **redundancies**) *n Br (dismissal)* licenciement *m*; **r. notice** avis *m* de licenciement; **r. pay** prime *f* de licenciement

redundant [rɪ'dʌndənt] *adj* **(a)** *Br (worker)* **to make sb r.** licencier qn; **to be made r.** être licencié(e) **(b)** *(superfluous)* inutile

reed [ri:d] *n* **(a)** *(plant)* roseau *m* **(b)** *(of musical instrument)* anche *f*

reef [ri:f] *n* récif *m*

reek [ri:k] **1** *n* relent *m*
2 *vi also Fig* **to r.** *(of sth)* puer (qch)

reel [ri:l] **1** *n* **(a)** *Br (for film, thread)* bobine *f*; *(for fishing line)* moulinet *m* **(b)** *(dance, music)* quadrille *m*
2 *vi (sway)* chanceler; *Fig* **my head is reeling** la tête me tourne
▸ **reel off** *vt sep (names, statistics)* débiter

▸ **re-elect** [ri:ɪ'lekt] *vt* réélire

re-election [ri:ɪ'lekʃən] *n* réélection *f*

re-enact [ri:ɪ'nækt] *vt* reconstituer

re-enter [ri:'entə(r)] **1** *vt* entrer à nouveau dans
2 *vi* rentrer

re-establish [ri:ɪ'stæblɪʃ] *vt* rétablir

re-examine [ri:ɪg'zæmɪn] *vt* réexaminer

ref [ref] *n* **(a)** *(abbr* **reference)** réf **(b)** *Fam (abbr* **referee)** arbitre *m*

refectory [rɪ'fektərɪ] *(pl* **refectories)** *n* réfectoire *m*

refer [rɪ'fɜ:(r)] *(pt & pp* **referred)** *vt* soumettre (**to** à); **to r. a patient to a specialist** envoyer un patient chez un spécialiste
▸ **refer to** *vt insep* **(a)** *(mention)* parler de; **she never**

refers to it elle n'en parle jamais **(b)** *(allude to)* faire allusion à; **referred to as...** appelé(e)... **(c)** *(consult)* consulter **(d)** *(apply to)* s'appliquer à

referee [refə'ri:] **1** *n* **(a)** *(in sport)* arbitre *m* **(b)** *(for job)* **please give the names of two referees** veuillez fournir deux références
2 *vt & vi* arbitrer

reference ['refərəns] *n* **(a)** *(consultation, source)* référence *f*; **for future r.** à titre d'information; **I can't do it without r. to Head Office** je ne peux pas le faire sans en référer au bureau central; **r. book** ouvrage *m* de référence; **r. number** *(numéro m de)* référence; **r. point, point of r.** point *m* de repère **(b)** *(allusion)* allusion *f*; **with r. to** *(in letter)* suite à **(c)** *(from employer)* lettre *f* de référence; **to give sb a r.** fournir une référence à qn

referendum [refə'rendəm] *n* référendum *m*

refill 1 *n* ['ri:fɪl] *(for notebook)* feuillets *fpl* de rechange; *(for pen)* cartouche *f*; *(for lighter)* recharge *f*; **would you like a r.?** *(of drink)* je te ressers?
2 *vt* [ri:'fɪl] *(glass)* remplir à nouveau; *(lighter, pen)* recharger

refine [rɪ'faɪn] *vt* **(a)** *(sugar, petroleum)* raffiner **(b)** *(improve)* perfectionner

refined [rɪ'faɪnd] *adj also Fig* raffiné(e)

refinement [rɪ'faɪnmənt] *n* **(a)** *(of manners, taste, person)* raffinement *m* **(b)** *(improvement)* perfectionnement *m*; **to make refinements to sth** perfectionner qch

refinery [rɪ'faɪnərɪ] *(pl* **refineries)** *n* raffinerie *f*

refit *n* ['ri:fɪt] *(of ship)* remise *f* en état
2 *vt* [ri:'fɪt] *(pt & pp* **refitted)** *(ship)* remettre en état

reflate [ri:'fleɪt] *vt Econ* relancer

reflation [ri:'fleɪʃən] *n Econ* relance *f*

reflect [rɪ'flekt] **1** *vt* **(a)** *(image, light)* réfléchir, refléter; **to be reflected (in)** se refléter ou se refléter (dans) **(b)** *Fig (portray)* refléter **(c)** *(think)* **to r. that...** se dire que
2 *vi* **(a)** *(think)* réfléchir (**on** à) **(b)** **to r. well/badly on sb/sth** faire honneur/du tort à qn/qch

reflection [rɪ'flekʃən] *n* **(a)** *(image, indication)* reflet *m*, *Fig* **it is no r. on your own capabilities** cela ne remet pas en cause vos compétences **(b)** *(thought)* réflexion *f*; **on r.** après réflexion

reflective [rɪ'flektɪv] *adj* **(a)** *(surface)* réfléchissant(e) **(b)** *(person)* réfléchi(e)

reflector [rɪ'flektə(r)] *n (on bicycle, vehicle)* catadioptre *m*

reflex ['ri:fleks] **1** *n* réflexe *m*
2 *adj* réflexe; **r. action** réflexe *m*; **r. camera** réflex *m*

reflexive [rɪ'fleksɪv] *adj Gram* **r. pronoun** pronom *m* réfléchi; **r. verb** verbe *m* pronominal réfléchi

reflexology [ri:flek'sɒlədʒɪ] *n* réflexologie *f*

reforestation [ri:fɒrɪ'steɪʃən] *n* reboisement *m*

reform [rɪ'fɔ:m] **1** *n* réforme *f*
2 *vt* réformer
3 *vi* se réformer

re-form ['ri:'fɔ:m] *vi (of organization, pop group)* se reformer

re-format ['ri:'fɔ:mæt] *(pt & pp* **re-formatted)** *vt Comptr (disk)* reformater

reformation [refə'meɪʃən] *n* réforme *f*; *Hist* **the R.** la Réforme

reformatory [rɪ'fɔ:mətərɪ] *(pl* **reformatories)** *n Am* centre *m* d'éducation surveillée

reformed [rɪ'fɔ:md] *adj (alcoholic, drug addict)* ancien(enne); **he's a r. character** il s'est assagi

reformer [rɪ'fɔ:mə(r)] *n* réformateur(trice) *m,f*

reformist [rɪ'fɔ:mɪst] *n & adj* réformiste *mf*

refract [rɪ'frækt] *vt* réfracter

refrain [rɪ'freɪn] **1** *n also Fig* refrain *m*
2 *vi* to r. from sth/doing sth s'abstenir de qch/de faire qch

re-freeze [ri:'fri:z] (*pt* re-froze [ri:'frəʊz], *pp* re-frozen [ri:'frəʊzən]) *vt* recongeler

refresh [rɪ'freʃ] *vt (of drink)* rafraîchir; *(of nap, holiday)* reposer; *(bath)* revigorer; *Comptr* actualiser; **to r. one's memory** se rafraîchir la mémoire; **to r. sb's glass** *(top up)* resservir à boire à qn

refreshing [rɪ'freʃɪŋ] *adj (breeze, drink)* rafraîchissant(e); *(nap, holiday)* reposant(e); *(bath)* revigorant(e); *Fig (honesty)* qui fait l'effet d'une bouffée d'air frais

refreshments [rɪ'freʃmənts] *npl* rafraîchissements *mpl*

refrigerate [rɪ'frɪdʒəreɪt] *vt* réfrigérer; **r. after opening** *(on packet)* à conserver au frais après ouverture

refrigeration [rɪfrɪdʒə'reɪʃən] *n* réfrigération *f*

refrigerator [rɪ'frɪdʒəreɪtə(r)] *n (domestic)* réfrigérateur *m*, frigidaire® *m*; *(industrial)* chambre *f* froide

refuel [ri:'fjʊəl] *(pt & pp* refuelled, *Am* refueled) **1** *vt (ship, aircraft)* ravitailler en carburant **2** *vi (of ship, aircraft)* se ravitailler en carburant

refuge ['refju:dʒ] *n (from danger, weather)* refuge *m*; *(for battered women)* foyer *m*; **to seek r.** chercher refuge; **to take r.** se réfugier

refugee [refjʊ'dʒi:] *n* réfugié(e) *m,f*; **r. camp** camp *m* de réfugiés; **r. status** statut *m* de réfugié

refund 1 *n* ['ri:fʌnd] remboursement *m*
2 *vt* [ri:'fʌnd] rembourser

refurbish [ri:'fɜ:bɪʃ] *vt* rénover

refusal [rɪ'fju:zəl] *n* refus *m*; **to give a flat r.** refuser catégoriquement; **to have first r. (on sth)** avoir la priorité (pour qch)

refuse¹ ['refju:s] *n (rubbish)* ordures *fpl*; **r. collection** ramassage *m* des ordures (ménagères); **r. disposal** traitement *m* des ordures; **r. dump** dépôt *m* d'ordures

refuse² [rɪ'fju:z] **1** *vt (invitation, offer)* refuser; *(request)* rejeter; **to r. to do sth** refuser de faire qch; **to r. sb sth** refuser qch à qn
2 *vi (of person)* refuser; *(of horse)* refuser l'obstacle

refute [rɪ'fju:t] *vt (argument, theory)* réfuter; *(allegation)* nier

regain [rɪ'geɪn] *vt (a) (get back)* retrouver, *(power, political seat)* reconquérir; **to r. possession of sth** rentrer en possession de qch; **to r. consciousness** revenir à soi; **to r. the lead** *(in contest)* reprendre l'avantage **(b)** *(reach again)* regagner

regal ['ri:gəl] *adj* royal(e)

regale [rɪ'geɪl] *vt* **to r. sb with sth** gratifier qn de qch

regalia [rɪ'geɪlɪə] *npl* insignes *mpl*

regard [rɪ'gɑ:d] **1** *n* **(a)** *(admiration)* respect *m*, estime *f*; **to hold sb in high r.** tenir qn en haute estime **(b)** *(consideration)* égard *m*; **out of r. for** par égard pour; **without r. to** sans tenir compte de **(c)** *(connection)* **in this r.** à cet égard; **in all regards** à tous égards; **with r. to** en ce qui concerne **(d) regards** *(good wishes)* amitiés *fpl*; **give her my regards** transmets-lui mes amitiés
2 *vt* **(a)** *(admire, respect)* estimer **(b)** *(consider)* **to r. sb/sth as** considérer qn/qch comme; **to r. sb/sth with suspicion** être soupçonneux(euse) à l'égard de qn/qch **(c)** *(concern)* concerner; **as regards...** en ce qui concerne..., concernant...

regarding [rɪ'gɑ:dɪŋ] *prep* en ce qui concerne, concernant

regardless [rɪ'gɑ:dlɪs] *adv* **(a)** *(despite everything)* quand même **(b) r. of** *(without considering)* sans tenir compte de; **r. of the expense** sans regarder à la dépense

regatta [rɪ'gætə] *n* régate *f*

regency ['ri:dʒənsɪ] (*pl* regencies) *n* régence *f*

regenerate [rɪ'dʒenəreɪt] **1** *(sector, city)* régénérer; *(interest, enthusiasm)* raviver
2 *vi* se régénérer

regeneration [rɪdʒenə'reɪʃən] *n* régénération *f*

regent ['ri:dʒənt] *adj & n* régent(e) *m,f*

reggae ['regeɪ] *n* reggae *m*

regime [reɪ'ʒi:m] *n* régime *m*

regiment ['redʒɪmənt] **1** *n* régiment *m*
2 *vt* enrégimenter

regimental [redʒɪ'mentəl] *adj* du régiment

regimented ['redʒɪmentɪd] *adj* très strict(e)

region ['ri:dʒən] *n* région *f*; *Fig* **in the r. of** environ

regional ['ri:dʒənəl] *adj* régional(e)

regionalism ['ri:dʒənəlɪzəm] *n* régionalisme *m*

register ['redʒɪstə(r)] **1** *n* registre *m*; *(at school)* cahier *m* d'appel; *(of voters)* liste f électorale; **to take the r.** *(at school)* faire l'appel; **r. of births, marriages and deaths** registre de l'état civil; **(cash) r.** caisse *f* (enregistreuse); *Br* **r. office** bureau *m* de l'état civil
2 *vt* **(a)** *(member, student)* inscrire; *(birth, marriage, death)* déclarer; *(complaint)* déposer; **to r. a protest** protester **(b)** *(temperature, speed)* enregistrer; *(astonishment, displeasure)* manifester **(c)** *(realize)* se rendre compte de **(d)** *(achieve)* *(victory, progress)* enregistrer
3 *vi* **(a)** *(for course)* s'inscrire; *(at hotel)* signer le registre; *(of voters)* s'inscrire sur les listes électorales **(b)** *Fam (of fact)* **I told him but it didn't r.** je lui ai dit mais il n'a pas enregistré

registered ['redʒɪstəd] *adj (charity)* reconnu(e) par l'État; *(childminder)* agréé(e); *(letter)* recommandé(e); **r. trademark** marque *f* déposée

registrar ['redʒɪstrɑ:(r)] *n* **(a)** *Br (record keeper)* officier *m* de l'état civil **(b)** *(in university) Am* responsable *mf* des inscriptions; *Br* secrétaire *mf* général(e) **(c)** *Br (in hospital)* chef *m* de clinique

registration [redʒɪs'treɪʃən] *n (of student)* inscription *f*; *(of voter)* inscription sur les listes électorales; *(of birth, death, marriage)* déclaration *f*; **r. number** *(of car)* numéro *m* d'immatriculation

registry office ['redʒɪstrɪ'ɒfɪs] *n* bureau *m* de l'état civil

regress [rɪ'gres] *vi* régresser

regression [rɪ'greʃən] *n* régression *f*

regressive [rɪ'gresɪv] *adj* régressif(ive)

regret [rɪ'gret] **1** *n* regret *m*; **to send one's regrets** *(apologies)* envoyer ses excuses; *(condolences)* envoyer ses condoléances
2 *vt (pt & pp* regretted) regretter; **to r. doing** *or* **having done sth** regretter d'avoir fait qch; **I r. to (have to) inform you that...** j'ai le regret de vous annoncer que...

regretful [rɪ'gretfʊl] *adj (voice, smile)* plein(e) de regret; *(person)* qui a des regrets

regrettable [rɪ'gretəbəl] *adj* regrettable

regroup [ri:'gru:p] **1** *vt* regrouper
2 *vi* se regrouper

regular ['regjʊlə(r)] **1** *n (in bar, restaurant)* habitué(e) *m,f*
2 *adj* **(a)** *(features, pulse, verb)* régulier(ère); **on a r. basis** régulièrement; **he comes twice a week, as r. as clockwork** il vient deux fois par semaine, c'est réglé comme du papier à musique **(b)** *(normal, habitual)* habituel(elle); *(in size)* moyen(enne); *(listener, viewer)* fidèle; *(customer)* régulier(ère); **she was a r. visitor to the house** elle venait régulièrement à la maison **(c)** *(army, soldier)* régulier(ère) **(d)** *Fam (for emphasis)* vrai(e)

regularity [regjʊ'lærɪtɪ] n régularité f
regulate ['regjʊleɪt] vt (a) (adjust) régler (b) (control) réglementer
regulation [regjʊ'leɪʃən] 1 n (a) (action) réglementation f (b) (rule) règlement m
2 adj (statutory) réglementaire
regulator ['regjʊleɪtə(r)] n régulateur m
regulatory [regjʊ'leɪtərɪ] adj de contrôle
regurgitate [rɪ'gɜːdʒɪteɪt] vt régurgiter; Fig recracher
rehabilitate [riːhə'bɪlɪteɪt] vt réhabiliter
rehabilitation [riːhəbɪlɪ'teɪʃən] n réhabilitation f
rehash Fam 1 n ['riːhæʃ] resucée f
2 vt [riː'hæʃ] (ideas, proposal) reprendre; (film, book) remanier
rehearsal [rɪ'hɜːsəl] n répétition f
rehearse [rɪ'hɜːs] vt & vi répéter
rehouse [riː'haʊz] vt reloger
reign [reɪn] 1 n règne m
2 vi also Fig régner
reigning ['reɪnɪŋ] adj (monarch) régnant(e); (champion) en titre
reimburse [riːɪm'bɜːs] vt rembourser
rein [reɪn] n also Fig rêne f; Fig to give sb free r. to do sth donner carte blanche à qn pour qu'il/elle fasse qch; Fig to give free r. to one's imagination donner libre cours à son imagination; Fig to keep a tight r. on sb tenir la bride haute à qn
reincarnate [riː'ɪnkɑːneɪt] vt to be reincarnated être réincarné(e)
reincarnation [riːɪnkɑː'neɪʃən] n réincarnation f
reindeer ['reɪndɪə(r)] n renne m
reinforce [riːɪn'fɔːs] vt also Fig renforcer; reinforced concrete béton m armé
reinforcement [riːɪn'fɔːsmənt] n renforcement m; also Fig reinforcements renforts mpl
reinsert [riːɪn'sɜːt] vt réinsérer
reinstate [riːɪn'steɪt] vt réintégrer
reinsurance [riːɪn'ʃʊərəns] n réassurance f
reinsure [riːɪn'ʃʊə(r)] vt réassurer
reinvent [riːɪn'vent] vt Fig to r. the wheel refaire ce qui a déjà été fait
reinvest [riːɪn'vest] vt réinvestir
reissue [riː'ɪʃuː] 1 n (of book, record) réédition f
2 vt (book, record) rééditer
reiterate [riː'ɪtəreɪt] vt réitérer
reiteration [riːɪtə'reɪʃən] n réitération f
reject 1 n ['riːdʒekt] (object) rebut m; Fam (person) inadapté(e) m,f
2 vt [rɪ'dʒekt] rejeter; (offer, goods) refuser
rejection [rɪ'dʒekʃən] n rejet m; (of offer, goods) refus m; to meet with r. être rejeté(e)
rejoice [rɪ'dʒɔɪs] vi se réjouir
rejoicing [rɪ'dʒɔɪsɪŋ] n réjouissance f
rejoin¹ [riː'dʒɔɪn] vt (a) (group, motorway) rejoindre; (race) reprendre (b) (join again) réintégrer
rejoin² [rɪ'dʒɔɪn] vt & vi (retort) répliquer, rétorquer
rejoinder [rɪ'dʒɔɪndə(r)] n réplique f
rejuvenate [rɪ'dʒuːvɪneɪt] vt rajeunir
rekindle [riː'kɪndəl] vt raviver
relapse 1 n ['riːlæps] rechute f
2 vi [rɪ'læps] rechuter; to r. into retomber dans
relate [rɪ'leɪt] 1 vt (a) (narrate) raconter (b) (connect) mettre en rapport (to avec)

2 vi (a) (be relevant) to r. to avoir rapport à (b) to r. to (understand) (person) avoir des affinités avec; (idea) comprendre
related [rɪ'leɪtɪd] adj (people, animals, languages) apparenté(e); (ideas, events, activities) lié(e)
relation [rɪ'leɪʃən] n (a) (relative) parent(e) m,f (b) (connection) rapport m; to bear no r. to n'avoir aucun rapport avec
relationship [rɪ'leɪʃənʃɪp] n (a) (between people) relation f; (romantic, sexual) relation amoureuse; (between countries) relations fpl; (within family) lien m de parenté; to have a good/bad r. with sb s'entendre/ne pas bien s'entendre avec qn (b) (connection) rapport m
relative ['relətɪv] 1 n (person) parent(e) m,f
2 adj (comparative) relatif(ive); r. to en rapport avec; Gram r. clause proposition f relative
relatively ['relətɪvlɪ] adv relativement
relativity [relə'tɪvɪtɪ] n Phys relativité f
relax [rɪ'læks] 1 vt (person) détendre; (muscles, discipline) relâcher; (law, control) assouplir; to r. one's grip (on) relâcher son étreinte (sur); Fig relâcher son emprise (sur)
2 vi (of person) se détendre; (of muscles) se relâcher; r.! (calm down) du calme!
relaxation [riːlæk'seɪʃən] n (a) (of person) détente f; (of discipline) relâchement m; (of control) assouplissement m (b) (as therapy) relaxation f; r. exercises/classes exercices mpl/cours mpl de relaxation
relaxed [rɪ'lækst] adj détendu(e)
relaxing [rɪ'læksɪŋ] adj relaxant(e)
relay 1 n ['riːleɪ] (of workers) équipe f de relais; to work in relays se relayer; r. (race) (course f de) relais m; Rad & TV r. station relais m
2 vt [rɪ'leɪ] retransmettre; (information) transmettre
release [rɪ'liːs] 1 n (a) (of prisoner) libération f; (of gas) émission f; (emotional) soulagement m (b) (of record, film) sortie f; to be on general r. (of film) être sorti(e) dans toutes les grandes salles de cinéma
2 vt (a) (prisoner) libérer; (gas, fumes) émettre; (balloon, bomb) lâcher; (funds) dégager; (brake) desserrer; to r. sb from an obligation dégager qn d'une obligation; to r. sb's hand lâcher la main de qn (b) (record, film) sortir; (news, information) communiquer
relegate ['relɪgeɪt] vt reléguer (to à); Br to be relegated (of team) descendre en division inférieure
relegation [relɪ'geɪʃən] n (of person) relégation f (to à); Br (of team) descente f en division inférieure
relent [rɪ'lent] vi (of storm, wind) se calmer; (of person) céder
relentless [rɪ'lentlɪs] adj (person, attitude) implacable; (rain, criticism) incessant(e)
relevance ['reləvəns] n pertinence f; to have r. to sth avoir un rapport avec qch
relevant ['reləvənt] adj (a) (apt) pertinent(e); to be r. (to sth) avoir un rapport (avec qch) (b) (appropriate) (chapter) correspondant(e); (authorities) compétent(e); (experience, qualifications) requis(e) (c) (topical) d'actualité
reliability [rɪlaɪə'bɪlɪtɪ] n (of person, information) sérieux m; (of machine) sûreté f, fiabilité f
reliable [rɪ'laɪəbəl] adj (person, machine) fiable; (information) sûr(e); from a r. source de source sûre
reliably [rɪ'laɪəblɪ] adv to be r. informed that... savoir de source sûre que...
reliance [rɪ'laɪəns] n (a) (dependence) dépendance f (on vis-à-vis de) (b) (trust) confiance f; to place r. on sb/sth faire confiance à qn/qch
reliant [rɪ'laɪənt] adj to be r. on être dépendant(e) de

relic ['relɪk] *n Rel* relique *f*; *Fig* vestige *m*
relief [rɪ'liːf] *n* (**a**) *(comfort)* soulagement *m*; **to bring r. to sb** soulager qn (**b**) *(help)* secours *m*, aide *f*; **r. fund** fonds *m* d'aide (**c**) *(replacement)* remplaçant(e) *m,f* (**d**) *(of besieged city, troops)* libération *f* (**e**) *(in art)* relief *m*; **in r.** en relief; *Fig* **to throw sth into r.** mettre qch en relief; **r. map** carte *f* en relief
relieve [rɪ'liːv] *vt* (**a**) *(alleviate)* soulager; *(boredom)* tromper; *(pressure)* réduire; *Euph* **to r. oneself** se soulager (**b**) *(replace)* remplacer (**c**) *(liberate)* libérer; **to r. sb of his duties** relever qn de ses fonctions; *Hum* **to r. sb of his wallet** soulager qn de son portefeuille
religion [rɪ'lɪdʒən] *n* religion *f*
religious [rɪ'lɪdʒəs] *adj also Fig* religieux(euse)
religiously [rɪ'lɪdʒəslɪ] *adv also Fig* religieusement
relinquish [rɪ'lɪŋkwɪʃ] *vt* *(hope, habit, thought)* abandonner; *(claim, share)* renoncer à; *Fig* **to r. one's hold on sb/sth** relâcher son emprise sur qn/qch
relish ['relɪʃ] **1** *n* (**a**) *(pleasure)* goût *m* (**for** pour); **to do sth with r.** faire qch avec délectation (**b**) *(pickle)* condiments *mpl*
2 *vt* savourer; **I didn't r. the idea** l'idée ne m'enthousiasmait guère
relive [riː'lɪv] *vt* revivre
relocate [riːləʊ'keɪt] **1** *vt* *(company)* transférer; *(person)* muter
2 *vi (of company)* être transféré(e); *(of person)* se déplacer
relocation [riːləʊ'keɪʃən] *n* déménagement *m*
reluctance [rɪ'lʌktəns] *n* réticence *f*; **to do sth with r.** faire qch à contrecœur
reluctant [rɪ'lʌktənt] *adj* *(smile, promise)* accordé(e) à contrecœur; **to be r. to do sth** être réticent(e) à faire qch
▸ **rely on, rely upon** [rɪ'laɪ] *(pt & pp relied) vt insep* (**a**) **to r. on sb (to do sth)** compter sur qn (pour faire qch) (**b**) *(be dependent on)* dépendre de
REM [ɑːriː'em] *n* *(abbr* rapid eye movement*)* mouvements *mpl* oculaires rapides
remain [rɪ'meɪn] *vi* (**a**) *(stay behind, continue to be)* rester (**b**) *(be left)* subsister; **it remains to be seen** cela reste à voir
remainder [rɪ'meɪndə(r)] *n* reste *m*
remaindered [rɪ'meɪndɜːd] *adj (book)* soldé(e)
remaining [rɪ'meɪnɪŋ] *adj* restant(e)
remains [rɪ'meɪnz] *npl (of meal, fortune)* restes *mpl*; *(of civilization, building)* vestiges *mpl*; (**human**) **r.** restes humains
remake 1 *n* ['riːmeɪk] *(of movie)* remake *m*
2 *vt* [riː'meɪk] *(pt & pp remade* [riː'meɪd]*) (movie)* faire un remake de
remand [rɪ'mɑːnd] *Law* **1** *n* **on r.** en détention préventive; **r. home** maison *f* de détention préventive
2 *vt* **to r. sb (in custody)** placer qn en détention préventive
remark [rɪ'mɑːk] **1** *n* remarque *f*; **to make** *or* **pass a r.** faire une remarque
2 *vt* faire remarquer
remarkable [rɪ'mɑːkəbəl] *adj* remarquable
remarkably [rɪ'mɑːkəblɪ] *adv* remarquablement
remarry [riː'mærɪ] *(pt & pp remarried) vi* se remarier
remedial [rɪ'miːdɪəl] *adj* (**a**) *(class)* de rattrapage; **r. education** rattrapage *m* scolaire (**b**) *(corrective)* **to take r. measures** prendre des mesures
remedy ['remɪdɪ] **1** *n* *(pl* remedies*) also Fig* remède *m*
2 *vt (pt & pp remedied)* remédier à
remember [rɪ'membə(r)] **1** *vt* (**a**) *(recall)* se souvenir de, se rappeler; **to r. doing sth** se souvenir d'avoir fait qch; **to r.**

to do sth penser à faire qch; **a night to r.** une nuit mémorable (**b**) *(commemorate)* commémorer; **to r. the dead** rendre hommage aux disparus (**c**) *(speak of)* **to r. sb to sb** rappeler qn au bon souvenir de qn
2 *vi* se souvenir, se rappeler; **as far as I r.** pour autant que je me souvienne
remembrance [rɪ'membrəns] *n* *Formal (memory)* souvenir *m*; **in r. of** en souvenir de; *Br* **R. Day** *or* **Sunday** = commémoration de la fin des deux guerres mondiales, ≃ le 11 novembre
remind [rɪ'maɪnd] *vt* **to r. sb of sth** rappeler qch à qn; **to r. sb to do sth** rappeler à qn de faire qch; **that reminds me…** à propos…
reminder [rɪ'maɪndə(r)] *n* rappel *m*
reminisce [remɪ'nɪs] *vi* évoquer des souvenirs; **to r. about sth** évoquer qch
reminiscence [remɪ'nɪsəns] *n* souvenir *m*
reminiscent [remɪ'nɪsənt] *adj* **to be r. of** rappeler
remiss [rɪ'mɪs] *adj* négligent(e); **it was very r. of him not to phone** c'était très négligent de sa part de ne pas téléphoner
remission [rɪ'mɪʃən] *n* (**a**) *Law* remise *f* de peine (**b**) *(of disease)* **to be in r.** être en phase de rémission
remit 1 *n* ['riːmɪt] *(area of authority)* attributions *fpl*
2 *vt* [rɪ'mɪt] *(pt & pp remitted) (payment)* remettre
remittance [rɪ'mɪtəns] *n* versement *m*
remnant ['remnənt] *n* reste *m*; *(of civilization, building)* vestige *m*; *(of cloth)* coupon *m*
remonstrate ['remənstreɪt] *vi* protester; **to r. with sb** faire des remontrances à qn
remorse [rɪ'mɔːs] *n* remords *m*; **to feel r.** avoir du *ou* des remords
remorseful [rɪ'mɔːsfʊl] *adj* plein(e) de remords
remorseless [rɪ'mɔːslɪs] *adj* impitoyable
remote [rɪ'məʊt] *adj* (**a**) *(far-off) (in space)* éloigné(e) (**from** de); *(in time)* lointain(e) (**from** de); **r. control** télécommande *f* (**b**) *(aloof)* distant(e) (**c**) *(chance, possibility)* vague; **the remotest chance/idea** la moindre chance/idée
remote-controlled [rɪ'məʊtkən'trəʊld] *adj* télécommandé(e)
remotely [rɪ'məʊtlɪ] *adv* (**a**) *(distantly)* **r. situated** isolé(e) (**b**) *(slightly)* vaguement; **not r.** pas du tout
remould ['riːməʊld] *n (tyre)* pneu *m* rechapé
removal [rɪ'muːvəl] *n* (**a**) *(of politician, official)* renvoi *m*; *(of control, doubt, threat)* suppression *f*; *(of stain)* nettoyage *m* (**b**) *Br (moving house)* déménagement *m*; **r. man** déménageur *m*; **r. van** camion *m* de déménagement
remove [rɪ'muːv] *vt* (**a**) *(take away) (thing)* enlever; *(doubt)* dissiper; *(stain)* faire partir; *(politician, official)* renvoyer; **to r. one's child from a school** retirer son enfant d'une école (**b**) *(take off) (coat, hat)* enlever, retirer; *(tyre)* démonter
remover [rɪ'muːvə(r)] *n* (**a**) *(for paint)* décapant *m*; *(for nail varnish)* dissolvant *m* (**b**) *Br* (**furniture**) **removers** déménageurs *mpl*
remunerate [rɪ'mjuːnəreɪt] *vt Formal* rémunérer
remuneration [rɪmjuːnə'reɪʃən] *n* *Formal* rémunération *f*
remunerative [rɪ'mjuːnərətɪv] *adj* *Formal* rémunérateur(trice)
renaissance [rɪ'neɪsəns] *n* renouveau *m*; **the R.** la Renaissance
renal ['riːnəl] *adj* rénal(e)
rename [riː'neɪm] *vt* rebaptiser

rend [rend] (*pt & pp* **rent** [rent]) *vt Lit (tear)* déchirer

render ['rendə(r)] *vt Formal* rendre; **to r.** homage to sb rendre hommage à qn; **to r.** sth into French rendre qch en français; **for services rendered** pour services rendus; **the news rendered her speechless** la nouvelle l'a laissée sans voix

rendezvous ['rɒndɪvuː] **1** *n* (*pl* **rendezvous** ['rɒndɪvuːz]) rendez-vous *m inv* **2** *vi* (*pt & pp* **rendezvoused** ['rɒndɪvuːd]) se retrouver

rendition [ren'dɪʃən] *n* interprétation *f*

renegade ['renɪgeɪd] *n* renégat(e) *m,f*

renege [rɪ'neɪg] *vi* **to r.** on sth revenir sur qch

renew [rɪ'njuː] *vt (passport, membership)* renouveler; *(activity, negotiations, library book)* reprendre; *(optimism, strength, interest)* raviver; *(speculation)* relancer

renewable [rɪ'njuːəbəl] *adj* renouvelable

renewal [rɪ'njuːəl] *n (of passport, membership)* renouvellement *m*; *(of activity, negotiations)* reprise *f*; *(of library book)* renouvellement de prêt; *(of optimism, interest)* regain *m*

rennet ['renɪt] *n* présure *f*

renounce [rɪ'naʊns] *vt* renoncer à; *(treaty)* dénoncer; *(friends, faith, principles)* renier

renovate ['renəveɪt] *vt* rénover

renovation [renə'veɪʃən] *n* rénovation *f*

renown [rɪ'naʊn] *n* renommée *f*

renowned [rɪ'naʊnd] *adj* renommé(e) **(for** pour)

rent¹ [rent] **1** *n (on flat, house)* loyer *m*; **for r.** à louer; *Br Fam* **r.** boy jeune prostitué *m* **2** *vt* louer

rent² *pt & pp of* **rend**

rental ['rentəl] *n* (**a**) *(hire)* location *f* (**b**) *(money) (for house)* loyer *m*; *(for car, equipment, TV)* location *f*; *(for telephone)* abonnement *m*

rent-free [rent'friː] **1** *adj* exempt(e) de loyer **2** *adv* sans payer de loyer

reopen [riː'əʊpən] **1** *vt* rouvrir *(talks)* reprendre; *Fig* **to r.** old wounds rouvrir une plaie **2** *vi (of talks)* reprendre; *(of shop, theatre)* rouvrir; **school reopens on August 21st** la rentrée des classes aura lieu le 21 août

reorder [riː'ɔːdə(r)] *vt* passer une nouvelle commande de

reorganization [riːɔːgənaɪ'zeɪʃən] *n* réorganisation *f*

reorganize [riː'ɔːgənaɪz] *vt* réorganiser

rep [rep] *n Fam (abbr* **representative)** VRP *m*

repaint [riː'peɪnt] *vt* repeindre

repair [rɪ'peə(r)] **1** *n* réparation *f*; **to be beyond r.** être irréparable; **to be in good/bad r.** être en bon/mauvais état; **to be under r.** être en réparation; **r.** shop atelier *m* de réparations **2** *vt* réparer

repairman [rɪ'peəmæn] *n* réparateur *m*

reparation [repə'reɪʃən] *n* (**a**) *Formal (compensation)* réparation *f*; **to make r.** for sth réparer qch (**b**) *(after war)* **reparations** réparations *fpl*

repartee [repɑː'tiː] *n* repartie *f*

repast [rɪ'pɑːst] *n Lit* repas *m*

repatriate [riː'pætrɪeɪt] *vt* rapatrier **(to** vers)

repatriation [riːpætrɪ'eɪʃən] *n* rapatriement *m*

repay [riː'peɪ] *(pt & pp* **repaid** [riː'peɪd]) *vt* (**a**) *(reimburse) (person, money)* rembourser (**b**) *(reward) (person)* remercier **(for** de); *(kindness)* payer de retour; *(loyalty)* récompenser

repayable [riː'peɪəbəl] *adj* remboursable

repayment [riː'peɪmənt] *n* remboursement *m*; **r.** plan calendrier *m* des paiements

repeal [rɪ'piːl] *vt* abroger

repeat [rɪ'piːt] **1** *n (of event)* répétition *f*; *(of TV or radio programme)* rediffusion *f*; **r.** prescription ≃ ordonnance *f* renouvelable **2** *vt* répéter; *(attempt)* renouveler; *(TV programme)* rediffuser; **to r.** oneself se répéter

repeated [rɪ'piːtɪd] *adj* répété(e)

repeatedly [rɪ'piːtɪdlɪ] *adv* à maintes reprises

repel [rɪ'pel] *(pt & pp* **repelled)** *vt also Fig* repousser

repellent [rɪ'pelənt] **1** *n (for insects)* anti-moustiques *m inv* **2** *adj (disgusting)* repoussant(e)

repent [rɪ'pent] **1** *vt* se repentir de **2** *vi* se repentir **(of** de)

repentance [rɪ'pentəns] *n* repentir *m*

repentant [rɪ'pentənt] *adj* repentant(e) **(of** de)

repercussion [riːpə'kʌʃən] *n* répercussion *f*

repertoire ['repətwɑː(r)] *n* répertoire *m*

repertory ['repətərɪ] *(pl* **repertories)** *n Th* répertoire *m*; **r.** company troupe *f* de répertoire

repetition [repɪ'tɪʃən] *n* répétition *f*; *(of attempt)* renouvellement *m*

repetitive [rɪ'petɪtɪv] *adj* répétitif(ive); **r.** strain injury = douleurs dans les bras et les mains dues à la répétition de certains mouvements

rephrase [riː'freɪz] *vt* reformuler

replace [rɪ'pleɪs] *vt* (**a**) *(put back)* to r. sth remettre qch à sa place; **to r.** the receiver *(on telephone)* raccrocher (**b**) *(substitute for)* remplacer

replacement [rɪ'pleɪsmənt] *n* (**a**) *(putting back)* remise *f* en place; *(substituting)* remplacement *m*; *Fin* **r.** cost coût *m* de remplacement; **r.** parts pièces *fpl* de remplacement; **r.** value valeur *f* de remplacement (**b**) *(person)* remplaçant(e) *m,f*

replay 1 *n* ['riːpleɪ] *(of match)* nouvelle rencontre *f*; **(action)** r. *(on TV)* = répétition d'une séquence précédente; *(at slow speed)* ralenti *m* **2** *vt* [riː'pleɪ] *(match)* rejouer

replenish [rɪ'plenɪʃ] *vt (cup, tank)* remplir à nouveau **(with** de); **to r.** one's supplies se réapprovisionner

replete [rɪ'pliːt] *adj Formal* rassasié(e) **(with** de)

replica ['replɪkə] *n* réplique *f*; *Fig (of person)* portrait *m*

replicate ['replɪkeɪt] *vt* reproduire

reply [rɪ'plaɪ] **1** *n (pl* **replies)** réponse *f*; **in r.** to your letter en réponse à votre lettre; **to say sth in r. (to sth)** répondre qch à qch; **there was no r.** *(on telephone)* ça ne répondait pas **2** *vt & vi (pt & pp* **replied)** répondre **(to** à)

report [rɪ'pɔːt] **1** *n* (**a**) *(account)* compte rendu *m*; *(analysis)* rapport *m*; *(in newspaper, on radio, television)* reportage *m*; **there are reports that...** il paraîtrait que...; **r.** card *(for primary school)* carnet *m* de notes; *(for secondary school)* bulletin *m* scolaire (**b**) *(sound)* détonation *f* **2** *vt (information)* rapporter; *(accident, theft)* signaler; **to r.** sb missing signaler la disparition de qn; **to r.** sb to the police/the authorities dénoncer qn à la police/aux autorités; **to r.** one's findings *(to sb)* faire un rapport (à qn) **3** *vi* (**a**) *(present oneself)* se présenter **(to** à); **to r.** for duty prendre son service (**b**) *(give account)* faire un rapport (on sur) **(c)** *(be accountable)* to r. to sb rendre compte à qn

reportedly [rɪ'pɔːtɪdlɪ] *adv* **he r.** said that... il aurait dit que …; **he is r.** resident in New York il résiderait à New York

reporter [rɪ'pɔːtə(r)] *n (for newspaper)* journaliste *mf*; *(on television, radio)* reporter *m*

repose [rɪ'pəʊz] *Formal* **1** *n* repos *m*
2 *vi* reposer

repository [rɪ'pɒzɪtərɪ] *(pl* **repositories)** *n (for books, furniture)* dépôt *m*

repossess [riːpə'zes] *vt* saisir

reprehensible [reprɪ'hensɪbəl] *adj* répréhensible

represent [reprɪ'zent] *vt* représenter; *(describe)* présenter

representation [reprɪzen'teɪʃən] *n (in Parliament)* représentation *f*; *(of facts)* exposé *m*; *Formal* **to make representations (to sb)** faire des démarches (auprès de qn)

representative [reprɪ'zentətɪv] **1** *n* représentant(e) *m,f*
2 *adj* représentatif(ive)

repress [rɪ'pres] *vt* réprimer; *(memories, feelings)* refouler; **to be repressed** *(of person)* être un(e) refoulé(e)

repression [rɪ'preʃən] *n* répression *f*; *(of memories, feelings)* refoulement *m*

repressive [rɪ'presɪv] *adj* répressif(ive)

reprieve [rɪ'priːv] **1** *n Law (cancellation)* commutation *f* de la peine capitale; *(postponement)* sursis *m*; *Fig* **to win a r.** *(of project, company)* bénéficier d'un sursis
2 *vt Law* **to r. sb** *(cancel punishment of)* commuer la peine capitale de qn en réclusion à perpétuité; *(postpone punishment of)* accorder un sursis à qn

reprimand ['reprɪmɑːnd] **1** *n (to child)* réprimande *f*; *(to employee)* avertissement *m*
2 *vt (child)* réprimander; *(employee)* avertir

reprint 1 *n* ['riːprɪnt] réimpression *f*
2 *vt* [riː'prɪnt] réimprimer

reprisal [rɪ'praɪzəl] *n* représailles *fpl*; **to take reprisals** exercer des représailles; **in r. for** en représailles à

reproach [rɪ'prəʊtʃ] **1** *n* reproche *m*; **a look of r.** un regard plein de reproche; **beyond** *or* **above r.** irréprochable
2 *vt* faire des reproches à; **to r. sb for** *or* **with sth** reprocher qch à qn; **to r. oneself** se reprocher qch

reproachful [rɪ'prəʊtʃfʊl] *adj (tone)* de reproche; *(look)* plein(e) de reproche

reprobate ['reprəbeɪt] *n* réprouvé(e) *m,f*; *Hum* dépravé(e) *m,f*

reproduce [riːprə'djuːs] **1** *vt* reproduire
2 *vi* se reproduire

reproduction [riːprə'dʌkʃən] *n* reproduction *f*; **r. furniture** copies *fpl* (de meubles anciens)

reproductive [riːprə'dʌktɪv] *adj* reproducteur(trice); **r. organs** organes *mpl* reproducteurs

reproof [rɪ'pruːf] *n Formal* réprobation *f*

reprove [rɪ'pruːv] *vt Formal (person)* réprimander; *(action)* condamner

reproving [rɪ'pruːvɪŋ] *adj Formal* réprobateur(trice)

reptile ['reptaɪl] *n* reptile *m*

reptilian [rep'tɪlɪən] *adj* reptilien(enne); *Fig (manner, looks)* de reptile

republic [rɪ'pʌblɪk] *n* république *f*

Republican [rə'pʌblɪkən] *n & adj (in US, Ireland)* républicain(e) *m,f*

republican [rə'pʌblɪkən] *n & adj* républicain(e) *m,f*

repudiate [rɪ'pjuːdɪeɪt] *vt Formal (offer)* rejeter; *(person, belief)* renier; *(wife)* répudier; *(rumour)* démentir

repudiation [rɪpjuːdɪ'eɪʃən] *n Formal (of offer)* rejet *m*; *(of person, belief)* reniement *m*; *(of wife)* répudiation *f*; *(of rumour)* démenti *m*

repugnant [rɪ'pʌgnənt] *adj* répugnant(e)

repulse [rɪ'pʌls] *vt* repousser

repulsive [rɪ'pʌlsɪv] *adj* repoussant(e)

reputable ['repjʊtəbəl] *adj* de bonne réputation

reputation [repjʊ'teɪʃən] *n* réputation *f*; **to have a good/bad r.** avoir (une) bonne/mauvaise réputation; **to have a r. for doing sth** avoir la réputation de faire qch; **to have a r. for frankness** avoir la réputation d'être franc (franche); **to live up to one's r.** être à la hauteur de sa réputation

repute [rɪ'pjuːt] **1** *n Formal* réputation *f*; **to be held in good r.** être estimé(e); **of r.** réputé(e)
2 *vt* **she is reputed to be wealthy/a genius** on la dit riche/géniale

reputedly [rɪ'pjuːtɪdlɪ] *adv* à ce qu'on dit

request [rɪ'kwest] **1** *n* demande *f* (**for** de); **available on r.** qui peut être obtenu(e) sur simple demande; **to make a r. (for)** faire une demande (de); **at sb's r.** à la demande de qn; **by popular r.** à la demande générale; **r. stop** *(for bus)* arrêt *m* facultatif
2 *vt* demander; **to r. sb to do sth** prier à qn de faire qch

requiem ['rekwɪəm] *n* requiem *m*; **r. (mass)** messe *f* de requiem

require [rɪ'kwaɪə(r)] *vt (of task, problem, situation)* requérir; *(of person)* avoir besoin de; **to be required to do sth** être tenu(e) de faire qch; **if required** si besoin est/était; **when required** quand il le faut/fallait/faudra

requirement [rɪ'kwaɪəmənt] *n (need)* exigence *f*; *(condition)* condition *f* (require); **to meet** *or* **satisfy sb's requirements** *(needs)* correspondre aux besoins de qn; *(demands)* satisfaire aux exigences de qn

requisite ['rekwɪzɪt] **1** *n* élément *m* essentiel
2 *adj* requis(e)

requisition [rekwɪ'zɪʃən] *vt* réquisitionner

rerun 1 *n* ['riːrʌn] *(on TV)* rediffusion *f*; *Fig (of situation, conflict)* répétition *f*
2 *vt* [riː'rʌn] *(pt* **reran** [riː'ræn]*, pp* **rerun)** **(a)** *(TV programme)* rediffuser **(b)** *(race)* courir de nouveau

resale [riː'seɪl] *n* revente *f*

reschedule [riː'ʃedjuːl] *vt* **(a)** *(meeting, flight) (change time of)* changer l'heure de; *(change date of)* changer la date de **(b)** *(debt)* rééchelonner

rescind [rɪ'sɪnd] *vt (law)* abroger; *(contract)* résilier

rescue [rɪ'skjuː] **1** *n* secours *m*; *(from drowning)* sauvetage *m*; **to come to sb's r.** venir au secours de qn; **r. services** secours *mpl*
2 *vt (from death)* sauver; *(from difficulty)* secourir

rescuer ['reskjuːə(r)] *n* sauveteur *m*

research [rɪ'sɜːtʃ] **1** *n* recherche *f*; **to do r.** faire de la recherche; **to do r. into sth** faire des recherches sur qch; **r. and development** recherche et développement *m*; **r. assistant/laboratory** assistant(e) *m,f*/laboratoire *m* de recherche
2 *vt* faire des recherches sur
3 *vi* faire des recherches (**into** sur)

researcher [rɪ'sɜːtʃə(r)] *n* chercheur(euse) *m,f*

resemblance [rɪ'zembləns] *n* ressemblance *f* (**to** avec); **to bear a r. to** ressembler à

resemble [rɪ'zembəl] *vt* ressembler à

resent [rɪ'zent] *vt* ne pas apprécier du tout

resentful [rɪ'zentfʊl] *adj* plein(e) de ressentiment; **to be** *or* **feel r.** éprouver du ressentiment

resentment [rɪ'zentmənt] *n* ressentiment *m*; **to feel r.** towards sb éprouver du ressentiment à l'égard de qn

reservation [rezə'veɪʃən] *n* (**a**) *(booking)* réservation *f*; **to make a r.** faire une réservation; **r. desk** bureau *m* des réservations (**b**) *(doubt)* réserve *f*; **to have reservations about** avoir des doutes sur (**c**) *(for Native Americans)* réserve *f*(indienne)

reserve [rɪ'zɜːv] **1** *n* (**a**) *(supply)* réserve *f*; **to draw on one's reserves** puiser dans ses réserves; **to keep sth in r.** garder qch en réserve (**b**) *(in sport)* remplaçant(e) *m,f*; *Mil* **the reserves** les réservistes *mpl* (**c**) *(for birds, nature)* réserve *f*(**d**) *(reticence)* réserve *f* **2** *vt (book, keep)* réserver; **to r. the right to do sth** se réserver le droit de faire qch; **to r. one's strength** ménager ses forces; **to r. judgement (on sth)** réserver son jugement (sur qch)

reserved [rɪ'zɜːvd] *adj* reserve(e)

reservist [rɪ'zɜːvɪst] *n Mil* réserviste *m*

reservoir ['rezəvwɑː(r)] *n (lake)* réservoir *m*; *Fig (of strength, courage)* réserve *f*

reset [riː'set] *(pt & pp* **reset**) *vt* (**a**) *(clock, watch)* mettre à l'heure; *(counter)* remettre à zéro; **r. button** bouton *m* de remise à zéro (**b**) *(fracture)* réduire

reshape [riː'ʃeɪp] *vt* réorganiser

reshuffle ['riːʃʌfəl] *n* réorganisation *f*; *Br Pol* (**Cabinet**) **r.** remaniement *m* (ministériel)

reside [rɪ'zaɪd] *vi* résider (**at/in** à/dans/en)

residence ['rezɪdəns] *n* (**a**) *(stay)* séjour *m*; **to take up r.** s'installer; **place of r.** lieu *m* de résidence; **r. permit** permis *m* de séjour (**b**) *Formal (home)* demeure *f*(**c**) *Br Univ* (**hall of**) **r.** résidence *f* universitaire

resident ['rezɪdənt] **1** *n (of country, street)* habitant(e) *m,f*; *(of hotel)* pensionnaire *mf*; **residents' association =** association de propriétaires ou de locataires d'un immeuble ou d'un quartier **2** *adj* **to be r. in Miami** résider à Miami

residential [rezɪ'denʃəl] *adj* (**a**) *(neighbourhood)* résidentiel(elle) (**b**) *(staff)* à demeure; **r. course =** stage qui nécessite un déplacement de plusieurs jours

residual [rɪ'zɪdjʊəl] *adj* résiduel(elle); *Fig (doubt, worry)* qui persiste; *(income)* net (nette)

residue ['rezɪdjuː] *n (remainder)* reste *m* (**b**) *Chem* résidu *m*

resign [rɪ'zaɪn] **1** *vt* (**a**) *(job, position)* démissionner de (**b**) **to r. oneself to sth/to doing sth** se résigner à qch/à faire qch **2** *vi* démissionner

resignation [rezɪg'neɪʃən] *n* (**a**) *(from job)* démission *f*; **to hand in one's r.** donner sa démission (**b**) *(attitude)* résignation *f*

resilience [rɪ'zɪliəns] *n (of material, metal)* élasticité *f*; *(of person, economy)* résistance *f*

resilient [rɪ'zɪliənt] *adj (material, metal)* élastique; *(person)* résistant(e)

resin ['rezɪn] *n* résine *f*

resist [rɪ'zɪst] **1** *vt* résister à; *Law* **to r. arrest** refuser d'obtempérer *(lors d'une arrestation)*; **to r. doing sth** s'empêcher de faire qch **2** *vi* résister

resistance [rɪ'zɪstəns] *n* résistance *f* (**to** à); **to put up** *or* **offer r.** offrir une résistance; **to meet with r.** rencontrer une résistance; **to take the line of least r.** adopter la solution de facilité; **r. fighter** résistant(e) *m,f*

resistant [rɪ'zɪstənt] *adj* **to be r. to sth** résister à qch

resistor [rɪ'zɪstə(r)] *n Elec* résistance *f*

resit [riː'sɪt] **1** *n* examen *m* de rattrapage; **to have to do**

resits devoir repasser des examens **2** *vt (pt & pp* **resat** [riː'sæt]) *(exam, driving test)* repasser

resolute ['rezəluːt] *adj* résolu(e); *(refusal, opposition)* clair(e)

resolution [rezə'luːʃən] *n* (**a**) *(decision, solution)* résolution *f*; **to pass** *or* **carry a r.** adopter une résolution (**b**) *(firmness)* fermeté *f*

resolve [rɪ'zɒlv] **1** *n* résolution *f* **2** *vt* (**a**) *(decide)* **to r. to do sth** *(of individual)* se résoudre à faire qch; *(of committee)* décider de faire qch (**b**) *(solve)* résoudre **3** *vi* **to r. on/against doing sth** se résoudre à faire/ne pas faire qch

resonance ['rezənəns] *n* résonance *f*

resonant ['rezənənt] *adj* qui résonne

resonate ['rezəneɪt] *vi* résonner

resort [rɪ'zɔːt] **1** *n* (**a**) *(recourse)* recours *m*; **without r. to** sans avoir recours à; **as a last r.** en dernier recours (**b**) *(holiday place)* lieu *m* de villégiature; **beach r.** station *f* balnéaire; **ski r.** station de sports d'hiver **2** *vi* **to r. to sth** recourir à qch; **to r. to doing sth** finir par faire qch

resound [rɪ'zaʊnd] *vi* résonner (**with** de)

resounding [rɪ'zaʊndɪŋ] *adj (crash, applause, failure)* retentissant(e); *(success)* éclatant(e)

resource [rɪ'zɔːs] **1** *n* ressource *f*; **r. management** gestion *f* des ressources **2** *vt* financer

resourceful [rɪ'zɔːsfʊl] *adj* ingénieux(euse)

respect [rɪ'spekt] **1** *n* (**a**) *(admiration, consideration)* respect *m*; **to have r. for** avoir du respect pour; **treat the sea with r.** soyez prudent à la mer; **with all due r.** sauf le respect que je vous dois; **to pay one's last respects to sb** rendre les derniers hommages à qn (**b**) *(aspect)* égard *m*; **in many respects** à bien des égards; **in some** *or* **certain respects** à certains égards; **in all respects** *or* **every r.** à tous les égards; **with r. to, in r. of** concernant **2** *vt* respecter

respectability [rɪspektə'bɪlɪtɪ] *n* respectabilité *f*

respectable [rɪ'spektəbəl] *adj (decent, fairly large)* respectable; *(fairly good)* honorable

respectably [rɪ'spektəblɪ] *adv* (**a**) *(honourably, decently)* de manière respectable; *(dressed)* convenablement (**b**) *(fairly well)* honorablement

respecter [rɪ'spektə(r)] *n* **to be no r. of** n'avoir aucun respect pour

respectful [rɪ'spektfʊl] *adj* respectueux(euse)

respective [rɪ'spektɪv] *adj* respectif(ive)

respectively [rɪ'spektɪvlɪ] *adv* respectivement

respiration [respɪ'reɪʃən] *n* respiration *f*

respirator ['respɪreɪtə(r)] *n* respirateur *m*; **to be on a r.** être branché(e) sur un respirateur

respiratory [rɪ'spɪrɪtərɪ] *adj* respiratoire

respite ['respaɪt] *n (rest)* répit *m*; *(delay)* sursis *m*

resplendent [rɪ'splendənt] *adj* resplendissant(e)

respond [rɪ'spɒnd] *vi (answer)* répondre (**to** à); *(react)* réagir (**to** à); **to r. (to treatment)** *(of patient)* bien réagir (au traitement)

respondent [rɪ'spɒndənt] *n* (**a**) *Law* défendeur(eresse) *m,f* (**b**) *(to questionnaire)* sondé(e) *m,f*

response [rɪ'spɒns] *n (answer)* réponse *f*; *(reaction)* réaction *f*; **in r. to** en réponse à; **the appeal met with a generous r.** le public a répondu généreusement à l'appel; **r. time** temps *m* de réponse

responsibility [rɪspɒnsɪ'bɪlɪtɪ] *(pl* **responsibilities**) *n* responsabilité *f* (**for** de); **to take** *or* **accept r. for sth** accepter la responsabilité de qch

responsible [rɪ'spɒnsɪbəl] *adj* responsable (**for** de); *(job)* à responsabilité; **to hold sb r.** tenir qn pour responsable

responsive [rɪ'spɒnsɪv] *adj (to kindness, praise)* sensible (**to** à); *(to idea, suggestion)* réceptif(ive) (**to** à)

rest¹ [rest] **1** *n* (**a**) *(repose)* repos *m*; **to have** *or* **take a r.** se reposer; *Euph* **to be at r.** reposer en paix; **to put** *or* **set sb's mind at r.** rassurer qn; *Br Fam* **give it a r.!** tu veux bien arrêter cinq minutes!; **to come to r.** *(of ball, car)* s'arrêter (**b**) *(support)* support *m* (**c**) *Mus (pause)* silence *m*
2 *vt* (**a**) *(cause to repose)* **to r. one's eyes/legs** se reposer les yeux/les jambes; **God r. his soul!** que Dieu ait son âme! (**b**) *(lean)* poser (**on** sur) (**c**) *(argument, hopes, confidence)* fonder (**on** sur); *Fig* **I r. my case!** sans commentaire!
3 *vi* (**a**) *(repose)* se reposer, prendre du repos; **I won't r. until she has been caught** je n'aurai de cesse qu'elle ne soit prise; **r. in peace** *(on gravestone)* qu'il/elle repose en paix (**b**) *(lean)* être posé(e) (**on** sur) (**c**) *(remain)* **to r. with sb** *(of decision, responsibility)* incomber à qn; **there the matter rests** l'affaire en est là; **I won't let it r. at that** je n'en resterai pas là; **r. assured...** soyez assuré que... (**d**) *(of argument, theory)* **to r. on** reposer sur

rest² *n* **the r.** *(remainder)* le reste; *(others)* les autres *mfpl*; **the r. of the time/the men** le reste du temps/des hommes; **the r. of them will stay here** les autres resteront ici

restaurant ['restrɒnt] *n* restaurant *m*; **r. car** *(in train)* wagon-restaurant *m*

restful ['restfʊl] *adj* reposant(e)

restive ['restɪv] *adj* agité(e)

restless ['restlɪs] *adj* agité(e); **to have a r. night** passer une nuit agitée

restoration [restə'reɪʃən] *n (of furniture, monarchy)* restauration *f*; *(of communications, law and order)* rétablissement *m*; *(of property)* restitution *f*

restore [rɪ'stɔː(r)] *vt (furniture, monarchy, faith, calm)* restaurer; *(communications, law and order, confidence)* rétablir; *(property)* restituer (**to** à); **to r. sb to health** redonner la santé à qn

restrain [rɪ'streɪn] *vt (person, dog)* maîtriser; *(passions)* refréner; *(anger, crowd)* contenir; **to r. sb from doing sth** retenir qn pour qu'il/elle ne fasse pas qch; **to r. oneself (from doing sth)** se retenir (de faire qch)

restrained [rɪ'streɪnd] *adj (person, manner)* réservé(e); *(tone, terms)* mesuré(e); *(style)* sobre

restraint [rɪ'streɪnt] *n* (**a**) *(moderation)* mesure *f*, modération *f*; **to show** *or* **exercise great r.** faire preuve d'une grande modération (**b**) *(restriction)* restriction *f*; **without r.** sans retenue

restrict [rɪ'strɪkt] *vt (person, freedom)* restreindre; **to r. oneself to sth/to doing sth** se limiter à qch/à faire qch

restricted [rɪ'strɪktɪd] *adj* restreint(e), limité(e); *(document)* secret(ète); **r. area** *Mil* zone *f* interdite; *(for parking)* zone bleue

restriction [rɪ'strɪkʃən] *n* restriction *f*; *(of speed)* limitation *f*; **to place restrictions on sth** apporter des restrictions à qch

restrictive [rɪ'strɪktɪv] *adj* restrictif(ive); *Ind* **r. practices** pratiques *fpl* restrictives

restroom ['restruːm] *n Am* toilettes *fpl*

restructure [riː'strʌktʃə(r)] *vt* restructurer

restructuring [riː'strʌktʃərɪŋ] *n* restructuration *f*

result [rɪ'zʌlt] **1** *n* résultat *m*; **as a r.** en conséquence; **as a r. of** à la suite de; **the r. is that...** il en résulte que...; **to**

yield *or* **show results** donner des résultats
2 *vi* **to r. from** résulter de; **to r. in** entraîner

resultant [rɪ'zʌltənt] *adj* résultant(e)

resume [rɪ'zjuːm] **1** *vt* reprendre; *(relations)* renouer; *(attempt)* renouveler; *(interest)* retrouver
2 *vi* reprendre

résumé ['rezjʊmeɪ] *n (summary)* résumé *m*; *Am (curriculum vitae)* curriculum vitae *m inv*

resumption [rɪ'zʌmpʃən] *n* reprise *f*

resurface [riː'sɜːfɪs] **1** *vt (road)* refaire le revêtement de
2 *vi also Fig* refaire surface

resurgent [rɪ'sɜːdʒənt] *adj* renaissant(e); *(economy)* qui connaît une reprise

resurrect [rezə'rekt] *vt Rel* ressusciter; *Fig (fashion)* remettre au goût du jour; *(argument)* ressortir; *(tradition)* faire renaître

resurrection [rezə'rekʃən] *n Fig* réapparition *f*; *Rel* **the R.** la Résurrection (du Christ)

resuscitate [rɪ'sʌsɪteɪt] *vt (person)* ranimer; *Fig (career)* redonner un nouvel élan à; *(scheme)* ressortir

retail ['riːteɪl] **1** *n Com* (vente *f* au) détail *m*; **r. outlet** magasin *m* de détail; **r. price** prix *m* de détail; *Econ* **r. price index** indice *m* des prix de détail; **r. trade** commerce *m* de détail
2 *vt (goods)* vendre au détail
3 *vi* se vendre (**at** à)

retailer ['riːteɪlə(r)] *n* détaillant(e) *m,f*

retain [rɪ'teɪn] *vt* (**a**) *(keep)* conserver, garder (**b**) *(hold in place)* maintenir; **retaining wall** mur *m* de soutènement (**c**) *(remember)* retenir

retainer [rɪ'teɪnə(r)] *n* (**a**) *(fee)* appointements *mpl* (**b**) *Old-fashioned (servant)* serviteur *m*, servante *f*

retaliate [rɪ'tælieɪt] *vi* riposter

retaliation [rɪtæli'eɪʃən] *n* représailles *fpl*; **in r. (for sth)** en représailles (à qch)

retard [rɪ'tɑːd] *vt* retarder

retarded [rɪ'tɑːdɪd] *adj* **(mentally) r.** arriéré(e)

retch [retʃ] *vi* avoir des haut-le-cœur

retention [rɪ'tenʃən] *n (of custom, practice)* maintien *m*; *(of fact, impression)* mémorisation *f*

retentive [rɪ'tentɪv] *adj (memory)* fidèle; *(person)* qui a (une) bonne mémoire

rethink 1 *n* [riː'θɪŋk] **to have a r. (about sth)** réfléchir à nouveau (à qch)
2 *vt* [riː'θɪŋk] *(pt & pp* **rethought** [riː'θɔːt]*)* repenser

reticent ['retɪsənt] *adj* peu communicatif(ive); **to be r. about sth** parler peu de qch

retina ['retɪnə] *n* rétine *f*

retinue ['retɪnjuː] *n* suite *f*, cortège *m*

retire [rɪ'taɪə(r)] **1** *vt* mettre à la retraite
2 *vi* (**a**) *(employee)* prendre sa retraite (**b**) *(withdraw)* se retirer; *(go to bed)* (aller) se coucher

retired [rɪ'taɪəd] *adj* retraité(e), à la retraite

retirement [rɪ'taɪəmənt] *n (from work, army)* retraite *f*; **to take early r.** prendre sa retraite anticipée; **to come out of r.** reprendre sa carrière; **r. age** l'âge *m* de la retraite; **r. pension** (pension *f* de) retraite

retiring [rɪ'taɪərɪŋ] *adj* (**a**) *(reserved)* réservé(e) (**b**) *(chairman, MP)* sortant(e); *(employee)* qui prend sa retraite; **r. age** l'âge *m* de la retraite

retort [rɪ'tɔːt] **1** *n (answer)* réplique *f*
2 *vt & vi* répliquer

retrace [rɪ'treɪs] *vt* **to r. one's steps** revenir sur ses pas

retract [rɪ'trækt] **1** *vt* (**a**) *(statement, offer)* revenir sur (**b**)

(claws, aircraft undercarriage) rentrer
2 *vi* **(a)** *(of person)* se rétracter **(b)** *(of claws, aircraft undercarriage)* rentrer
retractable [rɪ'træktəbəl] *adj* rétractable; *(antenna, aircraft undercarriage)* escamotable
retrain [riː'treɪn] **1** *vt* recycler
2 *vi* se recycler
retraining [riː'treɪnɪŋ] *n* recyclage *m*
retread ['riːtred] *n* pneu *m* rechapé
retreat [rɪ'triːt] **1** *n* **(a)** *(withdrawal)* retraite *f*; *also Fig* **to beat a (hasty) r.** battre en retraite **(b)** *(place)* retraite *f*
2 *vi* battre en retraite; *Fig* se réfugier
retrial [riː'traɪəl] *n Law* nouveau procès *m*
retribution [retrɪ'bjuːʃən] *n* châtiment *m*
retrieve [rɪ'triːv] *vt* récupérer; *Compu (file)* ouvrir
retriever [rɪ'triːvə(r)] *n (dog)* retriever *m*
retroactive [retrəʊ'æktɪv] *adj Formal* rétroactif(ive)
retrograde ['retrəgreɪd] *adj* rétrograde
retrospect ['retrəspekt] *n* **in r.** après coup, rétrospectivement
retrospective [retrə'spektɪv] **1** *n (exhibition)* rétrospective *f*
2 *adj* rétrospectif(ive); *(measure, decision)* à effet rétroactif
return [rɪ'tɜːn] **1** *n* **(a)** *(of person, peace, season, tennis service)* retour *m*; *(of goods)* renvoi *m*; **on my r.** à mon retour; **by r. of post** par retour du courrier; **in r. (for)** en échange (de); **to do sth in r.** faire qch en retour; **many happy returns (of the day)!** bon anniversaire! **r. journey** *(voyage m de)* retour; **r. match** match *m* retour; **r. ticket** (billet *m*) aller et retour *m* **(b)** *Fin (profit)* rapport *m*; **to bring a good r.** rapporter un bon bénéfice; **r. on investment** retour *m* sur investissement
2 *vt* **(a)** *(give or send back)* rendre; **to r. a favour** rendre la pareille; **r. to sender** *(on letter)* retour à l'envoyeur; **to r. service** *(in tennis)* renvoyer le service; **to r. sb's call** *(on phone)* rappeler qn; *Law* **to r. a verdict of guilty/not guilty** déclarer l'accusé(e) coupable/non coupable **(b)** *Fin (profit)* rapporter
3 *vi (come back)* revenir; *(go back)* retourner; **to r. to work** reprendre son travail
returnable [rɪ'tɜːnəbəl] *adj (bottle)* consigné(e)
reunification [riːjuːnɪfɪ'keɪʃən] *n* réunification *f*
reunify [riː'juːnɪfaɪ] *(pt & pp* reunified) *vt* réunifier
reunion [riː'juːnɪən] *n* réunion *f*
reunite [riːjuː'naɪt] *vt* réconcilier; **to be reunited with sb** retrouver qn
reusable [riː'juːzəbəl] *adj* réutilisable
reuse [riː'juːz] *vt* réutiliser
Rev *Rel (abbr* **Reverend) R.** Gray le révérend Gray
rev [rev] *Fam* **1** *n (abbr* **revolution)** tour *m*; **r. counter** compte-tours *m inv*
2 *vt (pt & pp* revved) **(to) r. the engine** faire monter le régime (du moteur)
revalue [riː'væljuː] *vt Fin* réévaluer
revamp [riː'væmp] *vt Fam (image)* rajeunir; *(company)* restructurer; *(house)* retaper
reveal [rɪ'viːl] *vt* révéler
revealing [rɪ'viːlɪŋ] *adj (sign, comment)* révélateur(trice); *(clothing)* qui ne cache pas grand-chose
revel ['revəl] *(pt & pp* **revelled,** *Am* **reveled)** *vi* faire la fête; **to r. in sth** savourer qch
revelation [revə'leɪʃən] *n* révélation *f*; **(the Book of) Revelations** l'Apocalypse *f*
reveller, *Am* **reveler** ['revələ(r)] *n* fêtard(e) *m,f*

revenge [rɪ'vendʒ] **1** *n (punishment)* vengeance *f*; *(getting one's own back)* revanche *f*; **to take** *or* **get r. (on sb)** se venger (de qn); *Prov* **r. is sweet** ça fait du bien de se venger!
2 *vt* venger
revenue ['revənjuː] *n* revenu *m*; *(from sales)* recettes *fpl*
reverberate [rɪ'vɜːbəreɪt] *vi* **(a)** *(of sound)* résonner **(b)** *(of news, rumour)* se propager
reverberation [rɪvɜːbə'reɪʃən] *n* **(a)** *(sound)* réverbération *f* **(b)** *(of news, rumour)* répercussion *f*
revere [rɪ'vɪə(r)] *vt* révérer
reverence ['revərəns] *n* révérence *f*
Reverend ['revərənd] *adj Rel* révérend; **Right R.** très révérend
reverential [revə'renʃəl] *adj* révérencieux(euse)
reverie ['revərɪ] *n* rêverie *f*
reversal [rɪ'vɜːsəl] *n (of opinion, policy)* revirement *m*; *(of roles)* renversement *m*; *(of fortune)* revers *m*; *Law (of decision)* annulation *f*
reverse [rɪ'vɜːs] **1** *n* **(a)** *(opposite)* contraire *m*; **quite the r.!** bien au contraire! **(b)** *(of coin)* revers *m*; *(of fabric)* envers *m* **(c)** *(defeat)* échec *m*; *(misfortune)* revers *m*; **to suffer a r.** *(defeat)* subir un échec; *(misfortune)* subir un revers **(d)** *(gear)* marche *f* arrière; **to put the car into r.** passer la marche arrière
2 *adj* inverse; **in r. order** en ordre inverse; **the r. side** *(of coin)* le revers; *(of fabric)* l'envers *m*; **r.-charge call** communication *f* en PCV; **r. gear** marche *f* arrière
3 *vt* **(a)** *(order, policy, roles)* inverser; *(decision)* revenir sur; *(situation, trend)* renverser; **Br to r. the charges** appeler en PCV **(b)** *(vehicle)* **to r. the car** faire marche arrière
reversible [rɪ'vɜːsəbəl] *adj* **(a)** *(jacket)* réversible **(b)** *(decree)* révocable; *(surgery)* réversible; **not r.** *(decision)* irrévocable; *(surgery)* irréversible
▸ revert [rɪ'vɜːt] *vt insep* revenir à; **to r. to type** reprendre ses vieilles habitudes
review [rɪ'vjuː] **1** *n* **(a)** *(of policy, salary)* révision *f*; *(of situation)* examen *m*; **to be under r.** faire l'objet d'une révision **(b)** *(of book, play, film)* critique *f* **(c)** *Mil* revue *f*
2 *vt* **(a)** *(policy, salary)* réviser; *(situation)* faire le point sur **(b)** *(book, play, film)* faire la critique de **(c)** *Mil (troops)* passer en revue
reviewer [rɪ'vjuːə(r)] *n (of book, play, film)* critique *mf*
revile [rɪ'vaɪl] *vt Formal* vilipender
revise [rɪ'vaɪz] **1** *vt* **(a)** *(text, law)* réviser; *(decision)* réexaminer; **to r. one's opinion (of)** changer d'opinion (à l'égard de) **(b)** *Br (for exam) (subject, notes)* réviser
2 *vi Br (for exam)* réviser, faire des révisions
revision [rɪ'vɪʒən] *n* **(a)** *(of text, law)* révision *f* **(b)** *Br (for exam)* révisions *fpl*
revisionism [rɪ'vɪʒənɪzəm] *n Pol* révisionnisme *m*
revisit [riː'vɪzɪt] *vt (place)* revisiter; *(person)* retourner voir
revitalize [riː'vaɪtəlaɪz] *vt (person)* revigorer; *(arts, industry)* donner un nouvel essor à
revival [rɪ'vaɪvəl] *n (of person)* réanimation *f*; *(of hopes)* renaissance *f*; *(of industry, custom, fashion)* renouveau *m*; *(of play)* reprise *f*
revive [rɪ'vaɪv] **1** *vt (person)* ranimer; *(industry, hopes, custom)* faire renaître; *(fashion)* relancer
2 *vi (of person)* reprendre connaissance; *(of industry)* connaître un renouveau; *(of hopes)* renaître
revoke [rɪ'vəʊk] *vt (law)* abroger; *(decision)* revenir sur; *(privilege)* abolir; **to r. sb's licence** retirer son permis à qn
revolt [rɪ'vəʊlt] **1** *n* révolte *f*; **to be in r.** être en révolte
2 *vt (disgust)* dégoûter
3 *vi (rebel)* se révolter **(against** contre)

revolting [rɪ'vəʊltɪŋ] *adj (disgusting)* dégoûtant(e)

revolution [revə'luːʃən] *n* (**a**) *(radical change)* révolution *f* (**b**) *(turn)* tour *m*, révolution *f*

revolutionary [revə'luːʃənərɪ] *(pl* **revolutionaries**) *n & adj* révolutionnaire *mf*

revolutionize [revə'luːʃənaɪz] *vt* révolutionner

revolve [rɪ'vɒlv] *vi* tourner (**around** autour de); *Fig* **to r. around sth** s'articuler autour de qch

revolver [rɪ'vɒlvə(r)] *n* revolver *m*

revolving [rɪ'vɒlvɪŋ] *adj (chair)* pivotant(e); *(platform)* tournant(e); *Fin (credit)* revolving *inv*; **r. door** porte *f* à tambour

revue [rɪ'vjuː] *n Th* revue *f*

revulsion [rɪ'vʌlʃən] *n* dégoût *m*

reward [rɪ'wɔːd] **1** *n* récompense *f*; **as a r. for** en récompense de
2 *vt* récompenser (**for** de *ou* pour)

rewarding [rɪ'wɔːdɪŋ] *adj* enrichissant(e), intéressant(e)

rewind [riː'waɪnd] *(pt & pp* **rewound** [riː'waʊnd]) *vt (tape, film)* rembobiner

rewire [riː'waɪə(r)] *vt* refaire l'installation électrique de

reword [riː'wɜːd] *vt* reformuler

rework [riː'wɜːk] *vt* retravailler

rewrite [riː'raɪt] *(pt* **rewrote** [riː'rəʊt], *pp* **rewritten** [riː'rɪtən]) *vt* réécrire

Reykjavik ['rekjəvɪk] *n* Reykjavik

RFU [ɑːref'juː] *n Br Sp (abbr* **Rugby Football Union**) = fédération britannique de rugby

rhapsodic(al) [ræp'sɒdɪk(əl)] *adj (prose, description)* dithyrambique; *(person)* enthousiaste

rhapsodize ['ræpsədaɪz] *vi* s'extasier (**over** *or* **about** sur)

rhapsody ['ræpsədɪ] *(pl* **rhapsodies**) *n Mus* rhapsodie *f*; **to go into rhapsodies over sth** s'extasier sur qch

rhesus ['riːsəs] *n* **r.** factor facteur *m* rhésus; **r. positive/negative** rhésus *m* positif/négatif; **r. monkey** rhésus *m*

rhetoric ['retərɪk] *n* rhétorique *f*; **the speech was nothing but empty r.** le discours ne consistait qu'en de belles phrases creuses

rhetorical [rɪ'tɒrɪkəl] *adj (style, question)* rhétorique; *(term)* de rhétorique

rheumatic [ruː'mætɪk] *adj (pain)* rhumatismal(e); *(joint)* atteint(e) de rhumatisme; **r. fever** rhumatisme *m* articulaire aigu

rheumatoid arthritis ['ruːmətɔɪdɑːθ'raɪtɪs] *n* polyarthrite *f* rhumatoïde

Rhine [raɪn] *n* **the R.** le Rhin

rhinestone ['raɪnstəʊn] *n* faux diamant *m*

rhino ['raɪnəʊ] *(pl* **rhinos**) *n Fam* rhinocéros *m*

rhinoceros [raɪ'nɒsərəs] *n* rhinocéros *m*

Rhodes [rəʊdz] *n* Rhodes

rhododendron [rəʊdə'dendrən] *n* rhododendron *m*

rhomboid ['rɒmbɔɪd] *n* rhomboïde *m*

rhombus ['rɒmbəs] *(pl* **rhombuses** *or* **rhombi** ['rɒmbaɪ]) *n* losange *m*

Rhone [rəʊn] *n* **the R.** le Rhône

rhubarb ['ruːbɑːb] *n* rhubarbe *f*; **r. jam/tart** confiture *f*/ tarte *f* à la rhubarbe

rhyme [raɪm] **1** *n (sound)* rime *f*; *(poem)* vers *mpl*; **without r. or reason** sans rime ni raison
2 *vi* rimer (**with** avec); **rhyming slang** = argot cockney où les mots sont remplacés par des locutions choisies pour la rime

rhythm ['rɪðəm] *n* rythme *m*; **r. method** *(of contraception)* méthode *f* du calendrier

rhythmic(al) ['rɪðmɪk(əl)] *adj* rythmé(e), cadencé(e)

rib [rɪb] **1** *n* (**a**) *(of person, animal)* côte *f* (**b**) *(of umbrella)* baleine *f*
2 *vt (pt & pp* **ribbed**) *Fam (tease)* taquiner (**about** à propos de)

ribald ['rɪbəld, 'raɪbəld] *adj* grivois(e), paillard(e)

ribbed [rɪbd] *adj (fabric, sweater)* à côtes

ribbon ['rɪbən] *n (for hair, typewriter)* ruban *m*; *(of land)* bande *f* étroite; **to tear sth to ribbons** déchiqueter qch; *Fig (criticize)* éreinter qch

ribcage ['rɪbkeɪdʒ] *n* cage *f* thoracique

riboflavin(e) [raɪbəʊ'fleɪvɪn] *n Chem* riboflavine *f*

rice [raɪs] *n* riz *m*; **r. field** *or* **paddy** rizière *f*; **r. pudding** riz au lait

rich [rɪtʃ] **1** *npl* **the r.** les riches *mpl*; **riches** *(wealth)* richesses *fpl*
2 *adj* riche; *(harvest, supply)* abondant(e); *(colour)* intense; *(voice)* chaud(e); **to be r. in sth** être riche en qch; *Fam* **that's r. coming from you!** venant de toi, c'est un peu fort!

richly ['rɪtʃlɪ] *adv* richement; **r. deserved** bien mérité(e)

Richter Scale ['rɪktə'skeɪl] *n* échelle *f* de Richter

rick¹ [rɪk] *n (of hay, straw)* meule *f*

rick² *vt* **to r. one's neck** attraper un torticolis; **to r. one's back** se donner un tour de reins

rickets ['rɪkɪts] *npl* rachitisme *m*; **to have r.** être rachitique

rickety ['rɪkɪtɪ] *adj Fam (furniture, staircase)* branlant(e); *(alliance, alibi)* boiteux(euse)

ricochet ['rɪkəʃeɪ] **1** *n* ricochet *m*
2 *vi (pt & pp* **ricochetted** ['rɪkəʃeɪd]) ricocher (**off** sur)

rid [rɪd] *(pt* **rid**, *pp* **rid** *or* **ridden** ['rɪdən]) *vt* **to r. sb of sth** débarrasser qn de qch; **to get r. of sth** se débarrasser de qch

riddance ['rɪdəns] *n Fam* **good r.!** bon débarras!

ridden ['rɪdən] *pp of* **rid**, **ride**

riddle ['rɪdəl] **1** *n (puzzle)* devinette *f*; *(mystery)* énigme *f*
2 *vt* **to r. sb/sth with bullets** cribler qn/qch de balles; **riddled with mistakes** truffé(e) de fautes

ride [raɪd] **1** *n* (**a**) *(on bicycle, in car)* tour *m*; *(on horse)* promenade *f*; **to go for a r.** aller faire un tour; **to give sb a r.** *(in car)* conduire qn en voiture; **it's only a short r. away** ce n'est pas très loin; *Fig* **she was given a rough r.** on lui en a fait voir de toutes les couleurs; *Fig* **to take sb for a r.** mener qn en bateau; *(at funfair)* attraction *f*
2 *vt (pt* **rode**, *pp* **ridden** ['rɪdən]) *(horse, bicycle)* monter à; *(bus, train)* prendre
3 *vi (on horse)* faire du cheval; *(on bicycle)* faire de la bicyclette; *Fig* **to be riding high** connaître une période de succès; *Fam Fig* **to let it r.** laisser courir

▸ **ride out** *vt sep (problem, crisis)* survivre à; *Fig* **to r. out the storm** surmonter la crise

rider ['raɪdə(r)] *n* (**a**) *(on horse)* cavalier(ère) *m,f*; *(on bicycle)* cycliste *mf*; *(on motorbike)* motocycliste *mf* (**b**) *Law (to document, treaty)* annexe *f*; *(to bill)* clause *f* additionnelle

ridge [rɪdʒ] *n (of mountain)* crête *f*; *(of roof)* faîte *m*; *(on surface)* strie *f*; *Met* **r. of high pressure** dorsale *f* barométrique

ridicule ['rɪdɪkjuːl] **1** *n* ridicule *m*; **to hold sb/sth up to r.** tourner qn/qch en ridicule
2 *vt* ridiculiser, tourner en ridicule

ridiculous ['rɪdɪkjʊləs] *adj* ridicule; **to make sb/sth look r.** rendre qn/qch ridicule; **to make oneself look r.** se rendre ridicule, se ridiculiser

riding ['raɪdɪŋ] n équitation f; **to go r.** faire du cheval; **r. boots** bottes fpl de cheval; **r. crop** or **whip** cravache f; **r. school** école f d'équitation

rife [raɪf] adj **to be r.** être très répandu(e); (of rumours) aller bon train

riffraff ['rɪfræf] n racaille f

rifle[1] ['raɪfəl] n fusil m; **r. range** champ m de tir; (at funfair) stand m de tir; **r. shot** coup m de fusil

rifle[2] vt (house, office) mettre sens dessus dessous; (pockets, drawer) fouiller dans

rifleman ['raɪfəlmən] n Mil fusilier m

rift [rɪft] n (in earth, rock) fissure f; (in relationship) rupture f; (difference of opinion) désaccord m

rig [rɪg] **1** n (a) (of ship) gréement m (b) (oil) **r.** derrick m; (at sea) plate-forme f pétrolière **2** vt (pt & pp **rigged**) (a) (ship) gréer (b) Fam (election, contest) truquer
► **rig out** vt sep Fam **to be rigged out in** être attifé(e) de
► **rig up** vt sep monter, installer

Riga ['riːgə] n Riga

rigging ['rɪgɪŋ] n (of ship) gréement m

right [raɪt] **1** n (a) (morality) bien m, to be in the **r.** avoir raison; **to set things to rights** arranger les choses (b) (entitlement) droit m; **to have the r. to do sth** avoir le droit de faire qch; **to be within one's rights** être dans son droit; **by rights** en principe; **by r.** de droit; **to be famous in one's own r.** être soi-même une célébrité; **the r. to vote** le droit de vote; **r. of way** (on land) droit de passage; (on road) priorité f (c) (right-hand side) droite f, côté m droit; **on** or **to the r.** à droite; **on my r.** à ou sur ma droite; **the r.** (in politics) la droite
2 adj (a) (correct) exact(e), bon (bonne); (word) juste; **to be r.** (of person) avoir raison; **to keep on the r. side of sb** veiller à ne pas se mettre qn à dos; **to be on the r. lines** être sur la bonne voie (b) (morally good) bien inv; **to do the r. thing** faire ce qu'il faut (c) (appropriate) bon (bonne); **the r. thing to do** la meilleure chose à faire; **to know the r. people** connaître les gens qu'il faut; **to be in the r. place at the r. time** se trouver là au bon moment (d) (mentally, physically well) **I'm not feeling quite r.** je ne me sens pas très bien; **to be as r. as rain** être en parfaite santé; **no one in his r. mind would do that** aucune personne sensée ne ferait cela; **he's not quite r. in the head** il n'a pas toute sa tête (e) Br Fam (for emphasis) véritable; **I felt a r. fool** je me suis vraiment senti stupide; **my hair was in a r. mess** mes cheveux étaient complètement en bataille (f) (right-hand) droit(e); **on the r. side** à ou sur la droite; Pol **the r. wing** l'aile f droite (g) Math **r. angle** angle m droit
3 adv (a) (straight) (tout) droit; **to put things r.** arranger les choses; **to put sb r.** détromper qn (b) **r. away** (immediately) sur-le-champ, immédiatement; **I'll be r. back** je reviens tout de suite; **r. now** (immediately) tout de suite; (at the moment) en ce moment (c) (completely) **to go r. through sth** traverser qch de part en part; **to go r. up to sb** se diriger (tout) droit vers qn; **to turn r. round** se retourner; **r. at the top/back** tout en haut/à l'arrière (d) (exactly) **r. here/there** juste ici/là; **r. in the middle** en plein milieu; **r. behind** juste derrière; Fig **to be r. behind sb** soutenir qn à fond (e) (answer) correctement; (guess) juste; **to understand/ remember r.** bien comprendre/se souvenir (f) (well) **I'm sure it'll all come r. for you** je suis sûr que

tout s'arrangera pour vous; Fam **to see sb r.** veiller à ce que qn ne soit pas à court d'argent; **it was a mistake, r. enough** c'était bien une erreur
(g) (look, turn) à droite; Fig **r., left and centre** de tous les côtés
4 vt (a) (put upright) redresser
(b) (redress) **to r. a wrong** réparer un tort

right-angled ['raɪtæŋgəld] adj à angle droit; (triangle) rectangle

righteous ['raɪtʃəs] adj (person) droit(e), vertueux(euse); (indignation) vertueux(euse)

rightful ['raɪtfʊl] adj (heir, owner) légitime; (share) auquel (à laquelle) on a droit

right-hand ['raɪthænd] adj de droite; (corner, side) droit(e); **r. bend** virage m à droite; **r. drive** conduite f à droite; **on the r. side** à droite; **to be sb's r. man** être le bras droit de qn

right-handed [raɪt'hændɪd] **1** adj droitier(ère)
2 adv de la main droite

right-hander [raɪt'hændə(r)] n (person) droitier(ère) m,f

rightly ['raɪtlɪ] adv (correctly) bien; (justifiably) à juste titre; **I don't r. know why...** je ne sais pas exactement pourquoi...; **r. or wrongly** à tort ou à raison; **... and r. so** ... et non sans raison

right-minded [raɪt'maɪndɪd], **right-thinking** [raɪt-'θɪŋkɪŋ] adj sensé(e)

right-wing [raɪt'wɪŋ] adj Pol de droite

right-winger [raɪt'wɪŋə(r)] n Pol (man) homme m de droite; (woman) femme f de droite

rigid ['rɪdʒɪd] adj rigide; Fig (person, ideas) inflexible; Br Fam **to be bored r.** s'ennuyer ferme

rigidity [rɪ'dʒɪdɪtɪ] n rigidité f

rigmarole ['rɪgmərəʊl] n Fam (process) procédure f compliquée; (speech) long discours m

rigor mortis ['rɪgə(r) 'mɔːtɪs] n rigidité f cadavérique

rigorous ['rɪgərəs] adj rigoureux(euse)

rigour ['rɪgə(r)] n rigueur f

rigout ['rɪgaʊt] n Fam (outfit) tenue f

rile [raɪl] vt Fam agacer

rim [rɪm] n (of cup, bowl) bord m; (of wheel) jante f; (of spectacles) monture f

rind [raɪnd] n (of fruit) écorce f; (of cheese) croûte f; (of bacon) couenne f

ring[1] [rɪŋ] **1** n (a) (for finger) (with stone) bague f; (without stone) anneau m; (for keys) porte-clés m inv; **the rings** (in gymnastics) les anneaux; **r. binder** classeur m à anneaux; **r. finger** annulaire m (b) (of people, chairs) cercle m; (on stove) brûleur m; (stain) marque f; **to have rings under one's eyes** avoir des cernes sous les yeux; Fig **to run rings round sb** surpasser qn; **r. road** périphérique m (c) (for boxing, wrestling) ring m (d) (of criminals) bande f; (of spies) réseau m
2 vt (surround) encercler

ring[2] **1** n (sound) (of doorbell, telephone) sonnerie f; (of small bell, coins) tintement m; **there was a r. at the door** on sonna à la porte; Br Fam **to give sb a r.** passer un coup de fil à qn; **to have a r. of truth** avoir l'air vrai(e); **the name has a familiar r. to it** ce nom me dit quelque chose
2 vt (pt **rang** [ræŋ], pp **rung** [rʌŋ]) (bell) sonner; (alarm) déclencher; Br (on phone) appeler; **to r. the doorbell** sonner à la porte; Fig **that rings a bell** cela me dit quelque chose; Fig **to r. the changes** introduire des changements
3 vi (a) (of bell, telephone) sonner; **to r. at the door** sonner à la porte; Fig **to r. true** avoir l'air vrai(e); **to r. false** sonner faux (b) (resonate) (of ears) bourdonner; **to r. with** (of street, room) retentir de (c) (make a phone call) appeler

▶ **ring back** *vt sep (on phone)* rappeler

▶ **ring off** *vi (on phone)* raccrocher

▶ **ring out** *vi (of voice, shout)* retentir

▶ **ring up** *vt sep* **(a)** *(on phone)* téléphoner à, appeler **(b)** *(on cash register)* enregistrer; **to r. up a profit** enregistrer un bénéfice

ringleader ['rɪŋliːdə(r)] *n (of strike)* meneur(euse) *m,f; (of gang)* chef *m* de bande

ringlet ['rɪŋlɪt] *n* anglaise *f*

ringmaster ['rɪŋmɑːstə(r)] *n* ≃ Monsieur *m* Loyal

ring-pull ['rɪŋpʊl] *n* bague *f* (d'ouverture)

ringside ['rɪŋsaɪd] *n* at the r. près du ring; **to have a r. seat** avoir une place au premier rang; *Fig* être aux premières loges

ringworm ['rɪŋwɜːm] *n Med* teigne *f*

rink [rɪŋk] *n (for roller skating)* piste *f; (for ice skating)* patinoire *f*

rinse [rɪns] **1** *n* to give sth a r. rincer qch
2 *vt (clothes, dishes)* rincer; **to r. one's hands/hair** se rincer les mains/les cheveux

▶ **rinse out** *vt sep* rincer

Rio (de Janeiro) ['riːəʊ(dɪdʒəˈneərəʊ)] *n* Rio (de Janeiro)

riot ['raɪət] **1** *n (uprising)* émeute *f; Fig* a r. of colour une explosion de couleurs; **to run r.** se déchaîner; **her imagination was running r.** elle s'imaginait toutes sortes de choses; **to read sb the r. act** passer un savon à qn; r. police police *f* anti-émeute, ≃ CRS *mpl*
2 *vi* faire une émeute; *(of prisoners)* se mutiner

rioter ['raɪətə(r)] *n* émeutier(ère) *m,f*

rioting ['raɪətɪŋ] *n* émeutes *fpl*

riotous ['raɪətəs] *adj (party, behaviour, event)* tapageur(euse); r. living vie *f* déréglée

RIP [ɑːraɪˈpiː] *(abbr* Rest In Peace) qu'il/elle repose en paix

rip [rɪp] **1** *n* déchirure *f*
2 *vt (pt & pp ripped)* déchirer; **to r. sth to pieces** *(cloth)* mettre qch en lambeaux; *(paper)* déchirer qch en mille morceaux; *Fig (criticize)* mettre qch en pièces
3 *vi* **(a)** *(of cloth, paper)* se déchirer **(b)** *Fam* to let r. *(in performance)* se déchaîner; **to let r. at sb** s'en prendre violemment à qn

▶ **rip off** *vt sep* **(a)** *(tear)* arracher **(b)** *Fam (swindle)* arnaquer; *(steal)* piquer

▶ **rip open** *vt sep* to r. open a letter ouvrir une lettre en déchirant l'enveloppe

▶ **rip up** *vt sep* **(a)** *(letter)* déchirer **(b)** *(floorboards)* arracher; *(pavement)* creuser des trous dans

ripe [raɪp] *adj (fruit)* mûr(e); *(cheese)* fait(e) à point; **to live to a r. old age** vivre jusqu'à un âge avancé; **the time is r. (to do sth)** le temps est venu (de faire qch)

ripen ['raɪpən] *vi* mûrir; *(of cheese)* se faire

rip-off ['rɪpɒf] *n Fam* arnaque *f*

riposte [rɪˈpɒst] *n* riposte *f*, réplique *f*

ripple ['rɪpəl] **1** *n (on water)* ride *f; (of applause, laughter)* vague *f; (of excitement)* frémissement *m*
2 *vi (of water)* se rider; **laughter rippled through the audience** des vagues de rires ont parcouru le public

rise [raɪz] **1** *n* **(a)** *(in price, temperature, pressure)* hausse *f; (pay)* r. augmentation *f* (de salaire); **to be on the r.** *(of prices)* être en hausse; *(of crime, inflation)* être en augmentation; **the r. and fall of** la grandeur et la décadence de
(b) *(of leader, party)* ascension *f; r.* to power accession *f* au pouvoir
(c) *(in road, ground)* éminence *f*

(d) *(idioms)* to give r. to sth donner lieu à qch; *Fam* to take a r. out of sb faire enrager qn
2 *vi (pt* rose [rəʊz], *pp* risen ['rɪzən]) **(a)** *(get up)* se lever; *(after falling)* se relever; *Fam* r. and shine! debout là-dedans!
(b) *(of smoke, balloon, ground)* monter; *(of sun, moon)* se lever; *(in career)* monter; **a murmur rose from the crowd** un murmure s'éleva de la foule; **to r. to the occasion** se montrer à la hauteur de la situation; **to r. to the position of managing director** accéder au poste de P-DG; **to r. to power** accéder au pouvoir; **to r. in sb's esteem** grandir dans l'estime de qn
(c) *(of temperature)* s'élever, monter; *(of price)* augmenter; **my spirits rose** je repris courage; **her voice rose in anger** elle a élevé la voix sous l'effet de la colère
(d) *(revolt)* se soulever; **to r. in arms** prendre les armes; **to r. in protest (against sth)** se soulever (contre qch)

▶ **rise above** *vt insep (problem, criticism)* surmonter

▶ **rise up** *vi (revolt)* se soulever; **to r. up in arms** prendre les armes; **to r. up in protest (against sth)** se soulever (contre qch)

risible ['rɪzɪbəl] *adj* risible

rising ['raɪzɪŋ] **1** *n (revolt)* soulèvement *m*
2 *adj (sun)* levant; *(temperature)* en hausse; *(prices, inflation)* en augmentation; *(artist, politician)* qui monte; *Fig* r. star étoile *f* montante

risk [rɪsk] **1** *n* risque *m*; **to take a r.** prendre un risque; **at r. (life, person)** en danger; *(job)* menacé(e); **to put one's health at r.** risquer de s'abîmer la santé; **at the r. of doing sth** au risque de faire qch; **to run the r. of doing sth** courir le risque de faire qch; **at one's own r.** à ses risques et périls; r. assessment évaluation *f* des risques; r. capital capital *m* à risque; r. management gestion *f* des risques
2 *vt* **(a)** *(life, reputation)* risquer; **to r. one's neck** risquer sa peau **(b)** *(take the chance of)* to r. failure risquer d'échouer; **to r. death** risquer sa vie; **I can't r. going** je ne peux pas prendre le risque d'y aller; **they r. losing all their money** ils risquent de perdre tout leur argent

risky ['rɪskɪ] *adj* risqué(e)

risotto [rɪˈzɒtəʊ] *(pl* risottos) *n* risotto *m*

risqué ['rɪskeɪ] *adj* osé(e)

rissole ['rɪsəʊl] *n* croquette *f*

rite [raɪt] *n* rite *m*

ritual ['rɪtjʊəl] **1** *n* rituel *m*
2 *adj* rituel(elle)

ritzy ['rɪtsɪ] *adj Fam* chic *inv*

rival ['raɪvəl] **1** *n & adj* rival(e) *m,f*
2 *vt (pt & pp rivalled, Am rivaled) (compete with)* rivaliser avec; *(equal)* égaler

rivalry ['raɪvəlrɪ] *n* rivalité *f*

river ['rɪvə(r)] *n* rivière *f; (flowing into sea)* fleuve *m; Fig (of blood)* flot *m*

riverbed ['rɪvəbed] *n* lit *m* de la rivière

riverside ['rɪvəsaɪd] *n* bord *m* de l'eau; r. villa villa *f* au bord de l'eau

rivet ['rɪvɪt] **1** *n* rivet *m*
2 *vt* river; **to be riveted (by)** être fasciné(e) (par); *Fig* to be riveted to the spot *(with fear, surprise)* être cloué(e) sur place

riveting ['rɪvɪtɪŋ] *adj Fig* fascinant(e)

Riviera [rɪvɪˈeərə] *n* the (French) R. la Côte d'Azur

RN [ɑːˈren] *(abbr* Royal Navy) = marine nationale britannique

RNA [ɑːrenˈeɪ] *n (abbr* ribonucleic acid) ARN *m*

RNLI [ɑːrenelˈaɪ] *n Br (abbr* Royal National Lifeboat

Institution) ≃ Société *f* nationale de sauvetage en mer

roach [rəʊtʃ] *n* **(a)** *(fish)* gardon *m* **(b)** *Am Fam (cockroach)* cafard *m*

road [rəʊd] *n* route *f; (in town)* rue *f;* **they live across** *or* **over the r.** ils habitent en face; **by r.** par la route; **to be off the r.** *(of car)* être en panne; **down/up the r.** un peu plus loin dans la rue; *Fam* **one for the r.** *(final drink)* un petit dernier pour la route; **to be on the r.** *(of salesman)* être sur la route; *(of pop group)* être en tournée; **after three hours on the r.** après trois heures de route; **to be on the r.** to **recovery/ruin** être en voie de guérison/ruine; *Fig* **to be on the right r.** être sur la bonne voie; *Fam* **let's get this show on the r.!** allez, c'est parti, on y va!; **a few years down the r.** dans quelques années; *Fig* **to come to the end of the r.** *(of relationship)* toucher à sa fin; **r. accident** accident *m* de la route; **r. conditions** états *mpl* des routes; *Fam* **r. hog** chauffard *m;* **r. map** carte *f* routière; **r. rage** violence *f* au volant; **r. sign** panneau *m* de signalisation; *Br* **r. tax** ≃ vignette *f* (automobile); **r. works** *or* **repairs** travaux *mpl* de voirie

roadblock ['rəʊdblɒk] *n* barrage *m* routier

roadside ['rəʊdsaɪd] *n* bord *m* de la route; **r. bar/hotel** bar *m*/hôtel *m* situé en bord de route

road-test ['rəʊdtest] *vt (car)* essayer sur route

roadway ['rəʊdweɪ] *n* chaussée *f*

roadworthy ['rəʊdwɜːðɪ] *adj* en état de rouler

roam [rəʊm] **1** *vt (streets, world)* parcourir; *(seas)* sillonner **2** *vi* **to r. (about)** errer; **to r. about the streets** traîner dans les rues

roar [rɔː(r)] **1** *n (of person, crowd)* hurlement *m; (of animal, engine)* rugissement *m; (of sea, wind)* mugissement *m; (of cars)* vacarme *m* **2** *vi (of person, crowd)* hurler; *(of animal, engine)* rugir; *(of sea, wind)* mugir; *(of cars)* vrombir; **to r. with laughter** hurler de rire

roaring ['rɔːrɪŋ] *adj* **r. drunk** ivre mort(e); **a r. fire** une belle flambée; **a r. success** un succès fou; **to do a r. trade** faire des affaires en or

roast [rəʊst] **1** *n (piece of meat)* rôti *m* **2** *adj* rôti(e) **3** *vt* **(a)** *(meat, potatoes)* faire rôtir; *(nuts, coffee)* faire griller **(b)** *Fam (criticize)* éreinter

roasting ['rəʊstɪŋ] *Fam* **1** *n* **to give sb a r.** *(reprimand)* passer un savon à qn; *(criticize)* descendre qn en flammes **2** *adj* **r.(-hot)** brûlant(e); **it's r. in here** il fait une chaleur à crever ici

rob [rɒb] *(pt & pp* robbed) *vt (bank)* dévaliser; *(person)* voler; *(house)* cambrioler; **to r. sb of sth** *(money, jewellery)* voler qch à qn; *Fig (youth, opportunity)* priver qn de qch

robber ['rɒbə(r)] *n* voleur(euse) *m,f*

robbery ['rɒbərɪ] *(pl* robberies) *n* vol *m*

robe [rəʊb] *n (of priest, judge)* robe *f; Am (dressing gown)* robe de chambre

robin ['rɒbɪn] *n* rouge-gorge *m*

robot ['rəʊbɒt] *n* robot *m*

robotics [rəʊ'bɒtɪks] *n* robotique *f*

robust [rəʊ'bʌst] *adj (person)* robuste; *(material, suitcase)* solide; *(defence, speech)* musclé(e)

rock [rɒk] **1** *n* **(a)** *(substance)* roche *f; (large stone)* rocher *m; Fig* **to be on the rocks** *(of marriage, company)* être en pleine débâcle; **on the rocks** *(drink)* avec des glaçons; **the R. of Gibraltar** le Rocher de Gibraltar; **to reach** *or* **hit r. bottom** toucher le fond; **r. climbing** varappe *f;* **r. face** paroi *f* rocheuse; **r. garden** rocaille *f;* **r. pool** ≃ flaque d'eau dans les rochers à marée basse; **r. salt** sel *m* gemme; **r. solid**

solide comme le roc **(b)** *Br (sweet)* = sucrerie en forme de bâton parfumée à la menthe **(c)** *(rocking motion)* **to give the cradle a r.** balancer un peu le berceau **(d)** *(music)* rock *m;* **r. and roll** rock-and-roll *m;* **r. concert** concert *m* de rock; **r. group** groupe *m* de rock; **r. singer** chanteur(euse) *m,f* de rock **2** *vt (boat, chair)* balancer; *(building)* secouer; **to r. a baby to sleep** bercer un enfant pour qu'il s'endorme; *Fig* **to r. the boat** faire des histoires; *Fig* **the country has been rocked by these revelations** le pays a été secoué par ces révélations **3** *vi (sway)* se balancer; *(of building)* trembler; **to r. with laughter** être secoué(e) par un fou rire

rock-bottom ['rɒkbɒtəm] *adj* **r. prices** prix *mpl* incroyables

rocker ['rɒkə(r)] *n* **(a)** *(chair)* fauteuil *m* à bascule; *Br Fam* **to be off one's r.** être givré(e) **(b)** *(musician, fan)* rocker(euse) *m,f*

rockery ['rɒkərɪ] *(pl* rockeries) *n* rocaille *f*

rocket ['rɒkɪt] **1** *n* fusée *f; Fig* **to give sb a r.** engueuler qn; **r. launcher** lance-fusées *m inv* **2** *vi (of prices, inflation, unemployment)* monter en flèche

rockfall ['rɒkfɔːl] *n* éboulement *m*

rock-hard [rɒk'hɑːd] *adj* dur(e) comme (de la) pierre

Rockies ['rɒkɪz] *npl* **the R.** les Rocheuses *fpl*

rocky ['rɒkɪ] *adj* **(a)** *(path, soil)* rocailleux(euse); **the R. Mountains** les Montagnes *fpl* Rocheuses **(b)** *Fig (economy, relationship)* instable

rod [rɒd] *n (wooden)* baguette *f; (metal)* tige *f; (for curtain)* tringle *f; (for fishing)* canne *f* à pêche; *Fig* **to rule with a r. of iron** gouverner d'une main de fer; *Fig* **to make a r. for one's own back** se préparer des ennuis

rode [rəʊd] *pt of* ride

rodent ['rəʊdənt] *n* rongeur *m*

rodeo ['rəʊdɪəʊ] *(pl* rodeos) *n* rodéo *m*

roe¹ [rəʊ] *n* **r. (deer)** chevreuil *m*

roe² [rəʊ] *n (of fish)* œufs *mpl* de poisson

roger ['rɒdʒə(r)] *exclam (in radio message)* bien reçu!

roger² *vt Br very Fam (have sex with)* baiser

rogue [rəʊg] *n (dishonest)* filou *m; (mischievous)* coquin(e) *m,f;* **r. elephant** éléphant *m* solitaire

roguish ['rəʊgɪʃ] *adj* canaille

role [rəʊl] *n* rôle *m; Fig* **to play an important/a leading r.** jouer un rôle important/prépondérant (dans qch); **r. model** modèle *m*

role-playing ['rəʊlpleɪɪŋ] *n* jeu *m* de rôle

roll [rəʊl] **1** *n* **(a)** *(of paper)* rouleau *m; (of fat)* bourrelet *m; (of banknotes)* liasse *f;* **a r. of film** une pellicule (photo) **(b)** *(bread)* petit pain *m;* **ham r.** ≃ sandwich *m* au jambon **(c)** *(of drum, thunder)* roulement *m* **(d)** *(movement)* roulis *m; Fam* **to be on a r.** avoir la chance de son côté **(e)** *(list)* liste *f;* **r. call** appel *m; Mil* **r. of honour** liste de ceux qui sont morts pour la patrie **2** *vt (a) (ball)* faire rouler; **to r. sth along the ground** faire rouler qch sur le sol; **to r. one's eyes** lever les yeux au ciel; **to r. one's r's** rouler les r; **the animal rolled itself into a ball** l'animal se mit en boule **(b)** *(lawn)* passer au rouleau; *(road)* cylindrer; *(metal)* laminer **(c)** *(cigarette)* rouler **3** *vi (of ball, ship)* rouler; *(of camera)* tourner; *Fig* **heads will r.** il y a des têtes qui vont tomber; *Br Fam* **to be rolling in money, to be rolling in it** rouler sur l'or; *Fig* **to start the ball rolling** mettre les choses en route **(b)** *(of thunder)* gronder

▸ **roll down 1** vt sep (sleeves) redescendre; (blind, car window) descendre
2 vi (of tears, sweat) couler

▸ **roll on** vi Fam **r. on Friday/Christmas!** vivement vendredi/Noël!

▸ **roll over** vi (of person) (once) se retourner; (several times) se rouler; (of car) (once) capoter; (several times) faire des tonneaux

▸ **roll up 1** vt sep (newspaper) rouler; (sleeves) retrousser; (blind, car window) remonter; **to r. sth up in paper** envelopper qch dans du papier
2 vi Fam (arrive) rappliquer; **r. up!, r. up!** venez nombreux!

rolled-up [rəʊl'dʌp] adj (sleeves, trousers) retroussé(e); (umbrella) replié(e); (newspaper) roulé(e)

roller ['rəʊlə(r)] n (for paint, garden) rouleau m; (for hair) bigoudi m; **r. blind** store m (à cylindre); **r. coaster** montagnes fpl russes; **r. skates** patins mpl à roulettes

rollerblades ['rəʊləbleɪdz] npl patins mpl en ligne

rollerblading ['rəʊləbleɪdɪŋ] n **to go r.** faire du patin à roulettes (avec des patins en ligne)

roller-skate ['rəʊləskeɪt] vi faire du patin à roulettes

roller-skating ['rəʊləskeɪtɪŋ] n **to go r.** faire du patin à roulettes

rolling ['rəʊlɪŋ] adj (hills, fields) ondulant(e); (sea, waves) gros (grosse); (thunder) qui gronde; **r. mill** (for steel) laminoir m; **r. pin** rouleau m à pâtisserie; Rail **r. stock** matériel m roulant

rollneck ['rəʊlnek] adj (sweater) à col roulé

roll-on ['rəʊlɒn] adj (a) **r. (deodorant)** déodorant m à bille (b) Naut **r.-roll-off ferry** ferry m de type roll-on-roll-off

rollover ['rəʊləʊvə(r)] n (in lottery) = à la loterie nationale, situation où, personne n'ayant gagné le gros lot, celui-ci est ajouté à l'enjeu du tirage suivant

roll-top desk ['rəʊltɒp'desk] n bureau m à cylindre

roll-up ['rəʊlʌp] n Fam (cigarette) cigarette f roulée

roly-poly ['rəʊlɪ'pəʊlɪ] adj Br Fam (plump) grassouillet(ette)

ROM [rɒm] n Comptr (abbr **read only memory**) mémoire f morte

Roman ['rəʊmən] **1** n Romain(e) m,f
2 adj romain(e); **R. Catholic** catholique; **R. nose** nez m aquilin; **R. numerals** chiffres mpl romains

roman ['rəʊmən] Typ **1** n romain m
2 adj romain(e)

romance ['rəʊmæns, rə'mæns] n (a) (book) roman m d'amour; (film) histoire f d'amour (b) (love affair) aventure f (c) (charm) charme m

Romania [rə'meɪnɪə] n la Roumanie

Romanian [rə'meɪnɪən] **1** n (a) (person) Roumain(e) m,f (b) (language) roumain m
2 adj roumain(e)

romantic [rəʊ'mæntɪk, rə'mæntɪk] **1** n romantique mf
2 adj romantique; (scheme, notion) romanesque

romanticism [rəʊ'mæntɪsɪzəm] n romantisme m

romanticize [rə'mæntɪsaɪz] vt (incident) romancer; (idea, war) présenter sous un jour romantique

Romany ['rəʊmənɪ] **1** n (pl **Romanies**) (a) (person) Tzigane mf (b) (language) tzigane m
2 adj tzigane

Rome [rəʊm] n Rome; **R. wasn't built in a day** Paris ne s'est pas fait en un jour; **when in R.(, do as the Romans do)** il faut adopter les usages de l'endroit où l'on se trouve

romp [rɒmp] **1** n **to have a r.** chahuter

2 vi **to r. (about** or **around)** s'ébattre; **to r. through an exam** réussir un examen les doigts dans le nez

romper ['rɒmpə(r)] n **r. suit, rompers** barboteuse f

roof [ru:f] **1** n (of building, car) toit m; (of tunnel, cave) plafond m; **to have a r.** over one's head avoir un endroit où vivre; **to live under one** or **the same r.** vivre sous le même toit; Fam **to hit the r.** sortir de ses gonds; Fam **to go through the r.** connaître une flambée; **r. of the mouth** voûte f du palais; **r. garden** jardin m aménagé sur le toit; **r. rack** galerie f
2 vt couvrir

roofing ['ru:fɪŋ] n toiture f; **r. material** matériaux mpl de couverture

rooftop ['ru:ftɒp] n toit m; Fig **to shout sth from the rooftops** crier qch sur les toits

rook [rʊk] n (bird) freux m; (in chess) tour f

rookery ['rʊkərɪ] (pl **rookeries**) n colonie f de freux

rookie ['rʊkɪ] n Am Fam bleu m

room [ru:m] **1** n (a) (in house) pièce f; (bedroom, in hotel) chambre f; (large, public) salle f; **r. and board** chambre et pension; **r. service** service m dans les chambres; **r. temperature** température f ambiante (b) (space) place f; **there's no r. to move** il n'y a pas de place; **to make r. (for sb)** faire de la place (pour qn); **there's no r. for doubt** cela ne fait aucun doute; **there is r. for improvement** ça pourrait être mieux
2 vi Am **to r. with sb** partager une chambre avec qn

roomy ['ru:mɪ] adj spacieux(euse); (clothes) ample

roost [ru:st] **1** n perchoir m; **to rule the r.** faire la loi
2 vi se percher; Fig **her actions have come home to r.** ses actions se sont retournées contre elle

rooster ['ru:stə(r)] n coq m

root [ru:t] **1** n (a) (of plant, tooth, word, hair) racine f; **to pull up by the roots** (plant) déraciner; also Fig **to take r.** prendre racine; **they destroyed the party r. and branch** ils ont entièrement détruit le parti; Fig **to put down roots** s'intégrer; Fig **to get back to one's roots** retrouver ses racines; Am **r. beer** = boisson gazeuse aux extraits de plantes; **r. crops** racines comestibles; **r. vegetables** légumes mpl à racine comestible (b) (origin) origine f; Prov **money is the r. of all evil** l'argent est la source de tous les maux
2 vt **to be rooted to the spot** être figé(e) sur place
3 vi (a) **to r. about** or **around (for sth)** fouiller (pour trouver qch) (b) Am **to r. for sb** appuyer qn

▸ **root for** vt insep (support) être pour

▸ **root out** vt sep supprimer

rope [rəʊp] **1** n (a) (also Fig) corde f; (of pearls) sautoir m; (of onions) chapelet m; **r. ladder** échelle f de corde (b) (idioms) **to be on the ropes** (of company) battre de l'aile; **to learn the ropes** apprendre les ficelles; **to show sb the ropes** former qn; **to give sb plenty of r.** donner du mou à qn
2 vt (fasten) lier (avec une corde) (**to** à); **they roped themselves together** (for climbing) ils se sont encordés

▸ **rope in** vt insep Fam (recruit) recruter; **to get roped in to do sth** se laisser convaincre de faire qch

▸ **rope off** vt sep **to r. sth off** interdire l'accès de qch avec une corde

rop(e)y ['rəʊpɪ] adj Br Fam (unreliable) pas terrible; (ill) patraque

rosary ['rəʊzərɪ] (pl **rosaries**) n Rel chapelet m; **to say one's r.** dire son chapelet

rose¹ [rəʊz] **1** n (a) (flower) rose f; (on watering can) pomme f; **r. bed** parterre m de rosiers; **r. bush** rosier m; **r. garden** roseraie f; **r. window** rosace f (b) (idioms) **life isn't**

a bed of roses tout n'est pas rose dans la vie; **to come up roses** se passer à merveille

2 *adj (colour)* rose

rose² *pt of* **rise**

rosé ['rəʊzeɪ] *n* rosé *m*

rosebud ['rəʊzbʌd] *n* bouton *m* de rose

rose-coloured, *Am* **rose-colored** ['rəʊzkʌləd], **rose-tinted** ['rəʊz-tɪntɪd] *adj* **to see things through r. glasses** *or* **spectacles** voir la vie en rose

rosehip ['rəʊzhɪp] *n* gratte-cul *m*

rosemary ['rəʊzmərɪ] *n* romarin *m*

rosette [rəʊ'zet] *n* rosette *f*

rosewater ['rəʊzwɔːtə(r)] *n* eau *f* de rose

rosewood ['rəʊzwʊd] *n* bois *m* de rose

roster ['rɒstə(r)] *n* liste *f* de service

rostrum ['rɒstrəm] *(pl* **rostrums** *or* **rostra** ['rɒstrə]) *n (for speaker)* estrade *f*; *(for prizewinner)* podium *m*

rosy ['rəʊzɪ] *adj (pink)* rose; *(complexion)* de rose; *Fig (future)* prometteur(euse)

rot [rɒt] **1** *n* (a) *(in house, wood)* pourriture *f*; *Fig* **the r. has set in** ça se gâte; *Fig* **to stop the r.** empêcher la situation de se dégrader (b) *Fam (nonsense)* bêtises *fpl*

2 *vt (pt & pp* **rotted**) (faire) pourrir

3 *vi* pourrir; **to r. in prison** moisir en prison

rota ['rəʊtə] *n* roulement *m*

rotary ['rəʊtərɪ] **1** *(pl* **rotaries**) *Am (roundabout)* rond-point *m*

2 *adj* rotatif(ive)

rotate [rəʊ'teɪt] **1** *vt* (a) *(turn)* faire tourner (b) *(alternate) (duties)* remplir à tour de rôle; *(crops)* alterner

2 *vi* (a) *(turn)* tourner (b) *(in job)* remplir des fonctions à tour de rôle

rotation [rəʊ'teɪʃən] *n* (a) *(of planet)* rotation *f* (b) *(in job)* roulement *m*; *(of crops)* alternance *f*; **by or in r.** à tour de rôle

rote [rəʊt] *n* **by r.** par cœur; **r. learning** apprentissage *m* par cœur

rotor ['rəʊtə(r)] *n* rotor *m*

rotten ['rɒtən] *adj* (a) *(wood, egg, fruit)* pourri(e) (b) *Br Fam (bad)* nul (nulle); *(weather)* pourri(e); **to feel r.** *(ill)* ne pas se sentir dans son assiette; *(guilty)* ne pas être fier(ère) (about de); **to have r. luck** avoir la guigne (c) *(unpleasant)* dégueulasse; **a r. trick** un tour de cochon

rottweiler ['rɒtvaɪlə(r)] *n* rottweiler *m*

rotund [rəʊ'tʌnd] *adj* rond(e)

rouble ['ruːbəl] *n* rouble *m*

rouge [ruːʒ] *n Old-fashioned* rouge *m* (à joues)

rough [rʌf] **1** *n* (a) *(in golf)* rough *m* (b) *(difficulty)* **you have to take the r. with the smooth** on ne peut pas tout avoir dans la vie

2 *adj* (a) *(surface, skin)* rugueux(euse); *(terrain)* accidenté(e)

(b) *(unrefined) (manners)* fruste; *Fig* **a r. diamond** un cœur d'or sous des dehors frustes; **r. draft** brouillon *m*; **r. sketch** ébauche *f*

(c) *Br Fam (ill)* **to feel/look r.** se sentir/avoir l'air patraque

(d) *(violent)* brutal(e); *(crossing, sea)* agité(e)

(e) *(harsh) (voice)* rude; *(wine, spirits)* âpre; *Fam* **it was r. on her** c'était dur pour elle; **r. justice** justice *f* sommaire

(f) *(approximate)* approximatif(ive); **at a r. guess** à vue de nez; **I've got a r. idea of what he wants** j'ai une petite idée de ce qu'il veut

3 *adv* **to play r.** jouer avec brutalité; *Fig* ne pas faire de cadeaux; *Fam* **to sleep r.** coucher à la dure

4 *vt Fam* **to r. it** vivre à la dure

▸ **rough up** *vt sep Fam (beat up)* tabasser

roughage ['rʌfɪdʒ] *n* fibres *fpl* (alimentaires)

rough-and-ready [rʌfən'redɪ] *adj (meal, accommodation)* sommaire; *(person)* rustre

rough-and-tumble [rʌfən'tʌmbəl] *n* bousculade *f*; *Fig* **the r. of politics** le monde sans pitié de la politique

roughly ['rʌflɪ] *adv* (a) *(violently)* brutalement; **to treat sb r.** rudoyer qn (b) *(crudely)* grossièrement (c) *(approximately)* à peu près; **r. (speaking)** en gros

roughness ['rʌfnɪs] *n* (a) *(of surface, skin)* rugosité *f* (b) *(of behaviour)* rudesse *f*

roughshod ['rʌfʃɒd] *adv* **to ride r. over sth** ne faire aucun cas de qch

rough-spoken [rʌf'spəʊkən] *adj* au langage grossier

roulette [ruː'let] *n* roulette *f*; **r. table** table *f* de roulette; **r. wheel** roulette

round [raʊnd] **1** *n* (a) *(slice) (of bread)* tranche *f* (b) *(stage of match)* manche *f*; *(stage of tournament)* tour *m*; *(in boxing)* round *m*; *(of golf)* partie *f*; **to get/be through to the next r.** se qualifier/s'être qualifié(e) pour le tour suivant (c) *(of talks, visits)* série *f*; *(of drinks)* tournée *f*; **r. of applause** applaudissements *mpl*; **to give sb a r. of applause** applaudir qn

(d) **to do one's rounds** *(of doctor)* faire ses visites; **to do the rounds** *(of rumour, illness)* circuler; **the daily r.** *(of tasks)* le train-train quotidien

(e) *Mil (bullet)* balle *f*

(f) *Mus* canon *m*

2 *adj* rond(e); **to have r. shoulders** avoir le dos rond; **a r. dozen** une douzaine exactement; **in r. figures** en arrondissant; **r. table (conference)** table *f* ronde; **r. trip** aller (et) retour *m*

3 *adv* autour; **all (the) year r.** toute l'année; **all r.** *(on the whole)* dans l'ensemble; **the wrong way r.** à l'envers; **the right way r.** *(not back to front)* à l'endroit; *(in the correct order)* dans le bon ordre; **the other way r.** *(in the other direction)* dans l'autre sens, **do it the other way r.** fais l'inverse; **to go r.** *(to sb's house)* passer (chez qn); **to invite sb r.** inviter qn

4 *prep* (a) *(position)* autour de; **r. here** dans le coin (b) *(motion)* **to look r. a room** parcourir une pièce du regard; **to travel r. the world** parcourir le monde; **to go r. an obstacle** contourner un obstacle, **to go r. the corner** *(of person)* tourner le coin; *(of vehicle)* prendre le virage; **it's just r. the corner** c'est juste au coin (de la rue); *Fig* **to drive or send sb r. the bend** rendre qn maboul(e)

(c) *(approximately)* **r. about** environ; **r. about midday** vers midi

5 *vt* (a) *(make round)* arrondir

(b) *(obstacle)* contourner; *(corner)* tourner

▸ **round down** *vt sep (figure)* arrondir au chiffre inférieur

▸ **round off** *vt sep (conclude)* conclure

▸ **round up** *vt sep* (a) *(cattle)* rassembler; *(criminals, suspects)* ramasser (b) *(figure)* arrondir au chiffre supérieur

roundabout ['raʊndəbaʊt] **1** *n* (a) *(at fairground)* manège *m* (b) *(for cars)* rond-point *m*

2 *adj (approach, route)* détourné(e); **to approach a subject in a r. way** aborder une question de biais

rounders ['raʊndəz] *n Br* = jeu similaire au base-ball

roundly ['raʊndlɪ] *adv (praise, condemn)* vivement; *(beat)* sévèrement

round-trip [raʊnd'trɪp] *adj Am (ticket)* aller (et) retour

roundup ['raʊndʌp] *n (of criminals)* rafle *f*; *(of events, news)* résumé *m*

rouse [raʊz] *vt* réveiller; **to r. oneself (to do sth)** se secouer (et faire qch); **to r. sb to action** pousser qn à agir; **to r. sb to anger** susciter la colère de qn

rousing ['raʊzɪŋ] *adj (music, speech)* exaltant(e); *(welcome, cheers)* enthousiaste

rout [raʊt] **1** *n* déroute *f*
2 *vt* mettre en déroute
▸ **rout out** *vt sep (get rid of)* se débarrasser de

route [ruːt] **1** *n (of traveller)* itinéraire *m*; *(of plane, ship)* route *f*; *(of bus, parade)* parcours *m*; *Fig (to success)* voie *f* (**to** de)
2 *vt (parcel, goods)* acheminer; *(bus, train, flight)* faire passer

routine [ruː'tiːn] **1** *n* **(a)** *(habit)* routine *f*; **the daily r.** le train-train quotidien **(b)** *(of performer, comedian)* numéro *m*; *Fam Fig* **don't give me that r.** arrête ton numéro **(c)** *Comptr* sous-programme *m*
2 *adj* **(a)** *(normal)* de routine **(b)** *(dull)* routinier(ère)

routinely [ruː'tiːnlɪ] *adv* systématiquement

rove [rəʊv] **1** *vt* parcourir
2 *vi* rôder, vagabonder; **her eyes roved around the room** son regard parcourait la pièce

row¹ [rəʊ] *n (line)* rangée *f*; **in a r.** en rang; **two Sundays in a r.** deux dimanches d'affilée; **in the front r.** *(of seats)* au premier rang

row² **1** *n (in boat)* promenade *f* en canot; **to go for a r.** canoter
2 *vt (boat)* faire aller à la rame; *(person)* transporter en canot
3 *vi (in boat)* ramer

row³ [raʊ] **1** *n* **(a)** *(noise)* vacarme *m*; *(protest)* tollé *m* **(b)** *(quarrel)* dispute *f*; **to have a r. (with sb)** se disputer (avec qn)
2 *vi (quarrel)* se disputer (**about** à propos de)

rowan ['raʊən] *n* sorbier *m*

rowboat ['rəʊbəʊt] *n Am* bateau *m* à rames

rowdy ['raʊdɪ] **1** *n (pl* **rowdies)** chahuteur(euse) *m,f*
2 *adj (person)* chahuteur(euse); *(event, party)* bruyant(e); **to be r.** chahuter

rower ['rəʊə(r)] *n* rameur(euse) *m,f*

rowing ['rəʊɪŋ] *n* canotage *m*; *(as sport)* aviron *m*; **r. boat** bateau *m* à rames; **r. machine** rameur *m*

royal ['rɔɪəl] **1** *adj* royal(e); *Fig (splendid)* princier(ère); **His/Her R. Highness** Son Altesse Royale; **r. blue** bleu roi *m inv*; **the R. Family** la famille royale; **r. flush** *(in cards)* quinte *f* royale; **r. jelly** gelée *f* royale; **R. Mail** = la Poste britannique; **the R. Navy** = la marine nationale britannique
2 *n Fam* membre *m* de la famille royale; **the Royals** la famille royale

royalist ['rɔɪəlɪst] *n & adj* royaliste *mf*

royally ['rɔɪəlɪ] *adv (entertain, welcome)* royalement

royalty ['rɔɪəltɪ] *n* **(a)** *(rank, position)* royauté *f*; **to be r.** faire partie de la famille royale; **to be treated like r.** être traité(e) royalement **(b)** **royalties** *(for author, singer)* droits *mpl* d'auteur

RP [ɑː'piː] *n Ling (abbr* **received pronunciation)** = prononciation de l'anglais considérée comme la norme

RPI [ɑːpiː'aɪ] *n Econ (abbr* **retail price index)** indice *m* des prix de détail

rpm [ɑːpiː'em] *n Aut (abbr* **revolutions per minute)** tr/min

R & R [ɑːrən'ɑː(r)] *n Mil (abbr* **rest and recreation)** permission *f*

RRP [ɑːrɑː'piː] *n Com (abbr* **recommended retail price)** prix *m* conseillé

RS [ɑː'res] *n Br (abbr* **Royal Society)** ≃ Académie *f* des Sciences

RSA [ɑːres'eɪ] *n (abbr* **Republic of South Africa)** Afrique *f* du Sud

RSI [ɑːres'aɪ] *n (abbr* **repetitive strain injury)** = douleurs dans les bras et les mains dues à la répétition de certains mouvements

RSVP [ɑːresviː'piː] *(abbr* **répondez s'il vous plaît)** *(on invitation)* RSVP

Rt Hon *Br Parl (abbr* **Right Honourable)** = formule accolée au nom des ministres et anciens ministres

rub [rʌb] **1** *n* **to give sth a r.** frotter qch; *Fig* **there's the r.!** voilà le hic!
2 *vt (pt & pp* **rubbed)** frotter; **to r. one's hands** se frotter les mains; *Fig* **to r. shoulders with sb** côtoyer qn; *Fam* **to r. sb up the wrong way** prendre qn à rebrousse-poil
3 *vi (of straps, shoes)* frotter **(against** contre)
▸ **rub along** *vi Fam* **(a)** *(manage)* se débrouiller **(b)** *(get on)* s'entendre (**with** avec)
▸ **rub in** *vt sep (lotion, ointment)* faire pénétrer; *Fam* **to r. it in** retourner le couteau dans la plaie
▸ **rub off** **1** *vt sep (dirt, stain)* enlever en frottant; *(writing)* effacer
2 *vi* partir, s'enlever; *Fig* **to r. off on sb** *(of manners, enthusiasm)* déteindre sur qn
▸ **rub out** *vt sep* **(a)** *(erase)* effacer **(b)** *Fam (murder)* buter

rubber ['rʌbə(r)] *n* **(a)** *(substance)* caoutchouc *m*; **r. ball/gloves** balle *f*/gants *mpl* en caoutchouc; **r. band** élastique *m*; **r. dinghy** canot *m* pneumatique; **r. plant** caoutchouc *m*; **r. ring** bouée *f*; **r. stamp** tampon *m* **(b)** *(eraser)* gomme *f*; *(for blackboards)* brosse *f* **(c)** *Am Fam (condom)* capote *f*

rubber-stamp [rʌbə'stæmp] *vt Fig (approve)* approuver sans discussion

rubbery ['rʌbərɪ] *adj* caoutchouteux(euse)

rubbish ['rʌbɪʃ] *Br* **1** *n* **(a)** *(refuse)* détritus *mpl*; *(from house)* ordures *fpl*; *(junk)* cochonneries *fpl*; **r. bag** sac *m* poubelle; **r. bin** poubelle *f*; **r. collection** ramassage *m* des ordures; **r. dump** dépotoir *m*; *Fig* **to throw sb/sth on the r. heap** mettre qn/qch au rancart **(b)** *Fam (nonsense)* idioties *fpl*; **that book/movie is a load of r.** ce livre/film est nul; **r.!** n'importe quoi!
2 *vt Fam (book, plan)* descendre en flammes

rubble ['rʌbəl] *n* décombres *mpl*

rubella [ruː'belə] *n* rubéole *f*

rubric ['ruːbrɪk] *n* instructions *fpl*

ruby ['ruːbɪ] **1** *n (pl* **rubies)** rubis *m*
2 *adj (colour)* rubis

ruck¹ [rʌk] *n* **(a)** *(in rugby)* mêlée *f* ouverte **(b)** *(fight)* bagarre *f*

ruck² **1** *n (in cloth)* faux pli *m*
2 *vi* **to r. up** *(of sheet)* se froisser

rucksack ['rʌksæk] *n* sac *m* à dos

ructions ['rʌkʃənz] *npl Fam* grabuge *m*

rudder ['rʌdə(r)] *n* gouvernail *m*

rude [ruːd] *adj* **(a)** *(impolite)* impoli(e) **(b)** *(vulgar)* grossier(ère); *(gesture)* obscène **(c)** *(primitive)* rudimentaire **(d)** *(shock, surprise)* **to receive a r. awakening** être brutalement rappelé(e) à la réalité **(e)** *(vigorous)* **to be in r. health** jouir d'une santé robuste

rudeness ['ruːdnɪs] *n* **(a)** *(impoliteness)* impolitesse *f* **(b)** *(vulgarity)* grossièreté *f*

rudimentary [ruːdɪ'mentərɪ] *adj* rudimentaire

rudiments ['ruːdɪmənts] *npl* rudiments *mpl*

rue [ruː] *vt Lit* regretter amèrement; **I r. the day I met her** je maudis le jour où je l'ai rencontrée

rueful ['ruːfʊl] *adj (voice, smile)* de regret; *(person)* qui a des regrets

ruff [rʌf] *n (on costume)* fraise *f*

ruffle ['rʌfəl] *vt (water)* troubler; *(hair)* ébouriffer; **to r.**

sb's feathers froisser qn; **to r. sb's composure** faire perdre contenance à qn

rug [rʌg] *n* (**a**) *(carpet)* tapis *m; Fig* **to pull the r. from under sb's feet** couper l'herbe sous le pied à qn (**b**) *(blanket)* couverture *f*

rugby ['rʌgbɪ] *n* rugby *m;* **r. ball** ballon *m* de rugby; **r. league** rugby à treize; **r. player** rugbyman *m;* **r. tackle** plaquage *m;* **r. union** rugby à quinze

rugby-tackle ['rʌgbɪ'tækəl] *vt* **to r. sb** plaquer qn au sol

rugged ['rʌgɪd] *adj* *(ground, country)* accidenté(e); *(features, manner)* rude; **r. good looks** beauté *f* un peu rude

rugger ['rʌgə(r)] *n Fam (rugby)* rugby *m*

ruin ['ruːɪn] **1** *n* ruine *f;* **to fall into ruin(s)** tomber en ruine(s); **it will be the r. of him** ça le perdra
2 *vt (suit, shoes)* abîmer; *(person)* ruiner; *(meal, evening, holiday)* gâcher; **to r. one's health** se ruiner la santé; **to r. one's eyesight** s'user la vue; **tourism has ruined the beach** le tourisme a défiguré la plage; **a ruined castle** un château en ruine(s)

ruinous ['ruːɪnəs] *adj (expensive)* ruineux(euse)

rule [ruːl] **1** *n* (**a**) *(principle)* règle *f; (regulation)* règlement *m;* **rules** *(of club, school)* règlement; **as a r.** en règle générale; **to make it a r. to do sth** se faire un principe de faire qch; **rules and regulations** règles; *Ind* **to work to r.** faire la grève du zèle; **it's against the rules** c'est contraire au règlement; **as a r. of thumb** pour avoir une idée approximative; **r. book** règlement (**b**) *(government)* autorité *f* (**c**) *(for measuring)* règle *f*
2 *vt* (**a**) *(country, people)* gouverner; **to let sth r. one's life** laisser qch dominer toute sa vie; *Fig* **to r. the roost** commander (**b**) *(decide, decree)* décider; **to be ruled illegal** être décrété(e) illégal(e) (**c**) *(paper)* régler
3 *vi* (**a**) *(of monarch)* régner (**b**) *(of judge)* statuer (**on** sur); **to r. in favour of/against sb** décider en faveur de/contre qn

▸ **rule out** *vt sep* exclure

ruler ['ruːlə(r)] *n* (**a**) *(of country)* dirigeant(e) *m,f* (**b**) *(for measuring)* règle *f*

ruling ['ruːlɪŋ] **1** *n (of judge, umpire)* décision *f*
2 *adj* (**a**) *(party)* au pouvoir; *(class)* dirigeant(e) (**b**) *(passion)* dominant(e); *(consideration)* premier(ère)

rum¹ [rʌm] *n (drink)* rhum *m*

rum² *adj Br Fam (strange)* bizarre; *(suspect)* louche

Rumania [ruːˈmeɪnɪə] = **Romania**

Rumanian [ruːˈmeɪnɪən] = **Romanian**

rumble ['rʌmbəl] **1** *n (of thunder, gunfire, traffic)* grondement *m; (of voices)* bourdonnement *m; (of stomach)* gargouillement *m;* **rumbles of discontent** murmures *mpl* de protestation
2 *vt Fam (find out) (person)* deviner le jeu de; *(plot)* découvrir
3 *vi (of thunder, traffic)* gronder; *(of stomach)* gargouiller

rumbustious [rʌmˈbʌstjəs] *adj* exubérant(e)

ruminant ['ruːmɪnənt] *n Zool* ruminant *m*

ruminate ['ruːmɪneɪt] *vi Formal* **to r. (about** *or* **on sth)** ruminer (qch)

rummage ['rʌmɪdʒ] **1** *vi* **to r. about** *or* **around** *(for sth)* farfouiller (à la recherche de qch); **to r. through sth** fouiller qch
2 *n Am* **r. sale** vente *f* de charité

rumour ['ruːmə(r)] **1** *n* rumeur *f*, bruit *m;* **r. has it... on** raconte que...; **there's a r. going round that...** le bruit court que...
2 *vt* **it is rumoured that...** le bruit court que...; **he is rumoured to be very rich/in hiding** le bruit court qu'il est très riche/qu'il se cache

rump [rʌmp] *n* (**a**) *(of animal)* croupe *f; Fam (of person)* postérieur *m;* **r. steak** romsteck *m* (**b**) *(of political party, assembly)* restant *m*

rumple ['rʌmpəl] *vt (clothes, sheets)* friper, froisser; *(hair)* ébouriffer

rumpus ['rʌmpəs] *n Fam (noise)* chahut *m;* **to kick up** *or* **cause a r. (about sth)** faire un scandale (à propos de qch)

run [rʌn] **1** *n* (**a**) *(act of running)* course *f;* **at a r. en courant;** **to go for a r.** aller courir; **to be on the r.** être en fuite; *Fig* **we've got them on the r.** nous les avons mis en déroute; **to give sb the r. of the house** mettre sa maison à la disposition de qn; *Fam* **to make a r. for it** *(escape)* se tirer; *(to catch train)* se grouiller; *Fam* **to give sb a r. for his money** donner du fil à retordre à qn; *Fam* **to have the runs** avoir la courante
(**b**) *(trip)* trajet *m; (for pleasure)* balade *f;* **to go for a r.** *(in car)* aller se balader en voiture
(**c**) *Com (of book)* tirage *m; (of product)* série *f*
(**d**) *(sequence, series)* série *f; (in cards)* suite *f;* **a r. of good luck** une période faste; **a r. of bad luck** une série de malheurs; **in the short/long r.** à court/long terme
(**e**) *Fin (on currency, stock exchange)* ruée *f* (**on** sur); *(on bank)* retrait *m* massif
(**f**) *(in stocking)* échelle *f*
(**g**) *(in cricket, baseball)* point *m*
(**h**) *(for skier)* piste *f*
(**i**) *(for chickens, rabbits)* enclos *m*
(**j**) *Mus* roulade *f*
2 *vt (pt* ran [ræn], *pp* run) (**a**) *(distance, race)* courir; **to r. an errand** faire une course; **to allow things to r. their course** laisser les choses aller; **to r. sb close** talonner qn; *Fam* **to be r. off one's feet** être débordé(e)
(**b**) *Br (drive)* **to r. sb into town** conduire qn en ville
(**c**) *(drugs, arms)* faire le trafic de
(**d**) *(machine)* faire fonctionner; *(tests)* effectuer; *Comptr (program)* exécuter
(**e**) *(business)* diriger; *(hotel)* tenir; *(car)* avoir; **to r. sb's life for them** dire à qn comment vivre sa vie
(**f**) *(cables, pipes)* faire passer; **to r. one's fingers over/through sth** passer la main sur/dans qch; **to r. one's eye over sth** parcourir qch du regard
(**g**) *(water, bath)* faire couler
(**h**) **to r. a temperature** avoir de la température
(**i**) **to r. a deficit** enregistrer un déficit
(**j**) **to r. an article** publier un article
3 *vi* (**a**) *(of person)* courir; **to r. up/down the street** monter/descendre la rue en courant; **to r. about** courir çà et là; **I'll just r. across/round to the shop** je fais un saut à l'épicerie; **to r. after sb** courir après qn; **to r. for help** courir chercher de l'aide; **to r. in/out** entrer/sortir en courant
(**b**) *(flee)* s'enfuir, se sauver; **r. for it!** sauve qui peut!
(**c**) *(compete in race)* courir; **to r. for President** se présenter aux présidentielles
(**d**) *(flow)* couler; **the river runs into a lake** la rivière se jette dans un lac; **my nose is running** j'ai le nez qui coule; **my blood ran cold** mon sang se glaça
(**e**) **to r. aground** *(of ship)* s'échouer; *Fig (of project, economy)* échouer
(**f**) *(of contract, lease)* courir; *(of play)* être à l'affiche; **it runs in the family** c'est de famille; **the total ran to $2,000** le montant total s'élevait à 2000 dollars
(**g**) *(of bus, train)* circuler; **to be running late** *(of bus, train)* avoir du retard; *(of person)* être en retard
(**h**) *(operate) (of machine)* marcher, fonctionner; *(of engine)* tourner; **to r. on gas/electricity** marcher *ou* fonctionner au gaz/à l'électricité; **to r. off the mains** marcher sur secteur; **the car runs on diesel** la voiture roule au diesel; **things are running smoothly** tout marche comme sur des roulettes

(i) *(of road, railway)* passer; **the line runs along the coast** la ligne suit *ou* longe la côte

(j) feelings *or* **tempers are running high** les esprits sont échauffés; **to be running low** *(of funds, supplies)* s'épuiser; **to r. dry** *(of river)* s'assécher

(k) *(of colour, dye)* déteindre

▸ **run away** *vi (of person)* s'enfuir, se sauver **(from** de); **to r. away from home** faire une fugue; *Fig* **to r. away from the facts** refuser l'évidence; *Fig* **don't r. away with the idea that…** ne va pas t'imaginer que…

▸ **run down 1** *vt sep* **(a)** *(in car)* renverser **(b)** *(find)* dénicher **(c)** *(criticize)* dénigrer **(d)** *(reduce) (production, stocks)* diminuer, réduire; *(industry, factory)* fermer progressivement

2 *vi (of battery)* se décharger

▸ **run in** *vt sep* **(a)** *Fam (arrest)* pincer **(b)** *(engine)* roder

▸ **run into** *vt insep* **(a)** *(collide with)* rentrer dans; *Fig (difficulties)* rencontrer; **to r. into trouble** s'attirer des ennuis **(b)** *(meet by chance)* tomber sur

▸ **run off 1** *vt sep (print)* imprimer; *(photocopy)* photocopier; **to r. off a copy of sth** faire une copie de qch

2 *vi (of person)* s'enfuir, se sauver **(with** avec)

▸ **run on** *vi* **(a)** *(of meeting)* durer **(b)** *Fam (talk a lot)* parler sans arrêt

▸ **run out** *vi (of lease, contract)* expirer; *(of money, supplies)* s'épuiser; **to have run out of sth** ne plus avoir de qch; **time is running out** il ne reste plus beaucoup de temps; *Fig* **to r. out of steam** *(of person, project)* s'essouffler

▸ **run over 1** *vt sep (in car)* renverser, écraser

2 *vt insep (speech, lines)* revoir

3 *vi (of speech, TV programme)* déborder

▸ **run to** *vt insep (amount to)* s'élever à; **we can't r. to a new car** *(afford)* nous ne pouvons pas nous permettre d'acheter une nouvelle voiture

▸ **run up** *vt sep* **(a)** *(debts)* accumuler **(b)** *(flag)* hisser **(c)** *(clothes)* confectionner à la hâte

run-around ['rʌnəraʊnd] *n Fam* **to give sb the r.** faire tourner qn en bourrique

runaway ['rʌnəweɪ] **1** *n* fugitif(ive) *m,f; (child)* fugueur(euse) *m,f*

2 *adj (prisoner, slave)* en fuite; *(train, lorry)* fou (folle); *(inflation)* galopant(e); *(victory)* remporté(e) haut la main; *(success)* fou (folle)

rundown ['rʌndaʊn] *n (summary)* résumé *m*; **to give sb a r. (on sth)** mettre qn au courant (de qch)

run-down [rʌn'daʊn] *adj (building)* délabré(e); *(person)* fatigué(e)

rung¹ [rʌŋ] *n (of ladder)* échelon *m*; *Fig* **on the bottom/ top r.** tout en bas/en haut de l'échelle

rung² *pp of* **ring**²

run-in ['rʌnɪn] *n Fam* **to have a r. with sb** avoir un accrochage avec qn

runner ['rʌnə(r)] *n* **(a)** *(athlete)* coureur(euse) *m,f; (messenger)* coursier(ère) *m,f; (for drugs, guns)* passeur(euse) *m,f* **(b) r. bean** haricot *m* d'Espagne **(c)** *(on sleigh)* patin *m; (on drawer)* glissière *f* **(d)** *Br Fam* **to do a r.** se tirer

runner-up [rʌnə'rʌp] *(pl* **runners-up)** *n* suivant(e) *m,f; (in second place)* second(e) *m,f*

running ['rʌnɪŋ] **1** *n* **(a)** *(activity)* course *f*; **to go r.** courir; *Fig* **to be out of the r.** *(in competition, race)* n'avoir aucune chance; **to be in the r.** avoir des chances; **to make all the r.** *(in relationship)* prendre toutes les initiatives; *Am Pol* **r. mate** = candidat à la vice-présidence accompagnant dans sa campagne le candidat à la présidence des États-Unis; **r. shoe** chaussure *f* de course; **r. track** piste *f* **(b)** *(of*

machine, car) **r. costs** frais *mpl* d'entretien **(c)** *(management)* gestion *f*

2 *adj (battle, feud)* incessant(e); *Fam* **(go) take a r. jump!** va voir ailleurs si j'y suis!; **r. board** *(on car)* marchepied *m*; **r. commentary** commentaire *m* en direct; **r. repairs** petites réparations *fpl*; **r. sore** plaie *f* qui suppure; **to keep a r. total (of sth)** comptabiliser (qch) au fur et à mesure; **r. water** eau *f* courante

runny ['rʌnɪ] *adj (liquid)* liquide; **to have a r. nose** avoir le nez qui coule

run-off ['rʌnɒf] *n* **(a)** *(election)* deuxième tour *m; (contest)* manche *f* pour départager deux candidats **(b)** *(from fields)* eaux *fpl* de ruissellement

run-of-the-mill [rʌnəvðə'mɪl] *adj* ordinaire

runt [rʌnt] *n* **(a)** *(of litter)* **the r.** le (la) plus faible de la portée **(b)** *(weak person)* avorton *m*

run-up ['rʌnʌp] *n (before jump)* course *f* d'élan; **the r. to the wedding/the election** la période précédant le mariage/les élections

runway ['rʌnweɪ] *n* piste *f*

rupee [ruːˈpiː] *n* roupie *f*

rupture ['rʌptʃə(r)] **1** *n* rupture *f*

2 *vt (relations)* rompre; *(container)* faire éclater

3 *vi also Med* éclater

rural ['rʊərəl] *adj* rural(e)

ruse [ruːz] *n* ruse *f*

rush¹ [rʌʃ] *n (plant)* jonc *m*; **r. matting** natte *f* (de jonc)

rush² [rʌʃ] **1** *n* **(a)** *(hurry)* **what's the r.?** pourquoi tant de hâte?; **to be in a r.** être pressé(e); **to do sth in a r.** faire qch à toute vitesse; **there's no r.** il n'y a rien qui presse; **to make a r. for sth** se précipiter vers qch; **r. hour** heures *fpl* de pointe; **a r. job** *(urgent)* un travail urgent; *(hurried)* un travail bâclé **(b)** *(surge) (of air)* bouffée *f; (of water)* flot *m* soudain; *(of requests)* flot **(c)** *(demand)* ruée *f*; **there's been a r. on tickets** les gens se sont rués sur les billets **(d)** *Cin* **rushes** rush(e)s *mpl*

2 *vt* **(a)** *(hurry) (task)* faire à la hâte; *(person)* bousculer; **to r. sb into doing sth** bousculer qn pour qu'il/elle fasse qch; **to be rushed off one's feet** être débordé(e) **(b)** *(transport quickly)* transporter d'urgence **(c)** *(attack)* prendre d'assaut

3 *vi (move quickly)* se ruer **(at/towards** sur/vers); *(act quickly)* se dépêcher; **the blood rushed to her head** le sang lui est monté à la tête; **to r. to do sth** s'empresser de faire qch; **to r. into doing sth** faire qch sans réfléchir

▸ **rush about, rush around** *vi* courir à droite et à gauche

▸ **rush in** *vi (enter)* entrer précipitamment

▸ **rush off** *vi* partir précipitamment

▸ **rush out 1** *vt sep (book)* publier à la hâte

2 *vi (exit)* sortir précipitamment

▸ **rush through 1** *vt sep (bill)* faire passer à la hâte; *(decision)* prendre à la hâte

2 *vt insep (book)* lire à toute vitesse; *(meal, work)* expédier

rusk [rʌsk] *n* gros biscuit *m (pour bébés)*

russet ['rʌsɪt] **1** *n (colour)* brun *m* roux

2 *adj* brun roux *inv*

Russia ['rʌʃə] *n* la Russie

Russian ['rʌʃən] **1** *n* **(a)** *(person)* Russe *mf* **(b)** *(language)* russe *m*

2 *adj* russe; **R. roulette** roulette *f* russe

rust [rʌst] **1** *n* rouille *f*

2 *adj (colour)* rouille *inv*

3 *vi* rouiller

rustic ['rʌstɪk] *adj* rustique

rustle¹ ['rʌsəl] **1** *n (of leaves, paper)* bruissement *m*

2 *vt (leaves, paper)* faire bruire

3 *vi (of leaves, paper)* bruire
rustle² *vt (cattle)* voler
▸ **rustle up** *vt sep Fam (meal, snack)* improviser; **to r. up support** rassembler des partisans
rustler ['rʌslə(r)] *n (cattle thief)* voleur(euse) *m,f* de bétail
rustproof ['rʌstpruːf] *adj (paint)* antirouille *inv*; *(metal)* inoxydable
rusty ['rʌstɪ] *adj also Fig* rouillé(e); *(colour)* rouille *inv*
rut¹ [rʌt] *n (groove)* ornière *f*; *Fig* **to be (stuck) in a r.** être prisonnier(ère) de la routine

rut² **1** *n (of stag)* rut *m*
2 *vi (pt & pp rutted)(of stag)* être en rut
rutabaga [ruːtə'beɪgə] *n Am* rutabaga *m*
ruthless ['ruːθlɪs] *adj* impitoyable
RV [ɑː'viː] *n Am (abbr recreational vehicle)* mobile home *m*
Rwanda [rə'wændə] *n* le Rwanda
Rwandan [rə'wændən] **1** *n* Rwandais(e) *m,f*
2 *adj* rwandais(e)
rye [raɪ] *n* seigle *m*; **r. bread** pain *m* de seigle

S

S, s [es] *n* (**a**) *(letter)* S, s *m inv* (**b**) *(abbr* **south**) S

Sabbath ['sæbəθ] *n (Jewish)* (jour *m* du) sabbat *m*; *(Christian)* jour du seigneur

sabbatical [sə'bætɪkəl] *Univ* **1** *n* congé *m* sabbatique; **to be on s.** être en congé sabbatique **2** *adj (term, year)* sabbatique

sable ['seɪbəl] **1** *n (animal)* zibeline *f*; **s. coat** manteau *m* de *ou* en zibeline **2** *adj Lit (black)* noir(e)

sabotage ['sæbətɑːʒ] **1** *n* sabotage *m* **2** *vt* saboter

saboteur [sæbə'tɜː(r)] *n* saboteur(euse) *m,f*

sabre ['seɪbə(r)] *n* sabre *m*

sac [sæk] *n Biol* sac *m*

saccharin ['sækərɪn] *n* saccharine *f*

saccharine ['sækərɪn] *adj Pej (smile, words)* mielleux(euse); *(film)* à l'eau de rose

sachet ['sæʃeɪ] *n* sachet *m*

sack¹ [sæk] **1** *n* (**a**) *(bag)* sac *m*; *Fam* **to hit the s.** se pieuter (**b**) *Br Fam (dismissal)* renvoi *m*; **to give sb the s.** virer qn; **to get the s.** se faire virer **2** *vt Fam (dismiss)* virer

sack² **1** *n (plundering)* sac *m* **2** *vt (plunder)* mettre à sac

sacking ['sækɪŋ] *n* (**a**) *(textile)* grosse toile *f* (**b**) *Fam (dismissal)* renvoi *m*

sacrament ['sækrəmənt] *n Rel* sacrement *m*; **to take** *or* **receive the sacraments** communier

sacred ['seɪkrɪd] *adj* sacré(e); *Fig* **s. cow** *(belief, institution)* véritable institution *f*

sacrifice ['sækrɪfaɪs] **1** *n* sacrifice *m*; **to make sacrifices** faire des sacrifices **2** *vt* sacrifier (**to** à); **to s. oneself** se sacrifier

sacrificial [sækrɪ'fɪʃəl] *adj* sacrificiel(elle); *Fig* **s. lamb** *or* **victim** bouc *m* émissaire

sacrilege ['sækrɪlɪdʒ] *n also Fig* sacrilège *m*

sacrilegious [sækrɪ'lɪdʒəs] *adj also Fig* sacrilège

sacristan ['sækrɪstən] *n Rel* sacristain *m*

sacrosanct ['sækrəʊsæŋkt] *adj* sacro-saint(e)

SAD [sæd] *n Med (abbr* **Seasonal Affective Disorder**) dépression *f* saisonnière

sad [sæd] *adj* (**a**) *(unhappy, depressing)* triste; **to make sb s.** attrister qn (**b**) *Fam (pathetic)* pitoyable

sadden ['sædən] *vt* attrister

saddle ['sædəl] **1** *n (on horse, bicycle)* selle *f*; **to be in the s.** être en selle; *Fig* être aux commandes **2** *vt (horse)* seller; *Fam Fig* **to s. sb with sb/sth** refiler qn/

qch à qn; **to get saddled with sb/sth** se retrouver avec qn/qch sur les bras

saddlebag ['sædəlbæg] *n* sacoche *f*

sadism ['seɪdɪzəm] *n* sadisme *m*

sadist ['seɪdɪst] *n* sadique *mf*

sadistic [sə'dɪstɪk] *adj* sadique

sadly ['sædlɪ] *adv* (**a**) *(unhappily)* tristement (**b**) *(unfortunately)* malheureusement (**c**) *(greatly)* **to be s. mistaken** se tromper lourdement; **he is s. missed** il nous/ leur/*etc* manque beaucoup

sadness ['sædnɪs] *n* tristesse *f*

sadomasochism [seɪdəʊ'mæsəkɪzəm] *n* sadomasochisme *m*

sadomasochist [seɪdəʊ'mæsəkɪst] *n* sadomasochiste *mf*

SAE [eseɪ'iː] *n (abbr* **stamped addressed envelope**) enveloppe *f* timbrée

safari [sə'fɑːrɪ] *n* safari *m*; **to go on s.** faire un safari; **s. jacket** saharienne *f*; **s. park** réserve *f* d'animaux sauvages

safe [seɪf] **1** *adj* (**a**) *(not in danger)* en sécurité; *(house, activity)* sûr(e); *(topic of conversation)* sans danger; **s. from sth** à l'abri de qch; **s. and sound** sain et sauf (saine et sauve); **as s. as houses** qui ne présente aucun risque; *Prov* **better s. than sorry** deux précautions valent mieux qu'une (**b**) *(not dangerous)* **it is s. to say that everyone enjoyed themselves** on peut dire sans risque de se tromper que ça a plu à tout le monde; **it's a s. bet that...** il y a fort à parier que...; **at a s. distance** à distance respectueuse; **in s. hands** entre de bonnes mains; **to wish sb a s. journey** souhaiter bon voyage à qn; **...to be on the s. side** ...pour plus de sûreté; **s. house** *(for spies)* cachette *f* sûre; **s. sex** rapports *mpl* sexuels protégés **2** *n (for money)* coffre-fort *m* **3** *adv* **to play (it) s.** ne pas prendre de risques

safe-conduct [seɪf'kɒndʌkt] *n* sauf-conduit *m*

safeguard ['seɪfgɑːd] **1** *n* garantie *f* **2** *vt* sauvegarder **3** *vi* **to s. against sth** se protéger contre qch

safekeeping [seɪf'kiːpɪŋ] *n* **in s.** en lieu sûr; **to give sth to sb for s.** confier qch à la garde de qn

safely ['seɪflɪ] *adv* (**a**) *(without risk)* en toute sécurité; *(drive)* prudemment; **to arrive s.** *(of person)* bien arriver; *(of goods)* arriver sans dommage (**b**) *(with certainty)* avec certitude

safety ['seɪftɪ] *n* sûreté *f*; **for s.'s sake** pour plus de sûreté; **to be s. conscious** se préoccuper beaucoup de la sécurité; *Prov* **(there's) s. in numbers** plus on est nombreux, moins on court de risques; **s. belt** ceinture *f* de sécurité; **s. catch** cran *m* de sûreté; **s. glass** verre *m* de sécurité; **s. matches** allumettes *fpl* de sûreté; **s. measures** mesures *fpl* de sûreté; **s. net** filet *m*; *Fig* mesure *f* de sécurité; **s. pin** épingle *f* de sûreté; *also Fig* **s. valve** soupape *f* de sûreté

saffron ['sæfrən] **1** *n* safran *m*
2 *adj* safran *inv*

sag [sæg] *(pt & pp* **sagged**) *vi (of roof, bridge)* s'affaisser; *(of flesh)* être flasque; *(of rope)* pendre; *(of breasts)* être tombant(e); *(of prices, support)* baisser

saga ['sɑːgə] *n also Fig (story)* saga *f*

sagacious [sə'geɪʃəs] *adj Formal* sagace

sagacity [sə'gæsɪtɪ] *n Formal* sagacité *f*

sage¹ [seɪdʒ] **1** *n (wise man)* sage *m*
2 *adj (person, conduct)* sage

sage² *n (herb)* sauge *f*

Sagittarius [sædʒɪ'teərɪəs] *n (sign of zodiac)* le Sagittaire; **to be (a) S.** être (du) Sagittaire

Sahara [sə'hɑːrə] *n* **the S. (Desert)** le Sahara

said [sed] *pt & pp of* **say**

sail [seɪl] **1** *n (on boat)* voile *f*; *(of windmill)* aile *f*; **to set s.** prendre la mer; **to go for a s.** faire un tour en voilier
2 *vi (of ship, person)* naviguer; *(start voyage)* prendre la mer; *Fig* **the clouds sailed by** les nuages passaient dans le ciel; *Fig* **the ball sailed over the wall** la balle est passée par-dessus le mur; *Fig* **to s. close to the wind** jouer avec le feu; *Fam* **to s. through an examination** réussir un examen les doigts dans le nez

sailing ['seɪlɪŋ] *n (activity)* voile *f*; *(departure)* appareillage *m*; **to go s.** faire de la voile; *Br* **s. boat/ship** voilier *m*

sailor ['seɪlə(r)] *n* marin *m*; **to be a good/bad s.** avoir/ne pas avoir le pied marin; **s. suit** costume *m* marin *(d'enfant)*

saint [seɪnt] *n* saint(e) *m,f*; **All Saints' (Day)** la Toussaint; **S. Bernard** *(dog)* saint-bernard *m inv*

saintly ['seɪntlɪ] *adj (life, behaviour)* de saint; *(smile)* d'ange

sake [seɪk] *n* **for the s. of sb, for sb's s.** *(for the good of)* pour le bien de qn; *(out of respect for)* par égard de qn; **for God's** *or* **heaven's s.!** mais bon sang!; **for the s. of peace** pour avoir la paix; **for old times'** **s.** en souvenir du passé; **this is just talking for talking's s.** c'est parler pour parler; **let's say, for the s. of argument…** admettons que…

salacious [sə'leɪʃəs] *adj* salace

salad ['sæləd] *n* salade *f*; **s. bowl** saladier *m*; *Fig* **s. days** années *fpl* de jeunesse; **s. dressing** = vinaigrette ou sauce pour salade

salamander ['sæləmændə(r)] *n* salamandre *f*

salami [sə'lɑːmɪ] *n* salami *m*

salaried ['sælərɪd] *adj* salarié(e)

salary ['sælərɪ] *(pl* **salaries**) *n* salaire *m*; **s. earner** salarié(e) *m,f*; **s. grade** échelon *m* de salaire; **s. scale** échelle *f* des salaires

sale [seɪl] *n* **(a)** *(action, event)* vente *f*; **for s.** à vendre; **to put sth up for s.** mettre qch en vente; **on s.** en vente; *Br* **sales assistant** vendeur(euse) *m,f*; **sales department** service *m* commercial; **sales drive** campagne *f* de vente; **sales force** force *f* de vente; **sales forecast** prévision *f* des ventes; **sales manager** directeur(trice) *m,f* commercial(e); **sales pitch** arguments *mpl* de vente; **sales target** objectif *m* de vente; **s. price** prix *m* de vente **(b)** *(at reduced prices)* soldes *mpl*; **the sales** les soldes; **in the sales** en solde

saleable ['seɪləbəl] *adj* vendable

saleroom ['seɪlruːm] *n* salle *f* des ventes

salesclerk ['seɪlzklɑːk] *n Am* vendeur(euse) *m,f*

salesgirl ['seɪlzgɜːl] *n* vendeuse *f*

salesman ['seɪlzmən] *n (for company)* représentant *m*; *(in shop)* vendeur *m*

salesmanship ['seɪlzmənʃɪp] *n* technique *f* de vente

salesperson ['seɪlzpɜːsən] *(pl* **salespeople**) *n (for company)* représentant(e) *m,f*; *(in shop)* vendeur(euse) *m,f*

saleswoman ['seɪlzwʊmən] *n (for company)* représentante *f*; *(in shop)* vendeuse *f*

salient ['seɪlɪənt] *adj (feature)* marquant(e); *(point)* essentiel(elle)

saline ['seɪlaɪn] *adj* salin(e); **s. drip** perfusion *f* de solution saline; **s. solution** solution *f* saline

saliva [sə'laɪvə] *n* salive *f*

salivate ['sælɪveɪt] *vi also Fig* saliver

sallow ['sæləʊ] *adj* jaunâtre

► **sally forth** ['sælɪ] *(pt & pp* **sallied**) *vi Lit* partir

salmon ['sæmən] *(pl* **salmon**) *n* saumon *m*; **s. (pink)** *(rose m)* saumon; **s. trout** truite *f* saumonée

salmonella [sælmə'nelə] *n* salmonelle *f*

salon ['sælɒn] *n* **(beauty) s.** institut *m* de beauté; **(hairdressing) s.** salon *m* de coiffure

saloon [sə'luːn] *n* **(a)** *(room)* salle *f*; *Am (bar)* bar *m* **(b)** *Br* **s. (car)** berline *f*

SALT [sɔːlt] *n (abbr* **Strategic Arms Limitation Talks**) SALT *m*

salt [sɔːlt] **1** *n (a) (mineral)* sel *m*; **s. flat** marais *m* salant; **s. mine** mine *f* de sel **(b)** *(idioms)* **to be worth one's s.** être à la hauteur; **to rub s. in sb's wounds** remuer le couteau dans la plaie; **the s. of the earth** le sel de la terre **(c)** *Fam* **an old s.** *(sailor)* un vieux loup de mer
2 *adj* **s. beef** bœuf *m* salé; **s. cod** morue *f* salée; **s. water** eau *f* salée
3 *vt (food)* saler; *(roads)* sabler

► **salt away** *vt sep (money)* mettre de côté

saltcellar ['sɔːltselə(r)] *n* salière *f*

salt-free ['sɔːltfriː] *adj* sans sel

saltpetre [sɔːlt'piːtə(r)] *n* salpêtre *m*

saltwater ['sɔːltwɔːtə(r)] *adj (lake)* salé(e); *(fish)* de mer

salty ['sɔːltɪ] *adj* salé(e)

salubrious [sə'luːbrɪəs] *adj Formal* salubre

salutary ['sæljʊtərɪ] *adj* salutaire

salute [sə'luːt] **1** *n* salut *m*; **to take the s.** passer les troupes en revue
2 *vt also Fig* saluer
3 *vi* faire un salut

salvage ['sælvɪdʒ] **1** *n (of ship)* sauvetage *m*; *(of waste material)* récupération *f*; **s. vessel** bateau *m* de sauvetage
2 *vt also Fig* sauver

salvation [sæl'veɪʃən] *n* salut *m*; **S. Army** Armée *f* du Salut

salve [sælv] *vt* **to s. one's conscience** se donner bonne conscience

salver ['sælvə(r)] *n (tray)* plateau *m* (de présentation)

salvo ['sælvəʊ] *(pl* **salvos** *or* **salvoes**) *n also Fig* salve *f*; *(of questions)* flot *m*; *(of insults)* torrent *m*

Samaritan [sə'mærɪtən] *n also Fig* **the Good S.** le bon Samaritain; **the Samaritans** ≃ S.O.S. Amitié

same [seɪm] **1** *adj* **the s. man** le même homme; **the s. woman** la même femme; **the s. children** les mêmes enfants; **in the s. way** de la même façon; *Fig* **to go the s. way** prendre le même chemin; **the s. day** le même jour; **the** *or* **that (very) s. day** *(for emphasis)* le jour même; **it all comes to the s. thing** cela revient au même; **at the s. time** *(regularly)* au même moment; *(simultaneously)* en même temps, à la fois

2 *pron* **the s.** le même, la même; *(plural)* les mêmes; **I would have done the s.** j'aurais fait la même chose *ou* pareil; **if it's all the s. to you** si cela vous est égal; *Fam* **(the) s. again?** *(in pub)* la même chose?; *Fam* **s. here!** *(so do I)* moi aussi!; *(neither do I)* moi non plus!; *(I did the same thing)* pareil!; **the house isn't the s. without her** la maison n'est plus la même sans elle **3** *adv* **to think/feel the s.** penser/ressentir la même chose; **to look the s.** *(of two things)* sembler pareils; **to taste the s.** avoir le même goût; **all the s.** *(nevertheless)* tout de même

sameness ['seɪmnɪs] *n* monotonie *f*

Samoa [sə'məʊə] *n* Samoa *m*

Samoan [sə'məʊən] **1** *n* **(a)** *(person)* Samoan(e) *m,f* **(b)** *(language)* samoan *m* **2** *adj* samoan(e)

samosa [səm'əʊsə] *n* samosa *m*

sample ['sɑːmpəl] **1** *n* échantillon *m*; *(of blood, urine)* prélèvement *m* **2** *vt* **(a)** *(food, experience)* goûter **(b)** *(public opinion)* sonder **(c)** *(piece of music)* sampler

sanatorium [sænə'tɔːrɪəm] *(pl* **sanatoria** [sænə'tɔːrɪə]) *n* sanatorium *m*

sanctify ['sæŋ(k)tɪfaɪ] *vt* sanctifier; *Fig* consacrer

sanctimonious [sæŋ(k)tɪ'məʊnɪəs] *adj* moralisateur(trice)

sanction ['sæŋ(k)ʃən] **1** *n* **(a)** *(penalty)* sanction *f*; **to impose sanctions on a country** imposer des sanctions à un pays **(b)** *Formal (consent)* consentement *m*, accord *m* **2** *vt Formal (consent to)* sanctionner

sanctity ['sæŋ(k)tɪtɪ] *n* sainteté *f*; *Fig (of life, marriage)* caractère *m* sacré

sanctuary ['sæŋ(k)tj(ʊ)ərɪ] *n Rel* sanctuaire *m*; *(for fugitive, refugee)* refuge *m*, asile *m*; *(for birds, wildlife)* réserve *f*; **to seek/find s.** chercher/trouver refuge

sand [sænd] **1** *n* sable *m*; **s. castle** château *m* de sable; **s. dune** dune *f* **2** *vt* **(a)** *(smooth with sandpaper)* poncer **(b)** *(cover with sand)* sabler

sandal ['sændəl] *n* sandale *f*

sandbag ['sændbæg] *n* sac *m* de sable

sandbank ['sændbæŋk] *n* banc *m* de sable

sandblast ['sændblɑːst] *vt* décaper à la sableuse

sandpaper ['sændpeɪpə(r)] **1** *n* papier *m* de verre **2** *vt* poncer, passer au papier de verre

sandpit ['sændpɪt] *n* bac *m* à sable

sandstone ['sændstəʊn] *n* grès *m*

sandstorm ['sændstɔːm] *n* tempête *f* de sable

sandwich ['sændwɪtʃ] **1** *n* sandwich *m*; **ham s.** sandwich au jambon; *Br* **s. course** stage *m* de formation (professionnelle) en alternance **2** *vt* **to be sandwiched between** *(of layer)* être intercalé(e) entre; *(of person, building)* être coincé(e) entre

sandy ['sændɪ] *adj* **(a)** *(earth)* sablonneux(euse); *(beach)* de sable **(b)** *(hair)* blond roux *inv*

sane [seɪn] *adj (person)* sain(e) d'esprit; *(action, remark)* sensé(e)

San Franciscan ['sænfrən'sɪskən] **1** *n* habitant(e) *m,f* de San Francisco **2** *adj* de San Francisco

San Francisco ['sænfrən'sɪskəʊ] *n* San Francisco

sang [sæŋ] *pt of* **sing**

sanguine ['sæŋgwɪn] *adj* optimiste

sanitary ['sænɪtərɪ] *adj* **(a)** *(clean)* hygiénique **(b)** *(relating to hygiene)* sanitaire; *Br* **s. towel,** *Am* **s. napkin** serviette *f* hygiénique

sanitation [sænɪ'teɪʃən] *n* installations *fpl* sanitaires

sanitize ['sænɪtaɪz] *vt* expurger

sanity ['sænɪtɪ] *n* santé *f* mentale

sank [sæŋk] *pt of* **sink²**

San Marino [sænmə'riːnəʊ] *n* Saint-Marin

Santa (Claus) ['sæntə('klɔːz)] *n* le père Noël

sap¹ [sæp] *n (of plant)* sève *f*

sap² *n Fam (gullible person)* andouille *f*

sap³ *(pt & pp* **sapped**) *vt (weaken)* saper

sapling ['sæplɪŋ] *n* jeune arbre *m*

sapper ['sæpə(r)] *n Mil* soldat *m* du génie

sapphire ['sæfaɪə(r)] *n* saphir *m*

Sarajevo [særə'jeɪveʊ] *n* Sarajevo

sarcasm ['sɑːkæzəm] *n* sarcasme *m*

sarcastic [sɑː'kæstɪk] *adj* sarcastique

sarcastically [sɑː'kæstɪklɪ] *adv* de manière sarcastique; *(speak)* d'un ton sarcastique

sarcophagus [sɑː'kɒfəgəs] *(pl* **sarcophagi** [sɑː'kɒfəgaɪ]) *n* sarcophage *m*

sardine [sɑː'diːn] *n* sardine *f*; *Fam Fig* **to be packed like sardines** être serrés(es) comme des sardines

Sardinia [sɑː'dɪnɪə] *n* la Sardaigne

Sardinian [sɑː'dɪnɪən] **1** *n* Sarde *mf* **2** *adj* sarde

sardonic [sɑː'dɒnɪk] *adj* sardonique

sari ['sɑːrɪ] *n* sari *m*

sarong [sə'rɒŋ] *n* paréo *m*

sartorial [sɑː'tɔːrɪəl] *adj Formal* vestimentaire

SAS [eseɪ'es] *n Br (abbr* **Special Air Service**) = service d'intervention spécial de l'Armée britannique

sash [sæʃ] *n (around waist)* large ceinture *f* de tissu; *(around shoulder)* écharpe *f*; **s. cord** corde *f* (actionnant une fenêtre à guillotine); **s. window** fenêtre *f* à guillotine

Sat *(abbr* **Saturday**) samedi

sat [sæt] *pt & pp of* **sit**

Satan ['seɪtən] *n* Satan

satanic [sə'tænɪk] *adj* satanique, diabolique

satchel ['sætʃəl] *n* cartable *m*

sate [seɪt] *vt Formal* assouvir

satellite ['sætəlaɪt] *n* satellite *m*; **s. dish** antenne *f* parabolique; **s. (state)** (État *m*) satellite; **s. television** télévision *f* par satellite; **s. town** ville *f* satellite

satiate ['seɪʃɪeɪt] *vt Formal* assouvir

satin ['sætɪn] *n* satin *m*

satire ['sætaɪə(r)] *n* satire *f*

satirical [sə'tɪrɪkəl] *adj* satirique

satirist ['sætɪrɪst] *n* écrivain *m* satirique

satirize ['sætɪraɪz] *vt* faire la satire de

satisfaction [sætɪs'fækʃən] *n* satisfaction *f*; **to have the s. of doing sth** avoir la satisfaction de faire qch

satisfactory [sætɪs'fæktərɪ] *adj* satisfaisant(e)

satisfied ['sætɪsfaɪd] *adj* satisfait(e)

satisfy ['sætɪsfaɪ] *(pt & pp* **satisfied**) *vt* **(a)** *(meet needs of) (person, curiosity)* satisfaire; *(condition)* remplir **(b)** *(convince)* convaincre, persuader

saturate ['sætʃəreɪt] *vt* saturer; **to s. the market** saturer le marché; **saturated fats** graisses *fpl* saturées

saturation [sætʃə'reɪʃən] *n* saturation *f*; **to reach s. point** arriver à saturation; *Mil* **s. bombing** bombardement *m* intensif

Saturday ['sætədɪ] *n* samedi *m*; **this S.** samedi prochain *ou* qui vient; **on S.** samedi; **on S. morning/afternoon/ evening** samedi matin/après-midi/soir; **on Saturdays** le samedi; **every S.** tous les samedis; **every other S.** un samedi sur deux; **last S.** samedi dernier; **the S.** before **last** pas samedi dernier mais celui d'avant; **next S.** samedi prochain; **the S. after next, a week on S., S. week** le samedi d'après, samedi en huit; **the following S.** le samedi suivant; **S.'s paper** le journal de samedi; **S. job** petit boulot *m (du samedi)*

Saturn ['sætɜːn] *n (planet)* Saturne *f*

sauce [sɔːs] *n* (a) *(for food)* sauce *f;* **tomato/chocolate s.** sauce tomate/au chocolat; **s. boat** saucière *f* (b) *Fam (impudence)* culot *m*

saucepan ['sɔːspən] *n* casserole *f*

saucer ['sɔːsə(r)] *n* soucoupe *f*

saucy ['sɔːsɪ] *adj Fam (impertinent)* insolent(e); *(risqué)* coquin(e)

Saudi ['saʊdɪ] **1** *n (person)* Saoudien(enne) *m,f; Fam (country)* l'Arabie *f* Saoudite
   2 *adj* saoudien(enne)

Saudi Arabia ['saʊdɪə'reɪbɪə] *n* l'Arabie *f* Saoudite

Saudi Arabian ['saʊdɪə'reɪbɪən] **1** *n* Saoudien(enne) *m,f*
   2 *adj* saoudien(enne)

sauna ['sɔːnə] *n* sauna *m;* **to have a s.** aller au sauna

saunter ['sɔːntə(r)] **1** *n* balade *f;* **to go for a s.** partir en balade
   2 *vi* **to s. (along)** flâner

sausage ['sɒsɪdʒ] *n* saucisse *f; Br Fam* **not a s.** *(nothing)* que dalle; *Br Hum* **you silly s.!** patate, va!; *Fam* **s. dog** saucisson *m* à pattes; **s. meat** chair *f* à saucisse

sauté ['səʊteɪ] **1** *adj* sauté(e)
   2 *vt (pt &pp* **sautéed)** faire sauter

savage ['sævɪdʒ] **1** *n Old-fashioned* sauvage *mf*
   2 *adj (animal, person)* féroce, brutal(e); *(attack, criticism)* violent(e)
   3 *vt (attack physically)* attaquer; *Fig (criticize)* descendre en flammes

savagely ['sævɪdʒlɪ] *adv (beat, attack)* sauvagement; *Fig (criticize)* violemment, avec virulence

savanna(h) [sə'vænə] *n* savane *f*

save¹ [seɪv] *prep Formal (except)* hormis

save² [seɪv] **1** *vt* (a) *(rescue)* sauver; **to s. sb's life** sauver la vie à qn; *Fam* **she can't play tennis to s. her life** elle joue au tennis comme un pied; *Fam* **to s. one's (own) neck** *or* **skin** sauver sa peau; **to s. sb from falling** empêcher qn de tomber; **to s. a goal** arrêter un but; **God s. the King/the Queen!** vive le Roi/la Reine! (b) *(keep for future)* garder, conserver; *(money)* mettre de côté; *Comptr* sauvegarder; **to s. oneself for sth** se réserver pour qch (c) *(not waste) (money, space)* économiser; *(time)* gagner; **s. your breath** économise ton souffle *ou* ta salive (d) *(spare)* **to s. sb sth** éviter qch à qn; **to s. sb (from) doing sth** éviter à qn de faire qch
   2 *vi* faire des économies **(for/on** pour/sur)
   3 *n (of goalkeeper)* arrêt *m;* **to make a s.** arrêter un but
   ▸ **save up** *vi* mettre de l'argent de côté **(for** pour)

saver ['seɪvə(r)] *n* épargnant(e) *m,f*

saving ['seɪvɪŋ] **1** *n* (a) *(economy)* économie *f* (b) *(money saved)* économies *fpl;* **to live off one's savings** vivre sur ses économies; **savings account** compte *m* d'épargne; **savings bank** caisse *f* d'épargne
   2 *adj* **her/its s. grace** ce qui la/le sauve; **the movie has one s. grace** une seule chose sauve le film

saviour, *Am* **savior** ['seɪvjə(r)] *n* sauveur *m;* **the S.** le Sauveur

savour, *Am* **savior** ['seɪvə(r)] **1** *n* saveur *f*
   2 *vt also Fig* savourer
   3 *vi Formal* **to s. of** sentir

savoury, *Am* **savory** ['seɪvərɪ] *adj* (a) *(food)* salé(e) (b) *(conduct)* honorable

saw¹ [sɔː] *pt of* **see²**

saw² **1** *n (tool)* scie *f*
   2 *vt (pp* **sawn** [sɔːn] *or* **sawed)** scier
   ▸ **saw off** *vt sep* scier
   ▸ **saw up** *vt sep* découper à la scie

sawdust ['sɔːdʌst] *n* sciure *f*

sawmill ['sɔːmɪl] *n* scierie *f*

sawn [sɔːn] *pp of* **saw²**

sawn-off shotgun ['sɔːnɒf'ʃɒtgʌn] *n* fusil *m* à canon scié

sax [sæks] *n Fam (saxophone)* sax *m*

Saxon ['sæks(ə)n] **1** *n* (a) *(person)* Saxon(onne) *m,f* (b) *(language)* saxon *m*
   2 *adj* saxon(onne)

Saxony ['sæksənɪ] *n* Saxe *f*

saxophone ['sæksəfəʊn] *n* saxophone *m*

saxophonist [sæk'sɒfənɪst] *n* saxophoniste *mf*

say [seɪ] **1** *vt (pt & pp* **said** [sed]) dire; *(of clock, watch)* indiquer; **to s. sth to sb** dire qch à qn; **it says that...** *(of text, sign)* il y a écrit que...; **I wouldn't s. no to a glass of wine** je prendrais volontiers un verre de vin; **I didn't s. a word** je n'ai pas dit un mot; **it's not for me to s.** ce n'est pas à moi de le dire; **there's no saying what might happen if...** inutile de vous dire ce qui se passerait si...; **what have you got to s. for yourself?** as-tu une excuse valable?; **there's a lot to be said for living in the country** il y a bien des avantages à vivre à la campagne; **you're honest, I'll s.** that for you tu es honnête, je te l'accorde; **it says a lot about her** ça en dit long sur sa personne; **don't s. you've forgotten already!** ne me dis pas que tu as déjà oublié!; **you can s. that again!, you said it!** c'est le cas de le dire!; **need I s. more?** ai-je besoin d'en dire plus?; **they s. that..., it is said that...** on dit que...; **s. we won first prize** supposons que nous gagnions le premier prix; **if I had, s., $100,000** si j'avais, mettons, 100 000 dollars
   2 *vi* **I'm not saying** je ne dirai rien; **as they s.** comme on dit; **I s.! dis-donc!; I'll s.!** absolument!, tout à fait!; *Fam* **you don't s.!** sans blague!
   3 *n* **to have one's s.** avoir son mot à dire; **to have a s./no s. in sth** avoir/ne pas avoir voix au chapitre concernant qch

saying ['seɪɪŋ] *n* maxime *f;* **as the s. goes** comme dit la maxime

say-so ['seɪsəʊ] *n Fam (permission)* permission *f*

scab [skæb] *n* (a) *(on skin)* croûte *f* (b) *Fam (strikebreaker)* jaune *mf*

scabbard ['skæbəd] *n* fourreau *m,* gaine *f*

scabies ['skeɪbiːz] *n* gale *f*

scaffold ['skæfəld] *n (outside building)* échafaudage *m;* *(for execution)* échafaud *m*

scaffolding ['skæfəldɪŋ] *n* échafaudage *m*

scald [skɔːld] **1** *n* brûlure *f*
   2 *vt* ébouillanter; **to s. one's hand** s'ébouillanter la main

scalding ['skɔːldɪŋ] *adj* brûlant(e)

scale¹ [skeɪl] **1** *n (on fish, reptile)* écaille *f;* *(in pipes, kettle)* dépôt *m* calcaire
   2 *vt (fish)* écailler

scale² [skeɪl] **1** *n* (a) *(of instrument)* gamme *f;* *(of salaries)* barème *m;* **on a s. of one to ten** sur une échelle allant de un à dix (b) *(of map, drawing)* échelle *f; Fig (of problem, changes)* étendue *f;* **to s.** à la bonne échelle; **s. model** modèle *m* réduit (c) *(of ruler, thermometer)* graduation *f*

scale³ *vt (climb)* escalader

▸ **scale down** *vt sep (reduce)* revoir à la baisse

▸ **scale up** *vt sep (increase)* augmenter

scales [skeɪlz] *npl* **(set of) s.** *(for kitchen)* balance *f; (for bathroom)* pèse-personne *m*

scallop ['skæləp] **1** *n* **(a)** *(shellfish)* coquille *f* Saint-Jacques **(b)** *(in sewing)* feston *m*
2 *vt (in sewing)* festonner

scallywag ['skælɪwæg] *n Fam* coquin(e) *m,f*

scalp [skælp] **1** *n* cuir *m* chevelu; *(as war trophy)* scalp *m*
2 *vt (in war)* scalper

scalpel ['skælpəl] *n* scalpel *m*

scaly ['skeɪlɪ] *adj (fish)* écailleux(euse); *(skin)* squameux(euse)

scam [skæm] *n Fam* arnaque *f,* magouille *f*

scamp [skæmp] *n (rascal)* coquin(e) *m,f*

scamper ['skæmpə(r)] *vi* gambader, galoper

▸ **scamper away, scamper off** *vi* détaler, partir en courant

scampi ['skæmpɪ] *n* scampi *mpl*

scan [skæn] **1** *vt (pt & pp* **scanned)** **(a)** *(examine closely)* scruter; *Comptr* balayer; *Med* faire une scanographie de; *(with ultrasound)* faire une échographie de **(b)** *(glance at)* parcourir
2 *n Med* scanographie *f; (with ultrasound)* échographie *f*

scandal ['skændəl] *n* **(a)** *(outrage)* scandale *m;* **to create** *or* **cause a s.** créer *ou* provoquer un scandale **(b)** *(gossip)* ragots *mpl*

scandalize ['skændəlaɪz] *vt* scandaliser, choquer

scandalous ['skændələs] *adj* scandaleux(euse)

Scandinavia [skændɪ'neɪvɪə] *n* la Scandinavie

Scandinavian [skændɪ'neɪvɪən] **1** *n* Scandinave *mf*
2 *adj* scandinave

scanner ['skænə(r)] *n Med & Comptr* scanner *m*

scant [skænt] *adj* insuffisant(e)

scantily ['skæntɪlɪ] *adv* insuffisamment, sommairement; **s. dressed** *or* **clad** légèrement vêtu(e)

scanty ['skæntɪ] *adj (dress)* léger(ère); *(amount, information)* maigre, limité(e)

scapegoat ['skeɪpɡəʊt] *n* bouc *m* émissaire

scar [skɑ:(r)] **1** *n also Fig* cicatrice *f;* **s. tissue** tissu *m* cicatriciel
2 *vt (pt & pp* **scarred)** marquer de cicatrices; *Fig* marquer; **to be scarred for life** garder des cicatrices toute sa vie; *Fig* être marqué(e) à vie
3 *vi (of wound)* laisser une cicatrice

scarce ['skeəs] *adj* rare; *Fam* **to make oneself s.** filer

scarcely ['skeəslɪ] *adv* à peine; **she could s. speak** elle pouvait à peine parler; **s. ever/anyone** presque jamais/personne; **it is s. likely that…** il est peu probable que…

scarcity ['skeəsɪtɪ], **scarceness** ['skeəsnɪs] *n* manque *m,* pénurie *f*

scare ['skeə(r)] **1** *n* frayeur *f;* **pollution s.** alerte *f* à la pollution; **you gave me an awful s.** tu m'as fait une belle frayeur
2 *vt* effrayer; *Fam* **to s. the life out of sb, to s. the living daylights out of sb** faire une de ces trouilles à qn
3 *vi* s'effrayer

▸ **scare away, scare off** *vt sep* faire fuir

scarecrow ['skeəkrəʊ] *n* épouvantail *m*

scared [skeəd] *adj* effrayé(e); **to be s. of sb/sth** avoir peur de qn/qch; **to be s. stiff, to be s. to death** être mort(e) de peur

scaremongering ['skeəmʌŋɡərɪŋ] *n* alarmisme *m*

scarf [skɑ:f] *(pl* **scarves** [skɑ:vz]) *n (long)* écharpe *f; (square)* foulard *m*

scarlet ['skɑ:lɪt] **1** *n* écarlate *f*
2 *adj* écarlate; *Fig* **to go** *or* **turn s.** *(with anger, embarrassment)* devenir rouge; **s. fever** scarlatine *f*

scarper ['skɑ:pə(r)] *vi Br Fam* ficher le camp, se tailler

scary ['skeərɪ] *adj Fam* effrayant(e)

scat [skæt] *exclam Fam* fiche le camp!, dégage!

scathing ['skeɪðɪŋ] *adj (remark, sarcasm)* acerbe; **to be s. about sb/sth** faire des remarques acerbes sur qn/qch

scatological [skætə'lɒdʒɪkəl] *adj* scatologique

scatter ['skætə(r)] **1** *vt (clouds, demonstrators)* disperser, éparpiller; *(corn, seed)* jeter *ou* semer à la volée; *(crumbs, papers)* laisser traîner
2 *vi (of crowd)* se disperser

scatterbrain ['skætəbreɪn] *n Fam* tête *f* de linotte

scatty ['skætɪ] *adj Br Fam* farfelu(e)

scavenge ['skævɪndʒ] **1** *vt* récupérer
2 *vi* **to s. for sth** fouiller pour trouver qch; **to s. in the dustbins** fouiller dans *ou* faire les poubelles

scavenger ['skævɪndʒə(r)] *n (animal)* charognard *m; Fig (person)* fouilleur(euse) *m,f* de poubelles

scenario [sɪ'nɑ:rɪəʊ] *(pl* **scenarios)** *n* **(a)** *(of film)* scénario *m* **(b)** *(situation)* hypothèse *f*

scene [si:n] *n* **(a)** *(in book, film, play)* scène *f; also Fig* **a touching/terrifying s.** une scène touchante/terrifiante; *also Fig* **behind the scenes** dans les coulisses; *Th* **s. shifter** machiniste *mf* **(b)** *(of event)* lieu *m,* endroit *m;* **a change of s.** un changement de décor; **to arrive** *or* **come on the s.** faire son apparition; **the s. of the crime/accident** le lieu du crime/de l'accident; **a s. of devastation** un spectacle de dévastation; **I can picture the s.** j'imagine la scène; *Fam* **it's not my s.** ce n'est pas mon truc **(c)** *(fuss)* scandale *m;* **to make a s.** faire un scandale

scenery ['si:nərɪ] *n* **(a)** *(in play)* décor(s) *m(pl)* **(b)** *(landscape)* paysage *m; Fam* **to need a change of s.** avoir besoin de changer d'air

scenic ['si:nɪk] *adj* pittoresque; **s. railway** petit train *m* (touristique); **s. route** route *f* touristique

scent [sent] **1** *n* **(a)** *(smell)* odeur *f* **(b)** *(perfume)* parfum *m* **(c)** *(in hunting)* fumet *m;* **to pick up the s.** trouver la piste; **to be on the s. of sth** être sur la trace de qch; **to lose the s.** perdre la trace; **she threw her pursuers off the s.** elle sema ses poursuivants
2 *vt* **(a)** *(smell)* flairer; *Fig* **to s. danger** flairer le danger **(b)** *(perfume)* parfumer

sceptic ['skeptɪk] *n* sceptique *mf*

sceptical ['skeptɪkəl] *adj* sceptique

sceptically ['skeptɪklɪ] *adv* avec scepticisme

scepticism ['skeptɪsɪzəm] *n* scepticisme *m*

sceptre ['septə(r)] *n* sceptre *m*

schedule ['ʃedju:l, *Am* 'skedju:l] **1** *n* **(a)** *(plan)* programme *m,* calendrier *m; Am (for trains, buses)* horaire *m;* **on s.** *(train, bus)* à l'heure; *(person)* dans les temps; **to be behind/ahead of s.** être en retard/en avance sur le programme; **to go according to s.** se dérouler comme prévu; **to work to a tight s.** avoir un emploi du temps serré **(b)** *Com (list of prices)* barème *m*
2 *vt* prévoir; **we're scheduled to arrive on Sunday** nous devons arriver dimanche; **the museum is scheduled to open in August** l'ouverture du musée est prévue pour le mois d'août

scheduled ['ʃedju:ld, *Am* 'skedju:ld] *adj* prévu(e); **s. flight** vol *m* régulier

schematic [skɪ'mætɪk] *adj* schématique

scheme 389 Scots

scheme [skiːm] **1** *n (arrangement, system)* arrangement *m*; *(plan)* plan *m*; *(plot)* machination *f*, complot *m*; **in the (great)** **s.** of things dans le fond; *Br* **(housing)** **s.** lotissement *m* **2** *vi Pej* comploter, intriguer

schilling [ˈʃɪlɪŋ] *n* schilling *m*

schism [ˈs(k)ɪzəm] *n* schisme *m*

schizoid [ˈskɪtsɔɪd] *n & adj* schizoïde *mf*

schizophrenia [skɪtsəʊˈfriːnɪə] *n* schizophrénie *f*

schizophrenic [skɪtsəʊˈfrenɪk] *n & adj* schizophrène *mf*

schmaltzy [ˈʃmɔːltsɪ] *adj Fam* à l'eau de rose, cucul *inv*

scholar [ˈskɒlə(r)] *n (learned person)* érudit(e) *m,f*

scholarly [ˈskɒləlɪ] *adj* érudit(e)

scholarship [ˈskɒləʃɪp] *n* **(a)** *(learning)* érudition *f*, savoir *m* **(b)** *(grant)* bourse *f* (d'études)

scholastic [skəˈlæstɪk] *adj Formal* scolaire

school¹ [skuːl] **1** *n* **(a)** *(for children)* école *f*; **to go to s.** aller à l'école; **s. of art, art s.** école d'art; **of s. age** d'âge scolaire; **s. bag** cartable *m*; *Br* **s. board** conseil *m* d'administration de l'établissement; **s. book** manuel *m ou* livre *m* scolaire; **s. day** journée *f* d'école *ou* scolaire; **s. friend** camarade *mf* d'école; *Br* **s. leaver** = jeune qui vient de terminer ses études secondaires; **s. report** *(for primary school)* carnet *m* de notes, *(for secondary school)* bulletin *m* scolaire; **s. uniform** uniforme *m* scolaire; **s. year** année *f* scolaire **(b)** *Am (college, university)* faculté *f*, université *f* **(c)** *(of artists, thinkers)* école *f*; **s. of thought** école de pensée; *Fig* **he's one of the old s.** il est de la vieille école **2** *vt (educate)* scolariser; *(train)* former, entraîner; **to s. sb in sth** former qn à qch

school² *n (of fish)* banc *m*

schoolboy [ˈskuːlbɔɪ] *n* écolier *m*, élève *m*

schoolchild [ˈskuːltʃaɪld] *n* écolier(ère) *m,f*, élève *mf*

schoolfellow [ˈskuːlfeləʊ] *n* camarade *mf* de classe

schoolgirl [ˈskuːlgɜːl] *n* écolière *f*, élève *f*

schooling [ˈskuːlɪŋ] *n* scolarité *f*, éducation *f*

schoolmaster [ˈskuːlmɑːstə(r)] *n* *Formal (primary)* instituteur *m*, maître *m* d'école; *(secondary)* professeur *m*

schoolmate [ˈskuːlmeɪt] *n* camarade *mf* de classe

schoolmistress [ˈskuːlmɪstrɪs] *n* *Formal (primary)* institutrice *f*, maîtresse *f* d'école; *(secondary)* professeur *m*

schoolroom [ˈskuːlruːm] *n* salle *f* de classe

schoolteacher [ˈskuːltiːtʃə(r)] *n* *(primary)* instituteur(trice) *m,f*; *(secondary)* professeur *m*

schooner [ˈskuːnə(r)] *n* **(a)** *(ship)* schooner *m* **(b)** *(glass)* grand verre *m* (à xérès)

sciatica [saɪˈætɪkə] *n* sciatique *f*

science [ˈsaɪəns] *n* science *f*; **she's good at s.** elle est bonne en sciences; **s. fiction** science-fiction *f*; **s. teacher** professeur *m* de sciences

scientific [saɪənˈtɪfɪk] *adj* scientifique

scientist [ˈsaɪəntɪst] *n* scientifique *mf*

sci-fi [ˈsaɪfaɪ] *Fam* **1** *n* SF *f* **2** *adj* SF

Scilly [ˈsɪlɪ] *n* **the S. Isles, the Scillies** les Sorlingues *fpl*

scimitar [ˈsɪmɪtə(r)] *n* cimeterre *m*

scintillating [ˈsɪntɪleɪtɪŋ] *adj* brillant(e)

scissors [ˈsɪzəz] *npl* ciseaux *mpl*; **a pair of s.** une paire de ciseaux

sclerosis [skləˈrəʊsɪs] *n* *Med* sclérose *f*

scoff [skɒf] **1** *vt Br Fam (eat)* bouffer **2** *vi (mock)* se moquer (**at** de)

scold [skəʊld] *vt* gronder

scone [skɒn] *n* scone *m*

scoop [skuːp] **1** *n* **(a)** *(device) (for ice cream)* cuillère *f* à glace; *(for flour, sugar)* pelle *f*; *(for mashed potato)* cuillère *f* **(b)** *(portion) (of ice cream)* boule *f*; *(of mashed potato)* portion *f* **(c)** *Fam (in journalism)* scoop *m* **2** *vt* **(a)** *(with hands, spoon)* ramasser **(b)** *(story)* publier en exclusivité ▸ **scoop up** *vt sep* ramasser

scoot [skuːt] *vi Fam* **to s.** (off *or* away) filer

scooter [ˈskuːtə(r)] *n (for child)* trottinette *f*; *(small motorbike)* scooter *m*

scope [skəʊp] *n (of action)* possibilité *f*; *(of enquiry)* étendue *f*, portée *f*; **to give s. for...** *(interpretation, explanation)* laisser le champ libre à...

scorch [skɔːtʃ] **1** *vt* roussir; **scorched earth policy** politique *f* de la terre brûlée **2** *n* **s. mark** brûlure *f*

scorcher [ˈskɔːtʃə(r)] *n Fam (hot day)* **it's been a s.** ça a été la canicule

scorching [ˈskɔːtʃɪŋ] *adj (day, weather)* torride; *(sun)* brûlant(e)

score [skɔː(r)] **1** *n* **(a)** *(in sport, quiz)* score *m*; **there was still no s.** personne n'avait encore marqué; **to keep the s.** compter les points; *Fam Fig* **to know the s.** connaître le topo **(b)** *(line)* rayure *f*, entaille *f* **(c)** *(quarrel)* **to have a s. to settle with sb** avoir un compte à régler avec qn **(d)** *(reason, grounds)* **on that s.** à ce sujet, sur ce point **(e)** *(in music)* partition *f* **(f)** *Old-fashioned (twenty)* **a s.** vingt; *Fam* **scores of** *(a lot)* des tas de **2** *vt* **(a)** *(in sport)* marquer; **to s. a hit** *(hit target)* atteindre la cible; *Fig (of person, film)* remporter un grand succès; *Fig* **to s. points off sb** avoir le dessus **(b)** *(cut line in)* entailler **(c)** *Fam (buy)* **to s. drugs** se procurer de la drogue **3** *vi* **(a)** *(score a goal)* marquer un but **(b)** *Fam (sexually)* faire une touche; *(buy drugs)* se procurer de la drogue ▸ **score off** *vt sep (delete)* biffer, barrer ▸ **score out** *vt sep (delete)* biffer, barrer

scoreboard [ˈskɔːbɔːd] *n* tableau *m* d'affichage (des scores)

scorecard [ˈskɔːkɑːd] *n* carte *f* de score

scorer [ˈskɔːrə(r)] *n* marqueur(euse) *m,f*

scorn [skɔːn] **1** *n* mépris *m*; **to pour s. on sb/sth** n'avoir que du mépris pour qn/qch **2** *vt* mépriser

scornful [ˈskɔːnfʊl] *adj* méprisant(e); **to be s. of sb/sth** considérer qn/qch avec mépris

Scorpio [ˈskɔːpɪəʊ] *n (sign of zodiac)* Scorpion *m*; **to be (a) S.** être (du) Scorpion

scorpion [ˈskɔːpɪən] *n* scorpion *m*

Scot [skɒt] *n* Écossais(e) *m,f*

Scotch [skɒtʃ] **1** *n (whisky)* scotch *m* **2** *adj* **S. broth** = potage écossais à base de légumes et d'orge perlé; *Am* **S. tape®** scotch® *m*; **S. terrier** scotch-terrier *m*; **S. whisky** scotch *m*

scotch [skɒtʃ] *vt (rumour)* étouffer

scot-free [ˈskɒtˈfriː] *adj Fam* **to get off s.** s'en tirer sans la moindre punition

Scotland [ˈskɒtlənd] *n* l'Écosse *f*

Scots [skɒts] **1** *n (dialect)* écossais *m* **2** *adj* écossais(e)

Scotsman ['skɒtsmən] n Écossais m

Scotswoman ['skɒtswʊmən] n Écossaise f

Scottie dog ['skɒtɪ'dɒg] n Fam scotch-terrier m

Scottish ['skɒtɪʃ] adj écossais(e); S. terrier scotch-terrier m

scoundrel ['skaʊndr(ə)l] n crapule f; Fam (child) coquin(e) m,f

scour ['skaʊə(r)] vt (a) (pot, surface) récurer, frotter (b) (area, house) ratisser, fouiller

scourer ['skaʊərə(r)] n tampon m à récurer

scourge [skɜːdʒ] n fléau m

scout [skaʊt] 1 n (a) (boy) s. (boy-)scout m, éclaireur m; (girl) s. éclaireuse f; (talent) s. dénicheur(euse) m,f de talents (b) (action) to have a s. around (for sth) chercher (qch)
2 vi to s. for talent dénicher des talents

scoutmaster ['skaʊtmɑːstə(r)] n chef m scout

scowl [skaʊl] 1 n regard m noir
2 vi lancer des regards noirs (at à)

scrabble ['skræbəl] vi to s. about or around for sth chercher qch à tâtons

scraggy ['skrægɪ] adj maigre, décharné(e)

scram [skræm] (pt & pp scrammed) vi Fam se tirer

scramble ['skræmbəl] 1 n (a) (rush) ruée f; (struggle) bousculade f (for pour)
2 vt (signal) brouiller
3 vi to s. for sth se précipiter pour qch; to s. up a hill gravir une colline avec les mains

scrambled eggs ['skræmbəld'egz] npl œufs mpl brouillés

scrap¹ [skræp] 1 n (a) (of material, paper) bout m; (of information) bribe f; (of evidence) semblant m; scraps (of food) restes mpl; a s. of truth une once de vérité; s. paper (papier m) brouillon m (b) s. (metal) ferraille f; s. merchant or dealer ferrailleur m; to sell sth for s. vendre qch à la casse
2 vt (pt & pp scrapped) (car) envoyer à la casse; (submarine, missile) mettre au rebut; (project) abandonner

scrap² Fam 1 n (fight) bagarre f; to have a s., to get into a s. se bagarrer
2 vi (fight) se bagarrer

scrapbook ['skræpbʊk] n album m (de coupures de presse etc)

scrape [skreɪp] 1 n (a) (action) coup m de grattoir; (mark) éraflure f; (sound) raclement m; to give sth a s. donner un coup de grattoir à qch (b) Fam to get into a s. se mettre dans le pétrin
2 vt (a) (skin, side of car) érafler; (dirt, wallpaper, vegetables) gratter; to s. one's plate clean nettoyer son assiette; Fig to s. the bottom of the barrel être tombé(e) bien bas (b) (barely obtain) to s. a living arriver tout juste à vivre; to s. a pass (in exam) passer de justesse
3 vi (a) (make sound) gratter, grincer (b) (barely manage) to s. home (in contest) réussir de justesse; to s. into college passer de justesse à l'université

▶ **scrape through** vt insep passer de justesse

▶ **scrape together** vt sep (money, resources) parvenir à rassembler

scraper ['skreɪpə(r)] n (tool) grattoir m

scrapheap ['skræphiːp] n tas m de ferraille; Fig to be on the s. être au rebut

scrappy ['skræpɪ] adj (performance) décousu(e); (knowledge) limité(e)

scratch [skrætʃ] 1 n (a) (on skin) égratignure f; (on record, furniture) rayure f; (by claw) griffure f (b) (action) to give

one's arm a s. se gratter le bras (c) Fam (idioms) to start from s. recommencer à zéro; to come up or be up to s. être à la hauteur; to bring sth/sb up to s. mettre qch/qn à niveau
2 adj (meal, team) improvisé(e)
3 vt (a) (skin) (by accident) égratigner; (to relieve itching) gratter; (with claw, nail) griffer; (glass, record) rayer; to s. oneself se gratter; to s. one's arm se gratter le bras; Fig you s. my back and I'll s. yours un service en vaut un autre; Fig we've only scratched the surface of the problem nous n'avons fait que survoler le problème (b) (write, draw) griffonner (c) (in sport) retirer
4 vi (of person) se gratter; (of pen, new clothes) gratter; (of thorns) piquer; the cat was scratching at the door le chat grattait à la porte

▶ **scratch out** vt sep (number, name) rayer; Fig to s. sb's eyes out arracher les yeux à qn

scratchcard ['skrætʃkɑːd] n = carte de loterie à gratter

scratchy ['skrætʃɪ] adj (garment, towel) qui gratte; (record) rayé(e)

scrawl [skrɔːl] 1 n (writing) gribouillage m
2 vt & vi gribouiller

scrawny ['skrɔːnɪ] adj maigrelet(ette)

scream [skriːm] 1 n (a) (of person) hurlement m; screams of laughter éclats mpl de rire (b) Fam (good fun) it/he was a s. c'était/il était tordant
2 vt hurler; the headlines screamed "guilty" le mot "coupable" s'étalait en gros à la une des journaux
3 vi hurler; the car screamed past la voiture est passée en rugissant; to s. with pain hurler de douleur; to s. with laughter se tordre de rire

screamingly ['skriːmɪŋlɪ] adv Fam s. funny tordant(e)

scree [skriː] n éboulis m

screech [skriːtʃ] 1 n (a) (of bird, person) cri m strident; (of brakes) crissement m; (of laughter) éclat m
2 vt hurler
3 vi (of bird) pousser des cris stridents; (of person) hurler; (of brakes) crisser; the truck screeched to a halt le camion s'est arrêté dans un crissement de pneus

screen [skriːn] n (a) (barrier) écran m; (folding) paravent m; s. door moustiquaire f (b) (of TV, computer, in cinema) écran m; the big/small s. le grand/petit écran; s. actor/actress acteur m/actrice f de cinéma; Comptr s. saver économiseur m d'écran; Cin s. test bout m d'essai; Aut s. wash liquide m lave-glace
2 vt (a) (protect) protéger; to s. sth from view cacher qch aux regards (b) (film) projeter; (TV programme) diffuser (c) (test) (for security) effectuer une enquête sur; (for disease) tester

screening ['skriːnɪŋ] n (a) Cin projection f (b) (for security) enquête f; (for disease) dépistage m

screenplay ['skriːnpleɪ] n Cin scénario m

screenwriter ['skriːnraɪtə(r)] n Cin scénariste mf

screw [skruː] 1 n (a) (for fixing) vis f; Fam Fig she's got a s. loose elle a une case en moins; Fam Fig to put the screws on sb faire pression sur qn; s. top (of bottle, jar) couvercle m qui se visse (b) (propeller) hélice f (c) very Fam (prison officer) maton(onne) m,f (d) Vulg (sex) to have a s. s'envoyer en l'air
2 vt (a) (fix) visser; to s. one's face into a smile se forcer à sourire; Fam to s. money out of sb extorquer de l'argent à qn (b) Vulg (have sex with) baiser; go and s. yourself! va te faire foutre!
3 vi Vulg (have sex) baiser

▶ **screw around** vi Vulg baiser à droite et à gauche

▶ **screw on** 1 vt sep (attach) visser; Fam she's got her head screwed on elle a la tête sur les épaules
2 vi (of lid) se visser

▶ **screw up 1** *vt sep* (**a**) *(paper)* froisser; **to s. up one's face** faire la grimace; *Fig* **to s. up one's courage** prendre son courage à deux mains (**b**) *very Fam (spoil)* foutre en l'air
2 *vi very Fam (fail)* cafouiller
screwdriver ['skru:draɪvə(r)] *n* tournevis *m*
scribble ['skrɪbəl] **1** *n* gribouillage *m*
2 *vt & vi* griffonner
scribe [skraɪb] *n* scribe *m*
scrimmage ['skrɪmɪdʒ] *n* (**a**) *(pushing)* bousculade *f* (**b**) *Am (in football)* mêlée *f*
scrimp [skrɪmp] *vi* **to s. (and save)** se serrer la ceinture
script [skrɪpt] *n* (**a**) *(for play)* texte *m*; *(for film, TV programme)* script *m*; *(in exam)* copie *f* d'examen (**b**) *(handwriting)* script *m*
Scripture ['skrɪptʃə(r)] *n* (Holy) S., the Scriptures les saintes Écritures *fpl*
scriptwriter ['skrɪptraɪtə(r)] *n Cin & TV* scénariste *mf*
scroll [skrəʊl] **1** *n* (**a**) *(of paper, parchment)* rouleau *m* (**b**) *Archit* volute *f*
2 *vi Comptr* défiler
▶ **scroll down** *vi Comptr* défiler vers le bas
▶ **scroll up** *vi Comptr* défiler vers le haut
scrooge [skru:dʒ] *n* avare *mf*
scrotum ['skrəʊtəm] *n* scrotum *m*
scrounge [skraʊndʒ] *Fam* **1** *n* **to be on the s.** venir quémander
2 *vt* **to s. sth from** *or* **off sb** taper qch à qn
3 *vi* **to s. off sb** vivre aux crochets de qn
scrounger ['skraʊndʒə(r)] *n Fam* parasite *m*
scrub [skrʌb] **1** *n* (**a**) *(bushes)* broussailles *fpl* (**b**) *(wash)* **to give sth a (good) s.** (bien) frotter qch (**c**) *(for skin, face)* gommage *m*
2 *vt (pt & pp scrubbed)* (**a**) *(floor)* frotter; *(pots)* récurer; **to s. one's hands** bien se frotter les mains (**b**) *Fam (cancel)* annuler
▶ **scrub up** *vi Med* se brosser les mains
scrubber ['skrʌbə(r)] *n (for dishes)* tampon *m* à récurer
scrubbing brush ['skrʌbɪŋ'brʌʃ] *n* brosse *f* en chiendent
scrubland ['skrʌblænd] *n* brousse *f*
scruff [skrʌf] *n* (**a**) **by the s. of the neck** par la peau du cou (**b**) *Fam (unkempt person)* **he's a bit of a s.** il n'est pas très soigné
scruffily ['skrʌfɪlɪ] *adv* **to be s. dressed** être dépenaillé(e)
scruffy ['skrʌfɪ] *adj (person)* peu soigné(e); *(clothes)* miteux(euse)
scrum [skrʌm] *n (in rugby)* mêlée *f*; *Fig* bousculade *f*; **s. half** demi *m* de mêlée
scrumptious ['skrʌm(p)ʃəs] *adj Fam* fameux(euse)
scrunch [skrʌntʃ] **1** *vt (paper)* froisser en boule; *(can, cigarette)* écraser
2 *vi* crisser
scrunchie ['skrʌntʃɪ] *n (for hair)* chouchou *m*
scruple ['skru:pəl] *n* scrupule *m*; **to have no scruples** n'avoir aucun scrupule
scrupulous ['skru:pjʊləs] *adj* scrupuleux(euse)
scrupulously ['skru:pjʊləslɪ] *adv* scrupuleusement
scrutineer [skru:tɪ'nɪə(r)] *n* scrutateur(trice) *m,f*
scrutinize ['skru:tɪnaɪz] *vt (document, contract)* éplucher; *(votes)* vérifier
scrutiny ['skru:tɪnɪ] *n (of document, votes)* examen *m* minutieux; **to come under s.** être examiné(e)

scuba ['sku:bə] *n* **s. diver** plongeur(euse) *m,f* sous-marin(e); **s. diving** plongée *f* sous-marine
scuff [skʌf] **1** *n* **s. mark** éraflure *f*
2 *vt (shoe)* érafler
scuffle ['skʌfəl] **1** *n* échauffourée *f*
2 *vi* se bagarrer
scull [skʌl] **1** *n (oar)* aviron *m*
2 *vi* ramer
scullery ['skʌlərɪ] *n Br* arrière-cuisine *f*
sculpt [skʌlpt] *vt* sculpter
sculptor ['skʌlptə(r)] *n* sculpteur *m*
sculpture ['skʌlptʃə(r)] **1** *n* sculpture *f*
2 *vt* sculpter
scum [skʌm] *n (a) (layer of dirt)* crasse *f*; *(froth)* écume *f* (**b**) *very Fam Pej (person)* ordure *f*; *(people)* racaille *f*; **the s. of the earth** le rebut de la société
scupper ['skʌpə(r)] *vt (ship, project)* couler
scurrilous ['skʌrɪləs] *adj* calomnieux(euse)
scurry ['skʌrɪ] *vi (dash)* courir
▶ **scurry away, scurry off** *vi* se sauver
scurvy ['skɜ:vɪ] *n Med* scorbut *m*
scuttle¹ ['skʌtəl] **1** *n (coal)* **s.** seau *m* à charbon
2 *vt (ship, plan)* saborder
scuttle² *vi (run)* courir
▶ **scuttle away, scuttle off** *vi* déguerpir
scythe [saɪð] **1** *n* faux *f*
2 *vt* faucher
SDLP [esdi:el'pi:] *n Br (abbr Social Democratic Labour Party)* = parti démocrate d'Irlande du Nord en faveur de la réunification de l'Irlande
SE [es'i:] *n (abbr southeast)* SE
sea [si:] *n* mer *f*; **by the s.** au bord de la mer; **to go to s.** *(become a sailor)* devenir marin; *Fig* **a s. of people** une marée humaine; **heavy seas** mer démontée; **on the high seas, out at s.** en haute mer; **to find** *or* **get one's s. legs** s'habituer au roulis; *Fig* **to be all at s.** être complètement perdu(e); **s. air** air *m* marin; **s. anemone** anémone *f* de mer; **s. battle** bataille *f* navale; **s. breeze** brise *f* de mer; **s. change** changement *m* radical; *Fam* **(old) s. dog** (vieux) loup *m* de mer; **s. horse** hippocampe *m*; *Naut* **s. lane** couloir *m* maritime; **s. level** niveau *m* de la mer; **s. lion** otarie *f*; **s. salt** sel *m* de mer; **s. urchin** oursin *m*; **s. voyage** voyage *m* en mer
seaboard ['si:bɔ:d] *n* côte *f*
seaborne ['si:bɔ:n] *adj (trade)* maritime; *(invasion)* naval(e)
seafarer ['si:feərə(r)] *n* marin *m*
seafaring ['si:feərɪŋ] *adj (people)* de navigateurs
seafood ['si:fu:d] *n* fruits *mpl* de mer
seafront ['si:frʌnt] *n* front *m* de mer
seagoing ['si:gəʊɪŋ] *adj (boat)* de mer
seagull ['si:gʌl] *n* mouette *f*
seal¹ [si:l] *n (animal)* phoque *m*
seal² **1** *n* (**a**) *(stamp)* sceau *m*; **to give one's s. of approval to sth** donner son approbation à qch; **to set the s. on sth** *(on alliance, friendship)* sceller qch; *(on victory, defeat)* confirmer qch (**b**) *(device)* joint *m* (d'étanchéité); *(on food container)* = fermeture garantissant la fraîcheur d'un produit
2 *vt (document, envelope)* cacheter; *(with official seal)* sceller; *(jar)* fermer hermétiquement; *(joint)* assurer l'étanchéité de; **to s. sb's fate** décider du sort de qn; **my lips are sealed** je ne dirai rien
▶ **seal in** *vt sep* enfermer

▸ **seal off** *vt sep (area)* boucler; *(people)* isoler

sealing wax ['si:lɪŋ'wæks] *n* cire *f* à cacheter

sealskin ['si:lskɪn] *n* peau *f* de phoque

seam [si:m] *n* (**a**) *(of garment)* couture *f*; *(in metalwork)* soudure *f*; **to be coming apart at the seams** *(of clothing)* craquer de partout; *Fig (of plan, organization)* s'effondrer (**b**) *(of coal)* veine *f*

seaman ['si:mən] *n Naut* marin *m*

seamanship ['si:mənʃɪp] *n Naut* qualités *fpl* de navigateur

seamstress ['semstrɪs] *n* couturière *f*

seamy ['si:mɪ] *adj* sordide

seance ['seɪɒns] *n* séance *f* de spiritisme

seaplane ['si:pleɪn] *n* hydravion *m*

seaport ['si:pɔ:t] *n* port *m* maritime

sear [sɪə(r)] *vt (skin)* brûler; *(meat)* saisir; *Fig* **the image was seared on her memory** l'image était gravée dans sa mémoire

search [sɜ:tʃ] **1** *n* recherches *fpl*; *(of building, room)* fouille *f*; **to have a s. for sth** chercher qch; **in s. of** à la recherche de; **to make a s.** faire des recherches; *Comptr* **to do a s.** faire une recherche; **s. party** équipe *f* de secours; *Law* **s. warrant** mandat *m* de perquisition **2** *vt (person, place)* fouiller; *Comptr (file, directory)* rechercher dans; *Fam* **s. me!** je n'en ai pas la moindre idée! **3** *vi* chercher; **to s. for sth** chercher qch; *Comptr* **s. and replace** rechercher et remplacer

searching ['sɜ:tʃɪŋ] *adj (examination)* minutieux(euse); *(look)* pénétrant(e)

searchlight ['sɜ:tʃlaɪt] *n* projecteur *m*

searing ['sɪərɪŋ] *adj (pain, heat)* fulgurant(e); *(criticism, indictment)* virulent(e)

seascape ['si:skeɪp] *n Art* marine *f*

seashell ['si:ʃel] *n* coquillage *m*

seashore ['si:ʃɔ:(r)] *n* rivage *m*

seasick ['si:sɪk] *adj* **to be s.** avoir le mal de mer

seasickness ['si:sɪknɪs] *n* mal *m* de mer

seaside ['si:saɪd] *n* **the s.** le bord de la mer; **at the s.** au bord de la mer; **s. resort** station *f* balnéaire

season¹ ['si:zən] *n* saison *f*; *(of films)* cycle *m*; **S.'s Greetings** meilleurs vœux de fin d'année; **the high s.** *(for tourism)* la haute saison; **strawberries are out of s.** ce n'est pas la saison des fraises; **s. ticket** abonnement *m*

season² *vt* (**a**) *(with salt, pepper)* assaisonner; *(with spice)* épicer (**b**) *(wood)* faire sécher

seasonable ['si:zənəbəl] *adj* **s. weather** un temps de saison

seasonal ['si:zənəl] *adj (work, fluctuations)* saisonnier(ère)

seasoned ['si:zənd] *adj* (**a**) *(food)* assaisonné(e); **a highly s. dish** un plat très relevé (**b**) *(wood)* sec (sèche) (**c**) *(person)* expérimenté(e); *(soldier)* aguerri(e)

seasoning ['si:zənɪŋ] *n Culin* assaisonnement *m*

seat [si:t] **1** *n* (**a**) *(chair)* chaise *f*; *(on bus, train, in theatre, cinema)* place *f*, siège *m*; *(in Parliament)* siège *m*; **to take a s.** s'asseoir; **s. belt** ceinture *f* de sécurité (**b**) *(part of chair, toilet)* siège *m*; *(of trousers)* fond *m* (**c**) *(centre) (of government)* siège *m*; **a s. of learning** un haut lieu du savoir; **country s.** *(of aristocrat)* demeure *f* familiale **2** *vt* (**a**) *(cause to sit) (child)* asseoir; *(guests)* faire asseoir; **to be/remain seated** être/rester assis(e); *Formal* **please be seated** veuillez vous asseoir (**b**) *(accommodate)* **the bus seats thirty** il y a trente places assises dans le bus; **this table seats six** on tient six à cette table; **the hall seats 150** la salle compte 150 places

seating ['si:tɪŋ] *n (seats)* sièges *mpl*; *(positioning)* placement *m*; **s. capacity** nombre *m* de places assises; **s. plan** plan *m* de table

SEATO ['si:təʊ] *n (abbr* **Southeast Asia Treaty Organization)** OTASE *f*

seaway ['si:weɪ] *n* route *f* (maritime)

seaweed ['si:wi:d] *n* algues *fpl*

seaworthy ['si:wɜ:ðɪ] *adj* en état de naviguer

sebaceous [sɪ'beɪʃəs] *adj* sébacé(e)

sec¹ *(abbr* **second(s))** s.

sec² [sek] *n Fam (second)* **I'll be there in a s.** j'arrive tout de suite; **wait a s.!** attends une seconde!

secateurs [sekə'tɜ:z] *npl* sécateur *m*

secede [sɪ'si:d] *vi* faire sécession (**from** de)

secession [sɪ'seʃən] *n* sécession *f*

secluded [sɪ'klu:dɪd] *adj (place)* reculé(e); *(life)* de reclus(e)

seclusion [sɪ'klu:ʒən] *n* isolement *m*

second¹ ['sekənd] *n (of time)* seconde *f*; **I won't be a s.** j'en ai pour deux secondes; **s. hand** *(of clock)* trotteuse *f*

second² **1** *n* (**a**) *(in series)* deuxième *mf*, second(e) *m,f*; **Edward the S.** Edward II; **I was s. in the race** je suis arrivé deuxième à la course (**b**) *(of month)* deux *m*; **the s. of May** le deux mai (**c**) *Com* **seconds** articles *mpl* défectueux (**d**) *(in duel)* témoin *m*; *(in boxing)* soigneur *m* (**e**) *Br Univ* **to get a s.** *(in degree)* ≃ avoir sa licence avec mention assez bien (**f**) **s. (gear)** seconde *f* (**g**) *Fam* **anyone for seconds?** *(at meal)* quelqu'un pour le rab? **2** *adj* deuxième, second(e); **twenty-s.** vingt-deuxième; **ninety-s.** quatre-vingt-douzième; **to be s. to none** être sans égal(e); **s. in command** *Mil* commandant *m* en second; *(in organization)* adjoint(e) *m,f*; **the s. largest city in England** la deuxième ville d'Angleterre; **a s. Hopper/Camus** un nouveau Hopper/Camus; **on s. thoughts** tout bien réfléchi; **to have s. thoughts (about sth)** ne plus être très sûr(e) (de qch); *Fig* **to play s. fiddle to sb** être dans l'ombre de qn; **it's s. nature to her** elle le fait automatiquement; **to get one's s. wind** trouver un second souffle; **s. chance** deuxième chance *f*; **to be in one's s. childhood** être retombé(e) en enfance; **s. class** *(on train)* deuxième classe *f*; *Rel* **the S. Coming** le second avènement; **s. cousin** petit(e) cousin(e) *m,f*; **s. floor** *Br* deuxième étage *m*, *Am* premier étage *m*; **s. language** seconde langue *f*; **s. name** nom *m* de famille; *Law* **s. offence** récidive *f*; **s. opinion** deuxième avis *m*; *Gram* **s. person** deuxième personne *f*; **s. sight** don *m* de double vue; **s. violin** second violon *m*; **the S. World War** la Seconde Guerre mondiale

second³ *vt (motion)* appuyer

second⁴ [sɪ'kɒnd] *vt (officer, employee)* détacher (**from/to** de/à)

secondary ['sekəndərɪ] *adj* secondaire; **s. school** établissement *m* secondaire

second-best ['sekənd'best] **1** *n* pis-aller *m*; **to content oneself with s.** se contenter d'un pis-aller **2** *adv* **to come off s.** être battu(e)

second-class ['sekənd'klɑ:s] **1** *adj (ticket, carriage)* de deuxième classe; **s. citizen** citoyen(enne) *m,f* de second rang; *Br Univ* **s. degree** licence *f* avec mention assez bien; **s. mail** courrier *m* au tarif lent **2** *adv* **to travel s.** voyager en seconde classe

seconder ['sekəndə(r)] *n* = personne qui appuie une motion

second-guess ['sekənd'ges] *vt* to s. sb anticiper ce que qn va faire

second-hand ['sekənd'hænd] **1** *adj (car, clothes)* d'occasion **2** *adv (buy)* d'occasion; to hear news s. avoir des nouvelles de seconde main

secondly ['sekəndlɪ] *adv* deuxièmement

secondment [sɪ'kɒndmənt] *n* to be on s. être en détachement

second-rate ['sekəndreɪt] *adj* médiocre

secrecy ['siːkrɪsɪ] *n* secret *m*; in s. en secret; to swear sb to s. faire jurer le silence à qn

secret ['siːkrɪt] **1** *n* secret *m*; to do sth in s. faire qch secrètement; I make no s. of it je ne m'en cache pas; it's no s. tout le monde le sait **2** *adj* secret(ète); to keep sth s. from sb cacher qch à qn; s. agent agent *m* secret; s. police police *f* secrète; s. service services *mpl* secrets; the S. Service = service de sécurité du président américain; *also Fig* s. weapon arme *f* secrète

secretarial [sekrə'teərɪəl] *adj (work)* administratif(ive); *(job, college, course)* de secrétariat

secretariat [sekrə'teərɪət] *n* secrétariat *m*

secretary ['sekrətərɪ] *n* (a) *(in office)* secrétaire *mf* (b) *Br Pol* ministre *m*

secretary-general ['sekrətərɪ'dʒenərəl] *n Pol* secrétaire *m* général

secrete [sɪ'kriːt] *vt* (a) *(discharge)* secréter (b) *(hide)* cacher

secretion [sɪ'kriːʃən] *n* sécrétion *f*

secretive ['siːkrɪtɪv] *adj* secret(ète); to be s. about sth faire des cachotteries à propos de qch

secretly ['siːkrɪtlɪ] *adv* secrètement

sect [sekt] *n* secte *f*

sectarian [sek'teərɪən] *adj* sectaire

sectarianism [sek'teərɪənɪzəm] *n* sectarisme *m*

section ['sekʃən] **1** *n* (a) *(in general)* partie *f*; *(of road, railway)* tronçon *m*; *(of machine)* élément *m*; *(of organization)* département *m*; *(in orchestra)* section *f*; *(of law, treaty)* article *m*; all sections of society toutes les catégories sociales (b) *(of soldiers)* section *f* (c) *(cross-section)* coupe *f* **2** *vt (cut)* sectionner

sector ['sektə(r)] *n* secteur *m*

secular ['sekjʊlə(r)] *adj (history, art)* laïque; *(music)* profane

secure [sɪ'kjʊə(r)] **1** *adj* (a) *(free from anxiety)* en sécurité; s. in the knowledge that... ayant l'assurance que... (b) *(investment, place)* sûr(e); *(foothold)* ferme; *(nomination, future)* assuré(e); *(load, rope)* bien attaché(e); *(foundations, lock)* solide **2** *vt* (a) *(make safe) (position, future)* assurer (b) *(fasten) (load)* bien amarrer; *(door, window)* bien fermer (c) *(obtain) (support, promise, loan)* obtenir

securely [sɪ'kjʊəlɪ] *adv* (a) *(stored, hidden)* en toute sécurité; *(protected)* bien (b) *(firmly)* solidement; the door was s. fastened la porte était bien fermée

security [sɪ'kjʊərɪtɪ] *n* (a) *(stability, safety)* sécurité *f*; s. of tenure sécurité de l'emploi; the S. Council le Conseil de sécurité; s. forces forces *fpl* de sécurité; s. guard garde *m*; s. officer agent *m* de sécurité; to be a s. risk être un danger pour la sécurité (b) *Fin (for loan)* garantie *f* (c) *Fin* securities titres *mpl*

sedan [sɪ'dæn] *n* (a) *Am (car)* berline *f* (b) s. chair chaise *f* à porteurs

sedate [sɪ'deɪt] **1** *adj* tranquille **2** *vt* donner des calmants à

sedately [sɪ'deɪtlɪ] *adv* tranquillement

sedation [sɪ'deɪʃən] *n* under s. sous calmants

sedative ['sedətɪv] *n* sédatif *m*, calmant *m*

sedentary ['sedəntrɪ] *adj* sédentaire

sediment ['sedɪmənt] *n* sédiment *m*

sedition [sɪ'dɪʃən] *n* sédition *f*

seditious [sɪ'dɪʃəs] *adj* séditieux(euse)

seduce [sɪ'djuːs] *vt (sexually)* séduire; *Fig* to s. sb into doing sth persuader qn de faire qch

seducer [sɪ'djuːsə(ɪ)] *n* séducteur(trice) *m,f*

seduction [sɪ'dʌkʃən] *n* séduction *f*

seductive [sɪ'dʌktɪv] *adj (look)* séducteur(trice); *(argument, offer)* séduisant(e)

see[1] [siː] *n Rel* évêché *m*

see[2] *(pt* saw [sɔː], *pp* seen [siːn]) **1** *vt* (a) *(with eyes, perceive)* voir; now s. what you've done! regarde ce que tu as fait!; s. page 50 voir page 50; to be seeing things *(hallucinate)* avoir des visions; it has to be seen to be believed il faut le voir pour le croire; to s. sb do *or* doing sth voir qn faire qch; I can't s. a way out of this problem je ne vois pas comment on peut s'en sortir; could you s. your way to lending me $50? cela te serait-il possible de me prêter 50 dollars?; to s. sense *or* reason entendre raison; the city has seen many changes la ville a connu de grands changements; I don't know what you s. in her je ne vois pas ce que tu lui trouves; it remains to be seen whether... reste à savoir si...; I'll s. what I can do je vais voir ce que je peux faire
(b) *(understand)* voir; I s. what you mean je vois ce que tu veux dire; I don't s. the point je n'en vois pas l'intérêt (c) *(envisage, imagine)* imaginer, voir; what do you s. happening next? à ton avis, qu'est-ce qui va se passer maintenant?; I can't s. them arriving before six ça m'étonnerait qu'ils arrivent avant six heures; I can't s. you as a boxer je t'imagine mal en boxeur
(d) *(make sure)* I shall s. that he comes je ferai en sorte qu'il vienne; s. that this doesn't happen again! fais en sorte que ça ne se reproduise pas!
(e) *(meet) (person, doctor, solicitor)* voir; I'm seeing Alison tomorrow je vois Alison demain; s. you (soon)! à bientôt!
(f) *(accompany)* to s. sb home accompagner qn chez lui; to s. sb to the door accompagner qn jusqu'à la porte
2 *vi* (a) *(with eyes)* voir; s. for yourself à toi de juger; we shall s. nous verrons bien
(b) *(understand)* comprendre; ah, I s.! ah, je vois!
(c) *(consider)* let me s.!, let's s.! voyons!; have you got a free room? – let me s. avez-vous une chambre libre? – voyons voir
(d) *(find out)* I'll go and s. je vais voir
▸ **see about** *vt insep* (a) *(deal with)* s'occuper de (b) *(consider)* voir; *Fam* we'll (soon) s. about that! c'est ce qu'on va voir!
▸ **see in** *vt sep* to s. in the New Year fêter le Nouvel An
▸ **see off** *vt sep* (a) *(say goodbye to)* dire au revoir à (b) *(attacker)* faire fuir
▸ **see out** *vt sep* accompagner jusqu'à la porte; I'll s. myself out inutile de me raccompagner
▸ **see through 1** *vt sep (project, policy)* mener à bien **2** *vt insep (person, lie, plan)* percer à jour
▸ **see to** *vt insep (deal with)* s'occuper de; to get sth seen to *(machine, roof)* faire réparer qch; *(wound, injury)* faire examiner qch; I'll s. to it that you're not disturbed je ferai en sorte que tu ne sois pas dérangé

seed [siːd] **1** *n* (a) *(for sowing)* graine *f*; *(of fruit)* pépin *m*; to go *or* run to s. *(of plant)* monter en graine; s. corn blé *m* de semence; *Fig* capital *m* initial; s. merchant grainetier(ère) *m,f*; s. potatoes pommes *fpl* de terre de semence (b) *Sp (in*

tournament) tête *f* de série **(c)** *Lit (semen)* semence *f*
2 *vt* **(a)** *(remove seeds from)* épépiner **(b)** *(lawn)* ensemencer **(c)** *(in tournament)* **seeded players** joueurs *mpl* classés tête de série
3 *vi (of plant)* monter en graine
seedless ['si:dlɪs] *adj* sans pépins
seedling ['si:dlɪŋ] *n* plant *m*
seedy ['si:dɪ] *adj* **(a)** *(shabby) (person, hotel, area)* miteux(euse) **(b)** *Fam (unwell)* mal fichu(e)
seeing ['si:ɪŋ] **1** *conj* **s.** *(that or how)...* étant donné que...
2 *n* **s.** is believing voir c'est croire
seek [si:k] *(pt & pp* **sought** [sɔ:t]) *vt* **(a)** *(look for) (thing lost, job)* chercher; *(sb's friendship, promotion)* essayer d'obtenir **(b)** *(request)* **to s. sth from sb** demander qch à qn; **to s. sb's advice** demander conseil à qn **(c)** *(try)* **to s. to do sth** essayer de faire qch
▸ **seek after** *vt insep* **to be much sought after** être très recherché(e)
▸ **seek out** *vt sep (person)* dénicher
seem [si:m] *vi* sembler; **to s.** tired avoir l'air fatigué(e); **do what seems best** fais au mieux; **it seemed like a dream** j'avais l'impression de rêver; **I s. to have heard her name somewhere** il me semble avoir entendu son nom quelque part; **I can't s. to get it right** je n'y arrive pas; **it seems (that)..., it would s. that...** il semble que...+ *subjunctive*; **it seems to me that...** il me semble que...; **it seems or would s. so** il paraît; **it seems or would s. not** il paraît que non
seeming ['si:mɪŋ] *adj* apparent(e)
seemingly ['si:mɪŋlɪ] *adv* apparemment
seemly ['si:mlɪ] *adj Formal* bienséant(e)
seen [si:n] *pp of* **see²**
seep [si:p] *vi* suinter; **to s. into sth** s'infiltrer dans qch
seepage ['si:pɪdʒ] *n (oozing)* suintement *m*; *(into surface)* infiltration *f*
seer [sɪə(r)] *n Lit* voyant(e) *m,f*
seesaw ['si:sɔ:] **1** *n* tapecul *m*
2 *vi Fig (of prices)* être en dents de scie
seethe [si:ð] *vi (of liquid)* bouillonner; *(of street)* grouiller **(with** de**)**; **to be seething (with anger)** bouillir (de rage)
see-through ['si:θru:] *adj* transparent(e)
segment 1 ['segmənt] segment *m*; *(of orange)* quartier *m*
2 *vt* [seg'ment] *(orange)* couper en quartiers; *(line)* segmenter
segmentation [segmen'teɪʃən] *n Econ* segmentation *f*
segregate ['segrɪgeɪt] *vt* séparer **(from** de**)**; *(prisoner)* isoler **(from** de**)**
segregation [segrɪ'geɪʃən] *n* ségrégation *f*; *(of prisoner)* isolement *m*
Seine [seɪn] *n* **the S.** la Seine
seismic ['saɪzmɪk] *adj* sismique
seismograph ['saɪzməgrɑ:f] *n* sismographe *m*
seismology [saɪz'mɒlədʒɪ] *n* sismologie *f*
seize [si:z] *vt* **(a)** *(grab) & Fig (opportunity)* saisir; **to s. hold of** saisir **(b)** *(city, territory)* s'emparer de; *(drugs, stolen goods)* saisir
▸ **seize on, seize upon** *vt insep* sauter sur
▸ **seize up** *vi (of engine, back)* se bloquer
seizure ['si:ʒə(r)] *n* **(a)** *(of land, city)* prise *f*; *Law (of property, drugs)* saisie *f* **(b)** *Med* crise *f*
seldom ['seldəm] *adv* rarement; **I s. see her** je la vois rarement; **s. have I seen such courage** j'ai rarement vu un tel courage

select [sɪ'lekt] **1** *adj (exclusive)* sélect(e); **a s. few** quelques privilégiés(ées)
2 *vt* sélectionner
selected [sɪ'lektɪd] *adj* choisi(e)
selection [sɪ'lekʃən] *n* sélection *f*, choix *m*; **to make a s.** faire un choix; **a wide s.** un grand choix
selective [sɪ'lektɪv] *adj* sélectif(ive)
selector [sɪ'lektə(r)] *n (of team)* sélectionneur(euse) *m,f*
self [self] *(pl* **selves** [selvz]) *n* **(a)** *(individual)* **he's quite his old s. again** il est redevenu comme avant; **she was her usual cheerful s.** comme à son habitude, elle était gaie **(b)** *Psy* **the s.** le moi
self-addressed envelope ['selfə'drest'envələʊp] *n* enveloppe *f* libellée à ses nom et adresse
self-appointed ['selfə'pɔɪntɪd] *adj* **he's the s. spokesman** il s'est proclamé porte-parole
self-assured ['selfə'ʃʊəd] *adj* plein(e) d'assurance
self-catering ['self'keɪtərɪŋ] *adj (holiday)* en appartement meublé; *(accommodation)* meublé(e)
self-centred ['self'sentəd] *adj* égocentrique
self-confessed ['selfkən'fest] *adj* **he's a s. liar/cheat** il est menteur/tricheur de son propre aveu
self-confidence ['self'kɒnfɪdəns] *n* confiance *f* en soi
self-confident ['self'kɒnfɪdənt] *adj* plein(e) d'assurance
self-conscious ['self'kɒnʃəs] *adj* timide, gêné(e)
self-contained ['selfkən'teɪnd] *adj (person)* réservé(e); *(apartment)* indépendant(e)
self-contradictory ['selfkɒntrə'dɪktərɪ] *adj* qui contient des contradictions
self-control ['selfkən'trəʊl] *n* maîtrise *f* de soi
self-deception ['selfdɪ'sepʃən] *n* aveuglement *m*
self-defeating ['selfdɪ'fi:tɪŋ] *adj* qui va à l'encontre du but recherché
self-defence, *Am* **self-defense** ['selfdɪ'fens] *n* autodéfense *f*; *Law* légitime défense *f*; **in s.** en état de légitime défense
self-denial ['selfdɪ'naɪəl] *n* abnégation *f*
self-destruct ['selfdɪ'strʌkt] *vi* s'autodétruire
self-determination ['selfdɪtɜ:mɪ'neɪʃən] *n* autodétermination *f*
self-discipline ['self'dɪsɪplɪn] *n* autodiscipline *f*
self-doubt ['self'daʊt] *n* manque *m* de confiance en soi
self-effacing ['selfɪ'feɪsɪŋ] *adj* effacé(e)
self-employed ['selfɪm'plɔɪd] *adj* indépendant(e)
self-esteem [selfə'sti:m] *n* confiance *f* en soi
self-evident ['self'evɪdənt] *adj* évident(e)
self-explanatory ['selfɪk'splænətərɪ] *adj* **to be s.** se passer d'explications
self-expression ['selfɪk'spreʃən] *n* expression *f* individuelle
self-government ['self'gʌvənmənt] *n* autonomie *f*
self-help ['self'help] *n* **s. group** groupe *m* d'entraide
self-important ['selfɪm'pɔ:tənt] *adj* suffisant(e)
self-indulgent ['selfɪn'dʌldʒənt] *adj* complaisant(e)
self-inflicted ['selfɪn'flɪktɪd] *adj* que l'on s'inflige à soi-même
self-interest ['self'ɪntərest] *n* intérêt *m* personnel
selfish ['selfɪʃ] *adj* égoïste
selfishness ['selfɪʃnɪs] *n* égoïsme *m*
self-knowledge ['self'nɒlɪdʒ] *n* connaissance *f* de soi
selfless ['selflɪs] *adj* désintéressé(e)
self-made man ['selfmeɪd'mæn] *n* self-made-man *m*

self-pity ['self'pɪtɪ] *n* apitoiement *m* sur son propre sort; **to be full of s.** s'apitoyer sur son sort

self-portrait ['self'pɔːtrət] *n* autoportrait *m*

self-possessed ['selfpə'zest] *adj* qui a une grande maîtrise de soi

self-preservation ['selfprezə'veɪʃən] *n* instinct for s. instinct *m* de conservation

self-raising flour ['selfreɪzɪŋ'flaʊə(r)], *Am* **self-rising flour** ['selfraɪzɪŋ'flaʊə(r)] *n* = farine contenant de la levure chimique

self-reliant ['selfrɪ'laɪənt] *adj* indépendant(e)

self-respect ['selfrɪ'spekt] *n* amour-propre *m*

self-respecting ['selfrɪ'spektɪŋ] *adj* qui se respecte

self-restraint ['selfrɪs'treɪnt] *n* retenue *f*, maîtrise *f* de soi

self-righteous ['self'raɪtʃəs] *adj* suffisant(e)

self-rising flour ['selfraɪzɪŋ'flaʊə(r)] *n Am* = **self-raising flour**

selfsame ['selfseɪm] *adj* the s. day le même jour exactement; the s. thing la même chose exactement

self-satisfied ['self'sætɪsfaɪd] *adj* suffisant(e), content(e) de soi

self-service ['self'sɜːvɪs] 1 *n* self-service *m* 2 *adj* self-service

self-starter ['self'stɑːtə(r)] *n (person)* personne *f* très motivée

self-styled ['selfstaɪld] *adj* prétendu(e), soi-disant *inv*

self-sufficient ['selfsə'fɪʃənt] *adj (person)* indépendant(e); *(country)* auto-suffisant(e)

self-taught ['self'tɔːt] *adj* autodidacte

sell [sel] *(pt & pp* sold [səʊld]) 1 *vt* vendre; **to s. sb sth, to s. sth to sb** vendre qch à qn; **scandal sells newspapers** le scandale fait vendre les journaux; *Fig* **to s. oneself** *(present oneself)* se vendre, *Fig* **to s. sb an idea** faire accepter une idée à qn; *Fig* **to s. sb down the river** trahir qn 2 *vi (of product)* se vendre; *(of person)* vendre; **to s. like hot cakes** se vendre comme des petits pains

▸ **sell off** *vt sep* liquider

▸ **sell out** 1 *vt sep* **(a) to be sold out** *(of book, item)* être épuisé(e); *(of show, concert)* afficher complet; **the tickets are sold out** il n'y a plus de billets **(b)** *(betray)* trahir, vendre 2 *vi* **(a) to s. out of sth** ne plus avoir de qch **(b)** *(betray beliefs)* se vendre

▸ **sell up** *vi (sell home, business)* tout vendre

sell-by date ['selbaɪdeɪt] *n Br* date *f* limite de vente

seller ['selə(r)] *n* vendeur(euse) *m,f*; *Econ* s.'s market marché *m* favorable au vendeur

selling ['selɪŋ] *n* vente *f*; s. point atout *m*; s. price prix *m* de vente

sell-off ['selɒf] *n (of state-owned company)* vente *f*

Sellotape® ['seləteɪp] *n* Scotch® *m*

sellotape ['seləteɪp] *vt* scotcher

sell-out ['selaʊt] *n* **(a)** *(event)* the play was a s. il n'y avait plus de places pour cette pièce, la pièce a joué à guichets fermés **(b)** *(betrayal)* trahison *f*

semantic [sɪ'mæntɪk] *adj* sémantique

semantics [sɪ'mæntɪks] *n* sémantique *f*

semaphore ['seməfɔː(r)] *n* signaux *mpl* à bras

semblance ['sembləns] *n* semblant *m*

semen ['siːmen] *n* sperme *m*

semester [sɪ'mestə(r)] *n* semestre *m*

semi ['semɪ] *n Br Fam (semi-detached house)* maison *f* jumelée

semiautomatic ['semɪɔːtə'mætɪk] *adj* semi-automatique

semicircle ['semɪsɜːkəl] *n* demi-cercle *m*

semicircular ['semɪ'sɜːkjʊlə(r)] *adj* semi-circulaire, en demi-cercle

semicolon ['semɪ'kəʊlən] *n* point-virgule *m*

semiconductor ['semɪkən'dʌktə(r)] *n Elec* semi-conducteur *m*

semiconscious ['semɪ'kɒnʃəs] *adj* à demi conscient(e)

semidetached ['semɪdɪ'tætʃt] 1 *n* maison *f* jumelée 2 *adj* jumelé(e)

semifinal ['semɪ'faɪnəl] *n* demi-finale *f*

semifinalist ['semɪ'faɪnəlɪst] *n* demi-finaliste *mf*

seminal ['semɪnəl] *adj* majeur(e), de première importance

seminar ['semɪnɑː(r)] *n* séminaire *m*

semi-precious ['semɪ'preʃəs] *adj* semi-précieux(euse)

semiquaver ['semɪkweɪvə(r)] *n Mus* double croche *f*

semi-skimmed [semɪ'skɪmd] *adj Br (milk)* demi-écrémé(e)

Semite ['semaɪt] *n* Sémite *mf*

Semitic [sɪ'mɪtɪk] *adj (language)* sémitique; *(people)* sémite

semitone ['semɪtəʊn] *n Mus* demi-ton *m*

semitropical ['semɪ'trɒpɪkəl] *adj* semi-tropical(e)

semolina [semə'liːnə] *n* semoule *f*

Senate ['senɪt] *n* the S. le Sénat

senator ['senətə(r)] *n* sénateur *m*

send [send] *(pt & pp* sent [sent]) *vt (letter, message, person)* envoyer; **to s. sb sth, to s. sth to sb** envoyer qch à qn; **to s. sb home** renvoyer qn chez soi; **to s. sb to prison** envoyer qn en prison; **to s. sb on an errand** envoyer qn faire une course; *Fig* **to s. sb/sth flying** envoyer qn/qch valser; **to s. sb into fits of laughter** faire rire qn aux larmes

▸ **send away 1** *vt sep (person)* renvoyer 2 *vi* **to s. away for sth** se faire envoyer qch

▸ **send back** *vt sep* renvoyer

▸ **send down** *vt sep Br* **(a)** *(expel from university)* renvoyer **(b)** *Fam (send to prison)* mettre en taule **(for** pour**)**

▸ **send for** *vt insep (help, supplies)* envoyer chercher; *(doctor)* faire venir

▸ **send in** *vt sep* envoyer

▸ **send off** *vt sep* **(a)** *(letter, order)* expédier, envoyer **(b)** *(player)* expulser 2 *vi* **to s. off for sth** se faire envoyer qch

▸ **send on** *vt sep (ahead)* expédier; *(later)* faire suivre

▸ **send out 1** *vt sep* envoyer 2 *vi* **to s. out for sth** envoyer chercher qch

▸ **send up** *vt sep Br Fam (parody)* se moquer de

sender ['sendə(r)] *n* expéditeur(trice) *m,f*

send-off ['sendɒf] *n Fam* **to give sb a good s.** faire des adieux en règle à qn

send-up ['sendʌp] *n Br Fam* parodie *f*, pastiche *m*

Senegal [senɪ'gɔːl] *n* le Sénégal

Senegalese [senɪgə'liːz] 1 *n (person)* Sénégalais(e) *m,f* 2 *adj* sénégalais(e)

senile ['siːnaɪl] *adj* sénile; s. dementia démence *f* sénile

senility [sɪ'nɪlɪtɪ] *n* sénilité *f*

senior ['siːnjə(r)] 1 *n* **(a)** *(in age)* to be sb's s. être l'aîné(e) de qn; she's three years his s. elle est son aînée de trois ans **(b)** *(in rank)* supérieur(e) *m,f* 2 *adj* **(a)** *(in age)* aîné(e); Alan Spencer, S. Alan Spencer père; he's two years s. to me il a deux ans de plus que moi;

s. citizen personne *f* du troisième âge **(b)** *(in rank, position)* supérieur(e); **s. officer** officier *m* supérieur; **s. partner** *(in company)* associé(e) *m,f* principal(e)

seniority [siːnɪˈrɪtɪ] *n (in age, length of service)* ancienneté *f; (in rank)* supériorité *f*

sensation [senˈseɪʃən] *n* **(a)** *(feeling)* sensation *f;* **a tingling/burning s.** une sensation de picotement/brûlure **(b)** *(excitement)* **to cause a s.** faire sensation

sensational [senˈseɪʃənəl] *adj* sensationnel(elle)

sensationalism [senˈseɪʃənəlɪzəm] *n* sensationnalisme *m*

sense [sens] **1** *n* **(a)** *(faculty)* sens *m;* **to come to one's senses** *(recover consciousness)* revenir à soi; *(see reason)* revenir à la raison; **s. of direction** sens de l'orientation; **s. of duty** sens du devoir; **s. of hearing** ouïe *f;* **s. of humour** sens de l'humour **(b)** *(rationality)* bon sens *m*, intelligence *f;* **there's no s. in staying/leaving** ça ne sert à rien de rester/partir **(c)** *(feeling)* sentiment *m;* **to lose all s. of time/reality** perdre toute notion du temps/de la réalité; **a s. of achievement** un sentiment de satisfaction **(d)** *(meaning)* sens *m*, signification *f;* **to make s.** être logique; **to make no s.** n'avoir aucun sens; **to make s. of sth** comprendre qch; **in a s.** dans un sens

2 *vt (perceive)* sentir, deviner; **to s. that** sentir que

senseless [ˈsenslɪs] *adj* **(a)** *(unconscious)* sans connaissance **(b)** *(pointless)* absurde

sensibilities [sensɪˈbɪlɪtɪz] *npl* susceptibilité *f*

sensible [ˈsensɪbəl] *adj* **(a)** *(rational)* sensé(e) **(b)** *(practical)* pratique **(c)** *Formal (aware)* **to be s. of sth** être sensible à qch

sensibly [ˈsensɪblɪ] *adv (rationally)* raisonnablement

sensitive [ˈsensɪtɪv] *adj* **(a)** *(person)* sensible **(to** à) **(b)** *(subject, issue)* délicat(e); *(document, information)* confidentiel(elle)

sensor [ˈsensə(r)] *n* détecteur *m*

sensory [ˈsensərɪ] *adj* sensoriel(elle); **s. organs** organes *mpl* sensoriels

sensual [ˈsensjʊəl] *adj* sensuel(elle)

sensuality [sensjʊˈælɪtɪ] *n* sensualité *f*

sensuous [ˈsensjʊəs] *adj* sensuel(elle)

sent [sent] *pt & pp of* **send**

sentence [ˈsentəns] **1** *n* **(a)** *(phrase)* phrase *f* **(b)** *(in prison)* peine *f;* **to pass s.** prononcer la sentence

2 *vt (criminal)* condamner **(to** à)

sententious [senˈtenʃəs] *adj Formal* sentencieux(euse)

sentient [ˈsentɪənt] *adj* sensible

sentiment [ˈsentɪmənt] *n* **(a)** *(opinion)* sentiment *m;* **my sentiments exactly** je suis tout à fait du même avis **(b)** *(sentimentality)* sentimentalité *f*

sentimental [sentɪˈmentəl] *adj* sentimental(e)

sentimentality [sentɪmenˈtælɪtɪ] *n* sentimentalité *f*, sensiblerie *f*

sentry [ˈsentrɪ] *n* sentinelle *f;* **to be on s. duty** être de garde; **s. box** guérite *f*

Seoul [səʊl] *n* Séoul

Sep *(abbr* **September)** septembre

separable [ˈsepərəbəl] *adj* séparable

separate 1 *adj* [ˈsepərət] *(parts)* séparé(e), distinct(e); *(box, room, document)* à part; *(occasion, attempt, entrance)* différent(e); *(organization)* indépendant(e); **raw and cooked meats should be kept s.** la viande crue et la viande cuite doivent être conservées séparément; **to lead s. lives** avoir chacun sa vie; *also Fig* **they went their s. ways** ils sont partis chacun de leur côté

2 *vt* [ˈsepəreɪt] séparer **(from** de)

3 *vi* [ˈsepəreɪt] se séparer **(from** de)

separation [sepəˈreɪʃən] *n* séparation *f*

separatist [ˈsepərətɪst] *n Pol* séparatiste *mf*

sepia [ˈsiːpɪə] *n* sépia *f*

sepsis [ˈsepsɪs] *n* infection *f*

Sept *(abbr* **September)** septembre

September [sepˈtembə(r)] *n* septembre *m; see also* **May**

septet [sepˈtet] *n* septuor *m*

septic [ˈseptɪk] *adj* septique; **to go s.** s'infecter; **s. tank** fosse *f* septique

septicaemia, *Am* **septicemia** [septɪˈsiːmɪə] *n* septicémie *f*

sepulchre, *Am* **sepulcher** [ˈsepəlkə(r)] *n Formal* sépulcre *m*

sequel [ˈsiːkwəl] *n* (a) *(book, film)* suite *f* **(to** de) **(b)** *(result)* conséquence *f* **(to** de)

sequence [ˈsiːkwəns] *n* **(a)** *(order)* ordre *m*, suite *f;* **in s.** par ordre; **out of s.** dans le désordre **(b)** *(of numbers, events)* suite *f*, série *f; (in film)* séquence *f*

sequential [sɪˈkwenʃəl] *adj* séquentiel(elle)

sequestrate [sɪˈkwestreɪt] *vt Law* séquestrer

sequestration [siːkweˈstreɪʃən] *n Law* mise *f* sous séquestre

sequin [ˈsiːkwɪn] *n* paillette *f*

sequoia [seˈkwɔɪə] *n* séquoia *m*

Serbia [ˈsɜːbɪə] *n* la Serbie

Serb [ˈsɜːb], **Serbian** [ˈsɜːbɪən] **1** *n* Serbe *mf*

2 *adj* serbe

Serbo-Croat [ˈsɜːbəʊˈkrəʊæt] **1** *n* serbo-croate *m*

2 *adj* serbo-croate

serenade [serəˈneɪd] **1** *n* sérénade *f*

2 *vt* chanter une sérénade à

serene [sɪˈriːn] *adj* serein(e)

serenity [sɪˈrenɪtɪ] *n* sérénité *f*

serf [sɜːf] *n Hist* serf (serve) *m,f*

serfdom [ˈsɜːfdəm] *n Hist* servage *m*

serge [sɜːdʒ] *n* serge *f*

sergeant [ˈsɑːdʒənt] *n (in police)* brigadier *m; Mil* sergent *m*

sergeant-major [sɑːdʒəntˈmeɪdʒə(r)] *n* sergent-major *m*

serial [ˈsɪərɪəl] **1** *n (in magazine)* roman-feuilleton *m; (on TV)* feuilleton *m*

2 *adj* d'une série, en série; **s. killer** tueur(euse) *m,f* en série; **s. number** numéro *m* de série

serialize [ˈsɪərɪəlaɪz] *vt (in magazine)* publier en feuilleton; *(on TV)* adapter en feuilleton

series [ˈsɪəriːz] *(pl* **series)** *n* série *f*

serious [ˈsɪərɪəs] *adj (person)* sérieux(euse); *(situation, problem, injury)* grave; **to be s. about doing sth** envisager sérieusement de faire qch; **are you s.?** tu parles sérieusement?; *Fam* **s. money** un bon paquet d'argent

seriously [ˈsɪərɪəslɪ] *adv* **(a)** *(in earnest)* sérieusement; **to take s./sth s.** prendre qn/qch au sérieux; **to take oneself too s.** se prendre trop au sérieux; **you can't s. expect…** sérieusement, vous ne pensez pas que… **(b)** *(gravely, critically)* gravement

sermon [ˈsɜːmən] *n also Fig* sermon *m*

serpent [ˈsɜːpənt] *n Lit* serpent *m*

serpentine [ˈsɜːpəntaɪn] *adj Lit* qui serpente, sinueux(euse)

serrated [seˈreɪtɪd] *adj* en dents de scie

serum [ˈsɪərəm] *n* sérum *m*

servant [ˈsɜːvənt] *n* domestique *mf*

serve [sɜːv] **1** vt (**a**) (country, cause) servir; **to s. one's own interests** servir ses propres intérêts (**b**) (be useful to) servir à, être utile à; **to s. a purpose** avoir une utilité; **it doesn't s. my purpose** cela ne me sert à rien; **it has served me well** ça m'a fait de l'usage; **if my memory serves me right** si ma mémoire est bonne (**c**) (prison sentence) purger; (apprenticeship) faire (**d**) (meal, customer, drink) servir; **s. chilled** (on food, drink) servir frais; **serves four** (on packet, in recipe) pour quatre personnes (**e**) Law **to s. sb with a summons** remettre une assignation à qn (**f**) (**it**) **serves her right!** bien fait pour elle! **2** vi servir; **to s. as** (be used as) servir de **3** n (in tennis) service m; (**it's**) **your s.!** à toi de servir!

▸ **serve up** vt sep servir

server ['sɜːvə(r)] n (**a**) (in tennis) serveur(euse) m,f (**b**) Comptr serveur m

service ['sɜːvɪs] **1** n (**a**) (with army, firm) service m; Mil **the services** les forces fpl armées; **to do sb a s.** rendre un service à qn; **to be at sb's s.** être au service de qn; **to be of s. to sb** être utile à qn; **to offer one's services** offrir ses services (**b**) (in shop, restaurant) service m; **s. included/not included** service compris/non compris; **s. charge** service; **s. industry** industrie f de services; Br **s. lift** ascenseur m de service (**c**) (system) **postal/air/train s.** service m postal/aérien/des trains (**d**) (maintenance) (of machine) entretien m; (of car) révision f; **s. area** (on motorway) aire f de service; **s. station** (on motorway) station-service f (**e**) (in church) service m, office m (**f**) (in tennis) service m; **s. line** ligne f de service (**g**) Old-fashioned **to be in/go into s.** (of servant) être/devenir domestique **2** vt (machine) entretenir; (car) réviser

serviceable ['sɜːvɪsəbl] adj (**a**) (in working order) en état de marche (**b**) (durable) résistant(e)

serviceman ['sɜːvɪsmən] n militaire m

servicewoman ['sɜːvɪswʊmən] n femme f soldat

serviette [sɜːvɪ'et] n Br serviette f (de table)

servile ['sɜːvaɪl] adj servile, obséquieux(euse)

serving ['sɜːvɪŋ] n (portion) portion f; **s. hatch** passe-plat m

servitude ['sɜːvɪtjuːd] n servitude f, asservissement m

servo ['sɜːvəʊ] **1** n (pl **servos**) Fam (servomechanism) servomécanisme m **2** adj **s. brake** servofrein m

sesame ['sesəmɪ] n (**a**) **s. oil** huile f de sésame; **s. seeds** graines fpl de sésame (**b**) **open s.!** sésame, ouvre-toi!

session ['seʃən] n (**a**) (period of activity) séance f, session f (**b**) (meeting) séance f; **to be in s.** siéger (**c**) (university, school term) trimestre m; (university year) année f universitaire; (school year) année f scolaire

set [set] **1** n (**a**) (of keys) jeu m; (of saucepans) série f, assortiment m; (of books) collection f; (of tyres) train m; (of problems, rules, symptoms) ensemble m; **s. of teeth** dentition f (**b**) (of people) cercle m (**c**) (TV, radio) poste m (**d**) (in theatre) décor m; (in cinema) plateau m (**e**) (in tennis) set m; **s. point** balle f de set **2** adj (**a**) (fixed) (look) figé(e); (ideas) déterminé(e); (price) fixe; **to be s. in one's ways** tenir à ses habitudes; **s. menu** menu m; **s. phrase** expression f figée; **s. piece** (in play, film) morceau m de bravoure; (in sport) tactique f (**b**) (ready) **to be (all) s. for sth/to do sth** être (fin) prêt(e) pour qch/à faire qch

(**c**) (determined) **to be (dead) s. on sth** avoir fixé son choix sur qch; **to be (dead) s. on doing sth** être fermement décidé(e) à faire qch; **to be dead s. against** être formellement opposé(e) à **3** vt (pt & pp **set**) (**a**) (place) placer, mettre; (jewel) sertir; **to s. the table** mettre la table; **to s. a trap (for sb)** tendre un piège (à qn); **the novel/film is set in Boston** le roman/film se passe à Boston (**b**) (fix) (date, day, limit, price) fixer, déterminer; (watch) régler; (alarm clock) mettre; (record) établir; **to s. a value on sth** estimer la valeur de qch; **to s. the scene** planter le décor (**c**) (cause to start) **to s. sb thinking** faire réfléchir qn; **to s. sb free** libérer qn; **to s. sth on fire** mettre le feu à qch (**d**) (task) fixer; (essay, homework) donner (**e**) (bone, fracture) réduire **4** vi (**a**) (of sun, moon) se coucher (**b**) (become firm) (of jelly, concrete) prendre; (of broken bone) se ressouder

▸ **set about** vt insep (**a**) (task, job) se mettre à, to **s. about doing sth** se mettre à faire qch (**b**) (attack) attaquer

▸ **set against** vt sep (**a**) (cause to oppose) **to s. sb against sb** monter qn contre qn (**b**) (compare) **to s. sth against sth** comparer qch à qch (**c**) (deduct) **to s. expenses against tax** déduire les dépenses des impôts

▸ **set apart** vt sep distinguer (**from** de)

▸ **set aside** vt sep (**a**) (put down, disregard) laisser de côté (**b**) (save) (money) mettre de côté; (time) réserver

▸ **set back** vt sep (**a**) (delay) retarder (**b**) Fam (cost) coûter

▸ **set down** vt sep (put down) poser, laisser; **to s. sth down in writing** coucher qch par écrit

▸ **set forth** vi Lit (depart) partir, se mettre en route

▸ **set in** vi (of winter, mood) s'installer; (of fog, night) tomber; (of infection) se déclarer

▸ **set off 1** vt sep (**a**) (bomb, explosion, alarm) déclencher; (argument, chain of events) provoquer; **to s. sb off (laughing)** faire éclater qn de rire; **to s. sb off (crying)** faire éclater qn en sanglots (**b**) (enhance) mettre en valeur, rehausser **2** vi (depart) partir, se mettre en route

▸ **set out 1** vt sep (arrange) disposer **2** vi (**a**) (depart) partir, se mettre en route; (in job, task) démarrer (**b**) (intend) **to s. out to do sth** avoir l'intention de faire qch

▸ **set to** vi (**a**) (start working) s'y mettre (**b**) Fam (start arguing) recommencer à se disputer

▸ **set up 1** vt sep (**a**) (statue) ériger; (tent, barrier) monter; (roadblock) mettre en place (**b**) (meeting) arranger; (company) créer; (system) mettre en place; **to s. up house** ou **home** s'installer; **to s. sb up in business (as)** installer qn (comme) (**c**) (trick, frame) monter un coup contre; **to be set up** être victime d'un coup monté **2** vi (establish oneself) s'installer (**as** comme); **to s. up in business (as)** s'installer (comme)

▸ **set upon** vt insep (attack) attaquer

setback ['setbæk] n revers m, échec m

set-square ['setskweə(r)] n équerre f (à dessin)

settee [se'tiː] n canapé m

setter ['setə(r)] n (dog) setter m

setting ['setɪŋ] **1** n (**a**) (of story, film) cadre m (**b**) (of sun) coucher m (**c**) (on machine) réglage m (**d**) **s. lotion** lotion f pour mise en plis **2** adj (sun) couchant(e)

settle ['setl] **1** vt (**a**) (put in place) installer; **to s. oneself** s'installer (**b**) (nerves) calmer; **to s. one's stomach** calmer ses douleurs d'estomac (**c**) (day, venue) décider, régler (**d**) (problem, dispute, bill) régler; **to s. one's affairs** régler ses

affaires; *Fam* **that settles it!** c'est décidé!; *Law* **to s. a matter out of court** régler une affaire à l'amiable **(e)** *(colonize)* coloniser
2 *vi* **(a)** *(of bird, insect)* se poser; *(of dust, liquid, beer)* se déposer **(b)** *(of person, family)* s'installer, s'établir; *(of crowd)* se calmer, s'apaiser; **to s. into an armchair** s'installer confortablement dans un fauteuil **(c)** *Law* **to s. out of court** régler l'affaire à l'amiable
▸ **settle down 1** *vt sep* **(a)** *(make comfortable)* installer **(b)** *(make calm)* calmer
2 *vi* **(a)** *(make oneself comfortable)* s'installer confortablement; **to s. down to work** se mettre au travail **(b)** *(become quieter, more disciplined)* s'assagir; **to s. down with sb** mener une vie stable avec qn **(c)** *(of situation, excitement)* se calmer
▸ **settle for** *vt insep* accepter, se contenter de
▸ **settle in** *vi (in new home)* s'installer; *(in new school, job)* s'adapter
▸ **settle on** *vt insep* se décider pour, choisir
▸ **settle up** *vi (pay bill)* régler
settled ['setəld] *adj (person, life)* rangé(e), établi(e); *(weather)* stable
settlement ['setəlmənt] *n* **(a)** *(of problem, dispute, bill)* règlement *m*; **to reach a s.** parvenir à un accord **(b)** *(village)* village *m*
settler ['setlə(r)] *n* colon *m*
set-to ['set'tuː] *n Fam* bagarre *f*
setup ['setʌp] *n Fam (arrangement)* système *m*
seven ['sevən] **1** *n* sept *m inv*
2 *adj* sept; **the s. deadly sins** les sept péchés capitaux; *Lit* **to sail the s. seas** parcourir les mers; *see also* **eight**
seventeen [sevən'tiːn] **1** *n* dix-sept *m inv*
2 *adj* dix-sept; *see also* **eight**
seventeenth [sevən'tiːnθ] **1** *n* **(a)** *(fraction)* dix-septième *m* **(b)** *(in series)* dix-septième *mf* **(c)** *(of month)* dix-sept *m inv*
2 *adj* dix-septième; *see also* **eighth**
seventh ['sevənθ] **1** *n* **(a)** *(fraction)* septième *m* **(b)** *(in series)* septième *mf* **(c)** *(of month)* sept *m inv*
2 *adj* septième; **to be in s. heaven** être au septième ciel; *see also* **eighth**
seventieth ['sevəntɪɪθ] **1** *n* **(a)** *(fraction)* soixante-dixième *m* **(b)** *(in series)* soixante-dixième *mf*
2 *adj* soixante-dixième
seventy ['sevəntɪ] **1** *n* soixante-dix *m inv*
2 *adj* soixante-dix; *see also* **eighty**
sever ['sevə(r)] *vt (arm, finger)* couper, trancher; *Fig (link, relationship)* rompre
several ['sevərəl] **1** *adj* plusieurs
2 *pron* plusieurs; **s. of us/them** plusieurs d'entre nous/ eux
severance ['sevərəns] *n* rupture *f*; **s. pay** indemnité *f* de licenciement
severe [sɪ'vɪə(r)] *adj (person, punishment, criticism)* sévère; *(pain)* vif (vive); *(illness, injury)* grave; *(winter)* rude; *(weather)* très mauvais(e); *(style)* austère, sévère
severity [sɪ'verɪtɪ] *n (of person, punishment, criticism)* sévérité *f*; *(of pain)* intensité *f*; *(of injury, illness)* gravité *f*; *(of winter)* rigueur *f*; *(of style)* austérité *f*, sévérité
sew [səʊ] *(pp* **sewn** [səʊn]*)* *vt & vi* coudre
▸ **sew up** *vt sep* **(a)** *(stitch)* coudre **(b)** *Fam* **it's all sewn up** *(decided, settled)* l'affaire est dans le sac
sewage ['suːɪdʒ] *n* eaux *fpl* usées *ou* d'égout; **s. disposal** évacuation *f* des eaux usées; **s. works** champ *m* d'épandage
sewer ['suːə(r)] *n* égout *m*; *Fam* **to have a mind like a s.** avoir l'esprit mal tourné

sewing ['səʊɪŋ] *n (activity)* couture *f*; *(work)* ouvrage *m*; **s. machine** machine *f* à coudre
sewn [səʊn] *pp of* **sew**
sex [seks] *n* sexe *m*; **to have s. with sb** faire l'amour avec qn; **s. appeal** sex-appeal *m*; **s. education** éducation *f* sexuelle; **s. life** vie *f* sexuelle; **s. maniac** obsédé(e) *m,f* sexuel(elle); **s. shop** sex-shop *m*; **s. symbol** sex-symbol *m*
sexagenarian [seksədʒɪ'neərɪən] *n* séxagénaire *mf*
sexism ['seksɪzəm] *n* sexisme *m*
sexist ['seksɪst] *n & adj* sexiste *mf*
sextant ['sekstənt] *n* sextant *m*
sextet [seks'tet] *n* sextuor *m*
sexton ['sekstən] *n* sacristain *m*, bedeau *m*
sexual ['seksjʊəl] *adj* sexuel(elle); **s. assault** agression *f* sexuelle; **s. discrimination** discrimination *f* sexuelle; **s. harassment** harcèlement *m* sexuel; **s. intercourse** rapports *mpl* sexuels; **s. reproduction** reproduction *f* sexuée
sexuality [seksjʊ'ælɪtɪ] *n* sexualité *f*
sexually ['seksjʊəlɪ] *adv* sexuellement; **s. transmitted disease** maladie *f* sexuellement transmissible
sexy ['seksɪ] *adj Fam* sexy *inv*; *Fig (car, hi-fi)* branché(e)
Seychelles [seɪ'ʃelz] *npl* **the S.** les Seychelles *fpl*
Sgt *(abbr* **Sergeant)** Sgt
sh [ʃ] *exclam* chut!
shabbily ['ʃæbɪlɪ] *adv* **(a)** *(furnished, dressed)* pauvrement **(b)** *(treat, behave)* avec mesquinerie
shabbiness ['ʃæbɪnɪs] *n* **(a)** *(of person, clothes, area)* apparence *f* miteuse **(b)** *(of treatment, behaviour)* mesquinerie *f*
shabby ['ʃæbɪ] *adj* **(a)** *(dingy, worn out)* miteux(euse) **(b)** *(behaviour, treatment)* minable, mesquin(e)
shack [ʃæk] *n* cabane *f*, hutte *f*
▸ **shack up** *vi Fam* **to s. up with sb** être *ou* vivre à la colle avec qn
shackle ['ʃækəl] **1** *n* **shackles** chaînes *fpl*, fers *mpl*
2 *vt (prisoner)* enchaîner
shade [ʃeɪd] **1** *n* **(a)** *(shadow)* ombre *f*; **in the s.** à l'ombre; *Fig* **to put sb in the s.** éclipser qn; **shades of** *(reminders, suggestions)* réminiscences *fpl* de **(b)** *(of colour, meaning, opinion)* nuance *f*, ton *m*; **a s. better/longer** un tout petit mieux/plus long **(c)** *Fam* **shades** *(sunglasses)* lunettes *fpl* de soleil
2 *vt (from sun)* **to s. one's eyes** se protéger les yeux
shaded ['ʃeɪdɪd] *adj* **(a)** *(garden, path)* à l'ombre, ombragé(e) **(b)** *(area on diagram, map)* hachuré(e)
shading ['ʃeɪdɪŋ] *n (on drawing)* ombres *fpl*; *(on diagram, map)* hachure *f*
shadow ['ʃædəʊ] **1** *n* ombre *f*; **to cast a s.** projeter une ombre; *Fig* **to cast a s. over sth** jeter une ombre sur qch; **to be a s. of one's former self** n'être plus que l'ombre de soi-même; **without a s. of doubt** sans l'ombre d'un doute; **the s. of death/war** le spectre de la mort/de la guerre; **to have shadows under one's eyes** avoir des cernes, avoir les yeux cernés
2 *adj Br Pol* **S. Cabinet** cabinet *m* fantôme; **S. Minister** ministre *mf* fantôme
3 *vt (follow)* filer, prendre en filature
shadowy ['ʃædəʊɪ] *adj (dark)* ombragé(e); *(form, outline)* vague
shady ['ʃeɪdɪ] *adj* **(a)** *(garden, lane)* ombragé(e) **(b)** *Fam (suspicious)* louche
shaft [ʃɑːft] **1** *n* **(a)** *(of golf club, tool)* manche *m*; *(of light)* rayon *m* **(b)** *(of mine)* puits *m*; *(for lift)* cage *f*
2 *vt very Fam (cheat)* entuber

shag¹ [ʃæg] n (tobacco) tabac m

shag² Br Vulg **1** n (sexual intercourse) **to have a s.** baiser **2** vt & vi (pt & pp **shagged**) baiser

shagged [ʃægd] adj very Fam (exhausted) crevé(e)

shaggy ['ʃægɪ] adj (hairy) hirsute; Fam **s. dog story** histoire f sans queue ni tête

shah [ʃɑː] n schah m

shake [ʃeɪk] **1** n (a) (action) secousse f; **to give sb/sth a s.** secouer qn/qch; Fig **to give oneself a s.** se secouer; Fam **to have the shakes** avoir la tremblote; Fam **in two shakes (of a lamb's tail)** en un rien de temps; Fam **to be no great shakes** ne pas casser trois pattes à un canard (b) **(milk) s.** (milk-)shake m **2** vt (pt **shook** [ʃʊk], pp **shaken** ['ʃeɪkən]) (person, box, bottle) secouer; (building) faire trembler, ébranler; Fig **to s. sb's faith/trust** ébranler la foi/la confiance de qn; **to s. one's head** faire non de la tête; **to s. one's fist at sb** menacer qn du poing; **to s. hands with sb** serrer la main à qn; **to s. hands on a deal** conclure un accord par une poignée de mains **3** vi (a) (of person, building, voice) trembler; **to s. like a leaf** trembler comme une feuille (b) Fam **to s. on it** (shake hands) toper; **s. on it!** tope là!

▸ **shake off** vt sep (illness, depression) sortir de; (pursuer) semer

▸ **shake up** vt sep (a) (upset) secouer (b) (reorganize) réorganiser de fond en comble

shaken ['ʃeɪkən] pp of **shake**

Shakespearean [ʃeɪksˈpɪərɪən] adj shakespearien(ne)

shake-up ['ʃeɪkʌp] n Fam (reorganization) chambardement m

shakily ['ʃeɪkɪlɪ] adv (walk) d'un pas vacillant; (write) d'une main tremblante; (speak) d'une voix tremblante

shaky ['ʃeɪkɪ] adj (table, ladder) branlant(e); (handwriting) tremblé(e); (voice) tremblant(e); (health, position) précaire

shale [ʃeɪl] n schiste m argileux

shall [stressed ʃæl, unstressed ʃəl]

> On trouve généralement **I/you/he**/etc **shall** sous leurs formes contractées **I'll/you'll/he'll**/etc. La forme négative correspondante est **shan't**, que l'on écrira **shall not** dans des contextes formels.

modal aux v **(a)** (with first person) (expressing future tense) **I s. be there** j'y serai; **where s. I sit?** où veux-tu que je m'asseye?; **I s. not** or **shan't be able to come** je ne pourrai pas venir; **as we s. see** comme nous le verrons **(b)** (making suggestions, offers) **s. I make some coffee?** veux-tu que je fasse du café?; **let's go in, s. we?** entrons, tu veux bien? **(c)** Formal (with 2nd and 3rd person) (expressing determination) **you s. pay for this!** tu me le paieras! **(d)** (indicating general truth) **all members s. be entitled to vote** tous les membres auront le droit de vote

shallot [ʃəˈlɒt] n échalote f

shallow ['ʃæləʊ] adj **(a)** (water, dish) peu profond(e); **s. end** (of swimming pool) petit bain m **(b)** Fig (person, mind) superficiel(elle)

sham [ʃæm] **1** n (trial, election) comédie f, farce f; (person) imposteur m **2** adj feint(e) **3** vt (pt & pp **shammed**) feindre, simuler **4** vi faire semblant

shamble ['ʃæmbəl] vi **to s. along** marcher en traînant les pieds

shambles ['ʃæmblz] n désordre m, pagaille f; **this place is a s.!** quel désordre!, quelle pagaille!

shambolic [ʃæmˈbɒlɪk] adj Fam bordélique

shame [ʃeɪm] **1** n **(a)** (disgrace, guilt) honte f; **to my s. à ma grande honte**; **s. on you!** tu devrais avoir honte!; **to put sb to s.** faire honte à qn **(b)** (pity) dommage m; **it's a s. (that...)** c'est dommage (que... + subjunctive); **what a s.!** quel dommage! **2** vt **(a)** (cause to feel ashamed) faire honte à; **to s. sb into doing sth** obliger qn à faire qch en lui faisant honte **(b)** (bring shame on) couvrir de honte

shamefaced ['ʃeɪmfeɪst] adj honteux(euse), penaud(e)

shameful ['ʃeɪmfʊl] adj honteux(euse), scandaleux(euse)

shamefully ['ʃeɪmfəlɪ] adv honteusement

shameless ['ʃeɪmlɪs] adj impudique; **to be s. about doing sth** n'avoir aucun scrupule à faire qch

shammy ['ʃæmɪ] n **s. (leather)** peau f de chamois

shampoo [ʃæmˈpuː] **1** n shampoing m **2** vt **to s. one's hair** se faire un shampoing

shamrock ['ʃæmrɒk] n trèfle m

shandy ['ʃændɪ] n Br panaché m

shank [ʃæŋk] n (of lamb, beef) jarret m

shan't [ʃɑːnt] = **shall not**

shanty¹ ['ʃæntɪ] n (hut) baraque f, cabane f; **s. town** bidonville m

shanty² n (song) chanson f de marins

shape [ʃeɪp] **1** n **(a)** (form) forme f; **what s. is it?** quelle forme cela a-t-il?; **to be the same s. as...** avoir la même forme que...; **to take s.** (of plan) prendre forme; Fig **in any s. or form** quel (quelle) qu'il (elle) soit; Fig **in the s. of** sous la forme de; (person) en la personne de **(b)** (condition) **to be in good/bad s.** (of person) être en bonne/mauvaise forme; (of company, economy) bien/mal marcher; **to get into/keep in s.** (of person) retrouver/garder la forme **2** vt **(a)** (clay) modeler; (wood) façonner **(b)** Fig (perception, events, future) influencer; (character) former

▸ **shape up** vi (of person) progresser; (of team, plans) prendre forme

shapeless ['ʃeɪplɪs] adj informe

shapely ['ʃeɪplɪ] adj bien fait(e)

shard [ʃɑːd] n (of glass) éclat m; (of pottery) tesson m

share [ʃeə(r)] **1** n **(a)** (portion) part f; **in equal shares** en parts égales; **to have a s. in sth** avoir une part dans qch; **to do one's s.** mettre la main à la pâte; also Fig **to get one's fair s. of sth** avoir sa part de qch **(b)** Fin action f; **s. capital** capital m social; **s. certificate** certificat m ou titre m d'actions **2** vt partager **3** vi partager; **to s. in sth** partager qch; **s. and alike!** chacun sa part!

▸ **share out** vt sep partager, répartir

shareholder ['ʃeəhəʊldə(r)] n Fin actionnaire mf

shareholding ['ʃeəhəʊldɪŋ] n Fin actionnariat m

shark [ʃɑːk] n also Fig requin m

sharp [ʃɑːp] **1** adj **(a)** (knife) bien aiguisé(e); (pencil) bien taillé(e); (scissors, razor) qui coupe bien; (point) aigu(uë); (claws) acéré(e) **(b)** (features) anguleux(euse); (turning, rise, fall) brusque; (photo, outline, focus) net (nette); (contrast) marqué(e); (hearing) fin(e); (eyesight) perçant(e); Fig **in the s. end** être en première ligne **(c)** (intelligent) vif (vive) **(d)** (harsh) (voice, words) cinglant(e); (person) mordant(e); **to have a s. tongue** être mordant **(e)** (taste, sauce) acide; (sound) perçant(e); (pain, wind) vif (vive) **(f)** (in music) **C s.** do dièse

2 *adv* (**a**) *(punctually)* pile; **at four o'clock s.** à quatre heures pile *ou* précises
(**b**) *(immediately)* **to turn s. left/right** tourner tout de suite à gauche/à droite
(**c**) *(idioms) Fam* **look s.!** grouille-toi!
3 *n (in music)* dièse *m*

sharpen ['ʃɑːpən] *vt* (**a**) *(knife, tool)* aiguiser; *(pencil)* tailler (**b**) *(pain)* accentuer; *(passion, desire)* exacerber; **to s. one's wits** faire travailler sa matière grise

sharpener ['ʃɑːpənə(r)] *n (for knife)* aiguisoir *m* (à couteaux); *(for pencil)* taille-crayon *m*

sharp-eyed ['ʃɑːpaɪd] *adj* observateur(trice)

sharply ['ʃɑːplɪ] *adv* (**a**) *(contrast)* nettement (**b**) *(rise, fall, brake)* brusquement

sharpness ['ʃɑːpnɪs] *n* (**a**) *(of knife)* tranchant *m* (**b**) *(of outline, photo)* netteté *f* (**c**) *(of mind, hearing, sight)* acuité *f* (**d**) *(of voice, words)* brusquerie *f* (**e**) *(of pain)* acuité *f*; *(of wind)* âpreté *f*

sharpshooter ['ʃɑːpʃuːtə(r)] *n* tireur *m* d'élite

sharp-sighted [ʃɑːp'saɪtɪd] *adj* observateur(trice)

sharp-tongued [ʃɑːp'tʌŋd] *adj* mordant(e)

shat [ʃæt] *pt of* **shit**

shatter ['ʃætə(r)] **1** *vt* (**a**) *(glass, bone)* briser en mille morceaux; *Fig (hopes, silence, nerves)* briser; *(health)* ruiner (**b**) *Fam* **to be shattered** *(stunned)* être accablé(e); *(exhausted)* être crevé(e)
2 *vi* se briser en mille morceaux

shattering ['ʃætərɪŋ] *adj* (**a**) *(defeat)* accablant(e); **it was a s. blow** ça a été un coup terrible (**b**) *Fam (stunning)* accablant(e); *(exhausting)* crevant(e)

shatterproof ['ʃætəpruːf] *adj (glass)* Sécurit®; *(windscreen, door)* en verre Sécurit®

shave [ʃeɪv] **1** *n* **to have a s.** se raser; *Fig* **that was a close s.** il était moins une
2 *vt* (**a**) *(face, legs)* raser; **to s. one's legs** se raser les jambes (**b**) *(wood)* raboter
3 *vi* se raser

▸ **shave off** *vt sep* se raser

shaven ['ʃeɪvən] *adj* rasé(e)

shaver ['ʃeɪvə(r)] *n* rasoir *m* électrique

shaving ['ʃeɪvɪŋ] *n* (**a**) **s. brush** blaireau *m*; **s. foam** mousse *f* à raser (**b**) *(piece of wood)* copeau *m*; *(piece of metal)* rognure *f*

shawl [ʃɔːl] *n* châle *m*

she [ʃiː] **1** *pron* elle; **she's Scottish** elle est écossaise; **SHE hasn't got it!** ce n'est pas elle qui l'a!
2 **it's a s.** *(of animal)* c'est une femelle

sheaf [ʃiːf] *(pl* **sheaves** [ʃiːvz]*) n (of corn)* gerbe *f*; *(of papers)* liasse *f*

shear [ʃɪə(r)] *(pp* **shorn** [ʃɔːn] *or* **sheared**) **1** *vt (sheep)* tondre; *Fig* **to be shorn of sth** être dépouillé(e) de qch
2 *vi (cut)* **to s. through sth** couper qch

shears [ʃɪəz] *npl* cisailles *fpl*

sheath [ʃiːθ] *n* (**a**) *(for sword, knife)* fourreau *m*; *(for electric cable)* gaine *f*; **s. knife** couteau *m* à gaine (**b**) *(contraceptive)* préservatif *m*

shed[1] [ʃed] *n (in garden)* abri *m*, remise *f*; *(in factory)* atelier *m*

shed[2] *(pt & pp* **shed**) *vt (leaves)* perdre; *(tears)* verser; **to s. its skin** *(of snake)* muer; **to s. light on sth** jeter de la lumière sur qch; **to s. weight** perdre du poids; **to s. its load** *(of lorry)* perdre son chargement

she'd [ʃiːd] = **she had**, **she would**

sheen [ʃiːn] *n (on metal, silk)* lustre *m*; *(on hair)* brillant *m*

sheep [ʃiːp] *(pl* **sheep**) *n* mouton *m*

sheepdog ['ʃiːpdɒg] *n* chien *m* de berger

sheepfold ['ʃiːpfəʊld] *n* parc *m* à moutons

sheepish ['ʃiːpɪʃ] *adj* penaud(e)

sheepskin ['ʃiːpskɪn] *n* peau *f* de mouton; **s. jacket** veste *f* en peau de mouton

sheer [ʃɪə(r)] *adj* (**a**) *(pure)* pur(e); **it's s. madness** c'est de la folie pure; **by s. chance** tout à fait par hasard (**b**) *(steep)* à pic *inv* (**c**) *(stockings, fabric)* très fin(e)

sheet [ʃiːt] *n* (**a**) *(on bed)* drap *m*; *(of paper)* feuille *f*; *(of glass, ice, metal)* plaque *f*; *(of flame)* rideau *m*; **s. lightning** éclair *m* en nappe(s); **s. metal** tôle *f*; **s. music** partitions *fpl*

sheetfeed ['ʃiːtfiːd] *n Comptr* avancement *m* du papier

sheik(h) [ʃeɪk] *n* cheikh *m*

shekel ['ʃekəl] *n* shekel *m*

shelf [ʃelf] *(pl* **shelves** [ʃelvz]*) n* (**a**) *(in cupboard, bookcase)* étagère *f*; **(set of) shelves** étagère; *Fig* **to be left on the s.** rester vieille fille; *Com* **s. life** *(of goods)* durée *f* de conservation avant vente (**b**) *(of cliff, rock face)* rebord *m*

shell [ʃel] **1** *n* (**a**) *(of snail, oyster, egg, nut)* coquille *f*; *(of lobster, tortoise)* carapace *f*; *(on beach)* coquillage *m*; *Fig* **to come out of one's s.** sortir de sa coquille (**b**) *(of building)* carcasse *f* (**c**) *(bomb)* obus *m*; **s. shock** psychose *f* traumatique *(à la suite d'une explosion)*
2 *vt* (**a**) *(nuts)* décortiquer; *(peas)* écosser; *(eggs)* écaler (**b**) *(bombard)* bombarder

▸ **shell out** *Fam* **1** *vt sep (money)* casquer
2 *vi* **to s. out (for sth)** casquer (pour qch)

she'll [ʃiːl] = **she will**, **she shall**

shellfire ['ʃelfaɪə(r)] *n* tirs *mpl* d'obus

shellfish ['ʃelfɪʃ] *n (crustacean)* crustacé *m*; *(mollusc)* coquillage *m*; *(as food)* fruits *mpl* de mer

shelling ['ʃelɪŋ] *n* bombardement *m*

shellshocked ['ʃelʃɒkt] *adj (soldier)* commotionné(e) *(à la suite d'une explosion)*; *Fig* sous le choc

shelter ['ʃeltə(r)] **1** *n (place, protection)* abri *m*; **to take s.** se mettre à l'abri, s'abriter
2 *vt* abriter *(from* de); *(criminal, refugee)* accueillir
3 *vi* s'abriter, se mettre à l'abri *(from* de)

sheltered ['ʃeltəd] *adj (place)* abrité(e); *(life, childhood)* protégé(e); *Br* **s. housing** = logements spécialement conçus pour les personnes âgées

shelve [ʃelv] *vt (postpone)* mettre au placard

shelving ['ʃelvɪŋ] *n* étagères *fpl*

shepherd ['ʃepəd] **1** *n* berger *m*; **s.'s pie** ≃ hachis *m* Parmentier
2 *vt (sheep)* garder; *Fig (people)* guider, conduire

shepherdess [ʃepə'des] *n* bergère *f*

sherbet ['ʃɜːbət] *n Br (powder)* poudre *f* acidulée; *Am (sorbet)* sorbet *m*

sheriff ['ʃerɪf] *n Br* = plus haut fonctionnaire du comté, dont le rôle est essentiellement protocolaire; *Scot* ≃ juge *m* au tribunal de grande instance; *Am* sherif *m*

sherry ['ʃerɪ] *n* sherry *m*, xérès *m*

she's [ʃiːz] = **she has**, **she is**

Shetland ['ʃetlənd] *n* **the S. Islands, the Shetlands** les (îles *fpl*) Shetland *fpl*; **S. pony** poney *m* des Shetland

shield [ʃiːld] **1** *n (of knight)* & *Fig (protection)* bouclier *m*; *(police badge)* badge *m*; *(trophy)* trophée *m* en forme d'écusson
2 *vt (protect)* protéger *(from* de); **to s. one's eyes** se protéger les yeux

shift [ʃɪft] **1** *n* (**a**) *(change of position)* changement *m*; **a s. in meaning** un glissement de sens; **a s. to the right/left** *(in politics)* un revirement à droite/gauche; **s. key** *(on typewriter, computer)* touche *f* des majuscules (**b**) *(period)* poste *m*; *(workers)* équipe *f*; **to work (in) shifts** avoir un travail posté (**c**) **s. (dress)** robe *f* chasuble

2 *vt* (**a**) *(move)* déplacer; *(stain)* enlever, faire partir; **to s. the blame onto sb** rejeter la responsabilité sur qn (**b**) *Fam (sell)* écouler

3 *vi (move)* bouger; *(of stain)* partir; *Fam (move quickly)* foncer

shiftless [ˈʃɪftlɪs] *adj* fainéant(e)

shiftwork [ˈʃɪftwɜːk] *n* travail *m* posté

shifty [ˈʃɪftɪ] *adj (person)* louche; *(look)* fuyant(e)

shilling [ˈʃɪlɪŋ] *n* shilling *m*

shimmer [ˈʃɪmə(r)] **1** *n (of light)* scintillement *m*; *(of water)* miroitement *m*; *(of silk)* chatoiement *m*

2 *vi (of light)* scintiller; *(of water)* miroiter; *(of silk)* chatoyer

shimmering [ˈʃɪmərɪŋ] *adj (light)* scintillant(e); *(water)* miroitant(e); *(silk)* chatoyant(e)

shin [ʃɪn] *n* tibia *m*; **s. guard** *or* **pad** *(in sport)* jambière *f*

▸ **shin up** *(pt & pp* **shinned)** *vt insep (climb)* grimper à

shinbone [ˈʃɪnbəʊn] *n* tibia *m*

shindy [ˈʃɪndɪ] *n Fam (din)* boucan *m*; **to kick up a s.** faire du boucan

shine [ʃaɪn] **1** *n* (**a**) brillant *m*, éclat *m* (**b**) *(idioms)* **to take the s. off sth** faire perdre son éclat à qch, ternir qch; *Fam* **to take a s. to sb** prendre qn en affection

2 *vt (pt & pp* **shone** [ʃɒn]) (**a**) *(light, torch)* braquer (**on** sur) (**b**) *(pt & pp* **shined)** *(polish)* faire briller

3 *vi (pt & pp* **shone)** briller; *Fig* **to s. at sth** briller en qch; **her face shone with joy** son visage rayonna de joie

shiner [ˈʃaɪnə(r)] *n Fam (black eye)* œil *m* au beurre noir

shingle [ˈʃɪŋɡəl] *n* (**a**) *(wooden tile)* bardeau *m* (**b**) *(pebbles)* galets *mpl*

shingles [ˈʃɪŋɡəlz] *n (disease)* zona *m*; **to have s.** avoir un zona

shining [ˈʃaɪnɪŋ] *adj* brillant(e); *Fig* **a s. example (of)** un parfait exemple (de)

shiny [ˈʃaɪnɪ] *adj* brillant(e)

ship [ʃɪp] **1** *n* navire *m*; *Fig* **when my s. comes in** quand je serai riche

2 *vt (pt & pp* **shipped)** *(transport)* transporter, *(send)* expédier; *(take on board)* embarquer

▸ **ship off** *vt sep Fam* expédier

shipboard [ˈʃɪpbɔːd] *n Naut* **on s.** à bord

shipbuilder [ˈʃɪpbɪldə(r)] *n* constructeur *m* naval

shipbuilding [ˈʃɪpbɪldɪŋ] *n* construction *f* navale; **the s. industry** (l'industrie *f* de) la construction navale

shipload [ˈʃɪpləʊd] *n* cargaison *f*; *Fig* **by the s.** en masse

shipmate [ˈʃɪpmeɪt] *n Naut* camarade *m* de bord

shipment [ˈʃɪpmənt] *n* cargaison *f*

shipowner [ˈʃɪpəʊnə(r)] *n* armateur *m*

shipping [ˈʃɪpɪŋ] *n (ships)* navires *mpl*; **s. agent** *(person)* agent *m* maritime; *(company)* agence *f* maritime; **s. lane** voie *f* de navigation

shipshape [ˈʃɪpʃeɪp] *adj* rangé(e), en ordre

shipwreck [ˈʃɪprek] **1** *n (disaster)* naufrage *m*; *(ship)* épave *f*

2 *vt* **to be shipwrecked** faire naufrage

shipwrecked [ˈʃɪprekt] *adj* naufragé(e)

shipwright [ˈʃɪpraɪt] *n Naut (company)* constructeur *m* naval; *(worker)* ouvrier(ère) *m,f* de chantier naval

shipyard [ˈʃɪpjɑːd] *n* chantier *m* naval

shire [ˈʃaɪə(r)] *n* comté *m*; **s. horse** shire *m*

shirk [ʃɜːk] **1** *vt (task)* éviter de faire; *(obligation, responsibility)* se dérober à

2 *vi (avoid work)* tirer au flanc

shirker [ˈʃɜːkə(r)] *n* tire-au-flanc *mf inv*

shirt [ʃɜːt] *n* chemise *f*; *Fam* **keep your s. on!** on se calme!

shirtmaker [ˈʃɜːtmeɪkə(r)] *n* fabricant(e) *m,f* de chemises

shirtsleeves [ˈʃɜːtsliːvz] *npl* **to be in s.** être en bras de chemise

shirt-tail [ˈʃɜːtteɪl] *n* pan *m* de chemise

shirty [ˈʃɜːtɪ] *adj Br Fam* en rogne; **to get s. (with sb)** se mettre en rogne (contre qn)

shit [ʃɪt] *Vulg* **1** *n* (**a**) *(excrement)* merde *f*; *(mess)* bordel *m*; *(nonsense)* conneries *fpl*; **to have a s.** chier (**b**) *(nasty man)* salaud *m*; *(nasty woman)* salope *f* (**c**) *(idioms)* **to talk s.** dire des conneries; **to be a s.** être dans la merde; **he doesn't give a s.** il n'en a rien à foutre; **to beat the s. out of sb** casser la gueule à qn; **to scare the s. out of sb** foutre une de ces trouilles à qn

2 *vt (pt & pp* **shitted** *or* **shat** [ʃæt]) **to s. oneself** chier dans son froc

3 *vi* chier

4 *exclam* merde!

shitty [ˈʃɪtɪ] *adj Vulg* (**a**) *(nappies, trousers)* dégueulasse (**b**) *(weather, job)* merdique, *(behaviour, remark)* dégueulasse; **to feel s.** *(ill)* avoir la tête dans le cul; *(guilty)* se sentir merdeux(euse)

shiver [ˈʃɪvə(r)] **1** *n (of cold, fear)* frisson *m*; **to send shivers down sb's spine** donner le frisson à qn

2 *vi* frissonner, trembler (**with** de)

shoal [ʃəʊl] *n (of fish)* banc *m*; *Fig (of people)* foule *f*

shock¹ [ʃɒk] *n (of hair)* crinière *f*

shock² **1** *n* (**a**) *(impact)* choc *m*, *(of earthquake)* secousse *f*; **s. absorber** amortisseur *m*; **s. tactics** tactique *f* de choc; *Mil* **s. troops** troupes *fpl* de choc; *also Fig* **s. wave** onde *f* de choc (**b**) *(emotional blow)* choc *m*, coup *m*; **I got a real s. when I saw him again** cela m'a vraiment fait un choc de le revoir; **to be in s.** être en état de choc (**c**) *(electric)* décharge *f* (électrique); **s. therapy** *(treatment m par)* électrochocs *mpl*

2 *vt (surprise, startle)* stupéfier; *(scandalize)* choquer; **to s. sb into doing sth** pousser qn à faire qch en lui faisant peur

shocked [ʃɒkt] *adj (startled)* stupéfié(e); *(scandalized)* choqué(e)

shocking [ˈʃɒkɪŋ] *adj* (**a**) *(scandalous)* choquant(e); **s. pink** rose *m* bonbon (**b**) *(very bad)* atroce

shockproof [ˈʃɒkpruːf] *adj (watch)* antichoc *inv*

shoddy [ˈʃɒdɪ] *adj (goods)* de mauvaise qualité; *(workmanship)* mal fait(e); *(conduct)* méprisable

shoe [ʃuː] **1** *n* chaussure *f*; *(horseshoe)* fer *m* (à cheval); *Fig* **I wouldn't like to be in her shoes** je n'aimerais pas être à sa place; *Fig* **put yourself in my shoes** mets-toi à ma place; **s. polish** cirage *m*; *Br* **s. shop,** *Am* **s. store** magasin *m* de chaussures

2 *vt (pt & pp* **shod** [ʃɒd] *or* **shoed)** *(horse)* ferrer

shoebrush [ˈʃuːbrʌʃ] *n* brosse *f* à chaussures

shoehorn [ˈʃuːhɔːn] *n* chausse-pied *m*

shoelace [ˈʃuːleɪs] *n* lacet *m* (de chaussure)

shoemaker [ˈʃuːmeɪkə(r)] *n (manufacturer)* bottier *m*; *(seller)* chausseur *m*

shoeshine [ˈʃuːʃaɪn] *n Am (person)* cireur *m* de chaussures

shoestring [ˈʃuːstrɪŋ] *n* (**a**) *Fam* **on a s.** avec trois fois rien (**b**) *Am (shoelace)* lacet *m* de (chaussure)

shone [ʃɒn] *pt & pp of* **shine**

shoo [ʃuː] *exclam* ouste!

▸ **shoo away, shoo off** *vt sep* chasser

shook [ʃʊk] *pt of* **shake**

shoot [ʃuːt] **1** *vt* (*pt & pp* **shot** [ʃɒt]) (**a**) *(fire) (bullet)* tirer; *(arrow) & Fig (glance)* lancer
(**b**) *to* **s. sb** *(wound)* blesser qn par balle; *(kill)* tuer qn par balle; *(execute)* fusiller qn; **to be shot in the arm** recevoir une balle dans le bras; **to** **s. rabbits/grouse** chasser le lapin/la grouse; *Fig* **to** **s. oneself in the foot** compromettre ses chances
(**c**) *(film, TV programme)* tourner
(**d**) *(pass rapidly)* **to s. the rapids** franchir les rapides; **to s. the lights** *(in car)* brûler *ou* griller le feu rouge
(**e**) **to s. dice/pool** jouer aux dés/au billard
2 *vi* (**a**) *(with gun)* tirer (**at** sur); *(in football)* tirer, shooter
(**b**) *(move rapidly)* **he shot into/out of the house** il se précipita dans/hors de la maison; **the pain shot up her left side** elle ressentit soudain une vive douleur au côté gauche
3 *n* (**a**) *(of plant)* pousse *f*
(**b**) *(hunting party)* chasse *f*
▸ **shoot down** *vt sep (person)* descendre; *(plane)* abattre
▸ **shoot off** *vi (leave quickly)* filer
▸ **shoot out** *vi (emerge quickly)* jaillir
▸ **shoot up** *vi* (**a**) *(of plant)* pousser vite; *(of child)* monter en graine; *(of buildings)* pousser comme des champignons (**b**) *(of rocket)* s'élever; *(of prices)* monter *ou* grimper en flèche (**c**) *Fam (with drugs)* se shooter

shooting ['ʃuːtɪŋ] **1** *n* (**a**) *(gunfire)* coups *mpl* de feu; *(incident)* fusillade *f*. **s. stick** canne-siège *f* (**b**) *(of film, TV programme)* tournage *m*
2 *adj* **s. star** étoile *f* filante

shoot-out ['ʃuːtaʊt] *n* fusillade *f*

shop [ʃɒp] **1** *n* (**a**) *(for goods)* magasin *m*; **s. assistant** vendeur(euse) *m,f*; **s. window** vitrine *f* (**b**) *Fam* **to do a s.** *(go shopping)* faire ses courses (**c**) *(workshop)* atelier *m*; *Fig* **the s. floor** les ouvriers *mpl* (**d**) *(idioms) Fam* **to talk s.** parler boutique; *Fam Fig* **all over the s.** *(everywhere)* un peu partout; *Fig* **his explanation was all over the s.** son explication ne tenait pas debout; **my hair was all over the s.** j'étais coiffé n'importe comment; **at the interview he was all over the s.** à l'entretien, il a raconté n'importe quoi
2 *vt* (*pt & pp* **shopped**) *Br Fam (betray)* balancer
3 *vi* faire ses courses; **to go shopping** faire des courses; *(for food)* faire ses courses; **to s. around** comparer les prix

shopgirl ['ʃɒpɡɜːl] *n* vendeuse *f*

shopkeeper ['ʃɒpkiːpə(r)] *n* commerçant(e) *m,f*

shoplifter ['ʃɒplɪftə(r)] *n* voleur(euse) *m,f* à l'étalage

shoplifting ['ʃɒplɪftɪŋ] *n* vol *m* à l'étalage

shopper ['ʃɒpə(r)] *n* client(e) *m,f*

shopping ['ʃɒpɪŋ] *n* courses *fpl*; **to do the s.** faire les courses; **to do one's s.** faire ses courses; **s. bag** sac *m* à provisions, cabas *m*; **s. basket** panier *m* (à provisions); *Br* **s. centre**, *Am* **s. mall** centre *m* commercial; **s. list** liste *f* des courses; **s. trolley** chariot *m*

shore [ʃɔː(r)] *n* *(of sea)* rivage *m*; *(of lake)* bord *m*; **on s.** à terre; **to go on s.** *(from ship)* débarquer
▸ **shore up** *vt sep (house, wall)* étayer; *Fig (reputation)* consolider

shoreline ['ʃɔːlaɪn] *n* littoral *m*

shorn [ʃɔːn] *pp of* **shear**

short [ʃɔːt] **1** *adj* (**a**) *(physically)* court(e); *(person)* petit(e); **Bill is s. for William** Bill est le diminutif de William; **the s. answer is "no"** c'est tout simplement "non"; **to have a s. temper** *or* **fuse** être coléreux(euse); **s. story** nouvelle *f*
(**b**) *(in time)* court(e), bref (brève); **in s.** en bref; **to make s. work of sb/sth** expédier qn/qch; **s. and sweet** clair(e) et net (nette)

(**c**) *(abrupt)* brusque, sec (sèche) (**with** avec)
(**d**) *(insufficient, lacking)* insuffisant(e); **to be in s. supply** manquer; **to be s. of sth** être à court *ou* manquer de qch; **I'm 50 cents s.** il me manque 50 cents; **little** *or* **not far s. of** *(almost)* pas loin de; **he's not far s. of forty** il n'est pas loin de la quarantaine; **it was nothing s. of miraculous that she survived** c'est vraiment un miracle qu'elle ait survécu
2 *adv* (**a**) *(suddenly)* **to stop s.** s'arrêter net; **to bring sb up s.** arrêter net qn
(**b**) *(in length, duration)* **to stop s. of doing sth** se retenir tout juste de faire qch; **to cut sb s.** couper la parole à qn, interrompre qn; **to cut sth s.** abréger qch
(**c**) *(without)* **to go s. (of sth)** se priver (de qch)
(**d**) *(insufficiency)* **to be running s. of sth** n'avoir presque plus de qch; **to fall s. of sth** *(target)* ne pas atteindre qch; *(expectations)* ne pas répondre à qch; *Fig* **to sell sb s.** rouler qn; **to be taken** *or* **caught s.** être pris(e) d'un besoin pressant
3 *n Fam* (**a**) *(short film)* court-métrage *m*
(**b**) *(drink)* alcool *m* fort
(**c**) *(short circuit)* court-circuit *m*

shortage ['ʃɔːtɪdʒ] *n* pénurie *f*; **food s.** pénurie de nourriture; **housing s.** crise *f* du logement; **to have no s. of sth** ne pas manquer de qch

shortbread ['ʃɔːtbred], **shortcake** ['ʃɔːtkeɪk] *n* sablés *mpl* au beurre

short-change [ʃɔːt'tʃeɪndʒ] *vt (in shop)* ne pas rendre assez de monnaie à; *Fig (cheat)* escroquer

short-circuit [ʃɔːt'sɜːkɪt] **1** *n* court-circuit *m*
2 *vt also Fig* court-circuiter
3 *vi* se mettre en court-circuit

shortcomings ['ʃɔːtkʌmɪŋz] *npl* défauts *mpl*

shorten ['ʃɔːtən] *vt (skirt, text)* raccourcir; *(visit, task)* abréger

shortfall ['ʃɔːtfɔːl] *n* manque *m*, insuffisance *f*

shorthaired ['ʃɔːtheəd] *adj (cat, dog)* à poil(s) court(s); *(person)* aux cheveux courts

shorthand ['ʃɔːthænd] *n* sténographie *f*, sténo *f*; **s. typist** sténodactylo *mf*

short-haul ['ʃɔːthɔːl] *adj* moyen-courrier

shortlist ['ʃɔːtlɪst] **1** *n* = liste de candidats après une première sélection
2 *vt* **to be shortlisted (for sth)** être parmi les candidats retenus (à qch)

short-lived [ʃɔːt'lɪvd] *adj* de courte durée

shortly ['ʃɔːtlɪ] *adv* (**a**) *(soon)* bientôt; **s. after(wards)** peu (de temps) après (**b**) *(abruptly)* sèchement

short-range ['ʃɔːtreɪndʒ] *adj (missile)* de courte portée

shorts [ʃɔːts] *npl (short trousers)* short *m*

short-sighted [ʃɔːt'saɪtɪd] *adj* myope; *Fig* peu clairvoyant(e)

short-sleeved [ʃɔːt'sliːvd] *adj* à manches courtes

shortstop ['ʃɔːtstɒp] *n Am Sp* bloqueur *m*

short-tempered [ʃɔːt'tempəd] *adj* coléreux(euse)

short-term ['ʃɔːttɜːm] *adj* à court terme

shot [ʃɒt] **1** *n* (**a**) *(act of firing, sound)* coup *m* (de feu); **to fire a s.** tirer; *Fig* **like a s.** sans hésiter; *Fig* **to take a s. in the dark** tenter le coup; *Fig* **to call the shots** faire la loi; **s. put** lancer *m* du poids (**b**) *(marksman)* tireur *m* (**c**) *(in football, rugby)* coup *m* de pied; *(in basketball)* lancer *m*; **good s.!** bien joué! (**d**) *(photograph)* photo *f*; *(of film, TV programme)* prise *f* de vue, plan *m* (**e**) *Fam (injection)* piqûre *f* (**f**) *(attempt)* tentative *f*, essai *m*; **to have a s. at sth/at doing sth** essayer qch/de faire qch (**g**) *(drink)* petit verre *m*
2 *pt & pp of* **shoot**

shotgun ['ʃɒtgʌn] n fusil m de chasse; Fam **s. wedding** mariage m forcé (lorsque la future mariée est enceinte)

should [ʃʊd]

> La forme négative **should not** s'écrit **shouldn't** en forme contractée.

modal aux v (a) (expressing obligation, desirability) **you s.** do it at once vous devriez le faire tout de suite; **you s.** have **come earlier** vous auriez dû venir plus tôt; **she shouldn't have told them** elle n'aurait pas dû leur dire (b) (expressing probability) **the weather s.** improve from now on le temps devrait s'améliorer à partir de maintenant; **she s.** have arrived by this time elle devrait être arrivée à l'heure qu'il est (c) (in exclamations, rhetorical questions) **why s.** you suspect me? pourquoi me soupçonnez-vous?; **who s.** I meet but Britney! et qui a-t-il fallu que je rencontre? Britney!; **he apologized** – **I s.** think so, too! il s'est excusé – j'espère bien! (d) (in subordinate clauses) **he ordered that they s.** be released il a ordonné leur libération; **she insisted that he s.** meet her parents elle a insisté pour qu'il rencontre ses parents (e) (in conditional clauses) **if he s.** come or Formal **s.** he come, let me know s'il vient, fais-le-moi savoir (f) (expressing opinions, preferences) **I s.** like a drink je prendrais bien un verre; **I s.** imagine he was rather angry j'imagine qu'il était plutôt en colère; **I shouldn't be surprised if...** cela ne m'étonnerait pas si...

shoulder ['ʃəʊldə(r)] **1** n (of person, meat) épaule f; to **stand s. to s.** (of two people) se tenir l'un(e) contre l'autre; Fig to **rub shoulders with sb** côtoyer qn; Fig to **be looking over one's s.** être constamment sur ses gardes; Fig to **cry on sb's s.** pleurer sur l'épaule de qn; **s. bag** (sac m) besace f; **s. blade** omoplate f; **s. pad** épaulette f; **s. strap** (of bag) bandoulière f; (of garment) bretelle f

2 vt (a) (push) to **s. one's way through a crowd** se frayer un passage à travers la foule à coups d'épaule; to **s. sb aside** écarter qn d'un coup d'épaule (b) (put on shoulder) mettre sur son épaule; Fig to **s. the responsibility** endosser la responsabilité

shouldn't ['ʃʊdnt] = should not

shout [ʃaʊt] **1** n cri m; **shouts of laughter** des éclats mpl de rire; **give me a s. when you're ready** appelle-moi quand tu seras prêt

2 vt crier; to **s. sth at sb** crier qch à qn

3 vi crier; to **s. at sb** crier après qn; to **s. for help** crier au secours; Fig to **have something to s. about** pouvoir être fier(ère) de qch

▸ **shout down** vt sep to **s. sb down** huer qn

shouting ['ʃaʊtɪŋ] n cris mpl

shove [ʃʌv] **1** n poussée f; to **give sb/sth a s.** pousser qn/qch

2 vt & vi pousser

▸ **shove around** vt sep Fam (bully) chahuter

▸ **shove off** vi Fam (leave) dégager

shovel ['ʃʌvəl] **1** n pelle f

2 vt (pt & pp shovelled) pelleter; Fam to **s. food into one's mouth** enfourner de la nourriture

shovelful ['ʃʌvəlfʊl] n pelletée f

show [ʃəʊ] **1** n (a) (exhibition) exposition f; to **be on s.** être exposé(e); to **put sth on s.** exposer qch; **s. house** maison f témoin; **s. jumper** cavalier(ère) m,f (spécialisée) dans le jumping); **s. jumping** jumping m; Pej **s. trial** procès m à grand spectacle

(b) (concert, play) spectacle m; (on TV, radio) émission f; Fig to **run the s.** commander; **s. business** show-business m, monde m du spectacle; **s. girl** girl f; Fam to **be a s.**

stopper être le clou du spectacle

(c) (act of showing) démonstration f, manifestation f; **s. of hands** vote m à main levée; **it's all s.** tout ça, c'est de la comédie; to **do sth for s.** faire qch pour épater la galerie; Fam **good s.!** (well done) bravo!

2 vt (pp shown [ʃəʊn]) (a) (display) montrer; (picture) exposer; (courage, talent) faire preuve de; to **s. sb sth**, to **s. sth to sb** montrer qch à qn; Fig to **s. one's cards** or one's **hand** abattre ses cartes; **they had nothing to s. for all that work** ils avaient fait tout ce travail pour rien; **he won't s. his face round here again** on ne le reverra pas de sitôt; to **s. oneself** se montrer; to **s. a profit/a loss** enregistrer un bénéfice/une perte; **you're showing your age** ça ne te rajeunit pas!; to **s. oneself to be...** se révéler...

(b) (indicate) montrer, indiquer

(c) (prove, demonstrate) démontrer, prouver; **it goes to s. that...** cela montre bien que...

(d) (teach) montrer; to **s. sb how to do sth** montrer à qn comment faire qch

(e) (film) montrer; (TV programme) diffuser

(f) (escort, lead) to **s. sb the way** montrer le chemin à qn; to **s. sb to his/her room** conduire qn à sa chambre; to **s. sb round the town** faire visiter la ville à qn

3 vi (a) (be visible) se voir

(b) (of film) passer

show in vt sep (escort in) faire entrer

▸ **show off 1** vt sep exhiber

2 vi frimer

▸ **show out** vt sep (escort out) reconduire, raccompagner

▸ **show up 1** vt sep (a) (reveal) révéler (b) (embarrass) faire honte à

2 vi (a) (stand out) ressortir, se voir (b) Fam (arrive) se pointer

showbiz ['ʃəʊbɪz] n Fam show-biz m, monde m du spectacle

showcase ['ʃəʊkeɪs] n vitrine f

showdown ['ʃəʊdaʊn] n confrontation f

shower ['ʃaʊə(r)] **1** n (a) (of rain) averse f; (of stones, insults) pluie f (b) (for washing) douche f; to **have** or **take a s.** prendre une douche; **s. cap** bonnet m de douche; **s. curtain** rideau m de douche; **s. gel** gel m douche; **s. head** pomme f de douche (c) Br Fam (group) **what a s.!** quelle bande de crétins!

2 vt to **s. sb with sth**, to **s. sth on sb** couvrir qn de qch

3 vi (take a shower) se doucher

showery ['ʃaʊərɪ] adj pluvieux(euse)

showing ['ʃəʊɪŋ] n (exhibition) exposition f; (of film) séance f

showman ['ʃəʊmən] n (at circus) forain m; Fig cabotin m

showmanship ['ʃəʊmənʃɪp] n sens m du spectacle

shown [ʃəʊn] pp of **show**

show-off ['ʃəʊɒf] n Fam frimeur(euse) m,f

showpiece ['ʃəʊpiːs] n joyau m

showroom ['ʃəʊruːm] n magasin m

showy ['ʃəʊɪ] adj voyant(e)

shrank [ʃræŋk] pt of **shrink**

shrapnel ['ʃræpnəl] n éclats mpl d'obus

shred [ʃred] **1** n lambeau m; **in shreds** en lambeaux; to **tear sth to shreds** mettre qch en lambeaux; Fig (criticize) mettre en pièces; Fig **there isn't a s. of evidence** il n'y a pas l'ombre d'une preuve

2 vt (pt & pp shredded) (documents) déchiqueter; (food) couper grossièrement

shredder ['ʃredə(r)] n (for paper) déchiqueteuse f

shrew [ʃruː] n (a) (animal) musaraigne f (b) (nagging woman) mégère f

shrewd [ʃruːd] adj (person) perspicace; (decision) judicieux(euse)

shrewdly ['ʃruːdlı] adv judicieusement

shriek [ʃriːk] 1 n cri m strident; **shrieks of laughter** hurlements mpl de rire; **to give a s.** pousser un cri strident 2 vt hurler 3 vi pousser un cri strident; **to s. with laughter** hurler de rire

shrift [ʃrıft] n **to give sb short s.** envoyer qn promener

shrill [ʃrıl] adj strident(e), aigu(uë)

shrimp [ʃrımp] n crevette f

shrine [ʃraın] n (tomb) tombeau m; (place) lieu m de pèlerinage; Fig mausolée m

shrink [ʃrıŋk] 1 vt (pt shrank [ʃræŋk], pp shrunk [ʃrʌŋk]) faire rétrécir 2 vi (a) (of material) rétrécir; (of income, budget) diminuer, se réduire (b) (move back) **to s. from sth** se dérober devant qch; **to s. from doing sth** répugner à faire qch 3 n Fam (psychiatrist) psy mf

shrinkage ['ʃrıŋkıdʒ] n (of material) rétrécissement m; Fig (in sales, profit) diminution f

shrink-wrapped [ʃrıŋk'ræpt] adj emballé(e) sous film plastique

shrivel ['ʃrıvəl] (pt & pp shrivelled, Am shriveled) 1 vt dessécher 2 vi se dessécher

► **shrivel up** vi se dessécher

shroud [ʃraʊd] 1 n linceul m; Fig (of mystery, darkness) voile m 2 vt Fig **to be shrouded in sth** être enveloppé(e) de qch

Shrove Tuesday ['ʃraʊv'tjuːzdı] n Mardi m gras

shrub [ʃrʌb] n arbuste m

shrug [ʃrʌg] 1 n haussement m d'épaules 2 vt (pt & pp shrugged) **to s. one's shoulders** hausser les épaules 3 vi hausser les épaules

► **shrug off** vt sep ignorer

shrunk [ʃrʌŋk] pp of **shrink**

shrunken ['ʃrʌŋkən] adj rétréci(e)

shudder ['ʃʌdə(r)] 1 n (of person) frisson m 2 vi (of person) frissonner; (of vehicle) vibrer; **I s. to think!** j'ai des frissons quand j'y pense!

shuffle ['ʃʌfəl] 1 n (a) **to walk with a s.** marcher en traînant les pieds (b) **to give the cards a s.** battre les cartes 2 vt (papers) brasser; (cards) battre 3 vi (when walking) traîner les pieds

shun [ʃʌn] (pt & pp shunned) vt fuir, éviter

shunt [ʃʌnt] vt (train, carriages) aiguiller; Fam Fig (people) transbahuter

shush [ʃʊʃ] 1 vt faire taire 2 exclam chut!

shut [ʃʌt] 1 adj fermé(e); Fam **to keep one's mouth s.** se taire 2 vt (pt & pp shut) fermer; **to s. the door on sb** fermer la porte au nez de qn; **to s. one's finger in the door** se coincer le doigt dans la porte; Fam **s. your mouth!** ferme-la! 3 vi (of door) se fermer; (of shop) fermer

► **shut down 1** vt sep fermer; (production) arrêter 2 vi fermer

► **shut in** vt sep (confine) enfermer

► **shut off** vt sep (a) (electricity, water, funds) couper (b) (road, exit) fermer (c) (isolate) isoler (from de)

► **shut out** vt sep (a) (exclude) exclure; (light, view) bloquer (b) (keep outside) empêcher d'entrer; **to s. oneself out** s'enfermer dehors

► **shut up 1** vt sep (a) (confine) enfermer (b) (close) fermer (c) Fam (silence) faire taire 2 vi Fam (be quiet) se taire

shutdown ['ʃʌtdaʊn] n (of factory) fermeture f

shut-eye ['ʃʌtaı] n Fam roupillon m; **to get some s.** roupiller

shutter ['ʃʌtə(r)] n (a) (on window) volet m; (of shop) store m; **to put up the shutters** (of shop) fermer le magasin (b) (in camera) obturateur m

shuttle ['ʃʌtəl] 1 n (a) (in sewing, train, bus, plane) navette f; **s. service** service m de navettes (b) (in badminton) volant m 2 vt véhiculer 3 vi faire la navette (**between** entre)

shuttlecock ['ʃʌtəlkɒk] n volant m

shy [ʃaı] 1 adj timide; **to be s. of sb** être intimidé(e) par qn; **to be s. of doing sth** éviter de faire qch à tout prix 2 vi (pt &pp shied) (of horse) s'effaroucher (**at** devant)

► **shy away** vi **to s. away from sth/from doing sth** éviter qch/de faire qch

shyly ['ʃaılı] adv timidement

Siamese [saıə'miːz] 1 n (pl Siamese) (cat) siamois m 2 adj siamois(e); **S. cat** chat m siamois; **S. twins** (boys) frères mpl siamois; (girls) sœurs fpl siamoises

Siberia [saı'bıərıə] n la Sibérie

Siberian [saı'bıərıən] 1 n Sibérien(enne) m,f 2 adj sibérien(enne)

sibling ['sıblıŋ] n (brother) frère m; (sister) sœur f; **s. rivalry** rivalité f entre frères et sœurs

sic [sık] adv sic

Sicilian [sı'sılıən] 1 n Sicilien(enne) m,f 2 adj sicilien(enne)

Sicily ['sısılı] n la Sicile

sick [sık] 1 adj (a) (ill) malade; **to be s.** (be ill) être malade; (vomit) vomir; **to feel s.** avoir envie de vomir; Fig **it makes me s.!** ça me dégoûte!; Fig **to be worried s.** se faire un sang d'encre; **s. bay** infirmerie f; **s. leave** congé m de maladie; **s. note** (from parents) mot m d'absence; (from doctor) certificat m médical; **s. pay** indemnité f de maladie (b) (fed up) **to be s. of sb/sth** en avoir assez de qn/qch; **to be s. and tired** or **s. to death of sb/sth** en avoir ras le bol de qn/qch (c) (humour, joke) de mauvais goût; (person) malsain(e); **to have a s. mind** avoir l'esprit dérangé 2 n Fam (vomit) vomi m 3 npl **the s.** les malades mpl

► **sick up** vt sep Br Fam (vomit) vomir

sicken ['sıkən] 1 vt (make ill) rendre malade; Fig (disgust) écœurer 2 vi **to be sickening for something** couver quelque chose

sickening ['sıknıŋ] adj écœurant(e)

sickle ['sıkəl] n faucille f

sickly ['sıklı] adj (a) (person, complexion) maladif(ive); (plant) rabougri(e); (colour, light, smile) faible (b) (taste, sentiment) écœurant(e); **s. sweet** douceâtre

sickness ['sıknıs] n (illness) maladie f; (nausea) écœurement m

sickroom ['sıkruːm] n chambre f de malade

side [saıd] 1 n (a) (of person, animal, object) côté m; (of mountain) flanc m, versant m; **by sb's s.** aux côtés de qn; **by s. s.** côte à côte; Fam **to split one's sides (laughing)** se tordre de rire; **s. door/entrance** porte f/entrée f latérale

(b) *(of record)* face *f*; *(paper)* côté *m*
(c) *(adjacent area)* côté *m*; **on this/that s.** **(of)** de ce côté
(de); **on the other s.** **(of)** de l'autre côté (de); **from all sides,**
from every s. de toutes parts; **to move from s. to s.**
osciller; **the left-/right-hand s.** le côté gauche/droit; **to**
lean to one s. se pencher sur le côté; **to stand to one s.** se
tenir à l'écart; **s. dish** plat *m* d'accompagnement; **s. salad**
salade *f*; **s. view** vue *f* latérale
(d) *(aspect)* côté *m*; **to look on the bright/gloomy s.** **(of**
things) voir le bon/mauvais côté (des choses)
(e) *(in game)* camp *m*; *(in dispute)* côté *m*; **to be on sb's s.**
être du côté de qn; **to take sides** prendre parti; **to change**
sides changer de camp; **he had let the s. down** il nous/
les/*etc* avait laissés tomber
(f) *(secondary)* **s. effects** effets *mpl* secondaires; **s. issue**
question *f* d'intérêt secondaire; **s. road** petite route *f*; **s.**
street ruelle *f*
(g) *(idioms)* **on his mother's s.** *(of family)* du côté de sa
mère; **to put sth to one s.** mettre qch de côté; **to take sb**
to one s. prendre qn à part; **to be on the wrong s. of**
forty avoir plus de quarante ans; **to get on the right s. of**
sb se faire bien voir de qn; **to get on the wrong s. of sb**
prendre qn à rebrousse-poil; **it's a bit on the expensive/**
long s. c'est un peu cher/long; **to do sth on the s.** *(as extra*
job) faire qch pour arrondir ses fins de mois; *Fam* **to have a**
bit on the s. *(of man)* avoir une maîtresse; *(of woman)* avoir
un amant
  2 *vi* **to s. with** prendre le parti de; **to s. against** prendre
parti contre
sideboard ['saɪdbɔːd] *n* buffet *m*
sideboards ['saɪdbɔːdz] *npl (facial hair)* pattes *fpl*
sidecar ['saɪdkɑː(r)] *n* side-car *m*
sidekick ['saɪdkɪk] *n Fam* acolyte *m*
sidelight ['saɪdlaɪt] *n* feu *m* de position
sideline ['saɪdlaɪn] *n* **(a)** *(of football, rugby pitch)* ligne *f* de
touche; *Fig* **to sit on the sidelines** rester sur la touche **(b)**
(business, sport) à-côté *m*; **we sell posters as a s.** nous
vendons également des posters
side-saddle ['saɪdsædəl] *adv* **to ride s.** monter en
amazone
sideshow ['saɪdʃəʊ] *n (at fair)* attraction *f*; *Fig*
événement *m* mineur
side-splitting ['saɪdsplɪtɪŋ] *adj Fam* tordant(e)
sidestep ['saɪdstep] *(pt & pp* **sidestepped**) **1** *vt (tackle,*
player) éviter; *Fig (question)* éluder
  2 *vi (in boxing)* esquiver
sideswipe ['saɪdswaɪp] *n* remarque *f* désobligeante
sidetrack ['saɪdtræk] *vt* distraire
sidewalk ['saɪdwɔːk] *n Am* trottoir *m*
sideways ['saɪdweɪz] **1** *adj (look, movement)* de côté
  2 *adv (move, walk)* latéralement; *(turn, fall, lean)* sur le côté
siding ['saɪdɪŋ] *n (on railway)* voie *f* de garage
sidle ['saɪdəl] *vi* **to s. up to sb** se glisser vers qn
siege [siːdʒ] *n* siège *m*; **to lay s. to a town** assiéger une
ville; **under s.** assiégé(e); **to have a s. mentality** se sentir
persécuté(e)
Sierra Leone [sɪˈerəlɪˈəʊn] *n* la Sierra Leone
sieve [sɪv] *n* crible *m*; *(in kitchen)* passoire *f*; *Fam* **to have**
a memory like a s. avoir la tête comme une passoire
  2 *vt* tamiser
sift [sɪft] **1** *vt (flour, sugar)* tamiser
  2 *vi Fig* **to s. through sth** passer qch au crible
sigh [saɪ] **1** *n* soupir *m*
  2 *vi* soupirer; *(of wind)* gémir
sight [saɪt] **1** *n* **(a)** *(faculty)* vue *f*; **to lose one's s.** perdre la
vue

(b) *(act of seeing)* **to catch s. of sb/sth** apercevoir qn/qch;
to lose s. of sb/sth perdre qn/qch de vue; **I hate the s. of**
him je ne peux pas le voir; **I can't stand the s. of blood** je
ne supporte pas la vue du sang; **to shoot on s.** tirer à vue;
at first s. à première vue; **it was love at first s.** ça a été le
coup de foudre; **to know sb by s.** connaître qn de vue; **to**
buy sth s. unseen acheter qch sans l'avoir vu
  (c) *(range of vision)* **to come into s.** apparaître; **in s.** en
vue; **to keep sb in s.** garder un œil sur qn; **out of s.**
caché(e); **to put sth out of s.** cacher qch; **to keep out of s.**
se cacher; *Prov* **out of s., out of mind** loin des yeux, loin
du cœur
  (d) *(of instrument, gun)* viseur *m*; *Fig* **to have sb/sth in**
one's sights avoir qn/qch en vue; *Fig* **to have** *or* **set one's**
sights on sb/sth avoir des vues sur qn/qch
  (e) *(spectacle)* spectacle *m*; **you're/it's a s.** for sore eyes
c'est un plaisir de te voir/de voir ça; *Fam* **to look a s.** ne pas
être beau (belle) à voir; **sights** *(of city)* attractions *fpl*
touristiques
  (f) *Fam (for emphasis)* **a damn s. easier/longer** bien plus
facile/long (longue)
  2 *vt (see)* apercevoir
sighted ['saɪtɪd] **1** *npl* **the s.** les voyants *mpl*
  2 *adj (person)* voyant(e)
sighting ['saɪtɪŋ] *n* several sightings of the fugitive
have been reported on a aperçu le fugitif à plusieurs
reprises; **there have been several UFO sightings in the**
area on a aperçu plusieurs ovnis dans les parages
sightless ['saɪtləs] *adj* aveugle
sight-read ['saɪtriːd] *(pt & pp* **sight-read** ['saɪtred]) *vt & vi*
déchiffrer
sightseeing ['saɪtsiːɪŋ] *n* tourisme *m*; **to go s.** faire du
tourisme
sightseer ['saɪtsiːə(r)] *n* touriste *mf*
sign [saɪn] **1** *n* **(a)** *(gesture, symbol, indication)* signe *m*; **to**
make a s. to sb faire un signe à qn; **it's a sure s. that...** on
peut être sûr que...; **a s. of the times** un signe des temps;
there's no s. of an improvement il n'y a rien qui annonce
une quelconque amélioration; **there's no s. of it/him** je ne
le vois nulle part; **she gave no s. of having heard** elle n'a
pas semblé avoir entendu; **all the signs are that...** tout
laisse à penser que...; **the equipment showed signs of**
having been used on voyait que l'équipement avait déjà
été utilisé; **s. language** langage *m* des sourds-muets **(b)**
(notice) panneau *m*; *(of pub, shop)* enseigne *f*; *(on road)*
follow the signs for Albany suivre la direction d'Albany
  2 *vt* **(a)** *(write signature on)* signer **(b)** *(in sign language)* dire
en langage des sourds-muets **(c)** *(in sport)* engager
  3 *vi* **(a)** *(write signature)* signer **(b)** *(in sport)* signer (**for**
avec)
▸ **sign away** *vt sep (rights)* renoncer à
▸ **sign for** *vt insep (delivery, parcel)* signer un reçu pour
▸ **sign in** *vi (in factory)* pointer; *(in hotel)* signer le registre
en arrivant
▸ **sign off** *vi* **(a)** *(of radio, TV presenter)* terminer l'émission
(b) *(close letter)* finir sa lettre
▸ **sign on** *vi Fam (for unemployment benefit)* *(initially)*
s'inscrire au chômage; *(regularly)* pointer
▸ **sign out** *1 vt sep* **to s. sth out** *(book, equipment)* signer
un registre pour emprunter qch
  2 *vi (from hotel)* signer le registre à son départ
▸ **sign up** *vi* **(a)** *(register)* s'inscrire (**for** à) **(b)** *(of soldier)*
s'engager
signal ['sɪgnəl] **1** *n* signal *m*; *Fig* **to send the wrong**
signals ne pas être clair(e); **s. box** poste *m* d'aiguillage; **s.**
flare fusée *f* éclairante; **s. rocket** fusée *f* de signalisation

2 vt (pt & pp **signalled**, Am **signaled**) (**a**) (make gesture to) faire signe à; **to s. sb to do sth** faire signe à qn de faire qch (**b**) (be sign of) être le signe de **3** vi (**a**) (make gesture) faire signe (**to** à) (**b**) (in car) clignoter

signalman ['sɪgnəlmən] (pl **signalmen**) n aiguilleur m

signatory ['sɪgnətərɪ] (pl **signatories**) n signataire mf

signature ['sɪgnətʃə(r)] n signature f; **s. tune** (of radio, TV programme) indicatif m

signboard ['saɪnbɔːd] n enseigne f

signet ring ['sɪgnɪt'rɪŋ] n chevalière f

significance [sɪg'nɪfɪkəns] n (**a**) (importance) importance f; **of great s.** d'une grande importance; **of no s.** sans importance (**b**) (meaning) signification f

significant [sɪg'nɪfɪkənt] adj (important) important(e), considérable; (meaningful) significatif(ive); **s. other** ami(e) m,f

significantly [sɪg'nɪfɪkəntlɪ] adv (**a**) (appreciably) nettement; **to vary/change s.** varier/changer considérablement (**b**) (meaningfully) d'une manière significative; **s., no one mentioned it** fait révélateur, personne n'en a parlé

signify ['sɪgnɪfaɪ] (pt & pp **signified**) vt signifier

signpost ['saɪnpəʊst] **1** n poteau m indicateur; Fig indice m
2 vt signaliser

Sikh [siːk] n & adj sikh mf

silage ['saɪlɪdʒ] n ensilage m

silence ['saɪləns] **1** n silence m; **to listen/watch in s.** écouter/regarder en silence; Prov **s. is golden** le silence est d'or
2 vt faire taire

silencer ['saɪlənsə(r)] n (on car, gun) silencieux m

silent ['saɪlənt] adj (person, place) silencieux(euse); (letter) muet(ette); **to fall s.** se taire; **to remain** or **keep s.** garder le silence; **s. film** or **movie** film m muet; **s. majority** majorité f silencieuse; **s. protest** manifestation f silencieuse

silently ['saɪləntlɪ] adv silencieusement

silhouette [sɪluːˈet] **1** n silhouette f
2 vt **she was silhouetted against the light** sa silhouette se détachait à contre-jour

silica ['sɪlɪkə] n silice f

silicon ['sɪlɪkən] n silicium m; **s. chip** puce f électronique

silk [sɪlk] n soie f; **s. screen printing** sérigraphie f

silkworm ['sɪlkwɜːm] n ver m à soie

silky ['sɪlkɪ] adj soyeux(euse); (voice) suave

sill [sɪl] n (of window) rebord m

silliness ['sɪlɪnɪs] n stupidité f

silly ['sɪlɪ] **1** adj idiot(e), stupide; **the s. thing is that...** ce qui est idiot, c'est que...; **to look s.** avoir l'air ridicule; **to say/do something s.** dire/faire une bêtise; **to laugh/worry oneself s.** mourir de rire/d'inquiétude; **to knock sb s.** assommer qn
2 n Fam bêta(asse) m,f

silo ['saɪləʊ] (pl **silos**) n silo m

silt [sɪlt] n vase f
▸ **silt up** vi s'envaser

silver ['sɪlvə(r)] **1** n (**a**) (metal) argent m; Prov **every cloud has a s. lining** à quelque chose malheur est bon; **s. haired** aux cheveux argentés; **s. (medal)** médaille f d'argent; **s. paper** papier m d'argent; **s. plate** (coating) plaqué m argent; (articles) argenterie f; **the s. screen** le grand écran; **s. wedding** noces fpl d'argent (**b**) Br (coins) pièces fpl d'argent (**c**) (silverware) argenterie f
2 adj (**a**) (made of silver) en argent (**b**) Br **s.(-coloured)**, Am **s.(-colored)** argenté(e)

silver-plated [sɪlvəˈpleɪtɪd] adj plaqué(e) argent

silversmith ['sɪlvəsmɪθ] n orfèvre mf

silverware ['sɪlvəweə(r)] n argenterie f

silverwork ['sɪlvəwɜːk] n orfèvrerie f

silvery ['sɪlvərɪ] adj (colour) argenté(e); (sound) argentin(e)

simian ['sɪmɪən] adj simien(enne)

similar ['sɪmɪlə(r)] adj semblable, similaire (**to** à); **s. in appearance/size** d'apparence/de taille semblable; **they are very s.** ils se ressemblent beaucoup

similarity [sɪmɪˈlærɪtɪ] (pl **similarities**) n ressemblance f

similarly ['sɪmɪləlɪ] adv de la même façon

simile ['sɪmɪlɪ] n comparaison f

simmer ['sɪmə(r)] **1** n at a s. à feu doux
2 vt mijoter
3 vi mijoter; Fig (of revolt, discontent) couver; **to s. with rage** bouillonner de rage
▸ **simmer down** vi Fam se calmer

simper ['sɪmpə(r)] vi minauder

simple ['sɪmpəl] adj (**a**) (easy) simple; **in s. terms** dit simplement; **the s. truth** la vérité pure et simple (**b**) (unintelligent) simplet(ette)

simple-minded [sɪmpəl'maɪndɪd] adj (person) d'esprit; (ideas, belief) naïf(ive)

simpleton ['sɪmpəltən] n simple mf d'esprit

simplicity [sɪm'plɪsɪtɪ] n simplicité f

simplification [sɪmplɪfɪˈkeɪʃən] n simplification f

simplify ['sɪmplɪfaɪ] (pt & pp **simplified**) vt simplifier

simplistic [sɪm'plɪstɪk] adj simpliste

simply ['sɪmplɪ] adv (**a**) (in simple manner) simplement (**b**) (absolutely) absolument (**c**) (just) simplement; **it's s. a question of time** c'est une simple question de temps; **you s. have to ask** vous n'avez qu'à demander

simulate ['sɪmjʊleɪt] vt simuler

simulated ['sɪmjʊleɪtɪd] adj (leather, marble) faux (fausse); (surprise, anger) simulé(e)

simulation [sɪmjʊ'leɪʃən] n simulation f

simultaneous [sɪməl'teɪnɪəs, Am saɪməl'teɪnɪəs] adj simultané(e); **s. broadcast** retransmission f simultanée; **s. translation** traduction f simultanée

simultaneously [sɪməl'teɪnɪəslɪ, Am saɪməl'teɪnɪəslɪ] adv simultanément

sin [sɪn] **1** n péché m; Old-fashioned or Hum **to be living in s.** (of unmarried couple) vivre dans le péché; Fam **it would be a s. to...** ce serait un crime de...
2 vi (pt & pp **sinned**) pécher

since [sɪns] **1** adv depuis; **long s.** depuis longtemps
2 prep depuis; **s. June/2002** depuis le mois de juin/2002; **s. then** depuis
3 conj (**a**) (in time) depuis que; **it's a long time. I saw her** cela fait longtemps que je ne l'ai pas vue (**b**) (because) puisque

sincere [sɪn'sɪə(r)] adj sincère

sincerely [sɪn'sɪəlɪ] adv sincèrement; Br **Yours s.**, Am **sincerely (yours)** (ending letter) Veuillez agréer, Monsieur/Madame, l'expression de mes salutations distinguées

sincerity [sɪn'serɪtɪ] n sincérité f; **in all s.** en toute sincérité

sinecure ['saɪnɪkjʊə(r)] n sinécure f

sinew ['sɪnjuː] n tendon m

sinewy ['sɪnjuːɪ] adj musclé(e)

sinful ['sɪnfʊl] adj (act, life) coupable; (waste) scandaleux(euse); **s. person** pécheur(eresse) m,f

sing [sɪŋ] (pt **sang** [sæŋ], pp **sung** [sʌŋ]) **1** vt (song) chanter **2** vi (of person, bird, kettle) chanter ▸ **sing out** vi (sing loudly) chanter fort

Singapore [sɪŋə'pɔ:(r)] n Singapour

Singaporean [sɪŋə'pɔ:rɪən] **1** n Singapourien(enne) m,f **2** adj singapourien(enne)

singe [sɪndʒ] vt roussir

singer ['sɪŋə(r)] n chanteur(euse) m,f; **s. songwriter** auteur-compositeur-interprète m

singing ['sɪŋɪŋ] n chant m; **his s. is awful** il chante atrocement; **s. lessons** cours mpl de chant; **to have a fine s. voice** chanter admirablement

single ['sɪŋɡəl] **1** adj (**a**) (just one) seul(e); **every s. day** tous les jours; **not a s. one** pas un(e); **don't say a s. word** ne dis pas un mot; **s. cream** ≃ crème f fraîche liquide; Fin **s. currency** monnaie f unique; Econ **s. European market** marché m unique européen (**b**) (not double) **in s. figures** inférieur à dix; **in s. file** en file indienne; **s. bed** lit m à une place; **s. room** chambre f pour une personne (**c**) (not married) célibataire; **s. mother** mere f célibataire; **s. parent** parent m isolé; **s. parent family** famille f monoparentale

2 n (**a**) (record) single m (**b**) (ticket) aller m simple (**c**) (hotel room) chambre f pour une personne (**d**) **singles** (in tennis) simple m

▸ **single out** vt sep distinguer; **she was singled out for praise** on n'a choisi de faire des compliments qu'à elle

single-breasted ['sɪŋɡəl'brestɪd] adj (jacket, suit) droit(e)

single-decker ['sɪŋɡəl'dekə(r)] n autobus m sans impériale

single-handedly ['sɪŋɡəl'hændɪdlɪ] adv tout(e) seul(e)

single-minded ['sɪŋɡəl'maɪndɪd] adj (person) résolu(e); (determination, conviction) farouche

single-sex school ['sɪŋɡəl'seks'sku:l] n école f non mixte

singlet ['sɪŋɡlɪt] n maillot m de corps

single-track railway ['sɪŋɡəl'træk'reɪlweɪ] n chemin m de fer à une seule voie

singsong ['sɪŋsɒŋ] **1** n (**a**) (voice, tone) voix f chantante (**b**) Fam (singing session) **to have a s.** chanter en chœur **2** adj (voice, tone) chantant(e)

singular ['sɪŋɡjʊlə(r)] **1** n Gram singulier m; **in the s.** au singulier **2** adj (**a**) Gram singulier(ère) (**b**) (remarkable) remarquable

singularly ['sɪŋɡjʊləlɪ] adv remarquablement

Sinhalese [sɪnə'li:z] **1** n (pl **Sinhalese**) (**a**) (person) Cinghalais(e) m,f (**b**) (language) cinghalais m **2** adj cinghalais(e)

sinister ['sɪnɪstə(r)] adj sinistre

sink[1] [sɪŋk] n (in kitchen) évier m; (in bathroom) lavabo m

sink[2] (pt **sank** [sæŋk], pp **sunk** [sʌŋk]) **1** vt (**a**) (ship) couler; **to be sunk in thought** être perdu(e) dans ses pensées; Fam Fig **to be sunk** être fichu(e) (**b**) (well) creuser; **to s. one's teeth into sth** mordre à pleines dents dans qch; **to s. money into sth** investir des capitaux dans qch **2** vi (in water, mud) couler; **her heart sank** son cœur s'est serré; **his spirits sank** il a perdu tout son courage; **to s. into sb's memory** (of information) se graver dans la mémoire de qn; **to s. into oblivion** tomber dans l'oubli; **to s. into a deep sleep** sombrer dans un profond sommeil; **to s. into an armchair** s'affaler dans un fauteuil; **to s. to the ground** s'effondrer par terre; **to s. in sb's estimation** baisser dans l'estime de qn; **how could you s. so low?** comment peux-tu tomber aussi bas?

▸ **sink in** vi (of liquid) pénétrer; (of information) être

assimilé(e); Fig **it hasn't sunk in yet** je n'ai/il n'a/etc pas encore digéré la nouvelle

sinking ['sɪŋkɪŋ] **1** n (**a**) (of ship) naufrage m (**b**) Fin **s. fund** fonds m d'amortissement **2** adj (feeling) d'angoisse; **with a s. heart** avec un serrement de cœur

sinner ['sɪnə(r)] n pécheur(eresse) m,f

sinuous ['sɪnjʊəs] adj (river, curves) sinueux(euse); (snake, dancer) qui ondule; (movement) ondulant(e)

sinus ['saɪnəs] n sinus m

sinusitis [saɪnə'saɪtɪs] n sinusite f

sip [sɪp] **1** n petite gorgée f; **to take a s. (of sth)** boire une petite gorgée (de qch) **2** vt (pt & pp **sipped**) siroter **3** vi **to s. at sth** siroter qch

siphon ['saɪfən] **1** n siphon m **2** vt siphonner ▸ **siphon off** vt sep (liquid) siphonner; Fig (money, supplies) détourner

sir [sɜ:(r)] n (**a**) (form of address) monsieur m; **Dear S./Sirs** (in letter) Monsieur/Messieurs (**b**) (title) **S. Clyde** sir Clyde (title de noblesse masculin)

sire ['saɪə(r)] **1** n (**a**) (father of animal) père m (**b**) Old-fashioned (address to sovereign) sire m **2** vt engendrer

siren ['saɪərən] n sirène f

sirloin ['sɜ:lɔɪn] n **s.** (steak) steak m d'aloyau

sissy ['sɪsɪ] n Fam (weak male) poule f mouillée; (effeminate male) garçon m efféminé

sister ['sɪstə(r)] n (**a**) (sibling, nun) sœur f; **s. company** société f sœur; **s. ship** sister-ship m (**b**) (nurse) infirmière-chef f

sisterhood ['sɪstəhʊd] n (**a**) (community of nuns) communauté f religieuse (**b**) (solidarity) solidarité f féminine

sister-in-law ['sɪstərɪnlɔ:] (pl **sisters-in-law**) n belle-sœur f

sisterly ['sɪstəlɪ] adj fraternel(elle)

sit [sɪt] (pt & pp **sat** [sæt]) **1** vt (**a**) **to s. a child on one's knee** asseoir un enfant sur ses genoux (**b**) Br (exam) passer **2** vi (**a**) (of person) s'asseoir; **to be sitting** être assis(e); **to be sitting reading** être assis en train de lire; **s.!** (to dog) assis!; Fam **to s. tight** (not move) ne pas bouger de sa place; (not take action) ne rien faire (**b**) (of assembly, court) siéger; **to s. on a jury** faire partie d'un jury (**c**) (of object) **to be sitting on the radiator/outside** être sur le radiateur/dehors

▸ **sit about, sit around** vi rester assis(e) à ne rien faire

▸ **sit back** vi (**a**) (lean back) **to s. back in one's chair** s'installer confortablement sur sa chaise (**b**) Fam (relax) se détendre; (not intervene) ne rien faire

▸ **sit down 1** vt sep asseoir; Fam **s. yourself down!** assieds-toi donc! **2** vi s'asseoir; **to be sitting down** être assis(e)

▸ **sit in** vi (at meeting) assister (**on** à)

▸ **sit on** vt insep Fam (**a**) (not deal with) laisser traîner (**b**) (repress) remballer

▸ **sit out** vt sep (not participate in) ne pas participer à **2** vi (in garden) s'asseoir dehors

▸ **sit through** vt insep rester jusqu'au bout de

▸ **sit up** vi (**a**) (straighten one's back) se redresser; (from lying position) s'asseoir (**b**) Fig **to make sb s. up (and take notice)** secouer qn (**b**) (not go to bed) veiller

sitar ['sɪtɑ:(r)] n sitar m

sitcom ['sɪtkɒm] n sitcom m

site [saɪt] **1** n (**a**) (of building) emplacement m;

(archaeological) site *m* **(b) (building) s.** chantier *m* (de construction)
2 *vt* situer

sit-in ['sɪtɪn] *n* occupation *f* des locaux

sitting ['sɪtɪŋ] **1** *n (of committee, for portrait)* séance *f*; *(for meal)* service *m*; **at one s.** d'un trait; *Br* **s. room** *(in house)* salon *m*
2 *adj* **(a)** *(seated)* assis(e); *Fam Fig* **s. duck** *or* **target** cible *f* facile **(b)** *(current) Pol* **s. member** député *m* en exercice; **s. tenant** locataire *mf* dans les lieux

situate ['sɪtjʊeɪt] *vt* situer

situated ['sɪtjʊeɪtɪd] *adj* situé(e)

situation [sɪtjʊ'eɪʃən] *n* **(a)** *(circumstances)* situation *f*; **s. comedy** *(on TV)* sitcom *m* **(b)** *(job)* **situations vacant/wanted** *(in advertisements)* offres *fpl*/demandes *fpl* d'emploi **(c)** *(location)* emplacement *m*

sit-up ['sɪtʌp] *n* **to do sit-ups** faire des abdominaux

six [sɪks] **1** *n* six *m inv*; *Fam* **it's s. of one and half a dozen of the other** c'est kif-kif; **at sixes and sevens** sens dessus dessous; *Fam* **to knock sb for s.** étendre qn
2 *adj* six; *see also* **eight**

six-figure ['sɪks'fɪgə(r)] *adj* **a s. sum** une somme à six chiffres

six-shooter ['sɪksʃuːtə(r)] *n* six-coups *m inv*

sixteen [sɪks'tiːn] **1** *n* seize *m inv*
2 *adj* seize; *see also* **eight**

sixteenth [sɪks'tiːnθ] **1** *n* **(a)** *(fraction)* seizième *m* **(b)** *(in series)* seizième *mf* **(c)** *(of month)* seize *m inv*
2 *adj* seizième; *see also* **eighth**

sixth [sɪksθ] **1** *n* **(a)** *(fraction)* sixième *m* **(b)** *(in series)* sixième *mf* **(c)** *(of month)* six *m inv*
2 *adj* sixième; *Br Sch* **the s. form** ≃ les classes *fpl* de première et de terminale; *Br Sch* **s. former** ≃ élève *mf* de première ou de terminale; **s. sense** sixième sens *m*; *see also* **eighth**

sixtieth ['sɪkstɪɪθ] **1** *n* **(a)** *(fraction)* soixantième *m* **(b)** *(in series)* soixantième *mf*
2 *adj* soixantième

sixty ['sɪkstɪ] **1** *n* soixante *m inv*
2 *adj* soixante; *see also* **eighty**

size [saɪz] *n (of person, clothes)* taille *f*; *(of shoe)* pointure *f*; *(of place, object)* dimensions *fpl*; *(of country)* superficie *f*; *(of problem, undertaking)* ampleur *f*; *Fam* **that's about the s. of it** c'est à peu près ça; **s. 10 shoes** ≃ des chaussures du 44; **to try sth (on) for s.** essayer qch pour voir si la taille convient
▸ **size up** *vt sep (person)* jauger; *(situation)* évaluer

sizeable ['saɪzəbəl] *adj* non négligeable; *(improvement)* net (nette)

sizzle ['sɪzəl] **1** *n* grésillement *m*
2 *vi* grésiller

skate¹ [skeɪt] *n (fish)* raie *f*

skate² **1** *n* patin *m*; *Fam Fig* **to get one's skates on** se dépêcher
2 *vi (on ice skates)* faire du patin à glace; *(on roller skates)* faire du roller; *Fig* **to s. round sth** tourner autour de qch
▸ **skate over** *vt insep (deal with superficially)* survoler

skateboard ['skeɪtbɔːd] *n* planche *f* à roulettes

skater ['skeɪtə(r)] *n* patineur(euse) *m,f*

skating ['skeɪtɪŋ] *n* patinage *m*; **s. rink** *(for ice skating)* patinoire *f*; *(for roller skating)* piste *f*

skeletal ['skelɪtəl] *adj* squelettique

skeleton ['skelɪtən] *n (of person)* squelette *m*; *(of building)* charpente *f*; *Fig* **to have a s. in the cupboard** *or* **closet**

avoir un secret honteux; **s. staff/crew** personnel *m*/équipage *m* réduit; **s. key** passe-partout *m inv*

sketch [sketʃ] **1** *n* **(a)** *(drawing, description)* croquis *m*; **s. pad** bloc *m* à dessin **(b)** *(on stage, TV)* sketch *m*
2 *vt also Fig* esquisser
▸ **sketch in** *vt sep also Fig* esquisser
▸ **sketch out** *vt sep* ébaucher

sketchbook ['sketʃbʊk] *n* carnet *m* de croquis

sketchily ['sketʃɪlɪ] *adv* vaguement

sketchy ['sketʃɪ] *adj* vague **(about** à propos de)

skew [skjuː] **1** *n* **on the s.** de travers
2 *vt (distort)* fausser

skewer ['skjuːə(r)] **1** *n* brochette *f*
2 *vt* embrocher

ski [skiː] **1** *n* ski *m*; **s. boots** chaussures *fpl* de ski; **s. instructor** moniteur(trice) *m,f* de ski; **s. jump** saut *m* à skis; **s. jumper** sauteur(euse) *m,f* à ski; **s. lift** remontée *f* mécanique; **s. pants** fuseau *m*; **s. resort** station *f* de ski; **s. run** *or* **slope** piste *f* de ski; **s. stick** bâton *m* de ski
2 *vi (pt & pp skied)* skier, faire du ski

skid [skɪd] **1** *n* **(a)** *(of car)* dérapage *m*; **to go into a s.** faire un dérapage **(b)** *(idioms) Fam* **to put the skids under sb/sth** faire accélérer qn/qch; *Fam* **to be on the skids** battre de l'aile; *Am Fam* **to be on s. row** être à la rue
2 *vi (pt & pp skidded)* déraper

skier ['skiːə(r)] *n* skieur(euse) *m,f*

skiing ['skiːɪŋ] *n* ski *m*; **to go s.** aller faire du ski; **s. instructor** moniteur(trice) *m,f* de ski

skilful, *Am* **skillful** ['skɪlfʊl] *adj* habile

skilfully, *Am* **skillfully** ['skɪlfʊlɪ] *adv* habilement

skill [skɪl] *n (ability)* qualités *fpl*; *(technique)* compétence *f*, connaissances *fpl*

skilled [skɪld] *adj (person, work)* qualifié(e); **to be s. in doing sth** être habile à faire qch; **s. worker** ouvrier(ère) *m,f* qualifié(e)

skillful, skillfully *Am* = **skilful, skilfully**

skim [skɪm] *(pt & pp skimmed)* **1** *vt* **(a)** *(milk)* écrémer; *(soup)* écumer **(b)** *(surface)* effleurer; **to s. stones on water** faire des ricochets
2 *vi* **to s. along** *or* **over the ground** voler au ras du sol; **to s. over the water** raser la surface de l'eau;
▸ **skim off** *vt sep (fat, cream)* enlever; *Fig (money)* ponctionner
▸ **skim through** *vt insep (novel, document)* lire en diagonale

skimmed milk ['skɪmd'mɪlk], *Am* **skim milk** ['skɪm'mɪlk] *n* lait *m* écrémé

skimp [skɪmp] **1** *vt* lésiner sur; *(work)* bâcler
2 *vi* **to s. on sth** lésiner sur qch

skimpy ['skɪmpɪ] *adj (meal)* maigre; *(clothes)* étriqué(e)

skin [skɪn] **1** *n* **(a)** *(of person, animal, fruit, on milk, sauce)* peau *f*; **to be all s. and bone** n'avoir que la peau et les os; *Fam* **to jump out of one's s.** sauter au plafond; **by the s. of one's teeth** de justesse; **to save one's (own) s.** sauver sa peau; *Fam* **to get under sb's s.** taper sur les nerfs de qn; *Fam* **it's no s. off my nose** je m'en balance; **s. cancer** cancer *m* de la peau; **s. complaint** problème *m* de peau; **s. cream** crème *f* pour la peau; **s. disease** maladie *f* de peau; **s. diving** plongée *f* sous-marine; *Am Fam* **s. flick** *(porn film)* film *m* porno; *Med* **s. graft** greffe *f* de peau **(b)** *Fam (skinhead)* skin *m*
2 *vt (pt & pp skinned) (animal)* écorcher; *(tomato)* peler; **to s. one's knees** s'écorcher les genoux
▸ **skin up** *vi Br very Fam* rouler un pétard

skincare ['skɪnkeə(r)] *n* soins *mpl* de la peau

skinflint ['skɪnflɪnt] *n Fam* radin(e) *m,f*
skinhead ['skɪnhed] *n* skinhead *mf*
skinny ['skɪnɪ] *adj* maigre
skint [skɪnt] *adj Br Fam* fauché(e)
skintight ['skɪntaɪt] *adj* moulant(e)
skip¹ [skɪp] **1** *n (jump)* saut *m*
2 *vt (pt & pp* skipped) *(meal, page, stage)* sauter
3 *vi (of lambs, children)* gambader; *(with rope)* sauter à la corde
skip² *n (for rubbish)* benne *f*
skipper ['skɪpə(r)] **1** *n (of ship, team)* capitaine *m*
2 *vt Fam* commander
skipping ['skɪpɪŋ] *n* saut *m* à la corde; **s. rope** corde *f* à sauter
skirmish ['skɜːmɪʃ] **1** *n Mil* escarmouche *f*; *Fig* accrochage *m*
2 *vi* s'engager dans une escarmouche
skirt [skɜːt] **1** *n* jupe *f*
2 *vt (village, hill)* contourner; **to s. (a)round a problem** contourner un problème
skirting board ['skɜːtɪŋbɔːd] *n Br* plinthe *f*
skit [skɪt] *n* satire *f*
skittish ['skɪtɪʃ] *adj* espiègle
skittle ['skɪtəl] *n* quille *f*
skive [skaɪv] *vi Br Fam* tirer au flanc
▸ **skive off** *vi Br Fam* s'esquiver
skiver ['skaɪvə(r)] *n Br Fam* tire-au-flanc *m inv*
skivvy ['skɪvɪ] *(pl* skivvies) *n Br Pej* bonne *f* à tout faire
skulduggery [skʌl'dʌgərɪ] *n* magouille *f*
skulk [skʌlk] *vi* rôder
skull [skʌl] *n* crâne *m*; **s. and crossbones** tête *f* de mort
skullcap ['skʌlkæp] *n* calotte *f*
skunk [skʌŋk] *n (animal)* moufette *f*; *Fam Pej (person)* mufle *m*
sky [skaɪ] *n* ciel *m*; *Fam* **the s.'s the limit** tout est possible; *Fam* **to praise sb to the skies** porter qn aux nues; **s. high** *(price, costs)* astronomique
sky-blue [skaɪ'bluː] *adj* bleu ciel *inv*
skydiver ['skaɪdaɪvə(r)] *n* parachutiste *mf* qui pratique la chute libre
skydiving ['skaɪdaɪvɪŋ] *n* parachutisme *m* en chute libre
skylark ['skaɪlɑːk] *n* alouette *f* des champs
skylight ['skaɪlaɪt] *n* lucarne *f* faîtière
skyline ['skaɪlaɪn] *n (horizon)* horizon *m*; *(of city)* silhouette *f*
skyscraper ['skaɪskreɪpə(r)] *n* gratte-ciel *m inv*
slab [slæb] *n (of stone, concrete)* dalle *f*; *(of cake)* tranche *f*; *(of meat)* pavé *m*; *(of chocolate)* plaque *f*; *(in mortuary)* table *f* d'autopsie
slack [slæk] **1** *adj* **(a)** *(not tight)* mou (molle); **trade is s.** le commerce marche mal; **in s. periods** en période creuse **(b)** *(careless)* négligent(e)
2 *n* **to take up the s.** *(in rope)* tendre la corde; *Fig* prendre le relais
3 *vi Fam* se relâcher
▸ **slack off** *vi (of rain)* se calmer; *(of trade, demand)* se ralentir
slacken ['slækən] **1** *vt (pace)* ralentir; *(rope)* détendre
2 *vi (of person, rope)* se relâcher; *(of speed)* se ralentir; *(of storm, wind)* se calmer; *(of energy, enthusiasm)* retomber
▸ **slacken off** *vi (of rain)* se calmer; *(of trade, demand)* se ralentir
slacker ['slækə(r)] *n Fam* flemmard(e) *m,f*

slackness ['slæknɪs] *n* **(a)** *(negligence)* négligence *f*; *(laziness)* fainéantise *f* **(b)** *(of rope)* mou *m* **(c)** *(of business)* stagnation *f*
slacks [slæks] *npl (trousers)* pantalon *m*
slag [slæg] *n* **(a)** *(from coalmine)* scories *fpl*; **s. heap** terril *m* **(b)** *Br very Fam Pej (woman)* salope *f*
▸ **slag off** *(pt & pp* slagged) *vt sep Br very Fam (criticize)* débiner
slain [sleɪn] **1** *npl* **the s.** les morts *mpl*
2 *pp of* **slay**
slake [sleɪk] *vt Lit* **to s. one's thirst** étancher sa soif
slalom ['slɑːləm] *n* slalom *m*
slam [slæm] **1** *vt (pt & pp* slammed) **(a)** *(door)* claquer; *(lid, drawer)* fermer violemment; **to s. the door in sb's face** claquer la porte au nez de qn; **to s. sth down** flanquer qch **(b)** *Fam (criticize)* éreinter
2 *vi (of door)* claquer; **to s. on the brakes** freiner à fond
3 *n (of door)* claquement *m*
slander ['slɑːndə(r)] **1** *n* calomnie *f*
2 *vt* calomnier
slanderous ['slɑːndərəs] *adj* calomnieux(euse)
slang [slæŋ] *n* argot *m*
slant [slɑːnt] **1** *n* **(a)** *(slope)* pente *f* **(b)** *(point of view)* perspective *f*; *(bias)* parti *m* pris; **to put a s. on sth** présenter qch d'une manière partiale
2 *vt* **(a)** *(set at angle)* incliner **(b)** *(bias)* présenter avec parti pris
3 *vi (slope)* être incliné(e)
slanting ['slɑːntɪŋ] *adj (roof)* en pente; *(writing)* penché(e)
slap [slæp] **1** *n (with hand)* claque *f*; *also Fig* **a s. in the face** une gifle; **to get a s. on the wrist** *(reprimand)* se faire taper sur les doigts
2 *adv Fam* **s. (bang) in the middle** en plein milieu
3 *vt (pt & pp* slapped) donner une claque à; **to s. sb's face, to s. sb in the face** gifler qn; **to s. sb on the back** donner une tape dans le dos à qn; *Fig* **to s. sb down** remettre qn à sa place; **to s. some paint on sth** passer un coup de peinture sur qch
slapdash ['slæpdæʃ] *adj* brouillon(onne)
slapstick ['slæpstɪk] *n* **s. (comedy)** comique *m* tarte à la crème
slap-up ['slæpʌp] *adj Br Fam* **s. meal** gueuleton *m*
slash [slæʃ] **1** *n* **(a)** *(cut)* coupure *f*, balafre *f* **(b)** *Typ* barre *f* oblique **(c)** *Br very Fam* **to have/go for a s.** pisser/aller pisser un coup
2 *vt* **(a)** *(cut)* tailler, balafrer; *(reduce)* réduire considérablement; **prices slashed** *(sign)* prix sacrifiés
slat [slæt] *n* latte *f*
slate [sleɪt] *n* **(a)** *(stone)* ardoise *f*; **s. grey** ardoise *m inv*; **s. quarry** ardoisière *f* **(b)** *(idioms) Fam* **put it on the s.** mettez-le-moi sur mon ardoise; **to wipe the s. clean** faire table rase
2 *vt Fam (criticize)* éreinter
slaughter ['slɔːtə(r)] **1** *n (of animals)* abattage *m*; *(of people)* massacre *m*
2 *vt (animals)* abattre; *(people)* massacrer; *Fam (defeat heavily)* massacrer
slaughterhouse ['slɔːtəhaʊs] *n* abattoir *m*
Slav [slɑːv] *n* Slave *mf*
slave [sleɪv] **1** *n* esclave *mf*; *Fam Fig* **s. driver** négrier *m*; **s. labour** travail *m* de forçat; **s. trade** commerce *m* des esclaves
2 *vi* trimer (over sur); **I've been slaving over a hot stove all day** j'ai passé ma journée aux fourneaux
slaver ['slævə(r)] *vi* baver

slavery ['sleɪvərɪ] *n* esclavage *m*

Slavic ['slɑːvɪk] *adj* slave

slavish ['sleɪvɪʃ] *adj* servile

Slavonic [slə'vɒnɪk] *adj* slave

slay [sleɪ] (*pt* **slew** [sluː], *pp* **slain** [sleɪn]) *vt Lit (kill)* tuer

sleaze [sliːz] *n Fam (a) (immorality)* côté *m* scabreux **(b)** *(in politics)* scandales *mpl*

sleazy ['sliːzɪ] *adj Fam* sordide

sledge [sledʒ], *Am* **sled** [sled] **1** *n* luge *f; (for transporting)* traîneau *m*
2 *vi (Am pt & pp* **sledded**) faire de la luge

sledgehammer ['sledʒhæmə(r)] *n* masse *f; Fig* **to use a s. to crack a nut** avoir recours à des moyens démesurés

sleek [sliːk] *adj (hair)* lisse et brillant(e); *(manner)* mielleux(euse)
▸ **sleek down** *vt sep* **to s. down one's hair** se lisser les cheveux

sleep [sliːp] **1** *n* **(a)** *(rest)* sommeil *m*; **to go to s.** s'endormir; **to put sb to s.** *(anaesthetize)* endormir qn; **to put an animal to s.** *(kill)* faire piquer un animal; *Fig* **to send sb to s.** *(bore)* endormir qn; **I won't lose any s. over it** cela ne va pas m'empêcher de dormir; **to walk in one's s.** être somnambule; **to talk in one's s.** parler en dormant; **my hand has gone to s.** je ne sens plus ma main **(b)** *(in eye)* **to have s. in one's eyes** avoir les yeux chassieux
2 *vi (pt & pp* **slept** [slept]) dormir; *Euph* **to s. with sb** coucher avec qn; **I slept through the alarm** je n'ai pas entendu le réveil; **I'll s. on it** la nuit porte conseil; **to s. rough** dormir à la dure
3 *vt* **the apartment sleeps four** on peut dormir à quatre dans l'appartement; **I haven't slept a wink all night** je n'ai pas fermé l'œil de la nuit
▸ **sleep around** *vi Fam* coucher à droite et à gauche
▸ **sleep in** *vi* ne pas se réveiller à l'heure
▸ **sleep off** *vt sep* **to s. off a hangover** cuver son vin
▸ **sleep together** *vi* coucher ensemble

sleeper ['sliːpə(r)] *n* **(a)** *(person)* dormeur(euse) *m,f;* **to be a light/heavy s.** avoir le sommeil léger/lourd **(b)** *Rail (train)* train-couchettes *m; Br (on track)* traverse *f*

sleepily ['sliːpɪlɪ] *adv* d'un air endormi

sleeping ['sliːpɪŋ] **1** *n* **s. arrangements** couchage *m;* **s. bag** sac *m* de couchage; **s. car** *(on train)* wagon-lit *m;* **s. pill** somnifère *m*
2 *adj* endormi(e); *Prov* **let s. dogs lie** ne réveillez pas le chat qui dort; **s. partner** *(in company)* commanditaire *m; Br* **s. policeman** *(in road)* ralentisseur *m*

sleepless ['sliːplɪs] *adj* **to have a s. night** ne pas fermer l'œil de la nuit

sleepwalk ['sliːpwɔːk] *vi* être somnambule

sleepwalker ['sliːpwɔːkə(r)] *n* somnambule *mf*

sleepy ['sliːpɪ] *adj* somnolent(e); **to be** *or* **feel s.** avoir sommeil

sleet [sliːt] **1** *n* neige *f* fondue
2 *vi* **it's sleeting** il tombe de la neige fondue

sleeve [sliːv] *n* **(a)** *(of shirt, jacket)* manche *f; Fig* **he's still got something up his s.** il n'a pas encore dit son dernier mot **(b)** *(of record)* pochette *f*

sleeveless ['sliːvlɪs] *adj* sans manches

sleigh [sleɪ] *n* traîneau *m*

sleight [slaɪt] *n* **s. of hand** tour *m* de passe-passe

slender ['slendə(r)] *adj* **(a)** *(person, figure)* svelte; *(waist)* fin(e) **(b)** *(hope)* mince; *(income)* maigre; *(majority)* faible; **of s. means** qui a peu de moyens

slept [slept] *pt & pp of* **sleep**

sleuth [sluːθ] *n Fam* limier *m*

slew [sluː] *pt of* **slay**

slice [slaɪs] **1** *n (of bread, meat, cake)* tranche *f; (of pizza)* part *f; (of cheese)* lamelle *f; (of salami)* rondelle *f; Fig* **a s. of the profits** une part des bénéfices
2 *vt* **(a)** *(bread, meat, cake)* couper en tranches; *(cheese)* couper en lamelles; *(salami)* couper en rondelles; **to s. sth in two** *or* **in half** couper qch en deux **(b)** *(in sport)* slicer
▸ **slice off** *vt sep* couper
▸ **slice through** *vt insep* trancher
▸ **slice up** *vt sep* couper en tranches

sliced bread ['slaɪst'bred] *n* pain *m* en tranches; *Fam* **it's the best thing since s.** on n'a rien fait de mieux depuis l'invention du fil à couper le beurre

slick [slɪk] **1** *adj* **(a)** *(campaign, event)* bien mené(e) **(b)** *Pej (reply, person, manner)* habile **(c)** *(surface, tyre)* lisse
2 *n (oil)* **s.** marée *f* noire
▸ **slick back** *vt sep* **to s. one's hair back** se lisser les cheveux

slide [slaɪd] **1** *n* **(a)** *(fall) (in prices, popularity)* chute *f; Math* **s. rule** règle *f* à calcul **(b)** *(in playground)* toboggan *m* **(c)** *(for microscope)* lame *f; (photographic)* diapositive *f; Br* **s. projector** projecteur *m* de diapositives **(d)** *Br (for hair)* barrette *f*
2 *vt (pt & pp* **slid** [slɪd]) glisser; **s. the lid off** faites glisser le couvercle
3 *vi* **(a)** *(slip) (of person)* glisser; *(of door, hatch)* coulisser; **the door slid open** la porte coulissante s'est ouverte; *Fig* **to let things s.** laisser les choses se dégrader; **to s. down a rope** glisser le long d'une corde **(b)** *(move quietly)* se glisser

sliding ['slaɪdɪŋ] *adj* coulissant(e); **s. door** porte *f* coulissante; **s. scale** échelle *f* mobile

slight [slaɪt] **1** *adj* **(a)** *(small, unimportant)* léger(ère); **the slightest danger/interest** pas le moindre danger/intérêt; **not in the slightest** pas du tout **(b)** *(person)* menu(e)
2 *n (affront)* affront *m*
3 *vt* blesser

slightly ['slaɪtlɪ] *adv* **(a)** *(to a small degree)* légèrement **(b)** **s. built** menu(e)

slim [slɪm] **1** *adj (person)* mince, svelte; *(book, chance, hope)* mince; *(majority)* faible
2 *vi (pt & pp* **slimmed**) faire un régime
▸ **slim down** *vt sep Fig (budget, company)* réduire
▸ **slim down** *vi (of person)* perdre du poids; *(of company)* réduire ses effectifs

slime [slaɪm] *n (mud)* vase *f; (of snail, slug)* bave *f*

slimmer ['slɪmə(r)] *n* personne *f* qui fait un régime amaigrissant

slimming ['slɪmɪŋ] *n* **s. can be bad for you** les régimes amaigrissants peuvent être dangereux pour la santé; **s. diet** régime *m* amaigrissant; **s. product** produit *m* amaigrissant

slimy ['slaɪmɪ] *adj (frog, snail)* visqueux(euse); *(person)* mielleux(euse)

sling [slɪŋ] **1** *n* **(a)** *(for injured arm)* écharpe *f* **(b)** *(weapon)* fronde *f*
2 *f (pt & pp* **slung** [slʌŋ]) *(throw)* lancer; **to s. sth over one's shoulder** mettre qch sur son épaule; *Br Fam Fig* **s. your hook!** dégage!
▸ **sling out** *vt sep Fam (throw away)* balancer; *(person)* vider

slingshot ['slɪŋʃɒt] *n Am* lance-pierres *m inv*

slink [slɪŋk] *(pt & pp* **slunk** [slʌŋk]) *vi* **to s. off** *or* **away** s'éclipser

slinky ['slɪŋkɪ] *adj (dress)* long (longue) et sexy

slip [slɪp] **1** *n* **(a)** *(fall)* chute *f; (of land)* glissement *m; (in prices, standards)* chute

(b) *(error)* erreur *f*; **a s. of the pen/tongue** un lapsus **(c) to give sb the s.** semer qn **(d)** *(of paper)* bout *m* de papier; *(printed)* bordereau *m* **(e) a s. of a girl** un petit bout de femme; **a s. of a lad** un gamin **(f)** *Br Aut* **s. road** bretelle *f* **(g)** *(garment)* combinaison *f*; **(pillow) s.** taie *f* d'oreiller **2** *vt* *(pt & pp* **slipped)** **(a)** *(escape)* **her name has slipped my mind** son nom m'échappe; **the ship slipped its moorings** le bateau a quitté son mouillage **(b)** *(put)* glisser; **to s. sth into the conversation** glisser qch dans la conversation; **to s. a coat on/off** enfiler/quitter un manteau **(c) to s. a disc** se faire une hernie discale **3** *vi* **(a)** *(slide)* *(of person, foot)* glisser; *(of prices, popularity)* chuter; **to s. from sb's hands** *or* **grasp** glisser des mains de qn; *Fig* **to s. through sb's fingers** glisser entre les doigts de qn; **to let one's guard/concentration s.** relâcher sa vigilance/concentration **(b)** *(move quickly)* **to s. into sth** *(bed, room, shoes)* se glisser dans qch; *(clothes)* enfiler qch; **to s. out of sth** *(clothes)* quitter qch **(c)** *(make mistake)* faire une erreur; **you're slipping!** tu baisses! **(d) to let sth s.** *(words, information)* lâcher qch

▸ **slip away** *vi* *(leave)* s'éclipser

▸ **slip by** *vi* *(of time, years)* passer vite

▸ **slip out** *vi* *(escape)* s'échapper; **to s. out to the shop** faire un saut au magasin

▸ **slip through** *vi* *(of mistake)* échapper à l'attention

▸ **slip up** *vi* *(make mistake)* se planter

slip-on ['slɪpɒn] **1** *n Fam* **slip-ons** chaussures *fpl* sans lacets **2** *adj* *(shoes)* sans lacets

slipper ['slɪpə(r)] *n* pantoufle *f*

slippery ['slɪpərɪ] *adj* glissant(e); *(person)* fuyant(e); *Fig* **to be on a s. slope** être sur une pente savonneuse

slippy ['slɪpɪ] *adj* glissant(e)

slipshod ['slɪpʃɒd] *adj* *(work)* bâclé(e)

slipstream ['slɪpstriːm] *n* sillage *m*

slip-up ['slɪpʌp] *n* bourde *f*

slipway ['slɪpweɪ] *n* *Naut* *(for repairs)* cale *f* de construction; *(for launching)* cale de lancement

slit [slɪt] **1** *n* fente *f* **2** *vt* *(pt & pp* **slit)** fendre; **to s. sth open** ouvrir qch; **to s. sb's throat** couper la gorge à qn

slither ['slɪðə(r)] *vi* glisser

sliver ['slɪvə(r)] *n* *(of ham, cheese)* mince tranche *f*; *(of wood, glass)* éclat *m*

slob [slɒb] *n Fam* *(untidy person)* dégueulasse *mf*; *(lazy person)* flemmard(e) *m,f*

slobber ['slɒbə(r)] *vi* baver

sloe [sləʊ] *n* *(fruit)* prunelle *f*; **s. gin** alcool *m* de prunelles

slog [slɒg] *Fam* **1** *vi* *(pt & pp* **slogged)** *(work hard)* trimer **(at** sur) **2** *n* **it was a bit of a s.** ça a été dur; **it's a long s.** *(walk)* ça fait une trotte

slogan ['sləʊgən] *n* slogan *m*

sloop [sluːp] *n* *(ship)* sloop *m*

slop [slɒp] **1** *n* **(a)** *(pig food)* pâtée *f* **(b)** *Fam (sentimentality)* sensiblerie *f* **2** *vt* *(pt & pp* **slopped)** renverser **3** *vi* se renverser

slope [sləʊp] **1** *n* pente *f*

▸ **slope off** *vi Fam* se tailler

sloping ['sləʊpɪŋ] *adj* *(roof, ground)* en pente; *(handwriting)* penché(e); **s. shoulders** épaules *fpl* tombantes

sloppy ['slɒpɪ] *adj* **(a)** *(careless)* *(person)* sans soin; *(attitude)* négligé(e); *(work)* bâclé(e) **(b)** *Fam (sentimental)* sentimental(e)

slosh [slɒʃ] *vi* *(of liquid)* clapoter; *(spill)* se renverser

sloshed [slɒʃt] *adj Fam (drunk)* bourré(e)

slot [slɒt] **1** *n* *(in box, machine)* fente *f*; *(in schedule, list)* créneau *m*; **s. machine** *(for vending)* distributeur *m* automatique; *(for gambling)* machine *f* à sous **2** *vt* *(pt & pp* **slotted)** *(part)* insérer

▸ **slot in 1** *vt sep* *(into schedule)* caser **2** *vi* *(of part)* rentrer; *(into team)* s'intégrer

sloth [sləʊθ] *n* **(a)** *(laziness)* paresse *f* **(b)** *(animal)* paresseux *m*

slothful ['sləʊθfʊl] *adj* paresseux(euse)

slouch [slaʊtʃ] **1** *n Fam* **he's no s.** il n'est pas empoté **2** *vi* *(on chair)* être avachi(e); **she slouched out of the room** elle est sortie de la pièce en traînant les pieds; **don't s.!** tiens-toi droit!

slough [slʌf] *vt* **to s. its skin** *(of reptile)* muer

Slovak ['sləʊvæk] **1** *n* **(a)** *(person)* Slovaque *mf* **(b)** *(language)* slovaque *m* **2** *adj* slovaque

Slovakia [sləʊ'vækɪə] *n* la Slovaquie

Slovakian [sləʊ'vækɪən] **1** *n* Slovaque *mf* **2** *adj* slovaque

Slovene ['sləʊviːn] **1** *n* **(a)** *(person)* Slovène *mf* **(b)** *(language)* slovène *m* **2** *adj* slovène

Slovenia [sləʊ'viːnɪə] *n* la Slovénie

Slovenian [sləʊ'viːnɪən] **1** *n* Slovène *mf* **2** *adj* slovène

slovenly ['slʌvənlɪ] *adj* *(untidy)* négligé(e); *(careless)* négligent(e)

slow [sləʊ] **1** *adj* *(not fast, stupid)* lent(e); **business is s.** les affaires tournent au ralenti; **my watch is s.** ma montre a du retard, **to be s.** *(to do sth)* être lent à faire qch; **to be s. off the mark** *(in race)* être lent à démarrer; *(to understand)* être lent à la détente; *Culin* **in a s. oven** à four doux; **we're making s. progress** nous avançons lentement; **she's a s. worker** elle travaille lentement; *Aut* **s. lane** voie *f* lente; *Cin & TV* **(in) s. motion** (au) ralenti *m*; **s. train** (train *m*) omnibus *m* **2** *adv* lentement **3** *vi* ralentir

▸ **slow down, slow up** *vt sep & vi* ralentir

slowcoach ['sləʊkəʊtʃ] *n Br Fam* lambin(e) *m,f*

slowly ['sləʊlɪ] *adv* lentement; **s. but surely** lentement mais sûrement

slowness ['sləʊnɪs] *n* lenteur *f*

slowpoke ['sləʊpəʊk] *n Am Fam* lambin(e) *m,f*

slow-witted ['sləʊ'wɪtɪd] *adj* à l'esprit lent

slow-worm ['sləʊwɜːm] *n* orvet *m*

SLR [esel'ɑː(r)] *n Phot* *(abbr* **single-lens reflex)** reflex *m* monoculaire

sludge [slʌdʒ] *n* vase *f*, boue *f*

slug [slʌg] *n* **(a)** *(mollusc)* limace *f* **(b)** *Fam (bullet)* balle *f* **(c)** *Fam (of drink)* goutte *f* **2** *vt* *(pt & pp* **slugged)** *Fam (hit)* cogner

sluggish ['slʌgɪʃ] *adj* *(person)* paresseux(euse); *(business, market)* au ralenti

sluice [sluːs] **1** *n* **(a)** *(channel)* canal *m* **(b)** *(sluicegate)* écluse *f*

2 *vt* **to s.** sth down/out laver qch à grande eau

sluicegate ['slu:sgeɪt] *n* écluse *f*

slum [slʌm] **1** *n (district)* quartier *m* délabré; *(shantytown)* bidonville *m*; *(house)* taudis *m*
2 *vt (pt & pp* **slummed) to s. it** s'encanailler

slumber ['slʌmbə(r)] **1** *n* **(a)** *Lit* sommeil *m* **(b)** *Am* **s. party** = soirée entre fillettes, où les invitées restent dormir chez leur hôte
2 *vi* dormir

slump [slʌmp] **1** *n (in prices, sales)* effondrement *m*; *(economic depression)* crise *f* (économique)
2 *vi (of person, economy, prices)* s'effondrer

slung [slʌŋ] *pt & pp of* **sling**

slunk [slʌŋk] *pt & pp of* **slink**

slur [slɜː(r)] **1** *n* **(a)** *(insult)* insulte *f*; **to cast a s. on sb's reputation** entacher la réputation de qn **(b)** *(in speech)* **there was a s. in her voice** elle avait du mal à articuler
2 *vt (pt & pp* **slurred)** mal articuler

slurp [slɜːp] *vt & vi (drink)* boire bruyamment; *(eat)* manger bruyamment

slush [slʌʃ] *n* **(a)** *(snow)* neige *f* fondue **(b)** *Pol* **s. fund** caisse *f* noire **(c)** *Fam (sentimentality)* sensiblerie *f*

slut [slʌt] *n (promiscuous woman)* salope *f*

sluttish ['slʌtɪʃ] *adj (slovenly)* négligé(e)

sly [slaɪ] **1** *adj* **(a)** *(cunning)* rusé(e) **(b)** *(dishonest)* sournois(e) **(c)** *(mischievous)* espiègle
2 *n* **on the s.** en douce

smack [smæk] **1** *n* **(a)** *(blow)* claque *f*; *(on bottom)* fessée *f*; *(sound)* claquement *m*; **a s. in the face** une gifle **(b)** *Fam (heroin)* héro *f*
2 *adv Fam* **to bump s. into a tree** rentrer en plein dans un arbre
3 *vt (hit)* donner une claque à; *(on bottom)* donner une fessée à; **to s. one's lips** faire claquer ses lèvres
▸ **smack of** *vt insep (suggest)* avoir des relents de

smacker ['smækə(r)] *n Fam* **(a)** *(kiss)* grosse bise *f* **(b) 50 smackers** *(pounds)* 50 livres; *(dollars)* 50 dollars

small [smɔːl] **1** *adj* **(a)** *(not large)* petit(e); **to make sth smaller** rapetisser qch; *Fig* **it made me feel s.** *(inconsequential)* je me suis senti tout petit; **the s. hours** le petit matin; *Journ* **s. ads** petites annonces *fpl*; **s. arms** armes *fpl* portatives; **s. business** petite entreprise *f*; **s. businessman** petit entrepreneur *m*; **s. letters** *(not capitals)* minuscules *fpl*; **s. talk** banalités *fpl* **(b)** *(not important)* peu important(e); **it's s. wonder that... ce** n'est pas très étonnant que...; **in a s. way** à sa façon; *Fam* **to be s. beer** *(of money)* être que dalle; **s. change** petite monnaie *f*; **s. fry** menu fretin *m*
2 *adv (chop)* menu; *(write)* petit; **to think s.** voir petit
3 *n* **(a) the s. of the back** la chute des reins **(b)** *Fam* **smalls** *(underwear)* sous-vêtements *mpl*

smallholder ['smɔːlhəʊldə(r)] *n* petit(e) exploitant(e) *m,f*

smallholding ['smɔːlhəʊldɪŋ] *n* petite exploitation *f*

small-minded [smɔːl'maɪndɪd] *adj* étroit(e) d'esprit

smallness ['smɔːlnɪs] *n* petitesse *f*

smallpox ['smɔːlpɒks] *n* variole *f*

small-scale ['smɔːlskeɪl] *adj (model)* réduit(e); *(research, project)* à petite échelle

small-time ['smɔːltaɪm] *adj Fam (criminal, businessman)* petit(e)

smarmy ['smɑːmɪ] *adj Pej* mielleux(euse)

smart [smɑːt] **1** *adj* **(a)** *(clever, sharp) (person)* futé(e); *(decision, move)* habile; **don't get s. with me** n'essaie pas de faire le malin avec moi; *Fam* **s. aleck** petit malin *m*; **s. bomb** bombe *f* intelligente; **s. card** carte *f* à puce **(b)**

(elegant) (clothes) élégant(e); *(hotel, area)* chic *inv*; **the s. set** le beau monde; **to be a s. dresser** bien s'habiller **(c)** *(quick) (pace, work)* rapide; **look s. (about it)!** et que ça saute! **(d)** *Fam (excellent)* génial(e); *(pretty)* canon *inv*
2 *vi (sting) (of wound, graze)* brûler; *(of eyes)* piquer; *Fig (of person)* être piqué(e) au vif
▸ **smarten up** ['smɑːtən] **1** *vt sep* égayer; **to s. oneself up** se faire beau
2 *vi (improve)* se reprendre

smarty-pants ['smɑːtɪpænts] *(pl* **smarty-pants)** *n Fam* petit(e) malin(igne) *m,f*

smash [smæʃ] **1** *n* **(a)** *(blow)* coup *m*; *(noise)* fracas *m*; *(collision)* collision *f*; *(in tennis)* smash *m*; **s. (hit)** *(record, film)* gros succès *m*
2 *vt* **(a) to s. sth (to pieces)** fracasser qch; **to s. sth open** défoncer qch; **to s. down a door** défoncer une porte **(b)** *(ruin)* anéantir; **to s. a drugs ring** démanteler un réseau de trafiquants de drogue; **she smashed the world record** elle a pulvérisé le record du monde
3 *vi* **(a)** *(strike)* **to s. into sth** s'écraser contre qch; **to s. (into pieces)** éclater (en morceaux)
▸ **smash up** *vt sep (room, car, furniture)* saccager

smash-and-grab raid [smæʃən'græb'reɪd] *n Br* pillage *m* de vitrines

smashed [smæʃt] *adj Fam (drunk)* pété(e)

smashing ['smæʃɪŋ] *adj* **(a)** *(blow)* violent(e) **(b)** *Br Fam (excellent)* génial(e); **we had a s. time!** on s'est éclatés!

smattering ['smætərɪŋ] *n* notions *fpl*

smear [smɪə(r)] **1** *n* **(a)** *(stain)* tache *f*; *Med* **s. test** frottis *m* **(b)** *(slander)* propos *m* diffamatoire; **s. campaign** campagne *f* de diffamation
2 *vt* **(a)** *(stain)* tacher; *(spread)* enduire, barbouiller; *(smudge) (paint)* salir **(b)** *(slander)* calomnier

smell [smel] **1** *n* **(a)** *(sense)* odorat *m* **(b)** *(odour)* odeur *f*; **there's a bad s.** ça sent mauvais; **to have a s. of sth** sentir qch
2 *vt (pt & pp* **smelled** *or* **smelt** [smelt]) *also Fig* sentir; *Fig* **I s. a rat** ça sent l'embrouille
3 *vi* sentir; *(stink)* sentir mauvais; **to s. of sth** sentir qch; **his breath smells** il a une mauvaise haleine

smelly ['smelɪ] *adj* qui sent mauvais

smelt [smelt] **1** *vt (ore)* fondre
2 *pt & pp of* **smell**

smile [smaɪl] **1** *n* sourire *m*; **to give sb a s.** sourire à qn; **she was all smiles** elle était tout sourire; **to take** *or* **wipe the s. off sb's face** passer l'envie de sourire à qn
2 *vi* sourire (**at** à); **fortune smiled on them** la fortune leur sourit; **s.!** *(for photograph)* un petit sourire!

smiling ['smaɪlɪŋ] *adj* souriant(e)

smirk [smɜːk] **1** *n* sourire *m* en coin
2 *vi* sourire en coin

smite [smaɪt] *(pt* **smote** [sməʊt], *pp* **smitten** ['smɪtən]) *vt* **(a)** *Lit (strike)* frapper **(b) smitten with terror** terrorisé(e); **smitten with remorse** envahi(e) par les remords

smith [smɪθ] *n* forgeron *m*

smithereens [smɪðə'riːnz] *npl* **to smash/blow sth to s.** réduire qch en miettes

smithy ['smɪðɪ] *(pl* **smithies)** *n* forge *f*

smitten ['smɪtən] **1** *adj (in love)* très épris(e) (**with** de)
2 *pp of* **smite**

smock [smɒk] *n* blouse *f*

smog [smɒg] *n* smog *m*

smoke [sməʊk] **1** *n* fumée *f*; **to have a s.** fumer une cigarette; *Fig* **to go up in s.** partir en fumée; *Prov* **there's no s. without fire** il n'y a pas de fumée sans feu; **s. bomb** bombe *f* fumigène; **s. detector** détecteur *m* de fumée; **s.**

Fig **s. screen** rideau *m* de fumée; **s. signals** signaux *mpl* de fumée
2 *vt* **(a)** *(cigarette)* fumer; **to s. a pipe** fumer la pipe **(b)** *(meat, fish)* fumer
3 *vi* **(a)** *(of person)* fumer **(b)** *(of chimney, oil)* fumer
▸ **smoke out** *vt sep (insects)* enfumer; *Fig (rebels)* débusquer
smoked [sməʊkt] *adj* fumé(e); **s. glass** verre *m* fumé; **s. salmon** saumon *m* fumé
smokeless ['sməʊklɪs] *adj* **s. fuel** combustible *m* non polluant; **s. zone** = zone où l'usage de combustible polluant n'est pas autorisé
smoker ['sməʊkə(r)] *n* fumeur(euse) *m,f*; **to be a cigarette/pipe s.** fumer des cigarettes/la pipe; **to be a heavy s.** être un grand fumeur; **s.'s cough** toux *f* de fumeur
smoking ['sməʊkɪŋ] *n* **s. can damage your health** fumer *ou* le tabac nuit à la santé; **no s.** *(sign)* défense de fumer; **s. compartment** compartiment *m* fumeurs; **s. jacket** veste *f* d'intérieur; **s. room** salle *f* fumeurs
smoky ['sməʊkɪ] *adj (atmosphere, room)* enfumé(e); *(fire)* qui dégage de la fumée; *(surface)* noirci(e) par la fumée; *(taste)* de fumée
smolder *Am* = **smoulder**
smooch [smuːtʃ] *vi Fam* se bécoter
smooth [smuːð] **1** *adj* **(a)** *(not rough)* lisse; *(sea)* calme; *(sauce)* homogène; *(skin, wine, whisky)* doux (douce); *(style)* coulant(e); *(flight, crossing)* calme; **a s. shave** un rasage de près **(b)** *(person, manner)* onctueux(euse); **he's a s. talker** c'est un beau parleur; **to be a s. operator** savoir y faire **(c)** *(without problems)* sans problèmes; **to get off to a s. start** commencer sans problèmes
2 *vt (feathers, hair)* lisser; *(pillow, sheet, clothing)* défroisser; *(surface)* égaliser; **to s. the way for sb** faciliter les choses à qn; **to s. the way for sth** faciliter qch
▸ **smooth back** *vt sep* **to s. back one's hair** lisser ses cheveux en arrière
▸ **smooth down** *vt sep* lisser
▸ **smooth out** *vt sep (map, sheets)* défroisser, *(crease)* faire disparaître; *Fig (difficulty)* aplanir
▸ **smooth over** *vt sep (difficulties)* aplanir; *(differences)* atténuer; **to s. things over** arranger les choses
smoothly ['smuːðlɪ] *adv* sans problèmes; **to go s.** se passer sans problèmes
smoothness ['smuːðnɪs] *n (of skin, wine, whisky)* douceur *f*; *(of surface)* aspect *m* lisse; *(of flight, crossing)* calme *m*; *(of sauce)* homogénéité *f*
smooth-talking ['smuːð'tɔːkɪŋ] *adj* mielleux(euse)
smote [sməʊt] *pt of* **smite**
smother ['smʌðə(r)] *vt* **(a)** *(person, fire, yawn)* étouffer; **to s. sb with kisses** couvrir qn de baisers **(b)** *(cover)* **to s. sth in sth** recouvrir qch de qch
smoulder, *Am* **smolder** ['sməʊldə(r)] *vi (of fire)* couver; *Fig* **to s. with anger/passion** se consumer de colère/passion
smudge [smʌdʒ] **1** *n* tache *f*
2 *vt (ink, lipstick)* étaler; *(drawing)* maculer
3 *vi (of ink, lipstick)* s'étaler
smug [smʌg] *adj* suffisant(e)
smuggle ['smʌgəl] *vt (arms, drugs)* faire de la contrebande de; **to s. sth in/out** faire entrer/sortir qch en contrebande; **to s. sb in/out** faire entrer/sortir qn clandestinement; **to s. sth through customs** passer qch en fraude à la douane
smuggler ['smʌglə(r)] *n* contrebandier(ère) *m,f*; *(of drugs)* trafiquant(e) *m,f*
smuggling ['smʌglɪŋ] *n* contrebande *f*; *(of drugs)* trafic *m*

smut [smʌt] *n* **(a)** *(soot)* tache *f* de suie **(b)** *(obscenity)* cochonneries *fpl*
smutty ['smʌtɪ] *adj* **(a)** *(dirty)* sale, noirci(e) **(b)** *(obscene)* cochon(onne)
snack [snæk] **1** *n* casse-croûte *m inv*; **to have a s. grignoter** quelque chose; **s. bar** snack-bar *m*
2 *vi* **to s. on** grignoter qch
snag [snæg] **1** *n (problem)* problème *m*
2 *vt (pt & pp snagged) (clothing)* faire un accroc à
snail [sneɪl] *n* escargot *m*; **at a s.'s pace** *(move)* comme un escargot; *(change, learn, progress)* très lentement; *Fam* **s. mail** courrier *m* escargot, = terme humoristique désignant les services postaux par opposition aux messageries électroniques
snake [sneɪk] **1** *n* serpent *m*; *Fig* **s. in the grass** traître(esse) *m,f*; **snakes and ladders** ≃ jeu *m* de l'oie; **s. charmer** charmeur(euse) *m,f* de serpent
2 *vi (of road, river)* serpenter
snakebite ['sneɪkbaɪt] *n* morsure *f* de serpent
snakeskin ['sneɪkskɪn] *n* peau *f* de serpent
snap [snæp] **1** *n* **(a)** *(bite)* coup *m* de dents **(b)** *(sound)* craquement *m*, **a s. of the fingers** un claquement de doigts **(c)** *(of weather)* **a cold s.** une brusque vague de froid **(d)** *Fam (photograph)* photo *f* **(e)** *Br (card game)* = jeu de cartes dont le but est de crier "snap" lorsque l'on pose sur la table une carte similaire à celle qui vient d'être posée; *Fam* **I'm going to Miami – s.!** je vais à Miami – tiens, moi aussi!
2 *adj (judgement, decision)* hâtif(ive); **to call a s. election** procéder à une élection surprise
3 *vt (pt & pp snapped)* **(a)** *(break)* casser net; **to s. sth in two** casser qch en deux **(b)** **to s. one's fingers** faire claquer ses doigts **(c)** *(say sharply)* dire sèchement **(d)** *Fam (take photograph of)* prendre en photo
4 *vi* **(a)** *(break cleanly)* casser net, *(break noisily)* casser avec un bruit sec **(b)** *(bite)* **to s. (at)** essayer de mordre; **to s. shut** *(of jaws, lid)* se refermer avec un bruit sec **(c)** *(speak abruptly)* parler sèchement **(at** à) **(d)** *(idioms)* **to s. out of it** *(of depression, apathy)* se secouer; *(of sulk)* arrêter de faire la tête
▸ **snap off** *vt sep* **(a)** *(break)* casser net **(b)** *Fam* **to s. sb's head off** rembarrer qn
2 *vi* casser net
▸ **snap up** *vt sep* **(a)** *(seize in jaws)* attraper **(b)** *(buy, take quickly)* rafler
snapdragon ['snæpdrægən] *n* gueule-de-loup *f*
snappy ['snæpɪ] *adj Fam (style, prose)* vif (vive); *(slogan)* accrocheur(euse); **to be a s. dresser** s'habiller toujours à la mode; **make it s.!** *(be quick)* au trot!
snapshot ['snæpʃɒt] *n Fam (photograph)* photo *f*
snare [sneə(r)] **1** *n* collet *m*; *Fig* piège *m*; **s. drum** caisse *f* claire
2 *vt* prendre au collet; *Fig* prendre au piège
snarl [snɑːl] **1** *n* grognement *m*
2 *vi* grogner *(at* après)
▸ **snarl up** *vi* être paralysé(e)
snarl-up ['snɑːlʌp] *n (of traffic)* bouchon *m*; *(in system)* paralysie *f*
snatch [snætʃ] **1** *n (of conversation)* bribe *f*; **to sleep in snatches** avoir un sommeil fragmenté; **a s. of music** quelques notes de musique
2 *vt* **(a)** *(grab)* saisir; **to s. something to eat** avaler quelque chose à la hâte; **to s. some sleep** dormir un peu **(b)** *(steal, abduct) (wallet, bag)* arracher; *(person)* enlever
3 *vi* **to s. at sth** essayer de saisir qch
▸ **snatch away** *vt sep* arracher
snazzy ['snæzɪ] *adj Fam* sympa *inv*

sneak [sni:k] **1** n **(a)** Fam (telltale) mouchard(e) m,f **(b)** to get a **s.** preview of sth voir qch en avant-première **2** vt (pt & pp sneaked, Am snuck [snʌk]) to **s.** sth past sb passer qch subrepticement devant qn; to **s.** sb in/out faire entrer/sortir qn subrepticement; to **s.** a glance at sb jeter un coup d'œil furtif à qn **3** vi **(a)** (tell tales) rapporter **(b)** (move furtively) se déplacer furtivement; to **s.** past sb passer furtivement devant qn; to **s.** in/out entrer/sortir furtivement
▸ **sneak away, sneak off** vi s'esquiver

sneaker ['sni:kə(r)] n Am (running shoe) chaussure f de sport

sneaky ['sni:kɪ] adj sournois(e)

sneer [snɪə(r)] **1** n (expression) sourire m méprisant **2** vt **"who do you think you are?,"** he sneered "tu te prends pour qui?", dit-il d'un air méprisant **3** vi ricaner; to **s.** at sb/sth se moquer de qn/qch

sneering ['snɪərɪŋ] **1** n (laughter) ricanement m; (remarks) sarcasmes mpl **2** adj méprisant(e)

sneeze [sni:z] **1** n éternuement m **2** vi éternuer; Fam Fig it's not to be sneezed at il ne faut pas cracher dessus

snicker ['snɪkə(r)] Am **1** n ricanement m **2** vi ricaner

snide [snaɪd] adj méprisant(e)

sniff [snɪf] **1** vt **(a)** (smell) sentir; (detect) flairer **(b)** (inhale) (air) respirer; (cocaine, glue) sniffer **2** vi renifler; (disdainfully) avoir une moue de dédain; Fam it's not to be sniffed at il ne faut pas cracher dessus **3** n to take a **s.** at sth sentir qch; with a **s.** of disgust avec une moue de dégoût
▸ **sniff out** vt sep (of dog) découvrir à l'odeur; Fig (of investigator) découvrir

sniffer dog ['snɪfədɒg] n chien m renifleur

sniffle ['snɪfəl] **1** n (slight cold) petit rhume m; to have the sniffles avoir un petit rhume **2** vi **(a)** (sniff repeatedly) renifler **(b)** (cry quietly) pleurer (doucement)

sniffy ['snɪfɪ] adj Fam (disdainful) dédaigneux(euse); to be **s.** about sth éprouver du dédain pour qch

snifter ['snɪftə(r)] n Fam Old-fashioned (drink) petit verre m

snigger ['snɪgə(r)] **1** n ricanement m étouffé **2** vi ricaner

snip [snɪp] **1** n **(a)** (cut) petite entaille f **(b)** (piece cut off) bout m **(c)** Br Fam (bargain) (bonne) affaire f **2** vt (pt & pp snipped) couper
▸ **snip off** vt sep couper

snipe¹ [snaɪp] (pl snipe) n (bird) bécassine f

snipe² vi (shoot) tirer (d'une position cachée); to **s.** at sb tirer sur qn (d'une position cachée); Fig (criticize) critiquer qn de façon malveillante

sniper ['snaɪpə(r)] n tireur(euse) m,f embusqué(e)

snippet ['snɪpɪt] n (of information, conversation) bribe f; a **s.** of news une nouvelle brève

snitch [snɪtʃ] Fam **1** n **(a)** (informer) mouchard(e) m,f **(b)** (nose) pif m **2** vi moucharder; to **s.** on sb moucharder qn

snivel ['snɪvəl] (pt & pp snivelled, Am sniveled) vi pleurnicher

snivelling, Am **sniveling** ['snɪvəlɪŋ] adj pleurnicheur(euse)

snob [snɒb] n snob mf

snobbery ['snɒbərɪ] n snobisme m

snobbish ['snɒbɪʃ] adj snob inv

snog [snɒg] Br Fam **1** n to have a **s.** se bécoter **2** vi (pt & pp snogged) se bécoter

snooker ['snu:kə(r)] **1** n (game) = billard qui se joue avec vingt-deux billes **2** vt to **s.** (in game) laisser qn dans une position difficile; Fig mettre qn dans l'embarras

snoop [snu:p] Fam **1** n **(a)** (person) fouineur(euse) m,f **(b)** (look) to have a **s.** (around) jeter un coup d'œil **2** vi fouiner, fureter

snooper ['snu:pə(r)] n Fam fouineur(euse) m,f

snooty ['snu:tɪ] adj Fam prétentieux(euse)

snooze [snu:z] Fam **1** n petit somme m; to have a **s.** faire un petit somme **2** vi faire un petit somme

snore [snɔ:(r)] **1** n ronflement m **2** vi ronfler

snoring ['snɔ:rɪŋ] n ronflements mpl

snorkel ['snɔ:kəl] **1** n tuba m **2** vi (pt & pp snorkelled, Am snorkeled) nager sous l'eau avec un tuba

snort [snɔ:t] **1** n (of person) grognement m; (of horse) ébrouement m **2** vt Fam (drugs) sniffer **3** vi (of person) grogner; (of horse) s'ébrouer

snot [snɒt] n Fam morve f

snotty ['snɒtɪ] adj Fam **(a)** (nose) qui coule **(b)** (arrogant) arrogant(e)

snout [snaʊt] n (of pig) groin m; (of other animal) museau m; Fam (of person) pif m

snow [snəʊ] **1** n neige f; **s.** blindness cécité f des neiges; **s.** line limite f des neiges éternelles **2** vi neiger; it's snowing il neige
▸ **snow in** vt sep to be snowed in être bloqué(e) par la neige
▸ **snow under** vt sep to be snowed under (with) (work) être débordé(e) (de); (invitations, offers) être submergé(e) (de)

snowball ['snəʊbɔ:l] **1** n boule f de neige; **s.** fight bataille f de boules de neige; Fam she hasn't a **s.'s** chance (in hell) elle n'a pas la moindre chance **2** vi Fig faire boule de neige

snowboarding ['snəʊbɔ:dɪŋ] n snowboard m; to go **s.** faire du snowboard

snowbound ['snəʊbaʊnd] adj bloqué(e) par la neige

snowcapped ['snəʊkæpt] adj couronné(e) de neige

snowdrift ['snəʊdrɪft] n congère f

snowdrop ['snəʊdrɒp] n (flower) perce-neige m ou f inv

snowfall ['snəʊfɔ:l] n chute f de neige

snowflake ['snəʊfleɪk] n flocon m de neige

snowman ['snəʊmæn] n bonhomme m de neige

snowmobile ['snəʊməʊbi:l] n (enclosed) autoneige f; (open) motoneige f

snowplough, Am **snowplow** ['snəʊplaʊ] n chasse-neige m inv

snowshoe ['snəʊʃu:] n raquette f

snowstorm ['snəʊstɔ:m] n tempête f de neige

snowsuit ['snəʊsu:t] n combinaison f de ski (pour enfants)

Snow White ['snəʊ'waɪt] n **S.** and the Seven Dwarfs Blanche-Neige et les sept nains

snowy ['snəʊɪ] adj (landscape, field) enneigé(e); (weather) neigeux(euse); (day) de neige

SNP [esen'pi:] n Br Pol (abbr Scottish National Party) = parti politique écossais indépendantiste

Snr *(abbr* **Senior)** Jonathan Pye-Finch S. Jonathan Pye-Finch père

snub [snʌb] **1** *n (refusal)* rebuffade *f; (insult)* affront *m* **2** *vt (pt & pp* **snubbed)** snober

snub nose [ˈsnʌbˈnəʊz] *n* nez *m* retroussé

snuck [snʌk] *Am pt & pp of* **sneak**

snuff [snʌf] **1** *n* tabac *m* à priser **2** *vt (candle)* moucher; *Br Fam* **to s. it** *(die)* casser sa pipe ▸ **snuff out** *vt sep (candle)* moucher; *(life, opposition)* mettre fin à

snuffbox [ˈsnʌfbɒks] *n* tabatière *f*

snuffle [ˈsnʌfəl] **1** *n (sniff)* reniflement *m* **2** *vi (sniff)* renifler

snug [snʌg] *adj* **(a)** *(place)* douillet(ette); *(person)* bien au chaud **(b)** *(tight fitting)* bien ajusté(c) ▸ **snuggle up** [ˈsnʌgəl] *vi* **to s.** up to sb se blottir contre qn

snugly [ˈsnʌglɪ] *adv (comfortably)* confortablement; **to fit s.** être bien ajusté(e)

so [səʊ] **1** *adv* **(a)** *(to such an extent)* tellement, si **(that** que); **I was so angry (that) I almost hit him** j'étais tellement en colère que j'ai failli le frapper; **he's not so clever as she is** il n'est pas aussi intelligent qu'elle; **it isn't so very old** il n'est pas si vieux; **I'm not so sure of that** je n'en suis pas si sûr; **so much money/many people** tant *ou* autant d'argent/de gens; **it was difficult, so much so that…** c'était difficile, à tel point que… **(b)** *(for emphasis)* tellement; **I was so disappointed!** j'étais tellement déçu!; **we enjoyed ourselves so much!** nous nous sommes tellement amusés! **(c)** *(expressing agreement)* **you're late – so I am!** tu es en retard – ah oui, tu as raison!; **that's Tony Blair! – so it is!** c'est Tony Blair! – ah oui, tu as raison! **(d)** *(referring to statement already mentioned)* **I hope so** j'espère bien; **I think so** je crois; **I suppose so** je le suppose; **so I believe** c'est ce que je crois; **I told you so!** je vous l'avais bien dit!; **I'm not very organized – so I see!** je ne suis pas très bien organisé – c'est ce que je vois!; **so be it!** soit! **(e)** *(also)* **so am I** moi aussi; **so do we** nous aussi; **so can they** eux aussi; **so is my brother** mon frère aussi **(f)** *(in this way)* ainsi, **do it (like)** so fais-le comme ça; **and so on, and so forth** et ainsi de suite **2** *conj* **(a)** *(because of this)* donc; **she has a bad temper, so be careful** elle a mauvais caractère, donc fais attention **(b)** *(introducing remark)* alors, **so you're not coming?** alors, tu ne viens pas?; **so that's why!** alors, c'est pour ça!; **so (what)?** et alors?, et après? **(c)** **so as to** afin de; **we hurried so as not to be late** nous nous sommes dépêchés afin de ne pas être en retard **(d)** **so that** pour que + *subjunctive*; **she sat down so that I could see better** elle s'est assise pour que je puisse mieux voir; **we hurried so that we wouldn't be late** nous nous sommes dépêchés pour ne pas arriver en retard

soak [səʊk] **1** *vt (leave in water)* faire *ou* laisser tremper; *(make very wet)* tremper **(with** de) **2** *vi (of food, clothes)* tremper; **to leave sth to s.** faire *ou* laisser tremper qch ▸ **soak in** *vi (of liquid)* pénétrer ▸ **soak up** *vt sep (liquid)* absorber; *Fig* **to s. up the sun** prendre un bain de soleil

soaked [səʊkt] *adj* trempé(e); **s. to the skin** trempé(e) jusqu'aux os

so-and-so [ˈsəʊənsəʊ] *n Fam* **(a)** *(unspecified person)* untel (unetelle) *m,f;* **Mr S.** M. Untel; **Mrs S.** Mme Unetelle **(b)** *(annoying person)* **you little s.!** espèce de petit minable!; **the greedy old s.!** espèce de gourmand!

soap [səʊp] **1** *n* savon *m;* **a bar of s.** un morceau de savon; **s. (opera)** feuilleton *m* populaire; **s. powder** lessive *f* (en poudre) **2** *vt* savonner

soapbox [ˈsəʊpbɒks] *n* tribune *f* improvisée à l'extérieur

soapdish [ˈsəʊpdɪʃ] *n* porte-savon *m*

soapflakes [ˈsəʊpfleɪks] *npl* savon *m* en paillettes

soapsuds [ˈsəʊpsʌdz] *npl* mousse *f* de savon

soapy [ˈsəʊpɪ] *adj (water)* savonneux(euse); *(body)* couvert(e) de savon; *(taste, smell)* de savon

soar [sɔː(r)] *vi (of bird, plane) & Fig (of prices)* monter en flèche; *Fig (of building)* se dresser

soaring [ˈsɔːrɪŋ] *adj Fig (prices)* en forte hausse; *(building)* élancé(e)

sob [sɒb] **1** *n* sanglot *m; Fam* **s. story** histoire *f* larmoyante **2** *vi (pt & pp* **sobbed)** sangloter

s.o.b. [esəʊˈbiː] *n Am very Fam (abbr* **son of a bitch)** salaud *m*

sobbing [ˈsɒbɪŋ] *n* sanglots *mpl*

sober [ˈsəʊbə(r)] *adj* **(a)** *(not drunk)* qui n'a pas bu **(b)** *(sensible)* sobre ▸ **sober up** *vt sep & vi* dessoûler

sobering [ˈsəʊbərɪŋ] *adj (news, thought)* qui donne à réfléchir

sobriety [səˈbraɪətɪ] *n* sobriété *f*

Soc *n (abbr* **society)** club *m,* société *f*

so-called [səʊˈkɔːld] *adj* soi-disant *inv;* **s. digital multiplexes** ce que l'on appelle des bouquets numériques; **s. progress** de prétendus progrès

soccer [ˈsɒkə(r)] *n* football *m;* **s. match** match *m* de football

sociable [ˈsəʊʃəbəl] *adj* sociable

social [ˈsəʊʃəl] **1** *n* adj social(e); **s. class** classe *f* sociale; **s. climber** arriviste *mf; Pol* **s. democrat** social(e)-démocrate *m,f;* **s. intercourse** relations *fpl* avec les gens; **s. life** vie *f* sociale; **s. outcast** paria *m;* **s. sciences** sciences *fpl* humaines; **s. security** prestations *fpl* sociales; **the s. services** les services *mpl* sociaux; **s. work** assistance *f* sociale; **s. worker** assistant(e) social(e) *m,f* **2** *n (party)* fête *f*

socialism [ˈsəʊʃəlɪzəm] *n* socialisme *m*

socialist [ˈsəʊʃəlɪst] *n & adj* socialiste *mf*

socialite [ˈsəʊʃəlaɪt] *n* mondain(e) *m,f*

socialize [ˈsəʊʃəlaɪz] *vi* fréquenter des gens; **to s. with sb** fréquenter qn

socially [ˈsəʊʃəlɪ] *adv* socialement; **to see sb s.** fréquenter qn

society [səˈsaɪətɪ] *n (pl* **societies)** *n* **(a)** *(community)* société *f;* **(high) s.** haute société, (beau) monde *m* **(b)** *(club)* club *m,* société *f*

socioeconomic [səʊsɪəʊiːkəˈnɒmɪk] *adj* socioéconomique

sociological [səʊsɪəˈlɒdʒɪkəl] *adj* sociologique

sociologist [səʊsɪˈɒlədʒɪst] *n* sociologue *mf*

sociology [səʊsɪˈɒlədʒɪ] *n* sociologie *f*

sock [sɒk] **1** *n* **(a)** *(garment)* chaussette *f; Br Fam Fig* **to pull one's socks up** se secouer **(b)** *Fam (blow)* coup *m* de poing **2** *vt Fam (hit)* donner un coup de poing à; *Fig* **to s. it to sb** montrer à qn de quoi on est capable

sod¹ [sɒd] *n (of earth)* motte *f*

sod² **1** *n very Fam (man)* salaud *m; (woman)* salope *f;* **poor**

s.! pauvre bougre!; **s. all** que dalle; **S.'s law** la loi de l'emmerdement maximum
2 *vt Vulg* **s. it!** merde!; **s. you!** va te faire voir!; **s. the party, I'm tired** tant pis pour la soirée, je suis fatigué
▸ **sod off** *(pt & pp* **sodded)** *vi Br Vulg (go away)* aller se faire voir

soda ['səʊdə] *n* **(a) s. (water)** eau *f* de Seltz; **s. fountain** cafétéria *f* **(b)** *Am (fizzy drink)* boisson *f* gazeuse **(c)** *Chem* soude *f*

sodden ['sɒdən] *adj* trempé(e)

sodium ['səʊdɪəm] *n Chem* sodium *m*; **s. bicarbonate** bicarbonate *m* de soude; **s. chloride** chlorure *m* de sodium

sodomize ['sɒdəmaɪz] *vt* sodomiser

sodomy ['sɒdəmɪ] *n* sodomie *f*

sofa ['səʊfə] *n* canapé *m*; **s. bed** canapé-lit *m*

Sofia [səʊ'fiːə] *n* Sofia

soft [sɒft] *adj* **(a)** *(in texture)* mou (molle); *(ground)* meuble; *(pillow, carpet)* moelleux(euse); *(fabric, skin)* doux (douce); **s. cheese** fromage *m* frais; *Comptr* **s. copy** visualisation *f* sur écran; **s. furnishings** tissus *mpl* d'ameublement; *Comptr* **s. return** retour *m* de chariot conditionnel, changement *m* de ligne facultatif; *Anat* **s. tissue** parties *fpl* charnues; **s. toy** peluche *f*
(b) *(voice)* doux (douce); *(rain)* léger(ère); *(colour)* doux, tendre; **s. currency** devise *f* faible; **s. drinks** boissons *fpl* non alcoolisées; **s. drugs** drogues *fpl* douces; *Phot* **in s. focus** dans le flou artistique; *Fin* **s. loan** prêt *m* offrant des conditions avantageuses; *Com* **s. sell** méthode *f* de vente non agressive
(c) *(not strict)* indulgent(e), faible; **to have a s. spot for sb** avoir un faible pour qn; **to have a s. heart** avoir le cœur tendre
(d) *Fam (stupid)* idiot(e)
(e) *(easy) (job, life)* facile; *Fam* **to be a s. touch** être bonne pâte; **s. option** solution *f* de facilité

softback ['sɒftbæk] *n* livre *m* broché

softball ['sɒftbɔːl] *n Am* = sorte de base-ball joué sur un plus petit terrain avec une balle moins dure

soft-boiled ['sɒftbɔɪld] *adj (egg)* à la coque

soften ['sɒfən] **1** *vt (wax, butter)* ramollir; *(leather, fabric)* assouplir; *(skin, light)* adoucir; *Fig* **to s. the blow** amortir le choc
2 *vi (of wax, butter)* ramollir; *Fig (of person)* se radoucir; *(of opinions, resolve, stance)* devenir plus modéré(e)
▸ **soften up** *vt sep Fam (before attack)* affaiblir; *(before request)* amadouer

softener ['sɒfənə(r)] *n* adoucissant *m*

softhearted [sɒft'hɑːtɪd] *adj* qui se laisse facilement attendrir

softie ['sɒftɪ] *n Fam* = softy

softly ['sɒftlɪ] *adv (quietly, gently)* doucement; **to be s. lit** être légèrement éclairé(e)

softly-softly ['sɒftlɪ'sɒftlɪ] *adj Br Fam (approach, attitude)* en douceur

softness ['sɒftnɪs] *n (of ground)* consistance *f* meuble; *(of fabric, skin, voice)* douceur *f*

soft-pedal [sɒft'pedəl] *(pt & pp* **soft-pedalled,** *Am* **soft-pedaled)** *vi also Fig* mettre la pédale douce

soft-soap ['sɒftsəʊp] *vt Fam* amadouer

soft-spoken [sɒft'spəʊkən] *adj* qui a une voix douce

software ['sɒftweə(r)] *n Comptr* logiciel *m*; **s. package** progiciel *m*

softy ['sɒftɪ] *(pl* **softies)** *n Fam (gentle person)* bonne pâte *f*; *(coward)* froussard(e) *m,f*

soggy ['sɒgɪ] *adj* trempé(e)

soh [səʊ] *n Mus* sol *m*

soil [sɔɪl] **1** *n (earth)* terre *f*; **on Irish s.** sur le sol irlandais
2 *vt (clothes, sheet)* salir; *Fig* **to s. one's hands** se salir les mains

solace ['sɒləs] *n Lit* réconfort *m*

solar ['səʊlə(r)] *adj* solaire; **s. eclipse** éclipse *f* solaire; **s. plexus** plexus *m* solaire; **s. system** système *m* solaire

sold [səʊld] *pt & pp of* **sell**

solder ['səʊldə(r)] **1** *n* soudure *f*
2 *vt* souder

soldering iron ['səʊldərɪŋ'aɪən] *n* fer *m* à souder

soldier ['səʊldʒə(r)] **1** *n* soldat *m*
2 *vi* être soldat
▸ **soldier on** *vi* persévérer

sole¹ [səʊl] **1** *n (of foot)* plante *f*; *(of shoe)* semelle *f*
2 *vt (shoe)* ressemeler

sole² *n (fish)* sole *f*

sole³ *adj (only)* unique; *Com* **s. agent** agent *m* exclusif

solely ['səʊllɪ] *adv* uniquement

solemn ['sɒləm] *adj* solennel(elle)

solemnity [sə'lemnɪtɪ] *n* solennité *f*

sol-fa [sɒl'fɑː] *n Mus* solfège *m*

solicit [sə'lɪsɪt] **1** *vt (request)* solliciter, demander
2 *vi (of prostitute)* racoler

solicitor [sə'lɪsɪtə(r)] *n Br (for property, wills)* notaire *m*; *(in court cases)* avocat(e) *m,f*; **S. General** conseiller *m* juridique de la Couronne

solicitous [sə'lɪsɪtəs] *adj Formal* empressé(e); *(caring)* plein(e) de sollicitude; *(concerned)* soucieux(euse) **(for** de)

solid ['sɒlɪd] **1** *n* solide *m*; **solids** *(food)* aliments *mpl* solides
2 *adj* **(a)** *(not liquid)* solide; **s. food** aliments *mpl* solides; **s. fuel** combustible *m* solide **(b)** *(not hollow)* plein(e); *(gold, silver)* massif(ive); **made of s. brick** construit(e) entièrement en brique **(c)** *(worker)* sérieux(euse)
3 *adv* **ten hours s.** dix heures d'affilée

solidarity [sɒlɪ'dærɪtɪ] *n* solidarité *f*

solidify [sə'lɪdɪfaɪ] *(pt & pp* **solidified)** *vi* se solidifier

solidity [sə'lɪdɪtɪ] *n* solidité *f*

solidly ['sɒlɪdlɪ] *adv (firmly)* solidement; *(without interruption)* sans arrêt

solid-state [sɒlɪd'steɪt] *adj Elec* transistorisé(e)

soliloquy [sə'lɪləkwɪ] *(pl* **soliloquies)** *n* soliloque *m*

solitaire [sɒlɪ'teə(r)] *n (card game)* réussite *f*; *(board game, jewellery)* solitaire *m*

solitary ['sɒlɪtərɪ] *adj* **(a)** *(single)* seul(e) **(b)** *(alone)* solitaire; **s. confinement** isolement *m* cellulaire

solitude ['sɒlɪtjuːd] *n* solitude *f*

solo ['səʊləʊ] **1** *n (pl* **solos)** *(musical)* solo *m*
2 *adj (flight, crossing)* en solitaire; *(performance)* solo
3 *adv* en solitaire; **to go s.** *(of musician)* faire une carrière solo; *(of business partner)* s'établir à son compte

soloist ['səʊləʊɪst] *n* soliste *mf*

Solomon Islands ['sɒləmən'aɪləndz] *npl* **the S.** les îles *fpl* Salomon

solstice ['sɒlstɪs] *n* solstice *m*

soluble ['sɒljʊbəl] *adj* soluble

solution [sə'luːʃən] *n* solution *f*

solve [sɒlv] *vt* résoudre

solvency ['sɒlvənsɪ] *n* solvabilité *f*

solvent ['sɒlvənt] **1** *n* solvant *m*, dissolvant *m*; **s. abuse** = utilisation de solvants hallucinogènes comme stupéfiants
2 *adj (financially)* solvable

Somali [sə'mɑːlɪ] **1** n **(a)** (person) Somalien(enne) m,f **(b)** (language) somali m
2 adj somalien(enne)
Somalia [sə'mɑːlɪə] n la Somalie
sombre, Am somber ['sɒmbə(r)] adj sombre
some [sʌm] **1** pron **(a)** (certain quantity or number) there is/are s. over there il y en a là-bas; (a few) il y en a quelques-uns là-bas; **give me s.** (of them) donne-m'en; (a few) donne-m'en quelques-uns; **do you want s.?** en veux-tu?; (a few) en veux-tu quelques-uns?; **s. of my wine** un peu de mon vin; **s. of my clothes** quelques-uns de mes vêtements; **s. of the time** une partie du temps **(b)** (as opposed to others) certains mpl, certaines fpl; **s. say...** certains disent que..., il y en a qui disent que...; **s. of the guests** certains sont invités; **they went off, s. one way, s. another** ils sont partis, certains par là, d'autres par là-bas **2** adj **(a)** (certain quantity or number of) **s. wine** du vin; **s. ice cream** de la glace; **s. water** de l'eau; **s. books** des livres; (a few) quelques livres; **in s. ways** par certains côtés; **to s. extent** jusqu'à un certain point **(b)** (as opposed to other) certain(e); **s. people say...** certains disent que..., il y a des gens qui disent que... **(c)** (considerable quantity or number of) **I've been waiting for s. time/hours** ça fait un moment/plusieurs heures que j'attends; **s. distance away** assez loin; **s. miles away** à plusieurs kilomètres **(d)** (unspecified) **for s. reason or other** pour une raison ou pour une autre; **she'll come s. day** elle viendra un jour (ou l'autre); **at s. time in the future** plus tard; **in s. book or other** dans un livre quelconque; **s. fool left the door open** un imbécile a laissé la porte ouverte **(e)** Fam (for emphasis) **that was s. storm/meal!** quel orage/repas!, Ironic **s. hope!** je peux/il peut/etc toujours y compter!; Ironic **s. friend you are!** quel ami tu fais! **3** adv (approximately) environ; **s. three days** environ trois jours

somebody ['sʌmbədɪ] **1** pron quelqu'un; **she's s. you can trust** c'est quelqu'un en qui vous pouvez avoir confiance; **s.'s coming** on vient; **s. important/taller** quelqu'un d'important/de plus grand; **s. else** quelqu'un d'autre **2** n **she thinks she's s.** elle se croit importante; **I want to be s.** je veux devenir quelqu'un

somehow ['sʌmhaʊ] adv **(a)** (in some way or other) d'une façon ou d'une autre **(b)** (for some reason or other) pour une raison ou pour une autre

someone ['sʌmwʌn] pron = **somebody**

somersault ['sʌməsɔːlt] **1** n (on the ground) roulade f; (in the air) saut m périlleux **2** vi (of person) (on the ground) faire une roulade; (in the air) faire un saut périlleux; (of car) faire un tonneau

something ['sʌmθɪŋ] **1** pron quelque chose; **there's s. about him I don't like** il y a quelque chose chez lui que je n'aime pas; **s. tells me she'll be there** quelque chose me dit qu'elle sera là; **s. to drink/to eat/to read** quelque chose à boire/à manger/à lire; **s. blue/different/special** quelque chose de bleu/de différent/de spécial; **he's s. in publishing** il a un poste important dans l'édition; **in nineteen-fifty s.** dans les années cinquante; **she's eighty s.** elle a quatre-vingts ans et quelques; **what's his name?** – **John s.** John quelque chose; **what's his name?** – **John s.** comment s'appelle-t-il? – John quelque chose; **at least he apologized, that's s.!** au moins, il s'est excusé, c'est déjà ça!; **there's s. in what you say** il y a quelque chose d'intéressant dans ce que vous dites; **she has s. to do with what happened** elle a quelque chose à voir avec ce qui s'est passé; **that was quite s.!** ce n'était pas mal du tout!; **he's a mechanic or s.** like that il est mécanicien ou quelque chose comme ça; **she's got a cold or s.** (like that) elle a un rhume, je crois

2 adv **(a)** (expressing degree) **there's been s. of an improvement** il y a eu une certaine amélioration; **she's s. of a miser** elle est plutôt avare; **it's s. like a guinea pig** ça ressemble à un cobaye **(b)** (for emphasis) **it hurt s. awful!** ça faisait mal, quelque chose de bien! **3** n a little **s.** un petit quelque chose

sometime ['sʌmtaɪm] adv **see you s.** à un de ces jours; **s. last week** la semaine dernière; **s. before the winter** avant l'hiver; **you'll have to make up your mind s.** il faudra bien que tu te décides un jour; **s. soon** d'ici peu, bientôt; **s. or other** un jour ou l'autre

sometimes ['sʌmtaɪmz] adv quelquefois

somewhat ['sʌmwɒt] adv quelque peu, un peu

somewhere ['sʌmweə(r)] adv **(a)** (some place) quelque part; **s. else** ailleurs; **do you have s. to stay?** est-ce que tu as trouvé à te loger?; Fig **now we're getting s.!** nous voilà enfin sur la bonne route ou voie! **(b)** (approximately) environ; **she's s. around fifty** elle a environ cinquante ans; **it costs s. in the region of $500** cela coûte environ 500 dollars

somnolent ['sɒmnələnt] adj Formal somnolent(e)
son [sʌn] n fils m; Am very Fam **s. of a bitch** salaud m
sonar ['səʊnɑː(r)] n sonar m
sonata [sə'nɑːtə] n sonate f
song [sɒŋ] n **(a)** chanson f; **to burst** or **break into s.** se mettre à chanter; **s. book** livre m de chansons **(b)** (idioms) **to buy sth for a s.** acheter qch pour une bouchée de pain; **to make a s. and dance (about sth)** faire toute une histoire (de qch)
songbird ['sɒŋbɜːd] n oiseau m chanteur
songwriter ['sɒŋraɪtə(r)] n auteur-compositeur m
sonic ['sɒnɪk] adj sonique; **s. boom** bang m
son-in-law ['sʌnɪnlɔː] (pl **sons-in-law**) n gendre m
sonnet ['sɒnɪt] n sonnet m
sonny ['sʌnɪ] n Fam fiston m
sonorous ['sɒnərəs] adj (deep) sonore; (impressive) imposant(e)
soon [suːn] adv **(a)** (within a short time) bientôt; (in past) vite, **it will s. be the weekend** c'est bientôt le week-end; **she s. changed her mind** elle a vite changé d'avis; **s. after(wards)** peu après; **s. after four** peu après quatre heures; **no sooner had she left than...** elle n'était pas plus tôt partie que... **(b)** (early) tôt; **none too s.** pas trop tôt; **how s. can you get here?** quand pouvez-vous être ici au plus tôt?; **sooner or later** tôt ou tard; **the sooner the better** le plus tôt sera le mieux; **as s.** as aussitôt que dès que; **as s. as possible** aussitôt que possible, dès que possible **(c)** (expressing preference) **I would just as s. stay** j'aimerais autant rester; **I would sooner go it alone** je préférerais faire seul
soot [sʊt] n suie f
soothe [suːð] vt apaiser
soothing ['suːðɪŋ] adj apaisant(e)
soothsayer ['suːθseɪə(r)] n devin (devineresse) m,f
sooty ['sʊtɪ] adj (covered in soot) couvert(e) de suie; (black) noir(e) comme de la suie
sop [sɒp] n (concession) concession f (to à)
sophist ['sɒfɪst] n sophiste mf
sophisticated [sə'fɪstɪkeɪtɪd] adj (person, taste) raffiné(e); (style, humour) recherché(e); (machinery, technique) sophistiqué(e)
sophistication [səfɪstɪ'keɪʃən] n (of person, taste) raffinement m; (of style, humour) recherche f; (of machinery, technique) sophistication f

sophistry ['sɒfɪstrɪ] n (reasoning) sophistique f; (argument) sophisme m
sophomore ['sɒfəmɔ:(r)] n Am étudiant(e) m,f de deuxième année
soporific [sɒpə'rɪfɪk] adj Formal soporifique
sopping ['sɒpɪŋ] adj s. (wet) trempé(e)
soppy ['sɒpɪ] adj Fam sentimental(e)
soprano [sɒ'prɑ:nəʊ] (pl sopranos or soprani [sɒ'prɑ:ni:]) n (singer) soprano mf; s. voice voix f de soprano
sorbet ['sɔ:beɪ] n sorbet m
sorcerer ['sɔ:sərə(r)] n sorcier m
sorceress ['sɔ:sərɪs] n sorcière f
sorcery ['sɔ:sərɪ] n sorcellerie f
sordid ['sɔ:dɪd] adj sordide
sore [sɔ:(r)] 1 adj (a) (painful) douloureux(euse); to have a s. head/back avoir mal à la tête/au dos; my feet are s. mes pieds me font mal (b) Fam (annoyed) en colère (about à propos de); it's a s. point (with him) c'est un sujet douloureux (pour lui)
2 n (wound) plaie f
sorely ['sɔ:lɪ] adv (greatly) sérieusement; she will be s. missed elle nous/leur manquera beaucoup; to be s. in need of sth avoir vraiment besoin de qch; s. tempted sérieusement tenté(e)
sorrow ['sɒrəʊ] n chagrin m; to my great s. à mon grand regret
sorrowful ['sɒrəfʊl] adj triste
sorry ['sɒrɪ] adj (a) (regretful, disappointed) désolé(e); to be s. about sth être désolé de qch; to be s. one did sth regretter d'avoir fait qch; to say s. (to sb) s'excuser (auprès de qn); I'm s. you didn't like it je suis désolé que tu n'aies pas aimé; s. to keep you waiting désolé de vous faire attendre; I'm s. to hear (that)... je suis désolé d'apprendre que...; Fam you'll be s.! tu vas le regretter!; s.? (pardon?) pardon?
(b) (sympathetic) to feel s. for sb plaindre qn; to feel s. for oneself s'apitoyer sur son propre sort; I'm just feeling a bit s. for myself je suis juste un peu déprimé
(c) (pathetic) triste; to be a s. sight être dans un triste état; to be in a s. state être dans un triste état
sort [sɔ:t] 1 n (a) (kind) sorte f; all sorts of toutes sortes de; what s. of tree is it? qu'est-ce que c'est comme arbre?; that s. of thing ce genre de chose; she's that s. of person elle est comme ça; something of the s. quelque chose de ce genre; I did nothing of the s. je n'ai jamais fait ça; he's so interesting – he's nothing of the s.! il est vraiment intéressant – pas du tout!; it takes all sorts il faut de tout pour faire un monde; Fam she's a good s. c'est une brave fille; she's not the s. to give in easily elle n'est pas du genre à abandonner facilement; we don't want your s. here nous ne voulons pas de personnes de votre genre ici; to be out of sorts (unwell) être mal fichu(e); (in a bad mood) être de mauvaise humeur; coffee of a s. une espèce de café; an artist of sorts une espèce d'artiste
(b) Fam this is s. of embarrassing c'est plutôt gênant; I s. of expected it je m'y attendais un peu; do you like it? – s. of ça te plaît? – oui, plus ou moins
(c) (in order to organize) to have a s. through sth faire du tri dans qch
2 vt also Comptr trier
► **sort out** vt sep (a) (organize) ranger; to s. oneself out se reprendre (b) (problem) régler; Fam to s. sb out régler son compte à qn
sortie ['sɔ:ti:] n Mil sortie f; Fig escapade f
sorting ['sɔ:tɪŋ] n tri m; s. office bureau m de tri
SOS [esəʊ'es] n S.O.S. m; to send out an S. lancer un S.O.S.

soufflé ['su:fleɪ] n soufflé m; cheese s. soufflé au fromage
sought [sɔ:t] pt & pp of seek
sought-after ['sɔ:tɑ:ftə(r)] adj recherché(e)
soul [səʊl] n (a) (spirit) âme f; to sell one's s. vendre son âme au diable; Fig she's the s. of discretion c'est la discrétion même; Fig it lacks s. cela n'a pas d'âme; All Souls' Day le jour des Morts (b) (person) âme f, personne f; he's a good s. c'est une bonne personne; there wasn't a s. in the street il n'y avait pas âme qui vive dans la rue; poor s.! le/la pauvre! (c) (music) soul f
soul-destroying ['səʊldɪstrɔɪɪŋ] adj démoralisant(e)
soulful ['səʊlfʊl] adj émouvant(e)
soulless ['səʊllɪs] adj (person) insensible; (place) sans âme
soulmate ['səʊlmeɪt] n âme f sœur
soul-searching ['səʊlsɜ:tʃɪŋ] n examen m de conscience
sound¹ [saʊnd] 1 n son m; (noise) bruit m; not a s. could be heard on n'entendait pas un bruit; she likes the s. of her own voice elle aime s'écouter parler; to turn the s. up/down (on TV, radio) monter/baisser le son; Fig I don't like the s. of it cela ne me dit rien qui vaille; she's angry, by the s. of it elle est en colère, on dirait; s. barrier mur m du son; s. bite petite phrase f; s. effects bruitage m; s. engineer ingénieur m du son; s. wave onde f sonore
2 vt (a) (bell) sonner; also Fig (alarm) donner; to s. one's horn klaxonner (b) (pronounce) prononcer; the "h" is not sounded le "h" ne se prononce pas
3 vi (a) (make sound) (of trumpet, bell) sonner (b) (seem) avoir l'air, sembler; she sounds Spanish on dirait qu'elle est espagnole; that sounds like a good idea ça me semble une bonne idée; he sounds like a nice guy ça a l'air d'être un type bien; it sounds like Bach on dirait du Bach; that sounds like trouble! c'est signe de problèmes!; how does that s. to you? (referring to suggestion) qu'en pensez-vous?
► **sound off** vi Fam se plaindre (about de)
► **sound out** vt sep sonder (about à propos de)
sound² 1 adj (a) (healthy) sain(e); (in good condition) en bon état; to be of s. mind être sain d'esprit (b) (sensible, logical) (argument) valable; (basis) solide; (advice) bon (person) (c) (reliable) (investment) sûr(e); (business) sain(e); (person) compétent(e)
2 adv to be s. asleep être profondément endormi(e)
sounding board ['saʊndɪŋbɔ:d] n (on pulpit, stage) abat-voix m; Fig I use my brother as a s. j'utilise mon frère pour tester mes idées
soundings ['saʊndɪŋz] npl to take s. faire des sondages
soundly ['saʊndlɪ] adv (a) (solidly) solidement (b) (logically) judicieusement (c) (thoroughly) to sleep s. dormir profondément; to thrash sb s. donner une bonne correction à qn
soundproof ['saʊndpru:f] 1 adj insonorisé(e)
2 vt insonoriser
soundtrack ['saʊndtræk] n bande f sonore
soup [su:p] n soupe f; Fig to be in the s. être dans le pétrin; s. kitchen soupe populaire; s. ladle louche f; s. plate assiette f creuse; s. spoon cuillère f à soupe
► **soup up** vt sep Fam (engine) gonfler; (car) gonfler le moteur de
sour ['saʊə(r)] 1 adj (fruit, milk, taste) aigre; Fig (person) aigri(e); to turn s. (of milk) tourner; Fig (of situation, relationship) tourner à l'aigre, mal tourner; s. cream crème f aigre; Fig it was just s. grapes c'était par dépit
2 vt (milk) faire tourner; Fig (atmosphere, relationship) empoisonner

3 vi (of milk) tourner; Fig (of atmosphere, relationship) détériorer

source [sɔːs] n source f; (of unrest, discontent) origine f; (of infection) foyer m

sourly ['saʊəlɪ] adv avec aigreur

souse [saʊs] vt tremper

south [saʊθ] **1** n sud m; **to the s. of** au sud de **2** adj (coast, side) sud; (wind) du sud; **S. Africa** Afrique f du Sud; **S. African** sud-africain(e); (person) Sud-Africain(e) m,f; **S. America** Amérique f du Sud; **S. American** sud-américain(e); (person) Sud-Américain(e) m,f; **S. Carolina** la Caroline du Sud; **S. China Sea** mer f de Chine du Sud; **S. Dakota** le Dakota du Sud; **S. Korea** Corée f du Sud; **S. Korean** sud-coréen(enne); (person) Sud-Coréen(enne) m,f; **S. Pole** pôle m sud **3** adv au sud; (travel) vers le sud; **to face s.** (of house) être exposé(e) au sud

southbound ['saʊθbaʊnd] adj (train, traffic) en direction du sud; **s. carriageway** voie f sud

southeast [saʊθ'iːst] **1** n sud-est m **2** adj (side) sud-est; (wind) du sud-est **3** adv au sud-est; (travel) vers le sud-est

southeasterly [saʊθ'iːstəlɪ] **1** n (wind) vent m du sud-est **2** adj (direction) vers le sud-est; (wind) du sud-est

southeastern [saʊθ'iːstən] adj (region) (du) sud-est

southerly ['sʌðəlɪ] **1** n (wind) vent m du sud **2** adj (direction) vers le sud; (wind) du sud; **the most s. point** le point le plus au sud

southern ['sʌðən] adj (region, accent) du sud; **s. France** le sud de la France; **s. hemisphere** hémisphère m sud

southerner ['sʌðənə(r)] n habitant(e) m,f du Sud (de l'Angleterre)

south-facing ['saʊθ'feɪsɪŋ] adj exposé(e) au sud

south-southeast ['saʊθsaʊθ'iːst] adv au sud sud est; (travel) vers le sud-sud-est

south-southwest ['saʊθsaʊθ'west] adv au sud-sud-ouest; (travel) vers le sud-sud-ouest

southward ['saʊθwəd] **1** adj au sud **2** adv vers le sud

southwards ['saʊθwədz] adv vers le sud

southwest [saʊθ'west] **1** n sud-ouest m **2** adj (side) sud-ouest; (wind) du sud-ouest **3** adv au sud-ouest; (travel) vers le sud-ouest

southwesterly [saʊθ'westəlɪ] **1** n (wind) vent m du sud-ouest **2** adj (direction) vers le sud-ouest; (wind) du sud-ouest

southwestern [saʊθ'westən] adj (region) (du) sud-ouest

souvenir [suːvə'nɪə(r)] n souvenir m

sovereign ['sɒvrɪn] n & adj souverain(e) m,f

sovereignty ['sɒvrəntɪ] n souveraineté f

Soviet ['səʊvɪət] **1** n (person) Soviétique mf **2** adj soviétique; Formerly **the S. Union** l'Union f soviétique

sow¹ [saʊ] (pt sowed [saʊd], pp sown [saʊn] or sowed) vt (seeds) & Fig (discord, doubt) semer; (field) ensemencer (with en)

sow² [saʊ] n (female pig) truie f

sown [saʊn] pp of sow¹

soya ['sɔɪə] n soja m

soy sauce [sɔɪ'sɔːs] n sauce f de soja

sozzled ['sɒzəld] adj Br Fam (drunk) bourré(e); **to get s.** se cuiter

spa [spɑː] n (place) ville f d'eau; (spring) source f thermale

space [speɪs] **1** n (a) (room) place f; **to stare into s.** regarder dans le vide (b) (individual place) place f; (on printed form) espace m; **wide open spaces** grands espaces; **s. bar** (on keyboard) barre f d'espacement (c) (period of time) espace m; **in the s. of a year** en l'espace d'une année (d) (outer space) espace m; **the s. age** l'ère f spatiale; **s. rocket** fusée f spatiale; **s. shuttle** navette f spatiale; **s. suit** combinaison f spatiale; **s. travel** voyages mpl dans l'espace (e) (gap) espace m, vide m; (in timetable) trou m **2** vt espacer
▸ **space out** vt sep espacer

space-age ['speɪseɪdʒ] adj futuriste

spacecraft ['speɪskrɑːft] n vaisseau m spatial

spaceman ['speɪsmæn] n astronaute m

spaceship ['speɪsʃɪp] n vaisseau m spatial

spacing ['speɪsɪŋ] n espacement m; Typ **single/double s.** simple/double interligne m

spacious ['speɪʃəs] adj spacieux(euse)

spade [speɪd] n (a) (tool) bêche f; **to call a s. a s.** appeler un chat un chat (b) (in cards) pique m

spaghetti [spə'getɪ] n spaghetti mpl

Spain [speɪn] n l'Espagne f

span [spæn] **1** n (a) (of hand) empan m; (of wing) envergure f (b) (of arch) portée f; (of bridge) travée f (c) (period of time) période f (d) (of knowledge, interests) étendue f **2** vt (pt & pp spanned) (of bridge) franchir; Fig (of life, knowledge) couvrir

Spaniard ['spænjəd] n Espagnol(e) m,f

spaniel ['spænjəl] n épagneul m

Spanish ['spænɪʃ] **1** npl (people) **the S.** les Espagnols mpl **2** n (language) espagnol m **3** adj espagnol(e); **the S. Inquisition** l'Inquisition f espagnole

spank [spæŋk] **1** n **to give sb a s.** donner une claque sur les fesses à qn **2** vt donner une claque sur les fesses à

spanking ['spæŋkɪŋ] **1** n fessée f; **to give sb a s.** donner une fessée à qn **2** adv Fam **s. new** flambant neuf (neuve); **they had a s. good time** ils se sont rudement bien amusés

spanner ['spænə(r)] n Br clef f; Fig **to throw a s. in the works** compliquer les choses

spar¹ [spɑː(r)] n (on ship) espar m

spar² (pt & pp sparred) vi **to s. with sb** (in boxing) s'entraîner avec qn; (argue) se chamailler avec qn

spare ['speə(r)] **1** n (spare part) pièce f de rechange; (tyre) pneu m de rechange **2** adj (a) (available) disponible; (surplus) en trop, qui reste; (reserve) de rechange; **do you have a s. pen?** tu as un stylo à me prêter?; **to be spare** être en trop; **a s. moment** un moment de libre; **s. part** pièce f de rechange; **s. ribs** travers mpl de porc; **s. room** chambre f d'amis; **s. time** temps m (de) libre; **s. tyre** pneu m de rechange; Br Fam Fig (around waist) bourrelet m; **s. wheel** roue f de secours
(b) (frugal) (meal) frugal(e); (style) dépouillé(e); (room) austère
(c) Br Fam (angry) **to go s.** sortir de ses gonds **3** vt (a) (give away, go without) (person) se passer de; **to have no time to s.** ne pas avoir le temps; **can you s. the time?** avez-vous le temps?; **with five minutes to s.** avec cinq minutes d'avance; **to have a few moments to s.** disposer de quelques minutes; **can you s. me a few moments?** pouvez-vous m'accorder quelques minutes?; **could you s. me some coffee?** est-ce que tu peux me donner un peu de café?; **to s. a thought for sb** penser à qn (b) (avoid) **to s. no expense** ne pas regarder à la dépense

(c) *(save from)* **to s. sb sth** épargner qch à qn; **s. me the details!** épargnez-moi les détails!
(d) *(show mercy towards)* épargner; **to s. sb's life** épargner la vie de qn; **to s. sb's feelings** ménager les sentiments de qn
sparing ['speərɪŋ] *adj* économe (**with** avec); **to be s. with one's praise** être avare de louanges
sparingly ['speərɪŋlɪ] *adv* en petite quantité
spark [spɑːk] **1** *n (electrical, from fire)* étincelle *f*; *Fig (of intelligence, interest)* lueur *f*; *Fig* **sparks will fly** cela va faire des étincelles; *Fig* **s. plug** bougie *f*
2 *vi* jeter *ou* faire des étincelles
▸ **spark off** *vt sep* déclencher
sparkle ['spɑːkəl] **1** *n also Fig* éclat *m*
2 *vi (of light, eyes) & Fig (of person, conversation)* briller; *(of diamond)* scintiller
sparkler ['spɑːklə(r)] *n* **(a)** *(firework)* cierge *m* magique **(b)** *Fam (diamond)* diam *m*
sparkling ['spɑːklɪŋ] *adj (light, eyes) & Fig (person, conversation)* brillant(e); *(diamond)* scintillant(e); *(wine)* pétillant(e)
sparring partner ['spɑːrɪŋ'pɑːtnə(r)] *n (in boxing)* partenaire *mf* d'entraînement; *Fig* adversaire *mf*
sparrow ['spærəʊ] *n* moineau *m*
sparse [spɑːs] *adj* clairsemé(e)
sparsely ['spɑːslɪ] *adv (populated, furnished)* peu; **s. covered with trees** aux arbres clairsemés
spartan ['spɑːtən] *adj also Fig* spartiate
spasm ['spæzəm] *n* spasme *m*; *Fig (of coughing)* quinte *f*; *(of jealousy)* crise *f*
spasmodic [spæz'mɒdɪk] *adj (irregular)* irrégulier(ère)
spasmodically [spæz'mɒdɪklɪ] *adv (irregularly)* irrégulièrement
spastic ['spæstɪk] *n Med* handicapé(e) *m,f* moteur
spat¹ [spæt] *n Fam (quarrel)* querelle *f*
spat² *pt & pp of* **spit**²
spate [speɪt] *n (of letters, calls)* avalanche *f*; *(of crimes)* vague *f*
spatial ['speɪʃəl] *adj* spatial(e)
spatter ['spætə(r)] *vt* éclabousser (**with** avec)
spatula ['spætjʊlə] *n* spatule *f*
spawn [spɔːn] **1** *n (of frog, fish)* œufs *mpl*
2 *vt (give rise to)* engendrer
3 *vi (of frog, fish)* frayer
speak [spiːk] *(pt* **spoke** [spəʊk]*, pp* **spoken** ['spəʊkən]) **1** *vt* **(a)** *(utter)* dire **(b)** *(language)* parler
2 *vi (talk, give a speech)* parler (**to/about** à/de); **they're not speaking** *(to each other)* ils ne se parlent pas; **I know her to s. to** on se parle quelquefois; **legally/morally speaking** légalement/moralement parlant; **so to s.** pour ainsi dire; **who's speaking?** *(on phone)* qui est à l'appareil?; **Mr Wright? – yes, speaking** Mr Wright? – lui-même
▸ **speak for** *vt insep* **to s. for sb** *(on behalf of)* parler pour qn; **s. for yourself!** parle pour toi!; **the facts s. for themselves** les faits parlent d'eux-mêmes
▸ **speak out** *vi* parler franchement; **to s. out against sth** s'élever contre qch
▸ **speak up** *vi* **(a)** *(speak more loudly)* parler plus fort **(b)** *(speak in favour of)* **to s. up for sb/sth** parler en faveur de qn/qch; **to s. up for oneself** se défendre
speaker ['spiːkə(r)] *n* **(a)** *(at meeting)* intervenant(e) *m,f*; *(at conference)* conférencier(ère) *m,f*; **an Italian s.** une personne qui parle italien; **to be a slow/fast s.** parler lentement/vite; *Pol* **the S.** *Br* le Président de la Chambre des Communes; *Am* le Président du Congrès **(b)** *(loudspeaker)* enceinte *f*

speaking ['spiːkɪŋ] *adj (doll, robot)* parlant(e); **s. clock** horloge *f* parlante; **s. part** *(in play, film)* rôle *m* parlant
spear ['spɪə(r)] **1** *n* lance *f*
2 *vt* transpercer d'un coup de lance
spearhead ['spɪəhed] **1** *n also Fig* fer *m* de lance
2 *vt (attack, campaign)* être le fer de lance de
spearmint ['spɪəmɪnt] *n* menthe *f* verte
spec [spek] *n Br Fam* **on s.** à tout hasard
special ['speʃəl] **1** *adj* spécial(e); *(friend)* proche; *(reason, effort, attention)* particulier(ère); **what's so s. about November 19th?** qu'est-ce que le 19 novembre a de si spécial?; **s. agent** agent *m* secret; *Br* **S. Branch** = service de renseignements britannique; **s. delivery** envoi *m* en exprès; **s. effects** effets *mpl* spéciaux; **s. needs** difficultés *fpl* d'apprentissage; **s. offer** offre *f* spéciale; *Pol* **s. powers** pouvoirs *mpl* exceptionnels
2 *n (on menu)* plat *m* du jour
specialist ['speʃəlɪst] **1** *n* spécialiste *mf*; *Med* **heart s.** cardiologue *mf*; **lung s.** pneumologue *mf*
2 *adj (skills, equipment)* d'un spécialiste; *(shop)* spécialisé(e)
speciality [speʃɪ'ælɪtɪ] *(pl* **specialities**) *n* spécialité *f*
specialization [speʃəlaɪ'zeɪʃən] *n* spécialisation *f*
specialize ['speʃəlaɪz] *vi* se spécialiser (**in** en)
specially ['speʃəlɪ] *adv (expressly)* spécialement
specialty ['speʃəltɪ] *(pl* **specialties**) *n Am* spécialité *f*
species ['spiːʃiːz] *(pl* **species**) *n* espèce *f*
specific [spɪ'sɪfɪk] **1** *adj* précis(e) *(about* au sujet de); **to be s.,…** pour être précis,…; *Phys* **s. gravity** densité *f*
2 *npl* **specifics** détails *mpl*
specifically [spɪ'sɪfɪkəlɪ] *adv* **(a)** *(explicitly)* expressément **(b)** *(specially)* spécialement **(c)** *(precisely)* précisément
specification [spesɪfɪ'keɪʃən] *n* spécification *f*
specify ['spesɪfaɪ] *(pt & pp* **specified**) *vt* **(a)** *(state exactly)* préciser **(b)** *(stipulate)* stipuler
specimen ['spesɪmɪn] *n* **(a)** *(sample amount) (of handwriting, blood)* échantillon *m*; **s. copy** spécimen *m* **(b)** *(individual example)* spécimen *m*; *Fam* **he's an odd s.** c'est un drôle de spécimen
specious ['spiːʃəs] *adj* spécieux(euse)
speck [spek] *n (of dust)* grain *m*; *(of paint, ink)* petite tache *f*; **a s. of dirt** une poussière
speckled ['spekəld] *adj* tacheté(e) (**with** de)
specs [speks] *npl Fam (spectacles)* lunettes *fpl*
spectacle ['spektəkəl] *n* **(a)** *(show, sight)* spectacle *m*; **to make a s. of oneself** se donner en spectacle **(b)** **spectacles** *(glasses)* lunettes *fpl*
spectacular [spek'tækjʊlə(r)] **1** *n* production *f* à grand spectacle
2 *adj* spectaculaire
spectator [spek'teɪtə(r)] *n* spectateur(trice) *m,f*; **s. sport** sport *m* à grand public
spectre, Am specter ['spektə(r)] *n* spectre *m*
spectrum ['spektrəm] *(pl* **spectra** ['spektrə]*)* *n* spectre *m*; *Fig* éventail *m*
speculate ['spekjʊleɪt] *vi* **(a)** *(hypothesize)* faire des suppositions *(about* au sujet de) **(b)** *Fin* **to s. (on the Stock Market)** spéculer (à la Bourse)
speculation [spekjʊ'leɪʃən] *n* suppositions *fpl*
speculative ['spekjʊlətɪv] *adj* spéculatif(ive)
speculator ['spekjʊleɪtə(r)] *n Fin* spéculateur(trice) *m,f*
sped [sped] *pt & pp of* **speed**
speech [spiːtʃ] *n* **(a)** *(faculty)* parole *f*; **s. defect** or

impediment défaut *m* d'élocution; **s. therapist** orthophoniste *mf*; **s. therapy** orthophonie *f* (**b**) *(address)* discours *m*; **to give** *or* **make a s.** faire un discours; *Br Sch* **s. day** remise *f* des prix (**c**) *(way of speaking)* langue *f* (**d**) *Gram* **part of s.** partie *f* du discours

speechless ['spi:tʃlɪs] *adj* muet(ette) **(with** de**); to be left s.** rester sans voix

speechwriter ['spi:tʃraɪtə(r)] *n* personne *f* qui écrit des discours

speed [spi:d] **1** *n* (**a**) *(rapidity)* vitesse *f*; **the s. of light/ sound** la vitesse de la lumière/du son; **at s.** à toute vitesse; **to gather** *or* **pick up/lose s.** prendre/perdre de la vitesse; *Fam* **s. cop** motard *m*; **s. limit** limitation *f* de vitesse; **s. trap** contrôle *m* de vitesse (**b**) *(gear)* vitesse *f*; **five-s. gearbox** boîte *f* à cinq vitesses (**c**) *Fam (amphetamine)* amphés *fpl*, speed *m*
    2 *vi* (**a**) *(pt & pp* **sped** [sped] *or* **speeded**) *(move quickly)* **to s. along** foncer; **to s. away/out** partir/sortir à toute vitesse (**b**) *(exceed speed limit)* faire un excès de vitesse; **to be caught speeding** être arrêté pour excès de vitesse (**c**) *Fam* **to be speeding** *(under effect of amphetamines)* être sous amphés
    ▸ **speed off** *vi* partir à toute vitesse
    ▸ **speed up 1** *vt sep (person)* faire aller plus vite; *(work, project, process)* accélérer
    2 *vi* aller plus vite

speedboat ['spi:dbəʊt] *n* vedette *f*; *(with outboard motor)* hors-bord *m inv*

speedily ['spi:dɪlɪ] *adv* vite, rapidement

speeding ['spi:dɪŋ] *n* excès *m* de vitesse

speedometer [spi:'dɒmɪtə(r)] *n* compteur *m* de vitesse

speedway ['spi:dweɪ] *n* speedway *m*

speedy ['spi:dɪ] *adj* rapide

spell[1] [spel] *n (magic words)* formule *f* magique; **to cast a s. on sb** jeter un sort à qn; **to break the s.** rompre le charme; **to be under a s.** être envoûté(e); **to be under sb's s.** être sous le charme de qn

spell[2] *(pt & pp* **spelt** [spelt] *or* **spelled**) **1** *vt* (**a**) *(in writing)* écrire, orthographier; *(aloud)* épeler; **how do you s. it?** comment ça s'écrit? (**b**) *(signify)* signifier; **to s. disaster** être un désastre; **to s. trouble** être mauvais signe
    2 *vi* **he can s. well** il a une bonne orthographe; **he can't s.** il a une mauvaise orthographe
    ▸ **spell out** *vt sep (address, name)* épeler; *Fig (explain explicitly)* expliquer clairement; **do I have to s. it out for you?** est-ce qu'il faut que je te fasse un dessin?

spell[3] *n (period)* période *f*; **after a s. as a lawyer, he...** après avoir été avocat pendant un temps, il...; **a cold s.** une période de froid; **a good/bad s.** une bonne/mauvaise période

spellbound ['spelbaʊnd] *adj* fasciné(e)

spell-checker ['speltʃekə(r)] *n Comptr* correcteur *m* d'orthographe

speller ['spelə(r)] *n Am* manuel *m* d'orthographe

spelling ['spelɪŋ] *n* orthographe *f*; **to be good/bad at s.** être bon (bonne)/mauvais(e) en orthographe; **s. mistake** faute *f* d'orthographe

spelt [spelt] *pt & pp of* **spell**[2]

spend [spend] *(pt & pp* **spent** [spent]) *vt* (**a**) *(money)* dépenser; **to s. money on sb** dépenser de l'argent pour qn; **to s. money on sth** *(object)* dépenser de l'argent en qch; *(holidays, education)* dépenser de l'argent pour qch (**b**) *(time)* passer; **to s. time on sth/doing sth** passer du temps sur qch/à faire qch

spender ['spendə(r)] *n* **to be a big s.** être dépensier(ère)

spending ['spendɪŋ] *n* dépenses *fpl*; **s. money** argent *m*

de poche; **s. power** pouvoir *m* d'achat; **to go on a s. spree** faire des folies

spendthrift ['spendθrɪft] *n* dépensier(ère) *m,f*

spent [spent] **1** *adj (bullet, match)* utilisé(e); **to be a s. force** ne plus avoir d'influence
    2 *pt & pp of* **spend**

sperm [spɜ:m] *n (semen)* sperme *m*; **s. bank** banque *f* de sperme; **s. donor** donneur *m* de sperme; **s. whale** cachalot *m*

spermicide ['spɜ:mɪsaɪd] *n* spermicide *m*

spew [spju:] *vt & vi Fam (vomit)* dégobiller

sphere [sfɪə(r)] *n also Fig* sphère *f*; **that's outside my s.** ce n'est pas dans mes compétences; **s. of influence** sphère d'influence

spherical ['sferɪkəl] *adj* sphérique

sphincter ['sfɪŋktə(r)] *n Anat* sphincter *m*

sphinx [sfɪŋks] *n* sphinx *m*

spice [spaɪs] **1** *n (seasoning)* épice *f*; *Fig (excitement)* sel *m*, piquant *m*; **s. rack** présentoir *m* à épices
    2 *vt (food)* épicer; *Fig* **to s. sth up** *(make more exciting)* ajouter du piquant à qch

spick [spɪk] *n Am very Fam* = terme injurieux désignant une personne originaire d'Amérique latine

spick-and-span [spɪkən'spæn] *adj* impeccable

spicy ['spaɪsɪ] *adj (food)* épicé(e); *Fig (story, gossip)* croustillant(e)

spider ['spaɪdə(r)] *n* araignée *f*; **s.'s web** toile *f* d'araignée; **s. plant** chlorophytum *m*

spiel [ʃpi:l] *n Fam* baratin *m*

spike [spaɪk] **1** *n* pointe *f*; **spikes** *(running shoes)* pointes *fpl*
    2 *vt Fig* **to s. sb's guns** mettre des bâtons dans les roues de qn; **to s. sb's drink** ajouter de l'alcool à la boisson de qn

spiky ['spaɪkɪ] *adj (plant)* couvert(e) de piquants; *(hair)* en épis

spill [spɪl] **1** *n* **to take a s.** *(fall)* faire une chute
    2 *vt (pt & pp* **spilt** [spɪlt] *or* **spilled**) renverser; *Fig* **to s. the** **3** *vi (of liquid)* se répandre
    ▸ **spill over** *vi (of liquid)* déborder; *Fig (of conflict)* s'étendre

spillage ['spɪlɪdʒ] *n* déversement *m*

spilt [spɪlt] *pt & pp of* **spill**

spin [spɪn] **1** *n* (**a**) *(turning movement)* tournoiement *m*; **to go into a s.** *(of car)* faire un tête-à-queue; **s. doctor** = spécialiste en communication chargé de présenter l'information de façon à mettre en valeur un parti politique (**b**) *Fam (in car)* **to go for a s.** aller faire un tour (**c**) *(on ball)* effet *m*; **to put s. on a ball** donner de l'effet à une balle
    2 *vt (pt & pp* **spun** [spʌn]) (**a**) *(wool, cotton)* filer (**b**) *(wheel, top)* faire tourner, faire tournoyer; **to s. a coin** jouer à pile ou face (**c**) *(spin-dry)* essorer
    3 *vi* tourner, tournoyer; **my head's spinning** j'ai la tête qui tourne; **the room's spinning** la pièce tourne (autour de moi)
    ▸ **spin out** *vt sep (speech, debate)* faire traîner (en longueur); *(money)* faire durer

spinach ['spɪnɪtʃ] *n* épinards *mpl*

spinal ['spaɪnəl] *adj* vertébral(e); **s. column** colonne *f* vertébrale; **s. cord** moelle *f* épinière; **s. injury** lésion *f* de la colonne vertébrale

spindly ['spɪndlɪ] *adj (person)* chétif(ive); *(arms, legs)* maigre

spin-dry ['spɪn'draɪ] *(pt & pp* **spin-dried**) *vt* essorer

spin-dryer ['spɪn'draɪə(r)] *n* essoreuse *f*

spine [spaɪn] *n* (**a**) *(backbone)* colonne *f* vertébrale (**b**) *(of book)* dos *m* (**c**) *(of plant, hedgehog)* piquant *m*

spine-chilling ['spaɪntʃɪlɪŋ] *adj* à vous glacer le sang

spineless ['spaɪnlɪs] *adj (weak)* mou (molle)

spinney ['spɪnɪ] *(pl* **spinneys**) *n* bosquet *m*

spinning top ['spɪnɪŋ'tɒp] *n* toupie *f*

spinning wheel ['spɪnɪŋ'wiːl] *n* rouet *m*

spin-off ['spɪnɒf] *n* (**a**) *(result)* retombée *f* (**b**) *(TV programme)* = feuilleton tiré d'un film ou d'un autre feuilleton

spinster ['spɪnstə(r)] *n* vieille fille *f*

spiny ['spaɪnɪ] *adj* couvert(e) de piquants; **s. lobster** langouste *f*

spiral ['spaɪərəl] **1** *n* spirale *f*; **s. staircase** escalier *m* en colimaçon
2 *vi (pt & pp* **spiralled**) *(of smoke)* s'élever *ou* monter en spirale; *(of prices)* s'envoler

spire ['spaɪə(r)] *n (of church)* flèche *f*

spirit ['spɪrɪt] *n* (**a**) *(soul, being)* esprit *m*; **the Holy S.** le Saint-Esprit (**b**) *(mood, attitude)* esprit *m*; **to enter into the s. of sth** participer de bon cœur à qch; **to take sth in the right/wrong s.** bien/mal prendre qch; **to be in good/poor spirits** être de bonne humeur/déprimé(e); *Fam* **that's the s.!** à la bonne heure! (**c**) *(determination)* courage *m*; **to break sb's s.** entamer le courage de qn (**d**) **spirits** *(drinks)* spiritueux *mpl*; **s. lamp** lampe *f* à alcool; **s. level** niveau *m* (à bulle)
▸ **spirit away, spirit off** *vt sep* faire disparaître (comme par enchantement)

spirited ['spɪrɪtɪd] *adj (person, defence)* courageux(euse); *(reply)* énergique; *(performance)* plein de brio

spiritual ['spɪrɪtjʊəl] **1** *adj* spirituel(elle); **Ireland is my s. home** c'est en Irlande que je me sens vraiment chez moi
2 *n (Negro)* **s.** Negro spiritual *m*

spiritualism ['spɪrɪtjʊəlɪzəm] *n* spiritisme *m*

spirituality [spɪrɪtjʊ'ælɪtɪ] *n* spiritualité *f*

spit[1] [spɪt] *n* (**a**) *(for cooking)* broche *f* (**b**) *(of land)* pointe *f*

spit[2] **1** *n (saliva)* salive *f*; *(spittle)* crachat *m*; *Fam* **s. and polish** astiquage *m*
2 *vt (pt & pp* **spat** [spæt]) cracher
3 *vi (of person, cat)* cracher; *(of hot fat)* sauter; *Fig* **to be within spitting distance (of)** être à deux pas (de); **it's spitting** *(with rain)* il pleuvote
▸ **spit out** *vt sep* cracher; *Fam* **s. it out!** *(say what you want to)* allez, accouche!

spite [spaɪt] **1** *n* (**a**) *(malice)* dépit *m*; **out of s.** par dépit (**b**) **in s. of** malgré; **to do sth in s. of oneself** faire qch malgré soi
2 *vt* vexer

spiteful ['spaɪtfʊl] *adj* vexant(e)

spitting image ['spɪtɪŋ'ɪmɪdʒ] *n Fam* **he's the s. of his father** c'est son père tout craché

spittle ['spɪtəl] *n* crachat *m*

spiv [spɪv] *n Br very Fam* aigrefin *m*

splash [splæʃ] **1** *n* (**a**) *(of liquid)* éclaboussure *f*; *(sound)* plouf *m*; *Fam Fig* **to make a s.** faire sensation (**b**) *(of colour, light)* tache *f*
2 *vt* éclabousser (**with** de); **to s. one's face with water** se passer le visage à l'eau; **the photo was splashed across the front page** la photo était étalée à la une
3 *vi (of liquid, waves)* faire des éclaboussures
▸ **splash about, splash around** *vi* patauger
▸ **splash down** *vi (of spacecraft)* amerrir
▸ **splash out** *vt sep Fam* claquer des ronds (**on** en achetant)

splatter ['splætə(r)] **1** *n* éclaboussure *f*; *(sound)* crépitement *m*
2 *vt* éclabousser (**with** de)

splay [spleɪ] *vt* écarter

spleen [spliːn] *n* (**a**) *(part of body)* rate *f* (**b**) *Formal (anger)* mauvaise humeur *f*; **to vent one's s. (on sb)** passer sa mauvaise humeur (sur qn)

splendid ['splendɪd] *adj* magnifique

splendour, Am splendor ['splendə(r)] *n* splendeur *f*

splice [splaɪs] *vt (film)* coller; *(rope)* épisser; *Fam* **to get spliced** *(marry)* se caser

splint [splɪnt] *n* attelle *f*

splinter ['splɪntə(r)] **1** *n (of wood, glass)* éclat *m*; *(in finger)* écharde *f*; *(of bone)* esquille *f*; *Pol* **s. group** groupe *m* dissident
2 *vt* briser
3 *vi* se briser; *Fig (of political party)* se scinder

split [splɪt] **1** *n (in wood)* fente *f*; *(in group)* division *f*; *(in garment) (tear)* déchirure *f*; *(by design)* fente; **to do the splits** faire le grand écart
2 *adj* brisé(e); **s. ends** *(in hair)* fourches *fpl*; **s. peas** pois *mpl* cassés; **s. personality** dédoublement *m* de la personnalité; **s. screen** écran *m* divisé; **in a s. second** en quelques dixièmes de seconde
3 *vt (pt & pp* **split**) (**a**) *(wood)* fendre; *(cloth)* déchirer; *(seam)* faire craquer; *(group)* diviser; *(political party)* scinder; **to s. one's head open** se fendre le crâne; **to s. the vote** éparpiller les voix; *Fam* **to s. one's sides (laughing)** se tordre de rire; *Fig* **to s. hairs** couper les cheveux en quatre (**b**) *(share)* partager; **to s. the difference** partager la différence
4 *vi* (**a**) *(of wood)* se fendre; *(of cloth)* se déchirer; *(of seam)* craquer; *(of group)* se diviser; *(of political party)* se scinder; *Fam* **my head's splitting** j'ai un mal de tête atroce (**b**) *very Fam (leave)* se casser
▸ **split up 1** *vt sep (share out)* diviser, partager
2 *vi (of couple, group)* se séparer; **to s. up with sb** rompre avec qn

split-second ['splɪtsekənd] *adj (decision)* pris(e) en un rien de temps; *(timing)* au quart de seconde

splitting ['splɪtɪŋ] *adj* **to have a s. headache** avoir un mal de tête atroce

splodge [splɒdʒ] *n Fam* tache *f*

splutter ['splʌtə(r)] *vi (of person)* bredouiller; *(of engine)* tousser; *(of flame, candle)* crépiter

spoil [spɔɪl] *(pt & pp* **spoilt** [spɔɪlt] *or* **spoiled**) **1** *vt* (**a**) *(ruin)* gâcher; **to s. sb's fun** gâcher le plaisir de qn; **to s. sb's appetite** couper l'appétit à qn; *Pol* **spoilt ballot** vote *m* nul (**b**) *(indulge)* gâter; **to be spoilt for choice** avoir l'embarras du choix
2 *vi* (**a**) *(of food)* s'abîmer (**b**) **to be spoiling for a fight** chercher la bagarre

spoils [spɔɪlz] *npl (of war, crime)* butin *m*

spoilsport ['spɔɪlspɔːt] *n Fam* rabat-joie *mf inv*

spoilt [spɔɪlt] *pt & pp of* **spoil**

spoke[1] [spəʊk] *n (of wheel)* rayon *m*; *Fig* **to put a s. in sb's wheel** mettre des bâtons dans les roues à qn

spoke[2] *pt of* **speak**

spoken ['spəʊkən] *pp of* **speak**

spokesman ['spəʊksmən] *n* porte-parole *m*

spokesperson ['spəʊkspɜːsən] *n* porte-parole *m*

spokeswoman ['spəʊkswʊmən] *n* porte-parole *m*

sponge [spʌndʒ] **1** *n* éponge *f*; *Fig* **to throw in the s.** jeter l'éponge; **s. bag** trousse *f* de toilette; **s. cake** génoise *f*; **s. pudding** = sorte de génoise, cuite à la vapeur et servie avec une sauce au chocolat, de la confiture etc

2 vt **(a)** (wash) nettoyer avec une éponge **(b)** Fam (scrounge) taper **(off** or **from** à) **3** vi Fam (scrounge) taper les autres ▸ **sponge down** vt sep (wash) nettoyer avec une éponge ▸ **sponge off 1** vt sep (stain) faire partir d'un coup d'éponge **2** vt insep Fam (scrounge from) taper

sponger ['spʌndʒə(r)] n Fam tapeur(euse) m,f

spongy ['spʌndʒɪ] adj spongieux(euse)

sponsor ['spɒnsə(r)] **1** n sponsor m; (of student, club member) parrain m **2** vt sponsoriser; (student) financer les études de; (club member) parrainer; **sponsored walk** marche f parrainée

sponsorship ['spɒnsəʃɪp] n sponsoring m; (of student, club member) parrainage m; **s. deal** (for athlete, team) contrat m de sponsoring

spontaneity [spɒntə'neɪɪtɪ] n spontanéité f

spontaneous [spɒn'teɪnɪəs] adj spontané(e)

spoof [spu:f] n Fam (a) (parody) parodie f (**on** de) (**b**) (hoax) canular m

spook [spu:k] n Fam fantôme m

spooky ['spu:kɪ] adj Fam qui fait froid dans le dos

spool [spu:l] n bobine f

spoon [spu:n] **1** n cuillère f **2** vt to **s. sth onto sth** mettre qch sur qch avec une cuillère

spoon-feed ['spu:nfi:d] (pt & pp **spoon-fed** ['spu:nfed]) vt faire manger à la cuillère; Fig mâcher le travail de

spoonful ['spu:nfʊl] n cuillerée f

sporadic [spə'rædɪk] adj sporadique

spore [spɔ:(r)] n spore f

sport [spɔ:t] **1** n (a) (activity) sport m (b) Fam (person) to **be a (good) s.** (man) être un chic type; (woman) être une chic fille; **to be a bad s.** etre mauvais(e) joueur(euse) **2** vt (wear) arborer

sporting ['spɔ:tɪŋ] adj (a) (related to sport) sportif(ive) (b) (fair) chic inv; **to give sb a s. chance** donner sa chance à qn

sports [spɔ:ts] adj **s. car** voiture f de sport; **s. centre** complexe m sportif; **s. day** = compétition sportive annuelle organisée à l'école; **s. ground** terrain m de sport; Br **s. jacket** veste f sport; **s. page** page f des sports; **s. shop** magasin m de sports

sportsman ['spɔ:tsmən] n sportif m

sportsmanship ['spɔ:tsmənʃɪp] n esprit m sportif

sportsperson ['spɔ:tspɜ:sən] n sportif(ive) m,f

sportswoman ['spɔ:tswʊmən] n sportive f

sporty ['spɔ:tɪ] adj (person) sportif(ive); (car, clothing) de sport

spot [spɒt] **1** n (a) (place) endroit m; **on the s.** sur place; Fam to **put sb on the s.** prendre qn au dépourvu; Fam to **be in a (tight) s.** être dans le pétrin; **s. check** contrôle m surprise (b) (stain) tache f (c) (pimple) bouton m (d) (forming pattern on cloth) pois m; (on leopard) tache f (e) Br Fam (small amount) goutte f; **to have a s. of lunch** manger un morceau; **s. of bother** de petits problèmes mpl (f) (spotlight) projecteur m; (smaller) spot m (g) (on TV, radio, in show) numéro m **2** vt (pt & pp **spotted**) (a) (stain, mark) tacher (b) (notice) remarquer; (opportunity, opening) repérer; **to s. sb doing sth** apercevoir qn en train de faire qch; **well spotted!** bien vu!

spotless ['spɒtlɪs] adj impeccable; Fig (reputation) irréprochable

spotlight ['spɒtlaɪt] n projecteur m; (smaller) spot m; Fig **to be in the s.** être sous le feu des projecteurs

spot-on ['spɒt'ɒn] adj Fam tout à fait exact(e)

spotter plane ['spɒtə'pleɪn] n avion-espion m

spotty ['spɒtɪ] adj (pimply) boutonneux(euse)

spouse [spaʊz] n époux (épouse) m,f

spout [spaʊt] **1** n (of teapot, kettle) bec m; Fam Fig **to be up the s.** être fichu(e); (of economy, business) s'être cassé la figure; (pregnant) être enceinte **2** vt (water) faire jaillir; Fam Fig (speech, nonsense) débiter **3** vi (of liquid) jaillir; Fam Fig (of person) faire des discours

sprain [spreɪn] **1** n (injury) entorse f **2** vt to **s. one's ankle/wrist** se fouler la cheville/le poignet

sprang [spræŋ] pt of **spring**

sprat [spræt] n sprat m

sprawl [sprɔ:l] vi (of person) s'affaler; (of town) s'étendre

sprawling ['sprɔ:lɪŋ] adj (person) affalé(e); (town) tentaculaire

spray¹ [spreɪ] n (of flowers) bouquet m

spray² **1** n (a) (of liquid) fines gouttelettes fpl; (from sea) embruns mpl (b) (act of spraying) **to give sth a s.** (flowers, crops) pulvériser; (room) vaporiser (c) (device) bombe f; (for perfume) atomiseur m; **s. can** bombe aérosol; **s. gun** (for paint) pistolet m (à peinture) **2** vt (flowers, crops) pulvériser; (room) vaporiser; **to s. oneself with sth** (perfume, deodorant) se vaporiser qch; **to s. sb with sth** asperger qn de qch

spray-paint ['spreɪ'peɪnt] **1** n peinture f en bombe **2** vt (with spray can) peindre à la bombe; (with spray gun) peindre au pistolet

spread [spred] **1** n (a) (of idea, religion, language) diffusion f; (of disease) propagation f (b) (of products, ages) éventail m (c) (in newspaper) full-page s. pleine page f; **two-page s.** double page f (d) (paste) **cheese/chocolate s.** fromage m/chocolat m à tartiner (e) (of wings, sails) envergure f (f) Fam (big meal) festin m **2** vt (pt & pp **spread**) (a) (arms, legs) écarter; Fig **to s. one's wings** acquérir de l'indépendance (b) (sand, sawdust, terror) répandre; (rumour, disease, germs) propager; (payments) étaler (c) (butter, ointment) étaler; **to s. a surface with sth** étaler qch sur une surface **3** vi se répandre; (of rumour, disease, fire) se propager ▸ **spread out 1** vt sep (a) (map, newspaper) étaler (b) (troops) déployer **2** vt insep to **be spread out** (of fields, city) s'étendre **2** vi (of person) s'étendre; (of search party) se disperser

spreadsheet ['spredʃi:t] n Comptr tableur m

spree [spri:] n Fam to **go on a s.** (go drinking) prendre une cuite; **to go on a shopping** or **spending s.** faire des folies dans les magasins

sprig [sprɪg] n (of parsley) brin m; (of holly, mistletoe) branche f

sprightly ['spraɪtlɪ] adj alerte

spring [sprɪŋ] **1** n (a) (of water) source f (b) (season) printemps m; **in (the) s.** au printemps; **s. onion** ciboule f; **s. roll** rouleau m de printemps; **s. tide** grande marée f (c) (leap) bond m (d) (elasticity) élasticité f; **to walk with a s. in one's step** marcher d'un pas souple (e) (device) ressort m **2** vi (pt **sprang** [spræŋ], pp **sprung** [sprʌŋ]) (a) (reveal unexpectedly) **to s. sth on sb** annoncer qch à qn de but en blanc; **to s. a surprise on sb** faire une surprise à qn (b) (develop) **to s. a leak** commencer à fuir; (of boat) commencer à prendre l'eau (c) Fam (prisoner) faire évader **3** vi (a) (jump) bondir, sauter; **to s. to one's feet** se lever d'un bond; **to s. into action** passer rapidement à l'action; **to s. to life** (of person, town) s'animer; (of machine) se mettre en marche; **to s. to sb's defence** prendre vivement la défense de qn; **to s. open/shut** s'ouvrir/se fermer brusquement; **to s. to mind** venir à l'esprit (b) (originate) **to s. from sth** naître de qch (c) **to s. into existence** voir le jour; Fam **where did you s. from?** d'où sortez-vous?

▸ **spring up** *vi* (**a**) *(jump to one's feet)* se lever d'un bond (**b**) *(appear suddenly)* surgir; *(of wind)* se lever; *(of feeling)* prendre naissance

springboard ['sprɪŋbɔːd] *n also Fig* tremplin *m*

spring-clean [sprɪŋ'kliːn] **1** *n* grand nettoyage *m* **2** *vt* nettoyer à fond

spring-cleaning [sprɪŋ'kliːnɪŋ] *n* grand nettoyage *m*; **to do the s.** faire le grand nettoyage

springtime ['sprɪŋtaɪm] *n* printemps *m*

springy ['sprɪŋɪ] *adj* souple

sprinkle ['sprɪŋkəl] **1** *(of salt, flour)* pincée *f* **2** *vt (with liquid)* arroser, asperger (**with** de); *(with salt, flour)* saupoudrer (**with** de); **to s. liquid on sth** arroser ou asperger qch de liquide; **to s. salt/sugar on sth** saupoudrer qch de sel/sucre

sprinkler ['sprɪŋklə(r)] *n (for lawns)* arroseur *m*; *(as fire prevention)* sprinkler *m*

sprinkling ['sprɪŋklɪŋ] *n* **a s. of** *(liquid)* quelques gouttes de; *(salt, flour)* un peu de; *Fig (people)* quelques

sprint [sprɪnt] **1** *n (fast run)* sprint *m*; *(running race)* course *f* (de vitesse); **to put on a s.** piquer un sprint **2** *vi (run fast)* piquer un sprint; **to s. off** partir en courant

sprinter ['sprɪntə(r)] *n* sprinter(euse) *m,f*

sprocket ['sprɒkɪt] *n* **s. (wheel)** pignon *m*

sprout [spraʊt] **1** *n (of plant)* pousse *f*; **(Brussels) s.** chou *m* de Bruxelles **2** *vt (leaves, shoots)* faire; *Fam (moustache, beard)* se laisser pousser **3** *vi (of leaves, hair)* pousser

▸ **sprout up** *vi (of plant, child)* pousser; *(of new buildings, towns)* surgir

spruce¹ [spruːs] *n (tree)* épicéa *m*

spruce² *adj* impeccable

▸ **spruce up** *vt sep (room)* bien nettoyer; **to s. oneself up** se faire beau (belle)

sprung [sprʌŋ] **1** *adj (mattress)* à ressorts **2** *pp of* **spring**

spry [spraɪ] *adj* alerte

spud [spʌd] *n Fam (potato)* patate *f*

spun [spʌn] **1** *adj* **s. silk** schappe *f* **2** *pt & pp of* **spin**

spunk [spʌŋk] *n* (**a**) *Fam (courage)* cran *m* (**b**) *Vulg (semen)* sperme *m*

spur [spɜː(r)] **1** *n* (**a**) *(for riding)* éperon *m*; *Fig (stimulus)* motivation *f*; *Fig* **to win one's spurs** faire ses preuves; **on the s. of the moment** sur un coup de tête (**b**) *(of land, rock)* éperon *m* **2** *vt (pt & pp spurred) (horse)* éperonner; *Fig* **to s. sb on** stimuler qn; **to s. sb on to do sth** inciter qn à faire qch; *Fig* **to s. sb into action** inciter qn à agir

spurious ['spjʊərɪəs] *adj (argument, reasoning)* spécieux(euse); *(claim, story, charge)* sans fondement

spurn [spɜːn] *vt* repousser, rejeter

spurt [spɜːt] **1** *n (of liquid)* giclée *f*; *(of activity, energy)* regain *m*; *(increase in speed)* accélération *f*; **to do sth in spurts** faire qch par à-coups; **to put on a s.** accélérer **2** *vt* **the wound was spurting blood** le sang giclait de la blessure; **the pen spurted ink** l'encre giclait du stylo **3** *vi* (**a**) *(of liquid)* gicler (**b**) *(move quickly)* **to s. off** s'élancer brusquement

sputter ['spʌtə(r)] *vi (of engine)* toussoter; *(of flame, candle)* crépiter

spy [spaɪ] **1** *n* espion(onne) *m,f*; **s. plane** avion-espion *m*; **s. ring** réseau *m* d'espionnage; **s. satellite** satellite *m* espion

2 *vt (notice)* repérer **3** *vi* espionner, faire de l'espionnage; **to s. on sb** espionner qn

▸ **spy out** *vt sep Fig* **to s. out the land** tâter le terrain

Sq *(abbr* **Square)** pl

sq *(abbr* **square)** carré; **sq. ft.** *(abbr* **square foot** *or* **feet)** ≃ mètres *mpl* carrés

squabble ['skwɒbəl] **1** *n* querelle *f* **2** *vi* se quereller (**about** *or* **over** à propos de)

squabbling ['skwɒblɪŋ] *n* querelles *fpl*

squad [skwɒd] *n (of workmen)* équipe *f*; *(of athletes, footballers)* délégation *f*; *(of soldiers)* section *f*; *(of police)* brigade *f*; **s. car** voiture *f* de patrouille

squadron ['skwɒdrən] *n Mil (of planes)* escadron *m*; *(of ships)* escadrille *f*

squalid ['skwɒlɪd] *adj (dirty)* crasseux(euse); *(sordid)* sordide

squall [skwɔːl] **1** *n (of wind)* bourrasque *f* **2** *vi (cry)* pousser des hurlements

squalor ['skwɒlə(r)] *n (dirtiness)* crasse *f*; *(poverty)* misère *f* noire

squander ['skwɒndə(r)] *vt (money, resources, talents)* gaspiller; *(time)* perdre; *(fortune, inheritance)* dilapider; *(opportunity)* laisser passer

square [skweə(r)] **1** *n* (**a**) *(shape)* carré *m*; *(on chessboard, map)* case *f*; *Fig* **to be back at s. one** être de retour à la case départ (**b**) *Math* carré *m* (**c**) *(of town, village)* place *f* (**d**) *Fam (unfashionable person)* **to be a s.** être ringard(e) **2** *adj* (**a**) *(in shape)* carré(e) (**b**) *(right-angled)* **s. corner** angle *m* droit (**c**) *Math* carré(e); **s. root** racine *f* carrée (**d**) *Fam (unfashionable)* vieux jeu *inv* (**e**) *(idioms)* **to be s. with sb** être honnête avec qn; **that's us s.** nous sommes quittes; **to feel like a s. peg in a round hole** ne pas se sentir à sa place; **s. deal** arrangement *m* équitable; **s. meal** bon repas *m* **3** *adv* **to hit sb s. on the jaw** frapper qn en pleine mâchoire; **to look sb s. in the eye** regarder qn bien en face **4** *vt* (**a**) *(make square)* mettre en forme de carré; *Math (number)* élever au carré; **squared paper** papier *m* quadrillé (**b**) *(settle) (account, debt)* régler (**c**) *(arrange)* **to s. sth with sb** arranger qch avec qn **5** *vi (agree)* coller; **to s. with** correspondre à

▸ **square up** *vi* (**a**) *(settle debts)* régler ses comptes (**b**) *(of fighters)* se mettre en garde; *Fig* **to s. up to a problem/an opponent** faire face à un problème/un adversaire

squarely ['skweəlɪ] *adv* (**a**) *(directly)* **to hit sb s. in the chest/face** frapper qn en pleine poitrine/figure (**b**) *(honestly)* honnêtement

squash¹ [skwɒʃ] **1** *n* (**a**) *(crush)* cohue *f*; **it was a s.** on était serrés comme des sardines (**b**) *Br (drink)* **orange/lemon s.** ≃ sirop *m* d'orange/de citron (**c**) *(sport)* squash *m*; **s. court** court *m* de squash **2** *vt* écraser **3** *vi* **to s. into a room/car** s'entasser dans une pièce/voiture

squash² *n Am (vegetable)* courge *f*

▸ **squash up** *vi* se serrer

squat [skwɒt] **1** *n (illegally occupied dwelling)* squat *m* **2** *adj (person, object, building)* trapu(e) **3** *vi (pt & pp squatted)* (**a**) *(crouch down) (of person)* s'accroupir; *(of animal)* se tapir (**b**) *(occupy illegally)* squatter

squatter ['skwɒtə(r)] *n* squatter *m*

squaw [skwɔː] *n* squaw *f*

squawk [skwɔːk] **1** *n (of bird)* cri *m* rauque; *Fam (of person)* braillement *m* **2** *vi (of bird)* pousser un cri rauque; *Fam (of person)* brailler

squeak [skwi:k] **1** n (of animal, person) cri m aigu; (of door, hinges) grincement m; Fam **I don't want to hear another s.** out of you je ne veux plus vous entendre **2** vi (of animal, person) pousser un cri aigu; (of door, hinges) grincer; (of shoes) craquer

squeaky ['skwi:kɪ] adj (voice) aigu(uë); (door, hinges) qui grince; (shoes) qui craque; **s. clean** impeccable

squeal [skwi:l] **1** n (of person, animal) cri m perçant; (of brakes) crissement m **2** vt crier **3** vi (a) (of person, animal) pousser un cri perçant; (of brakes) crisser; Fam **to s. about sth** (complain) se lamenter au sujet de qch (b) very Fam (inform) moucharder; **to s. on sb** balancer qn

squeamish ['skwi:mɪʃ] adj de nature délicate; **to be s. about sth** ne pas supporter qch

squeeze [skwi:z] **1** n pression f; **to give sth a s.** presser qch; **to give sb a s.** (hug) serrer qn dans ses bras; **a s. of lemon** quelques gouttes de citron; Fam **it was a tight s.** nous étions serrés comme des sardines; Fam **to put the s. on sb** (pressurize) faire pression sur qn **2** vt (a) (press) presser; **to s. sb's hand** serrer la main à qn; Fig **to s. sb** (pressurize) faire pression sur qn (b) (squash) **to s. sth into sth** faire rentrer qch dans qch; **I think we can just s. you in** je pense qu'on peut vous trouver une place **3** vi **to s. into sth** s'entasser dans qch; **to s. past sb** se glisser devant qn; **s. up a bit!** serrez-vous un peu!

▸ **squeeze out** vt sep (juice) exprimer

squelch [skweltʃ] vi patauger; **to s. through the mud** avancer en pataugeant dans la boue

squib [skwɪb] n (firework) pétard m; Fig **to be a damp s.** être bidon inv

squid [skwɪd] (pl **squid**) n calmar m

squiggle ['skwɪgəl] n gribouillis m

squint [skwɪnt] **1** n (a) (eye defect) strabisme m; **to have a s.** loucher (b) (quick look) coup d'œil m; **to have a s. at** jeter un coup d'œil à **2** vi (a) (have eye defect) loucher (b) (narrow one's eyes) plisser les yeux; **to s. at** plisser les yeux pour voir

squire ['skwaɪə(r)] n (landowner) châtelain m; Hist écuyer m

squirm [skwɜ:m] vi (wriggle) se tortiller; Fig **to s. (with embarrassment)** être mal à l'aise

squirrel ['skwɪrəl] n écureuil m

squirt [skwɜ:t] **1** n (a) (of liquid) giclée f (b) Fam (insignificant person) petit(e) morveux(euse) m,f **2** vt (liquid) faire gicler; **to s. sth on sb/sth, to s. sb/sth with sth** asperger qn/qch de qch **3** vi (of liquid) **to s. out** gicler

Sr (abbr **Senior**) **Sr** Alan Spencer, **Sr** Alan Spencer père

Sri Lanka [sri:'læŋkə] n le Sri Lanka

Sri Lankan [sri:'læŋkən] **1** n Sri Lankais(e) m,f **2** adj sri lankais(e)

SSE (abbr **south-southeast**) sud-sud-est

SSW (abbr **south-southwest**) sud-sud-ouest

St (a) (abbr **Street**) rue f (b) (abbr **Saint**) st(e); **St Kitts and Nevis** Saint-Kitts-et-Nevis; **St Lucia** Sainte-Lucie; **St Petersburg** Saint-Petersbourg; **St Vincent and the Grenadines** Saint-Vincent-et-Grenadines

stab [stæb] **1** n (a) (with knife) coup m de couteau; Fig **a s. of pain** un élancement; **a s. of envy** un pincement de jalousie; **a s. of guilt** un accès de culpabilité (b) Fam (attempt) **to have a s. at sth/at doing sth** essayer qch/de faire qch **2** vt (pt & pp **stabbed**) (with knife) poignarder; (with other weapon) transpercer; **to s. sb to death** tuer qn d'un coup

de couteau; Fig **to s. sb in the back** poignarder qn dans le dos

stabbing ['stæbɪŋ] **1** n (attack) agression f au couteau **2** adj (pain) lancinant(e)

stability [stə'bɪlɪtɪ] n stabilité f

stabilize ['steɪbɪlaɪz] **1** vt stabiliser **2** vi se stabiliser

stabilizer ['steɪbɪlaɪzə(r)] n (on bicycle) stabilisateur m

stable¹ ['steɪbəl] **1** n écurie f; Fig **to lock the s. door after the horse has bolted** prendre des mesures trop tard **2** vt mettre à l'écurie

stable² adj stable

stack [stæk] **1** n (a) (pile) pile f; Fam **stacks of** des tas de (b) (chimney) cheminée f **2** vt empiler; **to be stacked with sth** (full of) être plein(e) de qch; **the odds were stacked against them** ils n'avaient aucune chance

stadium ['steɪdɪəm] (pl **stadiums** or **stadia** ['steɪdɪə]) n stade m

staff [stɑ:f] **1** n (a) (stick) bâton m (b) (personnel) personnel m; **teaching/nursing s.** personnel m enseignant/infirmier; Br **s. nurse** infirmier(ère) m,f diplômé(e); **s. room** (in school) salle f des professeurs (c) Mus (pl **staves** [steɪvz]) portée f **2** vt **the office is staffed by volunteers** le personnel du bureau est composé de volontaires; **the desk is staffed at all times** il y a toujours quelqu'un au bureau

stag [stæg] n (animal) cerf m; **s. beetle** cerf-volant m; Br **s. night** or **party** (before wedding) enterrement m de la vie de garçon

stage [steɪdʒ] **1** n (a) (platform) plate-forme f; (in theatre) scène f; **to go on the s.** faire du théâtre; Fig **to set the s. for sth** préparer le terrain à qch; **s. directions** indications fpl scéniques; **s. door** entrée f des artistes; **s. fright** trac m; **s. manager** régisseur m; **s. name** nom m de scène; **s. whisper** aparté m (b) (phase) stade m; **at this s. in... to do sth in stages** faire qch par étapes (c) **s. (coach)** diligence f **2** vt (play) monter, mettre en scène; Fig (demonstration, invasion) organiser

stagehand ['steɪdʒhænd] n machiniste m

stage-manage ['steɪdʒˌmænɪdʒ] vt (play) s'occuper de la régie de; Fig (event, demonstration) mettre en scène

stage-struck ['steɪdʒstrʌk] adj fou (folle) de théâtre

stagflation [stæg'fleɪʃən] n Econ stagflation f

stagger ['stægə(r)] **1** vt (a) (astound) stupéfier (b) (tea-breaks, holidays) échelonner **2** vi (stumble) tituber; **to s. along/in/out** marcher/entrer/sortir en titubant; **to s. to one's feet** se relever péniblement

stagnant ['stægnənt] adj stagnant(e)

stagnate [stæg'neɪt] vi stagner

stagnation [stæg'neɪʃən] n stagnation f

staid [steɪd] adj collet monté inv

stain [steɪn] **1** n (mark) tache f; (dye) teinture f; **s. remover** détachant m **2** vt (mark) tacher; (dye) teindre; Fig (reputation) salir

stained-glass ['steɪndglɑ:s] n vitrail m; **s. window** vitrail

stainless steel® ['steɪnlɪs'sti:l] n acier m inoxydable, inox® m

stair [steə(r)] n (single step) marche f; **stairs** (staircase) escalier m

staircase ['steəkeɪs] n escalier m

stairway ['steəweɪ] n escalier m

stairwell ['steəwel] *n* cage *f* d'escalier

stake [steɪk] **1** *n* (**a**) *(piece of wood)* pieu *m*; *(piece of metal)* piquet *m*; *(for plant)* tuteur *m*; **to be burnt at the s.** périr sur le bûcher (**b**) *(bet)* enjeu *m*; **to be at s.** être en jeu (**c**) *(share)* **to have a s. in sth** avoir des intérêts dans qch; *Fig* être concerné(e) par qch **2** *vt* (**a**) *(money)* miser (**on** sur); *Fig (one's reputation, job)* risquer (**on** sur); **I'd s. my life on it** j'en mettrais ma tête à couper (**b**) **to s. a claim (to sth)** revendiquer un droit (à qch)

stakeout ['steɪkaʊt] *n* surveillance *f*

stalactite ['stæləktaɪt] *n* stalactite *f*

stalagmite ['stæləgmaɪt] *n* stalagmite *f*

stale [steɪl] *adj* (**a**) *(bread, cake)* rassis(e); *(air)* confiné(e); *(smell)* âcre (**b**) *Fig (social life, politics)* sans intérêt; *(excuse, joke)* éculé(e); *(person)* blasé(e)

stalemate ['steɪlmeɪt] *n (in chess)* pat *m*; *(in negotiations)* impasse *f*; **to reach a s.** être dans l'impasse

stalk¹ [stɔːk] **1** *vt (suspect, wild animal)* traquer; *(obsessively)* harceler **2** *vi (walk angrily)* **to s. in/out** entrer/sortir d'un air furieux mais digne

stalk² *n (of plant, flower)* tige *f*; *(of fruit)* queue *f*

stalker ['stɔːkə(r)] *n* = admirateur obsessionnel qui harcèle une célébrité ou une de ses connaissances

stall [stɔːl] **1** *n* (**a**) *(in stable)* stalle *f*; *(for shower, toilet)* cabine *f* (**b**) *(in market)* étal *m*; *(at exhibition)* stand *m* (**c**) *Br* **the stalls** *(in theatre)* l'orchestre *m* **2** *vt (hold off)* faire patienter **3** *vi* (**a**) *(of car)* caler; *Fig (of campaign)* être interrompu(e) (**b**) *(delay)* **to s. (for time)** essayer de gagner du temps

stallion ['stæljən] *n* étalon *m*

stalwart ['stɔːlwət] **1** *n* fidèle *mf* **2** *adj* résolu(e)

stamen ['steɪmən] *n* étamine *f*

stamina ['stæmɪnə] *n* résistance *f* physique

stammer ['stæmə(r)] **1** *n* bégaiement *m*; **to have a s.** bégayer **2** *vi* bégayer **3** *vt* balbutier

▸ **stammer out** *vt sep* balbutier

stamp [stæmp] **1** *n (for letter)* timbre *m*; *(mark)* cachet *m*; *(device)* tampon *m*; *Fig* **to bear the s. of sth** porter l'empreinte de qch; *Fig* **s. of approval** aval *m*, approbation *f*; **s. album** album *m* de timbres; **s. collector** philatéliste *mf*; *Br Fin* **s. duty** droit *m* de timbre; **s. machine** distributeur *m* de timbres-poste **2** *vt* (**a**) *(document)* tamponner; **to s. the date on sth** tamponner la date sur qch; **stamped addressed envelope** enveloppe *f* timbrée libellée à ses noms et adresse (**b**) **to s. one's foot** taper du pied **3** *vi* **to s. on sth** *(on purpose)* écraser qch avec le pied; *(accidentally)* écraser qch du pied; **to s. off/out** partir/ sortir en tapant des pieds

▸ **stamp out** *vt sep* (**a**) *(resistance, dissent)* anéantir; *(poverty)* éradiquer (**b**) *(fire)* éteindre en piétinant

stampede [stæm'piːd] **1** *n* débandade *f*; **there was a s. for the door** il y a eu une ruée vers la porte **2** *vi* se ruer

stance [stɑːns] *n also Fig* position *f*

stand [stænd] **1** *n* (**a**) *(opinion)* position *f*; **to take a s. (on sth)** prendre position (sur qch) (**b**) *(of lamp, microphone)* pied *m*; *(for books, postcards)* présentoir *m* (**c**) *(stall) (outside)* étalage *m*; *(at exhibition)* stand *m* (**d**) *(at sports ground)* tribune *f*

(**e**) *(taxi rank)* station *f* **2** *vt (pt & pp* **stood** [stʊd]) (**a**) *(place)* poser; **to s. sth against sth** mettre qch contre qch (**b**) *(endure)* supporter; **to s. comparison with sb/sth** soutenir la comparaison avec qn/qch; **to s. one's ground** tenir bon (**c**) *(pay for)* **to s. sb a drink/meal** payer à boire/manger à qn (**d**) *(have)* **to s. a chance (of doing sth)** avoir des chances (de faire qch); **she doesn't s. a chance** elle n'a aucune chance (**e**) *Law* **to s. trial** passer en jugement **3** *vi* (**a**) *(of person) (get up)* se mettre debout; *(be upright)* être debout; *(remain upright)* rester debout; **to s. on one's head** faire le poirier; **I could hardly s.** je tenais à peine debout; **don't just s. there!** ne reste pas planté là les bras ballants!; **to s. fast** *or* **firm** tenir bon; **to s. still** *(of person)* se tenir immobile; **time seemed to s. still** le temps semblait s'être arrêté (**b**) *(of building)* se dresser; *(of object)* être, se trouver (**c**) *(be in situation)* **inflation/unemployment stands at...** le taux d'inflation/de chômage s'élève à...; **to s. in need of sth** avoir besoin de qch; **to s. to do sth** risquer de faire qch; **it stands to reason that...** il est clair que... (**d**) *(idioms)* **to be standing right behind sb** être avec qn; **to s. on one's own two feet** se débrouiller tout(e) seul(e); **I don't know where I s.** je ne sais pas à quoi m'en tenir; **to know how things s.** savoir où en sont les choses; **I s. corrected** autant pour moi; *Br* **to s. for Parliament** se présenter aux élections législatives; **the offer still stands** l'offre tient toujours

▸ **stand aside** *vi* s'écarter

▸ **stand back** *vi (move away)* reculer (**from** de); *Fig* prendre de la distance (**from** par rapport à)

▸ **stand by 1** *vt insep* (**a**) *(person, cause)* défendre, soutenir (**b**) *(promise, decision)* maintenir **2** *vi* (**a**) *(be ready)* **to s. by (for sth/to do sth)** *(of person)* se tenir prêt(e) (pour qch/à faire qch); *(of vehicle)* être prêt (pour qch/à faire qch) (**b**) *(not get involved)* rester sans rien faire

▸ **stand down** *vi (retire)* se retirer

▸ **stand for** *vt insep* (**a**) *(mean, represent)* vouloir dire (**b**) *(tolerate)* supporter

▸ **stand out** *vi* (**a**) *(be prominent)* ressortir; **to s. out in a crowd** se détacher dans la foule; *Fam* **it stands out a mile** ça se voit comme le nez au milieu de la figure (**b**) *(oppose)* **to s. out against sth** résister à qch

▸ **stand up 1** *vt sep* (**a**) *(put in upright position)* mettre à la verticale (**b**) *Fam* **to s. sb up** *(on date)* poser un lapin à qn **2** *vi* (**a**) *(get up)* se mettre debout; *(be standing)* être debout; *Fig* **to s. up for sb/sth** défendre qn/qch; *Fig* **to s. up to sb** tenir tête à qn (**b**) *(of argument, theory)* faire le poids; **to s. up to sth** résister à qch; **it'll never s. up in court** ça ne sera pas valable au tribunal

standard ['stændəd] **1** *n* (**a**) *(point of reference)* référence *f*; *(set requirement)* norme *f*; *(for weight, measurement)* étalon *m* (**b**) *(required level)* niveau *m*; **to be up to/below s.** être du/ en dessous du niveau requis; **s. of living** niveau de vie; **s. of accommodation** qualité *f* du logement (**c**) **standards** *(morals)* principes *mpl* moraux; **to have high/low standards** être/ne pas être exigeant(e) (**d**) *(flag)* étendard *m*; *also Fig* **s. bearer** porte-drapeau *m* **2** *adj* (**a**) *(design, size)* standard *inv*; *Math* **s. deviation** écart *m* type; **s. lamp** lampadaire *m*; **s. measure** mesure *f* étalon (**b**) *(usual)* habituel(elle); **S. English** anglais *m* standard; **s. practice** pratique *f* courante

standardization [stændədaɪ'zeɪʃən] *n* normalisation *f*

standardize ['stændədaɪz] *vt* normaliser

stand-by ['stændbaɪ] n (a) (fuel, food) réserve f; to have sth as a s. avoir qch en réserve; to be on s. (of troops, emergency services) être en état d'alerte (b) (for air travel) to be on s. être en stand-by; s. passenger passager(ère) m,f en stand-by; s. ticket billet m en stand-by

stand-in ['stændɪn] n remplaçant(e) m,f; (for actor) doublure f

standing ['stændɪŋ] 1 n (a) (status) réputation f (b) (duration) of long s. de longue date
2 adj (a) (upright) debout; to give sb a s. ovation se lever pour applaudir qn (b) (permanent) permanent(e); I have a s. invitation je peux y aller quand je veux; s. army armée f de métier; s. charges (on bill) frais mpl d'abonnement; s. joke plaisanterie f classique; Fin s. order virement m automatique

stand-offish [stænd'ɒfɪʃ] adj distant(e)

standpoint ['stændpɔɪnt] n point m de vue

standstill ['stændstɪl] n to be at a s. (of traffic) être immobilisé(e); (of production, economy) être paralysé(e); to come to a s. (of traffic) s'immobiliser; (of production) s'arrêter; (of economy) être paralysé(e)

stand-up ['stændʌp] adj (a) s. comedian comique m f de scène; s. comedy spectacle m comique (b) (fight, argument) en règle

stank [stæŋk] pt of stink

stanza ['stænzə] n strophe f

staple¹ ['steɪpəl] 1 n (for fastening paper) agrafe f; s. gun agrafeuse f
2 vt agrafer

staple² n (basic food) aliment m de base; (basic product) principale production f; Fig divorce cases are a s. of his law practice son cabinet s'occupe essentiellement de divorces

stapler ['steɪplə(r)] n agrafeuse f

star [stɑː(r)] 1 n (a) (heavenly body) étoile f; the Stars and Stripes (US flag) la bannière étoilée; Fig to reach for the stars essayer d'atteindre les sommets; Fig to see stars (after blow to head) voir trente-six chandelles; s. fruit carambole f; s. sign signe m du zodiaque (b) (famous person) star f, vedette f; s. player vedette f (c) Fam stars (horoscope) horoscope m
2 vt (pt & pp starred) (of film, play) avoir pour vedette
3 vi to s. in a movie/play jouer dans un film/une pièce

starboard ['stɑːbəd] n Naut tribord m

starch [stɑːtʃ] 1 n (for shirts, in food) amidon m
2 vt (shirt) amidonner

starchy ['stɑːtʃɪ] adj (a) (food) riche en féculents (b) Fam (person, manner) guindé(e)

stardom ['stɑːdəm] n célébrité f

stare [steə(r)] 1 n regard m fixe
2 vt to be staring sb in the face (be obvious) crever les yeux à qn
3 vi to s. at sb dévisager qn; to s. at sth regarder qch fixement; to s. into space regarder dans le vague; it's rude to s. ce n'est pas poli de dévisager les gens

starfish ['stɑːfɪʃ] n étoile f de mer

stark [stɑːk] 1 adj (contrast) net (nette); (light, colours) cru(e); (truth, facts) brut(e); (landscape) nu(e)
2 adv s. naked tout(e) nu(e); Fam s. staring mad complètement dingue

starkers ['stɑːkəz] adj Fam à poil

starlet ['stɑːlɪt] n (young actress) starlette f

starlight ['stɑːlaɪt] n lumière f des étoiles

starling ['stɑːlɪŋ] n étourneau m

starlit ['stɑːlɪt] adj étoilé(e)

starry ['stɑːrɪ] adj étoilé(e)

starry-eyed [stɑːrɪ'aɪd] adj naïf(ïve)

start [stɑːt] 1 n (a) (beginning) début m; (starting place, of journey, race) départ m; for a s. pour commencer; at the s. au début; from the s. dès le départ; from s. to finish du début à la fin; to make a s. on sth commencer qch; a second honeymoon will give us a fresh s. une deuxième lune de miel nous fera repartir d'un bon pied; to give sb a 60-metre s. (in race) laisser 60 mètres d'avance à qn (b) (sudden movement) sursaut m; to wake with a s. se réveiller en sursaut; to give sb a s. faire sursauter qn
2 vt (a) (begin) commencer; (conversation, talks) entamer; (fire) déclencher; (fashion, rumour) lancer; (business) monter; to s. doing sth, to s. to do sth commencer de faire qch; to s. crying/laughing/sneezing se mettre à pleurer/rire/éternuer; to get started démarrer (b) (machine, engine) mettre en marche, (car) démarrer
3 vi (a) (begin) commencer; to s. at the beginning commencer par le commencement; to s. by doing sth, to s. with sth commencer qch; to s. on sth commencer qch; she had started as a doctor elle avait commencé sa carrière comme médecin; to s. with au début, d'abord; now don't you s.! tu ne vas pas t'y mettre aussi! (b) (make sudden movement) sursauter (c) (begin journey) se mettre en route (b) (of car, engine) démarrer
▸ **start off** vt sep (argument, debate) commencer; to s. sb off (in business) aider qn à démarrer; (on a subject) lancer qn
2 vi (begin) commencer; (on journey) se mettre en route
▸ **start out** vi (begin) débuter; (on journey) se mettre en route
▸ **start up** 1 vt sep (car) démarrer; (machine) mettre en marche; (business) monter
2 vi (of engine) démarrer; to s. up in business monter son entreprise

starter ['stɑːtə(r)] n (a) (competitor) partant(e) m,f; (official) starter m (b) to be a late s. (of child) ne pas être très précoce, to be a slow s. (of person) être lent(e) à démarrer (c) (device) starter m (d) (in meal) hors-d'œuvre m inv; Fig for starters pour commencer

starting ['stɑːtɪŋ] n (a) (in sport) s. block starting-block m; s. line ligne f de départ; s. pistol pistolet m de starter (b) (initial) s. point or place point m de départ; s. price (in betting) cote f au départ; s. salary salaire m de départ

startle ['stɑːtəl] vt faire sursauter

startling ['stɑːtlɪŋ] adj (noise) effrayant(e); (news, event) incroyable

start-up ['stɑːtʌp] n (a) (of new business) ouverture f, lancement m; s. costs coûts mpl d'installation (b) (Internet company) start-up f, jeune pousse f

starvation [stɑː'veɪʃən] n privation f totale de nourriture; to die of s. mourir de faim; to be on a s. diet (not have enough to eat) n'avoir presque rien à manger; s. wages salaires mpl de misère

starve [stɑːv] 1 vt priver de nourriture; to s. sb to death faire mourir qn de faim; Fig to be starved of sth être privé(e) de qch
2 vi (lack food) souffrir de la faim; s. (to death) mourir de faim; Fam I'm starving je meurs de faim

starving ['stɑːvɪŋ] adj famélique

stash [stæʃ] Fam 1 n réserve f
2 vt planquer

state [steɪt] 1 n (a) (condition) état m; (situation) situation f; I'm not in a fit s. to travel je ne suis pas en état de voyager; s. of war/emergency état de guerre/d'urgence; s. of affairs situation f; s. of health état de santé; s. of mind état d'esprit; in a s. of terror terrifié(e); in a s. of shock en état de choc; to be in a terrible s. être dans un état lamentable; **to lie in s.** *(of dead person)* être exposé(e) au public **(b)** *(country, administrative region)* État *m*; *Fam* **the States** *(the USA)* les États-Unis; **s.** control étatisme *m*; *Am* **S.** Department ≃ ministère *m* des Affaires étrangères; **s.** occasion cérémonie *f* officielle; **s.** school école *f* publique; **s.** secret secret *m* d'État; **s.** sector secteur *m* public; **s.** visit visite *f* officielle

2 *vt (declare)* déclarer; *(address, age)* indiquer, préciser; **to s. the obvious** enfoncer une porte ouverte; **as stated earlier/above** comme mentionné précédemment/ci-dessus; **at the stated times** aux heures prévues

stateless ['steɪtlɪs] *adj* apatride

stately ['steɪtlɪ] *adj* imposant(e); **s. home** ≃ château *m*

statement ['steɪtmənt] *n* **(a)** *(of opinion)* déclaration *f*; *(of facts)* exposé *m*; **to make a s.** *(of spokesperson)* faire une déclaration; *(of witness)* faire une déposition; *Fig (of lifestyle, behaviour)* faire passer un message **(b)** *(from bank)* relevé *m* de compte

state-of-the-art [steɪtəvðɪˈɑːt] *adj* ultramoderne

state-owned ['steɪt'əʊnd] *adj (company)* d'État; *(property)* de l'État

statesman ['steɪtsmən] *n* homme *m* d'État

statesmanlike ['steɪtsmənlaɪk] *adj* digne d'un homme d'État

static ['stætɪk] **1** *adj* statique; **s. electricity** électricité *f* statique
2 *n* électricité *f* statique

station ['steɪʃən] **1** *n* **(a)** *(for trains)* gare *f*; **s. master** chef *m* de gare; *Am* **s. wagon** *(car)* break *m* **(b)** *(post)* poste *m*; **(police) s.** poste (de police); **(radio/television) s.** station *f* de radio/télévision **(c)** *(social condition)* condition *f*; **to have ideas above one's s.** ne pas avoir les moyens de ses ambitions
2 *vt (person)* placer; *(soldier, troops)* poster

stationary ['steɪʃənərɪ] *adj* immobile

stationer ['steɪʃənə(r)] *n* **s.'s (shop)** papeterie *f*

stationery ['steɪʃənərɪ] *n (writing materials)* papeterie *f*; *(writing paper)* papier *m* à lettres

statistic [stəˈtɪstɪk] *n* chiffre *m*; **statistics** statistiques *fpl*

statistical [stəˈtɪstɪkəl] *adj* statistique

statistician [stætɪsˈtɪʃən] *n* statisticien(enne) *m,f*

statue ['stætjuː] *n* statue *f*

statuesque [stætjʊˈesk] *adj* sculptural(e)

statuette [stætjʊˈet] *n* statuette *f*

stature ['stætʃə(r)] *n (physical build)* stature *f*; *(reputation)* envergure *f*, réputation *f*

status ['steɪtəs] *n (position, prestige)* statut *m*; *Comptr* **s. line** ligne *f* d'état; **s. report** rapport *m* de situation; **s. symbol** marque *f* de prestige

status quo ['steɪtəs'kwəʊ] *n* statu quo *m inv*

statute ['stætjuːt] *n* texte *m* de loi; **by s.** par la loi; **s. book** recueil *m* de lois

statutory ['stætjʊtərɪ] *adj* légal(e); **s. duty** obligation *f* légale; **s. holiday** jour *m* férié

staunch¹ [stɔːntʃ] *adj (resolute)* convaincu(e); *(supporter)* ardent(e)

staunch² *vt (blood)* étancher

staunchly ['stɔːntʃlɪ] *adv* résolument

stave [steɪv] *n* **(a)** *(of barrel)* douve *f* **(b)** *Mus* portée *f*

▸ **stave in** *(pt & pp staved or stove [stəʊv])* *vt sep* défoncer; *(ribs)* enfoncer

▸ **stave off** *vt sep (problem, disaster)* éviter; *(hunger)* tromper

stay [steɪ] **1** *vt (endure)* **to s. the course** *or* **distance** tenir la distance
2 *vi* **(a)** *(not move, remain)* rester; *Fam* **to s. put** rester tranquille; **to s. still** rester tranquille; **computers are here to s.** l'informatique est entrée dans les mœurs **(b)** *(reside temporarily)* séjourner; **I stayed five years in the States** j'ai passé cinq ans aux États-Unis; **to s. with sb** loger chez qn **(c)** *Scot (live)* habiter
3 *n* **(a)** *(visit)* séjour *m* **(b)** *Law & Fig* **s. of execution** sursis *m*

▸ **stay away** *vi* **to s. away from sb/sth** ne pas s'approcher de qn/qch; **to s. away from school** ne pas aller à l'école

▸ **stay in** *vi (not go out)* rester chez soi

▸ **stay on** *vi* rester

▸ **stay out** *vi* **(a)** *(not go home)* ne pas rentrer; **to s. out all night** ne pas rentrer de la nuit; **to s. out late** rentrer tard **(b)** *(of strikers)* continuer la grève **(c)** *(not interfere)* **to s. out of sth** ne pas se mêler de qch

▸ **stay up** *vi* ne pas aller se coucher

staying power ['steɪɪŋ'paʊə(r)] *n* endurance *f*

STD [estiː'diː] *n (abbr* **sexually transmitted disease)** MST *f*

stead [sted] *n* **to stand sb in good s.** être fort utile à qn; **in sb's s.** à la place de qn

steadfast ['stedfɑːst] *adj* dévoué(e); *(opponent, resistance)* constant(e)

steadily ['stedɪlɪ] *adv (change, grow)* progressivement; *(work)* assidûment; *(walk)* d'un pas régulier; *(look)* fixement; *(breathe, increase)* régulièrement

steady ['stedɪ] **1** *adj* **(a)** *(stable)* stable; **in a s. voice** d'une voix assurée **(b)** *(regular)* régulier(ère); *(progress)* constant(e); *(relationship)* durable; **to have a s. girlfriend** avoir une copine (attitrée); **to drive at a s. 50 mph** ≃ rouler à une vitesse régulière de 80 km/h
2 *adv* **to be going s.** sortir ensemble sérieusement; *Fam* **s. (on)!** du calme!
3 *vt* faire tenir; **to s. oneself** trouver son équilibre; **to s. one's nerves** se calmer; **to s. one's voice** contrôler sa voix

steak [steɪk] *n (beef)* steak *m*; *(of fish)* darne *f*

steal [stiːl] *(pt* **stole** [stəʊl], *pp* **stolen** ['stəʊlən]) **1** *vt* **(a)** *(thieve)* voler; **to s. sth from sb** voler qch à qn **(b)** *(idioms)* **to s. a glance at sb** jeter un coup d'œil à qn; **to s. the show** ravir la vedette
2 *vi* **(a)** *(thieve)* voler **(b)** *(move quietly)* **to s. away/in/out** s'en aller/rentrer/sortir sans faire de bruit; **to s. up on sb** s'approcher de qn sans faire de bruit; *Fig* prendre qn par surprise

stealth [stelθ] *n* ruse *f*

stealthily ['stelθɪlɪ] *adv* furtivement

stealthy ['stelθɪ] *adj* furtif(ive)

steam [stiːm] **1** *n* **(a)** *(vapour)* vapeur *f*; *(on glass)* buée *f*; **s. bath** bain *m* de vapeur; **s. engine** locomotive *f* à vapeur; **s. iron** fer *m* à vapeur; **s. shovel** pelleteuse *f* **(b)** *(idioms)* **to get up s.** prendre de l'élan; **to run out of s.** s'essouffler; **to let off s.** se défouler; **to do sth under one's own s.** faire qch tout(e) seul(e)
2 *vt (food)* faire cuire à la vapeur
3 *vi (give off steam)* fumer

▸ **steam open** *vt sep (envelope)* décacheter à la vapeur

▸ **steam up 1** *vt sep* **to get all steamed up (about sth)** *(of person)* se mettre dans tous ses états (à propos de qch)
2 *vi (of window, glasses)* s'embuer

steamer ['stiːmə(r)] *n* **(a)** *(ship)* bateau *m* à vapeur *m* **(b)** *(for food)* panier *m* de cuisson à la vapeur

steamroller ['stiːmrəʊlə(r)] **1** *n* rouleau *m* compresseur

2 *vt* **to s. sb into doing sth** forcer qn à faire qch

steamship ['sti:mʃɪp] *n* bateau *m* à vapeur

steamy ['sti:mɪ] *adj* **(a)** *(room)* plein(e) de vapeur; *(mirror)* embué(e) **(b)** *Fam (novel, film)* torride

steel [sti:l] **1** *n* acier *m*; **nerves of s.** nerfs *mpl* d'acier; **the s. industry** la sidérurgie; **s. band** steel band *m*; **s. mill** aciérie *f*; **s. wool** paille *f* de fer
2 *vt* **to s. oneself to do sth** s'armer de courage pour faire qch; **to s. oneself against sth** se blinder contre qch

steelworker ['sti:lwɜːkə(r)] *n* employé(e) *m,f* de la sidérurgie

steep¹ [sti:p] *adj* **(a)** *(path, hill)* pentu(e), escarpé(e), *(climb)* raide; *Fig (increase)* considérable **(b)** *Fam (expensive)* salé(e); *(unreasonable)* raide

steep² *vt (soak)* faire tremper; *Fig* **steeped in history/tradition** imprégné(e) d'histoire/de tradition

steeple ['sti:pəl] *n* clocher *m*

steeplechase ['sti:pəltʃeɪs] *n* steeple-chase *m*

steeplejack ['sti:pəldʒæk] *n* réparateur *m* de clochers et de cheminées d'usines

steer¹ [stɪə(r)] **1** *vt (car)* conduire; *(ship)* barrer; **to s. sb out of trouble** sortir qn du pétrin
2 *vi (of person)* conduire; *(of ship)* se diriger **(for vers)**; **to s. clear of sb/sth** éviter qn/qch

steer² *n (bull)* bouvillon *m*

steering ['stɪərɪŋ] *n (mechanism)* direction *f*; **s. column** colonne *f* de direction; *Pol* **s. committee** comité *m* d'organisation; **s. wheel** volant *m*

stem [stem] **1** *n (of plant)* tige *f*; *(of glass)* pied *m*; *(of pipe)* tuyau *m*; *(of word)* radical *m*
2 *vt (pt & pp* stemmed) *(halt)* stopper; **to s. the tide of sth** enrayer le flot de qch
3 *vi* **to s. from** provenir de

stench [stentʃ] *n* puanteur *f*

stencil ['stensəl] **1** *n* pochoir *m*
2 *vt (pt & pp* stencilled, *Am* stenciled) dessiner au pochoir

stenographer [stə'nɒgrəfə(r)] *n* sténographe *m,f*

step [step] **1** *n* **(a)** *(movement, sound)* pas *m*; **to take a s.** faire un pas; **s. by s.** pas à pas; *Fig* petit à petit; *also Fig* **to watch one's s.** faire attention où l'on met les pieds; **to keep in s.** *(in dance)* danser en mesure; *Fig* **to be out of s. (with sb)** être en décalage (par rapport à qn) **(b)** *(action, measure)* mesure *f*; **to take steps (to do sth)** prendre des mesures (pour faire qch); **the next s. is to...** la prochaine chose à faire, c'est de...; **a s. in the right direction** un pas dans la bonne direction **(c)** *(stage)* étape *f*; **at every s.** à chaque étape; **every s. of the way** sur toute la ligne **(d)** *(of staircase)* marche *f*; *(of stepladder)* échelon *m*; **(flight of) steps** escalier *m*; *(on outside of building)* perron *m* **(e)** *(exercise)* step *m*; **s. class** cours *m* de step
2 *vi (pt & pp* stepped) *(take a step)* faire un pas; *(walk)* marcher; **to s. on sth** marcher sur qch; **s. this way** venez par ici; *Fam Fig* **to s. on it** se grouiller

▸ **step back** *vi* reculer **(from** de), *Fig* prendre du recul **(from** par rapport à)
▸ **step down** *vi (resign)* démissionner
▸ **step forward** *vi (volunteer)* se porter volontaire
▸ **step in** *vi (intervene)* intervenir
▸ **step up** *vt sep (increase)* accélérer; *(pressure)* augmenter

stepbrother ['stepbrʌðə(r)] *n* = fils du conjoint d'un des parents

stepchild ['steptʃaɪld] *n (boy)* beau-fils *m*; *(girl)* belle-fille *f*

stepdaughter ['stepdɔːtə(r)] *n* belle-fille *f*

stepfather ['stepfɑːðə(r)] *n* beau-père *m*

stepladder ['steplædə(r)] *n* escabeau *m*

stepmother ['stepmʌðə(r)] *n* belle-mère *f*

stepparent ['steppeərənt] *n (father)* beau-père *m*; *(mother)* belle-mère *f*

steppe [step] *n* steppe *f*

stepsister ['stepsɪstə(r)] *n* = fille du conjoint d'un des parents

stepson ['stepsʌn] *n* beau-fils *m*

stereo ['sterɪəʊ] **1** *n (pl* stereos) *(equipment)* chaîne *f* stéréo; *(sound)* stéréo *f*; **in s.** en stéréo
2 *adj* stéréo *inv*

stereophonic [sterɪəʊ'fɒnɪk] *adj* stéréophonique

stereoscopic [sterɪəʊ'skɒpɪk] *adj* stéréoscopique

stereotype ['sterɪəʊtaɪp] *n* stéréotype *m*

stereotyped ['sterɪəʊtaɪpt] *adj* stéréotypé(e)

sterile ['steraɪl] *adj* stérile

sterility [ste'rɪlɪtɪ] *n* stérilité *f*

sterilization [sterɪlaɪ'zeɪʃən] *n* stérilisation *f*

sterilize ['sterɪlaɪz] *vt* stériliser

sterling ['stɜːlɪŋ] **1** *n (British currency)* livre *f* sterling
2 *adj* **(a)** *(silver)* fin(e) **(b)** *(effort, quality)* remarquable

stern¹ [stɜːn] *adj (person, look)* sévère

stern² *n (of boat)* poupe *f*

sternum ['stɜːnəm] *n (pl* sternums *or* sterna ['stɜːnə]) *n* sternum *m*

steroid ['stɪərɔɪd] *n* stéroïde *m*

stethoscope ['steθəskəʊp] *n* stéthoscope *m*

stevedore ['sti:vədɔː(r)] *n* docker *m*

stew [stju:] **1** *n* ragoût *m*; *Fam Fig* **to be in a s.** *(of person)* être dans le pétrin
2 *vt (meat)* faire cuire en ragoût; *(fruit)* faire de la compote de
3 *vi (of meat)* mijoter; *Fig* **to let sb s. (in his/her own juice)** laisser qn mariner

steward ['stjʊəd] *n (on estate)* régisseur *m*; *(on ship, plane)* steward *m*; *(at sporting event)* organisateur *m*; *(at demonstration)* membre *m* du service d'ordre

stewardess [stjʊə'des] *n (on ship, plane)* hôtesse *f*

stewed [stju:d] *adj* **s. beef** bœuf *m* en ragoût; *Br* **s. fruit** compote *f* de fruits; **this tea is s.** ce thé a trop infusé

stick¹ [stɪk] *n* **(a)** *(of wood, glue, chewing gum)* bâton *m*; *(for walking)* canne *f*; *(of celery, rhubarb)* tige *f*; *Fam Fig* **to get hold of the wrong end of the s.** comprendre de travers; *Fam* **she lives out in the sticks** elle habite dans un trou perdu; **s. insect** phasme *m* **(b)** *Fam (criticism)* **to give sb s.** *(for sth)* taper sur les doigts de qn (à cause de qch); **to take a lot of s.** se faire beaucoup critiquer

stick² *(pt & pp* stuck [stʌk]) **1** *vt* **(a)** *(insert)* **to s. sth in(to) sth** planter qch dans qch **(b)** *Fam (put)* mettre, poser **(c)** *(attach with glue)* coller **(d)** *Fam (endure)* supporter
2 *vi* **(a)** *(adhere)* coller; *Fig* **the name stuck** ce nom lui/leur/*etc* est resté; *Fig* **to s. in one's guns** ne pas en démordre; **to s. to the facts** s'en tenir aux faits; **to s. to one's principles** rester sur ses principes **(b)** *(become jammed)* se coincer; *Fig* **it sticks in my throat** c'est dur à avaler

▸ **stick around** *vi Fam* attendre
▸ **stick at** *vt insep (persevere with)* persévérer dans; **to s. at nothing** ne reculer devant rien
▸ **stick by** *vt insep (friend)* soutenir; *(promise, statement)* maintenir
▸ **stick out 1** *vt sep* **(a)** *(cause to protrude)* faire sortir; **to s.**

one's tongue out (at sb) tirer la langue (à qn); *Fam* **to s. one's neck out (for sb)** prendre des risques (pour qn) **(b)** *Fam (endure)* **to s. it out** tenir bon
2 *vi* **(a)** *(protrude)* ressortir; *(of ears)* être décollés(ées); *(of teeth)* avancer **(b)** *Fam (be noticeable)* se voir; **it sticks out a mile** *or* **like a sore thumb** ça se voit comme le nez au milieu de la figure
▸ **stick together 1** *vt sep* coller
2 *vi* **(a)** *(with glue)* être collé(e) **(b)** *(of friends)* rester ensemble
▸ **stick up 1** *vt sep (sign, poster)* mettre; *Fam* **s. 'em up!** haut les mains!
2 *vi (of building, hair)* se dresser
▸ **stick up for** *vt insep (person, rights)* prendre la défense de
▸ **stick with** *vt insep (not give up)* rester avec

sticker ['stɪkə(r)] *n* autocollant *m*

stick-in-the-mud ['stɪkɪnðəmʌd] *n Fam* rabat-joie *m inv*

stickleback ['stɪklbæk] *n* épinoche *f*

stickler ['stɪklə(r)] *n* **to be a s. for sth** être à cheval sur qch

stick-on ['stɪkɒn] *adj* autocollant(e)

stick-up ['stɪkʌp] *n Fam (robbery)* braquage *m*

sticky ['stɪkɪ] *adj* **(a)** *(substance)* collant(e); *(climate)* humide, moite; *(label)* adhésif(ive); *Fig* **to have s. fingers** avoir une tendance pickpocket; **s. tape** ruban *m* adhésif **(b)** *Fig (awkward)* délicat(e); **to come to a s. end** mal finir; *Fam* **to be on a s. wicket** être dans une situation délicate

stiff [stɪf] *adj* **(a)** *(rigid)* rigide; *(paste)* ferme; **as s. as a board** tout(e) raide; **to be bored s.** s'ennuyer à mourir; **to be scared s.** avoir une trouille bleue; **to be frozen s.** être frigorifié(e) **(b)** *(joint)* ankylosé(e); **to be s.** *(of person)* avoir des courbatures; **to have a s. neck** avoir un torticolis; **my arm is s.** j'ai le bras ankylosé **(c)** *(handle, hinge, drawer)* dur(e) **(d)** *(severe) (punishment, fine)* sévère; *(resistance)* opiniâtre; *(competition)* rude; *(exam)* dur(e); *(breeze)* fort(e); **a s. drink** une boisson forte **(e)** *(formal)* rigide; *(smile)* forcé(e)

stiffen ['stɪfən] **1** *vt* renforcer; *(paste)* épaissir
2 *vi* se raidir

stiffly ['stɪflɪ] *adv (bow)* avec raideur; *(answer, greet)* avec froideur

stifle ['staɪfəl] *vt also Fig* étouffer

stifling ['staɪflɪŋ] *adj* étouffant(e)

stigma ['stɪgmə] *(pl* **stigmas)** *n* honte *f*

stigmata [stɪg'mɑːtə] *npl (of saint)* stigmates *mpl*

stigmatize ['stɪgmətaɪz] *vt* stigmatiser

stile [staɪl] *n* échalier *m*

stiletto [stɪ'letəʊ] *(pl* **stilettos)** *n (dagger)* stylet *m*; *(shoe)* talon *m* aiguille; **s. heels** talons aiguille

still[1] [stɪl] **1** *adj (motionless)* immobile; *(calm)* calme; *(silent)* silencieux(euse); *(drink)* non gazeux(euse); **to stand s.** ne pas bouger; *Art* **s. life** nature *f* morte; *Prov* **s. waters run deep** il faut se méfier de l'eau qui dort
2 *vt* calmer, apaiser
3 *n* **(a) in the s. of the night** dans le silence de la nuit **(b)** *(photograph)* photo *f* de plateau

still[2] *adv* **(a)** *(up to given point in time)* toujours, encore; **she's s. alive** elle vit toujours; **I s. think/say that...** je continue de penser/dire que...; **I s. have 200 euros** il me reste encore 200 euros **(b)** *(nonetheless)* tout de même; **s., it could have been worse** enfin, ç'aurait pu être pire **(c)** *(even)* encore; **s. more/better** encore plus/mieux

still[3] *n (distilling equipment)* alambic *m*

stillbirth ['stɪlbɜːθ] *n* enfant *m* mort-né

stillborn ['stɪlbɔːn] *adj* mort-né(e)

stillness ['stɪlnɪs] *n* tranquillité *f*

stilt [stɪlt] *n (for walking)* échasse *f*; *(for building)* pilotis *m*

stilted ['stɪltɪd] *adj* qui manque de naturel

stimulant ['stɪmjʊlənt] *n* stimulant *m*

stimulate ['stɪmjʊleɪt] *vt* stimuler

stimulating ['stɪmjʊleɪtɪŋ] *adj* stimulant(e)

stimulation [stɪmjʊ'leɪʃən] *n* stimulation *f*

stimulus ['stɪmjʊləs] *(pl* **stimuli** ['stɪmjʊlaɪ]) *n* encouragement *m*; *(physiological)* stimulus *m inv*

sting [stɪŋ] **1** *n* **(a)** *(of bee)* dard *m*; *(of scorpion)* aiguillon *m*; *(wound)* piqûre *f* **(b)** *(sensation)* brûlure *f* **(c)** *(idioms)* **to have a s. in the tail** *(of story, proposal)* avoir une fin inattendue; **to take the s. out of sth** atténuer les effets de qch
2 *vt (pt & pp* **stung** [stʌŋ]) *(of bee, nettle)* piquer; *Fig (of remark)* blesser, piquer au vif; *Fig* **to s. sb into action** pousser qn à agir; *Fam Fig* **they stung him for $50** ils l'ont arnaqué de 50 dollars
3 *vi (of eyes, skin)* piquer

stinging ['stɪŋɪŋ] *adj (pain)* cuisant(e); *(remark, criticism)* cinglant(e); **s. nettle** ortie *f*

stingray ['stɪŋreɪ] *n* pastenague *f*

stingy ['stɪndʒɪ] *adj (person)* pingre; *(portion)* minuscule; **to be s. with one's praise** être avare de compliments

stink [stɪŋk] **1** *n (smell)* puanteur *f*; *Fam Fig* **to kick up a s. (about sth)** faire tout un scandale (à propos de qch)
2 *vi (pt* **stank** [stæŋk] *or* **stunk** [stʌŋk], *pp* **stunk**) **(a)** *(smell)* puer; **to s. of sth** puer qch; *Fam Fig* **to s. of corruption** sentir la corruption à plein nez **(b)** *Fam Fig (be of bad quality)* craindre

stinkbomb ['stɪŋkbɒm] *n* boule *f* puante

stinker ['stɪŋkə(r)] *n Fam (person)* peau *f* de vache; *(difficult task)* casse-tête *m*; **a s. of a cold** un rhume carabiné

stinking ['stɪŋkɪŋ] **1** *adj* puant(e); **a s. cold** un rhume carabiné
2 *adv Fam* **to be s. rich** être bourré(e) de fric

stint [stɪnt] **1** *n (period)* période *f*; *(share of work)* part *f* de travail; **to take a s. at the wheel** prendre le volant; **he had a two-year s. in the army** il a fait deux ans d'armée
2 *vt* épargner; **to s. oneself** se sacrifier
3 *vi* **to s. on sth** lésiner sur qch

stipend ['staɪpend] *n* traitement *m*

stipulate ['stɪpjʊleɪt] *vt* stipuler

stipulation [stɪpjʊ'leɪʃən] *n* stipulation *f*

stir [stɜː(r)] **1** *vt (pt & pp* **stirred)** **(a)** *(liquid, mixture)* remuer; *(leaves)* agiter **(b)** *Fig (person)* émouvoir, remuer; *(emotion)* réveiller; *(curiosity)* exciter; **to s. sb to do sth** inciter qn à faire qch; *Fam* **to s. oneself** se remuer; *Fam* **to s. it** *(make trouble)* envenimer les choses
2 *vi (move)* bouger, remuer
3 *n* **(a) to give sth a s.** remuer qch **(b)** *Fig* **to cause a s.** faire du bruit
▸ **stir up** *vt sep* **(a)** *(dust, leaves)* remuer **(b)** *Fig (rebellion, anger, resentment)* attiser; *(workers, crowd)* inciter à la révolte; **to s. up trouble** semer la zizanie; **to s. things up** envenimer les choses

stir-fry ['stɜːfraɪ] *(pt & pp* **stir-fried)** *vt Culin* faire sauter

stirrer ['stɜːrə(r)] *n Fam (trouble-maker)* semeur(euse) *m, f* de zizanie

stirring ['stɜːrɪŋ] **1** *n* **the first stirrings of** les premiers signes de
2 *adj (speech, film)* poignant(e)

stirrup ['stɪrəp] *n* étrier *m*

stitch [stɪtʃ] **1** n **(a)** (in sewing) point m; (in knitting) maille f; Med point (de suture); Fam **she didn't have a s. on** elle était nue comme un ver; Prov **a s. in time saves nine** un point à temps en vaut cent **(b)** (sharp pain) point m (de côté); **to get a s.** prendre un point **(c)** Fam **we were in stitches** (laughing) on était pliés
2 vt (clothing) coudre; Med recoudre
▸ **stitch up** vt sep Fam (falsely incriminate) faire porter le chapeau à

stoat [stəʊt] n hermine f

stock [stɒk] **1** n **(a)** (supply) provisions fpl; Com stock m; Com **while stocks last** jusqu'à épuisement des stocks; **to have sth in s.** avoir qch en stock; **to be out of s.** être épuisé(e); Fig **to take s.** faire le point; Com **s. control** gestion f des stocks; Com **s. list** inventaire m des stocks **(b)** (livestock) bétail m **(c)** Fin valeurs fpl, actions fpl; Fig **her s. is going up/down** sa cote est en hausse/baisse; **stocks and shares** valeurs mobilières; **s. exchange** Bourse f (des valeurs); **s. market** marché m des valeurs **(d)** (descent) of **German s.** de souche allemande **(e)** (of rifle) fût m **(f)** **stocks** (for punishment) pilori m **(g)** (in cooking) bouillon m; **s. cube** bouillon cube m
2 adj (argument, excuse) classique
3 vt **(a)** (goods) vendre **(b)** (supply) (shop) approvisionner (with en)
▸ **stock up** vi faire des provisions (with de)

stockade [stɒˈkeɪd] n palissade f

stockbroker [ˈstɒkbrəʊkə(r)] n Fin agent m de change

stockholder [ˈstɒkhəʊldə(r)] n Fin actionnaire mf

Stockholm [ˈstɒkhəʊm] n Stockholm

stocking [ˈstɒkɪŋ] n (garment) bas m

stockist [ˈstɒkɪst] n Com stockiste mf

stockpile [ˈstɒkpaɪl] **1** n réserves fpl
2 vt faire des réserves de

stockroom [ˈstɒkruːm] n réserve f, magasin m

stock-still [ˈstɒkˈstɪl] adv **to stand s.** se tenir complètement immobile

stocktaking [ˈstɒkteɪkɪŋ] n Com inventaire m des stocks; Fig **a s. exercise** un examen de situation

stocky [ˈstɒkɪ] adj trapu(e)

stodge [stɒdʒ] n Fam (food) aliments mpl bourratifs

stodgy [ˈstɒdʒɪ] adj (food) bourratif(ive); (book) indigeste

stoic [ˈstəʊɪk] n & adj stoïque mf

stoical [ˈstəʊɪkəl] adj stoïque

stoicism [ˈstəʊɪsɪzəm] n stoïcisme m

stoke [stəʊk] vt (fire, boiler) alimenter; Fig entretenir

STOL [stɒl] n Av (abbr short take-off and landing) ADAC m

stole[1] [stəʊl] n (garment) étole f

stole[2] pt of steal

stolen [ˈstəʊlən] **1** adj volé(e)
2 pp of steal

stolid [ˈstɒlɪd] adj impassible

stomach [ˈstʌmək] **1** n ventre m; (organ) estomac m; **on an empty s.** à jeun; Fig **it turns my s.** ça m'écœure; Fig **to have no s. for sth** ne pas avoir envie de qch; **to have (a) s. ache** avoir mal au ventre; (in organ) avoir mal à l'estomac; Med **s. pump** pompe f stomacale
2 vt Fig (tolerate) supporter

stomp [stɒmp] vi marcher en tapant des pieds; **to s. in/out** entrer/sortir en tapant des pieds

stone [stəʊn] **1** n **(a)** (material, piece of rock) pierre f; (smaller) caillou m; Fig **to leave no s. unturned** remuer ciel et terre; Fig **a s.'s throw from here** à deux pas d'ici; **the S. Age** l'âge m de pierre **(b)** (of fruit) noyau m **(c)** (unit of weight) = 6,35kg

2 adj en pierre; (jug) en grès
3 vt **(a)** (fruit) dénoyauter **(b)** (person) lapider

stone-cold [ˈstəʊnˈkəʊld] adj glacé(e)

stoned [stəʊnd] adj very Fam (on drugs) défoncé(e)

stone-dead [ˈstəʊnˈded] adj raide mort(e)

stone-deaf [ˈstəʊnˈdef] adj sourd(e) comme un pot

stonemason [ˈstəʊnmeɪsən] n maçon m

stonewall [stəʊnˈwɔːl] vi (in game) pratiquer un jeu défensif; (in inquiry) refuser de répondre

stoneware [ˈstəʊnweə(r)] n poterie f en grès

stonework [ˈstəʊnwɜːk] n maçonnerie f

stonily [ˈstəʊnɪlɪ] adv froidement

stony [ˈstəʊnɪ] adj (ground, beach) caillouteux(euse); Fig (look, silence) glacial(e); Fam Fig **to be s. broke** n'avoir pas un rond

stood [stʊd] pt & pp of stand

stooge [stuːdʒ] n (comedian's fall-guy) faire-valoir m; (minion) larbin m

stool [stuːl] n **(a)** (seat) tabouret m; Fig **to fall between two stools** être assis(e) entre deux chaises; Fam **s. pigeon** balance f, indic m **(b)** Med (faeces) selles fpl

stoop[1] [stuːp] **1** n **to have a s.** être voûté(e); **to walk with a s.** marcher le dos courbé
2 vi (bend down) se pencher; Fig **to s. to (doing)** sth s'abaisser à (faire) qch

stoop[2] n Am (of house) (with roof) véranda f; (without roof) perron m

stop [stɒp] **1** n **(a)** (halt) arrêt m; **to put a s. to sth** mettre fin à qch; **to come to a s.** s'arrêter; Aut **s. sign** stop m **(b)** (pause) (in work) pause f; (in journey) halte f; (of plane) escale f; (of train) arrêt m **(c)** (for bus, train) arrêt m **(d)** (full stop) point m; (in telegram) stop m **(e)** Mus (on organ) jeu m; Fig **to pull out all the stops** tout mettre en œuvre
2 vt (pt & pp stopped) **(a)** (halt) (person, vehicle) arrêter; (conversation, speaker) interrompre; (corruption, abuse) mettre fin à; Fin **to s. a cheque** faire opposition à un chèque; **s., thief!** au voleur! **(b)** (cease) arrêter; **to s. doing sth** arrêter de faire qch **(c)** (prevent) empêcher; **to s. sb from doing sth** empêcher qn de faire qch; **I couldn't s. myself** je n'ai pas pu m'en empêcher **(d)** (fill in) (hole, gap) boucher
3 vi **(a)** (halt) (of moving person, vehicle) s'arrêter **(b)** (cease) (of speaker, worker) s'arrêter; (of pain, bleeding) cesser; (of rain) s'arrêter, cesser; **she'll s. at nothing** rien ne l'arrêtera; **to s. short** s'arrêter net **(c)** (stay) rester
▸ **stop by** vi (of visit) passer; **I'll s. by your place tomorrow** je passerai chez toi demain
▸ **stop off** vi faire une halte
▸ **stop over** vi Av faire escale
▸ **stop up** vt sep (hole, sink, pipe) boucher

stopcock [ˈstɒpkɒk] n robinet m d'arrêt

stopgap [ˈstɒpgæp] n (thing, person) bouche-trou m; **s. measure** mesure f transitoire

stoplight [ˈstɒplaɪt] n Am Aut feux mpl (tricolores ou de signalisation)

stopover [ˈstɒpəʊvə(r)] n Av escale f

stoppage [ˈstɒpɪdʒ] n **(a)** (of flow, traffic) arrêt m; (strike) débrayage m **(b)** Fin (deduction) retenue f

stopper [ˈstɒpə(r)] n bouchon m

stop-press [ˈstɒpres] adj Journ de dernière minute

stopwatch [ˈstɒpwɒtʃ] n chronomètre m

storage [ˈstɔːrɪdʒ] n **(a)** (action) emmagasinage m; (space available) (espace m de) rangement m; **to put sth into s.** entreposer qch; **s. heater** radiateur m à accumulation; s.

space espace *m* de rangement; **s. tank** citerne *f* **(b)** *Comptr* mémoire *f*

store [stɔ:(r)] **1** *n* **(a)** *(supply) (of goods, food)* provision *f*; *Fig (of knowledge)* fonds *m*; **stores** réserves *fpl* **(b)** *(warehouse)* entrepôt *m* **(c)** *Am (shop)* magasin *m*; *also Br* **s. detective** vigile *m* **(d)** *(idioms)* **to hold** *or* **keep sth in s.** tenir *ou* garder qch en réserve; **I have a surprise in s. for her** je lui réserve une surprise; **to set great s. by sth** faire grand cas de qch
2 *vt (put in storage)* entreposer; *(food)* ranger; *(electricity, heat)* emmagasiner; **s. in a cool place** conserver au frais
▸ **store up** *vt sep* accumuler

storehouse ['stɔ:haʊs] *n* entrepôt *m*

storeroom ['stɔ:ru:m] *n (in office, factory)* réserve *f*; *(at home)* débarras *m*

storey, *Am* **story** ['stɔ:rɪ] *n* étage *m*; **a four-s. building** un immeuble de quatre étages

stork [stɔ:k] *n* cigogne *f*

storm [stɔ:m] **1** *n* **(a)** *(bad weather)* tempête *f*; *(thunderstorm)* orage *m*; *Fig* **a s. in a teacup** une tempête dans un verre d'eau; **s. cloud** nuée *f* d'orage; **s. door** double porte *f* **(b)** *Fig (scandal, of protest)* tempête *f*; *(of abuse)* bordée *f* **(c)** *Mil* **to take sth by s.** prendre qch d'assaut; *Fig* **she took Broadway by s.** elle a eu un succès foudroyant à Broadway; **s. troops** troupes *fpl* d'assaut
2 *vt (town, fortress)* prendre d'assaut
3 *vi (of person)* tempêter (**at sb** contre qn); **to s. in/out** entrer/sortir comme un ouragan

stormy ['stɔ:mɪ] *adj also Fig* orageux(euse)

story[1] ['stɔ:rɪ] *(pl* **stories)** *n* **(a)** *(account)* histoire *f*; *Fig* **to tell stories** *(lie)* raconter des histoires **(b)** *(plot) (of novel, play)* intrigue *f*, histoire *f* **(c)** *(in newspaper)* article *m* **(d)** *(idioms)* **that's quite another s.** ça c'est une autre histoire; **it's the same old s.** c'est toujours la même histoire; *Fam* **it's the s. of my life** je suis le/la spécialiste de ce genre de choses; **it's a long s.** c'est une longue histoire; **to cut a long s. short,...** bref, pour résumer...

story[2] *Am (of building)* = **storey**

storybook ['stɔ:rɪbʊk] *n* livre *m* d'histoires

storyteller ['stɔ:rɪtelə(r)] *n* conteur(euse) *m,f*

stout [staʊt] **1** *n (beer)* stout *f*, bière *f* brune forte
2 *adj* **(a)** *(fat)* corpulent(e) **(b)** *(solid) (door, shoes)* solide **(c)** *(brave) (person, resistance)* acharné(e)

stouthearted [staʊt'hɑ:tɪd] *adj Lit* vaillant(e)

stoutly ['staʊtlɪ] *adv (resist, maintain)* avec fermeté

stove [stəʊv] **1** *pt & pp of* **stave**
2 *n (for cooking)* cuisinière *f*; *(for heating)* poêle *m*

stow [stəʊ] *vt (put away)* ranger; *Naut* arrimer
▸ **stow away** *vi (on ship)* s'embarquer clandestinement

stowaway ['stəʊəweɪ] *n* passager(ère) *m,f* clandestin(e)

straddle ['strædəl] *vt (horse)* enfourcher; *(chair)* se mettre à califourchon sur; *Fig (period of time, subject)* couvrir

strafe [streɪf] *vt Mil* mitrailler en rase-mottes

straggle ['strægəl] *vi* **(a)** *(lag behind)* être à la traîne **(b)** *(of hair)* pendouiller

straggler ['stræglə(r)] *n* retardataire *mf*

straggly ['stræglɪ] *adj (hair)* épars(e)

straight [streɪt] **1** *adj* **(a)** *(level, not curved) (line, tie, skirt, picture, back)* droit(e); *(hair)* raide; **to keep a s. face** garder son sérieux; **to put things** *or* **matters s.** arranger les choses; **to put sb s. about sth** éclairer qn sur qch **(b)** *(consecutive)* consécutif(ive); **s. flush** *(in cards)* quinte *f* flush **(c)** *(honest) (person)* honnête; *(answer)* clair(e); **to be s. with sb** jouer franc jeu avec qn

(d) *(conventional)* conformiste; *Th* **s. man** faire-valoir *m* **(e)** *Fam (heterosexual)* hétéro **(f)** *(undiluted)* pur(e)
2 *adv* **(a)** *(in straight line)* droit; **sit up s.!** tiens-toi droit sur ton siège!; **to see s.** voir bien; **I can't think s.** je n'ai pas les idées claires; **to look s. ahead** regarder droit devant soi; **go s. on** allez tout droit; *Fig* **to go s.** *(of criminal)* se ranger **(b)** *(immediately)* immédiatement; **I'll be s. back** je reviens tout de suite; **s. away** *or* **off** tout de suite **(c)** *(directly)* directement; **to come** *or* **get s. to the point** aller droit au fait; **to come s. out with sth** dire qch tout net **3** *n* **(a)** **to keep to the s. and narrow** rester sur le droit chemin
(b) *(on running track, racecourse)* ligne *f* droite

straightaway ['streɪtəweɪ] *adv* tout de suite

straighten ['streɪtən] *vt (bent nail, rod)* redresser; *(picture)* remettre droit; *(tie, hat)* ajuster; **to s. one's back** se redresser
▸ **straighten out** *vt sep (problem)* régler; *(one's affairs)* mettre de l'ordre dans

straight-faced ['streɪt'feɪst] *adj* à l'air sérieux

straightforward [streɪt'fɔ:wəd] *adj* **(a)** *(honest)* direct(e), franc (franche) **(b)** *(simple)* simple

strain[1] [streɪn] **1** *n* **(a)** *(on rope, beam, economy, friendship)* tension *f*; *(on muscle, ankle)* foulure *f*; **to put a s. on** *(economy)* grever; *(friendship)* éprouver **(b)** *(mental stress)* stress *m*; **to be under a lot of s.** être très stressé(e)
2 *vt* **(a)** *(muscle, ankle)* se fouler; *(economy)* grever; *(friendship)* éprouver; **to s. one's back** se faire mal au dos; **to s. one's ears** tendre l'oreille **(b)** *Culin (liquid)* filtrer, passer; *(vegetables)* égoutter
3 *vi* **to s. at a rope** tirer sur une corde; *Fig* **to s. at the leash** ne plus tenir en place

strain[2] *n (variety) (of virus)* souche *f*; *(of plant)* variété *f*

strained [streɪnd] *adj (muscle)* froissé(e); *Fig (atmosphere, relationship)* tendu(e)

strainer ['streɪnə(r)] *n* passoire *f*

strait [streɪt] *n* détroit *m*; **the Straits of Gibraltar** le détroit de Gibraltar

straitlaced ['streɪt'leɪst] *adj* collet monté *inv*

strand[1] [strænd] *vt (ship)* échouer; **to be stranded** *(of person)* être bloqué(e)

strand[2] *n (of rope, cotton)* brin *m*; *(of hair)* mèche *f*; *Fig (of plot)* fil *m*

strange [streɪndʒ] *adj* **(a)** *(odd) (person, behaviour)* bizarre **(b)** *(unfamiliar)* inconnu(e)

strangely ['streɪndʒlɪ] *adv (behave, dress)* bizarrement; **s. enough,...** chose bizarre,...

strangeness ['streɪndʒnɪs] *n* **(a)** *(oddness)* bizarrerie *f* **(b)** *(unfamiliarity)* étrangeté *f*

stranger ['streɪndʒə(r)] *n (unknown person)* inconnu(e) *m,f*; *(from somewhere else)* étranger(ère) *m,f*; **I'm a s. here myself** je ne suis pas d'ici

strangle ['stræŋgəl] *vt also Fig* étrangler

stranglehold ['stræŋgəlhəʊld] *n Fig* **to have a s. on sth** avoir la mainmise sur qch

strangulation [stræŋgjʊ'leɪʃən] *n* strangulation *f*

strap [stræp] **1** *n (of leather, canvas)* sangle *f*, lanière *f*; *(on dress, bra)* bretelle *f*; *(for watch)* bracelet *m*; *(for shoe)* bride *f*
2 *vt (pt & pp* **strapped)** **to s. sth to sth** sangler qch à qch; *Fam* **to be strapped (for cash)** être un peu juste
▸ **strap in** *vt sep* attacher; **to s. oneself in** attacher sa ceinture de sécurité

strapless ['stræplɪs] *adj (dress, bra)* sans bretelles

strapping ['stræpɪŋ] *adj* costaud(e)

Strasbourg [ˈstræzbɜːg] n Strasbourg

strategic [strəˈtiːdʒɪk] adj stratégique

strategist [ˈstrætɪdʒɪst] n stratège m

strategy [ˈstrætɪdʒɪ] (pl **strategies**) n stratégie f

stratification [strætɪfɪˈkeɪʃən] n stratification f

stratosphere [ˈstrætəsfɪə(r)] n stratosphère f

stratum [ˈstrɑːtəm] (pl **strata** [ˈstrɑːtə]) n strate f; Fig couche f

straw [strɔː] n (a) (from wheat, for drinking) paille f; s. hat chapeau m de paille; Fig s. man homme m de paille; s. poll sondage m d'opinion (b) (idioms) to clutch or grasp at straws se raccrocher à de faux espoirs; that's the last s.! ça c'est le comble!

strawberry [ˈstrɔːbərɪ] (pl **strawberries**) n fraise f; s. jam confiture f de fraises

straw-coloured, Am **straw-colored** [ˈstrɔːkʌləd] adj jaune paille inv

stray [streɪ] **1** n (dog) chien m errant; (cat) chat m égaré **2** adj (animal) égaré(e), (dog) errant(e), (bullet) perdu(e) **3** vi (of person, animal) s'égarer, to s. from the point s'écarter du sujet

streak [striːk] **1** n (stripe) (of paint, dirt) traînée f; (of light) raɪ m; (in hair) mèche f; a s. of lightning un éclair; a s. of luck une période de chance; to be on a winning/losing s. être dans une période de chance/poisse; to have a mean/ cruel s. avoir tendance à être radin(e)/cruel(elle) **2** vt streaked with dirt plein(e) de traînées sales; streaked with tears strié(e) de larmes; his hair is streaked with silver ses cheveux sont parsemés de cheveux gris; to have one's hair streaked se faire faire des mèches **3** vi (a) (move quickly) to s. off partir à toute vitesse; to s. past passer en trombe (b) Fam (run naked) courir nu(e) (en public)

streaker [ˈstriːkə(r)] n Fam = personne qui court nue en public

streaky [ˈstriːkɪ] adj (surface, pattern) strié(e); s. bacon bacon m entrelardé

stream [striːm] **1** n (a) (brook) ruisseau m (b) (of light, blood, water) jet m; (of tears, insults) torrent m; (of people) flot m; to come on s. (of industrial plant) entrer en production **2** vt (a) (spurt) to s. blood ruisseler de sang (b) Br Sch to s. pupils répartir des élèves par niveau **3** vi (a) (of liquid) ruisseler; (of people) affluer; (of traffic) s'écouler; her eyes were streaming ses yeux étaient ruisselants de larmes (b) (of hair, banner) flotter

streamer [ˈstriːmə(r)] n banderole f

streamline [ˈstriːmlaɪn] vt (vehicle) caréner; Fig (system) rationaliser; (department) dégraisser

streamlined [ˈstriːmlaɪnd] adj (vehicle) caréné(e); Fig (system) rationalisé(e); (department) dégraissé(e)

street [striːt] n (a) rue f; on the s. dans la rue; s. fighting combats mpl de rue; s. lamp lampadaire m; s. map plan m (de la ville); s. market marché m de plein air; s. sweeper balayeur(euse) m,f; s. theatre théâtre m de rue; s. value (of drugs) valeur f à la revente (b) (idioms) to walk the streets (of prostitute) faire le tapin ou le trottoir; the man in the s. Monsieur Tout-le-Monde; Fam to be streets ahead dépasser tout le monde; that's right up my s. c'est tout à fait mon rayon; Fam to have s. cred être très branché(e)

streetcar [ˈstriːtkɑː(r)] n Am tramway m

streetwalker [ˈstriːtwɔːkə(r)] n racoleuse f

streetwise [ˈstriːtwaɪz] adj dégourdi(e)

strength [streŋθ] n (a) (of person, wind, emotion, currency) force f; (of rope, fabric) solidité f; (of light, alcohol, army)

puissance f; to be at full s. (of department, regiment) avoir des effectifs complets; to be under s. (of department, regiment) ne pas avoir des effectifs complets; in s. en force; to go from s. to s. aller de mieux en mieux; on the s. of sur la base de; on the s. of her qualifications grâce à ses diplômes (b) (strong point) point m fort

strengthen [ˈstreŋθən] **1** vt (wall, building) renforcer, consolider; (muscle) affermir; (friendship) consolider; (determination, position) renforcer **2** vi (of friendship) se consolider; (of determination) se renforcer; (of currency) se raffermir; (of wind) souffler plus fort

strenuous [ˈstrenjʊəs] adj (activity, lifestyle) fatigant(e); (effort, opposition) vigoureux(euse); (denial) énergique

strenuously [ˈstrenjʊəslɪ] adv (campaign, deny) énergiquement; (resist) vigoureusement

stress [stres] **1** n (a) (tension) (physical) tension f; (mental) stress m; to be under a lot of s. être très stressé(e); s. factor facteur m de stress (b) (emphasis) insistance f; Ling accentuation f; to put s. on sth insister sur qch **2** vt (emphasize) insister sur; Ling accentuer

stressful [ˈstresfʊl] adj stressant(e)

stretch [stretʃ] **1** n (a) (of body) to have a s. s'étirer; Fig by no s. of the imagination même avec beaucoup d'imagination; s. marks vergetures fpl (b) (of water, land) étendue f; (of road) tronçon m; (of time, silence) période f; at one s. d'une traite (c) at full s. (factory) au maximum de ses capacités **2** vt (a) (elastic) étirer; (belt, arm, hand) tendre; to s. the truth exagérer; to s. one's legs se dégourdir les jambes (b) (put demands on) pousser à son maximum; (resources) utiliser au maximum; (sb's patience) abuser de; we're fully stretched at the moment nous sommes au maximum de notre rendement en ce moment (c) (make last) (income, supplies) faire durer **3** vi (a) (of elastic) s'étendre; (of person, fabric) s'étirer (b) (of road, land, years) s'étendre; s'étaler (c) (of resources, budget) my budget won't s. to a new computer je n'ai pas les moyens de m'acheter un nouvel ordinateur ► **stretch out 1** vt sep (arm, hand) tendre **2** vi (of person) s'étirer (b) (of road, time) s'étaler, s'étendre

stretcher [ˈstretʃə(r)] n brancard m; s. bearer brancardier m

stretchy [ˈstretʃɪ] adj extensible

strew [struː] (pp strewed or strewn [struːn]) vt (objects) éparpiller; to be strewn with sth (of surface) être jonché(e) de qch

stricken [ˈstrɪkən] adj (with grief, guilt) accablé(e) (with de); (with illness, by disaster) frappé(e) (with par)

strict [strɪkt] adj (a) (person, instruction, discipline) strict(e); s. morals morale f sévère; a s. Moslem un musulman de stricte obédience (b) (meaning, minimum) strict(e); in strictest confidence en toute confidence

strictly [ˈstrɪktlɪ] adv (a) (severely, only) strictement (b) (exactly) strictement à proprement parler; not s. true pas tout à fait vrai(e)

strictness [ˈstrɪktnɪs] n (of discipline, rules) sévérité f

stride [straɪd] **1** n (a) pas m; (when running) foulée f (b) (idioms) to make great strides faire des pas de géant; to take sth in one's s. prendre qch calmement; to get into one's s. trouver son rythme **2** vi (pt strode [strəʊd], pp stridden [ˈstrɪdən]) to s. in/out entrer/sortir à grands pas

strident [ˈstraɪdənt] adj strident(e)

strife [straɪf] n conflits mpl

strike [straɪk] **1** n (a) (refusal to work) grève f; to be on s.

être en grève; **s. fund** = caisse de prévoyance permettant d'aider les grévistes; **s. pay** indemnité *f* de grève
  (b) *(discovery) (of ore, oil)* découverte *f*
  (c) *(blow)* coup *m*; *Mil* attaque *f*, raid *m*
  2 *vt (pt & pp* **struck** [str∧k]) **(a)** *(hit)* frapper; *(collide with)* heurter, taper contre; **to be struck by lightning** être frappé(e) par la foudre; **to s. sb in the face** frapper qn à la figure; **to s. a blow** donner un coup; *Fig* **to s. a blow for freedom** se battre pour défendre sa liberté; **the clock struck ten** l'horloge a sonné dix heures; *Fig* **to s. the right/wrong note** *(of speech, remark)* sonner juste/faux; **to s. terror into sb** frapper qn de terreur; **to be struck dumb/blind** être frappé(e) de mutisme/cécité; **he was struck dead by a heart attack** il a été emporté par une crise cardiaque
  (b) *(match)* craquer
  (c) *(coin, medal)* frapper
  (d) *(impress)* frapper; **she strikes me as a reasonable person** elle me paraît raisonnable; **it struck me that...** il m'a semblé que...
  (e) *(discover) (gold, oil)* découvrir; *Fam* **to s. it rich** faire fortune; *Fam* **to s. it lucky** avoir un coup de chance
  (f) *(reach) (bargain, deal)* conclure; **to s. a balance** trouver un équilibre
  3 *vi* **(a)** *(attack) (of enemy)* attaquer; *(of criminal)* frapper; *(of disaster, earthquake)* se produire; *(of clock)* sonner; **to s. home** *(of criticism)* faire mouche; **s. while the iron is hot** il faut battre le fer pendant qu'il est chaud
  (b) *(of workers)* faire grève
▸ **strike back** *vi (retaliate)* riposter
▸ **strike down** *vt sep (of disease)* terrasser; *(of bullet)* abattre
▸ **strike off** *vt sep (doctor, lawyer)* radier
▸ **strike out 1** *vt sep (delete)* rayer
  2 *vi* **(a)** *(hit out)* **to s. out at sb** essayer de frapper qn **(b)** *(leave)* s'élancer **(for** vers)
▸ **strike up** *vt sep (song)* entonner; *(conversation)* entamer; **to s. up a friendship (with sb)** se lier d'amitié (avec qn)
strikebreaker ['straɪkbreɪkə(r)] *n* briseur(euse) *m,f* de grève
striker ['straɪkə(r)] *n* **(a)** *(striking worker)* gréviste *mf* **(b)** *(in football)* buteur *m*
striking ['straɪkɪŋ] *adj* **(a)** *(similarity, appearance)* frappant(e), saisissant(e) **(b)** *(worker)* en grève
string [strɪŋ] **1** *n* **(a)** *(for tying)* ficelle *f*; *(of violin, tennis racket, bow)* corde *f*; *(of puppet)* fil *m*; *Mus* **the strings** *(in orchestra)* les cordes; *Fig* **to have more than one s. to one's bow** avoir plus d'une corde à son arc; *Fig* **with no strings attached** sans conditions; *Fig* **to pull strings** faire jouer ses relations; *Mus* **s. quartet** quatuor *m* à cordes **(b)** *(of onions, islands)* chapelet *m*; *(of words, shops, defeats)* série *f*; *Comptr* série *f*
  2 *vt (pp & pt* **strung** [str∧ŋ]) **(a)** *(violin)* monter; *(tennis racket)* corder; *(bow)* bander **(b)** *(pearls, beads)* enfiler
▸ **string along** *vt sep Fam* mener en bateau
▸ **string up** *vt sep Fam (hang) (criminal)* pendre
stringed [strɪŋd] *adj (instrument)* à cordes
stringent ['strɪndʒənt] *adj* rigoureux(euse)
strip[1] [strɪp] *n* **(a)** *(of cloth, paper)* bande *f*; *(of metal)* lame *f*; *Fam* **to tear sb off a s.** passer un savon à qn; **s. cartoon** bande *f* dessinée; **s. lighting** éclairage *m* au néon **(b)** *(of sports team)* tenue *f*
strip[2] **1** *n* **to do a s.** *(undress)* se déshabiller; *(for show)* faire un strip-tease; **s. club** boîte *f* de strip-tease; **s. poker** strip-poker *m*; **s. show** strip-tease *m*
  2 *vt (pt & pp* **stripped**) *(person)* déshabiller; *(bed)* défaire;

(paint) gratter; *(wallpaper)* décoller; **to s. sb of sth** dépouiller qn de qch
  3 *vi (undress)* se déshabiller
▸ **strip off 1** *vt sep (paint)* gratter; *(wallpaper)* décoller
  2 *vi (undress)* se déshabiller
stripe [straɪp] *n* **(a)** *(on cloth, animal's coat)* rayure *f*, raie *f* **(b)** *(indicating rank)* galon *m*
striped [straɪpt] *adj* à rayures, rayé(e)
stripling ['strɪplɪŋ] *n* tout jeune homme *m*
stripper ['strɪpə(r)] *n* strip-teaseuse *f*; **(male) s.** = homme qui se livre à un strip-tease
strip-search ['strɪpsɑːtʃ] **1** *n* fouille *f* corporelle
  2 *vt* **to s. sb** faire subir une fouille corporelle à qn
striptease ['strɪptiːz] *n* strip-tease *m*
strive [straɪv] *(pt* **strove** [strəʊv], *pp* **striven** ['strɪvən]) *vi* **to s. to do sth** s'efforcer de faire qch; **to s. for** *or* **after sth** se battre pour obtenir qch
strobe [strəʊb] *n Phys* stroboscope *m*; **s. lighting** lumières *fpl* stroboscopiques
strode [strəʊd] *pt of* **stride**
stroke [strəʊk] **1** *n* **(a)** *(blow, tennis shot)* coup *m*; *(in rowing, swimming) (style)* nage *f*; *(single movement)* mouvement *m*; **a brush s.** un coup de pinceau *(of clock, bell)* **on the s. of nine** à neuf heures sonnantes **(c)** *(caress)* caresse *f*; **to give sb/sth a s.** caresser qn/qch **(d)** *Med* attaque *f* **(e)** *(idioms)* **she hasn't done a s. of work** elle n'a rien fichu; **a s. of luck** un coup de chance; **a s. of genius** un trait de génie; **at a s.** d'un seul coup
  2 *vt (caress)* caresser
stroll [strəʊl] **1** *n* promenade *f*, tour *m*; **to go for a s.** aller se promener *ou* faire un tour
  2 *vi* se promener, flâner
strong [strɒŋ] **1** *adj* **(a)** *(physically, mentally)* fort(e); *(candidate, team)* bon (bonne); *(friendship, argument)* solide; **the pound is s. against the dollar** la livre est solide face au dollar **(b)** *(in degree) (colour, light, protest)* vif (vive); *(smell, drink, accent, possibility)* fort(e); *(resemblance)* grand(e); *(measures)* énergique; **s. language** grossièretés *fpl*; **s. point** point *m* fort **(c)** *(sturdy) (rope, chair, shoes)* solide
  2 *adv* **to be still going s.** bien se maintenir
  3 *npl* **the s.** les forts *mpl*
strong-arm tactics [strɒŋɑːm'tæktɪks] *npl* manière *f* forte
strong-box ['strɒŋbɒks] *n* coffre-fort *m*
stronghold ['strɒŋhəʊld] *n (fortress)* forteresse *f*; *Fig (of political party, religion)* bastion *m*
strongly ['strɒŋlɪ] *adv (oppose, endorse)* vigoureusement; *(believe)* fermement; **s. built** solide; **a s. worded letter** une lettre bien sentie; **to feel s. about sth** être convaincu(e) de qch
strongman ['strɒŋmæn] *n (in circus)* hercule *m* (de foire); *Fig (dictator)* homme *m* fort
strong-minded [strɒŋ'maɪndɪd] *adj* résolu(e)
strongroom ['strɒŋruːm] *n* chambre *f* forte
strong-willed [strɒŋ'wɪld] *adj* résolu(e)
strontium ['strɒntɪəm] *n Chem* strontium *m*
stroppy ['strɒpɪ] *adj Br Fam* hargneux(euse); **to get s.** monter sur ses grands chevaux
strove [strəʊv] *pt of* **strive**
struck [str∧k] *pt & pp of* **strike**
structural ['str∧ktʃərəl] *adj* structurel(elle); **s. damage** dégâts *mpl* de structure; **s. survey** = inspection pour vérifier la solidité d'un bâtiment
structurally ['str∧ktʃərəlɪ] *adv* structurellement
structure ['str∧ktʃə(r)] **1** *n* **(a)** *(of society, language, story)*

structure f (**b**) (building, monument) édifice m, construction f
2 vt structurer
struggle ['strʌgəl] **1** n lutte f (**for** pour); **without a s.**
sans résistance; **life is a s.** la vie est un combat
2 vi lutter (**for** pour); **to s. to do sth** lutter pour faire qch;
to be struggling (of person, company) avoir des difficultés
ou du mal
strum [strʌm] (pt & pp **strummed**) vt (guitar) gratter
strung [strʌŋ] pt & pp of **string**
strut[1] [strʌt] n (for frame) étai m; Av pilier m
strut[2] (pt & pp **strutted**) vi se pavaner
strychnine ['strɪkniːn] n strychnine f
stub [stʌb] **1** n (of pencil) bout m; (of cigarette) mégot m; (of
cheque) talon m
2 vt (pt & pp **stubbed**) **to s. one's toe** (**on** or **against**) se
cogner l'orteil (contre)
▸ **stub out** vt sep (cigarette) écraser
stubble ['stʌbəl] n (**a**) (in field) chaume m (**b**) (on face)
barbe f de plusieurs jours
stubborn ['stʌbən] adj (person) têtu(e); (determination,
resistance) farouche; (stain, infection) rebelle
stubbornness ['stʌbənnɪs] n (of person) entêtement m,
obstination f; (of determination, resistance) inflexibilité f
stubby ['stʌbɪ] adj court(e) et boudiné(e)
stucco ['stʌkəʊ] n stuc m
stuck [stʌk] **1** adj bloqué(e), coincé(e); **to get s.** être
coincé; (in mud, sand, with problem) s'enliser; **to be s. for**
sth être à court de qch; Fam **to be s.** with sb/sth ne pas
pouvoir se débarrasser de qn/qch
2 pt & pp of **stick**[2]
stuck-up ['stʌk'ʌp] adj Fam snob inv
stud[1] [stʌd] n (fastener) bouton-pression m; (on football,
rugby boots) crampon m, (earring) clou m d'oreille
stud[2] n (**a**) (farm) haras m; (stallion) étalon m (**b**) Fam
(man) étalon m
student ['stjuːdənt] n (at university) étudiant(e) m,f; (at
school) élève m,f; **law s.** étudiant(e) m,f en droit; **s. card** carte
f d'étudiant; **s. life** vie f étudiante; **s. nurse** élève
infirmier(ère); **s. teacher** enseignant(e) m,f stagiaire;
students' union (association) = association d'aide et de
services aux étudiants; (place) foyer m des étudiants
studied ['stʌdɪd] adj (manner, attitude) calculé(e)
studio ['stjuːdɪəʊ] (pl **studios**) n studio m; (of artist) atelier
m; TV **s. audience** public m présent lors de l'enregistrement; Br **s. flat**, Am **s. apartment** studio
studious ['stjuːdɪəs] adj studieux(euse)
study ['stʌdɪ] **1** n (**a**) (investigation, by artist) étude f; **to
make a s. of sth** faire une étude sur qch; **s. group** groupe
m d'étude; **s. trip** voyage m d'études (**b**) (room) bureau m,
cabinet m de travail
2 vt (pt & pp **studied**) (facts, evidence) examiner;
(behaviour, school subject) étudier; (university subject) faire
des études de
3 vi (revise) travailler; (be at university) faire des études
stuff [stʌf] **1** n (**a**) (objects, possessions) affaires fpl; **some
s.** (substance) un truc; Fam **he reads all that intellectual s.**
il lit tous ces trucs intellos; Fam **he writes good s.** c'est
bien, ce qu'elle écrit; Fam **he knows his s.** il s'y connaît;
Fam **that's the s.!** c'est bien! (**b**) (cloth) étoffe f
2 vt (fill) (cushion) rembourrer; (chicken, tomatoes) farcir;
(pocket) remplir; **to s. sth into sth** fourrer qch dans qch;
Fam **to s. oneself** s'empiffrer; Br very Fam **get stuffed!** va
te faire foutre!
stuffing ['stʌfɪŋ] n (for furniture) rembourrage m; (for
chicken) farce f; Fam **to knock the s. out of sb** ficher un
coup à qn

stuffy ['stʌfɪ] adj (**a**) (room) qui sent le renfermé (**b**)
(person) vieux jeu inv
stultifying ['stʌltɪfaɪɪŋ] adj abrutissant(e)
stumble ['stʌmbəl] **1** n faux-pas m
2 vi (when walking, speaking) trébucher
▸ **stumble across** vt insep (find) tomber par hasard sur
stump [stʌmp] **1** n (**a**) (of tree) souche f; (of arm, leg)
moignon m (**b**) (in cricket) piquet m (**c**) Am Fam (of
politician) **to be on the s.** être en campagne électorale
2 vt (baffle) laisser perplexe; **to be stumped for an
answer** ne pas savoir quoi répondre
▸ **stump up** vt insep Br Fam (pay) cracher
stumpy ['stʌmpɪ] adj court(e) et boudiné(e)
stun [stʌn] (pt & pp **stunned**) vt (make unconscious)
assommer; Fig (shock) abasourdir
stung [stʌŋ] pt & pp of **sting**
stunk [stʌŋk] pt & pp of **stink**
stunning ['stʌnɪŋ] adj (shocking) étourdissant(e);
(excellent) excellent(e); (beautiful) superbe
stunt[1] [stʌnt] vt (person) ralentir la croissance de; (growth)
ralentir
stunt[2] n (in film) cascade f; (for publicity) coup m de pub; **s.
man** cascadeur m
stupefy ['stjuːpɪfaɪ] (pt & pp **stupefied**) vt (of alcohol,
drugs) abrutir; (of news, behaviour) stupéfier
stupefying ['stjuːpɪfaɪɪŋ] adj stupéfiant(e)
stupendous [stjuː'pendəs] adj fantastique
stupid ['stjuːpɪd] adj bête, stupide; **the s.** TV **keeps
breaking down** cette saleté de télé est sans arrêt en
panne; **what a s. thing to do!** c'est vraiment idiot d'avoir
fait ça!
stupidity [stjuː'pɪdɪtɪ] n bêtise f, stupidité f
stupidly ['stjuːpɪdlɪ] adv bêtement
stupor ['stjuːpə(r)] n état m d'abrutissement
sturdy ['stɜːdɪ] adj (person, object) robuste; (opposition,
resistance) résolu(e)
sturgeon ['stɜːdʒən] n esturgeon m
stutter ['stʌtə(r)] **1** n bégaiement m
2 vi bégayer
sty[1] [staɪ] n (for pigs) & Fig porcherie f
sty[2], **stye** [staɪ] n (in eye) orgelet m
style [staɪl] **1** n (**a**) (manner, design) style m (**b**)
(sophistication) classe f; **to live in s.** mener grand train
2 vt (design) créer; (hair) coiffer
stylish ['staɪlɪʃ] adj élégant(e), chic inv
stylist ['staɪlɪst] n (hairdresser) coiffeur(euse) m,f
stylistic [staɪ'lɪstɪk] adj stylistique
stylized ['staɪəlaɪzd] adj stylisé(e)
stylus ['staɪləs] (pl **styluses** or **styli** ['staɪlaɪ]) n (for
engraving) style m; (on record player) pointe f de lecture
stymie ['staɪmɪ] vt Fam coincer
suave [swɑːv] adj affable; Pej mielleux(euse)
sub [sʌb] Fam **1** n (**a**) (abbr **subscription**) cotisation f (**b**)
(abbr **substitute**) remplaçant m,f (**c**) (abbr **submarine**)
sous-marin m (**d**) Journ (abbr **subeditor**) secrétaire mf de
rédaction
2 vt (pt & pp **subbed**) Journ (abbr **subedit**) mettre au point
3 vi (abbr **substitute**) **to s. for sb** remplacer qn
subaltern ['sʌbəltən] n Mil officier m subalterne
subcommittee ['sʌbkəmɪtɪ] n sous-comité m
subconscious [sʌb'kɒnʃəs] **1** n **the s.** l'inconscient m
2 adj inconscient(e)
subcontinent [sʌb'kɒntɪnənt] n sous-continent m

subcontract 1 n [sʌb'kɒntrækt] sous-traitance f
2 vt [sʌbkən'trækt] sous-traiter
subcontractor ['sʌbkəntræktə(r)] n sous-traitant m
subculture ['sʌbkʌltʃə(r)] n phénomène m de groupe
subdivision [sʌbdɪ'vɪʒən] n subdivision f
subdue [səb'dju:] vt (enemy, rioter) soumettre; (emotions) maîtriser
subdued [səb'dju:d] adj (person, event) inhabituellement calme; (light) tamisé(e); (sound, voice) bas (basse)
subedit ['sʌb'edɪt] vt Journ mettre au point
subeditor [sʌb'edɪtə(r)] n Journ secrétaire mf de rédaction
subhuman [sʌb'hju:mən] **1** n sous-homme m
2 adj inférieur(e) (aux humains)
subject 1 n ['sʌbdʒɪkt] (a) (of conversation, book, painting, photograph) sujet m; (at school, university) matière f; **while we're on the s.** à ce propos; **to change the s.** parler d'autre chose; **s. matter** (of letter) contenu m; (of book) sujet (b) Gram sujet m (c) (of monarch) sujet(ette) m,f
2 adj ['sʌbdʒɪkt] (a) (prone) **to be s. to** (illness) être sujet(ette) à; (fine, taxation) être passible de; **to be s. to jealousy/depression** avoir tendance à être jaloux(ouse)/dépressif(ive) (b) **s. to** (dependent on) sous réserve de
3 vt [səb'dʒekt] (control) soumettre, assujettir; **to s. sb to sth** (force to undergo) soumettre qn à qch
subjective [səb'dʒektɪv] adj subjectif(ive)
subjectivity [sʌbdʒek'tɪvɪtɪ] n subjectivité f
sub judice ['sʌb'dʒu:dɪsɪ] adj Law en instance
subjugate ['sʌbdʒʊgeɪt] vt assujettir
subjunctive [səb'dʒʌŋktɪv] Gram **1** n subjonctif m
2 adj subjonctif(ive)
sublet [sʌb'let] (pt & pp sublet) vt sous-louer
sublimate ['sʌblɪmeɪt] vt sublimer
sublime [sə'blaɪm] **1** adj sublime; (utter) suprême
2 n **from the s. to the ridiculous** du sublime au ridicule
subliminal [sʌb'lɪmɪnəl] adj subliminal(e)
sub-machine gun [sʌbmə'ʃi:ngʌn] n mitraillette f
submarine [sʌbmə'ri:n] n sous-marin m
submerge [səb'mɜ:dʒ] **1** vt (immerse) immerger; (cover) submerger; Fig **to be submerged in sth** être submergé(e) par qch
2 vi plonger
submersion [səb'mɜ:ʃən] n submersion f
submission [səb'mɪʃən] n (a) (to will, authority) soumission f; **to starve sb into s.** réduire qn à la soumission en le/la privant de nourriture; **to beat sb into s.** battre qn jusqu'à ce qu'il/elle se soumette (b) (of document) présentation f (c) (report) soumission f
submissive [səb'mɪsɪv] adj soumis(e)
submit [səb'mɪt] (pt & pp submitted) **1** vt soumettre (for à)
2 vi (to person, authority) se soumettre (to à)
subnormal [sʌb'nɔ:məl] adj arriéré(e)
subordinate 1 n [sə'bɔ:dɪnət] subordonné(e) m,f
2 adj (rank) subalterne; (role) secondaire; **to be s. to sb** être subordonné(e) à qn; Gram **s. clause** proposition f subordonnée
3 vt [sə'bɔ:dɪneɪt] subordonner
subordination [səbɔ:dɪ'neɪʃən] n subordination f
subplot ['sʌbplɒt] n intrigue f secondaire
subpoena [sə'pi:nə] Law **1** n citation f ou assignation f à comparaître
2 vt citer ou assigner à comparaître
subscribe [səb'skraɪb] vi (a) (to newspaper, magazine)

s'abonner (**to** à); (to charity, organization) être membre (**to** de) (b) **to s. to** (opinion, theory) souscrire à
subscriber [səb'skraɪbə(r)] n (to newspaper, magazine, telephone) abonné(e) m,f; (to charity, organization) membre m
subscript ['sʌbskrɪpt] n Typ indice m
subscription [sʌb'skrɪpʃən] n (to newspaper, magazine) abonnement m; (to charity, organization, club) cotisation f
subsection ['sʌbsekʃən] n subdivision f
subsequent ['sʌbsɪkwənt] adj ultérieur(e)
subservient [sʌb'sɜ:vɪənt] adj servile
subside [səb'saɪd] vi (of ground, building) s'affaisser; (of water) baisser; (of bump) dégonfler; (of storm, excitement, fever) s'apaiser; (of noise, pain) s'affaiblir
subsidence [səb'saɪdəns] n (of ground, building) affaissement m; (of water) baisse f
subsidiarity [sʌbsɪdɪ'ærɪtɪ] n subsidiarité f
subsidiary [sʌb'sɪdɪərɪ] **1** n (pl subsidiaries) (company) filiale f
2 adj subsidiaire
subsidize ['sʌbsɪdaɪz] vt subventionner
subsidy ['sʌbsɪdɪ] (pl subsidies) n subvention f
subsist [səb'sɪst] vi **to s. on** vivre de
subsistence [səb'sɪstəns] n subsistance f; **s. allowance** faux frais mpl; **s. wage** salaire m à peine suffisant pour vivre
substance ['sʌbstəns] n (a) (matter) substance f; **s. abuse** usage m de stupéfiants (b) (essential element) fond m (c) (solidity, worth) fondement m
substandard [sʌb'stændəd] adj de qualité inférieure
substantial [səb'stænʃəl] adj (a) (significant) important(e); (meal) substantiel(elle); **a s. number of** un nombre important de (b) (solid, robust) solide
substantially [səb'stænʃəlɪ] adv (a) (considerably) considérablement (b) (for the most part) pour l'essentiel; **they are s. the same** ils sont pareils dans l'ensemble (c) (solidly) solidement
substantiate [səb'stænʃɪeɪt] vt (statement) corroborer; (claim) justifier
substantive ['sʌbstəntɪv] **1** n Gram substantif m
2 adj important(e)
substitute ['sʌbstɪtju:t] **1** n (person) remplaçant(e) m,f; (foodstuff, drug) succédané m; **to be a s./no s. for** remplacer ne pas remplacer
2 vt **to s. A for B** remplacer B par A
3 vi **to s. for sb** remplacer qn
substitution [sʌbstɪ'tju:ʃən] n substitution f; (of person, player) remplacement m
subsume [sʌb'sju:m] vt Formal subsumer
subterfuge ['sʌbtəfju:dʒ] n subterfuge m
subterranean [sʌbtə'reɪnɪən] adj souterrain(e)
subtitle ['sʌbtaɪtəl] **1** n sous-titre m
2 vt sous-titrer
subtle ['sʌtəl] adj subtil(e)
subtlety ['sʌtəltɪ] (pl subtleties) n subtilité f
subtly ['sʌtəlɪ] adv subtilement
subtotal ['sʌbtəʊtəl] n sous-total m
subtract [səb'trækt] vt soustraire (**from** de)
subtraction [səb'trækʃən] n soustraction f
subtropical [sʌb'trɒpɪkəl] adj subtropical(e)
suburb ['sʌbɜ:b] n banlieue f; **the suburbs** la banlieue
suburban [sə'bɜ:bən] adj (a) (of suburb) de banlieue; (population, development) suburbain(e) (b) Pej (narrowminded) étriqué(e)

suburbia [sə'bɜːbɪə] *n* la banlieue

subversion [səb'vɜːʃən] *n* subversion *f*

subversive [səb'vɜːsɪv] *n & adj* subversif(ive) *m,f*

subvert [səb'vɜːt] *vt* renverser, subvertir

subway ['sʌbweɪ] *n* (**a**) *Br (underpass)* passage *m* souterrain (**b**) *Am (underground railway)* métro *m*

sub-zero [sʌb'zɪərəʊ] *adj* au-dessous de zéro

succeed [sək'siːd] **1** *vt (follow)* succéder à
2 *vi* (**a**) *(be successful)* réussir; **to s. in doing sth** réussir à faire qch (**b**) **to s. to the throne** monter sur le trône

succeeding [sək'siːdɪŋ] *adj (following)* suivant(e)

success [sək'ses] *n* réussite *f*, succès *m*; **to be a s.** avoir du succès; **s. story** réussite *f*

successful [sək'sesfʊl] *adj (person)* brillant(e); *(project, application)* couronné(e) de succès; **to be s.** réussir; **to be s. in doing sth** réussir à faire qch

successfully [sək'sesfəlɪ] *adv* avec succès

succession [sək'seʃən] *n* succession *f*, série *f*; **ten years in s.** dix années de suite

successive [sək'sesɪv] *adj* successif(ive); **on five s. Sundays** cinq dimanches consécutifs

successor [sək'sesə(r)] *n* successeur *m*

succinct [sʌk'sɪŋ(k)t] *adj* succinct(e)

succulent ['sʌkjʊlənt] **1** *adj (delicious)* succulent(e)
2 *n (plant)* plante *f* grasse

succumb [sə'kʌm] *vi* succomber (**to** à)

such [sʌtʃ] **1** *pron* tel (telle) *m,f*; **if s. were the case** si tel était le cas; **and s. et des choses comme ça; as s. en tant que tel; s. is life!** c'est la vie!
2 *adj* (**a**) *(like)*, pareil(eille); **s. a question** une telle question, une question pareille; **animals s. as the dog or the cat** des animaux tels que le chien ou le chat; **s. books as these, books s. as these** de tels livres, des livres pareils; **here's my apartment, s. as it is** voici ce qui me sert d'appartement, **s. as?** par exemple?, **do you have s. a thing as a hammer?** est-ce que tu aurais un marteau?; **there's no s. thing as aliens** les extraterrestres n'existent pas; **I said/did no s. thing** je n'ai rien dit/fait de tel; **in s. a way that** d'une façon telle que; **on s. and s. a day** tel jour
3 *adv* (**a**) *(in comparisons)* **s. a big house** une si *ou* aussi grande maison; **I had never heard s. good music** je n'avais jamais entendu de si bonne musique
(**b**) *(for emphasis)* **we had s. a good time** nous nous sommes tellement bien amusés; **it was s. a long time ago** ça fait tellement longtemps; **s. a lot of people** tant de gens

suchlike ['sʌtʃlaɪk] *pron* **...and s.** ...et autres

suck [sʌk] **1** *vt (lollipop, thumb)* sucer; *(liquid, air)* aspirer; *(mother's milk)* téter
2 *vi very Fam (be of bad quality)* être nul (nulle)
▸ **suck in** *vt sep* aspirer; *Fig* **to get sucked into sth** se laisser entraîner dans qch
▸ **suck up 1** *vt sep (liquid, dust)* aspirer
2 *vi very Fam* **to s. up to sb** lécher les bottes a qn

sucker ['sʌkə(r)] *n* (**a**) *(of octopus)* suçoir *m*; *(of plant)* rejeton *m* (**b**) *Fam (gullible person)* niais(e) *m,f*; **to be a s. for sth** craquer pour qch

suckle ['sʌkəl] **1** *vt* allaiter
2 *vi* téter

sucrose ['suːkrəʊs] *n* saccharose *m*

suction ['sʌkʃən] *n* succion *f*

Sudan [suː'dɑːn] *n* le Soudan

Sudanese [suːdə'niːz] **1** *npl (people)* **the S.** les Soudanais
2 *n* Soudanais(e) *m,f*
3 *adj* soudanais(e)

sudden ['sʌdən] *adj* soudain(e), subit(e); **all of a s.** tout à coup; *Fig* **s. death** *(in match, contest)* la mort subite

suddenly ['sʌdənlɪ] *adv* soudain, tout à coup; *(die, happen)* subitement

suddenness ['sʌdənnɪs] *n* soudaineté *f*

suds [sʌdz] *npl (of soap)* mousse *f*

sue [suː] **1** *vt* intenter un procès à (**for** en)
2 *vi* **to s. for divorce** entamer une procédure de divorce; **to s. for damages** demander des dommages-intérêts

suede [sweɪd] *n* daim *m*

suet ['suːɪt] *n* graisse *f* de rognon

Suez ['suːɪz] *n* **the S. Canal** le canal de Suez

suffer ['sʌfə(r)] **1** *vt* (**a**) *(loss, defeat, consequence)* subir; *(pain)* avoir (**b**) *(tolerate)* supporter; **she doesn't s. fools gladly** elle ne supporte pas les imbéciles
2 *vi (of person)* souffrir (**from** de); *(of health, work)* en pâtir

sufferance ['sʌf(ə)rəns] *n* **I'm just here on s.** on me tolère tout juste ici

sufferer ['sʌfərə(r)] *n* victime *f*

suffering ['sʌfərɪŋ] *n* souffrance *f*

suffice [sə'faɪs] *vi Formal* suffire

sufficient [sə'fɪʃənt] *adj* suffisant(e); **to be s.** suffire, être suffisant

sufficiently [sə'fɪʃəntlɪ] *adv* suffisamment

suffix ['sʌfɪks] *n Gram* suffixe *m*

suffocate ['sʌfəkeɪt] **1** *vt also Fig* étouffer
2 *vi* suffoquer

suffocating ['sʌfəkeɪtɪŋ] *adj* suffocant(e)

suffocation [sʌfə'keɪʃən] *n* suffocation *f*

suffrage ['sʌfrɪdʒ] *n* droit *m* de vote

suffragette [sʌfrə'dʒet] *n* suffragette *f*

suffuse [sə'fjuːz] *vt Lit (of light, liquid, colour)* inonder; *(of heat)* envahir

sugar ['ʃʊgə(r)] **1** *n* (**a**) *(food)* sucre *m*; **two sugars, please** deux sucres, s'il te plaît; **s. almond** dragée *f*; **s. beet** betterave *f* sucrière; **s. bowl** sucrier *m*; **s. cane** canne *f* à sucre; *Fam* **s. daddy** vieux *m* plein de fric *(qui entretient une jeune femme)*; **s. lump** morceau *m* de sucre; **s. plantation** plantation *f* de canne à sucre; **s. refinery** raffinerie *f* de sucre (**b**) *Fam (term of address)* mon trésor
2 *vt (coffee, tea)* sucrer; *Fig* **to s. the pill** dorer la pilule

sugar-coated [ʃʊgə'kəʊtɪd] *adj* recouvert(e) de sucre

sugar-free [ʃʊgə'friː] *adj* sans sucre

sugary ['ʃʊgərɪ] *adj* (**a**) *(containing sugar)* sucré(e) (**b**) *Fig (smile, tone)* mielleux(euse), doucereux(euse)

suggest [sə'dʒest] *vt* (**a**) *(propose)* suggérer (**b**) *(imply)* indiquer

suggestible [sə'dʒestɪbəl] *adj* influençable

suggestion [sə'dʒestʃən] *n* (**a**) *(proposal)* suggestion *f*; **suggestions box** boîte *f* à idées (**b**) *(insinuation, hint)* indication *f*; **there is no s. that...** rien ne dit que...; **a s. of** une pointe de

suggestive [sə'dʒestɪv] *adj* suggestif(ive); **to be s. of** évoquer

suicidal [sʊɪ'saɪdəl] *adj* suicidaire

suicide ['sʊɪsaɪd] *n* suicide *m*; **to commit s.** se suicider; **s. attempt** tentative *f* de suicide; **s. mission** mission *f* suicide; **s. note** lettre *f* *(laissée par un suicidé)*

suit [suːt] **1** *n* (**a**) *(clothing) (man's)* complet *m*; *(woman's)* tailleur *m*; **s. of armour** armure *f* complète (**b**) *(in cards)* couleur *f*; *Fig* **to follow s.** faire de même; *Fig* **politeness is not her strong s.** la politesse n'est pas son fort (**c**) *Law* procès *m*
2 *vt* (**a**) *(of clothes, colours)* aller à (**b**) *(of arrangement, time,*

job) convenir à; **to be suited to** *or* **for sth** *(purpose, job)* être fait(e) pour qch; **to s. sb down to the ground** convenir parfaitement à qn; **they are well suited** ils sont vraiment faits l'un pour l'autre; *Fam* **s. yourself** fais comme tu voudras **(c)** *(adapt)* **to s. sth to sth** adapter qch à qch

suitability [suːtəˈbɪlɪtɪ] *n* convenance *f*; *(of person)* aptitude *f*

suitable [ˈsuːtəbəl] *adj (clothes, subject)* convenable; *(candidate, date, title)* adéquat(e); **the movie is not s. for children** ce n'est pas un film pour les enfants

suitably [ˈsuːtəblɪ] *adv (behave, dress)* convenablement; **s. impressed/embarrassed** vraiment impressionné(e)/ gêné(e)

suitcase [ˈsjuːtkeɪs] *n* valise *f*

suite [swiːt] *n* **(a)** *(of rooms)* suite *f* **(b)** *(of furniture)* **(three-piece) s.** canapé *m* avec deux fauteuils assortis **(c)** *Mus* suite *f*

suitor [ˈsuːtə(r)] *n Old-fashioned (admirer)* soupirant *m*

sulfate, sulfide *etc Am* = **sulphate, sulphide** *etc*

sulk [sʌlk] **1** *n* **to be in a s.** bouder
2 *vi* bouder

sulky [ˈsʌlkɪ] *adj* boudeur(euse)

sullen [ˈsʌlən] *adj* renfrogné(e)

sully [ˈsʌlɪ] *vt Lit (reputation)* ternir; *Fig* **to s. one's hands (with sth)** se salir les mains (en faisant qch)

sulphate, *Am* **sulfate** [ˈsʌlfeɪt] *n Chem* sulfate *m*

sulphide, *Am* **sulfide** [ˈsʌlfaɪd] *n Chem* sulfure *m*

sulphur, *Am* **sulfur** [ˈsʌlfə(r)] *n Chem* soufre *m*; **s. dioxide** anhydride *m* sulfureux

sulphuric, *Am* **sulfuric** [sʌlˈfjʊərɪk] *adj Chem* sulfurique; **s. acid** acide *m* sulfurique

sultan [ˈsʌltən] *n* sultan *m*

sultana [sʌlˈtɑːnə] *n* raisin *m* de Smyrne

sultry [ˈsʌltrɪ] *adj (heat)* étouffant(e); *(weather)* lourd(e); *(look, smile)* sensuel(elle)

sum [sʌm] *n (amount of money)* somme *f*; *(mathematical problem)* problème *m*; **the s. of** la somme de; **s. total** somme totale

▸ **sum up** *(pt & pp* **summed) 1** *vt sep* **(a)** *(summarize)* résumer **(b)** *(assess quickly)* jauger, évaluer
2 *vi (summarize)* résumer

summarily [ˈsʌmərɪlɪ] *adv* sommairement

summarize [ˈsʌməraɪz] *vt* résumer

summary [ˈsʌmərɪ] **1** *n (pl* **summaries)** résumé *m*
2 *adj (brief)* sommaire

summer [ˈsʌmə(r)] **1** *n* été *m*; **in (the) s.** en été; **s. holidays** vacances *fpl* d'été; **s. school** cours *mpl* d'été
2 *vi* passer l'été

summerhouse [ˈsʌməhaʊs] *n (in garden)* pavillon *m*

summertime [ˈsʌmətaɪm] *n* été *m*

summery [ˈsʌmərɪ] *adj* d'été

summing-up [sʌmɪŋˈʌp] *n Law* résumé *m* des débats

summit [ˈsʌmɪt] *n* sommet *m*; **to hold a s.** tenir un sommet

summon [ˈsʌmən] *vt (person, meeting)* convoquer; *(police, doctor, help)* appeler, faire venir; *Law (witness)* assigner *ou* citer à comparaître

▸ **summon up** *vt sep* rassembler

summons [ˈsʌmənz] *Law* **1** *n (pl* **summonses** [ˈsʌmənzɪz]) assignation *f ou* citation *f* à comparaître
2 *vt* assigner *ou* citer à comparaître

sump [sʌmp] *n* **(a)** *(in engine)* carter *m* à huile **(b)** *(cesspool)* fosse *f* d'aisance

sumptuous [ˈsʌm(p)tjʊəs] *adj* somptueux(euse)

Sun *(abbr* **Sunday)** dimanche

sun [sʌn] **1** *n* soleil *m*; **in the s.** au soleil; **to catch the s.** prendre le soleil; **everything under the s.** tout ce qu'il est possible d'imaginer; **s. lamp** lampe *f* à bronzer; **s. lotion** lotion *f* solaire; **s. shield** *or* **visor** *(in car)* pare-soleil *m*
2 *vt (pt & pp* **sunned) to s. oneself** prendre le soleil

sunbathe [ˈsʌnbeɪð] *vi* se faire bronzer

sunbeam [ˈsʌnbiːm] *n* rayon *m* de soleil

sunbed [ˈsʌnbed] *n* lit *m* à ultraviolets

sunburn [ˈsʌnbɜːn] *n* coup *m* de soleil; **to have s.** avoir un coup de soleil

sunburnt [ˈsʌnbɜːnt], **sunburned** [ˈsʌnbɜːnd] *adj* **to be s.** avoir un coup de soleil

sundae [ˈsʌndeɪ] *n* coupe *f* glacée

Sunday [ˈsʌndeɪ] *n* dimanche *m*; **S. best** habits *mpl* du dimanche; **S. paper** journal *m* du dimanche; **S. school** ≃ catéchisme *m*; *see also* **Saturday**

sundial [ˈsʌndaɪəl] *n* cadran *m* solaire

sundown [ˈsʌndaʊn] *n* coucher *m* du soleil

sun-drenched [ˈsʌndren(t)ʃt] *adj* inondé(e) de soleil

sun-dried [ˈsʌndraɪd] *adj* séché(e) au soleil

sundry [ˈsʌndrɪ] **1** *n* **(a) all and s.** tout le monde **(b) sundries** *(items)* articles *mpl* divers; *(costs)* frais *mpl* divers
2 *adj* divers(e)

sunflower [ˈsʌnflaʊə(r)] *n* tournesol *m*; **s. oil** huile *f* de tournesol; **s. seeds** *(as snack)* graines *fpl* de tournesol

sung [sʌŋ] *pp of* **sing**

sunglasses [ˈsʌnglɑːsɪz] *npl* lunettes *fpl* de soleil

sunhat [ˈsʌnhæt] *n* chapeau *m* de soleil

sunk [sʌŋk] *pp of* **sink²**

sunken [ˈsʌŋkən] *adj (ship)* englouti(e); *(eyes)* enfoncé(e); *(rock)* immergé(e)

sunlight [ˈsʌnlaɪt] *n* lumière *f* du soleil; **in the s.** au soleil

sunlit [ˈsʌnlɪt] *adj* éclairé(e) par le soleil

sunny [ˈsʌnɪ] *adj* **(a)** *(day, place)* ensoleillé(e); **it's s.** il fait du soleil **(b)** *Fig (face)* radieux(euse); **to have a s. nature** être toujours content(e)

sunray lamp [ˈsʌnreɪˈlæmp] *n* lampe *f* à bronzer

sunrise [ˈsʌnraɪz] *n* lever *m* de soleil; **at s.** au lever du soleil, au soleil levant; *Econ* **s. industry** industrie *f* d'avenir

sunroof [ˈsʌnruːf] *n* toit *m* ouvrant

sunset [ˈsʌnset] *n* coucher *m* de soleil; **at s.** au coucher du soleil, au soleil couchant

sunshade [ˈsʌnʃeɪd] *n* parasol *m*

sunshine [ˈsʌnʃaɪn] *n* soleil *m*

sunspot [ˈsʌnspɒt] *n* **(a)** *(on sun)* tache *f* solaire **(b)** *Fam (holiday resort)* destination *f* ensoleillée

sunstroke [ˈsʌnstrəʊk] *n* insolation *f*; **to have s.** avoir une insolation

suntan [ˈsʌntæn] *n* bronzage *m*; **to have a s.** être bronzé(e); **s. lotion** lotion *f* solaire

suntrap [ˈsʌntræp] *n* coin *m* très ensoleillé

sup [sʌp] *(pt & pp* **supped)** *vt* boire à petites gorgées

super [ˈsuːpə(r)] **1** *adj Fam (excellent)* super *inv*
2 *n (petrol)* super *m*

superannuation [suːpərænjʊˈeɪʃən] *n Fin* retraite *f*

superb [suːˈpɜːb] *adj* excellent(e)

supercharger [ˈsuːpətʃɑːdʒə(r)] *n Aut & Av* compresseur *m*

supercilious [suːpəˈsɪlɪəs] *adj* hautain(e)

superconductor [suːpəkənˈdʌktə(r)] *n Phys* supraconducteur *m*

super-duper ['su:pə'du:pə(r)] adj Fam super, génial(e)
superego ['su:pərɪgəʊ] n Psy surmoi m
superficial [su:pə'fɪʃəl] adj superficiel(elle)
superficiality [su:pəfɪʃɪ'ælɪtɪ] n superficialité f
superficially [su:pə'fɪʃəlɪ] adv superficiellement
superfluous [su:'pɜ:fluəs] adj superflu(e)
superhuman [su:pə'hju:mən] adj surhumain(e)
superimpose [su:pərɪm'pəʊz] vt superposer
superintend [su:pərɪn'tend] vt (run) diriger; (supervise) surveiller
superintendent [su:pərɪn'tendənt] n (supervisor) directeur(trice) m,f; (police officer) ≃ commissaire m de police
superior [su:'pɪərɪə(r)] 1 adj (a) (better, more senior) supérieur(e) (b) (arrogant) (person) qui se croit supérieur(e); (tone, air, smile) de supériorité
2 n (senior) supérieur(e) m,f
superiority [su:pɪərɪ'ɒrɪtɪ] n supériorité f
superlative [su:'pɜ:lətɪv] 1 n Gram superlatif m
2 adj (a) (excellent) excellent(e) (b) Gram superlatif(ive)
superman ['su:pəmæn] n surhomme m
supermarket ['su:pəmɑ:kɪt] n supermarché m
supermodel ['su:pəmɒdəl] n top model m
supernatural [su:pə'nætʃərəl] 1 n the s. le surnaturel
2 adj surnaturel(elle)
superpower ['su:pəpaʊə(r)] n superpuissance f
supersede [su:pə'si:d] vt supplanter, détrôner
supersonic [su:pə'sɒnɪk] adj supersonique
superstar ['su:pəstɑ:(r)] n superstar f
superstition [su:pə'stɪʃən] n superstition f
superstitious [su:pə'stɪʃəs] adj superstitieux(euse)
superstore ['su:pəstɔ:(r)] n hypermarché m
superstructure ['su:pəstrʌktʃə(r)] n superstructure f
supertanker ['su:pətæŋkə(r)] n supertanker m
supervise ['su:pəvaɪz] vt (children) surveiller; (staff) superviser
supervision [su:pə'vɪʒən] n (of children) surveillance f; (of staff) supervision f
supervisor ['su:pəvaɪzə(r)] n (a) (in office) chef m de service; (in factory) chef m d'équipe (b) (for thesis) directeur m de thèse
supervisory [su:pə'vaɪzərɪ] adj de supervision
supine ['su:paɪn] 1 adj couché(e) sur le dos; Fig (inactive) mou (molle)
2 adv to lie s. être couché(e) sur le dos
supper ['sʌpə(r)] n (evening meal) dîner m; (snack before going to bed) = casse-croûte pris avant d'aller se coucher
supplant [sə'plɑ:nt] vt supplanter
supple ['sʌpəl] adj souple
supplement ['sʌplɪmənt] 1 n supplément m
2 vt compléter
supplementary [sʌplɪ'mentərɪ] adj supplémentaire
supplication [sʌplɪ'keɪʃən] n supplication f
supplier [sə'plaɪə(r)] n fournisseur(euse) m,f
supply [sə'plaɪ] 1 n (pl supplies) (stock) provision f; (act of supplying) approvisionnement m, fourniture f; a week's/month's s. of sth une provision de qch pour une semaine/un mois; water is in short s. on manque d'eau; Econ s. and demand l'offre f et la demande; s. lines lignes fpl de ravitaillement; s. ship ravitailleur m; s. teacher remplaçant(e) m,f, suppléant(e) m,f
2 vt (pt & pp supplied) (provide) fournir; to s. sb with sth fournir qch à qn

support [sə'pɔ:t] 1 n (a) (backing) soutien m; to give sb/sth s. appuyer qn/qch; in s. of (theory, claim) à l'appui de; (cause) en faveur de; s. band (at concert) première partie f (b) (person supporting) soutien m; (thing supporting) support m
2 vt (a) (hold up) supporter, soutenir; I supported her with my arm je lui ai donné le bras pour qu'elle s'appuie dessus (b) (encourage, aid) soutenir, apporter son soutien à; (team in sport) supporter (c) (sustain) pourvoir aux besoins de; to s. oneself subvenir à ses propres besoins
supporter [sə'pɔ:tə(r)] n (of opinion, party, policy) défenseur m, sympathisant(e) m,f; (of team) supporter m
supporting [sə'pɔ:tɪŋ] adj s. film film m qui passe en première partie; s. cast seconds rôles mpl
supportive [sə'pɔ:tɪv] adj d'un grand soutien
suppose [sə'pəʊz] vt supposer; I s. so/not je suppose que oui/non; s. or supposing he came back supposons qu'il revienne; I don't s. you'd consider selling it? je suppose que tu ne veux pas le vendre?; s. we change the subject? et si nous changions de sujet?
supposed [sə'pəʊzd] adj (a) (meant) to be s. to do sth être censé(e) faire qch; there's s. to be a meeting today il est censé y avoir une réunion aujourd'hui (b) (reputed) the play's s. to be very good il paraît que c'est une très bonne pièce
supposition [sʌpə'zɪʃən] n supposition f; on this s. that... en supposant que...
suppository [sə'pɒzɪtrɪ] (pl suppositories) n Med suppositoire m
suppress [sə'pres] vt (revolt) réprimer; (fact, evidence) faire disparaître, (emotions) refouler, (cough, smile) réprimer
suppressed [sə'prest] adj (emotion) refoulé(e)
suppression [sə'preʃən] n (of revolt) répression f; (of fact, evidence) dissimulation f; (of emotions) refoulement m
suppurate ['sʌpjʊreɪt] vi suppurer
supranational [su:prə'næʃənəl] adj supranational(e)
supremacy [su:'preməsɪ] n suprématie f
supreme [su:'pri:m] adj suprême; to make the s. sacrifice se sacrifier; Fig to reign s. régner; Mil S. Commander commandant m en chef; Am Law S. Court Cour f suprême
supremely [su:'pri:mlɪ] adv suprêmement
supremo [su:'pri:məʊ] (pl supremos) n Fam grand chef m
surcharge ['sɜ:tʃɑ:dʒ] 1 n supplément m
2 vt faire payer un supplément à
sure [ʃʊə(r)] 1 adj (a) sûr; to be s. of or about sth être sûr de qch; to do sth ne pas oublier de faire qch; to be s. of oneself être sûr de soi; to make s. of sth s'assurer de qch; to make s. that... s'assurer que...; I don't know for s. je ne suis pas absolument certain(e); that's for s. ça, c'est sûr; Fam s. thing! bien sûr!
2 adv (a) Am Fam (really) it s. is cold il fait vachement froid; are you happy? – I s. am tu es content? – ça oui (b) (yes) bien sûr (c) s. enough he was there il était bien là
surefooted [ʃʊə'fʊtɪd] adj to be s. avoir le pied sûr
surely ['ʃʊəlɪ] adv (a) (certainly) sûrement; s. you don't believe that! tu ne crois quand même pas ça!; s. not! c'est pas vrai! (b) (in a sure manner) slowly but s. lentement mais sûrement
surety ['ʃʊərətɪ] n Law caution f; to stand s. (for sb) se porter caution (pour qn)
surf [sɜ:f] 1 n surf m
2 vi (go surfing) faire du surf
3 vt Comptr to s. the Net naviguer sur l'Internet
surface ['sɜ:fɪs] 1 n surface f; Fig on the s. en apparence;

Fig beneath the s. au fond; s. **mail** courrier *m* par voie de terre; s. **tension** tension *f* de surface; s. **water** eaux *fpl* de surface
  2 *vt (road)* revêtir
  3 *vi (from water) & Fam Hum (from bed)* faire surface; *Fig (of person, emotion)* réapparaître

surface-to-air missile ['sɜːfɪstʊ'eə'mɪsaɪl] *n Mil* missile *m* sol-air

surface-to-surface missile ['sɜːfɪstə'sɜːfɪs'mɪsaɪl] *n Mil* missile *m* sol-sol

surfboard ['sɜːfbɔːd] *n* (planche *f* de) surf *m*

surfeit ['sɜːfɪt] *n* surabondance *f*

surfer ['sɜːfə(r)] *n* surfer *m*

surfing ['sɜːfɪŋ] *n* surf *m*; **to go s.** aller faire du surf

surge [sɜːdʒ] **1** *n (of electricity)* surtension *f*; *(of enthusiasm, support, demand)* sursaut *m*; *(of profits)* hausse *f* soudaine; *(of crowd)* ruée *f*
  2 *vi (of water, crowd)* déferler; *(of feeling)* monter

surgeon ['sɜːdʒən] *n* chirurgien *m*

surgery ['sɜːdʒərɪ] *n* **(a)** *(technique)* chirurgie *f*; *(operation)* intervention *f* chirurgicale; **to perform s. on sb** opérer qn **(b)** *Br (doctor's office)* cabinet *m* (de consultation); *(period)* heures *fpl* de consultation **(c)** *Br (of MP)* permanence *f*

surgical ['sɜːdʒɪkəl] *adj* chirurgical(e); *Fig* **with s. precision** avec une précision mathématique; **s. instruments** instruments *mpl* de chirurgie; *Br* **s. spirit** alcool *m* à 90°; *Mil* **s. strike** offensive *f* chirurgicale

Surinam ['sʊrɪnæm] *n* le Surinam

surly ['sɜːlɪ] *adj* revêche

surmise [sɜː'maɪz] *vt* conjecturer

surmount [sɜː'maʊnt] *vt* surmonter

surname ['sɜːneɪm] *n* nom *m* de famille

surpass [sɜː'pɑːs] *vt (person)* surpasser; *(record)* battre; *(expectation)* dépasser; **to s. oneself** se surpasser

surplice ['sɜːplɪs] *n Rel* surplis *m*

surplus ['sɜːpləs] **1** *n* surplus *m*; *Econ (of trade)* excédent *m*
  2 *adj (items)* en trop, en surplus; **to be s. to requirements** être en trop

surprise [sə'praɪz] **1** *n* surprise *f*; **to take sb by s.** prendre qn par surprise; **to give sb a s.** faire une surprise à qn; **it was no s.** cela n'a étonné personne
  2 *adj (attack, defeat)* surprise *inv*; **s. party** soirée *f* surprise
  3 *vt* surprendre, étonner; **I'm not surprised** ça ne m'étonne pas

surprising [sə'praɪzɪŋ] *adj* surprenant(e), étonnant(e)

surprisingly [sə'praɪzɪŋlɪ] *adv* étonnamment; **not s.** comme il fallait s'y attendre; **s. enough,...** chose surprenante...

surreal [sə'rɪəl] *adj (surrealist)* surréaliste; *(strange)* délirant(e)

surrealism [sə'rɪəlɪzəm] *n Art* surréalisme *m*

surrealist [sə'rɪəlɪst] *n & adj Art* surréaliste *mf*

surrender [sə'rendə(r)] **1** *n* **(a)** *(of army, weapons)* reddition *f*; **no s.!** nous ne nous rendrons pas! **(b)** *Fin* **s. value** valeur *f* de rachat
  2 *vt (town)* livrer; *(right, possessions)* abandonner; *(advantage)* perdre; **to s. control of sth** abandonner la direction de qch
  3 *vi* se rendre

surreptitious [sʌrəp'tɪʃəs] *adj* furtif(ive)

surrogate ['sʌrəgət] *n* substitut *m*; **s. mother** mère *f* porteuse

surround [sə'raʊnd] **1** *vt* entourer; *(of police)* cerner
  2 *n* encadrement *m*

surrounding [sə'raʊndɪŋ] *adj* environnant(e)

surroundings [sə'raʊndɪŋz] *npl* environnement *m*

surtax ['sɜːtæks] **1** *n* surtaxe *f*
  2 *vt* surtaxer

surveillance [sə'veɪləns] *n* surveillance *f*; **under s.** sous surveillance

survey **1** ['sɜːveɪ] **(a)** *(of subject, situation)* étude *f*; *(of opinions)* sondage *m* **(b)** *(of house)* expertise *f*; *(of land)* relevé *m*
  2 *vt* [sə'veɪ] **(a)** *(look at)* contempler **(b)** *(subject, situation)* étudier, examiner **(c)** *(house)* faire l'expertise de; *(land)* faire un relevé de

surveying [sɜː'veɪɪŋ] *n (of house)* expertise *f*; *(of land)* relevé *m*

surveyor [sə'veɪə(r)] *n (of building)* expert *m*; *(of land)* géomètre *mf*

survival [sə'vaɪvəl] *n* **(a)** *(continued existence)* survie *f*; *also Fig* **the s. of the fittest** la survie du plus apte; **s. kit** équipement *m* de survie **(b)** *(relic)* vestige *m*

survive [sə'vaɪv] **1** *vt (of person)* survivre à; *(of object)* résister à; **he is survived by a wife and two children** il laisse une épouse et deux enfants
  2 *vi* survivre

surviving [sə'vaɪvɪŋ] *adj (of person)* survivant(e); *(remains, copy)* restant(e)

survivor [sə'vaɪvə(r)] *n* survivant(e) *m,f*

susceptible [sə'septɪbəl] *adj* sensible **(to** à)

suspect 1 ['sʌspekt] suspect(e) *m,f*
  2 *adj* suspect(e)
  3 *vt* [sə'spekt] **(a)** *(person)* soupçonner **(b)** *(have intuition of)* se douter de; **to s. the truth** soupçonner la vérité **(c)** *(consider likely)* croire

suspend [sə'spend] *vt* **(a)** *(hang)* suspendre **(from** à) **(b)** *(service, employee, player)* suspendre; *(pupil)* renvoyer temporairement

suspended [sə'spendɪd] *adj* suspendu(e); **in s. animation** en hibernation; *Law* **s. sentence** condamnation *f* avec sursis

suspender [sə'spendə(r)] *n* **(a)** *Br (for stocking)* jarretelle *f*; *(for sock)* fixe-chaussette *m*; **s. belt** porte-jarretelles *m inv* **(b)** *Am* **suspenders** *(braces)* bretelles *fpl*

suspense [sə'spens] *n (uncertainty)* incertitude *f*; *(in film)* suspense *m*; **to keep sb in s.** tenir qn en haleine

suspension [sə'spenʃən] *n* **(a)** *(of car)* suspension *f*; **s. bridge** pont *m* suspendu **(b)** *(of service, employee)* suspension *f*; *(of pupil)* renvoi *m*

suspicion [sə'spɪʃən] *n* **(a)** *(belief of guilt)* soupçon *m*; **to be under s.** être soupçonné(e); **to be above s.** être au-dessus de tout soupçon; **to have one's suspicions about sb/sth** avoir des doutes sur qn/qch; **to arouse s.** éveiller les soupçons **(b)** *(small amount)* soupçon *m*

suspicious [sə'spɪʃəs] *adj (arousing suspicions)* suspect(e); *(having suspicions)* méfiant(e) **(of** or **about** à l'égard de); **to make sb s.** éveiller les soupçons de qn

suspiciously [sə'spɪʃəslɪ] *adv (behave)* d'une manière suspecte; *(ask)* avec méfiance; *Fam* **it looks s. like malaria** ça ressemble étrangement au paludisme

▸ **suss out** [sʌs] *vt sep Br Fam* piger; *(person)* cerner

sustain [sə'steɪn] *vt* **(a)** *(maintain)* soutenir; *(life)* maintenir; **a proper breakfast will s. you until lunchtime** un bon petit déjeuner vous permettra de tenir jusqu'à midi; *Law* **objection sustained** objection accordée **(b)** *(loss, damage)* subir; **to s. an injury** être blessé(e)

sustainable [sə'steɪnəbəl] *adj (growth, development)* durable

sustained [sə'steɪnd] *adj* soutenu(e); **s. applause** applaudissements *mpl* prolongés

sustenance ['sʌstɪnəns] *n* subsistance *f*

suture ['suːtʃə(r)] *n* suture *f*

svelte [svelt] *adj* svelte

SW *n* (**a**) (*abbr* **southwest**) SO (**b**) *Rad* (*abbr* **Short Wave**) OC

swab [swɒb] **1** *n* (*cotton wool*) tampon *m* **2** *vt* (*pt & pp* **swabbed**) (*wound*) nettoyer; (*floor*) laver

swag [swæg] *n very Fam* (*of thief*) butin *m*

swagger ['swægə(r)] **1** *n* démarche *f* balancée et crâneuse
2 *vi* (*strut*) se pavaner

swallow[1] ['swɒləʊ] **1** *n* (*of drink*) gorgée *f*; (*of food*) bouchée *f*
2 *vt* (**a**) (*food, drink*) avaler; *Fig* (*pride, anger*) ravaler; **to s. sth whole** avaler qch tout rond (**b**) *Fam* (*believe*) gober, avaler
3 *vi* avaler; **to s. hard** (*when nervous, afraid*) avaler sa salive

swallow[2] *n* (*bird*) hirondelle *f*; *Prov* **one s. doesn't make a summer** une hirondelle ne fait pas le printemps
▸ **swallow up** *vt sep Fig* (*company, country*) engloutir

swam [swæm] *pt of* **swim**

swamp [swɒmp] **1** *n* marais *m*
2 *vt* (*flood*) inonder; *Fig* **to be swamped with sth** être submergé(e) de qch

swan [swɒn] **1** *n* cygne *m*; *Fig* **s. song** chant *m* du cygne
2 *vi* (*pt & pp* **swanned**) *Fam* **to s. in/out/off** arriver/ sortir/partir tranquillement
▸ **swan about, swan around** *vi Fam* musarder

swank [swæŋk] *Fam* **1** *n* (*ostentation*) épate *f*; (*ostentatious person*) frimeur(euse) *m,f*
2 *vi* frimer

swanky ['swæŋkɪ] *adj Fam* chic *inv*

swap [swɒp] **1** *n* échange *m*; **to do a s.** faire un échange
2 *vt* (*pt & pp* **swapped**) **to s. sth for sth** échanger qch contre qch; **to s. places with sb** changer de place avec qn; **to s. insults/ideas** échanger des insultes/idées
3 *vi* échanger

swarm [swɔːm] **1** *n* (*of bees*) essaim *m*; (*of people*) nuée *f*
2 *vi* (*of bees*) essaimer; (*of people*) accourir en masse; **to be swarming with** (*of place*) grouiller de

swarthy ['swɔːðɪ] *adj* basané(e)

swashbuckling ['swɒʃbʌklɪŋ] *adj* de cape et d'épée

swastika ['swɒstɪkə] *n* svastika *m*

SWAT [swɒt] *n Am* (*abbr* **Special Weapons and Tactics**) **S. team** = groupe d'intervention d'élite de la police américaine

swat [swɒt] (*pt & pp* **swatted**) *vt* écraser

swatch [swɒtʃ] *n* échantillon *m*

swathe [sweɪð] **1** *n* (*of grass*) andain *m*; (*of material, land*) bande *f*; *Fig* **to cut a s. through sth** (*of fire, storm*) détruire qch sur son passage
2 *vt* envelopper (**in** de)

sway [sweɪ] **1** *n* (**a**) (*movement*) balancement *m* (**b**) (*influence*) influence *f*; **to be under sb's s.** être sous l'influence de qn; **to hold s. over sb/sth** tenir qn/qch sous sa domination
2 *vt* (*influence*) influencer
3 *vi* se balancer; **to s. from side to side** se balancer d'un côté à l'autre

Swazi ['swɑːzɪ] **1** *n* (**a**) (*person*) Swazi(e) *m,f* (**b**) (*language*) swazi *m*
2 *adj* swazi(e)

Swaziland ['swɑːzɪlænd] *n* le Swaziland

swear [sweə(r)] (*pt* **swore** [swɔː(r)], *pp* **sworn** [swɔːn]) **1** *vt* (*vow*) jurer; **to s. to do sth** jurer de faire qch; *Law* **to s. an oath** prêter serment
2 *vi* (*use swearwords*) jurer; **to s. at sb** injurier qn
▸ **swear by** *vt insep* (*have confidence in*) se fier à
▸ **swear in** *vt sep Law* (*jury, witness*) faire prêter serment à

swearing ['sweərɪŋ] *n* grossièretés *fpl*

swearword ['sweəwɜːd] *n* juron *m*, mot *m* grossier

sweat [swet] **1** *n* transpiration *f*, sueur *f*; *Fig* **to be in a s. about sth** avoir des sueurs froides à propos de qch; *very Fam* **no s.!** pas de problèmes!; **s. gland** glande *f* sudoripare
2 *vt Fam* **to s. buckets** être en nage; *Fig* **to s. blood** suer sang et eau
3 *vi* (**a**) (*perspire*) transpirer, suer; *Fam* **to s. like a pig** suer comme un bœuf (**b**) *Fam Fig* (*worry*) se faire de la bile; **to make sb s.** laisser mariner qn

sweatband ['swetbænd] *n* (*on head*) bandeau *m*; (*on wrist*) poignet *m*

sweater ['swetə(r)] *n* pullover *m*, pull *m*

sweatshirt ['swetʃɜːt] *n* sweatshirt *m*

sweatshop ['swetʃɒp] *n* = atelier de confection où l'on exploite le personnel

sweaty ['swetɪ] *adj* (*person*) en sueur; (*hands*) moite; (*clothes*) imprégné(e) de sueur; (*work*) qui fait transpirer

Swede [swiːd] *n* (*person*) Suédois(e) *m,f*

swede [swiːd] *n Br* (*vegetable*) rutabaga *m*

Sweden ['swiːdən] *n* la Suède

Swedish ['swiːdɪʃ] **1** *npl* (*people*) **the S.** les Suédois *mpl*
2 *n* (*language*) suédois *m*
3 *adj* suédois(e)

sweep [swiːp] **1** *n* (**a**) (*action*) coup *m* de balai; **to give sth a s.** donner un coup de balai à qch; *Fig* **at one s.** d'un seul coup; *Fig* **to make a clean s.** (*win everything*) tout gagner (**b**) (*movement*) **with a s. of the arm** d'un geste large (**c**) (*of land, hills*) étendue *f*; (*of road, river*) courbe *f*
2 *vt* (*pt & pp* **swept** [swept]) (**a**) (*floor, street*) balayer; (*chimney*) ramoner; **to be swept overboard** être emporté(e) par une vague (**b**) (*idioms*) **to s. sth under the carpet** tirer le rideau sur qch; **to s. the board** (*in competition*) tout gagner; **the latest craze to s. the country** la dernière folie qui a envahi le pays; *Fig* **to s. sb off their feet** faire perdre la tête à qn
3 *vi* (*with broom*) balayer (**b**) (*move rapidly*) **to s. in/out** faire une entrée/une sortie majestueuse; **to s. to power** être propulsé(e) au pouvoir
▸ **sweep aside** *vt sep* (*opposition, criticism*) écarter
▸ **sweep away** *vt sep* (*building*) emporter; *Fig* (*obstacle, difficulty*) balayer; *Fig* **to be swept away by sth** (*enthusiasm, passion*) être emporté(e) par qch
▸ **sweep up** *vt sep & vi* balayer

sweeper ['swiːpə(r)] *n* (**a**) (*carpet*) **s.** balai *m* mécanique (**b**) (*footballer*) arrière *mf* volant(e)

sweeping ['swiːpɪŋ] *adj* (*gesture*) large; (*statement*) généralisateur(trice); (*change, proposal*) radical(e)

sweepstake ['swiːpsteɪk] *n* sweepstake *m*

sweet [swiːt] **1** *adj* (**a**) (*sugary*) sucré(e); (*wine*) doux (*f* douce); **to taste s.** avoir un goût sucré; **as s. as honey** doux comme le miel; **s. tooth** aimer les sucreries; **s. pea** pois *m* de senteur; **s. potato** patate *f* douce; **s. william** œillet *m* de poète (**b**) (*smell*) agréable; (*sound*) doux (*f* douce) (**c**) (*pretty, kind*) adorable; **to whisper s. nothings to sb** dire des mots doux à qn
2 *n Br* (*piece of confectionery*) bonbon *m*; (*dessert*) dessert *m*; **s. shop** confiserie *f*

sweetbreads ['swiːtbredz] *npl* ris *m* (*de veau, d'agneau*)

sweet-and-sour [swiːtən'saʊə(r)] *adj* aigre-doux (aigre-douce)

sweetcorn ['swi:tkɔːn] *n* maïs *m*

sweeten ['swi:tən] *vt (food)* sucrer; *Fig* **to s. sb up** amadouer qn

sweetener ['swi:tənə(r)] *n* **(a)** *(in food)* édulcorant *m* **(b)** *Fam (bribe)* pot-de-vin *m*

sweetheart ['swi:thɑːt] *n (term of address) (to woman)* chérie *f; (to man)* chéri *m*

sweetie ['swi:tɪ] *n Fam* **(a)** *Br (piece of confectionery)* bonbon *m* **(b)** *(darling)* chou *m*; **he's such a s.** il est adorable

sweetly ['swi:tlɪ] *adv (sing)* d'une voix douce; *(smile, answer)* gentiment

sweetness ['swi:tnɪs] *n* douceur *f;* **to be all s. and light** être tout sucre tout miel

sweet-talk ['swi:t'tɔːk] *vt Fam* **to s. sb into doing sth** baratiner qn pour qu'il fasse qch

sweet-tempered [swi:t'tempəd] *adj* doux (douce)

swell [swel] **1** *vt (pp* **swollen** ['swəʊlən] or **swelled)** *(numbers, crowd)* gonfler
  2 *vi (of part of body)* enfler; *(of number, crowd)* grossir; *(of sea)* se soulever; **to s. with pride** se gonfler d'orgueil
  3 *n (of sea)* houle *f*
  4 *adj Am Fam (excellent)* super *inv*
▸ **swell up** *vi (part of body)* enfler

swelling ['swelɪŋ] *n* gonflement *m*, enflure *f;* **the s. had gone down** ça avait désenflé

sweltering ['sweltərɪŋ] *adj* étouffant(e)

swept [swept] *pt & pp of* **sweep**

swerve [swɜːv] **1** *n (of car)* embardée *f; (of player)* écart *m*
  2 *vi (of car, driver)* faire une embardée; *(of player)* faire un écart; *(of ball)* décrire une courbe

swift [swɪft] **1** *n (bird)* martinet *m*
  2 *adj* rapide

swift-footed ['swɪftfʊtɪd] *adj* rapide à la course

swiftly ['swɪftlɪ] *adv* rapidement, vite

swiftness ['swɪftnɪs] *n* rapidité *f*

swig [swɪg] *Fam* **1** *n* lampée *f;* **to take a s. from a bottle** boire un coup à une bouteille
  2 *vt (pt & pp* **swigged)** boire à grands traits

swill [swɪl] **1** *n (food) (for pigs)* pâtée *f; Pej (for people)* nourriture *f* infâme
  2 *vt Fam (drink)* écluser
▸ **swill about, swill around** *vi (of liquid)* se répandre
▸ **swill out** *vt sep (rinse)* rincer à grande eau

swim [swɪm] **1** *n* to go for *or* **have a s.** aller nager
  2 *vt (pt* **swam** [swæm], *pp* **swum** [swʌm]) nager; **to s. the breast stroke** nager la brasse; **to s. the Channel** traverser la Manche à la nage
  3 *vi* **(a)** nager; **to go swimming** aller nager; *Fig* **to s. across sth** traverser qch à la nage; *Fig* **to s. with the tide** suivre le courant **(b)** *(be dizzy)* **my head is swimming** j'ai la tête qui tourne

swimmer ['swɪmə(r)] *n* nageur(euse) *m,f*

swimming ['swɪmɪŋ] *n* natation *f;* **s. cap** bonnet *m* de bain; **s. costume** maillot *m* de bain; **s. lesson** cours *m* de natation; **s. pool** piscine *f;* **s. trunks** slip *m* de bain

swimmingly ['swɪmɪŋlɪ] *adv Fam* au mieux; **things are going s.** ça baigne

swimsuit ['swɪmsuːt] *n* maillot *m* de bain

swindle ['swɪndəl] **1** *n* escroquerie *f*
  2 *vt* escroquer; **to s. sb out of sth** soutirer qch à qn

swindler ['swɪndlə(r)] *n* escroc *m*

swine [swaɪn] *(pl* **swine)** *n* **(a)** *Lit (pig)* porc *m*; **s. fever** peste *f* porcine **(b)** *Fam (man)* salaud *m*; *(woman)* garce *f*

swing [swɪŋ] **1** *n* **(a)** *(movement) (of rope, chain)*

balancement *m; (in golf)* swing *m; Fam* **to take a s. at sb/ sth** balancer un coup de poing à qn/qch; **to be in full s.** battre son plein; *Fam* **to go with a s.** marcher comme sur des roulettes; *Fam* **to get into the s. of things** se mettre dans le bain; **s. door** porte *f* battante **(b)** *(change) (in opinion)* revirement *m* (in de); *(in economy)* fluctuation *f* (in de); *(in mood)* saute *f* (in de) **(c)** *(in playground)* balançoire *f; Fam* **it's swings and roundabouts** ce qu'on gagne d'un côté on le perd de l'autre
  2 *vt (pt & pp* **swung** [swʌŋ]) *(arms, racquet, axe)* balancer; **to s. one's hips** balancer les hanches; **to s. sb/sth onto one's shoulder** hisser qn/qch sur ses épaules; *Fam* **to s. it so that...** arranger les choses de manière à ce que... + subjunctive
  3 *vi* **(a)** *(move to and fro)* se balancer; **to s. open** *(of door)* s'ouvrir; **to s. into action** passer à l'action; *Fam* **he should s. for this** *(be hanged)* il mérite d'être pendu; *Fam* **the party was really swinging** la fête battait son plein **(b)** *(change direction)* virer; **to s. round** se retourner

swingeing ['swɪndʒɪŋ] *adj* énorme

swipe [swaɪp] **1** *vt* **(a)** *(through electronic reader)* passer dans un lecteur de cartes **(b)** *Fam (steal)* faucher
  2 *vi (hit)* **to s. at** essayer de frapper
  3 *n* **to take a s. at** *(aim blow at)* essayer de frapper; *Fig (criticize)* s'en prendre à

swirl [swɜːl] **1** *n (of cream)* spirale *f; (of smoke, leaves, dust)* tourbillon *m*
  2 *vt* remuer
  3 *vi* tourbillonner, tournoyer

swish [swɪʃ] **1** *n (of cane, whip)* sifflement *m; (of dress, silk)* froufrou *m*
  2 *adj Fam (elegant)* chic *inv*
  3 *vt (cane)* faire siffler; **to s. its tail** *(of animal)* remuer la queue
  4 *vi (of cane, whip)* siffler; *(of dress, silk)* froufrouter

Swiss [swɪs] **1** *npl* **the S.** *(people)* les Suisses *mpl*
  2 *adj* suisse; **S. army knife** couteau *m* suisse; **S. chard** bette *f;* **S. cheese plant** philodendron *m*; **s. roll** roulé *m*

switch [swɪtʃ] **1** *n* **(a)** *(electrical)* interrupteur *m* **(b)** *(change)* revirement *m*; **to make a s.** effectuer un changement **(c)** *(stick)* baguette *f*
  2 *vt* **(a)** *(change)* **to s. channels/jobs** changer de chaîne/ d'emploi; **they switched their attention to...** leur attention s'est portée sur...; **he's been switched to another department** il a été muté dans un autre service **(b)** *(exchange)* échanger
  3 *vi (change)* **to s. to** passer à; *Comptr* basculer vers
▸ **switch off 1** *vt sep (appliance, heating)* éteindre
  2 *vi* **(a)** *(of appliance, heating)* s'éteindre **(b)** *Fam (of person)* décrocher
▸ **switch on 1** *vt sep (appliance, heating)* allumer
  2 *vi (of appliance, heating)* s'allumer
▸ **switch over** *vi (change TV channel)* passer sur une autre chaîne; **to s. over to sth** passer à qch

switchback ['swɪtʃbæk] *n* route *f* en lacets

switchboard ['swɪtʃbɔːd] *n* standard *m*; **s. operator** standardiste *mf*

Switzerland ['swɪtsələnd] *n* la Suisse

swivel ['swɪvəl] **1** *n* pivot *m*; **s. chair** chaise *f* pivotante
  2 *vi (pt & pp* **swivelled)** pivoter

swizz [swɪz] *n Fam* arnaque *f*

swollen ['swəʊlən] **1** *pp of* **swell**
  2 *adj* enflé(e)

swoon [swuːn] *n* évanouissement *m*
  2 *vi* s'évanouir

swoop [swuːp] **1** *n (of bird, plane)* descente *f* en piqué; *(of police)* descente *f*

2 *vi (of bird, plane)* descendre en piqué ; *(of police)* faire une descente

swop [swɒp] = **swap**

sword [sɔːd] *n* épée *f*; **s. dance** danse *f* du sabre

swordfish ['sɔːdfɪʃ] *n* espadon *m*

swore [swɔː(r)] *pt of* **swear**

sworn [swɔːn] **1** *adj* **s. enemy** ennemi(e) *m,f* juré(e) **2** *pp of* **swear**

swot [swɒt] *Br Fam* **1** *n (studious pupil)* bûcheur(euse) *m,f* **2** *vi (pt & pp* **swotted***) (study hard)* bûcher ► **swot up on** *vt insep Br Fam (subject)* potasser

swum [swʌm] *pp of* **swim**

swung [swʌŋ] *pt & pp of* **swing**

sycamore ['sɪkəmɔː(r)] *n* sycomore *m*

sycophant ['sɪkəfənt] *n* flagorneur(euse) *m,f*

sycophantic [sɪkə'fæntɪk] *adj* flagorneur(euse)

Sydney ['sɪdnɪ] *n* Sydney

syllable ['sɪləbəl] *n* syllabe *f*

syllabus ['sɪləbəs] *n* programme *m*

sylph-like ['sɪlflaɪk] *adj Hum* **a s. woman** une sylphide

symbiotic [sɪmb(a)ɪ'ɒtɪk] *adj* symbiotique

symbol ['sɪmbəl] *n* symbole *m*

symbolic [sɪm'bɒlɪk] *adj* symbolique

symbolism ['sɪmbəlɪzəm] *n Art* symbolisme *m*

symbolist ['sɪmbəlɪst] *n & adj Art* symboliste *mf*

symbolize ['sɪmbəlaɪz] *vt* symboliser

symmetrical [sɪ'metrɪkəl] *adj* symetrique

symmetry ['sɪmɪtrɪ] *n* symétrie *f*

sympathetic [sɪmpə'θetɪk] *adj (understanding)* compréhensif(ive); *(compassionate)* compatissant(e); **to be s. to a proposal/cause** être favorable à une proposition/ cause

sympathize ['sɪmpəθaɪz] *vi* **(a)** *(show compassion)* compatir (**with** avec) **(b)** *(show understanding)* **to s. (with sb)** comprendre (qn)

sympathizer ['sɪmpəθaɪzə(r)] *n* sympathisant(e) *m,f*

sympathy ['sɪmpəθɪ] *n* **(a)** *(pity, compassion)* compassion *f*; **to have s. for sb** éprouver de la compassion pour qn **(b)** *(understanding, support)* sympathie *f*; **to feel s. for sb** éprouver de la sympathie pour qn; **s. strike** grève *f* de solidarité

symphony ['sɪmfənɪ] *n* symphonie *f*; **s. orchestra** orchestre *m* symphonique

symposium [sɪm'pəʊzɪəm] *(pl* **symposia** [sɪm'pəʊzɪə]*) n* symposium *m*

symptom ['sɪm(p)təm] *n also Fig* symptôme *m*

symptomatic [sɪm(p)tə'mætɪk] *adj* symptomatique

synagogue ['sɪnəgɒg] *n* synagogue *f*

sync [sɪŋk] *n Fam* synchronisation *f*; **in/out of s. (with)** synchrone/pas synchrone (avec)

synchronization [sɪŋkrənaɪ'zeɪʃən] *n* synchronisation *f*

synchronize ['sɪŋkrənaɪz] *vt* synchroniser

syncopation [sɪŋkə'peɪʃən] *n Mus* syncope *f*

syndicalism ['sɪndɪkəlɪzəm] *n Pol* syndicalisme *m*

syndicalist ['sɪndɪkəlɪst] *n & adj Pol* syndicaliste *mf*

syndicate 1 *n* ['sɪndɪkət] syndicat *m* **2** *vt* ['sɪndɪkeɪt] *Journ* publier simultanément dans plusieurs journaux; **syndicated columnist** journaliste *mf* d'agence

syndrome ['sɪndrəʊm] *n Fig* syndrôme *m*

synergy ['sɪnədʒɪ] *n* synergie *f*

synod ['sɪnəd] *n Rel* synode *m*

synonym ['sɪnənɪm] *n* synonyme *m*

synonymous [sɪ'nɒnɪməs] *adj* synonyme (**with** de)

synopsis [sɪ'nɒpsɪs] *(pl* **synopses** [sɪ'nɒpsiːz]*) n* résumé *m*; *(of film)* synopsis *m*

syntax ['sɪntæks] *n Ling* syntaxe *f*; *Comptr* **s. error** erreur *f* de syntaxe

synthesis ['sɪnθɪsɪs] *(pl* **syntheses** ['sɪnθɪsiːz]*) n* synthèse *f*

synthesize ['sɪnθəsaɪz] *vt* synthétiser

synthesizer ['sɪnθəsaɪzə(r)] *n* synthétiseur *m*

synthetic [sɪn'θetɪk] **1** *adj* synthétique **2** *n* **synthetics** synthétique *m*

syphilis ['sɪfɪlɪs] *n* syphilis *f*

syphon [saɪfən] = **siphon**

Syria ['sɪrɪə] *n* la Syrie

Syrian ['sɪrɪən] **1** *n* Syrien(enne) *m,f* **2** *adj* syrien(enne)

syringe [sɪ'rɪndʒ] **1** *n* seringue *f* **2** *vt (ears)* déboucher

syrup ['sɪrəp] *n* sirop *m*

syrupy ['sɪrəpɪ] *adj (smile, music)* sirupeux(euse)

system ['sɪstəm] *n* **(a)** *(structure)* système *m*; **the S.** *(established order)* le système; *Fam* **it was a shock to the s.** ça a été un choc; *Fam* **to get sb/sth out of one's s.** se sortir qn/qch de la tête **(b)** *Comptr* système *m*; **systems analyst** analyste *m* programmeur *f*

systematic [sɪstə'mætɪk] *adj* systématique

systematize ['sɪstəmətaɪz] *vt* systématiser

T, t [tiː] *n* (**a**) *(letter)* T, t *m inv* (**b**) *(idioms)* **that's you to a T** c'est tout à fait toi; **to suit sb to a T** convenir parfaitement à qn

t *(abbr* **ton(s))** t

TA [tiːˈeɪ] *n Br (abbr* **territorial army)** = armée de réserve, constituée de volontaires

ta [tɑː] *exclam Br Fam* merci!

tab [tæb] *n* (**a**) *(on garment)* étiquette *f*; *Fam* **to keep tabs on sb/sth** avoir qn/qch à l'œil (**b**) *(on typewriter, word processor)* tabulation *f*; **t. (key)** tabulateur *m* (**c**) *Am Fam (for meal, drinks)* addition *f* (**d**) *(of LSD, ecstasy)* pilule *f*

tabby [ˈtæbɪ] *n* **t. (cat)** chat *m* tigré

tabernacle [ˈtæbənækəl] *n (church)* temple *m*; *(on altar)* tabernacle *m*

table [ˈteɪbəl] **1** *n* (**a**) *(furniture)* table *f*; **to lay** *or* **set the t.** mettre *ou* dresser la table; **to clear the t.** débarrasser la table; **t. lamp** petite lampe *f*; **t. linen** linge *m* de table; **to have good/bad t. manners** bien/mal se tenir à table; **t. mat** set *m* de table; **t. salt** sel *m* de table; **t. tennis** tennis *m* de table; **t. wine** vin *m* de table (**b**) *(of facts, figures)* tableau *m*, table *f*; **t. of contents** table des matières; **twelve times t.** table de douze (**c**) *(idioms)* **the offer is still on the t.** l'offre tient toujours; **to turn the tables on sb** renverser les rôles

2 *vt* **to t. a motion/proposal** *Br (present)* présenter une motion/une proposition; *Am (postpone)* ajourner une motion/une proposition

tablecloth [ˈteɪbəlklɒθ] *n* nappe *f*

tablespoon [ˈteɪbəlspuːn] *n* cuillère *f* à soupe

tablet [ˈtæblɪt] *n* (**a**) *(pill)* cachet *m* (**b**) *(inscribed stone)* tablette *f* (**c**) *(of soap)* pain *m*

tableware [ˈteɪbəlweə(r)] *n* vaisselle *f*

tabloid [ˈtæblɔɪd] *n (newspaper)* tabloïd *m*; **the t. press** la presse populaire

taboo [təˈbuː] **1** *n (pl* **taboos)** tabou *m*
2 *adj* tabou(e)

tabular [ˈtæbjʊlə(r)] *adj* **in t. form** sous forme de tableau

tabulate [ˈtæbjʊleɪt] *vt* présenter sous forme de tableau

tachometer [tækˈɒmɪtə(r)] *n* compte-tours *m*

tacit [ˈtæsɪt] *adj* tacite

tacitly [ˈtæsɪtlɪ] *adv* tacitement

taciturn [ˈtæsɪtɜːn] *adj* taciturne

tack [tæk] **1** *n* (**a**) *(small nail)* clou *m*; *Am (drawing pin)* punaise *f* (**b**) *Naut (course)* bordée *f*; *Fig* **to change t.** changer de tactique
2 *vt* (**a**) *(fasten)* clouer; *Am (with drawing pin)* punaiser; *Fig* **to t. sth on** *(add)* rajouter qch (**b**) *(in sewing)* faufiler
3 *vi Naut* louvoyer

tackle [ˈtækəl] **1** *n* (**a**) *(equipment)* matériel *m*, équipement *m* (**b**) *(in football)* tacle *m*; *(in rugby)* placage *m*
2 *vt* (**a**) *(deal with) (problem)* s'attaquer à; *(subject)* aborder; **to t. sb about sth** *(confront)* confronter qn à propos de qch (**b**) *(in football)* tacler; *(in rugby)* plaquer

tacky [ˈtækɪ] *adj* (**a**) *(sticky)* collant(e) (**b**) *Fam (tasteless)* de mauvais goût; *(person)* vulgaire

tact [tækt] *n* tact *m*

tactful [ˈtæktfʊl] *adj (person)* qui a du tact; *(answer, remark)* diplomatique

tactic [ˈtæktɪk] *n* tactique *f*

tactical [ˈtæktɪkəl] *adj* tactique; *Pol* **t. voting** vote *m* utile

tactician [tækˈtɪʃən] *n* tacticien(enne) *m,f*

tactile [ˈtæktaɪl] *adj* tactile

tactless [ˈtæktlɪs] *adj* dépourvu(e) de tact

tactlessly [ˈtæktlɪslɪ] *adv* sans tact

tad [tæd] *n Fam* **a t.** un peu

tadpole [ˈtædpəʊl] *n* têtard *m*

Tadzhikistan [tædʒɪkɪˈstɑːn] *n* le Tadjikistan

taffeta [ˈtæfɪtə] *n* taffetas *m*

tag [tæg] **1** *n* (**a**) *(label)* étiquette *f*; *Gram* **t. question** tag *m* (**b**) *(game)* **to play t.** jouer à chat
2 *vt (pt & pp* **tagged)** *(label)* étiqueter
▸ **tag along** *vi* **she always tags along** elle me/le/*etc* suit partout; **to t. along with sb** venir avec qn
▸ **tag on** *vt sep* **to t. sth on** rajouter qch

Tagus [ˈteɪgəs] *n* **the T.** le Tage

Tahiti [tɑːˈhiːtɪ] *n* Tahiti *f*

Tahitian [təˈhiːʃən] **1** *n* Tahitien(enne) *m,f*
2 *adj* tahitien(enne)

tail [teɪl] **1** *n* (**a**) *(of animal, plane)* queue *f*; *(of shirt)* pan *m*; **heads or tails?** *(when tossing coin)* pile ou face?; **tails, t. coat** queue-de-pie *f*; **t. end** *(last part)* fin *f* (**b**) *(idioms)* **with one's t. between one's legs** la queue entre les jambes; *Fam* **to put a t. on sb** prendre qn en filature; *Fam* **to turn t.** tourner les talons
2 *vt Fam (follow)* filer
▸ **tail away, tail off** *vi* décliner; *(of voice)* baisser

tailback [ˈteɪlbæk] *n (traffic jam)* bouchon *m*

tailboard [ˈteɪlbɔːd], *Am* **tailgate** [ˈteɪlgeɪt] *n* hayon *m*

taillight [ˈteɪllaɪt] *n Am* feu *m* arrière

tailor [ˈteɪlə(r)] **1** *n* tailleur *m*; **t.'s dummy** mannequin *m*; **t.'s shop** atelier *m* de tailleur
2 *vt (suit)* faire; *Fig (speech, policy)* adapter (**to** à)

tailored [ˈteɪləd] *adj* ajusté(e)

tailor-made [ˈteɪləmeɪd] *adj also Fig* fait(e) sur mesure

tailplane ['teɪlpleɪn] *n Av* stabilisateur *m*

tailspin ['teɪlspɪn] *n Av* descente *f* en vrille; **to go into a t.** descendre en vrille; *Fig* paniquer

tailwind ['teɪlwɪnd] *n* vent *m* arrière

taint [teɪnt] **1** *n* contamination *f*; *Fig* tare *f* **2** *vt (contaminate)* contaminer; *Fig* souiller

Taiwan [taɪ'wɑːn] *n* Taiwan

Taiwanese [taɪwə'niːz] **1** *n* Taiwanais(e) *m,f* **2** *adj* taiwanais(e)

Tajikistan [tædʒɪkɪ'stɑːn] *n* Tadzhikistan

take [teɪk] **1** *vt (pt* took [tʊk], *pp* taken ['teɪkən]) **(a)** *(grasp)* prendre; **to t. hold of** prendre *ou* saisir; **to t. sb by the hand** prendre qn par la main; **to t. sb in one's arms** prendre qn dans ses bras; **to t. the opportunity to do sth** profiter de l'occasion pour faire qch
(b) *(remove)* prendre; **to t. sth away from sb** prendre qch à qn; **to t. sth out of sth** prendre qch dans qch
(c) *(tolerate)* supporter; **he can't t.** a joke il prend mal la plaisanterie; **I can't t.** *(it)* any more je n'en peux plus
(d) *(lead, carry)* amener; **to t. sb home/to the station** conduire qn chez lui/à la gare; **to t. sb to court** faire un procès à qn; **to t. the dog for a walk** aller promener le chien; **her job takes her all over the world** son travail l'amène à voyager dans le monde entier; **if you can get the money we'll t.** it from there quand tu auras l'argent on verra comment on procède
(e) *(go by) (bus, road, turning)* prendre
(f) *(require)* prendre; **it takes courage (to do)** il faut du courage (pour faire); **how long does it t.?** combien de temps cela prend-il?, **it took me an hour to get here** il m'a fallu une heure pour venir; **that will t. a lot of explaining** ça ne va pas être facile de se faire pardonner
(g) *(adopt) (precautions, measures)* prendre; **to t. legal advice** consulter un avocat; **to t. sth as an example** prendre qch comme exemple
(h) *(record) (temperature, notes)* prendre
(i) *(capture) (power, town, chess piece)* prendre; **to t. first prize** remporter le premier prix
(j) *(assume)* **I t. it (that)...** je suppose que...
(k) *(accept) (cheque, credit card)* accepter; **my car only takes unleaded** ma voiture ne marche qu'à l'essence sans plomb; **t. it or leave it!** c'est à prendre ou à laisser!; **to t. sth well/badly** prendre bien/mal qch; **to t. the wrong way** mal comprendre qch; **how much** *or* **what will you t. for it?** combien est-ce que tu en veux?; **you can t. it from me that...** je peux te garantir que...
(l) *(contain)* avoir une capacité de
(m) *(subject)* faire; *(course)* suivre; *(exam)* passer; **he takes them for math** il leur enseigne les maths
(n) *(in phrases)* **to t. a bath** prendre un bain; **to t. drugs** se droguer; **to t. fright** prendre peur; **to be taken ill** tomber malade; **to t. a look at sth** jeter un coup d'œil à qch; **to t. a photograph of sb/sth** prendre qn/qch en photo; **to t. a seat** s'asseoir; **to t. a walk** se promener
2 *vi (be successful) (of fire, plant cutting, dye)* prendre
3 *n* **(a)** *(of film, music)* prise *f*
(b) *(money)* recette *f*; *Fam* **to be on the t.** toucher des pots-de-vin

▸ **take after** *vt insep* ressembler à

▸ **take apart** *vt (machine, engine)* démonter; *(argument)* démolir

▸ **take away 1** *vt sep (remove)* enlever, retirer; *(deduct)* ôter; **to t. sth away from sb** enlever qch à qn; *Br* **sandwiches to t. away** sandwichs à emporter
2 *vi* **to t. away from the pleasure/value of sth** diminuer le plaisir/la valeur de qch

▸ **take back** *vt sep* **(a)** *(return)* ramener, rapporter; **that takes me back to my childhood** cela me rappelle mon

enfance **(b)** *(accept)* reprendre **(c)** *(withdraw)* retirer; **t. that back!** retire ce que tu viens de dire!

▸ **take down** *vt sep* **(a)** *(remove) (from shelf)* prendre; *(downstairs)* descendre; *(poster, decorations)* enlever **(b)** *(lower)* baisser; *Fam* **to t. sb down a peg or two** remettre qn à sa place **(c)** *(dismantle) (tent, scaffolding)* démonter; *(wall, barricade)* démolir **(d)** *(record)* noter; *(notes)* prendre

▸ **take for** *vt sep* **to t. sb for somebody else** prendre qn pour quelqu'un d'autre; **what do you t. me for?** pour qui est-ce que tu me prends?

▸ **take in** *vt sep* **(a)** *(lead, carry) (person)* faire entrer; *(harvest)* rentrer **(b)** *(orphan)* recueillir; *(lodger)* prendre **(c)** *(garment)* reprendre **(d)** *(include)* inclure, comprendre **(e)** *(understand)* saisir **(f)** *(deceive)* tromper, rouler

▸ **take off 1** *vt sep* **(a)** *(remove)* enlever; **to t. sth off** sb's hands retirer qch des mains de qn; **to t. years off sb** *(of clothes, diet)* rajeunir qn; **he took $10 off (the price)** il a baissé (le prix) de 10 dollars; **he never took his eyes off her** il ne lui a pas quittés des yeux **(b)** *(lead) (person)* emmener; **to t. oneself off** on aller **(c)** *(mimic)* imiter
2 *vi* **(a)** *(of plane)* décoller **(b)** *(of person)* se casser **(c)** *Fam (succeed)* prendre

▸ **take on** *vt sep* **(a)** *(task, responsibility)* assumer; *(problem)* s'occuper de; *(opponent)* défier; *(fuel, supplies)* prendre **(b)** *(employ)* embaucher **(c)** *(acquire)* prendre

▸ **take out** *vt sep* **(a)** *(remove)* sortir; *Fam* **to t. it** *or* **a lot out of sb** épuiser qn; **to t. it out on sb** passer sa colère sur qn **(b)** *(person)* inviter (à sortir) **(c)** *(obtain) (licence)* obtenir; *(insurance policy)* souscrire; *(subscription)* prendre

▸ **take over 1** *vt sep* **(a)** *(become responsible for) (job, business)* reprendre **(b)** *(take control of) (place)* envahir; *(company)* racheter
2 *vi* **(a)** *(assume power)* prendre le pouvoir **(b)** *(relieve)* prendre la relève (**from** de)

▸ **take to** *vt insep* **(a)** *(go to)* **to t. to one's heels** prendre ses jambes à son cou; **to t. to one's bed** s'aliter; **to t. to the hills** se réfugier dans les collines **(b)** *(adopt habit)* **to t. to doing sth** se mettre à faire qch **(c)** *(like)* **to t. to sb** se prendre d'affection pour qn

▸ **take up 1** *vt sep* **(a)** *(carry)* monter **(b)** *(lead) (person)* faire monter **(c)** *(lift)* enlever **(d)** *(shorten) (skirt, hem)* raccourcir **(e)** *(challenge)* relever; *(offer, suggestion)* accepter; **to t. sb up on an offer** accepter l'offre de qn **(f)** *(subject, problem)* parler de **(g)** *(assume) (position, post)* prendre **(h)** *(hobby, studies)* se mettre à; **we t. up the story just after...** nous reprenons l'histoire juste après... **(i)** *(space, time)* prendre
2 *vi* **to t. up with sb** se lier avec qn

▸ **take upon** *vt sep* **to t. it upon oneself to do sth** prendre sur soi de faire qch

takeaway ['teɪkəweɪ], *Am* **takeout** ['teɪkaʊt] **1** *n (food)* plat *m* à emporter; *(restaurant)* restaurant *m* qui fait des plats à emporter
2 *adj (food)* à emporter

take-home pay ['teɪkhəʊmpeɪ] *n* salaire *m* net

taken ['teɪkən] **1** *adj (a) (occupied)* pris(e) **(b)** *(impressed)* **I was very t. with him** il m'a fait très bonne impression
2 *pp of* **take**

takeoff ['teɪkɒf] *n* **(a)** *(imitation)* imitation *f*; **to do a t. of sb** imiter qn **(b)** *(of plane)* décollage *m*

takeout ['teɪkaʊt] *n & adj Am* = **takeaway**

takeover ['teɪkəʊvə(r)] *n* **(a)** *Com (of company)* rachat *m*; **t. bid** offre *f* publique d'achat **(b)** *(of government, country)* prise *f* de pouvoir

taker ['teɪkə(r)] *n* **any takers?** y a-t-il des amateurs? **there were no takers** il n'y a pas eu d'amateurs

taking ['teɪkɪŋ] n (a) **it's yours for the t.** tu n'as plus qu'à accepter (**b**) Com **takings** recette f

talc [tælk] n talc m

talcum powder ['tælkəmpaʊdə(r)] n talc m

tale [teɪl] n (a) (story) histoire f; (legend) conte m; **to live to tell the t.** survivre (**b**) (lie) histoire f, salades fpl (**c**) **to tell tales (on sb)** moucharder (qn)

talent ['tælənt] n (a) (person, ability) talent m; **t. scout** or **spotter** dénicheur(euse) m,f de talents (**b**) Br Fam (attractive women) belles nanas fpl; (attractive men) beaux mecs mpl

talented ['tæləntɪd] adj talentueux(euse)

talisman ['tælɪzmən] n talisman m

talk [tɔːk] **1** n (a) (conversation) conversation f; **to have a t. with sb** parler ou s'entretenir avec qn; Fam **to be all t. (and no action)** parler beaucoup (et ne pas faire grand-chose); **t. show** (on TV, radio) talk-show m (**b**) **talks** (negotiations) pourparlers mpl (**c**) (gossip) **there is some t. of him resigning** le bruit court qu'il va démissionner; **it's the t. of the town** on ne parle que de cela (**d**) (lecture) intervention f **2** vt (speak) parler; **to t. nonsense** dire des bêtises; **to t. business/politics** parler business/politique; **to t. sense** tenir des propos sensés; **to t. (some) sense into sb** faire entendre raison à qn; **she can t. her way out of anything** avec son bagou elle arrive toujours à se tirer d'affaire; **to t. sb into/out of doing sth** convaincre/dissuader qn de faire qch **3** vi (a) (speak) parler (**to/about** à/de); **to t. to oneself** parler tout(e) seul(e); **talking of embarrassing situations,...** à propos de situations embarrassantes,...; Fam **now you're talking!** voilà qui est mieux!; Fam **you can t.!**, **look who's talking!** tu peux parler! (**b**) (gossip) cancaner, jaser (**c**) (give lecture) faire une intervention (**on** sur)

▸ **talk back** vi répondre avec insolence

▸ **talk down** vt insep **to t. down to sb** parler à qn sur un ton de supériorité

▸ **talk over** vt sep discuter

talkative ['tɔːkətɪv] adj bavard(e)

talker ['tɔːkə(r)] n **he was never much of a t.** il n'a jamais été très bavard

talking ['tɔːkɪŋ] adj **t. book** livre m enregistré; **t. point** sujet m de conversation; Fam **t. shop** = organisation où l'on parle beaucoup mais où l'on agit peu

talking-to ['tɔːkɪŋtuː] n Fam savon m; **to give sb a t.** passer un savon à qn

tall [tɔːl] **1** adj (person) grand(e); (building) haut(e); **how t. are you?** combien est-ce que tu mesures?; **to be 2 metres t.** (of person) mesurer 2 mètres; (of object) faire 2 mètres de haut; Fig **that's a t. order** ça va être dur; Fig **a t. story** une histoire invraisemblable **2** adv **to walk** or **stand t.** marcher la tête haute

tallboy ['tɔːlbɔɪ] n commode f haute

Tallin(n) ['tælɪn] n Tallinn

tallow ['tæləʊ] n suif m

tally ['tælɪ] **1** n compte m; **to keep a t. of sth** tenir le compte de qch **2** vi (of figure, report) concorder

talon ['tælən] n serre f

tamarind ['tæmərɪnd] n (fruit) tamarin m; (tree) tamarinier m

tambourine [tæmbə'riːn] n tambourin m

tame [teɪm] **1** adj (a) (not timid or vicious) familier(ère); (domesticated) apprivoisé(e) (**b**) (unadventurous) timide;

(speech, attempt) mou (molle); (party, evening) morne **2** vt (animal) apprivoiser; Fig (emotion) dominer

tamely ['teɪmlɪ] adv (say, ask) timidement; (accept) docilement

Tamil ['tæmɪl] **1** n (a) (person) Tamoul(e) m,f (**b**) (language) tamoul m **2** adj tamoul(e)

▸ **tamper with** ['tæmpə(r)] vt insep toucher à; (lock) tripoter; (documents, records) trafiquer

tampon ['tæmpɒn] n tampon m (hygiénique)

tan¹ [tæn] n Math (abbr **tangent**) tan f, tg f

tan² [tæn] **1** n (a) (colour) marron m clair (**b**) (from sun) bronzage m **2** adj (colour) marron clair inv **3** vt (pt & pp **tanned**) (a) (of sun) (skin) hâler (**b**) (leather) tanner; Fam **to t. sb, to t. sb's hide** tanner le cuir à qn **4** vi (of person, skin) bronzer

tandem ['tændəm] n (a) (bicycle) tandem m (**b**) **to do sth in t.** faire qch à deux

tang [tæŋ] n (taste) saveur f acidulée; (smell) odeur f acidulée

tangent ['tændʒənt] n Math tangente f; Fig **to go off at a t.** changer de sujet

tangerine [tændʒə'riːn] **1** n (fruit, colour) mandarine f **2** adj (colour) mandarine inv

tangible ['tændʒɪbəl] adj tangible; Fig (real) évident(e); Fin **t. assets** biens mpl corporels

tangibly ['tændʒɪblɪ] adv manifestement

Tangier(s) [tæn'dʒɪə(r)(z)] n Tanger

tangle ['tæŋgəl] **1** n enchevêtrement m; **to be in a t.** être emmêlé(e); Fig (of person, figures, accounts) être embrouillé(e); **to get into a t.** s'emmêler; Fig (of person, figures, accounts) s'embrouiller **2** vt **to get tangled up in sth** se prendre dans qch; Fig se retrouver mêlé(e) à qch

▸ **tangle with** vt insep Fam s'en prendre à

tangled ['tæŋgəld] adj emmêlé(e); Fig embrouillé(e)

tango ['tæŋgəʊ] **1** n (pl **tangos**) (dance) tango m **2** vi danser le tango; Fam **it takes two to t.** chacun a sa part de responsabilité

tangy ['tæŋɪ] adj acidulé(e)

tank [tæŋk] n (a) (container) réservoir m (**b**) Mil tank m (**c**) **t. top** (garment) débardeur m

▸ **tank along** vi Fam foncer

▸ **tank up** vt sep Br very Fam **to be tanked up** être bourré(e); **to get tanked up** se prendre une biture

tankard ['tæŋkəd] n chope f

tanker ['tæŋkə(r)] n (ship) navire-citerne m; (lorry) camion-citerne m

tanned [tænd] adj bronzé(e)

tanner ['tænə(r)] n tanneur(euse) m,f

tannery ['tænərɪ] n tannerie f

tannin ['tænɪn] n tan(n)in m

tannoy® ['tænɔɪ] n système m de haut-parleurs; **over the t.** au haut-parleur

tantalize ['tæntəlaɪz] vt allécher (**with** avec)

tantalizing ['tæntəlaɪzɪŋ] adj alléchant(e)

tantamount ['tæntəmaʊnt] adj **t.** to équivalent(e) à

tantrum ['tæntrəm] n caprice m; **to throw a t.** faire un caprice

Tanzania [tænzə'nɪə] n la Tanzanie

Tanzanian [tænzə'nɪən] **1** n Tanzanien(enne) m,f **2** adj tanzanien(enne)

tap¹ [tæp] **1** *n* **(a)** *Br (for water, gas)* robinet *m*; **to be on t.** *(of beer)* être à la pression; *Fig (of person, information)* être toujours disponible; **t. water** eau *f* du robinet **(b) to put a t. on a phone** mettre un téléphone sur écoute
2 *vt (pt & pp* **tapped) (a)** *(tree)* inciser; *(resources)* puiser dans; *Fam* **to t. sb for money** taper de l'argent à qn **(b)** *(phone)* mettre sur écoute

tap² **1** *n* **(a)** *(light blow)* petit coup *m*; *(with hand)* tape *f* **(b) t.** **dancer** danseur(euse) *m,f* de claquettes; **t. dancing** claquettes *fpl*
2 *vt (pt & pp* **tapped)** donner un petit coup à; *(with hand)* donner une tape à
3 *vi* **to t. (at** *or* **on)** frapper doucement (à)

tape [teɪp] **1** *n* **(a)** *(ribbon)* ruban *m*; *(of paper)* bande *f*; **(adhesive** *or Fam* **sticky) t.** ruban *m* adhésif, Scotch® *m*; *Sp* **(finishing) t.** ligne f d'arrivée; **t. (measure)** mètre *m* **(b)** *(for recording)* bande *f*, *(cassette)* cassette *f*; **t. deck** platine *f* cassette; **t. recorder** magnétophone *m*; **t. recording** enregistrement *m*
2 *vt* **(a)** *(stick with tape)* scotcher; *Fig* **to have sb taped** connaître qn comme sa poche; **to have sth taped** avoir compris qch **(b)** *(record)* enregistrer

taper ['teɪpə(r)] **1** *n (candle)* bougie *f* filée
2 *vi* s'effiler; **to t. to a point** se terminer en pointe
▸ **taper off** *vi (of object)* s'effiler; *Fig (decrease)* s'amenuiser

tape-record ['teɪprɪkɔːd] *vt* enregistrer

tapestry ['tæpɪstrɪ] *n* tapisserie *f*

tapeworm ['teɪpwɜːm] *n* ver *m* solitaire

tapioca [tæpɪ'əʊkə] *n* tapioca *m*

tapping ['tæpɪŋ] *n (sound)* petits coups *mpl*

tar [tɑː(r)] **1** *n* **(a)** *(substance)* goudron *m* **(b)** *Fam Old-fashioned (sailor)* matelot *m*
2 *vt (pt & pp* **tarred)** goudronner; **to t. and feather sb** rouler qn dans le goudron et les plumes; *Fig* **we've been tarred with the same brush** on nous a mis dans le même sac

tarantula [tə'ræntjʊlə] *n* tarantule *f*

tardily ['tɑːdɪlɪ] *adv (late)* tardivement; *(slowly)* lentement
tardy ['tɑːdɪ] *adj (late)* tardif(ive); *(slow)* lent(e)

target ['tɑːgɪt] **1** *n* **(a)** *(of bullet, missile, joke)* cible *f*; **t. language** *(in translating)* langue *f* d'arrivée; **t. practice** exercices *mpl* de tir **(b)** *Fig (goal)* objectif *m*; **to set oneself a t.** se fixer un objectif; **to be on t. (to do sth)** être dans les temps (pour faire qch); **t. audience** type *m* d'écoute ciblé; **t. market** marché *m* ciblé
2 *vt* **(a)** *(aim)* **to t. sth at sth** *(missile)* diriger qch sur qch; *Fig (campaign, TV programme, benefits)* destiner qch à qch **(b)** *also Fig (aim at)* viser

tariff ['tærɪf] *n (tax)* tarif *m*, droit *m* de douane; *(price list)* tarif; **t. barrier** barrière *f* douanière

tarmac® ['tɑːmæk] **1** *n* macadam *m*; **the t.** *(runway)* le tarmac
2 *vt (pt & pp* **tarmacked)** goudronner

tarnish ['tɑːnɪʃ] **1** *vt also Fig* ternir
2 *vi* se ternir

tarot ['tærəʊ] *n* tarot *m*; **t. card** carte *f* de tarot

tarpaulin [tɑː'pɔːlɪn] *n* bâche *f*

tarragon ['tærəgən] *n* estragon *m*

tart [tɑːt] **1** *n* **(a)** *(cake) (large)* tarte *f*; *(small)* tartelette *f* **(b)** *Br Fam Pej (promiscuous woman, prostitute)* pute *f*
2 *adj* **(a)** *(in taste)* âpre **(b)** *(tone, remark)* aigrelet(ette)
▸ **tart up** *vt sep Fam (room, pub)* retaper; **to t. oneself up** se faire une beauté

tartan ['tɑːtən] *n* tartan *m*, écossais *m*; **t. tie/jacket** cravate *f*/veste *f* écossaise

Tartar ['tɑːtə(r)] *n* Tatar(e) *m,f*

tartar ['tɑːtə(r)] *n (on teeth)* tartre *m*

tartar(e) sauce ['tɑːtə'sɔːs] *n* sauce *f* tartare

tartly ['tɑːtlɪ] *adv* avec aigreur

task [tɑːsk] *n* tâche *f*; **to take sb to t. for sth/for doing sth** reprocher qch à qn/à qn d'avoir fait qch

taskforce ['tɑːskfɔːs] *n Mil* corps *m* expéditionnaire; *Fig* commission *f*

taskmaster ['tɑːskmɑːstə(r)] *n* **to be a hard t.** être très exigeant(e)

Tasmania [tæz'meɪnɪə] *n* la Tasmanie

Tasmanian [tæz'meɪnɪən] **1** *n* Tasmanien(enne) *m,f*
2 *adj* tasmanien(enne)

Tasman Sea ['tæzmən'siː] *n* **the T.** la mer de Tasman

tassel ['tæsəl] *n* gland *m*

taste [teɪst] **1** *n* **(a)** *(flavour, sense)* goût *m*; **t. bud** papille *f* gustative **(b)** *(sample) also Fig* **to have a t. of sth** goûter à qch; **a t. of things to come** un avant-goût des choses à venir; **to give sb a t. of his own medicine** rendre la pareille à qn **(c)** *(liking)* goût *m* **(for** pour); **to acquire** *or* **develop a t. for sth** prendre goût à qch; **add salt to t.** ajouter du sel à volonté; **violent films are not to my t.** les films violents ne me plaisent pas **(d)** *(judgement)* goût *m*; **in good/bad** *or* **poor t.** de bon/mauvais goût
2 *vt* **(a)** *(detect flavour of)* sentir (le goût de) **(b)** *(sample)* goûter; *Fig (happiness, success)* goûter à
3 *vi* **to t. of** *or* **like sth** avoir un goût de qch; **to t. good/ bad** être bon (bonne)/mauvais(e)

tasteful ['teɪstfʊl] *adj* de bon goût

tastefully ['teɪstfəlɪ] *adv* avec goût

tasteless ['teɪstlɪs] *adj* **(a)** *(food)* insipide **(b)** *(remark, clothes)* de mauvais goût

taster ['teɪstə(r)] *n* **(a)** *(person)* goûteur(euse) *m,f* **(b)** *(foretaste)* avant-goût *m*

tasty ['teɪstɪ] *adj* **(a)** *(food)* savoureux(euse) **(b)** *Br Fam (good-looking)* bien foutu(e)

tat [tæt] *n Fam* camelote *f*

ta-ta [tæ'tɑː] *exclam Br Fam* au revoir!

tatters ['tætəz] *npl also Fig* **in t.** en lambeaux

tattered ['tætəd] *adj* déguenillé(e)

tattle ['tætəl] **1** *n* potins *mpl*, commérages *mpl*
2 *vi* commérer

tattoo¹ [tə'tuː] *n* **(a)** *(on drum)* retraite *f* du soir **(b)** *(military show)* parade *f* militaire

tattoo² **1** *n (design)* tatouage *m*; **he has a t. on his arm** il a le bras tatoué
2 *vt* tatouer

tatty ['tætɪ] *adj Fam* minable

taught [tɔːt] *pt & pp of* **teach**

taunt [tɔːnt] **1** *n (words)* raillerie *f*
2 *vt* railler

Taurus ['tɔːrəs] *n* le Taureau; **to be (a) T.** être Taureau

taut [tɔːt] *adj* tendu(e)

tauten ['tɔːtən] **1** *vt* tendre
2 *vi* se tendre

tautness ['tɔːtnɪs] *n* tension *f*

tautological [tɔːtə'lɒdʒɪkəl] *adj* tautologique

tautology [tɔː'tɒlədʒɪ] *n* tautologie *f*

tavern ['tævən] *n* taverne *f*

tawdry ['tɔːdrɪ] *adj* **(a)** *(conduct, motive)* lâche **(b)** *(decor, jewellery)* tape-à-l'œil *inv*

tawny ['tɔːnɪ] *adj* fauve; **t. owl** chouette *f* hulotte

tax [tæks] **1** *n* impôt *m*, taxe *f*; **t. allowance** abattement *m* fiscal; **t. avoidance** évitement *m* fiscal; **t. bracket** tranche *f* d'imposition; **t. collector** percepteur(trice) *m,f*; **t. cut** réduction *f* d'impôt; *Br* **t. disc** ≃ vignette *f* automobile; **t. evasion** évasion *f* fiscale; **t. exile** = personne vivant à l'étranger pour échapper au fisc; **t. haven** paradis *m* fiscal; **t. incentive** incitation *f* fiscale; **t. inspector** inspecteur(trice) *m,f* des impôts; **t. relief** dégrèvement *m* fiscal; **t. return** déclaration *f* d'impôt

2 *vt* (**a**) *(subject to tax)* imposer, frapper d'un impôt (**b**) *(put under strain)* mettre à l'épreuve (**c**) *Formal (accuse)* **to t. sb with sth** taxer qn de qch

taxable ['tæksəbl] *adj* imposable

taxation [tæk'seɪʃən] *n* imposition *f*; **an increase in t.** une augmentation des impôts

tax-deductible [tæksdɪ'dʌktɪbəl] *adj* déductible des impôts

tax-free [tæks'friː] *adj* exempt(e) d'impôt

taxi ['tæksɪ] **1** *n* taxi *m*; **t. driver** chauffeur *m* de taxi; **t. rank** station *f* de taxi

2 *vi (of aircraft)* rouler

taxidermist ['tæksɪdɜːmɪst] *n* taxidermiste *mf*

taxing ['tæksɪŋ] *adj* ardu(e)

taxonomy [tæk'sɒnəmɪ] *n* taxonomie *f*

taxpayer ['tækspeɪə(r)] *n* contribuable *mf*

TB [tiː'biː] *n (abbr* **tuberculosis)** tuberculose *f*

T-bone steak [tiːbəʊn'steɪk] *n* côte *f* de bœuf à l'os

te [tiː] *n Mus* si *m*

tea [tiː] *n* (**a**) *(plant, drink)* thé *m*; *(herbal infusion)* tisane *f*; **t. break** ≃ pause-café *f*; **t. caddy** boîte *f* à thé; **t. cosy** couvre-théière *m*; **t. leaves** feuilles *fpl* de thé; **t. party** goûter *m*; **t. set** service *m* à thé; **t. strainer** passoire *f* à thé; **t. towel** torchon *m* (pour la vaisselle); **t. tray** plateau *m* (**b**) *Br (evening meal)* dîner *m*; **(afternoon) t.** thé *m*

teabag ['tiːbæg] *n* sachet *m* de thé

teach [tiːtʃ] *(pt & pp* **taught** [tɔːt]) **1** *vt* enseigner; **to t. sb sth, to t. sth to sb** enseigner qch à qn; **to t. sb (how) to do sth** apprendre à qn à faire qch; **to t. oneself sth** apprendre qch tout seul; *Am* **to t. school** enseigner; *Fig* **to t. sb a lesson** donner une leçon à qn; *Fam* **that'll t. him!** ça lui apprendra!

2 *vi* enseigner

teacher ['tiːtʃə(r)] *n (at primary school)* instituteur(trice) *m,f*; *(at secondary school)* professeur *m*, enseignant(e) *m,f*; **t.'s pet** chouchou(te) *m,f* du professeur; *Br* **t. training formation *f* pédagogique; *Br* **t. training college** ≃ IUFM *m*

teaching ['tiːtʃɪŋ] *n* (**a**) *(profession, action)* enseignement *m*; **t. hospital** CHU *m*; **t. practice** stage *m* pratique d'enseignement; **t. staff** personnel *m* enseignant (**b**) *(doctrine)* doctrine *f*

teacup ['tiːkʌp] *n* tasse *f* à thé

teak [tiːk] *n* teck *m*

team [tiːm] *n* équipe *f*; **a t. effort** un travail d'équipe; **t. games** jeux *mpl* d'équipe; **t. player** joueur(euse) *m,f* qui a l'esprit d'équipe; **t. spirit** esprit *m* d'équipe

▸ **team up** *vi* s'associer (**with** avec)

team-mate ['tiːmmeɪt] *n* coéquipier(ère) *m,f*

teamwork ['tiːmwɜːk] *n* travail *m* d'équipe

teamster ['tiːmstə(r)] *n Am (lorry driver)* routier *m*

teapot ['tiːpɒt] *n* théière *f*

tear¹ [tɪə(r)] *n* larme *f*; **in tears** en larmes; **t. duct** canal *m* lacrymal; **t. gas** gaz *m* lacrymogène

tear² [teə(r)] **1** *vt* *(pt* **tore** [tɔː(r)], *pp* **torn** [tɔːn]) *(rip)* déchirer; *(snatch)* arracher (**from** à); **to t. sth in two** *or* **in half** déchirer qch en deux; **to t. sth to pieces** déchirer qch

en mille morceaux; *Fig* démolir qch; *Fig* **to t. sb to pieces** mettre qn en pièces; **to be torn between two things** se sentir tiraillé(e) entre deux choses; *Fam* **that's torn it!** il ne manquait plus que ça!

2 *vi* (**a**) *(rip)* se déchirer (**b**) **to t. at sth** déchirer qch (**c**) *(move quickly)* **to t. along/past/away** aller/passer/partir à toute vitesse

3 *n* déchirure *f*

▸ **tear apart** *vt sep Fig* déchirer

▸ **tear away** *vt sep Fig* **to t. oneself away from sth** s'arracher de qch

▸ **tear down** *vt sep (building)* démolir; *(statue)* renverser; *(poster)* arracher

▸ **tear into** *vt insep* **to t. into sb** *(physically)* se jeter sur qn; *(verbally)* passer un savon à qn

▸ **tear off** *vt sep (remove)* arracher

2 *vi (run away)* se sauver à toute vitesse

▸ **tear out** *vt sep* arracher; *Fig* **to t. one's hair out** s'arracher les cheveux

▸ **tear up** *vt sep (document, photo)* déchirer; *(plant)* déraciner; *(floorboards)* enlever

tearaway ['teərəweɪ] *n* casse-cou *m inv*

teardrop ['tɪədrɒp] *n* larme *f*

tearful ['tɪəfʊl] *adj* en larmes; **in a t. voice** avec des larmes dans la voix

tearfully ['tɪəfəlɪ] *adv* en pleurant

tearjerker ['tɪədʒɜːkə(r)] *n Fam (film, book)* **it's a real t.** c'est complètement mélo

tearoom ['tiːruːm] *n* salon *m* de thé

tearstained ['tɪəsteɪnd] *adj* barbouillé(e) de larmes

tease [tiːz] **1** *vt* taquiner (**about** sur *ou* à propos de)

2 *vi* plaisanter

3 *n (person)* taquin(e) *m,f*

▸ **tease out** *vt sep* clarifier

teaser ['tiːzə(r)] *n Fam (problem)* colle *f*

teashop ['tiːʃɒp] *n* salon *m* de thé

teasing ['tiːzɪŋ] *n* taquinerie *f*

teaspoon ['tiːspuːn] *n* cuillère *f* à café

teat [tiːt] *n (of animal)* trayon *m*; *(of feeding bottle)* tétine *f*

teatime ['tiːtaɪm] *n (in the afternoon)* l'heure *f* du thé; *(in the evening)* l'heure du dîner

technical ['teknɪkəl] *adj* technique; *Br* **t. college** ≃ institut *m* universitaire; **t. drawing** *(school subject)* dessin *m* industriel; **t. hitch** incident *m* technique

technicality [teknɪ'kælɪtɪ] *n* détail *m* technique

technically ['teknɪklɪ] *adv* techniquement

technician [tek'nɪʃən] *n* technicien(enne) *m,f*

technique [tek'niːk] *n* technique *f*

technological [teknə'lɒdʒɪkəl] *adj* technologique

technology [tek'nɒlədʒɪ] *n* technologie *f*

teddy ['tedɪ] *n* **t. (bear)** ours *m* en peluche

tedious ['tiːdɪəs] *adj* ennuyeux(euse); *(task)* fastidieux(euse)

tedium ['tiːdɪəm] *n* ennui *m*

tee [tiː] *n (in golf)* tee *m*

▸ **tee off** *vi (in golf)* jouer le départ

teem [tiːm] *vi* (**a**) *(rain)* **to t. (down)** pleuvoir à verse (**b**) **to be teeming with sth** *(insects, ideas)* grouiller de qch

teeming ['tiːmɪŋ] *adj* grouillant(e)

teenage ['tiːneɪdʒ] *adj* adolescent(e)

teenager ['tiːneɪdʒə(r)] *n* adolescent(e) *m,f*

teen ['tiːn] *adj* adolescent(e); **t. idol** idole *f* des jeunes

teens [ti:nz] *npl* adolescence *f*; **to be in one's t.** être adolescent(e)

teensy(-weensy) ['ti:nzɪ('wi:nzɪ)] *adj Fam* tout(e) petit(e)

teeny-bopper ['ti:nɪbɒpə(r)] *n Fam* petite minette *f*

teeny(-weeny) ['ti:nɪ('wi:nɪ)] *adj Fam* tout(e) petit(e)

teeshirt ['ti:ʃɜ:t] *n* tee-shirt *m*

teeter ['ti:tə(r)] *vi* chanceler; *Fig* **to t. on the brink of sth** être au bord de qch

teeth [ti:θ] *pl of* **tooth**

teethe [ti:ð] *vi* **to be teething** faire ses dents

teething ['ti:ðɪŋ] *n* poussée *f* dentaire; *Fig* **t. troubles** *or* **problems** *(of project)* difficultés *fpl* initiales

teetotal [ti:'təʊtəl] *adj* qui ne boit jamais d'alcool

teetotaller, *Am* **teetotaler** [ti:'təʊtələ(r)] *n* = personne qui ne boit jamais d'alcool

TEFL ['tefəl] *n (abbr* **Teaching of English as a Foreign Language)** enseignement *m* de l'anglais langue étrangère

Teh(e)ran [teə'rɑːn] *n* Téhéran

tel *(abbr* **telephone)** tél

telecommunications [telɪkəmju:nɪ'keɪʃənz] *npl* télécommunications *fpl*

telecommuting [telɪkə'mju:tɪŋ] *n* télétravail *m*

teleconference [telɪ'kɒnfərəns] *n* téléconférence *f*

telegenic [telɪ'dʒenɪk] *adj* télégénique

telegram ['telɪgræm] *n* télégramme *m*

telegraph ['telɪgrɑːf] **1** *n* télégraphe *m*; **t. pole/wire** poteau *m*/fil *m* télégraphique
2 *vt* télégraphier

telegraphic [telɪ'græfɪk] *adj* télégraphique

telemarketing [telɪ'mɑːkɪtɪŋ] *n* télémarketing *m*

telepathic [telɪ'pæθɪk] *adj* télépathique

telepathy [tɪ'lepəθɪ] *n* télépathie *f*

telephone ['telɪfəʊn] **1** *n* téléphone *m*; **to be on the t.** *(talking)* être au téléphone; *Com* **t. banking** transactions *fpl* bancaires télématiques; **t. bill** facture *f* de téléphone; **t. box** cabine *f* téléphonique; **t. call** appel *m* téléphonique, coup *m* de téléphone; **t. directory** *or* **book** annuaire *m* (téléphonique); **t. exchange** central *m* téléphonique; **t. line** ligne *f* téléphonique; **t. number** numéro *m* de téléphone
2 *vt* téléphoner à
3 *vi* téléphoner

telephoto lens ['telɪfəʊtəʊlenz] *n* téléobjectif *m*

teleprinter ['telɪprɪntə(r)] *n* téléimprimeur *m*

telesales ['telɪseɪlz] *npl Com* téléventes *fpl*

telescope ['telɪskəʊp] *n* téléscope *m*

telescopic [telɪs'kɒpɪk] *adj* télescopique; **t. sight** *(of rifle)* lunette *f*

teleshopping ['telɪʃɒpɪŋ] *n* téléachat *m*

teletext ['telɪtekst] *n* Télétexte*m*

televise ['telɪvaɪz] *vt* téléviser

television [telɪ'vɪʒən] *n* télévision *f*; **on t.** à la télévision; **t. camera** caméra *f* de télévision; *Br* **t. licence** redevance *f* télévision; **t. programme** émission *f* de télévision; **t. screen** écran *m* de télévision; **t. set** téléviseur *m*, poste *m* de télévision

telex ['teleks] **1** *n* télex *m*
2 *vt (message)* télexer

tell [tel] *(pt & pp* **told** [təʊld]) **1** *vt* **(a)** *(say)* dire; *(story, joke)* raconter; **to t. sb sth, to t. sth to sb** dire qch à qn; **to t. the truth/a lie** dire la vérité/un mensonge; **to t. you the truth, I don't know** je t'avouerai que je ne sais pas; **can you t. me**

the way to the station? est-ce que vous pouvez m'indiquer le chemin de la gare?; **I told you so!** je te l'avais bien dit!; **you're telling me!** à qui le dis-tu!; **let me t. you, I was frightened** laisse-moi te dire que j'ai eu peur!; **to t. the time** *(of clock)* donner l'heure; **to t. sb the time** *(of person)* donner l'heure à qn; **he can't t. the time** il ne sait pas lire l'heure **(b)** *(discern)* **I could t.** he was lying je savais qu'il mentait; **you can t. she's lived abroad** ça se voit qu'elle a vécu à l'étranger; **there's no telling what she'll do next** qui sait ce qu'elle va inventer maintenant **(c)** *(distinguish)* **to t. sth from sth** distinguer qch de qch; **to t. two people/things apart** distinguer deux personnes/choses; **to t. right from wrong** discerner le bien du mal; **I can't t. the difference** je ne vois pas la différence **(d)** *(order)* **to t. sb to do sth** dire à qn de faire qch; **do as you're told!** fais ce qu'on te dit!; **I'm not asking you, I'm telling you!** ce n'est pas une question, c'est un ordre!; **he wouldn't be told** il refusait d'écouter ce qu'on lui disait **(e)** *Pol (votes)* compter; **all told** au total
2 *vi* **(a)** *(say)* dire; **that would be telling!** je ne veux pas cafarder! **(b)** *(discern)* dire; **it's difficult** *or* **hard to t.** c'est difficile à dire; **it's too early to t.** il est trop tôt pour se prononcer; **you never can t.** on ne sait jamais **(c)** *(have effect)* se faire sentir

▶ **tell off** *vt sep (scold)* **to t. sb off** disputer qn

▶ **tell on** *vt insep Fam (inform on)* dénoncer, balancer

teller ['telə(r)] *n* **(a)** *(of votes)* scrutateur(trice) *m,f* **(b)** *(in bank)* guichetier(ère) *m,f*

telling ['telɪŋ] **1** *n (of story)* narration *f*
2 *adj* **(a)** *(revealing)* révélateur(trice) **(b)** *(decisive)* qui porte

telling-off *n* réprimande *f*; **to give sb a t.** disputer qn

telltale ['telteɪl] **1** *n (person)* rapporteur(euse) *m,f*
2 *adj (revealing)* révélateur(trice)

telly ['telɪ] *n Br Fam* télé *f*; **on t.** à la télé; **t. addict** accro *mf* de la télé

temerity [tɪ'merɪtɪ] *n* témérité *f*, audace *f*; **to have the t. to do sth** avoir l'audace de faire qch

temp [temp] *Br Fam* **1** *n* intérimaire *mf*; **to be a t.** faire de l'intérim
2 *vi* faire de l'intérim

temper ['tempə(r)] *n* **(a)** *(mood)* humeur *f*; *(bad mood)* mauvaise humeur *f*; **to be in a good/bad t.** être de bonne/mauvaise humeur; **to have a short t.** être coléreux(euse); **to lose one's t.** se mettre en colère; **to fly into a t.** piquer une colère; *Fam* **t.,** **t.!** on se calme!; **to keep one's t.** garder son sang-froid *Fam* **t., t.!** on se calme! **(b)** *(of steel)* trempe *f*
2 *vt* **(a)** *(steel)* tremper **(b)** *(action)* tempérer

temperament ['tempərəmənt] *n* tempérament *m*, caractère *m*

temperamental [tempərə'mentəl] *adj* capricieux(euse)

temperance ['tempərəns] *n* **(a)** *(moderation)* modération *f* **(b)** *(abstinence from alcohol)* tempérance *f*; *Hist* **t. movement** mouvement *m* antialcoolique

temperate ['tempərət] *adj* **(a)** *Geog (climate, zone)* tempéré(e) **(b)** *Formal (language, criticism)* mesuré(e)

temperature ['temprətʃə(r)] *n* température *f*; **to take sb's t.** prendre la température de qn; **to have** *or* **to run a t.** avoir de la température

tempered ['tempəd] *adj (steel)* trempé(e)

tempest ['tempɪst] *n Lit* tempête *f*

tempestuous [tem'pestjʊəs] *adj* tempétueux(euse)

template ['templeɪt] *n* gabarit *m*; *Comptr* modèle *m*

temple¹ ['tempəl] *n (place of worship)* temple *m*

temple² n (side of head) tempe f

tempo ['tempəʊ] (pl **tempos** or **tempi** ['tempiː]) n Mus tempo m

temporal ['tempərəl] adj temporel(elle)

temporarily [tempə'reərɪlɪ] adv temporairement

temporary ['tempərərɪ] adj temporaire

tempt [tem(p)t] vt tenter; **to t. sb to do sth** inciter qn à faire qch; **to be tempted to do sth** être tenté(e) de faire qch; **to t. fate** tenter le diable

temptation [tem(p)'teɪʃən] n tentation f

tempting ['tem(p)tɪŋ] adj tentant(e)

temptress ['tem(p)trɪs] n Lit tentatrice f

ten [ten] **1** n (**a**) dix m inv (**b**) (idioms) **they're t. a penny** on en trouve à la pelle; **t. to one he'll find out** je te parie qu'il finira par le savoir
2 adj dix; **the T. Commandments** les dix commandements; see also **eight**

tenable ['tenəbəl] adj défendable

tenacious [te'neɪʃəs] adj tenace

tenacity [te'næsɪtɪ] n ténacité f

tenancy ['tenənsɪ] n location f; **t. agreement** bail m (de location)

tenant ['tenənt] n locataire mf

tend¹ [tend] vt (look after) s'occuper de

tend² vi pencher (**towards** vers); **to t. to do sth** avoir tendance à faire qch
▸ **tend to** vt insep (look after) s'occuper de

tendency ['tendənsɪ] n tendance f (**towards** à); **to have a t. to do sth** avoir tendance à faire qch

tendentious [ten'denʃəs] adj Formal tendancieux(euse)

tender¹ ['tendə(r)] n Naut navette f; Rail tender m

tender² adj (**a**) (affectionate) tendre (**b**) (sore) sensible (**c**) (meat) tendre (**d**) (young) **at the t. age of...** dès l'âge de...

tender³ **1** n Com (bid) offre f, soumission f; **to make** or **put in a t.** soumissionner
2 vt (services, money) offrir; (resignation) donner; (apology) présenter
3 vi Com **to t. for a contract** soumissionner à un appel d'offres

tenderhearted [tendə'hɑːtɪd] adj au cœur tendre

tenderly ['tendəlɪ] adv tendrement

tenderness ['tendənɪs] n (**a**) (affection) tendresse f (**b**) (soreness) sensibilité f (**c**) (of meat) tendreté f

tendon ['tendən] n tendon m

tendril ['tendrɪl] n vrille f

tenement ['tenɪmənt] n immeuble m

tenet ['tenət] n (principle) dogme m; (belief) croyance f

tenfold ['tenfəʊld] **1** adj décuple
2 adv dix fois plus; **to increase t.** être multiplié(e) par dix

tenner ['tenə(r)] n Br Fam (sum) dix livres fpl; (note) billet m de dix livres

tennis ['tenɪs] n tennis m; **t. ball** balle f de tennis; **t. club** club m de tennis; **t. court** court m de tennis; **t. elbow** tennis-elbow m; **t. player** joueur(euse) m,f de tennis; **t. racquet** or **racket** raquette f de tennis; **t. shoe** (chaussure f de) tennis m ou f

tenor ['tenə(r)] n (**a**) (singer) ténor m; **t. saxophone** saxophone m ténor (**b**) Formal (content, sense) teneur f

tenpin bowling ['tenpɪn'bəʊlɪŋ] n bowling m (jeu)

tense¹ [tens] n Gram temps m

tense² **1** adj (cord, person, situation) tendu(e); (voice) étranglé(e); (muscle) contracté(e)

2 vt (cord) tendre; (muscle) contracter; **to t. oneself** se raidir
3 vi se tendre, se raidir
▸ **tense up** vi se crisper

tensely ['tenslɪ] adv nerveusement

tension ['tenʃən] n tension f

tent [tent] n tente f; **t. peg** piquet m de tente; **t. pole** mât m de tente

tentacle ['tentəkəl] n tentacule m

tentative ['tentətɪv] adj (hesitant) hésitant(e), timide; (provisional) provisoire

tentatively ['tentətɪvlɪ] adv (hesitantly) timidement; (provisionally) provisoirement

tenterhooks ['tentəhʊks] npl **to be on t.** être sur des charbons ardents; **to keep sb on t.** mettre qn au supplice

tenth [tenθ] **1** n (**a**) (fraction) dixième m (**b**) (in series) dixième mf (**c**) (of month) dix m inv
2 adj dixième; see also **eighth**

tenuous ['tenjʊəs] adj (connection) ténu(e); (comparison) subtil(e); (argument) faible

tenure ['tenjə(r)] n (of land) fermage m; (of office) occupation f; (of university teaching job) titularisation f

tepid ['tepɪd] adj also Fig tiède

tequila [tɪ'kiːlə] n tequila f

term [tɜːm] **1** n (**a**) (word, expression) terme m; **I told her in no uncertain terms** je le lui ai dit carrément; **in terms of salary/pollution** en ce qui concerne le salaire/la pollution (**b**) **to be on good/bad terms (with sb)** (relations) être en bons/mauvais termes (avec qn); **to be on friendly terms with sb** avoir des relations amicales avec qn; **to be on speaking terms** (of two people) se parler; **to come to terms with sth** accepter qch; **in terms of** du point de vue de; **we should think in terms of leaving** il faudrait songer à partir
(**c**) (term (conditions) conditions fpl; (of contract) termes mpl; **terms of reference** (of commission) attributions fpl; **terms of payment** conditions de paiement (**d**) (at school, university) trimestre m; **t. of office** (of politician) mandat m; **t. of imprisonment** peine f de prison; **in the long/short t.** à long/court terme; **to have reached (full) t.** (of pregnancy) arriver à terme
2 vt appeler

terminal ['tɜːmɪnəl] **1** n (**a**) (of battery) pôle m, borne f (**b**) (rail, bus) terminus m; (at airport) terminal m (**c**) Comptr terminal m
2 adj terminal(e); (illness) en phase terminale

terminally ['tɜːmɪnəlɪ] adv **to be t. ill** être en phase terminale

terminate ['tɜːmɪneɪt] **1** vt (**a**) (employment, project) mettre fin à; (contract) résilier (**b**) (pregnancy) interrompre
2 vi (**a**) (of contract) prendre fin (**b**) (of bus, train) aller jusqu'à

termination [tɜːmɪ'neɪʃən] n (**a**) (of employment, project) fin f; (of contract) résiliation f (**b**) **t. (of pregnancy)** interruption f de grossesse

terminology [tɜːmɪ'nɒlədʒɪ] n terminologie f

terminus ['tɜːmɪnəs] (pl **terminuses** or **termini** ['tɜːmɪnaɪ]) n terminus m

termite ['tɜːmaɪt] n termite m

tern [tɜːn] n sterne f

Terr abbr **Terrace**

terrace ['terɪs] n (**a**) (beside house, on hillside) terrasse f (**b**) Br **the terraces** (in football ground) les gradins mpl (**c**) Br (of houses) = rangée de maisons attenantes

terraced ['terɪst] adj (a) (hillside) en terrasses (b) Br t. house = maison située dans une rangée d'habitations attenantes

terracotta ['terə'kɒtə] n terre f cuite

terrain [tə'reɪn] n terrain m

terrapin ['terəpɪn] n tortue f d'eau douce

terrestrial [tɪ'restrɪəl] adj terrestre

terrible ['terɪbəl] adj (shocking) terrible; (of poor quality) épouvantable

terribly ['terɪblɪ] adv (a) (badly) affreusement mal; (injured) très gravement (b) Fam (very) extrêmement

terrier ['terɪə(r)] n (dog) terrier m; Fig he's a real t. il n'abandonne jamais

terrific [tə'rɪfɪk] adj Fam (a) (excellent) super inv (b) (enormous) incroyable

terrifically [tə'rɪfɪklɪ] adv Fam (very) extrêmement

terrified ['terɪfaɪd] adj terrifié(e); to be t. of avoir une peur bleue de

terrify ['terɪfaɪ] vt terrifier

terrifying ['terɪfaɪɪŋ] adj terrifiant(e)

territorial [terɪ'tɔːrɪəl] adj territorial(e); (animal) qui défend son territoire; Br the T. Army = armée de réserve, constituée de volontaires; t. waters eaux fpl territoriales

territory ['terɪtərɪ] (pl territories) n territoire m; Fig (area of activity) domaine m

terror ['terə(r)] n terreur f; reign of t. régime m de terreur; Fam that child is a t. cet enfant est une vraie terreur

terrorism ['terərɪzəm] n terrorisme m

terrorist ['terərɪst] n & adj terroriste mf

terrorize ['terəraɪz] vt terroriser

terror-stricken ['terəstrɪkən] adj terrorisé(e)

terse [tɜːs] adj (person, reply) sec (sèche); (style, prose) concis(e)

terseness ['tɜːsnɪs] n (of person, reply) brusquerie f; (of style, prose) concision f

tertiary ['tɜːʃərɪ] adj tertiaire; t. education enseignement m supérieur

TESL ['tesəl] n (abbr Teaching of English as a Second Language) enseignement m de l'anglais deuxième langue

TESOL ['tiːsɒl] n (abbr Teaching of English to Speakers of Other Languages) enseignement m de l'anglais langue étrangère

test [test] 1 n (a) (trial, check) test m; to put sb/sth to the t. mettre qn/qch à l'épreuve; to pass the t. se montrer à la hauteur; to stand the t. of time résister à l'épreuve du temps; t. ban interdiction f des essais nucléaires; Law t. case précédent m; t. drive essai m sur route; t. flight vol m d'essai; t. pilot pilote m d'essai; t. tube tube m à essai, éprouvette f; t. tube baby bébé-éprouvette m (b) (examination) examen m; (driving) t. examen du permis de conduire; French/math t. examen de français/ maths (c) (in cricket, rugby) t. (match) match m international 2 vt (a) (examine) (pupil) interroger (on sur); (sight, hearing) examiner; to t. sb's knowledge tester les connaissances de qn; to t. sb for Aids faire subir à qn le test de dépistage du sida (b) (try out) tester, mettre à l'épreuve 3 vi to t. for Aids faire un test de dépistage du sida; to t. positive/negative (for drugs) être positif/négatif; (for Aids) être séropositif(ive)/séronégatif(ive)

▸ **test out** vt sep tester

testament ['testəmənt] n (a) Law (will) testament m (b) (tribute) preuve f (to de)

test-bed ['testbed] n banc m d'essai

test-drive ['testdraɪv] vt essayer

testicle ['testɪkəl] n testicule m

testify ['testɪfaɪ] Law 1 vt to t. that... attester que... 2 vi témoigner (for/against en faveur de/contre); Fig to t. to sth (be proof of) témoigner de qch

testily ['testɪlɪ] adv d'un ton irrité

testimonial [testɪ'məʊnɪəl] n (a) (character reference) références fpl (b) (in soccer) t. (match) = match en l'honneur d'un footballeur

testimony ['testɪmənɪ] n Law témoignage m, déposition f; Fig to be a t. to sth (proof of) témoigner de qch

testing ['testɪŋ] 1 n essai m; t. ground terrain m d'essai 2 adj éprouvant(e)

testis ['testɪs] (pl testes ['testiːz]) n testicule m

testosterone [tes'tɒstərəʊn] n testostérone f

testy ['testɪ] adj (person, mood) irritable; (tone, manner) irrité(e)

tetanus ['tetənəs] n tétanos m

tetchy ['tetʃɪ] adj Fam irritable

tether ['teðə(r)] 1 n (for tying animal) longe f; Fig to be at the end of one's t. être à bout 2 vt (animal) attacher

Texan ['teksən] 1 n Texan(e) m,f 2 adj texan(e)

Texas ['teksəs] n le Texas

Tex-Mex [teks'meks] adj tex-mex inv

text [tekst] n texte f; Comptr t. editor éditeur m de texte

textbook ['tekstbʊk] n manuel m; Fig a t. example (of) un parfait exemple (de)

textile ['tekstaɪl] 1 n textile m 2 adj textile

textual ['tekstjʊəl] adj de texte

texture ['tekstʃə(r)] n texture f

Thai [taɪ] 1 n (a) (person) Thaïlandais(e) (b) (language) thaï m 2 adj thaïlandais(e)

Thailand ['taɪlænd] n la Thaïlande

Thames [temz] n the T. la Tamise

than [ðæn, unstressed ðən] conj que; he's older t. me il est plus âgé que moi; he was taller t. I had expected il était plus grand que je (ne) l'imaginais; more/less t. ten plus/ moins de dix; more t. once plus d'une fois

thank [θæŋk] vt remercier; to t. sb for sth/for doing sth remercier qn pour qch/d'avoir fait qch; t. God! Dieu merci!; t. you merci; t. you very much merci beaucoup; no, t. you non merci; t. you for coming merci d'être venu; Ironic I'll t. you to mind your own business! je te prierai de te mêler de tes affaires!; also Ironic we have Mike to t. for this c'est à Mike que nous devons cela

thankful ['θæŋkfʊl] adj reconnaissant(e) (for de); to be t. that... être heureux(euse) que...

thankfully ['θæŋkfəlɪ] adv (a) (gratefully) avec gratitude (b) (fortunately) heureusement

thankless ['θæŋklɪs] adj ingrat(e)

thanks [θæŋks] 1 npl remerciements mpl; t. to (because of) grâce à; no t. to you/them! ce n'est pas grâce à toi/eux! 2 exclam Fam t.! merci!; Fam no t. non merci; t. for coming/your letter merci d'être venu/pour ta lettre; Fam Ironic t. for nothing! je te remercie!

thanksgiving [θæŋks'gɪvɪŋ] n action f de grâces; Am T. (Day) = 4ème jeudi de novembre, fête commémorant la première action de grâce des colons anglais

thank you ['θæŋkjʊ] n merci m, remerciement m; to say

t. to sb dire merci à qn, remercier qn; **t. letter** *or* **note** lettre *f* de remerciement

that [ðæt] **1** *demonstrative pron* (*pl* **those** [ðəʊz]) (**a**) (*subject*) ce, cela, ça (*in more informal contexts*); (*object*) cela, ça (*in more informal contexts*); **who's t.?** qui est-ce?; **what's t.?** qu'est-ce que c'est?; **t.'s pretty** c'est joli; **t.'s what she told me** c'est ce qu'elle m'a dit; **is t. all the luggage you're taking?** c'est tout ce que vous prenez comme bagages?; **t.'s where he lives** c'est là qu'il habite; **can you run as fast as t.?** tu peux courir aussi vite que ça?; **t.'s it!** c'est çal; **t.'s t.!** un point, c'est tout!

(**b**) (*as opposed to* **this**) celui-là (celle-là) *m,f*; **in a case like t.** dans un cas comme celui-là

2 *demonstrative adj* (*pl* **those**) (**a**) (*indicating person, thing*) ce (cette); **t. book** ce livre; **t. question** cette question; **t. man** cet homme

(**b**) (*as opposed to* **this**) ce…-là (cette…-là); **I prefer t. film** je préfère ce film-là; **take t. cup** prends cette tasse-là; **t. one** celui-là (celle-là)

3 *adv* **t. high/big** haut(e)/grand(e) comme ça; **I tasted it but it wasn't t. good** j'y ai goûté mais ce n'était pas si bon que ça; **I've never seen one t. good** je n'en ai jamais vu d'aussi bon que ça; **he's t. stupid he…** il est tellement stupide qu'il…

4 [*unstressed* ðət] *relative pron*

On peut omettre le pronom relatif **that** sauf s'il est en position sujet.

(**a**) (*subject*) qui; (*object*) que; **the letter t. came yesterday** la lettre qui est arrivée hier; **the woman t. I saw** la femme que j'ai vue

(**b**) (*with preposition*) **the person t. I gave it to** la personne à qui je l'ai donné; **the woman t. we're talking about** la femme dont nous parlons; **the room t. he's sleeping in** la chambre où il dort

(**c**) (*when*) où; **the day t. you arrived** le jour où tu es arrivé

5 [*unstressed* ðət] *conj*

Sauf dans la langue soutenue, la conjonction **that** est souvent omise.

que; **she said t. she would come** elle a dit qu'elle viendrait

thatch [θætʃ] **1** *n* (*on roof*) chaume *m*; *Fam* (*of hair*) tignasse *f*

2 *vt* (*roof*) couvrir de chaume; **thatched cottage** chaumière *f*; **thatched roof** toit *m* de chaume

thaw [θɔ:] **1** *n also Fig* dégel *m*

2 *vt* (*snow, ice*) faire fondre; (*food*) décongeler

3 *vi* (*of snow, ice*) fondre; (*of food*) se décongeler; *Fig* (*of person*) se dérider

▸ **thaw out** *vi* (*of lake*) dégeler; (*of food*) se décongeler; *Fig* (*of person*) se dérider

the [*before consonant sounds* ðə, *before vowel sounds* ðɪ, *stressed* ði:] *definite art* (**a**) (*singular*) le (la); (*plural*) les; **t. pen** le stylo; **t. house** la maison; **t. airport** l'aéroport; **t. summer** (*this summer*) cet été; (*every summer*) l'été; **to have t. measles/flu** avoir la rougeole/la grippe; **at t. time** à ce moment-là; **t. Europe of today** l'Europe d'aujourd'hui; *Fam* **how's t. knee?** et ce genou?

(**b**) (*denoting concept, group*) **t. poor/blind** les pauvres/aveugles; **t. Wilsons** les Wilson; **t. supernatural** le surnaturel

(**c**) (*with titles*) **Elizabeth t. First** Élisabeth I; **Catherine t. Great** la Grande Catherine

(**d**) (*with proportions, rates*) **to be paid by t. hour** être payé(e) à l'heure; **15 kilometres to t. litre** 15 kilomètres au litre

(**e**) (*in exclamations*) **t. arrogance/stupidity of it!** quelle arrogance/stupidité!

(**f**) [*stressed* ði:] **not THE Professor Branestorm?** pas le célèbre professeur Branestorm?; **it's THE car for this year** c'est LA voiture de cette année

(**g**) (*in comparisons*) **t. more… t. more…** plus… plus…; **t. sooner t. better** le plus tôt sera le mieux; **t. more I see him, t. less I like him** plus je le vois, moins je l'apprécie

(**h**) (*with dates*) **t. sixties** les années soixante; **t. eighteen hundreds** le dix-neuvième siècle

theatre, *Am* **theater** ['θɪətə(r)] *n* (**a**) (*drama, building*) théâtre *m*; **t. company** compagnie *f* théâtrale, troupe *f* de théâtre (**b**) *Br* (*operating*) **t.** salle *f* d'opération (**c**) (*area*) **t. of war** théâtre *m* des hostilités

theatre-goer, *Am* **theater-goer** ['θɪətəgəʊə(r)] *n* amateur(trice) *m,f* de théâtre

theatrical [θɪ'ætrɪkəl] *adj also Fig* théâtral(e); **t. company** compagnie *f* théâtrale, troupe *f* de théâtre

thee [ði:] *pron Lit or Rel* te; (*after preposition*) toi

theft [θeft] *n* vol *m*

theftproof ['θeftpru:f] *adj* (*lock*) antivol *inv*; (*vehicle*) muni(e) d'un dispositif antivol

their ['ðeə(r)] *possessive adj* (**a**) (*singular*) leur; (*plural*) leurs; **t. job** leur travail; **t. wives** leurs femmes; **it wasn't THEIR idea!** ce n'est pas eux qui en ont eu l'idée! (**b**) (*for parts of body*) **they hit t. heads** ils se sont cogné la tête (**c**) (*indefinite use*) **someone's left t. jacket** quelqu'un a oublié sa veste

theirs [ðeəz] *possessive pron* (**a**) (*singular*) le leur (la leur) *m,f*; (*plural*) les leurs; **our house is big, but t. is bigger** notre maison est grande, mais la leur est plus grande encore

(**b**) (*used attributively*) **this book is t.** ce livre est à eux/à elles; **a friend of t.** un de leurs amis; **where's that brother of t.?** où leur frère a-t-il bien pu passer?

(**c**) (*indefinite use*) **if anyone hasn't got t. they can use mine** si quelqu'un n'a pas le sien, il pourra utiliser le mien

theism ['θi:ɪzəm] *n Rel* théisme *m*

them [ðem, *unstressed* ðəm] *pron* (**a**) (*direct object*) les; **I hate t.** je les déteste; **I can understand their son but not THEM** je comprends leur fils, mais je ne les comprends pas

(**b**) (*indirect object*) leur; **I gave t. the book** je leur ai donné le livre; **I gave it to t.** je le leur ai donné

(**c**) (*after preposition*) eux (elles) *mpl,fpl*; **I'm thinking of t.** je pense à eux/elles

(**d**) (*as complement of verb* **to be**) eux (elles) *mpl,fpl*; **it's t.!** ce sont eux/elles!; **it was t. who did it** c'est eux/elles qui l'ont fait

(**e**) (*indefinite use*) **if anyone comes, tell t.…** si quelqu'un vient, dis-lui…

thematic [θi:'mætɪk] *adj* thématique

theme [θi:m] *n* thème *m*; **t. park** parc *m* à thème; **t. restaurant** restaurant *m* à thème; **t. song** *or* **tune** chanson *f* du générique

themselves [ðəm'selvz, *stressed* ðem'selvz] *pron* (**a**) (*reflexive*) **they hurt t.** ils se sont blessés

(**b**) (*emphatic*) eux-mêmes (elles-mêmes) *mpl,fpl*; **they t. have never…** eux-mêmes (elles-mêmes n'ont jamais…; **they told me t.** ils me l'ont dit eux-mêmes; **they're not t. today** ils ne sont pas dans leur état normal aujourd'hui

(**c**) (*after preposition*) **they live by t.** ils vivent seuls; **they bought it for t.** ils se le sont acheté; **they talk to t.** ils parlent tout seuls

then [ðen] **1** *adv* (**a**) (*at that time*) alors, à ce moment-là; **since t.** depuis ce moment-là), depuis (lors); **until t.** (*in future*) jusque-là; (*in past*) jusqu'à ce moment-là; **by t.** d'ici là; **there and t., t. and there** sur-le-champ

(**b**) (*next*) ensuite, puis; **what t.?** et alors, qu'est-ce qui va se passer?

(**c**) (*in that case*) alors; **if it rains, t. we get wet** s'il pleut, alors on va se mouiller

(d) *(therefore)* donc; **you already knew, t.?** donc, tu le savais déjà?
2 *adj* **the t.** President le Président de l'époque
thence [ðens] *adv Formal* de là
theologian [θi:ə'ləʊdʒ(ɪ)ən] *n* théologien(enne) *m,f*
theological [θi:ə'lɒdʒɪkəl] *adj* théologique
theology [θi:'ɒlədʒɪ] *n* théologie *f*
theorem ['θɪərəm] *n* théorème *m*
theoretical [θi:ə'retɪkəl] *adj* théorique
theoretically [θi:ə'retɪklɪ] *adv* théoriquement
theoretician [θi:ərɪ'tɪʃən] *n* théoricien(enne) *m,f*
theorist ['θi:ərɪst] *n* théoricien(enne) *m,f*
theorize ['θi:əraɪz] *vi* théoriser **(about** sur)
theory ['θi:ərɪ] *n* théorie *f*; **in t.** en théorie
therapeutic [θerə'pju:tɪk] *adj also Fig* thérapeutique
therapist ['θerəpɪst] *n* thérapeute *mf*
therapy ['θerəpɪ] *n* thérapie *f*
there [ðeə(r), *unstressed* ðə(r)] **1** *pron* **t. is/are** il y a; **t. was/ were** il y avait; **t.'s somebody at the door** il y a quelqu'un à la porte; **t. isn't/aren't any** il n'y en a pas; **t. are** *or Fam* **t.'s two left** il (en) reste deux; **t.'s a page missing** il manque une page; **t. comes a time when...** il arrive un moment où...
2 *adv* **(a)** *(in that place)* là; *(over there)* là-bas; **he isn't t.** il n'est pas là; **the weather's nice t.** il fait beau là-bas; **I'm going t.** tomorrow j'y vais demain; **give me that book t.** donne-moi ce livre-là; **do we have time to get t. and back?** avons-nous le temps d'y aller et de revenir?; **t. it is!** le voilà!; **t. you are!** *(I was looking for you)* te voilà!; *(when handing over something)* voilà!; *(expressing triumph, satisfaction)* tu vois!; **t. and then, then and t.** sur-le-champ; *Fam* **he's not all t.** il n'a pas toute sa tête
(b) *(at that point)* là; **t.'s the difficulty** voilà la difficulté; **we'll stop t. for today** nous nous arrêterons là pour aujourd'hui; *Fam* **you've got me t.!** alors là, vous me posez une colle!
3 *exclam* voilà!, **t., t.!** allons, allons!; **t., I told you so!** et voilà, je te l'avais bien dit!; **t. now, that wasn't so bad!** voilà, ce n'était pas si terrible!
thereabouts ['ðeərə'baʊts] *adv* **(a)** *(with place)* dans les environs; **he's from Edinburgh or t.** il est d'Édimbourg, ou quelque part par là **(b)** *(with number, quantity, distance)* environ, à peu près; **it costs $500 or t.** ça coûte environ ou à peu près 500 dollars
thereafter [ðeər'ɑ:ftə(r)] *adv Formal* après cela, par la suite
thereby ['ðeəbaɪ] *adv Formal* ainsi; **t. hangs a tale!** c'est une longue histoire!
therefore ['ðeəfɔː(r)] *adv* donc
thereupon [ðeərə'pɒn] *adv Formal* sur ce
thermal ['θɜːməl] **1** *n Met* ascendance *f* thermique
2 *adj* thermique; **t. energy** énergie *f* thermique; *Comptr* **t. paper** papier *m* thermique; **t. springs** sources *fpl* thermales; **t. underwear** sous-vêtements *mpl* en Thermolactyl®
thermodynamics [θɜːməʊdaɪ'næmɪks] *n* thermodynamique *f*
thermoelectric [θɜːməʊɪ'lektrɪk] *adj* thermoélectrique
thermometer [θə'mɒmɪtə(r)] *n* thermomètre *m*
Thermos® ['θɜːməs] *n* T. (flask) (bouteille *f*) Thermos® *f* ou *m*
thermostat ['θɜːməstæt] *n* thermostat *m*
thesaurus [θɪ'sɔːrəs] (*pl* **thesauruses** *or* **thesauri** [θɪ'sɔːraɪ]) *n* dictionnaire *m* de synonymes
these [ðiːz] **1** *demonstrative pron* ceux-ci (celles-ci)

mpl,fpl; **in cases like t.** dans des cas comme ceux-ci; **t. are the ones I want** voici ceux que je veux; **t. are my friends** je te présente mes amis
2 *demonstrative adj* **(a)** *(indicating people or things)* ces; **t. children** ces enfants **(b)** *(as opposed to those)* ces...-ci; **I like t. shoes** j'aime bien ces chaussures-ci; **t. ones** ceux-ci (celles-ci) *mpl,fpl*
thesis ['θiːsɪs] (*pl* **theses** ['θiːsiːz]) *n* thèse *f*
thespian ['θespɪən] *n Lit or Hum* comédien(enne) *m,f*
they [ðeɪ] *pron* **(a)** *(subject)* ils (elles) *mpl,fpl*; **they're Canadian** *(masculine)* ils sont canadiens; *(feminine)* elles sont canadiennes; **THEY haven't got it!** ce ne sont pas eux/ elles qui l'ont! **(b)** *(indefinite use)* somebody called – what did t. want? quelqu'un a appelé – qu'est-ce qu'il voulait?; **t. say that...** on dit que...
they'd [ðeɪd] = they had, they would
they'll [ðeɪl] = they will, they shall
they're [ðeə(r)] = they are
they've [ðeɪv] = they have
thick [θɪk] **1** *adj* **(a)** *(in general)* épais(aisse), *Lit* **be a metre t.** faire un mètre d'épaisseur; **the air was t. with smoke** l'air était empli d'une épaisse fumée, **the snow was t. on the ground** il y avait une épaisse couche de neige sur le sol; *Fig* **to be t. on the ground** *(plentiful)* être légion
(b) *(voice)* pâteux(euse); *(accent)* fort(e)
(c) *Br Fam (stupid)* bouché(e), **to be as t. as two short planks** *or* **as a brick** être bête comme ses pieds
(d) *(idioms)* **to have a t. skin** ne pas être susceptible; *Br* **to give sb a t. ear** donner une gifle à qn; *Fam* **to be as t. as thieves** s'entendre comme larrons en foire; *Br Fam* **that's a bit t.!** ça, c'est un peu fort!
2 *adv* **(a)** *(cut)* en tranches épaisses; *(spread)* **Fam to lay it on a bit t.** exagérer
3 *n* **in the t. of the forest** au beau milieu de la forêt; **to be in the t. of it** *or* **things** être au cœur de l'action; **through t. and thin** quoi qu'il arrive
thicken ['θɪkən] **1** *vt* épaissir
2 *vi* s'épaissir; *Hum* **the plot thickens...** les choses se compliquent...
thicket ['θɪkɪt] *n* fourré *m*
thickly ['θɪklɪ] *adv* **(a)** *(cut)* en tranches épaisses; *(spread)* en couche épaisse **(b)** *(populated)* fortement **(c)** *(speak)* d'une voix pâteuse
thickness ['θɪknɪs] *n* épaisseur *f*
thickset ['θɪk'set] *adj* trapu(e)
thick-skinned [θɪk'skɪnd] *adj Fig* peu susceptible
thief [θiːf] (*pl* **thieves** [θiːvz]) *n* voleur(euse) *m,f*
thieve [θiːv] *vt & vi* voler
thieving ['θiːvɪŋ] **1** *n* vol *m*
2 *adj* voleur(euse)
thigh [θaɪ] *n* cuisse *f*
thighbone ['θaɪbəʊn] *n* fémur *m*
thimble ['θɪmbəl] *n* dé *m* à coudre
thin [θɪn] **1** *adj* **(a)** *(person, wall)* mince; *(paper, slice, layer)* fin(e), mince; *(blanket, clothing)* léger(ère); *(book)* peu épais(aisse); **to get thinner** *(of person)* maigrir
(b) *(sparse)* *(hair, crowd, vegetation)* clairsemé(e); *(fog, mist)* léger(ère)
(c) *(soup, sauce)* liquide; *(paint)* dilué(e); *(blood)* appauvri(e)
(d) *(voice)* grêle
(e) *(idioms)* **to vanish into t. air** se volatiliser; **to have a t. time (of it)** avoir la vie dure; **to be t. on the ground** être rare; **it's just the t. end of the wedge** ce n'est qu'un début

2 *adv (cut)* en tranches fines *ou* minces; *Fig* **our forces/ resources are spread very t.** nos forces/ressources sont très éparpillées

3 *vt (pt & pp* **thinned)** *(paint)* diluer; *(sauce)* éclaircir

4 *vi (of crowd)* s'éclaircir; *(of fog, mist)* se lever; **his hair is thinning** il perd ses cheveux

thing [θɪŋ] *n* (**a**) *(action, remark, fact)* chose *f*; **the important t. is that...** l'important, c'est que...; **it's the only t. we can do** c'est tout ce que nous pouvons faire; **that's another t.** altogether c'est une autre affaire; **the t. is,...** le problème, c'est que...; **that was a silly t. to do/say** c'était stupide de faire/dire ça; **for one t.** d'abord; **what with one t. and another** avec tout ce qui s'est passé; **I don't know a t. about physics** je n'y connais rien en physique; **to know a t. or two (about sth)** s'y connaître (en qch); **to take things too seriously** prendre les choses trop au sérieux; **it's just one of those things** ce sont des choses qui arrivent; **things are going well/badly** les choses vont bien/mal; *Fam* **how are things?, how's things?** comment ça va?

(**b**) *(object)* chose *f*; *Fam* **what's that t.?** qu'est-ce que c'est que ce truc?; *Fam* **where's that wrench t. I was using?** où est cette espèce de clé dont je me servais tout à l'heure?; **things** *(belongings)* affaires *fpl*

(**c**) *Fam (person)* **you poor t.!** pauvre de toi!; **you lucky t.!** sacré veinard!; **you silly t.!** espèce d'idiot!

(**d**) *(idioms)* **to have a t. about sb/sth** *(like)* avoir un faible pour qn/qch; *(dislike)* avoir quelque chose contre qn/qch; **to have a t. about tidiness/punctuality** être très à cheval sur la propreté/la ponctualité; **it's not the done t.** ça ne se fait pas; **the latest t. in shoes** la dernière mode en matière de chaussures

thingummy ['θɪŋəmɪ], **thingumajig** ['θɪŋəmɪ-dʒɪg], **thingumabob** ['θɪŋəmɪbɒb] *n Br Fam (object)* truc *m*; *(person)* machin(e) *m,f*

think [θɪŋk] **1** *vt (pt & pp* **thought** [θɔːt]) (**a**) *(have in mind)* **to t. that...** penser que...; **what are you thinking?** à quoi penses-tu?; **to t. evil thoughts** avoir de mauvaises pensées; **to t. to do sth** penser à faire qch

(**b**) *(believe, have as opinion)* croire, penser; **he thinks he knows everything** il croit tout savoir; **anyone would t. she was asleep** on jurerait qu'elle dort; **who'd have thought it!** qui l'eût cru!; **what do you t.?** qu'en penses-tu?; **I t. so** je pense (que oui); **I don't t. so, I t. not** je ne pense pas, je pense que non; **I thought so, I thought as much** c'est ce que je pensais; **I should t. so, too!** j'espère bien!; **that's what you t.!** c'est ce que tu crois!; **what do you t. about that idea?** qu'est-ce que tu penses de cette idée?

(**c**) *(imagine)* imaginer; **I can't t. why/what/where...** je me demande bien pourquoi/ce que/où...; **t. what we could do with all that money!** imagine ce qu'on pourrait faire avec tout cet argent!; **to t. that he's only twenty!** et dire qu'il n'a que vingt ans

2 *vi* réfléchir, penser; **to t. ahead** voir loin; **to t. aloud** penser tout haut; **to t. long and hard before doing sth** bien réfléchir avant de faire qch; **to t. on one's feet** réagir vite; **it makes you t.** ça fait réfléchir; **you can t. again!** tu te fourres le doigt dans l'œil!

3 *n* **to have a t.** réfléchir; *Fam* **you've got another t. coming!** tu te fourres le doigt dans l'œil!

▸ **think about** *vt insep (have in mind, take into account)* penser à; *(consider)* réfléchir à; **to t. about doing sth** songer à faire qch; **it's quite cheap when you t. about it** ça n'est pas très cher quand on y pense; **that will give them something to t. about** voilà qui va leur donner matière à réflexion

▸ **think back to** *vt insep* repenser à

▸ **think of** *vt insep* (**a**) *(have in mind, take into account)*

penser à; **to t. of doing sth** songer à faire qch; **come to t. of it, I DID see her that night** maintenant que j'y pense, je l'ai effectivement vue ce soir-là; **what were you thinking of walking home alone?** qu'est-ce qui t'a pris de rentrer à pied tout seul? (**b**) *(have opinion about)* **what do you t. of this?** qu'est-ce que tu penses de cela?; **to t. well/badly of sb** avoir une bonne/mauvaise opinion de qn; **I don't t. much of the idea** cette idée ne me dit pas grand-chose (**c**) *(recall)* se rappeler; **I can't t. of the word** le mot m'échappe

▸ **think out** *vt sep* réfléchir à

▸ **think over** *vt sep* réfléchir à

▸ **think through** *vt sep* **to t. sth through** bien réfléchir à qch

▸ **think up** *vt sep* imaginer, inventer

thinker ['θɪŋkə(r)] *n* penseur *m*

thinking ['θɪŋkɪŋ] **1** *n (process of thought)* réflexion *f*; **to do some t.** réfléchir (**b**) *(opinion)* avis *m*, opinion *f*; **to my (way of) t.** à mon avis

2 *adj Br Hum* **the t. man's/woman's crumpet** une jolie fille/un beau mec avec quelque chose dans la tête

think-tank ['θɪŋktæŋk] *n* comité *m* d'experts

thinly ['θɪnlɪ] *adv* (**a**) *(cut)* en tranches fines *ou* minces; *(spread)* en couche fine *ou* mince (**b**) *(populated)* faiblement

thinner ['θɪnə(r)] *n* diluant *m*

thinness ['θɪnnɪs] *n (of person, wall)* minceur *f*; *(of paper, slice, layer)* finesse *f*; *(of liquid)* fluidité *f*; *(of blanket, clothing)* légèreté *f*

third [θɜːd] **1** *n* (**a**) *(fraction)* tiers *m inv* (**b**) *(in series)* troisième *mf* (**c**) *(of month)* trois *m inv* (**d**) *Mus* tierce *f* (**e**) *Br Univ* **to get a t.** *(in degree)* ≃ avoir sa licence avec mention passable

2 *adj* troisième; **t. degree burns** brûlures *fpl* au troisième degré; *Fam* **to give sb the t. degree** cuisiner qn; *Law* **t. party** tiers *m*, tierce personne *f*; **t. party cover** *(in insurance)* assurance *f* au tiers; **t. rate** *(mediocre)* très mauvais(e); **the T. World** le tiers-monde; *see also* **eighth**

thirdly ['θɜːdlɪ] *adv* troisièmement

thirst [θɜːst] **1** *n* soif *f*; *Fig* **the t. for sth** la soif de qch

2 *vi Fig* être assoiffé(e) (**for** de)

thirsty ['θɜːstɪ] *adj also Fig* assoiffé(e); **to be** *or* **feel t.** avoir soif; *Fam* **all this talking is t. work** ça donne soif de parler autant

thirteen [θɜːˈtiːn] **1** *n* treize *m inv*

2 *adj* treize; *see also* **eight**

thirteenth [θɜːˈtiːnθ] **1** *n* (**a**) *(fraction)* treizième *m* (**b**) *(in series)* treizième *mf* (**c**) *(of month)* treize *m inv*

2 *adj* treizième; *see also* **eighth**

thirtieth ['θɜːtɪɪθ] **1** *n* (**a**) *(fraction)* trentième *m* (**b**) *(in series)* trentième *mf* (**c**) *(of month)* trente *m inv*

2 *adj* trentième; *see also* **eighth**

thirty ['θɜːtɪ] **1** *n* trente *m inv*

2 *adj* trente; *see also* **eighty**

this [ðɪs] **1** *demonstrative pron (pl* **these** [ðiːz]) (**a**) *(subject)* ce, ceci; *(object)* ceci; **who's t.?** qui est-ce?; **what's t.?** qu'est-ce que c'est?; **t. is ridiculous!** c'est ridicule!; **t. leads me to believe that...** ceci me mène à croire que...; **we do it like t.** nous le faisons comme ceci; **t. is what she told me** voici ce qu'elle m'a dit; **listen to t.** écoute ça; **t. is Sarah Jervis** *(on telephone)* c'est Sarah Jervis à l'appareil; *(introducing another person)* je te présente Sarah Jervis; *Fam* **to talk about t. and that** parler de choses et d'autres (**b**) *(as opposed to that)* celui-ci (celle-ci) *m,f*; **in a case like t.** dans un cas comme celui-ci

2 *demonstrative adj (pl* **these)** (**a**) *(indicating person, thing)* ce (cette); **t. book** ce livre; **t. question** cette question; **t. man** cet homme

(**b**) *(as opposed to that)* ce...-ci (cette...-ci); **I prefer t. film**

je préfère ce film-ci; **take t.** cup prends cette tasse-ci; **t. one** celui-ci (celle-ci)
3 *adv* **t. high/big** haut(e)/grand(e) comme ça; **I didn't** think it would be **t.** good je ne pensais pas que ce serait aussi bon; **I've never seen one t.** good je n'en ai jamais vu d'aussi bon que ça; **t. much is certain,...** une chose est sûre,...

thistle ['θɪsəl] *n* chardon *m*

thither ['ðɪðə(r)] *adv Lit* hither and **t.** ça et là

thong [θɒŋ] *n* lanière *f*

thorax ['θɔːræks] *n Anat* thorax *m*

thorn [θɔːn] *n* épine *f*; *Fig* **to be a t.** in sb's flesh *or* side être un sujet d'irritation pour qn

thorny ['θɔːnɪ] *adj also Fig* épineux(euse)

thorough ['θʌrə] *adj* **(a)** *(search, cleaning, preparation)* minutieux(euse); *(knowledge, examination, revision)* approfondi(e); **to do** *or* **make a t.** job of sth faire qch très consciencieusement **(h)** *(work, worker)* consciencieux(euse) **(c)** *(complete)* intégral(e)

thoroughbred ['θʌrəbred] **1** *n* pur-sang *m inv*
2 *adj (horse)* pur-sang *inv*

thoroughfare ['θʌrəfeə(r)] *n* voie *f* de communication

thoroughgoing ['θʌrəgəʊɪŋ] *adj (search)* minutieux(euse); *(knowledge, revision)* approfondi(e)

thoroughly ['θʌrəlɪ] *adv* **(a)** *(with thoroughness)* à fond **(b)** *(completely)* tout à fait

thoroughness ['θʌrənɪs] *n* minutie *f*

those [ðəʊz] *(plural of that)* **1** *demonstrative pron* ceux-là (celles-là) *mpl,fpl*; **in cases like t.** dans des cas comme ceux-là, t. are the ones I want voilà ceux que je veux. **t. of us who...** ceux d'entre nous qui...
2 *demonstrative adj* ceux, **t.** ones ceux-là (celles-là) *mpl, fpl*

though [ðəʊ] **1** *conj* bien que + *subjunctive*; **t. I say so myself** sans fausse modestie; **strange t.** it **may seem** aussi étrange que cela puisse paraître; **even t.** même si; **as t.** comme si
2 *adv* pourtant

thought [θɔːt] **1** *n* **(a)** *(thinking, idea)* pensée *f*; **it's quite a t.!** *(pleasant)* le rêve!; *(unpleasant)* quelle horreur!; **what a kind t.!** quelle délicate attention!; **the very t. of it...** le simple fait d'y penser...; **I didn't give it another t.** je n'y ai plus pensé; **her thoughts were elsewhere** son esprit était ailleurs; **what are your thoughts on the matter?** quelle est votre opinion sur le sujet? **(b)** *(reflection)* réflexion *f*; **after much t.** après mûre réflexion; **to give some/no t.** to sth réfléchir/ne pas réfléchir à qch; **to be deep** *or* **lost in t.** être perdu(e) *ou* plongé(e) dans ses pensées **(c)** *(intention)* intention *f*; **to have no t.** of doing sth ne pas avoir l'intention de faire qch; **you must give up all thought(s) of seeing him** tu dois renoncer à le voir
2 *pt & pp of* **think**

thoughtful ['θɔːtfʊl] *adj* **(a)** *(pensive) (person)* pensif(ive); *(book, writer)* sérieux(euse) **(b)** *(considerate) (person)* attentionné(e); *(gesture, remark)* gentil(ille)

thoughtfully ['θɔːtfəlɪ] *adv* **(a)** *(pensively)* pensivement **(b)** *(considerately)* gentiment

thoughtless ['θɔːtlɪs] *adj* irréfléchi(e)

thought-out ['θɔːt'aʊt] *adj* **well/poorly t.** *(plan, scheme)* bien/mal étudié(e)

thought-provoking ['θɔːtprəvəʊkɪŋ] *adj* qui donne à réfléchir

thousand ['θaʊzənd] **1** *n* mille *m inv*; **one** *or* **a t.** mille; **thousands of people** des milliers de gens
2 *adj* mille *inv*; **a t.** years mille ans; **two t.** men deux mille hommes; *Fam* **to have a t.** and one things to do avoir mille choses à faire

thousandth ['θaʊzənθ] **1** *n* **(a)** *(fraction)* millième *m* **(b)** *(in series)* millième *mf*
2 *adj* millième

thrash [θræʃ] *vt (beat)* battre; *Fam Fig (defeat heavily)* écraser, battre à plate(s) couture(s)
▸ **thrash about, thrash around 1** *vt sep* **to t.** one's arms and legs about se débattre
2 *vi (move wildly)* se débattre
▸ **thrash out** *vt sep* discuter *ou* débattre de

thread [θred] **1** *n* **(a)** *(for sewing)* fil *m*; *Fig* **his life hung by a t.** sa vie ne tenait qu'à un fil; **to lose the t.** **(of sth)** perdre le fil (de qch) **(b)** *(of screw, bolt)* filetage *m*
2 *vt* **(a)** *(needle, beads)* enfiler **(b)** *(move)* **to t.** one's way between the cars se faufiler entre les voitures; **to t.** one's way through the crowd se frayer un chemin à travers la foule

threadbare ['θredbeə(r)] *adj (clothes)* élimé(e); *Fig (argument, joke)* éculé(e)

threat [θret] *n* menace *f*

threaten ['θretən] **1** *vt* menacer; **to t. to do sth** menacer de faire qch; **to t. sb with sth** menacer qn de qch
2 *vi* menacer

threatening ['θretənɪŋ] *adj (look, gesture)* menaçant(e); *(letter)* de menaces

three [θriː] **1** *n* trois *m inv*; **come with us – no, (two's company,)** t. **'s a crowd** viens avec nous – non, je me sentirais de trop
2 *adj* trois *inv*; *see also* **eight**

three-cornered [θriː'kɔːnəd] *adj* triangulaire

three-course meal ['θriːkɔːs'miːl] *n* repas *m* à trois plats *(entrée, plat principal, dessert)*

three-dimensional [θriːdaɪ'menʃənəl] *adj (object)* tridimensionnel(elle), en trois dimensions; *(character)* qui semble réel; *(film, picture)* en relief

threefold ['θriːfəʊld] **1** *adj* triple
2 *adv* **to increase t.** être multiplié(e) par trois

three-legged [θriː'legɪd] *adj (stool)* à trois pieds, **t. race** = course dont les participants sont attachés deux à deux par une jambe

three-piece ['θriːpiːs] *adj* **t. suit** *(costume m)* trois-pièce *m inv*; *Br* **t. suite** canapé *m* avec deux fauteuils assortis

three-point turn ['θriːpɔɪnt'tɜːn] *n* demi-tour *m* en trois manœuvres

threescore ['θriːskɔː(r)] *n Lit* soixante *inv*; **t. (years) and ten** soixante-dix *inv*

threesome ['θriːsəm] *n* groupe *m* de trois personnes

three-wheeler [θriː'wiːlə(r)] *n (car)* voiture *f* à trois roues; *(tricycle)* tricycle *m*

thresh [θreʃ] *vt* battre

threshold ['θreʃəʊld] *n also Fig* seuil *m*; **to cross the t.** franchir le seuil; *Fig* **to be on the t. of sth** être au seuil de qch

threw [θruː] *pt of* **throw**

thrice [θraɪs] *adv Lit* trois fois

thrift [θrɪft] *n* économie *f*, épargne *f*

thriftless ['θrɪftlɪs] *adj* dépensier(ère)

thrifty ['θrɪftɪ] *adj* économe

thrill [θrɪl] **1** *n (excitement)* sensation *f*; *(trembling)* frisson *m*; **to get a t. out of doing sth** adorer faire qch
2 *vt* exalter, donner des frissons à; **to be thrilled for sb/ with sth** être ravi(e) pour qn/de qch
3 *vi Lit* tressaillir, frissonner

thriller ['θrɪlə(r)] *n* thriller *m*

thrilling ['θrɪlɪŋ] *adj (story, film, match)* palpitant(e); *(idea, proposal, situation)* exaltant(e)

thrive [θraɪv] (*pt & pp* **thrived** [θraɪvd], *pt also* **throve** [θrəʊv]) *vi (of child, plant)* se développer; *(of adult)* s'épanouir; *(of business)* prospérer; **to t. on sth** *(stress, danger)* avoir besoin de qch pour s'épanouir

thriving ['θraɪvɪŋ] *adj (plant, person, animal)* vigoureux(euse); *(business)* prospère, florissant(e)

throat [θrəʊt] *n* **(a)** gorge *f*; **to clear one's t.** se racler la gorge, s'éclaircir la voix **(b)** *(idioms)* **to ram** *or* **shove sth down sb's t.** rebattre les oreilles à qn de qch; **to jump down sb's t.** sauter sur qn; **to be at each other's throats** se battre

throaty ['θrəʊtɪ] *adj* rauque

throb [θrɒb] **1** *n (of heart)* battement *m*; *(of pain)* élancement *m*; *(of engine)* vibration *f*
2 *vi (pt & pp* **throbbed**) *(of heart)* battre; *(of engine)* vibrer; **my head is throbbing** j'ai une douleur lancinante dans la tête

throes [θrəʊz] *npl* **t. of death, death t.** affres *fpl* de la mort, l'agonie *f*; **to be in the t. of sth/of doing sth** être en plein qch/en train de faire qch

thrombosis [θrɒm'bəʊsɪs] *(pl* **thromboses**) *n* thrombose *f*

throne [θrəʊn] *n* trône *m*

throng [θrɒŋ] **1** *n* foule *f*
2 *vt* se presser dans; **the streets were thronged with people** les rues étaient noires de monde
3 *vi* affluer, se presser; **to t. round sb** se presser autour de qn

throttle ['θrɒtəl] **1** *n (valve)* papillon *m* des gaz; *(accelerator)* manette *f* des gaz; **at full t.** à pleins gaz
2 *vt also Fig* étrangler

through [θruː] **1** *prep* **(a)** *(with place)* par, à travers; **to go t. a tunnel** passer par un tunnel; **to look t. a hole** regarder par un trou; **to come in t. the window** entrer par la fenêtre; **we went t. the park** nous sommes passés par le parc
(b) *(in the course of)* **all t. his life** toute sa vie durant; **halfway t. a book/film** à la moitié d'un livre/film; **to get t. sth** *(finish)* venir à bout de qch; *Fam* **he's been t. a lot** il en a bavé
(c) *(by means of)* par; **to send sth t. the post** envoyer qch par la poste; **I found out t. my brother/the newspaper** je l'ai appris par mon frère/le journal
(d) *(because of)* à cause de; **t. ignorance/carelessness** par ignorance/négligence
(e) *Am (up to)* **Tuesday t. Thursday** de mardi à jeudi
2 *adv* **(a)** *(to other side)* **to go t.** *(of bullet, nail)* traverser; **to let sb t.** laisser passer qn; **to get t. to the final** être en finale
(b) *(from start to finish)* **to sleep all night t.** dormir toute la nuit; **to read a book right t.** lire un livre tout entier; **he's bad t. and t.** il est vraiment méchant
(c) *(in contact)* **to get t. to sb** *(on phone)* joindre qn; **to put sb t. to sb** *(on phone)* passer qn à qn; *Fam* **I just can't get t. to him** *(make myself understood)* je n'arrive pas à le lui faire comprendre
3 *adj* **(a)** *(finished)* fini(e); **to be t. with sb/sth** en avoir fini avec qn/qch
(b) *(direct)* **t. train** train *m* direct

throughout [θruː'aʊt] **1** *prep (in every part of)* partout dans; *(during)* tout au long de; **t. the country** dans tout le pays; **t. her life** tout au long de sa vie, pendant toute sa vie
2 *adv (everywhere)* partout; *(the whole time)* tout le temps

throughput ['θruːpʊt] *n Com* débit *m*

throve [θrəʊv] *pt of* **thrive**

throw [θrəʊ] **1** *vt (pt* **threw** [θruː], *pp* **thrown** [θrəʊn]) **(a)** *(in general)* jeter, lancer; *(javelin, discus)* lancer; **to t. sth at sb/sth** lancer qch à qn/contre qch; **to t. sth in sb's face**

lancer qch à la figure de qn; *Fig* jeter qch à la figure de qn; **to t. sb forwards/backwards** projeter qn en avant/en arrière; *Fig* **to t. oneself into sth** *(after traumatic event)* se jeter dans qch; *(enthusiastically)* se lancer dans qch; **to t. oneself at sb** se jeter sur qn; **to t. sb into confusion** plonger qn dans l'embarras; **to t. a switch** appuyer sur un interrupteur; **to t. open the door** ouvrir la porte en grand; *Fam* **to t. one's weight about** *or* **around** la ramener
(b) *(image, shadow)* projeter **(on** sur); *Fig* **to t. light on sth** éclairer qch
(c) *(have)* **to t. a fit** piquer une crise; *Fam* **to t. a party** organiser une fête
(d) *(in wrestling)* renverser
(e) *(of horse)* désarçonner
(f) *Fam (disconcert)* désarçonner, déconcerter
2 *n* **(a)** *(in general)* jet *m*; *(of javelin, discus)* lancer *m*; *(in wrestling)* mise *f* à terre
(b) *(for furniture, bed)* jeté *m*
(c) *Fam* **$50 a t.** *(each)* 50 dollars chaque

▸ **throw away** *vt sep* **(a)** *(discard)* jeter **(b)** *(chance, life)* gâcher; *(money)* gaspiller

▸ **throw in** *vt sep* **(a)** *(in general)* jeter; *Fig* **to t. in the sponge** *or* **the towel** jeter l'éponge; *Fig* **to t. in one's lot with sb** s'associer avec qn **(b)** *(add)* placer; *(give as extra)* ajouter, donner en plus

▸ **throw out** *vt sep* **(a)** *(eject)* *(person)* exclure, mettre à la porte; *(thing)* jeter; *(proposal)* rejeter **(b)** *(emit)* *(light, heat)* émettre

▸ **throw together** *vt sep (assemble or gather hurriedly)* assembler à la hâte; *(make hurriedly)* faire à la hâte; **chance had thrown us together** le hasard nous avait réunis

▸ **throw up 1** *vt sep* **(a)** *(raise)* **to t. up one's hands** *(in horror, dismay)* lever les bras au ciel **(b)** *(reveal)* *(facts, information)* révéler **(c)** *(abandon)* *(career)* abandonner
2 *vi Fam (vomit)* vomir

throwaway ['θrəʊəweɪ] *adj* **(a)** *(disposable)* jetable **(b)** *(line, remark)* fait(e) sans y penser

throwback ['θrəʊbæk] *n Biol* régression *f* **(to** à); *Fig* retour *m* **(to** à)

throw-in ['θrəʊɪn] *n (in football)* remise *f* en jeu

thrown [θrəʊn] *pp of* **throw**

thru [θruː] = **through**

thrush[1] [θrʌʃ] *n (bird)* grive *f*

thrush[2] *n (disease)* muguet *m*

thrust [θrʌst] **1** *n* **(a)** *(forward movement)* mouvement *m* en avant; *(of army)* attaque *f* **(b)** *(of argument)* idée *f* principale **(c)** *(force of engine)* poussée *f*
2 *vt (pt & pp* **thrust**) **to t. sth into sth** enfoncer qch dans qch; **to t. one's way through the crowd** se frayer un chemin à travers la foule

▸ **thrust aside** *vt sep* repousser, écarter

▸ **thrust forward** *vt sep* pousser en avant; *Fig* **to t. oneself forward** se mettre en avant

▸ **thrust on** *vt sep* **to t. sth on sb** imposer qch à qn; **thrust himself on them** il s'est imposé

▸ **thrust out** *vt sep (arm, leg)* allonger; *(chest)* bomber; *(chin)* avancer

▸ **thrust upon** = **thrust on**

thrusting ['θrʌstɪŋ] *adj* entreprenant(e), dynamique

thruway ['θruːweɪ] *n Am* autoroute *f*

thud [θʌd] **1** *n* bruit *m* sourd
2 *vi* faire un bruit sourd; **to t. against sth** frapper qch avec un bruit sourd

thug [θʌg] *n* voyou *m*

thumb [θʌm] **1** *n* pouce *m*; *Fig* **she's got him under her t.** il est sous sa coupe; *Fam* **to be all thumbs** être

maladroit(e); *Fam* **to give sth the thumbs up/down** accepter/rejeter qch
2 *vt* **to t. one's nose at sb** faire un pied de nez à qn; *Fam* **to t. a lift** *or* **ride** faire de l'auto-stop; **a well thumbed book/ magazine** un livre/magazine qui a beaucoup servi
3 *vi* **to t. through a book/magazine** feuilleter un livre/ magazine

thumbnail ['θʌmneɪl] *n* ongle *m* du pouce; **t. sketch** description *f* rapide

thumbprint ['θʌmprɪnt] *n* empreinte *f* du pouce

thumbtack ['θʌmtæk] *n Am* punaise *f*

thump [θʌmp] **1** *n (blow)* coup *m*; *(sound)* bruit *m* sourd
2 *vt (hit)* cogner, frapper; *(put down heavily)* poser lourdement
3 *vi* (a) **to t. on sth** *(table, door)* cogner, frapper qch (b) *(walk heavily)* **to t. around** *or* **about** marcher à pas lourds (c) *(of heart)* battre la chamade

thumping ['θʌmpɪŋ] *Br Fam* **1** *adj* (a) *(very large)* énorme (b) *(headache)* lancinant(e)
2 *adv* **a t. great book/salary** un livre/un salaire énorme

thunder ['θʌndə(r)] **1** *n* tonnerre *m*; **with a face like t.** le visage déformé par la colère
2 *vi also Fig* tonner; **to t. along** *(of train, lorry)* passer dans un bruit de tonnerre

thunderbolt ['θʌndəbəʊlt] *n* éclair *m* suivi d'un coup de tonnerre

thunderclap ['θʌndəklæp] *n* coup *m* de tonnerre

thundercloud ['θʌndəklaʊd] *n* nuage *m* orageux

thunderous ['θʌndərəs] *adj (voice)* tonitruant(e); **t. applause** un tonnerre d'applaudissements

thunderstorm ['θʌndəstɔːm] *n* orage *m*

thunderstruck ['θʌndəstrʌk] *adj* abasourdi(e)

Thur *(abbr* **Thursday)** jeudi

Thursday ['θɜːzdɪ] *n* jeudi *m*; *see also* **Saturday**

thus [ðʌs] *adv Formal* (a) *(in this way, therefore)* ainsi (b) **t. far** *(in present)* jusqu'ici; *(in past)* jusque-là

thwart [θwɔːt] *vt* contrecarrer

thyme [taɪm] *n* thym *m*

thyroid ['θaɪərɔɪd] **1** *n* thyroïde *f*
2 *adj* thyroïde; **t. gland** thyroïde *f*

tiara [tɪ'ɑːrə] *n (jewellery)* diadème *m*

Tibet [tɪ'bet] *n* le Tibet

Tibetan [tɪ'betən] **1** *n* (a) *(person)* Tibétain(e) *m,f* (b) *(language)* tibétain *m*
2 *adj* tibétain(e)

tibia ['tɪbɪə] *n Anat* tibia *m*

tic [tɪk] *n* tic *m*

tick¹ [tɪk] *n (parasite)* tique *f*

tick² *n Br Fam (credit)* **to buy sth on t.** acheter qch à crédit

tick³ **1** *n* (a) *(of clock)* tic-tac *m inv*; *Fam (moment)* instant *m* (b) *(mark)* coche *f*; **to put a t. beside sth** cocher qch
2 *vt (mark)* cocher
3 *vi (of clock)* faire tic-tac; **the minutes were ticking by** *or* **away** les minutes passaient, *Fam* **I don't know what makes him t.** je ne sais pas ce qui se passe dans sa tête

▸ **tick off** *vt sep* (a) *(on list)* cocher (b) *Br Fam (reprimand)* passer un savon à (c) *Am Fam (irritate)* énerver

▸ **tick over** *vi (of engine)* tourner au ralenti; *(of business)* tourner

ticket ['tɪkɪt] **1** *n* (a) *(for train, plane, cinema, lottery)* billet *m*; *(for underground, bus)* ticket *m*; **(parking) t.** P-V *m*; **t. inspector** contrôleur(euse) *m,f*; **t. office** guichet *m*, billetterie *f*; **t. tout** revendeur(euse) *m,f* de billets (b) *(label)* **(price) t.** étiquette *f* (c) *Am Pol (list of candidates)*

liste *f* électorale; **she ran on an anti-corruption t.** elle a fondé son programme électoral sur la lutte contre la corruption (d) *Fam* **it was just the t.!** c'était juste ce qu'il fallait!
2 *vt (goods)* étiqueter

ticking ['tɪkɪŋ] *n* (a) *(of clock)* tic-tac *m inv* (b) *(fabric)* toile *f* à matelas

ticking off *n Br Fam (reprimand)* savon *m*; **to give sb a t.** passer un savon à qn

tickle ['tɪkəl] **1** *n* chatouillement *m*; **to have a t. in one's throat** avoir des picotements dans la gorge
2 *vt* chatouiller; *Fig (amuse)* amuser; **to t. sb's fancy** plaire à qn; **to be tickled pink** être ravi(e)
3 *vi* chatouiller

ticklish ['tɪklɪʃ] *adj* (a) *(person)* chatouilleux(euse) (b) *Fam (situation, problem)* délicat(e)

tidal ['taɪdəl] *adj* régi(e) par les marées; **t. energy** énergie *f* marémotrice; **t. wave** raz de marée *m inv*

tiddler ['tɪdlə(r)] *n Br Fam (small fish)* petit poisson *m*, *(child)* mioche *m*

tiddly ['tɪdlɪ] *adj Br Fam* (a) *(small)* minuscule (b) *(drunk)* paf *inv*

tiddlywinks ['tɪdlɪwɪŋks] *n* jeu *m* de puce

tide [taɪd] *n* marée *f*; *Fig (of events)* cours *m*; **high/low t.** marée haute/basse; *Fig* **to go against the t.** aller à contrecourant; *Fig* **the t. has turned** le vent a tourné

▸ **tide over** *vt sep* **to t. sb over** dépanner qn

tidemark ['taɪdmɑːk] *n (mark left by tide)* laisse *f* de haute mer; *Br Fam (in bath, around neck)* ligne *f* de crasse

tidings ['taɪdɪŋz] *npl Lit* nouvelles *fpl*

tidy ['taɪdɪ] **1** *adj* (a) *(room, house)* rangé(e), en ordre; *(hair)* bien coiffé(e); *(appearance, handwriting)* soigné(e); *(person) (in habits)* ordonné(e); *(in appearance)* soigné (b) *Fam (considerable)* joli(e)
2 *vt* ranger; *(garden)* nettoyer; **to t. one's hair** se recoiffer

▸ **tidy up** *vt sep & vi* ranger

tie [taɪ] **1** *n* (a) *(link)* lien *m* (b) *(garment)* cravate *f*; *(draw) (in match)* match *m* nul; **there was a t. for second place** *(in race, competition)* il y a eu égalité pour la deuxième place (d) *(match)* match *m*
2 *vt (shoelace, string)* attacher, nouer; **to t. a knot** faire un nœud; *Fam* **to t. the knot** se marier; **to t. sth to sth** attacher qch à qch; *Fig* **to have one's hands tied** avoir les mains liées; *Fig* **to be tied to one's desk** être cloué(e) à son bureau
3 *vi (in race, contest)* être à égalité; **to t. for first/second place** être premiers(ères)/deuxièmes ex aequo

▸ **tie back** *vt sep (hair, curtains)* relever

▸ **tie down** *vt sep (immobilize)* attacher; *Fig* **children t. you down** les enfants vous sont une contrainte; **she didn't want to feel tied down** elle voulait garder sa liberté

▸ **tie in** *vt (of facts, story)* concorder, cadrer

▸ **tie on** *vt* attacher

▸ **tie up** *vt sep* (a) *(person, animal)* attacher; *(parcel)* ficeler; *(boat)* amarrer (b) *(deal)* conclure; *(money)* immobiliser (c) *Fig* **to be tied up** *(busy)* être occupé(e)

tie-break(er) ['taɪbreɪk(ə(r))] *n (in tennis)* tie-break *m*; *(in quiz, competition)* question *f* subsidiaire

tie-in ['taɪɪn] *n (link)* lien *m*, rapport *m* (**with** avec); **a film/TV t.** = livre, jouet etc commercialisé à la suite d'un film ou d'une série télévisée

tier [tɪə(r)] *n (of theatre, stadium)* gradin *m*; *(of wedding cake)* étage *m*; *(administrative)* échelon *m*

tiff [tɪf] *n Fam* querelle *f*; **a lover's t.** une dispute d'amoureux

tiger ['taɪgə(r)] *n* tigre *m*

tight [taɪt] **1** *adj* (**a**) *(clothes, knot, screw)* serré(e); **to be a t.**
fit *(of clothes)* être un peu juste; **to keep a t.** hold *or* **grip on**
sth s'agripper à qch; **it was a t.** **squeeze** il a fallu se serrer
un peu; *Fig* **to be in a t.** **spot** *or* **corner** être dans une
mauvaise passe; *Fig* **to run a t.** **ship** bien mener sa barque
(**b**) *(competition, race, bend, schedule)* serré(e); *(restrictions)*
strict(e); **a t.** **finish** *(in race)* une arrivée disputée; *Fam*
money's a bit t. at the moment je suis un peu à court
d'argent en ce moment (**c**) *Fam (mean)* radin(e) (**d**) *Fam*
(drunk) bourré(e)
2 *adv (hold, squeeze)* fortement; *(seal, shut)* bien; **hold t.!**
tiens bon!; **sleep t.!** dors bien!

tighten ['taɪtən] **1** *vt (screw, knot)* serrer; *(rope)* tendre;
(restrictions, security) renforcer; *(conditions, rules)* durcir; **to**
t. **one's grip on sth** *(rope, handle)* resserrer sa prise sur qch;
Fig (power, organization) renforcer son emprise sur qch; *Fig*
to t. **one's belt** se serrer la ceinture
2 *vi (of knot, grip)* se resserrer; *(of rope)* se tendre
▸ **tighten** **up** *vt sep (screw)* resserrer; *(restrictions,*
security) renforcer

tightfisted [taɪt'fɪstɪd] *adj Fam* radin(e)

tightknit ['taɪt'nɪt] *adj (community)* uni(e)

tight-lipped ['taɪtlɪpt] *adj (silent)* peu bavard(e); *(angry)*
renfrogné(e)

tightly ['taɪtlɪ] *adv (hold, squeeze)* fortement; *(seal, shut)* bien

tightness ['taɪtnɪs] *n (of link, clothing)* étroitesse *f; (of*
regulations, security) rigueur *f*

tightrope ['taɪtrəʊp] *n* corde *f* raide; *Fig* **to walk a t.** être
sur la corde raide; **t.** **walker** funambule *mf*

tights [taɪts] *npl Br (garment)* collant *m*

tigress ['taɪgrɪs] *n* tigresse *f*

'til [tɪl] = **until**

tile [taɪl] **1** *n (on roof)* tuile *f; (on floor, wall)* carreau *m*
2 *vt (roof)* couvrir de tuiles; *(floor, wall)* carreler

tiled [taɪld] *adj (roof)* de tuiles; *(floor, wall)* carrelé(e)

till¹ [tɪl] *vt (field)* labourer

till² *n (cash register)* caisse *f; Fig* **to be caught with one's**
hand *or* **fingers in the t.** être pris(e) la main dans le sac

till³ = **until**

tiller ['tɪlə(r)] *n (on boat)* barre *f*

tilt [tɪlt] **1** *n* (**a**) *(angle)* inclinaison *f* (**b**) **at full t.** à toute
vitesse
2 *vt (head, chair)* incliner, pencher; **to t.** **the balance of**
opinion in favour of faire pencher l'opinion en faveur de
3 *vi* (**a**) *(incline)* pencher; **to t.** **backwards/forwards**
pencher vers l'arrière/vers l'avant (**b**) *Fig* **to t.** **at**
windmills se battre contre des moulins à vent
▸ **tilt over** *vi* basculer

timber ['tɪmbə(r)] *n Br (wood)* bois *m;* **t.** **merchant** marchand *m* de bois

time [taɪm] **1** *n* (**a**) *(in general)* temps *m; Fig* **to have no t.**
for sb/sth ne pas avoir de temps à perdre avec qn/qch; **to**
take t. prendre du temps; **to take one's t.** (doing sth)
prendre son temps (pour faire qch); **you took your t.!** tu as
pris ton temps!; **in one's own t.** *(out of working hours)*
pendant son temps libre; *(at one's own pace)* à son rythme;
in t. *(eventually)* avec le temps; **in t. for sth/to do sth** à
temps pour qch/pour faire qch; **in good t.** *(early)* à temps;
(in due course) en temps voulu; **all in good t.** chaque chose
en son temps; **she'll do it in her own good t.** elle le fera
quand elle le pourra; **now my t. is my own** maintenant, je
suis libre de mon temps; **in no t. at all, in next to no t.** en
un rien de temps; **t.'s getting on** l'heure avance; **t.'s up!**
c'est l'heure!; **t.** **will tell** l'avenir le dira; *Prov* **t. is money** le
temps, c'est de l'argent; *Fam* **to do t.** *(go to prison)* faire de la

taule; *also Fig* **t.** **bomb** bombe *f* à retardement; **to be in a t.**
warp être hors du temps
(**b**) *(period)* **in a short/long t.** dans peu de temps/
longtemps; **for some t.** pendant quelque temps; **in three**
weeks' t. dans trois semaines; **to take a long t.** **over sth/**
to do sth passer beaucoup de temps sur qch/à faire qch;
for the t. **being** pour le moment; **to have a good t.** bien
s'amuser; **to give sb a hard t.** faire passer un mauvais
moment à qn
(**c**) *(age)* époque *f;* **before my t.** avant ma naissance; **to be**
ahead of one's t. être en avance sur son temps; **to move**
with the times vivre avec son temps; **she was a good**
singer in her t. c'était une bonne chanteuse à son époque;
she's seen a few things in her t. elle a vu pas mal de
choses dans sa vie; **t.** **capsule** = conteneur rempli d'objets
que l'on enterre pour permettre aux générations futures de
comprendre comment on vivait à une époque donnée
(**d**) *(moment)* moment *m;* **at the t.** à ce moment-là; **at the**
present t. en ce moment; **at one t.** à une époque; **at no t.**
jamais, à aucun moment; **at the same t.** en même temps;
at times parfois, par moments; **this t.** **next year** l'année
prochaine à la même époque; **from t.** **to t.** de temps en
temps; **at this t.** **of (the) year** à cette époque de l'année;
the t. **has come to...** le moment est venu de...; *Fam* **not**
before t.! il était temps!; *Fam* **it's high t.** **(that)...** il est
grand temps que... + *subjunctive*
(**e**) *(on clock)* heure *f;* **what's the t.?** quelle heure est-il?; **to**
pass the t. **of day with sb** parler de la pluie et du beau
temps avec qn; *Fam* **he wouldn't give you the t. of day** il
n'est vraiment pas aimable; **this t.** **tomorrow** demain à la
même heure; **on t.** à l'heure; **it's t.** **we were going** il est
temps de partir; **t.** **difference** décalage *m* horaire; **t.** **lag**
décalage *f; Ind* **t.** **sheet** fiche *f* horaire; **t.** **switch** minuterie *f*
(**f**) *(occasion)* fois *f;* **three times** trois fois; **t.** **and t. again,**
t. **after t.** encore et encore
(**g**) *(in multiplication)* **four times two is eight** quatre fois
deux égalent huit; **three times as big/expensive as** trois
fois plus grand(e)/cher (chère) que
(**h**) *(in music)* mesure *f;* **to keep t.** rester en mesure
2 *vt* (**a**) *(meeting, visit)* prévoir
(**b**) *(remark, action)* **well timed** opportun(e); **badly timed**
mal venu(e)
(**c**) *(athlete, race)* chronométrer

time-consuming ['taɪmkənsjuːmɪŋ] *adj* qui prend du
temps

time-honoured, *Am* **time-honored** ['taɪmɒnəd]
adj consacré(e) (par l'usage)

timekeeper ['taɪmkiːpə(r)] *n (in competition)* chrono-
métreur *m*

timekeeping ['taɪmkiːpɪŋ] *n* (**a**) *(in factory)* contrôle *m*
de présence (**b**) *(punctuality)* ponctualité *f*

timeless ['taɪmlɪs] *adj* intemporel(elle)

timely ['taɪmlɪ] *adj* opportun(e)

time-out ['taɪmaʊt] *n (in sport)* temps *m* mort; *Fig* pause
f; **to take t.** faire une pause

timepiece ['taɪmpiːs] *n (clock)* pendule *f; (watch)* montre *f*

timer ['taɪmə(r)] *n* minuteur *m*

time-saving ['taɪmseɪvɪŋ] *adj* qui permet de gagner du
temps

timescale ['taɪmskeɪl] *n* période *f*

time-share ['taɪmʃeə(r)] *n (flat)* appartement *m* en
multipropriété; *(house)* maison *f* en multipropriété

timespan ['taɪmspæn] *n* laps *m* de temps

timetable ['taɪmteɪbəl] **1** *n (at school, university)* emploi
m du temps; *(for event, project)* calendrier *m; (for trains,*
buses) horaire *m;* **to work to a t.** suivre un emploi du
temps

2 *vt (talks, meeting)* fixer une date pour; *(classes)* établir un emploi du temps pour

time-wasting ['taɪmweɪstɪŋ] *n* perte *f* de temps

timid ['tɪmɪd] *adj* timide

timidity [tɪ'mɪdɪtɪ] *n* timidité *f*

timidly ['tɪmɪdlɪ] *adv* timidement

timing ['taɪmɪŋ] *n* (a) *(of announcement, election)* moment *m* choisi (**of** pour) (**b**) *(of remark, action)* **good t.** à-propos *m*; **bad t.** manque *m* d'à-propos; **perfect t.!** ça tombe bien! (**c**) *(of musician)* sens *m* du rythme

timorous ['tɪmərəs] *adj* timoré(e)

tin [tɪn] *n* (**a**) *(metal)* étain *m*; **t. mine** mine *f* d'étain; **t. plate** fer-blanc *m*; **t. soldier** soldat *m* de plomb (**b**) *(mould)* moule *m* (**c**) *(container)* boîte *f*; *(for biscuits, cakes)* boîte en fer; **t. opener** ouvre-boîte *m*

tinder ['tɪndə(r)] *n* petit bois *m*

tinderbox ['tɪndəbɒks] *n Fig* poudrière *f*

tinfoil ['tɪn'fɔɪl] *n* papier *m* aluminium

ting-a-ling ['tɪŋəlɪŋ] *n* dring, dring *m inv*

tinge [tɪn(d)ʒ] **1** *n (of colour, emotion)* pointe *f* **2** *vt* **tinged with** teinté(e) de

tingle ['tɪŋgəl] **1** *n (physical sensation)* picotement *m*; *(of fear)* frisson *m*; *(of excitement)* frémissement *m* **2** *vi* picoter; **to t. with fear** frissonner de peur; **to t. with excitement** frémir d'excitation

tingling ['tɪŋglɪŋ] *n* picotement *m*

tinker ['tɪŋkə(r)] **1** *n (travelling person)* rétameur *m* **2** *vi* **to t. with sth** bricoler qch

tinkle ['tɪŋkəl] **1** *n (of bell)* tintement *m* **2** *vi* tinter

tinned [tɪnd] *adj Br (food)* en boîte

tinnitus ['tɪnɪtəs] *n* acouphène *m*

tinny ['tɪnɪ] *adj (sound)* métallique

tinsel ['tɪnsəl] *n* guirlandes *fpl* de Noël

tint [tɪnt] **1** *n* teinte *f,* nuance *f; (in hair)* rinçage *m* **2** *vt* teinter

tiny ['taɪnɪ] *adj* minuscule; **a t. bit** un tout petit peu

tip¹ [tɪp] **1** *n (end)* bout *m*; **on the tips of one's toes** sur la pointe des pieds; **it's on the t. of my tongue** je l'ai sur le bout de la langue; *Fig* **that's just the t. of the iceberg** ce n'est que la partie visible de l'iceberg **2** *vt (pt & pp* **tipped**) **to be tipped with sth** avoir le bout recouvert de qch

tip² **1** *n* (**a**) *(payment)* pourboire *m* (**b**) *(piece of advice)* truc *m* **2** *vt* (*pt & pp* **tipped**) (**a**) *(give money to)* donner un pourboire à (**b**) *(predict)* **to t. a winner** *(in horse race)* pronostiquer un cheval gagnant; **to t. sb for success/promotion** prédire à qn le succès/une promotion; **the movie is tipped to win an Oscar** on pressent que ce film va gagner un Oscar

tip³ **1** *n (for rubbish)* & *Fig* dépotoir *m* **2** *vt (pt & pp* **tipped**) (**a**) *(pour) (rubbish)* déverser; *(liquid)* verser; **to t. sth over sb/sth** renverser qch sur qn/qch (**b**) **to t. the scales at 95 kg** peser 95 kg; *Fig* **to t. the scales or balance (in sb's favour)** faire pencher la balance (en faveur de qn)

▸ **tip off** *vt sep (warn)* avertir

▸ **tip out** *vt sep (empty)* vider; *(discard)* jeter

▸ **tip over 1** *vt sep* renverser **2** *vi* se renverser

▸ **tip up 1** *vt sep* renverser **2** *vi* basculer

tip-off ['tɪpɒf] *n Fam* tuyau *m*

Tipp-Ex® ['tɪpeks] **1** *n* Tipp-Ex® *m inv* **2** *vt* **to t. sth out** effacer qch avec du Tipp-Ex®

tipple ['tɪpəl] *n Fam* **what's your t.?** qu'est-ce que vous buvez habituellement?; **gin's her favourite t.** ce qu'elle préfère, c'est le gin

tipsy ['tɪpsɪ] *adj* pompette

tiptoe ['tɪptəʊ] **1** *n* **on t.** sur la pointe des pieds **2** *vi* marcher sur la pointe des pieds; **to t. in/out** entrer/sortir sur la pointe des pieds

tiptop ['tɪptɒp] *adj* excellent(e)

tirade [taɪ'reɪd] *n* diatribe *f*

tire¹ ['taɪə(r)] **1** *vt* fatiguer **2** *vi* se fatiguer; **to t. of sth/of doing sth** se lasser de qch/de faire qch

▸ **tire out** *vt sep (exhaust)* épuiser

tire² *Am* = **tyre**

tired ['taɪəd] *adj* fatigué(e); **to be t. of sth/of doing sth** en avoir assez de qch/de faire qch

tireless ['taɪəlɪs] *adj* infatigable

tiresome ['taɪəsəm] *adj* ennuyeux(euse)

tiring ['taɪərɪŋ] *adj* fatigant(e)

tissue ['tɪsjuː] *n* (**a**) *Biol* tissu *m* (**b**) *(paper handkerchief)* mouchoir *m* en papier; *Fig* **a t. of lies** un tissu de mensonges; **t. paper** papier *m* de soie

tit¹ [tɪt] *n (bird)* mésange *f*

tit² *n* **t. for tat** un prêté pour un rendu; **to give sb t. for tat** rendre à qn la monnaie de sa pièce

tit³ *n very Fam* (**a**) *(breast)* nichon *m*; **to get on sb's tits** courir sur le haricot à qn (**b**) *(idiot)* con (conne) *m,f*

titanic [taɪ'tænɪk] *adj (conflict, struggle)* titanesque

titanium [taɪ'teɪnɪəm] *n Chem* titane *m*

titbit ['tɪtbɪt] *n (snack)* morceau *m* de choix; *Fig* **t. of information** nouvelle *f*

titch [tɪtʃ] *n Br Fam (small person)* microbe *m*

titchy ['tɪtʃɪ] *adj Br Fam* minuscule

tit-for-tat [tɪtfə'tæt] *adj Fam (murder)* en représailles; **it's just t.** c'est un prêté pour un rendu

titillate ['tɪtɪleɪt] *vt* titiller

titillation [tɪtɪ'leɪʃən] *n* titillation *f*

title ['taɪtl] **1** *n* titre *m*; **the titles** le générique; **t. deeds** titres de propriété; **t. fight** combat *m* comptant pour le titre; **t. page** page *f* de titre; **t. role** *(in play, film)* rôle-titre *m*; **t. track** *(of album)* morceau *m* qui donne son titre à l'album **2** *vt* intituler

titled ['taɪtld] *adj (person)* titré(e)

titleholder ['taɪtlhəʊldə(r)] *n (in sport)* tenant(e) *m,f* du titre

titter ['tɪtə(r)] **1** *n* petit rire *m* **2** *vi* rire bêtement

tittle-tattle ['tɪtltætl] *Fam* **1** *n* potins *mpl*, cancans *mpl* **2** *vi* cancaner

titular ['tɪtjʊlə(r)] *adj* en titre

tizzy ['tɪzɪ] *n Fam* **to be in/get into a t.** être/se mettre dans tous ses états

T-junction ['tiːdʒʌŋkʃən] *n* carrefour *m* en T

TNT [tiːen'tiː] *n Chem (abbr* **trinitrotoluene)** TNT *m*

to [tuː, *unstressed* tə] **1** *prep* (**a**) *(towards)* à; **to go to church/school** aller à l'église/à l'école; **to go to France/Canada/the USA** aller en France/au Canada/aux États-Unis; **to go to sb's/sb's** aller chez qn; **to the left/right** à gauche/droite (**b**) *(until)* jusqu'à; **it's ten to (six)** il est (six heures) moins dix; **to count to ten** compter jusqu'à dix; **a year to the day** un an jour pour jour

(c) *(expressing indirect object)* **to give sth to sb** donner qch à qn; **to speak to sb** parler à qn
(d) *(with result)* **to my surprise/joy** à ma grande surprise/joie; **to my horror, I discovered that...** et, horreur!, je découvris que...
(e) *(expressing proportion)* **six votes to four** six voix contre quatre; **there are 1.5 euros to the pound** une livre vaut 1,5 euros
2 *particle* **(a)** *(with infinitive)* **to go** aller; **to have things to do** avoir des choses à faire; **it's too cold to go out** il fait trop froid pour sortir; **he came to help me** il est venu m'aider; **I want him to know** je veux qu'il sache; **she told me to stay** elle m'a dit de rester
(b) *(representing verb)* **I want/ought to** je veux/devrais le faire; **I was told to** on m'a dit de le faire

toad [təʊd] *n (animal)* crapaud *m*; *Fam Pej (man)* type *m* répugnant; *Br* **t. in the hole** = saucisses cuites au four dans de la pâte à crêpes

toadstool ['təʊdstuːl] *n* champignon *m* non comestible

toady ['təʊdɪ] *Fam* **1** *n* lèche-bottes *mf inv*
2 *vi* **to t. to sb** lécher les bottes de qn

toast [təʊst] **1** *n* **(a)** *(toasted bread)* pain *m* grillé; **a slice** *or* **piece of t.** un toast; **t. rack** porte-toasts *m inv* **(b)** *(tribute)* toast *m*; **to drink a t. to sb/sth** porter un toast à qn/qch
2 *vt* **(a)** *(bread)* (faire) griller; **toasted cheese** fromage *m* fondu; **toasted sandwich** sandwich *m* grillé **(b)** *(tribute)* porter un toast à

toaster ['təʊstə(r)] *n* grille-pain *m inv*

toastie ['təʊstɪ] *n Fam (toasted sandwich)* sandwich *m* grillé

tobacco [tə'bækəʊ] *(pl* **tobaccos)** *n* tabac *m*; **t. pouch** blague *f* à tabac

tobacconist [tə'bækənɪst] *n* marchand(e) *m,f* de tabac; *Br* **t.'s (shop)** (bureau *m* de) tabac *m*

toboggan [tə'bɒgən] **1** *n* luge *f*
2 *vi* faire de la luge

today [tə'deɪ] *adv* aujourd'hui; **a year ago t.** il y a juste un an aujourd'hui; **t.'s date** la date d'aujourd'hui; **t.'s paper** le journal du jour

toddle ['tɒdəl] *vi (of infant)* commencer à marcher; *Fam* **to t. off** ficher le camp

toddler ['tɒdlə(r)] *n* enfant *mf* qui commence à marcher

to-do [tə'duː] *n Fam* remue-ménage *m inv*; **what a t.!** quelle histoire!

toe [təʊ] **1** *n* **(a)** *(of foot)* orteil *m*, doigt *m* de pied; *(of sock, shoe)* bout *m*; **big/little t.** gros/petit orteil **(b)** *(idioms)* **to be on one's toes** être en alerte; **to keep sb on his toes** ne pas laisser de répit à qn; **to tread on sb's toes** marcher sur les pieds de qn
2 *vt* **to t. the line** bien se tenir

toehold ['təʊhəʊld] *n (in climbing)* prise *f* de pied; *Fig* **to gain a t. in the market** mettre un pied sur le marché

toenail ['təʊneɪl] *n* ongle *m* de pied

toffee ['tɒfɪ] *n* caramel *m* (au beurre); *Fam* **he can't sing for t.** il chante comme un pied; **t. apple** pomme *f* d'amour

tofu ['təʊfuː] *n* tofu *m*

together [tə'geðə(r)] **1** *adv* ensemble; **t. with** ainsi que, en même temps que
2 *adj Fam (person)* équilibré(e)

togetherness [tə'geðənɪs] *n* unité *f*, harmonie *f*

toggle ['tɒgəl] **1** *n (on coat)* olive *f*; *Comptr & Elec* **t. switch** commande *f* à bascule
2 *vi Comptr* basculer

Togo ['təʊgəʊ] *n* le Togo

Togolese [təʊgəʊ'liːz] **1** *n* Togolais(e) *m,f*
2 *adj* togolais(e)

togs [tɒgz] *npl Fam (clothes)* fringues *fpl*

toil [tɔɪl] **1** *n Lit* labeur *m*
2 *vi (work hard)* travailler dur; **to t. away at sth** peiner sur qch; **to t. up a hill** gravir péniblement une colline

toilet ['tɔɪlɪt] *n* **(a)** *(lavatory)* toilettes *fpl*; **to go to the t.** aller aux toilettes; **t. paper** papier *m* hygiénique; **t. roll** rouleau *m* de papier hygiénique; **t. seat** siège *m* des toilettes **(b)** *Old-fashioned (washing and dressing)* toilette *f*; **t. bag** trousse *f* de toilette; **t. soap** savon *m* de toilette

toiletries ['tɔɪlɪtrɪz] *npl* articles *mpl* de toilette

toilet-trained ['tɔɪlɪttreɪnd] *adj* propre

toilet-training ['tɔɪlɪttreɪnɪŋ] *n* apprentissage *m* de la propreté

token ['təʊkən] **1** *n* **(a)** *(symbol)* signe *m*, marque *f*; **as a t. of my appreciation** en témoignage de mon appréciation; **by the same t.** de même, pareillement **(b)** *(for vending machine)* jeton *m*
2 *adj (resistance, effort)* symbolique; **I was the t. woman on the committee** j'étais la seule femme de la commission, parce qu'il en fallait une

Tokyo ['təʊkɪəʊ] *n* Tokyo

told [təʊld] *pt & pp of* **tell**

tolerable ['tɒlərəbəl] *adj* **(a)** *(bearable)* tolérable, supportable **(b)** *(reasonably good)* acceptable

tolerance ['tɒlərəns] *n* tolérance *f*; **to have a high/low t. for sth** bien/mal tolérer qch

tolerant ['tɒlərənt] *adj* tolérant(e); **to be t. of sb/sth** tolérer qn/qch

tolerate ['tɒləreɪt] *vt* tolérer

toleration [tɒlə'reɪʃən] *n* tolérance *f*

toll¹ [təʊl] *n* **(a)** *(charge)* péage *m*; **t. bridge** pont *m* à péage; **t. road** route *f* à péage **(b)** *(of dead, injured)* nombre *m* de victimes; *Fig* **to take its t.** faire des dégâts

toll² **1** *vt (bell)* sonner
2 *vi (of bell)* sonner

toll-free [təʊl'friː] *Am* **1** *adj* **t. number** ≃ numéro *m* vert
2 *adv (call)* gratuitement

Tom [tɒm] *n Fam* **any T., Dick or Harry** le premier venu

tom [tɒm] *n Fam* matou *m*

tomahawk ['tɒməhɔːk] *n* tomahawk *m*

tomato [tə'mɑːtəʊ, *Am* tə'meɪtəʊ] *(pl* **tomatoes)** *n* tomate *f*; **t. juice** jus *m* de tomate; **t. ketchup** ketchup *m*; **t. purée** concentré *m* de tomates; **t. sauce** *(for pasta)* sauce *f* tomate; *(ketchup)* ketchup; **t. soup** soupe *f* à la tomate

tomb [tuːm] *n* tombe *f*

tomboy ['tɒmbɔɪ] *n* garçon *m* manqué

tombstone ['tuːmstəʊn] *n* pierre *f* tombale

tomcat ['tɒmkæt] *n* matou *m*

tome [təʊm] *n Formal* gros volume *m*

tomfoolery [tɒm'fuːlərɪ] *n Fam* bêtises *fpl*

tomorrow [tə'mɒrəʊ] **1** *n* demain *m*; *Fam* **to do sth like there's no t.** faire qch frénétiquement
2 *adv* demain; **t. morning/evening** demain matin/soir

tom-tom ['tɒmtɒm] *n* tam-tam *m*

ton [tʌn] *n (a)* *(weight)* tonne *f* (b) *(idioms) Fam* **to weigh a t.** peser une tonne; *Fam* **tons of** des tonnes de; *Fam* **to come down on sb like a t. of bricks** tomber dessus à qn

tone [təʊn] *n* **(a)** *(of voice)* ton *m*; *(quality of sound)* sonorité *f*; **don't speak to me in that t. of voice** ne me parle pas sur ce ton; **leave your name and number after the t.** *(on answering machine)* laissez votre nom et votre numéro de téléphone après le signal sonore; *Fig* **it set the t. for the evening** et le ton a été donné pour le reste de la soirée; *Fig*

to raise/lower the t. of the neighbourhood améliorer/faire baisser le standing du quartier **(b)** *(colour)* ton *m* ▸ **tone down** *vt sep (colour)* adoucir; *Fig (remarks)* modérer ▸ **tone up** *vt sep (muscles)* raffermir, tonifier

tone-deaf [təʊn'def] *adj* **to be t.** ne pas avoir d'oreille

Tonga ['tɒŋɡə] *n* les îles *fpl* Tonga

Tongan ['tɒŋɡən] **1** *n* **(a)** *(person)* Tonguien(enne) *m,f* **(b)** *(language)* tongan *m* **2** *adj* tonguien(enne)

tongs [tɒŋz] *npl* **(pair of) t.** pince *f*; **(curling) t.** *(for hair)* fer *m* à friser

tongue [tʌŋ] *n* **(a)** *(in mouth, of land, flame)* langue *f*; *(of shoe)* languette *f*; *(language)* langue *f*; **to stick one's t.** out tirer la langue; **t. twister** = mot ou phrase difficile à prononcer **(b)** *(idioms)* **hold your t.!** tiens ta langue!, tais-toi!; **have you lost your t.?** tu as perdu ta langue?; **to say sth t. in cheek** dire qch en plaisantant

tongue-tied ['tʌŋtaɪd] *adj* muet(ette)

tonic ['tɒnɪk] *n also Fig* tonique *m*; **t. (water)** Schweppes® *m*

tonight [tə'naɪt] **1** *(evening)* ce soir *m*; *(night)* cette nuit *f* **2** *adv (evening)* ce soir; *(night)* cette nuit

tonnage ['tʌnɪdʒ] *n Naut (of ship)* tonnage *m*

tonne [tʌn] *n* tonne *f*

tonsil ['tɒnsəl] *n* amygdale *f*; **to have one's tonsils out** se faire opérer des amygdales

tonsillitis [tɒnsɪ'laɪtɪs] *n* angine *f*; **to have t.** avoir une angine

too [tuː] *adv* **(a)** *(excessively)* trop; **t. many people** trop de gens; **I know her all** *or* **only t. well** je ne la connais que trop; **you're t. kind** vous êtes trop aimable; **he's not t. well** today il ne va pas trop bien aujourd'hui; **t. bad** tant pis; *Fam* **t. right!** et comment! **(b)** *(also)* aussi **(c)** *(moreover)* en plus

took [tʊk] *pt of* **take**

tool [tuːl] *n* **(a)** *(implement)* outil *m*; **(set of) tools** outillage *m*; **t. bag** trousse *f* à outils; *also Comptr* **t. box** boîte *f* à outils; **t. kit** trousse *f* à outils; **t. shed** remise *f* **(b)** *(means, instrument)* instrument *m*

toot [tuːt] **1** *n* coup *m* de Klaxon® **2** *vt* **to t. the horn** klaxonner; **to t. sb** klaxonner qn **3** *vi* klaxonner

tooth [tuːθ] *(pl* **teeth** [tiːθ]*)* *n* **(a)** *(of person, saw, comb)* dent *f*; **to cut a t.** percer une dent; **t. decay** carie *f* **(b)** *(idioms)* **to fight t. and nail** se défendre bec et ongles; **to lie through one's teeth** mentir effrontément; **in the teeth of opposition** malgré l'opposition; **armed to the teeth** armé(e) jusqu'aux dents; *Fam* **to get one's teeth into sth** se mettre à fond dans qch; *Fam* **to be sick to the back teeth with sb/sth** en avoir ras le bol de qn/qch; *Fam* **to be long in the t.** n'être plus tout jeune

toothache ['tuːθeɪk] *n* mal *m* de dents; **to have t.** avoir mal aux dents

toothbrush ['tuːθbrʌʃ] *n* brosse *f* à dents

toothless ['tuːθlɪs] *adj* édenté(e), sans dents; *Fig (powerless)* sans pouvoir

toothpaste ['tuːθpeɪst] *n* dentifrice *m*

toothpick ['tuːθpɪk] *n* cure-dents *m inv*

toothy ['tuːθɪ] *adj* **t. grin** large sourire *m*

top[1] [tɒp] *n (toy)* toupie *f*

top[2] **1** *n* **(a)** *(highest part) (of tree, mountain, tower, head)* sommet *m*; *(of page, map)* haut *m*; **at the t. of the stairs/street** en haut des escaliers/de la rue; **to be (at the) t. of the class** être premier(ère) de la classe; **from t. to bottom**

de haut en bas; *Fig* de fond en comble; **at the t. of one's voice** à tue-tête; **to go over the t.** *Mil* partir à l'assaut; *Fig* aller trop loin; *Fig* **over the t.** *(excessive)* exagéré(e); **to make it to the t.** parvenir au sommet **(b)** *(lid) (of box)* couvercle *m*; *(of bottle)* bouchon *m*; *(of pen)* capuchon *m* **(c)** *(surface)* dessus *m* **(d)** *(garment)* haut *m* **(e)** **on t.** dessus; **on t. of** sur; *Fig* **to be on t. of sth** maîtriser qch; **you mustn't let things get on t. of you** il ne faut pas se laisser dépasser par les événements; **to come out on t.** prendre le dessus; **to feel on t. of the world** se sentir en pleine forme **2** *adj* **(a)** *(highest) (shelf, drawer)* du haut; *(floor)* dernier(ère); **the t. people** *(in society)* les gens *mpl* en vue; *(in an organization)* la direction *f*; *Fam* **the t. brass** les gros bonnets *mpl*; **t. coat** *(of paint)* dernière couche *f*; **t. deck** *(of bus)* impériale *f*; *Fam Fig* **t. dog** chef *m*; **to feel on t. form** se sentir en pleine forme; *Aut* **t. gear** *(fourth)* quatrième *f* *(vitesse f)*; *(fifth)* cinquième *f* *(vitesse f)*; **t. hat** haut-de-forme *m*; **t. security** haute sécurité *f*; **t. speed** vitesse *f* de pointe; *Fig* **at t. speed** à toute vitesse **(b)** *(best, major)* premier(ère); **the t. ten** les dix premiers; **to come t. in sth** arriver premier en qch **3** *vt* **(a)** *(place on top of)* couvrir **(with** de); *(cake, ice cream)* napper; **and to t. it all** et pour couronner le tout **(b)** *(exceed)* dépasser **(c)** *(be at the top of)* être en tête de; **to t. the bill** être la tête d'affiche **(d)** *Br very Fam* **to t. oneself** *(commit suicide)* se foutre en l'air ▸ **top up** *vt sep (glass, tank)* remplir; *(sum of money)* compléter

top-heavy [tɒp'hevɪ] *adj (structure)* trop lourd(e) du haut, déséquilibré(e); *(organization)* aux dirigeants trop nombreux

topic ['tɒpɪk] *n* sujet *m*, thème *m*

topical ['tɒpɪk(ə)l] *adj* d'actualité

topless ['tɒplɪs] *adj (woman)* aux seins nus; **to go t.** faire du monokini

top-level ['tɒplevəl] *adj* au plus haut niveau

topmost ['tɒpməʊst] *adj* le (la) plus haut(e)

top-notch ['tɒpnɒtʃ] *adj Fam* de première classe

topography [tə'pɒɡrəfɪ] *n* topographie *f*

topping ['tɒpɪŋ] *n (for pizza)* garniture *f*; *(for cake, ice cream)* nappage *m*

topple ['tɒpəl] *vt* faire tomber, renverser **2** *vi* tomber

top-secret ['tɒpsiːkrɪt] *adj* top secret(ète)

topsoil ['tɒpsɔɪl] *n* couche *f* arable

topsy-turvy [tɒpsɪ'tɜːvɪ] *Fam* **1** *adj (untidy)* sens dessus dessous; *(confused)* tordu(e) **2** *adv (untidily)* sens dessus dessous

torch [tɔːtʃ] **1** *n* **(a)** *(burning)* torche *f*; *Fig* **to carry a t. for sb** aimer qn secrètement **(b)** *Br (electric)* lampe *f* de poche **2** *vt* incendier; mettre le feu à

torchlight ['tɔːtʃlaɪt] *n* **by t.** à la lumière d'une lampe de poche; **t. procession** retraite *f* aux flambeaux

tore [tɔː] *pt of* **tear**[2]

torment 1 *n* ['tɔːment] supplice *m*; **to be in t.** être au supplice **2** *vt* [tɔː'ment] tourmenter

tormentor [tɔː'mentə(r)] *n* bourreau *m*

torn [tɔːn] *pp of* **tear**[2]

tornado [tɔː'neɪdəʊ] *n* tornade *f*

Toronto [tə'rɒntəʊ] *n* Toronto

torpedo [tɔːˈpiːdəʊ] **1** n torpille f; **t. boat** torpilleur m, vedette f lance-torpilles
2 vt also Fig torpiller

torpid [ˈtɔːpɪd] adj engourdi(e), léthargique

torpor [ˈtɔːpə(r)] n torpeur f

torrent [ˈtɒrənt] n torrent m; Fig (of abuse, insults) flot m; **it's raining in torrents** il pleut à torrents

torrential [tɒˈrenʃəl] adj torrentiel(elle)

torrid [ˈtɒrɪd] adj also Fig torride

torso [ˈtɔːsəʊ] n torse m

tortoise [ˈtɔːtəs] n tortue f

tortoiseshell [ˈtɔːtəsʃel] n écaille f (de tortue); **t. (cat)** chat m noir, blanc et roux

tortuous [ˈtɔːtjʊəs] adj tortueux(euse)

torture [ˈtɔːtʃə(r)] **1** n torture f; Fig **it was sheer t.!** c'était un vrai supplice!; **t. chamber** chambre f de torture
2 vt also Fig torturer

Tory [ˈtɔːrɪ] n & adj Tory m, conservateur(trice) m,f

tosh [tɒʃ] n Br Fam bêtises fpl

toss [tɒs] **1** n (a) (of ball) lancer m; (of head) mouvement m brusque; **to decide sth on the t.** of a coin décider qch à pile ou face; **to argue the t.** discuter inutilement (**b**) Br very Fam **not to give a t.** s'en ficher
2 vt (throw) lancer; (pancake) faire sauter; (salad) remuer; **to t. sth to sb** lancer qch à qn; **to t. a coin** jouer à pile ou face; **to t. one's head** rejeter la tête en arrière; **the ship was tossed by the sea** le bateau était ballotté par la mer
3 vi **to t. (up) for sth** jouer qch à pile ou face; **to t. and turn** (in bed) se tourner et se retourner (pour trouver le sommeil)
▸ **toss about, toss around** vt sep (ship) ballotter; Fig (idea) lancer
▸ **toss off** vt sep (**a**) (write) expédier (**b**) Vulg (masturbate) **to t. oneself off** se branler; **to t. sb off** branler qn
▸ **toss out** vt sep jeter

tosser [ˈtɒsə(r)] n Br very Fam con (conne) m,f

toss-up [ˈtɒsʌp] n **to have a t.** jouer à pile ou face; Fam **it was a t. between Jamaica and Antigua** nous avons dû choisir entre la Jamaïque et Antigua; **it's a t. whether or not she'll say yes** je ne sais vraiment pas si elle va dire oui

tot [tɒt] n (**a**) (child) tout-petit m (**b**) (of drink) (petite) goutte f
▸ **tot up** vt sep additionner

total [ˈtəʊtəl] **1** n total m; **in t.** au total
2 adj total(e); **t. eclipse** éclipse f totale
3 vt (**a**) (sum) se monter à (**b**) Am Fam (wreck) bousiller

totalitarian [təʊtælɪˈteərɪən] adj totalitaire

totality [təʊˈtælɪtɪ] n totalité f

totally [ˈtəʊtəlɪ] adv totalement

tote[1] [təʊt] n (in betting) totalisateur m, totaliseur m

tote[2] vt Fam (carry) trimbal(l)er

totem pole [ˈtəʊtəmˈpəʊl] n totem m

totter [ˈtɒtə(r)] vi also Fig chanceler; **to t. in/out** entrer/ sortir d'un pas chancelant

toucan [ˈtuːkæn] n toucan m

touch [tʌtʃ] **1** n (**a**) (act of touching) toucher m, contact m; **I felt a t. on my shoulder** j'ai senti qu'on me touchait le l'épaule; **it was t. and go whether...** il n'était pas certain que... + subjunctive
(**b**) (sense) toucher m; (feel) contact m; **hard/soft to the t.** dur/doux au toucher; **he's lost his t.** il a perdu la main
(**c**) (detail) **there were some nice touches in the film** il y avait quelques bons passages dans le film
(**d**) (small amount) pointe f; **a t. (too) strong/short** un peu trop fort(e)/court(e); **to have a t. of flu** être un peu grippé(e)

(**e**) (communication) **to be/get in t. with sb** être/se mettre en contact avec qn; **to stay in/lose t. with sb** rester en/ perdre contact avec qn
(**f**) (in football, rugby) **in t.** en touche; **t. judge** juge m de touche
2 vt (physically, emotionally) toucher; (interfere with) toucher à; **to t. bottom** (of ship, economy) toucher le fond; Fam **t. wood!** je touche du bois!; **I never t. cigarettes** je ne touche jamais aux cigarettes; **you haven't touched your meal** tu n'as pas touché à ton repas; **the law can't t. her** la loi ne peut rien contre elle; Fig **there's nothing to t. it** c'est sans égal; **there's nothing to t. her** elle est imbattable
▸ **touch down** vi (of plane) atterrir
▸ **touch on** vt insep aborder
▸ **touch up** vt sep (**a**) (picture) retoucher (**b**) Br Fam (molest) peloter

touchdown [ˈtʌtʃdaʊn] n (**a**) (of plane) atterrissage m (**b**) (in American football) but m

touched [tʌtʃt] adj (**a**) (moved) touché(e), ému(e) (**b**) Fam (mad) toqué(e)

touching [ˈtʌtʃɪŋ] adj (moving) touchant(e), émouvant(e)

touchline [ˈtʌtʃlaɪn] n ligne f de touche

touch-sensitive screen [ˈtʌtʃˈsensɪtɪvˈskriːn] n Comptr écran m tactile

touchstone [ˈtʌtʃstəʊn] n pierre f de touche

touch-type [ˈtʌtʃtaɪp] vi taper au toucher

touchy [ˈtʌtʃɪ] adj (subject) délicat(e); (person) susceptible (**about** à propos de)

tough [tʌf] **1** adj (**a**) (strict, severe) dur(e); (resistant) résistant(e), solide; Fam **a t. guy** un dur à cuire; **to get t. (with sb)** se montrer plus sévère (avec qn) (**b**) (difficult) dur(e), difficile; (unfair) dur(e); Fam **t. luck!** pas de chance!; Ironic **t. tant pis!**
2 adv **to act t.** jouer au dur
3 n dur(e) m,f

toughen [ˈtʌfən] vt (person, skin) endurcir; (penalties, conditions) durcir; **toughened glass** verre m trempé

toughness [ˈtʌfnɪs] n (of meat, skin, conditions) dureté f; (of task) difficulté f; (of person) (strength) force f; (hardness) dureté f

toupee [ˈtuːpeɪ] n postiche m

tour [tʊə(r)] **1** n (by tourist) voyage m; (of building, town) visite f; (by pop group, theatre company) tournée f; **to go on a t.** (of tourist) faire un voyage organisé; **to go on t.** (of pop group, theatre company) partir en tournée; Mil **t. of duty** service m; **t. of inspection** tournée f d'inspection; **t. guide** (person) guide m f; **t. operator** voyagiste m
2 vt (country, hospital) visiter; (of pop group, theatre company) être en tournée à/en
3 vi (of tourist) faire du tourisme, voyager; (of pop group, theatre company) être en tournée

tour de force [tʊədəˈfɔːs] n tour m de force

tourism [ˈtʊərɪzəm] n tourisme m

tourist [ˈtʊərɪst] n touriste mf; **t. attraction** site m touristique; **t. class** classe f touriste; **t. (information) office** syndicat m d'initiative, office m du tourisme; Fam **t. trap** piège m à touristes

tournament [ˈtʊənəmənt] n tournoi m

tourniquet [ˈtʊənɪkeɪ] n Med garrot m

tousle [ˈtaʊzəl] vt ébouriffer

tout [taʊt] **1** n (ticket) **t.** revendeur(euse) m,f de billets (au marché noir)
2 vt (tickets, goods) revendre
3 vi **to t. for business** racoler des clients

tow [təʊ] **1** n **to give sb a t.** remorquer qn; **on t.** en

remorque; *Fam* **to have someone in t.** avoir qn dans son sillage; **t. truck** dépanneuse *f*
2 *vt* remorquer; **to t. a car away** enlever une voiture

toward [tə'wɔːd] = towards

towards [tə'wɔːdz] *prep* **(a)** *(in space, time)* vers **(b)** *(directed at) (of feelings, behaviour)* envers **(c)** *(contributing to)* to contribute **t.** the cost of sth participer au coût de qch; **10% of the budget will go t.** improving safety 10% du budget sera destiné à l'amélioration de la sécurité

towbar ['təʊbɑː(r)] *n* barre *f* de remorquage

towel ['taʊəl] **1** *n* serviette *f* (de toilette); **t. rail** porte-serviette *m*
2 *vt* **to t. oneself (dry)** se sécher, s'essuyer

towelling, *Am* **toweling** ['taʊəlɪŋ] *n* tissu-éponge *m*

tower ['taʊə(r)] **1** *n* tour *f*; *Fig* **a t. of strength** un roc; *Br* **t. block** tour; *Comptr* **t. system** tour
2 *vi* **to t. over sb/sth** dominer qn/qch

towering ['taʊərɪŋ] *adj* immense

town [taʊn] *n* ville *f*; **to go into t.** aller en ville, to go out on the **t.** faire la fête en ville; *Fam Fig* **to go to t. (on sth)** mettre le paquet (sur qch); **t. centre** centre-ville *m*; **t. clerk** secrétaire *mf* de mairie; **t. council** conseil *m* municipal; **t. hall** mairie *f*; **t. planner** urbaniste *mf*; **t. planning** urbanisme *m*

townsfolk ['taʊnzfəʊk] *npl* citadins *mpl*

township ['taʊnʃɪp] *n (in North America)* municipalité *f*; *(in South Africa)* township *f*

townspeople ['taʊnzpiːpəl] *npl* citadins *mpl*

towpath ['taʊpɑːθ] *n* chemin *m* de halage

towrope ['təʊrəʊp] *n* câble *m* de remorque

toxic ['tɒksɪk] *adj* toxique

toxin ['tɒksɪn] *n* toxine *f*

toy [tɔɪ] **1** *n* jouet *m*; **t. soldier** petit soldat *m*; **t. shop** magasin *m* de jouets
2 *vi* **to t. with sb** jouer avec qn; **to t. with an idea** caresser une idée; **to t. with sb's affections** jouer avec les sentiments de qn

toyboy ['tɔɪbɔɪ] *n Fam* jeune amant *m (d'une femme plus âgée)*

trace [treɪs] **1** *n* trace *f*; **without t.** sans laisser de traces; *Chem* **t. element** oligo-élément *m*
2 *vt* **(a)** *(diagram, picture)* tracer **(b)** *(person)* retrouver (la trace de); *(development, history)* retracer

trachea [trə'kiːə] *(pl* **tracheae** [trə'kiːiː]*) n Anat* trachée *f*

track [træk] **1** *n* **(a)** *(mark)* trace *f*, *(trail)* piste *f* **(b)** *(path)* piste *f*, chemin *m*; *(in athletics)* piste; *Sp* **t. and field events** épreuves *fpl* d'athlétisme; *Fig* **t. record** passé *m*; **t. shoes** chaussures *fpl* d'athlétisme **(c)** *(on record, CD)* morceau *m* **(d)** *(of tank, tractor)* chenille *f* **(e)** *(railway line)* voie *f* **(f)** *(idioms)* **to be on the right t.** être sur la bonne voie; **to keep t. of sth** surveiller qch; **to lose t. of sb** perdre qn de vue; **I've lost t. of how much money I've spent** je ne sais plus combien d'argent j'ai dépensé; **to stop sb in his tracks** stopper qn net; *Fam* **to make tracks** filer, mettre les voiles
2 *vt (animal)* suivre à la trace; *(missile)* suivre la trajectoire de; *(person)* traquer

▸ **track down** *vt sep (locate)* trouver

tracked [trækt] *adj (vehicle)* chenillé(e)

tracker dog ['trækə'dɒg] *n* chien *m* policier

tracksuit ['træks(j)uːt] *n* survêtement *m*; **t. top** veste *f* de survêtement; **t. trousers** *or* **bottoms** pantalon *m* de survêtement

tract¹ [trækt] *n* **(a)** *(of land)* étendue *f* **(b)** *Anat (respiratory, digestive)* appareil *m*

tract² *n (pamphlet)* tract *m*

tractable ['træktəbəl] *adj (person, animal)* docile

traction ['trækʃən] *n (force)* traction *f*; *Med* **to be in t.** être en extension; **t. engine** locomobile *f*

tractor ['træktə(r)] *n (vehicle)* tracteur *m*; *Comptr* **t. feed** alimentation *f* par entraînement

trade [treɪd] **1** *n* **(a)** *Com (commerce)* commerce *m*; **t. association** association *f* professionnelle; **t. deficit** déficit *m* commercial; **t. discount** remise *f* professionnelle; **t. embargo** embargo *m* commercial; **t. fair** foire *f* *ou* exposition *f* commerciale; **t. gap** déficit commercial; **t. name** *(of product)* nom *m* de marque; *(of firm)* raison *f* commerciale; *also Fig* **t. secret** secret *m* de fabrication; *Geog* **t. winds** alizés *mpl* **(b)** *(swap)* échange *m*; **to do a t.** faire un échange **(c)** *(profession)* métier *m*; **he's an electrician by t.** il est électricien (de son métier); **t. union** syndicat *m*; **t. unionist** syndicaliste *mf*
2 *vt* **to t. sth (for sth)** échanger qch (contre qch); **to t. places with sb** changer de place avec qn; **to t. insults/ blows** échanger des insultes/coups
3 *vi (commerce)* faire du commerce

▸ **trade in** *vt sep* faire reprendre

▸ **trade on** *vt insep (exploit)* profiter de

trade-in ['treɪdɪn] *n* reprise *f*

trademark ['treɪdmɑːk] *n* marque *f* (de fabrique); *Fig* signe *m* distinctif

trade-off ['treɪdɒf] *n* compromis *m*

trader ['treɪdə(r)] *n* commerçant(e) *m,f*, marchand(e) *m,f*; *(on stock exchange)* opérateur(trice) *m,f*

tradesman ['treɪdzmən] *n* commerçant(e) *m,f*

trading ['treɪdɪŋ] *n* **t. partner** partenaire *m* commercial; **t. post** comptoir *m* commercial; **t. stamp** timbre-prime *m*

tradition [trə'dɪʃən] *n* tradition *f*

traditional [trə'dɪʃənəl] *adj* traditionnel(elle)

traditionalist [trə'dɪʃənəlɪst] *n & adj* traditionaliste *mf*

traffic ['træfɪk] **1** *n* **(a)** *(vehicles)* circulation *f*, trafic *m*; **t. cone** cône *m* de signalisation; *Fam* **t. cop** agent *m* de la circulation; **t. island** refuge *m*; **t. jam** embouteillage *m*; *Br* **t. lights** feux *mpl* (tricolores *ou* de signalisation); **t. police** police *f* de la route; *Br* **t. warden** contractuel(elle) *m,f* **(b)** *(trade)* trafic *m*
2 *vt* faire le trafic de
3 *vi* faire du trafic (in de)

trafficker ['træfɪkə(r)] *n* trafiquant(e) *m,f*

tragedy ['trædʒɪdɪ] *n* tragédie *f*

tragic ['trædʒɪk] *adj* tragique

tragically ['trædʒɪklɪ] *adv* tragiquement

trail [treɪl] **1** *n* **(a)** *(of smoke, blood)* traînée *f*; **to be on the t. of sb/sth** être sur les traces *ou* la piste de qn/qch **(b)** *(path)* sentier *m*, piste *f*; **t. bike** moto *f* de cross
2 *vt (drag)* traîner
3 *vi* **(a)** *(drag)* traîner **(b)** *(move slowly)* se traîner **(c)** *(in sport, contest)* **to be trailing (behind)** être menée(e)

▸ **trail away, trail off** *vi (of voice)* se taire; *(of sound)* s'arrêter

trailblazer ['treɪlbleɪzə(r)] *n* pionnier(ère) *m,f*

trailer ['treɪlə(r)] *n* **(a)** *(vehicle)* remorque *f*; *Am (caravan)* camping-car *m* **(b)** *Br (for film, TV programme)* bande-annonce *f*

train [treɪn] **1** *n* **(a)** *(means of transport)* train *m* **(b)** *(series)* suite *f*, enchaînement *m*; **t. of thought** enchaînement d'idées **(c)** *(retinue)* suite *f* **(d)** *(of dress)* traîne *f*
2 *vt* **(a)** *(person)* former; *(animal)* dresser; **to t. sb for sth/ to do sth** former qn à qch/à faire qch **(b)** *(gun, telescope)* braquer (on sur)
3 *vi* **(a)** *(of athlete, soldier)* s'entraîner; **to t. as a nurse/ hairdresser** suivre une formation d'infirmière/de coiffeur

trained [treɪnd] *adj* **(a)** *(animal)* dressé(e) **(b)** *(teacher, nurse)* diplômé(e) **(c)** *(eye, ear)* exercé(e)

trainee [treɪˈniː] *n* stagiaire *mf*

trainer [ˈtreɪnə(r)] *n* **(a)** *(of athlete, team, racehorse)* entraîneur *m*; *(of animals)* dresseur(euse) *m,f* **(b)** *(shoe)* chaussure *f* de sport **(c) t. (aircraft)** avion-école *m*

training [ˈtreɪnɪŋ] *n (in sport)* entraînement *m*; *(for job)* formation *f*; **to be in t. (for)** *(of athlete, team)* s'entraîner (pour); **to be out of t.** manquer d'entraînement; **t. course** stage *m* (de formation); **t. officer** officier *m* instructeur

trainload [ˈtreɪnləʊd] *n a* **t. of** un train plein de

trainspotter [ˈtreɪnspɒtə(r)] *n Br* = personne dont le passe-temps est de noter les numéros des trains; *Fam Pej* **he's a bit of a t.** il est vraiment ringard

traipse [treɪps] *vi Fam* traîner

trait [treɪt] *n* trait *m* (de caractère)

traitor [ˈtreɪtə(r)] *n* traître(esse) *m,f*

trajectory [trəˈdʒektərɪ] *n* trajectoire *f*

tram [træm] *n Br* tramway *m*

tramline [ˈtræmlaɪn] *n* ligne *f* de tramway; **tramlines** *(in tennis)* lignes *fpl* de côté

tramp [træmp] **1** *n* **(a)** *Br (vagabond)* clochard(e) *m,f* **(b)** *Am very Fam (immoral woman)* traînée *f* **(c) t. (steamer)** tramp *m* **(d)** *(walk)* promenade *f*
2 *vt (country)* arpenter, parcourir
3 *vi* marcher (d'un pas lourd)

trample [ˈtræmpəl] **1** *vt* piétiner; **to t. sth underfoot** fouler qch aux pieds
2 *vi* **to t. on sb/sth** piétiner qn/qch

trampoline [ˈtræmpəˈliːn] *n* trampoline *m*

trance [trɑːns] *n* transe *f*; **to go into a t.** entrer *ou* se mettre en transe

tranquil [ˈtræŋkwɪl] *adj* tranquille, calme

tranquillity, *Am* **tranquility** [træŋˈkwɪlɪtɪ] *n* tranquillité *f*, calme *m*

tranquillizer, *Am* **tranquilizer** [ˈtræŋkwɪlaɪzə(r)] *n* tranquillisant *m*, calmant *m*

transaction [trænˈzækʃən] *n* transaction *f*, opération *f*

transatlantic [trænzətˈlæntɪk] *adj* transatlantique

transcend [trænˈsend] *vt (go beyond)* transcender; *(be superior to)* surpasser

transcendental [trænsenˈdentəl] *adj* transcendantal(e); **t. meditation** méditation *f* transcendantale

transcontinental [trænzkɒntɪˈnentəl] *adj* transcontinental(e)

transcribe [trænsˈkraɪb] *vt* transcrire

transcript [ˈtrænskrɪpt] *n* transcription *f*

transcription [trænsˈkrɪpʃən] *n* transcription *f*

transfer 1 *n* [ˈtrænsfɜː(r)] **(a)** *(move)* transfert *m*; *(of employee)* mutation *f*; *(of power)* passation *f*; **t. fee** *(for sportsman)* prime *f* de transfert; **t. lounge** *(in airport)* salle *f* de transit; **t. passenger** passager *m* en transit; *Comptr* **t. speed** vitesse *f* de transfert **(b)** *(sticker)* transfert *m*
2 *vt* [trænsˈfɜː(r)] transférer; *(employee)* muter; *(attention, affection)* déplacer
3 *vi* [trænsˈfɜː(r)] être transféré(e) **(to** dans); *(between planes, trains)* changer

transferable [trænsˈfɜːrəbəl] *adj* transmissible; **not t.** *(on ticket)* titre de transport nominal

transfigure [trænsˈfɪgə(r)] *vt* transfigurer

transfix [trænsˈfɪks] *vt* transpercer; *Fig* **to be transfixed with fear** être pétrifié(e) par la peur

transform [trænsˈfɔːm] *vt* transformer **(into** en)

transformation [trænsfəˈmeɪʃən] *n* transformation *f*

transformer [trænsˈfɔːmə(r)] *n Elec* transformateur *m*

transfusion [trænsˈfjuːʒən] *n* **(blood) t.** transfusion *f* (sanguine)

transgress [trænzˈgres] *Formal* **1** *vt (law)* transgresser, enfreindre
2 *vi (violate law)* transgresser la loi; *(sin)* pécher

transient [ˈtrænzɪənt] *adj* éphémère

transistor [trænˈzɪstə(r)] *n Elec* transistor *m*; **t. (radio)** transistor

transit [ˈtrænzɪt] *n* transit *m*; **in t.** en transit; **t. camp** camp *m* de transit; **t. visa** visa *m* de transit

transition [trænˈzɪʃən] *n* transition *f*; **the t. from sth to sth** le passage de qch à qch

transitional [trænˈzɪʃənəl] *adj* transitoire, de transition

transitive [ˈtrænzɪtɪv] *adj Gram* transitif(ive)

transitory [ˈtrænsɪtərɪ] *adj* transitoire

translate [trænzˈleɪt] **1** *vt* traduire **(from/into** de/en); *Fig* **to t. ideas into action** mettre ses idées en pratique
2 *vi (of person)* faire de la traduction; *(of word, expression)* se traduire **(as** par)

translation [trænzˈleɪʃən] *n (of language)* traduction *f*

translator [trænzˈleɪtə(r)] *n* traducteur(trice) *m,f*

transliterate [trænzˈlɪtəreɪt] *vt* transcrire

translucent [trænzˈluːsənt] *adj* translucide

transmission [trænzˈmɪʃən] *n (action)* transmission *f*; *(TV, radio programme)* émission *f*; **t. shaft** *(in vehicle)* arbre *m* de transmission

transmit [trænzˈmɪt] *vt* transmettre; *(TV, radio programme)* diffuser

transmitter [trænzˈmɪtə(r)] *n (emitter)* émetteur *m*; *(relay station)* réémetteur *m*

transparent [trænsˈpærənt] *adj* **(a)** *(see-through)* transparent(e) **(b)** *(obvious)* évident(e)

transpire [trænsˈpaɪə(r)] **1** *vt (become apparent)* **it transpired that…** il s'est avéré que…; **she transpired to be…** elle s'est avérée être…
2 *vi (happen)* arriver, se passer

transplant 1 *n* [ˈtrænsplɑːnt] *(of organ)* transplantation *f*, greffe *f*
2 *vt* [trænsˈplɑːnt] **(a)** *(organ)* transplanter, greffer **(b)** *(population)* transplanter

transport 1 *n* [ˈtrænspɔːt] transport *m*; *Br* **t. café** routier *m (restaurant)*; **t. costs** frais *mpl* de transport
2 *vt* [trænzˈpɔːt] transporter

transportation [trænzpɔːˈteɪʃən] *n* transport *m*; *Hist (as punishment)* transportation *f*

transporter [trænsˈpɔːtə(r)] *n (vehicle)* camion *m* pour transport d'automobiles

transpose [trænsˈpəʊz] *vt* transposer

transsexual [trænz)ˈseksjʊəl] *n* transsexuel(elle) *m,f*

Transvaal [ˈtrɑːnzvɑːl] *n* **the T.** le Transvaal

transverse [ˈtrænzvɜːs] *adj* transversal(e)

transvestite [trænzˈvestaɪt] *n* travesti *m*

trap [træp] **1** *n* **(a)** *(in hunting)* & *Fig* piège *m*; **to set a t.** tendre un piège; *Fig* **to walk** *or* **fall straight into the t.** tomber en plein dans le piège **(b)** *very Fam (mouth)* gueule *f* **2** *vt* piéger, prendre au piège; **to t. sb into saying/doing sth** faire dire/faire faire qch à qn en usant de ruse

trapdoor [træpˈdɔː(r)] *n* trappe *f*

trapeze [trəˈpiːz] *n* trapèze *m*; **t. artist** trapéziste *mf*

trapper [ˈtræpə(r)] *n* trappeur *m*

trappings [ˈtræpɪŋz] *npl* signes *mpl* extérieurs

trash [træʃ] *n* **(a)** *(worthless objects)* camelote *f*; *Am (refuse)* ordures *fpl*; *(people)* racaille *f*; *Fam* **that book/film is a**

load of t. ce livre/film est nul; *Am* **t. can** poubelle *f*
2 *vt Fam* (**a**) *(vandalize)* saccager (**b**) *(criticize)* descendre en flammes

trashy ['træʃɪ] *adj Fam* à la noix

trauma ['trɔːmə] *n* traumatisme *m*

traumatic [trɔː'mætɪk] *adj* traumatisant(e)

traumatize ['trɔːmətaɪz] *vt* traumatiser

travail ['træveɪl] *n Lit* labeur *m*

travel ['trævəl] **1** *n* voyage *m*; **on my travels** au cours de mes voyages; **I spend half my money on t.** *(to and from work)* la moitié de mon argent part dans les transports; **t. agency** agence *f* de voyages; **t. agent** agent *m* de voyages; **t. documents** titre *m* de transport; **t. writer** auteur *m* de récits de voyage
2 *vt (road, country)* parcourir
3 *vi* (**a**) *(of person)* voyager; *(vehicle, of light, sound, electricity)* se déplacer; **cheese doesn't t. well** le fromage supporte mal d'être transporté; *Fam* **(good) news travels fast** les nouvelles vont vite

traveller, *Am* **traveler** ['trævələ(r)] *n* voyageur(euse) *m,f*; *Br* **(new age) t.** voyageur new age; **t.'s cheque** chèque *m* de voyage

travelling, *Am* **traveling** ['trævəlɪŋ] **1** *n* déplacement *m*, **t. bag** sac *m* de voyage; **t. companion** compagnon *m* de voyage; **t. expenses** frais *mpl* de déplacement
2 *adj (performer, circus)* itinérant(e); **t. salesman** voyageur *m* de commerce

traverse [trə'vɜːs] *vt Lit* traverser

travesty ['trævəstɪ] *n* travestissement *m*; **t. of justice** simulacre *m* de justice

trawl [trɔːl] **1** *n* (**a**) *(net)* chalut *m* (**b**) *Fig (search)* **to carry out** *or* **make a t. through sth** passer qch au crible
2 *vt* (**a**) *(sea)* aller à la pêche au chalut en (**b**) *Fig (search through)* passer au crible
3 *vi* (**a**) *(fish)* pêcher au chalut (**b**) *Fig* **to t. through sth** passer qch au crible

trawler ['trɔːlə(r)] *n (ship)* chalutier *m*

tray [treɪ] *n* plateau *m*; *(in office)* corbeille *f*

treacherous ['tretʃərəs] *adj* traître

treachery ['tretʃərɪ] *n* traîtrise *f*

treacle ['triːkəl] *n* mélasse *f*

tread [tred] **1** *vt (pt* **trod** [trɒd], *pp* **trodden** ['trɒdən]) marcher sur; **to t. sth underfoot** fouler qch aux pieds; **to t. sth into the carpet** mettre qch sur le tapis (avec ses chaussures); **to t. the boards** *(appear on stage)* monter sur les planches; **to t. grapes** fouler le raisin; **to t. water** faire du surplace; *Fig (of company)* se maintenir à flot
2 *vi* marcher (**on** sur); *also Fig* **to t. on sb's toes** marcher sur les pieds de qn; *Fig* **to t. carefully** *or* **warily** y aller doucement
3 *n* (**a**) *(sound of footstep)* pas *m* (**b**) *(of tyre)* chape *f*

treadmill ['tredmɪl] *n (in gym)* tapis *m* roulant de jogging; *Fig (routine)* routine *f*

treason ['triːzən] *n* trahison *f*

treasonable ['triːzənəbəl] *adj* qui constitue un acte de trahison

treasure ['treʒə(r)] **1** *n also Fig* trésor *m*; **t. hunt** chasse *f* au trésor
2 *vt (person, possession)* tenir beaucoup à; *(memory)* chérir

treasurer ['treʒərə(r)] *n* trésorier(ère) *m,f*

treasure-trove ['treʒətrəʊv] *n Law & Fig* trésor *m*

treasury ['treʒərɪ] *n* trésorerie *f*; **the T.** *(government department)* ≃ le ministère des Finances; *Fin* **t. bond** ≃ bon *m* du Trésor

treat [triːt] **1** *n (pleasure)* plaisir *m*; *(gift)* cadeau *m*; **to give**

sb a t. faire plaisir à qn; **it's my t.** *(I'm paying)* c'est moi qui régale; *also Ironic* **you've got a real t. in store** attends-toi à une belle surprise; *Fam* **to work a t.** marcher à merveille
2 *vt* (**a**) *(person, illness, metal)* traiter; **to t. sth as a joke** prendre qch à la rigolade (**b**) *(give present to)* **to t. sb to sth** offrir qch à qn; **to t. oneself to sth** s'offrir qch; **I'll t. you** *(pay for you)* je t'invite; *Ironic* **she treated us to one of her tantrums** nous avons eu droit à une de ses colères
3 *vi Formal (negotiate)* **to t. with sb/sth** traiter avec qn/qch

treatise ['triːtɪs] *n* traité *m*

treatment ['triːtmənt] *n* traitement *m*; *Fam* **to give sb the t.** rosser qn

treaty ['triːtɪ] *n (international)* traité *m*; *(between individuals)* accord *m*, contrat *m*

treble ['trebəl] **1** *n Mus (person, voice)* soprano *m*
2 *adj (triple)* triple; *Mus* **t. clef** clef *f* de sol
3 *vt & vi* tripler

tree [triː] *n* arbre *m*; *Fig* **at the top of the t.** en haut de l'échelle; *Am Fam* **to be out of one's t.** débloquer; **t. trunk** tronc *m* d'arbre

treetop ['triːtɒp] *n* cime *f* d'un arbre

trek [trek] **1** *n (long walk)* randonnée *f* (pédestre); *Fig* **it's quite a t. to the shops** ça fait loin à pied jusqu'aux magasins
2 *vi* faire de la randonnée; *Fig* **to t. to the shops/home** se taper le chemin à pied jusqu'aux magasins/jusqu'à chez soi

trellis ['trelɪs] *n* treillis *m*, treillage *m*

tremble ['trembəl] **1** *n* tremblement *m*
2 *vi* trembler (**with** de)

tremendous [trɪ'mendəs] *adj* (**a**) *(enormous)* énorme (**b**) *Fam (excellent)* formidable

tremendously [trɪ'mendəslɪ] *adv (very)* extrêmement

tremor ['tremə(r)] *n* tremblement *m*

tremulous ['tremjʊləs] *adj (voice, hand)* tremblant(e); *(person, smile)* timide

trench [trentʃ] *n (ditch)* fossé *m*; *Mil* tranchée *f*; **t. coat** trench-coat *m*; **t. warfare** guerre *f* de tranchées

trenchant ['trentʃənt] *adj* tranchant(e)

trend [trend] *n (tendency)* tendance *f*; *(fashion)* mode *f*; **to set** *or* **start a t.** lancer une mode

trendsetter ['trendsetə(r)] *n* lanceur(euse) *m,f* de mode

trendy ['trendɪ] *Br Fam n & adj* branché(e) *m,f*

trepidation [trepɪ'deɪʃən] *n Formal* inquiétude *f*

trespass ['trespəs] *vi Law* s'introduire illégalement dans une propriété privée

trespasser ['trespəsə(r)] *n Law* intrus(e) *m,f*; **trespassers will be prosecuted** *(sign)* défense d'entrer sous peine de poursuites

tresses ['tresɪz] *npl Lit (hair)* chevelure *f*

trestle ['tresəl] *n* tréteau *m*; **t. table** table *f* à tréteaux

trial ['traɪəl] *n* (**a**) *Law* procès *m*; **to bring sb to t.** traduire qn en justice; **to be on t. (for)** passer en jugement (pour) (**b**) *(test)* essai *m*; **on t. à l'essai**; **by t. and error** par tâtonnements; **t. period** période *f* d'essai; **t. run** essai; **t. separation** *(of couple)* séparation *f* à l'essai (**c**) *(ordeal)* épreuve *f*

triangle ['traɪæŋgəl] *n* triangle *m*

triangular [traɪ'æŋgjʊlə(r)] *adj* triangulaire

triathlon [traɪ'æθlɒn] *n* triathlon *m*

tribal ['traɪbəl] *adj* tribal(e)

tribalism ['traɪbəlɪzəm] *n* tribalisme *m*

tribe [traɪb] *n* tribu *f*

tribesman ['traɪbzmən] *n* membre *m* d'une tribu

tribulation [trɪbjʊ'leɪʃən] n Formal malheur m

tribunal [traɪ'bjuːnəl] n Law tribunal m

tributary ['trɪbjʊtərɪ] n (of river) affluent m

tribute ['trɪbjuːt] n (a) (homage) hommage m; to pay t. to rendre hommage à (b) (testimony) our success is a t. to all your hard work c'est grâce à vos efforts soutenus que nous avons réussi

trice [traɪs] n in a t. en un clin d'œil

triceps ['traɪseps] n Anat triceps m

trick [trɪk] 1 n (a) (ruse) tour m; (practical joke) farce f; to play a t. on sb jouer un tour à qn; (practical joke) faire une farce à qn; t. photography truquage m; t. question question f piège (b) (by magician) tour m (c) (in card game) pli m (d) (idioms) to do the t. marcher; to know all the tricks connaître toutes les astuces; the tricks of the trade les ficelles du métier; she doesn't miss a t. rien ne lui échappe; he's been up to his old tricks again il a encore fait des siennes; Fam how's tricks? comment vas-tu?
2 vt (person) duper; to t. sb into doing sth amener qn à faire qch par la ruse

trickery ['trɪkərɪ] n duperie f, ruse f

trickle ['trɪkəl] 1 vt (liquid) faire couler goutte à goutte
2 vi (of liquid) couler goutte à goutte; to t. in/out (of people) entrer/sortir au compte-gouttes
3 n (of liquid) filet m; (of complaints, letters) petit nombre m; t.-down theory = théorie selon laquelle la richesse de quelques-uns finira par profiter à toute la société

tricky ['trɪkɪ] adj délicat(e)

tricycle ['traɪsɪkəl] n tricycle m

trident ['traɪdənt] n trident m

tried-and-tested ['traɪdən'testɪd] adj qui a fait ses preuves

trier ['traɪə(r)] n Fam to be a t. être persévérant(e)

trifle ['traɪfəl] n (a) (insignificant thing) broutille f (b) a t. wide/short un tantinet trop large/court(e) (c) Br (dessert) = dessert où alternent une couche de génoise imbibée d'alcool et de fruits en gelée et une couche de crème anglaise, et recouvert de chantilly
▸ **trifle with** vt insep plaisanter avec

trifling ['traɪflɪŋ] adj insignifiant(e)

trigger ['trɪgə(r)] 1 n (of gun) détente f; Fig (of change, decision) élément m déclencheur; Fam to be t. happy avoir la gâchette facile
2 vt déclencher
▸ **trigger off** vt sep déclencher

trigonometry [trɪgə'nɒmɪtrɪ] n trigonométrie f

trilby ['trɪlbɪ] n Br (chapeau m en) feutre m

trill [trɪl] 1 n trille m
2 vi triller

trillion ['trɪljən] n trillion m; Fam **trillions of** (lots of) un milliard de

trilogy ['trɪlədʒɪ] (pl **trilogies**) n trilogie f

trim [trɪm] 1 adj (a) (neat) soigné(e) (b) (slim) svelte
2 vt (pt & pp **trimmed**) (a) (cut) (hair) rafraîchir; (hedge) tailler, élaguer; (meat) parer; (budget) réduire (b) (decorate) orner, décorer (**with** de)
3 n (a) to give sb's hair a t. faire une coupe d'entretien à qn; to give the hedge a t. tailler la haie (b) to be/keep in t. (keep fit) être en/garder la forme
▸ **trim down** vt sep (text) élaguer; (company, expenditure) réduire

trimaran ['traɪməræn] n trimaran m

trimester [trɪ'mestə(r)] n trimestre m

trimming ['trɪmɪŋ] n (a) (on clothes) garniture f (b) **trimmings** (of meal) accompagnements mpl traditionnels

Trinidad and Tobago ['trɪnɪdædəntə'beɪgəʊ] n Trinité-et-Tobago

Trinity ['trɪnɪtɪ] n Rel the T. la Trinité

trinket ['trɪŋkɪt] n babiole f

trio ['triːəʊ] (pl **trios**) n trio m

trip [trɪp] 1 n (a) (journey) voyage m; (for one day) excursion f (b) Fam (on drugs) trip m (c) (stumble) faux pas m; t. **wire** fil m de détente
2 vt (pt & pp **tripped**) (a) (make stumble) faire un croche-pied à (b) to t. a switch déclencher un interrupteur
3 vi (a) (stumble) trébucher (b) (step lightly) marcher d'un pas léger; to t. off the tongue (of word, name) bien couler (c) Fam (on drugs) to be tripping être en plein trip
▸ **trip over 1** vt insep trébucher sur
2 vi trébucher
▸ **trip up 1** vt sep (cause to stumble) faire un croche-pied à; Fig (cause to make mistake) désarçonner
2 vi (stumble) trébucher

tripe [traɪp] n (food) tripes fpl; Fam (nonsense) foutaises fpl

triple ['trɪpəl] 1 adj triple; t. jump triple saut m
2 adv t. the number/amount trois fois le nombre/la quantité
3 vt & vi tripler

triplet ['trɪplɪt] n (a) (person) triplé(e) m,f (b) Mus triolet m

triplicate ['trɪplɪkət] n in t. en trois exemplaires

tripod ['traɪpɒd] n trépied m

Tripoli ['trɪpəlɪ] n Tripoli

trite [traɪt] adj banal(e)

triumph ['traɪəmf] 1 n triomphe m; in t. triomphant(e)
2 vi triompher (**over** de)

triumphant [traɪ'ʌmfənt] adj triomphant(e)

triumvirate [traɪ'ʌmvɪrɪt] n triumvirat m

trivet ['trɪvɪt] n (on open fire) trépied m; (stand) = support métallique surélevé pour plats chauds

trivia ['trɪvɪə] npl (unimportant details) détails mpl; (useless information) futilités fpl

trivial ['trɪvɪəl] adj (detail, matter) sans importance, insignifiant(e); (person) superficiel(elle)

trivialize ['trɪvɪəlaɪz] vt banaliser

trod [trɒd] pt of **tread**

trodden ['trɒdən] pp of **tread**

Trojan ['trəʊdʒən] Hist 1 n Troyen(cnne) m,f
2 adj de Troie, troyen(enne); T. **Horse** cheval m de Troie; the T. **War** la guerre de Troie

troll [trəʊl] n troll m

trolley ['trɒlɪ] (pl **trolleys**) n Br chariot m; Fam to be off one's t. débloquer; Am t. **car** tramway m

trollop ['trɒləp] n Old-fashioned or Hum gourgandine f, catin f

trombone [trɒm'bəʊn] n trombone m

trombonist [trɒm'bəʊnɪst] n trombone m

troop [truːp] n (a) **troops** (soldiers) troupes fpl (b) (of people) groupe m
2 vi t. in/out entrer/sortir en groupe

trooper ['truːpə(r)] n (soldier) cavalier m; Am (mounted policeman) membre m de la police montée; Fam to swear like a t. jurer comme un charretier

trophy ['trəʊfɪ] n trophée m

tropic ['trɒpɪk] n tropique m; the tropics les tropiques

tropical ['trɒpɪkəl] adj tropical(e)

trot [trɒt] 1 n trot m; at a t. au trot; Fam on the t. (consecutively) de suite; Fam to have the trots avoir la courante

2 *vi* (*pt & pp* **trotted**) *(of horse)* aller au trot; *(of person)* trotter

▶ **trot out** *vt sep Fam* débiter

Trotskyism ['trɒtskɪɪzəm] *n* trotskisme *m*

Trotskyist ['trɒtskɪɪst], **Trotskyite** ['trɒtskɪaɪt] *n & adj* trotskiste *mf*

trotter ['trɒtə(r)] *n (of pig)* pied *m*

trouble ['trʌbəl] **1** *n* (**a**) *(problem)* ennui *m*; **to have t. with sb/sth** avoir des problèmes avec qn/qch; **to have t. doing sth** avoir du mal à faire qch; **to be in/get into t.** avoir/s'attirer des ennuis; **to get sb into t.** attirer des ennuis à qn; **to get sb out of t.** tirer qn d'affaire; **to make t. (for sb)** créer des ennuis (à qn); **it's more t. than it's worth** le jeu n'en vaut pas la chandelle; *Fam* **man/woman t.** ennuis *mpl* de cœur (**b**) *(inconvenience)* problème *m*; **to go to the t. of doing sth** se donner la peine de faire qch; **it's not worth the t.** ça n'en vaut pas la peine; (**it's**) **no t.** (ça ne pose) aucun problème (**c**) *(disorder, unrest)* troubles *mpl*; **t. spot** point *m* chaud

2 *vt (worry)* inquiéter; *(inconvenience)* déranger

3 *vi* **to t. to do sth** se donner la peine de faire qch

troubled ['trʌbəld] *adj (person)* inquiet(ète); *(region)* agité(e) de troubles, *(period)* troublé(e)

trouble-free ['trʌbəlfriː] *adj* sans souci

troublemaker ['trʌbəlmeɪkə(r)] *n* semeur(euse) *m,f* de troubles

troubleshooter ['trʌbəlʃuːtə(r)] *n (for organizational problems)* expert *m*; *(for industrial disputes)* conciliateur(trice) *m,f*; *(for machines)* dépanneur(euse) *m,f*

troublesome ['trʌbəlsəm] *adj* pénible

trough [trɒf] *n (for food)* mangeoire *f*; *(for drink)* abreuvoir *m*; *(of wave, on graph)* creux *m*; *(in weather front)* dépression *f*

trounce [traʊns] *vt* battre à plates coutures

troupe [truːp] *n* troupe *f*

trouser press ['traʊzəˈpres] *n* presse-pantalon *m*

trousers ['traʊzəz] *npl* (**a**) *Br* pantalon *m* (**b**) *(idioms) Fam* **to wear the t.** porter la culotte; *Fam* **to be caught with one's t. down** être pris(e) en flagrant délit

trouser suit ['traʊzəˈsuːt] *n Br* tailleur-pantalon *m*

trousseau ['truːsəʊ] *n* trousseau *m*

trout [traʊt] *n (pl* **trout**) truite *f*

trowel ['traʊəl] *n* truelle *f*

truancy ['truːənsɪ] *n* absentéisme *m* scolaire

truant ['truːənt] *n (pupil)* élève *mf* qui fait l'école buissonnière; **to play t.** faire l'école buissonnière

truce [truːs] *n also Fig* trêve *f*; **to call a t.** demander une trêve

truck [trʌk] **1** *n* (**a**) *(lorry)* camion *m*; **t. driver** conducteur(trice) *m,f* de camion, camionneur *m*; *Am* **t. farm** exploitation *f* maraîchère; **t. stop** relais *m* routier (**b**) *(rail wagon)* wagon *m* (**c**) *Fam* **to have no t. with sb/sth** ne rien avoir à faire avec qn/qch

2 *vt (goods)* acheminer par camion

3 *vi Am (drive a truck)* être conducteur(trice) *m,f* de camion

trucker ['trʌkə(r)] *n Am (truck driver)* camionneur *m*

truculent ['trʌkjʊlənt] *adj* agressif(ive)

trudge [trʌdʒ] **1** *n* trajet *m* pénible

2 *vi* marcher péniblement, se traîner

true [truː] **1** *adj* (**a**) *(not fictional)* vrai(e); **to come t.** se réaliser; **to hold t. (for)** être vrai (de) (**b**) *(genuine)* véritable; **t. love** grand amour *m*; **t. north** le nord géographique (**c**) *(faithful)* fidèle; **to be t. to sb** être loyal(e) envers qn; **to be t. to sth** être fidèle à qch; **t. to**

life fidèle à la réalité; **t. to form** *or* **type** fidèle à soi-même (**d**) *(accurate)* exact(e)

2 *n* **out of t.** hors d'aplomb

truffle ['trʌfəl] *n* truffe *f*

truism ['truːɪzəm] *n* truisme *m*

truly ['truːlɪ] *adv* vraiment; **Yours t.** *(at end of letter)* = je vous prie d'agréer, Madame/Monsieur, l'expression de mes sentiments distingués; *Fam (myself)* mézigue

trump [trʌmp] **1** *n* atout *m*; **hearts are trumps** c'est atout cœur; *Fig* **to play one's t. card** jouer son atout; *Fam Fig* **to turn** *or* **come up trumps** sauver la mise

2 *vt* couper à l'atout

trumped up ['trʌmptʌp] *adj* fabriqué(e)

trumpet ['trʌmpɪt] **1** *n* trompette *f*; *Fig* **to blow one's own t.** vanter ses propres mérites

2 *vt (proclaim)* claironner

3 *vi (of elephant)* barrir

trumpeter ['trʌmpɪtə(r)] *n* trompettiste *mf*

truncate [trʌŋˈkeɪt] *vt* tronquer

truncheon ['trʌn(t)ʃən] *n Br* matraque *f*

trundle ['trʌndəl] **1** *vt* pousser péniblement

2 *vi* rouler péniblement

trunk [trʌŋk] *n* (**a**) *(of tree, body)* tronc *m*; *Br* **t. call** appel *m* interurbain; *Br* **t. road** route *f* nationale (**b**) *(case)* malle *f* (**c**) *Am (of car)* coffre *m* (**d**) *(of elephant)* trompe *f* (**e**) **trunks** *(swimming costume)* slip *m* de bain

truss [trʌs] **1** *n* (**a**) *(for hernia)* bandage *m* herniaire (**b**) *(for roof, bridge)* ferme *f*

2 *vt (tie up)* ligoter

▶ **truss up** *vt sep (person)* ligoter; *(chicken, turkey)* trousser

trust [trʌst] **1** *n* (**a**) *(faith)* confiance *f* (**in** en); **to put one's t. in sb/sth** se fier à qn/qch; **to take sth on t.** croire qch sur parole (**b**) *Law* **in t.** par fidéicommis; *Fin* **t. fund** fonds *m* en fidéicommis (**c**) *Com (group of companies)* trust *m*

2 *vt* (**a**) *(believe in)* faire confiance à; **to t. sb with sth** confier qch à qn; **to t. sb to do sth** laisser à qn le soin de faire qch; *Fam* **t. him to say that!** c'est bien de lui! (**b**) *Formal (hope)* **t. (that)…** espérer que…

3 *vi* **to t. in sb/sth** faire confiance à qn/qch; **to t. to luck** s'en remettre au hasard

trusted ['trʌstɪd] *adj* de confiance

trustee [trʌsˈtiː] *n Law (of fund, property)* fidéicommissaire *m*; *(of charity)* administrateur(trice) *m,f*

trusting ['trʌstɪŋ] *adj* qui fait confiance aux gens

trustworthy ['trʌstwɜːðɪ] *adj (person)* digne de confiance; *(thing)* fiable

trusty ['trʌstɪ] *adj* fidèle

truth [truːθ] *n* vérité *f*; **to tell the t.** dire la vérité

truthful ['truːθfʊl] *adj (person)* sincère; *(story)* véridique

try [traɪ] **1** *vt* (**a**) *(sample, attempt)* essayer; *(food, drink)* goûter (à); **to t. doing sth** essayer de faire qch; **I'll t. anything once** il faut tout essayer dans la vie (**b**) *Law (case, person)* juger; *(test)* tester; *(person)* mettre à l'épreuve; **to t. sb's patience** mettre la patience de qn à l'épreuve

2 *vi* essayer; **to t. harder** faire plus d'efforts; **just you t.!** essaie un peu pour voir!

3 *n* (**a**) *(attempt)* essai *m*; **to give sth a t.** essayer qch; **to have a t. at sth/at doing sth** essayer qch/de faire qch; **it's worth a t.** ça vaut le coup d'essayer (**b**) *(in rugby)* essai *m*

▶ **try on** *vt sep (clothes)* essayer (**b**) *Fam* **to t. it on (with sb)** tenter le coup (avec qn); *(sexually)* draguer (qn)

▶ **try out** *vt sep* essayer; **to t. sth out on sb** expérimenter qch sur qn

trying ['traɪɪŋ] *adj* difficile

tsar [zɑː(r)] *n* tsar *m*

tsarist ['zɑːrɪst] *n & adj* tsariste *mf*

tsetse ['t(s)etsɪ] *n* **t. (fly)** (mouche *f*) tsé-tsé *f inv*

T-shirt ['tiːʃɜːt] *n* tee-shirt *m*

tub [tʌb] *n* **(a)** *(for washing clothes)* baquet *m*; *(bath)* baignoire *f* **(b)** *(for food, plants)* pot *m*

tuba ['tjuːbə] *n* tuba *m*

tubby ['tʌbɪ] *adj Fam* boulot(otte)

tube [tjuːb] *n* **(a)** *(cylindrical container)* tube *m*; *(pipe)* tuyau *m*; *Fam* **to go down the tubes** *(of money)* être foutu en l'air; *(of work, plan)* tomber à l'eau **(b)** *Br Fam* **the t.** *(underground railway)* le métro; **t. station** station *f* de métro **(c)** *Am Fam (TV)* télé *f*

tuber ['tjuːbə(r)] *n* tubercule *m*

tuberculosis [tjʊbɜːkjʊ'ləʊsɪs] *n* tuberculose *f*

tubing ['tjuːbɪŋ] *n* tuyaux *mpl*

tubular ['tjuːbjʊlə(r)] *adj* tubulaire; **t. bells** carillon *m*

TUC [tiːjuː'siː] *n Br (abbr* **Trades Union Congress)** = confédération des syndicats britanniques

tuck [tʌk] **1** *n* **(a)** *(in sewing)* pli *m* **(b)** *Br Fam (food)* sucreries *fpl*; **t. shop** *(in school)* boutique *f* de friandises **(c)** *(in cosmetic surgery) (for face)* lifting *m*
2 *vt* **to t. one's shirt into one's pants** rentrer sa chemise dans son pantalon; **to t. sth under one's arm** mettre qch sous son bras; **to t. sb up in bed** border qn; **to t. sth into a drawer** glisser qch dans un tiroir
▸ **tuck in 1** *vt sep (sheets, child)* border; *(clothes)* rentrer
2 *vi Fam (start to eat)* attaquer
▸ **tuck into** *vt insep Fam (meal)* attaquer

Tudor ['tjuːdə(r)] **1** *n Hist* **the Tudors** les Tudor
2 *adj* des Tudor

Tue(s) *(abbr* **Tuesday)** mardi

Tuesday ['tjuːzdɪ] *n* mardi *m*; *see also* **Saturday**

tuft [tʌft] *n* touffe *f*

tug [tʌg] **1** *vt (pt & pp* **tugged)** **(a)** *(pull)* tirer sur **(b)** *(tow)* remorquer
2 *vi* to **t. at sth** tirer sur qch
3 *n* **(a)** *(pull)* **to give sth a t.** tirer sur qch **(b)** *(boat)* remorqueur *m*

tug-of-love [tʌgəv'lʌv] *n Br* = conflit de parents séparés à propos de la garde d'un enfant

tug-of-war [tʌgəv'wɔː(r)] *n (game)* lutte *f* (de traction) à la corde; *Fig* lutte acharnée

tuition [tjʊ'ɪʃən] *n* cours *mpl*, leçons *fpl*

tulip ['tjuːlɪp] *n* tulipe *f*

tum [tʌm] *n (in children's language)* ventre *m*

tumble ['tʌmbəl] **1** *vi (of person)* faire une chute; *Fig (of prices)* chuter
2 *n (fall)* chute *f*; **to take a t.** *(of person)* faire une chute; *Fig (of prices)* chuter
▸ **tumble down** *vi* s'écrouler

tumbledown ['tʌmbəldaʊn] *adj* qui tombe en ruines

tumble-drier [tʌmbəl'draɪə(r)] *n* sèche-linge *m inv*

tumble-dry ['tʌmbəldraɪ] *vt* faire sécher au sèche-linge

tumbler ['tʌmblə(r)] *n* verre *m* droit

tummy ['tʌmɪ] *n Fam* ventre *m*; **to have (a) t. ache** avoir mal au ventre

tumour, *Am* **tumor** ['tjuːmə(r)] *n* tumeur *f*

tumult ['tjuːmʌlt] *n* tumulte *m*

tumultuous [tjʊ'mʌltjʊəs] *adj* tumultueux(euse)

tuna ['tjuːnə] *n* thon *m*

tundra ['tʌndrə] *n* toundra *f*

tune [tjuːn] **1** *n* **(a)** air *m*, mélodie *f*; **to be in/out of t.** *(of person)* chanter juste/faux; *(of instrument)* être accordé(e)/désaccordé(e) **(b)** *(idioms)* **to be in t. with sb/sth** être en harmonie avec qn/qch; **to call the t.** commander; **to change one's t.** changer de discours; **to be in debt to the t. of $200** avoir 200 dollars de dettes
2 *vt (musical instrument)* accorder; *(engine, TV, radio)* régler
▸ **tune in** *vi* brancher son poste

tuneful ['tjuːnfʊl] *adj* mélodieux(euse)

tuneless ['tjuːnlɪs] *adj* discordant(e)

tuner ['tjuːnə(r)] *n* **(a)** *(person)* accordeur(euse) *m,f* **(b)** *(on TV, radio)* tuner *m*

tungsten ['tʌŋstən] *n* tungstène *m*; **t. steel** acier *m* au tungstène

tunic ['tjuːnɪk] *n* tunique *f*

tuning fork ['tjuːnɪŋfɔːk] *n* diapason *m*

Tunis ['tjuːnɪs] *n* Tunis

Tunisia [tjuː'nɪzɪə] *n* la Tunisie

Tunisian [tjuː'nɪzɪən] **1** *n* Tunisien(enne) *m,f*
2 *adj* tunisien(enne)

tunnel ['tʌnəl] **1** *n* tunnel *m*; **to have t. vision** souffrir d'un rétrécissement du champ visuel; *Fig* avoir des œillères
2 *vt (pt & pp* **tunnelled)** **to t. one's way out of prison** s'échapper de prison en creusant un tunnel
3 *vi* creuser un tunnel

turban ['tɜːbən] *n* turban *m*

turbine ['tɜːbaɪn] *n* turbine *f*

turbo-charged ['tɜːbəʊtʃɑːdʒd] *adj* turbocompressé(e)

turbo-charger ['tɜːbəʊtʃɑːdʒə(r)] *n* turbocompresseur *m*

turbojet ['tɜːbəʊdʒet] *n (engine)* turboréacteur *m*; *(plane)* avion *m* à turboréacteur

turboprop ['tɜːbəʊprɒp] *n (engine)* turbopropulseur *m*; *(plane)* avion *m* à turbopropulseur

turbot ['tɜːbət] *n* turbot *m*

turbulence ['tɜːbjʊləns] *n* turbulence *f*

turbulent ['tɜːbjʊlənt] *adj* agité(e)

turd [tɜːd] *n very Fam* **(a)** *(excrement)* étron *m* **(b)** *(person)* connard (connasse) *m,f*

tureen [tjʊə'riːn] *n* soupière *f*

turf [tɜːf] **1** *n (grass-covered earth)* gazon *m*; *Fam (territory)* territoire *m*; **t. accountant** bookmaker *m*
2 *vt* gazonner
▸ **turf out** *vt sep Br Fam (person)* vider; *(thing)* balancer

Turk [tɜːk] *n* Turc (Turque) *m,f*

Turkey ['tɜːkɪ] *n* la Turquie

turkey ['tɜːkɪ] *(pl* **turkeys)** *n* **(a)** *(bird)* dinde *f* **(b)** *Fam (bad play, film)* navet *m*

Turkish ['tɜːkɪʃ] **1** *n (language)* turc *m*
2 *adj* turc (turque); **T. bath** bain *m* turc; **T. delight** loukoum *m*

Turkmenistan [tɜːkmenɪ'stɑːn] *n* le Turkménistan

turmeric ['tɜːmərɪk] *n* curcuma *m*

turmoil ['tɜːmɔɪl] *n (of person)* émoi *m*; *(of country)* agitation *f*; **to be in (a) t.** *(of person)* être dans tous ses états; *(of country)* être en ébullition; **his mind was in t.** il était très troublé

turn [tɜːn] **1** *n* **(a)** *(of wheel, screw)* tour *m*; **the meat is done to a t.** la viande est cuite à point
(b) *(change of direction)* demi-tour *m*; *(in road)* virage *m*; **no right/left t.** *(on sign)* défense de tourner à droite/gauche; *Fig* **at every t.** à tout bout de champ; **to take a t. for the better** s'améliorer; **to take a t. for the worse** se détériorer; **events took an unexpected t.** les événe-

ments ont pris une tournure inattendue; **the t. of the century** le tournant du siècle; **the t.** of **the tide** le changement de marée; *Fig* le renversement de tendances (**c**) *(in game, queue)* tour *m*; **to take (it in) turns (to do sth)** se relayer (pour faire qch); **in t.** à tour de rôle (**d**) *Fam (fit)* crise *f* (**e**) *Th (performance)* numéro *m* (**f**) *(service)* **to do sb a good t.** rendre un service à qn; **one good t. deserves another** un service en vaut un autre (**g**) **t. of phrase** tournure *f* de phrase

2 *vt* (**a**) *(cause to move)* tourner; *Fam Fig* **without turning a hair** sans broncher; *Fam Fig* **success has turned her head** le succès lui a tourné la tête; **to t. sb's stomach** soulever le cœur à qn (**b**) *(direct)* **to t. the conversation to sb/sth** orienter la conversation sur qn/qch (**c**) *(go round)* **to t. the corner** tourner au coin de la rue; *Fig* passer le moment critique; **she's just turned thirty** elle vient d'avoir trente ans (**d**) *(change)* **to t. sth into sth** transformer qch en qch; **to t. sth green/black** verdir/noircir qch; **to t. sb against sb** monter qn contre qn (**e**) *(on lathe)* tourner

3 *vi* (**a**) *(rotate) (of wheel)* tourner; *(of person)* se retourner; **she turned to me** elle s'est tournée vers moi; **to t. to sb (for help/advice)** se tourner vers qn (pour obtenir de l'aide/des conseils); **to t. (to the) right/left** tourner à droite/gauche (**b**) *(change)* **to t. against sb** se retourner contre qn; **to t. nasty** *(of person)* devenir méchant(e); *(of situation)* mal tourner; **to t. red** devenir rougé; **to t. sour** *(of milk)* tourner; *Fig (of relationship)* tourner au vinaigre
▸ **turn away 1** *vt sep (refuse entry, help to)* refuser **2** *vi* se détourner
▸ **turn back 1** *vt sep (person)* refouler; *(sheets)* rabattre; **to t. the clocks back** retarder les pendules; *Fig* faire machine arrière **2** *vi* faire demi-tour; **t. back to page 5** revenez à la page 5
▸ **turn down** *vt sep* (**a**) *(volume, heat)* baisser (**b**) *(request, application)* rejeter, refuser
▸ **turn in 1** *vt sep (lost property)* rapporter à la police; *(person)* livrer à la police **2** *vi Fam (go to bed)* aller se pieuter
▸ **turn into** *vt insep (become)* devenir
▸ **turn off 1** *vt sep* (**a**) *(water, gas)* fermer; *(light, TV, engine)* éteindre (**b**) *Fam* **to t. sb off** dégoûter qn; *(sexually)* couper l'envie à qn **2** *vt insep* **to t. off the road** quitter la route **3** *vi (leave road)* sortir
▸ **turn on 1** *vt sep* (**a**) *(water, gas)* ouvrir; *(light, TV, engine)* allumer (**b**) *Fam* **to t. sb on** *(excite)* brancher; *(sexually)* exciter **2** *vt insep* (**a**) *(attack)* **to t. on sb** attaquer qn (**b**) *(depend on)* dépendre de
▸ **turn out 1** *vt sep* (**a**) *(light)* éteindre; *(gas)* fermer (**b**) *(eject)* mettre à la porte (**c**) *(pocket, container)* vider (**d**) *(produce)* produire, fabriquer; **to be well turned out** *(of person)* être élégant(e) **2** *vi* (**a**) *(appear, attend)* se déplacer (**b**) *(result)* se terminer; **to t. out to be** s'avérer (être); **it turns out that...** il se trouve que...
▸ **turn over 1** *vt sep* (**a**) *(change position of)* retourner; **to t. sth over in one's mind** retourner qch dans sa tête; *Fig* **to t. over a new leaf** tourner la page (**b**) *(hand in)* **to t. sb/sth over to sb** remettre qn/qch entre les mains de qn **2** *vi* (**a**) *(of person)* se retourner; *(of car)* faire un tonneau, capoter (**b**) *(change TV channels)* changer de chaîne
▸ **turn round** *vt sep (object)* retourner; *(situation)* renverser; *(company, economy)* remettre sur pied **2** *vi (of person)* se retourner

▸ **turn up 1** *vt sep* (**a**) *(collar)* relever; *(trousers)* retrousser (**b**) *(volume, heat)* mettre plus fort **2** *vi (of person)* arriver; *(of lost object)* réapparaître; **something is sure to t. up** quelque chose finira bien par se présenter
turnabout ['tɜːnəbaʊt] *n (in situation, opinion)* revirement *m*
turnaround ['tɜːnəraʊnd] *n* (**a**) *(in situation, opinion)* revirement *m* (**b**) *Com* **t. time** délai *m* d'exécution
turncoat ['tɜːnkəʊt] *n* renégat(e) *m,f*
turning ['tɜːnɪŋ] *n* (**a**) *(off road) (in country)* route *f* transversale; *(in town)* rue *f* transversale; **the second t. on the left** la deuxième rue à gauche (**b**) **t. circle** *(of car)* rayon *m* de braquage; *Fig* **t. point** tournant *m*
turnip ['tɜːnɪp] *n* navet *m*
turn-off ['tɜːnɒf] *n* (**a**) *(on road)* sortie *f* (**b**) *Fam* **to be a t.** être rébarbatif(ive); *(sexually)* couper l'envie
turn-on ['tɜːnɒn] *n Fam* **to be a t.** *(sexually)* être excitant(e)
turnout ['tɜːnaʊt] *n (attendance)* assistance *f*; *(at election)* taux *m* de participation
turnover ['tɜːnəʊvə(r)] *n* (**a**) *(of company)* chiffre *m* d'affaires (**b**) *(cake)* chausson *m*; **apple t.** chausson *m* aux pommes
turnpike ['tɜːnpaɪk] *n Am (road)* autoroute *f*
turnstile ['tɜːnstaɪl] *n* tourniquet *m*
turntable ['tɜːnteɪbəl] *n* platine *f*
turn-up ['tɜːnʌp] *n* (**a**) *Br (on trousers)* revers *m* (**b**) *Fam* **what a t. for the books!** quel événement!
turpentine ['tɜːpəntaɪn] *n* essence *f* de térébenthine
turquoise ['tɜːkwɔɪz] **1** *n* (**a**) *(stone)* turquoise *f* (**b**) *(colour)* turquoise *m* **2** *adj* turquoise *inv*
turret ['tʌrɪt] *n* tourelle *f*; **(gun) t.** *(on ship, tank)* tourelle *f*
turtle ['tɜːtəl] *n Br* tortue *f* de mer; *Am* tortue *f*; **to turn t.** *(of ship)* chavirer; **t. dove** tourterelle *f*; **t. soup** potage *m* à la tortue
turtleneck ['tɜːtəlnek] *n Am* col *m* montant; **t. sweater** pull *m* à col montant
Tuscan ['tʌskən] *adj* toscan(e)
Tuscany ['tʌskənɪ] *n* la Toscane
tusk [tʌsk] *n* défense *f*
tussle ['tʌsəl] **1** *n* empoignade *f*; **to have a t. (with sb)** *(physically)* se battre (avec qn); *(verbally)* se disputer (avec qn) **2** *vi (physically)* se battre; *(verbally)* se disputer
tutor ['tjuːtə(r)] **1** *n (at university)* directeur(trice) *m,f* d'études; *(for private lessons)* professeur *m* particulier **2** *vt* **to t. sb (in sth)** donner des leçons particulières (de qch) à qn
tutorial [tjuːˈtɔːrɪəl] *n Br Univ* travaux *mpl* dirigés
tux [tʌks] *n Fam* smoking *m*
tuxedo [tʌkˈsiːdəʊ] *n* smoking *m*
TV [tiːˈviː] *n (television)* télé *f*, TV *f*; **TV dinner** plateau *m* télé, **TV movie** téléfilm *m*
TVP [tiːviːˈpiː] *n (abbr* **textured vegetable protein)** protéine *f* végétale texturée
twaddle ['twɒdəl] *n Fam* fadaises *fpl*
twang [twæŋ] **1** *n (sound)* vibration *f*; *(nasal voice)* ton *m* nasillard **2** *vi (of string)* vibrer
tweak [twiːk] **1** *n* **to give sth a t.** *(nose)* pincer qch; *(ear)* tirer qch; *Fam Fig (statistics, mechanism)* ajuster légèrement qch **2** *vt (nose)* pincer; *(ear)* tirer; *Fam Fig (statistics, mechanism)* ajuster légèrement

twee [twiː] *adj Br Fam Pej* cucul (la praline) *inv*

tweed [twiːd] *n* tweed *m*; **tweeds** *(suit)* costume *m* de tweed

tweet [twiːt] **1** *n* pépiement *m*
2 *vi* pépier

tweezers ['twiːzəz] *npl* pince *f* à épiler

twelfth [welfθ] **1** *n* **(a)** *(fraction)* douzième *m* **(b)** *(in series)* douzième *mf* **(c)** *(of month)* douze *m inv*
2 *adj* douzième; **T. Night** ≃ la fête des Rois; *see also* **eighth**

twelve [twelv] **1** *n* douze *m inv*; **half past t.** *(in the afternoon)* douze heures trente, midi et demi; *(at night)* zéro heures trente, minuit et demi
2 *adj* douze; *see also* **eight**

twentieth ['twentɪɪθ] **1** *n* **(a)** *(fraction)* vingtième *m* **(b)** *(in series)* vingtième *mf* **(c)** *(of month)* vingt *m inv*
2 *adj* vingtième; *see also* **eighth**

twenty ['twentɪ] **1** *n* vingt *m inv*
2 *adj* vingt; **to have t.-t. vision** avoir dix sur dix à chaque œil; *see also* **eighty**

twenty-first ['twentɪ'fɜːst] **1** *n* **(a)** *(in series)* vingt et unième *mf* **(b)** *(of month)* vingt et un *m inv*
2 *adj* vingt et unième

twenty one ['twentɪ'wʌn] **1** *n* vingt et un *m inv*
2 *adj* vingt et un

twerp [twɜːp] *n Br Fam* crétin(e) *m,f*

twice [twaɪs] *adv* deux fois; **t. a week** deux fois par semaine; **t. as big (as)** deux fois plus grand (que); **it would cost t. as much elsewhere** ça coûterait le double ailleurs; **t. over** à deux reprises; **to think t. before doing sth** réfléchir à deux fois avant de faire qch; **he didn't have to be asked t.** il ne s'est pas fait prier

twiddle ['twɪdəl] **1** *vt* tripoter; **to t. one's thumbs** se tourner les pouces
2 *vi* **to t. with sth** tripoter qch

twig¹ [twɪg] *n (small branch)* brindille *f*

twig² *(pt & pp* **twigged)** *vt & vi Br Fam* piger

twilight ['twaɪlaɪt] *n* crépuscule *m*

twin [twɪn] **1** *n* jumeau(elle) *m,f*; **t. brother** frère *m* jumeau; **t. sister** sœur *f* jumelle
2 *adj (paired)* jumeau(elle), jumelé(e); **t. beds** lits *mpl* jumeaux; **t.-engine(d) aircraft** avion *m* bimoteur
3 *vt (pt & pp* **twinned)** *(town)* jumeler

twine [twaɪn] **1** *n (string)* ficelle *f*
2 *vt* **to t. sth around sb/sth** enrouler qch autour de qn/qch

twinge [twɪn(d)ʒ] *n (of pain)* élancement *m*; **a t. of conscience** un léger remords

twinkle ['twɪŋkəl] **1** *vi (of star, light)* scintiller; *(of eyes)* pétiller
2 *n (of star, light)* scintillement *m*; *(of eyes)* pétillement *m*

twirl [twɜːl] **1** *n (movement)* tournoiement *m*
2 *vt* faire tournoyer
3 *vi (of person)* tournoyer

twist [twɪst] **1** *n (a) (action)* tour *m*; **to give sth a t.** *(to open)* dévisser qch; *(to close)* visser qch **(b)** *(bend)* tortillement *m*; **twists and turns** *(in road)* tours *mpl* et détours; *Fig (of events)* rebondissements *mpl*; *Br Fam* **to be round the t.** être cinglé(e) **(c)** *(in story, plot)* tour *m* inattendu **(d)** **a t. of lemon** une rondelle de citron **(e)** *(dance)* **the t.** le twist
2 *vt (hair, rope, thread)* tordre, tortiller; *Fig (words, meaning)* déformer; **to t. one's ankle** se fouler la cheville; **to t. sb's arm** tordre le bras à qn; *Fig* forcer la main à qn; *Fig* **to t. the knife (in the wound)** retourner *ou* remuer le couteau dans la plaie
3 *vi (of smoke)* faire des volutes; *(of road)* faire des lacets; **to t. and turn** *(of road)* être en lacets

▸ **twist off 1** *vt sep (lid)* dévisser
2 *vi* se dévisser

twisted ['twɪstɪd] *adj also Fig* tordu(e)

twister ['twɪstə(r)] *n* **(a)** *Br Fam (dishonest person)* escroc *m* **(b)** *Am (tornado)* tornade *f*

twit [twɪt] *n Fam* andouille *f*

twitch [twɪtʃ] **1** *n (pull)* coup *m* sec; **to have a nervous t.** avoir un tic (nerveux)
2 *vt (pull)* tirer d'un coup sec
3 *vi (of muscle, limb, face)* se contracter nerveusement

twitter ['twɪtə(r)] **1** *vi (of bird)* gazouiller; *Fig (of person)* jacasser
2 *n (of bird)* gazouillis *m*

two [tuː] **1** *n (pl* **twos)** deux *m*; **to break/fold sth in t.** casser/plier qch en deux; **to walk in twos** *or* **t. by t.** marcher deux par deux; *Fig* **to put t. and t. together** faire le rapprochement; *Fam* **that makes t. of us** comme ça, on est deux
2 *adj* deux; *see also* **eight**

two-bit ['tuː'bɪt] *adj Am Fam (cheap)* de quatre sous

two-dimensional [tuːdaɪ'menʃənəl] *adj* à deux dimensions; *Fig (character, film)* simpliste

two-faced ['tuː feɪst] *adj* hypocrite

twofold ['tuːfəʊld] *adj* double

two-legged [tuː'legɪd] *adj* bipède

two-piece ['tuːpiːs] *adj (suit, swimsuit)* deux pièces

two-pin ['tuːpɪn] *adj (plug, socket)* à deux fiches

twosome ['tuːsəm] *n* couple *m*

two-time ['tuːtaɪm] *vt Fam (boyfriend, girlfriend)* tromper

two-way ['tuːweɪ] *adj* **t. mirror** miroir *m* sans tain; **t. radio** poste *m* émetteur-récepteur

tycoon [taɪ'kuːn] *n* magnat *m*

type [taɪp] **1** *n* **(a)** *(kind)* type *m*, genre *m*; *Fam* **he's not my t.** ce n'est pas mon genre de mec **(b)** *Typ* caractères *mpl*; **in bold t.** en caractères gras
2 *vt & vi* taper (à la machine)
▸ **type up** *vt sep* taper (à la machine)

typecast ['taɪpkɑːst] *(pt & pp* **typecast)** *vt* **to be typecast** être cantonné(e) dans un rôle

typeface ['taɪpfeɪs] *n* police *f* de caractères

typescript ['taɪpskrɪpt] *n* tapuscrit *m*

typesetter ['taɪpsetə(r)] *n* typographe *mf*

typewriter ['taɪpraɪtə(r)] *n* machine *f* à écrire

typhoid ['taɪfɔɪd] *n* **t. (fever)** (fièvre *f*) typhoïde *f*; **to have t.** avoir la typhoïde

typhoon [taɪ'fuːn] *n* typhon *m*

typhus ['taɪfəs] *n* typhus *m*

typical ['tɪpɪkəl] *adj* typique; **that's t. (of him/her)!** ça ne m'étonne pas (de lui/d'elle)!

typify ['tɪpɪfaɪ] *(pt & pp* **typified)** *vt* caractériser

typing ['taɪpɪŋ] *n* dactylographie *f*, frappe *f*; **t. error** faute *f* de frappe; **t. paper** papier *m* machine; **t. pool** équipe *f* de dactylos; **t. speed** vitesse *f* de frappe

typist ['taɪpɪst] *n* dactylo *mf*

typographic(al) [taɪpə'græfɪk(əl)] *adj* typographique

typography [taɪ'pɒgrəfɪ] *n* typographie *f*

tyrannical [tɪ'rænɪkəl] *adj* tyrannique

tyrannize ['tɪrənaɪz] *vt* tyranniser

tyranny ['tɪrənɪ] *n* tyrannie *f*

tyrant ['taɪrənt] *n* tyran *m*

tyre, *Am* **tire** ['taɪə(r)] *n* pneu *m*; **t. marks** traces *fpl* de pneu; **t. pressure** pression *f* des pneus

tzar [zɑː(r)], **tzarist** ['zɑːrɪst] = tsar, tsarist

U

U, u [ju:] *n (letter)* U, u *m inv*; **U bend** tuyau *m* U; **U boat** sous-marin *m* allemand; **U turn** *(in car)* demi-tour *m*; *Fig* virage *m* à 180 degrés

UAE [ju:eɪ'i:] *n (abbr* **United Arab Emirates)** EAU *mpl*

UB40 [ju:bi:'fɔ:tɪ] *n Br* – carte de pointage de demandeur d'emploi

ubiquitous [ju:'bɪkwɪtəs] *adj* omniprésent(e)

UCAS ['ju:kæs] *n Br (abbr* **Universities and Colleges Admissions Service)** = centre national d'inscriptions à l'université

UDA [ju:di:'eɪ] *n Br Pol (abbr* **Ulster Defence Association)** = groupement paramilitaire protestant d'Irlande du Nord

udder ['ʌdə(r)] *n* pis *m*, mamelle *f*

UDI [ju:di:'aɪ] *n Pol (abbr* **Unilateral Declaration of Independence)** déclaration *f* unilatérale d'indépendance

UEFA [ju:'eɪfə] *n (abbr* **Union of European Football Associations)** UEFA *f*

UFO [ju:ef'əʊ] *n (abbr* **unidentified flying object)** OVNI *m*

Uganda [ju:'gændə] *n* l'Ouganda *m*

Ugandan [ju:'gændən] **1** *n* Ougandais(e) *m,f*
2 *adj* ougandais(e)

ugh [ʌχ] *exclam* berk!

ugly ['ʌglɪ] *adj* **(a)** *(in appearance)* laid(e); *Fig* **u. duckling** vilain petit canard *m* **(b)** *(unpleasant)* désagréable, déplaisant(e)

UHF [ju:eɪtʃ'ef] *n (abbr* **ultra-high frequency)** UHF

UHT [ju:eɪtʃ'ti:] *adj (abbr* **ultra-heat-treated)** UHT

UK [ju:'keɪ] *n (abbr* **United Kingdom)** *(written)* RU; *(spoken)* Royaume-Uni *m*

Ukraine [ju:'kreɪn] *n* the **U.** l'Ukraine *f*

Ukrainian [ju:'kreɪnɪən] **1** *n* **(a)** *(person)* Ukrainien(enne) *m,f* **(b)** *(language)* ukrainien *m*
2 *adj* ukrainien(enne)

ukulele [ju:kə'leɪlɪ] *n* ukulélé *m*

ulcer ['ʌlsə(r)] *n* ulcère *m*; *(in mouth)* aphte *m*

ulcerate ['ʌlsəreɪt] **1** *vt* ulcérer
2 *vi* s'ulcérer

ulna ['ʌlnə] *n* cubitus *m*

Ulster ['ʌlstə(r)] *n* l'Ulster *m*

ulterior [ʌl'tɪərɪə(r)] *adj* ultérieur(e); **u. motive** arrière-pensée *f*

ultimate ['ʌltɪmət] **1** *adj* **(a)** *(last)* final(e) **(b)** *(supreme, best)* absolu(e); **the u. holiday** les vacances idéales
2 *n Fam* **the u. (in)** le summum (de)

ultimately ['ʌltɪmɪtlɪ] *adv* **(a)** *(finally)* finalement **(b)** *(basically)* en fin de compte

ultimatum [ʌltɪ'meɪtəm] *n* ultimatum *m*

ultra- ['ʌltrə] *pref* ultra-

ultramarine [ʌltrəmə'ri:n] *n* bleu *m* outremer

ultramodern [ʌltrə'mɒdən] *adj* ultramoderne

ultrasound ['ʌltrəsaʊnd] *n* ultrasons *mpl*

ultraviolet [ʌltrə'vaɪələt] *adj* ultraviolet(ette)

Ulysses ['ju:lɪsi:z] *n* Ulysse *m*

umbilical cord [ʌm'bɪlɪkəlkɔ:d] *n* cordon *m* ombilical

umbrage ['ʌmbrɪdʒ] *n* **to take u. (at sth)** prendre ombrage (de qch)

umbrella [ʌm'brelə] *n* parapluie *m*; *Fig* **under the u. of** sous les auspices de; **u. organization** organisme *m* de tutelle; **u. stand** porte-parapluie *m*

umpire ['ʌmpaɪə(r)] **1** *n* arbitre *m*
2 *vt* arbitrer

umpteen [ʌmp'ti:n] *adj Fam* je ne sais combien de

umpteenth [ʌmp'ti:nθ] *adj Fam* énième

UN [ju:'en] *n (abbr* **United Nations)** ONU *f*

unabashed [ʌnə'bæʃt] *adj* imperturbable

unable [ʌn'eɪbəl] *adj* **to be u. to do sth** être incapable de faire qch

unabridged [ʌnə'brɪdʒd] *adj* intégral(e)

unacceptable [ʌnək'septəbəl] *adj* inacceptable

unaccompanied [ʌnə'kʌmpənɪd] **1** *adj (person)* non accompagné(e); *(violin, singer)* sans accompagnement **2** *adv (travel)* seul(e); *(play, sing)* sans accompagnement

unaccomplished [ʌnə'kʌmplɪʃt] *adj* médiocre

unaccountable [ʌnə'kaʊntəbəl] *adj* **(a)** *(not answerable)* **to be u. (to sb)** ne pas avoir de comptes à rendre (à qn) **(b)** *(puzzling)* inexplicable

unaccounted [ʌnə'kaʊntɪd] *adj* **to be u. for** *(of person)* ne pas être retrouvé(e)

unaccustomed [ʌnə'kʌstəmd] *adj* **(a)** *(not used)* **to be u. to sth/to doing sth** ne pas être habitué(e) à qch/à faire qch **(b)** *(not usual)* inhabituel(elle)

unacknowledged [ʌnək'nɒlɪdʒd] **1** *adj* non reconnu(e)
2 *adv* **to go u.** *(of talent, achievement)* ne pas être reconnu(e)

unacquainted [ʌnə'kweɪntɪd] *adj* **to be u. with sb/sth** ne pas connaître qn/qch

unadulterated [ʌnə'dʌltəreɪtɪd] *adj* **(a)** *(food)* naturel(elle) **(b)** *(total, sheer)* pur(e)

unadventurous [ʌnəd'ventʃərəs] *adj* peu audacieux(euse)

unaffected [ʌnə'fektɪd] *adj* **(a)** *(sincere)* simple **(b)** *(not touched)* **to be u. (by sth)** ne pas être affecté(e) (par qch)

unaffiliated [ˌʌnəˈfɪlɪeɪtɪd] *adj* non affilié(e)
unafraid [ˌʌnəˈfreɪd] *adj* to be u. ne pas avoir peur
unaided [ʌnˈeɪdɪd] *adv* sans aide
unaltered [ʌnˈɔːltəd] *adj* inchangé(e)
unambiguous [ˌʌnæmˈbɪgjʊəs] *adj* sans équivoque
unambitious [ˌʌnæmˈbɪʃəs] *adj* sans ambition
unanimity [ˌjuːnəˈnɪmɪtɪ] *n* unanimité *f*
unanimous [juːˈnænɪməs] *adj* unanime
unanimously [juːˈnænɪməslɪ] *adv* à l'unanimité
unannounced [ˌʌnəˈnaʊnst] **1** *adj* non annoncé(e) **2** *adv* sans prévenir
unanswerable [ʌnˈɑːnsərəbəl] *adj* irréfutable
unanswered [ʌnˈɑːnsəd] **1** *adj* sans réponse **2** *adv* to go u. *(of question, letter)* rester sans réponse
unappealing [ˌʌnəˈpiːlɪŋ] *adj* peu attrayant(e)
unappetizing [ʌnˈæpɪtaɪzɪŋ] *adj* peu appétissant(e)
unappreciated [ˌʌnəˈpriːʃɪeɪtɪd] *adj* non reconnu(e)
unapproachable [ˌʌnəˈprəʊtʃəbəl] *adj* inaccessible
unarmed [ʌnˈɑːmd] *adj* non armé(e); **u. combat** combat *m* à mains nues
unashamed [ˌʌnəˈʃeɪmd] *adj (joy, greed)* non dissimulé(e); **he's u. about his background** il n'a absolument pas honte de ses origines
unassailable [ˌʌnəˈseɪləbəl] *adj (castle, position)* imprenable; *(argument, theory)* inattaquable
unassuming [ˌʌnəˈsjuːmɪŋ] *adj* sans prétention
unattached [ˌʌnəˈtætʃt] *adj* **(a)** *(not connected)* détaché(e) **(b)** *(without partner)* sans attaches
unattainable [ˌʌnəˈteɪnəbəl] *adj* inaccessible
unattractive [ˌʌnəˈtræktɪv] *adj* peu attrayant(e)
unauthorized [ʌnˈɔːθəraɪzd] *adj* non autorisé(e)
unavailable [ˌʌnəˈveɪləbəl] *adj* non disponible; **to be u.** ne pas être disponible
unavailing [ˌʌnəˈveɪlɪŋ] *adj* vain(e)
unavoidable [ˌʌnəˈvɔɪdəbəl] *adj* inévitable
unaware [ˌʌnəˈweə(r)] *adj* ignorant(e); **to be u. of sth** ignorer qch
unawares [ˌʌnəˈweəz] *adv* **to catch sb u.** prendre qn au dépourvu
unbalanced [ʌnˈbælənst] *adj* **(a)** *(person)* instable **(b)** *(biased)* partial(e)
unbearable [ʌnˈbeərəbəl] *adj* insupportable
unbeatable [ʌnˈbiːtəbəl] *adj* imbattable
unbecoming [ˌʌnbɪˈkʌmɪŋ] *adj (behaviour)* inconvenant(e); *(dress)* peu seyant(e)
unbeknown(st) [ˌʌnbɪˈnəʊn(st)] *adv* **u. to me/him** à mon/son insu
unbelievable [ˌʌnbɪˈliːvəbəl] *adj* incroyable
unbending [ʌnˈbendɪŋ] *adj* inflexible
unbias(s)ed [ʌnˈbaɪəst] *adj* impartial(e)
unblock [ʌnˈblɒk] *vt (sink, pipe)* déboucher; *(road)* dégager
unborn [ˈʌnbɔːn] *adj (child)* à naître
unbounded [ʌnˈbaʊndɪd] *adj* sans bornes
unbreakable [ʌnˈbreɪkəbəl] *adj* **(a)** *(glass, toy)* incassable **(b)** *(promise, rule)* sacré(e)
unbridled [ʌnˈbraɪdəld] *adj* débridé(e)
unbroken [ʌnˈbrəʊkən] *adj* **(a)** *(intact)* intact(e) **(b)** *(uninterrupted)* ininterrompu(e)
unburden [ʌnˈbɜːdən] *vt* **to u. oneself to sb** se confier à qn
unbusinesslike [ʌnˈbɪznɪslaɪk] *adj* peu professionnel(elle)

unbutton [ʌnˈbʌtən] *vt* déboutonner
uncalled-for [ʌnˈkɔːldfɔː(r)] *adj (of behaviour, remark)* déplacé(e); *(insult)* gratuit(e)
uncanny [ʌnˈkænɪ] *adj* étrange, troublant(e)
uncaring [ʌnˈkeərɪŋ] *adj* indifférent(e)
unceasing [ʌnˈsiːsɪŋ] *adj* incessant(e)
uncertain [ʌnˈsɜːtən] *adj* incertain(e); **to be u. about sth** ne pas être certain(e) de qch; **it is u.** on ne sait pas si…; **in no u. terms** en termes on ne peut plus clairs
uncertainty [ʌnˈsɜːtəntɪ] *(pl* **uncertainties)** *n* incertitude *f*
unchallenged [ʌnˈtʃælɪndʒd] *adj* incontesté(e)
unchanged [ʌnˈtʃeɪndʒd] *adj* inchangé(e)
unchanging [ʌnˈtʃeɪndʒɪŋ] *adj* immuable
uncharacteristic [ˌʌnkærəktəˈrɪstɪk] *adj* inhabituel(elle)
uncharitable [ʌnˈtʃærɪtəbəl] *adj* peu charitable
uncharted [ʌnˈtʃɑːtɪd] *adj* inexploré(e)
unchecked [ʌnˈtʃekt] **1** *adj* **(a)** *(not restrained)* incontrôlé(e) **(b)** *(not verified)* non vérifié(e) **2** *adv* **to go u.** rester incontrôlé(e)
uncivil [ʌnˈsɪvɪl] *adj* impoli(e)
uncivilized [ʌnˈsɪvɪlaɪzd] *adj* non civilisé(e)
unclaimed [ʌnˈkleɪmd] *adj* non réclamé(e); **to go u.** ne pas être réclamé(e)
uncle [ˈʌŋkəl] *n* oncle *m*; *Am* **U. Sam** l'oncle Sam
unclean [ʌnˈkliːn] *adj* sale, souillé(e)
unclear [ʌnˈklɪə(r)] *adj* vague
unclothed [ʌnˈkləʊðd] *adj* nu(e)
uncoil [ʌnˈkɔɪl] *vt* dérouler
uncombed [ʌnˈkəʊmd] *adj* pas peigné(e)
uncomfortable [ʌnˈkʌmfətəbəl] *adj* inconfortable; *(silence)* gêné(e); **to feel u.** *(physically)* ne pas être à l'aise; *(ill at ease)* être mal à l'aise
uncommitted [ˌʌnkəˈmɪtɪd] *adj* indécis(e)
uncommon [ʌnˈkɒmən] *adj* peu commun(e)
uncommunicative [ˌʌnkəˈmjuːnɪkətɪv] *adj* peu communicatif(ive)
uncomplicated [ʌnˈkɒmplɪkeɪtɪd] *adj* simple, non compliqué(e)
uncomplimentary [ˌʌnkɒmplɪˈmentərɪ] *adj* peu flatteur(euse)
uncomprehending [ˌʌnkɒmprɪˈhendɪŋ] *adj* **to be u. of sth** ne pas comprendre qch; **with an u. look** l'air perplexe
uncompromising [ʌnˈkɒmprəmaɪzɪŋ] *adj (person, opposition)* intransigeant(e)
unconcealed [ˌʌnkənˈsiːld] *adj* non dissimulé(e)
unconcerned [ˌʌnkənˈsɜːnd] **1** *adj* indifférent(e); **to be u. about sth** ne pas s'inquiéter de qch **2** *adv* avec indifférence
unconditional [ˌʌnkənˈdɪʃənəl] *adj* sans condition
unconfirmed [ˌʌnkənˈfɜːmd] *adj* non confirmé(e)
unconnected [ˌʌnkəˈnektɪd] *adj* sans lien
unconscious [ʌnˈkɒnʃəs] **1** *adj* **(a)** *(having fainted)* sans connaissance; *(asleep)* profondément endormi(e) **(b)** *(unaware)* inconscient(e); **to be u. of sth** ne pas avoir conscience de qch **2** *n* **the u.** l'inconscient *m*
unconsciously [ʌnˈkɒnʃəslɪ] *adv* inconsciemment
unconstitutional [ˌʌnkɒnstɪˈtjuːʃənəl] *adj* inconstitutionnel(elle)
uncontaminated [ˌʌnkənˈtæmɪneɪtɪd] *adj* non contaminé(e)

uncontested [ʌnkən'testɪd] adj incontesté(e)
uncontrollable [ʌnkən'trəʊləbəl] adj incontrôlable
uncontroversial [ʌnkɒntrə'vɜːʃəl] adj anodin(e)
unconventional [ʌnkən'venʃənəl] adj nonconformiste
unconvinced [ʌnkən'vɪnst] adj sceptique
unconvincing [ʌnkən'vɪnsɪŋ] adj peu convaincant(e)
uncooked [ʌn'kʊkt] adj cru(e)
uncool [ʌn'kuːl] adj Fam ringard(e)
uncooperative [ʌnkəʊ'ɒpərətɪv] adj peu coopératif(ive)
uncoordinated [ʌnkəʊ'ɔːdɪneɪtɪd] adj qui manque de coordination
uncork [ʌn'kɔːk] vt déboucher
uncorroborated [ʌnkə'rɒbəreɪtɪd] adj non corroboré(e)
uncountable [ʌn'kaʊntəbəl] adj indénombrable
uncouth [ʌn'kuːθ] adj fruste
uncover [ʌn'kʌvə(r)] vt also Fig découvrir
uncritical [ʌn'krɪtɪkəl] adj peu critique; **to be u. of sb/ sth** ne pas être critique envers qn/qch
UNCTAD ['ʌŋktæd] n Econ (abbr **United Nations Conference on Trade and Development**) CNUCED f
unction ['ʌŋkʃən] n Rel onction f
unctuous ['ʌŋktjʊəs] adj Pej onctueux(euse)
uncultivated [ʌn'kʌltɪveɪtɪd] adj inculte
uncultured [ʌn'kʌltʃəd] adj inculte
uncut [ʌn'kʌt] adj (gem) brut(e); (text, film) intégral(e)
undamaged [ʌn'dæmɪdʒd] adj intact(e)
undated [ʌn'deɪtɪd] adj non daté(e)
undaunted [ʌn'dɔːntɪd] adj qui n'est pas impressionné(e); **to be u. by sth** ne pas se laisser impressionner par qch
undecided [ʌndɪ'saɪdɪd] adj (a) (question, problem) sans réponse; **that's still u.** aucune décision n'a encore été prise (b) (person) indécis(e) (**about** à propos de)
undefeated [ʌndɪ'fiːtɪd] adj invaincu(e)
undefended [ʌndɪ'fendɪd] adj sans défense
undemanding [ʌndɪ'mɑːndɪŋ] adj (job) peu prenant(e); (person) peu exigeant(e)
undemocratic [ʌndemə'krætɪk] adj antidémocratique
undemonstrative [ʌndɪ'mɒnstrətɪv] adj peu démonstratif(ive)
undeniable [ʌndɪ'naɪəbəl] adj indéniable
undeniably [ʌndɪ'naɪəblɪ] adv indéniablement
under ['ʌndə(r)] **1** prep (a) (beneath) sous; **u. the table/ the stairs** sous la table/l'escalier; Fam **to be u. the weather** ne pas être dans son assiette (b) (less than) moins de; **he's u. thirty** il a moins de trente ans; **children u. five** les enfants de moins de cinq ans (c) (under the control of) sous; **he had fifty men u. him** il avait cinquante hommes sous ses ordres; **Spain u. Franco** l'Espagne de Franco (d) (subject to) **to be u. orders to do sth** avoir pour ordre de faire qch; **u. the terms of the agreement** d'après les termes de l'accord; **u. these conditions** dans ces conditions; **u. the circumstances** dans ces circonstances; **u. repair/observation** en réparation/ observation; **to be u. investigation** faire l'objet d'une enquête; **to get u. way** (of meeting, campaign) commencer **2** adv (a) (underneath) dessous; (underwater) sous l'eau; **to go u.** (of company) faire faillite (b) (less) au-dessous; **children of five and u.** les enfants de cinq ans et au-dessous

underachiever [ʌndərə'tʃiːvə(r)] n = personne qui ne tire pas profit de ses capacités intellectuelles
under-age [ʌndər'eɪdʒ] adj mineur(e); **u.** drinking consommation f d'alcool par les mineurs; **u. sex** relations fpl sexuelles entre personnes mineures
undercarriage ['ʌndəkærɪdʒ] n train m d'atterrissage
undercharge [ʌndə'tʃɑːdʒ] vt se tromper dans l'addition de (à l'avantage du client); **he undercharged me by $5** il aurait dû me faire payer 5 dollars de plus
underclass ['ʌndəklɑːs] n sous-prolétariat m
underclothes ['ʌndəkləʊðz] npl sous-vêtements mpl
underclothing ['ʌndəkləʊðɪŋ] n sous-vêtements mpl
undercoat ['ʌndəkəʊt] n sous-couche f
undercook [ʌndə'kʊk] vt ne pas faire cuire assez longtemps
undercover ['ʌndəkʌvə(r)] **1** adj secret(ète) **2** adv clandestinement
undercurrent ['ʌndəkʌrənt] n (in sea) courant m sous-marin; Fig (of emotion, unrest) courant sous-jacent
undercut [ʌndə'kʌt] (pt & pp undercut) vt vendre moins cher que
underdeveloped [ʌndədɪ'veləpt] adj sous-développé(e)
underdog ['ʌndədɒg] n (a) (in contest) outsider m (b) (in society) **the u.** les opprimés mpl
underestimate 1 n [ʌndər'estɪmɪt] sous-estimation f **2** vt [ʌndər'estɪmeɪt] sous-estimer
underexposed ['ʌndərɪks'pəʊzd] adj sous-exposé(e)
underfed [ʌndə'fed] adj sous-alimenté(e)
underfoot [ʌndə'fʊt] adv sous les pieds; **it's slippery u.** le sol est glissant; **to trample sth u.** piétiner qch
underfunding [ʌndə'fʌndɪŋ] n insuffisance f de financement
undergarment ['ʌndəgɑːmənt] n sous-vêtement m
undergo [ʌndə'gəʊ] (pt **underwent** [ʌndə'went], pp **undergone** [ʌndə'gɒn]) vt (change) connaître; (test) subir; **to u. surgery** être opéré(e); **to u. treatment** (of patient) suivre un traitement
undergraduate [ʌndə'grædjʊɪt] n étudiant(e) m,f qui prépare une licence
underground 1 adj ['ʌndəgraʊnd] (a) (below ground) souterrain(e) (b) (clandestine) clandestin(e) **2** adv [ʌndə'graʊnd] (a) (below ground) sous terre (b) **to go u.** (into hiding) passer dans la clandestinité **3** n ['ʌndəgraʊnd] (a) Br (railway system) métro m (b) (resistance movement) mouvement m de résistance
undergrowth ['ʌndəgrəʊθ] n broussailles fpl
underhand ['ʌndəhænd] adj sournois(e)
underlain ['ʌndəleɪn] pp of **underlie**
underlay ['ʌndəleɪ] n (for carpet) thibaude f
underlie [ʌndə'laɪ] (pt **underlay** [ʌndə'leɪ], pp **underlain** [ʌndə'leɪn]) vt sous-tendre
underline [ʌndə'laɪn] vt also Fig souligner
underlying [ʌndə'laɪɪŋ] adj sous-jacent(e)
undermanning [ʌndə'mænɪŋ] n manque m de main-d'œuvre
undermentioned [ʌndəmenʃənd] adj Formal ci-dessous
undermine [ʌndə'maɪn] vt (weaken) saper
underneath [ʌndə'niːθ] **1** prep sous **2** adv dessous **3** n **the u.** le dessous
undernourished [ʌndə'nʌrɪʃt] adj sous-alimenté(e)

underpaid [ʌndə'peɪd] *adj* sous-payé(e)

underpants ['ʌndəpænts] *npl* slip *m*

underpass ['ʌndəpɑːs] *n* passage *m* souterrain

underperform [ʌndəpə'fɔːm] *vi Fin (of shares, investment)* ne pas être performant(e)

underpin [ʌndə'pɪn] *(pt & pp* **underpinned)** *vt* étayer

underpopulated [ʌndə'pɒpjʊleɪtɪd] *adj* sous-peuplé(e)

underprivileged [ʌndə'prɪvɪlɪdʒd] *adj* défavorisé(e)

underqualified [ʌndə'kwɒlɪfaɪd] *adj* sous-qualifié(e)

underrate [ʌndə'reɪt] *vt* sous-estimer

underside ['ʌndəsaɪd] *n* dessous *m*

undersized [ʌndə'saɪzd] *adj* trop petit(e)

underskirt ['ʌndəskɜːt] *n* jupon *m*; *(full-length)* combinaison *f*

understaffed [ʌndə'stɑːft] *adj* **to be u.** manquer de personnel

understand [ʌndə'stænd] *(pt & pp* **understood** [ʌndə'stʊd]) **1** *vt* **(a)** *(comprehend)* comprendre; **to make oneself understood** se faire comprendre; **they u. each other** ils se comprennent **(b)** *(believe, assume)* **to u. that** croire que; **I u. that you're coming to work here** j'ai appris que vous venez travailler ici; **to give sb to u. that** laisser entendre à qn que; **are we to u. that...?** devons-nous en conclure que...?
2 *vi* comprendre

understandable [ʌndə'stændəbəl] *adj* compréhensible

understandably [ʌndə'stændəblɪ] *adv* naturellement

understanding [ʌndə'stændɪŋ] **1** *n* **(a)** *(comprehension, sympathy)* compréhension *f* **(b)** *(agreement)* accord *m*; **to come to** *or* **to reach an u.** parvenir à un accord; **on the u. that** à condition que + *subjunctive*
2 *adj* compréhensif(ive)

understatement [ʌndə'steɪtmənt] *n* **that's an u.!** c'est peu dire!

understood [ʌndə'stʊd] *pt & pp of* **understand**

understudy ['ʌndəstʌdɪ] *n* doublure *f*

undertake [ʌndə'teɪk] *(pt* **undertook** [ʌndə'tʊk], *pp* **undertaken** [ʌndə'teɪkən]) *vt* entreprendre; **to u. to do sth** entreprendre de faire qch

undertaker ['ʌndəteɪkə(r)] *n* entrepreneur *m* de pompes funèbres

undertaking [ʌndə'teɪkɪŋ] *n* **(a)** *(enterprise)* entreprise *f* **(b)** *(promise)* engagement *m*, promesse *f*

undertone ['ʌndətəʊn] *n* *(low voice)* voix *f* basse; *Fig (hint, suggestion)* fond *m*

undertook [ʌndə'tʊk] *pt of* **undertake**

undertow ['ʌndətəʊ] *n* ressac *m*

undervalue [ʌndə'væljuː] *vt (property)* sous-évaluer; *Fig (person, ability)* sous-estimer

underwater 1 *adj* ['ʌndəwɔːtə(r)] de plongée
2 *adv* [ʌndə'wɔːtə(r)] sous l'eau

underwear ['ʌndəweə(r)] *n* sous-vêtements *mpl*

underweight [ʌndə'weɪt] *adj* trop maigre

underwent [ʌndə'went] *pt of* **undergo**

underworld ['ʌndəwɜːld] *n* **(a)** *(in mythology)* **the U.** les Enfers *mpl* **(b)** *(of criminals)* pègre *f*

underwrite ['ʌndəraɪt] *(pt* **underwrote** [ʌndə'rəʊt], *pp* **underwritten** [ʌndə'rɪtən]) *vt* souscrire

underwriter ['ʌndəraɪtə(r)] *n (in insurance)* souscripteur *m*

underwritten [ʌndə'rɪtən] *pp of* **underwrite**

underwrote [ʌndə'rəʊt] *pt of* **underwrite**

undeserved [ʌndɪ'zɜːvd] *adj* immérité(e)

undeserving [ʌndɪ'zɜːvɪŋ] *adj* peu méritant(e); **to be u. of sth** ne pas mériter qch

undesirable [ʌndɪ'zaɪərəbəl] *n & adj* indésirable *mf*

undetected [ʌndɪ'tektɪd] **1** *adj* non détecté(e)
2 *adv* **to go u.** passer inaperçu(e)

undetermined [ʌndɪ'tɜːmɪnd] *adj* indéterminé(e)

undeterred [ʌndɪ'tɜːd] **1** *adj* **to be u. (by sth)** ne pas se laisser décourager (par qch)
2 *adv* sans se laisser décourager

undeveloped [ʌndɪ'veləpt] *adj* non développé(e); *(land)* inexploité(e)

undid [ʌn'dɪd] *pt of* **undo**

undies ['ʌndɪz] *npl Fam* sous-vêtements *mpl*

undigested [ʌndaɪ'dʒestɪd] *adj also Fig* non digéré(e)

undignified [ʌn'dɪgnɪfaɪd] *adj* indigne

undiluted [ʌndaɪ'luːtɪd] *adj (liquid)* non dilué(e); *Fig (emotion)* pur(e)

undiminished [ʌndɪ'mɪnɪʃt] *adj* intact(e)

undiplomatic [ʌndɪplə'mætɪk] *adj* peu diplomate

undisciplined [ʌn'dɪsɪplɪnd] *adj* indiscipliné(e)

undisclosed [ʌndɪs'kləʊzd] *adj* non révélé(e)

undiscovered [ʌndɪs'kʌvəd] **1** *adj* inconnu(e)
2 *adv* **to go/continue u.** rester ignoré(e)

undiscriminating [ʌndɪs'krɪmɪneɪtɪŋ] *adj* **to be u.** manquer de discernement

undisputed [ʌndɪs'pjuːtɪd] *adj* incontesté(e)

undistinguished [ʌndɪs'tɪŋgwɪʃt] *adj* médiocre

undisturbed [ʌndɪs'tɜːbd] *adj (sleep)* paisible; **to leave sth u.** ne pas toucher à qch

undo [ʌn'duː] *(pt* **undid** [ʌn'dɪd], *pp* **undone** [ʌn'dʌn]) *vt* **(a)** *(mistake, damage)* réparer; *Comptr (command)* annuler **(b)** *(knot, button, shoelaces)* défaire; *(parcel, zip)* ouvrir; *(bra, dress)* dégrafer

undoing [ʌn'duːɪŋ] *n* ruine *f*; **her curiosity was her u.** c'est sa curiosité qui l'a perdue

undone [ʌn'dʌn] *pp of* **undo**

undoubted [ʌn'daʊtɪd] *adj* indubitable

undoubtedly [ʌn'daʊtɪdlɪ] *adv* indubitablement

undreamed-of [ʌn'driːmdɒv], **undreamt-of** [ʌn'dremtɒv] *adj* inimaginable

undress [ʌn'dres] **1** *vt* déshabiller; **to get undressed** se déshabiller
2 *vi* se déshabiller
3 *n* **in a state of u.** *(naked)* nu(e); *(nearly naked)* en petite tenue

undue [ʌn'djuː] *adj* excessif(ive)

undulate ['ʌndjʊleɪt] *vi* onduler

undulation [ʌndjʊ'leɪʃən] *n* ondulation *f*

unduly [ʌn'djuːlɪ] *adv* trop

unearned [ʌn'ɜːnd] *adj (reward, punishment)* immérité(e); *Fin* **u. income** rentes *fpl*

unearth [ʌn'ɜːθ] *vt (buried object)* déterrer; *Fig (information, secret)* mettre à jour

unearthly [ʌn'ɜːθlɪ] *adj* **(a)** *(supernatural)* mystérieux(euse) **(b)** *Fam* **at an u. hour** à une heure impossible; **an u. din** *or* **racket** un vacarme de tous les diables; **for some u. reason** pour une raison étrange

unease [ʌn'iːz] *n* malaise *m*

uneasily [ʌn'iːzɪlɪ] *adv* d'un air gêné

uneasy [ʌn'iːzɪ] *adj (person)* mal à l'aise; *(sleep)* agité(e); *(silence)* gêné(e)

uneconomical [ʌniːkə'nɒmɪkəl] *adj* peu économique

uneducated [ʌn'edjʊkeɪtɪd] *adj* sans instruction; **to be u.** ne pas avoir d'instruction

unemotional [ʌnɪ'məʊʃənəl] *adj* impassible

unemployable [ʌnɪm'plɔɪəbəl] *adj* inemployable

unemployed [ʌnɪm'plɔɪd] **1** *npl* **the u.** les sans-emploi *mpl*, les chômeurs *mpl* **2** *adj* sans emploi, au chômage

unemployment [ʌnɪm'plɔɪmənt] *n* chômage *m*; *Br* **u. benefit** allocation ƒ chômage

unending [ʌn'endɪŋ] *adj* interminable

unendurable [ʌnɪn'djʊərəbəl] *adj* insupportable

unenlightened [ʌnɪn'laɪtənd] *adj (person)* peu éclairé(e)

unenlightening [ʌnɪn'laɪtnɪŋ] *adj* obscur(e)

unenterprising [ʌn'entəpraɪzɪŋ] *adj* qui manque d'initiative

unenthusiastic [ʌnɪnθjuːzɪ'æstɪk] *adj* peu enthousiaste

unenviable [ʌn'envɪəbəl] *adj* peu enviable

unequal [ʌn'iːkwəl] *adj* inégal(e)

unequivocal [ʌnɪ'kwɪvəkəl] *adj* sans équivoque

unerring [ʌn'ɜːrɪŋ] *adj* infaillible

UNESCO [juː'neskəʊ] *n (abbr* **United Nations Educational, Scientific and Cultural Organization**) UNESCO ƒ

unethical [ʌn'eθɪkəl] *adj* contraire à l'éthique

uneven [ʌn'iːvən] *adj* inégal(e)

uneventful [ʌnɪ'ventfʊl] *adj* sans histoires

unexceptionable [ʌnɪk'sepʃənəbəl] *adj* tout à fait convenable

unexceptional [ʌnɪk'sepʃənəl] *adj* qui n'a rien d'exceptionnel

unexciting [ʌnɪk'saɪtɪŋ] *adj* peu intéressant(e)

unexpected [ʌnɪkə'pektɪd] *adj* inattendu(e), imprévu(e)

unexplained [ʌnɪks'pleɪnd] *adj* inexpliqué(e)

unexplored [ʌnɪks'plɔːd] *adj* inexploré(e)

unfailing [ʌn'feɪlɪŋ] *adj* à toute épreuve

unfair [ʌn'feə(r)] *adj* injuste; **to be u. to sb** être injuste envers qn; **to have an u. advantage (over sb)** être injustement favorisé(e) (par rapport à qn); *Com* **u. competition** concurrence ƒ déloyale; *Law* **u. dismissal** licenciement *m* abusif

unfairly [ʌn'feəlɪ] *adv (act, treat)* injustement; *(share, distribute)* inéquitablement; *(dismiss)* abusivement

unfairness [ʌn'feənɪs] *n* injustice ƒ

unfaithful [ʌn'feɪθfʊl] *adj* infidèle

unfamiliar [ʌnfə'mɪlɪə(r)] *adj* **(a)** *(unknown)* inconnu(e) **(b)** *(unacquainted)* **to be u. with** ne pas connaître

unfashionable [ʌn'fæʃənəbəl] *adj* démodé(e)

unfasten [ʌn'fɑːsən] **1** *vt* défaire **2** *vi* se défaire

unfathomable [ʌn'fæðəməbəl] *adj* insondable

unfavourable, *Am* **unfavorable** [ʌn'feɪvərəbəl] *adj* défavorable; *(moment)* peu propice

unfeeling [ʌn'fiːlɪŋ] *adj* insensible

unfinished [ʌn'fɪnɪʃt] *adj* inachevé(e); **to have (some) u. business (with sb)** avoir des affaires à régler (avec qn)

unfit [ʌn'fɪt] *adj* **(a)** *(unsuitable)* inapte; **to be u. to do sth** être incapable de faire qch; **he's u. for the job** il est incapable d'assumer ce travail; **u. for human consumption** impropre à la consommation; **u. mother** mère ƒ indigne **(b)** *(physically)* qui n'est pas en forme; **to be u.** ne pas être en forme

unflagging [ʌn'flægɪŋ] *adj (optimism, courage, enthusiasm)* inépuisable; *(attention, interest)* sans faille

unflappable [ʌn'flæpəbəl] *adj* imperturbable

unflattering [ʌn'flætərɪŋ] *adj* peu flatteur(euse)

unflinching [ʌn'flɪnʃɪŋ] *adj (courage)* inépuisable; *(resolve, loyalty, support)* à toute épreuve

unfold [ʌn'fəʊld] **1** *vt* **(a)** *(newspaper, map)* déplier **(b)** *(intentions, proposal)* dévoiler **2** *vi (of story, events)* se développer, se dérouler

unforced [ʌn'fɔːst] *adj* naturel(elle)

unforeseeable [ʌnfɔː'siːəbəl] *adj* imprévisible

unforeseen [ʌnfɔː'siːn] *adj* imprévu(e)

unforgettable [ʌnfə'getəbəl] *adj* inoubliable

unforgivable [ʌnfə'gɪvəbəl] *adj* impardonnable

unforgiving [ʌnfə'gɪvɪŋ] *adj* implacable, impitoyable

unforthcoming [ʌnfɔːθ'kʌmɪŋ] *adj* réticent(e)

unfortunate [ʌn'fɔːtʃənɪt] *adj (person)* malchanceux(euse); *(accident, event)* fâcheux(euse), regrettable; **it is u. that...** il est fâcheux *ou* regrettable que... + *subjunctive*

unfortunately [ʌn'tɔːtʃənɪtlɪ] *adv* malheureusement

unfounded [ʌn'faʊndɪd] *adj* infondé(e), sans fondement

unfriendly [ʌn'frendlɪ] *adj (person)* peu sympathique; *(reception, tone, look)* froid(e)

unfulfilled [ʌnfʊl'tɪld] *adj (promise)* non tenu(e); *(desire, ambition)* insatisfait(e); *(potential)* non réalisé(e); **to feel u.** se sentir insatisfait

unfunny [ʌn'fʌnɪ] *adj* qui n'a rien de drôle

unfurl [ʌn'fɜːl] **1** *vt* déployer **2** *vi* se déployer

unfurnished [ʌn'fɜːnɪʃt] *adj* non meublé(e)

ungainly [ʌn'geɪnlɪ] *adj* disgracieux(euse)

ungenerous [ʌn'dʒenərəs] *adj (person)* qui manque de générosité; *(remark)* pas gentil(ille)

ungodly [ʌn'gɒdlɪ] *adj* impie; *Fam* **at an u. hour** à une heure impossible

ungovernable [ʌn'gʌvənəbəl] *adj (people, country)* ingouvernable; *(feelings)* irrépressible

ungracious [ʌn'greɪʃəs] *adj* peu aimable

ungrateful [ʌn'greɪtfʊl] *adj* ingrat(e)

ungrudging [ʌn'grʌdʒɪŋ] *adj* accordé(e) de bon cœur; **to be u. in one's praise** être élogieux(euse) avec ses compliments

unguarded [ʌn'gɑːdɪd] *adj* **(a)** *(place)* sans surveillance **(b)** *(remark)* irréfléchi(e); **in an u. moment** dans un moment d'inattention

unhampered [ʌn'hæmpəd] *adj* non entravé(e) **(by par)**

unhappily [ʌn'hæpɪlɪ] *adv* **(a)** *(unfortunately)* malheureusement **(b)** *(sadly)* sans joie, sans bonheur

unhappiness [ʌn'hæpɪnɪs] *n* tristesse ƒ

unhappy [ʌn'hæpɪ] *adj* **(a)** *(sad)* triste, malheureux(euse) **(b)** *(worried)* **to be u. about doing sth** ne pas vouloir faire qch **(c)** *(not pleased)* mécontent(e) **(with** de**) (d)** *(unfortunate)* malheureux(euse), regrettable

unharmed [ʌn'hɑːmd] *adj* indemne

UNHCR [juːeneɪtʃsiː'ɑː(r)] *n (abbr* **United Nations High Commission for Refugees**) HCR *m*

unhealthy [ʌn'helθɪ] *adj* **(a)** *(person)* maladif(ive); *(environment, climate)* malsain(e) **(b)** *(unwholesome)* malsain(e)

unheard-of [ʌn'hɜːdɒv] *adj* **(a)** *(unknown)* inconnu(e) **(b)** *(unprecedented)* inouï(e); **it was u. in my youth!** c'était inconcevable dans ma jeunesse!

unheeded [ʌn'hiːdɪd] *adj* ignoré(e); **to go u.** rester ignoré

unhelpful [ʌn'helpful] *adj (person)* peu serviable; *(criticism, advice)* de peu d'utilité

unhesitating [ʌn'hezɪteɪtɪŋ] *adj (support)* résolu(e), ferme; *(reply, reaction)* immédiat(e)

unhindered [ʌn'hɪndəd] **1** *adj (progress)* sans encombres; **to be u. by sth** *(doubts, worry)* ne pas être gêné(e) par qch
2 *adv* sans encombres

unhinged [ʌn'hɪndʒd] *adj (mad)* déséquilibré(e)

unhip [ʌn'hɪp] *adj Fam (untrendy)* ringard(e)

unholy [ʌn'həʊlɪ] *adj* impie; *Fam* **an u. mess/racket** une pagaille/un bruit invraisemblable; **u. alliance** alliance *f* contre nature

unhurt [ʌn'hɜːt] *adj* indemne

unhygienic [ʌnhaɪ'dʒiːnɪk] *adj* contraire à l'hygiène; *(person)* qui manque d'hygiène

UNICEF ['juːnɪsef] *n (abbr* **United Nations International Children's Emergency Fund)** UNICEF *m*

unicorn ['juːnɪkɔːn] *n* licorne *f*

unidentified [ʌnaɪ'dentɪfaɪd] *adj* non identifié(e); **u. flying object** objet *m* volant non identifié

unification [juːnɪfɪ'keɪʃən] *n* unification *f*

uniform ['juːnɪfɔːm] **1** *n* uniforme *m*
2 *adj (colour, size)* uniforme; *(temperature)* constant(e)

uniformity [juːnɪ'fɔːmɪtɪ] *n* uniformité *f*

uniformly ['juːnɪfɔːmlɪ] *adv* uniformément

unify ['juːnɪfaɪ] *(pt & pp* **unified) 1** *vt* unifier
2 *vi* s'unifier

unilateral [juːnɪ'lætərəl] *adj* unilatéral(e)

unimaginable [ʌnɪ'mædʒɪnəbəl] *adj* inimaginable

unimaginative [ʌnɪ'mædʒɪnətɪv] *adj* qui manque d'imagination, peu imaginatif(ive)

unimpaired [ʌnɪm'peəd] *adj* intact(e)

unimportant [ʌnɪm'pɔːtənt] *adj* sans importance

unimpressed [ʌnɪm'prest] *adj* qui n'est pas impressionné(e); *(unconvinced)* qui n'est pas convaincu(e)

uninformed [ʌnɪn'fɔːmd] *adj* mal informé(e) **(about** sur)

uninhabitable [ʌnɪn'hæbɪtəbəl] *adj* inhabitable

uninhabited [ʌnɪn'hæbɪtɪd] *adj* inhabité(e)

uninhibited [ʌnɪn'hɪbɪtɪd] *adj (person)* sans complexes; *(feeling)* non refréné(e)

uninitiated [ʌnɪ'nɪʃɪeɪtɪd] *adj* non initié(e)

uninspiring [ʌnɪn'spaɪrɪŋ] *adj* peu stimulant(e)

unintelligible [ʌnɪn'telɪdʒɪbəl] *adj* inintelligible

unintended [ʌnɪn'tendɪd] *adj* involontaire

unintentional [ʌnɪn'tenʃənəl] *adj* involontaire

uninterested [ʌn'ɪntərestɪd] *adj* indifférent(e)

uninteresting [ʌn'ɪntərestɪŋ] *adj* inintéressant(e)

uninterrupted [ʌnɪntə'rʌptɪd] *adj* ininterrompu(e)

uninvited [ʌnɪn'vaɪtɪd] **1** *adj (comment, advice)* non désiré(e); **u. guest** invité(e)-surprise *m,f*
2 *adv* sans invitation

uninviting [ʌnɪn'vaɪtɪŋ] *adj* peu attrayant(e); *(food)* peu appétissant(e)

union ['juːnjən] *n* **(a)** *(between countries, people)* union *f*; **the U. Jack** l'Union Jack *m* (drapeau du Royaume-Uni) **(b)** *(trade union)* syndicat *m*

unionist ['juːnjənɪst] *n* **(a)** *(supporter of trade union)* syndicaliste *mf* **(b)** *(in Northern Ireland)* unioniste *mf*

unionize ['juːnjənaɪz] *vt* syndiquer

unique [juː'niːk] *adj* unique; **to be u. to** être propre à

unisex ['juːnɪseks] *adj* unisexe

unison ['juːnɪsən] *n* **in u.** *(sing, play)* à l'unisson; *(speak, reply)* en même temps

unit ['juːnɪt] *n* **(a)** *(in general)* unité *f*; **u. of measurement** unité de mesure; *Com* **u. price** prix *m* à l'unité; *Fin* **u. trust** fonds *m* commun de placement, SICAV *f* **(b)** *(part of system, machine)* bloc *m*, élément *m* **(c)** *(in hospital)* service *m*, département *m*; *(in army)* unité *f* **(d)** *(of furniture)* élément *m*

unitary ['juːnɪtərɪ] *adj* unitaire

unite [juː'naɪt] **1** *vt* unir, rassembler
2 *vi* s'unir; **to u. in doing sth** s'unir pour faire qch

united [juː'naɪtɪd] *adj* uni(e); **the U. Arab Emirates** les Émirats *mpl* arabes unis; **the U. Kingdom** le Royaume-Uni; **the U. Nations** les Nations *fpl* unies; **the U. States (of America)** les États-Unis *mpl* (d'Amérique)

unity ['juːnɪtɪ] *n* unité *f*

univ *(abbr* **university)** univ

universal [juːnɪ'vɜːsəl] *adj* universel(elle); **u. suffrage** suffrage *m* universel

universally [juːnɪ'vɜːsəlɪ] *adv* universellement

universe ['juːnɪvɜːs] *n* univers *m*

university [juːnɪ'vɜːsɪtɪ] *n* université *f*

UNIX ['juːnɪks] *n* Comptr *(abbr* **Uniplexed Information and Computing System)** UNIX *m*

unjust [ʌn'dʒʌst] *adj* injuste

unjustifiable [ʌndʒʌstɪ'faɪəbəl] *adj* injustifiable

unjustified [ʌn'dʒʌstɪfaɪd] *adj* injustifié(e)

unkempt [ʌn'kem(p)t] *adj* négligé(e)

unkind [ʌn'kaɪnd] *adj* pas gentil(ille); **to be u. to sb** ne pas être gentil avec qn

unkindly [ʌn'kaɪndlɪ] *adv* méchamment; **to take u. to sth** mal accepter qch

unknowingly [ʌn'nəʊɪŋlɪ] *adv* inconsciemment

unknown [ʌn'nəʊn] **1** *adj* inconnu(e); *Fig* **to be an u. quantity** rester une inconnue; **the U. Soldier** le Soldat inconnu
2 *adv* **u. to me/us** à mon/notre insu
3 *n (person)* inconnu(e) *m,f*; **the u.** l'inconnu *m*

unlace [ʌn'leɪs] *vt* délacer, défaire

unladylike [ʌn'leɪdɪlaɪk] *adj (person)* qui ne se conduit pas comme une jeune fille; *(behaviour)* qui n'est pas digne d'une jeune fille

unlawful [ʌn'lɔːful] *adj* illégal(e), illicite

unleaded [ʌn'ledɪd] **1** *adj* sans plomb
2 *n* sans plomb *m*

unleash [ʌn'liːʃ] *vt (dog)* détacher, lâcher; *Fig (emotion, criticism)* susciter

unleavened [ʌn'levənd] *adj* sans levain

unless [ʌn'les] *conj* à moins que + *subjunctive*; **u. I hear to the contrary** sauf avis contraire

unlike [ʌn'laɪk] *prep* **to be u. sb/sth** ne pas être comme qn/qch; **he's not u. his sister** il ressemble assez à sa sœur; **he, u. his father,...** lui, à la différence de son père,...; **it's u. her to do such a thing** cela ne lui ressemble pas de faire une chose pareille

unlikely [ʌn'laɪklɪ] *adj* improbable; *(story, explanation)* invraisemblable; **it's u. to happen** il est peu probable que cela se produise; **she's u. to do it** il est peu probable qu'elle le fasse; **in the u. event of an emergency** dans le cas fort peu probable d'un urgence

unlimited [ʌn'lɪmɪtɪd] *adj* illimité(e), sans limites; **u. mileage** *(of hired car)* ≃ kilométrage *m* illimité

unlisted [ʌn'lɪstɪd] *adj* **(a)** *Fin* non inscrit(e) à la cote **(b)** *Am Tel (phone number)* qui est sur liste rouge

unlit [ʌn'lɪt] *adj (fire, cigarette)* non allumé(e); *(place)* non éclairé(e)

unload [ʌn'ləʊd] **1** *vt (boat, gun, goods)* décharger; *Fig* **to u. one's problems onto sb** se soulager de ses problèmes en en parlant à qn **2** *vi (of lorry, ship)* décharger

unlock [ʌn'lɒk] *vt (door)* ouvrir; *Fig (mystery)* dévoiler, révéler

unlovable [ʌn'lʌvəbəl] *adj* peu attachant(e)

unloved [ʌn'lʌvd] *adj* mal aimé(e)

unlovely [ʌn'lʌvlɪ] *adj* déplaisant(e)

unluckily [ʌn'lʌkɪlɪ] *adv* malheureusement

unlucky [ʌn'lʌkɪ] *adj (coincidence, decision)* malheureux(euse); *(day)* de malchance; **to be u.** *(of person)* être malchanceux(euse); *(of thing)* porter malheur

unmanageable [ʌn'mænɪdʒəbəl] *adj (person, situation)* difficile; *(hair)* impossible à coiffer

unmanly [ʌn'mænlɪ] *adj (effeminate)* efféminé(e); peu viril(e); *(cowardly)* lâche

unmanned [ʌn'mænd] *adj (spaceship)* inhabité(e)

unmarked [ʌn'mɑːkt] *adj* **(a)** *(grave)* sans inscription; **u. (police) car** voiture *f* (de police) banalisée **(b)** *(uncorrected)* non corrigé(e)

unmarried [ʌn'mærɪd] *adj* non marié(e)

unmask [ʌn'mɑːsk] *vt* démasquer

unmentionable [ʌn'menʃənəbəl] *adj* à ne pas mentionner

unmistakable [ʌnmɪs'teɪkəbəl] *adj* caractéristique

unmitigated [ʌn'mɪtɪɡeɪtɪd] *adj* total(e), absolu(e)

unmoved [ʌn'muːvd] **I** *adj* **to be u. by sth** rester insensible à qch; **he was u. by her** elle le laissait complètement indifférent **2** *adv* sans broncher

unnamed [ʌn'neɪmd] *adj (person)* anonyme; *(thing)* sans nom

unnatural [ʌn'nætjərəl] *adj* **(a)** *(abnormal)* anormal(e) **(b)** *(affected)* affecté(e)

unnecessary [ʌn'nesɪsərɪ] *adj* inutile, superflu(e)

unnerve [ʌn'nɜːv] *vt* troubler

unnerving [ʌn'nɜːvɪŋ] *adj* troublant(e)

unnoticed [ʌn'nəʊtɪst] **1** *adj* inaperçu(e) **2** *adv* **to pass** *or* **go u.** passer inaperçu(e)

UNO [juːen'əʊ] *n (abbr* **United Nations Organization)** ONU *f*

unobservant [ʌnəb'zɜːvənt] *adj* peu observateur(trice)

unobserved [ʌnəb'zɜːvd] **1** *adj* inaperçu(e) **2** *adv* **to do sth u.** faire qch sans être vu(e)

unobstructed [ʌnəb'strʌktɪd] *adj* dégagé(e); *(pipe)* non obstrué(e)

unobtainable [ʌnəb'teɪnəbəl] *adj* impossible à obtenir

unobtrusive [ʌnəb'truːsɪv] *adj* discret(ète)

unoccupied [ʌn'ɒkjʊpaɪd] *adj (person)* qui n'est pas occupé(e); *(seat)* libre; *(house)* inhabité(e), inoccupé(e)

unofficial [ʌnə'fɪʃəl] *adj* officieux(euse), non officiel(elle); *Ind* **u. strike** grève *f* sauvage

unopened [ʌn'əʊpənd] *adj* non ouvert(e)

unopposed [ʌnə'pəʊzd] **1** *adj* sans opposition; **to be u.** ne pas rencontrer d'opposition **2** *adv* **to go u.** ne pas rencontrer d'opposition

unorthodox [ʌn'ɔːθədɒks] *adj* peu orthodoxe

unpack [ʌn'pæk] **1** *vt (suitcase)* défaire; *(contents)* déballer; *(box)* ouvrir **2** *vi* défaire ses bagages

unpaid [ʌn'peɪd] *adj* **(a)** *(work, volunteer)* non rémunéré(e) **(b)** *(bill, debt)* impayé(e)

unpalatable [ʌn'pælətəbəl] *adj (food)* qui n'est pas très bon (bonne); *Fig (truth)* désagréable à entendre

unparalleled [ʌn'pærəleld] *adj* incomparable, sans pareil(eille)

unpardonable [ʌn'pɑːdənəbəl] *adj* impardonnable

unpatriotic [ʌnpætrɪ'ɒtɪk, ʌnpeɪtrɪ'ɒtɪk] *adj (person)* peu patriote; *(song, remark)* antipatriotique

unperturbed [ʌnpə'tɜːbd] **1** *adj* **to be u. by sth** ne pas se laisser perturber par qch **2** *adv* imperturbablement

unplanned [ʌn'plænd] *adj* imprévu(e); *(pregnancy)* accidentel(elle)

unpleasant [ʌn'plezənt] *adj* désagréable, déplaisant(e)

unpleasantness [ʌn'plezəntnɪs] *n* **(a)** *(unpleasant nature)* côté *m* désagréable **(b)** *(ill-feeling)* désagréments *mpl*

unplug [ʌn'plʌɡ] *(pt & pp* **unplugged)** *vt* débrancher

unpolished [ʌn'pɒlɪʃt] *adj (shoes, surface)* non ciré(e); *Fig (performance, style)* imparfait(e)

unpolluted [ʌnpə'luːtɪd] *adj* non pollué(e)

unpopular [ʌn'pɒpjʊlə(r)] *adj* impopulaire; **she's very u. with the boss at the moment** elle n'est pas dans les bonnes grâces du patron en ce moment

unpopularity [ʌnpɒpjʊ'lærɪtɪ] *n* impopularité *f*

unpredictable [ʌnprɪ'dɪktəbəl] *adj* imprévisible

unprejudiced [ʌn'predʒʊdɪst] *adj (view, person)* impartial(e)

unprepared [ʌnprɪ'peəd] *adj (speech)* improvisé(e); **to be u. for sth** être mal préparé(e) à qch; *(not expect)* ne pas s'attendre à qch

unprepossessing [ʌnpriːpə'zesɪŋ] *adj* peu avenant(e)

unpresentable [ʌnprɪ'zentəbəl] *adj* qui n'est pas présentable

unpretentious [ʌnprɪ'tenʃəs] *adj* sans prétention(s)

unprincipled [ʌn'prɪnsɪpəld] *adj* sans scrupules

unprintable [ʌn'prɪntəbəl] *adj* licencieux(euse)

unproductive [ʌnprə'dʌktɪv] *adj* improductif(ive)

unprofessional [ʌnprə'feʃənəl] *adj* qui n'est pas professionnel(elle)

unprofitable [ʌn'prɒfɪtəbəl] *adj* peu rentable

unpromising [ʌn'prɒmɪsɪŋ] *adj* peu prometteur(euse)

unpronounceable [ʌnprə'naʊnsəbəl] *adj* imprononçable

unprotected [ʌnprə'tektɪd] *adj* sans protection; *(sex)* non protégé(e)

unprovoked [ʌnprə'vəʊkt] *adj* gratuit(e)

unpublished [ʌn'pʌblɪʃt] *adj* inédit(e)

unpunished [ʌn'pʌnɪʃt] **1** *adj* impuni(e) **2** *adv* **to go u.** rester impuni(e)

unqualified [ʌn'kwɒlɪfaɪd] *adj* **(a)** *(doctor, teacher)* non qualifié(e); **to be u. to do sth** ne pas être qualifié pour faire qch **(b)** *(support)* inconditionnel(elle), sans réserve; *(disaster, success)* total(e), complet(ète)

unquestionable [ʌn'kwestjənəbəl] *adj* indubitable, incontestable

unquestioning [ʌn'kwestjənɪŋ] *adj (trust, obedience)* absolu(e), aveugle

unravel [ʌn'rævəl] *(pt & pp* **unravelled) 1** *vt (wool, knitting)* défaire; *(threads)* démêler; *Fig (plot)* dénouer; *(mystery)* éclaircir **2** *vi (of wool, knitting)* se défaire; *Fig (of plan)* péricliter; *(of mystery)* s'éclaircir

unreadable [ʌnˈriːdəbəl] *adj* illisible

unreal [ʌnˈrɪəl] *adj* irréel(elle)

unrealistic [ʌnrɪəˈlɪstɪk] *adj* irréaliste

unreasonable [ʌnˈriːzənəbəl] *adj* déraisonnable

unrecognizable [ʌnrekəgˈnaɪzəbəl] *adj* méconnaissable

unrecognized [ʌnˈrekəgnaɪzd] **1** *adj* méconnu(e) **2** *adv* **to go u.** rester méconnu(e)

unrecorded [ʌnrɪˈkɔːdɪd] *adj* non enregistré(e)

unrefined [ʌnrɪˈfaɪnd] *adj* (**a**) *(sugar, petrol)* non raffiné(e) (**b**) *(person, taste)* qui manque de raffinement

unregistered [ʌnˈredʒɪstəd] *adj (birth)* non déclaré(e)

unrelated [ʌnrɪˈleɪtɪd] *adj* **to be u.** *(of events)* ne pas avoir de rapport; *(of people)* n'avoir aucun lien de parenté

unrelenting [ʌnrɪˈlentɪŋ] *adj* incessant(e); *(person)* tenace

unreliable [ʌnrɪˈlaɪəbəl] *adj* peu fiable

unrelieved [ʌnrɪˈliːvd] *adj (pain)* constant(e)

unremarkable [ʌnrɪˈmɑːkəbəl] *adj* quelconque

unremitting [ʌnrɪˈmɪtɪŋ] *adj* inlassable, infatigable

unrepentant [ʌnrɪˈpentənt] *adj* impénitent(e)

unreported [ʌnrɪˈpɔːtɪd] **1** *adj* non signalé(e) **2** *adv* **to go u.** ne pas être signalé(e)

unrepresentative [ʌnreprɪˈzentətɪv] *adj* non représentatif(ive)

unrepresented [ʌnreprɪˈzentɪd] *adj* non représenté(e)

unrequited love [ˈʌnrɪkwaɪtɪdˈlʌv] *n* amour *m* non partagé

unreserved [ʌnrɪˈzɜːvd] *adj* (**a**) *(praise, support)* sans réserve (**b**) *(seat, table)* non réservé(e)

unresponsive [ʌnrɪˈspɒnsɪv] *adj* sans réaction; **to be u. to sth** être insensible à qch

unrest [ʌnˈrest] *n* agitation *f*, troubles *mpl*

unrestricted [ʌnrɪˈstrɪktɪd] *adj* illimité(e); *(access)* libre

unrewarding [ʌnrɪˈwɔːdɪŋ] *adj (financially)* qui ne rapporte pas; *(intellectually)* ingrat(e)

unripe [ʌnˈraɪp] *adj* qui n'est pas mûr(e)

unrivalled [ʌnˈraɪvəld] *adj* sans pareil(eille), incomparable

unromantic [ʌnrəˈmæntɪk] *adj* peu romantique

unruffled [ʌnˈrʌfəld] *adj* imperturbable

unruly [ʌnˈruːlɪ] *adj (child, hair)* indiscipliné(e); *(crowd)* incontrôlé(e)

unsaddle [ʌnˈsædəl] *vt (horse)* desseller

unsafe [ʌnˈseɪf] *adj* (**a**) *(in danger)* en danger (**b**) *(dangerous)* dangereux(euse)

unsaid [ʌnˈsed] *adj* **to leave sth u.** passer qch sous silence; **it's better left u.** il vaut mieux garder le silence là-dessus

unsalted [ʌnˈsɔːltɪd] *adj* sans sel; **u. butter** beurre *m* doux

unsatisfactory [ʌnsætɪsˈfæktərɪ] *adj* peu satisfaisant(e)

unsatisfying [ʌnˈsætɪsfaɪɪŋ] *adj* peu satisfaisant(e)

unsavoury [ʌnˈseɪvərɪ] *adj (person, place)* peu recommandable; *(reputation)* sale

unscathed [ʌnˈskeɪðd] *adj* indemne

unscheduled [ʌnˈʃedjuːld] *adj* imprévu(e)

unscientific [ʌnsaɪənˈtɪfɪk] *adj* non scientifique

unscramble [ʌnˈskræmbəl] *vt* décoder

unscrew [ʌnˈskruː] **1** *vt* dévisser **2** *vi* se dévisser

unscrupulous [ʌnˈskruːpjʊləs] *adj (person)* sans scrupules; *(action)* malhonnête

unseat [ʌnˈsiːt] *vt (rider)* désarçonner; *Fig (MP)* faire perdre son siège à; *(leader)* faire tomber

unseemly [ʌnˈsiːmlɪ] *adj* inconvenant(e), indécent(e)

unseen [ʌnˈsiːn] **1** *adj* invisible; **u. translation** traduction *f* à vue **2** *adv* **to do sth u.** faire qch sans qu'on vous voie

unselfconscious [ʌnselfˈkɒnʃəs] *adj* naturel(elle)

unselfish [ʌnˈselfɪʃ] *adj* généreux(euse)

unsentimental [ʌnsentɪˈmentəl] *adj (person)* peu sentimental(e); *(book, film)* dénué(e) de tout sentimentalisme

unsettle [ʌnˈsetəl] *vt* perturber

unshakeable [ʌnˈʃeɪkəbəl] *adj* inébranlable

unshaven [ʌnˈʃeɪvən] *adj* pas rasé(e)

unsightly [ʌnˈsaɪtlɪ] *adj* laid(e)

unsigned [ʌnˈsaɪnd] *adj* non signé(e)

unskilful [ʌnˈskɪlf(ʊ)l] *adj* maladroit(e), malhabile

unskilled [ʌnˈskɪld] *adj* non qualifié(e)

unsociable [ʌnˈsəʊʃəbəl] *adj (by nature)* sauvage; **she's feeling rather u. at the moment** elle n'a pas envie de voir du monde en ce moment

unsold [ʌnˈsəʊld] *adj* invendu(e)

unsolicited [ʌnsəˈlɪsɪtɪd] *adj* non sollicité(e)

unsolved [ʌnˈsɒlvd] *adj* non résolu(e)

unsophisticated [ʌnsəˈfɪstɪkeɪtɪd] *adj* simple

unsound [ʌnˈsaʊnd] *adj* (**a**) *(health)* précaire; *Law* **to be of u. mind** ne pas jouir de toutes ses facultés mentales (**b**) *(decision, advice)* peu judicieux(euse); *(investment)* hasardeux(euse)

unsparing [ʌnˈspeərɪŋ] *adj* **to be u. of one's time/with one's advice** ne pas être avare de son temps/de ses conseils

unspeakable [ʌnˈspiːkəbəl] *adj* indescriptible

unspecified [ʌnˈspesɪfaɪd] *adj* non spécifié(e)

unspoilt [ʌnˈspɔɪlt] *adj (beach, landscape)* préservé(e)

unspoken [ʌnˈspəʊkən] *adj (fear, threat)* inexprimé(e); *(agreement)* tacite

unsporting [ʌnˈspɔːtɪŋ], **unsportsmanlike** [ʌnˈspɔːtsmənlaɪk] *adj* qui n'est pas fair-play

unstable [ʌnˈsteɪbəl] *adj* instable

unsteady [ʌnˈstedɪ] *adj (table, chair)* bancal(e); *(hand, voice)* mal assuré(e); **to be u. on one's feet** ne pas être très solide sur ses jambes

unstinting [ʌnˈstɪntɪŋ] *adj (praise, effort)* sans réserve

unstressed [ʌnˈstrest] *adj Ling* inaccentué(e)

unstuck [ʌnˈstʌk] *adj Fam* **to come u.** *(of person, plan)* se casser la figure

unsubstantiated [ʌnsəbˈstænʃɪeɪtɪd] *adj (accusation)* sans fondement

unsuccessful [ʌnsəkˈsesfʊl] *adj* **to be u.** *(of person, project)* ne pas réussir

unsuccessfully [ʌnsəkˈsesfəlɪ] *adv* en vain, sans succès

unsuitable [ʌnˈsuːtəbəl] *adj (candidate)* inadéquat(e); *(friend)* pas convenable; *(time)* inopportun(e); *(choice)* inapproprié(e); **to be u. for sth** ne pas convenir à qch; **this film is u. for children** ce n'est pas un film pour les enfants

unsuited [ʌnˈsuːtɪd] *adj* **to be u. to sth** ne pas être fait(e) pour qch; **to be u.** *(of couple)* être mal assorti(e)

unsupported [ʌnsəˈpɔːtɪd] *adj* (**a**) *(statement, charges)* sans fondement (**b**) *(structure)* non soutenu(e)

unsure [ʌnˈʃʊə(r)] adj incertain(e), peu sûr(e); **to be u.** of or about sth ne pas être sûr de qch

unsurpassed [ʌnsəˈpɑːst] adj inégalé(e)

unsuspected [ʌnsəsˈpektɪd] adj insoupçonné(e)

unsuspecting [ʌnsəsˈpektɪŋ] adj qui ne se doute de rien

unsweetened [ʌnˈswiːtənd] adj non sucré(e), sans sucre ajouté

unswerving [ʌnˈswɜːvɪŋ] adj à toute épreuve

unsympathetic [ʌnsɪmpəˈθetɪk] adj peu compatissant(e) (**to** à); (to cause, request) insensible (**to** à)

unsystematic [ʌnsɪstəˈmætɪk] adj non systématique

untainted [ʌnˈteɪntɪd] adj (food) qui n'a pas été contaminé(e); (reputation) qui n'a pas été entaché(e)

untalented [ʌnˈtæləntɪd] adj peu doué(e)

untamed [ʌnˈteɪmd] adj (animal) sauvage

untangle [ʌnˈtæŋgəl] vt demeler; Fig (plot) denouer

untapped [ʌnˈtæpt] adj inexploité(e)

untenable [ʌnˈtenəbəl] adj (position) intenable; (theory) indefendable

untested [ʌnˈtestɪd] adj (drug, product) non testé(e); (method, system) qui n'a pas été mis(e) à l'épreuve

unthinkable [ʌnˈθɪŋkəbəl] adj impensable, inconcevable

untidiness [ʌnˈtaɪdɪnɪs] n désordre m

untidy [ʌnˈtaɪdɪ] adj (person) désordonné(e); (place) en désordre

untie [ʌnˈtaɪ] vt (knot, shoelaces) défaire; (string) dénouer; (person, animal) détacher

until [ʌnˈtɪl] **1** prep jusqu'à; **u. June** jusqu'en juin; **u. now** jusqu'a present; **not u. tomorrow** pas avant demain; **I didn't see her u. Sunday** c'est seulement dimanche que je l'ai vue
2 conj jusqu'à ce que + subjunctive; **u. she gets back** jusqu'à ce qu'elle revienne; **don't move u. I tell you** ne bouge pas avant que je (ne) te le dise

untimely [ʌnˈtaɪmlɪ] adj (death) prématuré(e); (remark) inopportun(e); (moment) mauvais(e)

untiring [ʌnˈtaɪərɪŋ] adj infatigable, inlassable

untold [ʌnˈtəʊld] adj (wealth, beauty) immense

untouchable [ʌnˈtʌtʃəbəl] **1** n intouchable mf; Fig paria m
2 adj intouchable

untouched [ʌnˈtʌtʃt] adj qui n'a pas été touché(e), **to leave sth u.** ne pas toucher à qch

untoward [ʌntəˈwɔːd] adj fâcheux(euse), malencontreux(euse)

untrained [ʌnˈtreɪnd] adj (animal) non dressé(e); (person) sans formation

untranslatable [ʌntrænsˈleɪtəbəl] adj intraduisible

untried [ʌnˈtraɪd] adj (a) (person, system) qui n'a pas encore fait ses preuves (**b**) Law (person, case) non jugé(e)

untroubled [ʌnˈtrʌbəld] adj tranquille, calme; **to be u. by sth** ne pas être perturbé(e) par qch

untrue [ʌnˈtruː] adj (a) (false) faux (fausse) (**b**) (unfaithful) infidèle (**to** à)

untrustworthy [ʌnˈtrʌstwɜːðɪ] adj (person) qui n'est pas digne de confiance; (information) qui n'est pas fiable

untruth [ʌnˈtruːθ] n mensonge m

untruthful [ʌnˈtruːθfʊl] adj (person) menteur(euse); (story, reply) mensonger(ère)

unusable [ʌnˈjuːzəbəl] adj inutilisable

unused adj (a) [ʌnˈjuːzd] (not in use) inutilisé(e) (**b**) (never yet used) neuf (neuve) (**c**) [ʌnˈjuːst] (unaccustomed) **to be u.**

to sth/to doing sth ne pas avoir l'habitude de qch/de faire qch

unusual [ʌnˈjuːʒʊəl] adj (not common) inhabituel(elle); (strange) bizarre, étrange; **it's u. of her to be late** c'est rare qu'elle arrive en retard

unusually [ʌnˈjuːʒʊəlɪ] adv exceptionnellement

unvaried [ʌnˈveərɪd] adj monotone

unvarnished [ʌnˈvɑːnɪʃt] adj non verni(e), Fig **the u. truth** la vérité pure et simple

unveil [ʌnˈveɪl] vt also Fig dévoiler

unverifiable [ʌnˈverɪfaɪəbəl] adj invérifiable

unvoiced [ʌnˈvɔɪst] adj (a) Ling non voisé(e) (**b**) (unspoken) inexprimé(e)

unwaged [ʌnˈweɪdʒd] **1** npl **the u.** ceux qui n'ont pas d'activité rémunérée
2 adj qui n'a pas d'activité rémunérée

unwanted [ʌnˈwɒntɪd] adj non désiré(e); **to feel u.** se sentir de trop

unwarranted [ʌnˈwɒrəntɪd] adj injustifié(e)

unwary [ʌnˈweərɪ] adj sans méfiance

unwavering [ʌnˈweɪvərɪŋ] adj (devotion) inébranlable; (loyalty, support) à toute épreuve; (gaze) fixe

unwelcome [ʌnˈwelkəm] adj (visit, visitor) importun(e); (news) facheux(euse); **to make sb feel u.** faire sentir à qn qu'il n'est pas le bienvenu

unwell [ʌnˈwel] adj souffrant(e)

unwholesome [ʌnˈhəʊlsəm] adj malsain(e)

unwieldy [ʌnˈwiːldɪ] adj (object) difficile à manier; Fig (system, method) lourd(e)

unwilling [ʌnˈwɪlɪŋ] adj réticent(e); **to be u. to do sth** être réticent à faire qch

unwillingness [ʌnˈwɪlɪŋɪs] n réticence f

unwind [ʌnˈwaɪnd] (pt & pp unwound [ʌnˈwaʊnd]) **1** vt (string, wool) dérouler
2 vi (a) (of string, wool) se dérouler (**b**) Fam (relax) se détendre, se relaxer

unwise [ʌnˈwaɪz] adj (person) imprudent(e); (decision, action) peu judicieux(euse)

unwitting [ʌnˈwɪtɪŋ] adj involontaire

unworkable [ʌnˈwɜːkəbəl] adj infaisable

unworthy [ʌnˈwɜːðɪ] adj indigne (**of** de)

unwrap [ʌnˈræp] (pt & pp unwrapped) vt déballer

unwritten [ʌnˈrɪtən] adj (language) non écrit(e); (agreement) verbal(e); **it's an u. rule that...** il est entendu que...

unyielding [ʌnˈjiːldɪŋ] adj inflexible

unzip [ʌnˈzɪp] (pt & pp unzipped) vt ouvrir (la fermeture Éclair®)

up [ʌp] **1** adv (a) (with motion) **to come/go up** monter; **to go up to sb** s'approcher de qn; **to go up north** aller au nord; **to put one's hand up** lever la main; **to put a poster up** accrocher un poster; **petrol has gone up in price** l'essence a augmenté
(**b**) (with position) en haut; **up here** ici; **up there** là-haut; **up above** au-dessus; **further up** plus haut; **petrol is up in price** l'essence a augmenté
(**c**) (ahead) **to be one goal/five points up** avoir un but/cinq points d'avance
(**d**) (in phrases with to) **up to now/the age of five** jusqu'à maintenant/l'âge de cinq ans; **what are the children up to?** que fabriquent les enfants?; **she's up to something** elle prépare quelque chose; **what have you been up to?** qu'est-ce que tu devines?; **it's up to you** (you decide) c'est à vous de décider; **he's not up to the job** il n'est pas à la hauteur de la

tâche; **I don't feel up to it** je ne m'en sens pas capable; **it's not up to much** *(not very good)* ce n'est pas extraordinaire **2** *prep* **(a)** *(with motion)* **to go up the stairs/the street** monter les escaliers/la rue; **to run up the stairs/the street** monter les escaliers/la rue en courant; **to climb up a hill** monter à une colline; *Vulg* **up yours!** va te faire foutre!

(b) *(with position)* **to be up a tree/ladder** être dans un arbre/sur une échelle; **to live up the street (from sb)** habiter plus haut dans la rue (que qn); *Fig* **to be up against sth** avoir affaire à qch **3** *adj* **(a)** *(out of bed)* levé(e); **I was up at six** j'étais levé à six heures; **we were up all night** nous sommes restés debout toute la nuit; **to be up and about** être debout; *(after illness)* être sur pied **(b)** *(finished)* **the two weeks were up** les deux semaines étaient terminées; **(your) time's up** c'est terminé **(c)** *Fam (wrong)* **something's up** quelque chose ne va pas; **what's up?** qu'est-ce qu'il y a?; **what's up with her?** qu'est-ce qu'elle a? **(d)** *(idiom)* **to be up and running** *(of machine, system)* être opérationnel(elle) **4** *n* **ups and downs** des hauts et des bas **5** *vt Fam (price, offer)* augmenter **6** *vi Fam* **to up and go** *or* **leave** filer

up-and-coming [ˈʌpəndˈkʌmɪŋ] *adj* qui monte

upbeat [ʌpˈbiːt] *adj* optimiste

upbraid [ʌpˈbreɪd] *vt* réprimander; **to u. sb for sth** reprocher qch à qn; **to u. sb for doing sth** reprocher à qn d'avoir fait qch

upbringing [ˈʌpbrɪŋɪŋ] *n* éducation *f*

update 1 *n* [ˈʌpdeɪt] mise *f* à jour, actualisation *f* **2** *vt* [ʌpˈdeɪt] mettre à jour, actualiser; **to u. sb on sth** mettre qn au courant de qch

upend [ʌpˈend] *vt* renverser

upfront [ʌpˈfrʌnt] **1** *adj Fam (frank)* franc (franche), direct(e) **2** *adv (in advance)* d'avance

upgrade 1 *n* [ˈʌpgreɪd] *Comptr (of hardware)* augmentation *f* de puissance; *(of software)* nouvelle version *f* **2** *vt* [ʌpˈgreɪd] **(a)** *(improve)* améliorer; *(promote)* promouvoir **(b)** *Comptr (hardware)* augmenter la puissance de; *(software)* acquérir la dernière version de

upheaval [ʌpˈhiːvəl] *n* bouleversement *m*

uphill [ˈʌphɪl] **1** *adj* qui monte; *Fig (struggle)* ardu(e), pénible **2** *adv* **to go u.** monter

uphold [ʌpˈhəʊld] *(pt & pp* **upheld** [ʌpˈheld]*) vt (opinion, principle)* soutenir; *(decision)* maintenir; **to u. the law** faire respecter la loi

upholstered [ʌpˈhəʊlstəd] *adj* tapissé(e)

upholstery [ʌpˈhəʊlstərɪ] *n* tapisserie *f*; *(in car)* sièges *mpl*

upkeep [ˈʌpkiːp] *n* entretien *m*

uplift 1 *n* [ˈʌplɪft] élévation *f* morale *ou* spirituelle **2** *vt* [ʌpˈlɪft] élever

uplifting [ʌpˈlɪftɪŋ] *adj* édifiant(e)

up-market [ˈʌpmɑːkɪt] *adj (product)* haut de gamme *inv*; *(area, place)* chic *inv*

upon [əˈpɒn] *prep* sur

upper [ˈʌpə(r)] **1** *adj* supérieur(e); **u. class** aristocratie *f*; **to get/have the u. hand** prendre/avoir le dessus; *Br Pol* **the U. House** la Chambre des Lords **2** *n (of shoe)* empeigne *f*; *Fam* **to be on one's uppers** manger de la vache enragée

upper-class [ˈʌpəklɑːs] *adj* aristocratique

upper-crust [ˈʌpəkrʌst] *adj Fam* aristo

uppermost [ˈʌpəməʊst] *adj* le (la) plus haut(e); *Fig* **it was u. in my mind** c'était la première de mes préoccupations

uppity [ˈʌpɪtɪ] *adj Fam* crâneur(euse); **to get u.** crâner

upright [ˈʌpraɪt] **1** *adj* **(a)** *(vertical)* droit(e); **u. piano** piano *m* droit; **u. vacuum cleaner** aspirateur *m* balai **(b)** *(honest)* droit(e) **2** *adv* droit **3** *n (beam)* montant *m*

uprising [ˈʌpraɪzɪŋ] *n* soulèvement *m*, révolte *f*

uproar [ˈʌprɔː(r)] *n (noise, protest)* tumulte *m*; **the house was in an u.** ce fut le tumulte dans la maison

uproarious [ʌpˈrɔːrɪəs] *adj (noisy)* tonitruant(e); *(funny)* hilarant(e)

uproot [ʌpˈruːt] *vt* déraciner

upset 1 *vt* [ʌpˈset] *(pt & pp* **upset**) **(a)** *(liquid, container)* renverser **(b)** *(person, plans, schedule)* bouleverser **2** *n* [ˈʌpset] *(disturbance)* bouleversement *m*; *(surprise)* défaite *f*; **to have a stomach u.** avoir l'estomac dérangé **3** *adj* [ʌpˈset, ˈʌpset] *(unhappy)* bouleversé(e) **(about** par); **to have an u. stomach** avoir l'estomac dérangé

upsetting [ʌpˈsetɪŋ] *adj* bouleversant(e)

upshot [ˈʌpʃɒt] *n* conséquence *f*, résultat *m*

upside down [ˈʌpsaɪdˈdaʊn] **1** *adj* à l'envers **2** *adv* à l'envers; **to turn sth u.** retourner qch; *Fig* mettre qch sens dessus dessous

upstage [ʌpˈsteɪdʒ] **1** *adv Th (move)* vers le fond de scène; **u. of sb/sth** à l'arrière-plan par rapport à qn/qch **2** *vt Th & Fig* éclipser, voler la vedette à

upstairs *n* [ʌpˈsteəz] étage *m* **2** *adj* [ˈʌpsteəz] de l'étage du dessus; **u. neighbours** les voisins du dessus; **the u. bathroom** la salle de bains du haut **3** *adv* [ʌpˈsteəz] en haut; **to come/go u.** monter; **he lives u.** il habite à l'étage au-dessus

upstanding [ʌpˈstændɪŋ] *adj* droit(e)

upstart [ˈʌpstɑːt] *n* parvenu(e) *m,f*

upstream [ʌpˈstriːm] *adv* en amont; *(with movement)* vers l'amont

upsurge [ˈʌpsɜːdʒ] *n* vague *f*

upswing [ˈʌpswɪŋ] *n* amélioration *f* **(in** de); *(in economy)* redressement *m* **(in** de)

uptake [ˈʌpteɪk] *n Fam* **to be quick on the u.** piger vite; **to be slow on the u.** être lent(e) à la détente

uptight [ʌpˈtaɪt] *adj Fam (nervous)* tendu(e), crispé(e); *(inhibited)* coincé(e)

up-to-date [ʌptəˈdeɪt] *adj* **(a)** *(most recent)* à jour; *(news)* récent(e); **to bring sb u. (on sth)** mettre qn au courant (de qch) **(b)** *(modern)* à la mode

up-to-the-minute [ʌptəðəˈmɪnɪt] *adj (news, information)* de dernière minute; *(style, fashion)* dernier cri *inv*

upturn [ˈʌptɜːn] *n* amélioration *f* **(in** de); *(in economy)* redressement *m* **(in** de)

upturned [ˈʌptɜːnd] *adj (bucket, box)* retourné(e); *(nose)* retroussé(e)

upward [ˈʌpwəd] **1** *adj* vers le haut; **u. mobility** ascension *f* sociale; **an u. trend** une tendance à la hausse **2** *adv* = **upwards**

upwardly mobile [ˈʌpwədlɪˈməʊbaɪl] *adj* qui connaît une ascension sociale rapide

upwards [ˈʌpwədz] *adv* vers le haut; **from $100 u.** à partir de 100 dollars; **u. of** plus de

Urals [ˈjʊərəlz] *npl* **the U.** l'Oural *m*

uranium [jʊ'reɪnɪəm] *n* uranium *m*

Uranus [jʊ'reɪnəs] *n (planet)* Uranus *f*

urban ['ɜːbən] *adj* urbain(e); **u. legend** *or* **myth** = anecdote souvent inventée mais qui passe pour vraie; **u. renewal** rénovations *fpl* urbaines; **u. sprawl** étalement *m* urbain

urbane [ɜː'beɪn] *adj* urbain(e), courtois(e)

urbanization [ɜːbənaɪˈzeɪʃən] *n (process)* urbanisation *f*

urchin ['ɜːtʃɪn] *n* galopin(e) *m,f*

Urdu ['ʊədu:] *n* ourdou *m*

urethra [jʊ'riːθrə] *n* urètre *m*

urge [ɜːdʒ] **1** *n* terrible envie *f*; **to have an u. to do sth** avoir très envie de faire qch **2** *vt* (**a**) *(encourage)* **to u. sb to do sth** presser qn de faire qch (**b**) *(recommend)* conseiller; **to u. that sth be done** insister pour que qch soit fait

► **urge on** *vt sep* encourager; **to u. sb on to do sth** encourager qn à faire qch

urgency ['ɜːdʒənsɪ] *n* urgence *f*; **it's a matter of u.** il y a urgence

urgent ['ɜːdʒənt] *adj* urgent(e); **to be in u. need of sth** avoir un besoin urgent de qch

urgently ['ɜːdʒəntlɪ] *adv* d'urgence

urinal [jə'raɪnəl] *n* urinoir *m*

urinary ['jʊərɪnərɪ] *adj* urinaire

urinate ['jʊərɪneɪt] *vi* uriner

urine ['jʊərɪn] *n* urine *f*

urn [ɜːn] *n* urne *f*; (**tea**) **u.** fontaine *f* (à thé)

urology [jʊ'rɒlədʒɪ] *n* Med urologie *f*

Uruguay ['jʊərəgwaɪ] *n* l'Uruguay *m*

Uruguayan [jʊərəˈgwaɪən] **1** *n* Uruguayen(enne) *m,f* **2** *adj* uruguayen(enne)

us *[stressed* ʌs, *unstressed* əs] *pron* (**a**) *(direct object)* nous; **she hates us** elle nous déteste; **she can understand our son but not us** elle comprend notre fils, mais nous, elle ne nous comprend pas (**b**) *(indirect object)* nous; **she gave us the book** elle nous a donné le livre; **she gave it to us** elle nous l'a donné (**c**) *(after preposition)* nous; **she's thinking of us** elle pense à nous (**d**) *(as complement of verb* **to be***)* nous; **it's us!** c'est nous!; **it was us who did it** c'est nous qui l'avons fait

US [juː'es] **1** *n (abbr* **United States***)* **the US** les USA *mpl* **2** *adj (forces, officials)* américain(e), des États-Unis

USA [juːes'eɪ] *n* (**a**) *(abbr* **United States of America***)* **the U.** les USA *mpl* (**b**) *Am (abbr* **United States Army***)* armée *f* de terre des États-Unis

usable ['juːzəbəl] *adj* utilisable

USAF [juːeseɪ'ef] *n* Am *(abbr* **United States Air Force***)* armée *f* de l'air des États-Unis

usage ['juːsɪdʒ] *n* usage *m*

use 1 *n* [juːs] (**a**) *(utilization)* utilisation *f*, emploi *m*; **to make (good) u. of sth** faire (bon) usage de qch; **to be in u.** être utilisé(e); **not in u., out of u.** hors d'usage (**b**) *(ability, permission to use)* usage *m*; **to have the u. of sth** pouvoir utiliser qch; **she has full u. of her faculties** elle jouit de toutes ses facultés (**c**) *(usefulness)* **to be of u.** être utile; **can I be of any u. to you?** puis-je vous être d'une quelconque utilité?; **it's not much u.** cela ne sert pas à grand-chose; **to have no u. for sth** ne pas avoir l'usage de qch; *Fam* **he's no u.** il n'est bon à rien; **it's no u.** cela ne sert à rien; **it's no u. crying** cela ne sert à rien de pleurer; **what's the u. of worrying?** à quoi bon s'inquiéter? **2** *vt* [juːz] (**a**) *(utilize)* utiliser, se servir de; *(force, diplomacy)* avoir recours à; *Fam* **u. your head!** réfléchis un peu!; *Fam* **I could u. a drink** une boisson ne me ferait pas de mal (**b**) *(exploit)* utiliser, se servir de (**c**) *(consume) (petrol, electricity)* consommer; **who's used all the milk?** qui a pris tout le lait? **3** *v aux* **used to** ['juːstə] *(translated by imperfect of main verb)* **we used to live in France** (autrefois,) nous vivions en France; **I didn't u. to like him** avant, je ne l'aimais pas; **do you travel much?** – **I used to** tu voyages beaucoup? – autrefois, oui

► **use up** *vt sep (food, fuel)* finir; *(ideas)* épuiser; *(money)* dépenser

use-by date ['juːzbaɪdeɪt] *n* date *f* limite de consommation

used *adj* (**a**) [juːzd] *(second-hand)* d'occasion (**b**) [juːst] *(accustomed)* **to be u. to sth/to doing sth** être habitué(e) à qch/à faire qch; **to get u. to sb/sth** s'habituer à qn/qch

useful ['juːsfʊl] *adj* utile; **to make oneself u.** se rendre utile

usefully ['juːsfəlɪ] *adv* utilement

usefulness ['juːsfʊlnɪs] *n* utilité *f*

useless ['juːslɪs] *adj* (**a**) *(not useful)* inutile; **to be worse than u.** ne servir strictement à rien (**b**) *(incompetent)* nul (nulle) **(at** en*)*

user ['juːzə(r)] *n (of road, dictionary)* utilisateur(trice) *m,f*; *(of telephone)* usager *m*; *(of drugs)* consommateur(trice) *m,f*

user-friendly [juːzə'frendlɪ] *adj* convivial(e)

usher ['ʌʃə(r)] **1** *n (in court)* huissier *m*; *(in theatre, cinema)* ouvreur *m*; *(at wedding)* placeur *m* **2** *vt* **to u. sb in/out** faire entrer/sortir qn

usherette [ʌʃə'ret] *n* ouvreuse *f*

USIA [juːesaɪ'eɪ] *n* Am *(abbr* **United States Information Agency***)* renseignements *mpl* généraux américains

USN [juːes'en] *n* Am *(abbr* **United States Navy***)* marine *f* de guerre des États-Unis

USP [juːes'piː] *n* Com *(abbr* **unique selling point** *or* **proposition***)* avantage *m* unique

USS [juːes'es] *n* Am *(abbr* **United States Ship***)* U. Lexington le Lexington *(bâtiment de la marine américaine)*

USSR [juːeses'ɑː(r)] *n* Formerly *(abbr* **Union of Soviet Socialist Republics***)* URSS *f*

usual ['juːʒʊəl] **1** *adj* habituel(elle); **you're not your u. cheery self today** tu n'es pas aussi gai que d'habitude aujourd'hui; **earlier/later than u.** plus tôt/tard que d'habitude; **as u.** comme d'habitude **2** *n* Fam *(drink)* **the u., sir?** comme d'habitude, monsieur?

usually ['juːʒʊəlɪ] *adv* habituellement, d'habitude; **he was more than u. polite** il était plus poli que d'habitude

usurer ['juːʒərə(r)] *n* usurier(ère) *m,f*

usurp [juː'zɜːp] *vt* usurper

usurper [juː'zɜːpə(r)] *n* usurpateur(trice) *m,f*

usury ['juːʒʊrɪ] *n* usure *f*

utensil [juː'tensəl] *n* ustensile *m*

uterus ['juːtərəs] *(pl* **uteri** ['juːtəraɪ]*)* *n* utérus *m*

utilitarian [juːtɪlɪ'teərɪən] **1** *adj (approach, design)* utilitaire; *(in philosophy)* utilitariste **2** *n (in philosophy)* utilitariste *mf*

utility [juː'tɪlɪtɪ] *n* (**a**) *(usefulness)* utilité *f*; Comptr **program** (programme *m*) utilitaire *m*; **u. room** pièce *f* de rangement (**b**) *(public)* **utilities** services *mpl* (publics) (**c**) *Am* **utilities** *(service charges)* charges *fpl*

utilize ['juːtɪlaɪz] *vt* utiliser, se servir de

utmost ['ʌtməʊst] **1** *n* **to the u.** au plus haut point; **to do one's u. (to do sth)** faire de son mieux (pour faire qch) **2** *adj* (**a**) *(greatest)* **the u.** le (la) plus grand(e); **it is of the u.**

importance that... il est de la plus haute importance que... + *subjunctive* (**b**) *(furthest)* **to the u. ends of the earth** au bout du monde

utopia [ju:'təʊpɪə] *n* utopie *f*

utopian [ju:'təʊpɪən] **1** *n* utopiste *mf* **2** *adj* utopique

utter¹ ['ʌtə(r)] *adj* total(e); **it's u. madness** c'est de la folie pure; **it's u. nonsense** c'est complètement absurde

utter² *vt (cry)* pousser; *(word)* prononcer

utterance ['ʌtərəns] *n (act)* énonciation *f*; *(words spoken)* paroles *fpl*, déclaration *f*

utterly ['ʌtəlɪ] *adv* complètement, tout à fait

uttermost ['ʌtəməʊst] *adj* = **utmost**

UV [ju:'vi:] *adj Phys (abbr* **ultra-violet**) UV *inv*; **UV rays** UV *mpl*

uvula ['ju:vjələ] *n* luette *f*

Uzbekistan [ʊzbekɪ'stɑːn] *n* l'Ouzbékistan *m*

V, v [viː] n **(a)** (letter) V, v m inv: **V-sign** (for victory) signe m de la victoire; (as insult) cornes fpl **(b)** (abbr **very**) t **(c)** (abbr **versus**) contre **(d)** (abbr **verse**) (pl **vv**) V

V (abbr **volt**) V

VA [viː'eɪ] n Am (abbr **Veterans Administration**) ≃ ministère m des Anciens Combattants

vacancy ['veɪkənsɪ] n **(a)** (position, job) poste m vacant **(b)** (at hotel) chambre f libre ou à louer; **no vacancies** (sign) complet

vacant ['veɪkənt] adj **(a)** (seat, space) libre, inoccupé(e) **(b)** (expression, look) absent(e)

vacantly ['veɪkəntlɪ] adv d'un air absent

vacate [və'keɪt] vt (seat, flat) libérer, quitter; (one's post) démissionner de

vacation [və'keɪʃən] n Br Univ & Am vacances fpl; Am **to take a v.** prendre des vacances

vaccinate ['væksɪneɪt] vt vacciner

vaccination [væksɪ'neɪʃən] n vaccination f

vaccine ['væksiːn] n vaccin m

vacillate ['væsɪleɪt] vi hésiter **(between** entre**)**

vacuous ['vækjʊəs] adj (person, look) vide, sans expression; (book, remark) dénué(e) de sens

vacuum ['vækjʊm] **1** n Phys vacuum m; Fig vide m; **v. cleaner** aspirateur m; **v. flask** Thermos® f **2** vt (room) passer l'aspirateur dans **3** vi passer l'aspirateur

vacuum-packed [vækjʊm'pækt] adj (emballé(e)) sous vide

vagabond ['vægəbɒnd] n vagabond(e) m,f

vagary ['veɪgərɪ] n caprice m

vagina [və'dʒaɪnə] n vagin m

vagrancy ['veɪgrənsɪ] n vagabondage m

vagrant ['veɪgrənt] n vagabond(e) m,f

vague [veɪg] adj (idea, feeling) vague; (shape, outline) flou(e), indistinct(e); **I haven't the vaguest idea** je n'en ai pas la moindre idée

vaguely ['veɪglɪ] adv vaguement

vagueness ['veɪgnɪs] n imprécision f, flou m

vain [veɪn] **1** adj **(a)** (conceited) vaniteux(euse) **(b)** (hopeless) vain(e) **2** n **in v.** en vain

vale [veɪl] n Lit val m, vallée f; Fig **v. of tears** vallée de larmes

valency ['veɪlənsɪ] n Chem valence f

valentine ['væləntaɪn] n **v. (card)** carte f de la Saint-Valentin; **V.'s Day** la Saint-Valentin

valet ['væleɪ] n valet m de chambre

valiant ['vælɪənt] adj Lit vaillant(e)

valiantly ['vælɪəntlɪ] adv vaillamment

valid ['vælɪd] adj valable; **v. for one year** valable un an; **no longer v.** périmé(e)

validate ['vælɪdeɪt] vt (document) valider; (theory) con firmer

validation [vælɪ'deɪʃən] n (of document) validation f; (of theory) confirmation f

validity [və'lɪdɪtɪ] n validité f

valise [væ'liːz] n Am mallette f

valley ['vælɪ] n vallée f

valour, Am **valor** ['vælə(r)] n bravoure f

valuable ['væljʊəbəl] **1** adj (object) de valeur; (advice, time, contribution) précieux(euse) **(to** à**) 2** n **valuables** objets mpl de valeur

valuation [væljʊ'eɪʃən] n **(a)** (act) estimation f **(b)** (price) évaluation f

value ['væljuː] **1** n **(a)** (worth) valeur f; **to be of v.** avoir de la valeur; **to be good/poor v. (for money)** être d'un bon/ mauvais rapport qualité-prix; **to set a v.** upon sth estimer la valeur de qch; **to the v. of** pour une valeur de, **to make a v. judgment** faire un jugement de valeur **(b) values** (principles) valeurs fpl **2** vt **(a)** (evaluate) estimer **(b)** (appreciate) apprécier

value-added tax ['væljuːædɪd'tæks] n taxe f sur la valeur ajoutée

valued ['væljuːd] adj précieux(euse)

valueless ['væljʊlɪs] adj sans valeur

valve [vælv] n (in body) valve f; Tech soupape f

vampire ['væmpaɪə(r)] n vampire m; **v. bat** vampire

van¹ [væn] n **(a)** (vehicle) camionnette f, fourgonnette f; **v. driver** chauffeur m de camionnette **(b)** Br Rail fourgon m

van² = **vanguard**

Vancouver [væn'kuːvə(r)] n Vancouver

vandal ['vændəl] n vandale mf

vandalism ['vændəlɪzəm] n vandalisme m

vandalize ['vændəlaɪz] vt saccager

vane [veɪn] n girouette f

vanguard ['vængɑːd] n avant-garde f; **to be in the v. of** être à l'avant-garde de

vanilla [və'nɪlə] n vanille f; **v. essence, v. extract** extrait m de vanille; **v. ice cream** glace f à la vanille

vanish ['vænɪʃ] vi disparaître

vanishing ['vænɪʃɪŋ] *adj* **to do a v. act** disparaître dans la nature; **v. point** point *m* de fuite

vanity ['vænɪtɪ] *n* vanité *f*; **v. case** vanity-case *m*, mallette *f* de toilette

vanquish ['væŋkwɪʃ] *vt Lit* vaincre

vantage point ['vɑːntɪdʒ'pɔɪnt] *n* point *m* de vue; *Fig* position *f* objective

Vanuatu [vænuːˈætuː] *n* Vanuatu *m*

vapid ['væpɪd] *adj* insipide

vapor ['veɪpə(r)] *Am* = **vapour**

vaporize ['veɪpəraɪz] **1** *vt* vaporiser
  2 *vi* se vaporiser

vapour, *Am* **vapor** ['veɪpə(r)] *n* vapeur *f*; **v. trail** traînée *f* de condensation

variable ['veərɪəbəl] **1** *n* variable *f*
  2 *adj* variable

variance ['veərɪəns] *n* désaccord *m*; **to be at v. with sb/sth** être en désaccord avec qn/qch

variant ['veərɪənt] **1** *n* variante *f*
  2 *adj* différent(e)

variation [veərɪˈeɪʃən] *n* variation *f*

varicose vein ['værɪkəʊsˈveɪn] *n* varice *f*

varied ['veərɪːd] *adj* varié(e)

variegated ['veərɪɡeɪtɪd] *adj* panaché(e)

variety [vəˈraɪətɪ] *n* (**a**) *(diversity)* variété *f*; **a v. of** toutes sortes de; *Prov* **v. is the spice of life** la diversité est le sel de la vie (**b**) *(of plant)* variété *f* (**c**) *(in theatre, on TV)* variétés *fpl*; **v. show** spectacle *m* de variétés

various ['veərɪəs] *adj* *(different)* divers(e); *(several)* plusieurs

variously ['veərɪəslɪ] *adv* **v. described as a hero or a rogue** parfois décrit comme un héros, d'autres fois comme un escroc

varnish ['vɑːnɪʃ] **1** *n* vernis *m*
  2 *vt* vernir

▸ **varnish over** *vt sep Fig* maquiller, dissimuler

vary ['veərɪ] **1** *vt* varier
  2 *vi* varier (**in/with** en/selon)

varying ['veərɪɪŋ] *adj* qui varie, variable

vase [*Br* vɑːz, *Am* veɪz] *n* vase *m*

vasectomy [vəˈsektəmɪ] *n* vasectomie *f*; **to have a v.** subir une vasectomie

Vaseline® ['væsəliːn] *n* vaseline *f*

vast [vɑːst] *adj* immense

vastly ['vɑːstlɪ] *adv* à l'extrême; *(superior)* infiniment

VAT [viːeɪˈtiː] *n (abbr* **value added tax)** TVA *f*

vat [væt] *n (container)* cuve *f*, bac *m*

Vatican ['vætɪkən] *n* **the V.** le Vatican; **V. City** la cité du Vatican, le Vatican

vaudeville ['vɔːdəvɪl] *n* music-hall *m*

vault¹ [vɔːlt] *n* (**a**) *(roof)* voûte *f* (**b**) *(cellar)* cave *f*; *(for burial)* caveau *m*; *(of bank)* chambre *f* forte, salle *f* des coffres

vault² *vt & vi* sauter

vaulted ['vɔːltɪd] *adj (ceiling)* voûté(e)

vaulting horse ['vɔːltɪŋ'hɔːs] *n* cheval *m* d'arçons

vaunt [vɔːnt] *vt* vanter; **his much vaunted reputation as...** sa réputation tant vantée de...

VC [viːˈsiː] *n* (**a**) *(abbr* **Vice-Chairman)** vice-président *m* (**b**) *(abbr* **Victoria Cross)** = la plus haute distinction militaire britannique

VCR [viːsiːˈɑː(r)] *n Am (abbr* **video cassette recorder)** magnétoscope *m*

VD [viːˈdiː] *n (abbr* **venereal disease)** maladie *f* vénérienne

VDU [viːdiːˈjuː] *n Comptr (abbr* **visual display unit)** moniteur *m*

veal [viːl] *n* veau *m*

vector ['vektə(r)] *n* vecteur *m*

veer ['vɪə(r)] *vi* virer; **to v. to the left/right** virer à gauche/droit

▸ **veer round** *vi* tourner, changer de direction; *Fig* **she has veered round to our point of view** elle s'est ralliée à notre point de vue

veg [vedʒ] *npl Br Fam (abbr* **vegetables)** légumes *mpl*

vegan ['viːɡən] *n & adj* végétalien(enne) *m,f*

vegetable ['vedʒtəbəl] *n* (**a**) légume *m*; **v. garden** potager *m* (**b**) *(brain-damaged person)* légume *m*

vegetarian [vedʒɪ'teərɪən] *n & adj* végétarien(enne) *m,f*

vegetate ['vedʒɪteɪt] *vi* végéter

vegetation [vedʒɪ'teɪʃən] *n* végétation *f*

veggie ['vedʒɪ] *n & adj Br Fam (abbr* **vegetarian)** végétarien(enne) *m,f*

vehemence ['viːɪməns] *n* véhémence *f*

vehement ['viːɪmənt] *adj* véhément(e)

vehicle ['viːɪkəl] *n also Fig* véhicule *m*

vehicular [vɪˈhɪkjʊlə(r)] *adj* de véhicules; **v. traffic** circulation *f* automobile

veil [veɪl] **1** *n also Fig* voile *m*; *Fig* **to draw a v. over sth** jeter un voile sur qch; *Fig* **under a v. of secrecy** sous le voile du secret
  2 *vt* voiler; *Fig* **veiled in secrecy** secret(ète)

veiled [veɪld] *adj also Fig* voilé(e)

vein [veɪn] *n* (**a**) *(in body, wood, marble)* veine *f*; *(in leaf)* nervure *f*; *(in rock)* filon *m* (**b**) *(idioms)* **and now, in a lighter v....** et maintenant, dans un registre plus léger...; **in similar v.** de la même veine

Velcro® ['velkrəʊ] *n (bande f)* Velcro® *m*

vellum ['veləm] *n* vélin *m*; **v. (paper)** papier *m* vélin

velocity [vɪ'lɒsɪtɪ] *n* vélocité *f*

velvet ['velvɪt] *n* velours *m*; **v. skirt** jupe *f* en velours

velveteen [velvɪ'tiːn] *n* velvantine *f*

velvety ['velvɪtɪ] *adj* velouté(e)

venal ['viːnəl] *adj* vénal(e)

vendetta [ven'detə] *n* vendetta *f*; **to carry on a v. against sb** mener une vendetta contre qn

vending machine ['vendɪŋmə'ʃiːn] *n* distributeur *m* automatique

vendor ['vendɔː(r)] *n* vendeur(euse) *m,f*

veneer [vəˈnɪə(r)] *n* placage *m*; *Fig* vernis *m*, apparence *f*

venerable ['venərəbəl] *adj* vénérable

venerate ['venəreɪt] *vt* vénérer

veneration [venə'reɪʃən] *n* vénération *f*

venereal [vɪ'nɪərɪəl] *adj* vénérien(enne); **v. disease** maladie *f* vénérienne

Venetian [vɪ'niːʃən] **1** *n* Vénitien(enne) *m,f*
  2 *adj* vénitien(enne); **V. blind** store *m* vénitien

Venezuela [vene'zweɪlə] *n* le Vénézuela

Venezuelan [vene'zweɪlən] **1** *n* Vénézuélien(enne) *m,f*
  2 *adj* vénézuélien(enne)

vengeance ['vendʒəns] *n* vengeance *f*; **to take v. on sb** se venger de qn; *Fig* **with a v.** de plus belle; **the disease has returned with a v.** la maladie est revenue avec d'autant plus d'acuité

vengeful ['vendʒfʊl] *adj* vengeur(eresse)

venial ['vi:nɪəl] adj véniel(elle)

Venice ['venɪs] n Venise

venison ['venɪsən] n venaison f

venom ['venəm] n also Fig venin m

venomous ['venəməs] adj also Fig venimeux(euse)

vent [vent] **1** n conduit m; Fig to give **v. to sth** donner ou laisser libre cours à qch **2** vt to **v. one's anger (on)** décharger sa colère (sur)

ventilate ['ventɪleɪt] vt ventiler, aérer

ventilation [ventɪ'leɪʃən] n ventilation f, aération f

ventilator ['ventɪleɪtə(r)] n **(a)** Tech ventilateur m **(b)** Med respirateur m; **to be on a v.** être branché(e) sur respirateur

ventriloquism [ven'trɪləkwɪzəm] n ventriloquie f

ventriloquist [ven'trɪləkwɪst] n ventriloque mf; **v.'s dummy** poupée f de ventriloque

venture ['ventʃə(r)] **1** n entreprise f hasardeuse; (in business) entreprise; Fin **v. capital** capital risque m **2** vt risquer; **to v. to do sth** se risquer à faire qch; Prov **nothing ventured, nothing gained** qui ne risque rien n'a rien **3** vi s'aventurer ▸ **venture on, venture upon** vt insep s'aventurer dans

venue ['venju:] n (for meeting, concert) salle f; (for football match) stade m

Venus ['vi:nəs] n (planet) Vénus f

veracity [və'ræsɪtɪ] n Formal véracité f

veranda(h) [və'rændə] n véranda f

verb [vɜːb] n verbe m

verbal ['vɜːbəl] adj verbal(e); **v. abuse** insultes fpl verbales

verbalize ['vɜːbəlaɪz] vt verbaliser

verbally ['vɜːbəlɪ] adv verbalement

verbatim [vɜː'beɪtɪm] **1** adj textuel(elle) **2** adv mot pour mot

verbiage ['vɜːbɪɪdʒ] n verbiage m

verbose [vɜː'bəʊs] adj verbeux(euse)

verbosity [vɜː'bɒsɪtɪ] n verbosité f

verdict ['vɜːdɪkt] n also Fig verdict m; **to return a v. of guilty/not guilty** rendre un verdict de culpabilité/non-culpabilité

verge [vɜːdʒ] n (of road) bord m; Fig **on the v. of sth** au bord de qch; (victory, defeat) à deux doigts de qch; Fig **to be on the v. of doing sth** être sur le point de faire qch ▸ **verge on** vt insep friser

verger ['vɜːdʒə(r)] n (in Church of England) bedeau m

verifiable [verɪ'faɪəbəl] adj vérifiable

verification [verɪfɪ'keɪʃən] n vérification f

verify ['verɪfaɪ] (pt & pp verified) vt vérifier

verisimilitude [verɪsɪ'mɪlɪtju:d] n Formal vraisemblance f

veritable ['verɪtəbəl] adj Formal véritable

vermilion [və'mɪljən] **1** n vermillon m **2** adj vermillon inv

vermin ['vɜːmɪn] npl also Fig vermine f

vermouth ['vɜːməθ] n vermouth m

vernacular [və'nækjʊlə(r)] **1** n langue f vernaculaire **2** adj vernaculaire

verruca [ve'ru:kə] n verrue f plantaire

versatile ['vɜːsətaɪl] adj polyvalent(e)

versatility [vɜːsə'tɪlɪtɪ] n polyvalence f

verse [vɜːs] n **(a)** (poetry) vers mpl **(b)** (stanza) strophe f **(c)** (of Bible) verset m

versed [vɜːst] adj **to be (well) v. in sth** être versé(e) dans qch

version ['vɜːʃən] n version f

versus ['vɜːsəs] prep **(a)** (in law, sport) contre **(b)** (compared to) comparé(e) à

vertebra ['vɜːtɪbrə] (pl vertebrae ['vɜːtɪbri:]) n vertèbre f

vertebral column ['vɜːtɪbrəl'kɒləm] n colonne f vertébrale

vertebrate ['vɜːtɪbrɪt] **1** n vertébré m **2** adj vertébré(e)

vertex ['vɜːteks] (pl vertices ['vɜːtɪsi:z]) n sommet m

vertical ['vɜːtɪkəl] **1** n verticale f **2** adj vertical(e)

vertically ['vɜːtɪklɪ] adv à la verticale

vertigo ['vɜːtɪgəʊ] n vertige m

verve [vɜːv] n verve f

very ['verɪ] **1** adv **(a)** (extremely) très; **v. little** très peu; **v. much** beaucoup, **are you hungry? – yes, v.** as-tu faim? – oui, très; Rad **v. high frequency** hyperfréquences fpl **(b)** (emphatic use) **the v. first/last** le (la) tout(e) premier(ère)/dernier(ère); **the v. best** tout ce qu'il y a de mieux; **at the v. most/least** tout au plus/moins, **at the v. earliest/latest** au plus tôt/tard; **the v. same** exactement le même; **I v. nearly died** j'ai bien failli mourir; **the v. next day** le lendemain même **2** adj (emphatic use) **this v. room** cette pièce même; **this v. day** aujourd'hui même; **those were her v. words** c'est ce qu'elle a dit mot pour mot; **at the v. beginning** au tout début; **the v. thought of it!** rien que d'y penser!

vessel ['vesəl] n **(a)** (ship) vaisseau m **(b)** (container) récipient m

vest [vest] n Br (undershirt) maillot m de corps; Am (waistcoat) gilet m

vested ['vestɪd] adj **to have a v. interest in sth/in doing sth** avoir un intérêt personnel dans qch/à faire qch

vestibule ['vestɪbju:l] n hall m

vestige ['vestɪdʒ] n vestige m

vestments ['vestmənts] npl Rel habits mpl sacerdotaux

vestry ['vestrɪ] n Rel sacristie f

vet¹ [vet] n (veterinary surgeon) vétérinaire mf

vet² [vet] (pt & pp vetted) vt effectuer une enquête sur

vet³ n Am Fam Mil (veteran) ancien combattant m; Fig vétéran m

veteran ['vetərən] **1** n Mil ancien combattant m; Fig vétéran m **2** adj de longue date

veterinarian [vetərɪ'neərɪən] n Am vétérinaire mf

veterinary ['vetərɪnərɪ] adj vétérinaire; **v. medicine** médecine f vétérinaire; Formal **v. surgeon** vétérinaire mf

veto ['vi:təʊ] **1** n (pl vetoes) veto m; **right or power of v.** droit m de veto; **to impose a v. on sth** mettre son veto à qch **2** vt mettre son veto à

vetting ['vetɪŋ] n enquête f personnelle

vex [veks] vt contrarier

vexation [vek'seɪʃən] n (annoyance) contrariété f

vexed [vekst] adj **(a)** (annoyed) très contrarié(e) **(b)** **v. question** question f controversée

VHF [vi:eɪtʃ'ef] n (abbr very high frequency) VHF f

VHS [vi:eɪtʃ'es] n (abbr video home system) VHS m

via ['vaɪə] prep par, via

viability [vaɪə'bɪlɪtɪ] n viabilité f

viable ['vaɪəbəl] adj viable

viaduct ['vaɪədʌkt] *n* viaduc *m*

vibes [vaɪbz] *npl Fam* ambiance *f*; **I got good/bad v. from her** je la sentais/je ne la sentais pas bien

vibrant ['vaɪbrənt] *adj* très actif(ive)

vibrate [vaɪ'breɪt] *vi* vibrer

vibration [vaɪ'breɪʃən] *n* vibration *f*

vibrator [vaɪ'breɪtə(r)] *n* vibromasseur *m*

vicar ['vɪkə(r)] *n (in Church of England)* pasteur *m*

vicarage ['vɪkərɪdʒ] *n* presbytère *m*

vicarious [vaɪ'keərɪəs, vɪ-] *adj* indirect(e)

vice¹ [vaɪs] *n (immorality, immoral activity)* vice *m*; **the V. Squad** ≃ la brigade des mœurs

vice² *n (tool)* étau *m*

vice-chairman [vaɪs'tʃeəmən] *n* vice-président(e) *m,f*

vice-president [vaɪs'prezɪdənt] *n* vice-président(e) *m,f*

viceroy ['vaɪsrɔɪ] *n* vice-roi *m*

vice versa [vaɪs'vɜːsə] *adv* vice versa

vicinity [vɪ'sɪnɪtɪ] *n* **in the v. (of)** dans les alentours (de); **a sum in the v. of $10 000** un chiffre aux alentours de 10 000 dollars

vicious ['vɪʃəs] *adj (violent)* violent(e); *(malicious, cruel)* malveillant(e); **v. circle** cercle *m* vicieux

vicissitudes [vɪ'sɪsɪtjuːdz] *npl Formal* vicissitudes *fpl*

victim ['vɪktɪm] *n* victime *f*; **to be the v. of sth** être victime de qch

victimization [vɪktɪmaɪ'zeɪʃən] *n* brimades *fpl*

victimize ['vɪktɪmaɪz] *vt (bully)* prendre comme tête de Turc; *(penalize)* pénaliser

victor ['vɪktə(r)] *n* vainqueur *m*

Victorian [vɪk'tɔːrɪən] **1** *n* Victorien(enne) *m,f*
2 *adj* victorien(enne)

victorious [vɪk'tɔːrɪəs] *adj* victorieux(euse); **to be v. over sb** vaincre qn

victory ['vɪktərɪ] *n* victoire *f*; **v. celebrations** = fêtes pour célébrer une victoire

victuals ['vɪtəlz] *npl Old-fashioned (food)* victuailles *fpl*

video ['vɪdɪəʊ] **1** *n (pl* **videos)** *(medium)* vidéo *f*; *(cassette)* (cassette *f*) vidéo; *(recorder)* magnétoscope *m*; **v. camera** caméra *f* vidéo; **v. cassette** *or* **tape** cassette *f* vidéo; **v. (cassette) recorder** magnétoscope; **v. game** jeu *m* vidéo; **v. nasty** = film vidéo à contenu très violent ou pornographique
2 *vt* **(a)** *(on video recorder)* enregistrer **(b)** *(on camcorder)* filmer en vidéo

vie [vaɪ] *(pt & pp* **vied** [vaɪd]) *vi* **to v. with sb (for sth/to do sth)** rivaliser avec qn (pour qch/pour faire qch)

Vienna [vɪ'enə] *n* Vienne

Viennese [vɪə'niːz] **1** *n* Viennois(e) *m,f*
2 *adj* viennois(e)

Vietnam [vɪet'næm] *n* le Viêt Nam; **the V. War** la guerre du Viêt Nam

Vietnamese [vɪetnə'miːz] **1** *npl (people)* **the V.** les Vietnamiens *mpl*
2 *n* **(a)** *(person)* Vietnamien(enne) *m,f* **(b)** *(language)* vietnamien *m*
3 *adj* vietnamien(enne)

view [vjuː] **1** *n* **(a)** *(sight, scene, prospect)* vue *f*; **a room with a v.** une chambre avec vue; **to have a good v. of sth** avoir une belle vue de qch; **in full v. of** sous les yeux de; *Fig* **in v. of** *(considering)* compte tenu de, étant donné **(b)** *(opinion)* opinion *f*; **in my v.** à mon avis **(c)** *(intention)* intention *f*; **with this in v.** dans cette intention; **with a v. to doing sth** dans l'intention de faire qch
2 *vt* **(a)** *(look at)* voir; *(prospective property, exhibition)*

---

visiter **(b)** *(consider)* voir, considérer; **to v. sth with horror/interest** envisager qch avec horreur/intérêt

viewer ['vjuːə(r)] *n* **(a)** *(of TV)* téléspectateur(trice) *m,f* **(b)** *(for slides)* visionneuse *f*

viewfinder ['vjuːfaɪndə(r)] *n* viseur *m*

viewpoint ['vjuːpɔɪnt] *n* point *m* de vue

vigil ['vɪdʒɪl] *n* veillée *f*; **to keep v.** veiller

vigilance ['vɪdʒɪləns] *n* vigilance *f*

vigilant ['vɪdʒɪlənt] *adj* vigilant(e)

vigilante [vɪdʒɪ'læntɪ] *n* = membre d'une milice privée

vignette [vɪn'jet] *n (photo, picture)* buste *m* sur un fond dégradé; *(short essay)* court portrait *m*

vigor ['vɪgə(r)] *Am* = **vigour**

vigorous ['vɪgərəs] *adj* vigoureux(euse)

vigour, *Am* **vigor** ['vɪgə(r)] *n* vigueur *f*

Viking ['vaɪkɪŋ] **1** *n* Viking *mf*
2 *adj* viking *inv*

vile [vaɪl] *adj (weather, person, thought)* abominable; *(food, drink)* infecte; *(temper)* exécrable

vilification [vɪlɪfɪ'keɪʃən] *n* calomnie *f*

vilify ['vɪlɪfaɪ] *(pt & pp* **vilified)** *vt* calomnier

villa ['vɪlə] *n* villa *f*

village ['vɪlɪdʒ] *n* village *m*; **v. idiot** idiot *m* du village

villager ['vɪlɪdʒə(r)] *n* villageois(e) *m,f*

villain ['vɪlən] *n (scoundrel)* scélérat *m*; *Hum* **the v. of the piece** le/la coupable

villainous ['vɪlənəs] *adj* diabolique

villainy ['vɪlənɪ] *n* infamie *f*

Vilnius ['vɪlnɪəs] *n* Vilnius

vindicate ['vɪndɪkeɪt] *vt (decision, action)* donner raison à; *(right, claim)* justifier

vindication [vɪndɪ'keɪʃən] *n (of decision, action)* bien-fondé *m*; *(of right, claim)* justification *f*

vindictive [vɪn'dɪktɪv] *adj* vindicatif(ive)

vine [vaɪn] *n* vigne *f*; **v. leaf** feuille *f* de vigne

vinegar ['vɪnɪgə(r)] *n* vinaigre *m*

vineyard ['vɪnjəd] *n* vigne *f*

vintage ['vɪntɪdʒ] *n (year)* année *f*; *(wine)* cru *m*; *Fig* **a v. year (for)** une grande année (pour); **v. car** = voiture construite entre 1919 et 1930; **v. wine** vin *m* de cru

vinyl ['vaɪnɪl] *n* vinyle *m*

viola [vɪ'əʊlə] *n* alto *m*

violate ['vaɪəleɪt] *vt (agreement)* violer; *(rule, law)* enfreindre

violation [vaɪə'leɪʃən] *n* violation *f*

violence ['vaɪələns] *n* violence *f*

violent ['vaɪələnt] *adj* violent(e); **to take a v. dislike to sb/sth** se prendre d'une aversion violente pour qn/qch

violently ['vaɪələntlɪ] *adv* violemment; *(die)* de mort violente; **to be v. sick** être pris(e) de violents vomissements

violet ['vaɪələt] **1** *n* **(a)** *(flower)* violette *f* **(b)** *(colour)* violet *m*
2 *adj Br* **v.(-coloured),** *Am* **v.(-colored)** violet(ette)

violin [vaɪə'lɪn] *n* violon *m*

violinist [vaɪə'lɪnɪst] *n* violoniste *mf*

VIP [viːaɪ'piː] *n (abbr* **very important person)** VIP *mf*; **V. lounge** salon *m* de luxe; **to get V. treatment** recevoir un accueil princier

viper ['vaɪpə(r)] *n* vipère *f*

viral ['vaɪrəl] *adj* viral(e)

virgin ['vɜːdʒɪn] **1** *n* vierge *mf*; **the (Blessed) V.** la Sainte

Vierge; the V. Islands les îles *fpl* Vierges
2 *adj* vierge

Virginia [vəˈdʒɪnjə] *n* la Virginie

virginity [vəˈdʒɪnɪtɪ] *n* virginité *f*

Virgo [ˈvɜːgəʊ] *n (sign of zodiac)* la Vierge; **to be (a) V.** être Vierge

virile [ˈvɪraɪl] *adj* viril(e)

virility [vɪˈrɪlɪtɪ] *n* virilité *f*

virology [vaɪˈrɒlədʒɪ] *n* virologie *f*

virtual [ˈvɜːtjʊəl] *adj* **(a)** quasi; **it's a v. impossibility** c'est quasiment impossible **(b)** *Comptr* virtuel(elle); **v. reality** réalité *f* virtuelle

virtually [ˈvɜːtjʊəlɪ] *adv* quasiment, pratiquement

virtue [ˈvɜːtjuː] *n* **(a)** *(goodness)* vertu *f*; **by v. of** en vertu de, **to make a v. of necessity** faire de nécessité vertu **(b)** *(advantage)* avantage *m*

virtuoso [vɜːtjʊˈəʊzəʊ] *(pl* **virtuosos** *or* **virtuosi** [vɜːtjʊˈəʊziːl]) *n* virtuose *mf*

virtuous [ˈvɜːtjʊəs] *adj* vertueux(euse)

virulent [ˈvɪr(j)ʊlənt] *adj* virulent(e)

virus [ˈvaɪrəs] *n Med & Comptr* virus *m*

visa [ˈviːzə] *n* visa *m*

vis-à-vis [ˈviːzɑːviː] *prep* par rapport à, vis-à-vis de

visceral [ˈvɪsərəl] *adj* viscéral(e)

viscount [ˈvaɪkaʊnt] *n* vicomte *m*

viscous [ˈvɪskəs] *adj* visqueux(euse)

visibility [vɪzɪˈbɪlɪtɪ] *n* visibilité *f*

visible [ˈvɪzɪbəl] *adj* visible

visibly [ˈvɪzɪblɪ] *adv* visiblement

vision [ˈvɪʒən] *n* **(a)** *(eyesight)* vue *f*; **to have good/poor v.** avoir une bonne/mauvaise vue **(b)** *(foresight, imagination)* clairvoyance *f* **(c)** *(apparition)* vision *f*; **I had visions of having to walk all the way home** je me suis vu devoir rentrer à la maison à pied

visionary [ˈvɪʒənərɪ] *(pl* **visionaries)** *n & adj* visionnaire *mf*

visit [ˈvɪzɪt] **1** *n* visite *f*; **to pay sb a v.** rendre visite à qn; **to be on a v.** être en visite
2 *vt (person)* rendre visite à; *(museum, monument)* visiter
3 *vi* **to be visiting** être de passage

visiting [ˈvɪzɪtɪŋ] **1** *n* **v. card** carte *f* de visite; **v. hours** heures *fpl* de visite; **v. rights** *(of divorced parent)* droits *mpl* de visite
2 *adj* **v. professor** professeur *m* invité

visitor [ˈvɪzɪtə(r)] *n* visiteur(euse) *m,f*; **visitors' book** livre *m* d'or

visor [ˈvaɪzə(r)] *n* visière *f*

vista [ˈvɪstə] *n* vue *f*; *Fig* perspective *f*

visual [ˈvɪʒʊəl] *adj* visuel(elle); **v. aid** support *m* visuel; **v. arts** arts *mpl* plastiques; *Comptr* **v. display unit** console *f* de visualisation

visualize [ˈvɪʒʊəlaɪz] *vt (imagine)* visualiser, se représenter; *(foresee)* envisager

visually [ˈvɪʒʊəlɪ] *adv* visuellement; **v. impaired** malvoyant(e)

vital [ˈvaɪtəl] *adj* **(a)** *(essential)* vital(e); **v. organ** organe *m* vital; *Hum* **v. statistics** *(of woman)* mensurations *fpl* **(b)** *(vigorous)* vigoureux(euse)

vitality [vaɪˈtælɪtɪ] *n* vitalité *f*

vitally [ˈvaɪtəlɪ] *adv* **supplies are v. needed** on a un besoin vital de vivres; **v. important** d'une importance vitale

vitamin [*Br* ˈvɪtəmɪn, *Am* ˈvaɪtəmɪn] *n* vitamine *f*; **with added vitamins** vitaminé(e)

vitreous [ˈvɪtrɪəs] *adj* **v. enamel** émail *m* vitrifié; **v. humour** humeur *f* vitrée

vitriol [ˈvɪtrɪəl] *n also Fig* vitriol *m*

vitriolic [vɪtrɪˈɒlɪk] *adj* au vitriol

vituperative [vɪˈtjuːpərətɪv] *adj Formal* injurieux(euse)

viva [ˈvaɪvə] *n* **v. (voce)** oral *m*

vivacious [vɪˈveɪʃəs] *adj* enjoué(e)

vivacity [vɪˈvæsɪtɪ] *n* vivacité *f*

vivid [ˈvɪvɪd] *adj* vif (vive); *(memory)* clair(e)

vividly [ˈvɪvɪdlɪ] *adv* vivement; *(remember)* clairement; *(describe)* de manière vivante

vivisection [vɪvɪˈsekʃən] *n* vivisection *f*

vixen [ˈvɪksən] *n* renarde *f*

viz [vɪz] *adv (abbr* **videlicet)** à savoir

VOA [viːəʊˈeɪ] *n Am (abbr* **Voice of America)** = station de radio américaine de diffusion mondiale

vocabulary [vəˈkæbjʊlərɪ] *n* vocabulaire *m*

vocal [ˈvəʊkəl] **1** *adj* **(a)** *(relating to the voice)* vocal(e); **v. cords** cordes *fpl* vocales **(b)** *(outspoken)* franc (franche); **to be v. about sth** se faire entendre à propos de qch
2 *npl* **vocals** chant *m*; **on vocals** au chant

vocalist [ˈvəʊkəlɪst] *n* chanteur(euse) *m,f*

vocation [vəʊˈkeɪʃən] *n* vocation *f*; **to have a v. (for sth)** avoir une vocation (pour qch)

vocational [vəʊˈkeɪʃənəl] *adj* professionnel(elle)

vocative [ˈvɒkətɪv] *n* vocatif *m*

vociferous [vəˈsɪfərəs] *adj* bruyant(e)

vociferously [vəˈsɪfərəslɪ] *adv* bruyamment

vodka [ˈvɒdkə] *n* vodka *f*

vogue [vəʊg] *n* vogue *f*; **to be in v.** être en vogue

voice [vɔɪs] **1** *n* **(a)** *(of person)* voix *f*; **to raise/lower one's v.** élever/baisser la voix; **at the top of one's v.** à tue-tête; **I've lost my v.** je n'ai plus de voix; **v. box** larynx *m* **(b)** *Gram* **active/passive v.** voix f active/passive **(c)** *(idioms)* **the v. of reason** la voix de la raison; **with one v.** d'une seule voix; **to make one's v. heard** se faire entendre; **these reforms would give small parties a v.** ces réformes donneraient voix au chapitre aux petits partis
2 *vt* **(a)** *(opinion, feelings)* exprimer **(b)** *(consonant)* sonoriser

voiced [vɔɪst] *adj (consonant)* sonore

voiceless [ˈvɔɪslɪs] *adj (consonant)* sans voix

voice-over [ˈvɔɪsəʊvə(r)] *n* voix *f* off

void [vɔɪd] **1** *n* vide *m*; **to fill the v.** combler le vide
2 *adj* **(a)** *(devoid)* **v. of** dépourvu(e) de **(b)** *Law (deed, contract)* **(null and) v.** nul (nulle) et non avenu(e)

volatile [ˈvɒlətaɪl] *adj* **(a)** *(person)* inconstant(e); *(situation)* explosif(ive); *(economy, market)* instable **(b)** *Chem* volatil(e)

volcanic [vɒlˈkænɪk] *adj* volcanique

volcano [vɒlˈkeɪnəʊ] *(pl* **volcanoes)** *n* volcan *m*

vole [vəʊl] *n* campagnol *m*

volition [vəˈlɪʃən] *n Formal* **of one's own v.** de son propre gré

volley [ˈvɒlɪ] *n* **(a)** *(of gunfire, blows, stones)* volée *f*; *Fig (of insults)* bordée *f* **(b)** *(in tennis)* volée *f*

volleyball [ˈvɒlɪbɔːl] *n* volley(-ball) *m*

volt [vəʊlt] *n* volt *m*

voltage [ˈvəʊltɪdʒ] *n* voltage *m*

volte-face [vɒltˈfɑːs] *n* volte-face *f inv*

voluble [ˈvɒljʊbəl] *adj* volubile

volubly [ˈvɒljʊblɪ] *adv* avec volubilité

volume ['vɒlju:m] n (a) (book) volume m, tome m; Fig to speak volumes (about) (of action, expression) en dire long (sur) (b) (amount, space occupied) volume m; (of work) quantité f (c) (loudness) volume m; to turn the v. up/down (on TV, radio) monter/baisser le volume; v. control bouton m de réglage du volume

voluminous [və'lju:mɪnəs] adj (garment) ample; (container) volumineux(euse)

voluntarily [vɒlʌn'teərɪlɪ] adv de plein gré

voluntary ['vɒləntərɪ] adj volontaire; v. redundancy départ m volontaire; v. work travail m bénévole

volunteer [vɒlən'tɪə(r)] 1 n volontaire mf; (for charity) bénévole mf
2 vt (information) donner spontanément; (advice) offrir; to v. to do sth se porter volontaire pour faire qch
3 vi (a) (for military service) s'engager (b) (to help, for charity) se porter volontaire (for pour)

voluptuous [və'lʌptjʊəs] adj voluptueux(euse)

vomit ['vɒmɪt] 1 n vomi m
2 vt & vi vomir

voodoo ['vu:du:] n vaudou m

voracious [və'reɪʃəs] adj vorace

vortex ['vɔːteks] (pl vortices ['vɔːtɪsi:z]) n vortex m; Fig tourbillon m

vote [vəʊt] 1 n (choice) vote m; (election) scrutin m; (paper) voix f; to put sth to the v. soumettre qch au vote; to take a v. on sth voter sur qch; to have the v. avoir le droit de vote; they got 48% of the v. ils ont remporté 48% des voix; the party has increased its share of the v. le parti a amélioré ses résultats aux élections; v. of confidence vote de confiance; v. of no confidence motion f de censure; to propose a v. of thanks faire un discours de remerciement
2 vt to v. Republican voter républicain; to v. to do sth voter pour faire qch; to v. sth down voter contre qch; to v. sb in élire qn; to v. sb out ne pas réélire qn; I v.

(that) we go je propose qu'on y aille
3 vi voter (for/against pour/contre); to v. on sth voter sur qch

voter ['vəʊtə(r)] n électeur(trice) m,f

voting ['vəʊtɪŋ] 1 n scrutin m; v. booth isoloir m; v. rights droits mpl de vote
2 adj (member) votant(e)

votive ['vəʊtɪv] adj Rel votif(ive)

▸ **vouch for** [vaʊtʃ] vt insep (person) se porter garant(e) de; (quality, truth) attester de

voucher ['vaʊtʃə(r)] n coupon m, bon m; (gift) v. chèque-cadeau m

vow [vaʊ] 1 n vœu m; to make a v. faire un vœu; to take a v. of chastity/silence faire vœu de chasteté/silence
2 vt jurer; to v. to do sth jurer de faire qch; to v. that jurer que

vowel ['vaʊəl] n voyelle f; v. sound son m vocalique

voyage ['vɔɪɪdʒ] n voyage m

voyager ['vɔɪɪdʒə(r)] n voyageur(euse) m,f

vs (abbr versus) contre

VSO [vi:es'əʊ] n Br (abbr Voluntary Service Overseas) ≃ service m de la coopération

VTOL [vi:ti:əʊ'el] n (abbr vertical take-off and landing) ADAV m

VTR [vi:ti:'ɑ:(r)] n (abbr video tape recorder) magnétoscope m

vulgar ['vʌlgə(r)] adj vulgaire; Math v. fraction fraction f ordinaire

vulgarity [vʌl'gærɪtɪ] n vulgarité f

vulnerability [vʌlnərə'bɪlɪtɪ] n vulnérabilité f

vulnerable ['vʌlnərəbəl] adj vulnérable

vulture ['vʌltʃə(r)] n also Fig vautour m

vulva ['vʌlvə] (pl vulvas or vulvae ['vʌlvi:]) n vulve f

W, w [ˈdʌbəljuː] *n* **(a)** *(letter)* W. w *m inv* **(b)** *(abbr* **west)** O

W *n (abbr* **watt(s))** W

WAAF [wæf] *n (abbr* **Women's Auxiliary Air Force)** = groupe de femmes, auxiliaires de l'armée de l'air britannique durant la Seconde Guerre mondiale

wacky [ˈwækɪ] *adj Fam* farfelu(e)

wad [wɒd] *n (of cotton wool)* morceau *m*; *(of paper, bank notes)* liasse *f*

wadding [ˈwɒdɪŋ] *n* ouate *f*

waddle [ˈwɒdəl] *vi* se dandiner

wade [weɪd] *vi (in water)* marcher dans l'eau; **to w. across a stream** traverser une rivière à gué; *Fam Fig* **to w. in** intervenir

► **wade into** *vt insep Fam Fig (task)* s'attaquer à; *(person)* tomber sur

wader [ˈweɪdə(r)] *n* **(a)** *(bird)* échassier *m* **(b) waders** *(boots)* bottes *fpl* de pêcheur

wafer [ˈweɪfə(r)] *n* **(a)** *(biscuit)* gaufrette *f* **(b)** *Rel (for communion)* hostie *f*

wafer-thin [weɪfəˈθɪn] *adj* ultramince

waffle¹ [ˈwɒfəl] *n (food)* gaufre *f*

waffle² *Br Fam* **1** *n* remplissage *m*
2 *vi* faire du remplissage

waft [wɒft] **1** *vt (smell, sound)* porter
2 *vi (of smell, sound)* parvenir

wag¹ [wæg] **1** *vt (pt & pp* **wagged)** agiter, remuer; **to w. one's finger at sb** menacer qn du doigt; **to w. its tail** *(of dog)* remuer la queue
2 *vi* frétiller, remuer; **its tail was wagging** *(of dog)* il remuait la queue; *Fam* **tongues will w.** les langues vont aller bon train
3 *n (action)* frétillement *m*; **with a w. of its tail** la queue frétillante

wag² *n Fam (joker)* farceur(euse) *m,f*

wage [weɪdʒ] **1** *n (pay)* **wage(s)** salaire *m*, paie *f*; **w. claim** revendication *f* salariale; **w. cut** diminution *f* de salaire; **w. differential** écart *m* salarial; **w. earner** salarié(e) *m,f*; **w. freeze** gel *m* des salaires; **w. packet** *(envelope)* enveloppe *f* de paie; *(money)* paie
2 *vt* **to w. war (on)** faire la guerre (à); **to w. a campaign against drugs** mener une campagne anti-drogue

wager [ˈweɪdʒə(r)] **1** *n* pari *m*
2 *vt* parier

waggle [ˈwægəl] *vt & vi* remuer

wag(g)on [ˈwægən] *n (horse-drawn)* charrette *f*; *Br (for railway freight)* wagon *m* (découvert); *Fam Fig* **to be on the w.** être au régime sec; **to fall off the w.** se remettre à boire

---

waif [weɪf] *n (abandoned child)* enfant *mf* abandonné(e); *(very thin girl)* fille *f* excessivement maigre; **waifs and strays** *(children)* enfants *mpl* abandonnés; *(animals)* animaux *mpl* abandonnés

wail [weɪl] **1** *n (of person)* gémissement *m*; *(of siren)* hurlement *m*
2 *vi (of person)* gémir, pousser des gémissements; *(of siren)* hurler

waist [weɪst] *n* taille *f*

waistband [ˈweɪstbænd] *n* ceinture *f*

waistcoat [ˈweɪskəʊt] *n Br* gilet *m*

waistline [ˈweɪstlaɪn] *n* taille *f*; **to watch one's w.** surveiller sa ligne

wait [weɪt] **1** *n* attente *f*; **to have a long w.** attendre longtemps, **to lie in w. for sb** guetter qn
2 *vt* attendre; **to w. one's turn** attendre son tour
3 *vi* **(a)** attendre **to w. for sb/sth** attendre qn/qch; **to keep sb waiting** faire attendre qn; **I can't w. to see her** j'ai vraiment hâte de la voir; **repairs while you w.** *(sign)* réparations minute; **we must w. and see** on verra bien **(b) to w. at table** *(serve)* faire le service

► **wait about, wait around** *vi* attendre

► **wait on** *vt insep (serve)* servir; **to w. on sb hand and foot** être aux petits soins pour qn

► **wait up** *vi* **to w. up for sb** attendre qn pour aller se coucher

waiter [ˈweɪtə(r)] *n* serveur *m*

waiting [ˈweɪtɪŋ] *n* attente *f*; **to play the w. game** faire de l'attentisme; **w. list** liste *f* d'attente; **w. room** salle *f* d'attente

waitress [ˈweɪtrɪs] *n* serveuse *f*

waive [weɪv] *vt (rights, claim)* renoncer à; *(rule)* ignorer

wake¹ [weɪk] *n (of ship)* sillage *m*; *Fig* **in the w. of sth** à la suite de qch; *Fig* **to follow in sb's w.** suivre l'exemple de qn

wake² *n (on night before funeral)* veillée *f* de corps

wake³ *(pt* **woke** [wəʊk] *or* **waked**, *pp* **woken** [ˈwəʊkən] *or* **waked) 1** *vt* réveiller
2 *vi* se réveiller

► **wake up 1** *vt sep* réveiller
2 *vi* se réveiller; *Fig* **to w. up to sth** prendre conscience de qch

wakeful [ˈweɪkfʊl] *adj* **(a)** *(sleepless)* éveillé(e); **to have a w. night** ne pas fermer l'œil de la nuit **(b)** *(vigilant)* vigilant(e)

waken [ˈweɪkən] *vt* réveiller

wakey [ˈweɪkɪ] *exclam Fam* **w., w.!** réveille-toi!

Wales [weɪlz] *n* le pays de Galles

walk [wɔːk] **1** n **(a)** *(short)* promenade f; *(long)* marche f; **it's a long w.** c'est loin à pied; **it's a ten-minute w.** c'est à dix minutes à pied; **to go for a w.** aller se promener **(b)** *(gait)* démarche f; **I know her by her w.** je la reconnais à sa démarche **(c)** *(speed)* **at a w.** au pas **(d)** *(path)* avenue f **(e)** *(profession, situation)* **people from all walks of life** des gens de tous les milieux **2** vt **to w. the dog** promener le chien; **to w. sb home** raccompagner qn; **to w. the streets** battre le pavé; *Euph (of prostitute)* faire le trottoir **3** vi *(move on foot)* marcher; *(as opposed to riding, driving)* aller à pied; *(for exercise, pleasure)* se promener (à pied); **to w. home** rentrer à pied

▸ **walk away** vi s'en aller; *Fig* **to w. away from trouble** éviter les ennuis; *Fig* **to w. away with a medal** remporter une médaille

▸ **walk in** vi entrer

▸ **walk into** vt insep **(a)** *(enter)* entrer dans **(b)** *(collide with)* rentrer dans

▸ **walk off** vi s'en aller; **to w. off with sth** *(steal)* partir avec qch; *(win easily)* remporter qch

▸ **walk out** vi **(a)** *(leave)* sortir; **to w. out on sb** quitter qn **(b)** *(go on strike)* se mettre en grève

▸ **walk over** vt insep *Fam* **to w. all over sb** marcher sur les pieds de qn

walkabout ['wɔːkəbaʊt] n *(of politician)* bain m de foule

walker ['wɔːkə(r)] n marcheur(euse) m, f

walkie-talkie [wɔːkɪ'tɔːkɪ] n talkie-walkie m

walk-in closet ['wɔːkɪn'klɒzɪt] n *(for clothes)* débarras m; *(for food)* cellier m

walking ['wɔːkɪŋ] **1** n marche f; **w. frame** déambulateur m; **w. shoes** chaussures fpl de marche; **w. stick** canne f **2** adj **at a w. pace** au pas; *Fam* **she's a w. dictionary** c'est un dictionnaire ambulant; **the w. wounded** les blessés mpl en état de marcher

Walkman® ['wɔːkmən] n baladeur m, Walkman® m

walk-on part ['wɔːkɒn'pɑːt] n *(in film, play)* rôle m de figurant(e)

walkout ['wɔːkaʊt] n *(strike)* débrayage m; *(from meeting)* départ m en signe de protestation

walkover ['wɔːkəʊvə(r)] n *Fam* **it was a w.!** c'était du gâteau!

walkway ['wɔːkweɪ] n passage m (couvert)

wall [wɔːl] n **(a)** *(of building, room)* mur m; **the Berlin W.** le mur de Berlin; **the Great W. of China** la grande muraille de Chine; **w. cupboard** placard m mural; **w. hanging** tenture f murale **(b)** *(idioms)* **a w. of silence** un mur de silence; **to go to the w.** faire faillite; *Fam* **to drive sb up the w.** rendre qn dingue; *Fam* **it's like talking to a brick w.!** c'est comme parler à un mur

▸ **wall in** vt sep entourer

▸ **wall off** vt sep séparer

▸ **wall up** vt sep murer

wallaby ['wɒləbɪ] n wallaby m

wallet ['wɒlɪt] n portefeuille m

wallflower ['wɔːlflaʊə(r)] n *(plant)* giroflée f; *Fig* **to be a w.** *(of person)* faire tapisserie

Walloon [wɒ'luːn] **1** n **(a)** *(person)* Wallon(onne) m, f **(b)** *(language)* wallon m **2** adj wallon(onne)

wallop ['wɒləp] *Fam* **1** n beigne f, grand coup m **2** vt filer un grand coup à

walloping ['wɒləpɪŋ] *Fam* **1** n raclée f **2** adv *(for emphasis)* super; **a w. great lie** un mensonge gros comme ça

wallow ['wɒləʊ] vi se vautrer; **to w. in self-pity** s'apitoyer sur son propre sort

wallpaper ['wɔːlpeɪpə(r)] **1** n papier m peint **2** vt tapisser

wall-to-wall ['wɔːltəwɔːl] adj **w. carpeting** moquette f; *Fig* **w. coverage** couverture f complète

wally ['wɒlɪ] n *Br Fam (idiot)* andouille f

walnut ['wɔːlnʌt] n *(fruit)* noix f; *(tree, wood)* noyer m

walrus ['wɔːlrəs] *(pl* **walruses)** n morse m

waltz [wɔːlts] **1** n valse f **2** vi **(a)** *(dance)* valser **(b)** *Fam (move confidently)* **to w. in/out** entrer/sortir avec désinvolture; *Fam* **to w. off with sth** partir avec qch

WAN ['dʌbəljuːˈeɪˈen] n *Comptr (abbr* **wide area network)** grand réseau m

wan [wɒn] adj blême

wand [wɒnd] n baguette f

wander ['wɒndə(r)] **1** vt *(streets)* traîner dans; *(world)* courir **2** vi **(a)** *(roam)* errer; **to w. around the town** se promener dans la ville; **she had wandered off the path** elle s'était éloignée du chemin **(b)** *(verbally)* radoter; *(mentally)* dérailler; **to w. from the subject** s'écarter du sujet **3** n balade f; **to go for a w.** aller faire un tour

wanderer ['wɒndərə(r)] n vagabond(e) m, f

wandering ['wɒndərɪŋ] adj *(person, life)* errant(e); *(tribe)* nomade

wanderlust ['wɒndəlʌst] n soif f de voyages

wane [weɪn] **1** vi *(of moon)* décroître; *(of popularity, enthusiasm, power)* décliner **2** n **to be on the w.** *(of moon)* décroître; *(of popularity, enthusiasm, power)* être en déclin

wangle ['wæŋɡəl] vt *Fam* se débrouiller pour avoir; **to w. sth sth, to w. sth for sb** se débrouiller pour avoir qch à qn; **to w. it so that** se débrouiller pour que + *subjunctive*

wank [wæŋk] *Br Vulg* **1** vi se branler **2** n branlette f; **to have a w.** se branler

wanker ['wæŋkə(r)] n *Br Vulg* connard m

want [wɒnt] **1** vt **(a)** *(wish, desire)* vouloir; **to w. to do sth** vouloir faire qch; **to w. sb to do sth** vouloir que qn fasse qch; **that's the last thing I w.** nous ne voulons surtout pas cela; **I know when I'm not wanted** je sais quand je suis de trop; **what does she w. with me?** qu'est-ce qu'elle me veut? **(b)** *Fam (need)* avoir besoin de; **the lawn wants cutting** la pelouse a besoin d'être tondue; **you w. to be careful with him** il faut que tu fasses attention avec lui **(c)** *(seek)* **to be wanted by the police** être recherché(e) par la police; **you're wanted on the phone** on te demande au téléphone **2** vi **to w. for nothing** ne manquer de rien **3** n **(a)** *(need)* besoin m **(b)** *(lack)* manque m **(of** de); **for w. of sth/of doing sth** faute de qch/de faire qch; **for w. of anything better** faute de mieux

wanting ['wɒntɪŋ] adj **to be w. in sth** manquer de qch; **to be found w.** *(of person)* se révéler incapable; *(of thing)* laisser à désirer

wanton ['wɒntən] adj **(a)** *(unjustified)* gratuit(e) **(b)** *(unrestrained)* dévergondé(e); *(sexually)* licencieux(euse)

war [wɔː(r)] n guerre f; **to be at w. (with)** être en guerre (avec); **to go to w. (with/over)** entrer en guerre (contre/à propos de); *Fig* **w. of words** altercation f; *Fam Fig* **you look as if you've been in the wars** tu es dans un bel état!; **w. correspondent** correspondant(e) mf de guerre; **w. criminal** criminel m de guerre; **w. cry** cri m de guerre; **w. games** *Mil* manœuvres fpl; *(with model soldiers)* wargame m; **w. memorial** monument m aux morts

warble ['wɔːbəl] **1** n gazouillement m
2 vi gazouiller
warbler ['wɔːblə(r)] n fauvette f
ward [wɔːd] n (**a**) (in hospital) salle f (**b**) (electoral division) circonscription f (**c**) Law **w. of court** pupille mf sous tutelle judiciaire
▸ **ward off** vt sep (blow) éviter; (danger) chasser
warden ['wɔːdən] n (of institution, hostel) directeur(trice) m,f; (of park) gardien(enne) mf
warder ['wɔːdə(r)] n Br (of prison) gardien(enne) m,f
wardrobe ['wɔːdrəʊb] n (**a**) (cupboard) armoire f (**b**) (clothes) garde-robe f; **to have a large w.** avoir une garde-robe importante (**c**) (theatrical costumes) costumes mpl; **w. mistress** habilleuse f
warehouse ['weəhaʊs] n entrepôt m
wares [weə(r)z] npl articles mpl
warfare ['wɔːfeə(r)] n guerre f
warhead ['wɔːhed] n ogive f
warhorse ['wɔːhɔːs] n Fig **an old w.** un vétéran
warily ['weərɪlɪ] adv avec une prudence circonspecte
wariness ['weərɪnɪs] n prudence f circonspecte
warlike ['wɔːlaɪk] adj guerrier(ère)
warm [wɔːm] **1** adj (**a**) (in temperature) chaud(e); **to be w.** (of person) avoir chaud; (of object, water, clothing) être chaud; **it's w.** (of weather) il fait chaud; **you're getting warmer** (in guessing game) tu chauffes (**b**) (kind, friendly) chaleureux(euse)
2 vt chauffer; **to w. oneself by the fire** se chauffer près du feu
3 vt **to w. to sb** se prendre de sympathie pour qn; **to w. to sth** se laisser séduire par qch
▸ **warm up 1** vt sep (food) réchauffer
2 vi (**a**) (of person, room) se réchauffer (**b**) (of dancer, athlete) s'échauffer (**c**) (of engine) chauffer
warm-blooded [wɔːm'blʌdɪd] adj à sang chaud
warm-hearted [wɔːm'hɑːtɪd] adj chaleureux(euse)
warmly ['wɔːmlɪ] adv (**a**) (dress) chaudement (**b**) (applaud, thank) chaleureusement
warmonger ['wɔːmʌŋgə(r)] n belliciste mf
warmth [wɔːmθ] n chaleur f
warm-up ['wɔːmʌp] n (of dancer, athlete) échauffement m
warn [wɔːn] vt avertir, prévenir; **to w. sb about sb/sth** mettre qn en garde contre qn/qch; **to w. sb about doing sth** dire à qn de ne pas faire qch; **to w. sb not to do sth** déconseiller à qn de faire qch; **you have been warned!** te voilà prévenu!
warning ['wɔːnɪŋ] n (**a**) (caution) avertissement m; (against danger) mise f en garde; **to give sb a w.** donner un avertissement à qn; (against danger) mettre qn en garde; Fig **w. sign** signe m (**b**) (advance notice) avis m; **without w.** sans prévenir
warp [wɔːp] **1** vt (**a**) (wood, metal) gauchir (**b**) (person, mind) pervertir
2 vi (of wood, metal) gauchir
warpath ['wɔːpɑːθ] n Fam **to be on the w.** en vouloir à tout le monde
warped [wɔːpt] adj (**a**) (wood, metal) gauchi(e) (**b**) (person, mind) perverti(e)
warrant ['wɒrənt] **1** n Law mandat m; Mil **w. officer** adjudant m
2 vt (**a**) (justify) justifier (**b**) (guarantee) garantir
warranty ['wɒrəntɪ] (pl **warranties**) n garantie f; **under w.** sous garantie

warren ['wɒrən] n (of rabbit) garenne f; Fig (of streets) labyrinthe m
warring ['wɔːrɪŋ] adj en guerre
warrior ['wɒrɪə(r)] n guerrier(ère) m,f
Warsaw ['wɔːsɔː] n Varsovie; Formerly **the W. Pact** le pacte de Varsovie
warship ['wɔːʃɪp] n navire m de guerre
wart [wɔːt] n verrue f; **warts and all** (biography, portrait) sans complaisance
warthog ['wɔːthɒg] n phacochère m
wartime ['wɔːtaɪm] n temps m de guerre; **in w.** en temps de guerre
wary ['weərɪ] adj méfiant(e); **to be w. of sth/sb** se méfier de qch/qn
was [wɒz] pt of **be**
wash [wɒʃ] **1** n (action) lavage m; **to have a w.** se laver; **to give sth a w.** laver qch; **your shirt is in the w.** ta chemise est au lavage; Fig **it will all come out in the w.** tout va s'arranger (**b**) (of ship) remous m
2 vt (**a**) (clean) laver; **to w. oneself** se laver; **to w. one's face/one's hands** se laver la figure/les mains; Fig **to w. one's hands of sth** se laver les mains de qch; **to wash one's hands of sb** ne plus se préoccuper de qn (**b**) (carry) **to w. sb/sth ashore** rejeter qn/qch sur le rivage; **he was washed out to sea** il a été emporté par la mer
3 vi (wash oneself) se laver; Fam **that won't w.!** ça ne marche pas!
▸ **wash away** vt sep emporter
▸ **wash down** vt sep (**a**) (walls, car) laver à grande eau (**b**) (pill) faire descendre (with avec); **to w. down one's dinner with a bottle of wine** arroser son dîner d'une bouteille de vin
▸ **wash off 1** vt sep enlever
2 vi partir
▸ **wash out 1** vt sep (**a**) (cup, bottle) rincer (**b**) (stain, dirt) faire partir; **to be completely washed out** (exhausted) être complètement lessivé(e); (pale) être pâle de fatigue
2 vi (of stain, dirt) partir
▸ **wash up 1** vt sep (**a**) Br (clean) laver (**b**) (carry ashore) rejeter sur le rivage
2 vi (**a**) Br (do dishes) faire la vaisselle (**b**) Am (have a wash) se débarbouiller
washbasin ['wɒʃbeɪsən] n (cuvette f de) lavabo m
washboard ['wɒʃbɔːd] n planche f à laver
washbowl ['wɒʃbəʊl] n (small) cuvette f; (large) bassine f
washcloth ['wɒʃklɒθ] n Am (face cloth) lingette f
washer ['wɒʃə(r)] n (**a**) Fam (for clothes) machine f à laver (**b**) (for screw) rondelle f; (made of rubber) joint m
washer-dryer [wɒʃə'draɪə(r)] n machine f à laver qui fait sèche-linge
wash(-)hand basin ['wɒʃhænd'beɪsən] n lavabo m
washing ['wɒʃɪŋ] n (**a**) (action) lavage m; **to do the w.** faire la lessive; **w. line** corde f à linge; **w. machine** machine f à laver; **w. powder** poudre f à laver, lessive f (en poudre) (**b**) (dirty clothes) linge m sale; (clean clothes) linge (propre)
Washington ['wɒʃɪŋtən] n Washington; **W. (State)** l'État m de Washington; **W. DC** Washington
washing-up [wɒʃɪŋ'ʌp] n Br vaisselle f; **to do the w.** faire la vaisselle; **w. bowl** cuvette f; **w. liquid** liquide f vaisselle
washout ['wɒʃaʊt] n Fam bide m
washroom ['wɒʃruːm] n Am toilettes fpl
wasn't [wɒznt] = was not
wasp [wɒsp] n guêpe f

waspish ['wɒspɪʃ] *adj* **to be w.** avoir une langue de vipère

wastage ['weɪstɪdʒ] *n* gaspillage *m*

waste [weɪst] **1** *n* (**a**) *(of food, effort)* gaspillage *m*; *(of time, money)* perte *f*; **to go to w.** être gaspillé(e) (**b**) *(rubbish)* déchets *mpl*; **w. disposal unit** broyeur *m* d'ordures (**c**) **wastes** *(desert)* étendues *fpl* désertiques **2** *adj (heat, fuel)* gaspillé(e); *(water)* usé(e) **3** *vt (money)* gaspiller; *(time)* perdre; *(opportunity)* gâcher; **to w. no time doing sth** ne pas perdre de temps pour faire qch; *Prov* **w. not, want not** il ne faut pas gaspiller
▸ **waste away** *vi* dépérir

wasted ['weɪstɪd] *adj* (**a**) *(effort)* gaspillé(e); *(opportunity)* gâché(e) (**b**) *Fam (drunk)* bourré(e); *(on drugs)* défoncé(e)

wasteful ['weɪstfʊl] *adj* **to be w.** *(of process, practice)* ne pas être rentable; *(of person)* être gaspilleur(euse)

wasteland ['weɪstlænd] *n* désert *m*

wastepaper [weɪst'peɪpə(r)] *n* vieux papiers *mpl*; **w. basket/bin** corbeille *f* à papier

waster ['weɪstə(r)] *n Fam (idle person)* bon (bonne) *m,f* à rien

wasting disease ['weɪstɪŋdɪ'ziːz] *n* maladie *f* dégénérative

watch [wɒtʃ] **1** *n* (**a**) *(timepiece)* montre *f* (**b**) *(period of guard duty)* garde *f*; *(guard)* sentinelle *f*; **to be on w.** monter la garde; **to keep a close w. on sb/sth** surveiller qn/qch de près **2** *vt* (**a**) *(observe)* regarder; **to w. television** regarder la télévision; **to w. sb doing sth** regarder qn faire qch (**b**) *(keep an eye on)* surveiller (**c**) *(be careful of)* faire attention à; **w. your language** *or* **your mouth!** surveille ton langage!; *Fam* **w. it!** attention! **3** *vi* regarder
▸ **watch out** *vi* faire attention; **w. out!** attention!
▸ **watch out for** *vt insep* (**a**) *(look for) (person)* guetter; *(thing)* chercher (**b**) *(be on guard for)* faire attention à
▸ **watch over** *vt insep* veiller sur

watchdog ['wɒtʃdɒg] *n* chien *m* de garde; *Fig (organization)* organisme *m* de contrôle

watchful ['wɒtʃfʊl] *adj* vigilant(e)

watchmaker ['wɒtʃmeɪkə(r)] *n* horloger(ère) *m,f*

watchman ['wɒtʃmən] *n* gardien *m*

watchstrap ['wɒtʃstræp] *n* bracelet *m* de montre

watchtower ['wɒtʃtaʊə(r)] *n* tour *f* de guet

watchword ['wɒtʃwɜːd] *n* mot *m* d'ordre

water ['wɔːtə(r)] **1** *n* (**a**) eau *f*; **to pass w.** *(urinate)* uriner; **w. bed** matelas *m* d'eau; **w. biscuit** = biscuit sec non salé; **w. bottle** gourde *f*; **w. chestnut** macre *f*; *Old-fashioned* **w. closet** waters *mpl*; **w. heater** chauffe-eau *m*; **w. level** niveau *m* d'eau; **w. lily** nénuphar *m*; **w. meter** compteur *m* d'eau; **w. pistol** pistolet *m* à eau; **w. polo** water-polo *m*; **w. rat** rat *m* d'eau; **w. skiing** ski *m* nautique; **w. wings** brassards *mpl* de natation (**b**) *(idioms)* **to spend money like w.** jeter l'argent par les fenêtres; **the argument doesn't hold w.** cet argument ne tient pas debout; **to keep one's head above w.** garder la tête hors de l'eau; **that's all w. under the bridge now** c'est de l'histoire ancienne **2** *vt* (**a**) *(fields, plants)* arroser (**b**) *(horse)* donner à boire à **3** *vi (of eyes)* pleurer; **it makes my mouth w.** ça me met l'eau à la bouche; **my mouth is watering** j'en ai l'eau à la bouche
▸ **water down** *vt sep (liquid, chemical)* diluer; *Fig (criticism, legislation)* atténuer

waterborne ['wɔːtəbɔːn] *adj (goods)* transporté(e) par voie d'eau; *(disease)* d'origine hydrique

watercourse ['wɔːtəkɔːs] *n* cours *m* d'eau

watercolour, *Am* watercolor ['wɔːtəkʌlə(r)] *n* aquarelle *f*

watercress ['wɔːtəkres] *n* cresson *m* (de fontaine)

waterfall ['wɔːtəfɔːl] *n* cascade *f*

waterfowl ['wɔːtəfaʊl] *(pl* **waterfowl)** *n* gibier *m* d'eau

waterfront ['wɔːtəfrʌnt] *n (by river)* bord *m* de l'eau; *(by sea)* front *m* de mer

watering can ['wɔːtərɪŋ'kæn] *n* arrosoir *m*

watering hole ['wɔːtərɪŋ'həʊl] *n (for animals)* point *m* d'eau; *Fam (bar)* bar *m*

waterlogged ['wɔːtəlɒgd] *adj (shoes, clothes)* trempé(e); *(land)* détrempé(e)

watermark ['wɔːtəmɑːk] *n* filigrane *m*

watermelon ['wɔːtəmelən] *n* pastèque *f*

waterproof ['wɔːtəpruːf] **1** *adj* imperméable; *(watch, joint, seal)* étanche; *(make-up)* waterproof *inv*; *(sun lotion)* résistant(e) à l'eau **2** *n (raincoat)* imperméable *m* **3** *vt* imperméabiliser

water-resistant ['wɔːtərɪzɪstənt] *adj (watch)* étanche; *(fabric)* qui résiste à l'eau

watershed ['wɔːtəʃed] *n Geog* ligne *f* de partage des eaux; *Fig (turning point)* tournant *m*

waterside ['wɔːtəsaɪd] *n* bord *m* de l'eau

water-ski ['wɔːtəskiː] *vi (pt & pp* **water-skied)** faire du ski nautique

watertight ['wɔːtətaɪt] *adj (seal)* hermétique; *(compartment)* étanche; *Fig (argument, alibi)* inattaquable

waterway ['wɔːtəweɪ] *n* voie *f* navigable

waterworks ['wɔːtəwɜːks] *n* station *f* hydraulique; *Br Euph (urinary system)* voies *fpl* urinaires; *Fam* **to turn on the w.** *(cry)* se mettre à pleurer comme une madeleine

watery ['wɔːtərɪ] *adj (soup)* trop liquide; *(beer, tea, coffee)* insipide, fade; *(eyes)* qui pleure; *(colour)* délavé(e)

watt [wɒt] *n* watt *m*

wattage ['wɒtɪdʒ] *n* puissance *f* en watts

wave [weɪv] **1** *n* (**a**) *(of water, dislike, crime)* vague *f*; *Fig* **to make waves** faire des vagues (**b**) *(gesture)* signe *m* (de la main); **to give sb a w.** faire signe à qn (**c**) *(in hair)* ondulation *f* (**d**) *(in physics)* onde *f* **2** *vt (arm, flag)* agiter; *(stick)* brandir; **to w. one's arms about** agiter les bras; **to w. goodbye to sb** faire au revoir de la main à qn **3** *vi* (**a**) *(of person)* faire signe; **to w. to sb** faire signe à qn (**b**) *(of flag)* flotter au vent
▸ **wave aside** *vt insep Fig (objection, criticism)* écarter

waveband ['weɪvbænd] *n* bande *f* de fréquences

wavelength ['weɪvleŋθ] *n* longueur *f* d'ondes; *Fig* **to be on the same w.** être sur la même longueur d'ondes

waver ['weɪvə(r)] *vi (of person)* vaciller; *(of voice)* trembler; *(of courage)* faiblir

waverer ['weɪvərə(r)] *n* indécis(e) *m,f*

wavy ['weɪvɪ] *adj* ondulé(e)

wax¹ [wæks] **1** *n (for candles, polishing)* cire *f*; *(in ear)* cérumen *m* **2** *vt (polish)* cirer

wax² *vi* (**a**) *(of moon)* croître (**b**) *(become)* **to w. lyrical (about sth)** devenir lyrique (à propos de qch)

waxed [wækst] *adj* ciré(e)

waxen ['wæksən] *adj (complexion)* de cire

waxwork ['wækswɜːk] *n* **w. (dummy)** mannequin *m* de cire; **waxworks** musée *m* de cire

way [weɪ] **1** *n* (**a**) *(route) & Fig* chemin *m*; **the w. in** l'entrée *f;* **the w. out** la sortie; **the w. to the station** le chemin pour aller à la gare; **to ask sb the w.** demander son chemin à qn; **to show sb the w.** montrer le chemin à qn; **to lose one's w.** se perdre; **to know one's w. about** savoir se débrouiller; **on the w.** en chemin, en route; *Fam* **they've got a baby on the w.** ils ont un bébé en route; **I must be on my w.** je dois partir; **out of the w.** isolé(e); *Fig* **to go out of one's w. to help sb** se mettre en quatre pour aider qn; *Fig* **to find a w. out of a problem** trouver une issue à un problème; *Fig* **she is well on the w. to success** elle est bien partie pour réussir; **to make one's w.** to a place se diriger vers un endroit; **to make one's w. through the crowd** se frayer un chemin à travers la foule; *Fig* **to make w. for sb** laisser la place à qn; *Fig* **to make one's w. in the world** réussir dans la vie; *also Fig* **to stand in sb's w.** barrer le passage à qn; *also Fig* **to be/get in the w.** gêner; *also Fig* **to get out of the w.** s'écarter; *also Fig* **to keep out of the w.** se tenir à l'écart

   (b) *(manner)* manière *f,* façon *f;* **in this w.** de cette manière; **to do things in one's own w.** faire les choses à sa manière; **I don't like the w. things are going** je n'aime pas la façon dont les choses tournent; **one w. or another** d'une manière ou d'une autre; **to find a w. of doing sth** trouver un moyen de faire qch; **to get into the w. of doing sth** s'habituer à faire qch; **to have a w. with children/animals** savoir s'y prendre avec les enfants/animaux; **to get one's (own) w.** arriver à ses fins; **to get used to sb's ways** se faire aux habitudes de qn

   (c) *(distance)* **to go a part of the w.** faire un bout de chemin; **to go all the w.** aller jusqu'au bout; *Fig* **I'm with you all the w.** je suis tout à fait d'accord avec toi; **Las Vegas is a long w. from New York** Las Vegas est loin de New York; **we've still got a long w. to go** nous avons encore du chemin à faire; **to be a little/long w. off** être proche/loin

   (d) *(direction)* direction *f,* sens *m;* **which w....?** dans quel sens...?; **this/that w.** par ici/là; *Fig* **to look the other w.** se boucher les yeux; *Fam* **down or round our w.** chez nous; *Fig* **it works both ways** cela marche dans les deux sens; **to split sth three ways** partager qch en trois

   (e) *(street)* rue *f*

   (f) *(respect)* égard *m;* **in a w.** d'une certaine manière; **in every w.** en tous points; **in no w.** en aucune façon

   (g) *(state, condition)* **to be in a good w.** bien aller; **to be in a bad w.** être mal en point

   2 *adv Fam* **w. back in the 1920s** dans les années vingt; **Sarah and I go w. back** Sarah et moi sommes des amis de longue date; **w. ahead** devant tout le monde; **w. down south** tout au sud; **your guess was w. out** tu étais loin de la vérité

wayfarer ['weɪfeərə(r)] *n* voyageur(euse) *m,f*

waylay [weɪ'leɪ] *(pt & pp* **waylaid** [weɪ'leɪd]) *vt (attack)* agresser; *Fig (stop)* arrêter au passage

way-out [weɪ'aʊt] *adj Fam (person)* excentrique; *(ideas, beliefs)* curieux(euse)

wayside ['weɪsaɪd] *n* bord *m* de la route; *Fig* **to fall by the w.** se retrouver à la traîne

wayward ['weɪwəd] *adj* difficile

WBA [dʌbəlju:bi:'eɪ] *n (abbr* **World Boxing Association)** WBA *f,* = association mondiale de boxe

WC [dʌbəlju:'si:] *n (abbr* **water closet)** WC *mpl*

we [wi:] *pron* nous; **we're Irish** nous sommes irlandais; **we haven't got it!** ce n'est pas nous qui l'avons!; **as we say in England** comme on dit en Angleterre; **we French are...** nous autres Français, nous sommes...

weak [wi:k] *adj (person, currency, character)* faible; *(heart)* fragile; *(argument, excuse)* peu convaincant(e); *(tea, coffee)* peu fort(e); **to grow w.** s'affaiblir; **to be w. at sth** *(school subject)* être faible en qch; *Fig* **to go w. at the knees** avoir les jambes en coton; *Fig* **w. spot** point *m* faible

weaken ['wi:kən] **1** *vt* affaiblir
   2 *vi* s'affaiblir

weak-kneed [wi:k'ni:d] *adj Fig* mou (molle)

weakling ['wi:klɪŋ] *n* mauviette *f,* faible *mf*

weakly ['wi:klɪ] *adv* faiblement

weakness ['wi:knɪs] *n* faiblesse *f;* **to have a w. for sb/sth** avoir un faible pour qn/qch

weak-willed [wi:k'wɪld] *adj* sans volonté

weal [wi:l] *n* trace *f* de coup

wealth [welθ] *n* richesse *f; Fig* **a w. of sth** une abondance de qch

wealthy ['welθɪ] **1** *npl* **the w.** les riches
   2 *adj* riche

wean [wi:n] *vt (baby)* sevrer; *Fig* **to w. sb off sth** *(bad habit)* faire passer qch à qn; *(alcohol, drugs)* sevrer qn de qch

weapon ['wepən] *n* arme *f*

wear [weə(r)] **1** *vt (pt* **wore** [wɔ:(r)], *pp* **worn** [wɔ:n]) **(a)** *(garment, glasses)* porter; **to w. black** porter du noir; **to w. one's hair up** avoir les cheveux relevés **(b)** *(erode)* user; **to w. a hole in sth** faire un trou dans qch **(c)** *Fam (believe, accept)* avaler
   2 *vi (of clothing)* s'user; **to w. thin** s'user; *Fig* **that excuse is wearing thin** cette excuse ne prend plus; **my patience is wearing thin** je suis à bout de patience; **to w. smooth** devenir lisse; **to w. well** *(of clothing, person, film)* bien vieillir
   3 *n* **(a)** *(clothing)* vêtements *mpl;* **evening w.** habits *mpl* de soirée; **children's w.** vêtements pour enfants **(b)** *(use)* usure *f;* **to get a lot of w. out of sth** porter qch longtemps; *Fam* **to be the worse for w.** être bien éméché(e); **w. and tear** usure *f* naturelle
   ▸ **wear away 1** *vt sep* user
   2 *vi* s'user
   ▸ **wear down** *vt sep* user; *Fig* **to w. sb down** avoir qn à l'usure
   2 *vi* s'user
   ▸ **wear off** *vi (of pain)* disparaître; *(of effect)* cesser; *(of anaesthetic)* cesser de faire effet; **the novelty soon wore off** l'attrait de la nouveauté n'a pas duré
   ▸ **wear on** *vi (of time)* s'écouler
   ▸ **wear out** *vt sep* user; **to w. oneself out** s'épuiser

wearily ['wɪərɪlɪ] *adv* avec lassitude

weariness ['wɪərɪnɪs] *n* lassitude *f*

wearing ['weərɪŋ] *adj* lassant(e)

wearisome ['wɪərɪsəm] *adj* fatigant(e)

weary ['wɪərɪ] **1** *adj* las (lasse); **to be w. of sth/of doing sth** être las de qch/de faire qch; **to grow w. of sth** se lasser de qch
   2 *vt* fatiguer, lasser
   3 *vi* se lasser **(of** de)

weasel ['wi:zəl] *n* belette *f*

weather ['weðə(r)] **1** *n* **(a)** *(atmospheric conditions)* temps *m;* **what's the w. like?** quel temps fait-il?; **the w. is good/bad** il fait beau/mauvais; **in this w.** par un temps pareil; **w. permitting** si le temps le permet; **w. forecast** prévisions *fpl* météorologiques; **w. map** *or* **chart** carte *f* météorologique **(b)** *(idioms)* **to make heavy w. of sth** faire tout un plat de qch; **to be under the w.** se sentir patraque
   2 *vt* **(a)** *(rock)* éroder **(b)** *(problem, situation)* surmonter; *Fig* **to w. the storm** tenir le coup
   3 *vi (of rock)* s'éroder

weatherbeaten ['weðəbi:tən] *adj (person, face)* hâlé(e); *(cliff, rock)* battu(e) par les vents

weathercock ['weðəkɒk] *n* girouette *f*

weathergirl ['weðəgɜ:l] *n* présentatrice *f* de la météo

weatherman ['weðəmæn] *n* présentateur *m* de la météo

weatherproof ['weðəpruːf] *adj* résistant(e) aux intempéries

weave [wiːv] **1** *vt* (*pt* **wove** [wəʊv] *or* **weaved**, *pp* **woven** ['wəʊvən]) tisser; *Fig* **a skilfully woven plot** une intrigue bien ficelée
2 *vi* tisser; *Fig* **to w. through the traffic** se faufiler parmi les voitures
3 *n* (*pattern*) tissage *m*

weaver ['wiːvə(r)] *n* tisserand(e) *m,f*

weaving ['wiːvɪŋ] *n* tissage *m*

web [web] *n* (**a**) (*of spider*) toile *f*; *Fig* (*of lies*) tissu *m*; (*of intrigue*) nid *m* (**b**) (*of duck, frog*) palmure *f* (**c**) *Comptr* **the W.** le Web; **w. site** site *m* Web

webbed [webd] *adj* (*foot*) palmé(e)

webbing ['webɪŋ] *n* (*on chair, bed*) sangles *fpl*

web-footed [web'fʊtɪd] *adj* palmipède

we'd [wiːd] = **we had, we would**

Wed (*abbr* **Wednesday**) mercredi

wed [wed] (*pt & pp* **wedded**) **1** *vt* épouser; *Fig* **to be wedded to sth** être totalement dévoué(e) à qch
2 *vi* se marier

wedding ['wedɪŋ] *n* mariage *m*; **w. anniversary** anniversaire *m* de mariage; **w. breakfast** repas *m* de noces; **w. cake** gâteau *m* de mariage; **w. day** jour *m* du mariage; **w. dress** robe *f* de mariée; **w. night** nuit *f* de noces; **w. ring** alliance *f*

wedge [wedʒ] **1** *n* (*for door, wheel*) cale *f*; (*of cake*) part *f*; (*of cheese*) morceau *m*; *Fig* **it has driven a w. between them** ça les a éloignés l'un de l'autre
2 *vt* coincer; **to w. a door open** maintenir une porte ouverte avec une cale

wedlock ['wedlɒk] *n Law* mariage *m*; **to be born out of w.** naître de parents non mariés

Wednesday ['wenzdɪ] *n* mercredi *m*; *see also* **Saturday**

wee¹ [wiː] *adj Scot* (*small*) petit(e); **a w. bit** un petit peu

wee² *Br Fam* **1** *n* pipi *m*; **to do a w.** faire pipi
2 *vi* faire pipi

weed [wiːd] **1** *n* (**a**) (*plant*) mauvaise herbe *f* (**b**) *Pej* (*weak person*) mauviette *f*
2 *vt* désherber

▸ **weed out** *vt sep Fig* éliminer

weedkiller ['wiːdkɪlə(r)] *n* désherbant *m*

weedy ['wiːdɪ] *adj Pej* (*person*) malingre

week [wiːk] *n* semaine *f*; **next/last w.** la semaine prochaine/dernière; **once/twice a w.** une fois/deux fois par semaine; **within a w.** sous huitaine; **w. in w. out** chaque semaine; **tomorrow/Friday w.** demain/vendredi en huit

weekday ['wiːkdeɪ] *n* jour *m* de semaine

weekend [wiːk'end] *n* week-end *m*; *Br* **at** *or Am* **on the w.** ce week-end; (*every weekend*) le week-end; **w. break** week-end

weekly ['wiːklɪ] **1** *n* (*magazine*) hebdomadaire *m*
2 *adj* hebdomadaire
3 *adv* chaque semaine; **twice w.** deux fois par semaine

weeknight ['wiːknaɪt] *n* soir *m* de semaine

weep [wiːp] *vi* (*pt & pp* **wept** [wept]) pleurer
2 *vt & vi* (*pt & pp* **wept** [wept]) pleurer

weeping ['wiːpɪŋ] **1** *n* pleurs *mpl*
2 *adj* qui pleure; **w. willow** saule *m* pleureur

weepy ['wiːpɪ] *adj Fam* (*book, film*) mélo; **to be w.** (*of person*) avoir envie de pleurer

wee(-)wee ['wiːwiː] *n Fam* pipi *m*; **to do a w.** faire pipi

weft [weft] *n* trame *f*

weigh [weɪ] **1** *vt* (**a**) (*measure*) peser (**b**) (*consider*) mesurer; **to w. sth against sth** mettre qch en balance avec qch (**c**) *Naut* **to w. anchor** lever l'ancre
2 *vi* (*of person, parcel*) peser; **how much do you w.?** combien tu pèses?; **it's weighing on my conscience** ça me pèse sur la conscience; **her experience weighed in her favour** son expérience a fait pencher la balance en sa faveur

▸ **weigh down** *vt sep* lester; *Fig* **to be weighed down with sth** (*grief, responsibilities*) être accablé(e) de qch

▸ **weigh in** *vi* (*of boxer, jockey*) être pesé(e); **to w. in at 75 kilos** peser 75 kilos

▸ **weigh out** *vt sep* peser

▸ **weigh up** *vt sep* (*consider*) mesurer

weighbridge ['weɪbrɪdʒ] *n* pont-bascule *m*

weight [weɪt] **1** *n* (**a**) poids *m*; **they're the same w.** ils font le même poids; **to lose/put on w.** perdre/prendre du poids; **to have a w. problem** avoir un problème de poids; **weights and measures** poids et mesures; **w. training** entraînement *m* aux haltères (**b**) (*idioms*) **to throw one's w. about** affirmer son autorité; **to pull one's w.** faire sa part de travail; **that's a w. off my mind** ça m'ôte un poids; **to carry w.** avoir du poids
2 *vt Fig* **to be weighted in favour of sb/sth** peser en faveur de qn/qch

▸ **weight down** *vt sep* (*to keep in place*) maintenir avec un poids; (*to make sink*) lester

weighting ['weɪtɪŋ] *n Fin* pondération *f*; *Br* **London w.** (*in salary*) indemnité *f* de résidence à Londres

weightless ['weɪtlɪs] *adj* (*astronaut*) en apesanteur; (*conditions*) d'apesanteur

weightlifter ['weɪtlɪftə(r)] *n* haltérophile *mf*

weightlifting ['weɪtlɪftɪŋ] *n* haltérophilie *f*

weighty ['weɪtɪ] *adj* (*heavy*) lourd(e); *Fig* (*serious, important*) grave

weir [wɪə(r)] *n* barrage *m*

weird [wɪəd] *adj* bizarre

weirdo ['wɪədəʊ] (*pl* **weirdos**) *n Fam* type *m* bizarre

welcome ['welkəm] **1** *adj* (*person, news, change*) bienvenu(e); **to make sb w.** faire un bon accueil à qn; **to feel w.** se sentir le (la) bienvenu(e); **she's always w.** elle est toujours la bienvenue; **w. home!** ça fait plaisir de te revoir!; **w. to Scotland!** bienvenue en Écosse!; **you're w.** to borrow it n'hésite pas à l'emprunter si tu veux
2 *vt* (*person*) souhaiter la bienvenue à; (*news, change*) accueillir favorablement; (*opportunity*) profiter de
3 *n* accueil *m*; **to give sb a warm w.** faire un accueil chaleureux à qn

welcoming ['welkəmɪŋ] *adj* accueillant(e)

weld [weld] **1** *n* soudure *f*
2 *vt* souder

welder ['weldə(r)] *n* soudeur(euse) *m,f*

welding ['weldɪŋ] *n* soudure *f*

welfare ['welfeə(r)] *n* (**a**) (*wellbeing*) bien-être *m*; *Br* **W. State** l'État *m* providence; **w. work** assistance *f* sociale (**b**) *Am* (*social security*) **to be on w.** recevoir l'aide sociale

we'll [wiːl] = **we will, we shall**

well¹ [wel] *n* (*for water, oil*) puits *m*; (*for lift, stairwell*) cage *f*

▸ **well up** *vi* (*of tears*) monter

well² [wel] (*comparative* **better** ['betə(r)], *superlative* **best** [best]) **1** *adj* bien; **to be w.** aller bien; **to get w.** se remettre; **it's just as w....** heureusement que...; **that's all very w., but...** tout ça, c'est très bien, mais...; **it's all very w. for you to say that** c'est facile pour toi de dire ça
2 *adv* (**a**) (*satisfactorily*) bien; **to speak w. of sb** dire du

bien de qn; **I did as w. as I could** j'ai fait de mon mieux; **w. done!** bravo!; **you would do w.** to keep quiet about it vous feriez bien de vous taire à ce sujet; **he apologized, as w.** il s'est excusé, et c'était bien la moindre des choses; **very w.! *(OK)*** très bien!

(b) *(for emphasis)* **to be w.** able to do sth être parfaitement capable de faire qch; **to be w.** aware of sth avoir parfaitement conscience de qch; **to leave w.** alone ne pas s'en mêler; *Fam* **to be w. in with sb** être dans les petits papiers de qn; **it is w. known that...** il est bien connu que...; **it's w. worth the effort** ça vaut vraiment la peine; **I can w. believe it** je n'ai aucun mal à le croire; **w. before/after** bien avant/après

(c) as w. *(also)* aussi, également; **she has a flat in town as w. as a house in the country** elle a un appartement en ville ainsi qu'une maison à la campagne

3 *exclam (expressing surprise, enquiry)* eh bien!; *(expressing resignation, qualifying previous remark)* enfin; **w.**, **who would have believed it!** eh bien, qui l'eût cru!; **w.**, **who was it?** eh bien, qui était-ce?; **w.**, **if you must!** enfin, si tu es vraiment obligé!, **he's nice, w.** sometimes il est gentil, enfin quelquefois

well-adjusted [welə'dʒʌstɪd] *adj* équilibré(e)
well-advised [weləd'vaɪzd] *adj* sage; **you'd be w.** to start studying tu ferais bien de commencer à étudier
well-appointed [welə'pɔɪntɪd] *adj* bien équipé(e)
well-argued [wel'ɑːɡjuːd] *adj* bien argumenté(e)
well-balanced [wel'bælənst] *adj* équilibré(e)
well-behaved [welbɪ'heɪvd] *adj* sage
wellbeing ['welbiːɪŋ] *n* bien-être *m*
well-built [wel'bɪlt] *adj (building)* solide; *(person)* bien bâti(e)
well-chosen [wel'tʃeʊzən] *adj* bien choisi(e)
well-disposed [weldɪs'pəʊzd] *adj* **to be w. towards sb** être bien disposé(e) envers qn; **to be w. towards sth** être favorable à qch
well-dressed [wel'drest] *adj* bien habillé(e)
well-earned [wel'ɜːnd] *adj* bien mérité(e)
well-fed [wel'fed] *adj* bien nourri(e)
well-founded [wel'faʊndɪd] *adj* fondé(e)
well-heeled [wel'hiːld] *adj Fam* cossu(e)
well-informed [welɪn'fɔːmd] *adj* bien informé(e)
wellington ['welɪŋtən] *n Br* **wellingtons, w. boots** bottes *fpl* en caoutchouc
well-intentioned [welɪn'tenʃənd] *adj* bien intentionné(e)
well-kept [wel'kept] *adj (garden)* bien entretenu(e); *(secret)* bien gardé(e)
well-known [wel'nəʊn] *adj* connu(e)
well-loved [wel'lʌvd] *adj* très aimé(e)
well-made [wel'meɪd] *adj* bien fait(e)
well-meaning [wel'miːnɪŋ] *adj* bien intentionné(e)
well-nigh ['welnaɪ] *adv* pratiquement
well-off [wel'ɒf] *adj Br (wealthy)* riche; *Fig* **you don't know when you're w.** tu ne connais pas ton bonheur
well-paid [wel'peɪd] *adj* bien payé(e)
well-read [wel'red] *adj* cultivé(e)
well-spoken [wel'spəʊkən] *adj* qui s'exprime bien
well-timed [wel'taɪmd] *adj* opportun(e)
well-to-do [weltə'duː] *adj* aisé(e)
wellwisher ['welwɪʃə(r)] *n* sympathisant(e) *m,f*
well-worn [wel'wɔːn] *adj (garment)* très usé(e); *(argument)* éculé(e)
well-written [wel'rɪtən] *adj* bien écrit(e)

Welsh [welʃ] **1** *npl (people)* **the W.** les Gallois *mpl*
2 *n (language)* gallois *m*
3 *adj* gallois(e); **W. dresser** vaisselier *m*
Welshman ['welʃmən] *n* Gallois *m*
Welshwoman ['welʃwʊmən] *n* Galloise *f*
welt [welt] *n* trace *f* de coup
welter ['weltə(r)] *n (of forms, details)* masse *f*; *(of ideas, activities)* multitude *f*
welterweight ['weltəweɪt] *n Sp* poids *m* welter
wench [wentʃ] *n Old-fashioned or Hum* jeune fille *f*, jeune femme *f*
wend [wend] *vt Lit* **to w. one's way homewards** prendre le chemin du retour
went [went] *pt of* **go**
wept [wept] *pt & pp of* **weep**
we're [wɪə(r)] = **we are**
were [wɜː(r)] *pt of* **be**
weren't [wɜːnt] = **were not**
werewolf ['wɪəwʊlf] *(pl* **werewolves** ['wɪəwʊlvz]) *n* loup-garou *m*
west [west] **1** *n* ouest *m*; **to the w. (of)** à l'ouest (de), the **W.** l'Occident *m*, l'Ouest *m*
2 *adj (coast, side)* ouest *inv*; *(wind)* d'ouest; **W. Africa** l'Afrique *f* de l'Ouest; **the W. Bank** la Cisjordanie; **the W. Country** le sud-ouest de l'Angleterre; **the W. End** = quartier chic de Londres et Glasgow où l'on trouve théâtres et restaurants; *Formerly* **W. Germany** l'Allemagne *f* de l'Ouest; **W. Indian** antillais(e); *(person)* Antillais(e) *m,f*; **the W. Indies** les Antilles *fpl*; **the W. Side** = les quartiers ouest de New York; **W. Virginia** la Virginie occidentale
3 *adv* à l'ouest; *(travel)* vers l'ouest; *Fam Fig* **to go w.** *(of TV, car)* rendre l'âme
westbound ['westbaʊnd] *adj (train, traffic)* en direction de l'ouest
westerly ['westəlɪ] **1** *n (wind)* vent *m* d'ouest
2 *adj (point)* à l'ouest; *(wind)* d'ouest, qui vient de l'ouest; **in a w. direction** vers l'ouest
western ['westən] **1** *n (film)* western *m*; *(novel)* roman-western *m*
2 *adj (region)* de l'ouest; *(in politics, sociology)* occidental(e); **w. France** l'ouest *m* de la France; **W. Europe** l'Europe *f* de l'Ouest; **the W. Isles** *(of Scotland)* les Hébrides *fpl*; **W. Samoa** les Samoa *fpl* occidentales; **W. Samoan** samoan(e); *(person)* Samoan(e) *m,f*
westernized ['westənaɪzd] *adj* occidentalisé(e)
westward ['westwəd] **1** *adj (in the west)* à l'ouest, dans l'ouest
2 *adv* = **westwards**
westwards ['westwədz] *adv (face, point)* à l'ouest; *(go, travel)* vers l'ouest
wet [wet] **1** *adj* **(a)** *(not dry)* mouillé(e); *(weather)* pluvieux(euse); **to get w.** se mouiller; **the ink/paint was still w.** l'encre/la peinture n'était pas sèche; *Fig* **w. blanket** rabat-joie *mf*; **w. paint** *(sign)* peinture fraîche; **w. suit** combinaison *f* de plongée **(b)** *Br Fam (feeble)* minable
2 *vt (pt & pp of* **wet** *or* **wetted)** mouiller; **to w. the bed** faire pipi au lit; **to w. oneself** mouiller sa culotte
3 *n* **(a)** *(dampness)* humidité *f*; *(rain)* pluie *f* **(b)** *Br Pol* modéré(e) *m,f*
WEU [dʌbəljuːiːˈjuː] *n (abbr* **Western European Union)** UEO *f*
we've [wiːv] = **we have**
whack [wæk] *Fam* **1** *n* **(a)** *(blow)* grand coup *m*; **to give sb/sth a w.** donner un grand coup à qn/qch **(b)** *(share)* part *f*
2 *vt* **(a)** *(hit)* donner un grand coup à; **to w. sb on** *or* **over**

the head donner un grand coup sur la tête de qn (**b**) *Am very Fam (murder)* liquider
whacked [wækt] *adj Fam (exhausted)* nase, vanné(e)
whacking ['wækɪŋ] *adv Fam* **a w. great increase/fine** une vache d'augmentation/d'amende
whale [weɪl] *n* baleine *f; Fam* **to have a w. of a time** s'éclater
whaler ['weɪlə(r)] *n* baleinier *m*
whaling ['weɪlɪŋ] *n* pêche *f* ou chasse *f* à la baleine
wharf [wɔːf] (*pl* **wharves** [wɔːvz]) *n* quai *m*
what [wɒt] **1** *pron* (**a**) *(in questions) (subject)* qu'est-ce qui; *(object)* qu'est-ce que, que; *(after preposition)* quoi; **w.'s happening?** qu'est-ce qui se passe?; **w. do you want?** qu'est-ce que tu veux?, que veux-tu?; **w. are you thinking about?** à quoi penses-tu?; **w.'s that?** qu'est-ce que c'est?; **w.'s it to you?** qu'est-ce que ça peut vous faire?; **w. for?** *(for what purpose?)* pour quoi faire?; *(why?)* pourquoi?; **w.'s a modem for?** à quoi ça sert, un modem?; **w. did he do that for?** pourquoi est-ce qu'il a fait ça?; **w.'s French for "dog?"** comment dit-on "dog" en français?; **w.'s he like?** comment est-il?; **w. about the money I lent you?** et l'argent que je vous ai prêté?; **w. about a cup of tea?** et si on prenait une tasse de thé?; **w. about me?** et moi?; **if that doesn't work, w. then?** si ça ne marche pas, qu'est-ce qui reste?; *Fam* **w. of it?** et alors?; *Fam* **are you coming or w.?** tu viens ou quoi?

(**b**) *(in relative constructions) (subject)* ce qui; *(object)* ce que; **I don't know w. has happened** je ne sais pas ce qui s'est passé; **I can't remember w. you told me** je ne me souviens plus de ce que tu m'as dit; **w. is surprising is that…** ce qu'il y a de surprenant, c'est que…; **w. I like is…** ce que j'aime, c'est…; *Fam* **he knows w.'s w.** il sait ce qu'il en est; *Fam* **to give sb w. for** frotter les oreilles à qn

2 *adj* (**a**) *(in questions)* quel (quelle); *(plural)* quels (quelles); **w. time is it?** quelle heure est-il?; **tell me w. time it is** dis-moi l'heure qu'il est; **show me w. CDs you want** montre-moi quels CDs tu veux

(**b**) *(in relative constructions)* **I'll give you w. money I have** je vais vous donner l'argent que j'ai; **he took w. little food was left** il a pris le peu de nourriture qui restait

(**c**) *(in exclamations)* **w. an idea!** quelle idée!; **w. a fool he is!** qu'il est bête!; **w. a lot of people!** quel monde!

3 *exclam* quoi?; **w. next!** et quoi encore!

what-d'ye-call-her ['wɒtjəkɔːlə(r)] *n Fam (person)* Machine *f*
what-d'ye-call-him ['wɒtjəkɔːlɪm] *n Fam (person)* Machin *m*
what-d'ye-call-it ['wɒtjəkɔːlɪt] *n Fam (thing)* machin *m*, truc *m*
whatever [wɒt'evə(r)] **1** *pron* (**a**) *(no matter what)* quoi que + *subjunctive*; **w. it is, w. it may be** quoi que ce soit; **w. happens** quoi qu'il arrive (**b**) *(anything)* ce que; **do w. you like** fais ce que tu veux; **give him w. he wants** donne-lui tout ce qu'il veut; **w. you say** comme tu voudras (**c**) *(in questions)* **w. does that mean?** qu'est-ce que ça peut bien vouloir dire?

2 *adj* (**a**) *(no matter what)* **take w. food you want** prends toute la nourriture que tu veux; **pay w. price they ask** donne-leur le prix qu'ils en demandent, quel qu'il soit (**b**) *(emphatic)* **for no reason w.** sans aucune raison; **nothing w.** absolument rien

what's-her-name ['wɒtsəneɪm], **what's-his-name** ['wɒtsɪzneɪm], **what's-its-name** ['wɒtsɪtsneɪm] = **what-d'ye-call-her/him/it**
whatsit ['wɒtsɪt] *n Fam* machin *m*, truc *m*
whatsoever [wɒtsəʊ'evə(r)] *adj* **for no reason w.** sans aucune raison; **none w.** aucun(e); **nothing w.** absolument rien

wheat [wiːt] *n* blé *m*; **w. germ** germe *m* de blé
wheaten ['wiːtən] *adj (loaf, roll)* de blé ou froment
wheatfield ['wiːtfiːld] *n* champ *m* de blé
wheedle ['wiːdəl] *vt* **to w. sth out of sb** soutirer qch à qn par des cajoleries; **to w. sb into doing sth** amadouer qn pour qu'il/elle fasse qch
wheel [wiːl] **1** *n* (**a**) *(on car, bike, pram)* roue *f*; *(on trolley, suitcase)* roulette *f* (**b**) *(steering wheel)* volant *m*; **to be at the w.** être au volant
2 *vt (push)* pousser
3 *vi (turn)* **to w.** *(about or around)* *(of person)* se retourner brusquement; *(of plane)* tourner
wheelbarrow ['wiːlbærəʊ] *n* brouette *f*
wheelbase ['wiːlbeɪs] *n* empattement *m*
wheelchair ['wiːltʃeə(r)] *n* fauteuil *m* roulant
-wheeled [wiːld] *suff* **two/three/four-w.** à deux/trois/quatre roues
wheeling and dealing ['wiːlɪŋən'diːlɪŋ] *n* tractations *fpl*
wheeze [wiːz] **1** *n* (**a**) *(noise)* respiration *f* sifflante (**b**) *Fam (trick)* astuce *f*, combine *f*
2 *vi (breathe heavily)* respirer péniblement
whelk [welk] *n* bulot *m*
whelp [welp] *n* petit *m*
when [wen] **1** *adv (in questions)* quand; **w. will you come?** quand viendras-tu?; **tell me w. it happened** dis-moi quand cela s'est produit; *Fam* **say w.!** *(when pouring drink)* tu me dis stop!
2 *conj* (**a**) *(with time)* quand, lorsque; **w. I came into the room** quand ou lorsque je suis entré dans la pièce; **tell me w. you've finished** dis-moi quand tu auras terminé; **what's the good of talking w. you never listen?** à quoi sert de parler puisque tu n'écoutes jamais? (**b**) *(whereas)* alors que
whence [wens] *adv Lit* d'où
whenever [wen'evə(r)] **1** *conj* (**a**) *(every time that)* chaque fois que; **I go w. I can** j'y vais aussi souvent que je peux (**b**) *(no matter when)* n'importe quand; **come w. you like** viens quand tu veux
2 *adv* (**a**) *(referring to unspecified time)* n'importe quand; **Sunday, Monday or w.** dimanche, lundi ou n'importe quel autre jour (**b**) *(in questions)* **w. did you do that?** quand est-ce que tu as fait ça?
where [weə(r)] **1** *adv (in questions)* où; **w. are you going?** où vas-tu?; **w. does he come from?** d'où vient-il?; **tell me w. she is** dis-moi où elle est; **w. would we be if…?** que serions-nous devenus si…?
2 *conj* où; **I'll stay w.** je suis en reste (là) où je suis; **that's w. he lives** c'est là qu'il habite; **that is w. you are mistaken** c'est là que vous vous trompez; **they went to Paris, w. they stayed a week** ils sont allés à Paris, où ils ont séjourné une semaine
whereabouts 1 *npl* ['weərəbaʊts] **nobody knows her w., her w. are unknown** personne ne sait où elle est
2 *adv* [weərə'baʊts] *(emphatic)* où
whereas [weə'ræz] *conj* alors que, tandis que
whereby [weə'baɪ] *adv Formal* par lequel (par laquelle)
whereupon [weərə'pɒn] *conj Lit* sur quoi
wherever [weə'revə(r)] **1** *conj* (**a**) *(everywhere that)* où que; **I seek the w. I go** où que j'aille, je le vois; **w. possible** partout où cela est possible (**b**) *(no matter where)* n'importe où; **we'll go w. you want** nous irons où tu voudras
2 *adv* (**a**) *(referring to unknown or unspecified place)* **at home, in the office or w.** chez soi, au bureau ou n'importe où; **it's in Coatbridge, w. that is** c'est à Coatbridge, mais je ne sais pas où se trouve Coatbridge

(b) *(in questions)* **w. can she be?** où peut-elle bien être?

wherewithal ['weərwɪðɔːl] *n* **to have the w.** *(to do sth)* avoir les moyens (de faire qch)

whet [wet] *(pt & pp* **whetted)** *vt (tool, blade, appetite)* aiguiser

whether ['weðə(r)] *conj* **(a)** *(with indirect questions)* si; **I don't know w. it's true** je ne sais pas si c'est vrai **(b)** *(conditional)* **w. she comes or not we shall leave** qu'elle vienne ou non, nous partirons

whew [hjuː] *exclam (of relief)* ouf!; *(of fatigue)* pff!; *(of astonishment)* dis donc!

whey [weɪ] *n* petit-lait *m*

which [wɪtʃ] **1** *pron* **(a)** *(in questions)* lequel (laquelle) *m,f*; *(plural)* lesquels (lesquelles) *mpl,fpl*; **w. (one) is better?** lequel est le meilleur?; **w. of you is going?** qui d'entre vous y va?; **I can never remember w. is w.** je ne me rappelle jamais la différence

(b) *(relative) (subject)* qui; *(object)* que; **the house w. is for sale** la maison qui est à vendre; **the film w. I saw last week** le film que j'ai vu la semaine dernière

(c) *(referring back to whole clause) (subject)* ce qui; *(object)* ce que; **they're getting divorced, w. surprises me** ils vont se divorcer, ce qui m'étonne; **she was back in London, w. I didn't know** elle était de retour à Londres, ce que je ne savais pas

(d) *(with prepositions)* **behind/in front of w.** derrière/devant lequel (laquelle); **beside/above w.** à côté/au-dessus duquel (de laquelle); **the countries w. we are going to** les pays où nous allons; **the town w. we live in** la ville où nous habitons; **after w. he went out** après quoi, il est sorti

2 *adj* **(a)** *(in questions)* quel (quelle); *(plural)* quels (quelles); **w. colour do you like best?** quelle couleur préferez-vous?; **w. way do we go?** de quel côté allons-nous?; **w. one?** lequel (laquelle)?; **w. ones?** lesquels (lesquelles)?

(b) *(in relative constructions)* **I was there for a week, during w. time** j'y suis resté une semaine, période pendant laquelle...; **she came at two, by w. time I had eaten** elle est arrivée à deux heures, heure à laquelle j'avais déjà déjeuné

whichever [wɪtʃ'evə(r)] **1** *pron* **(a)** *(no matter which)* quel (quelle) que soit celui (celle) qui; **w. you choose, I'm sure she'll like it** quel que soit celui que tu choisisses, je suis sûr que ça lui plaira **(b)** *(any)* **take w. you want** prends celui (celle) que tu voudras **(c)** *(according to which)* **come on Saturday or Sunday, w. suits you** viens samedi ou dimanche, suivant ce qui t'arrange

2 *adj (no matter which)* **take w. book you like best** choisis le livre que tu préfères

while [waɪl] **1** *n* **(a)** *(time)* **a w.** un moment; **after/in a w.** après/dans un moment; **a short** *or* **little w. ago** il y a un petit moment; **a good w., quite a w.** un bon moment; **a long w.** longtemps; **once in a w.** de temps en temps **(b)** **it's not worth my w.** ça n'en vaut pas la peine; **it's not worth my w. going** ça ne vaut pas la peine que j'y aille; **I'll make it worth your w.** vous serez récompensé de votre peine

2 *conj* **(a)** *(during the time that)* pendant que; **w. reading I fell asleep** je me suis endormi en lisant **(b)** *(as long as)* tant que; **it won't happen w. I'm in charge!** ça ne se produira pas tant que ce sera moi le responsable! **(c)** *(although)* bien que + *subjunctive*; **w. I admit it's difficult,...** bien que j'admette que ce soit difficile... **(d)** *(whereas)* alors que; **one wore white, w. the other was in black** l'un portait du blanc, alors que l'autre était en noir

▶ **while away** *vt sep* **to w. away the time** passer le temps

whilst [waɪlst] *conj Br* = **while 2**

whim [wɪm] *n* lubie *f*, fantaisie *f*; **to do sth on a w.** faire qch sur un coup de tête

whimper ['wɪmpə(r)] **1** *n* gémissement *m*, geignement *m*; *Fig* **without a w.** sans broncher
2 *vi* gémir, geindre

whimsical ['wɪmzɪkəl] *adj (person, behaviour)* fantasque; *(remark, story)* saugrenu(e)

whine [waɪn] **1** *n (of person, animal)* gémissement *m*; *(of machine)* grincement *m*
2 *vi also Fig* gémir **(about** à propos de)

whinge [wɪndʒ] *vi* pleurnicher

whinny ['wɪnɪ] **1** *n* hennissement *m*
2 *vi* hennir

whip [wɪp] **1** *n* **(a)** *(for punishment)* fouet *m* **(b)** *Pol* chef *m* de file
2 *vt (pt & pp* **whipped)** **(a)** *(beat with whip)* fouetter; **whipped cream** crème *f* fouettée; *Fig* **she whipped the crowd into a frenzy** son discours rendit la foule frénétique **(b)** *Fam (defeat)* battre à plates coutures **(c)** *Fam (steal)* faucher

▶ **whip off** *vt sep Fam (clothes)* ôter rapidement

▶ **whip out** *vt sep Fam* sortir soudainement

▶ **whip round** *vi Fam (turn quickly)* se retourner brusquement

▶ **whip up** *vt sep* **(a)** *(support, enthusiasm)* susciter; *(audience)* galvaniser **(b)** *(prepare quickly) (dish, meal)* préparer en vitesse fait

whiplash ['wɪplæʃ] *n* lésion *f* des cervicales

whippersnapper ['wɪpəsnæpə(r)] *n Fam* garnement *m*

whippet ['wɪpɪt] *n* whippet *m*

whipround ['wɪpraʊnd] *n Fam* **to have a w. (for sb)** organiser une collecte (pour qn)

whirl [wɜːl] **1** *n also Fig* tourbillon *m*; **the social w.** le tourbillon de la vie mondaine; *Fam* **my head's in a w.** j'ai la tête qui tourne; *Fam* **let's give it a w.** on va tenter le coup
2 *vt* **to w. sb/sth around** faire tournoyer qn/qch
3 *vi* tourbillonner; **my head's whirling** j'ai la tête qui tourne

▶ **whirl along** *vi (of car, train)* filer à toute vitesse

▶ **whirl round** *vi* se retourner brusquement

whirlpool ['wɜːlpuːl] *n* tourbillon *m*; **w. bath** bain *m* à remous

whirlwind ['wɜːlwɪnd] *n* tourbillon *m*; **w. romance** passion *f* enivrante; **w. tour** visite *f* éclair

whirr [wɜː(r)] **1** *n* ronflement *m*
2 *vi* ronfler

whisk [wɪsk] **1** *n* batteur *m*, fouet *m*
2 *vt* **(a)** *(eggs)* battre **(b)** *(move quickly)* **to w. sb into hospital** transporter qn d'urgence à l'hôpital **3** *vi (move quickly)* **she whisked past me** elle est passée devant moi comme un éclair

▶ **whisk away, whisk off** *vt sep (person)* emmener rapidement; *(object)* enlever rapidement

whisker ['wɪskə(r)] *n* **whiskers** *(of cat, mouse)* moustaches *fpl*; *(of man)* favoris *mpl*; *Fam* **to win by a w.** gagner de justesse

whisky, *Am* **whiskey** ['wɪskɪ] *n* whisky *m*

whisper ['wɪspə(r)] **1** *n* chuchotement *m*; **to speak in a w.** chuchoter
2 *vt* chuchoter; **to w. sth to sb** chuchoter qch à qn; **it's being whispered that...** le bruit court que...
3 *vi* chuchoter; **to w. to sb** chuchoter à l'oreille de qn

whist [wɪst] n whist m

whistle ['wɪsəl] **1** n (**a**) (noise) sifflement m (**b**) (musical instrument) flageolet m; (of referee, policeman) sifflet m
2 vt (tune) siffler
3 vi siffler; Fam **he can w. for his money** s'il compte récupérer son argent, il peut toujours courir

whistle-stop tour ['wɪsəlstɒp'tʊə(r)] n tournée f rapide

Whit [wɪt] n Pentecôte f; **W. Sunday** la Pentecôte

whit [wɪt] n **it doesn't matter a w.** ça n'a aucune importance; **it won't make a w. of difference** ça ne changera absolument rien

white [waɪt] **1** n (**a**) (colour, of egg, eye) blanc m; **w. doesn't suit her** le blanc ne lui va pas (**b**) (person) Blanc (Blanche) m,f
2 adj blanc (blanche); **a w. man** un Blanc; **a w. woman** une Blanche; **to turn** or **go w.** (person) devenir blême; (object, hair) blanchir; **w. with fear** vert(e) de peur; **w. as a ghost/sheet** pâle comme la mort/un linge; **w. chocolate** chocolat m blanc; **w. coffee** café m au lait; Fig **w. elephant** = chose coûteuse et peu rentable; **w. fish** poisson m à chair blanche; **w. flag** drapeau m blanc; **w. flour** farine f blanche; **the W. House** la Maison-Blanche; **w. lie** pieux mensonge m; **w. meat** viande f blanche; Pol **w. paper** livre m blanc; **w. sauce** sauce f blanche; **w. spirit** white-spirit m; **w. stick** canne f blanche; **w. tie** (formal dress) tenue f de soirée; **w. wedding** mariage m en blanc

whitebait ['waɪtbeɪt] n friture f

white-collar worker ['waɪtkɒlə'wɜːkə(r)] n col m blanc

white-haired ['waɪt'heəd] adj aux cheveux blancs

Whitehall ['waɪthɔːl] n = rue de Londres où se trouvent les ministères

white-hot ['waɪt'hɒt] adj chauffé(e) à blanc

whiteness ['waɪtnɪs] n blancheur f

whitewash ['waɪtwɒʃ] **1** n (paint) badigeon m à la chaux; Fig (cover-up) blanchiment m
2 vt (paint) badigeonner à la chaux; Fig (cover up) blanchir

whither ['wɪðə(r)] adv Lit **w. Europe/education?** où va l'Europe/l'enseignement?

whiting ['waɪtɪŋ] n (fish) merlan m

whitish ['waɪtɪʃ] adj blanchâtre

Whitsun ['wɪtsən] n Pentecôte f

whittle ['wɪtəl] vt tailler (au couteau); Fig **to w. sth down** réduire qch
▸ **whittle away** vt sep Fig **to w. sth away** réduire qch à presque rien

whizz [wɪz] **1** n Fam (expert) crack m; **w. kid** jeune prodige m
2 vi (of bullet) siffler; (of person, car) passer à toute vitesse; **to w. through a book/meal** lire un livre/manger à toute vitesse

WHO [dʌbəljuːeɪtʃ'əʊ] n (abbr **World Health Organization**) OMS f

who [huː] pron (**a**) (in questions) qui; **w. is it?** qui est-ce?; **w. with?** avec qui?; **do you know w. she is?** sais-tu qui elle est?; **w.'s speaking?** (on phone) qui est à l'appareil?; **w. did you say was there?** qui était là, déjà?; **w. does he think he is?** pour qui se prend-il?
(**b**) (relative) qui; **the people w. came yesterday** les gens qui sont venus hier; **those w. have already paid can leave** ceux qui ont déjà payé peuvent s'en aller; **Louise's father, w. is a lawyer, was there** le père de Louise, qui est avocat, était la

whodun(n)it [huːˈdʌnɪt] n Fam polar m

whoever [huːˈevə(r)] pron (**a**) (no matter who) qui que +

subjunctive; **w. you are** qui que vous soyez; **w. wrote that letter** la personne qui a écrit cette lettre; Fam **ask Simon or Cris or w.** demande à Simon ou à Cris ou à n'importe qui d'autre (**b**) (anyone that) celui (celle) qui; **w. finds it may keep it** celui qui le trouvera pourra le garder (**c**) (in questions) **w. can that be?** qui cela peut-il être?

whole [həʊl] **1** adj (**a**) (entire, intact) entier(ère); **the w. truth** toute la vérité; **the w. world** le monde entier; **a w. week** toute une semaine, une semaine entière; **to swallow sth w.** avaler qch sans le mâcher; Fig avaler qch; **w. milk** lait m entier (**b**) Fam (for emphasis) **a w. lot of** tout un tas de; **the w. lot of you** vous tous
2 n totalité f, ensemble m; **the w. of the village/the money** tout le village/l'argent; **as a w.** dans sa totalité; **on the w.** dans l'ensemble

wholefood ['həʊlfuːd] n aliments mpl complets; **w. store** magasin m bio

wholehearted [həʊl'hɑːtɪd] adj sans réserve, total(e)

wholemeal ['həʊlmiːl] adj **w. bread** pain m complet; **w. flour** farine f complète

wholesale ['həʊlseɪl] **1** adj de gros; Fig (large-scale) à grande échelle
2 adv en gros; Fig (on a large scale) à grande échelle
3 n (vente f en) gros m

wholesaler ['həʊlseɪlə(r)] n grossiste mf

wholesome ['həʊlsəm] adj (food, entertainment) sain(e); (person) comme il faut

wholly ['həʊllɪ] adv entièrement

whom [huːm] pron Formal (**a**) (in questions) qui; **w. did you see?** qui avez-vous vu?; **for/to/of w.?** pour/à/de qui? (**b**) (relative) que; **the woman w. you saw** la femme que vous avez vue; **the man w. you gave the money to** l'homme à qui vous avez donné l'argent; **the person of w. we were speaking** la personne dont nous parlions; **the men, both of w. were quite young,...** les hommes, tous deux assez jeunes...

whoop [wuːp] **1** n cri m de joie
2 vi crier de joie

whoopee 1 [ˈwʊpiː] Fam **to make w.** (have fun) faire la bombe; (have sex) faire crac-crac
2 exclam [wʊ'piː] youpi!

whooping cough ['huːpɪŋ'kɒf] n coqueluche f

whoops [wuːps] exclam houp-là!

whopper ['wɒpə(r)] n Fam (**a**) (huge thing) truc m énorme (**b**) (lie) gros bobard m

whopping ['wɒpɪŋ] adj Br Fam **w. (great)** énorme

whore [hɔː(r)] n very Fam putain f

whorehouse ['hɔːhaʊs] n bordel m

whose [huːz] **1** possessive pron (in questions) à qui; **w. are these shoes?** à qui sont ces chaussures?; **w. is this?** à qui est-ce?; **tell me w. they are** dis-moi à qui ils sont
2 possessive adj (**a**) (in questions) à qui; **w. gloves are these?** à qui sont ces gants?; **w. daughter are you?** de qui es-tu la fille? (**b**) (relative) dont; **the student w. work I showed you** l'étudiant dont je t'ai montré le travail; **the man to w. wife I gave the money** l'homme à la femme de qui j'ai donné l'argent

why [waɪ] **1** adv (**a**) (in questions) pourquoi; **w. didn't you say so?** pourquoi ne l'as-tu pas dit?; **w. get angry?** pourquoi se mettre en colère?; **w. not?** pourquoi pas? (**b**) (in suggestions) **w. don't you phone him?** pourquoi ne lui téléphones-tu pas?; **w. don't I come with you?** pourquoi est-ce que je ne viendrais pas avec toi?; **w. not sell the car?** pourquoi ne pas vendre la voiture?
2 conj pourquoi; **I'll tell you w. I don't like her** je vais vous dire pourquoi je ne l'aime pas; **that's w....** voilà pourquoi...; **the reason w....** la raison pour laquelle...

3 *n* the whys and wherefores (of sth) le pourquoi et le comment (de qch)

4 *exclam* w., it's David! mais voilà David!

WI [dʌblju:'aɪ] *n* Br (abbr Women's Institute) = association de femmes en milieu rural qui organise diverses activités

wick [wɪk] *n* (**a**) (of lamp, candle) mèche *f* (**b**) Br Fam to get on sb's w. taper sur les nerfs à qn

wicked ['wɪkɪd] *adj* (**a**) (evil) méchant(e); Fig (dreadful) affreux(euse) (**b**) Fam (excellent) génial(e)

wickedness ['wɪkɪdnɪs] *n* méchanceté *f*

wicker ['wɪkə(r)] *n* osier *m*

wickerwork ['wɪkəwɜ:k] *n* vannerie *f*

wicket ['wɪkɪt] *n* (in cricket) guichet *m*

wicketkeeper ['wɪkɪtki:pə(r)] *n* (in cricket) gardien *m* de guichet

wide [waɪd] **1** *adj* (**a**) (broad) large; to be 100 metres w. faire 100 mètres de large; in the whole w. world dans le monde entier (**b**) (extensive) vaste

2 *adv* w. open (eyes, mouth, door) grand ouvert(e); to be w. open to criticism prêter le flanc à la critique; w. apart très espacé(e); (legs) très écarté(e); w. awake complètement réveillé(e); the shot went w. la balle est passée à côté; Fig w. of the mark loin de la vérité

wide-angle ['waɪdæŋgəl] *adj* grand angle *inv*

wide-eyed ['waɪdaɪd] *adj* aux yeux écarquillés

widely ['waɪdlɪ] *adv* (**a**) (extensively) largement; it is w. believed that... beaucoup de gens pensent que...; w. known connu(e) de tout le monde (**b**) (at a distance) w. spaced très espacé(e)

widen ['waɪdən] **1** *vt* agrandir; (garment) élargir; Fig (influence, scope) étendre; to w. one's horizons élargir son horizon

2 *vi* s'élargir; (of gap, eyes) s'agrandir

▸ **widen out** *vi* s'élargir

widespread ['waɪdspred] *adj* répandu(e)

widow ['wɪdəʊ] **1** *n* veuve *f*; w.'s pension allocation *f* veuvage

2 *vt* to be widowed devenir veuf (veuve)

widowed ['wɪdəʊd] *adj* veuf (veuve)

widower ['wɪdəʊə(r)] *n* veuf *m*

width [wɪdθ] *n* largeur *f*

wield [wi:ld] *vt* (sword, pen) manier (**b**) (power, influence) exercer

wife [waɪf] (pl wives [waɪvz]) *n* femme *f*, épouse *f*

wifely ['waɪflɪ] *adj* de bonne épouse

wig [wɪg] *n* perruque *f*

wiggle ['wɪgəl] **1** *n* trémoussement *m*

2 *vt* remuer

3 *vi* se trémousser

wiggly ['wɪglɪ] *adj* Fam (line) ondulé(e)

wigwam ['wɪgwæm] *n* wigwam *m*

wild [waɪld] **1** *adj* (**a**) (not domesticated) (animal, flower, countryside) sauvage; Fig it was a w. goose chase ça n'a rien donné; Fam w. horses wouldn't drag it out of me rien au monde ne me le ferait dire; Fig to sow one's w. oats jeter sa gourme; the W. West le Far West

(**b**) (unrestrained) (wind) violent(e); (weather) très mauvais(e); (hair) en bataille; (child) turbulent(e); (enthusiasm) délirant(e); (promise, rumour) insensé(e); w. eyes regard *m* fou; to be w. (person) mener une vie agitée; to drive sb w. rendre qn fou (folle)

(**c**) (random) it was just a w. guess j'ai dit ça au hasard; Comptr & Fig w. card joker *m*

(**d**) Fam (enthusiastic) to be w. about sb/sth être dingue de qn/qch

---

(**e**) Fam (excellent) génial(e)

2 *adv* to grow w. (of plant) pousser à l'état sauvage; to run w. être livré(e) à soi-même; the audience went w. le public s'est déchaîné

3 *n* in the w. à l'état sauvage; in the wilds en pleine brousse

wildcat ['waɪldkæt] *n* chat *m* sauvage; Ind w. strike grève *f* sauvage

wilderness ['wɪldənɪs] *n* région *f* sauvage; Fig (overgrown garden) jungle *f*; Fig to be in the w. être en pleine traversée du désert

wildfire ['waɪldfaɪə(r)] *n* to spread like w. se répandre comme une traînée de poudre

wildfowl ['waɪldfaʊl] (pl wildfowl) *n* gibier *m* d'eau

wildlife ['waɪldlaɪf] *n* nature *f*; w. park réserve *f* naturelle; w. programme (on *T V*) émission *f* sur les animaux

wildly ['waɪldlɪ] *adv* (**a**) (cheer, applaud) frénétiquement; to rush about w. courir dans tous les sens (**b**) (guess) au hasard (**c**) (for emphasis) extrêmement; (inaccurate, exaggerated) complètement

wildness ['waɪldnɪs] *n* (of countryside, animal) état *m* sauvage; (of wind, waves) fureur *f*; (of applause) frénésie *f*; (of ideas, words) extravagance *f*

wilful ['wɪlfʊl] *adj* (**a**) (stubborn) têtu(e) (**b**) (deliberate) délibéré(e); Law w. murder homicide *m* volontaire

wilfully ['wɪlfəlɪ] *adv* (**a**) (stubbornly) avec entêtement (**b**) (deliberately) délibérément

will¹ [wɪl] **1** *n* (**a**) (resolve, determination) volonté *f* (to do sth) de faire); at w. à volonté!; (cry) à la demande; (fire) au hasard; Mil fire at w.! feu à volonté; to show good w. faire preuve de bonne volonté; with the best w. in the world avec la meilleure volonté du monde; Prov where there's a w. there's a way quand on veut, on peut (**b**) (document) testament *m*; the last w. and testament of... les dernières volontés de...; to make one's w. faire son testament

2 *vt* (**a**) (wish) to w. sb to do sth souhaiter ardemment que qn fasse qch; to w. oneself to do sth faire un effort de volonté pour faire qch (**b**) (leave in one's will) to w. sth to sb léguer qch à qn par testament

will²

On trouve généralement **I/you/he**/etc **will** sous leurs formes contractées **I'll/you'll/he'll**/etc. La forme négative correspondante est **won't**, que l'on écrira **will not** dans des contextes formels.

modal aux v (**a**) (expressing future tense) **I'll do it tomorrow** je le ferai demain; **it won't take long** ça ne prendra pas longtemps; **when w. he be coming?** quand viendra-t-il?; **I'll have finished by five** j'aurai fini avant cinq heures; **w. you be there? – yes I w./no** I won't tu seras là? – oui/non; **you'll write to me, won't you?** tu m'écriras, n'est-ce pas? (**b**) (expressing wish, determination) **I won't allow it!** je ne le permettrai pas!; **you help me?** tu veux bien m'aider?; **she won't let me see him** elle refuse que je le voie; **won't you sit down?** vous ne voulez pas vous asseoir?; **be quiet, w. w.!** tais-toi, s'il te plaît!; **if she WILL insist on doing everything herself...** si elle continue à tout vouloir faire elle-même...; **WILL you shut up!** tais-toi, je te dis!; **it won't open** ça ne s'ouvre pas (**c**) (expressing general truth) **these things w. happen** ça arrive parfois; **the restaurant w. seat a hundred people** le restaurant peut accueillir cent personnes (**d**) (expressing conjecture) **you'll be tired** vous devez être fatigué; **they'll be home by now** ils ont dû arriver chez eux maintenant

William ['wɪlɪəm] *n* W. the Conqueror Guillaume le Conquérant

willie ['wɪlɪ] n Fam (penis) zizi m

willies ['wɪlɪz] npl Fam **to have the w.** avoir la trouille; **to give sb the w.** flanquer la trouille à qn

willing ['wɪlɪŋ] adj (assistant, participant) plein(e) de bonne volonté; **he was a w. accomplice** c'est de son plein gré qu'il est devenu complice; **to be w. to do sth** bien vouloir faire qch; **to show w.** faire preuve de bonne volonté

willingly ['wɪlɪŋlɪ] adv (voluntarily) de son plein gré; (with pleasure) volontiers

willingness ['wɪlɪŋnɪs] n bonne volonté f

will-o'-the-wisp [wɪləðə'wɪsp] n also Fig feu m follet

willow ['wɪləʊ] n w. (tree) saule m

willpower ['wɪlpaʊə(r)] n volonté f

willy ['wɪlɪ] n Fam (penis) zizi m

willy-nilly ['wɪlɪ'nɪlɪ] adv bon gré, mal gré

wilt [wɪlt] vi (of plant) se flétrir; Fig (of person) fatiguer

wily ['waɪlɪ] adj rusé(e)

wimp [wɪmp] n Fam mauviette f

wimpish ['wɪmpɪʃ] adj Fam mauviette

win [wɪn] **1** n victoire f
2 vt (pt & pp won [wʌn]) (a) (battle, race, prize) gagner; **to w. an argument** avoir le dernier mot; Fam **you can't w. them all, you w. some you lose some** on ne peut pas toujours être gagnant (b) (popularity, recognition) acquérir; (confidence, love) gagner (c) (parliamentary seat, election) remporter
3 vi gagner; Fam **you can't w.** j'aurai/tu auras/etc toujours tort; **OK, you w.!** bon, d'accord!
▸ **win back** vt sep reconquérir
▸ **win out** vi réussir
▸ **win over, win round** vt sep persuader
▸ **win through** vi réussir

wince [wɪns] **1** n grimace f
2 vi **to w. (with pain/embarrassment)** grimacer de douleur/d'embarras

winch [wɪntʃ] **1** n treuil m
2 vt hisser

wind¹ [wɪnd] **1** n (a) (air current) vent m; **to sail into** or **against the w.** naviguer vent debout; Fig **to sail close to the w.** (take risks) jouer avec le feu; (be risqué) friser l'indécence; **w. energy** or **power** énergie f éolienne; **w. instrument** instrument m à vent; **w. tunnel** soufflerie f (b) (breath) souffle m; **let me get my w. back** laisse-moi reprendre mon souffle (c) (abdominal) gaz m, vent m; **to have w.** avoir des gaz; **to break w.** lâcher un vent (d) (idioms) Fam **to put the w. up sb** faire une peur bleue à qn; **to take the w. out of sb's sails** couper l'herbe sous le pied à qn; **to get w. of sth** avoir vent de qch
2 vt **to w. sb** (with punch) couper la respiration à qn

wind² [waɪnd] (pt & pp **wound** [waʊnd]) **1** vt (a) (thread, string) enrouler (**round** autour de) (**b**) (handle) tourner; (clock, watch) remonter; **to w. a cassette on/back** faire avancer/rembobiner une cassette
2 vi (of path, river) serpenter
▸ **wind down 1** vt sep (a) (car window) baisser (**b**) (reduce) (production) réduire progressivement; (company) fermer progressivement
2 vi (of person) se calmer; (of meeting) tirer à sa fin; Fam (of person) se détendre, décompresser
▸ **wind up 1** vt sep (a) (car window) remonter (**b**) (finish) (speech, meeting) terminer (**c**) Fam (tease) faire marcher; (annoy) mettre en boîte
2 vi (a) (end speech, meeting) terminer (**b**) Fam (end up) finir; **to w. up doing sth** finir par faire qch; **she'll w. up in prison** elle va finir en prison

windbag ['wɪndbæg] n Fam moulin m à paroles

windbreak ['wɪndbreɪk] n brise-vent m inv

windcheater ['wɪndtʃiːtə(r)] n (jacket) coupe-vent m inv

windchill factor ['wɪndtʃɪlfæktə(r)] n = abaissement de la température dû au vent

winder ['waɪndə(r)] n (on watch) remontoir m; (on car door) lève-glace m inv

windfall ['wɪndfɔːl] n (fruit) fruit m abattu par le vent; Fig (money) aubaine f; Fin **w. profits** (of company) bénéfices mpl inattendus

winding ['waɪndɪŋ] adj (path, stream) sinueux(euse); (staircase) en colimaçon

windmill ['wɪndmɪl] n moulin m à vent

window ['wɪndəʊ] n (a) (of house) & Comptr fenêtre f; (of vehicle) vitre f; glace f; (of shop) vitrine f; **w. box** jardinière f; **w. cleaner** laveur(euse) m,f de carreaux; **w. frame** châssis m; **w. ledge** rebord m de fenêtre; **w. seat** (in vehicle, plane) place f côté fenêtre (**b**) (idioms) **to provide a w. on sth** procurer une ouverture sur qch; **w. of opportunity** ouverture f; Fam **that's my holiday out of the w.** voilà mes vacances fichues en l'air

window-dressing ['wɪndəʊdresɪŋ] n (in shop) vitrine f; Fig façade f

windowpane ['wɪndəʊpeɪn] n vitre f, carreau m

window-shopping ['wɪndəʊʃɒpɪŋ] n **to go w.** faire du lèche-vitrines

windowsill ['wɪndəʊsɪl] n rebord m de fenêtre

windpipe ['wɪndpaɪp] n trachée f

windscreen ['wɪndskriːn], Am **windshield** ['wɪndʃiːld] n pare-brise m inv; **w. wiper** essuie-glace m inv

windsock ['wɪndsɒk] n Av manche f à air

windsurf ['wɪndsɜːf] vi faire de la planche à voile

windsurfing ['wɪndsɜːfɪŋ] n planche f à voile; **to go w.** faire de la planche à voile

windswept ['wɪndswept] adj (hillside, scene) balayé(e) par le vent; (hair) décoiffé(e) par le vent; (person) échevelé(e)

wind-up ['waɪndʌp] n Fam plaisanterie f

windward ['wɪndwəd] adj au vent; **the W. Islands** les îles fpl du Vent

windy¹ ['wɪndɪ] adj (day) venteux(euse); (place) venté(e); **I hate w. weather** je déteste le vent

windy² ['waɪndɪ] adj (road) sinueux(euse)

wine [waɪn] **1** n vin m; **w. bar** bar m à vin; **w. bottle** bouteille f de vin; **w. box** cubitainer m de vin; **w. cellar** cave f à vin; **w. gum** bonbon m à la gomme; **w. list** carte f des vins; **w. tasting** dégustation f; **w. vinegar** vinaigre m de vin
2 vt **to w. and dine sb** inviter qn dans de bons restaurants

wineglass ['waɪnglɑːs] n verre m à vin

wing [wɪŋ] **1** n (a) (of bird, plane) aile f; Fig **to take sb under one's w.** prendre qn sous son aile; Fig **to spread** or **stretch one's wings** élargir son horizon; **w. nut** papillon m (**b**) (of car) aile f; **w. mirror** rétroviseur m extérieur (**c**) (of building, hospital) aile f (**d**) (in football, rugby) (player) ailier m; (area) aile f (**e**) **the wings** (in theatre) les coulisses fpl; Fig **to be waiting in the wings** attendre son heure (**f**) Pol **the left/right w.** l'aile f gauche/droite
2 vt (a) (injure) (bird) blesser à l'aile; (person) blesser au bras (**b**) Fam (improvise) **to w. it** improviser (**c**) (fly) **to w. its way towards sth** (of bird) voler vers qch; Fig **my letter should be winging its way towards you** j'ai posté ma lettre, tu devrais l'avoir bientôt

winger ['wɪŋə(r)] n (in football, rugby) ailier m

wingspan ['wɪŋspæn] n envergure f

wink [wɪŋk] **1** *n* clin *m* d'œil; **to give sb a w.** faire un clin d'œil à qn; *Fam* **to tip sb the w.** refiler un tuyau à qn; *Fam* **I didn't sleep a w.** je n'ai pas fermé l'œil **2** *vi* cligner de l'œil; *(of star, light)* clignoter ▸ **wink at** *vt insep (person)* faire un clin d'œil à; *Fig (offence, illegal practice)* fermer les yeux sur

winkle ['wɪŋkəl] *n (mollusc)* bigorneau *m* ▸ **winkle out** *vt sep Fam* **to w. sth out of sb** soutirer qch à qn

winner ['wɪnə(r)] *n* gagnant(e) *m,f*; **this book will be a w.** ce livre est assuré d'avoir du succès

winning ['wɪnɪŋ] **1** *npl* **winnings** gains *mpl* **2** *adj* **(a)** *(victorious)* gagnant(e); **w. post** poteau *m* d'arrivée **(b)** *(attractive)* charmant(e)

winnow ['wɪnəʊ] *vt* vanner

wino ['waɪnəʊ] *(pl* **winos)** *n Fam (alcoholic)* soûlot(ote) *m,f*

winsome ['wɪnsəm] *adj* charmant(e)

winter ['wɪntə(r)] **1** *n* hiver *m*; **in (the) w.** en hiver; **w. break** vacances *fpl* d'hiver; **w. clothing** vêtements *mpl* d'hiver; **w. sports** sports *mpl* d'hiver **2** *vi* passer l'hiver

wintertime ['wɪntətaɪm] *n* hiver *m*

wint(e)ry ['wɪnt(ə)rɪ] *adj (weather)* d'hiver; *Fig (hostile)* glacial(e)

wipe [waɪp] **1** *n* **(a)** *(action)* **to give sth a w.** essuyer qch **(b)** *(moist tissue)* lingette *f* **2** *vt* **(a)** *(table, plate)* essuyer; **to w. one's nose** s'essuyer le nez; **to w. one's hands (on)** s'essuyer les mains (avec); **to w. one's shoes (on)** s'essuyer les pieds (sur); *Fam Fig* **to w. the floor with sb** ne faire qu'une bouchée de qn **(b)** *(recording, tape)* effacer ▸ **wipe away** *vt sep (tears)* essuyer; *(mark)* enlever ▸ **wipe off** *vt sep (remove), Fam* **that'll w. the smile off his face!** ça lui fera passer l'envie de rire! **2** *vi (of train)* partir ▸ **wipe out** *vt sep (a) (erase)* effacer; *(debt)* liquider **(b)** *(destroy)* décimer ▸ **wipe up** *vt sep* essuyer

wiper ['waɪpə(r)] *n* essuie-glace *m inv*

wire ['waɪə(r)] **1** *n* **(a)** *(of metal)* fil *m* de fer; *(electrical)* fil (électrique); **w. brush** brosse *f* métallique; **w. fence** clôture *f* en fil de fer; **w. mesh** toile *f* métallique; **w. wool** paille *f* de fer **(b)** *Am (telegram)* télégramme *m* **(c)** *(idioms) Fam* **to get one's wires crossed** s'emmêler les pinceaux; **the tournament went right down to the w.** l'issue du tournoi a été incertaine jusqu'au bout **2** *vt* **(a)** *(house)* faire l'installation électrique de; **to w. sth to sth** *(connect electrically)* relier qch à qch; *(attach with wire)* attacher qch à qch avec du fil de fer **(b)** *(send telegram to)* télégraphier à

wirecutters ['waɪəkʌtəz] *npl* **(pair of) w.** pince *f* coupante

wireless ['waɪəlɪs] *n Old-fashioned* **w. (set)** (poste *m* de) TSF *f*

wiretapping ['waɪətæpɪŋ] *n* mise *f* sur écoute d'une ligne téléphonique

wiring ['waɪərɪŋ] *n* installation *f* électrique

wiry ['waɪərɪ] *adj (hair)* crépu(e); *(person)* petit(e) et musclé(e)

wisdom ['wɪzdəm] *n* sagesse *f*; **w. tooth** dent *f* de sagesse

wise [waɪz] *adj (knowledgeable)* sage; *(advisable)* prudent(e); *Fam Pej* **a w. guy** un gros malin; **the Three W. Men** les Rois *mpl* mages; **it's easy to be w. after the event** c'est facile de savoir ce qui s'est bien ou pas bien après

coup; **to be none the wiser** ne pas être plus avancé(e); *Fam* **to get w. to sb** se rendre compte de qch; *Fam* **to get w. to sth** percer qn à jour ▸ **wise up** *vi Fam* **to w. up to sb** voir qn sous son vrai jour; **to w. up to sth** se rendre compte de qch; **w. up!** ouvre les yeux!

-wise [waɪz] *suff Fam (with reference to)* **health-/salary-/** *etc* **w.** du point de vue de la santé/du salaire

wisecrack ['waɪzkræk] *Fam* **1** *n* vanne *f*, blague *f* **2** *vi* sortir des vannes

wisely ['waɪzlɪ] *adv* sagement

wish [wɪʃ] **1** *n* **(a)** *(desire)* désir *m*; *(thing desired)* vœu *m*; **to make a w.** faire un vœu; **to do sth against sb's wishes** faire qch contre le souhait de qn **(b)** *(greeting)* **best wishes** meilleurs vœux; *(in letter)* amicalement **2** *vt* **(a)** *(want)* désirer; **to w. to do sth** désirer faire qch; **to w. sb well** souhaiter à qn que tout se passe bien; **to w. sb luck/a pleasant journey** souhaiter bonne chance/bon voyage à qn; **to w. sth on sb** souhaiter qch à qn **(b)** *(want something impossible, unlikely)* **I w. she could come** j'aurais bien aimé qu'elle vienne; **I w. I had seen it!** j'aurais bien voulu voir ça!; **I w. I hadn't left so early** je regrette d'être parti aussi tôt; **I w. she wouldn't say things like that** je préférerais qu'elle s'abstienne de dire des choses pareilles; **w. you were here!** *(on postcard)* je pense bien à toi **3** *vi* **to w. for sth** souhaiter qch; **what more could you w. for?** que souhaiter de plus?; **as you w.** comme tu voudras

wishbone ['wɪʃbəʊn] *n* bréchet *m*

wishful ['wɪʃfʊl] *adj* **that's w. thinking** tu te fais/il se fait/*etc* des illusions

wishy-washy ['wɪʃɪwɒʃɪ] *adj Fam* mou (molle); *(couleur)* délavé(e)

wisp [wɪsp] *n (of straw, wool)* brin *m; (of hair)* mèche *f; (of smoke, cloud)* traînée *f*

wistful ['wɪstfʊl] *adj* nostalgique

wit [wɪt] *n* **(a)** *(intelligence, presence of mind)* esprit *m*; **to have the w. to do sth** être assez intelligent(e) pour faire qch; **to have quick wits** avoir l'esprit vif; **to have lost one's wits** avoir perdu l'esprit; **to have/keep one's wits about one** rester très vigilant(e); **to be at one's wits' end** ne plus savoir que faire; **to live by one's wits** vivre d'expédients; **to scare sb out of their wits** faire une peur bleue à qn **(b)** *(humour)* esprit *m* **(c)** *(witty person)* **(man)** homme *m* d'esprit; *(woman)* femme *f* d'esprit

witch [wɪtʃ] *n* sorcière *f*; **w. doctor** sorcier *m*

witchcraft ['wɪtʃkrɑːft] *n* sorcellerie *f*

witch-hunt ['wɪtʃhʌnt] *n Pol* chasse *f* aux sorcières

with [wɪð] *prep* **(a)** *(expressing accompaniment)* avec; **w. me/him** avec moi/lui; **to live w. one's parents** vivre chez ses parents; **I was left w. nothing to do** je me suis retrouvé sans rien à faire **(b)** *(having)* **the girl w. glasses/curly hair** la fille aux lunettes/aux cheveux bouclés; **w. one's hands in one's pockets** les mains dans les poches **(c)** *(expressing association)* **to be pleased w. sb** être content(e) de qn; **to be angry w. sb** être en colère contre qn; **to fight/compete w. sb** se battre/être en concurrence avec qn; **to be amorous w. sb** être amoureux(euse) de qn; **covered w. mud** couvert(e) de boue **(d)** *(expressing manner)* **w. pleasure/difficulty** avec plaisir/difficulté; **to say sth w. a smile** dire qch avec un sourire **(e)** *(expressing instrument, agent)* **to hit sb w. sth** frapper qn avec qch; **to cut sth w. a knife** couper qch avec un couteau; **it's pouring w. rain** il pleut à verse **(f)** *(because of)* **to tremble w. rage** trembler de rage; **to cry w. happiness** pleurer de joie; **w. her money, she can**

surely afford it avec l'argent qu'elle a, elle peut bien se permettre ça
(**g**) *(expressing simultaneity)* **to improve w. age** s'améliorer avec l'âge; **w. those words, he left** sur ces mots, il partit; **w. Christmas coming,...** puisque c'est bientôt Noël,...
(**h**) *(idioms)* **to be w. it** être dans le vent; **get w. it!** *(wake up)* réveille-toi!; *(face reality)* ouvre les yeux!; **I'm w. you** *(I support you)* je suis avec vous; **I'm not w. you** *(I don't understand)* je ne vous suis pas

withdraw [wɪð'drɔː] *(pt* **withdrew** [wɪð'druː], *pp* **withdrawn** [wɪð'drɔːn]) **1** *vt* retirer (**from** de)
2 *vi* se retirer (**from** de); **to w. in favour of sb** se désister en faveur de qn; **to w. into oneself** se replier sur soi-même

withdrawal [wɪð'drɔːəl] *n* retrait *m*; **to make a w.** *(from bank)* faire un retrait; **w. symptoms** symptômes *mpl* de manque; **to have w. symptoms** être en (état de) manque

withdrawn [wɪð'drɔːn] *adj* replié(e) sur soi-même

wither ['wɪðə(r)] *vi (of plant)* se flétrir; *(of limb)* s'atrophier

withered ['wɪðəd] *adj (plant)* flétri(e); *(limb)* atrophié(e)

withering ['wɪðərɪŋ] *adj (look)* foudroyant(e); *(tone)* cinglant(e)

withhold [wɪð'həʊld] *(pt & pp* **withheld** [wɪð'held]) *vt (consent, help)* refuser; *(money)* retenir; *(truth)* cacher; *(information)* faire de la rétention de

within [wɪð'ɪn] **1** *prep* (**a**) *(inside)* à l'intérieur de; **problems w. the company** des problèmes au sein de l'entreprise (**b**) *(not beyond)* **w. 10 miles of the town** ≃ à moins de 16 km de la ville; **w. a radius of** dans un rayon de; **w. limits** jusqu'à un certain point; **w. reason** dans des limites raisonnables; **to stay w. budget** rester dans les limites du budget; **to come w. an inch of doing sth** bien faillir faire qch (**c**) *(with expressions of time)* **w. an hour/a year** en moins d'une heure/d'un an; **w. minutes** en quelques minutes; **w. the next five years** *(in the space of)* *(in future)* au cours des cinq années à venir; *(in past)* au cours des cinq années suivantes; *(before the end of) (in future)* avant cinq ans; *(in past)* en moins de cinq ans; **they died w. a few days of each other** ils sont morts à quelques jours d'intervalle
2 *adv* à l'intérieur; **from w.** de l'intérieur

without [wɪð'aʊt] **1** *prep* sans; **w. any money/difficulty** sans argent/difficulté; **w. doing sth** sans faire qch; **do it w. him knowing** fais-le sans qu'il le sache; **it goes w. saying that...** il va sans dire que...; **to do** *or* **go w. sth** se passer de qch
2 *adv* **to do** *or* **go w.** se priver

withstand [wɪð'stænd] *(pt & pp* **withstood** [wɪð'stʊd]) *vt* supporter

witless ['wɪtlɪs] *adj (person, remark)* stupide; **to scare sb w.** faire une peur bleue à qn

witness ['wɪtnɪs] **1** *n* (**a**) *(person)* témoin *m*; **to call sb as w.** citer qn comme témoin; **w. for the defence/ prosecution** témoin à décharge/charge; **w. box** barre *f* des témoins (**b**) *(testimony)* **to bear w. (to sth)** témoigner (de qch)
2 *vt* être témoin de; *Fig* **this town has witnessed many battles** cette ville a été le théâtre de nombreuses batailles
3 *vi Law* **to w. to sth** témoigner de qch

witter ['wɪtə(r)] *vi Fam* **to w. (on)** bavasser

witticism ['wɪtɪsɪzəm] *n* mot *m* d'esprit

wittily ['wɪtɪlɪ] *adv* avec esprit

wittingly ['wɪtɪŋlɪ] *adv* sciemment

witty ['wɪtɪ] *adj* spirituel(elle), plein(e) d'esprit

wives [waɪvz] *pl of* **wife**

wizard ['wɪzəd] *n* magicien *m*; *Fig* as *m*

wizened ['wɪzənd] *adj* ratatiné(e)

wk *(abbr* **week)** semaine

wobble ['wɒbəl] *vi (of chair, table)* branler; *(of building, jelly)* trembler; *(of person)* être chancelant(e)

wobbly ['wɒblɪ] **1** *n Fam* **to throw a w.** piquer une crise
2 *adj (chair, table)* bancal(e); *(shelf, ladder)* branlant(e); *(person)* chancelant(e)

woe [wəʊ] *n Lit* malheur *m*; *Hum* **w. betide you if you're late** malheur à toi si tu es en retard

woebegone ['wəʊbɪgɒn] *adj* abattu(e)

woeful ['wəʊfʊl] *adj* (**a**) *(sad)* affligé(e) (**b**) *(very bad)* déplorable

wog [wɒg] *n Br very Fam* = terme injurieux désignant une personne qui n'est pas blanche

wok [wɒk] *n* poêle *f* chinoise

woke [wəʊk] *pt of* **wake**[3]

woken ['wəʊkən] *pp of* **wake**[3]

wolf [wʊlf] *(pl* **wolves** [wʊlvz]) *n* (**a**) loup *m*; **w. cub** louveteau *m*; **w. whistle** = sifflement admiratif au passage de quelqu'un (**b**) *(idioms)* **I don't earn much but it keeps the w. from the door** je ne gagne pas beaucoup mais je ne manque de rien; **to throw sb to the wolves** abandonner qn à son sort; **a w. in sheep's clothing** un loup déguisé en brebis; **to cry w.** crier au loup
▶ **wolf down** *vt sep* engloutir

woman ['wʊmən] *(pl* **women** ['wɪmɪn]) *n* femme *f*; **women's magazine** magazine *m* féminin; **women's movement** mouvement *m* de libération de la femme; **women's page** page *f* des lectrices; *Euph* **women's problems** des trucs *mpl* de femme; **w. doctor** femme médecin *f*; **w. driver** conductrice *f*

womanizer ['wʊmənaɪzə(r)] *n* coureur *m* (de jupons)

womanly ['wʊmənlɪ] *adj* féminin(e)

womb [wuːm] *n* utérus *m*

women ['wɪmɪn] *pl of* **woman**

womenfolk ['wɪmɪnfəʊk] *n* femmes *fpl*

won [wʌn] *pt & pp of* **win**

wonder ['wʌndə(r)] **1** *n* (**a**) *(miracle)* miracle *m*, merveille *f*; **to work** *or* **do wonders** faire des miracles; **it's a w. (that)...** c'est un miracle que... + *subjunctive*; **(it's) no w....** ce n'est pas étonnant que... + *subjunctive*; **w. drug** remède *m* miracle (**b**) *(astonishment)* émerveillement *m*; **in w.** avec émerveillement
2 *vt* se demander; **one wonders whether...** c'est à se demander si...; **I was wondering if you were free tonight** je voulais savoir si tu étais libre ce soir
3 *vi* (**a**) *(be curious)* se demander; *Fam* **I w. about her sometimes!** je me pose parfois des questions à son sujet! (**b**) *Lit (be amazed)* s'étonner (**at** de)

wonderful ['wʌndəfʊl] *adj* merveilleux(euse), formidable

wonky ['wɒŋkɪ] *adj Fam* déglingué(e)

won't [wəʊnt] = **will not**

wont [wəʊnt] *Formal* **1** *n* habitude *f*; **as is her w.** comme à son habitude
2 *adj* **to be w. to do sth** avoir l'habitude de faire qch

woo [wuː] *(pt & pp* **wooed**) *vt* (**a**) *Lit (woman)* courtiser (**b**) *Fig (supporters, investors)* attirer

wood [wʊd] *n* (**a**) *(forest, material)* bois *m*; **w. carving** sculpture *f* sur bois (**b**) *(idioms)* **she can't see the w. for the trees** elle s'y perd dans les détails; **we're not out of the woods yet** nous ne sommes pas encore tirés d'affaire; **touch w.!** je touche du bois!

woodbine ['wʊdbaɪn] *n (plant)* vigne *f* vierge

woodcock ['wʊdkɒk] *n* bécasse *f*

woodcut ['wʊdkʌt] *n* gravure *f* sur bois

woodcutter ['wʊdkʌtə(r)] n bûcheron m

wooded ['wʊdɪd] adj boisé(e)

wooden ['wʊdən] adj (made of wood) en bois; Fig (unexpressive) impassible; **w. spoon** cuillère f de bois; Fig **to get the w. spoon** (in contest) arriver dernier au classement

woodland ['wʊdlənd] n bois mpl

woodlouse ['wʊdlaʊs] (pl **woodlice** ['wʊdlaɪs]) n cloporte m

woodpecker ['wʊdpekə(r)] n pic m

woodpile ['wʊdpaɪl] n tas m de bois

woodshed ['wʊdʃed] n remise f à bois

woodwind ['wʊdwɪnd] n Mus the w. (instruments) les bois mpl; **w. instrument** bois m

woodwork ['wʊdwɜːk] n (craft) travail m du bois; (in house) boiserie f; Fig **to come** or **crawl out of the w.** faire soudain surface

woodworm ['wʊdwɜːm] n ver m à bois

woof [wʊf] **1** n aboiement m
2 exclam ouah!

wool [wʊl] n laine f; Fam **to pull the w. over sb's eyes** embobiner qn

woollen, Am **woolen** ['wʊlən] **1** n woollens lainages mpl
2 adj (garment) en laine

woolly, Am **wooly** ['wʊlɪ] **1** n Fam (garment) woollies lainages mpl
2 adj (garment) en laine; Fig (idea, theory) nébuleux(-euse)

woozy ['wuːzɪ] adj Fam dans les vapes

wop [wɒp] n very Fam rital(e) m,f. = terme raciste désignant un Italien

word [wɜːd] **1** n (a) (in general) mot m; **w. for w.** mot pour mot; **in a w.** en un mot; **in other words** autrement dit; **not in so many words** pas en ces termes-là; **not a w.** pas un mot; **in one's own words** à sa façon; **I can't put it into words** je n'arrive pas à trouver les mots; **he's a man of few words** c'est un homme qui parle peu; **I couldn't get a w. in (edgeways)** je n'ai pas pu placer un mot; **the w. of God** la parole de Dieu; **I'll take your w. for it** je te crois sur parole; **to take sb at his/her w.** prendre qn au mot; **it was too ridiculous for words** c'était d'un ridicule sans nom; **my w.!** ma parole!
(b) (remarks, conversation) **to have a w. with sb** parler à qn; **to have words with sb** avoir des mots avec qn; **just say the w.** tu n'as qu'à me faire signe; **you're putting words into my mouth** tu me fais dire des choses que je n'ai pas voulu dire; **you took the words right out of my mouth** c'est justement ce que j'allais dire; **to put in a good w. for sb** glisser un mot en faveur de qn; **he never has a good w. for anyone** il ne peut pas s'empêcher de dire du mal des gens; **a w. of warning** une mise en garde; **a w. of advice** un petit conseil
(c) (news) **to receive w. from sb** avoir des nouvelles de qn; **to send sb w. of sth** faire part à qn de qch; **the w. is that...** on raconte que...; **by w. of mouth** de bouche à oreille
(d) (promise) parole f; **w. of honour** parole d'honneur; **to give sb one's w.** donner sa parole à qn; **to keep one's w.** tenir sa promesse; **to go back on one's w.** manquer à sa parole
(e) words (lyrics) paroles fpl
2 vt (express in words) formuler

wording ['wɜːdɪŋ] n formulation f

word-processing [wɜːd'prəʊsesɪŋ] n Comptr traitement m de texte

word-processor ['wɜːdprəʊsesə(r)] n Comptr machine f à traitement de texte

wordy ['wɜːdɪ] adj prolixe

wore [wɔː(r)] pt of wear

work [wɜːk] **1** n (a) (labour) travail m; **to be at w.** on sth travailler à ou sur qch; **to get to w.** se mettre au travail; **w. in progress** (sign) travaux; Comptr **w. station** poste m de travail
(b) (task) travail m; **to put a lot of w. into sth** beaucoup travailler à qch; **to have one's w. cut out (to do sth)** avoir du mal (à faire qch); **to make quick** or **short w. of sth** venir rapidement à bout de qch; **good w.!** c'est du bon travail!
(c) (literary, artistic) œuvre f; **a w. of art** une œuvre d'art
(d) (employment) travail m; **to be out of w.** être sans travail; **w. permit** permis m de travail
(e) Ind **works council** comité m d'entreprise; **works outing** sortie f organisée par le comité d'entreprise
(f) works (construction) travaux mpl; **road works ahead** (sign) attention travaux
(g) works (mechanism) mécanisme m
(h) Fam **the works** (everything) le grand jeu; **to give sb the works** (beating) passer qn à tabac; (luxury treatment) jouer le grand jeu à qn
2 vt (a) (person) **to w. sb hard** exiger beaucoup de qn; **to w. oneself to death** se tuer au travail
(b) (operate) (machine) faire fonctionner
(c) (bring about) (miracle, cure, change) opérer; **to w. it** or **things so that** faire en sorte que
(d) (move) **to w. one's hands free** se libérer les mains; **to w. one's way through a book/list** avancer progressivement dans la lecture d'un livre/dans une liste
(e) (exploit) (mine, quarry) exploiter; (land) travailler
3 vi (a) (of person) travailler; **to w. against sb/in sb's favour** jouer en la défaveur/la faveur de qn
(b) (function) (of machine, system) marcher, fonctionner
(c) (have effect) (of medicine) faire effet; (of plan, method) marcher
▸ **work in** vt sep (include) introduire, glisser
▸ **work off** vt sep (anger) évacuer; **he worked off 5 kilos** il a perdu 5 kilos en faisant de l'exercice
▸ **work on 1** vt insep **to w. on sth** travailler à ou sur qch
2 vi (continue to work) continuer à travailler
▸ **work out 1** vt sep (cost, total) calculer; (answer) trouver; **to w. out how to do sth** trouver comment faire qch; **I'm sure we can w. this thing out** je suis sûr qu'on peut arranger ça
2 vi (a) (turn out) **to w. out well/badly (for sb)** bien/mal se passer (pour qn); **it all worked out in the end** finalement, tout s'est arrangé (b) (total) arriver à (c) (exercise) s'entraîner
▸ **work up** vt sep (a) (develop) **to w. up enthusiasm/ interest for sth** s'enthousiasmer pour/s'intéresser à qch; **I worked up an appetite** ça m'a ouvert l'appétit (b) (excite) **to get worked up (about sth)** se mettre dans tous ses états (à propos de qch)
▸ **work up to** vt insep se préparer à

workable ['wɜːkəbəl] adj possible

workaday ['wɜːkədeɪ] adj de tous les jours

workaholic [wɜːkə'hɒlɪk] n Fam bourreau m de travail

workbench ['wɜːkbentʃ] n établi m

workday ['wɜːkdeɪ] n Am jour m ouvrable

worker ['wɜːkə(r)] n travailleur(euse) m,f. (in industry) ouvrier(ère) m,f; **to be a fast/slow w.** travailler vite/ lentement; **w. bee** ouvrière f; **w. participation** participation f des travailleurs à la gestion

workforce ['wɜːkfɔːs] n main-d'œuvre f

workhouse ['wɜːkhaʊs] n Hist asile m des pauvres

working ['wɜːkɪŋ] **1** *n* **(a)** *(operation) (of machine)* fonctionnement *m* **(b) workings** *(mechanism)* mécanisme *m* **2** *adj (person)* qui travaille; **to have a w. knowledge of sth** avoir de bonnes bases en qch; **in w. order** en état de marche; **the w. class** la classe ouvrière; **w. clothes** vêtements *mpl* de travail; **w. hours** heures *fpl* de travail; **w. lunch** déjeuner *m* d'affaires; **w. majority** majorité *f* suffisante; **w. model** maquette *f* animée; **w. party** groupe *m* de travail

working-class ['wɜːkɪŋ'klɑːs] *adj* ouvrier(ère); *(accent)* prolétaire

workload ['wɜːkləʊd] *n* charge *f* de travail

workman ['wɜːkmən] *n* ouvrier *m*

workmanlike ['wɜːkmənlaɪk] *adj* de professionnel

workmanship ['wɜːkmənʃɪp] *n* travail *m*; **a fine piece of w.** du beau travail

workout ['wɜːkaʊt] *n* séance *f* d'entraînement

workplace ['wɜːkpleɪs] *n* lieu *m* de travail

workshop ['wɜːkʃɒp] *n* atelier *m*

workshy ['wɜːkʃaɪ] *adj* fainéant(e)

worktop ['wɜːktɒp] *n (in kitchen)* plan *m* de travail

work-to-rule ['wɜːktə'ruːl] *n Ind* grève *f* du zèle

world [wɜːld] *n* **(a)** *(the earth)* monde *m*; **the best/ biggest in the w.** le (la) meilleur(e)/plus grand(e) du monde; **the w. over, all over the w.** dans le monde entier; **the W. Bank** la Banque mondiale; **w. champion** champion(onne) *m,f* du monde; **the W. Cup** la Coupe du monde; **w. map** mappemonde *f*; **w. music** world music *f*; **w. record** record *m* du monde; **W. Series** = championnat national américain de base-ball; **W. War One/Two** la Première/Seconde *ou* Deuxième Guerre mondiale **(b)** *(sphere of activity)* **the literary/political/business w.** le monde littéraire/politique/des affaires **(c)** *(society)* **man/woman of the w.** homme *m*/femme *f* d'expérience; **to go up in the w.** faire du chemin; **to come down in the w.** déchoir; **to have the w. at one's feet** avoir le monde à ses pieds **(d)** *(for emphasis)* **to do sb the w. of good** faire le plus grand bien à qn; **a w. of difference** une différence énorme; **to think the w. of sb** admirer énormément qn; **they carried on for all the w. as if nothing had happened** ils ont continué comme si de rien n'était **(e)** *(idioms)* **she's not long for this w.** elle n'en a plus pour longtemps; **to bring a child into the w.** mettre un enfant au monde; **to have the best of both worlds** avoir tous les avantages et aucun des inconvénients; **she lives in a w. of her own** elle vit dans un monde à elle; *Fam* **it's out of this w.** c'est extraordinaire; **not for (anything in) the w.** pour rien au monde; **it's a small w.!** le monde est petit!; **what is the w. coming to?** où va-t-on?

world-beater ['wɜːldbiːtə(r)] *n* leader *m* mondial

world-famous ['wɜːld'feɪməs] *adj* célèbre dans le monde entier

worldly ['wɜːldlɪ] *adj (pleasure, goods)* matériel(elle)

worldly-wise ['wɜːldlɪ'waɪz] *adj* qui a de l'expérience

world-weary ['wɜːldwɪərɪ] *adj* désabusé(e)

worldwide ['wɜːldwaɪd] **1** *adj* mondial(e); *Comptr* **the W. Web** le Worldwide Web **2** *adv* dans le monde entier

worm [wɜːm] **1** *n* ver *m*; *(maggot)* asticot *m*; **to have worms** *(of person, animal)* avoir des vers; *Fig* **the w. has turned** il/elle/*etc* a fini par se rebiffer **2** *vt* **(a)** *(animal)* traiter contre les vers **(b) to w. one's way out of a situation** réussir à se tirer d'une situation; **to w. oneself into sb's favour/confidence** s'insinuer dans les bonnes grâces/la confiance de qn; **to w. a secret out of sb** arracher un secret à qn

wormeaten ['wɜːmiːtən] *adj (wood)* vermoulu(e); *(fruit)* véreux(euse)

worn [wɔːn] *pp of* wear

worried ['wʌrɪd] *adj* inquiet(ète); **to be w. about sb** être inquiet pour qn; **I'm w. about his safety** je m'inquiète pour sa sécurité; **he's w. about failing his exams** il a peur de rater ses examens

worrier ['wʌrɪə(r)] *n* anxieux(euse) *m,f*

worry ['wʌrɪ] **1** *n* souci *m*; **that's the least of my worries** c'est le cadet de mes soucis **2** *vt (pt & pp* **worried)** *(cause anxiety to)* inquiéter; **to w. oneself sick (about sth)** se faire un sang d'encre (à propos de qch) **3** *vi* s'inquiéter, se faire du souci; **to w. about sb** s'inquiéter pour qn; **to w. about the future** s'inquiéter pour l'avenir; **to w. about doing sth** avoir peur de faire qch; **not to w.!** ce n'est pas grave!; **there's/it's nothing to w. about** il n'y a pas de quoi s'inquiéter

worrying ['wʌrɪɪŋ] *adj* inquiétant(e)

worse [wɜːs] **1** *adj (comparative of* bad*)* pire **(than** que**)**; **there's nothing w. than...** il n'y a rien de pire que...; **to get w.** aller en empirant; **things could be w.** les choses pourraient aller plus mal; **and to make matters w.** et, pour tout arranger...; **to go from bad to w.** aller de mal en pis; **I'm none the w. for it** je ne m'en porte pas plus mal; **to be the w. for drink** être éméché(e); *Fam* **to be the w. for wear** *(of car, book)* être en mauvais état; *(of drunk person)* être dans un sale état; **w. luck!** quelle poisse! **2** *adv (comparative of* badly*)* plus mal; **you could do w.** tu aurais pu tomber plus mal; **I don't think any w. of her for it** elle n'a pas pour autant baissé dans mon estime; **he is w. off than before** sa situation a empiré **3** *n* there was w. to come le pire restait à venir; **I've seen w.** j'ai vu pire; **a change for the w.** une détérioration

worsen ['wɜːsən] **1** *vt* aggraver **2** *vi* empirer

Worship ['wɜːʃɪp] *n (title)* **His/Her W.** *(referring to mayor)* monsieur/madame le maire; *(referring to magistrate)* monsieur/madame le juge

worship ['wɜːʃɪp] **1** *n (of deity)* vénération *f*, culte *m*; *(of person)* adoration *f*; **place of w.** lieu *m* de culte **2** *vt (pt & pp* **worshipped)** *(deity)* vénérer; *(person)* adorer

worst [wɜːst] **1** *adj (superlative of* bad*)* the w. le (la) pire; **the w. film I've ever seen** le plus mauvais film que j'aie jamais vu; **her w. mistake** sa plus grave erreur; **the w. thing was...** le pire, c'était que... **2** *adv (superlative of* badly*)* le plus mal; **the elderly are the w. off** ce sont les personnes âgées qui sont le plus mal loties **3** *n* **the w.** le pire; **the w. that could happen** le pire qui puisse arriver; **the w. of it is that...** le pire dans tout ça, c'est que...; **if the w. comes to the w.** au pire; *Fam* **do your w.!** essaie un peu pour voir!; **the w. is over** on a passé le plus dur

worst-case scenario ['wɜːstkeɪsɪ'nɑːrɪəʊ] *(pl* **worst-case scenarios)** *n* le pire qui puisse se produire

worsted ['wʊstɪd] *n* peigné *m*

worth [wɜːθ] **1** *prep* **(a)** *(having a value of)* **to be w.** valoir qch; **how much is it w.?** combien est-ce que cela vaut?; **that's my opinion, for what it's w.** c'est mon opinion, elle vaut ce qu'elle vaut; **he's w. millions** il est millionnaire; **he was pulling for all he was w.** il tirait de toutes ses forces **(b)** *(meriting)* **the museum is w. a visit** le musée vaut le détour; **this book is not w. buying** ce livre ne vaut pas la peine d'être acheté; **it's w./it isn't w. it** ça en vaut/ça n'en vaut pas la peine; **it's w. thinking about** ça vaut le coup d'y réfléchir **2** *n* valeur *f*; **give me $20 w. of gas** donnez-moi pour 20 dollars d'essence; **to get one's money's w.** en avoir pour son argent

worthless ['wɜːθlɪs] *adj* **to be w.** *(of object)* ne rien valoir; *(of person)* être un(e) bon (bonne) à rien

worthwhile [wɜːθ'waɪl] *adj* **to be w.** valoir la peine *ou* le coup

worthy ['wɜːðɪ] **1** *adj (person, life)* digne; **to be w. of sth** être digne de qch
2 *n* notable *m*

would [wʊd]

> On trouve généralement **I/you/he/**etc **would** sous leurs formes contractées **I'd/you'd/he'd/**etc. La forme négative correspondante est **wouldn't**, que l'on écrira **would not** dans des contextes formels.

modal aux v **(a)** *(expressing conditional tense)* **she w. come if you invited her** elle viendrait si vous l'invitiez; **if he had let go, he w. have fallen** s'il avait lâché prise, il serait tombé; **if she had asked me, I w. have refused** si elle m'avait demandé, j'aurais refusé; **w. you do it? – yes I w./ no I wouldn't** tu le ferais? – oui/non; **you wouldn't do it, w. you?** tu ne le ferais pas, dis?
(b) *(expressing wish, determination)* **w. you pass the butter, please?** pourrais-tu passer le beurre, s'il te plaît?, **w. you like a drink?** tu veux boire quelque chose?; **she wouldn't let me speak to him** elle m'empêchait de lui parler; **be quiet, w. you!** tais-toi, s'il te plaît!; **the car wouldn't start** la voiture ne démarrait pas
(c) *(for emphasis)* **you would insist on going!** il fallait que tu insistes pour y aller!; **I forgot – you w.!** j'ai oublié – c'est bien (de) toi!
(d) *(expressing past habit)* **she w. often return home exhausted** il lui arrivait souvent de rentrer épuisée; **there w. always be some left over** il en restait toujours
(e) *(in reported speech)* **she told me she w. be there** elle m'a dit qu'elle serait là; **I said I w. do it** j'ai dit que je le ferais
(f) *(expressing conjecture)* **w. that be my scarf you're wearing?** est-ce que, par hasard, ce serait mon écharpe que vous portez?; **they w. have been tired after their journey** ils devaient être fatigués après leur voyage; **I wouldn't know** je n'en ai aucune idée

would-be ['wʊdbiː] *adj (actor, artist)* en puissance

wouldn't ['wʊdnt] = **would not**

wound¹ [wuːnd] **1** *n* blessure *f*
2 *vt also Fig* blesser; **to w. sb's feelings** blesser qn, heurter la sensibilité de qn

wound² [waʊnd] *pt & pp of* **wind²**

wounded ['wuːndɪd] **1** *adj* blessé(e)
2 *npl* **the w.** les blessés *mpl*

wounding ['wuːndɪŋ] *adj* blessant(e)

wove [wəʊv] *pt of* **weave**

woven ['wəʊvən] *pp of* **weave**

wow [waʊ] *Fam* **1** *vt* séduire, emballer
2 *exclam* la vache!

WP [dʌbəljuː'piː] *n Comptr* **(a)** *(abbr* **word-processor)** *(machine)* machine *f* à traitement de texte; *(software)* logiciel *m* de traitement de texte **(b)** *(abbr* **word-processing)** *(skill)* traitement *m* de texte

WPC [dʌbəljuːpiː'siː] *n Br (abbr* **woman police constable)** = femme agent de police

wpm [dʌbəljuːpiː'em] *(abbr* **words per minute)** mots par minute

WRAC [ræk] *n Br Mil (abbr* **Women's Royal Army Corps)** = section féminine de l'armée britannique

wrangle ['ræŋgəl] **1** *n* dispute *f*
2 *vi* se disputer **(about** *or* **over** à propos de)

wrap [ræp] **1** *n (shawl)* châle *m*; *Fig* **to keep sth under wraps** garder qch secret
2 *vt (pt & pp* **wrapped)** envelopper, emballer **(in** dans); **to w. sth around sth** enrouler qch autour de qch; *Fig* **wrapped in mystery** enveloppé(e) de mystère
▸ **wrap up 1** *vt sep* **(a)** *(parcel, present)* envelopper; *Fig* **to be wrapped up in sth** être absorbé(e) par qch **(b)** *Fam (bring to an end)* conclure
2 *vi (dress warmly)* s'emmitoufler

wrapper ['ræpə(r)] *n (of sweet)* papier *m*

wrapping ['ræpɪŋ] *n* emballage *m*; **w. paper** papier *m* d'emballage

wrath [rɒθ] *n Lit* courroux *m*

wreak [riːk] *vt* **to w. havoc** faire des ravages; **to w. vengeance on sb** assouvir sa vengeance sur qn

wreath [riːθ] *n* couronne *f*

wreathe [riːð] *vt Lit* couronner

wreck [rek] **1** *n (ship, car, train, plane)* épave *f*; *Fig* **to be a physical/nervous w.** être physiquement/nerveusement au bout du rouleau
2 *vt (ship)* faire faire naufrage à; *(car)* démolir; *(room, house)* saccager; *Fig (plans, hopes, happiness)* ruiner, anéantir; *(marriage, career)* ruiner; **to w. one's health** ruiner la santé

wreckage ['rekɪdʒ] *n* épave *f*

wrecker ['rekə(r)] *n Am (salvage vehicle)* dépanneuse *f*

wren [ren] *n* troglodyte *m*

wrench [rentʃ] **1** *n* **(a)** *(pull) (to ankle, shoulder)* faux mouvement *m*; *Fig (emotional)* déchirement *m* **(b)** *(tool)* clef *f*
2 *vt* **to w. one's ankle/shoulder** se fouler la cheville/ l'épaule; **to w. sth out of sb's hands** arracher qch des mains de qn

wrest [rest] *vt* **to w. sth from sb** arracher qch à qn

wrestle ['resəl] *vi (with person)* lutter (**with** contre); *Fig* **to w. with sth** se débattre avec qch

wrestler ['reslə(r)] *n* lutteur(euse) *m,f*

wrestling ['reslɪŋ] *n* lutte *f*, catch *m*; **w. match** match *m* de catch

wretch [retʃ] *n* malheureux(euse) *m,f*

wretched ['retʃɪd] *adj* **(a)** *(very bad)* atroce **(b)** *(unhappy)* démoralisé(e) **(c)** *Fam (for emphasis)* **I can't find the w. key!** je ne trouve pas cette maudite clé!

wriggle ['rɪgəl] **1** *vt* **to w. one's way out of a situation** se sortir d'une situation
2 *vi* **(about)** gigoter, se tortiller; **to w. out of sth** couper à qch; **he managed to w. out of paying me back** il s'est débrouillé pour ne pas me rembourser

wring [rɪŋ] *vt (pt & pp* **wrung** [rʌŋ]) *(clothes)* essorer; **to w. one's hands** se tordre les mains; **to w. sb's neck** tordre le cou à qn; *Fam* **I'd like to w. his neck** j'ai envie de lui tordre le cou; *Fig* **to w. sth from sb** réussir à arracher qch à qn
▸ **wring out** *vt sep (clothes)* essorer

wringer ['rɪŋə(r)] *n* essoreuse *f*; *Fam Fig* **to put sb through the w.** faire passer un mauvais quart d'heure à qn

wringing ['rɪŋɪŋ] *adj* **w. (wet)** trempé(e)

wrinkle ['rɪŋkəl] **1** *n (on skin, paper)* ride *f*; *(in cloth)* faux pli *m*
2 *vi* se froisser

wrinkled ['rɪŋkəld] *adj (skin)* ridé(e); *(clothes, fabric)* froissé(e)

wrinkly ['rɪŋklɪ] *adj* fripé(e)

wrist [rɪst] *n* poignet *m*

wristwatch ['rɪstwɒtʃ] *n* montre-bracelet *f*

writ [rɪt] *n Law* ordre *m*, assignation *f*; **to serve a w.** on sb assigner qn en justice

write [raɪt] (*pt* wrote [rəʊt], *pp* written ['rɪtən]) **1** *vt* (*answer, name*) écrire; (*cheque*) faire; *Am* **to w. sb** écrire à qn; **she had guilt written all over her face** la culpabilité se lisait sur son visage **2** *vi* écrire; *Br* **to w.** **to sb** écrire à qn; *Fam* **it's nothing to w. home about** ça n'a rien d'extraordinaire ► **write away for** *vt insep* **to w. away for sth** écrire pour recevoir qch ► **write back** *vi* répondre ► **write down** *vt sep* noter ► **write in 1** *vt sep (insert)* inscrire **2** *vi (send letter)* écrire ► **write off 1** *vt sep* (**a**) *(debt)* annuler (**b**) *Fam (car)* bousiller (**c**) *Fam (person)* enterrer; **to w. sth off as a mistake** considérer qch comme une erreur **2** *vi* **to w. off for sth** écrire pour recevoir qch ► **write out** *vt sep (instructions, recipe)* noter; (*cheque*) faire ► **write up** *vt sep (notes, thesis)* rédiger; (*diary, journal*) tenir

write-off ['raɪtɒf] *n* (**a**) *Fam (car)* **to be a w.** être bon (bonne) pour la casse (**b**) *(of debt)* annulation *f*

write-protected ['raɪtprə'tektɪd] *adj Comptr* protégé(e) en écriture

writer ['raɪtə(r)] *n (by profession)* écrivain *m*, auteur *m*; *(of article, book)* auteur

write-up ['raɪtʌp] *n (of play)* critique *f*

writhe [raɪð] *vi* se tordre (**in** de)

writing ['raɪtɪŋ] *n* (**a**) *(action, profession)* écriture *f*; **w. desk** bureau *m*, secrétaire *m*; **w. paper** papier *m* à lettres (**b**) *(handwriting)* écriture *f*; **in w.** par écrit (**c**) *(thing written)* écrit *m*; *Fig* **the w. is on the wall** la fin est proche

written ['rɪtən] **1** *adj* écrit(e); **w. consent** consentement *m* par écrit; **w. examination** écrit *m*, épreuve *f* écrite **2** *pp of* **write**

WRNS [renz] *n Br Mil (abbr* **Women's Royal Naval Service**) = section féminine de la marine britannique

wrong [rɒŋ] **1** *n (immoral action)* mal *m*; **to know right from w.** distinguer le bien du mal; *Ironic* **he can do no w.** il est parfait; **to do sb w.** faire du tort à qn; *Prov* **two wrongs don't make a right** on ne répare pas le mal

par le mal; **to be in the w.** être dans son tort **2** *adj* (**a**) *(morally bad)* mauvais(e); **stealing is w.** c'est mal de voler; **it was w. of you not to tell me** ce n'est pas bien de ta part de ne pas me l'avoir dit (**b**) *(incorrect, mistaken)* mauvais(e); **to be w.** *(of person)* avoir tort; **my watch is w.** ma montre n'est pas à l'heure; **don't get the w. idea** ne te fais pas de fausses idées; **I did/ said the w. thing** j'ai fait/dit ce qu'il ne fallait pas; *Fig* **to go the w. way about doing sth** mal s'y prendre pour faire qch; *Fig* **to get on the w. side of sb** se faire mal voir de qn; **you've got the w. number** *(on phone)* vous vous êtes trompé de numéro (**c**) *(amiss)* **what's w.?** qu'est-ce qui ne va pas?; **what's w. with her?** qu'est-ce qu'elle a?; **is anything w.?** quelque chose ne va pas?; **there's something w. with the car** il y a quelque chose qui ne va pas dans cette voiture; *Fam* **he's w. in the head** il ne tourne pas rond **3** *adv* (**a**) *(morally)* mal; **to do w.** mal agir (**b**) *(incorrectly)* mal; **to go w.** se gâter; **where did I go w.?** qu'est-ce que j'ai fait qui n'allait pas?; **don't get me w., I like her** je n'ai pas dit que je ne l'aimais pas **4** *vt* faire du tort à, léser

wrongdoer ['rɒŋduːə(r)] *n* auteur *m* d'un tort

wrongdoing ['rɒŋduːɪŋ] *n (immoral action)* méfait *m*; *(crime)* infraction *f*

wrongful ['rɒŋfʊl] *adj* arbitraire; **w. dismissal** licenciement *m* abusif

wrong-headed [rɒŋ'hedɪd] *adj* buté(e), borné(e)

wrongly ['rɒŋlɪ] *adv* (**a**) *(unjustly)* à tort (**b**) *(incorrectly)* incorrectement

wrote [rəʊt] *pt of* **write**

wrought-iron ['rɔːt'aɪən] *adj* en fer forgé

wrought-up ['rɔːt'ʌp] *adj* **to be w.** être dans tous ses états

wrung [rʌŋ] *pt & pp of* **wring**

wry [raɪ] *adj* ironique

wt *(abbr* **weight**) p.

WW *(abbr* **World War**) **WWI/II** la Première/Deuxième *ou* Seconde Guerre mondiale

WWF [dʌbəljuːdʌbəljuːʹef] *n (abbr* **World Wildlife Fund, Worldwide Fund for Nature**) WWF *m*

WYSIWYG ['wɪzɪwɪg] *n Comptr (abbr* **what you see is what you get**) WYSIWYG *m*

X, x [eks] *n (letter)* X, x *m inv*; **for x number of years** pendant x années; *Formerly* **X (certificate) film** film *m* X

xenon ['zenɒn] *n Chem* xénon *m*

xenophobia [zenə'fəʊbɪə] *n* xénophobie *f*

xenophobic [zenə'fəʊbɪk] *adj* xénophobe

Xerox® ['zɪərɒks] **1** *n (machine)* photocopieur *m; (copy)* photocopie *f*

2 *vt* photocopier

XL ['eks'el] *(abbr* **extra large)** XL

Xmas ['eksməs] *n (abbr* **Christmas)** Noël *m*

X-ray ['eksreɪ] **1** *n (radiation)* rayon *m* X; *(picture)* radio *f;* **to have an X.** passer une radio

2 *vt* radiographier

xylophone ['zaɪləfəʊn] *n* xylophone *m*

Y, y [waɪ] *n (letter)* Y, y *m inv*; **Y-fronts** slip *m* ouvert
yacht [jɒt] *n (sailing boat)* voilier *m*; *(large private boat)* yacht *m*; **y. club** club *m* de voile; **y. race** régate *f*
yachting ['jɒtɪŋ] *n* voile *f*; **to go y.** faire de la voile
yachtsman ['jɒtsmən] *n* navigateur *m*
yachtswoman ['jɒtswʊmən] *n* navigatrice *f*
yak [jæk] *n* yack *m*
yam [jæm] *n Br* igname *f*; *Am* patate *f* douce
Yank [jæŋk], **Yankee** ['jæŋkɪ] *n Br Fam (person from the USA)* Ricain(e) *m,f*; *Am Fam (person from north-eastern states of the USA)* habitant(e) *m,f* des États du Nord
yank [jæŋk] *Fam* **1** *n* **to give sth a y.** tirer qch d'un coup sec
2 *vt* tirer d'un coup sec; **to y. sth open/out** ouvrir/arracher qch d'un coup sec
yap [jæp] *(pt & pp* **yapped)** *vi (of dog)* japper; *Fam (of person)* jacasser
yard¹ [jɑːd] *n (unit of measurement)* = 0,914 m, yard *m*
yard² *n* **(a)** *(of house, school, farm)* cour *f*; *Am (garden)* jardin *m* **(b)** *(for working)* chantier *m*; **(builder's) y.** chantier de construction **(c)** *(for storage)* dépôt *m* de marchandises
yardstick ['jɑːdstɪk] *n (standard)* point *m* de référence
yarn [jɑːn] *n* **(a)** *(thread, wool)* fil *m* (à tricoter) **(b)** *Fam (story)* histoire *f* à dormir debout; **to spin a y.** raconter une histoire
yawn [jɔːn] **1** *n* bâillement *m*; *Fam (boring thing)* plaie *f*
2 *vi* **(a)** *(of person)* bâiller **(b)** *(of chasm)* béer
yd *(abbr* **yard(s))** yard *m*
ye [jiː] **1** *pron Lit* = **you**
2 *definite art Lit or Hum* = **the**
yea [jeɪ] **1** *n* **yeas and nays** voix *fpl* pour et voix contre
2 *adv Lit* = **yes**
yeah [jeə] *adv Fam* ouais
year [jɪə(r)] *n (twelve-month period)* an *m*; *(referring to duration)* année *f*; **in the y. 2002** en 2002; **this y.** cette année; **last/next y.** l'année dernière/prochaine; **every y.** chaque année, tous les ans; **twice a y.** deux fois par an; **to earn $50,000 a y.** gagner 50 000 dollars par an; **to be ten years old** avoir dix ans; **he got five years** *(prison sentence)* il en a pris pour cinq ans; **for many years** pendant des années; **y. in y. out** chaque année; **over the years** au fil des ans, avec les années; **years ago** il y a des années; **it's years since I saw him, I haven't seen him for** *or* **in years** ça fait des années que je ne l'ai pas vu; **from her earliest years** dès son plus jeune âge; **to be getting on in years** prendre de l'âge
yearbook ['jɪəbʊk] *n* almanach *m*
yearlong ['jɪəlɒŋ] *adj* d'un an

yearly ['jɪəlɪ] **1** *adj* annuel(elle)
2 *adv* annuellement; **twice y.** deux fois par an
yearn [jɜːn] *vi* **to y. for sth** désirer qch ardemment; **to y. to do sth** brûler de faire qch
yearning ['jɜːnɪŋ] *n* désir *m* ardent
yeast [jiːst] *n* levure *f*
yell [jel] **1** *n* hurlement *m*; **to give a y.** pousser un hurlement
2 *vt & vi* hurler
yellow ['jeləʊ] **1** *n* jaune *m*
2 *adj* **(a)** *(in colour)* jaune; **to turn** *or* **go y.** jaunir; **y. card** *(in football)* carton *m* jaune; **y. fever** fièvre *f* jaune; **the Y. Pages®** les Pages *fpl* Jaunes; **the Y. River** le fleuve Jaune **(b)** *Fam (cowardly)* trouillard(e)
3 *vi* jaunir
yelp [jelp] **1** *n* jappement *m*
2 *vi* japper
Yemen ['jemən] *n* le Yémen
Yemeni ['jemənɪ] **1** *n* Yéménite *mf*
2 *adj* yéménite
yen¹ [jen] *n (Japanese currency)* yen *m*
yen² *n* **to have a y. for sth/to do sth** avoir envie de qch/de faire qch
Yerevan [jerə'væn] *n* Erevan
yes [jes] **1** *adv* oui; *(after negative question)* si; **haven't you read the book? – y.(, I have)** tu n'as pas lu ce livre? – mais si
2 *n* oui *m inv*
yes-man ['jesmæn] *n Fam* béni-oui-oui *m inv*
yesterday ['jestədeɪ] **1** *n* hier *m*
2 *adv* hier; **y. morning/evening** hier matin/soir
yet [jet] **1** *adv* **(a)** *(still)* encore; **I haven't finished y.** je n'ai pas encore fini; **don't go y.** ne pars pas tout de suite; **I'll catch her y.!** je finirai bien par l'attraper!; **as y.** jusqu'à présent; **not y.** pas encore; **y. again** encore une fois; **y. more** encore plus; **y. another mistake** encore une erreur **(b)** *(in questions)* **have they decided y.?** est-ce qu'ils ont décidé?
2 *conj* cependant; **small y. strong** petit(e) mais fort(e); **and y. I like her** et pourtant, elle me plaît
yeti ['jetɪ] *n* yéti *m*
yew [juː] *n* if *m*
YHA *n (abbr* **Youth Hostels Association)** = association des auberges de jeunesse
Yiddish ['jɪdɪʃ] **1** *n* yiddish *m*
2 *adj* yiddish *inv*
yield [jiːld] **1** *n (of field, shares)* rendement *m*; *(of mine)* production *f*

2 *vt* (**a**) *(interest)* rapporter; *(results)* donner; **to y. a profit** rapporter (**b**) *(territory, right)* céder **3** *vi* *(surrender)* se rendre; **to y. to force** céder devant la force; **to y. to reason** se rendre à la raison; **to y. to temptation** céder à la tentation

yippee [jɪ'piː] *exclam* youpi!

YMCA [waɪɛmsiː'eɪ] *n* (*abbr* **Young Men's Christian Association**) = association chrétienne proposant hébergement et activités sportives

yob [jɒb], **yobbo** ['jɒbəʊ] (*pl* **yobbos** *or* **yobboes**) *n Fam* loubard *m*

yodel ['jəʊdəl] (*pt & pp* **yodelled**) *vi* iodler

yoga ['jəʊgə] *n* yoga *m*

yoghurt, yogurt ['jɒgət] *n* yaourt *m*

yoke [jəʊk] **1** *n* (**a**) *(for oxen) & Fig* joug *m* (**b**) *(for carrying)* palanche *f* **2** *vt (oxen)* atteler; *Fig* **to be yoked to sth** être lié(e) à qch

yokel ['jəʊkəl] *n Pej or Hum* péquenaud(e) *m,f*

yolk [jəʊk] *n* jaune *m* (d'œuf)

yonder ['jɒndə(r)] *adv* (**over**) **y.** là bas

yonks [jɒŋks] *npl Fam* une éternité; **it was y. ago** ça fait une paye

Yorkshire pudding ['jɔːkʃɪə'pʊdɪŋ] *n* = croquette de pâte à frire servie avec le rosbif

you [juː] *pron* (**a**) *(subject) (familiar)* tu; *(formal, familiar plural)* vous; **you're late** tu es/vous êtes en retard; **have you got it?** c'est toi qui l'as/vous qui l'avez? (**b**) *(direct object) (familiar)* te; *(formal, familiar plural)* vous; **I hate y.** je te/vous déteste; **I love y.** je t'aime/je vous aime; **I can understand your son but not you** je comprends ton fils, mais toi, je ne te comprends pas (**c**) *(indirect object) (familiar)* te; *(formal, familiar plural)* vous; **I gave y. the book** je t'ai/vous ai donné le livre; **I gave it to y.** je te/vous l'ai donné (**d**) *(after preposition) (familiar)* toi; *(formal, familiar plural)* vous; **I'm thinking of y.** je pense à toi/vous (**e**) *(as complement of verb* **to be**) *(familiar)* toi; *(formal, familiar plural)* vous; **it's y.** c'est toi/vous; **it was y. who did it** c'est toi qui l'as fait/vous qui l'avez fait (**f**) *(impersonal)* on; **y. never know** on ne sait jamais; **y. have to be careful with her** il faut faire attention avec elle, **smoking is bad for y.** fumer est mauvais pour la santé (**g**) *(in apposition)* **y. men/French** vous les hommes/les Français; **y. idiot!** espèce d'idiot! (**h**) *(with imperative)* **y. sit down here** toi, tu t'assois ici; **don't y. dare!** je t'interdis de le faire! (**i**) *(with interjections)* **silly y.!** que tu es bête!; **poor y.!** pauvre de toi!

you'd [juːd] = you had, you would

you-know-who [juːnəʊ'huː] *n* qui-tu-sais

you'll [juːl] = you will, you shall

young [jʌŋ] **1** *adj* jeune; **she's younger than me** elle est plus jeune que moi; **she's two years younger than me** elle a deux ans de moins que moi; **you're only y.** once on n'a pas tous les jours vingt ans; **when I was a y. man/woman** quand j'étais jeune; **in his younger days** dans sa jeunesse; **the night is y.!** la soirée ne fait que commencer!; **y. people** les jeunes *mpl*; **she's y. for her age** elle fait plus jeune que son âge; **y. in spirit** *or* **at heart** jeune d'esprit **2** *npl* (**a**) *(people)* **the y.** les jeunes *mpl* (**b**) *(animals)* petits *mpl*

youngster ['jʌŋstə(r)] *n* jeune *mf*

your [jɔː(r)] *possessive adj* (**a**) *(with singular possession) (familiar)* ton (ta); *(formal, familiar plural)* votre; *(with plural possession) (familiar)* tes; *(formal, familiar plural)* vos; **y. job** ton/votre travail; **y. wife** ta/votre femme; **y. parents** tes/

vos parents; **it wasn't YOUR idea!** ce n'est pas toi qui en as eu l'idée! (**b**) *(for parts of body)* **did you hit y. head?** vous vous êtes cogné la tête? (**c**) *(impersonal)* **you should buy y. ticket first** on doit acheter son billet d'abord; **smoking is bad for y. health** fumer est mauvais pour la santé; *Fam* **y. average American** l'Américain moyen

you're [jɔː(r)] = you are

yours [jɔːz] *possessive pron* (**a**) *(replacing singular possession) (familiar)* le tien (la tienne) *m,f*; *(formal, familiar plural)* le vôtre (la vôtre) *m,f*; *(replacing plural possession) (familiar)* les tiens (les tiennes) *mpl,fpl*; *(formal, familiar plural)* les vôtres *mfpl*; **my house is big, but y. is bigger** ma maison est grande, mais la tienne est plus grande encore (**b**) *(used attributively)* **this book is y.** ce livre est à toi/à vous; **a friend of y.** un de tes/vos amis; **where's that brother of y.?** où ton frère a-t-il bien pu passer?

yourself [jɔː'self] *pron* (**a**) *(reflexive)* **did you hurt y.?** *(familiar)* tu t'es blessé?; *(formal)* vous vous êtes blessé? (**b**) *(emphatic) (familiar)* toi-même; *(formal)* vous-même; **you y. have never...** vous même n'avez jamais...; **you told me y.** vous me l'avez dit **today** tu n'es pas dans ton état normal aujourd'hui (**c**) *(after preposition)* **do you live by y.?** vous vivez seul(e)?; **did you buy it for y.?** vous l'avez acheté pour vous-même?; **do you talk to y.?** tu parles tout(e) seul(e)?

yourselves [jɔː'selvz] *pron* (**a**) *(reflexive)* **have you hurt y.?** vous vous êtes blessé(e)s? (**b**) *(emphatic)* vous-mêmes; **you y. have never...** vous-mêmes n'avez jamais...; **you told me y.** vous me l'avez dit **you mémée; you're not y. today** vous n'êtes pas dans votre état normal aujourd'hui (**c**) *(after preposition)* **do you live by y.?** vous vivez seuls(es)?; **did you buy it for y.?** vous l'avez acheté pour vous-mêmes?; **do you talk to y.?** vous parlez tout(es) seuls(es)?

youth [juːθ] *n* (**a**) *(period)* jeunesse *f* (**b**) *(young man)* adolescent *m*, jeune *m* (**c**) *(young people)* jeunes *mpl*; **y. club** centre *m* de loisir pour les jeunes; **y. hostel** auberge *f* de jeunesse

youthful ['juːθfʊl] *adj (person, looks)* jeune; *(enthusiasm)* juvénile

you've [juːv] = you have

yowl [jaʊl] **1** *n* hurlement *m* **2** *vi* hurler

yo-yo® ['jəʊjəʊ] (*pl* **yo-yos**) *n* yo-yo® *m*

yr *(abbr* **year**) année *f*

yuan [juː'æn] *n* yuan *m*

yucca ['jʌkə] *n* yucca *m*

yuck [jʌk] *exclam Fam* berk!

yucky ['jʌkɪ] *adj Fam* berk *inv*

Yugoslav ['juːgəʊslɑːv] **1** *n* Yougoslave *mf* **2** *adj* yougoslave

Yugoslavia [juːgəʊ'slɑːvɪə] *n* la Yougoslavie

Yugoslavian [juːgəʊ'slɑːvɪən] *adj* yougoslave

yuletide ['juːltaɪd] *n* Noël *m*

yummy ['jʌmɪ] *adj Fam* délicieux(euse)

yuppie ['jʌpɪ] *n* yuppie *mf*; **y. area** quartier *m* riche et branché; *Fam* **y. flu** syndrome *m* de la fatigue chronique

YWCA [waɪdʌbəlju:siː'eɪ] *n* (*abbr* **Young Women's Christian Association**) = association chrétienne proposant hébergement et activités sportives

Z

Z, z [zed, *Am* ziː] *n (letter)* Z, z *m inv*
Zaire [zɑːˈɪə(r)] *n* le Zaïre
Zairean [zɑːˈɪərɪən] **1** *n* Zaïrois(oise) *m,f*
2 *adj* zaïrois(oise)
Zambia [ˈzæmbɪə] *n* la Zambie
Zambian [ˈzæmbɪən] **1** *n* Zambien(enne) *m,f*
2 *adj* zambien(enne)
zany [ˈzeɪnɪ] *adj* loufoque
zap [zæp] (*pt & pp* **zapped**) *Fam* **1** *vt* **(a)** *(destroy, disable)* éliminer **(b)** *Comptr (delete)* effacer
2 *vi* **(a)** *(change TV channel)* zapper **(b)** *(move quickly)* **to z. in/out/off** entrer/sortir/partir à toute pompe
zapper [ˈzæpə(r)] *n Fam (TV remote control)* télécommande *f*
zeal [ziːl] *n* zèle *m*
zealot [ˈzelət] *n* fanatique *mf*
zealous [ˈzeləs] *adj* zélé(e); *(campaigner, supporter)* fervent(e)
zebra [ˈziːbrə, ˈzebrə] *n* zèbre *m*; *Br* **z. crossing** passage *m* pour piétons
zeds [zedz] *npl Fam (sleep)* **to catch some z.** piquer un roupillon
zenith [ˈzenɪθ] *n also Fig* zénith *m*; **at the z. of her powers/influence** au sommet de son pouvoir/influence
zephyr [ˈzefə(r)] *n* zéphyr *m*
zero [ˈzɪərəʊ] **1** *n (pl* **zeros**) zéro *m*; **30 degrees below z.** 30 degrés en dessous de zéro
2 *adj Fam* aucun(e); **to have z. charm** n'avoir aucun charme
3 *vi* **to z. in on sb** foncer sur qn; **to z. in on sth** se concentrer sur qch
zero-rated [ˈzɪərəʊreɪtɪd] *adj Fin (for VAT)* exonéré(e) de TVA
zest [zest] *n* **(a)** *(enjoyment)* enthousiasme *m* **(b)** *(of orange, lemon)* zeste *m*
zigzag [ˈzɪgzæg] **1** *n* zigzag *m*
2 *vi (pt & pp* **zigzagged**) zigzaguer
zilch [zɪltʃ] *n Fam* que dalle
Zimbabwe [zɪmˈbɑːbweɪ] *n* le Zimbabwe
Zimbabwean [zɪmˈbɑːbweɪən] **1** *n* Zimbabwéen(enne) *m,f*

2 *adj* zimbabwéen(enne)
zinc [zɪŋk] *n* zinc *m*
Zionism [ˈzaɪənɪzəm] *n* sionisme *m*
Zionist [ˈzaɪənɪst] *n & adj* sioniste *mf*
zip [zɪp] **1** *n* **(a)** *Br* **z. (fastener)** fermeture *f* Éclair® **(b)** *Fam (vigour)* punch *m* **(c)** *Am* **z. code** code *m* postal
2 *vi (pt & pp* **zipped**) **to z. past** *(of car)* passer en trombe; *(of bullet)* passer en sifflant
▸ **zip through** *vt insep Fam* **I zipped through the book** j'ai lu le livre à toute vitesse; **we zipped through the work** nous avons fait le travail à toute vitesse
▸ **zip up 1** *vt sep (clothes)* remonter la fermeture Éclair® de
2 *vi* se fermer par une fermeture Éclair®
zipper [ˈzɪpə(r)] *n Am* fermeture *f* Éclair®
zippy [ˈzɪpɪ] *adj Fam* plein(e) de punch
zit [zɪt] *n Fam* bouton *m*
zither [ˈzɪðə(r)] *n* cithare *f*
zodiac [ˈzəʊdɪæk] *n* zodiaque *m*
zombie [ˈzɒmbɪ] *n* zombi *m*
zone [zəʊn] **1** *n* zone *f*
2 *vt* diviser en zones
zonked (out) [zɒŋkt(ˈaʊt)] *adj Fam (exhausted)* cassé(e); *(drugged)* défoncé(e); *(drunk)* pété(e)
zoo [zuː] *n* zoo *m*
zoological [zəʊəˈlɒdʒɪkəl] *adj* zoologique; **z. garden(s)** jardin *m* zoologique
zoologist [zəʊˈɒlədʒɪst] *n* zoologiste *mf*
zoology [zəʊˈɒlədʒɪ] *n* zoologie *f*
zoom [zuːm] **1** *n* **(a)** *(noise)* vrombissement *m* **(b)** **z. lens** zoom *m*
2 *vi Fam* **(a)** *(move quickly)* **to z. in/out/past** entrer/sortir/ passer comme une flèche **(b)** *(increase quickly)* monter en flèche
▸ **zoom in** *vi (of camera)* faire un zoom avant **(on** sur)
zucchini [zuːˈkiːnɪ] *n (pl* **zucchini** *or* **zucchinis**) *n Am* courgette *f*
Zulu [ˈzuːluː] **1** *n* Zoulou(e) *m,f*
2 *adj* zoulou(e)

French Grammar

Contents

1 Glossary of grammatical terms

ADJECTIVE

An adjective provides supplementary information about a noun, describing what something is like, eg a *small* house, a *red* car, an *interesting* pastime.

ADVERB

Adverbs are normally used with a verb to add extra information by indicating how the action is done (adverbs of manner), when, where or with how much intensity the action is done (adverbs of time, place and intensity), or to what extent the action is done (adverbs of quantity). Adverbs may also be used with an adjective or another adverb, eg a *very* attractive girl, *very* well.

AGREEMENT

In French, words such as adjectives, articles and pronouns must agree in number and gender with the noun or pronoun to which they refer. This means that their spelling changes according to the number of the noun (singular or plural) and according to its gender (masculine or feminine).

ANTECEDENT

The antecedent of a relative pronoun is the word or words to which the relative pronoun refers. The antecedent is usually found directly before the relative pronoun, eg in the sentence *I know the man who did this*, **the man** is the antecedent of *who*.

APPOSITION

A word or a clause is said to be in apposition to another when it is placed directly after it without any joining word, eg *Mr Jones, our bank manager, rang today*.

ARTICLE

See DEFINITE ARTICLE, INDEFINITE ARTICLE and PARTITIVE ARTICLE.

ASPIRATE H

If a word begins with an aspirate h in French, it means that there is no liaison between it and the word preceding it, eg in **les haricots** the **s** of **les** is not pronounced. Similarly, there is no contraction in spelling, eg **la haine** and not **l'haine**. See SILENT H.

AUXILIARY

The French auxiliary verbs are **avoir** (*to have*) and **être** (*to be*). They are used to make up the first part of compound tenses, the second part being a past participle, eg j'*ai* mangé, il *est* allé.

CARDINAL

Cardinal numbers are numbers such as *one, two, ten, fourteen*, as opposed to ORDINAL numbers, eg *first, second*.

CLAUSE

A clause is a group of words which contains at least a subject and a verb: he said is a clause. A clause often contains more than this basic information, eg he said this to her yesterday. Sentences can be made up of several clauses, eg he said/he'd call me/if he were free. See SENTENCE.

COMPARATIVE

The comparative forms of adjectives and adverbs allow two things, persons or actions to be compared. In English, *more ... than, ...er than, less ... than* and *as ... as* are used for comparison.

COMPOUND

Compound tenses are verb tenses consisting of more than one element. In French, the compound tenses of a verb are formed by the auxiliary verb and the past participle: j'ai visité, il est venu.

CONDITIONAL

This mood is used to describe what someone would do, or something that would happen if a condition were fulfilled, eg *I* **would come** if I were well; the chair **would have broken** if he had sat on it.

CONJUGATION

The conjugation of a verb is the set of different forms taken in the particular tenses of that verb.

Glossary of grammatical terms

CONJUNCTION Conjunctions are used to link different clauses. They may be coordinating or subordinating. Coordinating conjunctions are words like *and, but, or*; subordinating conjunctions are words like *because, after, although*.

DEFINITE ARTICLE The definite article is *the* in English and *le, la* and *les* in French.

DEMONSTRATIVE Demonstrative adjectives such as *this, that, these* and pronouns such as *this one, that one* are used to point out a particular person or object.

DIRECT OBJECT A direct object is a noun or a pronoun which in English follows a verb without any linking preposition, eg *I met a friend*.

ELISION Elision consists in replacing the last letter of certain words (*le, la, je, me, te, se, de, que*) with an apostrophe before a word starting with a vowel or a silent h, eg *l'eau, l'homme, j'aime*.

ENDING The ending of a verb is determined by the person (1st/2nd/3rd) and number (singular/plural) of its subject. In French, most tenses have six different endings. See PERSON and NUMBER.

EXCLAMATION An exclamation is a word or sentence used to express surprise or wonder, eg *what!, how!, how lucky!, what a nice day!*

FEMININE See GENDER.

GENDER The gender of a noun indicates whether the noun is masculine or feminine (all French nouns are either masculine or feminine).

IDIOMATIC EXPRESSIONS Idiomatic expressions (or idioms) are expressions which cannot normally be translated word for word. For example, *it's raining cats and dogs* is translated by *il pleut des cordes*.

IMPERATIVE This mood is used for giving orders, eg *eat!, don't go!*

INDEFINITE Indefinite pronouns and adjectives are words that do not refer to a definite person or object, eg *each, someone, every*.

INDEFINITE ARTICLE The indefinite article is *a* in English and *un, une* and *des* in French.

INDICATIVE The indicative is the normal form of a verb as in *I like, he came, we are trying*. It is opposed to the subjunctive, conditional and imperative.

INDIRECT OBJECT An indirect object is a pronoun or noun which follows a verb indirectly, with a linking preposition (usually **to**), eg *I spoke to **my friend/him***.

INFINITIVE The infinitive is the basic form of the verb as found in dictionaries. Thus *to eat, to finish, to take* are infinitives. In French, the infinitive is recognizable by its ending (**-er, -ir** or **-re**, eg *manger, finir, prendre*).

INTERROGATIVE Interrogative words are used to ask a question. This may be a direct question (**when** *will you arrive?*) or an indirect question (*I don't know* **when** *he'll arrive*). See QUESTION.

MASCULINE See GENDER.

MOOD This is the name given to the four main areas within which a verb is conjugated. See INDICATIVE, SUBJUNCTIVE, CONDITIONAL, IMPERATIVE.

NOUN A noun is a word or group of words which refers to a living creature, a thing, a place or an abstract idea, eg *postman, cat, shop, passport, life*.

NUMBER The number of a noun indicates whether the noun is singular or plural. A singular noun refers to one single person or thing, eg *boy, train* and a plural noun to more than one, eg *boys, trains*.

ORDINAL Ordinal numbers are *first, second, third, fourth* and all other numbers which end in **-th**. In French, all ordinal numbers, except for *premier* (first) and *second* (second), end in **-ième**.

Glossary of grammatical terms

PARTITIVE ARTICLE The partitive articles are *some* and *any* in English and *du, de la, de l'* and *des* (as in **du** *pain*, **de la** *confiture*, **de l'***eau*, **des** *bananes*) in French.

PASSIVE A verb is used in the passive when the subject of the verb does not perform the action but is subjected to it. The passive is formed with the verb *to be* and the past participle of the verb, eg *he was rewarded.*

PAST PARTICIPLE The past participle of a verb is the form which is used after **to have** in English, eg *I have* **eaten**, *I have* **said**, *you have* **tried**.

PERSON In any tense, there are three persons in the singular (1st: *I* ... , 2nd: *you* ... , 3rd: *he/she* ...), and three in the plural (1st: *we* ... , 2nd: *you* ... , 3rd: *they* ...). See also ENDING.

PERSONAL PRONOUNS Personal pronouns stand for a noun. They usually accompany a verb and can be either the subject (*I, you, he/she/it, we, they*) or the object of the verb (*me, you, him/her/it, us, them*).

PLURAL See NUMBER.

POSSESSIVE Possessive adjectives and pronouns are used to indicate possession or ownership. They are words like *my/mine, your/yours, our/ours.*

PREPOSITION Prepositions are words such as *with, in, to, at.* They are followed by a noun or a pronoun.

PRESENT PARTICIPLE The present participle is the verb form which ends in **-ing** in English and **-ant** in French.

PRONOUN This is a word which stands for a noun. The main categories of pronouns are:

* **Relative pronouns** (eg *who, which, that*)

* **Interrogative pronouns** (eg *who?, what?, which?*)

* **Demonstrative pronouns** (eg *this, that, these*)

* **Possessive pronouns** (eg *mine, yours, his*)

* **Personal pronouns** (eg *you, him, us*)

* **Reflexive pronouns** (eg *myself, himself*)

* **Indefinite pronouns** (eg *something, all*)

QUESTION There are two question forms: direct questions stand on their own and require a question mark at the end, eg *when will he come?*; indirect questions are introduced by a clause and require no question mark, eg *I wonder when he will come.*

REFLEXIVE Reflexive verbs 'reflect' the action back onto the subject, eg *I dressed myself.* They are always found with a reflexive pronoun and are much more common in French than in English.

SENTENCE A sentence is a group of words made up of one or more clauses (see CLAUSE) and which makes a complete grammatical structure. The end of a sentence is indicated by a punctuation mark (usually a full stop, a question mark or an exclamation mark).

SILENT H The term 'silent **h**' is actually misleading since an **h** is never pronounced in French. The point is that when a silent **h** occurs, any preceding vowel is not pronounced either. For example, the **h** in *j'habite* is silent (note the *j'*). The **h** in *je hurle*, however, is aspirate, and so there is no contraction in spelling.

SIMPLE TENSE Simple tenses are tenses in which the verb consists of one word only, eg *j'habite, Maurice partira.*

SINGULAR See NUMBER.

SUBJECT The subject of a verb is the noun or pronoun which performs the action. In the sentences, *the train left early* and *she bought a record*, **the train** and **she** are the subjects.

SUBJUNCTIVE The subjunctive is a verb form which is rarely used in English, eg *if I were you*, *God save the Queen*, but common in French.

SUPERLATIVE The superlative is the form of an adjective or an adverb which, in English, is marked by *the most ...* , *the ...est* or *the least ...*

TENSE Verbs are used in tenses, which tell us whether an action takes place in the present, the past or the future.

VERB A verb is a word which describes the performance of an action, eg *to sing*, *to work*, *to watch* or the existence of a state, eg *to be*, *to have*, *to hope*.

---

2 Articles

A THE DEFINITE ARTICLE

1 Forms

In English, there is only one form of the definite article: **the**. In French, there are three forms, depending on the gender and number of the noun following the article:

- with a masculine singular noun: **le**
- with a feminine singular noun: **la**   } the
- with a plural noun (masc or fem): **les**

Masc Sing	Fem Sing	Plural
le chauffeur	**la** secrétaire	**les** étudiants
the driver	*the secretary*	*the students*
le salon	**la** cuisine	**les** chambres
the living-room	*the kitchen*	*the bedrooms*

Note: **le** and **la** both change to **l'** before a vowel or a silent **h**:

	Masculine	Feminine
Before Vowel	**l'**avion	**l'**odeur
	the plane	*the smell*
Before Silent H	**l'**homme	**l'**hôtesse
	the man	*the hostess*

Pronunciation: the **s** of **les** is pronounced **z** when the noun following it begins with a vowel or a silent **h**.

2 Forms with the prepositions 'à' and 'de'

When the definite article is used with **à** or **de**, the following spelling changes take place:

a) with **à** (to, at)

à + le	→	**au**
à + les	→	**aux**

à + la and **à + l'** do not change

au restaurant	**aux** enfants
at/to the restaurant	*to the children*
à la plage	**à l'**aéroport
at/to the beach	*at/to the airport*

Pronunciation: the **x** of **aux** is pronounced **z** when the noun following it begins with a vowel or a silent **h**.

b) with **de** (of, from)

de + le	→	**du**
de + les	→	**des**

de + la and **de + l'** do not change

du directeur
of/from the manager

des chômeurs
of/from the unemployed

de la région	**de l'**usine
of/from the area	*of/from the factory*

Pronunciation: the **s** of **des** is pronounced **z** when the noun following it begins with a vowel or a silent **h**.

3 Use

As in English, the definite article is used when referring to a particular person or thing, or particular persons or things:

les amis dont je t'ai parlé
the friends I told you about

le café est prêt
the coffee is ready

However, the definite article is used far more frequently in French than in English. It is used in particular in the following cases where English uses no article:

a) when the noun is used in a general sense

i) to refer to all things of a kind:
vous acceptez **les** chèques?
do you take cheques?

le sucre est mauvais pour **les** dents
sugar is bad for the teeth

ii) to refer to abstract things:
le travail et **les** loisirs
work and leisure

la musique classique
classical music

iii) when stating likes and dislikes:

j'aime **la** viande mais je préfère **le** poisson
I like meat, but I prefer fish

je déteste **les** tomates
I hate tomatoes

b) with geographical names

i) continents, countries and areas:

le Canada	**la** France	**l'**Europe
Canada	*France*	*Europe*
la Bretagne	l'Afrique	
Brittany	*Africa*	

les États-Unis
the United States

But: the article **la** is omitted with the prepositions **en** and **de** when used with feminine country names:

j'habite **en** France   il vient **d'**Italie
I live in France   *he comes from Italy*

With masculine country names, the corresponding prepositions **à** and **de** follow the normal rules:

j'habite **au** Portugal/**aux** États-Unis
I live in Portugal/in the United States

je viens **du** Japon/**des** Pays-Bas
I come from Japan/the Netherlands

A very few country names do not require an article, eg **Panamá**, **Cuba**, **Taïwan**, **Singapour**.

ii) mountains, lakes and rivers:

le mont Everest   **le** lac de Genève
Mount Everest   *Lake Geneva*

c) with names of seasons

l'automne	*autumn/Am fall*
l'hiver	*winter*
le printemps	*spring*
l'été	*summer*

But: en automne/été/hiver
        in autumn/summer/winter

au printemps   un jour d'été
in spring   *a summer's day*

d) with names of languages

j'apprends **le** français
I'm learning French

But: ce film est en anglais
        this film is in English

e) with parts of the body

j'ai **les** cheveux roux   ouvrez **la** bouche
I've got red hair   *open your mouth*

les mains en l'air!
hands up!

l'homme à **la** barbe noire
the man with the black beard

f) with names following an adjective

le petit Pierre   **la** pauvre Isabelle
little Pierre   *poor Isabelle*

g) with titles

le docteur Coste
Doctor Coste

le commandant Cousteau
Captain Cousteau

h) with days of the week to express regular occurrences

que fais-tu **le** samedi?
what do you do on Saturdays?

le docteur reçoit **le** lundi et **le** vendredi
the doctor sees patients on Mondays and Fridays

i) with names of subjects or leisure activities

les maths
maths

l'histoire et **la** géographie
history and geography

la natation, **la** lecture, **le** football
swimming, reading, football

j) in expressions of price, quantity etc

c'est combien **le** kilo/**la** douzaine/**la** bouteille?
how much is it for a kilo/dozen/bottle?

B THE INDEFINITE ARTICLE

1 Forms

In French, there are three forms of the indefinite article, depending on the number and gender of the noun it accompanies:

● with a masculine singular noun: **un** *a*
● with a feminine singular noun: **une** *a*
● with a plural noun (masc or fem): **des** *some*

Note: **des** is often not translated in English:

il y a **des** nuages dans le ciel
there are clouds in the sky

2 Use

a) On the whole, the French indefinite article is used in the same way as its English equivalent:

un homme	**une** femme
a man	*a woman*

des hommes/femmes
(some) men/women

un livre	**une** tasse
a book	*a cup*

des livres/tasses
(some) books/cups

b) However, the English indefinite article is not always translated in French:

i) when stating someone's profession or occupation:

mon père est **architecte**
my father is an architect

elle est **médecin**
she is a doctor

Note, however, that the article is used after **c'est**, **c'était** etc:

c'est un acteur célèbre
he's a famous actor

ce sont des fraises
these are strawberries

ii) with nouns in apposition:

Madame Leclerc, **employée de bureau**
Mrs Leclerc, an office worker

iii) after **quel** in exclamations:

quel **dommage**!	quelle **surprise**!
what a pity!	*what a surprise!*

c) In negative sentences, **de** (or **d'**) is used instead of **un, une, des**:

je n'ai pas **d'**amis
I don't have any friends

je n'ai plus **de** voiture
I don't have a car any more

d) In French (but not in English), the indefinite article is used with abstract nouns followed by an adjective:

avec **une patience remarquable**
with remarkable patience

elle a fait **des progrès étonnants**
she's made amazing progress

Note, however, that the article is not used when there is no adjective:

avec **plaisir**	sans **hésitation**
with pleasure	*without hesitation*

C THE PARTITIVE ARTICLE

1 Forms

There are three forms of the French partitive article, which corresponds to 'some'/'any' in English:

- with a masculine singular noun: **du**
- with a feminine singular noun: **de la**
- with plural nouns (masc or fem): **des**

du vin	**de la** bière	**des** fruits
some wine	*some beer*	*some fruit*

Note that **de l'** is used in front of masculine or feminine singular nouns beginning with a vowel or a silent **h**:

de l'argent	**de l'**eau	**de l'**helium
some money	*some water*	*some helium*

2 Use

a) On the whole, the French partitive article is used as in English. However, English tends to omit the partitive article where French does not:

achète **du** pain
buy (some) bread

vous avez **du** beurre?
do you have (any) butter?

je voudrais **de la** viande
I'd like some meat

tu veux **de la** soupe?
do you want (any) soup?

tu dois manger **des** légumes
you must eat (some) vegetables

as-tu acheté **des** poires?
did you buy any pears?

b) The partitive article is replaced by **de** (or **d'**) in the following cases:

i) in negative expressions:

il n'y a plus **de** café
there isn't any coffee left

je n'ai pas **de** frères
I don't have any brothers

nous n'avons plus **d'**argent
we don't have any money

je n'ai pas **d'**enfants
I don't have any children left

Note, however, that when the clause is introduced by **c'est**, **il est** etc, the partitive article remains:

ce n'est pas **du** cuir, c'est **du** plastique
it's not leather, it's plastic

ii) after expressions of quantity (see also p73):

il boit trop **de** café
he drinks too much coffee

il gagne assez **d'**argent
he earns enough money

iii) after **avoir besoin de**:

j'ai besoin **d'**argent
I need (some) money

tu as besoin **de** timbres?
do you need (any) stamps?

iv) where an adjective is followed by a plural noun:

de petites villes
(some) small towns

d'énormes mensonges
outrageous lies

Note, however, that if the adjective comes after the noun, **des** does not change:

des résultats encourageants
encouraging results

3 Partitive or definite article?

When no article is used in English, it is not always clear which is the right article in French: **le/la/les** or **du/de la/des**.

If **some/any** can be inserted before the English noun, the French partitive article should be used. But if the noun is used in a general sense and inserting **some/any** in front of the English noun does not make sense, the definite article must be used:

did you buy fish? (ie any fish)
tu as acheté **du** poisson?

yes, I did; I like fish (ie fish in general)
oui; j'aime **le** poisson

3 Nouns

A noun is a word or group of words which refers to a person, an animal, a thing, a place or an abstract idea.

A GENDER

All French nouns are either masculine or feminine; there is no neuter as in English. Though no absolute rule can be stated, the gender can often be determined either by the meaning or the ending of the noun.

1 Masculine

a) *by meaning*

i) words referring to men and male animals:

un homme	**le boucher**	**le tigre**
a man	*the butcher*	*the tiger*

ii) names of common trees and shrubs:

le chêne	**le sapin**	**le laurier**
the oak	*the fir tree*	*the laurel*

iii) days, months, seasons:

lundi	**mars**	**le printemps**
Monday	*March*	*spring*

iv) languages:

le français	**le polonais**	**le russe**
French	*Polish*	*Russian*

v) rivers and countries not ending in a silent **e**:

le Danemark	**le Portugal**	**le Nil**
Denmark	*Portugal*	*the Nile*

Note, however, that there are exceptions to this rule:

le Danube	**le Rhône**	**le Mexique**
the Danube	*the Rhone*	*Mexico*

b) *by ending*

-acle	le spectacle *(show)*
	But: une débâcle *(shambles)*
-age	le fromage *(cheese)*
	But: la cage *(cage)*, une image *(picture)*, la nage *(swimming)*, la page *(page)*, la plage *(beach)*, la rage *(rage, rabies)*
-é	le marché *(market)*
	But: nouns ending in **-té** and **-tié** are usually feminine (see 2b)
-eau	le chapeau *(hat)*
	But: l'eau *(water)*, la peau *(skin)*
-ège	le piège *(trap)*, le collège *(secondary school)*
-ème	le thème *(theme, topic)*
	But: la crème *(cream)*
-isme,	le communisme *(communism)*, le
-asme	tourisme *(tourism)*, l'enthousiasme *(enthusiasm)*
-o	le numéro *(the number)*
	But: la dynamo *(dynamo)* and

most abbreviated expressions: une auto *(car)*, la météo *(weather forecast)*, la photo *(photograph)*, la radio *(radio)*, la sténo *(short hand)*, la stéréo *(stereo)*

Nouns ending in a consonant are usually *masculine.*

Notable exceptions are:

i) most nouns ending in **-tion, -sion, -ation, -aison, -ison**

ii) most abstract nouns ending in **-eur** (see 2b)

iii) the following nouns ending in a consonant:

la clef *(key)*
la nef *(nave)*
la soif *(thirst)*
la faim *(hunger)*
la fin *(end)*
la façon *(manner)*
la leçon *(lesson)*
la boisson *(drink)*
la moisson *(harvest)*
la rançon *(ransom)*
la mer *(sea)*
la cuiller *(spoon)*
la chair *(flesh)*
la basse-cour *(farmyard)*
la cour *(yard)*
la tour *(tower)*
la brebis *(ewe)*
une fois *(once)*
la vis *(screw)*
la souris *(mouse)*
la part *(share)*
la plupart *(majority, most)*
la dent *(tooth)*
la dot *(dowry)*
la forêt *(forest)*
la jument *(mare)*
la mort *(death)*
la nuit *(night)*
la croix *(cross)*
la noix *(nut)*
la paix *(peace)*
la perdrix *(partridge)*
la toux *(cough)*
la voix *(voice)*

2 Feminine

a) *by meaning*

i) words referring to women and female animals:

la mère   **la bonne**   **la génisse**
the mother   *the maid*   *the heifer*

ii) names of rivers and countries ending with a silent **e**:

la Seine   **la Russie**   **la Belgique**
the Seine   *Russia*   *Belgium*

iii) saints' days and festivals:

la Toussaint   la Pentecôte
All Saints' Day   Whitsun

Note, however, that **Noël** *(Christmas)* is masculine except when used with the definite article: **à la Noël** *(at Christmas)*

b) *by ending*

-ace   la place *(square, seat)*
         But: un espace *(space)*
-ade   la salade *(salad)*
         But: le grade *(degree, rank)*, le stade *(stadium)*
-ance,   la puissance *(power)*, la danse
-anse   *(dancing)*
-ée   la soirée *(evening)*, la journée
         (day)
         But: le musée *(museum)*, le lycée
         (secondary school)
-ence,   une évidence *(evidence)*, la
-ense   défense *(defence)*
         But: le silence *(silence)*
-ère   la lumière *(light)*
         But: le mystère *(mystery)*, le
         caractère *(character)*
-eur   la peur *(fear)*
         But: le bonheur *(happiness)*, le
         chœur *(choir)*, le cœur *(heart)*, un
         honneur *(honour)*, le labeur *(toil)*,
         le malheur *(misfortune)*
-ie   la pluie *(rain)*
         But: le génie *(genius)*, un incendie
         (fire), le parapluie *(umbrella)*
-ière   la bière *(beer)*
         But: le cimetière *(cemetery)*
-oire   la gloire *(glory)*
         But: le laboratoire *(laboratory)*, le
         pourboire *(tip)*
-tion, -sion, -ation, -aison, -ison
         la fiction *(fiction)*, la nation
         (nation), la raison *(reason)*, la
         prison *(prison)*
-té   la bonté *(goodness)*
         But: le côté *(side)*, le comté
         (county), le traité *(treaty)*, le pâté
         (pâté)
-tié   la moitié *(half)*, la pitié *(pity)*

Most nouns ending in a silent **e** following two consonants are feminine:

la botte *(boot)*, la couronne *(crown)*, la

Nouns

terre (earth), la masse (mass), la lutte (struggle)

But: le verre (glass), le parterre (flower bed), le tonnerre (thunder), un intervalle (interval), le carrosse (carriage)

3 Difficulties

a) Some nouns may have either gender depending on the sex of the person to whom they refer:

un artiste	**une artiste**
a (male) artist	a (female) artist
le Russe	**la Russe**
the Russian (man)	the Russian (woman)

similarly:

un aide/une aide an assistant
un camarade/une camarade a friend
un domestique/une domestique a servant
un enfant/une enfant a child
un malade/une malade a patient
un propriétaire/une propriétaire an owner

b) Others have only one gender for both sexes:

un ange	**un amateur**	**un auteur**
an angel	an amateur	an author

une connaissance	**une dupe**
an acquaintance	a dupe

un écrivain	**le médecin**
a writer	the doctor

le peintre	**une personne**
the painter	a person

la recrue	**le sculpteur**
the recruit	the sculptor (sculptress)

la sentinelle	**le témoin**
the sentry	the witness

la vedette	**la victime**
the (film) star	the victim

Note, however, that modern French tends to use feminine forms for many different functions. **La ministre, la juge** and **la professeur** can now be commonly found in the press, and new forms such as **une écrivaine** have also begun to appear.

c) The following nouns change meaning according to gender:

	MASCULINE	FEMININE
aide	male assistant	assistance, female assistant

crêpe	mourning band	pancake
critique	critic	criticism
faux	forgery	scythe
livre	book	pound
manche	handle	sleeve
manœuvre	labourer	manoeuvre
mémoire	memorandum	memory
mode	method, way	fashion
mort	dead man	death
moule	mould	mussel
page	pageboy	page
pendule	pendulum	clock
physique	physique	physics
poêle	stove	frying pan
poste	post (job), set	post office
somme	nap	sum
tour	trick, tour	tower
trompette	trumpeter	trumpet
vapeur	steamer	steam
vase	vase	silt
voile	veil	sail

d) A few words vary in gender according to their usage. The plural noun **gens** is regarded as feminine when it follows an adjective, and masculine when it precedes it:

de bonnes **gens**	des **gens** ennuyeux
good people	boring people

amour, délice and **orgue** are masculine when used in the singular and feminine when used in the plural:

un **amour** de jeunesse
an old flame

des **amours** malheureuses
unhappy love affairs

un **délice** inoubliable
an unforgettable delight

des **délices** infinies	les grandes **orgues**
infinite delights	the great organ

un **orgue** électrique
an electric organ

e) City names

Some city names are traditionally feminine:

La Rochelle	**La Haye**
La Rochelle	The Hague

Alger la Blanche
Algiers, the white city

Others are masculine in everyday usage:

le Paris des années 30
Paris in the 30s

le Londres de mon souvenir
the London I remember

le vieux Nice
old Nice

Berlin fut totalement **détruit**
Berlin was completely destroyed

In literary French, however, city names are feminine:
Caen fut **prise** après de terribles bombardements
Caen was taken after a terrible bombardment

B THE FORMATION OF FEMININES

The feminine of nouns may be formed in the following ways:

1 By adding an **e** to the masculine form:

un ami	**une amie**
a (male) friend	*a (female) friend*
un Hollandais	**une Hollandaise**
a Dutchman	*a Dutch woman*

Note that nouns which end in **-e** in the masculine form do not change:

un élève	**une élève**
a (male) pupil	*a (female) pupil*

Note also that the addition of an **e** often entails an alteration of the masculine form:

i) nouns ending in **-t** and **-n** double the final consonant:

le chien	la chie**nne** *(dog/bitch)*
le chat	la cha**tte** *(cat)*

ii) nouns ending in **-er** add a grave accent to the **e** immediately preceding the **r**:
un ouvrier
une ouvri**ère** *(workman/female worker)*

iii) nouns ending in **-eur** change into **-euse**:
le vendeur
la vend**euse** *(male/female shop assistant)*

However, a few nouns ending in **-eur** change into **-eresse**:
le pécheur
la péch**eresse** *(sinner)*

iv) nouns ending in **-teur** change into **-teuse** or **-trice** according to the following guidelines:

if the stem of the word is also that of a present participle the feminine form ends in **-euse**:

le chanteur
la chant**euse** *(male/female singer)*

if the stem is not that of a present participle, the feminine form ends in **-trice**:

le lecteur
la lec**trice** *(male/female reader)*

v) nouns ending in **-f** change into **-ve**:
le veuf
la veu**ve** *(widower/widow)*

vi) nouns ending in **-x** change into **-se**:
un époux
une épou**se** *(husband/wife)*

vii) nouns ending in **-eau** change into **-elle**:
le jumeau
la jum**elle** *(male/female twin)*

2 By using a different word (as in English):

le beau-fils	**la belle-fille** *(son-/daughter-in-law)*
le beau-père	**la belle-mère** *(father-/mother-in-law)*
le bélier	**la brebis** *(ram/ewe)*
le bœuf	**la vache** *(ox/cow)*
le canard	**la cane** *(drake/duck)*
le cheval	**la jument** *(horse/mare)*
le cerf	**la biche** *(stag/hind)*
le coq	**la poule** *(cock/hen)*
le fils	**la fille** *(son/daughter)*
le frère	**la sœur** *(brother/sister)*
un homme	**une femme** *(man/woman)*
un jars	**une oie** *(gander/goose)*
le mâle	**la femelle** *(male/female)*
le neveu	**la nièce** *(nephew/niece)*
un oncle	**une tante** *(uncle/aunt)*
le parrain	**la marraine** *(godfather/godmother)*
le père	**la mère** *(father/mother)*
le porc	**la trule** *(pig/sow)*
le roi	**la reine** *(king/queen)*

3 By adding the word **femme** (or **femelle** for animals):
une **femme** médecin *(doctor)*
un perroquet **femelle** *(female parrot)*

4 *Irregular feminine forms*

un abbé	**une abbesse** *(abbot/abbess)*
un âne	**une ânesse** *(donkey)*
le comte	**la comtesse** *(count/countess)*
le dieu	**la déesse** *(god/goddess)*
le duc	**la duchesse** *(duke/duchess)*
un Esquimau	**une Esquimaude** *(Eskimo)*
le fou	**la folle** *(madman/mad woman)*

Nouns

un Grec	une **Grecque** (Greek)	le genou	les gen**oux** knee
un héros	une **héroïne** (hero/heroine)	le hibou	les hib**oux** owl
un hôte	une **hôtesse** (host/hostess)	le joujou	les jouj**oux** toy
le maître	la **maîtresse** (master/mistress)	le pou	les p**oux** louse
le prêtre	la **prêtresse** (priest/priestess)		
le prince	la **princesse** (prince/princess)	b) Other nouns ending in **-ou** add **s**:	
le tigre	la **tigresse** (tiger/tigress)	le clou	les clou**s** nail
le Turc	la **Turque** (Turk)		
le vieux	la **vieille** (old man/old woman)		

C THE FORMATION OF PLURALS

1 Most nouns form their plural by adding **s** to the singular:

le vin	les vin**s** wine
un étudiant	des étudiant**s** student

2 Nouns ending in **-s**, **-x** or **-z** remain unchanged:

le bras	**les bras** arm
la voix	**les voix** voice
le nez	**les nez** nose

3 Nouns ending in **-au**, **-eau** and **-eu** add **x** to the singular:

le tuyau	les tuy**aux** drainpipe
le bateau	les bat**eaux** boat
le jeu	les j**eux** game
But: le landau	les land**aus** pram
le bleu	les bl**eus** bruise
le pneu	les pn**eus** tyre

4 Nouns ending in **-al** change to **-aux**:

le journal	les journ**aux** newspaper
But: le bal	les b**als** dance
le carnaval	les carnav**als** carnival
le festival	les festiv**als** festival

5 Nouns ending in **-ail** change to **-aux**:

le bail	les b**aux** lease
le travail	les trav**aux** work
le vitrail	les vitr**aux** stained-glass window
But: le détail	les détail**s** detail
l'épouvantail	les épouvant**ails** scarecrow
l'éventail	les éventa**ils** fan
le rail	les rail**s** rail

6 Nouns ending in **-ou**:

a) Seven nouns ending in **-ou** add **x** in the plural:

le bijou	les bij**oux** jewel
le caillou	les caill**oux** pebble
le chou	les ch**oux** cabbage

7 Plural of compound nouns:

Each noun ought to be checked individually in a dictionary:

eg le chou-fleur	**les choux-fleurs** cauliflower
le beau-père	**les beaux-pères** father-in-law
But: un essuie-glace	**des essuie-glaces** windscreen wiper
le tire-bouchon	**les tire-bouchons** corkscrew

8 Irregular plurals:

un œil	des **yeux** eye
le ciel	les **cieux** sky
Monsieur	**Messieurs** Mr
Madame	**Mesdames** Mrs
Mademoiselle	**Mesdemoiselles** Miss

9 Collective nouns:

a) Some nouns are singular in French but plural in English:

le bétail	cattle
la recette	takings
la police	police

la police a arrêté certains grévistes
the police have arrested some strikers

b) Others are plural in French but singular in English:

le nouvelles	news
les capitaux	capital
les cheveux	hair

les nouvelles sont bonnes
the news is good

10 Proper nouns:

a) Ordinary family names are invariable:

j'ai rencontré **les Leblanc**
I met the Leblancs

b) Historical names add **-s**:

les Stuarts	**les Bourbons**	**les Tudors**
the Stuarts	*the Bourbons*	*the Tudors*

4 Adjectives

Adjectives usually accompany a noun (or a pronoun) and provide extra information about what someone or something is like:

une **grande** ville	un film **intéressant**
a large city	*an interesting film*
elle est **espagnole**	c'était **ennuyeux**
she is Spanish	*it was boring*

A AGREEMENT OF ADJECTIVES

In French, adjectives agree in number and gender with the noun or pronoun to which they refer. Therefore French adjectives have four different forms which are determined by the noun they accompany.

- masculine singular (basic form, found in the dictionary)
- feminine singular
- masculine plural
- feminine plural

un passeport **vert**	une voiture **verte**
a green passport	*a green car*
des gants **verts**	des chaussettes **vertes**
green gloves	*green socks*

Note that if two singular words share the same adjective, the adjective will be in the plural:

un foulard et un bonnet **rouges**
a red scarf and (a red) hat

If one of these words is feminine and the other masculine, the adjective will be in the masculine plural:

une robe et un manteau **noirs**
a black dress and (a black) coat

B FEMININE FORMS OF ADJECTIVES

1 General rule

Add the letter **e** to the masculine singular form:

MASCULINE	FEMININE
grand	grand**e**
amusant	amusant**e**
anglais	anglais**e**
bronzé	bronzé**e**

un livre amusant	une histoire amusant**e**
an amusing book	*an amusing story*
il est bronzé	elle est bronzé**e**
he is suntanned	*she is suntanned*

2 Adjectives already ending in -e

These do not change:

MASCULINE	FEMININE
rouge	rouge
jeune	jeune
malade	malade

mon père est **malade**
my father is ill

ma mère est **malade**
my mother is ill

3 Others

The spelling of some adjectives changes when the **e** is added:

a) The following masculine endings generally double the final consonant before adding **e**:

MASCULINE ENDING	FEMININE ENDING
-el	-elle
-eil	-eille
-en	-enne
-on	-onne
-as	-asse
-et	-ette

MASCULINE		FEMININE
réel	*(real)*	réelle
cruel	*(cruel)*	cru**elle**
pareil	*(similar)*	par**eille**
ancien	*(old)*	anci**enne**
italien	*(Italian)*	itali**enne**
bon	*(good)*	b**onne**
gras	*(greasy)*	gr**asse**
bas	*(low)*	b**asse**
muet	*(dumb)*	mu**ette**
net	*(clear)*	n**ette**

un problème actuel	la vie actuelle
a topical problem	*present-day life*
un bon conseil	c'est une bonne recette
good advice	*it's a good recipe*

Note, however, that the feminine ending of some common adjectives in **-et** is **-ète** instead of **-ette**:

MASCULINE		FEMININE
complet	*(complete)*	compl**ète**
incomplet	*(incomplete)*	incompl**ète**
concret	*(concrete)*	concr**ète**
discret	*(discreet)*	discr**ète**

Adjectives

inquiet	*(worried)*	inqui**ète**
secret	*(secret)*	secr**ète**

b) MASCULINE IN -er		FEMININE IN -ère
cher	*(dear)*	ch**ère**
fier	*(proud)*	fi**ère**
dernier	*(last)*	derni**ère**

c) MASCULINE IN -x		FEMININE IN -se
heureux	*(happy)*	heur**euse**
malheureux	*(unhappy)*	malheur**euse**
sérieux	*(serious)*	séri**euse**
jaloux	*(jealous)*	jal**ouse**
But: doux	*(soft)*	**douce**
faux	*(false)*	**fausse**
roux	*(red-haired)*	**rousse**
vieux	*(old)*	**vieille**

d) MASCULINE IN -eur		FEMININE IN -euse
menteur	*(lying)*	ment**euse**
trompeur	*(deceitful)*	tromp**euse**

This rule, however, applies only when the stem of the adjective is also the stem of a present participle (eg **mentant, trompant**). The following five adjectives simply add an **e** to the feminine, **-eur** becoming **-eure**:

MASCULINE		FEMININE
extérieur	*(external)*	extérieur**e**
intérieur	*(internal)*	intérieur**e**
inférieur	*(inferior)*	inférieur**e**
supérieur	*(superior)*	supérieur**e**
meilleur	*(better)*	meilleur**e**

The feminine ending of the remaining adjectives in **-teur** is **-trice**:

MASCULINE		FEMININE
protecteur	*(protective)*	protec**trice**
destructeur	*(destructive)*	destruc**trice**

e) MASCULINE IN -f		FEMININE IN -ve
neuf	*(new)*	neu**ve**
vif	*(lively)*	vi**ve**
naïf	*(naive)*	naï**ve**
actif	*(active)*	acti**ve**
passif	*(passive)*	passi**ve**
positif	*(positive)*	positi**ve**
bref	*(brief)*	br**ève**
		(note the **è***)*

f) MASCULINE IN -c		FEMININE IN -che or -que
blanc	*(white)*	blan**che**
franc	*(frank)*	fran**che**
sec	*(dry)*	s**èche**
		(note the **è***)*

public	*(public)*	publi**que**
turc	*(Turkish)*	tur**que**
grec	*(Greek)*	gre**cque**
		(note the **c***)*

g) The following five common adjectives have an irregular feminine form and two forms for the masculine singular; the second masculine form, based on the feminine form, is used before words starting with a vowel or a silent **h**:

MASCULINE	FEMININE	MASCULINE 2
beau	**belle**	**bel** *(beautiful)*
nouveau	**nouvelle**	**nouvel** *(new)*
vieux	**vieille**	**vieil** *(old)*
fou	**folle**	**fol** *(mad)*
mou	**molle**	**mol** *(soft)*

un beau lac	une **belle** vue
a beautiful lake	*a beautiful view*

un **bel** enfant
a beautiful child

un nouveau disque	la **nouvelle** année
a new record	*the new year*

un **nouvel** ami
a new friend

un vieux tableau	la **vieille** ville
an old painting	*the old town*

un **vieil** homme
an old man

h) Other irregular feminines:

MASCULINE		FEMININE
favori	*(favourite)*	**favorite**
gentil	*(nice)*	**gentille**
nul	*(no)*	**nulle**
frais	*(fresh)*	**fraîche**
malin	*(shrewd)*	**maligne**
sot	*(foolish)*	**sotte**
long	*(long)*	**longue**
aigu	*(sharp)*	**aiguë**
ambigu	*(ambiguous)*	**ambiguë**
chic	*(elegant)*	**chic**
châtain	*(chestnut)*	**châtain**

C PLURALS OF ADJECTIVES

1 General rule

The masculine and feminine plural of adjectives is formed by adding an **s** to the singular form:

un vélo neuf	des vélos neuf**s**
a new bike	*new bikes*

Adjectives

une belle fleur	de belles fleurs
a beautiful flower	beautiful flowers
le livre intéressant	les livres intéressants
the interesting book	the interesting books

2 Adjectives ending in -s or -x

If the masculine singular ends in **-s** or **-x**, the plural form does not take an **s**:

il est heureux	ils sont **heureux**
he's happy	they are happy
un touriste anglais	des touristes **anglais**
an English tourist	English tourists

3 Others

A few masculine plurals are irregular (the feminine plurals are all regular):

a) **SINGULAR IN -al**		**PLURAL IN -aux**
normal	(normal)	normaux
brutal	(brutal)	brutaux
loyal	(loyal)	loyaux
But: fatal	(fatal)	fatals
natal	(native)	natals
naval	(naval)	navals

Note that the adjective **final** (final) has two masculine plural forms: **finals** and **finaux**.

b) **SINGULAR IN -eau**		**PLURAL IN -eaux**
beau	(beautiful)	beaux
nouveau	(new)	nouveaux

D POSITION OF ADJECTIVES

1 Unlike English adjectives, French adjectives usually follow the noun:

un métier intéressant
an interesting job

des parents modernes
modern parents

Adjectives of colour and nationality always follow the noun:

des chaussures rouges
red shoes

le drapeau britannique
the British flag

2 However, the following common adjectives generally come before the noun:

beau	beautiful
bon	good
court	short
gentil	nice
grand	big, tall
gros	fat
haut	high
jeune	young
joli	pretty
long	long
mauvais	bad
méchant	nasty, naughty
meilleur	better
moindre	lesser, least
petit	small
pire	worse
vieux	old
vilain	nasty, ugly

3 Some adjectives have a different meaning according to their position:

	BEFORE NOUN	AFTER NOUN
ancien	former	ancient
brave	good	brave
certain	some	sure
cher	dear	expensive
dernier	last (final)	last (latest)
grand	great (people only)	big, tall
même	same	very
pauvre	poor (pitiable)	poor (not rich)
propre	own	clean
seul	single, only	alone, lonely
simple	mere	simple
vrai	real	true

mon **ancien** métier
my former job
un tableau **ancien**
an old painting

un **brave** type
a nice fellow
un homme **brave**
a brave man

un **certain** charme
a certain charm
un fait **certain**
a definite fact

chère Brigitte
dear Brigitte
un cadeau **cher**
an expensive present

la **dernière** séance
the last performance
le mois **dernier**
last month

une **grande** vedette
a great star
un homme assez **grand**
a fairly tall man

le **même** endroit
the same place
la vérité **même**
the truth itself

mon **pauvre** ami!
my poor friend!
des gens **pauvres**
poor people

mon **propre** frère
my own brother
une chambre **propre**
a clean room

mon **seul** espoir
my only hope
un homme **seul**
a lonely man

(15)

un **simple** employé des goûts **simples**
an ordinary employee simple tastes

un **vrai** casse-pieds une histoire **vraie**
a real bore a true story

If a noun is accompanied by several adjectives, the same rules apply to each of them:

le **bon vieux** temps un **joli** foulard **rouge**
the good old days a pretty red scarf

E COMPARATIVE AND SUPERLATIVE OF ADJECTIVES

Persons or things can be compared by using:

1. *the comparative form of the adjective:*
   more ... than
   ...er than
   less ... than
   not as ... as
   as ... as

2. *the superlative form of the adjective:*
   the most ...
   the ...est
   the least ...

1 The comparative

The French comparative is formed as follows:

plus ... (que)
more ... (than), ... er (than)

plus long   **plus** cher
longer   *more expensive*

moins ... (que)
less ... (than), not as ... (as)

moins long   **moins** récent
less long   *less recent*

aussi ... (que)
as ... (as)

aussi bon   **aussi** important
as good   *as important*

une **plus grande** maison
a larger house

un village **plus ancien**
an older village

le football est-il **plus populaire que** le rugby?
is football more popular than rugby?

ces gants sont **moins** chauds **que** les autres
these gloves are less warm than the other ones

elle est beaucoup/bien **moins** patiente **que** lui
she's far less patient than he is

le problème de la pollution est tout **aussi** grave
the pollution problem is just as serious

2 The superlative

a) *Formation*

le/la/les plus ...   *the most ... , the ...est*
le/la/les moins ...   *the least ...*

le plus grand pays **la plus grande** ville
the largest country   the largest city

les plus grands acteurs
the greatest actors

les plus grandes voitures
the largest cars

b) *Word order*

i) The normal rules governing word order of adjectives apply. When a superlative adjective comes after the noun, the article is used twice, before the noun and before the adjective:

   le plat **le plus délicieux**
   the most delicious dish

   l'histoire **la plus passionnante**
   the most exciting story

ii) When a possessive adjective is used, there are two possible constructions, depending on the position of the adjective:

   ma plus forte matière
   my best subject

   or: mon besoin le plus **urgent** est de trouver un emploi
   my most urgent need is to find a job

c) 'in' is normally translated by **de**:

   la plus jolie maison **du** quartier/**de la** ville
   the prettiest house in the area/town

   le restaurant le plus cher **de** France
   the most expensive restaurant in France

   Note that verbs following the superlative usually take the subjunctive (see p50).

3 Irregular comparatives and superlatives

ADJECTIVE	COMPARATIVE	SUPERLATIVE
bon	**meilleur**	**le meilleur**
good	*better*	*best*

mauvais	pire	le pire
bad	**plus mauvais**	**le plus mauvais**
	worse	*the worst*
petit	**moindre**	**le moindre**
small	**plus petit**	**le plus petit**
	smaller, lesser	*the smallest,*
		the least

Note that **pire** and **le pire** are, strictly speaking, the correct comparative and superlative forms of mauvais. Plus mauvais and le plus mauvais can also be found in everyday French, however, with a slight difference in meaning: **pire** and **le pire** express the absolute (ie one cannot conceive of a worse example of ...) while plus mauvais and le plus mauvais indicate a comparison of a lesser degree:

il n'y a pas de **pire** professeur que lui
he is the worst teacher of all

c'est **la pire** chose qui pouvait lui arriver
it's the worst thing that could happen to him

ma note est **plus mauvaise** que la tienne
my mark is worse than yours

c'est **le plus mauvais** élève de la classe
he's the worst pupil in the class

Note, too, that **moindre** usually means 'less in importance', and **plus petit** 'less in size':

le **moindre de** mes soucis
the least of my worries

elle est **plus petite** que moi
she is smaller than I (am)

F ADJECTIVES OF NATIONALITY

1 French, unlike English, does not use capital letters for adjectives of nationality. Only nouns indicating nationality are written with a capital letter in French:

une voiture anglaise une **Anglaise**
an English car   *an English woman*

2 An adjective of nationality in English is sometimes best translated by a genitive construction in French:

l'ambassade de France
the French embassy

l'équipe de France de rugby
the French rugby team

l'équipe de Nantes
the Nantes team

l'équipe de Glasgow
the Glasgow/Glaswegian team

le championnat de France
the French league

la Coupe de France de football
the French football cup

la Grand Prix du Brésil
the Brazilian Grand Prix

la terre de France
French soil

la couronne de France
the French crown, the crown of France

les côtes de France
the French coastline

une grammaire de l'anglais
an English grammar

---

5 Adverbs

Adverbs are normally used with a verb to express:

		ADVERBS OF
how		*manner*
when		*time*
where	an action is	*place*
with how much	done	*intensity*
intensity		
to what extent		*quantity*

A ADVERBS OF MANNER

These are usually formed by adding **-ment** to the adjective (like **-ly** in English):

1 If the adjective ends in a consonant, **-ment** is added to its feminine form:

ADJECTIVE	ADVERB
(masc, fem)	
doux, douce *(soft)*	**doucement**
	(softly)
franc, franche *(frank)*	**franchement**
	(frankly)
final, finale *(final)*	**finalement**
	(finally)

2 If the adjective ends in a vowel, **-ment** is added to its masculine form:

Adverbs

ADJECTIVE	ADVERB
absolu (absolute)	**absolument** (absolutely)
désespéré (desperate)	**désespérément** (desperately)
vrai (true)	**vraiment** (truly)
simple (simple)	**simplement** (simply)
But: **gai** (cheerful)	**gaiement** or **gaîment** (cheerfully)
nouveau (new)	**nouvellement** (newly)
fou (mad)	**follement** (madly)

3 Many adverbs have irregular forms:

a) Some change the **e** of the feminine form of the adjective to **é** before adding **-ment**:

ADJECTIVE	ADVERB
commun (common)	**communément** (commonly)
précis (precise)	**précisément** (precisely)
profond (deep)	**profondément** (deeply)
énorme (enormous)	**énormément** (enormously)
aveugle (blind)	**aveuglément** (blindly)

b) Adjectives which end in **-ent** and **-ant** change to **-emment** and **-amment**. Note that both endings are pronounced like **amant**:

ADJECTIVE	ADVERB
prudent (careful)	**prudemment** (carefully)
évident (obvious)	**évidemment** (obviously)
brillant (brilliant)	**brillamment** (brilliantly)
But: **lent** (slow)	**lentement** (slowly)

4 Some adverbs are completely irregular, including some of the most commonly used ones:

ADJECTIVE	ADVERB
bon (good)	**bien** (well)
bref (brief)	**brièvement** (briefly)
gentil (kind)	**gentiment** (kindly)
mauvais (bad)	**mal** (badly)
meilleur (better)	**mieux** (better)

5 Some adjectives are also used as adverbs in

certain set expressions:

parler **bas/haut** or **fort**	to speak softly/loudly
coûter/payer **cher**	to cost/pay a lot
s'arrêter **net**	to stop short
couper **court**	to cut short
voir **clair**	to see clearly
marcher **droit**	to walk straight
travailler **dur**	to work hard
chanter **faux/juste**	to sing off key/in tune
sentir **mauvais/bon**	to smell bad/good
refuser **net**	to refuse point blank

6 After verbs relating to saying something or looking at something in French an adverbial phrase is often preferred to an adverb:

'tu m'écriras?' dit-il **d'une voix triste**
'will you write to me?' he said sadly

elle nous a regardés **d'un air dédaigneux**
she looked at us disdainfully

7 English adverbs may be expressed in French by a preposition followed by a noun:

sans soin	*carelessly*
avec fierté	*proudly*
avec amour	*lovingly*

B ADVERBS OF TIME

These are not usually formed from adjectives. The commonest ones are the following:

alors	*then*
après	*afterwards*
aujourd'hui	*today*
aussitôt	*at once*
bientôt	*soon*
d'abord	*first*
déjà	*already*
demain	*tomorrow*
encore	*still, again*
pas encore	*not yet*
enfin	*at last, finally*
hier	*yesterday*
parfois	*sometimes*
rarement	*seldom*
souvent	*often*
tard	*late*
tôt	*early*
toujours	*always*
tout de suite	*immediately*

il mange **encore**!
he's still eating!

tu as **déjà** essayé?
have you tried before?

c'est **déjà** Noël!
it's Christmas already!

elle n'est pas **encore** arrivée
she hasn't arrived yet

C ADVERBS OF PLACE

Like adverbs of time, these are not usually
formed from adjectives. The commonest ones
are the following:

ailleurs	*somewhere else, elsewhere*
ici	*here*
là	*there*
loin	*far away*
dessus	*on top, on it*
au-dessus	*over, above*
dessous	*underneath*
au-dessous	*below*
dedans	*inside*
dehors	*outside*
devant	*in front, ahead*
derrière	*behind*
partout	*everywhere*

ne restez pas **dehors**!
don't stay outside!

mon nom est marqué **dessus**
my name is written on it

qu'est-ce qu'il y a **dedans**?
what's inside?

passez **devant**
go in front

D ADVERBS OF INTENSITY AND QUANTITY

These may be used with a verb, an adjective or
another adverb. The commonest ones are the
following:

à peine	*hardly*
assez	*enough, quite*
autant	*as much/many*
beaucoup	*a lot, much/many*
combien	*how much/many*
comme	*how*
moins	*less*
plus	*more*
presque	*nearly*
peu	*little*
seulement	*only*
si	*so*
tant	*so much/many*
tellement	*so much/many*
très	*very*
trop	*too, too much/many*

un peu   *a little*

vous avez **assez** bu!
you've had enough to drink!

il ne fait pas **assez** chaud
it's not warm enough

nous avons **beaucoup** ri
we laughed a lot

comme c'est amusant!
how funny!

je vais **un peu** mieux
I'm feeling a little better

c'est **si** fatigant!
it's so tiring!

elle parle **trop**   il est **très** timide
she talks too much *he's very shy*

Note that all of these adverbs, except **à peine**,
comme, **presque**, **si**, **très** and **seulement**,
may be followed by **de** and a noun to express a
quantity (see p73).

E POSITION OF ADVERBS

1 Adverbs usually follow verbs:

je vais **rarement** au théâtre
I seldom go to the theatre

comme vous conduisez **prudemment**
you do drive carefully!

2 With compound tenses, shorter adverbs
usually come between the auxiliary and the
past participle:

j'ai **enfin** terminé   il me l'a **déjà** dit
I have finished at last *he's already told me*

nous y sommes **souvent** allés
we've often gone there

elle avait **beaucoup** souffert
she had suffered a lot

3 Adverbs of place and many adverbs of time,
however, follow the past participle:

je l'ai rencontré **hier**
I met him yesterday

elle avait cherché **partout**
she had looked everywhere

mettez-le **dehors**   tu t'es couché **tard**?
put it outside   *did you go to bed late?*

4 Adverbs usually come before adjectives or
other adverbs, as in English:

très rarement   **trop** vite
very seldom   *too quickly*

elle est **vraiment** belle
she is really beautiful

F COMPARATIVE AND SUPERLATIVE OF ADVERBS

1 The comparative and superlative of adverbs are formed in the same way as those of adjectives:

ADVERB	COMPARATIVE	SUPERLATIVE
souvent	**plus** souvent **(que)**	**le plus** souvent
often	*more often (than)*	*(the) most often*
	moins souvent **(que)**	**le moins** souvent
	less often (than) *not as often (as)*	*(the) least often*
	aussi souvent (que)	
	as often (as)	

Note that the superlative of the adverb always takes the masculine singular article **le**:

je le vois **plus souvent qu'**avant
I see him more often than I used to

il conduit **moins prudemment que** moi
he drives less carefully than I do
he doesn't drive as carefully as I do

c'est lui qui conduit **le moins prudemment**
he's the one who drives the least carefully

je sais cuisiner **aussi bien que** toi!
I can cook as well as you!

Note:

a) 'as ... as possible' is translated either by **aussi ... que possible** or by **le plus ... possible**:

as far as possible
aussi loin **que possible**
le plus loin **possible**

b) after a negative, **aussi** is often replaced by **si**:

pas **si** vite!
not so fast!

c) In French, the idea of 'not so', 'not as' is often expressed by **moins** *(less)*:

parle **moins** fort!
don't talk so loud!

2 Irregular comparatives and superlatives

ADVERB	COMPARATIVE	SUPERLATIVE
beaucoup	**plus**	**le plus**
much, a lot	*more*	*(the) most*
bien	**mieux**	**le mieux**
well	*better*	*(the) best*
mal	**pis** **plus mal**	**le pis** **le plus mal**
badly	*worse*	*(the) worst*
peu	**moins**	**le moins**
little	*less*	*(the) least*

il est **mieux** payé que moi
he is better paid than me

c'est lui **le mieux** payé
he's the best paid

Note:

a) **mieux/le mieux** must not be confused with **meilleur/le meilleur** which are adjectives, used in front of a noun.

elle chante **mieux** que toi
she sings better than you (do)

c'est elle qui chante **le mieux**
she sings best

elle est **meilleure** chanteuse que toi
she is a better singer than you

c'est **la meilleure** chanteuse
she is the best singer

b) **pis/le pis** are only found in certain set expressions or in literary French:

tant **pis**
too bad

de mal en **pis**
from bad to worse

il n'y a rien de **pis** que cela
there is nothing worse than that

on en dit **pis** que pendre
nobody has a good word to say about it

6 Pronouns and corresponding adjectives

A DEMONSTRATIVES

1 Demonstrative adjectives

a) *CE*

ce is often used to point out a particular person or thing, or persons or things. It is followed by the noun to which it refers and agrees in number and gender with that noun:

- with a masculine singular noun:
  ce (cet)   *this/that*
- with a feminine singular noun:
  cette   *this/that*
- with a plural noun (masc or fem):
  ces   *these/those*

ce roman m'a beaucoup plu
I really liked this novel

il a neigé **ce** matin
it snowed this morning

cette chanson m'énerve
that song gets on my nerves

cette fois, c'est fini!
this time, it's over!

tu trouves que **ces** lunettes me vont bien?
do you think these glasses suit me?

cet is used instead of **ce** in front of a masculine singular word that begins with a vowel or a silent **h**:

cet été   **cet** hôtel
this summer   *that hotel*

b) *-CI and -LÀ*

French does not have separate words to distinguish between 'this' and 'that'. However, when a particular emphasis is being placed on a person or object, or when a contrast is being made between persons or objects, **-ci** and **-là** are added to the noun:

-ci translates the idea of   *this/these*
-là translates the idea of   *that/those*

je suis très occupé ces jours**-ci**
I'm very busy these days

que faisiez-vous ce soir**-là**?
what were you doing that evening?

tu préfères cette robe**-ci** ou cette robe**-là**?
do you prefer this dress or that dress?

2 Demonstrative pronouns

Demonstrative pronouns are used instead of a noun with **ce/cette/ces**. They are:

celui, celle, ceux, celles
ce
ceci, cela, ça

a) *CELUI*

celui agrees in number and gender with the noun it refers to. It has four different forms:

	MASCULINE	**FEMININE**
SINGULAR	celui	celle
PLURAL	ceux	celles

celui, celle, ceux and **celles** cannot be used on their own. They are used:

● with **-ci** or **-là**, for emphasis or for contrast:

celui-ci   **celle-ci** *this (one)*
celui-là   **celle-là** *that (one)*
ceux-ci   **celles-ci** *these (ones)*
ceux-là   **celles-là** *those (ones)*

J'aime bien ce maillot mais **celui-là** est moins cher
I like this swimsuit, but that one is cheaper

je voudrais ces fleurs – lesquelles? **celles-ci** ou **celles-là**?
I'd like these flowers – which ones? these or those?

● with **de** + noun, to express possession:

je préfère mon ordinateur à **celui** de Jean-Claude
I prefer my computer to Jean-Claude's

range ta chambre plutôt que **celle** de ta sœur
tidy your own bedroom rather than your sister's

mes parents sont moins sévères que **ceux** de Nicole
my parents aren't as strict as Nicole's

les douches municipales sont mieux que **celles** du camping
the public showers are better than those at the campsite

● with the relative pronouns **qui, que, dont** to introduce a relative clause (for use of these relative pronouns, see p33).

Pronouns and corresponding adjectives

celui/celle/ceux/celles qui *the one(s)*
who/which
celui/celle/ceux/celles que *the one(s)*
whom/which
celui/celle/ceux/celles dont *the one(s) of*
which/whose

lequel est ton père? **celui qui** a une
moustache?
*which one is your father? the one with the
moustache?*

regarde cette voiture! **celle qui** est garée
au coin
*look at that car! the one which is parked at
the corner*

deux filles, **celles qu'**il avait rencontrées la
veille
two girls, the ones he had met the day before

voilà mon copain, **celui dont** je t'ai parlé
l'autre jour
*here's my friend, the one I told you about the
other day*

b) *CE*

ce (meaning 'it' or 'that') is normally used
with the verb **être**:

c'est   ce serait
it's/that's   it/that would be

c'était
it/that was

Note that **ce** changes to **c'** before an **e** or an
é.

● with a noun or pronoun, **ce** is used to
identify people or things, or to emphasize
them; it is translated in a variety of ways:
qu'est-ce que **c'**est? – **c'**est mon billet
d'avion
what's that? – it's my plane ticket

qui est-**ce**? – **c'**est moi
who is it? – it's me

ce doit être lui
that must be him

c'est un artiste bien connu
he's a well-known artist

c'était une bonne idée
it was a good idea

ce sont mes amis   **c'**est la dernière fois!
they're my friends   it's the last time!

c'est elle qui l'a fait
she's the one who did it

c'est celui que j'ai vu

he's the one I saw

ce sont des gens   **ce** ne sont pas mes
sympathiques   chaussures
they're nice people   those aren't my shoes

● before an adjective, **ce** is used to refer to
an idea, an event or a fact which has already
been mentioned; it does not refer to any
specific noun:
c'était formidable   **ce** serait amusant
it was great   it would be funny

oui, **c'**est vrai   **c'**est sûr?
yes, that's true   is that definite?

ce n'est pas grave
it doesn't matter/it's not serious

c'est bon à entendre **c'**est exact!
that's good to hear   that's right!

c'est rare qu'il pleuve en juin
it doesn't often rain in June

Note that the translation of **it** is an area of
some difficulty for students of French, as it
is sometimes translated by **ce** and sometimes by **il/elle**; see p83 for further
information.

c) *CECI, CELA, ÇA*

ceci *(this)*, **cela** *(that)* and **ça** *(that)* are used
to refer to an idea, an event, a fact or an
object. They never refer to a particular noun
already mentioned.
non, je n'aime pas **ça**!
no, I don't like that!

ah, bon? **cela** m'étonne
really? that surprises me

ça, c'est un acteur!
that's what I call an actor!

souvenez-vous de **ceci**
remember this

ça m'est égal   **ça** alors!
I don't mind   well, really!

cela ne vous regarde pas
that's none of your business

buvez **ceci**, **ça** vous fera du bien
drink this, it'll do you good

cela s'appelle comment, en anglais?
what do you call this in English?

Note that **ceci** is not very common in
French; **cela** and **ça** are often used to
translate 'this' as well as 'that'; **ça** is used far
more frequently than **cela** in spoken French.

B INDEFINITE ADJECTIVES AND PRONOUNS

1 Indefinite adjectives

They are:

MASCULINE	FEMININE	
autre(s)	autre(s)	*other*
certain(s)	certaine(s)	*certain*
chaque	chaque	*each, every*
même(s)	même(s)	*same*
plusieurs	plusieurs	*several*
quelque(s)	quelque(s)	*some*
tel(s)	telle(s)	*such*
tout (tous)	toute(s)	*all, every*

Note that, when used as indefinite adjectives, all the above adjectives are placed before the nouns to which they refer. **Certain** and **même** can be found after the noun but they will then have a different meaning (see p15).

a) *CHAQUE and PLUSIEURS*

chaque *(each)* is always singular, **plusieurs** *(several)* always plural; the feminine form is the same as the masculine form:

chaque personne   j'y vais **chaque** jour
each person   *I go there every day*

plusieurs années   il a **plusieurs** amis
several years   *he's got several friends*

b) *AUTRE, MÊME and QUELQUE*

autre *(other)*, **même** *(same)* and **quelque** *(some)* agree in number with the noun that follows; the feminine is the same as the masculine:

je voudrais un **autre** café
I'd like another coffee

d'**autres** couleurs   **quelque** temps après
other colours   *some time later*

la **même** taille   les **mêmes** touristes
the same size   *the same tourists*

à **quelques** kilomètres
a few kilometres away

c) *CERTAIN, TEL and TOUT*

certain *(certain, some)*, **tel** *(such)* and **tout** *(all)* agree in number and gender with the noun; they have four different forms:

un **certain** charme   une **certaine** dame
a certain charm   *a certain lady*

à **certains** moments **certaines** personnes
at (certain) times   *some people*

un **tel** homme   une **telle** aventure
such a man   *such an adventure*

de **tels** avantages   de **telles** difficultés
such advantages   *such difficulties*

quoi! tu as mangé **tout** le fromage et **tous** les fruits?
what! you've eaten all the cheese and all the fruit?

toute la journée   **toutes** mes matières
all day long   *all my subjects*

Note:

i) **tel**: the position of the article **un/une** with **tel** is not the same as in English: **un tel homme** = *such a man.*

ii) **tel** cannot qualify another adjective; when it is used as an adverb, 'such' is translated by **si** or **tellement**:

c'était un si bon repas/un repas **tellement** bon!
it was such a good meal!

iii) **tous les/toutes les** are often translated by 'every':

tous les jours   **toutes** les places
every day   *all seats, every seat*

2 Indefinite pronouns

a) These are:

MASCULINE	FEMININE	
aucun	aucune	*none, not any*
autre(s)	autre(s)	*another one, other ones*
certains	certaine(s)	*certain, some*
chacun	chacune	*each one, every one*
on		*everyone, one, someone, you, they, people, we*
personne		*nobody*
plusieurs	plusieurs	*several (ones)*
quelque chose		*something, anything*
quelqu'un		*someone*
quelques-uns	quelques-unes	*some, a few*
rien		*nothing*
tout (tous)	toute(s)	*everything, every one, all*

pas celui-là, l'**autre**
not that one, the other one

Pronouns and corresponding adjectives

où sont les **autres**?
where are the others?

certains disent que ...
some say that ...

personne n'est venu
no one came

qui est là? – **personne**
who's there? – nobody

qu'as-tu? – **rien**
what's wrong? – nothing

plusieurs d'entre eux
several of them

chacun pour soi!
every man for himself!

il manque **quelque chose**?
is anything missing?

dis **quelque chose**!
say something!

quelqu'un l'a averti
someone warned him

il y a **quelqu'un**?   c'est **tout**, merci
is anyone in?   *that's all, thanks*

j'ai **tout** oublié
I've forgotten everything

elles sont **toutes** arrivées
they've all arrived

allons-y **tous** ensemble
let's all go together

b) Points to note

i) **aucun(e)**, **personne** and **rien**: these can be used on their own, but they are more often used with a verb and the negative word **ne** (see Negative Expressions, p78):
personne n'habite ici
no one lives here

il **n'**y a **rien** à manger
there's nothing to eat

ii) **aucun(e)**, **un(e) autre**, **d'autres**, **certain(e)s**, **plusieurs** and **quelques-un(e)s**: when these pronouns are used as direct objects, the pronoun **en** must be used before the verb:
je n'**en** ai lu **aucun**
I haven't read any (of them)

donne-m'**en** une **autre**
give me another one

j'**en** ai vu **d'autres** qui étaient moins chers
I saw other ones which were cheaper

j'**en** connais **certains** il y **en** a **plusieurs**
I know some of them   there are several

tu m'**en** donnes **quelques-uns**?
will you give me a few?

achètes-**en quelques-unes**
buy a few

iii) **personne, quelque chose, rien, plusieurs**: when these are followed by an adjective, the preposition **de** (or **d'**) must be used in front of the adjective:
il n'y a **personne de** libre
there's no one available

quelque chose de mieux
something better

il y en avait **plusieurs de** cassés
several of them were broken

rien de grave
nothing serious

iv) **autre** is commonly used in the following expressions:
quelqu'un d'**autre**   rien d'**autre**
someone else   *nothing else*

quelque chose d'**autre**
something else

c) *ON*

This pronoun is used in a variety of ways in French. It can mean:

i) *one/you/they/people* in a general sense:
en France, **on** roule à droite
in France, they drive on the right

on ne sait jamais
you/one never know(s)

on ne doit pas mentir
you shouldn't lie

ii) *someone* (an undefined person)
In this sense, **on** is often translated by the passive (see p59):
on me l'a déjà dit
someone's already told me
I've already been told

on vous l'apportera
someone will bring it to you
it will be brought to you

iii) *we*

In spoken French, **on** is frequently used instead of **nous**; although it refers to a plural subject, it is followed by the third person singular:

qu'est-ce qu'**on** fait?
what shall we do?

fais vite, **on** t'attend!
hurry up, we're waiting for you!

Note that in compound tenses with the auxiliary **être**, the agreement of the past participle with **on** is optional:

on est **allé** au cinéma
on est **allés** au cinéma
we went to the cinema

on est **rentré** en taxi
on est **rentrées** en taxi
we went home by taxi

C INTERROGATIVE AND EXCLAMATORY ADJECTIVES AND PRONOUNS

1 The interrogative adjective QUEL?

a) Forms

quel *(which, what)* agrees in number and gender with the noun it refers to. It has four forms:

● with a masculine singular noun: **quel?**
● with a feminine singular noun: **quelle?**
● with a masculine plural noun: **quels?**
● with a feminine plural noun: **quelles?**

b) Direct questions:

quel est votre passe-temps favori?
what's your favourite pastime?

quelle heure est-il?
what time is it?

quels jours as-tu de libres?
which days have you got free?

quelles affaires comptes-tu prendre avec toi?
what/which things do you intend to take with you?

c) Indirect questions:

je ne sais pas **quel** CD choisir
I don't know which CD to choose

il se demande **quelle** veste lui va le mieux
he's wondering which jacket suits him best

2 The exclamatory adjective QUEL!

quel! has the same forms as the interrogative adjective **quel?**:

quel dommage!   **quelle** belle maison!
what a pity!   *what a beautiful house!*

quels imbéciles!   **quelles** jolies
what idiots!   chaussures!
                    what lovely shoes!

3 Interrogative pronouns

These are:

lequel/laquelle/   *which (one(s))?*
lesquels/lesquelles?
qui?   *who?/whom?*
que?   *what?*
quoi?   *what?*
ce qui   *what*
ce que   *what*

ce qui and **ce que** are used only in indirect questions; all other interrogative pronouns can be used both in direct and indirect questions.

a) LEQUEL?

i) forms

lequel *(which?, which one?)* agrees in gender and in number with the noun it stands for:

● with a masculine singular noun.
lequel? *which (one)?*
● with a feminine singular noun:
laquelle? *which (one)?*
● with a masculine plural noun:
lesquels? *which (ones)?*
● with a feminine plural noun:
lesquelles? *which (ones)?*

After the prepositions **à** and **de**, the following changes occur:

à + lequel?   →   auquel?
à + lesquels?   →   auxquels?
à + lesquelles?   →   auxquelles?

de + lequel?   →   duquel?
de + lesquels?   →   desquels?
de + lesquelles?   →   desquelles?

Note that **à/de + laquelle?** do not contract.

ii) direct questions:

je cherche un hôtel; **lequel** recommandez-vous?
I'm looking for a hotel; which one do you recommend?

Pronouns and corresponding adjectives

nous avons plusieurs couleurs; vous préférez **laquelle**?
we have several colours; which one do you prefer?

lesquels de ces livres sont à toi?
which of these books are yours?

je voudrais essayer ces chaussures – **lesquelles**?
I would like to try these shoes on – which ones?

iii) indirect questions:

demande-lui **lequel** de ces ordinateurs est le moins cher
ask him/her which (one) of these computers is the cheapest

c'est dans une de ces rues mais je ne sais plus **laquelle**
it's in one of these streets, but I can't remember which one

b) *QUI?*

qui *(who?, whom?)* is used to refer to people; it can be both subject and object and can be used after a preposition:
qui t'a accompagné?
who came/went with you?

qui as-tu appelé?   c'est pour **qui**?
who did you call?   who is it for?

tu y vas avec **qui**?
who are you going with?

pour **qui** vous prenez-vous?
who do you think you are?

à **qui** l'as-tu donné?
who did you give it to?

Note that **qui** does not contract to **qu'** before a vowel or a silent **h**:
qui est-ce qu'elle attend?
who is she waiting for?

qui? can be replaced by **qui est-ce qui?** (subject) or **qui est-ce que?** (object) in direct questions:
qui est-ce qui veut du café?
who wants coffee?

qui est-ce que tu as vu?
who did you see?

avec **qui est-ce que** tu sors ce soir?
who are you going out with tonight?

Note, however, that **qui** cannot be replaced by **qui est-ce qui** or **qui est-ce que** in indirect questions:

j'aimerais savoir **qui** vous a dit ça
I'd like to know who told you that

elle se demandait de **qui** étaient les fleurs
she was wondering who the flowers were from

For more details on the use of **qui/que** as relative pronouns, see p33.

c) *QUE?*

que *(what?)* is used to refer to things. It is only used in direct questions, is always a direct object and cannot be used after prepositions:
que désirez-vous?   **qu'**a-t-il dit?
what do you wish?   what did he say?

que? is rather formal and is usually replaced by **qu'est-ce qui?** or **qu'est-ce que?** in spoken French.

Note that **que** becomes **qu'** before a vowel or a silent **h**.

d) *QU'EST-CE QUI?*

qu'est-ce qui? *(what?)* is used as the subject of a verb; it cannot refer to a person:
qu'est-ce qui t'est arrivé?
what happened to you?

qu'est-ce qui la fait rire?
what makes her laugh?

e) *QU'EST-CE QUE?*

qu'est-ce que? *(what?)* replaces **que?** as the object of a verb; it becomes **qu'est-ce qu'** before a vowel or a silent **h**:
qu'est-ce que tu aimes lire?
what do you like reading?

qu'est-ce qu'il va faire pendant les vacances?
what's he going to do during the holidays?

f) *QUOI?*

quoi? *(what?)* refers to things; it is used:

i) instead of **que** or **qu'est-ce que** after a preposition:
à **quoi** penses-tu?
what are you thinking about?

dans **quoi** l'as-tu mis?
what did you put it in?

ii) in indirect questions:
demandez-lui de **quoi** il a besoin
ask him what he needs

je ne sais pas à **quoi** ça sert
I don't know what it's for

g) CE QUI, CE QUE

ce qui and **ce que** *(what)* are only used in indirect questions; they replace **qu'est-ce qui** and **(qu'est-ce) que**.

They are used in the same way as the relative pronouns **ce qui** and **ce que** (see p35).

i) **ce qui** is used as the subject of the verb in the indirect question (**ce qui** is the subject of **s'est passé** in the following example):

nous ne saurons jamais **ce qui s'est passé**
we'll never know what happened

ii) **ce que** (**ce qu'** before a vowel or a silent **h**) is used as the object of the verb in the indirect question (**ce que** is the object of **il faisait** in the following example):

je n'ai pas remarqué **ce qu'il faisait**
I didn't notice what he was doing

D PERSONAL PRONOUNS

There are four categories of personal pronouns:

- subject pronouns
- object pronouns
- disjunctive pronouns
- reflexive pronouns

For reflexive pronouns, see p42.

1 Subject pronouns

Person	Singular		Plural	
1st	**je (j')**	*I*	**nous**	*we*
2nd	**tu**	*you*	**vous**	*you*
3rd	**il**	*he, it*	**ils**	*they*
	elle	*she, it*	**elles**	*they*
	on	*one, we, they*		

Note:

a) **je** changes to **j'** before a vowel or a silent **h**:

j'ai honte
I'm ashamed

j'adore les frites
I love chips

j'habite en Écosse
I live in Scotland

b) **tu** and **vous**

vous can be plural or singular; it is used when speaking to more than one person (plural), or to a stranger or an older person (singular):

pourriez-**vous** m'indiquer la gare?
could you show me the way to the station?

vous venez, les gars?
are you coming, guys?

tu is used when speaking to a friend, a relative, a younger person, or someone else you know well:

tu viens, Marc?
are you coming, Marc?

c) **il/ils**, **elle/elles** may refer to people, animals or things, and must be of the same gender as the noun they replace:

ton stylo? **il** est là
your pen? there it is

ta montre? **elle** est là
your watch? there it is

tes gants? **ils** sont là
your gloves? there they are

tes lunettes? **elles** sont là
your glasses? there they are

When referring to several nouns of different genders, French uses the masculine plural **ils**:

j'ai trouvé dans mon sac un stylo et une montre. **Ils** ne m'appartiennent pas
I found a pen and a watch in my bag. They don't belong to me

d) **on**: see p24.

2 Object pronouns

There are three types of object pronouns:

- direct object pronouns
- indirect object pronouns
- the pronouns **en** and **y**

a) *Forms*

	Person	Direct	Indirect
Sing	1st	**me (m')**	**me (m')**
		me	*(to) me*
	2nd	**te (t')**	**te (t')**
		you	*(to) you*
	3rd	**le (l')**	**lui**
		him, it	*(to) him*
		la (l')	**lui**
		her, it	*(to) her*
Plur	1st	**nous**	**nous**
		us	*(to) us*
	2nd	**vous**	**vous**
		you	*(to) you*
	3rd	**les**	**leur**
		them	*(to) them*

Pronouns and corresponding adjectives

Note:

i) **me**, **te**, **le** and **la** change to **m'**, **t'** and **l'** before a vowel or a silent **h**:

il **m'**énerve!
he gets on my nerves!

je **m'**habituerai à lui
I'll get used to him

ii) **te** and **vous**: the same distinction should be made as between the subject pronouns **tu** and **vous** (see D 1b).

iii) **le** is sometimes used in an impersonal sense to refer to a fact, a statement or an idea which has already been expressed; it is usually not translated in English:

j'irai aux États-Unis un jour; en tout cas je **l'**espère
I'll go to the States one day; I hope so anyway

elle a eu un bébé – je **le** sais, elle me **l'**a dit
she's had a baby – I know, she told me

iv) when used as an indirect object pronoun, **lui** can be masculine or feminine:

pose-**lui** la question
ask him/her the question

j'ai décidé de **lui** offrir un cadeau
I've decided to give him/her a present

v) when they are used with imperatives, **moi** and **toi** are used instead of **me** and **te**, except when **en** follows:

écris-**moi** bientôt   donne **m'en**
write to me soon   *give me some*

b) *Position*

In French, object pronouns come immediately before the verb they refer to. With a compound tense, they come before the auxiliary:

on **t'**attendra ici
we'll wait for you here

je **l'**ai rencontrée en ville
I met her in town

Note that when there are two verbs, the pronoun comes immediately before the verb to which it refers:

j'aimerais **lui** demander
I'd like to ask him/her

tu **l'**as entendu chanter?
have you heard him sing?

In positive commands (the affirmative imperative) the pronoun follows the verb and is joined to it by a hyphen:

regarde-**les**!   parle-**lui**!
look at them!   *speak to him/her!*

dis-**nous** ce qui s'est passé
tell us what happened

c) *Direct pronouns and indirect pronouns*

i) Direct object pronouns replace a noun which directly follows the verb. They answer the question 'who(m)?' or 'what?'
WHO(M) did you see?
qui as-tu vu?

I saw my friend; I saw him
j'ai vu mon ami; je **l'**ai vu

tu **me** connais   je **les** ai trouvés
you know me   *I found them*

j'aime **le** voir danser
I like to see him dance

ne **nous** ennuie pas!
don't bother us!

ii) Indirect object pronouns replace a noun which follows the verb with a linking preposition (usually **à**, to whom?). They answer the question 'who to?'
WHO did you speak to?
à qui as-tu parlé?

I spoke to Marc; I spoke to him
j'ai parlé à Marc; je **lui** ai parlé

elle **lui** a menti   je **te** donne ce CD
she lied to him/her   *I'm giving this CD to you*

je ne **leur** parle plus
I'm not talking to them any more

iii) **le/la/les** or **lui/leur**?

Direct pronouns differ from indirect pronouns only in the 3rd person and great care must be taken to use the correct one.

English indirect object pronouns often look like direct objects; this becomes obvious when the object is placed at the end of the clause, after a linking preposition:
I showed him your photo = I showed your photo to him
je lui ai montré ta photo

This is particularly the case with the following verbs:
acheter   *to buy*
offrir   *to offer, to give*

donner	to give
prêter	to lend
montrer	to show
vendre	to sell

je **lui ai** acheté un livre
I bought him/her a book= I bought a book for him/her

ne **leur** prête pas mes affaires
don't lend them my things = don't lend my things to them

Some verbs take a direct object in English and an indirect object in French (see p62):
je ne **lui** ai rien dit
I didn't tell him/her anything

je **leur** demanderai
I'll ask them

tu **lui** ressembles   téléphone-**leur**
you look like him/her   phone them

Some verbs take a direct object in French and an indirect object in English (see p62):
je **l'**attends   écoutez-**les**!
I'm waiting for him/her   listen to them!

d) Order of object pronouns

When several object pronouns are used together, they come in the following order:

i) Before the verb:

1	me	te		nous	vous
2		le	la		les
3			lui	leur	

il **me l'**a donné
he gave it to me

je vais **vous les** envoyer
I'll send them to you

ne **la leur** vends pas   je **le lui** ai acheté
don't sell it to them   *I bought it for him/her*

ii) After the verb:

With a positive command (the affirmative imperative), the order is as follows:

1	le	la		les	
2	moi (m')	toi (t')		nous	vous
3		lui		leur	

apporte-**les-moi**!   prête-**la-nous**!
bring them to me!   *lend it to us!*

dites-**le-lui**!   rends-**la-leur**!
tell him/her!   *give it back to them!*

3 The pronoun EN

a) Use

en is used instead of **de** + noun. Since **de** has a variety of meanings, **en** can be used in a number of ways:

i) It means 'of it/them', but also 'with it/them', 'about it/them', 'from it/there', 'out of it/there':

tu es sûr du prix? – j'**en** suis sûr
are you sure of the price? – I'm sure of it

je suis content de ce cadeau; j'**en** suis content
I'm pleased with this present; I'm pleased with it

elle est folle des animaux; elle **en** est folle
she's crazy about animals; she's crazy about them

il est descendu du train; il **en** est descendu
he got off the train; he got off it

il revient de Paris; il **en** revient
he's coming back from Paris; he's coming back from there

ii) Verbal constructions

Particular care should be taken with verbs and expressions which are followed by de + noun. Since de is not always translated in the same way, **en** may have a number of meanings:

il a envie **de ce livre**; il **en** a envie
he wants this book; he wants it

je te remercie **de ton aide**; je t'**en** remercie
thank you for your help; thank you for it

tu as besoin **de ces papiers**? tu **en** as besoin?
do you need these papers? do you need them?

elle a peur **des chiens**; elle **en** a peur
she's afraid of dogs; she's afraid of them

tu te souviens **de ce film**? tu t'**en** souviens?
do you remember this film? do you remember it?

iii) 'some'/'any'

en replaces the partitive article (**du, de la, des**) + noun; it means 'some'/'any':

tu veux **du café**? – non, je n'**en** veux pas
do you want (any) coffee? – no, I don't want any

Pronouns and corresponding adjectives

j'achète **des fruits**? – non, j'**en** ai chez moi
shall I buy (some) fruit? – no, I've got some at home

il y a **de la place**? – **en** voilà là-bas
is there any room? – there's some over there

iv) Expressions of quantity

en must be used with expressions of quantity not followed by a noun. It replaces **de** + noun and means 'of it/them', but is seldom translated in English:

tu as pris assez **d'argent**? tu **en** as pris assez?
did you take enough money? did you take enough?

vous avez combien **de frères**? – j'**en** ai deux
how many brothers do you have? – I've got two

j'ai fini **mes cigarettes**; je vais **en** acheter un paquet
I've finished my cigarettes; I'm going to buy a packet

b) *Position*

Like object pronouns, **en** comes immediately before the verb, except with positive commands (the affirmative imperative), where it comes after the verb and is linked to it by a hyphen:

j'**en** veux un kilo
I want a kilo (of it/them)

j'**en** ai marre!
I'm fed up (with it)!

prends-**en** assez!
take enough (of it/them)!

laisses-**en** aux autres!
leave some for the others!

When used in conjunction with other object pronouns, it always comes last:

ne m'**en** parlez pas!
don't tell me about it!

je vous **en** donnerai
I'll give you some

prête-lui-**en**!   gardez-nous-**en**!
lend him/her some!   *keep some for us!*

4 The pronoun Y

a) *Use*

y is used instead of **à** + noun, but never refers to a person. It is used:

i)   As the indirect object of a verb. Since the preposition **à** is translated in a variety of ways in English, **y** may have various meanings (*it, of it/them, about it/them* etc*):

tu joues **au tennis**? – non, j'**y** joue rarement
do you play tennis? – no, I seldom play (it)

je pense à **mon pays natal**; j'**y** pense souvent
I'm thinking about my home country; I often think about it

il s'intéresse **à la photo**; il s'**y** intéresse
he's interested in photography; he's interested in it

ii) To mean 'there':
j'ai passé deux jours **à Londres**; j'**y** ai passé deux jours
I spent two days in London; I spent two days there

il est allé **en Grèce**; il **y** est allé
he went to Greece; he went there

Note that **y** must always be used with the verb **aller** *(to go)* when the place is not mentioned in the clause. It is often not translated in English:

comment vas-tu **à l'école**? – j'**y** vais en bus
how do you get to school? – I go (there) by bus

allons-**y**!   on **y** va demain
let's go!   *we're going (there) tomorrow*

iii) To replace the prepositions **en**, **dans**, **sur** + noun; **y** then means 'there', 'in it/them', 'on it/them':

je voudrais vivre **en France**; je voudrais **y** vivre
I'd like to live in France; I'd like to live there

je les ai mis **dans ma poche**; je les **y** ai mis
I put them in my pocket; I put them there

sur la table? – non, je ne l'**y** vois pas
on the table? no, I don't see it there

b) *Position*

Like other object pronouns, **y** comes immediately before the verb, except with a positive command (the affirmative imperative), where it must follow the verb:

j'**y** réfléchirai
I'll think about it

il s'**y** est habitué
he got used to it

pensez-**y**!
think about it!

n'**y** allez pas!
don't go!

When used with other object pronouns, **y** comes last:

il va nous **y** rencontrer
he'll meet us there

je l'**y** ai vu hier
I saw him there yesterday

5 Disjunctive pronouns

a) *Forms*

PERSON	SINGULAR	PLURAL
1st	**moi** *me*	**nous** *us*
2nd	**toi** *you*	**vous** *you*
3rd (masculine)	**lui** *him*	**eux** *them*
(feminine)	**elle** *her*	**elles** *them*
(impersonal)	**soi** *oneself*	

Note:

i) **toi/vous**: the same difference should be made as between **tu** and **vous** (see p27).

ii) **soi** is used in an impersonal, general sense to refer to indefinite pronouns and adjectives (**on**, **chacun**, **tout le monde**, **personne**, **chaque** etc); it is mainly found in set phrases, such as:

chacun pour **soi**
every man for himself

cela va de **soi**
that goes without saying

b) *Use*

Disjunctive pronouns, also called emphatic pronouns, are used instead of object pronouns when referring to persons in the following cases:

i) In answer to a question, alone or in a phrase without a verb.

qui est là? – **moi**
who's there? – me

j'ai aimé ce film; et **toi**?
I liked that film; did you?

qui préfères-tu, lui ou elle? – **elle**, bien sûr
who do you prefer, him or her? – her, of course

ii) After **c'est/ce sont**, **c'était/c'étaient** etc:

ouvrez, c'est **moi**!
open up, it's me!

non, ce n'était pas **lui**
no, it wasn't him

iii) After a preposition:

vous allez chez **lui**?
are you going to his place?

tu y vas avec **elle**?
are you going with her?

regarde devant **toi**!   oh, c'est pour **moi**?
look in front of you!   oh, is that for me?

iv) With verbal constructions. Special care should be taken when the verb is followed by a preposition:

tu peux compter sur **moi**
you can count on me

quoi! tu as peur de **lui**?
what! you're afraid of him?

il m'a parlé de **toi**
he told me about you

je pense souvent à **vous**
I often think about you

Note that emphatic pronouns are only used when referring to people. In other cases **y** or **en** must be used.

v) For emphasis, particularly when two pronouns are contrasted. The unstressed subject pronoun is usually included:

vous, vous m'énervez!
you get on my nerves!

lui, il joue bien; elle, non
he plays well; she doesn't

moi, je n'aime pas l'hiver
I don't like winter

eux, ils sont partis
they've left

vi) In the case of multiple subjects (two pronouns or one pronoun and one noun):

lui et son frère sont dans l'équipe
he and his brother are in the team

ma famille et **moi** allons très bien
my family and I are very well

vii) As the second element of a comparison:

il est plus sympa que **toi**
he is nicer than you

elle chante mieux que **lui**
she sings better than he does

Pronouns and corresponding adjectives

viii) Before a relative pronoun:

c'est lui que j'aime
he's the one I love

c'est toi qui l'as dit
you're the one who said it

lui qui n'aime pas le vin blanc en a bu
six verres
*he who doesn't like white wine had six
glasses*

ix) With **-même(s)** (*-self, -selves*), **aussi** (*too*),
seul (*alone*):

faites-le **vous-mêmes**
do it yourselves

j'irai **moi-même**
I'll go myself

lui aussi est parti   **elle seule** le sait
he too went away   *she alone knows*

x) To replace a possessive pronoun (see E2):

c'est le mien; il est à moi
it's mine; it belongs to me

cette valise n'est pas à lui?
doesn't that suitcase belong to him?

E POSSESSIVE ADJECTIVES AND PRONOUNS

1 Possessive adjectives

a) *Forms*

Possessive adjectives always come before
their related noun. Like other adjectives,
they agree in gender and number with the
noun; the masculine and feminine plural
forms are identical:

SINGULAR		PLURAL	
MASC	FEM	(MASC AND FEM)	
mon	ma	mes	*my*
ton	ta	tes	*your*
son	sa	ses	*his/her/its/ one's*
notre	notre	nos	*our*
votre	votre	vos	*your*
leur	leur	leurs	*their*

j'ai mis **mon argent** et **mes affaires**
dans **mon sac**
I've put my money and my things in my bag

notre rue est assez calme
our street is fairly quiet

ce sont **vos amis**
they're your friends

comment va **ton frère?** et **ta sœur?** et
tes parents?
*how's your brother? and your sister? and
your parents?*

Note that **mon/ton/son** are used instead of
ma/ta/sa when the next word starts with a
vowel or silent **h**:

mon ancienne maison
my old house

ton amie Christine
your friend Christine

son haleine sentait l'alcool
his/her breath smelled of alcohol

b) *Use*

i) The possessive adjective is repeated
before each noun and agrees in number
and gender with it:

mon père et **ma mère** sont sortis
my mother and father have gone out

ii) **son/sa/ses**

son, sa and **ses** can all mean 'his', 'her' or
'its'. In French, the form of the adjective is
determined by the gender and number of
the noun that follows, and not by the
possessor:

il m'a prêté **sa mobylette** et **son
casque**
he lent me his moped and his helmet

elle s'entend bien avec **sa mère** mais pas
avec **son père**
*she gets on well with her mother, but not
with her father*

elle vit pour **son travail**; lui pour **ses
enfants**
she lives for her job; he lives for his children

iii) **ton/ta/tes** and **votre/vos**

The two sets of words for 'your', **ton/ta/
tes** and **votre/vos**, correspond to the two
different forms of **tu** and **vous**; they must
not be used together with the same person:

tu as parlé à **ton patron?**
have you spoken to your boss?

Monsieur, vous oubliez **votre
parapluie!**
*excuse me, sir, you've forgotten your
umbrella!*

iv) In French, the possessive adjective is
replaced by the definite article (**le/la/les**)
with the following:

● parts of the body:

il s'est essuyé **les mains**
he wiped his hands

elle a haussé **les épaules**
she shrugged (her shoulders)

● descriptive phrases at the end of a clause, where English adds 'with':

il marchait lentement, **les mains** dans **les poches**
he was walking slowly, with his hands in his pockets

elle l'a regardé partir, **les larmes aux yeux**
she watched him leave with tears in her eyes

2 Possessive pronouns

SINGULAR		PLURAL	
MASC	FEM	(MASC AND FEM)	
le mien	la mienne	les mien(ne)s	*mine*
le tien	la tienne	les tien(ne)s	*yours*
le sien	la sienne	les sien(ne)s	*his/ hers/its*
le nôtre	la nôtre	les nôtres	*ours*
le vôtre	la vôtre	les vôtres	*yours*
le leur	la leur	les leurs	*theirs*

Possessive pronouns are used instead of a possessive adjective + noun. They agree in gender and in number with the noun they stand for, and not with the possessor (it is particularly important to remember this when translating 'his' and 'hers'):

j'aime bien ton **appartement** mais je préfère **le mien**
I quite like your flat, but I prefer mine

on prend quelle **voiture**? **la mienne** ou **la tienne**?
which car shall we take? mine or yours?

comment sont vos **profs**? **les nôtres** sont sympas
what are your teachers like? ours are nice

j'avais mon **passeport** mais Brigitte avait oublié **le sien**
I had my passport, but Brigitte had forgotten hers

j'ai gardé ma **moto** mais Paul a vendu **la sienne**
I've kept my motorbike but Paul has sold his

à or **de** + possessive pronoun

The prepositions **à** and **de** combine with the articles **le** and **les** in the usual way:

à + le mien	→	au mien
à + les miens	→	aux miens
à + les miennes	→	aux miennes
de + le mien	→	du mien
de + les miens	→	des miens
de + les miennes	→	des miennes

demande à tes parents, j'ai déjà parlé **aux miens**
ask your parents, I've already spoken to mine

leur appartement ressemble beaucoup **au nôtre**
their flat is very similar to ours

j'aime bien les chiens mais j'ai peur **du tien**
I like dogs, but I'm afraid of yours

Note that after the verb **être**, the possessive pronoun is often replaced by **à** + disjunctive pronoun (see p31):

à qui est cette écharpe? – elle est **à moi**
whose scarf is this? – it's mine

ce livre est **à toi**? – non, il est **à elle**
is this book yours? – no, it's hers

c'est à qui? à vous ou **à lui**?
whose is this? yours or his?

F RELATIVE PRONOUNS

1 Definition

Relative pronouns are words which introduce a relative clause. In the sentence:

I bought the book which you recommended

'which' is the relative pronoun, 'which you recommended' is the relative clause and 'the book' is the antecedent (ie the noun to which the relative pronoun refers).

2 Form

Relative pronouns are:

qui *who/which*	**lequel** *which*
que *who(m)/which*	**dont** *of which/whose*
quoi *what*	**ce qui** *what*
où *where*	**ce que** *what*

qui, **que**, **quoi**, **lequel**, **ce qui** and **ce que** can also be used as interrogative pronouns (see p25) and must not be confused with them.

Pronouns and corresponding adjectives

3 Use

a) *QUI*

qui is used as the subject of a relative clause. It means:

i) 'who', 'that' (referring to people):

est-ce que tu connais le monsieur **qui** habite ici?
do you know the man who lives here?

ce n'est pas lui **qui** a menti
he's not the one who lied

ii) 'which', 'that' (referring to things):

tu as pris le journal **qui** était sur la télé?
did you take the paper which/that was on the TV?

b) *QUE*

que (which contracts to **qu'** before a vowel or a silent **h**) is used as the object of a relative clause; it is often not translated. It means:

i) 'who(m)', 'that' (referring to people):

la fille **que** j'aime ne m'aime pas
the girl (that) I love doesn't love me

ii) 'which', 'that' (referring to things):

j'ai perdu le briquet **qu'**il m'a offert
I've lost the lighter (which/that) he gave me

c) *QUI or QUE?*

qui (subject) and **que** (object) are translated by the same words in English (who, which, that). To use the correct pronoun in French, it is essential to know whether a relative pronoun is the object or the subject of the relative clause:

i) when the verb of the relative clause has its own subject, the object pronoun **que** must be used:

c'est un passe-temps **que** j'adore
it's a pastime (that) I love (the subject of 'adore' is 'je')

ii) otherwise the relative pronoun is the subject of the verb in the relative clause and the subject pronoun **qui** must be used:

j'ai trouvé un manteau **qui** me plaît
I've found a coat that I like (the subject of 'plaît' is 'qui')

d) *LEQUEL*

i) *forms*

lequel *(which)* has four different forms, as it must agree with the noun to which it refers:

	SINGULAR	PLURAL
MASCULINE	lequel	lesquels
FEMININE	laquelle	lesquelles

which

lequel etc combines with the prepositions **à** and **de** as follows:

à + **lequel**	→	**auquel**
à + **lesquels**	→	**auxquels**
à + **lesquelles**	→	**auxquelles**
de + **lequel**	→	**duquel**
de + **lesquels**	→	**desquels**
de + **lesquelles**	→	**desquelles**

à + **laquelle** and **de** + **laquelle** do not change.

quels sont les sports **auxquels** tu t'intéresses?
what sports are you interested in?

voilà le village près **duquel** on campait
here's the village which we camped near

ii) **qui** or **lequel** with a preposition

When a relative pronoun follows a preposition, the pronoun used is either **qui** or **lequel**. In English, the relative pronoun is seldom used and the preposition is frequently placed after the verb or at the end of the sentence.

qui is generally used after a preposition when referring to people:

où est la fille **avec qui** je dansais?
where's the girl I was dancing with?

montre-moi la personnne **à qui** tu as vendu ton vélo
show me the person you sold your bike to

lequel is often used after a preposition when referring to things:

l'immeuble **dans lequel** j'habite est très moderne
the building (which) I live in is very modern

je ne reconnais pas la voiture **avec laquelle** il est venu
I don't recognize the car (which) he came in

lequel is also used when referring to persons after the prepositions **entre** *(between)* and **parmi** *(among)*:

elle observait les invités **parmi lesquels** elle ne reconnaissait personne
she was watching the guests, none of whom she recognized

il y avait deux candidats, **entre lesquels** nous avons dû choisir
there were two candidates, between whom we had to choose

e) DONT

dont is frequently used instead of **de qui**, **duquel** etc. It means:

i) of which/of whom:
un métier **dont** il est fier
a job (which) he is proud of

Care must be taken with verbs that are normally followed by de + object: **de** is not always translated by 'of' in English, and is sometimes not translated at all (see section on verbal constructions p B53):
voilà les choses **dont** j'ai besoin
here are the things (which) I need

les gens **dont** tu parles ne m'intéressent pas
I'm not interested in the people you're talking about

l'enfant **dont** elle s'occupe n'est pas le sien
the child she is looking after is not hers

ii) whose

dont is also used to translate the English pronoun 'whose'. In French, the construction of the clause that follows **dont** differs from English in two ways:

the noun which follows **dont** is used with the definite article (**le, la, les, l'**):
mon copain, **dont le père** a eu un accident
my friend, whose father had an accident

the word order in French is **dont** + subject + verb + object:
je te présente Hélène, **dont tu connais déjà le frère**
this is Hélène, whose brother you already know

c'était dans une petite rue **dont j'ai oublié le nom**
it was in a small street the name of which I've forgotten

Note that **dont** cannot be used after a preposition:
une jolie maison, près de laquelle il y a un petit lac
a pretty house, next to which there is a small lake

f) OÙ

i) **où** generally means 'where':
l'hôtel **où** on a logé était très confortable
the hotel where we stayed was very comfortable

ii) **où** often replaces a preposition + **lequel**, and means 'in/to/on/at which' etc:
c'est la maison **où** je suis né
that's the house in which/where I was born

une soirée **où** il a invité tous ses amis
a party to which he invited all his friends

iii) **où** is also used to translate 'when' after a noun referring to time:
le jour **où**   la fois **où**
the day when   the time when

le moment **où**
the moment when

tu te rappelles le soir **où** on a raté le dernier métro?
do you remember the evening when we missed the last train?

le jour **où** j'ai eu mon permis de conduire
the day when I got my driving licence

g) CE QUI, CE QUE

ce is used before **qui** and **que** when the relative pronoun does not refer to a specific noun. Both **ce qui** and **ce que** mean 'that which', 'the thing which', and are usually translated by 'what':

i) **ce qui**

ce qui is followed by a verb without a subject (**qui** is the subject):
ce qui s'est passé ne vous regarde pas
what happened is none of your business

ce qui m'étonne, c'est sa patience
what surprises me is his patience

Note that in French, this structure requires a comma between the two clauses, and the second clause must be introduced by **c'est/c'était/ce sera** depending on the tense being used.

ii) **ce que**

ce que (**ce qu'** before a vowel or a silent **h**) is followed by a verb with its own subject (**que** is the object):
fais **ce que** tu veux   c'est **ce qu'**il a dit?
do what you want   is that what he said?

ce que vous me demandez est
impossible
what you're asking me is impossible

iii) **tout ce qui/que**

tout is used in front of **ce qui/que** in
the sense of 'all that', 'everything that':

c'est **tout ce que** je veux
that's all I want

tout ce que tu as fait
everything you did

tu n'as pas eu de mal; c'est **tout ce qui**
compte
you weren't hurt; that's all that matters

iv) **ce qui/que** are often used in indirect
questions (see p27):

je ne sais pas **ce qu'**ils vont dire
I don't know what they'll say

v) when referring to a previous clause, **ce
qui** and **ce que** are translated by 'which':

elle est en retard, **ce qui** arrive souvent
she's late, which happens often

vi) **ce qui/que** are used with a preposition;
ce qui is used as the subject of the verb
in the relative clause and **ce que** is used
as the object of the verb in the relative
clause:

ce n'est pas étonnant, après **ce qui** nous
est arrivé
*it's not surprising, after what happened to
us*

il y a du vrai dans **ce que** vous dites
there is some truth in what you say

When a preposition is required by the verb
in the relative clause, eg penser à,
s'expliquer sur, **quoi** is used instead of **ce
que** and comes after the preposition:

c'est ce **à quoi** je pensais
that's what I was thinking about

voici ce **sur quoi** il devra s'expliquer
this is what he'll have to explain

ce dont is used instead of **de + ce que**
when **de** is the preposition required by the
verb in the relative clause, eg avoir peur
de, avoir besoin de:

c'est **ce dont** j'avais peur
that's what I was afraid of

tu as trouvé **ce dont** tu avais besoin?
did you find what you needed?

7 Verbs

A REGULAR CONJUGATIONS

1 Conjugations

There are three main conjugations in French,
which are determined by the infinitive endings.
The first conjugation verbs, by far the largest
category, end in **-er**, eg aimer and will be
referred to as **-er** verbs; the second conjugation verbs end in **-ir**, eg finir and will be
referred to as **-ir** verbs; the third conjugation
verbs, the smallest category, end in **-re**, eg
vendre and will be referred to as **-re** verbs.

2 Simple tenses

The simple tenses in French are:

- present
- imperfect
- future
- conditional
- past historic
- present subjunctive
- imperfect subjunctive

For the use of the different tenses, see p45.

3 Formation of tenses

The tenses are formed by adding the following
endings to the stem of the verb (usually the
stem of the infinitive) as set out in the following section:

a) PRESENT: stem of the infinitive + the
following endings:

-er verbs	-ir verbs	-re verbs
-e, -es, -e,	-is, -is, -it,	-s, -s, ø,
-ons, -ez,	-issons, -issez,	-ons, -ez, -ent
-ent	-issent	

AIMER	FINIR	VENDRE
j'aime	je finis	je vends
tu aimes	tu finis	tu vends
il aime	il finit	il vend
elle aime	elle finit	elle vend
nous aimons	nous finissons	nous vendons
vous aimez	vous finissez	vous vendez
ils aiment	ils finissent	ils vendent
elles aiment	elles finissent	elles vendent

b) IMPERFECT: stem of the first person plural
of the present indicative (ie the 'nous' form
minus **-ons**) + the following endings:

-ais, -ais, -ait, -ions, -iez, -aient

j'aim**ais**	je finiss**ais**	je vend**ais**
tu aim**ais**	tu finiss**ais**	tu vend**ais**
il aim**ait**	il finiss**ait**	il vend**ait**
elle aim**ait**	elle finiss**ait**	elle vend**ait**
nous aim**ions**	nous finiss**ions**	nous vend**ions**
vous aim**iez**	vous finiss**iez**	vous vend**iez**
ils aim**aient**	ils finiss**aient**	ils vend**aient**
elles aim**aient**	elles finiss**aient**	elles vend**aient**

Note that the only irregular imperfect is être:
j'étais etc.

c) FUTURE: infinitive + the following endings:
-ai, -as, -a, -ons, -ez, -ont

Note that verbs ending in **-re** drop the final **e** of the infinitive.

j'aimer**ai**	je finir**ai**	je vendr**ai**
tu aimer**as**	tu finir**as**	tu vendr**as**
il aimer**a**	il finir**a**	il vendr**a**
elle aimer**a**	elle finir**a**	elle vendr**a**
nous aimer**ons**	nous finir**ons**	nous vendr**ons**
vous aimer**ez**	vous finir**ez**	vous vendr**ez**
ils aimer**ont**	ils finir**ont**	ils vendr**ont**
elles aimer**ont**	elles finir**ont**	elles vendr**ont**

d) CONDITIONAL: infinitive + the following endings:
-ais, -ais, -ait, -ions, -iez, -aient

Note that verbs ending in **-re** drop the final **e** of the infinitive.

j'aimer**ais**	je finir**ais**	je vendr**ais**
tu aimer**ais**	tu finir**ais**	tu vendr**ais**
il aimer**ait**	il finir**ait**	il vendr**ait**
elle aimer**ait**	elle finir**ait**	elle vendr**ait**
nous aimer**ions**	nous finir**ions**	nous vendr**ions**
vous aimer**iez**	vous finir**iez**	vous vendr**iez**
ils aimer**aient**	ils finir**aient**	ils vendr**aient**
elles aimer**aient**	elles finir**aient**	elles vendr**aient**

e) PAST HISTORIC: stem of the infinitive + the following endings:

-er verbs	**-ir** verbs	**-re** verbs
-ai, -as, -a, -âmes, -âtes, -èrent	**-is, -is, -it, -îmes, -îtes, -irent**	**-is, -is, -it, -îmes, -îtes, -irent**

j'aim**ai**	je fin**is**	je vend**is**
tu aim**as**	tu fin**is**	tu vend**is**
il aim**a**	il fin**it**	il vend**it**
elle aim**a**	elle fin**it**	elle vend**it**
nous aim**âmes**	nous fin**îmes**	nous vend**îmes**
vous aim**âtes**	vous fin**îtes**	vous vend**îtes**
ils aim**èrent**	ils fin**irent**	ils vend**irent**
elles aim**èrent**	elles fin**irent**	elles vend**irent**

f) PRESENT SUBJUNCTIVE: stem of the first person plural of the present indicative (ie the 'nous' form minus -ons) + the following endings:
-e, -es, -e, -ions, -iez, -ent

j'aim**e**	je finiss**e**	je vend**e**
tu aim**es**	tu finiss**es**	tu vend**es**
il aim**e**	il finiss**e**	il vend**e**
elle aim**e**	elle finiss**e**	elle vend**e**
nous aim**ions**	nous finiss**ions**	nous vend**ions**
vous aim**iez**	vous finiss**iez**	vous vend**iez**
ils aim**ent**	ils finiss**ent**	ils vend**ent**
elles aim**ent**	elles finiss**ent**	elles vend**ent**

g) IMPERFECT SUBJUNCTIVE: stem of the first person singular of the past historic + the following endings:

-er verbs	**-ir** verbs	**-re** verbs
-asse, -asses, -ât, -assions, -assiez, -assent	**-isse, -isses, -ît, -issions, -issiez, -issent**	**-isse, -isses, -ît, -issions, -issiez, -issent**

j'aim**asse**	je fin**isse**	je vend**isse**
tu aim**asses**	tu fin**isses**	tu vend**isses**
il aim**ât**	il fin**ît**	il vend**ît**
elle aim**ât**	elle fin**ît**	elle vend**ît**
nous aim**assions**	nous fin**issions**	nous vend**issions**
vous aim**assiez**	vous fin**issiez**	vous vend**issiez**
ils aim**assent**	ils fin**issent**	ils vend**issent**
elles aim**assent**	elles fin**issent**	elles vend**issent**

B STANDARD SPELLING IRREGULARITIES

Spelling irregularities affect only **-er** verbs.

1 Verbs ending in -cer and -ger

a) Verbs ending in **-cer** require a cedilla under the **c** (**ç**) before an **a** or an **o** to preserve the soft sound of the **c**: eg commencer (to begin); il commença (he began).

b) Verbs ending in **-ger** require an **-e** after the **g** before an **a** or an **o** to preserve the soft sound of the **g**: eg manger (to eat); je mangeais (I was eating).

Changes to **-cer** and **-ger** verbs occur in the following tenses: present, imperfect, past historic, imperfect subjunctive and present participle.

Verbs

COMMENCER

PRESENT

je commence	je mange
tu commences	tu manges
il commence	il mange
elle commence	elle mange
nous commençons	nous mangeons
vous commencez	vous mangez
ils commencent	ils mangent
elles commencent	elles mangent

MANGER

IMPERFECT

je commençais	je mangeais
tu commençais	tu mangeais
il commençait	il mangeait
elle commençait	elle mangeait
nous commencions	nous mangions
vous commenciez	vous mangiez
ils commençaient	ils mangeaient
elles commençaient	elles mangeaient

PAST HISTORIC

je commençai	je mangeai
tu commenças	tu mangeas
il commença	il mangea
elle commença	elle mangea
nous commençâmes	nous mangeâmes
vous commençâtes	vous mangeâtes
ils commencèrent	ils mangèrent
elles commencèrent	elles mangèrent

IMPERFECT SUBJUNCTIVE

je commençasse	je mangeasse
tu commençasses	tu mangeasses
il commençât	il mangeât
elle commençât	elle mangeât
nous commençassions	nous mangeassions
vous commençassiez	vous mangeassiez
ils commençassent	ils mangeassent
elles commençassent	elles mangeassent

PRESENT PARTICIPLE

commençant   mangeant

2 Verbs with other -er endings

a) Verbs ending in -eler

Verbs ending in **-eler** double the **l** before a silent **e** (ie before **-e**, **-es**, **-ent** of the present indicative and subjunctive, and throughout the future and present conditional): eg appeler *(to call)*.

PRESENT INDICATIVE	**PRESENT SUBJUNCTIVE**
j'appelle	j'appelle
tu appelles	tu appelles
il appelle	il appelle
elle appelle	elle appelle
nous appelons	nous appelions
vous appelez	vous appeliez
ils appellent	ils appellent
elles appellent	elles appellent

FUTURE	**CONDITIONAL**
j'appellerai	j'appellerais
tu appelleras	tu appellerais
il appellera	il appellerait
elle appellera	elle appellerait
nous appellerons	nous appellerions
vous appellerez	vous appelleriez
ils appelleront	ils appelleraient
elles appelleront	elles appelleraient

Note, however, that some verbs in **-eler**, including the following, are conjugated like acheter (see p39):

celer	*to conceal*
congeler	*to (deep-)freeze*
déceler	*to detect, to reveal*
dégeler	*to defrost*
geler	*to freeze*
harceler	*to harass*
marteler	*to hammer*
modeler	*to model*
peler	*to peel*

b) Verbs ending in -eter

Verbs ending in **-eter** double the **t** before a silent **e** (ie before **-e**, **-es**, **-ent** of the present indicative and subjunctive, and throughout the future and conditional): eg jeter *(to throw)*.

PRESENT INDICATIVE	**PRESENT SUBJUNCTIVE**
je jette	je jette
tu jettes	tu jettes
il jette	il jette
elle jette	elle jette
nous jetons	nous jetions
vous jetez	vous jetiez
ils jettent	ils jettent
elles jettent	elles jettent

FUTURE	**CONDITIONAL**
je jetterai	je jetterais
tu jetteras	tu jetterais
il jettera	il jetterait
elle jettera	elle jetterait
nous jetterons	nous jetterions
vous jetterez	vous jetteriez
ils jetteront	ils jetteraient
elles jetteront	elles jetteraient

Note, however, that some verbs in **-eter**, including the following, are conjugated like acheter (see below):

crocheter   *to pick (lock)*
fureter   *to ferret about*
haleter   *to pant*
racheter   *to buy back*

c) *Verbs ending in* **-oyer** *and* **-uyer**

In verbs ending in **-oyer** and **-uyer** the **y** changes to **i** before a silent **e** (ie before **-e**, **-es**, **-ent** of the present indicative and subjunctive, and throughout the future and conditional): eg employer *(to use)* and ennuyer *(to bore)*.

PRESENT INDICATIVE	PRESENT SUBJUNCTIVE
j'emploie	j'emploie
tu emploies	tu emploies
il emploie	il emploie
elle emploie	elle emploie
nous employons	nous employions
vous employez	vous employiez
ils emploient	ils emploient
elles emploient	elles emploient

FUTURE	CONDITIONAL
j'emploierai	j'emploierais
tu emploieras	tu emploierais
il emploiera	il emploierait
elle emploiera	elle emploierait
nous emploierons	nous emploierions
vous emploierez	vous emploieriez
ils emploieront	ils emploieraient
elles emploieront	elles emploieraient

Note that envoyer *(to send)* and renvoyer *(to dismiss)* have an irregular future and conditional: j'enverrai, j'enverrais; je renverrai, je renverrais.

d) *Verbs ending in* **-ayer**

In verbs ending in **-ayer**, eg balayer *(to sweep)*, payer *(to pay)*, essayer *(to try)*, the change from **y** to **i** is optional:

eg je balaie	or	je balaye
je paie	or	je paye
j'essaie	or	j'essaye

e) *Verbs in* **e-** + *consonant* + **-er**

Verbs like acheter, enlever, mener, peser change the (last) **e** of the stem to **è** before a silent **e** (ie before **-e**, **-es**, **-ent** of the present indicative and subjunctive and throughout the future and conditional):

PRESENT INDICATIVE	PRESENT SUBJUNCTIVE
j'achète	j'achète
tu achètes	tu achètes
il achète	il achète
elle achète	elle achète
nous achetons	nous achetions
vous achetez	vous achetiez
ils achètent	ils achètent
elles achètent	elles achètent

FUTURE	CONDITIONAL
j'achèterai	j'achèterais
tu achèteras	tu achèterais
il achètera	il achèterait
elle achètera	elle achèterait
nous achèterons	nous achèterions
vous achèterez	vous achèteriez
ils achèteront	ils achèteraient
elles achèteront	elles achèteraient

Verbs conjugated like acheter include:

achever *to complete*
amener *to bring*
celer *to conceal*
crever *to burst*
crocheter *to pick (lock)*
élever *to raise*
emmener *to take away*
enlever *to remove*
étiqueter *to label*
fureter *to ferret about*
geler *to freeze*
haleter *to pant*
harceler *to harass*
lever *to lift*
marteler *to hammer*
mener *to lead*
modeler *to model*
peler *to peel*
peser *to weigh*
se promener *to go for a walk*
semer *to sow*
soulever *to lift*

f) *Verbs in* **é-** + *consonant* + **-er**

Verbs like espérer *(to hope)* change é to è before a silent **e** in the present indicative and subjunctive. Note, however, that in the future and conditional é is retained.

PRESENT INDICATIVE	PRESENT SUBJUNCTIVE
j'espère	j'espère
tu espères	tu espères
il espère	il espère
elle espère	elle espère

nous espérons
vous espérez
ils espèrent
elles espèrent

nous espérions
vous espériez
ils espèrent
elles espèrent

FUTURE	CONDITIONAL
j'espérerai	j'espérerais
tu espéreras	tu espérerais
il espérera	il espérerait
elle espérera	elle espérerait
nous espérerons	nous espérerions
vous espérerez	vous espéreriez
ils espéreront	ils espéreraient
elles espéreront	elles espéreraient

Verbs conjugated like espérer include verbs in **-éder**, **-érer**, **-éter** etc:

accéder	to accede to
céder	to yield
célébrer	to celebrate
compléter	to complete
considérer	to consider
décéder	to die
digérer	to digest
gérer	to manage
inquiéter	to worry
libérer	to free
opérer	to operate
pénétrer	to penetrate
persévérer	to persevere
posséder	to possess
précéder	to precede
préférer	to prefer
protéger	to protect
récupérer	to recover
refréner	to curb
régler	to rule
régner	to reign
répéter	to repeat, to rehearse
révéler	to reveal
sécher	to dry
succéder	to succeed
suggérer	to suggest
tolérer	to tolerate

C AUXILIARIES AND THE FORMATION OF COMPOUND TENSES

1 Formation

a) The two auxiliary verbs **avoir** and **être** are used with the past participle of a verb to form compound tenses.

b) *The past participle*

The regular past participle is formed by taking the stem of the infinitive and adding the following endings:

-er	-ir	-re
aim(er) + **é**	fin(ir) + **i**	vend(re) + **u**
aimé	**fini**	**vendu**

For the agreement of past participles see p58.

c) *Compound tenses*

In French there are seven compound tenses: perfect, pluperfect, future perfect, past conditional (conditional perfect), past anterior, perfect subjunctive, pluperfect subjunctive.

2 Verbs conjugated with AVOIR

PERFECT	PLUPERFECT
present of **avoir** + past participle	imperfect of **avoir** + past participle
j'ai aimé	j'avais aimé
tu as aimé	tu avais aimé
il a aimé	il avait aimé
elle a aimé	elle avait aimé
nous avons aimé	nous avions aimé
vous avez aimé	vous aviez aimé
ils ont aimé	ils avaient aimé
elles ont aimé	elles avaient aimé

FUTURE PERFECT	PAST CONDITIONAL
future of **avoir** + past participle	conditional of **avoir** + past participle
j'aurai aimé	j'aurais aimé
tu auras aimé	tu aurais aimé
il aura aimé	il aurait aimé
elle aura aimé	elle aurait aimé
nous aurons aimé	nous aurions aimé
vous aurez aimé	vous auriez aimé
ils auront aimé	ils auraient aimé
elles auront aimé	elles auraient aimé

PAST ANTERIOR

past historic of **avoir** + past participle

j'eus aimé
tu eus aimé
il eut aimé
elle eut aimé
nous eûmes aimé
vous eûtes aimé
ils eurent aimé
elles eurent aimé

PERFECT SUBJUNCTIVE	PLUPERFECT SUBJUNCTIVE
present subjunctive of **avoir** + past participle	imperfect subjunctive of **avoir** + **past** participle
j'aie aimé	j'eusse aimé
tu aies aimé	tu eusses aimé
il ait aimé	il eût aimé
elle ait aimé	elle eût aimé
nous ayons aimé	nous eussions aimé
vous ayez aimé	vous eussiez aimé
ils aient aimé	ils eussent aimé
elles aient aimé	elles eussent aimé

3 Verbs conjugated with ÊTRE

PERFECT	PLUPERFECT
present of **être** + past participle	imperfect of **être** + past participle
je suis arrivé(e)	j'étais arrivé(e)
tu es arrivé(e)	tu étais arrivé(e)
Il est arrivé	il était arrivé
elle est arrivée	elle était arrivée
nous sommes arrivé(e)s	nous étions arrivé(e)s
vous êtes arrivé(e)(s)	vous étiez arrivé(e)(s)
ils sont arrivés	ils étaient arrivés
elles sont arrivées	elles étaient arrivées

FUTURE PERFECT	PAST CONDITIONAL
future of **être** + past participle	conditional of **être** + past participle
je serai arrivé(e)	je serais arrivé(e)
tu seras arrivé(e)	tu serais arrivé(e)
il sera arrivé	il serait arrivé
elle sera arrivée	elle serait arrivée
nous serons arrivé(e)s	nous serions arrivé(e)s
vous serez arrivé(e)(s)	vous seriez arrivé(e)(s)
ils seront arrivés	ils seraient arrivés
elles seront arrivées	elles seraient arrivées

PAST ANTERIOR

past historic of **être** + past participle

je fus arrivé(e)
tu fus arrivé(e)
il fut arrivé
elle fut arrivée
nous fûmes arrivé(e)s
vous fûtes arrivé(e)(s)
ils furent arrivés
elles furent arrivées

PERFECT SUBJUNCTIVE	PLUPERFECT SUBJUNCTIVE
present subjunctive of **être** + past participle	imperfect subjunctive of **être** + past participle
je sois arrivé(e)	je fusse arrivé(e)
tu sois arrivé(e)	tu fusses arrivé(e)
il soit arrivé	il fût arrivé
elle soit arrivée	elle fût arrivée
nous soyons arrivé(e)s	nous fussions arrivé(e)s
vous soyez arrivé(e)(s)	vous fussiez arrivé(e)(s)
ils soient arrivés	ils fussent arrivés
elles soient arrivées	elles fussent arrivées

4 AVOIR or ÊTRE?

a) *Verbs conjugated with* **avoir**

The compound tenses of most verbs are formed with **avoir**:

j'**ai** marqué un but
I scored a goal

elle **a** dansé toute la nuit
she danced all night

b) *Verbs conjugated with* **être**

i) all reflexive verbs (see p42):

je me **suis** baigné
I had a bath

ii) the following verbs (mainly of motion):

aller	*to go*
arriver	*to arrive*
descendre	*to go/come down*
entrer	*to go/come in*
monter	*to go/come up*
mourir	*to die*
naître	*to be born*
partir	*to leave*
passer	*to go through, to drop in*
rester	*to remain*
retourner	*to return*
sortir	*to go/come out*
tomber	*to fall*
venir	*to come*

and most of their compounds:

revenir	*to come back*
devenir	*to become*
parvenir	*to reach, to manage to*
rentrer	*to return home*
remonter	*to go up again*
redescendre	*to go down again*

Verbs

Note, however, that **prévenir** *(to warn)* and **subvenir** *(to provide for)* are conjugated with **avoir**:

je t'**avais** prévenu!
I did warn you!

elle **avait** subvenu à toutes les dépenses
she met all the expenses

Note too that **passer** can also be conjugated with **avoir**:

il **a** passé par Paris
he went via Paris

Some of the verbs listed above can take a direct object. In such cases they are conjugated with **avoir** and will have a different meaning:

descendre	to take/bring down, to go down *(the stairs, a slope)*
monter	to take/bring up, to go up *(the stairs, a slope)*
rentrer	to take/bring/put in
retourner	to turn over
sortir	to take/bring out

les élèves **sont sortis** à midi
the pupils came out at midday

les élèves **ont sorti** leurs livres
the pupils took out their books

elle n'**est** pas encore **descendue**
she hasn't come down yet

elle **a descendu** un vieux tableau du grenier
she brought an old painting down from the loft

elle **a descendu** l'escalier
she came down the stairs

les prisonniers **sont montés** sur le toit
the prisoners climbed on to the roof

le garçon **a monté** les bouteilles de vin de la cave
the waiter brought the bottles of wine up from the cellar

nous **sommes rentrés** tard
we got home late

j'**ai rentré** la voiture dans le garage
I put the car in the garage

je **serais retourné** à Paris
I would have returned to Paris

le jardinier **a retourné** le sol
the gardener turned over the soil

ils **sont sortis** de la piscine
they got out of the swimming pool

il **a sorti** les mains de ses poches
he took his hands out of his pockets

D REFLEXIVE VERBS

1 Definition

Reflexive verbs are so called because they 'reflect' the action back onto the subject. Reflexive verbs are always accompanied by a reflexive pronoun, eg in the following sentence:

I look at myself in the mirror

'myself' is the reflexive pronoun.

je lave la voiture   je me lave
I'm washing the car   *I'm washing myself*

j'ai couché le bébé
I put the baby to bed

je me suis couché
I went to bed (I put myself to bed)

2 Reflexive pronouns

They are:

PERSON	SINGULAR	PLURAL
1st	**me (m')** *myself*	**nous** *ourselves*
2nd	**te (t')** *yourself*	**vous** *yourself/selves*
3rd	**se (s')** *himself, herself, itself, oneself*	**se (s')** *themselves*

Note:

a) **m'**, **t'** and **s'** are used instead of **me**, **te** and **se** in front of a vowel or a silent **h**:

tu **t'**amuses? – non, je **m'**ennuie
are you enjoying yourself? – no, I'm bored

il **s'**habille dans la salle de bain
he gets dressed in the bathroom

b) French reflexive pronouns are often not translated in English:

je **me** demande si ...
I wonder if ...

ils **se** moquent de moi
they're making fun of me

c) Plural reflexive pronouns can also be used to express reciprocal actions; in this case they are translated by 'each other' or 'one another':

nous **nous** détestons
we hate one another

Verbs

ils ne **se** parlent pas
they're not talking to each other

d) **se** can mean 'ourselves' or 'each other'
when it is used with the pronoun **on**
meaning 'we' (see p24):

on s'est perdu   on se connaît
we got lost   *we know each other*

3 Position of reflexive pronouns

Reflexive pronouns are placed immediately
before the verb, except in positive commands,
where they follow the verb and are linked to
it by a hyphen:

tu **te** dépêches?   dépêchons-**nous**!
will you hurry up?   *let's hurry!*

ne **t'**inquiète pas   ne **vous** fiez pas à lui
don't worry   *don't trust him*

Note that reflexive pronouns change to
disjunctive pronouns in positive commands:

elle doit **se** reposer   repose-**toi**
she needs to rest   *have a rest*

4 Conjugation of reflexive verbs

a) *Simple tenses*

These are conjugated in the same way as
non-reflexive verbs, except that a reflexive
pronoun is used.

b) *Compound tenses*

These are conjugated using the auxiliary
être followed by the past participle of the
verb.

Full conjugation tables are given in the
second part of this supplement.

5 Agreement of the past participle

a) In most cases, the reflexive pronoun is a
direct object and the past participle of the
verb agrees in number and in gender with
the reflexive pronoun:

il s'est **trompé**   elle s'est **endormie**
he made a mistake   *she fell asleep*

ils se sont **excusés**   elles se sont **assises**
they apologized   *they sat down*

b) When the reflexive pronoun is used as an
indirect object, the past participle does not
change:

nous nous sommes **écrit**
we wrote to each other

elle se l'est **acheté**
she bought it for herself

elles se sont **parlé**
they spoke to each other

les années se sont **succédé**
one year followed another

When the reflexive verb has a direct object,
the reflexive pronoun is the indirect object
of the reflexive verb and the past participle
does not agree with it:

Caroline s'est **tordu** la cheville
Caroline sprained her ankle

vous vous êtes **lavé** les mains, les filles?
did you wash your hands, girls?

elles se sont **égratigné** les genoux
they scratched their knees

6 Common reflexive verbs

s'en aller   s'éloigner (de)
to go away   *to move away (from)*

se moquer de   s'amuser
to laugh at   *to have fun*

s'endormir   s'occuper de
to fall asleep   *to take care of*

s'appeler   s'ennuyer
to be called   *to be bored*

se passer   s'approcher (de)
to happen   *to come near*

s'étonner (de)   se passer de
to be surprised (at) *to do without*

s'arrêter   s'excuser (de)
to stop   *to apologize (for)*

se promener   s'asseoir
to go for a walk   *to sit down*

se fâcher   se rappeler
to get angry/fall out *to remember*

s'attendre à   s'écrier
to expect   *to cry out/exclaim*

se raser   se baigner
to shave   *to have a bath*

s'habiller   se renseigner
to get dressed   *to make enquiries*

se battre   se hâter
to fight   *to hurry*

se ressembler   se blesser
to look alike   *to hurt oneself*

s'inquiéter   se retourner
to worry   *to turn round*

se coucher   s'installer
to go to bed   *to settle down*

se réveiller   se débarrasser de
to wake up   *to get rid of*

Verbs

se laver	se sauver
to wash	*to run away*
se demander	se lever
to wonder	*to get up*
se souvenir (de)	se dépêcher
to remember	*to hurry*
se mêler de	se taire
to meddle with	*to be/keep quiet*
se déshabiller	se mettre à
to undress	*to start*
se tromper	se diriger vers
to be mistaken	*to move towards*
se mettre en route	se trouver
to set off	*to be (situated)*

E IMPERSONAL VERBS

1 Conjugation

Impersonal verbs are used only in the third person singular and in the infinitive. The subject is always the impersonal pronoun **il** (= it).

il neige   **il** y a du brouillard
it's snowing   *it's foggy*

2 List of impersonal verbs

a) *verbs describing the weather:*

i) **faire** + adjective:

il fait beau/chaud   **il fait** frais/froid
it's fine/warm   *it's cool/cold*

il fera beau demain
the weather will be good tomorrow

il va faire très froid
it will be very cold

ii) **faire** + noun:

il fait beau temps
the weather is nice

il fait mauvais temps
the weather is bad

il fait jour   **il fait** nuit
it's daylight   *it's dark*

iii) other impersonal verbs and verbs used impersonally to describe the weather:

il gèle	(geler)	*it's freezing*
il grêle	(grêler)	*it's hailing*
il neige	(neiger)	*it's snowing*
il pleut	(pleuvoir)	*it's raining*
il tonne	(tonner)	*there's thunder*

Note that some of these verbs may be used personally:

je gèle
I'm freezing

iv) **il y a** + noun:

il y a des nuages	*it's cloudy*
il y a du brouillard	*it's foggy*
il y a du verglas	*it's icy*

b) **être**

i) **il est** + noun:

il est cinq heures
it's five o'clock

il était une fois un géant
once upon a time there was a giant

ii) **il est** + adjective + **de** + infinitive:

il est difficile **de**	*it's difficult to*
il est facile **de**	*it's easy to*
il est nécessaire **de**	*it's necessary to*
il est inutile **de**	*it's useless to*
il est possible **de**	*it's possible to*

il est difficile **d'**en parler
it's difficult to talk about it

Note that the indirect object pronoun in French corresponds to the English 'for me', 'for him' etc:

il m'est difficile d'en parler
it's difficult for me to talk about it

iii) **il est** + adjective + **que**:

il est douteux **que**	*it's doubtful that*
il est évident **que**	*it's clear that*
il est possible **que**	*it's possible that*
il est probable **que**	*it's probable that*
il est peu probable **que**	*it's unlikely that*
il est vrai **que**	*it's true that*

Note that **que** may be followed by the indicative or the subjunctive (see p49):

il est probable **qu'il ne viendra pas**
he probably won't come

il est peu probable **qu'il vienne**
it's unlikely that he'll come

c) **arriver**, **se passer** (to happen)

il est arrivé une chose curieuse
a strange thing happened

que **se passe-t-il**?
what's happening?

d) **exister** (to exist), **rester** (to remain), **manquer** (to be missing)

il existe trois exemplaires de ce livre
there are three copies of this book

il me **restait** un euro
I had one euro left

il me **manque** 4 euros
I am 4 euros short

e) **paraître, sembler** *(to seem)*
il paraîtrait/semblerait qu'il ait changé d'avis
it would appear that he has changed his mind

il paraît qu'il va se marier
it seems he's going to get married

il me **semble** que le professeur s'est trompé
it seems to me that the teacher has made a mistake

f) other common impersonal verbs

i) **s'agir de** *(to be a matter of)* may be followed by a noun, a pronoun or an infinitive:
il s'agit de ton avenir
it's about your future

de quoi **s'agit-il?**
what's it about?

Il s'agit de trouver le coupable
we must find the culprit

ii) **falloir** *(to be necessary)* may be followed by a noun, an infinitive or the subjunctive:
il faut deux heures pour aller à Paris
it takes two hours to get to Paris

il me **faut** plus de temps
I need more time

il faudra rentrer plus tôt ce soir
we'll have to come home earlier tonight

il faut que tu parles à Papa
you have to speak to Dad

iii) **suffire** *(to be enough)* may be followed by a noun, an infinitive or the subjunctive:
il suffit de peu de choses pour être heureux
it doesn't take much to be happy

il suffit de passer le pont
you just have to cross the bridge

il suffira qu'ils te donnent le numéro de téléphone
they will only have to give you the telephone number

iv) **valoir mieux** *(to be better)* may be followed by an infinitive or the subjunctive:

il vaudrait mieux prendre le car
it would be better to take the coach

il vaut mieux que vous ne sortiez pas seule le soir
you'd better not go out alone at night

F TENSES

For the formation of the different tenses, see p36 and p38.

Note that French has no continuous tenses (as in 'I am eating', 'I was going', 'I will be arriving'). The 'be' and '-ing' parts of English continuous tenses are not translated as separate words. Instead, the equivalent tense is used in French:

je mange
I am eating

je mangerai
I will be eating

1 PRESENT

The present is used to describe what someone does/something that happens regularly, or what someone is doing/something that is happening at the time of speaking.

a) *regular actions*
Il travaille dans un bureau
he works in an office

je **lis** rarement le journal
I seldom read the paper

b) *continuous actions*
ne le dérangez pas, il **travaille**
don't disturb him, he's working

je ne peux pas venir, je **garde** mon petit frère
I can't come, I'm looking after my little brother

Note that the continuous nature of the action can also be expressed by using the phrase **être en train de** *(to be in the process of)* + infinitive:
je suis en train de cuisiner
I'm (busy) cooking

c) *immediate future*
je **pars** demain
I'm leaving tomorrow

However, the present cannot be used after **quand** and other conjunctions of time when the future is implied (see p47):
je le ferai **quand j'aurai** le temps
I'll do it when I have the time

Verbs

d) *general truths*

la vie **est** dure
life is hard

2 IMPERFECT

The imperfect is a past tense used to express what someone was doing or what someone used to do, or to describe something in the past. The imperfect refers particularly to something that continued over a period of time, as opposed to something that happened at a specific point in time.

a) *continuous actions*

The imperfect describes an action that was happening, often when something else took place:

il **prenait** un bain quand le téléphone a sonné
he was having a bath when the phone rang

excuse-moi, je **pensais** à autre chose
I'm sorry, I was thinking of something else

Note that the continuous nature of the action can be emphasized by using **être en train de** + infinitive:

j'étais en train de faire le ménage
I was (busy) doing the housework

b) *regular actions in the past*

je le **voyais** souvent quand il **habitait** dans le quartier
I used to see him often when he lived in this area

quand il était plus jeune il **voyageait** beaucoup
when he was younger he used to travel a lot

c) *description in the past*

il **faisait** beau ce jour-là
the weather was good that day

c'**était** formidable!
it was great!

elle **portait** une robe bleue
she wore a blue dress

elle **donnait** sur la rue
it looked onto the street

3 PERFECT

The perfect tense is a compound past tense, used to express single actions which have been completed. What someone did, has done or has been doing, or something that has happened or has been happening are all expressed using the perfect tense:

je l'**ai envoyé** lundi
I sent it on Monday

on **est sorti** hier soir
we went out last night

tu **t'es** bien **amusé**?
did you have a good time?

je ne l'**ai** pas **vu** de toute la journée
I haven't seen him all day

j'**ai lu** toute la journée
I've been reading all day

tu **as** déjà **mangé**?
have you eaten?

In English, the simple past ('did', 'went', 'prepared') is used to describe both single and repeated actions in the past. In French, the perfect only describes single actions in the past, while repeated actions are expressed by the imperfect (they are sometimes signposted by 'used to'). Thus 'I went' should be translated 'j'allais' or 'je suis allé' depending on the nature of the action:

après dîner, **je suis allé** en ville
after dinner I went into town

l'an dernier, **j'allais** plus souvent au théâtre
last year I went to the theatre more often

4 PAST HISTORIC

This tense is used in the same way as the perfect tense, to describe a single, completed action in the past (what someone did or something that happened). It is a literary tense, not common in everyday spoken French; it is found mainly as a narrative tense in written form:

le piéton ne **vit** pas arriver la voiture
the pedestrian didn't see the car coming

5 PLUPERFECT

This compound tense is used to express what someone had done/had been doing or something that had happened or had been happening:

il n'**avait** pas **voulu** aller avec eux
he hadn't wanted to go with them

elle était essoufflée parce qu'elle **avait couru**
she was out of breath because she'd been running

However, the pluperfect is not used as in English with **depuis** *(for, since)*, or with **venir**

de + infinitive (*to have just done something*).
For details see p B31:

il **neigeait** depuis une semaine
it had been snowing for a week

les pompiers **venaient d'**arriver
the firemen had just arrived

6 FUTURE

This tense is used to express what someone
will do or will be doing or something that will
happen or will be happening:

je **ferai** la vaisselle demain
I'll do the dishes tomorrow

j'**arriverai** tard
I'll be arriving late

Note that the future and not the present, as in
English, is used in time clauses introduced by
quand *(when)* or other conjunctions of time
where the future is implied (see section 11):

il **viendra** quand il le **pourra**
he'll come when he can

French makes frequent use of **aller** + infinitive
(to be about to do something) to express the
immediate future:

je **vais** vous **expliquer** ce qui s'est passé
I'll explain (to you) what happened

il **va déménager** la semaine prochaine
he's moving house next week

7 FUTURE PERFECT

This compound tense is used to describe what
someone will have done or will have been
doing in the future or to describe something
that will have happened in the future:

j'**aurai** bientôt **fini**
I will soon have finished

In particular, it is used instead of the English
perfect in time clauses introduced by **quand**
or other conjunctions of time where the future
is implied (see section 11):

appelle-moi **quand tu auras fini**
call me when you've finished

on rentrera **dès qu'on aura fait** les
courses
*we'll come back as soon as we've done the
shopping*

8 PAST ANTERIOR

This tense is used instead of the pluperfect to
express an action that preceded another action

in the past (ie a past in the past). It is usually
introduced by a conjunction of time (translated
by 'when', 'as soon as', 'after' etc) and the main
verb is in the past historic:

il se coucha dès qu'ils **furent partis**
he went to bed as soon as they'd left

à peine **eut**-elle **raccroché** que le
téléphone sonna
*she'd hardly hung up when the telephone
rang*

9 Use of tenses with 'depuis' (for, since)

a) The present must be used instead of the
perfect to describe actions which started in
the past and are still continuing:

il **habite** ici depuis trois ans
he's been living here for three years

elle t'**attend** depuis ce matin
she's been waiting for you since this morning

Note, however, that the perfect, not the
present, is used when the clause is negative
or when the action has been completed:

il **n'a pas pris** de vacances depuis
longtemps
he hasn't taken any holidays for a long time

j'**ai fini** depuis un bon moment
I've been finished for quite a while

Note:

i) **il y a ... que** or **voilà ... que** are also
used with the present tense to translate
'for':
it's been ringing for ten minutes
ça sonne depuis dix minutes
il y a dix minutes que ça sonne
voilà dix minutes que ça sonne

ii) **depuis que** is used when 'since' introduces a clause, ie when there is a verb
following **depuis**:
elle dort **depuis que** vous êtes partis
she's been sleeping since you left

iii) Do not confuse **depuis** *(for, since)* and
pendant *(for, during)*: **depuis** refers to
the starting point of an action which is still
going on and **pendant** refers to the
duration of an action which is over and is
used with the perfect:
il vit ici **depuis** deux mois
he's been living here for two months

il a vécu ici **pendant** deux mois
he lived here for two months

b) The imperfect must be used instead of the pluperfect to describe an action which had started in the past and was still going on at a given time:

elle le **connaissait** depuis son enfance
she had known him since her childhood

il **attendait** depuis trois heures quand on est arrivé
he had been waiting for three hours when we arrived

Note, however, that if the sentence is negative or if the action has been completed, the pluperfect and not the imperfect is used:

je n'**étais** pas **allé** au théâtre depuis des années
I hadn't been to the theatre for years

il **était parti** depuis peu
he'd been gone for a short while

Note:

i) **il y avait ... que** + imperfect is also used to translate 'for':

she'd been living alone for a long time
elle habitait seule depuis longtemps
il y avait longtemps **qu'**elle habitait seule

ii) **depuis que** is used when 'since' introduces a clause; if it describes an action which was still going on at the time, it can be followed by the imperfect, otherwise it is followed by the pluperfect:

il pleuvait **depuis que** nous **étions** en vacances
it had been raining since we had been on holiday

il pleuvait **depuis que** nous **étions arrivés**
it had been raining since we arrived

iii) Do not confuse **depuis** and **pendant**: **depuis** refers to the starting point of an action which is still going on and **pendant** refers to the duration of an action which is over; **pendant** is used with the pluperfect:

j'y travaillais **depuis** un an
I had been working there for a year

j'y avais travaillé **pendant** un an
I had worked there for a year

10 Use of tenses with 'venir de'

venir de + infinitive means 'to have just done'.

a) If it describes something that has just happened, it is used in the present instead of the perfect:

l'avion **vient d'**arriver
the plane has just arrived

je **viens de** te le dire!
I've just told you!

b) If it describes something that had just happened, it is used in the imperfect instead of the pluperfect:

le film **venait de** commencer
the film had just started

je **venais de** rentrer
I'd just got home

11 Use of tenses after conjunctions of time

quand	*when*
tant que	*as long as*
dès/aussitôt que	*as soon as*
lorsque	*when*
pendant que	*while*

Verbs which follow these conjunctions must be used in the following tenses:

a) future instead of present:

je te téléphonerai **quand** je **serai** prêt
I'll phone you when I'm ready

elle ira le voir **dès qu'**elle le **pourra**
she'll go to see him as soon as she can

b) future perfect instead of perfect when the future is implied:

on rentrera **dès qu'**on **aura fini** les courses
we'll come back as soon as we've done the shopping

je t'appellerai **dès qu'**il **sera arrivé**
I'll call you as soon as he's arrived

c) conditional present/perfect instead of perfect/pluperfect in indirect speech:

il a dit qu'il sortirait **quand** il **aurait fini**
he said that he would come out when he had finished

For the tenses of the subjunctive and conditional, see G1 and G3.

G MOODS

1 THE SUBJUNCTIVE

In everyday spoken French, the only two subjunctive tenses that are used are the present and the perfect. The imperfect and the pluperfect subjunctive are found mainly in literature or in texts of a formal nature.

The subjunctive is always preceded by the conjunction **que** and is used in subordinate clauses when the subject of the subordinate clause is different from the subject of the main verb.

Some clauses introduced by **que** take the indicative. The subjunctive must be used after the following:

a) Verbs of emotion:

être content que *to be pleased that*
être désolé que *to be sorry that*
être étonné que *to be surprised that*
être heureux que *to be happy that*
être surpris que *to be surprised that*
être triste que *to be sad that*
avoir peur que ... ne *to be afraid/to fear that*
craindre que ... ne *to be afraid/to fear that*
regretter que *to be sorry that*

Ils étaient contents que j'aille les voir
they were pleased (that) I went to visit them

je serais très étonné qu'il **mente**
I would be very surprised if he was lying

je regrette que tu ne **puisses** pas y aller
I'm sorry (that) you can't go

Note that **ne** is used after several verbs in the subjunctive mood but it does not have a negative meaning in itself and is not translated in English:

je crains que l'avion **ne soit** en retard
I'm afraid (that) the plane will be late

j'ai bien peur qu'il **ne soit** déjà trop tard
I'm very much afraid (that) it's already too late

pour éviter que la situation **ne s'aggrave**
to prevent the situation from getting any worse

b) Verbs of wishing and willing:

aimer que *to like*
désirer que *to wish (that)*
préférer que *to prefer (that)*
souhaiter que *to wish (that)*
vouloir que *to want*

Note that in English, such verbs are often used in the following type of construction: verb of willing + object + infinitive (eg I'd like you to listen); this type of construction

is impossible in French, where a subjunctive clause has to be used:

je souhaite que tu **réussisses**
I hope you will succeed

il aimerait que je lui **écrive** plus souvent
he'd like me to write to him more often

voulez-vous que je vous y **amène** en voiture?
would you like me to drive you there?

préférez-vous que je **rappelle** demain?
would you rather I called back tomorrow?

c) Impersonal constructions (expressing necessity, possibility, doubt, denial, preference):

il faut que
it is necessary (that) (must)
il est nécessaire que
it is necessary that (must)
il est important que
it is important (that)
il est possible que
it is possible that (may)
il se peut que
it is possible that (may)
il est impossible que
it is impossible (that) (can't)
il est douteux que
it is doubtful whether
il est peu probable que
it is unlikely that
il semble que
it seems (that)
il est préférable que
it is preferable (that)
il vaut mieux que
it is better (that) (had better)
c'est dommage que
it is a pity (that)

Note that these expressions may be used in any appropriate tense:

il faut absolument que je le leur **dise**
I simply must tell them

il était important que tu le **saches**
it was important that you should know

il se pourrait qu'elle **change** d'avis
she might change her mind

il est peu probable qu'ils s'y **intéressent**
they're unlikely to be interested in that

il semble qu'elle **ait** raison
she appears to be right

il vaudrait mieux que tu ne **promettes** rien
you'd better not promise anything

Verbs

c'est dommage que vous vous **soyez**
manqués
it's a pity you missed each other

d) Some verbs and impersonal constructions
expressing doubt or uncertainty (mainly
used negatively or interrogatively):
douter que
to doubt (that)
(ne pas) croire que
(not) to believe (that)
(ne pas) penser que
(not) to think (that)
(ne pas) être sûr que
(not) to be sure that
il n'est pas certain que
it isn't certain that
il n'est pas évident que
it isn't obvious that
il n'est pas sûr que
it isn't certain that
il n'est pas vrai que
it isn't true that

je doute fort qu'il **veuille** t'aider
*I very much doubt whether he'll want to help
you*

croyez-vous qu'il y **ait** des places libres?
do you think there are any seats available?

on n'était pas sûr que ce **soit** le bon
endroit
we weren't sure that it was the right place

il n'était pas certain qu'elle **puisse** gagner
it wasn't certain whether she could win

e) **attendre que** (to wait until someone does
something or something happens, to wait for
someone to do something or for something
to happen):
attendons qu'il **revienne**
let's wait until he comes back

f) Some subordinating conjunctions:

bien que	*although*
quoique	*although*
sans que	*without*
pour que	*so that*
afin que	*so that*
à condition que	*provided that*
pourvu que	*provided that*
jusqu'à ce que	*until*
en attendant que	*until*
avant que ... (ne)	*before*
à moins que ... (ne)	*unless*
de peur que ... ne	*for fear that*
de crainte que ... ne	*for fear that*

de sorte que	*so that*
de façon que	*so that*
de manière que	*so that*

Note that when **ne** is shown in brackets, it
may follow the conjunction, although it is
seldom used in spoken French; it does not
have a negative meaning, and is not
translated in English.

il est allé travailler bien qu'il **soit** malade
he went to work although he was ill

elle est entrée sans que je la **voie**
she came in without me seeing her

voilà de l'argent pour que tu **puisses** aller
au cinéma
*here's some money so that you can go to the
cinema*

d'accord, pourvu que tu me **promettes** de
ne pas le répéter
*all right, as long as you promise not to tell
anyone*

tu l'as revu avant qu'il **(ne) parte**?
did you see him again before he left?

je le ferai demain, à moins que ce **(ne) soit**
urgent
I'll do it tomorrow, unless it's urgent

elle n'a pas fait de bruit de peur qu'il **ne
se réveille**
she didn't make any noise in case he woke

parle moins fort de sorte qu'elle **ne** nous
entende pas
talk more quietly so that she doesn't hear us

Note that when **de façon/manière que**
(so that) expresses a result, as opposed to a
purpose, the indicative is used instead of the
subjunctive:

il a fait du bruit de sorte qu'elle l'**a
entendu**
*he made some noise, and as a result she
heard him*

g) A superlative or adjectives like **premier**
(first), **dernier** *(last)*, **seul** *(only)* followed by
qui or **que**:
c'était le coureur le plus rapide que j'**aie**
jamais vu
he was the fastest runner I ever saw

Note, however, that the indicative is used
with a statement of fact rather than the
expression of an opinion:
c'est lui qui me l'**a dit**
it was he who told me

h) Negative and indefinite pronouns (eg **rien**, **personne**, **quelqu'un**) followed by **qui** or **que**:

je ne connais personne qui **fasse** aussi bien les crêpes
I don't know anyone who can make such good crêpes

il n'y a aucune chance qu'il **réussisse**
he hasn't got a chance of succeeding

ils cherchent quelqu'un qui **puisse** garder le bébé
they're looking for someone who can look after the baby

2 AVOIDING THE SUBJUNCTIVE

Note, however, that the subjunctive is not used if the verbs in both clauses have the same subject. The infinitive will be used in the subordinate clause instead, sometimes introduced by a preposition (**à** or **de**) (see p54).

a) **de** + infinitive replaces the subjunctive after:

i) verbs of emotion:
j'ai été étonné **d'apprendre** la nouvelle
I was surprised to hear the news

il regrette **de** ne pas **être arrivé** plus tôt
he's sorry he didn't arrive earlier

tu as peur **de** ne pas **avoir** assez d'argent?
are you worried you won't have enough money?

ii) **attendre** *(to wait)* and **douter** *(to doubt)*:
j'attendrai **d'avoir bu** mon café
I'll wait until I've drunk my coffee

iii) most impersonal constructions:
il serait préférable **de** les en **informer** tout de suite
it would be better to let them know immediately

il est indispensable **de parler** une langue étrangère
it's essential to be able to speak a foreign language

iv) most conjunctions:
il est resté dans la voiture **afin de** ne pas **se mouiller**
he stayed in the car so as not to get wet

j'ai lu **avant de m'endormir**
I read before falling asleep

tu peux sortir **à condition de rentrer**

avant minuit
you can go out, as long as you're back before midnight

b) **à** + infinitive replaces the subjunctive after:

i) **de façon/manière**
mets la liste sur la table **de manière à** ne pas l'**oublier**
put the list on the table so that you won't forget it

ii) **premier, seul, dernier**
il a été **le seul à s'excuser**
he was the only one who apologized

c) The infinitive without any linking preposition replaces the subjunctive after:

i) verbs of wishing and willing:
Je voudrais **sortir** avec toi
I'd like to go out with you

ii) **il faut, il vaut mieux**:
il vous **faudra prendre** des chèques de voyage
you'll have to take some traveller's cheques

il lui **a fallu recommencer** à zéro
he had to start all over again

il **vaudrait mieux** lui **apporter** des fleurs que des bonbons
it would be better to take her flowers than sweets

Note that **il faut** + infinitive is used to state a generality. If one particular person etc is the subject of the action, an indirect object is used:

il **faut réserver à** l'avance
you have to book in advance

il lui **faut se dépêcher**
he has to hurry

iii) verbs of thinking:
je ne **crois** pas le **connaître**
I don't think I know him

tu **penses être** chez toi à cinq heures?
do you think you'll be home at five?

iv) **pour** and **sans**:
le car est reparti **sans** nous **attendre**
the coach left without waiting for us

j'économise **pour pouvoir** acheter une moto
I'm saving up to buy a motorbike

Verbs

3 THE CONDITIONAL

a) *The conditional present*

i) The conditional present is used to describe what someone would do or would be doing, or what would happen (if something else were to happen):

si j'avais de l'argent, je **ferais** le tour du monde
if I had money, I would travel around the world

Note that when the main verb is in the conditional present, the verb after **si** is in the imperfect.

ii) It is also used in indirect questions or reported speech instead of the future:

il ne m'a pas dit s'il **viendrait**
he didn't tell me whether he would come

b) *The conditional perfect (or past conditional)*

The conditional perfect or past conditional is used to express what someone would have done or would have been doing or what would have happened:

si j'avais su, je n'**aurais** rien **dit**
if I had known, I wouldn't have said anything

qu'**aurais**-je **fait** sans toi?
what would I have done without you?

Note that if the main verb is in the conditional perfect, the verb introduced by **si** is in the pluperfect.

c) *Tenses after* **si**

The tense of the verb introduced by **si** is determined by the tense of the verb in the main clause:

MAIN VERB	VERB FOLLOWING 'SI'
conditional present	→ imperfect
conditional perfect	→ pluperfect

je te le **dirais** si je le **savais**
I would tell you if I knew

je te l'**aurais dit** si je l'**avais su**
I would have told you if I had known

The conditional and the future should never be used with **si** unless **si** means 'whether' (ie when it introduces an indirect question):

je me demande **si** j'y **serais arrivé** sans toi
I wonder if I would have managed without you

4 THE IMPERATIVE

a) *Definition*

The imperative is used to give commands or polite instructions, or to make requests or suggestions; these can be positive ('do!') or negative ('don't!'):

mange ta soupe! n'**aie** pas peur!
eat your soup!   *don't be afraid!*

partons!   **entrez**!
let's go!   *come in!*

faites attention! n'**hésitez** pas!
be careful!   *don't hesitate!*

tournez à droite à la poste
turn right at the post office

b) *Forms*

The imperative has only three forms, which are the same as the **tu**, **nous** and **vous** forms of the present tense, but without the subject pronoun:

	-ER VERBS	-IR VERBS	-RE VERBS
'tu' form:	**regarde** watch	**choisis** choose	**attends** wait
'nous' form:	**regardons** let's watch	**choisissons** let's choose	**attendons** let's wait
'vous' form:	**regardez** watch	**choisissez** choose	**attendez** wait

Note:

i) The **-s** of the **tu** form of **-er** verbs is dropped, except when **y** or **en** follow the verb:

parle-lui!   **parles-en** avec lui
speak to him!   *speak to him about it*

achète du sucre! **achètes-en** un kilo
buy some sugar!   *buy a kilo (of it)*

ii) The distinction between the subject pronouns **tu** and **vous** (see p27) applies to the **tu** and **vous** forms of the imperative:

prends ta sœur avec toi
take your sister with you

prenez le plat du jour, Monsieur; c'est du poulet rôti
have today's special, sir; it's roast chicken

ouvrez vos livres à la page 24
open your books at page 24

c) *Negative commands*

In negative commands, the verb is placed between **ne** and **pas** (or the second part of other negative expressions):

ne fais pas ça!   **ne dites rien**!
don't do that!   *don't say anything!*

d) *Imperative with object pronouns*

In positive commands, object pronouns come after the verb and are attached to it by a hyphen. In negative commands, they come before the verb (see p27):

dites-moi ce qui s'est passé
tell me what happened

attendons-les!
let's wait for them

prends-en bien soin, ne l'abîme pas!
take good care of it, don't damage it!

ne **le leur dis** pas!
don't tell them (that)!

ne **les écoutez** pas
don't listen to them

e) *Imperative of reflexive verbs*

The position of the reflexive pronoun of reflexive verbs is the same as that of object pronouns:

tais toi!   **levez-vous!**
be quiet!   *get up!*

méfiez-vous de lui   **arrêtons-nous** ici
don't trust him   *let's stop here*

ne **nous plaignons** pas
let's not complain

ne **t'approche** pas plus!
don't come any closer!

f) *Alternatives to the imperative*

i) infinitive

the infinitive is often used instead of the imperative in written instructions and in recipes:

s'adresser au concierge
see the caretaker

ne pas **fumer**
no smoking

verser le lait et bien **mélanger**
pour in the milk and mix well

ii) subjunctive

as the imperative has no third person (singular or plural), **que** + subjunctive is used for giving orders in the third person:

que personne ne me **dérange!**
don't let anyone disturb me!

qu'il **entre!**
let him (come) in!

qu'elle **parte**, je m'en fiche!
I don't care if she goes!

g) *Idiomatic usage*

The imperative is used in spoken French in many set phrases. Here are some of the most common ones:

allons donc!   **dis/dites** donc!
you don't say!   *by the way!*
                hey! (protest)

tiens/tenez!   **tiens!** voilà le facteur
here you are!   *ah! here comes the*
                postman

tiens (donc)!   **tiens! tiens!**
(oh) really?   *well, well!*

voyons!   **voyons** donc!
come (on) now!   *let's see now*

H THE INFINITIVE

1 The infinitive is the basic form of the verb. It is recognizable by its ending, which is found in three forms corresponding to the three conjugations: **-er**, **-ir**, **-re**.

These endings give the verb the meaning 'to ...':

acheter   **choisir**   **vendre**
to buy   to choose   to sell

Note that although this applies as a general rule, the French infinitive will often be translated by a verbal construction ending in -ing (see p82).

2 Uses of the infinitive

The infinitive can follow a preposition, a verb, a noun, a pronoun, an adverb or an adjective.

a) *After a preposition*

The infinitive can be used after some prepositions (**pour**, **avant de**, **sans**, **au lieu de**, **afin de** etc):

sans **attendre**   avant de **partir**
without waiting   *before leaving*

b) *After a verb*

There are three main constructions when a verb is followed by an infinitive:

i) Verbs followed by the infinitive with no linking preposition:

● verbs of wishing and willing, eg:

vouloir   to want
souhaiter   to wish
désirer   to wish, to want
espérer   to hope

Verbs

voulez-vous **manger** maintenant ou plus tard?
do you want to eat now or later?

je souhaite **parler** au directeur
I wish to speak to the manager

● verbs of seeing, hearing and feeling, eg:

voir	to see
écouter	to listen to
regarder	to watch
sentir	to feel, to smell
entendre	to hear

je l'ai vu **jouer**
I've seen him play

tu m'as regardé **danser**?
did you watch me dance?

j'ai entendu quelqu'un **crier**
I heard someone shout

● verbs of motion, eg:

aller	to go
monter	to go/come up
venir	to come
entrer	to go/come in
rentrer	to go/come home
sortir	to go/come out
descendre	to go/come down

je viendrai te **voir** demain
I'll come and see you tomorrow

il est descendu **laver** la voiture
he went down to wash the car

va **acheter** le journal
go and buy the paper

Note that in English, 'to come' and 'to go' may be linked to the verb that follows by 'and'; 'and' is not translated in French.

aller + infinitive can be used to express a future action:

qu'est-ce que tu **vas faire** demain?
what are you going to do tomorrow?

● modal auxiliary verbs (see p60)

● verbs of liking and disliking, eg:

aimer	to like
adorer	to love
aimer mieux	to prefer
détester	to hate
préférer	to prefer

tu aimes **voyager**?
do you like travelling?

je déteste **aller** à la campagne
I hate going to the country

j'adore **faire** la grasse matinée
I love having a lie-in

j'aime mieux **attendre**
I'd rather wait

● some impersonal verbs (see p44)

● a few other verbs, eg:

compter	to intend to
sembler	to seem
laisser	to let, to allow
faillir	'to nearly' (do)
oser	to dare

ils l'ont laissé **partir**
they let him go

je n'ose pas le leur **demander**
I daren't ask them

tu sembles **être** malade
you seem to be ill

je compte **partir** demain
I intend to leave tomorrow

j'ai failli **manquer** l'avion
I nearly missed the plane

● in the following set expressions:

aller chercher	to go and get, to fetch
envoyer chercher	to send for
entendre dire (que)	to hear (that)
entendre parler de	to hear about
laisser tomber	to drop
venir chercher	to come and get
vouloir dire	to mean

va **chercher** ton argent
go and get your money

j'**ai entendu dire** qu'il était journaliste
I've heard that he's a journalist

tu **as entendu parler** de ce film?
have you heard about this film?

ne le **laisse** pas **tomber**!
don't drop it!

ça **veut dire** 'demain'
it means 'tomorrow'

ii) Verbs followed by **à** + infinitive:

A list of these is given on p62:

je dois aider ma mère à **préparer** le déjeuner
I must help my mother prepare lunch

il commence à **faire** nuit
it's beginning to get dark

alors, tu t'es décidé à y **aller**?
so you've made up your mind to go?

je t'invite à **venir** chez moi pour les
vacances de Noël
*you are welcome to come to my house for
the Christmas holidays*

je passe mon temps à **lire** et à **regarder**
la télé
I spend my time reading and watching TV

cela sert à **ouvrir** les bouteilles
this is used for opening bottles

iii) Verbs followed by **de** + infinitive:

A list of these is given on p62:

je crois qu'il s'est arrêté de **pleuvoir**
I think it's stopped raining

tu as envie de **sortir**?
do you feel like going out?

le médecin a conseillé à Serge de **rester**
au lit
the doctor advised Serge to stay in bed

j'ai décidé de **rester** chez moi
I decided to stay at home

essayons de **faire** du stop
let's try and hitch-hike

demande à Papa de t'**aider**
ask Dad to help you

n'oublie pas d'en **acheter**!
don't forget to buy some!

je vous prie de m'**excuser**
please forgive me

tu as fini de m'**ennuyer**?
will you stop annoying me?

je t'interdis d'y **aller**
I forbid you to go

j'ai refusé de le **faire**
I refused to do it

il vient de **téléphoner**
he's just phoned

c) *After a noun, a pronoun, an adverb or an
adjective*

There are two possible constructions:

i) with the linking preposition **à**:

il avait plusieurs clients à **voir**
he had several customers to see

c'est difficile à **dire**
it's difficult to say

une maison à **vendre**
a house for sale

j'ai des examens à **préparer**
I've got exams to prepare

il nous a indiqué la route à **suivre**
he showed us the road to follow

il n'y a pas de temps à **perdre**
there's no time to lose

c'était une occasion à **ne pas manquer**
it was an opportunity not to be missed

● **à** conveys the idea of something to
do or to be done after the following:

beaucoup	*a lot*
plus	*more*
tant	*so much*
trop	*too much*
assez	*enough*
moins	*less*
rien	*nothing*
tout	*everything*
quelque chose	*something*

il y a trop de livres à **lire**
there are too many books to read

il n'y a rien à **ajouter**
there's nothing further to add

elle a quelque chose à **nous annoncer**
she has something to tell us

● **à** is used in a passive sense (when
something is being done) and after **c'est**:

un livre agréable à **lire**
a pleasant book to read

il est facile à **satisfaire**
he is easily satisfied

c'est intéressant à **savoir**
that's interesting to know

c'était impossible à **faire**
it was impossible to do

ii) with the linking preposition **de**:
je suis content **de** te **voir**
I am pleased to see you

● **de** is used after nouns of an abstract
nature, usually with the definite article, eg:

l'habitude de	*the habit of*
l'occasion de	*the opportunity to*
le temps de	*the time to*
le courage de	*the courage to*

Verbs

l'envie de	*the desire to*
le besoin de	*the need to*
le plaisir de	*the pleasure of*
le moment de	*the time to*

il n'avait pas l'habitude **d'être** seul
he wasn't used to being alone

je n'ai pas le temps **de** leur **expliquer**
I don't have time to explain it to them

avez-vous eu l'occasion **de** la **rencontrer?**
did you have the opportunity to meet her?

ce n'est pas le moment **de** le **déranger**
now is not the time to disturb him

je n'ai pas eu le courage **de** te le **dire**
I didn't have the courage to tell you

● **de** is used after **il est** in an impersonal sense (see p44):

il est intéressant **de savoir** que ...
it is interesting to know that ...

For information on the use of **c'est** and **il est**, see p83.

● **de** is used after many adjectives, and is frequently used to translate 'of' in English, eg:

certain/sûr de	*certain of/to*
capable de	*capable of*
incapable de	*incapable of*
coupable de	*guilty of*

j'étais sûr **de réussir**
I was sure of succeeding

il est incapable **d'**y **arriver** seul
he is incapable of managing on his own

● **de** is also used with adjectives relating to emotions and states of mind, eg:

content de	*pleased/happy to*
surpris/étonné de	*surprised to*
fier de	*proud to*
heureux de	*happy to*
fâché de	*annoyed to/at*
triste de	*sad to*
gêné de	*embarrassed to*
désolé de	*sorry for/to*

j'ai été très content **de recevoir** ta lettre
I was very pleased to get your letter

elle sera surprise **de** vous **voir**
she will be surprised to see you

nous avons été très tristes **d'apprendre** la nouvelle
we were very sad to hear the news

Note, however, that **à** is used with **prêt à** *(ready to)* and **disposé à** *(willing to)*:

es-tu prêt **à partir?**
are you ready to go?

je suis tout disposé **à** vous **aider**
I'm very willing to help you

d) **faire** + *infinitive*

faire is followed by an infinitive without any linking preposition to express the sense of 'having someone do something' or 'having something done'; two constructions are possible, depending on whether there are one or two objects:

i) when only one object is used, it is a direct object:

je dois le **faire réparer**
I must have it fixed

il veut **faire repeindre** sa voiture
he wants to have his car resprayed

cette veste est sale, il faut la **faire nettoyer**
this jacket's dirty, I'll have to have it cleaned

tu m'as **fait attendre!**
you kept me waiting!

je le **ferai parler**
I'll make him talk

Note the following set expressions:

faire entrer	*to show in*
faire venir	*to send for*

faites entrer ce monsieur
show this gentleman in

je vais **faire venir** le docteur
I'll send for the doctor

ii) when both **faire** and the following infinitive have an object, the object of **faire** is indirect:

elle **m'a fait prendre** une douche
she made me take a shower

je **leur ai fait ranger** leur chambre
I made them tidy their room

e) *Infinitive used as subject of another verb:*

trouver un emploi n'est pas facile
finding a job isn't easy

devenir pilote était mon rêve
my dream was to become a pilot

3 The perfect infinitive

a) *Form*

The perfect or past infinitive is formed with

the infinitive of the auxiliary **avoir** or **être** as appropriate (see p40), followed by the past participle of the verb, eg:

avoir mangé
to have eaten

être allé
to have gone

s'**être** levé
to have got up

b) *Use*

i) after the preposition **après** *(after)*:

après avoir attendu une heure, il est rentré chez lui
after waiting for an hour, he went back home

j'ai compris la remarque **après avoir relu** le livre
I understood the remark after reading the book again

ii) after certain verbs:

se souvenir de   to remember
remercier de   to thank for
regretter de   to regret, to be
           sorry for
être désolé de   to be sorry for

je vous remercie de m'**avoir invité**
thank you for inviting me

Il regrettait de leur **avoir menti**
he was sorry he had lied to them

tu te souviens d'**avoir fait** cela?
do you remember doing this?

I PARTICIPLES

1 The present participle

a) *Formation*

Like the imperfect, the present participle is formed by using the stem of the first person plural of the present tense (the **nous** form without the **-ons** ending) to which **ant** (like English 'ing') is added. The following three verbs, however, have irregular present participles:

INFINITIVE	PRESENT PARTICIPLE
avoir *to have*	**ayant** *having*
être *to be*	**étant** *being*
savoir *to know*	**sachant** *knowing*

b) *Use as an adjective*

Used as an adjective, the present participle agrees in number and in gender with its noun or pronoun:

un travail **fatigant**   la semaine **suivante**
tiring work   *the following week*

ils sont très **exigeants**
they're very demanding

des nouvelles **surprenantes**
surprising news

c) *Use as a verb*

The present participle is used far less frequently in French than in English, and English present participles in '-ing' are often not translated by a participle in French (see p82).

i) Used on its own, the present participle corresponds to the English present participle:

ne **voulant** plus attendre, ils sont partis sans moi
not wanting to wait any longer, they left without me

pensant bien faire, j'ai insisté
thinking I was doing the right thing, I insisted

ii) **en** + present participle

When the subject of the present participle is the same as that of the main verb, this structure is often used to express simultaneous actions (ie 'while doing something'), manner (ie 'by doing something') and to translate English phrasal verbs expressing motion.

● simultaneous actions

In English this structure is translated by:
while/when/on + present participle (eg 'on arriving')
while/when/as + subject + verb (eg 'as he arrived')

il est tombé **en descendant** l'escalier
he fell as he was going down the stairs

en le voyant, j'ai éclaté de rire
when I saw him, I burst out laughing

elle lisait le journal **en attendant** l'autobus
she was reading the paper while waiting for the bus

Note that the adverb **tout** is often used before **en** to emphasize the fact that the actions are simultaneous, especially when there is an element of contradiction:

Verbs

elle écoutait la radio **tout en faisant** ses devoirs
she was listening to the radio while doing her homework

tout en protestant, je les ai suivis
under protest, I followed them

● manner

When expressing how an action is done, **en** + participle is translated by 'by' + participle, eg:

il gagne sa vie **en vendant** des voitures d'occasion
he earns his living (by) selling second-hand cars

j'ai trouvé du travail **en lisant** les petites annonces
I found a job by reading the classified ads

● phrasal verbs of motion

en + present participle is often used to translate English phrasal verbs expressing motion, where the verb expresses the means of motion and a preposition expresses the direction of movement (eg 'to run out', 'to swim across').

In French, the English preposition is translated by a verb, while the English verb is translated by **en** + present participle.

il est sorti du magasin **en courant**
he ran out of the shop

elle a traversé la route **en titubant**
she staggered across the road

2 The past participle

a) *Forms*

For the formation of the past participle see p40.

b) *Use*

The past participle is mostly used as a verb in compound tenses or in the passive, but it can also be used as an adjective. In either case, there are strict rules of agreement to be followed.

i) When it is used as an adjective, the past participle always agrees with the noun or pronoun to which it refers:

un pneu **crevé**   ils étaient **épuisés**
a burst tyre   *they were exhausted*

une pomme **pourrie**
a rotten apple

des photos **prises** à la nuit tombée
photos taken at nightfall

Note that in French, the past participle is used as an adjective to describe postures or attitudes of the body, where English uses the present participle. The most common of these are:

accoudé	*leaning on one's elbows*
accroupi	*squatting*
agenouillé	*kneeling*
allongé	*lying (down)*
appuyé (contre)	*leaning (against)*
couché	*lying (down)*
étendu	*lying (down)*
penché	*leaning (over)*
(sus)pendu	*hanging*

il est **allongé** sur le lit
he's lying on the bed

une femme **assise** devant moi
a woman sitting in front of me

ii) In compound tenses:

● With the auxiliary **avoir** the past participle agrees in number and gender with the direct object only when the direct object comes before the participle, ie in the following cases:

in a clause introduced by the relative pronoun **que**:

le jeu vidéo que j'ai **acheté**
the video game I bought

la valise qu'il a **perdue**
the suitcase he lost

with a direct object pronoun:

je ne trouve pas la disquette; où l'as-tu **mise**?
I can't find the floppy disk; where did you put it?

merci pour tes suggestions, je les ai **trouvées** très utiles
thank you for your suggestions; I found them very useful

in a clause introduced by **combien de**, **quel** or **lequel**:

combien de pays as-tu **visités**?
how many countries have you visited?

laquelle avez-vous **choisie**?
which one did you choose?

Note that if the direct object comes after the past participle, the participle remains in the masculine singular form:

on a **rencontré** des gens très sympathiques
we met some very nice people

● With the auxiliary **être** the past participle agrees with the subject of the verb:

quand est-elle **revenue**?
when did she come back?

elle était déjà **partie**
she'd already left

ils sont **passés** te voir?
did they come to see you?

elles sont **restées** là
they stayed here

Note that this rule also applies when the verb is in the passive:

elle a été **arrêtée**
she's been arrested

● With reflexive verbs the past participle normally agrees with the reflexive pronoun if the pronoun is a direct object; since the reflexive pronoun refers to the subject, the number and gender of the past participle are determined by the subject:

Jacques s'est **trompé**
Jacques made a mistake

Marie s'était **levée** tard
Marie had got up late

ils se sont **disputés**?
did they have an argument?

elles se sont **vues**
they saw each other

Michèle et Marie, vous vous êtes **habillées**?
Michèle and Marie, have you got dressed yet?

Note, however, that the past participle does not agree when the reflexive pronoun is an indirect object:

elles se sont **écrit**
they wrote to each other

elle s'est **lavé** les cheveux
she washed her hair

ils se sont **serré** la main
they shook hands

J THE PASSIVE

1 Formation

The passive is used when the subject does not perform the action, but is subjected to it, eg:

the house has been sold
he was made redundant

Passive tenses are formed with the corresponding tense of the verb **être** ('to be', as in English), followed by the past participle of the verb, eg:

j'**ai été invité**
I was invited

The past participle must agree with its subject, eg:

il **sera puni**   elle **a été renvoyée**
he will be punished   *she has been dismissed*

ils **seront déçus**
they will be disappointed

elles **ont été vues**
they were seen

2 Avoidance of the passive

The passive is far less common in French than in English. In particular, an indirect object cannot become the subject of a sentence in French; the following sentence, where 'he' is an indirect object, has no equivalent in French:

he was given a book (ie a book was given to him)

In general, French tries to avoid the passive wherever possible. This can be done in several ways.

a) *By using the pronoun* **on**

on m'a volé mon portefeuille
my wallet has been stolen

on construit une nouvelle piscine
a new swimming pool is being built

en France, **on boit** beaucoup de vin
a lot of wine is drunk in France

b) *By making the agent the subject of the verb*

If the agent, that is the real subject, is mentioned in English, it can become the subject of the French verb:

la nouvelle va les surprendre
they will be surprised by the news

mon correspondant m'a invité
I've been invited by my penfriend

mon cadeau te plaît?
are you pleased with my present?

c) *By using a reflexive verb*

Reflexive forms can be created for a large

Verbs

number of verbs, particularly in the third person:

elle **s'appelle** Anne
she is called Anne

ton absence va **se remarquer**
your absence will be noticed

ce plat **se mange** froid
this dish is eaten cold

cela ne **se fait** pas ici
that isn't done here

d) *By using* **se faire** + *infinitive (when the subject is a person)*

il **s'est fait renverser** par une voiture
he was run over by a car

je **me suis fait couper** les cheveux
I've had my hair cut

K MODAL AUXILIARY VERBS

The modal auxiliary verbs are always followed by the infinitive. They express an obligation, a probability, an intention, a possibility or a wish rather than a fact.

The five modal auxiliary verbs are: **devoir**, **pouvoir**, **savoir**, **vouloir** and **falloir**.

1 Devoir (for conjugation see the Conjugation Tables) is used to express the following:

a) *obligation*

nous **devons** arriver à temps
we must arrive in time

nous **avions dû** partir
we had (had) to go

demain tu **devras** prendre le bus
tomorrow you'll have to take the bus

j'**ai dû** avouer que j'avais tort
I had to admit that I was wrong

In the conditional, **devoir** may be used for advice, ie to express what should be done (conditional present) or should have been done (conditional past):

vous **devriez** travailler davantage
you ought to/should work harder

tu ne **devrais** pas marcher sur l'herbe
you shouldn't walk on the grass

tu **aurais dû** tout avouer
you should have admitted everything

tu n'**aurais** pas **dû** manger ces champignons
you shouldn't have eaten those mushrooms

Note that the French infinitive is translated by a past participle in English: **manger** = eaten.

b) *probability*

il **doit** être en train de dormir
he must be sleeping (he's probably sleeping)

j'**ai dû** me tromper de chemin
I must have taken the wrong road

Note that in a past narrative sequence in the distant past, 'must have' is translated by a pluperfect in French:

il dit qu'il **avait dû** se tromper de chemin
he said he must have taken the wrong road

c) *intention, expectation*

je **dois** aller chez le dentiste
I am supposed to go to the dentist

le train **doit** arriver à 19h30
the train is due to arrive at 7.30 p.m.

2 Pouvoir (for conjugation see the Conjugation Tables) is used to express the following:

a) *capacity/ability*

il **peut** rester plusieurs jours sans dormir
he can go without sleep for several days

cette voiture **peut** faire du 150
this car can go up to 93 mph

il était si faible qu'il ne **pouvait** pas sortir de son lit
he was so weak that he couldn't get out of bed

b) *permission*

puis-je entrer?
may I come in?

puis-je vous offrir du thé?
may I offer you some tea?

c) *possibility*

cela **peut** arriver
it can happen

ça **peut** n'avoir aucune importance
it might not be at all important

Note that **pouvoir** + the infinitive is usually replaced by **peut-être** + the finite tense, eg il s'est peut-être trompé de livres (*he may have taken the wrong books*).

In the conditional, **pouvoir** is used to express something that could or might be (conditional present) or that could or might have been (conditional past):

tu **pourrais** t'excuser
you might apologize

j'**aurais pu** vous prêter mon téléphone portable
I could have lent you my mobile phone

Note that with verbs of perception, eg **entendre** *(to hear)*, **sentir** *(to feel, to smell)*, **voir** *(to see)*, **pouvoir** is often omitted.

j'**entendais** le bruit des vagues
I could hear the sound of the waves

3 **Savoir** (for conjugation see the Conjugation Tables) is used to express 'to know how to':

je **sais/savais** conduire une moto
I can/used to be able to ride a motorbike

elle **sait** parler plusieurs langues
she can speak several languages

4 **Vouloir** (for conjugation see the Conjugation Tables) is used to express the following:

a) *desire*

je **veux** partir
I want to go

voulez-vous danser avec moi?
will you dance with me?

b) *wish*

je **voudrais** être riche
I wish I were rich

je **voudrais** trouver un travail intéressant
I'd like to find an interesting job

j'**aurais voulu** te donner un coup de poing
I would have liked to punch you

c) *intention*

il **a voulu** sauter par la fenêtre
he tried to jump out of the window

Note that **veuillez**, the imperative of **vouloir**, is used as a polite form to express a request *('would you please ... ')*:

veuillez ne pas déranger
please do not disturb

5 **Falloir** (for conjugation see the Conjugation Tables) is used to express necessity:

il **faut** manger pour vivre
you must eat to live

il **faudrait** y aller tout de suite
we should go right away

il **aurait fallu** apporter des sandwichs
we should have brought sandwiches

Note that some of the above verbs can also be used without infinitive constructions in which case they have a different meaning, eg **devoir** = *to owe*, **savoir** = *to know*.

je te **dois** 20 euros
I owe you 20 euros

elle le **sait** par cœur
she knows it by heart

L VERBAL CONSTRUCTIONS

There are two main types of verbal construction:

1 Verbs followed by an infinitive

There are three main types of construction when a verb is followed by an infinitive. For examples of all three types, see p53.

a) *Verbs followed by an infinitive without any linking preposition*

These include verbs of wishing and willing, of movement and of perception:

adorer *to love*	aimer *to like*	aimer mieux *to prefer*
aller *to go (and)*	compter *to intend to*	descendre *to go down (and)*
désirer *to wish*	détester *to hate*	devoir *to have to*
écouter *to listen to*	entendre *to hear*	entrer *to go in (and)*
envoyer *to send*	espérer *to hope to*	faire *to make*
falloir *to have to*	laisser *to let*	monter *to go up (and)*
oser *to dare*	pouvoir *to be able to*	préférer *to prefer to*
regarder *to watch*	rentrer *to go in/back (and)*	savoir *to know how to*
sembler *to seem to*	sentir *to feel*	sortir *to go out (and)*
souhaiter *to wish to*	valoir mieux *to be better to*	
venir *to come (and)*	voir *to see*	vouloir *to want to*

Verbs

b) *Verbs followed by* **à** + *infinitive*

aider à	*to help (to do)*
s'amuser à	*to enjoy (doing)*
apprendre à	*to learn (to do)*
s'apprêter à	*to get ready (to do)*
arriver à	*to manage (to do)*
s'attendre à	*to expect (to do)*
autoriser à	*to allow (to do)*
chercher à	*to try (to do)*
commencer à	*to start (doing)*
consentir à	*to agree (to do)*
consister à	*to consist in (doing)*
continuer à	*to continue (to do)*
se décider à	*to make up one's mind (to do)*
encourager à	*to encourage (to do)*
enseigner à	*to teach how (to do)*
forcer à	*to force (to do)*
s'habituer à	*to get used (to doing)*
hésiter à	*to hesitate (to do)*
inciter à	*to prompt (to do)*
s'intéresser à	*to be interested in (doing)*
inviter à	*to invite (to do)*
se mettre à	*to start (doing)*
obliger à	*to force (to do)*
parvenir à	*to succeed (in doing)*
passer son temps à	*to spend one's time (doing)*
perdre son temps à	*to waste one's time (doing)*
persister à	*to persist in (doing)*
pousser à	*to urge (to do)*
se préparer à	*to get ready (to do)*
renoncer à	*to give up (doing)*
rester à	*to be left (to do)*
réussir à	*to manage (to do)*
servir à	*to be used for (doing)*
songer à	*to think of (doing)*
tarder à	*to delay/be late in (doing)*
tenir à	*to be keen (to do)*

c) *Verbs followed by* **de** + *infinitive:*

accepter de	*to agree (to do)*
accuser de	*to accuse of (doing)*
achever de	*to finish (doing)*
s'arrêter de	*to stop (doing)*
avoir besoin de	*to need (to do)*
avoir envie de	*to feel like (doing)*
avoir peur de	*to be afraid (to do)*
cesser de	*to stop (doing)*
se charger de	*to undertake (to do)*
commander de	*to order (to do)*
conseiller de	*to advise (to do)*
se contenter de	*to make do with (doing)*

craindre de	*to be afraid (to do)*
décider de	*to decide (to do)*
déconseiller de	*to advise against (doing)*
défendre de	*to forbid (to do)*
demander de	*to ask (to do)*
se dépêcher de	*to hasten (to do)*
dire de	*to tell (to do)*
dissuader de	*to dissuade from (doing)*
s'efforcer de	*to strive (to do)*
empêcher de	*to prevent (from doing)*
s'empresser de	*to hasten (to do)*
entreprendre de	*to undertake (to do)*
essayer de	*to try (to do)*
s'étonner de	*to be surprised (at doing)*
éviter de	*to avoid (doing)*
s'excuser de	*to apologize for (doing)*
faire semblant de	*to pretend (to do)*
feindre de	*to pretend (to do)*
finir de	*to finish (doing)*
se garder de	*to be careful not to (do)*
se hâter de	*to hasten (to do)*
interdire de	*to forbid (to do)*
jurer de	*to swear (to do)*
manquer de	*'to nearly' (do)*
menacer de	*to threaten (to do)*
mériter de	*to deserve (to do)*
négliger de	*to fail (to do)*
s'occuper de	*to undertake (to do)*
offrir de	*to offer (to do)*
omettre de	*to omit (to do)*
ordonner de	*to order (to do)*
oublier de	*to forget (to do)*
permettre de	*to allow (to do)*
persuader de	*to persuade (to do)*
prier de	*to ask (to do)*
promettre de	*to promise (to do)*
proposer de	*to offer (to do)*
recommander de	*to recommend (to do)*
refuser de	*to refuse (to do)*
regretter de	*to be sorry (to do)*
remercier de	*to thank for (doing)*
résoudre de	*to resolve (to do)*
risquer de	*to risk (doing)*
se souvenir de	*to remember (doing)*
suggérer de	*to suggest (doing)*
supplier de	*to implore (to do)*
tâcher de	*to try (to do)*
tenter de	*to try (to do)*
venir de	*to have just (done)*

2 Verbs followed by an object

In general, verbs which take a direct object in French also take a direct object in English, and verbs which take an indirect object in French (ie verb + preposition + object) also take an indirect object in English.

There are, however, some exceptions:

a) *Verbs followed by an indirect object in English but not in French* (the English preposition is not translated):

attendre	*to wait for*
chercher	*to look for*
demander	*to ask for*
écouter	*to listen to*
espérer	*to hope for*
payer	*to pay for*
regarder	*to look at*
reprocher	*to blame for*

on a demandé **l'addition**
we asked for the bill

j'attendais **l'autobus**
I was waiting for the bus

je cherche **mon frère**
I'm looking for my brother

tu écoutes **la radio**?
are you listening to the radio?

b) *Verbs which take a direct object in English, but an indirect object in French:*

convenir à	*to suit*
se fier à	*to trust*
jouer à	*to play (game, sport)*
jouer de	*to play (musical instrument)*
obéir à	*to obey*
désobéir à	*to disobey*
pardonner à	*to forgive*
renoncer à	*to give up*
répondre à	*to answer*
résister à	*to resist*
ressembler à	*to resemble (to look like)*
téléphoner à	*to telephone*

tu peux te fier **à moi**
you can trust me

tu joues souvent **au tennis**?
do you often play tennis?

il joue bien **de la guitare**
he plays the guitar well

tu as répondu **à ma lettre**?
did you answer my letter?

téléphonons **au médecin**
let's phone the doctor

obéis **à ton père**!
obey your father!

c) *Verbs which take a direct object in English but **de** + indirect object in French:*

s'apercevoir de	*to notice*
s'approcher de	*to come near*
avoir besoin de	*to need*
changer de	*to change*
douter de	*to doubt*
se douter de	*to suspect*
s'emparer de	*to seize, to grab*
jouir de	*to enjoy*
manquer de	*to lack, to miss*
se méfier de	*to mistrust*
se servir de	*to use*
se souvenir de	*to remember*
se tromper de ...	*to get the wrong ...*

je dois changer **de train**?
do I have to change trains?

il ne s'est aperçu **de rien**
he didn't notice anything

méfiez-vous **de lui**
don't trust him

je me servirai **de ton vélo**
I'll use your bike

tu te souviens **de Jean**?
do you remember Jean?

il s'est trompé **de numéro**
he got the wrong number

d) *Some verbs take **à** or **de** before an object, whereas their English equivalent uses a different preposition:*

i) Verb + **à** + object:

croire à	*to believe in*
s'intéresser à	*to be interested in*
penser à	*to think of/about*
songer à	*to think of*
rêver à	*to dream of/about*
servir à	*to be used for*

je m'intéresse **au football** et **à la course automobile**
I'm interested in football and in motor-racing

à quoi penses-tu?
what are you thinking about?

ça sert **à quoi**?
what is this used for?

ii) Verb + **de** + object:

dépendre de	*to depend on*
être fâché de	*to be annoyed at*
féliciter de	*to congratulate for*
parler de	*to speak of/about*
remercier de	*to thank for*

rire de	*to laugh at*
traiter de	*to deal with, to be about*
vivre de	*to live on*

cela dépendra **du temps**
it'll depend on the weather

il m'a parlé **de toi**
he told me about you

tu l'as remercié **du cadeau** qu'il t'a fait?
did you thank him for the present he gave you?

3 Verbs followed by one direct object and one indirect object

a) In general, these are verbs of giving or lending, and their English equivalents are constructed in the same way, eg:

donner quelque chose à quelqu'un
to give something to someone

il a vendu son ordinateur à son voisin
he sold his computer to his neighbour

Note that after such verbs, the preposition 'to' is often omitted in English but **à**, however, cannot be omitted in French. Particular care must be taken when object pronouns are used with these verbs (see p27).

b) With verbs expressing 'taking away', **à** is translated by 'from' (qn stands for 'quelqu'un' and *sb* for 'somebody'):

acheter à qn	*to buy from sb*
cacher à qn	*to hide from sb*
demander à qn	*to ask sb for*
emprunter à qn	*to borrow from sb*
enlever à qn	*to take away from sb*
ôter à qn	*to take away from sb*
prendre à qn	*to take from sb*
voler à qn	*to steal from sb*

à qui as-tu emprunté cela?
who did you borrow this from?

il l'a volé **à son frère**
he stole it from his brother

4 Verb + indirect object + 'de' + infinitive

Some verbs which take a direct object in English are followed by **à** + object + **de** + infinitive in French:

commander à qn de faire	*to order sb to do*
conseiller à qn de faire	*to advise sb to do*
défendre à qn de faire	*to forbid sb to do*
demander à qn de faire	*to ask sb to do*

dire à qn de faire	*to tell sb to do*
ordonner à qn de faire	*to order sb to do*
permettre à qn de faire	*to allow sb to do*
promettre à qn de faire	*to promise sb to do*
proposer à qn de faire	*to offer to do for sb, to suggest to sb to do*

je **leur** ai conseillé **de** ne pas essayer
I advised them not to try

demande **à ton fils de** t'aider
ask your son to help you

j'ai promis **à mes parents de** ne jamais recommencer
I promised my parents never to do this again

8 Prepositions

Prepositions in both French and English can have many different meanings, which presents considerable difficulties for the translator. The following guide to the most common prepositions sets out the generally accepted meanings on the left, with a description of their use in brackets, and an illustration. The main meanings are given first. Prepositions are listed in alphabetical order.

à

at	(place)	**au** troisième arrêt *at the third stop*
	(date)	**à** Noël *at Christmas*
	(time)	**à** trois heures *at three o'clock*
	(idiom)	**au** hasard **au** travail *at random* *at work*
in	(place)	**à** Montmartre **à** Lyon *in Montmartre* *in Lyons*
		au supermarché *in the supermarket*
		à la campagne *in the country*
		au lit *in bed*
		au loin *in the distance*

	(manner)	**à la** française *in the French way*
		à ma façon *my way*
to	(place)	aller **au** théâtre *to go to the theatre*
		aller **à** Londres *to go to London*
	(+ infinitive)	c'est facile **à** faire *it is easy to do (see p54)*
away from	(distance)	**à** 3 km d'ici *3 km away*
by	(means)	aller **à** vélo *to go by bike*
		je l'ai reconnu **à** ses habits *I recognized him by his clothing*
	(manner)	fait **à** la main *hand-made*
	(rate)	**à** la centaine *by the hundred*
		100 km **à** l'heure *100 km per hour*
for/up to	(+ pronoun)	c'est **à** vous de jouer *it's your turn*
		c'est **à** nous de te le dire *it's up to us to tell you*
	(purpose)	une tasse **à** café *a coffee cup*
from		il l'a caché **à** ses parents *he hid it from his parents*
his/her/my/etc	(possessive)	son sac **à** elle *her bag*
on	(means)	aller **à** cheval/**à** pied *to go on horseback/on foot*
	(place)	**à** la page 12 *on page 12*
		à droite/**à** gauche *on/to the right/left*
	(time)	**à** cette occasion *on this occasion*
with	(descriptive)	un homme **aux** cheveux blonds *a man with blond hair*

| | | l'homme **à** la valise
the man with the case |
| | (idiom) | **à** bras ouverts
with open arms |

For use of the preposition **à** with the infinitive see Verbal Constructions p61.

après

after	(time)	**après** votre arrivée *after your arrival*
	(sequence)	24 ans **après** la mort du président *24 years after the death of the President*
		je suis allé au lit **après** avoir fini le livre *I went to bed after I finished the book*
		après s'être séparée de son mari *after separating from her husband*

auprès de

| *beside* | | il s'assit **auprès de** sa mère
he sat down beside his mother |
| *compared to* | | ce n'est rien **auprès de** ce que tu as fait
it's nothing compared to what you've done |

avant

before	(time)	**avant** cet après-midi *before this afternoon*
		avant ce soir *before tonight*
		avant de s'asseoir *before sitting down*
	(preference)	la famille **avant** tout *the family comes first (above all else)*

avec

| *with* | (association) | je viendrai **avec** lui
I'll come with him |
| | (means) | elle marche **avec** une canne
she walks with a stick |

Prepositions

chez

at	(place)	**chez** moi/toi
		at/to my/your house
		chez mon oncle
		at my uncle's
		chez le pharmacien
		at the chemist's
among		**chez** les Écossais
		among the Scots
about		ce qui m'énerve **chez** toi, c'est ...
		what annoys me about you is ...
in		**chez** Sartre
		in Sartre's work

contre

against	(place)	**contre** le mur
		against the wall
with	(after verb)	je suis fâché **contre** elle
		I'm angry with her
for		elle a échangé un billet **contre** des pièces
		she changed a note for coins

dans

in	(position)	**dans** ma serviette
		in my briefcase
	(time)	je pars **dans** deux jours
		I'm leaving in two days' time
	(idiom)	**dans** l'attente de vous voir
		looking forward to seeing you
from	(removal)	prendre quelque chose **dans** l'armoire
		to take something from the cupboard
on	(position)	**dans** le train
		on the train
out of	(idiom)	boire **dans** un verre
		to drink out of a glass

de

from	(place)	je suis venu **de** Glasgow
		I have come from Glasgow
	(date)	**du** 5 février au 10 mars
		from 5 February to 10 March
		d'un week-end à l'autre
		from one weekend to another
of	(adjectival)	un cri **de** triomphe
		a shout of triumph
	(contents)	une tasse **de** café
		a cup of coffee
	(cause)	mourir **de** faim
		to die of hunger
	(measurement)	long **de** 3 mètres
		3 metres long
	(time)	ma montre retarde **de** 10 minutes
		my watch is 10 minutes slow
	(price)	le montant est **de** 20 euros
		the total is 20 euros
	(possessive)	le père **de** mon ami
		my friend's father
	(adjectival)	les vacances **de** Pâques
		the Easter holidays
	(after 'quelque chose')	quelque chose **de** bon
		something good
	(after 'rien')	rien **de** nouveau
		nothing new
	(after 'personne')	personne **d'**autre
		nobody else
	(quantity)	beaucoup **de**, peu **de**
		many, few
by	(idiom)	je le connais **de** vue
		I know him by sight
in	(manner)	**de** cette façon
		in this way
	(after superlatives)	la plus haute montagne **d'**Écosse
		the highest mountain in Scotland
on	(position)	**de** ce côté
		on this side
than	(comparative)	moins **de** 2 euros
		less than 2 euros
		plus **de** 3 litres
		more than 3 litres

to (after adjectives) ravi **de** vous voir
delighted to see you

il est facile **de** se tromper
it is easy to make a mistake

(after verbs) s'efforcer **de**
to try to

with (cause) tomber **de** fatigue
to drop with exhaustion

depuis

for (time) j'étudie le français **depuis** 3 ans
I have been studying French for 3 years

j'étudiais le français **depuis** 3 ans
I had been studying French for 3 years

je n'y ai pas joué **depuis** des années
I haven't played for years

from (place) **depuis** ma fenêtre, je vois la mer
from my window I can see the sea

(time) **depuis** le matin jusqu'au soir
from morning till evening

since **depuis** dimanche
since Sunday

derrière

behind (place) **derrière** la maison
behind the house

dès

from (time) **dès** six heures
from six o'clock onwards

dès 1934
as far back as 1934

dès le début
from the beginning

dès maintenant
from now on

(place) **dès** Édimbourg
from (the moment of leaving) Edinburgh

devant

in front of (place) **devant** l'école
in front of the school

before (place) sur la table **devant** eux
on the table before them

en

in (place) être **en** ville
to be in town

en Angleterre
in England

(colour) un mur peint **en** jaune
a wall painted yellow

(material) une montre **en** or
a gold watch

by (means) **en** auto/**en** avion
by car/by plane

(dates, seasons) **en** quelle année?
in what year?

en 2004 **en** juillet
in 2004 *in July*

en été
in the summer

(dress) **en** jupe
in a skirt

(language) **en** chinois
in Chinese

(time) j'ai fait mes devoirs **en** 20 minutes
I did my homework in 20 minutes

like, as il s'est habillé **en** femme
he dressed as a woman

on (idiom) **en** vacances
on holiday

en moyenne
on average

(+ present participle) **en** faisant
on/while/by doing

Note that en is not used with the definite article except in certain expressions: en l'an 2020 (*in the year 2020*), en l'honneur de (*in honour of*) and en la présence de (*in the presence of*).

Prepositions

en tant que

as/in one's capacity as	**en tant que** professeur *as a teacher*

entre

among		être **entre** amis *to be among friends*
between	(place)	**entre** Londres et Paris *between London and Paris*
	(time)	**entre** 6 et 10 heures *between 6 and 10 o'clock*
	(idiom)	**entre** nous *between you and me*
in	(punctuation)	**entre** guillemets *in inverted commas*
		entre parenthèses *in brackets*

d'entre

of/from among	certains **d'entre** eux *some of them*

envers

to/towards	être bien disposé **envers** quelqu'un *to be well-disposed towards someone*

hors de

out of	**hors de** danger *out of danger*

jusque

up to/as far as	(place)	**jusqu'à** la frontière espagnole *as far as the Spanish border*
	(time)	**jusqu'**ici **jusque**-là *up to now* *up till then*
till		**jusqu'à** demain *till tomorrow*

malgré

in spite of	**malgré** la chaleur *in spite of the heat*

par

by	(agent)	la décision fut prise **par** le président *the decision was made by the President*
	(means of transport)	**par** le train *by train*
	(distributive)	trois fois **par** semaine *three times a week*
		deux **par** deux *two by two*
	(place)	**par** ici/là *this/that way*
in/on	(weather)	**par** un temps pareil *in such weather*
		par un beau jour d'hiver *on a beautiful winter's day*
through/out of	(place)	regarder **par** la fenêtre *to look out of the window*
		jette-le **par** la fenêtre *throw it out of the window*
to/on		tomber **par** terre *to fall to the ground*
		étendu **par** terre *lying on the ground*
	(+ infinitive)	commencer/finir **par** faire *to begin/end by doing*

parmi

among	**parmi** mes ennemis *among my enemies*

pendant

for	(time)	il l'avait fait **pendant** 5 ans *he had done it for 5 years*
during		**pendant** l'été *during the summer*

pour

for	ce livre est **pour** vous *this book is for you*
	mourir **pour** la patrie *to die for one's country*

(purpose) c'est **pour** cela que je suis venu
that's why I've come

(emphatic) **pour** moi, cet argument ne tient pas
if you ask me, this argument isn't valid

(time) j'en ai **pour** une heure
it'll take me an hour

je suis en vacances **pour** 2 semaines
I'm on holiday for 2 weeks

(**pour** stresses intention and future time: see **depuis** and **pendant**, pp 67 and 68)

(idiom) c'est bon **pour** la santé
it's good for your health

to (+ infinitive) il était trop paresseux **pour** réussir ses examens
he was too lazy to pass his exams

près de

near (place) **près du** marché
near the market

nearly (time) il est **près de** minuit
it's nearly midnight

(quantity) **près de** cinquante
nearly fifty

quant à

as for **quant à** moi
as for me

sans

without (+ noun) **sans** espoir
without hope

(+ pronoun) je n'irai pas **sans** vous
I won't go without you

(+ infinitive) **sans** parler
without speaking

sans s'arrêter
without stopping

sauf

except for ils sont tous partis, **sauf** John
everyone left except John

barring **sauf** accidents/**sauf** imprévu
barring accidents/the unexpected

selon

according to **selon** le président
according to the President

selon moi
in my opinion

sous

under (physical) **sous** la table
under the table

(governed by) **sous** Élisabeth II
under Elizabeth II

in (weather) **sous** la pluie
in the rain

(idiom) **sous** peu
before long/shortly

sous la main
to hand

sous tous rapports
in all respects

sous mes yeux
before my eyes

sur

on/upon (place) le chat est **sur** le toit
the cat's on the roof

off je l'ai pris **sur** l'étagère
I took it off the shelf

out of neuf **sur** dix
(proportion) *nine out of ten*

une semaine **sur** trois
one week in three

over (place) le pont **sur** la Loire
the bridge over the Loire

l'emporter **sur** quelqu'un
to prevail over someone

about (idiom) une enquête **sur** ...
an enquiry about ...

at **sur** ces paroles
at these words

Conjunctions

	sur ce, il est sorti
	at this he went out
by	quatre mètres **sur** cinq
	four metres by five
in	**sur** un ton amer
	in a bitter tone (of voice)

vers

towards	(place)	**vers** le nord
		towards the north
	(time)	**vers** la fin du match
		towards the end of the match
about	(time)	**vers** 10 heures
		about 10 o'clock

voici/voilà

here	le **voici** qui vient
	here he comes
there	**voilà** où il demeure
	that's where he lives

---

9 Conjunctions

Conjunctions are words or expressions which link words, phrases or clauses. They fall into two categories, coordinating conjunctions and subordinating conjunctions:

A COORDINATING CONJUNCTIONS

1 Definition

These link two similar words or groups of words, eg nouns, pronouns, adjectives, adverbs, prepositions, phrases or clauses. The principal coordinating conjunctions (or adverbs used as conjunctions) are:

et	**mais**	**ou**
and	*but*	*or*
ou bien	**soit**	**ni**
or (else)	*either*	*neither*
alors	**aussi**	**donc**
then	*therefore*	*then, therefore*
puis	**car**	**or**
then (next)	*for (because)*	*now*

cependant	**néanmoins**	**pourtant**
however	*nevertheless*	*yet, however*
toutefois		
however		

il est malade **mais** il ne veut pas aller au lit
he's ill but he won't go to bed

il faisait beau **alors** il est allé se promener
it was nice weather so he went for a walk

2 Repetition

a) Some coordinating conjunctions are repeated:

soit ... soit ...	*either ... or ...*
ou (bien) ... ou (bien) ...	*either ... or ...*

prenez **soit** l'un **soit** l'autre
take one or the other

soit tu viens avec nous, **soit** tu restes ici mais tu te décides
either you come with us or you stay here, but you have to decide

ou tu t'habitues **ou** tu démissionnes
either you get used to it or you resign

ni ... ni ...	*neither ... nor ...*

le vieillard n'avait **ni** amis **ni** argent
the old man had neither friends nor money

b) **et** and **ou** can be repeated in texts of a literary nature:

et ... et ...	*both ... and ...*
ou ... ou ...	*either ... or ...*

elle ne cessa **et** de crier **et** de pleurer
she didn't stop shouting and crying

ou c'est lui **ou** c'est moi !
it's either him or me!

3 Aussi

aussi means 'therefore' only when placed before the verb. The subject pronoun is placed after the verb.

il pleuvait, **aussi** Pascal n'est-il pas sorti
it was raining, so Pascal didn't go out

When **aussi** follows the verb it means 'also':

j'ai **aussi** emporté des pulls, au cas où
I also brought some jumpers, just in case

B SUBORDINATING CONJUNCTIONS

These join a subordinate clause to another clause, usually a main clause. The principal subordinating conjunctions are:

comme	as
parce que	because
puisque	since
ainsi que	(just) as
à mesure que	as
tant que	as long as
avant que	before
après que	after
jusqu'à ce que	until
depuis que	since
pendant que	while
tandis que	whereas
si	if
à moins que	unless
pourvu que	provided
quoique	although
bien que	although
quand	when
lorsque	when
dès que	as soon as
aussitôt que	as soon as
pour que	in order that
afin que	so that
de sorte que	so that
de façon que	so that
de peur que	for fear
(+ ne)	that, lest

Note that some subordinating conjunctions require the subjunctive (see p50).

C QUE

1 Coordinating (see pp 16 and 20)

que is a coordinating conjunction when used in comparisons:

il est plus fort **que** moi
he is stronger than I

elle est plus courageuse **que** tu ne crois
she's braver than you think

2 Subordinating

a) *meaning 'that':*

elle dit **qu'**elle l'a vu
she says she has seen him

je pense **que** tu as raison
I think you're right

il faut **que** tu viennes
you'll have to come

il paraît **qu'**elle a gagné
it seems she's won

b) *replacing another conjunction:*

When a conjunction introduces more than one verb, **que** usually replaces the second subordinating conjunction and any subsequent ones to avoid repetition:

comme il était tard et **que** j'étais fatigué, je suis rentré
as it was late and I was tired, I went home

s'il fait beau et **que** tu es libre, nous irons à la piscine
if the weather's nice and you're free, we'll go to the swimming pool

nous sortirons lorsque nous aurons déjeuné et **que** tu te seras reposé
we'll go out when we've had lunch and you've had a rest

---

10 Numbers and quantities

A CARDINAL NUMBERS

0	zéro	**40**	quarante
1	un (une)	**50**	cinquante
2	deux	**60**	soixante
3	trois	**70**	soixante-dix
4	quatre	**71**	soixante et onze
5	cinq	**72**	soixante-douze
6	six	**80**	quatre-vingt(s)
7	sept	**90**	quatre-vingt-dix
8	huit	**99**	quatre-vingt-dix-neuf
9	neuf	**100**	cent
10	dix	**101**	cent un(e)
11	onze	**102**	cent deux
12	douze	**121**	cent vingt et un(e)
13	treize	**122**	cent vingt-deux
14	quatorze	**200**	deux cents
15	quinze	**201**	deux cent un(e)
16	seize	**1000**	mille
17	dix-sept	**1988**	mille neuf cent
18	dix-huit		quatre-vingt-huit
19	dix-neuf	**2000**	deux mille
20	vingt	**10 000**	dix mille
30	trente	**1 000 000**	un million

Note:

a) **un** is the only cardinal number which agrees with the noun in gender:

un kilo
a kilo

une pomme
an apple

Numbers and quantities

b) hyphens are used in compound numbers between 17 and 99 except where **et** is used (this also applies to compound numbers after 100: **cent vingt-trois** 123).

c) **cent** and **mille** are not preceded by **un** as in English (one hundred).

d) **vingt** and **cent** multiplied by a number take an **s** when they are not followed by another number.

il a quatre-**vingts** ans
he's eighty

elle a remporté quatre-**vingt**-deux victoires
she has notched up eighty-two wins

c'est une civilisation vieille de huit **cents** ans
it's a civilization which is eight hundred years old

ce livre compte trois **cent** cinq pages
this book has three hundred and five pages

e) **mille** is invariable.

trente **mille** personnes ont assisté à la rencontre
thirty thousand people went to the match

B ORDINAL NUMBERS

		abbreviation
1st	premier/première	1er/1ère
2nd	deuxième/second	2^e
3rd	troisième	3^e
4th	quatrième	4^e
5th	cinquième	5^e
6th	sixième	6^e
7th	septième	7^e
8th	huitième	8^e
9th	neuvième	9^e
10th	dixième	10^e
11th	onzième	11^e
12th	douzième	12^e
13th	treizième	13^e
14th	quatorzième	14^e
15th	quinzième	15^e
16th	seizième	16^e
17th	dix-septième	17^e
18th	dix-huitième	18^e
19th	dix-neuvième	19^e
20th	vingtième	20^e
21st	vingt et unième	21^e
22nd	vingt-deuxième	22^e
30th	trentième	30^e
100th	centième	100^e
101st	cent unième	101^e
200th	deux centième	200^e

1000th	millième	1000^e
10,000th	dix millième	10 000^e

Note:

a) ordinal numbers are formed by adding -**ième** to cardinal numbers, except for **premier** and **second**; **cinq**, **neuf** and numbers ending in -**e** undergo slight changes: **cinquième**, **neuvième**, **onzième**, **douzième** etc.

b) ordinal numbers agree with the noun in gender and number:

le **Premier** ministre
the Prime Minister

la **première** fleur du printemps
the first flower of spring

c) there is no elision with **huitième** and **onzième**:

le **huitième** jour
the eighth day

du **onzième** candidat
of the eleventh candidate

d) cardinal numbers are used for monarchs, except for 'first':

Charles **deux**   Charles **premier**
Charles II   *Charles I*

C FRACTIONS AND PROPORTIONS

1 Fractions

Fractions are expressed as in English: cardinal followed by ordinal:

deux cinquièmes
two fifths

But: ¼ **un quart**
½ **un demi, une demie**

⅓ **un tiers**
¾ **trois quarts**

2 Decimals

The English decimal point is conveyed by a comma in French:

un virgule huit (1,8)
one point eight (1.8)

3 Approximate numbers

une huitaine   une dizaine
about eight   *about ten*

une trentaine   une centaine
some thirty   *about a hundred*

But: un millier
about a thousand

Note that **de** is used when the approximate number is followed by a noun:

une **vingtaine d'**enfants
about twenty children

4 Arithmetic

Addition:	deux **plus** quatre	$2 + 4$
Subtraction:	cinq **moins** deux	$5 - 2$
Multiplication:	trois **fois** cinq	3×5
Division:	six **divisé par** deux	$6\ 4\ 2$
Square:	deux **au carré**	2^2
Power:	deux **puissance** six	2^6

D MEASUREMENTS AND PRICES

1 Measurements

a) *Dimensions*

long(ue)/de longueur/de long
long
profond(e)/de profondeur/de profond
deep
épais(se)/d'épaisseur
thick
haut(e)/de hauteur/de haut
high

la salle de classe **est longue de 12 mètres**
la salle de classe **a/fait 12 mètres de longueur/de long**
the classroom is 12 metres long

ma chambre **fait quatre mètres sur trois**
my bedroom is about four metres by three

b) *Distance*

à quelle distance sommes-nous de la gare?
how far are we from the station?

nous sommes **à deux kilomètres** de la gare
we are two kilometres from the station

combien y a-t-il d'ici à Blois?
how far is it to Blois?

2 Price

ce pull m'a coûté 50 euros
this sweater cost me 50 euros

j'ai payé ce pull 50 euros
I paid 50 euros for this sweater

des pommes à 2 euros le kilo
apples at 2 euros a kilo

du vin blanc à 5 euros la bouteille
white wine at 5 euros a bottle

cela fait/revient à 6 euros
that comes to 6 euros

ils coûtent 4 euros pièce
they cost 4 euros each

E EXPRESSIONS OF QUANTITY

Quantity may be expressed by an adverb of quantity, eg 'a lot', 'too much' or by a noun which names the actual quantity involved, eg 'a bottle', 'a dozen'.

1 Expression of quantity + 'de' + noun

Before a noun, adverbs and other expressions of quantity are followed by **de** (**d'** before a vowel or a silent **h**) and never by **du**, **de la** or **des**, except for bien des and **la plupart du/des**:

assez de *enough*	**autant de** *as much/many*
beaucoup de *a lot of/much/many*	**combien de** *how much/many*
moins de *less/fewer*	**plus de** *more*
peu de *little/few*	**un peu de** *a little*
tant de *so much/many*	**tellement de** *so much/many*
bien du/de la/des *many/a lot of*	**la plupart du/de la/des** *most*
trop de *too much/many*	

il y a **assez de** fromage?
is there enough cheese?

autant de gens
as many people

je n'ai pas **beaucoup de** temps
I haven't got much time

il y a **combien de** pièces?
how many rooms are there?

j'ai mis **moins de** temps que lui
I took less time than him

Expressions of time

mange **plus de** légumes!
eat more vegetables!

peu de gens le savent
not many people know that

tu veux **un peu de** pain?
would you like a little bread?

il y a **tant d**'années
so many years ago

j'ai **tellement de** travail
I've got so much work

bien des gens
a good many people

la plupart des Français
most French people

tu as **bien de** la patience
you have a lot of patience

il y a **trop de** voitures
there are too many cars

2 Noun expressing quantity + 'de' + noun

une boîte de *a box/tin/can/jar of*	**une bouteille de** *a bottle of*
une bouchée de *a mouthful of (food)*	**une cuillerée de** *a spoonful of*
une douzaine de *a dozen*	**une gorgée de** *a mouthful of (drink)*
un kilo de *a kilo of*	**un litre de** *a litre of*
une livre de *a pound of*	**un morceau de** *a piece of*
un paquet de *a packet of*	**une paire de** *a pair of*
une part de *a share/helping of*	**une tasse de** *a cup of*
une tranche de *a slice of*	**un verre de** *a glass of*

je voudrais **une boîte de** thon et **un litre de** lait
I'd like a tin of tuna and a litre of milk

il y a **une boîte de** limonade dans le frigo
there's a can of lemonade in the fridge

j'ai pris **deux parts de** choucroute
I took two helpings of sauerkraut

il a mangé **une douzaine d'**œufs et **six morceaux de** poulet
he ate a dozen eggs and six pieces of chicken

3 Expressions of quantity used without a noun

When an expression of quantity is not followed by a noun, **de** is replaced by the pronoun **en** (see p29):

il y avait beaucoup de neige; il y **en** avait beaucoup
there was a lot of snow; there was a lot (of it)

elle a mangé trop de chocolats; elle **en** a trop mangé
she's eaten too many chocolates; she's eaten too many (of them)

11 Expressions of time

A THE TIME

quelle heure est-il? *what time is it?*

a) *Full hours*
il est midi/minuit
it is 12 noon or midday/midnight

il est une heure
it is 1 o'clock

b) *Half-hours*
il est minuit **et demi(e)**
it is 12.30 a.m.

il est midi **et demi(e)**
it is 12.30 p.m.

il est une heure **et demie**
it is 1.30

c) *Quarter-hours*
il est deux heures **un/le quart**
it is a quarter past two

il est deux heures **moins et quart**
it is a quarter to two

d) *Minutes*
il est quatre heures **vingt-trois**
it is 23 minutes past 4

il est cinq heures **moins vingt**
it is 20 to 5

Note that **minutes** is usually omitted; **heures** is never omitted.

e) *A.m. and p.m.*

du matin	de l'après-midi/du soir
a.m., in the morning	*p.m., in the evening*

il est sept heures moins dix du soir
t is 7.10 p.m. or in the evening

il est sept heures dix du matin
it is 6.50 a.m. or in the morning

The 24-hour clock is commonly used:
dix heures trente
10.30 a.m.

quatorze heures trente-cinq
2.35 p.m.

dix-neuf heures dix
7.10 p.m.

Note that times are often abbreviated as
follows:
dix-neuf heures dix 19h10

B THE DATE

1 Names of months, days and seasons

à) *Months*

janvier	*January*
février	*February*
mars	*March*
avril	*April*
mai	*May*
juin	*June*
juillet	*July*
août	*August*
septembre	*September*
octobre	*October*
novembre	*November*
décembre	*December*

b) *Days of the week*

lundi	*Monday*
mardi	*Tuesday*
mercredi	*Wednesday*
jeudi	*Thursday*
vendredi	*Friday*
samedi	*Saturday*
dimanche	*Sunday*

c) *Seasons*

le printemps	*spring*
l'été	*summer*
l'automne	*autumn*
l'hiver	*winter*

For prepositions used with the seasons see
p6.

Note that in French, months and days are
masculine and do not have a capital letter
unless they begin a sentence.

2 Dates

a) Cardinals (eg **deux**, **trois**) are used for the
dates of the month except the first:

le **quatorze** juillet
the fourteenth of July

le **deux** novembre
the second of November

But: le **premier** février
the first of February

The definite article is used as in English;
French does not use prepositions ('on' and
'of' in English):

je vous ai écrit **le** trois mars
I wrote to you on the third of March

b) **mil** *(a thousand)* is used instead of **mille** in
dates from 1001 onwards:

mil neuf cent quatre-vingt sept
nineteen hundred and eighty-seven

l'an deux **mil** deux
the year two thousand and two

3 Année, journée, matinée, soirée

Année, **journée**, **matinée**, **soirée** (the feminine forms of **an**, **jour**, **matin** and **soir**) are
usually found in the following cases:

a) *when duration is implied:*

pendant une année
for a (whole) year

toute la journée
all day long, the whole day

dans la matinée
in the (course of the) morning

passer une soirée
to spend an evening

l'année scolaire/universitaire
the school/academic year

b) *with an ordinal number or an indefinite
expression:*

la deuxième année
the second year

dans sa vingtième année
in his twentieth year

plusieurs/quelques années
several/a few years

bien des/de nombreuses années
many years

environ une année
about a year

Expressions of time

c) *with an adjective:*

de bonnes/mauvaises années
good/bad years

C IDIOMATIC EXPRESSIONS

à cinq heures	*at five o'clock*
à onze heures environ	*(at) about eleven o'clock*
vers minuit	*(at) about midnight*
vers (les) dix heures	*(at) about ten o'clock*
il est six heures passées	*it's past six o'clock*
à quatre heures précises ou **pile**	*at exactly four o'clock*
sur le coup de trois heures	*on the stroke of three*
à partir de neuf heures	*from nine o'clock onwards*
peu avant sept heures	*shortly before seven*
peu après sept heures	*shortly after seven*
tôt ou tard	*sooner or later*
au plus tôt	*at the earliest*
au plus tard	*at the latest*
il est tard	*it is late*
il est en retard	*he is late*
il se lève tard	*he gets up late*
il est arrivé en retard	*he arrived late*
le train a vingt minutes de retard	*the train is twenty minutes late*
ma montre retarde de six minutes	*my watch is six minutes slow*
ma montre avance de six minutes	*my watch is six minutes fast*
ce soir	*this evening, tonight*
demain soir	*tomorrow evening, tomorrow night*
hier soir	*yesterday evening, last night*
samedi soir	*Saturday evening*
je sors samedi soir	*I'm going out on Saturday night or evening*
dans la soirée de samedi	*on Saturday evening*
dans la nuit de samedi (à dimanche)	*during Saturday night*
demain matin	*tomorrow morning*
hier matin	*yesterday morning*
lundi matin	*Monday morning*
j'y vais lundi matin	*I'm going there on Monday morning*
demain en huit	*tomorrow week*
le lendemain	*the next day*
le lendemain matin	*the next morning*
hier matin	*yesterday morning*

la semaine dernière	*last week*
la semaine prochaine	*next week*
la semaine qui vient	*this coming week*
je l'ai vu l'autre samedi	*I saw him the other Saturday*
lundi	*on Monday*
le lundi	*on Mondays*
je commence lundi	*I'm starting (on) Monday*
il vient le lundi	*he comes on Mondays, he comes on a Monday*
vient un lundi	*come one Monday*
un lundi sur deux	*every other Monday, every second Monday*
tous les lundis	*every Monday*
tous les lundis soirs	*every Monday evening or night*
tous mes lundis	*all my Mondays*
lundi en huit	*a week on Monday, Monday week*
lundi en quinze	*a fortnight on Monday*
il y a trois semaines	*three weeks ago*
il vient l'après-midi	*he comes in the afternoon(s)*
viens un après-midi	*come one afternoon*
une demi-heure	*a half-hour, half an hour*
un quart d'heure	*a quarter of an hour*
trois quarts d'heure	*three quarters of an hour*
passer son temps (à faire)	*to spend one's time (doing)*
perdre son temps	*to waste one's time*
de temps en temps	*from time to time*
de temps à autre	*from time to time*
dans les temps	*on time*
au début de l'après-midi/de la soirée, en début d'après-midi/de soirée	*in the early afternoon/evening*
je te téléphonerai en début de matinée	*I'll phone you first thing in the morning*
au début du mois	*at the beginning of the month*
j'ai une réunion de la matinée ou **en milieu de matinée**	*I have a meeting mid-morning*
au milieu (du mois)	*in the middle of*
de juin, (à la) mi-juin	*June, mid-June*
au milieu de l'hiver	*in the middle of winter, midwinter*
j'ai une réunion à la fin de la matinée ou **en fin de matinée**	*I have a meeting late morning*

à la fin de l'hiver	at the end of the winter
on en reparlera fin ou janvier ou à la fin du mois de janvier	we'll talk about it again at the end of January
quel jour sommes-nous aujourd'hui?	what day is it today?
le combien sommes-nous aujourd'hui?	what's the date today?, what's today's date?
nous sommes/c'est le trois avril	it's the third of April
aujourd'hui nous sommes samedi	today is Saturday, it's Saturday today
vendredi 11 janvier 2004	Friday, 11 January 2004
nous nous sommes vus le vendredi 11 janvier	we saw each other on Friday, 11th January
le vendredi treize juillet	Friday the thirteenth of July
en février/au mois de février	in February/in the month of February
en février 2004	in February 2004
l'été 2004	in the summer of 2004, in summer 2004
en 2004	in 2004
dans les années soixante	in the sixties, in the 60s, in the 1960s
au début/à la fin des années soixante	in the early/late sixties
au dix-septième siècle	in the seventeenth century
au XVIIᵉ	in the 17th century
le jour de l'An	New Year's Day
avoir treize ans	to be thirteen (years old)
être âgé de quatorze ans	to be fourteen (years old)
elle fête ses vingt ans	she's celebrating her twentieth birthday
elle a une vingtaine d'années	she's around twenty (years old)
un plan quinquennal	a five-year plan
une année bissextile	a leap year
une année civile	a calendar year
une année-lumière	a light year

12 The sentence

A WORD ORDER

Word order is usually the same in French as in English, except in the following cases:

1 Adjectives

Many French adjectives follow the noun (see p15):

de l'argent **suisse**   j'ai les yeux **bleus**
(some) Swiss money   I've got blue eyes

2 Adverbs

In simple tenses, adverbs usually follow the verb (see p19):

j'y vais **rarement**   il fera **bientôt** nuit
I seldom go there   it will soon be dark

3 Object pronouns

Object pronouns usually come before the verb (see p27):

je **t'**attendrai   il **la lui** a vendue
I'll wait for you   he sold it to him

4 Noun phrases

Noun phrases are formed differently in French (see p85):

une chemise en coton
a cotton shirt

le père de mon copain
my friend's father

5 Exclamations

The word order is not affected after **que** or **comme** (unlike after 'how' in English):

que tu es bête!   **qu'il fait froid!**
you are silly!   it's so cold!
(how silly you are!)

comme il chante mal!
he sings so badly!

comme c'est beau!
that's so beautiful!

6 DONT

dont must be followed by the subject of the clause it introduces; compare:

l'ami **dont** j'ai perdu l'adresse
the friend whose address I lost

l'ami **dont** l'adresse a changé
the friend whose address has changed

The sentence

7 Inversion

In certain cases, the subject of a French clause is placed after the verb. Word order is effectively that of an interrogative sentence (see p80). This occurs:

a) *after the following, when they occur at the beginning of a clause:*

à peine	**aussi**	**peut-être**
hardly	*therefore*	*maybe, perhaps*

à peine Alain était-il sorti qu'il a commencé à pleuvoir
Alain had barely gone out when it started raining

il y avait une grève du métro, **aussi a-t-il pris** un taxi
there was an underground strike, so he took a taxi

peut-être vont-ils téléphoner plus tard
maybe they'll phone later

But: Alain **était à peine sorti** qu'il a commencé à pleuvoir
ils vont peut-être téléphoner plus tard

b) *when a verb of saying follows direct speech:*

'si tu veux,' **a répondu Marie**
'if you want,' Marie replied

'attention!' **a-t-elle crié**
'watch out!' she shouted

'j'espère que non,' **dit-il**
'I hope not,' he said

'répondez!' **ordonna-t-il**
'answer!' he ordered

B NEGATIVE EXPRESSIONS

1 Main negative words

a)
ne ... pas	*not*
ne ... point	*not (literary)*
ne ... plus	*no more/longer, not ... any more*
ne ... jamais	*never*
ne ... rien	*nothing, not ... anything*
ne ... guère	*hardly*

b)
ne ... personne	*nobody, no one, not ... anyone*
ne ... que	*only*
ne ... ni (ni ... ni)	*neither ... nor*
ne ... aucun(e)	*no, not any, none*
ne ... nul(le)	*no*
ne ... nulle part	*nowhere, not ... anywhere*

Note:

i) **ne** becomes **n'** before a vowel or a silent **h**.

ii) **aucun** and **nul**, like other adjectives and pronouns, agree with the word they refer to; they are used only in the singular.

2 Position of negative expressions

a) *with simple tenses and with the imperative*

Negative words enclose the verb: **ne** comes before the verb, and the second part of the negative expression comes after the verb:

je **ne** la connais **pas**
I don't know her

n'insistez **pas!**
don't insist!

je **n'**ai **plus** d'argent
I haven't any money left

tu **ne** le sauras **jamais**
you'll never know

ne dis **rien**	il **n'**y a **personne**
don't say anything	*no one's here*

je **n'**avais **que** 3 euros
I only had 3 euros

il **n'**est **nulle part**
it isn't anywhere

tu **n'**as **aucun** sens de l'humour
you have no sense of humour

il **n'**est **ni** bête **ni** crédule
he's neither stupid nor gullible

b) *with compound tenses*

With **ne ... pas** and the other expressions in list 1a), the word order is: **ne** + auxiliary + **pas** + past participle:

il n'est pas revenu
he didn't come back

je n'ai plus essayé
I didn't try any more

je n'avais jamais vu Paris
I had never seen Paris

on n'a rien fait
we haven't done anything

With **ne ... personne** and the other expressions in list 1b), the word order is: **ne** + auxiliary + past participle + **personne/que/ni** etc:

il ne l'a dit à personne
he didn't tell anyone

tu n'en as acheté qu'un?
did you only buy one?

je n'en ai aimé aucun
I didn't like any of them

il n'est allé nulle part
he hasn't gone anywhere

c) *with the infinitive*

i) **ne ... pas** and the other expressions in list 1a) are placed together before the verb:

je préfère **ne pas y aller**
I'd rather not go

essaye de **ne rien perdre**
try not to lose anything

ii) **ne ... personne** and the other expressions in list 1b) enclose the infinitive:

il a été surpris de **ne voir personne**
he was surprised not to see anybody

j'ai décidé de **n'en acheter aucun**
I decided not to buy any of them

d) *at the beginning of a sentence*

When **personne, rien, aucun** and **ni ... ni ...** begin a sentence, they are followed by **ne**:

personne ne le sait
nobody knows

rien n'a changé
nothing has changed

ni Paul **ni** Simone **ne** sont venus
neither Paul nor Simone came

aucun secours **n'**est arrivé
no help arrived

3 Combination of negative expressions

Negative expressions can be combined:

ne ... plus jamais
ne ... plus rien   **ne ... jamais rien**
ne ... plus personne   **ne ... jamais personne**
ne ... plus ni ... ni   **ne ... jamais ni ... ni**
ne ... plus que   **ne ... jamais que**

on **ne** l'a **plus jamais** revu
we never saw him again

il **n'**y a **plus rien**
there isn't anything left

plus personne ne viendra
no one will come any more

tu ne dis **jamais rien**
you never say anything

je ne bois **jamais que** de l'eau
I only ever drink water

je ne vois **jamais personne**
I never see anybody

je ne pardonnerai **jamais ni n'**oublierai
I will never forgive nor forget

4 Negative expressions without a verb

a) **pas**

pas *(not)* is the most common of all negatives; it is frequently used without a verb:

tu l'aimes? – **pas** beaucoup
do you like it?   not much

ah non, **pas** lui!
oh no, not him!

non merci, **pas** pour moi
no thanks, not for me

un roman **pas** très long
not a very long novel

lui, il viendra, mais **pas** moi
he will come, but I won't

j'aime ça; **pas** toi?
I like that; don't you?

b) **ne**

ne is not used when there is no verb:

qui a crié? – **personne**
who shouted? – nobody

jamais de la vie!   **rien** du tout
not on your life!   *nothing at all*

rien! je ne veux **rien!**
nothing! I want nothing!

c) **non**

non *(no)* is always used without a verb:

tu aimes la natation? – **non,** pas du tout
do you like swimming? – no, not at all

tu viens, oui ou **non**? – je crois que **non**
are you coming, yes or no? – I don't think so

Note that **non plus** means 'neither':

je ne le crois pas – moi **non plus**
I don't believe him – neither do I

je n'ai rien mangé – nous **non plus**
I haven't eaten anything – neither have we

The sentence

C DIRECT AND INDIRECT QUESTIONS

1 Direct questions

There are three ways of forming direct questions in French:

a) *subject + verb (+ question word)*

The word order remains the same as in statements (subject + verb) but the intonation changes: the voice is raised at the end of the sentence. This is by far the most common question form in conversational French:

tu l'as acheté où?
where did you buy it?

je peux téléphoner d'ici?
can I phone from here?

vous prendrez quel train?
which train will you take?

tu me fais confiance?
do you trust me?

c'était comment? la gare est près d'ici?
what was it like? *is the station near here?*

le train part à quelle heure?
what time does the train leave?

cette robe me va?
does this dress suit me?

b) *(question word)* + **est-ce que** + *subject + verb*

This question form is also very common in conversation:

qu'est-ce que tu as?
what's the matter with you?

est-ce qu'il est là?
is he in?

est-ce que ton ami s'est amusé?
did your friend have a good time?

où est-ce que vous avez mal?
where does it hurt?

c) *inversion*

This question form is the most formal of the three, and the least commonly used in conversation:

i) If the subject is a pronoun, the word order is as follows:

(question word) + verb + hyphen + subject
où allez-vous?
where are you going?

voulez-vous commander?
do you wish to order?

quand est-il arrivé?
when did he arrive?

avez-vous bien dormi?
did you sleep well?

ii) If the subject is a noun, a pronoun referring to the noun is inserted after the verb, and linked to it with a hyphen:

(question word) + noun subject + verb + hyphen + pronoun
où ton père travaillait-il?
where did your father work?

Nicole en veut-elle?
does Nicole want any?

iii) **-t-** is inserted before **il** and **elle** when the verb ends in a vowel:

comment **va-t-il** voyager?
how will he travel?

aime-t-elle le café?
does she like coffee?

pourquoi **a-t-il** refusé?
why did he refuse?

Marie **viendra-t-elle**?
will Marie be coming?

Note that when a question word is used, modern French will often just invert the verb and the noun subject, without adding a pronoun; no hyphen is then necessary:

où travaille ton père?
where does your father work?

2 Indirect questions

a) *Definition*

Indirect questions follow a verb and are introduced by an interrogative word, eg:

ask him when he will arrive
I don't know why he did it

b) *Word order*

i) The word order is usually the same as in statements: question word + subject + verb:

je ne sais pas s'il voudra
I don't know if he'll want to

dis-moi où tu l'as mis
tell me where you put it

il n'a pas dit quand il appellerait
he didn't say when he would phone

ii) If the subject is a noun, the verb and subject are sometimes inverted:

demande-leur où est le camping
ask them where the campsite is

But: je ne comprends pas comment l'accident s'est produit
I don't understand how the accident happened

il ne savait pas pourquoi elle avait l'air triste
he didn't know why she looked sad

3 Translation of English question tags

Examples of question tags are: isn't it? aren't you? doesn't he? won't they? haven't you? is it? did you? and so on. Question tags are not used in French as often as they are in English. Some of them can, however, be translated in the following ways:

a) **n'est-ce pas?**

n'est-ce pas? is used at the end of a sentence when confirmation of a statement is expected:

c'était très intéressant, **n'est-ce pas?**
it was very interesting, wasn't it?

tu voudrais partir en vacances, **n'est-ce pas?**
you'd like to go on holiday, wouldn't you?

vous n'arriverez pas trop tard, **n'est-ce pas?**
you won't be arriving too late, will you?

b) **hein?** *and* **non?**

In conversation **hein?** and **non?** are often used after affirmative statements instead of **n'est-ce pas**:

il fait beau, **hein?**
the weather's nice, isn't it?

il est amusant, **non?**
he's funny, isn't he?

D ANSWERS ('YES' AND 'NO')

1 OUI, SI *and* NON

a) **oui** and **si** mean 'yes' and are equivalent to longer affirmative answers such as 'yes, it is', 'yes, I will', 'yes, he has' etc:

tu m'écriras? – **oui**, bien sûr!
will you write to me? – (yes) of course I will

b) **non** means 'no' and is equivalent to longer

negative answers such as 'no, it isn't', 'no, I didn't' etc:

c'était bien? – **non**, on s'est ennuyé
was it good? – no, it wasn't, we were bored

2 OUI *or* SI?

oui and **si** both mean 'yes', but **oui** is used to answer an affirmative question, and **si** to contradict a negative question:

cette place est libre? – **oui**
is this seat free? – yes (it is)

tu n'aimes pas lire? – **si**, bien sûr!
don't you like reading? – yes, of course (I do)

13 Translation problems

A GENERAL TRANSLATION PROBLEMS

1 French words not translated in English

Some French words are not translated in English, particularly:

a) *Articles*

Definite and indefinite articles are not always translated (see p5):

dans **la** société moderne
in modern society

les gens en ont assez!
people have had enough!

ah non! encore du riz! je déteste **le** riz!
oh no! rice again! I hate rice!

b) **que**

que meaning 'that' as a conjunction (see p71) or 'that'/'which'/'whom' as a relative pronoun (see p33) cannot be omitted in French:

j'espère **que** tu vas mieux
I hope you're better

elle pense **que** c'est vrai
she thinks it's true

celui **que** j'ai vu
the one I saw

c'est un pays **que** j'aime
it's a country I like

c) *Prepositions*

Some French verbs are followed by a preposition (+ indirect object) when their English equivalent takes a direct object without a preposition (see p62):

elle a téléphoné **au médecin**
she phoned the doctor

tu l'as dit **à ton père?**
did you tell your father?

d) **le**

When **le** *(it)* is used in an impersonal sense (see p28), it is not translated:

oui, je **le** sais   dis-**le**-lui
yes, I know   *tell him*

2 English words not translated in French

Some English words are not translated in French, for example:

a) *Prepositions*

i) with verbs which take an indirect object in English, but a direct object in French (see p63):

tu l'as payé **combien?**
how much did you pay for it?

écoutez cette chanson
listen to this song

ii) in certain expressions (see p76):

je viendrai te voir **lundi soir**
I'll come and see you on Monday night

b) *'can'*

'can' + verb of hearing or seeing (see p61):

je ne **vois** rien!
I can't see anything!

tu **entends** la musique?
can you hear the music?

3 Other differences

a) *English phrasal verbs*

Phrasal verbs are verbs which, when followed by a preposition, take on a different meaning, eg 'to give up', 'to walk out'. They do not exist in French and are translated by simple verbs or by expressions:

to give up	to run away	to run across
abandonner	s'enfuir	traverser en courant

b) *English possessive adjectives*

English possessive adjectives (my, your etc)

are translated by the French definite article (le/la/les) when parts of the body are mentioned (see p33):

brush your teeth   he hurt his foot
brosse-toi **les** dents   il s'est fait mal **au** pied

c) *'from'*

'from' is translated by **à** with verbs referring to taking something away (see p64):

he hid it from his parents
il l'a caché **à** ses parents

borrow some from your dad
empruntes-en **à** ton père

B SPECIFIC TRANSLATION PROBLEMS

1 Words ending in -ing

The English verbal form ending in -ing is translated in a number of ways in French:

a) *by the appropriate French tense (see p45):*

he's speaking *(present tense)*	il parle
he was speaking *(imperfect)*	il parlait
he will be speaking *(future)*	il parlera
he has been speaking *(perfect)*	il a parlé
he had been speaking *(pluperfect)*	il avait parlé
he would be speaking *(conditional)*	il parlerait

b) *by a French present participle (see p57)*

i) as an adjective:

un livre **amusant**   c'est **effrayant**
a funny book   *it's frightening*

ii) as a verb, with **en** (while/on/by doing something; see p57):

'ça ne fait rien', dit-il **en souriant**
'it doesn't matter', he said smiling

j'ai vu mes copains **en sortant** du lycée
I saw my friends when I was coming out of school

Note, however, that **en** + present participle cannot be used when the two verbs have different subjects, eg:

I saw my brother coming out of school
j'ai vu mon frère sortir du lycée/qui sortait du lycée

c) *by a present infinitive (see p53):*

i) after a preposition:

au lieu de **rire**   avant de **traverser**
instead of laughing   *before crossing*

ii) after verbs of perception:

je l'ai entendu **appeler**
I heard him calling

je l'ai vue **entrer**
I saw her going in

iii) after verbs of liking and disliking:

j'adore **faire** du camping
I love camping

tu aimes **lire?**
do you like reading?

iv) after verbs followed by **à** or **de**:

tu passes tout ton temps **à ne rien faire**
you spend all your time doing nothing

il a commencé **à neiger**
it started snowing

continuez **à travailler**
go on working

tu as envie **de sortir?**
do you feel like going out?

il doit finir **de manger**
he must finish eating

v) when an English verb in -ing is the subject of another verb:

attendre serait inutile
waiting would be pointless

écrire est une corvée!
writing is a real chore!

vi) when an English verb in -ing follows 'is' or 'was' etc:

mon passe-temps favori, c'est de **lire**
my favourite pastime is reading

d) *by a perfect infinitive* (see p56)

i) after **après** *(after)*:

j'ai pris une douche **après avoir nettoyé** ma chambre
I had a shower after cleaning my room

ii) after certain verbs:

regretter   **remercier de**
to regret   *to thank for*

se souvenir de
to remember

j'ai regretté de leur en **avoir parlé**
I regretted speaking to them about it

il m'a remercié d'**être allé** le chercher
he thanked me for going to pick him up

e) *by a noun*

particularly when referring to sports, activities, hobbies etc:

le ski	**la natation**	**l'équitation**
skiing	swimming	horse-riding
la voile	**le patinage**	**le canoë**
sailing	skating	canoeing
la lecture	**la planche à voile**	
reading	windsurfing	
la cuisine	**la boxe**	
cooking	boxing	
la lutte	**la marche à pied**	
wrestling	walking	

2 IT IS (IT'S)

'it is' (it's) can be translated in three ways in French:

a) **il** *or* **elle** (see p27)

il or **elle** are used with the verb **être** to translate 'it is', 'it was' etc (+ adjective) when referring to a particular masculine or feminine noun (a thing, a place etc):

merci de ta carte; **elle était** très amusante
thanks for your card; it was very funny

regarde ce blouson; **il n'est** vraiment pas cher
look at this jacket; it really isn't that expensive

b) **ce** (see p22)

ce (**c'** before a vowel) is used with the verb **être** to translate 'it is', 'it was' etc in two cases:

i) If **être** is followed by a word which is not an adjective on its own, ie by a noun, a pronoun, an expression of place etc:

c'était ta voix   **c'est** le tien?
it was your voice   *is it yours?*

c'est une grande maison
it's a big house

c'est moi! c'est Claude!
it's me! it's Claude!

c'est en France que tu vas?
is it France you're going to?

c'est pour lundi
it's for Monday

ii) If **être** is followed by an adjective which refers to something previously mentioned, such as an idea, an event or a fact, but not to a specific noun:

l'homme n'ira jamais sur Saturne; **ce n'est** pas possible
Man will never go to Saturn; it's not possible

j'ai passé mes vacances en Italie; **c'était** formidable!
I spent my holidays in Italy; it was great!

oh, je m'excuse! – **ce n'est** pas grave
oh, I'm sorry! – it's all right

c) **il** (see p44)

il is used to translate 'it is', 'it was' etc in three cases:

i) With **être** followed by an adjective + **de** or **que**, ie referring to something that follows, but not to a specific noun:
il est impossible **de** connaître l'avenir
it's impossible to know the future

il est évident **que** tu ne me crois pas
it's obvious you don't believe me

ii) To describe the weather (see p44):
il y a du vent   **il faisait** très froid
it's windy   *it was very cold*

iii) With **être** to tell the time and in phrases relating to the time of day, or in such expressions as **il est temps de** (it's time to):
il est deux heures du matin
it's two in the morning

il est tard!
it's late!

il est temps de partir
it's time to go

Note that with other expressions of time, **c'est** is used:
c'est lundi ou mardi aujourd'hui?
is it Monday or Tuesday today?

c'était l'été
it was summer

3 TO BE

Although 'to be' is usually translated by **être**, it can also be translated in the following ways:

a) **avoir**

i) **avoir** is used instead of **être** in many set expressions:
avoir faim/soif   *to be hungry/thirsty*
avoir chaud/froid *to be warm/cold*

avoir peur/honte   *to be afraid/ashamed*
avoir tort/raison *to be wrong/right*

ii) **avoir** is also used for age:
quel âge **as-**tu?   j'**ai** vingt-cinq ans
how old are you?   *I'm twenty-five*

b) **aller**

aller is used for describing health:
je **vais** mieux   tout le monde **va** bien
I am/feel better   *everyone's fine*

c) **faire**

faire is used in many expressions to describe the weather (see p44):
il **fait** beau   il **fera** chaud
the weather's nice   *it will be hot*

Note that **il y a** can also be used to describe the weather, but only before **du/de la/des**:
il y a du vent/**des** nuages/**de** la tempête
it's windy/cloudy/stormy

d) *untranslated*

'to be' is not translated when it is the first part of an English continuous tense; instead, the appropriate tense is used in French (see p45):
I'm having a bath   *he was driving slowly*
je prends un bain   il conduisait lentement

4 ANY

'any' can be translated in three different ways:

a) **du/de la/des** *or* **de** (see p7)

The partitive article is used with a noun in negative and interrogative sentences:
il ne mange jamais **de** viande
he never eats meat

tu veux **du** pain?
do you want any bread?

b) **en** (see p27)

en is used to translate 'any' when it occurs without a noun in negative and interrogative sentences:
je n'en **ai** pas   il **en** reste?
I haven't got any   *is there any left?*

c) **n'importe quel(le)/quel(le)s** *or* **tout(e)/tou(te)s**

these are used to translate 'any' (and 'every') when they mean 'no matter which':
il pourrait arriver à **n'importe quel** moment
he could arrive any time

prends **n'importe quelle** couleur, je les aime toutes
take any colour, I like them all

5 ANYONE, ANYTHING, ANYWHERE

Like 'any', these can be translated in different ways:

a) *in interrogative sentences:*

il y a **quelqu'un?**
is anyone in?

tu l'as vu **quelque part?**
did you see it anywhere?

il a dit **quelque chose?**
did he say anything?

b) *in negative sentences:*

il n'y a **personne**   je n'ai **rien** fait
there isn't anyone   *I didn't do anything*

je ne le vois **nulle part**
I can't see it anywhere

c) *in the sense of 'any' (and 'every'), 'no matter which':*

n'importe qui peut le faire
anyone can do that

il croit **n'importe quoi**
he believes anything

j'irai **n'importe où n'importe quand**
I'll go anywhere   anytime

6 YOU, YOUR, YOURS, YOURSELF

French has two separate sets of words to translate 'you', 'your', 'yours', 'yourself':

● **tu, te (t'), toi, ton/ta/tes, le tien** etc

● **vous, votre/vos, le vôtre** etc

For their respective meanings and uses, see p27.

a) **tu** *etc*

tu, te, ton etc correspond to the **tu** form of the verb (second person singular) and are used when speaking to one person you know well (a friend, a relative) or to someone younger. They represent the familiar form of address:

si **tu** viens au concert avec **ton** copain, je **t'**achète deux places; une pour **toi** et une pour lui
if you're coming to the concert with your boyfriend, I'll get you two tickets; one for you and one for him

b) **vous** *etc*

vous, vos etc correspond to the **vous** form of the verb (second person plural) and are used:

i) when speaking to more than one person:
dépêchez-**vous**, les gars! **Vous** allez manquer le train
hurry up, boys! You'll miss the train

ii) when speaking to one person you do not know well or to someone older. They represent the formal or polite form of address:
je regrette, Monsieur, mais **vous** ne pouvez pas garder **votre** chien avec **vous** dans ce restaurant
I'm sorry, sir, but you can't keep your dog with you in this restaurant

c) when speaking or writing to one person, you must not mix words from both sets, but decide whether you are being formal or familiar, and use the same form of address throughout:

Cher Michel,
Merci pour **ta** lettre. Comment vas-**tu?** ...
Dear Michel,
Thanks for your letter. How are you? ...

Monsieur,
Pourriez-**vous** me réserver une chambre dans **votre** hôtel pour le 8 juin?
Dear Sir,
Could you book a room for me in your hotel for 8th June?

vous etc and **tu** etc can only be used together when **vous** is plural (ie when it refers to more than one person):
tu sais, Jean, **toi** et **ta** sœur, **vous vous** ressemblez
you know, Jean, you and your sister look like each other

7 Noun phrases

A noun phrase is a combination of two nouns used together to name things or people. In English, the first of these nouns is used to describe the second one, eg 'a love story'. In French, however, the position of the two nouns is reversed, so that the describing noun comes second and is linked to the first one by the preposition **de** (or **d'**):

une histoire **d'**amour   une feuille **d'**impôts
a love story   *a tax form*

un magasin **de** disques   un acteur **de** cinéma
a record shop   *a film actor*

un arrêt **d'**autobus   un film **d'**aventure
a bus stop   *an adventure film*

un coup **de** soleil   une boule **de** neige
sunstroke   *a snowball*

un roman **de** science-fiction
a science-fiction novel

un match **de** football   un conte **de** fées
a football match   *a fairy tale*

le château **d'**Édimbourg
Edinburgh castle

un joueur **de** rugby
a rugby player

un employé **de** bureau
an office worker

Note that when the describing noun refers to a type of material, the preposition **en** is often used instead of **de**:

un pull **en** laine   un pantalon **en** cuir
a woollen jumper   *leather trousers*

une bague **en** or   un sac **en** plastique
a gold ring   *a plastic bag*

8 Possession

In English, possession is often expressed by using a noun phrase and tagging 's at the end of the first word, eg:

my friend's cat

This is translated in French by: object + **de** + possessor:

le chat **de mon ami**

Note the use of the article **le/la/les**.

le fiancé de ma sœur
my sister's fiancé

les amis de Claire
Claire's friends

les événements de **la** semaine dernière
last week's events

When 's is used to refer to someone's house or shop etc, it is translated by the preposition **chez**:

je téléphone de **chez** Paul
I'm telephoning from Paul's (house)

chez le dentiste
at/to the dentist's

French Conjugation Tables

Full listings of the conjugations of French regular -**er**, -**ir** and -**re** verbs are given on pages (88) and (89). On the following pages you will find a list of model irregular verbs. Numbers after verbs in the French-English side of the dictionary, eg [20], refer you to these tables where you will find their irregular forms.

The more common verbs such as **aller**, **avoir**, **être** and **faire** are shown in full for all persons and all tenses. In other cases, where complete forms have not been shown they follow the pattern indicated by the first person singular and/or plural.

As the perfect tense is always formed simply by **avoir** or **être** plus the past participle, this has not been shown apart from the verbs mentioned above. Similarly, the conditional tense can always be formed in the same way as the future tense but with the endings -**ais**, -**ais**, -**ait**, -**ions**, -**iez** and -**aient**. When not shown, the imperative has the same form as the present tense ("tu", "nous" and "vous" forms).

French Conjugation Tables

INDICATIVE

Present	Imperfect	Perfect	Past Historic	Future

REGULAR -er verb aimer

Present	Imperfect	Perfect	Past Historic	Future
j'aime	j'aimais	j'ai aimé	j'aimai	j'aimerai
tu aimes	tu aimais	tu as aimé	tu aimas	tu aimeras
il aime	il aimait	il a aimé	il aima	il aimera
nous aimons	nous aimions	nous avons aimé	nous aimâmes	nous aimerons
vous aimez	vous aimiez	vous avez aimé	vous aimâtes	vous aimerez
ils aiment	ils aimaient	ils ont aimé	ils aimèrent	ils aimeront

REGULAR -ir verb choisir

Present	Imperfect	Perfect	Past Historic	Future
je choisis	je choisissais	j'ai choisi	je choisis	je choisirai
tu choisis	tu choisissais	tu as choisi	tu choisis	tu choisiras
il choisit	il choisissait	il a choisi	il choisit	il choisira
nous choisissons	nous choisissions	nous avons choisi	nous choisîmes	nous choisirons
vous choisissez	vous choisissiez	vous avez choisi	vous choisîtes	vous choisirez
ils choisissent	ils choisissaient	ils ont choisi	ils choisirent	ils choisiront

REGULAR -re verb attendre

Present	Imperfect	Perfect	Past Historic	Future
j'attends	j'attendais	j'ai attendu	j'attendis	j'attendrai
tu attends	tu attendais	tu as attendu	tu attendis	tu attendras
il attend	il attendait	il a attendu	il attendit	il attendra
nous attendons	nous attendions	nous avons attendu	nous attendîmes	nous attendrons
vous attendez	vous attendiez	vous avez attendu	vous attendîtes	vous attendrez
ils attendent	ils attendaient	ils ont attendu	ils attendirent	ils attendront

CONDITIONAL Present	SUBJUNCTIVE Present	Imperfect	IMPERATIVE	PARTICIPLE Present	Past
j'aimerais	j'aime	j'aimasse		aimant	aimé
tu aimerais	tu aimes	tu aimasses	aime		
il aimerait	il aime	il aimât			
nous aimerions	nous aimions	nous aimassions	aimons		
vous aimeriez	vous aimiez	vous aimassiez	aimez		
ils aimeraient	ils aiment	ils aimassent			
je choisirais	je choisisse	je choisisse		choisissant	choisi
tu choisirais	tu choisisses	tu choisisses	choisis		
il choisirait	il choisisse	il choisît			
nous choisirions	nous choisissions	nous choisissions	choisissons		
vous choisiriez	vous choisissiez	vous choisissiez	choisissez		
ils choisiraient	ils choisissent	ils choisissent			
j'attendrais	j'attende	j'attendisse		attendant	attendu
tu attendrais	tu attendes	tu attendisses	attends		
il attendrait	il attende	il attendît			
nous attendrions	nous attendions	nous attendissions	attendons		
vous attendriez	vous attendiez	vous attendissiez	attendez		
ils attendraient	ils attendent	ils attendissent			

French Conjugation Tables

INDICATIVE

Present	Imperfect	Perfect	Past Historic	Future

1. avoir

Present	Imperfect	Perfect	Past Historic	Future
j'ai	j'avais	j'ai eu	j'eus	j'aurai
tu as	tu avais	tu as eu	tu eus	tu auras
il a	il avait	il a eu	il eut	il aura
nous avons	nous avions	nous avons eu	nous eûmes	nous aurons
vous avez	vous aviez	vous avez eu	vous eûtes	vous aurez
ils ont	ils avaient	ils ont eu	ils eurent	ils auront

2. être

Present	Imperfect	Perfect	Past Historic	Future
je suis	j'étais	j'ai été	je fus	je serai
tu es	tu étais	tu as été	tu fus	tu seras
il est	il était	il a été	il fut	il sera
nous sommes	nous étions	nous avons été	nous fûmes	nous serons
vous êtes	vous étiez	vous avez été	vous fûtes	vous serez
ils sont	ils étaient	ils ont été	ils furent	ils seront

3a. absoudre

Present	Imperfect	Perfect	Past Historic	Future
j'absous	j'absolvais		j'absolus	j'absoudrai
il absout				
nous absolvons				

3b. résoudre *follows the above pattern except for the following*

Present	Imperfect	Perfect	Past Historic	Future
			je résolus	

4a. accroître

Present	Imperfect	Perfect	Past Historic	Future
j'accrois	j'accroissais		j'accrus	j'accroîtrai
il accroît				
nous accroissons				

4b. croître *follows the above pattern except for the following*

Present	Imperfect	Perfect	Past Historic	Future
je croîs			je crûs	

5. accueillir

Present	Imperfect	Perfect	Past Historic	Future
j'accueille	j'accueillais		j'accueillis	j'accueillerai
nous accueillons				

6. acheter

Present	Imperfect	Perfect	Past Historic	Future
j'achète	j'achetais		j'achetai	j'achèterai
nous achetons				
ils achètent				

7. acquérir

Present	Imperfect	Perfect	Past Historic	Future
j'acquiers	j'acquérais		j'acquis	j'acquerrai
il acquiert				
nous acquérons				
ils acquièrent				

8. aller

Present	Imperfect	Perfect	Past Historic	Future
je vais	j'allais	je suis allé	j'allai	j'irai
tu vas	tu allais	tu es allé	tu allas	tu iras
il va	il allait	il est allé	il alla	il ira
nous allons	nous allions	nous sommes allés	nous allâmes	nous irons
vous allez	vous alliez	vous êtes allés	vous allâtes	vous irez
ils vont	ils allaient	ils sont allés	ils allèrent	ils iront

| CONDITIONAL | SUBJUNCTIVE | | IMPERATIVE | PARTICIPLE | |
| Present | Present | Imperfect | | Present | Past |

CONDITIONAL Present	SUBJUNCTIVE Present	Imperfect	IMPERATIVE	PARTICIPLE Present	Past
j'aurais	j'aie	j'eusse		ayant	eu
tu aurais	tu aies	tu eusses	aie		
il aurait	il ait	il eût			
nous aurions	nous ayons	nous eussions	ayons		
vous auriez	vous ayez	vous eussiez	ayez		
ils auraient	ils aient	ils eussent			
je serais	je sois	je fusse		étant	été
tu serais	tu sois	tu fusses	sois		
il serait	il soit	il fût			
nous serions	nous soyons	nous fussions	soyons		
vous seriez	vous soyez	vous fussiez	soyez		
ils seraient	ils soient	ils fussent			
	j'absolve	*not used*		absolvant	absous (oute)
	nous absolvions				
					résolu
	j'accroisse	j'accrusse		accroissant	accru
	nous accroissions	nous accrussions			
		je crûsse			crû
	j'accueille	j'accueillisse		accueillant	accueilli
	nous accueillions	nous accueillissions	accueille accueillons		
		vous accueilliez			
	j'achète	j'achetasse		achetant	acheté
	nous achetions	nous achetassions			
	j'acquière	j'acquisse		acquérant	acquis
	nous acquérions	nous acquissions			
j'irais	j'aille	j'allasse		allant	allé
tu irais	tu ailles	tu allasses	va		
il irait	il aille	il allât			
nous irions	nous allions	nous allassions	allons		
vous iriez	vous alliez	vous allassiez	allez		
ils iraient	ils aillent	ils allassent			

French Conjugation Tables

Present	Imperfect	Perfect	Past Historic	Future
9. appeler				
j'appelle nous appelons ils appellent	j'appelais		j'appelai	j'appellerai
10a. s'asseoir				
je m'assieds/ assois il s'assied/assoit nous nous asseyons/ assoyons	je m'asseyais/ assoyais		je m'assis	je m'assiérai/assoirai
10b. surseoir *follows pattern of oi forms of* **s'asseoir**				
				je surseoirai
11. battre				
je bats il bat nous battons	je battais		je battis	je battrai
12. boire				
je bois il boit nous buvons ils boivent	je buvais		je bus	je boirai
13. bouillir				
je bous il bout nous bouillons	je bouillais		je bouillis	je bouillirai
14. choir				
je chois il chut ils choient			il chût	
15. clore				
je clos il clôt ils closent				je clorai
16. commencer				
je commence nous commençons vous commencez ils commencent	je commençais		je commen- çai	je commencerai
17. conclure				
je conclus il conclut nous concluons	je concluais		je conclus	je conclurai

CONDITIONAL Present	SUBJUNCTIVE Present	Imperfect	IMPERATIVE	PARTICIPLE Present	Past
	j'appelle nous appelions	j'appelasse nous appelassions		appelant	appelé
	je m'asseye/ assoie	je m'assisse		asseyant/ assoyant	assis
	nous nous asseyions/ assoyions	nous nous assissions			
je surseoirais					
	je batte	je battisse		battant	battu
	nous battions	nous battissions			
	je boive	je busse		buvant	bu
	nous buvions	nous bussions			
	je bouille	je bouillisse		bouillant	bouilli
	nous bouillions	nous bouillissions			
					chu
	je close				clos
	nous closions				
	je commence	je commençasse		commençant	commencé
	nous commencions	nous commençassions			
	je conclue	je conclusse		concluant	conclu
	nous concluions	nous conclussions			

French Conjugation Tables

Present	Imperfect	Perfect	Past Historic	Future
18. conduire				
je conduis	je conduisais		je conduisis	je conduirai
il conduit				
nous conduisons				
19a. confire				
je confis	je confisais		je confis	je confira
il confit				
nous confisons				
19b. suffire PAST PARTICIPLE suffi (invariable)				
20. connaître				
je connais	je connaissais		je connus	je connaîtrai
il connaît				
nous connaissons				
21. coudre				
je couds	je cousais		je cousis	je coudrai
il coud				
nous cousons				
22. courir				
je cours	je courais		je courus	je courrai
il court				
nous courons				
23. craindre				
je crains	je craignais		je craignis	je craindrai
il craint				
nous craignons				
24. créer				
je crée	je créais		je créai	je créerai
nous créons				
25. croire				
je crois	je croyais		je crus	je croirai
il croit				
nous croyons				
ils croient				
26. devoir				
je dois	je devais		je dus	je devrai
il doit				
nous devons				
ils doivent				
27a. dire				
je dis	je disais		je dis	je dirai
il dit				
nous disons				
vous dites				

CONDITIONAL	SUBJUNCTIVE		IMPERATIVE	PARTICIPLE	
Present	Present	Imperfect		Present	Past
je conduise	je conduisisse			conduisant	Rlconduit
nous conduisions	nous conduisissions				
je confise	je confisse			confisant	confit
nous confisions	nous confissions				
je connaisse	je connusse			connaissant	connu
nous connaissions	nous connussions				
je couse	je cousisse			cousant	cousu
nous cousions	nous cousissions				
je coure	je courusse			courant	couru
nous courions	nous courussions				
je craigne	je craignisse			craignant	craint
nous craignions	nous craignissions				
je crée	je créasse			créant	créé
nous créions	nous créassions				
je croie	je crusse			croyant	cru
nous croyions	nous crussions				
je doive	je dusse			devant	dû (due), dus (dues)
nous devions	nous dussions				
je dise	je disse			disant	dit
nous disions	nous dissions				

French Conjugation Tables

Present	Imperfect	Perfect	Past Historic	Future

27b. contredire, interdire etc PRESENT vous contredisez, interdisez

28. distraire

Present	Imperfect	Perfect	Past Historic	Future
je distrais	je distrayais			je distrairai
il distrait				
nous distrayons				
ils distraient				

29. dormir

Present	Imperfect	Perfect	Past Historic	Future
je dors	je dormais		je dormis	je dormirai
il dort				
nous dormons				

30. écrire

Present	Imperfect	Perfect	Past Historic	Future
j'écris	j'écrivais		j'écrivis	j'écrirai
il écrit				
nous écrivons				

31a. émouvoir

Present	Imperfect	Perfect	Past Historic	Future
j'émeus	j'émouvais		j'émus	j'émouvrai
il émeut				
nous émouvons				
ils émeuvent				

31b. mouvoir PAST PARTICIPLE mû (mue), mus (mues)

32. employer

Present	Imperfect	Perfect	Past Historic	Future
j'emploie	j'employais		j'employai	j'emploierai
nous employons				
ils emploient				

33. envoyer

Present	Imperfect	Perfect	Past Historic	Future
j'envoie	j'envoyais		j'envoyai	j'enverrai
nous envoyons				
ils envoient				

34. espérer

Present	Imperfect	Perfect	Past Historic	Future
j'espère	j'espérais		j'espérai	j'espérerai
nous espérons				
ils espèrent				

35. faillir

Present	Imperfect	Perfect	Past Historic	Future
je faillis				je faillirai

36. faire

Present	Imperfect	Perfect	Past Historic	Future
je fais	je faisais	j'ai fait	je fis	je ferai
tu fais	tu faisais	tu as fait	tu fis	tu feras
il fait	il faisait	il a fait	il fit	il fera
nous faisons	nous faisions	nous avons fait	nous fîmes	nous ferons
vous faites	vous faisiez	vous avez fait	vous fîtes	vous ferez
ils font	ils faisaient	ils ont fait	ils firent	ils feront

37. falloir

Present	Imperfect	Perfect	Past Historic	Future
il faut	il fallait		il fallut	il faudra

| CONDITIONAL | SUBJUNCTIVE | | IMPERATIVE | PARTICIPLE | |
Present	Present	Imperfect		Present	Past
	je distraie			distrayant	distrait
	nous distrayions				
	je dorme	je dormisse		dormant	dormi
	nous dormions	nous dormissions			
	j'écrive	j'écrivisse		écrivant	écrit
	nous écrivions	nous écrivissions			
	j'émeuve	j'émusse		émouvant	ému
	nous émouvions	nous émussions			
	j'emploie	j'employasse		employant	employé
	nous employions	nous employassions			
	j'envoie	j'envoyasse		envoyant	envoyé
	nous envoyions	nous envoyassions			
	j'espère	j'espérasse		espérant	espéré
	nous espérions	nous espérassions			
				faillant	failli
je ferais	je fasse	je fisse		faisant	fait
tu ferais	tu fasses	tu fisses	fais		
il ferait	il fasse	il fît			
nous ferions	nous fassions	nous fissions	faisons		
vous feriez	vous fassiez	vous fissiez	faites		
ils feraient	ils fassent	ils fissent			
	il faille	il fallût			fallu

French Conjugation Tables

INDICATIVE

Present	Imperfect	Perfect	Past Historic	Future
38. fuir				
je fuis	je fuyais		je fuis	je fuirai
il fuit				
nous fuyons				
ils fuient				
39. geler				
je gèle	je gelais		je gelai	je gèlerai
nous gelons	nous gelions			
ils gèlent				
40. gésir				
je gis	je gisais			
il gît				
nous gisons				
41. haïr				
je hais	je haïssais		je haïs	je haïrai
il hait				
nous haïssons				
42. jeter				
je jette	je jetais		je jetai	je jetterai
nous jetons				
ils jettent				
43. joindre				
je joins	je joignais		je joignis	je joindrai
nous joignons				
44. lire				
je lis	je lisais		je lus	je lirai
nous lisons				
45. manger				
je mange	je mangeais		je mangeai	je mangerai
nous mangeons				
46. mener				
je mène	je menais		je menai	je mènerai
nous menons				
ils mènent				
47. mettre				
je mets	je mettais		je mis	je mettrai
il met				
nous mettons				
48. moudre				
je mouds	je moulais		je moulus	je moudrai
il moud				
nous moulons				

CONDITIONAL Present	SUBJUNCTIVE Present	Imperfect	IMPERATIVE	PARTICIPLE Present	Past
je fuie	je fuisse			fuyant	fui
nous fuyions	nous fuissions				
je gèle	je gelasse			gelant	gelé
	nous gelassions				
				gisant	
je haïsse	je haïsse			haïssant	haï
nous haïssions	nous haïssions				
je jette	je jetasse			jetant	jeté
nous jetions	nous jetassions				
je joigne	je joignisse			joignant	joint
nous joignions	nous joignissions				
je lise	je lusse			lisant	lu
nous lisions	nous lussions				
je mange	je mangeasse			mangeant	mangé
nous mangions	nous mangeassions				
je mène	je menasse			menant	mené
nous menions	nous menassions				
je mette	je misse			mettant	mis
nous mettions	nous missions				
je moule	je moulusse			moulant	moulu
nous moulions	nous moulussions				

French Conjugation Tables

Present	Imperfect	Perfect	Past Historic	Future
49. mourir				
je meurs il meurt nous mourons ils meurent	je mourais		je mourus	je mourrai
50a. naître				
je nais il naît nous naissons	je naissais		je naquis	je naîtrai
50b. paître no PAST HISTORIC; PAST PARTICIPLE pu (invariable; rare)				
50c. repaître as paître but PAST HISTORIC je repus				
51. ouïr				
j'ois il oit nous oyons ils oient	j'oyais		j'ouïs	j'ouïrai
52. ouvrir				
j'ouvre nous ouvrons	j'ouvrais		j'ouvris	j'ouvrirai
53. payer				
je paie/paye nous payons ils paient/payent	je payais		je payai	je paierai/payerai
54. peindre				
je peins il peint nous peignons	je peignais		je peignis	je peindrai
55a. plaire				
je plais il plait	je plaisais nous plaisions		je plus	je plairai
55b. taire PRESENT il tait				
56. pleuvoir				
il pleut	il pleuvait		il plut	il pleuvra
57. pouvoir				
je peux/puis il peut nous pouvons	je pouvais		je pus	je pourrai
58. prendre				
je prends il prend nous prenons ils prennent	je prenais		je pris	je prendrai

CONDITIONAL Present	SUBJUNCTIVE Present	Imperfect	IMPERATIVE	PARTICIPLE Present	Past
	je meure	je mourusse		mourant	mort
	nous mourions	nous mourussions			
	je naisse	je naquisse		naissant	né
	nous naissions	nous naquissions			
	j'oie	j'ouïsse		oyant	ouï
	nous oyions				
	j'ouvre			ouvrant	ouvert
			ouvre		
	nous ouvrions		ouvrons		
			ouvrez		
	je paie/paye	je payasse		payant	payé
	nous payions	nous payassions			
	je peigne	je peignisse		peignant	peint
	nous peignions	nous peignissions			
	je plaise	je plusse		plaisant	plu
	nous plaisions	nous plussions			
				pleuvant	plu
	il pleuve	il plût			
	je puisse	je pusse		pouvant	pu
	nous puissions	nous pussions			
	je prenne	je prisse		prenant	pris
	nous prenions	nous prissions			

French Conjugation Tables

Present	Imperfect	Perfect	Past Historic	Future
59. protéger				
je protège	je protégeais		je protégeai	je protégerai
nous protégeons				
ils protègent				
60. recevoir				
je reçois	je recevais		je reçus	je recevrai
il reçoit				
nous recevons				
ils reçoivent				
61. rire				
je ris	je riais		je ris	je rirai
il rit				
nous rions				
62. savoir				
je sais	je savais		je sus	je saurai
il sait				
nous savons				
63. servir				
je sers	je servais		je servis	je servirai
il sert				
nous servons				
64a. sortir				
je sors	je sortais		je sortis	je sortirai
il sort				
nous sortons				
64b. mentir PAST PARTICIPLE is invariable				
65. suivre				
je suis	je suivais		je suivis	je suivrai
il suit				
nous suivons				
66. supplier				
je supplie	je suppliais		je suppliai	je supplierai
nous supplions				
67. tressaillir				
je tressaille	je tressaillais		je tressaillis	je tressaillirai
nous tressaillons				
68. vaincre				
je vaincs	je vainquais		je vainquis	je vaincrai
il vainc				
nous vainquons				
69. valoir				
je vaux	je valais		je valus	je vaudrai
il vaut				
nous valons				

CONDITIONAL	SUBJUNCTIVE		IMPERATIVE	PARTICIPLE	
Present	Present	Imperfect		Present	Past
	je protège nous protégions	je protégeasse nous protégeassions		protégeant	protégé
	je reçoive nous recevions	je reçusse nous reçussions		recevant	reçu
	je rie nous riions	je risse nous rissions		riant	ri
	je sache nous sachions	je susse nous sussions	sache sachons sachez	sachant	su
	je serve nous servions	je servisse nous servissions		servant	servi
	je sorte nous sortions	je sortisse nous sortissions		sortant	sorti
	je suive nous suivions	je suivisse nous suivissions		suivant	suivi
	je supplie nous suppliions	je suppliasse nous suppliassions		suppliant	supplié
	je tressaille nous tressaillions	je tressaillisse nous tressaillissions		tressaillant	tressailli
	je vainque nous vainquions	je vainquisse nous vainquissions		vainquant	vaincu
	je vaille nous valions	je valusse nous valussions		valant	valu

French Conjugation Tables

INDICATIVE

Present	Imperfect	Perfect	Past Historic	Future
70. venir				
je viens il vient nous venons ils viennent	je venais		je vins	je viendrai
71. vêtir				
je vêts il vêt nous vêtons	je vêtais		je vêtis	je vêtirai
72. vivre				
je vis il vit nous vivons	je vivais		je vécus	je vivrai
73a. voir				
je vois il voit nous voyons ils voient	je voyais		je vis	je verrai

73b. pourvoir *follows the above pattern except for the following*

			je pourvus	je pourvoirai

73c. prévoir *follows the above pattern except for the following*

			je prévus	je prévoirai

Present	Imperfect	Perfect	Past Historic	Future
74. vouloir				
je veux il veut nous voulons ils veulent	je voulais		je voulus	je voudrai

French Conjugation Tables

CONDITIONAL Present	SUBJUNCTIVE Present	Imperfect	IMPERATIVE	PARTICIPLE Present	Past
	je vienne	je vinsse		venant	venu
	nous venions	nous vinssions			
	je vête	je vêtisse		vëtant	vêtu
	nous vêtions	nous vêtissions			
	je vive	je vécusse		vivant	vécu
	nous vivions	nous vécussions			
	je voie	je visse		voyant	vu
	nous voyions	nous vissions			

je pourvoirais

je prévoirais

	je veuille	je voulusse		voulant	voulu
	nous voulions	nous voulussions	vcuille veuillons		
			veuillez		

A, a [ɑ] *nm inv* A, a; **connaître un sujet de A à Z** to know a subject inside out; **prouver qch par A plus B** to prove sth in a logical *or* scientific fashion

A [ɑ] *nf (abrév* **autoroute) A1** *Br* ≃ M1, *Am* ≃ I1

a *voir* **avoir**

à [a] *prép*

> **à + le** contracts to form **au** [o], **à + les** contracts to form **aux** [a]

(a) *(indique la direction)* to; **aller/venir à Paris** to go/come to Paris; **aller à la pêche** to go fishing; **partir au Venezuela** to leave for Venezuela; **rentrer à la maison** to go/come home; **au lit!** off to bed!

(b) *(indique la position)* at; **être à la maison/à la campagne/à Marseille** to be at home/in the countryside/in Marseilles; **j'habite au 3, place des Cardeurs** I live at number 3, place des Cardeurs; **à la page deux** *on* page two; **à deux kilomètres/dix minutes d'ici** two kilometres/ten minutes from here; **à la télévision** on (the) television; **un livre à la main** with a book in his/her hand

(c) *(dans l'expression du temps)* **à huit heures** at eight (o'clock); **au vingtième siècle** in the twentieth century; **à la tombée de la nuit** at nightfall; **au printemps** in the spring; **à mon arrivée** when I arrive/arrived; **le 2 au soir** on the evening of the 2nd; **à lundi/demain!** see you Monday/tomorrow!

(d) *(avec de)* to; **de Paris à Lyon** from Paris to Lyons; **du lundi au vendredi** from Monday to Friday, *Am* Monday to *or* thru Friday; **de 2 à 4** *(heure)* from 2 till *or* to 4; **de 10 à 15%** *(environ)* between 10 and 15%

(e) *(introduit le complément d'objet indirect)* to; **donner/prêter qch à qn** to give/lend sth to sb, to give/lend sb sth; **penser à qn /qch** to think of *or* about sb/sth

(f) *(indique l'appartenance)* **c'est à lui/à Pierre** it's his/Pierre's; *Fam* **un ami à moi** a friend of mine; **c'est à vous de...** *(il vous incombe de)* it's up to you to...; *(c'est votre tour de)* it's your turn to...; **à toi!** your turn!

(g) *(indique le moyen, la manière)* **à bicyclette** by bicycle; **à pied/cheval** on foot/horseback; **au crayon** in pencil; **à la française** in the French style; **fonctionner à l'électricité** to run on electricity; **jouer un air au violon** to play a tune on the violin

(h) *(distributif)* **faire qch à deux/trois** to do sth in twos/threes; **se mettre à plusieurs pour faire qch** to team up to do sth; **100 km à l'heure** 100 km an *or* per hour; **être payé à l'heure** to be paid by the hour

(i) *(indique la caractéristique)* **l'homme à la barbe/aux lunettes noires** the man with a beard/with the dark glasses; **un timbre à 50 cents** a 50-cent stamp

(j) *(indique le but)* **maison à vendre** house for sale; **à louer** *(sur panneau) Br* to let, *Am* to rent; **j'ai une lettre à écrire/des courses à faire** I've got a letter to write/some errands to run

(k) *(indique la conséquence)* **c'était à mourir de rire** it was hilarious; **laid à faire peur** hideously ugly; **c'est à se demander si...** you begin to wonder if...

abaisser [abese] **1** *vt* **(a)** *(levier, manette, pont-levis)* to lower; *(store)* to pull down **(b)** *(prix, coût, pression)* to reduce **(c)** *Litt (humilier)* to humble, to abase **(d)** *Culin (pâte)* to roll out

2 s'abaisser *vpr* **(a)** *(descendre)* to slope down **(b)** **s'a. à faire qch** to lower oneself to do sth

abandon [abãdɔ̃] *nm* **(a)** *(d'un enfant, d'un projet)* abandonment; **exiger l'a. des hostilités** to call for an end to hostilities; *Jur* **a. du domicile conjugal** desertion; *Mil* **a. de poste** desertion of one's post **(b)** *(en sport)* **gagner par a.** to win by default; **être contraint à l'a.** to be forced to withdraw **(c)** *(d'un lieu)* neglect; **à l'a.** neglected, **laisser qch à l'a.** to neglect sth **(d)** *(nonchalance)* abandon **(e)** *Ordinat* abort

abandonner [abãdɔne] **1** *vt* **(a)** *(personne, village)* to desert, to abandon; *(voiture)* to abandon; **a. le navire** to abandon ship; **a. le domicile conjugal** to desert the marital home; **mes forces m'abandonnent** my strength is failing me **(b)** *(privilège, pouvoir, combat)* to give up; *(projet)* to abandon; *(course)* to withdraw from; **a. ses études** to drop out (of school/university); **a. ses études de médecine** to give up medicine; *aussi Fig* **a. la partie** to throw in one's hand **(c)** *(céder)* to give (**à** to) **(d)** *Ordinat* to abort

2 *vi* **(a)** *(renoncer)* to give up **(b)** *(en sport)* to withdraw **3 s'abandonner** *vpr (se laisser aller)* to let oneself go; **s'a. au sommeil** to drift off to sleep

abasourdi, -e [abazurdi] *adj* stunned

abat-jour [abaʒur] *nm inv* lampshade

abats [aba] *nmpl Br* offal, *Am* variety meat; *(de volaille)* giblets

abattage [abataʒ] *nm* **(a)** *(d'animal)* slaughter, slaughtering **(b)** **avoir de l'a.** *(acteur, politicien)* to be full of go

abattant [abatã] *nm (d'une table)* flap; *(des toilettes)* lid

abattement [abatmã] *nm* **(a)** *(physique)* exhaustion **(b)** *(moral)* dejection, depression **(c)** *Fin* **a. (fiscal)** tax allowance

abattis [abati] *nmpl* **(a)** *(de volaille)* giblets **(b)** *très Fam* **numéroter ses a.** to start saying one's prayers

abattoir [abatwar] *nm* slaughterhouse, abattoir; *Fig* **envoyer qn à l'a.** to send sb to the slaughter

abattre [11] [abatr] **1** *vt* **(a)** *(faire tomber) (mur, cloison)* to knock down, to pull down; *(arbre)* to fell, to cut down; *(sujet: vent) (arbre)* to blow down; *(avion)* to bring down; **a. de la besogne** to get through a lot of work **(b)** *(tuer) (personne)* to kill; *(animal de boucherie)* to slaughter; *(animal malade ou dangereux)* to destroy; *Fig* **c'est l'homme à a.** he needs to be

removed (**c**) *Fig (fatiguer) (sujet: maladie)* to lay low; **la chaleur nous a complètement abattus** the heat drained us of all energy (**d**) *Fig (démoraliser)* to dishearten, to depress; **ne vous laissez pas a.!** keep your chin up! (**e**) *aussi Fig* **a. ses cartes** *ou* **son jeu** to lay one's cards on the table
2 s'abattre *vpr (arbre, mur)* to crash down (**sur** on); *(pluie)* to pour down (**sur** on); *(oiseau)* to swoop down (**sur** on)

abattu, -e [abaty] *adj* dejected, depressed

abbaye [abei] *nf* abbey

abbé [abe] *nm* (**a**) *(d'une abbaye)* abbot (**b**) *(prêtre)* priest; **j'en parlerai à Monsieur l'a.** I'll mention it to the priest; **l'a. Martin** Father Martin

abc [abese] *nm inv (rudiments)* basics

abcès [apsɛ] *nm* abscess; *Fig* **crever** *ou* **vider l'a.** to resolve the situation

abdiquer [abdike] *vt (trône)* to abdicate; *(droits)* to renounce, to surrender; **être contraint d'a.** to be forced to abdicate

abdomen [abdɔmɛn] *nm* abdomen

abdominal, -e, -aux, -ales [abdɔminal, -o] **1** *adj* abdominal
2 *nmpl* **abdominaux** stomach muscles; **faire des abdominaux** to do abdominal exercises *or* sit-ups

abdos [abdo] *nmpl Fam* stomach muscles; **faire des a.** to do abdominal exercises *or* sit-ups

abécédaire [abesedɛr] *nm* ABC, alphabet book

abeille [abɛj] *nf* bee

aberrant, -e [abɛrɑ̃, -ɑ̃t] *adj* absurd

aberration [abɛrasjɔ̃] *nf* aberration; **c'est une a.!** it's absurd!

abêtir [abetir] **1** *vt* **a. qn** to dull sb's mind
2 s'abêtir *vpr* to become stupid

abêtissant, -e [abetisɑ̃, -ɑ̃t] *adj* mind-numbing

abhorrer [abɔre] *vt Litt* to abhor

Abidjan [abidʒɑ̃] *n* Abidjan

abîme [abim] *nm (de l'océan)* abyss, depths; *Fig (entre deux personnes)* gulf; *Fig* **être au bord de l'a.** to be on the brink of disaster

abîmer [abime] **1** *vt (objet)* to spoil, to damage; *(vêtement, chaussures)* to ruin
2 s'abîmer *vpr (a) (fruit)* to go bad; *(objet)* to get damaged; *(vêtement, chaussures)* to get ruined (**b**) **s'a. les yeux** to ruin one's eyesight (**c**) *Litt* **s'a. en mer** to be engulfed by the sea

abject, -e [abʒɛkt] *adj Péj* contemptible, despicable

abjurer [abʒyre] *vt (religion)* to abjure

ablation [ablasjɔ̃] *nf* removal

ablette [ablɛt] *nf* bleak

ablutions [ablysjɔ̃] *nfpl Litt ou Hum* **faire ses a.** to perform one's ablutions

abnégation [abnegasjɔ̃] *nf* abnegation, self-sacrifice

aboiement [abwamɑ̃] *nm* bark; **des aboiements** barking

abois [abwa] *nmpl* **être aux a.** *(cerf)* to be at bay; *Fig* **il est aux a.** *(personne)* the net's closing in on him

abolir [abɔlir] *vt* to abolish

abolition [abɔlisjɔ̃] *nf* abolition

abominable [abɔminabl] *adj* appalling, abominable; *(crime)* heinous; *(odeur)* foul; **l'a. homme des neiges** the abominable snowman

abominablement [abɔminabləmɑ̃] *adv* abominably; *(laid)* hideously

abomination [abɔminasjɔ̃] *nf* abomination; *Litt* **avoir qn/qch en a.** to loathe sb/sth

abondamment [abɔ̃damɑ̃] *adv (parler, critiquer)* at length; **se servir a.** to help oneself to large amounts of food

abondance [abɔ̃dɑ̃s] *nf* abundance; *(d'informations, de détails)* wealth; **il y avait des fruits en a.** there was plenty of fruit; **vivre dans l'a.** to live a life of ease

abondant, -e [abɔ̃dɑ̃, -ɑ̃t] *adj* abundant, plentiful; *(repas)* hearty; *(pluie)* heavy; *(saignement)* profuse; **une chevelure abondante** a thick head of hair; **peu a.** *(récolte, chevelure)* poor; *(pluie)* light; *(repas)* frugal

abonder [abɔ̃de] *vi* (**a**) *(foisonner)* to be plentiful; **a. en qch** to abound in sth (**b**) **a. dans le sens de qn** to agree entirely with sb

abonné, -e [abɔne] **1** *nm,f (d'une revue)* subscriber; *(du gaz, de l'électricité)* consumer; *(de la SNCF, d'un théâtre)* season-ticket holder; **il n'y a pas d'a. au numéro que vous avez demandé** ≃ the number you have dialled has not been recognized
2 *adj* **être a. à qch** *(revue)* to have a subscription to sth; *(SNCF, théâtre)* to have a season ticket to sth; *Fam (être sujet à)* to be prone to sth

abonnement [abɔnmɑ̃] *nm (à une revue)* subscription (**à** to); *(de train, de théâtre)* season ticket; *(au téléphone)* line rental; **prendre un a.** *(à une revue)* to take out a subscription; *(pour le train, pour le théâtre)* to buy a season ticket

abonner [abɔne] **1** *vt* **a. qn à une revue** to take out a subscription to a magazine for sb
2 s'abonner *vpr (à une revue)* to take out a subscription (**à** to); *(au théâtre)* to buy a season ticket (**à** for)

abord [abɔr] *nm* (**a**) *(d'un lieu)* **l'île est d'un a. difficile** the island is not easily accessible (**b**) **abords** *(d'un bâtiment)* surroundings; *(d'une ville)* outskirts (**c**) *(d'une personne)* **être d'un a. facile/difficile** to be approachable/unapproachable; **au premier a., de prime a.** at first sight (**d**) **d'a., tout d'a.** *(pour commencer)* at first, to begin with; *(premièrement)* first (and foremost), in the first place; *Fam* **toi, d'a., je ne te parle plus!** I'm not talking to you anymore, so there!

abordable [abɔrdabl] *adj* (**a**) *(lieu)* accessible (**b**) *(prix)* affordable (**c**) *(personne)* approachable

abordage [abɔrdaʒ] *nm (pour attaquer)* boarding; *(pour s'amarrer)* coming alongside; **monter à l'a.** to board a ship

aborder [abɔrde] **1** *vt* (**a**) *(personne)* to approach; **se faire a.** to be approached (**b**) *(question)* to deal with; *(virage)* to approach (**c**) *(navire) (attaquer)* to board; *(se mettre le long de)* to come alongside
2 *vi* to land

aborigène [abɔriʒɛn] **1** *nmf (d'un pays)* native; **les aborigènes d'Australie** the (Australian) Aborigines
2 *adj* native, indigenous (**de** to); *(des peuplades australiennes)* Aboriginal

abortif, -ive [abɔrtif, -iv] *adj voir* **pilule**

abouler [abule] *très Fam* **1** *vt* to hand over
2 s'abouler *vpr* to turn up, to show up; **alors, tu t'aboules?** well, are you coming or not?

aboutir [abutir] *vi* (**a**) *(réussir)* to be successful; **ne pas a.** to fall through (**b**) *(dans l'espace)* **a. à/dans** *(sujet: personne)* to end up at/in; **a. à** *(sujet: chemin, escalier)* to lead to; *Fig (sujet: efforts, recherches)* to result in; **n'a. à rien** *(personne)* to get nowhere; *(efforts, recherches)* to come to nothing

aboutissants [abutisɑ̃] *nmpl voir* **tenant**

aboutissement [abutismɑ̃] *nm* result, outcome

aboyer [32] [abwaje] *vi* to bark

abracadabrant, -e [abrakadabrɑ̃, -ɑ̃t] *adj Fam (histoire)* cock-and-bull

abrasif, -ive [abrazif, -iv] *adj & nm* abrasive

abrégé [abreʒe] *nm* (**a**) *(livre)* **un a. d'histoire de France**

a short history of France; **un a. de philosophie** a short guide to philosophy (**b**) **écrire en a.** to write in abbreviated form

abréger [59] [abreʒe] *vt (article, exposé)* to shorten, to cut down; *(visite)* to cut short; *(mot)* to abbreviate; *Fam* **allez, abrège!** come on, get to the point!

abreuver [abrœve] **1** *vt (chevaux, bétail)* to water; *Fig* **a. qn d'injures** to shower sb with insults **2 s'abreuver** *vpr (cheval, bétail)* to drink

abreuvoir [abrœvwar] *nm (dans une rivière)* watering place; *(baquet)* drinking trough

abréviation [abrevjasjɔ̃] *nf* abbreviation

abri [abri] *nm* shelter; **mettre qn/qch à l'a.** to shelter sb/sth; **se mettre à l'a.** to (take) shelter; **être à l'a. (de qch)** to be sheltered (from sth); **être à l'a. du besoin** to have no financial worries; **personne n'est à l'a. d'une erreur** anybody can make a mistake; **a. antiatomique** fallout shelter; **a. à vélos** bike shed

abribus ® [abribys] *nm* bus shelter

abricot [abriko] **1** *nm* apricot **2** *adj inv* apricot-coloured

abricotier [abrikɔtje] *nm* apricot tree

abrier [abrije] *Can* **1** *vt* to wrap up (well) **2 s'abrier** *vpr* to wrap oneself up (well)

abriter [abrite] **1** *vt (protéger)* to shelter (**de** from) **2 s'abriter** *vpr* **s'a. (de la pluie)** to (take) shelter (from the rain); **s'a. (du soleil)** to shade oneself (from the sun)

abrogation [abrɔgasjɔ̃] *nf (d'une loi)* repeal

abroger [45] [abrɔʒe] *vt (loi)* to repeal

abrupt, -e [abrypt] *adj (rocher, pente)* steep; *Fig (manière)* abrupt, blunt; **d'un ton a.** abruptly

abruti, -e [abryti] **1** *nm,f Fam* idiot, fool **2** *adj* (**a**) *(hébété)* stupefied, dazed; **a. par l'alcool** stupefied with drink (**b**) *Fam (bête)* stupid, idiotic

abrutir [abrytir] **1** *vt (hébéter)* to daze; **a. qn de travail** to work sb to the point of exhaustion **2 s'abrutir** *vpr* **s'a. de travail** to work oneself into the ground; **on s'abrutit à trop regarder la télévision** too much television numbs the brain

abrutissant, -e [abrytisɑ̃, -ɑ̃t] *adj* mind-numbing; *(bruit)* wearing

ABS [abeɛs] *nm Aut* **(système) A.** ABS

abscisse [apsis] *nf Math* x-axis

abscons, -e [apskɔ̃, -ɔ̃s] *adj Litt* abstruse

absence [apsɑ̃s] *nf* (**a**) *(d'une personne)* absence; **en** *ou* **pendant mon a.** in *or* during my absence, while I am/was/ etc away (**b**) *(manque)* lack (**c**) **avoir des absences** to be prone to absent-mindedness; **dans un moment d'a.** in a moment of absent-mindedness

absent, -e [apsɑ̃, -ɑ̃t] **1** *adj* (**a**) *(qui n'est pas présent)* absent (**de** from) (**b**) *(inexistant)* missing (**c**) *(distrait)* **avoir un air a.** to be miles away **2** *nm,f* absentee; **les absents ont toujours tort** it's always those who aren't there who get the blame

absentéisme [apsɑ̃teism] *nm* absenteeism

absenter [apsɑ̃te] **s'absenter** *vpr (sortir)* to go away (**de** from); **elle a dû s'a. quelques minutes** she had to go out for a few minutes

absinthe [apsɛ̃t] *nf* absinthe

absolu, -e [apsɔly] **1** *nm* **l'a.** the absolute; **dans l'a.,... in** principle,...
2 *adj* absolute; *(règle)* hard-and-fast; **être dans l'impossibilité absolue de faire qch** to be quite unable to do sth

absolument [apsɔlymɑ̃] *adv* (**a**) *(complètement)* abso-

lutely; **a. pas!** absolutely not! (**b**) *(sans faute)* **vous devez a. y aller!** you simply MUST go!

absolution [apsɔlysjɔ̃] *nf Rel* absolution

absolvais *etc voir* **absoudre**

absorbant, -e [apsɔrbɑ̃, -ɑ̃t] *adj* (**a**) *(matériau)* absorbent (**b**) *(livre, tâche)* absorbing

absorber [apsɔrbe] *vt* (**a**) *(liquide)* to absorb, to soak up (**b**) *(nourriture)* to eat; *(boisson)* to drink; *(médicament)* to take (**c**) *(entreprise)* to take over (**d**) *(sujet: lecture)* to absorb, to engross; **son travail l'absorbe** she is absorbed *or* engrossed in her work; **être absorbé dans ses pensées** to be lost in thought

absorption [apsɔrpsjɔ̃] *nf* (**a**) *(de liquide)* absorption (**b**) *(de nourriture)* eating; *(d'une boisson)* drinking; *(d'un médicament)* taking (**c**) *(d'une entreprise)* takeover

absoudre [3a] [apsudr] *vt Litt ou Rel* **a. qn de qch** to forgive sb sth

abstenir [70] [apstənir] **s'abstenir** *vpr (ne pas voter)* to abstain (from voting); **s'a. de faire qch** to refrain from doing sth; **dans le doute, abstiens-toi** if in doubt, don't; **pas sérieux s'a.** *(dans une petite annonce)* no timewasters

abstention [apstɑ̃sjɔ̃] *nf* abstention

abstentionniste [apstɑ̃sjɔnist] *nmf* abstainer

abstinence [apstinɑ̃s] *nf* abstinence

abstraction [apstraksjɔ̃] *nf* (**a**) **faire a. de qch** to disregard sth; **a. faite de cette dépense** leaving aside this expense (**b**) *(idée abstraite)* abstract idea, abstraction

abstrait, -e [apstrɛ, -ɛt] **1** *adj* abstract **2** *nm* **dans l'a.** in the abstract

absurde [apsyrd] **1** *adj* absurd **2** *nm* **l'a.** *(d'une situation, d'une remarque)* absurdity; **démonstration par l'a.** reductio ad absurdum

absurdité [apsyrdite] *nf* (**a**) *(caractère absurde)* absurdity (**b**) *(chose absurde)* absurdity, piece of nonsense; **dire des absurdités** to talk nonsense

abus [aby] *nm (excès)* overindulgence (**de** in); **l'a. d'alcool** alcohol abuse; **l'a. de médicaments est dangereux** taking too much medication is dangerous (**b**) *(pratique)* abuse; *Fam* **il y a de l'a.!** that's going too far! (**c**) *Jur* **a. de biens sociaux** misappropriation of funds; **a. de confiance** breach of trust; **a. de pouvoir** abuse of power

abuser [abyze] **1** *vt Litt* to deceive **2 abuser de** *vt ind (exploiter, violer)* to take advantage of; **a. du tabac** to smoke too much; **a. de ses forces** to overexert oneself; **il ne faut pas a. des bonnes choses** good things should be enjoyed in moderation; **je ne voudrais pas a.** I don't want to cause you any inconvenience; **alors là, vous abusez!** this is a bit much! **3 s'abuser** *vpr* **si je ne m'abuse** if I'm not mistaken

abusif, -ive [abyzif, -iv] *adj* (**a**) *(emploi d'un mot)* incorrect (**b**) *(excessif)* excessive; *(mère)* possessive

abysse [abis] *nm* abyssal zone

acabit [akabi] *nm Péj* **du même a.** of that type

acacia [akasja] *nm* acacia

académicien, -enne [akademisjɛ̃, -ɛn] *nm,f* = member of the "Académie française"

académie [akademi] *nf (des lettres, des sciences, d'art)* academy; **l'A. française** = learned society responsible for promoting the French language and imposing standards (**b**) *(école)* school, academy; **a. de musique/dessin** music/ art school (**c**) *(dans l'Éducation nationale) Br* ≃ local education authority, *Am* ≃ school district

académique [akademik] *adj* (**a**) *Scol* = relating to a local education authority (**b**) *Péj (style)* conventional

acajou [akaʒu] **1** *nm* mahogany **2** *adj inv* reddish-brown

a cap(p)ella [akapela] *adv* a cappella

acariâtre [akarjɑtr] *adj* cantankerous

acarien [akarjɛ̃] *nm* dust mite

accablant, -e [akɑblɑ̃, -ɑ̃t] *adj* (**a**) *(responsabilités)* overwhelming; *(chaleur)* oppressive (**b**) *(témoignage)* damning

accablement [akɑbləmɑ̃] *nm* dejection, depression

accabler [akɑble] *vt* (**a**) *(sujet: chaleur, malheur)* to overwhelm; **a. qn de travail** to overload sb with work; **a. qn de reproches** to heap criticism on sb (**b**) *(sujet: témoignage)* to damn

accalmie [akalmi] *nf* lull

accaparer [akapare] *vt (personne, conversation)* to monopolize; *(places, morceaux de choix)* to grab

accéder [34] [aksede] **accéder à** *vt ind* (**a**) *(atteindre)* to reach, to get to (**b**) *Fig (responsabilités, rang)* to gain; **a. au trône** to accede to the throne (**c**) *(requête)* to comply with (**d**) *Ordinat (programme)* to access

accélérateur [akseleratœr] *nm (de voiture, d'ordinateur)* accelerator; **appuyer sur l'a.** to step on the accelerator; *Ordinat* **a. graphique** graphic(s) accelerator

accélération [akselerasjɔ̃] *nf* acceleration

accéléré, -e [akselere] **1** *nm Cin* **en a.** in accelerated motion
2 *adj* quick, fast; *(mouvement)* accelerated; **cours a.** crash course

accélérer [34] [akselere] **1** *vt* to speed up; *Fig* **a. le mouvement** to get a move on
2 *vi (en voiture)* to accelerate
3 **s'accélérer** *vpr* to accelerate, to speed up

accent [aksɑ̃] *nm* (**a**) *(sur une lettre)* accent; **a. aigu/grave/circonflexe** acute/grave/circumflex (accent); **e a. circonflexe** e circumflex (**b**) *(en phonétique)* stress; **a. tonique** (primary) stress (**c**) *(prononciation)* accent (**d**) *Fig (inflexion)* **avoir des accents de vérité** to have a ring of truth; **mettre l'a. sur qch** to stress *or* emphasize sth

accentuation [aksɑ̃tɥasjɔ̃] *nf* (**a**) *(en phonétique)* stress (**b**) *(à l'écrit)* accentuation (**c**) *(d'un phénomène)* intensification

accentué, -e [aksɑ̃tɥe] *adj* (**a**) *(syllabe)* stressed (**b**) *(lettre)* accented (**c**) *Fig (net)* pronounced, marked

accentuer [aksɑ̃tɥe] **1** *vt* (**a**) *(syllabe)* to stress (**b**) *(lettre)* to put an accent on (**c**) *Fig (renforcer)* to emphasize; *(avance)* to increase
2 **s'accentuer** *vpr* to become more pronounced *or* marked

acceptable [akseptabl] *adj* (**a**) *(recevable)* acceptable (**b**) *(passable)* satisfactory

acceptation [akseptasjɔ̃] *nf* acceptance

accepter [aksepte] *vt* to accept; **a. de faire qch** to agree to do sth; **il est hors de question que j'accepte** I can't possibly accept

acception [aksɛpsjɔ̃] *nf Formel* (**a**) *(d'un mot)* meaning, sense (**b**) **sans a. de race/de sexe** irrespective of race/sex

accès [aksɛ] *nm* (**a**) *(approche)* access, approach (à to); **être facile/difficile d'a.** to be easy/hard to reach; **avoir a. à qch** to have access to sth; **donner a. à qch** *(sujet: porte, chemin)* to lead to sth; *(sujet: ticket)* to allow entry to sth; **a. aux quais** *(sur panneau)* to the trains (**b**) *(d'une personne)* **être d'un a. facile/difficile** to be approachable/unapproachable (**c**) *(poussée)* fit, attack; **a. de colère** fit of rage; **a. de fièvre** bout of fever; **a. de toux** coughing fit (**d**) *Ordinat* access; **avoir a. à** to be able to access

accessible [aksesibl] *adj* (**a**) *(lieu, livre)* accessible; *(prix)* affordable (**b**) *(personne)* approachable

accession [aksesjɔ̃] *nf* **a. au pouvoir/au trône** accession (to power)/to the throne; **l'a. à la propriété** home ownership

accessoire [akseswar] **1** *nm (d'appareil ménager, de mode)* accessory; *Th* **accessoires** props
2 *adj* minor; **c'est a.** it's a minor detail

accessoirement [akseswarmɑ̃] *adv* if necessary, if need be; *(en plus)* also

accessoiriste [akseswarist] *nmf Th* prop man, *f* prop woman

accident [aksidɑ̃] *nm* (**a**) *(collision, malheur)* accident; **a. d'avion** plane *or* air crash; **a. de chemin de fer** train crash; **a. de la circulation** traffic accident; **a. de la route** road accident; **a. du travail** industrial accident; **a. de voiture** car accident *or* crash (**b**) *(événement inattendu)* mishap; **par a.** by accident, by chance; **a. de parcours** hitch (**c**) **a. de terrain** *(bosse)* bump; *(trou)* hole

accidenté, -e [aksidɑ̃te] **1** *nm,f* accident victim; **accidentés de la route** road accident victims
2 *adj* (**a**) *(terrain)* uneven (**b**) *(voiture)* damaged

accidentel, -elle [aksidɑ̃tɛl] *adj* accidental

accidentellement [aksidɑ̃tɛlmɑ̃] *adv (par hasard)* accidentally, by chance; *(mourir)* in an accident

acclamation [aklamasjɔ̃] *nf* cheer; **sous les acclamations de la foule** to the cheers of the crowd

acclamer [aklame] *vt* to cheer

acclimatation [aklimatasjɔ̃] *nf* acclimatization, *Am* acclimation (à to)

acclimater [aklimate] **1** *vt* to acclimatize, *Am* to acclimate (à to)
2 **s'acclimater** *vpr* to become *or* get acclimatized *or Am* acclimated (à to)

accointances [akwɛ̃tɑ̃s] *nfpl* contacts

accolade [akɔlad] *nf* (**a**) *(embrassade)* (formal) embrace; **donner l'a. à qn** to embrace sb (**b**) *(signe typographique)* curly bracket, brace

accoler [akɔle] *vt (mettre côte à côte)* to put side by side

accommodant, -e [akɔmɔdɑ̃, -ɑ̃t] *adj* accommodating

accommoder [akɔmɔde] **1** *vt (nourriture)* to prepare; *(restes)* to use up
2 *vi (œil)* to focus
3 **s'accommoder** *vpr* **s'a. de qch** to put up with sth

accompagnateur, -trice [akɔ̃paɲatœr, -tris] *nm,f* (**a**) *(pianiste)* accompanist (**b**) *(d'un voyage organisé)* courier, tour guide; *(d'une sortie scolaire)* accompanying adult

accompagnement [akɔ̃paɲmɑ̃] *nm* (**a**) *(de morceau de musique)* accompaniment; **chanter sans a.** to sing unaccompanied (**b**) *(légumes)* accompaniment

accompagner [akɔ̃paɲe] **1** *vt* (**a**) *(venir avec)* to come with, to accompany; *(aller avec)* to go with, to accompany; **il est venu accompagné d'une amie** he came with a friend (**b**) *(conduire)* **a. qn à la gare** to take sb to the station (**c**) *(chanteur)* to accompany (à on) (**d**) *(ajouter à)* **il a accompagné ses mots d'un sourire** he said it with a smile; **elle a accompagné son exposé de diapositives** she accompanied her talk with a slide show
2 **s'accompagner** *vpr* (**a**) **s'a. au piano** to accompany oneself on the piano (**b**) *(se produire simultanément)* **s'a. de qch** to be accompanied by sth

accompli, -e [akɔ̃pli] *adj (excellent)* accomplished

accomplir [akɔ̃plir] **1** *vt* (**a**) *(tâche)* to carry out; *(bonne action)* to do; *(exploit)* to accomplish; *(souhait, promesse)* to fulfil (**b**) *(terminer)* to complete, to finish
2 **s'accomplir** *vpr (souhait)* to come true

accord [akɔr] *nm* (**a**) *(traité)* agreement; *(non formel)* understanding; *(pour résoudre un conflit)* settlement; **arriver** *ou* **parvenir à un a.** to come to *or* reach an agreement (**b**) *(entente)* agreement (**sur** on); **être d'a.** to

qn to agree with sb; **se mettre d'a.** ou **tomber d'a. avec qn** to come to an agreement with sb; **(c'est) d'a.!** all right!, OK!; **d'un commun a.** by common consent, by mutual agreement; **faire qch en a. avec qn** to do sth in agreement with sb **(c)** *(autorisation)* consent **(d)** *Gram* agreement **(avec** with) **(e)** *(en musique)* chord; **a. parfait** common chord **accordéon** [akɔrdeɔ̃] *nm* accordion; *Fig* **en a.** *(chaussettes)* at half-mast

accordéoniste [akɔrdeɔnist] *nmf* accordionist, accordion player

accorder [akɔrde] **1** *vt* **(a) a. qch à qn** *(faveur)* to grant sb sth; *(augmentation, dommages-intérêts)* to award sb sth; *(prêt, découvert bancaire)* to authorize sth to sb; **a. son pardon à qn** to pardon sb; **a. la plus grande importance à qch** to attach the utmost importance to sth; **pouvez-vous m'a. quelques minutes?** can you spare me a few minutes?; *Formel* **je ne l'aime pas, je vous l'accorde** I don't like him, I must admit **(b)** *Gram* **a. qch avec qch** to make sth agree with sth **(c)** *(instrument de musique)* to tune; *Fig* **il taudrait a. nos violons** we'd better get our story straight **(d)** *(harmoniser) (couleurs)* to co-ordinate

2 s'accorder *vpr* **(a)** *(se mettre d'accord)* to agree, to come to an agreement **(avec/sur** with/on); **on s'accorde à penser que...** there is a general belief or it is generally believed that... **(b)** *(couleurs)* to go together **(c)** *Gram* to agree **(avec** with) **(d)** *(à soi-même)* **s'a. qch** to allow or give oneself sth

accordeur [akɔrdœr] *nm* (piano) tuner

accoster [akɔste] **1** *vt (personne)* to approach

2 *vi Naut* to dock

accotement [akɔtmɑ̃] *nm* **(a)** *(d'une route)* verge; **accotements non stabilisés** *(sur panneau)* soft verges **(b)** *(de voie ferrée)* shoulder

accouchement [akuʃmɑ̃] *nm* childbirth, delivery; **avoir un a. difficile** to have a difficult birth; **a. sans douleur** painless delivery

accoucher [akuʃe] **1** *vt* **a. qn** to deliver sb's baby **2 accoucher de** *vt ind* **(a)** *(enfant)* to give birth to; **elle doit a. dans un mois** her baby's due in a month **(b)** *Fam* **accouche!** come on, spit it out!

accoucheur [akuʃœr] *nm* **(médecin) a.** obstetrician

accoucheuse [akuʃøz] *nf* midwife

accouder [akude] **s'accouder** *vpr* **s'a. à** ou **sur qch** to lean one's elbow(s) on sth

accoudoir [akudwar] *nm* armrest

accouplement [akupləmɑ̃] *nm* *(d'animaux)* pairing, mating

accoupler [akuple] **s'accoupler** *vpr (animaux)* to mate

accourir [22] [akurir] *vi* to run up, to rush up

accoutrement [akutrəmɑ̃] *nm (tenue)* rig-out, get-up

accoutrer [akutre] **1** *vt* to rig out **(de** in) **2 s'accoutrer** *vpr* to rig oneself out **(de** in)

accoutumance [akutymɑ̃s] *nf (adaptation)* familiarization (**à** with); *(à l'alcool, à la drogue)* addiction; **créer une a.** to be addictive

accoutumé, -e [akutyme] *adj* usual; **comme à l'accoutumée** as usual

accoutumer [akutyme] **1** *vt* **a. qn à qch** to accustom sb to sth, to get sb used to sth **2 s'accoutumer** *vpr* **s'a. à** to get used or accustomed to sth

accréditer [akredite] *vt* **(a)** *(ambassadeur, journaliste)* to accredit **(b)** *(rendre plausible)* to substantiate

accro [akro] *adj Fam (drogué)* & *Fig* addicted (**à** to), hooked (**à** on)

accroc [akro] *nm* **(a)** *(à un tissu)* tear, catch **(b)** *Fig* hitch, snag; **sans a.** without a hitch

accrochage [akrɔʃaʒ] *nm* **(a)** *(accident)* minor accident **(b)** *(dispute)* row; *Mil* skirmish

accroche [akrɔʃ] *nf* slogan

accroche-cœur *(pl* **accroche-cœurs)** [akrɔʃkœr] *nm* kiss curl

accrocher [akrɔʃe] **1** *vt* **(a)** *(suspendre)* to hang up (**à** on); *(wagon)* to hitch on, to couple; *Fig* **une robe qui accroche le regard** an eye-catching dress; **avoir le cœur bien accroché** to have strong nerves or a strong stomach **(b)** *(abîmer) (vêtement)* to catch (**à** on); *(pare-chocs)* to clip **2** *vi (achopper)* to hit a stumbling block; **un titre qui accroche** an eye-catching title; *Fam* **ça n'a pas du tout accroché entre eux** they didn't hit it off at all; *Fam* **je n'accroche pas du tout en chimie** I just can't get into chemistry at all **3 s'accrocher** *vpr* **(a)** *aussi Fig (s'agripper)* **s'a. à qn/qch** to cling to sb/sth; *Fam* **accroche-toi, tu n'as pas fini entendu!** brace yourself, you haven't heard everything yet! **(b)** *Fam (persévérer)* to stick at it **(c)** *(voitures)* to crash into each other **(d)** *Fam (se disputer)* to have a row **(avec** with) **(e)** *(se fixer)* to fasten

accrocheur, -euse [akrɔʃœr, -øz] *adj* **(a)** *(tenace)* tenacious, stubborn **(b)** *(titre, slogan)* catchy

accroissement [akrwasmɑ̃] *nm* increase **(de** in)

accroître [akrwat] **1** *vt* to increase, to enlarge **2 s'accroître** *vpr* to increase, to grow

accroupir [akrupir] **s'accroupir** *vpr* to squat (down), to crouch (down); **être accroupi** to be squatting or crouching

accu [aky] *nm* battery

accueil [akœj] *nm (façon d'accueillir)* reception, welcome; *(lieu)* reception; **faire bon a. à qn** to welcome sb; **faire mauvais a. à qn** to give sb a cool reception

accueillant, -e [akœjɑ̃, -ɑ̃t] *adj* welcoming

accueillir [5] [akœjir] *vt* **(a)** *(personne, proposition)* to greet; **bien a. qn** to give sb a warm welcome; **nous avons été mal accueillis** we weren't given a very warm welcome; **le film a été mal accueilli par le public** the movie was badly received by the public **(b)** *(loger) (sujet, ami)* to put up; *(sujet: hôtel)* to accommodate

acculer [akyle] *vt* to drive back **(contre** against); *Fig* **a. qn à faire qch** to give sb no choice but to do sth; *Fig* **être acculé à la faillite** to be forced into bankruptcy

accumulateur [akymylatœr] *nm* *Él* battery

accumulation [akymylasjɔ̃] *nf* accumulation; *(d'énergie)* storage; **chauffage par a.** storage heating

accumuler [akymyle] **1** *vt* to accumulate, to amass; *(énergie)* to store; **a. les erreurs** to make a series of mistakes **2 s'accumuler** *vpr* to accumulate; *(nuages)* to gather, to build up; *Fin (intérêts)* to accrue; **les preuves s'accumulent contre elle** the evidence against her is growing

accusateur, -trice [akyzatœr, -tris] **1** *adj (regard, doigt)* accusing **2** *nm,f* accuser

accusation [akyzasjɔ̃] *nf* accusation; **lancer** ou **porter une a. contre qn** to make an accusation against sb; *Jur* **mettre qn en a.** to commit sb for trial

accusé, -e [akyze] **1** *adj (trait)* prominent, pronounced **2** *nm,f (d'un crime)* accused; *(au tribunal)* defendant **3** *nm* **a. de réception** *(pour une lettre)* acknowledgement (of receipt); *Ordinat* acknowledge, acknowledgement

accuser [akyze] *vt* **(a)** *(incriminer)* to accuse; **a. qn de qch/de faire qch** to accuse sb of sth/of doing sth **(b)** *(tendance, baisse)* to show; **a. le coup** to be obviously shaken **(c)** **a. réception de qch** to acknowledge (receipt of) sth **2 s'accuser** *vpr* **(a)** *(se déclarer coupable)* to confess **(de** to) **(b)** *(se renforcer)* to become more pronounced or marked

acerbe [asɛrb] *adj* acerbic; **d'un ton a.** sharply

acéré, -e [asere] *adj (lame)* sharp; *Fig (remarque)* cutting

acériculteur [aserikyltœr] *nm Can* maple syrup and sugar producer

acériculture [aserikyltyr] *nf Can* production of maple syrup and sugar

acétone [asetɔn] *nf* acetone

ACF [aseɛf] *nm (abrév* **Automobile Club de France)** = French motoring organization

achalandé, -e [aʃalɑ̃de] *adj* **magasin bien/mal a.** well/poorly stocked shop

achaler [aʃale] *vt Can* to annoy, to bother

acharné, -e [aʃarne] *adj (lutte, concurrence)* fierce; *(travail)* relentless; *(joueur)* inveterate

acharnement [aʃarnəmɑ̃] *nm* relentlessness; **avec a.** relentlessly; **se battre avec a.** to fight tooth and nail

acharner [aʃarne] **s'acharner** *vpr* **s'a. après** *ou* **contre** *ou* **sur qn** *(persécuter)* to be always after sb; **s'a. sur qn** *(sujet: meurtrier)* to savage sb; *(sujet: examinateur)* to give sb a hard time; **s'a. à faire qch** to try very hard to do sth

achat [aʃa] *nm* **(a)** *(action)* purchase, buying; **faire un a.** to make a purchase, to buy something; **faire l'a. de qch** to buy sth **(b)** *(ce qu'on a acheté)* purchase; **achats** *(provisions, paquets)* shopping; **aller faire ses achats** to go shopping

acheminement [aʃəminmɑ̃] *nm (de troupes)* transportation *(sur ou vers* to); *(de marchandises)* shipping *(sur ou vers* to); **a. du courrier** mail handling

acheminer [aʃəmine] **1** *vt (troupes)* to transport *(sur ou vers* to); *(marchandises)* to ship *(sur ou vers* to); *(courrier)* to handle
2 s'acheminer *vpr* **s'a. vers** to make one's way towards

acheter [6] [aʃəte] **1** *vt* **(a)** *(acquérir)* to buy, to purchase; **a. qch à qn** *(faire une transaction)* to buy sth from sb; *(en cadeau)* to buy sb sth; **je vais lui a. un livre** I'm going to buy him/her a book; **j'ai acheté ce livre 10 euros** I bought this book for 10 euros **(b)** *Fam (corrompre)* to buy off
2 s'acheter *vpr* **(a)** *(pour soi-même)* **je vais m'a. une glace** I'm going to buy (myself) an ice cream **(b)** *(être acheté)* **ça s'achète en pharmacie** you can buy it/them in any pharmacy; **l'amour, ça ne s'achète pas** you can't buy love

acheteur, -euse [aʃətœr, -øz] *nm,f* buyer, purchaser; **je suis a.!** I'm interested!

achevé, -e [aʃəve] *adj (artiste, style)* accomplished; *(travail)* perfect; **c'est d'un ridicule a.!** it's utterly ridiculous!

achèvement [aʃɛvmɑ̃] *nm* completion

achever [46] [aʃəve] **1** *vt* **(a)** *(finir) (discours)* to end, to conclude; *(travail)* to complete **(b)** *(tuer) (personne, proie)* to finish off; *(animal malade ou blessé)* to put out of its misery; *Fam* **ça m'a achevé!** that really finished me (off)!
2 s'achever *vpr (finir)* to end

achigan [aʃigɑ̃] *nm Can* (black) bass

achoppement [aʃɔpmɑ̃] *nm voir* **pierre**

acide [asid] **1** *adj* acid(ic); *(au goût)* sour
2 *nm* acid

acidité [asidite] *nf* acidity; *(au goût)* sourness

acidulé, -e [asidyle] *adj* slightly acid; **bonbons acidulés** acid drops

acier [asje] *nm* steel; **a. inoxydable** stainless steel

aciérie [asjeri] *nf* steelworks *(singulier)*

acné [akne] *nf* acne; **a. juvénile** acne

acolyte [akɔlit] *nm Péj* accomplice

acompte [akɔ̃t] *nm* deposit, down payment; **recevoir un a.** to receive something on account; **verser un a.** to make a down payment

acoquiner [akɔkine] **s'acoquiner** *vpr* to team up **(avec** with)

Açores [asɔr] *nfpl* **les A.** the Azores

à-côté *(pl* **à-côtés)** [akote] *nm* **(a)** *(élément secondaire)* side issue **(b)** *(financier)* extra

à-coup *(pl* **à-coups)** [aku] *nm* jolt; **travailler par à-coups** to work in fits and starts; **le moteur a des à-coups** the engine judders

acoustique [akustik] **1** *adj* acoustic
2 *nf (discipline)* acoustics *(singulier)*; *(qualité)* acoustics *(pluriel)*

acquéreur [akerœr] *nm* purchaser, buyer; **notre voiture n'a pas trouvé a.** we couldn't find a buyer for our car

acquérir [7] [akerir] *vt* **(a)** *(obtenir, prendre)* to acquire; **nous avons acquis la certitude de son innocence** we have established beyond doubt that he/she is innocent; **a. de la valeur** to increase in value **(b)** *(acheter)* to purchase, to buy

acquière, acquiers *etc voir* **acquérir**

acquiescer [16] [akjese] *vi* to acquiesce (à to); **a. d'un signe de tête** to nod in agreement

acquis, -e [aki, -iz] **1** *pp voir* **acquérir**
2 *adj (savoir, caractères)* acquired; **tenir qch pour a.** to take sth for granted; **son aide nous est acquise** we can take it for granted that he will help us; **cela est a.** that's been established
3 *nm (connaissances)* knowledge; **il ne fonctionne que sur ses acquis** he gets by on what he knows already; **les a. sociaux** social benefits

acquisition [akizisjɔ̃] *nf* **(a)** *(action)* acquisition; **faire l'a. de qch** *(acheter)* to purchase sth **(b)** *(bien acheté)* purchase

acquit [aki] *nm Com* receipt; **pour a.** received (with thanks), paid; **par a. de conscience** to ease one's conscience

acquittement [akitmɑ̃] *nm* **(a)** *Jur* acquittal **(b)** *(d'une dette)* payment

acquitter [akite] **1** *vt* **(a)** *(accusé)* to acquit **(b)** *(dette, facture)* to pay
2 s'acquitter *vpr* **s'a. d'une obligation/d'un devoir** to fulfil an obligation/a duty; **s'a. envers qn** to repay sb

acre [akr] *nm ou nf Can* acre

âcre [ɑkr] *adj (goût)* bitter, *(odeur)* acrid

acrobate [akrɔbat] *nmf* acrobat

acrobatie [akrɔbasi] *nf (art)* acrobatics *(singulier)*; **faire des acrobaties** to perform acrobatics; **a. aérienne** aerobatics *(singulier)*

acrobatique [akrɔbatik] *adj* acrobatic

acronyme [akrɔnim] *nm* acronym

Acropole [akrɔpɔl] *nf* **l'A.** the Acropolis

acrylique [akrilik] *adj & nm* acrylic

acte [akt] *nm* **(a)** *(action)* act; **faire a. d'autorité** to exercise one's authority; **faire a. de candidature à un emploi** to apply for a job; **faire a. de présence** to put in an appearance; **passer aux actes** to take action; **a. de terrorisme** terrorist act **(b)** *Jur* deed, title; **dont a.** duly noted or acknowledged; **prendre a. de qch** to take note of sth; *Formel* **nous prenons a. de votre candidature** we acknowledge your application; **a. d'accusation** bill of indictment, charges; **a. de propriété** title deed; **a. unique européenne** Single European Act; **a. de vente** bill of sale **(c)** *(certificat)* record; **a. de décès** death certificate; **a. d'état civil** = certificate of birth, marriage or death; **a. de mariage** marriage certificate; **a. de naissance** birth certificate (**d**) **actes** *(d'un procès, d'un colloque)* proceedings; *(d'un organisme scientifique)* transactions (**e**) *Th* act

acteur [aktœr] *nm* (**a**) *(artiste)* actor; a. de cinéma/de théâtre film/stage actor (**b**) *(d'un événement)* les différents acteurs de la négociation the different participants in or parties involved in the negotiations

actif, -ive [aktif, -iv] **1** *adj* (**a**) *(défenseur, participation, substance)* active; femme active working woman (**b**) *(énergique) (personne)* active (**c**) *Gram* active **2** *nm* (**a**) *Com* assets; *Fig* avoir qch à son a. to have sth to one's name; il faut mettre sa patience à son a. you have to give him credit for patience (**b**) *Gram* verbe à l'a. verb in the active voice

action [aksjɔ̃] *nf* (**a**) *(acte)* action, act; bonne/mauvaise a. good/bad deed (**b**) *(influence, effet) (d'une substance)* action, effect (**sur** on) (**c**) *(activité)* entrer en a. *(loi)* to come into force; mettre qch en a. to put sth into operation; passer à l'a. to take action, to act; homme d'a. man of action (**d**) *(histoire)* action; *TV & Cin* a.! action! (**e**) *Fin* share (**f**) *Jur* action; intenter une a. judiciaire *ou* en justice contre to take legal action against (**g**) *Mil* action

actionnaire [aksjɔnɛr] *nmf Fin* shareholder

actionner [aksjɔne] *vt (mettre en marche)* to start up, to turn on; *(faire fonctionner)* to operate, to drive

activement [aktivmɑ̃] *adv* actively

activer [aktive] **1** *vt* (**a**) *(accélérer)* to speed up; *(feu)* to stoke (**b**) *Ordinat* to activate; a. une option to select an option **2** *vi Fam* to get a move on **3** s'activer *vpr* to be busy

activiste [aktivist] *adj & nmf* activist

activité [aktivite] *nf* activity; en a. *(volcan)* active; *(usine)* in production; *(personne)* working

actrice [aktris] *nf* actress

actualisation [aktɥalizasjɔ̃] *nf (d'un texte, d'une méthode de travail)* updating

actualiser [aktɥalize] *vt (texte, méthode de travail)* to update

actualité [aktɥalite] *nf* l'a. the news, current affairs; l'a. politique française the current French political scene; cette question est toujours d'a. this is still a topical question; les actualités *(à la télé, à la radio)* the news; les actualités télévisées the television news

actuel, -elle [aktɥɛl] *adj* present, current; dans la situation actuelle as things are *or* stand at the moment

actuellement [aktɥɛlmɑ̃] *adv* at present, at the present time

acuité [akɥite] *nf (de la douleur)* acuteness; *(d'un argument)* pointedness; *(d'un son)* shrillness; a. visuelle/auditive keenness of vision/hearing

acuponcture, acupuncture [akypɔ̃ktyr] *nf* acupuncture

adage [adaʒ] *nm* adage, (common) saying; selon l'a. as the saying goes

adaptateur, -trice [adaptatœr, -tris] **1** *nm (dispositif)* adapter **2** *nm,f (d'une œuvre)* adapter

adaptation [adaptasjɔ̃] *nf* (**a**) *(à une situation)* adaptation (à to); faire un effort d'a. to try to adapt; faculté d'a. adaptability (**b**) *(d'une œuvre)* adaptation; a. théâtrale stage adaptation

adapter [adapte] **1** *vt* (**a**) *(ajuster)* to adapt (à to); est-ce vraiment adapté à la situation? is it really suitable for the situation? (**b**) *(œuvre)* to adapt **2** s'adapter *vpr* (**a**) *(s'acclimater)* to adapt (à to); savoir s'a.

to be very adaptable *or* flexible (**b**) *(être compatible)* la prise s'adapte à toutes les télévisions the plug fits all types of television

Addis-Abeba [adisabeba] *n* Addis Ababa

additif [aditif] *nm* (**a**) *(ajout)* addition (**b**) *(substance)* additive; sans additifs additive free

addition [adisjɔ̃] *nf* (**a**) *(fait d'ajouter)* addition, adding (à to); *(pour faire un total)* adding up; faire une a. to do a sum (**b**) *(extension)* addition, extension (**c**) *(au restaurant) Br* bill, *Am* check

additionnel, -elle [adisjɔnɛl] *adj* additional, extra; *Ordinat* add-on

additionner [adisjɔne] **1** *vt* to add (up); lait additionné d'eau watered-down milk; café additionné d'eau-de-vie coffee laced with brandy **2** s'additionner *vpr* to add up; aux longues heures de travail s'additionnent celles passées dans le métro along with the long working hours, there are those spent on the underground

adduction [adyksjɔ̃] *nf Tech* admission, intake; *Constr* a. d'eau canalization

adepte [adɛpt] *nmf (d'une doctrine, d'une personnalité)* follower; *(d'une activité)* enthusiast; faire des adeptes to attract a following

adéquat, -e [adekwa, -at] *adj (personne, lieu, expression, méthode)* appropriate, suitable; *(montant, quantité)* adequate

adéquation [adekwasjɔ̃] *nf* appropriateness, suitability

adhérence [aderɑ̃s] *nf* adhesion, adherence; *(de pneus)* grip

adhérent, -e [aderɑ̃, -ɑ̃t] **1** *adj (substance, propriétés)* adhesive **2** *nm,f* member

adhérer [adere] *vi* (**a**) *(coller)* to adhere, to stick (à to); a. à la route *(pneus)* to grip the road (**b**) a. à *(opinion, doctrine)* to subscribe to (**c**) *(s'inscrire)* a. à un parti to join a party

adhésif, -ive [adezif, -iv] **1** *adj* adhesive, sticky **2** *nm* adhesive

adhésion [adezjɔ̃] *nf* (**a**) *(accord)* support (à for) (**b**) *(inscription)* joining (à of)

ad hoc [adɔk] *adj & adv* ad hoc

adieu, -x [adjø] **1** *exclam* goodbye!, farewell!; dire a. à qn to say goodbye to sb; *Fam Fig* dire a. à qch to kiss *or* say goodbye to sth **2** *nm* farewell; faire ses adieux to say one's goodbyes; faire ses adieux à qn to say goodbye to sb

adipeux, -euse [adipø, -øz] *adj (tissu)* adipose; *(visage)* fat

adjacent, -e [adʒasɑ̃, -ɑ̃t] *adj* adjacent (à to)

adjectif [adʒɛktif] *nm* adjective

adjoint, -e [adʒwɛ̃, -ɛ̃t] **1** *adj* assistant, deputy **2** *nm,f* assistant; a. au maire deputy mayor

adjonction [adʒɔ̃ksjɔ̃] *nf* addition; produit sans a. de sucre product with no added sugar

adjudant [adʒydɑ̃] *nm Br* ≃ warrant officer class II, *Am* ≃ warrant officer (junior grade); a.-chef *Br* ≃ warrant officer class I, *Am* ≃ chief warrant officer

adjudication [adʒydikasjɔ̃] *nf* sale by auction

adjuger [adʒyʒe] **1** *vt* a. qch à qn *(prix, contrat)* to award sth to sb; *(aux enchères)* to knock sth down to sb; une fois, deux fois, trois fois, adjugé, vendu! going, going, gone! **2** s'adjuger *vpr* s'a. qch to appropriate sth

admettre [admɛtr] *vt (accueillir)* a. qn to admit sb, to let sb in; les chiens ne sont pas admis *(sur la porte d'un* *magasin)* no dogs allowed; **être admis à l'université** to obtain a place at university; **être admis à un concours** to pass an examination **(b)** *(accepter)* to allow; **je n'admets pas qu'on me mente** I won't tolerate being lied to; **cette règle n'admet aucune exception** there can be no exceptions to this rule **(c)** *(reconnaître)* to admit, to accept; **admettons que ce soit possible** assuming it's possible; **admettons que j'ai tort** *(pour clore une discussion)* I stand corrected

administrateur, -trice [administratœr, -tris] *nm,f* **(a)** *(d'une société, d'une banque)* director **(b)** *(de fondation)* trustee

administratif, -ive [administratif, -iv] *adj* administrative

administration [administrasjɔ̃] *nf* **(a)** *(d'affaires)* administration, management; *(d'un pays)* governing **(b)** *(ensemble des directeurs)* board of directors; *(d'une institution)* governing body **(c)** **l'A.** *(service public)* ≃ the Civil Service; *(fonctionnaires)* civil servants

administré, -e [administre] *nm,f* citizen

administrer [administre] *vt* **(a)** *(propriété)* to administer, to manage; *(pays)* to govern **(b)** *(justice)* to dispense; *Rel (sacrements)* to administer; *(remède)* to administer; **je vais lui a. une bonne correction** I'm going to give him/her a good hiding

admirable [admirabl] *adj* admirable; *(très compétent)* wonderful; **elle a été a. de courage** she showed admirable courage

admirablement [admirabləmã] *adv* admirably; *(très bien)* wonderfully; **a. bien** wonderfully

admirateur, -trice [admiratœr, -tris] *nm,f* admirer

admiratif, -ive [admiratif, -iv] *adj* admiring

admiration [admirasjɔ̃] *nf* admiration; **avoir de l'a. pour** to admire sb; **être en a. devant qch** to be filled with admiration for sth; **tomber en a. devant qch** to be stopped in one's tracks by the beauty of sth; **faire l'a. de tous** to be universally admired

admirer [admire] *vt* to admire

admis, -e [admi, -iz] **1** *adj* **(a)** *(autorisé à entrer)* admitted, allowed (in) **(b)** *(accepté)* allowed, accepted **2** *nm,f (à un examen)* successful candidate

admissible [admisibl] *adj* **(excuse, preuve, conduite)** admissible, allowable; **(candidats)** admissibles candidates who have qualified for the oral examination

admission [admisjɔ̃] *nf* **(a)** *(entrée)* admission (**à/dans** to) **(b)** *Tech* intake; *Aut* induction

ADN [adeɛn] *nm (abrév* **acide désoxyribonucléique)** DNA

ado [ado] *nmf Fam* teenager

adolescence [adɔlesɑ̃s] *nf* adolescence; **pendant mon a.** when I was a teenager

adolescent, -e [adɔlesɑ̃, -ɑ̃t] **1** *nm,f* adolescent, teenager **2** *adj* adolescent, teenage

adon [adɔ̃] *nm Can Fam* coincidence

adonner [adɔne] **s'adonner** *vpr* **s'a. à qch** to devote oneself to sth; **s'a. à la boisson** to be an alcoholic

adopter [adɔpte] *vt* **(a)** *(enfant)* to adopt **(b)** *(accepter)* to accept **(c)** *(choisir)* to adopt **(d)** *(projet de loi, résolution)* to adopt, to pass

adoptif, -ive [adɔptif, -iv] *adj (enfant)* adopted; *(parent)* adoptive

adoption [adɔpsjɔ̃] *nf* **(a)** *(d'un enfant)* adoption **(b)** *(d'une idée, d'une mode)* adoption; **mon pays d'a.** my adopted country **(c)** *(d'un projet de loi)* adoption, passing

adorable [adɔrabl] *adj* adorable, charming

adoration [adɔrasjɔ̃] *nf aussi Fig* adoration; **être en a. devant qn** to worship sb

adorer [adɔre] **1** *vt aussi Fig* to adore, to love; **j'adore monter à cheval** I love riding **2 s'adorer** *vpr* to adore each other

adosser [adose] **1** *vt* **a. qch à** *ou* **contre qch** to lean sth (with its back) against sth **2 s'adosser** *vpr* **s'a. à** *ou* **contre qch** to lean (back) against sth; **le village est adossé à la colline** the village stands at the foot of the hill

adoucir [adusir] **1** *vt* **(a)** *(voix, eau, linge, peau)* to soften; *(contraste, couleur)* to tone down; **sa nouvelle coiffure adoucit son visage** her new haircut softens her face **(b)** *(douleur, chagrin)* to ease; *Prov* **la musique adoucit les mœurs** music hath charms to soothe the savage breast **2 s'adoucir** *vpr* *(voix, ton)* to soften **(b)** *(personne, caractère)* to mellow

adoucissant, -e [adusisɑ̃, ɑ̃t] **1** *adj* softening **2** *nm (pour le linge)* fabric softener

adoucisseur [adusisœr] *nm* (water) softener

adr. *(abrév* **adresse)** address

adrénaline [adrenalin] *nf* adrenalin(e)

adresse [adrɛs] *nf* **(a)** *(coordonnées)* address; **changer d'a.** to change one's address; *Fig* **tu te trompes d'a.** you've come to the wrong person; **il connaît de bonnes adresses** *(de restaurants, de magasins)* he knows all the good places to go to; **je l'ai dit à l'a. de ceux qui...** I said it for the benefit of those who...; **a. électronique** e-mail address **(b)** *(habileté)* skill; *(savoir-faire)* diplomacy; **avec a.** skilfully **(c)** *Ordinat* address; **a. virtuelle** virtual address

adresser [adrese] **1** *vt* **(a)** *(lettre)* to address; **a. qch à qn** to send sth to sb **(b)** *(personne)* **on m'a adressé à vous** I have been referred to you **(c)** **a. qch à qn** *(compliments, remerciements)* to present sth to sb; **cette remarque était adressée à Martin** that remark was aimed at *or* meant for Martin; **a. un sourire à qn** to smile at sb; **a. la parole à qn** to speak to sb **2 s'adresser** *vpr* **s'a. à qn** *(sujet: personne)* to speak to sb; *(pour un renseignement)* to ask sb; *(sujet: remarque, recommandation)* to apply to sb; **s'a. ici** *(sur écriteau)* enquire within

Adriatique [adrijatik] *nf* **l'A.** the Adriatic

adroit, -e [adrwa, -at] *adj* **(a)** *(habile)* skilful *(réponse, diplomate)* shrewd, clever

adroitement [adrwatmã] *adv* skilfully

aduler [adyle] *vt* to worship

adulte [adylt] **1** *adj (personne)* adult, grown-up; *(plante, animal)* fully-grown **2** *nmf* adult, grown-up

adultère [adyltɛr] *nm* adultery

advenir [70] [advənir] *v impersonnel (aux* **être)** to happen; **or, il advint que...** it so happened that...; **quoi qu'il advienne** no matter what happens; **advienne que pourra** come what may

adverbe [adverb] *nm* adverb

adverbial, -e, -aux, -ales [advɛrbjal, -o] *adj* adverbial

adversaire [advɛrsɛr] *nmf* opponent; *(dans un conflit, dans une guerre)* enemy

adverse [advɛrs] *adj (équipe)* opposing; *Jur* **la partie a.** the other side

AELE [aəɛlə] *nf (abrév* **Association européenne de libre-échange)** **l'A.** EFTA

aérateur [aeratœr] *nm* ventilator

aération [aerasjɔ̃] *nf (d'une pièce)* ventilation

aérer [34] [aere] **1** *vt* **(a)** *(pièce, linge)* to air **(b)** *(texte, exposé)* to lighten **2 s'aérer** *vpr* to get some fresh air

aérien, -enne [aerjɛ̃, -ɛn] *adj* **(a)** *(défense, attaque,* *transport)* air (**b**) *(texture)* (light and) airy; *(grâce, allure)* ethereal (**c**) *(câble)* overhead; *(voie ferrée)* elevated

aérobic [aerɔbik] *nm* aerobics *(singulier)*

aérodrome [aerɔdrom] *nm* aerodrome, airfield

aérodynamique [aerɔdinamik] *adj (forme, voiture)* streamlined

aérogare [aerɔgar] *nf* (air) terminal

aéroglisseur [aerɔglisœr] *nm* hovercraft

aérogramme [aerɔgram] *nm* aerogramme, airmail letter

aéromodélisme [aerɔmɔdelism] *nm* making model aircraft

aéronautique [aerɔnotik] **1** *adj* aeronautic(al) **2** *nf* aeronautics *(singulier)*

aéronaval, -e, -als, -ales [aerɔnaval] **1** *adj (forces)* air and sea **2** *nf* l'**Aéronavale** *Br* ≃ the Fleet Air Arm, *Am* ≃ the Naval Air Service

aéronef [aerɔnef] *nm* aircraft

aérophagie [aerɔfaʒi] *nf* flatulence; **avoir** *ou* **faire de l'a.** to suffer from flatulence

aéroport [aerɔpɔr] *nm* airport

aéroporté, -e [aerɔpɔrte] *adj* airborne

aérosol [aerɔsɔl] *nm* aerosol; **vendu en a.** sold in spray form

aérospatial, -e, -aux, -ales [aerɔspasjal, -o] *adj* aerospace

aérostat [aerɔsta] *nm (montgolfière)* hot-air balloon; *(dirigeable)* airship

affabilité [afabilite] *nf* affability

affable [afabl] *adj* affable

affabulation [afabylasjɔ̃] *nf* fabrication

affabuler [afabyle] *vi* to make things up

affaiblir [afeblir] **1** *vt* (**a**) *(sujet: maladie)* to weaken (**b**) *(réduire)* to lessen, to reduce **2 s'affaiblir** *vpr (personne)* to get weaker; *(vue, ouïe)* to get worse, to deteriorate; *(sentiment)* to wane; *(son)* to grow fainter; **le sens du mot s'est affaibli** the word has lost much of its meaning

affaiblissement [afeblismɑ̃] *nm (d'une personne, d'un gouvernement, de l'économie)* weakening; *(d'un sentiment)* waning; *(d'une lumière, d'un son)* fading

affaire [afɛr] *nf* (**a**) *(occupation)* business, concern; **ce n'est pas votre a.** it's none of your business; **j'en fais mon a.** I'll handle it; **c'est une a. de goût** it's a matter *or* question of taste; **c'est l'a. d'une minute** it won't take a minute; **ça, c'est une autre a.** that's another matter; **avoir a. à qn** to be dealt with by sb; **s'il continue à mentir, il aura a. à moi!** if he carries on lying, he'll have me to deal with! (**b**) *(usage)* **cela fera parfaitement l'a.** that will do nicely; *Fam* **faire son a. à qn** to do sb in (**c**) *(histoire, problème)* affair, business; **une a. de pots-de-vin** a bribery scandal; **a. de cœur** love affair; **ça n'a pas été une mince a.** it wasn't easy; **c'est tout une a.** it's quite a business; **la belle a.!** big deal!; **ça ne change rien à l'a.** that doesn't change anything; **tirer qn d'a.** to get sb out of trouble; **ce n'est pas une a. d'État!** it's no big deal! (**d**) *(transaction)* deal; *(achat à bon marché)* bargain; **il a fait une a. en achetant cette voiture** he got a bargain when he bought that car; **faire a. avec qn** to make a deal with sb; **une a. en or** the bargain of the century (**e**) *(entreprise)* firm, business (**f**) **affaires** *(effets personnels)* things, belongings (**g**) **les affaires** *(activités commerciales)* business *(singulier)*; **comment vont les affaires?** how's business?; **il est dur en affaires** he's a hard-headed businessman; **les affaires sont les affaires** business is business

(**h**) **les Affaires étrangères** *Br* ≃ the Foreign (and Commonwealth) Office, *Am* ≃ the State Department

affairé, -e [afere] *adj* busy

affairer [afere] **s'affairer** *vpr* to busy oneself; **s'a. autour de qn** to fuss (a)round sb

affairiste [aferist] *nmf* wheeler-dealer

affaissement [afesmɑ̃] *nm (de terrain)* subsidence; *(du plancher, d'une poutre)* sagging

affaisser [afese] **s'affaisser** *vpr* (**a**) *(s'enfoncer) (terrain)* to subside; *(poutre, fauteuil)* to sag (**b**) *(tomber, s'écrouler)* to collapse

affalé, -e [afale] *adj* **être a. dans un fauteuil** to be slumped in an armchair

affaler [afale] **s'affaler** *vpr* to collapse

affamé, -e [afame] *adj* starving

affectation [afɛktasjɔ̃] *nf* (**a**) *Péj (pose)* affectation, affectedness; *(simulacre)* pretence, affectation; **avec a.** affectedly; **sans a.** unaffectedly (**b**) *(de fonds, de crédits, de locaux)* assignment, allocation; (**c**) *(à un poste)* appointment (à to); *(d'un soldat)* posting (à to) (**d**) *Ordinat (de touche)* assignment; **a. de mémoire** memory allocation

affecté, -e [afɛkte] *adj Péj (personne, manière)* affected

affecter [afɛkte] *vt* (**a**) *(fonds, crédits, locaux)* to assign (à to), to allocate (à to) (**b**) *(employé)* to appoint (à to); *(soldat)* to post (à to) (**c**) *(feindre)* to affect; **a. de faire qch** to pretend to do sth (**d**) *(émouvoir)* to affect, to move (**e**) *(frapper) (carrière, santé)* to affect, to have an effect on; **la grève a affecté plusieurs usines** the strike has affected *or* hit several factories

affectif, -ive [afektif, -iv] *adj* emotional, *Spéc* affective

affection [afɛksjɔ̃] *nf* (**a**) *(attachement)* affection (**pour** for); **prendre qn en a.** to become fond of sb; **avoir de l'a. pour qn** to be fond of sb (**b**) *Litt (maladie)* ailment

affectionner [afɛksjɔne] *vt* to be fond of; **votre cousin affectionné** *(dans une lettre)* your affectionate cousin

affectivité [afɛktivite] *nf* feelings

affectueusement [afɛktɥøzmɑ̃] *adv* affectionately; *(dans une lettre)* love (from)

affectueux, -euse [afɛktɥø, -øz] *adj* affectionate

afférent, -e [aferɑ̃, -ɑ̃t] *adj* **a. à** *(concernant)* relating to

affermir [afermir] **1** *vt* (**a**) *(muscles, chairs)* to tone (up) (**b**) *(pouvoir, position, autorité)* to strengthen, to consolidate **2 s'affermir** *vpr (chairs, muscles)* to tone up; *(pouvoir, position, autorité)* to be strengthened

affichage [afiʃaʒ] *nm* (**a**) *(pose d'affiches)* billsticking, billposting; **a. interdit** *(sur panneau)* stick no bills (**b**) *Ordinat* display; **montre à. digital** *ou* **numérique** digital watch; **a. à cristaux liquides** liquid crystal display

affiche [afiʃ] *nf* notice; *(de publicité)* poster; **être à l'a.** *(spectacle)* to be on; **être en tête d'a.** to be top of the bill; **a. électorale** election poster

afficher [afiʃe] **1** *vt* (**a**) *(annonce, poster)* to put up; *(prix, horaires, résultats)* to display; **défense d'a.** *(sur panneau)* stick no bills; **a. complet** *(spectacle)* to be sold out (**b**) *(mépris, indifférence)* to show, to display; *(savoir)* to flaunt; *(déficit, excédent)* to show (**c**) *Ordinat (message)* to display **2 s'afficher** *vpr* (**a**) *(personne)* to flaunt oneself (**b**) *(sur un écran)* to be displayed

affichette [afiʃɛt] *nf* small notice; *(publicitaire)* poster

afficheur [afiʃœr] *nm (personne)* billsticker, billposter; *(société)* publicity company

affilée [afile] **d'affilée** *adv* in a row; **cinq heures d'a.** five hours solid *or* at a stretch

affiler [afile] *vt* to sharpen

affiliation [afiljasjɔ̃] *nf* joining (à of)

affilier [66] [afilje] **s'affilier** *vpr* to join; **s'a. à un parti** to join a party

affiner [afine] **1** *vt* (**a**) *(métal)* to refine; *(fromage)* to mature (**b**) *(esprit)* to sharpen; *(goût)* to refine
2 s'affiner *vpr (goût)* to become more refined; (*visage)* to get thinner; *(traits)* to become better defined; *(esprit)* to become sharper

affinité [afinite] *nf* affinity (**entre** between)

affirmatif, -ive [afirmatif, -iv] **1** *adj* (**a**) *(réponse)* affirmative, positive; **faire un signe a. de la tête** to nod in agreement (**b**) *(personne)* positive
2 *nf* **dans l'affirmative** if so, if the answer is yes; **répondre par l'affirmative** to answer yes
3 *exclam* affirmative!

affirmation [afirmasjɔ̃] *nf* assertion

affirmer [afirme] **1** *vt* (**a**) *(soutenir)* to maintain; **il affirme vous connaître** he maintains that he knows you (**b**) *(manifester)* to assert; **a. sa volonté de faire qch** to declare one's willingness to do sth
2 s'affirmer *vpr (personnalité)* to assert itself; *(tendance, talent)* to be confirmed

affleurer [aflœre] *vi (récif)* to be near the surface; *Fig (mépris, racisme)* to come to the surface; *Géol (filon)* to outcrop

affliction [afliksjɔ̃] *nf* affliction

affligé, -e [afliʒe] *adj* (**a**) **être a. de** *(atteint)* to be afflicted with (**b**) *(peiné)* distressed

affligeant, -e [afliʒɑ̃, -ɑ̃t] *adj (nouvelle, vision)* distressing; *(bêtise, ignorance, résultats)* appalling

affliger [45] [afliʒe] **1** *vt* (**a**) *(atteindre)* to afflict; **région affligée par le choléra** area afflicted with cholera; **la nature l'a affligé d'un grand nez** nature has cursed him with a big nose (**b**) *(peiner) (sujet: nouvelle, événement)* to distress
2 s'affliger *vpr* to be distressed (**de** about)

affluence [aflyɑ̃s] *nf (de personnes)* crowd; *(de marchandises)* abundance

affluent [aflyɑ̃] *nm* tributary

affluer [aflye] *vi (liquide)* to flow (**vers/dans** to/into); *(sang)* to rush (**à** to); *(foule)* to flock (**vers** to)

afflux [afly] *nm (de sang)* rush; *(de visiteurs)* flood; *(de capitaux)* influx

affolant, -e [afɔlɑ̃, -ɑ̃t] *adj (spectacle, nouvelle)* distressing; *Fam* **c'est a.!** it's incredible!

affolé, -e [afɔle] *adj (personne)* panic-stricken

affolement [afɔlmɑ̃] *nm* panic; **pas d'a.!** don't panic!

affoler [afɔle] **1** *vt* to throw into a panic
2 s'affoler *vpr* (**a**) *(paniquer)* to panic (**b**) *(aiguille de boussole)* to spin (**c**) *(machine)* to race

affranchir [afrɑ̃ʃir] **1** *vt* (**a**) *(lettre, colis)* to put a stamp/stamps on; *(avec une machine)* to frank (**b**) *(esclave)* to free
2 s'affranchir *vpr (peuple, personne)* to free oneself (**de** from)

affranchissement [afrɑ̃ʃismɑ̃] *nm* (**a**) *(montant payé)* (de lettre, paquet) postage (**b**) *(d'un esclave)* freeing

affres [afr] *nfpl Litt (du doute, de la jalousie, de la faim)* pangs; **les a. de la mort** death throes

affréter [34] [afrete] *vt* to charter

affreusement [afrøzmɑ̃] *adv* horribly; **il parle a. mal l'anglais** his English is awful

affreux, -euse [afrø, -øz] *adj* (**a**) *(laid)* hideous (**b**) *(atroce) (nouvelle, pauvreté, crime)* dreadful (**c**) *Fam (épouvantable) (temps, migraine)* awful, dreadful; **qu'est-ce que ça a augmenté, c'est a.!** it's dreadful *or* shocking how the price has gone up!; **un a. jojo** a little horror

affriolant, -e [afrijɔlɑ̃, -ɑ̃t] *adj* alluring

affront [afrɔ̃] *nm* affront, insult; **faire un a. à qn** to affront *or* insult sb

affrontement [afrɔ̃tmɑ̃] *nm* clash, confrontation

affronter [afrɔ̃te] **1** *vt (adversaire, danger, mort)* to face, to confront; **a. la colère de qn** to brave the wrath of sb
2 s'affronter *vpr (ennemis)* to clash; *(équipes, joueurs)* to clash; **deux thèses s'affrontent** there are two conflicting theories

affubler [afyble] **1** *vt* **a. qn de qch** to get sb up in sth
2 s'affubler *vpr* **s'a. de qch** to get oneself up in sth

affût [afy] **1** **à l'affût** *adv* **être à l'a.** *(à la chasse)* to lie in wait; *Fig* **être à l'a. de qch** to be on the lookout for sth

affûter [afyte] *vt* to sharpen

afghan, -e [afgɑ̃, -an] **1** *adj* Afghan
2 *nm,f* **A.** Afghan
3 *nm (langue)* Afghan

Afghanistan [afganistɑ̃] *nm* **l'A.** Afghanistan

afin [afɛ̃] *adv* **a. de faire qch** (in order) to do sth, so as to do sth; **a. que** + *subjunctive* so that; **a. que les autres puissent le voir** so that the others may see it

AFNOR [afnɔr] *nf (abrév* **Association française de normalisation)** = French industrial standards authority, *Br* ≃ BSI, *Am* ≃ ANSI

a fortiori [aforsjori] *adv* all the more so

AF-P [aɛfpe] *nf (abrév* **Agence France-Presse)** = French international news agency

africain, -e [afrikɛ̃, -ɛn] **1** *adj* African
2 *nm,f* **A.** African

Afrique [afrik] *nf* **l'A.** Africa; **l'A. du Nord** North Africa; **l'A. du Sud** South Africa

afro-américain, -e (*mpl* **afro-américains**, *fpl* **afro-américaines)** [afroamerikɛ̃, -ɛn] **1** *adj* Afro-American, African American
2 *nm,f* **A.** Afro-American, African American

after-shave [aftœrʃɛv] **1** *nm inv* aftershave
2 *adj* **lotion a.** aftershave (lotion)

A.G. [aʒe] *nf (abrév* **assemblée générale)** AGM

agaçant, -e [agasɑ̃, -ɑ̃t] *adj* annoying, irritating

agacer [16] [agase] *vt* (**a**) *(énerver)* to annoy, to irritate; **il m'agace avec ses questions** he's getting on my nerves, asking all those questions (**b**) *(dents, nerfs)* to set on edge

agapes [agap] *nfpl Litt* feast; *Hum* **nous allons faire des a. chez Jeannot** we're going to have a real feast at Jeannot's

agate [agat] *nf (pierre)* agate; *(bille)* marble

âge [aʒ] *nm* (**a**) *(d'une personne)* age; **quel â. avez-vous?** how old are you?; **à ton â., je travaillais** when I was your age, I was working; **à l'â. de dix ans** at the age of ten; **on ne lui donne pas son â.** he doesn't look his age; **faire son â.** to look one's age; **un homme d'un grand â.** a very old man; **entre deux âges** middle-aged; **être en â. de faire qch**, **être d'â. à faire qch** to be old enough to do sth; **ce n'est plus de mon â.** I'm too old for that type of thing; **un whisky de quinze ans d'â.** a fifteen-year-old whisky; **l'â. adulte** adulthood; **l'â. bête** *ou* **ingrat** the awkward *or* difficult age; **â. mental** mental age; **une femme d'â. mûr** a mature woman; **avoir l'â. de raison** to have reached the age of reason (**b**) *(époque)* age; **l'â. de (la) pierre** the Stone Age; **l'â. d'or du cinéma muet** the golden age of silent movies

âgé, -e [aʒe] *adj* (**a**) *(qui a tel âge)* **être â. de dix ans** to be ten years old; **un enfant â. de deux ans** a two-year-old child (**b**) *(vieux)* old; **être plus/moins â. que qn** to be older/younger than sb

agence [aʒɑ̃s] *nf* agency; *(de banque)* branch; **a. immobilière** *Br* estate agent's *or* agency, *Am* real estate agency; **a. matrimoniale** marriage bureau; **A. nationale pour l'emploi** = French national employment bureau; **a. de presse** press *or* news agency; **a. de voyages** travel agent's *or* agency

agencement [aʒɑ̃smɑ̃] *nm (d'éléments)* arrangement; *(d'une maison, d'une pièce)* layout

agencer [16] [aʒɑ̃se] **1** *vt (éléments)* to arrange; *(maison, pièce)* to lay out, to design

2 s'agencer *vpr* **les parties du discours s'agencent bien/mal** the different parts of the speech hang/don't hang together well

agenda [aʒɛ̃da] *nm* diary; **a. électronique** personal organizer

agenouiller [aʒnuje] **s'agenouiller** *vpr* to kneel (down) (**devant** in front of)

agent [aʒɑ̃] *nm* (**a**) *(employé, espion)* agent; **a. (de police)** police officer; **pardon, Monsieur l'a.** excuse me, officer; **a. d'assurance(s)** insurance broker; **a. de change** stockbroker; **a. de la circulation** traffic policeman; **a. immobilier** *Br* estate agent, *Am* realtor; **a. secret** secret agent (**b**) *(facteur)* factor (**c**) *Gram* agent

agglomération [aglɔmerasjɔ̃] *nf (ville)* town, built-up area; **l'a. lyonnaise/parisienne** Lyons/Paris and its suburbs

aggloméré [aglɔmere] *nm* chipboard

agglomérer [34] [aglɔmere] **1** *vt* to bind together
2 s'agglomérer *vpr* to bind together

agglutiner [aglytine] **s'agglutiner** *vpr (personnes)* to congregate, to gather

aggravant, -e [agravɑ̃, -ɑ̃t] *adj* aggravating

aggravation [agravɑsjɔ̃] *nf (d'une maladie)* aggravation; *(du temps, d'un conflit)* worsening

aggraver [agrave] **1** *vt (situation, état de santé)* to make worse; *(difficultés)* to increase; **pour a. les choses** to make matters worse

2 s'aggraver *vpr (situation)* to get worse; *(état de santé)* to deteriorate; *(difficultés)* to increase

agile [aʒil] *adj* agile, nimble

agilement [aʒilmɑ̃] *adv* agilely, nimbly

agilité [aʒilite] *nf* agility

agios [aʒjo] *nmpl* bank charges

agir [aʒir] **1** *vi* (**a**) *(faire quelque chose)* to act; **bien/mal a. envers qn** to behave well/badly towards sb; **je n'aime pas sa façon ou manière d'a.** I don't like his behaviour (**b**) *(produire un effet) (médicament, substance)* to act (**sur** on); **a. sur le moral** to have a demoralizing effect (**c**) *Jur* **a. au nom de qn** to act on behalf of sb

2 s'agir de *v impersonnel* (**a**) *(être question de)* **de quoi s'agit-il?** what's it about?; **l'affaire dont il s'agit** the matter in hand; **il ne s'agit pas d'argent** it's not a question of money; **quand il s'agit d'aider, il est toujours occupé!** when it comes to helping, he always seems to be busy! (**b**) *(falloir)* **il s'agit de prendre une décision** we have to take a decision; **il s'agit de savoir si...** the question is whether...; **il s'agirait de se dépêcher** we've got to hurry

agissements [aʒismɑ̃] *nmpl* dealings

agitateur, -trice [aʒitatœr, -tris] *nm,f Pol* agitator

agitation [aʒitasjɔ̃] *nf (inquiétude)* agitation; *(bougeotte)* restlessness; *(troubles)* unrest

agité, -e [aʒite] *adj (mer)* rough; *(patient, nuit)* restless; *(sommeil)* troubled; *(enfant)* fidgety; *(époque)* unsettled; *(vie)* hectic

agiter [aʒite] **1** *vt* (**a**) *(mouchoir, drapeau, bras)* to wave; *(bouteille)* to shake; *(sujet: vent) (arbre, branches)* to sway; **a. la queue** *(chien)* to wag its tail; *(cheval)* to flick its tail (**b**) *(inquiéter)* to trouble; *(malade)* to excite

2 s'agiter *vpr* (**a**) *(bouger)* to fidget; *(s'affairer)* to bustle around; **s'a. dans son sommeil** to toss and turn in one's sleep (**b**) *(s'énerver)* to get excited

agneau, -x [aɲo] *nm* lamb; **(peau d')a.** lambskin

agnelle [aɲɛl] *nf* ewe lamb

agnostique [agnɔstik] *adj & nmf* agnostic

agonie [agɔni] *nf aussi Fig* death throes; **être à l'a.** to be at death's door; *Fig (régime)* to be in its death throes

agonisant, -e [agɔnizɑ̃, -ɑ̃t] **1** *adj* dying
2 *nm,f* dying person

agoniser [agɔnize] *vi* to be dying; *Fig (régime)* to be in its death throes

agoraphobie [agɔrafɔbi] *nf Méd* agoraphobia; **souffrir d'a.** to be agoraphobic

agrafe [agraf] *nf* (**a**) *(de bureau)* staple; *(de robe)* hook; *Méd* clip (**b**) *Constr* cramp (iron)

agrafer [agrafe] *vt* (**a**) *(avec une agrafeuse)* to staple; *(robe)* to fasten (**b**) *Fam (arrêter)* to bust; **se faire a.** to get busted

agrafeuse [agraføz] *nf* stapler

agraire [agrɛr] *adj (économie, société)* agrarian

agrandir [agrɑ̃dir] **1** *vt* (**a**) *(rendre plus grand)* to enlarge; *(maison, influence)* to extend; *(cercle de relations)* to widen (**b**) *(sujet: loupe, microscope)* to magnify; **ce papier peint agrandit la pièce** this wallpaper makes the room look bigger

2 s'agrandir *vpr (ville)* to grow, to get bigger; *(nombre, influence)* to increase; *(entreprise)* to expand

agrandissement [agrɑ̃dismɑ̃] *nm* (**a**) *(d'une maison)* extension; *(d'une ville)* growth; *(d'une entreprise)* expansion (**b**) *(cliché)* enlargement

agréable [agreabl] *adj (personne, endroit, journée)* nice, pleasant; *(apparence)* pleasing; **a. au goût** tasty; **a. à regarder** nice to look at

agréablement [agreablmɑ̃] *adv* pleasantly

agréer [24] [agree] *vt (fournisseur, équipement)* to approve; **veuillez a. l'expression de mes sentiments distingués** *(à une personne dont on connaît le nom)* yours sincerely; *(à une personne dont on ne connaît pas le nom)* yours faithfully

agrégation [agregasjɔ̃] *nf* **(le concours de) l'a.** = competitive examination for posts on the teaching staff of lycées and universities

agrégé, -e [agreʒe] **1** *adj* = who has passed the "agrégation" examination
2 *nm,f* = graduate who has passed the "agrégation" examination

agrément [agremɑ̃] *nm* (**a**) *(plaisir)* **voyage d'a.** pleasure trip; (**b**) *(charme)* **une ville sans a.** an unattractive town; (**c**) *(accord)* approval, consent

agrémenter [agremɑ̃te] *vt* **a. qch de** *(décorer)* to adorn sth with; **texte agrémenté de citations** text spiced with quotations

agrès [agrɛ] *nmpl* (**a**) *Sp* (gymnastics) apparatus; **faire des a.** to do apparatus work (**b**) *Naut* tackle

agresser [agrese] *vt* to attack; to assault; *(en paroles)* to attack; *(tympans)* to assault; *(yeux)* to hurt; *(peau)* to damage; **se faire a.** to be attacked; *(pour son argent)* to be mugged

agresseur [agresœr] *nm* attacker

agressif, -ive [agresif, -iv] *adj* aggressive

agression [agresjɔ̃] *nf (d'une personne)* attack, assault; *(pour son argent)* mugging; *(d'un pays)* act of aggression; **être victime d'une a.** to be mugged; **les agressions de la vie moderne** the stresses of modern life

agressivement [agresivmɑ̃] *adv* aggressively

agressivité [agresivite] *nf* aggressiveness

agricole [agrikɔl] *adj* agricultural; *(population)* farming; *(produits)* farm

agriculteur, -trice [agrikyltœr, -tris] *nm,f* farmer

agriculture [agrikyltyr] *nf* farming, agriculture

agripper [agripe] **1** *vt* to clutch **2 s'agripper** *vpr* to cling on **(à** to)

agroalimentaire [agroalimɑ̃tɛr] **1** *adj (industrie, secteur)* food **2** *nm* **l'a.** the food-processing industry

agronome [agrɔnɔm] *nmf* agronomist

agronomie [agrɔnɔmi] *nf* agronomy

agrume [agrym] *nm* citrus fruit

aguets [agɛ] **aux aguets** *adv* on the lookout; **être** *ou* **se tenir aux a.** to be on the lookout

aguichant, -e [agiʃɑ̃, -ɑ̃t] *adj* seductive

aguicher [agiʃe] *vt* to seduce

ahuri, -e [ayri] **1** *adj* astounded **2** *nm,f* numbskull

ahurissant, -e [ayrisɑ̃, -ɑ̃t] *adj* astounding

aide [ɛd] **1** *nf* help, assistance; **demander de l'a. à qn** to ask sb for help; **venir en a. à qn** to help sb; **appeler à l'a.** to call for help; **à l'a.!** help!; **à l'a. de qch** with the aid of sth; *Ordinat* **a. à la césure** hyphenation help; **a. de l'État** government aid; **a. humanitaire** aid; **a. judiciaire** legal aid; *Ordinat* **a. en ligne** on-line help; **a. sociale** *Br* social security, *Am* welfare **2** *nmf* assistant; **un a. de camp** an aide-de-camp; **une a. familiale** a home help; **une a. ménagère** a home help

aide-mémoire [ɛdmemwar] *nm inv* aide-mémoire

aider [ede] **1** *vt* to help; *(sujet: gouvernement)* to aid; **que puis-je faire pour vous a.?** how may I help you?; **je me suis fait a. par un ami** I got a friend to help me; **a. qn à faire qch** to help sb to do sth; **a. qn à monter/sortir** to help sb up/out; *Ironique* **tu veux que je t'aide?** stop that!; **elle n'aide jamais** she never helps (out) **2 aider à** *vt ind* to contribute towards; **a. à faire qch** to help to do sth **3 s'aider** *vpr* **(a)** *(soi-même)* **s'a. de qch** to use sth; **marcher en s'aidant d'une canne/de béquilles** to walk with the aid of a stick/crutches; *Prov* **aide-toi et le ciel t'aidera** God helps those who help themselves **(b)** *(l'un l'autre)* to help each other

aide-soignant, -e *(mpl* **aides-soignants,** *fpl* **aides-soignantes)** [ɛdswaɲɑ̃, ɑ̃t] *nm,f* nursing auxiliary

aïe [aj] *exclam (cri de douleur)* ow!, ouch!; *Fig* **a., j'ai fait une gaffe!** oh no, I've put my foot in it!

aïeul [ajœl] *nm,f Vieilli* grandfather, *f* grandmother; **aïeuls** grandparents

aïeux [ajø] *nmpl Litt* ancestors

aigle [ɛgl] *nm* eagle; *Fig* **ce n'est pas un a.** he's no genius; **avoir un œil d'a.** to be eagle-eyed

aiglefin [ɛgləfɛ̃] *nm* haddock

aigre [ɛgr] *adj (goût, lait)* sour; *Fig (propos)* cutting; **d'un ton a.** sharply

aigre-doux, -douce *(mpl* **aigres-doux,** *fpl* **aigres-douces)** [ɛgrədu, -dus] *adj (sauce)* sweet-and-sour; *Fig (remarque)* snide

aigrelet, -ette [ɛgrəlɛ, -ɛt] *adj (vin, goût)* (rather) sour; *(son, voix)* shrill

aigrette [ɛgrɛt] *nf* **(a)** *(d'un oiseau)* crest **(b)** *(panache)* plume

aigreur [ɛgrœr] *nf* **(a)** *(d'un goût)* sourness; *(d'une remarque)* sharpness, bitterness **(b)** *Méd* **aigreurs (d'estomac)** heartburn

aigri, -e [ɛgri] *adj* embittered

aigu, -uë [ɛgy] *adj* **(a)** *(douleur)* acute, sharp; *(regard)* penetrating; *(esprit)* keen; **avoir un sens a.** **de qch** to have a keen sense of sth **(b)** *(instrument)* sharp; *(angle)* acute **(c)** *(son)* high-pitched **(d)** *Méd* acute

aigue-marine *(pl* **aigues-marines)** [ɛgmarin] *nf* aquamarine

aiguillage [ɛgɥijaʒ] *nm* **(a)** *(manœuvre) Br* shunting, *Am* switching; *(appareil) Br* points, *Am* switches **(b)** *Fig* **faire une erreur d'a.** to take the wrong course

aiguille [ɛgɥij] *nf* **(a)** *(instrument, objet pointu)* needle; *Fig* **chercher une a. dans une botte de foin** to look for a needle in a haystack; **a. à coudre/repriser/tricoter** sewing/darning/knitting needle; *Méd* **a. hypodermique** hypodermic needle; **a. de pin** pine needle **(b)** *(de boussole, de compteur de vitesse)* needle; *(de montre, d'horloge)* hand; **petite a.** little hand; **grande a.** big hand **(c)** *(d'une église)* spire **(d)** *(sommet)* sharp peak

aiguiller [ɛgɥije] *vt (train) Br* to shunt, *Am* to switch; *Fig* **a. qn vers** *(profession)* to steer sb towards; **a. ses recherches vers** to direct one's investigations towards; **a. la police sur une fausse piste** to put the police off the scent; **il a été mal aiguillé dans ses études** he was badly advised about his studies

aiguilleur [ɛgɥijœr] *nm (de trains)* signalman; **a. du ciel** air-traffic controller

aiguillon [ɛgɥijɔ̃] *nm* **(a)** *(pique-bœuf)* goad; *Fig* spur **(b)** *(d'une guêpe)* sting

aiguiser [ɛgize] *vt* **(a)** *(outil, couteau)* to sharpen **(b)** *Fig (curiosité, jalousie)* to arouse; *(appétit)* to whet

aïkido [ajkido] *nm* aikido; **faire de l'a.** to do aikido

ail *(pl* **ails** [aj], *Vieilli* **aulx** [o]) *nm* garlic; *Can* **a. des bois** wild garlic

aile [ɛl] *nf* **(a)** *(d'oiseau, de papillon)* wing; *Fig* **battre de l'a.** to be struggling; **la peur nous donnait des ailes** fear lent us wings; *Fam* **avoir un coup dans l'a.** to have had a bit too much to drink **(b)** *(d'une voiture) Br* wing, *Am* fender; *(d'un bâtiment)* wing; *(d'une armée)* flank **(c)** *(d'un avion)* wing; *(d'un moulin)* sail; *(d'une hélice, d'une turbine)* blade **(d)** *(au football, au rugby)* wing

ailé, -e [ɛle] *adj* winged

aileron [ɛlrɔ̃] *nm* **(a)** *(d'oiseau)* pinion; *(de requin)* fin **(b)** *Av* aileron

ailette [ɛlɛt] *nf (d'une turbine, d'un ventilateur)* blade; *(d'une bombe, d'un missile)* wing, fin

ailier [ɛlje] *nm (au football)* winger; *(au rugby, au basket)* wing

aille *etc voir* **aller**

ailler [aje] *vt* to put garlic in

ailleurs [ajœr] *adv* **(a)** *(à un autre endroit)* elsewhere, somewhere else; *Fig* **être a., avoir l'esprit a.** to be miles away; **partout a.** everywhere else; *(n'importe où)* anywhere else; **nulle part a.** nowhere else; **vous mangerez ici comme nulle part a.** you'll eat better here than anywhere else; *Fam* **va voir a. si j'y suis!** take a hike! **(b)** **d'a.** *(de plus)* besides, anyway; *(au fait)* by the way **(c) par a.** *(par d'autres côtés)* in other respects; *(d'autre part)* moreover

ailloli [ajɔli] = **aïoli**

aimable [ɛmabl] *adj (gentil)* kind, nice; **vous êtes bien a., c'est très a. de votre part** it's very kind of you; **peu a.** *(personne)* not very nice; *(propos)* unkind

aimablement [ɛmabləmɑ̃] *adv* kindly

aimant¹ [ɛmɑ̃] *nm* magnet

aimant², -e [ɛmɑ̃, -ɑ̃t] *adj (personne)* loving

aimanter [ɛmɑ̃te] *vt* to magnetize

aimer [eme] **1** vt (a) (d'amour) to love (b) (apprécier, avoir de l'affection pour) to like; **a. beaucoup qn/qch** to like sb/sth a lot, to be fond of sb/sth; **a. bien qn/qch** to like sb/sth; **a. faire qch** to like doing sth; **j'aurais aimé le voir** I would like to have seen him; **je n'aime pas que tu fréquentes ces gens** I don't like you mixing with those people; **j'aime(rais) autant** ou **mieux rester ici** I would rather stay here; **j'aime autant qu'il ne m'attende pas** I would rather he didn't wait for me; **a. mieux** to prefer; **ah, j'aime mieux ça!** now that's more like it!; **Fam j'aime mieux pas** I'd rather not; **je vais prendre un pot – qui m'aime me suive!** I'm going for a drink – anyone want to join me? **2 aimer à** vt ind Litt **a. à faire qch** to take pleasure in doing sth; **j'aime à croire que...** I like to think (that)... **3 s'aimer** vpr (a) (l'un l'autre) to love each other (b) (être fier de soi) to be in love with oneself; **je ne m'aime pas dans cette veste** I don't like myself in this jacket

aine [ɛn] nf groin

aîné, -e [ene] **1** adj (de deux enfants) elder; (de plus de deux enfants) eldest **2** nm,f (de deux enfants) elder (child); (de plus de deux enfants) eldest (child); **nos aînés** our elders; **il est mon a.** he is older than me; **il est mon a. de deux ans** he is two years older than me

aînesse [ɛnɛs] nf voir **droit**

ainsi [ɛsi] adv (a) (de cette façon) like this, in this way; **c'est a. qu'il est devenu soldat** that's how he became a soldier; **et a. de suite** and so on, and so forth; **pour a. dire** so to speak, as it were; Rel **a. soit-il** amen (b) **a. (donc)** (alors) so; **a. vous ne venez pas?** so you're not coming? (c) (par exemple) for example, for instance (d) **a. que** (et) as well as, and

aïoli [ajɔli] nm Culin aïoli, garlic mayonnaise

air [ɛr] nm (a) (gaz) air; **cela manque d'a.** it's stuffy in here; **faire de l'a.** to let some air in; **sortir prendre l'a.** to go out for some fresh air; **laisser qch à l'a.** to leave sth uncovered; **au grand a.** in the fresh air; **en plein a.**, **à l'a. libre** outside; **concert en plein a.** open-air concert; **activités de plein a.** outdoor pursuits; Fam **allez, de l'a.!** go on, clear off!, **a. comprimé** compressed air; **avoir l'a. conditionné** to have air-conditioning (b) (ciel) **l'a.** the air; **s'élever dans les airs** to rise into the air; **regarder en l'a.** to look up (c) Fig (atmosphère) **changer d'a.** to have a change of scene; **il y a de la dispute/de l'orage dans l'a.** there's an argument/a storm brewing (d) (vent) **il y a** ou **il fait de l'a.** there's a breeze (e) (allure) look; (mine) expression; **avoir un drôle d'a.** to look odd or funny; **avoir l'a. triste/de s'ennuyer** to look sad/bored; Fam **avoir l'a. fin** to look daft; **tu as l'a. de ne pas comprendre** you look as if you don't understand; **n'avoir l'a. de rien** (travail) to look (deceptively) easy; **il n'a l'a. de rien, mais...** he doesn't look much, but...; **se donner** ou **prendre des airs** to give oneself airs; **ne prends pas tes grands airs!** don't get on your high horse!; **a. de famille** family likeness (f) (musique) tune; **un a. d'opéra** an (operatic) aria (g) (locutions) Fam **ficher qch en l'a.** to mess sth up; **mettre qch en l'a.** (en désordre) to make an awful mess of sth; **c'est dans l'a. du temps** it's the in-thing

air-air [ɛrɛr] adj inv Mil air-to-air

aire [ɛr] nf (a) (surface plane) area; **a. (de battage)** threshing floor; **a. d'atterrissage** (pour avions) landing strip; (pour hélicoptères) helipad; **a. de jeux** play area; **a. de lancement** (de fusée) launch pad; **a. de repos** (sur l'autoroute) rest area; **a. de stationnement** lay-by (b) (d'un champ, d'un triangle, d'un bâtiment) area; Fig **a. d'influence** sphere of influence (c) (d'un aigle) eyrie

airelle [ɛrɛl] nf (rouge) cranberry

air-sol [ɛrsɔl] adj inv Mil air-to-ground

aisance [ɛzɑ̃s] nf (a) (facilité, grâce) ease (b) (financière) vivre dans l'a. to live comfortably

aise [ɛz] **1** nf être à l'a. (bien installé) to be comfortable; (avoir beaucoup de place) to have plenty of room; (financièrement) to be comfortably off; (dans une situation) to feel comfortable or at ease; **on tient à l'a. à six dans cette voiture** this car holds six comfortably; Fam **à l'a.!** (c'est facile) easy!, **ne pas être à son a.**, **se sentir mal à l'a.** to feel uncomfortable; **mettre qn à l'a.** to put sb at his ease; **se mettre à l'a.** to make oneself comfortable; Ironique **elle peut en parler à son a.!** it's easy (enough) for her to say that!; **à ton a.!** suit yourself!; **prendre ses aises** to make oneself at home **2** adj Litt **être bien** ou **tout a. de faire qch** to be delighted to do sth

aisé, -e [eze] adj (a) (financièrement) comfortably off (b) (tâche, mouvements) easy

aisément [ezemɑ̃] adv easily

aisselle [ɛsɛl] nf armpit

Aix-la-Chapelle [ɛkslaʃapɛl] n Aachen, Aix-la-Chapelle

AJ [aʒi] nf (abrév **auberge de jeunesse**) youth hostel

ajonc [aʒɔ̃] nm gorse

ajouré, -e [aʒure] adj (pull) loose-knit; (broderie, en architecture) openwork

ajourner [aʒurne] vt (réunion, décision, voyage) to postpone, to put off; (après le début de la séance) to adjourn; Scol (candidat) to refer

ajout [aʒu] nm addition (à to)

ajouter [aʒute] **1** vt to add (à to); Ordinat (à une base de données) to append **2** ajouter à vt ind to add to **3** s'ajouter vpr **s'a.** à to be added to; **à ceci viennent s'a. les frais de déplacement** on top of this there are travel expenses (to be added)

ajustable [aʒystabl] adj adjustable

ajustage [aʒystaʒ] nm fitting

ajuster [aʒyste] **1** vt (a) (régler) (appareil, outil) to adjust; (chapeau, coiffure) to adjust; **a. le tir** to aim (b) (adapter) to fit (à to); (vêtement) to alter; **veste ajustée** fitted jacket **2** s'ajuster vpr (a) (personne) to straighten one's clothes (b) (s'adapter) **s'a.** à to fit; **s'a. sur** to fit onto

ajusteur [aʒystœr] nm fitter

alaise [alɛz] nf undersheet

alambic [alɑ̃bik] nm still

alambiqué, -e [alɑ̃bike] adj convoluted

alangui, -e [alɑ̃gi] adj languid

alarmant, -e [alarmɑ̃, -ɑ̃t] adj alarming; **son état est a.** his condition is giving serious cause for concern

alarme [alarm] nf alarm; **donner/sonner l'a.** to give/sound the alarm; **une fausse a.** a false alarm; **a. antivol** car alarm; **a. incendie** fire alarm

alarmer [alarme] **1** vt to alarm **2** s'alarmer vpr to get alarmed; **il n'y a pas lieu de s'a.** there is no cause for alarm

albanais, -e [albanɛ, -ɛz] **1** adj Albanian **2** nm,f **A.** Albanian **3** nm (langue) Albanian

Albanie [albani] nf **l'A.** Albania

albâtre [albatr] nm alabaster

albatros [albatros] nm albatross

albinos [albinos] adj & nmf albino

album [albɔm] nm album; **a. de timbres/de photos** stamp/photo album

albumen [albymɛn] *nm* Biol albumen
albumine [albymin] *nf* Chim albumin
alcalin, -e [alkalɛ̃, -in] *adj* Chim alkaline
alchimie [alʃimi] *nf* alchemy
alchimiste [alʃimist] *nm* alchemist
alcool [alkɔl] *nm* (**a**) Chim alcohol; **a. à 90°** Br surgical spirit, Am rubbing alcohol; **a. à brûler** methylated spirits (**b**) *(digestif)* liqueur; **l'a.** *(boissons alcoolisées)* alcohol; **il ne tient pas l'a.** he can't hold his drink; **l'a. au volant** drink-driving; **a. de poire** pear brandy
alcoolémie [alkɔlemi] *nf* **taux d'a.** blood alcohol level
alcoolique [alkɔlik] *adj & nmf* alcoholic; **être a.** to be an alcoholic
alcoolisé, -e [alkɔlize] *adj* alcoholic
alcoolisme [alkɔlism] *nm* alcoholism
alcolo [alkɔlo] *adj & nmf Fam* drunk; **être a.** to be a drunk
Alcotest® [alkɔtɛst] *nm* breathalyzer test; **faire passer un A. à qn** to breathalyze sb
alcôve [alkov] *nf* recess *(for bed)*
aléa [alea] *nm* hazard
aléatoire [aleatwar] *adj* random; *(résultat)* uncertain
alémanique [alemanik] *adj* **la Suisse a.** German-speaking Switzerland
ALENA [alena] *nm (abrév* **Accord de libre-échange nord-américain)** **l'A.** NAFTA
alentour [alɑ̃tur] **1** *adv* around, round about; **les villages a.** the surrounding villages
  2 alentours *nmpl (voisinage)* surroundings; **aux alentours** in the vicinity; **aux alentours de la ville/100 euros** in the vicinity of the town/100 euros; **aux alentours de midi** (some time) around midday
Aléoutiennes [aleusjɛn] *adj & nfpl* **les (îles) A.** the Aleutian Islands
alerte [alɛrt] **1** *nf* (**a**) *(avertissement)* alarm; **donner/sonner l'a.** to give/sound the alarm; **a. à la bombe** bomb scare (**b**) *(menace)* threat; *(problème de santé)* scare; **à la première a.** at the first sign of danger; **fausse a.** false alarm
  2 *adj (personne) (physiquement)* sprightly; *(mentalement)* alert; *(esprit, style)* lively; **d'un pas a.** at a brisk pace
  3 *(exclam)* look out!
alerter [alɛrte] *vt* to alert (**sur** to)
alèse [alɛz] = **alaise**
alevin [alvɛ̃] *nm* young fish
Alexandre [alɛksɑ̃dr] *npr* **A. le Grand** Alexander the Great
Alexandrie [alɛksɑ̃dri] *n* Alexandria
alexandrin [alɛksɑ̃drɛ̃] *nm* alexandrine
alezan, -e [alzɑ̃, -an] **1** *adj (cheval)* chestnut
  2 *nm* chestnut (horse)
algèbre [alʒɛbr] *nf* algebra
algébrique [alʒebrik] *adj* algebraic
Alger [alʒe] *n* Algiers
Algérie [alʒeri] *nf* **l'A.** Algeria
algérien, -enne [alʒerjɛ̃, -ɛn] **1** *adj* Algerian
  2 *nmf* **A.** Algerian
algérois, -e [alʒerwa, -az] **1** *adj* of Algiers
  2 *nmf* **A.** person from Algiers
algorithme [algɔritm] *nm* Math & Ordinat algorithm; Ordinat **a. de tri** sorting algorithm
algue [alg] *nf* piece of seaweed; **algues** seaweed
alias [aljɑs] *adv* alias
alibi [alibi] *nm* alibi

aliénation [aljenasjɔ̃] *nf* (**a**) *(de l'esprit)* alienation; Psy **a. mentale** insanity (**b**) *(de liberté)* loss; Jur *(des droits, de biens)* alienation
aliéné, -e [aljene] **1** *adj* insane
  2 *nm,f* insane person
aliéner [34] [aljene] **1** *vt* (**a**) *(personne)* to alienate; **ce commentaire vous a aliéné la sympathie de l'auditoire** you lost the audience's sympathy when you made that comment (**b**) Jur *(biens, droits)* to alienate
  2 s'aliéner *vpr* **s'a. la sympathie de l'électorat** to lose the goodwill of the electorate; **s'a. un ami** to alienate a friend
alignement [aliɲəmɑ̃] *nm* (**a**) *(opération)* alignment, aligning; Pol *(sur un pays, une politique)* alignment (**sur** with) (**b**) *(ligne)* line; **être dans l'a. de qch** to be in line with sth (**c**) *(de monolithes)* = line of standing stones
aligner [aliɲe] **1** *vt* (**a**) *(mettre en ligne)* to align, to line up; *(politique, monnaie)* to align (**sur** with) (**b**) *(mettre à la suite)* *(arguments)* to reel off; **je passe ma journée à a. des chiffres** I spend all day producing lists of figures
  2 s'aligner *vpr (se mettre en rang)* to line up; Pol *(sur un pays, une politique)* to align oneself (**sur** with); Fam **tu peux toujours t'a.!** not a chance!
aliment [alimɑ̃] *nm* (**a**) *(nourriture)* food (**b**) Jur **aliments** alimony
alimentaire [alimɑ̃tɛr] *adj* (**a**) *(plante)* edible; **habitudes alimentaires** eating habits; **l'industrie a.** the food industry (**b**) Fig **ce n'est qu'un travail a.** I just do this job to keep body and soul together
alimentation [alimɑ̃tasjɔ̃] *nf* (**a**) *(régime alimentaire)* diet; **avoir une a. équilibrée** to have a balanced diet; **(magasin d')a.** grocer's; **(rayon) a.** grocery department (**b**) *(action) (de personne, de plante, d'animal)* feeding; *(d'une ville, d'un marché)* supply; **l'a. d'une ville en eau** the water supply to a town (**c**) Tech *(d'une chaudière)* feeding; *(en électricité)* power supply; **a. papier** *(d'une imprimante)* sheetfeed, paper feed
alimenter [alimɑ̃te] **1** *vt (personne, plante, animal, chaudière)* to feed; *(cours d'eau)* to flow into; Fin *(compte)* to pay money into; Fig *(conversation)* to keep going; *(sentiment)* to fuel; **a. une usine en courant** to supply a factory with power
  2 s'alimenter *vpr* to eat
alinéa [alinea] *nm* (**a**) *(renfoncement)* indent (**b**) *(texte)* paragraph
aliter [alite] **s'aliter** *vpr* to take to one's bed; **être alité** *(temporairement)* to be confined to one's bed; *(grabataire)* to be bedridden
alizé [alize] *adj & nm* **les (vents) alizés** the trade winds
Allah [ala] *npr* Allah
allaitement [aletmɑ̃] *nm* feeding; *(d'un animal)* suckling; **a. au biberon** bottle-feeding; **a. maternel** breast-feeding
allaiter [alete] *vt (enfant)* to breast-feed; *(sujet: animal)* to suckle; **est-ce que vous allaitez?** are you breast-feeding?
allant [alɑ̃] *nm* **avoir de l'a.**, **être plein d'a.** to be full of energy
alléchant, -e [aleʃɑ̃, -ɑ̃t] *adj (offre)* tempting; *(odeur, plat)* appetizing
allécher [34] [aleʃe] *vt* to tempt
allée [ale] *nf* (**a**) *(dans un jardin)* path; *(devant une résidence)* driveway; *(dans une ville)* avenue; *(dans un supermarché, un cinéma)* aisle (**b**) **allées et venues** coming(s) and going(s); **faire des allées et venues** to go back and forth
allégation [alegasjɔ̃] *nf* allegation
allégé, -e [aleʒe] *adj (en matières grasses)* low-fat; *(en sucre)* low-sugar
allègement [alɛʒmɑ̃] *nm* (**a**) *(d'impôts, de charges)*

reduction; *(des emplois de temps scolaires)* streamlining; a.
fiscal tax relief (**b**) *(d'un véhicule, d'un fardeau)* lightening
alléger [59] [aleʒe] *vt* (**a**) *(impôts, charges)* to reduce;
(douleur, chagrin) to soothe (**b**) *(véhicule, fardeau)* to lighten;
(emploi du temps scolaire) to streamline
allégorie [alegɔri] *nf* allegory
allégorique [alegɔrik] *adj* allegorical
allègre [alɛgr] *adj* lively, cheerful; **d'un ton a.** cheerfully,
light-heartedly; **d'un pas a.** with a spring in one's step
allègrement [alɛgrəmɑ̃] *adv* cheerfully; *(marcher)* with
a spring in one's step; **il m'a a. refilé ses enfants pour le
week-end** he cheerfully palmed his children off on me for
the weekend
allégresse [alegrɛs] *nf* joy; **a. générale** general rejoicing
alléluia [aleluja] *nm & exclam Rel* hallelujah
Allemagne [almaɲ] *nf* **l'A.** Germany; *Anciennement* **l'A.
de l'Ouest/de l'Est** West/East Germany
allemand, -e [almɑ̃, -ɑ̃d] **1** *adj* German
2 *nmf* **A.** German; *Anciennement* **A. de l'Est/de l'Ouest**
East/West German
3 *nm (langue)* German
aller¹ [8] [ale] *(aux être)* **1** *vi* (**a**) *(se déplacer)* to go; a. à
Toulon to go to Toulon; **ce train va à Lille** this train goes to
Lille; a. à la pêche to go fishing; a. et venir to come and go
(**b**) *(sujet: chemin, route)* a. à to go to
(**c**) *(arriver)* a. jusqu'à *(dans l'espace)* to go as far as; *(dans le
temps)* to last until; **jusqu'où ira-t-il?** *(pour atteindre son but)*
to what lengths will he go?; a. jusqu'à faire qch to go so far
as to do sth
(**d**) *(fonctionner)* to go; *(bien fonctionner)* to go well, **si tu
touches à mes affaires, ça va a. mal!** touch my things and
there'll be trouble!, ça va *(comme ça)*, merci *(à table)* that's
enough, thanks; je vous en offre 20 euros francs, ça va?
I'll give you 20 euros for it, OK?; *Fam* **non mais ça va
pas(, la tête)!** are you crazy?
(**e**) *(se porter)* a. bien/mal to be well/ill; **comment allez-
vous?** how are you?; ça va? ça va! how's things? – OK!
(**f**) *(indique le but)* a. faire qch to go and do sth; a. se
coucher to go to bed; a. se promener to go for a walk; va
voir! go and see!; **n'allez pas vous imaginer que...** don't
you go thinking that...
(**g**) *(convenir)* a. à qn to suit sb; a. bien à qn *(vêtement,
couleur)* to look good on sb; a. (bien) avec qch *(vêtement,
couleur)* to go (well) with sth, to match sth; *Fam* **ça lui va
mal de donner des conseils** he's a fine one to be giving
advice
(**h**) *(se ranger, s'adapter)* **où vont les couteaux?** where do
the knives go *or* belong?; **un plat qui va au four** an
ovenproof dish
(**i**) *(agir)* **il est allé un peu vite dans cette affaire** he was
a bit hasty; *Fam* **vas-y doucement** take it easy; *Fam*
comme tu y vas! that's a bit much!
(**j**) *(locutions)* **y a.** *(partir)* to go; *(commencer)* to get on with
it; **allez!** *(pour encourager)* come on!; *(pour consoler)* come
now!; **allons!** *(pour encourager, réprimander)* come on!; ça
passera, va don't worry, you'll get over it; **va pour 500
euros/mardi prochain** 500 euros/next Tuesday, that's fine;
a. de soi to be obvious; a. sur ses quarante ans to be
nearing forty
2 *v aux* (**a**) *(indique le futur proche)* a. faire qch to be going
to do sth; **il va s'en occuper** he's going to deal with it;
j'allais m'endormir quand... I was about to fall asleep
when... (**b**) *(indique la progression)* a. en empirant to be
getting worse and worse
3 *v impersonnel* **il en va de même pour moi/lui** it's the
same for me/him
4 s'en aller *vpr* (**a**) *(personne)* to go (away) (**b**) *(tache)* to
come out; *(couleur)* to fade; *(peinture)* to flake off

aller² *nm* (**a**) *(trajet)* outward journey; **à l'a.** on the way
there (**b**) *(billet)* a. (**simple**) *Br* single (ticket), *Am* one-way
(ticket); a. (**et**) retour *Br* return (ticket), *Am* round-trip
(ticket); *Fam Fig* **un a. et retour** *(gifle)* a slap round the face
allergie [alɛrʒi] *nf* allergy; **avoir** *ou* **faire une a. à qch** to
be allergic to sth
allergique [alɛrʒik] *adj aussi Fig* allergic (**à** to)
allergologiste [alɛrgɔlɔʒist], **allergologue** [alɛr-
gɔlɔg] *nmf Méd* allergist
alliage [aljaʒ] *nm (métallique)* alloy
alliance [aljɑ̃s] *nf* (**a**) *(entente)* alliance; *(d'un couple)*
marriage; **parent par a.** relative by marriage (**b**) *(bague)*
wedding ring (**c**) *(combinaison)* (**de parfums, de couleurs**)
combination
allié, -e [alje] **1** *nmf (partisan)* ally; **parents et alliés**
extended family; *Hist* **les Alliés** the Allies
2 *adj* (**a**) *(nation)* allied (**b**) *Hist* Allied
allier [66] [alje] **1** *vt* (**a**) *(pays)* to ally; *(familles)* to unite by
marriage (**b**) *(métaux)* to alloy; *(couleurs)* to combine; a.
l'intelligence à la beauté to combine intelligence and
beauty
2 s'allier *vpr* (**a**) *(s'unir)* to become allies (**avec** with); **s'a.
contre qn/qch** to unite against sb/sth (**b**) *(goûts, parfums,
couleurs)* to combine
alligator [aligatɔr] *nm* alligator
allitération [aliterasjɔ̃] *nf* alliteration; a. en s alliteration
of the letter s
allô, allo [alo] *exclam* hello!
allocation [alɔkasjɔ̃] *nf* (**a**) *(d'argent, de terres)* allocation;
(de titres financiers) allotment (**b**) *(prestation financière)*
allowance; **les allocations (familiales)** child benefit; a.
(**de**) **chômage** unemployment benefit, (**b**) **logement**
housing benefit
allocs [alɔk] *nfpl Fam* child benefit
allocution [alɔkysjɔ̃] *nf* address
allongé, -e [alɔ̃ʒe] *adj* (**a**) *(forme, silhouette)* elongated;
avoir le visage a. to have a long face (**b**) *(couché)* **être a.** to
be lying down
allongement [alɔ̃ʒmɑ̃] *nm* (**a**) *(agrandissement)*
lengthening (**b**) *(dans le temps)* extension; a. de l'espérance de vie increase in life expectancy
allonger [45] [alɔ̃ʒe] **1** *vt* (**a**) *(rendre plus long)* to lengthen;
(vêtement) to let down; *(sauce)* to thin (down); **cette robe
vous allonge la silhouette** this dress makes you look
taller (**b**) *(bras)* to stretch out; *(cou)* to crane; **a. le pas** to
quicken one's pace; *Sp* **a. l'allure** to increase the pace (**c**)
(personne) to lie down (**d**) *(vacances, délai)* to extend (**e**) *Fam*
a. une gifle à qn to give sb a slap; a. le fric/100 euros to
hand over the money/100 euros
2 *vi (jours)* to get longer
3 s'allonger *vpr* (**a**) *(ombres, jours)* to get longer; *Fig*
(enfant) to grow (**b**) *(se coucher)* to lie down; *Fam* **s'a. (par
terre)** *(tomber)* to fall flat on the ground
allopathie [alɔpati] *nf Méd* allopathy
allouer [alwe] *vt* a. qch à qn *(salaire, indemnité, délai)* to
grant sb sth; *(actions, ration)* to allocate sb sth
allumage [alymaʒ] *nm (d'un feu)* lighting; *(d'une lampe)*
switching on; *(d'un moteur)* ignition
allume-cigare *(pl* allume-cigares*)* [alymsigar] *nm* cigar
lighter
allume-gaz [alymgaz] *nm inv* gas lighter
allumer [alyme] **1** *vt* (**a**) *(cigarette, briquet, feu)* to light;
(lampe, télévision, électricité) to switch on, to turn on;
(incendie) to start; a. (**la lumière**) to switch *or* turn the light
on; a. le salon to switch on the lights in the lounge;
laisser la cuisinière allumée to leave the cooker on (**b**) *Fig*

(passions) to arouse; *Fam (séduire)* to tease **2 s'allumer** *vpr (lumière, lampe, téléviseur)* to come on; **où est-ce que ça s'allume?** where's the on switch?

allumette [alymɛt] *nf* match

allumeuse [alymøz] *nf Fam* prick-teaser

allure [alyr] *nf* **(a)** *(vitesse)* speed; **à toute a.** at top speed **(b)** *(démarche)* walk, gait; *(manière de se tenir)* bearing; **avoir de l'a.** to be stylish; **avoir fière a.** to cut a fine figure; **avoir une drôle d'a.** to look funny; **avoir des allures de malfrat** to look like a crook

allusion [alyzjɔ̃] *nf* allusion (**à** to); **faire a. à** to refer to, to allude to

alluvial, -e, -aux, -ales [alyvjal, -o] *adj* alluvial

alluvions [alyvjɔ̃] *nfpl* alluvium

almanach [almana] *nm* almanac

aloès [alɔɛs] *nm* aloe

aloi [alwa] *nm* **de bon a.** *(succès)* deserved; *(plaisanterie)* in good taste; **de mauvais a.** *(succès)* undeserved; *(plaisanterie)* in bad taste

alors [alɔr] *adv* **(a)** *(à ce moment-là)* then; *(dans ce cas)* then, in that case; **jusqu'a.** (up) until then; **le ministre d'a.** the minister at the time; **et a.?** so what?; **et a., qu'il a répondu?** so what did he say?; *Fam* **a., tu viens?** so are you coming?; *Fam* **non mais a., pour qui il se prend, celui-là?** really, just who does he think he is?; *Fam* **ça a.!** wow!, no way! **(b)** *(donc)* so; **il n'était pas là, a. je suis revenu** he wasn't there, so I came back **(c)** **a. que** *(au moment où)* when; *(bien que)* even though; **il a une maison, a. que moi j'habite dans un appartement** he's got a house, whereas I live in an apartment

alouette [alwɛt] *nf* lark

alourdir [alurdir] **1** *vt (chose)* to make heavier; *Fig (phrase)* to make cumbersome; *(charges sociales)* to increase **2 s'alourdir** *vpr* to get heavy; *(taille)* to get bigger

aloyau, -x [alwajo] *nm* sirloin

alpaga [alpaga] *nm* alpaca

alpage [alpaʒ] *nm* mountain pasture

alpaguer [alpage] *vt très Fam* to collar; **se faire a. par qn** to get collared by sb

Alpes [alp] *nfpl* **les A.** the Alps; **les A. suisses** the Swiss Alps

alphabet [alfabɛ] *nm* alphabet

alphabétique [alfabetik] *adj* alphabetical

alphabétiquement [alfabetikmɑ̃] *adv* alphabetically

alphabétisation [alfabetizasjɔ̃] *nf* teaching of literacy

alphanumérique [alfanymerik] *adj* alphanumeric

alphapage [alfapaʒ] *nm* bleeper

alpin, -e [alpɛ̃, -in] *adj* alpine

alpinisme [alpinism] *nm* mountaineering, climbing; **faire de l'a.** to go mountaineering *or* climbing

alpiniste [alpinist] *nmf* mountaineer, climber

Alsace [alzas] *nf* **l'A.** Alsace

alsacien, -enne [alzasjɛ̃, -ɛn] **1** *adj* of Alsace, Alsatian **2** *nm,f* **A.** Alsatian

altercation [alterkasjɔ̃] *nf* altercation

alter ego [alterego] *nm inv* alter ego

altérer [34] [altere] *vt* **(a)** *(détériorer) (viande, vin)* to spoil; *(santé)* to damage **(b)** *(changer)* to affect

alternance [alternɑ̃s] *nf* alternation; *Pol* change of government; **en a.** alternately

alternateur [alternatœr] *nm Él* alternator

alternatif, -ive [alternatif, -iv] **1** *adj* **(a)** *(successif)* & *Él* alternating **(b)** *(de remplacement)* alternative **2** *nf* **alternative** alternative

alternativement [alternativmɑ̃] *adv* alternately, in turn

alterner [alterne] **1** *vt (cultures)* to rotate **2** *vi (se succéder)* to alternate (**avec** with); *(personnes)* to take turns (**avec** with)

altesse [altɛs] *nf* **son A. royale** His/Her Royal Highness

altier, -ère [altje, -ɛr] *adj* haughty

altimètre [altimɛtr] *nm* altimeter

altitude [altityd] *nf* altitude; **à basse/haute a.** at low/high altitude; **à 100 mètres d'a.** at an altitude of 100 metres; **en a.** at altitude; **prendre de l'a.** to climb

alto [alto] *Mus* **1** *nm (instrument)* viola **2** *nf (chanteuse)* alto

altruisme [altrɥism] *nm* altruism

altruiste [altrɥist] *adj* altruistic

aluminium [alyminjɔm] *nm* aluminium

alunir [alynir] *vi* to land on the moon

alunissage [alynisaʒ] *nm* moon landing

alvéole [alveɔl] *nf (de ruche)* cell; *(pulmonaire)* alveolus; *(de dent)* socket

amabilité [amabilite] *nf* kindness; **auriez-vous l'a. de me le faire savoir?** would you be so kind as to let me know?

amadouer [amadwe] *vt* to coax

amaigrir [amegrir] **1** *vt* to make thin; **la maladie l'a beaucoup amaigri** he's much thinner following his illness **2 s'amaigrir** *vpr* to get thinner

amaigrissant, -e [amegrisɑ̃, -ɑ̃t] *adj (régime)* slimming

amaigrissement [amegrismɑ̃] *nm (involontaire)* weight loss; *(volontaire)* slimming

amalgame [amalgam] *nm* combination

amalgamer [amalgame] *vt (confondre)* to lump together

amanché, -e [amɑ̃ʃe] *adj Can* **mal a.** badly dressed

amande [amɑ̃d] *nf (fruit)* almond; *(dans un noyau)* kernel; **des yeux en a.** almond(-shaped) eyes

amandier [amɑ̃dje] *nm* almond tree

amanite [amanit] *nf* **a. phalloïde** death cap; **a. tue-mouches** fly agaric

amant [amɑ̃] *nm* lover

amarrage [amaraʒ] *nm Naut* mooring

amarre [amar] *nf Naut* (mooring) rope; **rompre ses amarres** to break its moorings

amarrer [amare] *vt Naut* to moor

amaryllis [amarilis] *nf* amaryllis

amas [ama] *nm* heap, pile

amasser [amase] **1** *vt* to amass **2 s'amasser** *vpr (preuves, foule)* to build up; *(neige)* to pile up; *(troupes)* to mass

amateur [amatœr] **1** *nm* **(a)** *(passionné)* **a. de tennis/de jardinage** tennis/gardening enthusiast; **a. d'art** art lover; **a. de bons vins** connoisseur of fine wines; *Fig* **est-ce qu'il y a des amateurs?** any takers?; **avis aux amateurs!** anyone interested? **(b)** *(non professionnel)* amateur; **faire de la photo en a.** to be an amateur photographer; *Péj* **c'est du travail d'a.** it's amateurish work **2** *adj* **photographe a.** amateur photographer

amateurisme [amatœrism] *nm* amateurism

Amazone [amazon] *nf* **l'A.** the Amazon

amazone [amazon] *nf* **(a)** *(dans la mythologie)* **les Amazones** the Amazons **(b)** *(cavalière)* horsewoman; **monter en a.** to ride sidesaddle

Amazonie [amazɔni] *nf* **l'A.** the Amazon (Basin)

amazonien, -enne [amazɔnjɛ̃, -ɛn] *adj* Amazonian; *(forêt)* Amazon

ambages [ɑ̃baʒ] **sans ambages** *adv* without beating about the bush

ambassade [ɑ̃basad] *nf* embassy; **l'a. de France au Japon** the French embassy in Japan

ambassadeur, -drice [ɑ̃basadœr, -dris] **1** *nm,f* ambassador; **l'a. de France au Japon** the French ambassador to Japan; *Fig* **être l'a. de son pays** to be an ambassador for one's country **2** *nf* **ambassadrice** *(épouse)* ambassador's wife

ambiance [ɑ̃bjɑ̃s] *nf* atmosphere, ambience; *Fam* **mettre de l'a.** to liven things up; *Fam* **il y a de l'a.** ici there's a good atmosphere here

ambiant, -e [ɑ̃bjɑ̃, -ɑ̃t] *adj (gaieté, enthousiasme)* pervading; **température ambiante** room temperature

ambidextre [ɑ̃bidɛkstr] *adj* ambidextrous

ambigu, -uë [ɑ̃bigy] *adj* ambiguous

ambiguïté [ɑ̃bigɥite] *nf* ambiguity; **répondre sans a.** to give an unambiguous answer

ambitieux, -euse [ɑ̃bisjø, -øz] **1** *adj* ambitious **2** *nm,f* ambitious person

ambition [ɑ̃bisjɔ̃] *nf* ambition; **avoir de l'a.** to be ambitious; **j'ai l'a. de devenir journaliste** my ambition is to be a journalist

ambitionner [ɑ̃bisjɔne] *vt* to aspire to; **il ambitionne de gagner leTour de France** his ambition is to win theTour de France

ambivalent, -e [ɑ̃bivalɑ̃, -ɑ̃t] *adj* ambivalent

ambre [ɑ̃br] *nm (résine)* amber

ambulance [ɑ̃bylɑ̃s] *nf* ambulance

ambulancier, -ère [ɑ̃bylɑ̃sje, -ɛr] *nm,f* ambulance man, *f* ambulancewoman

ambulant, -e [ɑ̃bylɑ̃, -ɑ̃t] *adj* itinerant, travelling; *Fam* **c'est un dictionnaire a.** he's a walking dictionary

âme [ɑm] *nf* **(a)** *Rel & Phil* soul; *Fig (animateur)* moving spirit; **être artiste dans l'â.** to have an artistic temperament; **rendre l'â.** to give up the ghost; **aller comme une â. en peine** to wander around like a lost soul; **trouver l'â. sœur** to find one's soul mate; **de toute mon â.** with all my heart; **en mon â. et conscience** to the best of my knowledge and belief **(b)** *(personne)* **une bonne â.** a kind soul; **ils ne rencontrèrent â. qui vive** they didn't meet a (living) soul; **un hameau de cinquante âmes** a hamlet of fifty inhabitants; **â. damnée** devoted servant; *Hum* partner in crime **(c)** *(d'un câble)* core

amélioration [ameljɔrasjɔ̃] *nf* improvement; **apporter des améliorations à qch** to make improvements to sth

améliorer [ameljɔre] **1** *vt* to improve **2 s'améliorer** *vpr* to improve; **ça ne s'améliore pas** it's not getting any better

amen [amɛn] *nm inv* amen; *Fig* **dire a. à qch** to go along with sth

aménagement [amenaʒmɑ̃] *nm (changement)* adjustment; *(d'une pièce)* conversion (**en** into); *(d'une ville, d'une région)* development; **a. du temps de travail** flexibility of working hours; **a. du territoire** regional development, physical planning

aménager [45] [amenaʒe] *vt (changer)* to adjust; *(pièce, maison)* to convert (**en** into)

amende [amɑ̃d] *nf* **(a)** *(contravention)* fine; **avoir 50 euros d'a.** to get a 50-euro fine **(b)** **faire a. honorable** to apologize

amendement [amɑ̃dmɑ̃] *nm Pol* amendment

amender [amɑ̃de] **1** *vt (loi, texte)* to amend **2 s'amender** *vpr* to turn over a new leaf

amener [46] [amne] **1** *vt* **(a)** *(apporter)* to bring; **a. l'eau à**

ébullition to bring the water to the boil; **a. qn à faire qch** to get sb to do sth; *(sujet: circonstances)* to lead sb to do sth; … **ce qui nous amène à parler du chômage** … which brings us to the issue of unemployment **(b)** *(occasionner)* to bring about **(c)** *(tirer à soi)* to pull in; *(voile)* to lower **2 s'amener** *vpr Fam* to turn up; **amène-toi!** come here!

amenuiser [amənɥize] **1** *vt* to wear down **2 s'amenuiser** *vpr* to dwindle; *(écart)* to get smaller

amer, -ère [amɛr] *adj* bitter

amèrement [amɛrmɑ̃] *adv* bitterly

américain, -e [amerikɛ̃, -ɛn] **1** *adj* American **2** *nm,f* **A.** American

américaine *nf (langue)* American (English) **4** *nf* **américaine** *Culin* homard à l'américaine = lobster cooked in a tomato, white wine and brandy sauce

américaniser [amerikanize] **1** *vt* to Americanize **2 s'américaniser** *vpr* to become Americanized

américanisme [amerikanism] *nm Ling* Americanism

amerindien, -enne [amerɛ̃djɛ̃, -ɛn] *adj* Amerindian, American Indian **2** *nm,f* **A.** Amerindian, American Indian

Amérique [amerik] *nf* **l'A.** America; **l'A. centrale** Central America; **l'A. latine** Latin America; **l'A. du Nord/du Sud** North/South America

amerloque [amɛrlɔk] *nmf très Fam* American

amerrir [amerir] *vi* to make a landing at sea; *(vaisseau spatial)* to splash down

amerrissage [amerisaʒ] *nm* landing at sea; *(d'un vaisseau spatial)* splashdown

amertume [amɛrtym] *nf* bitterness

améthyste [ametist] *nf* amethyst

ameublement [amœbləmɑ̃] *nm* **(a)** *(action de meubler)* furnishing **(b)** *(meubles)* furniture

ameuter [amøte] *vt (gens)* to bring out; **elle va a. tout le voisinage si elle continue à hurler comme ça!** she'll have the whole neighbourhood out if she carries on shouting like that!

ami, -e [ami] **1** *nm,f* friend, **(petit) a.** boyfriend; **(petite) amie** girlfriend; **a. d'enfance** childhood friend; **a. intime** close friend **2** *adj* friendly; **être a. avec qn** to be friends with sb; **prendre qn pour a.** to befriend sb **(b)** **faites-moi l'a. de lui dire** would you be so kind as to tell him?; **mes amitiés à votre sœur** my best wishes to your sister

amiable [amjabl] *Jur* **1** *adj* amicable **2** **à l'amiable** *adv* out of court

amiante [amjɑ̃t] *nm* asbestos

amical, -e, -aux, -ales [amikal, -o] **1** *adj* friendly; **peu a.** unfriendly **2** *nf* **amicale** association

amicalement [amikalmɑ̃] *adv* in a friendly way

amidon [amidɔ̃] *nm* starch

amidonner [amidɔne] *vt* to starch

amincir [amɛ̃sir] **1** *vt* to make thinner; **cette robe t'amincit** that dress makes you look thinner **2 s'amincir** *vpr* to get thinner

amincissant, -e [amɛ̃sisɑ̃, -ɑ̃t] *adj (produit, crème)* slimming

amincissement [amɛ̃sismɑ̃] *nm (d'une personne)* slimming

aminé, -e [amine] *adj Chim* **acide a.** amino acid

amiral, -aux [amiral, -o] *nm* admiral

amitié [amitje] *nf* **(a)** *(sentiment)* friendship; **avoir de l'a. pour qn** to like sb; **se lier d'a. avec qn** to make friends with

ammoniaque [amɔnjak] *nf* ammonia

amnésie [amnezi] *nf* amnesia; **souffrir d'a.** to have amnesia

amnésique [amnezik] **1** *adj* amnesic; **être a.** to have amnesia
2 *nmf* amnesiac

amniocentèse [amnjosɛtɛz] *nf Méd* amniocentesis

amniotique [amnjɔtik] *adj* amniotic

amnistie [amnisti] *nf* amnesty

amnistier [66] [amnistje] *vt* to grant an amnesty to

amocher [amɔʃe] *Fam* **1** *vt (personne)* to beat up; *(objet)* to ruin; **se faire (sérieusement) a.** to get (badly) beaten up
2 s'amocher *vpr* to smash oneself up

amoindrir [amwɛ̃drir] **1** *vt* to diminish
2 s'amoindrir *vpr* to diminish

amollir [amɔlir] **1** *vt* to soften
2 s'amollir *vpr* to soften

amonceler [11] [amɔ̃sle] **1** *vt* to pile up; *(preuves)* to accumulate
2 s'amonceler *vpr* to pile up; *(preuves)* to accumulate

amoncellement [amɔ̃sɛlmɑ̃] *nm (pile)* heap, pile

amont [amɔ̃] *nm* upstream section; *aussi Ind* **en a. (de)** upstream (from); **la Seine en a. de Paris** the Seine above Paris

amoral, -e, -aux, -ales [amɔral, -o] *adj* amoral

amorçage [amɔrsaʒ] *nm* **(a)** *Ordinat* booting; **système d'a.** *(d'une bombe)* detonating system **(b)** *(pour pêcher)* baiting

amorce [amɔrs] *nf* **(a)** *(commencement)* beginning **(b)** *(détonateur)* detonator; *(d'une petite arme)* cap; **pistolet à amorces** cap gun **(c)** *(appât)* bait

amorcer [16] [amɔrse] **1** *vt* **(a)** *(commencer)* to begin **(b)** *Ordinat* to boot (up); **a. de nouveau** to reboot **(c)** *(bombe)* to arm **(d)** *(hameçon)* to bait
2 s'amorcer *vpr* **(a)** *(commencer)* to begin; *(tendance)* to develop **(b)** *Ordinat* to boot (up)

amorphe [amɔrf] *adj* lifeless, apathetic

amortir [amɔrtir] *vt* **(a)** *(bruit)* to deaden; *(chute)* to break; *(choc)* to absorb; *(au football)* to trap; *(au tennis)* to kill **(b)** *Fin (dette)* to pay off **(c)** *(rentabiliser)* **il a amorti sa nouvelle voiture en six mois** he recouped the cost of his new car in six months; **le matériel a été amorti dès la première année** the equipment started to pay for itself after the first year

amortissement [amɔrtismɑ̃] *nm* **(a)** *(de matériel)* depreciation **(b)** *(d'un bruit)* deadening; *(d'une chute)* breaking; *(d'un choc)* absorption **(c)** *Fin (d'une dette)* paying off

amortisseur [amɔrtisœr] *nm (d'une voiture)* shock absorber

amour [amur] **1** *nm* **(a)** *(sentiment)* love; **avec a.** lovingly; **être fou d'a. pour qn** to be madly in love with sb; **faire qch par a. pour qn** to do sth out of love for sb; **faire l'a. (avec)** to make love (with); **pour l'a. du Ciel!** for heaven's sake!; **l'a. maternel/filial** a mother's/child's love; **l'a. du prochain** love of one's neighbour; **le grand a.** true love **(b)** *(personne)* **mon a.** my love, my darling; **tu es un a.!** you're an angel!; **quel a. d'enfant!** what an adorable child!
2 *nfpl* **amours** *(vie amoureuse)* love life; **à tes amours!** *(en buvant)* your health!, cheers!; *(quand on éternue)* bless you!

amouracher [amuraʃe] **s'amouracher** *vpr* **s'a. de qn** to become infatuated with sb

amourette [amurɛt] *nf* fling

amoureusement [amurøzmɑ̃] *adv* lovingly

amoureux, -euse [amurø, -øz] **1** *nm,f (amateur)* **un a. de** a lover of
2 *nm (petit ami)* boyfriend; **un couple d'a.** a pair of lovers

3 *adj (soin, regard)* loving; **vie amoureuse** love life; **tomber a. (de)** to fall in love (with); **être a. de qn** to be in love with sb

amour-propre [amurprɔpr] *nm* self-respect, pride; **elle est blessée dans son a.** her pride is hurt

amovible [amɔvibl] *adj* detachable, removable; *Ordinat (disque dur)* removable

ampère [ɑ̃pɛr] *nm Él* ampere

amphés [ɑ̃fe] *nfpl Fam* speed

amphétamine [ɑ̃fetamin] *nf* amphetamine

amphi [ɑ̃fi] *nm Fam* lecture hall

amphibie [ɑ̃fibi] *adj* amphibious

amphibien [ɑ̃fibjɛ̃] *nm Zool* amphibian

amphithéâtre [ɑ̃fiteɑtr] *nm* **(a)** *(d'université)* lecture hall **(b)** *Archit* amphitheatre; **en a.** in a semicircle

amphore [ɑ̃fɔr] *nf* urn

ample [ɑ̃pl] *adj (robe, jupe)* full; *(geste)* sweeping; *Fig* **de plus amples renseignements** more detailed information; **jusqu'à plus a. informé** until further information is available

amplement [ɑ̃pləmɑ̃] *adv* amply, fully; **nous avons a. le temps** we have plenty of time; **c'est a. suffisant** it's more than enough

ampleur [ɑ̃plœr] *nf* **(a)** *(d'un vêtement)* fullness **(b)** *(importance)* scale, extent; **prendre de l'a.** to grow in size

ampli [ɑ̃pli] *nm Fam* amp

amplificateur [ɑ̃plifikatœr] *nm* amplifier

amplification [ɑ̃plifikasjɔ̃] *nf (d'un son)* amplification; *(d'une tendance, d'un phénomène)* intensification

amplifier [66] [ɑ̃plifje] **1** *vt (son)* to amplify; *(tendance, phénomène)* to intensify
2 s'amplifier *vpr (son)* to increase; *(tendance, phénomène)* to intensify

amplitude [ɑ̃plityd] *nf* **(a)** *(d'un désastre)* magnitude, scale **(b)** *(d'un geste)* fullness **(c)** *(variation)* range; **a. thermique** temperature range **(d)** *(d'une oscillation)* amplitude

ampoule [ɑ̃pul] *nf* **(a)** *(d'une lampe)* (light) bulb; **a. à baïonnette/vis** bayonet/screw-in light bulb **(b)** *(sur la peau)* blister **(c)** *(fiole)* phial

ampoulé, -e [ɑ̃pule] *adj* bombastic

amputation [ɑ̃pytasjɔ̃] *nf* amputation

amputer [ɑ̃pyte] *vt* to amputate; *Fig* to slash; **il fut amputé de la jambe gauche** his left leg was amputated

Amsterdam [amstɛrdam] *n* Amsterdam

amulette [amylet] *nf* amulet

amusant, -e [amyzɑ̃, -ɑ̃t] **1** *adj* amusing, funny; *(divertissant)* entertaining; *(bizarre)* weird
2 *nm* **le plus a., c'est que...** the funniest thing is that...

amuse-gueule [amyzgœl] *nm inv* appetizer

amusement [amyzmɑ̃] *nm* amusement

amuser [amyze] **1** *vt* to amuse; **cette histoire m'a beaucoup amusé** I found the story very amusing; **si tu crois que ça m'amuse!** do you think I enjoy it?
2 s'amuser *vpr (se distraire)* to amuse oneself; **bien s'a.** to have a good time; **s'a. avec qn** to play with sb; **s'a. à faire qch** to amuse oneself doing sth; **faire qch pour s'a.** to do sth for the fun of it

amuseur, -euse [amyzœr, -øz] *nm,f* entertainer

amygdales [amidal] *nfpl* tonsils; **se faire opérer des a.** to have one's tonsils out

an [ɑ̃] *nm* year; **l'an passé** *ou* **dernier** last year; **l'an prochain** next year; **tous les ans** every year; **tous les trois ans** every three years; **en l'an 2000** in the year 2000;

en l'a. de grâce 1492 in the year of Our Lord 1492; **dans trois ans** in three years' time, three years from now; **par an** per year; *Fin* per annum; **avoir dix ans** to be ten (years old); **bon an, mal an** on average over the years

anabolisant [anabɔlizɑ̃] *nm* anabolic steroid

anachronique [anakrɔnik] *adj* anachronistic

anachronisme [anakrɔnism] *nm* anachronism

anagramme [anagram] *nf* anagram

anal, -e, -aux, -ales [anal, -o] *adj* anal

analgésique [analʒezik] *nm* analgesic

anallergique [analɛrʒik] *adj* hypoallergenic

analogie [analɔʒi] *nf* analogy; **par a.** **avec** by analogy with

analogique [analɔʒik] *adj* (**a**) *(dictionnaire)* analogical (**b**) *Él* analogue

analogue [analɔg] *adj* similar (**à** to)

analphabète [analfabɛt] **1** *adj* illiterate **2** *nmf* illiterate person

analyse [analiz] *nf* (**a**) *(étude)* analysis; **en dernière a.** in the final analysis; **faire l'a. de qch** to analyse sth (**b**) *Méd* test; **a. de sang/d'urine** blood/urine test; **faire une a. de sang** to have a blood test (**c**) *Psy* (psycho)analysis

analyser [analize] *vt* to analyse; *Méd (sang, urine)* to test

analyseur [analizœr] *nm Ordinat* **a.** **logique** logic analyzer; *Ordinat* **a.** **syntaxique** parser

analyste [analist] *nmf Ordinat* analyst; *Psy* (psycho)-analyst

analyste-programmeur (*pl* **analystes-program-meurs**) [analistprɔgramœr] *nm Ordinat* systems analyst

analytique [analitik] *adj* analytical

ananas [anana(s)] *nm* pineapple

anarchie [anarʃi] *nf aussi Fig* anarchy

anarchique [anarʃik] *adj aussi Fig* anarchic

anarchisant, -e [anarʃizɑ̃, -ɑ̃t] *adj (discours)* advocating anarchy

anarchisme [anarʃism] *nm* anarchism

anarchiste [anarʃist] *adj & nmf* anarchist

anatomie [anatɔmi] *nf* anatomy

anatomique [anatɔmik] *adj* anatomical

ancestral, -e, -aux, -ales [ɑ̃sɛstral, -o] *adj* ancestral

ancêtre [ɑ̃sɛtr] *nmf* ancestor; *Fam (vieillard)* granddad, *f* grandma

anche [ɑ̃ʃ] *nf Mus* reed

anchois [ɑ̃ʃwa] *nm* anchovy

ancien, -enne [ɑ̃sjɛ̃, -ɛn] **1** *adj* (**a**) *(vieux)* old; **livre a.** antiquarian book; **meubles anciens** antique furniture; **dans l'a. temps** in the old days; **je suis plus a. que vous dans la profession** I've been in the profession longer than you (**b**) *(d'autrefois) (professeur, voisin)* former, old; *(voiture, maison)* old; **c'est un a.** **footballeur** he used to be a footballer; **a.** **combattant** *Br* ex-serviceman, *Am* veteran; **a. élève** former student; *Hist* **l'A.** **Régime** the Ancien Régime **2** *nm* (**a**) *Rel & Pol* elder (**b**) **l'a.** *(meubles)* antiques **3** *nm,f (par l'expérience)* **c'est un a. de la maison** he's been with the firm a long time

anciennement [ɑ̃sjɛnmɑ̃] *adv* formerly

ancienneté [ɑ̃sjɛnte] *nf* (**a**) *(âge)* age (**b**) *(expérience)* seniority; **avoir vingt ans d'a.** to have twenty years' service

ancrage [ɑ̃kraʒ] *nm Naut* anchoring

ancre [ɑ̃kr] *nf* anchor; **lever l'a.** to weigh anchor; **jeter l'a.** to anchor

ancrer [ɑ̃kre] **1** *vt (navire)* to anchor; **cette idée est profondément ancrée en lui** this idea is firmly rooted in his mind **2** **s'ancrer** *vpr Fig (idée, concept)* to become rooted

andalou, -se [ɑ̃dalu, -uz] **1** *adj* Andalusian **2** *nm,f* **A.** Andalusian

Andalousie [ɑ̃daluzi] *nf* l'A. Andalusia

Andes [ɑ̃d] *nfpl* **les A.** the Andes

andorran, -e [ɑ̃dɔrɑ̃, -an] **1** *adj* Andorran **2** *nm,f* **A.** Andorran

Andorre [ɑ̃dɔr] *nf* Andorra; **la principauté d'A.** the Principality of Andorra

Andorre-la-Vieille [ɑ̃dɔrlavjɛj] *n* Andorra la Vella

andouille [ɑ̃duj] *nf* (**a**) *Culin* = sausage made from pigs' intestines (**b**) *Fam (imbécile)* fool; **faire l'a.** to play the fool

andouillette [ɑ̃dujɛt] *nf Culin* = small sausage made from pigs' intestines

androgyne [ɑ̃drɔʒin] *adj* androgynous

âne [ɑn] *nm* (**a**) *(animal)* donkey; **à dos d'â.** by donkey (**b**) *Fam (idiot)* ass; *(ignare)* dunce

anéantir [aneɑ̃tir] *vt (ville)* to destroy; *(armée)* to crush; *(espoirs)* to shatter; **la nouvelle l'a anéantie** she was crushed by the news

anéantissement [aneɑ̃tismɑ̃] *nm* (**a**) *(d'une ville d'un empire)* destruction; *(d'un espoir)* shattering (**b**) *(abattement)* **dans un état d'a. total** completely crushed

anecdote [anɛkdɔt] *nf* anecdote

anecdotique [anɛkdɔtik] *adj* anecdotal

anémie [anemi] *nf* anaemia; **faire de l'a.** to have anaemia

anémique [anemik] *adj* anaemic; *Fig* feeble, weak

anémone [anemɔn] *nf* anemone; **a. de mer** sea anemone

ânerie [ɑnri] *nf (paroles)* stupid remark; *(acte)* stupid act; **dire des âneries** to talk rubbish; **faire des âneries** to behave stupidly

ânesse [ɑnɛs] *nf* she ass

anesthésie [anɛstezi] *nf* anaesthesia; **être sous a.** to be under anaesthetic; **a.** **générale/locale** general/local anaesthetic

anesthésier [66] [anɛstezje] *vt* to anaesthetize

anesthésiste [anɛstezist] *nmf Br* anaesthetist, *Am* anesthesiologist

aneth [anɛt] *nm* dill

ange [ɑ̃ʒ] *nm aussi Fig* angel; **un visage d'a.** an angelic face; **être aux anges** to be in seventh heaven; **un a.** **passe** someone must have walked over my grave; **a.** **gardien** guardian angel

angélique [ɑ̃ʒelik] **1** *adj* angelic **2** *nf Culin* angelica

angine [ɑ̃ʒin] *nf* sore throat; **a. de poitrine** angina (pectoris)

angiome [ɑ̃ʒjom] *nm Méd* angioma

anglais, -e [ɑ̃glɛ, -ɛz] **1** *adj* English; *(britannique)* British **2** *nm,f* **A.** Englishman, *f* Englishwoman; *(Britannique)* British man, *f* British woman; **les A.** the English; *(Britanniques)* the British **3** *nm (langue)* English **4** *adj* **anglaise** (**a**) *Fam* **filer à l'anglaise** to slip away (**b**) **anglaises** *(boucles)* ringlets

angle [ɑ̃gl] *nm* (**a**) *(d'une pièce, d'une rue, d'une table)* corner; **faire l'a.** **avec la rue du Bac** to intersect the rue du Bac; **la maison qui fait l'a.** the house on the corner (**b**) *(point de vue)* angle (**c**) *(en géométrie)* angle; **a.** **droit** right angle; **se couper à angles droits** to cross at right angles; *Aut* **a.** **mort** blind spot

Angleterre [ãglətɛr] *nf* l'A. England; *(Grande-Bretagne)* Britain

anglican, -e [ãglikã, -an] *adj & nm,f* Anglican

anglicisme [ãglisism] *nm* Anglicism

anglo-américain, -e *(mpl* **anglo-américains,** *fpl* **anglo-américaines)** [ãgloamerikɛ̃, -ɛn] *adj* Anglo-American

anglo-irlandais, -e *(mpl* **anglo-irlandais,** *fpl* **anglo-irlandaises)** [ãgloirlãdɛ, -ɛz] *adj* Anglo-Irish

anglo-normand, -e *(mpl* **anglo-normands,** *fpl* **anglo-normandes)** [ãglonɔrmã, -ãd] *adj voir* **île**

anglophone [ãglofɔn] **1** *adj* English-speaking **2** *nmf* English speaker

anglo-saxon, -onne *(mpl* **anglo-saxons,** *fpl* **anglo-saxonnes)** [ãglosaksõ, -ɔn] **1** *adj* Anglo-Saxon **2** *nm,f* A. Anglo-Saxon

angoissant, -e [ãgwasã, -ãt] *adj (nouvelle)* distressing; *(attente)* agonizing; *(film, livre)* frightening; *(situation)* alarming

angoisse [ãgwas] *nf* anguish, distress; *Méd* **une crise d'a.** an anxiety attack; *Fam* **c'est l'a.!** what a drag!

angoissé, -e [ãgwase] **1** *adj* anxious **2** *nm,f* anxious person

angoisser [ãgwase] **1** *vt* **a. qn** to make sb anxious **2** *vi Fam* to worry, to get worked up **3** **s'angoisser** *vpr* to get anxious; **s'a. pour un rien** to get worked up about nothing

Angola [ãgɔla] *nm* l'A. Angola

angolais, -e [ãgɔlɛ, -ɛz] **1** *adj* Angolan **2** *nm,f* A. Angolan

angora [ãgɔra] **1** *nm* (a) *(lapin)* angora rabbit; *(chat)* Persian cat (b) *(laine)* angora (wool) **2** *adj* angora

anguille [ãgij] *nf* eel; *Fig* **il y a a. sous roche** there's something going on

angulaire [ãgylɛr] *adj* angular

anguleux, -euse [ãgylø, -øz] *adj (visage)* angular; *(contours)* rugged

anicroche [anikrɔʃ] *nf* hitch, snag; **sans a.** without a hitch

animal, -e, -aux, -ales [animal, -o] **1** *nm aussi Fig* animal; **animaux de boucherie** animals raised for slaughter; **a. domestique** pet **2** *adj* animal

animalerie [animalri] *nf Can* pet shop

animalier, -ère [animalje, -ɛr] *adj* **parc a.** safari park; **peintre a.** wildlife painter

animateur, -trice [animatœr, -tris] *nm,f* (a) *(de télé, de radio)* presenter (b) *(dans un club)* leader

animation [animasjõ] *nf* (a) *(vie)* life; **une ville pleine d'a.** a lively town; **parler avec a.** to speak animatedly; **mettre de l'a. dans une soirée** to liven up a party (b) *(divertissement)* event; **faire de l'a.** *(de centre aéré)* to be an entertainment officer; *(de télé, de radio)* to be a presenter (c) *Cin* animation (d) *Météo* **a. satellite** satellite picture

animé, -e [anime] *adj (personne, discussion)* lively, animated; *(rue, quartier)* busy, bustling

animer [anime] **1** *vt* (a) *(sujet: désir, ambition)* to drive (b) *(conversation, soirée, quartier)* to liven up (c) *(débat)* to conduct; *(jeu télévisé)* to present **2** **s'animer** *vpr (personne)* to come to life; *(conversation, soirée)* to get more lively; *(visage)* to light up

animisme [animism] *nm* animism

animosité [animozite] *nf* animosity (**contre** towards), hostility (**contre** towards); **dire qch sans a.** to say sth calmly

anis [ani(s)] *nm (plante)* anise; **(sirop d')a.** aniseed cordial; **(graine d')a.** *(en cuisine)* aniseed; **à l'a.** aniseed-flavoured

anisette [anizɛt] *nf* anisette

Ankara [ãkara] *n* Ankara

ankylose [ãkiloz] *nf* stiffness, *Spéc* ankylosis

ankyloser [ãkiloze] **1** *vt* **être ankylosé** to be stiff **2** **s'ankyloser** *vpr* to get stiff; *Fig (dans un métier, des habitudes)* to get into a rut

annales [anal] *nfpl* annals; **les a. du bac** = past baccalauréat examination papers (with sample answers); **a. de géographie/littéraires** geographical/literary review; *Fig* **ça restera dans les a.** it will go down in history

anneau, -x [ano] *nm* (a) *(cercle, bague)* ring; *(de chaîne)* link; **a. nuptial** *ou* **de mariage** wedding ring; **a. de rideau** curtain ring; **les anneaux** *(en gymnastique)* the rings (b) *(d'un serpent)* coil (c) *Astron* ring

année [ane] *nf* year; **Bonne A.!** Happy New Year!; **une a. de vacances** a year's holiday; **d'a. en a.** year by year; **les années 90** the 90s; **en quelle a....?** in what year...?; **l'a. prochaine/dernière** next/last year; **elle entre dans sa trentième a.** she's just turned twenty-nine; **entrer en troisième a. de médecine** to start the third year of one's medical course; **a. civile** calendar year; **a. comptable** *Br* accounting *or* financial year, *Am* fiscal year

année-lumière *(pl* **années-lumière)** [anelymjɛr] *nf* light year; **à des années-lumière** *(étoile, planète)* light years away; *Fig* **nous sommes à des années-lumière l'un de l'autre** we're light years apart

annexe [anɛks] **1** *nf* (a) *(bâtiment)* annexe (b) *(de lettre)* enclosure; *(de livre, de rapport)* appendix; *(de projet de loi)* rider; *(de loi)* schedule; **en a. veuillez trouver...** please find enclosed... **2** *adj* (a) *(complémentaire) (pièces)* enclosed; *(revenus)* supplementary; *(industries)* subsidiary (b) *(mineur)* secondary

annexer [anɛkse] **1** *vt* (a) *(territoire)* to annex (b) *(document)* to append (**à** to); **pièces annexées** *(à une lettre)* enclosures **2** **s'annexer** *vpr* **s'a. qch** to get hold of sth for oneself

annexion [anɛksjõ] *nf* annexation

annihilation [aniilasjõ] *nf (d'une ville, d'une armée)* annihilation; *(d'efforts, d'espoirs)* destruction

annihiler [aniile] *vt (ville, armée)* to annihilate; *(efforts, espoirs)* to destroy

anniversaire [anivɛrsɛr] **1** *nm (d'une naissance)* birthday; *(d'une victoire, d'une mort)* anniversary; **bon** *ou* **joyeux a.!** happy birthday!; **gâteau/carte d'a.** birthday cake/card; **a. de mariage** wedding anniversary **2** *adj* anniversary; **date a.** anniversary

annonce [anõs] *nf* (a) *(déclaration)* announcement; *(par écrit)* notice; *(aux cartes)* declaration, bid; *Fig* sign, indication (**de** of) (b) *(publicitaire, de vente)* advert, advertisement; **passer une (petite) a. dans un journal** to put an advert in a newspaper; **petites annonces** *Br* small ads, *Am* want ads; **annonces classées** classified ads

annoncer [16] [anõse] **1** *vt* (a) *(déclarer)* to announce; **a. la nouvelle à qn** to tell sb the news (b) *(dans la presse) (soldes, exposition)* to advertise (c) *(indiquer)* to herald; **cela n'annonce rien de bon** things aren't looking too good (d) **a. qn** *(visiteur)* to show sb in; *(lors d'une occasion officielle)* to announce sb; **se faire a.** to give one's name **2** **s'annoncer** *vpr* (a) *(prévenir de sa visite)* to announce one's arrival (b) *(situation)* **cela s'annonce bien/mal** things aren't looking too bad/good; **l'avènement de la démocratie s'annonce dans plusieurs pays** there are signs in several countries that democracy is on the way

annonceur [anɔ̃sœr] *nm (de publicité)* advertiser
annonciateur, -trice [anɔ̃sjatœr, -tris] *adj* **signes annonciateurs de crise** signs that a crisis is on the way
Annonciation [anɔ̃sjasjɔ̃] *nf* **l'A.** the Annunciation
annotation [anɔtasjɔ̃] *nf* annotation; **faire des annotations dans un texte** to annotate a text
annoter [anɔte] *vt* to annotate
annuaire [anɥɛr] *nm (d'un organisme)* yearbook; *(liste d'adresses)* directory; **l'a. du téléphone** *ou* **téléphonique** the telephone directory; **je suis dans l'a.** I'm in the (phone) book; **a. électronique** electronic telephone directory; **a. des marées** tide table
annuel, -elle [anɥɛl] *adj* annual, yearly
annuellement [anɥɛlmɑ̃] *adv* annually, yearly
annuité [anɥite] *nf (sur un emprunt)* annual repayment
annulaire [anɥlɛr] **1** *nm* ring finger
2 *adj* annular, ring-shaped
annulation [anylasjɔ̃] *nf* **(a)** *(d'une commande, d'un rendez-vous, de vacances)* cancellation; *(d'une dette)* writing off; *(d'un mariage, d'un contrat)* annulment; *(d'un jugement)* quashing **(b)** *Ordinat* deletion; **a. d'entrée** *(commande)* cancel entry
annuler [anyle] **1** *vt* **(a)** *(commande, rendez-vous, vacances)* to cancel; *(dette)* to write off; *(mariage, contrat)* to annul; *(jugement)* to quash **(b)** *(remplacer)* to supersede **(c)** *Sp (but, essai)* to disallow
2 s'annuler *vpr* to cancel each other out
anoblir [anɔblir] *vt* to ennoble
anode [anɔd] *nf Él* anode
anodin, -e [anɔdɛ̃, -in] *adj (remarque)* harmless; *(personne)* insignificant; *(blessure, changement)* slight; *minor; (infection)* mild
anomalie [anɔmali] *nf* anomaly; *Méd* abnormality
ânon [anɔ̃] *nm* little donkey
ânonner [anɔne] *vt* to stumble through
anonymat [anɔnima] *nm* anonymity; **garder l'a.** to remain anonymous
anonyme [anɔnim] *adj* anonymous; *Fig (décor, intérieur)* impersonal
anorak [anɔrak] *nm* anorak
anorexie [anɔrɛksi] *nf* anorexia; **faire de l'a.** to suffer from anorexia; **a. mentale** anorexia nervosa
anorexique [anɔrɛksik] *adj & nmf* anorexic
anormal, -e, -aux, -ales [anɔrmal, -o] **1** *adj* **(a)** *(non conforme)* abnormal; *(mentalement)* educationally subnormal; **il fait une chaleur anormale** it's abnormally hot **(b)** *(injuste)* unfair; **il est a. que tu sois si peu payé** it's unfair that you're paid so little
2 *nm,f (mentalement)* educationally subnormal person
anormalement [anɔrmalmɑ̃] *adv* abnormally
ANPE [aɛnpeø] *nf (abrév* **Agence nationale pour l'emploi)** = French state employment agency
anse [ɑ̃s] *nf* **(a)** *(d'une cruche, d'un panier)* handle **(b)** *(crique)* cove
antagonisme [ɑ̃tagɔnism] *nm* antagonism
antagoniste [ɑ̃tagɔnist] **1** *nmf* antagonist
2 *adj (opinions, parties)* antagonistic
antalgique [ɑ̃talʒik] *adj & nm Méd* analgesic
antan [ɑ̃tɑ̃] **d'antan** *adj Litt* of yesteryear
antarctique [ɑ̃tarktik] **1** *nm* **l'A.** the Antarctic, Antarctica
2 *adj* Antarctic
antécédent [ɑ̃tesedɑ̃] *nm* **(a)** antécédents *(d'une personne)* previous history, past record; **il y a des antécédents cancéreux dans ma famille** my family has

a history of cancer; **avoir de bons/mauvais antécédents** to have a good/bad record; **antécédents médicaux** *Ling* antecedent
Antéchrist [ɑ̃tekrist] *nm* Antichrist
antédiluvien, -enne [ɑ̃tedilyvjɛ̃, -ɛn] *adj Hum* **ma télévision est antédiluvienne** my television is an antique
anténatal, -e, -als, -ales [ɑ̃tenatal] *adj Méd* antenatal
antenne [ɑ̃tɛn] *nf* **(a)** *(de radio)* aerial, antenna; *(d'un satellite, d'un robot)* antenna; **être à l'a.** to be on the air; **passer à l'a.** *(émission)* to be broadcast; *(personne)* to be on the television/radio; **rendre l'a.** to hand over; **à vous l'a.** over to you; **hors a.** off the air; **a. parabolique** (satellite) dish **(b)** *(d'un insecte)* antenna, feeler; *Fig* **avoir des antennes** *(de l'intuition)* to have a sixth sense **(c)** *Mil* **a. chirurgicale** field hospital **(d)** *(de société)* branch
antépénultième [ɑ̃tepenyltjɛm] *adj* antepenultimate
antérieur, -e [ɑ̃terjœr] *adj* **(a)** *(période)* former; *(date)* earlier; *(année)* previous; *(engagement)* prior; **tous ces événements sont antérieurs à la révolution** all these events took place before the revolution; **dans une vie antérieure** in a previous life **(b)** *(muscle)* anterior, *(membre)* fore
anthologie [ɑ̃tɔlɔʒi] *nf* anthology
anthracite [ɑ̃trasit] **1** *nm* **(a)** *(minerai)* anthracite **(b)** *(couleur)* charcoal grey
2 *adj inv* charcoal grey
anthropologie [ɑ̃trɔpɔlɔʒi] *nf* anthropology
anthropologiste [ɑ̃trɔpɔlɔʒist], **anthropologue** [ɑ̃trɔpɔlɔg] *nmf* anthropologist
anthropophage [ɑ̃trɔpɔfaʒ] **1** *nmf* cannibal
2 *adj* cannibalistic
anti [ɑ̃ti] *préf (contre)* anti-
antiadhésif, -ive [ɑ̃tiadezif, -iv] *adj (revêtement, poêle)* nonstick
2 *nm* antiadhesivo
antiaérien, -enne [ɑ̃tiaerjɛ̃, -ɛn] *adj* anti-aircraft
anti-âge [ɑ̃tiaʒ] *adj inv* anti-aging
antialcoolique [ɑ̃tialkɔlik] *adj (ligue)* temperance
antiatomique [ɑ̃tiatɔmik] *adj* antinuclear
antibactérien, -enne [ɑ̃tibakterjɛ̃, -ɛn] *adj* antibacterial
antibiotique [ɑ̃tibjɔtik] **1** *nm* antibiotic; **être sous antibiotiques** to be on antibiotics
2 *adj* antibiotic
antiblocage [ɑ̃tiblɔkaʒ] *adj inv Aut* **système a. (des roues)** anti-lock brakes
antibrouillard [ɑ̃tibrujar] *adj inv & nm Aut* **(phare) a.** fog lamp
antibruit [ɑ̃tibrɥi] *adj inv (mur)* soundproof; **lutte a.** noise abatement campaign
antibuée [ɑ̃tibɥe] *adj inv & nm Aut* **(dispositif) a.** demister
anticalcaire [ɑ̃tikalkɛr] *adj inv* **produit a.** *(pour machine à laver)* water softener
anticancéreux, -euse [ɑ̃tikɑ̃serø, -øz] *adj* **centre/ sérum a.** cancer hospital/serum
anticasseurs [ɑ̃tikasœr] *adj inv* **loi a.** = law banning violent behaviour during demonstrations
antichambre [ɑ̃tiʃɑ̃br] *nf* waiting room, antechamber
antichar [ɑ̃tiʃar] *adj Mil* anti-tank
antichoc [ɑ̃tiʃɔk] *adj inv* shock-proof
anticipation [ɑ̃tisipasjɔ̃] *nf* anticipation; **payer par a.** to pay in advance; **littérature d'a.** science fiction; **film d'a.** science-fiction film

anticipé, -e [ãtisipe] *adj (paiement)* advance; *(départ, retour)* early; **avec mes remerciements anticipés** thanking you in advance

anticiper [ãtisipe] **1** *vt (réaction, réponse)* to anticipate; *(action)* to forestall; *(tendance, résultat d'élections)* to forecast; **j'anticipais déjà le pire** I was expecting the worst **2** *vi* to anticipate, to look *or* think ahead; *(en sport, aux échecs)* to anticipate what one's opponent will do next; **n'anticipons pas** let's not look too far ahead; **a. sur qch** to anticipate sth

anticlérical, -e, -aux, -ales [ãtiklerikal, -o] *adj & nm,f* anticlerical

anticoagulant, -e [ãtikɔagylã, -ãt] *adj & nm* anticoagulant

anticolonialiste [ãtikɔlɔnjalist] *adj* anti-colonialist

anticommunisme [ãtikɔmynism] *nm* anticommunism

anticommuniste [ãtikɔmynist] *adj & nmf* anticommunist

anticonceptionnel, -elle [ãtikɔ̃sɛpsjɔnɛl] *adj (pilule)* contraceptive

anticonformiste [ãtikɔ̃fɔrmist] *adj & nmf* nonconformist

anticonstitutionnel, -elle [ãtikɔ̃stitysjɔnɛl] *adj* unconstitutional

anticorps [ãtikɔr] *nm* antibody

anticyclone [ãtisiklon] *nm Météo* anticyclone

antidater [ãtidate] *vt* to backdate, to antedate

antidémocratique [ãtidemɔkratik] *adj* undemocratic

antidépresseur [ãtideprɛsœr] *adj m & nm* antidepressant

antidérapant, -e [ãtiderapã, -ãt] *adj (pneu, route)* nonskid; *(semelle, tapis)* non-slip

antidopage [ãtidɔpaʒ], **antidoping** [ãtidɔpiŋ] *adj inv Sp* contrôle a. drug(s) test

antidote [ãtidɔt] *nm aussi Fig* antidote (**contre** for)

antiesclavagiste [ãtiɛsklavaʒist] *adj* anti-slavery

antifasciste [ãtifaʃist] *adj* anti-fascist

antifongique [ãtifɔ̃ʒik] **1** *adj* fungicidal **2** *nm* fungicide

antigel [ãtiʒɛl] *nm* antifreeze

antigrippal, -e, -aux, -ales [ãtigripal, -o] *adj* anti-flu

antihéros [ãtiero] *nm* antihero

antihistaminique [ãtiistaminik] *adj & nm Méd* antihistamine

anti-inflammatoire [ãtiɛ̃flamatwar] *adj & nm Méd* anti-inflammatory

anti-inflationniste [ãtiɛ̃flasjɔnist] *adj* anti-inflationary

antillais, -e [ãtijɛ, -ɛz] **1** *adj* West Indian **2** *nm,f* **A.** West Indian

Antilles [ãtij] *nfpl* **les A.** the West Indies

antilope [ãtilɔp] *nf* antelope

antimatière [ãtimatjɛr] *nf Phys* antimatter

antimilitariste [ãtimilitarist] *adj & nmf* antimilitarist

antimite [ãtimit] **1** *adj inv (produit)* moth-repellent; **bombe a.** moth spray **2** *nm* mothkiller

antinazi, -e [ãtinazi] *adj* anti-Nazi

antinomie [ãtinɔmi] *nf* antinomy

antinucléaire [ãtinykleɛr] *adj* anti-nuclear

Antiope® [ãtjɔp] *n* = French teletext system, providing subtitles for the deaf

antioxydant, -e [ãtiɔksidã, -ãt] *adj & nm* antioxidant

antipathie [ãtipati] *nf* antipathy; **avoir** *ou* **éprouver de l'a. pour qn** to dislike sb

antipathique [ãtipatik] *adj* unpleasant; **il m'est très a.** I don't like him at all

antipelliculaire [ãtipelikylɛr] *adj* shampooing a. dandruff shampoo

antiphrase [ãtifraz] *nf Ling* antiphrasis

antipodes [ãtipɔd] *nmpl Géog* antipodes; **être aux a. de** to be on the other side of the world from; *Fig* to be the exact opposite of

antipoison [ãtipwazɔ̃] *adj inv Méd* **centre a.** poisons unit

antiquaire [ãtikɛr] *nmf* antique dealer

antique [ãtik] *adj (de l'Antiquité)* ancient; *(mobilier)* antique; *Hum (voiture, télévision)* antiquated; **la Grèce/la Rome a.** ancient Greece/Rome

antiquité [ãtikite] *nf* (**a**) *Hist* **l'a.** grecque/romaine ancient Greek/Rome (**b**) **antiquités** *(meubles et objets anciens)* antiques; **magasin d'antiquités** antique shop (**c**) **antiquités** *(dans un musée)* antiquities

antirabique [ãtirabik] *adj Méd* anti-rabies

antiracisme [ãtirasism] *nm* anti-racism

antiraciste [ãtirasist] *adj* anti-racist

antiradar [ãtiradar] *nm* anti-radar device

antireflet [ãtirəflɛ] *adj inv* non-reflecting; *Ordinat* non-reflecting, antiglare

antirides [ãtirid] *adj inv* anti-wrinkle

antirouille [ãtiruj] **1** *adj inv* rustproofing **2** *nm* rustproofing agent

antiroulis [ãtiruli] *adj Aut* **barre a.** anti-roll bar

anti-scintillements [ãtisɛ̃tijmã] *adj inv Ordinat* flicker-free

antisèche [ãtisɛʃ] *nf Fam* crib sheet

antisémite [ãtisemit] **1** *adj* anti-Semitic **2** *nmf* anti-Semite

antisémitisme [ãtisemitism] *nm* anti-Semitism

antiseptique [ãtisɛptik] *adj & nm* antiseptic

antisocial, -e, -aux, -ales [ãtisɔsjal, -o] *adj* antisocial

antispasmodique [ãtispasmɔdik] *adj & nm Méd* antispasmodic

antitabac [ãtitaba] *adj inv* **lutte** *ou* **campagne a.** anti-smoking campaign

antiterroriste [ãtiterɔrist] *adj* anti-terrorist

antithèse [ãtitɛz] *nf* antithesis; *Fig* **être l'a. de** to be the opposite of

antitrust [ãtitrœst] *adj inv* anti-trust

antivariolique [ãtivarjɔlik] *adj Méd* **vaccin a.** smallpox vaccine

antivenimeux, -euse [ãtivənimø, -øz] *adj Méd* antivenin

antivol [ãtivɔl] **1** *adj inv (dispositif)* anti-theft **2** *nm* anti-theft device

antre [ãtr] *nm (caverne)* cave, cavern; *(d'animaux, de brigands)* den, lair; *Fig (d'une personne)* den

anus [anys] *nm* anus

Anvers [ãvɛr(s)] *n* Antwerp

anxiété [ãksjete] *nf* anxiety; **éprouver de l'a.** to feel anxious; **avec a.** anxiously

anxieux, -euse [ãksjø, -øz] **1** *adj* anxious, worried; **a. de faire qch** anxious to do sth **2** *nm,f* worrier

anxiolytique [ãksjɔlitik] *Méd* **1** *adj* anxiety-reducing **2** *nm* tranquillizer

AOC [ɑɔse] *nf* (*abrév* **appellation d'origine contrôlée**) = (guarantee of) high-quality wine from an identified vineyard

aorte [aɔrt] *nf* aorta

août [u(t)] *nm* August; **le quinze a.** *(fête)* Assumption Day; *voir aussi* **janvier**

aoûtat [auta] *nm Br* harvest mite, *Am* chigger

aoûtien, -enne [ausjɛ̃, -ɛn] *nm,f* August *Br* holiday-maker *or Am* vacationer

apache [apaʃ] **1** *nm* **A.** Apache **2** *adj* Apache

apaisant, -e [apɛzɑ̃, -ɑ̃t] *adj* soothing, calming

apaisement [apɛzmɑ̃] *nm (de la douleur)* alleviation; *(calme)* calm

apaiser [apeze] **1** *vt (personne)* to calm (down); *(douleur)* to soothe; *(faim)* to satisfy; *(soif)* to quench; *(craintes)* to allay **2** **s'apaiser** *vpr (personne)* to calm down; *(vent, douleur, craintes)* to subside

apanage [apanaʒ] *nm* prerogative; **elle croit avoir l'a. de la sagesse** she thinks she has a monopoly on wisdom

aparté [aparte] *nm* (**a**) *Th* aside; **en a.** in an aside (**b**) *(entre deux personnes)* private conversation; **en a.** in private

apartheid [aparted] *nm* apartheid

apathie [apati] *nf* apathy, listlessness

apathique [apatik] *adj* apathetic, listless

apatride [apatrid] *nmf* stateless person

APEC [apɛk] *nf* (*abrév* **Association pour l'emploi des cadres**) = employment agency for executives and graduates

apercevoir [60] [apɛrsɔvwar] **1** *vt* to see; *(soudain, rapidement)* to catch sight of; **laisser a.** qch to let sth show **2** **s'apercevoir** *vpr* **s'a. de qch** *(comprendre, réaliser)* to realize *or* notice sth, **s'a. que...** to realize *or* notice that

aperçu [apɛrsy] *nm (idée générale)* general idea; *Ordinat* **a. avant impression** print preview

apéritif [aperitif] *nm* aperitif; **prendre l'a.** to have a drink before the meal

apéro [apero] *Fam* = **apéritif**

apesanteur [apəzɑ̃tœr] *nf* weightlessness; **en (état d')a.** in weightless conditions

à-peu-près [apøprɛ] *nm inv* vague approximation; **il y a trop d'à.** **dans votre exposé** there is too much vagueness in your report

apeuré, -e [apœre] *adj* frightened, scared

apeurer [apœre] *vt* to frighten, to scare

aphasie [afazi] *nf Méd* aphasia

aphasique [afazik] *adj & nmf Méd* aphasic

aphone [afɔn] *adj Méd* voiceless; **elle était a. d'avoir trop crié** she'd lost her voice because she'd been shouting too much

aphorisme [afɔrism] *nm* aphorism; *Péj* platitude

aphrodisiaque [afrɔdizjak] *adj & nm* aphrodisiac

aphte [aft] *nm* mouth ulcer

aphteux, -euse [aftø, -øz] *adj* **fièvre aphteuse** foot-and-mouth disease

à-pic [apik] *nm inv* sheer face

apiculteur, -trice [apikyltœr, -tris] *nm,f* beekeeper

apiculture [apikyltyr] *nf* beekeeping

apitoiement [apitwamɑ̃] *nm* pity; **pas d'a.!** don't let pity get the better of you!

apitoyer [32] [apitwaje] **1** *vt* **a.** qn to move sb to pity **2** **s'apitoyer** *vpr* **s'a. sur (le sort de)** qn to feel sorry for sb; **s'a. sur soi-même** *ou* **sur son sort** to feel sorry for oneself

APL [apeɛl] *nf* (*abrév* **Aide personnalisée au logement**) housing benefit

aplanir [aplanir] **1** *vt (bois)* to plane; *(route)* to level; *Fig (difficultés)* to iron out **2** **s'aplanir** *vpr (sol)* to level out

aplati, -e [aplati] *adj (ballon, nez)* flat; *(figure géométrique)* oblate

aplatir [aplatir] **1** *vt (objet)* to flatten; **a. qch à coups de marteau** to hammer sth flat **2** **s'aplatir** *vpr (coiffure)* to go flat; *(chapeau)* to get flattened; **s'a. contre un mur** to flatten oneself against a wall; *Fig* **s'a. devant** qn to grovel to sb

aplomb [aplɔ̃] *nm* (**a**) *(ligne droite)* perpendicularity; **mettre qch d'a.** to stand sth up straight; **les étagères ne sont pas d'a.** the shelves aren't level; **je ne me sens pas d'a. aujourd'hui** I'm feeling out of sorts today; **remettre qn d'a.** to perk sb up (**b**) *(assurance)* (self-) confidence; *Péj* nerve; *Péj* **il ne manque pas d'a.** he's got a nerve

apnée [apne] *nf* **plonger en a.** to dive without breathing apparatus

apocalypse [apɔkalips] *nf* apocalypse; **l'A.** *(dans la Bible)* the Book of Revelation; *Fig* **d'a.** apocalyptic

apocalyptique [apɔkaliptik] *adj* apocalyptic

apogée [apɔʒe] *nm Astron* apogee; *Fig* **être à l'a.** **de sa carrière** to be at the height of one's career

apolitique [apɔlitik] *adj* apolitical

apollon [apɔlɔ̃] *nm (bel homme)* Adonis

apologie [apɔlɔʒi] *nf (défense)* apologia **(de** for); *(éloge)* eulogy; **faire l'a. de** *(louer)* to eulogize

apoplectique [apɔplɛktik] *adj & nmf Méd* apoplectic

apoplexie [apɔplɛksi] *nf Méd* apoplexy

a posteriori [apɔsterjɔri] *adv* with hindsight

apostolat [apɔstɔla] *nm (métier)* vocation

apostrophe [apɔstrɔf] *nf* (**a**) *(signe, figure de style)* apostrophe (**b**) *(interpellation)* rude remark

apostropher [apɔstrɔfe] **1** *vt (pour attirer l'attention)* to shout to; *(être impoli envers)* to shout at **2** **s'apostropher** *vpr* to shout at one another

apothéose [apɔteoz] *nf (consécration)* crowning glory; **finir en a.** to end spectacularly

apothicaire [apɔtikɛr] *nm Vieilli* apothecary; *Fig* **tenir des comptes d'a.** to know where every penny goes

apôtre [apotr] *nm* apostle; *Fig* **se faire l'a. de** qch to become an advocate of sth

Appalaches [apalaʃ] *nmpl* **les (monts) A.** the Appalachians

apparaître [20] [aparɛtr] *(aux être)* **1** *vi* (**a**) *(devenir visible)* to appear; **il lui est apparu en rêve** he came *or* appeared to her in a dream (**b**) *(phénomène, espèce)* to appear (**c**) *(vérité, solution)* to become apparent (**d**) *(sembler)* **il m'apparaît comme le seul capable d'y parvenir** he seems to me to be the only person capable of doing it **2** *v impersonnel* **il apparaît que...** it appears (that)...

apparat [apara] *nm* pomp, show; **tenue d'a.** ceremonial dress; **en grand a.** with great pomp and ceremony

appareil [aparɛj] *nm* (**a**) *(instrument)* apparatus; *Tél* **qui est à l'a.?** who's speaking? (**c**) *(avion)* aircraft, plane; *Anat* system; **a. de la justice** the legal system; **a. de production** *(industriel)* production facilities (**e**) *Anat* system; **a. digestif** digestive system; **a. génital** genital system; **a. respiratoire** respiratory system; **la plus simple a. in** one's birthday suit

appareillage [aparɛjaz] *nm* (**a**) *Naut* getting under way (**b**) *(matériel)* equipment; *Ind* plant

appareiller [aparɛje] *vi Naut* to get under way

apparemment [aparamɑ̃] *adv* apparently

apparence [aparɑ̃s] *nf* (**a**) *(aspect extérieur)* appearance, look; **un homme à l'a.** négligée/soignée an untidy-looking/a tidy-looking man; **en dépit des apparences** in spite of appearances (**b**) *(aspect trompeur)* **il ne faut pas se fier aux apparences** appearances can be deceptive; **il a l'air gentil, mais ce n'est qu'une a.** he seems nice, but it's only a façade; **en a.** outwardly; **pour sauver les apparences** to keep up appearances

apparent, -e [aparɑ̃, -ɑ̃t] *adj* (**a**) *(visible)* visible, apparent; **peu a.** hardly noticeable; **sans raison apparente** for no apparent reason (**b**) *(prétendu)* apparent; **sous cette apparente bonté se cache un grand égoïsme** beneath that kind exterior there lies great selfishness

apparenté, -e [aparɑ̃te] *adj* (**a**) *(par le mariage)* related; *(en rapport)* related, connected (**b**) *Pol* **candidat a. à un parti** = candidate who, though not a member of a party, can count on its support in an election

apparenter [aparɑ̃te] **s'apparenter** *vpr (ressembler)* to have something in common (**à** with)

appariteur [aparitœr] *nm (d'université)* porter

apparition [aparisjɔ̃] *nf* (**a**) *(manifestation)* appearance; **faire son a.** *(personne)* to make one's appearance (**b**) *(fantôme)* apparition; **avoir des apparitions** to see things

appartement [apartəmɑ̃] *nm Br* flat, *Am* apartment; *(dans un hôtel)* suite; **vivre en a.** to live in a flat; **les grands appartements** *(d'un château)* the state apartments

appartenance [apartənɑ̃s] *nf* belonging (**à** to); *(à un parti)* membership (**à** of)

appartenir [70] [apartənir] **appartenir à 1** *vt ind* (**a**) *(être possédé par)* to belong to (**b**) *(faire partie de) (club, parti, espèce)* to belong to, to be a member of; **elle appartient à une famille très riche** she comes from a very wealthy family
2 *v impersonnel* **il appartient au comité de prendre la décision** it is up to the committee to decide

appât [apɑ] *nm (de pêche)* bait; *Fig (du succès)* lure; **l'a. du gain** the lure of money

appâter [apɑte] *vt* (**a**) *(animaux)* to lure; *Fig (personne)* to entice (**b**) *(hameçon)* to bait

appauvrir [apovrir] **1** *vt* to impoverish
2 s'appauvrir *vpr* to get poorer; *(sol, langue)* to become impoverished

appeau, -x [apo] *nm* birdcall *(instrument)*

appel [apɛl] *nm* (**a**) *(invitation, sollicitation)* appeal; **faire a. à qn** to appeal to sb; *(plombier, médecin)* to send for sb; **faire a. à la générosité de qn** to appeal to sb's generosity; **cette formation fait a. à des connaissances commerciales** this training course calls for some knowledge of business; **faire a. à ses souvenirs** to search one's memory; **un a. à la révolte** a call to revolt; *Com* **lancer un a. d'offres** to invite bids
(**b**) *(cri)* call; **a. au secours** call for help; **faire un a. de phares à qn** to flash one's headlights at sb; *Fig* **a. du pied** veiled hint
(**c**) *(attirance)* call; **l'a. du large/de la nature** the call of the sea/of the wild; **a. d'air** *(courant d'air)* draught
(**d**) **a. (téléphonique)** (tele)phone call; **a. gratuit** *Br* freefone call, *Am* toll-free call
(**e**) *(pour vérifier)* **faire l'a.** to have a roll call; *Scol* to take the register; **manquer/répondre à l'a.** to be absent/present
(**f**) *Jur* appeal; **faire a. d'une décision** to appeal against a decision; *Fig* **être sans a.** *(décision)* to be final

(**g**) *Typ* **a. de note** reference figure
(**h**) *(pour sauter)* take-off
(**i**) *Ordinat* call; *(de commande)* selection

appelé [apɔle] *nm* (**a**) *Mil* conscript (**b**) *Fig* **il y a beaucoup d'appelés, mais peu d'élus** many are called, but few are chosen

appeler [apɔle] **1** *vt* (**a**) *(personne, chien)* to call (to); *(taxi)* to hail; **a. (qn) au secours** to call (to sb) for help; **il arrive qu'il appelle la nuit** he sometimes calls out in the night
(**b**) **a. qn (au téléphone)** to call sb, to ring sb (up); **a. un taxi/un médecin** to call or ring for a taxi/a doctor; **laissela a. la première** wait for her to call you
(**c**) *(faire venir)* to send for; *(ascenseur)* to call; **faire a. un médecin** to send for a doctor; **a. qn à faire qch** *(inviter)* to call on sb to do sth; *aussi Hum* **le devoir t'appelle** duty calls
(**d**) *(désigner)* to call
(**e**) **être appelé à faire qch** *(être destiné à)* to be destined to do sth; *(avoir l'obligation de)* to be called upon to do sth
(**f**) *(demander, réclamer) (solution, mesures)* to call for; *(critique)* to invite
2 en appeler à *vt ind* to appeal to
3 s'appeler *vpr* (**a**) *(avoir pour nom)* to be called; **comment vous appelez-vous?** what's your name?; **je m'appelle David** my name's David (**b**) *(se téléphoner)* **alors, on s'appelle, hein?** talk to you on the phone, okay?

appellation [apelasjɔ̃] *nf* name; *(de produit)* designation; **a. contrôlée** *(de vin)* guaranteed vintage; **a. d'origine** = guarantee of high-quality wine

appendice [apɛ̃dis] *nm* (**a**) *Anat* appendix; *Zool & Bot* appendage (**b**) *(d'un livre)* appendix

appendicite [apɛ̃disit] *nf* appendicitis; **une crise d'a.** appendicitis; **se faire opérer de l'a.** to have one's appendix out

appesantir [apəzɑ̃tir] **1** *vt (démarche)* to slow down; **les paupières appesanties par le sommeil** eyes heavy with sleep
2 s'appesantir *vpr (démarche)* to slow down; *Fig* **s'a. sur qch** *(sujet)* to dwell at length on sth

appétissant, -e [apetisɑ̃, -ɑ̃t] *adj (nourriture)* appetizing, tempting

appétit [apeti] *nm* (**a**) *(de nourriture)* appetite; **couper l'a. à qn** to spoil sb's appetite; **donner de l'a. à qn, mettre qn en a.** to give sb an appetite; **manger de bon a.** to tuck in; **avoir un a. d'oiseau** to have a poor appetite; **avoir bon ou un gros a.** to have a good appetite; **bon a.!** enjoy your meal!; *Prov* **l'a. vient en mangeant** it's only when you start eating that you realize you're hungry (**b**) *(désir) (de culture, de connaissances)* appetite (**de** for)

applaudimètre [aplodimɛtr] *nm* clapometer

applaudir [aplodir] **1** *vt* to applaud
2 *vi* to applaud, to clap
3 applaudir à *vt ind (décision, changement)* to applaud

applaudissements [aplodismɑ̃] *nmpl* applause, clapping; **un tonnerre** *ou* **une tempête d'a.** thunderous applause

applicable [aplikabl] *adj* applicable (**à** to)

applicateur [aplikatœr] *nm (dispositif)* applicator

application [aplikasjɔ̃] *nf* (**a**) *(de peinture, de pommade)* application (**b**) *(d'un règlement)* application; *(de la loi, d'une peine)* enforcement; **mettre une théorie en a.** to put a theory into practice; **mettre une loi en a.** to enforce a law; **entrer en a.** to come into force (**c**) *(emploi)* application (**d**) *(assiduité)* application; **travailler avec a.** to apply oneself to one's work (**e**) *Ordinat* application

applique [aplik] *nf (lampe)* wall light

appliqué, -e [aplike] *adj* (**a**) *(personne)* hard-working, diligent; *(écriture)* careful (**b**) *(sciences)* applied

appliquer [aplike] **1** vt (**a**) (mettre) to apply (**sur** to) (**b**) (utiliser) to apply (**à** to); (loi, peine) to enforce **2 s'appliquer** vpr (**a**) (se concentrer) to apply oneself (**à** to); **s'a. à faire qch** to take pains to do sth (**b**) **s'a. à** (concerner) to apply to (**c**) (se placer) to be applied

appoint [apwɛ̃] nm (**a**) (monnaie) exact money or change; **faire l'a.** to give the exact money (**b**) (revenu supplémentaire) extra income; **d'a.** (chauffage, éclairage) additional

appointements [apwɛ̃tmã] nmpl salary

apport [apɔr] nm (contribution) contribution (**à** to); Fin a. **en capital/numéraire** capital/cash contribution

apporter [apɔrte] vt (**a**) (porter) to bring (**à** to); (capitaux) to bring in; **je t'ai apporté le DVD** I've brought you the DVD (**b**) (mettre) a. **du soin à faire qch** to exercise care in doing sth (**c**) (bonheur, soulagement) to bring (**à** to); (preuve) to provide; (changements) to bring about; **ce travail ne m'apporte pas grand-chose** I don't get much out of this work

apposer [apoze] vt (affiche) to put up; (signature, scellés, sceau) to affix (**à** to)

apposition [apozisjɔ̃] nf (**a**) (d'un sceau, de scellés, de signature) affixing (**à** to) (**b**) Gram apposition; **en a. in apposition**

appréciable [apresjabl] adj (**a**) (visible) appreciable, noticeable (**b**) (non négligeable) considerable, appreciable (**c**) (agréable) (qualités) praiseworthy; (changement) welcome

appréciation [apresjasjɔ̃] nf (**a**) (évaluation) valuation (**b**) (opinion) judgement, opinion; (sur devoir scolaire) comment; **laisser qch à l'a. de qn** to leave sth to sb's discretion (**c**) (augmentation de valeur) appreciation

apprécier [66] [apresje] **1** vt (**a**) (température, distance, son) to estimate; (différences, nuances) to appreciate; **tu ne l'apprécies pas à sa juste valeur** you don't appreciate her true worth (**b**) (aimer) to like; Fam **elle n'a pas apprécié** she wasn't too pleased **2 s'apprécier** vpr (**a**) (personnes) to like each other (**b**) (monnaie) to appreciate

appréhender [apreãde] vt (**a**) Jur (arrêter) to arrest, to apprehend (**b**) (craindre) to dread; **a. de faire qch** to dread doing sth (**c**) (comprendre) to grasp

appréhensif, -ive [apreãsif, -iv] adj apprehensive

appréhension [apreãsjɔ̃] nf (crainte) apprehension (**de** about); **avoir une a.** to be apprehensive

apprendre [58] [aprãdr] **1** vt (**a**) (leçon, langue, instrument de musique) to learn; a. **à faire qch** to learn how to do sth; a. **vite/lentement** to be a fast/slow learner (**b**) (nouvelle) to hear; (mort, mariage) to hear of; a. **que...** to hear that... (**c**) (enseigner) a. **qch à qn** to teach sb sth; a. **à qn à faire qch** to teach sb how to do sth; Fam **je t'apprendrai à me parler sur ce ton!** I'll teach you to speak to me like that!; Fam **ça vous apprendra!** that'll teach you! (**d**) (informer de) a. **qch à qn** to tell sb sth; **vous ne m'apprenez rien!** you're telling me! **2 s'apprendre** vpr **ça s'apprend vite** it can be learned quickly; **ça s'apprend facilement** it's easy to learn

apprenti, -e [aprãti] nm,f apprentice; a. **menuisier** carpenter's apprentice; Fig **jouer les apprentis sorciers** to bite off more than one can chew

apprentissage [aprãtisaʒ] nm (**a**) (professionnel) training; (chez un artisan) apprenticeship; **être en a. chez qn** to be apprenticed to sb (**b**) (d'une matière, d'une langue) **l'a. de qch** learning sth; Fig **faire l'a. de qch** to learn about sth

apprêté, -e [aprete] adj (style, attitude) affected

apprêter [aprete] **1** vt (**a**) (repas) to prepare (**b**) (tissu, cuir) to finish **2 s'apprêter** vpr (se préparer) to get ready; **s'a. à faire qch** to get ready to do sth

apprivoisé, -e [aprivwaze] adj tame

apprivoiser [aprivwaze] **1** vt (animal) to tame; Fig (personne) to win over **2 s'apprivoiser** vpr (animal) to become tame; Fig (personne) to become more sociable

approbateur, -trice [aprɔbatœr, -tris] adj approving

approbation [aprɔbasjɔ̃] nf approval (**de** of); **le film a reçu l'a. du public** the movie was well received by the public; **pour a.** for approval

approchant [aprɔʃã] adj m **je n'ai jamais rien vu d'a.** I've never seen anything like it; **voilà ce qu'il a dit ou quelque chose d'a.** that's what he said, or something similar

approche [aprɔʃ] nf (**a**) (dans le temps) approach; à **l'a. de la vieillesse** as one approaches old age; **aux approches de la trentaine elle a voulu avoir des enfants** as she approached thirty she wanted children (**b**) (dans l'espace) à **son a.** as she approached; Fig **d'une a. difficile** (personne) unapproachable; (livre) hard to understand (**c**) (d'une question) approach (**de** to) (**d**) **approches** (d'une ville, d'un village) outskirts (**e**) Av approach

approcher [aprɔʃe] **1** vt (**a**) (mettre plus près) to bring up; a. **qch de qn/qch** to bring sth near (to) sb/sth (**b**) (venir près de) to approach, to get closer to; (aborder) to go up to **2** vi (**a**) (dans l'espace, dans le temps) to approach, to get closer; **l'heure ou le moment approche** it will soon be time; **la nuit approchait** it was beginning to get dark; **approche, je vais te montrer quelque chose** come (over) here, I've got something to show you; a. **de qn/qch** to approach sb/sth; Fig **a. du but** to be nearing one's goal; **il approche de la quarantaine** he's getting on for forty (**b**) Fig a. **de qch** (être semblable à) to be close to sth **3 s'approcher** vpr to approach, to get closer; **s'a. de qn/qch** to approach sb/sth; Fig **s'a. de qch** (être semblable à) to be close to sth

approfondi, -e [aprɔfɔ̃di] adj (recherche) detailed, extensive; (connaissance, enquête) thorough, in-depth

approfondir [aprɔfɔ̃dir] vt (examiner) to go thoroughly into

approprié, -e [aprɔprije] adj appropriate (**à** for)

approprier [66] [aprɔprije] **1** vt Belg (nettoyer) to clean; (ranger) to tidy **2 s'approprier** vpr **s'a. qch** for appropriate sth

approuver [apruve] vt (**a**) (décision, choix) to approve of; a. **qn (d'avoir fait qch)** to think sb is right (for to have done sth) (**b**) (facture, contrat, projet de loi) to approve

approvisionnement [aprɔvizjɔnmã] nm (**a**) (ravitaillement) (d'une ville, d'une armée) supplying (**en** with); (d'un magasin) stocking (**en** with) (**b**) **approvisionnements** (stocks) supplies

approvisionner [aprɔvizjɔne] **1** vt (**a**) (ville, armée, personne) to supply (**en** with); (magasin) to stock (**en** with) (**b**) (compte bancaire) to pay money into; **son compte en banque n'est plus approvisionné** his bank account is no longer in credit **2 s'approvisionner** vpr to get in supplies (**en** of); **s'a. chez qn** to get one's supplies from sb; (faire ses courses) to shop at sb's

approximatif, -ive [aprɔksimatif, -iv] adj (calcul, estimation) approximate; **un anglais a.** in broken English

approximation [aprɔksimasjɔ̃] nf approximation

approximativement [aprɔksimativmã] adv approximately

appt (abrév **appartement**) Br flat, Am apartment

appui [apɥi] nm (**a**) (support) support; **prendre a. sur qch** to lean on sth; **prendre a. sur le pied gauche**

(pour sauter) to take off from the left foot; **a. de fenêtre** window ledge *or* sill (**b**) *(moral)* support, backing; **à l'a. de qch** in support of sth; **preuves à l'a.** with supporting evidence

appui-tête *(pl* **appuis-tête)** [apɥitɛt] *nm* headrest

appuyé, -e [apɥije] *adj (plaisanterie, ironie)* laboured; **il lui lançait des regards appuyés** he was staring at him intently

appuyer [32] [apɥije] **1** *vt* (**a**) *(poser)* to lean, to rest (**contre** against) (**b**) *(appliquer)* **a. qch sur qch** to press sth on sth; **a. le pied sur la pédale de frein** to put one's foot on the brake (**c**) *Fig (demande, pétition, candidat)* to support, to back; *(proposition)* to second
2 *vi (presser)* to press; **a. sur un bouton** to press a button
3 s'appuyer *vpr* (**a**) *(reposer)* **s'a. sur/contre** to lean on/against; *Fig* **s'a. sur qch** *(être basé sur)* to be based on sth; *(se servir de)* to draw on sth (**b**) *Fam* **s'a. qch** *(corvée)* to get lumbered with sth

âpre [apr] *adj* (**a**) *(aigre)* bitter; *(vin)* rough (**b**) *(vent)* raw (**c**) *(concurrence)* fierce; **être â. au gain** to be money-grabbing

âprement [aprəmã] *adv* fiercely

après [aprɛ] **1** *prép* (**a**) *(dans le temps, dans l'espace)* after; **jour a. jour** day after day; **a. s'être rasé** after shaving; **a. vous, Monsieur/Madame!** after you!; *Fam* **courir a. qn** to run after sb; *Fig (faire la cour à)* to chase sb; **il est toujours a. moi** he's always nagging me; *Fam* **en avoir a. qn** to have it in for sb; **a. coup** after the event; **a. tout** after all (**b**) **d'a.** *(selon)* according to; **d'a. l'article 12** under article 12
2 *adv* afterwards; **six semaines a.** six weeks later; **a. que** after, when; **avec lui, la famille, ça passe a.** his family takes second place; **le jour d'a.** the next *or* following day; **et a.?** what happened next?; *Fam* **et puis a.?** so what?

après- [aprɛ] *préf* post-; **l'a.-68** the post-1968 period; **l'a.-Gorbatchev** the post-Gorbachev era

après-demain [aprɛdəmɛ̃] *adv* the day after tomorrow

après-guerre *(pl* **après-guerres)** [aprɛgɛr] *nm* post-war period

après-midi [aprɛmidi] *nm inv ou nf inv* afternoon; **trois heures de l'a.** three (o'clock) in the afternoon

après-rasage *(pl* **après-rasages)** [aprɛrazaʒ] *nm & adj inv* aftershave

après-ski *(pl* **après-skis)** [aprɛski] *nm* snowboot

après-soleil [aprɛsɔlɛj] *adj inv voir* **lait**

après-vente [aprɛvãt] *adj inv* **Com service a.** aftersales service

âpreté [aprəte] *nf* (**a**) *(aigreur)* bitterness; *(du vin)* roughness (**b**) *(du vent)* rawness (**c**) *(de la concurrence)* fierceness

a priori [aprijɔri] **1** *adv* in principle
2 *nm inv* preconception; **avoir des a. (contre/en faveur de qch)** to be prejudiced (against/in favour of sth); **être sans a.** to be impartial

apr. J.-C. *(abrév* **après Jésus-Christ)** AD

à-propos [aprɔpo] *nm (d'une remarque, d'une réaction)* appropriateness; **avoir l'esprit d'à.** to have presence of mind; **répondre avec à.** to give an appropriate reply

apte [apt] *adj* **a. à qch/à faire qch** fit for sth/for doing sth; *Mil* **a. au service** fit for military service

aptitude [aptityd] *nf (capacité)* aptitude, ability (**à** *ou* **pour** for)

aquaplanage [akwaplanaʒ], **aquaplaning** [akwaplaniŋ] *nm Aut* aquaplaning

aquarelle [akwarɛl] *nf* watercolour; **peindre à l'a.** to paint in watercolours

aquarium [akwarjɔm] *nm* aquarium

aquatique [akwatik] *adj* aquatic

aqueduc [akədyk] *nm* aqueduct

aqueux, -euse [akø, -øz] *adj Anat & Chim* aqueous; *(soupe)* watery

aquilin, -e [akilɛ̃, -in] *adj* aquiline

Aquitaine [akitɛn] *nf* **l'A.** Aquitaine

arabe [arab] **1** *adj (monde, littérature, pays)* Arab, Arabic; *(chiffres, langue)* Arabic; *(cheval)* Arab; *(coutumes, civilisation)* Arabian, Arabic
2 *nmf* **A.** Arab
3 *nm (langue)* Arabic

arabesque [arabɛsk] *nf* arabesque

arabica [arabika] *nm* arabica

Arabie [arabi] *nf* **l'A.** Arabia; **l'A. saoudite** Saudi Arabia

arable [arabl] *adj* arable

arachide [araʃid] *nf (plante)* peanut, groundnut; **huile d'a.** peanut *or* groundnut oil

araignée [arɛɲe] *nf* spider; *Fam* **avoir une a. au plafond** to have a screw loose; **a. de mer** spider crab

Aral [aral] *n voir* **mer**

arbalète [arbalɛt] *nf* crossbow

arbitrage [arbitraʒ] *nm* (**a**) *(au tennis)* umpiring; *(au football)* refereeing (**b**) *(dans un conflit)* arbitration

arbitraire [arbitrɛr] *adj* arbitrary

arbitrairement [arbitrɛrmã] *adv* arbitrarily

arbitre [arbitr] *nm* (**a**) *(au tennis)* umpire; *(au football)* referee (**b**) *(dans un conflit)* arbitrator (**c**) *Phil* **libre a.** free will

arbitrer [arbitre] *vt* (**a**) *(match de tennis)* to umpire; *(match de football)* to referee (**b**) *(conflit)* to arbitrate

arborer [arbore] *vt (porter, exhiber)* to wear, to sport

arborescence [arboresãs] *nf Ordinat* tree diagram

arborescent, -e [arboresã, -ãt] *adj* (**a**) *Bot* arborescent (**b**) *Math & Ordinat* **structure arborescente** tree diagram

arboriculteur, -trice [arbɔrikyltœr, -tris] *nm,f* tree grower

arboriculture [arbɔrikyltyr] *nf* tree growing

arbre [arbr] *nm* (**a**) *(végétal)* tree; *Fig* **les arbres cachent la forêt** you can't see the wood for the trees; **a. fruitier** fruit tree; **a. de Noël** Christmas tree (**b**) **a. généalogique** family tree; **faire son a. généalogique** to trace one's family tree (**c**) *Tech* shaft; **a. à cames** camshaft; **a. de transmission** transmission shaft

arbrisseau, -x [arbriso] *nm* shrub

arbuste [arbyst] *nm* shrub

arc [ark] *nm* (**a**) *(arme)* bow (**b**) *Archit & Anat* arch; **a. de triomphe** triumphal arch (**c**) *(de cercle)* arc; **assis en a. de cercle** sitting in a semicircle

arcade [arkad] *nf* (**a**) *Archit* archway; **arcades** *(d'une place)* arcade (**b**) *Anat* **a. sourcilière** arch of the eyebrows

arc-bouter [arkbute] **s'arc-bouter** *vpr* to brace oneself

arceau, -x [arso] *nm* (**a**) *(d'une voûte)* arch (**b**) *(au croquet)* hoop; **a. de sécurité** roll bar

arc-en-ciel *(pl* **arcs-en-ciel)** [arkãsjɛl] *nm* rainbow

archaïque [arkaik] *adj* archaic

archaïsme [arkaism] *nm* archaism

archange [arkãʒ] *nm* archangel

arche¹ [arʃ] *nf* **l'a. de Noé** Noah's ark

arche² *nf (d'un pont)* arch

archéologie [arkeɔlɔʒi] *nf* archaeology

archéologique [arkeɔlɔʒik] *adj* archaeological

archéologue [arkeɔlɔg] *nmf* archaeologist

archer [arʃe] *nm* archer

archet [arʃɛ] *nm* bow *(for violin)*

archétype [arketip] *nm* archetype; **c'est l'a. du père de famille** he is the archetypal father figure

archevêque [arʃəvɛk] *nm* archbishop

archiconnu, -e [arʃikɔny] *adj Fam* very well-known

archiduc [arʃidyk] *nm* archduke

archiduchesse [arʃidyʃɛs] *nf* archduchess

archifaux, -fausse [arʃifo, -fos] *adj Fam* dead wrong

Archimède [arʃimɛd] *npr* Archimedes

archipel [arʃipɛl] *nm* archipelago

architecte [arʃitɛkt] *nmf* architect

architectural, -e, -aux, -ales [arʃitɛktyral, -o] *adj* architectural

architecture [arʃitɛktyr] *nf aussi Ordinat* architecture; *Fig* otructure

architecturé, -e [arʃitɛktyre] *adj Ordinat* **a. autour de** with its architecture built around

archiver [arʃive] *vt (documents officiels)* to archive; *(lictures)* to file

archives [arʃiv] *nfpl* archives, records; **les a. nationales** ≃ the (Public) Record Office

archiviste [arʃivist] *nmf* archivist; *(employé de bureau)* filing clerk

arçon [arsɔ̃] *nm* oaddle bow

arctique [arktik] **1** *adj* arctic **2** *nm* **l'A.** the Arctic

ardemment [ardamɑ̃] *adv (aimer)* passionately; **désirer qch a.** to long for sth

ardent, -e [ardɑ̃, -ɑ̃t] *adj* **(a)** *(braises, soleil)* scorching, blazing; *(soif, fièvre)* raging **(b)** *(tempérament, jeunesse)* fiery; *(désir)* burning; *(lutte)* fierce

ardeur [ardœr] *nf* **(a)** *(enthousiasme)* ardour, fervour; **travailler avec a.** to work enthusiastically **(b)** *(du soleil, du feu)* intense heat

ardoise [ardwaz] *nf* **(a)** *(matière, plaque, pour écrire)* slate; **toit d'ardoises** slate roof **(b)** *Fam (compte)* tab; **il a des ardoises dans tous les bars de la ville** he owes money in every bar in town

ardu, -e [ardy] *adj* arduous

are [ar] *nm* are, = 100 m²

aréna [arena] *nf Can* = sports centre including an ice rink

arène [arɛn] *nf (d'amphithéâtre)* arena; *(de tauromachie)* bullring; **arènes** *(antiques)* amphitheatre; *Fig* **descendre dans l'a.** to enter the fray; *Fig* **l'a. politique** the political arena

arête [arɛt] *nf* **(a)** *(de poisson)* bone; **sans arêtes** boneless; **enlever les arêtes d'un poisson** to fillet a fish **(b)** *(du nez)* bridge **(c)** *(d'un solide)* edge **(d)** *Géog* ridge

argent [arʒɑ̃] **1** *nm* **(a)** *(métal)* silver; **bracelet d'a. ou en a.** silver bracelet **(b)** *(monnaie)* money; **en avoir pour son a.** to get one's money's worth; *Fig* **prendre qch pour a. comptant** to take sth at face value; *Prov* **l'a. ne fait pas le bonheur** money can't buy you happiness; **a. liquide** cash; **a. de poche** pocket money **(c)** *(couleur)* silver **2** *adj inv* silver

argenté, -e [arʒɑ̃te] *adj* **(a)** *(couleur)* silver **(b)** *(plaqué)* silver-plated

argenterie [arʒɑ̃tri] *nf* (silver) plate, silverware

argentin, -e [arʒɑ̃tɛ̃, -in] **1** *adj* Argentinian, Argentine **2** *nmf* **A.** Argentinian, Argentine

Argentine [arʒɑ̃tin] *nf* **l'A.** Argentina

argile [arʒil] *nf* clay

argileux, -euse [arʒilø, -øz] *adj* clayey

argot [argo] *nm* slang

argotique [argotik] *adj* slang, slangy

arguer [arge, argɥe] **arguer de** *vt ind Litt* **a. de qch** to give sth as a reason

argument [argymɑ̃] *nm* argument; **a. de vente** selling point

argumentaire [argymɑ̃tɛr] *nm* sales blurb

argumentation [argymɑ̃tasjɔ̃] *nf (arguments)* argument

argumenter [argymɑ̃te] *vi* to argue **(contre/en faveur de** against/for)

argus [argys] *nm* = guide to used car prices

aria [arja] *nf Mus* aria

aride [arid] *adj (pays)* arid, barren; *(œuvre, sujet)* dry

aridité [aridite] *nf* aridity, barrenness

aristocrate [aristɔkrat] *nmf* aristocrat

aristocratie [aristɔkrasi] *nf* aristocracy

aristocratique [aristɔkratik] *adj* aristocratic

Aristote [aristɔt] *npr* Aristotle

arithmétique [aritmetik] **1** *adj* arithmetical **2** *nf (matière, calculs)* arithmetic

arlequin [arləkɛ̃] *nm* l'h Harlequin

armagnac [armaɲak] *nm* Armagnac

armateur [armatœr] *nm* shipowner

armature [armatyr] *nf* framework; *(dans le béton)* reinforcement; *(de tente, d'abat-jour)* frame; *(de soutiengorge)* underwiring

arme [arm] *nf* **(a)** *(de combat)* arm, weapon; **peuple/ville en armes** nation/town in arms; **prendre les armes** to take up arms **(contre** against); **aux armes!** to arms!; **le métier ou la carrière des armes** the military profession; **passer qn par les armes** to send sb to the firing squad; *Fam* **passer l'a. à gauche** to snuff it, to kick the bucket; **faire ses premières armes** to cut one's spurs; **à armes égales** on equal terms; **avec armes et bagages** with bag and baggage; **a. blanche** knife; **a. à feu** firearm **(b)** *(section de l'armée)* service **(c)** **armes** *(blason)* (coat of) arms

armé, -e [arme] *adj* **(a)** *(muni d'une arme)* armed; **a. jusqu'aux dents** armed to the teeth; *aussi Fig* **être a. pour qch** to be armed with sth; *Fig* **être a. pour qch** *(préparé)* to be equipped for sth **(b)** *(renforcé)* fortified, strengthened

armée [arme] *nf aussi Fig* army; **être dans l'a.** to be in the army; **être à l'a.** to be doing one's military service; **l'a. de l'air** the air force; **a. de métier** professional army; **a. régulière ou active** regular army; **a. de réserve** reserves; **l'A. du salut** the Salvation Army; **l'a. de terre** the army

armement [arməmɑ̃] *nm* **(a)** *(action) (d'un pays, d'une région)* armament; *(d'une armée)* arming **(b)** **armements** *(armes)* armaments, weaponry **(c)** *(d'une arme à feu)* cocking; *(d'un appareil photo)* commissioning, fitting out

Arménie [armeni] *nf* **l'A.** Armenia

arménien, -enne [armenjɛ̃, -ɛn] *adj* Armenian **2** *nmf* **A.** Armenian **3** *nm (langue)* Armenian

armer [arme] **1** *vt* **(a)** *(munir d'armes)* to arm **(de** with); **je sors toujours armé** I always carry a weapon when I go out **(b)** *(navire)* to commission, to fit out **(c)** *(arme à feu)* to cock; *(appareil photo)* to set **2 s'armer** *vpr* to arm oneself; **s'a. de courage/de patience** to summon up one's courage/patience

armistice [armistis] *nm* armistice

armoire [armwar] *nf (placard) Br* cupboard, *Am* closet; *(pour les vêtements) Br* wardrobe, *Am* closet; **a. à glace** mirrored wardrobe; *Fam* **c'est une a.** à **glace** he's built like a tank; **a. de toilette** *ou* **de salle de bain** bathroom cabinet

armoiries [armwari] *nfpl* (coat of) arms

armure [armyr] *nf* armour

armurier [armyrje] *nm* (**a**) *(vendeur)* gun dealer (**b**) *(dans une caserne)* armourer

ARN [aɛrɛn] *nm* *(abrév* **acide ribonucléique)** RNA

arnaque [arnak] *nf Fam* rip-off; **c'est de l'a.!** what a rip-off!

arnaquer [arnake] *vt Fam* to rip off; **se faire a.** to get ripped off

arnaqueur, -euse [arnakœr, -øz] *nm,f Fam* rip-off merchant

arnica [arnika] *nm ou nf* arnica

aromate [arɔmat] *nm (herbe)* herb; *(épice)* spice

aromathérapie [arɔmaterapi] *nf* aromatherapy

aromatique [arɔmatik] *adj* aromatic

aromatisé, -e [arɔmatize] *adj* flavoured; **a. à l'orange** orange-flavoured

arôme [arom] *nm (parfum)* aroma; *(goût)* flavour; **crème glacée, a. vanille** vanilla ice cream

arpège [arpɛʒ] *nm Mus* arpeggio

arpent [arpɑ̃] *nm* = former land measurement approximately equivalent to one acre

arpenter [arpɑ̃te] *vt* (**a**) *(mesurer)* to survey, to measure (**b**) *(parcourir)* to pace up and down

arqué, -e [arke] *adj (sourcils)* arched; *(nez)* hooked; **jambes arquées** bow legs

arquer [arke] **s'arquer** *vpr* to bend, to curve

arrachage [araʃaʒ] *nm (de plantes)* uprooting; *(de pommes de terre)* lifting; *(d'une dent, d'un clou, de piquets)* pulling out

arraché [araʃe] *nm (en haltérophilie)* snatch; *Fig* **gagner à l'a.** to snatch victory; *Fig* **ils ont obtenu le contrat à l'a.** it was a struggle for them to get the contract

arrachement [araʃmɑ̃] *nm (peine)* wrench

arrache-pied [araʃpje] **d'arrache-pied** *adv* relentlessly

arracher [araʃe] **1** *vt* (**a**) *(arbre)* to uproot; *(légumes)* to lift; *(dent, mauvaises herbes, piquets)* to pull out; *(page)* to tear out; *(affiche)* to tear down; *(vêtement, membre, toit)* to tear off; **se faire a. une dent** to have a tooth out; **a. qch à qn/ des mains de qn** to snatch sth from sb/from sb's hands; *Fig* **je vais lui a. les yeux!** I'll scratch his eyes out! (**b**) *(obtenir)* **a. qch à qn** *(argent)* to get sth off sb; *(secret)* to drag sth out of sb; *(promesse, sourire)* to force sth out of sb; *Fig* **nous sommes finalement parvenus à lui a. quelques mots** nevertheless, we did manage to get a few words out of him (**c**) *(séparer)* **a. un enfant à sa mère** to take a child away from its mother; **a. qn à la mort** to snatch sb from the jaws of death; **a. qn à son travail** to tear sb away from his work (**d**) *Fam (sujet: alcool, piment)* **ça arrache!** it brings tears to your eyes!

2 s'arracher *vpr* (**a**) *(se disputer)* **s'a. qn/qch** to fight over sb/sth (**b**) *(se retirer)* **c'est à s'a. les cheveux!** it's enough to make you tear your hair out!; **s'a. à son travail** to tear oneself away from one's work (**c**) *très Fam (partir)* to hit the road

arracheur [araʃœr] *nm* **mentir comme un a. de dents** to lie through one's teeth

arraisonner [arɛzɔne] *vt* to stop and examine

arrangeant, -e [arɑ̃ʒɑ̃, -ɑ̃t] *adj* helpful

arrangement [arɑ̃ʒmɑ̃] *nm* (**a**) *(fait de disposer)* arranging; *(manière d'être disposé)* arrangement (**b**) *(accord)* agreement, settlement (**c**) *Mus* arrangement

arranger [45] [arɑ̃ʒe] **1** *vt* (**a**) *(meubles, fleurs)* to arrange; *(pièce, maison)* to put in order; *(cravate, col)* to straighten (**b**) *(réparer)* to repair (**c**) *(organiser)* to arrange, to organize; **j'ai tout arrangé** I've made all the arrangements (**d**) *(régler)* *(problème)* to settle; **cela n'arrangera rien** that won't help

things; *Ironique* **pour tout a., il s'est mis à pleuvoir** just to help matters, it started to rain (**e**) *Fam* **a. qn** *(maltraiter)* to give sb a going over; *(critiquer)* to tear sb to pieces (**f**) *(convenir à)* to suit; **faire qch pour a. qn** to do sth to help sb out (**g**) *Mus* to arrange

2 s'arranger *vpr* (**a**) *(s'organiser)* to manage; **arrangez-vous pour être là/finir à temps** make sure you're there/ you finish on time; *Fam* **je ne sais pas comment tu t'arranges, tu es toujours en retard** I don't know how you manage it, but you're always late (**b**) *(s'améliorer)* to work out; **ça ne s'arrange pas!** things aren't getting any better! (**c**) *(rectifier son apparence)* to tidy oneself up (**d**) *(se mettre d'accord)* to come to an agreement (**avec** with); **ça ne me regarde pas, arrange-toi avec elle** it's got nothing to do with me, sort it out with her (**e**) *(se contenter)* **s'a. de qch** to make do with sth

arrestation [arɛstasjɔ̃] *nf* arrest; **en état d'a.** under arrest

arrêt [arɛ] *nm* (**a**) *(interruption) (des combats, des hostilités, de la production)* stop; **Toulouse, dix minutes d'a.** *(en train)* this is Toulouse, there will be a ten-minute stop; **sans a.** continuously; **tomber en a. devant qn/qch** to stop and stare at sb/sth; **marquer un temps d'a.** to pause; **a. du cœur** heart failure; *Ordinat* **a. de défilement** scroll lock; *TV & Cin* **a. sur image** freeze frame; **a. de jeu** stoppage; **a. de travail** sick leave (**b**) *(de véhicule)* stop; **ne pas descendre avant l'a. complet du train** *(sur la portière)* do not get off before the train has come to a complete stop; **le train est sans a. jusqu'à Hendaye** the train is non-stop to Hendaye; **a. de bus** bus stop; **a. facultatif** request stop (**c**) *Jur* judgement; *aussi Fig* **a. de mort** death sentence

arrêté, -e [arete] **1** *adj (idées)* fixed

2 *nm (décret)* order, decree; **a. ministériel** ministerial order; **a. municipal** bylaw; **a. préfectoral** bylaw

arrêter [arete] **1** *vt* (**a**) *(personne, animal, véhicule)* to stop; *(machine, moteur, musique)* to turn off; *(fuite)* to stem; *(études)* to give up; **là je vous arrête, je ne suis pas d'accord!** I've got to stop you there, I don't agree!; **arrête-moi au carrefour** drop me off at the crossroads; **rien ne l'arrête** nothing will stop him; **a. de faire qch** to stop doing sth; **elle n'arrête pas de me déranger** she keeps disturbing me; **ce détail arrêta mon attention** this detail caught my attention (**b**) *(criminel)* to arrest (**c**) *(déterminer)* to decide; *(date, prix)* to fix

2 *vi (qn)* **arrête!** stop it!

3 s'arrêter *vpr* (**a**) *(cesser, s'immobiliser)* to stop; **s'a. de faire qch** to stop doing sth; **s'a. chez qn** to call in at sb's house (**b**) **s'.a. à qch** *(faire attention à)* to pay attention to sth

arrhes [ar] *nf pl* deposit

arrière [arjɛr] **1** *adj inv* back; **feu a.** rear light; **roue a.** rear or back wheel

2 *nm* (**a**) *(d'une maison, d'un avion)* back; *(d'un bateau)* stern; **à l'a. de la voiture** in the back of the car (**b**) *Mil* **l'a.** the rear; *Fig* **protéger ses arrières** to leave oneself a way out (**c**) *(au football, au rugby)* full back

3 *exclam* stand back!

4 en arrière *adv* (**a**) *(derrière)* behind; **rester en a.** to stay behind; **en a. de qn/qch** behind sb/sth (**b**) *(dans la direction inverse)* backwards; **pencher la tête en a.** to lean one's head back; **retourner en a.** to go or turn back

arriéré, -e [arjere] **1** *adj* (**a**) *(paiement)* overdue (**b**) *(dans ses idées, son développement)* backward

2 *nm* arrears

arrière-boutique (*pl* **arrière-boutiques**) [arjɛrbutik] *nf Br* back shop, *Am* back store

arrière-cour (*pl* **arrière-cours**) [arjɛrkur] *nf* backyard

arrière-garde (*pl* **arrière-gardes**) [arjɛrgard] *nf* rearguard

arrière-goût (*pl* arrière-goûts) [arjɛrgu] *nm aussi Fig* aftertaste

arrière-grand-mère (*pl* arrière-grands-mères) [arjɛrgrɑ̃mɛr] *nf* great-grandmother

arrière-grand-père (*pl* arrière-grands-pères) [arjɛrgrɑ̃pɛr] *nm* great-grandfather

arrière-grands-parents [arjɛrgrɑ̃parɑ̃] *nmpl* great-grandparents

arrière-pays [arjɛrpei] *nm inv* hinterland

arrière-pensée (*pl* arrière-pensées) [arjɛrpɑ̃se] *nf* ulterior motive

arrière-petite-fille (*pl* arrière-petites-filles) [arjɛrpɔtitfij] *nf* great-granddaughter

arrière-petit-fils (*pl* arrière-petits-fils) [arjɛrpɔtifis] *nm* great-grandson

arrière-petits-enfants [arjɛrpɔtizɑ̃fɑ̃] *nmpl* great-grandchildren

arrière-plan (*pl* arrière-plans) [arjɛrplɑ̃] *nm aussi Fig* background; **à l'a.** in the background

arrière-saison (*pl* arrière-saisons) [arjɛrsɛzɔ̃] *nf Br* late autumn; *Am* late fall

arrière-train (*pl* arrière-trains) [arjɛrtrɛ̃] *nm* (*d'un animal*) (hind)quarters; *Fam* (*d'une personne*) rump, rear

arrimer [arime] *vt* (**a**) *Naut* (*cargaison*) to stow (**b**) (*fixer*) to secure *or* fasten (**à** to)

arrivage [arivaʒ] *nm* consignment

arrivant, -e [arivɑ̃, -ɑ̃t] *nm,f* arrival; **les nouveaux arrivants** the new arrivals, the newcomers

arrivé, -e [arive] **1** *adj* **être a.** (*socialement*) to have arrived, to have made it
2 *nm,f* (*personne*) **le premier/dernier a.** the first/last (*person*) to arrive

arrivée [arive] *nf* (**a**) (*venue*) arrival; **depuis son a. au pouvoir** since he came to power; **à mon a.** when I arrive/arrived; **arrivées** (*sur panneau*) arrivals (**b**) *Tech* inlet (**c**) (*d'une course*) winning post, finish

arriver [arive] (*aux être*) **1** *vi* (**a**) (*venir*) to arrive; **a. à Lyon/en France** to arrive in Lyons/in France; **a. le premier/dernier** (*à une soirée*) to arrive first/last; **a. premier/second** (*dans un concours, une course*) to come first/second; **j'arrive!** (I'm coming!); **c'est à cette heure-là que tu arrives?** and what time do you call this?; **nous sommes presque arrivés** we're almost there
(**b**) (*atteindre*) **l'eau m'arrive aux genoux** the water comes up to my knees; **ses cheveux lui arrivent aux épaules** her hair comes down to her shoulders *or* is shoulder-length
(**c**) **en a. à faire qch** to get to the stage of doing sth; **c'est malheureux d'en a. là** it's a shame it's got to that stage; **j'en arrive à penser que.../me demander si...** I'm beginning to think.../wonder if...
(**d**) (*socialement*) to arrive, to make it
(**e**) (*parvenir*) **a. à un résultat** to achieve a result; **a. à faire qch** to manage to do sth; **je n'arrive pas à l'ouvrir** I can't open it; **il n'arrivera jamais à rien** he'll never make anything of himself
(**f**) (*se produire*) to happen (**à** to)
2 *v impersonnel* **quoi qu'il arrive** whatever happens; **il lui est arrivé quelque chose** something's happened to him; **il m'arrive d'y penser** I sometimes think about it; **il arrive à tout le monde de se tromper** anyone can make a mistake; **qu'est-ce qu'il t'arrive?** what's wrong (with you)?

arrivisme [arivism] *nm* unscrupulous ambition

arriviste [arivist] *nmf* social climber, arriviste

arrogance [arɔgɑ̃s] *nf* arrogance; **avec a.** arrogantly

arrogant, -e [arɔgɑ̃, -ɑ̃t] *adj* arrogant

arroger [45] [arɔʒe] **s'arroger** *vpr* **s'a. un droit/un privilège** to claim a right/a privilege

arrondi, -e [arɔ̃di] **1** *adj* (*objet, visage*) round
2 *nm* (**a**) (*forme*) roundness, rounded form (**b**) (*d'une jupe*) hemline

arrondir [arɔ̃dir] **1** *vt* (**a**) (*forme*) **a. qch** to make sth round; **cette coiffure lui arrondit le visage** that haircut makes her face look round; *Fig* **a. les angles** to smooth things over (**b**) (*chiffre, somme*) (*vers le haut*) to round up; (*vers le bas*) to round down; *Fam* **a. ses fins de mois** to supplement one's income; **a. à l'euro supérieur/inférieur** to round up/down to the nearest euro
2 s'arrondir *vpr* (*corps, visage*) to fill out

arrondissement [arɔ̃dismɑ̃] *nm* = administrative subdivision of Paris, Lyons and Marseilles

arrosage [arozaʒ] *nm* (*des plantes, du sol*) watering; (*des rues*) spraying; (*d'une pelouse*) sprinkling

arroser [aroze] **1** *vt* (**a**) (*plantes, sol*) to water; (*pelouse*) to sprinkle; (*rues*) to spray; (*rôti*) to baste; **région très peu arrosée** area with little rainfall; **a. qch d'essence** to douse sth in petrol (**b**) (*fêter*) to drink to; **un repas bien arrosé** a meal washed down with plenty of alcohol (**c**) (*sujet: rivière*) to flow through
2 s'arroser *vpr* (*se fêter*) **ça s'arrose!** that calls for a celebration!

arroseur [arozœr] *nm* (*appareil*) sprinkler

arrosoir [arozwar] *nm* watering can

arsenal, -aux [arsənal, -o] *nm* (**a**) *Mil* arsenal; **a. maritime** *ou* **de la marine** naval dockyard (**b**) *Fam* (*attirail*) gear

arsenic [arsənik] *nm* arsenic

art [ar] *nm* (**a**) (*esthétique*) art; **c'est du grand a.!** it's a work of art!; **le septième a.** cinema; **a.** dramatique drama, dramatic art; **les arts graphiques** graphic arts; **l'a.** lyrique opera; **arts martiaux** martial arts; **arts plastiques** fine art (**b**) (*savoir-faire*) **l'a. de faire qch** the art of doing sth; **cultiver l'a. de vivre** to enjoy the finer things in life; **préparer le café, c'est tout un a.** there's quite an art to making coffee; *Fig* **avoir l'a. de faire qch** to have a knack for doing sth

Arte [arte] *n* = French-German TV channel showing cultural programmes

artère [artɛr] *nf* (**a**) (*vaisseau*) artery (**b**) (*route*) arterial road; (*en ville*) main thoroughfare

artériel, -elle [arterjɛl] *adj* (*système, maladie*) arterial

artériosclérose [arterjoskleroz] *nf* hardening of the arteries, *Spéc* arteriosclerosis

arthrite [artrit] *nf* arthritis

arthrose [artroz] *nf* osteoarthritis

Arthur [artyr] *npr Fam* **je vais me faire appeler A.!** I'm going to get a real telling-off!

artichaut [artiʃo] *nm* artichoke

article [artikl] *nm* (**a**) *Com* item; **articles de toilette** toiletries; **faire l'a.** to make a sales pitch (**b**) *Journ* article; (*de dictionnaire*) entry (**c**) (*d'un traité, d'un règlement*) article (**d**) *Gram* article; **a.** défini/indéfini definite/indefinite article (**e**) **être à l'a. de la mort** to be on the point of death (**f**) *Ordinat* (*dans base de données*) record; (*commande*) command

articulaire [artikylɛr] *adj Anat* articular, articulatory

articulation [artikylasjɔ̃] *nf* (**a**) *Anat* & *Tech* joint (**b**) (*prononciation*) articulation (**c**) (*organisation*) structure

articuler [artikyle] **1** *vt* (**a**) (*idées, arguments*) to link (**b**) (*mots*) to articulate; **articule!** speak clearly!
2 s'articuler *vpr* (*pièces, idées*) to be linked; **les différentes parties du texte s'articulent bien** the

different parts of the text hang well together; **s'a.** autour de qch *(théorie)* to centre on sth

artifice [artifis] *nm* trick

artificiel, -elle [artifisjɛl] *adj* **(a)** *(non naturel)* artificial; *Fig (personne)* false; *(rire)* forced **(b)** *(arbitraire)* arbitrary

artificiellement [artifisjɛlmɑ̃] *adv* **(a)** *(de façon non naturelle)* artificially **(b)** *(arbitrairement)* arbitrarily

artificier [artifisje] *nm (fabricant)* firework manufacturer; *(dans un feu d'artifice)* master of ceremonies

artillerie [artijri] *nf* artillery; **a. légère/lourde** light/heavy artillery; **pièce d'a.** artillery cannon

artilleur [artijœr] *nm* artilleryman

artisan [artizɑ̃] *nm* craftsman, *f* craftswoman; *Fig* architect

artisanal, -e, -aux, -ales [artizanal, -o] *adj* traditionally-made; *(à la main)* hand-made; **métier a.** craft

artisanat [artizana] *nm* craft industry

artiste [artist] **1** *adj (tempérament, style)* artistic; **se donner un genre a.** to cultivate an arty image
2 *nmf* **(a)** *(personne créative)* artist **(b)** *(qui pratique un art)* artiste; *(musicien)* performer; *(acteur)* actor, *f* actress; *(chanteur)* singer; *(danseur)* dancer; **a. (peintre)** artist

artistique [artistik] *adj* artistic

as¹ *voir* avoir

as² [ɑs] *nm* **(a)** *(aux cartes)* ace; *(aux dominos, aux dés)* one; *Fam* **être ficelé** *ou* **fichu comme l'as de pique** to be dressed like a tramp; **être plein aux as** to be rolling in it; *Fam* **passer à l'as** to go out of the window **(b)** *Fam (champion)* pro; **as du volant** crack racing driver; **un as du bricolage** a DIY expert

ascendance [asɑ̃dɑ̃s] *nf (ancêtres)* ancestry

ascendant, -e [asɑ̃dɑ̃, -ɑ̃t] **1** *adj (échelle)* rising; *(mouvement, courant)* upward
2 *nm* **(a)** *(influence)* influence; **avoir de l'a. sur qn** to have influence over sb **(b)** *ascendants (ancêtres)* ancestry

ascenseur [asɑ̃sœr] *nm* **(a)** *(dans un bâtiment) Br* lift, *Am* elevator; *Fig* **je lui renverrai l'a.** I'll return the favour **(b)** *Ordinat* scroll box

ascension [asɑ̃sjɔ̃] *nf* **(a)** *(escalade)* ascent; **faire l'a. d'une montagne** to climb a mountain **(b)** *(progression)* **a. sociale** social climbing **(c)** *Rel* **(la fête** *ou* **le jeudi de) l'A.** Ascension Day

ascensionnel, -elle [asɑ̃sjɔnɛl] *adj (mouvement)* upward

ascète [asɛt] *nmf* ascetic

ascorbique [askɔrbik] *adj (acide)* ascorbic

aseptique [asɛptik] *adj* aseptic

aseptiser [asɛptize] *vt (blessure)* to sterilize; *(pièce)* to disinfect; *Fig & Péj* **un univers aseptisé** a sterile environment

asexué, -e [asɛksɥe], **asexuel, -elle** [asɛksɥɛl] *adj aussi Fig* asexual

ashkénaze [aʃkenaz] *adj & nmf* Ashkenazi

asiatique [azjatik] **1** *adj* oriental
2 *nmf* **A.** Oriental

Asie [azi] *nf* **l'A.** Asia; **l'A. centrale** Central Asia; **l'A. du Sud-Est** South-east Asia

asile [azil] *nm* **(a)** *(abri)* refuge; *Vieilli* **a. (d'aliénés)** mental hospital; **a. de nuit** night shelter; **a. de vieillards** old folk's home **(b)** *(statut)* **a. politique/diplomatique** political/diplomatic asylum; **demander l'a. politique** to ask for political asylum

asocial, -e, -aux, -ales [asɔsjal, -o] **1** *adj* asocial
2 *nm,f* asocial person

aspartam(e) [aspartam] *nm* aspartame

aspect [aspɛ] *nm* **(a)** *(air)* appearance, look **(b)** *(angle)* angle, point of view; **sous tous ses aspects** from every angle, from all points of view **(c)** *Gram* aspect

asperge [aspɛrʒ] *nf* **(a)** *(plante)* asparagus **(b)** *Fam (personne)* beanpole

asperger [45] [aspɛrʒe] **1** *vt (linge, plante)* to spray with water; **a. qn de qch** to splash sb with sth; **se faire a.** to get splashed
2 **s'asperger** *vpr* **s'a. de qch** to splash oneself with sth

aspérité [asperite] *nf* **(a)** *(d'une surface)* rough part **(b)** *(d'un caractère)* harshness

aspersion [aspɛrsjɔ̃] *nf* spraying

asphalte [asfalt] *nm* asphalt

asphyxiant, -e [asfiksjɑ̃, -ɑ̃t] *adj* asphyxiating, suffocating; **gaz a.** poison gas

asphyxie [asfiksi] *nf* asphyxiation

asphyxier [66] [asfiksje] **1** *vt* **(a)** *(personne, animal)* to asphyxiate **(b)** *Fig (économie, industrie)* to paralyse
2 **s'asphyxier** *vpr (suffoquer)* to choke; *(se suicider)* to gas oneself

aspirateur [aspiratœr] *nm* vacuum (cleaner); **passer l'a. dans la maison** to vacuum the house

aspiration [aspirasjɔ̃] *nf* **(a)** *(inhalation)* inhalation; *Tech (d'eau dans une pompe)* suction **(b)** *(désir)* yearning (**à** for); *(ambition)* aspiration (**à** for) **(c)** *Ling* aspiration

aspiré, -e [aspire] *adj Ling* aspirate(d)

aspirer [aspire] **1** *vt* **(a)** *(air, parfum)* to inhale, to breathe (in) **(b)** *(liquide)* to suck up **(c)** *Ling* to aspirate
2 **aspirer à** *vt ind* to aspire to; **a. à faire qch** to aspire to do sth

aspirine [aspirin] *nf* aspirin; **un cachet d'a.** an aspirin; **blanc comme un cachet d'a.** white as a ghost

assagir [asaʒir] **1** *vt* to quieten down
2 **s'assagir** *vpr* to settle down

assaillant, -e [asajɑ̃, -ɑ̃t] *nm,f* assailant, attacker

assaillir [67] [asajir] *vt* to assault, to attack; *Fig (sujet: difficultés, remords, doute)* to beset; **a. qn de questions** to bombard sb with questions; **il a été assailli par les journalistes** he was set upon by the journalists

assainir [asenir] *vt (maison, rivière)* to clean up; *(atmosphère)* to purify; *(marais)* to drain; *(économie)* to stabilize

assainissement [asenismɑ̃] *nm (d'une maison, d'une rivière)* cleaning up; *(de l'atmosphère)* purifying; *(d'un marais)* drainage; *(de l'économie)* stabilization

assaisonnement [asɛzɔnmɑ̃] *nm (de plat)* seasoning; *(de salade)* dressing

assaisonner [asɛzɔne] *vt (plat)* to season (**de** with); *(salade)* to dress; *Fam Fig* **se faire a.** to get a good telling-off

assassin, -e [asasɛ̃, -in] **1** *nm* murderer; *(d'une personnalité politique)* assassin; **à l'a.!** murder!
2 *adj* **(a)** *(méchant) (regard)* murderous; *(remarque)* crushing **(b)** *(provocant) (sourire, œillade)* provocative

assassinat [asasina] *nm* murder; *(d'une personnalité politique)* assassination

assassiner [asasine] *vt* to murder; *(personnalité politique)* to assassinate; *Fig (chanson, texte)* to murder; *(sujet: critique)* to crucify

assaut [aso] *nm (attaque)* assault, attack; *Mil* charge; **donner l'a. à** to storm, to launch an attack on; **prendre qch d'a.** *Mil* to storm sth; *Fig (buffet, guichets)* to make a run for sth

assèchement [aseʃmɑ̃] *nm (d'un terrain, d'un marécage)* drainage; *(d'un cours d'eau)* drying out

assécher [34] [aseʃe] **1** vt (terrain, marécage) to drain; (cours d'eau) to dry out **2** s'assécher vpr to dry up

ASSEDIC [asedik] nfpl (abrév Association pour l'emploi dans l'industrie et le commerce) = French unemployment benefits department; **toucher les A.** to be on Dr unemployment benefit or Am welfare

assemblage [asɑ̃blaʒ] nm **(a)** (de pièces détachées) assembly; (en menuiserie) joint; (en couture) making up; (de feuillets) collating **(b)** (structure) assembly

assemblée [asɑ̃ble] nf **(a)** (réunion) assembly; (plus petite) meeting; **a. générale** annual general meeting **(b)** Pol **l'A. nationale** the National Assembly, Br ≃ the House of Commons, Am ≃ the House of Representatives **(c)** (foule) crowd

assembler [asɑ̃ble] **1** vt **(a)** (machine, meuble en kit) to assemble, to put together; (feuillets) to collate **(b)** (pièces) to join **(c)** Ordinat (programme) to assemble; (modules) to link **2** s'assembler vpr (foule) to gather

assembleur [asɑ̃blœr] nm Ordinat assembler

asséner [34] [asene] vt **a. qch à qn** (coup) to deliver sth to sb; (remarque) to hurl sth at sb

assentiment [asɑ̃timɑ̃] nm assent

asseoir [aswar] **1** vt **(a)** (installer) (personne) to seat, to sit; **être assis** to be sitting **(b)** Fig (autorité, réputation) to establish **2** vi **faire a. qn** to ask sb to sit down or to take a seat **3** s'asseoir vpr to sit (down); (depuis la position allongée) to sit up; **s'a. sur une chaise/dans un fauteuil** to sit on a chair/in an armchair; Fam Fig **s'a. sur qch** not to give a damn about sth

assermenté [asermɑ̃te] adj sworn (in); (témoin) under or on oath; **fonctionnaire a.** sworn official; Hist (prêtre) non **a.** non-juring (priest)

assertion [asersjɔ̃] nf assertion

asservir [aservir] vt to enslave

asservissement [aservismɑ̃] nm enslavement; **a. à qn/qch** subjection to sb/sth

assesseur [asesœr] nm assessor

asseyais etc voir asseoir

assez [ase] adv **(a)** (suffisamment) enough; **a. grand/intelligent (pour faire qch)** big/clever enough (to do sth); **a. bien** well enough; (appréciation scolaire) fair; **tu as a. mangé** you've eaten enough; **a.!** that's enough!; **a. parlé!** that's enough talk!; **nous sommes a. de trois** three of us is enough **(b)** **a. de** enough, **il y a a. de café/de pâtes** there's enough coffee/pasta; **j'en ai a.** (suffisamment) I've got enough; (je suis agacé) I've had enough **(c)** (plutôt) quite, rather

assidu, -e [asidy] adj **(a)** (toujours présent) regular; **être a. aux cours** to attend classes regularly **(b)** (appliqué) diligent; **un soin a.** painstaking care **(c)** (attentionné) **être a. auprès de qn** to be attentive to sb; **faire une cour assidue à qn** to pay constant court to sb

assiduité [asidɥite] nf **(a)** (présence régulière) regularity; **a. aux cours** regular attendance at classes **(b)** (zèle) diligence **(c)** poursuivre qn de ses assiduités to force one's attentions on sb

assidûment [asidymɑ̃] adv **(a)** (régulièrement) regularly **(b)** (avec application) diligently

assied etc voir asseoir

assiéger [59] [asjeʒe] vt aussi Fig to besiege

assiéra etc voir asseoir

assiette [asjet] nf **(a)** (vaisselle) plate; (contenu) plateful; Culin **a. anglaise** assorted cold meats; **a. creuse** soup plate; **a. à dessert** dessert plate; **a. plate** dinner plate **(b)**

(d'un impôt, d'un taux) base **(c)** (d'un cavalier) seat **(d)** **ne pas être dans son a.** to be out of sorts

assiettée [asjete] nf plateful

assignation [asiɲasjɔ̃] nf **(a)** (d'une tâche) assignment (à to); (de fonds, d'une part) allotment (à to) **(b)** Jur summons; **a. à résidence** house arrest

assigner [asiɲe] vt **(a)** (tâche) to assign (à to); (fonds, part) to allot (à to) **(b)** Jur (témoin) to summon; **a. qn à résidence** to place sb under house arrest

assimilable [asimilabl] adj (comparable) comparable (à to)

assimilation [asimilasjɔ̃] nf **(a)** (absorption) & Fig assimilation **(b)** (comparaison) comparison (à with)

assimilé, -e [asimile] adj (de même nature) similar; **cadres et assimilés** executives and those in similar categories

assimiler [asimile] **1** vt **(a)** (aliment, connaissances, immigrés) to assimilate; **un élève qui a du mal a. a.** a pupil who finds it hard to take things in **(b)** (comparer) to compare (à with) **2** s'assimiler vpr **(a)** (immigré) to assimilate **(b)** (être comparable) to be comparable (à with)

assis, -e [asi, -iz] **1** pp voir asseoir **2** adj sitting, seated; **je travaille a. toute la journée** I spend the whole day at work sitting down; Fig **situation bien assise** a secure job

assise [asiz] nf (d'une théorie) basis, foundation

assises [asiz] nfpl **(a)** (congrès) conference **(b)** Jur **les a.** = French court dealing with serious crimes

assistanat [asistana] nm assistantship

assistance [asistɑ̃s] nf **(a)** (public) audience **(b)** (aide) assistance; **prêter a. à qn** to give sb assistance **(c)** **être à l'A. (publique)** to be in care

assistant, -e [asistɑ̃, -ɑ̃t] nm,f assistant; (de langue) language assistant; **a. metteur en scène** assistant director; **assistante maternelle** child minder; **assistante sociale** social worker

assisté, -e [asiste] **1** nm,f Péj person living on handouts **2** adj **a. par ordinateur** computer-aided

assister [asiste] **1** vt (personne) to assist **2** assister à vt ind to be (present) at, to attend; (accident) to witness; **je ne peux pas vous répondre, je n'ai pas assisté à la scène** I can't give you an answer, I wasn't there

associatif, -ive [asɔsjatif, -iv] adj mouvement a. association; **vie associative** community life

association [asɔsjasjɔ̃] nf **(a)** (groupe, société) association; Com partnership; **a. à but non lucratif** Br non-profit-making or Am not-for-profit organization; **A. européenne de libre-échange** European Free Trade Association; **a. de parents d'élèves** parent-teacher association; **a. sportive** sports club **(b)** (de mots, d'idées) association; (d'aliments, de substances, de couleurs) combination **(c)** Jur **a. de malfaiteurs** criminal conspiracy

associé, -e [asɔsje] **1** nm,f associate; Com partner **2** adj **membre a.** associate member

associer [66] [asɔsje] **1** vt **(a)** (lier) to combine (à with) **(b)** (mentalement) to associate (à with) **2** s'associer vpr **(a)** **s'a. à un projet** to join in a project; **s'a. à ou avec qn** (dans une lutte) to join forces with sb; Com to enter into partnership with sb **(b)** (se mêler) to combine (à with)

assoiffé, -e [aswafe] adj thirsty; Fig **a. de sang** bloodthirsty; **a. de savoir** thirsty for knowledge

assolement [asɔlmɑ̃] nm crop rotation

assombrir [asɔ̃brir] **1** vt to darken; (avenir) to cast a shadow over **2** s'assombrir vpr (ciel, visage) to darken, to cloud over; (personne) to become gloomy

assommant, -e [asɔmɑ̃, -ɑ̃t] *adj* very boring

assommer [asɔme] *vt* **a.** **qn** *(étourdir)* to knock sb senseless; *(engourdir)* to make sb lethargic; *(ennuyer)* to bore sb to death

Assomption [asɔ̃psjɔ̃] *nf* **(la fête de) l'A.** (the feast of) the Assumption

assonance [asɔnɑ̃s] *nf* assonance

assorti, -e [asɔrti] *adj* (**a**) *(en harmonie)* matching; **bien a.** well-matched; **mal a.** ill-matched; **veste avec jupe assortie** jacket with matching skirt; **le pull n'était pas a. à la jupe** the sweater didn't match the skirt (**b**) *(bonbons)* assorted, mixed (**c**) **bien a.** *(magasin)* well-stocked (**d**) *(accompagné)* **a. de** accompanied by

assortiment [asɔrtimɑ̃] *nm (de produits)* assortment

assortir [asɔrtir] *vt* (**a**) *(couleurs)* to match (**à** to) (**b**) *Com* to restock

assoupir [asupir] **s'assoupir** *vpr* to doze off

assouplir [asuplir] **1** *vt (chaussures, cuir, corps)* to make supple; *Fig (réglementation)* to relax
2 s'assouplir *vpr (chaussures, cuir, corps)* to get supple

assouplissant [asuplisɑ̃] *nm* fabric softener

assouplissement [asuplismɑ̃] *nm (du corps)* making supple; *Fig (de la réglementation)* relaxing; **exercices d'a., assouplissements** limbering-up exercises

assourdir [asurdir] *vt* (**a**) *(personne)* to deafen (**b**) *(son)* to deaden

assourdissant, -e [asurdisɑ̃, -ɑ̃t] *adj* deafening

assouvir [asuvir] *vt (faim, désir)* to satisfy

assouvissement [asuvismɑ̃] *nm (de la faim, du désir)* satisfaction

assoyant *voir* **asseoir**

assujettir [asyʒetir] *vt* (**a**) *(province)* to subjugate (**b**) *(soumettre)* **a. qn à qch** to subject sb to sth; **être assujetti à l'impôt** to be liable for tax (**c**) *(objet)* to fix, to fasten (**à** to)

assujettissement [asyʒetismɑ̃] *nm* (**a**) *(dépendance)* subjection (**à** to) (**b**) *(à l'impôt)* liability (**à** for)

assumer [asyme] **1** *vt* (**a**) *(responsabilité)* to assume, to take on; *(risque)* to take (**b**) *(accepter) (conséquences)* to take
2 *vi Fam* **tu vas devoir a.** you'll have to live with it
3 s'assumer *vpr* to come to terms with oneself

assurance [asyrɑ̃s] *nf* (**a**) *(confiance)* (self-)assurance (**b**) *(garantie)* assurance; **je vous donne l'a. que tout sera fini demain** I assure you that everything will be finished tomorrow; **demander/recevoir des assurances** to ask for/to receive assurance (**c**) *(contre le vol, les accidents)* insurance; **prendre une a.** to take out insurance; *Fam* **je vais écrire à mon a.** I'm going to write to my insurance company; **a. auto** car insurance; **a. maladie** health insurance; **a. au tiers** third-party insurance; **a. tous risques** comprehensive insurance; **a. sur la vie, a.-vie** life insurance; **a. vieillesse** retirement pension

assuré, -e [asyre] **1** *adj* (**a**) *(pas, voix)* firm; *(air, personne)* assured, confident; **d'une voix mal assurée** in an unsteady voice (**b**) *(succès, victoire)* guaranteed, certain
2 *nm,f* **l'a.** the insured; **les assurés sociaux** ≃ people who pay *Br* national insurance *or Am* social security

assurément [asyremɑ̃] *adv Vieilli* certainly

assurer [asyre] **1** *vt* (**a**) *(garantir)* to ensure, to guarantee; **a. une rente à qn** to settle an annuity on sb; **ma retraite m'assure de quoi vivre** my pension gives me enough to live on; **a. ses arrières** to leave oneself a way out (**b**) *(certifier)* **a. qch à qn, a. qn de qch** to assure sb of sth; **a. qn que** to assure sb that; **c'est bien vrai, je t'assure** it's absolutely true, I assure you (**c**) *(se charger de)* to be in charge of; **a. les fonctions de directeur de la production** to be production manager; **un service régulier est assuré**

entre Paris et Marseille there is a regular service between Paris and Marseilles; **j'assure la permanence ce matin** I'm on duty this morning; **a. la défense de qn** *(sujet: avocat)* to defend sb (**d**) *(immobiliser)* to steady; *(attacher)* to secure (**e**) *(par contrat d'assurance)* to insure (**contre** against)
2 *vi Fam* **a. en maths** to be brilliant at maths; **à l'entretien, j'ai assuré un max** I did brilliantly at the interview
3 s'assurer *vpr* (**a**) **s'a. de qch** *(vérifier)* to make sure of sth; **je vais m'en a.** I'll check (**b**) *(par contrat d'assurance)* to insure oneself (**contre** against); **s'a. au tiers/sur la vie** to take out third-party/life insurance (**c**) *(se procurer)* **s'a. la collaboration de qn** to secure sb's collaboration; **les Allemands se sont assuré la victoire** the Germans have assured of victory

assureur [asyrœr] *nm* insurer

astérisque [asterisk] *nm* asterisk

astéroïde [asterɔid] *nm* asteroid

asthmatique [asmatik] *adj & nmf* asthmatic

asthme [asm] *nm* asthma; **avoir de l'a.** to have asthma; **crise d'a.** asthma attack

asticot [astiko] *nm* maggot

asticoter [astikɔte] *vt Fam* to bug

astigmate [astigmat] *adj & nmf* astigmatic

astiquer [astike] *vt (faire briller)* to polish; *(récurer)* to scour; **a. sa maison** to get one's house spotlessly clean

astrakan [astrakɑ̃] *nm* astrakhan

astre [astr] *nm* star; **beau comme un a.** as pretty as a picture

astreignant, -e [astrɛɲɑ̃, -ɑ̃t] *adj* exacting, demanding

astreindre [54] [astrɛ̃dr] **1** *vt* **a. qn à faire qch** to compel *or* oblige sb to do sth
2 s'astreindre *vpr* **s'a. à un régime sévère** to strictly follow a diet; **s'a. à faire qch** to force oneself to do sth

astreinte [astrɛ̃t] *nf* constraint

astrologie [astrɔlɔʒi] *nf* astrology

astrologique [astrɔlɔʒik] *adj* astrological

astrologue [astrɔlɔg] *nmf* astrologer

astronaute [astrɔnot] *nmf* astronaut

astronautique [astrɔnotik] *nf* astronautics *(singulier)*

astronome [astrɔnɔm] *nmf* astronomer

astronomie [astrɔnɔmi] *nf* astronomy

astronomique [astrɔnɔmik] *adj aussi Fig* astronomical

astrophysique [astrɔfizik] *nf* astrophysics *(singulier)*

astuce [astys] *nf* (**a**) *(finesse)* shrewdness (**b**) *(truc)* trick; *(conseil)* tip; **il doit y avoir une a.** there must be a trick to it (**c**) *(plaisanterie)* witticism; *(jeu de mots)* pun; **je ne saisis pas l'a.** I don't get it

astucieusement [astysjøzmɑ̃] *adv* shrewdly

astucieux, -euse [astysjø, -øz] *adj (personne)* shrewd; *(solution)* clever

asymétrie [asimetri] *nf* asymmetry

asymétrique [asimetrik] *adj* asymmetrical

asynchrone [asɛ̃kron] *adj Ordinat* asynchronous

atavisme [atavism] *nm* atavism; **faire qch par a.** to do sth because it's in one's genes

atchoum [atʃum] *exclam* atishoo!

atelier [atəlje] *nm* (**a**) *(lieu)* workshop; *(dans une maison)* workroom; *(d'artiste)* studio; **a. de carrosserie** bodyshop; **a. de montage** assembly shop; *TV & Cin* **a. de production** production studio; **a. de réparations** repair shop (**b**) *(personnel)* workshop staff (**c**) *(groupe de travail)* work-group

atermoiements [atermwamɑ̃] *nmpl* procrastination

athée [ate] **1** *adj* atheistic
2 *nmf* atheist

athéisme [ateism] *nm* atheism

Athènes [aten] *n* Athens

athénien, -enne [atenjɛ̃, -ɛn] **1** *adj* Athenian **2** *nm,f* **A.** Athenian

athlète [atlɛt] *nmf* athlete

athlétique [atletik] *adj* athletic

athlétisme [atletism] *nm* athletics *(singulier)*; **épreuves d'a.** athletic events

atlantique [atlɑ̃tik] **1** *adj* Atlantic **2** *nm* **l'A.** the Atlantic (Ocean)

atlas [atlas] *nm (livre)* atlas

atmosphère [atmɔsfɛr] *nf aussi Fig* atmosphere

atmosphérique [atmɔsferik] *adj* atmospheric

atoca [atɔka] *nm Can* cranberry

atoll [atɔl] *nm* atoll

atome [atom] *nm* atom; *Fig* **avoir des atomes crochus avec qn** to hit it off with sb; **elle n'a pas un a. de bon sens** she doesn't have a bit of common sense

atomique [atɔmik] *adj* atomic

atomiser [atɔmize] *vt* (a) *(pulvériser)* to atomize (b) *(ville, région)* to destroy with nuclear weapons

atomiseur [atɔmizœr] *nm* atomizer, spray; **parfum en a.** perfume spray

atone [atɔn] *adj* (a) *(inerte)* lacklustre (b) *(voyelle)* unstressed

atours [atur] *nmpl Litt ou Hum* finery; **parée de ses plus beaux a.** in all her finery

atout [atu] *nm (aux cartes)* trump; *Fig* **asset. a. pique** spades are trumps; *aussi Fig* **avoir tous les atouts dans son jeu** to hold all the winning cards

âtre [ɑr] *nm Litt* hearth; **au coin de l'â.** by the fireplace

atriqué, -e [atrike] *adj Can* **mal a.** badly dressed

atroce [atrɔs] *adj (crime)* atrocious; *(douleur)* excruciating; *(odeur, cauchemar, repas)* dreadful, horrible; **j'avais une peur a. de le rencontrer** I dreaded meeting him

atrocement [atrɔsmɑ̃] *adv (cruellement)* atrociously; *(très mal)* dreadfully, horribly; **avoir a. mal** to be in dreadful pain; **sentir a. mauvais** to smell really horrible

atrocité [atrɔsite] *nf* atrocity

atrophie [atrɔfi] *nf* atrophy

atrophier [66] [atrɔfje] *vt* to atrophy **2 s'atrophier** *vpr* to atrophy

attabler [atable] **s'attabler** *vpr* to sit down at the/a table

attachant, -e [ataʃɑ̃, -ɑ̃t] *adj* engaging

attache [ataʃ] *nf* (a) *(lien)* fastener; *Fig* **attaches** *(amis)* links; *Fig* **sans attaches** unattached; **je n'avais plus aucune a. dans cette ville** there was nothing to keep me in the town (b) **avoir les attaches fines** *(chevilles et poignets)* to have delicate wrists and ankles

attaché, -e [ataʃe] **1** *adj* (a) *(fixé)* fastened; *(chien)* chained up (b) *(affectivement)* **a. à** attached to (c) *(dépendant)* **les avantages attachés à une fonction** the benefits attached to a post **2** *nm,f* attaché; **a. d'ambassade** attaché; **a. culturel** cultural attaché; **a. militaire** military attaché; **a. de presse** press officer

attaché-case *(pl* attachés-cases) [ataʃekɛz] *nm* attaché case

attachement [ataʃmɑ̃] *nm* attachment (à to)

attacher [ataʃe] **1** *vt* (a) **a. qch à qch** *(fixer)* to fasten sth to sth; *(avec de la ficelle, avec une corde)* to tie sth to sth; *(avec une chaîne)* to chain sth to sth; **a. ses cheveux** to tie one's hair back; **a. ses lacets** *ou* **chaussures** to do one's shoelaces

up (b) *(accorder)* **a. de l'importance/de la valeur à qch** to attach importance/great value to sth **2** *vi (dans une poêle, une casserole)* to stick to the pan; **une casserole qui n'attache pas** a non-stick saucepan **3 s'attacher** *vpr* (a) *(se fixer)* to be fastened (à to); **cette jupe s'attache par derrière** this skirt does up at the back (b) *(affectivement)* **s'a. à qn** to get attached to sb; **je ne veux pas m'a.** I don't want to commit myself (c) *(se concentrer)* **s'a. aux faits** to stick to the facts; **s'a. à faire qch** to strive to do sth (d) *(s'assurer)* **s'a. les services de qn** to procure sb's services

attaquant, -e [atakɑ̃, -ɑ̃t] **1** *nm,f Sp* attacker **2** *adj* attacking

attaque [atak] *nf* (a) *(agression, en sport)* attack; *aussi Fig* **passer à l'a.** to go on the offensive; **à l'a.!** attack!; **a. aérienne** air raid; **a. à main armée** armed robbery (b) *Fam* **être d'a.** to be on top form; **se sentir d'a. pour faire qch** to feel up to doing sth (c) *Méd (crise)* attack; **une a.** *(apoplexie)* a stroke; *(crise cardiaque)* a heart attack

attaquer [atake] **1** *vt* (a) *(physiquement, verbalement)* to attack; *(sujet: acide)* to attack; *Jur* **a. qn en justice** to bring an action against sb (b) *(repas, sujet, travail)* to tackle; *Fam* **on attaque?** *(à table)* shall we get stuck in? (c) *Mus (morceau)* to strike up; *(note)* to attack **2 s'attaquer** *vpr* **s'a. à** *(adversaire)* to attack; *(problème)* to tackle; **s'a. à plus fort que soi** to bite off more than one can chew

attardé, -e [atarde] **1** *nm,f* **a.** **(mental)** (mentally) retarded person **2** *adj* (a) *(qui flâne)* **il ne restait plus que quelques passants attardés** there were only a few people still about (b) *(vieux)* old-fashioned (c) *(mentalement)* (mentally) retarded

attarder [atarde] **s'attarder** *vpr* to linger; **s'a. à des détails** to dwell over details; **ne nous attardons pas sur ce point** let's not dwell on this point

atteignais *etc voir* atteindre

atteindre [54] [atɛ̃dr] **1** *vt* to reach; *(cible)* to hit; **être atteint d'une maladie** to be suffering from a disease; **il a été atteint dans son amour-propre** his pride has been wounded; **le poumon est atteint** the lung is affected; *Fig* **rien ne l'atteint** nothing affects him; *Fam* **il est très atteint** *(fou)* he's completely cracked **2** *vi* **a.** **à** *(but)* to reach; **a. à la perfection** to be close to perfection

atteinte [atɛ̃t] *nf (attaque)* **a.** attack on; **porter a. à** to undermine

attelage [atəlaʒ] *nm (animaux)* team

atteler [42] [atəle] **1** *vt (chevaux)* to harness; *(bœufs)* to yoke; **a. une voiture** to hitch up horses to a carriage **2 s'atteler** *vpr* **s'a. à une tâche** to buckle down to a task

attelle [atɛl] *nf* splint

attenant, -e [atənɑ̃, -ɑ̃t] *adj* adjoining; **a. à** adjoining

attendre [atɑ̃dr] **1** *vt* to wait for; **a. son tour** to wait one's turn; **a. un bébé** to be expecting (a baby); **se faire a.** *(personne)* to keep people waiting; **la réponse ne s'est pas fait a.** the reply wasn't long in coming; **je l'attends d'une minute à l'autre** I'm expecting him any minute now; **qch de qn/qch** to expect sth from sb/sth; **qu'est-ce que tu attends pour le lui dire?** what are you waiting for? go and tell him; **a. que qn fasse qch** to wait for sb to do sth; *Fig* **a. qn au tournant** to be waiting to catch sb out **2** *vi* to wait; **a. une heure** to wait (for) an hour; **sans plus a.** without further ado; **faire a. qn** to keep sb waiting; *Fam* **on ne va pas a. cent sept ans** we're not going to wait forever; **en attendant** meanwhile; *(néanmoins)* all the same; **en attendant son arrivée** until he arrives/arrived **3 s'attendre** *vpr* **s'a.** to expect sth; **je m'attends à**

tout I'm ready for anything; **je m'y attendais** I expected as much; **il fallait s'y a.** it was only to be expected; **je m'attendais à ce que tu le lui dises** I was expecting you to tell him

attendrir [atɑ̃driʀ] **1** *vt* (**a**) *(émouvoir)* to move; *(rendre indulgent)* to soften (**b**) *(viande)* to tenderize **2 s'attendrir** *vpr* to be moved (**sur** by)

attendrissant, -e [atɑ̃drisɑ̃, -ɑ̃t] *adj* moving

attendu, -e [atɑ̃dy] **1** *adj* expected; **le jour tant a. est arrivé** the long-awaited day arrived **2** *prép Formel* **a. les circonstances** considering the circumstances **3 attendu que** *conj Formel* considering that; *Jur* whereas

attentat [atɑ̃ta] *nm* attack; **a. à la bombe** bombing; **a. à la pudeur** indecent assault; **a. à la sûreté de l'État** high treason; **a. à la voiture piégée** car-bomb attack

attente [atɑ̃t] *nf* (**a**) *(fait d'attendre)* waiting; *(période)* wait; **être dans l'a. de qch** to be waiting for sth; **en a.** *(au téléphone)* on hold; *Ordinat* **liste de fichiers à imprimer en a.** print queue (**b**) *(espoir)* expectations; **contre toute a.** against all expectations; **répondre à l'a.** *ou* **aux attentes de qn** to live up to sb's expectations; **dans l'a. de votre réponse/de vous rencontrer** *(dans une lettre)* I look forward to receiving your reply/to meeting you

attenter [atɑ̃te] **attenter à** *vt ind* to make an attempt on; **a. à ses jours** to attempt suicide

attentif, -ive [atɑ̃tif, -iv] *adj* attentive; **être a. aux autres** to be attentive to others; **être a. à qch** to pay attention to sth; *(ses intérêts, sa santé)* to look after sth; **écouter d'une oreille attentive** to listen attentively

attention [atɑ̃sjɔ̃] *nf* (**a**) *(soin)* attention; **écouter avec a.** to listen attentively; **faire a. à qch** to pay attention to sth; *(sa santé, ses intérêts)* to look after sth; **il a fait a. de ne pas la blesser** he took care not to hurt her; **ne pas prêter la moindre a. à** to take no notice of; **(faites) a.!** look out!; **a. si je t'attrape!** if I catch you there'll be trouble!; **a., peinture fraîche** *(sur écriteau)* wet paint; **a. à la fermeture des portières, a. au départ!** stand clear of the doors, the train is about to depart!; **à l'a. de qn** *(sur une lettre)* for the attention of sb (**b**) *(amabilité)* attention; **être plein d'attentions envers qn** to be very attentive towards sb

attentionné, -e [atɑ̃sjɔne] *adj* attentive (**auprès de** towards)

attentisme [atɑ̃tism] *nm* wait-and-see policy

attentivement [atɑ̃tivmɑ̃] *adv* attentively

atténuation [atenɥasjɔ̃] *nf* *(d'un effet, de la douleur)* reduction; *(d'une lumière)* dimming; *(d'une couleur)* toning down; *(d'une chute)* breaking

atténuer [atenɥe] **1** *vt* *(effet, douleur)* to reduce; *(lumière)* to dim; *(couleur)* to tone down; *(chute)* to break **2 s'atténuer** *vpr* *(douleur)* to ease; *(lumière, couleurs, bruit)* to fade

atterrant, -e [aterɑ̃, -ɑ̃t] *adj* appalling

atterrer [atere] *vt* to appal

atterrir [aterir] *vi* to land; **a. en catastrophe** to make an emergency landing; *Fam* **a. dans un bar/en prison** to land up in a bar/in prison

atterrissage [aterisaʒ] *nm* landing; **a. en douceur** soft landing; **a. forcé** forced landing

attestation [atɛstasjɔ̃] *nf* certificate

attester [atɛste] *vt* *(témoigner)* to testify to; **a. que** to testify that; **aucun dictionnaire n'atteste l'existence de ce mot** there's no evidence of this word in any dictionary

attifer [atife] *Fam* **1** *vt* to dress (**de** in) **2 s'attifer** *vpr* to dress; **s'a. de qch** to put sth on

attirail [atiraj] *nm* paraphernalia

attirance [atirɑ̃s] *nf* attraction; **éprouver de l'a. pour** *ou* **envers qn** to be attracted to sb

attirant, -e [atirɑ̃, -ɑ̃t] *adj* attractive

attirer [atire] **1** *vt* (**a**) *(sujet: aimant, planète)* to attract; *Fig* **a. qn dans un piège** to lure sb into a trap; **a. qn dans un coin** to take sb into a corner; **a. l'attention de qn** *(sujet: chose)* to catch sb's attention; **a. l'attention de qn sur qch** to draw sb's attention to sth; **a. les regards** to catch the eye (**b**) *(séduire)* to attract; *(sujet: matière, pays)* to appeal to **2 s'attirer** *vpr* (**a**) *(mutuellement)* to be attracted to each other (**b**) *(sur soi)* **s'a. des critiques** to come in for criticism; **s'a. des ennuis** to get oneself into trouble; **s'a. la colère de qn** to incur sb's anger

attiser [atize] *vt* (**a**) *(feu)* to poke (**b**) *Fig (désir, colère, racisme)* to stir up

attitré, -e [atitre] *adj* (**a**) *(habituel)* usual (**b**) *(chargé d'une fonction)* appointed

attitude [atityd] *nf* (**a**) *(conduite, position)* attitude (**envers** *ou* **à l'égard de** towards); **tu as eu une a. déplorable** your behaviour was appalling (**b**) *(affectation)* pose

attouchement [atuʃmɑ̃] *nm* fondling; **se livrer à des attouchements sur qn** to fondle sb

attraction [atraksjɔ̃] *nf* (**a**) *(d'un aimant)* attraction; **l'a. terrestre** the earth's gravitational pull (**b**) *aussi Fig (spectacle)* attraction

attrait [atrɛ] *nm* attraction

attrape [atrap] *nf* *(farce)* trick

attrape-nigaud (*pl* **attrape-nigauds**) [atrapnigo] *nm* trick

attraper [atrape] **1** *vt* (**a**) *(capturer, saisir)* to catch; **se faire a.** to be caught; *Fam* **a. qn à faire qch** to catch sb doing sth (**b**) *(maladie)* to catch; **a. froid** to catch cold; **a. mal** to catch a chill (**c**) *(tromper)* **a. qn** to take sb in; **là, tu es bien attrapé** you really fell for it (**d**) *Fam (gronder)* **se faire a.** to get a good talking to **2 s'attraper** *vpr (maladie)* to be caught; *(habitude)* to be picked up

attrayant, -e [atrɛjɑ̃, -ɑ̃t] *adj* attractive; **peu a.** unattractive

attribuable [atribɥabl] *adj* attributable (**à** to)

attribuer [atribɥe] **1** *vt* (**a**) *(allouer)* to assign, to allot (**à** to); *(prix, récompense, bourse)* to award (**à** to) (**b**) *(œuvre, crime, erreur)* to attribute (**à** to); **a. de l'importance à qch** to attach importance to sth **2 s'attribuer** *vpr* **s'a. qch** to claim sth; **il s'en est attribué tout le mérite** he claimed all the credit for it

attribut [atriby] **1** *nm* attribute **2** *adj* attributive

attribution [atribysjɔ̃] *nf* (**a**) *(allocation)* assigning, allocation (**à** to); *(d'un prix, d'une récompense, d'une bourse)* awarding (**à** to); **attributions** *(fonctions)* duties; **entrer dans les attributions de qn** to be part of sb's duties (**b**) *(d'une œuvre, d'un crime, d'une erreur)* attribution (**à** to)

attristant, -e [atristɑ̃, -ɑ̃t] *adj* depressing

attrister [atriste] **1** *vt* to sadden; **cela m'attriste** it makes me sad **2 s'attrister** *vpr* to be saddened (**de** by)

attroupement [atrupmɑ̃] *nm* crowd; **provoquer un a.** to draw a crowd

attrouper [atrupe] **s'attrouper** *vpr* to gather

atypique [atipik] *adj* atypical

au [o] *voir* **à**

aubaine [obɛn] *nf* godsend; **profiter de l'a.** to take advantage of one's good luck

aube [ob] *nf* (**a**) *(matin)* dawn; **à l'a.** at dawn; *Fig* **l'a. de la civilisation** the dawn of civilization (**b**) *Rel* alb

aubépine [obepin] *nf* hawthorn; **fleurs d'a.** may blossom

auberge [ober3] *nf* inn; *Fig* **ici, c'est l'a. espagnole** there's not much provided here; *Fam* **on n'est pas sorti de l'a.** we're not out of the wood yet; **a. de jeunesse** youth hostel

aubergine [ober3in] *nf* (**a**) *(plante) Br* aubergine, *Am* egg-plant (**b**) *Fam (contractuelle) Br* (female) traffic warden, *Am* meter maid

aubergiste [ober3ist] *nmf* innkeeper

auburn [obœrn] *adj inv* auburn

aucun, -e [okœ̃, -yn] **1** *pron indéfini* (**a**) *(personne, rien)* none; **a. des deux** neither (of them); **a. d'entre eux** none of them; **je ne me fie à a. d'entre eux** I don't trust any of them (**b**) *Litt* **d'aucuns** some people **2** *adj indéfini* (**a**) *(négatif)* no, not any; **je n'en ai aucune idée** I've (got) no idea; **sans aucune exception** without any exception; **sans a. doute** without a doubt (**b**) *(positif)* any, **plus rapide qu'a. autre coureur** faster than any other runner

aucunement [okynmɑ̃] *adv* not at all, not in the slightest

audace [odas] *nf* (**a**) *(courage)* boldness, daring (**b**) *(culot)* audacity, impudence (**c**) *(originalité)* boldness (**d**) *(action audacieuse)* **avoir toutes les audaces** to do the most daring things

audacieusement [odasjøzmɑ̃] *adv* (**a**) *(avec courage)* boldly, daringly (**b**) *(avec culot)* impudently

audacieux, -euse [odasjø, -øz] *adj* (**a**) *(courageux)* bold, daring (**b**) *(culotté)* impudent (**c**) *(original)* bold

au-dedans [odədɑ̃] *adv* inside; **a. de** inside

au-dehors [odəɔr] *adv* outside; **a. de** outside

au-delà [odəla] **1** *nm* **l'a.** the next world **2** *prép* **a. de** beyond **3** *adv* beyond; **jusqu'à une certaine somme mais pas a.** up to a certain sum but no more

au-dessous [odəsu] *adv* below, underneath; **on en trouve à 50 euros et même a.** you can get them for 50 euros or even less; **a. de** *(dans l'espace)* below, under; *(nombre, somme)* under; *(dans une hiérarchie)* below; **15 degrés a.** de zéro 15 degrees below zero; *Fig* **être a. de tout** to be beneath contempt

au-dessus [odəsy] *adv* above; *(à l'étage supérieur)* upstairs; **une terrasse avec une marquise a.** a terrace with an awning over it; **500 euros et a.** 500 euros and upwards; **a. de** *(dans l'espace, dans une hiérarchie)* above, *(nombre, somme)* over; **a. de nos têtes** *(dans le ciel)* overhead; **c'est a. de mes forces** it's beyond me; **vivre a. de ses moyens** to live beyond one's means; *Fig* **je suis a. de ça** I'm above all that

au-devant [odəvɑ̃] **au-devant de** *prép* **aller/courir a. de qn** to go to meet sb; **aller a. des désirs de qn** to anticipate sb's wishes; **aller a. du danger** to court danger

audible [odibl] *adj* audible

audience [odjɑ̃s] *nf* (**a**) *(entrevue)* audience; *Jur* hearing; **l'a. est suspendue** the case is adjourned (**b**) *(intérêt)* **trouver a. auprès des jeunes** to find a following among young people (**c**) *(public)* audience

Audimat® [odimat] *nm (appareil)* = device for calculating television audience ratings; *(résultats)* audience ratings; **faire de l'A.** to increase audience ratings

audioconférence [odjokɔ̃ferɑ̃s] *nf* audioconference

audionumérique [odjonymerik] *adj* digital audio; **disque a.** compact disc

audiovisuel, -elle [odjovizɥɛl] **1** *adj* (**a**) *(méthodes)* audiovisual (**b**) *TV & Rad* television and radio **2** *nm TV & Rad* **l'a.** television and radio

auditeur, -trice [oditœr, -tris] *nm,f* (**a**) *(d'un programme de radio)* listener (**b**) *Univ* **suivre un cours en a. libre** = to follow a course without being officially registered as a student, *Am* to audit a course

auditif, -ive [oditif, -iv] *adj (nerf)* auditory; *(troubles)* hearing

audition [odisjɔ̃] *nf* (**a**) *(faculté)* hearing (**b**) *(de chanteur, d'acteur)* audition; **passer une a.** to have an audition (**c**) *Jur* **a. des témoins** examination of the witnesses

auditionner [odisjone] *vt & vi* to audition

auditoire [oditwar] *nm* (**a**) *(public)* audience (**b**) *Belg & Suisse* auditorium

auditorium [oditɔrjɔm] *nm* auditorium; *Rad & TV* recording studio

auge [oʒ] *nf (mangeoire)* trough

augmentation [ɔgmɑ̃tasjɔ̃] *nf* (**a**) *(accroissement)* increase (**de** in); **a.** *(de salaire) Br* (pay-)rise, *Am* raise; **demander une a.** to ask for a (pay-)rise; **être en a.** to be on the increase (**b**) *Ordinat* **a. de puissance** upgrade

augmenter [ɔgmɑ̃te] **1** *vt* to increase; **édition augmentée** enlarged edition; **a. qn** to raise sb's salary **2** *vi* to increase (**de** by)

augure [ogyr] *nm* (**a**) *(devin)* augur (**b**) *(présage)* omen; **de bon a.** auspicious; **de mauvais a.** ominous

augurer [ogyre] *vt* **a. bien/mal de qch** to augur well/ill for sth

auguste [ogyst] *adj* august

aujourd'hui [oʒurdɥi] *adv* (**a**) *(ce jour)* today; **le journal d'a.** today's paper; *Fam* **c'est pour a. ou pour demain?** I/ we haven't got all day! (**b**) *(à l'heure actuelle)* nowadays; today; **les jeunes gens d'a.** young people of today; **l'Europe d'a.** present-day Europe

aulne [on] *nm* alder

aumône [omon] *nf* alms; **demander l'a.** to ask for charity; **faire l'a. à qn** to give alms to sb

aumônier [omonje] *nm* chaplain

aune [on] *nm* alder

auparavant [oparavɑ̃] *adv (avant)* before(hand); *(d'abord)* first

auprès [oprɛ] **auprès de** *prép* (**a**) *(près de)* by, next to; **ambassadeur a. des Nations unies** ambassador to the United Nations (**b**) *(en comparaison de)* compared with (**c**) *(en s'adressant à)* **se renseigner a. de qn** to ask sb

auquel [okɛl] *voir* **lequel**

aura¹ [ɔra] *voir* **avoir**

aura² [ɔra] *nf* aura

auréole [ɔreol] *nf* (**a**) *(de saint, d'un astre)* halo; *Fig* **parer qn d'une a.** to idolize sb (**b**) *(trace)* ring

auréoler [ɔreole] *vt* **tout auréolé de gloire** crowned with glory

auriculaire [ɔrikylɛr] *nm* little finger

aurifère [ɔrifɛr] *adj* gold-bearing; **gisement a.** goldfield

Aurigny [ɔriɲi] *n* Alderney

aurore [ɔrɔr] *nf* dawn, daybreak; **à l'a.** at dawn; *Fam* **aux aurores** at the crack of dawn; **a. boréale** aurora borealis, northern lights

auscultation [ɔskyltasjɔ̃] *nf* auscultation

ausculter [ɔskylte] *vt (malade, cœur)* to listen to

auspices [ɔspis] *nmpl* **sous les a. de** *(sous l'égide de)* under the auspices of; **sous d'heureux a.** auspiciously; **sous de fâcheux a.** inauspiciously

aussi [osi] **1** *adv* (**a**) *(également)* too, as well; **lui a. il sait le faire** he, too, knows how to do it, he knows how to do it as well (**b**) *(tellement)* so; **une a. belle journée** such a nice day

(c) *(dans les phrases comparatives)* as; **a. grand que moi** as tall as me; **pas a. gros que** not as big as, not so big as; **a. bien que moi** as well as me **(d)** *(quelque)* however; **a. bizarre que cela soit** however odd it may be **2** *conj* therefore, so

aussitôt [osito] **1** *adv* immediately, straight away; **a. avant/après** immediately before/after; **a. après son retour je suis parti** as soon as he returned I left; **a. l'argent reçu je vous paierai** as soon as I get the money I'll pay you; **a. dit, a. fait** no sooner said than done **2** *conj* **a. que** as soon as

austère [ostɛr] *adj (vie, style)* austere; *(vêtement)* severe; *(expression)* stern

austérité [osterite] *nf (de la vie, d'un style)* austerity; *(d'un vêtement)* severity; *(d'une expression)* sternness; **mesures d'a.** austerity measures

austral, -e, -als *ou* **-aux** [ostral, -o] *adj* southern

Australasie [ostralazi] *nf* **l'A.** Australasia

Australie [ostrali] *nf* **l'A.** Australia

australien, -enne [ostraljɛ̃, -ɛn] **1** *adj* Australian **2** *nm,f* **A.** Australian

autant [otɑ̃] *adv* **(a)** *(tellement)* so much; **a. de** *(quantité)* so much; *(nombre)* so many; **je n'avais jamais vu a. de neige/ de voitures** I had never seen so much snow/so many cars **(b)** *(la même quantité, le même nombre)* **remettez-m'en encore a.** give me the same again; **il m'en veut, mais je lui en veux tout a.** he's angry with me, but I'm just as angry with him; **le coût de la vie a augmenté de 5% mais les salaires n'ont pas augmenté d'a.** the cost of living has increased by 5% but salaries have not risen by the same amount; **a. que** *(quantité)* as much as; *(nombre)* as many as; **a. que possible** as far as possible; **a. de ... que** *(quantité)* as much ... as; *(nombre)* as many ... as; **ils ont a. de terrain/ d'amis que vous** they have as much land/as many friends as you **(c)** *(de même)* **on ne peut pas en dire a. de tout le monde** you can't say the same for everybody; **essaie un peu d'en faire a.** try to do the same **(d)** *(locutions)* **a. elle est expansive, a. il est réservé** she's as extroverted as he is shy; **a. pour moi!** I stand corrected!; **(pour) a. que je sache** as far as I know, to the best of my knowledge; **ce sera a. de moins à payer** it will be that much less to pay; **a. rester ici** we may as well stay here; **a. dire que...** which amounts to saying that...; **j'aimerais a. aller au cinéma** I'd rather go to the cinema; **j'aime a. te dire que je n'étais pas contente!** I wasn't too happy, I can tell you!, ...**d'a. (plus) que**... ..., especially since...; **d'a. plus/ moins que** all the more/less because; **cela vous sera d'a. plus facile que vous êtes jeune** it will be that much easier for you since you are young; **pour a.** *(malgré cela)* for all that

autarcie [otarsi] *nf Pol* autarky; **vivre en a.** to be self-sufficient

autel [otɛl] *nm aussi Fig* altar; **conduire sa fille à l'a.** to give one's daughter away

auteur [otœr] *nm* **(a)** *(de livre)* author, writer; *(de chanson)* composer; *(de tableau)* painter **(b)** *(responsable)* author; *(d'un crime)* perpetrator; *(d'un projet)* instigator

authenticité [otɑ̃tisite] *nf* authenticity

authentification [otɑ̃tifikasjɔ̃] *nf* authentication

authentifier [66] [otɑ̃tifje] *vt* to authenticate

authentique [otɑ̃tik] *adj* authentic, genuine; *(fait, histoire)* true

authentiquement [otɑ̃tikmɑ̃] *adv* authentically, genuinely

autisme [otism] *nm* autism

autiste [otist] **1** *adj* autistic **2** *nmf* person with autism

auto [oto] *nf* car; **autos tamponneuses** bumper cars; **petite a.** *(jouet)* toy car

auto- *préf* auto-, self-

autoaccusation [otoakyzasjɔ̃] *nf* self-accusation

autobiographie [otobjografi] *nf* autobiography

autobiographique [otobjografik] *adj* autobiographical

autobronzant, -e [otobrɔ̃zɑ̃, -ɑ̃t] **1** *adj* self-tanning **2** *nm* self-tanning cream, self-tan

autobus [otobys] *nm* bus; **a. à impériale** double-decker (bus)

autocar [otokar] *nm* bus, *Br* coach; **a. de luxe** luxury coach

autocassable [otokasabl] *adj* **ampoule a.** break-open phial

autocensurer [otosɑ̃syre] **s'autocensurer** *vpr* to practise self-censorship

autochtone [otɔkton] **1** *nmf aussi Hum* native **2** *adj* native

autocollant, -e [otokɔlɑ̃, -ɑ̃t] **1** *adj* self-adhesive; *(enveloppe)* self-seal **2** *nm* sticker

autocorrecteur, -trice [otokɔrɛktœr, -tris] *adj Ordinat* self-correcting

autocouchette(s) [otokuʃet] *adj inv voir* **train**

autocrate [otokrat] *nmf* autocrat

autocratie [otokrasi] *nf* autocracy

autocratique [otokratik] *adj* autocratic

autocritique [otokritik] *nf* self-criticism; **faire son a.** to criticize oneself

autocuiseur [otokɥizœr] *nm* pressure cooker

autodafé [otodafe] *nm Hist* auto-da-fé

autodéfense [otodefɑ̃s] *nf* self-defence

autodestructeur, -trice [otodɛstryktœr, -tris] *adj* self-destructive

autodestruction [otodɛstryksjɔ̃] *nf* self-destruction

autodétermination [otodeterminasjɔ̃] *nf Pol* self-determination

autodidacte [otodidakt] **1** *adj* self-taught **2** *nmf* self-taught person

autodrome [otodrom] *nm* motor-racing track; *(pour les essais)* car-testing track

auto-école [pl **auto-écoles**) [otoekɔl] *nf* driving school

autofinancement [otofinɑ̃smɑ̃] *nm* self-financing

autofinancer [45] [otofinɑ̃se] **s'autofinancer** *vpr* to be self-financing

autofocus [otofokys] *adj & nm Phot* autofocus

autogéré, -e [otoʒere] *adj* self-managed

autogestion [otoʒɛstjɔ̃] *nf* self-management

autographe [otograf] *nm & adj* autograph

automate [otɔmat] *nm aussi Fig* automaton

automation [otɔmasjɔ̃] *nf* automation

automatique [otɔmatik] **1** *adj* automatic; **il est absent tous les lundis, c'est a.** he's off every Monday without fail **2** *nm* **(a)** *Tél* direct dialling **(b)** *(pistolet)* automatic

automatiquement [otɔmatikmɑ̃] *adv* automatically

automatisation [otɔmatizasjɔ̃] *nf* automation

automatiser [otɔmatize] *vt* to automate

automatisme [otɔmatism] *nm* **(a)** *(réflexe)* automatism; **agir par a.** to act automatically; **fermer la porte à double tour est devenu un a.** double-locking the door has become automatic **(b)** *(dispositif)* automatic device

automédication [otomedikasjɔ̃] *nf* self-medication
automitrailleuse [otomitrajøz] *nf* armoured car
automnal, -e, -aux, -ales [otɔnal, -o] *adj* autumnal
automne [otɔn] *nm* autumn, *Am* fall; **en a., à l'a.** in autumn, *Am* in the fall; **une soirée d'a.** an autumn evening, *Am* a fall evening; *Fig* **à l'a. de sa vie** in the autumn *or Am* fall of his/her life
automobile [otomɔbil] **1** *nf* **(a)** *(voiture)* car, *Am* automobile **(b)** *(industrie)* **l'a.** the car industry **2** *adj* **(a)** *(véhicule)* self-propelling **(b)** *(industrie, accessoires)* car, *Am* automobile
automobiliste [otomɔbilist] *nmf* motorist
autonettoyant, -e [otonetwajɑ̃, -ɑ̃t] *adj* **four a.** self-cleaning oven
autonome [otɔnɔm] *adj (état, région)* autonomous, self-governing; *(appareil)* self-contained; *(personne)* self-sufficient; *Ordinat* **calculateur a.** stand-alone (computer)
autonomie [otɔnɔmi] *nf* **(a)** *Pol* autonomy, self-government **(b)** *(de personne)* self-sufficiency **(c)** *(de voiture)* range; *(de batterie)* life; *Av* **a. (de vol)** range
autonomiste [otɔnɔmist] *nmf Pol* separatist
autoportrait [otopɔrtrɛ] *nm* self-portrait
autopsie [otɔpsi] *nf* autopsy, post-mortem; *Fig* **faire l'a. d'une œuvre** to dissect a work
autopsier [66] [otɔpsje] *vt* to perform an autopsy *or* a post-mortem on
autopunition [otopynisjɔ̃] *nf* self-punishment
autoradio [otoradjo] *nm* car radio
autorail [otoraj] *nm* railcar
autorégulation [otoregylɑsjɔ̃] *nf* self-regulation
autoreverse [otorivɛrs] *adj* **appareil a.** auto-reverse
autorisation [otorizɑsjɔ̃] *nf* **(a)** *(permission)* authorization, permission; **donner à qn l'a. de faire qch** to give sb permission to do sth; **demander à qn l'a. de faire qch** to ask (sb) permission to do sth; *Ordinat* **a. d'accès** access authorization; **a. de sortie du territoire** = parental authorization for a minor to travel abroad; *Av* **a. de vol** flight clearance **(b)** *(document)* authorization
autorisé, -e [otorize] *adj* **(a)** *(qualifié)* **tenir qch de source autorisée** to have sth from an authoritative source; **les milieux autorisés** official circles **(b)** *(permis)* permitted, allowed
autoriser [otorize] *vt* **(a)** *(permettre à)* **a. qn à faire qch** to authorize *or* permit sb to do sth **(b)** *(permettre)* **ces découvertes (nous) autorisent à penser que…** these discoveries entitle us to believe that…
autoritaire [otoritɛr] *adj* authoritarian
autoritairement [otoritɛrmɑ̃] *adv* in an authoritarian manner
autoritarisme [otoritarism] *nm* authoritarianism
autorité [otorite] *nf* **(a)** *(domination, fermeté)* authority; **avoir de l'a. sur qn** to have authority over sb; **faire qch d'a.** to do sth on one's own authority **(b)** *(poids)* **faire a. en qch** *(personne)* to be an authority on sth; **ce livre fait a.** this book is the authoritative work **(c)** *(gouvernement)* **les représentants de l'a.** the representatives of authority; **les autorités** the authorities **(d)** *(personne respectée)* authority
autoroute [otorut] *nf* **(a)** *Aut Br* motorway, *Am* freeway; **a. à péage** *Br* toll motorway, *Am* turnpike (road) **(b)** *Ordinat* **a. de l'information** information superhighway
autoroutier, -ère [otorutje, -ɛr] *adj* **réseau a.** *Br* motorway *or Am* freeway system
autosatisfaction [otosatisfaksjɔ̃] *nf* self-satisfaction
auto-stop [otostɔp] *nm* hitch-hiking, hitching; **faire de l'a.** to hitch-hike, to hitch; **prendre qn en a.** to give sb a lift;

faire le tour de l'Europe en a. to hitch-hike around Europe
auto-stoppeur, -euse *(mpl* **auto-stoppeurs,** *fpl* **auto-stoppeuses)** [otostɔpœr, -øz] *nmf* hitch-hiker, hitcher
autosuggestion [otosygʒɛstjɔ̃] *nf* auto-suggestion
autour [otur] *adv* around; **une ville avec des murs tout a.** a town with walls all around it; **a. de** *(dans l'espace)* around, round; *(environ)* about; *Fig* **discuter qch a. d'un verre** to discuss sth over a drink
autre [otr] **1** *adj indéfini* **(a)** *(différent)* other; **l'a. côté** the other side; **un a. jour** another day; **as-tu d'autres questions?** do you have any other questions?; **les choux et autres légumes** cabbages and other vegetables; **je l'ai vu l'a. jour/soir** I saw him the other day/evening **(b)** *(avec un pronom personnel)* **nous autres Français** we French (people); *Fam* **eh, vous autres, venez par ici!** hey, you lot, come over here! **(c)** *(locutions)* **a. chose** something else; **avez-vous a. chose à faire?** have you got anything else to do?; *Fig* **il est assez bon musicien, mais sa femme c'est autre c.l** he's not a bad musician, but his wife's in another league!; **a. part** somewhere else **2** *pron indéfini* **(a)** *(personne, chose)* the other (one); **et l'a. qui se plaint tout le temps!** and then there's him and his constant complaining!; *Fam* **comme dit l'a.** as the saying goes, as they say; **un a.** *(personne, chose)* another (one); **il n'est pas plus bête qu'un a.** he is no more stupid than an ordinary tourist; **c'était un touriste comme un a.** he was just an ordinary tourist; **c'est une raison comme une a.** it's as good a reason as any; **les autres** *(personnes, choses)* the others, the other ones; **tu devrais penser un peu aux autres** you should think of others a bit more; *Fam* **d'autres!** who do you think you're kidding?; *Fam* **j'en ai vu d'autres** I've seen worse than that **(b)** *(avec l'un, les uns)* **l'un et l'a.** both, **l'un dit ceci, l'a. dit** cela one says this and the other says that; **les uns disent ceci, les autres disent cela** some say this and others say that; **les uns et les autres** *(deux groupes)* both parties; **l'un ou l'a.** either; **c'est l'un ou l'autre** *(il faut choisir)* it's one or the other; **ni l'un ni l'a.** neither; **je ne les connais ni l'un ni l'a.** I don't know either of them; **ni les uns ni les autres** none of them; **je n'ai vu ni les uns ni les autres** I didn't see any of them; **l'un l'a.** each other, one another; **les autres** one another; **ils dépendent l'un de l'a.** they depend on each other; *Fig* **l'un dans l'a.** on the whole **(c)** *(avec chose)* **quelque chose d'a.** something else; *(dans une question)* **anything else; **rien d'autre** nothing else; **il n'y en a pas d'a.** there aren't any others; **personne d'a.** nobody else; **quelqu'un d'a.** somebody else; *(dans les questions)* anyone else; **que pouvait-il faire d'a.?** what else could he do?; **qui d'a. sera là?** who else will be there?
autrefois [otrəfwa] *adv* in the past, once; **d'a.** of long ago
autrement [otrəmɑ̃] *adv* **(a)** *(différemment)* differently; **il ne put faire a. que d'obéir** he had no alternative but to obey; **a. dit** in other words **(b)** *(sinon)* otherwise **(c)** *(bien plus)* far more; **a. dangereux (que)** far more dangerous (than) **(d)** *(pas a.* not particularly; **cela ne me surprend pas a.** that doesn't particularly surprise me
Autriche [otriʃ] *nf* **l'A.** Austria
autrichien, -enne [otriʃjɛ̃, -ɛn] **1** *adj* Austrian **2** *nm,f* **A.** Austrian
autruche [otryʃ] *nf* ostrich; **sac en a.** ostrich-skin handbag; *Fig* **avoir un estomac d'a.** to have a cast-iron stomach; **pratiquer la politique de l'a., faire l'a.** to bury one's head in the sand
autrui [otrɥi] *pron indéfini* others, other people; **ne fais pas à a. ce que tu ne voudrais pas qu'on te fît** do as you would be done by

auvent [ovã] *nm (toit)* porch roof; *(de tente)* canopy, awning

auvergnat, -e [overɲa, -at] **1** *adj* of the Auvergne **2** *nm,f* **A.** person from the Auvergne

aux [o] *voir* **à**

auxiliaire [ɔksiljɛr] **1** *adj* auxiliary **2** *nmf (aide)* assistant; *(dans les hôpitaux)* auxiliary; *(dans l'administration)* temporary worker; **a. familiale** mother's help **3** *nm Gram* auxiliary verb

auxquels, auxquelles [okɛl] *voir* **lequel**

av. *abrév* avenue

avachi, -e [avaʃi] *adj* **(a)** *(vêtement, bottes, canapé)* misshapen **(b)** *(personne, muscles)* flabby; **être a. dans un fauteuil** to be slumped in an armchair

avachir [avaʃir] **s'avachir** *vpr* **(a)** *(vêtement, bottes, canapé)* to lose its shape **(b)** *(personne) (physiquement)* to get flabby; *(moralement)* to let oneself go; **s'a. dans un fauteuil** to flop into an armchair

avais *etc voir* **avoir**

aval¹, -als [aval] *nm Fin (d'un effet de commerce)* endorsement; **a. bancaire** bank guarantee; *Fig* **donner son a. à un projet** to give a project one's backing *or* support

aval² *nm (d'un cours d'eau)* downstream section; *aussi Ind* **en a.(de)** downstream (from); **la Seine en a. de Paris** the Seine below Paris

avalanche [avalɑ̃ʃ] *nf* avalanche; *Fig (d'injures)* shower; *(de lettres, de compliments)* flood

avaler [avale] *vt* to swallow; *(goulûment) (nourriture)* to bolt; *(boisson)* to gulp down; *(croire)* to devour; **j'ai avalé de travers** it went down the wrong way; **je meurs de faim, je n'ai rien avalé depuis ce matin** I'm starving, I haven't had a thing to eat since this morning; **a. la fumée** to inhale; *Fig* **a. ses mots** to mumble; **a. une carte de crédit** *(distributeur automatique)* to eat up a credit card; **a. les kilomètres** to eat up the miles; **tu as avalé ta langue?** have you lost your tongue?

avaleur [avalœr] *nm* **a. de sabres** sword-swallower

avance [avɑ̃s] *nf* **(a)** *(progression)* advance; **a. rapide** *(sur magnétophone)* fast-forwarding **(b)** *(avantage)* lead; **avoir de l'a. sur qn** to be ahead of sb; **prendre de l'a. sur qn** to take the lead over sb; **avoir 2 minutes/2 km d'a.** to have a 2-minute/2-km lead over sb; **avoir un but/point d'a. (sur qn)** to be one goal/point ahead (of sb); *Scol* **avoir un an d'a.** to be a year ahead; **arriver avec cinq minutes d'a.** to arrive five minutes early; **d'a., à l'a., par a.** in advance; **en a.** early; **être en a.** ahead of time **(c)** *(d'argent)* advance; **faire une a. à qn** to give sb an advance **(d) faire des avances à qn** *(chercher à séduire)* to make advances to sb

avancé, -e [avɑ̃se] *adj* **(a)** *(dans l'espace)* advanced **(b)** *(précoce)* **être a. pour son âge** to be advanced for one's age **(c)** *(idées, technologie)* advanced **(d)** *(tardif)* **à une heure avancée de la nuit** late in the night; **à un âge a.** at an advanced age **(e)** *(presque à terme)* **un a stade a.** at an advanced stage; **mon travail est bien a.** I'm making good progress with my work; *Fig* **vous voilà bien a.!** a lot of good that's done you!

avancée [avɑ̃se] *nf* **(a)** *(saillie)* projection; *Constr* **a. du toit** eaves **(b)** *(de troupes, de la recherche)* advance

avancement [avɑ̃smɑ̃] *nm* **(a)** *(d'un projet)* progress; **état d'a. des travaux** progress report **(b)** *(promotion)* promotion; **avoir** *ou* **obtenir de l'a.** to be promoted **(c)** *Ordinat* **a. automatique** automatic feed; **a. ligne par ligne**

line feed; **a. du papier** paper feed; **a. par friction** friction feed

avancer [16] [avɑ̃se] **1** *vt* **(a)** *(mettre en avant)* to move forward; *(pion)* to advance; *(présenter) (main, verre, assiette)* to hold out; *Formel ou Hum* **l'automobile de Monsieur est avancée** Sir's carriage awaits **(b)** *Fig (thèse)* to advance, to put forward **(c)** *(dans le temps)* to bring forward; **a. sa montre d'une heure** to put one's watch forward one hour **(d)** *(argent)* **a. qch à qn** to advance sb sth; *(prêter)* to lend sb sth **(e)** *(faire progresser)* **à quoi cela vous avancera-t-il?** what good will that do you?; **ça ne t'avancera à rien de te mettre en colère** losing your temper won't get you anywhere; **ses réponses ne m'ont pas beaucoup avancé** his answers didn't leave me much the wiser **2** *vi* **(a)** *(aller de l'avant)* to move forward; *(armée)* to advance; **a. d'un pas** to take a step forward; **faire a. qn** to move sb along; **allez, avance! on va être en retard** come on, move it! we're going to be late **(b)** *(faire des progrès)* to progress; **alors, ça avance?** so, how's it coming along?; **faire a. les choses** to get things moving **(c)** *(montre)* to be fast; **ma montre avance d'une minute par jour** my watch gains a minute a day; **vous avancez de dix minutes** your watch is ten minutes fast **(d)** *(promontoire, toit)* to jut out **3 s'avancer** *vpr* **(a)** *(aller devant)* to move forward; **s'a. vers qch** to head towards sth; **s'a. d'un pas** to take a step forward **(b)** *(faire son travail à l'avance)* to get ahead **(c)** *Fig (s'engager hâtivement)* to commit oneself

avant [avɑ̃] **1** *prép* **(a)** *(dans le temps, dans l'espace)* before; **a. une heure** by one o'clock; *(dans moins d'une heure)* within an hour; **800 a. Jésus-Christ** 800 BC; **a. impôt** before tax; **je vous reverrai a. de partir** I'll see you before I leave; **ne fais rien a. d'être tout à fait sûr** don't do anything until you're absolutely sure; **je vous reverrai a. que vous (ne) partiez** I'll see you before you leave; **je serai parti a. que vous ayez fini** I'll have left by the time you've finished; **ne partez pas a. qu'on vous le dise** don't go until you are told; *Fam* **celle-là, a. qu'elle se décide!** she takes forever to make her mind up! **(b)** *(par ordre de priorité)* before; **faire passer qch a. le reste** to put sth before everything else; **pour lui, le travail passe a. tout** for him, work comes first; **a. tout** *(surtout)* above all; **a. toute chose** before anything else **2** *adv* **(a)** *(auparavant)* before; *(d'abord)* beforehand; **a. j'avais les cheveux longs** I used to have long hair; **tu ferais mieux de téléphoner a.** you'd better phone first; **le jour d'a.** the day before **(b)** *(dans l'espace)* **vous voyez l'église? sa maison est juste a.** you see the church? his house is just before you get to it **(c)** *Litt (loin)* far; *(tard)* late; *Fig* **poussons plus a. notre enquête** let's take our investigation(s) further **(d) en a.** *(devant les autres)* in front, ahead; *(se pencher, tomber)* forwards; *Mil* **en a., marche!** forward march!; **partir en a.** to go on ahead; **faire deux pas en a.** to take two steps forward; *Fig* **se mettre en a.** to push oneself forward; **en a. de** in front of **3** *adj inv* front **4** *nm* **(a)** *(d'un véhicule, d'une salle)* front; **à l'a.** *(d'un véhicule)* in the front; **aller de l'a.** to get on with it **(b)** *(en sport)* forward; **jouer a.** to be a forward

avantage [avɑ̃taʒ] *nm* **(a)** *(intérêt)* advantage; **cette solution ou présente l'a. d'être rapide** this solution has the advantage of being quick **(b)** *(supériorité)* advantage **(sur** over); **être à son a.** *(physiquement)* to look one's best **(c)** *(profit)* advantage; **tu aurais a. à être poli** you'd do well to be polite; **être/tourner à l'a. de qn** to be/to turn to sb's advantage; **tirer a. de qch** to turn sth to one's advantage; **a. fiscal** tax benefit; **a. en nature** benefit in kind; **avantages sociaux** social security benefits (**d**) *Sp* advantage; **prendre/conserver l'a.** to gain/retain the advantage

avantager [45] [avɑ̃taʒe] *vt* (**a**) *(favoriser)* **a. qn (par rapport à)** to give sb an advantage (over) (**b**) *(physiquement)* **a. qn** to show sb off to advantage

avantageux, -euse [avɑ̃taʒø, -øz] *adj* (**a**) *(offre)* attractive; *(conditions)* favourable; *(prix)* reasonable; *(produit)* good value (**b**) *(vaniteux) (ton)* superior

avant-bras [avɑ̃bra] *nm inv* forearm

avant-centre (*pl* avants-centres) [avɑ̃sɑ̃tr] *nm (au football)* centre forward

avant-coureur (*pl* avant-coureurs) [avɑ̃kurœr] *adj m voir* **signe**

avant-dernier, -ère (*mpl* avant-derniers, *fpl* avant-dernières) [avɑ̃dɛrnje, -ɛr] **1** *adj* last but one, second to last; **l'avant-dernière fois** the time before last
2 *nm,f* last but one, second to last

avant-garde (*pl* avant-gardes) [avɑ̃gard] *nf* (**a**) *Mil* advance guard (**b**) **l'a.** *(modernité)* the avant-garde; **d'a.** *(œuvre, théâtre)* avant-garde; **être à l'a. de la mode** to be at the cutting edge of fashion

avant-goût (*pl* avant-gouts) [avɑ̃gu] *nm* foretaste (**de** of)

avant-guerre (*pl* avant-guerres) [avɑ̃gɛr] *nm ou nf* pre-war period

avant-hier [avɑ̃tjɛr] *adv* the day before yesterday; **a. au soir** the evening before last

avant-poste (*pl* avant-postes) [avɑ̃pɔst] *nm Mil* outpost

avant-première (*pl* avant-premières) [avɑ̃prəmjɛr] *nf* preview; **(présenté) en a.** *(film, pièce)* previewed

avant-propos [avɑ̃propo] *nm inv* foreword, preface

avant-scène (*pl* avant-scènes) [avɑ̃sɛn] *nf Th* apron

avant-toit (*pl* avant-toits) [avɑ̃twa] *nm* eaves

avant-veille (*pl* avant-veilles) [avɑ̃vɛj] *nf* **l'a. (de qch)** two days before (sth)

avare [avar] **1** *adj* mean, miserly; *Fig* **il n'est pas a. de compliments** he's generous with his compliments
2 *nmf* miser

avarice [avaris] *nf* miserliness, avarice

avarie [avari] *nf* damage; **subir une a.** to be damaged

avarié, -e [avarje] *adj (nourriture)* rotten

avarier [66] [avarje] **s'avarier** *vpr (nourriture)* to go off, to go bad

avatar [avatar] *nm* (**a**) *(incarnation)* incarnation (**b**) *(mésaventure)* mishap, misadventure

avec [avɛk] **1** *prép* (**a**) *(en compagnie de)* with; **être gentil/méchant a. qn** to be nice/nasty to sb; **être bien/mal a. qn** *(s'entendre bien/mal)* to get on well/badly with sb; **je suis a. vous** *(je vous soutiens)* I'm right behind you; *Fam* **et a. ça?** *(chez le marchand)* anything else?
(**b**) *(indique la manière)* **a. enthousiasme** enthusiastically, with enthusiasm; **a. beaucoup de gentillesse** very kindly, with great kindness; **c'est a. émotion que j'accepte** I'm delighted to accept
(**c**) *(indique la simultanéité)* **diminuer a. l'âge** to decrease with age; **cela viendra a. le temps** it will come in time
(**d**) *(indique le moyen)* with; **ouvrir qch a. une clef** to open sth with a key; **j'ai eu un accident a. cette voiture** I had an accident in this car
(**e**) *(à cause de)* **a. tous les ennuis que j'ai en ce moment...** with all the problems I have at the moment...; **impossible de sortir a. cette pluie** it's impossible to go out in this rain

(**f**) *(en ce qui concerne)* **a. elle, on ne sait jamais** you never can tell with her
(**g**) **divorcer d'a. qn** to divorce sb
2 *adv Fam* **je suis venu a.** *(mon parapluie, mes gants)* I came with it/them; **il faut bien faire a.** I'll/we'll just have to put up with it

avenant, -e [avnɑ̃, -ɑ̃t] **1** *adj (personne, manières)* pleasant
2 *nm* (**a**) *(de police d'assurance)* endorsement (**b**) **le bâtiment est beau et le jardin est à l'a.** the building is beautiful and the garden is in keeping with it

avènement [avɛnmɑ̃] *nm (du Christ, d'une ère)* advent; *(d'un roi)* accession

avenir [avnir] *nm* future; **assurer l'a. de qn** to make provision for sb; **dans un très proche a.** in the very near future; **avoir de l'a.** *(personne, technique)* to have a future; **un métier d'a.** a career with good prospects; **un avocat d'a.** a lawyer with a great future; **à l'a.** in future

Avent [avɑ̃] *nm* **l'A.** Advent

aventure [avɑ̃tyr] *nf* (**a**) *(histoire)* adventure; **pour trouver des fruits en hiver, c'est tout une a.** it's quite a job finding fruit in winter (**b**) *(liaison)* (love) affair (**c**) **l'a.** *(le risque)* adventure; **tenter l'a.** to seek adventure; **partir à l'a.** to set off in search of adventure; *(sans préparation)* to set out without making plans (**d**) **dire la bonne a. à qn** to tell sb's fortune

aventurer [avɑ̃tyre] **s'aventurer** *vpr* to venture (**dans** into); **je ne m'aventurerai pas à dire que...** I wouldn't go so far as to say (that)...

aventureux, -euse [avɑ̃tyrø, -øz] *adj (vie, personne)* adventurous; *(projet)* risky

aventurier, -ère [avɑ̃tyrje, -ɛr] *nm,f* adventurer, *f* adventuress

avenue [avny] *nf* avenue

avérer [34] [avere] **s'avérer** *vpr (se révéler)* to prove to be; **il s'est avéré que...** it turned out that...

averse [avɛrs] *nf* shower; *Fig* **a. de neige** snow flurry

aversion [avɛrsjɔ̃] *nf* aversion (**pour** to), dislike (**pour** of); **prendre qn en a.** to take a dislike to sb

averti, -e [averti] *adj (bien informé)* (well-)informed; **vous voilà a.!** I don't say I didn't warn you!; *Prov* **un homme a. en vaut deux** forewarned is forearmed

avertir [avertir] *vt* **a. qn de qch** *(informer)* to inform sb of sth; *(d'un danger)* to warn sb of sth; **je vais me mettre en colère, je t'avertis!** I'm going to get angry, I'm warning you!

avertissement [avertismɑ̃] *nm* (**a**) *(avis préalable)* warning; **a. (au lecteur)** foreword (**b**) *(réprimande)* warning; *Sp (de l'arbitre)* warning, caution (**c**) *(signal)* warning sign

avertisseur [avertisœr] *nm (dispositif)* alarm; *(Klaxon®)* horn; **a. d'incendie** fire alarm

aveu, -x [avø] *nm* confession; **passer aux aveux** to make a confession; **je dois vous faire un a....** I must confess...; **de l'a. de tout le monde...** it is commonly acknowledged that...

aveuglant, -e [avœglɑ̃, -ɑ̃t] *adj* blinding, dazzling; *Fig (preuve)* blindingly obvious

aveugle [avœgl] **1** *adj aussi Fig* blind; **a. d'un œil** blind in one eye; **avoir une confiance a. en qn** to trust sb implicitly
2 *nmf* blind man, *f* blind woman; **les aveugles** the blind

aveuglement [avœgləmɑ̃] *nm (moral, mental)* blindness

aveuglément [avœglemɑ̃] *adv* blindly

aveugle-né, -e (*mpl* aveugles-nés, *fpl* aveugles-nées) [avœgləne] **1** *adj* blind from birth
2 *nm,f* person blind from birth

aveugler [avœgle] *vt aussi Fig* to blind; **aveuglé par la colère** blind with rage

aveuglette [avœglɛt] **à l'aveuglette** *adv* blindly; **aller à l'a.** to grope one's way

aviateur, -trice [avjatœr, -tris] *nm,f* aviator

aviation [avjasjɔ̃] *nf* (**a**) *(activité)* flying; **faire de l'a.** to go flying (**b**) *(secteur)* aviation; **a. civile/commerciale** civil/commercial aviation; **a. de tourisme** civil aviation (**c**) *Mil* air force

aviculteur, -trice [avikyltœr, -tris] *nm,f (de volailles)* poultry farmer

aviculture [avikyltyr] *nf (de volailles)* poultry farming

avide [avid] *adj* (**a**) *(passionné)* eager (**de** for); **a. de sang** bloodthirsty (**b**) *Péj (cupide)* greedy

avidement [avidmɑ̃] *adv (voracement)* greedily; *(avec passion)* eagerly

avidité [avidite] *nf (voracité, cupidité)* greed; *(passion)* eagerness; **avec a.** *(manger)* greedily; *(écouter, regarder)* eagerly

aviez *voir* avoir

avilir [avilir] **1** *vt (dégrader)* to degrade, to demean **2 s'avilir** *vpr (personne)* to demean oneself

avilissant, -e [avilisɑ̃, -ɑ̃t] *adj* degrading

avilissement [avilismɑ̃] *nm (dégradation)* degradation

aviné, -e [avine] *adj (personne)* inebriated; *(haleine)* reeking of wine

avion [avjɔ̃] *nm* plane, *Br* aeroplane, *Am* airplane; **par a.** *(sur lettre)* airmail; **voyager en a.** to travel by plane or by air; **a. charter** charter plane; **a. de chasse** fighter (plane); **a. gros-porteur** jumbo jet; **a. de ligne** airliner; **a. à réaction** jet (plane); **a. supersonique** supersonic plane; **a. de tourisme** private plane

avion-cargo *(pl* avions-cargos) [avjɔ̃kargo] *nm* freight plane, cargo plane

avions *voir* avoir

aviron [avirɔ̃] *nm* (**a**) *(rame)* oar; *Can* paddle (**b**) *(sport)* l'a. rowing; **faire de l'a.** to row

avironner [avirɔne] *vi Can* to paddle

avis [avi] *nm* (**a**) *(opinion)* opinion; **changer d'a.** to change one's mind; **les a. sont partagés** opinion is divided; **à mon a.** in my opinion; **être de l'a. de qn** to be of the same opinion as sb; **de l'a. de tous...** the general opinion is that...; **être d'a. de faire qch** to be of a mind to do sth; *Prov* **deux a. valent mieux qu'un** two heads are better than one (**b**) *(conseils)* advice (**c**) *(avertissement)* notice; **jusqu'à nouvel a.** until further notice; **sauf a. contraire** unless I/you/etc hear otherwise; **a. de livraison** delivery note; **a. de prélèvement** direct debit advice; **a. de réception** acknowledgement of receipt

avisé, -e [avize] *adj (sage)* sensible, wise; *(acheteur, consommateur)* shrewd; **tu serais bien/mal a. de...** you'd be well-/ill-advised to...

aviser [avize] **1** *vt (a) (informer)* **a. qn de qch** to inform sb of sth; **a. qn que...** to inform sb that... (**b**) *Fam (entrevoir)* to spot **2** *vi (prendre une décision)* to make up one's mind **3 s'aviser** *vpr* (**a**) *(se rendre compte)* **s'a. que** to notice that (**b**) *(oser)* **s'a. de faire qch** to get it into one's head to do sth; **et ne t'avise pas de recommencer!** don't you dare start again!

aviver [avive] *vt (couleurs)* to brighten up; *(passion, querelle, feu)* to stir up; *(appétit)* to sharpen

av. J.-C. *(abrév* avant Jésus-Christ) BC

avocat¹, -e [avɔka, -at] *nm,f* (**a**) *Jur* lawyer; **a. d'affaires** business lawyer; **a. général** assistant public prosecutor *(in a Court of Appeal)* (**b**) *Fig* advocate; **se faire l'a. du diable** to play devil's advocate

avocat² *nm (fruit)* avocado (pear)

avocette [avɔsɛt] *nf* avocet

avoine [avwan] *nf* (**a**) *(céréale)* oats (**b**) *Fam (argent)* dough

avoir¹ [avwar] **1** *v aux* to have; **je ne l'ai pas encore fini** I haven't finished it yet; **je te l'ai dit hier** I told you yesterday; **j'avais déjà vu ce film** I had already seen the film before; **il faut que je l'aie fini pour demain** I have to finish it by tomorrow
2 *vt* (**a**) *(posséder)* to have; **il a une fille** he has or he's got a daughter; **a. les yeux verts** to have green eyes; **a. une drôle de forme** to have a funny shape; **a. un rhume** to have a cold; **a. du diabète** to be diabetic; **a. mal au cœur** to feel sick; **j'ai le nez qui pique** I've got an itchy nose; **a. de l'ambition** to be ambitious; **a. de l'humour** to have a sense of humour; **a. 20 ans** to be 20 (years old); **a. de quoi manger** to have something to eat; **elle a Guy pour voisin** Guy is her neighbour; **qui as-tu comme prof de math?** who's your maths teacher?
(**b**) *(obtenir)* to get; **a. qn au téléphone** to speak to sb on the telephone; **a. son train** to catch one's train; **je l'ai eu pour 50 euros** I bought it for 50 euros; **j'ai eu mon bac en 1995** I passed my "bac" in 1995
(**c**) *(porter) (vêtement)* to wear; *(objet)* to carry
(**d**) *(faire)* **il a eu un sourire étrange** he smiled strangely
(**e**) *(atteindre) (cible)* to hit
(**f**) *Fam (duper) (personne)* to take for a ride, to con; **tu nous a bien eus!** you really had us going!; **se faire a.** to be conned; **se faire a. de 50 euros** to be conned out of 50 euros
(**g**) *(locutions)* **a. faim/froid** to be hungry/cold; **a. quelque chose à faire** to have something to do; **j'ai à faire** I've got things to do; **j'ai à lui parler** I've got to talk to him; **tu n'as qu'à le lui dire** just tell her; **tu en as pour combien de temps?** how long will you be?; **j'en ai pour 10 minutes** I'll be 10 minutes; **je n'en ai pas pour longtemps** I won't be long; **qu'est-ce que tu as?** what's wrong?; **j'ai que je suis fatigué** I'm tired, that's all; **qu'est-ce qu'il a à se plaindre sans arrêt?** why is he complaining all the time?; **on les aura!** we'll have them!
3 *il y a* **v** *impersonnel* there is/are; **il y a un problème** there's a problem; **il y a des problèmes** there are some problems; **il y a six ans** six years ago; **il y a un mois que je suis arrivé** I've been here for a month; **il n'y a qu'à le faire** we'll just have to do it; **il n'y a pas que ça dans la vie** there's more to life than that; **il n'y a pas de quoi!** don't mention it!; **qu'y a-t-il?, qu'est-ce qu'il y a?** what is it?, what's wrong?

avoir² *nm (d'une compagnie)* assets; *(d'un compte)* credit; *(dans un magasin)* voucher

avoisinant, -e [avwazinɑ̃, -ɑ̃t] *adj* neighbouring, nearby

avoisiner [avwazine] *vt* **une somme avoisinant les 500 euros** a sum in the region of 500 euros

avons *voir* avoir

avortement [avɔrtəmɑ̃] *nm* (**a**) *(chez une femme)* **a.** *(provoqué)* abortion; **a. spontané** miscarriage; **a. thérapeutique** termination for medical reasons (**b**) *(chez un animal)* casting (**c**) *Fig (d'un projet)* failure

avorter [avɔrte] **1** *vi* (**a**) *(subir une IVG)* to have an abortion; *(faire une fausse couche)* to miscarry (**b**) *(animal)* to cast (**c**) *Fig (projet)* to fall through
2 *vt (sujet: médecin)* to abort; **se faire a.** to have an abortion

avorteur, -euse [avɔrtœr, -øz] *nm,f* abortionist

avorton [avɔrtɔ̃] *nm Péj* runt

avoué¹ [avwe] *nm Jur Br* ≃ solicitor, *Am* ≃ attorney

avoué², -e *adj* (**a**) *(auteur, partisan)* confessed (**b**) *(but)* declared

avouer [avwe] **1** *vt (faute, crime)* to confess to, to own up to; **il a fini par a.** he finally confessed; **a. que** to admit that; **ceci me surprend, je l'avoue** this surprises me, I must confess; **il faut bien a. que...** it must be admitted that... **2 s'avouer** *vpr* **s'a. coupable** to admit one's guilt; **s'a. vaincu** to acknowledge defeat

avril [avril] *nm* April; **le premier a.** *(jour des farces)* April Fools' Day; *Prov* **en a., ne te découvre pas d'un fil** ne'er cast a clout till May is out; *voir aussi* **janvier**

axe [aks] *nm* (**a**) *(géométrique)* axis; **a. des abscisses/des ordonnées** x-/y-axis; **être dans l'a. de qch** to be in line with sth, **(grand) a.** *(routier)* main road; *Fig* **les grands axes de sa politique** the main thrust of his policy (**b**) *(de machine, de roue de vélo)* axle (**c**) *Hist* **l'A. (Rome-Berlin)** the (Rome-Berlin) Axis

axer [akse] *vt* to centre; **être axé sur** *ou* **autour de** to centre on

axiome [aksjom] *nm* axiom

ayant *etc voir* **avoir**

ayant droit *(pl* **ayants droit)** [εjādrwa] *nm Jur* beneficiary

ayatollah [ajatɔla] *nm* ayatollah

azalée [azale] *nf* azalea

Azerbaïdjan [azɛrbajdʒā] *nm* **l'A.** Azerbaijan

azerbaïdjanais, -e [azɛrbajdʒanɛ, -ɛz] **1** *adj* Azerbaijani **2** *nm,f* **A.** Azerbaijani

azéri, -e [azeri] **1** *adj* Azeri **2** *nm,f* **A.** Azeri

azimuts [azimyt] *nmpl Fam* **une campagne électorale tous a.** an all-out electoral campaign

azote [azɔt] *nm* nitrogen

AZT® [azɛdte] *nm Méd (abrév* **azidothymidine)** AZT

aztèque [aztɛk] **1** *adj* Aztec **2** *nmf* **A.** Aztec

azur [azyr] *nm Litt* (**a**) *(couleur)* azure (**b**) **l'a.** *(ciel)* the sky

azyme [azim] *adj m voir* **pain**

B, b [be] *nm inv* B, b
baba¹ [baba] *nm* b. au rhum rum baba; *Fam* elle l'a dans le b. she's had it
baba² *adj inv Fam* flabbergasted
baba cool (*pl* babas cool) [babakul] *nmf* hippie
Babel [babɛl] *n* la tour de B. the Tower of Babel
babil [babil] *nm (d'un enfant)* prattling; *(des oiseaux)* twittering; *(d'un ruisseau)* babbling
babiller [babije] *vi (enfant)* to prattle; *(oiseau)* to twitter; *(ruisseau)* to babble
babines [babin] *nfpl aussi Hum* chops; **d'avance, je m'en lèche les b.** my mouth's watering in anticipation
babiole [babjɔl] *nf* (a) *(bibelot)* knick-knack, trinket (b) *(broutille)* trifle
bâbord [babɔr] *nm* port (side); **à b.** to port
babouche [babuʃ] *nf* Turkish slipper
babouin [babwɛ̃] *nm* baboon
baboune [babun] *nf Can Fam* **faire la b.** to sulk
baby-boom (*pl* baby-booms) [bebibum] *nm* baby boom
baby-foot [babifut] *nm inv* table football
baby-sitter (*pl* baby-sitters) [bebisitœr] *nmf* baby-sitter
baby-sitting [bebisitiŋ] *nm* baby-sitting; **faire du b.** to baby-sit
bac¹ [bak] *nm* (a) *(bateau)* ferry(-boat) (b) *(récipient)* tank; *(d'imprimeur, de photographe)* tray; *Ordinat* b. d'alimentation sheet feed; **b. à glace** ice tray; **b. à légumes** salad drawer; *Belg* **b. à ordures** *Br* dustbin, *Am* garbage can; **b. de** *ou* **à papier** *(d'imprimante)* paper tray; **b. à sable** sandpit
bac² *Fam* = baccalauréat
baccalauréat [bakalɔrea] *nm* = secondary school examination qualifying for entry to university, *Br* ≃ A levels, *Am* ≃ high school diploma; **b. L** *ou* **littéraire** = arts-based "baccalauréat"; **b. S** *ou* **scientifique** = science-based "baccalauréat"
bacchantes [bakɑ̃t] *nfpl Hum* moustache
bâche [baʃ] *nf (toile)* tarpaulin
bachelier, -ère [baʃəlje, -ɛr] *nm,f* = student who has passed the "baccalauréat"
bâcher [baʃe] *vt* **b. qch** to cover sth with a tarpaulin
bachot [baʃo] *Fam Vieilli* = baccalauréat
bachotage [baʃɔtaʒ] *nm Fam Vieilli* cramming, *Br* swotting
bachoter [baʃɔte] *vi Fam Vieilli* to cram, *Br* to swot
bacille [basil] *nm Biol* bacillus
bâcler [bakle] *vt Fam* to botch
bacon [bekɔn] *nm* bacon

bactérie [bakteri] *nf* bacterium
bactériologique [bakterjɔlɔʒik] *adj* bacteriological; **guerre b.** germ warfare
badaboum [badabum] *exclam Fam* **et b., il est tombé!** he fell down, crash, bang, wallop!
badaud [bado] *nm (promeneur)* stroller; *(curieux)* rubberneck
badge [badʒ] *nm Br* badge, *Am* button
badigeonner [badiʒɔne] *vt* (a) *(surface)* to daub (de with); *(mur)* to whitewash; *Culin* to brush (de with) (b) *(gorge, plaie)* to paint (de with)
badin, -e [badɛ̃, -in] *adj* playful
badinage [badinaʒ] *nm* banter
badine [badin] *nf* switch
badiner [badine] *vi* to jest, to joke; **il ne badine pas avec la ponctualité** he's very strict about punctuality
badinerie [badinri] *nf* jest
badminton [badmintɔn] *nm* badminton
bâdrant, -e [badrɑ̃, -ɑ̃t] *adj Can* bothersome
bâdrer [badre] *vt Can* to bother
baffe [baf] *nf Fam* clout
baffle [bafl] *nm* baffle
bafouer [bafwe] *vt (personne)* to jeer at; *(règlement, autorité)* to flout
bafouiller [bafuje] *vt & vi* to stammer
bâfrer [bafre] *vi très Fam* to stuff oneself
bagage [bagaʒ] *nm* (a) *(sac, valise)* **bagages** luggage, baggage; **faire ses bagages** to pack one's bags; **b. à main** piece of hand luggage (b) *Fig (connaissances)* knowledge (en of)
bagagiste [bagaʒist] *nm* baggage handler
bagarre [bagar] *nf* fight, brawl; **chercher la b.** to look for a fight
bagarrer [bagare] **se bagarrer** *vpr Fam* to fight
bagarreur, -euse [bagarœr, -øz] *Fam* **1** *adj (personne, caractère)* aggressive **2** *nm,f* brawler
bagatelle [bagatɛl] *nf (chose sans importance)* trifle; **pour la b. de 50 euros** for a mere 50 euros
Bagdad [bagdad] *n* Baghdad
bagnard [baɲar] *nm* convict
bagne [baɲ] *nm Hist (prison)* convict prison; *(peine)* penal servitude
bagnole [baɲɔl] *nf Fam* car
bagou(t) [bagu] *nm* glibness; **avoir du b.** to have the gift of the gab

bague [bag] *nf* (a) *(bijou)* ring; *Fig* passer à qn la b. au doigt to marry sb; **b. de fiançailles** engagement ring (**b**) *(d'une boîte de conserve)* ring-pull; *(de cigare)* band (**c**) *(d'oiseau)* ring (**d**) *Tech* bush, ring; **b. de serrage** jubilee clip

baguenauder [bagnode] **1** *vi* to saunter around **2 se baguenauder** *vpr* to saunter around

baguer [bage] *vt (oiseau, arbre)* to ring

baguette [bagɛt] *nf (tige)* stick; *(de chef d'orchestre)* baton; *(pain)* baguette, French loaf; **baguettes** *(pour manger)* chopsticks; **mener** *ou* **faire marcher qn à la b.** to rule sb with a rod of iron; **b. magique** magic wand; **d'un coup de b. magique** with a wave of my/his/*etc* magic wand; **baguettes de tambour** drumsticks

bah [bɑ] *exclam* bah!

Bahamas [baamas] *nfpl* **les B.**, **l'archipel des B.** the Bahamas

Bahreïn [barajn], **Bahrayn** [barɛ̃] *n* Bahrain

bahut [bay] *nm* (**a**) *(coffre)* chest; *(buffet)* sideboard (**b**) *Fam (collège, lycée)* school

bai, -e [bɛ] *adj (cheval)* bay

baie¹ [bɛ] *nf Géog* bay; **la b. d'Hudson** Hudson Bay

baie² *nf* **b. vitrée** picture window

baie³ *nf (fruit)* berry

baignade [bɛɲad] *nf* (**a**) *(activité)* swimming, *Br* bathing; **b. interdite** *(sur panneau)* no swimming (**b**) *(endroit)* swimming *or Br* bathing place

baigner [beɲe] **1** *vt (pieds, œil, blessure)* to bathe; *(bébé, chien) Dr* to bath, *Am* to bathe; *(sujet: mer)* to wash; *(sujet: rivière)* to water; **être baigné de sueur** to be dripping with sweat; **visage baigné de larmes** face streaming with tears; **baigné de lumière** bathed in light **2** *vi (tremper)* to soak, to steep (**dans** in); **les légumes baignent dans la sauce** the vegetables are swimming in sauce; **il haignait dans son sang** he was lying in a pool of his own blood; *Fam* **ça baigne (dans l'huile)!** everything's hunky dory! **3 se baigner** *vpr* (**a**) *(se laver)* to have *or* take a bath (**b**) *(nager)* to have a swim

baigneur, -euse [bɛɲœr, øz] **1** *nmf* swimmer, *Br* bather **2** *nm (poupée)* doll

baignoire [bɛɲwar] *nf* (**a**) *(dans la salle de bains)* bath (**b**) *Th* ground-floor box

Baïkal [bajkal] *n voir* lac

bail [baj] *(pl* **baux** [bo]) *nm* lease; *Fam* **ça fait un b. que je ne l'ai pas vu** I haven't seen him for ages

bâillement [bɑjmɑ̃] *nm* yawn

bâiller [bɑje] *vi (a) (personne)* to yawn; *Fam* **b. à s'en** *ou* **se décrocher la mâchoire** to yawn one's head off (**b**) *(coutures, col)* to gape; *(porte)* to be ajar

bâillon [bɑjɔ̃] *nm* gag; **mettre un b. à qn** to gag sb

bâillonner [bɑjɔne] *vt aussi Fig* to gag

bain [bɛ̃] *nm* (**a**) *(pour se laver)* bath; **prendre un b.** to have *or* take a bath; *Fam Fig* **être/se mettre dans le b.** to be in/get into the swing of things; **b. de bouche** mouthwash; **faire un b. de bouche** to use mouthwash; **b. de boue** mud bath; **prendre un b. de foule** *(personnalité)* to go on a walkabout; **b. moussant** bubble bath; **prendre un b. de pieds** to soak one's feet; **prendre un b. de soleil** to sunbathe; **b. turc** Turkish bath; **b. de vapeur** steam bath (**b**) *(à la piscine)* **petit/grand b.** small/large pool (**c**) *(à la mer, en rivière)* swim, *Br* bathe; *Vieilli* **bains de mer** swimming in the sea (**d**) *Phot* bath (**e**) *Tex* dye

bain-marie [bɛ̃mari] *(pl* **bains-marie** [bɛ̃mari]) *nm* bain-marie *(cooking pan set over second pan of boiling water)*; **faire cuire qch au b.** to cook sth in a bain-marie

baïonnette [bajɔnɛt] *nf* bayonet

baisemain [bɛzmɛ̃] *nm* **faire le b. à qn** to kiss sb's hand

baiser¹ [beze] **1** *vt* (**a**) *Litt (embrasser)* to kiss (**b**) *Vulg (coucher avec)* to fuck (**c**) *Vulg (tromper)* to screw; **se faire b.** to get screwed **2** *vi Vulg* to fuck

baiser² *nm* kiss; **gros baisers** *(dans une lettre)* love and kisses, lots of love

baisse [bɛs] *nf* fall, drop (**de** in); **être en b.** *(température, actions)* to be falling; *(popularité)* to be on the decline

baisser [bese] **1** *vt* (**a**) *(rideau, store, vitre de voiture)* to lower; **b. la tête** to lower one's head; *(de honte, de découragement)* to hang one's head; **b. les yeux** to look down; *Fig* **b. les bras** to give in (**b**) *(lumière, son, chauffage)* to turn down; *(prix)* to lower; **b. la voix** to lower one's voice; **je vous prie de b. le ton!** please keep your voice down! **2** *vi* (**a**) *(diminuer) (température, niveau de l'eau, prix)* to fall; *(marée)* to ebb; **elle a baissé dans mon estime** she's gone down in my estimation (**b**) *(s'affaiblir) (malade)* to get weaker; *(enthousiasme)* to fall off; *(feu)* to burn low; *(vue, mémoire)* to fail; **le jour baisse** night is falling **3 se baisser** *vpr* to bend down; *(pour éviter un coup)* to duck; *Fig* **il n'y a qu'à se b. pour les ramasser** there are loads of them around

baissier [besje] *adj m voir* marché

bajoues [baʒu] *nfpl (d'animal)* chops; *Péj (d'une personne)* flabby cheeks

Bakou [baku] *n* Baku

bal *(pl* **bals**) [bal] *nm (populaire)* dance; *(élégant)* ball; **b. costumé** *ou* **masqué** fancy dress ball; **b. musette** = dance to accordion music; **b. populaire** = dance, usually outdoors, open to the public

balade [balad] *nf Fam (à pied)* walk; *(en voiture)* drive; *(à bicyclette, à moto)* ride; **faire une b.** *(à pied)* to go for a walk; *(en voiture)* to go for a drive; *(à bicyclette, à moto)* to go for a ride

balader [balade] *Fam* **1** *vt (personne, chien)* to take for a walk; *(avoir avec soi) (objet)* to drag around **2** *vi* **envoyer b. qn** to send sb packing **3 se balader** *vpr (à pied)* to go for a walk; *(en voiture)* to go for a drive; *(à bicyclette, à moto)* to go for a ride

baladeur, -euse [baladœr, -øz] **1** *adj Fam* **avoir les mains baladeuses** to have wandering hands **2** *nm* personal stereo, Walkman® **3** *nf* **baladeuse** *(lampe)* inspection lamp

baladin [baladɛ̃] *nm* strolling player

balafre [balafr] *nf* (**a**) *(coupure)* gash (**b**) *(cicatrice)* scar

balafré [balafre] *nm* scarface

balafrer [balafre] *vt* to gash; **visage balafré** scarred face

balai [balɛ] *nm* (**a**) *(de ménage)* broom; **passer le b.** to give the floor a sweep; **donner un coup de b.** *(balayer)* to give the floor a sweep; *Fig (dans une entreprise)* to have a shake-out; **du b.!** clear off!; **b. mécanique** carpet sweeper (**b**) *Aut (d'essuie-glace)* blade (**c**) *(percussion)* brush (**d**) *Fam (an)* **avoir quarante/cinquante balais** to be forty/fifty

balai-brosse *(pl* **balais-brosses**) [balɛbrɔs] *nm* long-handled scrubbing brush

balaise [balɛz] = **balèze**

balalaïka [balalaika] *nf* balalaika

balance [balɑ̃s] *nf* (**a**) *(appareil)* (pair of) scales; *(publique)* weighing machine; *Fig* **ce facteur pèse dans la b.** this factor carries some weight; **faire pencher la b.** to tip the scales (**b**) *Astron & Astrol* **la B.** Libra; **être B.** to be a Libran (**c**) *Écon* balance; **b. commerciale** balance of trade; **b. des paiements** balance of payments (**d**) *Fam (mouchard)* squealer

balancé, -e [balɑ̃se] *adj Fam* **être bien b.** *(personne)* to have a good figure

balancelle [balɑ̃sɛl] *nf (de jardin) Br* swing hammock, *Am* glider

balancement [balɑ̃smɑ̃] *nm* swaying

balancer [16] [balɑ̃se] **1** *vt* **(a)** *(bras, jambes, trompe, pendule)* to swing; *(hanches)* to sway **(b)** *Fam (projectile, objet)* to chuck, to throw; **b. des vannes/remarques (c)** *Com (compte)* to make snide/unpleasant remarks **(c)** *Com (compte)* to balance **(d)** *Fam (se débarrasser de) (objet)* to chuck *or* throw out; **b. qn** to dump sb; **elle a tout balancé** *(tout abandonné)* she's given it all up **(e)** *Fam (dénoncer)* to squeal on
2 *vi Litt (hésiter)* to waver
3 se balancer *vpr* **(a)** *(arbres, blés)* to sway; **se b. sur sa chaise** to rock backwards and forwards on one's chair; **se b. d'un pied sur l'autre** to rock from one foot to the other **(b)** *(sur une balançoire)* to swing **(c)** *très Fam* **je m'en balance!** I don't give a damn! **(d)** *Fam* **il s'est balancé du haut de la tour Eiffel** he chucked himself off the top of the Eiffel Tower

balancier [balɑ̃sje] *nm* **(a)** *(d'un funambule)* balancing pole **(b)** *(d'horloge)* pendulum

balançoire [balɑ̃swar] *nf (suspendue)* swing; *(bascule)* seesaw

balayage [balɛjaʒ] *nm* **(a)** *(pour nettoyer)* sweeping **(b)** *Rad, Él & TV* scanning

balayer [53] [balɛje] *vt* **(a)** *(nettoyer)* to sweep; *(saletés)* to sweep up; *Fig (objections, obstacles)* to brush aside; **le vent a balayé les nuages** the wind has swept the clouds away; *Fig* **b. devant sa porte** to put one's own house in order **(b)** *Rad, Él & TV* to scan; *(sujet: projecteurs)* to sweep

balayette [balɛjɛt] *nf* small brush

balayeur, -euse [balɛjœr, -øz] **1** *nm,f* road-sweeper
2 *nf* **balayeuse** *Can (aspirateur)* vacuum cleaner

balbutiement [balbysimɑ̃] *nm* **(a)** *(en parlant)* stammering **(b)** **balbutiements** *(d'une science, d'une discipline)* early stages

balbutier [66] [balbysje] **1** *vi* to stammer
2 *vt* to stammer (out)

balcon [balkɔ̃] *nm* **(a)** *(d'édifice)* balcony **(b)** *(dans un théâtre)* circle; **premier/deuxième b.** dress/upper circle

baldaquin [baldakɛ̃] *nm* canopy

Bâle [bɑl] *n* Basel

Baléares [balear] *nfpl* **les (îles) B.** the Balearic Islands

baleine [balɛn] *nf* **(a)** *(animal)* whale; **b. blanche/bleue** white/blue whale **(b)** *(d'un parapluie)* rib; *(d'un corset)* (whale)bone

baleineau, -x [balɛno] *nm* whale calf

baleinière [balɛnjer] *nf* whaleboat

balèze [balɛz] *adj Fam (grand et fort)* hefty; *(intelligent)* brainy; **b. en maths** brilliant at maths

balisage [balizaʒ] *nm* **(a)** *(signaux) Naut & Rad* beacons; *Av* lights **(b)** *(action) Naut & Rad* beaconing; *Av* lighting

balise [baliz] *nf Naut & Rad* beacon; *Av* light; *(de piste de ski, d'épave)* marker; *Ordinat* tag; *Naut* **b. flottante** buoy; *Rad* **b. radar** radar beacon

baliser [balize] *vt (chenal)* to beacon; *(aéroport)* to equip with lights; *(route)* to mark out with beacons; *(piste de ski)* to mark out

balistique [balistik] **1** *adj (missile)* ballistic
2 *nf* ballistics *(singulier)*

balivernes [balivern] *nfpl* nonsense

balkanisation [balkanizasjɔ̃] *nf aussi Fig* Balkanization

Balkans [balkɑ̃] *nmpl* **les B.** the Balkans

ballade [balad] *nf* ballad

ballant, -e [balɑ̃, -ɑ̃t] *adj (bras, jambes)* dangling

ballast [balast] *nm* **(a)** *Constr (d'une route, d'une voie ferrée)* ballast **(b)** *Naut* ballast tank

balle¹ [bal] *nf* **(a)** *(pour jouer)* ball; **jouer à la b.** to play ball; *Fig* **prendre** *ou* **saisir la b. au bond** to seize the opportunity; *Fig* **se renvoyer la b.** to pass the buck; *Fig* **la b. est dans votre camp** the ball's in your court; **b. de golf/de tennis** golf/tennis ball; **b. de break/de match break/match point (b)** *(d'arme)* bullet; **b. à blanc** blank; **b. perdue** stray bullet **(c)** *Fam* **balles** *(francs)* francs

balle² *nf (de coton, de laine)* bale

balle³ *nf (de blé)* husk

ballerine [balrin] *nf* **(a)** *(danseuse)* ballerina **(b)** *(chaussure)* pump

ballet [balɛ] *nm* ballet

ballon [balɔ̃] *nm* **(a)** *(aéronef)* balloon; **b. d'essai** pilot balloon **(b)** *(balle)* ball; **jouer au b.** to play with a ball; **b. de football** football; **le b. ovale** rugby; **le b. rond** *Br* football, *Am* soccer ball **(c)** *(pour boire)* **(verre) b.** round wine glass **(d)** **b. (de baudruche)** balloon; **souffler dans le b.** *(d'Alcotest®)* to blow into the bag; **b. d'oxygène** oxygen bottle

ballonné, -e [balɔne] *adj (ventre, personne)* bloated

ballon-sonde *(pl* **ballons-sondes)** [balɔ̃sɔ̃d] *nm Météo* sounding balloon

ballot [balo] *nm (a) (paquet)* bundle **(b)** *Fam (imbécile)* twit

ballottage [balɔtaʒ] *nm Pol* **il y a b.** there will be a second ballot

ballottement [balɔtmɑ̃] *nm (de train)* rocking; *(des passagers)* shaking; *(de navire)* tossing

ballotter [balɔte] **1** *vt (bateau)* to toss about; *(passagers)* to shake about; *Fig* **un enfant ballotté entre son père et sa mère** a child passed backwards and forwards between its father and mother
2 *vi (bagages, bateau)* to be tossed about; *(poitrine)* to bounce up and down

ball-trap [baltrap] *nm (sport)* clay-pigeon shooting

balluchon [balyʃɔ̃] *nm Fam (de vêtements)* bundle; **faire son b.** to pack one's bags

balnéaire [balneɛr] *adj voir* **station**

balourd, -e [balur, -urd] **1** *adj (personne)* oafish
2 *nm,f* clumsy oaf

balsa [balza] *nm* balsawood

balte [balt] **1** *adj* Baltic; **les pays Baltes** the Baltic states
2 *nmf* Balt

Baltique [baltik] *nf* **la (mer) B.** the Baltic (Sea)

baluchon [balyʃɔ̃] = **balluchon**

balustrade [balystrad] *nf* **(a)** *Archit* balustrade **(b)** *(clôture)* railing

bambin [bɑ̃bɛ̃] *nm Fam* toddler

bambou [bɑ̃bu] *nm (plante)* bamboo; *Fam* **c'est le coup de b.!** it's a rip-off!

bamboula [bɑ̃bula] *nf Fam* spree; **faire la b.** to live it up

ban [bɑ̃] *nm* **(a)** *(applaudissements)* round of applause **(b)** *bans (de mariage)* banns **(c)** **être au b. de la société** to be an outcast from society; **le b. et l'arrière-b.** *(tout le monde)* the world and his wife

banal, -e, -als, -ales [banal] *adj (objet, gens, occupation)* ordinary; *(idée, remarque, style)* trite, banal; *(accident, exemple)* common; **pas b.** unusual

banalisation [banalizasjɔ̃] *nf* **la b. de qch** the way sth is becoming more common

banaliser [banalize] **1** *vt (rendre commun)* to trivialize; **véhicule banalisé** unmarked police car
2 se banaliser *vpr* to become commonplace

banalité [banalite] *nf* **(a)** *(d'un objet, de gens, d'une occupation)* ordinariness; *(d'une idée, d'une remarque, d'un style)* triteness, banality; *(d'un accident, d'un exemple)* commonness **(b)** **banalités** platitudes

banane [banan] *nf* **(a)** *(fruit)* banana **(b)** *(coiffure)* quiff **(c)** *(petit sac) Br* bum bag, *Am* fanny pack

bananier, -ère [bananje, -ɛr] **1** *adj (plantation, production)* banana **2** *nm (arbre)* banana tree

banc [bã] *nm* **(a)** *(siège)* bench; **ils se sont connus sur les bancs de l'école** they got to know each other at school; **b. des accusés** dock; **b. d'église** pew; **b. des témoins** *Br* witness box, *Am* witness stand **(b)** *(de roche)* layer; *Can* **b. de neige** snowbank; **b. de sable** sandbank **(c)** *(de poissons)* shoal; **b. d'huîtres** oyster bed **(d)** *(établi)* (work)bench **(e)** **b. d'essai** *Ind* test bed; *Ordinat* benchtest; *Fig* testing ground; *Ordinat* **b. de mémoire** memory bank

bancaire [bãkɛr] *adj (opération)* banking; *(chèque, compte)* bank

bancal, -e, -als, -ales [bãkal] *adj (meuble)* wobbly; *Fig (raisonnement, projet)* unsound

bandage [bãdaʒ] *nm (pansement)* bandage; *(action)* bandaging

bandana [bãdana] *nm* bandana

bande¹ [bãd] *nf* **(a)** *(de tissu, de papier, de terre)* strip; *(motif)* stripe; **b. dessinée** comic strip **(b)** *(pansement)* bandage; **b. Velpeau®** crêpe bandage **(c)** *(magnétique)* tape; *(pellicule)* film; *Ordinat* **b. en cassettes** cassette tape; *Ordinat* **b. de défilement** scroll bar; *Ordinat* **b. de données** data tape; **b. originale** *(d'un film)* original soundtrack; **b. sonore** soundtrack **(d)** *Aut* **b. d'arrêt d'urgence** *Br* hard shoulder, *Am* shoulder; **b. médiane** *(sur la route)* central line; **b. de roulement** *(de pneu)* tread **(e)** *Rad* band **(f)** *(d'une mitrailleuse)* cartridge belt **(g)** *Naut* **donner de la b.** to list

bande² *nf (de personnes)* band, group; *(de voleurs)* gang, band; **faire b. à part** *(agir seul)* to do one's own thing; **viens avec nous, ne fais pas b. à part** come with us, don't stay all on your own; **faire qch en b.** to do sth in a group; **une b. d'incapables/d'imbéciles** a bunch of incompetents/idiots

bande-annonce *(pl* **bandes-annonces)** [bãdanɔs] *nf* trailer *(de* for)

bandeau, -x [bãdo] *nm* **(a)** *(pour les cheveux)* headband **(b)** *(sur les yeux)* blindfold; **mettre un b. à qn** to blindfold sb

bandelette [bãdlɛt] *nf (de tissu)* strip; **bandelettes** *(de momie)* bandages

bander [bãde] **1** *vt* **(a)** *(blessure, main)* to bandage; **b. les yeux à qn** to blindfold sb **(b)** *(ressort)* to tighten; *(arc)* to bend; *(muscles)* to flex **2** *vi Vulg* to have a hard-on

banderille [bãdrij] *nf* banderilla

banderole [bãdrɔl] *nf* banner

bande-son *(pl* **bandes-son)** [bãdsɔ̃] *nf* soundtrack

bandit [bãdi] *nm (escroc)* crook; *Vieilli (brigand)* bandit; **b. de grand chemin** highwayman

banditisme [bãditism] *nm* crime; **le grand b.** organized crime

bandoulière [bãduljɛr] *nf (d'un sac)* shoulder strap; **en b.** over one's shoulder

bang [bãg] *nm inv Av* sonic boom

Bangkok [bãkɔk] *n* Bangkok

Bangladesh [bãgladɛʃ, bɛ̃gladɛʃ] *nm* **le B.** Bangladesh

banjo [bãdʒo] *nm* banjo

banlieue [bãljø] *nf* suburbs; **la b. parisienne/lyonnaise** the suburbs of Paris/Lyons; **la grande/proche b.** the outer/inner suburbs; **vivre en b.** to live in the suburbs; **de b.** suburban

banlieusard, -e [bãljøzar, -ard] *nm,f* suburbanite

bannière [banjɛr] *nf* banner; **la b. étoilée** the Star-spangled Banner

bannir [banir] *vt (personne, idée)* to banish *(de* from); *(sujet de conversation)* to ban *(de* from); **vous devez b. le sucre de votre alimentation** you must exclude sugar from your diet

bannissement [banismã] *nm* banishment

banque [bãk] *nf* **(a)** *(établissement)* bank; **la b.** *(activité)* banking; **employé/directeur de b.** bank clerk/manager; **b. d'affaires** *Br* merchant bank, *Am* investment bank; **b. centrale** central bank; **la B. de France** the Bank of France; **la B. mondiale** the World Bank **(b)** *(au jeu)* bank; **faire sauter la b.** to break the bank **(c)** *Ordinat* **b. de données** data bank; *Méd* **b. d'organes/du sperme** organ/sperm bank

banquer [bãke] *vi Fam* to cough up

banqueroute [bãkrut] *nf Jur* bankruptcy; **faire b.** to go bankrupt

banquet [bãkɛ] *nm* banquet

banquette [bãkɛt] *nf (siège)* seat; **la b. arrière** *(d'une voiture)* the back seat

banquier, -ère [bãkje, -ɛr] *nm,f* banker

banquise [bãkiz] *nf* ice floe

bantou, -e [bãtu] **1** *adj* Bantu **2** *nm,f* Bantu

baobab [baɔbab] *nm* baobab (tree)

baptême [batɛm] *nm* **(a)** *Rel* baptism, christening; **donner le b. à qn** to baptize *or* christen sb **(b)** *(d'un navire)* christening; *(d'une cloche)* blessing **(c)** **b. de l'air** first flight; **b. du feu** baptism of fire

baptiser [batize] *vt* **(a)** *Rel* to baptize, to christen **(b)** *(nommer)* to name; *(surnommer)* to christen **(c)** *(navire)* to name; *(cloche)* to bless

baptismal, -e, -aux, -aux [batismal, -o] *adj* baptismal

baptistère [batistɛr] *nm Rel* baptistry

baquet [bakɛ] *nm (cuve)* tub

bar¹ [bar] *nm (café, comptoir)* bar

bar² *nm (poisson)* bass

bar³ *nm Phys* bar

barachois [baraʃwa] *nm Can (dans une rivière)* sandbar

baragouiner [baragwine] *Fam* **1** *vt (langue étrangère)* to speak badly; **qu'est-ce qu'il baragouine?** what's he jabbering on about? **2** *vi (dans une langue étrangère)* to jabber away; *(de façon incompréhensible)* to jabber (on)

baraque [barak] *nf* **(a)** *(cabane)* hut, shack; *(de forain)* stall, stand **(b)** *Fam (maison)* place

baraqué, -e [barake] *adj Fam* hefty

baraquement [barakmã] *nm* shacks; *Mil* camp

baratin [baratɛ̃] *nm Fam* **(a)** *(d'un vendeur)* sales talk, patter; *(d'un séducteur)* smooth talk **(b)** *(verbiage)* waffle

baratiner [baratine] *Fam* **1** *vt (sujet: vendeur)* to give the sales talk to; *(sujet: séducteur) Br* to chat up, *Am* to hit on **2** *vi* to waffle

baratineur, -euse [baratinœr, -øz] *nm,f Fam* smooth talker

baratte [barat] *nf* churn

Barbade [barbad] *nf* **la B.** Barbados

barbant, -e [barbã, -ãt] *adj Fam* boring

barbare [barbar] **1** *adj (cruel, sauvage)* barbaric **2** *nmf* barbarian

barbarie [barbari] *nf* (a) *(cruauté)* barbarity (b) *(manque de civilisation)* barbarism
barbarisme [barbarism] *nm* barbarism
barbe [barb] *nf* (a) *(d'homme)* beard; **b. de trois jours** stubble; *Fig* **à la b.** de qn right under sb's nose; **parler dans sa b.** to mutter, to mumble; **rire dans sa b.** to laugh up one's sleeve; *Fam* **quelle b.!** what a drag!; **b. à papa** *Br* candy floss, *Am* cotton candy (b) *(de chèvre, d'épi)* beard; *(de plume, d'hameçon)* barb (c) *Tech (de métal)* burr; *(de papier)* ragged edge
barbecue [barbəkju] *nm* barbecue; **faire un b.** to have a barbecue
barbelé [barbəle] **1** *adj m voir* **fil**
2 *nmpl* **barbelés** barbed wire
barber [barbe] *Fam* **1** *vt* **b.** qn to bore sb stiff
2 se barber *vpr* to be bored stiff
barbiche [barbiʃ] *nf* goatee (beard)
barbichette [barbiʃɛt] *nf Fam* small goatee (beard)
barbier [barbje] *nm* (a) *Vieilli* barber (b) *Can (coiffeur pour hommes)* (men's) hairdresser
barbiturique [barbityrik] *nm* barbiturate
barboter [barbɔte] **1** *vi* to splash about
2 *vt Fam (voler)* to pinch
barboteuse [barbɔtøz] *nf* romper-suit
barbouiller [barbuje] *vt* (a) *(salir)* to smear (**de** with); *(peindre)* to daub (b) *Fam* **b. l'estomac** *ou* **le cœur à qn** to make sb feel queasy; **se sentir barbouillé** to feel queasy
barbouze [barbuz] *nf Fam (agent secret)* secret agent
barbu, -e [barby] **1** *adj* bearded
2 *nm* bearded man
Barcelone [barsəlɔn] *n* Barcelona
barda [barda] *nm Fam* gear; *Mil* kit
barde¹ [bard] *nf Culin (sur un rôti)* bard
barde² *nm* bard
barder¹ [barde] *v impersonnel Fam* **ça va b.!** there's going to be trouble!
barder² *vt* (a) *Culin* to bard (b) **bardé de fer/cuir** steel-/leather-clad; **être bardé de décorations** to be covered with decorations; **être bardé de diplômes** to have a whole string of qualifications
barème [barɛm] *nm* (a) *(de notes, de salaires, de prix)* scale (b) *(pour calcul rapide)* ready reckoner
barge [barʒ] *nf (péniche)* barge
baril [baril] *nm (de vin, de pétrole)* barrel; *(de poudre)* keg; *(de lessive)* drum
barillet [barijɛ] *nm (de revolver)* cylinder
bariolé, -e [barjɔle] *adj* multicoloured
barjo(t) [barʒo] *adj Fam* nutty
barman [barman] *(pl* **barmans** *ou* **barmen** [barmɛn]) *nm Br* barman, *Am* bartender
baromètre [barɔmɛtr] *nm aussi Fig* barometer
baron [barɔ̃] *nm (seigneur)* baron; *Fig* **les barons de la finance/de l'industrie** financial/industrial tycoons
baronne [barɔn] *nf* baroness
baroque [barɔk] **1** *adj (architecture, art, musique)* baroque; *(idées)* bizarre, odd
2 *nm* **le b.** the Baroque
baroud [barud] *nm* **b. d'honneur** last stand
barouder [barude] *vi Fam (voyager)* to knock about
baroudeur [barudœr] *nm Fam* (a) *(combattant)* fighter (b) *(voyageur)* keen traveller
barouf(le) [baruf(l)] *nm Fam* din, row
barque [bark] *nf* boat; *Fig* **bien mener** *ou* **bien conduire**

sa b. to manage one's affairs well; *Fig* **c'est elle qui mène la b.** she's the boss
barquette [barkɛt] *nf* (a) *(pour plat à emporter)* container; *(de fruits)* punnet (b) *(gâteau)* pastry boat
barrage [baraʒ] *nm (sur l'eau)* dam; **b. de police** police roadblock; **b. routier** roadblock
barre [bar] *nf* (a) *(de métal)* bar, rod; *(de bois)* rod; **b. d'appui** *(d'une fenêtre)* rail; **b. de chocolat** bar of chocolate; **b. à mine** = metal bar used for breaking stone surfaces (b) *(pour la danse)* barre; *Sp* **barres asymétriques** asymmetric bars; **b. fixe** horizontal bar; **barres parallèles** parallel bars; **b. transversale** *(de but)* crossbar; *Fig* **placer la b. trop haut** to set too high a standard (c) *(trait)* line, stroke; *(d'un t)* cross; **b. oblique** oblique, slash; *Mus* **b. de mesure** bar (line) (d) *Naut (à l'arrière)* tiller; *(volant)* helm; *aussi Fig* **être à** *ou* **tenir la b.** to be at the helm (e) *Jur (de tribunal)* bar; **b. des témoins** *Br* witness box, *Am* witness stand; **être appelé à la b.** to be called to the witness box (f) *(de clavier)* **b. d'espacement** space bar (g) *Ordinat* **b. d'outils** tool bar; **b. de sélection** menu bar; **b. de titre** title bar
barreau, -x [baro] *nm* (a) *(d'une fenêtre, d'une cage)* bar; *(d'une échelle, d'une chaise)* rung; *Fig* **b. de chaise** fat cigar; **être derrière les barreaux** to be behind bars (b) *Jur* **le b.** the bar
barrer [bare] **1** *vt* (a) *(route, passage, chemin)* to block off; *(porte, fenêtre)* to bar; *Can (fermer à clef)* to lock; **route barrée** *(sur panneau)* road closed; **le b. le passage** *ou* **la route à qn** to bar sb's way (b) *(chèque)* to cross (c) *(mot, paragraphe)* to cross out (d) *Naut (bateau)* to steer; *(à l'aviron)* to cox (e) *Fam* **on est mal barrés** things don't look good
2 se barrer *vpr Fam* to clear off, to beat it
barrette [barɛt] *nf* (a) *(pour les cheveux) Br* (hair) slide, *Am* barrette (b) *(broche)* brooch (c) *Ordinat* **b. de mémoire vive** RAM module
barreur [barœr] *nm Naut* helmsman; *(à l'aviron)* cox
barricade [barikad] *nf* barricade
barricader [barikade] **1** *vt (rue, porte)* to barricade
2 se barricader *vpr* to barricade oneself in
barrière [barjɛr] *nf (obstacle)* barrier; *(clôture)* fence; *(d'un passage à niveau)* gate; *Aut* **b. de dégel** = ban on the use of a road by heavy traffic during a thaw; *Com* **barrières douanières** trade barriers; **la Grande B. de Corail** the Great Barrier Reef
barrique [barik] *nf* barrel; *Fam Fig* **plein** *ou* **rond comme une b.** blind drunk
barrir [barir] *vi (éléphant)* to trumpet
barrissements [barismɑ̃] *nmpl (d'un éléphant)* trumpeting
bar-tabac *(pl* **bars-tabacs)** [bartaba] *nm* = bar that also sells cigarettes and tobacco
baryton [baritɔ̃] *nm Mus* baritone
baryum [barjɔm] *nm Chim* barium
bas¹ [bɑ], **basse** [bɑs] **1** *adj* (a) *(dans l'espace, en quantité, en intensité)* low; *(marée)* low; **à b. prix** cheaply; **avoir la vue basse** to be short-sighted (b) *(dans une hiérarchie)* low; *Péj ou Hum* **le b. peuple** the hoi polloi; **les b. quartiers** the poor districts (c) *(note)* low; *(instrument de musique)* bass (d) *(dans le temps)* late; **le b. Moyen Âge** the late Middle Ages (e) *Péj (acte)* mean, low; *(besognes)* menial
2 *adv* (a) *(dans l'espace)* low (down); **voir plus b.** *(dans un article)* see below; *Fig* **mettre qn plus b. que terre** to treat

sb like dirt; **tomber b.** *(température, prix d'une action)* to plummet; *Fam* **b. les mains** *ou* **les pattes!** hands off!, keep your paws off!

(b) *(dans une hiérarchie)* low **(c)** *(parler)* quietly; *(chanter)* *(dans le registre)* low; *(doucement)* softly; **rire tout b.** to chuckle to oneself **(d) en b.** at the bottom; *(à l'étage inférieur)* downstairs; **les gens d'en b.** the people below *or* downstairs; **la tête en b.** upside down; **en b. de** at the bottom of **(e) à b. la dictature/la police!** down with dictatorship/ the police! **3** *nm (partie inférieure)* bottom; **l'étagère du b.** the bottom shelf; **le b. du dos** the small of the back; **au b. de** at the bottom of; **de b. en haut** upwards **4** *nf* **basse** *Mus* **(a)** *(partie)* bass part; *(voix, chanteur)* bass **(b)** *(contrebasse)* (double) bass; *(guitare)* bass (guitar)

bas² *nm (vêtement)* stocking; **b. de contention** elastic stocking; *Fig* **b. de laine** nest egg; **b. nylon** nylons; **b. résille** fishnet stocking; **b. à varices** support stocking

basalte [bazalt] *nm* basalt

basané, -e [bazane] *adj (bronzé)* tanned; *(tanné)* weatherbeaten; *(naturellement)* swarthy

bas-côté *(pl* **bas-côtés)** [bakote] *nm* **(a)** *(d'une route)* verge **(b)** *(d'une église)* (side) aisle

basculant, -e [baskylɑ̃, -ɑ̃t] *adj* **benne basculante** *(de camion)* tipping body; **pont b.** drawbridge

bascule [baskyl] *nf* **(a)** *(balançoire)* seesaw **(b)** *(balance)* weighing machine

basculer [baskyle] **1** *vt* **(a)** *(brouette, charrette)* to tip up; *(chargement)* to tip over **(b)** *Ordinat* to toggle **2** *vi* **(a)** *(tomber)* to topple over; **faire b.** *(personne)* to knock over; *(chargement)* to tip over; **le pays a basculé dans l'anarchie** the country tipped over into anarchy **(b)** *Ordinat* to toggle

base [baz] *nf* **(a)** *(partie inférieure)* base; *Fig (d'un syndicat, d'un parti politique)* rank and file; **b. de maquillage** foundation, base **(b)** *Mil (d'opérations)* base; **b. aérienne/ navale** air/naval base, **b. de lancement** launch site **(c)** *(principe)* basis; **jeter** *ou* **poser les bases de qch** to lay the foundations for sth; **de b.** basic; **denrées de b.** staple commodities; **à b. d'amidon/de gin** starch-/gin-based **(d)** *Math & Chim* base **(e)** *Ordinat* **b. de données** database

base-ball [bɛzbol] *nm* baseball

baser [baze] **1** *vt* to base; **être basé sur qch** to be based on sth **2 se baser** *vpr* **se b. sur qch** *(sujet: personne)* to base one's argument on sth; **sur quoi te bases-tu pour dire que…?** what basis do you have for saying that…?

bas-fond *(pl* **bas-fonds)** [bafɔ̃] *nm (dans la mer, la rivière)* shallow; **les bas-fonds** *(d'une ville)* the rough areas

basic [bazik] *nm Ordinat* BASIC

basilic [bazilik] *nm (plante)* basil

basilique [bazilik] *nf* basilica

basket [basket] **1** *nm ou nf (chaussure)* baseball boot **2** *nm (sport)* basketball

basket-ball [basketbol] *nm* basketball

basketteur, -euse [basketœr, -øz] *nm,f* basketball player

basque¹ [bask] **1** *adj* Basque **2** *nmf* **B.** Basque **3** *nm (langue)* Basque

basque² *nf (d'une veste)* tail; *Fig* **être toujours pendu aux basques de qn** to be always at sb's heels

bas-relief *(pl* **bas-reliefs)** [barəljɛf] *nm* bas-relief

basse [bas] *voir* **bas¹**

basse-cour *(pl* **basses-cours)** [baskur] *nf* **(a)** *(cour)* farmyard **(b)** *(volaille)* poultry

bassement [basmɑ̃] *adv* **être b. intéressé** to have one's own interests at heart

bassesse [bases] *nf* **(a)** *(d'une action, d'un caractère)* lowness **(b)** *(action)* low act

basset [base] *nm (chien)* basset (hound)

bassin [basɛ̃] *nm* **(a)** *(récipient)* basin, bowl; **b. (hygiénique)** bedpan **(b)** *(dans un jardin)* ornamental lake; *(de fontaine)* basin; *(réservoir)* tank; **petit b.** *(de la piscine)* children's pool; **grand b.** *(de la piscine)* large pool **(c)** *(d'un port)* dock, basin **(d)** *Géol* basin; **b. houiller** coal basin; **b. minier** mining area; **le B. parisien** the Paris Basin **(e)** *(partie du corps)* pelvis

bassine [basin] *nf* **(a)** *(en plastique)* basin, bowl; *(contenu)* basinful, bowlful **(b)** *(en cuivre)* pan; *(contenu)* panful

bassiner [basine] *vt Fam (ennuyer)* to bore stiff

bassiste [basist] *nmf (contrebassiste)* double bass player; *(guitariste)* bass guitarist

basson [basɔ̃] *nm (instrument)* bassoon **(b)** *(joueur)* bassoonist

basta [basta] *exclam Fam* that'll do!

bastide [bastid] *nf* **(a)** *(maison)* country house, *(ferme)* farm **(b)** *Hist (ville fortifiée)* fortified town

bastille [bastij] *nf* fortress, *Hist* **la B.** the Bastille; **la prise de la B.** the storming of the Bastille

bastingage [bastɛ̃gaʒ] *nm Naut (garde-corps)* rail

bastion [bastjɔ̃] *nm aussi Fig* bastion

baston [bastɔ̃] *nm ou nf Fam* punch-up

bastringue [bastrɛ̃g] *nm Fam* **(a)** *(dancing)* (seedy) dance hall **(b)** *(affaires)* gear, stuff; **et tout le b.** and the whole caboodle

bas-ventre *(pl* **bas-ventres)** [bavɑ̃tr] *nm* lower abdomen

bât [ba] *nm* packsaddle; *Fig* **c'est là que le b. blesse** there's the rub

bataclan [bataklɑ̃] *nm Fam (affaires)* stuff, gear; **et tout le b.** and the whole caboodle

bataille [bataj] *nf* **(a)** *(lutte)* battle, fight; *(électorale)* contest; **b. terrestre/aérienne/navale** land/air/naval battle; **cheveux en b.** dishevelled hair **(b)** *(jeu de cartes)* beggar-my-neighbour

batailler [bataje] *vi Fam* **b. pour faire qch** to battle to do sth

batailleur, -euse [batajœr, -øz] *adj* aggressive

bataillon [batajɔ̃] *nm Mil* battalion; *Fam* **b. de** a troop of

bâtard, -e [batar, -ard] **1** *adj (enfant)* illegitimate; *Péj (style, solution)* hybrid **2** *nm,f (enfant)* illegitimate child; *Péj* bastard **3** *nm (chien)* mongrel; *(pain)* = small French stick

batavia [batavja] *nf* batavia lettuce

bateau, -x [bato] **1** *nm* **(a)** *(embarcation)* boat; **b.** to go boating; **prendre le b.** to go/come by boat; **en** *ou* **par b.** by boat; *Fam Fig* **mener qn en b.** to take sb for a ride; **monter un b. à qn** to wind sb up; **b. à moteur** motorboat; **b. de pêche** fishing boat; **b. de plaisance** pleasure boat; **b. à vapeur** steamboat, steamer; **b. à voiles** *Br* sailing boat, *Am* sailboat [bato] *(sur le trottoir)* driveway entrance **(c)** **encolure b.** boat neck **2** *adj inv Fam (banal)* hackneyed

bateau-mouche *(pl* **bateaux-mouches)** [batomuʃ] *nm* river boat *(on the Seine)*

bateleur, -euse [batlœr, -øz] *nm,f Vieilli (jongleur)* juggler; *(acrobate)* acrobat

batelier, -ère [batəlje, -ɛr] *nm,f* boatman,f boatwoman; *(sur un bac)* ferryman,f ferrywoman

bat-flanc [baflɑ̃] *nm inv (dans un dortoir, une prison)* wooden partition

bâti, -e [bɑti] **1** *adj (personne)* être bien b. to be well-built; être mal b. to have an odd shape

2 *nm* (**a**) *Constr* frame, framework (**b**) *(en couture)* tacking, basting

batifoler [batifole] *vi Fam* to lark about

batik [batik] *nm* batik

bâtiment [bɑtimɑ̃] *nm* (**a**) *(immeuble)* building; b. d'habitation residential building (**b**) *(secteur)* le b. building; être dans le b. to be in the building trade (**c**) *Naut* ship; b. de guerre warship, battleship

bâtir [bɑtir] **1** *vt* (**a**) *(maison, ville)* to build; *Fig (fortune, hypothèse)* to build (up); (**se**) faire b. une maison to have a house built; terrain bâti developed *or* built-up site (**b**) *(en couture)* to tack, to baste

2 se bâtir *vpr* se b. une réputation (de) to build up a reputation (as)

bâtisse [bɑtis] *nf* ugly building

batiste [batist] *nf* batiste

bâton [bɑtɔ̃] *nm* (**a**) *(en bois, de colle, de craie)* stick; *(d'agent de police) Br* truncheon, *Am* nightstick; *(de majorette)* baton; mener une vie de b. de chaise to lead a wild life; mettre des bâtons dans les roues à qn to put a spoke in sb's wheel; parler à bâtons rompus to talk about this and that; conversation à bâtons rompus casual conversation; b. de rouge à lèvres lipstick; bâtons de ski ski sticks *or* poles (**b**) *(trait vertical)* vertical line

bâtonnet [bɑtɔnɛ] *nm* stick

batracien [batrasjɛ̃] *nm Zool* amphibian

battage [bataʒ] *nm* (**a**) *Fam (publicité)* hype; faire du b. autour de qch to hype sth up (**b**) *(du blé)* threshing

battant, -e [batɑ̃, -ɑ̃t] **1** *adj (pluie)* lashing; le cœur b. with a pounding heart

2 *nm,f (personne combative)* fighter

3 *nm* (**a**) *(d'une cloche)* clapper, tongue (**b**) *(d'une porte, d'un volet)* leaf; porte à double b. double door

batte [bat] *nf* bat; b. de base-ball baseball bat

battement [batmɑ̃] *nm* (**a**) *(de tambour)* beat, beating; *(de mains)* clapping; *(d'ailes, de voiles)* flapping; *(de porte)* banging; j'entendais les battements de son cœur I could hear his heart beating (**b**) *(entre deux événements)* gap; deux heures de b. a two-hour gap

batterie [batri] *nf* (**a**) *(dans un orchestre)* drums; être à la b. to be on drums (**b**) *Mil* battery; *Fig* dévoiler ses batteries to show one's hand; b. antiaérienne/antichars anti-aircraft/antitank battery (**c**) *(ensemble, groupe)* battery; *(de tests, de questions)* series; élevage en b. battery farming; poulet de b. battery chicken; b. de cuisine kitchen utensils (**d**) *Él* battery; fonctionner sur b. to be battery-operated *or* battery-powered; b. de secours emergency battery

batteur [batœr] *nm* (**a**) *(dans un groupe)* drummer (**b**) *(au cricket)* batsman; *(au base-ball)* batter, striker (**c**) *(de cuisine)* mixer

batteuse [batøz] *nf (machine agricole)* threshing machine, thresher

battoir [batwar] *nm* (**a**) *(pour les tapis)* carpet) beater; *(pour le linge)* beetle (**b**) *Fam (grande main)* great paw *or* mitt

battre [11] [batr] **1** *vt* (**a**) *(frapper) (personne, chien, tapis)* to beat; *(blé)* to thresh; *(métal)* to hammer; b. qn à coups de poings/avec une canne to punch/cane sb; b. le tambour to beat the drum; b. le rappel *Mil* to call to arms; *Fig* to call everyone together; b. la campagne to scour *or* comb the countryside; *(divaguer)* to wander; *Prov* il faut b. le fer quand il *ou* pendant qu'il est chaud strike while the iron is hot (**b**) *(cartes)* to shuffle; *(beurre)* to churn; *(œufs, préparation*

culinaire) to beat, to whisk; b. les blancs en neige to beat the whites until stiff (**c**) *(adversaire)* to beat; *(record)* to break; b. qn à plate(s) couture(s) to beat sb hollow; *Fig* b. tous les records to take some beating (**d**) *Mus* b. la mesure to beat time (**e**) *Naut* b. pavillon français/britannique to fly the French/British flag

2 *vi* (**a**) *(cœur)* to beat; *(porte, volet)* to bang; *(voile)* to flap; il a le cœur qui bat *(d'émotion)* his heart is pounding (**b**) b. en retraite to beat a retreat

3 battre de *vt ind* b. des mains to clap one's hands; b. des cils to flutter one's eyelashes

4 se battre *vpr aussi Fig* to fight (avec/contre with/ against); se b. comme des chiffonniers to fight like cat and dog; se b. au couteau to fight with knives; *très Fam* je m'en bats l'œil I don't give a damn

battu, -e [baty] *adj (femme, enfant)* battered; un air *ou* regard de chien b. a hangdog look; avoir les yeux battus to have dark circles under one's eyes

battue [baty] *nf (à la chasse)* beat; *(pour retrouver quelqu'un)* search

batture [batyr] *nf Can* sandbank

baud [bo] *nm Tél & Ordinat* baud

baudet [bodɛ] *nm* donkey; chargé comme un b. loaded down like a packhorse

baudrier [bodrije] *nm* shoulder strap; *(pour épée)* baldric; *(d'escalade)* harness

baudroie [bodrwa] *nf* monkfish

baudruche [bodryʃ] *nf* (ballon de) b. balloon

baume [bom] *nm aussi Fig* balm; mettre du b. au cœur de qn *(événement)* to be a consolation for sb

baux [bo] *voir* bail

bauxite [boksit] *nf* bauxite

bavard, -e [bavar, -ard] **1** *adj* (**a**) *(qui parle beaucoup)* chatty; *(style, essai)* wordy; il est b. comme une pie he'd talk the hind legs off a donkey (**b**) *(indiscret)* indiscreet

2 *nm,f* (**a**) *(qui parle beaucoup)* chatterbox (**b**) *(indiscret)* gossip

bavardage [bavardaʒ] *nm* (**a**) *(action)* chatting; *(commérage)* gossiping (**b**) bavardages *(paroles)* chat; *(commérage)* gossip

bavarder [bavarde] *vi (parler)* to chat; *(commérer)* to gossip

bavarois, -e [bavarwa, -az] **1** *adj* Bavarian

2 *nm,f* B. Bavarian

3 *nm Culin* bavarois, = dessert consisting of set custard and whipped cream mixed with fruit purée

bave [bav] *nf (de personne)* dribble; *(de chien)* slaver; *(de cheval, de chien enragé)* froth, foam; *(d'escargot)* slime; *(de crapaud)* spittle

baver [bave] *vi (personne)* to dribble; *(chien)* to slaver; *(chien enragé)* to foam at the mouth; *(stylo)* to leak, to run; *(encre)* to smudge; *Fam* en b. (des ronds de chapeaux) to have a hard time of it; *Fam* en faire b. (des ronds de chapeaux) à qn to give sb a hard time

bavette [bavɛt] *nf* (**a**) *(d'un bébé, d'un tablier)* bib (**b**) *Culin* skirt (of beef) (**c**) *Fam* tailler une b. to have a chat

baveux, -euse [bavø, -øz] **1** *adj (bouche, enfant)* dribbling; *(omelette)* runny

2 *nm,f Can (morveux)* pain, pest

Bavière [bavjɛr] *nf* la B. Bavaria

bavoir [bavwar] *nm* bib

bavure [bavyr] *nf* (**a**) *(tache)* smudge, smear (**b**) *(erreur)* slip-up; sans bavure(s) faultless; b. policière case of police misconduct

bayer [53] [baje] *vi* b. aux corneilles to stare into space

bazar [bazar] *nm* (**a**) *(marché)* bazaar (**b**) *(magasin)* general store (**c**) *Fam (désordre)* shambles *(singulier); (bruit)* racket; *(affaires)* stuff, gear; **et tout le b.** and the whole caboodle; **mettre du** *ou* **le b.** dans qch to make a shambles of sth

bazarder [bazarde] *vt Fam (se débarrasser de)* to get rid of; *(jeter)* to chuck out; *(vendre)* to flog

bazooka [bazuka] *nm* bazooka

BCBG [besebeʒe] *adj inv (abrév* **bon chic bon genre)** *Br* ≃ Sloany, *Am* ≃ preppy

BCG® [beseʒe] *nm Méd* BCG

BD [bede] *nf* (**a**) *(abrév* **bande dessinée)** comic strip, cartoon (**b**) *Ordinat (abrév* **base de données)** dbase

bd *abrév* boulevard

béant, -e [beɑ̃, -ɑ̃t] *adj (bouche, porte)* wide open; *(blessure, gouffre)* gaping

béat, -e [bea, -at] *adj Rel* blessed; *(heureux)* blissful; *Péj (niais)* inane; **être b. d'admiration** to be open-mouthed in admiration; **elle nous observait d'un air b.** she watched us open-mouthed

béatement [beatmɑ̃] *adv (sourire)* inanely

béatifier [66] [beatifje] *vt Rel* to beatify

béatitude [beatityd] *nf* (**a**) *Rel* beatitude (**b**) *(bonheur parfait)* bliss

beau, belle [bo, bɛl]

> **bel** is used before masculine singular nouns beginning with a vowel or h mute.

1 *adj* (**a**) *(d'apparence) (femme, enfant)* beautiful, good-looking; *(homme)* handsome, good-looking; *(objet, maison)* lovely, beautiful; **b. comme un dieu** like a Greek god; **ce n'est pas b. à voir** it's not a pretty sight; **se faire b.** to smarten oneself up; *Fam Fig* **te voilà b.!** you're in a real mess!

(**b**) *(de qualité) (œuvre, spectacle, discours)* fine; **avoir une belle situation** to have a good job

(**c**) *(moralement)* fine, noble; **un b. geste** a noble gesture; **ce n'est pas b. de mentir** it isn't nice to tell lies

(**d**) *(bien)* **c'est trop b. pour être vrai** it's too good to be true; **ce serait trop b.!** that would be too much (to hope for)!; **le plus b. jour de ma vie** the best day of my life

(**e**) *Ironique* **une belle grippe** a nasty dose of the flu; **une belle correction** a good thrashing; **te voilà dans un bel état!** look at the state of you!; **j'ai eu une belle peur** I was really scared; **vous avez fait du b. travail!** well done!; *très Fam* **un b. salaud** a real bastard; **j'en ai entendu de belles sur votre compte!** I've heard some unpleasant things about you!; **il en a fait de belles** he got up to some real tricks

(**f**) *(intensif)* **au b. milieu de la rue** right *or* bang in the middle of the road; **une belle somme** a tidy sum; **un b. poulet** a nice big chicken

(**g**) *(locutions)* **bel et bien** *(complètement)* well and truly; **il est bel et bien venu** he really did come; **il s'est bel et bien trompé** he has indeed made a mistake; **de plus belle** with a vengeance; **il reprit l'entraînement de plus belle** he resumed training with a vengeance *or* more enthusiastically than ever

2 *adv* **il fait b.** it's fine; **il ferait b. voir ça!** that'll be the day!; **j'ai b. le lui expliquer...** no matter how many times I explain it to him...; **j'ai b. pousser, la porte ne bouge pas** try as I might, I can't get the door to open

3 *nm* **le b.** *(beauté)* beauty; **mais le plus b. c'est que...** but the best bit *or* part is that ...; *Fam Ironique* **c'est du b.!** that's great!; **le temps est au b. (fixe)** the weather is set fair; *Fig* **avoir le moral au b. fixe** to be permanently in a good mood; **un vieux b.** an old roué; **faire le b.** *(chien)* to sit up and beg

4 *nf* **belle** (**a**) *(partie)* decider (**b**) *Hum (amie)* lady friend (**c**) *Fam* **se faire la b.** to run away; *(de prison)* to escape

beaucoup [boku] *adv* (**a**) *(intensément, en grande quantité)* a lot; **ça te plaît?** – **pas b.** do you like it? – **not much** *or* not a lot

(**b**) *(une grande quantité, un grand nombre)* **il reste encore b. à faire** there's still a lot to do; **c'est déjà b. qu'il veuille bien vous parler** it's quite something that he condescended to speak to you; **il y est pour b.** he has had a lot *or* a great deal to do with it; **b. pensent que...** a lot *or* many people think that...; **b. d'entre nous** a lot of *or* many of us; **de b.** *(de loin)* by far; **il s'en faut de b. que je sois riche** I'm far from rich

(**c**) **b. de** *(quantité)* a lot of; *(nombre)* a lot of, many; **b. de vin/chance** a lot of wine/luck; **b. de fautes** a lot of *or* many mistakes; **pas b. de** *(argent, courage)* not much; *(gens, problèmes)* not many; **avec b. de soin** with great care, very carefully; **j'en veux b.!** I want a lot!

(**d**) *(avec des comparatifs)* a lot, much; **b. moins/plus vite** a lot *or* much slower/faster; **il parle b. trop** he talks far too much; **b. moins d'enfants** a lot *or* far fewer children; **b. moins de temps** a lot *or* much less time

beauf [bof] *Fam* **1** *adj Péj* **il est un peu b.** he's a bit of a narrow-minded average Frenchman **2** *nm* (**a**) *(beau-frère)* brother-in-law (**b**) *Péj* = stereotypical narrow-minded, average Frenchman

beau-fils *(pl* beaux-fils) [bofis] *nm* (**a**) *(gendre)* son-in-law (**b**) *(après remariage)* stepson

beau-frère *(pl* beaux-frères) [bofrɛr] *nm* brother-in-law

beaujolais [boʒɔlɛ] *nm* Beaujolais

beau-père *(pl* beaux-pères) [bopɛr] *nm* (**a**) *(père du conjoint)* father-in-law (**b**) *(après remariage)* stepfather

beaupré [bopre] *nm Naut* bowsprit

beauté [bote] *nf* beauty; **être en b.** to be looking stunning; **de toute b.** stunning; **finir en b.** to end on a high note; **faire qch pour la b. du geste** to do sth for the sake of it; **se refaire une b.** to put one's face on

beaux-arts [bozar] *nmpl* fine art; **école des b., B.** art school

beaux-parents [boparɑ̃] *nmpl* parents-in-law

bébé [bebe] *nm* (**a**) *(nourrisson)* baby; **faire le b.** to behave like a baby; **être très b.** to be very babyish (**b**) *(animal)* **b. gazelle/lapin** baby gazelle/rabbit

bébé-éprouvette *(pl* bébés-éprouvette) [bebeepruvɛt] *nm* test-tube baby

bébelle [bebɛl] *nf Can (gadget)* gadget, *(bibelot)* ornament; *(jouet)* toy

bébête [bebɛt] *Fam* **1** *adj* silly **2** *nf* creepy-crawly

bec [bɛk] *nm* (**a**) *(d'oiseau, de tortue, de pieuvre)* beak (**b**) *Fam (bouche)* mouth; **il n'a pas ouvert le b. de la journée** he hasn't opened his mouth all day; **la clope au b.** with a smoke in one's mouth; **rester le b. dans l'eau** to be left high and dry; **b. fin** gourmet (**c**) *(de pot)* lip; *(de cafetière)* spout; *(d'instrument à vent)* mouthpiece; **b. Bunsen** Bunsen burner; **b. de gaz** *(réverbère)* gas lamp; **b. verseur** spout (**d**) *Can (baiser)* **donner un b. à qn** to give sb a kiss

bécane [bekan] *nf Fam (vélo)* bike; *(machine, ordinateur)* machine

bécarre [bekar] *adj & nm Mus* natural

bécasse [bekas] *nf* (**a**) *(oiseau)* woodcock (**b**) *Fam (idiote)* silly thing

bec-de-lièvre *(pl* becs-de-lièvre) [bɛkdəljɛvr] *nm* harelip

béchamel [beʃamɛl] *nf* (**sauce**) **b.** béchamel sauce

bêche [bɛʃ] *nf* spade

bêcher [beʃe] *vt* to dig, to turn over

bêcheur, -euse [beʃœr, -øz] *nm,f Fam (snob)* stuck-up person

bécosses [bekɔs] *nfpl Can Fam Br* bog, *Am* john

bécoter [bekɔte] *Fam* **1** *vt* to snog
2 se bécoter *vpr* to snog

becqueter [42] [bɛkte] **1** *vt (sujet: oiseau)* to peck at
2 *vi très Fam (personne)* to eat

becter [bɛkte] *vi =* **becqueter**

bedaine [bədɛn] *nf Fam* pot(-belly), paunch; **prendre de la b.** to get a pot(-belly) *or* a paunch

bédé [bede] *nf Fam* comic strip, cartoon

bedeau, -x [bədo] *nm* verger

bedon [bədɔ̃] *nm Fam* pot(-belly), paunch

bedonnant, -e [bədɔnɑ̃, -ɑ̃t] *adj Fam* pot-bellied, paunchy

bédouin, -e [bedwɛ̃, -in] **1** *adj* Bedouin
2 *nm,f* B. Bedouin

bée [be] *adj f* **bouche b.** open-mouthed; **j'en suis restée bouche b.** I was speechless; **regarder qch bouche b.** to gape at sth

beffroi [befrwa] *nm* belfry

bégaiement [begɛmɑ̃] *nm* stuttering, stammering

bégayer [53] [begeje] **1** *vi* to stutter, to stammer
2 *vt* to stammer (out)

bégonia [begɔnja] *nm* begonia

bègue [bɛg] **1** *adj* **être b.** to stutter, to stammer
2 *nmf* stutterer, stammerer

bégueule [begœl] *adj* prudish

béguin [begɛ̃] *nm Fam (personne)* crush; **avoir le b. pour qn** to have a crush on sb; **avoir le b. pour qch** to have taken a fancy to sth

BEI [beɑi] *nf (abrév* **Banque européenne d'investissement)** EIB

beige [bɛʒ] *adj & nm* beige

beigne¹ [bɛɲ] *nf Fam* clout

beigne² *nm Can* doughnut

beignet [bɛɲɛ] *nm (salé)* fritter; *(au sucre, à la confiture)* doughnut, donut; **b. de** *ou* **aux pommes** apple fritter

bel [bɛl] *voir* **beau**

bêlement [bɛlmɑ̃] *nm aussi Fig* bleat; **des bêlements** bleating

bêler [bɛle] *vi aussi Fig* to bleat

belette [bəlɛt] *nf* weasel

Belfast [bɛlfast] *n* Belfast

belge [bɛlʒ] **1** *adj* Belgian
2 *nmf* B. Belgian

belgicisme [bɛlʒisism] *nm (mot)* Belgian-French word; *(tournure)* Belgian-French expression

Belgique [bɛlʒik] *nf* **la B.** Belgium

Belgrade [bɛlgrad] *n* Belgrade

bélier [belje] *nm* **(a)** *(animal)* ram **(b)** *Mil* battering ram **(c)** *Astron & Astrol* **le B.** Aries; **être B.** to be (an) Aries

Belize [beliz] *nm* **le B.** Belize

belladone [beladɔn] *nf* belladonna, deadly nightshade

bellâtre [bɛlɑtr] *nm Péj* smoothie

belle [bɛl] *voir* **beau**

belle-famille *(pl* **belles-familles)** [bɛlfamij] *nf* in-laws

belle-fille *(pl* **belles-filles)** [bɛlfij] *nf* **(a)** *(épouse du fils)* daughter-in-law **(b)** *(après remariage)* stepdaughter

belle-mère *(pl* **belles-mères)** [bɛlmɛr] *nf* **(a)** *(mère du conjoint)* mother-in-law **(b)** *(après remariage)* stepmother

belle-sœur *(pl* **belles-sœurs)** [bɛlsœr] *nf* sister-in-law

belligérant, -e [beliʒerɑ̃, -ɑ̃t] **1** *adj* belligerent
2 *nm* **les belligérants** the warring nations

belliqueux, -euse [belikø, -øz] *adj (pays, peuple)* warlike; *(personne, humeur)* aggressive

belote [bəlɔt] *nf =* card game

bélouga [beluga], **béluga** [belyga] *nm* beluga whale

belvédère [bɛlvedɛr] *nm* **(a)** *(construction)* belvedere, gazebo **(b)** *(sur un site naturel)* viewpoint

bémol [bemɔl] *Mus* **1** *nm* flat; *Fam Fig* **mettre un b.** to tone it down
2 *adj* flat

ben [bɛ̃] *adv Fam* **b. oui!** well, yes!; **b. voilà, euh…** yeah, well, er…

bénédictin, -e [benediktɛ̃, -in] *adj, nm,f & nf* Benedictine

bénédiction [benediksjɔ̃] *nf Rel* blessing, benediction; *(d'une église)* consecration; *Fig* blessing

bénéfice [benefis] *nm* **(a)** *(gain)* profit; **b. d'exploitation** operating profit **(b)** *(avantage)* benefit, advantage; **tirer un certain b. de qch** to derive some benefit *or* advantage from sth; **avoir le b. de l'âge** to have the benefit of age; **accorder** *ou* **laisser le b. du doute à qn** to give sb the benefit of the doubt; **au b. de** *(œuvre charitable)* in aid of

bénéficiaire [benefisjɛr] **1** *adj Com (entreprise)* profit-making; *(compte)* in credit
2 *nmf (d'un chèque)* payee; *Jur* beneficiary

bénéficier [66] [benefisje] **bénéficier de** *vt ind* **(a)** *(profiter de)* to benefit from; **faire b. qn de son expérience** to give sb the benefit of one's experience **(b)** *(avoir)* to have; **cette carte d'abonnement vous fait b. d'une remise** this season ticket entitles you to a 20 per cent reduction

bénéfique [benefik] *adj* beneficial (**à** to)

Benelux [benelyks] *nm* **le B.** Benelux

benêt [bənɛ] **1** *adj m* simple
2 *nm* simpleton

bénévolat [benevɔla] *nm* voluntary work

bénévole [benevɔl] **1** *adj (travail, infirmière)* voluntary
2 *nmf* volunteer, voluntary worker

Bengale [bɛ̃gal] *nm* **le B.** Bengal

Bénin [benɛ̃] *nm* **le B.** Benin

bénin, -igne [benɛ̃, -iɲ] *adj (accident, opération)* minor; *(tumeur)* benign

béninois, -e [beninwa, -az] **1** *adj* Beninese
2 *nm,f* B. Beninese

bénir [benir] *vt aussi Fig* to bless; *(église)* to consecrate; **(que) Dieu vous bénisse!** (may) God bless you!; **être béni des dieux** to be blessed

bénit, -e [beni, -it] *adj voir* **eau, pain**

bénitier [benitje] *nm Rel* holy-water stoup

benjamin, -e [bɛ̃ʒamɛ̃, -in] *nm,f* **(a)** *(le/la plus jeune)* youngest **(b)** *Sp* junior *(10 to 12 years old)*

benjoin [bɛ̃ʒwɛ̃] *nm* (gum) benzoin, benjamin

benne [bɛn] *nf (de camion)* tipping *or* dump body; *(dans une mine)* tub, truck; *(de téléphérique)* (cable) car; **b. à ordures** bin lorry

benzine [bɛ̃zin] *nf* benzine

BEP [beape] *nm Scol (abrév* **brevet d'études professionnelles)** = vocational diploma taken at age eighteen

BEPC [beapese] *nm Anciennement Scol (abrév* **brevet d'études du premier cycle)** = school-leaving certificate taken at age fifteen

béquille [bekij] *nf* **(a)** *(pour marcher)* crutch; **marcher avec des béquilles** to be on crutches **(b)** *(d'un vélo, d'une moto)* stand

berbère [bɛrbɛr] **1** *adj* Berber
2 *nmf* **B.** Berber
3 *nm (langue)* Berber
bercail [bɛrkaj] *nm (de l'Église)* fold; *Hum* **rentrer au b.** to return to the fold
berçante [bɛrsɑ̃t] *adj f & nf Can* **(chaise) b.** rocking chair
berce [bɛrs] *nf Belg & Suisse (berceau)* cradle
berceau, -x [bɛrso] *nm (de bebé)* cradle; *Fig (d'une civilisation, d'un mouvement)* birthplace; **dès le b.** from the cradle, from birth; *Fam* **il les prend au b.** he's a cradle-snatcher
bercer [16] [bɛrse] **1** *vt* (**a**) *(bébé, passager)* to rock; *Fig* **mon enfance a été bercée par la musique de Debussy** I was brought up listening to Debussy (**b**) *Fig* **b. qn de promesses** to delude sb with promises **2 se bercer** *vpr* **se b. d'illusions** to delude oneself
berceuse [bɛrsøz] *nf (chanson)* lullaby
BERD [bɛrd] *nf (abrév* **Banque européenne pour la reconstruction et le développement)** EBRD
béret [berɛ] *nm* beret
bergamote [bɛrgamɔt] *nf* bergamot
berge[1] [bɛrʒ] *nf (bord)* bank
berge[2] *nf Fam* **il a quarante berges** he's forty
berger, -ère [bɛrʒe, -ɛr] **1** *nm,f* shepherd, *f* shepherdess **2** *nm (chien)* **b. allemand** German shepherd, *Br* Alsatian; **b. des Pyrénées** Pyrenean mountain dog **3** *nf* **bergère** *(fauteuil)* wing chair
bergerie [bɛrʒəri] *nf* sheepfold
bergeronnette [bɛrʒərɔnɛt] *nf* wagtail
Béring [bɛriŋ] *n voir* **détroit**
berk [bɛrk] *exclam* yuk!
Berlin [bɛrlɛ̃] *n* Berlin; **B.-Ouest/-Est** West/East Berlin
berline [bɛrlin] *nf Aut Br* (four-door) saloon, *Am* (four-door) sedan
berlingot [bɛrlɛ̃go] *nm* (**a**) *(bonbon) Br* boiled sweet, *Am* hard candy (**b**) *(de lait)* carton, *(de produit d'entretien)* pack
berlinois, -e [bɛrlinwa, -az] **1** *adj* from Berlin **2** *nm,f* **B.** Berliner
berlue [bɛrly] *nf Fam* **avoir la b.** to be seeing things
bermuda [bɛrmyda] *nm* Bermuda shorts, Bermudas
Bermudes [bɛrmyd] *nfpl* **les (îles) B.** Bermuda
bernard-l'(h)ermite [bɛrnarlɛrmit] *nm inv* hermit crab
Berne [bɛrn] *n* Bern
berne [bɛrn] **en berne** *adj Naut* at *Br* half mast *or Am* half staff; *Mil* furled
berner [bɛrne] *vt* to fool
bernois, -e [bɛrnwa, -az] **1** *adj* Bernese **2** *nm,f* **B.** Bernese
besace [bəzas] *nf (de mendiant)* bag; *(de pèlerin)* scrip; **sac b.** = large, soft handbag
bésef [bezɛf] = **bézef**
besogne [bəzɔɲ] *nf* job, task; **aller vite en b.** to get things done quickly; *Fig & Péj* to jump the gun
besoin [bəzwɛ̃] *nm* (**a**) *(nécessité)* need (**de qch** for sth); **avoir b. de qn/qch** to need sb/sth; **avoir b. de faire qch** to need to do sth; **j'ai b. que tu m'aides** I need you to help me; **éprouver le b. de faire qch** to feel the need to do sth; **pour les besoins de la cause** for the sake of the cause; **au b.** if necessary, if need be; **en cas de b.** if need be; **si b. est** if necessary, if need be (**b**) **faire ses besoins** *(personne)* to relieve oneself; *(animal)* to do its business (**c**) *(misère)* **être dans le b.** to be in need
bestial, -e, -aux, -ales [bɛstjal, -o] *adj* bestial
bestiaux [bɛstjo] *nmpl* livestock

bestiole [bɛstjɔl] *nf* small animal; *(insecte)* creepy-crawly
best-seller *(pl* **best-sellers)** [bɛstsɛlœr] *nm* best-seller
bêta, -asse [bɛta, -as] *Fam* **1** *adj* silly **2** *nm,f* silly-billy
bêtabloquant [bɛtablɔkɑ̃] *nm Méd* beta-blocker
bétail [betaj] *nm* livestock; **gros b.** cattle and horses
bétaillère [betajɛr] *nf* cattle truck
bêta-test *(pl* **bêta-tests)** [betatɛst] *nm Ordinat* beta test
bête [bɛt] **1** *adj* stupid, silly; **c'est b., on a loupé le film!** what a pity *or* a shame, we've missed the film!; **ce n'est pas b.** *(suggestion)* that's not a bad idea; **rester tout b.** *(décontenancé)* to be open-mouthed; *Fam* **être b. comme ses pieds** to be as thick as two short planks; **être b. à pleurer** to be pathetically stupid; **c'est b. comme chou, c'est tout b.** it's as easy as pie **2** *nf* (**a**) *(animal)* animal; **travailler comme une b.** to work flat out, **elle m'a regardé comme une b. curieuse** she looked at me as if I was from another planet; *Péj* **b. à concours** *Br* swot, *Am* grind; **b. à cornes** horned animal; **b. fauve** big cat; **b. féroce** wild animal; **b. noire** *(personne)* bête noire; *(chose)* pet hate; **b. de somme** beast of burden (**b**) *(insecte)* insect; *Fig* **chercher la petite b.** to nit-pick; **b. à bon Dieu** *Br* ladybird, *Am* ladybug
bêtement [bɛtmɑ̃] *adv (rire, regarder)* stupidly; **mourir b. to die** senselessly; **tout b.** quite simply purely and simply
bêtifier [66] [betifje] *vi (avec un enfant)* to use baby-talk
bêtise [betiz] *nf* (**a**) *(manque d'intelligence)* stupidity, silliness (**b**) *(action idiote)* stupid thing (to do); *(parole idiote)* stupid thing to say; **dire des bêtises** to talk nonsense (**c**) *(chose sans importance)* trivial thing; **se disputer pour des bêtises** to argue over nothing (**d**) *Can* **bêtises** *(injures)* insults (**e**) **bêtises de Cambrai** *Br* ≃ mint humbugs, *Am* ≃ hard mint candies
béton [betɔ̃] *nm* (**a**) *(matériau)* concrete; *Fig* **des muscles en b.** rock hard muscles; **un alibi en b.** a cast-iron alibi; **b. armé** reinforced concrete (**b**) *Fam* **laisse b.!** forget it!
bétonner [betɔne] *vt* to concrete
bétonneuse [betɔnøz], **bétonnière** [betɔnjɛr] *nf* cement mixer, concrete mixer
bette [bɛt] *nf* (Swiss) chard
betterave [bɛtrav] *nf* **b. (rouge)** *Br* beetroot, *Am* beet; **b. fourragère** mangel-wurzel; **b. sucrière** sugar beet
beuglement [bøgləmɑ̃] *nm (d'une vache)* moo; *(d'un taureau)* bellow; *(de la radio, de la télé)* blaring; **des beuglements** mooing/bellowing; **pousser des beuglements** *(personne)* to bellow
beugler [bøgle] **1** *vi (vache)* to moo; *(taureau, personne)* to bellow; *(radio, télé)* to blare **2** *vt (chanson)* to bawl out, to bellow out
beur [bœr] **1** *nmf* = North African born in France of immigrant parents **2** *adj inv* = of North Africans born in France of immigrant parents
beurre [bœr] *nm* butter; **au b.** *(pâtisserie)* made with butter; *Fam* **ça compte pour du b.** that doesn't count; *Fam* **faire son beurre** to make a packet; **ça mettra du b. dans les épinards** that will make life a bit easier; **elle veut le b. et l'argent du b.** she wants to have her cake and eat it; **b. de cacahouètes** peanut butter; **b. de cacao** cocoa butter; **b. salé/demi-sel** salted/slightly salted butter
beurré, -e [bœre] *adj très Fam (ivre)* plastered, legless
beurrer [bœre] *vt* to butter
beurrier [bœrje] *nm* butter dish
beuverie [bøvri] *nf* binge, drinking session
bévue [bevy] *nf* slip-up

Beyrouth [berut] n Beirut

bézef [bezɛf] adv Fam **il n'y en a pas b.** (pain, confiture) there's not much or a lot (of it); (légumes, livres) there aren't many or a lot (of them)

Bhoutan [butɑ̃] nm **le B.** Bhutan

bi- [bi-] préf bi-

biais [bjɛ] nm (a) (d'un mur) slant; **regarder qn de b.** to look sideways at sb; **en b.** at an angle; **tailler un tissu dans le b.** to cut material on the bias (**b**) (moyen) way; **par le b. de** through (**c**) (aspect) angle; **par quel b. envisager la chose?** from what angle should we look at the issue?

biaiser [bjeze] vi (ruser) to dodge the issue

biathlon [biatlɔ̃] nm biathlon

bibelot [biblo] nm curio, knick-knack

biberon [bibrɔ̃] nm (baby's or feeding) bottle; **nourrir** ou **élever un enfant au b.** to bottle-feed a child; **c'est l'heure du b.** it's the baby's feeding time

bibi¹ [bibi] nm (chapeau) (woman's) hat

bibi² pron Fam (moi) yours truly

bibine [bibin] nf Fam (boisson) dishwater

bibite [bibit] nf Can Fam bug, insect

bible [bibl] nf aussi Fig bible; **la B.** the Bible

bibliographie [biblijɔgrafi] nf bibliography

bibliographique [biblijɔgrafik] adj bibliographical

bibliophile [biblijɔfil] nmf book-lover

bibliothécaire [biblijɔtekɛr] nmf librarian

bibliothèque [biblijɔtɛk] nf (**a**) (bâtiment, salle) library; **b. municipale** public library; **b. de prêt** lending library; **b. universitaire** university library (**b**) (meuble) bookcase

biblique [biblik] adj biblical

Bic® [bik] **1** adj stylo B., pointe B. ballpoint (pen) **2** nm ballpoint (pen)

bicarbonate [bikarbɔnat] nm Chim bicarbonate; **b. de soude** bicarbonate of soda

bicentenaire [bisɑ̃tnɛr] nm Br bicentenary, Am bicentennial

biceps [bisɛps] nm biceps; Fam **avoir des b.** to have big biceps

biche [biʃ] nf (**a**) (animal) hind, doe (**b**) Fam **ma b.** darling

bicher [biʃe] vi Fam Vieilli (se réjouir) to be tickled pink

bichonner [biʃɔne] **1** vt (**a**) (préparer) to doll up (**b**) (soigner) to pamper **2 se bichonner** vpr to doll oneself up

bicolore [bikɔlɔr] adj two-colour(ed)

bicoque [bikɔk] nf Fam (maison) house, place

bicorne [bikɔrn] nm cocked hat

bicyclette [bisiklɛt] nf bicycle; **aller en ville à** ou **en b.** to cycle into town, to go into town by bicycle; **faire de la b.** to go cycling; **il ne sait pas faire de la b.** he can't ride a bicycle

bidasse [bidas] nm très Fam Br squaddie, Am G.I.

bide [bid] nm Fam (**a**) (ventre) belly; **avoir/prendre du b.** to have/develop a belly (**b**) (échec) **faire un b.** Br to flop, Am to bomb

bidet [bidɛ] nm (**a**) (de toilette) bidet (**b**) Hum (cheval) nag

bidimensionnel, -elle [bidimɑ̃sjɔnɛl] adj bidimensional

bidoche [bidɔʃ] nf très Fam meat

bidon [bidɔ̃] **1** adj inv Fam (excuse, argument) phoney, fake; (élections) rigged **2** nm (**a**) (d'huile, d'essence) can; (de lait) churn; (gourde) water bottle; **b. d'essence** petrol can, jerry can (**b**) Fam (ventre) belly (**c**) Fam (bluff) **c'est du b.** it's a load of crap

bidonnant, -e [bidɔnɑ̃, -ɑ̃t] adj Fam hilarious

bidonner [bidɔne] **se bidonner** vpr Fam to laugh one's head off

bidonville [bidɔ̃vil] nm shantytown

bidouiller [biduje] vt Fam to patch up; Ordinat (programme) to modify

bidule [bidyl] nm Fam thingy, whatsit; **B.** (personne) what's-his-name, f what's-her-name

bielle [bjɛl] nf Aut connecting rod, con-rod

biélorusse [bjelorys] **1** adj Byelorussian **2** nmf **B.** Byelorussian

Biélorussie [bjelorysi] nf **la B.** Belarus

bien [bjɛ̃] **1** adv (**a**) (convenablement) well; **un livre b. écrit** a well-written book; **écoutez-moi b.** listen carefully; Ironique **ça commence b.!** that's a good start!
(**b**) (moralement) right; **se conduire** ou **se tenir b.** to behave (well); **vous avez b. fait** you did the right thing; **tu fais b. de me le dire** it's a good thing you've told me; **tu ferais b. de te méfier** you would be wise to beware
(**c**) (emphatique) **regarder qn b. en face** to look sb right in the face; **c'est b. cela** that's right; **c'est b. une erreur** that's definitely a mistake; **est-ce b. le train pour Lille?** is this the right train for Lille?; **j'ai b. dû lire dix de ses livres** I must have read at least ten of his books; **j'irais b. avec vous mais...** I'd love to go with you but...; **j'y suis b. obligé** I just have to; **je sais b.** I'm well aware of it; **je vous l'avais b. dit!** I told you so!; **c'est b. ce que je pensais** that's what I thought; **nous verrons b.!** we'll see!; **qu'est-ce que ça peut b. être/vouloir dire?** what on earth can it be/mean?; **est-ce b. raisonnable?** is that really reasonable?; **B. à vous** (dans une lettre) Yours
(**d**) (très) very; **vous arrivez b. tard** you're very late; **que ce soit b. clair, je...** let's get this clear, I...
(**e**) (beaucoup) (réfléchir, changer) a lot, a great deal; **b. plus** much or a lot more; **b. moins** much or a lot less; **b. des gens** a lot of people; **b. d'autres** many others; **b. des fois** often; **avoir b. de la peine** ou **du mal à faire qch** to have a lot of difficulty doing sth; **tu as b. de la chance!** you're really lucky!
(**f**) (locutions) **b. que** although, though; **b. que je le sache** although I know it; **b. entendu, b. sûr, b. évidemment** of course; **b. sûr que je viendrai** of course I'll come; **b. sûr que non!** of course not!
2 exclam **eh b.!** well!; **b.! je vous appelle demain!** OK, I'll call you tomorrow!
3 adj inv (**a**) (satisfaisant) good; **c'est b.!** good!
(**b**) (à l'aise) comfortable; **être b. avec qn** (en bons termes) to be on good terms with sb; **se mettre b. avec qn** to get into sb's good books; Fam **nous voilà b.!** we're in a right mess!
(**c**) (en forme) well
(**d**) (moral) decent; **ce n'est pas b. de vous moquer de lui** it's not nice or kind of you to make fun of him
(**e**) (beau) (personne) good-looking, attractive; **elle est b. sur cette photo** she looks good in this photo
4 nm (**a**) Phil & Rel good; **le b. et le mal** good and evil, right and wrong; **faire le b.** to do good; **faire du b. à qn** to do sb good; **grand b. vous fasse!** much good may it do you!; **dire du b. de qn** to speak well of sb; **c'est pour ton b.** it's for your own good; **c'était en tout b. tout honneur** it was quite innocent
(**b**) (chose matérielle) possession; Jur assets; **biens** possessions, property; **avoir du b.** to have property; Prov **b. mal acquis ne profite jamais** ill-gotten gains never prosper; **biens de consommation** consumer goods; **biens immobiliers** ou **immeubles** real estate or property

bien-aimé, -e (mpl **bien-aimés**, fpl **bien-aimées**) [bjɛ̃neme] adj beloved

bien-être [bjɛ̃nɛtr] *nm* well-being

bienfaisance [bjɛ̃fəzɑ̃s] *nf* œuvre de **b.** charity, charitable organization

bienfaisant, -e [bjɛ̃fəzɑ̃, -ɑ̃t] *adj* (**a**) *(personne)* charitable (**b**) *(remède)* beneficial; *(vent, pluie)* refreshing

bienfait [bjɛ̃fɛ] *nm* (**a**) *(acte)* kindness (**b**) *(avantage)* benefit

bienfaiteur, -trice [bjɛ̃fɛtœr, -tris] *nm,f* benefactor, *f* benefactress

bien-fondé [bjɛ̃fɔ̃de] *nm* validity; *Jur* cogency

bienheureux, -euse [bjɛ̃nørø, -øz] *adj* blissful; *Rel* blessed

biennal, -e, -aux, -ales [bjenal, -o] *adj* biennial

bien-pensant, -e [bjɛ̃pɑ̃sɑ̃, -ɑ̃t] *(mpl* **bien-pensants,** *fpl* **bien-pensantes)** *adj & nm,f* conformist

bienséance [bjɛ̃seɑ̃s] *nf* propriety, decorum

bientôt [bjɛ̃to] *adv* soon; **il est b. deux heures** it's nearly two o'clock; **on est b. arrivés?** will we soon be there?; *Fam* **tu n'as pas b. fini?** have you quite finished?; **à b.!** see you soon!

bienveillance [bjɛ̃vɛjɑ̃s] *nf* kindness, avec **b.** kindly

bienveillant, -e [bjɛ̃vɛjɑ̃, -ɑ̃t] *adj* kind

bienvenu, -e [bjɛ̃vny] **1** *adj (remarque)* apposite; *(repas, explication)* welcome
2 *nm,f* **soyez le b.!** welcome!; **vous serez toujours la bienvenue** you're always welcome

bienvenue [bjɛ̃vny] **1** *nf* welcome; **souhaiter la b. à qn** to welcome sb
2 *exclam* welcome! (à to); *Can (de rien)* you're welcome!

bière¹ [bjɛr] *nf (boisson)* beer; *Fam* **ce n'est pas de la petite b.** it's no small thing; **b. blonde** *Br* lager, *Am* light beer; **b. brune** *Br* brown ale, *Am* dark beer; **b. pression** *Br* draught beer, *Am* draft beer

bière² *nf (cercueil)* coffin; **assister à la mise en b.** to be present when the body is placed in the coffin

biffer [bife] *vt* to cross out; **b. un nom d'une liste** to cross a name off a list

biffure [bifyr] *nf* crossing out

bifidus [bifidys] *nm* live culture

bifocal, -e, -aux, -ales [bifɔkal, -o] *adj (lentille)* bifocal; **lunettes bifocales** bifocals

bifteck [biftɛk] *nm* (beef)steak; **b. haché** *Br* mince, *Am* ground beef; *Fam* **gagner son b.** to earn one's bread and butter

bifurcation [bifyrkasjɔ̃] *nf* fork

bifurquer [bifyrke] *vi (route, chemin)* to fork; *(automobiliste)* to turn off; **bifurquez à droite** take the right fork

bigame [bigam] *adj* bigamous

bigamie [bigami] *nf* bigamy

bigarré, -e [bigare] *adj (tissu)* multicoloured; **une foule bigarrée** a motley crew

bigarreau, -x [bigaro] *nm* = type of cherry

bigler [bigle] *Fam* **1** *vi* (**a**) *(loucher)* to have a squint (**b**) **b. sur qch** to have a good look at sth
2 *vt (personne)* to eye up

bigleux, -euse [biglø, -øz] *adj Fam (qui louche)* cross-eyed; *(myope)* short-sighted

bigophone [bigɔfɔn] *nm Fam Br* blower, *Am* horn

bigorneau, -x [bigɔrno] *nm* winkle

bigot, -e [bigo, -ɔt] **1** *nm,f* (religious) bigot
2 *adj* sanctimonious

bigoterie [bigɔtri] *nf* (religious) bigotry

bigoudi [bigudi] *nm* (hair) curler *or* roller; **se mettre des bigoudis** to put one's hair in curlers

bigre [bigr] *exclam Fam Vieilli* gosh!

bigrement [bigrəmɑ̃] *adv Fam (très)* awfully; *(beaucoup)* a heck of a lot

bihebdomadaire [biɛbdɔmadɛr] *adj* twice-weekly

bijou, -x [biʒu] *nm* jewel; *Fig* gem; **des bijoux** jewellery, jewels; **b. de famille** family jewel; **un b. fantaisie** a piece of costume jewellery

bijouterie [biʒutri] *nf (boutique)* jeweller's (shop); *(commerce, fabrication)* jeweller's trade

bijoutier, -ère [biʒutje, -ɛr] *nm,f* jeweller

bikini® [bikini] *nm* bikini

bilan [bilɑ̃] *nm* (**a**) *Fin* balance sheet; **faire** *ou* **dresser un b.** to draw up a balance sheet; *Com* **déposer son b.** to file one's petition (in bankruptcy); *Com* **un dépôt de b.** a petition in bankruptcy; **b. comptable** balance sheet (**b**) *(appréciation) (d'une situation, de faits)* assessment, evaluation; *(résultats)* results; *(d'une catastrophe)* toll; **faire le b. de la situation** to take stock of the situation; **accident sur l'autoroute, b. trois morts** *(titre)* freeway pile-up, three dead; **b. de santé** complete check-up

bilatéral, -e, -aux, -ales [bilateral, -o] *adj* bilateral

bilboquet [bilbɔkɛ] *nm* cup-and-ball

bile [bil] *nf* bile; **décharger sa b. sur qn** to vent one's spleen on sb; *Fam* **se faire de la b. (pour)** to fret (about)

biler [bile] **se biler** *vpr Fam* to fret

biliaire [biljɛr] *adj* biliary

bilingue [bilɛ̃g] *adj* bilingual

billard [bijar] *nm* (**a**) *(jeu)* billiards; **faire un b.** *ou* **une partie de b.** to have a game of billiards; **b. américain** pool, **b. électrique** pinball (**b**) *(table)* billiard table (**c**) *Fam* **passer sur le b.** to go under the knife

bille¹ [bij] *nf* (**a**) *(de verre)* marble; *Fig* **reprendre ses billes** to pull out; *Fam* **toucher sa b. en qch** to know a thing or two about sth (**b**) *(de billard)* (billiard) ball; *Fig* **y aller b. en tête** *Tech* to bear about the bush (**c**) *Tech* ball (**d**) *très Fam (visage)* mug; **avoir une bonne b.** to look pleasant enough

bille² *nf (pièce de bois)* billet

billet [bijɛ] *nm* (**a**) *(argent)* **b. (de banque)** *Br* (bank)note, *Am* bill; **un b. de 50 euros** a 50-euro note; **un faux b.** a forged banknote; **le b. vert** the dollar; *Fam* **je te fiche mon b. qu'il ne viendra pas!** I bet my bottom dollar he won't come! (**b**) *(pour voyager, pour le cinéma)* ticket; **b. d'avion/ de train** plane/train ticket; **b. de première/de seconde** first-/second-class ticket; **b. simple** *Br* single *or Am* one-way ticket; **b. aller (et) retour** *Br* return *or Am* round-trip ticket (**c**) *Com & Fin (effet)* bill; **b. au porteur** bill payable to bearer (**d**) *Litt (lettre)* note; *Scol* **b. d'absence** absence slip; **b. doux** love letter; *Scol* **b. de retard** = note given to pupil who is late, specifying the time of arrival

billetterie [bijɛtri] *nf* (**a**) *(lieu)* ticket office (**b**) *(de billets de transport)* **b. automatique** ticket machine

billion [biljɔ̃] *nm* trillion

billot [bijo] *nm* block

bimensuel, -elle [bimɑ̃sɥɛl] **1** *adj Br* fortnightly, *Am* semimonthly
2 *nm Br* fortnightly *or Am* semimonthly magazine

bimestriel, -elle [bimɛstriɛl] *adj & nm* bimonthly

bimoteur [bimɔtœr] *adj & nm* (**avion**) **b.** twin-engine aircraft

binaire [binɛr] *adj Math* binary; **langage b.** binary notation

biner [bine] *vt* to hoe

binett¹ [binɛt] *nf (outil)* hoe

binette² [binɛt] *nf très Fam (visage)* mug

biniou [binju] *nm* Breton bagpipes

binoclard, -e [binɔklar, -ard] *nm,f Fam* specs wearer
binocle [binɔkl] *nm* pince-nez *inv*; *Fam* **binocles** *(lunettes)* specs
binôme [binom] *nm* (**a**) *Math* binomial (**b**) *Scol* travailler en b. to work in twos
bio [bjo] *adj inv Fam (produit, yaourt)* organic
biocarburant [bjokarbyrā] *nm* biofuel
biochimie [bjoʃimi] *nf* biochemistry
biodégradable [bjodegradabl] *adj* biodegradable
biographe [bjograf] *nmf* biographer
biographie [bjografi] *nf* biography
biographique [bjografik] *adj* biographical
bio-industrie *(pl* **bio-industries)** [bjoɛ̃dystri] *nf* biotechnology industry
biologie [bjɔlɔʒi] *nf* biology
biologique [bjɔlɔʒik] *adj* biological; *(sans engrais chimiques)* organic
biologiste [bjɔlɔʒist] *nmf* biologist
biomasse [bjomas] *nf* biomass
biophysique [bjofizik] *nf* biophysics *(singulier)*
biopsie [bjɔpsi] *nf* biopsy
biorythme [bjoritm] *nm* biorhythm
biosphère [bjosfɛr] *nf* biosphere
biotechnique [bjotɛknik], **biotechnologie** [bjotɛknolɔʒi] *nf* biotechnology
bip [bip] **1** *exclam* beep!
2 *nm* (**a**) *(son)* beep; **faire b.** to beep (**b**) *(appareil)* beeper, pager
biparti, -e [biparti], **bipartite** [bipartit] *adj* bipartite
bipède [bipɛd] *adj & nm* biped
biplace [biplas] *adj & nm Aut & Av* two-seater
biplan [biplā] *nm* biplane
bipolaire [bipolɛr] *adj Él & Phys* bipolar
bique [bik] *nf Fam* (**a**) *(chèvre)* nanny goat (**b**) *Péj (femme)* **vieille b.** old bag
biquet, -ette [bikɛ, -ɛt] *nm,f* (**a**) *(chevreau)* kid (**b**) *Fam* **mon b.** my pet
biréacteur [bireaktœr] *nm* twin-engine jet
birman, -e [birmā, -an] **1** *adj* Burmese
2 *nm,f* **B.** Burmese
3 *nm (langue)* Burmese
Birmanie [birmani] *nf* **la B.** Burma
bis¹, -e [bi, biz] *adj* greyish-brown
bis² [bis] *adv* (**a**) *Th* encore; *Mus* repeat (**b**) *(d'une adresse)* **7 b.** ≃ 7A
bisaïeul, -e [bizajœl] *nm,f Litt* great-grandfather, *f* great-grandmother
bisannuel, -elle [bizanɥɛl] *adj* biennial
bisbille [bisbij] *nf Fam* squabble; **être en b. avec qn** to be at odds with sb
biscornu, -e [biskɔrny] *adj* (**a**) *(chapeau)* misshapen; *(bâtiment, objet)* oddly shaped (**b**) *Fam (idées)* cranky; *(raisonnement, esprit)* tortuous
biscoteaux [biskoto] *nmpl Fam* biceps; **avoir des b.** to have bulging biceps
biscotte [biskɔt] *nf* rusk
biscuit [biskɥi] *nm* (**a**) *(gâteau)* Br biscuit, Am cookie; **b. à la cuiller** Br sponge finger, Am lady finger; **biscuits salés** crackers (**b**) *(porcelaine)* biscuit
bise¹ [biz] *nf (vent)* north wind
bise² *nf Fam (baiser)* kiss; **donner** *ou* **faire une b. à qn** to give sb a kiss; **se faire la b.** to give each other a

kiss; **grosses bises** *(sur une lettre)* love and kisses, lots of love
biseau, -x [bizo] *nm* (**a**) *(bord)* bevel; **taillé en b.** beveledged (**b**) *(outil)* bevel
biseauter [bizote] *vt* (**a**) *(tailler)* to bevel (**b**) *(cartes à jouer)* to mark
bisexualité [bisɛksɥalite] *nf* bisexuality
bisexuel, -elle [bisɛksɥɛl] *adj* bisexual
bismuth [bismyt] *nm* bismuth
bison [bizɔ̃] *nm* bison
Bison Futé [bizɔ̃fyte] *n* = organization which advises drivers of driving conditions on French motorways
bisou [bizu] *nm Fam* kiss
bisque [bisk] *nf Culin* **b. de homard** lobster bisque
bisquer [biske] *vi Fam* **faire b. qn** to wind sb up
bissectrice [bisɛktris] *nf* bisector
bisser [bise] *vt* (**a**) *(sujet: artiste) (chanson)* to give an encore of (**b**) *(sujet: spectateur) (chanson)* to call for an encore of; **b. un chanteur** to call on a singer to give an encore
bissextile [bisɛkstil] *adj* **année b.** leap year
bistouri [bisturi] *nm* lancet
bistro(t) [bistro] *nm Fam* bar
BIT [beite] *nm (abrév* **Bureau international du travail**) ILO
bit [bit] *nm Ordinat* bit; **b. d'arrêt** stop bit; **b. de contrôle** control bit; **b. de départ** start bit
bite [bit] *nf Vulg* cock
bitoniau [bitɔnjo] *nm Fam* thingy
bitte¹ [bit] = **bite**
bitte² *nf Naut* **b. d'amarrage** bollard
bitture [bityr] *nf très Fam* **prendre une b.** to get plastered
bitturer [bityre] **se bitturer** *vpr très Fam* to get plastered
bitume [bitym] *nm (revêtement)* asphalt
bitumer [bityme] *vt (route)* to asphalt
bitum(in)eux, -euse [bitym(in)ø, -øz] *adj* bituminous
biture [bityr] = **bitture**
biturer [bityre] = **bitturer**
bivouac [bivwak] *nm* bivouac
bivouaquer [bivwake] *vi* to bivouac
bizarre [bizar] *adj* strange, odd
bizarrement [bizarmā] *adv* strangely, oddly
bizarrerie [bizarri] *nf (d'une situation, d'une idée, d'une attitude)* strangeness, oddness; **bizarreries** oddities; *(d'une personne)* eccentricities
bizarroïde [bizarɔid] *adj Fam* weird
bizut [bizy] *nm Fam* = first-year student on whom practical jokes are played
bizutage [bizytaʒ] *nm Fam* = practical jokes played on first-year students
bizuter [bizyte] *vt Fam (étudiant)* to play practical jokes on
bizuth [bizy] = **bizut**
bla-bla [blabla] *nm Fam* claptrap
blackbouler [blakbule] *vt Fam (à un examen)* to fail; **faire b.** to fail, *Am* to flunk
blafard, -e [blafar, -ard] *adj* pallid
blague [blag] *nf* (**a**) *(plaisanterie)* joke; **faire une b. à qn** to play a joke on sb; **b. à part** joking apart; **sans b.?** No kidding? (**b**) *(mensonge)* **raconter des blagues** to lie
blaguer [blage] *vi Fam* to joke; **aimer b.** to like a joke
blagueur, -euse [blagœr, -øz] *Fam* **1** *adj* **il est très b.** he really likes a joke
2 *nm,f (qui dit des blagues)* joker; *(qui fait des blagues)* practical joker

blair [blɛr] *nm très Fam Br* conk, *Am* schnozzle

blaireau, -x [blɛro] *nm* (a) *(animal)* badger (b) *(pinceau)* shaving brush

blairer [blere] *vt Fam* **je ne peux pas le b.** I can't stand him

blâme [blɑm] *nm* (a) *(reproche)* blame (b) *(sanction)* reprimand

blâmer [blɑme] *vt* (a) *(désapprouver)* to blame (b) *(sanctionner)* to reprimand

blanc, blanche [blɑ̃, blɑ̃ʃ] **1** *adj* (a) *(couleur)* white; b. comme neige as white as snow (b) *(peau)* pale; *(pas bronzé)* white; **b. comme un linge** as white as a sheet (c) *(page)* blank (d) *(sourd)* **d'une voix blanche** in a toneless voice **2** *nm* (a) *(couleur)* white; **le b. est à la mode** white is in; **b. cassé** off-white (b) *(partie blanche)* *(d'une cible)* bull's-eye; **le b. des yeux** the whites of the eyes; **regarder qn dans le b. des yeux** to look sb straight in the eye; **b. d'œuf** egg white; **b. de poulet** chicken breast (c) *(espace)* blank (d) *(aux dominos)* blank (e) **chauffé à b.** white-hot; **tirer à b.** to fire a blank/blanks (f) *(linge)* **(articles de) b.** linen; **je lave le b. séparément** I wash my whites separately (g) *(vin)* white wine **3** *nm,f* B. White (man), *f* White (woman); **les Blancs** the Whites **4** *nf* **blanche** *Mus Br* minim, *Am* half note

blanc-bec *(pl* blancs-becs) [blɑ̃bɛk] *nm* total novice

blanchâtre [blɑ̃ʃatr] *adj* whitish

blanche [blɑ̃ʃ] *voir* blanc

Blanche-Neige [blɑ̃ʃnɛʒ] *npr* Snow White

blancheur [blɑ̃ʃœr] *nf* whiteness

blanchiment [blɑ̃ʃimɑ̃] *nm (d'argent)* laundering

blanchir [blɑ̃ʃir] **1** *vt* (a) *(rendre blanc)* to whiten; *(linge)* to launder; **b. à la chaux** to whitewash (b) *(disculper)* to clear (c) *(argent)* to launder (d) *Culin* to blanch **2** *vi* (a) *(devenir blanc)* to turn or go white; (b) *(pâlir)* to blanch

blanchissage [blɑ̃ʃisaʒ] *nm* (a) *(du linge)* laundering (b) *Can Sp* shutout

blanchissement [blɑ̃ʃismɑ̃] *nm* whitening

blanchisserie [blɑ̃ʃisri] *nf* laundry

blanchisseur, -euse [blɑ̃ʃisœr, -øz] *nm,f* laundryman,*f* laundrywoman

blanchon [blɑ̃ʃɔ̃] *nm Can* whitecoat *(seal pup)*

blanquette¹ [blɑ̃kɛt] *nf Culin* **b. (de veau)** = veal stew in a white sauce

blanquette² *nf* **b. de Limoux** = sparkling white wine from Limoux

blasé, -e [blaze] *adj* blasé

blason [blazɔ̃] *nm* coat of arms

blasphème [blasfɛm] *nm* blasphemy

blasphémer [34] [blasfeme] *vi* to blaspheme

blatte [blat] *nf* cockroach

blazer [blazɛr, blazœr] *nm* blazer

bld *abrév* boulevard

blé [ble] *nm* (a) *(céréale)* wheat, *Br* corn; **b. dur** durum wheat; **b. en herbe** wheat in the blade; *Fig* **manger son b. en herbe** to eat one's seed corn; *Can* **b. d'Inde** *Br* maize, *Am* (Indian) corn (b) *Fam (argent)* bread

bled [blɛd] *nm Fam (lieu isolé)* dump, hole; **dans un b. perdu** in the middle of nowhere

blême [blɛm] *adj (personne, matin)* pale; **b. de colère** livid with anger; **devenir b.** to turn or go pale

blêmir [blemir] *vi* to turn or go pale; **b. de colère** to turn livid with anger

blennorragie [blenoraʒi] *nf* gonorrhoea

blessant, -e [blesɑ̃, -ɑ̃t] *adj* hurtful

blessé, -e [blese] **1** *adj (par arme)* wounded; *(dans un accident)* injured; *(moralement)* hurt; **être b. dans son amour-propre** to have had one's pride hurt; **êtes-vous b.?** are you hurt? **2** *nm,f (victime d'un accident)* injured person; *(victime d'une agression)* wounded person; **les blessés** the injured/wounded

blesser [blese] **1** *vt* (a) *(par arme)* to wound; *(dans un accident)* to injure, to hurt; *(sujet: chaussures)* to hurt; **il a été blessé au bras** *(par arme)* he was wounded in the arm; *(dans un accident)* his arm was injured (b) *(moralement)* to hurt **2** **se blesser** *vpr (avec une arme)* to wound oneself; *(accidentellement)* to hurt or injure oneself **(avec** with); **se b. à la tête** *(avec une arme)* to wound oneself in the head; *(accidentellement)* to hurt one's head

blessure [blesyr] *nf (par arme)* wound; *(dans un accident)* injury; *Fig (morale)* wound, hurt

blette [blɛt] = **bette**

bleu, -e [blø] **1** *adj* blue; *(bifteck)* very rare; **b. de froid** blue with cold **2** *nm* (a) *(couleur)* blue; **le b. est à la mode** blue is in; **b. canard** peacock blue; **b. ciel** sky blue; **b. électrique** electric blue; **b. marine** navy (blue); **b. nuit** midnight blue; **b. de Prusse** Prussian blue; **b. roi** royal blue (b) *(ecchymose)* bruise; **se faire un b.** to bruise oneself (c) *Fam (novice)* novice; *Mil* rookie (d) *(fromage)* blue cheese; **b. d'Auvergne/de Bresse** = blue cheese from Auvergne/Bresse (e) **b. (de chauffe** *ou* **de travail)** overalls; *(salopette)* dungarees

bleuâtre [bløatr] *adj* bluish

bleuet [bluɛ] *nm* (a) *(plante)* cornflower (b) *Can (baie)* blueberry

bleuetière [bløtjɛr] *nf Can* blueberry field

bleuté, -e [bløte] *adj* bluish; *(verres)* blue-tinted

blindage [blɛ̃daʒ] *nm Mil* armour-plating

blindé, -e [blɛ̃de] **1** *adj* (a) *(véhicule militaire)* armoured, armour-plated; *(voiture)* bulletproof; **porte blindée** steel security door (b) *Fam* **je suis b.** I'm hardened to it **2** *nm Mil* armoured vehicle

blinder [blɛ̃de] *vt* (a) *(véhicule)* to armour-plate; *(porte)* to reinforce with steel (b) *Fam (personne)* to harden **(contre** to)

blini [blini] *nm* blini

blizzard [blizar] *nm* blizzard

bloc [blɔk] *nm* (a) *(de bois, de pierre)* block (b) *(de maisons)* block (c) *Pol* bloc; **faire b. (avec/contre qn)** to join forces (with/against sb) (d) *(de papier)* pad; **b. de papier à lettres** writing pad (e) *(ensemble d'éléments)* unit; **b. opératoire** operating theatre (f) *très Fam (FAM prison)* clink; **être au b.** to be in the clink (g) *Ordinat* block; **b. d'alimentation** secteur mains power unit; **b. de données** data block; **b. de touches** keypad (h) *(locutions)* **tout refuser en b.** to reject everything in its entirety; **serrer qch à b.** to screw sth as tightly as possible

blocage [blɔkaʒ] *nm* (a) *(d'un mécanisme)* jamming; *(des freins)* locking; *(des prix, des salaires)* freezing; *Psy (mental)* block; *Psy* **faire un b.** to get a (mental) block (b) *Ordinat (dans réseau)* lockout; **b. majuscule** caps lock

blockhaus [blɔkos] *nm* blockhouse

bloc-moteur *(pl* blocs-moteurs) [blɔkmɔtœr] *nm* engine block

bloc-notes *(pl* blocs-notes) [blɔknɔt] *nm* notepad

blocus [blɔkys] *nm* blockade; **lever/forcer le b.** to raise/run the blockade

blond, -e [blɔ̃, -ɔ̃d] **1** adj (cheveux) fair, blond; (personne) fair-haired, blond; (sable, blés) golden; **être b. comme les blés** (sujet: personne) to have golden-blond hair **2** nm,f (personne) **un b. a** fair-haired man; **une blonde** a blonde, a fair-haired woman; **une blonde décolorée** a peroxide blonde **3** nm (couleur) **b. cendré** ash blond; **b. platine** platinum blond; **b. vénitien** strawberry blond **4** nf **blonde** (**a**) (bière) Br lager, Am light beer (**b**) Can Fam (amie) girlfriend

blondinet, -ette [blɔ̃dinɛ, -ɛt] nm,f fair-haired child

blondir [blɔ̃dir] **1** vt (cheveux) to bleach **2** vi (cheveux, personne) to go or turn blond; **faire b. des oignons** to cook onions until they turn pale yellow

bloquer [blɔke] **1** vt (**a**) (mécanisme, porte) to jam; **il m'a bloqué contre un mur** he jammed me up against a wall; Fam **je suis bloqué à l'hôpital** I'm stuck in hospital (**b**) (réunir) to group together; (jours de congé) to lump together (**c**) (compte en banque) to block; (prix, salaires) to freeze (**d**) (route, ballon) to block; **b. le chemin** ou **le passage à qn** to block sb's way (**e**) Belg Fam (sujet) to bone up on (**f**) Psy **ça me bloque de me sentir observé** I get a (mental) block if I feel I'm being watched; **être bloqué** to have a (mental) block **2 se bloquer** vpr (**a**) (machine, ascenseur) to get stuck (**b**) Psy to get a (mental) block

blottir [blɔtir] **se blottir** vpr to snuggle up; **se b. contre qn/dans les bras de qn** to snuggle up to sb/in sb's arms; **blottis les uns contre les autres** huddled up together

blousant, -e [bluzɑ̃, -ɑ̃t] adj loose-fitting

blouse [bluz] nf (**a**) (tablier) overall; **b. de laboratoire/ blanche** lab/white coat (**b**) (de femme) blouse

blouser [bluze] **1** vt Fam (personne) to con **2** vi (corsage) to be loose-fitting

blouson [bluzɔ̃] nm (lumber-)jacket; (plus léger) blouson; **b. en** ou **de cuir** leather jacket; **b. d'aviateur** bomber jacket; Fam Vieilli **b. noir** young hoodlum (wearing a black leather jacket)

blue-jean [bludʒin] (pl **blue-jeans** [bludʒins]) nm Vieilli jeans

blues [bluz] nm blues

bluff [blœf] nm bluff; **y aller au b.** to try and bluff

bluffer [blœfe] **1** vt (aux cartes) to bluff; Fam (personne) to take in **2** vi (aux cartes) & Fam to bluff

blush [blœʃ] nm blusher

BN [beɛn] nf (abrév **Bibliothèque nationale**) = French national library, based in Paris

boa [bɔa] nm (**a**) (serpent) boa; **b. constricteur** boa constrictor (**b**) (en plumes) boa

boat people [botpipœl] nmpl boat people

bob [bɔb] nm Fam (chapeau) sun hat

bobard [bɔbar] nm Fam tall story

bobine [bɔbin] nf (**a**) (de ruban, de fil) reel; (de machine à coudre) bobbin; (de machine à écrire, d'appareil photo) spool; (de film, de papier) roll (**b**) Él coil (**c**) Fam (visage) mug

bobo [bobo] nm (langage enfantin) (coupure) cut; (piqûre) sting; **ça fait b.?** does it hurt?; **se faire b.** to hurt oneself

bobsleigh [bɔbslɛ(g)] nm bobsleigh

bocage [bɔkaʒ] nm bocage (countryside with many hedges, trees and small fields)

bocal, -aux [bɔkal, -o] nm jar; (aquarium) (fish)bowl

Boche [bɔʃ] nmf Fam Péj Kraut, = offensive term referring to a German

bock [bɔk] nm beer glass

body [bɔdi] nm (vêtement) body

body-building [bɔdibildiŋ] nm body building; **faire du b.** to do body building

bœuf [bœf, pl bø] **1** nm (**a**) (animal) bullock; (de trait) ox; Fam **on n'est pas des bœufs** we're not superhuman (**b**) (viande) beef; **b. bourguignon** bœuf bourguignon; Culin **b. mode** stewed beef (**c**) Fam (improvisation) jam session; **faire un b.** to jam **2** adj inv Fam **avoir un succès b.** to be incredibly successful; **faire un effet b.** to make a really big impression

bof [bɔf] exclam Fam **ça te plaît? – b., pas tellement** do you like it? – not really, no; **il est chouette, hein, mon nouveau pull? – b.** my new sweater's great, isn't it? – I guess

Bogota [bogota] n Bogota

bogue [bɔg] nf (**a**) (de châtaigne) Br burr, Am shuck (**b**) Ordinat bug; **dépourvu/plein de bogues** bug-free/ -ridden; **b. de logiciel** software bug

bohème [bɔɛm] **1** adj bohemian **2** nmf **mener une vie de b.** to lead a bohemian life

Bohème [bɔɛm] nf **la B.** Bohemia

bohémien, -enne [bɔemjɛ̃, -ɛn] nm,f gypsy

boire¹ [12] [bwar] **1** vt (**a**) (sujet: personne) to drink; Fig **b. les paroles de qn** to drink in sb's every word (**b**) (sujet: plante, matière poreuse) to soak up, to absorb **2** vi (personne) to drink; (plante) to soak up or absorb water; Can (bébé) to feed; **b. comme un trou** to drink like a fish; **b. à la bouteille** to drink from the bottle; **b. au succès de qn/qch** to drink to the success of sb/sth; **donner à b. à qn** to give sb a drink; **faire b. qn** to give sb something to drink; **faire b. les chevaux** to water the horses; Fig **il y a à b. et à manger là-dedans** it's a bit of a mixed bag; Prov **qui a bu boira** old habits die hard **3 se boire** vpr to be drunk

boire² nm **le b. et le manger** food and drink

bois [bwa] nm (**a**) (forêt) wood (**b**) (matériau) wood; **des meubles en b.** wooden furniture; Fig **elle n'est pas de b.** she's only human; Fig **je vais leur faire voir de quel b. je me chauffe!** I'll show them (what I'm made of)!; **petit b.** kindling; **b. de charpente** ou **de construction** Br timber, Am lumber; **b. de chauffage** firewood; **b. mort** deadwood; **b. de rose** rosewood (**c**) (de chaise, de raquette) frame; **faire un b.** (au tennis) to hit the ball off the frame; **b. de lit** bed frame (**d**) Mus **les b.** the woodwind (**e**) **les b.** (d'un cerf) the antlers

boisé, -e [bwaze] adj (région) wooded

boisement [bwazmɑ̃] nm afforestation

boiseries [bwazri] nfpl panelling

boisson [bwasɔ̃] nf drink; Can (spiritueux) hard liquor, spirits; **b. alcoolisée/non alcoolisée** alcoholic/soft drink; **b. chaude/fraîche** hot/cold drink; **b. gazeuse** fizzy drink

boîte [bwat] nf (**a**) (récipient) box; **des haricots en b.** canned or Br tinned beans; **mettre qch en b.** (marchandises) to box sth; (aliments) to can sth, Br to tin sth; Fam **mettre qn en b.** to pull sb's leg; **b. d'allumettes** (pleine) box of matches; (vide) matchbox; **b. à bijoux** jewel box; **b. de conserve** can, Br tin; **b. à couture** ou **ouvrage** sewing box; **b. à gants** glove compartment; **b. à** ou **aux lettres** Br postbox, Am mailbox; (chez soi) Br letterbox, Am mailbox; **b. à lettres électronique** mailbox; **b. à musique** music box; Av **b. noire** black box; **b. à outils** toolbox; **b. postale** Post Office Box; Aut **b. de vitesses** gearbox (**b**) Fam (entreprise) firm; (école) school (**c**) **b. (de nuit)** nightclub; **aller** ou **sortir en b.** to go clubbing

boiter [bwate] vi to limp

boiteux, -euse [bwatø, -øz] adj (personne, cheval,

explication) lame; *(raisonnement)* shaky; *(phrase)* badly constructed

boîtier [bwatje] *nm* case; *Phot* (camera) body; *Ordinat* **b. de commande** command box; *Ordinat* **b. commutateur** data switch

boitiller [bwatije] *vi* to limp slightly

boive *etc voir* **boire**

bol [bɔl] *nm* **(a)** *(récipient)* bowl **(b)** *(contenu)* bowl(ful), **prendre un b. d'air frais** *ou* **pur** to get a good breath of fresh air **(c)** *Fam (chance)* luck; **avoir du b.** to be lucky; **ne pas avoir de b.** to be unlucky; **manque de b., il était déjà parti!** just my luck, he'd already left! **(d) le B. d'or** = 24-hour motorcycle race

bolchevique [bɔlʃəvik, bɔlʃevik] *adj & nmf* Bolshevik

bolduc [bɔldyk] *nm* gift-wrap ribbon

bolée [bɔle] *nf* bowl(ful)

boléro [bɔlero] *nm (vêtement, pièce musicale)* bolero

bolet [bɔlɛ] *nm* bolotus

bolide [bɔlid] *nm (voiture)* racing car; **comme un b.** like a rocket

Bolivie [bɔlivi] *nf* la **B.** Bolivia

bolivien, -enne [bɔlivjɛ̃, -ɛn] **1** *adj* Bolivian **2** *nm,f* **B.** Bolivian

bolognais, -e [bɔlɔɲɛ, -ɛz] *adj* Bolognese; *Culin* **spaghetti bolognaise** spaghetti bolognese

Bologne [bɔlɔɲ] *n* Bologna

bombage [bɔ̃baʒ] *nm Fam (aérosol)* graffiti; **faire des bombages sur un mur** to spray-paint a wall (with graffiti)

bombance [bɔ̃bɑ̃s] *nf Fam* **faire b.** to feast

bombardement [bɔ̃bardəmɑ̃] *nm (avec des obus)* shelling; *(avec des bombes)* bombing; **b. aérien** air raid

bombarder [bɔ̃barde] *vt* **(a)** *(avec des obus)* to shell; *(avec des bombes)* to bomb, **b. qn de questions/de lettres** to bombard sb with questions/letters **(b)** *Fam* **on l'a bombardé ministre** he's been pitchforked into the post of minister

bombardier [bɔ̃bardje] *nm (avion)* bomber; *(aviateur)* bombardier

bombe [bɔ̃b] *nf* **(a)** *(explosif)* bomb; *Fig* **faire l'effet d'une b.** to be a bombshell; **b. atomique** atom(ic) bomb; **b. à eau** water bomb; *Culin* **b. glacée** bombe glacée; **b. H** H bomb; **b. à hydrogène** hydrogen bomb; **b. lacrymogène** tear-gas grenade; **b. à retardement** time bomb **(b)** *(atomiseur)* spray, aerosol **(c)** *(chapeau)* riding hat **(d)** *Fam* **faire la b.** to live it up

bombé, -e [bɔ̃be] *adj* bulging

bomber [bɔ̃be] **1** *vt (gonfler)* **b. qch** to cause sth to bulge; **b. le torse** to throw out one's chest; *Fig* to swagger (around) **2** *vi (mur)* to bulge; *(planche)* to warp

bombonne [bɔ̃bɔn] = **bonbonne**

bôme [bom] *nf Naut* boom

bon¹, bonne [bɔ̃, bɔn] **1** *adj* **(a)** *(agréable)* good; **passer une bonne soirée** to spend a pleasant evening; **l'eau est bonne** *(en se baignant)* the water's great, **de bons petits plats** nice little meals; **souhaiter une** *ou* **la bonne année à qn** to wish sb a happy New Year; **bonnes vacances!** have a good holiday!

(b) *(satisfaisant) (travail, qualité)* good; **c'est b.** *(d'accord)* that's fine; **c'est b., j'ai compris** all right *or* OK, I understand **(c)** *(correct)* right; **c'est la bonne réponse/le b. bus** that's the right answer/bus; **un intellectuel, au b. sens du terme** an intellectual in the true sense of the word **(d)** *(compétent)* good **(en** at); **un b. professeur/père** a good teacher/father **(e)** *(profitable) (investissement, conseil, idée)* good; **cet**

exercice est b. pour le dos this exercise is good for the back; **c'est b. à savoir** it's worth knowing; **il serait b. que vous lui en parliez** it would be a good idea if you spoke to her about it; **à quoi b.?** what's the point *or* the use?; **à quoi b. se plaindre?** what's the point *or* the use of complaining?; **quand b. vous semble** whenever you like **(f)** *(apte)* **b. à manger** fit *or* safe to eat; **b. pour le service** *Mil* fit for duty; *Fig* serviceable; **elle n'est bonne à rien** she's useless; **tu es b. pour une contravention** you're in for a fine

(g) *(valable) (billet, abonnement)* valid; **la balle est bonne** *(au tennis)* the ball is in *or* good; **les œufs sont-ils encore bons?** are the eggs still all right to eat? **(h)** *(moralement)* good; *(généreux)* good, kind **(envers** *ou* **avec** to) **(i)** *(en intensif)* good; **j'ai attendu deux bonnes heures** I waited for a good two hours; **il m'a fallu un b. moment pour comprendre** it took me a while to understand; **un b. rhume** a bad cold **(j)** *(locutions)* **elle est bien bonne!** that's a good one!; **il en a de bonnes!** he must be joking *or* kidding!; **avoir qn à la bonne** to have a soft spot for sb; **pour de b.** *(partir, revenir)* for good

2 *exclam (d'accord)* right!, fine!; **b., on y va?** right, shall we go?; **allons b.!** what!; **ah b., je ne le savais pas** really? I didn't know

3 *adv (sentir)* good, nice; **il fait b.** it's lovely; **un pays où il fait b. vivre** a country that's nice to live in

4 *nm,f* **les bons et les méchants** *(dans un film)* the goodies and the baddies; **un b. à rien** a good-for-nothing **5** *nm* **cela a du b.** it has some good points

bon² *nm* **(a)** *(papier)* voucher, coupon, **b. d'achat** *Br* gift voucher, *Am* gift certificate; **b. de commande** order form; **b. de garantie** guarantee; **b. de livraison** delivery note; **b. de réduction** money-off coupon **(b)** *Fin* bond; **b. du trésor** treasury bond

bonard, -e [bɔnar, -ard] *adj Fam* **c'est b.!** that's pretty good!

bonasse [bɔnas] *adj* soft, **d'un ton b.** meekly

bonbon [bɔ̃bɔ̃] *nm* **(a)** *(sucrerie) Br* sweet, *Am* candy; **b. à la menthe** mint **(b)** *Belg* biscuit

bonbonne [bɔ̃bɔn] *nf* demijohn; *(de gaz)* cylinder

bonbonnière [bɔ̃bɔnjɛr] *nf Br* sweet *or Am* candy box

bond [bɔ̃] *nm* **(a)** *(saut)* leap, jump; **faire un b.** to leap up; *Fig* to shoot up; **faire un b. en avant/en arrière** to leap forwards/back; **franchir qch d'un b.** to clear sth at one leap; **se lever d'un b.** **(b)** *(d'une balle)* bounce; **faire un b.** to leave sb in the lurch

bonde [bɔ̃d] *nf* **(a)** *(bouchon) (d'un évier, d'une baignoire)* plug; *(d'un tonneau)* bung; *(d'un bassin)* sluice gate **(b)** *(trou) (d'un évier, d'une baignoire)* plughole; *(d'un tonneau)* bunghole; *(d'un bassin)* drainage hole

bondé, -e [bɔ̃de] *adj* packed, crammed

bondir [bɔ̃dir] *vi* to leap, to jump; **b. sur** to pounce on; *Fig* **cela me fait b.** it makes me hopping mad

bon enfant [bɔ̃nɑ̃fɑ̃] *adj inv* easy-going

bonheur [bɔnœr] *nm* **(a)** *(bien-être)* happiness; **faire le b. de qn** to make sb happy **(b)** *(chance)* good fortune, (good) luck; **j'ai le b. de la connaître** I have the good fortune to know her; **porter b. à qn** to bring sb (good) luck; **il ne connaît pas son b.** he doesn't know how lucky he is; **par b.** luckily; **au petit b. (la chance)** at random **(c)** *Litt (réussite)* **avec b.** felicitously

bonhomie [bɔnɔmi] *nf* good-naturedness; **avec b.** good-naturedly

bonhomme [bɔnɔm] *(pl* **bonshommes** [bɔ̃zɔm]*) nm Fam* guy; **c'est un sacré b.** he's a hell of a guy; **on se retrouvera, mon b.!** I'll get even with you, my friend!; **aller**

son petit b. de chemin to be jogging along nicely; **b. de neige** snowman

boniche [bɔniʃ] *nf* maid, *Br* skivvy

bonification [bɔnifikasjɔ̃] *nf* (**a**) *(d'une terre, d'un vin)* improvement (**b**) *Com* bonus (**c**) *Sp* advantage

bonifier [66] [bɔnifje] **1** *vt (terre, caractère)* to improve **2 se bonifier** *vpr* to improve

boniment [bɔnimɑ̃] *nm* (**a**) *(discours)* sales talk, patter; *Fam* **faire du b. à qn** *Br* to chat sb up, *Am* to hit on sb (**b**) *Fam (mensonges)* tall story; **tout ça, c'est du b.** that's all claptrap

bonite [bɔnit] *nf* bonito

bonjour [bɔ̃ʒur] *nm* hello; *(le matin)* good morning; *(l'après-midi)* good afternoon; **dire b. à qn** to say hello/ good morning/good afternoon to sb; **dis b. à ta mère de ma part** say hello to your mother for me; **facile** *ou* **simple comme b.** easy as pie; *Fam* **b. l'ambiance!** there was one hell of an atmosphere!; *Fam* **b. la soirée!** what an evening!; *Fam* **le périphérique à six heures du soir, b.!** the *Br* ring road *or Am* beltway at six o'clock at night, forget it!

bon marché [bɔ̃marʃe] *adj inv* cheap; **acheter/vendre qch (à) b.** to buy/sell sth cheap(ly)

bonne [bɔn] **1** *voir* **bon**[1] **2** *nf (domestique)* maid, *Vieilli* maidservant; *Fam* **dis-donc, je ne suis pas ta b.!** I'm not your maid, you know!; **b. à tout faire** maid; **b. d'enfants** nanny

Bonne-Espérance [bɔnɛsperɑ̃s] *voir* **cap**

bonnement [bɔnmɑ̃] *adv* **tout b.** simply

bonnet [bɔnɛ] *nm* (**a**) *(coiffure)* hat; **c'est b. blanc et blanc b.** it's six of one and half a dozen of the other; **b. d'âne** dunce's cap; **b. de bain** bathing cap; **b. de nuit** nightcap; **b. de ski** ski hat (**b**) *(d'un soutien-gorge)* cup; **quelle profondeur de b.?** what size cup?

bonneterie [bɔnɛtri] *nf* (**a**) *(bas)* hosiery (**b**) *(commerce)* hosiery trade; *(magasin)* hosier's (shop)

bonniche [bɔniʃ] = **boniche**

bonsaï [bɔnzaj, bɔ̃zaj] *nm* bonsai

bonsoir [bɔ̃swar] *nm* good evening; *(quand on se quitte tard, quand on se couche)* goodnight; **dire b. à qn** to say good evening/goodnight to sb

bonté [bɔ̃te] *nf* (**a**) *(gentillesse)* kindness, goodness; **une femme d'une grande b.** a very kind woman; **un sourire plein de b.** a kind smile; **avoir la b. de faire qch** to be so good as to do sth; **faire qch par b. d'âme** to do sth out of the goodness of one's heart; *Vieilli* **b. divine!** good heavens! (**b**) *(acte)* **remercier qn pour ses bontés** to thank sb for his/ her kindness

bonus [bɔnys] *nm (prime de salaire)* bonus; *(d'assurance)* no-claims bonus

bon vivant [bɔ̃vivɑ̃] *adj m* **être b.** to enjoy life

bonze [bɔ̃z] *nm* Buddhist priest

bookmaker [bukmɛkœr] *nm* bookmaker

booléen, -enne [buleɛ̃, -ɛɛn] *adj Math & Ordinat* Boolean

boom [bum] *nm* boom

boomerang [bumrɑ̃g] *nm* boomerang

booter [bute] *vi Ordinat* **b. (sur le lecteur B)** to boot up (off the B drive)

boots [buts] *nmpl* ankle boots

borborygmes [bɔrbɔrigm] *nmpl* rumbling

bord [bɔr] *nm* (**a**) *(limite)* edge; *(d'un chapeau)* brim; *(d'une tasse, d'un verre)* rim; **un chapeau à larges bords** a wide-brimmed hat; **le b. du trottoir** *Br* the kerb, *Am* the curb; **sur le** *ou* **au b. de** *(route)* at the side of; *(lac, rivière)* beside; **aller au b. de la mer** to go to the seaside; **une maison en b. de mer** a house beside the sea; **au b. des larmes/de la catastrophe** on the verge of tears/of disaster; *Fam* **un peu voleur sur les bords** a bit light-fingered; **b. à b.** edge to edge; *Ordinat* **b. de reliure** inside margin (**b**) à **b. de** *(bateau, avion)* on board; **prendre qn à son b.** to take sb on board; **par-dessus b.** overboard; *Fig* **être du même b.** to be on the same side

bordages [bɔrdaʒ] *nmpl Can (glace)* inshore ice

bordeaux [bɔrdo] **1** *nm* Bordeaux (wine); **b. rouge** claret **2** *adj inv* maroon

bordée [bɔrde] *nf* (**a**) *Naut (de coups de feu)* broadside; *Fig* **b. de jurons** torrent of swearwords (**b**) *Fam* **être en b.** to be on a binge (**c**) *Can* **b. (de neige)** heavy snowfall

bordel [bɔrdɛl] *nm* **très** *Fam (hôtel de passe)* brothel; *(désordre)* mess; *(vacarme)* racket; **mettre** *ou* **foutre le b. dans qch** to make a mess of sth; **et tout le b.** and the whole damn lot; *Vulg* **b.!** shit!

bordelais, -e [bɔrdəlɛ, -ɛz] **1** *adj* of Bordeaux **2** *nm,f* **B.** = person from Bordeaux **3** *nm* **le B.** *(région)* the Bordeaux region

bordélique [bɔrdelik] *adj Fam (pièce, organisation)* shambolic; **être b.** *(personne)* to be a slob

border [bɔrde] *vt* (**a**) *(garnir)* **b. qch de** to edge sth with (**b**) *(sujet: arbres) (route)* to line; *(sujet: bateau) (côte)* to skirt (**c**) *(lit, draps)* to tuck in; **b. qn (dans son lit)** to tuck sb in

bordereau, -x [bɔrdəro] *nm (liste)* schedule; **b. de livraison** delivery note

bordure [bɔrdyr] *nf* (**a**) *(bord)* edge; *(d'un vêtement)* border; **en b. de route/de mer** by the roadside/the sea (**b**) *(d'un miroir, d'un tableau)* frame

boréal, -e, -als *ou* **-aux, -ales** [bɔreal, -o] *adj* northern

borgne [bɔrɲ] **1** *adj* (**a**) *(personne)* one-eyed; *(mur)* blind; *(fenêtre)* obstructed (**b**) *(louche)* shady **2** *nmf* one-eyed man, *f* one-eyed woman

borne [bɔrn] *nf* (**a**) *(limite)* boundary marker; *(pierre)* boundary stone; *Fig* **sans bornes** boundless; **b. d'incendie** *Br* (fire) hydrant, *Am* fireplug; **b. kilométrique** kilometre marker, ≈ milestone; **b. Fam (kilomètre)** kilometre (**c**) *Él* terminal (**d**) *Ordinat* **b. (interactive)** terminal

borné, -e [bɔrne] *adj (esprit)* narrow; *(personne)* narrow-minded

borne-fontaine [bɔrnfɔ̃tɛn] *(pl* **bornes-fontaines**) *nf Can (bouche d'incendie)* Br (fire) hydrant, *Am* fireplug

borner [bɔrne] **1** *vt (terrain)* to mark out **2 se borner** *vpr* (**a**) **se b. à qch/à faire qch** *(personne)* to restrict oneself to sth/to doing sth (**b**) **se b. à qch** *(choses)* to be limited to sth

borsalino [bɔrsalino] *nm* fedora

bosniaque [bɔsnjak] **1** *adj* Bosnian **2** *nmf* **B.** Bosnian

Bosnie [bɔsni] *nf* **la B.** Bosnia; **la B.-Herzégovine** Bosnia-Herzegovina

bosquet [bɔskɛ] *nm* copse, grove

bosse [bɔs] *nf* (**a**) *(d'un bossu, d'un chameau)* hump; *Fig* **avoir la b. du commerce/des maths** to have a good head for business/maths; *Fam* **il a roulé sa b.** he's knocked about a bit (**b**) *(sur la tête)* bump, lump; *(sur le sol)* bump; *(sur une piste de ski)* mogul; **se faire une b.** to get a bump

bosselé, -e [bɔsle] *adj (casserole, pare-chocs)* dented

bosser [bɔse] *Fam* **1** *vi* to work **2** *vt Scol Br* to swot up, *Am* to grind away at

bosseur, -euse [bɔsœr, -øz] *Fam* **1** *adj* hardworking **2** *nm,f* hard worker

bossu, -e [bɔsy] **1** *adj (personne)* hunchbacked; *(animal)* humped **2** *nm,f* hunchback

bot [bo] *adj m voir* **pied**

botanique [botanik] **1** *adj* botanical **2** *nf* botany

botaniste [botanist] *nmf* botanist

Botswana [botswana] *nm* **le B.** Botswana

botte¹ [bot] *nf (de fleurs, de carottes, de radis)* bunch; *(de foin, de paille)* bale

botte² *nf (chaussure)* boot; *Fig* **sous la b. de** under the heel of; *Fam* **en avoir plein les bottes (de)** to be fed up to the back teeth (with); **bottes de** *ou* **en caoutchouc** rubber boots, *Br* wellingtons; **bottes de cavalier** *ou* **de cheval** riding boots

botte³ *nf (en escrime)* thrust; **porter une b. à qn** to make a thrust at sb; *Fig* **b. secrète** secret weapon

botter [bote] *vt* **(a)** *(chausser)* **botté de cuir** wearing leather boots **(b)** *Fam* **b. les fesses** *ou* **le derrière à qn** to boot sb up the backside **(c)** *Fam (plaire à)* **ça me botte** it's cool

bottier [botje] *nm* bootmaker

bottillon [botijɔ̃] *nm* ankle boot

Bottin® [botɛ̃] *nm (annuaire téléphonique)* phone book, telephone directory, **B. mondain** ≃ Who's Who

bottine [botin] *nf* ankle boot

botulisme [botylism] *nm Méd* botulism

boubou [bubu] *nm* = long traditional African robe

bouc [buk] *nm (animal)* (billy) goat; *(barbe)* goatee (beard); *Fam* **puer comme un b., puer le b.** to stink to high heaven; **b. émissaire** scapegoat

boucan [bukɑ̃] *nm Fam* row, din; **faire du b.** to kick up a row

boucane [bukan] *nf Can* smoke

boucané, -e [bukane] *adj (teint)* weatherbeaten

boucanier [bukanje] *nm* buccaneer

bouche [buʃ] *nf* **(a)** *(de personne, d'animal)* mouth; **avoir/ parler la b. pleine** to have/to talk with one's mouth full; **une pipe à la b.** with a pipe in his mouth; *Fig* **faire la fine b.** to be fussy; **c'est une fine b.** he's a gourmet; **b. cousue!** mum's the word!; **de b. à oreille** by word of mouth **(b)** *(d'une rivière, d'un cratère, d'un four)* mouth; *(d'un fusil, d'un canon)* muzzle; **b. d'égout** manhole; **b. d'incendie** *Br* (fire) hydrant, *Am* fireplug; **b. de métro** *Br* underground *or Am* subway entrance

bouché, e [buʃe] *adj (conduite, rue)* blocked; *(temps)* cloudy, overcast; **j'ai le nez b.** my nose is stuffed up; **J'ai les oreilles bouchées** my ears are blocked up; *Fam* **être b.** *(personne)* to be dense; *Fam* **être b. à l'émeri** to be a complete moron

bouche-à-bouche [buʃabuʃ] *nm inv* mouth-to-mouth resuscitation, *Br* kiss of life; **faire du b. à qn** to give sb mouth-to-mouth resuscitation

bouchée [buʃe] *nf* **(a)** *(quantité)* mouthful; *Fig* **ne faire qu'une b. de qn/qch** to make short work of sb/sth; **acheter qch pour une b. de pain** to buy sth for a song; **mettre les bouchées doubles** to really get a move on **(b)** *Culin* **b. (au chocolat)** chocolate; **b. à la reine** chicken vol au-vent

boucher¹ [buʃe] **1** *vt (fente, trou)* to fill in; *(conduite, fenêtre)* to block up; *(vue)* to block; *(bouteille)* to cork; **b. le passage à qn** to block sb's way; *Fam* **elle/ça m'en a bouché un coin** she/that took the wind out of my sails **2 se boucher** *vpr (conduite)* to get blocked up; **se b. le nez** to hold one's nose; **se b. les oreilles** to put one's fingers in one's ears

boucher², -ère [buʃe, -ɛr] *nm,f aussi Fig* butcher

boucherie [buʃri] *nf (boutique)* butcher's (shop); *(activité)*

butchery; *Fig (massacre)* slaughter; **b. chevaline** horse butcher's (shop)

bouche-trou *(pl* **bouche-trous)** [buʃtru] *nm Fam* stopgap; **servir de b.** to act as a stopgap

bouchon [buʃɔ̃] *nm* **(a)** *(à vis)* cap, top; *(d'un tonneau)* stopper; **b. (de liège)** cork; **vin qui sent le b.** corked wine; *Aut* **b. de réservoir** *Br* petrol cap, *Am* fuel cap **(b)** *(embouteillage)* hold-up, traffic jam; **3 kilomètres de b.** a 3-kilometre tailback **(c)** *(d'une ligne de pêche)* float **(d)** *(de paille)* wisp **(e)** **tu pousses le b. un peu loin!** you're going a bit too far!

bouchonné, -e [buʃone] *adj* corked

bouchonner [buʃone] **1** *vt (cheval)* to rub down **2** *vi Fam* **ça bouchonne** *(sur la route)* there's congestion

bouchot [buʃo] *nm* mussel bank

boucle [bukl] *nf (de ceinture, de chaussure, de harnais)* buckle; **b. d'oreille** earring **(b)** *(nœud, méandre, looping)* loop; **faire une b.** *(en marchant, en voiture)* to loop back **(c)** *(de cheveux)* curl **(d)** *Sp* lap **(e)** *Ordinat* loop

bouclé, -e [bukle] *adj (cheveux)* curly; *(personne)* curly-haired; *Ordinat* **systeme b.** looped system

boucler [bukle] **1** *vt* **(a)** *(ceinture, valise)* to buckle; *Fam (affaire)* to finish off; **b. sa valise** *(se préparer à partir)* to pack one's bags; **avoir du mal à b. ses fins de mois** to struggle to make ends meet at the end of the month; *Fam* **boucle-la!** belt up! **(b)** *(quartier)* to seal off; *Fam (chambre, maison)* to lock up; *Fam (prisonnier)* to bang up **(c) b. la boucle** *Av* to loop the loop; *Fig* to come full circle **2** *vi (cheveux)* to be curly; *(personne)* to have curly hair

bouclette [buklɛt] *nf (de cheveux)* small curl; *(de laine, de moquette)* curl

bouclier [buklje] *nm aussi Fig* shield; **b. atomique** *ou* **nucléaire** nuclear shield; **b. thermique** *(d'engin spatial)* heat shield

Bouddha [buda] *npr* Buddha

bouddhisme [budism] *nm* Buddhism

bouddhiste [budist] *adj & nmf* Buddhist

bouder [bude] **1** *vi* to sulk **2** *vt* **b. qn/qch** to refuse to have anything to do with sb/sth; **en été, les Parisiens boudent les salles de cinéma** Parisians don't go to the movies in summer

boudeur, -euse [budœr, -øz] **1** *adj* sulky **2** *nm,f* sulky person

boudin [budɛ̃] *nm* **(a)** *(charcuterie)* **b. (noir)** *Br* black pudding, *Am* blood sausage; **b. blanc** white pudding **(b)** *(de pâte à modeler, de terre)* roll **(c)** *(traversin)* bolster **(d)** *Fam Péj (femme)* fat lump

boudiné, -e [budine] *adj* **(a)** **je suis b. dans ce pantalon** I'm bursting out of these trousers **(b)** *(doigts)* podgy

boudoir [budwar] *nm* **(a)** *(salon)* boudoir **(b)** *(biscuit) Br* sponge finger, *Am* lady finger

boue [bu] *nf* **(a)** *(terre détrempée)* mud; *Fig* **traîner qn dans la b.** to drag sb through the mud **(b)** *(dans une rivière)* silt; *(dans l'océan)* ooze

bouée [bwe] *nf Naut* buoy; *(pour nager)* rubber ring; **b. de sauvetage** lifebelt; *Fig* lifeline

boueux, -euse [buø, -øz] **1** *adj* muddy **2** *nm Fam Br* dustman, *Am* garbage man

bouffant, -e [bufɑ̃, -ɑ̃t] **1** *adj (manche)* puff(ed); *(jupe)* full; *(pantalon)* baggy; **cheveux bouffants** bouffant hair-do **2** *nm (des cheveux)* body

bouffe [buf] *nf Fam (nourriture)* grub; *(repas)* meal

bouffée [bufe] *nf* **(a)** *(de fumée)* puff; *(de parfum)* whiff; *(d'air)* breath; *aussi Fig* **une b. d'air pur** a breath of fresh air; *Méd* **b. de chaleur** *Br* hot flush, *Am* hot flash **(b)** *(d'éloquence, de colère)* outburst; *(d'orgueil)* fit

bouffer [bufe] **1** *vt Fam* **(a)** *(manger)* to eat; *Fig* **je l'aurais bouffé** I could have killed him; **elle se laisse b. par ses enfants/son travail** she has no time for anything but her children/her work; **b. du curé** to rant against the clergy; **elle a bouffé du lion!** she's full of beans! **(b)** *(argent, économies)* to blow; **b. de l'essence** *(voiture)* to be heavy on petrol
2 *vi* **(a)** *Fam (manger)* to eat **(b)** *(manche, jupe)* to puff out; *(cheveux)* to have body; **faire b. ses cheveux** to give body to one's hair
3 se bouffer *vpr Fam* **elles se bouffent constamment le nez** they're always having a go at each other

bouffi, -e [bufi] *adj (yeux, visage)* puffy, swollen; **b. d'orgueil** puffed up with pride

bouffon, -onne [bufɔ̃, -ɔn] **1** *nm* buffoon; *Hist* jester
2 *adj* farcical

bouge [buʒ] *nm Péj (maison)* hovel; *(bar)* dive

bougeoir [buʒwar] *nm (plat)* candleholder; *(haut)* candlestick

bougeotte [buʒɔt] *nf Fam* **avoir la b.** to be fidgety; *(envie de voyager)* to have itchy feet

bouger [45] [buʒe] **1** *vt* to move, to shift
2 *vi (remuer, se déplacer)* to move; **rester sans b.** to keep still; **ne bougeons plus!** *(pour une photo)* hold it there!; **je n'ai pas bougé (de chez moi) pendant deux jours** I haven't been out for two days; *Fig* **ce pull ne bouge pas au lavage** *(ne déteint pas)* this sweater doesn't run in the wash; *(ne rétrécit pas)* this sweater doesn't shrink in the wash; *Fam* **ça bouge pas mal, dans cette ville** it's quite a lively town
3 se bouger *vpr Fam (se déplacer)* to move; *(s'activer)* to get a move on; **bouge-toi de là!** shift yourself!

bougie [buʒi] *nf* **(a)** *(en cire)* candle; **s'éclairer à la b.** to use candles for lighting **(b)** *Aut* **b. (d'allumage)** spark plug

bougnat [buɲa] *nm Fam Vieilli* coal-merchant

bougnoul(e) [buɲul] *nmf* = racist term referring to a North African person

bougon, -onne [bugɔ̃, -ɔn] *Fam* **1** *adj* grumpy
2 *nm,f* grumbler

bougonner [bugɔne] *vi Fam* to grumble

bougre [bugr] *nm Fam* **(a)** *Vieilli (individu)* **le pauvre b.** the poor devil; **ce n'est pas un mauvais b.** he's not a bad sort **(b) b. d'imbécile** damn(ed) fool

bougrement [bugrəmã] *adv* damn(ed)

boui-boui *(pl* **bouis-bouis)** [bwibwi] *nm Fam* dingy café

bouillabaisse [bujabɛs] *nf* bouillabaisse *(Provençal fish soup)*

bouillant, -e [bujã, -ãt] *adj* **(a)** *(qui bout)* boiling; *(très chaud, fiévreux)* boiling hot **(b)** *Fig (ardent)* fiery

bouille [buj] *nf Fam (visage)* mug; **il a une bonne b.** he looks like a nice guy

bouilleur [bujœr] *nm* **b. de cru** home distiller

bouilli, -e [buji] **1** *adj* boiled
2 *nm* boiled meat; *Can* = beans, cabbage, potatoes, salt pork and ham cooked together for several hours; **b. de bœuf** boiled beef

bouillie [buji] *nf (pour bébés)* baby food; *(à base de céréales)* baby cereal; **b. de légumes** mashed vegetables; **réduire qch en b.** *(légumes, fruits)* to mash sth; *(au mixer)* to liquidize; *Fam (voiture, visage)* to smash sth up; *Fam* **mettre ou réduire qn en b.** to beat sb to a pulp

bouillir [13] [bujir] *vi* to boil; **faire b. qch** to boil sth; **b. de colère** to seethe with anger; **b. d'impatience** to burst with impatience; **cela me fait b.** that makes my blood boil

bouilloire [bujwar] *nf* kettle

bouillon [bujɔ̃] *nm* **(a)** *(d'un liquide en ébullition)* bubble;

bouillir à gros bouillons to boil hard; **le sang sortait à gros bouillons** the blood was gushing out **(b)** *Culin (liquide)* stock; *Fam* **boire un b.** *(en nageant)* to get a mouthful; *(professionnellement)* to come to grief; **b. cube** stock cube; **b. de culture** culture medium; **b. de légumes** vegetable stock

bouillonnant, -e [bujɔnã, -ãt] *adj* bubbling; *(torrent)* foaming; *Fig* **b. de colère** seething; *Fig* **b. de vie/d'idées** bubbling over with life/ideas

bouillonner [bujɔne] *vi (eau, soupe, bain)* to bubble; *(torrent)* to foam; **b. de colère** to seethe with anger; **b. d'idées** to bubble over with ideas

bouillotte [bujɔt] *nf* hot-water bottle

boul. *abrév* boulevard

boulanger, -ère [bulãʒe, -ɛr] *nm,f* baker

boulangerie [bulãʒri] *nf (magasin)* baker's (shop); *(industrie)* bakery trade; **b.-pâtisserie** baker's and confectioner's (shop)

boule [bul] *nf* **(a)** *(sphère)* ball; *Fam (tête)* nut; **se rouler ou se mettre en b.** *(animal)* to roll up into a ball; *Fig* **se mettre en b.** *(en colère)* to fly off the handle; *Fam* **avoir la b. à zéro** to be a skinhead; *Fam* **avoir les boules** *(être énervé)* to be pissed off; *(avoir peur)* to be wetting oneself; *Fam* **perdre la b.** to go off one's head; **b. de neige** snowball; *Fig* **faire b. de neige** to snowball; **c'est une b. de nerfs** he's/she's a bundle of nerves; **b. puante** stink bomb; **b. Quiès®** earplug **(b)** *(de pétanque, de bowling)* bowl; *(de billard)* ball; **jouer aux boules** to play bowls **(c)** *(de machine à écrire)* golf ball

bouleau, -x [bulo] *nm* (silver) birch; *(bois)* birch(wood)

bouledogue [buldɔg] *nm* bulldog

bouler [bule] *vi Fam* **envoyer b. qn** to send sb packing

boulet [bulɛ] *nm* **(a)** *(projectile)* **b. (de canon)** cannonball; **passer comme un b. (de canon)** to hurtle past; **tirer à boulets rouges sur qn** to go for sb hammer and tongs **(b)** *(de bagnard)* ball and chain; *Fig* **c'est un b. qu'il traînera toute sa vie** it'll be a millstone round his neck all his life

boulette [bulɛt] *nf* **(a)** *(de papier, de pâte)* small ball **(b)** *Culin* meatball **(c)** *Fam (gaffe)* *Br* boob, *Am* boo-boo

boulevard [bulvar] *nm* boulevard; **les Grands Boulevards** *(à Paris)* the main boulevards; **b. périphérique** *Br* ring road, *Am* beltway

bouleversant, -e [bulvɛrsã, -ãt] *adj (émouvant)* deeply moving; *(perturbant)* distressing

bouleversement [bulvɛrsəmã] *nm* **(a)** *(de projets, d'habitudes)* disruption; **bouleversements politiques/économiques** political/economic upheavals **(b)** *(d'une personne)* emotion

bouleverser [bulvɛrse] *vt* **(a)** *(projets, habitudes)* to disrupt; *(vie)* to turn upside down **(b)** *(émouvoir)* to move deeply; *(perturber)* to distress

boulier [bulje] *nm* abacus

boulimie [bulimi] *nf Méd* bulimia

boulimique [bulimik] *adj & nmf Méd* bulimic; **être b.** to be bulimic, to have bulimia

bouliste [bulist] *nmf* bowls player

boulocher [buloʃe] *vi (vêtement)* to pill

boulodrome [bulodrom] *nm* bowling alley

boulon [bulɔ̃] *nm* bolt

boulonner [bulɔne] **1** *vt* to bolt
2 *vi Fam (travailler)* to slog away

boulot¹, -otte [bulo, -ɔt] *adj Fam* tubby

boulot² [bulo] *Fam* **1** *nm (travail, lieu de travail)* work; *(emploi)* job; **allez, au b.!** come on, get to work!; **refaire les peintures dans une maison, c'est du b.** to repaint a whole house is quite a job; *Fig* **faire le sale b.** to do the dirty work **2** *adj inv* **être b.** to be a workaholic

boum [bum] **1** *exclam* bang!
2 *nm Fam* (**a**) *(bruit)* bang (**b**) *(succès)* le **b.** du multimédia/ de l'informatique the multimedia/computer boom; **en plein b.** in full swing
3 *nf Fam (fête)* party *(for young people)*
boumer [bume] *vi Fam Vieilli* **ça boume?** how's things?

bouquet¹ [bukɛ] *nm* (**a**) *(fleurs)* bunch of flowers; *(imposant)* bouquet; *(petit)* posy; *(d'arbres)* clump; **un b. de roses** a bunch/bouquet of roses; **le b. de la mariée** the bride's bouquet; *Culin* **b. garni** bouquet garni *(hunch of mixed herbs)* (**b**) *(d'un vin)* bouquet, nose (**c**) *(d'un feu d'artifice)* **b. (final)** grand finale; *Fam Fig* **ça, c'est le b.!** that takes the *Br* biscuit *or Am* cake! (**d**) *TV* **b. numérique** multiplex *(bundle of digital TV channels)*

bouquet² *nm (crevette)* prawn
bouquetin [buktɛ̃] *nm* ibex
bouquin [bukɛ̃] *nm Fam* book
bouquiner [bukine] *vi Fam* to read
bouquiniste [bukinist] *nmf* second-hand bookseller
bourbeux, -euse [burbø, -øz] *adj* muddy
bourbier [burbje] *nm aussi Fig* quagmire
bourbon [burbɔ̃] *nm (whisky)* bourbon
bourde [burd] *nf Fam* (**a**) *(balivernes)* fib (**b**) *(gaffe)* blunder; **faire une b.** to put one's foot in it
bourdon [burdɔ̃] *nm* (**a**) *(insecte)* bumblebee; *Fam* **avoir le b.** to be down (in the dumps) (**b**) *(cloche)* great bell (**c**) *Mus (de cornemuse)* drone; *(d'orgue)* bourdon stop
bourdonnement [burdɔnmɑ̃] *nm (d'insectes)* buzz(ing), *(de machine, de moteur)* hum(ming); **avoir des bourdonnements d'oreilles** to have a buzzing in one's ears
bourdonner [burdɔne] *vi (insectes, oreilles)* to buzz; *(machine, moteur)* to hum
bourg [bur] *nm* market town
bourgade [burgad] *nf* village
bourge [burʒ] *Fam* **1** *adj* (**a**) *(de la bourgeoisie)* upper-class (**b**) *Péj* snobby
2 *nmf* (**a**) *(de la bourgeoisie)* upper-class person (**b**) *Péj* snob
bourgeois, -e [burʒwa, -az] **1** *adj* (**a**) *(personne)* middle-class; **cuisine bourgeoise** home cooking (**b**) *Péj (conventionnel)* middle-class, bourgeois
2 *nmf* (**a**) *(de la classe moyenne)* middle-class person; **les grands/petits b.** the upper/lower middle class (**b**) *Hist (roturier)* commoner
bourgeoisie [burʒwazi] *nf* middle class, bourgeoisie; **la haute/petite b.** the upper/lower middle class
bourgeon [burʒɔ̃] *nm* bud; **en bourgeons** in bud
bourgeonner [burʒɔne] *vi* (**a**) *(plante, arbre)* to bud (**b**) *Fam (avoir des boutons)* to come out in spots
bourgmestre [burgmɛstr] *nm* burgomaster
Bourgogne [burgɔɲ] **1** *nf* **la B.** Burgundy
2 *nm* burgundy
bourguignon, -onne [burgiɲɔ̃, -ɔn] **1** *adj* Burgundian
2 *nm,f* **B.** Burgundian
bourlinguer [burlɛ̃ge] *vi (personne) (naviguer)* to sail the seven seas; *Fam (voyager)* to knock about
bourrade [burad] *nf* push, shove
bourrasque [burask] *nf* squall, gust (of wind); **b. de neige** snow flurry; **souffler en bourrasques** to gust
bourratif, -ive [buratif, -iv] *adj Fam* stodgy
bourre [bur] *nf* (**a**) *(pour rembourrer)* stuffing, padding; *(de coton, de soie)* waste (**b**) *(des bourgeons)* down (**c**) *(d'arme à feu)* wad (**d**) *Fam* **de première b.** first-rate; **à la b.** in a rush

bourré, -e [bure] *adj* (**a**) *(plein)* packed, crammed (**de** with); **b. à craquer** full to bursting; *Fam* **être b. de complexes** to have loads of complexes; *Fam* **être b. de fric** to be loaded (**b**) *très Fam (ivre)* wasted
bourreau, -x [buro] *nm* (**a**) *(exécuteur)* executioner; *(qui pend)* hangman; *(tortionnaire)* torturer (**b**) *Fig* tormentor; **b. des cœurs** ladykiller; *Hum* child-beater; *Hum* child tormentor; **b. de travail** workaholic
bourrée [bure] *nf (danse)* bourrée
bourrelé, -e [burle] *adj* **b. de remords** stricken with remorse
bourrelet [burlɛ] *nm Fam* **b. (de graisse)** *(au ventre)* spare tyre (**b**) *(contre les courants d'air)* weather strip, *Br* draught excluder
bourrer [bure] **1** *vt* (**a**) *(chaise, coussin)* to stuff, to pad (**b**) *(placard, sac)* to cram (**de** with); *(pipe)* to bourrer *(aliment)* it's filling; **b. qn de qch** *(gaver)* to fill sb up with sth; **b. qn de coups** to beat sb up; *Fam* **b. le crâne à qn** *(élève)* to stuff sb's head with facts; *(politiquement)* to brainwash sb; *Fam* **b. le mou à qn** to pull the wool over sb's eyes
2 se bourrer *vpr* (**a**) **se b. de qch** *(se gaver)* to stuff oneself with sth (**b**) *très Fam* **se b. la gueule** to get wasted
bourriche [buriʃ] *nf (d'huitres)* basket
bourrichon [buriʃɔ̃] *nm Fam* **se monter le b.** to get worked up
bourricot [buriko] *nm (small)* donkey
bourrin [burɛ̃] *nm Fam (cheval)* nag
bourrique [burik] *nf (ânesse)* female donkey; *Fam (personne têtue)* pigheaded individual; **faire tourner qn en b.** to drive sb crazy
bourru, -e [bury] *adj* surly
bourse [burs] *nf* (**a**) *(porte-monnaie)* purse; **la b. ou la vie!** your money or your life!; **sans b. délier** without spending a penny; **faire b. commune** to pool one's money (**b**) *Scol & Univ* **b. (d'études)** grant (**c**) *Fin* **la B. (des valeurs)** the Stock Exchange, the Stock Market; **jouer à la B.** to play the market; **b. de commerce** commodities exchange (**d**) *Anat* **bourses** scrotum
boursicoter [bursikɔte] *vi* to dabble on the Stock Market
boursier, -ère [bursje, -er] **1** *adj* (**a**) *Fin* Stock Exchange, Stock Market (**b**) *Scol & Univ* **étudiant b.** grant holder
2 *nm,f* (**a**) *Scol & Univ* grant holder (**b**) *Fin* (Stock Exchange) operator
boursouflé, -e [bursufle] *adj (visage, yeux)* swollen, puffy; *(peinture)* blistered; *Fig (style, discours)* turgid
bous *voir* **bouillir**
bousculade [buskylad] *nf (agitation)* pushing and shoving; **être pris dans la b.** to be caught up in the rush
bousculer [buskyle] **1** *vt* (**a**) *(pousser)* to jostle; *Fig (habitudes)* to disrupt; *(préjugés)* to overturn (**b**) *(presser)* to rush
2 se bousculer *vpr (foule)* to push and shove; **les idées se bousculaient dans sa tête** his head was buzzing with ideas; *Fig* **les candidats ne se bousculent pas au portillon** applicants aren't exactly fighting over the job
bouse [buz] *nf* **de la b.** (**de vache**) cow dung; **une b.** a cowpat
bouseux [buzø] *nm Fam Péj* yokel
bousiller [buzije] *Fam* **1** *vt (voiture, appareil photo)* to wreck; *(travail)* to botch (up), to bungle
2 se bousiller *vpr* **se b. la santé** to ruin one's health
boussole [busɔl] *nf* compass; **s'orienter à la b.** to use a compass to get one's bearings; *Fam Fig* **perdre la b.** to go off one's head
boustifaille [bustifaj] *nf très Fam* grub

bout¹ [bu] *voir* **bouillir**

bout² *nm* (**a**) *(extrémité)* end; **b. à b.** end to end; **de b. en b.**, **d'un b.** à **l'autre** *(dans l'espace)* from one end to the other; *(reprendre un travail, lire)* from start to finish; **à l'autre b.**, **au b. du fil** *(au téléphone)* on the other end; *Fig* **je n'en vois pas le b.** I'm nowhere near the end of it; *Fig* **voir le b. du tunnel** to see the light at the end of the tunnel; **au b. de la rue** at the end of the street; **aller au b. du monde** to go to the ends of the earth; *Fig* **ce n'est pas le b. du monde** it's not exactly difficult; **au b. d'une heure/de quelques jours** after an hour/a few days

(**b**) *(du doigt, du nez)* tip, end; *(d'une pipe)* mouthpiece; *(d'une chaussure)* toe; **b. filtre** *(d'une cigarette)* filter tip; **b. du sein** nipple

(**c**) *(morceau)* bit; **elle en connaît un b. sur la question** she knows a thing or two about it; **faire un b. de chemin** to go part of the way; **un b. de temps** a little while; *Fig* **b. de chou** little child; *Cin & TV* **b. d'essai** screen test

(**d**) *(locutions)* **être à b.** *(épuisé)* to be exhausted; *(exaspéré)* to be at the end of one's patience; **pousser qn à b.** to push sb too far; **être à b. d'arguments** to have run out of arguments; **venir à b. de qch** *(travail)* to get through sth; *(obstacle)* to overcome sth; **à b. de bras** at arm's length; *Fig* **porter une entreprise à b. de bras** to carry a firm; **à b. portant** point-blank; **on ne sait jamais par quel b. le prendre** it's hard to know how to handle him; **avoir un mot sur le b. de la langue** to have a word on the tip of one's tongue; **tenir le bon b.** to be well on the way to success

boutade [butad] *nf (trait d'esprit)* quip

boute-en-train [butãtrɛ̃] *nm inv* live wire

bouteille [butɛj] *nf* bottle; *(de gaz, d'oxygène)* cylinder; *(contenu)* bottle(ful); **c'est une bonne b.** it's a good bottle of wine; **mettre du vin en bouteilles** to bottle wine; *Fam* **prendre de la b.** to be getting long in the tooth

boutique [butik] *nf Br* shop, *Am* store; **fermer b.** to shut up shop; **b. hors taxes** duty-free *Br* shop *or Am* store; **b. de mode** clothes shop, boutique

boutiquier, -ère [butikje, -ɛr] *nm,f Br* shopkeeper, *Am* storekeeper

bouton [butɔ̃] *nm* (**a**) *(de fleur)* bud; **b. de rose** rosebud; **en b.** in bud (**b**) *(sur un vêtement)* button; *(de col)* stud; **boutons de manchette** cufflinks (**c**) *(de porte, de radio)* knob; *(qu'on pousse) & Ordinat* button; *(interrupteur)* switch; *Ordinat* **b. de réinitialisation** reset button (**d**) *(sur le visage)* spot

bouton-d'or *(pl* **boutons-d'or)** [butɔ̃dɔr] *nm* buttercup

boutonnage [butɔnaʒ] *nm* buttoning (up); **veste à double b.** double-breasted jacket

boutonner [butɔne] **1** *vt (vêtement)* to button (up), to fasten (up)
2 se boutonner *vpr (vêtement)* to button (up)

boutonneux, -euse [butɔnø, -øz] *adj* spotty

boutonnière [butɔnjɛr] *nf (de vêtement)* buttonhole; **porter une fleur à la b.** to wear a *Br* buttonhole *or Am* boutonnière

bouton-pression *(pl* **boutons-pression)** [butɔ̃presjɔ̃] *nm Br* press stud, *Am* snap fastener

bouture [butyr] *nf* cutting; **faire des boutures** to take cuttings

bouturer [butyre] *vt* to propagate by cuttings

bouvier, -ère [buvje, -ɛr] **1** *nm,f* cowherd
2 *nm (chien)* sheepdog

bouvreuil [buvrœj] *nm* bullfinch

bovin, -e [bɔvɛ̃, -in] **1** *adj aussi Fig* bovine
2 *nm Zool* bovine

bowling [buliŋ] *nm* (**a**) *(jeu)* (tenpin) bowling (**b**) *(lieu)* (tenpin) bowling alley

box *(pl* **boxes)** [bɔks] *nm (dans un dortoir)* cubicle; *(dans une écurie)* stall; *(garage)* lock-up (garage); *Jur* **b. des accusés** dock

boxe [bɔks] *nf* boxing; **faire de la b.** to box; **b. anglaise** boxing; **b. française** kick boxing

boxer¹ [bɔkse] **1** *vi* to box
2 *vt Fam (frapper)* to punch up

boxer² [bɔksɛr] *nm (chien)* boxer

boxeur [bɔksœr] *nm* boxer

box-office *(pl* **box-offices)** [bɔksɔfis] *nm* box office; **être en tête du b.** to be a box-office hit

boyau, -x [bwajo] *nm* (**a**) *(d'animal)* gut; *(corde)* (cat)gut (**b**) *(de vélo)* tubular tyre (**c**) *(allée)* narrow alleyway; *(de mine)* narrow gallery; *Mil* communication trench

boycott(age) [bɔjkɔt(aʒ)] *nm* boycott(ing)

boycotter [bɔjkɔte] *vt* to boycott

boy-scout *(pl* **boy-scouts)** [bɔjskut] *nm Vieilli* boy scout; *Fig* **mentalité de b.** boy-scout mentality

BP [bepe] *nf (abrév* **boîte postale)** PO Box

bracelet [braslɛ] *nm* (**a**) *(bijou)* bracelet; *(rigide)* bangle; *(de montre)* strap (**b**) *(élastique)* rubber *or* elastic band

bracelet-montre *(pl* **bracelets-montres)** [braslɛmɔ̃tr] *nm* wristwatch

braconnage [brakɔnaʒ] *nm* poaching

braconner [brakɔne] *vi* to poach

braconnier [brakɔnje] *nm* poacher

brader [brade] *vt (solder)* to sell off

braderie [bradri] *nf (liquidation)* clearance sale; *(vente par des particuliers) Br ≃* car boot sale, *Am ≃* garage sale; *(magasin)* discount store

braguette [bragɛt] *nf* flies

braille [braj] *nm* Braille; **lire en b.** to read Braille

braillements [brajmɑ̃] *nmpl* yelling; *(d'enfant)* howling

brailler [braje] **1** *vi* to yell; *(enfant)* to howl
2 *vt (chanson)* to bawl out; *(slogan)* to chant

braire [28] [brɛr] *vi (âne)* to bray; *Fam Fig* to yell

braise [brɛz] *nf (charbons)* (glowing) embers; **des yeux de b.** glowing eyes

braiser [brɛze] *vt Culin* to braise

bramer [brame] *vi (cerf)* to bell; *Fig (hurler)* to howl

brancard [brɑ̃kar] *nm* (**a**) *(d'une civière, d'une charrette)* shaft; *Fig* **ruer dans les brancards** to kick up a fuss (**b**) *(civière)* stretcher

brancardier, -ère [brɑ̃kardje, -ɛr] *nm,f* stretcher bearer

branchage [brɑ̃ʃaʒ] *nm (des arbres)* branches; **branchages** *(coupés)* cut branches

branche [brɑ̃ʃ] *nf* (**a**) *(d'un arbre)* branch; *(de céleri)* stick; *Fig (de l'industrie, de la science, d'une famille)* branch; *(professionnelle)* line of business; **la b. maternelle** the mother's side; *Fam* **vieille b.** old buddy (**b**) *(d'un compas)* leg; *(de lunettes)* side piece; *(d'un chandelier)* branch

branché, -e [brɑ̃ʃe] *adj Fam (à la mode)* cool, hip; **il est b. rugby/techno** he's really into rugby/techno music

branchement [brɑ̃ʃmɑ̃] *nm (sur un réseau)* connecting (up) **(sur** to); *(à une prise)* plugging in; *(assemblage de fils)* connection

brancher [brɑ̃ʃe] **1** *vt* (**a**) *(à un réseau)* to connect (up) **(sur** to); *(à une prise)* to plug in; *Fig* **b. qn sur un sujet** to get sb onto a subject (**b**) *Fam (plaire à)* **la peinture moderne, ça ne me branche pas tellement** I'm not really into modern art; **on va en boîte ce soir, ça te branche?** feel like going clubbing tonight?
2 se brancher *vpr* (**a**) *(appareil électrique)* to plug in (**b**) **se b. sur** *(une station de radio)* to tune in to

branchie [brɑ̃ʃi] *nf* gill

brandade [brɑ̃dad] *nf* Culin **b. (de morue)** = salt cod puréed with garlic, oil and cream

brandebourg [brɑ̃dbur] *nm* frog

brandir [brɑ̃dir] *vt* to brandish

brandy [brɑ̃di] *nm* brandy

branlant, -e [brɑ̃lɑ̃, -ɑ̃t] *adj (dent)* loose; *(chaise, escalier)* rickety

branle [brɑ̃l] *nm* **mettre qch en b.** *(processus)* to set sth in motion; **se mettre en b.** *(partir)* to get moving; *(entrer en fonctionnement)* to get going

branle-bas [brɑ̃lba] *nm inv* **b. (de combat)** *(agitation)* commotion

branlée [brɑ̃le] *nf* Fam thrashing; **prendre** *ou* **recevoir une b.** to get a thrashing

branler [brɑ̃le] **1** *vt* Vulg *(masturber)* to jerk off, Br to wank off; Fig **mais qu'est-ce qu'il branle?** what the hell's he up to?

2 *vi (dent)* to be loose; *(chaise, escalier)* to be rickety

3 se branler *vpr* Vulg *(se masturber)* to jerk off, Br to wank; Fig **je m'en branle!** I don't give a shit!

branleur, -euse [brɑ̃lœr, -øz] *nm,f* Vulg *(bon à rien)* nerd, Br wanker

braquage [brakaʒ] *nm* **(a)** Aut *(des roues)* turning; **(angle de) b.** steering lock **(b)** Fam *(vol)* hold-up; **faire un b.** to do a hold-up

braque [brak] *nm (chien)* pointer

braquer [brake] **1** *vt* **(a)** *(diriger)* to point **(sur** at); *(regard)* to fix **(sur** on) **(b)** *(rendre hostile)* **b. qn contre qn/qch** to turn sb against sb/sth **(c)** Fam *(banque)* to hold up

2 *vi* Aut to turn the *(steering)* wheel; **b. à fond** to apply full lock; **voiture qui braque mal** car that has a poor lock

3 se braquer *vpr* to dig one's heels in; **se b. contre qn** to set one's face against sb

braquet [brake] *nm* gear ratio; **changer de b.** to change gear

bras [bra] *nm* **(a)** *(membre)* arm; **donner le b. à qn** to give sb one's arm; **un panier au b.** with a basket on one's arm; **les b. croisés** with one's arms folded; Fig **rester les b. croisés** *(être passif)* to stand by doing nothing; **b. dessus, b. dessous** arm in arm; **être le b. droit de qn** to be sb's right-hand man; **accueillir qn à b. ouverts** to welcome sb with open arms; Fam **tomber sur qn à bras raccourcis** to get stuck into sb; Fig **avoir le b. long** to have a lot of influence; Fig **avoir qn/qch sur les b.** to have sb/sth on one's hands; **les b. m'en tombent!** I'm flabbergasted!; **en b. de chemise** in (one's) shirtsleeves; **une partie de b. de fer** an arm-wrestling match; **faire un b. d'honneur à qn** ≃ to give sb the finger **(b)** *(d'un fauteuil, d'un levier, d'une ancre)* arm; *(d'une grue)* jib; *(d'une croix)* limb; **b. de lecture** pickup arm **(c)** *(de fleuve)* arm; **b. de mer** arm of the sea

brasero [brazero] *nm* brazier

brasier [brazje] *nm (incendie)* blaze, inferno

Brasilia [brazilja] *n* Brasilia

bras-le-corps [bralkɔr] **à bras-le-corps** *adv* **saisir qn à b.** to seize sb round the waist; **prendre un problème à b.** to get to grips with a problem

brassage [brasaʒ] *nm* **(a)** *(de la bière)* brewing **(b)** *(mélange)* mixing

brassard [brasar] *nm* armband; **b. de deuil** black armband

brasse [bras] *nf* Sp *(style)* breaststroke; *(mouvement)* stroke; **nager la b.** to swim breaststroke; **b. coulée** = breaststroke in which face is submerged; **b. papillon** butterfly (stroke)

brassée [brase] *nf* armful

brasser [brase] *vt* **(a)** *(bière)* to brew **(b)** *(mélanger)* to mix; Fig **b. de l'argent** to handle large amounts of money; **b. de l'air** *ou* **du vent** to work without getting anything done

brasserie [brasri] *nf* **(a)** *(fabrique)* brewery; *(industrie)* brewing **(b)** *(restaurant)* brasserie

brasseur, -euse [brasœr, -øz] *nm,f* **(a)** *(fabricant de bière)* brewer **(b)** Fig **b. d'affaires** big businessman

brassière [brasjer] *nf* **(a)** *(de bébé)* Br vest, Am undershirt **(b)** *(soutien-gorge)* bra

Bratislava [bratislava] *n* Bratislava

bravade [bravad] *nf* bravado; **par b.** out of bravado

brave [brav] **1** *adj* **(a)** *(courageux)* brave, courageous **(b)** *(bon)* good; **de braves gens** good people **(c)** Péj **il est bien b.** *(pas futé)* he means well

2 *nm* **(a)** *(héros)* brave man **(b)** Vieilli **mon b.** my good man

bravement [bravmɑ̃] *adv* **(a)** *(courageusement)* bravely, courageously **(b)** *(avec résolution)* boldly

braver [brave] *vt* *(mort, danger)* to brave; *(personne, lois, règlements)* to defy

bravo [bravo] **1** *exclam* bravo!, *(dans un début)* hear, hear!; Ironique well done!

2 *nm* **un grand b.** à toute l'équipe technique a big hand for all the technical crew; **des bravos** cheers

bravoure [bravur] *nf* bravery, courage

Brazzaville [brazavil] *n* Brazzaville

break¹ [brɛk] *nm (voiture)* Br estate car, Am station wagon

break² *nm (pause)* & Sp break

brebis [brəbi] *nf* **(a)** *(animal)* ewe; Fig **b. galeuse** black sheep **(b)** Rel sheep

brèche [brɛʃ] *nf (dans un mur, une haie)* gap; *(dans la coque d'un bateau)* hole, Mil breach; Fig **être toujours sur la b.** to be always on the go; **battre qch en b.** to demolish sth

bréchet [breʃɛ] *nm* breastbone

bredouille [brəduj] *adj* empty-handed

bredouiller [brəduje] *vt & vi* to mumble, to mutter

bref, -ève [brɛf, brɛv] **1** *adj* brief, short; Ling *(voyelle)* short; **soyez b.!** be brief!

2 *adv* in short; **une cousine ou une tante, enfin b.,** quelqu'un de sa famille a cousin or an aunt, well anyway, one of his relatives; **l'actualité en b.** the news in brief

3 *nf* **brève** *(nouvelle)* short news item

brelan [brəlɑ̃] *nm* three of a kind; **b. d'as** three aces

breloque [brəlɔk] *nf (sur un bracelet)* charm

brème [brɛm] *nf* bream

Brême [brɛm] *n* Bremen

Brésil [brezil] *nm* **le B.** Brazil

brésilien, -enne [breziljɛ̃, -ɛn] **1** *adj* Brazilian

2 *nm,f* **B.** Brazilian

Bretagne [brətaɲ] *nf* **la B.** Brittany

bretelle [brətɛl] *nf* **(a)** *(de soutien-gorge, de robe)* (shoulder) strap; **(paire de) bretelles** *(pour pantalon)* (pair of) Br braces *or* Am suspenders **(b)** *(lanière)* strap; *(de fusil)* sling **(c)** *(route)* **b. (d'accès)** access road; **b. (d'autoroute)** Br slip road

breton, -onne [brətɔ̃, -ɔn] **1** *adj* Breton

2 *nm,f* **B.** Breton

3 *nm (langue)* Breton

bretzel [brɛdzɛl] *nm* pretzel

breuvage [brœvaʒ] *nm (potion)* potion; Hum *(boisson)* concoction

brève [brɛv] *voir* **bref**

brevet [brəvɛ] *nm (certificat)* certificate; *(diplôme)* diploma; Scol **b. (des collèges)** = general exam taken at fifteen; **b. d'études professionnelles** = vocational

diploma; **b. (d'invention)** patent; **b. de pilote** *Av* pilot's licence; *Mil* wings; **b. de technicien supérieur** = advanced vocational training certificate
breveter [42] [brəvte] *vt (invention)* to patent; **faire b. qch** to take out a patent on sth
bréviaire [brevjɛr] *nm Rel* breviary
briard [brijar] *nm (chien)* Briard
bribes [brib] *nfpl* **b. de conversation** snatches of conversation; **des b. de suédois** a few scraps of Swedish
bric-à-brac [brikabrak] *nm inv (vieux objets)* odds and ends, bric-à-brac; *(mélange)* jumble **(de** of); **(boutique de) b.** *Br* second-hand shop, *Am* thrift store
bric et de broc [brikedəbrɔk] **de bric et de broc** *adv* haphazardly
brick [brik] *nm (carton)* carton
bricolage [brikɔlaʒ] *nm* **(a)** *(travail)* do-it-yourself, *Br* DIY; **faire du b.** to do some do-it-yourself *or Br* DIY **(b)** *Péj (réparation)* botch-up
bricole [brikɔl] *nf (objet)* trinket; *(chose sans importance)* trifle; *Fam* **il va lui arriver des bricoles** he's/she's going to get into a pickle
bricoler [brikɔle] **1** *vt (construire)* to put together; *(réparer)* to tinker with
2 *vi* to do some do-it-yourself *or Br* DIY; **j'ai passé la matinée à b. dans la maison** I spent the morning doing odd jobs about the house
bricoleur, -euse [brikɔlœr, -øz] **1** *adj* **être b.** to be good with one's hands
2 *nm,f* handyman, *f* handywoman
bride [brid] *nf* **(a)** *(de harnais)* bridle; *Fig* **lâcher la b. à qn** to give sb free rein; *Fig* **avoir la b. sur le cou** to have a free rein; **aller à b. abattue** to ride full tilt **(b)** *(de boutonnière)* bar
bridé, -e [bride] *adj (yeux)* slanting
brider [bride] *vt (cheval)* to bridle; *(personne, passions, impulsion)* to curb, to restrain
bridge [bridʒ] *nm (jeu, prothèse)* bridge
brie [bri] *nm* Brie
brièvement [brievmã] *adv* briefly
brièveté [brievte] *nf* brevity, briefness
brigade [brigad] *nf* **(a)** *Mil* brigade; *(de police, de gendarmerie)* squad; **b. antigang** organized crime squad; *Hist* **Brigades internationales** International Brigades; **b. des stupéfiants** *ou Fam* **des stups** drug squad **(b)** *(d'ouvriers)* team
brigadier [brigadje] *nm* **(a)** *Mil* corporal; *(d'artillerie)* bombardier **(b) b. (de police)** (police) sergeant
brigand [brigã] *nm (bandit)* brigand; *(personne malhonnête)* crook
briguer [brige] *vt (honneur, poste)* to solicit
brillamment [brijamã] *adv* brilliantly
brillant, -e [brijã, -ãt] **1** *adj* **(a)** *(lumière, couleur)* bright, brilliant; *(pierre précieuse)* sparkling; *(cheveux, chaussures, cuir)* shiny; **b. de fièvre** bright with fever **(b)** *(carrière, élève, avenir)* brilliant; *(conversation)* sparkling
2 *nm* **(a)** *(d'un métal)* brilliance, brightness; *(d'une pierre précieuse)* sparkle; *(d'un papier, d'un tissu, de cheveux)* shininess **(b)** *(diamant)* brilliant **(c) b. à lèvres** lip gloss
brillantine [brijãtin] *nf* brilliantine
briller [brije] *vi* **(a)** *(soleil, étoiles, yeux)* to shine; *(bougie)* to glimmer; *(pierre précieuse)* to sparkle; *(eau, satin)* to shimmer; *(braises)* to glow; **faire b. ses chaussures** to shine *or* polish one's shoes; **des yeux qui brillent de colère/de joie** eyes shining with anger/happiness; **b. de mille feux** to sparkle brilliantly; *Prov* **tout ce qui brille**

n'est pas or all that glitters is not gold **(b)** *(exceller)* to shine; **b. par son absence** to be conspicuous by one's absence; **elle ne brille pas par sa ponctualité** she's not noted for her punctuality
brimade [brimad] *nf* instance of bullying; **faire subir des brimades à qn** to bully sb
brimbaler [brɛ̃bale] = **bringuebaler**
brimer [brime] *vt* to bully; **se sentir brimé** to feel victimized
brin [brɛ̃] **1** *nm* **(a)** *(de persil, de romarin)* sprig; *(de mimosa, de muguet)* spray; *(de paille)* wisp; **un b. d'herbe** a blade of grass **(b)** *Fam (petite quantité)* bit **(de** of); **un b. d'ironie/de jalousie** a touch of irony/jealousy; **faire un b. de toilette** to have a quick wash (and brush-up); **un beau b. de fille** a good-looking girl **(c)** *(de laine, corde, fil)* strand
2 *adv Fam* **un b.** a bit
brindille [brɛ̃dij] *nf* twig
bringue¹ [brɛ̃g] *nf Fam* **grande b.** *(fille)* beanpole
bringue² *nf Fam (fête)* binge; **faire la b.** to go on a binge
bringuebaler [brɛ̃gbale], **brinquebaler** [brɛ̃kbale] *vt & vi Fam* to shake about
brio [brijo] *nm* brilliance; **avec b.** brilliantly
brioche [brijɔʃ] *nf* brioche; *Fam Fig* **avoir/prendre de la b.** to have/develop a paunch
brioché, -e [brijɔʃe] *adj* **pain b.** = milk bread
brique [brik] **1** *nf* **(a)** *(de construction)* brick; **mur de** *ou* **en briques** brick wall **(b)** *Anciennement Fam (10 000 francs)* 10,000 francs
2 *adj inv* brick-red
briquer [brike] *vt (nettoyer)* to scrub down; *(pont de navire)* to holystone
briquet [brikɛ] *nm* (cigarette) lighter
briqueterie [briketri] *nf* brickyard
briquette [brikɛt] *nf* **(a)** *(petite brique)* small brick **(b)** *(de jus de fruit)* small carton **(c)** *(de charbon)* briquette
bris [bri] *nm (de verre, de scellés)* breaking; **b. de glaces** broken windows
brisant [brizã] *nm (écueil)* reef; **brisants** *(vagues)* breakers
brise [briz] *nf* breeze; *Naut* **forte b.** stiff breeze
brise-glace [brizglas] *nm inv (a) (navire)* ice breaker **(b)** *(d'une pile de pont)* ice breaker; *(d'un navire)* ice beam
brise-lames [brizlam] *nm inv* breakwater
briser [brize] **1** *vt (casser)* to break; *(opposition, résistance, espérances)* to crush; *(carrière)* to wreck; *(grève)* to break; **b. qn** *(sujet: effort, marche)* to shatter sb; **brisé par la douleur** broken by grief; **la voix brisée par l'émotion** his/her voice choked with emotion; **cela me brise le cœur** it breaks my heart
2 *se briser vpr (vagues, porcelaine, verre)* to break; *Fig (espoirs)* to be shattered
brise-tout [briztu] *nmf inv* clumsy person *(who is always breaking things)*
briseur, -euse [brizœr, -øz] *nm,f* **b. de grève** strike breaker
brise-vent [brizvã] *nm inv* windbreak
bristol [bristɔl] *nm* Bristol board; *(carte de visite)* visiting card
britannique [britanik] **1** *adj* British; **les îles Britanniques** the British Isles
2 *nmf* **B.** Briton; **les Britanniques** the British
broc [bro] *nm* pitcher, jug
brocante [brɔkãt] *nf (commerce)* secondhand trade; *(magasin)* secondhand shop; *(marché aux puces)* secondhand market

brocanteur, -euse [brɔkɑ̃tœr, -øz] *nm,f* secondhand dealer

brocarder [brɔkarde] *vt Litt* to gibe at

brocart [brɔkar] *nm* brocade

broche [brɔʃ] *nf* (a) *(pour rôtir)* spit; **faire cuire qch à la b.** to spit-roast sth (b) *(bijou)* brooch (c) *Tech, Él & Méd* pin

brocher [brɔʃe] *vt* (a) *(livre)* to stitch (b) *(tissu)* to brocade

brochet [brɔʃɛ] *nm* pike

brochette [brɔʃɛt] *nf (broche)* skewer; *(plat)* kebab

brochure [brɔʃyr] *nf* brochure, pamphlet

brocoli [brɔkɔli] *nm* broccoli; **des brocolis** broccoli

brodequin [brɔdkɛ̃] *nm* laced boot

broder [brɔde] *vt & vi aussi Fig* to embroider

broderie [brɔdri] *nf* (a) *(ouvrage)* piece of embroidery; **broderies** embroidery; **b. anglaise** broderie anglaise (b) *(activité)* embroidery

broie *voir* **broyer**

bromure [brɔmyr] *nm* bromide

bronche [brɔ̃ʃ] *nf* bronchial tube; **être fragile des bronches** to have a weak chest

broncher [brɔ̃ʃe] *vi* (a) *(réagir)* **sans b.** without batting an eyelid; **il n'a pas bronché** he didn't bat an eyelid (b) *(cheval)* to stumble

bronchite [brɔ̃ʃit] *nf* bronchitis; **avoir une b.** to have bronchitis

broncho-pneumonie *(pl* **broncho-pneumonies)** [brɔ̃kɔpnømɔni] *nf Méd* bronchopneumonia

bronzage [brɔ̃zaʒ] *nm (activité)* tanning; *(hâle)* (sun)tan; **b. intégral** all-over tan

bronze [brɔ̃z] *nm (métal, objet d'art)* bronze

bronzé, -e [brɔ̃ze] *adj (peau)* (sun)tanned; *Euph ou Péj (personne)* coloured

bronzer [brɔ̃ze] *vi (personne)* to go brown, to tan

bronzette [brɔ̃zɛt] *nf Fam* sunbathing; **faire b.** to do a bit of sunbathing

brosse [brɔs] *nf* (a) *(ustensile)* brush; **donner un coup de b. à qch** to give sth a brush; **donner un coup de b. à qn** to give sb's hair a brush; **avoir les cheveux en b.** to have a crew cut; *Fig* **manier la b. à reluire** to bow and scrape; **b. à cheveux** hairbrush; **b. à dents** toothbrush; **b. à habits** clothes brush; **b. à ongles** nailbrush (b) *(pinceau large)* (paint)brush

brosser [brɔse] **1** *vt (tapis, manteau, cheveux)* to brush; *(sol)* to scrub; *(cheval)* to brush down; *Belg* **b. un cours** to skip a class (b) *(décrire)* **b. un tableau optimiste de la situation** to paint an optimistic picture of the situation **2 se brosser** *vpr (se nettoyer)* to brush oneself down; **se b. les dents/les cheveux** to brush one's teeth/one's hair; *Fam* **tu peux toujours te b.!** not a chance!

brou [bru] *nm* (a) *(enveloppe)* husk, *Am* shuck (b) *(teinture)* **b. de noix** walnut stain

broue [bru] *nf Can* froth; *très Fam Fig* **faire *ou* péter de la b.** to talk big

brouette [bruɛt] *nf* wheelbarrow

brouhaha [bruaa] *nm* hubbub

brouillard [brujar] *nm* fog; **il y a du b.** it's foggy; *Fig* **être dans le b.** to be in a fog; **b. givrant** freezing fog

brouille [bruj] *nf* quarrel, disagreement

brouillé, -e [bruje] *adj* (a) *(teint)* blotchy (b) **être b. avec qn** to have fallen out with sb; **être b. avec les chiffres/la grammaire** to be hopeless with figures/at grammar

brouiller [bruje] **1** *vt* (a) *(rendre trouble) (idées)* to muddle up; *(vue)* to blur; **yeux brouillés de larmes** eyes blurred with tears; *Fig* **b. les cartes** to confuse the issue; *Fig* **b. les**

pistes to cover one's tracks (b) *(fâcher)* **b. qn avec qn** to set sb against sb (c) *Rad & Él (accidentellement)* to cause interference to; *(intentionnellement)* to jam **2 se brouiller** *vpr* (a) *(idées, dates)* to get muddled up (b) *(vue)* to get blurred (c) *(se détériorer)* **le temps se brouille** it's clouding over (d) *(se disputer)* to fall out (**avec qn** with sb)

brouillon, -onne [brujɔ̃, -ɔn] **1** *adj (mal organisé)* disorganized, unmethodical; *(mal présenté)* untidy **2** *nm (ébauche)* (rough) draft; *(papier)* **b.** *Br* scrap *or Am* scratch paper; **faire un exercice au b.** to do an exercise in rough, **(cahier de) b.** rough book; *Ordinat* **version b.** draft version

broussaille [brusaj] *nf* **broussailles** scrub; **en b.** *(cheveux)* tousled; *(sourcils)* bushy

broussailleux, -euse [brusajø, -øz] *adj (terrain)* scrubby; *(cheveux)* tousled, *(sourcils)* bushy

brousse [brus] *nf* **la b.** the bush

brouter [brute] **1** *vt (herbe)* to graze **2** *vt (a) (animal)* to graze (b) *(embrayage)* to judder

broutille [brutij] *nf* trifle

broyer [32] [brwaje] *vt (pierre, aliments, couleurs)* to grind; *(membre, main, personne)* to crush; *Fig* **b. du noir** to be down in the dumps

broyeur, -euse [brwajœr, -øz] **1** *adj (appareil)* grinding **2** *nm (machine)* grinder; **b. à ordures** *Br* waste *or Am* garbage disposal unit

bru [bry] *nf* daughter-in-law

brugnon [bryɲɔ̃] *nm* nectarine

bruine [brɥin] *nf* drizzle

bruiner [brɥine] *v impersonnel* to drizzle

bruire [brɥir] *vi Litt (feuilles, étoffe)* to rustle; *(ruisseau, vent)* to murmur

bruissement [brɥismɑ̃] *nm (des feuilles, d'une étoffe)* rustle, rustling *(d'un ruisseau, du vent)* murmur(ing)

bruit [brɥi] *nm* (a) *(son)* sound, noise; **b. de** *pas* (sound of) footsteps; **des bruits de voix** the sound of voices; **sans b.** without a sound (b) *(vacarme)* noise; **faire du b.** *(être bruyant)* to make a noise; *Fig (affaire, histoire)* to cause a sensation; **b. de fond** background noise; **beaucoup de b. pour rien** a lot of fuss over nothing (c) *(rumeur)* rumour; **faire courir un b.** to spread a rumour; **le b. court que…** rumour has it that…

bruitage [brɥitaʒ] *nm* sound effects

bruiteur, -euse [brɥitœr, -øz] *nm,f* sound-effects man, *f* woman

brûlant, -e [brylɑ̃, -ɑ̃t] *adj (plat, casserole)* red-hot; *(café)* boiling (hot); *(soleil)* scorching; *Fig* **b. de désir** burning with desire; **question brûlante** burning question; **le sujet est d'une actualité brûlante** it's one of the burning issues of the day

brûlé, -e [bryle] **1** *nm,f (accidenté)* burns victim; *Méd* **les grands brûlés** people with third-degree burns **2** *nm* sentir le b. to smell burnt; **une odeur de b.** a burnt smell; **avoir un goût de b.** to taste burnt

brûle-parfum *(pl* **brûle-parfums)** [brylparfœ̃] *nm* perfume burner

brûle-pourpoint [brylpurpwɛ̃] **à brûle-pourpoint** *adv* point-blank

brûler [bryle] **1** *vt* (a) *(sujet: flamme, acide)* to burn; *(sujet: eau bouillante)* to scald; *(sujet: fer à repasser)* to scorch; *(café)* to roast; **gazon brûlé par le soleil** lawn scorched by the sun; **être brûlé vif** *(dans un accident)* to be burnt alive; *(être supplicié)* to be burnt at the stake; **l'argent lui brûle les doigts** money burns a hole in his pocket (b) *(consommer)* *(électricité, combustible)* to use; *(calories)* to burn (c) **b. un**

feu rouge to go through a red light; **b.** un stop to go straight past a stop sign
2 *vi* (**a**) *(flamber, être carbonisé)* to burn; *(être très chaud)* to be red-hot; *(liquide)* to be boiling (hot); *(blessure)* to smart; **attention, ça brûle!** careful, it's hot!; **tu brûles** *(dans un jeu)* you're getting hot (**b**) *Fig* **b. de faire qch** to be burning to do sth; **b. d'impatience** to be bursting with impatience; **b. de désir** to be burning with desire
3 **se brûler** *vpr (par accident)* to burn oneself (**avec** on); **se b. la langue/la main** to burn one's tongue/hand

brûleur [brylœr] *nm* burner

brûlot [brylo] *nm Can (moustique)* gnat, midge

brûlure [brylyr] *nf (blessure)* burn; *(sensation)* burning; **b. de cigarette** cigarette burn; **brûlures d'estomac** heartburn

brume [brym] *nf* mist, haze; **b. de chaleur** heat haze

brumeux, -euse [brymø, -øz] *adj* misty, hazy; *Fig (idées, explication)* hazy

Brumisateur® [brymizatœr] *nm* atomizer, spray

brun, -e [brœ̃, bryn] **1** *adj (cheveux)* dark, brown; *(peau, personne) (naturellement)* dark; *(bronzé)* brown; **être b. de peau** to be dark-skinned
2 *nm,f (personne)* dark-haired man, *f* dark-haired woman
3 *nm (couleur)* brown
4 *nf* **brune** *(bière)* brown ale

brunante [brynãt] *nf Can* dusk

brunâtre [brynɑtr] *adj* brownish

Brunei [brynei] *nm* **le B.** Brunei

brunir [brynir] *vi (peau, personne)* to tan; *(cheveux)* to darken

brushing® [brœʃiŋ] *nm* blow-dry

brusque [brysk] *adj* abrupt

brusquement [bryskəmã] *adv* abruptly

brusquer [bryske] *vt* (**a**) **b. qn** *(être impoli envers)* to be abrupt with sb; *(maltraiter)* to treat sb harshly (**b**) *(hâter) (décision)* to rush; **il ne faut rien b.** we mustn't rush things

brusquerie [bryskəri] *nf* abruptness; **avec b.** abruptly

brut, -e [bryt] **1** *adj* (**a**) *(pétrole, minerai)* crude; *(sucre)* unrefined; *(pierre précieuse)* uncut; *(champagne)* extra-dry; *(cidre)* dry; **à l'état b.** in its raw state (**b**) *(bénéfice, poids, salaire)* gross
2 *nm* (**a**) *(pétrole)* crude (oil) (**b**) *(champagne)* extra-dry champagne
3 *adv* gross

brutal, -e, -aux, -ales [brytal, -o] *adj* (**a**) *(personne, paroles, manières)* brutal; *(choc)* violent; **être b. avec qn** to be rough with sb (**b**) *(changement)* abrupt

brutalement [brytalmã] *adv (violemment)* brutally; *(avec brusquerie)* roughly; *(soudainement)* abruptly

brutaliser [brytalize] *vt* to ill-treat

brutalité [brytalite] *nf (violence, brusquerie)* brutality; *(soudaineté)* abruptness; **brutalités** brutality

brute [bryt] *nf (personne violente)* brute; *(personne grossière)* boor; **taper sur qch comme une b.** to bang at sth like a madman; **une b. épaisse** a great brute; **grosse b.!** you big brute!

Bruxelles [brysɛl] *n* Brussels

bruxellois, -e [brysɛlwa, -az] **1** *adj* of Brussels
2 *nm,f* **B.** = person from Brussels

bruyamment [brɥijamã] *adv (parler, rire)* loudly; *(manger)* noisily

bruyant, -e [brɥijã, -ãt] *adj (rue, voisin)* noisy; *(rire, applaudissements)* loud

bruyère [bryjɛr] *nf (plante)* heather; *(terre)* heath; **pipe de b.** briar pipe; **terre de b.** peat

BTP [betepe] *nm (abrév* **bâtiment et travaux publics**) construction industry

BTS [betees] *nm (abrév* **brevet de technicien supérieur**) = advanced vocational training certificate

bu, -e *pp voir* **boire**

buanderie [bɥãdri] *nf* laundry (room)

bubonique [bybɔnik] *adj voir* **peste**

Bucarest [bykarɛst] *n* Bucharest

buccal, -e, -aux, -ales [bykal, -o] *adj* buccal; **par voie buccale** orally

bûche [byʃ] *nf* (**a**) *(morceau de bois)* log; **b. de Noël** Yule log (**b**) *Fam (chute)* fall; **prendre une b.** to come a cropper

bûcher¹ [byʃe] *nm* (**a**) *(pour le bois)* woodshed (**b**) *(supplice)* stake (**c**) *(funéraire)* (funeral) pyre

bûcher² *Fam Scol* **1** *vt Br* to swot up, *Am* to grind away at
2 *vi Br* to swot, *Am* to grind

bûcheron [byʃrɔ̃] *nm* woodcutter

bûcheur, -euse [byʃœr, -øz] *Fam Scol* **1** *adj* hard-working
2 *nm,f Br* swot, *Am* grind

bucolique [bykɔlik] *adj* pastoral

Budapest [bydapɛst] *n* Budapest

budget [bydʒɛ] *nm* budget

budgétaire [bydʒeter] *adj (dépenses, contrôle)* budgetary; *(année)* financial; **déficit/excédent b.** budget deficit/surplus

buée [bɥe] *nf (sur les vitres)* condensation; *(sur un miroir)* mist

Buenos Aires [bɥenɔzɛr] *n* Buenos Aires

buffet [byfɛ] *nm* (**a**) *(meuble) (bas)* sideboard; *(haut)* dresser (**b**) *(repas)* buffet; **b. campagnard** = cold buffet made with country produce; **b. froid** cold buffet (**c**) *Fam (ventre)* belly

buffle [byfl] *nm* buffalo

building [bildiŋ] *nm* tower block

buis [bɥi] *nm (arbre)* box (tree); *(bois)* box(wood)

buisson [bɥisɔ̃] *nm* bush

buissonnière [bɥisɔnjer] *adj f voir* **école**

bulbe [bylb] *nm* (**a**) *Bot* bulb (**b**) *Anat* **b. pileux** hair bulb; **b. rachidien** medulla oblongata (**c**) *Archit* onion dome

bulgare [bylgar] **1** *adj* Bulgarian
2 *nmf* **B.** Bulgarian
3 *nm (langue)* Bulgarian

Bulgarie [bylgari] *nf* **la B.** Bulgaria

bulldozer [byldozœr] *nm* bulldozer

bulle [byl] *nf* (**a**) *(d'air, de savon, stérile)* bubble; *(de bandes dessinées)* balloon; **faire des bulles** to blow bubbles; *Fam* **coincer la b.** to sleep, *Br* to kip; *Ordinat* **b. d'aide** tooltip (**b**) *(lettre du pape)* (papal) bull

buller [byle] *vi Fam* to laze around

bulletin [byltɛ̃] *nm (communiqué)* bulletin; *(d'entreprise)* newsletter; *(formulaire)* form; *Scol* **b. (scolaire)** (school) report; **b. blanc** blank ballot paper; **b. d'informations** news bulletin; **b. météorologique** weather report; **b. de paie** *ou* **de salaire** pay slip; *Méd* **b. de santé** medical report; **b. trimestriel** end-of-term report; **b. de vote** ballot paper; **b. (de vote) nul** spoiled ballot paper

bulletin-réponse *(pl* **bulletins-réponse**) [byltɛ̃repɔ̃s] *nm* reply form

bungalow [bœ̃galo] *nm* bungalow

bunker [bunkœr] *nm Mil* bunker; *(en golf) Br* bunker, *Am* sand trap

buraliste [byralist] *nmf* (**a**) *(de bureau de tabac)* tobacconist (**b**) *(dans un bureau)* clerk

bure [byr] *nf (étoffe)* frieze ; *(habit religieux)* frock
bureau, -x [byro] *nm* **(a)** *(meuble)* desk
 (b) *(lieu)* office ; *(à la maison)* study
 (c) *(comité)* committee
 (d) *(agence)* office ; **b. de change** bureau de change ; **b.
 d'études** design office ; *(de recherche)* R & D department ; **B.
 international du travail** International Labour Office ; **b.
 de poste** post office ; **b. de tabac** tobacconist's (shop)
 (e) *(organisme)* **b. d'aide sociale** welfare office
bureaucrate [byrokrat] *nmf* bureaucrat
bureaucratie [byrokrasi] *nf (système)* bureaucracy ;
 (ensemble des fonctionnaires) bureaucrats
bureaucratique [byrokratik] *adj* bureaucratic
Bureautique® [byrotik] *nf* office automation
burette [byʀɛt] *nf (pour l'huile)* oilcan ; *(de chimiste)* burette
burin [byʀɛ̃] *nm* **(a)** *(de graveur)* burin **(b)** *(pour découper)*
 (cold) chisel
buriné, -e [byʀine] *adj (visage)* seamed
Burkina [byrkina] *nm* **le B.** Burkina Faso
burkinabé [byrkinabe] **1** *adj* of Burkina Faso
 2 *nmf* **B.** = person from Burkina Faso
burlesque [byrlɛsk] **1** *adj* **(a)** *(ridicule)* ludicrous,
 ridiculous **(b)** *(film, genre)* burlesque
 2 *nm (genre)* **le b.** the burlesque
Burundi [burundi] *nm* **le B.** Burundi
bus [bys] *nm (autobus)* & *Ordinat* bus
buse [byz] *nf* buzzard
busqué, -e [byske] *adj (nez)* hook(ed)
buste [byst] *nm (torse)* chest ; *(seins, sculpture)* bust
bustier [bystje] *nm (corsage)* bustier , *(soutien-gorge)* long
 line (strapless) bra
but [by, byt] *nm* **(a)** *(objectif)* aim, goal ; *(intention)*
 purpose ; *(d'un trajet)* destination, goal ; **dans ce b.** with
 this aim in view ; **c'est le b. de l'opération** that's the point of

the operation ; **errer sans b.** to wander about aimlessly **(b)**
 Sp goal ; **marquer un b.** to score a goal ; **gagner/perdre
 (par) 3 buts à 1** to win/lose by 3 goals to 1 ; **les buts** *(zone)*
 the goal **(c) demander/dire qch de b. en blanc** to ask/say
 sth straight out
butane [bytan] *nm* butane
buté, -e [byte] *adj* stubborn, obstinate
butée [byte] *nf* **(a)** *(pièce)* **b. (d'arrêt)** stop **(b)** *Archit*
 abutment
buter [byte] **1** *vt* **(a)** *(braquer)* **b. qn** to put sb's back up **(b)**
 très Fam (tuer) to bump off
 2 *vi* **b. contre qch** *(cogner)* to bump into sth ; *(trébucher)* to
 stumble over sth ; **b. sur un problème/une difficulté** to
 come up against a problem/a difficulty
 3 se buter *vpr (s'entêter)* to dig one's heels in
buteur [bytœr] *nm (au football)* goalscorer ; *(au rugby)*
 kicker
butin [bytɛ̃] *nm (d'une armée)* booty ; *(de pillards)* spoils ; *(de
 voleur)* loot
butiner [bytine] **1** *vi (abeille)* to gather pollen
 2 *vt (sujet : abeille)* to gather pollen from ; *(renseignements)*
 to gather
butoir [bytwar] *nm Rail* buffer ; *(de porte)* door stop
butte [byt] *nf (colline)* hillock ; *Fig* **être en b. à qch** to be
 exposed to sth
buvable [byvabl] *adj* **(a)** *(potable)* drinkable **(b)** *(médicament)* to be taken orally
buvard [byvar] *nm (feuille)* sheet of blotting paper ; *(sous-
 main)* blotter ; **(papier) b.** blotting paper
buvette [byvɛt] *nf (dans une gare, à une fête)* refreshment
 bar
buveur, -euse [byvœr, -øz] *nmf* drinker ; **un gros b.** a
 heavy drinker
buviez *etc voir* **boire**

C

C, c [se] *nm inv* C, c; **c cédille** c cedilla

C (*abrév* **Celsius**) C

c' *voir* **ce**

CA [sea] *nm* (**a**) *Él* (*abrév* **courant alternatif**) AC (**b**) *Com* (*abrév* **chiffre d'affaires**) turnover

ça [sa] *pron démonstratif* (**a**) *(en désignant) (cela)* that; *(ceci)* this; **donne-moi ça** give that to me; **c'est bien vrai ça!** that's very true!; **écoute-moi ça!** just listen to this!; **ce n'est pas si facile que ça** it isn't as easy as that; **ça oui!** oh yes!; **à part ça** apart from that; **qui/quand/où ça?** who/when/where?; **c'est ça!** that's right!; *Ironique* if you say so!; **comment ça, elle est partie?** what do you mean she's gone?; **ça alors!, ça par exemple!** my goodness!; **ça y est, j'ai fini** that's it, I'm finished; **et insolent avec ça!** and you're/she's/*etc* rude as well! (**b**) *(sujet indéterminé)* it; **ça m'ennuie/me choque** it annoys/shocks me; **ça m'amuse** I find it funny; **ça me ferait plaisir** I'd enjoy it (**c**) *Fam* **ça criait dans tous les coins** there was shouting going on everywhere; *Hum* **ça travaille là-dedans!** you're not just a pretty face!

çà [sa] **çà et là** *adv* here and there

cabale [kabal] *nf* (**a**) *(complot, comploteurs)* cabal; **monter une c. contre qn** to plot against sb (**b**) *Rel* cabbala

cabalistique [kabalistik] *adj* cabbalistic

caban [kabɑ̃] *nm (de marin)* reefer jacket; *(d'officier)* pea jacket

cabane [kaban] *nf* (**a**) *(baraque)* hut; *(en rondins)* cabin; *(à outils)* shed; **c. à lapins** rabbit hutch; *Can* **c. à sucre** sugar shack (**b**) *très Fam (prison)* **en c.** in the clink; **faire de la c.** to do time

cabanon [kabanɔ̃] *nm* (**a**) *(petite cabane)* hut, shed (**b**) *(en Provence) (maison de campagne)* (country) cottage

cabaret [kabarɛ] *nm* cabaret

cabas [kaba] *nm* shopping bag

cabestan [kabɛstɑ̃] *nm* capstan

cabillaud [kabijo] *nm* (fresh) cod

cabine [kabin] *nf* *(de bateau, de vaisseau spatial)* cabin; **c. de pilotage** *(de petit avion)* cockpit; *(de gros avion)* flight deck (**b**) **c. de douche** *(pièce)* shower room; *(installation)* shower cubicle; **c. de bain(s)** *(de plage)* beach hut; *(de piscine)* changing cubicle; **c. d'essayage** fitting room (**c**) *(de grue, de locomotive, de camion)* cab; *(d'ascenseur) Br* cage, *Am* car; **c. téléphonique** phone box *or* booth

cabinet [kabinɛ] *nm* (**a**) *(petite pièce)* small room; *Fam* **les cabinets** *Br* the loo, *Am* the john; **c.** cubbyhole; **c. de toilette** (small) bathroom; **c. de travail** study (**b**) *(de pub)* agency; *(d'architectes, de notaire)* office; *(de médecin) Br* surgery, practice, *Am* office; **c. dentaire** dental surgery *or* practice (**c**) *(entreprise)* **c. conseil** consultancy; **c.**

juridique law firm (**d**) *Pol (d'un ministre)* departmental staff

câble [kɑbl] *nm* (**a**) *(fil)* cable; **c. métallique** wire cable (**b**) *Vieilli (message)* cable

câbler [kɑble] *vt* (**a**) *TV (ville, quartier)* to install cable television in (**b**) *Vieilli (message)* to cable

câblo-opérateur (*pl* **câblo-opérateurs**) [kɑblo-ɔperatœr] *nm* cable company

cabochard, -e [kabɔʃar, -ard] *Fam* **1** *adj* pigheaded **2** *nm,f* pigheaded person

caboche [kabɔʃ] *nf Fam (tête)* nut; **mets-le-toi dans la c.!** get that into your thick skull!

cabosser [kabɔse] *vt (métal, voiture)* to bash up; *(chapeau)* to bash in; **un vieux chapeau cabossé** a battered old hat

cabot [kabo] *nm Fam* (**a**) *(chien)* pooch (**b**) *(acteur)* ham (actor)

cabotage [kabɔtaʒ] *nm Naut* coasting

caboteur [kabɔtœr] *nm Naut* coaster

cabotin, -e [kabɔtɛ̃, -in] **1** *adj (acteur)* ham **2** *nm,f* (**a**) *(acteur)* ham (actor, *f* actress) (**b**) *(vantard)* show-off

cabrer [kabre] **se cabrer** *vpr (cheval)* to rear (up); *Fig (personne)* to recoil

cabriole [kabrijɔl] *nf (saut, bond)* caper; *(en danse)* cabriole; *(en équitation)* capriole; *(de gymnaste)* somersault; **faire des cabrioles** to caper about

cabriolet [kabrijɔlɛ] *nm* (**a**) *(auto)* convertible (**b**) *(voiture à cheval)* cabriolet

CAC [kak] *n (abrév* **Compagnie des agents de change**) **le C.-40** = the Paris Stock Exchange index

caca [kaka] *nm (langage enfantin) (excrément)* poo; **faire c.** to do a poo; **c. d'oie** yellowish green

cacah(o)uète [kakawɛt] *nf* peanut

cacao [kakao] *nm (boisson, poudre)* cocoa; *(fève)* cocoa bean

cacaoui [kakawi] *nm Can* long-tailed duck

cacatoès [kakatɔɛs] *nm* cockatoo

cacatois [kakatwa] *nm Naut (voile)* royal sail; **(mât de) c.** royal mast

cachalot [kaʃalo] *nm* sperm whale

cache [kaʃ] **1** *nf* hiding place; **c. d'armes** arms cache **2** *nm (sur un texte)* masking card

caché, -e [kaʃe] *adj* hidden; *(sentiment)* secret

cache-cache [kaʃkaʃ] *nm* **jouer à c.** to play hide-and-seek

cache-col [kaʃkɔl] *nm inv Vieilli* scarf

Cachemire [kaʃmir] *nm* **le C.** Kashmir

cachemire [kaʃmir] *nm (laine)* cashmere; **à impression c.** paisley

cache-nez [kaʃne] *nm inv* scarf

cache-pot [kaʃpo] *nm inv* flowerpot holder

cacher [kaʃe] **1** *vt* to hide; **il ne cache pas que…** he makes no secret of the fact that…; **c. qch à qn** *(omettre de lui dire)* to hide sth from sb; **pour ne rien te c.** to be completely open with you; **je ne vous cache pas que j'ai été surpris** I won't pretend (that) I wasn't surprised; **le mur nous cache la vue** the wall blocks our view
2 se cacher *vpr (personne, soleil)* to hide; **se c. de qn** to hide from sb; **sa timidité se cache derrière une certaine rudesse** his shyness is hidden behind a bluff exterior; **je ne m'en cache pas** I make no secret of it; **en se cachant** secretly; **sans se c.** openly

cache-sexe [kaʃsɛks] *nm inv* G-string; *(d'indigène)* apron

cachet [kaʃɛ] *nm* **(a)** *(médicament)* tablet, pill **(b)** *(tampon)* stamp; *(sceau)* seal; *(de fabricant)* (trade)mark; **c. de la poste** postmark **(c)** *(style) (d'un endroit)* character; *(d'un vêtement)* style **(d)** *(salaire)* fee

cacheter [42] [kaʃte] *vt* to seal

cachette [kaʃɛt] *nf* hiding place; **en c.** secretly; **boire en c.** *(habituellement)* to be a secret drinker; **faire qch en c. de qn** to do sth without sb's knowing

cachot [kaʃo] *nm* **(a)** *(cellule)* dungeon **(b)** *(isolement)* solitary confinement

cachotterie [kaʃɔtri] *nf* **faire des cachotteries** to be secretive

cachottier, -ère [kaʃɔtje, -ɛr] **1** *adj* secretive
2 *nm,f* secretive person; **petit c.!** you secretive little thing!

cachou [kaʃu] *nm (bonbon)* cachou *(liquorice sweet)*

cacophonie [kakɔfɔni] *nf* cacophony

cactus [kaktys] *nm* cactus

c-à-d. *(abrev* **c'est-à-dire)** i.e.

cadastre [kadastr] *nm (registre)* cadastre; *(administration)* cadastral survey office

cadavérique [kadaverik] *adj (teint)* deathly pale; *Méd* cadaveric

cadavre [kadavr] *nm* **(a)** *(de personne)* corpse, (dead) body; *(d'animal)* carcass, body; *Fam* **c'est un c. ambulant** he's a walking skeleton **(b)** *Fam (bouteille)* empty

caddie [kadi] *nm* **(a)** *Sp* caddie **(b)** *(chariot) Br* trolley, *Am* cart

cadeau, -x [kado] *nm* present, gift; *(avec un achat)* free gift; **en c.** as a present; **en c. avec** *(achat)* free with; **faire un c. à qn** to give sb a present; **faire c. de qch à qn** *(donner)* to give sb sth as a present; *Fam Fig* **il ne lui a pas fait de cadeaux** he didn't spare him/her; *Fam* **ton frère, ce n'est pas un c.** your brother's a real pain; **c'est un c. empoisonné** it's more trouble than it's worth

cadenas [kadna] *nm* padlock

cadenasser [kadnase] **1** *vt (porte, pièce)* to padlock
2 se cadenasser *vpr (personne)* to lock oneself away

cadence [kadɑ̃s] *nf (rythme régulier)* rhythm; *(vitesse)* rate; **en c.** in time; **c. de production** rate of production; **c. de tir** rate of fire

cadencé, -e [kadɑ̃se] *adj* **(a)** *(rythmé)* rhythmic(al); **marcher au pas c.** to walk in time **(b)** *Ordinat* **c. à** running at

cadet, -ette [kadɛ, -ɛt] **1** *adj (de deux)* younger; *(de plus de deux)* youngest
2 *nm,f* **(a)** *(de deux)* younger (one); *(de plus de deux)* youngest (one); **il est mon c. de deux ans** he's two years younger than I am; **c'est le c. de mes soucis** that's the least of my worries **(b)** *Sp* junior *(16 to 18 years old)* **(c)** *Hist & Mil* cadet

cadrage [kadraʒ] *nm Cin & Phot (de l'image)* centring; *(plan)* frame; *Ordinat* positioning

cadran [kadrɑ̃] *nm (d'horloge, de baromètre)* face; *(d'instrument, de téléphone)* dial; *Can (réveil)* alarm-clock; *Fig* **faire le tour du c.** *(dormir)* to sleep round the clock; *Aut* **cadrans (de bord)** display panels; **c. solaire** sundial

cadre [kadr] *nm* **(a)** *(de tableau, de porte, de vélo)* frame **(b)** *(domaine)* limits; *(structure)* framework; **dans le c. de** within the framework of **(c)** *(décor)* setting; **c. (de vie)** environment **(d)** *(dans un formulaire)* box; *Ordinat (pour graphique)* box; **c. réservé à l'administration** *(sur formulaire)* for official use only **(e)** *(dans une entreprise)* executive, manager; **les cadres** the management; *Mil* the officers; **c. moyen** middle manager; **c. supérieur** senior executive; **jeune c.** dynamic young executive **(f)** **être sur les cadres** to be a member of staff; **être rayé des cadres** to be dismissed

cadre-adresse *(pl* **cadres-adresses)** [kadradrɛs] *nm* address space

cadrer [kadre] **1** *vt (photo)* to centre; *(plan)* to frame; *Ordinat* to position
2 *vi (correspondre)* to tally **(avec** with)

cadreur [kadrœr] *nm TV & Cin* cameraman

caduc, caduque [kadyk] *adj* **(a)** *(feuille)* deciduous **(b)** *Jur (accord)* lapsed; *(loi)* null and void

caducée [kadyse] *nm* caduceus

CAF [seaɛf] *(abrév* **Caisse d'allocations familiales)** = child benefit office

cafard [kafar] *nm* **(a)** *(insecte)* cockroach **(b)** *Fam* **avoir le c.** *ou* **un coup de c.** to feel down *or* low **(c)** *Fam (rapporteur)* sneak

cafarder [kafarde] *vi Fam* **(a)** *(rapporter)* to sneak **(b)** *(avoir le cafard)* to feel down *or* low

cafardeur, -euse [kafardœr, -øz] *nm,f Fam* sneak

cafardeux, -euse [kafardø, -øz] *adj Fam* **se sentir** *ou* **être c.** to feel down *or* low

café [kafe] **1** *nm* **(a)** *(produit, boisson)* coffee; **glace au c.** coffee ice cream; **c. crème** white coffee; **c. décaféiné** decaffeinated coffee; **c. en grains** coffee beans; **c. au lait** white coffee; **c. liégeois** = coffee ice cream topped with whipped cream; **c. moulu** ground coffee; *Suisse* **c. nature** black coffee; **c. noir** black coffee; **c. en poudre** *ou* **instantané** instant coffee **(b)** *(bar)* café *(also serving alcoholic drinks)*; **c. tabac** = café-cum-tobacconist's
2 *adj inv (couleur)* **c. (au lait)** coffee-coloured

caféine [kafein] *nf* caffeine

cafétéria [kafeterja] *nf* cafeteria

café-théâtre *(pl* **cafés-théâtres)** [kafeteatr] *nm* = café where theatre performances take place

cafetier [kaftje] *nm* café owner

cafetière [kaftjɛr] *nf (récipient)* coffee pot; *(électrique)* coffee machine; **c. à pression** percolator

cafouillage [kafujaʒ] *nm Fam* **(a)** *(confusion)* muddle, shambles **(b)** *(de moteur de voiture)* misfiring

cafouiller [kafuje] *vi Fam* **(a)** *(personne)* to get into a muddle; *(projet)* to fall apart **(b)** *(moteur de voiture)* to misfire; *(poste de télévision)* to be on the blink

cage [kaʒ] *nf* **(a)** *(pour oiseaux, dans un zoo)* cage; *(pour poules)* coop; *(pour lapins)* hutch; **mettre un oiseau en c.** to put a bird in a cage; *Fam Fig* **c. à lapins** rabbit hutch **(b)** *(de foot)* goal **(c)** **c. d'ascenseur** lift *or Am* elevator shaft; **c. d'escalier** stairwell **(d)** *Anat* **c. thoracique** rib cage

cageot [kaʒo] *nm* **(a)** *(caisse)* crate **(b)** *Fam Péj (femme)* dog

cagibi [kaʒibi] *nm Fam* storage room

cagneux, -euse [kaɲø, -øz] *adj* **avoir les genoux c.** to have knock-knees, to be knock-kneed

cagnotte [kaɲɔt] *nf (caisse commune)* kitty; *(de jeux)* pool; *(économies)* nest egg

cagoule [kagul] *nf (de moine)* cowl; *(de pénitent, de terroriste)* hood

cahier [kaje] *nm* (**a**) *(livre)* notebook; *(d'écolier)* exercise book; **c. de brouillon** rough book; **c. de textes** homework book (**b**) *Typ* signature (**c**) *(d'un journal)* section (**d**) **Cahiers de...** *(revue)* Journal of... (**e**) *Com* **c. des charges** *(d'un contrat)* terms and conditions; *(de fabrication)* specifications

cahin-caha [kaɛ̃kaa] *adv Fam* **aller c.** *(se déplacer)* to struggle along; **ça va, la santé? – ça va, c.** how are you keeping? – oh, so-so

cahot [kao] *nm (secousse)* jolt

cahoter [kaɔte] **1** *vt* **être cahoté** *(dans un véhicule)* to be jolted about
2 *vi* to jolt along

cahoteux, -euse [kaɔtø, -øz] *adj* bumpy

cahute [kayt] *nf* shack

caïd [kaid] *nm Fam (chef de bande)* gang leader; **un c. de la drogue** a drugs baron; **faire le c., jouer les caïds** to act high and mighty

caillasse [kajas] *nf Fam* loose stones

caille [kɑj] *nf* quail; *Fam* **ma petite c.** my little dove

caillé [kɑje] *nm* curds

caillebotis [kɑjbɔti] *nm* (**a**) *Naut* grating (**b**) *(plancher)* duckboard

caillebotte [kɑjbɔt] *nf* curds

cailler [kɑje] **1** *vt (lait)* to curdle; *(sang)* to clot
2 *vi* (**a**) *(lait)* to curdle; *(sang)* to clot; **faire c. du lait** to curdle milk (**b**) *Fam* **ça caille** it's freezing
3 se cailler *vpr Fam* **on se (les) caille** it's freezing

caillot [kajo] *nm (de sang)* clot

caillou, -x [kaju] *nm* (**a**) *(petite pierre)* stone; *(sur la plage)* pebble (**b**) *Fam (pierre précieuse)* stone (**c**) *Fam (tête)* nut; **il n'a plus un poil sur le c.** he's as bald as a coot

caillouteux, -euse [kajutø, -øz] *adj (route)* stony; *(plage)* pebbly

caïman [kaimɑ̃] *nm* cayman

Caire [kɛr] *voir* **Le Caire**

cairote [kerɔt] **1** *adj* of Cairo
2 *nmf* **C.** person from Cairo, Cairene

caisse [kɛs] *nf* (**a**) *(pour marchandises)* case; *(à outils)* box; *(de champagne, de vin)* case; *(pour plantes)* tub; *(de fruits)* crate (**b**) *Com & Fin (coffre)* cash box; *(d'une caisse enregistreuse)* till; *(où l'on paie) (dans un magasin)* cash desk; *(dans un supermarché)* checkout; **les caisses de l'État** the coffers of the State; **tenir la c.** *(dans un restaurant, dans un magasin)* to be the cashier; **passer à la c.** *(se faire licencier)* to be paid off; *Fam (payer)* to pay; *Fam (se faire payer)* to be paid; **c. (enregistreuse)** cash register; *Pol* **c. noire** slush fund (**c**) *(argent)* cash (in hand); **faire la ou sa c.** to do the till (**d**) *(organisme)* **c. d'allocations familiales** *Br* ≃ Child Benefit office, *Am* ≃ Aid to Dependent Children office; **c. d'épargne** savings bank; *Can* **c. populaire** credit union; **c. primaire d'assurance maladie** = French government department dealing with health insurance; **c. de retraite** pension fund (**e**) *Mus* **c. claire** snare drum; **c. de résonance** sound box (**f**) *(de piano, d'horloge)* case; *(de véhicule)* body (**g**) *très Fam (voiture)* car

caissette [kɛsɛt] *nf* small box

caissier, -ère [kɛsje, -ɛr] *nm,f* cashier; *(dans un supermarché)* checkout operator

caisson [kɛsɔ̃] *nm* (**a**) *très Fam* **se faire sauter le c.** to blow one's brains out (**b**) *Archit* **plafond à caissons** coffered ceiling (**c**) *(de plongée)* caisson

cajoler [kaʒɔle] *vt* to cuddle

cajolerie [kaʒɔlri] *nf* cuddle

cajou [kaʒu] *nm voir* **noix**

cake [kɛk] *nm* fruit cake

cal *(pl* **cals)** [kal] *nm (durillon)* callus

calamar [kalamar] = **calmar**

calamine [kalamin] *nf (dépôt)* carbon deposits

calamité [kalamite] *nf (fléau)* calamity; *(malheur)* great misfortune; *Fam* **ce mec, c'est une vraie c.!** this guy is a walking disaster!

calamiteux, -euse [kalamitø -øz] *adj* calamitous

calandre [kalɑ̃dr] *nf* (**a**) *(machine)* calender (**b**) *Aut* radiator grille

calanque [kalɑ̃k] *nf* deep narrow creek *(in the Mediterranean)*

calcaire [kalkɛr] **1** *adj (sol, terrain)* chalky; *(roche)* calcareous; *(eau)* hard
2 *nm* (**a**) *Géol* limestone (**b**) *(dépôt)* fur

calcification [kalsifikasjɔ̃] *nf Méd* calcification

calciner [kalsine] **1** *vt (brûler)* to char; **calciné** *(trop cuit)* burnt to a cinder
2 se calciner *vpr* to burn

calcium [kalsjɔm] *nm* calcium

calcul¹ [kalkyl] *nm* (**a**) *(compte)* calculation; **faire un c.** to make a calculation (**b**) *Scol* **le c.** arithmetic; **c. mental** mental arithmetic (**c**) *Math* **c. différentiel/intégral** differential/integral calculus (**d**) *(prévision)* calculation; **agir par c.** to act from selfish motives; **faire un mauvais c.** to miscalculate

calcul² *nm Méd* stone, *Spéc* calculus; **c. biliaire/rénal** gall/kidney stone

calculateur, -trice [kalkylatœr, -tris] **1** *adj (personne, politique)* calculating
2 *nm Ordinat* (desktop) calculator; **c. (électronique)** (electronic) computer
3 *nf* **calculatrice (de poche)** (pocket) calculator

calculé, -e [kalkyle] *adj (insulte, risque)* calculated; *(méchanceté)* premeditated; *(insolence)* deliberate

calculer [kalkyle] **1** *vt (compter) (prix, superficie)* to work out, to calculate; *(comportement, propos)* to plan; *(conséquences, chances)* to weigh (up); **tout bien calculé** taking everything into account
2 *vi* to calculate; *Péj (économiser)* to count every penny

calculette [kalkylɛt] *nf* (pocket) calculator

Calcutta [kalkyta] *n* Calcutta

caldoche [kaldɔʃ] **1** *adj* White New Caledonian
2 *nmf* **C.** New Caledonian

cale¹ [kal] *nf Naut* (**a**) *(de navire)* hold; **à fond de c.** down in the hold (**b**) *(rampe)* **c. sèche** dry dock

cale² *nf (pour meuble, pour porte)* wedge; *(pour bloquer une roue)* chock

calé, -e [kale] *adj Fam* (**a**) *(personne)* **être c. en qch** to be well up in sth (**b**) *(problème, question, devoir)* tough

calebasse [kalbas] *nf* calabash

calèche [kalɛʃ] *nf* barouche

calecif [kalsif] *nm Fam Br* pants, *Am* shorts

caleçon [kalsɔ̃] *nm (pour homme)* boxer shorts; *(de femme)* leggings; *Vieilli* **c. de bain** bathing trunks; *Vieilli* **c. long** long johns

calédonien, -enne [kaledɔnjɛ̃, -ɛn] **1** *adj* Caledonian
2 *nm,f* **C.** Caledonian

calembour [kalɑ̃bur] *nm* pun, play on words; **faire des calembours** to make puns

calendes [kalɑ̃d] *nfpl* **renvoyer qch aux c. grecques** to put sth off indefinitely

calendrier [kalɑ̃drije] *nm* **(a)** *(système, tableau)* calendar **(b)** *(de voyage, de travail)* timetable

cale-pied (*pl* cale-pieds) [kalpje] *nm* toe clip

calepin [kalpɛ̃] *nm* notebook

caler¹ [kale] **1** *vt* **(a)** *(meuble, porte)* to wedge; *(roue)* to chock; *(chargement)* to secure; **c. un malade avec des coussins** to prop up a patient with cushions **(b)** *Fam (remplir)* **ça cale (l'estomac)** it fills you up; **je suis calé** I'm stuffed
2 *vi (moteur)* to stall
3 se caler *vpr (dans un fauteuil)* to settle oneself comfortably

caler² *vi* **(a)** *Fam (abandonner)* to give up **(b)** *Can (se dégarnir)* to have a receding hairline

calfater [kalfate] *vt Naut* to caulk

calfeutrer [kalføtre] **1** *vt* **(a)** *(brèches)* to block up **(b)** *(pièce, fenêtre)* to draught-proof
2 se calfeutrer *vpr (pour avoir chaud)* to make oneself cosy, *(pour être seul)* to shut oneself away

calibre [kalibr] *nm* **(a)** *(d'arme à feu, de tuyau, de balle)* calibre; *(d'œufs, de fruits)* grade; *Fig* **sa sœur est d'un autre c.** his sister is of quite a different calibre **(b)** *(outil)* gauge **(c)** *très Fam (revolver)* shooter

calibrer [kalibre] *vt (pièce)* to gauge; *(instrument de mesure)* to calibrate; *Com (œufs, fruits)* to grade

calice¹ [kalis] *nm Rel* chalice; *Fig* **boire le c. jusqu'à la lie** to drain the cup to the dregs

calice² *nm Bot* calyx

calife [kalif] *nm* caliph

Californie [kalifɔrni] *nf* **la C.** California

californien, -enne [kalifɔrnjɛ̃, -ɛn] **1** *adj* Californian
2 *nm,f* **C.** Californian

califourchon [kalifurʃɔ̃] **à califourchon** *adv* astride; **se mettre à c. sur qch** to sit astride sth

câlin, -e [kɑlɛ̃, -in] **1** *adj* affectionate
2 *nm* cuddle; **faire un c. à qn** to give sb a cuddle

câliner [kaline] *vt* to cuddle

calisson [kalisɔ̃] *nm* = lozenge-shaped sweet made of marzipan

calleux, -euse [kalø, -øz] *adj* callous

call-girl (*pl* call-girls) [kolgœrl] *nf* call girl

calligramme [kaligram] *nm* calligram

calligraphe [kaligraf] *nmf* calligrapher

calligraphie [kaligrafi] *nf* calligraphy

calmant, -e [kalmɑ̃, -ɑ̃t] *Méd* **1** *adj (pour les nerfs)* sedative; *(pour la douleur)* painkilling
2 *nm (pour les nerfs)* sedative; *(pour la douleur)* painkiller; **sous calmants** under sedation

calmar [kalmar] *nm* squid

calme [kalm] **1** *adj* **(a)** *(personne) (qui garde son sang-froid)* calm; *(tranquille)* quiet **(b)** *(mer)* calm; *(ciel)* clear; **les affaires sont calmes en août** business is quiet in August
2 *nm (absence d'agitation)* calm, calmness; *(sang-froid)* composure; *(du paysage)* peace and quiet; **être au c.** to have peace and quiet; **du c.!** *(taisez-vous)* quiet!; *(ne vous affolez pas)* calm down!; **garder/perdre son c.** to keep/lose one's composure; *Naut* **c. plat** dead calm; **c'est le c. plat dans ma vie sentimentale** my love life is non-existent

calmement [kalməmɑ̃] *adv* calmly

calmer [kalme] **1** *vt (personne)* to calm (down); *(craintes)* to calm; *(douleur)* to soothe; *(fièvre)* to reduce; *(soif)* to quench; *(faim)* to appease; *(ardeur, passion)* to cool
2 se calmer *vpr (personne)* to calm down; *(tempête, vent)* to die down; *(mer)* to become calm; *(pluie)* to ease off; *(douleur, fièvre)* to subside

calomnie [kalɔmni] *nf (en paroles)* slander; *(par écrit)* libel

calomnier [66] [kalɔmnje] *vt (en paroles)* to slander; *(par écrit)* to libel

calomnieux, -euse [kalɔmnjø, -øz] *adj (paroles)* slanderous; *(écrits)* libellous

calorie [kalɔri] *nf* calorie; **régime basses calories** low-calorie diet

calorifère [kalɔrifɛr] **1** *adj* heat-conveying
2 *nm Vieilli* (slow-combustion) stove; *Can* radiator

calorifique [kalɔrifik] *adj* calorific

calorifuge [kalɔrifyʒ] **1** *adj* (heat-)insulating
2 *nm* heat insulation; *(pour chaudière, tuyau)* lagging

calorique [kalɔrik] *adj* calorific

calot [kalo] *nm (coiffure militaire) Br* forage cap, *Am* garrison cap

calotte [kalɔt] *nf* **(a)** *(chapeau rond)* skullcap; *Rel* calotte; *(de chapeau)* crown; *très Fam Péj* **la c.** *(le clergé)* the clergy **(b)** *Fam (gifle)* clout **(c)** *Anat* **c. crânienne** skullcap **(d)** *Géol* **c. glaciaire** ice cap

calque [kalk] *nm (copie)* tracing; *Fig (de poème, de portrait)* exact copy; *(traduction)* calque; **prendre un c. de qch** to make a tracing of sth; **(papier) c.** tracing paper

calquer [kalke] *vt (reproduire)* to trace; *Fig* to copy exactly; **expression calquée sur l'anglais** expression copied from the English, **il calque sa conduite sur celle de son frère** he models his behaviour on his brother's

calumet [kalymɛ] *nm* peace pipe; *Fig* **fumer le c. de la paix** to bury the hatchet

calvados [kalvados] *nm* Calvados

calvaire [kalvɛr] *nm* **(a)** *(du Christ)* calvary; *Fig (épreuve pénible)* ordeal **(b)** *(croix)* calvary

calviniste [kalvinist] *adj & nmf* Calvinist

calvitie [kalvisi] *nf* baldness; **avoir un début de c.** to be starting to go bald; **c. précoce** premature baldness

camaïeu, -x [kamajø] *nm (peinture)* monochrome; *(gravure)* tint drawing; **un c. de bleu** *(papiers peints, vêtements)* different shades of blue

camarade [kamarad] *nmf* friend; *Pol (terme d'adresse)* comrade; **c. de classe** classmate; **c. d'école** school friend

camaraderie [kamaradri] *nf* camaraderie

cambiste [kɑ̃bist] *nmf Fin* foreign exchange dealer

Cambodge [kɑ̃bɔdʒ] *nm* **le C.** Cambodia

cambodgien, -enne [kɑ̃bɔdʒjɛ̃, -ɛn] **1** *adj* Cambodian
2 *nm,f* **C.** Cambodian

cambouis [kɑ̃bwi] *nm* dirty oil

cambré, -e [kɑ̃bre] *adj (pied)* with a high instep; *(personne)* with an arched back

cambrer [kɑ̃bre] **1** *vt (dos, pied)* to arch; **c. la taille** *ou* **les reins** to arch one's back
2 se cambrer *vpr* to arch one's back

cambrien, -enne [kɑ̃brijɛ̃, -ɛn] *Géol* **1** *adj* Cambrian
2 le C. the Cambrian period

cambriolage [kɑ̃brijɔlaʒ] *nm* burglary, break-in

cambrioler [kɑ̃brijɔle] *vt (maison, personne) Br* to burgle, *Am* to burglarize

cambrioleur, -euse [kɑ̃brijɔlœr, -øz] *nm,f* burglar

cambrousse [kɑ̃brus], **cambrouse** [kɑ̃bruz] *nf Fam* country; **en pleine c.** in the middle of nowhere

cambrure [kɑ̃bryr] *nf (du pied, du dos)* arch; **c. des reins** small of the back

cambuse [kɑ̃byz] *nf* **(a)** *Naut* storeroom **(b)** *très Fam Vieilli (chambre)* hole

came¹ [kam] *nf Tech* cam

came² *nf très Fam (drogue)* dope

camé, -e [kame] *très Fam* **1** *adj* high **2** *nm,f* junkie

camée [kame] *nm* cameo

caméléon [kamele5] *nm aussi Fig* chameleon

camélia [kamelja] *nm* camellia

camelote [kamlɔt] *nf Fam* **(a)** *(pacotille)* junk **(b)** *(marchandise)* stuff

camembert [kamãbɛr] *nm* **(a)** *(fromage)* Camembert **(b)** *(diagramme)* pie-chart

camer [kame] **se camer** *vpr très Fam* to do drugs; **se c. à l'héroïne** to do heroin

caméra [kamera] *nf Cin & TV* camera; **c. de télévision** television camera; **c. vidéo** video camera

cameraman [kameraman] *(pl* **cameramans** *ou* **cameramen** [kameramɛn]) *nm Cin & TV* cameraman

Cameroun [kamrun] *nm* **le C.** Cameroon

camerounais, -e [kamrunɛ, -ɛz] **1** *adj* Cameroonian **2** *nm,f* **C.** Cameroonian

Caméscope® [kameskɔp] *nm* camcorder

camion [kamjɔ̃] *nm Br* lorry, *Am* truck; **c. à benne** dump truck; **c. de déménagement** removal van; **c. de dépannage** breakdown truck; **c. frigorifique** *ou* **réfrigéré** refrigerated lorry

camion-benne *(pl* **camions-bennes)** [kamjɔ̃bɛn] *nm Br* dumper truck, *Am* dumpster

camion-citerne *(pl* **camions-citernes)** [kamjɔ̃sitɛrn] *nm Br* tanker, *Am* tank truck

camionnette [kamjɔnɛt] *nf* van; **c. de livraison** delivery van

camionneur [kamjɔnœr] *nm* **(a)** *(conducteur) Br* lorry driver, *Am* truck driver **(b)** *(transporteur) Br* haulier, *Am* trucker

camisole [kamizɔl] *nf* **(a)** *Can (tricot de corps) Br* vest, *Am* undershirt **(b)** *(chemise de nuit)* nightshirt **(c)** **c. de force** straitjacket

camomille [kamɔmij] *nf* camomile; *(tisane)* camomile tea

camouflage [kamuflaʒ] *nm Mil* camouflage; *(de la vérité, d'intentions)* disguising; *(de bénéfices)* concealment

camoufler [kamufle] **1** *vt Mil* to camouflage; *(vérité, intentions)* to disguise; *(bénéfices)* to conceal; **c. un meurtre en suicide** to make a murder look like suicide **2 se camoufler** *vpr* to camouflage oneself

camp [kɑ̃] *nm* **(a)** *(campement)* camp; **établir un c.** to pitch camp; **lever le c.** to strike camp; *Fam Fig (partir)* to hit the road; **c. (de vacances)** *Br* (children's) holiday camp, *Am* summer camp; **c. de concentration** concentration camp; **c. de loisirs** holiday camp; **c. de prisonniers** prison camp **(b)** *(parti)* camp, side **(c)** *(de jeux)* side; **faire deux camps** to form two teams

campagnard, -e [kɑ̃paɲar, -ard] *adj* country

campagne [kɑ̃paɲ] *nf* **(a)** *(par opposition à la ville)* country; *(paysage)* countryside; **à la c.** in the country; **en pleine c.** deep in the countryside; **en rase c.** in the open country **(b)** *Mil, Pol & Com* campaign; *Pol* **entrer en c.** to go on the campaign trail; **faire c.** to campaign for/against; **partir en c. contre le tabac** to launch an anti-smoking campaign; **c. électorale** election campaign; **c. de presse** press campaign; **c. publicitaire** *ou* **de publicité** advertising campaign

campanile [kɑ̃panil] *nm Archit* bell tower

campanule [kɑ̃panyl] *nf* campanula

campement [kɑ̃pmɑ̃] *nm (installation)* camp; *(lieu)* camping place; **établir un c.** to pitch camp

camper [kɑ̃pe] **1** *vi* **(a)** *(faire du camping)* to camp **(b)** *Fig (chez quelqu'un)* to camp out **2** *vt* **(a)** *Vieilli* **c. son chapeau sur sa tête** to plant one's hat on one's head **(b)** *(décrire)* to put in context; **c. un personnage** *(sujet: acteur)* to play a part effectively **3 se camper** *vpr* **se c. devant qn** to plant oneself in front of sb

campeur, -euse [kɑ̃pœr, -øz] *nm,f* camper

camphre [kɑ̃fr] *nm* camphor

camphré, -e [kɑ̃fre] *adj* camphorated

camping [kɑ̃piŋ] *nm* **(a)** *(activité)* camping; **faire du c.** to go camping; **c. à la ferme** farm camping; **c. sauvage** unauthorized camping **(b)** *(lieu)* camp site; **c. aménagé** camp site with facilities

camping-car *(pl* **camping-cars)** [kɑ̃piŋkar] *nm* camper

camping-caravaning [kɑ̃piŋkaravaniŋ] *nm* camping-caravanning

Camping-Gaz® [kɑ̃piŋgaz] *nm inv* camping stove

campus [kɑ̃pys] *nm* campus; **habiter sur le c.** to live on campus

camus [kamy] *adj m (nez)* flat

Canada [kanada] *nm* **le C.** Canada

Canadair® [kanadɛr] *nm* fire-fighting plane

canadianisme [kanadjanism] *nm Ling* Canadianism

canadien, -enne [kanadjɛ̃, -ɛn] **1** *adj* Canadian **2** *nm,f* **C.** Canadian **3** *nf* **canadienne** *(veste)* sheepskin jacket; *(tente)* ridge tent

canaille [kanaj] **1** *adj (chanson, paroles)* vulgar; *(air)* roguish **2** *nf (crapule)* scoundrel; **petite c.!** *(à un enfant)* you little devil!

canal, -aux [kanal, -o] *nm* **(a)** *(cours d'eau)* canal; **c. d'irrigation** irrigation canal; **le c. de Panama/de Suez** the Panama/Suez Canal **(b)** *(conduite)* conduit **(c)** *Anat & Bot* duct **(d)** *Rad & TV* channel; *TV* **C.+** = French pay television channel **(e)** *Fig (moyen)* channel; **par le c. de la poste** through the post **(f)** *Com* channel; **c. de distribution** distribution channel

canalisation [kanalizasjɔ̃] *nf* **(a)** *(conduite)* pipe; *(pour pétrole)* pipeline **(b)** *(de rivière)* canalization

canaliser [kanalize] *vt* **(a)** *(région, rivière)* to canalize **(b)** *(énergie)* to channel; *(trafic, foule)* to direct

canapé [kanape] *nm* **(a)** *(meuble)* sofa, couch; **c. convertible** sofa bed; **c. deux places** two-seater sofa **(b)** *(pour l'apéritif)* canapé

canapé-lit *(pl* **canapés-lits)** [kanapeli] *nm* sofa bed

canaque [kanak] **1** *adj* Kanak *(of New Caledonia)* **2** *nmf* **C.** Kanak *(from New Caledonia)*

canard [kanar] *nm* **(a)** *(oiseau)* duck; *(mâle)* drake; *Fam* **mon petit c.** my pet; **marcher en c.** to walk with one's feet turned out; **c. laqué** Peking duck; **c. à l'orange** duck à l'orange; **c. sauvage** wild duck **(b)** *Fam (journal)* rag **(c)** *(morceau de sucre)* = sugar lump dipped in coffee or alcoholic drink **(d)** *Mus* false note

canarder [kanarde] *vt Fam* to snipe at

canari [kanari] *nm* canary

Canaries [kanari] *nfpl* **les (îles) C.** the Canary Islands

canasson [kanasɔ̃] *nm Fam (cheval)* nag

cancan [kɑ̃kɑ̃] *nm* **(a)** **cancans** *(ragots)* gossip **(sur** about) **(b)** *(danse)* cancan

cancaner [kɑ̃kane] *vi* **(a)** *(médire)* to gossip **(sur** about) **(b)** *(canard)* to quack

cancanier, -ère [kɑ̃kanje, -ɛr] *Fam* **1** *adj* gossipy **2** *nm,f* gossip

cancer [kɑ̃sɛr] *nm* **(a)** *Méd & Fig* cancer; **c. du poumon/**

du sein lung/breast cancer; **avoir un c.** to have cancer (**b**) *Astron & Astrol* **le C.** Cancer; **être C.** to be (a) Cancer **cancéreux, -euse** [kãserø, -øz] **1** *adj (tumeur)* cancerous **2** *nmf* cancer sufferer **cancérigène** [kãseriʒɛn] *adj* carcinogenic; **produit c.** carcinogen **cancérologie** [kãserɔlɔʒi] *nf* cancerology **cancérologue** [kãserɔlɔg] *nmf* cancer specialist **cancre** [kãkr] *nm Fam* dunce **cancrelat** [kãkrəla] *nm* cockroach **candélabre** [kãdelabr] *nm (chandelier)* candelabra **candeur** [kãdœr] *nf* guilelessness; **un regard plein de c.** a guileless look **candi** [kãdi] *adj m voir* **sucre** **candidat, -e** [kãdida, -at] *nmf (à un poste)* applicant (à for); *(à un examen)* candidate (à for); **être c. aux élections** to stand *or* run for election **candidature** [kãdidatyr] *nf (aux élections)* candidature; *(à un poste)* application (à for); **poser sa c. à un poste** to apply for a post; **c. spontanée** unsolicited application **candide** [kãdid] *adj* guileless **candidement** [kãdidmã] *adv* guilelessly **candidose** [kãdidoz] *nf Méd* candidiasis **cane** [kan] *nf* (female) duck **caneton** [kantɔ̃] *nm* (male) duckling **canette**[1] [kanɛt] *nf (petite cane)* (female) duckling **canette**[2] = **cannette** **canevas** [kanva] *nm* (**a**) *(trame)* canvas (**b**) *(de film, de roman)* outline **caniche** [kaniʃ] *nm* poodle **canicule** [kanikyl] *nf* heatwave **canif** [kanif] *nm* penknife **canin, -e** [kanɛ̃, in] **1** *adj* canine; **exposition canine** dog show **2** *nf* canine canine (tooth) **caniveau, -x** [kanivo] *nm* gutter **cannabis** [kanabis] *nm* cannabis **cannage** [kanaʒ] *nm (partie en rotin)* canework **canne** [kan] *nf* (**a**) *(tige)* cane; **c. à pêche** fishing rod; **c. à sucre** sugar cane (**b**) *(pour s'appuyer)* (walking) stick; **blanche** white stick (**c**) *très Fam (jambe)* leg **canné, -e** [kane] *adj (chaise)* cane **canneberge** [kanberʒ] *nf* cranberry **cannelé, -e** [kanle] *adj (colonne)* fluted; *(pneu)* grooved **cannelle** [kanɛl] *nf* cinnamon; **bâton de c.** cinnamon stick; **à la c.** cinnamon(-flavoured) **cannellonis** [kanɛlɔni] *nmpl* cannelloni **cannelure** [kanlyr] *nf (rainure)* groove; *(de colonne)* fluting **cannette** [kanɛt] *nf* (**a**) *(petite bouteille)* bottle; *(boîte)* can (**b**) *Tex* spool **cannibale** [kanibal] **1** *nmf* cannibal **2** *adj (pratiques)* cannibalistic; **tribu c.** tribe of cannibals **cannibalisme** [kanibalism] *nm* cannibalism **canoë** [kanɔe] *nm* canoe; **faire du c.** to go canoeing **canoë-kayak** [kanɔekajak] *nm* canoeing **canon**[1] [kanɔ̃] *nm* (**a**) *(pièce d'artillerie)* gun; *Hist* cannon (**b**) *(de carabine)* barrel (**c**) *Anciennement (mesure)* = wine measure equivalent to 0.058 l; *Fam* **boire un c.** to have a glass of wine **canon**[2] **1** *nm* (**a**) *Rel & Fig (règle)* canon (**b**) *Mus* canon; **c. à**

deux/trois voix canon for two/three voices; **chanter qch en c.** to sing sth in canon (**c**) *Fam (personne)* babe **2** *adj inv Fam (beau)* gorgeous, hot **canonique** [kanɔnik] *adj* canonical; *Fig* **être d'un âge c.** to be advanced in years **canoniser** [kanɔnize] *vt Rel* to canonize **canonnade** [kanɔnad] *nf* gunfire; **une c.** a burst of gunfire **canot** [kano] *nm* *Naut* (**a**) *(petit bateau)* boat; **c. pneumatique** rubber dinghy; **c. de sauvetage** lifeboat (**b**) *Can (canoë)* canoe **canotage** [kanɔtaʒ] *nm* boating; *Can (en canoë)* canoeing; **faire du c.** to go boating/canoeing **canoter** [kanɔte] *vi Naut* to go boating; *Can (en canoë)* to go canoeing **canotier** [kanɔtje] *nm* (**a**) *(rameur)* rower (**b**) *(chapeau)* boater **cantal, -als** [kãtal] *nm* Cantal **cantate** [kãtat] *nf* cantata **cantatrice** [kãtatris] *nf (chanteuse d'opéra)* opera singer; *(de concert)* (concert) singer **cantine** [kãtin] *nf* (**a**) *(réfectoire)* canteen; *(à l'école)* dining hall; **déjeuner à la c.** *(de l'école)* to have school meals (**b**) *(malle)* trunk **cantique** [kãtik] *nm Rel* hymn; **le C. des cantiques** the Song of Solomon **canton** [kãtɔ̃] *nm (en France)* canton *(administrative division of a department)*; *(en Suisse)* canton *(semi-autonomous administrative region of Switzerland)*; *Can* **les cantons de l'Est** the Eastern Townships **cantonade** [kãtɔnad] **à la cantonade** *adv* to everybody present, *(au théâtre)* off **cantonais, -e** [kãtɔnɛ, -ɛz] **1** *adj* Cantonese **2** *nm f* **C.** Cantonese **3** *nm (langue)* Cantonese **cantonal, -e, -aux, -ales** [kãtɔnal, -o] *adj* cantonal; **les (élections) cantonales** the cantonal elections **cantonnement** [kãtɔnmã] *nm Mil (des troupes)* quartering; *(lieu)* quarters **cantonner** [kãtɔne] **1** *vt* (**a**) *Mil (troupes)* to quarter (**b**) **c. qn dans/à** to confine sb to **2** **se cantonner** *vpr (se limiter)* **se c. dans/à** to confine oneself to **cantonnier** [kãtɔnje] *nm* roadmender; *Rail* lineman **canular** [kanylar] *nm Fam* hoax; **monter un c.** to play a hoax **canule** [kanyl] *nf Méd* cannula **canyon** [kanjɔ̃] *nm* canyon; **le Grand C.** the Grand Canyon **CAO** [seao] *nf Ordinat (abrév* conception assistée par ordinateur*)* CAD **caoutchouc** [kautʃu] *nm* (**a**) *(substance)* rubber; **Mousse®** foam rubber; **c. synthétique** synthetic rubber (**b**) *(plante)* rubber plant **caoutchouteux, -euse** [kautʃutø, -øz] *adj Péj* rubbery **CAP** [seape] *nm (abrév* certificat d'aptitude professionnelle*)* = vocational training certificate **Cap** [kap] *voir* **Le Cap** **cap** [kap] *nm* (**a**) *Géog* cape, headland; **passer** *ou* **franchir** *ou* **doubler un c.** to round a cape; **quand on a franchi le c. de la quarantaine** when you've turned forty; **notre usine va passer le c. des mille employés** our factory will soon pass the thousand-employee mark; **le c. de Bonne-Espérance** the Cape of Good Hope; **le c. Horn** Cape Horn

(**b**) *Naut & Av (direction)* course; **mettre le c. sur...** to set course for...
capable [kapabl] *adj* (**a**) *(susceptible)* **être c.** de qch to be capable of sth; **être c.** de faire qch to be capable of doing sth, to be able to do sth; **il est c.** de tout he's capable of anything; **c. du meilleur comme du pire** capable of the best as well as the worst; **elle est bien c. d'oublier les clefs!** she's quite capable of forgetting the keys! (**b**) *(compétent)* capable, able (**c**) *Jur* competent (**de faire** to do)
capacité [kapasite] *nf* (**a**) *(contenance)* capacity; **c. d'accueil** *(d'un hôtel)* accommodation capacity (**b**) *(aptitude)* ability, capability; **de grandes capacités (intellectuelles)** great intellectual abilities; *Ordinat* **c. d'adressage** address capability; **c. de concentration** attention span; *Ordinat* **c. de mémoire** memory capacity (**c**) *Jur* capacity; **avoir c. pour faire qch** to be (legally) entitled to do sth (**d**) *Jur* **c. en droit** = certificate entitling holder to practise in some branches of the legal profession
cape [kap] *nf* *(vêtement)* cape; *(plus longue)* cloak; **film/roman de c. et d'épée** swashbuckling movie/novel; *Fig* **rire sous c.** to laugh up one's sleeve
capeline [kaplin] *nf (chapeau)* floppy hat
CAPES [kapɛs] *nm* *(abrév* **certificat d'aptitude au professorat de l'enseignement du second degré)** = postgraduate teaching certificate
CAPET [kapɛt] *nm* *(abrév* **certificat d'aptitude au professorat de l'enseignement technique)** = postgraduate technical teaching certificate
capétien, -enne [kapesjɛ̃, -ɛn] **1** *adj* Capetian **2** *nmpl* **les Capétiens** the Capetians
capharnaüm [kafarnaɔm] *nm* *Fam (pièce en désordre)* pigsty; *(désordre)* mess
capillaire [kapilɛr] **1** *adj* capillary **2** *nm* (**a**) *(plante)* maidenhair (fern) (**b**) *Anat* capillary
capillarité [kapilarite] *nf* *Phys* capillarity
capilotade [kapilɔtad] **en capilotade** *adv* **j'ai le dos en c.** my back's killing me
capitaine [kapitɛn] *nm* (**a**) *Mil & Naut* captain; *Av* *Br* flight lieutenant, *Am* captain; **c. de gendarmerie** police *Br* superintendent *or* *Am* captain; **c. des pompiers** fire chief; **c. de port** harbour master (**b**) *Sp* captain
capitainerie [kapitɛnri] *nf* harbour master's office
capital, -e, -aux, -ales [kapital, -o] **1** *adj* (**a**) *(essentiel)* major; **il est c. qu'il soit présent à la réunion** it is essential for him to be at the meeting (**b**) *Typ* **lettre capitale** capital letter **2** *nm* *Fin* capital; *Fig (culturel, artistique)* wealth; **posséder un c.** to have some capital; **capitaux propres** equity; **c. social** (issued) share capital **3** *nf* **capitale** (**a**) *(ville)* capital (city) (**b**) *Typ* capital; **écrire en capitales d'imprimerie** to write in block letters
capitalisable [kapitalizabl] *adj (intérêts)* capitalizable
capitalisation [kapitalizasjɔ̃] *nf (d'intérêts)* capitalization
capitaliser [kapitalize] **1** *vt (intérêts)* to capitalize **2** *vi* to save
capitalisme [kapitalism] *nm* capitalism
capitaliste [kapitalist] *adj & nmf* capitalist
capiteux, -euse [kapitø, -øz] *adj (vin, parfum)* heady; *(charme)* sensuous; *(femme)* alluring
capitonnage [kapitɔnaʒ] *nm (action, matière)* padding, stuffing
capitonné, -e [kapitɔne] *adj (siège, cellule)* padded
capitulation [kapitylasjɔ̃] *nf* surrender; **c. sans conditions** unconditional surrender
capituler [kapityle] *vi* to surrender

caporal, -aux [kapɔral, -o] *nm* *Mil* *Br* lance corporal, *Am* private first class
capot¹ [kapo] *nm* *Aut* *Br* bonnet, *Am* hood; *Av (de moteur d'avion)* cowl; *Naut (bâche)* tarpaulin; *Ordinat* **c. d'imprimante** printer hood
capot² *adj inv* **être c.** *(aux cartes)* to have made no tricks at all
capote [kapɔt] *nf* (**a**) *Aut (de décapotable)* *Br* hood, *Am* top; **baisser la c.** to put the hood down (**b**) *Mil (manteau)* greatcoat (**c**) *Fam* **c. (anglaise)** condom, rubber
capoté, -e [kapɔte] *adj* *Can* *Fam* annoyed
capoter [kapɔte] *vi* *Naut* to capsize; *Aut & Av* to overturn; *Fig (échouer) (projet)* to fall through
cappuccino [kaputʃino] *nm* cappuccino
câpre [kɑpr] *nf* caper
caprice [kapris] *nm* (**a**) *(fantaisie)* whim, caprice; **on lui passe tous ses caprices** they indulge his/her every whim; **par un c. du destin** by a whim of fate (**b**) *(crise de colère)* tantrum; **faire un c.** to throw a tantrum
capricieux, -euse [kaprisjø, -øz] *adj (personne, courant, vent)* capricious; *(moteur)* temperamental; *(temps)* changeable
capricorne [kaprikɔrn] *nm* (**a**) *(insecte)* capricorn beetle (**b**) *Astron & Astrol* **le C.** Capricorn; **être C.** to be (a) Capricorn
caprin, -e [kaprɛ̃, -in] *adj* *Zool* goat, *Spéc* caprine
capsule [kapsyl] *nf* (**a**) *Anat, Bot & Méd* capsule (**b**) *(de bouteille)* cap, top (**c**) **c. (spatiale)** (space) capsule
capter [kapte] *vt* (**a**) *(l'attention de quelqu'un)* to gain, to capture (**b**) *(courant électrique)* to pick up; *(eaux)* to harness (**c**) *Rad & Tél (messages, station)* to pick up
capteur [kaptœr] *nm* *Phys* sensor; *Ordinat* **c. photosensible** photosensitive sensor; **c. solaire** solar panel
captif, -ive [kaptif, -iv] *adj & nm,f* captive
captivant, -e [kaptivɑ̃, -ɑ̃t] *adj* captivating
captiver [kaptive] *vt* to captivate
captivité [kaptivite] *nf* captivity; **en c.** in captivity
capture [kaptyr] *nf* (**a**) *(d'un ennemi, d'un animal)* capture (**b**) *(proie)* catch (**c**) *Ordinat* **c. vidéo** video capture
capturer [kaptyre] *vt* to capture
capuche [kapyʃ] *nf* hood; *(de poche)* rainhood
capuchon [kapyʃɔ̃] *nm* (**a**) *(de manteau)* hood; *(de moine)* cowl (**b**) *(de stylo, de tube de dentifrice)* cap, top; *(de cheminée)* cowl
capucine [kapysin] *nf* nasturtium
capverdien, -enne [kapvɛrdjɛ̃, -ɛn] **1** *adj* of Cape Verde **2** *nm,f* **C.** = person from Cape Verde
Cap-Vert [kapvɛr] *nm* **le C., les îles du C.** Cape Verde
caquelon [kaklɔ̃] *nm* fondue dish
caquet [kakɛ] *nm* (**a**) *(de poules)* cackle (**b**) *Fam (bavardage)* prattle; **quel c. elle a!** she doesn't half prattle on!; **rabattre** *ou* **rabaisser le c. à qn** to shut sb up
caqueter [42] [kakte] *vi* (**a**) *(poule)* to cackle (**b**) *Fam (bavarder)* to prattle
car¹ [kar] *conj* for, because
car² *nm (véhicule)* bus, *Br* coach; **c. de police** police van; **c. de ramassage scolaire** school bus
carabine [karabin] *nf* rifle; **c. à air comprimé** air gun
carabiné, -e [karabine] *adj* *Fam (vent)* stiff; *(orage, fièvre)* violent; *(rhume)* stinking
carabinier [karabinje] *nm* (**a**) *(en Espagne)* frontier guard (**b**) *(en Italie)* carabiniere (**c**) *Hist* carabineer
Caracas [karakas] *n* Caracas

caraco [karako] *nm* camisole

caracoler [karakɔle] *vi (cheval)* to caracole; *Fam (sautiller)* to prance about

caractère [karaktɛr] *nm* (a) *(nature)* character, nature; *(détermination, style)* character; **avoir bon c.** to be good-natured; **avoir mauvais** *ou* **sale c.** to be bad-tempered; *Fam* **avoir un c. de cochon** to have a foul temper; **ce n'est pas dans son c. de...** it's not in his nature to... (b) *(attribut)* characteristic, feature; *(aspect)* nature, character; **publication à c. officiel** publication of an official nature; *Biol* **c. héréditaire/acquis** hereditary/acquired characteristic (c) *(signe)* character, letter; *Typ* **caractères** *(en métal)* type; **en petits caractères** in small print; **écrivez en caractères d'imprimerie** *(sur formulaire)* write in block letters (d) *Ordinat* character; **c. de changement de ligne** line feed character; **c. de changement de page** page break character; **c. de contrôle** control character; **c. d'effacement** delete character; **c. imprimable** printable character; **c. d'interruption** break character; **c. en mode point** bitmap character; **c. de retour arrière** backspace character; **c. à sept bits** seven-bit character

caractériel, -elle [karakterjɛl] *Psy* **1** *adj (troubles)* emotional; **enfant c.** problem child **2** *nmf* emotionally disturbed person; *(enfant)* problem child

caractérisé, -e [karakterize] *adj* **une rougeole caractérisée** a clear case of measles; **c'est de la méchanceté caractérisée** it's sheer spite

caractériser [karakterize] **1** *vt* to characterize; **la bonté qui la caractérise** her characteristic kindness **2 se caractériser** *vpr* **se c. par** to be characterized by

caractéristique [karakteristik] **1** *adj* characteristic **(de** of) **2** *nf (particularité)* characteristic, feature; **caractéristiques** *(d'une voiture, d'un avion)* specifications

carafe [karaf] *nf* (a) *(pour le vin, l'eau)* carafe; *(pour le whisky)* decanter (b) *Fam* **rester en c.** to be (left) stranded

carafon [karafɔ̃] *nm (pour le vin)* small carafe; *(pour le whisky)* small decanter

Caraïbes [karaib] *nfpl* **les C.** the Caribbean

carambolage [karābɔlaʒ] *nm* (multiple) pile-up

caramboler [karābɔle] **se caramboler** *vpr Fam* to collide

caramel [karamɛl] *nm* caramel

caraméliser [karamelize] *vt & vi* to caramelize

carapace [karapas] *nf aussi Fig* shell

carapater [karapate] **se carapater** *vpr Fam* to beat it

carat [kara] *nm* carat; **or (à) 18 carats** 18-carat gold; *Fam* **tu as jusqu'à sept heures, dernier c.** you've got until seven o'clock at the latest

caravanage [karavanaʒ] = **caravaning**

caravane [karavan] *nf* (a) *(de tourisme)* caravan, *Am* trailer (b) *(du désert)* caravan

caravaning [karavaniŋ] *nm* caravanning; **faire du c.** to go caravanning

carbonate [karbɔnat] *nm Chim* carbonate; **c. de soude** sodium carbonate; *(dans le commerce)* washing soda

carbone [karbɔn] *nm Chim* carbon; **c. 14** carbon-14; **datation au c. 14** carbon dating; **(papier) c.** carbon (paper)

carbonique [karbɔnik] *adj* carbonic; **gaz c.** carbon dioxide; **neige c.** dry ice

carbonisé, -e [karbɔnize] *adj (nourriture)* burnt to a cinder; *(corps)* charred; **mourir c.** to burn to death

carburant [karbyrā] *nm* fuel

carburateur [karbyratœr] *nm Aut* carburettor

carbure [karbyr] *nm Chim* carbide; **c. d'hydrogène** hydrogen carbide

carburer [karbyre] *vi* (a) *(moteur)* **mal c.** to be badly tuned (b) *Fam* **ça carbure ici** everyone here's working like mad; **il carbure au café** coffee keeps him going

carcajou [karkaʒu] *nm* wolverine

carcan [karkā] *nm Fig* yoke; **le c. des horaires** scheduling constraints

carcasse [karkas] *nf* (a) *(d'animal mort)* carcass; *Fam (de personne)* body (b) *(de maison, de bateau)* shell; **à c. radiale** *(pneu)* radial-ply

carcéral, -e, -aux, -ales [karseral, -o] *adj* prison

carcinogène [karsinɔʒɛn] *adj Méd* carcinogenic

cardan [kardā] *nm* universal joint

carder [karde] *vt* to card

cardiaque [kardjak] **1** *adj (arrêt, massage)* cardiac; **être c.** to have a heart condition **2** *nmf* person with a heart condition

cardigan [kardigā] *nm* cardigan

cardinal, -e, -aux, -ales [kardinal, -o] **1** *adj (point, nombre, vertu)* cardinal **2** *nm (religieux)* cardinal

cardiologie [kardjɔlɔʒi] *nf* cardiology

cardiologue [kardjɔlɔg] *nmf* cardiologist

cardio-vasculaire *(pl* cardio-vasculaires*)* [kardjɔvaskylɛr] *adj* cardiovascular

carême [karɛm] *nm* (a) *(période)* **le C.** Lent (b) *(jeûne)* fast; **faire c.** to fast

carence [karās] *nf (manque)* deficiency; **c. en vitamine E** vitamin E deficiency; **c. alimentaire** nutritional deficiency; **c. affective** emotional deprivation

carène [karɛn] *nf* hull

caréner [34] [karene] *vt* (a) *Naut* to careen (b) *Av & Aut* to streamline

caressant, -e [karesā, -āt] *adj* affectionate; **d'une voix caressante** affectionately

caresse [karɛs] *nf* caress; **faire des caresses à** *(personne)* to caress; *(animal)* to stroke

caresser [karese] *vt (personne)* to caress, *(animal)* to stroke; *Fig (espoir, rêve)* to cherish

car-ferry *(pl* car-ferrys*)* [karferi] *nm* car ferry

cargaison [kargɛzɔ̃] *nf* cargo; *Fam* **il est arrivé avec une c. de cadeaux** he arrived laden with presents

cargo [kargo] *nm Naut* freighter

cariatide [karjatid] *nf* caryatid

caribou [karibu] *nm* caribou

caricatural, -e, -aux, -ales [karikatyral, -o] *adj (récit, description)* caricatured

caricature [karikatyr] *nf* caricature

caricaturer [karikatyre] *vt* to caricature

caricaturiste [karikatyrist] *nmf* caricaturist

carie [kari] *nf* **c. (dentaire)** tooth decay, *Spéc* dental caries; **avoir une c.** to have a cavity

carié, -e [karje] *adj* decayed

carier [66] [karje] **se carier** *vpr* to rot, to decay

carillon [karijɔ̃] *nm* (a) *(sonnerie)* chimes; **c. électrique** doorbell (b) *(ensemble de cloches)* bells (c) *(horloge)* chiming clock

carillonner [karijɔne] **1** *vi (cloches)* to chime; **c. à la porte** to ring the (door)bell loudly **2** *vt (air)* to chime; *(fête religieuse)* to announce with a peal of bells

carioca [karjɔka] **1** *adj* of Rio de Janeiro
2 *nmf* **C.** person from Rio de Janeiro

caritatif, -ive [karitatif, -iv] *adj* charitable; **association caritative** charity

carlingue [karlɛ̃g] *nf* **(a)** *Av* cabin **(b)** *Naut* keelson

carmélite [karmelit] *nf* Carmelite (nun)

carmin [karmɛ̃] **1** *nm* carmine
2 *adj inv* carmine, crimson

carnage [karnaʒ] *nm* carnage

carnassier, -ère [karnasje, -ɛr] **1** *adj (animal)* flesh-eating; *Fig (sourire)* cruel
2 *nm* carnivore

carnaval, -als [karnaval] *nm* carnival; **un masque de c.** a carnival mask

carnet [karnɛ] *nm (cahier)* notebook; *(de tickets de métro)* = book of ten tickets; *Scol* **c. (de notes)** report card; **c. d'adresses** address book; **c. de chèques** *Br* cheque book, *Am* check book; *Scol* **c. de correspondance** = book of forms to be completed by parents of schoolchildren in the event of absence; *Journ* **c. mondain** society column; **c. de santé** health record; **c. de timbres** book of stamps

carnivore [karnivɔr] **1** *adj (animal)* carnivorous
2 *nm* carnivore

Caroline [karɔlin] *nf* **la C. du Nord/du Sud** North/South Carolina

carolingien, -enne [karɔlɛ̃ʒjɛ̃, -ɛn] **1** *adj* Carolingian
2 *nmpl* **les Carolingiens** the Carolingians

carotène [karɔtɛn] *nm* carotene

carotide [karɔtid] *nf* carotid

carotte [karɔt] **1** *nf* **(a)** *(légume)* carrot; **la c. et** *ou* **ou le bâton** the carrot and the stick; *Fam* **les carottes sont cuites** you've/he's/*etc* had it **(b)** *(enseigne)* = sign outside a tobacco store
2 *adj inv* **cheveux (roux) c.** carroty hair

carotter [karɔte] *vt Fam (objet, argent)* to pinch; **il m'a carotté 50 euros** he cheated me out of 50 euros

caroube [karub] *nf* carob (bean)

Carpates [karpat] *nfpl* **les C.** the Carpathians

carpe¹ [karp] *nm Anat* carpus

carpe² *nf* carp

carpette [karpɛt] *nf* rug; *Fam Péj* **c'est une vraie c.** he's a real doormat

carquois [karkwa] *nm* quiver

carre [kar] *nf (de patin, de ski)* edge

carré, -e [kare] **1** *adj* **(a)** *(figure, jardin, visage)* square; *(épaules)* square, broad **(b)** *Math* **20 mètres carrés** 20 square metres **(c)** *(tranché) (personne)* straightforward; **être c. en affaires** to be straightforward in one's business dealings
2 *nm* **(a)** *(forme)* square; *Can (place)* (public) square; **c. de soie** silk scarf; *Naut* **c. des officiers** wardroom; **c. de valets** *(aux cartes)* four jacks; **avoir une coupe au c.** *ou* **un c.** to have one's hair in a bob; *Fam* **faire la tête au c. à qn** to punch sb's face in **(b)** *Math (d'un nombre)* square; **élever au c.** to square; **le c. de six, six au c.** six squared **(c)** *Culin* **c. d'agneau** rack of lamb

carreau, -x [karo] *nm* **(a)** *(motif)* square; *(sur du tissu)* check; **tissu à carreaux** check(ed) material **(b)** *(de céramique)* tile **(c)** *(vitre)* (window) pane; *Fam* **carreaux** *(lunettes)* specs, glasses **(d)** *(cartes)* diamond; *(couleur)* diamonds; *Fam* **se tenir à c.** to keep a low profile **(e)** *(locutions) Fam* **rester sur le c.** *(être tué)* to be killed; *(être blessé)* to be badly injured; *(être éliminé)* to be given the boot

carreauté, -e [karote] *adj Can (chemise)* check(ed)

carrefour [karfur] *nm* **(a)** *(croisement)* crossroads

(singulier); *Fig* **être à un c.** to be at a crossroads **(b)** *(réunion)* forum

carrelage [karlaʒ] *nm (carreaux)* tiles; *(sol)* (tiled) floor

carreler [42] [karle] *vt* to tile

carrelet [karlɛ] *nm* plaice

carreleur [karlœr] *nm* tiler

carrément [karemɑ̃] *adv Fam* **(a)** *(franchement)* straight out; **vas-y c.** get on with it **(b)** *(très)* totally; **c'était c. immangeable** it was absolutely inedible

carrière¹ [karjɛr] *nf (profession)* career; **faire c. (dans)** to make a career (in)

carrière² *nf (lieu)* quarry

carriériste [karjerist] *nmf Péj* careerist

carriole [karjɔl] *nf* **(a)** *(petite charrette)* light cart **(b)** *Can* sleigh, sled

carrossable [karɔsabl] *adj (chemin, route)* suitable for motor vehicles

carrosse [karɔs] *nm* (horse-drawn) coach

carrosser [karɔse] *vt* to fit the body to; **une voiture bien carrossée** a sturdily built car

carrosserie [karɔsri] *nf (de voiture)* bodywork

carrossier [karɔsje] *nm* coachbuilder

carrousel [karuzɛl] *nm (d'une aérogare)* carousel

carrure [karyr] *nf (de personne)* build; *(de vêtement)* width across the shoulders; **un homme à la forte c.** a broad-shouldered man; *Fig* **un homme d'une c. exceptionnelle** a man of exceptional qualities

cartable [kartabl] *nm* school bag

carte [kart] *nf* **(a)** *(géographique)* map; *Naut* chart; **faire la c. d'une région** to map (out) an area; *Astrol* **c. du ciel** astronomical chart; **c. d'état-major** *Br* ≃ Ordnance Survey map, *Am* ≃ Geological Survey map; **c. routière** road map
(b) *(carton)* card; **c. (à jouer)** (playing) card; **jouer aux cartes** to play cards; **donner les cartes** to deal (the cards); *Fig* **donner c. blanche à qn** to give sb carte-blanche; *Fig* **jouer cartes sur table** to lay one's cards on the table; **c. d'anniversaire** birthday card; **c. maîtresse** trump card; **c. postale** postcard; **c. de visite** *(personnelle) Br* visiting *or Am* calling card; *(professionnelle)* business card; **c. de vœux** greetings card
(c) *(document officiel)* card; **c. d'abonnement** *(de bibliothèque)* library card; *(de transports, de théâtre)* season ticket; **c. d'adhérent** membership card; **c. d'électeur** voting card; **c. d'embarquement** boarding pass; **c. d'étudiant** student card; **c. de fidélité** loyalty card; *Aut* **c. grise** ≃ (vehicle) registration document; **c. d'identité** identity card; *Rail* **c. Jeunes** = reduced-rate railcard for young people, valid in certain European countries; **C. Orange** *(à Paris)* = combined monthly season ticket for the underground, bus and suburban train; **c. de presse** press card; **c. de Sécurité sociale** ≃ National Insurance Card; **c. de séjour** residence permit; *Rail* **C. Vermeil** = reduced-rate railcard for people over sixty within France; *Aut* **c. verte** green card
(d) *(document informatisé)* card; **c. bancaire** bank card; **c. Bleue®** debit card; **c. de crédit** credit card; **c. de paiement** payment card; **c. à puce** smart card; **c. de téléphone** phonecard
(e) *(de restaurant)* menu; **manger à la c.** to eat à la carte; **c. des vins** wine list
(f) *Ordinat* card; *(de clavier)* map; **c. accélératrice** accelerator card; **c. à circuit imprimé** *ou* **de circuits imprimés** printed circuit board, PCB; **c. à circuit(s) intégré(s)** integrated circuit card, IC card; **c. d'extension** expansion card *or* board; **c. mémoire** memory card; **c. mère** motherboard; **c. modem** modem card; **c. de polices**

de caractères font card; **c. processeur** processor card; **c. réseau** network card; **c. SCSI** SCSI card; **c. son** *ou* **sonore** sound card; **c. unité centrale** CPU board; **c. vidéo** video card; **c. vocale** voice card

carte-adaptateur (*pl* **cartes-adaptateurs**) [kart-adaptatœr] *nf Ordinat* **c. réseau** network adaptor card

cartel [kartɛl] *nm Écon* cartel; **c. de l'acier/de la drogue** steel/drug cartel

carte-lettre (*pl* **cartes-lettres**) [kartəlɛtr] *nf* lettercard

carter [kartɛr] *nm (d'engrenages)* casing; *(de bicyclette)* chain guard; *Aut (de vilebrequin)* crankcase

carte-réponse (*pl* **cartes-réponses**) [kartrepɔ̃s] *nf* reply card

carterie [kartəri] *nf* card *Br* shop *or Am* store

cartésien, -enne [kartezjɛ̃, -ɛn] *adj* (**a**) *Math* Cartesian (**b**) *(logique)* logical

cartilage [kartilaʒ] *nm* cartilage

cartilagineux, -euse [kartilaʒinø, -øz] *adj* cartilaginous; *(viande)* gristly

cartographe [kartəgraf] *nmf* cartographer

cartographie [kartəgrafi] *nf* cartography

cartomancien, -enne [kartɔmɑ̃sjɛ̃, -ɛn] *nm,f* fortuneteller *(who uses cards)*

carton [kartɔ̃] *nm* (**a**) *(matière)* cardboard; *(feuille)* piece of cardboard; **c. d'invitation** invitation (card); **c. jaune/rouge** *(au football)* yellow/red card (**b**) *(boîte)* (cardboard) box; **faire des cartons** to pack one's things up in cardboard boxes; **c. à chapeau(x)** hatbox (**c**) *Art (dessin)* cartoon, sketch; **c. à dessin** portfolio (**d**) *(locutions)* **faire un c.** *(au tir)* to have a shot; *Fam (sur quelqu'un)* to shoot somebody; *Fam (à un examen)* to pass with flying colours; *Fam Scol* (se) **prendre un c.** *(une mauvaise note)* to get a bad grade

cartonner [kartɔne] **1** *vt (livre)* to case; **livre cartonné** hardback (book)
2 *vi Fam (à l'école)* to get good grades (**en** in)

cartonneux, -euse [kartɔnø, -øz] *adj* like cardboard

carton-pâte [kartɔ̃pɑt] *nm* pasteboard

cartouche [kartuʃ] *nf (de fusil, de stylo, d'imprimante)* cartridge; *(de cigarettes)* carton

cartouchière [kartuʃjɛr] *nf* cartridge belt

caryatide [karjatid] = **cariatide**

cas [kɑ] *nm* (**a**) *(situation)* case, situation; *Jur & Méd* case; **c. particulier** exception; **envisager tous les c. possibles** to consider all the possibilities; **c'est le c. de le dire** you can say that again; **en pareil c.** in a similar situation; **si tel est votre c.** if that applies to you; **il parle trois langues mais ce n'est pas mon c.** he speaks three languages but I don't; *Fam* **c'est un c.!** he's unbelievable!; **un c. social** a person with social problems (**b**) *Gram* case (**c**) *(locutions)* **en aucun c.** under no circumstances, on no account; **en tout c., dans tous les c.** in any case, anyway; **dans ce c.** *(puisqu'il en est ainsi)* in that case; **dans tous les c. de figure** in all cases; **le c. échéant** if necessary, if need be; **selon le c.** as the case may be; **en c. d'urgence** in an emergency; **en c. de besoin** if need be; **j'ai pris un pull supplémentaire en c. de besoin** I took an extra sweater just in case; **au c. où il viendrait** in case he comes; *Fam* **je te le laisse au c. où** I'll leave it for you just in case; **faire grand c. de qn/qch** to have a high opinion of sb/sth; **faire peu de c. de qch** to have a low opinion of sth; **ne faire aucun c. de qch** to take no notice of sth

Casablanca [kazablɑ̃ka] *n* Casablanca

casanier, -ère [kazanje, -ɛr] *adj* home-loving; *Péj* stay-at-home

casaque [kazak] *nf (de jockey)* blouse; *Fig* **tourner c.** *(partir)* to turn tail; *(changer d'opinion)* to change sides

cascade [kaskad] *nf* (**a**) *(chute d'eau)* waterfall; *Fig* **des rires en c.** peals of laughter; *Ordinat* **ouvrir des fenêtres en c.** to cascade windows (**b**) *(au cinéma)* stunt

cascadeur, -euse [kaskadœr, -øz] *nm,f* stuntman, *f* stuntwoman

case [kɑz] *nf* (**a**) *(de tiroir)* compartment; *(de formulaire)* box; *(de mots croisés, de damier)* square; *Fam* **il lui manque une c., il a une c. de vide** he's got a screw loose; **c. départ** *(dans les jeux)* start; *Fig* **retour à la c. départ** back to square one (**b**) *(hutte)* hut (**c**) *Ordinat* button; *(en forme de boîte)* box

casemate [kazmat] *nf* blockhouse

caser [kaze] **1** *vt* (**a**) *(placer)* to fit in (**b**) *Fam* **c. qn** *(établir)* to fix sb up with a job; *(marier)* to marry sb off
2 se caser *vpr Fam (trouver un emploi)* to get oneself a job; *(se marier)* to get married and settle down

caserne [kazɛrn] *nf* barracks; **c. de pompiers** fire station

cash [kaʃ] *adv Fam* **payer c.** to pay cash (down)

cash-flow (*pl* **cash-flows**) [kaʃflo] *nm Com* cash flow

casier [kazje] *nm* (**a**) *(compartiment)* compartment; *(pour le courrier)* pigeonhole; *(à vêtements)* locker; **à bouteilles** bottle rack (**b**) *Jur* **c. judiciaire** police *or* criminal record; **avoir un c. (judiciaire)** to have a record (**c**) *(pour pêcher)* pot

casino [kazino] *nm* casino

Caspienne [kaspjɛn] *adj f voir* **mer**

casque [kask] *nm* (**a**) *(de soldat, de pompier)* helmet; *(de motocycliste)* (crash) helmet; **le port du c. est obligatoire** *(sur panneau)* safety helmets must be worn; **c. intégral** full-face crash helmet; **les Casques bleus** the Blue Berets (**b**) *(écouteurs)* headphones, headset (**c**) *(de salon de coiffure)* hairdryer

casqué, -e [kaske] *adj* helmeted

casquer [kaske] *vi Fam (payer)* to fork out

casquette [kaskɛt] *nf* cap

cassable [kasabl] *adj* breakable

cassant, -e [kasɑ̃, -ɑ̃t] *adj* brittle; *Fig (personne, ton)* brusque

cassation [kasasjɔ̃] *nf Jur* annulment

casse[1] [kas] *nf Typ* case; **bas/haut de c.** lower/uppercase

casse[2] *nf* (**a**) *(action de casser)* **il va y avoir de la c.** something may get broken; *Fam (des ennuis)* there'll be trouble; **aller ou partir à la c.** *(voiture)* to go for scrap (**b**) *(objets cassés)* breakages

casse[3] *nm très Fam (cambriolage)* break-in

cassé, -e [kase] *adj (objet, jambe)* broken; *(voix)* cracked; *très Fam (ivre)* wasted; *(drogué)* stoned

casse-cou [kasku] *nmf inv (personne)* reckless
2 *nmf inv (personne)* daredevil

casse-croûte [kaskrut] *nm inv* (**a**) *Fam (repas)* snack, bite (**b**) *Can (snack)* snack bar

casse-cul [kasky] *très Fam* **1** *adj inv* damn annoying
2 *nmf inv* pain in the *Br* arse *or Am* ass

casse-gueule [kasgœl] *très Fam* **1** *adj inv (endroit)* dangerous; *(entreprise)* risky
2 *nm inv (endroit)* danger spot; *(entreprise)* risky business

casse-noisettes [kasnwazɛt] *nm inv* nutcrackers

casse-noix [kasnwa] *nm inv* nutcrackers

casse-pieds [kaspje] *Fam* **1** *adj inv* damn annoying; **ce qu'il peut être c.!** he can be a real pain (in the neck)!
2 *nmf inv* pain (in the neck)

casse-pipe [kaspip] *nm inv Fam* **aller au c.** to go to the front

casser [kase] **1** *vt* (**a**) *(briser)* to break; *(noix)* to crack;

(voix) to strain; *(chaussures)* to break in; *Fam (personne)* to humiliate; **c. les prix** to slash prices; *aussi Fig* **c. le moral des troupes** to discourage the ranks; *Fig* **c. du sucre sur le dos de qn** to talk about sb behind his/her back; *Fam* **c. la croûte** *ou* **la graine** to have a bite to eat; *Fam* **ça ne casse pas trois pattes à un canard, ça ne casse pas des briques** it's nothing to write home about; *Fam* **c. la baraque** *(pièce, acteur)* to bring the house down; *Fam* **à tout c.** *(au maximum)* at the very most

(b) *Fam (locutions avec parties du corps)* **c. les pieds à qn** *(ennuyer)* to bore the pants off sb; *(agacer)* to get on sb's nerves; **ça fait deux mois qu'elle me casse les pieds pour que j'y aille** she's been bugging me to go for two months now; **c. les oreilles à qn** to deafen sb; **c. la figure** *ou très Fam* **la gueule à qn** to smash sb's face in; *Fam* **c. sa pipe** to bite the dust, to croak; *Vulg* **il nous casse les couilles, il nous les casse** he's a pain in the *Br* arse *or Am* ass

(c) *Jur (verdict)* to quash; *(mariage)* to annul; *(fiançailles)* to break off

2 *vi* **(a)** *(se briser)* to break; **attention, ça casse!** be careful, it's fragile!

(b) *Fam (se séparer)* to split up

3 se casser *vpr* **(a)** *(se briser)* to break

(b) se c. une *ou* **la jambe** to break one's leg; *Fig* **se c. le nez** to fail; *Fig* **se c. la tête** to rack one's brains; *Fam* **se c. la figure** *ou très Fam* **la gueule** *(tomber)* to fall flat on one's face; *(échouer)* to fail

(c) *Fam (se fatiguer)* **il ne s'est pas cassé pour m'aider** he didn't exactly strain himself helping me; *Vulg* **se c. le cul à faire qch** to bust a gut trying to do sth

(d) *Fam (partir)* to split, to clear off; **tu viens? on se casse** we're off, are you coming?; **casse-toi!** piss off!

casserole [kasrɔl] *nf* **(a)** *(de cuisine)* (sauce)pan; *très Fam* **passer à la c.** *(sexuellement)* to be given a good seeing-to; *(être tué)* to get bumped off **(b)** *Fam* **chanter comme une c.** to be a lousy singer

casse-tête [kastɛt] *nm inv* **(a)** *(jeu)* puzzle **(b)** *(problème)* headache

cassette [kasɛt] *nf* **(a)** *(magnétique)* cassette, tape; **enregistrer qch sur c.** to tape sth; **c. vidéo** video (cassette) **(b)** *Ordinat* **c. à bande magnétique** mag tape cassette

casseur, -euse [kasœr, -øz] *nm,f* **(a)** *(manifestant)* rioter **(b)** *très Fam (cambrioleur)* burglar

cassis [kasis] *nm* **(a)** *(baie)* blackcurrant **(b)** *(arbuste)* blackcurrant bush **(c)** *(liqueur)* cassis, blackcurrant liqueur

cassonade [kasɔnad] *nf* brown sugar

cassoulet [kasulɛ] *nm* cassoulet *(stew of beans, pork, goose etc, a speciality of Languedoc)*

cassure [kasyr] *nf* break; *Géol* fault

castagnettes [kastaɲɛt] *nfpl* castanets

caste [kast] *nf* caste

castillan, -e [kastijã, -an] **1** *adj* Castilian **2** *nm,f* **C.** Castilian **3** *nm (langue)* Castilian

Castille [kastij] *nf* **la C.** Castile

casting [kastiŋ] *nm Cin & Th* casting

castor [kastɔr] *nm* beaver

castrat [kastra] *nm Mus* castrato

castrer [kastre] *vt* to castrate; *(chat, chien)* to neuter

cataclysme [kataklism] *nm* cataclysm

cataclysmique [kataklismik] *adj* cataclysmic

catacombes [katakɔ̃b] *nfpl* catacombs

catadioptre [katadjɔptr] *nm (de véhicule)* reflector; *(sur la route)* cat's-eye®

catafalque [katafalk] *nm* catafalque

catalan, -e [katalã, -an] **1** *adj* Catalan **2** *nm,f* **C.** Catalan **3** *nm (langue)* Catalan

Catalogne [katalɔɲ] *nf* **la C.** Catalonia

catalogue [katalɔg] *nm* catalogue; **faire le c. de** to catalogue; **acheter sur c.** to buy things from a catalogue

cataloguer [katalɔge] *vt* to catalogue; *Fig & Péj* to label

catalyser [katalize] *vt aussi Fig* to catalyse

catalyseur [katalizœr] *nm aussi Fig* catalyst

catalytique [katalitik] *adj Chim* catalytic

catamaran [katamarã] *nm Naut* catamaran

Cataphote® [katafɔt] = **catadioptre**

cataplasme [kataplasm] *nm* poultice

catapulte [katapylt] *nf* catapult

catapulter [katapylte] *vt* to catapult; *Fig* **c. qn à un poste** to catapult sb into a job

cataracte [katarakt] *nf (maladie, chute d'eau)* cataract

catastrophe [katastrɔf] *nf* disaster, catastrophe; **c. ferroviaire/aérienne** rail/air disaster; **c'est la c.!** it's a disaster!; **c.! il est déjà là!** panic stations! he's here already!; **en c.** *(à toute vitesse)* in a mad rush *or* panic

catastrophé, -e [katastrɔfe] *adj Fam* stunned

catastrophique [katastrɔfik] *adj* disastrous, catastrophic

catch [katʃ] *nm* wrestling; **faire du c.** to wrestle

catcheur, -euse [katʃœr, -øz] *nm,f* wrestler

catéchisme [kateʃism] *nm* catechism

catégorie [kategɔri] *nf* category, type; *(d'hôtel, de personnel)* grade; *(de boxeur)* class; **c. sociale** social class; **c. socioprofessionnelle** socio-professional group

catégorique [kategɔrik] *adj (réponse, refus)* categoric(al); **je suis absolument c., c'est lui** I'm absolutely positive it's him

catégoriquement [kategɔrikmã] *adv* categorically

catégoriser [kategɔrize] *vt* to categorize

Cathares [katar] *nmpl Hist* **les C.** the Cathars

catharsis [katarsis] *nf* catharsis

cathédrale [katedral] *nf* cathedral

cathéter [kateter] *nm Méd* catheter

catho [kato] *adj Fam* Catholic

cathode [katɔd] *nf Él* cathode

cathodique [katɔdik] *adj Él* cathodic; **tube c.** cathode ray tube

catholicisme [katɔlisism] *nm* (Roman) Catholicism

catholique [katɔlik] **1** *adj* (Roman) Catholic; *Fam* **ce n'est pas très c.** it's a bit shady **2** *nmf* (Roman) Catholic

catimini [katimini] **en catimini** *adv* on the sly

catogan [katɔgã] *nm (nœud)* hair ribbon *(for ponytail)*; *(queue de cheval)* ponytail

Caucase [kokaz] *nm* **le C.** the Caucasus

caucasien, -enne [kokazjɛ̃, -ɛn] *adj* Caucasian

cauchemar [koʃmar] *nm aussi Fig* nightmare; **une vision de c.** a nightmarish vision; **faire un c.** to have a nightmare

cauchemarder [koʃmarde] *vi* to have nightmares

cauchemardesque [koʃmardɛsk] *adj* nightmarish

causal, -e, -als *ou* **-aux, -ales** [kozal, -o] *adj* causal

causant, -e [kozã, -ãt] *adj Fam* chatty

cause [koz] *nf* **(a)** *(origine)* cause; **quelle est la c. de son départ?** why is he leaving?; **il s'est mis en colère, et pour c.** he got angry, and with good reason; **fermé pour c. d'inventaire/de décès** *(sur panneau)* closed for stocktaking/due to bereavement; **à c. de** because of (**b**) *Jur* case; *Fig* **la c. est entendue** there's nothing more to be said; **être en c.** *(sujet à caution)* to be in question; **mettre qch en c.** to doubt sth, to question sth; **mettre qn en c.** *(impliquer)* to implicate sb; **mettre qn hors de c.** to clear sb; **en tout état de c.** in any case (**c**) *(parti)* cause; **faire c.** commune avec qn to join forces with sb

causer¹ [koze] *vt (provoquer)* to cause; **c. des ennuis à qn** to cause sb problems

causer² *vi* (**a**) *(parler)* to chat, to talk (**de** about); **c. affaires** to talk business; **c. avec** *ou* **à qn** to chat with sb; *Fam* **je ne lui cause plus!** I'm not talking to him!; *Ironique* **cause toujours(, tu m'intéresses)!** yeah, whatever! (**b**) *(cancaner)* to chat, to gossip; **on en cause au village** it's the talk of the village

causerie [kozri] *nf (discussion)* chat, talk (**b**) *(conférence)* (informal) talk

causette [kozɛt] *nf Fam* little chat; **faire la c.** *ou* **un brin de c. avec qn** to have a little chat with sb

causse [kos] *nm* = limestone plateau in central and southern France

caustique [kostik] *adj aussi Fig* caustic

cautériser [koterize] *vt* to cauterize

caution [kosjɔ̃] *nf* (**a**) *(pour appartement)* deposit; *Jur* bail; *Fig (appui)* support, backing; *Jur* **sous c.** on bail; **sujet à c.** *(information)* unconfirmed (**b**) *(personne)* guarantor

cautionner [kosjone] *vt (personne)* to stand surety for; *Jur* to stand bail for; *Fig (approuver)* to support, to back

cavalcade [kavalkad] *nf Fam (bousculade)* stampede

cavale [kaval] *nf Fam (évasion)* escape; **être en c.** to be on the run

cavaler [kavale] *vi Fam (se démener)* to rush around; *(fuir)* to run off; **c. après qn** to chase after sb

cavalerie [kavalri] *nf Mil* cavalry

cavaleur, -euse [kavalœr, -øz] *Fam* **1** *adj (homme)* womanizing; *(femme)* man-chasing
2 *nm,f (homme)* skirt-chaser; *(femme)* man-chaser

cavalier, -ère [kavalje, -ɛr] **1** *adj (manière, personne)* cavalier
2 *nm,f* (**a**) *(à cheval)* rider, horseman, *f* horsewoman (**b**) *(de bal)* partner; *Fig* **faire c. seul** to go it alone
3 *nm* (**a**) *(aux échecs)* knight (**b**) *(accompagnateur)* escort (**c**) *Ordinat* jumper

cavalièrement [kavaljɛrmɑ̃] *adv* in a cavalier manner

cave¹ [kav] *adj (joues, yeux)* hollow, sunken

cave² *nf (cellier)* cellar; **c. à charbon/vin** coal/wine cellar; *Fig* **de la c. au grenier** from top to bottom

caveau, -x [kavo] *nm* (**a**) *(petite cave)* small cellar (**b**) *(funéraire)* burial vault

caverne [kavɛrn] *nf* cave, cavern; **homme des cavernes** caveman

caverneux, -euse [kavɛrnø, -øz] *adj (voix)* deep

caviar [kavjar] *nm* caviar

caviarder [kavjarde] *vt* to censor

caviste [kavist] *nm* cellarman

cavité [kavite] *nf* cavity, hollow; **c. buccale** oral cavity

Cayenne [kajɛn] *n* (**a**) *(ville)* Cayenne (**b**) **poivre de C.** cayenne pepper

CC [sese] *nm (abrév* **compte courant)** CA

CCI [sesei] *nf (abrév* **Chambre de commerce et d'industrie)** Chamber of Commerce and Industry

CCP [sesepe] *nm (abrév* **compte courant postal, compte chèque postal)** *Br* ≃ Giro account, *Am* ≃ Post Office checking account

CD [sede] *nm* (**a**) *(abrév* **Compact Disc)** CD (**b**) *(abrév* **corps diplomatique)** CD

CDD [sedede] *nm (abrév* **contrat à durée déterminée)** fixed-term contract

CDI [sedei] *nm inv* (**a**) *(abrév* **centre des impôts)** tax office (**b**) *(abrév* **contrat à durée indéterminée)** permanent contract (**c**) *(abrév* **centre de documentation et d'information)** school library *(with special resources on how to find information)*

CD-I [sedei] *(abrév* **Compact Disc interactif**) CDI

CD-Rom [sederɔm] *nm inv* CD-ROM; **C. interactif** interactive CD-ROM

CE [seə] **1** *nm* (**a**) *(abrév* **Conseil de l'Europe)** Council of Europe (**b**) *(abrév* **cours élémentaire)** **CE1** = second year of primary school; **CE2** = third year of primary school
2 *nf (abrév* **Communauté européenne)** EC

ce¹ [sə] *pron démonstratif*

> **ce** becomes **c'** before a vowel.

(**a**) *(pour désigner)* **c'est mon père** that's my father; *(au téléphone)* it's my father; **ce sont** *ou Fam* **c'est mes amis** those are my friends; *(qui arrivent)* there are my friends; **c'était mon idée** it was my idea; **c'est le plus beau jour de ma vie** this is the best day of my life; **c'est moi** it's me; **qui est-ce?**, *Fam* **qui c'est?** who is it?; **c'est lui qui l'a écrit** HE wrote it; **qui a fait ça? – c'est moi!** who did that? – I did!; **c'est un bon traducteur** he's a good translator; **c'est la première voiture que j'aie eue** that was my first car; **c'est ici que je suis né** this is where I was born, I was born here; **c'est mardi aujourd'hui** today's Tuesday, it's Tuesday today; **c'était il y a longtemps** it was a long time ago (**b**) *(pour qualifier ou pour expliquer)* **c'est drôle/joli** it's funny/nice; **c'est exact!** that's right!; **c'est que maman est déjà partie** the thing is, Mum's already left; **s'il chante, (alors) c'est qu'il est de bonne humeur** if he's singing, it means he's in a good mood; *Fam* **c'est bizarre qu'il n'ait pas appelé!** it's strange that he hasn't called!; *Fam* **ce qui est pénible!** he's such a pain! (**c**) *(avec des pronoms relatifs)* **ce qui, ce que** what je **sais ce qui s'est passé** I know what happened; **ce que je crois, c'est que...** what I think is...; **voici ce dont il s'agit** this is what it's all about; **voilà ce à quoi j'avais pensé** this is what I thought of; **ce qui compte, c'est que...** what counts is that...; **j'ai appris tout ce qui se trouve dans le chapitre 4** I've learned everything in chapter 4; **j'ai oublié tout ce qu'elle m'a dit** I've forgotten everything she told me; **pour ce qui est de la qualité** with regards to or as regards quality (**d**) *(locutions)* **ce faisant** in so doing, whilst doing so; **il y est allé, et ce malgré mon interdiction** he went despite the fact that I had forbidden him; **sur ce, je m'en vais** on that note, I'm leaving; **... et, sur ce, il sortit son album de photos** ... whereupon he brought out his photo album

ce², cet, cette, ces [sə, sɛt, se] *adj démonstratif*

> **cet** is used before a masculine singular noun or adjective beginning with a vowel or mute h.

(**a**) *(par référence)* **ce garçon** this boy; **cet enfant** this child; **cette fille** this girl; **ces gens/animaux/couleurs** these people/animals/colours (**b**) *(en désignant)* **ce vin-ci** this wine; **ce vin-là** that wine; **ces voitures-ci** these cars; **ces voitures-là** those cars (**c**) *Fam (intensif)* **alors, cette lettre, tu me la montres?** so do I get to see this or that letter of yours?; **et ce café, il arrive?** is that coffee on its way or what?; **je lui ai envoyé une de ces lettres!** I wrote him such a letter!; **j'ai une de ces faims!** I'm so hungry!

ceci [səsi] *pron démonstratif* this; **c. (étant) dit** having said that; **c. n'explique pas cela** that's no explanation

cécité [sesite] *nf* blindness; **être atteint de c.** to be blind

CED [seəde] *nf* (*abrév* **Communauté européenne de défense**) EDC

céder [34] [sede] **1** *vt* (**a**) *(donner) (objet, droit)* to give up (**à** to); *(dans un testament)* to leave (**à** to); **c. sa place à qn** to give up one's seat to sb; **c. du terrain** to give ground; **cédez le passage** *(sur panneau) Br* give way, *Am* yield (**b**) *(vendre)* to sell; **à c.** *(sur panneau)* for sale
2 *vi* (**a**) *(plancher, branche)* to give way (**b**) *(se soumettre)* to give in (**devant** to)
3 céder à *vt ind (personne, tentation, revendication)* to give in to

Cedex [sedeks] *nm* (*abrév* **Courrier d'entreprise à distribution exceptionnelle**) = postal code ensuring rapid delivery of business mail

cédille [sedij] *nf* cedilla

cédrat [sedra] *nm (fruit)* citron

cèdre [sedr] *nm (arbre, bois)* cedar; **c. du Liban** cedar of Lebanon

CEE [seəə] *nf* (*abrév* **Communauté économique européenne**) EEC

CEEA [seəaa] *nf* (*abrév* **Communauté européenne de l'énergie atomique**) Euratom

cégep [seʒɛp] *nm Can* (*abrév* **collège d'enseignement général et professionnel**) = college of further education

CEI [seəi] *nf* (*abrév* **Communauté d'États indépendants**) CIS

ceindre [54] [sɛdr] *vt Litt* (**a**) *(épée)* to strap on (**b**) *(sujet: couronne)* to encircle

ceinture [sɛtyr] *nf* (**a**) *(accessoire)* belt; **être c. noire de judo** to be a black belt in judo; *Fam* **se serrer la c., faire c.** to tighten one's belt; **c. de chasteté** chastity belt; **c. de sécurité** seat belt; **attacher sa c. (de sécurité)** to fasten one's seat belt (**b**) *(taille) (de vêtement)* waistband; *(d'une personne)* waist; **frapper au-dessous de la c.** to hit below the belt (**c**) **la petite C.** = circular bus route around centre of Paris

ceinturer [sɛtyre] *vt* to grab around the waist

ceinturon [sɛtyrɔ̃] *nm* belt

cela [səla, sla] *pron démonstratif* that; **c'est pour c. que je viens** that's what I've come for or why I've come; **il y a deux ans de c.** that was two years ago; **et pourquoi c.?** why is that?; **s'il n'y avait que c.** if that were the only problem; **et avec c.?** *(dans un magasin)* (will there be) anything else?

célébration [selebrasjɔ̃] *nf* celebration

célèbre [selɛbr] *adj* famous (**pour** for); **se rendre c. par qch** to become famous for sth; **tristement c.** notorious

célébrer [34] [selebre] *vt* (**a**) *(fêter) (anniversaire, victoire, messe)* to celebrate (**b**) *(vanter)* **c. les mérites/le talent de qn** to extol sb's merits/talent

célébrité [selebrite] *nf (notoriété)* fame; *(personne)* celebrity

céleri [selri] *nm* celery; *Culin* **c. rémoulade** = grated celeriac in mayonnaise

céleri-rave (*pl* **céleris-raves**) [selrirav] *nm* celeriac

céleste [selɛst] *adj* (**a**) *(du firmament) (phénomènes, corps)* celestial, heavenly (**b**) *Rel* heavenly

célibat [seliba] *nm* single life; *(des prêtres)* celibacy

célibataire [selibatɛr] **1** *adj (non marié)* unmarried, single
2 *nm* bachelor; **un c. endurci** a confirmed bachelor
3 *nf* single woman

celle [sɛl] *voir* **celui**

cellier [selje] *nm* storeroom; *(cave)* cellar

Cellophane® [selofan] *nf* cellophane®; **sous C.** cellophane-wrapped

cellulaire [selyler] *adj* (**a**) *Biol* cell (**b**) *Jur* **régime c.** solitary confinement (**c**) *Tél* cellular

cellule [selyl] *nf* (**a**) *(d'une prison, d'un couvent)* cell (**b**) *Biol* cell; **c. nerveuse** nerve cell (**c**) *Fig (élément)* unit; *(de parti politique)* cell (**d**) *Él* **c. photoélectrique** photoelectric cell

cellulite [selylit] *nf* cellulite

Celluloïd® [selylɔid] *nm* celluloid®

cellulose [selyloz] *nf* cellulose

celte [sɛlt] **1** *adj* Celtic
2 *nmf* **C.** Celt

celtique [sɛltik] *adj & nm* Celtic

celui, celle [səlɥi, sɛl] (*mpl* **ceux** [sø], *fpl* **celles**) *pron démonstratif* the one; **mon pull et c. de Paul** my sweater and Paul's; **mes pulls et ceux de Paul** my sweaters and Paul's; **c. que je t'ai donné** the one I gave you; **celles dont je t'ai parlé** the ones I talked to you about; **c.-ci** this one; *(ce dernier)* the latter; **c.-là** that one; *(le premier)* the former; **ceux-ci** these ones; *(ces derniers)* the latter; **ceux-là** those ones; *(les premiers)* the former; **ah, c.-là, quel idiot!** he's such an idiot, that one!; **autre exemple, plus compliqué c.-là** another example, a more complicated one this time; **elle est bien bonne, celle-là!** that's a good one!

cendre [sɑ̃dr] *nf* ash(es); **faire cuire des pommes de terre sous la c.** to roast potatoes in the ashes; **réduire qch en cendres** to reduce sth to ashes; **cendres** *(après incinération)* ashes; *Rel* **le mercredi des Cendres** Ash Wednesday

cendré, -e [sɑ̃dre] *adj voir* **blond**

cendrée [sɑ̃dre] *nf Sp (piste)* cinder track; *(mâchefer)* cinders

cendrier [sɑ̃drije] *nm* ashtray

Cendrillon [sɑ̃drijɔ̃] *npr* Cinderella

Cène [sɛn] *nf* **la C.** the Last Supper

censé, -e [sɑ̃se] *adj* **être c. faire qch** to be supposed to do sth

censeur [sɑ̃sœr] *nm* (**a**) *Scol (d'un lycée) Br* deputy head, *Am* assistant principal (**b**) *(dans les médias)* censor (**c**) *Litt (juge)* critic

censure [sɑ̃syr] *nf (activité)* censorship; *(personnes)* (board of) censors

censurer [sɑ̃syre] *vt* (**a**) *(film, livre, scène)* to censor (**b**) *Litt (critiquer)* to censure

cent¹ [sɑ̃] **1** *adj* a *or* one hundred; **deux cents hommes** two hundred men; **deux c. cinquante** two hundred and fifty; **je te l'ai dit c. fois** I've told you a hundred times; **vous avez c. fois raison** you're absolutely right; *Fam* **je ne vais pas t'attendre (pendant) c. sept ans** I'm not going to wait for you forever; **faire les c. pas** to pace up and down; *Fam* **être aux c. coups** to be frantic; *Fam* **faire les quatre cents coups** to get up to all sorts of tricks
2 *nm* a hundred; **pour c.** per cent; **c. pour c.** a hundred per cent; *voir aussi* **trois**

cent² [sɛnt] *nm (monnaie)* cent

centaine [sɑ̃tɛn] *nf* **une c. (de)** about a hundred, a hundred *or* so; **des centaines de livres** hundreds of books; **plusieurs centaines de personnes** several hundred people

centaure [sɑ̃tɔr] *nm* centaur

centenaire [sɑ̃tnɛr] **1** *adj (personne, arbre)* hundred-year-old; **être c.** *(avoir cent ans)* to be a hundred (years old); *(avoir plus de cent ans)* to be over a hundred (years old); **plusieurs fois c.** hundreds of years old
2 *nmf* centenarian
3 *nm* centenary

centième [sɑ̃tjɛm] **1** *nmf, nm & adj* hundredth; *voir aussi* **cinquième**
2 *nf Th* hundredth performance

centigrade [sɑ̃tigrad] *adj* **degré c.** degree centigrade

centigramme [sɑ̃tigram] *nm* centigram

centilitre [sɑ̃tilitr] *nm* centilitre

centime [sɑ̃tim] *nm* centime; **je ne lui donnerai pas un c.!** I won't give him a *Br* penny *or Am* cent!

centimètre [sɑ̃timɛtr] *nm* (**a**) *(unité de mesure)* centimetre (**b**) *(ruban)* tape measure

centrafricain, -e [sɑ̃trafrikɛ̃, -ɛn] **1** *adj* of the Central African Republic **2** *nm,f* **C.** person from the Central African Republic

central, -e, -aux, -ales [sɑ̃tral, -o] **1** *adj* (**a**) *(au centre)* central (**b**) *(principal)* central, main (**c**) **(l'École) Centrale** = "Grande École" specializing in engineering **2** *nm* **c. téléphonique** telephone exchange **3** *nf* **centrale** (**a**) *(usine)* **centrale (électrique)** power station; **centrale thermique/nucléaire** thermal/nuclear power station (**b**) *(prison)* county jail (**c**) *(groupement)* **centrale (syndicale)** = group of affiliated labor unions; *Com* **centrale d'achat** (central) purchasing group

centralisation [sɑ̃tralizasjɔ̃] *nf* centralization

centraliser [sɑ̃tralize] *vt* to centralize

centralisme [sɑ̃tralism] *nm Pol* centralism

centre [sɑ̃tr] *nm* (**a**) *(milieu)* centre, **il se prend pour le c. du monde** he thinks the world revolves round him; **cette question est au c. du débat** this question is at the heart of the debate; *Phys* **c. de gravité** centre of gravity; **c. d'intérêt** centre of interest (**b**) *Pol* centre; **le c. droit/gauche** the centre right/left (**c**) *(au football)* *(passe)* cross; **faire un c.** to make a cross (**d**) *(organisme, lieu)* centre; **c. aéré** outdoor activity centre; **c. commercial** *Br* shopping centre, *Am* (shopping) mall; **c. culturel** arts centre; **c. hospitalier** hospital complex; **c. des impôts** tax office; **c. de loisirs** leisure centre; **c. de tri** sorting office

centrer [sɑ̃tre] *vt (ballon, mécanisme)* to centre; **c. une discussion sur un sujet** to focus a discussion on a subject

centre-ville *(pl* **centres-villes)** [sɑ̃travil] *nm* town centre; *(d'une grande ville) Br* city centre, *Am* downtown area; **habiter au c.** to live in the town centre

centrifuge [sɑ̃trify3] *adj* centrifugal

centrifuger [45] [sɑ̃trify3e] *vt* to centrifuge

centrifugeur [sɑ̃trify3œr] *nm,* **centrifugeuse** [sɑ̃trify3øz] *nf (en chimie, en biologie)* centrifuge; *(pour jus de fruits)* juice extractor

centripète [sɑ̃tripɛt] *adj* centripetal

centrisme [sɑ̃trism] *nm Pol* centrism

centriste [sɑ̃trist] *adj & nmf Pol* centrist

centuple [sɑ̃typl] *nm* **le c. de dix** a hundred times ten; **je te le rendrai au c.** I'll repay you a hundred times over

cep [sɛp] *nm* **c. (de vigne)** vine-stock

cépage [sepaʒ] *nm* variety of vine

cèpe [sɛp] *nm* cep

cependant [səpɑ̃dɑ̃] **1** *conj* however, nevertheless; **le directeur, c., n'est pas d'accord** the manager, however, does not agree; **c., vous ne m'avez pas averti** nevertheless, you didn't tell me **2** *adv Litt* meanwhile; **c. que** while

céphalée [sefale] *nf Méd* headache, *Spéc* cephalalgia

céramique [seramik] *nf (art)* ceramics *(singulier)*; *(matière, objet)* ceramic

cerceau, -x [sɛrso] *nm* hoop

cercle [sɛrkl] *nm* (**a**) *(figure)* circle; **en c.** in a circle; **c. vicieux** vicious circle; **décrire des cercles** *(avion, oiseau)* to circle (**b**) *(groupe de personnes)* circle (**c**) *(association)* club; **c. littéraire** literary society (**d**) *(objet circulaire)* hoop, ring (**e**) *Géog* **c. (polaire) arctique** Arctic Circle

cerclé, -e [sɛrkle] *adj* **lunettes cerclées d'écaille** horn-rimmed spectacles; **un tonneau c. de fer** a barrel with iron hoops

cercueil [sɛrkœj] *nm* coffin

céréale [sereal] *nf* cereal, grain; **céréales** *(au petit déjeuner)* cereal

céréalier, -ère [serealje, -ɛr] *adj (production, culture)* cereal; *(région)* cereal-growing

cérébral, -e, -aux, -ales [serebral, -o] *adj* cerebral; **hémorragie cérébrale** brain haemorrhage

cérémonial, -als [seremɔnjal] *nm* ceremonial

cérémonie [seremɔni] *nf* ceremony; **habit de c.** dress suit; **uniforme de c.** dress uniform; *Fig* **sans cérémonies** *(réception, repas)* informal; *(recevoir quelqu'un)* informally; *(renvoyer quelqu'un)* unceremoniously; **faire des cérémonies** to stand on ceremony; **sans plus de c.** without further ado

cérémonieux, -euse [seremɔnjø, -øz] *adj* ceremonious

cerf [sɛr] *nm* stag

cerfeuil [sɛrfœj] *nm* chervil

cerf-volant *(pl* **cerfs-volants)** [sɛrvolɑ̃] *nm* (**a**) *(jeu)* kite (**b**) *(insecte)* stag beetle

cerise [səriz] **1** *nf* cherry **2** *adj inv* cherry(-red)

cerisier [sərizje] *nm (arbre)* cherry tree; *(bois)* cherrywood

CERN [sɛrn] *nm (abrév* **Conseil européen pour la recherche nucléaire)** CERN

cerne [sɛrn] *nm* ring

cerné, -e [sɛrne] *adj* **avoir les yeux cernés** to have rings under one's eyes

cerner [sɛrne] *vt* (**a**) *(encercler)* to surround (**b**) *(définir) (problème)* to identify; **une personne difficile à c.** a difficult person to figure out

certain, -e [sɛrtɛ̃, -ɛn] **1** *adj (sûr)* certain; **il viendra, c'est c.** he'll definitely come; **être c. de qch** to be certain of sth; **aller à une mort certaine** to be heading for certain death **2** *adj indéfini (avant le nom)* certain; **il a un c. charme** he has a certain charm; **un c. temps** a while; **jusqu'à un c. point** up to a (certain) point; **d'une certaine façon** in a way; **dans une certaine mesure** to a certain extent; **d'un c. âge** elderly; **avoir un c. âge** to be getting on; **cela demande un c. courage** it takes some nerve/courage; **une certaine Isabelle** someone called Isabelle **3** *pron indéfini* **certains pensent que...** some (people) think (that)...; **certaines d'entre nous/vous** some of us/you

certainement [sɛrtɛnmɑ̃] *adv (probablement)* most probably; **c.!** of course!; **c. pas!** certainly not!

certes [sɛrt] *adv* certainly; **il n'est pas sans défauts, c., mais...** he has his faults, certainly, but...; **c. oui!** yes indeed!; **c. non!** certainly not!

certificat [sɛrtifika] *nm* certificate; **c. d'assurance** insurance certificate; **c. de garantie** certificate of guarantee; **c. médical** medical certificate; **c. de scolarité** school attendance record; **c. de travail** certificate of employment

certifié, -e [sɛrtifje] *adj* **professeur c.** = qualified (graduate) teacher

certifier [66] [sɛrtifje] *vt* (**a**) *(authentifier)* to certify; *(signature)* to witness (**b**) *(assurer)* **c. qch à qn** to assure sb of sth

certitude [sɛrtityd] *nf* certainty; **j'en ai la c.** I'm certain of it

cérumen [serymɛn] *nm* earwax, *Spéc* cerumen

cerveau, -x [sɛrvo] nm Anat & Fig brain; (esprit) mind, brains; Fam (personne intelligente) smart person; (d'un projet) mastermind

cervelas [sɛrvəla] nm saveloy

cervelet [sɛrvəlɛ] nm Anat cerebellum

cervelle [sɛrvɛl] nf Anat (substance) brain; se brûler ou se faire sauter la c. to blow one's brains out; il n'a rien dans la c. he's got nothing between his ears; avoir une c. de moineau to be bird-brained; Culin c. d'agneau lamb's brains

cervical, -e, -aux, -ales [sɛrvikal, -o] adj Anat cervical

CES [səəɛs] nm (a) (abrév contrat emploi-solidarité) = short-term contract subsidised by the government (b) (abrév collège d'enseignement secondaire) = former secondary school for pupils aged 12 to 15

ces [se] voir ce²

César [sezar] 1 npr Jules C. Julius Caesar 2 nm Cin = French cinema award

césarienne [sezarjɛn] nf Caesarean (section)

cessant, -e [sɛsɑ̃, -ɑ̃t] adj toutes affaires cessantes forthwith

cessation [sɛsasjɔ̃] nf cessation; c. des hostilités ceasefire; c. de paiements suspension of payments

cesse [sɛs] nf (a) sans c. constantly, continually (b) Litt il n'aura (pas) de c. qu'il ne réussisse he won't rest until he has succeeded

cesser [sese] 1 vi to stop, to cease; (vent) to die down; faire c. qch to put a stop to sth; il faudra que ça cesse this has to stop 2 vt (interrompre) to stop; Mil cessez le feu! cease fire!; c. de faire qch to stop doing sth

cessez-le-feu [seselfø] nm inv ceasefire

cession [sɛsjɔ̃] nf Jur transfer

c'est-à-dire [sɛtadir] conj that is (to say); vous l'avez prévenu? – eh bien, c. que non did you let him know? – well, actually, no; c. que je n'étais pas au courant the thing is that no one told me; il faut aller de l'avant! – c.? we must forge ahead! – what do you mean by that?

césure [sezyr] nf (en poésie) caesura; Ordinat break, hyphenation

cet [sɛt] voir ce²

cétacé [setase] nm cetacean

cette [sɛt] voir ce²

ceux [sø] voir celui

Ceylan [selɑ̃] n Ceylon

cf (abrév confer) cf

CFA [seɛfa] (abrév Communauté financière africaine) franc C. CFA franc

CFAO [seɛfao] nf (abrév conception et fabrication assistées par ordinateur) CADCAM

CFC [seɛfse] nm (abrév chlorofluorocarbone) CFC

CFDT [seɛfdete] nf (abrév Confédération française démocratique du travail) = French trade union

CFTC [seɛftese] nf (abrév Confédération française des travailleurs chrétiens) = French trade union

CGC [sezese] nf (abrév Confédération générale des cadres) = French trade union for managerial staff

CGT [sezete] nf (abrév Confédération générale du travail) = French trade union

chacal, -als [ʃakal] nm jackal; Fig vulture

chacun, -e [ʃakœ̃, -yn] pron indéfini (a) (chaque personne) each (one), every one; 5 euros c. 5 euros each; nous aurons pris c. notre chapeau each of us took our hat (b) (tout le monde) everyone, everybody; c. pour soi every man for

himself; c. ses goûts everyone to their own taste; c. son tour (dans une file d'attente) each in turn; c. son tour! wait your turn!; tout un c. everyone

chagrin, -e [ʃagrɛ̃, -in] 1 nm (peine) grief, sorrow; avoir du c. to be upset; avoir un gros c. (langage enfantin) to be very unhappy; faire du c. à qn to upset sb; un c. d'amour an unhappy love affair 2 adj Litt woeful; esprits chagrins malcontents

chagriner [ʃagrine] vt (peiner) to grieve; (contrarier) to bother

chahut [ʃay] nm Fam racket, din; faire du c. to make a racket

chahuter [ʃayte] Fam 1 vi (faire du tapage) to make a racket; (jouer brutalement) to be rowdy 2 vt (professeur) to bait; (orateur) to heckle; se faire c. (professeur) to get baited; (orateur) to get heckled

chai [ʃɛ] nm wine and spirits storehouse

chaîne [ʃɛn] nf (a) (pour attacher, pour décorer) chain; faire la c. to form a chain; chaînes Aut (snow) chains; Fig (contraintes) chains, shackles (b) (de transmission) chain; c. de vélo bicycle chain (c) (série) (d'hôtels, de magasins) chain; c. alimentaire food chain; c. de montagnes range or chain of mountains (d) TV channel; c. de télévision television channel (e) (dans l'industrie) c. (de montage) assembly line, production line; travail à la c. assembly line work; travailler à la c. to work on the assembly line (f) Tex warp (g) Ordinat string; c. de caractères character string; c. de recherche search string (h) c. (haute-fidélité) hi-fi

chaînette [ʃɛnɛt] nf small chain

chaînon [ʃɛnɔ̃] nm link; Fig le c. manquant the missing link

chair [ʃɛr] 1 nf (d'humain, d'animal, de fruit) flesh; en c. et en os in the flesh; être bien en c. to be plump; la c. est faible the flesh is weak; c. à canon cannon fodder; avoir la c. de poule to have Br goose pimples or Am goose bumps; donner la c. de poule à qn to give sb goose pimples; c. à saucisse sausagemeat; Fam Fig je vais en faire de la c. à saucisse I'll make mincemeat of him 2 adj inv (couleur) c. flesh-coloured

chaire [ʃɛr] nf (a) (dans une église) pulpit (b) Univ (fonction, tribune) chair; être titulaire d'une c. to hold a chair

chaise [ʃɛz] nf chair; Fig être assis ou très Fam avoir le cul entre deux chaises to be in an awkward position; Can c. berçante rocking chair; chaises musicales musical chairs; c. électrique electric chair; c. haute high chair; c. longue deckchair; c. à porteurs sedan chair; c. roulante wheelchair

chaland [ʃalɑ̃] nm barge

châle [ʃal] nm shawl

chalet [ʃalɛ] nm (a) (de montagne) chalet (b) Can cottage

chaleur [ʃalœr] nf (a) (température) heat; les grandes chaleurs the hot season; il fait une c. terrible it's terribly hot; coup de c. heatstroke (b) (d'une personne, d'une couleur, d'une voix, d'un accueil) warmth; c. humaine human warmth; avec c. warmly (c) Zool être en c. to be Br on heat or Am in heat

chaleureusement [ʃalørøzmɑ̃] adv warmly

chaleureux, -euse [ʃalørø, -øz] adj (accueil, atmosphère) warm; (paroles) glowing

challenge [ʃalɑ̃ʒ] nm (a) Sp tournament (b) (défi) challenge

challenger [tʃalɑ̃ʒœr] nm challenger

chaloupe [ʃalup] nf launch; (à rames) Br rowing boat, Am rowboat; c. à moteur motor launch; c. de sauvetage lifeboat

chaloupé, -e [ʃalupe] adj swaying

chalumeau, -x [ʃalymo] *nm* (a) *Tech Br* blowlamp, *Am* blowtorch (b) *Can* spout *(for collecting sap of maple tree)*

chalut [ʃaly] *nm* trawl; **pêcher au c.** to trawl

chalutier [ʃalytje] *nm* trawler

chamade [ʃamad] *nf* **battre la c.** to beat wildly

chamailler [ʃamaje] **se chamailler** *vpr* to squabble

chamailleur, -euse [ʃamajœr, -øz] **1** *adj* quarrelsome **2** *nm,f* squabbler

chamarré, -e [ʃamare] *adj* richly coloured

chambardement [ʃɑ̃bardəmɑ̃] *nm Fam* upheaval

chambarder [ʃɑ̃barde] *vt Fam (projets, maison)* to turn upside down

chambouler [ʃɑ̃bule] *vt Fam (projets, maison)* to turn upside down

chambranle [ʃɑ̃brɑ̃l] *nm (d'une porte, d'une fenêtre)* frame

chambre [ʃɑ̃br] *nf* (a) *(pièce)* bedroom; *(d'un hôtel)* room; **c. à un lit/deux lits** single/twin room; **vous auriez une c. (de) libre?** do you have any vacancies?; **faire c. à part** to sleep in separate rooms; **faire sa c.** to tidy (up) one's room; **garder la c.** to keep to one's room; **sportif/voyageur en c.** armchair sportsman/traveller; **c. d'amis** spare room; **c. de bonne** maid's room; **c. à coucher** *(pièce)* bedroom; *(mobilier)* bedroom furniture; **c. forte** strongroom; **c. frigorifique** *ou* **froide** cold store; **c. à gaz** gas chamber; **c. d'hôte** ≃ guest house; **c. meublée** furnished room, attic room (b) *Jur (d'un tribunal)* division; **c. d'accusation** Court of Criminal Appeal; **C. de commerce** Chamber of Commerce (c) *Pol* **la C.** the House; **siéger à la C.** to sit in the House; **C. des députés** = lower chamber of Parliament (d) *Tech (d'un fusil, d'un appareil photo)* chamber; **c. à air** inner tube

chambrée [ʃɑ̃bre] *nf* (a) *(occupants d'une chambre)* room(ful) (b) *Mil* barrack room

chambrer [ʃɑ̃bre] *vt* (a) **c. qch** *(bouteille, vin)* to bring sth to room temperature (b) *Fam* **c. qn** to pull sb's leg

chameau, -x [ʃamo] *nm* (a) *(animal)* camel (b) *Fam (homme)* bastard; *(femme)* bitch

chamelier [ʃaməlje] *nm* camel-driver

chamelle [ʃamɛl] *nf* she-camel

chamois [ʃamwa] *nm* (a) *(animal)* chamois (b) *Sp* **c. d'or/ d'argent/de bronze** = gold/silver/bronze skiing proficiency medal

champ [ʃɑ̃] *nm* (a) *(étendue)* field; **c. de blé** field of wheat, wheatfield; **prendre** *ou* **couper à travers champs** to cut across country; **à tout bout de c.** at every possible opportunity; *Fig* **laisser le c. libre à qn** to leave the field free for sb; **c. de bataille** battlefield; **c. de courses** *Br* racecourse, *Am* racetrack; **c. de foire** fairground; **mort** *ou* **tombé au c. d'honneur** killed in action; **c. de mines** minefield; **c. de tir** rifle range; *Mil* practice ground; *(d'un fusil)* field of fire (b) *Fig (portée)* scope; **c. d'action** field of activity; **élargir le c. de ses activités** to extend the scope of one's activities (c) *Phot* shot, picture; *(d'un instrument optique)* field; **être dans le c.** to be in shot; **c. visuel** field of vision (d) *Él & Rad* field; **c. magnétique** magnetic field (e) *Ordinat* field; **c. numérique** numeric field; **c. de texte** text field

champagne [ʃɑ̃paɲ] *nm* champagne

champenois, -e [ʃɑ̃pənwa, -az] **1** *adj* (a) *(de la région)* of Champagne (b) **méthode champenoise** champagne method **2** *nm,f* **C.** person from Champagne

champêtre [ʃɑ̃pɛtr] *adj* rustic, rural

champignon [ʃɑ̃piɲɔ̃] *nm* (a) *(plante)* mushroom; *Fig* **pousser comme un c.** *(enfant)* to shoot up; *(ville)* to mushroom; **c. atomique** mushroom cloud; **c. hallucino-**

gène magic mushroom; **c. de Paris** button mushroom; **c. vénéneux** poisonous mushroom, toadstool (b) *Méd* fungus (c) *Fam (accélérateur)* **appuyer sur le c.** *Br* to put one's foot down, *Am* to step on the gas

champion, -onne [ʃɑ̃pjɔ̃, -ɔn] **1** *nm,f* (a) *(dans une discipline)* champion; **le c. du monde d'escrime** the world fencing champion; *Fam* **c'est un c. du bricolage** he's a great handyman (b) *(d'une cause)* champion **2** *adj* (a) *Sp* **l'équipe championne du monde** the world champions (b) *Fam* great; **pour les gaffes, il est c.!** he's a great one for putting his foot in it!

championnat [ʃɑ̃pjɔna] *nm* championship

chance [ʃɑ̃s] *nf* (a) *(sort favorable)* (good) luck; **souhaiter bonne c. à qn** to wish sb luck; **bonne c.!** good luck!; **quelle c.!** what a stroke of luck!; **avec un peu de c....** with a bit of luck...; **avoir de la c.** to be lucky *or* fortunate; **ne pas avoir de c.** to be unlucky; **porter c. à qn** to bring sb luck; **c'est mon jour de c.** it's my lucky day; **c'est bien ma c.!** just my luck!; **pas de c.!** too bad!; **par c.** luckily, fortunately (b) *(possibilité)* chance; **avoir des chances de faire qch** to stand a (good) chance of doing sth; **avoir peu de chances de faire qch** to have little chance of doing sth; **donner une** *ou* **sa c. à qn** to give sb a chance; **elle a une c. sur deux de gagner** she has a fifty-fifty chance of winning, *Fam* **il y a des chances** probably; **il y a de grandes** *ou* **fortes chances (pour) qu'on le lui propose** there's every chance that she will be offered it

chancelant, -e [ʃɑ̃slɑ̃, -ɑ̃t] *adj (pas)* unsteady; *(mémoire)* shaky; *(santé)* delicate; *(pouvoir, gouvernement)* tottering; *(détermination)* wavering

chanceler [42] [ʃɑ̃sle] *vi (personne)* to stagger, to totter; *(objet)* to wobble; *(régime, gouvernement)* to totter; **l'uppercut le fit c.** the uppercut sent him reeling

chancelier [ʃɑ̃səlje] *nm Pol* chancellor; *(d'ambassade)* chief secretary

chancellerie [ʃɑ̃sɛlri] *nf* (a) *(d'une ambassade)* chancery (b) *(ministère de la Justice) Br* ≃ Lord Chancellor's Department, *Am* ≃ Department of Justice

chanceux, -euse [ʃɑ̃sø, -øz] *adj* lucky

chancre [ʃɑ̃kr] *nm Méd & Fig* canker

chandail [ʃɑ̃daj] *nm* sweater

Chandeleur [ʃɑ̃dlœr] *nf* **la C.** Candlemas

chandelier [ʃɑ̃dəlje] *nm (à une branche)* candlestick; *(à plusieurs branches)* candelabra

chandelle [ʃɑ̃dɛl] *nf* (a) *(bougie)* candle; **s'éclairer à la c.** to use candlelight; **un dîner aux chandelles** a candlelit dinner; **faire des économies de bouts de c.** to scrimp and save; **brûler la c. par les deux bouts** to burn the candle at both ends; **le jeu n'en vaut pas la c.** the game is not worth the candle; **tenir la c.** *Br* to play gooseberry, *Am* to feel like a fifth wheel; **voir trente-six chandelles** to see stars; **devoir une fière c. à qn** to owe sb a great debt *(en gymnastique)* **faire la c.** to do a shoulder stand (c) *Av (montée en)* **c.** vertical climb

chanfrein [ʃɑ̃frɛ̃] *nm (de cheval)* chamfer

change [ʃɑ̃ʒ] *nm Fin* exchange; **le c. est avantageux** the exchange rate is good; *Fig* **gagner/ne pas perdre au c.** to gain on/not to lose on the exchange (b) *Fig* **donner le c. à qn** to put sb off the scent (c) *(couche-culotte)* (complet) disposable *Br* nappy *or Am* diaper

changeant, -e [ʃɑ̃ʒɑ̃, -ɑ̃t] *adj (temps)* unsettled; **d'humeur changeante** moody

changement [ʃɑ̃ʒmɑ̃] *nm* (a) *(modification)* change; **ça va te faire un drôle de c.** it'll be quite a change for you; **c. de décor** scene change; *Fig* change of scenery (b) **c. de direction** *(sur un écriteau)* under new management (b) *(dans les transports)* change; **il y a un c. à Valence** you have to change at Valence **(c) c.** de vitesse *(action)* change of gear; *(levier) Br* gear lever, *Am* gear shift; *Ordinat* **c.** de ligne line feed

changer [ʃɑ̃ʒe] **1** *vt* **(a)** *(remplacer) (draps, couche de bébé, roue)* to change; **c.** qch contre qch to change *or* exchange sth for sth **(b)** *(enfant, bébé)* to change **(c)** *(convertir) (argent)* to change (**en** into) **(d)** *(transformer)* **c.** qn/qch en to change sb/sth into **(e)** *(modifier)* to change, to alter; **ça va les c.!** that'll be a change for them!; **ça lui changera les idées** that'll take his mind off things; **ça nous change du café du coin!** that makes a change from the local bar!; **cela ne change rien à l'affaire** that makes no difference; **sa nouvelle coiffure la change** she looks different with her new hairstyle; **mais cela change tout!** that changes everything!; **c.** qch de place to move sth **2** *vi* **(a)** *(se modifier)* to change; **c. en bien** *ou* **en mieux** to change for the better; **c. en mal** *ou* **en pire** to change for the worse; *Ironique* **pour c.** for a change **(b)** *(dans les transports)* to change **3 changer de** *vt ind* to change; **c. de train/de travail** to change trains/jobs; **c. de place avec qn** to change places with sb; **c. de coiffure** to change one's hairstyle; **c. de vêtements** to change (one's clothes), to get changed; **c. de couleur** to change colour; *Aut* **c. de vitesse** to change gear; **je te prie de c. de ton!** don't use that tone (of voice) with me!; *Fam Fig* **change de disque!** put another record on! **4 se changer** *vpr* **(a)** *(mettre d'autres vêtements)* to change **(b) se c. les idées** to change one's ideas **(c)** *(se transformer)* **se c. en** to change *or* turn into

chanoine [ʃanwan] *nm Rel* canon

chanson [ʃɑ̃sɔ̃] *nf* **(a)** *(air)* song; **la c. française** French songs; *Fam* **c'est toujours la même c.!** it's always the same old story!; *Fam* **on connaît la c.!** I've heard that one before!; **c. d'amour** love song; **c. à boire** drinking song **(b)** *(genre littéraire)* song; **c. de geste** chanson de geste

chansonnette [ʃɑ̃sɔnɛt] *nf* ditty

chansonnier [ʃɑ̃sɔnje] *nm* satirical cabaret singer

chant [ʃɑ̃] *nm* **(a)** *(chanson)* song; *(d'un instrument de musique, de la mer, du vent)* sound; *(d'un oiseau)* singing; *(du grillon, de la cigale)* chirping; *(du coq)* crowing; **au c. du coq** at cockcrow; *Fig* **c. du cygne** swan song; **c. funèbre** dirge; **c. de Noël** Christmas carol; **c. sacré** hymn **(b)** *(art)* singing; **leçon/professeur de c.** singing lesson/teacher; **apprendre le c.** to take singing lessons; **c. choral** choral singing; **c. grégorien** Gregorian chant **(c)** *(d'un poème)* canto

chantage [ʃɑ̃taʒ] *nm* blackmail; **faire du c.** to use blackmail; **il lui fait du c. au suicide** he's blackmailing her with suicide threats

chantant, -e [ʃɑ̃tɑ̃, -ɑ̃t] *adj (musique, air)* tuneful; *(accent, voix)* lilting

chanter [ʃɑ̃te] **1** *vt (chanson)* to sing; *Fam* **qu'est-ce que vous me chantez là?** what are you on about?; *Fam* **elle le chante sur tous les tons** she's always going on about it **2** *vi* **(a)** *(personne, oiseau)* to sing; *(coq)* to crow; *(grillon, cigale)* to chirp; **c. juste/faux** to sing in tune/out of tune **(b) faire c. qn** *(exercer un chantage sur)* to blackmail sb **(c)** *(plaire)* **viens, si ça te chante** come along, if you feel like it; **il vient quand ça lui chante** he comes when he feels like it

chanterelle¹ [ʃɑ̃trɛl] *nf Mus (corde)* top string

chanterelle² *nf (champignon)* chanterelle

chanteur, -euse [ʃɑ̃tœr, -øz] *nm,f* singer; **c. de charme** crooner; **c. des rues** street singer

chantier [ʃɑ̃tje] *nm* **(a)** *(lieu de construction)* (building) site; *(sur la route)* roadworks; **c. interdit au public** *(sur* *panneau)* no admittance to the public; **mettre qch en c.** to get sth under way; **c. naval** shipyard **(b)** *Fam (désordre)* **quel c.!** what a shambles!; **ils ont tout laissé en c.** they left the place in a complete shambles

chantilly [ʃɑ̃tiji] *nf* **(crème) c.** whipped cream

chantonner [ʃɑ̃tɔne] *vt & vi* to sing softly; *(sans paroles)* to hum

chantre [ʃɑ̃tr] *nm (défenseur)* champion

chanvre [ʃɑ̃vr] *nm* hemp; **c. indien** Indian hemp

chaos [kao] *nm* chaos

chaotique [kaɔtik] *adj* chaotic

chaparder [ʃaparde] *vt Fam* to pinch

chapardeur, -euse [ʃapardœr, -øz] *nm,f Fam* thief

chape [ʃap] *nf (de béton)* screed; *(d'un pneu)* tread; **la chaleur pèse sur la ville comme une c. de plomb** the heat lies on the town like a lead weight

chapeau, -x [ʃapo] *nm* **(a)** *(coiffure)* hat; *Fig* **porter le c.** to carry the can; *Fig* **tirer son c. à qn** to take off one's hat to sb; **c.!** well done!; **c. melon** *Br* bowler hat, *Am* derby; **c. mou** *Br* trilby, *Am* fedora; **c. de paille** straw hat **(b)** *(d'un champignon)* cap **(c)** *(partie supérieure) (de vol-au-vent, de bouchée à la reine)* lid; **prendre un virage sur les chapeaux de roues** to take a corner at top speed; **démarrer sur les chapeaux de roues** *(projet, soirée)* to get off to a cracking start **(d)** *Typ & Journ* lead-in

chapeauter [ʃapote] *vt (contrôler)* to head

chapelain [ʃaplɛ̃] *nm Rel* chaplain

chapelet [ʃaplɛ] *nm (de prière)* rosary; *Fig (d'invectives, d'insultes)* stream; *(d'objets)* string; **dire son c.** to say the rosary

chapelier, -ère [ʃapəlje, -ɛr] *nm,f* hatter

chapelle [ʃapɛl] *nf* chapel; **c. ardente** chapel of rest

chapelure [ʃaplyr] *nf* breadcrumbs

chaperon [ʃaprɔ̃] *nm* **(a)** *(personne)* chaperon **(b) le Petit C. rouge** Little Red Riding Hood

chaperonner [ʃaprɔne] *vt aussi Fig* to chaperon

chapiteau, -x [ʃapito] *nm* **(a)** *Archit (d'une colonne)* capital **(b)** *(d'un cirque)* big top; **sous c.** in a marquee

chapitre [ʃapitr] *nm* **(a)** *(d'un livre)* chapter; *(d'un budget)* item; **inscrire une somme au c. des recettes/dépenses** to enter a sum under revenue/expenditure; **elle est sévère sur le c. de la discipline** she is strict in the matter of discipline; **en voilà assez sur ce c.** that's enough of that; **et maintenant, au c. des faits divers...** and now for the news in brief... **(b)** *Rel (assemblée)* chapter; *Fig* **avoir voix au c.** to have a say in the matter

chapitrer [ʃapitre] *vt* **c. qn** *(réprimander)* to tell sb off; *(faire la morale à)* to lecture sb

chapon [ʃapɔ̃] *nm (coq)* capon

chaptaliser [ʃaptalize] *vt* to chaptalize

chaque [ʃak] *adj indéfini* each, every; **c. femme doit pouvoir travailler et élever ses enfants** every woman should be able to work as well as bring up her children; **ces livres coûtent 10 euros c.** these books cost 10 euros each; **c. chose à sa place** everything in its place; **c. chose en son temps** all in good time; **c. fois qu'il vient** whenever he comes; **j'y pense à c. instant** I think about it all the time

char [ʃar] *nm* **(a)** *Mil* **c. (d'assaut** *ou* **de combat)** tank **(b)** *(romain)* chariot **(c) c. de carnaval** float **(d)** *Can Fam (voiture)* car **(e)** *Sp* **c. à voile** sand yacht; **faire du c. à voile** to go sand yachting **(f)** *Fam* **arrête ton c.!** come off it!

charabia [ʃarabja] *nm Fam* gibberish

charade [ʃarad] *nf* = charade which is described rather than acted out

charançon [ʃarɑ̃sɔ̃] *nm* weevil

charbon [ʃarbɔ̃] *nm* (**a**) *(combustible)* coal; **c. (de bois)** charcoal; **chauffage au c.** coal-fired heating; *Fig* **être sur des charbons ardents** to be on tenterhooks (**b**) *Art* charcoal; **dessin au c.** charcoal drawing (**c**) *Méd (médicament)* charcoal

charbonnage [ʃarbɔnaʒ] *nm* (**a**) *(exploitation)* coal mining (**b**) **charbonnages** *(houillères)* collieries

charbonneux, -euse [ʃarbɔnø, -øz] *adj (noir)* coal-black; *(yeux)* smoky *(with black make-up)*

charbonnier, -ère [ʃarbɔnje, -ɛr] **1** *adj (industrie)* coal **2** *nm,f*(**a**) *(marchand de charbon)* coal merchant; *Prov* **c. est maître dans sa maison** *ou* **chez soi** a man is master in his own home (**b**) *Naut* coaler **3** *nf* **charbonnière** *(mésange)* great tit

charcuter [ʃarkyte] *Fam* **1** *vt* **c. qn** to hack sb about **2 se charcuter** *vpr* to cut oneself to ribbons; **se c. le menton/le doigt** to cut one's chin/finger to ribbons

charcuterie [ʃarkytri] *nf* (**a**) *(magasin)* pork butcher's (shop) (**b**) *(activité)* cooked meats trade (**c**) *(produits)* cooked meats

charcutier, -ère [ʃarkytje, -ɛr] *nm,f* (**a**) *(commerçant, fabricant)* pork butcher (**b**) *Fam Péj (chirurgien)* butcher

chardon [ʃardɔ̃] *nm (plante)* thistle

chardonneret [ʃardɔnrɛ] *nm* goldfinch

charentais, -e [ʃarɑ̃tɛ, -ɛz] **1** *adj* of Charente **2** *nm,f* **C.** person from Charente **3** *nf* **charentaise** *(chausson)* slipper

charge [ʃarʒ] *nf* (**a**) *(poids)* load; *(sur bateau)* cargo; *Fig* **être une c. pour qn** to be a burden to sb; **c. utile** *(d'un véhicule)* capacity (**b**) *(responsabilité)* responsibility; **être en c. de qch** to be in charge of sth; **prendre qn/qch en c.** to take charge of sb/ sth; **se prendre en c.** to be responsible for oneself (**c**) *(fonction)* office, *(d'avoué)* practice (**d**) *(obligation financière)* **être à la c. de qn** *(personne)* to be dependent on sb, *(appel, transport, réparations)* to be chargeable to sb; **avoir deux enfants à c.** to have two dependent children; **prendre un client en c.** *(taxi)* to pick up a fare; **être pris en c. à cent pour cent par la Sécurité sociale** to have one's medical expenses fully paid for by Social Security; **charges (locatives)** *(d'un appartement)* maintenance charges; **charges d'exploitation** operating costs; **charges sociales** *Br* ≃ national insurance contributions, *Am* ≃ social security charges *(paid by the employer)* (**e**) *(d'une arme, d'explosifs)* charge (**f**) *Constr (pression)* load (**g**) *Él (d'une batterie, d'une particule)* charge (**h**) *Mil* charge; *Fig* **revenir à la c.** to return to the attack (**i**) *Jur (preuve)* charge

chargé, -e [ʃarʒe] **1** *adj* (**a**) *(camion, navire)* loaded, laden *(de* with); *(revolver, appareil photo)* loaded; *Fig (style)* ornate; **la voiture est trop chargée** the car is overloaded; **être c. comme un bourricot** *ou* **un mulet** to be loaded down; **avoir la langue chargée** to have a furred tongue; **un regard c. de reconnaissance** a look full of gratitude (**b**) *(occupé) (journée, programme)* full (**c**) *(responsable)* **être c. de qch** *(mission)* to be entrusted with sth; *(tâche)* to be responsible for sth; **être c. de famille** to have family responsibilities; **être c. de faire qch** to be responsible for doing sth (**d**) *Phys* charged **2** *nm* **c. d'affaires** chargé-d'affaires; **c. de mission** official representative **3** *nm,f Univ* **c. de cours** = part-time lecturer; *Can* lecturer

chargement [ʃarʒəmɑ̃] *nm* (**a**) *(action)* loading; *Él (d'une batterie)* charging; **machine à laver à c. frontal** front-loading washing machine (**b**) *(marchandises)* load; *(sur bateau)* cargo

charger [45] [ʃarʒe] **1** *vt* (**a**) *(camion, navire, marchandises)* to load (**b**) *(remplir)* to fill (**de** with) (**c**) *(fusil, appareil photo)* to load; *Él (batterie)* to charge; *Ordinat* to load (up) (**d**) *(donner une responsabilité à)* **c. qn de qch** to entrust sb with sth; **c. qn de faire qch** to give sb the responsibility for doing sth (**e**) *(attaquer)* to charge (at) **2** *vi* (**a**) *Ordinat* to load up (**b**) *Mil* to charge **3 se charger** *vpr* (**a**) *(s'alourdir)* to weigh oneself down (**b**) **se c. de qn/qch** *(prendre la responsabilité de)* to take care of sb/sth; **se c. de faire qch** to undertake to do sth

chargeur [ʃarʒœr] *nm (d'arme)* magazine; *Phot* cartridge; *Él* (battery) charger; *Ordinat* loader; **c. automatique** self loader

chariot [ʃarjo] *nm* (**a**) *(petite charrette)* wagon; *(de supermarché)* trolley, *Am* cart; *(pour diapositives)* cartridge; *(pour la manutention)* truck; *(d'hôpital)* Br trolley, *Am* gurney; *Cin* dolly; *(d'une machine à écrire)* carriage; **c. à bagages** luggage trolley

charismatique [karismatik] *adj* charismatic

charisme [karism] *nm* charisma

charitable [ʃaritabl] *adj* charitable (**envers** towards); *(conseil)* friendly

charité [ʃarite] *nf* (**a**) *(altruisme)* charity; **faites-moi** *ou* **ayez la c. de...** please be kind enough to...; *Prov* **c. bien ordonnée commence par soi-même** charity begins at home (**b**) *(don)* charity; **faire la c. à qn** to give money to sb; **demander la c.** to ask for charity; **la c., Messieurs Dames** *(dans la rue)* can you spare some change, please?

charlatan [ʃarlatɑ̃] *nm Péj (mauvais médecin)* quack; *(escroc)* charlatan

Charles [ʃarl] *npr* **C.** Quint Charles the Fifth

charlot [ʃarlo] *nm Fam (personne peu sérieuse)* clown

charlotte [ʃarlɔt] *nf Culin* charlotte; **c. aux fraises/au chocolat** strawberry/chocolate charlotte

charmant, -e [ʃarmɑ̃, -ɑ̃t] *adj (personne, chose, soirée)* charming, delightful; *Ironique* **et voilà qu'il pleut, ah, c'est c.!** and now it's raining, wonderful!

charme[^1] [ʃarm] *nm* (**a**) *(attrait)* charm; **avoir du c.** to have charm; **c'est ce qui en fait le c.** that's what makes it so attractive; **faire du c. a qn** to turn on the charm with sb; **charmes** *(d'une femme)* charms; **vivre de ses charmes** to sell one's charms (**b**) *(magie)* spell; **être/tomber sous le c.** to be/fall under the charm; *Fig* **se porter comme un c.** to be as fit as a fiddle

charme[^2] *nm (arbre)* hornbeam

charmer [ʃarme] *vt* (**a**) *(plaire à)* to charm; **j'ai été charmé de vous rencontrer** it's been a pleasure to meet you (**b**) *(envoûter)* to charm

charmeur, -euse [ʃarmœr, -øz] **1** *nm,f* charmer; **c. de serpents** snake charmer **2** *adj (regard, sourire)* charming

charnel, -elle [ʃarnɛl] *adj* carnal

charnier [ʃarnje] *nm* mass grave

charnière [ʃarnjɛr] *nf (de porte, de fenêtre)* hinge; *Fig* **à la c. de deux grandes périodes** at the junction of two great eras; **époque/œuvre c.** transitional period/work

charnu, -e [ʃarny] *adj (partie du corps, lèvres)* fleshy; *(fruit)* pulpy; *Hum* **la partie charnue de son anatomie** his posterior

charognard [ʃarɔɲar] *nm* (**a**) *Zool* carrion-eater (**b**) *(exploiteur)* vulture

charogne [ʃarɔɲ] *nf* (**a**) *(d'animal)* carrion (**b**) *Fam (homme)* bastard; *(femme)* bitch

charpente [ʃarpɑ̃t] *nf (d'un bâtiment, d'un roman)* framework; *(du corps)* frame; **avoir une solide c.** *(personne)* to be solidly built

charpenterie [ʃarpɑ̃tri] *nf (métier)* carpentry

charpentier [ʃarpɑ̃tje] *nm* carpenter

charpie [ʃarpi] *nf* **mettre qch en c.** to tear sth to shreds; *Fam* **mettre qn en c.** to make mincemeat out of sb

charretier [ʃartje] *nm* **jurer comme un c.** to swear like a trooper

charrette [ʃarɛt] *nf* **(a)** *(véhicule)* cart **(b)** *(de licenciements)* round of redundancies **(c)** *Suisse Fam* **c. de Paul!** that darn Paul!

charrier [66] [ʃarje] **1** *vt* **(a)** *(transporter)* to cart **(b)** *(entraîner)* to carry along **(c)** *Fam (se moquer de)* **c. qn** *Br* to have sb on, *Am* to put sb on; **se faire c.** to be had on **2** *vi Fam (exagérer)* to go too far; **faut pas c.!** *(n'exagère pas)* that's a bit much!

charrue [ʃary] *nf* **(a)** *(pour labourer)* plough; *Fig* **mettre la c. avant les bœufs** to put the cart before the horse **(b)** *Can* snowplough

charte [ʃart] *nf* charter

charter [ʃartɛr] *nm (avion)* **c.** charter plane

chartreux, -euse [ʃartrø, -øz] **1** *nm,f Rel* Carthusian **2** *nf* **chartreuse (a)** *(couvent)* Carthusian monastery **(b)** *(alcool)* Chartreuse

chas [ʃa] *nm* eye

chasse [ʃas] *nf* **(a)** *(activité)* hunting; *(au fusil)* shooting; **aller à la c.** to go hunting/shooting; **la c. est ouverte/ fermée** the shooting season has begun/ended; *Prov* **qui va à la c. perd sa place** if you leave your place someone will take it; **c. à courre** hunting; **c. au lapin** rabbit shooting **(b)** *(événement)* hunt; *(au fusil)* shoot **(c)** *(réserve)* **c. gardée** private game preserve; *Fig (domaine)* preserve **(d)** *(poursuite)* chase; **donner la c. à qn/qch, prendre qn/qch en c.** to give chase to sb/sth; **c. à l'homme** manhunt; *Pol* **c. aux sorcières** witch hunt; **c. au trésor** treasure hunt **(e)** **c. (d'eau)** flush; **tirer la c. (d'eau)** to flush the toilet **(f)** **être en c.** *(chienne, chatte)* to be *Br* on heat *or Am* in heat

châsse [ʃas] *nf Rel* shrine

chassé-croisé *(pl* **chassés-croisés)** [ʃasekrwaze] *nm (de personnes)* comings and goings; *(de conversations)* babble

chasse-neige [ʃasnɛʒ] *nm inv* **(a)** *(engin)* snowplough **(b)** *(en ski)* snowplough; **descendre une piste en c.** to snowplough down a ski slope

chasser [ʃase] **1** *vt* **(a)** *(animaux)* to hunt; **c. le renard/la perdrix** to go foxhunting/partridge shooting **(b)** *(expulser)* to drive *or* chase away **(de** from); *(employé)* to dismiss; *(mouches)* to brush away; *(sujet: vent) (nuages)* to blow away; **je ne veux pas vous c. mais il est tard** I'm not trying to get rid of you but it's getting late; *Fig* **c. qn/qch de son esprit** to dismiss sb/sth from one's thoughts **2** *vi* **(a)** *(aller à la chasse)* to hunt, to go hunting; *(au fusil)* to shoot, to go shooting **(b)** *Aut* to skid

chasseur, -euse [ʃasœr, -øz] **1** *nm* **(a)** *(dans un hôtel) Br* pageboy, *Am* bellboy **(b)** *(avion de chasse)* fighter **(c)** *Mil* **les chasseurs alpins** the mountain light infantry **2** *nm* **(a)** hunter; **c. de primes** bounty hunter; *aussi Fig* **c. de têtes** headhunter

châssis [ʃasi] *nm* **(a)** *(charpente)* frame **(b)** *Art* stretcher **(c)** *(de jardin)* (cold) frame **(d)** *Aut* chassis

chaste [ʃast] *adj* chaste

chastement [ʃastəmɑ̃] *adv* chastely

chasteté [ʃastəte] *nf* chastity

chasuble [ʃazybl] *nf* **(a)** **(robe) c.** *Br* pinafore dress, *Am* jumper **(b)** *Rel* chasuble

chat, chatte [ʃa, ʃat] **1** *nm,f* cat; **petit c.** kitten; *Fam* **mon petit c., ma petite chatte** sweetie; *Fig* **il n'y avait pas un c.** there wasn't a soul there; **appeler un c. un c.** to call a spade a spade; **avoir un c. dans la gorge** to have a

frog in one's throat; **jouer au c. et à la souris avec qn** to play cat-and-mouse with sb; *Prov* **c. échaudé craint l'eau froide** once bitten, twice shy; **quand le c. n'est pas là, les souris dansent** when the cat's away the mice will play; **c. de gouttière** alley cat; **c. persan** Persian (cat); **c. sauvage** wildcat; *Can (raton laveur)* raccoon; **c. siamois** Siamese (cat) **2** *nf* **chatte** *Vulg (sexe féminin)* pussy

châtaigne [ʃatɛɲ] *nf* **(a)** *(fruit)* (sweet) chestnut **(b)** *très Fam (coup de poing)* clout; **flanquer une c. à qn** to clout sb; **se prendre une c.** *(décharge)* to get a shock

châtaignier [ʃatɛɲe] *nm (arbre, bois)* chestnut

châtain [ʃatɛ̃] **1** *adj (cheveux)* (chestnut-)brown; *(personne)* brown-haired **2** *nm* chestnut brown

château, -x [ʃato] *nm* **(a)** *(forteresse)* castle; *(manoir)* mansion; *(de famille aristocratique)* stately home; *(palais)* palace; **les châteaux de la Loire** the châteaux of the Loire; *Fig* **bâtir des châteaux en Espagne** to build castles in the sky; **c. de cartes** house of cards; **c. d'eau** water tower; **c. fort** castle **(b)** *(exploitation vinicole)* château; **mis en bouteille au c.** *(sur bouteille)* bottled at source

châtelain [ʃatlɛ̃] *nm (au Moyen Âge)* lord of the manor; *(propriétaire d'un château)* château owner

châtelaine [ʃatlɛn] *nf (au Moyen Âge)* lady of the manor; *(propriétaire d'un château)* (woman) château owner; *(épouse du propriétaire)* wife of a château owner

chat-huant *(pl* **chats-huants)** [ʃayɑ̃] *nm* tawny owl

châtié, -e [ʃatje] *adj (style)* polished; *(langage)* refined

châtier [66] [ʃatje] *vt Litt (personne)* to chastise; *Prov* **qui aime bien châtie bien** spare the rod and spoil the child

chatière [ʃatjɛr] *nf* **(a)** *(pour chat)* cat flap **(b)** *(pour aération)* ventilation hole

châtiment [ʃatimɑ̃] *nm* **(a)** *Litt* chastisement **(b)** **c. corporel** corporal punishment

chaton¹ [ʃatɔ̃] *nm* **(a)** *(petit chat)* kitten **(b)** *Bot* catkin

chaton² *nm* **(a)** *(d'une bague)* bezel **(b)** *(pierre)* stone

chatouille [ʃatuj] *nf* **faire des chatouilles à qn** to tickle sb; **craindre les chatouilles** to be ticklish

chatouiller [ʃatuje] *vt* to tickle; *Fig (curiosité)* to arouse; *(amour-propre)* to flatter; **ah, ça chatouille!** oh, that tickles!

chatouilleux, -euse [ʃatujø, -øz] *adj* ticklish; *Fig* sensitive **(sur** about)

chatoyant, -e [ʃatwajɑ̃, -ɑ̃t] *adj* shimmering; *(pierre, imagination)* sparkling

chatoyer [32] [ʃatwaje] *vi* to shimmer; *(pierre)* to sparkle

châtrer [ʃatre] *vt (homme, taureau)* to castrate; *(étalon)* to geld; *(chat)* to neuter

chatte [ʃat] *nf voir* **chat**

chatterton [ʃatɛrtɔ̃] *nm Br* insulating tape, *Am* friction tape

chaud, -e [ʃo, ʃod] **1** *adj* **(a)** *(modérément)* warm; *(intensément)* hot; *Fig (voix)* sultry; *(couleur)* warm; **la soupe est toute chaude** the soup is piping hot; **l'été est être c.** it'll be a hot summer; *Fig* there'll be a lot of unrest this summer; **l'alerte fut chaude** it was a close thing; **une nouvelle toute chaude** some hot news **(b)** *(passionné) (discussion)* heated; *(partisan)* keen; **elle n'est pas chaude pour le projet** she's not keen on the plans **2** *adv* **j'aime manger c.** I like my food hot **3** *nm (modéré)* warmth; *(intense)* heat; **garder** *ou* **tenir qch au c.** to keep sth warm; **chez soi, au c.** at home, in the warmth; **avoir c.** to be *or* feel hot; *Fam (échapper de justesse)* to have a narrow escape; **il fait c.** it's hot; *Fig* **cela ne me fait ni c. ni froid** it's all the same to me; **interroger les spectateurs à c.** to question the audience on the spot; **attraper un c. et froid** to catch a chill

chaudement [ʃodmɑ̃] *adv* *(s'habiller, féliciter, recommander)* warmly

chaudière [ʃodjɛr] *nf* *(de chauffage)* boiler; **c. à mazout/à gaz** oil-fired/gas boiler

chaudron [ʃodrɔ̃] *nm* cauldron

chaudronnier, -ère [ʃodrɔnje, -ɛr] *nm,f* boiler maker

chauffage [ʃofaʒ] *nm* *(d'une pièce, d'un bâtiment)* heating; *(appareils)* heating (system); *(dans une voiture)* heater; **c. à l'électricité/au gaz/au mazout** electric/gas/oil-fired heating; **c. central** central heating

chauffagiste [ʃofaʒist] *nm* heating engineer

chauffant, -e [ʃofɑ̃, -ɑ̃t] *adj voir* **couverture, plaque**

chauffard [ʃofar] *nm* reckless driver

chauffe-biberon *(pl* **chauffe-biberons)** [ʃofbibrɔ̃] *nm* bottle-warmer

chauffe-eau [ʃofo] *nm inv* water heater; **c. électrique** immersion heater

chauffe-plat *(pl* **chauffe-plats)** [ʃofpla] *nm* hot plate

chauffer [ʃofe] **1** *vt (pièce, bâtiment)* to heat (up); *(moteur)* to warm up; **c. une maison au gaz** to heat a house with gas; **la chambre n'est pas chauffée** there's no heating in the bedroom; *Fig* **c. son public** to warm up one's audience
2 *vi* **(a)** *(devenir chaud)* to heat up; **ce radiateur chauffe bien/mal** this radiator gives out/doesn't give out a lot of heat; **faire c. qch, mettre qch à c.** to heat sth up **(b)** *(s'échauffer) (moteur)* to overheat **(c)** *Fam* **ça va c. s'il est en retard!** there'll be trouble if he's late!; **tu chauffes!** *(dans un jeu)* you're getting warmer!
3 se chauffer *vpr* to warm oneself; **se c. (les muscles)** to warm up; **se c. au mazout/à l'électricité** to have oil fired/electric heating

chaufferette [ʃofrɛt] *nf (pour les pieds)* footwarmer

chaufferie [ʃofri] *nf* boiler room

chauffeur [ʃofœr] *nm (de voiture, de bus)* driver; *(employé)* chauffeur; **les chauffeurs du dimanche** Sunday drivers; **c. de camion** *Br* lorry driver, *Am* truck driver; **c. de taxi** taxi driver

chauffeuse [ʃoføz] *nf (fauteuil)* low armless chair

chauler [ʃole] *vt (murs)* to whitewash; *(terres)* to treat with lime

chaume [ʃom] *nm* **(a)** *(pour toits)* thatch **(b)** *(des céréales)* stubble

chaumière [ʃomjɛr] *nf (maison pauvre)* cottage; *(maison à toit de chaume)* thatched cottage

chaussée [ʃose] *nf (route)* roadway

chausse-pied *(pl* **chausse-pieds)** [ʃospje] *nm* shoehorn

chausser [ʃose] *vt* **1 (a)** *(chaussures, lunettes, skis)* to put on; **chaussé de pantoufles** wearing slippers; **elle chausse du 37** she takes a size 37 **(b)** *(mettre des chaussures à)* to put shoes on **(c)** *(aller à)* to fit; **chaussures qui chaussent bien** shoes that fit well
2 se chausser *vpr (mettre ses chaussures)* to put one's shoes on

chausses [ʃos] *nfpl (vêtement)* breeches

chaussette [ʃosɛt] *nf* sock; **en chaussettes** in one's socks; **laisser tomber qn comme une vieille c.** to cast sb aside like an old rag

chausseur [ʃosœr] *nm (magasin)* shoe shop; *(fabricant)* shoe manufacturer

chausson [ʃosɔ̃] *nm* **(a)** *(pantoufle)* slipper; *(de danse)* ballet shoe; *(de bébé)* bootee **(b)** *Culin* **c. aux pommes** apple *Br* turnover *or Am* popover

chaussure [ʃosyr] *nf* shoe; **(l'industrie de) la c.** the shoe industry; **chaussures de ville/de sport/habillées** town/sports/dress shoes; **chaussures à lacets** lace-up shoes;

chaussures de marche *ou* **de montagne** walking boots; **chaussures montantes** ankle boots; **chaussures de ski** ski boots; **chaussures à talons** high-heeled shoes; *Fig* **trouver c. à son pied** to find the right woman/man

chauve [ʃov] **1** *adj* bald
2 *nm* bald(-headed) man

chauve-souris *(pl* **chauves-souris)** [ʃovsuri] *nf* bat

chauvin, -e [ʃovɛ̃, -in] **1** *adj* chauvinistic
2 *nm,f* chauvinist

chauvinisme [ʃovinism] *nm* chauvinism

chaux [ʃo] *nf* lime; **blanchir un mur à la c.** to whitewash a wall; **c. vive** quicklime

chavirer [ʃavire] **1** *vi* **(a)** *(bateau)* to capsize; **faire c. un bateau** to capsize a boat **(b)** *(tourner)* **tout chavire autour de moi** everything's spinning
2 *vt (bouleverser)* to overwhelm

check-up [tʃɛkœp] *nm inv Méd* check-up; **se faire faire un c.** to have a check-up

chef [ʃɛf] *nm* **(a)** *(d'un parti politique, d'une bande)* leader; *(d'une tribu)* chief; *Fam (patron)* boss; **ingénieur/rédacteur en c.** chief engineer/editor; **se débrouiller comme un c.** to be getting on very well; **c. d'atelier** (shop) foreman; **c. d'entreprise** company head; **c. d'État** head of state; **c. de famille** head of the family; **c. de file** leader; **c. de gare** station manager; **le c. du gouvernement** the head of government; **c. d'orchestre** conductor; **c. de service** departmental head **(b)** *(cuisinier)* chef **(c)** *Jur* **c. d'accusation** charge **(d)** *(tête)* head; **faire qch de son propre c.** to do sth on one's own authority

chef-d'œuvre *(pl* **chefs-d'œuvre)** [ʃɛdœvr] *nm* masterpiece

chef-lieu *(pl* **chefs-lieux)** [ʃɛfljø] *nm* = administrative centre of a département

cheik(h) [ʃɛk] *nm* sheik(h)

chelem [ʃlɛm] *nm Sp* grand c. grand slam

chemin [ʃəmɛ̃] *nm* **(a)** *(route étroite)* path, track; **c. de grande randonnée** hiking trail; **c. de ronde** parapet walk, **c. de terre** track; **c. de traverse** path across the fields **(b)** *(itinéraire)* way **(de** to); *Fig (de la gloire, du bonheur)* road **(de** to); **en c.** on the way; **se mettre en c.** to set out *or* off; **nous ne pouvons pas nous arrêter en si bon c.** we can't give up now when we're doing so well; **ne pas y aller par quatre chemins** to get straight to the point; **prendre le c. des écoliers** to take the long way round; **suivre le droit c.** to stay on the straight and narrow **(c)** *(distance)* way; *aussi Fig* **avoir beaucoup de c. à faire** to have a long way to go; **nous avons fait la moitié du c. ensemble/à pied** we went half the way together/on foot; *Fig* **faire son c.** *(idée)* to gain ground **(d)** *Ordinat* path; **c. d'accès** path

chemin de fer *(pl* **chemins de fer)** [ʃəmɛ̃dfɛr] *nm Br* railway, *Am* railroad; *Ordinat (affichage)* thumbnail; **les chemins de fer** *(société d'exploitation) Br* the railway, *Am* the railroad

cheminée [ʃəmine] *nf* **(a)** *(dans une maison)* fireplace; *(dessus)* mantelpiece **(b)** *(conduit) (de maison, d'usine)* chimney; *(de bateau à vapeur)* funnel **(c)** *Géol* chimney

cheminement [ʃəminmɑ̃] *nm (de personnes)* movement; *Fig* **le c. de la pensée** the development of thought

cheminer [ʃəmine] *vi (personne)* to make one's way; *Fig (idée)* to gain ground

cheminot [ʃəmino] *nm Br* railwayman, *Am* railroader

chemise [ʃəmiz] *nf* **(a)** *(vêtement)* shirt; **c. à manches longues/courtes** long-/short-sleeved shirt; *Fig* **changer de qch comme de c.** to change sth at the drop of a hat; **c. de nuit** *(de femme)* nightdress; *(d'homme)* nightshirt **(b)** *(classeur)* folder

chemisette [ʃəmizɛt] *nf (d'homme)* short-sleeved shirt

chemisier [ʃəmizje] *nm* **(a)** *(corsage)* blouse **(b)** *(fabricant)* shirt-maker; *(marchand)* men's outfitter

chenal, -aux [ʃənal, -o] *nm (d'une rivière, d'un port)* channel

chenapan [ʃənapɑ̃] *nm Vieilli* scoundrel

chêne [ʃɛn] *nm* oak; **table en c.** massif solid oak table; **c. vert** holm oak

chêne-liège *(pl* **chênes-lièges)** [ʃɛnljeʒ] *nm* cork oak

chenet [ʃənɛ] *nm* firedog

chenil [ʃənil] *nm* **(a)** *(abri, élevage)* kennels **(b)** *Suisse (désordre)* shambles

chenille [ʃənij] *nf* **(a)** *(insecte)* caterpillar **(b)** *(de char, d'autoneige)* caterpillar track; **véhicule à chenilles** tracked vehicle **(c)** *(tissu)* chenille

chenu, -e [ʃəny] *adj Litt (personne, tête)* hoary; *(arbre)* leafless

cheptel [ʃɛptɛl] *nm (d'un agriculteur)* livestock

chèque [ʃɛk] *nm* **c.** **(bancaire)** *Br* cheque, *Am* check; **c. de 100 euros** cheque for 100 euros; **faire un c. à qn** to write sb a cheque; **payer qch par c.** to pay for sth by cheque; **c. barré** crossed cheque; **c. en blanc** blank cheque; *Fam* **c. en bois** rubber cheque; **c. sans provision** bad cheque; **j'ai fait un c. sans provision** my cheque bounced; **c. de voyage** traveller's cheque

chèque-cadeau *(pl* **chèques-cadeaux)** [ʃɛkkado] *nm* gift token

chèque-repas *(pl* **chèques-repas)** [ʃɛkrəpa], **chèque-restaurant** *(pl* **chèques-restaurant)** [ʃɛkrɛstɔrɑ̃] *nm* luncheon voucher

chéquier [ʃekje] *nm Br* cheque book, *Am* check book

cher, -ère [ʃɛr] **1** *adj* **(a)** *(coûteux)* dear, expensive; *Fam* **pas c.** cheap; **la vie est chère en ville** it's expensive to live in town **(b)** *(aimé)* dear; *Litt* **être c. à qn** to be dear to sb; **c'est mon vœu le plus c.** it's my dearest wish; **il a retrouvé sa chère maison/son c.** bureau he's back in his beloved house/office; **C. Monsieur** *(dans une lettre)* Dear Mr X; *(officiel)* Dear Sir
2 *adv* **payer qch cher./trop c.** to pay a high price/too much for sth; *Fam* **je l'ai eu pour pas c.** I got it cheap; **coûter c.** to cost a lot; **je donnerais c. pour savoir ce qu'il leur a dit** I'd give anything to know what he said to them
3 *nm,f* **mon c., ma chère** my dear

chercher [ʃɛrʃe] **1** *vt* **(a)** *(objet, personne, emploi, solution)* to look for; *(dans un dictionnaire)* to look up; *(dans ses souvenirs)* to try to think of; **c. qn du regard** *ou* **des yeux** to look around for sb; **c. ses mots** to search for words; **cherche!** *(à un chien)* fetch!; *Fig* **où va-t-il donc c. tout cela?** where on earth does he get that from?; **il l'a bien cherché** he was asking for it; **c. midi à quatorze heures** to look for problems where there are none **(b)** *(prendre)* **aller/venir c. qn/qch** to go/come and) fetch sb/sth **(c)** *(essayer)* **c. à faire qch** to try to do sth **(d)** *Fam (atteindre)* **cela va c. dans les 3 000 euros** you're talking about something like 3,000 euros **(e)** *Fam (provoquer)* to get at; **tu me cherches?** are you looking for a fight?
2 **se chercher** *vpr (chercher son identité)* to try to find oneself

chercheur, -euse [ʃɛrʃœr, -øz] *nm,f* **(a)** *(scientifique)* researcher **(b)** **c. d'or** gold digger

chère [ʃɛr] *nf Litt* **aimer la bonne c.** to be a lover of good food

chèrement [ʃɛrmɑ̃] *adv* **vendre c. sa peau** to sell one's life dearly

chéri, -e [ʃeri] **1** *adj* dear
2 *nm,f* darling; **mon c., ma chérie** darling

chérir [ʃerir] *vt Litt* to cherish

cherra *etc voir* **choir**

cherry *(pl* **cherrys** *ou* **cherries)** [ʃeri] *nm* cherry brandy

cherté [ʃɛrte] *nf* high cost; **la c. de la vie** the high cost of living

chérubin [ʃerybɛ̃] *nm aussi Fig* cherub

chétif, -ive [ʃetif, -iv] *adj (personne)* puny, sickly; *(arbuste)* stunted

cheval, -aux [ʃəval, -o] *nm* **(a)** *(animal)* horse; *Péj (femme)* carthorse; **à c.** on horseback; **monter à c.** to ride; *aussi Fig* **être à c. sur** **qch** to straddle sth; **être à c. sur l'étiquette** to be a stickler for etiquette; *Fam* **ce n'est pas un mauvais c.** he's not such a bad sort; **monter sur ses grands chevaux** to get on one's high horse; **petits chevaux** = type of board game; **c. d'arçons** (vaulting) horse; **c. à bascule** rocking horse; **c'est son c. de bataille** that's her hobby-horse; **chevaux de bois** *Br* roundabout, *Am* carousel; **c. de course** racehorse; **c. de labour** workhorse; **c. de trait** carthorse **(b)** *Aut* horsepower; **une automobile de 20 chevaux** a 20-horsepower car

chevalerie [ʃəvalri] *nf* **(a)** *(dignité)* knighthood **(b)** *(institution)* chivalry

chevalet [ʃəvalɛ] *nm* **(a)** *(de peintre)* easel; *(de menuisier, de charpentier)* trestle **(b)** *Mus (de violon)* bridge

chevalier [ʃəvalje] *nm* **(a)** *(seigneur)* knight; **c. servant** faithful admirer **(b)** **c. de la Légion d'honneur** chevalier

chevalière [ʃəvaljɛr] *nf* signet ring

chevalin, -e [ʃəvalɛ̃, -in] *adj* equine; *Fig (traits)* horsey

cheval-vapeur [ʃəvalvapœr] *(pl* **chevaux-vapeur** [ʃəvovapœr]) *nm* horsepower

chevauchée [ʃəvoʃe] *nf (course)* ride

chevaucher [ʃəvoʃe] **1** *vt (mur, chaise)* to straddle; *Litt (cheval, âne)* to ride
2 *vi Litt* to ride
3 **se chevaucher** *vpr* to overlap

chevelu, -e [ʃəvly] *adj Péj* long-haired

chevelure [ʃəvlyr] *nf* (head of) hair; **femme à la c. rousse/blonde** red-haired/blonde woman

chevet [ʃəvɛ] *nm* **(a)** *(tête de lit)* bedhead; **rester au c. de qn** to stay at sb's bedside **(b)** *Archit (d'une église)* chevet

cheveu, -x [ʃəvø] *nm* **(a)** *(poil)* hair; **avoir le c. terne** to have dull hair; **c. blanc** a grey hair; **arriver comme un c. sur la soupe** to come at a bad time; **il s'en est fallu d'un c. qu'il n'éclate de rire** he very nearly burst out laughing; **rater qch d'un c.** to miss sth by a whisker; **à un c. près, je ratais mon train** I caught my train by a hair's breadth **(b)** *Fam* **cheveux** hair; **avoir les cheveux longs/courts** to have long/short hair; **un vieillard à cheveux blancs** a white-haired old man; **argument tiré par les cheveux** far-fetched argument; **cheveux d'ange** *(pâtes)* angel-hair pasta

cheville [ʃəvij] *nf* **(a)** *(partie du corps)* ankle; *Fig* **il ne vous arrive pas à la c.** he can't hold a candle to you; *Fam Péj* **tu as les chevilles qui enflent** you're getting too big for your *Br* boots *ou Am* britches **(b)** *(pour accrocher)* peg; *(pour boucher un trou)* plug; *(de violon, de guitare)* peg; *Fam* **être en c. avec qn** to be in cahoots with sb; *Fig* **c. ouvrière** mainspring

chèvre [ʃɛvr] **1** *nf* goat; *Fam* **devenir c.** to go round the bend; *Fam* **rendre qn c.** to drive sb round the bend
2 *nm* goat's cheese

chevreau, -x [ʃəvro] *nm* kid; **gants en c.** kid gloves

chèvrefeuille [ʃɛvrəfœj] *nm* honeysuckle

chevreuil [ʃəvrœj] *nm* roe deer; *Can* deer; *(gibier)* venison

chevron [ʃəvrɔ̃] *nm* **(a)** *Constr (d'un toit)* rafter **(b)** *Mil* stripe, chevron **(c)** *(motif)* tissu à chevrons herringbone-pattern material

chevronné, -e [ʃəvrɔne] *adj (qui a de l'expérience)* experienced

chevrotant, -e [ʃəvrɔtɑ̃, -ɑ̃t] *adj (voix)* quavering

chevroter [ʃəvrɔte] *vi (voix)* to quaver

chevrotine [ʃəvrɔtin] *nf* buckshot

chewing-gum *(pl* **chewing-gums)** [ʃwiŋgɔm] *nm* chewing-gum

chez [ʃe] *prép* **(a)** *(dans la maison de)* il n'est pas **c.** lui he's not at home, he's not in; **elle est rentrée c.** elle she's gone home; **faites comme c.** vous make yourself at home; **je vais c.** mon trère I'm going to my brother's; **venez c.** nous come to our place; **il vit c.** nous he lives with us; **aller c.** le dentiste to go to the dentist; **chez…** *(sur une lettre)* c/o… **(b)** *(en, dans)* c'est devenu une habitude **c.** moi it's become a habit with me; **ce que j'admire c.** cet homme, c'est… what I admire about the man is…; **c.** les Espagnols, on dine tard the Spaniards have dinner late **(c)** *(au temps de)* during the time of **(d)** *(parmi)* among; **cette expression** est courante **c.** les jeunes this expression is common among young people

chez-soi [ʃeswa] *nm inv* son petit **c.** one's own little home

chialer [ʃjale] *vi très Fam* to blubber

chiant, -e [ʃjɑ̃, -ɑ̃t] *adj très Fam* damned annoying

chianti [kjɑ̃ti] *nm* Chianti

chiasse [ʃjas] *nf Vulg* avoir la **c.** *(la diarrhée)* to have the shits; *(avoir peur)* to be shit-scared

chic [ʃik] **1** *adj inv* **(a)** *(élégant)* stylish, smart; **les gens c.** the smart set **(b)** *Fam Vieilli (aimable)* decent **2** *nm* **(a)** *(savoir-faire)* avoir le **c.** pour faire qch to have the knack of doing sth **(b)** *(élégance)* style; **bon c. bon genre** *Br* ≃ Sloany, *Am* ≃ preppy **3** *exclam Fam Vieilli* **c. (alors)!** great!

Chicago [ʃikago] *n* Chicago

chicaner [ʃikane] **1** *vi (chercher querelle à)* to quibble with **(sur** about) **2** chicaner sur *vt ind* to quibble over **3 se chicaner** *vpr* to squabble

chicaneur, -euse [ʃikanœr, -øz], **chicanier, -ère** [ʃikanje, -ɛr] *nm,f* quibbler

chiche [ʃiʃ] *adj (repas)* scanty; *(personne)* mean; **être c. de louanges** to be sparing in one's praise; *Fam* **tu n'es pas c. d'y aller!** I bet you don't go!; *Fam* **c.!** *(pour défier)* I dare you!; *(pour relever le défi)* you're on!

chichement [ʃiʃmɑ̃] *adv* meanly

chichi [ʃiʃi] *nm Fam* **faire du c.** ou **des chichis** *(se donner des airs)* to put on airs; *(compliquer les choses)* to make a fuss; **repas sans c.** informal meal

chicorée [ʃikɔre] *nf* **(a)** *(plante)* chicory; **(frisée) c. sauvage** chicory **(b)** *(en poudre)* chicory

chicot [ʃiko] *nm (dent)* stump

chiée [ʃje] *nf très Fam* **(toute) une c.** de a hell of a lot of

chien, chienne [ʃjɛ̃, ʃjɛn] **1** *nm,f* dog, *f* bitch; **jeune c.** puppy, pup; **(attention) c.** méchant *(sur écriteau)* beware of the dog; **traiter qn comme un c.** to treat sb like a dog; *Fam* **quel temps de c.!** what foul weather!; *Fam* **vie de c.** dog's life; **être comme c.** et chat to fight like cat and dog; **entre c.** et loup at dusk; **se regarder en chiens de faïence** to stare at one another; **c. d'arrêt** pointer; **c. d'aveugle** guide dog; **c. de berger** sheepdog; **c. de chasse** retriever; **c. de garde** guard dog; **c. policier** police dog; **c. de race** pedigree dog; **c. savant** *(dans un cirque)* performing dog; *Fig* performing monkey; **c. de traîneau** husky **2** *nm* **(a)** *Fam (style)* **avoir du c.** to have a certain

something **(b)** *(d'un fusil)* hammer; **dormir en c.** de fusil to sleep curled up

chiendent [ʃjɛ̃dɑ̃] *nm* couch grass; **brosse en** ou **de c.** scrubbing brush; **pousser comme du c.** to sprout up

chien-loup *(pl* **chiens-loups)** [ʃjɛ̃lu] *nm* wolfhound

chienne [ʃjɛn] *nf voir* **chien**

chier [66] [ʃje] *vi Vulg* to shit, to crap; **faire c.** qn *(énerver)* to piss sb off; *(ennuyer)* to bore sb shitless; **se faire c.** *(s'ennuyer)* to be bored shitless; **se faire c.** (à faire qch) *(avoir du mal)* to bust a gut (doing sth); **je me suis fait c.** à l'attendre I did myself in waiting for him

chiffe [ʃif] *nf Fam* c'est une **c.** molle he's a drip

chiffon [ʃifɔ̃] *nm* rag; **c.** à poussière duster; **passer un coup de c.** to have a dust; **passer un coup de c.** sur qch to give sth a dust; *Fam* **parler chiffons** to talk clothes

chiffonner [ʃifɔne] **1** *vt* **(a)** *(robe, morceau de papier)* to crumple **(b)** *Fam (ennuyer)* to bother **2 se chiffonner** *vpr* to crumple

chiffonnier, -ère [ʃifɔnje, -ɛr] **1** *nm,f* rag picker; **se disputer comme des chiffonniers** to go at it hammer and tongs **2** *nm (meuble)* chiffonier

chiffrable [ʃifrabl] *adj* facilement/difficilement **c.** easy/difficult to calculate; **ne pas être c.** to be impossible to calculate

chiffre [ʃifr] *nm* **(a)** *(nombre)* figure, number; **chiffres arabes/romains** Arabic/Roman numerals; **nombre à trois chiffres** three-figure number; *Ordinat* **c. binaire** binary digit; *Ordinat* **c. ASCII** ASCII number **(b)** *(total)* total, **c. d'affaires (annuel)** *(annual)* turnover; **faire un c. d'affaires de 2 millions d'euros** to have a turnover of 2 million euros

chiffrement [ʃifrəmɑ̃] *nm Ordinat* **c. de données** data encryption

chiffrer [ʃifre] **1** *vt* **(a)** *(montant, coût)* to work out, to calculate; *(réparations)* to assess **(b)** **message** chiffré coded message **2 se chiffrer** *vpr* **se c.** à to add up to, to amount to

chignole [ʃiɲɔl] *nf* hand drill; *(électrique)* electric drill

chignon [ʃiɲɔ̃] *nm* bun, chignon; **se faire un c.** to put one's hair in a bun

chihuahua [ʃiwawa] *nm* chihuahua

chiite [ʃiit] *adj & nm,f Rel* Shiite

Chili [ʃili] *nm* le **C.** Chile

chili (con carne) [ʃili(kɔnkarne)] *nm Culin* chilli (con carne)

chilien, -enne [ʃiljɛ̃, -ɛn] **1** *adj* Chilean **2** *nm,f* **C.** Chilean

chimère [ʃimɛr] *nf (monstre)* chimera; *Fig (rêve)* pipe dream

chimie [ʃimi] *nf* chemistry

chimiothérapie [ʃimjoterapi] *nf Méd* chemotherapy; **faire une c.** to have chemotherapy

chimique [ʃimik] *adj* chemical

chimiste [ʃimist] *nmf* chemist; **ingénieur c.** chemical engineer

chimpanzé [ʃɛ̃pɑ̃ze] *nm* chimpanzee

chinchilla [ʃɛ̃ʃila] *nm (animal, fourrure)* chinchilla; **veste en c.** chinchilla jacket

Chine [ʃin] *nf* la **C.** China

chiné, -e [ʃine] *adj (tissu)* flecked

chiner [ʃine] **1** *vt Fam (personne)* to kid **2** *vi* to hunt for second-hand goods

chinetoque [ʃintɔk] *nmf très Fam* Chink, = racist term used to refer to a Chinese

chinois, -e [ʃinwa, -az] **1** *adj* Chinese **2** *nm,f* C. Chinese; **les C.** the Chinese **3** *nm* (a) *(langue)* Chinese; *Fam Fig* **c'est du c.** it's all Greek to me (b) *(ustensile)* conical strainer

chinoiserie [ʃinwazri] *nf* (a) *(objet)* Chinese curio (b) *Fam* **chinoiseries** *(complications)* pointless complications

chintz [ʃints] *nm* chintz; **des rideaux en c.** chintz curtains

chiot [ʃjo] *nm* puppy, pup

chiottes [ʃjɔt] *nfpl très Fam Br* bog, *Am* john

chiper [ʃipe] *vt Fam* to pinch, to swipe

chipie [ʃipi] *nf Fam* minx

chipolata [ʃipɔlata] *nf* chipolata (sausage)

chipoter [ʃipɔte] *vi* (a) *(picorer)* to pick at one's food (b) *(contester)* to quibble (**sur** about)

chips [ʃips] *nf Br* crisp, *Am* chip; **des (pommes) c.** *Br* crisps, *Am* chips

chique [ʃik] *nf* (a) *(de tabac)* quid (b) *Belg* sweet

chiqué [ʃike] *nm Fam* **faire du c.** to put on an act; **c'est du c.** it's all put on

chiquenaude [ʃiknod] *nf* flick; **d'une c.**, **il l'envoya sur le bureau** he flicked it onto the desk

chiquer [ʃike] **1** *vt* to chew **2** *vi* to chew tobacco

chiromancien, -enne [kirɔmɑ̃sjɛ̃, -ɛn] *nm,f* palmist

chirurgical, -e, -aux, -ales [ʃiryrʒikal, -o] *adj* surgical

chirurgie [ʃiryrʒi] *nf* surgery; **c. esthétique** plastic surgery

chirurgien [ʃiryrʒjɛ̃] *nm* surgeon

chirurgien-dentiste (*pl* **chirurgiens-dentistes**) [ʃiryrʒjɛ̃dɑ̃tist] *nm* dental surgeon

chiure [ʃjyr] *nf* **c. de mouche** fly-speck

ch-l. (*abrév* **chef-lieu**) = administrative centre of a "département"

chleuh, -e [ʃlø] *adj & nm,f très Fam* Kraut, = offensive term used to refer to a German

chlinguer [ʃlɛ̃ge] *vi très Fam* to stink

chlorate [klɔrat] *nm Chim* chlorate

chlore [klɔr] *nm* chlorine

chlorer [klɔre] *vt* to chlorinate

chlorhydrique [klɔridrik] *adj (acide)* hydrochloric

chlorofluorocarbure [klɔrɔflyɔrɔkarbyr] *nm Chim* chlorofluorocarbon

chloroforme [klɔrɔfɔrm] *nm* chloroform

chloroformer [klɔrɔfɔrme] *vt* to chloroform

chlorophylle [klɔrɔfil] *nf* chlorophyll

chlorure [klɔryr] *nm Chim* chloride; **c. de sodium** sodium chloride

chnoque [ʃnɔk] = **schnock**

choc [ʃɔk] *nm* (a) *(coup)* impact; *Fig (conflit)* clash; *(forte impression)* impact; *Écon* **c. pétrolier** oil crisis (b) *Méd* shock; **c. opératoire** post-operative shock (**c**) *(émotion brutale)* shock; **faire un c. à qn** to give sb a shock; **être en état de c.** to be in a state of shock; **être sous le c.** to be in shock (**d**) *(équipe de choc)* team of troubleshooters; **troupes de c.** shock troops

-choc [ʃɔk] *suff* **image-c.** shocking image; **prix-chocs** *(sur une vitrine)* rock-bottom prices

chochotte [ʃɔʃɔt] *nf Fam Péj* la-di-da type; *(homme)* namby-pamby; **faire sa c.** to put on airs

chocolat [ʃɔkɔla] **1** *nm* (a) *(produit)* chocolate; **gâteau au c.** chocolate cake; **c. blanc** white chocolate; **un c. (chaud)** a hot chocolate; **c. à cuire** cooking chocolate; **c. au lait** milk chocolate; **c. noir** *ou* **à croquer** plain *or* dark chocolate; **c. aux noisettes** hazelnut chocolate; **c. en poudre** drinking chocolate (b) *(bonbon)* chocolate **2** *adj inv* chocolate-coloured; *Fam* **être c.** to have lost out

chocolaté, -e [ʃɔkɔlate] *adj* chocolate

chocolatier, -ère [ʃɔkɔlatje, -ɛr] **1** *nm,f (fabricant)* chocolate-maker; *(vendeur)* chocolate-seller **2** *adj (industrie)* chocolate

chocottes [ʃɔkɔt] *nfpl Fam* **avoir les c.** to have the jitters

chœur [kœr] *nm* choir; *(d'opéra)* chorus; **les chœurs** the chorus; **chanter en c.** to sing in chorus; **répétez tous en c.** repeat all together now

choir [14] [ʃwar] *vi (aux* **être**) *Litt (tomber)* to fall; **se laisser c.** to sink down; *Fam* **laisser c.** qn to drop sb

choisi, -e [ʃwazi] *adj* (a) *(sélectionné)* **morceaux choisis de...** selected extracts from... (b) *(langage, termes)* careful

choisir [ʃwazir] *vt* to choose, to pick; **c. de faire qch** to choose to do sth; **il a bien choisi son moment!** he really picked his moment!; **à toi de c.**, **cette fois** it's your turn to choose now

choix [ʃwa] *nm* choice; **un grand c. de cravates** a wide choice *or* selection of ties; **avoir le c.** to have a choice; **faire son c.** to take one's pick; **faire le bon c.** to make the right choice; **mon c. est fait** I've made my choice; **laisser le c. à qn** to let sb choose; **viande ou poisson au c.** *(sur un menu)* choice of meat or fish; **de premier c.** top-grade; **de second c.** second-grade

choléra [kɔlera] *nm* cholera; **avoir le c.** to have cholera

cholestérol [kɔlesterɔl] *nm* cholesterol; **taux de c.** cholesterol level; *Fam* **avoir du c.** to have a high cholesterol level

cholestérolémie [kɔlesterɔlemi] *nf Méd* cholesterol level

chômage [ʃomaʒ] *nm* unemployment; **être au c.** to be unemployed, to be out of work; **toucher le c.** to claim unemployment benefit; **s'inscrire au c.** to register as unemployed; **le c. des jeunes** youth unemployment; **être en c. technique** to have been laid off

chômé, -e [ʃome] *adj* **jour c.** public holiday, *Br* bank holiday

chômer [ʃome] *vi* **vous n'avez pas chômé!** you certainly haven't been idle!

chômeur, -euse [ʃomœr, -øz] *nm,f* unemployed person; **les chômeurs** the unemployed

chope [ʃɔp] *nf (récipient)* beer mug; *(contenu)* ≃ pint

choper [ʃɔpe] *vt Fam* (a) *(arrêter, prendre)* to nab; **se faire c.** to get nabbed (b) *(maladie)* to catch

chopine [ʃɔpin] *nf Fam (bouteille)* half-litre bottle; **tu viens boire une c.?** are you coming for a drink?

choquant, -e [ʃɔkɑ̃, -ɑ̃t] *adj* shocking

choquer [ʃɔke] *vt* (a) *(indigner)* to shock (b) *(traumatiser)* **c. qn** to shake sb badly

choral, -e, -aux *ou* **-als, -ales** [kɔral] **1** *adj* choral **2** *nf* **chorale** *(club)* choral society; *(chanteurs)* choir

chorégraphe [kɔregraf] *nmf* choreographer

chorégraphie [kɔregrafi] *nf* choreography; **faire la c. d'un spectacle** to choreograph a show

chorégraphique [kɔregrafik] *adj* choreographic

choriste [kɔrist] *nmf* choir member; *(d'église)* chorister; *(d'opéra)* chorus member; *(d'un chanteur)* backing singer

chorizo [tʃorizo] *nm* chorizo

chorus [kɔrys] *nm (de jazz)* chorus

chose [ʃoz] **1** *nf* (**a**) *(objet, parole, événement)* thing; **il s'est passé une c.** incroyable something unbelievable has happened; **je vais te dire une c.** I'm going to tell you something; **il a très bien pris la c.** he took it very well (**b**) *(locutions)* **avant toute c.** first of all; **les choses étant ce qu'elles sont** with things as they are, **aller au fond des choses** to get to the heart of the matter; **bien faire les choses** to do things in style; **il ne fait pas les choses à moitié** he doesn't do things by halves; **parler de choses d'autres** to talk about this and that; **c'est c. faite** it's done; **de deux choses l'une, soit il parle, soit…** either he talks or…; **c. curieuse, personne n'en savait rien** curiously enough, nobody knew anything about it; **et, c. rare, il a demandé pardon** he apologized for once; **dites bien des choses de ma part à…** remember me to… **2** *nm Fam (truc)* whatsit, thingummy; **Monsieur/Madame C.** Mr/Mrs thingummy **3** *adj inv* **Fam se sentir tout c.** to feel a bit peculiar

chou¹, -x [ʃu] *nm* (**a**) *(légume)* cabbage; **faire ses choux gras de qch** to have a field day with sth, **faire c. blanc** to draw a blank; **mon petit c.** darling; **c. de Bruxelles** Brussels sprout; **c. rouge** red cabbage (**b**) *(gâteau)* **c. à la crème** cream puff

chou² *adj inv Fam* cute

chouchou, -oute [ʃuʃu, -ut] **1** *nm,f Fam* **c'est le c.** (**de la maîtresse**) he's teacher's pet; **c'est le c. de sa maman** he's his mother's little blue-eyed boy **2** *nm (pour les cheveux)* scrunchie

chouchouter [ʃuʃute] *vt Fam* to pamper; **elle aime se faire c.** she enjoys being pampered

choucroute [ʃukrut] *nf (chou)* sauerkraut; **c. (garnie)** = sauerkraut served with different types of sausages and bacon

chouette¹ [ʃwɛt] *nf (owl,* c. hulotte tawny owl; *Fam Péj* **une vieille c.** an old shrew

chouette² *Fam* **1** *adj* great, terrific; **il a été très c. avec elle** he's been really nice to her **2** *exclam* great!, terrific!

chou-fleur *(pl* **choux-fleurs**) [ʃuflœr] *nm* cauliflower; **oreille en c.** cauliflower ear

chouia [ʃuja] *nm Fam* **un c. (de qch)** a tiny bit (of sth)

chouraver [ʃurave], **chourer** [ʃure] *vt très Fam* to swipe; **se faire c. qch** to have sth swiped

choyer [32] [ʃwaje] *vt* to pamper

CHR [seaʃɛr] *nm (abrév* **centre hospitalier régional)** regional hospital

chrétien, -enne [kretjɛ̃, -ɛn] *adj & nm,f* Christian

chrétienté [kretjɛ̃te] *nf* Christendom

Christ [krist] *nm* (**a**) **le C.** Christ (**b**) *(crucifix)* **c.** crucifix

christianisme [kristjanism] *nm* Christianity

chromatique [krɔmatik] *adj* (**a**) *(des couleurs)* & *Mus* chromatic (**b**) *Biol* chromosomal

chrome [krom] *nm Chim* chromium; **chromes** *(d'une voiture)* chrome

chromé, -e [krome] *adj* chromium-plated; **acier c.** chrome steel

chromosome [krɔmozom] *nm* chromosome

chromosomique [krɔmozomik] *adj* chromosomal

chronique¹ [krɔnik] *adj* chronic

chronique² *nf* (**a**) *Journ* column; **tenir la c. sportive** to write the sports column (**b**) *(annale)* chronicle

chroniqueur, -euse [krɔnikœr, -øz] *nm,f Journ* columnist; **c. sportif** sports reporter

chrono [krɔno] *nm Fam* stopwatch; **faire du 220 km/h c.** to be timed at 220 kph

chronologie [krɔnɔlɔʒi] *nf* chronology

chronologique [krɔnɔlɔʒik] *adj* chronological

chronomètre [krɔnɔmɛtr] *nm (montre de précision)* chronometer; *(pour le sport)* stopwatch

chronométrer [34] [krɔnɔmetre] *vt Sp* to time

chrysalide [krizalid] *nf* chrysalis

chrysanthème [krizɑ̃tɛm] *nm* chrysanthemum

ch'timi [ʃtimi] **1** *nmf Fam* Northerner *(from Northern France)* **2** *nm (patois)* = dialect spoken in Northern France

CHU [seaʃy] *nm inv (abrév* **centre hospitalo-universitaire)** teaching hospital

chu *voir* **choir**

chuchotement [ʃyʃɔtmɑ̃] *nm* whisper; **des chuchotements** whispering

chuchoter [ʃyʃɔte] *vt & vi* to whisper

chuintement [ʃɥɛ̃tmɑ̃] *nm* hissing

chuinter [ʃɥɛ̃te] *vt (siffler)* to hiss

chut [ʃyt] *exclam* sh!, hush!

chute [ʃyt] *nf* (**a**) *(fait de tomber)* & *Fig* fall; *(diminution)* drop, fall; **faire une c. (de cheval/moto)** to have a fall (from one's horse/motorbike); **prévenir la c. des cheveux** to prevent hair loss; **il m'a entraîné dans sa c.** he has dragged me down with him; **c. libre** free fall; **descendre en c. libre** to be in free fall; **c. de neige** snowfall (**b**) **c. d'eau** waterfall; **les chutes Victoria/du Niagara** the Victoria/Niagara Falls (**c**) *(d'histoire drôle)* punchline (**d**) *(de tissu, de métal)* scrap; *(de bois)* off-cut

chuter [ʃyte] *vi (diminuer)* to fall, to drop; *Fam (tomber)* to fall *(down)*

Chypre [ʃipr] *n* Cyprus

chypriote [ʃiprijɔt] **1** *adj* Cypriot **2** *nmf* **C.** Cypriot

ci¹ [si] *adv* **ce livre-ci** this book, **ces jours-ci** these days, **de-ci de-là** here and there; **par-ci par-là** here and there

ci² *pron démonstratif Fam* **faire ci et ça** to do this and that

CIA [seia] *nf* **la C.** the CIA

ciao [tʃao] *exclam Fam* ciao!

ci-après [siaprɛ] *adv* below; *Jur* hereinafter

cibiste [sibist] *nmf* CB user

cible [sibl] *nf aussi Fig* target

ciblé, -e [sible] *adj* well-targeted

ciboire [sibwar] *nm Rel* ciborium

ciboulette [sibulɛt] *nf* chives

ciboulot [sibulo] *nm très Fam (tête)* nut; **se creuser le c.** to rack one's brains

cicatrice [sikatris] *nf aussi Fig* scar

cicatrisant, -e [sikatrizɑ̃, -ɑ̃t] *adj* healing

cicatrisation [sikatrizasjɔ̃] *nf* healing

cicatriser [sikatrize] **1** *vt & vi* to heal **2** **se cicatriser** *vpr* to heal

ci-contre [sikɔ̃tr] *adv* opposite

ci-dessous [sidəsu] *adv* below

ci-dessus [sidəsy] *adv* above

ci-devant [sidəvɑ̃] *adv Vieilli* formerly

CIDJ [seidezi] *nm (abrév* **centre d'information et de documentation de la jeunesse)** = library offering careers information and literature to young people

cidre [sidr] *nm Br* cider, *Am* hard cider; **c. bouché** = traditionally-made cider, fermented twice; **c. doux/brut** sweet/dry cider

Cie *(abrév* **compagnie)** Co

ciel [sjɛl] *nm* (**a**) *(air)* sky; **les ciels de Turner** Turner's skies; **à c. ouvert** open-air; **sous d'autres cieux** in other climes; **lever les bras/les yeux au c.** to raise one's arms/one's eyes heavenwards; *Fam* **être au septième c.** to be in seventh heaven; *Fam* **tomber du c.** (à qn) *(héritage)* to be a godsend (to sb); *(solution)* to come (to sb) out of the blue (**b**) *(pl* **cieux** [sjø]) *(paradis)* heaven; **il est au c.** he's in heaven; **notre Père qui êtes aux cieux** our Father which art in Heaven (**c**) **c. de lit** canopy

cierge [sjɛrʒ] *nm Rel* candle; **brûler un c.** to light a candle

cigale [sigal] *nf* cicada

cigare [sigar] *nm* (**a**) *(à fumer)* cigar (**b**) *très Fam (tête)* **ne rien avoir dans le c.** to be completely brainless

cigarette [sigarɛt] *nf* cigarette

ci-gît [siʒi] *voir* **gésir**

cigogne [sigɔɲ] *nf* stork

ciguë [sigy] *nf* hemlock

ci-inclus, -e *(mpl* **ci-inclus,** *fpl* **ci-incluses)** [siɛkly, -yz] **1** *adj* **la copie ci-incluse** the enclosed copy
2 *adv* (**vous trouverez**) **c. copie de votre lettre** please find enclosed a copy of your letter

ci-joint, -e *(mpl* **ci-joints,** *fpl* **ci-jointes)** [siʒwɛ̃, -ɛ̃t] **1** *adj* **les pièces ci-jointes** the enclosed documents
2 *adv* (**vous trouverez**) **c. copie de votre lettre** please find enclosed a copy of your letter

cil [sil] *nm* eyelash; **faux cils** false eyelashes

ciller [sije] *vi* to blink; *Fig* **il n'a pas cillé** he didn't bat an eyelid

cime [sim] *nf (d'une montagne)* summit; *(pic)* peak; *(d'un arbre, d'un mât)* top

ciment [simã] *nm* cement

cimenter [simãte] *vt aussi Fig* to cement

cimetière [simtjɛr] *nm* cemetery; *(d'église)* graveyard; **c. de voitures** scrapyard

ciné [sine] *nm Fam* movies

cinéaste [sineast] *nmf* film maker

ciné-club *(pl* **ciné-clubs)** [sineklœb] *nm* film club

cinéma [sinema] *nm* (**a**) *(art, industrie)* Br cinema, Am movies; **faire du c.** to be a film or movie actor; *Fam* **c'est du c.** it's all an act; *Fam* **arrête ton c.!** stop making such a fuss!; **c. d'art et d'essai** arthouse films; **c. muet** silent films; **c. parlant** talking films (**b**) *(salle)* Br cinema, Am movie theater; **aller au c.** to go to the cinema

CinémaScope® [sinemaskɔp] *nm* CinemaScope®

cinémathèque [sinematɛk] *nf* film library

cinématographie [sinematɔgrafi] *nf* cinematography

cinématographique [sinematɔgrafik] *adj* cinema, film

ciné-parc *(pl* **cinés-parcs)** [sinepark] *nm Can* drive-in movie theater

cinéphile [sinefil] **1** *adj* **être c.** to be a movie buff
2 *nmf* movie buff

cinéraire [sinerɛr] *adj (urne)* cinerary

cinétique [sinetik] *adj (énergie)* kinetic

cinglant, -e [sɛ̃glã, -ãt] *adj (pluie)* lashing; *(vent, remarque)* cutting

cinglé, -e [sɛ̃gle] *Fam* **1** *adj* crazy
2 *nm,f* nut, screwball

cingler¹ [sɛ̃gle] *vi Naut* **c. vers** to make for

cingler² *vt (frapper)* to lash; **la grêle lui cinglait le visage** the hail was stinging his face

cinoche [sinɔʃ] *nm Fam Br* cinema, *Am* movie theater

cinq [sɛk] **1** *adj inv* five
2 *nm inv* five; **recevoir qn c. sur c.** to receive sb loud and

clear; *Fam* **c'était moins c.** it was a close shave; *voir aussi* **trois**

cinquantaine [sɛ̃kɑ̃tɛn] *nf* **une c. de personnes** about fifty people, fifty or so people; **avoir la c.** to be about fifty

cinquante [sɛ̃kɑ̃t] *adj & nm inv* fifty; *voir aussi* **trois**

cinquantenaire [sɛ̃kɑ̃tnɛr] **1** *nm (anniversaire)* fiftieth anniversary
2 *adj* **être c.** to be fifty years old

cinquantième [sɛ̃kɑ̃tjɛm] *nmf, nm & adj* fiftieth; *voir aussi* **cinquième**

cinquième [sɛ̃kjɛm] **1** *adj* fifth; **le c. jour** the fifth day; **arriver c.** to finish fifth
2 *nmf* fifth; **le c. en partant de la droite** the fifth from the right; **arriver le c.** to finish fifth
3 *nm* (**a**) *(fraction)* fifth (**b**) *(étage)* fifth floor; **habiter au c.** to live on the Br fifth or Am sixth floor (**c**) *(arrondissement)* fifth arrondissement
4 *nf* (**a**) *(classe) Br* ≃ second year of secondary school, Am ≃ sixth grade (**b**) *(vitesse)* fifth (gear); **passer la c.** to go into fifth (gear)

cinquièmement [sɛ̃kjɛmmã] *adv* fifthly

cintre [sɛ̃tr] *nm* (coat)hanger

cintré, -e [sɛ̃tre] *adj (veste)* fitted; *(taille)* nipped-in

CIO [seio] *nm (abrév* **Comité international olympique**) IOC

cirage [siraʒ] *nm (shoe)* polish; *Fam* **être dans le c.** to be feeling woozy

circoncire [sirkɔ̃sir] *vt* to circumcise

circoncision [sirkɔ̃sizjɔ̃] *nf* circumcision

circonférence [sirkɔ̃ferãs] *nf* circumference; **avoir 10 centimètres de c.** to have a circumference of 10 centimetres

circonflexe [sirkɔ̃flɛks] *adj voir* **accent**

circonlocution [sirkɔ̃lɔkysjɔ̃] *nf* circumlocution; **parler par circonlocutions** to speak in a roundabout way

circonscription [sirkɔ̃skripsjɔ̃] *nf* division, district; **c. électorale** *(au niveau municipal)* ward; *(au niveau national)* constituency

circonscrire [30] [sirkɔ̃skrir] *vt Math* to circumscribe; *(encercler)* to encircle; *(incendie)* to contain

circonspect, -e [sirkɔ̃spɛ, -ɛkt] *adj* circumspect, cautious

circonstance [sirkɔ̃stãs] *nf* circumstance; **dans les circonstances actuelles** in the present circumstances; **en pareille c.** under such circumstances; **être à la hauteur des circonstances** to be equal to the occasion; **des paroles de c.** appropriate words; **habillé pour la c.** appropriately dressed; **circonstances aggravantes** aggravating circumstances; *Jur* **circonstances atténuantes** extenuating circumstances

circonstancié, -e [sirkɔ̃stãsje] *adj* detailed

circonstanciel, -elle [sirkɔ̃stãsjel] *adj voir* **complément**

circonvolution [sirkɔ̃vɔlysjɔ̃] *nf* convolution

circuit [sirkɥi] *nm* (**a**) *(chemin)* way; *(boucle)* tour; *Fig* **ça fait longtemps que je ne suis plus dans le c.** I've been out of circulation for ages; **c. touristique** (organized) tour (**b**) *(de course automobile, de cyclisme)* circuit; **c. automobile** racing circuit (**c**) *Él* circuit (**d**) *Tech* **c. de refroidissement** cooling system (**e**) *Ordinat* **c. de commande** command circuit; **c. imprimé** printed circuit; **c. intégré** integrated circuit; **c. de liaison** link circuit; **c. logique** logic circuit (**f**) *Écon* **c. de distribution** distribution network; **circuits de vente** commercial channels

circulaire [sirkyler] **1** *nf* circular
2 *adj* circular; **billet c.** round-trip ticket

circulation [sirkylasjɔ̃] *nf (d'autos, d'avions)* traffic; **c. interdite** *(sur panneau)* no thoroughfare; **c. aérienne** air traffic; **c. routière** road traffic **(b)** *(du sang, de l'information, des marchandises)* circulation; **mettre qch en c.** to put sth into circulation; **retirer un produit de la c.** to take a product off the market **(c)** *Fin (des billets, des capitaux)* circulation **(d)** *Pol & Écon* **libre c. des personnes et des biens** free movement of persons and goods

circulatoire [sirkylatwar] *adj* circulatory

circuler [sirkyle] *vi* **(a)** *(sang, air, rumeur)* to circulate; **faire c. un plat** to pass *or* hand a dish round; **faire c. une pétition** to circulate a petition **(b)** *(voyageur)* to travel; *(train, autobus)* to run; **on circule très mal dans Londres** it's very difficult to drive around in London; **circulez, il n'y a rien à voir!** move along now, there's nothing to see!

cire [sir] *nf* wax; *(pour le bois)* polish; *(dans l'oreille)* (ear)wax; **c. d'abeille** beeswax; **c. à cacheter** sealing wax; **personnage en c.** waxwork (model)

ciré [sire] *nm* oilskin

cirer [sire] *vt (chaussures, meubles)* to polish; *Fam* **c. les pompes à qn** to lick sb's boots; *très Fam* **il en a rien à c. (de tes histoires)** he doesn't give a damn (about your stories)

cireur, -euse [sirœr, -øz] **1** *nm,f (de chaussures)* shoeblack **2** *nf* **cireuse** *(machine)* (floor) polisher

cireux, -euse [sirø, -øz] *adj* waxy

cirque [sirk] *nm* **(a)** *(spectacle)* circus; *Fam* **quel c. dans ce bureau!** it's like a zoo in this office!; *Fam* **faire tout un c.** to make a scene **(b)** *Géol* corrie

cirrhose [siroz] *nf* **c. (du foie)** cirrhosis (of the liver); **avoir une c.** to have cirrhosis

cisaille [sizaj] *nf* **c., cisailles** *(de jardinier)* shears

cisailler [sizaje] *vt (branches, haie)* to prune

ciseau, -x [sizo] *nm* **(a)** *(de jardin)* shears; **(une paire de) ciseaux** *(pour papier, pour tissu)* (a pair of) scissors; **des ciseaux à ongles** nail scissors **(b)** *Sp* **sauter en ciseaux** to do a scissors jump **(c)** *Tech* chisel

ciseler [39] [sizle] *vt (or, argent)* to chase; *(marbre)* to chisel; *(bijou)* to engrave a design on

Cisjordanie [sisʒɔrdani] *nf* **la C.** the West Bank

cisjordanien, -enne [sisʒɔrdanjɛ̃, -ɛn] **1** *adj* from the West Bank **2** *nm,f* **C.** person from the West Bank

cistercien, -enne [sistɛrsjɛ̃, -ɛn] *adj & nm Rel* Cistercian

citadelle [sitadɛl] *nf* citadel

citadin, -e [sitadɛ̃, -in] **1** *nm,f* city-dweller **2** *adj* city

citation [sitasjɔ̃] *nf* **(a)** *(extrait)* quotation; **fin de c.** unquote **(b)** *Jur* **c. à comparaître** *(d'un accusé)* summons; *(d'un témoin)* subpoena

cité [site] *nf* **(a)** *(ville)* city **(b)** *(groupe d'immeubles)* (housing) *Br* estate *or Am* development; **c. universitaire** *Br* halls of residence, *Am* dormitory complex

cité-dortoir *(pl* cités-dortoirs*)* [sitedɔrtwar] *nf* dormitory town

citer [site] *vt* **(a)** *(rapporter)* to quote; *(auteur)* to quote (from); **c. qn en exemple** to quote sb as an example; **il a dit, je cite...** he said, and I quote,... **(b)** *(énumérer)* to name **(c)** *Jur (personne en justice)* to summons; *(témoin)* to subpoena **(d)** *Mil* **c. qn (à l'ordre du jour)** to mention sb in dispatches

citerne [sitɛrn] *nf* tank; **c. à mazout** oil tank

cithare [sitar] *nf (instrument moderne)* zither

citizen band [sitizənbɑ̃d] *nf* Citizens' Band, CB

citoyen, -enne [sitwajɛ̃, -ɛn] *nm,f* citizen; **c. d'honneur** freeman *(of a city)*

citoyenneté [sitwajɛnte] *nf* citizenship; **la c. française** French citizenship

citrique [sitrik] *adj (acide)* citric

citron [sitrɔ̃] *nm* **(a)** *(fruit)* lemon; **un c. givré** = lemon sorbet served inside the skin of a whole lemon; **un c. pressé** = freshly squeezed lemon juice served with water and sugar; **c. vert** lime **(b)** *Fam (tête)* nut

citronnade [sitrɔnad] *nf Br* lemon squash, *Am* lemonade

citronnelle [sitrɔnɛl] *nf (plante, huile)* citronella

citronnier [sitrɔnje] *nm* lemon tree

citrouille [sitruj] *nf* pumpkin

civelle [sivɛl] *nf* elver

civet [sive] *nm Culin* **c. de lapin** rabbit stew; **c. de lièvre** ≃ jugged hare

civière [sivjɛr] *nf* stretcher

civil, -e [sivil] **1** *adj* **(a)** *(du citoyen, non ecclésiastique)* civil **(b)** *(non militaire)* civilian; **dans la vie civile** in civilian life **(c)** *Jur (courtois)* civil **2** *nm* **(a)** *(personne) (non ecclésiastique)* layman, civilian **(b)** **dans le c.** in civilian life; **en c.** *(policier)* in plain clothes; *(militaire)* in civilian clothes **(c)** *Jur* **poursuivre qn au c.** to bring a civil action against sb

civilement [sivilmɑ̃] *adv* **(a)** *Jur* **se marier c.** to have a civil wedding **(b)** *Litt (avec courtoisie)* civilly

civilisation [sivilizasjɔ̃] *nf* civilization

civilisé, -e [sivilize] *adj* civilized

civilité [sivilite] *nf Litt* **(a)** *(courtoisie)* civility **(b)** **civilités** *(politesses)* courtesies

civique [sivik] *adj* civic; **avoir le sens c.** to have a sense of civic responsibility

civisme [sivism] *nm* sense of civic responsibility

clac [klak] *exclam (d'un fouet)* crack!; *(d'un objet qui se casse)* snap!; *(d'une porte)* slam!

clafoutis [klafuti] *nm* clafoutis *(fruit, usually cherries, baked in a dish of batter)*

claie [klɛ] *nf* **(a)** *(treillis)* rack **(b)** *(clôture)* fence

clair, -e [klɛr] **1** *adj* **(a)** *(transparent) (eau, teint, voix)* clear; **par temps c.** on a clear day **(b)** *(pièce, couleur)* light **(c)** *(sens, explication)* clear; **il a été très c. là-dessus** he was very clear about it; **il est c. qu'il a tort** he's clearly wrong; **être c. comme le jour** to be crystal clear; **avoir les idées claires** to have a clear head; **c'est c. et net** there are no two ways about it; *Fam* **un individu pas très c.** a bit of a shady character **(d)** *(soupe)* thin **2** *adv* clearly; **il fait c.** it's light; *Fig* **je commence à y voir c.** I'm beginning to understand **3** *nm* **(a)** *(lumière)* **c. de lune** moonlight; **au c. de lune** in the moonlight **(b)** **en c.** *(autrement dit)* in plain language; **émission en c.** non-encrypted broadcast **(c)** *Fig* **tirer une affaire au c.** to clear a matter up; **passer le plus c. de son temps à faire qch** to spend the better part of one's time doing sth

clairement [klɛrmɑ̃] *adv* clearly

claire-voie *(pl* claires-voies*)* [klɛrvwa] *nf* **(a)** *(treillage)* lattice; **à c.** open-work **(b)** *Archit* clerestory

clairière [klɛrjɛr] *nf* clearing, glade

clair-obscur *(pl* clairs-obscurs*)* [klɛrɔpskyr] *nm (en peinture)* chiaroscuro

clairon [klɛrɔ̃] *nm* **(a)** *(instrument)* bugle; **sonner le c.** to sound the bugle **(b)** *(joueur)* bugler

claironner [klɛrɔne] *vt (nouvelle)* to trumpet forth

clairsemé, -e [klɛrsəme] *adj (population, cheveux, gazon)* sparse; *(arbres)* scattered

clairvoyant, -e [klɛrvwajɑ̃, -ɑ̃t] *adj* perceptive

clamer [klame] *vt* to proclaim

clameur [klamœr] *nf* clamour; **une c.** de joie a shout of joy; **les clameurs de la foule** the clamour of the crowd

clamser [klamse] *vi très Fam (mourir)* to kick the bucket

clan [klɑ̃] *nm (tribu)* clan; *Péj (groupe)* clique

clandestin, -e [klɑ̃dɛstɛ̃, -in] **1** *adj (réunion, atelier)* clandestine; *(travailleur, immigré)* illegal; *(mouvement)* underground
2 *nmf (voyageur)* stowaway; *(immigré)* illegal immigrant; *(travailleur)* illegal worker

clandestinement [klɑ̃dɛstinmɑ̃] *adv (secrètement)* clandestinely; *(illégalement)* illegally

clandestinité [klɑ̃dɛstinite] *nf* **dans la c.** *(secrètement)* clandestinely; *(illégalement)* illegally; **entrer dans/sortir de la c.** to go into/to come out of hiding

clap [klap] *nm Cin* clapperboard; **c. de fin** end board

clapet [klapɛ] *nm* **(a)** *Tech* valve **(b)** *Fam* **ferme ton c.!** shut your trap!

clapier [klapje] *nm (rabbit)* hutch

clapoter [klapɔte] *vi* to lap

clapotis [klapɔti] *nm* lapping

claquage [klakaʒ] *nm (blessure)* pulled muscle; **se faire un c.** to pull a muscle

claque [klak] *nf* **(a)** *(gifle)* slap; **donner une c. à qn** to give sb a slap; *Fam Fig* **il va se prendre une c.** it'll be a slap in the face for him; **une paire de claques** a slap **(b)** *Fam* **j'en ai ma c.** I've had enough **(c)** *Can* **claques** galoshes

claqué, -e [klake] *adj Fam (fatigué) Br* shattered, *Am* bushed

claquement [klakmɑ̃] *nm (de porte)* slam(ming); *(de dents)* chattering; *(d'un fouet)* crack(ing); *(d'un drapeau)* flap(ping); *(de doigts)* snap(ping); *(de talons, de la langue)* click(ing); *(de sabots)* clatter(ing)

claquer [klake] **1** *vt* **(a)** *(porte)* to slam; **c. la langue** to click one's tongue **(b)** *Fam (dépenser)* to blow; **il claque un fric monstre chez le coiffeur** he spends a fortune at the hairdresser's
2 *vi* **(a)** *(porte)* to slam; *(drapeau)* to flap; *(talons)* to click; *(sabots)* to clatter; **c. des mains** to clap; **c. des doigts** to snap one's fingers; **elle claque des dents** her teeth are chattering; **faire c. sa langue** to click one's tongue **(b)** *(ampoule électrique)* to go; *Fam (personne)* to kick the bucket
3 se claquer *vpr* **se c. un muscle** to pull a muscle

claquettes [klakɛt] *nfpl* tap dancing; **faire des c.** to do tap dancing; **danseur de c.** tap dancer

clarification [klarifikasjɔ̃] *nf aussi Fig* clarification

clarifier [66] [klarifje] **1** *vt (liquide, situation)* to clarify
2 se clarifier *vpr (situation)* to become clear

clarinette [klarinɛt] *nf* clarinet

clarinettiste [klarinetist] *nmf* clarinettist

clarté [klarte] *nf* **(a)** *(lumière)* light **(b)** *(transparence)* clearness **(c)** *Fig (du style)* clarity; **avec c.** clearly; **manquer de c.** *(personne)* not to make oneself clear; *(texte, argument)* to be unclear

classe [klas] **1** *nf* **(a)** *(catégorie)* class; *(dans une hiérarchie)* grade; **c. affaires/économie** business/economy class; **c. d'âge** age group; **la c. dirigeante** the ruling class; **les classes moyennes** the middle class(es); **la c. ouvrière** the working class(es); **c. sociale** social class
(b) *(qualité)* class; **un sportif de c. internationale** a world-class sportsman; **avoir de la c.** *(personne)* to have class; *(objet, vêtement)* to be classy; *Fam* **ce type, c'est la c.!** he's got real class!
(c) *(à l'école) (niveau)* year; *(groupe d'élèves)* class; **les grandes classes, les classes supérieures** the senior school; **les petites classes** the junior school; **c. de mer/ de neige** school study trip to the seaside/to the mountains;

partir en **c.** de mer to go on a school study trip to the seaside; **c. préparatoire (aux grandes écoles)** = preparatory class for the entrance examinations for the Grandes Écoles; **c. verte** school study trip to the countryside
(d) *(leçon)* class; **la c. de chimie** the chemistry class; **aller en c.** to go to school; **être en c.** *(à l'école)* to be at school; *(en cours)* to be in class; **faire la c.** to teach
(e) *(pièce)* **(salle de) c.** classroom
(f) *Mil (de conscrits)* levy; **faire ses classes** to undergo basic training
2 *adj inv Fam* classy

classé, -e [klase] *adj (monument)* listed

classement [klasmɑ̃] *nm* **(a)** *(dans une classe ou une course)* position, place; *(liste d'équipes, de concurrents)* classification **(b)** *(des plantes)* classification; **être troisième au c.** to be in third place; **c. général** overall classification **(b)** *(rangement) (de documents)* filing; *(d'articles)* sorting out; **faire du c.** to do some filing; **c. (par ordre) alphabétique** alphabetical classification

classer [klase] **1** *vt* **(a)** *(classifier)* to classify; *(étudiants)* to grade; **être classés par pays** to be classified according to country **(b)** *(ranger) (documents)* to file; *(articles)* to sort out; **c. une affaire** to consider a matter closed; **c'est une affaire classée** the matter's closed
2 se classer *vpr* **se c. parmi les meilleurs** to rank among the best; *Sp* **se c. troisième** to be placed third

classeur [klasœr] *nm* **(a)** *(dossier)* ring binder **(b)** *(meuble)* filing cabinet **(c)** *Ordinat* filer

classicisme [klasisism] *nm* classicism

classification [klasifikasjɔ̃] *nf* classification; *Chim* **c. périodique des éléments** periodic table

classifier [66] [klasifje] *vt* to classify

classique [klasik] **1** *adj* **(a)** *(période)* classical; *(beauté)* classic **(b)** *(conventionnel) (vêtement, style, exemple, plaisanterie)* classic; *(arme, guerre)* conventional; *Fam* **c'est le coup c.** it's the same old story
2 *nm* **(a)** *(auteur)* classical author **(b)** *(œuvre, film, chanson)* classic; **c'est un c. du genre** it's a classic of its kind **(c)** *(style musical)* **le c.** classical music

claudication [klodikasjɔ̃] *nf* limp

claustrophobe [klostrɔfɔb] *adj* claustrophobic

claustrophobie [klostrɔfɔbi] *nf* claustrophobia

clavecin [klavsɛ̃] *nm* harpsichord

claveciniste [klavsinist] *nmf* harpsichordist

clavicule [klavikyl] *nf* collarbone, *Spéc* clavicle

clavier [klavje] *nm* keyboard; *Ordinat* **c. multifonction** multifunctional keyboard; **c. numérique** numerical or numeric keypad

claviste [klavist] *nmf Ordinat* keyboarder; *Typ* typesetter

clé [kle] = **clef**

clean [klin] *adj inv Fam* **(a)** *(BCBG)* clean-cut **(b)** *(qui ne se drogue pas)* clean

clébard [klebar], **clebs** [klɛps] *nm Fam* pooch

clef [kle] **1** *nf* **(a)** *(d'une porte, d'un cadenas)* key; **fermer qch à c.** to lock sth; **tenir/mettre qch sous c.** to keep/put sth under lock and key; **usine clefs en main** turnkey factory; **prix clefs en main** *(d'une voiture)* on-the-road price; *(d'une maison)* all-inclusive price; *Fig* **mettre la c. sous la porte** to move away; *(commerçant)* to shut up shop; **prendre la c. des champs** *(prisonnier)* to make a bid for freedom; **c. de contact** ignition key; **c. passe-partout** passkey, master key **(b)** *(outil)* spanner; **c. anglaise** monkey wrench; **c. à**

molette adjustable spanner; **c. plate** open-end *Br* spanner or *Am* wrench (**c**) *Mus (d'un instrument à cordes)* peg; *(d'un instrument à vent)* key; **c. de sol/de fa** treble/bass clef; **il y a une forte somme d'argent à la c.** there is a large sum of money at the end of it (**d**) *(moyen d'accès, solution)* **la c. du placard/mystère** the key to the cupboard/mystery (**e**) **c. de voûte** *(d'une arche)* keystone; *Fig* cornerstone (**f**) *Ordinat* key; *(du DOS)* switch; **c. de contrôle** control key; **c. gigogne** dongle; **c. à puce** computerized key 2 *adj (vital)* key; **un secteur(-)c. de la recherche** a key area of research

clématite [klematit] *nf* clematis

clémence [klemɑ̃s] *nf* (**a**) *(de la température)* mildness (**b**) *(d'un juge, d'un maître)* clemency (**envers** towards)

clément, -e [klemɑ̃, -ɑ̃t] *adj* (**a**) *(température)* mild (**b**) *(juge, maître)* clement (**envers** towards)

clémentine [klemɑ̃tin] *nf* clementine

Cléopâtre [kleɔpɑtr] *npr* Cleopatra

cleptomane [kleptɔman] *adj & nmf* kleptomaniac

cleptomanie [kleptɔmani] *nf* kleptomania

clerc [klɛr] *nm* (**a**) *(dans un bureau)* **c. de notaire** ≃ clerk (**b**) *Rel* cleric (**c**) *(d'un métier)* **il n'est pas besoin d'être grand c. pour...** you don't have to be a genius in order to...

clergé [klɛrʒe] *nm* clergy

clérical, -e, -aux, -ales [klerikal, -o] *adj* clerical

clic [klik] *nm* click; **faire c.** to click

clic-clac [klikklak] *nm inv* (**a**) *(d'un appareil photo)* click; *(des talons)* clack-click (**b**) *(canapé)* sofa bed

cliché [kliʃe] *nm* (**a**) *(photo)* photo; *(négatif)* negative (**b**) *(lieu commun)* cliché

client, -e [klijɑ̃, -ɑ̃t] *nm,f (d'un magasin, d'une entreprise)* customer; *(d'un médecin)* patient; *(d'un avocat)* client; *(d'un hôtel)* guest; *(d'un taxi)* fare; **lci, le c. est roi** the customer is always right

clientèle [klijɑ̃tɛl] *nf* (**a**) *(d'un magasin, d'une entreprise)* customers; *(d'un médecin, d'un avocat)* practice; *(d'un hôtel)* clientèle; *(d'un taxi)* fares; **c. de passage** passing trade (**b**) *(fait d'acheter)* custom; **accorder sa c. à** to give one's custom to

cligner [kliɲe] *vi* **c. des yeux** to blink; **c. de l'œil** to wink

clignotant, -e [kliɲɔtɑ̃, -ɑ̃t] 1 *adj (étoile)* twinkling; *(lumière)* flashing 2 *nm (de voiture) Br* indicator, *Am* flasher; **mettre son c. (à gauche/droite)** to indicate (left/right)

clignoter [kliɲɔte] *vi (étoile)* to twinkle; *(lumière, voyant)* to flash; *Ordinat (d'un marqueur)* to flash, to blink

climat [klima] *nm aussi Fig* climate; **sous des climats plus ensoleillés** in sunnier climes; **c. de détente** relaxed climate

climatique [klimatik] *adj (conditions)* climatic

climatisation [klimatizasjɔ̃] *nf* air conditioning

climatisé, -e [klimatize] *adj* air-conditioned

climatiser [klimatize] *vt* to air-condition

climatiseur [klimatizœr] *nm* air-conditioner

clin d'œil *(pl* clins d'œil) [klɛ̃dœj] *nm* wink; **faire un c. à qn** to wink at sb; **en un c.** in a flash

clinique [klinik] 1 *nf* (**a**) *(hôpital privé)* clinic (**b**) *(médecine)* clinical medicine 2 *adj* clinical

clinquant, -e [klɛ̃kɑ̃, -ɑ̃t] 1 *adj* flashy 2 *nm (éclat trompeur)* flashiness

clip [klip] *nm* (**a**) *(vidéo)* (music) video (**b**) *(bijou)* clip

clique [klik] *nf* (**a**) *Fam (gang)* clique, gang; **et toute la c.** and the rest of the gang (**b**) *(d'une fanfare militaire)* drum-and-bugle band

cliquer [klike] *vi Ordinat* to click (**sur** on); **c. deux fois** to double-click

cliques [klik] *nfpl Fam* **prendre ses c. et ses claques** to pack one's bags and go

cliqueter [42] [klikte] *vi (chaînes)* to rattle; *(épées, aiguilles à tricoter)* to click; *(monnaie, clefs)* to jingle

cliquetis [klikti] *nm (de chaînes)* rattling; *(de pièces de monnaie, de clefs)* jingling; *(d'épées, d'aiguilles à tricoter)* clicking

clitoris [klitɔris] *nm* clitoris

clivage [klivaʒ] *nm (dans la société)* divide; *(dans un parti politique)* split

cloaque [klɔak] *nm aussi Fig* cesspool

clochard, -e [klɔʃar, -ard] *nm,f* tramp, *Am* hobo

clochardiser [klɔʃardize] 1 *vt* to turn into a tramp 2 **se clochardiser** *vpr* to turn into a tramp

cloche [klɔʃ] 1 *nf* (**a**) *(d'église, de bétail)* bell; **déménager à la c. de bois** to do a moonlight flit; *Fig* **entendre plusieurs sons de c.** to hear several different versions of events (**b**) *(pour couvrir)* *Chim* bell jar; *(pour cultures)* cloche; *(pour garder au chaud)* dish cover; **c. à fromage(s)** covered cheese dish; **c. à plongeur** diving bell (**c**) *Fam (imbécile)* twit (**d**) **(chapeau) c.** cloche (hat) (**e**) *Fam* **être de la c.** *(être clochard)* to be a tramp *or Am* hobo 2 *adj Fam* stupid

cloche-pied [klɔʃpje] **à cloche-pied** *adv* **sauter à c.** to hop

clocher¹ [klɔʃe] *nm (d'une église)* bell tower, steeple

clocher² [klɔʃe] *vi Fam* **il y a quelque chose qui cloche** there's something wrong somewhere; **il y a quelque chose qui cloche dans son histoire** there's something not quite right about her story

clochette [klɔʃet] *nf* (**a**) *(petite cloche)* small bell (**b**) *(fleur)* bell-flower; *(corolle)* bell-shaped flower

clodo [klodo] *nm Fam* tramp, *Am* bum

cloison [klwazɔ̃] *nf* (**a**) *(entre des pièces)* partition (**b**) *Anat* **c. nasale** nasal septum

cloisonner [klwazɔne] *vt (pièce)* to partition (off); *Fig* to compartmentalize

cloître [klwatr] *nm* (**a**) *(partie d'un monastère)* cloister (**b**) *(bâtiment) (pour moines)* monastery; *(pour religieuses)* convent

cloîtrer [klwatre] 1 *vt Rel* to cloister; *Fig* to shut up *or* away; **nonne cloîtrée** nun in an enclosed order 2 **se cloîtrer** *vpr (moine)* to enter a monastery; *(religieuse)* to enter a convent; *Fig* to shut oneself away

clonage [klonaʒ] *nm Biol* cloning

clone [klon] *nm Biol* clone

clope [klɔp] *nf Fam (cigarette)* smoke

clopin-clopant [klɔpɛ̃klɔpɑ̃] *adv* **aller c.** to hobble along; *Fig (commerce)* to struggle along

clopiner [klɔpine] *vi* to hobble

clopinettes [klɔpinɛt] *nfpl Fam* **des c.** next to nothing; **travailler pour des c.** to work for peanuts

cloporte [klɔpɔrt] *nm (insecte)* woodlouse

cloque [klɔk] *nf* (**a**) *(sur la peau, sur la peinture)* blister; **faire des cloques** to blister (**b**) *très Fam* **être en c.** *(enceinte) Br* to be up the spout, to be knocked up

clore [15] [klɔr] 1 *vt (réunion, discussion)* to conclude, to end; *(débat, compte)* to close; *Ordinat* **c. une session** to log off, to log out 2 **se clore** *vpr (réunion, film, livre)* to end (**sur** with)

clos, -e [klo, kloz] 1 *pp voir* **clore** 2 *adj* (**a**) *(fermé) (porte, volets)* closed (**b**) *(achevé)* finished, concluded; **l'incident est c.** the matter is closed; **les**

inscriptions seront closes le 5 mars the closing date for applications is 5 March (**c**) *(clôturé) (jardin)* enclosed **3** *nm* enclosure; **c. (de vigne)** vineyard

clôture [klotyr] *nf* (**a**) *(barrière)* fence (**b**) *(d'une réunion, d'une discussion)* conclusion, end; *(d'un débat, d'un compte)* closing; **c. des inscriptions le 3 mars** closing date for applications is 3 March; **c. de la chasse** close of the hunting season; *Fin* **c. de l'exercice** end of the financial year (**c**) *(à la Bourse)* close; **à la c.** at the close (**d**) *Ordinat* close; **c. de session** logging off

clôturer [klotyre] **1** *vt* (**a**) *(champ, terrain)* to enclose, to fence in (**b**) *(session, débats)* to close (**c**) *Fin (comptes)* to close **2** *vi (valeur, indice)* **c. à** to close at

clou [klu] *nm* (**a**) *(pointe)* nail; **être maigre comme un c.** to be as thin as a rake; *Fam* **ça ne vaut pas un c.** it's not worth a penny; *Fam* **des clous!** not a sausage!; *Fam* **travailler pour des clous** to work for peanuts (**b**) *Culin* **c. de girofle** clove (**c**) *(d'un spectacle)* main attraction; **ça a été le c.** **de la soirée** it was the highlight of the evening (**d**) **clous** *(passage piéton) Br* the pedestrian crossing, *Am* the crosswalk (**e**) *Fam* (**vieux**) **c.** *(voiture)* old banger; *(vélo)* old boneshaker (**f**) *Fam* **mettre qn au c.** *(en prison)* to lock sb up; *Vieilli* **mettre qch au c.** *(en gage)* to pawn sth

clouer [klue] *vt* (**a**) *(au mur)* to nail up; *(ensemble)* to nail together; *(caisse)* to nail down; *Fam* **c. le bec à qn** to shut sb up (**b**) *Fig (immobiliser)* **c. qn au sol** to pin sb down; **rester cloué sur place** to be rooted to the spot; **être cloué au lit** to be stuck in bed

clouté, -e [klute] *adj (chaussures)* studded

clown [klun] *nm aussi Fig* clown; **faire le c.** to clown around

club [klœb] *nm* (**a**) *(culturel, sportif, politique)* club; **c. automobile** car club; **c. de foot** soccer club; **c. de vacances** *Br* holiday club, *Am* vacation center (**b**) *(canne de golf)* club

CM [seɛm] *nm (abrév* **cours moyen***)* = two-year subdivision of primary-level education in France (ages 10 to 11); **CM1** = fourth year of primary school; **CM2** = fifth year of primary school

cm *(abrév* **centimètre(s)***)* cm

CNPF [seɛnpeɛf] *nm (abrév* **Conseil national du patronat français***)* = national employers' association

CNRS [seɛnɛrɛs] *nm (abrév* **Centre national de la recherche scientifique***)* = national organization for scientific research

coach [kotʃ] *nm (entraîneur)* coach

coagulant, -e [kɔagylɑ̃, -ɑ̃t] **1** *adj* coagulating **2** *nm* coagulant

coagulation [kɔagylasjɔ̃] *nf* coagulation

coaguler [kɔagyle] **1** *vt & vi (sang)* to clot; *(lait)* to curdle **2 se coaguler** *vpr (sang)* to clot; *(lait)* to curdle

coaliser [kɔalize] **se coaliser** *vpr* to unite; *(partis, pays)* to form a coalition

coalition [kɔalisjɔ̃] *nf* (**a**) *(alliance)* coalition (**b**) *Fig & Péj* conspiracy; **former une c. contre** to join forces against

coaltar [koltar] *nm* coaltar; *Fam* **être dans le c.** to be in a daze

coasser [kɔase] *vi (grenouille)* to croak

coassurance [koasyrɑ̃s] *nf* mutual assurance

coauteur [kootœr] *nm* (**a**) *(d'un livre)* co-author (**b**) *Jur* accomplice

COB [kɔb] *nf Fin (abrév* **Commission des opérations de Bourse***)* = French Stock Exchange watchdog

cobalt [kɔbalt] *nm* cobalt

cobaye [kɔbaj] *nm aussi Fig* guinea pig

cobol [kɔbɔl] *nm Ordinat* COBOL

cobra [kɔbra] *nm* cobra

Coca® [kɔka] *nm inv Fam (boisson)* Coke®

coca [kɔka] **1** *nm (plante)* coca **2** *nf (feuilles)* coca

Coca-Cola® [kɔkakɔla] *nm inv* Coca-Cola®

cocagne [kɔkaɲ] *nf voir* **mât**

cocaïne [kɔkain] *nf* cocaine

cocaïnomane [kɔkainɔman] *nmf* cocaine addict

cocarde [kɔkard] *nf (insigne)* rosette; *Hist (sur un chapeau)* cockade

cocasse [kɔkas] *adj Fam* comical

coccinelle [kɔksinɛl] *nf* (**a**) *(insecte) Br* ladybird, *Am* ladybug (**b**) *(voiture)* beetle

coccyx [kɔksis] *nm* coccyx

coche [kɔʃ] *nm Vieilli* stagecoach; *Fam* **rater** *ou* **louper le c.** to miss the boat

cochenille [kɔʃnij] *nf* cochineal

cocher[1] [kɔʃe] *nm* coachman

cocher[2] *vt Br* to tick (off), *Am* to check

cochère [kɔʃɛr] *adj f voir* **porte**

cochon, -onne [kɔʃɔ̃, -ɔn] **1** *nm* (**a**) *(animal, personne sale)* pig; *(viande)* pork; **sale comme un c.** filthy; **gros** *ou* **gras comme un c.** as round as a barrel; **manger comme un c.** to eat like a pig; **tu écris comme un c.** your writing's an absolute mess; *Fig* **nous n'avons pas gardé les cochons ensemble!** but we hardly know each other!; *Fam Fig* **eh ben, mon c.!** you old devil!; **c. de lait** suck(l)ing pig (**b**) **c. d'Inde** guinea pig (**c**) *(personne malfaisante)* swine (**d**) *(personne grivoise)* dirty devil; **un vieux c.** a dirty old man **2** *adj (histoire, film)* dirty

cochonner [kɔʃɔne] *vt Fam (travail)* to bungle, to botch

cochonnerie [kɔʃɔnri] *nf* (**a**) *(chose sans valeur)* trash, rubbish (**b**) *(nourriture de mauvaise qualité)* muck (**c**) *(saleté)* mess; **faire des cochonneries** to make a mess (**d**) *(obscénité)* smutty remark; **dire des cochonneries** to say smutty things

cochonnet [kɔʃɔnɛ] *nm* (**a**) *(aux boules)* jack (**b**) *(petit cochon)* piglet

cocker [kɔkɛr] *nm* cocker spaniel

cockpit [kɔkpit] *nm Naut & Av* cockpit

cocktail [kɔktɛl] *nm (boisson) & Fig* cocktail; *(soirée)* cocktail party; **c. de fruits** fruit cocktail; **c. Molotov** Molotov cocktail

coco[1] [koko] *nm* (**a**) *(plante)* coconut (**b**) *Fam* **mets-toi ça dans le c.!** *(dans la tête)* get that into your thick skull!; *(dans l'estomac)* get that inside you!

coco[2] *nm* (**a**) *Fam (type)* **un drôle de c.** a strange character; **toi, mon c., je t'ai à l'œil** just watch it, buddy (**b**) *(terme d'affection)* **mon petit c.** sweetheart

coco[3] *adj & nmf Fam (communiste)* commie

cocon [kɔkɔ̃] *nm aussi Fig* cocoon; *Fig* **le c. familial** the family nest

cocorico [kɔkɔriko] **1** *exclam* cock-a-doodle-doo! **2** *nm (cri du coq)* cock-a-doodle-doo; *aussi Fig* **faire c.** to crow

cocoter [kɔkɔte] *vi Fam* to stink

cocotier [kɔkɔtje] *nm (arbre)* coconut palm

cocotte [kɔkɔt] *nf* (**a**) *(marmite)* large casserole dish (**b**) *(poule)* hen (**c**) *(pliage)* paper bird (**d**) *(terme d'affection)* **ma c.** darling (**e**) *Fam* **hue, c.!** gee up! (**f**) *Fam Vieilli* tart

Cocotte-Minute® *(pl* **Cocottes-Minute***)* [kɔkɔtminyt] *nf* pressure cooker

cocu, -e [kɔky] **1** *adj* **un mari c.** a cuckold; **je suis c./**

cocue my wife's/husband's cheating on me **2** *nm* cuckold; **faire c.** son mari to cheat on one's husband

cocufier [66] [kɔkyfje] *vt* to be unfaithful to

coda [kɔda] *nf Mus* coda

codage [kɔdaʒ] *nm* coding

code [kɔd] *nm* (**a**) *(symboles)* code; **mettre qch en c.** to put sth into code; **c. confidentiel** security code; *(d'une carte bancaire)* PIN; **c. postal** *Br* postcode, *Am* zip code (**b**) *Ordinat* code; **c. abrégé** shortcode; **c. d'accès** access code; **c. d'arrêt** stop code; **c. d'autorisation d'accès** access authorization code; **c. de caractère** character code; **c. de commande** command code; **c. de contrôle** control code; **c. de départ** start code; **c. d'erreur** error code; **c. d'imprimante** printer code; **c. natif** source code; **c. objet** object code; **c. source** source code (**c**) *(ensemble de lois, livre)* code; **passer le c.** *(du permis de conduire)* to sit the written part of one's driving test; **c. civil** civil code, ≃ common law; **c. de la nationalité** = laws governing French nationality; **c. pénal** penal code; **c. de la route** Highway Code; **c. du travail** employment legislation (**d**) *(phare)* **codes** *Br* dipped headlights, *Am* low beams; **se mettre en codes** *Br* to dip one's headlights, *Am* to switch on one's low beams; **rouler en codes** to drive with *Br* dipped headlights or *Am* low beams (**e**) *Biol* **c. génétique** genetic code

code-barres (*pl* **codes-barres**) [kɔdbar] *nm* bar code

codéine [kɔdein] *nf* codeine

coder [kɔde] *vt* to code

codétenu, -e [kɔdetny] *nm,f* fellow prisoner

CODEVI [kɔdevi] *nm* = type of instant-access savings account, money from which is invested in industrial development

codicille [kɔdisil] *nm Jur* codicil

codification [kɔdifikasjɔ̃] *nf Ordinat* **c. binaire** binary code; **c. décimale** decimal coding

codifier [66] [kɔdifje] *vt* to codify

codirecteur, -trice [kɔdirɛktœr, -tris] *nm,f* joint manager

coédition [kɔedisjɔ̃] *nf* joint publication

coefficient [kɔefisjɑ̃] *nm* coefficient; *Aut* **c. aérodynamique** *ou* **de pénétration dans l'air** drag coefficient

coentreprise [kɔɑ̃trəpriz] *nf* joint venture

coéquipier, -ère [koekipje, -ɛr] *nm,f* team-mate

coercitif, -ive [kɔɛrsitif, -iv] *adj* coercive

coercion [kɔɛrsjɔ̃] *nf* coercion

cœur [kœr] *nm* (**a**) *(organe)* heart; **être malade du c.** to have a weak heart; **être opéré à c. ouvert** to have open-heart surgery; **recevoir une balle en plein c.** to get a bullet right in the heart; **en (forme de) c.** heart-shaped (**b**) *(poitrine)* **serrer** *ou* **presser qn contre son c.** to hold sb close (**c**) *(estomac)* **avoir mal au c.** to feel sick; **soulever le c. à qn** to turn sb's stomach; *Fig* **avoir le c. solide** *ou* **bien accroché** to have a strong stomach (**d**) *(symbole de la bonté)* **avoir bon c.** to be kind-hearted; **ne pas avoir de c.** to be heartless; **avoir un c. d'or/de pierre** to have a heart of gold/stone; **avoir le c. sur la main** to be very generous; **à votre bon c., M'sieurs Dames** can you spare a few coins? (**e**) *(siège des sentiments)* **donner son c. à qn** to lose one's heart to sb; **de tout (son) c.** with all one's heart; **aller droit au c. de qn** to go straight to sb's heart; **avoir le c. brisé** to be broken-hearted; *Fig* **ça (me) fait mal au c.** it's sickening; **faire qch le c. léger** to do sth with a light heart; **avoir le c. gros** *ou* **serré** to have a heavy heart; **si tu aimes la viande, tu vas t'en donner à c. joie** if you like meat, you'll be able

to eat it to your heart's content; **ne pas porter qn dans son c.** to be not very fond of sb; **du fond du c.** from the bottom of one's heart; **au fond de mon c.** in my heart of hearts; *Prov* **le c. a ses raisons que la raison ne connaît point** the heart has its reasons (**f**) *(pensées intimes)* **dire ce qu'on a sur le c.** to say what's on one's mind; **en avoir le c. net** to get to the bottom of it; **ouvrir son c. à qn** to open one's heart to sb (**g**) **par c.** by heart; *Fam* **connaître qn par c.** to know sb inside out (**h**) *(courage)* courage; **ne pas avoir le c. de faire qch** not to have the heart to do sth; *Fam* **avoir du c. au ventre** to have plenty of guts (**i**) *(envie, désir)* **ils n'ont pas le c. à l'ouvrage** their hearts aren't in it; **le c. n'y est pas** his/my/*etc* heart isn't in it; **elle n'a plus le c. à rien** she hasn't the heart for anything any more; **avoir le c. à rire** to be in the mood for laughing; **si le c. vous en dit** if you feel like it; **avoir à c. de faire qch** to have one's heart set on doing sth; **ce projet lui tient à c.** this project is close to his heart; **de bon c.** *(volontiers)* willingly; *(rire)* heartily; **y aller de bon c.** to get down to it (**j**) *(personne)* **c'est un c. d'or** she's got a heart of gold, **merci, mon c.** thank you, darling (**k**) *(centre)* heart; *(d'un réacteur nucléaire)* core; **fromage fait à c.** ripe cheese; **au c. de l'hiver/l'été** in the depths of winter/height of summer; **au c. de la ville** in the heart of the town; **au c. du débat** at the heart of the debate; **c. d'artichaut** artichoke heart; *Fig* **avoir un c. d'artichaut** to fall in love with every girl/man one meets; **c. de palmier** palm heart (**l**) *(objet en forme de cœur)* heart; *(carte)* heart; *(couleur)* hearts

coexistence [kɔɛgzistɑ̃s] *nf* coexistence *(avec* with); *Pol* **c. pacifique** peaceful coexistence

coexister [kɔɛgziste] *vi* to coexist (**avec** with)

coffrage [kɔfraʒ] *nm (pour ouvrages en béton)* formwork

coffre [kɔfr] *nm* (**a**) *(meuble)* chest; **c. à jouets** toy box; **c. à linge** linen chest (**b**) *(pour objets de valeur)* safe; *(à la banque)* safe deposit box; **les coffres de l'État** the coffers of the State (**c**) *Fam* **avoir du c.** *(avoir du souffle)* to have a lot of puff; *(avoir de la voix)* to have a powerful voice (**d**) *(d'une voiture) Br* boot, *Am* trunk; **c. à bagages** *(d'un avion)* baggage compartment

coffre-fort (*pl* **coffres-forts**) [kɔfrəfɔr] *nm* safe

coffrer [kɔfre] *vt Fam (mettre en prison)* to put inside; **se faire c.** to get put inside

coffret [kɔfrɛ] *nm* (**a**) *(petit coffre)* box; **c. à bijoux** jewellery box (**b**) *(de livres, de disques)* box (**c**) *Ordinat* case

cogérant, -e [kɔʒerɑ̃, -ɑ̃t] *nm,f* joint manager

cogestion [kɔʒɛstjɔ̃] *nf* joint management

cogitation [kɔʒitasjɔ̃] *nf Hum* cogitation

cogiter [kɔʒite] *vi Hum* to cogitate

cognac [kɔɲak] *nm* cognac

cognement [kɔɲəmɑ̃] *nm (bruit)* banging; *(d'un moteur)* knocking

cogner [kɔɲe] **1** *vt* (**a**) *(heurter)* to knock (**b**) *Fam (battre)* to knock about **2** *vi* (**a**) *(buter)* to bang **(sur/contre** on); **sa tête a cogné contre le mur** he banged his head on the wall; **c. du poing sur la table** to bang one's fist on the table; **c. à une porte** to bang on a door (**b**) *Fam (frapper)* **il cogne dur** he knows how to use his fists; **se faire c. dessus** to get knocked about (**c**) *Fam* **ça cogne** *(il fait chaud)* it's scorching (**d**) *(moteur)* to knock **3 se cogner** *vpr* to bang oneself; **se c. à** *ou* **contre qch** to bang into sth; **se c. la tête contre qch** to bang one's head on sth; *Fig* **se c. la tête contre les murs** to bang one's head against a brick wall

cohabitation [kɔabitasjɔ̃] nf living together, cohabitation; Pol cohabitation

cohabiter [kɔabite] vi to live together; c. avec qn to live with sb

cohérence [kɔerɑ̃s] nf (d'une argumentation, d'un discours) coherence; (d'une attitude) consistency

cohérent, -e [kɔerɑ̃, -ɑ̃t] adj (argumentation, discours) coherent; (attitude) consistent

cohéritier, -ère [kɔeritje, -ɛr] nm,f joint heir, f joint heiress

cohésion [kɔezjɔ̃] nf cohesion

cohorte [kɔɔrt] nf (de gens) horde

cohue [kɔy] nf crowd

coi, coite [kwa, kwat] adj se tenir c. to keep quiet; en rester c. to be speechless

coiffe [kwaf] nf (coiffure régionale, religieuse) headdress

coiffé, -e [kwafe] adj (a) je ne suis pas encore coiffée I haven't done my hair yet; elle est bien coiffée her hair is lovely; il est mal c. his hair's a mess (b) être c. de qch to be wearing sth (on one's head)

coiffer [kwafe] 1 vt (a) (peigner) c. qn to do sb's hair; il coiffe bien he's a good hairdresser; se faire c. (chez/par qn) to have one's hair done (at sb's/by sb) (b) (mettre un chapeau à) c. qn de qch to put sth on sb's head; Fig c. sainte Catherine to be twenty-five and still unmarried (c) (service) to head (d) Sp & Fig se faire c. (au poteau) to be pipped at the post
  2 se coiffer vpr (a) (se peigner) to do one's hair (b) (mettre) se c. de qch to put sth on

coiffeur, -euse [kwafœr, -øz] 1 nm,f hairdresser
  2 nf coiffeuse (meuble) dressing-table

coiffure [kwafyr] nf (a) (coupe de cheveux) hairstyle (b) (activité) hairdressing (c) (chapeau) headgear; (de costume régional) headdress

coin [kwɛ̃] nm (a) (angle) corner; faire le c. to be on the corner; à tous les coins de rue on every street corner; aux quatre coins du monde in all corners of the earth; mettre un enfant au c. (pour le punir) to make a child stand in the corner; Fig rester dans son c. to keep to oneself; les coins et les recoins de qch the nooks and crannies of sth; je ne voudrais pas le rencontrer au c. d'un bois I wouldn't like to meet him on a dark night; Av & Rail c. fenêtre/couloir window/aisle seat; au c. du feu by the fire(side); lancer un regard en c. à qn to give sb a sidelong glance; sourire en c. half smile; regarder qn du c. de l'œil to look at sb out of the corner of one's eye (b) (endroit quelconque) spot, place; un petit c. tranquille a quiet little spot; Euph le petit c. the smallest room (in the house); dans un c. de ma mémoire in a corner of my mind; j'ai dû le mettre dans un c. I must have put it somewhere; chercher qch dans tous les coins to look high and low for sth (c) (voisinage) du c. local; il habite dans le c. he lives around here (d) (parcelle) patch; c. de ciel bleu patch of blue sky (e) (cale) wedge

coincé, -e [kwɛ̃se] adj (a) (fermeture, porte, mécanisme) jammed, stuck (b) Fam (inhibé) hung up (c) il faut que je paie, je suis c. I'll have to pay, I've no choice

coincer [16] [kwɛ̃se] 1 vt (a) (accidentellement) (tiroir, clef) to jam; j'ai coincé mes cheveux dans ma fermeture Éclair® I got my hair caught in my zip; la voiture est coincée entre deux camions (en stationnement) the car is boxed in by two lorries; être coincé (personne) (dans un embouteillage, un endroit) to be stuck; (être occupé) to be tied up (b) (volontairement) to wedge; elle l'a coincé dans le couloir she cornered him in the corridor; il m'a coincé (je n'ai pas su répondre) he had me cornered (c) Fam (arrêter) to bust; se faire c. to get busted
  2 vi (tiroir, mécanisme) to jam, to stick; Fam ça coince there's a hitch

3 se coincer vpr (tiroir, mécanisme) to jam, to stick; se c. le doigt dans la porte to catch one's finger in the door; je me suis coincé le dos my back's seized up

coïncidence [kɔɛ̃sidɑ̃s] nf coincidence

coïncider [kɔɛ̃side] vi (événements, versions) to coincide (avec with); leurs intérêts coïncident they have similar interests; tous les témoignages coïncident the witnesses all bear each other out

coin-coin [kwɛ̃kwɛ̃] 1 nm inv (des canards) quacking
  2 exclam quack! quack!

coin-cuisine (pl coins-cuisines) [kwɛ̃kɥizin] nm kitchen area

coïnculpé, -e [kɔɛ̃kylpe] nm,f co-defendant

coing [kwɛ̃] nm quince

coin-repas (pl coins-repas) [kwɛ̃rəpa] nm dining area

coït [kɔit] nm coitus

coite [kwat] voir coi

coke [kɔk] 1 nm (combustible) coke
  2 nf Fam (cocaïne) coke

col [kɔl] nm (a) (d'une robe, d'une chemise) collar; c. fourrure/de dentelle fur/lace collar; c. blanc (employé de bureau) white-collar worker; c. bleu (ouvrier) blue-collar worker; c. cheminée ou montant Br turtleneck, Am mock turtleneck; c. rond round neck; c. roulé Br polo neck, Am turtleneck; c. en V V-neck; faux c. false collar (b) (d'une bouteille) neck (c) Géog col (d) Anat (d'un os) neck; c. de l'utérus cervix

colchique [kɔlʃik] nm autumn crocus

coléoptère [kɔleɔptɛr] nm beetle, Spéc coleopteran

colère [kɔlɛr] nf anger; être en c. (contre qn) to be angry (with sb); mettre qn en c. to make sb angry; se mettre en c. to get angry; se mettre dans une c. bleue ou noire to fly into a towering rage; piquer une c. to fly into a rage; passer sa c. sur qn to take one's anger out on sb; avec c. angrily; Litt la c. de Dieu the wrath of God; c. froide cold fury

coléreux, -euse [kɔlerø, -øz], **colérique** [kɔlerik] adj (personne) quick-tempered; (disposition) irritable

colibri [kɔlibri] nm humming-bird

colifichet [kɔlifiʃɛ] nm trinket, knick-knack

colimaçon [kɔlimasɔ̃] nm voir escalier

colin [kɔlɛ̃] nm (merlu) hake; (lieu noir) coley

colin-maillard [kɔlɛ̃majar] nm blindman's-buff; jouer à c. to play blindman's-buff

colique [kɔlik] nf (a) (diarrhée) diarrhoea; avoir la c. to have diarrhoea (b) (douleur) coliques stomach pains, colic; c. néphrétique renal colic

colis [kɔli] nm parcel; par c. postal by parcel post

Colisée [kɔlize] nm le C. the Coliseum

colistier, -ère [kɔlistje, -ɛr] nm,f Pol fellow candidate

colite [kɔlit] nf Méd colitis

collabo [kɔlabo] nmf Fam Hist collaborator

collaborateur, -trice [kɔlabɔratœr, -tris] nm,f (a) (aide) assistant (b) Journ contributor (de to) (c) Hist collaborator

collaboration [kɔlabɔrasjɔ̃] nf (a) (aide) collaboration (à on); travailler en étroite c. (avec qn) to work closely (with sb) (b) Journ contribution (c) Hist collaboration

collaborer [kɔlabɔre] vi (a) (travailler ensemble) to collaborate (avec with); c. à qch (projet) to take part in sth; (journal) to contribute to sth (b) Hist to collaborate

collage [kɔlaʒ] nm (a) (d'affiches) sticking up; (de bois) gluing; (de papier) pasting (b) (composition) collage

collagène [kɔlaʒɛn] nm collagen

collant, -e [kɔlɑ̃, -ɑ̃t] 1 adj (a) (adhésif) sticky (b)

(poisseux) sticky **(c)** *(moulant)* skin-tight **(d)** *Fam (personne)* **qu'est-ce qu'il est c.!** you just can't shake him off!

2 *nm Br* (pair of) tights, *Am* pantihose; **c. de danse** dance tights

collation [kɔlasjɔ̃] *nf (repas)* light meal

colle [kɔl] *nf* **(a)** *(transparente)* glue; *(blanche)* paste; **c. à bois** woodworking glue; **c. forte** strong glue; **de la c. en pot/stick/tube** a pot/stick/tube of glue **(b)** *Fam (question difficile)* poser; **là, tu me poses une c.** you've got me there **(c)** *Fam (punition)* detention **(d)** *Fam (examen oral)* oral test **(e)** *très Fam* **vivre** *ou* **être à la c.** to be shacked up together

collecte [kɔlɛkt] *nf* collection; **faire une c.** (au profit de) to make a collection (in aid of)

collecter [kɔlɛkte] *vt* to collect

collecteur, -trice [kɔlɛktœr, -tris] **1** *nm,f* collector; **c. d'impôts** tax collector

2 *nm* **(a)** *(d'eaux pluviales)* main sewer **(b)** *Aut* **c. d'échappement** exhaust manifold

collectif, -ive [kɔlɛktif, -iv] **1** *adj (action, travail, responsabilité)* collective; *(billet)* group, *(licenciements)* mass

2 *nm* **(a)** *Fin* **c. budgétaire** bill of supply **(b)** *(association)* collective

collection [kɔlɛksjɔ̃] *nf* **(a)** *(action)* collecting; **faire la c. de qch** to collect sth **(b)** *(série) (de timbres, de papillons, d'œuvres d'art)* collection; *(de périodiques)* series; *(d'échantillons)* line; **j'en ai toute une c.** I've got a whole collection of them **(c)** *(de haute couture, de prêt-à-porter)* collection

collectionner [kɔlɛksjɔne] *vt* to collect

collectionneur, -euse [kɔlɛksjɔnœr, -øz] *nm,f* collector

collectivisme [kɔlɛktivism] *nm Écon* collectivism

collectivité [kɔlɛktivite] *nf* **(a)** *(groupe)* community **(b)** **collectivités locales** local communities

collège [kɔlɛʒ] *nm* **(a)** *(école)* school; **c. d'enseignement secondaire** = former secondary school for pupils aged 12 to 15; **c. d'enseignement technique** technical school, **le C. de France** the Collège de France *(prestigious higher education institution)* **(b)** *Pol* **c. électoral** electoral college

collégial, -e, -aux, -ales [kɔleʒjal, -o] **1** *adj* collegiate **2** *nf* **collégiale** collegiate church

collégien, -enne [kɔleʒjɛ̃, -ɛn] *nm,f* schoolboy, *f* schoolgirl; **je me suis fait avoir comme un c.** I fell for it like a fool

collègue [kɔlɛg] *nmf* **c. (de travail)** colleague

coller [kɔle] **1** *vt* **(a)** *(faire adhérer)* to stick (à/sur to/on); **il avait les cheveux collés par la sueur/la peinture** his hair was matted with sweat/paint; **il est resté collé à la télé toute la soirée** he was glued to the TV all evening **(b)** *(appuyer)* **c. qch à** *ou* **contre qch** to press sth against sth **(c)** *Fam (mettre)* to stick; **ils ont collé le bébé à la grand-mère** they've dumped the baby on the grandmother; **on m'a collé la comptabilité sans que j'aie dit oui** I got shoved in accounts without any say in the matter; **c. une gifle à qn** to slap sb in the face; **si tu continues, je t'en colle une!** if you don't stop, I'll slap you one!; **c. une contravention à qn** to slap a fine on sb **(d)** *Fam (retenir en punition)* to keep in; **se faire c.** to be kept in **(e)** *(refuser) (candidat)* to fail; **se faire c.** to fail **(f)** *Fam (suivre)* to follow closely; **il me colle!** he sticks to me like glue! **(g)** *Ordinat* to paste

2 *vi Fam* **(a)** *(coïncider)* to tally (avec with) **(b)** *(aller bien)* **ça colle!** that's OK!; **ça ne va pas c.** pour mercredi it's no go for Wednesday; **ça ne colle pas entre eux** they don't hit it off

3 **coller à** *vt ind aussi Fig* to stick to; *Fam* **c. aux fesses à qn** to stick to sb's tail; **sa réputation lui colle à la peau** he can't shake off his reputation

4 **se coller** *vpr* **(a)** *(adhérer les uns aux autres)* to stick **(b)** *(s'aplatir)* **se c. contre un mur** to flatten oneself against a wall; **se c. contre qn** to cling to sb; *Fam* **se c. devant la télé** to plonk oneself down in front of the TV; *Fam* **c'est encore toi qui t'y colles** you're landed with it again

collerette [kɔlrɛt] *nf* **(a)** *(de vêtement)* collar; *Hist (fraise)* ruff **(b)** *Bot (de champignon)* annulus **(c)** *(de tuyau)* flange

collet [kɔlɛ] *nm* **(a)** *(de vêtement)* collar; **saisir** *ou* **prendre qn au c.** to grab sb by the scruff of the neck; **mettre la main au c. à qn** *(l'arrêter)* to get hold of sb; **être c. monté** to be strait-laced **(b)** *(piège)* snare

colleter [42] [kɔlte] **se colleter** *vpr Fam* to tussle (**avec qn** with sb); **se c. avec qch** to grapple with sth

collier [kɔlje] *nm* **(a)** *(bijou)* necklace; **c. de perles** pearl necklace; **c. de fleurs** garland of flowers **(b)** *(de chien)* collar; *Fig* **donner un coup de c.** to put one's back into it **(c)** *(barbe)* **c. (de barbe)** fringe of beard **(d)** *Culin (de bœuf, de mouton)* neck **(e)** *Tech* collar; **c. de serrage** clamp collar **(f)** *Zool (d'oiseau)* collar

collimateur [kɔlimatœr] *nm Fig* **avoir qn dans le c.** to keep one's eye on sb

colline [kɔlin] *nf* hill

collision [kɔlizjɔ̃] *nf (entre véhicules, entre objets)* collision; **entrer en c. avec qch** to collide with sth; *Aut* **c. frontale/latérale** head-on/side-on collision

colloque [kɔlɔk] *nm (conférence)* seminar

collusion [kɔlyzjɔ̃] *nf* collusion

collutoire [kɔlytwar] *nm* throat spray

collyre [kɔlir] *nm* eyewash

colmater [kɔlmate] *vt* to fill in

colo [kɔlo] *nf Fam Br* (children's) holiday camp, *Am* summer camp

colocataire [kɔlokatɛr] *nmf Br* flatmate, *Am* roommate

Colomb [kɔlɔ̃] *npr* **Christophe C.** Christopher Columbus

colombage [kɔlɔ̃baʒ] *nm Constr* half-timbering; **maison à colombages** half-timbered house

colombe [kɔlɔ̃b] *nf* dove

Colombie [kɔlɔ̃bi] *nf* **la C.** Colombia

Colombie-Britannique [kɔlɔ̃bibritanik] *nf* **la C.** British Columbia

colombien, -enne [kɔlɔ̃bjɛ̃, -ɛn] **1** *adj* Colombian **2** *nm,f* **C.** Colombian

colombier [kɔlɔ̃bje] *nm (pigeonnier)* dovecote

colon [kɔlɔ̃] *nm* **(a)** *(pionnier)* settler, colonist **(b)** *(dans colonie de vacances)* child (at camp)

côlon [kolɔ̃] *nm* colon

colonel [kɔlɔnɛl] *nm (dans l'armée de terre)* colonel; *(dans l'armée de l'air)* Br group captain, *Am* colonel

colonial, -e, -aux, -ales [kɔlɔnjal, -o] **1** *adj* colonial **2** *nf Hist* **la coloniale** the Colonial Army

colonialisme [kɔlɔnjalism] *nm* colonialism

colonialiste [kɔlɔnjalist] *adj & nmf* colonialist

colonie [kɔlɔni] *nf* **(a)** *(territoire, immigrés)* colony **(b)** **c. (de vacances)** *Br* (children's) holiday camp, *Am* summer camp; **envoyer ses enfants en c.** to send one's children to camp

colonisation [kɔlɔnizasjɔ̃] *nf* colonization

coloniser [kɔlɔnize] *vt* to colonize

colonnade [kɔlɔnad] *nf* colonnade

colonne [kɔlɔn] *nf* **(a)** *(pilier)* column, pillar; **c. Morris** = dark-green ornate pillar used to advertise forthcoming events in Paris **(b)** *(file)* column; **en c. par deux/trois** in columns of two/three **(c)** *(d'un dictionnaire, d'un journal)* column **(d)** *(de fumée, de mercure)* column **(e)** *Anat* **c.**

vertébrale spine, spinal column (**f**) *Aut* **c. de direction** steering column

coloquinte [kɔlɔkɛ̃t] *nf (plante)* bitter apple

colorant, -e [kɔlɔrɑ̃, -ɑ̃t] **1** *adj* colouring **2** *nm* (**a**) *(pour teindre)* colorant (**b**) *(alimentaire)* colouring; **sans colorants** *(sur étiquette)* no artificial colouring

coloration [kɔlɔrasjɔ̃] *nf* (**a**) *(fait de colorer)* colouring; **se faire faire une c.** to have one's hair tinted (**b**) *(de la peau)* colouring (**c**) *Fig* **c. politique** political colour

coloré, -e [kɔlɔre] *adj* coloured; *(teint)* ruddy; *Fig (style)* colourful

colorer [kɔlɔre] **1** *vt* to colour; *Fig (récit)* to lend colour to; **c. qch en vert** to colour sth green **2 se colorer** *vpr (visage)* to become flushed

coloriage [kɔlɔrjaʒ] *nm (action)* colouring (in); *(dessin)* drawing; **album** *ou* **livre de c.** colouring (in) book

colorier [66] [kɔlɔrje] *vt* to colour (in)

coloris [kɔlɔri] *nm* shade

coloriser [kɔlɔrize] *vt Cin* to colourize

colossal, -e, -aux, -ales [kɔlɔsal, -o] *adj* colossal, huge

colosse [kɔlɔs] *nm (homme)* giant; *Fig* **un c. aux pieds d'argile** a giant with feet of clay

colostomie [kɔlɔstɔmi] *nf Méd* colostomy

colporter [kɔlpɔrte] *vt (marchandises)* to hawk; *(nouvelle, rumeurs)* to spread

colporteur, -euse [kɔlpɔrtœr, -øz] *nm,f* hawker

colt [kɔlt] *nm* Colt®

coltiner [kɔltine] **se coltiner** *vpr Fam* **se c. qn/qch** to get landed with sb/sth

colvert [kɔlvɛr] *nm* mallard

colza [kɔlza] *nm* rape

coma [kɔma] *nm* coma; **être/tomber dans le c.** to be in/ go into a coma

comateux, -euse [kɔmatø, -øz] **1** *adj* comatose **2** *nm,f* patient in a coma

combat [kɔ̃ba] *nm* (**a**) *Mil (bataille)* fight; *(activité)* combat; **c. aérien** dog fight; *aussi Fig* **c. d'arrière-garde** rearguard action; **c. naval** naval engagement (**b**) *(dispute)* fight; **c. de boxe** boxing match; **c. de coqs** cockfight (**c**) *Fig (lutte)* fight (**contre** against)

combatif, -ive [kɔ̃batif, -iv] *adj* combative

combativité [kɔ̃bativite] *nf* combativeness

combattant, -e [kɔ̃batɑ̃, -ɑ̃t] **1** *nm,f* combatant; **anciens combattants** veterans **2** *adj (troupes, unité)* fighting

combattre [11] [kɔ̃batr] **1** *vt (ennemi)* to fight (against); *(maladie, inflation, racisme)* to fight **2** *vi* to fight (**pour/contre** for/against)

combien [kɔ̃bjɛ̃] **1** *adv* (**a**) *(comme)* how (much); **j'ai pu constater c. tu avais changé** I could see how much you'd changed (**b**) *(en nombre)* how many; **c. sont-ils?** how many (of them) are there?; **c. de** how many; **c. de gens furent tués dans cette guerre!** what a lot of people were killed in that war! (**c**) *(en quantité, en poids)* how much; **ça fait c.?** *(d'argent)* how much is that?; **c. y a-t-il d'ici à Londres?** how far is it to London?; **à c. sommes-nous de Paris?** how far are we from Paris?; **c. mesure-t-il?** how tall is he?; **elle est enceinte - de c.?** she's pregnant - **how many months?**; **c. de** how much; **c. de temps** how long **2** *nm inv Fam* **le c. sommes-nous?** what's the date (today)?; **il y a un car tous les c.?** how often do the buses run?; **tu chausses du c.?** what size shoe do you take?

combientième [kɔ̃bjɛ̃tjɛm] *Fam* **1** *nmf* **c'est le c. sur la liste?** where is it on the list?

2 *adj* **tu as été reçu c. à l'examen?** where did you come in the exam?; **c'est la c. fois que tu viens?** how often have you been now?

combinaison [kɔ̃binɛzɔ̃] *nf* (**a**) *(assemblage)* combination; **la c. gagnante** *(au tiercé)* the winning combination; *Ordinat* **c. de touches** key combination (**b**) *(vêtement) (de travail)* Br boiler suit, Am coveralls; *Av* flying suit; *(de femme)* catsuit; *(sous-vêtement)* slip; **c. de plongée** wet suit; **c. de ski** ski suit

combine [kɔ̃bin] *nf Fam* trick; **il a une c. pour entrer sans payer** he knows a way of getting in without paying; **mettre qn dans la c.** to let sb in on it

combiné, -e [kɔ̃bine] **1** *adj (action, efforts)* combined **2** *nm* (**a**) **c. (téléphonique)** receiver (**b**) *(en ski)* **c. alpin** alpine competition

combiner [kɔ̃bine] **1** *vt* (**a**) *(unir)* to combine (**b**) *Fam (plan)* to concoct; **qu'est-ce que tu combines encore?** what are you cooking up now? **2 se combiner** *vpr* to combine

comble [kɔ̃bl] **1** *adj* (jam-)packed; **faire salle c.** *(au théâtre)* to have a full house **2** *nm* (**a**) *(maximum)* **le c.** the height of; *(du désespoir)* the depth of; **ça, c'est la** *ou* **un c.!** that's the last straw!; **être au c. de la joie** to be overjoyed (**b**) *Archit (en bois)* roof timbers; *(en métal)* roof structure; **les combles** *(grenier)* the attic; **loger sous les combles** to live in an attic

combler [kɔ̃ble] *vt* (**a**) *(puits, fossé, trou)* to fill in; *(perte)* to make good; *(découvert)* to pay off; *(lacune)* to fill; **c. son retard** to make up for lost time (**b**) *(satisfaire)* to satisfy; **c. qn de cadeaux** to shower sb with gifts; **un mari comblé** a happily married man

combustible [kɔ̃bystibl] **1** *nm* fuel **2** *adj* combustible

combustion [kɔ̃bystjɔ̃] *nf* combustion

comédie [kɔmedi] *nf (pièce, film, genre)* comedy; **jouer la c.** to act; *Fig* to put on an act; **allons, pas de c.!** *(caprice)* come on, stop your nonsense!; **c'est une vraie c. quand il faut aller à l'école** it's a real fuss when it's time to go to school; **c. de mœurs** comedy of manners; **c. musicale** musical

Comédie-Française [kɔmedifrɑ̃sɛz] *nf* **la C.** = state-run theatre company presenting plays from the established repertoire

comédien, -enne [kɔmedjɛ̃, -ɛn] **1** *nm,f (acteur)* actor, f actress; *Fig* **c'est une comédienne** she's always putting on an act; **comédiens ambulants** strolling players **2** *adj* **elle est très comédienne** she's always putting on an act

comédon [kɔmedɔ̃] *nm* blackhead

comestible [kɔmɛstibl] *adj* edible; **denrées comestibles** foodstuffs

comète [kɔmɛt] *nf* comet; *Fig* **tirer** *ou* **faire des plans sur la c.** to build castles in the air

comice [kɔmis] *nm* **c. agricole** agricultural association; **comices agricoles** *(foire)* agricultural show

comique [kɔmik] **1** *adj* (**a**) *(acteur, film, rôle)* comedy; **le genre c.** comedy (**b**) *(amusant)* comical, funny **2** *nm* (**a**) *(genre)* comedy; **c. de situation** situation comedy (**b**) *(acteur)* comic actor; *Péj (bouffon)* comedian (**c**) **le c. de l'histoire, c'est que...** the funny part is that...

comité [kɔmite] *nm* committee; **faire partie d'un c.** to sit on a committee; *Fig* **nous serons en petit c.** we'll just have a small get-together; **c. d'entreprise** works council; **C. international olympique** International Olympic Committee

commandant [kɔmɑ̃dɑ̃] *nm* (**a**) *(officier) (d'unité)* commander; *(de camp, de base)* commandant; *(de bateau)* captain *(whatever his rank); Av* **c. de bord** captain; **c. en chef** commander-in-chief; *Naut* executive officer **(b)** *(rang) (dans l'armée de terre)* major; *(dans l'armée de l'air)* Br squadron leader, *Am* major

commande [kɔmɑ̃d] *nf* **(a)** *Com* order; **faire** *ou* **passer une c.** to put in *or* place an order; **sur c.** to order; *Fig* at will; **on ne peut pas rire sur c.** you can't laugh to order; **ouvrage de c.** commissioned work **(b)** *(action, manette)* control; *(mécanisme)* drive; **c. à distance** remote control; **commandes** *(d'un avion)* controls; **prendre les commandes** *(d'un avion)* to take over the controls; *(d'une société)* to take control **(c)** *Ordinat* command; **c. d'annulation/d'effacement** undo/delete command; **à c. vocale** voice-activated

commandement [kɔmɑ̃dmɑ̃] *nm* **(a)** *(ordre)* Mil command; **à mon c.** when I give the command; *Rel* **les dix commandements** the Ten Commandments **(b)** *(pouvoir)* command; **avoir/prendre le c.** to be in/to take command; **c. suprême, haut c.** high command

commander [kɔmɑ̃de] **1** *vt* **(a)** *(diriger, ordonner)* to command; *Fam* **sans vous c., est-ce que vous pourriez fermer la porte?** I wonder if you'd mind closing the door **(b)** *(marchandises, dîner)* to order; *(peinture, ouvrage)* to commission; **c. qch à qn** to order/commission sth from sb **(c)** *(mouvement, valve)* to control; *(machine)* to drive **(d)** *Ordinat* to drive; **commandé par menu** menu-driven

2 *vi* **c. à qn de faire qch** to order sb to do sth; **qui est-ce qui commande ici?** who's in charge here?

3 se commander *vpr* **ces choses-là ne se commandent pas** *(sont incontrôlables)* these things are beyond our control

commanditaire [kɔmɑ̃diter] *adj & nm* Com **(associé) c.** Br sleeping *or* Am silent partner; **les commanditaires de l'attentat** the people behind the attack

commandite [kɔmɑ̃dit] *nf* Com **(société en) c.** mixed liability company

commandité [kɔmɑ̃dite] *adj & nm* Com **(associé) c.** active partner

commanditer [kɔmɑ̃dite] *vt* Com to finance; *(meurtre, attentat)* to be behind

commando [kɔmɑ̃do] *nm* *(groupe)* commando (unit)

comme [kɔm] **1** *adv* **(a)** *(devant un nom, un pronom)* like; **il n'est pas c. les autres** he isn't like the others; **c. ça** like that; *(du coup)* that way; **c'est c. ça, un point c'est tout!** too bad, that's the way it is!; **alors c. ça, vous venez de Genève?** you come from Geneva, don't you?; *Fam* **c. ça!** *(formidable)* great!, fab!; **quelque chose c. deux cents personnes** something like two hundred people

(b) *(devant une proposition)* as; **il écrit c.** il parle he writes as he speaks; **insolent c. il est…** insolent as he is…; **il leva la main c. pour me frapper** he lifted his hand as if *or* as though to strike me; **c. il faut** *(se conduire)* properly; **des gens très c. il faut** very respectable people; **c. si** as if, as though; **c. si je ne le savais pas!** as if I didn't know!

(c) *(dans des images)* as; **doux c. un agneau** (as) gentle as a lamb

(d) *(et)* **les femmes c. les hommes** men and women alike; **tout le monde fera la vaisselle, toi c. les autres** everyone's going to do the washing-up, and you're no exception

(e) *(tel que)* such as, like; **les bois durs c. le chêne** hard woods like *or* such as oak; **P c. pomme** P as in pomme

(f) *(en tant que)* as; **je l'ai eue c. professeur** she was my teacher; **qu'est-ce que vous avez c. desserts?** what have you got in the way of desserts?; **ce n'est pas mal c. film** it's not a bad movie

(g) *(en quelque sorte)* **elle a eu c. une hésitation** she seemed to hesitate; **j'étais c. hypnotisé** it was as if *or* as though I was hypnotized

(h) *(comment)* how; **tu sais bien c. il est** you know what

he's like; *Fam* **elle a fait les carreaux, faut voir c.!** you should see the way she's done the windows!

(i) *(exclamatif)* how; **c. tu as grandi!** how you've grown!; **elle est bête!** she's so stupid!; **c. elle a de beaux cheveux!** what lovely hair she has!

(j) *Fam (locutions)* **c'est tout c.** it amounts to the same thing; **c. ci c. ça** so-so; **c. qui dirait** as it were; **c. quoi** *(disant que)* to the effect that; *(ce qui prouve que)* which goes to show that; **drôle c. tout** as funny as anything

2 *conj* **(a)** *(puisque)* as, since; **c. vous êtes mon ami, je vais tout vous dire** as you're my friend I'll tell you everything

(b) *(alors que)* **c. il allait frapper, la porte s'ouvrit** he was just about to knock when the door opened

commémoratif, -ive [kɔmemɔratif, -iv] *adj (plaque, cérémonie)* commemorative; *(service)* memorial; **monument c.** memorial

commémoration [kɔmemɔrasjɔ̃] *nf* commemoration; **en c. de** in commemoration of

commémorer [kɔmemɔre] *vt* to commemorate

commencement [kɔmɑ̃smɑ̃] *nm* beginning, start; **au c.** at the beginning *or* start; **il faut un c. à tout** you've got to start somewhere; *Fam* **c'est le c. de la fin** it's the beginning of the end

commencer [10] [kɔmɑ̃se] **1** *vt* **(a)** *(entreprendre)* to begin, to start; *(traitement, régime)* to go on, to start; **nous avons mal commencé l'année** we've made a bad start to the year **(b)** *(être au début de)* to begin, to start

2 *vi* to begin, to start; **pour c., je dois vous dire…** to begin with, I must tell you…; *Ironique* **ça commence bien!** that's a good start!; **c. par qch/par faire qch** to begin *or* start with/by doing sth; **par où c.?** where shall I begin?; **à c. par…** beginning with…

3 commencer à *vt ind* **c. à faire qch** to begin *or* start to do sth, to begin *or* start doing sth; *Fam* **je commence à en avoir assez!** I've had just about enough!; *Fam* **ça commence à bien faire** it's getting a bit too much

comment [kɔmɑ̃] **1** *adv* how; **c. allez-vous?** how are you?; **c.?** *(pour faire répéter)* I beg your pardon?; **c. faire?** what can I/we/etc do?; **c. est-il, ce garçon?** what's this boy like?; **elle me dira c. faire** she'll tell me how to do it

2 *exclam* what!; **mais c. donc!** why, of course!; *Fam* **ça vous a plu? – et c.!** did you like it? – you bet I did!

commentaire [kɔmɑ̃ter] *nm* **(a)** *(remarque)* comment, remark; **faire des commentaires** to make comments; **cela se passe de c.** it speaks for itself; *Fam* **sans c.!** no comment!; *Scol* **c. de texte** textual commentary **(b)** *(à la radio, à la télévision)* commentary; **c. sportif** sports commentary

commentateur, -trice [kɔmɑ̃tatœr, -tris] *nm,f (à la radio, à la télévision)* commentator; **c. sportif** sports commentator

commenter [kɔmɑ̃te] *vt (expliquer, donner son avis sur)* to comment on; *(à la radio, à la télévision) (compétition)* to commentate on; **c. l'actualité** to comment on current affairs

commérage [kɔmeraʒ] *nm* (piece of) gossip; **commérages** gossip

commerçant, -e [kɔmersɑ̃, -ɑ̃t] **1** *nm,f* trader; *(qui tient un magasin)* shopkeeper; **petits commerçants** small traders

2 *adj* **quartier c.** shopping area; **rue très commerçante** busy shopping street; **il n'est pas très c.** he doesn't look after his customers very well

commerce [kɔmers] *nm* **(a)** **le c.** *(activité, secteur)* trade; *(affaires)* business; **ça se trouve dans le c.** you can buy it in the shops; **faire du c. avec** to do business with; **hors c.** not for (general) sale; **c. en** *ou* **de gros/de détail** wholesale/

retail trade; **c. intérieur/extérieur** home/foreign trade; **c. international** world trade; **c. maritime** seaborne trade; **le petit c.** small traders **(b)** *(magasin)* business

commercer [16] [kɔmɛrse] *vi* to trade **(avec** with)

commercial, -e, -aux, -ales [kɔmɛrsjal, -o] **1** *adj (rapports, pratiques)* business, commercial; *(embargo, tribunal)* trade; *(droit)* commercial; *Péj (film, chanson)* commercial; **suivre une formation commerciale** to do a business studies course
2 *nm,f* salesman, *f* saleswoman
3 *nf* **commerciale** *(voiture) Br* estate car, *Am* station wagon

commercialisation [kɔmɛrsjalizasjɔ̃] *nf* marketing

commercialiser [kɔmɛrsjalize] *vt (produit)* to market

commère [kɔmɛr] *nf* gossip

commettre [47] [kɔmɛtr] **1** *vt* **(a)** *(crime, péché, injustice)* to commit; *(erreur)* to make; *Hum* **il a déjà commis deux pièces de théâtre** he's already to blame for two plays **(b)** *Jur* **avocat commis d'office** counsel appointed by the court
2 se commettre *vpr Litt* **se c. avec qn** to compromise oneself by associating with sb

commis¹, -e *voir* **commettre**

commis² [kɔmi] *nm* **(a)** *(employé)* clerk; *(dans un magasin)* (shop) assistant **(b)** *Vieilli* **c. voyageur** commercial traveller

commisération [kɔmizerasjɔ̃] *nf* commiseration; **témoigner de la c. à qn** to commiserate with sb

commissaire [kɔmisɛr] *nm* **(a) c. (de police)** *Br* ≃ (police) superintendent, *Am* ≃ (police) captain **(b)** *Fin* **c. aux comptes** government auditor **(c)** *(membre d'une commission)* commissioner **(d)** *Sp* steward

commissaire-priseur *(pl* **commissaires-priseurs)** [kɔmisɛrprizœr] *nm* auctioneer

commissariat [kɔmisarja] *nm* **(a) c. (de police)** police station **(b)** *(fonction)* commissionership **(c)** *(service)* commission; **le C. à l'énergie atomique** the Atomic Energy Commission

commission [kɔmisjɔ̃] *nf* **(a)** *(course)* **faire les commissions** to go shopping **(b)** *(service)* errand; *(message)* message; **faire une c.** to run an errand; **faire une c. à qn** to give sb a message **(c)** *(comité)* commission, committee; **c. d'enquête** board of inquiry; **C. européenne** European Commission; **C. des opérations de Bourse** = French Stock Exchange watchdog **(d)** *(pourcentage) Com* commission; *Fin* brokerage; **être payé à la c.** to be paid on a commission basis; **c. bancaire** bank commission **(e)** *Fam* **la petite/grosse c.** number one/two

commissionnaire [kɔmisjɔner] *nm* **(a)** *(messager)* messenger; *(à l'hôtel, au théâtre)* commissionaire **(b)** *Com* (commission) agent

commissionner [kɔmisjɔne] *vt* to commission

commissures [kɔmisyr] *nfpl* **c. des lèvres** *ou* **de la bouche** corners of the mouth

commode [kɔmɔd] **1** *adj* **(a)** *(heure, lieu)* convenient; *(outil, système)* handy **(b) pas c.** *(difficile)* tricky **(c) pas c.** *(peu aimable)* awkward
2 *nf* chest of drawers

commodément [kɔmɔdemɑ̃] *adv (assis, installé)* comfortably

commodité [kɔmɔdite] *nf* **(a)** *(facilité)* convenience; **pour plus de c.** for greater convenience; **les commodités de la vie moderne** the comforts of modern life **(b)** *Vieilli* **commodités** *(toilettes) Br* toilet, *Am* rest room

commotion [kɔmɔsjɔ̃] *nf* **(a)** *Méd* **c. cérébrale** concussion **(b)** *(émotion)* shock

commotionner [kɔmɔsjɔne] *vt* **(a)** *Méd* to concuss **(b)** *(choquer)* to shake (up)

commuer [kɔmɥe] *vt Jur (peine)* to commute **(en** to)

commun, -e [kɔmœ̃, -yn] **1** *adj* **(a)** *(non exclusif)* common **(à** to); *(travail)* joint; *(ami)* mutual; **jardin c. à deux maisons** garden shared by two houses; **en c.** *(travailler)* together; *(vivre)* communally; **avoir qch en c.** *(se ressembler)* to have sth in common; **se mettre** *ou* **mettre de l'argent en c.** pour acheter un cadeau to club toget her to buy a present **(b)** *(répandu)* common; **il est d'une force peu commune** he's unusually strong **(c)** *(vulgaire)* common
2 *nm* **(a)** *(majorité)* **le c. des mortels** the ordinary man; **hors du c.** out of the ordinary **(b)** **communs** *(dépendances)* outbuildings

communal, -e, -aux, -ales [kɔmynal, -o] *adj (de la commune) (terrain, salle) Br* ≃ council, *Am* ≃ district; **école communale** ≃ local *Br* primary *or Am* elementary school

communautaire [kɔmynoter] *adj (en commun)* communal; *(de la Communauté européenne)* Community

communauté [kɔmynote] *nf* **(a)** *(collectivité) & Rel* community; *(de hippies)* commune; **vivre en c.** to live in a commune; **la C. économique européenne** the European Economic Community; **la C. d'États indépendants** the Commonwealth of Independent States **(b)** *(d'intérêts, d'idées)* similarity; *Jur* **être mariés sous le régime de la c.** to be married on the basis of a joint settlement of property

commune [kɔmyn] *nf* **(a)** *(municipalité)* commune *(smallest territorial division)* **(b)** *Hist* **la C.** the Commune *(in 1789 and 1871)*

communément [kɔmynemɑ̃] *adv* commonly

communiant, -e [kɔmynjɑ̃, -ɑ̃t] *nm,f Rel* communicant; **premier c.** person taking his first communion

communicatif, -ive [kɔmynikatif, -iv] *adj* **(a)** *(qui parle)* communicative; **peu c.** uncommunicative **(b)** *(rire, bonne humeur)* infectious

communication [kɔmynikasjɔ̃] *nf* **(a)** *(échange)* communication; **entrer** *ou* **se mettre en c. avec qn** to get in touch *or* in contact with sb; **toutes les communications sont coupées** all lines of communication are cut; **c. de masse** mass communication **(b)** **c. (téléphonique)** (telephone) call; **je vous passe la c.** I'll put you through; **la c. est mauvaise** the line is bad **(c)** *(message)* communication, message; **faire une c.** *(dans un colloque)* to read a paper

communier [66] [kɔmynje] *vi Rel* to receive Communion

communion [kɔmynjɔ̃] *nf* **(a)** *(communauté)* communion; **être en c. avec la nature** to commune with nature **(b)** *Rel* Communion; **première c.** first Communion; **c. solennelle** solemn Communion; **faire sa c.** to make one's first/solemn Communion

communiqué [kɔmynike] *nm* communiqué; **c. de presse** press release

communiquer [kɔmynike] **1** *vt* to communicate **(à** to); *(maladie)* to pass on **(à** to)
2 *vi* **(a)** *(être en relation)* to communicate **(avec** with) **(b)** *(pièce)* to communicate **(avec** with); **porte qui communique avec le jardin** door that leads into the garden
3 se communiquer *vpr (se transmettre)* to spread **(à** to)

communisme [kɔmynism] *nm* communism

communiste [kɔmynist] *adj & nmf* communist

commutateur [kɔmytatœr] *nm Él (bouton)* switch; *Ordinat* **c. de données** data switch

commutation [kɔmytasjɔ̃] *nf* **(a)** *Jur (de peine)* commutation **(b)** *(changement) & Gram* substitution; *(entre documents)* switching **(c)** *Ordinat* **c. de message/de paquets** message/packet switching

Comores [kɔmɔr] *nfpl* les **C.**, l'archipel des **C.** the Comoros **comorien, -enne** [kɔmɔrjɛ̃, -ɛn] **1** *adj* Comoran **2** *nmf* **C.** Comoran

compact, -e [kɔpakt] **1** *adj* (**a**) *(de petit format)* compact (**b**) *(masse, terre)* compact; *(foule)* dense **2** *nm (CD)* compact disc **Compact Disc®** *(pl* **Compact Discs)** [kɔpaktdisk] *nm* compact disc **compacter** [kɔpakte] *vt Ordinat (fichier, données)* to compress; *(base de données)* to pack **compacteur** [kɔpaktœr] *nm Ordinat* **c. de données** data compressor; **c. d'exécutables** execute file compressor **compagne** [kɔpaɲ] *nf* (**a**) *(camarade)* companion; **mes compagnes de captivité** my fellow captives (**b**) *(concubine)* partner **compagnie** [kɔpaɲi] *nf* (**a**) *(présence)* company; **tenir c. à qn** to keep sb company (**b**) *(groupe)* **et toute la c.** and everybody (**c**) *Com & Th* company; *Com* **Leclerc et C.** Leclerc and Company; **c. aérienne** airline; **c. d'assurances** insurance company; **c. maritime** shipping line; **c. pétrolière** oil company; **c. de transports** carrier (**d**) *Mil* company (**e**) *(de perdrix)* covey **compagnon** [kɔpaɲɔ̃] *nm* (**a**) *(camarade)* companion; **c. de voyage** travelling companion (**b**) *(ouvrier)* journeyman (**c**) *(concubin)* partner **comparable** [kɔparabl] *adj* comparable (**à** *ou* **avec** to *or* with); **ce n'est pas c.** there's no comparison **comparaison** [kɔparɛzɔ̃] *nf* (**a**) *(action de comparer)* comparison; **faire la c.** entre to make a comparison between; **c'est sans c. avec...** it can't be compared with...; **il est sans c. le plus grand** he is by far the tallest; **en c. de...** in comparison with...; **par c.** by comparison; **par c. avec** *ou* **à** compared with *or* to (**b**) *(figure de style)* simile **comparaître** [50a] [kɔparɛtr] *vi Jur* **c. (en justice)** to appear (in court); **être appelé à c.** to be summoned to appear **comparatif, -ive** [kɔparatif, -iv] **1** *adj* comparative **2** *nm Gram* comparative; **c. de supériorité/d'infériorité** comparative of greater/lesser degree **comparativement** [kɔparativmã] *adv* comparatively **comparé, -e** [kɔpare] *adj (anatomie, histoire, littérature)* comparative; **c. à** compared with *or* to **comparer** [kɔpare] **1** *vt* to compare (**à** *ou* **avec** to *or* with) **2 se comparer** *vpr* (**a**) *(soi-même)* **se c. à** *ou* **avec** to compare oneself to *or* with (**b**) *(être comparé)* **Händel ne peut pas se c. à Mozart** Handel can't be compared with Mozart **comparse** [kɔpars] *nmf Péj* associate **compartiment** [kɔpartimã] *nm (de wagon, de boîte, de tiroir)* compartment; **c. fumeurs** smoking compartment; **c. non-fumeurs** no-smoking compartment; **c. à bagages** *(d'autocar)* luggage compartment **compartimenter** [kɔpartimãte] *vt (diviser en espaces)* to partition; *Fig* **une société compartimentée** a compartmentalized society **comparution** [kɔparysjɔ̃] *nf Jur* appearance **compas** [kɔpa] *nm* (**a**) *Math* (pair of) compasses; *Fig* **avoir le c. dans l'œil** to have an accurate eye; **c. à pointes sèches** dividers (**b**) *Naut* compass **compassé, -e** [kɔpase] *adj* stiff, starchy **compassion** [kɔpasjɔ̃] *nf* compassion; **avec c.** compassionately **compatibilité** [kɔpatibilite] *nf* compatibility **compatible** [kɔpatibl] *adj aussi Ordinat* compatible (**avec** with)

compatir [kɔpatir] *vi* to sympathize; **c. au chagrin de qn** to sympathize with sb in his/her grief **compatissant, -e** [kɔpatisã, -ãt] *adj* compassionate, sympathetic **compatriote** [kɔpatriɔt] *nmf* compatriot **compensable** [kɔpãsabl] *adj (chèque)* clearable **compensation** [kɔpãsasjɔ̃] *nf* (**a**) *(d'une perte, d'un inconvénient)* compensation; **en c. de qch** as compensation for sth (**b**) *(de chèque)* clearing **compensé, -e** [kɔpãse] *adj* **chaussures à semelles compensées** platform shoes **compenser** [kɔpãse] **1** *vt* (**a**) *(perte, défaut)* to compensate for, to make up for (**b**) *(chèque)* to clear **2 se compenser** *vpr* to make up for each other **compère** [kɔpɛr] *nm Vieilli (camarade)* friend **compétence** [kɔpetãs] *nf* (**a**) *(capacité)* competence; **compétences** *(connaissances)* ability; **cela n'entre pas dans mes compétences** it's beyond my capabilities (**b**) *Jur (d'un tribunal, d'un maire)* competence; **cela n'est pas de sa c.** that doesn't come within her province **compétent, -e** [kɔpetã, -ãt] *adj* (**a**) *(capable)* competent; **en c. en qch** conversant with sth (**b**) *Jur (tribunal, autorité)* competent; **adressez-vous au service c.** apply to the relevant department **compétitif, -ive** [kɔpetitif, -iv] *adj* competitive **compétition** [kɔpetisjɔ̃] *nf* (**a**) *(rivalité)* competition; **être en c. avec qn** to compete with sb (**b**) *Sp (épreuve)* **c. (sportive)** *(sporting)* event; **faire de la c.** to go in for competitive sport **compétitivité** [kɔpetitivite] *nf* competitiveness **compilateur** [kɔpilatœr] *nm Ordinat* compiler; **c. croisé** cross-compiler **compilation** [kɔpilasjɔ̃] *nf* compilation **compiler** [kɔpile] *vt aussi Ordinat* to compile **complaire** [55a] [kɔplɛr] **se complaire** *vpr* **se c. dans qch/à faire qch** to delight or revel in sth/in doing sth **complaisance** [kɔplezãs] *nf* (**a**) *(bienveillance)* kindness; **faire qch par c.** to do sth out of kindness (**b**) *Péj (indulgence)* indulgence; **certificat médical de c.** = medical certificate to which one is not entitled (**c**) *(autosatisfaction)* complacency, smugness **complaisant, -e** [kɔplezã, -ãt] *adj* (**a**) *(bienveillant)* obliging, kind (**envers** towards) (**b**) *Péj (indulgent)* indulgent (**c**) *(satisfait)* complacent, smug **complément** [kɔplemã] *nm (reste)* rest, remainder; **demander un c. d'information** to ask for further information (**b**) *Gram* complement; **c. d'attribution** indirect object; **c. circonstanciel de temps/de manière** adverbial phrase of time/of manner; **c. de nom** possessive phrase; **c. d'objet direct/indirect** direct/indirect object **complémentaire** [kɔplemãter] *adj (couleur)* complementary; **pour tout renseignement c., s'adresser à...** for further information, apply to... **complet, -ète** [kɔplɛ, -ɛt] **1** *adj* (**a**) *(entier, intégral) (tenue, service)* complete, whole; **trois jours complets** three full *or* whole days; **formation très complète** thorough training; *Fam* **c'est c.!** that's the last straw! (**b**) *(détaillé)* full (**c**) *(absolu)* complete; **un c. abruti** a complete moron; **ce fut un échec c.** it was a complete failure (**d**) *(bus, salle de théâtre)* full; **c.** *(sur panneau) (parking)* full; *(pension, hôtel)* no vacancies (**e**) *(pain, pâtes)* wholemeal; *(riz)* brown **2** *nm* (-veston) suit; **est-ce que nous sommes au c.?** are we all here?; **j'ai invité la famille au (grand) c. pour Noël** I've invited the whole family for Christmas **complètement** [kɔplɛtmã] *adv* (**a**) *(terminé, guéri)* completely, totally; **je n'ai pas c.** fini I haven't quite finished (**b**) *(vraiment) (perdu, idiot)* completely, totally

compléter [34] [kɔplete] **1** *vt (collection, formation)* to complete; *(somme)* to make up; *(formulaire)* to complete, to fill in
2 se compléter *vpr* to complement one another

complexe [kɔplɛks] **1** *adj (compliqué)* complex
2 *nm* (**a**) *(ensemble de bâtiments, d'industries)* complex; **c. hôtelier** hotel complex; **c. sportif** sports complex (**b**) *(gêne)* hang-up; *Psy* complex; **avoir des complexes (à cause de qch)** to have a hang-up (about sth); **être sans c.** to have no hang-ups; **c. d'infériorité** inferiority complex; **c. d'Œdipe** Oedipus complex

complexé, -e [kɔplɛkse] *adj* hung up (**par** about)

complexer [kɔplɛkse] *vt* **c. qn** to give sb a hang-up

complexité [kɔplɛksite] *nf* complexity

complication [kɔplikasjɔ̃] *nf* (**a**) *(ennui)* complication; **faire des complications** to create complications (**b**) *(complexité)* complexity (**c**) *Méd* **complications** complications

complice [kɔplis] **1** *nmf* accomplice
2 *adj (regard, sourire)* knowing; **être c. de qch** to be party to sth

complicité [kɔplisite] *nf* complicity; **agir en c. avec qn** to act in collusion with sb; **accusé de c. de meurtre** accused of being an accessory to murder

compliment [kɔplimɑ̃] *nm* compliment; **faire des compliments à qn (sur qch)** to pay sb compliments (on sth); **(je vous fais) mes compliments!** I congratulate you!; *Ironique* **mes compliments!** congratulations!

complimenter [kɔplimɑ̃te] *vt* **c. qn pour** *(courage, présence d'esprit)* to congratulate sb on; **c. qn sur** *(toilette, coiffure)* to compliment sb on

compliqué, -e [kɔplike] *adj* complicated; **ce n'est pourtant pas c.!** it's quite simple!

compliquer [kɔplike] **1** *vt* to complicate; **c. les choses** to complicate matters
2 se compliquer *vpr (situation, problème)* to get complicated; **se c. l'existence** to make life complicated for oneself

complot [kɔplo] *nm* plot, conspiracy

comploter [kɔplɔte] **1** *vt* to plot
2 *vi* to plot (**contre** against); **c. de faire qch** to plot to do sth

comportement [kɔpɔrtəmɑ̃] *nm* behaviour; *Écon* **c. d'achat** buying behaviour

comporter [kɔpɔrte] **1** *vt* (**a**) *(être constitué de)* to consist of, to be made up of (**b**) *(contenir)* to contain (**c**) *(difficultés, inconvénients)* to involve
2 se comporter *vpr* (**a**) *(agir)* to behave (**vis-à-vis de** *ou* **envers** towards) (**b**) *(fonctionner) (voiture)* to handle

composant [kɔpozɑ̃] *nm* component

composante [kɔpozɑ̃t] *nf* component

composé, -e [kɔpoze] *adj & nm* compound

composer [kɔpoze] **1** *vt* (**a**) *(symphonie, poème)* to compose, to write; *(bouquet)* to make up (**b**) *(faire partie de)* to make up; **être composé de qch** to be made up *or* composed of sth (**c**) *(numéro de téléphone)* to dial (**d**) *Typ* to set (**e**) **c. son visage** to compose one's features
2 *vi* (**a**) *(s'entendre)* to compromise (**avec** with) (**b**) *Scol* to take a test
3 se composer *vpr* (**a**) **se c. de qch** to be made up *or* composed of sth (**b**) **se c. un visage de circonstance** to put on a suitable expression

composite [kɔpozit] *adj* composite

compositeur, -trice [kɔpozitœr, -tris] *nm,f* (**a**) *Mus* composer (**b**) *Typ* typesetter

composition [kɔpozisjɔ̃] *nf* (**a**) *(d'une symphonie, d'un poème)* composition, writing; **un poème de ma c.** a poem I wrote (myself) (**b**) *(éléments)* composition; *(d'un aliment)* ingredients; **la c. des équipes n'est pas encore connue** the teams haven't been announced yet (**c**) *(œuvre musicale, littéraire)* composition (**d**) *(rédaction)* essay; *(examen)* test (**e**) *(caractère)* **être de bonne c.** to be good-natured (**f**) *Typ* typesetting

compost [kɔpɔst] *nm* compost

composter [kɔpɔste] *vt (billet)* to cancel

compote [kɔpɔt] *nf* compote, stewed fruit; **c. de pommes** *Br* apple compote, stewed apples, *Am* applesauce; *Fam* **j'ai les jambes en c.** my legs feel like jelly

compotier [kɔpɔtje] *nm* fruit dish

compréhensible [kɔpreɑ̃sibl] *adj* (**a**) *(clair)* comprehensible (**par** to) (**b**) *(justifié)* understandable

compréhensif, -ive [kɔpreɑ̃sif, -iv] *adj* understanding

compréhension [kɔpreɑ̃sjɔ̃] *nf* (**a**) *(fait de comprendre)* comprehension, understanding (**b**) *(bienveillance)* understanding

comprendre [58] [kɔprɑ̃dr] **1** *vt* (**a**) *(par l'esprit)* to understand; **dois-je c. que…?** am I to understand that…?; **mal c. qn/qch** to misunderstand sb/sth; **je ne le comprends pas** *(il est étrange, il n'articule pas)* I can't understand him; **il faut la c.** you have to see things from her point of view; **je n'y comprends rien** I can't make head nor tail of it; **c'est à n'y rien c.** it's incomprehensible; **ne cherche pas, il n'y a rien à c.** don't even try to understand; **va y c. quelque chose!** YOU try to make head or tail of it!; **faire c. à qn que…** to give sb to understand that…; *(avec autorité)* to make it clear to sb that…; **se faire c.** to make oneself understood; **me suis-je bien fait c.?** have I made myself clear?; **elle comprend vite** she's quick on the uptake; **ça va, j'ai compris!** OK, I understand!; **tu comprends…** you see… (**b**) *(être composé de)* to consist of, to be made up of (**c**) *(inclure)* to include
2 se comprendre *vpr (l'un l'autre)* to understand each other; **ça se comprend** it's understandable; **je me comprends!** I know what I mean!

compresse [kɔpres] *nf* compress

compresser [kɔprese] *vt* to compress

compresseur [kɔpresœr] *nm* (**a**) *Tech (de gaz, de vapeur)* compressor; *(de moteur)* supercharger (**b**) *Ordinat* **c. de données** data compressor

compression [kɔmpresjɔ̃] *nf* (**a**) *(de gaz, de vapeur)* compression (**b**) *(réduction)* reduction; **c. des dépenses** spending cuts

comprimé, -e [kɔprime] **1** *adj (gaz)* compressed
2 *nm (médicament)* tablet; **un c. d'aspirine** an aspirin

comprimer [kɔprime] *vt* (**a**) *(gaz, air)* to compress; **cette jupe me comprime la taille** this skirt is too tight round my waist (**b**) *Fig (dépenses)* to reduce

compris, -e [kɔpri, -iz] **1** *pp voir* **comprendre**
2 *adj* (**a**) *(enregistré)* **bien c.** (fully) understood; **mal c.** misunderstood; **alors, c'est c.?** so, do you understand?; *Fam* **tu fais tes devoirs immédiatement, c.?** you'll do your homework right now, (is that) understood? (**b**) *(inclus)* included; **service non c.** service not included; **tout c.** all in; **y c.** including (**c**) *(situé)* **être c. entre** to be between

compromettant, -e [kɔprɔmetɑ̃, -ɑ̃t] *adj* compromising

compromettre [47] [kɔprɔmɛtr] **1** *vt* (**a**) *(personne, réputation)* to compromise; **être compromis dans qch** to be implicated in sth (**b**) *(sécurité, vacances, chances)* to jeopardize
2 se compromettre *vpr* to compromise oneself; **se c. dans qch** to be implicated in sth

compromis [kɔ̃prɔmi] *nm (arrangement)* compromise
compromission [kɔ̃prɔmisjɔ̃] *nf Péj* compromise
comptabiliser [kɔ̃tabilize] *vt (recettes, dépenses)* to enter in the accounts; *(points)* to count
comptabilité [kɔ̃tabilite] *nf* **(a)** *(livres)* accounts; *(technique)* book-keeping, accounting; **tenir la c.** to keep the accounts **(b)** *(service)* accounts department
comptable [kɔ̃tabl] **1** *adj (travail, technique)* book-keeping, accounting **2** *nmf* accountant; **c. agréé** *Br* chartered accountant, *Am* certified public accountant
comptage [kɔ̃taʒ] *nm* counting
comptant [kɔ̃tɑ̃] **1** *adv* **payer c.** to pay (in) cash **2** *nm* cash; **payer/acheter au c.** to pay (in)/buy for cash
compte [kɔ̃t] *nm* **(a)** *(dans une banque, chez un commerçant)* account; **comptes** *(comptabilité)* accounts; **tenir les comptes** to keep the accounts; **faire ses comptes** to do one's accounts; **verser une somme sur son c.** to pay a sum into one's account; **se mettre** *ou* **s'installer a son c.** to start one's own business; **faire qch pour le c. de qn** to do sth on sb's behalf; **c. en banque** *ou* **bancaire** bank account; **c. chèques** *Br* current account, *Am* checking account; **c. chèques postal** ≃ giro account; **c. courant** *Br* current account, *Am* checking account; **c. de dépôt** deposit account; **c. épargne** savings account; **c. joint** joint account **(b)** *(calcul)* calculation; **faire le c. de** *(dépenses)* to add up; *(temps restant)* to calculate; *(objets, personnes)* to count; **le c. y est** *(somme)* it's the right amount; *(objets, personnes)* they're all here; **c. à rebours** countdown **(c)** *(explication)* **demander des comptes à qn** to ask sb for an explanation; **rendre des comptes** to explain oneself; **je n'ai de comptes à rendre à personne** I'm not answerable to anyone; **rendre c. de qch** to account for sth **(d)** *(locutions) Fam* **avoir son c.** to have had enough; **être loin du c.** *(se tromper)* to be wide of the mark; *Fam* **régler son c. à qn** to sort sb out; **on réglera nos comptes plus tard** we'll settle scores later; **apprendre qch sur le c. de qn** to learn sth about sb; *Fam* **son c. est bon** he's for it; **tenir c. de qch** to take sth into account; **c. tenu de** considering; **s'en tirer à bon c.** to get off lightly; **y trouver son c.** to get something out of it; **à ce c.-là** in that case; **au bout du c., en fin de c.** in the end; **tout c. fait** all things considered; *Prov* **les bons comptes font les bons amis** pay your debts and keep your friends
compte-gouttes [kɔ̃tgut] *nm inv* dropper; *Fig* **au c.** in dribs and drabs
compter [kɔ̃te] **1** *vt* **(a)** *(dénombrer)* to count; **on ne compte plus les mécontents** we've lost count of the malcontents; *Fig* **c. les points** to watch from the sidelines **(b)** *(donner avec parcimonie)* **il compte chaque sou** he begrudges every penny he spends; **ses jours sont comptés** his days are numbered **(c)** *(inclure)* to include; **sans c....** not counting...; **sans c. que...** besides the fact that...; **je le compte parmi mes meilleurs amis** I number him among my best friends **(d)** *(prévoir)* to allow; **j'ai compté une bouteille par personne** I've allowed one bottle per person; **c. faire qch** *(espérer)* to expect to do sth; *(avoir intention de)* to intend to do sth **(e)** *(facturer)* **c. qch à qn** to charge sb for sth **2** *vi* **(a)** *(calculer)* to count; **dépenser sans c.** *(dépenser trop)* to spend money like water; **à c. du 1er janvier** (with effect) from 1 January **(b)** *(être parcimonieux)* to count the pennies **(c)** *(être important)* to count, to matter; **il compte beaucoup pour elle** he means a lot to her; **c. double** to count double; **à table, il compte pour deux** he eats enough for two **(d)** *(figurer)* **c. parmi les meilleurs** to rank among the best **(e)** **c. avec qn/qch** to reckon with sb/sth **(f)** **c. sur qn/qch** to count *or* rely on sb/sth; **j'y compte bien!** I

should hope so!; *Fam* **compte là-dessus et bois de l'eau!** you'll be lucky!
3 se compter *vpr* **les détournements de fonds se comptent par dizaines** there have been dozens of cases of embezzlement
compte rendu *(pl* **comptes rendus)** [kɔ̃trɑ̃dy] *nm* report; *(d'un roman, d'un film)* review; *(d'une réunion)* minutes
compte-tours [kɔ̃ttur] *nm inv* rev counter
compteur [kɔ̃tœr] *nm* meter; **c. d'eau/d'électricité/à gaz** water/electricity/gas meter; **c. (de) Geiger** Geiger counter; *Aut* **c. kilométrique** *Br* mileometer, *Am* odometer; *Aut* **c. de vitesse** speedometer
comptine [kɔ̃tin] *nf* nursery rhyme
comptoir [kɔ̃twar] *nm* **(a)** *(dans un magasin)* counter; *(dans un bar)* bar; **prendre une consommation au c.** to have a drink at the bar; **c. d'enregistrement** check-in desk; **c. d'information** information desk; **c. de réception** reception desk; **c. de vente** sales counter **(b)** *(dans un pays éloigné)* trading post
compulser [kɔ̃pylse] *vt (documents, livres)* to consult
comte [kɔ̃t] *nm* count; *(en Grande-Bretagne)* earl
comté [kɔ̃te] *nm* **(a)** *Hist* earldom **(b)** *(subdivision administrative)* county **(c)** *(fromage)* = type of hard cheese **(d)** *Can Pol* riding
comtesse [kɔ̃tɛs] *nf* countess
con, conne [kɔ̃, kɔn] **1** *adj très Fam* **(a)** *(stupide)* bloody stupid; *Fam* **être c. comme la lune** *ou* **un balai** to be as daft as a brush; **c'est con c.!** that's pretty smart! **(b)** *(facile)* **c'est tout c.!** it's dead easy! **2** *nm,f très Fam* stupid bastard; **faire le c.** to arse around; **pauvre c.!** stupid bastard!; **à la c.** *(ordinateur, voiture)* bloody useless; *(idée, histoire)* bloody stupid **3** *nm Vulg (sexe)* cunt
conard [kɔnar] *nm très Fam* jerk
conasse [kɔnas] *nf très Fam* silly bitch
concasser [kɔkase] *vt (roche)* to crush; *(poivre)* to grind
concave [kɔkav] *adj* concave
concéder [34] [kɔsede] *vt* **(a)** *(privilège, droit, terrain, concession)* **c. qch à qn** to grant sb sth, to grant sth to sb **(b)** *(reconnaître)* **c. qu'on a tort** to admit that one is wrong; **il fait chaud, je vous le concède** it's warm, I grant you **(c)** *Sp (point, but, victoire)* to concede
concentration [kɔsɑ̃trasjɔ̃] *nf* concentration
concentrationnaire [kɔsɑ̃trasjɔnɛr] *adj* of concentration camps; **la vie c.** life in a concentration camp
concentré, -e [kɔsɑ̃tre] **1** *adj* **(a)** *(solution)* concentrated; *(lait)* condensed **(b)** *(intellectuellement)* **il était très c.** he was concentrating hard **2** *nm Chim & Culin* concentrate; **c. de tomate** tomato purée
concentrer [kɔsɑ̃tre] **1** *vt (troupes, forces, efforts)* to concentrate; *(rayons du soleil)* to focus **2 se concentrer** *vpr* **(a)** *(être attentif)* to concentrate **(sur on) (b)** *(s'assembler)* *(foule)* to gather; **la population se concentre dans les grandes villes** the population is concentrated in the big cities
concentrique [kɔsɑ̃trik] *adj* concentric
concept [kɔsɛpt] *nm* concept
conception [kɔsɛpsjɔ̃] *nf* **(a)** *(d'un enfant, d'une idée)* conception **(b)** *(idée)* concept **(c)** *(création)* design; **c. assistée par ordinateur** computer-aided *or* -assisted design
concernant [kɔsɛrnɑ̃] *prép* concerning
concerner [kɔsɛrne] *vt* to concern; **en ce qui me concerne** as far as I am concerned; **cela ne vous concerne pas** *(cela ne vous regarde pas)* it's none of your business; *(vous n'êtes pas visé)* it doesn't concern you

concert [kɔsɛr] *nm* (a) *(de musique)* concert (b) *(accord)* **agir de c. avec qn** to act jointly with sb

concertation [kɔsɛrtasjɔ̃] *nf* consultation

concerté, -e [kɔsɛrte] *adj (action)* concerted

concerter [kɔsɛrte] **1** *vt (projet)* to devise together **2 se concerter** *vpr* to consult together

concertiste [kɔsɛrtist] *nmf* concert performer

concerto [kɔsɛrto] *nm* concerto

concession [kɔsɛsjɔ̃] *nf* (a) *(compromis)* concession; **faire des concessions** to make concessions; **sans concessions** uncompromising (b) *(attribution) (de terrain)* granting (c) *(terrain)* concession; *(au cimetière)* plot (d) *(droit exclusif de vente)* dealership

concessionnaire [kɔsɛsjɔnɛr] *nmf* dealer

concevable [kɔsəvabl] *adj* conceivable

concevoir [60] [kɔsəvwar] **1** *vt* (a) *(enfant, plan, idée)* to conceive; *(produit)* to design (b) *(comprendre)* to understand (c) *(éprouver)* **c. de l'amitié pour qn** to take a liking to sb. **2 se concevoir** *vpr* **ça se conçoit** that's understandable

concierge [kɔsjɛrʒ] *nmf (d'immeuble, d'appartements) & Scol Br* caretaker, *Am* janitor; *(dans un hôtel)* porter; *Fam* **c'est une vraie c.** she's a terrible gossip

concile [kɔsil] *nm Rel* council

conciliabule [kɔsiljabyl] *nm (conversation)* confab

conciliant, -e [kɔsiljɑ̃, -ɑ̃t] *adj* conciliatory

conciliation [kɔsiljasjɔ̃] *nf* reconciliation

concilier [66] [kɔsilje] **1** *vt (deux choses)* to reconcile; **c. sa vie professionnelle et sa vie de famille** to combine one's professional life with one's family life **2 se concilier** *vpr* (a) *(être compatible)* **se c. avec** to go with (b) **se c. qn** *ou* **la faveur de qn** to win sb's goodwill

concis, -e [kɔsi, -iz] *adj* concise

concision [kɔsizjɔ̃] *nf* conciseness; **avec c.** concisely

concitoyen, -enne [kɔsitwajẽ, -ɛn] *nm,f* fellow citizen

concluant, -e [kɔklyɑ̃, -ɑ̃t] *adj* conclusive; **peu c.** inconclusive

conclure [17] [kɔklyr] **1** *vt* (a) *(terminer)* to conclude, to end *(par with)* (b) *(accord, pacte)* to finalize; *(marché)* to clinch; **marché conclu!, affaire conclue!** it's a deal! (c) *(déduire)* to conclude *(de* from); **dois-je en c. que...?** am I to conclude that...? **2 conclure à** *vt ind* **ils ont conclu au suicide/meurtre** they concluded it was suicide/murder

conclusion [kɔklyzjɔ̃] *nf* (a) *(fin) (d'un discours, d'une réunion)* conclusion, end (b) *(déduction)* conclusion; **tirer une c. de qch** to draw a conclusion from sth; *Fam* **c., l'échafaudage s'est écroulé** the result was that the scaffolding collapsed

concocter [kɔkɔkte] *vt Fam* to concoct

concombre [kɔkɔbr] *nm* cucumber

concordance [kɔkɔrdɑ̃s] *nf* (a) *(de preuves, de témoignages, de dates)* tallying (b) *Gram* **c. des temps** sequence of tenses

concorder [kɔkɔrde] *vi (preuves, dates, témoignages)* to tally *(avec* with)

concourir [22] [kɔkurir] *vi* (a) *Sp* to compete (b) *(lignes)* to converge **2 concourir à** *vt ind* **c. à qch/à faire qch** to contribute to sth/to doing sth

concours [kɔkur] *nm* (a) *(compétition)* competition, contest; *(examen)* competitive examination; **c. agricole/ hippique** agricultural/horse show; **c. de beauté** beauty contest; **c. d'entrée** entrance examination *(to)* (b) *(aide)* aid, assistance (c) **c. de circonstances** combination of circumstances

concret, -ète [kɔkrɛ, -ɛt] *adj* concrete

concrètement [kɔkrɛtmã] *adv* in concrete terms

concrétiser [kɔkretize] **1** *vt (rêve)* to realize; *(projet, promesse)* to carry out **2 se concrétiser** *vpr* to materialize

conçu, -e *voir* **concevoir**

concubin, -e [kɔkybẽ, -in] *nm,f Jur* cohabitant

concubinage [kɔkybinaʒ] *nm* cohabitation; **vivre en c.** to cohabit

concupiscent, -e [kɔkypisɑ̃, -ɑ̃t] *adj* concupiscent

concurrence [kɔkyrɑ̃s] *nf* (a) *(rivalité, concurrents)* competition; **faire c. à** to compete with; **faire jouer la c.** to shop around (b) **jusqu'à c. de...** up to...

concurrencer [16] [kɔkyrɑse] *vt* to compete with

concurrent, -e [kɔkyrɑ̃, -ɑ̃t] **1** *adj (industries, produits)* competing, rival **2** *nm,f* (a) *Com* competitor (b) *(dans une épreuve, un concours)* competitor

concurrentiel, -elle [kɔkyrɑ̃sjɛl] *adj* competitive

condamnation [kɔdanasjɔ̃] *nf* (a) *Jur (jugement)* conviction *(pour* for); *(peine)* sentence *(à* to); **c. à mort** death sentence (b) *(critique)* condemnation

condamné, -e [kɔdane] **1** *adj (malade)* terminally ill **2** *nm,f* convicted person; **un c. à mort** a condemned man

condamner [kɔdane] *vt* (a) *Jur* to sentence *(à* to); **c. qn à 1000 euros d'amende** to fine sb 1,000 euros (b) *(obliger à)* **c. qn à qch** to force sb into sth; **être condamné à la solitude** to be condemned to loneliness; **je suis condamnée à les attendre** I have to wait for them (c) *(blâmer)* to condemn (d) *(porte)* to block up; *(pièce)* to seal up (e) *(interdire)* to forbid

condensateur [kɔdɑ̃satœr] *nm Él* condenser

condensation [kɔdɑ̃sasjɔ̃] *nf* condensation

condensé, -e [kɔdɑ̃se] **1** *adj* condensed **2** *nm* digest

condenser [kɔdɑ̃se] **1** *vt (article, récit)* to condense **2 se condenser** *vpr* to condense

condescendant, -e [kɔdesɑ̃dɑ̃, -ɑ̃t] *adj* condescending

condescendre [kɔdesɑ̃dr] *vi* **c. à faire qch** to condescend to do sth

condiment [kɔdimɑ̃] *nm* condiment

condisciple [kɔdisipl] *nmf Univ* fellow student; *Scol* schoolmate

condition [kɔdisjɔ̃] *nf* (a) *(stipulation)* condition; **sans c.** unconditionally; **à une c....** on one condition...; **à c. que tu viennes avec moi** providing that *or* on condition that you come with me; **tu peux y aller à c. de rentrer avant minuit** you can go providing that *or* on condition that you're home before midnight (b) **conditions** *(circonstances)* conditions; *(d'une vente, d'un accord)* terms; **dans ces conditions, je n'y vais pas** if that's the way it is, I'm not going; **conditions atmosphériques** atmospheric conditions; **conditions de paiement** terms of payment; **conditions de vie/travail** living/working conditions (c) *(état)* condition; **être en bonne/mauvaise c. physique** to be in good/bad shape (d) *(sort)* condition; **la c. humaine** the human condition; **les ouvriers/des paysans** the workers'/farmers' lot (e) *(classe sociale)* station, status

conditionnel, -elle [kɔdisjɔnɛl] **1** *adj* conditional **2** *nm Gram* conditional

conditionnement [kɔdisjɔnmɑ̃] *nm* (a) *(fait d'emballer, emballage)* packaging (b) *Psy* conditioning

conditionner [kɔdisjɔne] *vt* (a) *(être la condition de)* to govern (b) *(emballer)* to package (c) *Psy (personne)* to condition

condoléances [kɔ̃dɔleɑ̃s] *nfpl* condolences; **présenter ses c. à qn** to offer one's condolences to sb; **toutes mes c.** (please accept) my condolences

condominium [kɔ̃dɔminjɔm] *nm Pol* condominium

condor [kɔ̃dɔr] *nm* condor

conducteur, -trice [kɔ̃dyktœr, -tris] **1** *nm,f(d'une voiture, d'un train)* driver; *(de machine)* operator; **c. de travaux** clerk of works **2** *nm Él & Phys* conductor **3** *adj Él & Phys* conductive

conduction [kɔ̃dyksjɔ̃] *nf Él* conduction

conductivité [kɔ̃dyktivite] *nf Él* conductivity

conduire [18] [kɔ̃dɥir] **1** *vt* (a) *(emmener)* to take; *(en voiture)* to drive, to take (b) *(mener) (troupeau, aveugle)* to lead (c) *(entraîner)* **c. qn à faire qch** to lead sb to do sth; **c. qn au désespoir/suicide** to drive sb to despair/suicide (d) *(voiture, camion)* to drive; *(moto)* to ride; *(bateau)* to steer (e) *(acheminer) (eau, gaz)* to carry (f) *(diriger) (opérations)* to manage, to run **2** *vt* (a) *(en voiture)* to drive; *(en moto)* to ride; **elle conduit bien** she's a good driver (b) *(sujet: porte, couloir, études)* **c. à** to lead to **3 se conduire** *vpr (se comporter)* to behave; **se c. mal** *(d'un enfant)* to misbehave; **se c. bien/mal avec qn** to behave well/badly towards sb

conduit [kɔ̃dɥi] *nm* (a) *(tuyau)* conduit, pipe; **c. d'aération** air duct; **c. de ventilation** ventilation shaft (b) *Anat* **c. auditif** auditory canal

conduite [kɔ̃dɥit] *nf* (a) *(de voiture, de camion)* driving; *(de moto)* riding; **leçons de c.** driving lessons; **c. à gauche/droite** *(position du volant)* left-/right-hand drive; *(sur la route)* driving on the left/right; **c. accompagnée** = learning to drive accompanied by someone holding a full driving licence; **c. intérieure** *Br* saloon (car), *Am* sedan; **c. sur route** driving on the open road (b) *(des affaires, des opérations)* management, running; *(d'une armée)* command; *(de travaux)* supervision (c) *(comportement)* behaviour, conduct; *Hum* **s'acheter une c.** to turn over a new leaf (d) *(tuyau)* pipe; **c. d'eau/de gaz** water/gas main

cône [kon] *nm* cone

confection [kɔ̃fɛksjɔ̃] *nf* (a) *(d'un vêtement, d'un repas)* making (b) *(industrie)* (ready-made) clothing industry; **vêtements de c.** ready-made clothes

confectionner [kɔ̃fɛksjɔne] *vt* to make

confédération [kɔ̃federasjɔ̃] *nf* confederation; **la C. helvétique** the Swiss Confederation

conférence [kɔ̃ferɑ̃s] *nf* (a) *(congrès, colloque)* conference; **c. de presse** press conference; **c. au sommet** summit (conference) (b) *(exposé)* lecture; **faire une c. sur...** to give a lecture on...

conférencier, -ère [kɔ̃ferɑ̃sje, -ɛr] *nm,f* lecturer

conférer [34] [kɔ̃fere] **1** *vt (titre)* to confer (à on); **l'âge confère certains privilèges** age brings with it certain privileges **2** *vi* to confer (**avec** with)

confesser [kɔ̃fese] **1** *vt* (a) *Rel* to confess (b) *(reconnaître)* to confess, to admit **2 se confesser** *vpr* to confess; **(aller) se c.** to go to confession

confession [kɔ̃fɛsjɔ̃] *nf* (a) *Rel & Fig* confession; *Fam* **on lui donnerait le bon Dieu sans c.** he/she looks as though butter wouldn't melt in his/her mouth (b) *(croyance)* denomination

confessionnal, -aux [kɔ̃fɛsjɔnal, -o] *nm* confessional

confetti [kɔ̃feti] *nm* (piece of) confetti; **confettis** confetti

confiance [kɔ̃fjɑ̃s] *nf* (a) *(foi)* trust, confidence; **avoir c.**

en qn/qch, faire c. à qn/qch to trust sb/sth, to have confidence in sb/sth; **faites-moi c.** trust me; *Fam (croyez-moi)* believe me; **digne de c.** trustworthy; **de c.** *(mission)* of trust; *(personne)* trustworthy (b) *(assurance)* confidence; **c. en soi** self-confidence; **avoir c. en soi** to be self-confident

confiant, -e [kɔ̃fjɑ̃, -ɑ̃t] *adj* (a) *(qui fait confiance)* trusting (b) *(optimiste)* confident (**dans** in) (c) *(qui a confiance en soi)* self-confident

confidence [kɔ̃fidɑ̃s] *nf* confidence; **faire une c. à qn** to confide in sb; **mettre qn dans la c.** to let sb into the secret

confident, -e [kɔ̃fidɑ̃, -ɑ̃t] *nm,f* confidant, *f* confidante

confidentiel, -elle [kɔ̃fidɑ̃sjɛl] *adj* confidential

confidentiellement [kɔ̃fidɑ̃sjɛlmɑ̃] *adv* confidentially

confier [66] [kɔ̃fje] **1** *vt* (a) *(laisser)* **c. qch à qn** to entrust sb with sth; **je leur ai confié les enfants** I left the children with them (b) *(dire)* **c. qch à qn** to confide sth to sb; **c. un secret à qn** to share a secret with sb **2 se confier** *vpr* **se c. à qn** to confide in sb

configuration [kɔ̃figyrasjɔ̃] *nf* (a) *(disposition)* configuration; *(de bâtiment)* layout; **la c. du terrain** the lie of the land (b) *Ordinat* configuration; **c. matérielle** hardware configuration

configurer [kɔ̃figyre] *vt Ordinat* to configure

confiné, -e [kɔ̃fine] *adj* (a) *(atmosphère)* enclosed, *(air)* stale (b) *(enfermé)* shut up

confiner [kɔ̃fine] **1** *vt (enfermer)* to confine, to shut up **2 confiner à** *vt ind* to border on **3 se confiner** *vpr* **se c. chez soi** to shut oneself up indoors

confins [kɔ̃fɛ̃] *nmpl (de région, d'État)* confines, borders; **aux c. de** on the edge of

confirmation [kɔ̃firmasjɔ̃] *nf* confirmation

confirmer [kɔ̃firme] **1** *vt (nouvelle, jugement)* to confirm; **c. qn dans son opinion** to confirm sb in his/her opinion **2 se confirmer** *vpr (nouvelle, bruit)* to be confirmed; *(tendance)* to continue

confiserie [kɔ̃fizri] *nf* (a) *(magasin) Br* sweetshop, *Am* candy store (b) *(bonbon)* **confiseries** *Br* sweets, *Am* candy (c) *(secteur)* confectionery

confiseur, -euse [kɔ̃fizœr, -øz] *nm,f* confectioner

confisquer [kɔ̃fiske] *vt* to confiscate

confit, -e [kɔ̃fi, -it] **1** *adj (fruits)* crystallized, candied **2** *nm* **c. de canard** duck confit

confiture [kɔ̃fityr] *nf* jam; **c. de fraises** strawberry jam; **c. d'oranges** (orange) marmalade; *Fig* **ce serait donner de la c. aux cochons** that would be throwing pearls before swine

conflictuel, -elle [kɔ̃fliktɥel] *adj (témoignages, intérêts)* conflicting; **situation conflictuelle** situation of potential conflict; **ils ont des rapports conflictuels** they have a tempestuous relationship

conflit [kɔ̃fli] *nm* conflict; **c. armé** armed conflict; **conflits sociaux** industrial disputes

confluent [kɔ̃flyɑ̃] *nm* confluence; **au c. du Cher et de la Loire** where the Cher and the Loire meet

confondre [kɔ̃fɔ̃dr] **1** *vt* (a) *(personnes, noms, dates)* to confuse, to mix up; **je l'ai confondu avec Paul** I mistook him for Paul; **toutes catégories confondues** all categories taken together (b) *(sidérer)* to astound (c) *(démasquer)* to confound **2 se confondre** *vpr* (a) *(couleurs, formes)* to merge, to blend (**en** into) (b) *(être similaire) (intérêts)* to merge (c) *(se répandre)* **se c. en excuses** to apologize profusely; **se c. en remerciements** to be profuse in one's thanks

conforme [kɔ̃fɔrm] *adj* (a) *(identique)* **copie c. à l'original** exact copy; **pour copie c.** *(sur document)*

certified true copy; *Fig* **c'est la copie c. de sa sœur** she's the image of her sister (**b**) *(qui correspond)* **être à** to be in accordance with
conformément [kɔ̃fɔrmemɑ̃] **conformément à** *prép* in accordance with
conformer [kɔ̃fɔrme] **1** *vt* to model (**à** on)
2 se conformer *vpr* **se c. à qch** to conform to sth
conformisme [kɔ̃fɔrmism] *nm* conformism
conformiste [kɔ̃fɔrmist] *adj & nmf* conformist
conformité [kɔ̃fɔrmite] *nf (d'un produit aux normes)* compliance (**à** with); **en c. avec** in accordance with
confort [kɔ̃fɔr] *nm* comfort; **maison/hôtel tout c.** house/hotel with every modern convenience; **c. d'emploi** *(d'un ordinateur)* user-friendliness
confortable [kɔ̃fɔrtabl] *adj* comfortable
confortablement [kɔ̃fɔrtabləmɑ̃] *adv* comfortably; **installe-toi c.** make yourself comfortable
conforter [kɔfɔrte] *vt (position, avance)* to consolidate; **c. qn dans son opinion** to confirm sb's opinion
confrère [kɔ̃frɛr] *nm (de profession)* colleague; *(de société)* fellow member
confrérie [kɔ̃freri] *nf Rel* brotherhood
confrontation [kɔ̃frɔ̃tasjɔ̃] *nf* (**a**) *(face-à-face)* confrontation; *Fig (d'opinions, d'idéaux)* clash, conflict (**b**) *(comparaison)* comparison
confronter [kɔ̃frɔ̃te] *vt* (**a**) *(personnes)* to confront; **être confronté à** to be confronted with (**b**) *(comparer)* to compare
confucianisme [kɔ̃fysjanism] *nm* Confucianism
confus, -e [kɔ̃fy, -yz] *adj* (**a**) *(indistinct) (masse, explication, idées)* confused; *(bruit)* indistinct; *(style, texte)* obscure (**b**) *(embarrassé)* embarrassed
confusément [kɔ̃fyzemɑ̃] *adv* vaguely
confusion [kɔ̃fyzjɔ̃] *nf* (**a**) *(désordre)* confusion; **jeter la c. dans les esprits** to confuse people (**b**) *(méprise)* mix-up, confusion (**c**) *(gêne)* embarrassment
congé [kɔ̃ʒe] *nm* (**a**) *(vacances) Br* holiday, *Am* vacation; **en c.** on holiday; **un jour/une semaine de c.** a day/a week off; **congés payés** paid holiday (**b**) *(arrêt de travail)* leave; **c. de maladie** sick leave; **c. de maternité** maternity leave (**c**) *(avis de renvoi)* notice; **donner son c. à qn** to give sb his notice; **demander son c.** to hand in one's notice (**d**) **prendre c. de qn** to take one's leave of sb
congédier [66] [kɔ̃ʒedje] *vt* to dismiss
congélateur [kɔ̃ʒelatœr] *nm* freezer
congélation [kɔ̃ʒelasjɔ̃] *nf* freezing
congeler [39] [kɔ̃ʒle] **1** *vt (aliments)* to freeze **2 se congeler** *vpr* to freeze
congénital, -e, -aux, -ales [kɔ̃ʒenital, -o] *adj* congenital
congère [kɔ̃ʒɛr] *nf* snowdrift
congestion [kɔ̃ʒɛstjɔ̃] *nf* congestion; **c. cérébrale** stroke; **c. pulmonaire** congestion of the lungs
congestionné, -e [kɔ̃ʒɛstjɔne] *adj (visage)* flushed; *(routes)* congested
conglomérat [kɔ̃ɡlɔmera] *nm* conglomerate
Congo [kɔ̃ɡo] *nm* **le C.** the Congo
congolais, -e [kɔ̃ɡɔlɛ, -ɛz] **1** *adj* Congolese **2** *nm,f* **C.** Congolese **3** *nm (pâtisserie)* coconut cake
congratuler [kɔ̃ɡratyle] *vt* to congratulate
congre [kɔ̃ɡr] *nm* conger (eel)
congrégation [kɔ̃ɡreɡasjɔ̃] *nf Rel* congregation
congrès [kɔ̃ɡrɛ] *nm* conference; **le C.** *(aux États-Unis)* Congress

congru, -e [kɔ̃ɡry] *adj voir* **portion**
conifère [kɔnifɛr] *nm* conifer
conique [kɔnik] *adj* conical
conjecture [kɔ̃ʒɛktyr] *nf* conjecture
conjecturer [kɔ̃ʒɛktyre] *vi* to conjecture
conjoint, -e [kɔ̃ʒwɛ̃, -ɛ̃t] **1** *adj* joint **2** *nm* spouse; **les conjoints** the husband and wife
conjointement [kɔ̃ʒwɛ̃tmɑ̃] *adv* jointly
conjonctif, -ive [kɔ̃ʒɔ̃ktif, -iv] *adj* (**a**) *Gram* conjunctive (**b**) *Anat* connective
conjonction [kɔ̃ʒɔ̃ksjɔ̃] *nf* (**a**) *(union)* union; **la c. de nos efforts** our combined efforts (**b**) *Gram* conjunction; **c. de coordination/subordination** coordinating/subordinating conjunction
conjonctivite [kɔ̃ʒɔ̃ktivit] *nf* conjunctivitis
conjoncture [kɔ̃ʒɔ̃ktyr] *nf (situation)* circumstances, situation; **dans la c. actuelle** in the present circumstances
conjugaison [kɔ̃ʒyɡɛzɔ̃] *nf* (**a**) *(d'un verbe)* conjugation (**b**) *(union)* combination
conjugal, -e, -aux, -ales [kɔ̃ʒyɡal, -o] *adj (devoir)* conjugal; **bonheur c.** wedded bliss; **le domicile c.** the matrimonial home; **le lit c.** the marital bed; **la vie conjugale** married life
conjuguer [kɔ̃ʒyɡe] *vt* (**a**) *(verbe)* to conjugate (**b**) *(unir)* to combine
conjurer [kɔ̃ʒyre] **1** *vt* (**a**) *(implorer)* **c. qn de faire qch** to beg *or* implore sb to do sth; **je t'en conjure** I beg you (**b**) *(écarter) (danger, mauvais sort)* to avert, to ward off **2 se conjurer** *vpr* to conspire (together) (**contre** against)
connaissance [kɔnɛsɑ̃s] *nf* (**a**) *(fait de connaître)* knowledge; **avoir c. de qch** to be aware of sth; **prendre c. de qch** to acquaint oneself with sth; **à ma c.** to my knowledge; **en (toute) c. de cause** with full knowledge of the facts (**b**) *(contact)* **faire la c. de qn** to make sb's acquaintance; **faire c. avec qn** to get to know sb; **quelqu'un de ma c.** someone I know, an acquaintance of mine (**c**) *(personne)* acquaintance (**d**) *(savoir)* knowledge; **elle a de bonnes connaissances en chimie** she has a good knowledge of chemistry (**e**) *(conscience)* consciousness; **sans c.** unconscious
connaisseur, -euse [kɔnɛsœr, -øz] **1** *nm,f* connoisseur, expert **2** *adj* expert
connaître [20] [kɔnɛtr] **1** *vt* (**a**) *(personne, détails, endroit)* to know; **c. qn de nom/de vue** to know sb by name/by sight; **il n'y connaît rien** he doesn't know anything about it; **c'est ce film qui l'a fait c.** this is the movie that made his/her name; **tu connais la nouvelle?** have you heard the news?; **c'est mal le c.** you/they/etc don't know him; *Fam* **je connais la musique** *ou* **la chanson** I've heard it all before; *Fam* **si tu fais ça, je ne te connais plus** if you do that, I'll have nothing more to do with you (**b**) *(rencontrer)* to meet (**c**) *(éprouver) (famine, guerre civile)* to experience; *(amour, peur, faim)* to know; **c. des moments difficiles** to go through some difficult times; **c. un destin tragique** to have a tragic fate; **c. un succès considérable** to enjoy considerable success (**d**) *(avoir)* **ne pas c. de limites** to know no bounds **2 se connaître** *vpr* (**a**) **se c. (soi-même)** to know oneself (**b**) **s'y c. en qch** to know a lot about sth (**c**) *(se rencontrer)* to meet
connard [kɔnar] *= conard*
conne [kɔn] *voir* **con**
connecter [kɔnɛkte] *vt Él* to connect; *Ordinat* **connecté** on line; **connecté en anneau/bus/étoile** in a ring/bus/star configuration
connerie [kɔnri] *nf très Fam* (**a**) *(acte stupide)* **faire une**

c./des conneries to do a bloody stupid thing/some bloody stupid things (**b**) *(remarque stupide)* bloody stupid thing; **dire** *ou* **raconter des conneries** to talk bullshit (**c**) *(caractère stupide)* stupidity

connexion [kɔnɛksjɔ̃] *nf* connection

connivence [kɔnivɑ̃s] *nf* connivance; **agir/être de c. avec qn** to act/be in connivance with sb; **des regards de c.** conniving looks

connotation [kɔnɔtasjɔ̃] *nf* connotation

connu, -e [kɔny] **1** *adj (écrivain, chanteur)* well-known; **c'est bien c.!** everyone knows that! **2** *pp voir* **connaître**

conquérant, -e [kɔkerɑ̃, -ɑ̃t] **1** *adj (air)* triumphant **2** *nm,f* conqueror

conquérir [7] [kɔkerir] *vt (pays, territoire, sommet)* to conquer; *(marché)* to capture; **ils ont été conquis par son charme** they were won over by his charm

conquête [kɔkɛt] *nf* conquest; **faire la c. de** *(pays)* to conquer; *(personne)* to make a conquest of; **se lancer à la c. de** *(pouvoir)* to make a bid for; *(sommet)* to set out to conquer

conquis, -e *voir* **conquérir**

conquistador [kɔkistadɔr] *nm* conquistador

consacré, -e [kɔsakre] *adj (coutume)* established; **selon l'expression consacrée** as the saying goes; **c. par l'usage** sanctioned by usage

consacrer [kɔsakre] **1** *vt* (**a**) *Rel* to consecrate (**b**) *(temps, énergie)* **c. qch à** to devote sth to; **combien de temps pouvez-vous me c.?** how much time can you spare me? (**c**) *(entériner)* to establish **2 se consacrer** *vpr* **se c. à son travail/sa famille** to devote oneself to one's work/family

consanguin, -e [kɔsɑ̃gɛ̃, in] *adj* **frère c.** half-brother *(on the father's side)*; **sœur consanguine** half-sister *(on the father's side)*; **mariage c.** intermarriage

consciemment [kɔsjamɑ̃] *adv* consciously

conscience [kɔsjɑ̃s] *nf* (**a**) *(esprit)* consciousness; **perdre/reprendre c.** to lose/regain consciousness; **avoir/prendre c. de qch** to be/become aware *or* conscious of sth (**b**) *(morale)* conscience; **avoir bonne/mauvaise c.** to have a clear/bad conscience; **se donner bonne c.** to ease one's conscience; **avoir la c. tranquille, avoir sa c. pour soi** to have a clear conscience; **avoir qch sur la c.** to have sth on one's conscience (**c**) **c. professionnelle** professional integrity

consciencieusement [kɔsjɑ̃sjøzmɑ̃] *adv* conscientiously

consciencieux, -euse [kɔsjɑ̃sjø, -øz] *adj* conscientious

conscient, -e [kɔsjɑ̃, -ɑ̃t] *adj* (**a**) *(décision, choix)* conscious; **être c. de qch** to be aware *or* conscious of sth (**b**) *(lucide)* conscious

consécration [kɔsekrasjɔ̃] *nf* (**a**) *(d'une église, d'un évêque)* consecration; *(d'un prêtre)* ordination (**b**) *(aboutissement) (des efforts, d'une œuvre)* recognition; *(d'une carrière)* crowning moment

consécutif, -ive [kɔsekytif, -iv] *adj* consecutive; **c. à** resulting from

consécutivement [kɔsekytivmɑ̃] *adv* consecutively; **c. à** following

conseil [kɔsɛj] *nm* (**a**) *(recommandation)* piece of advice; **des conseils** advice; **donner un c. à qn** to give sb a piece of advice; **être de bon c.** to give good advice (**b**) *(assemblée)* council, committee; *(d'une entreprise)* board; *(réunion)* meeting; **c. d'administration** board of directors; **c. de classe** = staff meeting with participation of class

representatives to discuss school matters; **C. constitutionnel** = independent body which pronounces on the constitutionality of government decisions; **c. de discipline** disciplinary committee; **C. d'État** Council of State; **C. de l'Europe** Council of Europe; **C. général** regional council; **c. de guerre** *(réunion)* council of war; *(tribunal)* court martial; **le c. des ministres** ≃ the Cabinet; **c. municipal** local council; **Can C. national des autochtones du Canada** Native Council of Canada; **C. de sécurité** *(de l'ONU)* Security Council (**c**) *(personne)* consultant (**en** in)

conseiller¹ [kɔseje] *vt* (**a**) *(guider) (personne)* to advise (**b**) *(recommander)* **c. qch à qn** to recommend sth to sb; **c. à qn de faire qch** to advise sb to do sth; **il est conseillé de ne pas fumer** it is advisable not to smoke

conseiller², -ère [kɔseje, -er] *nm,f* (**a**) *(spécialiste)* adviser, consultant; **c. d'orientation** careers adviser; **c. technique** technical adviser (**b**) *Pol* **c. général** regional councillor; **c. municipal** local councillor

consensuel, -elle [kɔsɑ̃sɥel] *adj* consensual

consensus [kɔsɑ̃sys] *nm* consensus (**of opinion**)

consentant, -e [kɔsɑ̃tɑ̃, -ɑ̃t] *adj* consenting; **être c. to consent**

consentement [kɔsɑ̃tmɑ̃] *nm* consent; **donner son c. à qch** to give one's consent to sth; **divorce par c. mutuel** divorce by mutual consent

consentir [64a] [kɔsɑ̃tir] **1** *vi* to consent, to agree (**à qch/à faire qch**); **je consens (à ce) qu'il vienne** I consent to his coming **2** *vt* **c. un prêt à qn** to grant sb a loan; **c. une remise à qn** to allow sb a discount

conséquence [kɔsekɑ̃s] *nf* consequence; **une erreur sans c.** an inconsequential mistake; **tirer les conséquences de qch** to draw conclusions from sth; **la baisse des taxes a eu pour c. de créer des emplois** the tax reduction resulted in the creation of jobs; **agir en c.** to take appropriate action; **en c. (de quoi)** consequently

conséquent, -e [kɔsekɑ̃, -ɑ̃t] *adj* (**a**) *(cohérent)* consistent (**b**) *Fam (somme)* tidy (**c**) **par c.** consequently

conservateur, -trice [kɔservatœr, -tris] **1** *adj Pol* Conservative **2** *nm,f* (**a**) *(de musée)* curator; *(de bibliothèque)* librarian (**b**) *Pol* Conservative **3** *nm (alimentaire)* preservative; **sans c.** *(sur emballage)* free of preservatives

conservation [kɔservasjɔ̃] *nf (de fruits, de viande)* preserving; *(de bâtiments)* preservation; *(d'archives)* keeping

conservatoire [kɔservatwar] *nm (de musique, d'art dramatique)* school, academy; **le C. (de Paris)** the (Paris) Conservatoire; **le C. national des arts et métiers** = science and technology school in Paris

conserve [kɔserv] *nf (aliment)* canned *or Br* tinned food; *(en bocal)* preserve; *(boîte)* can, *Br* tin; **en c.** canned, *Br* tinned; *(en bocal)* preserved; **mettre qch en c.** to can sth, *Br* to tin sth; *(en bocal)* to preserve sth

conserver [kɔserve] **1** *vt* (**a**) *(aliment)* to keep; *(dans le sel, le vinaigre)* to preserve; **c. à l'abri de la lumière** *(sur emballage)* keep away from direct sunlight; **c. au froid** *(sur emballage)* keep in a cold place; **être bien conservé** *(personne)* to be well preserved (**b**) *(garder) (objet, emploi, sang-froid)* to keep; *(droits)* to retain; **c. un bon souvenir de qch** to have good memories of sth **2 se conserver** *vpr (aliment)* to keep

considérable [kɔsiderabl] *adj* considerable

considérablement [kɔsiderablᵊmɑ̃] *adv* considerably

considération [kɔsiderasjɔ̃] *nf* (**a**) *(examen)* **prendre qch en c.** to take sth into consideration; *(offre, demande)* *d'emploi)* to consider sth **(b)** *(estime)* regard, esteem; **agir avec/sans c.** to act considerately/inconsiderately; **jouir d'une grande c.** to be highly regarded **(c) considérations (sur)** *(observations)* observations (on); **je ne peux pas entrer dans ces considérations** I can't go into that

considérer [34] [kɔ̃sidere] **1** *vt* **(a)** *(étudier, regarder)* to consider; **tout bien considéré** all things considered **(b)** *(estimer)* **c. que** to consider that; **c. qn/qch comme...** to regard sb/sth as... **2 se considérer** *vpr* **se c. désavantagé** to consider oneself disadvantaged; **se c. comme un artiste/un révolutionnaire** to consider oneself an artist/a revolutionary

consigne [kɔ̃siɲ] *nf* **(a)** *(ordres)* orders; **avoir pour c. de...** to have orders to...; **passer la c.** to pass on the orders; **consignes en cas d'incendie** fire notice **(b)** *(punition)* Mil confinement to barracks; *Scol* detention **(c)** *(pour les bagages)* **c. (à bagages)** *Br* left-luggage office, *Am* check-room; **c. automatique** lockers **(d)** *(de bouteille)* deposit

consigner [kɔ̃siɲe] *vt* **(a)** *(bouteille, emballage)* to charge a deposit on **(b)** *(noter)* to record **(c)** *(punir)* *(soldat)* to confine to barracks; *(élève)* to keep in **(d)** *(laisser à la consigne)* Br to deposit in the left-luggage office, *Am* to check

consistance [kɔ̃sistɑ̃s] *nf (d'un corps)* consistency; **sans c.** *(pâte, fromage)* too soft; *Fig (personne)* bland; *(personnage de fiction)* insubstantial

consistant, -e [kɔ̃sistɑ̃, -ɑ̃t] *adj (substance)* firm; *(sauce, soupe)* thick; *(repas)* substantial; *(argument)* sound

consister [kɔ̃siste] *vi* **c. en qch** to consist of sth; **c. à faire qch** to consist in doing sth

consœur [kɔ̃sœr] *nf* (female) colleague

consolation [kɔ̃sɔlasjɔ̃] *nf* consolation, comfort

console [kɔ̃sɔl] *nf* console

consoler [kɔ̃sɔle] **1** *vt* to console, to comfort; **si ça peut te c.** if that's any consolation to you **2 se consoler** *vpr* to console oneself; *(l'un l'autre)* to console each other; **se c. d'une perte/d'un échec** to get over a loss/a failure; **elles se sont consolées mutuellement** they consoled each other

consolidation [kɔ̃sɔlidasjɔ̃] *nf* **(a)** *aussi* Fig *(renforcement)* strengthening **(b)** *Méd (d'une fracture)* knitting

consolider [kɔ̃sɔlide] **1** *vt* **(a)** *aussi* Fig *(renforcer)* to strengthen **(b)** *(fracture)* to knit **(c)** *Fin (dette)* to fund; *(bilan)* to consolidate **2 se consolider** *vpr* **(a)** *(régime)* to strengthen its position; *(amitié, liens)* to become stronger **(b)** *(fracture)* to knit

consommateur, -trice [kɔ̃sɔmatœr, -tris] *nm,f* Écon consumer; *(dans un restaurant, un café)* customer; **je suis un grand c. de café** I'm a great coffee drinker; *Écon* **c. final** end-user

consommation [kɔ̃sɔmasjɔ̃] *nf* **(a)** *(d'électricité, de pétrole, de nourriture)* consumption; *(d'une voiture)* (fuel) consumption; **faire une grande c. de qch** to consume great quantities of sth **(b)** *(dans un café)* drink **(c)** *(du mariage)* consummation

consommé, -e [kɔ̃sɔme] **1** *nm* Culin consommé **2** *adj* consummate

consommer [kɔ̃sɔme] **1** *vt* **(a)** *(électricité, pétrole, nourriture)* to consume; **à c. avant fin août** *(sur emballage)* best before end August; **cette voiture consomme trop (d'essence)** this car is heavy on fuel; **c. au bar** to drink at the bar **(b)** *(mariage)* to consummate **2 se consommer** *vpr* **ce plat se consomme froid** this dish is eaten cold

consonance [kɔ̃sɔnɑ̃s] *nf* Mus & Ling consonance; **langue à c. germanique** German-sounding language

consonne [kɔ̃sɔn] *nf* consonant

consortium [kɔ̃sɔrsjɔm] *nm* Com & Fin consortium

conspirateur, -trice [kɔ̃spiratœr, -tris] **1** *nm,f* conspirator **2** *adj* conspiratorial

conspiration [kɔ̃spirasjɔ̃] *nf* conspiracy, plot

conspirer [kɔ̃spire] *vi* **(a)** *(comploter)* to conspire, to plot **(contre** against) **(b)** *(contribuer)* to conspire **(à faire qch** to do sth)

constamment [kɔ̃stamɑ̃] *adv* constantly

constance [kɔ̃stɑ̃s] *nf* **(a)** *(dans une tâche)* perseverance; *(en amour)* constancy; **travailler avec c.** to work steadily **(b)** *(de la température, d'un phénomène)* constancy

constant, -e [kɔ̃stɑ̃, -ɑ̃t] **1** *adj (souci, température, va-et-vient)* constant; *(effort)* persistent; *(amitié, intérêt)* steady **(b)** *(personne)* **être c. dans ses opinions** to stick to one's opinions; **être c. dans ses amitiés** to be faithful to one's friends **2** *nf* **constante** *(en sciences)* constant

constat [kɔ̃sta] *nm* **(a)** *Jur* official report; **dresser un c. d'accident** to write out an accident report; **c. amiable** = report of road accident agreed by parties involved **(b)** *(bilan)* assessment; **faire un c. d'échec** to acknowledge failure

constatation [kɔ̃statasjɔ̃] *nf* **(a)** *(observation)* observation; **c'est une simple c.** it's a simple statement of fact **(b)** **constatations** *(d'une enquête)* findings

constater [kɔ̃state] *vt* **(a)** *(observer)* to note **(que** that); **vous pouvez c. vous-même qu'elle est partie** you can see for yourself that she's gone **(b)** *Jur (enregistrer)* to record; *(décès)* to certify; *(dégâts)* to assess

constellation [kɔ̃stelasjɔ̃] *nf* constellation

constellé, -e [kɔ̃stele] *adj* **un ciel c. d'étoiles** a star-studded sky

consternant, -e [kɔ̃stɛrnɑ̃, -ɑ̃t] *adj (nouvelle)* dismaying; **d'une bêtise consternante** appallingly stupid

consternation [kɔ̃stɛrnasjɔ̃] *nf* dismay, consternation; **jeter la c. dans/parmi** to fill with dismay; **à la c. générale** to everyone's dismay

consterner [kɔ̃stɛrne] *vt* to dismay

constipation [kɔ̃stipasjɔ̃] *nf* constipation

constipé, -e [kɔ̃stipe] *adj* constipated; *Fam (mal à l'aise)* ill at ease

constituer [kɔ̃stitɥe] **1** *vt* **(a)** *(composer)* to make up; **être constitué de** to be made up of **(b)** *(équivaloir à)* to constitute **(c)** *(comité, gouvernement, équipe)* to form; *(bibliothèque, fortune, stocks)* to build up; **c. une rente/une dot à qn** to settle an annuity/a dowry on sb **2 se constituer** *vpr (a) (devenir)* **se c. prisonnier** to give oneself up; *Jur* **se c. partie civile** to bring a civil suit for damages **(b)** *(se réunir)* **se c. en commission/en association** to form a committee/an association

constitution [kɔ̃stitysjɔ̃] *nf* **(a)** *(physique, d'un pays)* constitution; **avoir une bonne c.** to have a sound constitution **(b)** *(de comité, de société, de gouvernement)* formation; *(de stocks, de bibliothèque)* building up

constitutionnel, -elle [kɔ̃stitysjɔnɛl] *adj* constitutional

constructeur [kɔ̃stryktœr] *nm (bâtisseur)* builder; **c. automobile** car manufacturer; **c. naval** shipbuilder

constructif, -ive [kɔ̃stryktif, -iv] *adj* constructive

construction [kɔ̃stryksjɔ̃] *nf* **(a)** *(d'une maison, d'une route, d'un voilier)* building, construction; *(d'une phrase)* structure; **en c.** under construction; **c. navale** shipbuilding **(b)** *(bâtiment)* building

construire [18] [kɔ̃strɥir] **1** *vt* to build, to construct; *(roman, phrase, théorie)* to construct

2 se construire vpr Gram "bien que" se construit avec le
subjonctif "bien que" takes the subjunctive
consul [kɔsyl] nm consul; le **c.** de France the French
consul; **c. général** consul general
consulaire [kɔsylɛr] adj consular
consulat [kɔsyla] nm (lieu) consulate; (charge) consulship
consultant, -e [kɔsyltā, -āt] **1** nm,f consultant
2 adj consulting; **médecin c.** consultant
consultation [kɔsyltasjɔ̃] nf (**a**) (d'un expert, d'un
médecin) consultation; **le médecin est en c.** the doctor is
with a patient; **heures de c.** consulting or Br surgery hours
(**b**) (de livre) consultation (**c**) Pol **c. populaire** consultation
of the people
consulter [kɔsylte] **1** vt to consult
2 vi (docteur) to see patients, Br to take surgery
3 se consulter vpr to consult each other
consumer [kɔsyme] **1** vt (brûler) to consume; Fig
consumé par le remords consumed with remorse
2 se consumer vpr (brûler) to burn; Fig **se c. de désespoir**
to be consumed with despair
contact [kɔtakt] nm (**a**) (relation, personne) contact;
garder/perdre le **c.** avec qn to keep in touch/lose touch
with sb; prendre **c.** ou se mettre en **c.** avec qn to get in
touch or in contact with sb; **être/entrer en c. avec qn** to be
in/come into contact with sb; **être d'un c.** facile/difficile
to be approachable/unapproachable; **au c. de qn** through
spending time with sb (**b**) (toucher) contact; **au c.** agréable
pleasant to the touch; **être/entrer en c.** avec qch to be in/
come into contact with sth; **au c.** de qch on contact with
sth (**c**) Él contact (**d**) Aut contact; **mettre/couper le c.** to
switch on/off
contacter [kɔtakte] vt to contact
contagieux, -euse [kɔtaʒjø, -øz] adj (maladie, virus,
personne) contagious; (rire, enthousiasme) infectious
contagion [kɔtaʒjɔ̃] nf Méd contagion
container [kɔtɛnɛr] nm container
contamination [kɔtaminasjɔ̃] nf (pollution) contamination; Méd infection
contaminer [kɔtamine] vt (polluer) to contaminate; Méd
to infect
conte [kɔt] nm story, tale; **c. de fées** fairy tale; Fig **elle vit
un c. de fées** her life is a fairy tale
contemplatif, -ive [kɔtāplatif, -iv] adj & nm,f
contemplative
contemplation [kɔtāplasjɔ̃] nf contemplation; **être en
c. devant qch** to gaze at sth
contempler [kɔtāple] **1** vt to contemplate, to gaze at
2 se contempler vpr (soi-même) to gaze at oneself
contemporain, -e [kɔtāpɔrɛ̃, -ɛn] **1** adj (**a**) (moderne)
contemporary (**b**) (du même âge) contemporary (de with);
être c. de qn to be a contemporary of sb; **ils sont
contemporains** they are contemporaries
2 nm,f contemporary
contenance [kɔtnās] nf (**a**) (d'un récipient) capacity (**b**)
(allure) attitude, bearing; **faire qch pour se donner une c.**
to do sth to give an impression of composure; **faire bonne
c.** to put on a bold front; **perdre c.** to lose one's composure
contenant [kɔtnā] nm container
conteneur [kɔtnœr] nm container
contenir [70] [kɔtnir] **1** vt (**a**) (renfermer) to contain; **le
théâtre contient mille places** the theatre holds or seats a
thousand (**b**) (foule, ennemi) to contain, to keep in check;
(colère) to curb; (larmes) to hold back
2 se contenir vpr to contain oneself
content, -e [kɔtā, -āt] **1** adj (satisfait) happy, content (de
with); (joyeux) glad (**de faire** to do); **je suis très c. de vous**

voir I'm very pleased to see you; **être c. de soi** to be
pleased with oneself; **tu peux être c. de toi, tu as vu ce
que tu as fait!** I hope you're happy, just look what you've
done!; **non c. de mentir, il vole!** not content with lying, he
steals as well!; **je suis vraiment c. que vous soyez venu**
I'm so glad you've come; Fam **et si tu n'es pas c.**, c'est
pareil you can like it or lump it
2 nm **manger tout son c.** to eat one's fill; **avoir son c. de
qch** to have had one's fill of sth
contentement [kɔtātmā] nm (état) satisfaction,
contentment; **un sourire de c.** a contented smile
contenter [kɔtāte] **1** vt (personne) to satisfy, to please
2 se contenter vpr **se c. de qch/de faire qch** to content
oneself with sth/with doing sth; **se c. de peu** to be easily
satisfied; **je me contenterai de faire remarquer que...** I
will merely point out that...
contentieux [kɔtāsjø] nm (querelle) dispute; Jur
litigation; (service) legal department; **avoir un c. avec qn**
to be in dispute with sb
contenu, -e [kɔtny] **1** nm (d'un paquet, d'une bouteille,
d'une boîte) contents; (d'une lettre, d'un livre) content
2 adj (émotion) restrained
conter [kɔte] vt to tell; **elle ne s'en laisse pas c.** you can't
fool her
contestataire [kɔtɛstatɛr] **1** adj Pol anti-establishment;
(mécontent) rebellious
2 nmf Pol protester; (mécontent) rebel
contestation [kɔtɛstasjɔ̃] nf (**a**) (protestation) protest; **il
y a matière** ou sujet à **c.** there are grounds for dispute;
sans c. possible beyond dispute (**b**) Pol protest
conteste [kɔtɛst] **sans conteste** adv indisputably
contester [kɔtɛste] vt to dispute; **je lui conteste le droit
de...** I dispute his right to...; **elle est très contestée** she is
very controversial; **faire qch sans c.** to do sth without protest
conteur, -euse [kɔtœr, -øz] nm,f storyteller
contexte [kɔtɛkst] nm context; **dans le c. de** in the
context of; **hors c.** out of context
contigu, -ë [kɔtigy] adj (maisons, pièces) adjoining; **c. à
qch** adjoining sth
continent [kɔtinā] nm (**a**) (étendue) continent; **l'Ancien/
le Nouveau C.** the Old/the New World (**b**) (par rapport à
une île) mainland
continental, -e, -aux, -ales [kɔtinātal, -o] **1** adj
(climat, plateau) continental; (par rapport à une île) mainland
2 nm,f mainlander
contingent [kɔtɛ̃ʒā] nm (**a**) Mil contingent; **les soldats
du c.** the conscripted soldiers (**b**) (quota) quota
continu, -e [kɔtiny] adj (ligne, effort) continuous; (soin,
attention) constant; **en c.** continuously; Ordinat **papier en
c.** continuous paper
continuation [kɔtinyasjɔ̃] nf continuation; **bonne c.!**
all the best!
continuel, -elle [kɔtinyɛl] adj (ininterrompu) continuous; (qui se répète) continual
continuellement [kɔtinyɛlmā] adv (de façon ininter-
rompue) continuously; (de façon répétitive) continually
continuer [kɔtinye] **1** vt (études, efforts, politique) to
continue (with), to carry on with; (trait, route) to continue;
c. sa route ou **son chemin** to continue on one's way;
continuez! carry on!; **si tu continues comme ça,...** if
you carry on like that,...
2 vi to continue
3 continuer à ou **de** vt ind **c. à** ou **de faire qch** to continue
doing sth, to carry on doing sth; **je continue à** ou **de me
demander si...** I keep wondering if...
4 se continuer vpr to continue

continuité [kɔ̃tinɥite] *nf (d'une action)* continuity; *(d'une tradition, d'une politique)* continuation

contondant, -e [kɔ̃tɔ̃dɑ̃, -ɑ̃t] *adj* blunt

contorsion [kɔ̃tɔrsjɔ̃] *nf* contortion

contorsionner [kɔ̃tɔrsjɔne] **se contorsionner** *vpr* to contort oneself

contorsionniste [kɔ̃tɔrsjɔnist] *nmf* contortionist

contour [kɔ̃tur] *nm (silhouette)* outline

contourner [kɔ̃turne] *vt* to go round; *Fig (loi, difficulté)* to get round

contraceptif, -ive [kɔ̃traseptif, -iv] *Méd* **1** *adj* contraceptive **2** *nm* contraceptive; **c.** **oral** oral contraceptive

contraception [kɔ̃trasepsjɔ̃] *nf* contraception

contractant, -e [kɔ̃traktɑ̃, -ɑ̃t] *adj* *Jur (partie)* contracting

contracté, -e [kɔ̃trakte] *adj* **(a)** *(muscles, visage, personne)* tense **(b)** *Ling* contracted

contracter¹ [kɔ̃trakte] *vt* **(a)** *(alliance, dette)* to contract; *(assurance)* to take out **(b)** *(habitude, goût, manie)* to acquire; *(maladie)* to contract

contracter² **1** *vt (muscles, visage)* to tense; **visage contracté par la douleur** face drawn with pain **2** **se contracter** *vpr* **(a)** *(cœur, muscle)* to contract; *(personne)* to tense (up) **(b)** *Ling* to contract

contraction [kɔ̃traksjɔ̃] *nf* **(a)** *(d'un muscle, d'un gaz, d'un mot)* contraction; **contractions** *(à l'accouchement)* contractions **(b)** *Scol* **c. de texte** précis

contractuel, -elle [kɔ̃traktɥɛl] **1** *adj (obligations)* contractual; **agent c.** = contractor working for the local council **2** *nm,f (auxiliaire de police) Br* ≃ traffic warden, *Am* ≃ traffic policeman, *f* traffic policewoman

contracture [kɔ̃traktyr] *nf Méd* spasm

contradiction [kɔ̃tradiksjɔ̃] *nf* **(a)** *(opposition)* contradiction; **avoir l'esprit de c.** to be contrary; **il ne supporte pas la c.** he can't stand being contradicted **(b)** *(illogisme)* contradiction; **être en c. avec qch** to contradict sth; **être en c. avec soi-même** to contradict oneself

contradictoire [kɔ̃tradiktwar] *adj* contradictory **(avec** to); **débat c.** debate

contraignant, -e [kɔ̃trɛɲɑ̃, -ɑ̃t] *adj* restricting

contraindre [23] [kɔ̃trɛ̃dr] **1** *vt (obliger)* **c. qn à faire qch** to force or compel sb to do sth; **être contraint de faire qch** to be forced or compelled to do sth; **contraint et forcé** under duress **2** **se contraindre** *vpr* **se c. à faire qch** to force oneself to do sth

contrainte [kɔ̃trɛ̃t] *nf* **(a)** *(obligation, limitation, retenue)* constraint; **parler sans c.** to speak freely **(b)** *(force)* force; **obtenir qch par la c.** to get sth by force; **faire qch sous la c.** to do sth under duress **(c)** *Tech* stress

contraire [kɔ̃trɛr] **1** *adj* **(a)** *(opposé) (intérêts, avis)* conflicting; **vent c.** headwind; **c. à** contrary to; **en sens c.** in the opposite direction **(b)** *(défavorable)* **le sort nous/m' est c.** fate is against us/me **2** *nm* opposite; **le c. de** the opposite of; **son frère est tout le c. de lui** his brother is the exact opposite of him; **(bien) au c.** on the contrary

contrairement [kɔ̃trɛrmɑ̃] **contrairement à** *prép* contrary to; **c. à moi,...** unlike me,...

contralto [kɔ̃tralto] *nm Mus* contralto

contrariant, -e [kɔ̃trarjɑ̃, -ɑ̃t] *adj* **(a)** *(personne)* contrary; **elle n'est pas contrariante** she's easy-going; *Péj* she says yes to everything **(b)** *(situation)* annoying, irritating

contrarier [66] [kɔ̃trarje] *vt* **(a)** *(ennuyer)* to annoy, to irritate **(b)** *(contrecarrer) (projets, desseins)* to thwart, to frustrate

contrariété [kɔ̃trarjete] *nf* annoyance; **éprouver une vive c.** to feel extremely annoyed

contraste [kɔ̃trast] *nm* contrast; **faire c. (avec)** to contrast (with); **par c. avec** in contrast to; **effet de c.** contrasting effect

contrasté, -e [kɔ̃traste] *adj* **(a)** *(différencié)* contrasting; **photo bien/mal contrastée** photo with the right amount of/with not enough contrast **(b)** *Ordinat* highlighted

contraster [kɔ̃traste] *vi* to contrast **(avec** with)

contrat [kɔ̃tra] *nm* **(a)** *(accord)* contract, agreement; **passer un c. (avec qn)** to enter into an agreement (with sb); **c. d'assurance** contract of insurance; **c. collectif** collective agreement; **c. à durée déterminée/indéterminée** fixed-term/permanent contract; **c. emploi-solidarité** = short-term contract subsidized by the government; **c. de mariage** marriage contract; **c. de travail** *Br* contract of employment, *Am* labor contract **(b)** *(au bridge)* contract

contravention [kɔ̃travɑ̃sjɔ̃] *nf (envers un règlement)* contravention; *(amende)* fine; *(pour stationnement non autorisé) (amende)* parking fine; *(avis)* (parking) ticket

contre [kɔ̃tr] *prép* **(a)** *(se battre, jouer)* against; **se fâcher c. qn** to get angry with sb; **la campagne c. cette réforme** the campaign against this reform; **je n'ai rien c., je ne suis pas c.** I've got nothing against it; **par c.** on the other hand **(b)** *(pour se protéger de)* **sirop c. la toux** cough mixture; **être assuré c. le vol** to be insured against theft **(c)** *(en échange de)* (in exchange) for; **échanger une chose c. une autre** to exchange one thing for another **(d)** *(en proportion de)* to; **parier à quatre c. un** to bet four to one; **10 voix c. 2** 10 votes to 2 **(e)** *(en contact avec)* against; **s'appuyer c. qch** to lean against sth; **leur maison est tout c. la mienne** their house is right next to mine; **joue c. joue** cheek to cheek; **le radiateur est allumé, assieds-toi tout c.** the heater is on, sit right next to it **(f)** *(en dépit de)* **c. toute logique** against all logic; **c. toute attente** against all expectations **(g)** *(en comparaison de)* compared to; **la livre est à $1,86 c. $1,45 le mois dernier** the pound stands at $1.86 compared to $1.45 last month **2** *nm* **(a)** peser le pour et le c. to weigh up the pros and cons **(b)** *(au volley, au basket)* block

contre-allée *(pl* **contre-allées)** [kɔ̃trale] *nf* side road

contre-attaque *(pl* **contre-attaques)** [kɔ̃tratak] *nf* counter-attack

contre-attaquer [kɔ̃tratake] *vi* to counter-attack

contrebalancer [16] [kɔ̃trəbalɑ̃se] **1** *vt (poids)* to counterbalance; *(inconvénient)* to offset **2** **se contrebalancer** *vpr Fam* **se c. de qch** not to give a damn about sth

contrebande [kɔ̃trəbɑ̃d] *nf* **(a)** *(activité)* smuggling; **faire de la c.** to smuggle goods; **faire entrer des marchandises en c.** to smuggle in goods; **de c.** smuggled **(b)** *(marchandises)* contraband

contrebandier, -ère [kɔ̃trəbɑ̃dje, -ɛr] *nm,f* smuggler

contrebas [kɔ̃trəba] **en contrebas** *adv* (down) below; **en c. de** below

contrebasse [kɔ̃trəbas] *nf (instrument)* (double) bass; *(musicien)* (double) bass player

contrebassiste [kɔ̃trəbasist] *nmf* (double) bass player

contre-braquer [kɔ̃trəbrake] *vi Aut* to steer into the skid

contrecarrer [kɔ̃trəkare] *vt* to thwart
contrechamp [kɔ̃trəʃɑ̃] *nm Cin* reverse shot
contre-chant (*pl* **contre-chants**) [kɔ̃trəʃɑ̃] *nm Mus* counterpoint
contrecœur [kɔ̃trəkœr] **à contrecœur** *adv* reluctantly, unwillingly
contrecoup [kɔ̃trəku] *nm (conséquence)* repercussions
contre-courant [kɔ̃trəkurɑ̃] **à contre-courant** *adv (nager)* against the current; *(sur la route)* in the wrong direction; *Fig* **aller à c.** **de qch** to go against the current of sth
contredanse [kɔ̃trədɑ̃s] *nf Fam (amende)* parking fine; *(avis)* (parking) ticket; **flanquer une c. à qn** to give sb a (parking) ticket
contredire [27b] [kɔ̃trədir] **1** *vt* to contradict **2 se contredire** *vpr (soi-même)* to contradict oneself; *(l'un l'autre)* to contradict each other
contrée [kɔ̃tre] *nf Littér (région)* region; *(pays)* land
contre-emploi (*pl* **contre-emplois**) [kɔ̃trɑ̃plwa] *nm Th & Cin* miscasting; **utiliser qn à c.** to miscast sb
contre-enquête (*pl* **contre-enquetes**) [kɔ̃trɑ̃kɛt] *nf Jur* counter-inquiry
contre-espionnage [kɔ̃trɛspjɔnaʒ] *nm* counter-espionage
contre-exemple (*pl* **contre-exemples**) [kɔ̃trɛgzɑ̃pl] *nm* counter-example
contre-expertise (*pl* **contre-expertises**) [kɔ̃trɛkspɛrtiz] *nf* second valuation
contrefaçon [kɔ̃trəfasɔ̃] *nf* (a) *(pratique)* counterfeiting; *(de signature)* forging (b) *(produit)* fake, imitation
contrefaire [36] [kɔ̃trəfɛr] *vt* (a) *(voix, écriture)* to disguise (b) *(pièce, produit de marque)* to counterfeit; *(signature)* to forge
contreficher [kɔ̃trəfiʃe] **se contreficher** *vpr très Fam* **se c. de qch** not to give a damn about sth
contre-filet (*pl* **contre-filets**) [kɔ̃trəfilɛ] *nm Culin* sirloin
contrefort [kɔ̃trəfɔr] *nm* (a) *Archit* buttress (b) *Géog* **contreforts** foothills (c) *(de chaussure)* stiffener
contre-indication (*pl* **contre-indications**) [kɔ̃trɛdikasjɔ̃] *nf* contraindication
contre-interrogatoire (*pl* **contre-interrogatoires**) [kɔ̃trɛ̃terɔgatwar] *nm Jur* cross-examination
contre-jour (*pl* **contre-jours**) [kɔ̃trəʒur] *nm* (a) *(éclairage défavorable)* light from behind; **à c.** against the light (b) *Art, Cin & Phot* backlighting
contre-la-montre [kɔ̃trəlamɔ̃tr] *nm inv Sp* time-trial
contremaître, -esse [kɔ̃trəmɛtr, -ɛs] *nm,f* foreman, *f* forewoman
contre-manifestation (*pl* **contre-manifestations**) [kɔ̃trəmanifɛstasjɔ̃] *nf* counter-demonstration
contremarche [kɔ̃trəmarʃ] *nf (d'un escalier)* riser
contremarque [kɔ̃trəmark] *nf (au spectacle)* passout ticket
contre-mesure (*pl* **contre-mesures**) [kɔ̃trəməzyr] *nf* countermeasure
contre-offensive (*pl* **contre-offensives**) [kɔ̃trɔfɑ̃siv] *nf* counter-offensive
contrepartie [kɔ̃trəparti] *nf (compensation)* compensation; **en c. (de)** in return (for)
contre-performance (*pl* **contre-performances**) [kɔ̃trəpɛrfɔrmɑ̃s] *nf* substandard performance
contrepèterie [kɔ̃trəpɛtri] *nf* spoonerism
contre-pied [kɔ̃trəpje] *nm* (a) **prendre le c. de qch** *(faire le contraire)* to do the opposite of sth; *(dire le contraire)*

to take the opposite view to sth (b) *Sp* **prendre son adversaire à c.** to wrong-foot one's opponent; **prendre la balle à c.** to take the ball on the wrong foot
contreplaqué [kɔ̃trəplake] *nm* plywood
contre-plongée (*pl* **contre-plongées**) [kɔ̃trəplɔ̃ʒe] *nf Cin & TV* low-angle shot; **filmer qch en c.** to film sth from below
contrepoids [kɔ̃trəpwa] *nm aussi Fig* counterbalance; *Fig* **faire c. à qch** to counterbalance sth
contre-poil [kɔ̃trəpwal] **à contre-poil** *adv* the wrong way; *Fam* **prendre qn à c.** to rub sb up the wrong way
contrepoison [kɔ̃trəpwazɔ̃] *nm* antidote
contre-pouvoir (*pl* **contre-pouvoirs**) [kɔ̃trəpuvwar] *nm* anti-establishment force
contre-proposition (*pl* **contre-propositions**) [kɔ̃trəprɔpozisjɔ̃] *nf* counter-proposal
contrer [kɔ̃tre] *vt* (a) *(attaque, argument, personne)* to counter (b) *(au volley, au basket)* to block (c) *(aux cartes)* to double
contre-révolution (*pl* **contre-révolutions**) [kɔ̃trərevɔlysjɔ̃] *nf* counter-revolution
contre-révolutionnaire (*pl* **contre-révolutionnaires**) [kɔ̃trərevɔlysjɔner] *adj & nmf* counter-revolutionary
contresens [kɔ̃trəsɑ̃s] *nm* (a) *(mauvaise compréhension)* misinterpretation; *(mauvaise traduction)* mistranslation; **faire un c.** *(mal comprendre)* to make a mistake in interpretation; *(mal traduire)* to make a mistake in translation (b) *Aut* **à c.** the wrong way; **prendre une rue à c.** to go the wrong way down a street
contresigner [kɔ̃trəsiɲe] *vt* to countersign
contretemps [kɔ̃trətɑ̃] *nm* (a) *(ennui)* hitch, mishap (b) *Mus* off-beat; **à c.** off the beat; *Fig* **at the wrong moment**
contre-ténor (*pl* **contre-ténors**) [kɔ̃trətenɔr] *nm* counter-tenor
contre-torpilleur (*pl* **contre-torpilleurs**) [kɔ̃trətɔrpijœr] *nm* destroyer
contrevenant, -e [kɔ̃trəvənɑ̃, -ɑ̃t] *nm,f* offender
contrevenir [70] [kɔ̃trəvənir] **contrevenir à** *vt ind* to contravene
contrevent [kɔ̃trəvɑ̃] *nm (volet)* (outside) shutter
contrevérité [kɔ̃trəverite] *nf* untruth, falsehood
contribuable [kɔ̃tribɥabl] *nmf* taxpayer
contribuer [kɔ̃tribɥe] **contribuer à** *vt ind* to contribute to; **c. financièrement à qch** to contribute (money) to sth; **c. à faire qch** to help (to) do sth
contribution [kɔ̃tribysjɔ̃] *nf* (a) *(impôt)* tax; **contributions** *(à l'État)* taxes; *(à la collectivité locale)* Br rates, *Am* local taxes; **(bureau des) contributions** tax office, *Br* Inland Revenue, *Am* Internal Revenue; **contributions directes/indirectes** direct/indirect taxation; **c. sociale généralisée** = income-based tax deducted at source as a contribution to paying off the French social security budget deficit (b) *(collaboration, aide financière)* contribution (à to); **mettre qn à c.** to call on sb's services
contrit, -e [kɔ̃tri, -it] *adj* contrite
contrôle [kɔ̃trol] *nm* (a) *(vérification)* checking; *Scol* test; *Univ* **c. continu** continuous assessment; **c. douanier** customs control; **c. fiscal** tax inspection; **c. d'identité** identity check; **c. de police** police check; **c. radar** *(sur la route)* radar speed check; *Aut* **c. technique** inspection (b) *(surveillance) (d'opérations)* monitoring; *Fin* **c. des changes** exchange control; **sous c. judiciaire** on probation; **sous c. médical** under medical supervision; **c. des prix** price control (c) *(maîtrise)* control; **avoir le c. de qch** to have

control of sth, to be in control of sth; **perdre le c.** de son **véhicule** to lose control of one's vehicle; **c. de soi** self-control; **sous c. serbe** under Serb control; **c. des naissances** birth control (**d**) *Ordinat* **touche c.** control key; **c. d'accès** access control; **faire un c. croisé de** to cross-check

contrôler [kɔ̃trole] **1** *vt* (**a**) *(vérifier)* to check (**b**) *(surveiller) (opérations)* to monitor (**c**) *(maîtriser)* to control (**d**) *Ordinat* **contrôlé par le logiciel** software-controlled; **contrôlé par menu** menu-driven, menu-controlled **2 se contrôler** *vpr* to control oneself

contrôleur, -euse [kɔ̃trolœr, -øz] **1** *nm,f (dans les trains, les bus)* ticket inspector; **c. aérien** air-traffic controller; **c. des impôts** tax inspector **2** *nm Ordinat* **c. d'affichage** display *or* screen controller

contrordre [kɔ̃trɔrdr] *nm* countermand; **il y a c.** the orders have been changed; **sauf c.** unless otherwise directed

controverse [kɔ̃trɔvɛrs] *nf* controversy; **prêter à c.** to be controversial

controversé, -e [kɔ̃trɔvɛrse] *adj* controversial

contumace [kɔ̃tymas] **par contumace** *adv Jur* in absentia

contusion [kɔ̃tyzjɔ̃] *nf* bruise, *Spéc* contusion

contusionné, -e [kɔ̃tyzjɔne] *adj* bruised

convaincant, -e [kɔ̃vɛ̃kɑ̃, -ɑ̃t] *adj* convincing

convaincre [68] [kɔ̃vɛ̃kr] *vt* (**a**) *(persuader)* to convince (**de/que** of/that); **c. qn de faire qch** to persuade sb to do sth; **se laisser c.** to let oneself be persuaded (**b**) *(prouver la culpabilité de)* **être convaincu de vol** to be convicted *or* found guilty of theft

convaincu, -e [kɔ̃vɛ̃ky] *adj* convinced; *(pacifiste, partisan)* committed; **être c. de/que** to be convinced of/that; **d'un ton c.** with conviction

convalescence [kɔ̃valesɑ̃s] *nf* convalescence; **être en c.** to be convalescing

convalescent, -e [kɔ̃valɛsɑ̃, -ɑ̃t] *adj & nm,f* convalescent

convecteur [kɔ̃vɛktœr] *nm* convector (heater)

convenable [kɔ̃vnabl] *adj* (**a**) *(décent)* decent, respectable; **il n'est pas c. de parler fort** it is not polite to talk loudly (**b**) *(acceptable) (salaire, délai)* decent (**c**) *(approprié)* appropriate, suitable

convenablement [kɔ̃vnabləmɑ̃] *adv* decently

convenance [kɔ̃vnɑ̃s] *nf* (**a**) *(fait de convenir)* **pour (des raisons de) c. personnelle** for personal reasons; **trouver qch à sa c.** to find sth to one's liking; **il le fera à sa c.** he'll do it at his own convenience (**b**) **les convenances** the proprieties; **contraire aux convenances** improper

convenir [70] [kɔ̃vnir] **1 convenir à** *vt ind (aller à, plaire à)* to suit; **il est difficile de trouver le mot qui convient** it's hard to find the right word **2 convenir de** *vt ind* (**a**) *(reconnaître)* to admit; **j'ai eu tort, j'en conviens** I was wrong, I admit it; **il convient qu'il a eu tort** he admits that he was wrong (**b**) *(décider de)* to agree on; **c. de faire qch** to agree to do sth **3** *v impersonnel* (**a**) **il convient de...** *(il est souhaitable de)* it is advisable to...; *(il est de bon ton de)* it is proper to... (**b**) *(être décidé)* **il fut convenu qu'ils le feraient venir** it was agreed that they would send for him

convention [kɔ̃vɑ̃sjɔ̃] *nf* (**a**) *(accord)* agreement; **c. collective** collective agreement (**b**) *(règle arbitraire)* convention; **les conventions (sociales)** the (social) conventions; *Péj* **amabilité/sourire de c.** superficial courtesy/smile (**c**) *Pol (assemblée)* assembly

conventionné, -e [kɔ̃vɑ̃sjɔne] *adj (médecin, clinique)*

attached to the health system; **médecin non c.** private doctor

conventionnel, -elle [kɔ̃vɑ̃sjɔnɛl] *adj* (**a**) *(style, personne, armes)* conventional (**b**) *Jur (clause)* contractual

convenu, -e [kɔ̃vny] *adj* (**a**) *(décidé)* agreed; **comme c.** as agreed (**b**) *Péj (peu original)* conventional

convergence [kɔ̃vɛrʒɑ̃s] *nf* convergence

convergent, -e [kɔ̃vɛrʒɑ̃, -ɑ̃t] *adj* convergent

converger [45] [kɔ̃vɛrʒe] *vi (routes, lignes)* to converge (**vers** on); **c. vers** *(efforts)* to be focused on; **leurs opinions convergent** they are of like mind

conversation [kɔ̃vɛrsasjɔ̃] *nf* conversation; **être en grande c. (avec qn)** to be deep in conversation (with sb); **engager la c.** to start a conversation; **faire la c. (à qn)** to make conversation (with sb); **n'avoir aucune c.** to be a poor conversationalist; **c. téléphonique** telephone conversation

conversationnel, -elle [kɔ̃vɛrsasjɔnɛl] *adj Ordinat* **mode c.** conversational *or* interactive mode

converser [kɔ̃vɛrse] *vi Formel* to converse (**avec** with)

conversion [kɔ̃vɛrsjɔ̃] *nf* (**a**) *(changement)* conversion (**en** into); *Ordinat* **c. de fichier** file conversion (**b**) *(à une doctrine)* conversion (**à** to)

converti, -e [kɔ̃vɛrti] **1** *nm,f Rel* convert; *Fig* **prêcher un c.** to preach to the converted **2** *adj* converted

convertibilité [kɔ̃vɛrtibilite] *nf Fin* convertibility

convertible [kɔ̃vɛrtibl] **1** *adj* convertible (**en** into) **2** *nm (canapé)* sofa bed

convertir [kɔ̃vɛrtir] *vt* (**a**) *(changer)* to convert (**en** into) (**b**) *(à une doctrine)* to convert (**à** to) **2 se convertir** *vpr* (**a**) *(à une doctrine)* to be converted (**à** to) (**b**) **se c. en** *(se changer en)* to be converted into

convertisseur [kɔ̃vɛrtisœr] *nm Tech* converter; *Ordinat* **c. analogique numérique** digitizer

convexe [kɔ̃vɛks] *adj* convex

conviction [kɔ̃viksjɔ̃] *nf* (**a**) *(certitude)* conviction; **avoir la c. que...** to be convinced that... (**b**) **convictions** *(opinions)* convictions

convier [66] [kɔ̃vje] *vt Formel (inviter)* to invite (**à** to); **c. qn à faire qch** to invite sb to do sth

convive [kɔ̃viv] *nmf* guest

convivial, -e, -aux, -ales [kɔ̃vivjal, -o] *adj* convivial; *Ordinat* user-friendly

convivialité [kɔ̃vivjalite] *nf* conviviality; *Ordinat* user-friendliness

convocation [kɔ̃vɔkasjɔ̃] *nf* (**a**) *(lettre)* notice to attend; *Jur* summons; **c. à un examen** notification of an examination (**b**) *(d'une assemblée)* convening

convoi [kɔ̃vwa] *nm* (**a**) *(de véhicules, de troupes, de prisonniers)* convoy; **c. exceptionnel** *(sur un camion) (dangereux)* dangerous load; *(large)* wide load (**b**) *(train)* train; **c. de marchandises** goods *or* freight train; **c. postal** mail train (**c**) *(cortège)* **c. funèbre** funeral procession

convoiter [kɔ̃vwate] *vt (poste, richesse)* to covet; *(femme)* to lust after

convoitise [kɔ̃vwatiz] *nf* covetousness; **regarder qch avec c.** to look covetously at sth; **exciter les convoitises** to excite envy

convoler [kɔ̃vɔle] *vi Hum* **c. (en justes noces)** to marry

convoquer [kɔ̃vɔke] *vt* (**a**) *(assemblée)* to convene; **c. les actionnaires** to call the shareholders to a meeting (**b**) *(témoin)* to summon; *(employé)* to call in; **c. qn à un examen** to notify sb of an examination

convoyer [32] [kɔ̃vwaje] *vt (troupes)* to convoy; *(fonds)* to transport under armed guard

convoyeur [kɔ̃vwajœr] *nm* (**a**) *(personne)* **c.** de fonds security guard (**b**) *Ind* conveyer

convulser [kɔ̃vylse] **1** *vt* to convulse **2 se convulser** *vpr* to be convulsed

convulsif, -ive [kɔ̃vylsif, -iv] *adj* convulsive

convulsion [kɔ̃vylsjɔ̃] *nf* convulsion; **être pris de convulsions** to go into convulsions

convulsivement [kɔ̃vylsivmɑ̃] *adv* convulsively

cool [kul] *adj inv Fam* cool

coopérant, -e [kɔɔperɑ̃, -ɑ̃t] **1** *nm,f (à l'étranger)* aid worker **2** *nm (pendant le service militaire)* = man doing voluntary work overseas instead of military service

coopératif, -ive [kɔɔperatif, -iv] **1** *adj (société, personne)* co-operative **2** *nf* **coopérative** *(association, magasin)* co-operative, co-op; **coopérative d'achat** wholesale co-operative

coopération [kɔɔperasjɔ̃] *nf* (**a**) *(appui)* co-operation; **en c. avec qn** in co-operation with sb (**b**) *Pol* overseas development; *(service militaire)* = voluntary work overseas carried out as an alternative to military service

coopérer [34] [kɔɔpere] *vi* to co-operate (**à** in)

cooptation [kɔɔptasjɔ̃] *nf* co-option; **par c.** by co-option

coordinateur, -trice [kɔɔrdinatœr, -tris] = **coordonnateur**

coordination [kɔɔrdinasjɔ̃] *nf (d'un projet, des mouvements)* co-ordination

coordonnateur, -trice [kɔɔrdɔnatœr, -tris] *nm,f* co-ordinator

coordonné, -e [kɔɔrdɔne] **1** *adj (mouvement, efforts)* co-ordinated; *(draps, vêtements)* matching **2** *nmpl* **coordonnés** *(vêtements)* co-ordinates **3** *nfpl* **coordonnées** (**a**) *Math, Géog & Astron* coordinates (**b**) *(d'une personne)* address and phone number

coordonner [kɔɔrdɔne] *vt* to co-ordinate (**à** *ou* **avec** with)

copain, copine [kɔpɛ̃, kɔpin] *Fam* **1** *nm,f* (**a**) *(camarade)* pal, mate; **salut les copains!** *(en arrivant)* hi guys!; *(en partant)* see you guys!; **c. de classe** classmate (**b**) *(fiancé)* (petit) **c.** boyfriend; (petite) copine girlfriend **2** *adj* **ils sont très copains** they're great buddies; **être copains comme cochons** to be thick as thieves; **ils sont très c.-c.** they're very pally

copeau, -x [kɔpo] *nm (de bois, de chocolat)* shaving; *(de métal)* cutting

Copenhague [kɔpɛnag] *n* Copenhagen

copie [kɔpi] *nf* (**a**) *(double, manuscrit)* copy (**b**) *Scol (d'examen)* paper; **rendre c. blanche** to hand in a blank paper; **c. simple/double** single/double sheet of paper (**c**) *(d'une œuvre d'art)* copy, reproduction; *(d'un roman, d'un style)* imitation (**d**) *TV & Cin* copy (**e**) *Ordinat* **c. sur papier** hard copy, printout; **c. de sauvegarde** *ou* **de secours** backup (copy), security copy

copier [66] [kɔpje] *vt* (**a**) *(texte, musique, document informatique)* to copy; **c. qch au propre** *ou* **au net** to make a fair copy of sth, to copy sth out neatly (**b**) *(œuvre d'art)* to copy, to reproduce; *(personne, style)* to imitate (**c**) *(à un devoir sur table)* to copy (**sur** from)

copier-coller [kɔpjekɔle] *nm inv Ordinat* copy-and-paste

copieur, -euse [kɔpjœr, -øz] **1** *nm,f (élève)* copier **2** *nm (photocopieuse)* (photo)copier

copieusement [kɔpjøzmɑ̃] *adv (manger, boire)* copiously; **il s'est servi c.** he took a generous helping; **un repas c.** **arrosé** a meal washed down with a lot of wine; **je me suis fait c. insulter** I got quite a mouthful

copieux, -euse [kɔpjø, -øz] *adj (repas)* copious; *(portion, part, pourboire)* generous

copilote [kopilɔt] *nmf (d'avion)* co-pilot; *(de rallye automobile)* navigator

copinage [kɔpinaʒ] *nm Fam* obtenir un poste par **c.** to get a job through one's connections

copiste [kɔpist] *nmf (scribe)* copyist

coprésentateur, -trice [koprezɑ̃tatœr, tris] *nm,f* co-presenter

coprésidence [koprezidɑ̃s] *nf* co-chairmanship

coprésident, -e [koprezidɑ̃, -ɑ̃t] *nm,f* co-chairman, *f* co-chairwoman

coprocesseur [koprɔsesœr] *nm Ordinat* co-processor; **c.** arithmétique maths co-processor

coproduction [koprɔdyksjɔ̃] *nf* coproduction

coproduire [18] [koprɔdɥir] *vt* to coproduce

copropriétaire [koprɔprijeter] *nmf* co-owner, joint owner

copropriété [koprɔprijete] *nf* co-ownership, joint ownership; **acheter/posséder une maison en c.** to buy/own a house jointly

copte [kɔpt] **1** *adj* Coptic **2** *nmf* **C.** Copt

copulation [kɔpylasjɔ̃] *nf* copulation

copuler [kɔpyle] *vi* to copulate

copyright [kɔpirajt] *nm* copyright

coq¹ [kɔk] *nm* (**a**) *(oiseau)* cock, *Am* rooster; **jeune c.** Fig young upstart; **le c. gaulois** the French cockerel; *Fig* **le c. du village** the local Casanova; *Fig* **passer** *ou* **sauter du c. à l'âne** to jump from one subject to another; **être comme un c. en pâte** to be in clover; **c. de bruyère** capercaillie; **c. de combat** fighting cock; *Culin* **c. au vin** coq au vin *(chicken cooked in wine)* (**b**) *(girouette)* weathercock

coq² *nm Naut (ship's)* cook

coq-à-l'âne [kɔkalan] *nm inv* **faire un c.** to jump from one subject to another

coquard, coquart [kɔkar] *nm Fam* shiner, black eye

coque [kɔk] *nf* (**a**) *(d'une noix, d'un fruit)* shell; *Fig* **c. de noix** flimsy craft (**b**) *(d'un navire)* hull; *(d'un avion)* fuselage; *(d'une voiture)* body (**c**) *(mollusque)* cockle

coquelet [kɔklɛ] *nm* cockerel

coquelicot [kɔkliko] *nm* (red) poppy

coqueluche [kɔklyʃ] *nf (maladie)* whooping cough; **avoir la c.** to have whooping cough; **il est devenu la c. de ces dames** he's become a heart-throb

coquet, -ette [kɔkɛ, -ɛt] **1** *adj (ville, intérieur)* charming; **elle est coquette** she's very concerned about her appearance; *Fam* **une coquette somme** a tidy sum **2** *nf* **coquette** *Vieilli*

coquetier [kɔktje] *nm* egg-cup; *Fam* **gagner** *ou* **décrocher le c.** to hit the jackpot

coquetterie [kɔkɛtri] *nf* (**a**) *(vestimentaire)* consciousness of one's appearance; *Vieilli (désir de plaire)* coquetry; **avec c.** *(s'habiller)* stylishly (**b**) *Fam* **avoir une c. dans l'œil** to have a cast in one's eye

coquillage [kɔkijaʒ] *nm* (**a**) *(mollusque)* shellfish (**b**) *(coque vide)* shell

coquille [kɔkij] *nf* (**a**) *(de mollusque, d'œuf, de noix)* shell; *Fig* **rentrer dans/sortir de sa c.** to withdraw into/to come out of one's shell; *Fig* **c. de noix** flimsy craft; **c. d'œuf** *(couleur)* eggshell; **c. Saint-Jacques** *Culin* scallop; *(coquillage)* scallop shell (**b**) *Typ* misprint

coquillettes [kɔkijet] *nfpl* pasta shells

coquin, -e [kɔkɛ̃, -in] **1** *adj (sourire, air)* mischievous; *(sous-vêtement)* naughty; *(histoire)* risqué **2** *nm,f (garnement)* rascal

cor [kɔr] *nm* (**a**) *(instrument)* horn; **c. de chasse** hunting horn; **sonner du c.** to sound *or* blow the horn; *Fig* **réclamer qch à c. et à cri** to clamour for sth (**b**) *(durillon)* corn

corail, -aux [kɔraj, -o] **1** *nm* coral **2** *adj inv* **(rouge) c.** coral(-red)

Coran [kɔrɑ̃] *nm* **le C.** the Koran

coranique [kɔranik] *adj* Koranic

corbeau, -x [kɔrbo] *nm* (**a**) *(oiseau)* crow (**b**) *(auteur de lettres anonymes)* poison-pen letter writer

corbeille [kɔrbɛj] *nf* (**a**) *(panier)* basket; **c. à linge** laundry basket; **c. de mariage** wedding presents; **c. à ouvrage** workbasket; **c. à pain** breadbasket; **c. à papier** wastepaper basket (**b**) *(à la Bourse de Paris)* trading floor (**c**) *Th* dress circle (**d**) *Ordinat* wastebasket, *Am* trash

corbillard [kɔrbijar] *nm* hearse

cordage [kɔrdaʒ] *nm (corde)* rope; *(d'une raquette)* stringing; *Naut* **cordages** rigging

corde [kɔrd] *nf* (**a**) *(lien)* rope; **échelle de c.** rope ladder; **c. à linge** clothes *or* washing line; **c. lisse** climbing rope; **c. à nœuds** knotted climbing rope; **c. raide** tightrope; *Fig* **être sur la c. raide** to be walking a tightrope; **c. à sauter** *Br* skipping rope, *Am* jump-rope (**b**) *(d'instrument, de raquette)* string; **les cordes** *(d'un orchestre)* the strings; *Fig* **avoir plus d'une c. à son arc** to have more than one string to one's bow; *Fig* **j'ai dû toucher la c. sensible** I must have touched a raw nerve (**c**) *Sp* **tenir la c.** *(coureur)* to be on the inside; *(cheval)* to hug the rails; **les cordes** *(d'un ring)* the ropes (**d**) *Anat* **cordes vocales** vocal cords; *Fig* **ce n'est pas dans mes cordes** it's not in my line

cordeau, -x [kɔrdo] *nm (corde)* string; *Fig* **tiré au c.** as straight as a die

cordée [kɔrde] *nf (d'alpinistes)* roped party; **premier de c.** leader

cordelette [kɔrdəlɛt] *nf* cord

cordelière [kɔrdəljɛr] *nf (ceinture)* cord

cordial, -e, -aux, -ales [kɔrdjal, -o] **1** *adj (accueil, personne)* cordial **2** *nm (médicament)* tonic

cordialement [kɔrdjalmɑ̃] *adv* cordially; **détester c. qn** to heartily dislike sb; **bien c.** *(dans une lettre)* best wishes

cordier [kɔrdje] *nm (de violon)* tailpiece

cordillère [kɔrdijɛr] *nf* mountain range; **la c. des Andes** the Andes

cordon [kɔrdɔ̃] *nm* (**a**) *(lien)* cord, string; *Fig* **tenir les cordons de la bourse** to hold the purse-strings; *Anat* **c. ombilical** umbilical cord; *aussi Fig* **couper le c.** (ombilical) to cut the umbilical cord (**b**) *(de policiers, de soldats)* cordon

cordon-bleu (*pl* **cordons-bleus**) [kɔrdɔ̃blø] *nm Fam* cordon bleu (cook)

cordonnerie [kɔrdɔnri] *nf* (**a**) *(métier)* shoe-repairing (**b**) *(boutique)* shoe repair store

cordonnier, -ère [kɔrdɔnje, -ɛr] *nm,f* shoe repairer; *Prov* **les cordonniers sont toujours les plus mal chaussés** the shoemaker's children are always the worst shod

Corée [kɔre] *nf* **la C. du Nord/du Sud** North/South Korea

coréen, -enne [kɔreɛ̃, -ɛn] **1** *adj* Korean **2** *nm,f* **C.** Korean

Corfou [kɔrfu] *n* Corfu

coriace [kɔrjas] *adj* (**a**) *(viande)* tough (**b**) *(personne, adversaire)* tough

coriandre [kɔrjɑ̃dr] *nf* coriander

Corinthe [kɔrɛ̃t] *n voir* **raisin**

cormoran [kɔrmɔrɑ̃] *nm* cormorant

corne [kɔrn] *nf* (**a**) *(d'animal)* horn; **c. d'abondance** horn of plenty, cornucopia; **la C. de l'Afrique** the Horn of Africa (**b**) *(matériau)* horn; **peigne de c.** horn comb (**c**) *(d'un croissant)* end; **faire une c. à une page** to turn down the corner of a page (**d**) *(aux pieds, aux mains)* hard skin

corned-beef [kɔrnbif] *nm* corned beef

cornée [kɔrne] *nf* cornea

cornéen, -enne [kɔrneɛ̃, -ɛn] *adj* corneal

corneille [kɔrnɛj] *nf* crow

cornemuse [kɔrnəmyz] *nf* bagpipes

corner¹ [kɔrne] *vt* (**a**) *(page)* to turn down the corner of; *(abîmer)* to make dog-eared (**b**) *Fam* **c. qch aux oreilles de qn** to shout sth into sb's ear

corner² [kɔrnɛr] *nm (au football)* corner; **tirer un c.** to take a corner

cornet [kɔrnɛ] *nm (de papier)* cone; *(de marrons, de frites)* cornet; **mettre les mains en c.** to cup one's hands together; **c. (à pistons)** cornet; **c. de glace** ice cream cone

cornette [kɔrnɛt] *nf (coiffe)* cornet

cornettiste [kɔrnetist] *nmf* cornetist

corn flakes [kɔrnflɛks] *nmpl* cornflakes

corniaud [kɔrnjo] *nm* (**a**) *(chien)* mongrel (**b**) *Fam (personne)* twit

corniche [kɔrniʃ] *nf* (**a**) *(de bâtiment)* cornice (**b**) *(de rochers)* ledge; *(de glace, de neige)* cornice; **(route de) c.** coast road

cornichon [kɔrniʃɔ̃] *nm* gherkin

Cornouailles [kɔrnwaj] *nf* **la C.** Cornwall

cornu, -e [kɔrny] *adj (animal, diable)* horned

corollaire [kɔrɔlɛr] *nm (suite)* consequence

corolle [kɔrɔl] *nf* corolla

coron [kɔrɔ̃] *nm* mining village

coronaire [kɔrɔnɛr] *adj* coronary

coronarien, -enne [kɔrɔnarjɛ̃, -ɛn] *adj* coronary

corporation [kɔrpɔrasjɔ̃] *nf* corporate body

corporatiste [kɔrpɔratist] *adj* corporatist

corporel, -elle [kɔrpɔrɛl] *adj (punition)* corporal; *(besoins)* bodily; *(hygiène)* personal

corps [kɔr] *nm* (**a**) *(organisme)* body; **trembler de tout son c.** to tremble all over; **lutter c. à c.** to fight hand to hand; *Fig* **faire qch à son c. défendant** to do sth reluctantly; *Fig* **se jeter à c. perdu dans qch** to throw oneself into sth; *Fig* **se donner c. et âme à qn/qch** to give oneself body and soul to sb/sth (**b**) *(cadavre)* body, corpse (**c**) *Chim & Phys* body; *Astron* **c. céleste** heavenly body; **c. composé** compound; **c. gras** fat; **c. simple** element (**d**) *(consistance)* **avoir du c.** *(vin)* to have body; *Fig* **prendre c.** *(projet, idée)* to take shape (**e**) *(partie principale)* main part; *(d'un texte)* body; *Naut* **perdu c. et biens** lost with all hands; *Jur* **le c. du délit** the corpus delicti (**f**) *(groupe)* **c. d'armée** army corps; **c. de ballet** corps de ballet; **c. diplomatique** diplomatic corps; **c. électoral** electorate; **plaisanterie de c. de garde** barrackroom joke; **le c. médical** the medical profession; **c. de métier** trade; *Hist* corporation; **les grands c. de l'État** = the highest sections of the French administration *(Conseil d'État, Cour des comptes etc)*

corpulence [kɔrpylɑ̃s] *nf* stoutness, corpulence

corpulent, -e [kɔrpylɑ̃, -ɑ̃t] *adj* stout, corpulent

corpus [kɔrpys] *nm Jur & Ling* corpus

corpuscule [kɔrpyskyl] *nm* corpuscle

correct, -e [kɔrɛkt] *adj* (**a**) *(sans fautes)* correct (**b**) *(courtois) (personne)* correct; **cela n'est pas c. de sa part**

that's not right of him; **elle a été correcte avec moi** she behaved properly towards me (**c**) *Fam (acceptable) (repas, travail, salaire)* reasonable

correctement [kɔrɛktəmɑ̃] *adv* (**a**) *(sans faire d'erreur, décemment)* correctly (**b**) *Fam (de façon acceptable)* reasonably; **gagner c. sa vie** to make a reasonable living

correcteur, -trice [kɔrɛktœr, -tris] **1** *nm,f (de copies d'examen)* examiner; *(en typographie)* proofreader; *(dans la presse)* copy reader
2 *nm Ordinat* checker; **c. liquide** correcting fluid; *Ordinat* **c. d'orthographe** *ou* **orthographique** spellchecker
3 *adj (verres)* correcting

correction [kɔrɛksjɔ̃] *nf* (**a**) *(d'une faute)* correction; *Scol (d'un exercice)* correcting, marking; *Typ (d'épreuves)* proofreading (**b**) *(punition)* beating (**c**) *(décence, courtoisie)* correctness

correctionnel, -elle [kɔrɛksjɔnɛl] *Jur* **1** *adj* **peine correctionnelle** = penalty of more than five days' (but less than five years') imprisonment; **tribunal c.** criminal court
2 *nf* **correctionnelle** criminal court; **passer en correctionnelle** to go before the criminal court

corrélation [kɔrelasjɔ̃] *nf* correlation

correspondance [kɔrɛspɔ̃dɑ̃s] *nf* (**a**) *(lettres, échange de lettres)* correspondence (**b**) *(entre trains, avions)* connection; **assurer la c. avec...** *(train, bateau)* to connect with... (**c**) *(entre deux choses)* correspondence; *(d'idées, de principes)* conformity

correspondant, -e [kɔrɛspɔ̃dɑ̃, -ɑ̃t] **1** *adj* corresponding (**à** to)
2 *nm,f* (**a**) *(journaliste)* correspondent; **c. de guerre** war correspondent; **c. permanent à New York** New York correspondent (**b**) *(au téléphone)* caller; *(par lettre)* penfriend; **nous recherchons votre c.** *(au téléphone)* we're trying to connect you

correspondre [kɔrɛspɔ̃dr] *vi* (**a**) *(être conforme, équivaloir)* **c. à qch** to correspond to sth; **les vis et les écrous qui correspondent** the screws and the nuts that go with them (**b**) *(par lettres)* **c. avec qn** to correspond with sb

corrida [kɔrida] *nf* bullfight; *Fam (problèmes)* hassle; *Br* carry-on

corridor [kɔridɔr] *nm* corridor

corrigé, -e [kɔriʒe] **1** *adj* corrected; **en données corrigées des variations saisonnières** seasonally adjusted
2 *nm Scol (d'un exercice)* correct answers (**de** to); *(à la fin d'un ouvrage)* key

corriger [45] [kɔriʒe] **1** *vt* (**a**) *(erreur, faute d'orthographe, myopie, défauts)* to correct; *(exercice, examen)* to correct, to mark; *(épreuves typographiques)* to read; *(article de journal)* to sub-edit; **c. qn de qch** to cure sb of sth (**b**) *(pour punir)* **c. qn** to give sb a beating
2 **se corriger** *vpr (personne)* to mend one's ways; **se c. de qch** to cure oneself of sth

corroborer [kɔrɔbɔre] *vt* to corroborate

corroder [kɔrɔde] *vt* to corrode

corrompre [kɔrɔ̃pr] *vt* (**a**) *(personne, goût)* to corrupt (**b**) *(soudoyer)* to bribe

corrompu, -e [kɔrɔ̃py] *adj* corrupt

corrosif, -ive [kɔrozif, -iv] *adj* corrosive; *Fig (propos, humour)* caustic

corrosion [kɔrozjɔ̃] *nf (d'un métal)* corrosion

corruption [kɔrypsjɔ̃] *nf (perversion)* corruption; *(fait de soudoyer)* bribery

corsage [kɔrsaʒ] *nm* blouse

corsaire [kɔrsɛr] **1** *nm* (**a**) *Hist (navire, homme)* corsair (**b**) *(pantalon)* breeches
2 *adj* **pantalon c.** breeches

Corse [kɔrs] *nf* **la C.** Corsica

corse [kɔrs] **1** *adj* Corsican
2 *nmf* **C.** Corsican
3 *nm (langue)* Corsican

corsé, -e [kɔrse] *adj (vin)* full-bodied; *(sauce, plat)* spicy; *(café)* full-flavoured; *Fig (histoire)* spicy

corser [kɔrse] **1** *vt (plat)* to spice up; *Fig (récit)* to liven up
2 **se corser** *vpr (intrigue)* to thicken; **ça se corse** things are getting complicated

corset [kɔrsɛ] *nm* corset; **c. orthopédique** surgical corset

cortège [kɔrtɛʒ] *nm* procession; *Fig* **la vie de famille et son c. de problèmes** family life and its attendant problems; **c. funèbre** funeral cortège

cortex [kɔrtɛks] *nm Anat & Bot* cortex

corticoïde [kɔrtikɔid] *nm* corticoid

cortisone [kɔrtizɔn] *nf* cortisone

corvée [kɔrve] *nf* (**a**) *(obligation pénible)* chore; **je suis de c. de vaisselle ce soir** I'm on dishwashing duty tonight; **quelle c.!** what a drag! (**b**) *Mil* fatigue duty; **être de c.** to be on fatigue duty (**c**) *Hist* corvée

corvette [kɔrvɛt] *nf* corvette

coryza [kɔriza] *nm* head cold, *Spéc* coryza

cosaque [kɔzak] *nm* cossack

cosignataire [kosiɲatɛr] *adj & nmf* cosignatory

cosinus [kɔsinys] *nm* cosine

cosmétique [kɔsmetik] *adj & nm* cosmetic

cosmique [kɔsmik] *adj* cosmic

cosmologie [kɔsmɔlɔʒi] *nf* cosmology

cosmonaute [kɔsmɔnot] *nmf* cosmonaut

cosmopolite [kɔsmɔpɔlit] *adj* cosmopolitan

cosmos [kɔsmos] *nm (univers)* cosmos; *(espace)* outer space

cosse [kɔs] *nf (de petits pois)* pod

cossu, -e [kɔsy] *adj (maison, intérieur)* opulent; *(personne)* well-to-do

costard [kɔstar] *nm Fam* suit

Costa Rica [kɔstarika] *nm* **le C.** Costa Rica

costaud, -e [kɔsto, -od] **1** *adj (fort, solide)* sturdy
2 *nm,f* sturdy man, f woman

costume [kɔstym] *nm (habit)* costume; *(complet)* suit

costumé, -e [kɔstyme] *adj voir* **bal**

costumier, -ère [kɔstymje, -ɛr] *nm,f (de théâtre)* wardrobe master, f wardrobe mistress; *(de cinéma)* costume supervisor

cotation [kɔtasjɔ̃] *nf* **c. (en Bourse)** quotation (on the Stock Market)

cote [kɔt] *nf* (**a**) *(d'une action) (valeur)* quotation; *(liste)* share index; *(d'un cheval)* odds; **c. de popularité** popularity rating; *Fam* **avoir la c. (avec** *ou* **auprès de)** to be popular (with) (**b**) *(servant à classer)* classification mark (**c**) *(altitude)* altitude; **atteindre la c. d'alerte** *(fleuve)* to reach danger level; *Fig* to reach crisis point

coté, -e [kɔte] *adj* (**a**) *(estimé)* **bien/très/mal c.** highly/very highly/not highly thought of (**b**) **action cotée en Bourse** share quoted on the Stock Exchange; **être c. à 17 euros** to be trading at 17 euros; **être c. à l'argus** to be listed in the car buyer's guide

côte [kot] *nf* (**a**) *(os)* rib; **c. à c.** side by side; *Fam* **on lui voit les côtes** he's nothing but skin and bone; **c. d'agneau/de porc** lamb/pork chop; **c. de bœuf** rib of beef (**b**) *(de melon, de feuille)* rib; **tissu à côtes** ribbed material (**c**) *(d'une* *montagne)* slope; **monter/descendre une c.** to go up/down a hill **(d)** *(rivage)* coast; **la C.** *(d'Azur)* the (French) Riviera **côté** [kote] *nm* **(a)** *(du corps humain)* side; **couché sur le c.** lying on one's side; *Fig* **être aux côtés de qn** to be at sb's side **(b)** *(d'une route, d'un triangle, d'une feuille)* side; **de l'autre c.** **(de qch)** on the other side (of sth); **siège c. couloir/fenêtre** aisle/window seat; *Th* **c. jardin/cour** on stage left/right **(c)** *(aspect)* side; **il a de bons côtés** he's got a good side to him; **prendre la vie du bon c.** to look on the bright side of life **(d)** *(endroit)* **de tous côtés** *(cerné)* on all sides; *(affluer)* from all directions; **du c. de** *(près de)* near; **ils s'en allèrent chacun de son c.** they went their separate ways; **de quel c.?** *(direction)* which way?; *(position)* which side?; *Fig* **être du c. de qn** to be on sb's side; **mon oncle du c. maternel** my uncle on my mother's side; **d'un c...., d'un autre c....** on the one hand..., on the other hand... **(e)** *Fam (en ce qui concerne)* **c. argent, ça va** things are OK moneywise; **de ce c., il n'y a rien à craindre** there's nothing to worry about on that score **(f)** **à c.** *(près)* nearby; **à c. de** *(près de)* next to; *(comparé à)* compared with; **les voisins d'à c.** the next-door neighbours; **à c. l'un de l'autre** side by side; *Fig* **passer à c. de qch** to miss out on sth **(g)** **faire un saut de c.** to leap to one side *or* aside; *Fig* **mettre qch de c.** to put sth aside; *Fig* **laisser qn/qch de c.** to leave sb/sth out

coteau, -x [kɔto] *nm (versant)* hillside; *(colline)* hill

Côte d'Ivoire [kotdivwar] *nf* **la C.** the Ivory Coast

côtelé, -e [kotle] *adj voir* **velours**

côtelette [kotlɛt, kɔtlɛt] *nf* chop; **c. d'agneau/de porc** lamb/pork chop

coter [kɔte] *vt* **(a)** *(prix, actions)* to quote **(b)** *(documents)* to classify

côtier, -ère [kotje, -ɛr] *adj (fleuve, navigation)* coastal; *(pêche)* inshore

cotillon [kɔtijɔ̃] *nm* **accessoires de c., cotillons** party novelties

cotisation [kɔtizasjɔ̃] *nf* **(a)** *(à une caisse)* contribution; **cotisations de Sécurité Sociale** social security contributions **(b)** *(à un club)* subscription

cotiser [kɔtize] **1** *vi (à une caisse de retraite, à une mutuelle)* to contribute (**à** to) **2 se cotiser** *vpr* to club together

coton [kɔtɔ̃] **1** *nm* **(a)** *(plante, tissu)* cotton; **chemise 100% c.** 100% cotton shirt; *Fam* **filer un mauvais c.** *(financièrement, physiquement)* to be in a bad way **(b) c. (hydrophile)** *Br* cotton wool, *Am* absorbent cotton; **un c.** a piece of *Br* cotton wool *or Am* absorbent cotton; *Fig* **élever un enfant dans du c.** to wrap a child in cotton wool; *Fam* **j'ai les jambes en c.** my legs feel like jelly **2** *adj Fam* tough, tricky

cotonnade [kɔtɔnad] *nf* cotton fabric

cotonneux, -euse [kɔtɔnø, -øz] *adj (feuille)* downy; *(nuage)* fluffy; *(fruit)* mushy

Coton-Tige® *(pl* **Cotons-Tiges)** [kɔtɔ̃tiʒ] *nm* cotton bud

côtoyer [32] [kotwaje] *vt* **(a)** *(personnes)* to mix with **(b)** *(rivière, forêt)* to border on

cotte [kɔt] *nf* **c. de mailles** coat of mail

cou [ku] *nm* neck; **tendre le c.** to crane one's neck; **se jeter au c. de qn** to throw one's arms round sb's neck; *Fam* **endetté jusqu'au c.** up to one's eyes in debt

couac [kwak] *nm (fausse note)* false note; *Fig* discordant note; **faire un c.** to play a false note; *(chanteur)* to sing a false note

couchage [kuʃaʒ] *nm voir* **sac**

couchant, -e [kuʃɑ̃, -ɑ̃t] **1** *adj* **le soleil c.** the setting sun **2** *nm (ouest)* west; **dans la direction du c.** in a westerly direction

couche [kuʃ] *nf* **(a)** *(de peinture)* coat; *(de beurre, de crème, de poussière)* layer; *(classe sociale)* level; *Géol* layer, stratum; **la c. d'ozone** the ozone layer; *Fam* **il en tient une c.!** he's really stupid! **(b)** *(de bébé) Br* nappy, *Am* diaper **(c)** *Vieilli* **femme en couches** woman in labour; **mourir en couches** to die in childbirth **(d)** *Litt (lit)* bed

couché, -e [kuʃe] *adj* **(a)** *(allongé)* lying (down); *(au lit)* in bed **(b)** *(écriture)* slanting, sloping

couche-culotte *(pl* **couches-culottes)** [kuʃkylɔt] *nf* disposable *Br* nappy *or Am* diaper

coucher¹ [kuʃe] *nm* **(a)** *(fait d'aller au lit)* **l'heure du c.** bedtime **(b)** *(gîte)* accommodation **(c)** *(du soleil)* setting; **un superbe c. de soleil** a magnificent sunset; **au c. du soleil** at sunset

coucher² **1** *vt* **(a)** *(mettre au lit)* **c. qn** to put sb to bed **(b)** *(allonger, poser)* to lay down **(c)** *(écrire)* **c. qn sur son testament** to mention sb in one's will **2** *vi* **(a)** *(passer la nuit)* to sleep; *Fig* **c. sous les ponts** to sleep rough **(b)** *Fam* **c. avec qn** to sleep with sb; **c. ensemble** to sleep together **(c)** *(à un chien)* **couché!** (lie) down! **3 se coucher** *vpr* **(a)** *(au lit)* to go to bed; **aller se c.** to go to bed; *Fam* **se c. avec les poules** to go to bed early; *Prov* **comme on fait son lit, on se couche** as we make our bed, so we must lie in it **(b)** *(s'allonger)* to lie down; **se c. à plat ventre** to lie flat on one's stomach **(c)** **se c. sur le flanc** *(navire)* to keel over **(d)** *(soleil, lune)* to set, to go down

coucheries [kuʃri] *nf Fam* sleeping around

couchette [kuʃɛt] *nf (de navire)* bunk; *(de train)* couchette

coucheur [kuʃœr] *nm Fam* **c'est un mauvais c.** he's an awkward customer

couci-couça [kusikusa] *adv Fam* so-so

coucou [kuku] **1** *nm* **(a)** *(oiseau)* cuckoo **(b)** *(horloge)* cuckoo clock **(c)** *(plante)* cowslip **(d)** *Fam (avion)* old crate **2** *exclam (langage enfantin)* peekaboo!; *(bonjour)* cooee!

coude [kud] *nm* **(a)** *(articulation)* elbow; **être au c. à c.** to be neck and neck; **jouer des coudes** to push and shove; *Fig* **to manœuvre**; *Fig* **se serrer les coudes** to stick together; *Fig* **garder qch sous le c.** to hold on to sth; *Fam* **lever le c.** to booze **(b)** *(tournant)* sharp bend; *(de barre, de tuyau)* bend; *(d'arbre)* crank

coudé, -e [kude] *adj* bent

coudée [kude] *nf* **avoir les coudées franches** to have plenty of elbow room

cou-de-pied *(pl* **cous-de-pied)** [kudəpje] *nm* instep

coudre [21] [kudr] *vt (ourlet)* to sew; *(bouton)* to sew on; *(deux morceaux d'étoffe)* to sew together; *(jupe, plaie)* to sew up; **c. un bouton à une veste** to sew a button on a jacket; **je ne sais pas c.** I can't sew

coudrier [kudrije] *nm* hazel (tree)

couenne [kwan] *nf* rind

couette¹ [kwɛt] *nf (édredon)* duvet, continental quilt

couette² *nf (coiffure)* bunch; **se faire des couettes** to put one's hair in bunches

couille [kuj] *nf Vulg (testicule)* ball; *(problème)* balls-up

couillon, -onne [kujɔ̃, -ɔn] *nm,f très Fam (imbécile)* jackass

couillonner [kujɔne] *vt très Fam (personne)* to con; **se faire c.** to be conned

couiner [kwine] *vi (animal)* to squeak; *(enfant)* to whine

coulant, -e [kulɑ̃, -ɑ̃t] *adj (fromage)* runny; *Fig (style)* flowing; *Fam (personne)* easy-going

coulée [kule] *nf* **c. de boue** mudslide; **c. de lave** lava flow

couler [kule] **1** *vt* **(a)** *(liquide, cire, ciment)* to pour; *(métal, statue)* to cast **(b)** *(navire)* to sink; *Fig* **c. qn** to bring sb down **(c)** *(passer)* **c. des jours heureux** to lead a happy life; *Fam* **se la c. douce** to take things easy
2 *vi* **(a)** *(liquide, rivière)* to flow, to run; *(fromage, maquillage)* to run; **la sueur coule sur son front** sweat is trickling down his/her forehead; **cette affaire a fait c. beaucoup d'encre** a lot has been written about this affair; **faire c. un bain à qn** to run a bath for sb; *Fig* **c. de source** to be obvious **(b)** *(navire)* to sink, to go down; *(entreprise)* to go under **(c)** *(tonneau, stylo)* to leak; *(nez)* to run; **avoir le nez qui coule** to have a runny nose
3 se couler *vpr (se glisser)* to slip

couleur [kulœr] **1** *nf* **(a)** *(teinte, orientation politique)* colour; **de quelle c. est...?** what colour is...?; **de c.** coloured; **télévision/photographie en c.** *ou* **couleurs** colour television/photography; **les couleurs** *(linge)* coloureds; *Fig* **pour faire c. locale** to add a bit of local colour; *Fam* **elle nous en a fait voir de toutes les couleurs** she gave us a hard time; *Fam* **je n'en ai pas encore vu la c.** I've seen no sign of it yet **(b)** *(teint)* **prendre des couleurs** to get some colour in one's cheeks **(c)** *Mil* **couleurs** *(drapeau)* colours **(d)** **couleurs** *(d'un club, d'une écurie)* colours; **défendre les couleurs de** to represent **(e)** *(peinture)* paint; **une boîte de couleurs** a paintbox **(f)** *(aux cartes)* suit; **annoncer la c.** to call (trumps); *Fam* to lay one's cards on the table **(g)** *(en coiffure)* dye; **se faire une c.** *(soi-même)* to dye one's hair; *(chez le coiffeur)* to have one's hair dyed
2 *adj inv (télévision, pellicule)* colour; **une chevelure c. de feu** flame-coloured hair

couleuvre [kulœvr] *nf* **c. (à collier)** grass snake; *Fig* **avaler des couleuvres** *(se faire humilier)* to eat humble pie; *(être naïf)* to swallow anything

coulis [kuli] *nm* **c. de tomates/framboises** tomato/raspberry coulis

coulissant, -e [kulisɑ̃, -ɑ̃t] *adj* sliding

coulisse [kulis] *nf* **(a)** *(glissière)* runner; **porte à c.** sliding door **(b)** *Th* **les coulisses** the wings; **en coulisses, dans les coulisses** in the wings; *Fig* behind the scenes

coulisser [kulise] *vi* to slide

couloir [kulwar] *nm* **(a)** *(de maison)* corridor, passage; *(de train)* corridor; *(en athlétisme, en natation)* lane; *(au tennis) Br* tramlines, *Am* alley; **c. aérien** air corridor; **c. d'autobus** bus lane **(b)** *Géog* gully

coulommiers [kulɔmje] *nm* = type of soft cheese

coulpe [kulp] *nf* **battre sa c.** to beat one's breast

coup [ku] *nm* **(a)** *(choc)* blow; **donner un c. à qn** to hit sb; **se donner un c. contre qch** to knock against sth; **donner un c. de bâton à qn** to hit sb with a stick; **donner un c. de couteau à qn** to knife sb; **donner un c. de coude à qn** to nudge sb; **c. de pied** kick; **donner un c. de pied à qn/qch** to kick sb/sth; **c. de poing** punch; **donner un c. de poing à qn** to punch sb; **c. de poing américain** knuckle-duster; *Fig* **donner un c. de pouce à qn** to push sb; **c. de tête** header; *Fam* **faire qch sur un c. de tête** to do sth on the spur of the moment; **donner un c. de griffe à qn/qch** to claw at sb/sth; **rendre c. pour c.** to give as good as one gets; *Fig* **tous les coups sont permis** there are no holds barred; *Fig* **c'était un c. bas** that was below the belt; *Jur* **coups et blessures** grievous bodily harm
(b) *(choc émotionnel)* blow; **faire un c. à qn** to be a blow; **accuser le c.** to show that one has been affected; *Fam* **tenir le c.** to hold out; *Fam* **en prendre un c.** to be devastated; **un c. dur** a setback
(c) *(action soudaine, événement soudain)* **c. de vent** gust of wind; *Fam* **passer en c. de vent** to pay a flying visit;

donner un c. de frein to brake; **donner un c. de volant** to turn the wheel sharply; **donner un c. d'arrêt à qch** to call a halt to sth; *Fam* **prendre un c.** de vieux to age; *Fam* **avoir un c. de barre** *ou* **de pompe** to have the munchies; **c. de chance** *ou Fam* **de bol** *ou* **de pot** stroke of luck; *Fam* **avoir un c. de cœur pour qch** to absolutely love sth, **c. d'État** coup (d'État); *Fig* **ça a été le c. de foudre** it was love at first sight; **attraper un c. de froid** to catch a cold; *Fam* **pousser un c. de gueule** to yell; *Fam* **un c. de pub** a publicity stunt; **prendre un c. de soleil** to get sunburned; **c. de théâtre** coup de théâtre; *(dans la vie)* sudden turn of events
(d) *(bruit)* **c. de feu** shot; **c. de fusil** shot; **c. de sifflet** whistle; **c. de sonnette** ring; **c. de tonnerre** clap of thunder; **tirer deux coups** to fire twice; **l'horloge sonna trois coups** the clock struck three; *Fig* **sur le c. de midi** on the stroke of twelve; **les trois coups** *(au théâtre)* = the three knocks given just before the curtain rises
(e) *(influence)* **sous le c. de la colère** in a fit of anger; **tomber sous le c. de la loi** to be an offence
(f) *(essai)* attempt, go; *Fig* **réussir son c.** to be a great success; **d'un seul c.** in one go; **du premier c.** at the first attempt; *Fam* **à tous les coups, le patron va nous repérer** the boss is bound to see us; **il n'en est pas à son c. d'essai** it's not the first time he's done it; **c. de maître** master-stroke
(g) *(au golf)* stroke; *(aux échecs)* move; **c. droit** *(au tennis)* forehand; *Fig* **faire c. double** to kill two birds with one stone; **c. d'envoi** *(au football, au rugby)* kickoff; *Fig* **donner le c. d'envoi de qch** to launch sth; **c. franc** *(au football)* free kick; **c. de pied de réparation** penalty kick
(h) *Fam (tour, combine)* **réussir un bon c.** to do well for oneself; **faire un sale c. à qn** to play a dirty trick on sb; **être sur un c.** to be on to a good thing; **être dans le c.** *(impliqué)* to be involved; *(à la mode)* to be trendy, **c. fourré, c. de Jarnac** dirty trick; **c. monté** put-up job
(i) *Vulg* **tirer un c.** to have a screw
(j) *(locutions)* **tout à c., tout d'un c.** suddenly, all of a sudden; **à c. sûr** for certain, definitely; **au c. par c.** step by step; **c. sur c.** one after the other; **après c.** after the event; *Fam* **du c.** and so; **pleurer un bon c.** to have a good cry; **mourir sur le c.** to die on the spot; **sur le c., je n'ai pas compris** at the time I didn't understand; **faire les quatre cents coups** to sow one's wild oats; **donner le c. de grâce à qn** to finish sb off; **avoir le c. de main (pour faire qch)** to have the knack (of doing sth); **donner un c. de main à qn** to give sb a hand; *Fam* **boire un c.** to have a drink; *Fam* **avoir un c. dans le nez** to be smashed; *Fam* **valoir le c.** to be worth it; *Fam* **il va falloir en mettre un c.** we're going to have to pull out all the stops

coupable [kupabl] **1** *adj (personne)* guilty **(de** of**)**; *(action, négligence)* culpable; *(faiblesse)* reprehensible; **se sentir c. (de faire qch)** to feel guilty (about doing sth)
2 *nmf* culprit

coupant, -e [kupɑ̃, -ɑ̃t] *adj* sharp

coupe¹ [kup] *nf* **(a)** *(récipient)* bowl; **c. à champagne** champagne glass; *Fig* **la c. est pleine** that's the limit; *Prov* **il y a loin de la c. aux lèvres** there's many a slip 'twixt cup and lip **(b)** *(trophée)* cup; **la C. du monde de football** Football World Cup; **la c. Davis** the Davis Cup

coupe² *nf* **(a)** *(action)* *(du blé)* cutting; *(de tissu)* cutting out; *(d'arbres)* cutting down; **c. (de cheveux)** haircut; **acheter du fromage à la c.** to buy cheese from the fresh cheese counter; **c. sombre** *(dans une forêt)* slight thinning; *(du personnel, des dépenses)* drastic cut **(b)** *(d'un vêtement)* cut **(c)** *(plan)* section **(d)** *(aux cartes)* cut; *Fig* **être sous la c. de qn** to be under sb's thumb

coupé, -e [kupe] **1** *adj* **(a)** *(taillé)* cut; **un costume mal c.** a badly cut suit (**b**) *(au tennis)* une balle coupée a slice (**c**) *(castré) (chat)* neutered

2 *nm (voiture)* coupé; **c. sport** sports coupé

coupe-coupe [kupkup] *nm inv* machete

coupe-faim [kupfɛ̃] *nm inv* appetite suppressant

coupe-feu [kupfø] *nm inv* firebreak; **porte c.** fire-door

coupe-gorge [kupgɔrʒ] *nm inv (quartier)* dangerous area; *(bâtiment)* death trap

coupe-légumes [kuplegym] *nm inv* vegetable slicer

coupelle [kupɛl] *nf* (**a**) *(petite coupe)* small dish (**b**) *(de laboratoire)* cupel

coupe-ongles [kupɔ̃gl] *nm inv* nail clippers

coupe-papier [kuppapje] *nm inv* paper knife, letter opener

couper [kupe] **1** *vt* (**a**) *(trancher)* to cut; *(arbre)* to cut down; *(vêtement)* to cut out; **c. qch en morceaux** to cut sth up (into pieces); **c. qch en trois** to cut sth into three; **c. les cheveux à qn** to cut sb's hair; **c. la tête à qn** to cut off sb's head; **c. les cheveux en quatre** to split hairs; **un brouillard à c. au couteau** fog you could cut with a knife; **j'en donnerais ma main** *ou* **ma tête à c.** I'd stake my life on it (**b**) *(supprimer, raccourcir)* to cut; **c. dans le vif** to take drastic measures (**c**) *(traverser)* to cut across; **c. la route à qn** to cut in in front of sb; **c. à travers champs** to cut across country; **c. par le jardin** to cut through the garden (**d**) *(séparer)* to divide (**en deux** in two); **être coupé du monde** to be cut off from the outside world (**e**) *(interrompre) (personne)* to cut in on; *(son)* to turn right down; **c. l'eau** *(pour réparation)* to turn off the water; *(pour non-paiement)* to cut off the water; **c. le courant** *ou* **l'électricité** *(pour réparation)* to switch off the current; *(pour non-paiement)* to cut off the power; **c. le téléphone à qn** to cut off sb's telephone; **nous avons été coupés, la communication a été coupée** we were cut off; **c. le contact** *(d'une voiture)* to switch off the ignition; **c. l'appétit à qn** to spoil sb's appetite; **ces bas me coupent la circulation** these stockings are cutting off my circulation; *Fam* **ça te la coupe!** that's taken the wind out of your sails! (**f**) *(châtrer) (chat)* to neuter (**g**) **c. du vin** *(en mélangeant)* to blend wine; *(avec de l'eau)* to water down wine (**h**) *(paquet de cartes)* to cut; *(prendre avec l'atout)* to trump; **à toi de c.** it's your turn to cut; **c. à carreau** to trump with a diamond (**i**) *(au tennis) (balle)* to slice

2 *vi (être tranchant)* to be sharp

3 couper à *vt ind* (**a**) *Fam* **c. à qch** *(se dérober)* to get out of sth (**b**) **c. court à qch** to cut sth short

4 se couper *vpr* (**a**) *(se blesser)* to cut oneself; **se c. le** *ou* **au doigt** to cut one's finger; **se c. les veines** to slash one's wrists (**b**) *(tailler)* **se c. les ongles/les cheveux** to cut one's nails/hair (**c**) *(routes)* to intersect, to cross (**d**) **se c. de qn** to cut oneself off from sb

couper-coller [kupekɔle] *nm inv Ordinat* cut and paste

couperet [kuprɛ] *nm* (**a**) *(pour la viande)* cleaver (**b**) *(de la guillotine)* blade

couperose [kuproz] *nf* blotches

couperosé, -e [kuproze] *adj* blotchy

coupe-vent [kupvɑ̃] *nm inv* (**a**) *(dispositif)* windbreak (**b**) *(blouson) Br* windcheater, *Am* Windbreaker®

couple [kupl] *nm (de personnes)* couple; *(d'animaux)* pair; **vivre en c.** to live together; **un c. sans enfants** a childless couple

couplet [kuplɛ] *nm (de chanson)* verse; *Fam* tirade (**sur** about)

coupole [kupɔl] *nf* dome, cupola

coupon [kupɔ̃] *nm* (**a**) *(ticket)* **c. de réduction** money-off coupon (**b**) *(de tissu)* remnant (**c**) *Fin* **c. d'action** coupon

coupon-réponse *(pl* **coupons-réponse**) [kupɔ̃repɔ̃s] *nm* reply coupon

coupure [kupyr] *nf* (**a**) *(blessure)* cut (**b**) *(suppression)* cut (**c**) **c. (de courant)** power cut (**d**) *Fig (séparation)* break (**e**) **c. de journal** *ou* **de presse** newspaper *or* press cutting (**f**) *Fin* denomination; **50 000 euros en petites coupures** 50,000 euros in small notes *or* denominations

cour [kur] *nf* (**a**) *(de maison, de ferme)* yard; **c. d'honneur** main courtyard; **c. de récréation** *Br* playground, *Am* schoolyard (**b**) *(de souverain)* court; **vivre à la c.** to live at court (**c**) *(tribunal)* court; **Messieurs, la C.!** all rise!; **Haute C.** High Court *(for impeachment of president or ministers)*; **c. d'appel** court of appeal; **c. d'assises** court of assizes; **c. de cassation** ≃ Supreme Court of Appeal; **la C. des comptes** the Audit Office; **la C. internationale de justice** the International Court of Justice; **c. martiale** court martial; **passer en c. martiale (pour qch)** to be court-martialled (for sth); *Can* **la C. suprême** the Supreme Court (**d**) **faire la c. à qn** to court sb

courage [kuraʒ] *nm* courage, bravery; **avec c.** bravely, courageously; **perdre c.** to lose heart; **prendre son c. à deux mains** to pluck up courage; **avoir/se sentir le c. de ses opinions** to have the courage of one's convictions; **avoir/se sentir le c. de faire qch** to be/to feel up to doing sth; **bon c.!** good luck!

courageusement [kuraʒøzmɑ̃] *adv (bravement)* courageously, bravely; *(résolument)* with a will

courageux, -euse [kuraʒø, -øz] *adj* (**a**) *(brave)* courageous, brave (**b**) *(énergique)* energetic

courailler [kuraje] *vi Can Fam* to chase women

courailleur [kurajœr] *nm Can Fam* womanizer

couramment [kuramɑ̃] *adv* (**a**) *(parler)* fluently (**b**) *(généralement)* commonly; **ce mot s'emploie c.** this word is in common use

courant, -e [kurɑ̃, -ɑ̃t] **1** *adj* (**a**) *(commun)* common; **dans la vie courante** in everyday life (**b**) *(en cours)* current

2 *nm* (**a**) *(dans une rivière)* current; *Fig (tendance)* trend; **suivre/remonter le c.** to go with/against the current; **c. d'air** draught; **c. de pensée** way of thinking (**b**) *Él* **c. (électrique)** (electric) current; **c. continu/alternatif** direct/alternating current; *Fig* **le c. ne passe pas** we're/they're/you're not on the same wavelength (**c**) *(durée)* **dans le c. de** in the course of; **c. janvier** during the month of January (**d**) **être au c. (de qch)** to know (about sth); **mettre qn au c. (de qch)** to tell sb (about sth); **tenir qn au c. (de qch)** to keep sb up-to-date (on sth)

3 *nf* **courante** *Fam* **avoir la courante** to have the squits

courbatu, -e [kurbaty] *adj* aching (all over)

courbature [kurbatyr] *nf* ache; **avoir des courbatures** to be aching (all over)

courbaturé, -e [kurbatyre] *adj* aching (all over)

courbe [kurb] **1** *adj* curved

2 *nf* curve; *(graphe)* graph; **c. de niveau** contour (line); **c. des prix/des salaires** price/salary curve; **c. de température** temperature curve

courber [kurbe] **1** *vt* to bend; **c. la tête** to bow *or* bend one's head; *Fig* **c. l'échine** to submit

2 *vi* to bend

3 se courber *vpr (personne)* to bend down, to stoop; **se c. en deux** to bend double

courbette [kurbɛt] *nf (salut)* bow; *Fig* **faire des courbettes (à qn)** to bow and scrape (to sb)

courbure [kurbyr] *nf (d'une surface, d'une ligne)* curvature; *(d'un morceau de bois, du dos)* curve

coureur, -euse [kurœr, -øz] **1** *nm,f (à pied)* runner; **c.** *(automobile)* (racing) driver; **c. (cycliste)** (racing) cyclist **2** *adj (homme)* womanizing; *(femme)* manhunting **3** *nm* **c. (de jupons)** womanizer **4** *nf* **coureuse** *(dévergondée)* manhunter

courge [kurʒ] *nf* **(a)** *(plante) Br* marrow, *Am* squash **(b)** *Fam (imbécile)* wally

courgette [kurʒɛt] *nf Br* courgette, *Am* zucchini

courir [22] [kurir] **1** *vi* **(a)** *(personne)* to run; **monter/ descendre la colline en courant** to run up/down the hill; **arriver en courant** to come running (up); **je cours le prévenir** I'll run and warn him; **c. après sb/qch** to run after sb/sth; **c. après la gloire** to chase after glory; **c. à sa perte** to be heading for disaster; **l'assassin court toujours** the murderer is still at large; **ça ne court pas les rues** *(personnes)* they're not thick on the ground; *(objets)* you don't see that every day; *Fam* **tu peux toujours c.!** not a chance!; *Fam* **laisse c.!** forget it!; *Prov* **rien ne sert de c., il faut partir à point** slow and steady wins the race **(b)** *(se propager)* **le bruit court que…** rumour has it that…; **faire c. un bruit** to spread a rumour **(c)** *(eau, ruisseau)* to rush **(d)** *(participer à une course) (à pied)* to run; *(automobile)* to drive; *(cycliste)* to ride

2 *vt* **(a)** *(tenter)* **c. un risque** to run a risk **(b)** *Sp* **c. le 800 mètres** to run the 800 metres **(c)** *(parcourir, fréquenter)* **c. le monde** to roam the world; **c. les théâtres** to go to the theatre all the time **(d)** *(chasser)* **c. les filles** to chase women; *Fig* **c. deux lièvres à la fois** to have two irons in the fire

3 *v impersonnel* **il court des bruits sur lui** there are rumours going round about him

courlis [kurli] *nm* curlew

couronne [kurɔn] *nf* **(a)** *(de fleurs, de lauriers)* wreath; **c. funéraire** *ou* **mortuaire** (funeral) wreath **(b)** *(de souverain)* crown; *(de noble)* coronet; **la C. de France** the French Crown **(c)** *(monnaie)* crown **(d)** *(pain)* ring-shaped loaf; *(de dent)* crown; **se faire poser une c.** to have a tooth crowned

couronnement [kurɔnmã] *nm (de souverain)* coronation; *Fig (réussite)* crowning achievement

couronner [kurɔne] *vt* **(a)** *(sacrer)* to crown; *Fig* **mes efforts furent couronnés de succès** my efforts were crowned with success; **et pour c. le tout…** and to crown it all… **(b)** *(dent)* to crown

courra *etc voir* **courir**

courre [kur] *voir* **chasse**

courrier [kurje] *nm* **(a)** *(lettres)* mail, *Br* post; **c. électronique** e-mail; **c. interne** internal mail **(b)** *Journ* **c. du cœur** problem page; **c. des lecteurs** letters to the Editor **(c)** *Vieilli (messager)* courier

courroie [kurwa] *nf* **(a)** *(de cuir, de toile)* strap **(b)** *Méc* belt; **c. de transmission** driving belt; **c. de ventilateur** fanbelt

courroucé, -e [kuruse] *adj Litt* incensed

courroux [kuru] *nm Litt* ire, wrath

cours¹ [kur] *nm* **(a)** *(leçon) Univ* lecture; *Scol* lesson; *(ensemble des leçons)* course; **aller en c.** *Univ* to go to lectures; *Scol* to go to school; **prendre** *ou* **suivre un c.** to take *ou* do a course; **donner des c.** *Univ* to give lectures; *Scol* to give classes; **c. par correspondance** correspondence course; **c. intensif** crash course; **c. magistral** lecture; **c. particulier** private lesson; **c. du soir** evening class **(b)** *(classe)* **c. élémentaire** = two-year subdivision of primary-level education in France (ages 8 to 9); **c. moyen** = two-year subdivision of primary-level education in France (ages 10 to 11); **c. préparatoire** *Br* ≃ first year infants class, *Am* ≃ nursery school **(c)** *(de rivière, d'un astre)* course; **suivre le c. de ses pensées** to follow one's train of thought; **donner libre c. à qch** to give free rein to sth; **c. d'eau** waterway **(d)** *(évolution)* course; **suivre son c.** to run

its course; **en c.** *(affaires)* in hand; *(travaux)* in progress; *(année)* current; **en c. de route** on the way; **au c. de qch** in the course of sth **(e)** *(d'une monnaie)* currency; **avoir c.** *(monnaie)* to be legal tender; *(pratique)* to be current **(f)** *Fin (d'une action)* price; *(de devises)* rate; **c. des changes** exchange rates

cours² *voir* **courir**

course [kurs] *nf* **(a)** *Sp (épreuve)* race; *(discipline)* racing; **les courses (de chevaux)** the races; *Fam* **ça va encore être la c.** it's going to be another mad rush; **la c. aux armements** the arms race; **c. automobile** motor race; *(discipline)* motor racing; **c. de chevaux** horse race; *Sp & Fig* **c. contre la montre** race against the clock; **c. cycliste** cycle race; **c. de haies** *(en athlétisme)* hurdles; *(course de chevaux)* steeplechase; **c. d'obstacles** steeplechase; **c. à pied** race; *(discipline)* running; **c. de taureaux** *(corrida)* bullfight **(b)** *(action de courir)* running **(c)** *(achat)* **faire une c.** to get something from the shops; **courses** shopping; **faire des courses** to go shopping **(d)** *(trajet en taxi)* journey; *(prix)* **fare (e)** *(de planète, de projectile)* course

courser [kurse] *vt Fam* to chase after

coursier, -ère [kursje, -ɛr] *nm,f* messenger; *(en moto)* motorcycle courier

coursive [kursiv] *nf Naut* gangway

court¹, -e [kur, kurt] **1** *adj* short; *Fam* **10 euros, c'est un peu c.** 10 euros isn't very much **2** *adv* short; **pour faire c.** to cut a long story short; **on l'appelle Luc tout c.** people just call him Luc; **prendre qn de c.** *(en lui laissant peu de temps)* to give sb short notice; *(sans le prévenir)* to catch sb unawares; **à c. de qch** short of

court² *nm* **c. (de tennis)** (tennis) court

court³ *voir* **courir**

court-bouillon *(pl* **courts-bouillons)** [kurbujõ] *nm* court-bouillon

court-circuit *(pl* **courts-circuits)** [kursirkɥi] *nm* short circuit

court-circuiter [kursirkɥite] *vt Él & Fam Fig* to short-circuit

courtier, -ère [kurtje, -ɛr] *nm,f* broker; **c. d'assurances** insurance broker

courtisan [kurtizã] *nm* **(a)** *Hist* courtier **(b)** *Péj (flatteur)* sycophant

courtisane [kurtizan] *nf Litt* courtesan

courtiser [kurtize] *vt* **(a)** *(femme)* to court **(b)** *(flatter)* to fawn on

courtois, -e [kurtwa, -az] *adj (poli)* courteous **(envers** *ou* **avec** towards)

courtoisement [kurtwazmã] *adv* courteously

courtoisie [kurtwazi] *nf* courtesy **(envers** towards)

court-vêtu, -e *(mpl* **court-vêtus,** *fpl* **court-vêtues)** [kurvety] *adj* in a short skirt; **être c.** to be wearing a short skirt

couru, -e [kury] *adj* **(a)** *(lieu, spectacle)* popular **(b)** *Fam* **c'est c. (d'avance)** it's a sure thing

cousais *etc voir* **coudre**

couscous [kuskus] *nm* couscous

cousin¹, -e [kuzɛ̃, -in] *nm,f* cousin; **c. germain** first cousin

cousin² *nm (insecte)* mosquito

coussin [kusɛ̃] *nm* **(a)** *(de siège)* cushion; *Belg (oreiller)* pillow **(b)** **c. d'air** air cushion

coussinet [kusine] *nm* **(a)** *(coussin)* small cushion **(b)** *(d'animal)* pad

cousu¹, -e [kuzy] *adj* sewn; **c. (à la) main** hand-sewn; *Fam* **c'est du c. main** it's first-rate; **une histoire cousue de fil blanc** a blatant lie

cousu²,-e voir **coudre**

coût [ku] nm aussi Fig cost; **le c.** **de la vie** the cost of living

coûtant [kutɑ̃] adj m voir **prix**

couteau, -x [kuto] nm (**a**) (ustensile) knife; **être à couteaux tirés (avec qn)** to be at daggers drawn (with sb); Fig **avoir le c. sous la gorge** to have a gun at one's head; **c. de cuisine** kitchen knife; **c. à fromage** cheese-knife; **c. à pain** breadknife (**b**) (mollusque) razor shell (**c**) Fig **deuxième** ou **second c.** (en politique, dans la Mafia) minion

couteau-scie (pl couteaux-scies) [kutosi] nm serrated knife

coutelas [kutlɑ] nm large knife

coûter [kute] vi to cost; **combien ça coûte?** how much is it?, how much does it cost?; **ça coûte 75 euros** it costs 75 euros, it's 75 euros; **c. les yeux de la tête** to cost a fortune; **ça ne coûte rien d'essayer** there's no harm in trying; **c. cher** to cost a lot, to be expensive; **cela vous coûtera cher** it'll cost you a lot; Fig you'll pay for that; **c. la vie à qn** to cost sb his/her life; **ça m'a beaucoup coûté** it was very painful for me; **coûte que coûte** at all costs

coûteux, -euse [kutø, -øz] adj costly, expensive; **peu c.** inexpensive

coutume [kutym] nf (**a**) (habitude) custom; **avoir c. de faire qch** to be accustomed to doing sth; **plus aimable que de c.** nicer than usual; **comme de c.** as usual; **une fois n'est pas c.** it won't hurt for once (**b**) (tradition) custom

coutumier, -ère [kutymje, -ɛr] adj (**a**) (habituel) customary, usual (**b**) (personne) **il est c. du fait** it's not the first time he's done that (**c**) Jur **droit c.** common law

couture [kutyr] nf (**a**) (de vêtement) seam; Fig **examiner qn/qch sous toutes les coutures** to examine sb/sth from every angle (**b**) (activité) sewing, needlework; **faire de la c.** to sew

couturier [kutyrje] nm fashion designer; **grand c.** major fashion designer

couturière [kutyrjɛr] nf dressmaker

couvaison [kuvɛzɔ̃] nf incubation

couvée [kuve] nf (**a**) (œufs) clutch (**b**) (d'oisillons, d'enfants) brood

couvent [kuvɑ̃] nm (**a**) (communauté religieuse) (de femmes) convent; (d'hommes) monastery (**b**) (pensionnat) convent school

couver [kuve] **1** vt (**a**) (œufs) to sit on; Fig (personne) to mollycoddle; **c. qn des yeux** to look fondly at sb (**b**) (maladie) to be coming down with **2** vi (poule) to brood; (feu, passion) to smoulder, (émeute) to be brewing

couvercle [kuvɛrkl] nm lid; (qui se visse) cap, top

couvert¹, -e [kuvɛr, -ɛrt] **1** adj (**a**) (allée, marché) covered; (piscine) indoor; (ciel) overcast (**b**) (jonché, plein) **c. de** covered with or in (**c**) (habillé) covered up; **chaudement** ou **bien c.** warmly dressed (**d**) (ciel) overcast **2** pp voir **couvrir**

couvert² nm (**a**) (ustensiles) **un c. en argent** a silver knife, fork and spoon; **couverts** cutlery (**b**) (pour chaque convive) place setting; **mettre le c.** to set or Br lay the table; **mettre trois couverts** to set or Br lay the table for three (**c**) **sous le c. de** (sous l'apparence de) under the cover of

couverture [kuvɛrtyr] nf (**a**) (de lit) blanket; Fig **tirer la c. à soi** to take all the credit; **c. chauffante** electric blanket (**b**) (d'un livre, d'un magazine, d'un cahier) cover; **en c.** on the cover (**c**) (protection) **c. sociale** social security cover (**d**) (d'un bâtiment) roofing (**e**) (d'un événement médiatique) coverage

couveuse [kuvøz] nf (**a**) (pour nouveau-nés) incubator (**b**) (poule) brooder

couvre-chef (pl couvre-chefs) [kuvrəʃɛf] nm Hum hat

couvre-feu (pl couvre-feux) [kuvrəfø] nm Mil curfew

couvre-lit (pl couvre-lits) [kuvrəli] nm bedspread

couvre-pied(s) (pl couvre-pieds) [kuvrəpje] nm quilt

couvreur [kuvrœr] nm roofer

couvrir [52] [kuvrir] **1** vt (**a**) (casserole, meuble, livre) to cover (**de** with) (**b**) **c. qn de** (cadeaux, honneurs, compliments) to shower sb with (**c**) (protéger, justifier) to cover; **être couvert par ses supérieurs** to be acting with the authority of one's superiors (**d**) (parcourir, englober) & Journ to cover (**e**) (bruit, voix) to drown (out) (**f**) (sujet: assurance) to cover (**g**) Zool (femelle) to cover **2** **se couvrir** vpr (**a**) (pour sortir) to wrap up; (pour cacher sa nudité) to cover oneself up; (mettre son chapeau) to put on one's hat (**b**) (ciel) to cloud over; **le temps** ou **ça se couvre** it's clouding over (**c**) **se c. de** (honte, ridicule) to cover oneself with; **se c. de feuilles** (arbre) to come into leaf

cow-boy (pl cow-boys) [kobɔj] nm cowboy

coyote [kɔjɔt] nm coyote

CP [sepe] nm (abrév **cours préparatoire**) Br ≃ first year infants class, Am ≃ nursery school

CPAM [sepeaɛm] nf (abrév **caisse primaire d'assurance maladie**) = French social security department dealing with health insurance

cpp Ordinat (abrév **caractères par pouce**) cpi

cps Ordinat (abrév **caractères par seconde**) cps

crabe [krab] nm crab

crac [krak] **1** exclam (bruit de cassure) crack!; Fam **et c., est tombée malade!** and what do you know, she fell ill! **2** nm crack

crachat [kraʃa] nm gob of spit; **crachats** spit

craché, -e [kraʃe] adj Fam **c'est sa mère tout c., c'est le portrait (tout) c. de sa mère** he's the spitting image of his mother; **c'est lui tout c.!** that's just like him!

cracher [kraʃe] **1** vi (**a**) (personne) to spit; Fam Fig **ne pas c. sur qch** not to say no to sth; Fam Fig **c. dans la soupe** to bite the hand that feeds (**b**) (stylo) to splutter (**c**) (haut-parleur, téléphone, radio) to crackle **2** vt (**a**) (chewing-gum, nourriture) to spit out; **c. du sang** to spit blood (**b**) (fumée) to belch out (**c**) très Fam (somme d'argent) to cough up

cracheur, -euse [kraʃœr, -øz] nm,f **c. de feu** fire-eater

crachin [kraʃɛ̃] nm (fine) drizzle

crachoir [kraʃwar] nm spittoon; Fam Fig **tenir le c.** to monopolize the conversation; Fam Fig **tenir le c. à qn** to listen to sb rambling on and on

crachoter [kraʃɔte] vi (feu) to splutter; (radio, téléphone) to crackle

crack [krak] nm (**a**) Fam (personne) ace (**en** at) (**b**) (drogue) crack

cracker [krakœr] nm cracker

Cracovie [krakɔvi] n Cracow

cracra [krakra] adj inv Fam filthy

crade [krad], **cradingue** [kradɛ̃g], **crado** [krado] adj Fam filthy

craie [krɛ] nf (matière) chalk; (bâtonnet) stick of chalk

craignais etc voir **craindre**

craignos [krɛɲos] adj Fam (laid) hideous; (louche) dodgy

craindre [23] [krɛ̃dr] **1** vt (**a**) (redouter) to fear, to be afraid of; **ne craignez rien!** (n'ayez pas peur) don't be frightened!; (ne vous inquiétez pas) don't worry!; **je crains qu'il (ne) soit parti** I'm afraid he's left; **c. de faire qch** to be afraid of doing sth (**b**) (ne pas supporter) **ces plantes craignent le gel** these plants don't like frost; **craint l'humidité/la chaleur** (sur emballage) keep dry/cool

2 *vi Fam* **ça craint!** *(c'est ennuyeux)* what a pain!; *(c'est très laid)* it's hideous!; *(c'est louche)* it's dodgy

craint, -e *voir* **craindre**

crainte [krɛ̃t] *nf* fear; **de c.** de tomber for fear of falling; **de c. qu'on ne l'entende** for fear of being overheard; **soyez sans c., n'ayez c.** have no fear

craintif, -ive [krɛ̃tif, -iv] *adj* timid

cramer [krame] *Fam* **1** *vi & vt* to burn **2 se cramer** *vpr* to burn oneself; **se c. les doigts** to burn one's fingers

cramoisi, -e [kramwazi] *adj* crimson

crampe [krɑ̃p] *nf* cramp; **j'ai une c. à la jambe** I've got cramp in my leg; **crampes d'estomac** stomach cramps

crampon [krɑ̃pɔ̃] *nm* **(a)** *(de chaussure de sport)* stud; *(pour alpinisme)* crampon; **crampons** *(chaussures)* boots with studs **(b)** *Constr* cramp (iron) **(c)** *Fam (personne)* leech

cramponner [krɑ̃pɔne] **se cramponner** *vpr* to hold on; **se c. à** to hold on to; *Fig (vie, espoir)* to cling to; *(fonction)* to hang on to

cran [krɑ̃] *nm* **(a)** *(entaille)* notch; *(de ceinture)* hole; **serrer sa ceinture d'un c.** to take one's belt in a notch; **c. de sûreté** *ou* **d'arrêt** safety catch; **(couteau à) c. d'arrêt** *Br* flick knife, *Am* switchblade **(b)** *Fig (degré)* **avancer/reculer d'un c.** to go up/come down a notch **(c)** *Fam* **être à c.** to be wound up **(d)** *Fam (courage)* guts; **avoir du c.** to have guts **(e)** *(dans les cheveux)* crimp

crâne [krɑn] *nm* skull, *Spéc* cranium; *Fam* **avoir mal au c.** to have a headache; *Fam* **mets-toi ça dans le c.!** get that into your head!

crâner [krɑne] *vi Fam* to swagger, to show off

crâneur, -euse [krɑnœr, -øz] *Fam* **1** *adj* swaggering; **être c.** to be a show-off **2** *nm,f* show-off

crânien, -enne [krɑnjɛ̃, -ɛn] *adj Anat* cranial

crapahuter [krapayte] *vi Fam* **(a)** *(marcher)* to traipse about **(b)** *Mil (soldat)* to trudge along

crapaud [krapo] *nm* **(a)** *(animal)* toad **(b)** *(défaut)* flaw

crapule [krapyl] *nf* scoundrel, villain

crapuleux, -euse [krapylø, -øz] *adj voir* **crime**

craqueler [42] [krakle] **1** *vt* to crack **2 se craqueler** *vpr* to crack

craquement [krakmɑ̃] *nm (de branche)* crack; *(d'escalier, de plancher)* creak; **des craquements** cracking/creaking

craquer [krake] **1** *vi* **(a)** *(branche)* to crack; *(escalier, plancher)* to creak; **faire c. ses doigts** to crack one's fingers **(b)** *(se déchirer)* to rip; *(se casser)* to snap **(c)** *(perdre le contrôle de soi)* to crack up **(d)** *Fam (succomber)* **c. pour qn** to fall for sb; **ce mec me fait c.** I'm wild about the guy **2** *vt* **(a)** *(allumette)* to strike **(b)** *(déchirer)* to rip

crasse [kras] **1** *adj (ignorance)* crass **2** *nf* **(a)** *(saleté)* filth **(b)** *Fam (mauvais tour)* dirty trick; **faire une c. à qn** to play a dirty trick on sb

crasseux, -euse [krasø, -øz] *adj* filthy

cratère [kratɛr] *nm* crater

cravache [kravaʃ] *nf (riding)* crop; *Fig* **mener qn à la c.** to rule sb with a rod of iron

cravacher [kravaʃe] **1** *vt (cheval)* to use the crop on **2** *vi Fam (travailler vite)* to work like mad

cravate [kravat] *nf* tie; *Fam* **s'en jeter un derrière la c.** to knock back a drink

crawl [krol] *nm* crawl; **nager le c.** to do the crawl

crayeux, -euse [krɛjø, -øz] *adj (matière, teint)* chalky

crayon [krɛjɔ̃] *nm* **(a)** *(pour écrire)* pencil; **c. de couleur** coloured pencil, crayon; **c. gras** soft lead pencil; *Ordinat* **c.**

lumineux *ou* **optique** light pen **(b)** *(bâton)* stick; **c. à lèvres** lip pencil

créance [kreɑ̃s] *nf* debt; **c. douteuse** bad debt

créancier, -ère [kreɑ̃sje, -ɛr] *nm,f* creditor

créateur, -trice [kreatœr, -tris] **1** *adj (génie)* creative; **industrie créatrice d'emplois** job-creating industry **2** *nm,f* creator; *Rel* **le C.** the Creator

créatif, -ive [kreatif, -iv] *adj* creative

création [kreasjɔ̃] *nf* **(a)** *(fait de créer)* creation; **c. d'emplois** job creation **(b)** *(produit)* new product; *(d'un couturier)* creation **(c)** *(univers)* **la c.** creation **(d)** *(première représentation)* *(d'une pièce)* first production; *(d'un rôle)* creation; *(d'une œuvre musicale)* first performance

créativité [kreativite] *nf* creativity

créature [kreatyr] *nf* **(a)** *(être vivant)* creature; *Hum* **une c. de rêve** *(femme)* a georgeous creature **(b)** *Péj (protégé)* creature

crécelle [kresɛl] *nf* rattle; **une voix de c.** a rasping voice

crèche [krɛʃ] *nf* **(a)** *(garderie)* crèche, day nursery **(b)** *(de Noël)* crib

crécher [34] [kreʃe] *vi Fam* to live; *(temporairement)* to crash

crédibilité [kredibilite] *nf* credibility

crédible [kredibl] *adj* credible

crédit [kredi] *nm* **(a)** *(prêt)* credit; **à c.** on credit; **faire c. à qn** to give sb credit; **la maison ne fait pas c.** *(sur panneau)* we do not give credit; **c. à la consommation** consumer credit; **c. gratuit** interest-free credit; **c. immobilier** home loan, mortgage **(b)** *(en comptabilité)* credit side; **porter une somme au c. de qn** to credit sb with a sum **(c)** **crédits** *(somme d'argent)* funds **(d)** *Litt (influence)* credit

crédit-bail *(pl* **crédits-bails)** [kredibaj] *nm* leasing

créditer [kredite] *vt (a)* *Fin (compte)* to credit **(de** with**) (b)** *Fig* **c. qn de qch** to give sb credit for sth

créditeur, -trice [kreditœr, -tris] *adj (solde, compte)* credit; **être c.** to be in credit

crédit-relais *(pl* **crédits-relais)** [kredirəlɛ] *nm* bridging loan

credo [kredo] *nm inv* credo, creed

crédule [kredyl] *adj* credulous

crédulité [kredylite] *nf* credulity

créer [24] [kree] **1** *vt* **(a)** *(emplois, poste)* to create; *(entreprise)* to set up **(b)** *(œuvre, nouveau produit, vêtement)* to create **(c)** *(difficultés, problème)* to create (**à** for) **(d)** *(interpréter pour la première fois)* *(rôle)* to create; *(pièce de théâtre)* to produce for the first time; *(œuvre musicale)* to perform for the first time **2 se créer** *vpr* **(a)** *(être créé)* to be created **(b)** *(pour soi-même)* **se c. une clientèle** to build up a clientèle; **se c. des problèmes** to create problems for oneself

crémaillère [kremajɛr] *nf* **(a)** *(dans la cheminée)* trammel (hook); **pendre la c.** to have a housewarming (party)

crémant [kremɑ̃] *nm* slightly sparkling champagne

crémation [kremasjɔ̃] *nf* cremation

crématoire [krematwar] *adj voir* **four**

crématorium [krematɔrjɔm] *nm* crematorium

crème [krɛm] **1** *nf* **(a)** *(du lait, dessert)* cream; *Fig* **c'est la c. des hommes** he's the best of men; **c. anglaise** custard; **c. au beurre** = butter, sugar, eggs and cream, baked together and used as a cake filling; **c. brûlée** crème brûlée; **c. (au) caramel** caramel custard, crème caramel; **c. Chantilly** whipped cream *(with sugar added)*; **c. fouettée** whipped cream; **c. fraîche** crème fraîche; **c. glacée** ice cream; **c. pâtissière** confectioner's custard; **c. renversée** crème caramel *(turned out of its mould)* **(b)** *(produit cosmétique)* cream; **c. antirides** anti-wrinkle cream; **c. hydratante** moisturizing cream; **c. à raser** shaving cream **(c)** *(liqueur)* **c. de menthe** crème de menthe; **c. de cassis** cassis, blackcurrant liqueur **2** *nm Fam* coffee with milk, ≃ latte; **un grand c.** a large coffee with milk **3** *adj inv* cream(-coloured)

crémerie [kremri] *nf (magasin)* dairy

crémeux, -euse [kremø, -øz] *adj* creamy

crémier, -ère [kremje, -ɛr] *nm,f* dairyman, *f* dairy-woman

crémone [kremɔn] *nf* espagnolette

créneau, -x [kreno] *nm* **(a)** *(de rempart)* crenel **(b)** *(manœuvre)* **faire un c.** to reverse into a (parking) space **(c)** *Com* niche **(d)** *(dans un programme, un emploi du temps)* slot; **c. horaire** time slot

crénelé, -e [krenle] *adj* crenellated

créole [kreɔl] **1** *adj* Creole **2** *nmf* **C.** Creole **3** *nm (langue)* Creole **4** *nfpl* **créoles** *(boucles d'oreille)* hoop earrings

crêpe [krɛp] **1** *nf* pancake **2** *nm* **(a)** *(tissu)* crêpe **(b)** *(caoutchouc)* crêpe (rubber); **semelles (de) c.** crêpe soles

crêper [krepe] **1** *vt* **(a)** *(cheveux)* to backcomb **(b)** *(tissu)* to crimp **2 se crêper** *vpr Fam Fig* **se c. le chignon** to have a catfight

crêperie [krepri] *nf* pancake restaurant

crépi, -e [krepi] *adj & nm Constr* roughcast

crépir [krepir] *vt Constr* to roughcast

crépitement [krepitmã] *nm (du feu)* crackling

crépiter [krepite] *vi (feu)* to crackle

crépon [krepɔ̃] *nm (papier)* crêpe paper

crépu, -e [krepy] *adj* frizzy

crépuscule [krepyskyl] *nm aussi Fig* twilight

crescendo [kreʃendo] **1** *adv* crescendo; **aller c.** to get louder and louder; *Fig (difficultés)* to get worse and worse **2** *nm* crescendo

cresson [kresɔ̃, krasɔ̃] *nm* watercress

crétacé, -e [kretase] *Géol* **1** *adj* Cretaceous **2** *nm* **le C.** the Cretaceous period

Crète [krɛt] *nf* **la C.** Crete

crête [krɛt] *nf* **(a)** *(d'oiseau)* crest; *(de coq)* comb **(b)** *(de montagne, de vague, de toit)* crest

crétin, -e [kretɛ̃, -in] *nm,f Fam* cretin

crétois, -e [kretwa, -az] **1** *adj* Cretan **2** *nm,f* **C.** Cretan

cretonne [krətɔn] *nf* cretonne

cretons [krətɔ̃] *nmpl Can* potted pork

creuser [krøze] **1** *vt* **(a)** *(trou, tranchée, puits)* to dig; *Fig* **c. l'écart entre** to widen the gap between; *Fig* **c. un abîme entre deux personnes** to create a gulf between two people **(b)** *(évider)* to hollow (out); **c. la terre** to dig **(c)** *(problème, question)* to look into **(d)** *(donner faim à)* **c. qn** to give sb an appetite; **le grand air, ça creuse** the fresh air gives you an appetite **(e)** *(cambrer)* **c. les reins** to arch one's back **(f)** *(amaigrir)* **il avait le visage creusé par la fatigue/la maladie** his face was gaunt with exhaustion/illness **2** *vi* to dig **3 se creuser** *vpr* **(a)** *(s'agrandir) (écart)* to widen **(b)** **se c. (la tête** *ou* **la cervelle) (pour faire qch)** to rack one's brains (to do sth) **(c)** *(visage)* to grow hollow

creuset [krøzɛ] *nm* **(a)** *Chim* crucible **(b)** *Fig* melting pot

creux, -euse [krø, krøz] **1** *adj* **(a)** *(vide) (arbre, mur, dent)* hollow; *(chemin)* sunken; *Fig* **avoir le ventre c.** to be hungry

(b) *(période, heures)* off-peak **(c)** *(joues)* hollow; *(visage)* gaunt **(d)** *Péj (débat, discours, personne)* hollow **2** *adv* **sonner c.** to sound hollow; *Fig* to sound empty **3** *nm* **(a)** *(de la main, dans le sol, sur une route)* hollow; **le c. des reins** the small of the back **(b)** *(d'une vague, d'une courbe)* trough; *Fig* **être au c. de la vague** to have hit rock bottom **(c)** *Fam* **avoir un (petit) c.** to be feeling (a bit) peckish

crevaison [krəvɛzɔ̃] *nf (d'un pneu)* puncture, flat

crevant, -e [krəvã, -ãt] *adj Fam* **(a)** *(fatigant)* exhausting **(b)** *(drôle)* priceless

crevasse [krəvas] *nf* **(a)** *(sur la peau)* crack; **avoir des crevasses aux mains** to have chapped hands **(b)** *(dans un mur, le sol)* crack; *(dans un glacier)* crevasse

crevé, -e [krəve] *adj* **(a)** *(éclaté) (ballon, pneu)* burst **(b)** *Fam (fatigué)* dead beat **(c)** *très Fam (mort)* dead

crève [krɛv] *nf très Fam* **avoir la c.** *(gros rhume)* to have a stinking cold; **attraper la c.** to catch one's death of cold

crève-cœur [krɛvkœr] *nm inv* heartbreak; **c'est un c. de partir** it's heartbreaking to leave

crève-la-faim [krɛvlafɛ̃] *nm inv Fam* down-and-out

crever [46] [krəve] **1** *vt* **(a)** *(ballon, sac, pneu)* to burst; **c. un œil à qn** to put sb's eye out; *Fam* **me crève le cœur** I'm heartbroken about it; *Fig* **ça crève les yeux** it sticks out a mile; *Fig* **c. l'écran** to fill the screen with one's presence **(b)** *Fam (épuiser)* to wear out **(c)** *très Fam* **c. la dalle** to be starving **2** *vi* **(a)** *(éclater)* to burst; **mon pneu a** *ou Fam* **j'ai crevé** I've got a *Br* puncture *or Am* flat; **c. de** *(jalousie, orgueil)* to be bursting with **(b)** *(mourir) (bête, plante)* to die; *très Fam (personne)* to kick the bucket; *Fam* **il fait une chaleur à c.** it's boiling hot; *Fam* **c. d'envie de faire qch** to be dying to do sth; *Fam* **c. de faim** *(mourir)* to starve to death; *(avoir faim)* to be starving; *Fam* **c. de froid/de chaud** to be freezing/boiling; *Fam* **c. de rire** to split one's sides laughing; *Fam* **qu'il crève!** he can go to hell!; *Fam* **plutôt c.!** I'd rather die! **3 se crever** *vpr Fam* to wear oneself out

crevette [krəvɛt] *nf* **c. (rose)** prawn; **c. grise** shrimp

cri [kri] *nm* **(a)** *(d'une personne)* cry, shout; *(perçant)* scream; **j'ai entendu des cris** I heard shouting; *Fig* **pousser les hauts cris** to kick up a fuss; **c'est le c. du cœur** it's a cry from the heart; *Mil* **c. de guerre** war cry **(b)** *(d'un animal, d'un oiseau)* cry

criailler [kriaje] *vi (crier sans arrêt)* to bawl **(b)** *(faisan, pintade)* to cry; *(oie)* to honk

criant, -e [krijã, -ãt] *adj (erreur)* glaring; *(preuve, contraste)* striking; *(vérité)* obvious; *(abus, injustice)* blatant; **c. de vérité** *(témoignage, reportage)* obviously true

criard, -e [krijar, -ard] *adj* **(a)** *(aigu) (voix)* shrill **(b)** *(couleur)* loud **(c)** *(enfant)* noisy

crible [kribl] *nm* sieve; *Fig* **passer qch au c.** to go through sth with a fine-tooth comb

criblé, -e [krible] *adj* **c. de** *(trous, balles)* riddled with; *Fig* **être c. de dettes** to be up to one's eyes in debt

cric [krik] *nm* jack

cricket [kriket] *nm* cricket

criée [krije] *nf (vente)* (sale by) auction; *(salle)* auction room; *(dehors)* auction area; **à la c.** by auction

crier [66] [krije] **1** *vi* **(a)** *(personne)* to shout, to cry (out); *(fort)* to scream; *(parler très fort)* to shout; **c. de douleur** to cry out *or* scream with pain; **c. contre** *ou* **après qn** to shout at sb; **c. au secours** to shout for help; **c. au scandale** to protest, to be up in arms; **c. qch sur les toits** to shout sth from the rooftops **(b)** *(souris)* to squeak; *(oiseau)* to call **2** *vt (ordre, injures)* to shout (**à** at); **c. à qn de faire qch** to shout to sb to do sth; **c. son innocence** to protest one's innocence

crime [krim] *nm* (a) *Jur & Fig* crime; **ce n'est pas un c.!** it's not a crime!; **c. crapuleux** crime committed for financial gain; **c. d'État** treason; **crimes de guerre** war crimes; **c. contre l'humanité** crime against humanity (b) *(meurtre)* murder; **c. passionnel** crime of passion

criminalité [kriminalite] *nf* crime

criminel, -elle [kriminɛl] **1** *adj (acte)* criminal; *Fam* **ce serait c. de la jeter** it would be criminal to throw it away **2** *nm,f* (a) *(malfaiteur)* criminal; **c. de guerre** war criminal (b) *(assassin)* murderer

criminologie [kriminɔlɔʒi] *nf* criminology

crin [krɛ̃] *nm* horsehair; *Fig* **à tout c.**, **à tous crins** out-and-out

crinière [krinjɛr] *nf aussi Fig* mane

crinoline [krinɔlin] *nf* crinoline

crique [krik] *nf* creek

criquet [krikɛ] *nm* locust

crise [kriz] *nf* (a) *(marasme, période d'instabilité)* crisis; **c. de l'énergie** energy crisis; **c. du logement** housing crisis or shortage (b) *(d'une maladie)* attack; **c. cardiaque** heart attack; **c. de foie** bilious attack (c) *(accès)* **c. de colère** fit of anger; **c. de conscience** attack of conscience; **c. de larmes** crying fit; **c. de nerfs** attack of nerves, fit of hysterics; **la c. (de rire)!** what a hoot! (d) *Fam (colère)* fit of rage; **piquer** *ou* **faire une c.** to throw a fit

crispant, -e [krispã, -ãt] *adj Fam* irritating, annoying

crispé, -e [krispe] *adj (visage, personne)* tense; *(sourire, rire)* forced

crisper [krispe] **1** *vt* (a) *(poings, mains)* to clench; *(corps)* to tense (b) *(énerver)* to irritate, to annoy **2 se crisper** *vpr (muscle, visage)* to tense; *(sourire)* to become strained; *(personne)* to get tense

crissement [krismã] *nm (de la craie sur le tableau)* squeak; *(des pneus, des freins)* squeal; *(du gravier, de la neige)* crunch

crisser [krise] *vi (pneus, freins)* to squeal; *(gravier, neige)* to crunch; *(craie)* to squeak

cristal, -aux [kristal, -o] *nm* crystal; **c. de roche** rock crystal; **cristaux** *(verre)* crystal(ware); *(de sel, de glace)* crystals; *Tech* **cristaux liquides** liquid crystal

cristallin, -e [kristalɛ̃, -in] **1** *adj (a) (roche)* crystalline (b) *Fig (eau, voix)* crystal-clear; *(son, note)* ringing **2** *nm (de l'œil)* crystalline lens

cristalliser [kristalize] **1** *vi* to crystallize **2 se cristalliser** *vpr* to crystallize

critère [kriter] *nm* criterion; *Ordinat* **c. de tri** sort criterion

critérium [kriterjɔm] *nm Sp* heat

critique¹ [kritik] *adj (décisif, crucial)* critical

critique² **1** *adj (esprit, personne, édition)* critical **2** *nmf* critic; **c. d'art/de cinéma** art/film critic; **c. gastronomique** restaurant critic **3** *nf* (a) *(condamnation)* criticism; **si je peux me permettre de vous faire une c.,...** if I could just make one criticism,...; **il n'accepte pas la c.** he can't take criticism (b) *(article)* critical article; *Th & Cin* review; **faire la c. de qch** to review sth (c) **la c.** *(l'ensemble des critiques)* the critics

critiquer [kritike] *vt (personne, attitude)* to criticize (**pour** for); **ce n'est pas pour te c., mais...** I don't mean to criticize, but...; **c'est facile de c.** it's easy to criticize

croassement [krɔasmã] *nm* caw; **des croassements** cawing

croasser [krɔase] *vi* to caw

croate [krɔat] **1** *adj* Croatian **2** *nmf* **C.** Croat, Croatian

Croatie [krɔasi] *nf* **la C.** Croatia

croc [kro] *nm* (a) *(de loup, de chien)* fang; *Fam* **avoir les crocs** to be famished (b) *(crochet)* hook

croc-en-jambe *(pl* **crocs-en-jambe)** [krɔkãʒãb] *nm* trip; **faire un c. à qn** to trip sb up

croche [krɔʃ] *nf Mus Br* quaver, *Am* eighth note

croche-pied *(pl* **croche-pieds)** [krɔʃpje] = **croc-en-jambe**

crochet [krɔʃɛ] *nm* (a) *(pour accrocher)* hook; *Fig* **vivre aux crochets de qn** to live off sb (b) *(pour tricoter)* crochet hook; *(technique)* crochet; **faire du c.** to (do) crochet (c) *(détour)* **faire un c. (par)** *(personne)* to make a detour (through) (d) *Typ* square bracket; **entre crochets** in square brackets (e) *(coup de poing)* hook; **c. du gauche/du droit** left/right hook (f) *(d'un serpent)* fang

crocheter [39] [krɔʃte] *vt (serrure)* to pick; *(porte)* to pick the lock on

crochu, -e [krɔʃy] *adj (nez, bec)* hooked; *(doigts)* claw-like

crocodile [krɔkɔdil] *nm* crocodile; **en c.** *(sac, chaussures)* crocodile(-skin)

crocus [krɔkys] *nm* crocus

croire [25] [krwar] **1** *vt* (a) *(accepter, faire confiance à)* to believe; *Fam Ironique* **c'est ça, je te crois!** is that so?; *Fam* **faut pas c.!** don't you believe it!; **croyez-moi, ce n'était pas facile** believe (you) me, it wasn't easy; **à l'en c.,...** to hear him, you'd think...; **je n'en croyais pas mes yeux/mes oreilles** I couldn't believe my eyes/my ears (b) *(penser)* to think; **je crois que oui** I think so; **je crois que non** I don't think so; **vous croyez?** do you really think so?; **je vous croyais américain/riche** I thought you were American/rich; **j'ai cru nécessaire de...** I thought it necessary to...; **j'ai cru bien faire** I thought or believed I was doing the right thing; **elle ne croyait pas si bien dire** she didn't know how right she was; **je n'aurais pas cru cela de lui** I would never have thought it of him; **on croirait qu'il dort** you'd think he was asleep **2** *vi (avoir la foi)* to be a believer **3 croire à** *vt ind* (a) *(envisager)* **le médecin crut à une grippe** the doctor thought it was flu (b) *(accepter)* to believe; **veuillez c.** *ou* **je vous prie de c. à l'expression de mes sentiments distingués** *Br* yours sincerely, *Am* sincerely (yours) (c) *(avoir confiance en, adhérer à)* to believe in **4 croire en** *vt ind (personne, talent, Dieu)* to believe in **5 se croire** *vpr* **il se croit intelligent** he thinks he's clever; **il se croit tout permis** he thinks he can get away with anything; **on se serait cru en octobre** it felt like October; *Fam* **se c. sorti de la cuisse de Jupiter** to think a lot of oneself; *Fam* **il s'y croit** he thinks a lot of himself

croisade [krwazad] *nf Hist & Fig* crusade; **partir en c.** to go on a crusade

croisé, -e [krwaze] **1** *adj (manteau, veste)* double-breasted **2** *nm Hist* crusader

croisement [krwazmã] *nm* (a) *(carrefour)* crossroads *(singulier)*, intersection (b) *(d'animaux)* crossing; *(animal)* cross **(entre** between)

croiser [krwaze] **1** *vt* (a) *(couper)* *(ligne, route)* to cross; **c. le regard de qn** to meet sb's gaze (b) *(passer à côté de)* *(véhicule, personne)* to pass (c) *(mettre l'un sur l'autre)* **c. les jambes** to cross one's legs; **c. les bras** to fold one's arms; *Fig* **c. les doigts** to keep one's fingers crossed (d) *(animaux, espèces)* to cross(breed) **2** *vi (navire)* to cruise **3 se croiser** *vpr* (a) *(lignes, routes)* to cross, to intersect; *(regards)* to meet (b) *(personnes)* *(dans la rue)* to walk past each other; **se voir rapidement** to meet briefly; *(lettres)* to cross

croiseur [krwazœr] *nm Naut* cruiser

croisière [krwazjɛr] *nf* cruise; **faire une c.** to go on a cruise

croisillon [krwazijɔ̃] *nm* (**a**) *(de croix)* crosspiece (**b**) croisillons *(de fenêtre, de barrière)* latticework; *(sur une tarte)* lattice

croissais *etc voir* **croître**

croissance [krwasɑ̃s] *nf (d'un enfant)* & *Écon* growth; **en pleine c.** growing rapidly; **finir sa c.** *(enfant)* to stop growing

croissant[1], **-e** [krwasɑ̃, -ɑ̃t] *adj (plante, tendance, angoisse)* growing; *(ordre)* ascending; *(chaleur, température)* increasing

croissant[2] *nm* (**a**) *(arc de cercle)* crescent; **un c. de lune** a crescent moon; **en c.** crescent-shaped (**b**) *(pâtisserie)* croissant; **c. au beurre/ordinaire** croissant made with/without butter

croissant[3] *voir* **croître**

croître [4b] [krwatr] *vi* (**a**) *(enfant, plantes)* to grow (**b**) *(vente, chiffre)* to grow, to increase (**de** by); *(jours)* to get longer; *(lune)* to wax; **aller croissant** *(succès)* to grow and grow; *(suspense)* to get worse and worse

croix [krwa] *nf* cross; **signer d'une c.** to make one's mark; *Fam Fig* **faire une c. sur qch** to say goodbye to sth; **en (forme de) c.** cross-shaped; **les bras en c.** with one's arms stretched out at the sides; **c. de bois c. de fer, si je mens je vais en enfer** cross my heart and hope to die; **c'est la c. et la bannière** it's the devil of a job; **c. gammée** swastika; **la C.-Rouge** the Red Cross

croquant, -e [krokɑ̃, -ɑ̃t] *adj* crisp, crunchy

croque-au-sel [krokosɛl] **à la croque-au-sel** *adv* = raw and seasoned only with salt

croque-madame [krokmadam] *nm inv* = toasted cheese and ham sandwich topped with a fried egg

croque-monsieur [krokməsjø] *nm inv* = toasted cheese and ham sandwich

croque-mort (*pl* **croque-morts**) [krokmor] *nm Fam* undertaker's assistant

croquer [kroke] **1** *vt* (**a**) *(pomme, bonbon)* to crunch; *Fig (fortune, héritage)* to squander; **à sucer ou à c.** *(sur boîte de médicaments)* may be sucked or chewed; *Fig* **c. la vie à belles dents** to make the most of life; **il est à c.** *(enfant)* he looks good enough to eat; **joli** *ou* **mignon à c.** as pretty as a picture (**b**) *(faire un croquis de)* to sketch
2 *vi* (**a**) *(pomme, salade)* to be crunchy (**b**) *(mordre)* **c. dans** to bite into

croquet [kroke] *nm (jeu)* croquet

croquette [krokɛt] *nf (de pomme de terre, de viande, de poisson)* croquette; **croquettes** *(pour chien, chat)* biscuits

croquis [kroki] *nm* sketch; **faire un c. de qch** to make a sketch of sth

cross [kros] *nm (sport)* cross-country running; *(événement)* cross-country run

crosse [kros] *nf* (**a**) *(de fusil)* butt; *(de pistolet)* grip; *(d'évêque)* crook (**b**) *(de hockey)* stick; *Fam Fig* **chercher des crosses à qn** to try to pick a fight with sb

crotte [krot] *nf* (**a**) *(de cheval, de mouton, de lapin)* dung, droppings; **une c. de chien** dog dirt; *Fam* **c.!** blast! (**b**) **une c. de chocolat** a chocolate (**c**) *Vieilli (boue)* mud

crotter [krote] **1** *vt (chaussures, manteau)* to cover in mud
2 se crotter *vpr* to get covered in mud

crottin [krotɛ̃] *nm* (**a**) *(excrément) (de cheval)* dung (**b**) *(fromage)* crottin, = small goat's-milk cheese

croulant, -e [krulɑ̃, -ɑ̃t] **1** *adj (bâtiment)* crumbling
2 *nm,f très Fam* (**vieux**) **c.** (old) fogey

crouler [krule] *vi (bâtiment)* to crumble; **c. sous le poids de qch** to give way under the weight of sth; **c. sous le travail** to be snowed under with work; **la salle croulait sous les applaudissements** the audience brought the house down

croupe [krup] *nf* rump; **monter en c.** to ride behind

croupi, -e [krupi] *adj (eau)* stagnant

croupier [krupje] *nm* croupier

croupion [krupjɔ̃] *nm (d'oiseau)* rump; *(d'une volaille) Br* parson's *or Am* pope's nose

croupir [krupir] *vi* (**a**) *(eau)* to stagnate (**b**) *(végéter)* **c. en prison** to rot in prison

croupissant, -e [krupisɑ̃, -ɑ̃t] *adj (eau, vie)* stagnant

CROUS [krus] *nm (abrév* **Centre régional des œuvres universitaires et scolaires)** = organization responsible for student accommodation and catering etc

croustillant, -e [krustijɑ̃, -ɑ̃t] *adj* (**a**) *(biscuit, pâte)* crisp; *(pain)* crusty (**b**) *Fig (histoire, détails)* spicy

croustiller [krustije] *vi (biscuit, pâte)* to be crisp; *(pain)* to be crusty

croûte [krut] *nf* (**a**) *(de pain, de tarte)* crust; *(de fromage)* rind; *(d'une plaie)* scab; **la c. terrestre** the earth's crust; *Fam* **gagner sa c.** to earn one's bread and butter (**b**) *Fam (mauvaise peinture)* daub

croûton [krutɔ̃] *nm* (**a**) *(de pain)* end (**b**) *(dans la soupe, les salades)* crouton (**c**) *Fam* (**vieux**) **c.** old fossil

croyable [krwajabl] *adj* believable, credible; **ce n'est pas c.!** it's unbelievable!, it's incredible!

croyais *etc voir* **croire**

croyance [krwajɑ̃s] *nf* belief (**en** in)

croyant, -e [krwajɑ̃, -ɑ̃t] **1** *adj* **être c.** to be a believer
2 *nm,f* believer

CRS [seɛres] *nm (abrév* **compagnie républicaine de sécurité)** = French riot policeman; **les C.** = French riot police

cru[1], **-e** [kry] *adj* (**a**) *(viande, poisson, légumes)* raw; *(lait)* unpasteurized (**b**) *(couleur, lumière)* garish (**c**) *(licencieux) (langage)* crude (**d**) *(direct) (réponse, personne)* blunt (**e**) **monter à c.** to ride bareback

cru[2] *nm (terroir)* vineyard; *(vin)* wine; **un grand c.** a vintage wine; **du c.** local; *Fig* **une histoire de son (propre) c.** a story of his/her own invention

cru[3], **-e** *voir* **croire**

cruauté [kryote] *nf* (**a**) *(dureté)* cruelty (**envers** to) (**b**) *(acte)* (act of) cruelty

cruche [kryʃ] *nf* (**a**) *(récipient, contenu) Br* jug, *Am* pitcher; *Prov* **tant va la c. à l'eau qu'à la fin elle se casse** the pitcher has gone to the well once too often (**b**) *Fam (imbécile)* ass

cruchon [kryʃɔ̃] *nm (récipient, contenu)* small *Br* jug *or Am* pitcher

crucial, -e, -aux, -ales [krysjal, -o] *adj* crucial

crucifier [66] [krysifje] *vt* to crucify

crucifix [krysifi] *nm* crucifix

crucifixion [krysifiksjɔ̃] *nf* crucifixion

cruciforme [krysiform] *adj* cruciform; **vis/tournevis c.** Phillips® screw/screwdriver

cruciverbiste [krysivɛrbist] *nmf* crossword enthusiast

crudité [krydite] *nf* (**a**) **crudités** *(légumes)* assorted raw vegetables (**b**) *(d'une couleur, d'une lumière)* garishness (**c**) *(d'une expression)* crudeness

crue [kry] *nf (montée)* swelling; *(inondation)* flood; **rivière en c.** river in spate

cruel, -elle [kryɛl] *adj* cruel (**envers** *ou* **avec** to)

cruellement [kryɛlmɑ̃] *adv* cruelly; **être c. éprouvé** to be deeply affected; **faire c. défaut** to be sadly lacking

crûment [krymã] *adv* (**a**) *(parler) (sans détours)* bluntly; *(grossièrement)* crudely (**b**) **éclairé c.** garishly lit

crustacé [krystase] *nm* *Zool* crustacean; **crustacés** crustaceans; *Culin* seafood

cruzado [kruzado] *nm* cruzado

cryogénie [krijoʒeni] *nf* cryogenics *(singulier)*

cryptage [kriptaʒ] *nm* encoding

crypte [kript] *nf* crypt

crypté, -e [kripte] *adj (message) & TV* coded

crypter [kripte] *vt* to encode

CSA [seɛsa] *nm* *(abrév* **Conseil supérieur de l'audiovisuel)** = French broadcasting supervisory body

CSG [seɛsʒe] *nf (abrév* **Contribution sociale généralisée)** = income-based tax deducted at source as a contribution to paying off the French social security budget deficit

Cuba [kyba] *n* Cuba

cubain, -e [kybɛ̃, -ɛn] **1** *adj* Cuban **2** *nm,f* **C.** Cuban

cube [kyb] **1** *nm* cube; *(de jeu)* building block; **élever un nombre au c.** to cube a number **2** *adj (mètre, centimètre)* cubic

cubique [kybik] *adj* cubic

cubisme [kybism] *nm* cubism

cubitus [kybitys] *nm* ulna

cucul [kyky] *adj inv* *Fam* **c. (la praline)** *(personne, décoration)* twee; *(film, livre)* corny

cueillette [kœjɛt] *nf (action)* gathering, picking; *(fruits, noisettes, baies)* harvest

cueillir [5] [kœjir] *vt (fleurs, fruits)* to gather, to pick; *Fig* **la mort l'a cueilli en pleine jeunesse** he was cut down in his prime; *Fam* **c. qn** to pick sb up

cui-cui [kɥikɥi] **1** *nm* cheeping **2** *exclam* cheep!

cuiller, cuillère [kɥijɛr] *nf (a) (couvert)* spoon; *(contenu)* spoon(ful); *Fam Fig* **il n'y va pas avec le dos de la c.** he doesn't go in for half measures; *Fam Fig* **en deux ou trois coups de c. à pot** in two shakes (of a lamb's tail); *Fam* **être à ramasser à la petite c.** *(épuisé)* to be all in; *(déprimé)* to be down in the dumps; **c. à café, petite c.** teaspoon; **c. à soupe** tablespoon (**b**) *(pour la pêche)* spoon (bait); **pêcher la truite à la c.** to troll for trout

cuillerée [kɥijere] *nf* spoonful; **une c. à café** a teaspoonful; **une c. à soupe** a tablespoonful

cuir [kɥir] *nm* (**a**) *(matière)* leather; *(veste)* leather jacket; **chaussures/blouson en c.** leather shoes/jacket (**b**) *(d'un éléphant, d'un rhinocéros)* hide (**c**) **c. chevelu** scalp

cuirasse [kɥiras] *nf* (**a**) *(protection)* breastplate; *Fig* **trouver le défaut dans la c. de qn** to find the chink in sb's armour (**b**) *(d'un navire de guerre, d'un blindé)* armour (plating)

cuirassé [kɥirase] *nm* battleship

cuirassier [kɥirasje] *nm* cuirassier

cuire [18] [kɥir] **1** *vt* (**a**) *(aliment)* to cook; **c. qch à l'eau** to boil sth; **c. qch à la vapeur** to steam sth; **c. qch au four** to bake sth (**b**) *(briques, poterie)* to fire (**c**) *(chauffer) (sujet: soleil)* to bake **2** *vi* (**a**) *(aliments, plat)* to cook; **faire trop c. qch** to overcook sth; **faire c. qch à feu doux** to cook sth over a low heat (**b**) *(brûler)* **les joues me cuisent** my cheeks are burning (**c**) *Fam (avoir très chaud)* to be boiling **3** *v impersonnel* **il vous en cuira** you'll regret it

cuisais *etc voir* **cuire**

cuisant, -e [kɥizã, -ãt] *adj (douleur)* burning; *(froid)* biting; *(déception, échec)* bitter

cuisine [kɥizin] *nf* (**a**) *(pièce)* kitchen; *(sur un navire)* galley (**b**) *(art)* cooking, cookery; **faire la c.** to do the cooking; **bien faire la c.** to be a good cook; **c. au beurre/à l'huile** cooking with butter/oil; **la c. italienne/japonaise** Italian/Japanese cooking *or* cuisine (**c**) *Fam (magouilles)* scheming

cuisiner [kɥizine] **1** *vi* to cook; **bien c.** to be a good cook **2** *vt* (**a**) *(préparer)* to cook; **plats cuisinés** ready-cooked meals (**b**) *Fam (interroger)* to grill

cuisinier, -ère [kɥizinje, -ɛr] **1** *nm,f* cook **2** *nf* **cuisinière** stove; **cuisinière électrique/à gaz** electric/gas stove; **c. mixte** combined gas and electric stove

cuissardes [kɥisard] *nfpl (bottes de femme)* thigh boots; *(de pêche)* waders

cuisse [kɥis] *nf* thigh; **cuisses de grenouilles** frogs' legs; **c. de poulet** chicken leg, drumstick

cuisson [kɥisɔ̃] *nf* (**a**) *(d'aliments)* cooking; *(de pain, de gâteau)* baking; **temps de c.** cooking time; **c. à la vapeur** steaming (**b**) *(des briques, de la porcelaine)* firing

cuissot [kɥiso] *nm (de venaison)* haunch

cuistot [kɥisto] *nm Fam* cook

cuit, -e [kɥi, kɥit] *adj* (**a**) *(aliment)* cooked; **bien c.** well done; **c. à point** done to a turn; **trop c.** overcooked; **pas assez c.** undercooked; **c. au four** baked (**b**) *Fam Fig* **être c.** to have had it; **c'est c.!** we've had it!; **c'est du tout c.** it's a cinch

culte [kylt] *nf Fam* **avoir/prendre une c.** to be/get plastered

cuivre [kɥivr] *nm* (**a**) *(métal)* **c. (rouge)** copper; **c. jaune** brass; **les cuivres** *(objets)* copperware; *(en cuivre jaune)* brasses (**b**) *Mus* **les cuivres** the brass *(section)*

cuivré, -e [kɥivre] *adj (peau, teint) (naturellement)* copper-coloured; *(par le soleil)* bronzed

cul [ky] **1** *nm* (**a**) *Fam (d'une personne)* backside, butt; **rester** *ou* **tomber sur le c.** to be flabbergasted; **c'est à se taper le c. par terre** it's an absolute scream; **de c.** *(magazine, film)* porn; **être comme c. et chemise** to be as thick as thieves; *Vulg* **l'avoir dans le c.** to be screwed up; *Vulg* **en avoir plein le c.** to be pissed off; **avoir qn au c.** to have sb on one's tail (**b**) *Fam (chance)* **avoir du c.** to be jammy (**c**) *(d'un sac, d'un tonneau, d'une bouteille)* bottom; **boire c. sec** to down one's drink in one go; **c. sec!** bottoms up! **2** *adj Fam (personne, décoration)* twee; *(livre)* corny

culasse [kylas] *nf* (**a**) *(de fusil, de pistolet)* breech (**b**) *(de moteur)* cylinder head

culbute [kylbyt] *nf* (**a**) *(cabriole)* somersault; **faire la c.** to do a somersault (**b**) *(chute)* tumble; **faire la c.** to take a tumble

culbuter [kylbyte] **1** *vi (vase, statue)* to topple over; *(personne)* to take a tumble; *(voiture)* to overturn **2** *vt (objet)* to knock over

cul-de-jatte (*pl* **culs-de-jatte**) [kydʒat] *nmf* legless cripple

cul-de-poule [kydpul] *nm* **avoir la bouche en c.** to have pursed lips

cul-de-sac (*pl* **culs-de-sac**) [kydsak] *nm* dead end, cul-de-sac; *Fig* dead end

culinaire [kyliner] *adj* culinary

culminant, -e [kylminã, -ãt] *adj* **point c.** *(d'une chaîne de montagnes)* highest point; *(de la gloire, d'une carrière)* height, peak

culminer [kylmine] *vi* (**a**) **l'Everest culmine à 8848 mètres** Everest is 8,848 metres at its highest point (**b**) *(crise, tension)* to peak

culot [kylo] *nm Fam (audace)* cheek, nerve; **il a un de ces culots!** he's got a nerve!; **y aller au c.** to brazen it out (**b**) *(de douille, de cartouche)* base

culotte [kylɔt] *nf* (**a**) *(sous-vêtement) (de femme)* panties, knickers; *(d'enfant)* pants (**b**) *(pantalon)* **c. courte** short *Br* trousers *or Am* pants; **c. de cheval** jodhpurs; *Fam Fig* jodhpur thighs; **c. de golf** plus-fours; *Fam Fig* **c'est elle qui porte la c.** she's the one who wears the trousers; *Fam* **faire dans sa c.** to dirty one's pants; *Fig* to wet oneself (**c**) *(de bœuf)* rump

culotté, -e [kylɔte] *adj Fam* cheeky

culpabiliser [kylpabilize] **1** *vt* **c. qn** to make sb feel guilty **2** *vi* to feel guilty

culpabilité [kylpabilite] *nf* guilt

culte [kylt] *nm* (**a**) *(vénération)* worship; *Fig* cult; *Fig* **vouer un c. à qn** to (hero-)worship sb; **c. de la personnalité** personality cult (**b**) *(religion)* religion; **liberté du c.** freedom of worship

cul-terreux (*pl* **culs-terreux**) [kyterø] *nm Fam Péj* yokel, hick

cultivable [kyltivabl] *adj* suitable for cultivation

cultivateur, -trice [kyltivatœr, -tris] **1** *nm,f* farmer; **petits cultivateurs** small farmers **2** *nm (machine)* cultivator

cultivé, -e [kyltive] *adj* (**a**) *(terre, champs)* cultivated (**b**) *(personne)* cultured, cultivated

cultiver [kyltive] **1** *vt* (**a**) *(sol, champ)* to cultivate, to farm; *(plantes)* to grow (**b**) *(art, relations, amitié)* to cultivate **2 se cultiver** *vpr* to improve one's mind

culture [kyltyr] *nf* (**a**) *(du sol)* cultivation; *(de plantes)* growing; **cultures** land under cultivation (**b**) *(espèce cultivée)* crop (**c**) *(connaissances)* culture; **un homme d'une grande c.** a highly cultured man; **c. générale** general knowledge (**d**) *(civilisation)* culture (**e**) *Biol* **c. microbienne/de tissus** bacteria/tissue culture (**f**) **c. physique** physical training

culturel, -elle [kyltyrɛl] *adj* cultural

culturisme [kyltyrism] *nm* body-building

culturiste [kyltyrist] *nmf* body-builder

cumin [kymɛ̃] *nm* cumin

cumul [kymyl] *nm* **c. des fonctions** plurality of offices; **c. des traitements** drawing of more than one salary

cumulable [kymylabl] *adj (fonctions)* which can be held concurrently; *(traitements)* which can be drawn concurrently

cumulatif, -ive [kymylatif, -iv] *adj* cumulative

cumuler [kymyle] *vt* **c. des fonctions** to hold more than one office; **c. plusieurs traitements** to draw several salaries; **c. plusieurs emplois** to have several jobs

cumulo-nimbus [kymylonɛ̃bys] *nm inv* cumulonimbus

cumulus [kymylys] *nm inv* cumulus

cupide [kypid] *adj* avaricious

cupidité [kypidite] *nf* cupidity

Cupidon [kypidɔ̃] *npr* Cupid

curable [kyrabl] *adj (maladie)* curable

curaçao [kyraso] *nm* curaçao (liqueur)

curage [kyraʒ] *nm* cleaning out

curare [kyrar] *nm* curare

cure [kyr] *nf* (**a**) *(traitement)* (course of) treatment; **c. d'amaigrissement** (course of) slimming treatment; **faire une c. de désintoxication** *(alcoolique)* to receive treatment for alcohol dependency; *(toxicomane)* to receive treatment for drug dependency; **faire une c. de vitamines** to go/be on a course of vitamins; **faire une c. de fruits** to eat a lot of fruit; **faire une c. de repos/ de sommeil** to go/be on a rest cure/sleep cure (**b**) *(dans une ville d'eau)* **c. (thermale)** spa cure; **faire une c. to**

take the waters (**c**) *(fonction de curé)* office of a parish priest

curé [kyre] *nm* parish priest; **aller à l'école chez les curés** to be educated by priests

cure-dents [kyrdɑ̃] *nm inv* toothpick

curée [kyre] *nf (lutte)* scramble; **ce fut la c. entre les héritiers** the heirs started to fight over the spoils

cure-pipe (*pl* **cure-pipes**) [kyrpip] *nm* pipe-cleaner

curer [kyre] **1** *vt* to clean out **2 se curer** *vpr* **se c. les ongles/les oreilles** to clean one's nails/one's ears

curetage [kyrtaʒ] *nm (en chirurgie)* curettage

curieusement [kyrjøzmɑ̃] *adv* curiously (enough)

curieux, -euse [kyrjø, -øz] **1** *adj* (**a**) *(intéressé)* curious; **je serais c. de voir cela** I'd be curious to see that (**b**) *(indiscret)* curious, inquisitive (**c**) *(étrange)* curious, strange; **chose curieuse,...** curiously enough,... **2** *nm,f* inquisitive person; *(badaud)* onlooker

curiosité [kyrjozite] *nf* (**a**) *(intellectuelle)* curiosity; **avec c.** curiously (**b**) *(indiscrétion)* curiosity, inquisitiveness; **par c.** out of curiosity; *Prov* **la c. est un vilain défaut** curiosity killed the cat (**c**) *(objet)* curio; **les curiosités d'une ville** the interesting sights of a town

curiste [kyrist] *nmf* = patient taking a spa cure

curriculum vitae [kyrikylɔmvite] *nm inv Br* curriculum vitae, *Am* résumé

curry [kyri] *nm* curry; **poulet au c., c. de poulet** chicken curry

curseur [kyrsœr] *nm aussi Ordinat* cursor

cursif, -ive [kyrsif, -iv] *adj (écriture)* cursive

cursus [kyrsys] *nm Univ* degree course

cutané, -e [kytane] *adj* skin, *Spéc* cutaneous

cuti [kyti] *nf* skin test; **virer sa c.** to have a positive skin test; *Fam Fig* to change radically

cuti-réaction (*pl* **cuti-réactions**) [kytireaksjɔ̃] *nf* skin test

cutter [kœtœr, kytɛr] *nm* Stanley knife®

cuve [kyv] *nf (réservoir)* (storage) tank; *(de machine à laver)* tub; *(pour la fermentation des alcools, du vin)* vat; *(en photographie)* tank

cuvée [kyve] *nf* (**a**) *(quantité)* vatful (**b**) *(produit)* vintage; *Fig* batch

cuver [kyve] *vt Fam* **c. (son vin)** to sleep it off

cuvette [kyvɛt] *nf* (**a**) *(récipient)* basin, bowl (**b**) *(de W.-C.)* bowl (**c**) *Géog* basin

CV¹ [seve] *Aut (abrév* **cheval-vapeur**) hp

CV² *nm (abrév* **curriculum vitae**) *Br* CV, *Am* résumé

cyanure [sjanyr] *nm* cyanide

cybercafé [siberkafe] *nm* cybercafé

cyberespace [siberɛspas] *nm* cyberspace

cybernétique [sibernetik] **1** *adj* cybernetic **2** *nf* cybernetics *(singulier)*

cyclable [siklabl] *adj voir* **piste**

cyclamen [siklamen] *nm* cyclamen

cycle [sikl] *nm* (**a**) *(suite, mouvement)* cycle; **c. menstruel** menstrual cycle (**b**) *(dans l'éducation)* **premier/second c.** *Scol* lower/upper classes *(in secondary school)*; *Univ* first/ last two years *(of degree course)*; *Univ* **troisième c.** postgraduate studies; **c. I/II/III** = subdivisions of primary school (between the ages of 2 and 4, 5 and 7, and 8 and 10 respectively) (**c**) *(bicyclette)* cycle

cyclique [siklik] *adj* cyclical

cyclisme [siklism] *nm* cycling

cycliste [siklist] **1** nmfcyclist
2 adj voir **coureur, course**
cyclo-cross [siklokrɔs] nm inv cyclo-cross
cyclomoteur [siklomɔtœr] nm moped, scooter
cyclone [siklon] nm cyclone
cyclope [siklɔp] nm cyclops
cyclothymique [siklotimik] adj Psy cyclothymic
cyclotourisme [sikloturism] nm bicycle touring
cygne [siɲ] nm swan
cylindre [silɛdr] nm (**a**) aussi Aut cylinder; **une quatre
cylindres** a four-cylinder car (**b**) (rouleau) roller
cylindrée [silɛdre] nf (cubic) capacity; **petite/grosse
c.** (moto) motorbike with a small/large engine; (voiture)
car with a small/large engine
cylindrique [silɛdrik] adj cylindrical
cymbale [sɛbal] nf cymbal
cynique [sinik] **1** adj cynical
2 nmf cynic
cyniquement [sinikmɑ̃] adv cynically
cynisme [sinism] nm cynicism
cyprès [siprɛ] nm cypress (tree)
cypriote [siprijɔt] **1** adj Cypriot
2 nmf C. Cypriot
cyrillique [sirilik] adj (alphabet, caractères) Cyrillic
cystite [sistit] nf cystitis
cytoplasme [sitɔplasm] nm Biol cytoplasm

D¹, d [de] *nm inv* D, d

D² [de] *nf (abrév* **route départementale)** = designation of secondary road

DAB [deabe] *nm (abrév* **distributeur automatique de billets)** ATM

dactylo [daktilo] **1** *nmf (abrév* **dactylographe)** typist **2** *nf (abrév* **dactylographie)** typing

dactylographe [daktilograf] *nmf* typist

dactylographie [daktilografi] *nf* typing

dactylographier [66] [daktilografje] *vt* to type

dada [dada] *nm* **(a)** *(langage enfantin) (cheval)* gee-gee **(b)** *Fam (sujet favori)* hobby-horse

dadais [dadɛ] *nm Fam* **un grand d.** a great gawk

dague [dag] *nf (épée)* dagger

dahlia [dalja] *nm* dahlia

daigner [deɲe] *vt* **d. faire qch** to deign to do sth

daim [dɛ̃] *nm* **(a)** *(animal)* (fallow) deer; *(mâle)* buck **(b)** *(peau)* suede; **gants/veste en d.** suede gloves/jacket

dais [dɛ] *nm* canopy

Dakar [dakar] *n* Dakar

dalaï-lama [dalailama] *nm* dalai lama

dallage [dalaʒ] *nm (action, revêtement)* paving

dalle [dal] *nf* **(a)** *(de pierre)* paving stone; *(de marbre)* slab; *(de moquette, de lino)* tile **(b)** *Fam* **que d.** *(rien)* damn all; **j'y vois que d.** I can't see a damn thing **(c)** *Fam* **avoir** *ou* **crever la d.** to be starving

daller [dale] *vt* to pave

dalmatien, -enne [dalmasjɛ̃, -ɛn] *nm,f (chien)* Dalmatian

daltonien, -enne [daltɔnjɛ̃, -ɛn] **1** *adj* colour-blind **2** *nm,f* colour-blind person

daltonisme [daltɔnism] *nm* colour blindness

dam [dã] *nm* **au grand d. de qn** to the great displeasure of sb

damage [damaʒ] *nm (de la terre, de la neige)* packing down

Damas [damas] *n* Damascus

damas [damas] *nm* damask

dame [dam] *nf* **(a)** *(femme)* lady; **d. de compagnie** lady's companion; **d. d'honneur** lady-in-waiting **(b)** *(aux cartes, aux échecs)* queen; *(au jeu de dames)* king **(c)** **dames** *(jeu) Br* draughts, *Am* checkers

damer [dame] *vt* **(a)** *Fam Fig* **d. le pion à qn** to put one over on sb **(b)** *(terre, neige)* to pack down

dameuse [damøz] *nf* piste basher

damier [damje] *nm Br* draughtboard, *Am* checkerboard; **tissu à damiers** *Br* checked *or Am* checkered material

damnation [dɑnasjɔ̃] *nf* damnation

damné, -e [dɑne] **1** *adj* damned **2** *nm,f* damned soul; *Fig* **souffrir comme un d.** to suffer sheer torture

damner [dɑne] **1** *vt* to damn **2 se damner** *vpr* to damn oneself; **il se damnerait pour...** he'd sell his soul to the devil for...

Damoclès [damɔklɛs] *n voir* **épée**

dancing [dãsiŋ] *nm Vieilli* dance hall

dandinement [dãdinmã] *nm* waddle

dandiner [dãdine] **se dandiner** *vpr* to waddle; **se d. d'un pied sur l'autre** to shift from foot to foot

dandy [dãdi] *nm* dandy

Danemark [danmark] *nm* **le D.** Denmark

danger [dãʒe] *nm* danger; **être en d.** to be in danger; **mettre en d. la vie de qn** to endanger sb's life; **d. de mort** *(sur panneau)* danger of death; **hors de d.** out of danger; **d. public** public menace

dangereusement [dãʒrøzmã] *adv* dangerously

dangereux, -euse [dãʒrø, -øz] *adj* dangerous

danois, -e [danwa, -az] **1** *adj* Danish **2** *nm,f* **D.** Dane **3** *nm* **(a)** *(langue)* Danish **(b)** *(chien)* Great Dane

dans [dã] *prép* **(a)** *(à l'intérieur de)* in; **d. une boîte** in(side) a box; **il est d. sa chambre** he's in his room; **lire qch d. un journal** to read sth in a newspaper; **tomber d. l'escalier** to fall down the stairs; **il pleut d. tout le pays** it's raining all over the country; **être d. le commerce/l'informatique** to be in business/computers; **travailler d. le bruit/la saleté** to work in noisy/dirty surroundings **(b)** *(avec mouvement)* into; **il est entré d. leur chambre** he went into their room **(c)** *(exprime la temporalité)* in; **d. 30 ans** in 30 years, in 30 years' time **(d)** *(indique une provenance)* out of; **boire d. un verre** to drink out of a glass; **découper un article d. le journal** to cut an article out of the paper **(e)** *(indique une approximation)* **d. les trente ans/les 200 euros** about thirty (years old)/200 euros **(f)** *(pour indiquer un état)* in; **d. mon excitation/ma hâte** in my excitement/hurry

dansant, -e [dãsã, -ãt] *adj voir* **soirée, thé**

danse [dãs] *nf (ensemble de mouvements, musique)* dance; **la d.** *(art)* dancing; **d. classique** ballet; **d. folklorique** folk dance/dancing; *Méd* **d. de Saint-Guy** St Vitus's dance; **la d. du ventre** belly-dancing

danser [dãse] **1** *vi* to dance; **le bouchon/le bateau danse sur l'eau** the cork/the boat is bobbing up and down on the water; *Fig* **avec lui je ne sais jamais sur**

quel pied d. I never know where I am with him **2** vt (valse, tango) to dance

danseur, -euse [dɑ̃sœr, -øz] nm,f dancer; **d. (classique ou de ballet)** ballet-dancer; **d. étoile** lead dancer; **danseuse étoile** prima ballerina; **être en danseuse** (en cyclisme) to stand on the pedals

Danube [danyb] nm **le D.** the Danube

dard [dar] nm (d'insecte, de scorpion) sting

darder [darde] vt **il a dardé sur moi un regard furieux** he shot a furious look at me; **le soleil darde ses rayons** the sun is beating down

dare-dare [dardar] adv Fam at the double

darne [darn] nf (de poisson) steak

dartre [dartr] nf dry patch of skin

darwinisme [darwinism] nm Darwinism

datation [datasjɔ̃] nf dating

date [dat] nf date; **prendre d. pour qch** to fix a date for sth; **faire d.** to be a landmark; **amitié de fraîche/longue d.** recent/long-standing friendship; **je la connais de longue d.** I've known her (for) a long time; **d. limite** deadline; **d. limite de consommation/de vente/de fraîcheur** use-by/sell-by/best-before date; **d. de naissance** date of birth

dater [date] **1** vt (lettre) to date **2** vi **à d. du 15** as from the 15th; **ça date un peu** it's a bit dated; **ça ne date pas d'hier** that's nothing new

dateur [datœr] adj m **tampon ou timbre d.** date stamp

datte [dat] nf date

dattier [datje] nm date palm

dauphin [dofɛ̃] nm **(a)** (animal) dolphin **(b)** Hist D. Dauphin **(c)** Fig (successeur) heir apparent

daurade [dorad] nf sea bream

davantage [davɑ̃taʒ] adv more; **elle est jolie, mais tu l'es bien d.** she's pretty but you're even prettier; **nous ne resterons pas d.** we won't stay any longer

DCA [desea] nf Mil (abrév Défense contre avions) anti-aircraft defence

DD Ordinat (abrév disque dur) HD

DDASS [das] nf (abrév Direction départementale de l'action sanitaire et sociale) = local social work department, one of whose tasks is to deal with children who have been abandoned or ill-treated

DDT [dedete] nm (abrév dichlorodiphényltrichloréthane) DDT

de [də]

---

de becomes **d'** before vowel and h mute; **de + le** contracts to form **du**, and **de + les** to form **des**.

---

1 prép **(a)** (indique l'origine) from; **venir/être de** to come/be from; **sortir de chez soi** to leave the house; **l'idée est de vous** it's your idea; **de vous à moi...** between ourselves... **(b)** (indique une progression) **de ... à ...** from... to...; **du matin au soir** from morning till night; **de vingt à trente personnes** between twenty and thirty people; **de ... en ...** from ... to ...; **errer de ville en ville** to go from town to town **(c)** (introduit l'agent, l'auteur) by; (introduit l'instrument) with; **accompagné de ses amis** accompanied by his friends; **la statue est de Rodin** the statue is by Rodin; **armé de pierres** armed with stones; **couvert de puces** covered in fleas **(d)** (indique la manière) **d'un air amusé** with an amused expression; **d'une voix douce** gently, in a gentle voice **(e)** (indique la cause) **sauter de joie** to jump for joy; **resplendissant de santé** blooming with health **(f)** (introduit une mesure) **un enfant de dix ans** a child of ten, a ten-year-old child; **il est plus grand que moi de 5**

---

cm he's 5 cm taller than I am; **une pièce de 20 centimes** a 20-centime coin; **la terrasse fait 20 mètres de long** the terrace is 20 metres long; **20 euros de l'heure** 20 euros an hour **(g)** (indique l'appartenance) of; **le livre de Pierre** Pierre's book; **le toit de la maison** the roof of the house **(h)** (pour préciser la nature, la matière) **un problème d'algèbre** an algebra problem; **un hôtel de la rive gauche** a hotel on the left bank; **le journal d'hier** yesterday's paper; **à quatre heures de l'après-midi** at four (o'clock) in the afternoon; **une robe de soie** a silk dress; **un verre de vin** a glass of wine **(i)** (dans, parmi) of; **l'un d'eux** one of them; **le meilleur élève de la classe** the best pupil in the class; **la moitié de ses économies** half (of) her savings **(j)** (pendant) **je ne l'ai pas vu de la soirée** I haven't seen him all evening; **de nuit** by night **(k)** (introduit un infinitif) **il est honteux de mentir** it is shameful to lie; **j'aime mieux attendre que de me faire mouiller** I would rather wait than get wet **(l)** (pour insister) **c'est d'un ridicule!** it's utterly ridiculous! **(m)** (dans un titre) **de l'amour** (on) love **2** art partitif some; **je bois du café tous les matins** I drink coffee every morning; **donnez-moi du vin** give me some wine; **c'est du Mozart** it's Mozart; **avez-vous du sucre?** have you got any sugar? **3** art indéfini **je n'ai plus d'amis/de problèmes** I haven't got any friends/problems any more

dé¹ [de] nm (pour jouer) dice; **jouer aux dés** to play dice; **couper qch en dés** (légumes) to dice sth

dé² nm **dé (à coudre)** thimble

DEA [deəa] nm (abrév diplôme d'études approfondies) = postgraduate qualification which is a prerequisite for PhD candidates

dealer [dilœr] nm Fam (de drogue) dealer

déambulateur [deɑ̃bylatœr] nm walking frame

déambuler [deɑ̃byle] vi to stroll (about)

débâcle [debakl] nf **(a)** (d'un cours d'eau gelé) breaking up **(b)** Mil rout; Fig (d'une affaire, d'une monnaie) collapse

déballage [debalaʒ] nm **(a)** (action) unpacking **(b)** Fam (aveu) outpouring

déballer [debale] vt **(a)** (affaires, produits, caisses) to unpack **(b)** Fam (sa vie privée, ses sentiments) to pour out

débandade [debɑ̃dad] nf (d'une armée, d'une équipe) rout; **c'est la d. dans l'entreprise** the company's in disarray

débaptiser [debatize] vt (personne, rue) to rename

débarbouillage [debarbujaʒ] nm face wash

débarbouiller [debarbuje] **1** vt **d. qn** to wash sb's face **2** se débarbouiller vpr to wash one's face

débarbouillette [debarbujet] nf Can (face) flannel, face cloth, Am washrag

débarcadère [debarkader] nm landing stage; (pour les marchandises) wharf

débardeur [debardœr] nm **(a)** (vêtement) vest **(b)** (personne) docker, stevedore

débarquement [debarkəmɑ̃] nm **(a)** (de cargaison) unloading; (de passagers) landing **(b)** (de troupes) landing; Hist **le D.** the Normandy landings

débarquer [debarke] **1** vt (cargaison) to unload; (passagers) to land **2** vi **(a)** (d'un bateau, d'un avion) to disembark **(b)** Fam Fig to turn up; **il a toujours l'air de d.** he never seems to know what's going on

débarras [debara] nm **(a)** (endroit) junk room **(b)** Fam **bon d.!** good riddance!

débarrasser [debarase] **1** vt (table, bureau, pièce) to clear;

d. qn de qch to relieve sb of sth; *Fam Fig* **d. le plancher** to clear out
2 se débarrasser *vpr* **se d. de** to get rid of

débat [deba] *nm* debate; *Pol* **débats (parlementaires)** (parliamentary) proceedings

débattre [11] [debatr] **1** *vt (discuter)* to debate, to discuss; **prix à d.** price negotiable
2 débattre de *vt ind* to discuss
3 se débattre *vpr* to struggle; **se d. contre les difficultés** to be up against difficulties

débauche [deboʃ] *nf* debauchery; **lieu de d.** den of vice; *Fig* **une d. de couleurs** a riot of colour

débauché, -e [deboʃe] **1** *adj* debauched
2 *nm,f* debauchee

débaucher [deboʃe] *vt* **(a)** *(inciter à la débauche)* to corrupt **(b)** *(licencier)* to lay off

débecter [debɛkte] *vt très Fam* to sicken

débile [debil] **1** *adj* **(a)** *(qui manque de vigueur) (enfant)* sickly; *(corps)* weak; *(santé)* poor **(b)** *Fam (stupide)* stupid
2 *nmf* **d. mental** mental defective; *Fam Fig* complete idiot

débilitant, -e [debilitã, -ãt] *adj* debilitating; *Fig* demoralizing

débilité [debilite] *nf* **(a)** *(faiblesse)* debility; **d. mentale** mental deficiency **(b)** *Fam (stupidité)* stupidity

débiliter [debilite] *vt* to debilitate

débiner [debine] *Fam* **1** *vt* to run down
2 se débiner *vpr* to clear off

débit [debi] *nm* **(a)** *Fin* debit **(b)** *(ventes)* turnover **(c)** *(commerce)* **d. de boissons** bar; **d. de tabac** tobacconist's (shop) **(d)** *(de bois)* cutting up **(e)** *(d'une rivière, de liquide)* flow; *(d'une machine)* output; *Ordinat* **d. de données** data throughput **(f)** *(d'un orateur)* delivery; *Fam* **il a un de ces débits!** he's really got the gift of the gab!

débitant, -e [debitã, -ãt] *nm,f* **d. de boissons** bar owner; **d. de tabac** tobacconist

débiter [debite] *vt* **(a)** *(sujet: usine)* to produce; *(sujet: cours d'eau)* to have a flow rate of **(b)** *Fin (somme, compte)* to debit **(c)** *(bois, viande)* to cut up **(d)** *(vendre)* to sell **(e)** *Péj (dire)* to spout

débiteur, -trice [debitœr, -tris] **1** *adj (compte)* debit
2 *nm,f* debtor

déblaiement [deblɛmã] *nm* clearing

déblatérer [34] [deblatere] *vi Fam* **d. contre** *ou* **sur qn/ qch** to rail against sb/sth

déblayage [deblɛjaʒ] *nm* clearing

déblayer [53] [debləje] *vt* **(a)** *(terre, gravats, neige)* to clear **(b)** *(terrain)* to clear; *Fig* **d. le terrain** *(faire des préparatifs)* to prepare the ground

déblocage [deblɔkaʒ] *nm (d'une porte, d'un tiroir, d'un mécanisme)* unjamming; *(des prix, des salaires)* unfreezing

débloquer [deblɔke] **1** *vt* **(a)** *(porte, tiroir, mécanisme)* to unjam; *(prix, salaires)* to unfreeze; **d. des fonds** to release funds **(b)** *Psy* **d. qn** *(lui ôter ses complexes)* to rid sb of his/ her complexes; *(le rendre moins timide)* to make sb less inhibited
2 *vi Fam (être fou)* to be off one's rocker; *(raconter n'importe quoi)* to talk drivel; *(être gâteux)* to be gaga

déboguer [debɔge] *vt Ordinat* to debug

débogueur [debɔgœr] *nm Ordinat* debugger

déboires [debwar] *nmpl (déceptions)* disappointments; *(ennuis)* problems

déboisement [debwazmã] *nm* deforestation

déboiser [debwaze] *vt* to deforest

déboîtement [debwatmã] *nm* **(a)** *(d'un membre, d'une articulation)* dislocation **(b)** *(en voiture)* pulling out

déboîter [debwate] **1** *vt* **(a)** *(objets encastrés)* to disconnect **(b)** *(articulation, membre)* to dislocate
2 *vi (en voiture)* to pull out
3 se déboîter *vpr (articulation, membre)* to become dislocated; **se d. l'épaule/le genou** to dislocate one's shoulder/knee

débonnaire [debɔnɛr] *adj (personne)* good-natured, easy-going; **répondre d'un ton d.** to answer good-naturedly

débordant, -e [debɔrdã, -ãt] *adj (activité)* tireless; *(imagination)* boundless; **d. de santé/d'enthousiasme** bursting with health/with enthusiasm

débordé, -e [debɔrde] *adj* **d. (de travail)** snowed under (with work)

débordement [debɔrdəmã] *nm* **(a)** *(d'une rivière)* overflowing; *Fig (d'enthousiasme, de joie)* outburst **(b)** **débordements** excesses **(c)** *Mil (de l'ennemi)* outflanking

déborder [debɔrde] **1** *vi* **(a)** *(liquide, rivière)* to overflow; **l'eau déborde du vase** the vase is overflowing; **les papiers débordent de la corbeille** the wastepaper basket is overflowing with paper; **d. sur le temps prévu** to overrun **(b)** *Fig* **d. de vie** to be bursting with vitality; **d. d'imagination** to have boundless imagination
2 *vt (dépasser) (alignement)* to stick out from; *(limite)* to go beyond; *Mil (l'ennemi)* to outflank; *Sp (coureur)* to overtake; **cela déborde le cadre de...** that is beyond the scope of...

débouchage [debuʃaʒ] *nm* **(a)** *(d'un tuyau, d'un évier)* unblocking **(b)** *(d'une bouteille)* uncorking

débouché [debuʃe] *nm (professionnel)* opening, job opportunity; *Com* outlet

déboucher [debuʃe] **1** *vt* **(a)** *(tuyau, évier)* to unblock **(b)** *(bouteille)* to uncork
2 *vi (dans l'espace) (personne, voiture)* to emerge (**de** from), to come out (**de** of); **d. dans/sur** to lead to **(b)** *Fig* **d. sur qch** *(avoir pour résultat)* to lead to sth
3 se déboucher *vpr (tuyau, évier, oreilles)* to clear; **la bouteille se débouche facilement** the bottle opens easily

débouler [debule] *Fam* **1** *vt* **d. l'escalier** to race down the stairs
2 *vi* **(a)** *(descendre)* to race down **(b)** *(arriver)* to turn up

déboulonner [debulɔne] *vt* **(a)** *Tech* to unbolt; *(statue)* to take down **(b)** *Fam Fig (critiquer)* to debunk; *(de son poste)* to kick out

débourser [deburse] *vt (argent)* to lay out; **sans rien d.** without spending a penny

déboussoler [debusɔle] *vt Fam* to throw

debout [dəbu] *adv* **(a)** *(verticalement) (chose)* upright; *(personne)* standing; **cent ans plus tard, la maison est encore d.** the house is still standing a hundred years later; **elle est d. toute la journée** she's on her feet all day; **mettre qch d.** to stand sth up; **se mettre d.** to stand up; **rester d.** to stand; **tenir d.** *(objet)* to stay upright; *(personne)* to stay on one's feet; *Fig* **un argument qui ne tient pas d.** an argument that won't stand up; **se tenir d.** to stand; **conte** *ou* **histoire à dormir d.** cock-and-bull story **(b)** *(hors du lit)* **être d.** to be up; **allons, d.!** come on, get up!

débouter [debute] *vt Jur* to nonsuit

déboutonner [debutɔne] **1** *vt* to unbutton
2 se déboutonner *vpr (personne)* to undo one's coat/ jacket/etc; *(vêtement)* to unbutton; *Fig (se confier)* to open up

débraillé, -e [debraje] *adj* slovenly

débrancher [debrãʃe] *vt* to unplug

débrayage [debrɛjaʒ] *nm* **(a)** *Aut* declutching **(b)** *(grève)* stoppage

débrayer [53] [debreje] *vi* **(a)** *Aut* to release the clutch **(b)** *(se mettre en grève)* to stop work

débridé, -e [debride] *adj (passion)* unbridled; *(imagination)* vivid

débris [debri] **1** *nmpl (d'un avion, d'une voiture)* debris, wreckage; *(de verre, de bois)* fragments; *(de métal)* scrap *(metal)* **2** *nm Fam* **un vieux d.** an old wreck

débrouillard, -e [debrujar, -ard] *Fam* **1** *adj* resourceful **2** *nm,f* resourceful person

débrouillardise [debrujardiz] *nf* resourcefulness

débrouiller [debruje] **1** *vt (fil, mystère)* to unravel **2 se débrouiller** *vpr* to manage, to cope; *(dans une langue, un domaine)* to get by; **débrouillez-vous!** you'll just have to manage!; **elle s'est débrouillée pour rencontrer le directeur** she worked it so that she got to meet the director

débroussailler [debrusɑje] *vt* to clear of undergrowth; *Fig (question)* to clarify

débusquer [debyske] *vt* to flush out

début [deby] *nm* **(a)** *(commencement)* beginning, start; **au d. (de)** at the start or beginning (of); **nu tout d., tout au d.** at the very start *or* beginning; **dès le d.** from the start; **je le savais depuis le d.** I knew all along, **du d. à la fin** from start to finish; **en d. de** at the start of; **Hum il faut** *ou* **il y a un d. à tout** there's a first time for everything **(b)** *débuts (d'un acteur, d'un chanteur)* debut, first appearance; **faire ses débuts** to make one's debut; **en être à ses débuts** *(société, projet)* to be in its early stages **(c)** *Ordinat* home; **aller au d.** *(commande)* go top

débutant, -e [debytɑ̃, -ɑ̃t] **1** *adj* novice **2** *nm,f (dans une discipline)* beginner; **grand d.** complete beginner

débuter [debyte] **1** *vi* **(a)** *(commencer)* to begin, to start *(par with)* **(b)** *(dans le spectacle)* to make one's debut; *(dans la vie professionnelle)* to start out; **mal/bien d. dans la vie** to get off to a bad/good start in life **2** *vt Fam* to start, to begin *(par with)*

deçà [dəsa] **en deçà de** *prép (dans l'espace)* (on) this side of; **rester (très) en d. de la vérité** to be (very) short of the truth

déca [deka] *nm Fam (café)* decaf

décacheter [42] [dekaʃte] *vt* to unseal, to open

décadenasser [dekadnase] *vt* to take the padlock off

décadence [dekadɑ̃s] *nf (état)* decadence; *(processus)* decline; **tomber en d.** to go into decline

décadent, -e [dekadɑ̃, -ɑ̃t] *adj* decadent

décaféiné [dekafeine] *nm* decaffeinated coffee

décagonal, -e, -aux, -ales [dekagɔnal, -o] *adj* decagonal

décagone [dekagon] *nm Math* decagon

décalage [dekalaʒ] *nm* **(a)** *(désaccord)* gap **(b)** *(dans le temps)* time lag; **d. horaire** time difference; **souffrir du d. horaire** to have jet lag

décalaminer [dekalamine] *vt* to decoke

décalcification [dekalsifikasjɔ̃] *nf Méd* decalcification

décalcifier [66] [dekalsifje] *Méd* **1** *vt* to decalcify **2 se décalcifier** *vpr* to become decalcified

décalcomanie [dekalkɔmani] *nf (procédé) Br* transfer process, *Am* decal; *(image) Br* transfer, *Am* decal; **faire de la d.** to do *Br* transfers *or Am* decals

décaler [dekale] **1** *vt* **(a)** *(dans l'espace)* to move, to shift **(b)** *(dans le temps) (avancer)* to bring forward **(de** from) **(b)** *(reculer)* to put back **(de** by) **2 se décaler** *vpr* to move, to shift; **vous pourriez vous d. d'un rang/vers la gauche?** could you move up a row/ move to the left?

décalitre [dekalitr] *nm* decalitre

décalquer [dekalke] *vt* to trace

décamètre [dekamɛtr] *nm* decametre

décamper [dekɑ̃pe] *vi Fam* to clear off

décan [dekɑ̃] *nm* decan

décaniller [dekanije] *vi Fam* to clear off

décanter [dekɑ̃te] **1** *vt (vin)* to decant **2 se décanter** *vpr (vin)* to settle; *Fig (situation)* to become clearer

décapage [dekapaʒ] *nm (avec un produit)* stripping; *(au papier de verre)* sanding (down); *(d'un four)* cleaning

décapant, -e [dekapɑ̃, -ɑ̃t] **1** *adj* **(a)** **produit d.** *(pour vernis, peinture)* paint stripper; *(pour four)* oven cleaner **(b)** *Fig (humour)* caustic **2** *nm (pour vernis, peinture)* paint stripper; *(pour four)* oven cleaner

décaper [dekape] *vt* **(a)** *(avec un produit)* to strip; *(au papier de verre)* to sand (down); *(four)* to clean **(b)** *Fam Fig* **ça décape!** *(alcool)* it takes the roof of your mouth off!

décapeuse [dekapøz] *nf* scraper

décapitation [dekapitasjɔ̃] *nf* decapitation

décapiter [dekapite] *vt (personne)* to decapitate; *(arbre)* to pollard

décapotable [dekapɔtabl] **1** *adj* convertible; *(coupé)* drop head **2** *nf* convertible

décapoter [dekapɔte] *vt* to lower the top of

décapsuler [dekapsyle] *vt* to take the top off

décapsuleur [dekapsylœr] *nm* bottle opener

décarcasser [dekarkase] **se décarcasser** *vpr Fam* to sweat blood **(pour faire** to do)

décasyllabe [dekasilab] **1** *adj* decasyllabic **2** *nm* decasyllable

décathlon [dekatlɔ̃] *nm* decathlon

décati, -e [dekati] *adj (visage)* age-worn; *(personne)* decrepit

décatir [dekatir] **se décatir** *vpr* to become decrepit

décédé, -e [desede] *adj* deceased

décéder [34] [desede] *vi* to die

décelable [deslabl] *adj* detectable

déceler [39] [desle] *vt* **(a)** *(découvrir)* to detect **(b)** *(indiquer)* to indicate

décélération [deselerasjɔ̃] *nf* deceleration

décélérer [34] [deselere] *vi* to decelerate

décembre [desɑ̃br] *nm* December; *voir aussi* **janvier**

décemment [desamɑ̃] *adv* **(a)** *(convenablement) (se comporter)* properly; *(s'habiller)* decently **(b)** *(passablement)* reasonably well **(c)** *(raisonnablement)* reasonably; **je ne pouvais pas d. refuser** I couldn't reasonably refuse

décence [desɑ̃s] *nf* **(a)** *(bienséance) (de comportement)* propriety; *(d'habillement)* decency **(b)** *(tact)* decency; **avoir la d. de faire qch** to have the decency to do sth

décennal, -e, -aux, -ales [desenal, -o] *adj* ten-year

décennie [deseni] *nf* decade

décent, -e [desɑ̃, -ɑ̃t] *adj* **(a)** *(comportement)* proper; *(vêtements) (de comportement)* decent; **peu d.** improper/indecent **(b)** *(passable)* reasonable

décentralisation [desɑ̃tralizasjɔ̃] *nf* decentralization

décentraliser [desɑ̃tralize] *vt* to decentralize

décentrer [desɑ̃tre] **1** *vt* to move off centre **2 se décentrer** *vpr* to move off centre

déception [desɛpsjɔ̃] *nf (disappointment)* disappointment; **d. sentimentale** disappointment in love

décerner [deserne] *vt (prix, médaille)* to award **(à** to)

décès [desɛ] *nm* death; **fermé pour cause de d.** *(sur la porte d'un magasin)* closed due to bereavement

décevant, -e [desəvã, -ãt] *adj* disappointing

décevoir [60] [desəvwar] *vt* to disappoint; **il/ce voyage m'a beaucoup déçu** I was very disappointed in him/with the trip

déchaîné, -e [deʃene] *adj (passion)* unbridled; *(mer, vent)* raging; *(personne)* wild

déchaînement [deʃɛnmã] *nm (des éléments)* fury; *(des passions)* outburst

déchaîner [deʃene] **1** *vt (passions, colère)* to unleash; **d. l'hilarité** to provoke laughter
2 se déchaîner *vpr (tempête, vent)* to rage; *(personne)* to fly into a rage **(contre** with)

déchanter [deʃãte] *vi Fam* to become disillusioned

décharge [deʃarʒ] *nf* **(a)** *(tirs)* discharge **(b)** **d. (électrique)** (electric) shock; **d. d'adrénaline** rush of adrenaline **(c)** *(d'ordures)* **d. (publique)** *Br* rubbish *or Am* garbage dump; **d. interdite** *(sur panneau)* no dumping **(d)** *Jur (d'un accusé)* acquittal; *(d'une obligation)* discharge; *Fig* **dire qch à la d. de qn** to say sth in sb's defence

déchargement [deʃarʒəmã] *nm* unloading

décharger [45] [deʃarʒe] **1** *vt* **(a)** *(vider) (camion, bateau, cargaison)* to unload; *(sujet: camion) (sable, gravier)* to dump; *(arme à feu)* to fire, to discharge; *Fig* **d. sa conscience** to unburden one's conscience **(de** of) **(b)** *(soulager)* **d. qn de qch** *(tâche, responsabilité)* to relieve sb of sth; *Jur (d'une accusation)* to acquit sb of sth
2 se décharger *vpr* **(a)** *(personne)* **se d. d'une tâche/ d'une responsabilité sur qn** to offload a task/a responsibility onto sb **(b)** *(pile, batterie)* to go flat

décharné, -e [deʃarne] *adj (corps, membres, visage)* emaciated; *Fig (arbre)* bare

déchaussé, -e [deʃose] *adj* **(a)** *(sans chaussures)* barefoot **(b)** *(dent)* loose

déchausser [deʃose] **1** *vt (enlever ses chaussures à)* **d. qn** to take off sb's shoes; **d. ses skis** to take off one's skis
2 se déchausser *vpr (enlever ses chaussures)* to take off one's shoes **(b)** *(dent)* to work loose

dèche [dɛʃ] *nf Fam* **être dans la d.** to be totally broke; **c'est la d.** I'm/we're/*etc* totally broke

déchéance [deʃeãs] *nf* **(a)** *(physique, morale)* decline **(b)** *Jur (de droits)* forfeiture; **d. de l'autorité parentale** loss of parental rights

déchet [deʃɛ] *nm* **(a)** **déchets** waste; **déchets radioactifs/industriels** radioactive/industrial waste **(b)** *(perte)* **il y a du d.** there's some wastage **(c)** *Péj (personne)* down-and-out; **un d. de la société** a social outcast

déchiffrable [deʃifrabl] *adj* decipherable

déchiffrage [deʃifraʒ] *nm Mus* sight-reading

déchiffrement [deʃifrəmã] *nm* deciphering; *Ordinat* decryption

déchiffrer [deʃifre] *vt* **(a)** *(inscription, écriture, message)* to decipher; *(signaux)* to interpret; *Fig (pensées, sentiments, mystère)* to fathom **(b)** *(musique)* to sight-read

déchiqueté, -e [deʃikte] *adj* **(a)** *(irrégulier)* jagged **(b)** *(vêtements, papiers)* torn to shreds; *(corps) (dans une explosion)* blown to pieces

déchiqueter [42] [deʃikte] *vt (vêtements, papiers)* to tear to shreds; *(sujet: explosion) (corps)* to blow to pieces

déchirant, -e [deʃirã, -ãt] *adj (spectacle, adieux)* heartrending

déchiré, -e [deʃire] *adj aussi Méd & Fig* torn; **être d. entre deux personnes** to be torn between two people

déchirement [deʃirmã] *nm (peine)* heartbreak

déchirer [deʃire] **1** *vt* **(a)** *(accidentellement)* to tear; *(volontairement)* to tear up; *(enveloppe)* to tear open **(b)** *Fig (famille, pays)* to tear apart; *(silence)* to pierce; **des sons qui déchirent le tympan** ear-splitting sounds
2 se déchirer *vpr* **(a)** *(tissu, papier)* to tear **(b)** *Méd* **se d. un muscle** to tear a muscle **(c)** *Fig (couple)* to tear each other apart

déchirure [deʃiryr] *nf (dans un tissu)* & *Méd* tear; *Fig (peine)* heartbreak; **se faire une d. musculaire** to tear a muscle

déchoir [14] [deʃwar] *vi* **ce serait d. (que de...)** it would be demeaning (to...); **par ce mariage il déchoit de son rang** he is marrying beneath him

déchu, -e [deʃy] *adj (dépossédé) (roi)* deposed; **être d. de qch** *(droit, nationalité)* to be stripped of sth

décibel [desibɛl] *nm* decibel

décidé, -e [deside] *adj* **(a)** *(fixé)* settled **(b)** *(caractère, personne, manière)* determined; **d'un ton d.** in a decisive tone; **être d. à faire qch** to be determined to do sth

décidément [desidemã] *adv* really; **d. je n'ai pas de chance!, je n'ai d. pas de chance!** I really don't have any luck!

décider [deside] **1** *vt* **(a)** *(déterminer)* **d. que/quand/si** to decide that/when/if; **il fut décidé qu'on attendrait** it was decided that we/they/*etc* should wait; **c'est moi qui décide ici** I'm the one who makes the decisions here; **je déciderai pour toi** I'll decide for you **(b)** *(convaincre)* **d. qn à faire qch** to persuade sb to do sth
2 décider de *vt ind* **d. de qch** to decide on sth; **un événement qui a décidé de sa carrière** an event that determined his career; **d. de faire qch** to decide to do sth
3 se décider *vpr* **(a)** *(prendre une décision)* to make up one's mind, to come to a decision; **se d. à faire qch** to make up one's mind to do sth; **je ne peux pas me d. à le faire** I can't bring myself to do it; *Fig* **il ne se décide pas à faire beau** the weather can't make up its mind whether to be fine or not; **se d. pour qn/qch** to decide on sb/sth **(b)** *(problème, question)* to be settled

décideur, -euse [desidœr, -øz] *nm,f* decision-maker

décigramme [desigram] *nm* decigram

décilitre [desilitr] *nm* decilitre

décimal, -e, -aux, -ales [desimal, -o] **1** *adj* decimal
2 *nf* **décimale** decimal

décimer [desime] *vt* to decimate

décimètre [desimɛtr] *nm* decimetre; **double d.** *(règle)* ruler *(20 cm long)*

décisif, -ive [desizif, -iv] *adj (bataille, argument)* decisive; *(preuve)* conclusive; *(moment)* critical

décision [desizjɔ̃] *nf* **(a)** *(choix)* decision; *Jur* ruling; **arriver à/prendre une d.** to come to/to make a decision; **prendre la d. de faire qch** to decide to do sth; **la d. me m'appartient pas** it's not my decision **(b)** *(détermination)* determination; **avec d.** decisively; **esprit de d.** decisiveness

déclamation [deklamasjɔ̃] *nf (éloquence)* declamation

déclamatoire [deklamatwar] *adj Péj (style)* declamatory; *(discours)* bombastic

déclamer [deklame] *vt (discours, vers)* to declaim; *Péj* to spout

déclaration [deklarasjɔ̃] *nf* **(a)** *(annonce orale, écrite)* statement; **d. (d'amour)** declaration of love; **faire une** *ou* **sa d. à qn** to declare one's love to sb; **le chef de l'État a une importante d. à faire** the President has an important announcement to make; **faire une d. à la police** to make a statement to the police; **D. des droits de l'homme** Declaration of Human Rights; **d. de guerre** declaration of war; *Hist* **D. d'indépendance** Declaration of Independence; **d. de principe** statement of principle **(b)** *(acte* *officiel) (de naissance, de décès)* registration; *(à une compagnie d'assurances)* claim (**de** for); *(à la police)* report; **d. en douane** customs declaration; **d. d'impôts** tax return; **faire sa d. d'impôts** to fill in one's tax return; **d. de revenus** income tax return (**c**) *Ordinat* **d. de champ** field definition

déclaré, -e [deklare] *adj (ennemi, intention)* declared; *(partisan)* avowed

déclarer [deklare] **1** *vt (annoncer)* to declare; *(revenus, décès, naissance)* to register; *(à une compagnie d'assurances)* to make a claim for; *(à la police)* to report; **d. que** to declare (that); **d. forfait** *(en sport)* to scratch; **d. la guerre à qn** to declare war on sb; **rien à d.** *(en douane)* nothing to declare; **être déclaré coupable** to be found guilty **2 se déclarer** *vpr* (**a**) *(feu, maladie, guerre)* to break out (**b**) *(se prononcer)* **se d. pour/contre qch** to declare oneself in favour of/against sth (**c**) *(se dire)* **se d. satisfait/surpris** to declare oneself satisfied/surprised; **se d. coupable** to admit one's guilt (**d**) *(faire une déclaration d'amour)* to declare one's love

déclasser [deklase] *vt* (**a**) *(faire changer de classe) Sp* to relegate; *(hôtel)* to downgrade; *(passagers)* to transfer from one class to another (**b**) *(déranger)* to get out of order

déclenchement [deklɑ̃ʃmɑ̃] *nm (d'un appareil)* starting; *(d'un mécanisme)* activation; *(d'une sonnerie)* setting off; *(d'un événement)* triggering

déclencher [deklɑ̃ʃe] *vt (appareil)* to start; *(mécanisme)* to activate; *(sonnerie)* to set off; *(événement, critiques, questions)* to trigger; *Mil (attaque)* to launch

déclencheur [deklɑ̃ʃœr] *nm Phot* shutter release

déclic [deklik] *nm (bruit)* click; **la vue de cette photo a été pour elle un véritable d.** when she looked at the photo things fell into place

déclin [deklɛ̃] *nm (du talent, de la santé, d'une civilisation)* decline; *(de la beauté)* fading; *(du jour)* close; **être en d.** to be in decline, **le soleil est à son d.** the sun is setting; **au d. de sa vie** in her declining years

déclinaison [deklinɛzɔ̃] *nf Gram* declension

déclinant, -e [deklinɑ̃, -ɑ̃t] *adj (beauté, lumière)* fading; *(pouvoirs)* declining

décliner [dekline] **1** *vi (jour)* to draw to a close; *(talent, santé)* to decline; *(beauté)* to fade **2** *vt* (**a**) *Formel (refuser) (offre, invitation)* to decline; **d. toute responsabilité** to accept no liability (**b**) *Gram* to decline (**c**) *(réciter) (identité)* to state **3 se décliner** *vpr Gram* to be declined

déclivité [deklivite] *nf* slope, incline

décloisonnement [deklwazɔnmɑ̃] *nm* decompartmentalization

décloisonner [deklwazɔne] *vt* to decompartmentalize

déco [deko] *nf Fam (d'une pièce)* décor; *(métier)* (interior) decorating

décocher [dekɔʃe] *vt* (**a**) *(flèche)* to shoot; **d. un coup/une ruade à qn** to hit out at/to kick sb (**b**) *Fig (remarque)* to fire off (**à** at); *(sourire, œillade)* to flash (**à** at)

décoction [dekɔksjɔ̃] *nf* decoction

décodage [dekɔdaʒ] *nm* decoding

décoder [dekɔde] *vt* to decode

décodeur [dekɔdœr] *nm TV* decoder

décoiffer [dekwafe] *vt (ébouriffer)* **d. qn** to mess up sb's hair; **tu es tout décoiffé** your hair's in a mess; *Fam Fig* **un film qui décoiffe** a mind-blowing film **2 se décoiffer** *vpr* (**a**) *(se dépeigner)* to mess up one's hair (**b**) *(ôter son chapeau)* to remove one's hat

décoincer [16] [dekwɛ̃se] **1** *vt (tiroir, mécanisme)* to loosen; *Fam Fig (personne)* to loosen up

2 se décoincer *vpr (tiroir, mécanisme)* to loosen; *Fam Fig* (**personne**) to loosen up

déçois *etc voir* **décevoir**

décolérer [34] [dekɔlere] *vi* to calm down; **il ne décolérait pas** he was still angry; **il n'a pas décoléré depuis huit jours** he's been angry for a week

décollage [dekɔlaʒ] *nm* (**a**) *aussi Fig (démarrage)* takeoff (**b**) *(d'un timbre, de papier peint, d'une affiche)* peeling off

décollement [dekɔlmɑ̃] *nm* (**a**) *Méd* **d. de la rétine** detachment of the retina (**b**) *(d'un timbre, de papier peint, d'une affiche)* peeling off

décoller [dekɔle] **1** *vt (timbre, papier peint, affiche)* to peel off; **d. une enveloppe à la vapeur** to steam open an envelope; *Fam Fig* **d. qn de la télé/du bar** to tear sb away from the TV/the bar **2** *vi* (**a**) *(avion, fusée, économie)* to take off (**b**) *Fam (partir)* to leave; **bon, on décolle!** shall we get moving?; **je ne décollerai pas d'ici tant que...** I'm not budging until...; *Sp* **d. du peloton** to pull away from the pack **3 se décoller** *vpr (se détacher)* to peel off; *Méd (rétine)* to become detached

décolleté, -e [dekɔlte] **1** *adj (vêtement)* low-cut; **une femme très décolletée** a woman in a very low-cut dress; **robe décolletée dans le dos** dress cut low at the back **2** *nm (de vêtement)* low neckline; *(haut des seins)* cleavage

décolonisation [dekɔlɔnizasjɔ̃] *nf* decolonization

décoloniser [dekɔlɔnize] *vt* to decolonize

décolorant, -e [dekɔlɔrɑ̃, -ɑ̃t] **1** *adj* bleaching **2** *nm* bleaching agent

décoloration [dekɔlɔrasjɔ̃] *nf (d'un tissu)* fading; *(des cheveux)* bleaching; **se faire faire une d.** to have one's hair bleached

décolorer [dekɔlɔre] **1** *vt (tissu)* to fade; *(cheveux)* to bleach **2 se décolorer** *vpr (tissu)* to fade; **se d. les cheveux** to bleach one's hair

décombres [dekɔ̃br] *nmpl* ruins, debris

décommander [dekɔmɑ̃de] **1** *vt (réunion, dîner)* to cancel, to call off; *(invité)* to put off **2 se décommander** *vpr* to cancel

décomplexer [dekɔ̃plɛkse] *vt Fam* **d. qn** to cure sb of his/her hang-ups

décomposer [dekɔ̃poze] **1** *vt* (**a**) *(élément chimique)* to decompose; *(problème, phrase, mouvement)* to break down (**en** into) (**b**) *(matière organique)* to decompose (**c**) *(traits, visage)* to distort; **il est arrivé complètement décomposé** *(par l'émotion)* he arrived quite distraught **2 se décomposer** *vpr* (**a**) *(corps, viande, feuilles)* to decompose; *Fig (tomber en décadence)* to decay (**b**) *(visage, traits)* to become distorted

décomposition [dekɔ̃pozisjɔ̃] *nf* (**a**) *(d'un élément chimique)* decomposition; *(d'un problème, d'une phrase, d'un mouvement)* breaking down (**en** into) (**b**) *(de viande, de feuilles, de corps)* decomposition; *Fig (décadence)* decay

décompresser [dekɔ̃prese] **1** *vt Tech* to decompress; *Ordinat* to decompress, to unbundle, to uncrunch **2** *vi Fam* to unwind

décompression [dekɔ̃presjɔ̃] *nf* decompression; *Ordinat* decompression, unbundling; **avoir un accident de d.** *(plongeur)* to get the bends

décompte [dekɔ̃t] *nm (sur une somme à payer)* deduction; *(calcul)* calculation

décompter [dekɔ̃te] *vt* to deduct (**de** from)

déconcentrer [dekɔ̃sɑ̃tre] **1** *vt* (**a**) *(pouvoirs, administration)* to devolve, to decentralize (**b**) *(distraire)* to distract **2 se déconcentrer** *vpr* to lose concentration

déconcertant, -e [dekɔ̃sɛrtɑ̃, -ɑ̃t] *adj* disconcerting

déconcerté, -e [dekɔ̃sɛrte] *adj* disconcerted

déconcerter [dekɔ̃sɛrte] *vt* to disconcert

déconfit, -e [dekɔ̃fi, -it] *adj (personne, mine)* crestfallen

déconfiture [dekɔ̃fityr] *nf (échec)* defeat

décongeler [39] [dekɔ̃ʒle] *vt* to defrost, to thaw

décongestionner [dekɔ̃ʒɛstjɔne] *vt aussi Fig* to relieve congestion in

déconnecter [dekɔnɛkte] *vt (fil)* to disconnect; *Fig* **déconnecté de la réalité** out of touch with the real world

déconner [dekɔne] *vi très Fam* (a) *(dire des bêtises)* to talk garbage; *(faire des bêtises)* to piss around; **faire qch pour d.** *(pour rire)* to do sth for a laugh; **sans d., c'était super** no kidding, it was great; **sans d.!** *(en réponse)* no kidding! (b) *(mal fonctionner)* to play up

déconneur, -euse [dekɔnœr, -øz] *nm,f très Fam* clown

déconseiller [dekɔ̃seje] *vt* **d. qch à qn** to advise sb against sth; **d. à qn de faire qch** to advise sb against doing sth; **un livre à d. aux jeunes** an unsuitable book for young people; **il est déconseillé de faire qch** it is inadvisable to do sth

déconsidérer [34] [dekɔ̃sidere] **1** *vt* to discredit
2 se déconsidérer *vpr* to bring discredit on oneself

décontamination [dekɔ̃taminasjɔ̃] *nf* decontamination

décontaminer [dekɔ̃tamine] *vt* to decontaminate

décontenancer [16] [dekɔ̃tnɑ̃se] **1** *vt* to disconcert
2 se décontenancer *vpr* to become disconcerted

décontracté, -e [dekɔ̃trakte] *adj (ambiance, attitude, personne)* relaxed; *(vêtement)* casual; *Péj (désinvolte)* casual

décontraction [dekɔ̃traksjɔ̃] *nf* relaxation; **faire qch avec d.** to do sth casually

déconvenue [dekɔ̃vny] *nf Formel* disappointment; **quelle ne fut pas ma d. quand...** I was so disappointed when...

décor [dekɔr] *nm* (a) *(d'une maison, d'un restaurant)* décor (b) *Th, Cin & TV* **décors** set, scenery; **en d. naturel** on location; *Fam* **aller/envoyer qn dans le d.** *(en voiture)* to go/knock sb off the road (c) *(environnement)* surroundings; *Fig* **il aurait besoin d'un changement** *ou* **de changer de d.** he needs a change of scene

décorateur, -trice [dekɔratœr, -tris] *nm,f* (a) *(d'intérieur)* (interior) decorator (b) *Th* set designer

décoratif, -ive [dekɔratif, -iv] *adj* decorative; *(arbre)* ornamental; *Péj* **n'avoir qu'un rôle d.** to have a purely decorative role

décoration [dekɔrasjɔ̃] *nf* (a) *(d'une maison, d'un restaurant)* decoration; **faire de la d.** to decorate; **d. d'intérieur** interior decorating; **décorations de Noël** Christmas decorations (b) *(médaille)* decoration

décorer [dekɔre] *vt* (a) *(pièce, maison)* to decorate (**de** with) (b) *(médailler)* to decorate (**de** with)

décorticage [dekɔrtikaʒ] *nm (de crevettes, de noisettes)* shelling; *(de riz, d'orge)* hulling; *Fig (d'un texte, d'un auteur)* detailed analysis

décortiquer [dekɔrtike] *vt (crevettes, noisettes)* to shell; *(riz, orge)* to hull; *Fig (texte)* to analyse in detail

décorum [dekɔrɔm] *nm* decorum

découcher [dekuʃe] *vi* to stay out all night

découdre [21] [dekudr] **1** *vt (vêtement, poche, ourlet)* to unpick, to unstitch; *(bouton)* to take off
2 *vi* **en d.** to fight
3 se découdre *vpr (vêtement, poche, ourlet)* to come unstitched; *(bouton)* to come off

découler [dekule] *vi* to follow (**de** from); **il en découle que...** it follows that...

découpage [dekupaʒ] *nm* (a) *(de gâteau)* cutting up; *(de viande)* carving; *(de métaux, du cuir)* punching; *Ordinat (de fichier, d'image)* splitting; *Pol* **d. électoral** division into constituencies (b) *(image découpée)* cutout; **faire du d.** *ou* **des découpages** to do some cutting out (c) *Fig (d'un texte)* division (**en** into); *Cin (scénario)* shooting script

découpé, -e [dekupe] *adj (irrégulier)* jagged

découper [dekupe] **1** *vt* (a) *(gâteau, papier)* to cut up; *(viande)* to carve; *(métaux, cuir)* to punch; *Ordinat (fichier)* to split; *(disque dur)* to partition; **d. un article dans un journal** to cut an article out of a newspaper (b) *Fig (texte)* to divide (**en** into)
2 se découper *vpr* **se d. sur** to stand out against

décourageant, -e [dekuraʒɑ̃, -ɑ̃t] *adj (nouvelle, situation, travail)* disheartening; *(personne)* hopeless

découragement [dekuraʒmɑ̃] *nm* discouragement

décourager [45] [dekuraʒe] **1** *vt* (a) *(démoraliser)* to discourage, to dishearten; **se laisser d.** to be discouraged *or* disheartened (b) *(dissuader)* to discourage; **d. qn de faire qch** to discourage sb from doing sth
2 se décourager *vpr* to get discouraged *or* disheartened

décousu, -e [dekuzy] *adj (ourlet, poche, vêtement)* unstitched; *Fig (phrases, idées)* disjointed; *(conversation)* rambling; *(travail)* unmethodical

découvert, -e [dekuvɛr, -ɛrt] **1** *adj (épaules)* bare; *(terrain)* open; **dormir d.** to sleep without any covers; **la tête découverte** bareheaded
2 *nm* (a) *Fin* **d. (bancaire)** overdraft; **être à d. (de 2000 euros)** *(personne, compte)* to be overdrawn (by 2,000 euros) (b) **agir à d.** to act openly; **s'avancer à d.** to move forward without cover

découverte [dekuvɛrt] *nf* discovery; **aller** *ou* **partir à la d. de qch** to go off to explore sth; **faire une d.** to make a discovery; *Hum* **ce n'est pas une d.!** that's nothing new!

découvrir [52] [dekuvrir] **1** *vt* (a) *(trouver)* to discover (b) *(mettre à jour) (secret, complot)* to uncover; **d. qch à qn** *(projets, secrets)* to disclose *or* reveal sth to sb (c) *(apprendre à connaître) (domaine, art, sentiment)* to discover; *(personne)* to get to know (d) *(casserole, statue)* to uncover; *(dents, bras)* to bare; **une robe avec un décolleté qui découvre les épaules** an off-the-shoulder dress; *aussi Fig* **d. son jeu** to show one's hand (e) *(apercevoir)* to have a view of
2 se découvrir *vpr* (a) *(enlever son chapeau)* to take off one's hat (b) *(en dormant)* **le malade s'est découvert** the patient threw off his bedclothes (c) *(ciel)* to clear (d) *(se trouver)* to discover; **se d. des parents éloignés** to discover some distant relatives; **il s'est découvert un don pour la cuisine** he discovered he had a gift for cooking

décrasser [dekrase] **1** *vt* to clean; *Fam Fig* **d. qn** to knock the rough edges off sb
2 se décrasser *vpr* to clean oneself up; *Fig (en faisant de l'exercice)* to tone up

décrêper [dekrepe] *vt (cheveux)* to straighten

décrépit, -ite [dekrepi, -it] *adj (maison, mur, personne)* decrepit

décrépitude [dekrepityd] *nf* decrepitude; *(décadence)* decay

décret [dekrɛ] *nm* decree

décréter [34] [dekrete] *vt* (a) *Jur (état d'urgence, nomination)* to decree (b) *(décider)* **d. que** to vow (that)

décrié, -e [dekrije] *adj* disparaged

décrire [30] [dekrir] *vt* (a) *(représenter)* to describe (b) **d. un cercle** to circle; **d. une courbe** to curve

décrispation [dekrispasjɔ̃] *nf Pol* détente

décrisper [dekrispe] **1** *vt (personne)* to relax; *(atmosphère)* to lighten
2 se décrisper *vpr* to relax

décrocher [dekrɔʃe] **1** vt **(a)** (détacher) (vêtement d'une patère, rideaux, tableau) to take down (**de** from); (wagons) to uncouple; (combiné) to pick up; **d.** (le téléphone) (pour répondre) to pick up the phone; (pour ne pas être dérangé) to take the phone off the hook; **décrochez** (dans cabine téléphonique) lift the receiver (**b**) (recevoir) (poste, prix, contrat) to land; Fam **d. la timbale** to hit the jackpot
2 vi Fam **(a)** (ne plus se concentrer) to switch off; (être à la traîne) to fail to keep up (**b**) (arrêter de se droguer) to kick the habit
3 se décrocher vpr (rideau, tableau) to come unhooked (**de** from); (vêtement) to fall down (**de** from); (collier) to come undone; (wagon) to come uncoupled (**de** from); **se d. la mâchoire** to dislocate one's jaw

décrocheur, -euse [dekrɔʃœr, -øz] nmf Can dropout

décroiser [dekrwaze] vt (jambes, bras) to uncross

décroissant, -e [dekrwasɑ̃, -ɑ̃t] adj decreasing; **par ordre d.** in descending order

décroître [4a] [dekrwatr] vi (forces, population, nombre, intensité) to decrease; (journées) to draw in, to get shorter; (lune) to wane; (eaux) to subside; **aller (en) décroissant** to be decreasing

décrotter [dekrɔte] vt (chaussures, semelles) to clean the mud off; Fam Fig (personne) to knock the rough edges off

décrue [dekry] nf (de rivière) drop in level

décrypter [dekripte] vt to decipher

déçu, -e [desy] **1** pp voir **décevoir**
2 adj disappointed; Fig & Ironique **elle ne va pas être déçue (du voyage)** she's in for a disappointment

déculottée [dekylɔte] nf Fam hammering

déculotter [dekylɔte] **1** vt **d. qn** (enlever son slip) to take sb's underpants off; (enlever son pantalon) to take sb's Br trousers or Am pants off
2 se déculotter vpr (enlever son slip) to take one's underpants off; (enlever son pantalon) to take off one's Br trousers or Am pants; Fig (s'abaisser) to grovel (**devant** to)

déculpabiliser [dekylpabilize] **1** vt **d. qn** to stop sb feeling guilty
2 se déculpabiliser vpr to stop feeling guilty

décuple [dekypl] nm **le d. de qch** ten times sth

décupler [dekyple] **1** vt to increase tenfold; Fig **la terreur décupla ses forces** terror gave her the strength of ten people
2 vi to increase tenfold

dédaigner [dedeɲe] vt (offre) to scorn; (injure, conseil, gloire) to disregard; (personne) to despise; **il ne dédaigne pas un cigare de temps en temps** he is not averse to the occasional cigar

dédaigneusement [dedeɲøzmɑ̃] adv scornfully, disdainfully

dédaigneux, -euse [dedeɲø, -øz] adj scornful, disdainful (**de** of)

dédain [dedɛ̃] nm scorn, disdain (**pour qn/de qch** for sb/sth); **avec d.** scornfully, with disdain

dédale [dedal] nm aussi Fig maze

dedans [dədɑ̃] **1** adv inside; **la lettre est d.** the letter is inside; **c'est un bon film mais il y a trop de violence d.** it's a good film but there's too much violence in it; **de d.** (depuis l'intérieur) from inside; **en d.** (d'un objet) (on the) inside; (en son for intérieur) inwardly; **marcher les pieds en d.** to be pigeon-toed; **en d. de** inside
2 nm (d'une maison, d'une boîte) inside; **du d.** (depuis l'intérieur) from inside

dédicace [dedikas] nf **(a)** (de livre, de photo) dedication (**b**) (à la radio) dedication

dédicacer [16] [dedikase] vt **(a)** (signer) to sign (**à** for);

(écrire dans) (livre) to write a dedication in (**à** to); (photo) to write a dedication on (**à** to) (**b**) (chanson) to dedicate (**à** to)

dédier [66] [dedje] vt to dedicate (**à** to)

dédire [27a] [dedir] **se dédire** vpr **se d. d'une déclaration** to retract or to withdraw a statement; **se d. d'une promesse** to go back on one's word

dédommagement [dedɔmaʒmɑ̃] nm compensation; **50 000 euros de d.** 50,000 euros (in) compensation; **en d. de qch** in compensation for sth

dédommager [45] [dedɔmaʒe] vt (financièrement) to compensate (**de** for); **pour me d., il m'a invité au restaurant** he took me out for a meal to make up for it

dédouanement [dedwanmɑ̃] nm clearance through customs

dédouaner [dedwane] **1** vt (marchandise) to clear (through customs); Fig (personne) to clear
2 se dédouaner vpr to clear one's name

dédoublement [dedublamɑ̃] nm **d. de la personnalité** split personality

dédoubler [deduble] **1** vt (partager) to divide or split into two
2 se dédoubler vpr Psy to have a split personality; Hum **je ne peux pas me d.** I can't be in two places at once

dédramatiser [dedramatize] vt **d. qch** to make sth less dramatic

déductible [dedyktibl] adj deductible; **d. des impôts** tax-deductible

déduction [dedyksjɔ̃] nf **(a)** (soustraction, abattement) deduction; **d. faite de** after deducting (**b**) (conclusion) deduction

déduire [18] [deduir] vt **(a)** (enlever) to deduct (**de** from) (**b**) (conclure) to deduce (**de** from)

déesse [deɛs] nf goddess

défaillance [defajɑ̃s] nf **(a)** (insuffisance) (morale) failing; (physique) deficiency; (d'une machine) failure; **avoir des défaillances en** (intellectuelles) to have problems with; **courage sans d.** unfailing courage; **d. cardiaque** heart failure (**b**) (évanouissement) fainting fit; (faiblesse) feeling of weakness; **avoir une d.** (s'évanouir) to faint; (se sentir faible) to feel weak

défaillant, -e [defajɑ̃, -ɑ̃t] adj (**a**) (forces, mémoire, santé) failing; (cœur) weak; (voix) faltering (**b**) (qui s'évanouit) faint

défaillir [35] [defajir] vi (**a**) (faiblir) (mémoire, forces) to fail; **à cette nouvelle, son cœur défaillit** her heart sank at the news (**b**) (s'évanouir) to faint; **d. de faim/de bonheur** to feel faint with hunger/happiness

défaire [36] [defɛr] **1** vt **(a)** (ouvrir, détacher) to undo; (valise) to unpack; **d. le lit** (enlever les draps) to strip the bed; (le mettre en désordre) to rumple the bedclothes; **d. ses cheveux** to let one's hair down (**b**) (désassembler) (puzzle) to take apart; (ourlet) to undo
2 se défaire vpr (**a**) (se dénouer) (vêtement, nœud) to come undone; (cheveux) to come down (**b**) (se désagréger) (puzzle) to come apart; (ourlet) to come undone; Fig (alliance, mariage) to break up (**c**) **se d. de qn/qch** to get rid of sb/sth; **je ne veux pas m'en d.** I don't want to part with it (**d**) (s'altérer) (visage) to drop

défait, -e [defɛ, -ɛt] adj (traits, visage) haggard; **il est arrivé à l'hôpital, complètement d.** he arrived at the hospital in total distress

défaite [defɛt] nf defeat

défaitisme [defetism] nm defeatism

défaitiste [defetist] adj & nmf defeatist

défalquer [defalke] vt to deduct (**de** from)

défausser [defose] **se défausser** vpr (aux cartes) to

discard; **se d. à cœur** to discard a heart/some hearts; **se d. d'un dix** to discard a ten

défaut [defo] *nm* (**a**) *(imperfection) (d'une personne)* fault, shortcoming; *(d'une pierre précieuse, d'un verre, d'un tissu)* flaw; *(d'une machine)* defect; *(d'un raisonnement)* flaw; *(inconvénient)* drawback; **c'est là son moindre d.** that's the least of his faults; **sans d.** faultless, flawless; **prendre qn en d.** to catch sb napping; **d. de fabrication** manufacturing fault; **d. de prononciation** *ou* **d'élocution** speech impediment (**b**) *(manque)* lack; **le courage lui a fait d.** his courage failed him; **l'argent lui fait cruellement d.** she is very short of money; **le bon sens lui fait cruellement d.** he is sadly lacking in common sense; **ou à d.,...** or, failing that,...; **à d. de qch** for lack of sth; **à d. d'un salaire conséquent, elle a au moins un travail intéressant** she might not have a very good salary, but at least her work is interesting (**c**) *Jur* default; **faire d.** to default; **d. de paiement** default on payment (**d**) *Math* **total approché par d.** total rounded down; *Ordinat* **lecteur/clavier par d.** default drive/keyboard

défaveur [defavœr] *nf* **être en d. (auprès de qn)** to be in disfavour (with sb); **s'attirer la d. de qn** to incur sb's disfavour

défavorable [defavɔrabl] *adj* unfavourable (**à** to)

défavorisé, -e [defavɔrize] *adj (milieu, pays)* underprivileged

défavoriser [defavɔrize] *vt* to put at a disadvantage (**par rapport à** compared to)

défectif, -ive [defɛktif, -iv] *adj* defective

défection [defɛksjɔ̃] *nf* (**a**) *(d'un espion, d'un soldat)* defection (**b**) *(annulation)* cancellation

défectueux, -euse [defɛktɥø, -øz] *adj* defective, faulty

défendable [defɑ̃dabl] *adj* defensible

défendre [defɑ̃dr] **1** *vt* (**a**) *(soutenir)* to defend (**contre** against) (**b**) *(protéger) (personne, pays, propriété)* to defend (**contre** against *ou* from); *(intérêts)* to protect; **d. qn contre le froid** *ou* **du froid** to protect sb from the cold; *Fig* **d. son bifteck** to look after number one (**c**) *(interdire)* to forbid, to prohibit; **ce médicament est défendu aux enfants** this medicine must not be given to children; **d. à qn de faire qch** to forbid sb to do sth; **il m'est défendu de fumer** I'm not allowed to smoke; **il est défendu de fumer** smoking is prohibited

2 se défendre *vpr* (**a**) *(se protéger)* to defend oneself (**de** *ou* **contre** against); **se d. comme un beau diable** to fight like a mad thing (**b**) *Fam (se débrouiller)* **je me défends (en espagnol/en squash)** I can get by (in Spanish/at squash) (**c**) *(se justifier)* **ça se défend** there's something to be said for it (**d**) *(s'empêcher)* **se d. de faire qch** to refrain from doing sth; **on ne peut se d. de les aimer** you can't help liking them

défenestrer [defənɛstre] *vt* to defenestrate

défense¹ [defɑ̃s] *nf* (**a**) *(soutien) (d'une théorie, d'une politique, d'un accusé)* defence; **prendre la d. de qn** to come to sb's defence; **sans d.** defenceless; *Jur* **assurer la d. de qn** to defend sb; **qu'avez-vous à dire pour votre d.?** what do you have to say in your defence?; **d. des consommateurs** consumer protection (**b**) *(protection) (d'une personne, d'un pays, en sport)* defence; **d. aérienne/nationale/passive** air/national/civil defence; *Méd* **défenses immunitaires** immune defences (**c**) *(interdiction)* **d. d'entrer/de fumer** *(sur panneau)* no entry/smoking; **et d. d'en parler à ton père!** don't go telling your father about it!

défense² *nf (d'éléphant, de sanglier)* tusk

défenseur [defɑ̃sœr] *nm* (**a**) *(d'une personne, d'une ville, d'une cause, en sport)* defender; **jouer les défenseurs de la veuve et de l'orphelin** to protect the weak and oppressed (**b**) *Jur* counsel for the defence

défensif, -ive [defɑ̃sif, -iv] *adj* defensive **2** *nf* **être** *ou* **se tenir sur la défensive** to be on the defensive

déféquer [34] [defeke] *vi* to defecate

déférence [deferɑ̃s] *nf* deference (**pour** for)

déférer [34] [defere] *vt Jur* **d. une affaire à un tribunal** to refer a case to a court; **d. qn à la justice** to hand sb over to the police

déferlante [defɛrlɑ̃t] *adj f & nf* **(vague) d.** breaker

déferlement [defɛrləmɑ̃] *nm (des vagues)* breaking; *Fig (de personnes)* invasion; *(d'enthousiasme, de violence, de racisme)* wave

déferler [defɛrle] *vi (vagues)* to break; **la foule déferle dans les rues** the crowd is surging along the streets; **les vacanciers déferlent sur les routes** holiday-makers are taking to the roads in droves

défi [defi] *nm* (**a**) *(acte de provocation)* challenge (**à** to); **lancer** *ou* **jeter un d. à qn** to throw out a challenge to sb; **mettre qn au d. de faire qch** to defy sb to do sth; **relever un d.** to take up a challenge (**b**) *(bravade)* defiance

défiance [defjɑ̃s] *nf* mistrust

déficience [defisjɑ̃s] *nf* deficiency; **d. immunologique** immune deficiency

déficient, -e [defisjɑ̃, -ɑ̃t] **1** *adj* deficient; *(raisonnement, théorie)* weak **2** *nm,f* **d. moteur** person with motor deficiency; **d. mental** mentally deficient person

déficit [defisit] *nm* (**a**) *Fin* deficit; **être en d.** to be in deficit; **d. budgétaire/commercial** budget/trade deficit (**b**) *Méd (mental)* deficiency; **d. immunitaire** immunodeficiency

déficitaire [defisiter] *adj (entreprise)* loss-making; *(compte)* in debit; *(budget)* in deficit

défier [66] [defje] **1** *vt* (**a**) *(provoquer)* to challenge; **d. qn aux échecs** to challenge sb to a game of chess (**b**) *(inciter)* **d. qn de faire qch** to defy sb to do sth (**c**) *(braver) (personne, danger, mort)* to defy (**d**) *(résister à)* **d. l'imagination** to defy the imagination; **des prix qui défient toute concurrence** unbeatable prices **2 se défier** *vpr Litt* **se d. de** to mistrust

défigurer [defigyre] *vt (personne, paysage)* to disfigure; *Fig (vérité, sens)* to distort; *(pensée, intentions)* to misrepresent

défilé [defile] *nm* (**a**) *Géog* (mountain) pass (**b**) *(de manifestants)* march; *(de chars de carnaval)* procession; *Mil* parade; **un d. ininterrompu de touristes/voitures** an endless stream of tourists/cars; **d. aérien** flypast; **d. de mode** fashion show

défilement [defilmɑ̃] *nm Ordinat* scrolling

défiler¹ [defile] **se défiler** *vpr Fam (se dérober)* to slope off

défiler² *vi* (**a**) *(manifestants)* to march; *(chars de carnaval)* to drive in procession; *(touristes, voitures)* to stream; *Mil* to parade (**b**) *(avancer) (bande)* to wind on; *Ordinat* **faire d. un document** to scroll through a document; *Ordinat* **d. vers le bas/le haut** to scroll down/up (**c**) *(se succéder) (images, souvenirs)* to pass; **le paysage défile à toute vitesse** the countryside is speeding past

défini, -e [defini] *adj* (**a**) *(précis)* definite; **bien d.** clearly defined; *Ordinat* **d. par l'utilisateur** user-defined (**b**) *Gram* definite

définir [definir] **1** *vt* to define **2 se définir** *vpr (concept)* **se d. comme** to be defined as (**b**) *(soi-même)* to describe oneself (**comme** as)

définissable [definisabl] *adj* definable

définitif, -ive [definitif, -iv] *adj* (**a**) *(irrévocable) (jugement, décision, version)* final (**b**) *(pour toujours)*

(séparation, fermeture) permanent **(c)** *(qui fait autorité)* definitive **(d)** **en définitive** *(à la fin)* in the end
définition [definisjɔ̃] *nf* **(a)** *(d'un mot, de conditions)* definition; *(de mots croisés)* clue; **par d.** by definition **(b)** *(d'une image sur écran)* definition
définitivement [definitivmɑ̃] *adv (décider)* definitely; *(partir, s'installer)* for good; *(nommé)* permanently
défiscaliser [defiskalize] *vt* to exempt from tax
déflagration [deflagrasjɔ̃] *nf (explosion)* explosion
déflation [deflasjɔ̃] *nf Écon* deflation
déflecteur [deflɛktœr] *nm (d'une voiture) Br* quarterlight, *Am* vent
déflorer [deflɔre] *vt* **(a)** *(vierge)* to deflower **(b)** *Fig (sujet)* to spoil
défoliant [defɔljɑ̃] *nm* defoliant
défonce [defɔ̃s] *nf Fam* **la d.** getting high
défoncé, -e [defɔ̃se] *adj* **(a)** *(chemin)* bumpy **(b)** *Fam (drogué)* high
défoncer [defɔ̃se] **1** *vt (boîte, porte)* to smash in, *(matelas)* to ruin, *(mur)* to knock down, *(tonneau, bateau)* to stave in; *(chaussée)* to break up
2 se défoncer *vpr Fam* **(a)** *(se droguer)* to get high (**à** on) **(b)** *(faire un grand effort)* to sweat blood (**pour faire qch** to do sth)
déforestation [defɔrestasjɔ̃] *nf* deforestation
déformant, -e [defɔrmɑ̃, -ɑ̃t] *adj (glace)* distorting
déformation [defɔrmasjɔ̃] *nf (d'un membre)* deformation; *(d'un vêtement, de chaussures)* putting out of shape; *(du métal)* buckling, *(du bois)* warping; *(des traits, d'une image, des faits)* distortion; *(de propos)* twisting; **ne fais pas attention, c'est de la d. professionnelle!** don't worry, it's just my job!
déformer [defɔrme] **1** *vt (membre)* to deform; *(vêtement, chaussures)* to put out of shape; *(métal)* to buckle; *(bois)* to warp; *(traits, image, faits)* to distort; *(propos)* to twist; *(pensée)* to misrepresent
2 se déformer *vpr (corps, vêtement, chaussures)* to get out of shape; *(bois)* to warp; *(métal)* to buckle
défoulement [defulmɑ̃] *nm Fam* letting off steam, **avoir besoin de d.** to need to let off steam
défouler [defule] *Fam* **1** *vt (agressivité)* to vent (**sur** on); **d. qn** to help sb let off steam; **ça défoule** it helps you let off steam
2 se défouler *vpr* to let off steam; **se d. sur qn** to take it out on sb
défraîchi, -e [defreʃi] *adj (fleur, beauté)* faded; *(vêtement)* shabby
défrayer [defreje] *vt (rembourser)* **d. qn** to pay sb's expenses; **d. la chronique** to be widely talked about
défrichage [defriʃaʒ], **défrichement** [defriʃmɑ̃] *nm (de terrain)* clearing
défricher [defriʃe] *vt* to clear; *Fig (domaine)* to open up; *Fig* **d. le terrain** to prepare the ground
défriser [defrize] *vt (cheveux)* to straighten; *Fam Fig (agacer)* to bug
défroisser [defrwase] *vt* to smooth out
défroqué, -e [defrɔke] *adj* defrocked
défunt, -e [defœ̃, -œ̃t] **1** *adj* **mon d. mari** my late husband; *Litt* **des amours défuntes** lost loves
2 *nmf* deceased; **prier pour les défunts** to pray for the dead
dégagé, -e [degaʒe] *adj (ton, air)* casual; *(ciel, route)* clear; *(vue)* open; **une coupe avec la nuque très dégagée** a haircut that is very short at the back
dégagement [degaʒmɑ̃] *nm* **(a)** *(d'une route, des*

poumons) clearing **(b)** *(au football)* clearance **(c)** *(de vapeur, de gaz, de chaleur)* emission
dégager [45] [degaʒe] **1** *vt* **(a)** *(libérer)* to free (**de** from); *(d'une voiture accidentée, de décombres)* to pull clear (**de** of); **une robe qui dégage les épaules** an off-the-shoulder dress **(b)** *(désencombrer) (route, passage)* to clear; *Fam* **dégage!** clear off! **(c)** *Fam (enlever)* to clear away; **tu vas me d. toutes ces bricoles de tes étagères** I want you to clear all these odds and ends off your shelves **(d)** *(laisser échapper) (vapeur, odeur, chaleur)* to emit; *Fig (impression)* to give off **(e)** *(au football)* **d. (le ballon) en touche** to kick the ball into touch **(f)** *Fin (crédits)* to release; *(profit)* to show
2 se dégager *vpr* **(a)** *(se libérer)* to free oneself (**de** from); *(d'une situation difficile)* to extricate oneself (**de** from) **(b)** *(se débloquer) (ciel, nez)* to clear **(c)** *(gaz, odeur, chaleur)* to be given off (**de** by); *Fig* **le magnétisme qui se dégage d'elle** the magnetism she radiates
dégaine [degɛn] *nf Fam (démarche)* peculiar gait; *(apparence)* strange appearance
dégainer [degene] *vt* to draw
dégarni, -e [degarni] *adj (personne)* balding; **avoir le front d.** to have a receding hairline
dégarnir [degarnir] **1** *vt (frigidaire, rayons)* to empty
2 se dégarnir *vpr (personne)* to go bald; *(arbre)* to lose its leaves; *(salle)* to empty; *(rayons)* to be emptied
dégât [degɑ] *nm* damage; **faire du d.** *ou* **des dégâts** to cause damage, *Fig* **limiter les dégâts** to limit the damage; **dégâts des eaux** water damage; **dégâts matériels** material damage
dégel [deʒɛl] *nm Météo & Pol* thaw; *Écon (des prix, des salaires, des crédits)* unfreezing
dégeler [39] [deʒle] **1** *vt (a) (réchauffer)* to thaw; *(surgelé)* to defrost; *Fig (public)* to warm up; **d. l'atmosphère** to make the atmosphere less chilly **(b)** *Écon (prix, salaires, crédits)* to unfreeze
2 *vi (étang, surgelé)* to thaw; **faire d. qch** *(surgelé)* to defrost sth
3 *v impersonnel* to thaw
4 se dégeler *vpr* **(a)** *(étang)* to thaw **(b)** *Fig (atmosphère)* to become less chilly
dégénératif, -ive [deʒeneratif, -iv] *adj* degenerative
dégénéré, -e [deʒenere] **1** *adj* **(a)** *(arriéré)* mentally defective **(b)** *(dépravé)* degenerate
2 *nmf* **(a)** *(arriéré)* mental defective **(b)** *(dépravé)* degenerate
dégénérer [34] [deʒenere] *vi (mal tourner) (situation, conversation)* to degenerate (**en** into); **son rhume a dégénéré en bronchite** his cold developed into bronchitis
dégénérescence [deʒeneresɑ̃s] *nf Méd & Fig* degeneration
dégingandé, -e [deʒɛ̃gɑ̃de] *adj* gangling, lanky
dégivrage [deʒivraʒ] *nm* **(a)** *(action) (d'un pare-brise)* de-icing; *(d'un réfrigérateur)* defrosting **(b)** *(dispositif) (d'un pare-brise)* de-icer; *(d'un réfrigérateur)* defroster
dégivrer [deʒivre] *vt (pare-brise)* to de-ice; *(réfrigérateur)* to defrost
déglacer [deglase] *vt Culin (poêle à frire)* to deglaze
déglinguer [deglɛ̃ge] *Fam* **1** *vt (appareil)* to bust; *Fam* **moto est toute déglinguée** my motorcycle is falling to pieces
2 se déglinguer *vpr (appareil)* to go wrong; *(véhicule)* to fall to pieces
déglutir [deglytir] *vi* to swallow
déglutition [deglytisjɔ̃] *nf* swallowing
dégobiller [degɔbije] *très Fam* **1** *vi* to puke
2 *vt* to puke up

dégonflé, -e [degɔ̃fle] **1** adj **(a)** (pneu, ballon) flat **(b)** Fam (lâche) chicken
2 nm,f Fam chicken
dégonfler [degɔ̃fle] **1** vt (pneu, ballon) to let the air out of, to deflate
2 vi (partie du corps) to go down
3 se dégonfler vpr **(a)** (pneu, ballon) to go flat **(b)** Fam (personne) to chicken out
dégorger [45] [degɔrʒe] **1** vt **(a)** (évacuer) to discharge; **la rue a dégorgé un flot de gens** a crowd of people surged from the street **(b)** (passage, tuyau, évier) to unblock
2 vi **faire d. des concombres** = to remove water from cucumbers by sprinkling them with salt
dégot(t)er [degɔte] vt Fam to dig up
dégouliner [deguline] vi (liquide) to trickle; **je dégouline** I'm dripping wet
dégoupiller [degupije] vt to pull the pin out of
dégourdi, -e [degurdi] **1** adj smart, bright
2 nm,f **c'est un d.** he's a smart one
dégourdir [degurdir] **1** vt (membres) to remove the stiffness from; Fig **d. qn** to teach sb a thing or two
2 se dégourdir vpr **(a)** (membres) **se d. les jambes** to stretch one's legs **(b)** Fig to learn a thing or two
dégoût [degu] nm **(a)** (aversion) disgust, distaste; **éprouver du d. pour qch** to be disgusted by sth; **prendre qch en d.** to take a strong dislike to sth **(b)** (lassitude) weariness; **le d. de la vie** world-weariness
dégoûtant, -e [degutɑ̃, -ɑ̃t] **1** adj disgusting
2 nm,f disgusting person; **un vieux d.** a dirty old man
dégoûté, -e [degute] **1** adj **(a)** (écœuré) (air) disgusted; Ironique **vous n'êtes pas d.!** you're not fussy! **(b)** (choqué) disgusted **(c)** (las) weary; **être d. de qch** to be sick of sth
2 nm,f **faire le d.** to turn up one's nose
dégoûter [degute] vt **d. qn** (physiquement) to turn sb's stomach; (moralement) to disgust sb, to make sb sick; **d. qn de qch** to put sb off sth; **c'est à vous d. de l'Italie/des hommes!** it's enough to put you off Italy/men for life!
dégoutter [degute] **dégoutter de** vt ind (laisser couler) to drip with
dégradant, -e [degradɑ̃] adj degrading
dégradation [degradasjɔ̃] nf (d'un monument) defacement; (de matériel scolaire, de l'environnement) damage (**de** to); Fig (de la santé, de relations, d'une situation) deterioration
dégradé [degrade] nm (de couleurs) gradation; **se faire faire un d.** (chez le coiffeur) to have one's hair layered; Ordinat **d. de couleur** colour scale
dégrader [degrade] **1** vt **(a)** (abîmer) (monument) to deface; (matériel, maison) to damage; Ordinat (données) to corrupt **(b)** Fig (humilier) to degrade **(c)** Mil to demote
2 se dégrader vpr **(a)** (se détériorer) (santé, relations, situation) to deteriorate; (bâtiment) to fall into disrepair **(b)** (s'abaisser) to degrade oneself
dégrafer [degrafe] **1** vt (vêtement, bracelet) to undo
2 se dégrafer vpr **(a)** (vêtement, bracelet) to come undone **(b)** (femme) to undo one's dress
dégraissage [degrɛsaʒ] nm (d'une entreprise) downsizing
dégraisser [degrese] **1** vt (bouillon) to skim the fat off; Fig (entreprise) to downsize; **d. les effectifs** to cut back on staff
2 vi (entreprise) to downsize
degré [dəgre] nm **(a)** (d'un angle, de chaleur) degree; (de boisson alcoolisée) proof; **combien de degrés fait ce whisky?** what proof is this whisky?; **d. Celsius/Fahrenheit** degree Celsius/Fahrenheit **(b)** (stade, niveau) stage; **d. de parenté** family relationship; **cousins au second d.** second cousins; **brûlure au deuxième/**

troisième d. second/third degree burn; **au plus haut d.** (extrêmement) in the extreme; **jusqu'à un certain d.** up to a point; **par degrés** by degrees; **prendre une plaisanterie au premier d.** to take a joke seriously **(c)** (d'escalier) step; (d'échelle) rung
dégressif, -ive [degresif, -iv] adj **tarif d.** tapering rate; **impôt d.** degressive taxation
dégrèvement [degrɛvmɑ̃] nm **d. (fiscal)** tax relief
dégriffé, -e [degrife] **1** adj = with its designer label removed and reduced in price
2 nm = reduced-price designer item with its label removed
dégringolade [degrɛ̃gɔlad] nf Fam (chute) tumble; Fig (d'une entreprise) collapse; (des prix, des cours) slump (**de** in)
dégringoler [degrɛ̃gɔle] Fam **1** vt to rush down
2 vi (personne) to tumble; Fig (entreprise) to collapse; (prix, cours) to slump
dégripper [degripe] vt (mécanisme) to unjam
dégriser [degrize] vt to sober up; Fig to bring down to earth
dégrossir [degrosir] vt (bois) to trim; (pierre) to roughhew; Fig (travail) to rough out; **d. qn** to knock the rough edges off sb; **être mal dégrossi** to be uncouth
dégrouper [degrupe] vt to divide into groups
déguenillé, -e [degəniʒe] adj ragged
déguerpir [degɛrpir] vi to clear off; **faire d. qn** to chase sb away
dégueulasse [degœlas] très Fam **1** adj (sale) filthy; (mauvais, désagréable) disgusting; **c'est pas d.** (bon) it's not bad at all; **être d. avec qn** to be mean to sb; **se balader en d.** to go around in sloppy old clothes
2 nmf **un gros d.** (sale) a filthy pig; (débauché) a filthy swine
dégueulasser [degœlase] vt très Fam to mess up
dégueuler [degœle] vi très Fam to puke
dégueulis [degœli] nm très Fam puke
déguisé, -e [degize] adj (pour tromper) disguised; (pour s'amuser) dressed up; **avec une joie non déguisée** with unconcealed delight
déguisement [degizmɑ̃] nm (pour tromper) disguise; (pour s'amuser) fancy dress
déguiser [degize] **1** vt **(a)** (costumer) to dress up; **d. qn en clown** to dress sb up as a clown **(b)** (voix, écriture, vérité, pensée) to disguise
2 se déguiser vpr (pour tromper) to disguise oneself; (pour s'amuser) to dress up; **se d. en cow-boy** to dress up as a cowboy
dégurgiter [degyrʒite] vt aussi Fig to regurgitate
dégustation [degystasjɔ̃] nf tasting; **d. de vin** wine tasting; **d. d'huîtres** (panneau devant un restaurant) oysters served here
déguster [degyste] vt **(a)** (tester) (vin, alcool) to taste **(b)** (savourer) (aliment, livre) to savour **(c)** très Fam **toute sa vie, elle a dégusté** (souffert) she's had a rough time of it all her life; **tu vas d.!** you're in for it!
déhanché, -e [deɑ̃ʃe] adj lopsided
déhanchement [deɑ̃ʃmɑ̃] nm (en marchant) swaying of the hips; (à l'arrêt) standing with one's weight on one foot
déhancher [deɑ̃ʃe] **se déhancher** vpr (en marchant) to sway one's hips; (à l'arrêt) to stand with one's weight on one foot
dehors [dəɔr] **1** adv (à l'extérieur) outside; (en plein air) out of doors; (pas chez soi) out; Fam **ficher** ou **foutre qn d.** to kick sb out; **ne pas mettre le nez** ou **les pieds d.** not to set foot outside; **en d.** (s'ouvrir, tourner) outwards; **marcher les**

pieds en d. to walk with one's feet turned out; **en d. de** *(à l'extérieur de)* outside; *(à part)* apart from; **rester en d. d'une dispute** to keep out of an argument; **en d. du sujet** *(remarque)* irrelevant **2** *nm* **(a)** *(extérieur)* outside; **au d.** on the outside; *(se pencher, se répandre)* out **(b)** *(apparence)* **une maison aux d. imposants** a house with an imposing exterior; **sous des d. aimables** under a pleasant exterior

déhoussable [deusabl] *adj (canapé, siège)* with loose covers

déjà [deʒa] *adv* **(a)** *(dès maintenant)* already; *(si tôt)* yet; **il est d. trois heures** it's already three o'clock; **faut-il que vous partiez d.?** do you have to go so soon? **(b)** *(auparavant)* before; **j'avais d. vu ce film** I'd seen that movie before; **d. en 1800** as early as 1800 **(c)** *(intensif)* **j'aurais dû le faire il y a d. trois jours** I should have done it three days ago as it is; **c'est d. ça!, c'est d. pas mal!** that's not bad at all!; **vous avez d. trop de travail** you have too much work as it is; **d. que je n'en ai pas beaucoup, si tu m'en prends la moitié…** I haven't got much as it is, so if you take half… **(d)** *(interrogatif)* **qu'est-ce que vous faites, d.?** what did you say your job was?; **c'est quoi, d., ton nom?** what was your name again?

déjanter [deʒɑ̃te] **1** *vi très Fam (être fou)* to be off one's rocker; *(devenir fou)* to flip one's lid **2 se déjanter** *vpr (pneu)* to come off the rim

déjà-vu [deʒavy] *nm inv* **une impression de d.** a feeling of déjà vu; **c'est du d.** *(ce n'est pas original)* it's the same old thing

déjeuner [deʒœne] **1** *nm* **(a)** *(repas de midi)* lunch; **prendre son d.** to have lunch; **d. d'affaires/de travail** business/working lunch **(b)** *(repas du matin)* **(petit) d.** breakfast **(c)** *(tasse et soucoupe)* breakfast cup and saucer **2** *vi* **(a)** *(le matin)* to have breakfast **(b)** *(à midi)* to have lunch; **nous avons les Marchand à d. dimanche** the Marchands are coming for lunch on Sunday; **d. d'un sandwich** to have a sandwich for lunch

déjouer [deʒwe] *vt (complot, plans)* to foil

délabré, -e [delabre] *adj (bâtiment, meuble)* dilapidated; *(santé)* ruined

délabrement [delabrəmɑ̃] *nm (d'un bâtiment, d'un meuble)* dilapidated state; *(d'une entreprise)* ruin; **dans un état de grand d.** *(bâtiment)* in a state of total disrepair

délabrer [delabre] **se délabrer** *vpr (bâtiment)* to fall into disrepair; *(meuble)* to fall to pieces; *(entreprise)* to go to rack and ruin; *(santé)* to deteriorate

délacer [16] [delase] **1** *vt (chaussures)* to untie; *(corset)* to unlace **2 se délacer** *vpr (chaussures)* to come untied; *(corset)* to come unlaced; *(femme)* to unlace one's corset

délai [dele] *nm* **(a)** *(laps de temps)* time allowed; **dans un d. de dix jours** within ten days; **il faut compter un d. de dix jours** you should allow ten days; **respecter** *ou* **tenir les délais** to meet the deadline; **dans les délais** on time; **dans les plus brefs délais** as soon as possible; **après-demain dernier d.** by the day after tomorrow at the very latest; **d. de livraison: un mois** delivery within one month; **d. de paiement** *(fixé par contrat)* term of payment **(b)** *(prolongation)* extension; **laisser à qn un d. de réflexion** to give sb time to think; **sans d.** without delay, immediately

délaisser [delese] *vt (abandonner)* to desert, to abandon; *(négliger)* to neglect

délassant, -e [delɑsɑ̃] *adj (bain, massage)* relaxing; *(lecture)* entertaining

délassement [delɑsmɑ̃] *nm* relaxation

délasser [delɑse] **1** *vt* to relax **2 se délasser** *vpr* to relax

délateur, -trice [delatœr, -tris] *nm,f* informer

délation [delasjɔ̃] *nf* denouncement

délavé, -e [delave] *adj (tissu, jean)* faded; *(couleur)* watery

délayage [delejaʒ] *nm Péj* padding

délayer [53] [deleje] *vt* **(a)** *(poudre)* to add water to; *(peinture)* to thin; *(liquide)* to water down; **d. de la farine dans du lait** to mix flour with milk **(b)** *Fig (discours, texte)* to pad out

Delco® [delko] *nm Aut* distributor

délectable [delɛktabl] *adj* delectable

délecter [delɛkte] **se délecter** *vpr* **se d. de qch/à faire qch** to take delight in sth/in doing sth

délégation [delegasjɔ̃] *nf* **(a)** *(action de déléguer) (de représentants)* delegation; **agir par d.** to act on the authority invested in one; **d. de pouvoir** delegation of authority **(b)** *(groupe)* delegation

délégué, -e [delege] *nm,f* delegate; *Scol* **d. (de classe)** class representative *(at class meetings)*; **d. du personnel** staff representative; **d. syndical** union representative; *(d'usine)* shop steward

déléguer [34] [delege] *vt* **(a)** *(personne)* to delegate **(b)** *(transmettre) (pouvoirs)* to delegate (**à** to); **c'est un patron qui sait d.** he's a boss who knows how to delegate

délestage [delɛstaʒ] *nm (d'un navire, d'un ballon)* unballasting; **pour assurer le d. des grandes artères** to relieve congestion on the main roads

délester [delɛste] *vt (navire, ballon)* to unballast; *(voie de communication)* to relieve congestion on; *aussi Hum* **d. qn de qch** to relieve sb of sth

délibération [deliberasjɔ̃] *nf* **(a)** *(débat)* deliberation; **être en d.** to be under discussion **(b)** *(réflexion)* deliberation; **après mûre d.** after careful consideration

délibéré, -e [delibere] **1** *adj (intentionnel)* deliberate **2** *nm Jur (de juges)* consultation

délibérément [deliberemɑ̃] *adv* deliberately

délibérer [34] [delibere] *vi* **(a)** *(discuter)* to deliberate *(de ou sur on)*; *Jur (jury)* to consider its verdict **(b)** *(réfléchir)* to deliberate

délicat, -e [delika, -at] *adj* **(a)** *(fragile, fin, difficile)* delicate; *(peau)* sensitive; *(travail)* fine **(b)** *(raffiné) (goûts)* refined; *(gestes)* graceful; *(plat)* sophisticated; **avoir le palais d.** to have a discerning palate **(c)** *(plein de tact)* tactful; **quelle attention délicate!** how thoughtful!; **peu d.** *(peu scrupuleux)* unscrupulous **(d)** *(exigeant)* fussy; **faire le d.** turn up one's nose

délicatement [delikatmɑ̃] *adv* *(légèrement)* gently; *(finement)* finely

délicatesse [delikatɛs] *nf* **(a)** *(d'un objet)* fragility; *(d'une fleur, d'un tissu, d'un coloris)* delicacy; *(de la peau)* sensitivity; *(de la santé)* frailty **(b)** *(des goûts)* refinement; *(des gestes)* gracefulness; *(d'un plat)* sophistication; **avec d.** *(légèrement)* gently; *(finement)* finely **(c)** *(difficulté)* delicacy **(d)** *(tact)* tact; **avec d.** tactfully

délice [delis] *nm (plaisir)* delight; **ce gâteau est un vrai d.** this cake is absolutely delicious

délices [delis] *nfpl Litt ou Hum* delights; **faire ses d. de qch** to delight in sth

délicieusement [delisjøzmɑ̃] *adv* *(agréablement)* delightfully; **d. bon** *(plat)* absolutely delicious

délicieux, -euse [delisjø, -øz] *adj (nourriture, sensation, chaleur)* delicious; *(personne, robe)* delightful

délictueux, -euse [deliktɥø, -øz] *adj Jur* **acte d.** offence

délié, -e [delje] **1** *adj (taille)* slim; *(doigts)* nimble **2** *nm (de l'écriture)* thin stroke

délier [66] [delje] **1** *vt* to untie; **d. qn d'une promesse** to release sb from a promise; *Fig* **le vin lui a délié la langue** the wine loosened his tongue **2 se délier** *vpr (se défaire)* to come untied; *Fig* **sa langue s'est déliée** he/she found his/her tongue

délimiter [delimite] *vt (territoire)* to demarcate; *(responsabilité, sujet)* to define

délinquance [delɛ̃kɑ̃s] *nf* delinquency; **d. juvénile** juvenile delinquency; **la petite d. des banlieues** petty crime in the suburbs

délinquant, -e [delɛ̃kɑ̃, -ɑ̃t] **1** *adj* delinquent **2** *nm,f* offender; **d. juvénile** juvenile delinquent

déliquescence [delikesɑ̃s] *nf Péj (d'une civilisation, des mœurs)* decay; **tomber en d.** to fall into decay

déliquescent, -e [delikesɑ̃] *adj Péj (civilisation, mœurs)* decadent

délirant, -e [delirɑ̃, -ɑ̃t] *adj Méd* delirious; *Fig (joie, imagination)* frenzied; **c'est d. de leur demander de tout payer!** it's crazy asking them to pay for everything!

délire [delir] *nm* **(a)** *Méd* delirium; **avoir le d.** to be delirious; *Fig* **c'est du d.!** it's crazy!; **d. de grandeur** delusions of grandeur; **d. de persécution** persecution complex **(b)** *(frénésie)* frenzy; **foule en d.** frenzied crowd; *Fam* **cette soirée, c'est le d.!** it's a wild party!

délirer [delire] *vi (être malade)* to be delirious; *(dire n'importe quoi)* to rave

delirium tremens [delirjɔmtremɛ̃s] *nm* delirium tremens; **avoir le d.** to have delirium tremens

délit [deli] *nm* offence; **d. de fuite** failure to report an accident; **d. d'initié** insider dealing *or* trading

délivrance [delivrɑ̃s] *nf* **(a)** *(soulagement)* relief; **leur départ fut une vraie d.** it was a real relief when they left **(b)** *(accouchement)* delivery **(c)** *(d'un certificat, d'un passeport, d'un permis)* issue

délivrer [delivre] **1** *vt* **(a)** *(libérer) (captif, otage)* to rescue; *(ville)* to liberate; *(peuple)* to set free; **d. qn de ses liens** to free sb from his bonds **(b)** *(soulager)* **d. qn d'un secret trop lourd** to share the burden of a secret with sb; **d. qn d'un grand poids** to take a weight off sb's shoulders **(c)** *(remettre) (marchandises)* to deliver; *(certificat, passeport, permis)* to issue **2 se délivrer** *vpr* to free oneself (**de** from)

délocalisation [delɔkalizasjɔ̃] *nf* relocation

déloger [45] [delɔʒe] *vt (envahisseur)* to drive out (**de** from); *(locataire)* to evict; *(objet coincé)* to dislodge (**de** from)

déloyal, -e, -aux, -ales [delwajal, -o] *adj (ami)* disloyal, unfaithful; *(adversaire, pratique, concurrence)* unfair; *(coup)* illegal

delta [dɛlta] *nm* **(a)** *(d'un fleuve)* delta **(b)** *Av* **(aile) d.** delta wing

deltaplane [dɛltaplan] *nm* hang-glider; **faire du d.** to go hang-gliding

déluge [delyʒ] *nm (de pluie)* downpour; *(d'injures)* torrent; *(de larmes)* flood; *Rel* **le D.** the Flood; **noyer qn sous un d. de compliments** to shower sb with compliments; **après moi le d.!** when I'm gone I don't care what happens!

déluré, -e [delyre] *adj (vif)* sharp, smart; *Péj (provocant)* forward

démagogie [demagɔʒi] *nf* demagogy

démagogique [demagɔʒik] *adj* demagogic

démagogue [demagɔg] *nmf* demagogue

demain [dəmɛ̃] **1** *adv* tomorrow; **d. soir** tomorrow evening; **d. en huit** a week tomorrow, tomorrow week; **à**

d.! see you tomorrow!; **le journal de d.** tomorrow's paper; *Fam* **ce n'est pas pour d., ce n'est pas d. la veille** that won't happen for a long time yet; *Fig* **d. il fera jour** tomorrow is another day; *Fig* **de d.** *(de l'avenir)* of tomorrow **2** *nm* tomorrow; **tu as tout d. pour y réfléchir** you've got all tomorrow to think about it

demande [dəmɑ̃d] *nf* **(a)** *(requête)* request (**de** for); *(formulaire)* application form; **faire une d. de qch** *(de permis, de prêt)* to apply for sth; **faire qch à** *ou* **sur la d. de qn** to do sth at sb's request; **à la d. générale** by popular demand; **sur d.** on request; **demandes d'emploi** *(titre de rubrique)* situations wanted; **d. (en mariage)** proposal (of marriage); **faire sa d. (en mariage)** to propose; **d. de rançon** ransom demand **(b)** *Écon* demand; **d. des consommateurs** consumer demand **(c)** *Jur* **d. en divorce** divorce petition; **d. de dommages-intérêts** claim for damages **(d)** *(besoin) (de soins, d'affection)* need

demander [dəmɑ̃de] **1** *vt* **(a)** *(réclamer) (augmentation, addition, preuves)* to ask for; *(dommages et intérêts)* to claim; **d. qch à qn** to ask sb for sth; *(service)* to ask sb; **d. à qn de faire qch** to ask sb to do sth; **d. à manger/boire** to ask for something to eat/drink; **d. son avis à qn** to ask sb's opinion; **d. le divorce** to apply for a divorce; **d. la main de qn** to ask for sb's hand (in marriage); **d. qn en mariage** to propose to sb; **d. la parole** to ask to speak; **d. la permission de faire qch** to ask (for) permission to do sth; **combien demandez-vous de l'heure?** how much do you charge an hour?; **combien en demande-t-elle?** how much is she asking for it?; **je ne demande pas mieux que de vous aider** I'll be only too pleased to help you; **il ne demande que ça** he'd be only too pleased; *Hum* **que demande le peuple?** what more could I/he/*etc* ask?; **je ne demande qu'une seule chose, qu'on me laisse tranquille** all I ask is to be left alone; **on demande un maçon** *(dans une petite annonce)* builder wanted; **être très demandé** to be in great demand; **il n'y a qu'à** *ou* **il suffit de d.** you/he/*etc* only have/has to ask **(b)** *(nécessiter) (tact, réflexion, attention)* to require; **ça demande de gros sacrifices** great sacrifices are called for **(c)** *(exiger)* to demand; **en d. trop à qn** to ask too much of sb; **d. l'impossible** to ask the impossible **(d)** *(s'enquérir de) (prix, cause, raison)* to ask; **d. qch à qn** to ask sb sth; **il m'a demandé de tes nouvelles** he asked after you; *Fam* **je ne t'ai rien demandé!** I didn't ask for your advice!; **je vous (le) demande, je vous demande un peu!** I ask you! **(e)** *(appeler) (médecin, prêtre)* to ask for; **on vous demande** you're wanted; **on vous demande au téléphone** there's a call for you **2 demander à** *vt ind* **d. à faire qch** to ask to do sth; **les suspects ne demandaient qu'à parler** the suspects were only too willing to speak; **demande à ce qu'on vienne te chercher** ask someone to come and collect you **3 se demander** *vpr* to wonder, to ask oneself; **c'est à se d. si...** it makes you wonder whether...; **des choses comme ça, ça ne se demande pas!** you don't ask that sort of question!

demandeur, -euse [dəmɑ̃dœr, -øz] *nm,f* **d. d'asile** asylum seeker; **d. d'emploi** job seeker

démangeaison [demɑ̃ʒɛzɔ̃] *nf* itch; **avoir une d.** to have an itch, to be itching; **j'ai des démangeaisons aux les jambes** my legs are itchy

démanger [45] [demɑ̃ʒe] *vi* to itch; **l'épaule me démange** my shoulder's itching; *Fig* **méfie-toi, la main me démange!** watch out *or* you'll feel the back of my hand!; **ça me démange de lui dire ce que je pense** I'm itching to tell him/her what I think

démantèlement [demɑ̃tɛlmɑ̃] *nm* breaking up

démanteler [39] [demɑ̃tle] *vt* to break up

démantibuler [demɑ̃tibyle] *Fam* **1** *vt* to break up **2 se démantibuler** *vpr* to come to pieces

démaquillage [demakijaʒ] *nm* removal of make-up

démaquillant, -e [demakijɑ̃] **1** *adj* cleansing **2** *nm* cleanser; **d. pour les yeux** eye make-up remover

démaquiller [demakije] **1** *vt* **d. qn** to remove sb's make-up **2 se démaquiller** *vpr* to remove one's make-up; **se d. les yeux** to remove one's eye make-up

démarcation [demarkasjɔ̃] *nf* demarcation

démarchage [demarʃaʒ] *nm* (*porte-à-porte*) door-to-door selling; **d. électoral** canvassing; **d. par téléphone** telesales

démarche [demarʃ] *nf* (**a**) (*allure*) gait, walk (**b**) (*requête*) step; **faire une d. auprès de qn** to approach sb; **faire les démarches nécessaires pour faire qch** to take the necessary steps to do sth (**c**) *Fig* (*cheminement*) process; **d. intellectuelle** thought process

démarcher [demarʃe] *vt* to canvass for

démarcheur, -euse [demarʃœr, -øz] *nm,f* door-to-door salesman, *f* saleswoman

démarque [demark] *nf Com* markdown; **la d. inconnue** shrinkage

démarquer [demarke] **1** *vt* (*marchandises*) to mark down **2 se démarquer** *vpr Sp* to lose one's marker; *Fig* **se d. de qn** (*se distinguer*) to distinguish oneself from sb

démarrage [demaraʒ] *nm* (*d'un moteur*) starting; (*d'un projet, d'une campagne publicitaire*) start-up; **au d.** (*d'un véhicule*) when moving off; **faire un d.** (*coureur*) to put on a spurt; *Ordinat* **d. à chaud/froid** warm/cold boot; **d. en côte** hill start

démarrer [demare] **1** *vi* (**a**) (*véhicule*) to move off; (*moteur*) to start; (*conducteur*) to drive off (**b**) (*commencer*) to start; **bien/mal d.** to get off to a good/bad start (**c**) (*commencer à réussir*) to take off **2** *vt* to start; *Ordinat* to boot (up), to start up

démarreur [demarœr] *nm Aut* starter (motor)

démasquer [demaske] *vt aussi Fig* to unmask

démâter [demate] **1** *vt* to dismast **2** *vi* to lose its mast

démêlant [demelɑ̃] *adj m & nm* (**produit**) **d.** conditioner

démêlé [demele] *nm* disagreement (**avec** with); **avoir des démêlés avec la justice** to be in trouble with the law

démêler [demele] **1** *vt* (*fil, laine, cheveux*) to untangle; (*mystère*) to unravel; **d. le vrai du faux** to disentangle the truth from the lies **2 se démêler** *vpr* **se d. de** to extricate oneself from

démembrement [demɑ̃brəmɑ̃] *nm* (*d'un empire*) breaking up; (*d'une propriété agricole*) division

démembrer [demɑ̃bre] *vt* (*empire*) to break up; (*propriété agricole*) to divide (up)

déménagement [demenaʒmɑ̃] *nm* move; **c'est pour quand le d.?** when are you/we/*etc* moving?

déménager [45] [demenaʒe] **1** *vi* (**a**) (*personne, entreprise*) to move; **où déménage-t-il?** where's he moving to?; **d. à la cloche de bois** to leave in the middle of the night; *Fam* **allez, déménagez!** beat it! (**b**) *Fam Fig* (*musique*) to be mind-blowing; (*cocktail*) to pack a punch **2** *vt* (*meubles*) to move

déménageur [demenaʒœr] *nm Br* removal man, *Am* furniture mover; **avoir des épaules de d.** to have strong broad shoulders

démence [demɑ̃s] *nf* insanity; *Méd* dementia; *Fam* **c'est de la d.!** it's madness!

démener [46] [demne] **se démener** *vpr* (**a**) (*s'agiter*) to thrash about; **se d. comme un beau diable** (*pour se libérer*) to thrash out (**b**) (*se dépenser*) to exert oneself

dément, -e [demɑ̃, -ɑ̃t] **1** *adj* (*fou*) insane; *Fam* (*formidable*) terrific; *Fam* **c'est d.!** it's unreal! **2** *nm,f* lunatic; *Méd* demented person

démenti [demɑ̃ti] *nm* denial; *Journ* disclaimer; **opposer un d. formel à qch** to issue a firm denial of sth

démentiel, -elle [demɑ̃sjɛl] *adj* (*idée, projet*) insane; *Fam* (*incroyable*) crazy

démentir [64a] [demɑ̃tir] **1** *vt* to deny; (*être en contradiction avec*) to belie **2 se démentir** *vpr* (*cesser*) **leur honnêteté ne s'est jamais démentie** they've always been unfailing in their honesty

démerder [demɛrde] **se démerder** *vpr très Fam* to get by, to manage; **démerde-toi tout seul!** sort it out yourself!; **elle est assez grande pour se d. seule** she's old enough to take care of herself; **elle se démerde pas mal en cuisine/tennis** she's not a bad cook/tennis player; **se d. pour faire qch** to manage to do sth

démériter [demerite] *vi* to be at fault; **je ne vois pas en quoi il a démérité** I don't see how he is at fault

démesure [deməzyr] *nf* excess

démesuré, -e [deməzyre] *adj* (*en taille*) enormous; (*orgueil, ambition*) excessive

démesurément [deməzyremɑ̃] *adv* enormously

démettre¹ [47] [demɛtr] **1** *vt* **il m'a démis l'épaule** he dislocated my shoulder **2 se démettre** *vpr* **se d. l'épaule/le genou** to dislocate one's shoulder/knee

démettre² **1** *vt* **d. qn de ses fonctions** to remove sb from his/her post **2 se démettre** *vpr* **se d. de ses fonctions** to resign from one's post

demeurant [dəmœrɑ̃] **au demeurant** *adv* (*malgré tout*) for all that, (*d'ailleurs*) after all

demeure [dəmœr] *nf* (**a**) (*château*) mansion; *Litt* (*résidence*) (*place of*) residence; *Euph* **dernière d.** last resting place (**b**) **mettre qn en d. de faire qch** to instruct sb to do sth; *Jur* to give sb notice to do sth (**c**) **à d.** permanently

demeuré, -e [dəmœre] **1** *adj Vieilli* mentally retarded; *Fam Péj* halfwitted **2** *nm,f Vieilli* mentally retarded person; *Fam Péj* halfwit

demeurer [dəmœre] *vi* (**a**) (*aux* être) (*rester*) to remain; **d. convaincu que...** to remain convinced that...; **d. fidèle à qn** to remain faithful to sb; **demeurons-en là** let's leave it at that; **il n'en demeure pas moins que...** the fact remains that... (**b**) *Formel* (*aux* avoir) (*habiter*) to reside

demi, -e [dəmi] **1** *adj* (**a**) (*après un nom*) **deux heures et demie** (*durée*) two and a half hours; (*moment*) half past two; **un litre/kilo et d.** a litre/kilo and a half; **il gagne deux fois et demie ce que je gagne** he earns two and a half times as much as I do (**b**) (*avant un nom ou un adjectif*) half; **une d.-cuillère de sucre** half a teaspoon of sugar **2** *nm* (**a**) (*moitié*) half (**b**) (*bière*) **un d.** ≃ a beer (**c**) *Sp* (*au football*) midfielder; **d. de mêlée** (*au rugby*) scrum half; **d. d'ouverture** (*au rugby*) fly half **3** *nf* **demie** (*heure*) **il est la demie** it's half past; **à la demie** at half past **4** *adv* half; **d. plein** half full; **à d. mort** half dead; **faire les choses à d.** to do things by halves; **croire qn à d.** to half believe sb; **ouvrir qch à d.** to half open sth

demiard [dəmjar] *nm Can* half pint

demi-cercle (*pl* demi-cercles) [dəmisɛrkl] *nm* semicircle, half circle; **en d.** in a semicircle

demi-dieu (*pl* demi-dieux) [dəmidjø] *nm* demigod

demi-douzaine (pl **demi-douzaines**) [dəmiduzɛn] nf half-dozen; **une d.** d'œufs/de **tomates** half a dozen eggs/tomatoes

demi-droite (pl **demi-droites**) [dəmidrwat] nf Math half-line

demi-écrémé, -e (mpl **demi-écrémés**, fpl **demi-écrémées**) [dəmiekreme] adj Br semi-skimmed, Am part-skim

demi-finale (pl **demi-finales**) [dəmifinal] nf semifinal

demi-fond [dəmifɔ̃] nm inv Sp **(course de) d.** middle-distance race

demi-frère (pl **demi-frères**) [dəmifrɛr] nm half-brother

demi-gros [dəmigro] nm inv **(commerce de) d.** cash and carry

demi-heure (pl **demi-heures**) [dəmijœr] nf **une d.** half an hour; **toutes les demi-heures** every half-hour

demi-jour (pl **demi-jours**) [dəmiʒur] nm half-light

demi-journée (pl **demi-journées**) [dəmiʒurne] nf half-day

démilitariser [demilitarize] vt to demilitarize

demi-litre (pl **demi-litres**) [dəmilitr] nm half-litre; **un d. de vin** half a litre of wine

demi-lune (pl **demi-lunes**) [dəmilyn] nf half-moon

demi-mesure (pl **demi-mesures**) [dəmiməzyr] nf (compromis) half-measure

demi-mort, -e (mpl **demi-morts**, fpl **demi-mortes**) [dəmimɔr, -mɔrt] adj half-dead

demi-mot [dəmimo] **à demi-mot** adv **comprendre à d.** to take the hint; **nous nous comprenons à d.** we know how each other's mind works

déminage [deminaʒ] nm mine clearance; (en mer) minesweeping

déminer [demine] vt to clear of mines

démineur [deminœr] nm (personne) bomb disposal expert; (navire) minesweeper

demi-pause (pl **demi-pauses**) [dəmipoz] nf Mus Br minim rest, Am half-note rest

demi-pension [dəmipɑ̃sjɔ̃] nf (à l'hôtel) Br half-board, Am breakfast and one meal; **sept jours en d.** seven days Br half-board or Am breakfast and one meal; Scol **être en d.** to be a Br day boarder or Am day student

demi-pensionnaire (pl **demi-pensionnaires**) [dəmipɑ̃sjɔnɛr] nmf (écolier) Br day boarder, Am day student

demi-portion (pl **demi-portions**) [dəmipɔrsjɔ̃] nf Fam Péj weed

demi-queue (pl **demi-queues**) [dəmikø] adj & nm **(piano) d.** baby grand (piano)

démis, -e [demi, -iz] adj dislocated

demi-saison (pl **demi-saisons**) [dəmisɛzɔ̃] nf spring or autumn; **vêtements de d.** spring or autumn clothes

demi-sel [dəmisɛl] adj inv (beurre) slightly salted; **fromage d.** = slightly salted cream cheese

demi-sœur (pl **demi-sœurs**) [dəmisœr] nf half-sister

demi-sommeil (pl **demi-sommeils**) [dəmisɔmɛj] nm half-sleep

demi-soupir (pl **demi-soupirs**) [dəmisupir] nm Mus Br quaver rest, Am eighth-note rest

démission [demisjɔ̃] nf resignation; Fig renunciation; **donner sa d.** to hand in one's resignation

démissionnaire [demisjɔnɛr] adj resigning

démissionner [demisjɔne] vi to resign (**de** from); Fig to give up

demi-tarif [dəmitarif] **1** nm (pl **demi-tarifs**) half-price

2 adj inv **billet d.** (de transports) half-fare (ticket); (de spectacle) half-price ticket

demi-teinte (pl **demi-teintes**) [dəmitɛ̃t] nf halftone; Fig **être tout en demi-teintes** to be subtle in character

demi-ton (pl **demi-tons**) [dəmitɔ̃] nm Mus Br semitone, Am half step

demi-tour (pl **demi-tours**) [dəmitur] nm half-turn; (en voiture) Mil about-turn; **faire d.** to turn back; **faire un d.** (en voiture) to do a U-turn; Mil **d. droite!** right about-turn!

démiurge [demjyrʒ] nm demiurge

demi-volée (pl **demi-volées**) [dəmivɔle] nf (au tennis, au football) half-volley

démobilisation [demɔbilizasjɔ̃] nf (a) (de troupes) demobilization (b) Fig (désintérêt) apathy

démobiliser [demɔbilize] vt (a) (troupes) to demobilize (b) Fig (désintéresser) to demotivate

démocrate [demɔkrat] **1** adj democratic **2** nmf democrat

démocrate-chrétien, -enne (mpl **démocrates-chrétiens**, fpl **démocrates-chrétiennes**) [demɔkrat-kretjɛ̃, -ɛn] adj & nm,f Pol Christian Democrat

démocratie [demɔkrasi] nf democracy

démocratique [demɔkratik] adj democratic

démocratiquement [demɔkratikmɑ̃] adv democratically

démocratisation [demɔkratizasjɔ̃] nf democrati-zation

démocratiser [demɔkratize] **1** vt to democratize **2 se démocratiser** vpr to become (more) democratic

démodé, -e [demɔde] adj old-fashioned

démoder [demɔde] **se démoder** vpr to go out of fashion

démographie [demɔgrafi] nf demography

démographique [demɔgrafik] adj demographic

demoiselle [dəmwazɛl] nf (a) (jeune fille) young lady; **d. de compagnie** lady's companion; **d. d'honneur** (d'une mariée) bridesmaid (b) (célibataire) single woman; **c'est une vieille d.** she's never married (c) (insecte) dragonfly

démolir [demɔlir] vt (a) (abattre) to demolish, to pull down; (mettre en pièces) to demolish, to wreck; **d. une porte à coups de hache** to smash in a door with an axe; **l'alcool lui a démoli le foie** alcohol has ruined his/her liver (b) Fig (théorie, adversaire) to demolish; (autorité) to undermine; (auteur, cinéaste, roman, film) to slate (c) Fam (battre) to beat up; **d. le portrait à qn** to smash sb's face in; **se faire d. (le portrait)** to get beaten up

démolition [demɔlisjɔ̃] nf demolition; **chantier de d.** demolition site; **entreprise de d.** demolition contractors; **en d.** being demolished

démon [demɔ̃] nm aussi Fig demon, devil; **le d.** the Devil; **le d. de midi** the mid-life crisis

démoniaque [demɔnjak] adj demonic; Fig (pervers) fiendish

démonstratif, -ive [demɔ̃stratif, -iv] **1** adj (affectueux) & Gram demonstrative **2** nm Gram demonstrative

démonstration [demɔ̃strasjɔ̃] nf (a) Math demonstration; **d. par l'absurde** reductio ad absurdum; **faire la d. de qch** to demonstrate sth (b) (d'appareil) demonstration; **être en d.** to be a display model (c) (manifestation) show; **d. de force** show of force; **faire de grandes démonstrations d'amitié** to make a great show of friendship

démontable [demɔ̃tabl] adj that can be dismantled

démontage [demɔ̃taʒ] nm dismantling

démonté, -e [demɔ̃te] adj (mer) raging

démonter [demɔ̃te] **1** vt (a) (machine, meuble, tente) to dismantle; (pneu) to remove (b) Fam (déconcerter) to throw; **se laisser d.** to get thrown **2 se démonter** vpr (a) (machine, meuble) to come apart (b) Fam **elle ne s'est pas démontée pour si peu** she wasn't so easily thrown

démontrable [demɔ̃trabl] adj demonstrable

démontrer [demɔ̃tre] vt to demonstrate; Fam **d. qch par A plus B** to prove sth conclusively

démoralisant, -e [demɔralizɑ̃, -ɑ̃t] adj demoralizing

démoralisation [demɔralizasjɔ̃] nf demoralization

démoraliser [demɔralize] **1** vt to demoralize **2 se démoraliser** vpr to become demoralized

démordre [demɔrdr] démordre de vt ind **ne pas d. de qch** to stick to sth; **elle n'en démord pas** she's sticking to her guns

démotiver [demɔtive] vt to demotivate; **se laisser d. par qch** to be put off by sth

démoulage [demulaʒ] nm (d'un moulage) removal from the mould; (d'un gâteau) turning out

démouler [demule] vt (moulage) to remove from the mould; (gâteau) to turn out

démuni, -e [demyni] adj penniless

démunir [demynir] **1** vt **d. qn de qch** to deprive sb of sth **2 se démunir** vpr **se d. de qch** to part with sth

démystification [demistifikasjɔ̃] nf demystification

démystifier [66] [demistifje] vt to demystify

dénatalité [denatalite] nf fall in the birth rate

dénationaliser [denasjɔnalize] vt to denationalize

dénaturé, -e [denatyre] adj (a) (parents, goût, mœurs) unnatural (b) Chim denatured

dénaturer [denatyre] vt (faits, propos) to distort; Chim to denature

dénégation [denegasjɔ̃] nf denial

déneiger [4b] [deneʒe] vt to clear the snow from

déneigeuse [deneʒøz] nf Can snowblower

déni [deni] nm Jur **d. de justice** denial of justice

déniaiser [denjeze] vt Fam **d. qn** (dépuceler) to take away sb's innocence; (dégourdir) to open sb's eyes

dénicher [deniʃe] vt Fam (objet) to unearth; (personne) to track down

denier [dənje] nm (a) Hist (monnaie française) denier; Fig **deniers** funds (b) (de bas) **bas de 30 deniers** 30-denier stockings

dénier [66] [denje] vt (a) (nier) (faute, responsabilité) to deny (b) (refuser) **d. à qn le droit de faire qch** to deny sb the right to do sth

dénigrement [denigrəmɑ̃] nm denigration; **une campagne de d.** a smear campaign

dénigrer [denigre] vt to denigrate

dénivelé [denivle] nm difference in level

dénivellation [denivɛlasjɔ̃] nf difference in level

dénombrable [denɔ̃brabl] adj countable

dénombrer [denɔ̃bre] vt to count

dénominateur [denɔminatœr] nm Math denominator; **le plus petit d. commun** the lowest common denominator

dénomination [denɔminasjɔ̃] nf designation

dénommé, -e [denɔme] adj **un d. Gérard** someone by the name of Gérard

dénoncer [16] [denɔ̃se] **1** vt (a) (trahir) (malfaiteur) to denounce (à to); (élève) to tell on (à to) (b) (protester contre)

(abus) to denounce (c) (annuler) (traité, contrat) to terminate **2 se dénoncer** vpr (malfaiteur) to give oneself up (à to); (élève) to own up (à to)

dénonciation [denɔ̃sjasjɔ̃] nf denunciation

dénoter [denɔte] vt to denote, to indicate

dénouement [denumɑ̃] nm (d'un livre) ending; (d'une pièce) dénouement; (d'une affaire) outcome

dénouer [denwe] **1** vt (nœud) to untie, to undo; (cheveux) to undo, to let down; Fig (intrigue) to unravel **2 se dénouer** vpr (nœud) to come undone; (cheveux) to come down

dénoyauter [denwajɔte] vt Br to stone, Am to pit

denrée [dɑ̃re] nf foodstuff; **denrées alimentaires** foodstuffs; **denrées de consommation courante** staple foods; **denrées périssables** perishable goods

dense [dɑ̃s] adj dense

densité [dɑ̃site] nf (a) (de population) & Phys density (b) Ordinat **à double d.** double-density

dent [dɑ̃] nf (a) (d'homme, d'animal) tooth; **faire ses dents** (enfant) to be teething; **se faire les dents sur qch** (chat, enfant) to cut one's teeth on sth; **manger du bout des dents** to pick at one's food; **mordre à belles dents dans qch** to take a good bite out of sth; **parler entre ses dents** to mumble, to mutter; Fig **se casser les dents sur qch** to come a cropper over sth; aussi Fig **serrer les dents** to grit one's teeth; Fig **avoir les dents longues** to have great ambitions; Fig **avoir la d. dure** to have a sharp tongue; Fig **il n'a pas desserré les dents de la soirée** he hasn't opened his mouth all evening; Fam **être sur les dents** (épuisé) to be worn out; (surmené) to be overworked; Fam **avoir une d. contre qn** to have a grudge against sb; Fam **avoir la d.** to be starving; **d. de lait/de sagesse** milk/wisdom tooth (b) (de peigne, de scie) tooth; (de roue) cog; (de fourchette) prong; (de timbre) perforation; **en dents de scie** serrated; Fig (évolution, progrès) uneven

dentaire [dɑ̃ter] adj dental

denté, -e [dɑ̃te] adj Tech toothed; (feuille) jagged

dentelé, -e [dɑ̃tle] adj (rivage, feuille) jagged

dentelle [dɑ̃tɛl] nf lace; **robe de ou en d.** lace dress; **des crêpes d.** very thin pancakes; Fam **ne pas faire dans la d.** (en paroles) not to beat about the bush; (en actions) not to mess about

dentellière [dɑ̃təljer] nf (personne) lacemaker

dentelure [dɑ̃tlyr] nf (d'un rivage, d'une feuille) jagged outline; **dentelures** (d'un timbre) perforations

dentier [dɑ̃tje] nm (set of) false teeth, dentures

dentifrice [dɑ̃tifris] **1** nm toothpaste **2** adj **pâte d.** toothpaste

dentiste [dɑ̃tist] nmf dentist

dentition [dɑ̃tisjɔ̃] nf (a) (croissance) dentition (b) (denture) set of teeth

denture [dɑ̃tyr] nf set of teeth

dénudé, -e [denyde] adj (campagne, arbre, fil) bare

dénuder [denyde] **1** vt (colline, arbre, fil) to strip; **cette robe dénude le dos** this dress leaves the back bare **2 se dénuder** vpr (a) (colline) to grow bare; (arbre) to lose its leaves (b) (se déshabiller) to strip (naked)

dénué, -e [denye] adj **d. de** (intelligence, intérêt) devoid of; **d. de tout fondement** totally without foundation

dénuement [denymɑ̃] nm destitution; **être dans le d.** to be destitute

déodorant [deɔdɔrɑ̃] nm deodorant

déodoriser [deɔdɔrize] vt to deodorize

déontologie [deɔ̃tɔlɔʒi] nf professional code of ethics

dépannage [depanaʒ] nm (d'une machine) (emergency)

repairs; *(remorquage)* recovery; *Ordinat* trouble-shooting; **service de d.** breakdown service

dépanner [depane] *vt (machine)* to repair; *Fam (personne)* to help out (**de** with)

dépanneur [depanœr] *nm* (**a**) *(de voitures)* breakdown mechanic; *(de téléviseurs)* (television) repairman (**b**) *Can (magasin) Br* corner shop, *Am* convenience store

dépanneuse [depanøz] *nf Br* breakdown lorry, *Am* wrecker

dépareillé, -e [depareje] *adj (gant)* odd; *(service de table)* incomplete

déparer [depare] *vt* to spoil, to mar; **ce tableau ne dépare pas dans le salon** this painting goes very well in the living room

départ [depar] *nm* (**a**) *(d'une personne, d'un véhicule, d'un bateau)* departure; **les grands départs** the great holiday exodus; **être sur le d.** to be on the point of leaving; **excursions au d. de Biarritz** trips departing from Biarritz; **je regrette votre d.** I'm sorry you're leaving; **d. volontaire** *(d'employé)* voluntary redundancy (**b**) *(d'une course)* start; **ligne de d.** starting line; **faux d.** false start; **donner le d. (d'une course)** to give the starting signal (for a race); *aussi Fig* **prendre un bon/mauvais d.** to get off to a good/bad start (**c**) *(début)* start, beginning; **salaire de d.** starting salary; **au d.** at first, to start with

départager [45] [departaʒe] *vt* to decide between

département [departəmɑ̃] *nm* (**a**) *(de la France)* department *(division of local government)* (**b**) *(dans un ministère)* department; **le d. d'allemand** *(d'une faculté)* the German department

départemental, -e, -aux, -ales [departəmãtal, -o] **1** *adj* departmental **2** *nf* **départementale** secondary road, *Br* B road

départir [64a] [departir] **se départir** *vpr Litt* **il ne s'est jamais départi de sa bonne humeur** his good humour never deserted him

dépassé, -e [depase] *adj* (**a**) *(démodé) (vêtement, technique)* old-fashioned (**b**) *(perdu)* overwhelmed; **être d. par les événements** to be overtaken by events

dépassement [depasmã] *nm* (**a**) *(en voiture) Br* overtaking, *Am* passing (**b**) *Fin* **il y a un d. de crédit de plusieurs millions** the budget has been exceeded by several million

dépasser [depase] **1** *vt* (**a**) *(aller plus loin que)* to go past (**b**) *(doubler) Br* to overtake, *Am* to pass (**c**) *(excéder) (limite de vitesse, temps imparti, poids)* to exceed; **d. la date limite de vente** *(produit)* to be past its sell-by date; **d. dix minutes** to last longer than ten minutes; **ne pas d. la dose prescrite** *(sur notice)* do not exceed the stated dose; **cela dépasse l'entendement** it's beyond belief (**d**) *(surpasser)* to outstrip; **d. qn d'une tête** to stand a head taller than sb; **d. qn en beauté** to be more beautiful than sb; **d. les espérances de qn** to exceed sb's expectations (**e**) *(exagérer)* **d. les bornes** to overstep the mark; **cela me dépasse** it's beyond me **2** *vi* (**a**) *(en voiture) Br* to overtake, *Am* to pass (**b**) *(se voir)* to stick out (**de** of); *(jupon)* to show **3 se dépasser** *vpr* to surpass oneself

dépassionner [depasjone] *vt (débat)* to take the heat out of

dépatouiller [depatuje] **se dépatouiller** *vpr Fam* to cope, to manage

dépaysé, -e [depeize] *adj* out of one's element

dépaysement [depeizmã] *nm (positif)* change of scene; *(négatif)* disorientation

dépayser [depeize] *vt (positivement)* to be a change of scene for; *(négativement)* to disorientate

dépecer [16/34] [depəse] *vt (sujet: boucher)* to cut up; *(sujet: animal)* to tear up

dépêche [depɛʃ] *nf* dispatch; **d. d'agence** agency news item

dépêcher [depeʃe] **1** *vt (messager)* to dispatch **2 se dépêcher** *vpr* to hurry; **dépêchez-vous!** hurry up!; **se d. de faire qch** to hurry to do sth; **dépêche-toi de finir ton travail** hurry up and finish your work

dépeindre [54] [depɛ̃dr] *vt* to depict

dépenaillé, -e [depənaje] *adj* ragged

dépénalisation [depenalizasjɔ̃] *nf* decriminalization

dépénaliser [depenalize] *vt* to decriminalize

dépendance [depãdãs] *nf* (**a**) *(asservissement)* dependence (**à** on); **être sous la d. de qn** to be under sb's domination (**b**) *(bâtiment)* outbuilding

dépendant, -e [depãdã, -ãt] *adj* dependent (**de** on)

dépendre [depãdr] *vi* to depend (**de** on); **cela ne dépend pas de nous** it's not up to us; *Fam* **cela dépend (des fois)** it depends

dépens [depã] *nmpl* (**a**) **aux d. de** at the expense of; **apprendre qch à ses d.** to learn sth to one's cost (**b**) *Jur* **être condamné aux d.** to be ordered to pay costs

dépense [depãs] *nf* (**a**) *(frais)* expenditure, expense; **dépenses** spending; **les dépenses du ménage** household expenses; **faire des dépenses** to spend money; **pousser (les gens) à la d.** to encourage people to spend; **il ne regarde pas à la d.** he spares no expense (**b**) **d. physique** physical exertion

dépenser [depãse] **1** *vt (de l'argent)* to spend; *Fig* **d. toute son énergie (à faire qch)** to use up all one's energy (in doing sth) **2** *vi* to spend (money); **d. sans compter** to spend lavishly **3 se dépenser** *vpr* to burn up energy

dépensier, -ère [depãsje, -ɛr] *adj* extravagant

déperdition [depɛrdisjɔ̃] *nf (de chaleur, d'énergie)* loss

dépérir [deperir] *vi (personne)* to waste away; *(plante)* to wither; *(arbre)* to decay

dépêtrer [depetre] *Fam* **1** *vt* **d. qn de qch** to free sb from sth **2 se dépêtrer** *vpr (se dégager)* to free oneself (**de** from); *Fig* **se d. de qch** to get oneself out of sth; *Fig* **se d. de qn** to get rid of sb

dépeuplement [depœpləmã] *nm (d'un pays)* depopulation

dépeupler [depœple] **1** *vt (pays)* to depopulate **2 se dépeupler** *vpr (pays)* to become depopulated

déphasé, -e [defaze] *adj* (**a**) *Él* out of phase (**b**) *Fam (désorienté)* disoriented

dépiauter [depjote] *vt Fam (animal)* to skin; *Fig* **d. un texte** to pull a text to pieces

dépilatoire [depilatwar] *adj* **crème d.** hair-removing cream

dépistage [depistaʒ] *nm (d'une maladie)* screening; **d. du sida** AIDS screening

dépister [depiste] *vt (gibier, criminel)* to track down; *(maladie)* to detect

dépit [depi] *nm* (**a**) *(ressentiment)* spite; **par d.** out of spite (**b**) **en d. de** in spite of, despite; **en d. du bon sens** contrary to common sense

dépité, -e [depite] *adj* annoyed

déplacé, -e [deplase] *adj* (**a**) *(dérangé)* out of place; **avoir une vertèbre déplacée** to have a slipped disc (**b**) *(inconvenant) (observation)* uncalled-for

déplacement [deplasmã] *nm* (**a**) *(réarrangement)* moving; *(mutation)* transfer; **d. de vertèbre** slipped disc; *Ordinat* **d. du curseur** cursor movement; *Ordinat* **d. entre fichiers** movement between files (**b**) *(voyage)* travel;

déplacements travel; **être en d.** to be on a (business) trip; *Fig* **valoir le d.** to be worth the trip

déplacer [16] [deplase] **1** *vt (objet)* to move; *(fonctionnaire, service)* to transfer; *Fig* **d. le problème** *(volontairement)* to avoid the issue; *(involontairement)* to miss the point **2 se déplacer** *vpr* (**a**) *(changer de place)* to move around (**b**) *(voyager)* to travel (**c**) **se d. une vertèbre** to slip a disc

déplafonner [deplafɔne] *vt (prix, crédit)* to remove the ceiling on

déplaire [55a] [deplɛr] **1** *vi* **d. à qn** *(irriter)* to displease sb; **cet homme/cette maison me déplaît** I don't like that man/that house; **cela ne me déplairait pas** I wouldn't mind; *Ironique* **ne vous/leur en déplaise** whether you/they like it or not **2 se déplaire** *vpr* **il se déplaît à Londres** he doesn't like it in London; **elle ne se déplaît pas à Londres** she quite likes it in London

déplaisant, -e [deplɛzɑ̃, -ɑ̃t] *adj* unpleasant

déplaisir [deplezir] *nm* displeasure, annoyance; **à son grand d.** to his great annoyance

dépliant [deplijɑ̃] *nm* leaflet; *(d'un livre)* fold-out page

déplisser [deplise] **1** *vt* to take the creases out of **2 se déplisser** *vpr* to lose its creases

déploiement [deplwamɑ̃] *nm (d'ailes)* spreading; *(de troupes)* deployment; *Fig (de force)* display

déplorable [deplɔrabl] *adj* deplorable

déplorer [deplɔre] *vt* to deplore; **nous devrons travailler plus, (et) je le déplore, mais...** we'll have to do more work, I'm sorry to say, but...; **d. la mort de qn** to mourn sb's death; **d. la perte de qch** to lament the loss of sth

déployer [32] [deplwaje] **1** *vt (journal, carte)* to unfold, to open out; *(voiles, ailes)* to spread; *(troupes, police)* to deploy; *Fig* to display **2 se déployer** *vpr (voile)* to unfurl; *(troupes, police)* to deploy

déplumé, -e [deplyme] *adj* featherless; *Fam (chauve)* bald

déplumer [deplyme] **se déplumer** *vpr (oiseau)* to moult; *Fam (personne)* to go bald

dépoitraillé, -e [depwatraje] *adj Fam* with one's shirt open

dépoli, -e [depɔli] *adj (verre)* frosted

dépolitiser [depɔlitize] *vt* to depoliticize

dépolluer [depɔlye] *vt* to clean up

déportation [depɔrtasjɔ̃] *nf (en camp de concentration)* internment

déporté, -e [depɔrte] *nm,f (de camp de concentration)* internee

déporter [depɔrte] *vt* **d. qn** to send sb to a concentration camp

déposer [depoze] **1** *vt* (**a**) *(mettre à terre)* to put down; *aussi Fig* **d. les armes** to lay down one's arms (**b**) *(laisser)* *(personne)* to drop (off); **d. qch chez qn** to drop sth off at sb's house; **d. une gerbe sur une tombe** to lay a wreath on a grave; **d. un baiser sur le front de qn** to plant a kiss on sb's forehead; **d. la clé à la réception** to leave the key at reception; **d. une caution** to leave a deposit; **d. de l'argent (à la banque)** to deposit money (at the bank); *Jur* **d. une plainte (contre qn)** to lodge a complaint (against sb); *Pol* **d. un projet de loi** to introduce a bill (**c**) *(marque, brevet)* to register; **marque déposée** registered trademark (**d**) *(monarque)* to depose **2** *vi Jur* **d. (en justice)** to give evidence (**contre** against) **3 se déposer** *vpr (substance)* to settle

dépositaire [depozitɛr] *nmf* (**a**) *(de papiers)* depositary; *Fig (d'un secret)* guardian (**b**) *Com (de produits)* agent

déposition [depozisjɔ̃] *nf* (**a**) *Jur* statement *(made by*

witness); **faire/recueillir une d.** to make/take a statement (**b**) *(d'un monarque)* deposing

déposséder [34] [deposede] *vt* to dispossess, to deprive (**de** of)

dépôt [depo] *nm* (**a**) *(action)* depositing; *(somme)* deposit; **faire un d.** *(à la banque)* to make a deposit; **mettre qch en d.** to put sth into storage; *Fin* **d. d'espèces** cash deposit; *Jur* **d. légal** registration of copyright; *Fin* **d. à vue** cash deposit (**b**) *(entrepôt)* depot; *(de trains)* engine shed; *(prison)* prison; **d. de munitions** munitions depot; **d. d'ordures** *Br* rubbish dump, *Am* garbage dump (**c**) *(substance)* deposit; *(limon)* silt; *(de bouilloire)* fur

dépoter [depɔte] *vt (plantes)* to repot

dépotoir [depɔtwar] *nm (dépôt d'ordures)* dump; *Fam (chambre)* dump; *(classe)* dumping ground

dépôt-vente *(pl* **dépôts-ventes)** [depovɑ̃t] *nm* second-hand shop *(where clothes are sold on commission)*

dépouille [depuj] *nf* (**a**) *(d'animal)* skin, hide; **d. (mortelle)** *(mortal)* remains (**b**) **dépouilles** *(trésor de guerre)* spoils, booty

dépouillé, -e [depuje] *adj (style)* bald; *(arbre)* bare

dépouillement [depujmɑ̃] *nm* (**a**) *(examen)* **d. du scrutin** counting of the votes; **d. du courrier** sorting through the mail (**b**) *(pauvreté)* poverty; *(sobriété)* austerity

dépouiller [depuje] **1** *vt* (**a**) *(priver)* to deprive (**de** of); **d. qn de ses vêtements** to strip sb; **se faire d.** *(dans une affaire)* to lose all one's money (**b**) *(examiner)* *(courrier)* to sort through; **d. le scrutin** to count the votes (**c**) *(animal)* to skin **2 se dépouiller** *vpr* **se d. de qch** to rid oneself of sth; **les arbres se dépouillent de leurs feuilles** the trees are shedding their leaves

dépourvu, -e [depurvy] *adj* (**a**) **d. de qch** devoid of sth (**b**) **être pris au d.** to be caught off *(guard)* guard

dépoussiérer [34] [depusjere] *vt* to dust; *Fig (institution)* to dust down

dépravation [depravasjɔ̃] *nf* depravity

dépravé, -e [deprave] **1** *adj* depraved **2** *nm,f* degenerate

dépraver [deprave] *vt* to deprave

dépréciation [depresjasjɔ̃] *nf* depreciation

déprécier [66] [depresje] **1** *vt* to undervalue **2 se déprécier** *vpr (valeurs, marchandises)* to depreciate

déprédation [depredasjɔ̃] *nf* depredation

dépressif, -ive [depresif, -iv] *adj* depressive

dépression [depresjɔ̃] *nf* (**a**) *(creux)* depression, **d. (atmosphérique)** low, trough (**b**) *Psy* depression; **faire la d.** to be suffering from depression; **faire une d.** to be depressed; **d. nerveuse** nervous breakdown

dépressurisation [depresyrizasjɔ̃] *nf* depressurization

dépressuriser [depresyrize] *vt (avion)* to depressurize

déprimant, -e [deprimɑ̃, -ɑ̃t] *adj* depressing

déprime [deprim] *nf Fam* depression; **avoir un (petit) coup de d.** to be feeling (a bit) low

déprimé, -e [deprime] *adj Psy* depressed

déprimer [deprime] **1** *vt (démoraliser)* to depress **2** *vi Fam* to be feeling low

déprogrammer [deprɔgrame] *vt (émission)* to cancel; *Ordinat* to remove from a program

dépuceler [42] [depysle] *vt Fam* to deflower

depuis [dəpɥi] **1** *prép* (**a**) *(indiquant le point de départ)* **hier/cet après-midi/2002** since yesterday/this afternoon/2002; **d. l'âge de cinq ans** from the age of five; **d. leur rencontre** since they met; **d. ce temps-là** since then; **quand êtes-vous ici?** how long have you been here?

(**b**) *(durée)* for; **je suis ici d. trois jours** I've been here for three days; **d. combien de temps êtes-vous mariés?** how long have you been married (for)?; **il l'aime d. toujours** he has always loved her; **d. longtemps** for a long time; **d. la nuit des temps** since the dawn of time (**c**) *(lieu)* from; **il ne m'a pas parlé d. Caen** he hasn't spoken to me since (we left) Caen **2** *adv* since (then) **3** *conj* **d. que** since; **d. que le monde est monde** since the world began

député [depyte] *nm Pol* deputy, *Br* ≃ MP, *Am* ≃ Representative (**de** for); **d. du Parlement européen** Member of the European Parliament, MEP

déraciné, -e [derasine] **1** *adj* uprooted **2** *nm,f* person who has been uprooted

déraciner [derasine] *vt (arbre, personne)* to uproot

déraillement [derɑjmɑ̃] *nm* derailment

dérailler [derɑje] *vi* (**a**) *(train, tram)* to leave the rails; **faire d. un train** to derail a train (**b**) *Fam (personne)* to talk nonsense

dérailleur [derɑjœr] *nm (de bicyclette)* derailleur (gears)

déraison [derezɔ̃] *nf Litt* folly

déraisonnable [derezɔnabl] *adj* foolish

déraisonner [derezɔne] *vi Litt* to talk nonsense

dérangé, -e [derɑ̃ʒe] *adj (fou)* deranged

dérangeant, -e [derɑ̃ʒɑ̃, -ɑ̃t] *adj (film, personnage)* disturbing

dérangement [derɑ̃ʒmɑ̃] *nm* (**a**) *(gêne)* trouble; **je ne veux pas vous causer de d.** I don't want to put you to any trouble; **excusez-moi pour le d.** I'm sorry to trouble you (**b**) *(panne)* **la ligne est en d.** the line is out of order

déranger [45] [derɑ̃ʒe] **1** *vt* (**a**) *(papiers, livres)* to disturb; *(pièce)* to mess up (**b**) *(gêner) (personne)* to disturb; **ne pas d.** *(sur panneau)* do not disturb; **cela vous dérange si je ferme la porte?** would you mind if I closed the door?; **si cela ne vous dérange pas** if that's all right by you; *Ironique* **je ne te dérange pas trop?** am I in your way?; *Fam* **et alors, ça te dérange?** what's it to you? (**c**) *(perturber)* to upset; **avoir le cerveau dérangé** to be deranged **2** *vi (choquer)* to be disturbing **3** **se déranger** *vpr* **merci de vous être dérangé** thank you for your trouble; **ne vous dérangez pas pour moi** please don't go to any trouble on my account

dérapage [derapaʒ] *nm (en voiture)* skid; *(à skis)* sideslip; *Fig* mistake; *Fig* **le d. des prix** spiralling prices

déraper [derape] *vi (voiture)* to skid; *(à skis)* to sideslip; *Fig (prix)* to be rising uncontrollably

dératé, -e [derate] *nm,f Fam* **courir comme un d.** to run flat out

dératiser [deratize] *vt* **d. qch** to clear sth of rats

derechef [dərəʃef] *adv Litt* once more

déréglé, -e [deregle] *adj (mécanisme)* not working properly

déréglement [dereglǝmɑ̃] *nm (d'un mécanisme)* malfunctioning; **d. hormonal** hormone disorder

dérégler [34] [deregle] **1** *vt (mécanisme)* to cause to malfunction **2** **se dérégler** *vpr (mécanisme)* to go wrong; **elle s'est déréglé le système digestif** she's ruined her digestive system

dérider [deride] **1** *vt* to cheer up **2** **se dérider** *vpr* to cheer up

dérision [derizjɔ̃] *nf* derision; **tourner qch en d.** to deride sth

dérisoire [derizwar] *adj (salaire, somme)* derisory; *(prix)* rock-bottom

dérivatif [derivatif] *nm* distraction (**à** from)

dérivation [derivasjɔ̃] *nf* (**a**) *(route, cours d'eau)* diversion; *Él* **monté en d.** shunt connected (**b**) *Math* derivation

dérive [deriv] *nf Naut & Av* drift; **à la d., en d.** adrift; **la d. des continents** continental drift

dérivé, -e [derive] **1** *adj* (**a**) *(sens, fonction)* derived; **produit d.** *Chim* by-product; *Fin* derivative (**b**) *Él* **courant d.** shunt current **2** *nf Math* **dérivée** derivative

dériver¹ [derive] **1** *vt* (**a**) *(cours d'eau)* to divert; *Él (courant)* to shunt (**b**) *Math (fonction)* to derive **2** **dériver de** *vt ind (mot)* to be derived from

dériver² *vi Naut & Av* to drift

dériveur [derivœr] *nm Naut* sailing dinghy *(with centre-board)*

dermatite [dɛrmatit] *nf Méd* dermatitis

dermato [dɛrmato] *nmf Fam* dermatologist

dermatologie [dɛrmatɔlɔʒi] *nf* dermatology

dermatologique [dɛrmatɔlɔʒik] *adj* dermatological

dermatologiste [dɛrmatɔlɔʒist], **dermatologue** [dɛrmatɔlɔg] *nmf* dermatologist

derme [dɛrm] *nm* dermis

dernier, -ère [dɛrnje, -ɛr] **1** *adj* (**a**) *(ultime)* last; *(marquant la fin)* final; **au d. moment** at the last moment (**b**) *(passé)* last; *(le plus récent) (livre, nouvelles, mode)* latest; **au cours des dernières années** over the past or last few years (**c**) *(dans l'espace)* last; **le d. rang** the back or last row; **la dernière marche de l'escalier** *(en haut)* the top step; *(en bas)* the bottom step; **au d. étage** on the top floor (**d**) *Litt (extrême)* utmost; **de la dernière importance** of the utmost importance; **c'est du d. chic** it's the height of elegance (**e**) *(le pire)* worst; **de d. ordre** very inferior; **être reçu d. au concours** to come last in the competition; **c'était la dernière chose à faire** that's the last thing you/he/*etc* should have done **2** *nm,f* (**a**) *(dans un classement)* last; **les six derniers** the last six; **arriver dans les derniers** to be one of the last to finish; **il est arrivé le d.** *ou* **bon d.** he came in last; **c'est le d. de sa classe** he's bottom of his class; *Fam* **c'est le d. de mes soucis** that's the least of my worries (**b**) *(dans une chronologie) (l'ultime)* last; *(le plus récent)* latest; **le d. en date** the most recent; **ce d. répondit...** the latter answered...; **c'est toujours le d. à sortir** he's always last out; **comment va la petite dernière?** how's the little one? (**c**) *Péj* **on la traite comme la dernière des dernières** they treat her like the lowest of the low; **c'est vraiment le d. des lâches** he's the world's biggest coward **3** *nf* **dernière** (**a**) *(spectacle)* last night (**b**) *(nouveauté)* **tu as entendu la dernière de ton frère?** have you heard the latest about your brother? **4** *adv* **en d.** last (of all); **il sort toujours en d.** he's always last out

dernièrement [dɛrnjɛrmɑ̃] *adv* lately, recently

dernier-né, dernière-née *(mpl* **derniers-nés,** *fpl* **dernières-nées)** [dɛrnjene, dɛrnjɛrne] *nm,f* youngest (child)

dérobade [derɔbad] *nf* (**a**) *(esquive)* evasion (**b**) *(d'un cheval)* swerve

dérobé, -e [derɔbe] *adj* (**a**) *(escalier, porte)* hidden, secret (**b**) *(volé)* stolen

dérobée [derɔbe] **à la dérobée** *adv* secretly, on the sly; **regarder qn à la d.** to steal a glance at sb

dérober [derɔbe] **1** *vt* (**a**) *(voler)* to steal (**à** from) (**b**) *(cacher)* to hide (**à** from); **d. qn à la curiosité des autres** to keep sb away from prying eyes

2 se dérober vpr (a) (s'échapper) to slip away (à from); **se d.** à la curiosité de qn to avoid sb's prying eyes (b) (manquer) (sol, jambes) to give way (sous beneath) (c) (de cheval) to swerve

dérogation [derɔgasjɔ̃] nf exemption (à from); Jur waiver; (à une loi) derogation (à of)

déroger [45] [derɔʒe] vi **d. à l'usage/à la loi** to depart from custom/the law

dérouillée [deruje] nf très Fam hammering

dérouiller [deruje] **1** vi très Fam (a) (être battu) to get a hammering (b) (souffrir) to have a hard time of it **3 se dérouiller** vpr Fam **se d. les jambes** to stretch one's legs

déroulement [derulmã] nm (d'événement) unfolding; **pendant tout le d. de la cérémonie** throughout the ceremony

dérouler [derule] **1** vt (rouleau) to unroll; (store) to let down; (câble) to unwind; Ordinat **d. un menu** to pull down a menu **2 se dérouler** vpr (a) (rouleau) to unroll; (store) to come down; (câble) to unwind (b) Fig (événement) to unfold; **la manifestation s'est déroulée dans le calme** the demonstration passed off peacefully

déroutant, -e [derutã, -ãt] adj disconcerting

déroute [derut] nf aussi Fig rout; **l'ennemi fut mis en d.** the enemy was routed

dérouter [derute] vt (a) (navire, avion) to divert, to reroute (b) (égarer) (poursuivants) to throw off the scent (c) Fig (étonner) to throw

derriere [dɛrjɛr] **1** prép behind; **les uns d. les autres** one behind the other; **sortir de d. un buisson** to come out from behind a bush; aussi Fig **les autres sont loin d. elle** the others are way behind her; Fig **il faut toujours être d. elle** you always have to be at her back; Fig **c'est lui qui est d. tout ça** he's the one behind it all **2** adv behind; **aller ou monter d.** (en voiture) to sit in the back **3** nm (a) (de bâtiment) back, rear; **le mur de d.** the back wall (b) (de personne) behind, backside; (d'animal) hindquarters; **recevoir des coups de pied dans le ou au d.** to get kicked in the behind

des [de] voir **de, un**

dès [dɛ] prép (à partir de) from; **d. 1840** as far back as 1840; **d. le matin** first thing in the morning; **d. leur arrivée** as soon as they arrive/arrived; **d. maintenant, d. à présent** from now on; **d. que tu seras là** as soon as you're here; **d. lors** (dans le temps) from then on; (par conséquent) consequently; **d. lors que...** since...

désabusé, -e [dezabyze] adj disillusioned

désaccord [dezakɔr] nm disagreement; **être en d. avec qn (sur qch)** to disagree with sb (about sth)

désaccordé, -e [dezakɔrde] adj out of tune

désaccoutumer [dezakutyme] **se désaccoutumer** vpr to get out of the habit (**de** of)

désaffecté, -e [dezafɛkte] adj disused

désaffection [dezafɛksjɔ̃] nf disaffection (à l'égard de with)

désagréable [dezagreabl] adj unpleasant

désagrégation [dezagregasjɔ̃] nf (désintégration) disintegration

désagréger [59] [dezagreʒe] **1** vt (désintégrer) to cause to disintegrate **2 se désagréger** vpr to disintegrate

désagrément [dezagremã] nm (a) (gêne) trouble (b) (souci, aspect négatif) problem

désaltérant, -e [dezaltɛrã, -ãt] adj thirst-quenching

désaltérer [34] [dezaltere] **1** vt **d. qn** to quench sb's thirst; **c'est une boisson qui désaltère** it's a thirst-quenching drink **2 se désaltérer** vpr to quench one's thirst

désambiguïser [dezãbigɥize] vt (situation) to clarify; (mot) to disambiguate

désamorçage [dezamɔrsaʒ] nm (a) (d'une bombe, d'un conflit) defusing (b) (d'une pompe) draining

désamorcer [16] [dezamɔrse] vt (a) (bombe, conflit, querelle) to defuse (b) (pompe) to drain

désappointer [dezapwɛ̃te] vt Litt to disappoint

désapprobateur, -trice [dezaprɔbatœr, -tris] adj disapproving

désapprobation [dezaprɔbasjɔ̃] nf disapproval

désapprouver [dezapruve] vt to disapprove of

désarçonner [dezarsɔne] vt (a) (jeter bas) to unseat, to throw (b) Fig (déconcerter) to throw

désargenté, -e [dezarʒãte] adj Fam (personne) broke

désarmant, -e [dezarmã, -ãt] adj disarming

désarmé, -e [dezarme] adj (profondément touché) disarmed; (sans défenses) defenceless, helpless

désarmement [dezarmɔmã] nm (a) (d'un pays, d'une région) disarmament; **d. unilatéral** multilateral disarmament (b) (de soldats) disarming

désarmer [dezarme] **1** vt (a) (malfaiteur) to disarm (b) Fig (toucher profondément) to disarm (c) (navire) to lay up **2** vi (a) (pays, région) to disarm (b) (cesser) **sa colère ne désarme pas** he is still angry

désarroi [dezarwa] nm confusion; **jeter qn dans le d.** to throw sb into confusion; **il est en plein d. ou dans un grand d.** he's in a state of utter confusion

désarticuler [dezartikyle] **1** vt to dislocate **2 se désarticuler** vpr to contort oneself; **se d. l'épaule** to dislocate one's shoulder

désastre [dezastr] nm disaster

désastreux, -euse [dezastrø, -øz] adj disastrous

désavantage [dezavãtaʒ] nm disadvantage; **avoir un d. par rapport à qn** to be at a disadvantage compared with sb; **voir qn à son d.** to see sb in an unfavourable light

désavantager [45] [dezavãtaʒe] vt to put at a disadvantage, to disadvantage; **être désavantagé par rapport à qn** to be at a disadvantage compared with sb

désavantageux, -euse [dezavãtaʒø, -øz] adj disadvantageous

désaveu [dezavø] nm (a) (reniement) disowning (b) (condamnation) disapproval

désavouer [dezavwe] vt (a) (renier) to disown (b) (condamner) to disapprove of (c) Jur (enfant) to disown

désaxé, -e [dezakse] nm,f unbalanced person

desceller [desele] vt (a) (pierre) to loosen (b) (acte, document) to unseal

descendance [desãdãs] nf (a) (filiation) descent (b) (postérité) descendants

descendant, -e [desãdã, -ãt] **1** adj (mouvement) downward **2** nm,f descendant

descendre [desãdr] **1** vi (aux être) (a) (en s'approchant) to come down; (en s'éloignant) to go down; **d. de qch** to come down from sth; **faire d. qn de qch** to get sb down from sth; **aider qn à d.** to help sb down; **d. à 150 m de profondeur** to go down to a depth of 150 m; **d. en dessous des dix secondes** to get below ten seconds; **d. à Marseille/dans le Midi** to go down to Marseilles/to the South; Fig **d. dans la rue** to take to the streets (b) (d'un escalier) (en s'approchant) to come downstairs; (en *s'éloignant)* to go downstairs; **d. à la cave** to go down to the cellar

(**c**) *(d'un véhicule)* **d. d'un train/d'une voiture** to get off a train/out of a car; **d. de cheval/de vélo/de moto** to dismount; **tout le monde descend!** *(au terminus)* all change!

(**d**) *(baisser) (marée)* to go out; **faire d. la fièvre** to reduce fever

(**e**) *(tomber) (brouillard)* to come down

(**f**) *(s'étendre)* to go down; *(route, rue)* to go downhill; **d. jusqu'à la taille/jusqu'aux chevilles** to come down to the waist/to the ankles; **ce chemin descend au village** this path goes down to the village

(**g**) *(loger)* **d. chez qn** to stay with sb; **d. à l'hôtel** to stay at a hotel

(**h**) *Fig (venir)* **d. de** to be descended from

2 *vt (aux* **avoir**) (**a**) *(dévaler)* **d. un escalier/la rue/la rivière** *(en s'éloignant)* to go down a staircase/the street/the river; *(en s'approchant)* to come down a staircase/the street/the river

(**b**) *(porter vers le bas) (en s'éloignant)* to take down; *(en s'approchant)* to bring down; **d. la poubelle** to take the garbage down; **peux-tu me d. ma veste?** can you bring me down my jacket?

(**c**) *(abaisser) (store, étagère)* to lower

(**d**) *Fam (abattre) (avion, personne)* to shoot down

(**e**) *Fam (consommer) (repas, boisson)* to put away; **qu'est-ce qu'il descend!** he's really knocking it back!

descente [desɑ̃t] *nf* (**a**) *(action de descendre)* descent; **d. en rappel** abseiling

(**b**) *(sortie)* **accueillir qn à sa d. du train** to meet sb off the train

(**c**) *(incursion)* raid; **d. de police** police raid

(**d**) *(route en pente)* slope; **ralentir dans la d.** to slow down when going downhill

(**e**) *(en ski) (course)* downhill (race); **faire de la d.** to do downhill (skiing)

(**f**) **d. de lit** bedside rug

(**g**) *(tuyau)* downpipe

(**h**) *Fam* **il a une bonne d.** he can really put it away

descriptible [dɛskriptibl] *adj* describable

descriptif, -ive [dɛskriptif, -iv] **1** *adj* descriptive **2** *nm* description

description [dɛskripsjɔ̃] *nf* description; **faire la d. de** to give a description of; **d. de poste** job description

désembourber [dezɑ̃burbe] *vt* to pull out of the mud

désembuage [dezɑ̃bɥaʒ] *nm* demisting

désemparé, -e [dezɑ̃pare] *adj (personne)* at a loss

désemparer [dezɑ̃pare] *vi* **sans d.** without stopping

désemplir [dezɑ̃plir] *vi* **ne pas d.** to be always full

désenchanté, -e [dezɑ̃ʃɑ̃te] *adj (personne)* disillusioned; *(sourire)* wistful

désenchantement [dezɑ̃ʃɑ̃tmɑ̃] *nm* disillusion

désenchanter [dezɑ̃ʃɑ̃te] *vt* to disillusion

désenclaver [dezɑ̃klave] *vt (région)* to open up

désencombrer [dezɑ̃kɔ̃bre] *vt (passage)* to clear (**de** of)

désendettement [dezɑ̃dɛtmɑ̃] *nm* debt clearing

désenfler [dezɑ̃fle] *vi* to go down, to become less swollen

désengagement [dezɑ̃gaʒmɑ̃] *nm* disengagement

désengager [45] [dezɑ̃gaʒe] **1** *vt* to free (**de** from) **2 se désengager** *vpr* to free oneself (**de** from)

désensabler [dezɑ̃sable] *vt* (**a**) *(chenal, port)* to clear of sand (**b**) *(bateau)* to get off the sand; *(voiture)* to dig out of the sand

désensibiliser [desɑ̃sibilize] *vt aussi Fig* to desensitize

désépaissir [dezepesir] *vt* (**a**) *(sauce)* to thin down (**b**) *(cheveux)* to thin out

déséquilibre [dezekilibr] *nm* imbalance; **être en d.** to be unsteady

déséquilibré, -e [dezekilibre] **1** *adj* unbalanced **2** *nm,f* unbalanced person

déséquilibrer [dezekilibre] *vt* (**a**) *(objet, personne)* to throw off balance (**b**) *Psy* to unbalance

désert, -e [dezɛr, -ɛrt] **1** *adj (lieu)* deserted; *(pays, région)* uninhabited **2** *nm* desert; **d. culturel** cultural desert *or* wasteland; **le d. de Gobi** the Gobi Desert; **d. de sable** sandy desert

déserter [dezɛrte] **1** *vt* (**a**) *(lieu, fonction)* to desert; **Mil d. son poste** to desert one's post (**b**) *Fig (cause)* to desert, to abandon **2** *vi (soldat)* to desert

déserteur [dezɛrtœr] *nm* deserter

désertification [dezɛrtifikasjɔ̃] *nf* (**a**) *(transformation en désert)* desertification (**b**) *(dépeuplement)* depopulation

désertion [dezɛrsjɔ̃] *nf* desertion

désertique [dezɛrtik] *adj* desert

désespérant, -e [dezɛsperɑ̃, -ɑ̃t] *adj (situation, personne)* hopeless; **être d'une lenteur/bêtise désespérante** to be incredibly slow/stupid

désespéré, -e [dezɛspere] **1** *adj* (**a**) *(qui ne laisse aucun espoir)* desperate; *(inconsolable)* in despair (**b**) *(exprimant le désespoir)* desperate (**c**) *(extrême) (mesure, solution)* desperate **2** *nm,f* desperate person

désespérément [dezɛsperemɑ̃] *adv* desperately

désespérer [34] [dezɛspere] **1** *vt (personne)* to drive to despair **2** *vi* to despair **3** **désespérer de** *vt ind* to despair of; **d. de faire qch** to despair of doing sth; **il ne désespère pas d'y arriver** he hasn't given up hope of getting there **4 se désespérer** *vpr* to despair

désespoir [dezɛspwar] *nm* despair; **être au d.** to be in despair; **être à d. faire qch** to be extremely sorry to do sth; **faire ou être le d. de qn** *(personne)* to be the despair of sb; **réduire qn au d.** to drive sb to despair

déshabillé [dezabije] *nm* negligee

déshabiller [dezabije] **1** *vt (personne)* to undress; **d. qn du regard** to undress sb with one's eyes **2 se déshabiller** *vpr* (**a**) *(pour être nu)* to undress, to take off one's clothes (**b**) *(ôter son manteau)* to take off one's coat

déshabituer [dezabitɥe] **1** *vt* **d. qn de qch/de faire qch** to get sb out of the habit of sth/doing sth **2 se déshabituer** *vpr* **se d. de qch/de faire qch** to get out of the habit of sth/of doing sth

désherbage [dezɛrbaʒ] *nm* weeding

désherbant [dezɛrbɑ̃] *nm* weedkiller

désherber [dezɛrbe] *vt* to weed

déshérité, -e [dezerite] **1** *adj (démuni)* deprived **2** *nm,f* **les déshérités** the underprivileged

déshériter [dezerite] *vt* to disinherit

déshonneur [dezɔnœr] *nm* dishonour

déshonorant, -e [dezɔnɔrɑ̃, -ɑ̃t] *adj* dishonourable

déshonorer [dezɔnɔre] **1** *vt* to disgrace; **se croire/sentir déshonoré de faire qch** to think/feel it beneath oneself to do sth **2 se déshonorer** *vpr* to disgrace oneself

déshumaniser [dezymanize] *vt* to dehumanize

déshydratation [dezidratasjɔ̃] *nf* dehydration

déshydraté, -e [dezidrate] *adj* dehydrated

déshydrater [dezidrate] **1** *vt* to dehydrate **2 se déshydrater** *vpr* to become dehydrated

desiderata [deziderata] *nmpl* desiderata

design [dizajn] **1** *nm* **(a)** *(stylique)* design; **d. industriel** industrial design **(b)** *(conception)* design **2** *adj inv* designer; **un intérieur d.** a designer interior

désignation [dezijɲasjɔ̃] *nf* **(a)** *(appellation)* designation **(b)** *(choix)* appointment

désigner [deziɲe] *vt* **(a)** *(montrer)* to point out; **d. qn/qch du doigt** to point to sb/sth **(b)** *(dénommer)* to refer to **(c)** *(choisir)* to designate, to appoint **(d) il est tout désigné pour le faire** he's just the man for the job

désillusion [dezilyzjɔ̃] *nf* disillusion

désillusionner [dezilyzjɔne] *vt* to disillusion

désincrustant, -e [dezɛ̃kryɔtɑ̃, ɑ̃t] **1** *adj* **(a)** *Tech (substance)* scaling **(b)** *(masque, savon)* cleansing **2** *nm* **(a)** *Tech* scale preventive **(b)** *(savon)* cleanser

désindustrialisation [dezɛ̃dystrijalizasjɔ̃] *nf* deindustrialization

désinence [dezinɑ̃s] *nf* Gram ending

désinfectant, -e [dezɛ̃fɛktɑ̃, -ɑ̃t] *adj & nm* disinfectant

désinfecter [dezɛ̃fɛkte] *vt* to disinfect

désinfection [dezɛ̃fɛksjɔ̃] *nf* disinfection

désinflation [dezɛ̃flasjɔ̃] *nf* Écon disinflation

désinformation [dezɛ̃fɔrmasjɔ̃] *nf* disinformation

désinformer [dezɛ̃fɔrme] *vt* to disinform

désintégration [dezɛ̃tegrasjɔ̃] *nf* **(a)** *(des roches)* weathering **(b)** *(d'un groupe, de la famille)* break-up **(c)** *Phys (de matière)* disintegration

désintégrer [34] [dezɛ̃tegre] **1** *vt* **(a)** *(roches)* to weather **(b)** *(groupe, famille)* to break up **(c)** *Phys (matière)* to disintegrate; *(atome)* to split **2 se désintégrer** *vpr* **(a)** *(roches)* to weather **(b)** *(groupe, famille)* to break up **(c)** *Phys (matière)* to disintegrate

désintéressé, -e [dezɛ̃terese] *adj* disinterested

désintéresser [dezɛ̃terese] **se désintéresser** *vpr* **se d. de qn/qch** *(ne pas s'y intéresser)* to have no interest in sb/sth; *(s'en détacher)* to lose interest in sb/sth

désintérêt [dezɛ̃tere] *nm* disinterest

désintoxication [dezɛ̃tɔksikasjɔ̃] *nf* Méd detoxification

désintoxiquer [dezɛ̃tɔksike] **1** *vt (alcoolique, drogué)* to treat for alcoholism/drug addiction **2 se désintoxiquer** *vpr* **(a)** *(alcoolique, drogué)* to come off alcohol/drugs **(b)** *Fig (se remettre en forme)* to clean out one's system; *(perdre une habitude)* to get out of the habit

désinvolte [dezɛ̃vɔlt] *adj* **(a)** *(négligent)* casual, offhand **(b)** *(à l'aise)* *(manière)* unselfconscious; *(mouvements)* easy

désinvolture [dezɛ̃vɔltyr] *nf* **(a)** *(excès de liberté)* casualness; **avec d.** casually **(b)** *(naturel)* *(de manières)* unselfconsciousness; *(de mouvement)* ease

désir [dezir] *nm* **(a)** *(souhait)* desire; **selon le d. de qn** in accordance with sb's wishes; **prendre ses désirs pour des réalités** to indulge in wishful thinking; **tes désirs sont des ordres** your wish is my command **(b) d. (sexuel)** (sexual) desire

désirable [dezirabl] *adj* desirable

désirer [dezire] *vt* **(a)** *(souhaiter)* to wish; **d. faire qch** to wish to do sth; **je désire qu'il vienne** I want him to come; **cela laisse à d.** it leaves a lot to be desired; **elle se fait d.** *(elle n'arrive pas)* she's keeping us waiting; **que désirez-vous?**, *Fam* **vous désirez?** *(dans un magasin)* can I help you?; *(qu'est-ce que je vous sers?)* what would you like? **(b)** *(sexuellement)* to desire

désireux, -euse [dezirø, øz] *adj* **être d. de faire qch** to be anxious to do sth

désistement [dezistəmɑ̃] *nm* withdrawal

désister [deziste] **se désister** *vpr* to withdraw

désobéir [dezɔbeir] *vi* to disobey; **d. à qn/qch** to disobey sb/sth

désobéissance [dezɔbeisɑ̃s] *nf* disobedience **(à** to)

désobéissant, -e [dezɔbeisɑ̃, -ɑ̃t] *adj* disobedient **(à** to)

désobligeant, -e [dezɔbliʒɑ̃, -ɑ̃t] *adj* disagreeable

désodorisant, -e [dezɔdɔrizɑ̃, -ɑ̃t] *adj & nm* deodorant

désodoriser [dezɔdɔrize] *vt* to deodorize

désœuvré, -e [dezœvre] *adj* idle

désœuvrement [dezœvrəmɑ̃] *nm* idleness; **par d.** for something to do

désolant, -e [dezɔlɑ̃, -ɑ̃t] *adj* **(a)** *(affligeant)* distressing **(b)** *(contrariant)* annoying

désolé, -e [dezɔle] *adj* **(a)** *(navré)* sorry; **je suis d. de vous déranger** I'm sorry to disturb you; **d., je n'ai pas le temps** sorry, I haven't got the time **(b)** *(affligé)* upset **(c)** *(région)* desolate

désoler [dezɔle] **1** *vt* **(a)** *(navrer)* to upset **(b)** *(affliger)* to distress **2 se désoler** *vpr* to be upset

désolidariser [desɔlidarize] **se désolidariser** *vpr* **se d. de** to dissociate oneself from

désopilant, -e [dezɔpilɑ̃, -ɑ̃t] *adj* hilarious

désordonné, -e [dezɔrdɔne] *adj* **(a)** *(chambre, bureau, personne)* untidy **(b)** *(désorganisé) (personne, article, pensées)* disorganized **(c)** *(vie)* disorderly

désordre [dezɔrdr] *nm* **(a)** *(manque d'ordre)* untidiness, mess; **en d.** untidy; **mettre qch en d.** to make a mess of sth **(b)** *(manque d'organisation)* disorder **(c)** *(trouble)* commotion; **mettre le d. dans une réunion** to disrupt a meeting **(d)** *(agitation)* **désordres** disturbances **(e)** Méd disorder

désorganisation [dezɔrganizasjɔ̃] *nf* disorganization

désorganiser [dezɔrganize] *vt* to disrupt

désorienté, -e [dezɔrjɑ̃te] *adj* **(a)** *(égaré)* disorientated **(b)** *(déconcerté)* bewildered

désorienter [dezɔrjɑ̃te] *vt (déconcerter)* to bewilder

désormais [dezɔrmɛ] *adv* from now on, in future

désosser [dezɔse] **1** *vt (viande, poisson)* to bone **2 se désosser** *vpr* to contort oneself

despote [dɛspɔt] *nm aussi Fig* despot

despotique [dɛspɔtik] *adj* despotic

desquamation [dɛskwamasjɔ̃] *nf* peeling, Spéc desquamation

desquels, desquelles [dekɛl] *voir* **lequel**

DESS [deɔeses] *nm (abrév* diplôme d'études supérieures spécialisées*)* = postgraduate diploma lasting one year

dessaisir [desezir] **1** *vt* **(a)** *(déposséder)* **d. qn de qch** to confiscate sth from sb **(b) d. un juge d'une affaire** to withdraw a judge from a case **2 se dessaisir** *vpr* **se d. de qch** to relinquish sth, to part with sth

dessaler [desale] **1** *vt* **(a)** *(viande, poisson)* to remove the salt from *(by soaking)*; *(eau de mer)* to desalinate **(b)** Fam **d. qn** to teach sb a thing or two **2** *vi* **(a)** *(voilier)* to capsize **(b)** **mettre qch à d.** *(viande, poisson)* to soak sth to remove the salt **3 se dessaler** *vpr* Fam to learn a thing or two

dessaouler [desule] Fam = **dessoûler**

dessèchement [desɛʃmɑ̃] *nm (de la peau)* drying up; *(de la végétation)* withering

dessécher [34] [deseʃe] **1** *vt* **(a)** *(déshydrater)* *(peau)* to dry up; *(végétation)* to wither

2 **se dessécher** *vpr(peau)* to dry up; *(végétation)* to wither

dessein [desɛ̃] *nm* intention, purpose; **dans ce d.** with this intention; **à d.** intentionally; **dans le d.** de faire qch with the intention of doing sth

desseller [desele] *vt (cheval)* to unsaddle

desserrer [desere] **1** *vt* (**a**) *(relâcher) (vis, ceinture, nœud)* to loosen; *(frein à main)* to release (**b**) *(décrisper) (poing)* to unclench; *(étreinte)* to relax; *Fig* **il n'a pas desserré les dents** he didn't open his mouth
2 se desserrer *vpr* (**a**) *(vis, ceinture, nœud)* to come loose (**b**) *(étreinte)* to relax

dessert [desɛr] *nm* dessert; **qu'est-ce qu'il y a comme** *ou* **au d.?** what's for dessert?

desserte [desɛrt] *nf (meuble)* sideboard

desservir¹ [63] [desɛrvir] *vt* (**a**) *(passer par) (ville, localité)* to serve; **ce train dessert les gares de...** *(annonce)* this train stops at...; **ville bien desservie** town with good public transport (**b**) *(conduire à) (pièce)* to lead to

desservir² **1** *vt* (**a**) *(débarrasser) (table)* to clear (**b**) *(nuire à)* **d. qn** to do sb a disservice
2 *vi (débarrasser la table)* to clear away

dessiller [desije] *vt Fig & Litt* **d. les yeux de qn** to open sb's eyes

dessin [desɛ̃] *nm* (**a**) *(technique, art)* drawing; **faire du d.** to draw; (**b**) *(représentation)* drawing; **faire un d.** to do a drawing; *Fam Fig* **faire un d. à qn** to spell it out for sb; *Cin* **d. animé** cartoon; **d. humoristique** cartoon (**c**) *(motif) (sur tissu)* design, pattern (**d**) *(contour) (de la bouche, du visage)* outline

dessinateur, -trice [desinatœr, -tris] *nm,f* (**a**) *(artiste)* drawer; **d. de bandes dessinées** cartoonist; **d. humoristique** cartoonist (**b**) *(concepteur)* designer (**c**) *Tech* **d. industriel** draughtsman

dessiner [desine] **1** *vt* (**a**) *(faire un dessin de)* to draw; **d. à l'encre/à la craie** to draw in ink/chalk (**b**) *(concevoir)* to design (**c**) *Fig (tracer) (lignes)* to outline; **vêtement qui dessine la taille** garment that shows off the waist; **visage bien dessiné** finely chiselled face
2 se dessiner *vpr* (**a**) *(apparaître)* to stand out; **se d. à l'horizon** to stand out on the horizon; **un sourire se dessine sur ses lèvres** a smile flickers over her lips (**b**) *Fig (prendre forme) (changement, résultat)* to become apparent; *(projet)* to take shape

dessoûler [desule] *vt & vi Fam* to sober up

dessous [dəsu] **1** *adv* (**a**) *(sous)* underneath (**b**) **en d.** underneath; **l'appartement d'en d.** the downstairs flat, the flat downstairs; **en d. de** below; **tu es très en d. de la vérité** you're not even close; *Fam* **être en d. de tout** to be worse than useless (**c**) **prendre/porter qch par (en) d.** to take hold of/carry sth from underneath; *Fig* **regarder qn par en d.** to look at sb furtively
2 *nm (partie inférieure) (d'une assiette, d'une table)* underside; *(du pied)* bottom; **les gens du d.** the people below; **avoir le d.** to get the worst of it
3 *nmpl* (**a**) *(partie cachée) (d'une affaire)* hidden side (**b**) *(sous-vêtements)* underwear

dessous-de-plat [dəsudpla] *nm inv* table mat

dessous-de-table [dəsudtabl] *nm inv* backhander; **verser un d. à qn** to give sb a backhander

dessous-de-verre [dəsudvɛr] *nm inv* coaster; *(en carton)* beer mat

dessus [dəsy] **1** *adv* on (it/them); **il a marché d.** he trod on it; **mais il n'y a pas l'adresse d.** but the address isn't on it
2 *nm* (**a**) *(d'une table, du pied)* top; *(d'une assiette)* upper side; **l'étage du d.** the top floor (**b**) *Fig* **avoir le d.** to have the upper hand; **reprendre le d.** *(se remettre)* to get over it

dessus-de-lit [dəsydli] *nm inv* bedspread

déstabiliser [destabilize] *vt* to destabilize

destin [dɛstɛ̃] *nm* fate, destiny

destinataire [dɛstinater] *nmf (d'une lettre)* addressee; *(de marchandises)* consignee; *(mandat postal)* payee

destination [dɛstinasjɔ̃] *nf* destination; **trains/vols à d. de La Rochelle** trains/flights to La Rochelle; **arriver à d.** to reach one's destination

destinée [dɛstine] *nf* (**a**) *(vie)* destiny (**b**) *Litt* **être promis à de grandes** *ou* **hautes destinées** to be destined for great things (**c**) *(fatalité)* fate, destiny

destiner [dɛstine] **1** *vt* (**a**) *(réserver)* **d. qch à qn** *(bien, somme d'argent, emploi)* to intend sth for sb (**b**) *(adresser)* **être destiné à qn** *(remarque, paquet)* to be meant for sb (**c**) *(assigner)* **d. une somme d'argent à qch** to allot *or* assign a sum of money to sth; **cet argent est destiné à la recherche contre le cancer** this money is going towards cancer research (**d**) *(concevoir pour)* **destiné à** (intended) for (**e**) *(vouer)* **d. qn à qch** to destine sb for sth; *Litt* **le sort les destinait à se rencontrer** they were destined to meet
2 se destiner *vpr* **se d. à qch** to intend to take up sth

destituer [dɛstitɥe] *vt (renvoyer) (officier)* to discharge; *(fonctionnaire)* to remove from office; *(souverain)* to depose

destitution [dɛstitysjɔ̃] *nf (d'un officier)* discharge; *(d'un fonctionnaire)* removal from office; *(d'un souverain)* deposition

destructeur, -trice [dɛstryktœr, -tris] *adj* destructive

destruction [dɛstryksjɔ̃] *nf* destruction

désuet, -ète [desɥɛ, -ɛt] *adj* (**a**) *(dépassé)* obsolete (**b**) *(démodé)* old-fashioned

désuétude [desɥetyd] *nf* disuse; **tomber en d.** *(mot, expression)* to become obsolete

désuni, -e [dezyni] *adj (famille, amis, amants)* divided

désunir [dezynir] *vt (personnes, famille)* to divide

désynchronisé, -e [desɛ̃krɔnize] *adj* out of synch

détachable [detaʃabl] *adj* detachable

détachant, -e [detaʃɑ̃, -ɑ̃t] **1** *adj* stain-removing
2 *nm* stain remover

détaché, -e [detaʃe] *adj* (**a**) *(ton, air, manière)* detached (**b**) *(fonctionnaire)* seconded

détachement [detaʃmɑ̃] *nm* (**a**) *(indifférence)* detachment (**de** from) (**b**) *(d'un fonctionnaire)* secondment; **être en d.** to be on secondment (**c**) *(troupes)* detachment

détacher¹ [detaʃe] **1** *vt* (**a**) *(défaire) (étiquette, page perforée)* to detach; *(ceinture, liens)* to undo; *(rideau)* to take down; *(wagon)* to uncouple; **d. ses yeux de qch** to take one's eyes off sth (**b**) *(libérer) (prisonnier, animal)* to untie (**c**) *(déléguer) (fonctionnaire)* to second; *(militaire)* to detach (**d**) *Fig* **d. qn de qch** to turn sb away from sth (**e**) *(faire sonner)* **d. les syllabes d'un mot** to pronounce each syllable of a word separately; *Mus* **d. les notes** to detach the notes
2 se détacher *vpr* (**a**) *(étiquette, bouton, page)* to come off; *(ceinture)* to come undone; *(écorce)* to peel off (**b**) *(se libérer) (animal)* to get loose (**c**) *Fig* **se d. de qn** (en devenant adulte) to break away from sb; *(par manque d'intérêt)* to grow apart from sb; **se d. de qch** to turn one's back on sth (**d**) *(se séparer) (groupe de coureurs)* to break away (**e**) *(ressortir)* to stand out (**sur** against)

détacher² *vt (nettoyer)* to remove the stains from

détail [detaj] *nm* (**a**) *(élément)* detail (**b**) *(énumération) (d'un compte, d'un inventaire)* items; *(d'une facture)* breakdown; **elle m'a fait le d. de sa soirée** she gave me a detailed account of her party; *Fam Fig* **il n'a pas fait de d.!** he didn't make any exceptions!; *Fam Fig* **il n'a pas fait dans le d.** he didn't go into detail; **en d.** in detail; **se perdre dans les détails** to get bogged down in detail (**c**) *Com* retail; **vendre/acheter au d.** to sell/buy retail

détaillant, -e [detajã, -ãt] *nm,f Com* retailer

détaillé, -e [detaje] *adj (récit, description)* detailed; *(facture)* itemized

détaler [detale] *vi Fam (personne)* to take off; **faire d. qn** to send sb packing

détartrage [detartraʒ] *nm* (a) *(de dents)* scaling; **se faire faire un d.** to have one's teeth scaled (b) *(de bouilloire, de cafetière, de chaudière)* descaling

détartrer [detartre] *vt* (a) *(dents)* to scale (b) *(bouilloire, cafetière, chaudière)* to descale

détaxe [detaks] *nf* tax refund

détaxer [detakse] *vt* to exempt from tax; **marchandises détaxées** duty-free goods

détectable [detɛktabl] *adj* detectable

détecter [detɛkte] *vt* to detect

détecteur, -trice [detɛktœr, -tris] **1** *adj* detecting **2** *nm* detector; **d. de faux billets** forged banknote detector; **d. de fumée** smoke detector; **d. de mensonges** lie detector; **d. de mines** mine detector, *Ordinat* **d. virus** virus detector

détection [detɛksjõ] *nf* detection; *Ordinat* **d. d'erreurs** error detection; *Ordinat* **d. virale** virus detection

détective [detɛktiv] *nm* detective; **d. privé** private detective

déteindre [54] [detɛ̃dr] *vi (tissu)* to run (**sur** over); **d. au lavage** to run in the wash; *Fig* **cela a déteint sur eux** it's rubbed off on them

dételer [42] [detle] **1** *vt (chevaux)* to unharness; *(bœufs)* to unyoke **2** *vi Fam* to stop working; **sans d.** non-stop

détendre [detɑ̃dr] **1** *vt* (a) *(relâcher) (corde)* to slacken; *(arc)* to unbend; *(ressort)* to release (b) *(décontracter) (personne)* to relax; **la musique me détend** music relaxes me (c) **d. l'atmosphère** to make the atmosphere less tense **2 se détendre** *vpr* (a) *(corde)* to slacken; *(arc)* to unbend; *(ressort)* to lose its tension (b) *(se relaxer) (personne, visage)* to relax (c) *(atmosphère, situation)* to become less tense

détendu, -e [detɑ̃dy] *adj (personne, conversation)* relaxed

détenir [70] [detnir] *vt* (a) *(avoir en sa possession) (passeport, titres, pouvoir, record du monde)* to hold; *(secret, preuve)* to have (b) *(garder prisonnier)* to hold

détente [detɑ̃t] *nf* (a) *(relaxation)* relaxation (b) *Pol* détente (c) *(d'une arme)* trigger (d) *(d'un athlète)* spring; **avoir de la d.** to jump well (e) *(d'un gaz)* expansion (f) **être dur** *ou* **long à la d.** to be slow on the uptake

détenteur, -trice [detɑ̃tœr, -tris] *nm,f (d'argent, de titres, de record)* holder; *(d'arme)* possessor

détention [detɑ̃sjõ] *nf* (a) *(de titres)* holding; *(d'armes)* possession (b) *(incarcération)* detention; **d. provisoire** detention pending trial

détenu, -e [detny] *nm,f* prisoner

détergent, -e [detɛrʒã, -ãt] *adj & nm* detergent

détérioration [deterjɔrasjõ] *nf* deterioration

détériorer [deterjɔre] **1** *vt* to damage **2 se détériorer** *vpr* to deteriorate

déterminant, -e [detɛrminã, -ãt] **1** *adj* decisive **2** *nm* (a) *Ling* determiner (b) *Math* determinant

détermination [detɛrminasjõ] *nf* (a) *(fermeté)* determination (b) *(d'une date, d'un lieu, d'un prix)* fixing; *(du sang, d'une bactérie)* typing

déterminé, -e [detɛrmine] *adj* (a) *(résolu)* determined; **être d. à faire qch** to be determined to do sth (b) *(défini)* specific

déterminer [detɛrmine] **1** *vt* (a) *(définir)* to determine, to fix; *(sang, bactérie)* to type (b) *(décider)* **d. qn à faire qch** to

induce sb to do sth (c) *(causer) (changement)* to cause; *(action, décision)* to determine (d) *Gram* to determine **2 se déterminer** *vpr* **se d. à faire qch** to make up one's mind to do sth

déterré, -e [detere] *nm,f Fam* **avoir une mine de d.** to look like death warmed up

déterrer [detere] *vt aussi Fig* to dig up

détestable [detɛstabl] *adj* foul

détester [detɛste] **1** *vt* to detest, to hate; **je déteste me lever tôt** I hate getting up early; **ne pas d. faire qch** to quite like doing sth **2 se détester** *vpr (soi-même)* to hate oneself; *(l'un l'autre)* to hate each other

détonant, -e [detɔnã, -ãt] **1** *adj aussi Fig* explosive **2** *nm* explosive

détonateur [detɔnatœr] *nm* detonator; *Fig* **servir de d. à qch** to spark sth off

détonation [detɔnasjõ] *nf (bruit)* explosion; *(bruit d'arme à feu)* bang

détoner [detɔne] *vi (explosif)* to detonate; **faire d. qch** to detonate sth

détonner [detɔne] *vi* (a) *(chanteur)* to sing out of tune; *(instrumentiste)* to play out of tune (b) *(trancher) (couleurs)* to clash; **il détonne dans ce milieu** he's out of place in that environment

détordre [detɔrdr] *vt (fil)* to untwist

détour [detur] *nm* (a) *(parcours)* detour; **faire un d. (par)** to make a detour (via); **valoir le d.** *(site)* to be worth the trip (b) *Fig (biais)* roundabout means; **user de détours pour faire qch** to do sth in a roundabout way; **sans d.** without beating about the bush (c) *(tracé) (d'une route, d'une rivière)* bend; **faire un d.** to bend; *Fig* **au d. de la conversation** in the course of the conversation

détourné, -e [deturne] *adj aussi Fig* roundabout, indirect

détournement [deturnəmã] *nm* (a) **d. d'avion** hijacking (b) *(d'un cours d'eau)* diversion (c) **d. de fonds** embezzlement

détourner [deturne] **1** *vt* (a) *(circulation, rivière)* to divert; *(avion)* to hijack (b) *(éloigner)* **d. qn de** *(ami, famille)* to take sb away from; *(préoccupation, engagement)* to divert sb from; **d. qn du droit chemin** to lead sb astray; **d. l'attention de qn** to divert or distract sb's attention; **d. la conversation** to change the subject; **les soupçons** to avert suspicion (c) *(voler) (fonds)* to embezzle (à from) (d) *(tourner)* **d. la tête** to turn one's head away; **d. les yeux** *ou* **le regard** to look away **2 se détourner** *vpr aussi Fig* to turn away (**de** from)

détracteur, -trice [detraktœr, -tris] *nm,f* detractor

détraqué, -e [detrake] **1** *adj (appareil)* out of order; *(estomac)* upset; *(temps)* unsettled; *Fam (personne) (psychologiquement)* unhinged **2** *nm,f Fam* maniac

détraquer [detrake] **1** *vt (appareil)* to put out of order; *(santé)* to ruin; *(estomac)* to upset **2 se détraquer** *vpr (appareil, santé)* to break down; *(temps)* to become unsettled; **se d. l'estomac** to upset one's stomach

détrempé, -e [detrɑ̃pe] *adj (terre, sol)* sodden, waterlogged

détresse [detrɛs] *nf* (a) *(angoisse)* distress (b) *(dénuement)* financial difficulties (c) *(perdition)* **en d.** *(navire)* in distress; *(voiture, avion)* in difficulties

détriment [detrimã] *nm* **au d. de** to the detriment of; **je l'ai appris à mon d.** I found it out to my cost

détritus [detritys] *nm Br* rubbish, *Am* garbage

détroit [detrwa] *nm* strait; **le d. de Béring** the Bering Strait; **le d. de Gibraltar** the Strait of Gibraltar

détromper [detrɔ̃pe] **1** *vt* **d. qn** to put sb right (**sur** about) **2 se détromper** *vpr* to realize that one was wrong; **détrompez-vous!** think again!

détrôner [detrone] *vt* (**a**) *(monarque)* to dethrone (**b**) *(théorie, méthode, produit)* to supersede

détrousser [detruse] *vt Hum* **d. qn** to relieve sb of his valuables

détruire [18] [detrɥir] **1** *vt* (**a**) *(anéantir) (espoir, mariage, santé)* to ruin, to wreck (**b**) *(démolir) (édifice, empire, avion)* to destroy (**c**) *(tuer)* to kill **2 se détruire** *vpr (se faire du mal)* to ruin one's health

dette [dɛt] *nf aussi Fig* debt; **avoir des dettes** to be in debt; **être couvert** *ou* **criblé de dettes** to be crippled with debt; **d. extérieure** foreign debt; **la d. publique** *ou* **de l'État** the National Debt; **payer sa d. à la société** to pay one's debt to society

DEUG [dœg] *nm (abrév* **diplôme d'études universitaires générales**) = degree gained after a two-year course

deuil [dœj] *nm* (**a**) *(décès)* bereavement; **il y a eu un d. dans leur famille** there has been a death in their family (**b**) *(tristesse)* mourning; **être en d.** to be in mourning; **journée de d. national** day of national mourning (**c**) *(tenue)* **porter le d. (de qn)** to be in mourning (for sb); **prendre/quitter le d.** to go into/come out of mourning; *Fam Fig* **avoir les ongles en d.** to have dirty fingernails (**d**) **faire son d. de qch** to give sth up as lost

Deutsche Mark [dɔjtʃmark, døtʃmark] *nm Anciennement* Deutschmark

deux [dø] **1** *adj inv* (**a**) *(chiffre)* two; **d. fois** twice; **des d. côtés du fleuve** on either side *or* on both sides of the river; **tous (les) d.** both; **tous les d. jours** every other day, every two days; **nous/vous/eux d.** the two of us/you/them; **vivre à d.** to live together; **les ordinateurs et moi, ça fait d.** I know absolutely nothing about computers (**b**) *(peu de)* **c'est à d. pas d'ici** it's only a short distance away, it's two minutes away; **je reviens dans d. minutes** I'll be back in a minute; **tu peux venir? – d. secondes!** can you come here? – just a minute! **2** *nm inv* two; **casser qch en d.** to break sth in two; **marcher par d.** to walk in pairs *or* twos; *(dans une procession)* to march two abreast; *Fam* **en moins de d.** in next to no time; *voir aussi* **trois**

deuxième [døzjɛm] *adj & nmf* second; *voir aussi* **cinquième**

deuxièmement [døzjɛmmɑ̃] *adv* secondly

deux-mâts [døma] *nm* two-master

deux-pièces [døpjɛs] *nm* (**a**) *(maillot de bain)* two-piece (swimsuit) (**b**) *(tailleur)* two-piece (**c**) *(appartement)* two-room *Br* flat *or Am* apartment

deux-points [døpwɛ] *nm* colon

deux-roues [døru] *nm* two-wheeled vehicle

deux-temps [døtɑ̃] *nm (moteur)* two-stroke (engine)

deuzio [døzjo] *adv Fam* second

dévaler [devale] **1** *vt (escalier, pente)* to hurtle down **2** *vi (personne, pierres)* to hurtle down; *(eau, lave, boue)* to rush down

dévaliser [devalize] *vt* (**a**) *(cambrioler) (banque)* to rob; *(maison)* to burgle; *Fig (commerçant)* to clean out (**b**) *(vider) (réfrigérateur, placard)* to raid

dévalorisation [devalorizasjɔ̃] *nf* (**a**) *(action) (de la monnaie)* devaluation; *(de marchandises)* marking down; *(résultat) (de la monnaie)* depreciation; *(de marchandises)* mark-down (**b**) *Fig (d'une personne, d'une politique)* discrediting; *(d'un diplôme, d'une profession)* devaluation

dévaloriser [devalorize] **1** *vt* (**a**) *(monnaie)* to devalue (**b**) *(personne, politique)* to discredit; *(qualification, diplôme)* to devalue **2 se dévaloriser** *vpr* (**a**) *(monnaie)* to depreciate (**b**) *(personne)* to put oneself down

dévaluation [devalɥasjɔ̃] *nf Fin* devaluation

dévaluer [devalɥe] **1** *vt (monnaie)* to devalue **2 se dévaluer** *vpr* to fall in value

devancer [16] [dəvɑ̃se] *vt (être devant) (concurrent)* to be/get ahead of; **d. son époque** to be ahead of one's time (**b**) *(arriver avant)* to arrive before (**c**) *(prévoir) (personne, critiques)* to forestall; *(demande)* to anticipate (**d**) *(faire avant) Mil* **d. l'appel** to enlist before call-up; *Fin* **d. une échéance** to settle an account early

devant [dəvɑ̃] **1** *prép* (**a**) *(en face de, en avant de)* in front of; **assis d. moi** sitting in front of me; **marcher droit d. soi** to walk straight on; **regardez d. vous!** look where you're going!; **passer d. qn/qch** *(dans la rue)* to go past sb/sth; **passer d. qn** *(dans une file d'attente)* to go in front of sb; **avoir du temps/de l'argent d. soi** to have time/money to spare; **tu as la vie d. toi** you've got your whole life ahead of you; **d. derrière** back to front (**b**) *(face à)* **d. le danger** in the face of danger; **égaux d. la loi** equal in the eyes of the law **2** *adv* (**a**) *(en face)* in front; **je cherchais la poste et j'étais juste d.** I was looking for the post office when I was standing right in front of it; **où est Thierry? – je crois qu'il est d.** where's Thierry? – he's up ahead, I think (**b**) *(en avant) (dans les premiers rangs)* at the front; *(en voiture)* in the front; **aller d.** to go in front; **marcher/courir d.** to walk on/run on ahead; **passez d.!** you go ahead of me! **3** *nm* front; *Fig* **prendre les devants** to make the first move

devanture [dəvɑ̃tyr] *nf (vitrine)* window; *(façade)* front

dévastateur, -trice [devastatœr, -tris] *adj* devastating

dévastation [devastasjɔ̃] *nf* devastation

dévaster [devaste] *vt* to devastate

déveine [devɛn] *nf Fam* bad luck; **être dans la d.** to be down on one's luck

développement [devlɔpmɑ̃] *nm* development; *(de pellicule)* developing; *(en cyclisme)* gear ratio; **en plein d.** *(entreprise, pays)* growing fast; **développements** *(d'une affaire)* developments; *Fig* **se lancer dans de grands développements** to go into detailed explanation

développer [devlɔpe] **1** *vt* to develop **2 se développer** *vpr* to develop; *(s'étendre)* to spread

devenir[1] [dəvnir] *nm Litt* (**a**) *(évolution)* evolution; **être en perpétuel d.** to be constantly evolving (**b**) *(futur)* future

devenir[2] [70] *(aux être) vi* to become; **il devint général** he became a general; **il était devenu (un) homme** he had grown into a man; **ça devient difficile** it's getting difficult; **d. vieux** to get *or* grow old; **d. fou** to go mad; **c'est à d. fou!** it's enough to drive you mad!; **d. tout rouge** to go all red; **que devient-il?** how is he getting on?; **qu'est-il devenu?** what's become of him?

dévergondé, -e [devɛrgɔ̃de] **1** *adj* shameless **2** *nm,f* shameless person

dévergonder [devɛrgɔ̃de] **se dévergonder** *vpr* to get into bad ways

déversement [devɛrsəmɑ̃] *nm (écoulement)* discharge; *(action)* pouring

déverser [devɛrse] **1** *vt* (**a**) *(eau)* to pour; *(sable, gravier, déchets)* to dump; *Fig (touristes, voyageurs)* to disgorge (**b**) **d. sa colère sur qn** to vent one's anger on sb; **d. des insultes sur qn** to shower sb with abuse **2 se déverser** *vpr (rivière)* to empty (**dans** into)

dévêtir [71] [devetir] **1** *vt* to undress
2 se dévêtir *vpr* to undress
devez *voir* **devoir**
déviation [devjɑsjɔ̃] *nf* (**a**) *(itinéraire modifié)* Br diversion, Am detour (**b**) *(modification)* deviation (*par rapport à* from)
dévier [66] [devje] **1** *vt* (**a**) *(circulation)* to divert (**b**) *(balle, coup)* to deflect
2 *vi (véhicule, missile)* to veer (**vers** towards); *(balle)* to deflect (**vers** towards); **d. de sa route** *(véhicule, missile)* to veer off course; *Fig* **d. de son sujet** to digress
devin [dəvɛ̃] *nm* soothsayer; *Fam* **je ne suis pas d.!** I 'm not a mind-reader!
deviner [dəvine] *vt (énigme, secret)* to guess; *(futur)* to predict; *(pensée)* to read; **devine qui j'ai vu** guess who I saw; *Fam* **je ne pouvais pas d.!** how was I supposed to know?
devinette [dəvinɛt] *nf* riddle; **poser une d. à qn** to ask sb a riddle
devis [dəvi] *nm* estimate, quote; **faire faire un d. pour qch** to get an estimate or a quote for sth
dévisager [45] [deviʒaʒe] *vt* to stare at
devise [dəviz] *nf* (**a**) *(d'une personne)* motto (**b**) *(monnaie)* currency; **devises étrangères** foreign currency; **d. forte** hard currency (**c**) *(en héraldique)* device
deviser [dəvize] *vi Litt* to converse
dévisser [devise] **1** *vt* to unscrew
2 *vi (alpiniste)* to fall
3 se dévisser *vpr* to unscrew; *(par accident)* to come unscrewed; *Fig* **se d. la tête** ou **le cou** to screw one's head round
de visu [devizy] *adv* with one's own eyes
dévitaliser [devitalize] *vt (dent)* to remove the nerve from
dévoiler [devwale] **1** *vt (visage, statue, plaque)* to unveil; *Fig (nom, secret, complot)* to disclose
2 se dévoiler *vpr (secret, complot)* to come to light
devoir¹ *nm* (**a**) *(obligation)* duty; **faire qch par d.** to do sth out of a sense of duty; **un homme/une femme de d.** a man/a woman with a sense of duty; **faire** ou **remplir son d.** (**envers**) to do one's duty (by); **il est de mon d. de vous le dire** it is my duty to tell you (**b**) *(exercices) (en classe)* test; **devoirs** *(à la maison)* homework; **faire ses devoirs** to do one's homework; **devoirs de vacances** holiday homework (**c**) *Formel* **rendre les derniers devoirs à qn** to pay one's last respects to sb
devoir² [26] **1** *vt (être redevable de)* **d. qch à qn** to owe sb sth, to owe sth to sb; **il me doit cent euros** he owes me a hundred euros; **je lui dois bien cela** it's the least I can do for him, I owe him that at least
2 *v aux* (**a**) *(indique l'obligation)* **d. faire qch** to have to do sth; **vous devez être là à midi** you must or you have to be there by noon; **elle a cru d. refuser** she thought it advisable to refuse; **les commandes doivent être adressées à...** orders should be sent to...; **vous devriez rester** you should stay, you ought to stay; **il aurait dû m'avertir** he should have warned me, he ought to have warned me
(**b**) *(indique la nécessité)* **tu dois absolument lui en parler** you really must talk to him about it; **finalement, j'ai dû céder** I had to give way in the end; **il ne devait plus les revoir** *(il ne les reverrait plus)* he was (destined) never to see them again; **cela devait arriver!** it was bound to or it had to happen!
(**c**) *(indique l'intention)* **je devais partir lundi, mais...** I was meant to leave on Monday, but...; **le train doit arriver à midi** the train is due (to arrive) at twelve o'clock

(**d**) *(indique la supposition)* **vous devez être fatigué** you must be tired; **il ne doit pas avoir plus de 50 ans** he can't be more than 50; **il a dû me prendre pour un autre** he must have mistaken me for someone else; **la pollution devrait s'accroître d'ici la fin du siècle** pollution is expected to increase by the end of the century
3 se devoir *vpr* **je me dois à ma famille/mon travail** I must devote myself to my family/my work; **je me dois de le faire** it's my duty to do it; **comme il se doit** as is (only) right and proper
dévolu, -e [devɔly] **1** *adj (somme, responsabilités)* assigned (**à** to)
2 *nm* **jeter son d. sur** to set one's heart on
devons *voir* **devoir**
dévorant, -e [devɔrɑ̃, -ɑ̃t] *adj (jalousie, passion)* consuming; *(envie)* overwhelming; *(curiosité)* burning; **avoir une faim dévorante** to be ravenous
dévorer [devɔre] *vt* (**a**) *(proie, nourriture, livre)* to devour; **être dévoré par les moustiques** to be eaten alive by mosquitoes; **d. qn des yeux** ou **du regard** to devour sb with one's eyes (**b**) *Fig (détruire)* **l'ambition/la jalousie la dévore** she is consumed by ambition/jealousy; **dévoré de remords** consumed with remorse (**c**) *Fig (fortune, kilomètres)* to eat up
dévot, -e [devo, -ɔt] **1** *adj* devout
2 *nm,f* dévout person
dévotion [devosjɔ̃] *nf* (**a**) *(ferveur)* devoutness (**b**) *(adoration)* devotion; **avoir une d. pour** to be devoted to (**c**) **dévotions** *(prières)* devotions
dévoué, -e [devwe] *adj* devoted (**à** to)
dévouement [devumɑ̃] *nm* (**a**) *(abnégation)* devotion to duty (**b**) *(amour)* devotion (**à** to); **avec d.** devotedly
dévouer [devwe] **se dévouer** *vpr (se sacrifier)* to volunteer (**pour faire qch** to do sth); *(se consacrer)* to devote oneself (**à** to); **il faut que quelqu'un se dévoue** somebody has to do it
dévoyé, -e [devwaje] *adj & nm,f* delinquent
dévoyer [32] [devwaje] **se dévoyer** *vpr Litt* to go astray
devra *etc voir* **devoir**
dextérité [dɛksterite] *nf* dexterity, skill; **avec d.** skilfully
DGSE [deʒeɛsə] *nf (abrév* **direction générale de la sécurité extérieure)** = French military intelligence service, *Br* ≃ MI6, *Am* ≃ CIA
diabète [djabɛt] *nm* diabetes; **avoir du d.** to have diabetes
diabétique [djabetik] *adj & nmf* diabetic
diable [djɑbl] *nm* (**a**) *(démon)* devil; **le d.** the Devil; **un petit d.** *(enfant)* a little devil; **avoir une faim de tous les diables** to be absolutely ravenous; **un bruit de tous les diables** a hell of a din; *Fig* **avoir le d. au corps** to be possessed; *Fig* **tirer le d. par la queue** to live from hand to mouth; **au d. l'avarice!** to hell with the expense!; **allez au d.!** go to hell!, **au d. vauvert** miles away; **que le d. l'emporte!** he can go to hell!; **c'est bien le d. si...** it would be surprising if... (**b**) *(marque la surprise, l'agacement)* **d.!** goodness me!; **où d. est-elle allée?** where the devil has she gone?; **que d.!** for goodness sake! (**c**) *(chariot)* (two-wheeled) trolley (**d**) *(jouet)* jack-in-the-box
diablement [djɑbləmɑ̃] *adv Fam* damned
diablesse [djɑblɛs] *nf (démon, méchante femme)* she-devil; *Vieilli (jeune fille)* devil
diablotin [djɑblɔtɛ̃] *nm* imp
diabolique [djɑbɔlik] *adj* diabolical
diabolo [djɑbɔlo] *nm (boisson)* **d. menthe/fraise** mint/strawberry syrup and lemonade
diadème [djadɛm] *nm* tiara

diagnostic [djagnɔstik] *nm* diagnosis; **faire un d.** to make a diagnosis; **ce médecin a un d. très sûr** this doctor makes very reliable diagnoses; *Ordinat* **d. d'autotest** self-test diagnosis

diagnostiquer [djagnɔstike] *vt* to diagnose

diagonal, -e, -aux, -ales [djagɔnal, -o] **1** *adj* diagonal **2** *nf* **diagonale** diagonal; **en diagonale** diagonally; *Fig* **lire qch en diagonale** to skim through sth

diagonalement [djagɔnalmã] *adv* diagonally

diagramme [djagram] *nm* diagram

dialecte [djalɛkt] *nm* dialect

dialectique [djalɛktik] **1** *adj* dialectical **2** *nf* dialectics *(singulier)*

dialogue [djalɔg] *nm* dialogue; *(conversation)* conversation; **c'est un d. de sourds** it's a dialogue of the deaf; *Ordinat* **mode de d.** interactive mode

dialoguer [djalɔge] *vi* to communicate; *(avec un ordinateur)* to interact

dialyse [djaliz] *nf Méd* dialysis

diamant [djamã] *nm* diamond

diamantaire [djamãtɛr] *nm (tailleur)* diamond cutter; *(vendeur)* diamond merchant

diamétralement [djametralmã] *adv* **d. opposés** diametrically opposed

diamètre [djamɛtr] *nm* diameter

diapason [djapazɔ̃] *nm Mus* **(a)** *(note)* pitch; *Fig* **se mettre au d.** to fall in with the others **(b)** *(appareil)* tuning fork

diaphane [djafan] *adj* diaphanous

diaphragme [djafragm] *nm* diaphragm

diapo [djapo] *nf Fam* slide

diapositive [djapozitiv] *nf* slide

diarrhée [djare] *nf* diarrhoea; **avoir la d.** to have diarrhoea

diaspora [djaspɔra] *nf* diaspora

diatonique [djatɔnik] *adj* diatonic

diatribe [djatrib] *nf* diatribe **(contre** against)

dichotomie [dikɔtɔmi] *nf* dichotomy

dico [diko] *nm Fam* dictionary

Dictaphone® [diktafɔn] *nm* Dictaphone®

dictateur [diktatœr] *nm* dictator

dictatorial, -e, -aux, -ales [diktatɔrjal, -o] *adj* dictatorial

dictature [diktatyr] *nf* dictatorship

dictée [dikte] *nf* dictation; **écrire qch sous la d. de qn** to write sth at sb's dictation; **d. musicale** musical dictation

dicter [dikte] *vt* to dictate

diction [diksjɔ̃] *nf* diction

dictionnaire [diksjɔnɛr] *nm* dictionary; **d. électronique** electronic dictionary; **d. de langue** language dictionary

dicton [diktɔ̃] *nm* saying

didactique [didaktik] **1** *adj* **(a)** *(ouvrage, voyage)* educational **(b)** *(terme, langage)* technical **2** *nf* didactics *(singulier)*

dièse [djɛz] *Mus* **1** *nm* sharp **2** *adj* sharp; **fa d.** F sharp

diesel [djezɛl] **1** *adj* **moteur d.** diesel engine **2** *nm (carburant)* diesel **3** *nf (voiture)* diesel

diète [djɛt] *nf (partielle)* diet; *(totale)* fast; **être à la d.** *(partielle)* to be on a diet; *(totale)* to be fasting

diététicien, -enne [djetetisjɛ̃, -ɛn] *nm,f* dietitian

diététique [djetetik] **1** *adj (menu, repas)* diet; *(magasin, restaurant)* health food **2** *nf* dietetics *(singulier)*

dieu, -x [djø] **1** *nm* **(a)** *(divinité)* god; *Fam* **comme un d.** *(chanter, jouer)* like a god **(b)** *(dans la religion chrétienne)* **D.** God; **le bon D.** God; **D. merci!, D. soit loué!** thank God!; **D. sait si j'ai travaillé** God knows I've worked hard enough; **D. seul le sait** God only knows **2** *exclam* **mon D.!** (good) God!; **D. qu'elle est petite!** God, she's small!; *Fam* **c'est pas D. possible!** it's just not possible!; *Fam* **bon D.!** for God's sake!; *très Fam* **nom de D.!** Christ almighty!

diffamation [difamasjɔ̃] *nf (paroles)* slander; *(écrits)* libel; **procès en d.** slander/libel trial

diffamatoire [difamatwar] *adj (paroles)* slanderous; *(écrits)* libellous

différé, -e [difere] **1** *adj Ordinat* **traitement d.** off-line processing **2** *nm* **en d.** *(émission)* pre-recorded

différemment [diferamã] *adv* differently

différence [diferãs] *nf* difference **(entre** between); **d. d'âge/de prix** age/price difference; **faire la d. (entre)** to make a distinction (between); **cela ne fait aucune** *ou* **pas de d.** it makes no difference; **à la d. de** unlike

différenciation [diferãsjasjɔ̃] *nf* differentiation

différencier [66] [diferãsje] **1** *vt* to differentiate **(de** *ou* **d'avec** from) **2** *se* **différencier** *vpr* **(a)** *(être différent)* to differ **(de/par** from/in) **(b)** *(chercher à être différent)* to differentiate oneself **(de** from)

différend [diferã] *nm* difference of opinion, disagreement **(entre** between); *Jur* dispute; **avoir un d. avec qn** to have a disagreement with sb

différent, -e [diferã, -ãt] *adj* different **(de** from); **différents cas** *(plusieurs)* various cases

différentiel, -elle [diferãsjɛl] **1** *adj & nm* differential **2** *nf* **différentielle** *Math* differential

différer [34] [difere] **1** *vt (jugement, paiement)* to defer; *(décision, départ)* to postpone **2** *vi (être différent)* to differ **(par** in)

difficile [difisil] **1** *adj* difficult; *(exigeant)* fussy; **le plus d. est fait** the most difficult part is over; **il est d. de le joindre** it's difficult to contact him; **il m'est d. d'accepter** it's difficult for me to accept; **être d. à vivre** to be difficult to get on with; **être d. sur qch** to be particular about sth **2** *nmf* **faire le d.** to be fussy

difficilement [difisilmã] *adv* with difficulty, not easily; **on peut d. le lui dire** you can hardly tell him that

difficulté [difikylte] *nf* difficulty; **être en d.** to be in difficulty *or* trouble; **faire des difficultés** to create difficulties; **avoir de la d. à faire qch** to have difficulty (in) doing sth; **avoir des difficultés en espagnol** to have difficulties with Spanish

difforme [difɔrm] *adj* deformed, misshapen

difformité [difɔrmite] *nf* deformity

diffus, -e [dify, -yz] *adj (lumière)* diffuse; *(impression, souvenir)* vague

diffuser [difyze] *vt* **(a)** *(lumière, chaleur)* to diffuse; *(livres)* to distribute; *(idée, nouvelle)* to spread **(b)** *(émission)* to broadcast

diffuseur [difyzœr] *nm (de lumière, de chaleur)* diffuser; **d. de parfum** room freshener

diffusion [difyzjɔ̃] *nf* **(a)** *(de lumière, de chaleur)* diffusion; *(de livres)* distribution; *(d'une idée, d'une nouvelle)* spreading **(b)** *(d'une émission)* broadcasting

digérer [34] [diʒere] *vt* **(a)** *(aliment)* to digest; **je ne digère pas le lait** I can't digest milk **(b)** *(assimiler intellectuellement)* to digest; *Fam (accepter)* to swallow

digeste [diʒɛst] *adj Fam aussi Fig* easily digestible

digestif, -ive [diʒɛstif, -iv] **1** *adj* digestive **2** *nm* liqueur

digestion [diʒɛstjɔ̃] *nf* digestion; **avoir une d.** difficile to have problems with one's digestion

digital¹, -e, -aux, -ales [diʒital, -o] *adj (numérique)* digital

digital², -e, -aux, -ales 1 *adj voir* **empreinte 2** *nf* **digitale** *Bot* digitalis

digne [diɲ] *adj (a) (méritant)* **d. de** worthy of; **d. d'éloges** praiseworthy; **d. de foi** reliable; **être d. de faire qch** to be fit to do sth **(b)** *(approprié)* **d. de** worthy of; **peu d. de qn** unworthy of sb; **d. de ce nom** worthy of the name; *Hum* **tu es bien le d. fils de ton père** you're your father's son all right **(c)** *(grave)* dignified

dignement [diɲəmɑ̃] *adv* **(a)** *(avec dignité)* with dignity **(b)** *(de façon appropriée)* fittingly; **être d. récompensé** to be justly rewarded

dignitaire [diɲitɛr] *nm* dignitary

dignité [diɲite] *nf* dignity

digression [digrɛsjɔ̃] *nf* digression; **faire une d.** to digress

digue [dig] *nf (dans un port)* dike; *(contre l'érosion)* sea wall

dilapider [dilapide] *vt (fortune)* to squander; *(fonds publics)* to embezzle

dilatation [dilatasjɔ̃] *nf* **(a)** *(des pupilles)* dilation; *(de l'estomac)* distension **(b)** *(d'un gaz)* expansion

dilater [dilate] **1** *vt* **(a)** *(pupilles)* to dilate; *(estomac)* to distend **(b)** *(gaz)* to expand **2 se dilater** *vpr* **(a)** *(pupilles)* to dilate; *(estomac)* to distend **(b)** *(gaz)* to expand

dilemme [dilɛm] *nm* dilemma

dilettante [diletɑ̃t] *nmf* dilettante; **faire qch en d.** to dabble in sth

diligence [diliʒɑ̃s] *nf* **(a)** *(véhicule)* (stage)coach **(b)** *Litt (soin)* diligence

diligent, -e [diliʒɑ̃, -ɑ̃t] *adj Litt (zélé)* diligent

diluant [dilɥɑ̃] *nm* thinner

diluer [dilɥe] *vt (boisson)* to dilute; *(peinture)* to thin down; *Fig (discours, dissertation)* to pad out

dilution [dilysjɔ̃] *nf (de peinture)* thinning down; *(d'une boisson)* dilution

diluvien, -enne [dilyvjɛ̃, -ɛn] *adj (pluies)* torrential

dimanche [dimɑ̃ʃ] *nm* Sunday; **le d. des Rameaux/de Pâques** Palm/Easter Sunday; *Fig* **conducteur du d.** Sunday driver; *voir aussi* **samedi**

dîme [dim] *nf Hist* tithe

dimension [dimɑ̃sjɔ̃] *nf* **(a)** *(grandeur)* dimension, size; **à deux/trois dimensions** two-/three-dimensional; **prendre les dimensions de qch** *(objet)* to take the measurements of sth **(b)** *(importance)* magnitude **(c)** *(aspect)* dimension

diminué, -e [diminɥe] *adj* **être d.** to have gone downhill

diminuer [diminɥe] **1** *vt* **(a)** *(réduire)* to reduce, to decrease **(b)** *(affaiblir)* to weaken **(c)** *(dénigrer) (personne)* to belittle; *(action)* to undermine **2** *vi* to decrease; *(fièvre)* to drop **3 se diminuer** *vpr* to belittle oneself

diminutif, -ive [diminytif, -iv] *adj & nm* diminutive

diminution [diminysjɔ̃] *nf* reduction, decrease

dinar [dinar] *nm* dinar

dinde [dɛ̃d] *nf* **(a)** *(volaille, viande)* turkey **(b)** *Fam (femme sotte)* silly goose

dindon [dɛ̃dɔ̃] *nm* turkey (cock); *Fig* **être le d. de la farce** to be made a fool of

dindonneau, -x [dɛ̃dɔno] *nm* turkey poult

dîner¹ [dine] *nm* **(a)** *(repas du soir)* dinner; *(soirée)* dinner party; **il y a du risotto pour le** *ou* **au** *ou* **à d.** it's risotto for dinner **(b)** *(repas de midi)* lunch

dîner² *vi* **(a)** *(le soir)* to have dinner, to dine; **il dîna d'une tranche de jambon** he had a slice of ham for dinner **(b)** *(à midi)* to have lunch

dînette [dinɛt] *nf (service)* doll's teaset; **jouer à la d.** to have a dolls' tea party

dingo [dɛ̃go] *adj Fam* crazy

dingue [dɛ̃g] *Fam* **1** *adj* **(a)** *(fou)* crazy; **être d. de qn/qch** to be crazy about sb/sth **(b)** *(incroyable)* incredible **2** *nmf (fou)* nutcase; **être un d. de moto/cinéma** to be a motorcycle/movie nut

dinguer [dɛ̃ge] *vi Fam* **aller d. contre qch** to go crashing into sth; **envoyer d. qn** *(éconduire)* to send sb packing; **envoyer d. qch** to send sth flying

dinosaure [dinozɔr] *nm aussi Fig* dinosaur

diocèse [djɔsɛz] *nm Rel* diocese

diode [djɔd] *nf Él* diode; **d. électroluminescente** light-emitting diode

dioxyde [diɔksid] *nm Chim* dioxide; **d. de carbone** carbon dioxide

diphtérie [difteri] *nf Méd* diphtheria; **avoir la d.** to have diphtheria

diphtongue [diftɔ̃g] *nf Ling* diphthong

diplomate [diplɔmat] **1** *adj* diplomatic **2** *nm Culin* ≃ trifle **3** *nmf* diplomat

diplomatie [diplɔmasi] *nf* **(a)** *(habileté)* diplomacy; **user de d.** to be diplomatic **(b)** *(service)* diplomatic service

diplomatique [diplɔmatik] *adj* diplomatic

diplomatiquement [diplɔmatikmɑ̃] *adv* diplomatically

diplôme [diplom] *nm* diploma; *Univ* degree; **avoir des diplômes** to have qualifications

diplômé, -e [diplome] **1** *adj* qualified; *Univ* graduate; **un ingénieur d. de l'École polytechnique** an engineering graduate of the École Polytechnique **2** *nm,f* holder of a diploma; *Univ* graduate

dire¹ [dir] *nm* **au d. de qn** according to sb; **selon ses dires** according to him/her

dire² [27a] **1** *vt* **(a)** *(exprimer)* to say; **comment dit-on "soleil" en anglais?** how do you say "soleil" in English?; **il ne savait plus quoi d.** he didn't know what to say; **je sais ce que je dis!** I know what I'm talking about!; **laisse-les d.,** **ils sont stupides!** let them talk, they're stupid!; **elle a dit qu'elle arriverait en retard** she said she would be late; **comment dirais-je?** how shall I put it?; **comme on dit** as the saying goes; **cela dit…** having said that…; **il est un peu lent, pour ne pas d. complètement idiot** he's a bit slow, or to put it bluntly he's a complete idiot; **qui dit mieux?** *(à une vente aux enchères)* any advance?; **c'est vite dit** it's easier said than done

(b) *(communiquer)* **d. qch à qn** to tell sb sth; **d. à qn que…** to tell sb (that)…; **je t'ai déjà dit que oui!** I've already said yes!; **je vous l'avais bien dit!** I told you so!; *Fam* **c'est elle, je te dis** it's her, I tell you; **je lui ai fait d. de venir** I sent for him; **elle ne se le fit pas d. deux fois** she didn't wait to be told twice

(c) *(ordonner)* **d. à qn de faire qch** to tell sb to do sth; **faites ce qu'on vous dit** do as you're told; **taisez-vous, j'ai dit!** be quiet, I said!

(d) *(prétendre)* to say; **à ce qu'elle dit** according to her; **on le dit mort** he is said to have died

(e) *(langage enfantin) (rapporter)* to tell; **je vais le d. à ma**

mère I'm going to tell my mum on you

(f) *(décider)* **disons à quatre heures** let's say four o'clock; **il est dit que je resterai célibataire** I'm destined to stay single

(g) *(penser)* **alors, qu'est-ce que tu en dis?** well, what do you think?; **qu'est-ce que tu dirais d'aller au cinéma?** how about going to the cinema?; **on dirait qu'il pleut** it looks as if it's raining; **on dirait du Mozart** it sounds like Mozart; **on dirait du gin** *(au goût)* it tastes like gin; **on aurait dit qu'elle était hypnotisée** it looked as if she was hypnotized; **et d. que...!** and to think (that)...!

(h) *(objecter)* to say; **j'ai eu une augmentation conséquente, je n'ai rien à d.** I got a decent rise, I can't complain; **vous avez beau d.,...** you can say what you like, but...; **ce n'est pas pour d., mais...** I don't want to be rude, but...

(i) *(indiquer) (sujet: statistiques)* to show; **que dit le baromètre?** what does the barometer say?; **qu'est-ce qui vous dit qu'il viendra?** what makes you think he'll come?; **ce nom ne me dit rien** the name doesn't ring a bell; **quelque chose me dit que...** something tells me (that)...

(j) *(plaire)* **ça te dit de partir en vacances avec nous?** do you fancy coming on holiday with us?; **ça ne me dit trop rien de manger italien** I don't really fancy Italian food; **ça ne me dit rien qui vaille** I don't like the look of it

(k) *(prière, messe)* to say; *(poésie)* to recite

(l) *(signifier)* **qui dit bordeaux dit bon vin** Bordeaux is synonymous with good wine

(m) *(locutions)* **c'est (tout) d.** need I say more?; **c'est d. s'il t'aime** that shows how much he loves you; **c'est beaucoup d.** that's saying (quite) a lot; **c'est peu d.** that's putting it mildly; **il n'y a pas à d.,...** there are no two ways about it,...; **pour ainsi d.** so to speak, as it were; **pour tout (vous) d.,...** to be honest (with you),...; **quelques jours, je ne dis pas, mais un mois!** a few days, that's fair enough, but a whole month!; **Fam je te dis pas la tête qu'il a faite!** you should have seen his face!; **Fam je ne te dis que ça** say no more, enough said; **c'est moi qui vous le dis** let me tell you, believe me; **Fam à qui le dites-vous!** you're telling ME!; **vous m'en direz tant!** you don't say!; **Fam je ne te le fais pas d.!** tell me something I don't know!; **Fam tu l'as dit (, bouffi)!** you can say that again!; **cela va sans d.** that goes without saying; **dis donc!** *(au fait)* hey!; *(marque la surprise)* gosh!; *(marque l'indignation)* do you mind!; **tu me le donnes, dis?** give it to me, yeah?

2 se dire *vpr* **(a)** *(l'un à l'autre)* **on se dit bonjour** we say hello

(b) *(penser)* **se d. que...** to think that...; **dis-toi bien que ça aurait pu être plus grave** it could have been worse, you know; **je me disais bien que je l'avais déjà vu quelque part** I knew I'd seen him somewhere before

(c) *(être exprimé)* **comment ça se dit en anglais?** how do you say that in English?; **ça se dit en français?** can you say that in French?

(d) *(se prétendre)* **elle se dit suisse** she says she's Swiss

direct, -e [dirɛkt] **1** *adj* direct
2 *nm* **(a)** *(à la radio, à la télévision)* live broadcasting; **en d. de** live from **(b)** *(en boxe)* jab; **d. du droit/du gauche** straight right/left **(c)** *(train)* direct train **(pour** to)
3 *adv Fam* straight

directement [dirɛktəmɑ̃] *adv* **(a)** *(sans détour)* straight **(b)** *(sans intermédiaire)* directly

directeur, -trice [dirɛktœr, -tris] **1** *nm,f* **(a)** *(d'un magasin, d'un service)* manager; **d. artistique** *(d'un film)* artistic director; *(à la télévision)* production designer; *(d'un journal)* art editor; **d. commercial** sales director; **d. général** *(d'une entreprise)* managing director; **d. de la rédaction** editorial director; **d. des ressources humaines** *ou* **du personnel** human resources manager **(b)** *(d'une école) Br* headmaster, *f* headmistress, *Am* principal **(c)** *(d'une prison) Br* governor,

Am warden **(d)** *Univ* **d. de thèse** thesis supervisor
2 *adj* *(équipe, instances)* management; *(idée)* main; *(principe, force)* guiding

direction [dirɛksjɔ̃] *nf* **(a)** *(d'une entreprise, d'un théâtre)* management; *(d'une école)* running; *(d'un parti, d'un pays)* leadership; **sous la d. de qn** under the supervision of sb; *(orchestre)* conducted by sb **(b)** *(ensemble des cadres)* management; **d. générale** general management; **d. des ressources humaines** *ou* **du personnel** *(service)* personnel department **(c)** *(orientation)* direction; **toutes/autres directions** *(sur panneau)* all/other directions; **quelle d. ont-ils prise?** which way did they go?; **le train en d. de Reims** the train to Reims, the Reims train **(d)** *(d'un véhicule)* steering; **d. assistée** power steering

directive [dirɛktiv] *nf* directive

directoire [dirɛktwar] *nm* **(d'une société anonyme)** board of directors

dirham [diram] *nm* dirham

dirigeable [diriʒabl] *adj & nm* **(ballon) d.** dirigible, airship

dirigeant, -e [diriʒɑ̃, ɑ̃t] **1** *adj voir* **classe**
2 *nm,f* *(d'un parti, d'un pays)* leader; *(d'une entreprise)* manager; **d. syndical** union leader

diriger [45] [diriʒe] **1** *vt* **(a)** *(entreprise, équipe, projet)* to manage, to run; *(pays, parti)* to lead; *(séance)* to conduct; *(travaux)* to supervise; *(acteurs)* to direct; *(orchestre)* to conduct **(b)** *(arme, télescope, lumière)* to point **(sur** at) **(c)** *(pas)* to direct **(vers** towards); *(regard)* to turn **(vers** to); *(attention)* to turn **(sur** to); *(conversation)* to steer **(sur** onto) **(d)** *(orienter professionnellement)* to steer **(sur** *ou* **vers** towards)
2 se diriger *vpr* **(a)** *(aller)* **se d. vers** *(endroit)* to head for; *(personne)* to go up to; *(carrière, secteur)* to go into **(b)** *(s'orienter)* to find one's way around

dirigisme [diriʒism] *nm* state control

disais *etc voir* **dire**

discernement [disɛrnəmɑ̃] *nm* *(jugement)* discernment; **sans d.** rashly

discerner [disɛrne] *vt* **(a)** *(percevoir)* to make out **(b)** *(différencier)* **d. qch de** to distinguish sth from **(c)** *(deviner)* to discern

disciple [disipl] *nmf* disciple

disciplinaire [disipliner] *adj* disciplinary

discipline [disiplin] *nf* *(ordre, matière)* discipline

discipliné, -e [disipline] *adj* disciplined

discipliner [disipline] **1** *vt* *(enfant)* to control
2 se discipliner *vpr* to discipline oneself

disc-jockey *(pl* **disc-jockeys)** [diskʒɔke] *nm* disc jockey

discographie [diskɔgrafi] *nf* discography

discontinu, -e [diskɔ̃tiny] *adj* intermittent; *(ligne)* broken

discontinuer [diskɔ̃tinɥe] **sans discontinuer** *adv* without stopping

disconvenir [70] [diskɔ̃vnir] *vi Litt* **ne pas d. de qch** not to deny sth

discordant, -e [diskɔrdɑ̃, ɑ̃t] *adj* **(a)** *(son, bruit)* discordant **(b)** *(couleurs)* clashing; *(opinions)* conflicting

discorde [diskɔrd] *nf* discord; **semer la d.** to make trouble

discothèque [diskɔtɛk] *nf* **(a)** *(boîte de nuit)* disco **(b)** *(organisme)* record library; *(collection)* record collection

discount [diskunt] *nm* *(rabais)* discount

discourir [22] [diskurir] *vi* **d. sur qch** to discourse on sth; *Péj* to air one's opinions on sth

discours [diskur] *nm* **(a)** *(allocution)* speech; **prononcer**

ou faire un d. to make a speech; **d. de clôture/ d'ouverture** closing/opening speech (**b**) *Gram* speech; **d. indirect/direct** reported *or* indirect/direct speech (**c**) *(paroles)* talk; **il m'a tenu un grand d.** sur la tolérance he gave me a great long speech about tolerance; **tous ces beaux d. ne nous avancent à rien** all this talking isn't getting us anywhere

discrédit [diskredi] *nm* discredit; **jeter le d.** sur qn to bring discredit on sb

discréditer [diskredite] **1** *vt* to discredit **2 se discréditer** *vpr (personne)* to discredit oneself; **se d.**

auprès de *ou* **aux yeux de qn** to discredit oneself with sb

discret, -ète [diskrɛ, -ɛt] *adj* (**a**) *(plein de retenue)* discreet; **tu sauras rester d.?** you'll keep it to yourself, won't you? (**b**) *(sobre) (personne)* unassuming; *(vêtements)* simple; *(maquillage)* natural (**c**) *(endroit)* quiet

discrètement [diskrɛtmɑ̃] *adv* (**a**) *(avec retenue)* discreetly; **il lui a parlé d.** he had a quiet word with him/ her (**b**) *(sobrement) (habillé)* simply; **être d. maquillée** to be wearing natural make-up

discrétion [diskresjɔ̃] *nf* (**a**) *(retenue)* discretion (**b**) *(sobriété)* simplicity; **avec d.** *(s'habiller)* simply; *(se maquiller)* discreetly (**c**) **champagne à d.** unlimited champagne

discrimination [diskriminasjɔ̃] *nf* discrimination; **d. raciale/sexuelle** racial/sexual discrimination

discriminatoire [diskriminatwar] *adj* discriminatory

disculper [diskylpe] **1** *vt* to exonerate (**de** from) **2 se disculper** *vpr* to exonerate oneself (**de** from)

discussion [diskysjɔ̃] *nf* discussion; **avoir une d.** (**sur** *ou* **à propos de**) to have a discussion (about); **pas de d., au travail!** don't argue, get to work!

discutable [diskytabl] *adj* questionable

discutailler [diskytaje] *vi Fam Péj* to quibble

discuté, -e [diskyte] *adj (question)* disputed; *(livre, sujet)* much discussed

discuter [diskyte] **1** *vt (examiner)* to discuss; *(contester)* to question; *Fam* **d. le coup, d. le bout de gras** to have a chat **2** *vi* (**a**) *(parler)* to discuss; **d. avec qn sur** *ou* **de qch** to discuss sth with sb (**b**) *(protester)* to argue **3 se discuter** *vpr* **ça se discute** that's debatable

dise *etc voir* **dire**

disette [dizɛt] *nf* food shortage

diseuse [dizøz] *nf* **d. de bonne aventure** fortune teller

disgrâce [disgras] *nf* **tomber en d.** to fall into disfavour

disgracieux, -euse [disgrasjø, -øz] *adj (personne)* ungainly; *(visage, moue)* ugly

disjoindre [43] [disʒwɛ̃dr] **1** *vt* to separate **2 se disjoindre** *vpr* to come apart

disjoint, -e [disʒwɛ̃, -ɛ̃t] *adj (pièces)* separated

disjoncter [disʒɔ̃kte] **1** *vt (circuit électrique)* to break **2** *vi (circuit électrique)* to fuse; *Fam Fig* to crack up

disjoncteur [disʒɔ̃ktœr] *nm* circuit breaker

dislocation [dislɔkasjɔ̃] *nf (d'une articulation)* dislocation

disloquer [dislɔke] **1** *vt* (**a**) *(épaule, genou)* to dislocate (**b**) *(empire, État)* to break up **2 se disloquer** *vpr (empire, État)* to break up; **se d. l'épaule** to dislocate one's shoulder

disparaître [20] [disparɛtr] *vi* (**a**) *(devenir invisible)* to disappear, to vanish; **d. dans la foule** to disappear into the crowd; *Fam* **d. de la circulation** to drop out of circulation; *Fam* **disparais!** clear off! (**b**) *(mourir)* to die (**c**) *(douleur, sentiment)* to disappear; *(maladie, tradition)* to die out; **faire d. qch** to get rid of sth

disparate [disparat] *adj (éléments)* disparate; *(couleurs, objets, mobilier)* ill-matched

disparité [disparite] *nf (d'éléments)* disparity; *(de couleurs, d'objets, de mobilier)* mismatch; *(des salaires, des revenus)* inequality

disparition [disparisjɔ̃] *nf* (**a**) *(absence)* disappearance (**b**) *(décès)* death

disparu, -e [dispary] **1** *adj (personne)* missing; **être porté d.** to be reported missing **2** *nm,f (mort)* dead person; *(absent)* missing person

dispensaire [dispɑ̃sɛr] *nm* community health centre

dispense [dispɑ̃s] *nf* (**a**) *(d'une obligation)* exemption (**b**) *(certificat)* certificate of exemption

dispenser [dispɑ̃se] **1** *vt* (**a**) **d. qn de qch/de faire qch** to exempt sb from sth/from doing sth; **se faire d. de qch** to be excused *or* let off sth; *Euph* **je vous dispense de vos commentaires** you can keep your remarks to yourself (**b**) *(soins, charité, faveurs)* to dispense **2 se dispenser** *vpr* **se d. de qch/de faire qch** to get out of sth/of doing sth; **tu pourrais te d. de ce genre de commentaire!** you can keep that sort of remark to yourself!

dispersé, -e [disperse] *adj (épars)* scattered

disperser [disperse] **1** *vt (foule, famille, feuilles)* to scatter **2 se disperser** *vpr (nuages, foule, famille)* to scatter, to disperse, *Fig (intellectuellement)* to spread oneself too thinly

dispersion [dispersjɔ̃] *nf (de manifestants, de nuages, d'une armée)* scattering, dispersal; *Fig (inattention)* lack of focus

disponibilité [disponibilite] *nf* (**a**) *(d'une personne, de places, d'un capital)* availability; **d. d'esprit** receptiveness (**b**) *(d'un fonctionnaire)* leave of absence; **être en d.** to be on leave of absence (**c**) *Fin* **disponibilités** available funds

disponible [disponibl] *adj* (**a**) *(personne, place, capital)* available; **êtes-vous d. ce soir?** are you free tonight? (**b**) *(fonctionnaire)* on leave of absence

dispos, -e [dispo, -oz] *adj (personne)* fit and well

disposé, -e [dispoze] *adj (personne)* **être bien/mal d.** to be in a good/bad mood; **être bien d. envers qn** to feel well disposed towards sb; **être d. à faire qch** to feel disposed *or* willing to do sth

disposer [dispoze] **1** *vt* (**a**) *(objets, fleurs)* to arrange; *(table)* to lay, to set (**b**) **d. qn à (faire) qch** to dispose *or* incline sb to (do) sth **2** *vi* (**a**) *Formel* **vous pouvez d.** you may go (**b**) *(décider) Prov* **l'homme propose, Dieu dispose** man proposes, God disposes **3** *se disposer vt ind* to have at my disposal; **les renseignements dont je dispose** the information at my disposal; **le droit des peuples à la d. d'eux-mêmes** the right of people to self-determination **4** *se disposer vpr* **se d. à faire qch** to get ready to do sth

dispositif [dispozitif] *nm* (**a**) *(appareil)* device (**b**) *(ensemble de moyens)* system; **d. policier** police presence (**c**) *Ordinat* **d. d'alimentation** power unit; *(pour papier)* sheet feed; **d. d'alimentation papier** *(d'une imprimante)* sheet feed, paper feed

disposition [dispozisjɔ̃] *nf* (**a**) *(arrangement)* arrangement (**b**) *(disponibilité)* **à la d. de qn** at sb's disposal (**c**) *(tendance)* tendency (**à** to) (**d**) *(intentions)* **être dans de bonnes/mauvaises dispositions** to be in a good/bad mood; **être dans de bonnes dispositions à l'égard de qn** to be favourably disposed towards sb (**e**) *(dons)* **avoir des dispositions pour qch** to have an aptitude for sth (**f**) **dispositions** *(préparatifs)* arrangements; **prendre des dispositions pour faire qch** to make arrangements to do sth; **prendre ses dispositions** to make arrangements (**g**) *Jur* **dispositions** *(d'une loi)* clauses

disproportion [disprɔpɔrsjɔ̃] *nf* disproportion (**entre** between)

disproportionné, -e [disprɔpɔrsjɔne] *adj* disproportionate (**par rapport à** to)

dispute [dispyt] *nf* quarrel, argument

disputé, -e [dispyte] *adj (question)* controversial; *(match)* hard-fought; **ce poste sera très d.** there will be a lot of competition for this post

disputer [dispyte] **1** *vt* (**a**) *(match)* to play; *(combat)* to fight (**b**) *(se battre pour)* **d. qch à qn** to fight with sb over sth (**c**) *Fam (réprimander)* to tell off; **se faire d.** to get told off
2 se disputer *vpr* (**a**) *(se quereller)* to quarrel, to argue (**pour/avec** over/with) (**b**) *(avoir lieu)* **le match se disputera demain** the match will be played tomorrow (**c**) *(se battre pour)* **se d. qch** to fight over sth

disquaire [disker] *nmf* record dealer

disqualification [diskalifikasjɔ̃] *nf* disqualification

disqualifier [66] [diskalifje] *vt (sportif)* to disqualify

disque [disk] *nm* (**a**) *(enregistrement)* record; **mettre un d.** to play a record; **d. audionumérique** compact disc; **d. compact** compact disc, CD; **d. compact vidéo** video compact disc; **d. laser** laser disc (**b**) *Ordinat* disk; **d. amovible** removable disk; **d. dur** hard disk; **d. fixe** fixed disk (**c**) *(cartilage)* disc (**d**) *(objet rond)* disc; **d. de stationnement** parking disc (**e**) *(en sport)* discus (**f**) *Tech* disc; **d. d'embrayage** clutch plate

disquette [disket] *nf Ordinat* diskette, floppy (disk); **sur d.** on diskette, on floppy; **d. de démonstration**, *Fam* **d. démo** demo disk; **d. haute densité** high-density disk; **d. optique** optical disk, floptical disk

dissection [diseksjɔ̃] *nf aussi Fig* dissection

dissemblable [disɑ̃blabl] *adj* dissimilar

dissémination [diseminasjɔ̃] *nf (de graines, de peuple)* scattering; *(de germes)* spreading

disséminer [disemine] **1** *vt (graines, peuple)* to scatter; *(germes)* to spread; **les écoles sont très disséminées** the schools are very thin on the ground
2 se disséminer *vpr* to be scattered

dissension [disɑ̃sjɔ̃] *nf* dissension

disséquer [34] [diseke] *vt aussi Fig* to dissect

dissertation [disertasjɔ̃] *nf* essay

disserter [diserte] *vi (parler)* **d. sur qch** to discourse on sth, *Péj* to hold forth on sth; *(écrire)* to write about sth

dissidence [disidɑ̃s] *nf* dissidence; **la d.** *(les opposants)* the dissidents

dissident, -e [disidɑ̃, -ɑ̃t] **1** *adj (en politique)* dissident; *(en religion)* dissenting
2 *nm,f (en politique)* dissident; *(en religion)* dissenter

dissimulateur, -trice [disimylatœr, -tris] **1** *adj* dissembling
2 *nm,f* dissembler

dissimulation [disimylasjɔ̃] *nf* (**a**) *(hypocrisie)* dissembling, deceit; **agir avec d.** to act in an underhand way (**b**) *(des sentiments, de la vérité)* concealment

dissimuler [disimyle] **1** *vt* to cover up, to conceal; *(sujet: rideau)* to screen off; **d. qch à qn** to conceal sth from sb; **avec un plaisir non dissimulé** with unconcealed delight
2 se dissimuler *vpr* to be hidden

dissipation [disipasjɔ̃] *nf* (**a**) *(de craintes, de soupçons)* dispelling; *(d'un malentendu)* clearing up; **après d. des brouillards matinaux** after the early fog has cleared (**b**) *(à l'école)* unruly behaviour (**c**) *Litt (débauche)* dissipation

dissipé, -e [disipe] *adj* (**a**) *(élève)* unruly (**b**) *Litt (débauché)* dissipated

dissiper [disipe] **1** *vt* (**a**) *(nuages)* to disperse; *(brouillard)*

to clear; *(malentendu)* to clear up; *(craintes, soupçons)* to dispel (**b**) *(distraire)* to lead astray
2 se dissiper *vpr* (**a**) *(nuages)* to disperse; *(brouillard)* to clear; *(craintes, soupçons)* to vanish (**b**) *(se laisser distraire)* to be unruly

dissociable [disɔsjabl] *adj* separable

dissocier [66] [disɔsje] **1** *vt* to separate
2 se dissocier *vpr* **se d. de qch** to dissociate oneself from sth

dissolu, -e [disɔly] *adj Litt* dissolute

dissolution [disɔlysjɔ̃] *nf* (**a**) *(d'un parlement, d'un mariage)* dissolution; *(d'une association)* breaking up (**b**) *(dans un liquide)* dissolving

dissolvais *etc voir* **dissoudre**

dissolvant, -e [disɔlvɑ̃, -ɑ̃t] *adj & nm* (**produit**) **d.** solvent; *(pour ongles)* nail polish remover

dissonant, -e [disɔnɑ̃, -ɑ̃t] *adj (sons)* dissonant; *Fig* clashing

dissoudre [3a] [disudr] **1** *vt* (**a**) *(substance)* to dissolve (**b**) *(parlement, mariage)* to dissolve; *(association)* to break up
2 se dissoudre *vpr (substance)* to dissolve; *(association)* to break up

dissuader [disɥade] *vt* **d. qn de faire qch** to dissuade sb from doing sth

dissuasif, -ive [disɥazif, -iv] *adj* deterrent; *(prix)* prohibitive; **avoir un effet d.** to be a deterrent

dissuasion [disɥazjɔ̃] *nf* dissuasion; *Mil* **force de d.** deterrent

dissymétrie [disimetri] *nf* asymmetry

distance [distɑ̃s] *nf* distance; **suivre qn à d.** to follow sb at a distance; **à quelle d. sommes-nous de la ville?** how far are we from the town?; **à une courte d. (de)** a short distance away (from); **à d.** *(déclencher)* by remote control; *(rester, observer)* at a distance; *aussi Fig* **tenir qn à d.** to keep sb at a distance; **conserver** *ou* **garder ses distances, se tenir à d.** to hold oneself aloof; **prendre ses distances, prendre de la d.** to stand back; *Sp & Fig* **tenir la d.** to go the distance

distancer [16] [distɑ̃se] *vt aussi Fig* to outstrip, to outdistance; **se laisser d.** to fall *or* lag behind; **d. qn de deux points/de 10 mètres** to go two points/10 metres ahead of sb

distant, -e [distɑ̃, -ɑ̃t] *adj* (**a**) *(éloigné)* distant; **nos deux maisons sont distantes d'un kilomètre** our two houses are a kilometre apart (**b**) *Fig (froid)* distant, standoffish (**avec** with)

distendre [distɑ̃dr] **1** *vt (corde, élastique, vêtement)* to stretch; *(muscle)* to strain
2 se distendre *vpr (corde, élastique, vêtement)* to stretch; *(muscle)* to slacken

distillation [distilasjɔ̃] *nf* distillation

distiller [distile] *vt* (**a**) *(alcool, pétrole)* to distil; **eau distillée** distilled water (**b**) *(poison)* to distil; *Fig (colère, ennui)* to exude

distillerie [distilri] *nf (lieu)* distillery; *(procédé)* distilling

distinct, -e [distɛ̃, -ɛ̃kt] *adj* (**a**) *(séparé)* distinct, separate (**de** from) (**b**) *(clair) (silhouette, voix)* distinct, clear

distinctement [distɛ̃ktəmɑ̃] *adv* distinctly, clearly

distinctif, -ive [distɛ̃ktif, -iv] *adj* distinctive

distinction [distɛ̃ksjɔ̃] *nf* (**a**) *(différence)* distinction; **faire une d. entre deux choses** to make a distinction between two things; **sans d.** without distinction, indiscriminately; **sans d. de race ou de couleur** regardless of race or colour (**b**) *(élégance)* distinction; **avoir de la d.** to be distinguished

distingué, -e [distɛ̃ge] adj distinguished
distinguer [distɛ̃ge] **1** vt (**a**) (différencier) to distinguish (de from); **il a appris à d.** les champignons he has learnt how to tell the various kinds of mushroom apart; **on peut à peine les d. l'un de l'autre** you can hardly tell them apart (**b**) (discerner) (objet, silhouette) to make out; (personne) to pick out; **d. une nuance d'amertume dans la voix de qn** to detect a trace of bitterness in sb's voice
2 se distinguer vpr (**a**) (s'illustrer) to distinguish oneself (par by); **on ne peut vraiment pas dire qu'il se distingue par son intelligence** he hardly stands out as being very intelligent (**b**) (se différencier) **se d. de qn/qch (par)** to be distinguishable from sb/sth (by) (**c**) (être perçu) **au loin se distinguait la côte** the coastline could be made out in the distance
distinguo [distɛ̃go] nm distinction; **faire un d. entre** to make a distinction between
distordre [distɔrdr] vt to distort
distorsion [distɔrsjɔ̃] nf distortion; (entre deux facteurs, deux salaires) imbalance
distraction [distraksjɔ̃] nf (**a**) (inattention) absent-mindedness; **par d.** inadvertently, absent-mindedly (**b**) (loisir) activity; **ça manque de distractions le soir** there's nothing to do at night
distraire [28] [distrer] **1** vt (**a**) (détourner) to distract (de from) (**b**) (divertir) to entertain, to amuse
2 se distraire vpr (s'occuper) to amuse oneself; (se détendre) to enjoy oneself
distrait, -e [distrɛ, -ɛt] adj (**a**) (étourdi) absent-minded; **d'un air d.** absent-mindedly (**b**) (inattentif) inattentive; **d'une oreille distraite** with only half an ear
distraitement [distrɛtmɑ̃] adv absent-mindedly
distrayais etc voir distraire
distrayant, -e [distrɛjɑ̃, -ɑ̃t] adj entertaining
distribuer [distribɥe] vt (**a**) (donner) (prix, bonbons, provisions, vivres) to distribute (à to); (dividendes) to pay (à to); (cartes) to deal (à to); (courrier) to deliver (à to); (eau, gaz, électricité) to supply (à to); (sourires, compliments) to bestow (à on); **d. des coups** to lash out with one's fists (**b**) (répartir) (tâches) to allocate; **d. les rôles** to cast a play (**c**) (commercialiser) to distribute
distributeur, -trice [distribytœr, -tris] **1** nm,f Com distributor; **d. agréé** authorized distributor
2 nm (appareil) (vending) machine; **d. (automatique) de billets** ATM; **d. (automatique) de boissons/de cigarettes** drinks/cigarette machine
distribution [distribysjɔ̃] nf (**a**) (remise) distribution; (de lettres, de marchandises) delivery; **la d. des prix** (à l'école) prizegiving (**b**) (répartition) (de tâches) allocation; (d'une maison, d'un appartement) layout; (d'un film, d'une pièce) (action) casting; (acteurs) cast (**c**) Com distribution; **grande d.** large-scale distribution (**d**) (approvisionnement) supply; **d. des eaux** water supply
district [distrikt] nm district
dit, -e [di, dit] **1** pp voir dire
2 adj (**a**) (décidé) **à l'heure dite** at the agreed time (**b**) (appelé) known as
dithyrambique [ditirɑ̃bik] adj eulogistic
diurétique [djyretik] adj & nm diuretic
diurne [djyrn] adj diurnal
diva [diva] nf diva
divagations [divagasjɔ̃] nfpl raving
divaguer [divage] vi to rave
divan [divɑ̃] nm divan, couch
divergence [divɛrʒɑ̃s] nf (de lignes, de rayons) divergence; (d'opinions) difference

divergent, -e [divɛrʒɑ̃, -ɑ̃t] adj (lignes) divergent; (opinions) differing
diverger [45] [divɛrʒe] vi (opinions, lignes, rayons) to diverge (de from)
divers, -e [divɛr, -ɛrs] adj (**a**) (différents) varied; **d.** (rubrique) miscellaneous (**b**) (plusieurs) various; **diverses solutions sont possibles** there are various possible solutions
diversement [divɛrsəmɑ̃] adv in various ways
diversification [divɛrsifikasjɔ̃] nf diversification
diversifier [66] [divɛrsifje] **1** vt (économie, cultures, activités) to diversify; (intérêts, couleurs) to vary
2 se diversifier vpr (entreprise, activités) to diversify
diversion [divɛrsjɔ̃] nf diversion; **faire d.** to create a diversion
diversité [divɛrsite] nf (variété) variety, diversity
divertir [divɛrtir] **1** vt (amuser) to entertain, to amuse
2 se divertir vpr to enjoy oneself; **se d. de qch** to laugh at sth
divertissant, -e [divɛrtisɑ̃, -ɑ̃t] adj amusing, entertaining
divertissement [divɛrtismɑ̃] nm (**a**) (amusement) entertainment, amusement (**b**) Mus divertimento
dividende [dividɑ̃d] nm Math & Fin dividend
divin, -e [divɛ̃, -in] adj aussi Fig divine; **le d. Enfant** the Holy Child
divinement [divinmɑ̃] adv divinely
divinité [divinite] nf (**a**) (nature de Dieu) divinity (**b**) (dieu) deity
diviser [divize] **1** vt (**a**) (partager) to divide (en/entre into/among), **d. 15 par 3** to divide 15 by 3 (**b**) (opposer) to divide; **l'opinion est divisée au sujet de cette affaire** opinion on the matter is divided; **d. pour mieux régner** divide and rule
2 se diviser vpr to divide (en into); **l'examen se divise en trois parties** the examination is divided into three parts; **le chemin se divise en deux** the road divides or forks
diviseur [divizœr] nm Math divisor
divisible [divizibl] adj divisible
division [divizjɔ̃] nf (**a**) (séparation) & Math division (en into); **faire une d.** to do a division; Biol **d. cellulaire** cell division; **d. du travail** division of labour (**b**) (partie) part, section; Mil division; **d. blindée** armoured division (**c**) (désaccord) division
divisionnaire [divizjɔnɛr] nm (police) superintendent
divorce [divɔrs] nm divorce; Fig (désaccord) gulf; **demander le d.** to ask for a divorce; **obtenir le d.** to get a divorce
divorcé, -e [divɔrse] **1** adj divorced
2 nm,f divorcee
divorcer [16] [divɔrse] vi to get divorced, to get a divorce; **d. d'avec** ou **de qn** to divorce sb
divulgation [divylgasjɔ̃] nf disclosure (de of)
divulguer [divylge] vt to divulge, to disclose
dix [dis] adj & nm inv ten; voir aussi trois
dix-huit [dizɥit] adj & nm inv eighteen; voir aussi trois
dix-huitième [dizɥitjɛm] nmf, nm & adj eighteenth; voir aussi cinquième
dixième [dizjɛm] nmf, nm & adj tenth; voir aussi cinquième
dixit [diksit] **d. Paul** so Paul says
dix-neuf [diznœf] adj & nm inv nineteen; voir aussi trois
dix-neuvième [diznœvjɛm] nmf, nm & adj nineteenth; voir aussi cinquième

dix-sept [dis(s)ɛt] *adj & nm inv* seventeen; *voir aussi* **trois**

dix-septième [dis(s)ɛtjɛm] *nmf, nm & adj* seventeenth; *voir aussi* **cinquième**

dizaine [dizɛn] *nf* **une d. (de)** about ten, ten or so; *Math* **la colonne des dizaines** the tens column

Djibouti [dʒibuti] *n* Djibouti

do [do] *nm inv (note)* C; *(chantée)* doh

doberman [dɔbɛrman] *nm* doberman

docile [dɔsil] *adj (enfant, animal)* docile

docilement [dɔsilmɑ̃] *adv* docilely

docilité [dɔsilite] *nf* docility

dock [dɔk] *nm* (**a**) *(bassin)* dock (**b**) *(entrepôt)* warehouse

docker [dɔkɛr] *nm* docker

docte [dɔkt] *adj Litt* learned

docteur [dɔktœr] *nm* (**a**) *(médecin)* doctor (**b**) *Univ* **être d. ès lettres/ès sciences** to have a doctorate in arts/science; **être d. en droit** to have a doctorate in law

doctoral, -e, -aux, -ales [dɔktɔral, -o] *adj Péj (air, ton)* pompous

doctorat [dɔktɔra] *nm Univ* doctorate; **d. d'État** = highest postgraduate research degree; **d. de 3ᵉ cycle** ≃ PhD

doctoresse [dɔktɔrɛs] *nf Vieilli* lady doctor

doctrine [dɔktrin] *nf* doctrine

document [dɔkymɑ̃] *nm* document

documentaire [dɔkymɑ̃tɛr] *adj & nm* documentary

documentaliste [dɔkymɑ̃talist] *nmf (d'archives)* archivist; *(dans les écoles)* librarian

documentation [dɔkymɑ̃tasjɔ̃] *nf (action)* research; *(documents)* documentation (**sur** on)

documenté, -e [dɔkymɑ̃te] *adj (personne)* well-informed; *(étude, thèse)* documented

documenter [dɔkymɑ̃te] **se documenter** *vpr* to gather information *or* material (**sur** on)

dodeliner [dɔdəline] *vi* **il dodelinait de la tête** his head kept nodding

dodo [dodo] *nm (langage enfantin)* **faire d.** to sleep; **aller au d.** to go to bye-byes

dodu, -e [dɔdy] *adj* plump, chubby

doge [dɔʒ] *nm Hist* doge

dogmatique [dɔgmatik] *adj* dogmatic

dogmatisme [dɔgmatism] *nm* dogmatism

dogme [dɔgm] *nm* dogma

dogue [dɔg] *nm* mastiff

doigt [dwa] *nm* (**a**) *(de la main)* finger; **d. de pied** toe; **le petit d.** the little finger; **lever le d.** *(en classe)* to put one's hand up; **porter une bague au d.** to wear a ring on one's finger; **faire signe à qn du d.** to beckon to sb; **être comme les (deux) doigts de la main** to be very close; **on peut les compter sur les doigts de la main** you can count them on the fingers of one hand; *Fig* **se faire taper sur les doigts** to get a rap over the knuckles; **filer** *ou* **glisser entre les doigts de qn** to slip through sb's fingers; **vous avez mis le d. dessus** you've put your finger on it; **obéir à qn au d. et à l'œil** to obey sb blindly; **savoir qch sur le bout des doigts** to have sth at one's fingertips; **mon petit d. me l'a dit** a little bird told me; **avoir des doigts de fée** to have nimble fingers; *Fig* **ne pas lever** *ou* **bouger le petit d.** not to lift a finger; *Fam* **tu te mets le d. dans l'œil (jusqu'au coude)** you couldn't be more wrong (if you tried); *Fam* **faire qch les doigts dans le nez** to do sth standing on one's head; *Fam* **gagner les doigts dans le nez** to win hands down

(**b**) *(petite quantité) (d'alcool)* drop; **être à deux doigts de**

qch/de **faire qch** to be within a hair's breadth of sth/of doing sth

doigté [dwate] *nm* (**a**) *Mus (d'un morceau de musique)* fingering (**b**) *Fig (adresse)* dexterity; *(tact)* tact

dois, doive *etc voir* **devoir**

doléances [dɔleɑ̃s] *nfpl* complaints

dollar [dɔlar] *nm* dollar

dolmen [dɔlmɛn] *nm* dolmen

domaine [dɔmɛn] *nm* (**a**) *(propriété)* estate, property; **être du d. public** to be in the public domain; **d. skiable** skiing area (**b**) *(matière)* field, domain; **c'est du d. du possible** it's within the realms of possibility

domanial, -e, -aux, -ales [dɔmanjal, -o] *adj* state-owned

dôme [dom] *nm Archit & Géog* dome

domestication [dɔmɛstikasjɔ̃] *nf* domestication

domestique [dɔmɛstik] **1** *adj (vie, soucis, querelle)* domestic; *(tâches, déchets)* household; **accidents domestiques** accidents in the home
2 *nmf* servant

domestiquer [dɔmɛstike] *vt (animal)* to domesticate; *(éléments)* to harness

domicile [dɔmisil] *nm* (place of) residence, home; **sans d. fixe** of no fixed abode; **travailler à d.** to work from home; **livrer à d.** to do home deliveries; *Jur* **d. conjugal** marital home

domicilié, -e [dɔmisilje] *adj* **d. à** resident at

dominant, -e [dɔminɑ̃, -ɑ̃t] **1** *adj (opinion)* prevailing; *(couleur, trait, idée)* dominant; *Biol* **caractère d.** dominant characteristic
2 *nf* **dominante** *(ce qui domine)* chief characteristic; **j'ai choisi du tissu à dominante rouge** I chose fabric that is mainly red

dominateur, -trice [dɔminatœr, -tris] *adj (personne, ton, attitude)* domineering

domination [dɔminasjɔ̃] *nf* domination (**sur** over); **être sous la d. de qn** to be dominated by sb

dominer [dɔmine] **1** *vt* (**a**) *(assujettir) (personne)* to dominate; *(empire)* to rule over (**b**) *(surpasser) (adversaire, concurrent)* to surpass (**c**) *(prédominer dans)* to be the dominant feature of (**d**) *(maîtriser) (timidité, passions, larmes, sujet)* to master; *(paresse, envie)* to overcome; *(match)* to dominate; **d. la situation** to keep the situation under control (**e**) *(surplomber)* to dominate; **de leur terrasse, on domine la mer** their balcony overlooks the sea
2 *vi* (**a**) *(l'emporter)* to be dominant (**b**) *(prédominer)* to predominate
3 se dominer *vpr* to control oneself

dominicain, -e [dɔminikɛ̃, -ɛn] **1** *adj* Dominican
2 *nm,f* (**a**) *Rel* Dominican (**b**) *(de la République Dominicaine)* **D.** Dominican

dominical, -e, -aux, -ales [dɔminikal, -o] *adj* Sunday; **repos d.** day of rest; **ouverture dominicale des magasins** Sunday opening

Dominique [dɔminik] *nf* **la D.** Dominica

domino [dɔmino] *nm (plaquette)* domino; **jouer aux dominos** to play dominoes

dommage [dɔmaʒ] *nm* (**a**) *(préjudice)* harm; **causer un d. à qn** to do sb harm; **d. corporel** physical injury; **dommages et intérêts, dommages-intérêts** damages; **d. matériel** material damage (**b**) **dommages** *(dégâts matériels)* damage (**c**) **(quel) d.!** what a pity!, what a shame!; **c'est (bien) d. qu'elle ne soit pas venue** it's a (great) pity that she didn't come

dommageable [dɔmaʒabl] *adj* detrimental (**à** to)

dompter [dɔ̃(p)te] *vt (fauve, fleuve, nature)* to tame; *(sentiments, passions, personne)* to subdue

dompteur, -euse [dɔ̃(p)tœr, -øz] *nm,f* tamer

DOM-TOM [dɔmtɔm] *nmpl (abrév* **départements et territoires d'outre-mer)** = French overseas departments and territories

DON [deœn] *nm Ordinat (abrév* **disque optique numérique) CD**

don [dɔ̃] *nm* **(a)** *(cadeau)* gift; *(à un musée, une œuvre)* donation; **faire d. à qn de qch** to make a gift of sth to sb; **d. du sang/de sperme** blood/sperm donation; *Fig* **d. du ciel** godsend; **le d. de soi** self-sacrifice **(b)** *(aptitude)* gift, talent; *aussi Ironique* **avoir le d. de faire qch** to have a knack for doing sth

donateur, -trice [dɔnatœr, -tris] *nm,f* donor

donation [dɔnasjɔ̃] *nf* donation

donc [dɔ̃k] *conj* **(a)** *(marque la conséquence)* so **(b)** *(emphatique)* **tu le savais d. depuis le début?** so you knew from the start?; **que voulez-vous d.?** whatever do you want?; **mais taisez-vous d.!** do be quiet!; **allons d.!** come on! **(c)** *(après interruption ou digression)* **je disais d. que...** I was saying, then, that...

dondon [dɔ̃dɔ̃] *nf Fam Péj* **grosse d.** great lump of a woman/girl

donjon [dɔ̃ʒɔ̃] *nm* keep

don Juan *(pl* **dons Juans)** [dɔ̃ʒɥɑ̃] *nm* Don Juan

donne [dɔn] *nf (aux cartes)* deal

donné, -e [dɔne] *adj* **(a)** *(offert)* given; *Fam* **c'est d.** it's dirt cheap, *Fam* **ce n'est pas d.** it doesn't come cheap **(b)** *(défini)* given; **à un moment d.** *(dans le passé)* at one point; *(dans le futur)* at some point; **étant d. la situation** given the situation; **étant d. que...** seeing that...

donnée [dɔne] *nf* **(a)** *(élément)* piece of information; **avoir toutes les données du problème** to have all the data *or* information on the problem **(b)** *Ordinat* **données** data; **données numériques** digital data

donner [dɔne] **1** *vt* **(a)** *(offrir, distribuer)* to give; **d. qch à qn** to give sth to sb, to give sb sth; **d. à boire à qn** to give sb something to drink; **d. à manger à** *(animal)* to feed; **c'est à qui de d.?** *(aux cartes)* whose deal is it? **(b)** *(faire don de) (temps, vie)* to give; *(corps, organe)* to donate; **d. son sang** to give blood **(c)** *(céder; Fam (dénoncer)* to grass on **(à** to); **en d. à qn pour son argent** to give sb their money's worth **(d)** *(payer)* **je lui donne 20 euros de l'heure** I pay him 20 euros an hour; **je vous en donne 500 euros** I'll give you 500 euros for it **(e)** *(confier)* **d. qch à qn à garder** to give sb sth to look after; **d. un vêtement à nettoyer** to hand in a garment to be dry-cleaned **(f)** *(avis, ordre, conseil)* to give; **d. l'heure à qn** to tell sb the time; **tu lui donneras le bonjour de ma part** say hello to her for me; **d. des ou de ses nouvelles à qn** to keep in touch with sb **(g)** *(chance, délai, occasion)* to give; **je vous donne une semaine, pas plus** I'll give you a week and no more **(h)** *(causer)* **d. de l'appétit à qn** to give sb an appetite; **d. des boutons à qn** to bring sb out in a rash; **d. mal à la tête à qn** to give sb a headache; **d. faim/sommeil/chaud à qn** to make sb hungry/sleepy/hot; **d. du souci à qn** to cause sb worry; **toute cette histoire m'a donné à réfléchir** the whole business made me think again **(i)** *(produire) (récoltes)* to yield; *(fruits)* to bear; **les blés vont d. cette année** there will be a good crop of wheat this year; **ça n'a rien donné** nothing came of it; **qu'est-ce que ça donne?** *(comment ça se présente?)* how does it look? **(j)** *(administrer)* to give; **d. un baiser/une gifle à qn** to give sb a kiss/slap in the face; **tu peux d. un coup de**

balai dans la cuisine? can you give the kitchen a sweep? **(k)** *(bal, dîner, conférence)* to give; *(pièce de théâtre)* to put on, to perform; **qu'est-ce qu'on donne au cinéma?** what's on at the cinema? **(l)** *(attribuer)* **je lui donne vingt ans** I'd say she's twenty; **les médecins lui donnent deux mois (à vivre)** the doctors give him two months (to live) **(m)** *(maladie)* to give **2** *vi (cogner)* **d. de la tête contre qch** to hit one's head against sth; *Fig* **je ne savais pas où d. de la tête** I didn't know where to start **3** *v impersonnel* **le spectacle le plus épouvantable qu'il m'ait été donné de voir** the most horrifying sight I've ever been unfortunate enough to witness; **il n'est pas donné à tout le monde d'être écrivain** not everyone can be a writer **4** **donner dans** *vt ind* **(a)** *(tomber)* **d. dans le piège** *ou* **le panneau** to fall into the trap **(b)** *(avoir un penchant pour)* to have a tendency to **5** **donner sur** *vt ind (sujet: fenêtre)* to look onto; *(sujet: porte)* to lead into **6** **se donner** *vpr* **(a)** *(faire don de soi)* to give of oneself; **se d. à qch** to devote oneself to sth; **se d. en spectacle** to make an exhibition of oneself **(b)** *(à soi-même)* **se d. un coup de peigne/brosse** to give one's hair a quick comb/brush; **se d. un coup de marteau sur le pouce** to hit one's thumb with a hammer; **se d. le temps de réfléchir** to give oneself time to think; **se d. pour tâche de faire qch** to set oneself the task of doing sth **(c)** *Litt (sexuellement)* to give oneself (à to) **(d)** *(l'un l'autre)* **se d. des coups** to exchange blows; **se d. des baisers** to kiss (each other)

donneur, -euse [dɔnœr, -øz] *nm,f* **(a)** *(d'organe)* donor; **d. de sang** blood donor **(b)** *(aux cartes)* dealer

dont [dɔ̃] *pron relatif* **(a)** *(introduit le complément du verbe)* **la famille d. je descends** the family I'm descended from; **la façon d. il me regardait** the way (in which) he looked at me; **le livre d. j'ai besoin** the book (that) I need; **un film d. on parle beaucoup** a film that is being talked about a lot; **l'homme d. elle se moque** the man she's making fun of **(b)** *(introduit le complément du nom)* **la dame d. je connais la fille** the woman whose daughter I know; **la maison d. on voit le toit** the house whose roof can be seen; **un livre d. voici le résumé** a book of which this is a summary; **quelques-uns étaient là, d. votre sœur** there were a few people there, including your sister **(c)** *(introduit le complément de l'adjectif)* **la femme d. il est amoureux** the woman he is in love with; **le groupe d'enfants d. vous êtes responsable** the group of children you are responsible for

dopage [dɔpaʒ] *nm* doping; *(de sportif)* drug-taking

doper [dɔpe] **1** *vt (droguer)* to dope **2** **se doper** *vpr* to take drugs

dorade [dɔrad] *nf* sea bream

doré, -e [dɔre] **1** *adj* **(a)** *(recouvert d'or)* gilded, gilt; **d. sur tranche** gilt-edged **(b)** *(couleur d'or) (blé, lumière, peau, cheveux)* golden; *(gâteau passé au jaune d'œuf)* glazed; *(viande, pommes de terre, gâteau)* browned **2** *nm Can (poisson)* wall-eyed pike, yellow pike

dorénavant [dɔrenavɑ̃] *adv* from now on

dorer [dɔre] **1** *vt (a) (recouvrir d'or)* to gild; *Fig* **d. la pilule à qn** to sweeten the pill for sb **(b)** *(donner une couleur dorée à) (peau)* to turn golden; *(gâteau)* to glaze; *(viande, pommes de terre)* to brown **2** *vi (plat, gâteau)* to brown **3** **se dorer** *vpr* **se d. au soleil** to sunbathe; *Fig* **se d. la pilule** to catch some rays

dorloter [dɔrlɔte] *vt* to pamper, to coddle

dormant, -e [dɔrmɑ̃, -ɑ̃t] *adj* eaux dormantes stagnant water

dormeur, -euse [dɔrmœr, -øz] *nm,f (personne endormie)* sleeper; **être un gros d.** to need a lot of sleep

dormir [29] [dɔrmir] *vi* (a) *(sommeiller)* to sleep; **elle dort** she's sleeping, she's asleep; **d. profondément** to be fast asleep; **je n'ai pas dormi de la nuit** I didn't sleep a wink (all night); **le café m'empêche de d.** coffee keeps me awake; *Fam* **ce n'est pas ça qui va m'empêcher de d.** I won't lose any sleep over it; **d. à poings fermés, d. comme un loir** to sleep like a log; **ne d. que d'un œil** to sleep with one eye open; **vous pouvez d. tranquille** *ou* **sur vos deux oreilles** you can rest easy; **avoir envie de d.** to be *or* feel sleepy; **d. debout** to be asleep on one's feet; *Prov* **qui dort, dîne** he who sleeps forgets his hunger (b) *Fig (ville, forêt)* to be sleeping; *(capitaux)* to lie idle

dorsal, -e, -aux, -ales [dɔrsal, -o] *adj* dorsal

dortoir [dɔrtwar] *nm* dormitory

dorure [dɔryr] *nf* (a) *(couche d'or)* gilding (b) *(ornement)* gilt

doryphore [dɔrifɔr] *nm* Colorado beetle

DOS [dɔs] *nm Ordinat* DOS

dos [do] *nm* (a) *(d'une personne, d'un animal)* back; **sur le d.** on one's back; **je n'ai rien à me mettre sur le d.** I haven't a thing to wear; **à d. d'âne** on a donkey; **je ne l'ai vu que de d.** I only saw him from the back; **d. à d.** back to back; **faire le gros d.** *(chat)* to arch its back; **faire qch derrière** *ou* **dans le d. de qn** to do sth behind sb's back; *Fam* **je l'ai tout le temps sur le d.** she's always on my back; **s'enrichir sur le d. de qn** to get rich off sb; **avoir bon d.** *(personne)* to have a broad back; **elle a bon d., la grève des postes, dis plutôt que tu n'as pas écrit** why don't you admit you haven't written instead of blaming it on the postal strike?; *Fam* **en avoir plein le d.** to be sick of it, to be fed up with it; **se mettre qn à d.** to get sb's back up; **tourner le d. à qn** *(debout)* to stand with one's back to sb; *(assis)* to sit with one's back to sb; *(volontairement)* to turn one's back on sb; **dès qu'il a le d. tourné** as soon as his back is turned (b) *(d'une chaise, d'une page, d'un chèque, de la main)* back; *(d'un livre)* spine; **voir au d.** (please) turn over, PTO (c) **d. (crawlé)** backstroke

dosage [dozaʒ] *nm (d'ingrédients)* proportioning; *(de médicaments)* dosage

dos-d'âne [dodan] *nm inv* bump; **pont en d.** humpbacked bridge

dose [doz] *nf (d'un élément dans un mélange)* proportion; *(de médicament)* dose; *Fig* **à petites doses** in small doses; *Fam* **il faut une sacrée d. de culot pour faire cela** it takes a hell of a nerve to do that; **forcer la d.** to overdo it; *Fam* **avoir sa d. (de qch)** to have had more than enough (of sth)

doser [doze] *vt (médicament, ingrédient)* to measure out

doseur [dozœr] *nm* measure

dossard [dosar] *nm* number *(worn by competitor)*

dossier [dosje] *nm* (a) *(d'un siège)* back (b) *(documents)* file, dossier; *(d'un prisonnier, d'un malade, d'un élève)* record; *(chemise)* folder, file; *Ordinat* file; **constituer un d. sur qn/qch** to build up a file on sb/sth; *Ordinat* **d. système** system folder (c) *Fig (sujet)* question

dot [dɔt] *nf* dowry

dotation [dɔtasjɔ̃] *nf (fonds) (d'hôpital, de collège)* endowment; *(versés à un chef d'État)* allowance

doter [dɔte] *vt (équiper)* to equip (de with); **elle est dotée d'une intelligence remarquable** she is endowed with great intelligence

douairière [dwɛrjɛr] *adj & nf* dowager

douane [dwan] *nf* customs; **passer à la d.** to go through customs; **droits de d.** customs duty

douanier, -ère [dwanje, -ɛr] **1** *adj* customs; **union douanière** customs union; **barrières douanières** tariff barriers **2** *nm* customs officer

doublage [dublaʒ] *nm* (a) *(d'un vêtement)* lining (b) *(d'un film, d'une voix)* dubbing; *(par une doublure)* doubling

double [dubl] **1** *adj* (a) *(quantité, lit, chambre)* double; **en d. exemplaire** in duplicate; **fermer une porte à d. tour** to double-lock a door; **avoir la d. nationalité** to have dual nationality; *Mus* **d. croche** *Br* semi-quaver, *Am* sixteenth note; *Ordinat* **d. densité** double density; **d. mètre** two-metre rule; **d. vitrage** double glazing (b) *(ambigu)* **mener une d. vie** to lead a double life; **mot à d. sens** ambiguous word **2** *adv* double **3** *nm* (a) **le d. (de)** *(quantité, prix)* twice as much (as); *(nombre)* twice as many (as); **dix est le d. de cinq** ten is two times five; **mettre qch en d.** to fold sth in two *or* half (b) *(exemplaire)* duplicate, copy; *(d'une clef)* duplicate; *Ordinat* backup; **avoir qch en d.** to have two of sth; **faire qch en d.** *(lettre, devoir)* to make two copies of sth (c) *(personne)* double (d) *(au tennis)* **d. messieurs/dames/mixte** men's/ladies'/mixed doubles

doublé, -e [duble] **1** *adj* (a) *(veste, gants)* lined (de with) (b) *(film)* dubbed **2** *nm (victoires)* double

doublement¹ [dubləmɑ̃] *adv* doubly

doublement² [dubləmɑ̃] *nm (d'un nombre, d'une somme, d'une lettre)* doubling

doubler [duble] **1** *vt* (a) *(multiplier par deux)* to double (b) *(plier)* to fold in two *or* in half (c) *(vêtement)* to line (d) *(film, voix)* to dub; *(sujet: acteur)* to dub the voice of; *(sujet: cascadeur)* to stand in for (e) *(passer) (véhicule)* *Br* to overtake, *Am* to pass (f) *Fam (trahir)* to double-cross **2** *vi* (a) *(population, salaire)* to double; **d. de valeur** to double in value (b) *(véhicule)* *Br* to overtake, *Am* to pass **3 se doubler** *vpr* **se doubler de** to be coupled with

doublure [dublyr] *nf* (a) *(d'un vêtement, d'un sac)* lining (b) *(au théâtre)* understudy; *(au cinéma)* stand-in

douce [dus] *voir* **doux**

douceâtre [dusɑtr] *adj (saveur)* sickly sweet; *(ton)* smarmy

doucement [dusmɑ̃] *adv (délicatement)* gently; *(bas)* softly; **allez-y d.!** gently does it!; *Fam* **(allez-y) d. avec le champagne!** go easy on the champagne!

doucereux, -euse [dusrø, -øz] *adj (personne, voix, ton)* smarmy

douceur [dusœr] *nf* (a) *(d'un son, d'une matière)* softness; *(d'un climat)* mildness; *(du miel, d'un parfum)* sweetness (b) *(de caractère)* gentleness; *(d'un sourire)* sweetness; **traiter qn avec d.** to treat sb gently; **en d.** gently; **la voiture a démarré en d.** the car started smoothly (c) *douceurs (sucreries)* *Br* sweets, *Am* candy

douche [duʃ] *nf* shower; **prendre une d.** to have *or* take a shower; *Fig* **avec lui, c'est la d. écossaise** you never know where you are with him; *Fig* **d. froide** terrible disappointment

doucher [duʃe] **1** *vt (pour laver)* **d. qn** to give sb a shower **2 se doucher** *vpr* to have *or* take a shower

doudoune [dudun] *nf (anorak)* padded jacket

doué, -e [dwe] *adj* gifted, talented; **être d. pour** to have a gift for

douille [duj] *nf (d'une ampoule)* lamp socket; *(d'une cartouche)* case

douillet, -ette [dujɛ, -ɛt] *adj* (a) *(lit)* cosy (b) *(délicat)* **ne sois pas si d.!** don't be such a baby!

douillettement [dujɛtmɑ̃] *adv (confortablement)* cosily

douleur [dulœr] *nf (physique)* pain; *(diffuse)* ache; *(morale)* sorrow, grief; **nous avons la d. de vous faire part de…** we regret to inform you of…; *Fam* **j'ai compris ma d.** my worst fears came true

douloureux, -euse [dulurø, -øz] *adj* **(a)** *(coup, maladie, opération)* painful; *(au contact)* sore, tender; **mon dos est d.** my back is aching **(b)** *(perte, événement)* sad; *(séparation, circonstances)* painful

doute [dut] *nm* **(a)** *(incertitude)* doubt; **être dans le d.** (au sujet de qch) to be doubtful (about sth); **mettre qch en d.** to question sth, to cast doubt on sth; **mettre en d. la parole de qn** to doubt sb's word; **il n'y a pas de** *ou* **aucun d.** there's no doubt about it; **sans d.** no doubt, probably; **sans aucun d.** without (any) doubt **(b)** *(soupçon)* doubt; **avoir des doutes sur** *ou* **au sujet de qn/qch** to have doubts about sb/sth

douter [dute] **1** *vi* to doubt; **d. de qn/qch** to doubt sb/sth; **elle ne doute de rien** she isn't backward in coming forward; **j'en doute** I doubt it

2 *vt* **je doute qu'il soit assez fort** I doubt whether he's strong enough; **je n'ai jamais douté que tu viendrais** I never doubted that you'd come

3 se douter *vpr* **se d. de qch** to suspect sth; **je m'en doutais (bien)** I thought as much; *Fam* **on s'en serait douté!** I might have known!

douteux, -euse [dutø, -øz] *adj* **(a)** *(incertain)* doubtful **(b)** *(suspect)* dubious; **vêtements d.** *ou* **d'une propreté douteuse** clothes that are none too clean; **d'un goût d.** *(plaisanteries, vêtements)* in dubious taste

douve [duv] *nf (d'un château)* moat

Douvres [duvr] *n* Dover

doux, douce [du, dus] **1** *adj* **(a)** *(au toucher)* soft; *(au goût)* mild **(b)** *(couleur, son, lumière)* soft; *(climat, hiver, tabac)* mild; *(vin, cidre)* sweet; *(pente)* gentle; **médecines douces** alternative medicine **(c)** *(nature, regard, voix)* gentle; **faire les yeux d. à qn** to make sheep's eyes at sb; **d. comme un agneau** as gentle as a lamb

2 *adv Fam* **filer d.** to toe the line

3 *nf* **douce** *Fam* **en d.** on the quiet

douzaine [duzɛn] *nf* **une d. (de)** *(environ)* around a dozen, a dozen or so; **trois douzaines d'œufs** three dozen eggs

douze [duz] *adj & nm inv* twelve; *voir aussi* **trois**

douzième [duzjɛm] *nmf, nm & adj* twelfth; *voir aussi* **cinquième**

doyen, -enne [dwajɛ̃, -ɛn] *nm,f* **(a)** *(personne la plus âgée)* most senior member **(b)** *(d'une faculté)* dean

drachme [drakm] *nf* drachma

draconien, -enne [drakɔnjɛ̃, -ɛn] *adj (règlement)* draconian; *(régime)* very strict

dragage [dragaʒ] *nm (nettoyage)* dredging

dragée [draʒe] *nf (confiserie)* sugared almond; *(médicament)* sugar-coated pill

dragon [dragɔ̃] *nm* **(a)** *(animal mythologique, femme acariâtre)* dragon **(b)** *(soldat)* dragoon

draguer [drage] **1** *vt* **(a)** *(nettoyer)* to dredge **(b)** *Fam (hommes, femmes)* to chat up, *Am* to hit on

2 *vi Fam* to go on the pull

dragueur, -euse [dragœr, -øz] **1** *nm (bateau)* dredger; **d. de mines** minesweeper

2 *nm,f Fam* **c'est un d.** he's always hitting on women

drain [drɛ̃] *nm* **(a)** *(conduit)* drain **(b)** *Méd* drainage tube

drainage [drenaʒ] *nm (d'un champ, d'une plaie)* draining

drainer [drene] *vt (sol, abcès)* to drain

dramatique [dramatik] **1** *adj* **(a)** *(de théâtre)* dramatic; **auteur d.** playwright **(b)** *(grave)* tragic

2 *nf* TV drama

dramatiser [dramatize] *vt* to dramatize

dramaturge [dramatyrʒ] *nm* dramatist, playwright

drame [dram] *nm* **(a)** *(genre littéraire, pièce)* drama **(b)** *Fig* tragedy; **faire un d. de qch** to make a drama out of sth

drap [dra] *nm* **(a)** *(linge)* **d. (de lit)** sheet; **d. de dessous/dessus** bottom/top sheet; *Fig* **être dans de beaux draps** to be in a real mess; **d. de bain** bath sheet **(b)** *(tissu)* cloth **(c)** *Belg (serviette)* towel

drapeau, -x [drapo] *nm* flag; *Fig* **être sous les drapeaux** to serve in the armed forces; **d. blanc** white flag; **d. tricolore** tricolour

draper [drape] **1** *vt (étoffe)* to drape

2 se draper *vpr* **se d. dans** to drape oneself in

draperie [drapri] *nf (tenture)* drapery

drap-housse *(pl* **draps-housses)** [draus] *nm* fitted sheet

drapier, -ère [drapje, -ɛr] **1** *nm,f (marchand)* draper; *(fabricant)* cloth manufacturer

2 *adj* cloth

drastique [drastik] *adj* drastic

drave [drav] *nf Can (de rondins)* drive

draver [drave] *vt Can (rondins)* to float, to drive

draveur [dravœr] *nm Can* driver, raftsman

Dresde [drɛzd] *n* Dresden

dressage [dresaʒ] *nm (d'un animal)* training; *(d'un cheval)* breaking in

dresser [drese] **1** *vt* **(a)** *(élever)* to put up, to erect; **d. la tête** to raise or lift one's head; *(pour regarder)* to look up; **d. les oreilles** to prick up *or* cock its ears; *Fig* **d. l'oreille** to prick up one's ears **(b)** *(plan, rapport, liste)* to prepare, to draw up **(c)** *(animal)* to train **(à faire qch** to do sth); *(cheval)* to break in; *Fam* **ça va le d.!** that'll put him in his place! **(d)** *(exciter)* **d. qn contre qn** to set sb against sb

2 se dresser *vpr* **(a)** *(se lever)* to stand up, to rise **(b)** *(monument)* to stand, *(montagne)* to rise up; *Fig* **les obstacles qui se dressent sur notre chemin** the obstacles that stand in our way

dresseur, -euse [dresœr, -øz] *nm,f (d'animaux)* trainer

dribble [dribl] *nm* dribble

dribbler [drible] **1** *vi* to dribble

2 *vt (joueur)* to dribble round

drille [drij] *nm Fam* **c'est un joyeux d.** he's always good for a laugh

drogue [drɔg] *nf* **(a)** *(stupéfiant)* drug; **d. dure/douce** hard/soft drug **(b)** *Vieilli (médicament)* medicine

drogué, -e [drɔge] *nm,f* drug addict

droguer [drɔge] **1** *vt* **(a)** *(victime)* to drug; *(cheval)* to dope **(b)** *(malade)* to dose with drugs

2 se droguer *vpr* to take drugs; **se d. à qch** to be on sth

droguerie [drɔgri] *nf* hardware *Br* shop *or Am* store

droguiste [drɔgist] *nmf* hardware dealer

droit¹, -e [drwa, drwat] **1** *adj* **(a)** *(rectiligne, vertical)* straight; **se tenir d.** *(debout)* to stand (up) straight; *(assis)* to sit (up) straight; **d. comme un I** *ou* **un piquet** as straight as a poker **(b)** *(honnête)* upright

2 *nf* **droite** straight line

3 *adv* **écrire/marcher d.** to write/walk straight; **aller d. devant soi** to go straight ahead; **aller d. au but** to get straight to the point; **aller à la catastrophe** to be heading straight for disaster; **c'est tout d.** it's straight ahead

droit², -e [drwa, drwat] *adj (main, jambe, gant)* right; **du côté d.** on the right-hand side

2 *nf* **droite (a)** *(côté)* right; **tourner à droite** to turn (to the) right; **rouler à droite** to drive on the right; **le placard de droite** the right-hand cupboard, the cupboard on the right; **à ma droite, l'abbaye** to *or* on my right is the abbey; *Fig* **courir à droite et à gauche** to run about all over the place (**b**) *Pol* **la droite** the right (wing); **de droite** *(candidat, journal)* right-wing; **voter à droite** to vote for the right **droit³** *nm* (**a**) *(prérogative)* right; **avoir d. à qch** to have a right to sth; **avoir le d. de faire qch** to have the right to do sth; **être dans son (bon) d.** to be within one's rights; **avoir des droits sur qn/qch** to have rights over sb/sth; **tous droits (de reproduction) réservés** *(sur livre)* all rights reserved; **de quel d. me critiques-tu?** what gives you the right to criticize me?; **d. d'aînesse** birthright; **d. d'asile** right of asylum; **avoir un d. de regard sur qch** to have the right to know about sth; **d. de réponse** right of reply; **d. de visite** *(d'un parent)* visiting rights; **d. de vote** right to vote; **les droits de l'homme** human rights (**b**) *(en argent)* fee; *(imposition)* duty; *(taxe)* tax; **droits d'auteur** royalties; **droits de douane** (customs) duty; **d. d'entrée** admission fee; **droits d'inscription** registration fee; **droits de succession** death duties; **d. de timbre** stamp duty (**c**) *Jur* law; **faire son d.** to study law; **d. administratif** administrative law; **d. des affaires** business law; **d. canon** canon law; **d. civil** civil law; **d. commercial** commercial law; **d. commun** ordinary law; **d. communautaire** Community law; **d. constitutionnel** constitutional law; **d. international** international law; **d. pénal** criminal law; **d. privé** private law; **d. public** public law; **d. du travail** labour law

droitier, -ère [drwatje, -ɛr] **1** *adj* right-handed **2** *nm,f* right-handed person

droiture [drwatyr] *nf* rectitude

drôle [drol] *adj* (**a**) *(amusant)* funny (**b**) *(étrange)* funny; **un d. de type** a funny sort; **faire une d. de tête** to pull a face; *Fam* **ça ma fait tout d. de te voir ici** it feels really funny seeing you here

drôlement [drolmɑ̃] *adv* funnily; *Fam (très)* terribly; *Fam* **les prix ont d. augmenté** prices have gone up an awful lot; *Fam* **elle est d. bien** *(remarquable)* she's a terrific person; *(belle)* she's great-looking

drôlerie [drolri] *nf* funniness

dromadaire [drɔmadɛr] *nm* dromedary

dru, -e [dry] **1** *adj (herbe, blé, cheveux, barbe)* thick; *(pluie)* heavy **2** *adv* **pousser d.** to grow thickly; **tomber d.** *(pluie)* to fall heavily

druide [drɥid] *nm* druid

DST [dɛɛste] *nf (abrév* **Direction de la surveillance du territoire**) = internal state security department, *Br* ≃ MI5, *Am* ∼ CIA

DTP [detepe] *nm (abrév* **diphtérie, tétanos, polio**) diphtheria, tetanus and polio vaccination

du [dy] *voir* **de**

dû, due *(mpl* **dus,** *fpl* **dues**) [dy] **1** *pp voir* **devoir 2** *adj* (**a**) *(que l'on doit)* due, owed; **en port dû** carriage forward (**b**) *(causé)* **être dû à qch** to be due to sth (**c**) **en bonne et due forme** in due form **3** *nm* **due**

dualisme [dɥalism] *nm* dualism

dualité [dɥalite] *nf* duality

dubitatif, -ive [dybitatif, -iv] *adj* doubtful

Dublin [dyblɛ̃] *n* Dublin

dublinois, -e [dyblinwa, -az] **1** *adj* of Dublin **2** *nm,f* **D.** Dubliner

duc [dyk] *nm* duke

ducal, -e, -aux, -ales [dykal, -o] *adj* ducal

duché [dyʃe] *nm* duchy

duchesse [dyʃɛs] *nf* (**a**) *(femme)* duchess (**b**) **pommes**

(de terre) d. duchesse potatoes *(mashed, shaped and baked)*

due *voir* **dû**

duel [dɥɛl] *nm* duel; **se battre en d.** to fight a duel

dulcinée [dylsine] *nf Litt ou Hum* ladylove

dûment [dymɑ̃] *adv* duly

dumping [dœmpiŋ] *nm* dumping; **faire du d.** to dump

dune [dyn] *nf* dune

Dunkerque [dœ̃kɛrk] *n* Dunkirk

duo [dɥo] *nm (chanson)* duet; *(de comiques, de musiciens)* duo

duodénum [dɥɔdenɔm] *nm* duodenum

dupe [dyp] **1** *nf* dupe **2** *adj* **être d. (de)** to be taken in (by)

duper [dype] *vt* to dupe, to fool

duperie [dypri] *nf* deception

duplex [dyplɛks] *nm* (**a**) **(émission en) d.** link-up (**b**) *(appartement) Br* maisonette, *Am* duplex

duplicata [dyplikata] *nm* duplicate

duplication [dyplikasjɔ̃] *nf* (**a**) *Biol* doubling (**b**) *Ordinat* **d. de logiciel** software copying

duplicité [dyplisite] *nf* duplicity

dur, -e [dyr] **1** *adj* (**a**) *(rigide)* hard; *(viande)* tough; *(pain)* stale (**b**) *(difficile, pénible) (travail, hiver)* hard; *(scène, film)* distressing (**c**) *(sévère, cruel)* harsh (**avec** with) (**d**) *Fam* **être d. de la feuille** to be hard of hearing **2** *nm,f Fam (personne)* tough type; *Pol* hard liner; **un d. à cuire** a hard-boiled type; **jouer les durs** to act tough **3** *nm* **bâtiment en d.** permanent building **4** *nf Fam* **élever qn à la dure** to bring sb up the hard way **5** *adv (travailler)* hard

durable [dyrabl] *adj* lasting

durablement [dyrabləmɑ̃] *adv* for a long time

duraille [dyraj] *adj Fam* hard

durant [dyrɑ̃] *prép* **a. le mois de mai** during May; **d. plusieurs années** for several years; **d. toute sa vie, sa vie d.** throughout his life; **parler des heures d.** to talk for hours on end

durcir [dyrsir] **1** *vt aussi Fig* to harden **2** *vi* to harden **3** **se durcir** *vpr aussi Fig* to harden

durcissement [dyrsismɑ̃] *nm aussi Fig* hardening

durée [dyre] *nf (d'un règne, d'une guerre, d'un séjour)* duration, length; *(d'une note)* length, value; **de courte d.** *(bonheur, soulagement)* short lived; **de longue d.** *(chômage)* long-term; **d. de projection** *(d'un film)* running time; **d. de validité** *(d'un billet)* period of validity; **d. de vie** *(de personne)* lifespan; *(d'une pile)* life; *(d'une machine)* useful life; **d. de vol** flight time

durement [dyrmɑ̃] *adv (répondre, parler)* harshly; **éprouvé** sorely tried

durer [dyre] *vi* to last; **voilà trois mois que cela dure** it's been going on for three months; **ça ne peut pas d.** this can't go on; *Hum* **faire d. le plaisir** to prolong the agony

dureté [dyrte] *nf* (**a**) *(rigidité)* hardness; *(d'une viande)* toughness (**b**) *(d'un hiver)* severity (**c**) *(cruauté)* *(d'une personne)* harshness; **parler avec d.** to speak harshly

durillon [dyrijɔ̃] *nm (de la main)* callus; *(du pied)* corn

Durit® [dyrit] *nf* hose (connection)

DUT [deyte] *nm (abrév* **diplôme universitaire de technologie**) = post-baccalauréat technical qualification awarded after two years

duvet [dyvɛ] *nm* (**a**) *(poil)* down (**b**) *(sac de couchage)* sleeping bag (**c**) *Suisse* duvet, quilt

duveteux, -euse [dyvtø, -øz] *adj* downy

dynamique [dinamik] **1** *adj* dynamic **2** *nf* **(a)** *(science)* dynamics *(singulier)* **(b)** *(progrès)* dynamic

dynamiser [dinamize] *vt* to energize

dynamisme [dinamism] *nm* dynamism

dynamite [dinamit] *nf* dynamite

dynamiter [dinamite] *vt* to dynamite

dynamo [dinamo] *nf* dynamo

dynastie [dinasti] *nf* dynasty

dysenterie [disãtri] *nf* dysentery

dysfonctionnement [disfɔ̃ksjɔnmã] *nm* dysfunction

dyslexie [disleksi] *nf* dyslexia

dyslexique [disleksik] *adj* dyslexic

E, e [ə] *nm inv* E, e

E (*abrév* **Est**) E

EAO [əao] *nm inv* (*abrév* **enseignement assisté par ordinateur**) CAL

eau, -x [o] *nf* (**a**) *(liquide)* water; **laver qch à grande e.** to wash sth down; **prendre l'e.** to let in water; **avoir l'e. courante** to have running water; *Fig* **mettre de l'e. dans son vin** to tone it down a bit; *Fig* **apporter de l'e. au moulin de qn** to strengthen sb's case; *Fig* **dans ces eaux-là** or thereabouts; *Fam* **s'en aller en e. de boudin** to go down the tubes; *Fam* **il y a de l'e. dans le gaz** there's trouble brewing; **e. bénite** holy water; **e. de Cologne** eau de Cologne; **e. douce** fresh water; **e. de Javel** bleach; **e. lourde** heavy water; **e. de mer** *ou* **salée** salt water; **e. minérale** mineral water; **e. oxygénée** hydrogen peroxide; **e. de pluie** rainwater; **e. du robinet** tap water; *Fig* **roman/film à l'e. de rose** sentimental novel/film; **e. de source** spring water; **eaux thermales** hot springs; **e. de toilette** toilet water; *aussi Fig* **e. de vaisselle** dishwater (**b**) *(étendue)* water; **au bord de l'e.** by the water's edge; **tomber à l'e.** to fall into the water; *Fig* to fall through; *Fig* **se jeter à l'e.** to take the plunge; **les eaux territoriales françaises** French waters (**c**) *(sécrétion)* **être tout en e.** to be dripping with perspiration; **j'en ai l'e. à la bouche!** my mouth's watering!; **elle a perdu les eaux** her waters have broken (**d**) **un diamant de la plus belle e.** a diamond of the first water

eau-de-vie (*pl* **eaux-de-vie**) [odvi] *nf* brandy

eau-forte (*pl* **eaux-fortes**) [ofɔrt] *nf* (*estampe*) etching

ébahi, -e [ebai] *adj* astounded

ébats [eba] *nmpl* frolicking; **é. amoureux** lovemaking

ébattre [11] [ebatr] **s'ébattre** *vpr* to frolic

ébauche [eboʃ] *nf* (*dessin*) rough sketch; *(d'un roman)* outline; *(d'une lettre)* draft; *Fig* **l'é. d'un sourire** the ghost of a smile

ébaucher [eboʃe] *vt (tableau, roman)* to rough out; *(lettre)* to draft; *Fig* **é. un sourire** to give a faint smile; *Fig* **é. un geste** to make a movement

ébène [ebɛn] *nf* ebony; **(d'un noir) d'é., (noir) é.** jet black

ébéniste [ebenist] *nmf* cabinet maker

éberlué, -e [ebɛrlɥe] *adj* flabbergasted

éblouir [ebluir] *vt aussi Fig* to dazzle

éblouissant, -e [ebluisɑ̃, -ɑ̃t] *adj aussi Fig* dazzling; **d'une beauté éblouissante** dazzlingly beautiful

éblouissement [ebluismɑ̃] *nm* dazzle, glare; *(malaise)* fit of dizziness; *Fig* **ce fut un é.** it was dazzling

éborgner [ebɔrɲe] *vt* **é. qn** to put sb's eye out

éboueur [ebwœr] *nm Br* dustman, *Am* garbage man

ébouillanter [ebujɑ̃te] **1** *vt* to scald
2 s'ébouillanter *vpr* to scald oneself

éboulement [ebulmɑ̃] *nm* (**a**) *(écroulement)* collapse; *(de mine)* cave-in; **deux personnes sont mortes dans l'é. de la falaise** two people were killed when the cliff collapsed (**b**) *(gravats)* mass of fallen rocks

ébouler [ebule] **s'ébouler** *vpr (falaise, remblai)* to collapse; *(tunnel)* to cave in

éboulis [ebuli] *nm* mass of fallen rocks

ébouriffé, -e [eburife] *adj (cheveux, personne)* dishevelled

ébouriffer [eburife] *vt (cheveux)* to ruffle; **é. qn** to ruffle sb's hair

ébranler [ebrɑ̃le] **1** *vt aussi Fig* to shake
2 s'ébranler *vpr* to move off

Èbre [ɛbr] *nm* **l'È.** the Ebro

ébrécher [34] [ebreʃe] *vt (verre, porcelaine)* to chip; *(lame)* to nick

ébriété [ebriete] *nf* **en état d'é.** in a state of inebriation

ébrouer [ebrue] **s'ébrouer** *vpr* (**a**) *(cheval)* to snort (**b**) *(chien)* to shake itself

ébruiter [ebrɥite] **1** *vt (secret)* to give away; *(nouvelle)* to spread
2 s'ébruiter *vpr (nouvelle)* to spread

EBS [øbeɛs] *nf* (*abrév* **encéphalite bovine spongiforme**) BSE

ébullition [ebylisjɔ̃] *nf* boiling; **arriver à é.** to come to the boil; **amener qch à é.** to bring sth to the boil; *Fig* **en é.** in turmoil

écaille [ekaj] *nf (de poisson)* scale; *(de tortue, d'huître)* shell; *(de peinture)* flake; **peigne en é.** tortoiseshell comb; **des lunettes d'é.** *ou* **en é.** tortoiseshell-rimmed glasses

écailler [ekaje] **1** *vt* (**a**) *(poisson)* to scale (**b**) *(huître)* to open
2 s'écailler *vpr (émail)* to chip (off); *(peinture)* to peel (off)

écarlate [ekarlat] *adj* scarlet; *Fig* **devenir é.** to go bright red

écarquiller [ekarkije] *vt* **é. les yeux** to open one's eyes wide

écart [ekar] *nm* (**a**) *(entre deux chiffres)* difference (**entre** between); *(en distance, en temps, dans un classement)* gap (**entre** between); **ils ont trois ans d'é.** there's a three-year gap between them; **é. de niveau** *(dans une classe)* difference in ability; **é. de salaires** salary *ou* pay differential (**b**) **faire le grand é.** to do the splits (**c**) *(déviation)* **faire un é.** *(personne)* to jump aside; *(cheval)* to shy; *(voiture)* to swerve; *Fig* **écarts de conduite**

misbehaviour; *Fig* **écarts de langage** bad language (**d**) **mettre qn à l'é.** to keep sb out of things; **tenir qn à l'é. de qch** to keep sb out of sth; **se tenir à l'é.** to keep out of things; **un terrain à l'é.** de la ville a piece of land away from the town

écarté, -e [ekarte] *adj (bras, pieds)* apart; *(yeux)* widely spaced; **avoir les dents écartées** to be gap-toothed

écarteler [39] [ekartəle] *vt* to quarter; *Fig* **être écartelé (entre)** to be torn (between)

écartement [ekartəmã] *nm (distance)* space, gap

écarter [ekarte] **1** *vt* (**a**) *(séparer) (doigts, bras, jambes)* to spread; *(rideaux)* to draw (back); *(personnes, objets)* to move apart (**b**) *(repousser) (objet, branches)* to move aside; *(danger, soupçons)* to avert; **é. qn/qch de** to move sb/sth away from; **é. qn de son chemin** to push sb out of one's way (**c**) *(exclure) (candidat, proposition)* to turn down

  2 s'écarter *vpr* (**a**) *(se séparer) (personnes)* to move apart, *(foule)* to part; *(routes)* to diverge (**b**) *(s'éloigner) (piéton)* to move away (**de** from); *(voiture)* to swerve (**de** from); *Fig* **s'é. du sujet** to wander from the subject

ecchymose [ekimoz] *nf* bruise

ecclésiastique [eklezjastik] **1** *adj* ecclesiastical   **2** *nm* clergyman

écervelé, -e [esɛrvəle] **1** *adj* scatterbrained   **2** *nm,f* scatterbrain

ECG [əseʒe] *nm Méd (abrév* **électrocardiogramme**) ECG

échafaud [eʃafo] *nm* scaffold; *Fig* **monter à l'é.** to go to the scaffold

échafaudage [eʃafodaʒ] *nm* scaffolding; **des échafaudages** scaffolding

échafauder [eʃafode] *vt (empiler)* to pile up; *Fig (système, argumentation)* to put together

échalas [eʃala] *nm Fam* **grand é.** beanpole

échalote [eʃalɔt] *nf* shallot

échancré, -e [eʃãkre] *adj* low-cut

échancrer [eʃãkre] *vt* to cut out the neckline of

échancrure [eʃãkryr] *nf (décolleté)* low neckline

échange [eʃãʒ] *nm* (**a**) *(d'objets, de prisonniers, d'idées)* exchange; **voulez-vous (me) faire l'é.?** could you exchange it/them (for me)?; **recevoir/donner qch en é. (de qch)** to receive/give sth in exchange (for sth); **de violents échanges** *(physiques)* violent clashes; *(verbaux)* violent exchanges; **échanges culturels** cultural exchanges (**b**) **échanges commerciaux** trade; **échanges internationaux** international trade (**c**) *(au tennis)* rally; **faire des échanges** to knock up (**d**) *Ordinat* **é. de données** data exchange; **é. de données informatisé** electronic data interchange

échanger [45] [eʃãʒe] *vt (objets, articles)* to exchange, to swap (**contre** for); *Fig (coups, idées)* to exchange; *(injures)* to trade

échangeur [eʃãʒœr] *nm* interchange

échantillon [eʃãtijõ] *nm* sample; **prélever un é. de qch** to take a sample of sth; **é. gratuit** free sample

échantillonnage [eʃãtijɔnaʒ] *nm* (**a**) *(action)* sampling (**b**) *(échantillons)* selection of samples

échantillonner [eʃãtijɔne] *vt (pour sondage)* to sample

échappatoire [eʃapatwar] *nf* way out

échappée [eʃape] *nf* (**a**) *(de coureurs)* breakaway; **être dans l'é.** to be part of the breakaway group (**b**) *(espace libre)* **une é. sur la mer** a sea view

échappement [eʃapmã] *nm* (**a**) *(de voiture)* exhaust; **des gaz d'é.** exhaust fumes (**b**) *Ordinat* escape

échapper [eʃape] **1 échapper à** *vt ind* **é. à qn** *(sujet: personne)* to get away from sb; **é. à qch** *(punition, mort)* to

escape sth; *(corvée)* to get out of sth; **son nom m'échappe** her name escapes me; **ça m'échappe** it escapes me; **rien ne lui échappe** he doesn't miss a thing; **la victoire nous a échappé** victory eluded us; **la bouteille m'a échappé des mains** the bottle slipped out of my hands

  2 *vi* **laisser é.** *(personne, animal)* to let escape; *(objet)* to drop; *(de l'air)* to let out; *(de la vapeur)* to let off; *(larme)* to let fall; *(secret, soupir, cri)* to let out; *(détail)* to overlook

  3 *vt* **il l'a échappé belle** he had a narrow escape

  4 s'échapper *vpr* (**a**) *(s'évader)* to escape (**de** from) (**b**) *(sortir) (eau, gaz)* to escape (**de** from); **un cri s'échappa de ses lèvres** she let out a cry

écharde [eʃard] *nf* splinter

écharpe [eʃarp] *nf* scarf; **l'é. tricolore** the tricolour sash; **avoir le bras en é.** to have one's arm in a sling

écharper [eʃarpe] *vt Fam* **se faire é.** to get torn to pieces

échasse [eʃas] *nf* (**a**) *(bâton)* stilt; **être monté sur des échasses** to be on stilts (**b**) *(oiseau)* stilt

échassier [eʃasje] *nm* wader

échaudé, -e [eʃode] *adj Fig* **être é.** to get one's fingers burnt

échauffement [eʃofmã] *nm* (**a**) *(d'un moteur)* overheating (**b**) *(excitation)* overexcitement (**c**) *(d'athlète)* warm-up

échauffer [eʃofe] **1** *vt* (**a**) *(moteur)* to overheat (**b**) *(exciter)* **é. les esprits** to get people worked up; *Fam* **é. les oreilles à qn** to get up sb's nose (**c**) *(athlète)* to warm up   **2 s'échauffer** *vpr* (**a**) *(moteur)* to get overheated (**b**) *(athlète)* to warm up

échauffourée [eʃofure] *nf* brawl; *Mil* skirmish

échéance [eʃeãs] *nf (de dette, de facture)* date of payment; **à courte/longue é.** *(prêt)* short-/long-term; **venir à é.** to fall due; **faire face à ses échéances** to meet one's financial obligations; *Fig* **une é. électorale** an election

échéancier [eʃeãsje] *nm* (**a**) *(livre)* billbook (**b**) *(calendrier)* timetable

échéant [eʃeã] *adj m voir* **cas**

échec [eʃɛk] *nm* (**a**) *(défaite)* failure; *(revers)* setback; **subir un é.** *(défaite)* to fail; *(revers)* to suffer a setback; *L'an* **mettre en é.** *(au hockey)* to check; **faire é. à qch** to foil sth; **faire é. à qn** to frustrate sb; **l'é. scolaire** doing badly at school (**b**) *(jeu)* **échecs** chess; **é.!** check!; **é. et mat!** checkmate!

échelle [eʃɛl] *nf* (**a**) *(pour grimper)* ladder; **l'é. des pompiers** the fireman's ladder; *Fig* **l'é. sociale** the social ladder; *Fig* **é. des salaires** salary scale; **é. des valeurs** scale of values; **faire la courte é. à qn** to give sb *Br* a leg up or *Am* a boost; **six sur l'é. de Richter** six on the Richter scale (**b**) *(d'une carte)* scale; **l'é. est de 1/10 000** the scale is 1:10,000; **sur une grande é.** on a large scale; **à l'é. nationale** on a national scale; *Ordinat* **intégration à grande/petite é.** large-/small-scale integration (**c**) *(dans un collant) Br* ladder, *Am* run; **faire une é. à son collant** *Br* to ladder one's tights, *Am* to get a run in one's pantyhose

échelon [eʃlõ] *nm* (**a**) *(d'une échelle)* rung (**b**) *(d'une hiérarchie)* grade; **gravir tous les échelons** to climb to the top of the ladder (**c**) *(niveau)* level; **à l'é. national** on a national level; **à tous les échelons** at every level

échelonnement [eʃlɔnmã] *nm* (**a**) *(de paiements)* spreading; *(de vacances)* staggering (**b**) *(d'objets)* spacing

échelonner [eʃlɔne] **1** *vt* (**a**) *(paiements)* to spread; *(vacances)* to stagger (**b**) *(objets)* to space out   **2 s'échelonner** *vpr* (**a**) **les paiements s'échelonnent sur deux ans** the payments are spread over two years (**b**) *(objets)* to be spaced out

écheveau, -x [eʃvo] *nm (de fil)* skein; *Fig* **démêler l'é. d'une affaire compliquée** to untangle a complicated business

échevelé, -e [eʃəvle] *adj (personne)* dishevelled; *Fig (course)* mad

échevin [eʃəvɛ̃] *nm Belg* deputy mayor

échine [eʃin] *nf* (**a**) *(colonne vertébrale)* spine, backbone (**b**) *(de porc)* loin

échiner [eʃine] **s'échiner** *vpr* **s'é. à faire qch** to wear oneself out doing sth

échiquier [eʃikje] *nm (d'échecs)* chessboard

écho [eko] *nm* (**a**) *(bruit)* echo; **il y a de l'é.** there's an echo; *Fig* **trouver un é.** to get a response; *Fig* **se faire l'é. de qch** to echo sth; *Fig* **j'en ai eu de très bons échos** I've had some very good feedback (**b**) **les échos** *(de journal)* gossip column

échographie [ekografi] *nf* (ultrasound) scan; **passer une é.** to have a scan

échoir [14] [eʃwar] **1** *vi (dette)* to fall due; *(investissement)* to mature **2 échoir à** *vt ind* to fall to

échoppe [eʃɔp] *nf* shop

échotier, -ère [ekɔtje, -ɛr] *nm,f* gossip columnist

échouer [eʃwe] **1** *vi* (**a**) *(navire)* to run aground; *(baleine)* to get stranded; **navire échoué** stranded ship; *Fam* **é. dans un bar** to land up in a bar (**b**) *(rater) (projet, personne)* to fail; **é. à un examen** to fail an exam; **faire é.** *(projet)* to wreck; *(complot)* to foil **2** *vt (navire)* to beach **3 s'échouer** *vpr (navire)* to run aground; *(baleine)* to get stranded

éclabousser [eklabuse] *vt* to splash, to spatter (**avec** with)

éclaboussure [eklabusyr] *nf* splash

éclair [eklɛr] **1** *nm* (**a**) *(lumière)* flash; *(pendant un orage)* flash of lightning; **éclairs** lightning; **être rapide comme l'é.** to be as quick as a flash; *Fig* **en un é.** in a flash (**b**) *Fig (de lucidité, de génie)* flash; **lancer des éclairs** *(yeux)* to flash (**c**) *(gâteau)* éclair **2** *adj inv (visite, attaque)* lightning

éclairage [eklɛraʒ] *nm* lighting; *(par projecteurs)* floodlighting

éclairagiste [eklɛraʒist] *nmf (de cinéma, de théâtre)* lighting technician

éclaircie [eklɛrsi] *nf* sunny spell

éclaircir [eklɛrsir] **1** *vt* (**a**) *(rendre plus clair) (couleur, cheveux)* to lighten; *(teint)* to clear (**b**) *(rendre moins épais) (sauce)* to thin (**c**) *Fig (élucider) (mystère)* to clear up **2 s'éclaircir** *vpr* (**a**) *(temps, ciel)* to clear; *(visage)* to brighten up (**b**) *(se dissiper) (brouillard)* to clear; *Fig (mystère)* to be cleared up (**c**) *(cheveux)* to thin (**d**) **s'é. la voix** to clear one's throat

éclaircissement [eklɛrsismɑ̃] *nm* (**a**) *(explication)* explanation; **demander (à qn) des éclaircissements sur qch** to ask (sb) for an explanation of sth (**b**) *(de cheveux)* lightening

éclairé, -e [eklere] *adj* lit; *Fig* enlightened

éclairer [eklere] **1** *vt* (**a**) *(pièce, vitrine)* to light; **e. qn to** give sb some light; **éclairé au néon** neon-lit; *Fig* **é. qch d'un jour nouveau** to shed or throw new light on sth; *Fig* **un sourire éclairait son visage** a smile lit up her face (**b**) *Fig (informer)* to enlighten; *Fam* **é. la lanterne de qn (sur qch)** to put sb in the picture (about sth) **2** *vi* **cette lampe éclaire mal** this lamp doesn't give much light **3 s'éclairer** *vpr* (**a**) *(personne)* **s'é. au pétrole/gaz** to use oil lamps/gaslight; **s'é. à la bougie** to use candles for lighting (**b**) *(devenir lumineux) (bâtiment, visage)* to light up (**c**) *Fig* **tout s'éclaire!** everything's becoming clear!

éclaireur, -euse [eklɛrœr, -øz] **1** *nm Mil* scout; *Mil & Fig* **partir en é.** to go off for a scout around **2** *nm,f* (boy) scout, *f* (girl) guide

éclat [ekla] *nm* (**a**) *(fragment) (de bois, de verre)* splinter; *(de pierre)* chip; **é. d'obus** piece of shrapnel; **des éclats d'obus** shrapnel; **des éclats de verre** *(bris)* broken glass; *(projeté)* flying glass; **voler en éclats** to shatter (**b**) *(son)* **é. de rire** burst of laughter; **partir d'un grand é. de rire** to burst out laughing; **éclats de rire** roar with laughter; *un* é. **de voix** loud voices (**c**) *Fig (scandale)* scandal (**d**) *(du soleil)* glare; *(d'un diamant)* flash; *(de couleurs)* brilliance; **l'é. de ses yeux** the sparkle in his/her eyes; *Fig* **l'é. de la jeunesse** the bloom of youth (**e**) *(d'une cérémonie, d'une époque)* splendour; **action** *ou* **coup d'é.** brilliant feat

éclatant, -e [eklatɑ̃, -ɑ̃t] *adj* (**a**) *(lumière, couleur, succès)* brilliant; *(teint)* glowing; *(preuve)* striking; **être é. de santé** to be glowing with health; **être dans une forme éclatante** to be on brilliant form (**b**) *(son, rire)* loud

éclaté, -e [eklate] *adj (vision)* fragmented

éclatement [eklatmɑ̃] *nm (d'un obus, d'un pneu)* bursting; *(d'un verre)* shattering; *Fig (d'un groupe)* break-up

éclater [eklate] **1** *vi* (**a**) *(exploser) (obus, pneu, ballon)* to burst; *(verre)* to shatter; *Fig (groupe)* to break up; **faire é. qch** to burst/shatter sth; **faire é. un pétard** to let off a firework (**b**) *Fig* **é. de rire** to burst out laughing; **é. en sanglots** to burst into tears; **é. en applaudissements** to burst into applause (**c**) *(se déclencher) (guerre, incendie)* to break out; *(orage, scandale)* to break **2** *vt Fam* **é. la tête à qn** to smash sb's head in **3 s'éclater** *vpr Fam* to have a really good time

éclectique [eklektik] *adj* eclectic

éclipse [eklips] *nf (de soleil, de lune)* eclipse

éclipser [eklipse] **1** *vt aussi Fig* to eclipse **2 s'éclipser** *vpr Fam (s'esquiver)* to slip away

éclopé, -e [eklɔpe] **1** *adj* lame **2** *nm,f* lame person

éclore [15] [eklɔr] *vi* (**a**) *(œuf, poussin)* to hatch (**b**) *(fleur)* to open

éclosion [eklozjɔ̃] *nf* (**a**) *(d'œuf, de poussin)* hatching (**b**) *(de fleurs)* opening

écluse [eklyz] *nf* lock; **(porte d')é.** lock gate

éclusier, -ère [eklyzje, -ɛr] *nm,f* lock keeper

écœurant, -e [ekœrɑ̃, -ɑ̃t] *adj* (**a**) *(nourriture)* nauseating; *Fig (révoltant)* disgusting (**b**) *Fam (décourageant)* sickening

écœurement [ekœrmɑ̃] *nm* (**a**) *(nausée)* nausea; *Fig (indignation)* disgust; **manger qch jusqu'à l'é.** to eat sth until one feels sick (**b**) *Fam (découragement)* discouragement

écœurer [ekœre] *vt* (**a**) **é. qn** *(donner la nausée à)* to make sb feel sick; *Fig (indigner)* to disgust sb (**b**) *Fam (décourager)* to sicken

école [ekɔl] *nf* (**a**) *(établissement, enseignement)* school; **être à l'é.** to be at school; **aller à l'é.** to go to school; **reprendre l'é.** to go back to school; **faire l'é. buissonnière** to play *Br* truant *or Am* hookey; *Fig* **être à bonne é.** to be in good hands; *Fam* **je n'ai pas é. aujourd'hui** I don't have any classes today; **les grandes écoles** = university-level colleges specializing in professional training; **É. des beaux-arts** = art school in Paris; **é. de commerce** business school; **é. de conduite** driving school; **é. de danse** dancing school; **é. de dessin** art school; **é. hôtelière** hotel school; **é. libre** independent *or* private school; **é. maternelle** nursery school; **é. militaire** military academy; **é. de musique** music school; **É. nationale d'administration** = university-level college preparing students for senior posts in law and economics;

Anciennement **é. normale** teacher training college; **É. normale supérieure** = university-level college preparing students for senior posts in teaching; **é. primaire** *(bâtiment) Br* primary school, *Am* elementary school; *(enseignement) Br* primary education, *Am* elementary education; **é. privée** private school; **é. publique** *Br* state *or Am* public school **(b)** *(de pensée, d'art)* school; **faire é.** to win a following

écolier, -ère [ekɔlje, -er] *nm,f* schoolchild, schoolboy, *f* schoolgirl *(at primary school)*

écolo [ekɔlo] *adj & nmf Fam* green

écologie [ekɔlɔʒi] *nf* ecology

écologique [ekɔlɔʒik] *adj* ecological

écologiste [ekɔlɔʒist] *adj & nmf* environmentalist

écomusée [ekomyze] *nm* living museum *(showing man in his natural and social environment)*

éconduire [18] [ekɔdɥir] *vt Litt* **(a)** *(congédier)* to dismiss **(b)** *(refuser) (prétendant)* to reject

économat [ekɔnɔma] *nm* **(a)** *(fonction)* bursarship **(b)** *(bureau)* bursar's office

économe [ekɔnɔm] **1** *adj* economical, thrifty **2** *nmf (de collège)* bursar **3** *nm* **(couteau) é.** potato peeler

économie [ekɔnɔmi] *nf* **(a)** *(système)* economy; **é. dirigée** planned economy; **é. libérale** open market economy; **é. de marché** market economy **(b)** *(gain)* saving; *(vertu)* economy, thrift; **avoir le sens de l'é.** to be thrifty; **faire une é. de temps/de 20%** to save time/20%; **faire l'é. d'un coup de fil** to save oneself a phone call **(c) économies** savings; **faire des économies** to save money; **faire des économies de chauffage** to save money on heating; **faire des économies d'énergie** to save energy; **prendre sur ses économies** to dip into one's savings; **il n'y a pas de petites économies** every little helps

économique [ekɔnɔmik] *adj* **(a)** *(relatif à l'économie)* economic **(b)** *(avantageux)* economical

économiser [ekɔnɔmize] *vt (argent, temps, énergie)* to save; *(électricité, nourriture)* to economize on, to save on; **é. ses forces** to conserve one's strength; **é. sa salive** to save one's breath; **é. pour ses vacances** to save up for one's holidays

économiste [ekɔnɔmist] *nmf* economist

écoper [ekɔpe] **1** *vt (barque)* to bale (out); **nous avons dû é.** we had to bale out **2** *vt ind Fam (être puni)* **é. d'une amende/de cinq ans de prison** to get a fine/five years in prison; **c'est encore moi qui vais é.** I'm going to get the blame again

écorce [ekɔrs] *nf* **(a)** *(d'arbre)* bark; *(d'orange)* peel **(b) l'é. terrestre** the earth's crust

écorché, -e [ekɔrʃe] **1** *nm* anatomical model **2** *nm,f Fig* **é. (vif)** tortured soul

écorcher [ekɔrʃe] **1** *vt* **(a)** *(animal)* to skin; *(criminel)* to flay **(b)** *(érafler)* to graze; *Fig (nom)* to mispronounce; *Fig* **é. les oreilles à qn** to grate on sb's ears **2 s'écorcher** *vpr* to graze oneself; **s'é. le coude** to graze one's elbow

écorchure [ekɔrʃyr] *nf* graze

écorner [ekɔrne] *vt (meuble)* to damage the corner(s) of; *(livre)* to dog-ear

écossais, -e [ekɔse, -ez] **1** *adj* Scottish; *(whisky)* Scotch; **une jupe écossaise** a tartan skirt **2** *nm,f* **É.** Scot **3** *nm (tissu)* tartan

Écosse [ekɔs] *nf* **l'É.** Scotland

écosser [ekɔse] *vt* to shell

écosystème [ekosistɛm] *nm* ecosystem

écot [eko] *nm* **payer son é.** to pay one's share

écoulement [ekulmã] *nm* **(a)** *(de liquide)* flow **(b)** *(de blessure)* discharge **(c)** *(de marchandises)* sale **(d)** *(du temps)* passage

écouler [ekule] **1** *vt (marchandises, faux billets)* to dispose of **2 s'écouler** *vpr* **(a)** *(liquide)* to flow out, to run out **(de** of**) (b)** *(marchandises)* to sell **(c)** *(temps)* to pass

écourter [ekurte] *vt (robe, texte)* to shorten; *(visite, discours)* to cut short

écoute [ekut] *nf* **(a)** *(d'une radio)* être à l'é. (de) to be listening in (to); **rester à l'é.** to stay tuned; **heure de grande é.** *Rad* peak listening time; *TV* prime time; **indice d'é.** ratings; **écoutes téléphoniques** telephone tapping **(b)** être à l'é. des autres to be willing to lend a sympathetic ear

écouter [ekute] **1** *vt* **(a)** *(entendre)* to listen to; **é. qn jusqu'au bout** to hear sb out; **savoir é.** to be a good listener; **é. aux portes** to listen at doors; **faire é. qch à qn** to play sb sth; **écoutez!** listen! **(b)** *(suivre) (personne)* to listen to; **é. sa conscience** to listen to one's conscience **2 s'écouter** *vpr* **il s'écoute trop** he coddles himself; **si je m'écoutais** if I did what I wanted; **s'é. parler** to like the sound of one's own voice

écouteur [ekutœr] *nm (du téléphone)* earpiece; **écouteurs** *(casque)* headphones

écoutille [ekutij] *nf Naut* hatchway

écouvillon [ekuvijɔ] *nm (pour bouteille, biberon)* bottle brush

écrabouiller [ekrabuje] *vt Fam* to squash, to crush; **se faire é. par une voiture** to get flattened by a car

écran [ekrã] *nm* **(a)** *(de télévision, de cinéma)* screen; **porter une pièce à l'é.** to adapt a play for the screen; **prochainement sur vos écrans** coming soon to a cinema near you; **le grand/petit é.** the big/small screen; **é. panoramique** wide screen; **é. plat** flat screen **(b)** *Ordinat* screen, display; **à l'é.** on screen; **é. d'accueil** logo screen; **é. couleur** colour screen *or* display; **é. à cristaux liquides** liquid crystal screen; **é. à fenêtres** split screen; **é. monochrome** monochrome screen; **é. rétro-éclairé** back-lit screen; **é. tactile** touch-sensitive screen **(c)** *(pour protéger)* screen; **on ne peut pas voir le lac car les arbres font é.** you can't see the lake because it's screened by the trees; **é. de fumée** smoke screen; **é. total** sun block

écrasant, -e [ekrazã, -ãt] *adj (poids, défaite, responsabilité)* crushing; *(majorité, victoire)* overwhelming

écrasé, -e [ekraze] *adj (nez)* flat

écraser [ekraze] **1** *vt* **(a)** *(fruit, ail, membre)* to crush; *(insecte)* to squash; *(cigarette)* to stub out; *(piéton, chien)* to run over; **se faire é.** *(par une voiture)* to get run over; *Fam* **é. l'accélérateur** *ou* **le champignon** to put one's foot down **(b)** *(vaincre) (adversaire, troupes)* to crush **(c)** *Fam* **en é.** to sleep like a log **(d)** *très Fam* **écrase!** shut it! **2 s'écraser** *vpr (avion)* to crash **(b)** *Fam (ne rien dire)* to keep quiet

écrémage [ekremaʒ] *nm (sélection)* creaming off

écrémer [34] [ekreme] *vt (lait)* to skim; *Fig (sélectionner)* to cream off the best of

écrevisse [ekrəvis] *nf* crayfish

écrier [66] [ekrije] **s'écrier** *vpr* to cry out, to exclaim

écrin [ekrɛ̃] *nm* (jewel) case

écrire [30] [ekrir] **1** *vt (lettre, livre, chanson)* to write; *(noter)* to write down; **é. à qn** to write to sb; **é. un mot à qn** to drop sb a line; **jour sb à qn il a écrit de venir** I've written asking them to come; **il écrit bien** his handwriting is good; *(écrivain)* he writes well; **ce stylo écrit très bien** this pen writes very well

2 s'écrire vpr (a) (s'orthographier) to be spelt; **comment ça s'écrit?** how do you spell it? (b) (correspondre) to write to each other

écrit [ekri] nm (a) **mettre qch par é.** to put sth down in writing (b) (texte) (written) document; **écrits** (œuvre) writings (c) (examen) written examination

écriteau, -x [ekrito] nm notice

écritoire [ekritwar] nf writing case

écriture [ekrityr] nf (a) (système, caractères) writing; Ordinat write (b) (façon d'écrire) (hand)writing; **elle a une belle é.** she has good handwriting (c) (littérature) writing; TV & Cin é. **de scénarios** scriptwriting (d) **écritures** (comptabilité) accounts; **tenir les écritures** to keep the accounts (e) Rel **l'É. sainte, les saintes Écritures** the Scriptures

écrivain [ekrivɛ̃] nm writer; é. **public** (public) letter writer

écrivais etc voir **écrire**

écrou [ekru] nm (de boulon) nut

écrouer [ekrue] vt Jur to imprison

écroulé, -e [ekrule] adj Fam é. **(de rire)** doubled up with laughter

écroulement [ekrulmã] nm collapse

écrouler [ekrule] **s'écrouler** vpr (bâtiment, prix, empire) to collapse; (espoirs) to crumble away; **s'é. sur une chaise** to flop onto a chair; **s'é. de fatigue** to collapse with exhaustion

écru, -e [ekry] adj (beige) ecru; (naturel) unbleached

ecstasy [ekstazi] nf ecstasy

ECU, ÉCU [eky] nm Anciennement (abrév **European Currency Unit**) ECU

écu [eky] nm (a) Hist crown (b) (bouclier) shield

écueil [ekœj] nm (rocher) reef; Fig (danger) pitfall

écuelle [ekɥɛl] nf bowl

éculé, -e [ekyle] adj (chaussure) down-at-heel; Fig (plaisanterie, argument) hackneyed

écume [ekym] nf (bave, sur la mer) foam; (sur la soupe, la confiture) scum; **avoir l'é. à la bouche** to be foaming at the mouth; é. **(de mer)** (magnésite) meerschaum

écumer [ekyme] **1** vt (a) (soupe, confiture) to skim (b) (piller) to plunder; Fig (parcourir) to scour; é. **les mers** (pirates) to scour the seas
2 vi é. **(de rage)** to foam (with rage)

écumoire [ekymwar] nf skimmer; Fig **troué comme une é.** riddled with holes

écureuil [ekyrœj] nm squirrel

écurie [ekyri] nf stable; é. **(de courses)** (de chevaux, de voitures) (racing) stable

écusson [ekysɔ̃] nm (a) (armoiries) escutcheon (b) (de tissu) badge

écuyer, -ère [ekɥije, -ɛr] **1** nm Hist (gentilhomme) squire
2 nm,f rider; é. **de cirque** circus rider

eczéma [egzema] nm eczema; **avoir** ou **faire de l'é.** to have eczema

édam [edam] nm Edam

edelweiss [edɛlvɛs] nm edelweiss

Éden [edɛn] nm **l'É.** Eden; Fig **un é.** a paradise

édenté, -e [edɑ̃te] adj toothless

EDF [ødeɛf] nf (abrév **Électricité de France**) French electricity company

EDI [ødei] nm Ordinat (abrév **échange de données informatisé**) EDI

édifiant, -e [edifjɑ̃, -ɑ̃t] adj edifying

édification [edifikasjɔ̃] nf (a) (d'un monument) erection;

Fig (d'un empire, d'une fortune) building up (b) (instruction morale) edification

édifice [edifis] nm building; Fig **apporter sa pierre à l'é.** to make a contribution; Fig **l'é. social** the social fabric

édifier [66] [edifje] vt (a) (monument) to erect; Fig (empire, fortune) to build up (b) (instruire) to edify

Édimbourg [edɛ̃bur] n Edinburgh

édit [edi] nm Hist edict

éditer [edite] vt (a) (publier) to publish (b) (commenter) (texte) to edit (c) Ordinat to edit; **pouvant être édité** editable

éditeur, -trice [editœr, -tris] **1** nm,f (a) (d'une maison d'édition) publisher (b) (commentateur) editor
2 nm Ordinat (de programme) editor; é. **d'icônes** icon editor; é. **de logiciel** software company; é. **de texte** text editor

édition [edisjɔ̃] nf (a) (activité) publishing (b) (texte, exemplaire) edition; Hum **où est le café? – dans le placard, troisième é.!** where's the coffee? – for the third time, it's in the cupboard!; é. **originale** first edition (c) (d'un journal) edition; **dernière é.** final edition; é. **spéciale** special edition (d) Ordinat editing; é. **de liens** linking; é. **pleine page** full page editing; é. **électronique** electronic publishing

édito [edito] nm Fam editorial, Br leader

éditorial, -e, -aux, -ales [editorjal, -o] **1** adj editorial
2 nm editorial

éditorialiste [editorjalist] nmf editorial writer

édredon [edrədɔ̃] nm eiderdown

éducateur, -trice [edykatœr, -tris] nm,f teacher; é. **spécialisé** special needs teacher

éducatif, -ive [edykatif, -iv] adj educational

éducation [edykasjɔ̃] nf (a) (enseignement) education; (par les parents) upbringing; **faire l'é. de qn** to educate sb; é. **manuelle et technique** handicraft classes; **l'É. nationale** the Department of Education; é. **physique** physical training or education; é. **religieuse** religious instruction; é. **sexuelle** sex education (b) (savoir-vivre) good manners; **avoir de l'é.** to have good manners; **manquer d'é.** to have no manners (c) Fig (des réflexes, du goût) training

édulcorant, -e [edylkɔrɑ̃, -ɑ̃t] **1** adj sweetening
2 nm sweetener; é. **de synthèse** artificial sweetener

édulcorer [edylkɔre] vt (discours, compte rendu) to water down; (roman pornographique) to tone down

éduquer [edyke] vt (a) (donner un enseignement à) (enfant, peuple) to educate; (élever) to bring up; **mal éduqué** ill-mannered (b) Fig (réflexes, goût) to train

EEG [øøʒe] nm (abrév **électroencéphalogramme**) EEG

effaçable [efasabl] adj erasable

effacé, -e [efase] adj (a) (personne, manières) self-effacing (b) (menton) receding

effacement [efasmã] nm (a) (d'un mot, d'un message, d'une bande) erasing; Ordinat deletion; (d'une tache) removal; (par le temps) (d'une inscription) wearing away; (des souvenirs) fading (b) (d'une personne) self-effacement

effacer [16] [efase] **1** vt (a) (mot, enregistrement, bande) to erase; (tableau) to clean; Ordinat (données) to erase, to delete; (écran) to clear; (tache, traces) to remove; (sujet: temps) (inscription) to wear away (b) Fig é. **qch de sa mémoire** to erase sth from one's memory; **on efface tout et on recommence** we'll wipe the slate clean and make a fresh start
2 s'effacer vpr (a) (disparaître) (inscription) to wear away; Fig (sentiment, souvenir) to fade (away) (b) (s'écarter) to move aside; Fig (se faire discret) to keep in the background

effaceur [efasœr] *nm* e. **(d'encre)** ink eraser

effarant, -e [efarɑ̃, -ɑ̃t] *adj* astounding

effaré, -e [efare] *adj* astounded

effarement [efarmɑ̃] *nm* astonishment

effarer [efare] *vt* to astound

effaroucher [efaruʃe] **1** *vt* **(a)** *(effrayer)* to scare; *(faire reculer)* to scare away **(b)** *(choquer)* to shock
  2 s'effaroucher *vpr* **(a)** *(s'effrayer)* to take fright **(de** at) **(b)** *(s'offusquer)* to be shocked **(de** by)

effectif, -ive [efɛktif, -iv] **1** *adj (réel)* effective
  2 *nm (employés)* staff; *(d'un club, d'un bataillon)* strength; *(d'une classe)* size

effectivement [efɛktivmɑ̃] *adv* **(a)** *(en effet)* actually; c'est joli, hein? – e.! it's pretty, isn't it? – yes it is! **(b)** *(réellement, de manière effective)* actually

effectuer [efɛktɥe] **1** *vt (mouvement, opération)* to perform; *(paiement, parcours, calcul, réservation)* to make; *(démarches)* to take; *(commande)* to place
  2 s'effectuer *vpr (mouvement, opération)* to be performed; *(paiement, parcours)* to be made

efféminé, -e [efemine] *adj* effeminate

effervescence [efɛrvesɑ̃s] *nf* excitement; être en e. *(ville, bureau)* to be buzzing with excitement

effervescent, -e [efɛrvesɑ̃, -ɑ̃t] *adj (médicament)* effervescent

effet [efɛ] *nm* **(a)** *(résultat, conséquence)* effect **(sur** on); avoir pour e. de faire qch to have the effect of doing sth; faire e. to take effect; à cet e. with that in mind; rester *ou* demeurer sans e. to have no effect; sous l'e. de l'alcool/la drogue under the influence of alcohol/drugs; les feuilles sont tombées sous l'e. de la chaleur the heat caused the leaves to drop off; e. pervers undesired effect; *Méd* side effect; e. de serre greenhouse effect; e. secondaire side effect; *Ordinat* e. de transition melt
  (b) *(impression)* impression; quel e. ça te fait qu'elle revienne? how do you feel about her coming back?; ne faire aucun e. à qn to make no impression on sb; elle me fait l'e. d'une fille plutôt équilibrée she strikes me as being a fairly well-balanced girl; il me fait de l'e. he does something for me; faire un drôle d'e. à qn to give sb a funny feeling; faire bon/mauvais e. (à qn) to make a good/bad impression (on sb)
  (c) *(but recherché)* manquer son e. *(plaisanterie)* to fall flat; faire des effets de voix to make striking use of one's voice; *Cin* effets spéciaux special effects; e. de style stylistic effect
  (d) *(application)* prendre e. to take effect
  (e) *(au tennis)* spin; donner de l'e. à une balle to put spin on a ball
  (f) *Fin* bill; e. de commerce bill of exchange
  (g) effets **(personnels)** *(affaires)* belongings
  (h) en e., je m'en souviens yes, I do remember; en e., c'est ce que je me suis dit that's just what I thought; mais c'est monstrueux! – en e.! it's abominable! – isn't it just!; j'ai dû partir, en e. j'étais pressé I had to leave because I was in a hurry

effeuiller [efœje] *vt (fleur)* to pull the petals off; *(sujet: vent) (arbre)* to blow the leaves off; *Fig* e. la marguerite to play "he/she loves me, he/she loves me not"

efficace [efikas] *adj (méthode, remède)* effective; *(personne)* efficient

efficacement [efikasmɑ̃] *adv (avec succès)* effectively; *(de façon productive)* efficiently

efficacité [efikasite] *nf (d'une méthode, d'un remède)* effectiveness; *(d'une personne)* efficiency

effigie [efiʒi] *nf* effigy; à l'e. de qn bearing the image of sb

effilé, -e [efile] *adj (frange)* ragged; *(doigts)* tapering; *(outil, lame)* tapered; *(amandes)* slivered

effilocher [efiloʃe] s'effilocher *vpr* to fray

efflanqué, -e [eflɑ̃ke] *adj* skinny

effleurement [eflœrmɑ̃] *nm* light touch

effleurer [eflœre] *vt (frôler)* to touch lightly; *(accidentellement)* to brush (against); *(surface de l'eau)* to skim; *Fig (sujet)* to touch on; cette idée ne m'a jamais effleuré the idea never crossed my mind

effluent [eflyɑ̃] *nm* e. urbain (sewage) effluent; effluents radioactifs radioactive waste

effluve [eflyv] *nm* emanation

effondré, -e [efɔ̃dre] *adj (peiné)* grief-stricken; *(déçu)* shattered

effondrement [efɔ̃drəmɑ̃] *nm (d'un bâtiment, d'un mur, d'un toit)* collapse; *Fig (d'un plan)* falling through; *(d'un empire, des prix)* collapse; *(d'une personne)* dejection

effondrer [efɔ̃dre] s'effondrer *vpr (bâtiment, mur, toit)* to collapse; *Fig (plan)* to fall through; *(empire, prix)* to collapse; *(personne)* to go to pieces

efforcer [16] [efɔrse] s'efforcer *vpr* s'e. de faire qch to do one's best to do sth

effort [efɔr] *nm* **(a)** *(physique, intellectuel)* effort; allons, encore un (petit) e. come on, try again; son médecin lui a interdit tout e. her doctor has forbidden any exertion; sans e. effortlessly; faire un e. (pour faire qch) to make an effort (to do sth); faire des efforts to make an effort; faire l'e. de faire qch to make the effort to do sth; après l'e., le réconfort I/you/*etc* deserve this; il est partisan du moindre e. he doesn't believe in exerting himself **(b)** *Tech* strain, stress

effraction [efraksjɔ̃] *nf* *Jur* breaking and entering; entrer par e. to break in

effraie [efrɛ] *nf (oiseau)* barn owl

effranger [45] [efrɑ̃ʒe] **1** *vt* to fray
  2 s'effranger *vpr* to fray

effrayant, -e [efrɛjɑ̃, -ɑ̃t] *adj* frightening; *(chaleur, appétit)* tremendous

effrayer [53] [efreje] **1** *vt (faire peur à)* to frighten, to scare; *(inquiéter)* to alarm
  2 s'effrayer *vpr* to be frightened **(de** at); elle s'effraie pour un rien the least little thing frightens her

effréné, -e [efrene] *adj (passion, luxe)* unbridled; *(galop, course)* frantic

effritement [efritmɑ̃] *nm (d'un mur, d'un revêtement)* crumbling; *(de la roche)* weathering; *Fig (de l'autorité, d'une majorité, de fonds)* erosion

effriter [efrite] **1** *vt (pain, fromage)* to crumble; *(roche)* to weather
  2 s'effriter *vpr (mur, revêtement)* to crumble; *(roche)* to weather; *Fig (autorité, majorité, fonds)* to be eroded

effroi [efrwa] *nm Litt* dread

effronté, -e [efrɔ̃te] *adj (personne, manières)* impudent; *(mensonge, menteur)* brazen

effrontément [efrɔ̃temɑ̃] *adv* impudently; *(mentir)* brazenly

effronterie [efrɔ̃tri] *nf (d'une personne, de manières)* impudence; *(d'un mensonge)* brazenness

effroyable [efrwajabl] *adj* dreadful

effroyablement [efrwajabləmɑ̃] *adv* dreadfully

effusion [efyzjɔ̃] *nf* **(a)** e. de sang bloodshed **(b)** *(exubérance)* effusiveness; avec e. effusively

égailler [egaje] s'égailler *vpr* to disperse

égal, -e, -aux, -ales [egal, -o] **1** *adj* **(a)** *(équivalent)* equal (à to); la partie n'est pas égale they/we/you are not evenly matched; **ils sont de force/d'intelligence égale** they are equally strong/intelligent; **à surface égale, je préfère mon appartement au leur** square foot for square foot, I prefer my flat to theirs (**b**) *(constant) (respiration, son)* even; *(allure, pouls)* steady; *(sol)* level; *(climat)* equable; **être d'humeur égale** to be even-tempered; **rester é. à soi-même** to be still one's old self (**c**) **cela m'est é.** it's all the same to me; *(cela ne m'intéresse pas)* I don't care **2** *nm,f* equal; **être l'é. de qn** to be sb's equal; **traiter qn d'é. à é.** to treat sb as an equal; **sans é.** unequalled

également [egalmɑ̃] *adv (aussi)* as well, too

égaler [egale] *vt (personne, score, record)* to equal; **deux et deux égalent quatre** two and two equal four

égalisation [egalizasjɔ̃] *nf* (**a**) *(équilibrage)* equalization; *Sp* (**but/point d')é.** equalizer (**b**) *(d'une surface)* levelling

égaliser [egalize] **1** *vt* (**a**) *(salaires, pression)* to equalize; *(cheveux)* to trim (**b**) *(sol)* to level **2** *vi Sp* to equalize

égalitaire [egalitɛr] *adj* egalitarian

égalité [egalite] *nf* (**a**) *(entre des quantités, des personnes)* equality; *(au tennis)* deuce; **être à é.** *(équipes)* to be level; **é. des chances** equal opportunities; **é. des salaires** equal pay (**b**) *(constance) (de la respiration, d'un son)* evenness; *(de l'allure, du pouls)* steadiness; *(du sol)* levelness; *(du climat)* equability; **é. d'humeur** even-temperedness

égard [egar] *nm* (**a**) *(respect)* consideration; **par é. pour qn** out of consideration for sb; **égards** *(attentions)* consideration (**b**) *(aspect)* **à cet é.,...** in this respect,...; **je n'ai pas d'opinion à cet é.** I've no opinion on that score; **à certains/tous les égards** in some/all respects (**c**) *(locutions)* **à l'é. de qn** towards sb; **eu é. à** considering

égaré, -e [egare] *adj* (**a**) *(personne, animal)* lost (**b**) *(hagard) (air, regard)* distraught

égarement [egarmɑ̃] *nm* (**a**) *(folie)* distraction (**b**) **égarements** *(dérèglements de conduite)* wild behaviour

égarer [egare] **1** *vt (objet)* to mislay; *(personne) (volontairement)* to mislead; *(soupçons)* to avert **2 s'égarer** *vpr* (**a**) *(se perdre) (personne, lettre)* to get lost (**b**) *(sortir du sujet)* to wander from the point

égayer [53] [egeje] **1** *vt (personne)* to cheer up; *(conversation)* to liven up; *(pièce, vêtement)* to brighten up **2 s'égayer** *vpr (s'animer)* to cheer up

Égée [eʒe] *n voir* **mer**

égérie [eʒeri] *nf* muse

égide [eʒid] *nf* **sous l'é. de** under the aegis of

églantier [eglɑ̃tje] *nm* wild rose (bush)

églantine [eglɑ̃tin] *nf* wild rose

églefin [egləfɛ̃] *nm* haddock

église [egliz] *nf* (**a**) *(bâtiment)* church; **aller à l'é.** *(à la messe)* to go to church; **se marier à l'é.** to get married in church, to have a church wedding (**b**) **l'É.** the Church; **l'É. catholique** the Catholic Church; **l'É. anglicane** the Church of England, the Anglican Church

ego [ego] *nm inv* ego

égocentrique [egosɑ̃trik] **1** *adj* self-centred, egocentric **2** *nmf* self-centred person

égoïsme [egɔism] *nm* selfishness, egoism

égoïste [egɔist] **1** *adj* selfish, egoistic **2** *nmf* selfish person, egoist

égorger [45] [egɔrʒe] *vt* to cut the throat of

égosiller [egozije] **s'égosiller** *vpr (en parlant)* to shout oneself hoarse; *(en chantant)* to sing at the top of one's voice

égout [egu] *nm* sewer

égoutier [egutje] *nm* sewerman

égoutter [egute] **1** *vt* to drain **2** *vi* **laisser é. qch** to leave sth to drain **3 s'égoutter** *vpr* to drain

égouttoir [egutwar] *nm* (**a**) *(dans l'évier)* draining board; *(mobile)* drainer (**b**) *(passoire)* colander

égratigner [egratiɲe] **1** *vt* to scratch; *Fig* to have a dig at **2 s'égratigner** *vpr* to scratch oneself; **s'é. la joue** to scratch one's cheek

égratignure [egratiɲyr] *nf* scratch; *Fig* dig

égrener [46] [egrəne] *vt* (**a**) *(maïs, pois)* to shell; *(grappe)* to pick the grapes off (**b**) *Fig* **é. son chapelet** to tell one's beads

égrillard, -e [egrijar, -ard] *adj* bawdy

Égypte [eʒipt] *nf* **l'É.** Egypt

égyptien, -enne [eʒipsjɛ̃, -ɛn] **1** *adj* Egyptian **2** *nm,f* **É.** Egyptian

eh [e] *exclam* hey!; **eh bien** well; **eh oui!** that's right!

éhonté, -e [eɔ̃te] *adj* shameless

éjaculation [eʒakylasjɔ̃] *nf* ejaculation; **é. précoce** premature ejaculation

éjaculer [eʒakyle] *vi* to ejaculate

éjectable [eʒɛktabl] *adj* **siège é.** ejector seat

éjecter [eʒɛkte] *vt (cartouche, pilote)* to eject; *Fam (expulser)* to throw out (**de** of)

éjection [eʒɛksjɔ̃] *nf (d'une cartouche, du pilote)* ejection; *Fam (expulsion)* throwing out

élaboration [elabɔrasjɔ̃] *nf (d'un plan, d'une idée)* development; *(d'une constitution, d'une loi)* drawing up

élaboré, -e [elabɔre] *adj (technique, machine)* sophisticated; *(plan)* elaborate

élaborer [elabɔre] *vt (plan, idée)* to develop; *(constitution, loi)* to draw up

élagage [elagaʒ] *nm aussi Fig* pruning

élaguer [elage] *vt aussi Fig* to prune

élan¹ [elɑ̃] *nm* (**a**) *(course)* run-up; *(vitesse)* momentum; *Fig (impulsion)* boost; **prendre de l'é.** *ou* **son é.** to take a run-up; **saut sans/avec é.** standing/running jump; *Fig* **d'un seul é.** all in one go; *Fig* **emporté par son é.** carried away (**b**) *(transport) (d'enthousiasme)* burst; *(de tendresse, de passion)* surge (**c**) *(ferveur)* fervour

élan² *nm (cerf)* elk

élancé, -e [elɑ̃se] *adj* slim, slender

élancement [elɑ̃smɑ̃] *nm (douleur)* shooting pain

élancer [16] [elɑ̃se] **1** *vi* **la jambe m'élance** I've got shooting pains in my leg **2 s'élancer** *vpr (se précipiter)* to rush forward; *Sp* to take a run-up

élargir [elarʒir] **1** *vt* (**a**) *(route, rue)* to widen; *(vêtement)* to let out; *(trou)* to enlarge (**b**) *Fig (groupe, gamme de produits)* to expand; *(connaissances, débat)* to broaden (**c**) *Jur (prisonnier)* to release **2** *vi Fam (personne)* to get bigger **3 s'élargir** *vpr* (**a**) *(route, rue)* to widen; *(chaussures, vêtement)* to stretch; *(trou)* to enlarge (**b**) *Fig (groupe, gamme de produits)* to expand; *(connaissances, débat)* to broaden

élargissement [elarʒismɑ̃] *nm* (**a**) *(d'une route, d'une rue)* widening; *(d'un trou)* enlargement (**b**) *Fig (d'un groupe, d'une gamme de produits)* expansion; *(des connaissances, d'un débat)* broadening (**c**) *Jur (d'un prisonnier)* release

élastique [elastik] **1** *adj (corps, matière)* elastic; *Fig (démarche)* springy; *(règlement, principes)* flexible; *(conscience)* accommodating **2** *nm* (**a**) *(pour la couture)* elastic (**b**) *(de bureau)* elastic *or* rubber band (**c**) *(jeu)* **jouer à l'é.** to play elastics

électeur, -trice [elɛktœr, -tris] nm,f voter, elector; **mes électeurs** the people who voted for me
élection [elɛksjɔ̃] nf (a) (d'un candidat) election; **élections législatives** general election; **élections municipales** local elections; **é. présidentielle, élections présidentielles** presidential election (b) (choix) **mon pays d'é.** my adopted country
électoral, -e, -aux, -ales [elɛktɔral, -o] adj (campagne, comité, promesses) election
électorat [elɛktɔra] nm voters, electorate; **l'é. communiste/féminin** communist/female voters
électricien, -enne [elɛktrisjɛ̃, -ɛn] nm,f electrician
électricité [elɛktrisite] nf electricity; (installation) wiring; Fig **il y a de l'é. dans l'air** the atmosphere is electric; **é. statique** static (electricity)
électrifier [66] [elɛktrifje] vt (chemin de fer) to electrify; (village) to bring electricity to
électrique [elɛktrik] adj aussi Fig electric
électrisant, -e [elɛktrizɑ̃, -ɑ̃t] adj (exaltant) electrifying
électriser [elɛktrize] vt aussi Fig to electrify
électroaimant [elɛktroɛmɑ̃] nm electromagnet
électrocardiogramme [elɛktrokardjɔgram] nm electrocardiogram
électrochoc [elɛktroʃɔk] nm electric shock; **traitement par électrochocs** electric shock treatment; **faire des électrochocs à qn** to give sb electric shock treatment
électrocuter [elɛktrɔkyte] **1** vt to electrocute; **se faire é.** to be electrocuted
2 s'électrocuter vpr to electrocute oneself
électrocution [elɛktrokysjɔ̃] nf electrocution
électrode [elɛktrɔd] nf electrode
électroencéphalogramme [elɛktroɑ̃sefalɔgram] nm electroencephalogram
électrogène [elɛktroʒɛn] adj **groupe é.** generating unit
électrolyse [elɛktrɔliz] nf electrolysis
électroménager [elɛktromenaʒe] **1** adj m **appareils électroménagers** household appliances
2 nm household appliances
électron [elɛktrɔ̃] nm electron
électronicien, -enne [elɛktrɔnisjɛ̃, -ɛn] nm,f electronics engineer
électronique [elɛktrɔnik] **1** adj (composant, jeu) electronic; (microscope, télescope) electron; (industrie) electronics
2 nf electronics (singulier)
électrophone [elɛktrɔfɔn] nm record player
élégamment [elegamɑ̃] adv (vêtu, maquillée) elegantly, smartly
élégance [elegɑ̃s] nf (d'une personne, d'un restaurant, d'un style) elegance, smartness; (d'un geste, d'un comportement) courtesy; (d'une méthode, d'une solution) neatness; **habillé avec é.** elegantly or smartly dressed; **savoir perdre avec é.** to be a good loser
élégant, -e [elegɑ̃, -ɑ̃t] adj (vêtements, restaurant, style) elegant, smart; (geste, comportement) courteous; (méthode, solution) neat; **un procédé peu é.** callous behaviour
élégie [eleʒi] nf elegy
élément [elemɑ̃] nm (a) (partie) (d'une structure, d'un problème) element; (meuble) unit; Ordinat **é. de menu** menu item (b) (personne) element; **j'ai de bons éléments dans ma classe** I've got some good pupils in my class (c) (naturel) element; **les quatre éléments** the four elements; **é. être dans son é.** to be in one's element (d) Chim element (e) (d'une batterie, d'un accumulateur) cell
élémentaire [elemɑ̃tɛr] adj (a) (de base) (connaissance,

cours, problème) elementary; (minimal) (habitation) basic; **c'est é.!** (évident) it's elementary! (b) Chim & Phys elementary
éléphant [elefɑ̃] nm elephant; **é. mâle/femelle** bull/cow elephant; **é. de mer** sea elephant; **é. d'Afrique/d'Asie** African/Indian elephant
éléphanteau, -x [elefɑ̃to] nm baby elephant
élevage [elvaʒ] nm (a) (production) breeding; (d'abeilles, de volaille) keeping; **faire de l'é.** (de bétail) to breed cattle; **é. intensif/en batterie** intensive/battery farming (b) (ferme) cattle farm
élévateur, -trice [elevatœr, -tris] **1** adj **chariot é.** fork-lift truck
2 nm (appareil) elevator
élévation [elevasjɔ̃] nf (a) (action d'élever) (du niveau d'eau, de la voix, des prix, de la température) raising; (d'une statue) erection; Rel (de l'hostie) elevation (b) (dans l'air) rising (up) (c) (augmentation) rise (de in) (d) Litt (des sentiments) nobility (e) Archit (projection) elevation (f) (relief) rise
élevé, -e [elve] adj (a) (haut, important) high; (rythme, pouls) rapid; Fig (style, esprit) elevated (b) (éduqué) **bien/mal é.** well-/ill-mannered; **c'est très mal é. de parler la bouche pleine** it's very bad manners to speak with your mouth full
élève [elɛv] nmf student, pupil; **é. infirmière** student nurse; Mil **é. officier** cadet
élever[1] [46] [elve] vt (a) (éduquer) to bring up, to raise; **bébé élevé au sein/au biberon** breast-/bottle-fed baby (b) (faire l'élevage de) (bétail, volailles, volaille) to keep
élever[2] **1** vt (a) (faire monter) (niveau d'eau, voix, prix, température) to raise; **é. un nombre au carré/au cube** to square/cube a number; **é. un nombre à la puissance 4** to raise a number to the power of 4 (b) (dresser) (monument, statue) to erect; (bras, poing, yeux) to raise; Fig (objection) to raise (c) (rehausser) (plafond, plancher) to raise; **e. qch de 20 cm** to raise sth by 20 cm (d) (promouvoir) to promote (au rang de to) (e) (édifier) (esprit) to improve; **é. le débat** to raise the tone of the debate
2 s'élever vpr (a) (avec mouvement) to rise (up); (cri) to go up (b) (se dresser) (bâtiment, montagnes) to stand (c) (monter) (température, prix) to rise (d) (protester) **s'é.** to rise up against (e) **s'é. à** (atteindre) to amount to
éleveur, -euse [elvœr, -øz] nm,f (de bovins) cattle farmer; **é. de chevaux/chiens** horse/dog breeder; **é. de moutons/poulets** sheep/poultry farmer
elfe [ɛlf] nm elf
éligibilité [eliʒibilite] nf eligibility
éligible [eliʒibl] adj eligible
élimé, -e [elime] adj worn, threadbare
élimination [eliminasjɔ̃] nf elimination; **procéder par é.** to use a process of elimination
éliminatoire [eliminatwar] adj **cinq est une note é.** five counts as a fail; **il a eu une note é.** he didn't get a pass mark; (épreuve) é. qualifying heat
éliminer [elimine] vt (candidat, suspect, toxines) to eliminate (de from); Sp (pour faute, dopage) to disqualify; (possibilité, théorie) to rule out; **faites de l'exercice pour é.** do some exercise to clear your system
élire [44] [elir] vt (a) (candidat, représentant) to elect (b) **é. domicile** to take up residence
élisabéthain [elizabetɛ̃] nf Ling elizabethan
élite [elit] nf (de. (personnel) top; (régiment) crack
élitisme [elitism] nm elitism
élitiste [elitist] adj & nmf elitist
élixir [eliksir] nm elixir

elle [ɛl] *pron personnel* (**a**) *(sujet) (personne)* she; *(chose, animal)* it; **ton amie viendra-t-e.?** is your friend coming?; **e., e. n'aurait pas levé le petit doigt** SHE wouldn't have raised a finger; **la France, e., a exprimé clairement sa position** France, for its part, has clearly expressed its position; **si j'étais e., je me méfierais** if I were her, I'd be careful (**b**) *(objet direct) (personne)* her; *(chose)* it; **et e., tu l'oublies?** and what about her, have you forgotten her? (**c**) *(avec préposition) (personne)* her; *(chose, animal)* it; **dis-le-lui, à e.** tell HER; **ce n'est pas à moi, c'est à e.** it's not mine, it's hers; **elle possède une entreprise à e.** she has her own company; *Fam* **une relation à e.** a relation of hers; **e. ne pense qu'à e.** she only thinks about herself (**d**) *(dans les comparaisons)* her; **il boit plus qu'e.** he drinks more than she does *or* than her

elle-même [ɛlmɛm] *pron personnel (personne)* herself; *(chose, animal)* itself

elles [ɛl] *pron personnel* (**a**) *(sujet)* they; **nos chambres sont-e. prêtes?** are our rooms ready?; **e., e. seraient déjà parties** THEY would have left by now; **mes filles, e., ont fait des études** my daughters, for their part, have been to university; **si j'étais e., je me méfierais** if I were them, I'd be careful (**b**) *(objet direct)* them; **et e., tu les oublies?** and what about them, have you forgotten them? (**c**) *(avec préposition)* them; *(réfléchi)* themselves; **dis-le-leur, à e.** tell THEM; **cette voiture est à e.** this car is theirs; **e. ont un appartement à e.** they have their own flat; *Fam* **un parent à e.** a relative of theirs (**d**) *(dans les comparaisons)* them; **je mange plus qu'e.** I eat more than they do *or* than them

elles-mêmes [ɛlmɛm] *pron personnel* themselves

ellipse [elips] *nf* (**a**) *Gram* ellipsis (**b**) *(courbe)* ellipse

elliptique [eliptik] *adj* elliptical

élocution [elɔkysjɔ̃] *nf* diction

éloge [elɔʒ] *nm* (**a**) *(louange)* praise; **faire l'é. de qn/qch** to praise sb/sth; **digne d'éloges** praiseworthy (**b**) *(discours)* eulogy; **é. funèbre** funeral oration

élogieux, -euse [elɔʒjø, -øz] *adj (discours, article)* complimentary; **parler de qn/qch en termes é.** to speak very highly of sb/sth

éloigné, -e [elwaɲe] *adj (dans l'espace, dans le temps)* distant, remote; *(parent)* distant; **ils sont éloignés d'un kilomètre** they're one kilometre apart; **être é. de qch** to be a long way (away) from sth; **se tenir é. de** to keep away from

éloignement [elwaɲmɑ̃] *nm* (**a**) *(séparation)* separation; **l'é. est difficile à vivre** being apart is difficult (**b**) *(distance) (dans l'espace, dans le temps)* distance, remoteness

éloigner [elwaɲe] **1** *vt* (**a**) *(dans l'espace) (personne, objet)* to move away (**de** from); *(moustiques)* to keep away; **ce trajet nous éloigne du centre-ville** this route takes us away from the centre of town (**b**) *(distraire, détourner) (crainte, pensée)* to dismiss; *(soupçons)* to avert; *(personne) (de son travail, d'une autre personne)* to keep away (**de** from) **2 s'éloigner** *vpr* (**a**) *(s'écarter)* to move away (**de** from); *(partir)* to go away (**de** from); *(orage)* to pass (**b**) *(se distraire, se détourner)* **s'é. de** *(vérité, sujet)* to wander from; *(famille, amis)* to distance oneself from; *(dans un couple)* to grow away from

élongation [elɔ̃gasjɔ̃] *nf* pulled muscle; **se faire une é.** to pull a muscle

éloquence [elɔkɑ̃s] *nf (expressivité)* eloquence

éloquent, -e [elɔkɑ̃, -ɑ̃t] *adj aussi Fig* eloquent; **ces chiffres sont éloquents** these figures speak for themselves

élu, -e [ely] **1** *adj (à un poste)* elected; *Rel* chosen **2** *nm,f* (**a**) *Rel* **les élus** the chosen ones (**b**) *(responsable)* elected representative (**c**) *Hum* **qui est l'heureuse élue?** who's the lucky lady?; **l'é. de son cœur** her beloved

élucider [elyside] *vt* to elucidate

élucubrations [elykybrasjɔ̃] *nfpl Péj* flights of fancy

éluder [elyde] *vt* to evade

Élysée [elize] *nm* (**le palais de**) **l'É.** the Élysée Palace *(residence of the President of the French Republic)*

émacié, -e [emasje] *adj* emaciated

émail, -aux [emaj, -o] *nm* enamel; *(sur porcelaine)* glaze; **en é.** *(ustensile de cuisine)* enamel

émaillé, -e [emaje] *adj* (**a**) *(métal, ustensile de cuisine)* enamelled (**b**) *(porcelaine)* glazed (**c**) *Fig* **é. de** *(plein de)* studded with

émanation [emanasjɔ̃] *nf* **émanations** emanations; **émanations toxiques** toxic fumes; *Fig* **être l'é. de qch** to emanate from sth

émancipation [emɑ̃sipasjɔ̃] *nf* emancipation; *Fig (de l'esprit, de la pensée)* liberation

émancipé, -e [emɑ̃sipe] *adj* emancipated

émanciper [emɑ̃sipe] **1** *vt* to emancipate **2 s'émanciper** *vpr* to become emancipated

émaner [emane] **émaner de** *vt ind aussi Fig* to emanate from

émarger [45] [emarʒe] **1** *vi* to draw one's salary **2** *vt (apposer ses initiales sur)* to initial; *(signer)* to sign

émasculation [emaskylasjɔ̃] *nf* emasculation

émasculer [emaskyle] *vt* to emasculate

emballage [ɑ̃balaʒ] *nm* (**a**) *(action)* packing; *(dans du papier)* wrapping; **e. sous vide** vacuum-packing (**b**) *(contenant)* packaging; *(papier)* wrapping

emballé, -e [ɑ̃bale] *adj Fam (enthousiaste)* mad keen (**par** on)

emballer [ɑ̃bale] **1** *vt* (**a**) *(empaqueter)* to pack; *(dans du papier)* to wrap; *(pour la vente)* to package (**b**) *(moteur)* to race (**c**) *Fam (enthousiasmer)* to grab **2 s'emballer** *vpr* (**a**) *(moteur)* to race; *(cheval)* to bolt (**b**) *Fam (s'enthousiasmer)* to get carried away (**c**) *(cours, monnaie)* to spiral out of control

embarcadère [ɑ̃barkader] *nm* landing stage

embarcation [ɑ̃barkasjɔ̃] *nf* (small) boat

embardée [ɑ̃barde] *nf (d'une voiture)* swerve; *(d'un bateau)* yaw; **faire une e.** *(voiture)* to swerve; *(bateau)* to yaw

embargo [ɑ̃bargo] *nm* embargo; **mettre l'e. sur** to put an embargo on; **lever l'e. sur** to lift the embargo on

embarquement [ɑ̃barkəmɑ̃] *nm (de passagers)* boarding; *(de marchandises)* loading; **e. immédiat porte 5** *(annonce)* now boarding through gate 5

embarquer [ɑ̃barke] **1** *vt* (**a**) *(passagers)* to take on board; *(marchandises)* to load (**b**) *Fam (emporter)* to take (with one) (**c**) *Fam (entraîner) (en week-end, au cinéma)* to take off; *(arrêter) Br* to nick, *Am* to bust; **se laisser e. dans** *(affaire, discussion)* to get caught up in **2** *vi (sur un bateau) (monter)* to go on board, to board; *(pour une destination)* to embark **3 s'embarquer** *vpr* (**a**) *(sur un bateau) (monter)* to go on board, to board; *(pour une destination)* to embark (**b**) *Fam Fig* **s'e. dans** *(entreprise, discussion)* to embark on

embarras [ɑ̃bara] *nm* (**a**) *(situation difficile)* **mettre qn dans l'e.** to put sb in an awkward situation; **tirer qn d'e.** to get sb out of an awkward situation; **n'avoir que l'e. du choix** to be spoilt for choice (**b**) *(difficulté financière)* **être dans l'e.** to be in financial difficulties (**c**) *(gêne)* embarrassment (**d**) *(obstacle)* être un e. pour qn to be a bother to sb (**e**) *Méd* e. gastrique upset stomach

embarrassant, -e [ãbarasã, -ãt] *adj* (**a**) *(qui gêne)* *(question, situation)* embarrassing (**b**) *(qui encombre)* cumbersome

embarrassé, -e [ãbarase] *adj* (**a**) *(gêné)* embarrassed; je suis très e. de devoir leur dire I'm very embarrassed about having to tell them (**b**) *(encombré)* *(table, pièce)* cluttered (**de** with); **avoir les mains embarrassées** to have one's hands full

embarrasser [ãbarase] **1** *vt* (**a**) *(gêner)* to embarrass (**b**) *(encombrer)* *(table, pièce)* to clutter up (**de** with); **e. qn** *(vêtement, achats)* to hamper sb; *(empêcher le passage de)* to be in sb's way
2 s'embarrasser *vpr (s'encombrer)* **s'e. de** to burden oneself with; *Fig* **elle ne s'embarrasse pas de scrupules** she doesn't bother herself with scruples

embauche [ãboʃ] *nf* (**a**) *(action)* taking on, hiring (**b**) *(emploi)* employment

embaucher [ãboʃe] **1** *vt* to take on, to hire; **l'entreprise embauche en ce moment** the company is currently recruiting people
2 s'embaucher *vpr* to get taken on

embaumer [ãbome] *vt* (**a**) *(corps)* to embalm (**b**) *(répandre une odeur de)* to be fragrant with; **son parfum embaumait la pièce** the scent of her perfume filled the room; **le jasmin embaumait** there was a fragrant smell of jasmine

embaumeur [ãbomœr] *nm (de corps)* embalmer

embellie [ãbɛli] *nf (éclaircie)* bright spell; *Naut* calm spell, lull; *Fig (de l'économie, d'une situation etc)* improvement; **courte e.** bright interval

embellir [ãbelir] **1** *vt (pièce, parc, personne)* to make more attractive; *Fig (histoire, vérité)* to embellish
2 *vi* to grow more attractive

embellissement [ãbelismã] *nm (d'un lieu)* improvement; *(d'un récit)* embellishment

emberlificoter [ãberlifikɔte] *Fam* **1** *vt* (**a**) *(fil)* to tangle up (**b**) *(duper)* to take in
2 s'emberlificoter *vpr* **s'e. dans** *(vêtements, mensonges)* to get tangled up in

embêtant, -e [ãbetã, -ãt] *adj Fam* annoying

embêtement [ãbetmã] *nm Fam* problem; **faire des embêtements à qn** to make trouble for sb

embêter [ãbete] *Fam* **1** *vt (contrarier, agacer)* to annoy; *(ennuyer)* to bore
2 s'embêter *vpr (s'ennuyer)* to be bored; *Ironique* **tu ne t'embêtes pas!** you don't do badly for yourself!; **s'e. à faire qch** *(prendre la peine de le faire)* to bother doing sth

emblée [ãble] **d'emblée** *adv* right away, straight away

emblématique [ãblematik] *adj* emblematic; *Fig* symbolic

emblème [ãblɛm] *nm aussi Fig* emblem

embobiner [ãbɔbine] *vt Fam (duper)* to take in

emboîter [ãbwate] **1** *vt (assembler)* to fit together; **e. qch dans qch** to fit sth into sth; **e. le pas à qn** to follow close on sb's heels; *Fig* to follow sb's lead
2 s'emboîter *vpr* to fit together

embolie [ãbɔli] *nf* embolism; **e. gazeuse/pulmonaire/ cérébrale** air/pulmonary/cerebral embolism

embonpoint [ãbɔpwɛ̃] *nm* stoutness; **avoir/prendre de l'e.** to be/get stout

embouché, -e [ãbuʃe] *adj Fam* **mal e.** foul-tempered

embouchure [ãbuʃyr] *nf* (**a**) *(d'un instrument à vent)* mouthpiece (**b**) *(d'un cours d'eau)* mouth

embourber [ãburbe] **s'embourber** *vpr* (**a**) *(véhicule)* to get stuck in the mud (**b**) *Fig & Péj* to get bogged down

embourgeoisement [ãburʒwazmã] *nm (d'une personne)* attainment of middle-class respectability; *(d'un quartier)* gentrification

embourgeoiser [ãburʒwaze] **s'embourgeoiser** *vpr (personne)* to become middle-class; *(quartier)* to become gentrified

embout [ãbu] *nm (d'un parapluie, d'une canne)* tip; *(d'un tuyau)* nozzle

embouteillage [ãbutɛjaʒ] *nm* traffic jam, hold-up

embouteiller [ãbutɛje] *vt* to clog up

emboutir [ãbutir] *vt* (**a**) *(véhicule)* to crash into (**b**) *(métal)* to stamp

embranchement [ãbrãʃmã] *nm* (**a**) *(croisement)* junction; *(bifurcation)* *(d'une route)* fork (**b**) *(voie secondaire)* *(de route)* side road; *(de chemin de fer)* branch line (**c**) *Bot & Zool* subkingdom

embraser [ãbraze] *Litt* **1** *vt* (**a**) *(incendier)* to set ablaze (**b**) *(éclairer)* to set aglow (**c**) *Fig (exalter) (foule)* to set alight
2 s'embraser *vpr* (**a**) *(prendre feu)* to blaze up (**b**) *(rougeoyer)* to glow

embrassade [ãbrasad] *nf* embrace, hug

embrasser [ãbrase] **1** *vt* (**a**) *(donner un baiser à)* to kiss (**b**) *(étreindre)* to embrace, to hug; **qui trop embrasse mal étreint** one shouldn't spread oneself too thinly (**c**) *(adopter) (religion, doctrine, cause)* to embrace; *(carrière)* to take up (**d**) *(englober) (sujets, questions)* to embrace, to take in; **e. qch du regard** to take sth in at a glance
2 s'embrasser *vpr* to kiss (each other)

embrasure [ãbrazyr] *nf Constr* aperture; **se tenir dans l'e. de la porte** to stand in the doorway

embrayage [ãbrɛjaʒ] *nm* (**a**) *(mécanisme)* clutch (**b**) *(action)* engaging the clutch

embrayer [ãbrɛje] *vi* (**a**) *Aut* to engage the clutch (**b**) *Fam (commencer)* to get going (**sur** on)

embrigadement [ãbrigadmã] *nm* dragooning (**dans** into)

embrigader [ãbrigade] *vt* to dragoon (**dans** into)

embringuer [ãbrɛ̃ge] *Fam* **1** *vt* **e. qn dans qch** to get sb mixed up in sth
2 s'embringuer *vpr* **s'e. dans qch** to get mixed up in sth

embrocher [ãbrɔʃe] *vt* (**a**) *Culin (viande)* to put on a spit (**b**) *Fam (transpercer)* **e. qn** to skewer sb

embrouillamini [ãbrujamini] *nm Fam* muddle

embrouillé, -e [ãbruje] *adj* (**a**) *(fils)* tangled (**b**) *Fig (idées, raisonnement, esprit)* muddled; *(affaire)* complicated

embrouiller [ãbruje] **1** *vt* (**a**) *(fils)* to tangle (up) (**b**) *Fig (personne, situation, idées)* to muddle (up)
2 s'embrouiller *vpr (personne, idées)* to get muddled (up)

embroussaillé, -e [ãbrusaje] *adj (allée, jardin)* overgrown; *(cheveux)* messed up

embrumé, -e [ãbryme] *adj* (**a**) *(horizon)* hazy; *(esprit)* fuddled

embruns [ãbrœ̃] *nmpl* spray

embryologie [ãbrijɔlɔʒi] *nf* embryology

embryon [ãbrijɔ̃] *nm* embryo

embryonnaire [ãbrijɔnɛr] *adj* embryonic

embûches [ãbyʃ] *nfpl* traps; **semé d'e.** full of pitfalls

embuer [ãbɥe] *vt (miroir, vitre)* to mist up; **yeux embués de larmes** eyes misted over with tears

embuscade [ãbyskad] *nf* ambush; **tendre une e. à qn** to set an ambush for sb; **tomber dans une e.** to be ambushed

embusquer [ãbyske] **s'embusquer** *vpr* **(a)** *(se mettre en embuscade)* to lie in ambush **(b)** *(se faire affecter loin du front)* to get a cushy posting

éméché, -e [eme∫e] *adj Fam* tipsy

émeraude [emrod] **1** *nf (pierre)* emerald
2 *nm & adj inv* emerald green

émergence [emɛrʒãs] *nf (apparition)* emergence

émerger [45] [emɛrʒe] *vi* **(a)** *(apparaître)* to emerge **(de** from) **(b)** *Fam (se lever)* to surface

émeri [emri] *nm* emery; **papier** *ou* **toile é.** emery paper

émérite [emerit] *adj* **(a)** *(expert)* highly skilled **(b)** *(professeur)* emeritus

émerveillement [emɛrvɛjmã] *nm* wonder

émerveiller [emɛrveje] **1** *vt (enchanter)* to fill with wonder; **être émerveillé par** to marvel at
2 s'émerveiller *vpr* **s'é. de** *ou* **devant** *(s'enchanter de)* to marvel at

émetteur, -trice [emetœr, -tris] **1** *adj* **(a)** *Fin (banque, organisme)* issuing **(b)** *Rad* **poste é.** transmitter; **station émettrice** transmitting station
2 *nm* transmitter

émettre [47] [emɛtr] **1** *vt* **(a)** *(cri, rot, soupir)* to give; *(son, lumière)* to give out, to emit; *(fumée, chaleur)* to give off, to emit **(b)** *Fig (opinion, objection, idée)* to voice **(c)** *Rad & TV* to transmit, to broadcast **(d)** *(billets de banque, actions, timbres-poste)* to issue
2 *vi Rad & TV* to transmit, to broadcast

émeu [emø] *nm* emu

émeus, émeut *voir* **émouvoir**

émeute [emøt] *nf* riot

émeutier, -ère [emøtje, -ɛr] *nm,f* rioter

émeuve *etc voir* **émouvoir**

émietter [emjete] **1** *vt* **(a)** *(pain)* to crumble **(b)** *Fig (domaine, empire)* to break up
2 s'émietter *vpr (pain, roche)* to crumble

émigrant, -e [emigrã, -ãt] *nm,f* emigrant

émigration [emigrasjɔ̃] *nf* emigration

émigré, -e [emigre] **1** *nm,f* emigrant; *Hist* émigré
2 *adj (travailleur, population)* migrant

émigrer [emigre] *vi* to emigrate

émincer [16] [emɛ̃se] *vt (viande, légumes)* to slice thinly

éminemment [eminamã] *adv* eminently

éminence [eminãs] *nf* **(a)** *(de relief)* hill **(b)** *Rel* **É.** Eminence; *Fig* **l'é. grise** the éminence grise

éminent, -e [eminã, -ãt] *adj (personne)* eminent; **il nous a rendu d'éminents services** he rendered us outstanding service

émir [emir] *nm* emir

émirat [emira] *nm* emirate; **les Émirats arabes unis** the United Arab Emirates

émissaire [emisɛr] *nm (envoyé)* emissary

émission [emisjɔ̃] *nf* **(a)** *(de son, de substance)* emission **(b)** *Rad & TV (action)* transmission, broadcasting; *(ce qui est diffusé)* programme **(c)** *(de billets de banque, d'actions, de timbres-poste)* issue

emmagasiner [ãmagazine] *vt (marchandises)* to store; *(électricité, chaleur, connaissances)* to store up

emmailloter [ãmajote] *vt (nourrisson)* to swaddle

emmancher [ãmã∫e] **1** *vt* **(a)** *(outil)* to fit a handle on **(b)** *(tuyaux)* to fit together; *(pièce)* to fit **(dans** into)
2 s'emmancher *vpr (pièces)* to fit together; *Fam Fig* **bien/ mal s'e.** to get off to a good/bad start

emmanchure [ãmã∫yr] *nf* armhole

emmêler [ãmɛle] **1** *vt (fils, cheveux)* to tangle

2 s'emmêler *vpr (fils, cheveux)* to get tangled; *Fam* **s'e. les pédales** *ou* **les pinceaux** to get all muddled up

emménager [45] [ãmenaʒe] *vi* to move in

emmener [46] [ãmne] *vt* **(a)** *(prendre avec soi) (personne)* to take; *(prisonnier)* to take away; *Fam (objet)* to take; **e. qn en voiture** to give sb a *Br* lift *or Am* ride **(b)** *(entraîner) (équipier, peloton, sprint)* to lead

emmenthal [emɛ̃tal] *nm* Emmenthal

emmerdant, -e [ãmɛrdã, -ãt] *adj très Fam* bloody annoying

emmerdement [ãmɛrdəmã] *nm très Fam* bloody nuisance; **avoir des emmerdements** to have a hell of a lot of trouble

emmerder [ãmɛrde] **1** *vt très Fam* **e. qn** *(contrarier, agacer)* to get on sb's nerves; *(ennuyer)* to bore sb stiff; **je l'emmerde!** sod him!
2 s'emmerder *vpr très Fam* to be bored stiff; **s'e. à faire qch** *(prendre la peine de le faire)* to bother doing sth; *Ironique* **tu ne t'emmerdes pas!** you're not doing badly for yourself!; *(tu as du culot)* you've got a nerve!

emmerdeur, -euse [ãmɛrdœr, -øz] *nm,f très Fam* pain in the arse

emmitoufler [ãmitufle] **1** *vt* to wrap up **(dans** in)
2 s'emmitoufler *vpr* to wrap oneself up **(dans** in)

emmurer [ãmyre] *vt* to wall up

émoi [emwa] *nm (trouble)* emotion; *(plaisir)* excitement; **être (tout) en é.** *(troublé)* to be in a flutter

émollient, -e [emoljã, -ãt] *adj & nm* emollient

émoluments [emolymã] *nmpl* remuneration

émonder [emɔ̃de] *vt (arbre, texte)* to prune

émotif, -ive [emotif, -iv] **1** *adj* emotional
2 *nm,f* emotional person

émotion [emosjɔ̃] *nf* emotion; *(frayeur)* fright; **donner des émotions à qn** to give sb a real fright

émotivité [emotivite] *nf* **être d'une grande é.** to be highly emotional

émoulu, -e [emuly] *adj* **frais é. de l'université** fresh out of *Br* university *or Am* school

émoussé, -e [emuse] *adj (pointe, lame)* blunt; *Fig (sentiment, intérêt)* blunted

émoustiller [emustije] *vt* to arouse

émouvant, -e [emuvã, -ãt] *adj* moving

émouvoir [31a] [emuvwar] **1** *vt (toucher)* to move, to touch; *(troubler)* to upset
2 s'émouvoir *vpr (être touché)* to be moved *or* touched; **s'é. de qch** *(s'en inquiéter)* to be concerned about sth

empailler [ãpaje] *vt* **(a)** *(animal)* to stuff **(b)** **e. une chaise** to bottom a chair with straw

empaler [ãpale] **1** *vt* to impale
2 s'empaler *vpr* to impale oneself

empaqueter [42] [ãpakte] *vt* to pack

emparer [ãpare] **s'emparer** *vpr* **s'e. de** *(lieu, personne, objet)* to seize; *(sujet : sentiment, doute)* to take hold of

empâter [ãpate] **1** *vt* to bloat
2 s'empâter *vpr* to become bloated

empattement [ãpatmã] *nm* **(a)** *(d'une voiture)* wheelbase **(b)** *Typ* serif

empêché, -e [ãpe∫e] *adj (retenu)* held up, detained

empêchement [ãpe∫mã] *nm* hitch; **il a eu un e.** something came up

empêcher [ãpe∫e] **1** *vt (action, événement)* to prevent, to stop; *(mouvement, passage)* to obstruct; **e. qn de faire qch** to prevent *or* stop sb (from) doing sth; *Fam* **ça ne m'empêchera pas de dormir** I won't lose any sleep over it; **il n'y a rien qui t'en empêche** there's nothing stopping you; **cela n'empêche que...**, **il n'empêche que...** all the same,...; *Fam* **(il) n'empêche** all the same **2 s'empêcher** *vpr* **je ne peux pas m'en e.** I can't help it; **je ne pouvais pas m'e.** de rire I couldn't help laughing **empêcheur, -euse** [ɑ̃pɛʃœr, -øz] *nm,f Fam* **e. de tourner en rond** spoilsport

empennage [ɑ̃penaʒ] *nm* (*de flèche*) feathering, feathers; *(d'avion)* tail section

empereur [ɑ̃prœr] *nm* emperor

empesé, -e [ɑ̃pəze] *adj* (**a**) *(col, chemise)* starched (**b**) *Fig (personne, air, style)* stiff

empester [ɑ̃pɛste] **1** *vt (frigo, pièce)* to stink out; **e. l'alcool/le parfum/le fromage** to stink of alcohol/perfume/cheese **2** *vi* to stink

empêtrer [ɑ̃petre] **s'empêtrer** *vpr* to get entangled; **s'e. les pieds dans qch** to get one's feet caught in sth; *Fig* **s'e. dans** *(explications, mensonges)* to get tangled up in; *Fig* **s'e. dans une affaire** to get mixed up in a business; **s'e. de qn** to land oneself with sb

emphase [ɑ̃faz] *nf* pomposity; **avec e.** pompously

emphatique [ɑ̃fatik] *adj* pompous

emphysème [ɑ̃fizɛm] *nm* emphysema

empiècement [ɑ̃pjɛsmɑ̃] *nm (d'un vêtement)* yoke

empiétement [ɑ̃pjetmɑ̃] *nm* encroachment (**sur** on)

empiéter [34] [ɑ̃pjete] *vi* **e. sur** *(terrain, horaire, vie privée)* to encroach on

empiffrer [ɑ̃pifre] **s'empiffrer** *vpr Fam* to stuff oneself (**de** with)

empiler [ɑ̃pile] **1** *vt (livres, bois, boîtes)* to stack, to pile (up) **2 s'empiler** *vpr* (*livres, dossiers*) to pile up (**b**) *(passagers)* **s'e. dans** to cram into

empire [ɑ̃pir] *nm* (**a**) *Hist & Fig* empire; **un e. commercial** a business empire; **pas pour un e.!** not for all the tea in China!; **le premier E.**, **l'E.** the First Empire; **le second E.** the Second Empire; **style/meubles E.** Empire style/furniture (**b**) *Litt (influence)* influence; **avoir de l'e. sur qn** to have influence over sb; **faire qch sous l'e. de la boisson/de la colère** to do sth under the influence of drink/in a fit of anger

empirer [ɑ̃pire] *vi* to worsen, to get worse

empirique [ɑ̃pirik] *adj* empirical

emplacement [ɑ̃plasmɑ̃] *nm* (**a**) *(endroit)* site, location; *(sur un marché, dans un parking)* space (**b**) *Ordinat* slot; **e. pour carte d'extension** expansion slot; **e. (pour) périphériques** extension slot

emplafonner [ɑ̃plafɔne] *vt Fam* to crash into

emplâtre [ɑ̃plɑtr] *nm* (**a**) *(pansement)* plaster (**b**) *Fam (personne)* drip

emplette [ɑ̃plɛt] *nf* purchase; **faire ses emplettes** to go shopping; **faire l'e. de qch** to purchase sth

emplir [ɑ̃plir] **1** *vt* to fill (**de** with) **2 s'emplir** *vpr* to fill (up) (**de** with)

emploi [ɑ̃plwa] *nm* (**a**) *(utilisation)* use; **prêt à l'e.** ready to use; **e. du temps** timetable, schedule; **faire double e.** to be redundant (**b**) *(situation)* job; *(embauche)* employment; **être sans e.** to be out of work, to be unemployed; **la crise/situation de l'e.** the employment crisis/situation; *Fig* **il a le physique** *ou* **la tête** *ou Fam* **la gueule de l'e.** he looks the part

employé, -e [ɑ̃plwaje] *nm,f* employee; **e. de banque** bank clerk; **e. de bureau** office worker; **e. de maison** domestic employee

employer [32] [ɑ̃plwaje] **1** *vt* (**a**) *(utiliser) (outil, mot, technique, force)* to use; **e. les grands moyens** to take drastic measures; **e. son temps à faire qch** to spend one's time doing sth (**b**) *(faire travailler) (personne)* to employ; **elle l'emploie comme secrétaire** she employs her as a secretary **2 s'employer** *vpr* (**a**) *(personne)* **s'e. à faire qch** to work on doing sth; **je m'y emploie** I'm working on it (**b**) *(être utilisé)* to be used

employeur, -euse [ɑ̃plwajœr, -øz] *nm,f* employer

empocher [ɑ̃pɔʃe] *vt* to pocket

empoignade [ɑ̃pwaɲad] *nf Fam* dust-up

empoigne [ɑ̃pwaɲ] *nf voir* **foire**

empoigner [ɑ̃pwaɲe] **1** *vt* to grab (hold of) **2 s'empoigner** *vpr* to have a dust-up

empoisonnant, -e [ɑ̃pwazɔnɑ̃, -ɑ̃t] *adj Fam* irritating

empoisonnement [ɑ̃pwazɔnmɑ̃] *nm* (**a**) *(par une substance nocive)* poisoning (**b**) *Fam (ennui)* problem

empoisonner [ɑ̃pwazɔne] **1** *vt* (**a**) *(avec une substance nocive)* (personne, nourriture, lieu) to poison; *Fig* **empoisonné** *(paroles)* poisonous (**b**) *(empester) (lieu)* to stink out (**c**) *Fam (irriter)* **e. qn** to get on sb's nerves (**d**) *(altérer) (existence, relations)* to poison; **e. la vie de qn** to make sb's life a misery **2 s'empoisonner** *vpr* to poison oneself

emporté, -e [ɑ̃pɔrte] *adj* quick-tempered

emportement [ɑ̃pɔrtəmɑ̃] *nm* anger

emporte-pièce [ɑ̃pɔrtəpjɛs] à l'emporte-pièce *adj* *(jugement, style)* incisive

emporter [ɑ̃pɔrte] **1** *vt* (**a**) *(prendre avec soi)* to take; **plats à e.** take-away meals (**b**) *(transporter)* to take away (**c**) *(entraîner) (sujet: courant)* to sweep away; *(sujet: vent)* to blow off; **il a eu une jambe emportée par un obus** a shell took one of his legs off; **e. qn** *(maladie)* to carry sb off; **e. la bouche** *ou Fam* **la gueule** *(moutarde, plat épicé)* to take the roof of your mouth off; *Fig* **se laisser e. par la colère/son imagination** to give way to anger/one's imagination **(gagner)** to win; *(prédominer)* to prevail; **l'e. sur qn** to beat sb; **l'e. sur qch** to prevail over sth **2 s'emporter** *vpr* to lose one's temper (**contre qn** with sb)

empoté, -e [ɑ̃pɔte] *Fam* **1** *adj* clumsy **2** *nm,f* clumsy idiot

empourprer [ɑ̃purpre] **1** *vt* to tinge with crimson **2 s'empourprer** *vpr* to turn crimson

empoussiéré, -e [ɑ̃pusjere] *adj* dusty

empreinte [ɑ̃prɛ̃t] *nf* (**a**) *(trace) (de pas)* footprint; *(d'animal)* track; **e. digitale** fingerprint; **e. génétique** genetic fingerprint (**b**) *Fig (de l'éducation, du milieu)* stamp, mark

empressé, -e [ɑ̃prese] **1** *adj (prévenant)* attentive *nm,f Péj* **faire l'e. auprès de** to dance attendance on sb

empressement [ɑ̃prɛsmɑ̃] *nm* (**a**) *(prévenance)* attentiveness (**b**) *(hâte)* eagerness; **à faire qch** to do sth); **il montre peu d'e.** à faire les travaux he seems very eager to do the work; **avec e.** eagerly; **mettre beaucoup d'e. à faire qch** to hasten to do sth

empresser [ɑ̃prese] **s'empresser** *vpr* (**a**) *(se dépêcher)* **s'e. de faire qch** to hasten to do sth (**b**) *(être prévenant)* **s'e. auprès de qn** to be attentive to sb

emprise [ɑ̃priz] *nf* hold (**sur** over); **sous l'e. de la colère** in a fit of anger

emprisonnement [ɑ̃prizɔnmɑ̃] *nm* imprisonment; **peine d'e.** prison sentence

emprisonner [ɑ̃prizɔne] *vt* to imprison

emprunt [ɑ̃prœ̃] *nm* (**a**) *(action)* borrowing (**b**) *(somme)* loan; **faire un e.** *(auprès d'une banque)* to take out a loan; **e. d'État** government loan; **lancer un e.** to issue a bond (**c**) *Ling* borrowing

emprunté, -e [ɑ̃prœ̃te] *adj* self-conscious, awkward

emprunter [ɑ̃prœ̃te] *vt* (**a**) *(objet, argent)* to borrow (**à** from) (**b**) *(route, chemin)* to take

emprunteur, -euse [ɑ̃prœ̃tœr, -øz] *nm,f* borrower

empuantir [ɑ̃pyɑ̃tir] *vt (lieu)* to stink out

ému, -e [emy] **1** *pp voir* **émouvoir**
2 *adj (touché)* moved, touched; *(intimidé)* nervous; **voix émue** voice filled with emotion; **garder un souvenir é. de qch** to have fond memories of sth

émulation [emylasjɔ̃] *nf aussi Ordinat* emulation

émule [emyl] *nmf* emulator; **j'ai fait des émules** people followed my example

émuler [emyle] *vt Ordinat* to emulate

émulsifiant [emylsifjɑ̃] *nm* emulsifier

émulsion [emylsjɔ̃] *nf* emulsion

en¹ [ɑ̃] *prép* (**a**) *(indique la date ou la durée)* in; **en 1800** in 1800; **en hiver/été** in winter/summer; **en une minute/trois jours** in a minute/three days
(**b**) *(indique la destination)* to; **aller en Espagne** to go to Spain; **partir en vacances** to go on *Br* holiday *or Am* vacation
(**c**) *(indique le lieu)* in; **vivre en France** to live in France; **en altitude** at altitude; **se promener en forêt** to walk in the forest; **en pleine mer** out at sea; **il y a quelque chose en lui qui me déplaît** there's something about him I don't like
(**d**) *(indique le moyen)* by; **en voiture/avion/train** by car/plane/train
(**e**) *(décrit un état)* in; **écrit en français** written in French; **en ruines** ruined; **être en colère/en larmes** to be angry/crying; **être en transe/en danger** to be in a trance/in danger; **être en arrêt maladie** to be on sick leave; **en trois parties** in three parts; **montre en or/en argent** gold/silver watch; **disponible en rouge/38** available in red/in size 38; **être bon en physique** to be good at physics; **payer en francs** to pay in francs; **la même chose en mieux/en moins bien** the same thing but better/but not as good
(**f**) *(indique une transformation, une progression)* into; **traduire qch en français** to translate sth into French; **transformer une chambre en bureau** to convert a bedroom into an office; **casser qch en deux** to break sth in two *or* in half; **peindre qch en rouge** to paint sth red; **réduire qch en poudre** to reduce sth to a powder; **se mettre en colère** to get angry; **aller de ville en ville** to go from town to town; **de jour en jour** by the day; **changer en bien/mal** to change for the better/for the worse
(**g**) *(en tant que)* as; **parler à qn en ami** to speak to sb as a friend; **parler en connaisseur** to speak as an expert; **agir en traître** to be disloyal
(**h**) *(avec un participe présent)* **entrer en criant** to come in shouting; **il s'est coupé en se rasant** he cut himself shaving; **c'est impoli de lire en mangeant** it's rude to read while you're eating; **traverser en courant** to run across; **répondre en maugréant** to grumble in reply; **dire qch en plaisantant** to say sth as a joke; **elle s'est cassé la jambe en tombant** she fell and broke her leg; **c'est en s'entraînant qu'il s'améliorera** he'll only get better if he practises

en² *pron* (**a**) *(avec les adjectifs construits avec de)* **il en est bien capable** he's quite capable of it; **et ta voiture? — j'en suis très content** how's your car? — I'm very pleased with it
(**b**) *(avec les verbes construits avec de)* **qu'en penses-tu?** what do you think of it?; **je ne m'en souviens plus** I can't remember; **on en reparlera** we'll talk about it later;

j'espère en tirer 200 euros I hope to get 200 euros for it
(**c**) *(remplace le complément du nom)* **nous en avons la possibilité** we can do it; **elle en a mangé un morceau** she ate a piece of it; **j'en ai acheté trois kilos** I bought three kilos
(**d**) *(remplace le nom)* **il y en a plusieurs** there are several of them; **elle en a cassé deux** she broke two of them; **est-ce que tu en veux?** do you want some?; **je n'en ai jamais vu** I've never seen one/any; **est-ce de l'argent? — non, ce n'en est pas** is it silver? — no, it's not
(**e**) *(indique la cause)* **il en a perdu la raison** it made him lose his mind; **j'en suis tout retourné** I'm really upset about it
(**f**) *Fam (pour insister)* **il en a fait une histoire!** he made such a fuss about it; **des balayeurs, il en faut** someone has to sweep the streets
(**g**) *(indique la provenance)* from there; **justement, j'en viens** I've just come from there

ENA [ena] *nf (abrév* **École nationale d'administration**) = university-level college preparing students for senior posts in law and economics

enamourer [ɑ̃namure] **s'enamourer** *vpr* **s'e. de** to become enamoured of

énarque [enark] *nmf* = graduate of the "ENA"

encabaner [ɑ̃kabane] **s'encabaner** *vpr Can* to shut oneself away

encadré [ɑ̃kadre] *nm (dans un texte)* box; *Ordinat* **e. graphique** graphics box; *Ordinat* **e. texte** text box

encadrement [ɑ̃kadrəmɑ̃] *nm* (**a**) *(cadre)* frame; **dans l'e. de la porte** in the doorway (**b**) *(fonction) (de personnel)* management; *(d'élèves, d'enfants)* supervision; *(personnes qui encadrent) (du personnel)* management; *Mil* officers (**c**) *Écon* **e. du crédit** credit squeeze

encadrer [ɑ̃kadre] *vt* (**a**) *(tableau, photo)* to frame (**b**) *(entourer) (mots, paragraphe)* to circle; **encadré par deux gendarmes** flanked by two policemen (**c**) *(guider) (personnel, équipe)* to manage; *(enfants, handicapés)* to supervise; *Mil (soldats)* to officer (**d**) *Fam (supporter)* **je ne peux pas l'e.** I can't stand him/her

encadreur, -euse [ɑ̃kadrœr, -øz] *nm,f* picture framer

encaissé, -e [ɑ̃kese] *adj (vallée)* deep; *(rivière)* with steep sides; *(route)* cut into the hillside

encaissement [ɑ̃kɛsmɑ̃] *nm* (**a**) *(d'un chèque)* cashing; *(d'argent)* collection (**b**) *(d'une vallée)* depth

encaisser [ɑ̃kese] *vt* (**a**) *(chèque)* to cash; *(argent)* to collect (**b**) *Fam (supporter) (coups, critiques)* to take; **je ne peux pas l'e.** I can't stand her; **il sait e.** he can take it; **qu'est-ce qu'il a encaissé!** he took a lot of punishment!

encanailler [ɑ̃kanaje] **s'encanailler** *vpr* to slum it

encart [ɑ̃kar] *nm (feuille)* insert; **e. publicitaire** advertising insert

en-cas [ɑ̃ka] *nm inv* snack

encastrable [ɑ̃kastrabl] *adj (machine à laver, cuisinière)* that can be built in

encastré, -e [ɑ̃kastre] *adj* built-in

encastrer [ɑ̃kastre] **1** *vt* to build in
2 **s'encastrer** *vpr (éléments)* to fit together; *(machine à laver, cuisinière)* to fit (**dans** into); **la voiture s'est encastrée sous un camion** the car embedded itself under a truck

encaustique [ɑ̃kɔstik] *nf* wax, polish

enceinte¹ [ɑ̃sɛ̃t] *nf* (**a**) *(mur)* (surrounding) wall; *(palissade)* fence (**b**) *(espace)* enclosure; *(d'église, de couvent)* precinct(s); **dans l'e. du parc** within the park (**c**) *(baffle)* **e. (acoustique)** speaker

enceinte² *adj f* pregnant; **e. de cinq mois** five months pregnant; **être e. de jumeaux** to be pregnant with or expecting twins; **elle est e. de Laurent** she's pregnant by Laurent

encens [ãsã] nm incense

encenser [ãsãse] vt **e. qn** to praise sb to the skies

encensoir [ãsãswar] nm censer

encéphalite [ãsefalit] nf encephalitis; **e. bovine spongiforme** bovine spongiform encephalopathy

encéphalogramme [ãsefalɔgram] nm encephalogram

encercler [ãsɛrkle] vt (a) (ennemi, lieu) to encircle, to surround (b) (mot) to circle, to ring

enchaînement [ãʃɛnmã] nm (a) (série) (d'événements, de circonstances) series, chain (b) (liaison) (d'idées, de séquences) linking (c) (en danse) sequence (of steps); (en ballet) enchaînement (d) Ordinat concatenation

enchaîner [ãʃene] **1** vt (a) (animal, prisonnier) to chain up; Fig (peuple) to enslave; (presse) to curb; **e. qn à** to chain sb (up) to (b) (lier) (épisodes, séquences) to link (up)
2 vi to move on; **e. sur un sujet** to move on to a subject
3 s'enchaîner vpr (a) (personne) s'e. à to chain oneself (up) to (b) (séquences, épisodes) to be linked together; **les événements se sont enchaînés rapidement** events happened very quickly

enchanté, -e [ãʃãte] adj (a) (ravi) delighted (de with), e. (de faire votre connaissance)! pleased to meet you! (b) (magique) enchanted

enchantement [ãʃãtmã] nm (a) (sortilège) (magic) spell; **comme par e.** as if by magic (b) (ravissement, merveille) delight

enchanter [ãʃãte] vt (a) (ravir) to delight; **cette idée ne l'enchante pas** she's not keen on the idea (b) (ensorceler) to bewitch

enchanteur, -eresse [ãʃãtœr, -trɛs] **1** adj (sourire) bewitching; (spectacle, endroit) enchanting, delightful
2 nm (a) (sorcier) sorcerer (b) Fig (charmeur) charmer
3 nf **enchanteresse** sorceress

enchâsser [ãʃase] vt (a) (bijou) to set (b) (relique) to enshrine

enchère [ãʃɛr] nf bid; **les enchères** the bidding; **vente aux enchères** auction; **faire monter les enchères** to up the bidding; Fig to raise the stakes; **vendre qch aux enchères** to sell sth at auction

enchérir [ãʃerir] vi to make a higher bid; **e. sur qn** to outbid sb; Fig to go one better than sb

enchevêtré, -e [ãʃəvetre] adj (branchages, fils, explications) tangled

enchevêtrement [ãʃəvetrəmã] nm (de fils, branchages) tangle

enchevêtrer [ãʃəvetre] **1** vt (fils, branchages) to tangle (up)
2 s'enchevêtrer vpr (fils) to get tangled (up)

enclave [ãklav] nf enclave

enclenchement [ãklãʃmã] nm (d'une vitesse, d'un mécanisme) engaging

enclencher [ãklãʃe] **1** vt (vitesse, mécanisme) to engage; Fig (processus) to get under way
2 s'enclencher vpr (vitesse, mécanisme) to engage; Fig (processus) to get under way

enclin, -e [ãklɛ̃, -in] adj **être e. à faire qch** to be inclined to do sth; **être e. à la paresse/la méfiance** to be inclined to be lazy/distrustful

enclos [ãklo] nm (espace) enclosure; (pour chevaux) paddock

enclume [ãklym] nf anvil; Fig **être entre le marteau et l'e.** to be between the devil and the deep blue sea

encoche [ãkɔʃ] nf notch; Ordinat **e. de protection contre l'écriture** write-protect notch

encodage [ãkodaʒ] nm Ling & Ordinat encoding

encoder [ãkode] vt Ling & Ordinat to encode

encoignure [ãkwaɲyr] nf (a) (d'une pièce) corner (b) (meuble) corner cupboard

encoller [ãkɔle] vt (papier peint) to paste

encolure [ãkɔlyr] nf (a) (d'animal) neck; **gagner d'une e.** to win by a neck (b) (tour de cou) collar size (c) (d'un vêtement) neck

encombrant, -e [ãkɔ̃brã, -ãt] adj (meuble, valise, paquet) cumbersome, bulky; Fig (personne, témoin) undesirable

encombre [ãkɔ̃br] nm **sans e.** without mishap

encombrement [ãkɔ̃brəmã] nm (a) (état) (d'une pièce) clutter; (de lignes téléphoniques) jamming; (embouteillage) traffic jam (b) (volume) (d'un objet) (overall) dimensions (c) Ordinat **faible e. sur le disque dur** low use of hard disk space

encombrer [ãkɔ̃bre] **1** vt (pièce) to clutter (up); (passage, route) to block; (lignes téléphoniques) to jam; **tu m'encombres, sors d'ici!** you're getting under my feet, get out!
2 s'encombrer vpr **s'e. de** (colis, équipement) to load oneself down with; Fig (obligations, personne) to saddle oneself with

encontre [ãkɔ̃tr] **à l'encontre de** prép aller à l'e. de to go against

encorbellement [ãkɔrbɛlmã] nm corbelled structure

encorder [ãkɔrde] **s'encorder** vpr to rope up

encore [ãkɔr] adv (a) (toujours) still; **pas e.** not yet; **elle n'est pas e. arrivée** she hasn't arrived yet; **je n'avais e. jamais vu ça** I'd never seen that before; **qu'il m'appelle par mon prénom, passe e., mais...** his calling me by my first name is one thing, but...; **e. heureux que les enfants n'aient pas été là!** it's just as well the children weren't there!
(b) (davantage) more: **en voulez-vous e.?** would you like some more?; **e. une tasse de café** another cup of coffee; **e. trois mois** three more months, another three months; **e. plus/moins** even more/less; **e. plus froid** even colder; **c'est e. pire/mieux** it's even worse/better; **mais e.?** and apart from that?
(c) (de nouveau) again; **il a e. cassé un verre** he's broken another glass; **qu'est-ce qu'il a e. fait?** what's he done this time?; **quoi e.?** now what?; **et puis quoi e.?** is that all?; **e. une fois** once more, once again; **e. vous!** you again!
(d) (restrictif) **si e.... if only...; il vous en donnera 10 euros, et e.!** he'll give you 10 euros for it, if that!; **et là..., ce n'est même pas sûr** even then, it's not certain; **e. faudrait-il qu'elle accepte/qu'il le sache!** she has to agree/he has to know about it first!
(e) (seulement) only; **hier e. elle me disait que...** only yesterday she was telling me that...
(f) **e. que** although, even though

encorner [ãkɔrne] vt to gore

encourageant, -e [ãkuraʒã, -ãt] adj encouraging

encouragement [ãkuraʒmã] nm encouragement; **des encouragements** encouragement

encourager [45] [ãkuraʒe] vt (a) (personne) to encourage; (athlète, équipe) to cheer on; **e. qn à faire qch** to encourage sb to do sth (b) (promouvoir) (arts) to encourage

encourir [22] [ãkurir] vt to incur

encrasser [ãkrase] **1** vt (vêtements, mains) to dirty; Aut (bougie) to soot up; (moteur) to clog
2 s'encrasser vpr to get dirty; Aut (bougie) to soot up; (moteur) to get clogged

encre [ãkr] *nf* ink; *Fig* **nuit d'e.** inky black night; **e. de Chine** Indian ink; **e. sympathique** invisible ink

encrier [ãkrije] *nm* inkpot; *(de pupitre)* inkwell

encroûter [ãkrute] **s'encroûter** *vpr Fam (personne)* to get into a rut

enculé, -e [ãkyle] *nm,f Vulg Br* arsehole, *Am* asshole

enculer [ãkyle] *vt Vulg* to bugger; **va te faire e.!** fuck off!; *Fig* **e. les mouches** to nit-pick

encyclique [ãsiklik] *nf Rel* encyclical

encyclopédie [ãsiklɔpedi] *nf* encyclopedia

encyclopédique [ãsiklɔpedik] *adj* encyclopedic

endémie [ãdemi] *nf* endemic disease

endémique [ãdemik] *adj* endemic

endetté, -e [ãdɛte] *adj* in debt; **très e.** heavily in debt

endettement [ãdɛtmã] *nm* debt

endetter [ãdɛte] **1** *vt* **e. qn** to get sb into debt
2 s'endetter *vpr* to get into debt

endeuiller [ãdœje] *vt (famille, nation)* to plunge into mourning; *(événement)* to cast a gloom over

endiablé, -e [ãdjable] *adj (personne, musique, rythme)* wild

endiguer [ãdige] *vt* **(a)** *(cours d'eau)* to dyke (up) **(b)** *Fig (révolte, inflation, chômage)* to contain

endimanché, -e [ãdimãʃe] *adj* in one's Sunday best

endive [ãdiv] *nf* chicory

endocrine [ãdɔkrin] *adj (glande)* endocrine

endoctrinement [ãdɔktrinmã] *nm* indoctrination

endoctriner [ãdɔktrine] *vt* to indoctrinate

endolori, -e [ãdɔlɔri] *adj* painful

endommager [45] [ãdɔmaʒe] *vt* **(a)** *(abîmer)* to damage **(b)** *Ordinat* to corrupt

endormi, -e [ãdɔrmi] **1** *adj* **(a)** *(qui dort) (personne)* sleeping; *(voix, village)* sleepy; **être e.** *(personne)* to be asleep *or* sleeping; **avoir l'air e.** to look sleepy **(b)** *(inerte, lent) (personne)* sluggish **(c)** *Fig (passion, intérêt)* dormant
2 *nm,f (personne inerte, lente)* slowcoach

endormir [29] [ãdɔrmir] **1** *vt* **(a) e. qn** *(bébé)* to send sb to sleep; *(anesthésier)* to put sb to sleep; *(ennuyer)* to send sb to sleep **(b)** *(apaiser) (douleur)* to deaden
2 s'endormir *vpr* to fall asleep, to go to sleep

endossable [ãdosabl] *adj (chèque)* endorsable

endossement [ãdosmã] *nm (d'un chèque)* endorsement

endosser [ãdose] *vt* **(a)** *(vêtement)* to put on **(b)** *(responsabilité)* to assume **(c)** *(chèque)* to endorse

endroit [ãdrwa] *nm* **(a)** *(lieu)* place, spot; **à quel e.?** where?; **c'est à cet e. que...** this is where...; **par endroits** here and there, in places **(b)** *(d'un vêtement)* right side; **à l'e.** the right way round

enduire [18] [ãdɥir] **1** *vt* to coat, to cover **(de** with)
2 s'enduire *vpr* **s'e. de** to cover oneself with

enduit [ãdɥi] *nm* coating; *(pour boucher)* filler

endurance [ãdyrãs] *nf* **(a)** *(physique)* stamina **(b)** *Sp* **épreuve/course d'e.** endurance race

endurant, -e [ãdyrã, -ãt] *adj* tough

endurci, -e [ãdyrsi] *adj* **(a)** *(dur) (personne)* hard **(b)** *(invétéré) (criminel)* hardened; *(célibataire)* confirmed

endurcir [ãdyrsir] **1** *vt* **(a)** *(moralement)* to harden **(b)** *(physiquement)* to toughen (up)
2 s'endurcir *vpr* **(a)** *(moralement)* to become hard **(b)** *(physiquement)* to toughen up

endurer [ãdyre] *vt* to endure, to bear

enduro [ãdyro] *nm Sp* enduro

énergétique [enɛrʒetik] *adj* **(a)** *(nourriture)* energy-giving **(b)** *(ressources, besoins)* energy

énergie [enɛrʒi] *nf* **(a)** *(dynamisme)* energy; **mettre toute son é. à qch/à faire qch** to devote all one's energy to sth/to doing sth; **avec é.** *(nier)* strongly; *(refuser, répondre)* forcefully; **sans é.** *(enfant)* listless; *(jouer)* listlessly **(b)** *(force)* energy, power; **é. hydroélectrique** hydroelectric power; **é. nucléaire** *ou* **atomique** nuclear power; **é. solaire** solar power *or* energy

énergique [enɛrʒik] *adj* **(a)** *(personne)* energetic, dynamic; *(geste)* brisk; *(visage)* strong **(b)** *(mesures)* strong; *(remède)* powerful

énergiquement [enɛrʒikmã] *adv (nier)* strongly; *(refuser)* forcefully; **serrer é. la main à qn** to shake sb's hand warmly

énergumène [enɛrgymɛn] *nmf* eccentric

énervant, -e [enɛrvã, -ãt] *adj* irritating

énervé, -e [enɛrve] *adj (agacé)* irritated; *(excité)* edgy, agitated

énervement [enɛrvəmã] *nm (agacement)* irritation; *(excitation)* agitation

énerver [enɛrve] **1** *vt* **é. qn** *(agacer)* to get on sb's nerves, to irritate sb; *(exciter)* to make sb nervous
2 s'énerver *vpr* to get worked up

enfance [ãfãs] *nf (jeunesse)* childhood; *(de garçon)* boyhood; *(de fille)* girlhood; **la petite e.** early childhood; *Fam* **c'est l'e. de l'art** it's child's play

enfant [ãfã] *nmf* child; **faire l'e.** to act like a child; **je l'ai connu e.** I knew him when he was a child; **il lui a fait un e.** she had a child by him; **viens ici, mon e.** come here, my child; *Fam* **il n'y a plus d'enfants!** children are so precocious nowadays!; **e. en bas âge** infant; **e. bleu** blue baby; *Rel* **e. de chœur** altar boy; *Fig* **ce n'est pas un e. de chœur** he's no angel; **e. terrible** enfant terrible; **e. trouvé** foundling; **e.unique** only child

enfantement [ãfãtmã] *nm Litt* childbirth

enfanter [ãfãte] *vt Litt* to give birth to

enfantillages [ãfãtijaʒ] *nmpl* childish behaviour; **faire des e.** to be childish

enfantin, -e [ãfãtɛ̃, -in] *adj (voix)* child's; *(littérature)* children's; *(très facile)* childishly simple; *Péj (remarque, conduite)* childish

enfarger [ãfarʒe] *vi Can* to trip

enfariné, -e [ãfarine] *adj (visage, cheveux)* covered with flour; *Fam* **arriver la gueule enfarinée** to arrive in all innocence *or* quite unsuspecting

enfer [ãfer] *nm aussi Fig* **l'e.** hell; **aller à un train d'e.** to go like a bat out of hell; *Fig* **elle a vécu un véritable e.** she's been through sheer hell; *Fam* **c'est l'e. pour se garer ici** it's hell trying to park here; *Fam* **une soirée d'e.** one hell of a party; **l'e. est pavé de bonnes intentions** the road to hell is paved with good intentions

enfermement [ãferməmã] *nm* imprisonment

enfermer [ãferme] **1** *vt (personne, chose)* to shut up; **e. qn/qch à clef** to lock sb/sth up; **je suis enfermé toute la journée** I'm cooped up all day; *Fam* **elle est bonne à e.** she should be locked up
2 s'enfermer *vpr* to shut oneself up; **s'e. à clef** to lock oneself in; *Fig* **s'e. dans le silence** to retreat into silence

enferrer [ãfere] **s'enferrer** *vpr Fig* to get tangled up (**dans** in)

enfiévré, -e [ãfjevre] *adj (front, imagination)* fevered

enfiévrer [34] [ãfjevre] **1** *vt (personne, imagination)* to excite
2 s'enfiévrer *vpr* to get excited

enfilade [ãfilad] *nf (de portes, de pièces)* series; **être en e.** to be adjoining

enfiler [ãfile] **1** *vt* **(a)** *(aiguille, perles)* to thread **(b)** *(vêtements)* to slip on

2 s'enfiler vpr (**a**) (gants, bottes) to go on (**b**) Fam (boisson, nourriture) to put away

enfin [ɑ̃fɛ̃] adv (**a**) (en dernier lieu) finally, lastly (**b**) (à la fin) at last, finally (**c**) (de résignation) e., n'en parlons plus! look, let's forget about it!, e., ce qui est fait est fait! what's done is done! (**d**) (d'exaspération) e. quoi, tu n'as plus dix ans! for God's sake, you're not ten years old!; mais e., je te l'avais dit! but I told you, for God's sake! (**e**) (d'hésitation, pour résumer) well; e., je ne dis pas non, mais... well, I'm not saying no, but...; elle n'est pas mal, e. pour son âge she's not bad, for her age that is; e. (bref), c'était la panique! in short, it was panic!

enflammé, -e [ɑ̃flame] adj (**a**) (brindille, torche, allumette) burning (**b**) (joues) (de froid) glowing; (de fièvre, de gêne) burning (**c**) Fig (discours) fiery, passionate

enflammer [ɑ̃flame] **1** vt (**a**) (mettre le feu à) to set light to; (allumette) to strike (**b**) Fig (imagination) to stir; la colère enflammait son regard her eyes were blazing with anger
2 s'enflammer vpr (**a**) (prendre feu) to catch fire (**b**) Fig (imagination) to be stirred

enflé, -e [ɑ̃fle] adj (rivière, membre) swollen

enfler [ɑ̃fle] **1** vt (**a**) (rivière, membre) to swell; e. les joues to puff out one's cheeks (**b**) Fig (exagérer) (histoire, succès) to exaggerate
2 vi (membre) to swell (up)

enflure [ɑ̃flyr] nf (**a**) (d'un membre) swelling (**b**) très Fam (imbécile) jerk

enfoiré, -e [ɑ̃fware] nm,f Vulg bugger, bastard

enfoncé, -e [ɑ̃fɔ̃se] adj (yeux) deep-set

enfoncement [ɑ̃fɔ̃smɑ̃] nm (dans le sol) dip; (dans un mur) recess

enfoncer [16] [ɑ̃fɔ̃se] **1** vt (**a**) (clou) to bang in; (pieu) to drive in; (aiguille) to stick in, to push in; e. un couteau dans qch to stick a knife into sth; e. la main dans sa poche to thrust one's hand into one's pocket; e. son chapeau sur sa tête to jam one's hat on one's head (**b**) (porte) to break down (**c**) Fam (personne) to humiliate
2 s'enfoncer vpr (clou, couteau) to go in; (bateau) to sink; s'e. dans son fauteuil to sink into one's armchair; s'e. dans un bois to go into the depths of a wood; Fam enfonce-toi ça dans le crâne! can't you get it into your thick head?

enfouir [ɑ̃fwir] **1** vt to bury (dans/sous in/under)
2 s'enfouir vpr to bury oneself

enfourcher [ɑ̃furʃe] vt (cheval, vélo) to get on, to mount

enfourner [ɑ̃furne] vt (pain) to put in the oven; (poteries, briques) to put in the kiln; Fam (manger) to stuff down

enfreindre [54] [ɑ̃frɛ̃dr] vt to infringe, to break

enfuir [38] [ɑ̃fɥir] **s'enfuir** vpr to run away (de from); (d'une prison) to escape (de from)

enfumé, -e [ɑ̃fyme] adj (pièce, atmosphère) smoky

enfumer [ɑ̃fyme] vt (**a**) (pièce) to fill with smoke (**b**) (personne, abeilles) to smoke out

enfuyais etc voir **enfuir**

engagé, -e [ɑ̃gaʒe] **1** adj (littérature, écrivain) committed
2 nm (soldat) e. (volontaire) volunteer

engageant, -e [ɑ̃gaʒɑ̃, -ɑ̃t] adj (manière, sourire) engaging

engagement [ɑ̃gaʒmɑ̃] nm (**a**) (promesse) undertaking, commitment; prendre un e. to enter into an undertaking; prendre l'e. de faire qch to undertake to do sth; tenir ses engagements to honour one's commitments; sans e. (de votre part) without obligation (on your part) (**b**) (à une cause) commitment (**c**) (coup d'envoi) (au football, au rugby) kick-off; (au hockey) bully-off; (au basket) tip-off (**d**)

(commencement) start; (de poursuites) institution (**e**) (d'un employé) appointment; (d'un soldat) enlistment

engager [45] [ɑ̃gaʒe] **1** vt (**a**) (lier) to commit; e. sa parole to give one's word; cela ne vous engage à rien it doesn't commit you to anything; cela n'engage que moi that's just my opinion (**b**) (mettre en gage) to pawn (**c**) (embaucher) (employé) to appoint; (soldat) to enlist (**d**) (commencer) (conversation, négociations) to begin, to start; (poursuites) to institute; e. la partie to start the match; la partie est maintenant bien engagée the match is now well under way (**e**) (introduire) (clef) to insert (dans) (**f**) (inciter) e. qn à faire qch to urge sb to do sth
2 s'engager vpr (**a**) (promettre) s'e. à faire qch to promise to do sth, to undertake to do sth (**b**) (prendre position) to commit oneself (**c**) (se lancer) s'e. dans une aventure to get involved in an adventure (**d**) (soldat) to enlist, to join up (**e**) (pénétrer) s'e. dans une rue to turn into a street; s'e. dans une forêt to enter a forest (**f**) (commencer) (négociations, conversation) to begin

engeance [ɑ̃ʒɑ̃s] nf Fam crew, bunch

engelure [ɑ̃ʒlyr] nf chilblain

engendrer [ɑ̃ʒɑ̃dre] vt to father; Fig (maladie, pauvreté) to cause

engin [ɑ̃ʒɛ̃] nm (machine) machine; (outil) device; Fam (objet) thing; e. blindé armoured vehicle; e. de mort deadly weapon; e. spatial spacecraft

englober [ɑ̃glɔbe] vt to include (dans in)

engloutir [ɑ̃glutir] vt (**a**) (avaler) (boisson) to gulp down; (nourriture) to wolf down (**b**) (submerger) (bateau, village) to submerge, Fig (fortune) to swallow up

engoncé, -e [ɑ̃gɔ̃se] adj il avait l'air e. dans son manteau his coat looked too tight for him

engorgement [ɑ̃gɔrʒmɑ̃] nm (blocage) blocking; (d'un marché) glutting

engorger [45] [ɑ̃gɔrʒe] **1** vt (bloquer) to block, to clog; (marché) to glut
2 s'engorger vpr (tuyau) to be blocked or clogged

engouement [ɑ̃gumɑ̃] nm craze (pour for)

engouffrer [ɑ̃gufre] **1** vt Fam (nourriture) to devour
2 s'engouffrer vpr s'e. dans to rush in to; le vent s'engouffra par la porte the wind rushed in through the door

engourdi, -e [ɑ̃gurdi] adj numb (par with)

engourdir [ɑ̃gurdir] **1** vt (**a**) (membre) to numb (**b**) (douleur) to dull
2 s'engourdir vpr to go numb, to go to sleep

engourdissement [ɑ̃gurdismɑ̃] nm numbness

engrais [ɑ̃grɛ] nm fertilizer

engraisser [ɑ̃grese] **1** vt (animaux, personne) to fatten up
2 vi Fam to get fatter

engranger [45] [ɑ̃grɑ̃ʒe] vt (céréales) to bring in; Fig to build up

engrenage [ɑ̃grənaʒ] nm (**a**) (roues dentées) gears (**b**) Fig (d'événements) chain; l'e. de la violence the cycle of violence; être pris dans un e. to get caught up in a system; mettre le doigt dans l'e. to get caught up in it

engrosser [ɑ̃grose] vt très Fam (femme) to knock up; faire e. (par) to get knocked up (by)

engueulade [ɑ̃gœlad] nf Fam (réprimande) telling-off; (querelle) row

engueuler [ɑ̃gœle] Fam **1** vt e. qn to give sb an earbashing; se faire e. to get an earbashing; e. qn comme du poisson pourri to call sb every name under the sun
2 s'engueuler vpr to have a row

enguirlander [ɑ̃girlɑ̃de] vt (**a**) Fam e. qn to give sb an earbashing; **se faire e.** to get an earbashing **(b)** *(décorer)* to garland **(de** with)

enhardir [ɑ̃ardir] **1** *vt* to embolden

2 s'enhardir *vpr* to become bolder; **s'e. à faire qch** to pluck up the courage to do sth

énième [enjɛm] *adj* **après une é.** tentative after countless attempts; **pour la é.** fois for the nth time

énigmatique [enigmatik] *adj* enigmatic

énigme [enigm] *nf (mystère)* enigma, mystery; *(devinette)* riddle

enivrant, -e [ɑ̃nivrɑ̃, -ɑ̃t] *adj (parfum)* heady; *(vitesse)* exhilarating

enivrement [ɑ̃nivrəmɑ̃] *nm* **(a)** *(par l'alcool)* intoxication **(b)** *Fig* exhilaration

enivrer [ɑ̃nivre] **1** *vt* **(a)** *(soûler)* to intoxicate, to make drunk **(b)** *Fig (exalter)* to exhilarate; **enivré par le succès** intoxicated with success

2 s'enivrer *vpr (se soûler)* to become intoxicated **(de** with), to get drunk **(de** on)

enjambée [ɑ̃ʒɑ̃be] *nf* stride; **marcher à grandes enjambées** to stride along

enjambement [ɑ̃ʒɑ̃bmɑ̃] *nm* enjambment

enjamber [ɑ̃ʒɑ̃be] *vt (obstacle)* to step over; *(sujet: pont) (rivière)* to span

enjeu, -x [ɑ̃ʒø] *nm (au jeu)* stake; *Fig (d'une guerre)* stakes; **quel est l'e. de cette élection?** what's at stake in this election?

enjoignais *etc voir* **enjoindre**

enjoindre [43] [ɑ̃ʒwɛ̃dr] *vt Litt* **e. à qn de faire qch** to enjoin sb to do sth

enjôler [ɑ̃ʒole] *vt* to cajole

enjôleur, -euse [ɑ̃ʒolœr, -øz] *adj* cajoling

2 *nm,f* charmer

enjoliver [ɑ̃ʒɔlive] *vt* to embellish

enjoliveur [ɑ̃ʒɔlivœr] *nm* hubcap

enjoué, -e [ɑ̃ʒwe] *adj* playful

enjouement [ɑ̃ʒumɑ̃] *nm* playfulness

enlacement [ɑ̃lasmɑ̃] *nm* **(a)** *(de rubans, de branches)* intertwining **(b)** *(étreinte)* embrace

enlacer [16] [ɑ̃lase] **1** *vt* **(a)** *(rubans, branches)* to intertwine **(b)** *(étreindre)* to embrace

2 s'enlacer *vpr (s'étreindre)* to embrace

enlaidir [ɑ̃ledir] **1** *vt (personne)* to make ugly, to disfigure; *(paysage, ville)* to disfigure

2 s'enlaidir *vpr* to make oneself look ugly

enlevé, -e [ɑ̃lve] *adj (style)* lively

enlèvement [ɑ̃lɛvmɑ̃] *nm* **(a)** *(de meubles, d'une tache)* removal, removing; *(de bagages)* collection; **e. des ordures** *Br* rubbish *or Am* garbage collection **(b)** *(kidnapping)* kidnapping, abduction

enlever [46] [ɑ̃lve] **1** *vt* **(a)** *(vêtements, couvercle)* to remove, to take off; *(meubles)* to remove, to take away; *(tapis)* to take up; *(rideaux)* to take down; *(papier peint, étiquette, tache)* to remove; **e. qch à qn** to take sth away from sb; **elle me l'a enlevé des mains** she took it from me; **e. à qn la garde d'un enfant** to remove a child from sb's care; **e. à qn le goût de qch** to take away sb's taste for sth **(b)** *(kidnapper)* to kidnap, to abduct **(c)** *(remporter) (prix)* to carry off; *(victoire, contrat)* to win

2 s'enlever *vpr (couvercle, peinture)* to come off; *(tache)* to come out

enlisement [ɑ̃lizmɑ̃] *nm* sinking

enliser [ɑ̃lize] **1** *vt* **e. une voiture** to get a car stuck

2 s'enliser *vpr (personne, voiture)* to get stuck; *Fig* **s'e. dans ses explications** to get bogged down in explanations

enluminure [ɑ̃lyminyr] *nf* illumination

enneigé, -e [ɑ̃neʒe] *adj (montagne, champ, route)* snow-covered; *(village)* snowbound

enneigement [ɑ̃neʒmɑ̃] *nm* snow cover

ennemi, -e [ɛnmi] **1** *nm,f* enemy; **se faire un e. de qn** to make an enemy of sb; **passer à l'e.** to defect; *Prov* **le mieux est l'e. du bien** it's better to leave well alone; **e. public numéro un** public enemy number one

2 *adj* **en pays e.** in enemy country

ennui [ɑ̃nɥi] *nm* **(a)** *(souci)* worry; *(problème)* problem; **avoir des ennuis** *(soucis)* to be worried; *(problèmes)* to have problems; **avoir des ennuis de santé** to have health problems; **avoir des ennuis avec la police** to be in trouble with the police; **attirer des ennuis à qn** to get sb into trouble; **faire des ennuis à qn** to bother sb **(b)** *(lassitude)* boredom; **il est d'un e.!** his conversation is so boring!

ennuyé, -e [ɑ̃nɥije] *adj* **(a)** *(contrarié)* annoyed **(de** about) **(b)** *(las)* bored

ennuyer [32] [ɑ̃nɥije] **1** *vt* **(a)** *(contrarier)* to bother; **cela vous ennuierait-il d'attendre?** would you mind waiting? **(b)** *(agacer)* to annoy, to irritate **(c)** *(lasser)* to bore **(avec** with)

2 s'ennuyer *vpr* to be bored; **qu'est-ce qu'on s'ennuie ici!** it's so boring here!; **s'e. à cent sous de l'heure** to be bored to death

ennuyeux, -euse [ɑ̃nɥijø, -øz] *adj* **(a)** *(contrariant)* annoying, irritating; **comme c'est e.!** it's so annoying! **(b)** *(lassant)*

énoncé [enɔ̃se] *nm* **(a)** *(des faits)* statement; *(d'une sentence)* pronouncement **(b)** *(d'une question)* wording

énoncer [16] [enɔ̃se] *vt (opinion, conditions)* to state

énonciation [enɔ̃sjasjɔ̃] *nf (de faits)* statement

enorgueillir [ɑ̃nɔrɡœjir] **1** *vt* to make proud

2 s'enorgueillir *vpr* **s'e. de qch/de faire qch** to pride oneself on sth/on doing sth

énorme [enɔrm] *adj* enormous, huge

énormément [enɔrmemɑ̃] *adv (lire, travailler, pleurer)* an awful lot; **je le regrette é.** I'm extremely sorry; **s'amuser é.** to have a great time; **il n'a pas é. d'argent** he hasn't got a huge amount of money

énormité [enɔrmite] *nf* **(a)** *(d'une demande, d'un crime)* enormity, outrageousness **(b)** *(d'une personne, d'une somme)* huge size **(c)** *(erreur)* glaring mistake; *(propos choquants)* outrageous statement

enquérir [7] [ɑ̃kerir] **s'enquérir** *vpr* to inquire **(de** about)

enquête [ɑ̃kɛt] *nf* **(a)** *(recherches)* inquiry; *(de journalistes, de policiers)* investigation **(sur** into); *Fam* **faire sa petite e.** to do a bit of investigating **(b)** *(sondage)* survey

enquêter [ɑ̃kete] *vi* **(a)** *(faire des recherches)* to hold an inquiry; *(police, journaliste)* to investigate; **e. sur qch** to investigate sth **(b)** *(faire un sondage)* to conduct a survey **(sur/auprès de** into/among)

enquêteur, -trice [ɑ̃kɛtœr, -tris] *nm,f* **(a)** *(policier)* investigator **(b)** *(sondeur)* researcher

enquiers, enquiert *voir* **enquérir**

enquiquinant, -e [ɑ̃kikinɑ̃, -ɑ̃t] *adj Fam (agaçant)* irritating, annoying

enquiquiner [ɑ̃kikine] *vt Fam (agacer)* to irritate, to annoy

enquiquineur, -euse [ɑ̃kikinœr, -øz] *nm,f Fam* nuisance, pain

enquis, -e *voir* **enquérir**

enraciné, -e [ɑ̃rasine] *adj (habitude, haine)* deep-rooted, deep-seated

enraciner [ārasine] **s'enraciner** *vpr aussi Fig* to take root

enragé, -e [āraʒe] **1** *adj (animal)* rabid **2** *nm,f Fam* fanatic

enrager [45] [āraʒe] *vi* to be furious; **e. de devoir faire qch** to be really angry at having to do sth; **faire e. qn** *(taquiner)* to tease sb

enrayer [āreje] [53] **1** *vt (machine)* to jam; *Fig (épidémie)* to check; *(inflation)* to curb **2 s'enrayer** *vpr (machine)* to jam

enrégimenter [āreʒimāte] *vt Péj (dans une organisation)* to enrol

enregistrement [ārəʒistrəmā] *nm* **(a)** *(d'une naissance, d'un acte)* registration; *(de bagages)* check-in **(b)** *(disque)* recording; **e. vidéo** video recording; **e. sur bande/ cassette** tape/cassette recording **(c)** *Ordinat (de données)* logging, recording; **e. de transactions** transaction logging

enregistrer [ārəʒistre] **1** *vt* **(a)** *(naissance, acte)* to register; *(bagages)* to check in; **les meilleures ventes jamais enregistrées** the best sales ever recorded **(b)** *(disque, émission)* to record, to tape; *(données)* to store; *Ordinat* **programme enregistré** stored programme **(c)** *Fam (mémoriser)* to note, to register **2 s'enregistrer** *vpr (personne)* to record oneself

enregistreur, -euse [ārəʒistrœr, -øz] *adj (appareil)* recording

enrhumé, -e [āryme] *adj* **être e.** to have a cold

enrhumer [āryme] **s'enrhumer** *vpr* to catch a cold

enrichi, -e [āriʃi] *adj* **(a)** *(personne)* wealthy **(b)** *(céréales)* enriched *(en blé)*

enrichir [āriʃir] **1** *vt (personne, pays)* to make richer; *Fig (collection)* to enhance *(de with)* **2 s'enrichir** *vpr* **(a)** *(personne, pays)* to get richer; *Fig (collection)* to be enhanced **(de** by) **(b)** **s'e. l'esprit** to improve one's mind

enrichissant, -e [āriʃisā, -āt] *adj (expérience)* rewarding

enrichissement [āriʃismā] *nm (en argent)* acquiring of wealth

enrober [ārɔbe] *vt* **(a)** *(bonbon)* to coat **(de** with) **(b)** *Hum* **il est un peu enrobé** he's a bit chubby

enrôlement [ārolmā] *nm* enrolment; *(d'un soldat)* enlistment

enrôler [ārole] **1** *vt* to enrol, to recruit; *(soldat)* to enlist **2 s'enrôler** *vpr* to enrol; *(soldat)* to enlist

enroué, -e [ārwe] *adj* hoarse, husky; **avoir la voix enrouée** to have a husky voice

enrouer [ārwe] **1** *vt (voix, personne)* to make hoarse **2 s'enrouer** *vpr* to get hoarse

enrouler [ārule] **1** *vt* **(a)** *(rouler) (carte, tapis)* to roll up; *(câble, ruban)* to wind **(b)** *(envelopper)* to wrap up **(dans** in) **2 s'enrouler** *vpr* **(a)** *(serpent)* to coil up; *(fil)* to wind **(b)** **s'e. dans une couverture** to wrap oneself up in a blanket

ENS [əenes] *nf (abrév* **École normale supérieure)** = university-level college preparing students for senior posts in teaching

ensablement [āsabləmā] *nm* **(a)** *(d'un port)* silting up **(b)** *(dépôt) (dû à l'eau)* sandbank; *(dû au vent)* sand dune

ensabler [āsable] **1** *vt (port)* to silt up **2 s'ensabler** *vpr* **(a)** *(véhicule)* to get stuck in the sand **(b)** *(port)* to silt up

ensanglanter [āsāglāte] *vt* to cover with blood; **des mains ensanglantées** bloodstained *or* bloody hands; **un festival ensanglanté par un attentat** a festival marred by an attempted murder

enseignant, -e [āsɛɲā, -āt] **1** *nm,f* teacher **2** *adj* **le corps e.** the teaching profession

enseigne [āsɛɲ] **1** *nf* **(a)** *(panonceau)* sign; **e. lumineuse** illuminated sign; *Fig* **nous sommes tous logés à la même e.** we're all in the same boat **(b)** *Litt* **à telle e. que... so** much so that... **2** *nm* **e. (de vaisseau)** *Br* sub-lieutenant, *Am* ensign

enseignement [āsɛɲmā] *nm* **(a)** *(profession)* teaching; **être dans l'e.** to be a teacher **(b)** *(formation)* education; *Fig* **tirer un e. de qch** to learn a lesson from sth; **e. assisté par ordinateur** computer-aided learning; **e. par correspondance** distance learning; **e. primaire/ secondaire** primary/secondary education; **e. professionnel/technique** vocational/technical education; **e. supérieur** higher education

enseigner [āsɛɲe] **1** *vt* to teach; **e. qch à qn** to teach sb sth **2** *vi* to be a teacher, to teach

ensemble [āsābl] **1** *adv* together, **aller bien e.** *(personnes)* to be well matched; *(couleurs)* to go together; **ils sont partis tous e.** they left en masse; *Hum* **ne répondez pas tous e.** don't all answer at once **2** *nm* **(a)** *(totalité)* **l'e. des personnes présentes** all the people present; **l'e. de sa fortune** his whole fortune; **dans l'e.** on the whole **(b)** *(unité)* unity; **avec un parfait e.** *(répondre)* as one; *(danser)* in unison **(c)** *(groupe) (de gens)* group; *(d'objets, de faits)* set; *(de services)* package **(d)** *(tenue)* outfit; **e. pantalon** *Br* trouser suit, *Am* pant suit **(e)** *(immeubles)* block; **grand e.** residential estate **(f)** *Math* set

ensemblier [āsāblije] *nm* interior designer; *(pour la télévision)* set designer

ensemencer [16] [āsəmāse] *vt (a) (champ)* to sow **(b)** *Biol* to culture

ensevelir [āsəvlir] *vt Litt* to bury

ensoleillé, -e [āsɔleje] *adj* sunny

ensoleillement [āsɔlɛjmā] *nm* **en raison de l'e. d'une pièce** because the room gets a lot of sun; **cinq heures d'e. par jour** five hours of sunshine a day; **jouir d'un e. exceptionnel** to get a lot of sun

ensommeillé, -e [āsɔmeje] *adj* sleepy

ensorceler [42] [āsɔrsəle] *vt* to cast *or* put a spell on; *Fig* to bewitch, to captivate

ensorcellement [āsɔrsɛlmā] *nm (action)* bewitching; *(état)* bewitchment; *Fig (charme)* charm

ensuite [āsɥit] *adv (plus tard)* later; *(puis)* then, next; **et e., qu'est-ce qu'on fait?** what do you do next?; *Fam* **d'abord, c'est très cher, et e. ça ne te va pas du tout** for one thing it's very expensive, and for another it doesn't suit you at all

ensuivre [65] [āsɥivr] **s'ensuivre** *vpr* **jusqu'à ce que mort s'ensuive** until dead; **il s'ensuit que...** it follows that...; **et tout ce qui s'ensuit** and all that goes with it

entacher [ātaʃe] *vt (réputation)* to sully

entaille [ātaj] *nf* **(a)** *(dans du bois)* notch; *(longue)* groove **(b)** *(blessure)* gash; **se faire e. au doigt** to cut one's finger open

entailler [ātaje] *vt (blesser)* to gash

entame [ātam] *nf* **(a)** *(de pain, de jambon)* first slice **(b)** *(aux cartes)* lead

entamer [ātame] *vt* **(a)** *(blesser)* to cut into; *Fig (conviction, détermination)* to undermine **(b)** *(commencer) (pain, jambon)* to start on; *(bouteille, pot de confiture)* to open; *(travail, recherches, conversation, négociations)* to start; *(démarches)* to initiate; *(poursuites)* to institute **(c)** *(aux cartes)* **e. à trèfle** to open clubs

entartrer [ātartre] **1** *vt (chaudière)* to fur (up) **2 s'entartrer** *vpr (chaudière)* to fur (up); *(dents)* to scale up

entassement [ātasmā] *nm* **(a)** *(de pierres) (action)* piling up; *(tas)* pile **(b)** *(de passagers, de bétail)* crowding together

entasser [ɑ̃tase] **1** *vt* (**a**) *(pierres, livres, vêtements)* to pile up (**b**) *(passagers, bétail)* to crowd together **2 s'entasser** *vpr* (**a**) *(objets)* to pile up (**b**) *(personnes)* to crowd together

entendement [ɑ̃tɑ̃dmɑ̃] *nm* **dépasser l'e.** to be beyond comprehension

entendeur [ɑ̃tɑ̃dœr] *nm* **à bon e., salut!** mark my words!

entendre [ɑ̃tɑ̃dr] **1** *vt* (**a**) *(ouïr)* to hear; **je n'entends rien (de ce que tu dis)** I can't hear a thing (you're saying); **je l'entends rire** I can hear him laughing; **e. dire que...** to hear that...; **e. qn dire qch** to hear sb say sth; **e. parler de** *(connaître l'existence de)* to hear of; *(être au courant de)* to hear about; **elle ne veut pas en e. parler!** she doesn't want to hear another word about it!; **il va m'e.!** I'll give him a talking-to!; **elle répétait à qui voulait l'e. que...** she'd tell anyone who'd listen that...; *Fam* **ce qu'il ne faut pas e.!** I've heard it all now!
(**b**) *(écouter)* *(témoin, suppliant)* to hear; **e. qn en confession** to hear sb's confession; **à vous e.,** il a eu tort from what you say, he was in the wrong; **il n'a rien voulu e.** he wouldn't listen; **que Dieu vous entende** may God answer your prayers
(**c**) *(comprendre)* to understand; **laisser e. qch** to imply sth; **elle m'a laissé e. que...** she gave me to understand that...; **ce n'est pas ainsi qu'il l'entend** he doesn't see it like that
(**d**) *(vouloir dire)* to mean; **qu'entendez-vous par là?** what do you mean by that?
(**e**) *(vouloir)* **e. faire qch** to intend *or* mean to do sth; **faites comme vous l'entendez** do as you think best; **il ne l'entendait pas ainsi** he wouldn't hear of it
2 *vi* to hear; **e. mal** to be hard of hearing; **j'ai mal entendu!** *(je n'ai pas entendu)* I didn't hear you properly!; *(je suis choqué)* I don't think I heard you right!; **tu entends?** *(menace)* got it?
3 s'entendre *vpr* (**a**) *(sympathiser)* to get on (**avec** with) (**b**) *(se mettre d'accord)* to agree; **entendons-nous bien!** let's be clear about this!
(**c**) *(être entendu)* to be heard; **on ne s'entend plus ici** you can't hear yourself think in here
(**d**) *(être compris)* to be understood
(**e**) **s'e. aux affaires** to have a good head for business; **il s'y entend** he knows what he's talking about

entendu, -e [ɑ̃tɑ̃dy] *adj* (**a**) *(complice)* *(sourire)* knowing; **d'un air e.** knowingly (**b**) *(décidé)* (**c'est**) **e.!** fine!, all right! (**c**) **bien e.** of course

entente [ɑ̃tɑ̃t] *nf* (**a**) *(accord)* agreement, understanding (**entre** between) (**b**) *(harmonie)* **bonne e.** harmony

entériner [ɑ̃terine] *vt* to ratify

entérite [ɑ̃terit] *nf Méd* enteritis

enterrement [ɑ̃tɛrmɑ̃] *nm* (**a**) *(mise en terre)* burial (**b**) *(cérémonie)* funeral; *Fam* **faire une tête d'e.** to look miserable (**c**) *(cortège)* funeral procession

enterrer [ɑ̃tere] **1** *vt* (**a**) *(trésor, corps)* to bury; *Hum* **il nous enterrera tous** he'll outlive us all (**b**) *Fig (projet)* to scrap; *(affaire)* to bury; **e. sa vie de garçon** to have a *Br* stag *or Am* bachelor party
2 s'enterrer *vpr Fig* to hide oneself away

entêtant, -e [ɑ̃tetɑ̃, -ɑ̃t] *adj (parfum, musique)* heady

en-tête [pl **en-têtes**] [ɑ̃tɛt] *nm* heading; *Ordinat* header

entêté, -e [ɑ̃tete] **1** *adj* obstinate, stubborn
2 *nm,f* obstinate *or* stubborn person

entêtement [ɑ̃tɛtmɑ̃] *nm* obstinacy, stubbornness; **e. à faire qch** persistence in doing sth

entêter [ɑ̃tete] **s'entêter** *vpr* to persist; **s'e. à faire qch** to persist in doing sth

enthousiasmant, -e [ɑ̃tuzjasmɑ̃, -ɑ̃t] *adj* exciting

enthousiasme [ɑ̃tuzjasm] *nm* enthusiasm (**pour** for); **avec e.** enthusiastically; **sans e.** unenthusiastically

enthousiasmer [ɑ̃tuzjasme] **1** *vt (personne)* to fill with enthusiasm
2 s'enthousiasmer *vpr* to get enthusiastic (**pour** about)

enthousiaste [ɑ̃tuzjast] **1** *adj* enthusiastic
2 *nmf* enthusiast

enticher [ɑ̃tiʃe] **s'enticher** *vpr* **s'e. de qn/qch** to become infatuated with sb/sth

entier, -ère [ɑ̃tje, -ɛr] **1** *adj* (**a**) *(complet)* whole, entire; **la France entière** the whole of France; **il a mangé le gâteau tout e.** he ate the whole cake; **des heures entières** for hours on end; **le mystère reste e.** the mystery remains unsolved (**b**) *(responsabilité)* full; *(confiance)* complete; **jouir d'une entière liberté** to have absolute freedom; **donner entière satisfaction à qn** *(produit)* to give sb complete satisfaction (**c**) *(sans compromis)* *(personne)* uncompromising
2 *nm* (**a**) **elle a lu le livre en e.** she read the whole book; **le pays dans son e.** the whole country (**b**) *Math (nombre)* integer, whole number

entièrement [ɑ̃tjɛrmɑ̃] *adv* entirely; **je ne l'ai pas lu e.** I didn't read all of it

entité [ɑ̃tite] *nf* entity

entonner [ɑ̃tɔne] *vt* to start singing

entonnoir [ɑ̃tɔnwar] *nm* funnel

entorse [ɑ̃tɔrs] *nf* sprain, wrench; **se faire une e. au poignet** to sprain one's wrist; *Fig* **faire une e. au règlement** to bend the rules

entortiller [ɑ̃tɔrtije] **1** *vt (envelopper)* to wrap (**dans** in); *(enrouler)* to wind (**autour de** round)
2 s'entortiller *vpr* (**a**) *(serpent, lierre)* to coil (**autour de** round) (**b**) *(s'empêtrer)* to get tangled up (**dans** in) (**c**) *(s'enrouler)* to wrap oneself up (**dans** in)

entour [ɑ̃tur] *nm* **à l'e. de** round

entourage [ɑ̃turaʒ] *nm (amis)* circle (of friends); *(de ministre, de souverain)* entourage; **dans son e. proche** amongst those close to him

entourer [ɑ̃ture] **1** *vt* (**a**) *(border, enceindre)* to surround (**de** with) (**b**) *(être autour de)* to surround; **les gens qui vous entourent** the people around *or* about you; **le monde qui nous entoure** the world about us; **entouré de mystère** shrouded in mystery; **un rang de perles entourait son cou** she had a string of pearls round her neck (**c**) *(soutenir)* *(personne)* to rally round; **elle est très entourée** she has a lot of people she can turn to for support
2 s'entourer *vpr* **s'e. d'amis/de belles choses** to surround oneself with friends/with beautiful things

entourloupe [ɑ̃turlup], **entourloupette** [ɑ̃turlupɛt] *nf Fam* dirty trick; **faire une e. à qn** to play a dirty trick on sb

entournure [ɑ̃turnyr] *nf Fam* **être gêné aux entournures** *(mal à l'aise)* to feel awkward; *(financièrement)* to feel the pinch

entracte [ɑ̃trakt] *nm* intermission

entraide [ɑ̃trɛd] *nf* mutual aid

entraider [ɑ̃trede] **s'entraider** *vpr* to help one another

entrailles [ɑ̃traj] *nfpl* entrails

entrain [ɑ̃trɛ̃] *nm* get-up-and-go; **être plein d'e.** to be full of life; **travailler avec e.** to beaver away; **faire qch sans e.** to do sth half-heartedly

entraînant, -e [ɑ̃trɛnɑ̃, -ɑ̃t] *adj (air, rythme)* lively

entraînement [ɑ̃trɛnmɑ̃] *nm* (**a**) *(en sport)* training; **un e.** a training session; **à l'e.** in training; **avoir de l'e.** to be well trained; **manquer d'e.** to be out of practice (**b**) *Tech* drive

entraîner [ãtrene] **1** *vt* (**a**) *(sujet: rivière)* to carry away; *(sujet: locomotive)* to pull; **e. qn quelque part** to take sb off somewhere; **il l'a entraîné dans sa chute** he dragged him down with him (**b**) *(exercer une influence sur)* to influence; **e. qn à faire qch** to lead sb to do sth; **e. qn dans un piège** to lure sb into a trap; **se laisser e.** to allow oneself to be led astray (**c**) *(causer)* *(dépense, modification)* to entail, to lead to; **e. un retard** to result in a delay (**d**) *(athlète, équipe)* to coach, to train; *(cheval)* to train; **e. qn à faire qch** to train sb to do sth (**e**) *Tech* to drive **2 s'entraîner** *vpr (athlète)* to train; **s'e. à faire qch** to practise doing sth

entraîneur [ãtrenœr] *nm (d'un athlète, d'une équipe)* coach; *(d'un cheval)* trainer

entraîneuse [ãtrɛnøz] *nf* (**a**) *(de boîte de nuit)* hostess (**b**) *(d'un athlète, d'une équipe)* coach; *(d'un cheval)* trainer

entrapercevoir [60] [ãtrapɛrsəvwar] *vt* to catch a fleeting glimpse of

entrave [ãtrav] *nf (obstacle)* hindrance, impediment (**à** to)

entraver [ãtrave] *vt* (**a**) *(mouvement, processus)* to hinder, to impede (**b**) *Fam* **j'y entrave que dalle** it beats me

entre [ãtr] *prép* (**a**) *(au milieu de)* between; *Fig* **e. les deux** *(ni l'un ni l'autre)* in between; **être e. la vie et la mort** to hover between life and death; **être e. deux âges** to be middle aged; *Fig* **faire qch e. deux portes** to do sth in passing (**b**) *(parmi)* among(st); **hésiter e. plusieurs solutions** to hesitate between several solutions; **plusieurs d'e. nous** several of us; **être dangereux e. tous** to be extremely dangerous; **e. autres** among others (**c**) *(rapport réciproque)* *(deux personnes)* between; *(plus de deux personnes)* among(st); **se marier e. cousins** to intermarry with cousins; **ils se battent e. eux** they fight with each other; **qu'y a-t-il e. eux exactement?** what exactly is going on between them?; **soit dit e. nous** between you and me; *Fam* **il faut que je te parle e. quat'z'yeux** I've got to talk to you in private (**d**) *(dans)* **tenir qch e. ses mains** to hold sth in one's hands; **ces murs** within these walls (**e**) *(à travers)* through; **se faufiler e. les arbres** to thread one's way through the trees

entrebâillement [ãtrəbajmã] *nm* **par l'e. de la porte** through the half-open door

entrebâiller [ãtrəbaje] *vt (porte, fenêtre)* to half-open; **la porte était entrebâillée** the door was ajar

entrechat [ãtrəʃa] *nm (pas de danse)* entrechat

entrechoquer [ãtrəʃɔke] **1** *vt* to knock together; **e. des verres** to chink glasses **2 s'entrechoquer** *vpr* to knock against one another; *(verres)* to chink

entrecôte [ãtrəkot] *nf* rib steak

entrecouper [ãtrəkupe] *vt* to interrupt (**de** with)

entrecroiser [ãtrəkrwaze] **1** *vt (ligne)* to intersect; *(fils)* to interlace **2 s'entrecroiser** *vpr (lignes, routes)* to intersect; *(fils)* to interlace

entre-déchirer [ãtrədeʃire] **s'entre-déchirer** *vpr* to tear each other to pieces

entre-deux-guerres [ãtrədøgɛr] *nm inv* **l'e.** the interwar period

entre-dévorer [ãtrədevɔre] **s'entre-dévorer** *vpr* to devour one another or each other

entrée [ãtre] *nf* (**a**) *(action)* entry, entrance; *(de marchandises)* import; **faire son e.** to make one's entrance; **l'e. de la Norvège dans d'UE** Norway's entry into the EU; **avant mon e. à l'université** before I went to university; **e. en scène** entrance (on to the stage); **e. en fonction** assumption of one's duties; **e. en matière** introduction; **e. en vigueur** coming into force; *Fig* **à l'e. de l'hiver** at the beginning of winter; *Fig* **d'e. (de jeu)** from the outset (**b**) *(accès)* admission, admittance **(dans** *ou* **de** to); **avoir ses entrées dans un lieu** to have contacts in a place; **e. à l'hôpital** admission into hospital; **e. interdite** *(sur panneau)* no admittance, no entry; **e. libre** *(dans un musée)* admission free; *(dans une boutique)* browsers welcome (**c**) *(voie d'accès)* way in, entrance (**de** to); *(vestibule)* entrance hall; **e. des artistes** stage door; **e. principale** main entrance; **e. de service** service entrance (**d**) *(hors-d'œuvre)* starter (**e**) **faire 1000 entrées** *(film)* to sell 1,000 tickets (**f**) *Ordinat (processus)* input, entry; *(information)* entry; *(touche)* enter (key); **données d'e.** input (data); **e. (par le) clavier** keyboard input; **e. de gamme** entry level; **e. de papier** paper input; **e./sortie** input/output; **e./sortie parallèles** parallel input/output

entrefaites [ãtrəfɛt] *nfpl* **sur ces e.** at that moment

entrefilet [ãtrəfile] *nm* short (news) item

entrejambe [ãtrəʒãb] *nm* crotch

entrelacer [16] [ãtrəlase] **1** *vt (rubans, branches)* to intertwine; *Ordinat* **écran entrelacé** interlaced screen **2 s'entrelacer** *vpr* to intertwine

entrelacs [ãtrəla] *nm* interlaced design, tracery

entrelarder [ãtrəlarde] *vt Culin (viande)* to lard; *Fig* **e. un discours de citations** to lace a speech with quotations

entremêler [ãtrəmele] **1** *vt* to interweave (**de** with) **2 s'entremêler** *vpr* to be interwoven

entremets [ãtrəmɛ] *nm* dessert, *Br* sweet

entremetteur, -euse [ãtrəmɛtœr, -øz] *nm,f* go-between

entremise [ãtrəmiz] *nf* intervention; **par l'e. de qn** through sb

entrepont [ãtrəpɔ̃] *nm* 'tweendecks; *(pour voyageurs)* steerage

entreposer [ãtrəpoze] *vt* to store; *(marchandises)* to warehouse

entrepôt [ãtrəpo] *nm* warehouse

entreprenant, -e [ãtrəprənã, -ãt] *adj* enterprising; *(auprès des femmes)* forward

entreprendre [58] [ãtrəprãdr] *vt* (**a**) *(commencer)* to undertake; **e. des démarches** to take steps; **e. de faire qch** to undertake to do sth (**b**) *(entretenir)* **e. qn sur qch** to engage sb in conversation about sth

entrepreneur, -euse [ãtrəprənœr, -øz] *nm,f* (**a**) *(dans le bâtiment)* contractor (**b**) *(patron)* entrepreneur (**c**) **e. de pompes funèbres** *Br* undertaker, *Am* mortician

entrepris, -e *voir* **entreprendre**

entreprise [ãtrəpriz] *nf* (**a**) *(action, initiative)* enterprise, undertaking; **e. libre** free enterprise (**b**) *(firme)* company, firm; **e. privée** private company; **e. publique** public corporation

entrer [ãtre] **1** *vi (aux être)* (**a**) *(aller)* to go in, to enter; *(venir)* to come in, to enter; **e. dans qch** to go/come into sth, to enter sth; **e. dans une voiture/un ascenseur** to get into a car/lift; **e. par la fenêtre** to get in *or* enter through the window; **e. en courant** to run in; **e. sans payer** to get in without paying; **e. en gare** to come into the station; **e. au port** to come into harbour; **laisser e. qn/qch** to let sb/sth in; **empêcher qn d'e.** to keep sb out; **faire e. qch** to show sb in; *(sujet: secrétaire, majordome)* to show sb in; **faire e. qch dans une pièce** to get sth into a room; *Th* **Hamlet entre en scène** enter Hamlet; **entrez!** come/go in! (**b**) *(pénétrer)* *(eau, air)* to go/come in; **le clou entra dans le mur** the nail went into the wall; **la clef n'entre pas dans la serrure** the key won't go in the lock (**c**) *(heurter)* **e. dans qch** to go into sth, to run into sth; *Fam* **e. dans le décor** to go off the road

(d) *(faire tenir)* **faire e. qch dans qch** to insert sth in sth; **on n'y entrera jamais à vingt** we'll never get twenty people in; **il n'entre pas dans le carton** it won't go in the box

(e) *(devenir membre)* **e. dans l'armée** to join the army; **e. en religion** to take (holy) orders; **e. chez Renault** to start working for Renault; **e. au service de qn** to enter sb's service; **e. dans l'UE** to join the EU

(f) *(être admis)* **e. à l'université** to go to university; **e. à l'hôpital** to go into hospital; **e. en maternelle** to start nursery school

(g) *(faire partie de)* **e. dans une catégorie** to fall into a category; **e. dans la légende** to become a legend; **e. dans l'histoire** to go down in history; **e. en ligne de compte** to be taken into account; **e. dans les projets de qn** to be part of sb's plans; **e. dans la vie de qn** to come into sb's life; **e. dans la composition de qch** to go into the making of sth; **cela n'entre pas dans mes idées** I don't go along with that

(h) *(commencer)* **e. dans une colère terrible** to get extremely angry; **e. en campagne** *Mil* to take the field; *Pol* to go on the campaign trail; **e. en guerre** to enter the war; **e. en fonction** to take up one's duties; **e. en vigueur** to come into force *or* effect; **e. dans la vie active** to start one's working life; **e. dans une ère nouvelle** to enter a new era; **e. dans les détails** to go into detail; **on entre dans l'hiver** winter is just beginning

(i) *Fam (se concentrer)* **e. dans un match** to get into a match

(j) *Ordinat* to log in *or* on

2 *vt (aux avoir)* **(a)** *(introduire)* **e. des marchandises en fraude** to smuggle in goods

(b) *(enfoncer)* **e. ses ongles dans le cou de qn** to sink one's nails into sb's neck

(c) *Ordinat (données)* to enter, to input; *(au clavier)* to key in

3 *v impersonnel* **il n'entre pas dans mes projets de le faire** it's not part of my plans to do it

entresol [ɑ̃trəsɔl] *nm* mezzanine (floor)

entre-temps [ɑ̃trətɑ̃] *adv* meanwhile, in the meantime

entretenir [70] [ɑ̃trətənir] **1** *vt* **(a)** *(soigner) (maison, jardin, routes, machine)* to maintain; **une moquette facile à e.** a carpet which is easy to look after; **e. sa forme** to keep fit **(b)** *(payer pour) (famille, maîtresse)* to maintain, to support **(c)** *(maintenir)* **e. une correspondance avec qn** to keep up a correspondence with sb; **e. de bonnes relations avec qn** to remain on good terms with sb **(d)** *(parler à)* **e. qn de qch** to converse with sb about sth

2 *s'entretenir* *vpr* **s'e. avec qn (de qch)** to converse with sb (about sth)

entretenu, -e [ɑ̃trətny] *adj* **(a)** **bien/mal e.** *(maison, jardin)* well-kept/badly kept **(b)** **une femme entretenue** a kept woman

entretien [ɑ̃trətjɛ̃] *nm* **(a)** *(soins) (d'une maison, d'un jardin, des routes, d'une machine)* maintenance; **facile/difficile d'e., d'e. facile/difficile** easy/difficult to maintain; **produits d'e.** (household) cleaning materials **(b)** *(subsistance) (d'une famille, d'une armée)* support, maintenance **(c)** *(conversation)* conversation; *(audience)* interview; **entretiens** *(négociations)* discussions, talks

entre-tuer [ɑ̃trətɥe] **s'entre-tuer** *vpr* to kill each other

entreverrai *etc voir* **entrevoir**

entrevoir [73a] [ɑ̃trəvwar] *vt (rapidement)* to catch sight of, to catch a glimpse of; *(indistinctement)* to make out; **e. des difficultés** to foresee difficulties

entrevoyons *etc voir* **entrevoir**

entrevu, -e *voir* **entrevoir**

entrevue [ɑ̃trəvy] *nf (rendez-vous)* interview; *(réunion)* meeting

entrouvert, -e [ɑ̃truvɛr, -ɛrt] *adj* half-open

entrouvrir [52] [ɑ̃truvrir] **1** *vt* to half-open **2** *s'entrouvrir* *vpr* to half-open

entuber [ɑ̃tybe] *vt Fam (duper)* to con; **se faire e.** to be conned

énumération [enymerɑsjɔ̃] *nf* listing

énumérer [34] [enymere] *vt* to list

envahir [ɑ̃vair] *vt (pays)* to invade; *(marché)* to flood; **un jardin envahi par les mauvaises herbes** a garden overgrown with weeds; *Fig* **un doute m'a envahi** I was overcome with doubt; *Fam* **e. qn** *(sujet: personne)* to intrude on sb

envahissant, -e [ɑ̃vaisɑ̃, -ɑ̃t] *adj (plantes)* invasive; *(odeur)* overwhelming; *Fam (personne)* intrusive

envahisseur [ɑ̃vaisœr] *nm* invader

enveloppant, -e [ɑ̃vlɔpɑ̃, -ɑ̃t] *adj* **(a)** *(couvrant)* **regard e.** look that takes/took everything in **(b)** *Fig (séduisant) (manières)* captivating

enveloppe [ɑ̃vlɔp] *nf* **(a)** *(de lettre)* envelope; **e. à fenêtre** window envelope; **envoyer qch sous e.** to send sth under cover; *Fig* **e. budgétaire** budget; *Fig* **l'e. de la recherche** the research budget **(b)** *(de paquet)* wrapping **(c)** *(de graines)* husk **(d)** *Fig (apparence)* **sous une e. de rudesse** beneath a rough exterior

enveloppé, -e [ɑ̃vlɔpe] *adj Fam* **bien e.** *(personne)* well-padded

envelopper [ɑ̃vlɔpe] **1** *vt* **(a)** *(marchandises, bébé)* to wrap (up); **enveloppé dans des bandages** swathed in bandages **(b)** *(entourer)* **e. qch du regard** to take sth in with one's gaze; **la nuit nous enveloppa** darkness closed in on us; **enveloppé de mystère/brume** shrouded in mystery/mist

2 *s'envelopper* *vpr* **s'e. dans une couverture** to wrap oneself up in a blanket

envenimer [ɑ̃vənime] **1** *vt (plaie)* to make septic; *Fig (querelle, discussion)* to embitter

2 *s'envenimer* *vpr (plaie)* to turn septic; *Fig (querelle, discussion)* to get acrimonious

envergure [ɑ̃vɛrgyr] *nf* **(a)** *(d'un oiseau, d'un avion)* wingspan **(b)** *Fig (ampleur)* scope; **de grande e., d'e.** *(réforme)* far-reaching; *(opération)* large-scale **(c)** *(de personne)* calibre; **manquer d'e.** to be of a low calibre

enverrai *etc voir* **envoyer**

envers¹ [ɑ̃vɛr] *nm (d'un document, d'une assiette)* back; *(d'une médaille, d'une pièce)* reverse; **à l'e.** *(l'extérieur à l'intérieur)* inside out; *(de haut en bas)* the wrong way up; *(devant derrière)* the wrong way round, back to front; *Fig* **l'e. du décor** the other side of the picture; *Fam* **c'est le monde à l'e.!** what's the world coming to!

envers² *prép* towards; **e. et contre tous** in the face of all opposition

envi [ɑ̃vi] **à l'envi** *adv* **faire qch à l'e.** to vie with one another in doing sth

enviable [ɑ̃vjabl] *adj* enviable

envie [ɑ̃vi] *nf* **(a)** *(désir)* desire; *(caprice)* craving *(de* for); **avoir (très) e. de qch/de faire qch** to (really) want sth/to do sth; **avoir e. de dormir** to feel sleepy; **être pris d'une terrible e. de rire** to have a terrible urge to laugh; **donner à qn l'e. de faire qch** to make sb want to do sth; **il a e. que je le fasse** he wants me to do it; **je vais lui ôter l'e. de s'amuser** I'll stop her messing around; **cette robe me fait e.** I'm tempted by this dress; **faire e. à qn** *(sujet: personne)* to tempt sb; *Fam* **ça lui a pris comme une e. de pisser** he just got a sudden urge **(b)** *(jalousie)* envy; **regarder qch avec e.** to look enviously at sth **(c)** *(au doigt)* hangnail; *(sur la peau)* birthmark

envier [66] [ãvje] *vt* to envy; **e. qch à qn** to envy sb sth; **n'avoir rien à e. à personne** to have no cause to be envious of anyone

envieux, -euse [ãvjø, -øz] **1** *adj* envious (**de** of) **2** *nm,f* envious person; **faire des e.** to make people envious

environ [ãvirɔ̃] **1** *adv (à peu près)* about, around **2 environs** *nmpl (alentours)* surrounding area; **aux** *ou* **dans les environs de Grenoble** in the vicinity of Grenoble; **aux environs de cinq heures** round about five o'clock

environnant, -e [ãvirɔnã, -ãt] *adj* surrounding

environnement [ãvirɔnmã] *nm* (**a**) *(milieu)* environment (**b**) *Ordinat* environment; **e. partagé** shared environment

environner [ãvirɔne] **1** *vt* to surround; **environné de qch** surrounded by sth **2 s'environner** *vpr* **s'e. de** to surround oneself with

envisageable [ãvizaʒabl] *adj* conceivable

envisager [45] [ãvizaʒe] *vt (considérer) (question, situation, solution)* to consider; *(projeter) (conséquence, événement)* to envisage; **e. l'avenir** to foresee the future; **e. de faire qch** to consider doing sth

envoi [ãvwa] *nm* (**a**) *(action)* sending; **e. recommandé** recorded delivery (**b**) *(colis)* parcel; *(lettre)* letter; *(marchandises)* consignment (**de** of)

envol [ãvɔl] *nm (d'avion)* take-off; *(d'oiseau)* taking off

envolée [ãvɔle] *nf* flight; **Fig e. lyrique** flight of fancy; **Fig l'e. du dollar** the soaring price of the dollar

envoler [ãvɔle] **s'envoler** *vpr* (**a**) *(oiseau)* to fly away; *(avion)* to take off; **Je m'envole dans une heure** my plane leaves in an hour; **Fig s'e. dans les sondages** to shoot up the opinion polls (**b**) *(emporté par le vent) (chapeau)* to blow off; *(papiers)* to blow away (**c**) **Fam** *(disparaître) (personne, sac)* to vanish

envoûtant, -e [ãvutã, -ãt] *adj (fascinant)* bewitching

envoûtement [ãvutmã] *nm aussi Fig* bewitchment

envoûter [ãvute] *vt aussi Fig* to bewitch

envoyé, -e [ãvwaje] *nm,f (messager)* messenger; *(d'un gouvernement)* envoy; **e. spécial** *(journaliste)* special correspondent

envoyer [33] [ãvwaje] **1** *vt* to send; *(lancer)* to throw; **e. qch par courrier** to mail sth, Br to post sth; **e. qch à qn** to send sb sth; *(lancer)* to throw sth to sb; **e. un baiser à qn** to blow sb a kiss; **e. chercher qn** to send for sb; **e. qn faire qch** to send sb to do sth; **Fam e. promener** *ou* **balader** *ou* **paître qn, e. qn sur les roses** to send sb packing; **Fam je vais tout e. promener** I'm going to chuck it all in; **Fig e. des fleurs à qn** to pat sb on the back **2 s'envoyer** *vpr* (**a**) *(l'un l'autre)* **ils s'envoient des cartes postales** they send postcards to each other (**b**) **Fam s'e. un verre de vin** to knock back a glass of wine; **très Fam s'e. qn** to screw sb; **très Fam s'e. en l'air** to have a screw

envoyeur, -euse [ãvwajœr, -øz] *nm,f* sender; **retour à l'e.** return to sender

enzyme [ãzim] *nf* enzyme; **lessive aux enzymes** biological washing powder

éolien, -enne [eɔljɛ̃, -ɛn] **1** *adj* **énergie éolienne** wind energy; **moteur é.** wind-powered engine **2** *nf* **éolienne** wind turbine

épagneul, -e [epaɲœl] *nm,f* spaniel; **é. breton** Brittany spaniel

épais, -aisse [epɛ, -ɛs] **1** *adj* thick; **é. de deux mètres** two metres thick; **Fam elle n'est pas bien épaisse** she hasn't got much on her

2 *adv* (**a**) *(pousser)* thick(ly) (**b**) **Fam** *(beaucoup)* **il n'y en a pas é.** there's not much of it **3** *nm* **au plus é.** de la forêt in the depths of the forest

épaisseur [epesœr] *nf* thickness; **Fig** *(d'une personne)* depth; **avoir deux mètres d'é.** to be two metres thick

épaissir [epesir] **1** *vt (sauce, peinture)* to thicken; *(ombre, mystère)* to deepen **2** *vi (sauce)* to thicken; *(personne)* to fill out **3 s'épaissir** *vpr (cheveux, brouillard, sauce)* to thicken; *(personne)* to fill out; *(ombre, mystère)* to deepen

épaississant [epesisã] *nm (substance)* thickener

épaississement [epesismã] *nm (du brouillard, d'une sauce)* thickening

épanchement [epɑ̃fmã] *nm* (**a**) *Méd* **é. de synovie** water on the knee (**b**) *Fig (de sentiments)* outpouring

épancher [epɑ̃fe] **1** *vt* **é. sa bile** to vent one's spleen; **é. son cœur** to pour out one's heart **2 s'épancher** *vpr (personne)* to pour out one's heart

épandre [epɑ̃dr] **s'épandre** *vpr Litt* to spread (**sur** over)

épanoui, -e [epanwi] *adj (fleur)* in full bloom; *(visage, sourire)* beaming; *(personne)* well-adjusted

épanouir [epanwir] **1** *vt (fleur, pétales)* to open out **2 s'épanouir** *vpr (a) (fleur)* to bloom (**b**) *(visage)* to light up (**c**) *(personne)* to blossom

épanouissant, -e [epanwisã, -ãt] *adj (travail, vie)* fulfilling

épanouissement [epanwismã] *nm* (**a**) *(action) (d'une fleur)* blooming; *(d'un visage)* lighting up; *(d'une personne)* blossoming (**b**) *(plénitude)* full bloom

épargnant, -e [eparɲã, -ãt] *nm,f* saver

épargne [eparɲ] *nf* (**a**) *(action, vertu)* saving (**b**) *(sommes)* savings (**c**) *(épargnants)* **l'é. privée** private investors

épargner [eparɲe] **1** *vt* (**a**) *(argent, provisions)* to save (**b**) *(énergie, temps)* to save; **é. à qn la peine de faire qch** to save sb the trouble of doing sth; **épargne-moi les détails!** (**c**) *(prisonnier)* to spare **2** *vi (sauce)* to save (**sur** on) **3 s'épargner** *vpr* **s'é. la peine de faire qch** to save oneself the trouble of doing sth

éparpiller [eparpije] **1** *vt (objets, foule)* to scatter **2 s'éparpiller** *vpr (objets, foule)* to scatter; *Fig (personne)* to take on too much

épars, -e [epar, -ars] *adj (maisons)* scattered; *(végétation, population, informations)* sparse; *(cheveux)* thin

épatant, -e [epatã, -ãt] *adj Fam* splendid

épaté, -e [epate] *adj Fam* dumbfounded

épater [epate] *vt Fam* to astound

épaule [epol] *nf* shoulder; **être large d'épaules** to be broad-shouldered; *Culin* **é. d'agneau** shoulder of lamb

épauler [epole] **1** *vt (fusil)* to raise to one's shoulder (**b**) *(aider)* **é. qn** to back sb up **2** *vi* to take aim

épaulette [epolɛt] *nf* (**a**) *(rembourrage)* shoulder pad (**b**) *(bretelle)* shoulder strap

épave [epav] *nf aussi Fig* wreck

épée [epe] *nf* sword; *Sp* épée; **coup d'é.** swordthrust; *Fig* **un coup d'é. dans l'eau** a wasted effort; *Fig* **une é. de Damoclès** a Sword of Damocles

épeler [42] [eple] *vt & vi* to spell

éperdu, -e [eperdy] *adj (regard)* distraught; *(amour)* passionate

éperdument [eperdymã] *adv (aimer)* madly; **é. amoureux** head over heels in love, madly in love; *Fam* **je m'en fiche é.** I couldn't care less

éperlan [eperlã] *nm* smelt

éperon [eprɔ̃] *nm* spur

éperonner [eprɔne] *vt* to spur on

épervier [epɛrvje] *nm* sparrowhawk

éphèbe [efɛb] *nm* Adonis

éphémère [efemɛr] **1** *adj* short-lived, ephemeral **2** *nm* mayfly

épi [epi] *nm* (**a**) *(de grain)* ear; *(de fleur)* spike; **é. de maïs** corncob (**b**) *(de cheveux)* tuft of hair

épice [epis] *nf* spice; **quatre épices** allspice

épicé, -e [epise] *adj* spicy

épicéa [episea] *nm* spruce

épicentre [episɑ̃tr] *nm* epicentre

épicer [epise] *vt* to spice

épicerie [episri] *nf* (**a**) *(magasin)* grocer's (shop); **é. fine** delicatessen (**b**) *(produits)* groceries (**c**) *Can Fig* **liste d'é.** *(de griefs)* shopping list

épicier, -ère [episje, -ɛr] *nm,f* grocer

épicurien, -enne [epikyrjɛ̃, -ɛn] **1** *adj* epicurean; *Phil* Epicurean **2** *nm,f* epicure; *Phil* Epicurean

épidémie [epidemi] *nf* epidemic

épidémique [epidemik] *adj* epidemic

épiderme [epidɛrm] *nm* skin, *Spéc* epidermis

épidermique [epidɛrmik] *adj* epidermal; *Fig* **une réaction é.** a kneejerk reaction

épier [epje] *vt (espionner) (personne, activités)* to spy on; *(observer) (signe, occasion)* to watch out for

épilation [epilasjɔ̃] *nf (des jambes)* removal of unwanted hair; *(des sourcils)* plucking

épilatoire [epilatwar] *adj (crème)* hair-removing

épilepsie [epilɛpsi] *nf* epilepsy; **crise d'é.** epileptic fit

épileptique [epilɛptik] *adj & nmf* epileptic

épiler [epile] **1** *vt (jambes)* to remove the unwanted hair from; *(sourcils)* to pluck **2 s'épiler** *vpr* **s'é. les jambes** to remove the unwanted hair from one's legs; **s'é. les sourcils** to pluck one's eyebrows; **s'é. les jambes à la cire** to wax one's legs

épilogue [epilɔg] *nm* epilogue

épiloguer [epilɔge] *vi* to hold forth (**sur** about)

épinard [epinar] *nm (plante)* spinach; **épinards** spinach; **épinards en branches** leaf spinach

épine [epin] *nf (piquant)* thorn; *(d'un animal)* spine, prickle; *Fig* **tirer une é. du pied à qn** *(tirer d'embarras)* to get sb out of a mess; *(soulager)* to relieve sb's mind; **é. dorsale** backbone

épinette [epinɛt] *nf* (**a**) *Can Bot* spruce (**b**) *(instrument)* spinet

épineux, -euse [epinø, -øz] *adj (arbuste, problème)* thorny; *(poisson)* spiny

épingle [epɛ̃gl] *nf (à) pin;* **attacher qch avec des épingles** *(cheveux)* to pin sth up; *(tissu, feuilles)* to pin sth together; *Fig* **tirer son é. du jeu** to extricate oneself; *Fig* **être tiré à quatre épingles** to be dressed up to the nines; *Fig* **chercher une é. dans une botte de foin** to look for a needle in a haystack; *Fig* **monter qch en é.** to make too much of sth; **é. à chapeau** hatpin; **é. à cheveux** hairpin; **virage en é. à cheveux** hairpin *Br* bend *or Am* turn; **é. à linge** clothes *Br* peg *or Am* pin; **é. de** *ou* **à nourrice, é. de sûreté** safety pin

épingler [epɛ̃gle] *vt* (**a**) *(attacher)* to pin (**à**/**sur** to/on) (**b**) *Fam (arrêter)* to nab; **se faire é.** to get nabbed

épinoche [epinɔʃ] *nf* stickleback

Épiphanie [epifani] *nf Rel* **l'É.** Epiphany

épique [epik] *adj* epic

épiscopal, -e, -aux, -ales [episkɔpal, -o] *adj* episcopal

épiscopat [episkɔpa] *nm (fonction, évêques)* episcopate

épisode [epizɔd] *nm aussi Fig* episode

épisodique [epizɔdik] *adj (intermittent)* occasional; *(accessoire)* minor

épisodiquement [epizɔdikmɑ̃] *adv* occasionally

épistémologie [epistemɔlɔʒi] *nf* epistemology

épistolaire [epistɔlɛr] *adj* epistolary; **être en relation é. avec qn** to correspond with sb

épitaphe [epitaf] *nf* epitaph

épithélium [epiteljɔm] *nm* epithelium

épithète [epitɛt] *nf* epithet; *Gram* attribute

épître [epitr] *nf* epistle

éploré, -e [eplɔre] *adj* tearful

épluchage [eplyʃaʒ] *nm* peeling; *Fig* detailed examination

épluche-légumes [eplyʃlegym] *nm inv* potato peeler

éplucher [eplyʃe] *vt (peler)* to peel; *Fig (texte, journal)* to go through in detail

épluchette [eplyʃɛt] *nf Can* **é. de blé d'Inde** corn-husking party

épluchure [eplyʃyr] *nf (pelure)* peeling

éponge [epɔ̃ʒ] **1** *nf* sponge; **donner un coup d'é. à qch** to wipe sth with a sponge; **d'un coup d'é.** with a sponge; *Fig* **jeter l'é.** *(à la boxe)* to throw in the towel; *Fig* **passer l'é.** to forget all about it **2** *adj inv* **tissu é.** (terry) towelling; **serviette é.** terry towel

éponger [45] [epɔ̃ʒe] **1** *vt* (**a**) *(liquide)* to mop up (**b**) *(surface)* to sponge (down); *(le front de quelqu'un)* to mop (**c**) *Fig (déficit)* to mop up **2 s'éponger** *vpr* **s'é. le front** to mop one's brow

épopée [epɔpe] *nf aussi Fig* epic

époque [epɔk] *nf* (**a**) *(historique)* era, age; *Géol* period; **la Belle É.** ≃ the Edwardian era; **quelle é. (nous vivons)!** what times we live in!; **être de son é.** to be in tune with the times; **meubles d'é.** period furniture (**b**) *(moment précis)* time; **à l'é.** at the time

épouiller [epuje] *vt* to delouse

époumoner [epumɔne] **s'époumoner** *vpr (en criant)* to shout oneself hoarse; *(en chantant)* to sing oneself hoarse

épouse [epuz] *nf* wife

épouser [epuze] *vt* to marry; *Fig (cause)* to espouse; *Fig* **é. la forme de qch** to take on the exact shape of sth

épousseter [42] [epuste] *vt* to dust

époustouflant, -e [epustuflɑ̃, -ɑ̃t] *adj Fam* astounding

époustoufler [epustufle] *vt Fam* to astound

épouvantable [epuvɑ̃tabl] *adj* dreadful, appalling

épouvantail [epuvɑ̃taj] *nm (de jardin)* scarecrow; *Péj (personne laide)* fright; *(personne terrifiante)* bogy

épouvante [epuvɑ̃t] *nf* terror

épouvanté, -e [epuvɑ̃te] *adj* terror-stricken

épouvanter [epuvɑ̃te] *vt* to terrify

époux [epu] *nm* husband; **les é.** the married couple; **les é. Bertier** Mr and Mrs Bertier

éprendre [58] [eprɑ̃dr] **s'éprendre** *vpr* **s'é. de qn** to fall in love with sb

épreuve [eprœv] *nf* (**a**) *(essai)* test; **mettre qn/qch à l'é.** to put sb/sth to the test; **à l'é. du feu** fireproof; **à l'é. des balles** bulletproof; **un courage à toute é.** unfailing courage; **être mis à rude é.** *(personne, patience)* to be severely tested; **les bateaux furent mis à rude é. par la tempête** the boats took a battering from the storm; *Fig* **é. de force** trial of strength (**b**) *(examen) (écrit)* (examination) paper; *(oral)* test **(c)** *(d'athlétisme)* event; **é. contre la montre** time trial; **é. éliminatoire** heat **(d)** *(adversité)* trial, ordeal; **dans l'é.** in adversity **(e)** *Typ* proof **(f)** *Phot* print

épris, -e [epri, -iz] *adj* **(a) é. de qn** in love with sb **(b) é. de qch** passionate about sth

éprouvant, -e [epruvã, -ãt] *adj* trying

éprouvé, -e [epruve] *adj* **(a)** *(testé) (remède)* proven, welltried; *(matériaux)* tested **(b)** *(famille)* sorely tried; *(région)* hard-hit

éprouver [epruve] *vt* **(a)** *(essayer) (méthode, personne, courage)* to test **(b)** *(ressentir) (sensation, sentiment, douleur)* to feel **(c)** *(subir) (perte)* to suffer; *(difficultés)* to meet with

éprouvette [epruvεt] **1** *nf* test tube **2** *adj* **bébé é.** test-tube baby

EPS [əpeεs] *nf (abrév* **éducation physique et sportive)** PE

épuisant, -e [epɥizã, -ãt] *adj* exhausting

épuisé, -e [epɥize] *adj* **(a)** *(très fatigué)* exhausted **(b)** *(sol)* exhausted **(c)** *(livre, édition)* out of print; *(marchandises)* sold out

épuisement [epɥizmã] *nm* **(a)** *(fatigue)* exhaustion; **danser jusqu'à l'é.** to dance till one drops **(b)** *(d'un sol, d'un stock, de ressources)* exhaustion; **jusqu'à. é. des stocks** while stocks last

épuiser [epɥize] **1** *vt* **(a)** *(fatiguer)* to exhaust **(b)** *(sol, stock, ressources, sujet)* to exhaust **2 s'épuiser** *vpr* **(a)** *(se fatiguer)* to exhaust oneself, to wear oneself out; **s'é. à faire qch** to wear oneself out doing sth **(b)** *(source)* to dry up; *(stock, ressources)* to run out

épuisette [epɥizεt] *nf* landing net

épuration [epyrasjõ] *nf (de l'eau, du gaz)* purification; *(du pétrole, d'un minerai)* refining; *Fig (d'une langue)* refining; *Pol* purge

épurer [epyre] *vt (eau, gaz)* to purify; *(pétrole, minerai)* to refine; *Fig (langue)* to refine; *Pol (parti)* to purge

équarrir [ekarir] *vt* **(a)** *(bois, pierre)* to square **(b)** *(animal)* to quarter

équarrissage [ekarisaʒ] *nm* **(a)** *(du bois, de la pierre)* squaring **(b)** *(d'animaux)* quartering

Équateur [ekwatœr] *nm* **l'É.** Ecuador

équateur [ekwatœr] *nm* equator; **sous l'é.** at the equator

équation [ekwasjõ] *nf* equation; **é. du premier/ deuxième degré** simple/quadratic equation

équatorial, -e, -aux, -ales [ekwatɔrjal, -o] *adj* equatorial

équatorien, -enne [ekwatɔrjɛ̃, -εn] **1** *adj* Ecuadorian **2** *nm,f* **É.** Ecuadorian

équerre [ekεr] *nf* **é. (à dessin)** set square; **en é., à l'é.** at right angles; **d'é.** square, straight

équestre [ekεstr] *adj (statue, sports)* equestrian; *(exercices)* horseriding

équidés [ekɥide, ekide] *nmpl* horse family; *Spéc* Equidae

équidistant, -e [ekɥidistã, -ãt] *adj* equidistant **(de** from)

équilatéral, -e, -aux, -ales [ekɥilateral, -o] *adj* equilateral

équilibrage [ekilibraʒ] *nm* balancing

équilibre [ekilibr] *nm* **(a)** *(d'un corps, d'un objet)* balance; **mettre qch en é.** to balance sth; **perdre l'é.** to lose one's balance; **faire perdre l'é. à qn** to throw sb off balance; **faire de l'é. sur qch** to balance on sth; **être en é.** to be precariously balanced **(b)** *(mental)* (mental) balance, equilibrium **(c) budget en é.** balanced budget; **é. budgétaire** balanced budget **(d)** *(d'un ensemble)* balance

équilibré, -e [ekilibre] *adj (chargement, alimentation)* balanced; *(personne)* well-balanced; *(vie)* stable

équilibrer [ekilibre] **1** *vt (charge, composition)* to balance; *(bateau, avion)* to trim; **é. un budget** to balance a budget **2 s'équilibrer** *vpr (l'un l'autre)* to balance each other out

équilibriste [ekilibrist] *nmf (funambule)* tightrope walker

équinoxe [ekinɔks] *nm* equinox

équipage [ekipaʒ] *nm* **(a)** *(d'un navire, d'un avion)* crew; **les hommes d'é.** the crew; **les membres de l'é.** the crew **(b)** *(voiture et chevaux)* equipage

équipe [ekip] *nf* **(a)** *Sp* team; **une é. de rugby** a rugby team **(b)** *(de chercheurs, de médecins)* team; *(d'ouvriers)* gang; *(à l'usine)* shift; *Mil* working party; **faire é. avec qn** to team up with sb; **é. dirigeante** management team; **é. de jour/ nuit** day/night shift; **é. de secours** rescue team

équipée [ekipe] *nf (frasque)* escapade; *(promenade, voyage)* jaunt

équipement [ekipmã] *nm* **(a)** *(action) (d'un atelier, d'une cuisine)* equipping, fitting out **(b)** *(matériel)* equipment; *(de soldat)* kit **(c)** *(installations)* facilities; **équipements collectifs** public facilities; *Ordinat* **é. informatique** computer equipment

équiper [ekipe] **1** *vt (atelier, cuisine)* to equip, to fit out **(de** with); *(sportif, armée)* to equip **(de** with); **avec cuisine équipée** *(appartement)* with cooking facilities **2 s'équiper** *vpr* to equip oneself **(de** with)

équipier, -ère [ekipje, -εr] *nm,f* team member

équitable [ekitabl] *adj* fair

équitablement [ekitabləmã] *adv* fairly

équitation [ekitasjõ] *nf* (horse)riding; **faire de l'é.** to go (horse)riding

équivalence [ekivalãs] *nf* equivalence; *Univ* **avoir/ obtenir une é.** to have/get an equivalent diploma

équivalent, -e [ekivalã, -ãt] **1** *adj* equivalent **(à** to) **2** *nm* equivalent; **sans é.** without equal

équivaloir [69] [ekivalwar] *vi* **é. à qch** *(valoir)* to be equivalent to sth, *(revenir à)* to amount to sth

équivaut *voir* **équivaloir**

équivoque [ekivɔk] **1** *adj* **(a)** *(ambigu) (terme, attitude)* equivocal, ambiguous **(b)** *(douteux) (conduite, passé)* dubious **2** *nf* ambiguity; **sans é.** *(réponse, situation)* unequivocal; *(répondre)* unequivocally

érable [erabl] *nm (arbre, bois)* maple; **sirop d'é.** maple syrup

érablière [erablijεr] *nf Can* maple grove

éradication [eradikasjõ] *nf* eradication

éradiquer [eradike] *vt* to eradicate

érafler [erafle] **1** *vt (genou)* to graze; *(cuir)* to scuff; *(bois, meuble)* to scratch **2 s'érafler** *vpr* **s'é. le coude** to graze one's elbow

éraflure [eraflyr] *nf (au genou)* graze; *(sur cuir)* scuff mark; *(sur bois, sur meuble)* scratch

éraillé, -e [eraje] *adj* **(a)** *(voix)* hoarse **(b)** *(surface)* scratched

ère [εr] *nf* era; **en l'an 1150 de notre è.** in the year 1150 AD; **avant notre è.** BC

érection [erεksjõ] *nf* **(a)** *(construction)* erection **(b)** *(gonflement)* erection; **être en é.** *(personne)* to have an erection; *(verge)* to be erect

éreintant, -e [erε̃tã, -ãt] *adj Fam* exhausting

éreinté, -e [erε̃te] *adj Fam* exhausted

éreinter [erε̃te] **1** *vt* **(a)** *(fatiguer) (personne, animal)* to exhaust, to wear out **(b)** *(critiquer) (livre, auteur)* to pull to pieces **2 s'éreinter** *vpr* **s'é. à faire qch** to wear oneself out doing sth

érémiste [eʀemist] = RMiste

Erevan [eʀevan] *n* Yerevan

ergot [eʀgo] *nm* (**a**) *(d'un coq)* spur (**b**) *(d'un chien)* dewclaw (**c**) *Tech* pin

ergoter [eʀgɔte] *vi* to quibble (**sur** about)

Érié [eʀje] *n voir* lac

ériger [45] [eʀiʒe] **1** *vt* (**a**) *(dresser) (statue, temple, mât)* to erect (**b**) *(créer) (tribunal)* to establish, to set up (**c**) *Fig* **é. qn en qch** to set sb up as sth; **é. qch en qch** to elevate sth to the status of sth **2 s'ériger** *vpr* **s'é. en qch** to set oneself up as sth

ermitage [eʀmitaʒ] *nm* hermitage

ermite [eʀmit] *nm* hermit; **vivre en e.** to live the life of a recluse

érogène [eʀɔʒen] *adj* erogenous

érosion [eʀozjɔ̃] *nf* erosion

érotique [eʀɔtik] *adj* erotic

érotisme [eʀɔtism] *nm* eroticism

errance [eʀɑ̃s] *nf Litt* roving, wandering

errant, -e [eʀɑ̃, -ɑ̃t] *adj* *(vie)* roving, wandering; **chevalier e.** knight-errant; **chien e.** stray dog

errata [eʀata] *nmpl voir* erratum

erratique [eʀatik] *adj* erratic

erratum [eʀatɔm] (*pl* **errata** [eʀata]) *nm* erratum

errements [eʀmɑ̃] *nmpl* bad ways; **retomber dans ses e. passés** to fall back into one's bad old ways

errer [eʀe] *vi (marcher)* to wander; **e. par les rues** to roam the streets; **e. comme une âme en peine** to wander about like a lost soul

erreur [eʀœʀ] *nf* (**a**) *(faute)* mistake, error; **faire** *ou* **commettre une e.** to make a mistake; **faire e.** to be mistaken; **être dans l'e.** to be mistaken; **induire qn en e.** to mislead sb; **par e.** by mistake; **sauf e. de ma part** if I'm not mistaken; **il y a e. sur la personne** you've/they've/*etc* got the wrong person; **il n'y a pas d'e. (possible)** there's no doubt about it; **l'e. est humaine** to err is human; **e. de calcul** miscalculation; **e. de jeunesse** youthful indiscretion; **e. judiciaire** miscarriage of justice; **e. de jugement** error of judgement (**b**) *Ordinat* error; **message d'e.** error message; **correction des erreurs** error correction; **e. d'analyse (syntaxique)** parse error; **e. disque** disk error; **e. d'échantillonnage** sampling error; **e. d'écriture** write error; **e. de lecture** read error; **e. de logiciel** software *or* system error; **e. de programmation** programming error; **e. de saisie** keying error

erroné, -e [eʀɔne] *adj* erroneous

ersatz [eʀzats] *nm inv* ersatz, substitute

éructer [eʀykte] **1** *vi* to belch **2** *vt Fig* **é. des injures** to hurl abuse

érudit, -e [eʀydi, -it] **1** *adj* erudite, scholarly **2** *nm,f* scholar

érudition [eʀydisjɔ̃] *nf* erudition, scholarship

éruption [eʀypsjɔ̃] *nf* (**a**) *(d'un volcan)* eruption; **entrer en é.** to erupt (**b**) *(de boutons)* rash

érythème [eʀitem] *nm Méd* rash; **é. fessier** *Br* nappy *or Am* diaper rash; **é. solaire** sunburn

Érythrée [eʀitʀe] *nf* l'É. Eritrea

érythréen, -enne [eʀitʀeɛ̃, -ɛn] **1** *adj* Eritrean **2** *nm,f* É. Eritrean

E/S *Ordinat (abrév* **entrée/sortie)** I/O

ès [es] *prép* **docteur ès lettres/sciences** ≃ PhD; **licencié ès lettres** ≃ BA; **licencié ès sciences** ≃ BSc

esbroufe [esbʀuf] *nf Fam* bluffing; **faire de l'e.** to bluff

escabeau, -x [eskabo] *nm* (**a**) *(tabouret)* stool (**b**) *(marchepied)* stepladder

escadre [eskadʀ] *nf Naut* squadron; *Av* **e. aérienne** wing; **chef d'e.** *Naut* squadron commander; *Av* wing commander

escadrille [eskadʀij] *nf* (**a**) *Naut* flotilla (**b**) *Av (unité)* flight

escadron [eskadʀɔ̃] *nm* (**a**) *Mil* squadron; **chef d'e.** major (**b**) *Av* squadron (**c**) *Fig (groupe) (de journalistes)* troop, band

escalade [eskalad] *nf* (**a**) *(d'un mur, d'une falaise)* climbing, scaling; *Sp* climbing; **faire de l'e.** to go climbing (**b**) *Fig (d'une guerre, des prix, de la violence)* escalation

escalader [eskalade] *vt* to climb, to scale

escalator® [eskalatɔʀ] *nm* escalator

escale [eskal] *nf* (**a**) *(arrêt)* stopover; **faire e.** *(en bateau)* to put into port; *(en avion)* to touch down; **faire e. à Marseille** *(en bateau)* to put in at Marseilles; *(en avion)* to stop over at Athens; **vol sans e.** nonstop flight; **e. technique** refuelling stop (**b**) *(lieu) (pour bateau)* port of call; *(pour avion)* stopover

escalier [eskalje] *nm (marches)* stairs; *(cage)* staircase; **dans l'e., dans les escaliers** on the stairs; **monter en e.** *(en ski)* to sidestep; **e. en colimaçon** spiral staircase; **e. mécanique, e. roulant,** *Can* **e. mobile** escalator; **e. de secours** fire escape; **e. de service** backstairs

escalope [eskalɔp] *nf* escalope

escamotable [eskamɔtabl] *adj (antenne, train d'atterrissage, phares)* retractable; *(meuble)* foldaway

escamotage [eskamɔtaʒ] *nm* (**a**) *(par un illusionniste)* vanishing (**b**) *(d'un train d'atterrissage)* retraction (**c**) *Fig (d'un problème)* dodging

escamoter [eskamɔte] *vt* (**a**) **e. qch** *(sujet: illusionniste)* to make sth vanish (**b**) *(voler)* to sneak off with (**c**) *(train d'atterrissage)* to retract (**d**) *Fig (problème)* to dodge

escampette [eskɑ̃pet] *nf Fam* **prendre la poudre d'e.** to make off

escapade [eskapad] *nf* jaunt; **faire une e.** to go on a jaunt

escarbille [eskaʀbij] *nf* cinder

escargot [eskaʀgo] *nm* snail; **aller à une allure d'e.** *ou* à la vitesse d'un e. to go at a snail's pace; **marcher comme un e.** to walk at a snail's pace; *Fig* **opération e.** = slowing down of traffic by protesting truck drivers

escarmouche [eskaʀmuʃ] *nf* skirmish

escarpé, -e [eskaʀpe] *adj (route, montagne)* steep

escarpement [eskaʀpəmɑ̃] *nm (versant)* steep slope; *Géog* escarpment

escarpin [eskaʀpɛ̃] *nm* pump, *Br* court shoe

escarpolette [eskaʀpɔlet] *nf Vieilli (balançoire)* swing

escarre [eskaʀ] *nf Méd* scab; *(dû aux draps)* bedsore

escient [esjɑ̃] *nm* **à bon e.** wisely; **à mauvais e.** unwisely

esclaffer [esklafe] **s'esclaffer** *vpr* to burst out laughing, to roar with laughter

esclandre [esklɑ̃dʀ] *nm (scandale, tapage)* scene; **faire** *ou* **causer un e.** to make a scene

esclavage [esklavaʒ] *nm* slavery; **réduire qn en e.** to enslave sb

esclavagisme [esklavaʒism] *nm* slavery; *(doctrine)* pro-slavery

esclave [esklav] **1** *nmf* slave; **être vendu comme e.** to be sold into slavery; *Fig* **être l'e. de qn/qch** to be a slave to sb/sth **2** *adj Fig* **être e. de ses habitudes** to be a slave to one's habits

escogriffe [eskɔgʀif] *nm* **(grand) e.** beanpole

escompte [eskɔ̃t] *nm* discount; *Fin* **taux d'e.** (bank) discount rate

escompter [ɛskɔ̃te] *vt (espérer)* to expect, to anticipate *(que* that); **e. faire qch** to expect to do sth

escorte [ɛskɔrt] *nf* escort; **sous (bonne) e.** under escort

escorter [ɛskɔrte] *vt* to escort

escouade [ɛskwad] *nf Mil* squad

escrime [ɛskrim] *nf Sp* fencing; **faire de l'e.** to fence

escrimer [ɛskrime] **s'escrimer** *vpr* to fight; **s'e. à faire qch** to struggle to do sth

escrimeur, -euse [ɛskrimœr, -øz] *nm,f* fencer

escroc [ɛskro] *nm* crook, swindler

escroquer [ɛskrɔke] *vt (personne)* to swindle, to cheat; **e. qch à qn, e. qn de qch** to swindle *or* to cheat sb out of sth

escroquerie [ɛskrɔkri] *nf (action)* swindling; *(résultat)* swindle; *(délit)* fraud; *Fam* **mais c'est de l'e.!** it's a rip-off!

escudo [ɛskydo] *nm* escudo

eskimo [ɛskimo] = esquimau

ésotérique [ezɔterik] *adj* esoteric

espace [ɛspas] *nm* **(a)** *(étendue, distance)* space; **laisser de l'e.** to leave space; **e. blanc** space; **E. économique européen** European economic area; **e. publicitaire** advertising space; **e. de rangement** storage space; **e. vital** living space; **espaces verts** green spaces **(b)** *(durée)* **en l'e. d'un mois** within a month **(c)** *(atmosphère)* space; **e. aérien** airspace **(d)** *Math* space; **e. à trois/quatre dimensions** three-/four-dimensional space **(e)** *Ordinat* **e. disque** disk space; **e. mémoire** memory space; **e. de stockage** storage space

espacement [ɛspasmɑ̃] *nm (action)* spacing out; *(résultat)* spacing; *(distance)* space; *Ordinat* **e. arrière** backspace

espacer [16] [ɛspase] **1** *vt (objets, paiements, visites)* to space out
2 s'espacer *vpr* **(a)** *(visites, lettres)* to become less frequent **(b)** *(personnes)* **espacez-vous** space yourselves out

espace-temps *(pl* **espaces-temps)** [ɛspastɑ̃] *nm Math & Phys* space-time (continuum)

espadon [ɛspadɔ̃] *nm* swordfish

espadrille [ɛspadrij] *nf* espadrille

Espagne [ɛspaɲ] *nf* l'E. Spain

espagnol, -e [ɛspaɲɔl] **1** *adj* Spanish
2 *nm,f* **E.** Spaniard; **les Espagnols** the Spanish
3 *nm (langue)* Spanish

espagnolette [ɛspaɲɔlɛt] *nf* window catch *(long vertical bar with pivoting central catch)*

espalier [ɛspalje] *nm* **(a)** *(mur)* espalier wall **(b)** *(de gymnase)* wall bars

espèce [ɛspɛs] *nf* **(a)** *(sorte)* kind, sort; **les gens de son e.** people like her, people of her kind; **de la pire e.** of the worst sort; **cela n'a aucune e. d'importance** that's of no importance whatsoever; *Fam* **cette e. d'idiot** that stupid idiot; *Fam* **e. d'idiot!** you idiot! **(b)** *Jur* **cas d'e.** specific case; **la loi applicable en l'e.** the law applicable to the case in point **(c)** **espèces** *(argent)* cash; **payer en espèces** to pay in cash; **espèces sonnantes et trébuchantes** hard cash **(d)** *Bot & Zool* species; **l'e. humaine** the human race, mankind

espérance [ɛsperɑ̃s] *nf* hope; **dans l'e. de faire qch** in the hope of doing sth; **dans l'e. que...** in the hope that...; **au-delà de nos espérances** beyond our expectations; **répondre aux espérances de qn** to live up to sb's expectations; **e. de vie** life expectancy

espérer [34] [ɛspere] **1** *vt* to hope for; **e. faire qch** to hope to do sth; **e. que** to hope that; **je ne vous espérais plus** I'd given you up
2 *vi* **j'espère bien** I hope so; **espérons!** let's hope so!

espiègle [ɛspjɛgl] *adj* mischievous

espion, -onne [ɛspjɔ̃, -ɔn] *nm,f* spy

espionnage [ɛspjɔnaʒ] *nm* espionage, spying; **faire de l'e.** to spy; **l'e. industriel** industrial espionage

espionner [ɛspjɔne] **1** *vt* to spy on
2 *vi* to spy

esplanade [ɛsplanad] *nf* esplanade

espoir [ɛspwar] *nm* **(a)** *(espérance)* hope; **avoir l'e. de faire qch** to have hopes of doing sth; **avoir bon e.** to be full of hope; **reprendre e.** to become hopeful again; **nourrir l'e. de faire qch** to live in hope of doing sth; **tous les espoirs sont permis** things look hopeful, *Ironique* **l'e. fait vivre** hope springs eternal **(b)** *(personne)* hope; **un e. du tennis américain** one of the most promising American tennis players

esprit [ɛspri] *nm* **(a)** *(intellectuel)* mind; **avoir l'e. large/ étroit** to be broad-/narrow-minded; **avoir l'e. tranquille** to be easy in one's mind; **avoir l'e. mal tourné** to have a dirty mind; **avoir l'e. d'analyse/scientifique** to have an analytical/a scientific (turn of) mind; **perdre l'e.** to go out of one's mind, **reprendre ses esprits** to regain consciousness; **elle avait l'e.** ailleurs her thoughts were elsewhere, **elle n'a pas l'e. à ce qu'elle fait** her mind isn't on what she's doing; **je n'ai pas l'e. à plaisanter** I'm not in the mood for joking, **une pareille idée ne me serait jamais venue à l'e.** such an idea would never have crossed my mind; **qu'avez-vous à l'e.?** what are you thinking about?
(b) *(attitude mentale)* spirit; **avoir mauvais e.** to be a malicious sort; **faire du mauvais e.** to be malicious; **e. de caste** class-consciousness; **e. de clocher** parochialism; **e. de compétition** competitive spirit; **e. de corps** esprit de corps; **e. d'entreprise** enterprise spirit; **e. d'équipe** team spirit; **e. de famille** family feeling
(c) *(humour)* wit; **avoir de l'e.** to be witty; **mots** *ou* **traits d'e.** witticisms; **faire de l'e.** to display one's wit
(d) *(personne)* person, **un e. fort** a freethinker, *Prov* **les grands esprits se rencontrent** great minds think alike
(e) *(sens)* spirit; **l'e. de la loi** the spirit of the law
(f) *(fantôme)* spirit; **e., es-tu là?** *(dans une séance de spiritisme)* is there anybody there?; **e. frappeur** poltergeist
(g) *Chim* (volatile) spirit

esquif [ɛskif] *nm* skiff; **un frêle e.** a frail barque

esquimau, -aude, -x, -audes [ɛskimo, -od] **1** *adj* Eskimo, *Am* Inuit
2 *nm,f* **E.** Eskimo, *Am* Inuit
3 *nm (glace)* **E.®** *Br ≃* choc-ice *(on a stick)*, *Am ≃* ice-cream bar

esquinté, -e [ɛskɛ̃te] *adj Fam (abîmé)* knackered

esquinter [ɛskɛ̃te] *Fam* **1** *vt (abîmer)* to damage; *(blesser)* to hurt
2 s'esquinter *vpr (s'abîmer)* **s'e. la jambe** to hurt one's leg; **s'e. la santé/les yeux (à faire qch)** to ruin one's health/eyes (doing sth)

esquisse [ɛskis] *nf (dessin)* sketch; *Fig (d'un projet, d'un roman)* outline; *(d'un sourire)* suggestion

esquisser [ɛskise] **1** *vt (dessiner)* to sketch, *Fig (plan, roman)* to outline; *Fig* **e. un sourire** to give a slight smile
2 s'esquisser *vpr (idée, projet)* to take shape

esquiver [ɛskive] **1** *vt aussi Fig* to dodge, to evade
2 s'esquiver *vpr* to slip away

essai [ɛsɛ] *nm* **(a)** *(tentative)* try; **faire un e.** to have a try **(b)** *(test) (d'un produit, d'une voiture)* test, trial; **à l'e.** on a trial basis; *Ordinat* **e. approfondi** beta test; **e. nucléaire** nuclear test; *Ordinat* **e. de performance** benchmark **(c)** *(ouvrage)* essay **(d)** *(au rugby)* try

essaim [ɛsɛ̃] *nm aussi Fig* swarm

essaimer [eseme] *vi (abeilles)* to swarm; *Fig (population, famille)* to spread; *(entreprise)* to expand

essayage [esɛjaʒ] *nm* fitting

essayer [53] [eseje] **1** *vt* (**a**) *(pour la première fois) (gadget, restaurant)* to try (out); *(voiture)* to test-drive; *(vin, plat)* to try, to taste; *(vêtement, chaussures)* to try on (**b**) *(tester) (machine, produit)* to test (**c**) *(tenter)* **e. de faire qch** to try to do sth
2 s'essayer *vpr* **s'e. à qch/à faire qch** to try one's hand at sth/at doing sth

ESSEC [esɛk] *nf (abrév* **École supérieure des sciences économiques et commerciales)** = university-level business school

essence [esɑ̃s] *nf* (**a**) *(combustible) Br* petrol, *Am* gas(oline); **e. ordinaire** *Br* two-star petrol, *Am* regular gas; **e. sans plomb** unleaded (*Br* petrol *or Am* gas) (**b**) *(extrait) (de plantes, de café)* essence; **e. de térébenthine** spirits of turpentine (**c**) *(caractère fondamental)* essence; **par e.** essentially (**d**) *(espèce)* species

essentiel, -elle [esɑ̃sjɛl] **1** *adj* (**a**) *(nécessaire)* essential, necessary (**à/pour** for) (**b**) *(principal) (condition, caractère)* essential; *(raison)* basic, main
2 *nm* **l'e.** *(le plus important)* the main thing; *(le minimum)* the essentials; **l'e. de** *(la majeure partie de)* the majority of

essentiellement [esɑ̃sjelmɑ̃] *adv* (**a**) *(principalement)* essentially, mainly (**b**) *(par nature)* essentially

esseulé, -e [esœle] *adj* isolated

essieu, -x [esjø] *nm* axle

essor [esɔr] *nm* (**a**) *(d'un oiseau)* flight; **prendre son e.** to fly off (**b**) *Fig (d'une industrie, d'une économie)* (rapid) growth; **en plein e.** booming; **prendre son e.** to take off

essorage [esɔraʒ] *nm (à la machine)* spin-drying; *(à la main)* wringing

essorer [esɔre] *vt (vêtements) (à la machine)* to spin(-dry); *(à la main)* to wring out; *(salade)* to spin

essoreuse [esɔrøz] *nf (à tambour)* spin-drier

essoufflé, -e [esufle] *adj* out of breath

essoufflement [esufləmɑ̃] *nm* breathlessness; *Fig (de l'économie, d'une activité)* running down

essouffler [esufle] **1** *vt* to make out of breath
2 s'essouffler *vpr* to get out of breath; *Fig (économie, activité)* to run down

essuie-glace *(pl* **essuie-glaces)** [esɥiglas] *nm Br* windscreen *or Am* windshield wiper

essuie-mains [esɥimɛ̃] *nm inv* hand towel

essuie-tout [esɥitu] *nm inv* kitchen paper

essuyer [32] [esɥije] **1** *vt* (**a**) *(surface)* to wipe; *(liquide)* to wipe up; *(larmes)* to wipe away; **e. la vaisselle** to dry the dishes, to dry up (**b**) *(subir) (défaite, perte, insultes)* to suffer; *(refus)* to meet with; *(tempête)* to run into
2 s'essuyer *vpr* to wipe oneself; *(après un bain)* to dry oneself; **s'e. la bouche/les yeux** to wipe one's mouth/eyes

est¹ [ɛ] *voir* **être²**

est² [ɛst] **1** *nm* east; **un vent d'e.** an easterly wind; **le vent d'e.** the east wind; **à l'e.** in the east; **à l'e. de** (to the) east of; *Géog & Pol* **l'E.** the East
2 *adj inv (côte, face, régions)* eastern

estafilade [estafilad] *nf* gash

estaminet [estaminɛ] *nm Belg* (small) café

estampe [estɑ̃p] *nf* print

estampille [estɑ̃pij] *nf (sur un document)* stamp; *(sur un produit)* mark

est-ce que [ɛskə] *adv interrogatif* **e. je peux entrer?** can I come in?; **est-ce qu'il est là?** is he here?; **e. tu la connais?** do you know her?

esthète [ɛstɛt] *nmf* aesthete

esthéticien, -enne [ɛstetisjɛ̃, -ɛn] *nm,f* beautician

esthétique [ɛstetik] **1** *adj* aesthetic; *(beau)* aesthetically pleasing
2 *nf (beauté)* aesthetic quality

estimable [estimabl] *adj* (**a**) *(digne de respect)* estimable (**b**) *(assez bon)* fairly good

estimation [estimasjɔ̃] *nf* (**a**) *(détermination) (d'un prix, d'une distance, d'un poids)* estimation; *(de marchandises, d'une œuvre d'art)* valuation; *(de dommages, de besoins)* assessment (**b**) *(valeur, quantité estimée)* estimate

estime [estim] *nf* (**a**) *(respect)* esteem, regard; **avoir de l'e. pour qn/qch** to esteem sb/sth; **baisser/remonter dans l'e. de qn** to go down/up in sb's estimation; **avoir un succès d'e.** to be a critical (though not a popular) success (**b**) *Naut* **à l'e.** by dead reckoning

estimer [estime] **1** *vt* (**a**) *(déterminer) (prix, distance, poids)* to estimate; *(marchandises, œuvre d'art)* to value; *(dommages, besoins)* to assess (**b**) *(considérer)* to consider, to think (**que** that); **il n'a pas estimé nécessaire de me prévenir** he didn't consider it necessary to warn me (**c**) *(respecter) (personne)* to have a high opinion of; **e. qn à sa juste valeur** to value sb
2 s'estimer *vpr* **s'e. satisfait/heureux** to consider oneself satisfied/lucky

estival, -e, -aux, -ales [estival, -o] *adj* summer

estivant, -e [estivɑ̃, -ɑ̃t] *nm,f Br* holidaymaker, *Am* vacationer

estocade [estɔkad] *nf aussi Fig* death-blow; **donner l'e. à** to deal the death-blow to

estomac [estɔma] *nm* (**a**) *(ventre)* stomach; **avoir l'e. vide** to have an empty stomach; **avoir l'e. dans les talons** to be starving (**b**) *Fam Fig (courage)* guts

estomaquer [estɔmake] *vt Fam* to flabbergast

estomper [estɔ̃pe] **1** *vt Art (dessin)* to shade off; *Fig (paysage, contour, souvenir)* to blur
2 s'estomper *vpr (paysage, contour, souvenir)* to become blurred; *(peine)* to ease; *(rides)* to be smoothed out

Estonie [estɔni] *nf* **l'E.** Estonia

estonien, -enne [estɔnjɛ̃, -ɛn] **1** *adj* Estonian
2 *nm,f* **E.** Estonian
3 *nm (langue)* Estonian

estourbir [esturbir] *vt Fam* (**a**) *(tuer)* to bump off (**b**) *(étonner)* to astound

estrade [estrad] *nf* platform

estragon [estragɔ̃] *nm* tarragon

estropié, -e [estrɔpje] **1** *adj* crippled
2 *nm,f* cripple

estropier [66] [estrɔpje] *vt* (**a**) *(personne)* to cripple, to maim (**b**) *Fig (morceau de musique, langue étrangère)* to murder; *(mot, nom)* to mispronounce; *(texte)* to mutilate

estuaire [estɥɛr] *nm* estuary

estudiantin, -e [estydjɑ̃tɛ̃, -in] *adj* student

esturgeon [estyrʒɔ̃] *nm* sturgeon

et [e] **1** *conj* (**a**) *(exprime l'addition, la simultanéité)* and; **et son frère et sa sœur** both his brother and his sister; **et d'un, il pleut, et de deux, je n'ai pas envie d'y aller** in the first place it's raining, and in the second place I don't want to go; **j'aime le chocolat, et vous?** I like chocolate, do you?; **et moi, alors?** what about me? (**b**) *(dans les nombres, les heures)* **vingt/trente et un** twenty-/thirty-one; **une livre et demie** a pound and a half; **il est quatre heures et demie/et quart** it's half/quarter past four
2 *nm (symbole)* **et commercial** ampersand

ETA [ətea] *nf (abrév* **Euskadi ta Askatasuna)** ETA

étable [etabl] *nf* cowshed

établi¹ [etabli] *nm* workbench

établi²,-e *adj* established; **considérer qch comme une chose établie** to take sth for granted

établir [etablir] **1** *vt* (**a**) *(paix, relations, principe)* to establish; *(agence)* to set up; *(camp)* to pitch; *(prix)* to fix; *(devis, liste)* to draw up; *(record)* to set (**b**) *(démontrer)* to establish, to prove (**c**) *(autorité, réputation)* to establish (**sur on**)
2 s'établir *vpr* (**a**) *(dans une ville, un pays)* to settle (**b**) *(pour exercer un métier)* to set up in business (**c**) *(s'instaurer)* to become established

établissement [etablismã] *nm* (**a**) *(de la paix, de relations, d'un principe)* establishment; *(d'une agence)* setting up; *(d'un camp)* pitching; *(d'un prix)* fixing; *(d'un devis, d'une liste)* drawing up (**b**) *(démonstration)* establishment (**c**) *(installation)* *(d'une personne)* settlement (**d**) *(institution)* establishment, institution; **é. bancaire** bank; **é. de crédit** credit institution; **é. financier** financial institution; **é. hospitalier** hospital, **é. scolaire** school (**e**) *(entreprise)* business, firm, **les établissements** Henry Henry & Co

étage [etaʒ] *nm* (**a**) *(d'un bâtiment)* floor, storey; **à deux étages** two-storeyed; **au troisième é.** on the *Br* third *or Am* fourth floor; **à l'é.** upstairs (**b**) *(d'un terrain)* level; *(d'un gâteau)* tier (**c**) *(d'une fusée)* stage

étager [45] [etaʒe] **s'étager** *vpr* to rise in tiers

étagère [etaʒɛr] *nf* *(meuble)* (set of) shelves; *(planche)* shelf

étai [etɛ] *nm Constr* prop

étain [etɛ̃] *nm* (**a**) *(métal)* tin (**b**) *(matériau pour vaisselle)* pewter; **un é.** a piece of pewter

étais, était *voir* **être²**

étal *(pl* **étals)** [etal] *nm* (**a**) *(au marché)* stall (**b**) *(de boucher)* butcher's block

étalage [etalaʒ] *nm* (**a**) *(vitrine)* window display (**b**) *Fig (ostentation)* display; **faire é. de son savoir/sa richesse** to show off one's knowledge/wealth

étalagiste [etalaʒist] *nmf* window dresser

étalement [etalmã] *nm (dans le temps)* staggering (**sur over**)

étaler [etale] **1** *vt* (**a**) *(étendre)* *(journal, papiers)* to spread out; *(nappe, beurre)* to spread; *(peinture, pommade)* to apply (**sur** to); *(cartes)* to lay down (**b**) *Fig (montrer)* *(richesse, connaisances)* to show off; *(vie privée)* to make a display of; **é. une affaire au grand jour** to make a matter public (**c**) *(dans le temps)* to stagger (**sur** over)
2 s'étaler *vpr* (**a**) *(village, parc)* to spread out (**b**) *(dans le temps)* to be spread (**sur** over); *(se vautrer)* to sprawl (**d**) *Fam (tomber)* to fall flat on the ground; **s'é. de tout son long** to fall flat on one's face

étalon¹ [etalɔ̃] *nm (cheval)* stallion

étalon² *nm (de mesure, monétaire)* standard; *Fig (modèle)* yardstick; *Écon* **l'é.-or** the gold standard

étamine [etamin] *nf Bot* stamen

étanche [etãʃ] *adj (bateau, récipient)* watertight; *(montre, bottes)* waterproof

étanchéité [etãʃeite] *nf (d'un bateau, d'un récipient)* watertightness; *(d'une montre, de bottes)* waterproofness

étancher [etãʃe] *vt* (**a**) *(liquide)* to stop the flow of; *(sang)* to staunch (**b**) *(soif)* to quench

étang [etã] *nm* pond, pool

étant *voir* **être²**

étape [etap] *nf* (**a**) *(lieu)* stopover; **faire é.** to stop; *Fig* **brûler les étapes** *(dans la hiérarchie)* to shoot to the top; *(dans une tâche)* to cut corners (**b**) *(distance)* stage (**c**) *Fig (phase)* stage, step; **par étapes** in stages

---

état [eta] *nm* (**a**) *(façon d'être)* state, condition; *Phys* state; **l'é. des routes** road conditions; **à l'é. solide/naturel** in its solid/natural state; **à l'é. neuf** as good as new; **à l'é. pur** *(substance)* unalloyed; *Fig (bêtise, incompétence)* sheer, downright; **dans l'é. actuel des choses** as things stand; **être dans un triste é.** to be in a sorry state; **être dans tous ses états** to be in a state; **en bon/mauvais é.** in good/bad condition; **remettre qch en é.** to repair sth; *(moteur)* to overhaul sth; **laisser les choses en l'é.** to leave things as they are; **être en é. de marche** to be in working order; *(voiture)* to be roadworthy; **être/se sentir en é. de faire qch** to be/feel up to doing sth; **é. d'alerte** state of alert; **faire qch sans états d'âme** *(sans scrupules)* to have no qualms about doing sth; **é. de choses** state of affairs; **é. d'esprit** state of mind; **c'est un é. de fait** it's an undeniable fact; **l'é. de guerre a été déclaré** a state of war has been declared; **é. de santé** state of health; **être dans un é. second** to be spaced out; **en é. de siège** martial law; **é. d'urgence** state of emergency
(**b**) *Vieilli ou Hum (profession)* **épicier de son é.** grocer by trade
(**c**) *(autorité centrale)* **l'É.** the State; **É. membre** member state
(**d**) *(inventaire)* *(des dépenses, des ventes)* statement; **faire é. de qch** to mention sth; **é. civil** *(à la mairie)* register office; **é. des lieux** inventory of fixtures *(in rented premises)*; **états de service** service record
(**e**) *Hist* **les États généraux** the States General
(**f**) *Ordinat* **é. d'attente** wait state; **en é. de veille** in standby mode

étatique [etatik] *adj* state

étatiser [etatize] *vt* to bring under state control

état-major *(pl* **états-majors)** [etamaʒɔr] *nm* (**a**) *Mil (officiers)* (general) staff; *(lieu)* headquarters (**b**) *(d'une firme)* management; *(d'un parti politique)* leadership

États-Unis [etazyni] *nmpl* **les É. (d'Amérique)** the United States (of America)

étau, -x [eto] *nm* (**a**) *Tech* vice (**b**) *Fig (restrictions)* stranglehold; **l'é. se resserre** the net is closing in

étayer [53] [eteje] *vt* (**a**) *(mur, plafond)* to shore up (**b**) *Fig (argumentation, théorie)* to support

etc [ɛtsetera] *adv* etc

et cætera, et cetera [ɛtsetera] *adv* et cetera

été¹ [ete] *nm* summer; **en é.** in (the) summer; **un jour d'é.** a summer's day; **é. indien** Indian summer

été² *voir* **être²**

éteindre [54] [etɛ̃dr] **1** *vt (incendie, bougie, cigarette)* to put out, to extinguish; *(gaz)* to turn off; *(lumière, radio, radiateur)* to switch off, to turn off; **éteins dans la chambre, s'il te plaît** can you switch the light off in the bedroom, please
2 s'éteindre *vpr* (**a**) *(incendie, cigarette, lampe)* to go out (**b**) *(passion)* to fade; *(son, rires, voix)* to die away (**c**) *(disparaître)* *(personne)* to pass away; *(race)* to die out

éteint, -e [etɛ̃, -ɛ̃t] *adj* (**a**) **être é.** *(incendie, cigarette)* to be out; *(lampe, électricité, radio)* to be off (**b**) *(race, famille, volcan)* extinct (**c**) *(terne)* *(couleur)* dull; *(regard)* blank; *(voix)* faint; *(personne)* subdued

étendard [etãdar] *nm* (**a**) *(drapeau)* standard (**b**) *Fig (symbole)* **lever l'é. de la révolte** to raise the standard of revolt; **se ranger sous l'é. de qn** to join sb's camp

étendoir [etãdwar] *nm (à linge)* clothes-line

étendre [etãdr] **1** *vt* (**a**) *(déployer)* *(carte, nappe)* to spread out; *(linge)* to hang up; *(beurre, pommade, ailes)* to spread; *(pâte)* to roll out; **é. les bras** to open one's arms wide; *Fam* **se faire é.** *(être assommé)* to be knocked out; *(à un examen)* to fail (**b**) *(coucher)* to lay down (**c**) *(influence, pouvoir,*

connaissances) to extend (**à** to) (**d**) (diluer) to dilute (**e**) Ordinat (mémoire) to upgrade
2 s'étendre vpr (**a**) (s'allonger) to lie down (**b**) (aller) to stretch (**c**) (incendie, épidémie, grève) to spread; (pouvoir, influence, connaissances) to grow (**d**) (s'attarder) **s'é. sur un sujet** to dwell on a subject

étendu, -e [etɑ̃dy] **1** adj (**a**) (large, important) (plaine, connaissances) extensive; (pouvoirs) far-reaching (**b**) (bras, jambes) outstretched (**c**) (personne) lying (**d**) (dilué) diluted (**de** with)
2 nf **étendue** (d'un champ, d'une région) area; (d'une grève, d'une épidémie, d'un problème) scale, extent; (d'eau, de sable, de terre) expanse; (des connaissances, du vocabulaire, des pouvoirs) range

éternel, -elle [etɛrnɛl] **1** adj eternal; (discussion, bavardages) never-ending; **tu es un é. mécontent** you're never satisfied
2 nm (**a**) **l'É.** (Dieu) the Lord; Hum **c'est un grand fumeur/ paresseux devant l'É.** he's an incurable smoker/incurably lazy (**b**) **l'é. féminin** the archetypal female

éternellement [etɛrnɛlmɑ̃] adv for ever; (reconnaissant) eternally; **elle est é. mécontente** she's never satisfied

éterniser [etɛrnize] **s'éterniser** vpr (durer) to drag on (for ever); (chez quelqu'un) to outstay one's welcome

éternité [etɛrnite] nf eternity; **il y a une é. ou des éternités que je ne vous ai vu** I haven't seen you for ages

éternuement [etɛrnymɑ̃] nm sneeze

éternuer [etɛrnɥe] vi to sneeze

êtes voir **être²**

éther [etɛr] nm ether

éthéré, -e [etere] adj ethereal

Éthiopie [etjɔpi] nf **l'É.** Ethiopia

éthiopien, -enne [etjɔpjɛ̃, -ɛn] **1** adj Ethiopian
2 nm,f **É.** Ethiopian

éthique [etik] **1** adj ethical
2 nf ethics (singulier)

ethnie [ɛtni] nf ethnic group

ethnique [ɛtnik] adj ethnic

ethnologie [ɛtnɔlɔʒi] nf ethnology

ethnologique [ɛtnɔlɔʒik] adj ethnological

ethnologue [ɛtnɔlɔg] nmf ethnologist

éthylique [etilik] adj **alcool é.** ethyl alcohol; **coma é.** alcohol-induced coma

éthylisme [etilism] nm Méd alcoholism

étiez voir **être²**

étincelant, -e [etɛ̃slɑ̃, -ɑ̃t] adj sparkling; (étoile) twinkling

étinceler [42] [etɛ̃sle] vi (diamant, métal, lac) to sparkle; (étoile) to twinkle; (yeux) (de joie) to sparkle (**de** with); (de colère) to glint (**de** with)

étincelle [etɛ̃sɛl] nf aussi Fig spark; **lancer des étincelles** to throw out sparks; (diamant, yeux) to sparkle; Fig **ça va faire des étincelles** sparks will fly; **avoir une é. de génie** to have a stroke of genius

étioler [etjɔle] **s'étioler** vpr (plante) to wilt; (personne) to grow sickly; (esprit, mémoire) to deteriorate

étions voir **être²**

étiqueter [42] [etikte] vt aussi Fig to label (**comme** as)

étiquette [etikɛt] nf (**a**) (sur une valise, un produit) label (**b**) Fig (d'une personne) label; **coller une é. à qn** to label sb; **é. politique** political affiliation (**c**) (protocole) **l'é.** etiquette

étirer [etire] **1** vt to stretch
2 s'étirer vpr (personne, tissu, vêtement) to stretch; (journée, réunion) to drag on (for ever)

étoffe [etɔf] nf material, fabric; Fig **avoir l'é. d'un chef d'État** to have the makings of a statesman; **avoir l'é. d'un héros** to be the stuff heroes are made of

étoffer [etɔfe] **1** vt (discours, livre, personnage) to flesh out
2 s'étoffer vpr (personne) to fill out

étoile [etwal] nf (**a**) (astre) star; **un ciel sans étoiles** a starless sky; **coucher ou dormir à la belle é.** to sleep out (in the open); **né sous une bonne/mauvaise é.** born under a lucky/an unlucky star; **l'é. du berger** (vue le matin) the morning star; (vue le soir) the evening star; **é. filante** shooting star; **l'é. Polaire** the Pole star (**b**) (ornement, objet) star; (astérisque) asterisk; **hôtel trois étoiles** three-star hotel; **é. de David** Star of David (**c**) (vedette) star (**d**) **é. de mer** starfish (**e**) Ordinat **connecté en é.** in a star configuration

étoilé, -e [etwale] adj (**a**) (ciel, nuit) starry (**b**) (pare-brise) starred

étonnamment [etɔnamɑ̃] adv surprisingly

étonnant, -e [etɔnɑ̃, -ɑ̃t] adj surprising; **ce n'est pas é. qu'il soit fatigué** it's not surprising that he's tired; **chose étonnante, elle est arrivée à l'heure** amazingly enough, she arrived on time

étonné, -e [etɔne] adj surprised (**de** at)

étonnement [etɔnmɑ̃] nm surprise; **à mon grand é.** to my amazement

étonner [etɔne] **1** vt to surprise; **elle n'est pas venue? ça m'étonne** she didn't come? I'm surprised; Fam **alors ça, ça m'étonnerait!** that'll be the day!; **ça m'étonne de toi** I'm surprised at you; Fam **tu m'étonnes!** you don't say!; **tu m'étonneras toujours!** you never cease to amaze me!
2 s'étonner vpr to be surprised (**de** at); **je ne m'étonne plus de rien** nothing surprises me any more

étouffant, -e [etufɑ̃, -ɑ̃t] adj (air, chaleur, atmosphère) stifling; (temps) oppressive

étouffe-chrétien [etufkretjɛ̃] Fam **1** adj inv stodgy
2 nm inv **c'est de l'é., cette tarte** this tart is pure stodge

étouffée [etufe] **à l'étouffée 1** adj braised
2 adv **cuire qch à l'é.** to braise sth

étouffement [etufmɑ̃] nm (asphyxie) suffocation

étouffer [etufe] **1** vt (**a**) (personne) to suffocate; Euph **ce ne sont pas les scrupules qui l'étouffent** she's not exactly overscrupulous (**b**) Fig (cri, bâillement, rire) to stifle; (son) to muffle; (feu) to smother; (révolte) to suppress; (scandale, affaire) to hush up
2 vi to suffocate; **é. de rire/colère** to choke with laughter/anger; **on étouffe ici** it's stuffy in here
3 s'étouffer vpr to suffocate; (en mangeant) to choke (**avec** on)

étourderie [eturdəri] nf (**a**) (caractère) absentmindedness (**b**) (faute) careless mistake

étourdi, -e [eturdi] **1** adj (distrait) scatterbrained
2 nm,f scatterbrain

étourdir [eturdir] vt (assommer) to stun, to daze; Fig (sujet: vin, éloges) to make dizzy

étourdissant, -e [eturdisɑ̃, -ɑ̃t] adj (bruit) deafening; (nouvelles, succès) staggering; (beauté) stunning

étourdissement [eturdismɑ̃] nm **avoir un é.** to feel dizzy

étourneau, -x [eturno] nm starling

étrange [etrɑ̃ʒ] adj strange, odd; **chose é., il est revenu** strangely enough, he came back

étrangement [etrɑ̃ʒmɑ̃] adv strangely, oddly; **ressembler é. à qch** to look suspiciously like sth

étranger, -ère [etrɑ̃ʒe, -ɛr] **1** adj (**a**) (d'un autre pays) foreign (**b**) (inconnu) strange, unfamiliar (**à** to) (**c**) (extérieur) **des éléments étrangers** outsiders; **elle est étrangère à**

cette société/au projet she isn't involved with this company/the plan **2** *nm,f* **(a)** *(d'un autre pays)* foreigner **(b)** *(d'un autre groupe)* stranger, outsider **3** *nm* **l'é.** *(pays étrangers)* foreign countries; **aller/vivre à l'é.** to go/live abroad

étrangeté [etrɑ̃ʒte] *nf* strangeness, oddness

étranglé, -e [etrɑ̃gle] *adj (passage, vallée)* narrow; *(voix)* choked; *Méd (hernie)* strangulated

étranglement [etrɑ̃gləmɑ̃] *nm* **(a)** *(d'une personne)* strangling, strangulation; **mourir par é.** to be strangled **(b)** *(partie resserrée) (d'une rivière)* narrow part; *(d'une route)* bottleneck

étrangler [etrɑ̃gle] **1** *vt* **(a)** *(personne)* to strangle; *Fig (ruiner)* to cripple **(b)** *(resserrer) (taille, tube)* to constrict **2 s'étrangler** *vpr* **(a)** *(en mangeant)* to choke **(avec** on**), s'é. de colère/rire** to choke with anger/laughter **(b)** *(voix)* to choke; **les mots s'étranglèrent dans sa gorge** the words stuck in her throat

étrave [etrav] *nf Naut* stem

être¹ [etr] *nm (personne, âme)* being; **un e. cher** a loved one; **c'est un é. méprisable** he's a despicable creature; **ê. humain** human being; **ê. vivant** living creature

être² [2] **1** *vi* **(a)** *(indique la nature)* to be; **ê. avocat/ dentiste** to be a lawyer/dentist; **ceci est un reptile** this is a reptile **(b)** *(indique l'état)* to be; **ê. bien/mal** *(en bonne/mauvaise santé)* to be well/ill; **le temps est à l'orage** there's a storm brewing **(c)** *(indique le lieu)* to be; **elle est chez elle** she's at home; **Mombasa est au Kenya** Mombasa is in Kenya; **j'en suis au chapitre IV** I'm on chapter IV; **où en es-tu dans ton travail?** how far have you got with your work?; **je ne sais plus où j'en suis** I don't know what I'm doing any more; **j'en suis à me demander si...** I'm beginning to wonder whether... **(d)** *(indique le moment)* **nous sommes mercredi/le 16** it's Wednesday/the 16th today **(e)** *(indique l'appartenance)* **ê. à qn** to belong to sb; *Fig* **je suis à vous** I'm all yours; **elle est de la famille** she's one of the family **(f)** *(indique la provenance)* to be; **je suis de Lyon/du sud** I'm from Lyons/from the South; **l'enfant n'est pas de lui** it's not his child; **ce tableau est de Renoir** this picture is by Renoir **(g)** *(indique l'obligation)* **ceci est à lire pour demain** this has to be read for tomorrow; **ce film est à voir absolument** this film is unmissable **(h)** *(aller)* to go; **as-tu déjà été à Chicago?** have you ever been to Chicago?; *Fam* **ça a été** it went OK **(i)** *(exister)* to be; **la plus belle voiture qui soit** the most beautiful car in the world; *Litt* **elle n'est plus** she is no longer with us **(j)** *(locutions)* **ê. tout le temps à se plaindre/à médire** to be always complaining/criticizing; **ne serait-ce que** if only **2** *v aux* **(a)** *(avec des verbes à l'actif)* to have/to be; **je suis sorti hier soir** I went out last night; **es-tu déjà allé en Afrique?** have you ever been to Africa?; **elle est née en 1967** she was born in 1967; **j'étais parti très tôt** I had left very early; **il serait mieux avec les cheveux courts** he would look better with short hair; **ils se sont aimés** they loved each other; **nous nous étions trompés** we had made a mistake **(b)** *(avec des verbes au passif)* to be; **nous y sommes/ étions toujours bien reçus** we are/were always warmly welcomed **3** *v impersonnel* to be; **il est cinq heures** it's five (o'clock); **il est difficile de juger** it's hard to tell; **il m'est impossible de vous répondre** it's impossible for me to give you an answer

étreindre [54] [etrɛ̃dr] *vt* to embrace; *(sujet: peur, douleur)* to grip

étreinte [etrɛ̃t] *nf (embrassade)* embrace; *(sexuelle)* coupling

étrenner [etrene] *vt (objet)* to use for the first time, to christen; *(vêtement)* to wear for the first time

étrennes [etren] *nfpl* New Year's gift; *(pour facteur, éboueur)* ≃ Christmas bonus

étrier [etrije] *nm* **(a)** *(en équitation)* stirrup; **vider les étriers** to be thrown; *Fig* **mettre le pied à l'é. à qn** to give sb a helping hand **(b)** *(sur table d'examen)* stirrup

étriller [etrije] *vt* **(a)** *(cheval)* to curry **(b)** *Fig (critiquer)* to pan

étriper [etripe] **1** *vt (poisson, volaille)* to gut; *Fam Fig* **je vais l'é.!** I'll murder him! **2 s'étriper** *vpr Fam (se battre)* to tear each other apart

étriqué, -e [etrike] *adj* **(a)** *(vêtement)* tight **(b)** *Fig (esprit, vie)* narrow

étroit, -e [etrwa, -at] *adj* **(a)** *(peu large)* narrow; *Fig* **avoir l'esprit é.** to be narrow-minded **(b)** *(serré)* tight, *Fig (liens, collaboration, surveillance)* close **(c)** *(logement, pièce)* poky; **être à l'é.** to be cramped for room

étroitement [etrwatmɑ̃] *adv (nouer, tenir)* tightly; *Fig (unir, collaborer, surveiller)* closely

étroitesse [etrwates] *nf* narrowness; *(d'un logement, d'une pièce)* pokiness; *Fig* **é. d'esprit** narrow-mindedness

étron [etrɔ̃] *nm* piece of excrement

étrusque [etrysk] **1** *adj* Etruscan **2** *nmf* **É.** Etruscan

étude [etyd] *nf* **(a)** *(examen)* study, survey; **mettre qch à l'é.** to study or investigate sth; **é. de cas** case study; **é. de faisabilité** feasibility study; **faire une é. de marché** to do market research **(b)** *études (éducation)* studies; **j'ai arrêté mes études à seize ans** I left school when I was sixteen; **faire des études (de chinois/de droit)** to study (Chinese/ law); **elle a fait ses études à Oxford** she studied at Oxford **(c)** *Scol (heure)* study period; *(salle)* study room **(d)** *(morceau de musique, peinture)* study **(e)** *(bureau)* office

étudiant, -e [etydjɑ̃, -ɑ̃t] **1** *nm,f* student; **é. en médecine/en droit** medical/law student; **é. de première/seconde année** first-/second-year student, *Am* freshman/sophomore **2** *adj (vie, mouvement)* student

étudié, -e [etydje] *adj* **(a)** *(recherché) (tenue)* carefully chosen **(b)** *Péj (affecté)* studied **(c)** *Com* **prix très étudiés** very reasonable prices

étudier [66] [etydje] **1** *vt* to study; *(leçon)* to prepare **2** *vi* to study **3 s'étudier** *vpr (l'un l'autre)* to study each other

étui [etɥi] *nm* case; *(de revolver)* holster; **é. à lunettes** glasses case

étuve [etyv] *nf* **(a)** *(aux thermes)* steam room; *Fig* oven **(b)** *(pour sécher)* drying oven; *(pour stériliser)* sterilizer

étuvée [etyve] **à l'étuvée 1** *adj* braised **2** *adv* **cuire qch à l'é.** to braise sth

étymologie [etimɔlɔʒi] *nf* etymology

EU [əy] *nmpl (abrév* États-Unis) USA

eu, -e *pp voir* avoir¹

eucalyptus [økaliptys] *nm* eucalyptus

eucharistie [økaristi] *nf Rel* **l'e.** the Eucharist

euh [ø] *exclam* er!

eunuque [ønyk] *nm* eunuch

euphémisme [øfemism] *nm* euphemism

euphorie [øfɔri] *nf* euphoria

euphorique [øfɔrik] *adj* euphoric

euphorisant, -e [øfɔrizɑ̃, -ãt] **1** adj (effet, atmosphère) exhilarating; (médicament) antidepressant; (drogue) that produces a feeling of euphoria **2** nm antidepressant; (drogue) drug that produces a feeling of euphoria

Euphrate [øfrat] nm l'E. the Euphrates

eurasien, -enne [ørazjɛ̃, -ɛn] **1** adj Eurasian **2** nm,f E. Eurasian

eurêka [øreka] exclam eureka!

euro [øro] nm (monnaie) Euro

euro- [øro] préf Euro-

eurocrate [ørokrat] nmf Eurocrat

eurodevise [ørodəviz] nf Eurocurrency

eurodollar [ørodɔlar] nm Eurodollar

Europe [ørɔp] nf l'E. Europe; l'E. **centrale** central Europe; l'E. de l'Est/de l'Ouest Eastern/Western Europe; l'E. du Nord Northern Europe; l'E. **occidentale** Western Europe; l'E. **verte** European Community agriculture

européen, -enne [øropeɛ̃, -ɛn] **1** adj European **2** nm,f E. European

eurosceptique [ørosɛptik] nmf Pol Eurosceptic

Eurovision [ørovizjɔ̃] nf Eurovision

eut voir avoir[1]

euthanasie [øtanazi] nf euthanasia

eux [ø] pron personnel (a) (sujet) they; ils apprécient mon travail, e.! THEY like my work!; les enfants, e., se sont amusés the children, for their part, enjoyed themselves; si j'étais e., je me méfierais if I were them, I'd be careful (b) (objet direct) them; et e., tu les oublies? and what about them, have you forgotten them? (c) (avec préposition) them; (réfléchi) themselves; dis-le-leur, à e. tell THEM; les deux maisons sont à e. both houses are theirs; ils ont leurs méthodes à e. they have their own methods; Fam un copain à e. a friend of theirs (d) (dans les comparaisons) them; je dépense plus qu'e. I spend more than they do or than them

eux-mêmes [ømɛm] pron personnel themselves

évacuation [evakɥasjɔ̃] nf (a) (de matières du corps) discharge; (des eaux de pluie, des eaux usées) drainage (b) (de personnes, d'un lieu) evacuation

évacuer [evakɥe] vt (a) (matières du corps) to discharge; (eaux de pluie, eaux usées) to drain off (b) (personnes, lieu) to evacuate; faire é. une salle to evacuate a hall (c) Fig (problème) to solve

évadé, -e [evade] nm,f escaped prisoner

évader [evade] s'évader vpr aussi Fig to escape (de from)

évaluation [evalɥasjɔ̃] nf (d'une propriété, d'un bien) valuation; (de dommages) assessment; (d'un poids, d'un nombre, des risques) estimation

évaluer [evalɥe] vt (propriété, bien) to value; (dommages) to assess; (poids, nombre, risques) to estimate

évangéliser [evɑ̃ʒelize] vt to evangelize

évangéliste [evɑ̃ʒelist] nm (prédicateur) evangelist; (de la Bible) Evangelist

évangile [evɑ̃ʒil] nm Rel l'É. the Gospel; Fig prendre qch pour parole d'é. to take sth as gospel (truth)

évanoui, -e [evanwi] adj unconscious; tomber é. to fall down in a faint

évanouir [evanwir] s'évanouir vpr (a) (perdre conscience) to faint (b) (disparaître) to fade (away)

évanouissement [evanwismɑ̃] nm (syncope) fainting fit

évaporation [evapɔrasjɔ̃] nf evaporation

évaporé, -e [evapɔre] Péj **1** adj scatterbrained **2** nm,f airhead

évaporer [evapɔre] s'évaporer vpr (a) (liquide) to evaporate (b) Fig (disparaître) to vanish (into thin air)

évasé, -e [evaze] adj (récipient) wide-mouthed; (jupe) flared

évaser [evaze] s'évaser vpr to widen; (jupe) to be flared

évasif, -ive [evazif, -iv] adj evasive

évasion [evazjɔ̃] nf (a) (fuite) escape (de from); é. de capitaux flight of capital; é. fiscale tax evasion (b) Fig (distraction) escapism; avoir besoin d'é. to need to escape

Ève [ɛv] npr Eve; Fam je ne le connais ni d'È. ni d'Adam I don't know him from Adam

évêché [eveʃe] nm (diocèse) bishopric; (palais) bishop's palace

éveil [evɛj] nm awakening; être en é. to be alert

éveillé, -e [eveje] adj (a) (non endormi) awake (b) (vif) alert

éveiller [eveje] **1** vt (a) (curiosité, soupçons, jalousie) to arouse; (intelligence, imagination) to stimulate (b) Litt (personne) to wake **2** s'éveiller vpr (a) Litt (personne) to awake (b) Fig (curiosité, soupçons, jalousie) to be aroused; (intelligence, imagination) to develop

événement [evɛnmɑ̃] nm event; attendre la suite des événements to wait and see what happens; créer l'é. to make big news; Hum quand il fait la vaisselle, c'est (tout) un é. it's a major event when he does the dishes

éventail [evɑ̃taj] nm (a) (pour se rafraîchir) fan; en é. fan-shaped (b) (choix) range

éventaire [evɑ̃tɛr] nm (a) (étal) stall (b) (d'un marchand ambulant) tray

éventé, -e [evɑ̃te] adj (vin, parfum) stale; (bière) flat

éventer [evɑ̃te] **1** vt (a) (avec un éventail) to fan (b) (secret, complot) to discover **2** s'éventer vpr (a) (avec un éventail) to fan oneself (b) (vin, parfum) to go stale; (bière) to go flat

éventrer [evɑ̃tre] vt (personne, animal) to disembowel; (colis, matelas) to rip open; (fût, boîte) to break open

éventualité [evɑ̃tɥalite] nf (a) (circonstance) eventuality; parer à toute é. to be prepared for all eventualities; dans l'é. de in the event of (b) (possibilité) possibility

éventuel, -elle [evɑ̃tɥel] adj possible

éventuellement [evɑ̃tɥelmɑ̃] adv possibly; j'aurais é. besoin de votre concours I may need your help

évêque [evɛk] nm bishop

Everest [evɔrɛst] nm l'E., le mont E. (Mount) Everest

évertuer [evɛrtɥe] s'évertuer vpr s'é. à faire qch to endeavour to do sth

éviction [eviksjɔ̃] nf (d'un rival, d'une tête de parti) ousting; (d'un locataire) eviction

évidemment [evidamɑ̃] adv of course, obviously

évidence [evidɑ̃s] nf (a) (d'un fait, de la vérité) obviousness; c'est une é.! obviously!; nier l'é. to deny the obvious; se rendre à l'é. to face facts; de toute é., à l'é. obviously (b) en é. (visible) in a prominent position; mettre qch en é. (phénomène) to highlight sth; se mettre en é. to try to get oneself noticed

évident, -e [evidɑ̃, -ãt] adj obvious; tu crois qu'on va réussir? – c'est é.! do you think we'll succeed? – of course (we will)!; elle va se rendre compte, c'est é. she's bound to notice; Fam c'est pas é.! (pas facile) it's not so easy!

évider [evide] vt to hollow out

évier [evje] nm sink

évincer [16] [evɛ̃se] vt (rival) to oust (de from)

éviter [evite] **1** vt (a) (s'écarter de) to avoid; é. de faire qch to avoid doing sth; il faut é. qu'il le voie he mustn't be allowed to see it; **évite que ça se sache** don't let it get out (**b**) *(épargner)* **é. qch à qn** to save *or* spare sb sth; **ça m'évitera d'avoir à le faire** it will save me having to do it **2 s'éviter** *vpr* (**a**) **s'é. qch** to avoid sth (**b**) *(se fuir mutuellement)* to avoid each other

évocateur, -trice [evɔkatœr, -tris] *adj* evocative (**de** of)

évocation [evɔkasjɔ̃] *nf* evocation

évolué, -e [evɔlɥe] *adj (société)* advanced; *(personne)* broadminded; *Ordinat (langage)* high-level

évoluer [evɔlɥe] *vi* (**a**) *(se déplacer)* to move around; *Fig* **é. dans le milieu des artistes** to move in artistic circles (**b**) *(se développer)* to develop (**c**) *Ordinat* **faire é.** to upgrade

évolutif, -ive [evɔlytif, -iv] *adj* progressive; *Ordinat* upgradeable

évolution [evɔlysjɔ̃] *nf* (**a**) *(développement)* development (**b**) *Biol* evolution (**c**) **évolutions** *(déplacements)* movements

évoquer [evɔke] *vt* (**a**) *(se remémorer) (passé)* to recall, to evoke (**b**) *(faire penser à)* to be reminiscent of; **son nom ne m'évoque rien** her name means nothing to me (**c**) *(aborder)* to touch on, to mention (**d**) *(par la magie)* to call up, to invoke

ex [cks] *nmf Fam* ex

ex- [ɛks] *préf* ex-; **ex-femme/-ministre** ex-wife/-minister

exacerbation [ɛgzasɛrbasjɔ̃] *nf* exacerbation

exacerber [ɛgzasɛrbe] **1** *vt* to exacerbate **2 s'exacerber** *vpr* to become acute

exact, -e [ɛgzakt] *adj* (**a**) *(quantité, poids, nombre)* exact, precise; *(rapport, description)* exact, accurate; *(mot, réponse, heure, date)* right, correct; **c'est e.** *(vrai)* it's quite true; **il s'appelle bien Vivien? - e.** his name's Vivien? - that's right! (**b**) *(ponctuel)* punctual, on time

exactement [ɛgzaktəmɑ̃] *adv* exactly

exactions [ɛgzaksjɔ̃] *nfpl* atrocities

exactitude [ɛgzaktityd] *nf* (**a**) *(précision, fidélité)* exactness; *(justesse)* correctness (**b**) *(ponctualité)* punctuality; *Prov* **l'e. est la politesse des rois** punctuality is the politeness of kings

ex æquo [ɛgzɛko] **1** *adj inv* **être e.** to tie, to be equally placed (**avec** with) **2** *nmf inv* **il y a deux e.** there's a two-way tie; **départager les e.** to break the tie **3** *adv* **être troisième e.** to tie for third place

exagération [ɛgzaʒerasjɔ̃] *nf* exaggeration

exagéré, -e [ɛgzaʒere] *adj (récit, geste)* exaggerated; *(prix, salaire, pessimisme)* excessive; **il n'est pas e. de dire que...** it's no exaggeration to say that...

exagérément [ɛgzaʒeremɑ̃] *adv* excessively

exagérer [34] [ɛgzaʒere] **1** *vt* to exaggerate; **il ne faut rien e.**, **n'exagérons rien** let's not exaggerate **2** *vi (amplifier)* to exaggerate; *(abuser)* to go too far

exaltant, -e [ɛgzaltɑ̃, -ɑ̃t] *adj* stirring

exaltation [ɛgzaltasjɔ̃] *nf (excitation)* intense excitement

exalté, -e [ɛgzalte] **1** *adj (discours, sentiment)* impassioned; *(personne)* fanatical **2** *nm,f* fanatic

exalter [ɛgzalte] *vt* (**a**) *(exciter) (imagination)* to stir; *(ressentiment, orgueil)* to intensify (**b**) *(louer) (personne)* to exalt

exam [ɛgzam] *nm Fam* exam

examen [ɛgzamɛ̃] *nm* (**a**) *(d'un document, de faits)* examination; *(d'une machine)* checking; *(d'un local)* inspection; *(d'une demande)* consideration; **e. de conscience** soul-searching (**b**) **e. (médical)** (medical) examination; **e. de la vue** sight *or* eye test (**c**) *Scol & Univ* exam, examination; **e.**

blanc mock exam; **e. d'entrée** entrance exam; **e. de passage** *Br* end-of-year exam, *Am* final exam

examinateur, -trice [ɛgzaminatœr, -tris] *nm,f* examiner

examiner [ɛgzamine] **1** *vt* (**a**) *(étudier) (document, faits)* to examine; *(machine)* to check; *(local)* to inspect; *(demande)* to consider (**b**) *(observer)* to examine; *(horizon)* to scan; **e. qn de la tête aux pieds** to eye sb up and down (**c**) *(patient)* to examine; **se faire e. par un médecin** to be examined by a doctor **2 s'examiner** *vpr* (**a**) *(dans une glace)* to examine oneself (**b**) *(l'un l'autre)* to examine each other

exaspérant, -e [ɛgzasperɑ̃, -ɑ̃t] *adj* exasperating

exaspération [ɛgzasperasjɔ̃] *nf* exasperation

exaspérer [34] [ɛgzaspere] *vt* (**a**) *(personne)* to exasperate (**b**) *Litt (douleur, sentiment)* to aggravate

exaucement [ɛgzosmɑ̃] *nm* granting

exaucer [16] [ɛgzose] *vt* (**a**) *(souhait)* to grant (**b**) **e. qn** to grant sb's wish

excavateur [ɛkskavatœr] *nm* excavator, (mechanical) digger

excavation [ɛkskavasjɔ̃] *nf* (**a**) *(trou)* excavation; *(creusée par une bombe)* crater (**b**) *(action)* excavation

excavatrice [ɛkskavatris] *nf* = excavateur

excédant, -e [ɛksedɑ̃, -ɑ̃t] *adj* exasperating

excédent [ɛksedɑ̃] *nm* surplus; **budget en e.** surplus budget; **e. de poids** excess weight; **e. de bagages** excess baggage; **être en e.** to show a surplus

excédentaire [ɛksedɑ̃tɛr] *adj (production, poids)* excess; *(budget)* surplus; **balance commerciale e.** trade surplus

excéder [34] [ɛksede] *vt* (**a**) *(quantité, somme, limite)* to exceed; *(forces, compétences)* to be beyond; **e. ses pouvoirs** to exceed one's powers (**b**) *(irriter)* to exasperate

excellence [ɛkselɑ̃s] *nf* excellence; *Scol* **prix d'e.** class prize *(for all-round standard)*; **par e.** par excellence; **Son/Votre E.** *(titre)* His/Her/Your Excellency

excellent, -e [ɛkselɑ̃, -ɑ̃t] *adj* excellent (**en** at)

exceller [ɛksele] *vi* to excel (**en** at)

excentré, -e [ɛksɑ̃tre] *adj (a) (quartier)* outlying (**b**) *Tech* off centre

excentricité [ɛksɑ̃trisite] *nf (de caractère, acte bizarre)* eccentricity

excentrique [ɛksɑ̃trik] **1** *adj (bizarre)* eccentric **2** *nmf (personne)* eccentric

excepté, -e [ɛksɛpte] **1** *prép* except, apart from **2 les femmes exceptées** except for *or* apart from women

excepter [ɛksɛpte] *vt* to except (**de** from); **sans e. les enfants** not forgetting the children

exception [ɛksɛpsjɔ̃] *nf* exception (**à** to); **c'est l'e. qui confirme la règle** it's the exception that proves the rule; **à quelques exceptions près** with a few exceptions; **un être d'e.** an exceptional person

exceptionnel, -elle [ɛksɛpsjɔnɛl] *adj* exceptional; **ne rien avoir d'e.** to be nothing special

exceptionnellement [ɛksɛpsjɔnɛlmɑ̃] *adv* exceptionally

excès [ɛksɛ] *nm (excédent)* excess; **pécher par e. de zèle** to be overzealous; **avec e.** excessively; **sans e.** in moderation; **jusqu'à l'e.** to excess, excessively; **tomber dans l'e. inverse** to go to the other extreme; **e. de vitesse** speeding; **faire un e. de vitesse** to speed (**b**) *(abus)* excess; **faire des e.** to overindulge

excessif, -ive [ɛksɛsif, -iv] *adj (excessive)*; **il est e.** he does things to excess

excessivement [ɛksɛsivmɑ̃] *adv (extrêmement)* extremely; *(avec excès)* excessively

excision [ɛksizjɔ̃] *nf* excision

excitant, -e [ɛksitɑ̃, -ɑ̃t] **1** *adj (fascinant, provocant)* exciting; *(tonique)* stimulating **2** *nm* stimulant

excitation [ɛksitasjɔ̃] *nf* (**a**) *(incitation)* incitement (**à** to) (**b**) *(état)* excitement (**c**) *Méd* excitation

excité, -e [ɛksite] **1** *adj* excited **2** *nm,f (personne)* hothead

exciter [ɛksite] **1** *vt* (**a**) *(attiser) (curiosité, jalousie, pitié)* to arouse (**b**) *(encourager)* to urge on; **e. qn à la révolte** to incite sb to revolt (**c**) *(énerver)* to excite (**d**) *(nerf, muscle)* to excite **2 s'exciter** *vpr* to get excited

exclamation [ɛksklamasjɔ̃] *nf* exclamation

exclamer [ɛksklame] **s'exclamer** *vpr* **s'e. de qch** *(joie, douleur)* to cry out with sth; **"jamais!" s'exclama-t-il** "never!" he exclaimed

exclu, -e [ɛkskly] **1** *adj* (**a**) *(non compris)* TVA **exclue** excluding sales tax (**b**) *(impensable)* out of the question; **il est e. qu'elle vienne avec nous** there's no question of her coming with us **2** *nm,f* outcast

exclure [17] [ɛksklyr] *vt* (**a**) *(expulser)* **e. qn de qch** *(parti, école)* to expel sb from sth; *(fonction publique)* to remove sb from sth; *(salle, réunion)* to eject sb from sth (**b**) *(mettre à l'écart)* **e. qn de qch** to exclude sb from sth (**c**) *(ne pas considérer) (hypothèse, solution)* to rule out; **cela n'exclut pas que vous puissiez enseigner** that doesn't rule out the possibility of your teaching

exclusif, -ive [ɛ́ksklyzif, -iv] *adj* exclusive; *(but, mission)* sole; **être e. dans ses amitiés** to be selective in one's choice of friends

exclusion [ɛksklyzjɔ̃] *nf* (**a**) *(d'un parti, d'une école)* expulsion; *(d'une fonction publique)* removal; *(d'une salle, d'une réunion)* ejection (**de** from) (**b**) **à l'e. de** with the exception of

exclusivement [ɛksklyzivmɑ̃] *adv* exclusively

exclusivité [ɛksklyzivite] *nf* (**a**) *(droit)* exclusive rights (**de** to); **en e.** exclusively; **film en première e.** recent release; *Fig* **ne pas avoir l'e. de l'intelligence** not to have a monopoly on intelligence (**b**) *(information)* exclusive, scoop

excommunier [66] [ɛkskɔmynje] *vt* to excommunicate

excréments [ɛkskremɑ̃] *nmpl* excrement

excrétion [ɛkskresjɔ̃] *nf* (**a**) *(action)* excretion (**b**) **excrétions** *(déchets)* excreta

excroissance [ɛkskrwasɑ̃s] *nf* excrescence

excursion [ɛkskyrsjɔ̃] *nf (en car, en voiture)* excursion, trip; *(d'une journée)* day trip; *(de plusieurs jours)* tour; **faire une e., partir en e.** to go on a trip/a tour

excursionniste [ɛkskyrsjɔnist] *nmf* day-tripper, *Am* excursionist

excusable [ɛkskyzabl] *adj* excusable, forgivable

excuse [ɛkskyz] *nf* (**a**) *(raison)* excuse; **trouver des excuses à qn** to find excuses for sb; **ce n'est pas une e.!** that's no excuse! (**b**) **excuses** *(regrets)* apology; **faire** *ou* **présenter ses excuses à qn** to make one's apologies to sb

excuser [ɛkskyze] **1** *vt* (**a**) *(justifier) (personne, action)* to excuse; **e. qn auprès de qn** to apologize for sb to sb (**b**) *(pardonner) (personne, erreur, colère)* to excuse; **excusez-moi** *(j'ai fait une faute)* I'm sorry; *(pour attirer l'attention)* excuse me; **excuse-moi de te déranger** I'm sorry to disturb you; **excuse-moi de ne pas t'avoir téléphoné** I'm sorry I didn't call you; *Formel* **je vous prie de m'e.** I do beg

your pardon; **tu es tout excusé** there's no need to apologize; *Hum* **excusez du peu!** if you please! (**c**) *(dispenser)* to excuse; **se faire e.** to ask to be excused **2 s'excuser** *vpr* to apologize; **s'e. auprès de qn** to apologize to sb; **s'e. de qch/de faire qch** to apologize for sth/for doing sth; **je m'excuse!** I'm sorry!

exécrable [ɛgzekrabl] *adj* atrocious

exécrer [34] [ɛgzekre] *vt Litt* to loathe

exécutable [ɛgzekytabl] *adj* executable

exécutant, -e [ɛgzekytɑ̃, -ɑ̃t] *nm,f* (**a**) *(employé)* subordinate; **ce n'est qu'un simple e.** he just carries out orders (**b**) *(musicien)* performer

exécuter [ɛgzekyte] **1** *vt* (**a**) *(effectuer) (travail, ordres)* to carry out; *(danse, morceau de musique)* to perform; *(peinture)* to execute (**b**) *Ordinat (programme)* to run; *(commande)* to execute (**c**) *(mettre à mort)* to execute; *Fam (battre)* to slaughter; *Fam (critiquer)* to savage **2 s'exécuter** *vpr* to comply

exécuteur, -trice [ɛgzekytœr, -tris] *nm,f Jur* **e. testamentaire** executor; **exécutrice testamentaire** executrix

exécutif, -ive [ɛgzekytif, -iv] **1** *adj (pouvoir)* executive **2** *nm* **l'e.** the executive

exécution [ɛgzekysjɔ̃] *nf* (**a**) *(d'un travail, d'ordres)* carrying out; *(d'une danse, d'un morceau de musique)* performance; *(d'une peinture)* execution; **mettre qch à e.** to carry sth out (**b**) *Ordinat* execution (**c**) *(mise à mort)* execution

exécutoire [ɛgzekytwar] *adj* (**a**) **jugement e.** enforceable decision (**b**) **formule e.** executory formula

exégèse [ɛgzeʒez] *nf* exegesis

exemplaire¹ [ɛgzɑ̃plɛr] *adj* (**a**) *(comportement, courage)* exemplary (**b**) *(punition)* exemplary

exemplaire² *nm (livre, gravure)* copy; **en deux/trois exemplaires** in duplicate/triplicate; **photocopier qch en vingt exemplaires** to make twenty photocopies of sth; **le livre a été tiré à dix mille exemplaires** ten thousand copies of the book were printed

exemple [ɛgzɑ̃pl] *nm* (**a**) *(modèle)* example (**pour** for); **donner l'e. (à qn)** to set (sb) an example; **suivre l'e. de qn** to follow sb's example; **prendre qn en e.** to model oneself on sb; **citer qn/qch en e.** to quote sb/sth as an example; **faire un e.** *(en punissant)* to set an example (**b**) *(cas, mot, phrase)* example; **être l'e. même de la bêtise** to be stupidity itself (**c**) **par e.** for example, for instance; *Fam* **ah ça par e.!** *(stupeur)* oh no!

exempt, -e [ɛgzɑ̃, -ɑ̃t] *adj* **e. de** *(service militaire)* exempt from; *(danger, problème)* free from; **e. de droits de douane** duty-free; **sa remarque n'était pas exempte d'une certaine amertume** her remark wasn't without a trace of bitterness

exempter [ɛgzɑ̃te] *vt (dispenser)* to exempt (**de** from)

exemption [ɛgzɑ̃psjɔ̃] *nf* exemption (**de** from)

exercé, -e [ɛgzɛrse] *adj (œil, oreille)* trained; *(main)* practised

exercer [16] [ɛgzɛrse] **1** *vt* (**a**) *(entraîner) (corps, esprit, mémoire)* to train; **e. qn à qch/à faire qch** to train sb in sth/to do sth (**b**) *(user de) (autorité, talent, droit)* to exercise; **e. une influence sur qn** to exert an influence on sb; **e. une pression sur qn/qch** to exert pressure on sb/sth; **e. un contrôle sur qch** to exercise control over sth (**c**) *(profession)* to practise; **e. ses fonctions** to carry out one's duties; **e. le métier de journaliste** to work as a journalist **2** *vi (médecin, juriste)* to practise **3 s'exercer** *vpr* (**a**) *(s'entraîner)* to practise; **s'e. à qch/à faire qch** to practise sth/doing sth (**b**) *(se manifester) (autorité, pouvoir)* to make itself felt

exercice [ɛgzɛrsis] *nm* (**a**) *(entraînement sportif ou scolaire)* exercise; **faire des exercices** to do (some) exercises; **prendre de l'e.** to (take) exercise **(b)** *Mil* drill; **être à l'e.** to be on parade **(c)** *(du pouvoir, d'un droit)* exercise **(d)** *(d'une profession)* practice; **dans l'e. de ses fonctions** in the exercise of one's duties; **être en e.** *(avocat, médecin)* to be in practice; *(président)* to be in office; **le président en e.** the incumbent president **(e) l'e. du culte** public worship **(f)** *(en comptabilité) Br* financial year, *Am* fiscal year

exergue [εgzεrg] *nm (de médaille)* inscription; *(d'un texte)* epigraph; **en e.** *(citation)* as an epigraph

exfoliant, -e [εksfɔljã, -ãt] **1** *adj* exfoliating **2** *nm* exfoliant

exhaler [εgzale] **1** *vt (odeur)* to give off; *Fig (joie, colère)* to give vent to; *Fig* **cette maison exhale la tristesse** this house exudes sadness **2 s'exhaler** *vpr (odeur)* to be given off

exhausser [εgzose] *vt (mur, édifice)* to heighten; **e. une maison d'un étage** to add a storey to a house

exhaustif, -ive [εgzostif, -iv] *adj* exhaustive

exhiber [εgzibe] **1** *vt* **(a)** *(documents, passeport)* to produce **(b)** *Péj (savoir, richesses)* to show off, to flaunt **2 s'exhiber** *vpr* to flaunt oneself

exhibition [εgzibisjõ] *nf Péj (de savoir, de richesses)* flaunting

exhibitionniste [εgzibisjɔnist] *nmf* exhibitionist

exhortation [εgzɔrtasjõ] *nf* exhortation **(a to)**

exhorter [εgzɔrte] *vt* **e. qn à qch/à faire qch** to exhort sb to sth/to do sth

exhumation [εgzymasjõ] *nf (d'un corps)* exhumation; *(d'un trésor, de vestiges)* excavation

exhumer [εgzyme] *vt (corps)* to exhume; *(trésor, vestiges)* to excavate

exigeant, -e [εgziʒã, -ãt] *adj (personne, travail)* exacting

exigence [εgziʒãs] *nf* **(a)** *(caractère)* exacting nature **(b)** *(condition)* demand

exiger [45] [εgziʒe] *vt* **(a)** *(demander qn insistant)* to demand **(de** from); **e. que qch soit fait** to demand that sth be done **(b)** *(nécessiter) (soin, action)* to require

exigible [εgziʒibl] *adj (dette, impôt)* payable

exigu, -ë [εgzigy] *adj* cramped, tiny

exiguïté [εgziguite] *nf* crampedness

exil [εgzil] *nm* exile; **envoyer qn en e.** to send sb into exile; **être en e.** to be in exile

exilé, -e [εgzile] *nm,f* exile

exiler [εgzile] **1** *vt* to exile **(de** from) **2 s'exiler** *vpr* to go into exile; *Fig* **s'e. de la ville** to cut oneself off from the town

existant, -e [εgzistã, -ãt] *adj* existing

existence [εgzistãs] *nf* **(a)** *Phil (être)* existence **(b)** *(vie)* life; **mener une e. tranquille** to lead a quiet life; **dans l'e.** in life **(c)** *(présence)* existence **(de** of) **(d)** *(durée) (d'une institution)* life

existentialisme [εgzistãsjalism] *nm Phil* existentialism

existentiel, -elle [εgzistãsjεl] *adj* existential

exister [εgziste] **1** *vi* to exist; **rien n'existe pour lui que l'art** art is all that matters to him; **et l'amitié, cela existe, non?** there's such a thing as friendship, isn't there? **2** *v impersonnel* **il existe** there is/are

exode [εgzɔd] *nm* exodus; **e. des cerveaux** brain drain; **e. rural** rural depopulation

exonération [εgzɔnerasjõ] *nf* exemption; **e. fiscale** tax exemption

exonérer [34] [εgzɔnere] *vt (personne)* to exempt; *(marchandises)* to exempt from tax; **être exonéré d'impôts** to be exempt from tax

exorbitant, -e [εgzɔrbitã, -ãt] *adj (prix, demande)* exorbitant

exorbité, -e [εgzɔrbite] *adj (yeux)* protruding; *Fig* **ils regardaient, les yeux exorbités** they watched with bulging eyes

exorciser [εgzɔrsize] *vt aussi Fig* to exorcize

exorcisme [εgzɔrsism] *nm* exorcism

exotique [εgzɔtik] *adj* exotic; **poisson e.** tropical fish

expansé, -e [εkspãse] *adj (polystyrène)* expanded

expansif, -ive [εkspãsif, -iv] *adj (exubérant)* expansive

expansion [εkspãsjõ] *nf* **(a)** *(de gaz, de l'univers)* expansion; **l'univers en e.** the expanding universe **(b)** *(développement) (d'une ville, d'une industrie)* expansion; **taux d'e.** growth rate; **être en pleine e.** *(d'une économie, d'une entreprise)* to be booming

expansionnisme [εkspãsjɔnism] *nm* expansionism

expatriation [εkspatrijasjõ] *nf* expatriation

expatrié, -e [εkspatrije] *adj & nm,f* expatriate

expatrier [66] [εkspatrije] **1** *vt (personne)* to expatriate **2 s'expatrier** *vpr* to leave one's country

expectative [εkspεktativ] *nf* **être dans l'e.** to be waiting to see what happens

expectorant, -e [εkspεktɔrã, -ãt] *adj & nm* expectorant

expectorer [εkspεktɔre] *vt* to expectorate

expédient [εkspedjã] *nm* expedient; **vivre d'expédients** to live by one's wits

expédier [66] [εkspedje] *vt* **(a)** *(envoyer)* to send, to dispatch; **e. qch par bateau/par avion/par le train** to send sth by sea/air/rail **(b)** *(se débarrasser de)* to dispose of; **elle les a expédiés en colonie de vacances** she packed them off to camp **(c)** *(faire rapidement) (tâche)* to deal promptly with; *(devoirs, dissertation)* to dash off; **e. les affaires courantes** to deal with day-to-day matters

expéditeur, -trice [εkspeditœr, tris] **1** *nm,f* sender **2** *adj (bureau, gare)* dispatching

expéditif, -ive [εkspeditif, -iv] *adj* hasty

expédition [εkspedisjõ] *nf* **(a)** *(envoi)* dispatch, sending **(b)** *(marchandises)* consignment **(c)** *(voyage, opération militaire) Fig* expedition; **partir en e.** to go on an expedition

expéditionnaire [εkspedisjɔner] *adj Mil* expeditionary

expérience [εksperjãs] *nf* **(a)** *(pratique)* experience; **avoir de l'e.** to have experience; **avoir l'e. de qch** to have experience of sth; **savoir qch par e.** to know sth from experience; **faire l'e. de qch** to experience sth; **tenter l'e.** to give it a try **(b)** *(test scientifique)* experiment; **e. en laboratoire** laboratory experiment; **faire une e. (sur)** to carry out an experiment (on)

expérimental, -e, -aux, -ales [εksperimãtal, -o] *adj* experimental

expérimentalement [εksperimãtalmã] *adv* experimentally

expérimentation [εksperimãtasjõ] *nf* experimentation; **e. sur l'homme** human experiments

expérimenté, -e [εksperimãte] *adj* experienced

expérimenter [εksperimãte] *vt (remède, vaccin)* to test, to try out **(sur** on)

expert, -e [εkspεr, -εrt] **1** *adj* expert, skilled **(en/dans** in); **être e. en la matière** to be an expert on the subject **2** *nm* expert; *(d'assurance)* valuer

expert-comptable *(pl* **experts-comptables)** [εkspεrkõtabl] *nm Br* ≃ chartered accountant, CA, *Am* ≃ certified public accountant, CPA

expertise [εkspεrtiz] *nf* **(a)** *(évaluation) (d'une objet)* valuation; *(de dommages)* assessment **(b)** *(rapport)* expert's report **(de** on) **(c)** *(compétence)* expertise

expertiser [ɛkspɛrtize] *vt (œuvre d'art)* to value; *(dommages)* to assess

expiation [ɛkspjasjɔ̃] *nf* expiation (**de** of)

expiatoire [ɛkspjatwar] *adj* expiatory

expier [66] [ɛkspje] *vt* to atone for, to expiate

expiration [ɛkspirasjɔ̃] *nf* (**a**) *(respiration)* breathing out (**b**) *(d'un contrat, d'un bail) Br* expiry, *Am* expiration; **venir** *ou* **arriver à e.** to expire

expirer [ɛkspire] **1** *vi* (**a**) *Litt (mourir)* to expire (**b**) *(contrat, bail)* to expire (**c**) *(respirer)* to breathe out
2 *vt* to breathe out

explicatif, -ive [ɛksplikatif, -iv] *adj* explanatory; **notice explicative** directions for use

explication [ɛksplikasjɔ̃] *nf* explanation; **donner une e. à qch** to give an explanation for sth; **exiger des explications** to demand an explanation; **avoir une e. avec qn** *(discuter)* to talk things over with sb; *(se disputer)* to have it out with sb; **e. de textes** textual analysis

explicite [ɛksplisit] *adj* explicit

explicitement [ɛksplisitmɑ̃] *adv* explicitly

expliquer [ɛksplike] **1** *vt* to explain; *(texte)* to analyse
2 s'expliquer *vpr* (**a**) *(communiquer ses idées, se justifier)* to explain oneself; **je m'explique** let me explain (**b**) *(comprendre)* **je ne m'explique pas pourquoi il...** I can't understand why he... (**c**) *(être explicable)* **cela s'explique facilement** that's easily explained; **tout s'explique!** there's a reason for everything! (**d**) *(se parler)* to talk things over; **s'e. avec qn** *(discuter)* to talk things over with sb; *(se disputer)* to have it out with sb

exploit [ɛksplwa] *nm* feat

exploitant, -e [ɛksplwatɑ̃, -ɑ̃t] *nm,f* (**a**) **e. (agricole)** farmer; **petits exploitants** small farmers (**b**) *Cin* exhibitor

exploitation [ɛksplwatasjɔ̃] *nf* (**a**) *(d'une mine, d'une forêt)* working; *(d'une ligne de chemin de fer, d'une ferme)* running; *(d'une terre)* farming; *(des ressources naturelles, d'un brevet)* & *Fig Péj* exploitation; *Ordinat* **système d'e.** operating system; *Fig* **c'est de l'e.!** it's exploitation! (**b**) *(entreprise)* concern; **e. agricole** farm; **e. minière** mine

exploiter [ɛksplwate] *vt* (**a**) *(mine, forêt)* to work; *(ressources naturelles, brevet)* to exploit; *(ligne de chemin de fer, ferme)* to run; *(terre)* to farm; *Fig (situation, talent, idée)* to exploit (**b**) *Péj (abuser de) (personne)* to exploit

exploiteur, -euse [ɛksplwatœr, -øz] *nm,f Péj* exploiter

explorateur, -trice [ɛksplɔratœr, -tris] *nm,f (personne)* explorer

exploration [ɛksplɔrasjɔ̃] *nf* exploration; **partir en e.** to go off exploring

exploratoire [ɛksplɔratwar] *adj* exploratory

explorer [ɛksplɔre] *vt* to explore

exploser [ɛksploze] *vi* (**a**) *(bombe, avion, chaudière)* to explode; **faire e. une bombe** to explode a bomb (**b**) *Fig (se mettre en colère)* to explode

explosif, -ive [ɛksplozif, -iv] **1** *adj aussi Fig* explosive
2 *nm* explosive

explosion [ɛksplozjɔ̃] *nf aussi Fig* explosion; **une e. de joie** an outburst of joy; **e. démographique** population explosion

exponentiel, -elle [ɛkspɔnɑ̃sjɛl] **1** *adj* exponential
2 *nf* **exponentielle** exponential

export [ɛkspɔr] *nm* export; *Ordinat* **e. de données** data export

exportateur, -trice [ɛkspɔrtatœr, -tris] **1** *adj* exporting; **pays e. de vin** wine-exporting country
2 *nm,f* exporter

exportation [ɛkspɔrtasjɔ̃] *nf (action)* export(ation);

(produit) export; *Ordinat (d'un fichier)* exporting; *Ordinat (données exportées)* exported data

exporter [ɛkspɔrte] *vt aussi Ordinat* to export (**vers** to)

exposant, -e [ɛkspozɑ̃, -ɑ̃t] **1** *nm,f (artiste, firme)* exhibitor
2 *nm* (**a**) *Math* exponent (**b**) *Typ (chiffre, lettre)* superscript; **3 en e.** superscript 3

exposé [ɛkspoze] *nm (de faits, d'une situation)* account; *Scol & Univ* talk; **après un bref e. de la situation** after outlining the situation; **faire un e.** to give a talk

exposer [ɛkspoze] **1** *vt* (**a**) *(montrer) (marchandises)* to display; *(œuvres d'art)* to exhibit (**b**) *(expliquer) (raisons, projet)* to set out; *(griefs, point de vue)* to air; **je leur ai exposé ma situation** I explained my situation to them (**c**) *(présenter)* **e. qch à la lumière/au soleil** to expose sth to the light/to the sun; **e. un film** to expose a film; **e. qn à la critique/au danger** to expose sb to criticism/to danger; **exposé au nord** facing north
2 s'exposer *vpr* **s'e. au danger** to put oneself in danger; **s'e. à la critique/à des poursuites** to lay oneself open to criticism/to prosecution; **ne t'expose pas trop longtemps** don't stay in the sun too long

exposition [ɛkspozisjɔ̃] *nf* (**a**) *(action) (de marchandises, de fleurs)* display; *(d'œuvres d'art)* exhibition (**b**) *(de musée)* exhibition (**c**) *(salon, foire)* exhibition, show; **l'E. universelle** the World Fair (**d**) *(de faits, de raisons)* exposition (**e**) *(au froid, au danger)* exposure (**à** to); *(d'une maison)* aspect; *Phot* exposure

exprès¹, -esse [ɛksprɛs] *adj (explicite)* express

exprès² *adj inv* **lettre/paquet e.** special delivery letter/parcel; **en e.** by special delivery

exprès³ [ɛksprɛ] *adv (à dessein)* on purpose, deliberately; *(spécialement)* specially; **j'ai déclenché l'alarme sans le faire e.** I set off the alarm without meaning to; **c'est fait e.** it's deliberate; **on dirait un fait e.** you'd think it was done on purpose; **comme (par) un fait e., il pleuvait** wouldn't you know it, it was raining

express [ɛksprɛs] **1** *adj (train)* express
2 *nm* (**a**) *(train)* express (**b**) *(café)* espresso

expressément [ɛkspresemɑ̃] *adv* (**a**) *(catégoriquement)* expressly (**b**) *(spécialement)* specially

expressif, -ive [ɛkspresif, -iv] *adj* expressive

expression [ɛkspresjɔ̃] *nf* (**a**) *(d'un sentiment, opinion)* expression; *(du visage)* expression, look; **l'e. de son visage** the expression or look on her face; **sans e.** expressionless; **e. corporelle** self-expression through movement (**b**) *(locution)* expression (**c**) *Math* expression; *Fig* **réduit à sa plus simple e.** reduced to its simplest form; *Ordinat* **e. logique** logical expression

expressionnisme [ɛkspresjɔnism] *nm* expressionism

exprimable [ɛksprimabl] *adj* expressible

exprimer [ɛksprime] **1** *vt* (**a**) *(sentiment, opinion)* & *Math* to express (**b**) *(jus)* to squeeze (**de** from)
2 s'exprimer *vpr (en parlant, en agissant)* to express oneself; **s'e. par gestes** to use sign language; **si je peux m'e. ainsi** if I can put it like that; **le président ne s'est pas encore exprimé sur ce sujet** the president has yet to voice an opinion on the matter

expropriation [ɛksprɔprijasjɔ̃] *nf* expropriation

exproprier [66] [ɛksprɔprije] *vt* to expropriate

expulser [ɛkspylse] *vt (étranger)* to deport, to expel (**de** from); *(locataire)* to evict (**de** from); *(élève, membre de parti)* to expel (**de** from); *(joueur)* to send off

expulsion [ɛkspylsjɔ̃] *nf (d'un étranger)* deportation (**de** from); *(d'un locataire)* eviction (**de** from); *(d'un élève, d'un membre de parti)* expulsion (**de** from); *(d'un joueur)* sending off

expurger [45] [εkspyrʒe] *vt* to expurgate

exquis, -e [εkski, -iz] *adj* exquisite; *(personne, sourire, temps)* delightful

exsangue [εksɑ̃g, εgzɑ̃g] *adj (patient, visage)* anaemic; *Fig (pays, région)* bled white

extase [εkstɑz] *nf* (**a**) *Rel & Psy* ecstasy (**b**) *(admiration)* rapture, ecstasy; **être en e. devant qn/qch** to be in raptures over sb/sth

extasier [66] [εkstɑzje] **s'extasier** *vpr (s'exclamer)* to go into raptures (**sur/devant** about/over); *(être en extase)* to be in raptures (**sur/devant** about/over)

extatique [εkstatik] *adj* ecstatic

extenseur [εkstɑ̃sœr] **1** *adj m (muscle)* extensor **2** *nm (appareil)* chest expander

extensible [εkstɑ̃sibl] *adj* (**a**) *(métal)* tensile; *(vêtement, tissu)* stretch (**b**) *Ordinat* upgradeable

extensif, -ive [εkstɑ̃sif, -iv] *adj* culture extensive extensive farming

extension [εkstɑ̃sjɔ̃] *nf* (**a**) *(d'un muscle, d'un ressort)* stretching; **être en e.** *(ressort)* to be released; *(gymnaste)* to be fully stretched (**b**) *Fig (d'un territoire, d'une firme)* expansion; *(d'un contrat)* extension; *(d'une maladie, d'une langue)* spread; **prendre de l'e,** *(entreprise)* to expand; *(maladie, incendie)* to spread (**c**) **par e.** by extension (**d**) *Ordinat* expansion; **e. mémoire** memory upgrade

exténuer [εkstenɥe] **1** *vt* to exhaust **2 s'exténuer** *vpr* **s'e. à faire qch** to exhaust oneself doing sth

extérieur, -e [εksterjœr] **1** *adj* (**a**) *(surface, partie)* outer, external; *(escalier, éclairage, intérêts)* outside; *(signe, fragilité)* outward; *(facteur, cause)* external; **le monde e.** the outside world; **sans aide extérieure** without outside help (**b**) *(étranger) (commerce, politique)* foreign, external **2** *nm* (**a**) *(d'un bâtiment, d'une boîte)* outside, exterior; **vu de l'e.** seen from the outside; **à l'e.** *(d'un bâtiment)* outside; *(d'une boîte)* on the outside; **à l'e. de la gare/ville** outside the station/town; *Fig* **juger de l'e.** to judge by appearances; **match à l'e.** away match; **jouer à l'e.** to play away (**b**) **l'e.** *(pays étrangers)* foreign countries; **à l'e.** abroad; **de l'e.** from abroad; **à l'e.** *Cin* location shot; **tourner en e.** to film on location

extérieurement [εksterjœrmɑ̃] *adv* (**a**) *(dehors)* on the outside, externally (**b**) *(en apparence)* outwardly

extérioriser [εksterjorize] **1** *vt (sentiment)* to express; *Psy* to externalize **2 s'extérioriser** *vpr (sentiment)* to express itself; *(personne)* to express oneself

exterminateur, -trice [εksterminatœr, -tris] **1** *adj (rage)* destructive **2** *nmf* exterminator

extermination [εksterminasjɔ̃] *nf* extermination

exterminer [εkstermine] *vt* to exterminate

externat [εksterna] *nm* (**a**) *(école)* day school (**b**) *(élèves)* day pupils (**c**) *(à l'hôpital)* non-resident (medical) studentship

externe [εkstern] **1** *adj* (**a**) *(surface, partie)* external, outer; *(cause)* external; *Ordinat* **dispositif e.** external device; **à usage e.** *(médicament)* for external use only (**b**) **élève e.** day pupil **2** *nmf* (**a**) *(élève)* day pupil (**b**) *(étudiant en médecine)* **e. (des hôpitaux)** non-resident medical student, *Am* extern

extincteur [εkstɛ̃ktœr] *nm* fire extinguisher

extinction [εkstɛ̃ksjɔ̃] *nf* (**a**) **e. des feux** lights out (**b**) *(d'une espèce)* extinction (**c**) **e. de voix** loss of voice; **avoir une e. de voix** to have lost one's voice

extirper [εkstirpe] **1** *vt (plante)* to root up; *Fig (vices)* to eradicate, to root out; **e. qn de son lit** to drag sb out of bed; **je n'ai pas pu lui e. le moindre renseignement** I couldn't get a single piece of information out of him **2 s'extirper** *vpr* **s'e. de qch** to extricate oneself from sth; **s'e. de son lit** to drag oneself out of bed

extorquer [εkstorke] *vt (argent, promesse)* to extort (**à** from)

extorsion [εkstorsjɔ̃] *nf* extortion; **e. de fonds** extortion of funds

extra [εkstra] **1** *adj inv* (**a**) *(de qualité supérieure)* topquality (**b**) *Fam (remarquable)* great, neat **2** *nm inv* (**a**) *(gâterie)* (special) treat; **s'offrir un e.** to treat oneself (**b**) *(serviteur)* extra hand; **faire des e. chez qn** to do occasional work for sb

extra- [εkstra] *préf* extra-

extraconjugal, -e, -aux, -ales [εkstrakɔ̃ʒygal, -o] *adj* extramarital

extracteur [εkstraktœr] *nm* extractor

extraction [εkstraksjɔ̃] *nf aussi Math* extraction; *(d'une balle)* removal; *Fig* **de haute/basse e.** of noble/humble extraction

extrader [εkstrade] *vt* to extradite

extradition [εkstradisjɔ̃] *nf* extradition

extrafin, -e [εkstrafɛ̃, -in] *adj* (**a**) *(petit pois)* extra-fine (**b**) *(de qualité supérieure)* top-quality

extrafort, -e [εkstrafor, -ort] *adj* extra-strong **2** *nm* bias binding

extraire [28] [εkstrɛr] **1** *vt aussi Math* to extract (**de** from); *(balle)* to remove (**de** from); *(épingle, clou)* to pull out (**de** of); *(personne)* to free (**de** from); **cette citation est extraite de...** this quotation is taken from... **2 s'extraire** *vpr* **s'e. de qch** to extricate oneself from sth

extrait [εkstrɛ] *nm* (**a**) *(essence)* extract (**b**) *(de texte, de film)* extract; *(d'un acte)* abstract; **e. de casier judiciaire** – documentary evidence showing whether one has a criminal record; **e. de naissance** birth certificate

extralucide [εkstralysid] *adj & nmf* (**voyante**) **e.** clairvoyant

extraordinaire [εkstraordinɛr] *adj* (**a**) *(spécial) (mesures, messager, mission)* special (**b**) *(étonnant, remarquable)* extraordinary; *Fam (excellent)* fantastic; **cela n'a rien d'e.** that's nothing out of the ordinary; **si par e.** if by some remote chance

extraordinairement [εkstraordinɛrmɑ̃] *adv* extraordinarily

extraplat, -e [εkstrapla, -at] *adj (montre, calculette)* slimline

extrapoler [εkstrapole] *vi* to extrapolate

extrascolaire [εkstraskolɛr] *adj (activités)* extracurricular

extraterrestre [εkstraterɛstr] *adj & nmf* extraterrestrial

extra-utérin, -e [εkstrayterɛ̃, -in] *adj voir* grossesse

extravagance [εkstravagɑ̃s] *nf* (**a**) *(d'un comportement, de vêtements)* extravagance; *(d'une personne)* eccentricity; **faire des extravagances** to behave extravagantly; **dire des extravagances** to talk wildly (**b**) *(action, remarque)* piece of nonsense

extravagant, -e [εkstravagɑ̃, -ɑ̃t] *adj (idée, comportement, vêtements, prix)* extravagant; *(personne)* eccentric

extraverti, -e [εkstraverti] *adj & nmf* extrovert

extrême [εkstrɛm] **1** *adj* (**a**) *(point, limite)* furthest; *(jeunesse, vieillesse, froid, plaisir)* extreme; **en cas d'e. urgence** if it's extremely urgent; **d'une maigreur**

extremely thin; *Pol* **e. droite/gauche** far *or* extreme right/ left (**b**) *(excessif)* extreme **2** *nm* extreme; **passer d'un e. à l'autre** to go from one extreme to the other; **prudent à l'e.** cautious in the extreme

extrêmement [ɛkstrɛmmɑ̃] *adv* extremely

extrême-onction (*pl* **extrêmes-onctions**) [ɛkstrɛmɔ̃ksjɔ̃] *nf Rel* extreme unction

Extrême-Orient [ɛkstrɛmɔrjɑ̃] *nm* **l'E.** the Far East

extrémisme [ɛkstremism] *nm* extremism

extrémité [ɛkstremite] *nf* (**a**) *(bout)* *(d'une jambe, d'une corde)* end; *(d'un doigt)* tip; *(d'une aiguille, d'une épée)* point;

les extrémités *(pieds et mains)* the extremities (**b**) *(acte désespéré)* extreme act; **en venir à des extrémités** to resort to extreme measures (**c**) *(situation désespérée)* extremity; **être à la dernière e.** to be on the point of death

exubérance [ɛgzyberɑ̃s] *nf (d'une personne)* exuberance; *(d'une végétation)* lushness; **avec e.** exuberantly

exubérant, -e [ɛgzyberɑ̃, -ɑ̃t] *adj (personne, joie)* exuberant; *(végétation)* lush

exultation [ɛgzyltasjɔ̃] *nf* exultation

exulter [ɛgzylte] *vi* to exult, to rejoice

exutoire [ɛgzytwar] *nm* outlet (**à** for)

ex-voto [ɛksvɔto] *nm inv Rel* votive offering

F, f [ɛf] *nm inv* F, f; **un F2/F3** *(appartement)* a two-/three-roomed *Br* flat *or Am* apartment

F (a) *(abrév* **franc(s))** F, fr **(b)** *(abrév* **Fahrenheit)** F

fa [fa] *nm inv (note de musique)* F; *(chantée)* fa

fable [fabl] *nf* **(a)** *(récit)* fable **(b)** *(invention)* story

fabricant, -e [fabrikã, -ãt] *nm,f* manufacturer

fabrication [fabrikasjõ] *nf (industrielle)* manufacture; *(manuelle)* making; **f. artisanale** production by craftsmen; **bombe de f. artisanale** home-made bomb; **f. assistée par ordinateur** computer-aided manufacture; **de f. française** French-made

fabrique [fabrik] *nf* factory

fabriquer [fabrike] *vt* **(a)** *(industriellement)* to manufacture; *(manuellement)* to make; *Fam* **qu'est-ce qu'elle fabrique?** what's she up to? **(b)** *(inventer)* to make up, to fabricate

fabulation [fabylasjõ] *nf* fantasizing

fabuleusement [fabyløzmã] *adv* fabulously

fabuleux, -euse [fabylø, -øz] *adj* fabulous

fac [fak] *nf Fam Br* uni, *Am* school; **à la f.** at *Br* uni *or Am* school; **être en f. d'allemand** to be studying German at *Br* uni *or Am* school

façade [fasad] *nf aussi Fig* façade

face [fas] *nf* **(a)** *(visage)* face; *Fig* **perdre/sauver la f.** to lose/save face
(b) *(d'un disque)* side; *(d'une pièce de monnaie)* head (side); **changer un disque de f.** to turn a record over
(c) *Fig (aspect)* side; **changer la f. des choses** to change the face of things
(d) *(locutions)* **f. à** *(dans l'espace)* facing; *(difficultés, situation)* faced with; *(adversaire)* confronted with; **f. à f. (avec)** face to face (with); **faire f. à** *(lieu, personne)* to face, to be opposite; *(responsabilités, dépenses)* to meet; *(situation, difficultés)* to face up to; **de f.** face on; *(attaquer)* from the front; **en f.** opposite; *(de l'autre côté de la rue)* across the road; **regarder qn en f.** to look sb in the face; **dire à qn qch en f.** to tell sb sth to his face; **la maison (d')en f.** the house across the road; **en f. de** opposite, facing; **l'un en f. de l'autre** opposite *or* facing each other

face-à-face [fasafas] *nm inv (public)* face-to-face debate; *(privé)* one-to-one meeting

facétie [fasesi] *nf Litt* joke

facétieux, -euse [fasesjø, -øz] *adj Litt (personne)* mischievous

facette [faset] *nf aussi Fig* facet; **à facettes** facetted; *(personnalité)* multi-faceted

fâché, -e [faʃe] *adj* **(a)** *(en colère)* angry **(contre** with) **(b)** *(brouillé)* on bad terms **(avec** with); *Fam* **elle est fâchée**

avec la chimie she's hopeless at chemistry **(c)** *(contrarié)* sorry; **je ne suis pas f. que ça soit terminé** I'm not sorry that it's finished

fâcher [faʃe] **1** *vt (mettre en colère)* to make angry, to anger **2 se fâcher** *vpr* **(a)** *(se mettre en colère)* to get angry **(contre** with) **(b)** *(se brouiller)* to fall out **(avec** with)

fâcheux, -euse [faʃø, -øz] *adj* unfortunate

facho [faʃo] *adj & nmf Fam* fascist

faciès [fasjes] *nm* features

facile [fasil] **1** *adj* **(a)** *(simple)* easy; **être f. à faire** to be easy to do; **c'est f. à dire** that's easily said; **f. d'emploi** easy to use **(b)** *(agréable)* easy-going; **être f. à vivre** to be easy to get on with **(c)** *Péj (superficiel)* facile **(d)** *Péj (femme, fille)* easy **2** *adv Fam (au moins)* easily

facilement [fasilmã] *adv* easily

facilité [fasilite] *nf* **(a)** *(simplicité)* easiness; **choisir la f.** to take the easy way out **(b)** *(aisance)* ease; **avoir des facilités pour qch** to have a talent for sth **(c)** **facilités de paiement** payment facilities

faciliter [fasilite] *vt* to make easier; **f. qch à qn** to make sth easier for sb

façon [fasõ] *nf* **(a)** *(manière)* way, manner; **faire qch à sa f.** to do sth (in) one's own way; **de cette f.** (in) this way; **de f. à faire qch** so as to do sth; **de f. à ce qu'il t'entende** so that he hears you; **de telle f. que** in such a way that; **d'une** *ou* **de f. générale** generally speaking; **d'une f.** *ou* **d'une autre** one way or another; **de toute f.** anyway, in any case; *Formel* **vous ne me dérangez en aucune f.** you're not disturbing me in the least; **c'est une f. de parler** in a manner of speaking; **je ne tolère pas ces façons de parler!** I won't tolerate that sort of language! **(b)** *(imitation)* **f. cuir** imitation leather **(c)** **façons** *(comportement)* manners, behaviour; **en voilà des façons!** what a way to behave!; **faire des façons** *(minauder)* to put on airs; **faire des façons pour accepter qch** to make a fuss about accepting sth; **sans façons** *(personne, repas)* unpretentious; **non merci, sans façons!** no thanks, really!

façonner [fasone] *vt* **(a)** *(travailler)* to shape **(b)** *(fabriquer)* to make **(c)** *Fig (personne, caractère)* to mould

fac-similé *(pl* **fac-similés)** [faksimile] *nm* facsimile

facteur¹, -trice [faktœr, -tris] **1** *nm,f (employé des Postes) Br* postman, *Am* mailman **2** *nm (de pianos, de clavecins)* maker; *(d'orgues)* builder

facteur² *nm* **(a)** *(élément)* factor; **le f. temps** the time factor **(b)** *Math* factor

factice [faktis] *adj* **(a)** *(faux)* imitation **(b)** *Fig (sourire)* forced; *(gaieté)* false

faction [faksjõ] *nf* **(a)** *(groupe)* faction **(b)** *Mil* guard duty; **être de** *ou* **en f.** to be on guard duty

factotum [faktɔtɔm] *nm* factotum

factuel, -elle [faktɥɛl] *adj* factual

facturation [faktyrasjɔ̃] *nf* invoicing, billing

facture¹ [faktyr] *nf* (**a**) *(style) (d'une œuvre)* construction; *(d'un artiste)* style (**b**) *(de pianos, de clavecins)* making; *(d'orgues)* building

facture² *nf (document)* invoice, bill; **faire** *ou* **dresser une f.** to make out an invoice; **f. d'électricité/de gaz** electricity/gas bill; **f. détaillée** itemized invoice

facturer [faktyre] *vt* to invoice

facturette [faktyrɛt] *nf* credit card sales slip

facultatif, -ive [fakyltatif, -iv] *adj* optional

faculté [fakylte] *nf* (**a**) *(de médecine, de droit)* faculty (**b**) *(pouvoir)* capacity (**de** for) (**c**) **facultés mentales** faculties; **ne plus avoir toutes ses facultés** to no longer have all one's faculties

fada [fada] *Fam* **1** *adj* crazy **2** *nmf* nutcase, *Am* wacko

fadaise [fadɛz] *nf* silly remark; **dire des fadaises** to talk nonsense

fadasse [fadas] *adj Fam* insipid

fade [fad] *adj* insipid

fadeur [fadœr] *nf* insipidness

fagot [fago] *nm* bundle of firewood; *Fig* **de derrière les fagots** *(bouteille de vin)* for special occasions; *(compliment, idée)* remarkable

fagoté, -e [fagote] *adj Péj* **mal/bizarrement f.** badly/oddly dressed

faiblard, -e [fɛblar, -ard] *adj Fam* a bit weak

faible [fɛbl] **1** *adj* (**a**) *(physiquement, moralement)* weak; (**b**) *(raisonnement, plaisanterie)* weak; **être f. en qch** *(élève)* to be weak at sth (**c**) *(voix, odeur, lumière)* faint; *(vent)* light; **et le terme est f.!** and that's putting it mildly! (**d**) *(quantité)* small; *(prix, revenu)* low; *(avantage, chance, espoir)* slight; *(vitesse)* low; **à une f. hauteur/profondeur** not very high up/deep down **2** *nmf* weakling; **les faibles d'esprit** the feeble-minded **3** *nm* **avoir un f. pour qn/qch** to have a soft spot for sb/a weakness for sth

faiblement [fɛbləmɑ̃] *adv (résister, protester)* weakly, feebly; *(éclairer)* faintly

faiblesse [fɛblɛs] *nf* (**a**) *(physique, morale)* weakness; **avoir la f. de faire qch** to be weak enough to do sth; **donner des signes de f.** *(appareil)* to be showing signs of wear and tear; *(personne)* to be looking weak (**b**) *(médiocrité)* weakness (**en** at) (**c**) *(malaise)* **avoir une f.** to feel faint

faiblir [fɛblir] *vi* (**a**) *(devenir faible) (personne, monnaie)* to weaken; *(lumière)* to grow weaker; *(vent)* to drop (**b**) *(niveau scolaire)* to decrease; *(élève)* to get weaker

faïence [fajɑ̃s] *nf* (**a**) *(matière)* earthenware (**b**) *(objet)* piece of earthenware; **faïences** earthenware

faïencerie [fajɑ̃sri] *nf* (**a**) *(articles)* earthenware (**b**) *(fabrique)* pottery (works) (**c**) *(commerce)* pottery (trade)

faille [faj] *nf* (**a**) *(dans un raisonnement)* flaw; *(dans une amitié)* rift; **sans f.** *(raisonnement)* flawless; *(fidélité)* unwavering (**b**) *Géol* fault

faillir [fajir] *vt* (**a**) **j'ai failli tomber** I nearly *or* almost fell; **j'ai bien failli me noyer** I very nearly drowned **2 faillir à** *vt ind Litt (réputation)* not to live up to; *(devoir)* to fail in

faillite [fajit] *nf* (**a**) *(d'entreprise)* bankruptcy; **être en f.** to be bankrupt; **faire f.** to go bankrupt (**b**) *(échec)* failure

faim [fɛ̃] *nf* hunger; **avoir f.** to be hungry; *Fig* **avoir f. de qch** to hunger for sth; *Fam* **avoir une grosse/petite f.** to be

very hungry/a bit hungry; **avoir une f. de loup** to be ravenous; **rester sur sa f.** to remain hungry; *Fig* to be left unsatisfied

fainéant, -e [fɛneɑ̃, -ɑ̃t] **1** *adj* lazy, idle **2** *nmf* idler

fainéanter [fɛneɑ̃te] *vi* to idle about

fainéantise [fɛneɑ̃tiz] *nf* laziness, idleness

faire [36] [fɛr] **1** *vt* (**a**) *(fabriquer, produire)* to make; *(tache, trace)* to leave; **f. du bruit** to make some noise; **f. de la fumée** to give off smoke; **f. une erreur** to make a mistake; **f. du blé/de la vigne** to grow wheat/grapes; *Fam* **des femmes comme ça, on n'en fait plus** they don't make women like that any more; **f. un enfant à qn** to make sb pregnant; **f. des compliments à qn** to compliment sb; **je ferai de lui un homme/un avocat** I'll make a man/a lawyer of him; **qu'est-ce que je vais f. de lui?** what am I going to do with him?; **qu'est-ce que tu vas f. de ce vieux bidon?** what are you going to do with that old can?; **qu'est-ce que j'ai fait de mes clés?** what have I done with my keys?

(**b**) *(effectuer) (changements, effort, grimace, mouvement)* to make; **f. le ménage/la vaisselle** to do the housework/the washing-up; **f. un pas en avant** to step forward; **faire demi-tour** to turn round; **f. une école de commerce** to study at a business school; **f. une licence** to study for a degree; **c'est moi qui fais tout ici** I have to do everything round here; **voilà une bonne chose de faite** that's one thing out of the way; **ce qui est fait est fait** what's done is done; **c'est bien fait pour elle** it serves her right

(**c**) *(occasionner)* **f. de la peine à qn** to hurt sb; **qu'est-ce que tu lui as fait?** what have you done to her? *Fam* **f. des ennuis à qn** to make trouble for sb; **ça m'a fait quelque chose/un choc** it upset/shocked me; **ça a fait du scandale** it caused a scandal; **ça ne fait rien** it doesn't matter; **qu'est-ce que ça peut faire?** what difference does it make?; **ça fait mauvais effet** it gives a bad impression; **le médicament n'a pas fait effet** the medicine didn't take effect

(**d**) *(changer)* **on ne peut rien y f.** nothing can be done about it; *Fam* **rien à f.!** nothing doing!

(**e**) *(subir)* to have; **f. une dépression** to have depression; *Fam* **f. une pneumonie/une grippe** to have pneumonia/(the) flu; *Fam* **il m'a encore fait une grippe!** he's gone and got the flu again!

(**f**) *(pratiquer)* **f. du tennis/football** to play tennis/soccer; **f. de la voile** to sail; **f. du violon/piano** to play the violin/the piano; **f. du japonais/de l'allemand** to do Japanese/German

(**g**) *(constituer)* to make; **il ferait un excellent mari/pompier** he would make an excellent husband/fireman; **f. l'affaire** to do the trick; **c'est cela qui fait ton charme** that's what gives you your charm; **cette chambre fait aussi bureau** this bedroom also serves as an office

(**h**) *(s'occuper à)* to do; **qu'est-ce qu'il fait dans la vie?** what does he do for a job?; **qu'est-ce que tu fais demain?** what are you doing tomorrow?; **f. des études** to study; **qu'est-ce que tu fais ici?** what are you doing here?

(**i**) *(parcourir)* to do; **f. 100 kilomètres par jour** to do 100 kilometres a day; **f. la fuite toute la ville pour te retrouver** he searched the whole town for her; **f. du cent à l'heure** to do 100 km/h

(**j**) *(indique une mesure, une quantité)* to be; **la table fait 1 mètre de long** the table is 1 metre long; **deux et deux font quatre** two and two are *or* make four; **combien ça fait en dollars?** how much is that in dollars?; **le bébé fait cinq kilos** the baby weighs five kilos

(**k**) *(agir comme)* **f. l'imbécile** to play the fool; **f. l'innocent** to play the innocent; **f. l'important** to act important; **il fait celui qui n'a pas entendu** he pretends he hasn't heard

(**l**) *(sembler)* to look; **il fait jeune/français** he looks young/French (**m**) *(dire)* to say; "**à demain!**", **fit-elle** "see you tomorrow!", she said; **ça a fait plouf** it went splash (**n**) *(suivi d'un infinitif)* **f. voir qch à qn** to show sb sth; **f. traverser qn** to help sb across; **f. faire qch à qn** to make sb do sth; **elle m'a fait ranger ma chambre** she made me tidy up my bedroom; **f. réparer qch** to get *or* have sth repaired; **f. construire une maison** to have a house built; **elle ne fait que se plaindre** she's always complaining; **je ne fais que répéter ses paroles** I'm just repeating what she said (**o**) *(pour remplacer un verbe)* **il devait arroser les plantes mais il ne l'a pas fait** he was meant to water the plants but he didn't; **mais faites donc!** please do!

2 *vi* (**a**) *(agir)* to do; **f. vite** to be quick; **fais comme tu voudras** do as you like; **f. pour le mieux** to do one's best; **f. comme chez soi** to make oneself at home; **comment f.?** how can I/we do it?; *Fam* **il faut f. avec** it'll have to do (**b**) *Fam (faire ses besoins)* to go to the toilet

3 *v impersonnel* (**a**) *(indique un état)* to be; **il fait froid/chaud** it's cold/hot; **il fait beau** it's nice; **il fait 15 degrés** it's 15 degrees; **il fait jour/nuit** it's light/night (**b**) *(indique la distance, la durée)* **ça fait un mois qu'il est parti** he's been gone for a month; **ça fait une heure que je t'attends** I've been waiting for you for an hour; **ça fait 500 kilomètres que nous roulons** we've been driving for 500 kilometres

4 **se faire** *vpr* (**a**) *(avoir lieu)* **finalement ça ne s'est jamais fait** nothing happened in the end; **comment se fait-il que...?** how is it that...? (**b**) *(être pratiqué)* to be done; **ça se fait beaucoup cette année** it's the in thing this year (**c**) *(être acceptable)* **ça se fait** it's the done thing; **ça ne se fait pas** it's not the done thing (**d**) *(être fabriqué)* to be made (**e**) *(se confectionner)* **se f. un lit** to make a bed for oneself; **se f. une bibliothèque** to build up a library; **se f. un sandwich** to make oneself a sandwich; **se f. les ongles** to do one's nails (**f**) *(fromage, vin)* to mature; *(chaussures)* to wear in (**g**) *(provoquer)* **se f. mal** to hurt oneself; **se f. une entorse au poignet** to sprain one's wrist; **se f. du souci** to worry; **se f. une opinion** to form an opinion; **se f. des amis/des ennemis** to make friends/enemies; *Fam* **s'en f.** to worry; **elle ne s'en fait pas celle-là!** *(elle a du culot)* she's got a nerve!; *(elle a beaucoup d'argent)* she hasn't got a care in the world! (**h**) *(s'ériger en)* **se f. le défenseur des opprimés** to become established as a defender of the oppressed (**i**) *(devenir)* **se f. vieux** to get old; **se f. beau** to do oneself up; **se f. moine** to become a monk; **il se fait tard** it's getting late (**j**) *(avec un infinitif)* **se f. insulter** to get abused; **se f. couper les cheveux** to have one's hair cut; **se f. prêter qch** to borrow sth; **se f. refaire le nez** to have a nose job (**k**) *(s'habituer)* **se f. à qch** to get used to sth (**l**) *(l'un l'autre)* **se f. des cadeaux** to give each other presents; **se f. des reproches** to blame each other (**m**) *Fam* **il faut se le f. celui-là!** what a pain in the neck!

faire-part [fɛrpar] *nm inv* announcement

faire-valoir [fɛrvalwar] *nm inv (personne)* foil

fair-play [fɛrplɛ] **1** *adj inv* **être f.** to play fair **2** *nm* fair play

fais *voir* faire

faisabilité [fəzabilite] *nf* feasibility

faisable [fəzabl] *adj* feasible

faisan [fəzã] *nm* pheasant

faisandé, -e [fəzãde] *adj (gibier)* high

faisane [fəzan] *adj f & nf* **(poule) f.** hen pheasant

faisceau, -x [fɛso] *nm* (**a**) *(rayons)* beam; **f. hertzien**

electromagnetic wave; **f. lumineux** beam of light (**b**) *Fig (de preuves)* body

faiseur, -euse [fəzœr, -øz] **1** *nm,f* maker; **f. d'embarras** fusspot; **f. de miracles** miracle worker **2** *nf* **faiseuse d'anges** backstreet abortionist

faisons *voir* faire

faisselle [fɛsɛl] *nf (fromage)* = type of soft white cheese; *(récipient)* cheese drainer

fait¹, -e *pp voir* faire

fait², -e [fɛ, fɛt] *adj* (**a**) *(fabriqué)* **tout f.** *(idée, expression)* fixed (**b**) *(adapté)* **être f. pour qn/qch** to be made for sb/sth; **ils sont faits l'un pour l'autre** they're made for each other; **être f. pour faire qch** *(personne)* to be cut out to do sth (**c**) *(bâti)* *Litt ou Hum* **être bien f. de sa personne** to be good-looking (**d**) *(maquillé)* **avoir les ongles/les yeux faits** wearing nail polish/eye make-up (**e**) *(fromage)* ripe

fait³ *nm* (**a**) *(acte)* act; **les faits et gestes de qn** sb's every move; **prendre qn sur le f.** to catch sb in the act *or* red-handed; **prendre f. et cause pour qn** to stand up for sb (**b**) *(réalité)* fact; **le f. d'habiter en ville** living in town; **mettre qn devant le f. accompli** to present sb with a fait accompli; **c'est un f. acquis** it's an established fact (**c**) *(point précis)* **aller droit au f.** to get straight to the point; **en venir au f.** to come to the point (**d**) *(événement)* event; **un f. nouveau** a new development; **un f. divers** a news item; **faits divers** *(rubrique)* ≃ news in brief (**e**) *(locutions)* **au f.** by the way; **en f., de f.** in fact, as a matter of fact; **de ce f.** for that reason

faîte [fɛt] *nm* (**a**) *(d'un toit)* ridge; *(d'un arbre, d'une maison)* top; *(d'une montagne)* summit (**b**) *Fig* **le f. de la gloire** the height of glory

faites *voir* faire

faitout *nm*, **fait-tout** *nm inv* [fɛtu] stewpot

fakir [fakir] *nm* fakir

falaise [falɛz] *nf* cliff

fallacieux, -euse [talasjø, -øz] *adj (prétexte)* false; *(argument, raisonnement)* specious; *(apparence)* misleading

falloir [37] [falwar] **1** *v impersonnel* (**a**) *(être nécessaire)* **faut-il tout cela?** is all that necessary?; **je l'ai fait parce qu'il le fallait** I did it because I had to; **il lui faut un nouveau pardessus** he needs a new coat; **il me faudrait un kilo de pommes de terre** I need a kilo of potatoes; **je lui ai tout donné, qu'est-ce qu'il lui faut de plus!** I've given him everything, what more does he want!; **il m'a fallu une semaine pour le faire** it took me a week to do it; **il faut partir** I/we/you/*etc* must go *or* have to go; **il lui faut se dépêcher** she has to hurry; **il fallait le dire!** why didn't you say so?; **je vous en prie, il ne fallait pas!** you shouldn't have!; **il faudrait qu'elle reste** she ought to stay; **il ne faudrait pas que je vous mette en retard** I'd better not make you late; **il faut toujours que tu fasses des histoires!** why do you always have to cause such a fuss!; **il a fallu qu'elle le raconte à tout le quartier** she had to go and tell the whole neighbourhood! (**b**) *(locutions)* *Fam* **il faut ce qu'il faut** you might as well do things in style!; **il faut voir** *(il faut attendre)* we'll have to wait and see; *(il faut réfléchir)* I/we will have to think about it; *Fam* **elle l'a répondu, faut voir comment!** you wouldn't believe the way she answered him! **2** **s'en falloir** *vpr* **il s'en est fallu de peu** *ou* **peu s'en est fallu qu'elle ne meure** she very nearly died; **15 euros ou peu s'en faut** the best part of 15 euros; **loin** *ou* **tant s'en faut** far from it

fallu *voir* falloir

falot¹ [falo] *nm (lanterne)* lantern

falot², **-e** [falo, -ɔt] *adj* dreary, drab

falsification [falsifikasjɔ̃] *nf (de documents, de comptes)* falsification; *(d'une signature)* forging

falsifier [66] [falsifje] *vt (document, comptes)* to falsify; *(signature)* to forge

falzar [falzar] *nm Fam Br* trousers, *Am* pants

famé, **-e** [fame] *adj* **mal f.** disreputable

famélique [famelik] *adj* half-starved

fameusement [famøzmɑ̃] *adv Fam (très)* incredibly

fameux, **-euse** [famø, -øz] *adj* **(a)** *(célèbre)* famous **(pour** for); **c'est donc ça, ton f. régime!** so this is your famous diet! **(b)** *Fam (excellent)* brilliant; **pas f.** not much good

familial, **-e**, **-aux**, **-ales** [familjal, -o] **1** *adj (vie, atmosphère)* family; *(entreprise, hôtel)* family-run; *(paquet, format)* family-size
2 *nf* **familiale** *(auto) Br* estate car, *Am* station wagon

familiariser [familjarize] **1** *vt* **f. qn avec qch** to familiarize sb with sth, to get sb used to sth
2 se familiariser *vpr* **se f. avec qch** *(en le pratiquant)* to familiarize oneself with sth; *(en s'y habituant)* to get used to sth; *(lieu)* to get to know sth

familiarité [familjarite] *nf* **(a)** *(désinvolture)* informality **(b) familiarités** *(libertés)* familiarities

familier, **-ère** [familje, -ɛr] **1** *adj* **(a)** *(désinvolte)* informal **(avec** with) **(b)** *(langage, expression)* colloquial **(c)** *(connu)* familiar **(à** to)
2 *nm,f (client)* regular visitor **(de** to)

familièrement [familjɛrmɑ̃] *adv* familiarly; **parler f. à qn** to be familiar with sb

famille [famij] *nf* **(a)** *(proches)* family; **de bonne f.** from a good family; **en f.** with one's family; **c'est de f.** it runs in the family; *Fam* **un repas des familles** a cosy little meal; **f. monoparentale** one-parent family; **f. nombreuse** large family **(b)** *(d'animaux, de langues, de plantes)* family; **f. littéraire/politique** literary/political circle

famine [famin] *nf* famine; **crier f.** to be starving

fan [fan], **fana** [fana] *nmf Fam* fan

fanal, **-aux** [fanal, -o] *nm (lanterne)* lantern

fanatique [fanatik] **1** *adj* fanatical **(de** about)
2 *nmf* fanatic; **f. de tennis** tennis fanatic

fanatiser [fanatize] *vt* to make fanatical

fanatisme [fanatism] *nm* fanaticism

faner [fane] **1** *vi (fleur)* to wither; *Fig (beauté, teint)* to fade
2 se faner *vpr (fleur)* to wither; *Fig (beauté, teint)* to fade

fanes [fan] *nfpl (de carottes, de radis)* tops

fanfare [fɑ̃far] *nf (orchestre)* brass band; **réveil en f.** brutal awakening

fanfaron, **-onne** [fɑ̃farɔ̃, -ɔn] **1** *adj* boastful
2 *nm,f* braggart; **faire le f.** to brag, to boast

fanfaronnades [fɑ̃farɔnad] *nfpl* bragging, boasting

fanfaronner [fɑ̃farɔne] *vi* to brag, to boast

fanfreluches [fɑ̃frəlyʃ] *nfpl Péj* frills

fange [fɑ̃ʒ] *nf Litt* mire

fanion [fanjɔ̃] *nm (d'un club)* pennant; *(balise)* flag; **fanions** *(guirlandes)* bunting

fanon [fanɔ̃] *nm (de baleine)* whalebone

fantaisie [fɑ̃tezi] **1** *adj inv* **collants f.** patterned tights; **kirsch f.** kirsch-flavoured liqueur
2 *nf* **(a)** *(envie)* whim; **faire qch à sa f.** to do sth as the fancy takes one **(b)** *(créativité)* imagination **(c)** *(œuvre musicale)* fantasia

fantaisiste [fɑ̃tezist] **1** *adj (personne)* eccentric;

(interprétation) fanciful; *(horaires, mode de vie)* unorthodox
2 *nmf (comédien)* variety artist

fantasmagorique [fɑ̃tasmagɔrik] *adj* phantasmagorical

fantasme [fɑ̃tasm] *nm* fantasy

fantasmer [fɑ̃tasme] *vi* to fantasize **(sur** about)

fantasque [fɑ̃task] *adj* whimsical

fantassin [fɑ̃tasɛ̃] *nm* foot soldier, infantryman

fantastique [fɑ̃tastik] **1** *adj* **(a)** *(littérature, conte, film)* fantasy **(b)** *Fam (excellent)* fantastic **(c)** *(créature)* fantastic
2 *nm* **le f.** the fantastic; *(littérature)* fantasy literature

fantoche [fɑ̃tɔʃ] **1** *nm* puppet
2 *adj* **gouvernement f.** puppet government

fantomatique [fɑ̃tɔmatik] *adj* ghostly

fantôme [fɑ̃tom] **1** *nm* ghost, phantom
2 *adj (ville, train)* ghost

fanzine [fɑ̃zin] *nm* fanzine

faon [fɑ̃] *nm* fawn

far [far] *nm* **f. breton** = custard tart with prunes

faramineux, **-euse** [faraminø, -øz] *adj Fam* phenomenal

farandole [farɑ̃dɔl] *nf* farandole

farce [fars] *nf* **(a)** *(tour)* (practical) joke, prank; **faire une f. à qn** to play a (practical) joke on sb; **magasin de farces et attrapes** joke shop **(b)** *(préparation culinaire)* stuffing **(c)** *(pièce de théâtre)* farce

farceur, **-euse** [farsœr, -øz] **1** *adj* mischievous
2 *nm,f* (practical) joker, prankster

farcir [farsir] **1** *vt* **(a)** *(volaille, légume)* to stuff **(b)** *Fam (remplir)* to cram **(de** with)
2 se farcir *vpr Fam* **se f. qch** *(corvée)* to get landed with sth; **se f. qn** *(supporter)* to put up with sb

fard [far] *nm* make-up; *Fam* **piquer un f.** to go red; **f. à joues** blusher; **f. à paupières** eye shadow

fardeau, **-x** [fardo] *nm* load; *Fig* burden

farder [farde] **1** *vt (maquiller)* to make up
2 se farder *vpr* to put on one's make-up; **se f. les yeux** to put eye shadow on

farfadet [farfadɛ] *nm* goblin

farfelu, **-e** [farfəly] *Fam* **1** *adj (personne, idée)* weird
2 *nm,f* weirdo

farfouiller [farfuje] *vi Fam* to rummage **(dans** through)

farine [farin] *nf* flour; **f. de blé** wheat flour; **f. de maïs** *Br* cornflour, *Am* cornstarch

farineux, **-euse** [farinø, -øz] **1** *adj* **(a)** *Péj (pommes de terre, banane)* floury **(b)** *(contenant de la fécule)* starchy
2 *nmpl* starchy food

farniente [farnjɛnte] *nm* idleness

farouche [faruʃ] *adj* **(a)** *(animal)* timid; *(personne)* shy **(b)** *(haine, air, regard)* fierce

farouchement [faruʃmɑ̃] *adv* fiercely

fart [fart] *nm (ski)* wax

fascicule [fasikyl] *nm (d'une publication)* instalment; *(brochure)* brochure

fascinant, **-e** [fasinɑ̃, -ɑ̃t] *adj* fascinating

fascination [fasinasjɔ̃] *nf* fascination

fasciner [fasine] *vt* **(a)** *(impressionner)* to fascinate **(b)** *(charmer)* to captivate

fascisme [faʃism] *nm* fascism

fasciste [faʃist] *adj & nmf* fascist

fasse *etc voir* **faire**

faste¹ [fast] *nm* splendour

faste² *adj (jour)* lucky; *(période)* good

fast-food (*pl* **fast-foods**) [fastfud] *nm* fast-food restaurant

fastidieux, -euse [fastidjø, -øz] *adj* tedious

fastoche [fastɔʃ] *adj Fam* dead easy

fastueux, -euse [fastɥø, -øz] *adj* sumptuous

fat [fa(t)] *nm* conceited person

fatal, -e, -als, -ales [fatal] *adj* (a) *(mortel)* fatal; *Fig* fatal (à for); **le choc lui a été f.** the shock killed him; *Ordinat* **erreur fatale** fatal error (b) *(inévitable)* inevitable

fatalement [fatalmɑ̃] *adv* inevitably

fatalisme [fatalism] *nm* fatalism

fataliste [fatalist] **1** *adj* fatalistic **2** *nmf* fatalist

fatalité [fatalite] *nf* (a) *(malédiction)* bad luck (b) *(inévitabilité)* inevitability

fatidique [fatidik] *adj* fateful

fatigant, -e [fatigɑ̃, -ɑ̃t] *adj* (a) *(épuisant)* tiring; **c'est f. pour le cœur/les yeux** it's a strain on the heart/the eyes (b) *(ennuyeux)* tiresome

fatigue [fatig] *nf* tiredness; **tomber** *ou* **être mort de f.** to be dead tired; **f. nerveuse** nervous exhaustion; **f. oculaire** eyestrain

fatigué, -e [fatige] *adj* (a) *(las)* tired; **f. par sa promenade** tired from one's walk; **f. par le voyage** travel-weary; **f. de qn/qch** tired of sb/sth; **f. de faire qch** tired or weary of doing sth (b) *(estomac, foie)* upset; *(cœur)* strained

fatiguer [fatige] **1** *vt* (a) *(personne)* to tire (out); *(yeux, cœur)* to strain; *(estomac, foie)* to upset; *Ironique* **si ça ne te fatigue pas trop** if it's not too much of an effort (b) *(ennuyer)* to wear out (c) *Fam* **f. la salade** to toss the salad **2** *vi (personne)* to get tired; *(moteur, voiture)* to labour **3** **se fatiguer** *vpr* (a) *(s'épuiser)* to get tired; **se f. à faire qch** to tire oneself out doing sth; **se f. les yeux/le cœur** to strain one's eyes/heart; *Ironique* **tu ne t'es pas fatigué** you didn't exactly strain yourself; **ne te fatigue pas, je m'en charge** don't bother, I'll see to it (b) *(se lasser)* **se f. de qn/qch** to get tired of sb/sth

fatras [fatra] *nm* jumble, muddle

faubourg [fobur] *nm* suburb

fauche [foʃ] *nf Fam* thieving; **il y a de la f.** there are thieves about

fauché, -e [foʃe] *adj Fam* **f. (comme les blés)** (flat) broke

faucher [foʃe] *vt* (a) *(herbe, champ)* to mow; *(blé)* to reap (b) *(piéton)* to mow down; **se faire f. par une voiture** to be mown down by a car (c) *Fam (voler)* to pinch; **se faire f. qch** to get sth pinched

faucheur, -euse [foʃœr, -øz] *nmf (de blé)* reaper; *(d'herbe)* mower **2** *nm (insecte) Br* harvestman, *Am* daddy-long-legs **3** *nf* **faucheuse** *(machine) (pour le blé)* reaper; *(pour l'herbe)* mower; **la Faucheuse** *(la Mort)* the Grim Reaper

faucheux [foʃø] *nm Br* harvestman, *Am* daddy-long-legs

faucille [fosij] *nf* sickle; **la f. et le marteau** the hammer and sickle

faucon [fokɔ̃] *nm* falcon, hawk; **f. pèlerin** peregrine falcon

faudra *etc voir* **falloir**

faufiler [fofile] **1** *vt* to tack, to baste **2** **se faufiler** *vpr (à travers la foule)* to work one's way (à travers through); **il s'était faufilé parmi les invités** he had slipped in with the guests

faune [fon] *nf (animaux)* fauna, animal life; *Fig & Péj* **la f. des boîtes de nuit** the nightclub set; **elle fréquente une f. étrange** she mixes with a strange crowd

faussaire [fosɛr] *nmf* forger

fausse [fos] *adj voir* **faux¹**

faussement [fosmɑ̃] *adv* (a) *(injustement)* wrongly, falsely (b) *(de façon hypocrite)* deceptively

fausser [fose] **1** *vt* (a) *(clef, axe)* to buckle, to bend (b) *(réalité, résultat)* to distort (c) **f. compagnie à qn** to give sb the slip **2** **se fausser** *vpr* (a) *(voix)* to become strained (b) *(clef, axe)* to buckle, to bend

fausset [fosɛ] *nm Mus* falsetto

fausseté [foste] *nf* (a) *(d'une information, d'un raisonnement)* falseness (b) *(hypocrisie)* duplicity

faut *voir* **falloir**

faute [fot] *nf* (a) *(erreur)* mistake, error; *(au football)* foul; *(au tennis)* fault; **faire une f.** to make a mistake *or* an error; **être en f.** to be at fault, prendre qn en f. to catch sb out; **c'est de ma f.!** it's my fault!; **f. d'étourderie** *ou* **d'inattention** careless mistake; **f. de français** grammatical mistake; **f. de frappe** typing mistake; **f. d'orthographe** spelling mistake; **f. professionnelle** professional misconduct (b) *(manque)* **sans f.** without fail; **f. de temps** for lack of time; **f. de mieux** for lack *or* want of anything better; **f. de quoi** failing which, otherwise; **ce n'est pas f. d'avoir essayé** it's not for want of trying

fauteuil [fotœj] *nm* (a) *(siège)* armchair, easy chair; **f. à bascule** rocking chair; **f. d'orchestre** seat in the *Br* stalls *or Am* orchestra; **f. pivotant** swivel chair; **f. roulant** wheelchair (b) *Fig (à l'Académie française)* seat

tauteur [fotœr] *nm* **t. de troubles** troublemaker

fautif, -ive [fotif, -iv] *adj* (a) *(coupable)* at fault, in the wrong (b) *(incorrect)* faulty **2** *nm,f (coupable)* person at fault *or* in the wrong

fauve [fov] **1** *adj* (a) *(roux)* fawn (b) *(odeur)* musky (c) *(en peinture)* Fauvist **2** *nm* (a) *(grand félin)* big cat, **sentir le f.** to smell of sweat (b) *(couleur)* fawn (c) *(en peinture)* Fauvist

fauvette [fovɛt] *nf* warbler

fauvisme [fovism] *nm* Fauvism

faux¹, fausse [fo, fos] **1** *adj* (a) *(incorrect)* wrong; **c'est un f. problème** that's not the real problem; **f. ami** false friend; **faire une fausse couche** to have a miscarriage; **faire une fausse note** to hit a wrong note; **faire fausse route** to take the wrong road; *Fig* to be on the wrong track; **faire un f. sens** *(en traduisant)* to give an inaccurate translation; *(en français)* to give an inaccurate definition (b) *(mensonger)* false, untrue; *Fam* **c'est un f. jeton** *ou* **cul** he's two-faced; **f. témoignage** perjury (c) *(injustifié) (alerte, espoirs)* false (d) *(postiche)* false (e) *(billet, pièce, document)* forged; *(tableau, bijoux)* fake; *(plafond)* false (f) *Péj (hypocrite)* false **2** *adv (chanter, sonner)* out of tune, off key; *Fig* **sonner f.** not to ring true **3** *nm* (a) *(tableau, sculpture)* fake (b) *(document)* forgery; **f. en écriture** forgery

faux² *nf* scythe

faux-filet (*pl* **faux-filets**) [fofilɛ] *nm* sirloin

faux-fuyant (*pl* **faux-fuyants**) [fofɥijɑ̃] *nm (prétexte)* subterfuge

faux-monnayeur (*pl* **faux-monnayeurs**) [fomɔnɛjœr] *nm* forger, counterfeiter

faux-semblant (*pl* **faux-semblants**) [fosɑ̃blɑ̃] *nm* pretence, sham

faveur [favœr] *nf* (a) *(considération)* favour; **avoir la f. de qn** to be in favour with sb; **de f.** *(marques)* of favour; *(régime, traitement)* special (b) *(privilège)* favour; **faire une f. à qn** to do sb a favour (c) **être en f. de qch** *(être favorable à)* to be in

favour of sth; **en ma/sa f.** *(à mon/son avantage)* in my/her favour, to my/her advantage **(d)** *(ruban)* favour
favorable [favɔrabl] *adj* favourable **(à** to)
favorablement [favɔrabləmɑ̃] *adv* favourably
favori, -ite [favɔri, -it] *adj & nm,f* favourite
favoris [favɔri] *nmpl* sideburns
favorisé, -e [favɔrize] *adj (milieu, famille)* fortunate
favoriser [favɔrize] *vt* **(a)** *(avantager) (personne)* to favour **(b)** *(encourager) (croissance, emploi)* to encourage, to promote
favoritisme [favɔritism] *nm* favouritism
fax [faks] *nm (appareil)* fax (machine); *(message)* fax; **envoyer qch par f.** to send sth by fax, to fax sth; **f. modem** fax modem
faxer [fakse] *vt* to fax
fayot [fajo] *nm Fam* **(a)** *(haricot sec)* bean **(b)** *(élève)* crawler
fayotage [fajotaʒ] *nm Fam* crawling
fayoter [fajote] *vi Fam* to crawl
fébrile [febril] *adj aussi Fig* feverish
fébrilement [febrilmɑ̃] *adv* feverishly
fébrilité [febrilite] *nf* feverishness
fécond, -e [fekɔ̃, -ɔ̃d] *adj (femme, femelle, terre, imagination)* fertile; *(écrivain)* prolific; *Fig* **f. en qch** *(période, moment)* full of sth
fécondation [fekɔ̃dasjɔ̃] *nf (d'une femme, d'une femelle)* impregnation; *(d'un œuf, d'un ovule)* fertilization; **f. artificielle** artificial insemination; **f. in vitro** in vitro fertilization
féconder [fekɔ̃de] *vt (femme, femelle)* to impregnate; *(œuf, ovule)* to fertilize
fécondité [fekɔ̃dite] *nf* **(a)** *(d'une femme, d'une femelle)* fertility **(b)** *(d'un écrivain)* productiveness
fécule [fekyl] *nf* starch
féculent, -e [fekylɑ̃, -ɑ̃t] **1** *adj* starchy **2** *nm* starchy food
FED [efəde] *nm (abrév* **Fonds européen de développement)** EDF
FEDER [fedɛr] *nm (abrév* **Fonds européen de développement régional)** ERDF
fédéral, -e, -aux, -ales [federal, -o] *adj* federal
fédéralisme [federalism] *nm* federalism
fédéraliste [federalist] *adj & nmf* federalist
fédérateur, -trice [federatœr, -tris] *adj* federal
fédération [federasjɔ̃] *nf* federation
fédéré, -e [federe] *adj* federate
fée [fe] *nf* fairy; *Hum* **une f. du logis** a wonderful home-maker
feed-back [fidbak] *nm* feedback
féerie [feri, feeri] *nf (spectacle magnifique)* enchanting display
féerique [ferik, feerik] *adj (personnage, monde)* fairy; *(vision)* enchanting
feignais *etc voir* **feindre**
feignant, -e [fɛɲɑ̃, -ɑ̃t] *Fam* **1** *adj* bone idle **2** *nm,f* idler
feindre [54] [fɛ̃dr] *vt (maladie, sentiment)* to feign; **inutile de f.** it's no use pretending; **f. de faire qch** to pretend to do sth
feint, -e [fɛ̃, fɛ̃t] *adj (maladie, joie)* feigned
feinte [fɛ̃t] *nf* **(a)** *(ruse)* ruse **(b)** *(au football, au rugby)* dummy
feinter [fɛ̃te] **1** *vt Fam (duper)* to take in **2** *vi (au football, au rugby)* to dummy

fêlé, -e [fele] *adj* **(a)** *(verre, voix)* cracked **(b)** *Fam (fou)* crackers, nuts
fêler [fele] *vt* to crack
félicitations [felisitasjɔ̃] *nfpl* congratulations **(pour** on)
féliciter [felisite] **1** *vt* to congratulate **(de/pour** on); **f. qn d'avoir fait qch** to congratulate sb on having done sth **2 se féliciter** *vpr* **se f. de qch/d'avoir fait qch** to congratulate oneself on sth/on having done sth
félin, -e [felɛ̃, -in] *adj & nm* feline
fêlure [felyr] *nf* crack
femelle [fəmɛl] *adj & nf* female
féminin, -e [feminɛ̃, -in] **1** *adj (personne, charme, visage)* feminine; *(hormone, population, sexe)* female; *(équipe, magazine, mode)* women's **2** *nm Grammaire* feminine; **au f.** in the feminine
féminiser [feminize] **1** *vt* **(a)** *(ouvrir aux femmes)* to increase the number of women in **(b)** *(rendre efféminé)* to make effeminate **2 se féminiser** *vpr* **(a)** *(profession, institution, carrière)* to attract more women **(b)** *(homme)* to become effeminate
féminisme [feminism] *nm* feminism
féministe [feminist] *adj & nmf* feminist
féminité [feminite] *nf* femininity
femme [fam] *nf* **(a)** *(adulte de sexe féminin)* woman; **des femmes, de la f.** *(libération, émancipation, droits)* women's; **la f. de ma vie** the love of my life; **elle est très f.** she's very feminine; *Fam* **une bonne f.** a woman; **f. d'affaires** businesswoman; **f. de chambre** *(dans un hôtel)* (chamber)maid; **f. fatale** femme fatale; **f. au foyer** housewife; **f. de ménage** cleaning lady; **f. du monde** society woman; **f. de tête** forceful woman **(b)** *(épouse)* wife
femmelette [famlɛt] *nf Péj (homme)* weakling
fémur [femyr] *nm* thighbone, *Spéc* femur
FEN [fɛn] *nf (abrév* **Fédération de l'Éducation Nationale)** = largest French teachers' union
fenaison [fənɛzɔ̃] *nf* haymaking
fendant, -e [fɑ̃dɑ̃, -ɑ̃t] *adj Fam* hilarious
fendiller [fɑ̃dije] **1** *vt (bois, vernis)* to crack; *(peau, lèvres)* to chap **2 se fendiller** *vpr (bois, vernis)* to crack; *(peau, lèvres)* to chap
fendre [fɑ̃dr] **1** *vt* **(a)** *(bois)* to split; *(pierre, sol)* to crack; **f. le cœur à qn** to break sb's heart **(b)** *(traverser) (flots, mer)* to plough through; *(air)* to cut through **2 se fendre** *vpr* **(a)** *(bois)* to split; *(pierre, sol)* to crack **(b)** *Fam* **se f. de qch** *(d'une somme)* to fork out sth; *(d'un cadeau)* to fork out on sth; **tu ne t'es pas fendu** *(ce n'était pas cher)* it didn't break the bank; *(tu ne t'es pas fatigué)* you didn't strain yourself **(c)** *Fam* **se f. la pipe** *ou* **la pêche** *ou* **la poire** to split one's sides (laughing)
fendu, -e [fɑ̃dy] *adj (jupe)* slit
fenêtre [fənɛtr] *nf* **(a)** *(ouverture)* window; **f. à guillotine** sash window **(b)** *Ordinat* window; **f. d'aide** help window; **f. déroulante** pull-down window
fennec [fenɛk] *nm* fennec
fenouil [fənuj] *nm* fennel
fente [fɑ̃t] *nf* **(a)** *(dans le bois)* split; *(dans le sol, dans un mur)* crack **(b)** *(d'une tirelire, d'une boîte aux lettres)* slot
féodal, -e, -aux, -ales [feɔdal, -o] *adj* feudal
féodalité [feɔdalite] *nf* feudalism
fer [fɛr] *nm* **(a)** *(métal)* iron; *Fig* **de f.** *(discipline, volonté)* iron; *(santé)* cast-iron; **croire qch dur comme f.** to believe very firmly in sth; **f. forgé** wrought iron **(b)** *(objet en fer)* **f. à cheval** horseshoe; *Fam* **les quatre fers en l'air** flat on one's back; *Fig* **f. de lance** spearhead **(c)** *(outil)* **f. à repasser** iron

donner un coup de f. à qch to iron sth; **marquer qch au f. rouge** to brand sth; **f. à souder** soldering iron **(d) fers** *(chaînes)* irons
ferai *etc voir* **faire**
fer-blanc *(pl* **fers-blancs)** [fɛrblɑ̃] *nm* tin(plate); **en f.** tin
ferblanterie [fɛrblɑ̃tri] *nf* **(a)** *(commerce)* tinplate trade **(b)** *(articles)* tinware
férié, -e [ferje] *adj* **lundi prochain est f.** next Monday is a (public) holiday
férir [ferir] *vt* **sans coup f.** without any difficulty
ferme¹ [fɛrm] **1** *adj* **(a)** *(dur)* firm **(b)** *Jur* **trois ans de prison f., trois ans fermes** three years' imprisonment **2** *adv (travailler)* hard; *(discuter)* keenly; **s'ennuyer f.** to be bored stiff
ferme² *nf* farm; **produits de la f.** farm produce
fermé, -e [fɛrme] *adj* **(a)** *(porte, récipient, boutique)* closed, shut; *(route)* closed **(b)** *(expression, visage)* impassive; **être f. à qch** *(ne pas être sensible à)* to have no appreciation of sth **(c)** *(société, club, milieu)* exclusive, select
fermement [fɛrməmɑ̃] *adv* firmly
ferment [fɛrmɑ̃] *nm aussi Fig* ferment
fermentation [fɛrmɑ̃tasjɔ̃] *nf* fermentation
fermenter [fɛrmɑ̃te] *vi* to ferment
fermer [fɛrme] **1** *vt* **(a)** *(porte, boîte, livre)* to close, to shut, *(maison)* to shut up; *(rideaux)* to close, to draw; *(vêtement)* to fasten, to do up; *(parenthèse)* to close; *(enveloppe)* to seal; **f. sa porte à qn** to close one's door to sb; **f. les yeux/la bouche** to close one's eyes/one's mouth; *Fig* **les yeux sur qch** to turn a blind eye to sth; *Fam* **je n'ai pas fermé l'œil** I didn't sleep a wink; *Fam* **f. sa gueule, la f.** to shut up, to shut one's mouth **(b)** *(frontière, pays)* to close off **(c)** *(robinet, eau, électricité)* to turn off **(d)** *(compte bancaire)* to close **(e)** *(entreprise) (temporairement)* to close, to shut; *(définitivement)* to close down; **f. boutique** to shut up shop **(f)** *Ordinat (fichier, fenêtre)* to close; *(commande)* to end **2** *vi* **(a)** *(porte, boîte)* to close, to shut, **f. bien/mal** to close/ not to close properly **(b)** *(entreprise, magasin) (temporairement)* to close, to shut; *(définitivement)* to close down **3 se fermer** *vpr* **(a)** *(porte, boîte, yeux)* to close, to shut; *(vêtement)* to fasten, to do up **(b)** *(visage)* to freeze; *(personne)* to clam up
fermeté [fɛrməte] *nf* firmness; **avec f.** firmly
fermeture [fɛrmətyr] *nf* **(a)** *(d'une porte)* closing, shutting; *(d'une route, d'une frontière, d'un débat)* closing **(b)** *(cessation d'activité)* closing; **heure de f.** closing time **(c)** *(d'un compte bancaire)* closing **(d) f. Éclair®** *ou* **à glissière** *Br* zip, *Am* zipper **(e)** *Ordinat (d'un fichier, d'une fenêtre)* closing; *(d'une commande)* ending
fermier, -ère [fɛrmje, -ɛr] **1** *adj (poulet)* free-range; *(beurre)* dairy **2** *nm,f* farmer
fermoir [fɛrmwar] *nm* clasp
féroce [ferɔs] *adj (animal, personne, critique)* ferocious; *(joie, moquerie)* savage; *(appétit)* ravenous
férocement [ferɔsmɑ̃] *adv* ferociously
férocité [ferɔsite] *nf* ferocity
Féroé [ferɔe] *nfpl* **les (îles) F.** the Faroe Islands, the Faroes
ferraille [fɛrɑj] *nf* **(a)** *(débris de fer)* scrap (iron); **mettre qch à la f.** to put sth on the scrap heap **(b)** *Fam (petite monnaie)* small change
ferré, -e [fɛre] *adj* **(a)** *(chaussure)* hobnailed; *(canne)* metal-tipped **(b)** *(calé)* **être f. en qch** to be well up in sth
ferrer [fɛre] *vt* **(a)** *(cheval)* to shoe **(b)** *(poisson)* to strike
ferreux, -euse [fɛrø, -øz] *adj* ferrous
ferronnerie [fɛrɔnri] *nf* **(a)** *(objets)* **f. (d'art)** (decorative)

ironwork **(b)** *(travail)* ironwork **(c)** *(atelier)* ironworks *(singulier)*
ferronnier, -ère [fɛrɔnje, -ɛr] *nm,f* **f. (d'art)** worker in wrought iron
ferroviaire [fɛrɔvjɛr] *adj (réseau, trafic, ligne) Br* railway, *Am* railroad; *(transports)* rail
ferrugineux, -euse [fɛryʒinø, -øz] *adj* ferruginous
ferrure [fɛryr] *nf* **(a)** *(garniture)* fitting **(b)** *(d'un cheval)* shoeing
ferry [fɛri] *nm* ferry
ferry-boat *(pl* **ferry-boats)** [fɛribot] *nm* ferry
fertile [fɛrtil] *adj aussi Fig* fertile; *Fig* **f. en qch** *(période)* full of sth
fertilisation [fɛrtilizasjɔ̃] *nf* fertilization
fertiliser [fɛrtilize] *vt* to fertilize
fertilité [fɛrtilite] *nf* fertility
féru, -e [fery] *adj* **f. de qch** passionately interested in sth
férule [feryl] *nf Litt* **être sous la f. de qn** to be under sb's sway
fervent, -e [fɛrvɑ̃, -ɑ̃t] **1** *adj* fervent; *(Catholique)* devout **2** *nm,f* devotee **(de** of**)**
ferveur [fɛrvœr] *nf* fervour; **avec f.** fervently
fesse [fɛs] *nf* buttock; **fesses** *Br* bottom, *Am* butt
fessée [fese] *nf* spanking; **donner une f. à qn** to give sb a spanking
fessier, -ère [fesje, -ɛr] **1** *adj (muscle)* buttock, *Spéc* gluteal **2** *nm (muscle)* gluteal muscle
festif, -ive [fɛstif, -iv] *adj* festive
festin [fɛstɛ̃] *nm* feast, banquet
festival, -als [fɛstival] *nm* festival; **le f. d'Avignon** = theatre festival held in Avignon, **le f. de Cannes** the Cannes film festival
festivités [fɛstivite] *nfpl* festivities
feston [fɛstɔ̃] *nm* **(a)** *(en broderie)* scallop; **à festons** scalloped **(b)** *(guirlande) & Archit* festoon
festoyer [fɛstwaje] *vi* to feast
feta [feta] *nf* feta (cheese)
fêtard, -e [fɛtar, -ard] *nm,f Fam* party animal
fête [fɛt] *nf* **(a)** *(célébration publique)* fête, fair; *(événement culturel)* festival; **f. foraine** funfair; **la f. des Mères/Pères** Mother's/Father's Day; **la f. de la Musique** = annual music festival held on 21 June; **la f. des Rois** Twelfth Night **(b)** *(soirée)* party; **organiser** *ou* **faire une f.** to have a party **(c)** *(manifestation de joie)* **en f.** in a festive mood; **avoir le cœur en f.** to be over the moon; *Fam* **faire la f.** to party; **être de la f.** to be one of the party; **faire f. à qn** to make a fuss of sb **(d)** *(du saint dont on porte le nom)* saint's day; *Ironique* **ça va être ta f.!** you're in for it! **(e)** *(jour chômé)* holiday; **les fêtes (de fin d'année)** the Christmas and New Year holidays; **f. légale** *Br* bank holiday, *Am* legal holiday; **f. nationale** national holiday; **la f. du Travail** Labour Day
Fête-Dieu *(pl* **Fêtes-Dieu)** [fɛtdjø] *nf* **la F.** Corpus Christi
fêter [fete] *vt* **(a)** *(anniversaire, événement)* to celebrate **(b)** *(personne)* to fête
fétiche [fetiʃ] **1** *adj* lucky **2** *nm (objet de culte)* fetish; *(mascotte)* mascot
fétichisme [fetiʃism] *nm* fetishism
fétide [fetid] *adj* fetid
fétu [fety] *nm* **f. (de paille)** wisp of straw
feu¹, -x [fø] **1** *nm* **(a)** *(élément, flammes, incendie)* fire; **mettre (le) f. à qch** to set fire to sth; **prendre f.** to catch fire; **allumer** *ou* **faire un f.** to make a fire; **au f.!** fire!; **en f.** *(lieu)* on fire; *Fig (joues, visage)* burning; **mettre une ville à**

f. et à sang to ransack a town; **être tout f.** to tout flamme to be burning with enthusiasm; **faire f.** de tout bois to use every available means; **ne pas faire long f.** not to last long; **dans le f.** de l'action in the heat of the action; *Fig* sous le **f.** des projecteurs in the limelight; *Vulg* avoir le **f.** au cul *(être pressé)* to be in a mad rush; *(sexuellement)* to be always gagging for it; **f. d'artifice** *(spectacle)* fireworks display; **f. de Bengale** Bengal light; **f. de camp** campfire; **f. de cheminée** fire in the hearth; **f. follet** will-o'-the-wisp; **f. de forêt** forest fire; **f. de joie** bonfire; *Fig* **f. de paille** flash in the pan (**b**) *(pour allumer une cigarette)* **avez-vous du f.?** have you got a light?

(**c**) *(brûleur)* burner; **à f. doux** *ou* **à petit f.** over a low heat; **à f. vif** over a high heat

(**d**) *(sur la chaussée)* **f. rouge/vert** red/green light; **feux de signalisation** *ou* **tricolores** traffic lights; *Fig* **donner le f. vert à qn** to give sb the green light

(**e**) *(phare)* **feux de brouillard** *ou* **antibrouillard** fog lamps; **feux de croisement** dipped headlights, *Am* low beams; **feux de détresse** hazard (warning) lights; **feux de position** sidelights; **feux de stationnement** parking lights

(**f**) *(tirs)* **faire f.** to fire, to shoot; **ouvrir le f.** to open fire; *Fig* **être pris entre deux feux** to be caught in the crossfire

2 *adj inv* **noir et f.** black-and-tan

feu², **-e** *adj* **f. M. Laroque** the late Mr Laroque; **f. mon mari** my late husband

feuillage [fœjaʒ] *nm* leaves, foliage

feuille [fœj] *nf* (**a**) *(de plante, d'arbre)* leaf; **f. morte** dead leaf; **f. de vigne** fig leaf (**b**) *(de papier)* sheet; **f. volante** loose sheet (**c**) *(journal)* paper; *Péj* **f. de chou** rag (**d**) *(document)* **f. d'impôt** tax return; **f. de maladie** = form given by doctor to patient for claiming reimbursement from Social Security; **f. de paie** *ou* **paye** payslip; **f. de soins** medical expenses claim form (**e**) *Ordinat* **f. de calcul** spreadsheet

feuillet [fœjɛ] *nm* leaf

feuilleté, **-e** [fœjte] **1** *adj* (**a**) *(pâte)* flaky (**b**) *(verre)* laminated

2 *nm* **f. au jambon/au fromage** ham/cheese pasty

feuilleter [42] [fœjte] *vt* (**a**) *(livre)* to leaf through (**b**) *Ordinat* **f. en arrière** to page up; **f. en avant** to page down

feuilleton [fœjtɔ̃] *nm* serial; **f. télévisé** television serial

feuillu, **-e** [fœjy] **1** *adj* (**a**) *(ayant beaucoup de feuilles)* leafy (**b**) *Bot* broad-leaved

2 *nm Bot* broad-leaved tree

feutre [føtr] *nm* (**a**) *(matière)* felt (**b**) *(chapeau)* felt hat (**c**) *(stylo)* felt-tip (pen)

feutré, **-e** [føtre] *adj* (**a**) *(garni de feutre)* felt(-covered) (**b**) *(assourdi)* muffled; **à pas feutrés** stealthily (**c**) *(vêtement)* matted

feutrer [føtre] **1** *vt* (**a**) *(garnir de feutre)* to cover with felt (**b**) *(assourdir)* to muffle (**c**) *(vêtement)* to mat

2 *vi (vêtement)* to felt

3 se feutrer *vpr (vêtement)* to felt

feutrine [føtrin] *nf* felt

fève [fɛv] *nf* (**a**) *(plante, graine)* broad bean (**b**) *(dans la galette des Rois)* charm (**c**) *Can (haricot)* bean

février [fevrije] *nm* February; *voir aussi* **janvier**

FF *nm (abrév* **franc(s) français)** FF

FFI [ɛfɛfi] *nfpl Hist (abrév* **Forces françaises de l'intérieur)** = French Resistance forces in France during World War Two

FFL [ɛfɛfɛl] *nfpl Hist (abrév* **Forces françaises libres)** Free French Army

fiabilité [fjabilite] *nf* reliability

fiable [fjabl] *adj* reliable

fiacre [fjakr] *nm* hackney carriage

fiançailles [fjɑ̃sɑj] *nfpl* engagement

fiancé, **-e** [fjɑ̃se] *nm,f* fiancé, *f* fiancée

fiancer [16] [fjɑ̃se] **se fiancer** *vpr* to get engaged (**avec** to); **être fiancés** to be engaged

fiasco [fjasko] *nm* fiasco

fibre [fibr] *nf* fibre; *Fig* **avoir la f. maternelle** to have strong maternal feelings; **f. optique** fibre optics *(singulier)*; **f. de verre** fibreglass

fibreux, **-euse** [fibrø, -øz] *adj (tissu)* fibrous; *(viande)* stringy

fibrome [fibrom] *nm* fibroma

fibroscopie [fibrɔskɔpi] *nf Méd* fibre-optic endoscopy

ficelé, **-e** [fisəle] *adj Fam* (**a**) *(construit)* **bien/mal f.** *(scénario)* well/poorly put together (**b**) *(habillé)* got up

ficeler [42] [fisəle] *vt* (**a**) *(attacher)* to tie up (**b**) *Fam (construire)* to put together

ficelle [fisɛl] *nf* (**a**) *(cordelette)* string; *Fig* **les ficelles du métier** the tricks of the trade (**b**) *(pain)* = very thin baguette

fiche¹ [fiʃ] *nf* (**a**) *(formulaire)* form; **f. d'état civil** = administrative record of birth details and marital status; **f. de paie** payslip; **f. signalétique** information sheet (**b**) *(carte)* (index) card; **mettre qch sur fiches** to card-index sth; **f. cartonnée** index card; **f. cuisine** *(dans un magazine)* recipe card (**c**) *(prise)* plug; *(broche)* pin (**d**) *Ordinat* **f. d'état** report form

fiche² = **ficher³**

ficher¹ [fiʃe] *vt (mettre sur fiches) (informations)* to file; *(personne)* to put on file

ficher² **1** *vt (enfoncer)* **f. qch dans qch** to stick sth into sth

2 se ficher *vpr (balle, clou)* **se f. dans qch** to go into sth

ficher³ *Fam* **1** *vt* (**a**) *(mettre)* to stick; **f. qn par terre** to send sb sprawling; **f. qch par terre** *(exprès)* to chuck sth on the floor; *(accidentellement)* to knock sth over; *Fig* to mess sth up; **f. qn à la porte** to kick sb out; **f. une gifle à qn** to give sb a slap in the face (**b**) *Fam (faire)* to do; **qu'est-ce que tu fiches?** what are you up to? (**c**) *Fam* **f. le camp** to clear off

2 se ficher *vpr* (**a**) *(se mettre)* **se f. un coup** to wallop oneself; **se f. par terre** to go sprawling; **se f. dedans** to screw up (**b**) *(se moquer)* **se f. de qn** to poke fun at sb; **se f. du monde** to take the piss; **se f. de qch** not to give a damn about sth; **je m'en fiche** I don't give a damn

fichier [fiʃje] *nm* (**a**) *(ensemble de fiches)* (card-index) file (**b**) *(boîte)* card-index box; *(meuble)* card-index cabinet (**c**) *Ordinat* file

fichu¹, **-e** [fiʃy] *adj Fam* (**a**) *(insupportable)* damn; *(caractère)* rotten (**b**) *(abîmé)* **être f.** to have had it; **c'est f. maintenant!** *(c'est raté)* we can forget it!; **c'est f. pour dimanche** we can forget Sunday (**c**) **être bien/mal f.** *(bien/mal bâti)* to have/not to have a nice body; *(bien/mal conçu)* to be well/badly designed; **être mal f.** *(malade)* to be under the weather (**d**) *(capable)* **être f. de faire qch** to be capable of doing sth

fichu² *nm* headscarf

fictif, **-ive** [fiktif, -iv] *adj* fictitious

fiction [fiksjɔ̃] *nf* fiction

ficus [fikys] *nm* ficus

fidèle [fidɛl] **1** *adj* (**a**) *(ami, époux)* faithful; *(lecteur, auditeur, client)* regular; **être f. à qn** to be faithful to sb; **être f. à qch** to be loyal or true to sth; *Fig* **être f. au poste** to be always there (**b**) *(copie, traduction, récit)* faithful (**à** to); *(mémoire, souvenir)* reliable

2 *nmf* (**a**) *(croyant)* believer; **les fidèles** the faithful; *(à l'église)* the congregation (**b**) *(partisan)* loyal supporter (de

of) (**c**) *(d'un programme télévisé)* regular viewer (**de** of); *(d'un programme radio)* regular listener (**de** to)
fidèlement [fidɛlmɑ̃] *adv* faithfully
fidélisation [fidelizasjɔ̃] *nf* **f. de la clientèle** building of customer loyalty
fidéliser [fidelize] *vt* to win the loyalty of; **f. la clientèle** to create customer loyalty
fidélité [fidelite] *nf* (**a**) *(d'un époux, d'un ami)* faithfulness (**à** to); *(d'un client, à un principe)* loyalty (**à** to) (**b**) *(d'une traduction, d'une reproduction)* faithfulness
Fidji [fidʒi] *nfpl* **les îles F.** Fiji
fiduciaire [fidysjɛr] *adj Fin* **monnaie f.** paper money
fief [fjɛf] *nm* fief; *Fig* **un f. du parti socialiste** a Socialist stronghold
fieffé, -e [fjefe] *adj* inveterate
fiel [fjɛl] *nm aussi Fig* gall
fier¹, fière [fjɛr] **1** *adj* (**a**) *(satisfait)* proud (**de** of); **être f. de faire qch** to be proud to do sth; **f. comme un paon** proud as a peacock (**b**) *(hautain, noble)* proud **2** *nm,f* **Péj faire le f.** to put on airs
fier² [66] [fje] **se fier** *vpr* **se f. à qn/qch** *(avoir confiance en)* to trust sb/sth; *(compter sur)* to rely on sb/sth
fièrement [fjɛrmɑ̃] *adv* proudly
fierté [fjɛrte] *nf* (**a**) *(satisfaction)* pride; **tirer f. de qch** to take pride in sth (**b**) *(amour-propre)* pride
fiesta [fjɛsta] *nf Fam* wild party
fièvre [fjɛvr] *nf* (**a**) *(élévation de la température)* fever; **avoir de la f.** to have a fever or a temperature; **elle a 40 de f.** she's got a temperature of 40 degrees; **avoir une f. de cheval** to have a raging fever (**b**) *(excitation)* frenzy
fiévreusement [fjevrøzmɑ̃] *adv* feverishly
fiévreux, -euse [fjevrø, -øz] *adj aussi Fig* feverish
fifre [fifr] *nm (instrument)* fife
figé, -e [fiʒe] *adj* (**a**) *(locution)* set (**b**) *(sourire)* fixed (**c**) *(sauce)* congealed
figer [45] [fiʒe] **1** *vt* (**a**) *(immobiliser)* to paralyze; **figé sur place** rooted to the spot (**b**) *(solidifier)* to congeal **2 se figer** *vpr* *(huile, sauce)* to congeal; *(regard, traits, sourire)* to freeze
fignoler [fiɲɔle] *vt Fam* to put the finishing touches to; **il ne reste plus qu'à** it's just a matter now of adding the finishing touches
figue [fig] *nf* fig; **f. de Barbarie** prickly pear
figuier [figje] *nm* fig tree; **f. de Barbarie** prickly pear
figurant, -e [figyrɑ̃, -ɑ̃t] *nm,f (dans une pièce de théâtre)* walk-on; *(dans un film)* extra
figuratif, -ive [figyratif, -iv] *adj* figurative
figuration [figyrasjɔ̃] *nf* **faire de la f.** to play bit parts
figure [figyr] *nf* (**a**) *(visage)* face; **faire bonne f.** to make a good impression; **faire f. d'intellectuel/de patriarche** to be seen as an intellectual/a patriarchal figure (**b**) *(représentation)* figure; *aussi Fig* **f. de proue** figurehead (**c**) *(personnage)* figure (**d**) *(en danse, en patinage artistique)* figure; **figures imposées** compulsory figures; **figures libres** freestyle (**e**) *Ling* **f. de rhétorique** figure of speech; **f. de style** stylistic device
figuré, -e [figyre] **1** *adj (sens)* figurative **2** *nm* **au f.** in the figurative sense
figurer [figyre] **1** *vt* to represent **2** *vi* (**a**) *(apparaître)* to appear (**sur/dans** on/in) (**b**) *(faire partie)* to figure (**parmi** among) **3 se figurer** *vpr* **se f. que** to imagine that
figurine [figyrin] *nf* figurine
fil [fil] *nm* (**a**) *(brin, de toile d'araignée)* thread; **de f. en**

aiguille little by little, bit by bit; *Fig* **ne tenir qu'à un f.** to hang by a thread; **f. conducteur** unifying thread; **f. à coudre** (sewing) thread; **f. dentaire** dental floss; **f. d'Écosse** lisle thread; **f. à plomb** plumb line (**b**) *(métallique, électrique)* wire; *Fig* **donner du f. à retordre à qn** to give sb trouble; **f. de fer** wire; **f. de fer barbelé** *Br* barbed wire, *Am* barb wire (**c**) *Fam (téléphone)* **au bout du f.** on the line; **coup de f.** call; **donner** *ou* **passer un coup de f. à qn** to give sb a call, to call sb (up) (**d**) *(cours)* **au f. de l'eau** with the current; **au f. des jours/semaines** with the passing days/weeks; **perdre/reprendre le f. de qch** to lose/pick up the thread of sth (**e**) *(tissu)* linen (**f**) *(tranchant)* edge
filament [filamɑ̃] *nm* (**a**) *(d'une ampoule électrique)* filament (**b**) *(de viande)* fibre (**c**) *Biol* filament
filandreux, -euse [filɑ̃drø, -øz] *adj (viande, légumes)* stringy
filant, -e [filɑ̃, -ɑ̃t] *adj voir* **étoile**
filasse [filas] **1** *nf* tow **2** *adj inv* tow-coloured
filature [filatyr] *nf* (**a**) *(fabrique)* (spinning) mill (**b**) *(surveillance)* shadowing; **prendre qn en f.** to shadow sb
file [fil] *nf* (**a**) *(queue) Br* queue, *Am* line; **en f. indienne** in single file; **quatre jours à la f.** four days in a row; **f. (d'attente)** *Br* queue, *Am* line (**b**) *(sur la route)* lane; **se garer en double f.** to double-park (**c**) *Ordinat* **f. d'attente** print queue
filé, -e [file] *adj* (**a**) *(bas, collant)* with a run, *Br* laddered (**b**) *(verre)* spun
filer [file] **1** *vt* (**a**) *(coton, verre)* to spin (**b**) *Fam (donner)* **f. qch à qn** to give sb sth (**c**) *(surveiller) (suspect)* to shadow, to tail (**d**) *(bas, collant)* to put a run in, *Br* to ladder (**e**) **f. le parfait amour** to live love's dream **2** *vi* (**a**) *(passer vite) (temps)* to fly; *(véhicule)* to speed along; **f. entre les mains** *ou* **les doigts à qn** *(argent)* to run through sb's fingers like water; *(personne)* to slip through sb's fingers (**b**) *Fam (partir)* **il faut que je file** I must dash; **allez, file!** off you go! (**c**) *(bas, collant)* to run, *Br* to ladder
filet¹ [filɛ] *nm* (**a**) *(de lumière)* thin streak; *(d'air)* thin stream; *(d'eau)* trickle (**b**) *(petite quantité)* dash (**c**) *(d'une vis)* thread (**d**) *(de viande, de poisson)* fillet; **f. mignon** filet mignon *(small fillet steak)*
filet² [filɛ] *nm* (**a**) *(en mailles)* net; **f. à bagages** luggage rack; **f. à papillons** butterfly net; **f. de pêche** fishing net; **f. à provisions** string bag (**b**) *(au cirque)* (safety) net; **travailler sans f.** *(trapéziste)* to work without a net; *Fig* to take risks (**c**) *(au tennis)* net
filial, -e, -aux, -ales [filjal, -o] **1** *adj* filial **2** *nf* **filiale** subsidiary (company)
filiation [filjasjɔ̃] *nf* (**a**) *(lien de parenté)* filiation (**b**) *Fig (relation)* relationship (**avec** to)
filière [filjɛr] *nf* (**a**) *(voie obligée)* channels (**b**) *(domaine d'études)* field of study; **suivre une f. scientifique/commerciale** to study scientific/business subjects (**c**) *(organisation clandestine)* network
filiforme [filiform] *adj* spindly
filigrane [filigran] *nm (dessin)* watermark; *Fig* **en f.** implicit
filin [filɛ̃] *nm* rope
fille [fij] *nf* (**a**) *(descendante)* daughter (**b**) *(enfant)*; **petite f.** little girl (**c**) *(femme)* **salut les filles!** hi, girls!; **f. de joie** prostitute; **jeune f.** girl; **vieille f.** old maid
fillette [fijɛt] *nf* little girl
filleul, -e [fijœl] *nm,f* godson, *f* goddaughter
film [film] *nm* (**a**) *(œuvre)* film, movie; **f. d'action** action

film; **f. d'animation** animated film; **f. d'aventures** adventure film; **f. d'épouvante** *ou* **d'horreur** horror film; **f.** policier detective film (**b**) *(déroulement)* **revoir le f. de sa vie** to see one's life flashing before one's eyes (**c**) *(emballage)* film; **f. alimentaire** clingfilm

filmer [filme] *vt* to film

filmographie [filmɔgrafi] *nf* filmography

filon [filɔ̃] *nm* (**a**) *(de minéraux)* vein, seam (**b**) *Fam* **trouver le f.** to strike it rich

filou [filu] *nm (escroc)* rogue; *(enfant)* rascal

fils [fis] *nm* son; **f. de famille** young man of good social standing; *Péj* **f. à papa** daddy's boy

filtrage [filtraʒ] *nm* (**a**) *(contrôle)* screening (**b**) *(d'un liquide)* filtering

filtrant, -e [filtrã, -ãt] *adj (pouvoir)* filtering; *(verres, papier)* filter

filtre [filtr] *1 adj (cigarette, café, papier)* filter
2 *nm* filter; **f. à air** air filter; **f. à café** coffee filter; *Phot* **f. coloré** colour filter; *Ordinat* **f. écran** screen filter

filtrer [filtre] **1** *vt* (**a**) *(liquide, son, lumière)* to filter (**b**) *(informations, visiteurs)* to screen
2 *vi (liquide)* to filter (**à travers** through); *(nouvelle)* to leak out; **laisser f. qch** to let sth filter through; *Fig* to leak sth

fin¹ [fɛ̃] *nf* (**a**) *(conclusion)* end; **f. janvier** at the end of January; **à la f.** in the end; *Fam* **tu m'ennuies à la f.!** you're really annoying me!; **en f. de qch, à la f. de qch** at the end of sth; **chômeur en f. de droits** = unemployed person about to lose their entitlement to benefit; **mettre f. à qch** to put an end to sth; **prendre f.** to come to an end; **toucher** *ou* **tirer à sa f.** to draw to a close; **avoir des fins de mois difficiles** to be always short of money at the end of the month; **f. de série** discontinued line (**b**) *(mort)* end, death (**c**) *(but)* end, aim; **arriver** *ou* **parvenir à ses fins** to achieve one's ends; **à cette f.** to this end; **à toutes fins utiles** just in case (**d**) *Ordinat* **f. de ligne** line end; **f. de page** pagebreak; **f. de session** logoff

fin², fine [fɛ̃, fin] **1** *adj* (**a**) *(papier, tranche, taille)* thin; *(cheveux, sable, pointe)* fine; **une petite pluie fine** drizzle (**b**) *(traits)* fine (**c**) *(de première qualité)* fine (**d**) **fines herbes** mixed herbs (**e**) **un f. connaisseur** a connoisseur (**f**) *(vue, odorat)* keen; **avoir l'ouïe fine** to have keen hearing (**g**) *(subtil)* subtle (**h**) **le f. mot de l'histoire** the truth of the matter
2 *nm* **le f. du f.** the ultimate
3 *adv* (**a**) **f. prêt** all ready (**b**) *(finement)* finely

final, -e *ou* **-aux, -ales** [final, -o] *adj* final

finale [final] **1** *nf* (**a**) *(compétition sportive)* final; **aller/être en f.** to go through to/to be in the finals (**b**) *(de mot)* final syllable
2 *nm (d'un morceau de musique)* finale

finalement [finalmã] *adv* in the end, finally

finaliser [finalize] *vt* to finalize

finaliste [finalist] *adj & nmf* finalist

finalité [finalite] *nf* (**a**) *(objectif)* aim (**b**) *(en biologie)* finality

finance [finãs] *nf* (**a**) *(profession)* finance; **la haute f.** high finance (**b**) *(argent)* **moyennant f.** for a fee; **finances** finances

financement [finãsmã] *nm* financing

financer [16] [finãse] *vt* to finance

financier, -ère [finãsje, -ɛr] **1** *adj* financial
2 *nm* financier

financièrement [finãsjɛrmã] *adv* financially

finasser [finase] *vi Fam* to resort to trickery

finaud, -e [fino, -od] **1** *adj* crafty
2 *nm,f* crafty devil

fine [fin] *nf* ≃ brandy

finement [finmã] *adv* (**a**) *(adroitement)* cleverly (**b**) *(délicatement)* finely

finesse [fines] *nf* (**a**) *(minceur)* fineness; *(de la taille)* slenderness, slimness (**b**) *(d'un visage)* fineness; *(d'un travail fait à la main)* delicacy (**c**) *(subtilité)* subtlety

fini, -e [fini] **1** *adj* (**a**) *(usé, à bout)* finished (**b**) *Péj (imbécile, escroc)* absolute (**c**) *(espace, temps, nombre)* finite
2 *nm (d'un objet manufacturé)* finish

finir [finir] **1** *vt* to finish; *(vie)* to end; **f. son assiette** to finish what's on one's plate
2 *vi* to end, to finish; **f. bien/mal** to end well/badly; *(film, roman)* to have a happy/sad ending; **mal f.** *(personne)* to come to a bad end; **f. de faire qch** to finish doing sth; **f. par faire qch** to end up doing sth; **en f.** *(avec)* endless; **pour f.** *(en résumé)* to cut a long story short; *(finalement)* in the end

finish [finiʃ] *nm inv* finish

finition [finisjɔ̃] *nf* finishing touch; **travail de f.** finishing touches; **les finitions de ce manteau sont mal faites** this coat is badly finished

finlandais, -e [fɛ̃lãdɛ, -ɛz] **1** *adj* Finnish
2 *nm,f* **F.** Finn

Finlande [fɛ̃lãd] *nf* **la F.** Finland

finnois, -e [finwa, -az] **1** *adj* Finnish
2 *nm (langue)* Finnish

fiole [fjɔl] *nf (flacon)* phial

fioriture [fjɔrityr] *nf (dessin)* flourish

fioul [fjul] *nm* fuel oil

firmament [firmamã] *nm Litt* firmament

firme [firm] *nf* firm

FIS [fis] *nm (abrév* **Front islamique du salut**) **le F.** the Islamic Salvation Front

fisc [fisk] *nm Br* ≃ Inland Revenue, *Am* ≃ Internal Revenue

fiscal, -e, -aux, -ales [fiskal, -o] *adj* tax

fiscaliser [fiskalize] *vt* to tax

fiscalité [fiskalite] *nf* tax system

fissure [fisyr] *nf aussi Fig* crack

fissurer [fisyre] **1** *vt* to crack; *Fig* to split
2 se fissurer *vpr* to crack; *Fig* to split

fiston [fistɔ̃] *nm Fam* son, lad

FIV [ɛfive] *nf (abrév* **fécondation in vitro**) IVF

fivete [fivɛt] *nf (abrév* **fécondation in vitro et transfert embryonnaire**) GIFT

fixateur, -trice [fiksatœr, -tris] *Phot* **1** *adj* fixing
2 *nm* fixer

fixatif [fiksatif] *nm* fixative

fixation [fiksasjɔ̃] *nf* (**a**) *(action)* fixing (**b**) *(de skis)* (ski) binding (**c**) *(obsession)* fixation; **faire une f. sur qn/qch** to become fixated on sb/sth

fixe [fiks] **1** *adj* (**a**) *(immobile) (étagère, planche, regard)* fixed (**b**) *(arrêté) (prix, frais)* fixed
2 *nm* fixed salary

fixement [fiksəmã] *adv* fixedly; **regarder f. qn/qch** to stare at sb/sth

fixer [fikse] **1** *vt* (**a**) *(immobiliser)* to fix; **f. son attention/son regard sur qch** to focus one's attention/one's gaze on sth; **f. qn (du regard)** to stare at sb (**b**) *(déterminer) (date, heure, rendez-vous)* to fix; *(prix, salaire)* to set (**à** at); **f. son choix sur qch** to decide on sth (**c**) *(informer)* **maintenant, tu es fixé** now you know
2 se fixer *vpr* (**a**) *(s'installer)* to settle down (**b**) **son choix s'est fixé sur celui-ci** she decided on this one (**c**) **se f. un objectif** to set oneself a target

fixité [fiksite] *nf (du regard)* fixedness
fjord [fjɔrd] *nm* fjord
flacon [flakɔ̃] *nm* (small) bottle
flagada [flagada] *adj inv Fam* washed-out
flageller [flaʒele] *vt* to flog, to whip
flageoler [flaʒɔle] *vi (jambes)* to shake, to tremble
flageolet [flaʒɔlɛ] *nm (haricot)* flageolet (bean)
flagornerie [flagɔrnəri] *nf Péj* fawning, toadying
flagrant, -e [flagrɑ̃, -ɑ̃t] *adj* flagrant, blatant; **en f. délit** red-handed; **être pris en f. délit d'adultère** to be caught in flagrante
flair [flɛr] *nm* sense of smell; **avoir du f.** to have a good sense of smell; *Fig* to have good intuition
flairer [flere] *vt aussi Fig* to smell
flamand, -e [flamɑ̃, -ɑ̃d] *1 adj* Flemish
2 *nm,f* **F.** Fleming
3 *nm (langue)* Flemish
flamant [flamɑ̃] *nm* **f. rose** flamingo
flambant [flɑ̃bɑ̃] *adv* **f. neuf** brand new
flambeau, -x [flɑ̃bo] *nm (torche)* torch; *Fig* **passer le f. à qn** to pass the torch on to sb
flambée [flɑ̃be] *nf* **(a)** *(feu)* blaze **(b)** *(de violence)* flare-up; *(des prix)* upsurge
flamber [flɑ̃be] **1** *vi* **(a)** *(brûler)* to blaze **(b)** *Fam (parier)* to gamble for big money
2 *vt* **(a)** *(volaille)* to singe **(b)** *(crêpes)* to flambé
flambeur, -euse [flɑ̃bœr, -øz] *nm,f Fam* big-time gambler
flamboyant, -e [flɑ̃bwajɑ̃, -ɑ̃t] *adj* **(a)** *(regard)* blazing; **d'un rouge f.** flaming red **(b)** *Archit* flamboyant
flamboyer [flɑ̃bwaje] *vi* to blaze
flamme [flam] *nf* **(a)** *(feu)* flame; **en flammes** on fire, ablaze; *Fig* **descendre qn/qch en flammes** to shoot sb/sth down in flames **(b)** *Fig (enthousiasme)* fire **(c)** *Litt (amour)* passion
flammèche [flamɛʃ] *nf* spark
flan [flɑ̃] *nm (dessert)* custard tart
flanc [flɑ̃] *nm* side; *(d'une armée)* flank; **être sur le f.** *(malade)* to be laid up; *(épuisé)* to be worn out; *Fam* **tirer au f.** to shirk, *Br* to skive
flancher [flɑ̃ʃe] *vi Fam* to give in
Flandre [flɑ̃dr] *nf* **la F., les Flandres** Flanders
flanelle [flanɛl] *nf* flannel
flâner [flɑne, flane] *vi* **(a)** *(se promener)* to stroll, to saunter **(b)** *(perdre son temps)* to hang about
flânerie [flɑnri, flanri] *nf (promenade)* stroll
flâneur, -euse [flɑnœr, flanœr, -øz] *nm,f (promeneur)* stroller
flanquer¹ [flɑ̃ke] *vt (accompagner)* **flanqué de** flanked by
flanquer² *Fam* **1** *vt* **(a)** *(jeter)* to chuck; **f. qn à la porte** *ou* **dehors** to kick sb out; *(licencier)* to fire sb, *Br* to sack sb **(b)** **f. qch à qn** *(coup de pied, gifle)* to give sb sth; **f. la trouille** *ou* **les jetons à qn** to put the wind up sb
2 se flanquer *vpr* **se f. par terre** to go sprawling
flapi, -e [flapi] *adj Fam* dead beat
flaque [flak] *nf (d'huile, de sang)* pool; **f. (d'eau)** puddle
flash [flaʃ] *nm* **(a)** *(sur un appareil photo)* flash **(b)** *(à la radio, à la télévision)* flash; **f. d'information** newsflash; **f. publicitaire** commercial
flash-back [flaʃbak] *nm inv* flashback
flasher [flaʃe] *vi Fam* **f. sur qn/qch** to fall for sb/sth in a big way

flasque¹ [flask] *adj (chair)* flabby
flasque² *nf* flask
flatter [flate] **1** *vt* **(a)** *(complimenter)* to flatter **(b)** *(avantager)* to flatter **(c)** *(caresser) (animal)* to stroke
2 se flatter *vpr* to flatter oneself; **se f. de faire qch** to pride oneself on doing sth; **je ne m'en flatterais pas** it's not something I'd be proud of
flatterie [flatri] *nf* flattery
flatteur, -euse [flatœr, -øz] **1** *adj (remarque, portrait, couleur)* flattering; *(personne)* full of flattery
2 *nm,f* flatterer
flatulence [flatylɑ̃s] *nf* flatulence
FLE [flə] *nm (abrév français langue étrangère)* French as a foreign language
fléau, -x [fleo] *nm* **(a)** *(calamité)* scourge; *Fig (chose pénible)* pain **(b)** *(à céréales)* flail **(c)** *(d'une balance à plateaux)* beam
fléchage [fleʃaʒ] *nm* signposting
flèche [flɛʃ] *nf* **(a)** *(projectile, signe)* arrow; **partir comme une f.** to shoot off; **monter en f.** *(avion, prix)* to shoot up **(b)** *(attaque verbale)* jibe **(c)** *(d'une église)* spire **(d)** *Ordinat* **f. de défilement** scroll arrow; **flèches verticales** up and down arrow keys
flécher [34] [fleʃe] *vt (route, direction)* to arrow; **itinéraire fléché** signposted route
fléchette [fleʃɛt] *nf* dart; **jouer aux fléchettes** to play darts
fléchir [fleʃir] **1** *vt* **(a)** *(bras, jambe, genou)* to bend **(b)** *(émouvoir)* to sway
2 *vi* **(a)** *(ployer) (branche)* to bend; *(jambes)* to give way; *(poutre)* to sag **(b)** *(faiblir)* to weaken **(c)** *(baisser) (prix, devises)* to fall
fléchissement [fleʃismɑ̃] *nm* **(a)** *(du genou)* bending; *(d'une poutre)* sagging **(b)** *(de prix, de devises, de résultats)* drop **(de** in)
flegmatique [flɛgmatik] *adj* phlegmatic
flegme [flɛgm] *nm* phlegm
flemmard, -e [flemar, -ard] *Fam* **1** *adj* lazy
2 *nm,f* lazybones
flemmarder [flemarde] *vi Fam* to laze about
flemmardise [flemardiz] *nf Fam* laziness
flemme [flɛm] *nf Fam* laziness; **j'ai la f. (de le faire)** I can't be bothered (to do it)
flétan [fletɑ̃] *nm* halibut
flétri, -e [fletri] *adj* withered
flétrir [fletrir] **1** *vt (peau, plantes)* to wither
2 se flétrir *vpr (visage, plantes)* to wither
fleur [flœr] *nf* **(a)** *(plante)* flower; **à fleurs** *(tissu)* floral; **en fleurs** *(arbre)* in flower; **être f. bleue** to be a romantic; *Fam* **faire une f. à qn** to do sb a favour; **fleurs des champs** wild flowers **(b)** *(locutions)* **dans la f. de l'âge** in the prime of life; **la fine f. de qch** the cream of sth; **à f. d'eau** just above the surface of the water; **avoir les nerfs à f. de peau** to be all on edge
fleurdelisé [flœrdəlize] *nm Can (drapeau du Québec)* flag of Quebec
fleurer [flœre] *vt Litt* to smell of
fleuret [flœrɛ] *nm (épée)* foil
fleurette [flœrɛt] *nf Vieilli* **conter f. à qn** to whisper sweet nothings to sb
fleuri, -e [flœri] *adj* **(a)** *(couvert de fleurs) (arbre)* in flower **(b)** *(orné de fleurs) (tissu, robe)* floral; *(vaisselle)* flower-patterned **(c)** *(style)* flowery
fleurir [flœrir] **1** *vi* **(a)** *(plantes)* to flower **(b)** *(art, commerce)* to flourish

2 vt (table) to decorate with flowers; (tombe) to lay flowers on

fleuriste [flœrist] nmf (commerçant) florist

fleuron [flœrɔ̃] nm (d'une collection) jewel

fleuve [flœv] nm river; **le f. Jaune** the Yellow River

flexibilité [flɛksibilite] nf aussi Fig flexibility

flexible [flɛksibl] **1** adj aussi Fig flexible **2** nm (tuyau) hose(pipe)

flexion [flɛksjɔ̃] nf (fléchissement) bending

flibustier [flibystje] nm buccaneer

flic [flik] nm Fam cop

flingue [flɛ̃g] nm Fam shooter

flinguer [flɛ̃ge] Fam **1** vt to gun down **2 se flinguer** vpr to blow one's brains out

flippant, -e [flipɑ̃, -ɑ̃t] adj Fam (déprimant) grim; (effrayant) creepy

flipper¹ [flipœr] nm (appareil) pinball machine; (jeu) pinball; **jouer au f.** to play pinball

flipper² [flipe] vi Fam (déprimer) to feel down

flirt [flœrt] nm (a) (amourette) flirtation (b) (personne) boyfriend, f girlfriend

flirter [flœrte] vi to flirt (avec with)

FLN [ɛfɛlɛn] nm (abrév Front de libération nationale) National Liberation Front (in Algeria)

FLNC [ɛfɛlɛnse] nm (abrév Front de libération nationale de la Corse) Corsican liberation front

FLNKS [ɛfɛlɛnkɑs] nm (abrév Front de libération nationale kanak et socialiste) Kanak national liberation front (in New Caledonia)

flocon [flɔkɔ̃] nm flake; **flocons d'avoine** oat flakes; **f. de neige** snowflake

floconneux, -euse [flɔkɔnø, -øz] adj fluffy

flonflons [flɔ̃flɔ̃] nmpl tiddly-om-pom-pom

flop [flɔp] nm Fam flop; **faire un f.** to flop

flopée [flɔpe] nf Fam une f. ou des flopées de qch loads of sth, masses of sth

floraison [flɔrɛzɔ̃] nf flowering

floral, -e, -aux, -ales [flɔral, -o] adj floral

floralies [flɔrali] nfpl flower show

flore [flɔr] nf flora; **f. intestinale** intestinal flora

Floride [flɔrid] nf la F. Florida

florilège [flɔrilɛʒ] nm anthology

florin [flɔrɛ̃] nm florin

florissant, -e [flɔrisɑ̃, -ɑ̃t] adj (affaire) flourishing; (santé) blooming

flot [flo] nm (a) (marée) flood (tide) (b) (quantité importante) stream (de of) (c) Litt les flots (la mer) the waves (d) (locutions) couler à flots to flow freely; être à f. (bateau) to be afloat; Fig (personne) to have one's head above water

flottaison [flɔtɛzɔ̃] nf floating

flotte [flɔt] nf (a) (bateaux) fleet (b) Fam (pluie) rain (c) Fam (eau) water

flottement [flɔtmɑ̃] nm (a) (d'un drapeau) fluttering (b) (d'une monnaie) fluctuation (c) (hésitation) wavering

flotter [flɔte] **1** vi (a) (embarcation) to float; Fig elle flotte dans sa robe her dress is far too baggy for her (b) (drapeau) to flutter; **f. au** ou **dans le vent** (cheveux) to stream in the wind **2** v impersonnel Fam **il flotte** it's raining

flotteur [flɔtœr] nm float

flottille [flɔtij] nf (de bateaux) flotilla

flou, -e [flu] **1** adj (a) (contour, photographie) blurred, fuzzy (b) (idée, réponse) vague

2 nm (d'un contour, d'une photographie) fuzziness; (d'une idée, d'une réponse) vagueness; **f. artistique** (en photographie) soft-focus effect; Fig deliberate vagueness

flouer [flue] vt Fam to swindle

flouse, flouze [fluz] nm Fam (argent) cash, Am bucks

fluctuant, -e [flyktɥɑ̃, -ɑ̃t] adj fluctuating

fluctuation [flyktɥasjɔ̃] nf fluctuation

fluctuer [flyktɥe] vi to fluctuate

fluet, -ette [flɥɛ, -ɛt] adj thin

fluide [flɥid] **1** adj (liquide) fluid; (circulation) flowing freely; (style, pensée) flowing **2** nm (a) (substance) fluid (b) (pouvoir surnaturel) occult power

fluidifier [66] [flɥidifje] vt (sang) to thin

fluidité [flɥidite] nf (d'un corps) fluidity; (de la circulation) free flow

fluo [flyo] adj inv Fam fluorescent

fluor [flyɔr] nm fluorine

fluorescent, -e [flyɔresɑ̃, -ɑ̃t] adj fluorescent

flûte [flyt] **1** nf (a) (instrument) flute; **f. à bec** recorder; **f. de Pan** panpipes; **f. traversière** concert flute (b) (pain) small French stick (c) (verre) f. à champagne champagne flute **2** exclam Fam damn!

flûtiste [flytist] nmf Br flautist, Am flutist

fluvial, -e, -aux, -ales [flyvjal, -o] adj river; (alluvions) fluvial

flux [fly] nm (a) (de paroles) flow (b) (marée montante) flow; **f. et le reflux** the ebb and flow; **f. migratoire** flow of migrants (c) (électrique, magnétique) flux

fluxion [flyksjɔ̃] nf inflammation; **f. de poitrine** pneumonia

FM [ɛfɛm] nf (abrév frequency modulation) FM

FMI [ɛfɛmi] nm (abrév Fonds monétaire international) IMF

FN [ɛfɛn] nm (abrév Front national) = French political party of the extreme right

FNSEA [ɛfɛnɛsəa] nf (abrév Fédération nationale des syndicats d'exploitants agricoles) = French farmers' union

FO [ɛfo] nf (abrév Force ouvrière) = French trade union formed out of the split with communist CGT in 1948

foc [fɔk] nm jib

focal, -e, -aux, -ales [fɔkal, -o] adj focal

focaliser [fɔkalize] **1** vt to focus (sur on) **2 se focaliser** vpr to focus (sur on)

fœtal, -e, -aux, -ales [fetal, -o] adj foetal

fœtus [fetys] nm foetus

fofolle [fɔfɔl] adj voir foufou

foi [fwa] nf (a) (confiance) faith, trust; **avoir f. en qn/qch** to have faith in sb/sth; **les candidatures devront nous parvenir avant le 1er mars, le cachet de la poste faisant f. ≃** applications should be postmarked no later than March 1 (b) (croyance religieuse) faith; **avoir/perdre la f.** to have/lose faith (c) (locutions) **bonne f.** sincerity; **mauvaise f.** insincerity; **être de bonne/mauvaise f.** to be sincere/insincere; **ma f., oui!** yes indeed!

foie [fwa] nm liver; **très** Fam **avoir les foies** to be scared shitless; **f. gras** foie gras; **f. de veau/volaille** calf's/chicken liver

foin [fwɛ̃] nm (fourrage) hay; **faire les foins** to make hay; Fam **faire du f.** (causer un scandale) to kick up a fuss; (faire du bruit) to make a din

foire [fwar] nf (a) (fête foraine) funfair; Fam **faire la f.** to muck about; *Fam* c'est la f., ici it's bedlam in here; f. d'empoigne free-for-all (b) *(salon international, professionnel)* (trade) fair

foirer [fware] *vi très Fam* to be a cock-up

foireux, -euse [fwarø, -øz] *adj très Fam (projet, affaire)* hopeless

fois [fwa] *nf* time; **une f.** once; **il était une f. un roi** once upon a time there was a king; **deux f.** twice; **deux f. par jour/mois** twice a day/month; **ça coûte trois f. rien** it costs next to nothing; **trois f. trois neuf** three times three is nine; **trois f. plus grand** three times as big; **neuf f. sur dix** nine times out of ten; **combien de f.?** how many times?, how often?; **toutes les f. ou chaque f.** que every time (that), whenever; **encore une f.** once more, once again; **une (bonne) f.** pour toutes once and for all; **une f.** que once, as soon as; **pour cette f.** this once; **pour une f.** for once; **pour une f.** que j'étais à l'heure, **personne n'était là** the one time I was on time and no one was there; **à la f.** utile et pas cher both useful and inexpensive; **une chose à la f.** one thing at a time; **l'autre f.** *(il y a peu)* the other day; *Fam* des f. *(parfois)* sometimes; *Fam* des f. qu'il viendrait in case he comes; *Fam* non, mais des f.! really now!

foison [fwazɔ̃] *nf* à f. in abundance

foisonnement [fwazɔnmɑ̃] *nm (abondance)* abundance

foisonner [fwazɔne] *vi* to abound **(de ou en in); f. d'idées** *(personne)* to have plenty of ideas

fol [fɔl] *voir* **fou**

folâtre [fɔlatr] *adj (personne)* playful

folâtrer [fɔlatre] *vi (personne)* to romp, to frolic

foldingue [fɔldɛ̃g] *adj Fam* crazy

follichon, -onne [fɔliʃɔ̃, -ɔn] *adj Fam* ce n'est pas f. it's not much fun

folie [fɔli] *nf* madness; **aimer qn à la f.** to be madly in love with sb; **aimer qch à la f.** to adore sth; **faire des folies** *(faire des achats extravagants)* to go mad; c'est de la f.! it's madness!; **c'est de la f. douce** it's sheer madness; **la f. des grandeurs** delusions of grandeur

folio [fɔljo] *nm* folio

folk [fɔlk] *adj & nm* folk

folklo [fɔlklo] *adj inv Fam (personne)* eccentric; *(endroit, soirée)* bizarre

folklore [fɔlklɔr] *nm* folklore

folklorique [fɔlklɔrik] *adj (a) (costume)* traditional; *(danse)* folk (b) *Fam (personne)* eccentric; *(endroit, soirée)* bizarre

folle [fɔl] *adj voir* **fou**

follement [fɔlmɑ̃] *adv* madly

follet [fɔlɛ] *adj m voir* **feu**

fomenter [fɔmɑ̃te] *vt* to foment

foncé, -e [fɔ̃se] *adj* dark

foncer [16] [fɔ̃se] **1** *vt* to darken **2** *vi* (a) *(s'assombrir)* to darken (b) *(se hâter)* to get a move on; **f. sur qn/qch** *(se précipiter sur)* to swoop on sb/sth (c) *Fam (s'y mettre)* to get one's head down

fonceur, -euse [fɔ̃sœr, -øz] *Fam* **1** *adj* go-getting **2** *nm,f* go-getter

foncier, -ère [fɔ̃sje, -ɛr] *adj* (a) *(impôt, crédit)* land (b) *(fondamental)* fundamental, basic

foncièrement [fɔ̃sjɛrmɑ̃] *adv* fundamentally, basically

fonction [fɔ̃ksjɔ̃] *nf* (a) *(poste)* office; **entrer en fonctions, prendre ses fonctions** to take up one's duties; **être en f.** to be in office; **de f.** *(voiture, appartement)* company; **la f. publique** the civil service (b) *(rôle)* function; **faire f. de qch** to act as sth (c) *Ordinat* **f. de**

comptage de mots word count facility; **f. d'éditeur de texte** text editing feature; **f. multimédia** multimedia facility; **f. recherche et remplacement** search and replace function; **f. de sauvegarde** save function (d) **en f. de** according to

fonctionnaire [fɔ̃ksjɔnɛr] *nmf* civil servant; **haut f.** senior civil servant

fonctionnel, -elle [fɔ̃ksjɔnɛl] *adj* functional

fonctionnement [fɔ̃ksjɔnmɑ̃] *nm (d'une machine)* working, functioning; **en état de f.** in (good) working order; *Ordinat* **f. en réseau** networking

fonctionner [fɔ̃ksjɔne] *vi (machine, mécanisme)* to work, to function; *Ordinat* to run; **faire f. qch** to operate sth

fond [fɔ̃] *nm* (a) *(d'un récipient, de la mer, de l'océan)* bottom; *(d'un espace clos, de la gorge)* back; **la pièce du f.** the room at the end, the far room; **au fin f. de qch** in the depths of sth; **il n'en reste qu'un f.** there's only a drop left; **du f. du cœur** from the bottom of one's heart; **tu connais le f. de ma pensée** you know what my feelings really are; **à f.** *(à bloc)* all the way; *(complètement)* thoroughly; *(totalement)* totally; **à f. de train** at full tilt; *Fam* **à f. la caisse** *(très vite)* hell for leather; **au f., dans le f.** when it comes down to it, **de f. en comble** from top to bottom; **f. d'artichaut** artichoke heart; **f. de bouteille** *(contenu)* dregs; **f. de teint** foundation (b) *(substance essentielle)* **le f. du problème** the heart of the problem; **avoir un bon/mauvais f.** to be basically a good/bad person; **le f. et la forme** form and content (c) *(arrière-plan)* background; **f. sonore** background music

fondamental, -e, -aux, -ales [fɔ̃damɑ̃tal, -o] *adj* basic, fundamental

fondamentalement [fɔ̃damɑ̃talmɑ̃] *adv* fundamentally, basically

fondamentalisme [fɔ̃damɑ̃talism] *nm* fundamentalism

fondamentaliste [fɔ̃damɑ̃talist] *nmf* fundamentalist

fondant, -e [fɔ̃dɑ̃, -ɑ̃t] **1** *adj* (a) *(neige)* melting (b) *(poire)* that melts in the mouth; *(viande)* very tender **2** *nm (bonbon, dessert)* fondant

fondateur, -trice [fɔ̃datœr, -tris] **1** *adj (mythe)* underlying; **membre f.** founder member **2** *nm,f* founder

fondation [fɔ̃dasjɔ̃] *nf* (a) *(d'une ville, d'un hôpital)* founding (b) *(établissement)* foundation (c) **fondations** *(d'une construction)* foundations

fondé, -e [fɔ̃de] **1** *adj (reproches, doutes)* well-founded, justified; **être f. à faire qch** to have good reason to do sth **2** *nm,f* **f. de pouvoir** agent *(holding power of attorney); (mandant)* proxy

fondement [fɔ̃dmɑ̃] *nm* foundation

fonder [fɔ̃de] **1** *vt* (a) *(créer) (ville, hôpital)* to found; *(société, journal)* to start, to set up; **f. un foyer** to start a family (b) *(baser)* **f. qch sur qch** to base sth on sth; **f. de grands espoirs sur qn** to pin one's hopes on sb **2 se fonder** *vpr* **se f. sur qch** *(sujet: remarque, théorie)* to be based on sth; **sur quoi se fonde-t-il pour le nier?** what are his grounds for denying it?; **pour son livre, elle s'est fondée sur plusieurs articles** she based her book on several articles

fonderie [fɔ̃dri] *nf (usine)* foundry

fondre [fɔ̃dr] **1** *vt* (a) *(rendre liquide) (métal)* to melt *(sucre, cire)* to dissolve; *(fabriquer)* to cast (b) *(combiner) (couleurs)* to blend; *(sociétés)* to merge **2** *vi* (a) *(se liquéfier)* to melt; *(sucre)* to dissolve; **faire f. qch** to melt sth; *(sucre)* to dissolve; **f. dans la bouche** to melt in the mouth; **f. en larmes** to dissolve into tears; *Fig* je

fonds my heart melts (**b**) *Fig (diminuer)* to melt away (**c**) *Fam (maigrir)* to lose weight
3 fondre sur *vt ind* to swoop on
4 se fondre *vpr* **se f. dans** to merge into

fonds [fɔ̃] **1** *nm* (**a**) *(capital)* funds; *(organisme)* fund; **prêter son argent à f. perdu** to lend one's money without security; **f. commun de placement** mutual fund; **F. européen de développement** European Development Fund; **F. européen de développement régional** European Regional Development Fund; **F. monétaire international** International Monetary Fund; **f. de roulement** working capital (**b**) *(d'un musée, d'une bibliothèque)* collection; *(ressources)* resource (**c**) **f. de commerce** business
2 *nmpl (ressources financières)* funds; **être en f.** to be in funds; **f. publics** government funds; *(valeurs)* government stocks

fondu [fɔ̃dy] *nm* (**a**) *(de couleurs)* blending (**b**) *Cin* fadeout; **f. enchaîné** dissolve

fondue [fɔ̃dy] *nf* **f. (savoyarde)** (cheese) fondue; **f. bourguignonne** fondue bourguignonne, = fondue consisting of cubes of raw beef cooked in hot oil

fongicide [fɔ̃ʒisid] **1** *adj* fungicidal
2 *nm* fungicide

font *voir* **faire**

fontaine [fɔ̃tɛn] *nf (source naturelle)* spring; *(construction publique)* fountain

fonte [fɔ̃t] *nf* (**a**) *(de métaux)* melting down; **la f. des neiges** the thaw (**b**) *(alliage)* cast iron; **poêle en f.** cast-iron stove (**c**) *Typ* font

fonts [fɔ̃] *nmpl* **f. baptismaux** font

foot [fut] *nm Fam Br* football, *Am* soccer

football [futbol] *nm Br* football, *Am* soccer

footballeur, -euse [futbolœr, -øz] *nm,f Br* footballer, *Am* soccer player

footing [futiŋ] *nm* jogging; **faire du f.** to go jogging

for [fɔr] *nm* **dans** *ou* **en son f. intérieur** in one's heart of hearts, deep (down) inside

forage [fɔraʒ] *nm* drilling, boring

forain, -e [fɔrɛ̃, -ɛn] **1** *adj voir* **fête, marchand**
2 *nm* fairground stallholder

forçat [fɔrsa] *nm (prisonnier)* convict

force [fɔrs] *nf* (**a**) *(vigueur)* strength; **ne pas se sentir/ne pas être de f. à faire qch** not to feel/not to be up to doing sth; **de f. égale, de même f.** equally matched; **dans la f. de l'âge** in the prime of life; **être à bout de forces** to have no strength left; **c'est au-dessus de ses forces** it's too much for him; **de toutes ses forces** *(pousser, frapper)* with all one's strength; *(vouloir)* with all one's heart; **f. de caractère** strength of character; **c'est une f. de la nature** *(personne)* she's a force to be reckoned with; **les forces vives du pays** the country's resources (**b**) *(violence)* force; **faire qch de force** *ou* **par la f.** to do sth by force; **par la f. des choses** through force of circumstance (**c**) *(puissance)* **f. centrifuge/centripète** centrifugal/centripetal force; *aussi Fig* **f. d'inertie** inertia; **f. motrice** motive power; *Fig* driving force (**d**) *(organisation)* **les forces armées** the armed forces; **les forces aériennes** the airforce; **f. de dissuasion** deterrent; **f. de frappe** strike force; **les forces de police** *ou* **de l'ordre** the police (force) (**e**) *(locutions)* **à f.** in the end; **à f. de volonté** through sheer willpower; **à f. d'insister, tu vas finir par m'agacer** if you keep going on about it, I'm going to get annoyed; **en f.** in force

forcé, -e [fɔrse] *adj* forced; *Fam* **c'est f.!** it's inevitable!

forcément [fɔrsemɑ̃] *adv* inevitably; **elle sera f. déçue** she's bound to be disappointed; **pas f.** not necessarily

forcené, -e [fɔrsəne] **1** *adj (partisan, individualisme)* fanatical; *(haine, lutte)* frenzied
2 *nm,f* maniac

forceps [fɔrsɛps] *nm* forceps

forcer [16] [fɔrse] **1** *vt* (**a**) *(obliger)* to force; **f. qn à faire qch** to force sb to do sth; **f. la main à qn** to force sb's hand; **f. le respect/l'admiration** to command respect/admiration (**b**) *(faire céder)(porte)* to force (open) (**c**) *(voix)* to strain; *Fig* **f. la dose** to overdo it
2 *vi (appuyer, tirer)* to force it; *(se surmener)* to overdo it; *Fam* **f. sur qch** to overdo sth
3 se forcer *vpr (s'obliger)* to force oneself (**à faire qch** to do sth)

forcing [fɔrsiŋ] *nm Fam* sustained pressure; **faire du f.** to put on a lot of pressure

forcir [fɔrsir] *vi (vent, tempête)* to get stronger

forer [fɔre] *vt* to drill, to bore

forestier, -ère [fɔrɛstje, -ɛr] **1** *adj (zone, chemin)* forest; **exploitation forestière** *(activité)* forestry
2 *nm* forester

forêt [fɔrɛ] *nf* forest; **F.-noire** *(gâteau)* Black Forest gateau; **f. vierge** virgin forest

foreuse [fɔrøz] *nf* drill

forfait¹ [fɔrfɛ] *nm (crime)* heinous crime

forfait² *nm* (**a**) *(contrat)* fixed-price contract; **travailler au f.** to do fixed-price work (**b**) **être au f.** *(fiscalement)* to pay an estimated amount of tax (**c**) *(prix global)* all-in price; **f. week-end** weekend package (**d**) *(de ski)* pass

forfait³ *nm voir* **déclarer**

forfaitaire [fɔrfɛtɛr] *adj (indemnités)* basic; *(prix)* all-in

forfanterie [fɔrfɑ̃tri] *nf* bragging

forge [fɔrʒ] *nf* forge

forger [45] [fɔrʒe] **1** *vt* (**a**) *(métal)* to forge; *Fig (caractère)* to form (**b**) *(inventer) (histoire, excuse)* to make up
2 se forger *vpr* **se f. une réputation** to carve out a reputation for oneself

forgeron [fɔrʒərɔ̃] *nm* (black)smith

formaliser [fɔrmalize] **1** *vt* to formalize
2 se formaliser *vpr* to take offence (**de** at)

formalisme [fɔrmalism] *nm* formalism

formalité [fɔrmalite] *nf* formality; **les formalités d'usage** the usual formalities

format [fɔrma] *nm* format; *Ordinat* **f. d'écran** screen format; *Ordinat* **f. de fichier** file format; *Ordinat* **f. d'impression** print format; **f. de papier** paper format; **f. de poche** pocket format

formatage [fɔrmataʒ] *nm Ordinat* formatting

formater [fɔrmate] *vt Ordinat* to format

formateur, -trice [fɔrmatœr, -tris] **1** *adj* formative
2 *nm,f* trainer

formation [fɔrmasjɔ̃] *nf* (**a**) *(de roches, d'un mot)* formation; *(du caractère)* forming (**b**) *(éducation)* training; **f. continue** *ou* **permanente** continuing education; **f. professionnelle** vocational training; **être en f.** to be undergoing training (**c**) *(groupe)* group

forme [fɔrm] *nf* (**a**) *(configuration)* shape, form; **formes** *(d'une femme)* curves; **en f. d'une croix** in the shape of a cross; **en f. de L** L-shaped; **sous f. de qch** in the form of sth; **sous toutes ses formes** in all its forms; **sans f.** shapeless; **prendre f.** to take shape (**b**) *(manière)* form; **en bonne et due f.** in due form; **sans autre f. de procès** without further ado (**c**) *(convention)* **de pure f.** purely formal; **pour la f.** as a matter of form; **dans les formes** in the accepted way (**d**) *(bonne santé physique)* form; **être en (pleine) f.** to be on (top) form

formel, -elle [fɔrmɛl] *adj* **(a)** *(personne)* positive; *(ordre)* express; *(démenti, refus)* flat; *(interdiction)* strict **(b)** *(apparent)* formal **(c)** *(soutenu)* formal

formellement [fɔrmɛlmã] *adv* **(a)** *(interdire)* strictly; *(affirmer)* categorically; *(identifier)* positively **(b)** *(du point de vue de la forme)* formally

former [fɔrme] **1** *vt* **(a)** *(créer) (gouvernement, projet)* to form **(b)** *(constituer)* to form; **ils forment une bonne équipe/un beau couple** they make a good team/a lovely couple **(c)** *(tracer) (lettre)* to form **(d)** *(entraîner)* to train **(e)** *(développer) (caractère)* to form; *(esprit, goût, jugement)* to develop
2 se former *vpr* **(a)** *(apparaître)* to form; *(association, liens)* to be formed **(b)** *(mûrir) (goût)* to develop **(c)** *(apprendre son métier)* to train oneself

Formica® [fɔrmika] *nm* Formica®; **en F.** Formica®

formidable [fɔrmidabl] *adj* **(a)** *(fantastique)* great, fantastic **(b)** *(gigantesque)* tremendous

formol [fɔrmɔl] *nm* formalin

formulaire [fɔrmylɛr] *nm* form; **remplir un f.** to fill in *or* out a form; *Ordinat* **f. de saisie** input form

formulation [fɔrmylasjɔ̃] *nf* formulation, wording

formule [fɔrmyl] *nf* **(a)** *(expression)* expression, phrase; **selon la f. consacrée** as the expression goes; **f. magique** magic formula; **f. de politesse** polite phrase; *(au début d'une lettre)* standard opening; *(à la fin d'une lettre)* standard ending **(b)** *(solution)* method; **nouvelle f.** *(menu, abonnement)* new-style **(c)** *(en mathématique, en chimie)* formula **(d)** *(automobile)* **f. 1/2** Formula 1/2

formuler [fɔrmyle] *vt* to formulate

forniquer [fɔrnike] *vi* to fornicate

FORPRONU [fɔrprɔny] *nf* *(abrév* **Forces de protection des Nations unies)** la F. UNPROFOR

forsythia [fɔrsisja] *nm* forsythia

fort, -e [fɔr, fɔrt] **1** *adj* **(a)** *(vigoureux)* strong; **f. comme un Turc** *ou* **un bœuf** as strong as an ox; **c'est une forte tête** she's very strong-minded; **c'est plus f. que moi!** I can't help it!; *Fam* **c'est un peu f.!** that's a bit much!; **le plus f., c'est que...** the best of it is,... **(b)** *(doué)* **être f. en qch** to be good at sth **(c)** *(boisson, odeur, vent, lumière, accent)* strong; *(mer)* heavy; *(voix)* loud **(d)** *(robuste) (personne)* large **(e)** *(considérable) (somme d'argent)* large; *(pente)* steep; **il y a de fortes chances (pour) que ça réussisse** there's a good chance it will work
2 *adv* **(a)** *(parler, crier, chanter)* loud, loudly; *(frapper, tirer)* hard; *(sentir)* strong; *Fam* **y aller f.** to overdo it; *Fam* **faire (très) f.** to do (really) brilliantly **(b)** *(très)* very **(c)** *(beaucoup)* very much; **avoir f. à faire (avec qn/qch)** to have one's work cut out (with sb/sth)
3 *nm* **(a)** *(spécialité)* strong point **(b)** *(citadelle)* fort **(c)** **au plus f. de qch** *(hiver)* in the depths of sth; *(été, épidémie, tempête)* at the height of sth

fortement [fɔrtəmã] *adv* **(a)** *(avec force) (tirer, pousser)* hard **(b)** *(intensément) (désirer, souhaiter, influencer)* strongly; *(impressionner, irriter)* greatly; *(insister)* firmly **(c)** *(très) (épicé)* highly; *(conseillé)* strongly

forteresse [fɔrtərɛs] *nf* fortress

fortifiant, -e [fɔrtifjã, -ãt] **1** *adj (nourriture, boisson)* fortifying
2 *nm* tonic

fortification [fɔrtifikasjɔ̃] *nf* fortification

fortifier [66] [fɔrtifje] *vt (ville, mur)* to fortify; *(muscles, corps, sentiment)* to strengthen

fortuit, -e [fɔrtɥi, -it] *adj* chance, fortuitous

fortune [fɔrtyn] *nf* **(a)** *(richesse)* fortune; **faire f.** to make one's fortune **(b)** *(hasard)* fortune, chance; **de f.** *(moyens,* *installation)* makeshift; **faire contre mauvaise f. bon cœur** to make the best of it

fortuné, -e [fɔrtyne] *adj (riche)* wealthy

forum [fɔrɔm] *nm* forum

fosse [fos] *nf* **(a)** *(creux)* pit; **f. d'aisances** cesspool; **f. aux lions** lions' den; **f. d'orchestre** orchestra pit; **f. septique** septic tank **(b)** *(tombe)* grave; **f. commune** mass grave

fossé [fose] *nm (le long de la route)* ditch; *(autour d'un château)* moat; *Fig (entre personnes)* gulf

fossette [fosɛt] *nf* dimple

fossile [fɔsil] **1** *adj* fossil
2 *nm* *Fam aussi Fig* fossil

fossoyeur [foswajœr] *nm* gravedigger; *Fig* destroyer

fou, folle [fu, fɔl] *nm*

fol is used before masculine singular nouns beginning with a vowel or h mute.

1 *adj* **(a)** *(dément)* mad, insane; **f. de joie** beside oneself with joy; **f. à lier** raving mad; **être f. (amoureux) de qn/qch** to be mad about sb/sth **(b)** *(énorme)* tremendous; *(prix)* exorbitant **(c)** *(incroyable)* incredible **(d)** *(train)* runaway; *(boussole, aiguille)* crazy; **f. rire** uncontrollable laugh; **avoir un** *ou* **le f. rire** to have the giggles
2 *nm,f* madman, *f* madwoman; *Fam* **comme un f.** like mad; **entrer/sortir comme un f.** to storm in/out; **faire le f.** to play *or* act the fool; **un f. furieux** a maniac; **un f. du volant** a reckless driver; *Prov* **plus on est de fous, plus on rit** the more the merrier
3 *nm* **(a)** *(aux échecs)* bishop **(b)** *(bouffon)* jester **(c)** **f. de Bassan** gannet

foudre [fudr] **1** *nf* lightning; *Litt* **s'attirer les foudres de qn** to bring down sb's wrath on one
2 *nm* **un f. de guerre** a great warrior; *Fig* **ce n'est pas un f. de guerre** he's no bright spark

foudroyant, -e [fudrwajã, -ãt] *adj (maladie)* violent; *(crise cardiaque)* massive; *(révélation, nouvelle)* devastating; *(succès)* stunning; *(vitesse, progrès)* lightning; *(regard)* withering

foudroyer [32] [fudrwaje] *vt* to strike; **être foudroyé** to be struck by lightning; **f. qn du regard** to give sb a withering look

fouet [fwe] *nm (pour punir)* whip; *(de cuisine)* whisk; **de plein f.** head-on

fouetter [fwete] **1** *vt* **(a)** *(punir)* to whip; *Fam* **il n'y a pas de quoi f. un chat** it's nothing to make a fuss about; *Fam* **avoir d'autres chats à f.** to have other fish to fry **(b)** *(cingler)* to lash (against) **(c)** *(battre) (œufs)* to beat, to whisk; *(crème)* to whip
2 *vi Fam (puer)* to stink

foufou, fofolle [fufu, fɔfɔl] *adj Fam* daft

fougasse [fugas] *nf* = type of flat bread often made with olives, herbs, bacon etc and traditionally cooked in wood ash

fougère [fuʒɛr] *nf* fern

fougue [fug] *nf* fire, spirit

fougueusement [fugøzmã] *adv (s'élancer)* impetuously; *(s'embrasser)* passionately

fougueux, -euse [fugø, -øz] *adj (personne, tempérament)* fiery, ardent; *(cheval)* spirited

fouille [fuj] *nf* **(a)** *(recherche)* search; **faire une f.** to make a search **(b)** **fouilles** *(archéologiques)* excavations, dig **(c)** *Fam (poche)* pocket

fouillé, -e [fuje] *adj (approfondi)* detailed

fouiller [fuje] **1** *vt* **(a)** *(maison, personne)* to search **(b)** *(problème)* to go thoroughly into
2 *vi* to search **(dans** in)

fouillis [fuji] *nm* jumble, muddle

fouine [fwin] *nf* stone marten

fouiner [fwine] *vi* to nose about (**dans** in)

foulard [fular] *nm* scarf

foule [ful] *nf (de gens)* crowd; **il ne supporte pas la f.** he can't stand crowds; *Fig* **une f. de qch** lots of sth

foulée [fule] *nf (d'un coureur)* stride; *Fig* **dans la f., j'ai vérifié les comptes** while I was at it, I checked the accounts

fouler [fule] **1** *vt (sol)* to tread; *(raisins)* to press; *Fig* **f. qch aux pieds** to trample sth underfoot
2 se fouler *vpr* (**a**) **se f. la cheville** to sprain one's ankle (**b**) *Fam (se fatiguer)* to strain oneself

foulure [fulyr] *nf* sprain

four [fur] *nm* (**a**) *(de cuisine)* oven; **f. à gaz/électrique/à micro-ondes** gas/electric/microwave oven; **cuit au f.** *(pain)* baked; *(viande)* roasted; **il fait noir comme dans un f.** it's pitch black; **on ne peut être à la fois au f. et au moulin** you can't be in two places at once (**b**) **petits fours** *(gâteaux)* petits fours (**c**) *(industriel)* kiln; *Hist* **les fours crématoires** the gas ovens (**d**) *Fam (fiasco)* flop; **faire un f.** to flop

fourbe [furb] **1** *adj* deceitful
2 *nmf* cheat

fourbi [furbi] *nm Fam* (**a**) *(désordre)* mess (**b**) *(truc)* thingy

fourbu, -e [furby] *adj* exhausted

fourche [furʃ] *nf* (**a**) *(outil)* fork (**b**) *(de bicyclette, sur une route)* fork; *(des cheveux)* split end; **faire une f.** to fork

fourcher [furʃe] *vi* **sa langue a fourché** she made a slip of the tongue

fourchette [furʃɛt] *nf* (**a**) *(ustensile)* fork; *Fam* **avoir un joli** *ou* **bon coup de f.** to have a hearty appetite (**b**) *(écart)* bracket; **f. de prix** price bracket

fourchu, -e [furʃy] *adj* forked; **avoir les cheveux fourchus** to have split ends

fourgon [furgɔ̃] *nm* (**a**) *(véhicule)* van; **f. cellulaire** *Br* police van, *Am* patrol wagon; **f. funèbre** *ou* **funéraire** hearse (**b**) *(d'un train)* **f. à bétail** cattle truck

fourgonnette [furgɔnɛt] *nf* small van

fourguer [furge] *vt Fam* **f. qch à qn** to unload sth onto sb

fourmi [furmi] *nf* ant; *Fig (personne travailleuse)* busy bee; **avoir des fourmis (dans les jambes)** to have pins and needles (in one's legs)

fourmilière [furmiljer] *nf* anthill

fourmillement [furmijmɑ̃] *nm* (**a**) *(sensation)* pins and needles (**b**) *(agitation)* swarming

fourmiller [furmije] **1** *vi* to swarm, to teem
2 fourmiller de *vt ind* to swarm with, to teem with

fournaise [furnɛz] *nf* furnace

fourneau, -x [furno] *nm* (**a**) *(de cuisine)* stove; **être aux fourneaux** to be cooking (**b**) *(de verrier, de fondeur)* furnace (**c**) *(d'une pipe)* bowl

fournée [furne] *nf aussi Fig* batch

fourni, -e [furni] *adj* (**a**) *(magasin)* **bien/mal f.** well/poorly stocked (**b**) *(barbe, sourcils)* bushy; **peu f.** sparse

fournil [furni] *nm* bakehouse

fournir [furnir] **1** *vt* (**a**) *(approvisionner)* to supply (**en** with) (**b**) *(procurer)* **f. qch à qn** to provide sb with sth (**c**) *(présenter) (preuve, alibi)* to provide; *(documents)* to provide; **pièces à f.** required documents (**d**) *(effort)* to make
2 se fournir *vpr* **se f. en qch** to get in supplies of sth; **se f. chez qn** to get one's supplies from sb

fournisseur, -euse [furnisœr, -øz] *nm,f* supplier; *Ordinat* **f. d'accès** access provider

fournitures [furnityr] *nfpl* **f. de bureau** office supplies; **f. scolaires** educational stationery

fourrage [furaʒ] *nm* fodder

fourrager[1] [45] [furaʒe] *vi Fam (fouiller)* to rummage (**dans** in)

fourrager[2], **-ère** [furaʒe, -ɛr] *adj (plante)* fodder

fourreau, -x [furo] *nm* (**a**) *(d'épée)* sheath, scabbard; *(de parapluie)* cover (**b**) *(robe)* **f.** sheath dress; **jupe f.** pencil skirt

fourrer [fure] **1** *vt* (**a**) *(gâteau, bonbon)* to fill (**à** with); **bonbon fourré** *Br* soft-centred sweet, *Am* soft-centered candy (**b**) *Fam (mettre)* to stick
2 se fourrer *vpr Fam* **où est-il allé se f.?** where's he got to?; **ne pas savoir où se f.** not to know where to put oneself; **se f. dans une sale affaire** to get involved in a nasty business

fourre-tout [furtu] **1** *adj inv (placard)* junk; **un texte/ une loi f.** a jumble of a text/a law
2 *nm inv* (**a**) *(pièce)* junk room; *(placard)* junk cupboard (**b**) *(sac) Br* holdall, *Am* carryall

fourreur [furœr] *nm* furrier

fourrière [furjɛr] *nf* pound; **mettre en f.** *ou* **à la f.** *(voiture)* to impound; *(chien)* to put in the pound

fourrure [furyr] *nf* fur; **de** *ou* **en f.** fur

fourvoyer [32] [furvwaje] *Litt* **se fourvoyer** *vpr* to lose one's way; *Fig* to go astray

foutaise [futɛz] *nf Fam* bullshit

foutoir [futwar] *nm Fam* dump

foutre [futr] *très Fam* **1** *vt* (**a**) *(mettre)* to stick; **f. qch par terre** to chuck sth on the ground; **f. qn à la porte** to kick sb out; **f. qch en l'air** *(le faire échouer)* to screw sth up (**b**) *(faire)* to do; **ne rien f.** to do damn all; **je n'en ai rien à f.!** I couldn't give a damn!; **qu'est-ce que ça peut f.?** what the hell does it matter? (**c**) *(donner) (correction, gifle)* to give; **f. la trouille à qn** to put the wind up sb (**d**) *(locutions)* **f. le camp** to piss off; **fous(-moi) le camp!** piss off!; **je t'en foutrais, du champagne!** champagne, you'll be bloody lucky!; *Vulg* **va te faire f.!** fuck off!
2 se foutre *vpr* (**a**) *(se mettre)* **se f. un coup** to bang oneself; **se f. par terre** to go sprawling; **se f. dedans** to screw up (**b**) **se f. (de la gueule de) qn** *(se moquer de)* to take the piss out of sb; **se f. du monde** to take the piss (**c**) **se f. de qn/qch** *(être indifférent à)* not to give a damn about sb/sth; **je m'en fous** I don't give a damn

foutu, -e [futy] *adj Fam* (**a**) *(maudit)* damn (**b**) *(en mauvais état, perdu)* **être f.** to have had it; **c'est f.!** forget it! (**c**) **être bien/mal f.** *(bien/mal bâti)* to have/not to have a nice body; *(bien/mal conçu)* to be well/badly designed; **être mal f.** *(malade)* to be under the weather (**d**) *(capable)* **être f. de faire qch** to be quite likely to do sth

fox [fɔks], **fox-terrier** *(pl* **fox-terriers**) [fɔksterje] *nm* fox terrier

foyer [fwaje] *nm* (**a**) *(domicile)* home; **le f. conjugal** the marital home (**b**) *(famille)* family (**c**) *(résidence) (d'étudiants)* residence; *(de travailleurs, de délinquants)* hostel (**d**) *(de chaleur, d'infection)* source; *(d'incendie, de conflits)* seat (**e**) *(âtre)* hearth (**f**) *(de lunettes)* focus

fracas [fraka] *nm* crash

fracassant, -e [frakasɑ̃, -ɑ̃t] *adj (bruit)* deafening; *(nouvelle, révélation)* shattering; *(succès)* resounding

fracasser [frakase] **1** *vt* to smash
2 se fracasser *vpr* to smash

fraction [fraksjɔ̃] *nf* (**a**) *(partie)* part (**b**) *Math* fraction

fractionnement [fraksjɔnmɑ̃] *nm* splitting up

fractionner [fraksjɔne] **1** *vt* to split up
2 se fractionner *vpr* to split up

fracture [fraktyr] *nf* fracture; **f. du crâne** fractured skull; *Fig* **f. sociale** social fracture

fracturer [fraktyre] **1** *vt* (**a**) *(serrure, porte)* to break open (**b**) *(os)* to fracture **2 se fracturer** *vpr* **se f. le tibia** to fracture one's tibia

fragile [fraʒil] *adj (matériau, objet)* fragile; *(santé, estomac, équilibre)* delicate; *(personne) (physiquement)* frail; *(mentalement)* sensitive; *(bonheur)* precarious; *(hypothèse)* shaky

fragiliser [fraʒilize] *vt* to weaken

fragilité [fraʒilite] *nf (d'un matériau, d'un objet)* fragility; *(d'une personne) (physique)* frailty; *(mentale)* sensitivity; *(du bonheur)* precariousness; *(d'une hypothèse)* shakiness; *(de la santé, de l'estomac, d'un équilibre)* delicacy

fragment [fragmɑ̃] *nm (d'un objet, de conversation, fragment, (d'un livre)* extract; *(de vérité)* shred

fragmentaire [fragmɑ̃tɛr] *adj* fragmentary

fragmenter [fragmɑ̃te] *vt* to fragment

fraîche [frɛʃ] *adj voir* **frais¹**

fraîchement [frɛʃmɑ̃] *adv* (**a**) *(recevoir, accueillir)* coolly (**b**) *(récemment)* newly

fraîcheur [frɛʃœr] *nf (de la température, d'un accueil)* coolness; *(d'aliments, du teint)* freshness

fraîchir [frɛʃir] *vi (temps)* to freshen

frais¹, fraîche [frɛ, frɛʃ] **1** *adj* (**a**) *(vent, air, accueil)* cool (**b**) *(aliments, fleurs, teint)* fresh; **f. et dispos** hale and hearty (**c**) *(souvenir, nouvelles)* recent; *(encre, peinture)* wet **2** *adv* **servir/boire f.** *(sur étiquette)* serve/drink chilled; **f. émoulu de** fresh out of **3** *nm* **prendre le f.** to get a breath of fresh air; **mettre/ conserver qch au f.** to put/keep sth in a cool place; **il fait f.** it's cool **4** *nf* **à la fraîche** in the cool part of the day

frais² *nmpl* expenses, costs; **faire de gros f.** to go to great expense; **tous f. payés** all expenses paid; **rentrer dans ses f.** to cover one's expenses; *Fig* **faire les f. de qch** *(être victime de)* to pay the price for sth; **faire les f. de la conversation** to keep the conversation going; **faire qch à ses f.** to do sth at one's own expense; **aux f. de la société** at the company's expense; **aux f. de la princesse** at the firm's/government's/*etc* expense; **à grands/peu de f.** at great/little cost; **se mettre en f.** to go to great expense; **en être pour ses f.** to have been wasting one's time; **f. de déplacement** travelling expenses; **f. généraux** overheads; **f. d'inscription** membership fee; **f. de port** postage and packing; **f. de scolarité** school fees; **faux f.** incidental expenses

fraise¹ [frɛz] *nf (fruit)* strawberry; **f. des bois** wild strawberry

fraise² *nf (de dentiste)* drill

fraise³ *nf (collerette)* ruff

fraisier [frɛzje] *nm* (**a**) *(plante)* strawberry plant (**b**) *(gâteau)* strawberry cream cake

framboise [frɑ̃bwaz] *nf* raspberry

framboisier [frɑ̃bwazje] *nm* raspberry bush

franc¹ [frɑ̃] *nm* franc; *Anciennement* **f. français/belge** French/Belgian franc; **f. CFA** CFA franc; **ancien/nouveau f.** old/new franc; **f. suisse** Swiss franc; **f. symbolique** nominal sum

franc², franche [frɑ̃, frɑ̃ʃ] **1** *adj* (**a**) *(sincère)* frank (**b**) *(zone, ville, port)* free (**c**) *(net) (couleur)* pure; *(rupture)* clean **2** *adv (parler)* frankly

français, -e [frɑ̃sɛ, -ɛz] **1** *adj* French **2** *nm,f* **F.** Frenchman, *f* Frenchwoman; **les F.** the French **3** *nm (langue)* French; **parler f.** to speak French;

(correctement) to speak properly; *Fam* **tu ne comprends pas le f.?** don't you understand plain English?

France [frɑ̃s] *nf* **la F.** France; *TV* **F. 2/3** = second/third French state-owned TV channel

Francfort [frɑ̃kfɔr] *n* Frankfurt

franche [frɑ̃ʃ] *adj voir* **franc**

franchement [frɑ̃ʃmɑ̃] *adv* (**a**) *(sincèrement)* frankly (**b**) *(tout à fait, vraiment)* really (**c**) *(carrément)* **y aller f.** to get on with it

franchir [frɑ̃ʃir] *vt (obstacle, difficulté)* to get over; *(porte)* to go through; *(fossé)* to jump (over); *(ligne d'arrivée, rivière, frontière)* to cross; *Fig (cap, seuil, niveau)* to pass

franchise [frɑ̃ʃiz] *nf* (**a**) *(sincérité)* frankness; **en toute f.** quite frankly (**b**) *(exonération)* exemption; **f. postale** postage paid (**c**) *(d'assurance)* *Br* excess, *Am* deductible (**d**) *Com* franchise

franchouillard, -e [frɑ̃ʃujar, -ard] *adj Fam* typically French

franciscain, -e [frɑ̃siskɛ̃, -ɛn] *adj & nm,f* Franciscan

franciser [frɑ̃size] *vt* to gallicize

franc-maçon (*pl* francs-maçons) [frɑ̃masɔ̃] *nm* freemason

franc-maçonnerie [frɑ̃masɔnri] *nf* freemasonry

franco [frɑ̃ko] *adv* (**a**) *Com (franchement)* **y aller f.** to get on with it (**b**) *Com* **f. (de port)** postage paid; **f. à bord** on board

francophile [frɑ̃kɔfil] *adj & nmf* Francophile

francophobe [frɑ̃kɔfɔb] *adj & nmf* Francophobe

francophone [frɑ̃kɔfɔn] **1** *adj* French-speaking **2** *nmf* French speaker

francophonie [frɑ̃kɔfɔni] *nf* French-speaking world

franc-parler [frɑ̃parle] *nm* outspokenness; **avoir son f.** to speak one's mind

franc-tireur (*pl* francs-tireurs) [frɑ̃tirœr] *nm (combattant)* irregular (soldier); *Fig* maverick

frange [frɑ̃ʒ] *nf* fringe

frangin, -e [frɑ̃ʒɛ̃, -in] *nm,f Fam* brother, *f* sister

frangipane [frɑ̃ʒipan] *nf* = almond-flavoured confectioner's custard

franglais [frɑ̃glɛ] *nm* Franglais

franquette [frɑ̃kɛt] *nf* **à la bonne f.** without ceremony, informally

frappant, -e [frapɑ̃, -ɑ̃t] *adj* striking

frappe [frap] *nf* (**a**) *(sur un clavier d'ordinateur)* keying; *(sur une machine à écrire)* typing; *Ordinat* **f. en continu** type-ahead; *Ordinat* **f. au kilomètre** continuous input (**b**) *(de monnaie)* minting (**c**) *(au base-ball)* hit; *(au football)* kick; *(en boxe)* punch (**d**) *Fam (voyou)* hoodlum

frappé, -e [frape] *adj* (**a**) *(champagne)* chilled; *(café)* iced (**b**) *Fam (fou)* crazy

frapper [frape] **1** *vt* (**a**) *(donner un ou des coups à)* to hit, to strike; *Fig (faire une forte impression sur)* to strike (**b**) *(monnaie)* to mint (**c**) *(champagne)* to put on ice **2** *vi* (**a**) *(donner un coup)* to strike, to hit; **f. du poing sur la table** to bang (on) the table; **f. des mains** *ou* **mains** to clap (one's hands); **f. à la porte** to knock on *or* at the door; **f. tu frappes à la bonne/mauvaise porte** you've come to the right/wrong place; **entrez sans f.** *(sur écriteau)* go straight in **3** *se frapper* *vpr Fam (s'en faire ou du souci)* to get oneself worked up

frasques [frask] *nfpl* carryings-on

fraternel, -elle [fratɛrnɛl] *adj* fraternal, brotherly

fraterniser [fratɛrnize] *vi* to fraternize

fraternité [fratɛrnite] *nf* fraternity, brotherhood

fratricide [fratrisid] **1** *adj* fratricidal
2 *nmf (personne)* fratricide
3 *nm (crime)* fratricide

fraude [frod] *nf* fraud; **passer qch en f.** to smuggle sth in; **f. électorale** electoral fraud; **f. fiscale** tax evasion

frauder [frode] **1** *vt (douane)* to defraud; **f. le fisc** to evade tax
2 *vi* to cheat (**sur** on)

fraudeur, -euse [frodœr, -øz] *nm,f* defrauder

frauduleux, -euse [frodylø, -øz] *adj* fraudulent

frayer [53] [freje] **1** *vi (poisson)* to spawn; *Fig* **f. avec qn** to mix with sb
2 se frayer *vpr* **se f. un chemin** to clear a way (for oneself)

frayeur [frejœr] *nf* fright; **faire une f. à qn** to give sb a fright

fredaines [frədɛn] *nfpl* pranks, escapades

fredonner [frədɔne] *vt & vi* to hum

free-lance [frilɑ̃s] **1** *adj inv* freelance
2 *nm (travail)* freelance work; **travailler en f.** to work freelance
3 *nmf (pl* **free-lances**) freelance, freelancer

freezer [frizœr] *nm* freezer compartment

frégate [fregat] *nf* **(a)** *(oiseau)* frigate bird **(b)** *(navire)* frigate

frein [frɛ̃] *nm* **(a)** *(de voiture)* brake; **donner un coup de f.** to put on the brakes; *Fig* **mettre un f. à qch** to curb sth; **freins à disque** disc brakes; **f. à main** *Br* handbrake, *Am* parking brake; **f. moteur** engine brake **(b)** *(mors)* bit

freinage [frɛnaʒ] *nm* braking

freiner [frene] **1** *vt* **(a)** *(véhicule, processus)* to slow down; *(chute)* to break; *(inflation, production)* to curb **(b)** *(personne)* to restrain
2 *vi* to brake

frelaté, -e [frəlate] *adj (vin)* adulterated

frelater [frəlate] *vt* to adulterate

frêle [frɛl] *adj* frail

frelon [frəlɔ̃] *nm* hornet

freluquet [frəlykɛ] *nm Fam* whippersnapper

frémir [fremir] *vi* **(a)** *(personne)* to tremble (**de** with) **(b)** *(eau chaude)* to simmer; *(feuillage)* to rustle

frémissant, -e [fremisɑ̃, -ɑ̃t] *adj (eau)* simmering; *(voix)* trembling; *(feuillage)* rustling

frémissement [fremismɑ̃] *nm* **(a)** *(de peur)* shudder; *(de plaisir, de joie)* thrill; *(de colère, d'impatience)* quiver **(b)** *(de l'eau)* simmering; *(des feuilles)* rustle

french cancan [pl **french cancans**) [frɛnʃkɑ̃kɑ̃] *nm* cancan

frêne [frɛn] *nm* ash

frénésie [frenezi] *nf* frenzy

frénétique [frenetik] *adj* frenzied

frénétiquement [frenetikmɑ̃] *adv* frenziedly

fréquemment [frekamɑ̃] *adv* frequently

fréquence [frekɑ̃s] *nf* frequency; **basse/haute f.** low/high frequency

fréquent, -e [frekɑ̃, -ɑ̃t] *adj* frequent

fréquentable [frekɑ̃tabl] *adj* **des gens peu fréquentables** people you wouldn't want to associate with; **un endroit peu f.** a place you wouldn't want to be seen in

fréquentation [frekɑ̃tasjɔ̃] *nf* **(a)** *(d'un lieu)* frequenting; **la f. de qn** seeing sb regularly **(b)** *(relations)* company; **avoir de mauvaises fréquentations** to keep bad company

fréquenté, -e [frekɑ̃te] *adj* **très f.** very busy; **bien/mal f.** of good/ill repute

fréquenter [frekɑ̃te] **1** *vt* **(a)** *(lieu)* to frequent **(b)** *(personne)* *(voir régulièrement)* to see regularly; *(sortir avec)* to go out with
2 se fréquenter *vpr (se voir régulièrement)* to see each other regularly; *(sortir ensemble)* to go out with each other

frère [frɛr] **1** *adj (pays, peuple)* fellow
2 *nm* brother; **faux f.** false friend; **frères d'armes** brothers-in-arms

frérot [frero] *nm Fam* kid brother

fresque [frɛsk] *nf* fresco

fret [frɛ, frɛt] *nm* freight

frétillant, -e [fretijɑ̃, -ɑ̃t] *adj (poisson)* wriggling; *(personne) (de joie)* quivering (**de** with)

frétiller [fretije] *vi (poisson, personne)* to wriggle; **f. de joie** to quiver with joy

fretin [frətɛ̃] *nm aussi Fig* **menu f.** small fry

freudien, -enne [frødjɛ̃, -ɛn] *adj* Freudian

freux [frø] *nm* rook

FRF *(abrév* **franc(s) français)** FF

friable [frijabl] *adj* crumbly

friand, -e [frijɑ̃, -ɑ̃d] **1** *adj* **être f. de qch** to be fond of sth
2 *nm (salé)* = small savoury pastry; *(sucré)* = small almond cake

friandise [frijɑ̃diz] *nf* titbit, delicacy

fric [frik] *nm Fam (argent)* cash

fricassée [frikase] *nf (ragoût)* fricassee; *Belg* fried egg and bacon

friche [friʃ] *nf* fallow land; **en f.** fallow; **f. industrielle** industrial wasteland

frichti [friʃti] *nm Fam* grub

fricot [friko] *nm Fam* grub; **faire le f.** to do the cooking

fricoter [frikɔte] *Fam* **1** *vt* **(a)** *(manigancer)* to cook up **(b)** *(plat)* to cook
2 *vi (avoir des activités suspectes)* to be on the fiddle

friction [friksjɔ̃] *nf* **(a)** *(massage)* rubdown; *(du cuir chevelu)* scalp massage **(b)** *(heurt)* friction

frictionner [friksjɔne] *vt (partie du corps)* to rub; *(personne)* to rub down

Frigidaire® [friʒidɛr] *nm* fridge

frigide [friʒid] *adj* frigid

frigidité [friʒidite] *nf* frigidity

frigo [frigo] *nm Fam* fridge

frigorifié, -e [frigɔrifje] *adj Fam (personne)* frozen stiff

frigorifier [66] [frigɔrifje] *vt (aliment)* to refrigerate

frigorifique [frigɔrifik] *adj voir* **camion**

frileux, -euse [frilø, -øz] *adj (personne)* sensitive to the cold; *(attitude, réponse)* timid; **elle est très frileuse** she really feels the cold

frime [frim] *nf Fam* show

frimer [frime] *vi Fam* to show off

frimeur, -euse [frimœr, -øz] *nm,f Fam* show-off

frimousse [frimus] *nf Fam* sweet little face

fringale [frɛ̃gal] *nf Fam (faim)* hunger; *Fig (envie)* craving (**de** for); **avoir la f.** to be starving

fringant, -e [frɛ̃gɑ̃, -ɑ̃t] *adj (personne)* dashing

fringuer [frɛ̃ge] *Fam* **1** *vt* to dress
2 se fringuer *vpr* to get dressed

fringues [frɛ̃g] *nfpl Fam* gear

fripé, -e [fripe] *adj* crumpled

friper [fripe] **1** *vt* to crumple
2 se friper *vpr* to get crumpled
friperie [fripri] *nf* second-hand clothes *Br* shop *or Am* store
fripes [frip] *nfpl* second-hand clothes
fripier, -ère [fripje, -ɛr] *nm,f* second-hand clothes dealer
fripon, -onne [fripɔ̃, -ɔn] *Fam* **1** *adj* mischievous
2 *nm,f* rascal
fripouille [fripuj] *nf Fam* rogue
friqué, -e [frike] *adj Fam* loaded
frire [19a] [frir] **1** *vt* to fry
2 *vi* to fry; **faire f.** qch to fry sth
Frisbee® [frizbi] *nm* Frisbee®
frise [friz] *nf* frieze
frisé, -e [frize] **1** *adj (cheveux)* curly; *(personne)* curly-haired
2 *nf* frisée *(salade)* curly endive
friser [frize] **1** *vt* (a) *(cheveux)* to curl (b) *(approcher)* **f. la catastrophe** to come within an inch of disaster
2 *vi (cheveux)* to curl, *(personne)* to have curly hair
frisette [frizɛt] *nf (de cheveux)* small curl
frisotter [frizɔte] **1** *vt (cheveux)* to frizz
2 *vi* to be frizzy
frisquet, -ette [friskɛ, -ɛt] *adj Fam* chilly; **il fait f.** it's chilly
frisson [frisɔ̃] *nm (de froid, de peur)* shiver; *(de plaisir)* thrill; **avoir des frissons** to shiver; **donner des frissons** *ou* **le f. à** qn *(de peur)* to give sb the shivers
frissonner [frisɔne] *vi* (a) *(personne) (de froid, de peur)* to shiver (b) *Litt (feuillage)* to quiver; *(eau)* to ripple
frit, -e [fri, frit] **1** *adj* fried
2 *nf* frite (a) *(de pomme de terre) Br* chip, *Am* (French) fry (b) *Fam* **avoir la frite** to be on form
friteuse [fritøz] *nf* deep frier; **f. électrique** electric frier
friture [frityr] *nf* (a) *(mode de cuisson)* frying (b) *(corps gras)* frying fat (c) *(aliments)* fried food; **f. (de poissons)** fried fish (d) *Rad & Tél* crackling (e) *Belg (friterie) Br* chip stall, *Am* French fry vendor
frivole [frivɔl] *adj* frivolous
frivolité [frivɔlite] *nf* frivolity
froc [frɔk] *nm* (a) *Fam (pantalon) Br* trousers, *Am* pants (b) *(habit religieux)* habit
froid, -e [frwa, frwad] **1** *adj aussi Fig* cold
2 *adv* **boire/manger qch f.** to drink/eat sth cold
3 *nm* cold; **les grands froids** the coldest part of the winter; **il fait f.** it's cold; *Fam* **il fait un f. de canard** it's freezing (cold); *Fig* **ça fait f. dans le dos** it sends a shiver down your spine; **avoir f.** to be cold; **j'ai f. aux mains** my hands are cold, I've got cold hands; *Fig* **ne pas avoir f. aux yeux** to have plenty of nerve; **à f.** *(répondre)* off the top of one's head; *(humour)* deadpan; **être en f. (avec qn)** to be on bad terms (with sb); **prendre f.** to catch cold
froidement [frwadmɑ̃] *adv (accueillir, recevoir)* coldly; *(abattre)* cold-bloodedly; *(répondre)* coolly
froideur [frwadœr] *nf* coldness; **avec f.** coldly
froissement [frwasmɑ̃] *nm* (a) *(bruit)* rustle (b) *(de muscle)* straining
froisser [frwase] **1** *vt* (a) *(tissu, papier)* to crumple, to crease (b) *Fig (sentiment, personne)* to offend
2 se froisser *vpr* (a) *(tissu)* to crease, to crumple (b) **se f. un muscle** to strain a muscle (c) *Fig (personne)* to take offence **(de** at)
frôlement [frolmɑ̃] *nm (contact)* brushing (contre against); *(son)* rustle
frôler [frole] **1** *vt* (a) *(effleurer)* to brush (against), to touch

lightly (b) *Fig (la mort, la catastrophe)* to come close to; *(le ridicule)* to border on
2 se frôler *vpr* to brush (against) each other
fromage [frɔmaʒ] *nm* (a) *(produit laitier)* cheese; *Fam Fig* **faire tout un f. de** qch to make a great fuss about sth; **f. blanc** fromage frais; **f. de chèvre** goat's cheese; **f. frais** soft cheese; **f. à pâte molle/dure** soft/hard cheese; **f. à tartiner** cheese spread (b) **f. de tête** *Br* brawn, *Am* headcheese
fromager, -ère [frɔmaʒe, -ɛr] **1** *adj* cheese
2 *nm,f (commerçant)* cheese seller; *(fabricant)* cheese-maker
fromagerie [frɔmaʒri] *nf (lieu de fabrication)* cheese dairy; *(magasin)* cheese shop
froment [frɔmɑ̃] *nm* wheat
fronce [frɔ̃s] *nf* gather
froncement [frɔ̃smɑ̃] *nm* **f. de(s) sourcils** frown
froncer [16] [frɔ̃se] *vt* (a) *(nez, front)* to wrinkle; **f. les sourcils** to frown (b) *(tissu)* to gather
fronde [frɔ̃d] *nf* (a) *(arme)* sling; *(jouet) Br* catapult, *Am* slingshot (b) *(révolte)* rebellion
frondeur, -euse [frɔ̃dœr, -øz] **1** *adj* rebellious
2 *nm,f* rebel
front [frɔ̃] *nm* (a) *(partie du visage)* forehead (b) *(avant)* front; **faire f.** to face up to things; **faire f. à** qn/qch to face up to sb/sth; **de f.** *(marcher, avancer)* side by side; *(heurter, aborder un problème)* head-on; **mener plusieurs choses de f.** to have several things on the go at once; **f. de mer** seafront (c) *(audace)* **avoir le f. de faire** qch to have the nerve to do sth (d) *Mil & Météo* front
frontal, -e, -aux, -ales [frɔ̃tal, -o] *adj* (a) *(attaque, choc)* head-on; **machine à laver à chargement f.** front-loading washing machine (b) *Ordinat* front-end; **ordinateur f.** front end (c) *(os)* frontal
frontalier, -ère [frɔ̃talje, -ɛr] **1** *adj (région)* border, frontier
2 *nm,f (habitant)* person living near the border; *(travailleur)* cross-border commuter
frontière [frɔ̃tjer] **1** *adj (ville, poste)* border, frontier
2 *nf (entre pays)* border, frontier; *Fig (des langues)* boundary; *(de la connaissance)* frontier
frontispice [frɔ̃tispis] *nm* frontispiece
fronton [frɔ̃tɔ̃] *nm* (a) *(sur monument)* pediment (b) *(de pelote basque)* fronton
frottement [frɔtmɑ̃] *nm (d'une chose contre une autre)* rubbing; *Tech* friction (b) *(heurt)* friction
frotter [frɔte] **1** *vt* to rub; *(allumette)* to strike; *(parquet)* to scrub
2 *vi* to rub (contre against)
3 se frotter *vpr* to rub oneself; *aussi Fig* **se f. les mains** to rub one's hands; *Fig* **se f. à** qn/qch to be in contact with sb/sth; *Fig* **se f. à** qn *(l'attaquer)* to meddle with sb
frottis [frɔti] *nm Méd* smear; **f. vaginal** cervical smear
froufrou [frufru] *nm* (a) *(bruit)* rustling (b) froufrous *(vêtements)* frills
froufrouter [frufrute] *vi* to rustle
froussard, -e [frusar, -ard] *adj & nm,f Fam* chicken
frousse [frus] *nf Fam* fear; **avoir la f.** to be scared
fructifier [66] [fryktifje] *vi (arbres, idée)* to bear fruit; *(terre)* to be productive; *(placements, capital)* to yield a profit; **faire f. qch** *(idée, projet)* to bring sth to fruition
fructose [fryktoz] *nm* fructose
fructueux, -euse [fryktчø, -øz] *adj* fruitful, profitable
frugal, -e, -aux, -ales [frygal, -o] *adj* frugal
frugalité [frygalite] *nf* frugality

fruit [frɥi] *nm aussi Fig* fruit; **des fruits** (some) fruit; **un f.** some fruit, a piece of fruit; **fruits confits** crystallized fruit; *Fig* **le f. défendu** the forbidden fruit; **fruits de mer** seafood; **f. de la passion** passion fruit; **fruits rouges** red berries and currants; **fruits secs** dried fruit

fruité, -e [frɥite] *adj* fruity

fruitier, -ère [frɥitje, -ɛr] **1** *adj voir* **arbre**
2 *nm,f* fruit seller, *Br* fruiterer

frusques [frysk] *nfpl Fam* gear

fruste [fryst] *adj (style, personne)* rough

frustrant, -e [frystrɑ̃, -ɑ̃t] *adj* frustrating

frustration [frystrasjɔ̃] *nf* frustration

frustré, -e [frystre] **1** *adj* frustrated
2 *nm,f* frustrated person

frustrer [frystre] *vt* **(a)** *(décevoir)* to frustrate **(b)** *(priver)* **f. qn de qch** to deprive sb of sth

FTP [ɛftepe] *nmpl (abrév* **Francs-tireurs et partisans**) = French Communist resistance group in the Second World War

fuchsia [fyʃja] **1** *adj inv* **(rose) f.** fuchsia
2 *nm (fleur, couleur)* fuchsia

fuel [fjul] *nm* fuel oil

fugace [fygas] *adj* fleeting

fugitif, -ive [fyʒitif, -iv] **1** *adj (fugace)* fleeting
2 *nm,f* fugitive, runaway

fugue [fyg] *nf* **(a)** *(composition musicale)* fugue **(b)** *(d'un enfant)* **faire une f.** to run away

fuguer [fyge] *vi* to run away

fugueur, -euse [fygœr, -øz] **1** *adj* who runs away a lot
2 *nm,f* runaway

fui *voir* **fuir**

fuir [38] [fɥir] **1** *vt (pays)* to flee; *(personne)* to run away from; *(guerre)* to escape; *(responsabilités)* to shirk
2 *vi* **(a)** *(s'échapper)* to run away, to flee **(devant** from); **f. de son pays** to flee one's country **(b)** *(robinet, gaz, eau)* to leak **(c)** *(s'écouler rapidement)* to fly by

fuis, fuit *voir* **fuir**

fuite [fɥit] *nf* **(a)** *(escapade)* flight **(devant** from); *Fig (devant des difficultés, des problèmes)* avoidance **(devant** of); **prendre la f.** to take flight; **être en f.** to be on the run; **mettre qn en f.** to put sb to flight; **la f. des capitaux** the flight of capital; **la f. des cerveaux** the brain drain **(b)** *(de liquide, de gaz, d'informations)* leak

fulgurant, -e [fylgyrɑ̃, -ɑ̃t] *adj* **(a)** *(attaque, changement, rapidité)* lightning; *(succès)* spectacular **(b)** *(douleur)* searing

fulminer [fylmine] *vi* to fulminate **(contre** against)

fumant, -e [fymɑ̃, -ɑ̃t] *adj* **(a)** *(âtre, cendres)* smoking; *(potage)* steaming **(b)** *Fam (remarquable)* **faire un coup f.** to pull off a masterstroke

fumé, -e [fyme] *adj* **(a)** *(poisson, viande)* smoked **(b)** *(verres)* tinted

fume-cigare [fymsigar] *nm inv* cigar holder

fumée [fyme] *nf (de feu, de cigarette)* smoke; *(d'un liquide chaud)* steam

fumer [fyme] **1** *vt* **(a)** *(poisson, viande)* to smoke **(b)** *(tabac, cigarette)* to smoke; **f. la pipe** to smoke a pipe
2 *vi* **(a)** *(feu, moteur)* to smoke; *(liquide, plat)* to steam **(b)** *(fumeur)* to smoke; **f. comme un pompier** *ou* **un sapeur** to smoke like a chimney

fumet [fymɛ] *nm (d'un mets)* aroma

fumeur, -euse [fymœr, -øz] *nm,f* smoker; **fumeurs** *(sur panneau)* smoking

fumeux, -euse [fymø, -øz] *adj (idées, explications, projets)* hazy

fumier [fymje] *nm* **(a)** *(engrais)* manure, dung **(b)** *très Fam (injure)* bastard

fumigation [fymigasjɔ̃] *nf* fumigation; *Méd* inhalation

fumiste [fymist] **1** *nmf Fam (sur qui on ne peut compter)* clown
2 *nm (technicien)* heating engineer
3 *adj Fam* unreliable

fumisterie [fymistəri] *nf* **(a)** *(métier)* heating engineering **(b)** *Fam (farce)* con

fumoir [fymwar] *nm* smoking room

funambule [fynɑ̃byl] *nmf* tightrope walker

funboard [fœnbɔrd] *nm* funboard

funèbre [fynɛbr] *adj* **(a)** *(cérémonie, marche)* funeral; **hymne** *ou* **chant f.** dirge **(b)** *(lugubre)* funereal

funérailles [fyneraj] *nfpl* funeral; **f. nationales** state funeral

funéraire [fynerɛr] *adj (dépenses, urne)* funeral; **pierre f.** tombstone, gravestone

funeste [fynɛst] *adj* **(a)** *(erreur, conséquences, influence)* disastrous **(b)** *Litt (accident)* fatal

funiculaire [fynikylɛr] *nm* funicular (railway)

fur [fyr] *nm* **au f. et à mesure** as one goes along, bit by bit; **au f. et à mesure de leurs recherches** as they progressed with their research

furax [fyraks] *adj inv Fam* livid

furet [fyrɛ] *nm* ferret

fureter [39] [fyrte] *vi (chercher)* to ferret about

fureur [fyrœr] *nf* **(a)** *(colère)* fury, rage **(b)** *(passion)* passion; **faire f.** to be all the rage

furibard, -e [fyribar, -ard] *adj Fam* livid

furibond, -e [fyribɔ̃, -ɔ̃d] *adj* furious

furie [fyri] *nf* **(a)** *(rage)* fury; **en f.** infuriated; **la f. du jeu** passion for gambling **(b)** *Fig (femme)* shrew; **comme une f.** like a wild thing

furieux, -euse [fyrjø, -øz] **1** *adj* **(a)** *(en colère)* furious **(contre** with); *Fig (tempête)* raging; *(combat)* violent **(b)** *Fam (intense) (envie)* tremendous

furoncle [fyrɔ̃kl] *nm* boil

furtif, -ive [fyrtif, -iv] *adj* furtive, stealthy

furtivement [fyrtivmɑ̃] *adv* furtively, stealthily; **entrer f.** to sneak in

fusain [fyzɛ̃] *nm (crayon, dessin)* charcoal

fuseau, -x [fyzo] *nm* **(a)** *(pantalon)* ski pants **(b)** *(pour filer la laine)* spindle; *(pour faire de la dentelle)* bobbin **(c)** **f. horaire** time zone

fusée [fyze] *nf* **(a)** *(projectile)* rocket **il est parti comme une f.** he shot off like a rocket; **f. éclairante** flare **(b)** *(d'axe)* spindle; *Aut* stub axle

fuselage [fyzlaʒ] *nm (d'un avion)* fuselage

fuselé, -e [fyzle] *adj (colonne, doigts)* tapering; *(voiture)* streamlined

fuser [fyze] *vi* **des rires/cris fusèrent de toutes parts** laughter was/cries were suddenly heard from all sides

fusible [fyzibl] *nm* fuse

fusil [fyzi] *nm* **(a)** *(arme)* gun, rifle; **f. à air comprimé** air gun; **f. de chasse** shotgun; **f. à lunette** rifle with telescopic sight; *Fig* **changer son f. d'épaule** to change tack; **coup de f.** gunshot; *Fam* **c'est le coup de f. dans ce restaurant** the prices in this restaurant are extortionate **(c)** *(pour aiguiser)* steel

fusilier [fyzilje] *nm* fusilier; **f. marin** marine

fusillade [fyzijad] *nf (tir)* gunfire

fusiller [fyzije] *vt* **(a)** *(par un peloton d'exécution)* to shoot *Fig* **f. qn du regard** to look daggers at sb **(b)** *Fam (abîmer)* to wreck

fusil-mitrailleur (*pl* fusils-mitrailleurs) [fyzimitrajœr] *nm* light machine-gun

fusion [fyzjɔ̃] *nf* (**a**) *(par la chaleur)* melting, *Spéc* fusion; *(en métallurgie)* smelting; **point de f.** melting point; **métal/roche en f.** molten metal/rock (**b**) *(de sociétés)* merger; *Ordinat* **f. de fichiers** file merge

fusionner [fyzjɔne] *vi* & *vt aussi Ordinat* to merge

fustiger [45] [fystiʒe] *vt (critiquer)* to castigate

fût [fy] *nm* (**a**) *(tonneau)* cask, barrel (**b**) *(d'arbre)* bole (**c**) *(de colonne)* shaft (**d**) *(de fusil)* stock

futaie [fytɛ] *nf* forest *(producing timber from full-grown trees)*

futal, -als [fytal], **fute** [fyt] *nm Fam Br* trousers, *Am* pants

futé, -e [fyte] **1** *adj* crafty
 2 *nm,f* crafty devil

futile [fytil] *adj (argument, occupation, prétexte)* trivial, trifling; *(personne)* frivolous

futilement [fytilmɑ̃] *adv* frivolously

futilité [fytilite] *nf* triviality

futur, -e [fytyr] **1** *adj* future; **un f. artiste** a budding artist; **mon f. emploi/appartement** my next job/flat; **mon f. mari** my husband-to-be
 2 *nm,f* **Ilum mon f./ma future** my intended
 3 *nm* (**a**) *(avenir)* future (**b**) *Gram* future (tense); **au f. in the** future (tense); **f. antérieur** future perfect

futurisme [fytyrism] *nm* futurism

futuriste [fytyrist] **1** *adj* futuristic
 2 *nmf* futurist

fuyant, -e [fɥijɑ̃, -ɑ̃t] *adj* (**a**) *(ligne, menton)* receding; **lignes fuyantes** perspective lines (**b**) *(personne, attitude)* evasive; *(yeux)* shifty

fuyard, -e [fɥijar, -ard] *nm,f* fugitive, runaway

fuyez *etc voir* **fuir**

G

G, g [ʒe] *nm inv* G, g; **le G7** the G7

g. (**a**) *(abrév* **gauche**) L (**b**) *(abrév* **gramme(s)**) g

gabardine [gabardin] *nf* gabardine

gabarit [gabari] *nm* (**a**) *(dimension)* size (**b**) *Fam (corpulence)* **un grand/petit g.** a huge/tiny man, *f* woman (**c**) *(valeur)* calibre (**d**) *(instrument)* gauge (**e**) *Ordinat* template

Gabon [gabɔ̃] *nm* **le G.** Gabon

gabonais, -e [gabɔnɛ, -ɛz] **1** *adj* Gabonese **2** *nm,f* **G.** Gabonese

gâcher [gɑʃe] *vt* (**a**) *(gaspiller)* to waste (**b**) *(gâter) (plaisir, soirée)* to spoil (**c**) *(mélanger) (mortier, plâtre)* to mix

gâchette [gɑʃɛt, gaʃɛt] *nf* trigger; *Fam* **avoir la g.** **facile** to be trigger-happy; **appuyer sur la g.** to pull the trigger

gâchis [gɑʃi] *nm* waste

gadget [gadʒɛt] *nm* gadget

gadoue [gadu] *nf* mud

gaélique [gaelik] *adj & nm* Gaelic

gaffe [gaf] *nf* (**a**) *Fam (maladresse)* blunder; **faire une g.** to put one's foot in it (**b**) *(perche)* boathook (**c**) *Fam* **faire g.** to be careful

gaffer [gafe] **1** *vt (objet flottant)* to hook; *(poisson)* to gaff **2** *vi Fam* to put one's foot in it

gaffeur, -euse [gafœr, -øz] *nm,f Fam* blunderer

gag [gag] *nm* gag

gaga [gaga] *adj Fam* gaga

gage [gaʒ] *nm* (**a**) *(chez le prêteur sur gages)* pledge; *Fig (garantie)* guarantee; **laisser qch en g.** to leave sth as security; **mettre qch en g.** to pawn sth (**b**) *(preuve)* token; **en g. de notre amitié** as a token of our friendship (**c**) *(dans un jeu)* forfeit (**d**) *Vieilli (salaire)* **gages** wages

gager [45] [gaʒe] *vt Litt* **g. que...** to wager that...

gageure [gaʒyr] *nf* (**a**) *(action difficile)* challenge (**b**) *Litt (pari)* wager

gagnant, -e [gaɲɑ̃, -ɑ̃t] **1** *adj* winning **2** *nm,f* winner; **partir g.** to have a strong probability of winning

gagne-pain [gaɲpɛ̃] *nm inv* livelihood

gagne-petit [gaɲpəti] *nmf inv* low wage earner

gagner [gaɲe] **1** *vt* (**a**) *(remporter) (course, prix, guerre)* to win; **rien n'est encore gagné!** it's not in the bag yet! (**b**) *(comme rémunération)* to earn; **g. sa vie** to earn one's living (**c**) *(obtenir)* to gain; **g. du temps** *(aller plus vite)* to save time; *(temporiser)* to gain time; **g. de l'espace** to save space; **chercher à g. du temps** to play for time; **c'est toujours ça de gagné** that's something, anyway; **tu as tout à g.** you've got everything to gain; **et moi, qu'est-ce que j'y gagne?** and what do I get out of it? (**d**) *(se concilier)* **g. qn à une cause** to win sb over to a cause; **g. la confiance/l'estime de qn** to win *or* gain sb's confidence/respect (**e**) *(atteindre) (ville, sortie, porte)* to reach, to get to; *(sujet: maladie, infection)* to spread to; *(sujet: sentiment, sommeil)* to overcome; **le rire gagna l'assemblée tout entière** laughter spread through the whole audience (**f**) *(s'étendre à) (sujet: feu, épidémie)* to spread to; **g. du terrain** to gain ground (**g**) *(battre)* **g. qn de vitesse** to outstrip sb

2 *vi* (**a**) *(être vainqueur)* to win; **g. haut la main** to win hands down (**b**) *(profiter)* **g. à qch/à faire qch** to benefit from sth/from doing sth; **g. à être connu** to improve with acquaintance; **j'ai gagné au change** I got the best of the deal (**c**) *(croître)* to increase; **g. en intensité/en vigueur** to increase in intensity/in strength

gagneur, -euse [gaɲœr, -øz] *nm,f* winner

gai, -e [ge] *adj* cheerful; **g. comme un pinson** happy as a lark; *Fam* **être un peu g.** *(ivre)* to be tipsy; *Ironique* **ça va être g.!** that'll be fun!

gaiement [gemɑ̃] *adv* cheerfully; *Ironique* **allons-y g.!** let's get on with it!

gaieté [gete] *nf* cheerfulness, gaiety; **je ne le fais pas de g. de cœur** I don't enjoy doing it

gaillard, -e [gajar, -ard] **1** *adj* (**a**) *(vigoureux) (personne)* strong; *(vieillard)* sprightly (**b**) *(jovial) (humeur)* merry; *(grivois) (histoire, commentaire)* bawdy

2 *nm* (**a**) *(homme)* hearty type; **un grand et solide g.** a great strapping man; **toi mon g., tu ne perds rien pour attendre!** just you wait, chum! (**b**) *Naut* **g. d'avant** forecastle; **g. d'arrière** poop

gaîment [gemɑ̃] = **gaiement**

gain [gɛ̃] *nm* (**a**) *(succès)* winning; **avoir** *ou* **obtenir g. de cause** to win one's case; **donner g. de cause à qn** to decide in favour of sb (**b**) *(profit)* gain, profit; **l'appât du g.** the lure of money (**c**) *(économie)* **ça fait un sacré g. de temps/de place** that saves an awful lot of time/space (**d**) **gains** *(au jeu)* winnings; *(à la Bourse)* profit

gaine [gɛn] *nf* (**a**) *(étui)* sheath (**b**) *Anat & Bot* sheath (**c**) *(sous-vêtement)* girdle

gainer [gene] *vt* to sheathe (**de** in)

Gal *Mil (abrév* **Général**) Gen

gala [gala] *nm* gala; **en habit** *ou* **tenue de g.** in gala dress; *Fig* in one's best clothes

galamment [galamɑ̃] *adv* gallantly

galant, -e [galɑ̃, -ɑ̃t] **1** *adj (homme)* gallant; **rendez-vous g.** romantic rendezvous **2** *nm Vieilli & Litt* gallant

galanterie [galɑ̃tri] *nf* gallantry; **dire des galanteries à qn** to pay sb compliments

Galapagos [galapagos] *nfpl* **les (îles) G.** the Galapagos (Islands)

galaxie [galaksi] *nf* galaxy

galbe [galb] *nm* curve

galbé, -e [galbe] *adj* shapely

gale [gal] *nf* **(a)** *Méd* scabies; *Fig* **je n'ai pas la g.!** I haven't got the plague! **(b)** *(de chien, de chat)* mange **(c)** *Bot* scab

galère [galɛr] *nf* **(a)** *(navire)* galley **(b)** *Fam (situation pénible)* hassle; **je me suis mis dans une g. pas possible** I got myself into a terrible mess; **être dans la même g.** to be in the same boat

galérer [34] [galere] *vi Fam* to have a hard time

galerie [galri] *nf* **(a)** *(passage, salle)* gallery; *Can (véranda)* porch; **g. d'art/de portraits** art/portrait gallery; **g. marchande** shopping arcade, *Am* mall **(b)** *(dans une mine)* gallery; *(de taupe)* tunnel **(c)** *(de voiture)* roof rack **(d)** *(de théâtre)* balcony; *Fig* **c'est pour (épater) la g.** it's just showing off

galérien [galerjɛ̃] *nm* galley slave

galet [galɛ] *nm* **(a)** *(caillou)* pebble; **plage de galets** shingle beach **(b)** *Tech* roller

galette [galɛt] *nf* **(a)** *(crêpe de blé noir)* buckwheat pancake; **g. des Rois** = cake traditionally eaten on Twelfth Night **(b)** *(biscuit rond sablé)* butter *Br* biscuit or *Am* cookie **(c)** *Fam (argent)* cash

galeux, -euse [galø, -øz] *adj (chien)* mangy; *(mur)* peeling

Galice [galis] *nf* **la G.** Galicia

galicien, -enne [galisjɛ̃, -ɛn] **1** *adj* Galician **2** *nm,f* **G.** Galician

Galilée¹ [galile] *nf (région)* **la G.** Galilee

Galilée² *npr* Galileo

galimatias [galimatja] *nm* gibberish

galion [galjɔ̃] *nm* galleon

galipette [galipɛt] *nf Fam* somersault; **faire des galipettes** to do somersaults; *(ébats amoureux)* to fool around

galipote [galipɔt] *nf Can* **courir la g.** to chase women

Galles [gal] *voir* **pays**

gallicisme [galisism] *nm* Gallicism

gallois, -e [galwa, -az] **1** *adj* Welsh **2** *nm,f* **G.** Welshman, *f* Welshwoman; **les G.** the Welsh **3** *nm (langue)* Welsh

gallon [galɔ̃] *nm* gallon

gallo-romain, -e *(mpl* **gallo-romains,** *fpl* **gallo-romaines)** [galorɔmɛ̃, -ɛn] *adj* Gallo-Roman

galoche [galɔʃ] *nf* clog *(with leather upper)*

galon [galɔ̃] *nm* **(a)** *(en couture)* braid **(b)** *(de militaire)* stripe; *Fam* **prendre du g.** to get promoted

galop [galo] *nm* gallop; **au g.** at a gallop; *Fig* **allez, au travail et au g.!** come on, to work, and be quick about it!; **g. d'essai** trial run

galopade [galɔpad] *nf* **(a)** *(de cheval)* gallop **(b)** *(de personnes)* stampede

galopant, -e [galɔpɑ̃, -ɑ̃t] *adj (inflation)* galloping; **phtisie galopante** galloping consumption

galoper [galɔpe] *vi* to gallop

galopin [galɔpɛ̃] *nm Fam* urchin; **espèce de petit g.!** you little rascal!

galure [galyr], **galurin** [galyrɛ̃] *nm Fam* hat

galvaniser [galvanize] *vt* to galvanize

galvauder [galvode] **1** *vt (nom, réputation)* to bring into disrepute; *(talents, dons)* to prostitute; *(mot)* to overuse **2 se galvauder** *vpr* to damage one's reputation

gambade [gɑ̃bad] *nf* leap

gambader [gɑ̃bade] *vi* to leap *or* frisk about

gambas [gɑ̃bas] *nfpl* large prawns

gamberger [45] [gɑ̃bɛrʒe] *vi Fam* to think hard

gambette [gɑ̃bɛt] *nf Fam (jambe)* pin

Gambie [gɑ̃bi] *nf* **la G.** the Gambia

gamelle [gamɛl] *nf (de soldat)* mess tin; *(d'ouvrier)* billy(can); *(d'animal)* bowl; *Hum (assiette)* plate; *Fam aussi Fig* **(se) ramasser** *ou* **(se) prendre une g.** to come a cropper

gamète [gamɛt] *nm* gamete

gamin, -e [gamɛ̃, -in] **1** *nm,f (enfant)* kid; **une gamine de neuf ans** a girl of nine **2** *adj* **(a)** *(jeune)* **elle était encore toute gamine** she was still just a child **(b)** *(puéril)* childish

gaminerie [gaminri] *nf (acte)* childish prank; *(compor tement)* childishness

gamme [gam] *nf* **(a)** *(de couleurs, de prix, d'articles)* range; **produit bas/haut de g.** bottom-of-the-range/top-of-the-range product **(b)** *Mus* scale

gammée [game] *adj f voir* **croix**

ganache [ganaʃ] *nf* **(a)** *Fam (imbécile)* **vieille g.** old fool **(b)** *(d'un cheval)* lower jaw

Gand [gɑ̃] *n* Ghent

gang [gɑ̃g] *nm* gang

Gange [gɑ̃ʒ] *nm* **le G.** the Ganges

ganglion [gɑ̃glijɔ̃] *nm* ganglion; **j'ai des ganglions** I've got swollen glands

gangrène [gɑ̃grɛn] *nf* **(a)** *Méd* gangrene **(b)** *Fig* canker

gangrener [46] [gɑ̃grəne] **1** *vt* **(a)** *Méd* to turn gangrenous **(b)** *Fig* to corrupt **2 se gangrener** *vpr* **(a)** *Méd* to go gangrenous **(b)** *Fig* to become corrupt

gangster [gɑ̃gstɛr] *nm* gangster

gangstérisme [gɑ̃gsterism] *nm* gangsterism

gangue [gɑ̃g] *nf (de minéral)* gangue; *(couche) (de boue, de glace)* layer; *Fig (carcan)* straitjacket

gant [gɑ̃] *nm* glove; **g. de boxe** boxing glove; **gants de caoutchouc** rubber gloves; **g. de toilette** ≃ facecloth; *Fig* **cela vous va comme un g.** it fits you like a glove; **prendre** *ou* **mettre des gants avec qn** to handle sb with kid gloves; **jeter le g. à qn** to throw down the gauntlet to sb; **relever le g.** to take up the gauntlet

ganté, -e [gɑ̃te] *adj (personne)* wearing gloves; *(main)* gloved

gantelet [gɑ̃tlɛ] *nm* gauntlet

garage [garaʒ] *nm (pour se garer, pour les réparations)* garage; **g. de** *ou* **à bicyclettes** bicycle shed; **g. d'autobus** bus depot; *Can* **vente de g.** garage sale

garagiste [garaʒist] *nmf (propriétaire)* garage owner; *(mécanicien)* garage mechanic

garant, -e [garɑ̃, -ɑ̃t] *nm,f* guarantor; **se porter g. de qn** *(à la banque)* to stand guarantor for sb; **se porter g. de qch** to vouch for sth

garantie [garɑ̃ti] *nf* **(a)** *(précaution)* guarantee, safeguard **(contre** against) **(b)** *(de produit)* guarantee; **être sous g.** to be under guarantee **(c)** *(certitude)* guarantee

garantir [garɑ̃tir] *vt* **(a)** *(promettre)* to guarantee; **g. à qn que** to give sb a guarantee that; **je te le garantis** I can vouch for it **(b)** *Fin (émission d'actions)* to underwrite; *(emprunt)* to secure **(c)** *(protéger)* to protect **(de** from)

garce [gars] *nf Fam* bitch

garçon [garsɔ̃] *nm* **(a)** *(enfant mâle, fils)* boy; *(jeune homme)* young man; **un mauvais g.** a bad sort; **vieux g.** confirmed bachelor; **g. manqué** tomboy **(b)** *(serveur)* waiter; **g. d'ascenseur** *Br* lift attendant, *Am* elevator operator; **g. de café** waiter; **g. d'honneur** ≃ best man

garçonne [garsɔn] *nf* **être coiffée à la g.** to have an urchin cut

garçonnet [garsɔnɛ] *nm* little boy

garçonnière [garsɔnjer] *nf* bachelor *Br* flat *or Am* apartment

garde¹ [gard] *nf* **(a)** *(protection)* care; *Jur* **g. des enfants** *(après un divorce)* custody of the children **(b)** *(surveillance)* guarding; **être de g.** to be on duty; **monter la g.** to mount guard; **médecin de g.** duty doctor; **pharmacie de g.** emergency chemist **(c)** *(méfiance)* **mettre qn en g. contre qn/qch** to warn sb against sb/sth; **être** *ou* **se tenir sur ses gardes** to be on one's guard; **prendre g. à qn/qch** to watch out for sb/sth; **prendre g. que... (ne)** + *subjunctive* to be careful that...; **prendre g. de ne pas faire qch** to be careful not to do sth **(d)** *(groupe de soldats)* **la g.** the guard; **g. d'honneur** guard of honour; **la G. républicaine** the Republican Guard *(of Paris)* **(e)** *Jur* **g. à vue** police custody; **il a été mis/est resté en g. à vue** he was put/was held in police custody **(f)** *(en boxe, en escrime)* guard; **se mettre en g.** to take one's guard; **en g.!** on guard! **(g)** *Aut* **g. au sol** ground clearance **(h)** *(d'une épée)* hilt

garde² **1** *nm* **(a)** *(soldat) (sentinelle)* guard; *(dans une garde)* guardsman; **g. mobile** = member of the security police **(b)** *(dans un domaine particulier)* **g. champêtre** rural policeman; **g. du corps** bodyguard; **g. forestier** *Br* forest warden, *Am* ranger **(c)** **le g. des Sceaux** the (French) Minister of Justice **2** *nmf* **g. de nuit** *(pour un malade)* night nurse *(privately employed)*; **g. d'enfants** childminder

garde-à-vous [gardavu] *nm inv* *Mil* (position of) attention; **se mettre/être au g.** to stand to attention; **g.!** attention!

garde-barrière *(pl* **gardes-barrière(s))** [gardəbarjer] *nmf Br* level-crossing *or Am* grade-crossing keeper

garde-boue [gardəbu] *nm inv* mudguard

garde-chasse *(pl* **gardes-chasse(s))** [gardəʃas] *nm* game-keeper

garde-chiourme *(pl* **gardes-chiourme(s))** [gardə-ʃjurm] *nm (personne autoritaire et brutale)* martinet

garde-côte *(pl* **garde-côtes)** [gardəkot] *nm (bateau)* coastguard vessel

garde-feu [gardəfø] *nm inv* fireguard

garde-fou *(pl* **garde-fous)** [gardəfu] *nm (mur)* parapet; *(rambarde)* railing; *Fig* safeguard

garde-malade *(pl* **gardes-malade(s))** [gardəmalad] *nmf* nurse

garde-manger [gardəmãʒe] *nm inv* larder

garde-meuble *(pl* **garde-meubles)** [gardəmœbl] *nm* furniture repository; **mettre une table au g.** to put a table into storage

gardénia [gardenja] *nm* gardenia

garder [garde] **1** *vt* **(a)** *(conserver)* to keep; **g. qn à dîner** to get sb to stay for dinner; **g. la chambre** to keep to *or* stay in one's room; **devoir g. le lit** to be confined to bed; **g. la tête froide** to keep a cool head **(b)** *(surveiller) (maison, sac, enfants)* to look after, to mind; *Jur* **g. à vue** to hold sb in custody **(c)** *(protéger)* to protect (**de** from); **que Dieu nous garde!** God protect us!
2 se garder *vpr* **(a)** *(se méfier)* **se g. de qn/qch** to beware of sb/sth **(b)** *(s'abstenir)* **se g. de faire qch** to be careful not to do sth **(c)** *Fam (conserver)* **tes réflexions, tu peux te les g.!** you can keep your thoughts to yourself! **(d)** *(se conserver) (denrées)* to keep

garderie [gardəri] *nf Br* day nursery, *Am* daycare center;

(dans un magasin, une université) *Br* crèche, *Am* baby-sitting service; *(le soir, après l'école)* childminding service

garde-robe *(pl* **garde-robes)** [gardərɔb] *nf (armoire, vêtements)* wardrobe

gardien, -enne [gardjɛ̃, -ɛn] *nm,f (concierge)* caretaker, *Am* janitor; *(de musée, de parking)* attendant; *Fig (de libertés, traditions)* guardian; **g. de but** goalkeeper; **g. de nuit** night watchman; **g. de la paix** policeman; **g. de prison** prison *Br* warder *or Am* guard; **gardienne d'enfants** childminder

gardiennage [gardjɛnaʒ] *nm (d'un bâtiment)* caretaking; *(de locaux)* guarding; **société de g.** security firm

gardon [gardɔ̃] *nm* roach; *Fig* **frais comme un g.** fresh as a daisy

gare¹ [gar] *nf* station; **g. maritime** harbour station; **g. marchandises** goods station; **g. routière** bus station; **g. de triage** marshalling yard

gare² *exclam* **(a)** *(menace)* **g. à toi si on l'apprend** woe betide you if anyone finds out; *Fam* **si je te reprends à voler de l'argent, g. à tes fesses!** if I catch you stealing money again, you've had it! **(b)** *(attention)* **g. aux orties!** mind the nettles!; **sans crier g.** without warning

garer [gare] **1** *vt (voiture)* to park
2 se garer *vpr* **(a)** *(automobiliste)* to park **(b)** **se g. de qn/qch** to steer clear of sb/sth; *Fam* **garez-vous!** get out of the way!

gargariser [gargarize] **se gargariser** *vpr* to gargle; *Fam Péj* **se g. de qch** to revel in sth

gargarisme [gargarism] *nm (produit)* mouthwash; *(action)* gargling

gargote [gargɔt] *nf Péj* cheap restaurant

gargouillement [gargujmã] *nm* gurgling; *(d'estomac)* rumbling

gargouiller [garguje] *vi* **(a)** *(eau)* to gurgle **(b)** *(estomac)* to rumble

gargouillis [garguji] = **gargouillement**

garnement [garnəmã] *nm* scamp, rascal

garni, -e [garni] *adj* **(a)** **bien g.** *(bourse)* well-lined **(b)** *(plat, viande)* with vegetables

garnir [garnir] *vt* **(a)** *(munir)* to fit out (**de** with); *(commode, tiroir)* to line; *(siège) (rembourrer)* to stuff; *(couvrir)* to cover **(b)** *(embellir) (robe, chapeau)* to trim (**de** with) **(c)** *Culin (plat)* to garnish **(d)** *(remplir)* to fill (**de** with); *(cave)* to stock (**de** with)

garnison [garnizɔ̃] *nf* garrison; **ville de g.** garrison town

garniture [garnityr] *nf* **(a)** *(ornement) (d'un chapeau, d'une robe)* trimming; **g. de lit** bedding; **g. de cheminée** mantelpiece ornaments **(b)** *(d'un plat)* garnish; *(légumes)* vegetables; *(d'un vol-au-vent)* filling **(c)** *Aut* **g. d'embrayage** clutch lining; **g. de frein** brake lining; *(de disque de frein)* brake pad

Garonne [garɔn] *nf* **la G.** the Garonne

garrigue [garig] *nf* scrubland *(typical of southern France)*

garrocher [garɔʃe] *vt Can très Fam* to throw

garrot¹ [garo] *nm* **(a)** *Méd* tourniquet **(b)** *(supplice)* garrotte

garrot² *nm (de quadrupède)* withers; **mesurer 1,20 m au g.** to be 12 hands high

garrotter [garɔte] *vt (prisonnier)* to tie up; *Fig (opposants)* to muzzle

gars [gɑ] *nm Fam (jeune homme)* lad; *(homme)* guy

Gascogne [gaskɔn] *nf* **la G.** Gascony

gas-oil, gasoil [gazɔjl, gazwal] *nm* diesel oil

gaspillage [gaspijaʒ] *nm (d'argent, de nourriture, de temps)* wasting; **c'est du g.** it's a waste

gaspiller [gaspije] *vt* to waste

gastéropode [gasterɔpɔd] *nm Zool* gastropod

gastrique [gastrik] *adj* gastric; **embarras g.** upset stomach

gastrite [gastrit] *nf Méd* gastritis

gastro-entérite (*pl* gastro-entérites) [gastroᾱterit] *nf Méd* gastroenteritis

gastro-entérologue (*pl* gastro-entérologues) [gastroᾱterɔlɔg] *nmf Méd* gastroenterologist

gastro-intestinal, -e, -aux, -ales [gastro-ἐtεstinal, -o] *adj Méd* gastrointestinal

gastronome [gastrɔnɔm] *nmf* gastronome, gourmet

gastronomie [gastrɔnɔmi] *nf* gastronomy

gastronomique [gastrɔnɔmik] *adj* gastronomic

gastropode [gastrɔpɔd] *nm Zool* gastropod

gâté, -e [gɑte] *adj* (**a**) *(pourri)* *(fruit, dents)* bad (**b**) *Fig (enfant)* spoilt

gâteau, -x [gɑto] *nm* cake; **faire un g.** to make *or* bake a cake; *Fam* **c'est du g.** it's a piece of cake; *Fam* **ce n'est pas du g.** it's no easy thing; *Fam* **se partager le g.** to share out the cake; **g. d'anniversaire** birthday cake; **g. de riz** rice pudding; **g. sec** *Br* biscuit, *Am* cookie

gâter [gɑte] **1** *vt* (**a**) *(gâcher)* to spoil (**b**) *(choyer) (personne)* to spoil; **on n'est pas gâtés!** just our luck!
2 se gâter *vpr (affaires, temps)* to take a turn for the worse; *(aliment)* to go bad

gâterie [gɑtri] *nf (petit cadeau, friandise)* treat

gâteux, -euse [gɑtø, -øz] *Fam* **1** *nm,f* old dodderer
2 *adj (sénile)* senile; **avec leurs petits-enfants, ils sont complètement g.** they're totally besotted with their grandchildren

gâtisme [gɑtism] *nm* senility

GATT [gat] *nm Écon (abrév* **General Agreement on Tariffs and Trade**) le G. GATT

gauche [goʃ] **1** *adj* (**a**) *(par opposition à droit)* left (**b**) *(maladroit) (personne, attitude, démarche, style)* awkward, clumsy (**c**) *Tech (déformé)* warped
2 *nf* (**a**) *(côté)* left; **à ma g.** on my left; **le tiroir de g.** the left-hand drawer; **à g. (de)** on the left (of); **tournez à g.** turn left; **conduire à g.** to drive on the left; *Fam* **mettre de l'argent à g.** to put some money away (**b**) *Pol* **la g.** the left; **politique/gouvernement de g.** left-wing politics/ government; **voter à g.** to vote for the left
3 *nm (en boxe)* left; **un crochet du g.** a left hook; **un direct du g.** a straight left

gaucher, -ère [goʃe, -εr] **1** *adj* left-handed
2 *nm,f* left-hander

gauchisant, -e [goʃizᾱ, -ᾱt] *adj* **être g.** to have left-wing tendencies

gauchisme [goʃism] *nm* leftism

gauchiste [goʃist] *adj & nmf* leftist

gaufre [gofr] *nf* waffle

gaufrette [gofrεt] *nf* wafer (biscuit)

Gaule [gol] *nf* **la G.** Gaul

gaule [gol] *nf* pole; *(pour pêcher)* fishing rod

gauler [gole] *vt* (**a**) *(arbre fruitier, noyer)* to beat; *(fruits, noix)* to bring down *(using a pole)* (**b**) *Fam (attraper)* to bust; **se faire g.** to get busted

gaullisme [golism] *nm* Gaullism

gaulliste [golist] *adj & nmf* Gaullist

gaulois, -e [golwa, -az] **1** *adj* Gallic; **esprit g.** bawdy humour
2 *nm,f* **les G.** the Gauls
3 *nf* **Gauloise®** Gauloise *(popular brand of cigarette)*

gauloiserie [golwazri] *nf (plaisanterie)* bawdy joke; *(caractère)* bawdiness

gausser [gose] **se gausser** *vpr Litt* **se g. de qn** to mock sb; **vous vous gaussez!** you jest!

gaver [gave] **1** *vt (engraisser) (volaille)* to force-feed; *(personne) (de nourriture)* to stuff (**de** with); *Fig* **g. qn de qch** to force-feed sb sth
2 se gaver *vpr Fam* to stuff oneself (**de** with), *Fig* **se g. de romans policiers/jeux vidéo** to read detective novels/ play video games till they're coming out of one's ears

gaz [gaz] *nm* gas; *Fam* **il y a de l'eau dans le g.** things aren't going too well; *Fam* **mettre les g.** *Br* to put one's foot down, *Am* to step on the gas; *Av* to open up the throttle; **avoir des g.** to have wind; **g. carbonique** carbon dioxide; **g. de combat** poison gas; **g. d'échappement** exhaust fumes; **g. à effet de serre** greenhouse gas; **g. hilarant** laughing gas; **g. lacrymogène** tear gas; **g. naturel** natural gas; **g. de ville** town gas; **avoir le g. de ville** to be connected to the gas supply

Gaza [gaza] *n* **la bande de G.** the Gaza Strip

gaze [gaz] *nf* gauze

gaze, -e [gaze] **1** *adj* gassed
2 *nm,f (poison)* gas victim

gazéifier [66] [gazeifje] *vt* to gasify; *(boissons)* to carbonate

gazelle [gazεl] *nf* gazelle

gazer [gaze] **1** *vt (asphyxier)* to gas
2 *vi Fam* **ça gaze!** everything's OK!; **ça gaze?** how's things?

gazette [gazεt] *nf (journal)* newspaper

gazeux, -euse [gazø, -øz] *adj* (**a**) *(eau, boisson)* fizzy (**b**) *Chim* gaseous

gazinière [gazinjεr] *nf* gas cooker

gazoduc [gazɔdyk, gazɔdyk] *nm* gas pipeline

gazole [gazɔl] *nm* diesel oil

gazomètre [gazɔmεtr] *nm* gasometer

gazon [gazɔ̃] *nm* (**a**) *(herbe)* grass, turf (**b**) *(surface)* lawn

gazonner [gazɔne] *vt* to turf

gazouillement [gazujmᾱ] *nm (des oiseaux)* twittering, chirping; *(d'un bébé)* gurgling; *(d'un ruisseau)* babbling

gazouiller [gazuje] *vi (oiseau)* to twitter, to chirp; *(bébé)* to gurgle; *(eau)* to babble

gazouillis [gazuji] = **gazouillement**

GDF [ʒedeεf] *nm (abrév* **Gaz de France**) = French gas company

geai [ʒε] *nm* jay

géant, -e [ʒeᾱ, -ᾱt] **1** *adj* (**a**) *(arbre, écran)* giant, gigantic; *(paquet)* giant(-size) (**b**) *Fam (formidable)* **c'est g.!** it's fantastic!
2 *nm,f* giant; *Fig* **avancer** *ou* **aller à pas de g.** to make great strides

geignard, -e [ʒεɲar, -ard] *Fam* **1** *adj* whining
2 *nm,f* whiner

geindre [54] [ʒε̃dr] *vi* (**a**) *(gémir)* to moan, to groan (**de** with) (**b**) *Fam (se plaindre constamment)* to whine

gel [ʒεl] *nm* (**a**) *(verglas)* frost; *Fig* **g. des négociations** suspension of negotiations; **g. des prix/salaires** price/ wage freeze (**b**) *(produit cosmétique)* gel; **g. douche** shower gel

gélatine [ʒelatin] *nf* gelatine

gélatineux, -euse [ʒelatinø, -øz] *adj* gelatinous

gelé, -e [ʒəle] *adj* (**a**) *(lac, rivière)* frozen; *(plante)* frostnipped (**b**) *Méd (orteil, doigt)* frostbitten (**c**) *(très froid)* frozen; **j'ai les pieds gelés/les mains gelées** my feet/ hands are frozen (**d**) *(bloqué) (fonds)* frozen; *(négociations)* suspended

gelée [ʒəle] *nf* (**a**) *(gel)* frost; **g. blanche** hoarfrost (**b**) *Culin* jelly; **g. royale** royal jelly

geler [39] [ʒəle] **1** *vt* (**a**) *(lac, rivière, liquide)* to freeze; **fleurs/salades gelées par le froid** flowers/lettuces nipped by the frost (**b**) *Fin (bloquer) (crédits, capital)* to freeze **2** *vi (lac, rivière)* to freeze (over); **on gèle dans cette salle** it's freezing in this room **3** *v impersonnel* **il gèle** it's freezing; **il gèle à pierre fendre** it's freezing hard; **il a gelé blanc cette nuit** there was a frost last night **4 se geler** *vpr Fam* to freeze

gélifiant [ʒelifjɑ̃] *nm* gelling agent

gélule [ʒelyl] *nf* capsule

gelure [ʒəlyr] *nf* frostbite

Gémeaux [ʒemo] *nmpl Astron & Astrol* Gemini; **être G.** to be (a) Gemini

gémir [ʒemir] *vi (personne)* to groan, to moan (**de** with); *(vent)* to moan

gémissant, -e [ʒemisɑ̃, -ɑ̃t] *adj (personne)* groaning; *(voix)* wailing

gémissement [ʒemismɑ̃] *nm (d'une personne)* groan, moan; *(de vent)* moaning

gemme [ʒɛm] *nf* (**a**) *(pierre)* gem(stone) (**b**) *(résine)* pine resin

gênant, -e [ʒɛnɑ̃, -ɑ̃t] *adj* (**a**) *(témoin, situation, silence)* awkward; *(bruit, lumière)* irritating (**b**) *(encombrant) (objet)* cumbersome

gencive [ʒɑ̃siv] *nf* gum

gendarme [ʒɑ̃darm] *nm* gendarme, policeman; **jouer aux gendarmes et aux voleurs** to play cops and robbers; *Fam* **faire le g.** to lay down the law; **g. couché** sleeping policeman; **g. mobile** = member of the flying squad

gendarmerie [ʒɑ̃darməri] *nf* (**a**) *(corps) (en France)* gendarmerie, police force; **g. mobile** = flying squad; **g. nationale** national police force; **la G. royale du Canada** the Royal Canadian Mounted Police (**b**) *(lieu)* gendarmes' headquarters

gendre [ʒɑ̃dr] *nm* son-in-law

gène [ʒɛn] *nm* gene

gêne [ʒɛn] *nf* (**a**) *(confusion)* embarrassment; **ressentir de la g.** to feel embarrassed; **où (il) y a de la g.,** *(il n')y a pas de plaisir* we don't need to stand on ceremony (**b**) *(dérangement)* inconvenience (**c**) *(difficulté physique)* discomfort; **g. respiratoire** breathing difficulties (**d**) *(manque d'argent)* **être dans la g.** to be in financial difficulties

gêné, -e [ʒene] *adj* (**a**) *(embarrassé)* embarrassed; *Fam* **il n'est pas g., lui!** he's got a nerve! (**b**) *(serré)* **il se sentait g. dans son uniforme** he felt uncomfortable in his uniform (**c**) *(qui manque d'argent)* in financial difficulties

généalogie [ʒenealɔʒi] *nf* genealogy

généalogique [ʒenealɔʒik] *adj* genealogical; **arbre g.** family tree

gêner [ʒene] **1** *vt* (**a**) *(perturber) (sujet: bruit, fumée, chaleur)* to bother; *(opérations, déroulement)* to hamper; **g. la circulation** to hold up the traffic; **g. le passage** to be in the way; **pousse-toi, tu me gênes!** move over, you're in my way!; **ça te gêne si je fume?** do you mind if I smoke?; **cela ne te gênerait pas de me prêter ta voiture?** would you mind lending me your car?; **ce qui me gêne, c'est que…** what bothers me is that…; **sa présence me gêne** I feel awkward in her presence (**b**) *(être source d'inconfort)* **cette ceinture/ce col me gêne** this belt/this collar is uncomfortable (**c**) *(embarrasser)* to embarrass; **ça me gênerait de le rencontrer** I'd feel uncomfortable meeting him; *Fam* **et alors, ça te gêne?** what's it to you? **2 se gêner** *vpr* (**a**) **je ne me suis pas gêné pour le lui dire** I didn't hesitate to tell him so; **elle aurait tort de se g.** she

shouldn't feel bad about it; *aussi Ironique* **ne vous gênez pas pour moi!** don't mind me! (**b**) *(dans un lieu)* to be in each other's way

général, -e, -aux, -ales [ʒeneral, -o] **1** *adj* general; **assemblée/amnistie générale** general assembly/amnesty; **l'intérêt g.** the general interest; **à la surprise générale** to everyone's surprise; **à la demande générale** by popular request; **d'une façon générale** generally speaking; **en g.** *(globalement)* in general; *(habituellement)* as a rule, generally **2** *nm* (**a**) *Mil* general (**b**) *(ce qui est universel)* **passer du g. au particulier** to go from the general to the particular **3** *nf* **générale** (**a**) *Th* dress rehearsal (**b**) *(femme de général)* general's wife

généralement [ʒeneralmɑ̃] *adv* generally

généralisation [ʒeneralizasjɔ̃] *nf* generalization

généraliser [ʒeneralize] **1** *vt* to generalize; *Méd* **un cancer généralisé** a generalized cancer **2** *vi* to generalize **3 se généraliser** *vpr (utilisation, usage, phénomène)* to become widespread; *(conflit, grève)* to spread

généraliste [ʒeneralist] *adj & nmf* (**médecin**) **g.** *Br* general practitioner, GP, *Am* family practitioner

généralité [ʒeneralite] *nf* (**a**) *(notion générale)* generality; **s'en tenir à des généralités** to confine oneself to generalities (**b**) *(majorité)* **la g. de** the majority of

générateur, -trice [ʒeneratœr, -tris] **1** *adj (machine)* generating; *(organe)* generative; **être g. de** to generate **2** *nm* generator; *Ordinat* **g. de caractères** character generator; **g. d'effets numériques** digital effects generator; **g. d'effets spéciaux** (special) effects generator; **g. graphique** graphics generator **3** *nf* **génératrice** generator

génération [ʒenerasjɔ̃] *nf* (**a**) *(classe d'âge, degrés de filiation)* generation (**b**) *(action de produire)* generation; *Biol* **g. spontanée** spontaneous generation

générer [34] [ʒenere] *vt* to generate

généreusement [ʒenerøzmɑ̃] *adv* generously

généreux, -euse [ʒenerø, -øz] *adj* generous; **une terre généreuse** a fertile soil; **elle a des formes généreuses** she has generous curves

générique [ʒenerik] **1** *adj* generic **2** *nm Cin & TV* credits; **g. de fin** closing credits

générosité [ʒenerozite] *nf* generosity; **avec g.** generously

Gênes [ʒɛn] *n* Genoa

genèse [ʒənɛz] *nf* genesis; **la G.** Genesis

genêt [ʒənɛ] *nm* broom

généticien, -enne [ʒenetisjɛ̃, -ɛn] *nm,f* geneticist

génétique [ʒenetik] **1** *adj* genetic **2** *nf* genetics *(singulier)*

gêneur, -euse [ʒenœr, -øz] *nm,f* nuisance

Genève [ʒənɛv] *n* Geneva

genevois, -e [ʒənvwa, -az] **1** *adj* Genevan **2** *nm,f* **G.** Genevan

genévrier [ʒənevrije] *nm* juniper

génial, -e, -aux, -ales [ʒenjal, -o] *adj* (**a**) *(invention, œuvre, artiste)* brilliant (**b**) *Fam (extraordinaire)* fantastic, great

génialement [ʒenjalmɑ̃] *adv* brilliantly

génie¹ [ʒeni] *nm* (**a**) *(qualité, personne)* genius; **avoir du g.** to be a genius; **une idée/invention de g.** a brilliant idea/invention; **un trait de g.** a stroke of genius; **avoir le g. de qch/pour faire qch** to have a genius for sth/for doing sth (**b**) *(être mythique)* genie; **son bon/mauvais g.** his good/evil genius

génie² *nm Mil* le (corps du) g. ≃ the Engineers; **g.** civil civil engineering; *(corps)* civil engineers; **g.** **génétique** genetic engineering

genièvre [ʒənjɛvr] *nm (fruit)* juniper berry; *(arbre)* juniper (tree)

génique [ʒenik] *adj Méd* **thérapie g.** gene therapy

génisse [ʒenis] *nf* heifer

génital, -e, -aux, -ales [ʒenital, -o] *adj (glandes, hormones)* genital

géniteur, -trice [ʒenitœr, -tris] *nm,f Hum* parent

génocide [ʒenɔsid] *nm* genocide

génoise [ʒenwaz] *nf (gâteau)* sponge cake

génome [ʒenom] *nm Biol* genome

génotype [ʒenɔtip] *nm Biol* genotype

genou, -x [ʒənu] *nm* knee; **enfoncé jusqu'aux genoux dans la boue** knee-deep in mud; **avoir les genoux en dedans** to be knock-kneed; **être à genoux** to be kneeling (down), to be on one's knees; **se mettre à genoux** to kneel (down); *Fig* **être à genoux devant qn** to worship sb; *Fig* **demander qch à genoux** to ask for sth on bended knee; *Fig* **être sur les genoux** to be on one's last legs; **tenir un enfant sur ses genoux** to hold a child on one's knee *or* one's lap

genouillère [ʒənujɛr] *nf (protection du genou)* kneepad; *Méd* knee bandage

genre [ʒɑr] *nm* **(a)** *(sorte)* kind, sort; **en tout g., en tous genres** of all kinds; **très bon dans son g.** very good in its own way; **c'est ce qu'on fait de mieux dans le g.** it's the best of its kind; **c'est tout à fait son g.** **d'arriver en retard** it's just like him to be late; **ce n'est pas le g. (de femme) à** se plaindre she's not the sort (of woman) to complain; **tu vois le g.** you know the sort; **un vin blanc g. sauternes** a Sauternes-type white wine **(b)** *(artistique, littéraire)* genre; **le g. comique** comedy **(c)** *(race)* **le g. humain** the human race **(d)** *(goût)* **ça fait bon/mauvais g.** it's in good/bad taste **(e)** *Gram* gender

gens [ʒɑ̃] *nmpl (individus)* people; **les g. du pays** *ou* **du coin** the local people, **jeunes g.** *(garçons et filles)* young people; *(jeunes hommes)* young men; **g. de lettres** men and women of letters; **g. du voyage** *(artistes)* travelling players; *(gitans)* travellers

gent [ʒɑ̃] *nf Vieilli ou Hum* **la g. féminine/masculine** the fair/male sex

gentiane [ʒɑ̃sjan] *nf (plante)* gentian

gentil, -ille [ʒɑ̃ti, -ij] *adj* **(a)** *(aimable)* kind, nice **(avec** to); *(sage)* good; **sois g., ferme la fenêtre** do me a favour and close the window **(b)** *(considérable)* **une gentille somme** a nice little sum

gentilhomme [ʒɑ̃tijɔm] *(pl* **gentilshommes** [ʒɑ̃tizɔm])* *nm* gentleman

gentillesse [ʒɑ̃tijɛs] *nf (bonté)* kindness; **auriez-vous la g. de...?** would you be kind as to...?; **elle a eu la g. de venir elle-même** she was kind enough to come herself; **dire des gentillesses à qn** to say kind things to sb

gentillet, -ette [ʒɑ̃tijɛ, -ɛt] *adj Péj (roman, film)* pleasant enough

gentiment [ʒɑ̃timɑ̃] *adv (aimablement)* kindly; *(sagement)* nicely

génuflexion [ʒenyflɛksjɔ̃] *nf* genuflexion; **faire une g.** to genuflect

géo [ʒeo] *nf Fam Scol* geog

géographe [ʒeɔgraf] *nmf* geographer

géographie [ʒeɔgrafi] *nf* geography

géographique [ʒeɔgrafik] *adj* geographic(al)

geôle [ʒol] *nf Litt* jail

geôlier, -ère [ʒolje, -ɛr] *nm,f Litt* jailer

géologie [ʒeɔlɔʒi] *nf* geology

géologique [ʒeɔlɔʒik] *adj* geological

géologue [ʒeɔlɔg] *nmf* geologist

géomètre [ʒeɔmɛtr] *nm (arpenteur)* **g.** (land) surveyor

géométrie [ʒeɔmetri] *nf* geometry; **g. dans l'espace** solid geometry; **à g. variable** *(avion)* swing-wing; *Fig* that varies according to circumstances

géométrique [ʒeɔmetrik] *adj* geometric(al)

géophysicien, -enne [ʒeofizisjɛ̃, -ɛn] *nm,f* geophysicist

géophysique [ʒeofizik] **1** *adj* geophysical **2** *nf* geophysics *(singulier)*

géopolitique [ʒeopɔlitik] **1** *adj* geopolitical **2** *nf* geopolitics *(singulier)*

Géorgie [ʒeɔrʒi] *nf* **la G.** *(aux États-Unis, dans le Caucase)* Georgia

géorgien, -enne [ʒeɔrʒjɛ̃, -ɛn] **1** *adj* Georgian **2** *nm,f G.** Georgian

géostationnaire [ʒeostasjɔnɛr] *adj voir* **satellite**

géothermie [ʒeotɛrmi] *nf* geothermics *(singulier)*

géothermique [ʒeotɛrmik] *adj* geothermal

gérance [ʒerɑ̃s] *nf* management; **prendre un commerce en g.** to take over the management of a business

géranium [ʒeranjɔm] *nm* geranium

gérant, -e [ʒerɑ̃, -ɑ̃t] *nm,f* manager

gerbe [ʒɛrb] *nf (de blé)* sheaf; *(d'étincelles)* shower; *(d'eau)* spray; **g. (de fleurs)** spray of flowers

gerber [ʒɛrbe] *vi Vulg (vomir)* to puke, to barf

gercé, -e [ʒɛrse] *adj* chapped

gercer [16] [ʒɛrse] **1** *vt & vi* to chap **2 se gercer** *vpr* to chap

gerçure [ʒɛrsyr] *nf* **avoir des gerçures (aux mains/ lèvres)** to have chapped hands/lips

gérer [34] [ʒere] *vt* to manage

gériatrie [ʒerjatri] *nf Méd* geriatrics *(singulier)*

gériatrique [ʒerjatrik] *adj Méd* geriatric

germain, -e [ʒɛrmɛ̃, -ɛn] *adj voir* **cousin**

germanique [ʒɛrmanik] *adj* **(a)** *Hist (relatif aux Germains)* Germanic **(b)** *(allemand)* German **(c)** *(langue)* Germanic

germanophone [ʒɛrmanɔfɔn] **1** *adj* German-speaking **2** *nmf* German speaker

germe [ʒɛrm] *nm (embryon, virus)* germ; *(de pomme de terre)* eye; *Fig* **les germes de** *(origine)* the seeds of; **germes de soja** bean sprouts

germer [ʒɛrme] *vi (plante, idée)* to germinate; *(pommes de terre)* to sprout

germination [ʒɛrminasjɔ̃] *nf Biol* germination

gérondif [ʒerɔ̃dif] *nm Gram* gerund; *(cas latin)* gerundive

gérontologie [ʒerɔ̃tɔlɔʒi] *nf Méd* gerontology

gérontologue [ʒerɔ̃tɔlɔg] *nmf Méd* gerontologist

gésier [ʒezje] *nm* gizzard

gésir [40] [ʒezir] *vi Litt* to lie; **ci-gît...** *(sur une tombe)* here lies...

gestation [ʒɛstasjɔ̃] *nf Biol* gestation; *Fig* **en g.** in preparation

geste [ʒɛst] *nm (mouvement)* gesture; **faire un g.** to make a gesture; **pas un g. ou je tire!** one move and I'll shoot!; **il lui montra la porte d'un g.** he motioned her towards the door; **d'un g. de la main** with a wave of the hand; **écarter qn d'un g.** to wave sb aside; **joindre le g. à la parole** to suit the action to the word **(b)** *(action)* gesture; **un beau g.** a fine gesture; **faire un g.** to make a gesture

gesticuler [ʒɛstikyle] *vi* to gesticulate

gestion [ʒɛstjɔ̃] *nf* management; *Ordinat* **g. de bases de données** database management; *Ordinat* **g. des couleurs** colour management; **g. d'entreprise** business management; *Ordinat* **g. de fichiers** file management; *Ordinat* **g. de mémoire** memory management; *Ordinat* **g. sonore** sound handling, sound management; **g. des stocks** stock control

gestionnaire [ʒɛstjɔnɛr] **1** *nmf (dirigeant)* administrator **2** *nm Ordinat* manager, driver; **g. de fichiers** file manager; **g. de périphérique** device driver; **g. de projets** project management package; **g. de réseau** network manager

gestuel, -elle [ʒɛstɥɛl] **1** *adj* gestural **2** *nf* **gestuelle** body language

geyser [ʒezɛr] *nm* geyser

Ghana [gana] *nm* **le G.** Ghana

ghanéen, -enne [ganeɛ̃, -ɛn] **1** *adj* Ghanaian **2** *nm,f* **G.** Ghanaian

ghetto [geto] *nm* ghetto

gibecière [ʒibsjɛr] *nf (de chasseur)* game bag

gibelotte [ʒiblɔt] *nf Culin* **g. (de lapin)** = rabbit stew made with white wine

gibet [ʒibɛ] *nm* gibbet, gallows *(singulier)*

gibier [ʒibje] *nm* game; *aussi Fig* **gros g.** big game; **g. à plumes** game birds; **g. à poil** game animals; *Fig* **g. de potence** gallows bird

giboulée [ʒibule] *nf* sudden shower; **giboulées de mars** ≃ April showers

Gibraltar [ʒibraltar] *n* Gibraltar

giclée [ʒikle] *nf (d'eau, de sang)* spurt

gicler [ʒikle] *vi (eau, sang)* to spurt out; *(boue)* to splash up

gicleur [ʒiklœr] *nm Aut* jet

gifle [ʒifl] *nf aussi Fig* slap in the face; **donner une g. à qn** to give sb a slap in the face

gifler [ʒifle] *vt (sujet: personne)* to slap in the face; *(sujet: vent)* to lash

gigahertz [ʒigaɛrts] *nm Phys* gigahertz

gigantesque [ʒigɑ̃tɛsk] *adj* gigantic

gigaoctet [ʒigaɔktɛ] *nm Ordinat* gigabyte

GIGN [ʒeiʒɛɛn] *nm (abrév* **Groupe d'intervention de la gendarmerie nationale)** = special task force of the "gendarmerie", *Br* ≃ SAS, *Am* ≃ SWAT

gigogne [ʒigɔɲ] *adj* **tables gigognes** nest of tables; **lits gigognes** beds that fit one underneath the other; **poupées gigognes** set of (Russian) dolls

gigolo [ʒigɔlo] *nm Fam* gigolo

gigot [ʒigo] *nm (d'agneau, de mouton)* leg

gigoter [ʒigɔte] *vi* to wriggle, to fidget

gigue¹ [ʒig] *nf (danse)* jig

gigue² [ʒig] *nf Fam* **une grande g.** *(fille)* a beanpole (of a girl)

gilet [ʒilɛ] *nm (sans manches) Br* waistcoat, *Am* vest; *(veste en laine)* cardigan; **g. pare-balles** bulletproof vest; **g. de sauvetage** life jacket

gin [dʒin] *nm* gin; **g. tonic** gin and tonic

gingembre [ʒɛ̃ʒɑ̃br] *nm* ginger

gingivite [ʒɛ̃ʒivit] *nf Méd* gingivitis

ginseng [ʒɛsɑ̃, ʒinsɑ̃g] *nm* ginseng

girafe [ʒiraf] *nf* giraffe; *Fig (personne)* beanpole

giratoire [ʒiratwar] *adj (mouvement)* gyratory

girofle [ʒirɔfl] *nm voir* **clou**

giroflée [ʒirɔfle] *nf* stock

girolle [ʒirɔl] *nf* chanterelle (mushroom)

giron [ʒirɔ̃] *nm (partie du corps)* lap; *Fig* bosom

gironde [ʒirɔ̃d] *adj f Fam* curvy; *Péj* on the plump side

girondin, -e [ʒirɔ̃dɛ̃, -in] **1** *adj* of the Gironde **2** *nm,f* **G.** person from the Gironde

girouette [ʒirwɛt] *nf aussi Fig* weathercock

gisais *etc voir* **gésir**

gisement [ʒizmɑ̃] *nm (de minerai)* deposit; **g. de pétrole** oilfield

gît *voir* **gésir**

gitan, -e [ʒitɑ̃, -an] **1** *adj* gypsy **2** *nm,f* gypsy **3** *nf* **Gitane®** Gitane® *(popular brand of cigarette)*

gîte¹ [ʒit] *nm* **(a)** *(logement)* lodging; **offrir le g. et le couvert à qn** to offer sb board and lodging **(b)** *(en montagne, à la campagne)* **g. d'étape** = transit accommodation for hikers, cyclists etc; **g. rural** gîte, = self-catering holiday cottage or apartment **(c)** *(du lièvre)* form **(d)** *Culin* shank

gîte² *nf Naut* list; **donner de la g.** to list

gîter [ʒite] *vi Naut* to list

givre [ʒivr] *nm* frost

givré, -e [ʒivre] *adj* **(a)** *(couvert de givre)* covered with frost **(b)** *Fam (fou)* mad, crazy

glabre [glabr] *adj (rasé)* clean-shaven; *(imberbe) (personne)* smooth-chinned; *(visage)* hairless

glaçage [glasaʒ] *nm (d'un gâteau)* icing

glaçant, -e [glasɑ̃, -ɑ̃t] *adj (manières, accueil)* frosty

glace [glas] *nf* **(a)** *(eau à l'état solide)* ice; *Fig* **rester de g.** to remain impassive; *Fig* **rompre la g.** to break the ice; **g. pilée** crushed ice **(b)** *(de voiture)* window **(c)** *(miroir)* mirror; **g. sans tain** two-way mirror **(d)** *(crème glacée)* ice cream; **g. à la vanille/à la fraise** vanilla/strawberry ice cream; **g. à l'italienne** soft ice cream

glacé, -e [glase] *adj* **(a)** *(rivière, lac)* frozen **(b)** *(très froid) (pièce, eau, personne)* freezing (cold); *(avec des glaçons) (café)* iced; **j'ai les mains glacées** my hands are freezing **(c)** *Fig (accueil, politesse, regard)* frosty **(d)** *(brillant) (papier, épreuve)* glossy **(e)** *Culin (fruits)* glacé

glacer [16] [glase] **1** *vt (a) (refroidir, intimider)* to chill; *Fig* **à vous g. le sang** spine-chilling **(b)** *(gâteau)* to ice **2 se glacer** *vpr (sang)* to run cold

glaciaire [glasjɛr] *adj Géol (vallée)* glacial; **période g.** Ice Age

glacial, -e, -als *ou* **-aux, -ales** [glasjal, -o] *adj (température, froid, air, vent)* freezing, icy; *Fig (ton, attitude, sourire)* frosty; *(personne)* cold

glacier¹ [glasje] *nm (étendue de glace)* glacier

glacier² *nm (vendeur)* ice-cream seller; *(fabricant)* ice-cream maker

glacière [glasjɛr] *nf (de pique-nique)* cool box; **cette chambre est une vraie g.!** this room's like an icebox!

glaçon [glasɔ̃] *nm (pour rafraîchir une boisson)* ice cube; *(pendant)* icicle; *Fig (personne)* cold fish; **glaçons** *(sur une rivière)* ice; **avec ou sans glaçons?** with or without ice?; **un whisky avec des glaçons** a whisky on the rocks; **j'ai les pieds comme des glaçons** my feet are like blocks of ice

gladiateur [gladjatœr] *nm* gladiator

glaïeul [glajœl] *nm* gladiolus; **des glaïeuls** gladioli

glaire [glɛr] *nf (crachat)* phlegm; **g. cervicale** cervical mucus

glaise [glɛz] *nf* **(terre) g.** clay

glaive [glɛv] *nm (épée)* broadsword; *Fig (symbole)* sword

gland [glɑ̃] *nm* **(a)** *(de chêne)* acorn **(b)** *(de passementerie)* tassel **(c)** *Anat* glans **(d)** *très Fam (personne) Br* prat, *Am* jerk

glande [glɑ̃d] *nf (organe)* gland; *très Fam* **foutre les**

glandes à qn *(énerver)* to piss sb off; *(mettre mal à l'aise)* to put the wind up sb; **glandes lacrymales** tear glands

glander [glɑ̃de] *vi très Fam (ne rien faire)* to loaf around; *(attendre)* to hang around; **mais qu'est-ce qu'il glande?** *(que fait-il?)* what the hell's he up to?; **j'en ai rien à g.** I don't give a shit

glandeur, -euse [glɑ̃dœr, -øz] *nm,f très Fam* layabout

glandouiller [glɑ̃duje] *vi très Fam (ne rien faire)* to loaf around, *(attendre)* to hang around

glandulaire [glɑ̃dyler], **glanduleux, -euse** [glɑ̃dylø, -øz] *adj* glandular

glaner [glane] *vt aussi Fig* to glean

glapir [glapir] *vi (chien)* to yap; *(renard)* to bark; *(personne, radio)* to shriek

glapissements [glapismɑ̃] *nmpl (d'un chien)* yapping; *(d'un renard)* barking; *(d'une personne, de la radio)* shrieking

glas [glɑ] *nm* knell; **sonner le g.** to toll the knell; *Fig* **sonner le g. de qch** to sound the death knell for sth

glaucome [glokom] *nm Méd* glaucoma

glauque [glok] *adj (eau)* murky; *(ambiance, personne)* creepy

glissade [glisad] *nf* sliding; *(de patineur)* gliding; *(pas de danse)* glissade; **faire une g./des glissades** to slide

glissant, -e [glisɑ̃, -ɑ̃t] *adj* slippery; *Fig* **être sur un terrain g.** to be on dangerous ground

glisse [glis] *nf* **sports de g.** = sports involving sliding motion, such as skiing, surfing, windsurfing

glissement [glismɑ̃] *nm (action)* sliding; *(variation électorale)* swing **(à to)**; **g. de sens** shift in meaning; **g. de terrain** landslide; *(moins important)* landslip

glisser¹ [glise] **1** *vi* **(a)** *(par accident)* to slip; *(roue)* to skid; **le couteau lui a glissé des mains** the knife slipped out of her hands; *Av* **g. sur l'aile** to sideslip **(b)** *(volontairement)* to slide; **se laisser g. le long d'une corde** to slide down a rope; *Ordinat* **faire g.** *(pointeur)* to drag **(c)** *(avancer régulièrement)* to glide; *Fig (dans le sommeil, vers le désespoir)* to slip **(d)** **g. sur** *(sujet)* to skip over **(e)** *(avoir une surface glissante)* to be slippery

2 *vt (introduire)* to slip; **g. un mot à l'oreille de qn** to drop a word in sb's ear

3 se glisser *vpr* to slip **(dans into)**

glisser² *nm Ordinat* **g. d'icônes** icon drag

glissière [glisjer] *nf* **(a)** *Tech* runner, slide; **à g.** sliding **(b)** **g. de sécurité** crash barrier **(c)** *Ind (pour le charbon)* chute

global, -e, -aux, -ales [global, -o] *adj (somme)* total; *(paiement)* lump; *(vision)* overall; *Scol* **méthode globale** word recognition method

globalement [globalmɑ̃] *adv* overall

globalité [globalite] *nf* **prendre un problème dans sa g.** to tackle a problem as a whole

globe [glob] *nm* **(a)** *(sphère)* globe; **g. oculaire** eyeball **(b)** *(terre)* globe; **faire le tour du g.** to go round the world; **g. terrestre** *(terre)* earth; *(mappemonde)* globe **(c)** *(en verre)* *(d'une pendule)* glass dome

globe-trotter *(pl* **globe-trotters)** [globtrotœr] *nmf* globetrotter

globulaire [globyler] *adj Méd* **numération g.** blood count

globule [globyl] *nm (du sang)* corpuscle; **globules blancs/rouges** white/red corpuscles

globuleux, -euse [globylø, -øz] *adj (yeux)* protruding

gloire [glwar] *nf* **(a)** *(renom)* glory; **tirer g. de qch** to glory in sth **(b)** *(personne célèbre)* celebrity; **il est la g. de notre école** he is the pride of our school **(c)** *(manifestation de respect)* **rendre g. à** to glorify; **g. à...!** glory to...!; **à la g. de qn** in praise of sb

glorieux, -euse [glorjø, -øz] *adj* glorious; **être promis à un avenir g.** to have a glorious future ahead of one; *Fam* **ce n'est pas très g.** *(pas très bon)* it's not exactly brilliant

glorifier [66] [glorifje] **1** *vt* to glorify

2 se glorifier *vpr* **se g. de qch/de faire qch** to glory in sth/in doing sth

gloriole [glorjol] *nf Fam* **faire qch par g.** to do sth in order to show off

glose [gloz] *nf (explication)* gloss

gloser [gloze] **gloser sur** *vt ind (discourir sur)* to ramble on about

glossaire [gloser] *nm (ouvrage)* glossary

glotte [glot] *nf Anat* glottis

glouglou [gluglu] *nm* **(a)** *(bruit d'un liquide)* gurgle; **faire g.** to gurgle **(b)** *(cri de la dinde)* gobble

gloussements [glusmɑ̃] *nmpl (d'une poule)* clucking; *(d'une dinde)* gobbling; *(d'une personne)* chuckling

glousser [gluse] *vi (poule)* to cluck; *(dinde)* to gobble; *(personne)* to chuckle

glouton, -onne [glutɔ̃, -ɔn] **1** *adj* greedy, gluttonous

2 *nm,f* glutton

3 *nm (animal)* wolverine

gloutonnement [glutɔnmɑ̃] *adv* greedily

gloutonnerie [glutɔnri] *nf* gluttony, greed

glu [gly] *nf (colle)* glue

gluant, -e [glyɑ̃, -ɑ̃t] *adj* slimy

glucide [glysid] *nm* carbohydrate

glucose [glykoz] *nm* glucose

gluten [glyten] *nm* gluten; **sans g.** gluten-free

glycémie [glisemi] *nf Méd* glycaemia

glycérine [gliserin] *nf* glycerine

glycine [glisin] *nf (plante)* wisteria

gnangnan [nɑ̃nɑ̃] *adj inv Fam (personne)* drippy; *(livre, film)* soppy

gnognot(t)e [nɔnɔt] *nf Fam (mauvaise qualité)* **c'est de la g.** it's garbage; **c'est pas de la g., cette voiture** that car's quite something

gnole, gnôle [nol] *nf Fam* hooch

gnome [gnom] *nm* gnome; *Fig & Péj (homme)* midget

gnon [nɔ̃] *nm Fam (coup de poing)* thump; **se prendre un g.** to get thumped

GO 1 *Rad (abrév* **grandes ondes)** LW

2 [ʒeo] *nm (abrév* **gentil organisateur)** activity organizer *(at Club Méditerranée holiday villages)*

Go *nm Ordinat (abrév* **gigaoctet(s))** GB

go [go] **tout de go** *adv* straight away

goal [gol] *nm* goalkeeper

gobelet [gɔblɛ] *nm (en argent, en étain)* tumbler; **g. en plastique/carton** plastic/paper cup

gober [gɔbe] *vt (nourriture)* to gulp down; *Fig (croire)* to swallow

goberger [gɔbɛrʒe] **se goberger** *vpr Fam* to have a good time

Gobi [gɔbi] *n voir* **désert**

godasse [gɔdas] *nf Fam* shoe

godelureau, -x [gɔdlyro] *nm Péj & Vieilli* popinjay

godet [gɔdɛ] *nm* **(a)** *(récipient)* pot; *Fam* **boire un g.** to have a jar **(b)** *(d'une noria)* scoop; *(d'un excavateur, d'une roue à eau)* bucket **(c)** *(d'une jupe)* **à godets** flared

godiche [gɔdiʃ] *Fam* **1** *adj* clumsy

2 *nf* clumsy oaf

godille [gɔdij] *nf* **(a)** *Naut* scull; **avancer à la g.** to scull **(b)** *(en ski)* wedeln; **faire de la g.** to wedeln

godiller [gɔdije] vi (a) Naut to scull (b) (en ski) to wedeln

godillot [gɔdijo] nm Mil boot; Fam (gros soulier) clodhopper

goéland [gɔelɑ̃] nm gull

goélette [gɔelɛt] nf (navire) schooner

goémon [gɔemɔ̃] nm wrack

gogo¹ [gogo] à gogo adv Fam galore

gogo² nm Fam sucker, mug

goguenard, -e [gɔgnar, -ard] adj mocking

goguette [gɔgɛt] nf Fam être en g. (faire la noce) to be out for a good time

goinfre [gwɛ̃fr] Fam **1** nmf pig
2 adj piggish

goinfrer [gwɛ̃fre] se goinfrer vpr Fam to pig oneself (de on)

goinfrerie [gwɛ̃frəri] nf piggishness

goitre [gwatr] nm Méd goitre

golden [gɔldɛn] nf Golden Delicious (apple)

golf [gɔlf] nm golf; (terrain de) g. golf course; g. miniature miniature golf

golfe [gɔlf] nm gulf, bay; le G. the Gulf; le g. Persique the Persian Gulf; les États ou les pays du G. the Gulf States; le g. du Bengale the Bay of Bengal; le g. de Gascogne the Bay of Biscay; le g. du Mexique the Gulf of Mexico

golfeur, -euse [gɔlfœr, -øz] nm,f golfer

Gomina® [gɔmina] nf hair cream

gominé, -e [gɔmine] adj plastered-down

gommage [gɔmaʒ] nm (a) (pour effacer) rubbing out, erasing (b) (nettoyage de la peau) face scrub; se faire un g. to give oneself a face scrub

gomme [gɔm] nf (a) (pour effacer) eraser, Br rubber (b) (substance) gum; g. à mâcher chewing gum (c) Fam (locutions) mettre (toute) la g. to get a move on; (en voiture) to step on it; à la g. useless

gommé, -e [gɔme] adj (papier, enveloppe) gummed

gommer [gɔme] vt (effacer) to rub out, to erase; Fig (souvenir) to erase

gond [gɔ̃] nm (de porte) hinge; sortir de ses gonds (porte) to come off its hinges; Fig to fly off the handle

gondole [gɔ̃dɔl] nf (barque, présentoir) gondola

gondoler [gɔ̃dɔle] **1** vi (bois, disque) to warp; (papier) to crinkle
2 se gondoler vpr (a) (bois, disque) to warp; (papier) to crinkle (b) Fam (rire) to fall about laughing

gondolier [gɔ̃dɔlje] nm gondolier

gonflable [gɔ̃flabl] adj inflatable

gonflage [gɔ̃flaʒ] nm g. (des pneus) tyre pressure

gonflant, -e [gɔ̃flɑ̃, -ɑ̃t] adj (a) (coiffure) bouffant (b) très Fam (énervant) maddening

gonflé, -e [gɔ̃fle] adj (a) (boursouflé) swollen (b) Fam être g. (personne) to have a lot of nerve; c'est g., ce qu'il a fait là what he did took some nerve; g. à bloc (sûr de soi) raring to go

gonflement [gɔ̃fləmɑ̃] nm (d'une partie du corps) swelling

gonfler [gɔ̃fle] **1** vt (a) (pneu, ballon, matelas pneumatique) to blow up, to inflate; (ses joues) to puff out; (sujet: vent) (voiles) to fill (b) (faire augmenter de volume) to swell (c) Fig (grossir) (résultats, conséquences) to exaggerate; Fam (moteur) to soup up (d) très Fam (énerver) g. qn to get up sb's nose or Br on sb's tits
2 vi to swell; (gâteau, pâte) to rise
3 se gonfler vpr (voiles, poumons) to fill; Fig se g. de joie (cœur) to fill with joy

gonflette [gɔ̃flɛt] nf Fam Péj pumping iron; faire de la g. to pump iron

gong [gɔ̃g] nm (a) (percussion) gong (b) (en boxe) bell; Fig sauvé par le g. saved by the bell

gonzesse [gɔ̃zes] nf très Fam chick, Br bird

goret [gɔrɛ] nm piglet; Fam (enfant malpropre) little pig

gorge [gɔrʒ] nf (a) (gosier, cou) throat; avoir mal à la g. to have a sore throat; avoir la g. serrée to have a lump in one's throat; Fig cela m'est resté en travers de la g. it stuck in my throat; trancher la g. à qn to cut sb's throat; Fig être pris à la g. to be in a stranglehold; faire des gorges chaudes de qch to laugh sth to scorn; rire à la g. déployée to roar with laughter (b) Litt (poitrine) bosom (c) (vallée) gorge (d) (d'une poulie) groove

gorgé, -e [gɔrʒe] adj une éponge gorgée d'eau a sponge full of water; sol g. d'eau waterlogged earth

gorgée [gɔrʒe] nf mouthful; boire qch à petites gorgées to sip sth; avaler qch d'une g. to swallow sth in one gulp

gorger [45] [gɔrʒe] se gorger vpr to gorge oneself (de on or with); se g. d'eau (sol) to get waterlogged

gorgonzola [gɔrgɔ̃zɔla] nm Gorgonzola

gorille [gɔrij] nm (animal) gorilla; Fam (garde du corps) gorilla

gosier [gozje] nm throat; Fam avoir la g. sec to be parched

gosse [gɔs] nmf (a) Fam (enfant) kid (b) Fam être beau g. to be good-looking (c) Can Fam gosses balls

gosser [gɔse] vt Can Fam to whittle

gotha [gɔta] nm le g. du show-business/de la finance the showbusiness/financial elite

gothique [gɔtik] **1** adj Gothic; écriture g. Gothic script
2 nm (style) Gothic

gouache [gwaʃ] nf gouache

gouailleur, -euse [gwajœr, -øz] adj (ton) bantering

gouda [guda] nm Gouda

goudron [gudrɔ̃] nm tar; goudrons (dans les cigarettes) tar

goudronner [gudrɔne] vt to tar

gouffre [gufr] nm abyss; Géol sinkhole; Br swallow hole; Fig être au bord du g. to be on the edge of the abyss; Fig cette voiture est un g. this car just swallows up money

gougère [guʒɛr] nf Culin gougère (choux pastry with cheese)

gouine [gwin] nf très Fam dyke, = offensive term used to refer to a lesbian

goujat [guʒa] nm boor

goujon [guʒɔ̃] nm (poisson) gudgeon

goulache, goulasch [gulaʃ] nm goulash

goulée [gule] nf (de liquide) gulp; (d'air) lungful

goulet [gulɛ] nm (défilé) gully; g. d'étranglement bottleneck

gouleyant, -e [gulejɑ̃, -ɑ̃t] adj (vin) easy-drinking

goulot [gulo] nm (d'une bouteille) neck; boire au g. to drink straight from the bottle

goulu, -e [guly] **1** adj greedy, gluttonous
2 nm,f glutton

goulûment [gulymɑ̃] adv greedily

goupille [gupij] nf (d'une grenade) pin

goupiller [gupije] Fam **1** vt (arranger) to fix (up)
2 se goupiller vpr bien se g. to work out well; ça s'est mal goupillé it didn't work out

goupillon [gupijɔ̃] nm (a) (pour eau bénite) sprinkler (b) (pour biberons, bouteilles) bottle brush

gourd, -e [gur, gurd] *adj* numb (with cold)
gourde [gurd] **1** *nf* (**a**) *(récipient)* flask (**b**) *Fam (femme niaise)* airhead
2 *adj Fam* dizzy
gourdin [gurdɛ̃] *nm* club, cudgel
gourer [gure] se gourer *vpr Fam Br* to boob, *Am* to goof; **se g. d'adresse/de jour** to get the wrong address/day
gourgane [gurgan] *nf Can* broad bean
gourmand, -e [gurmɑ̃, -ɑ̃d] **1** *adj (personne)* who likes his/her food; *Fig (intéressé, regard)* greedy
2 *nmf* person who likes his/her food; **quel g.!** he certainly likes his food!
gourmandise [gurmɑ̃diz] *nf* (**a**) *(d'une personne)* love of food; *Fig* **avec g.** greedily (**b**) **gourmandises** *(sucreries)* delicacies
gourmet [gurme] *nm* gourmet; **un fin g.** a great gourmet
gourmette [gurmɛt] *nf (bracelet)* chain (bracelet)
gourou [guru] *nm aussi Fig* guru
gousse [gus] *nf (de haricot, de petit pois)* pod; **g. d'ail** clove of garlic; **g. de vanille** vanilla pod
gousset [gusɛ] *nm (poche)* fob (pocket)
goût [gu] *nm* (**a**) *(saveur)* taste; **avoir un g. de café/ d'alcool** to taste of coffee/alcohol; **manquer de g.**, **ne pas avoir de g.** to be tasteless (**b**) *(sens)* taste (**c**) *(préférence, convenance)* taste; **avoir des goûts de luxe** to have expensive tastes; **trouver qn/qch à son g.** to find sb/sth to one's taste; **avoir du g. pour** *ou* **le g. de qch** to have a taste for sth; **elle n'a plus (de) g. à rien** she doesn't want to do anything any more; **faire qch par g.** to do sth because one likes to; **prendre g. à qch** to acquire a taste for sth; **chacun ses goûts** each to his own; **des goûts et des couleurs on ne discute pas, tous les goûts sont dans la nature** there's no accounting for taste (**d**) *(discernement, jugement)* taste; **s'habiller avec g.** to have good dress sense; **de bon g.** tasteful; **d'un g.** douteux in doubtful taste; **de mauvais g.** in bad taste (**e**) *(style)* **quelque chose dans ce g.-là** something of that sort
goûter¹ [gute] *nm (afternoon)* tea; **l'heure du g.** teatime
goûter² **1** *vt* (**a**) *(essayer) (nourriture, boisson)* to taste, to try (**b**) *(apprécier)* to enjoy, to appreciate
2 *vi (à quatre heures)* to have tea
3 **goûter de** *vt ind (aliment)* to taste, to try; *Fig* to have a taste of
goûteur, -euse [gutœr, -øz] *nmf* taster
goutte [gut] **1** *nf* (**a**) *(de liquide)* drop; **couler g. à g.** to drip; **il suait à grosses gouttes** the sweat was pouring off him; *Fig* **c'est la g. d'eau qui fait déborder le vase** it's the straw that breaks/broke the camel's back; *Fam* **avoir la g. au nez** to have a runny nose; **se ressembler comme deux gouttes d'eau** to be as like as two peas in a pod (**b**) *(petite quantité)* drop; **encore une g. de café?** a drop more coffee?; *Fam* **boire la g.** to have a nip (**c**) *Méd* gout; **gouttes** *(pour les yeux, les oreilles)* drops
2 *adv Vieilli* **je n'y vois/entends g.** I can't see/understand anything
goutte-à-goutte [gutagut] *nm inv Méd Br* drip, *Am* IV; **on lui a mis un g.** she was put on *Br* a drip *or Am* an IV
gouttelette [gutlɛt] *nf* droplet
goutter [gute] *vi* to drip
gouttière [gutjɛr] *nf* (**a**) *(le long du toit)* gutter (**b**) *(le long du mur)* drainpipe
gouvernail [guvɛrnaj] *nm Naut* rudder; **tenir le g.** to be at the helm
gouvernant, -e [guvɛrnɑ̃, -ɑ̃t] **1** *adj (classe, parti)* governing, ruling
2 *nm* **les gouvernants** those in power

gouvernante [guvɛrnɑ̃t] *nf (d'enfants)* governess; *(d'une personne, d'un hôtel)* housekeeper
gouverne [guvɛrn] *nf* (**a**) *Av* gouvernes control surfaces (**b**) **pour votre g.** for your guidance
gouvernement [guvɛrnəmɑ̃] *nm* government; **sous le g. Jospin** during Jospin's term of office
gouvernemental, -e, -aux, -ales [guvɛrnəmɑ̃tal, -o] *adj* government; *(parti)* governing
gouverner [guvɛrne] **1** *vt* (**a**) *(diriger) (pays)* to govern, to rule; **un parti qui gouverne depuis des années** a party which has been in power for years (**b**) *(bateau)* to steer
2 **se gouverner** *vpr* **le droit des peuples à se g. eux-mêmes** the right of peoples to self-government
gouverneur [guvɛrnœr] *nm* governor; *Can* **G. Général** governor-general; *Can* **Lieutenant-G.** lieutenant-governor
goyave [gɔjav] *nf* guava
GR [ʒeɛr] *nm (abrév* **sentier de) grande randonnée)** = designation for long-distance footpath
grabat [graba] *nm* pallet
grabataire [grabatɛr] **1** *adj* bedridden
2 *nmf* bedridden invalid
grabuge [grabyʒ] *nm Fam* rumpus; **il va y avoir du g.** there'll be a rumpus
grâce [grɑs] *nf* (**a**) *(charme)* grace; **avec g.** gracefully (**b**) **g. à qn/qch** *(avec l'aide de)* thanks to sb/sth (**c**) *Litt (bienveillance, faveur)* favour; **faites-moi la g. d'oublier cette histoire** do me the favour of forgetting this matter; **trouver g. aux yeux de qn** to find favour in sb's eyes; **de g.!** for pity's sake! (**d**) *(volonté)* **de bonne g.** willingly, **de mauvaise g.** unwillingly, grudgingly (**e**) *(acquittement)* pardon; **demander** *ou* **crier g.** to beg for mercy; **faire g. à qn de qch** *(dette, tâche)* to let sb off sth; **je vous fais g. des détails** I'll spare you the details; **g. présidentielle** presidential pardon (**f**) *(remerciements)* **rendre g. à** to give thanks to (**g**) *Rel* grace
gracier [66] [grasje] *vt* to pardon
gracieusement [grasjøzmɑ̃] *adv* (**a**) *(avec grâce)* gracefully (**b**) *(aimablement)* graciously (**c**) *(gratuitement)* free of charge
gracieux, -euse [grasjø, -øz] *adj* (**a**) *(qui a du charme)* graceful (**b**) *(aimable)* gracious (**c**) *(gratuit)* à titre g. free of charge
gracile [grasil] *adj* slender
gradation [gradasjɔ̃] *nf* gradation
grade [grad] *nm (dans l'armée, dans l'administration)* rank; **monter en g.** to be promoted; *Fam* **en prendre pour son g.** to be hauled over the coals
gradé, -e [grade] *nmf Mil* non-commissioned officer, NCO
gradin [gradɛ̃] *nm (d'amphithéâtre, de stade)* row of seats; **les gradins** *(d'un stade) Br* the terraces, *Am* the bleachers
graduation [graduasjɔ̃] *nf* graduation
gradué, -e [gradue] *adj* (**a**) *(qui porte une graduation)* graduated (**b**) *(progressif) (exercices, problèmes)* graded
graduel, -elle [graduɛl] *adj* gradual
graduellement [graduɛlmɑ̃] *adv* gradually
graduer [gradue] *vt* (**a**) *(diviser en degrés)* to graduate (**b**) *(augmenter)* to increase gradually
graffiti [grafiti] *nm* piece of graffiti; **des graffitis** graffiti
grailler [graje] *vi très Fam (manger)* to eat
graillon [grajɔ̃] *nm* **sentir le g.** to smell of burnt fat
grain¹ [grɛ̃] *nm* (**a**) *(graine, fruit, céréales)* grain; **g. de café** coffee bean; **g. de poivre** peppercorn; **g. de raisin** grape (**b**) *(de sable, de poudre)* grain; *(de poussière)* speck; *(de chapelet)* bead; *Fig* **un g. de qch** *(un peu de)* a hint of sth;

pas un g. de bon sens/de vérité not a grain of common sense/of truth; *Fam* **il a un g.** he's not quite right in the head; **mettre son g. de sel** to stick one's oar in; **g. de beauté** mole (**c**) *(d'un tissu, d'une photographie)* grain; *(de la peau)* rough side

grain² *nm Naut* squall; *Fig* **veiller au g.** to keep a weather eye open

graine [grɛn] *nf* seed; **monter en g.** to run to seed; *Fig (personne)* to shoot up; **regarde un peu ce qu'a fait ton cousin et prends-en de la g.!** just look at what your cousin's done and take a leaf out of his book!; **c'est de la mauvaise g.** he's a bad lot; **g. de voyou/voleur** little lout/thief

graissage [grɛsaʒ] *nm (d'une machine, d'un engrenage)* greasing

graisse [grɛs] *nf (d'animal, de personne)* fat; *(lubrifiant)* grease; **graisses animales/végétales** animal/vegetable fat

graisser [grɛse] *vt (machine, engrenage)* to grease; *(bottes)* to oil; **g. la patte à qn** to grease sb's palm

graisseux, -euse [grɛsø, -øz] *adj* (**a**) *(taché de graisse)* greasy (**b**) *(tumeur, tissu)* fatty

grammaire [gramɛr] *nf* (**a**) *(science, règles)* grammar; **faute/règle de g.** grammatical error/rule (**b**) *(livre)* grammar (book)

grammairien, -enne [gramɛrjɛ̃, -ɛn] *nm,f* grammarian

grammatical, -e, -aux, -ales [gramatikal, -o] *adj* grammatical

gramme [gram] *nm* gram; *aussi Fig* **pas un g. de** not an ounce of

grand, -e [grɑ̃, grɑ̃d] **1** *adj* (**a**) *(en taille)* big, large; *(en hauteur)* tall; *(en longueur)* long; *Phot* **g. angle** wide-angle lens

(**b**) *(principal)* chief, main; **grandes lignes** *(de train)* main lines

(**c**) *(adulte, plus âgé)* big

(**d**) *(en quantité, intensité) (bruit)* loud; *(coup)* heavy; *(froid)* severe; *(différence, catastrophe)* big; **le g. amour** true love; **un acteur sans g. talent** a rather untalented actor; **il fait g. jour** it's broad daylight; **c'est un g. buveur** he's a big drinker; **les grands blessés** the seriously wounded

(**e**) *(puissant, prestigieux)* great; **une grande dame de la littérature** a great literary lady

(**f**) *(dans un titre, un grade)* grand; **g. prêtre** high priest; **g. reporter** chief reporter

2 *adv* **ouvrir g. la bouche/la fenêtre** to open one's mouth/the window wide; **g. ouvert** wide open

3 *nm,f* **les grands** *(enfants)* the older ones; **grands et petits** old and young, grown-ups and children; **les grands de ce monde** those in high places; **les grands du pétrole** the oil giants; **mon g.** mate, pal; **ma grande** dear

grand-chose [grɑ̃ʃoz] **1** *pron indéfini* **pas g.** not much; **ce ne sont que quelques fleurs, ce n'est pas g.** it's just a few flowers, nothing much

2 *nmf inv Fam (personne)* **un pas g.** a dead loss

grand-duc *(pl* **grands-ducs)** [grɑ̃dyk] *nm (noble)* grand duke; *Fam* **faire la tournée des grands-ducs** to go out on the town

grand-duché *(pl* **grands-duchés)** [grɑ̃dyʃe] *nm* grand duchy

Grande-Bretagne [grɑ̃dbrətaɲ] *nf* **la G.** Great Britain

grande-duchesse *(pl* **grandes-duchesses)** [grɑ̃ddyʃɛs] *nf* grand duchess

grandement [grɑ̃dmɑ̃] *adv (beaucoup)* greatly; **se tromper g.** to be greatly mistaken; **avoir g. le temps** to have ample time; **avoir g. de quoi vivre** to have plenty to live on

grandeur [grɑ̃dœr] *nf* (**a**) *(taille)* size; *(d'un arbre)* height, size; **g. nature** life-size (**b**) *(importance)* importance (**c**) *Math* magnitude (**d**) *(gloire)* greatness, grandeur; **g. et décadence d'un empire** rise and fall of an empire (**e**) *(des sentiments)* nobility; **g. d'âme** magnanimity

grand-guignol [grɑ̃giɲɔl] *nm Péj* **c'est du g.** it's all blood and gore

grandiloquence [grɑ̃dilɔkɑ̃s] *nf* grandiloquence

grandiloquent, -e [grɑ̃dilɔkɑ̃, -ɑ̃t] *adj* grandiloquent

grandiose [grɑ̃djoz] *adj* imposing

grandir [grɑ̃dir] **1** *vi (en taille)* to grow; *(en âge)* to grow up; *(en importance)* to increase, to grow

2 *vt* **g. qn** *(sujet: talons)* to make sb look taller; *Fig (sujet: expérience, épreuve)* to improve sb's standing

3 *se grandir* *vpr (en taille)* to make oneself taller

grandissant, -e [grɑ̃disɑ̃, -ɑ̃t] *adj* growing

grand-mère *(pl* **grand-mères** *ou* **grands-mères)** [grɑ̃mɛr] *nf* grandmother; *Fam (vieille femme)* old dear

grand-oncle *(pl* **grands-oncles** [grɑ̃zɔ̃kl]) *nm* great-uncle

grand-peine [grɑ̃pɛn] **à grand-peine** *adv* with great difficulty

grand-père *(pl* **grands-pères)** [grɑ̃pɛr] *nm* grandfather; *Fam (vieil homme)* granddad

grand-route *(pl* **grand-routes)** [grɑ̃rut] *nf* main road

grand-rue *(pl* **grand-rues)** [grɑ̃ry] *nf* high street, main street

grands-parents [grɑ̃parɑ̃] *nmpl* grandparents

grand-tante *(pl* **grand-tantes** *ou* **grands-tantes)** [grɑ̃tɑ̃t] *nf* great-aunt

grand-voile *(pl* **grand-voiles** *ou* **grands-voiles)** [grɑ̃vwal] *nf* mainsail

grange [grɑ̃ʒ] *nf* barn

granit(e) [granit] *nm* granite

granule [granyl] *nm* granule

granulé [granyle] *nm* granule

granuleux, -euse [granylø, -øz] *adj* granular

graphe [graf] *nm* graph

graphie [grafi] *nf Ling* written form

graphique [grafik] **1** *adj* graphic

2 *nm* diagram; *(sur un axe)* graph; *Ordinat* graphic; *Ordinat* **g. de gestion** management chart; **g. à** *ou* **en barres** bar chart

graphisme [grafism] *nm* (**a**) *(écriture)* handwriting (**b**) *Art (style)* style of drawing

graphiste [grafist] *nmf* graphic designer

graphite [grafit] *nm* graphite

graphologie [grafɔlɔʒi] *nf* graphology

graphologue [grafɔlɔg] *nmf* graphologist

grappe [grap] *nf (de raisin)* bunch; *(de fleurs, de gens)* cluster; *Vulg* **lâche-moi la g.!** piss off!

grappiller [grapije] *vt (renseignements)* to glean; *(argent)* to make on the side

grappin [grapɛ̃] *nm Naut* grappling hook *or* iron; *Fam Fig* **mettre le g. sur qn/qch** to get one's hands on sb/sth

gras, grasse [grɑ, grɑs] **1** *adj* (**a**) *(nourriture, tissu)* fatty (**b**) *(gros) (personne, animal)* fat; *(poulet)* plump (**c**) *(graisseux) (chiffon, cheveux, peau)* greasy (**d**) *(épais) (terre)* heavy, clayey; *(crayon)* soft lead; *(toux)* loose; *(rire)* throaty (**e**) *Typ* bold; **caractères g.** bold type (**f**) *Fig (bénéfices, récompense)* handsome; **faire la grasse matinée** to have a lie-in (**g**) *(graveleux) (histoire)* dirty, smutty

2 *adv* **manger g.** to eat fatty food

3 *nm* (**a**) *(de la jambe, du bras)* fleshy part (**b**) *(du jambon, de la viande)* fat (**c**) *Typ* bold; **en g.** in bold

gras-double *(pl* **gras-doubles**) [gradubl] *nm* tripe
grassement [grasmã] *adv (récompenser, payer)* handsomely
grasseyer [graseje] *vi* = to pronounce one's r's at the back of the throat
grassouillet, -ette [grasuje, -ɛt] *adj* plump, chubby
gratifiant, -e [gratifjã, -ãt] *adj* rewarding, gratifying
gratification [gratifikasjɔ̃] *nf* (**a**) *(prime)* bonus (**b**) *(satisfaction)* gratification
gratifier [66] [gratifje] *vt* (**a**) **g. qn de qch** *(récompense)* to present sb with sth; *Ironique (sourire)* to bestow sth on sb (**b**) *(valoriser)* to gratify
gratin [gratẽ] *nm* (**a**) *(plat)* gratin *(baked dish with a topping of grated cheese and sometimes breadcrumbs)*; **au g.** au gratin; **chou-fleur au g.** cauliflower cheese; **g. dauphinois** gratin dauphinois, = sliced potatoes baked with cream and browned on top (**b**) *Fam Fig* **le g.** *(le beau monde)* the upper crust
gratiné, -e [gratine] **1** *adj* (**a**) *(au gratin)* au gratin *(topped with grated cheese and sometimes breadcrumbs)* (**b**) *Fam Fig (addition)* huge; *(examen, problème)* tough **2** *nf* **gratinée** *Culin* onion soup au gratin
gratiner [gratine] **1** *vt* to brown **2** *vi* **faire g. qch** to brown sth
gratis [gratis] **1** *adv* free (of charge) **2** *adj* free
gratitude [gratityd] *nf* gratitude
gratouiller [gratuje] *vt Fam (démanger)* **ça (me) gratouille** it makes me itch
gratte [grat] *nf Can* snowplough
gratte-ciel [gratsjɛl] *nm inv* skyscraper
gratte-papier [gratpapje] *nm inv Péj* pen-pusher
gratter [grate] **1** *vt (avec les ongles)* to scratch; *(avec un objet)* to scrape; *(effacer) (mot, inscription)* to scratch out, *(tache)* to scrape off; *Fam* **ça me gratte** it makes me itch; **pull qui gratte** scratchy jumper; *Fig* **g. les fonds de tiroir** to scrape around for money **2** *vi* **g. à la porte** to tap lightly at the door **3 se gratter** *vpr* to scratch oneself; **se g. jusqu'au sang** to scratch oneself raw; **se g. la tête/l'oreille** to scratch one's head/ear; *très Fam* **tu peux toujours te g.!** you can take a running jump!
grattoir [gratwar] *nm* scraper; *(de boîte d'allumettes)* striking surface
grattouiller [gratuje] = **gratouiller**
gratuit, -e [gratɥi, -it] *adj* (**a**) *(billet, entrée, échantillon)* free; **à titre g.** free of charge (**b**) *(acte, violence)* gratuitous
gratuité [gratɥite] *nf* (**a**) *(fait de ne pas payer)* **la g. de l'enseignement/des soins hospitaliers** free education/hospital care (**b**) *(d'un acte, de la violence)* gratuitousness
gratuitement [gratɥitmã] *adv* (**a**) *(sans payer)* free (of charge) (**b**) *(sans motif)* gratuitously
gravats [grava] *nmpl* rubble
grave [grav] **1** *adj* (**a**) *(sérieux, dramatique)* serious; **ce n'est pas g.** *(ça n'a pas d'importance)* it doesn't matter; **un accident qui a fait deux blessés graves** an accident in which two people were seriously injured (**b**) *(solennel)* *(visage, ton, expression)* grave, solemn (**c**) *(note, voix)* low, deep **2** *nm* **le g., les graves** *(notes)* the low notes; **les graves** *(sur une chaîne stéréo)* the bass
graveleux, -euse [gravlø, -øz] *adj* (**a**) *(histoire, chanson)* smutty, dirty (**b**) *(terre)* gravelly
gravement [gravmã] *adv* (**a**) *(malade, blessé)* seriously (**b**) *(avec dignité)* gravely, solemnly

graver [grave] *vt (matériau, motif)* to engrave; *(sur bois)* to carve; *(disque)* to make; *Fig* **rester gravé dans la mémoire de qn** to be engraved on sb's memory
graveur, -euse [gravœr, -øz] *nm,f* engraver; **g. sur bois** woodcarver
gravier [gravje] *nm* gravel
gravillon [gravijɔ̃] *nm (caillou)* piece of gravel; **du g., des gravillons** gravel; **gravillons** *(sur panneau)* loose chippings
gravir [gravir] *vt* to climb; *Fig* **g. les échelons** to climb the ladder
gravissime [gravisim] *adj* extremely serious
gravitation [gravitasjɔ̃] *nf* gravitation
gravité [gravite] *nf* (**a**) *Phys* gravity (**b**) *(solennité)* gravity (**c**) *(importance)* seriousness; **sans g.** *(blessure, problème)* minor
graviter [gravite] *vi* **g. autour de qch** to orbit sth; *Fig* **g. autour de qn** to hover around sb
gravure [gravyr] *nf* (**a**) *(action)* engraving; **g. sur bois** woodcarving (**b**) *(ouvrage)* engraving; **g. sur bois** woodcut; *Fig* **c'est une vraie g. de mode** she dresses like a fashion model
gré [gre] *nm* (**a**) *(goût)* **à mon/son g.** for my/his/her liking (**b**) *(volonté)* **contre son g.** against one's will; **de son propre g., de son plein g.** of one's own free will; **de bon g.** willingly, gladly; **bon g. mal g.** whether we/you/etc like it or not; **faites-le venir de g. ou de force** make him come whether he wants to or not; **au g. des flots** at the mercy of the waves; **au g. des événements/des circonstances** *(agir, changer d'avis)* according to how events turn out/to the circumstances (**c**) *Formel (gratitude)* **nous vous saurions g. de bien vouloir...** we would be grateful if you would kindly...
grec, grecque [grɛk] **1** *adj* Greek **2** *nm,f* **G.** Greek **3** *nm (langue)* Greek; **g. ancien/moderne** ancient/modern Greek **4** *nf* **grecque** (**a**) *Culin* **à la grecque** *(légumes)* = marinated in olive oil, lemon juice and herbs and served cold (**b**) *(motif)* Greek key pattern
Grèce [grɛs] *nf* **la G.** Greece
gredin, -e [grədẽ, -in] *nm,f Fam Vieilli* rascal
gréement [gremã] *nm Naut* rigging
greffe¹ [grɛf] *nf* (**a**) *(de peau, de tissu)* graft; *(d'organe)* transplant; **g. du cœur/du rein** heart/kidney transplant (**b**) *Bot (action)* grafting; *(bouture)* graft
greffe² *nm Jur* clerk of the court's office
greffé, -e [grɛfe] *nm,f Méd* **g. cardiaque** *ou* **du cœur** heart transplant patient
greffer [grɛfe] *vt (peau, tissu, bouture)* to graft; *(organe)* to transplant
greffier [grɛfje] *nm Jur* clerk (of the court)
greffon [grɛfɔ̃] *nm (de tissu, de peau)* graft; *(d'organe)* transplant; *(bouture)* graft
grégaire [greger] *adj* gregarious; **l'instinct g.** the herd instinct
grège [grɛʒ] *adj (beige)* whitish-beige
grégorien, -enne [gregorjẽ, -ɛn] *adj* Gregorian
grêle¹ [grɛl] *adj (jambes, mains)* skinny; *(tige, silhouette)* slender; *(voix, son)* shrill
grêle² *nf aussi Fig* hail
grêlé, -e [grele] *adj (peau)* pockmarked
grêler [grele] *v impersonnel* to hail
grêlon [grɛlɔ̃] *nm* hailstone
grelot [grəlo] *nm* (small) bell

grelotter [grǝlɔte] *vi* to shiver (**de** with)
Grenade [grǝnad] *nf (aux Antilles)* **la G.** Grenada
grenade [grǝnad] *nf* (**a**) *(projectile)* grenade; **g.** lacry-mogène tear-gas grenade (**b**) *(fruit)* pomegranate
grenadine [grǝnadin] *nf* grenadine
grenaille [grǝnɑj] *nf* (**a**) *(plombs)* shot (**b**) *Belg* **grenailles errantes** *(sur panneau)* loose chippings
grenat [grǝna] **1** *nm* garnet
2 *adj inv* dark red
grenier [grǝnje] *nm* (**a**) *(sous les combles)* attic (**b**) *(pour grain, fourrage)* granary; **g. à blé** wheat loft; **g. à foin** hay-loft
grenouille [grǝnuj] *nf (animal)* frog; *Fig & Péj* **g. de bénitier** Bible basher
grenouillère [grǝnujer] *nf (pour bébé)* Babygro®
grès [grɛ] *nm* (**a**) *(pierre)* sandstone (**b**) *(céramique)* stoneware; **cruche en g.** stoneware jug
grésil [grezil, grezi] *nm* fine hail
grésillement [grezijmɑ̃] *nm (du feu, d'une radio)* crackling; *(de l'huile)* sizzling
grésiller [grezije] *vi (feu, radio)* to crackle; *(huile)* to sizzle
gressin [gresɛ̃] *nm* bread stick
grève¹ [grɛv] *nf (arrêt du travail)* strike; **se mettre en g.** to go out on strike, to strike; **être en g., faire g.** to be on strike; **g. des Postes** postal strike; **g. de la faim** hunger strike; **g. générale** general strike; **g. sauvage** wildcat strike; **g. sur le tas** sit-down strike; **g. tournante** staggered strike; **g. du zèle** work-to-rule, go-slow
grève² *nf (le long de la mer)* shore; *(d'un fleuve)* bank
grever [46] [grǝve] *vt (pouvoir d'achat)* to restrict; *(budget)* to put a strain on
gréviste [grevist] *nmf* striker; **g. de la faim** hunger striker
gribouillage [gribujaʒ] *nm (écriture)* scribble, scrawl; *(dessin)* doodle
gribouiller [gribuje] *vt & vi (écrire)* to scrawl, to scribble; *(dessiner)* to doodle
gribouillis [gribuji] = gribouillage
grief [grijef] *nm* grievance, ground for complaint; **faire** *ou* **tenir g. à qn de qch** to hold sth against sb
grièvement [grijɛvmɑ̃] *adv* seriously, badly
griffe [grif] *nf* (**a**) *(d'animal)* claw; **faire ses griffes** *(chat)* to sharpen its claws; *Fig* **montrer les griffes** to show one's claws; **arracher qn des griffes de qn** to snatch sb out of sb's clutches (**b**) *(sur un bijou)* claw (**c**) *(sur vêtements)* label; *Fig (style)* stamp
griffé, -e [grife] *adj (vêtement)* designer
griffer [grife] *vt* to scratch
griffon [grifɔ̃] *nm* (**a**) *(chien)* griffon (**b**) *(créature mythique)* griffin
griffonner [grifɔne] *vt & vi (écrire)* to scrawl, to scribble; *(dessiner)* to sketch quickly
griffure [grifyr] *nf* scratch
grignoter [griɲɔte] **1** *vt* to nibble; *Fig (libertés)* to erode; *(capital, économies)* to eat into
2 *vi* to nibble
gril [gril] *nm (de cuisine) Br* grill, *Am* broiler; **faire cuire qch sur le g.** to grill *or Am* broil sth; *Fig* **être sur le g.** to be on tenterhooks
grillade [grijad] *nf (viande)* piece of grilled meat; *(poisson)* piece of grilled fish; **faire des grillades** to have a barbecue
grillage [grijaʒ] *nm (de fenêtre, de porte)* wire mesh; *(clôture)* wire netting

grillagé, -e [grijaʒe] *adj (fenêtre)* covered with wire mesh; *(jardin)* surrounded with wire netting
grille [grij] *nf* (**a**) *(à l'entrée d'un parc, d'un jardin)* gate; *(clôture basse)* railings (**b**) *(d'une cage, d'une fenêtre)* screen, netting; *Aut* **g. de radiateur** radiator grille (**c**) *(d'un évier, d'un égout)* grating, grate (**d**) *(tableau) (de mots croisés)* grid; *Rad & TV* **g. des programmes** programme schedule; **g. des salaires** salary scale
grille-pain [grijpɛ̃] *nm inv* toaster
griller [grije] **1** *vt* (**a**) *(rôtir) (viande)* to grill, *Am* to broil; *(pain)* to toast; *(café, marrons)* to roast; *(ampoule, fusible)* to blow; *Fam (cigarette)* to smoke (**c**) *Fam (dépasser)* **g. un concurrent** to leave a competitor standing; **g. un feu rouge** to jump the lights (**d**) *Fam (discréditer)* **il est grillé** his game's up
2 *vi* (**a**) *(viande)* to grill, *Am* to broil; *(pain)* to toast; *(marrons)* to roast; *Fig* **g. d'impatience** to be burning with impatience (**b**) *(ampoule, fusible)* to blow
3 se griller *vpr* **se g. au soleil** to roast in the sun; *Fam* **se g. auprès de qn** to blot one's copybook with sb
grillon [grijɔ̃] *nm* cricket
grimaçant, -e [grimasɑ̃, -ɑ̃t] *adj* grimacing
grimace [grimas] *nf* grimace; **faire une g. (à qn)** to make *or* pull a face (at sb); **faire la g.** to make *or* pull a face; **faire une g. de douleur** to wince with pain
grimacer [16] [grimase] *vi* to make *or* pull a face; **g. de douleur** to wince with pain
grimer [grime] **1** *vt* to make up
2 se grimer *vpr* to put one's make-up on
grimpant, -e [grɛ̃pɑ̃, -ɑ̃t] *adj (plante)* climbing
grimpe [grɛ̃p] *nf Fam* rock-climbing; **faire de la g.** to go rock-climbing
grimpée [grɛ̃pe] *nf (stiff)* climb
grimper [grɛ̃pe] **1** *vi aussi Fig* to climb; **g. aux arbres** to climb trees; **ça grimpe** it's steep
2 *vt (montagne, escalier)* to climb; *Fig* **g. les échelons** to climb the ladder
grimpeur, -euse [grɛ̃pœr, -øz] *nm,f* climber
grinçant, -e [grɛ̃sɑ̃, -ɑ̃t] *adj (qui grince)* creaking; *Fig (caustique)* caustic
grincement [grɛ̃smɑ̃] *nm (d'une porte, de roues)* creaking; **grincements de dents** grinding of teeth; *Fig* gnashing of teeth
grincer [16] [grɛ̃se] *vi (porte, roues)* to creak; **g. des dents** to grind one's teeth; *Fig* to gnash one's teeth
grincheux, -euse [grɛ̃ʃø, -øz] **1** *adj* grumpy
2 *nm,f* grumpy person
gringalet [grɛ̃galɛ] **1** *nm* weakling
2 *adj m* puny
griotte [grijɔt] *nf* morello (cherry)
grippal, -e, -aux, -ales [gripal, -o] *adj* **soulage états grippaux** *(sur médicament)* relieves flu symptoms
grippe [grip] *nf* (**a**) *(maladie)* flu; **avoir la g.** to have (the) flu; **g. intestinale** gastric flu (**b**) **prendre qn/qch en g.** to take a dislike to sb/sth
grippé, -e [gripe] *adj* (**a**) *(malade)* **être g.** to have (the) flu (**b**) *(moteur, mécanisme)* seized-up
grippe-sou *(pl* **grippe-sous** *ou* **grippe-sou)** [gripsu] *nm* skinflint, miser
gris, -e [gri, griz] **1** *adj* (**a**) *(couleur, temps)* grey; **il fait g. ce matin** it's a grey *or* dull morning; **g. ardoise** slate grey; **g. perle** pearl grey (**b**) *(ivre)* tipsy
2 *nm* (**a**) *(couleur)* grey; *Ordinat* **tons de g.** shades of grey; **s'habiller en g.** to wear grey (**b**) *(tabac)* shag
grisaille [grizɑj] *nf (caractère morne)* dreariness

grisant, -e [grizɑ̃, -ɑ̃t] *adj (succès, atmosphère)* intoxicating; *(aventure, soirée)* exhilarating

grisâtre [grizɑtr] *adj* greyish

grisé [grize] *nm Ordinat* grey tone

griser [grize] **1** *vt* (**a**) *(enivrer)* to make tipsy; *Fig* to intoxicate (**b**) *Ordinat* to shade
2 se griser *vpr* **se g. de qch** *(air pur)* to get drunk on sth; *(paroles)* to get carried away by sth

grisonnant, -e [grizɔnɑ̃, -ɑ̃t] *adj (cheveux, personne)* greying; **avoir les tempes grisonnantes** to be greying at the temples

grisonner [grizɔne] *vi (cheveux, personne)* to go grey

grisou [grizu] *nm* firedamp; **coup de g.** firedamp explosion

grive [griv] *nf* thrush

grivois, -e [grivwa, -az] *adj* bawdy

grivoiserie [grivwazri] *nf (plaisanterie)* bawdy joke; *(histoire)* bawdy story; *(acte)* rude gesture

grizzli, grizzly [grizli] *nm* grizzly (bear)

Groenland [grɔɛnlɑ̃d] *nm* **le G.** Greenland

grog [grɔg] *nm* hot toddy

groggy [grɔgi] *adj inv Fam* groggy

grogne [grɔɲ] *nf Fam* discontent

grognement [grɔɲmɑ̃] *nm (d'un cochon)* grunt; *(d'un chien, d'un ours, d'une personne)* growl; **pousser des grognements** to grunt/to growl

grogner [grɔɲe] *vi* (**a**) *(gronder) (cochon)* to grunt; *(chien, personne)* to growl (**b**) *(protester)* to grumble

grognon [grɔɲɔ̃] *adj* grumpy

groin [grwɛ̃] *nm* snout

grol(l)e [grɔl] *nf très Fam* shoe

grommeler [42] [grɔmle] *vt & vi* to mutter

grommellements [grɔmɛlmɑ̃] *nmpl* muttering

grondement [grɔ̃dmɑ̃] *nm* (**a**) *(d'un chien)* growl (**b**) *(du tonnerre)* rumble; *(d'un torrent, des vagues, d'un moteur)* roar; *(des canons)* booming

gronder [grɔ̃de] **1** *vi* (**a**) *(chien)* to growl (**b**) *(tonnerre)* to rumble; *(torrent, vagues, moteur)* to roar; *(canons)* to boom; **la révolte/le mécontentement gronde** there are rumblings of rebellion/discontent
2 *vt (réprimander)* to scold, to tell off

groom [grum] *nm Br* page, *Am* bellhop

gros, grosse [gro, gros] **1** *adj* (**a**) *(corpulent)* big, fat (**b**) *(important, abondant)* big; *(rhume)* bad; *(dépenses, averse, mer)* heavy; *(somme)* large; *(faute)* serious; **g. buveur/mangeur** big drinker/eater; **avoir un g. chagrin** to be very upset; **la plus grosse partie de qch** the majority of sth; **un mensonge g. comme une maison** a whopper of a lie; *très Fam* **g. lard** big fat slob; *Fam* **g. nigaud** *ou* **bêta!** you fool!; *Fam* **g. bonnet, grosse légume** big shot, bigwig (**c**) *(épais) (morceau, caractères)* big, large; *(toile)* coarse; *(pull, chaussettes, corde)* thick; *(chaussures)* strong, stout (**d**) *(peu subtil) (voix)* gruff; *(rire)* coarse; **c'est un peu g.!** that's a bit much!; **g. mot** swearword (**e**) *Mus* **grosse caisse** bass drum
2 *adv (beaucoup) (gagner, rapporter, risquer)* a lot; **je donnerais g. pour savoir qui a fait ça** I'd give a lot to know who did that
3 *nm,f* **fat man**, *f* **fat woman**
4 *nm* (**a**) *(partie la plus importante)* bulk; **le g. de** the majority of; **le plus g. est fait** the bulk of the work has been done (**b**) *Com* wholesale (trade); **faire du g.** to sell wholesale; **de g.** *(commerce, boucher)* wholesale (**c**) **en g.** *(en grosses lettres)* in big *or* large letters; *Com* wholesale; *(approximativement)* roughly; **en g. et** en détail

groseille [grozɛj] *nf* **g. (rouge)** redcurrant; **g. à maquereau** gooseberry

groseillier [grozeje] *nm* redcurrant bush; **g. à maquereau** gooseberry bush

grosse [gros] *voir* **gros**

grossesse [grosɛs] *nf* pregnancy; **g. extra-utérine** ectopic pregnancy; **g. nerveuse** phantom pregnancy; **g. à risque** high-risk pregnancy

grosseur [grosœr] *nf* (**a**) *(taille, volume)* size (**b**) *Méd* lump

grossier, -ère [grosje, -ɛr] *adj* (**a**) *(impoli) (personne)* rude (**envers** to); *(langage, plaisanterie)* crude; **un g. personnage** an uncouth individual (**b**) *(peu raffiné) (nourriture, tissu)* coarse, rough; *(dessin)* crude, rough; *(goûts, traits du visage)* coarse; *(ruse)* crude (**c**) *(important) (erreur)* gross

grossièrement [grosjɛrmɑ̃] *adv* (**a**) *(de façon impolie)* rudely (**b**) *(sans raffinement)* crudely (**c**) *(approximativement)* roughly

grossièreté [grosjɛrte] *nf* (**a**) *(incorrection)* coarseness (**b**) *(parole grossière)* rude word (**c**) *(caractère rudimentaire) (d'un dessin) crudeness; (d'un tissu, des goûts)* coarseness

grossir [grosir] **1** *vi (personne, animal)* to put on weight, to get fatter; *(mer)* to get rough; *(rivière)* to swell; **g. de cinq kilos** *(personne)* to put on five kilos
2 *vt (sujet: loupe, microscope)* to magnify; *Fig (exagérer)* to exaggerate; **g. qn** *(sujet: vêtement)* to make sb look fat; **g. les rangs de qch** to swell the ranks of sth

grossissant, -e [grosisɑ̃, -ɑ̃t] *adj* **miroir g.** distorting mirror

grossissement [grosismɑ̃] *nm* (**a**) *(augmentation de taille)* increase in size (**b**) *(pouvoir grossissant)* magnification

grossiste [grosist] *nmf* wholesaler

grosso modo [grosomɔdo] *adv* roughly; **g. c'est une comédie** broadly speaking it's a comedy

grotesque [grɔtɛsk] *adj* ludicrous, ridiculous

grotte [grɔt] *nf* cave; **g. artificielle** grotto

grouillant, -e [grujɑ̃, -ɑ̃t] *adj* swarming (**de** with)

grouiller [gruje] **1** *vi (se presser)* to swarm around; **g. de** to swarm with
2 se grouiller *vpr Fam* to get a move on

groupe [grup] *nm* (**a**) *(de gens, de choses)* group; *(de musiciens)* group, band; **en g.** in a group; **se mettre par groupes de trois** to get into *or* form groups of three; *Pol* **le G. des 7** the Group of Seven; **g. d'âge** age group; *Ordinat* **g. de discussion** discussion group; *Scol* **g. de niveau** stream; *Pol* **g. de pression** pressure group (**b**) *(industriel, de presse)* group; *(hospitalier, scolaire)* complex (**c**) *Gram* **g. verbal/nominal** verbal/nominal group (**d**) *Mil* **g. de combat** unit (**e**) *Méd* **g. sanguin** blood group (**f**) *Él* **g. électrogène** generator

groupement [grupmɑ̃] *nm (association)* group; **g. d'achat** purchasing co-operative; **g. de consommateurs** consumer group

grouper [grupe] **1** *vt* to group (together); *(moyens, ressources)* to pool
2 se grouper *vpr (dans une association)* to form a group; *(dans un lieu)* to gather; **rester groupés** to keep together

groupie [grupi] *nf Fam* groupie

groupuscule [grupyskyl] *nm* small group

gruau [gryo] *nm* **g. (d'avoine)** groats; **(farine de) g.** (fine) wheat flour

grue [gry] *nf* (**a**) *(oiseau)* crane; **faire le pied de g.** to hang about (**b**) *(machine)* crane; *TV & Cin* cherry picker (**c**) *très Fam Vieilli (prostituée)* tart

gruger [45] [gryʒe] *vt (rouler)* to swindle

grumeau, -x [grymo] *nm (dans une sauce, une pâte)* lump

grumeleux, -euse [grymlø, -øz] *adj (sauce, pâte)* lumpy

gruyère [gryjɛr] *nm* Gruyère (cheese)

Guadeloupe [gwadlup] *nf* la **G.** Guadeloupe

guadeloupéen, -enne [gwadlupeɛ̃, -ɛn] **1** *adj* of Guadeloupe **2** *nm,f* **G.** person from Guadeloupe

Guatemala [gwatemala] *nm* le **G.** Guatemala

guatémaltèque [gwatemaltɛk] **1** *adj* Guatemalan **2** *nmf* **G.** Guatemalan

gué [ge] *nm* ford; **passer une rivière à g.** to ford a river

guéguerre [gegɛr] *nf Fam* squabble

guenilles [gənij] *nfpl* (old) rags; **en g.** in rags

guenon [gənɔ̃] *nf* female monkey

guépard [gepar] *nm* cheetah

guêpe [gɛp] *nf* wasp; *Fam* **pas folle, la g.!** she's nobody's fool!

guêpier [gepje] *nm* wasps' nest; *Fig (situation)* sticky situation

guêpière [gepjɛr] *nf* basque

guère [gɛr] *adv* **ne ... g.** *(pas beaucoup)* not much; *(pas longtemps)* hardly, scarcely; **il n'a g. d'argent/d'amis** he hasn't got much money/many friends; **il n'y a g. qu'elle qui soit au courant** she's about the only one who knows what's going on; **il ne mange g. que des pâtes** he eats hardly anything but pasta; **il n'y a g. plus de six ans** just over six years ago; **et celui-là, comment le trouvez-vous? – g. mieux!** and what do you think of that one? – not much better!

guéri, -e [geri] *adj aussi Fig* cured (**de** of)

guéridon [geridɔ̃] *nm* pedestal table

guérilla [gerija] *nf* guerrilla warfare

guérillero [gerijero] *nm* guerrilla

guérir [gerir] **1** *vt (personne, maladie)* to cure; *Fig* **g. qn de qch** *(timidité, habitude)* to cure sb of sth **2** *vi (personne)* to get better, to recover; *(blessure)* to heal **3** **se guérir** *vpr (soi-même)* to cure oneself; *Fig* **se g. de qch** *(timidité, habitude)* to cure oneself of sth

guérison [gerizɔ̃] *nf (rétablissement)* recovery

guérissable [gerisabl] *adj* curable

guérisseur, -euse [gerisœr, -øz] **1** *nm,f* healer **2** *nm (d'une tribu)* medicine man

guérite [gerit] *nf Mil* sentry box

guerre [gɛr] *nf* (**a**) *(conflit)* war; *(technique)* warfare; **en temps de g.** in wartime; **être en g. (contre)** to be at war (with); **faire la g.** *(soldat)* to fight; **la drôle de g.** the phoney war; **la Grande G.** the Great War; **la Première/la Seconde G. mondiale** the First/Second World War, World War One/ Two; **la g. de 14** the 1914–**18 War**; **la g. de 70** the Franco-Prussian War; **la g. d'Algérie** the Algerian War of Independence; **la g. de Cent Ans** the Hundred Years' War; **g. civile** civil war; **la g. de Corée** the Korean War; **g. éclair** blitzkrieg; **la g. d'Espagne** the Spanish Civil War; **la g. froide** the cold war; **la g. du Golfe** the Gulf War; **la g. d'Indochine** the first Indo-Chinese War *(1946–1954)*; **g. sainte** holy war; **la g. de Sécession** the American Civil War; **la g. du Viêt Nam** the Vietnam War (**b**) *(locutions)* **elle fait la g. à son fils pour qu'il ne fume pas** she's fighting a running battle with her son about smoking; **faire la g. à qch** to wage war on sth; **partir en g. contre qch** to declare war on sth; **il est en g. ouverte contre sa hiérarchie** there's open war between him and his superiors; **à la g. comme à la g.** we'll/you'll/*etc* have to do the best we/you/*etc* can; **c'est de bonne g.** that's fair enough; **de g. lasse** for the sake of peace and quiet

guerrier, -ère [gɛrje, -ɛr] **1** *adj* warlike; *(chant)* war **2** *nm,f* warrior

guerroyer [32] [gɛrwaje] *vi Litt* to wage war (**contre** on)

guet [gɛ] *nm* **poste de g.** lookout post; **faire le g.** to be on the lookout

guet-apens (*pl* **guets-apens**) [gɛtapɑ̃] *nm (piège)* ambush; *Fig* trap; **tomber dans un g.** to be ambushed; *Fig* to fall into a trap

guêtre [gɛtr] *nf* gaiter

guetter [gete] *vt (occasion)* to watch out for; *(proie)* to lie in wait for; **le surmenage/la dépression le guette** overwork/depression will get him in the end

gueulante [gœlɑ̃t] *nf très Fam* **pousser une g.** to kick up a stink

gueulard, -e [gœlar, -ard] *très Fam* **1** *adj (personne)* loudmouthed; *(bébé)* screaming; *(couleur)* garish **2** *nm,f (personne)* loudmouth; *(bébé)* screaming kid

gueule [gœl] *nf* (**a**) *(d'un animal)* mouth; *Fig* **se jeter dans la g. du loup** to put one's head in the lion's mouth (**b**) *très Fam (bouche)* mouth; **ça emporte** *ou* **arrache la g.** it takes the roof of your mouth off; **une grande g.** *(personne)* a loudmouth; **(ferme) ta g.!** shut your mouth *or* face!, shut it!; **avoir la g. de bois** to have a hangover (**c**) *très Fam (visage)* mug, face; **avoir une sale g.** *(mine patibulaire)* to look shady; *(mauvaise mine)* to look rotten; **faire la g.** to sulk; **faire la g. à qn** to be in a huff with sb; **faire une g. d'enterrement** to look really pissed off; **se foutre de** *ou* **se payer la g. de qn** to take the piss out of sb; **(s')en prendre plein la g.** to get a right mouthful (of abuse) (**d**) *Fam (allure)* **avoir une drôle de g.** to look odd; **ce tableau a de la g.** that's some picture

gueuler [gœle] *très Fam* **1** *vi* to yell, to bawl; *(radio, télévision)* to blare; *(protester)* to kick up a fuss; **si je suis en retard, ça va g. à la maison** if I'm late, I'll get an earbashing when I get home **2** *vt* to bawl out, to yell out

gueuleton [gœltɔ̃] *nm Fam* blowout; **faire un g.** to have a blowout

gueux, gueuse [gø, gøz] *nm,f Vieilli (mendiant)* beggar

gueuze, gueuse [gøz] *nf* = type of strong double-fermented Belgian beer

gugusse [gygys] *nm Fam* clown; **faire le g.** to act the fool

gui [gi] *nm* mistletoe

guibol(l)e [gibɔl] *nf Fam (jambe)* pin, leg

guichet [giʃɛ] *nm* (**a**) *(de gare, de poste, de banque)* window; *(de théâtre)* box office; **on joue à guichets fermés** the performance is sold out; **g. automatique** *(de banque)* cash dispenser (**b**) *(de porte de prison)* hatch; *(de confessionnal)* grille (**c**) *(au cricket)* wicket

guichetier, -ère [giʃtje, -ɛr] *nm,f (de gare)* ticket clerk; *(de poste, de banque)* counter clerk

guide [gid] *nm* (**a**) *(personne)* guide; **g. de haute montagne** mountain guide; **g.-interprète** bilingual tour guide (**b**) *(manuel)* guide (book); **g. de conversation** phrasebook; **g. gastronomique** restaurant guide; **g. touristique** tourist guide **2** *nf (scout) Br* (Girl) Guide, *Am* Girl Scout

guider [gide] *vt* to guide; **se laisser g. par son intuition** to be guided by one's intuition

guidon [gidɔ̃] *nm* handlebars

guigne[1] [giɲ] *nf (cerise)* sweet cherry; *Fam* **se soucier de qn/qch comme d'une g.** not to give a fig about sb/sth

guigne[2] *nf Fam (malchance)* bad luck; **avoir la g.** to be out of luck

guigner [giɲe] *vt Fam (avoir des vues sur)* to have one's eye on

guignol [giɲɔl] *nm* **(a)** *(personnage)* ≃ Punch **(b)** *Péj (personne)* clown, joker; **faire le g.** to clown around **(c)** *(spectacle)* ≃ Punch and Judy show

Guillaume [gijom] *npr* **G. le Conquérant** William the Conqueror

guillemets [gijmɛ] *nmpl* inverted commas, quotation marks; **entre g.** in inverted commas, in quotation marks

guilleret, -ette [gijrɛ, -ɛt] *adj* jaunty, lively

guillotine [gijɔtin] *nf* guillotine

guillotiner [gijɔtine] *vt* to guillotine

guimauve [gimov] *nf (confiserie)* marshmallow; *Fig & Péj* **c'est de la g.** it's pure schmaltz

guimbarde [gɛbard] *nf* **(a)** *Fam (vieille voiture)* jalopy **(b)** *(instrument de musique)* Jew's harp

guindé, -e [gɛ̃de] *adj (personne, air)* stiff, *(atmosphère)* strained; *(style)* stilted; *(réception)* posh

Guinée [gine] *nf* **la G.** Guinea; **la G. équatoriale** Equatorial Guinea

Guinée-Bissau [ginebiso] *nf* **la G.** Guinea Bissau

guinéen, -enne [gineɛ̃, -ɛn] **1** *adj* Guinean **2** *nmf* **G.** Guinean

guingois [gɛgwa] **de guingois** *adv* askew, lopsided

guinguette [gɛgɛt] *nf* riverside café

guirlande [girlɑ̃d] *nf (de fleurs)* garland; **g. lumineuse** string of lights; **g. de Noël** piece of tinsel; **g. de papier** paper chain

guise [giz] *nf* **faire qch à sa g.** to do sth as one likes; **n'en faire qu'à sa g.** to do just as one likes; **en g. de** by way of

guitare [gitar] *nf* guitar; **g. basse** bass guitar; **g. électrique** electric guitar; **g. sèche** acoustic guitar

guitariste [gitarist] *nmf* guitarist

gus [gys] *nm Fam* guy

gustatif, -ive [gystatif, -iv] *adj* **papilles gustatives** taste buds

guttural, -e, -aux, -ales [gytyral, -o] *adj* guttural

Guyana [gɥijana] *nm* **le G.** Guyana

guyanais, -e [gɥijanɛ, -ɛz] **1** *adj* Guianese **2** *nmf* **G.** Guianese

Guyane [gɥijan] *nf* **la G.** Guiana; **la G. française** French Guiana

gym [ʒim] *nf Fam* gym

gymkhana [ʒimkana] *nm* rally

gymnase [ʒimnaz] *nm* gymnasium

gymnaste [ʒimnast] *nmf* gymnast

gymnastique [ʒimnastik] *nf* gymnastics; *Fig* **il faut faire toute une g. pour sortir de cette auto** you have to be a contortionist to get out of this car; **g. respiratoire** breathing exercises; **g. rythmique** eurhythmics *(singulier)*

gynécologie [ʒinekɔlɔʒi] *nf* gynaecology

gynécologique [ʒinekɔlɔʒik] *adj* gynaecological

gynécologue [ʒinekɔlɔg] *nmf* gynaecologist

gypse [ʒips] *nm* gypsum

gyrophare [ʒirofar] *nm* flashing light

H, h [aʃ] *nm inv* H, h; **h.** **aspiré** aspirate h; **h muet** mute h
***ha** [ɑ] *exclam* ah!; **ha, ha!** *(rire)* ha-ha!
habile [abil] *adj* (**a**) *(personne)* skilful; *(manœuvre, film, roman)* clever; **être h.** de ses mains to be good with one's hands; **être h.** en affaires to be a good businessman/ businesswoman (**b**) *Jur* **h. à faire qch** able to do sth
habilement [abilmɑ̃] *adv* skilfully
habileté [abilte] *nf* skill
habiliter [abilite] *vt Jur* **h. qn à faire qch** to enable sb to do sth
habillage [abijaʒ] *nm* (**a**) *(d'une personne)* dressing (**b**) **h. intérieur** *(d'une voiture)* trim (**c**) *TV & Rad* station identification
habillé, -e [abije] *adj* (**a**) *(vêtu)* dressed; **h. en femme/ cow-boy** dressed (up) as a woman/cowboy; **s'endormir tout h.** to go to sleep with one's clothes on (**b**) *(élégant) (personne, tenue)* smart; **soirée habillée** formal occasion
habillement [abijmɑ̃] *nm* (**a**) *(vêtements)* clothes (**b**) *(industrie)* clothing industry
habiller [abije] **1** *vt* (**a**) *(vêtir)* to dress; **h. qn en soldat/ cow-boy** to dress sb up as a soldier/cowboy (**b**) *(fournir en vêtements)* to clothe (**c**) *(garnir)* to cover (**d**) *(aller à)* **un rien t'habille** you look good in anything
2 s'habiller *vpr* (**a**) *(se vêtir)* to get dressed, to dress; **elle s'habille n'importe comment** she wears any old thing; **comment vous habillez-vous pour la soirée?** what are you wearing to the party?; **s'h. en femme/cow-boy** to dress up as a woman/cowboy (**b**) *(se fournir)* **elle s'habille chez un jeune couturier** she buys her clothes from a young designer (**c**) *(élégamment)* to dress up
habilleur, -euse [abijœr, -øz] *nm,f* dresser
habit [abi] *nm* (**a**) *(vêtement)* habits clothes; **habits du dimanche** Sunday best (**b**) *(tenue)* **h. (de soirée)** evening dress, tails; **l'h. vert** = the green coat worn by a member of the "Académie française" (**c**) *(religieux)* habit; *Prov* **l'h. ne fait pas le moine** appearances can be deceptive
habitable [abitabl] *adj* (in)habitable
habitacle [abitakl] *nm* *(d'un avion)* cockpit; *(d'une voiture)* passenger compartment
habitant, -e [abitɑ̃, -ɑ̃t] **1** *nm,f* (**a**) *(d'une ville)* inhabitant, resident; *(d'une maison)* occupant; **loger chez l'h.** *(en voyage)* to stay with local people (**b**) *Can (fermier)* small-scale farmer
2 *adj Can Péj* **il est un peu h.** he's a bit of a hick
habitat [abita] *nm* *(d'un animal, d'une plante)* habitat; *(de personnes) (mode de peuplement)* settlement; *(conditions de logement)* housing conditions

habitation [abitasjɔ̃] *nf* (**a**) *(fait de résider)* living; **locaux à usage d'h.** premises for residential use (**b**) *(lieu)* dwelling; **h. à loyer modéré** *Br* ≃ council flat/house, *Am* ≃ public housing unit
habiter [abite] **1** *vt (maison, lieu)* to live in; *Fig (âme, personne)* to possess; **la région n'est pas habitée** the area is uninhabited
2 *vi* to live (**à/en** in)
habitude [abityd] *nf* (**a**) *(comportement répété)* habit; **avoir l'h. ou avoir pour h. de faire qch** to be in the habit of doing sth; **ça ne la gênera pas, elle a l'h.** that won't bother her, she's used to it; **avoir l'h. de qch** to be used to sth; **prendre l'h. de faire qch** to get into the habit of doing sth; **faire qch par h.** to do sth out of habit; **ce n'est pas dans mes habitudes** I don't make a habit of it; **d'h.** usually; **meilleur/plus tôt que d'h.** better/earlier than usual; **comme d'h.** as usual (**b**) **habitudes** *(coutumes)* customs
habitué, -e [abitɥe] *nm,f* *(d'une maison)* regular visitor; *(d'un restaurant, d'un magasin)* regular (customer)
habituel, -elle [abitɥel] *adj* usual, customary
habituellement [abitɥelmɑ̃] *adv* usually
habituer [abitɥe] **1** *vt* **h. qn à qch/à faire qch** to get sb used to sth/to doing sth; **être habitué à qn/à qch/à faire qch** to be used or accustomed to sb/to sth/to doing sth
2 s'habituer *vpr* **s'h. à qn/à qch/à faire qch** to get used or accustomed to sb/to sth/to doing sth
***hâbleur, -euse** [ablœr, -øz] *adj* boastful
***hache** [aʃ] *nf* axe; *Fig* **enterrer la h. de guerre** to bury the hatchet
***haché, -e** [aʃe] **1** *adj* (**a**) *(viande) Br* minced, *Am* ground; *(légumes, herbes)* chopped (**b**) *(style, phrases)* jerky
2 *nm Br* mince, *Am* ground meat
***hacher** [aʃe] *vt* to chop (up); *(viande) (dans un hachoir) Br* to mince, *Am* to grind; **h. menu qch** to chop sth (up) finely; *Fig* **h. qn menu (comme chair à pâté)** to make mincemeat of sb; *Fig* **se faire h.** *(se faire battre)* to be massacred
***hachette** [aʃɛt] *nf* hatchet
***hachis** [aʃi] *nm* **h. d'herbes** chopped herbs; **h. Parmentier** ≃ cottage pie; **h. de viande** *Br* mince, *Am* ground meat
***hachisch** [aʃiʃ] *nm* hashish
***hachoir** [aʃwar] *nm* (**a**) *(couteau)* chopper (**b**) *(machine) Br* mincer, *Am* grinder
***hachurer** [aʃyre] *vt* to hatch
***hachures** [aʃyr] *nfpl* hatching
***hagard, -e** [agar, -ard] *adj* *(visage)* haggard; *(expression, regard, yeux)* wild

The symbol * indicates that the initial **h** is aspirate and that hence there is no liaison, eg **les haricots** [leariko] and not [lezariko], or contraction in spelling, eg **la haine** and not **l'haine**.

*haie [ɛ] *nf* (a) *(clôture)* hedge; **h.** vive quickset hedge (**b**) *(en athlétisme)* hurdle; *(en équitation)* fence; **400 mètres haies** 400 metre hurdles (**c**) *(d'arbres, de pieux, de curieux)* line, row; **h. d'honneur** guard of honour

*haillons [ɑjɔ̃] *nmpl (vêtements)* rags; **en h.** in rags (and tatters)

*haine [ɛn] *nf* hate, hatred; **sa h. de/pour** his hatred of/for; *très Fam* **avoir la h.** *(être révolté)* to be full of rage; *(être furieux)* to be bloody furious

*haineux, -euse [ɛnø, -øz] *adj* full of hatred

*haïr [41] [air] **1** *vt* to hate **2 se haïr** *vpr (soi-même)* to hate oneself; *(l'un l'autre)* to hate each other

*hais *voir* haïr

*haïssable [aisabl] *adj* hateful

*hait *voir* haïr

Haïti [aiti] *n* Haiti

haïtien, -enne [aisjɛ̃, -ɛn] **1** *adj* Haitian **2** *nmf* H. Haitian

*halage [alaʒ] *nm* towing

*hâle [ɑl] *nm* (sun)tan

*hâlé, -e [ɑle] *adj* (sun)tanned

haleine [alɛn] *nf* breath; **avoir mauvaise h.** to have bad breath; **courir à perdre h.** to run until one is out of breath; **reprendre h.** to get one's breath (back); **tenir qn en h.** to keep sb in suspense; **hors d'h.** out of breath, breathless; **travail de longue h.** long job

*haler [ale] *vt* to tow

*haletant, -e [alɑtɑ̃, -ɑ̃t] *adj (coureur, malade, voix)* panting, gasping; *Fig (suspense)* unbearable; **respiration haletante** panting, gasping

*halètement [alɛtmɑ̃] *nm (d'un coureur, d'un malade)* panting, gasping

*haleter [ɔlte] *vi (coureur, malade)* to pant, to gasp

*hall [ol] *nm (d'une maison)* entrance hall; *(d'un hôtel)* foyer, lobby; *(d'un aéroport)* lounge; **h. d'accueil** reception hall; **h. d'entrée** entrance hall; **h. de gare** station concourse; *Péj* **littérature/roman de h. de gare** trashy literature/novel

*halle [al] *nf* (covered) market; **h. au poisson** fish market

*hallebarde [albard] *nf* halberd; *Fam* **il pleut** *ou* **tombe des hallebardes** it's raining cats and dogs

hallucinant, -e [alysinɑ̃, -ɑ̃t] *adj (extraordinaire)* striking; *(incroyable)* incredible

hallucination [alysinasjɔ̃] *nf* hallucination; **avoir des hallucinations** *(malade, ivrogne)* to have hallucinations; *Fig (se tromper)* to see things

halluciner [alysine] *vi (avoir des hallucinations)* to hallucinate; *Fam Fig* **j'hallucine!** I don't believe it!

hallucinogène [alysinɔʒɛn] **1** *adj* hallucinogenic **2** *nm* hallucinogen

*halo [alo] *nm aussi Fig* halo

halogène [alɔʒɛn] *nm Chim* halogen; **(lampe à) h.** halogen lamp

*halte [alt] *nf* (**a**) *(arrêt)* stop; **faire h.** to stop; **h.(-là)!** stop!; *Fig* **h.-là, je ne suis pas d'accord!** hold on, I don't agree!; **h. à l'armement!** stop the arms build-up! (**b**) *(lieu)* stopping place

*halte-garderie (*pl* **haltes-garderies**) [altəgardəri] *nf* crèche

haltère [altɛr] *nm* dumbbell

haltérophile [alterɔfil] *nmf* weightlifter

haltérophilie [alterɔfili] *nf* weightlifting

*hamac [amak] *nm* hammock

*Hambourg [ɑ̃bur] *n* Hamburg

*hamburger [ɑ̃burgœr] *nm* burger

*hameau, -x [amo] *nm* hamlet

hameçon [amsɔ̃] *nm* (fish-)hook; *Fig* **mordre à l'h.** to swallow the bait

*hammam [amam] *nm* Turkish baths

*hampe [ɑ̃p] *nf (d'un drapeau)* pole

*hamster [amster] *nm* hamster

*hanche [ɑ̃ʃ] *nf* hip

*hand [ɑ̃d] *nm Fam* handball

*handball [ɑ̃dbal] *nm* handball

*handballeur, -euse [ɑ̃dbalœr, -øz] *nmf* handball player

*handicap [ɑ̃dikap] *nm (physique, mental)* disability; *Fig* handicap; *Fig* **partir avec un h.** to start at a disadvantage

*handicapé, -e [ɑ̃dikape] **1** *adj* disabled **2** *nmf* disabled person; **les handicapés** the disabled; **h. mental** mentally handicapped person; **h. moteur** person with motor impairment

*handicaper [ɑ̃dikape] *vt (physiquement, mentalement)* to disable; *Fig* to handicap

*hangar [ɑ̃gar] *nm* shed; *(pour les trains, les bus)* depot; *(pour les avions)* hangar; **h. à bateaux** boathouse

*hanneton [antɔ̃] *nm* cockchafer; *Fam* **pas piqué des hannetons** *(difficile)* tough; *(bon, beau)* incredible

Hanoi [anɔj] *n* Hanoi

*Hanovre [anɔvr] *n* Hanover

*hanté, -e [ɑ̃te] *adj* haunted

*hanter [ɑ̃te] *vt (sujet: fantôme, pensée)* to haunt; *Fig (bars, musées)* to hang round

*hantise [ɑ̃tiz] *nf* obsession; **avoir la h. de qch** to really dread sth

*happer [ape] *vt (dans sa gueule, son bec)* to snap up; *(sujet: véhicule)* to hit

*hara-kiri [arakiri] *nm* hara-kiri; **(se) faire h.** to commit hara-kiri

*harangue [arɑ̃g] *nf* harangue

*haranguer [arɑ̃ge] *vt* to harangue

*haras [ara] *nm* stud farm

*harassant, -e [arasɑ̃, ɑ̃t] *adj* exhausting

*harassé, -e [arase] *adj* exhausted

*harasser [arase] *vt* to exhaust

*harcèlement [arsɛlmɑ̃] *nm* harassment; **h. sexuel** sexual harassment

*harceler [39/42] [arsɔle] *vt (importuner)* to harass; *(insister auprès de)* to pester; **h. qn de questions** to pester sb with questions; **être harcelé de remords/regrets** to be plagued by remorse/regrets

*harde [ard] *nf (de cerfs)* herd

*hardes [ard] *nfpl (haillons)* rags

*hardi, -e [ardi] *adj (audacieux, original)* bold; *(osé)* brazen

*hardiesse [ardjɛs] *nf (audace, originalité)* boldness; *(caractère osé)* brazenness

*hardiment [ardimɑ̃] *adv (avec audace)* boldly

*hard-rock [ardrɔk] *nm* hard rock

*harem [arɛm] *nm* harem

*hareng [arɑ̃] *nm* herring; **h. saur** smoked herring

*harfang [arfɑ̃] *nm Can* snowy owl

The symbol ***** indicates that the initial **h** is aspirate and that hence there is no liaison, eg **les haricots** [leariko] and not [lezariko], or contraction in spelling, eg **la haine** and not **l'haine**.

*hargne [arɲ] *nf* bad temper; **avec h.** bad-temperedly

*hargneux, -euse [arɲø, -øz] *adj (personne)* bad-tempered; **d'un ton h.** bad-temperedly

*haricot [ariko] *nm* **(a)** *(légume)* bean; **haricots en grains** dried beans; *Fam* **c'est la fin des haricots** we've/they've/ *etc* had it now; *Fam* **courir sur le h. à qn** *Br* to get up sb's nose, *Am* to tee sb off; **h. beurre** butter bean; **h. blanc** haricot bean; **h. rouge** *or* kidney bean; **h. vert** green bean **(b)** *Culin* **h. de mouton** mutton stew

*harissa [arisa] *nf Culin* harissa *(hot pepper purée)*

*harki [arki] *nm* harki *(Algerian soldier who fought on the French side during the Franco-Algerian War)*

harmonica [armɔnika] *nm* harmonica, mouth organ

harmonie [armɔni] *nf* **(a)** *(accord)* & *Mus* harmony; **être en h. avec qch** to be in harmony with sth; **vivre en h.** to live in harmony **(b)** *(fanfare)* brass band

harmonieux, -euse [armɔnjø, -øz] *adj* harmonious

harmonique [armɔnik] *adj Mus* harmonic

harmonisation [armɔnizasjɔ̃] *nf* harmonization

harmoniser [armɔnize] **1** *vt* to harmonize **(avec)** **2 s'harmoniser** *vpr* to go well together

harmonium [armɔnjɔm] *nm* harmonium

*harnachement [arnaʃmɑ̃] *nm* **(a)** *(action)* harnessing **(b)** *(harnais)* harness; *Fig (vêtements)* get-up

*harnacher [arnaʃe] *vt (cheval)* to harness; *Fig* **il fallait voir comment elle était harnachée** you should have seen the ridiculous outfit she was wearing

*harnais [arnɛ] *nm* **(a)** *(de cheval)* harness **(b)** **h. de sécurité** *(d'alpiniste, d'élagueur)* safety harness

*haro [aro] *nm* **crier h. sur** to rail against; **crier h. sur le baudet** to scream for blood

*harpe [arp] *nf* harp

*harpie [arpi] *nf aussi Fig* harpy

*harpiste [arpist] *nmf* harpist

*harpon [arpɔ̃] *nm* harpoon; **pêche au h.** harpoon fishing

*harponner [arpɔne] *vt* **(a)** *(poisson)* to harpoon **(b)** *Fam (sujet: police)* to nab; *(sujet: importun)* to corner

*hasard [azar] *nm* **(a)** *(sort)* chance, luck; **coup de h.** stroke of luck; **par un heureux h.** by a happy coincidence; **ne rien laisser au h.** to leave nothing to chance; **le h. fait bien les choses!** what a stroke of luck!; **au h.** *(choisir, répondre)* at random; *(marcher)* aimlessly; **au h. de ses voyages/lectures** in the course of her travels/reading; **à tout h.** *(par précaution)* just in case; *(pour voir)* on the off chance; **par h.** by accident, by chance; **si par h. vous le voyez** if you (should) happen to see him; **comme par h.** as if by chance **(b)** **hasards** *(dangers)* hazards

*hasarder [azarde] **1** *vt (opinion, remarque)* to venture **2 se hasarder** *vpr (dans l'obscurité, dans la jungle)* to venture; **se h. à faire qch** to risk doing sth

*hasardeux, -euse [azardø, -øz] *adj* risky, hazardous

*hasch [aʃ] *nm Fam* hash, pot

*haschisch [aʃiʃ] *nm* hashish

*hâte [ɑt] *nf* haste; **avoir h. de faire qch** *(avoir envie)* to be eager to do sth; **à la h.** hastily; **en h.** in a hurry, hurriedly

*hâter [ɑte] **1** *vt (accélérer)* to hasten; *(avancer)* to bring forward **2 se hâter** *vpr* to hurry; **se h. de faire qch** to hurry to do sth

*hâtif, -ive [ɑtif, -iv] *adj (trop rapide)* hasty

*hâtivement [ɑtivmɑ̃] *adv* hastily

*hauban [obɑ̃] *nm* **(a)** *Naut* shroud **(b)** *(d'un pont)* stay

*hausse [os] *nf* rise, increase **(de** in); **être en h.** to be rising; **être à la h.** *(marché)* to be rising; **jouer à la h.** *(en Bourse)* to speculate on a rising market

*haussement [osmɑ̃] *nm* **h. d'épaules** shrug; **avec un h. de sourcils** with raised eyebrows

*hausser [ose] **1** *vt* to raise; **h. la voix/les sourcils** to raise one's voice/eyebrows; **h. les épaules** to shrug (one's shoulders) **2 se hausser** *vpr* to raise oneself (up); **se h. sur la pointe des pieds** to stand on tiptoe

*haussier [osje] *adj m voir* **marché**

*haut, -e [o, ot] **1** *adj* **(a)** *(dans l'espace, en quantité, en intensité)* high; **une femme de haute taille** a tall woman; **un mur h. de deux mètres** a two-metre high wall **(b)** *(dans une hiérarchie)* high; **la haute couture** high fashion; **les hauts salaires** the highly paid; **un athlète de h. niveau** a top-ranking athlete; **une montre de haute précision** a high-precision timepiece; **de hauts faits** daring deeds **(c)** *(note)* high **(d)** *(dans le temps)* early; **le h. Moyen Âge** the early Middle Ages **(e)** **h. en couleur** *(récit, personnage)* colourful **2** *adv* **(a)** *(dans l'espace)* high; **comme il est dit plus h.** as mentioned above; **h. les mains!** hands up! **gagner h. la main** to win hands down; **h. les cœurs!** cheer up! **(b)** *(dans une hiérarchie)* highly **(c)** *(dans la gamme)* high **(d)** *(fort)* **dire qch tout h.** to say sth out loud; **dire tout h. ce que tout le monde pense tout bas** to say what everyone is thinking (but is too afraid to say) **(e)** **en h.** at the top; *(à l'étage supérieur)* upstairs; **les gens d'en h.** the people above or upstairs; **en h. de** at the top of **3** *nm* **(a)** *(hauteur)* **le mur fait 3 mètres de h.** the wall is 3 metres high **(b)** *(partie supérieure)* top; **l'étagère du h.** the top shelf; **regarder qn de h. en bas** to look sb up and down; **connaître des hauts et des bas** to have one's ups and downs **(c)** *(corsage)* top **4** *nf Fam* **haute** upper crust

*hautain, -e [otɛ̃, -ɛn] *adj* haughty

*hautbois [obwa] *nm* oboe

*haut-commissariat *(pl* **hauts-commissariats)** [okɔmisarja] *nm* high commission

*haut-de-chausses *(pl* **hauts-de-chausses)** [odəʃos] *nm* breeches

*haut-de-forme *(pl* **hauts-de-forme)** [odəfɔrm] *nm* top hat

*haute-contre *(pl* **hautes-contre)** [otkɔ̃tr] *nm* counter tenor

*haute-fidélité [otfidelite] *nf* hi-fi; **chaîne h.** hi-fi (system)

*hautement [otmɑ̃] *adv (très)* highly

*hauteur [otœr] *nf* **(a)** *(dimension)* height **(b)** *(altitude)* altitude; **prendre de la h.** to climb, to gain height; **à la h. de qch** *(dans l'espace)* level with sth; **à la h. du Mans** near Le Mans; *Fig* **être** *ou* **se montrer à la h. de qch** to be equal to *or* up to sth; **être à la h.** to be up to it; **à h. des yeux** at eye level; **l'eau nous arrivait à h. des épaules** the water came up to our shoulders; **à h. de deux millions** to contribute two million **(c)** *(d'une note de musique)* pitch

*haut-fond *(pl* **hauts-fonds)** [ofɔ̃] *nm* shallow

*haut-fourneau *(pl* **hauts-fourneaux)** [ofurno] *nm* blast furnace

The symbol ***** indicates that the initial **h** is aspirate and that hence there is no liaison, eg **les haricots** [leariko] and not [lezariko], or contraction in spelling, eg **la haine** and not **l'haine**.

*haut-le-cœur [olǝkœr] nm inv avoir un h. to retch; cette vision me donna un h. the sight of it made me feel sick

*haut-parleur (pl haut-parleurs) [oparlœr] nm (loud)-speaker

*Havane [avan] **1** voir **La Havane** **2** nm **h.** Havana (cigar)

*hâve [ɑv] adj (visage) gaunt; (joues) sunken

*havre [ɑvr] nm Litt haven

Hawaii [awai] n Hawaii

hawaiien, -enne [awajẽ, -ɛn] **1** adj Hawaiian **2** nm,f **H.** Hawaiian

*Haye [ɛ] voir **La Haye**

*hayon [ajɔ̃] nm (d'une voiture) hatchback

HCR [aʃseɛr] nm (abrév **Haut-Commissariat des Nations unies pour les réfugiés**) UNHCR

*hé [e] exclam (pour interpeller) hey!

hebdo [ɛbdo] nm Fam weekly; **h. télé** TV magazine show

hebdomadaire [ɛbdɔmadɛr] adj & nm weekly

hébergement [ebɛrʒǝmɑ̃] nm (d'un ami) putting up; (d'un sans-abri, d'un réfugié) taking in; (d'un fugitif) harbouring

héberger [45] [ebɛrʒe] vt (ami) to put up; (sans-abri, réfugié) to take in; (fugitif) to harbour

hébété, -e [ebete] adj dazed

hébreu, -x [ebrø] **1** adj m Hebrew **2** nm (langue) Hebrew; Fam **c'est de l'h. pour moi** it's all Greek to me **3** nmpl **les Hébreux** the Hebrews

Hébrides [ebrid] nfpl **les H.** the Hebrides

HEC [aʃøøe] nf (abrév **Hautes études commerciales**) = prestigious business school in Paris

hécatombe [ekatɔ̃b] nf (tuerie) slaughter, massacre; Fig **ça a été une h. cette année à l'examen!** the exam results were disastrous this year!

hectare [ɛktar] nm hectare

hectogramme [ɛktɔgram] nm hectogram

hectolitre [ɛktɔlitr] nm hectolitre

hectomètre [ɛktɔmɛtr] nm hectometre

hédonisme [edɔnism] nm hedonism

hédoniste [edɔnist] **1** adj hedonistic **2** nmf hedonist

hégémonie [eʒemɔni] nf hegemony

*hein [ẽ] exclam Fam (a) (pour faire répéter) eh?, what? (b) (pour insister) **c'est drôle, h.?** it's funny, isn't it?; **ne refais jamais ça, h.!** don't ever do that again, OK?; **h. qu'il fait bien la cuisine!** he does cook well, doesn't he?

*hélas [elɑs] exclam unfortunately

*héler [34] [ele] vt to hail

hélice [elis] nf (a) (d'un hélicoptère, d'un bateau) propeller (b) Math & Biol helix

hélico [eliko] nm Fam chopper

hélicoïdal, -e, -aux, -ales [elikɔidal, -o] adj helical

hélicoptère [elikɔptɛr] nm helicopter

héliomarin, -e [eljɔmarẽ, -in] adj Méd **cure héliomarine** = course of treatment based on sun and sea air; **centre h.** = seaside convalescent home where heliotherapy is used

héliothérapie [eljɔterapi] nf Méd heliotherapy

héliport [elipɔr] nm heliport

héliporté, -e [elipɔrte] adj (matériel) transported by helicopter; (troupes) airborne

hélium [eljɔm] nm helium

*Helsinki [ɛlsinki] n Helsinki

helvétique [ɛlvetik] adj Swiss

hématie [emasi] nf Biol red blood corpuscle

hématologie [ematɔlɔʒi] nf Méd haematology

hématome [ematom] nm bruise, Spéc haematoma; **se faire un h.** to bruise oneself

hémicycle [emisikl] nm **l'h.** (de l'Assemblée nationale) the chamber

hémiplégie [emipleʒi] nf Méd hemiplegia

hémiplégique [emipleʒik] adj & nm f Méd hemiplegic

hémisphère [emisfɛr] nm hemisphere; **l'h. Nord/Sud** the Northern/Southern hemisphere

hémisphérique [emisferik] adj hemispheric(al)

hémistiche [emistiʃ] nm hemistich

hémoglobine [emɔglɔbin] nf haemoglobin; Fig (dans un film) blood and gore

hémophile [emɔfil] Méd **1** adj haemophilic **2** nm haemophiliac

hémophilie [emɔfili] nf Méd haemophilia

hémorragie [emɔraʒi] nf haemorrhage, bleeding; Fig (des capitaux) drain; **h. interne** internal bleeding

hémorroïdes [emɔrɔid] nfpl haemorrhoids, piles

*henné [ene] nm henna; **se faire un h.** to henna one's hair

*hennir [enir] vi to neigh, to whinny; Fig (personne) to bray

*hennissement [enismɑ̃] nm neigh, whinny; **hennissements** neighing, whinnying; Fig braying

hépatique [epatik] adj Méd hepatic

hépatite [epatit] nf hepatitis

héraldique [eraldik] **1** adj heraldic **2** nf heraldry

herbage [ɛrbaʒ] nm pasture

herbe [ɛrb] nf (a) (de gazon) grass; Fig **couper l'h. sous le pied à qn** to cut the ground from under sb's feet; **en h.** (céréale) green; Fig (débutant) budding (b) (plante) herb; **fines herbes** mixed herbs; **omelette/fromage aux fines herbes** omelette/cheese with herbs; **mauvaise h.** weed; **herbes folles** wild grass; Can **h. à la puce** poison ivy (c) Fam (drogue) grass

herbeux, -euse [ɛrbø, -øz] adj grassy

herbicide [ɛrbisid] adj & nm (produit) **h.** weedkiller

herbier [ɛrbje] nm (collection) herbarium

herbivore [ɛrbivɔr] Zool **1** adj herbivorous **2** nm herbivore

herboriser [ɛrbɔrize] vi to collect plants

herboriste [ɛrbɔrist] nmf herbalist

herboristerie [ɛrbɔristɔri] nf (boutique) herbalist's (shop); (commerce) herb trade

herbu, -e [ɛrby] adj grassy

herculéen, -enne [ɛrkyleẽ, -ɛn] adj Herculean

*hère [ɛr] nm **pauvre h.** poor creature

héréditaire [erediter] adj (maladie, titre) hereditary; **c'est h.!** it runs in the family!

hérédité [eredite] nf Biol heredity; **avoir une lourde h.** to come from a family with a history of mental/physical illness

hérésie [erezi] nf heresy; Fig **c'est une h.** ou **de l'h.!** that's sacrilege!

hérétique [eretik] **1** adj heretical
2 nmf heretic
*hérissé, -e [erise] adj **(a)** (cheveux) spiky; (moustache) bristly **(b)** (garni) **h.** de bristling with
*hérisser [erise] **1** vt **(a)** (ses plumes) to ruffle up; **h. ses poils** to bristle **(b)** Fig (mettre en colère) **h. qn** to get sb's back up
2 se hérisser vpr (animal) to bristle; (poils, cheveux) to stand on end; Fig (personne) to bristle
*hérisson [eris5] nm hedgehog
héritage [erita3] nm inheritance; Fig (spirituel, intellectuel) heritage; **faire un h.** to come into an inheritance
hériter [erite] **1** vt to inherit **(de** from)
2 hériter de vt ind (fortune, objet, qualité) to inherit; **h. de qn** to receive an inheritance from sb; Fig **h. de qn/qch** (se retrouver avec) to be landed with sb/sth
héritier, -ère [eritje, -εr] nm,f heir, f heiress **(de** to)
hermaphrodite [εrmafrɔdit] nm & adj hermaphrodite
hermétique [εrmetik] adj **(a)** (récipient) hermetically sealed; (joint) (à l'air) airtight; (à l'eau) watertight **(b)** Fig (abscons) abstruse; (visage) impenetrable; **être h. à qch** to be impervious to sth
hermétiquement [εrmetikmɑ̃] adv hermetically
hermine [εrmin] nf (animal) stoat; (fourrure) ermine
*hernie [εrni] nf hernia; **h. discale** slipped disc
héroïne¹ [erɔin] nf (personnage) heroine
héroïne² nf (drogue) heroin
héroïnomane [erɔinɔman] nmf heroin addict
héroïque [erɔik] adj heroic
héroïquement [erɔikmɑ̃] adv heroically
héroïsme [erɔism] nm heroism
*héron [erɔ̃] nm heron; **h. cendré** grey heron
*héros [ero] nm hero; **mourir en h.** to die a hero's death
herpès [εrpεs] nm Méd herpes; (buccal) cold sore
*herse [εrs] nf **(a)** (pour labourer) harrow **(b)** (de forteresse) portcullis
hertz [εrts] nm hertz
hésitant, -e [ezitɑ̃, -ɑ̃t] adj hesitant
hésitation [ezitasjɔ̃] nf hesitation; **avec h.** hesitatingly; **sans h.** without hesitation
hésiter [ezite] vi to hesitate **(sur/entre** over/between); **je ne sais pas, j'hésite** I don't know, I can't make up my mind; **h. à faire qch** to hesitate to do sth
hétéro [etero] adj & nmf Fam straight, hetero
hétéroclite [eterɔklit] adj motley
hétérogène [eterɔ3εn] adj mixed
hétérogénéité [eterɔ3eneite] nf heterogeneity
hétérosexualité [eterɔseksɥalite] nf heterosexuality
hétérosexuel, -elle [eterɔseksɥεl] adj & nm,f heterosexual
*hêtre [εtr] nm beech
*heu [ø] exclam er
heure [œr] nf **(a)** (soixante minutes) hour; **25 euros l'h. ou de l'h.** 25 euros an hour; Scol **h. de cours** period; **heures supplémentaires** overtime
(b) (de la journée) time; **à h. fixe** at regular intervals; **à toute h.** at any time; **h. du jour ou de la nuit** at any hour of the day or night; **quelle h. est-il?** what time is it?, what's the time?; **quelle h. avez-vous?** what time do you make it?; **il est deux heures** it's two o'clock; **quatre heures moins dix** ten to four; **trois heures vingt** twenty past three; **vingt heures quarante** eight forty pm; **à**

quelle h....? what time...?; **ils devraient être arrivés à l'h. qu'il est** they ought to have arrived by now; **être à l'h.** (personne) to be on time; (montre) to be right; **mettre sa montre à l'h.** to set one's watch; **à la bonne h.!** marvellous!; **de bonne h.** early; **heures d'affluence** peak hours; **heures de bureau** office hours; **h. d'été** Br summer time, Am daylight-saving time; **heures d'ouverture** opening hours; **heures de pointe** rush hour
(c) (moment précis) time; **l'h. du dîner/déjeuner** dinner/lunch time; **il est ou c'est l'h. (de faire qch)** it's time (to do sth); **son h. est venue** his time has come; **avoir son h. de gloire** to have one's moment of glory; **l'h. H** zero hour
(d) (moment présent) **l'h. est grave** these are difficult times; **à l'h. actuelle** currently; **pour l'h.** for the present, for the time being; Litt **sur l'h.** at once
heureusement [œrøzmɑ̃] adv **(a)** (par bonheur) fortunately, luckily; **h. que j'étais là** it's a good thing I was there **(b)** (avec succès) successfully
heureux, -euse [œrø, -øz] **1** adj **(a)** (satisfait) happy (de with); **être h. en ménage** to be happily married; **vivre h.** to live happily; **être h. de faire qch** to be happy to do sth; **h. anniversaire!** happy birthday! **(b)** (favorable) successful; (juste) (formule, style) apt; (choix) happy **(c)** (favorisé) lucky; **h. au jeu/en amour** lucky at cards/in love; **s'estimer h. (de faire qch)** to consider oneself lucky (to do sth) **(d)** (situation) **c'est h. que vous soyez libre** it's a good thing you're free; Fam **encore h. (qu'il ait gardé le ticket de caisse)!** it's just as well (he held on to the receipt)!
2 nm,f **si tu le lui donnes, tu vas faire un h.** if you give it to him, you'll make him a happy man; **faire des h.** to make some people happy
*heurt [œr] nm (choc) collision; Fig (conflit) clash; **sans heurts** smoothly, without a hitch
*heurter [œrte] **1** vt **(a)** (cogner) to hit; (entrer en collision avec) to collide with **(b)** (choquer) to offend
2 vi **h. contre qch** to hit sth
3 se heurter vpr **(a)** (se cogner) to collide (à ou contre with); Fig **se h. à qch** to meet with sth **(b)** (couleurs, intérêts, personnes) to clash
*heurtoir [œrtwar] nm (door) knocker
hévéa [evea] nm rubber tree
hexagonal, -e, -aux, -ales [εgzagɔnal, -o] adj hexagonal; Fig French
hexagone [εgzagɔn] nm hexagon; Fig **l'H.** France
hiatus [jatys] nm **(a)** Ling & Anat hiatus **(b)** (décalage) gap
hibernation [ibεrnasjɔ̃] nf hibernation
hiberner [ibεrne] vi to hibernate
*hibou, -x [ibu] nm owl
*hic [ik] nm inv Fam **voilà le h.!** that's the snag!; **le h., c'est que...** the snag is...
*hideusement [idøzmɑ̃] adv hideously
*hideux, -euse [idø, -øz] adj hideous
hier [jεr] adv yesterday; **h. matin/soir** yesterday morning/evening; **je m'en souviens comme si c'était h.** I remember it as if it were yesterday; **le journal d'h.** yesterday's paper; **cela ne date pas d'h.** that's nothing new; **je ne suis pas né d'h.** I wasn't born yesterday
*hiérarchie [jerarʃi] nf hierarchy
*hiérarchique [jerarʃik] adj hierarchical; **c'est mon supérieur h.** he's immediately above me in rank; **par la voie h.** through the official channels
*hiérarchisé, -e [jerarʃize] adj hierarchical
*hiéroglyphe [jerɔglif] nm hieroglyph
*hi-fi [ifi] adj inv & nf inv hi-fi

The symbol ***** indicates that the initial **h** is aspirate and that hence there is no liaison, eg **les haricots** [leariko] and not [lezariko], or contraction in spelling, eg **la haine** and not **l'haine**.

*hi-han [iɑ̃] *exclam* hee-haw!

hilarant, -e [ilarɑ̃, -ɑ̃t] *adj* hilarious

hilare [ilar] *adj* grinning

hilarité [ilarite] *nf* hilarity, mirth; **provoquer l'h.** générale to be the source of much hilarity

Himalaya [imalaja] *nm* **l'H.** the Himalayas

*hindi [indi] *nm* Hindi

hindou, -e [ɛ̃du] **1** *adj* Hindu **2** *nm,f* H. Hindu

hindouisme [ɛ̃duism] *nm* Hinduism

*hippie [ipi] *adj & nmf* hippy

hippique [ipik] *adj* **concours h.** horse show; **sport h.** equestrianism

hippisme [ipism] *nm* horse riding; *(courses)* horse racing

hippocampe [ipɔkɑ̃p] *nm* sea horse

hippodrome [ipɔdrom] *nm Br* racecourse, *Am* racetrack

hippopotame [ipɔpɔtam] *nm* hippopotamus

*hippy [ipi] = **hippie**

hirondelle [irɔdɛl] *nf* swallow; *Prov* **une h. ne fait pas le printemps** one swallow doesn't make a summer; **h. de mer** tern

hirsute [irsyt] *adj (personne)* hairy; *(barbe)* shaggy; *(cheveux)* unkempt

hispanique [ispanik] *adj* Hispanic

hispano-américain, -e *(mpl* hispano-américains, *fpl* hispano-américaines) [ispanɔamerikɛ̃, -ɛn] **1** *adj* Spanish-American **2** *nm,f* H. Spanish-American, Hispanic

hispanophone [ispanɔfɔn] **1** *adj* Spanish-speaking **2** *nmf* Spanish speaker

*hisser [ise] **1** *vt* to hoist (up); **ho! hisse!** heave ho! **2 se hisser** *vpr* to heave oneself up; **se h. sur la pointe des pieds** to stand on tiptoe; *Fig* **se h. jusqu'au pouvoir** to rise to power

histogramme [istɔgram] *nm* bar chart, histogram

histoire [istwar] *nf* **(a)** *(discipline)* history; **l'h. de France** French history; **h. de l'art** history of art; **sachez, pour la petite h., que...** let me tell you in passing that...; *Fig* **c'est de l'h. ancienne** that's all ancient history **(b)** *(récit)* story; *Fam (mensonge)* fib, story; **raconter des histoires** *(mentir)* to tell fibs; **c'est toujours la même h.** it's always the same old story; **c'est une autre h.** it's quite a different matter; **il m'est arrivé une drôle d'h.** a funny thing happened to me; **elle l'a dit, h. de dire quelque chose** she said it just for the sake of saying something; **c'est toute une h.** *(à raconter)* it's a long story; **c'est une h. de fous!** it's crazy! **(c)** *(problème)* fuss; **c'est toute une h. pour lui faire prendre son bain** it's quite a business getting her to have a bath; *Fam* **en voilà une h.!** what a fuss!, what a song and dance!; **faire des histoires** to make a fuss; **s'attirer des histoires** to get oneself into trouble; **faire des histoires à qn** to make trouble for sb; **au lit, et pas d'histoires!** off to bed now, and no fuss!

histologie [istɔlɔʒi] *nf* histology

historien, -enne [istɔrjɛ̃, -ɛn] *nm,f* historian

historique [istɔrik] **1** *adj (qui concerne l'histoire)* historical; *(important)* historic **2** *nm* historical account; *Ordinat (de document)* log; **faire l'h. des événements** to give a chronological account of events

historiquement [istɔrikmɑ̃] *adv* historically

*hit-parade *(pl* hit-parades) [itparad] *nm* charts

HIV [aʃive] *nm* HIV

hiver [ivɛr] *nm* winter; **en h.** in winter; **une soirée d'h.** a winter's night; **h. nucléaire** nuclear winter

hivernal, -e, -aux, -ales [ivɛrnal, -o] *adj* winter; *(temps)* wintry

hiverner [ivɛrne] *vi* to overwinter

*HLM [aʃɛlɛm] *nm ou nf (abrév* habitation à loyer modéré) *Br* ≃ block of council flats, *Am* ≃ low-rent apartment building

*hochement [ɔʃmɑ̃] *nm* **h. de tête** *(négatif)* shake of the head; *(affirmatif)* nod

*hocher [ɔʃe] *vt* **h. la tête** *(pour dire non)* to shake one's head; *(pour dire oui)* to nod

*hochet [ɔʃɛ] *nm* (child's) rattle

*hockey [ɔkɛ] *nm* **(a)** *(sport)* hockey; **h. sur gazon** *Br* hockey, *Am* field hockey; **h. sur glace** ice hockey, *Am* hockey **(b)** *Can (crosse)* ice hockey stick

*holà [ɔla] **1** *exclam (pour appeler)* stop!, hold on!; **h., on se calme, hein!** hey, cool it, OK? **2** *nm* **mettre le h. à qch** to put a stop to sth

*holding [ɔldiŋ] *nm* holding company

*hold-up [ɔldœp] *nm inv Fam* hold-up

*hollandais, -e [ɔlɑ̃dɛ, -ɛz] **1** *adj* Dutch **2** *nm,f* H. Dutchman, *f* Dutchwoman; **les H.** the Dutch **3** *nm (langue)* Dutch

*Hollande [ɔlɑ̃d] *nf* **la H.** Holland

holocauste [ɔlɔkost] *nm* holocaust

hologramme [ɔlɔgram] *nm* hologram

holographie [ɔlɔgrafi] *nf* holography

*homard [ɔmar] *nm* lobster

homélie [ɔmeli] *nf* homily

homéopathe [ɔmeɔpat] *nmf* homoeopath

homéopathie [ɔmeɔpati] *nf* homoeopathy

homéopathique [ɔmeɔpatik] *adj* homoeopathic

Homère [ɔmɛr] *npr* Homer

homicide [ɔmisid] **1** *adj* homicidal **2** *nm* homicide; **h. involontaire** *ou* **par imprudence** manslaughter *(through negligence)*

hommage [ɔmaʒ] *nm* homage; **rendre h. à qn** to pay homage to sb; **hommages** respects; **mes hommages!** how do you do!

hommasse [ɔmas] *adj Péj* mannish

homme [ɔm] *nm* **(a)** *(adulte)* man; **rayon hommes** men's department; **parler à qn d'h. à h.** to have a man-to-man talk with sb; **il n'est pas h. à laisser passer cela** he's not the sort of man to let something like that happen; **comme un seul h.** in unison; *Fam* **mon h.** my man; **jeune h.** young man; **h. d'affaires** businessman; **h. de barre** helmsman; **h. de confiance** right-hand man; **h. d'église** man of the church; **h. d'équipage** crewman; **h. d'État** statesman; **h. à femmes** ladies' man; **h. de loi** lawyer; **h. de main** henchman; **h. du monde** gentleman; **h. de paille** figurehead; **h. de peine** labourer; **h. politique** politician; **h. à tout faire** handyman; **h. de troupe** private **(b)** *(genre humain)* man, mankind; **de mémoire d'h.** within living memory

homme-grenouille *(pl* hommes-grenouilles) [ɔmgrɔnuj] *nm* frogman

homme-orchestre *(pl* hommes-orchestres) [ɔmɔrkɛstr] *nm* one-man band

homme-sandwich *(pl* hommes-sandwichs) [ɔmsɑ̃dwitʃ] *nm* sandwich man

homo [ɔmo] *adj & nmf* gay

The symbol ***** indicates that the initial **h** is aspirate and that hence there is no liaison, eg **les haricots** [leariko] and not [lezariko], or contraction in spelling, eg **la haine** and not **l'haine**.

homogène [ɔmɔʒɛn] *adj* homogeneous

homogénéisation [ɔmɔʒeneizasjɔ̃] *nf* homogenization

homogénéiser [ɔmɔʒeneize] *vt* to homogenize

homogénéité [ɔmɔʒeneite] *nf* homogeneity

homologue [ɔmɔlɔg] *nmf* counterpart, opposite number

homologuer [ɔmɔlɔge] *vt (accord, décision, record)* to ratify; *(testament)* to prove

homonyme [ɔmɔnim] **1** *nm (mot)* homonym **2** *nmf (personne)* namesake

homosexualité [ɔmɔsɛksɥalite] *nf* homosexuality

homosexuel, -elle [ɔmɔsɛksɥɛl] *adj & nm,f* homosexual

***Honduras** [ɔ̃dyras] *nm* **le H.** Honduras

***hondurien, -enne** [ɔ̃dyrjɛ̃, -ɛn] **1** *adj* Honduran **2** *nm,f* **H.** Honduran

***Hongrie** [ɔ̃gri] *nf* **la H.** Hungary

***hongrois, -e** [ɔ̃grwa, -az] **1** *adj* Hungarian **2** *nm,f* **H.** Hungarian **3** *nm (langue)* Hungarian

honnête [ɔnɛt] *adj* **(a)** *(intègre) (personne, conduite)* honest; **peu h.** dishonest; **être h. avec soi-même** to be honest with oneself **(b)** *(décent) (vie, gens)* decent; *(intentions)* honourable **(c)** *(acceptable) (prix, note, résultat)* fair; **un repas/film h.** sans plus an OK meal/movie, but nothing to write home about

honnêtement [ɔnɛtmɑ̃] *adv* **(a)** *(avec intégrité) (agir, se comporter)* honestly **(b)** *(franchement)* to be honest; **h., qu'est-ce que tu en penses?** be honest, what do you think? **(c)** *(raisonnablement)* decently

honnêteté [ɔnɛtte] *nf* **(a)** *(intégrité)* honesty **(b)** *(décence)* decency

honneur [ɔnœr] *nm* honour; **mettre un point d'h. à faire qch** to make it a point of honour to do sth; **déclarer/ jurer sur l'h. que…** to state/swear on one's honour that…; **sauver l'h.** to save one's honour; **en tout bien tout h.** with no ulterior motive; **en l'h. de qn** in sb's honour; **à qui ai-je l'h.?** to whom have I the honour (of speaking)?; *Fam* **en quel h. devrais-je t'aider?** give me one good reason why I should help you!; **à vous l'h.** after you; **être à l'h.** to have pride of place; **c'est tout à ton h.** it's to your credit; **faire h. à qn/qch** to be a credit to sb/sth; **faire h. à un repas** to do justice to a meal; **rechercher les honneurs** to court fame

***honnir** [ɔnir] *vt* to disgrace

honorable [ɔnɔrabl] *adj* **(a)** *(profession, personne, intentions)* honourable **(b)** *(performance, résultat)* creditable, respectable

honorablement [ɔnɔrabləmɑ̃] *adv* **(a)** *(de façon respectable)* honourably **(b)** *(correctement)* **il s'en est h. tiré** he did quite creditably; **gagner h. sa vie** to earn a good living

honoraire [ɔnɔrɛr] **1** *adj (fonction, membre)* honorary **2** *nmpl* **honoraires** fee, fees

honorer [ɔnɔre] **1** *vt* **(a)** *(rendre hommage à)* to honour; **h. qn de sa confiance** to put one's trust in sb **(b)** *(acquitter) (facture, dette, engagements)* to honour **(c)** *(valoir de l'estime à) (personne, chose)* to be a credit to **(d)** *Hum (sexuellement)* to service **2** **s'honorer** *vpr* **s'h. de qch/d'avoir fait qch** to pride oneself on sth/on having done sth

honorifique [ɔnɔrifik] *adj* honorary

***honoris causa** [ɔnɔriskoza] *adj* honoris causa; **docteur h.** doctor honoris causa, honorary doctor

***honte** [ɔ̃t] *nf* **(a)** *(sentiment)* shame; **à ma grande h.** to my shame; **sans h.** shamelessly; **avoir h. (de)** to be ashamed (of); **avoir h. pour qn** to feel embarrassed for sb; **faire h. à qn** to make sb ashamed **(b)** *(chose scandaleuse)* disgrace; **c'est une h.!** it's a disgrace!

***honteux, -euse** [ɔ̃tø, -øz] *adj* **(a)** *(personne)* ashamed **(b)** *(conduite, acte)* shameful, disgraceful; **c'est h.!** it's a disgrace!

***hop** [ɔp] *exclam* **allez h., saute!** go on, jump!; **allez h., tout le monde dehors!** come on, everybody out!; **h.-là!** oops(-a-daisy)!

hôpital, -aux [ɔpital, -o] *nm* hospital; **h. de campagne** field hospital; **h. de jour** day hospital; **h. militaire** military hospital; **h. psychiatrique** psychiatric hospital

***hoquet** [ɔkɛ] *nm* hiccup; **avoir le h.** to have the hiccups

***hoqueter** [42] [ɔkəte] *vi* to hiccup

horaire [ɔrɛr] **1** *adj* hourly **2** *nm* **(a)** *(des services de transport)* timetable, schedule; **être en retard sur l'h.** to be running late **(b)** *(emploi du temps)* timetable, schedule; **h. variable** *ou* **flexible** flexible hours, flexitime; **horaires de travail** working hours

***horde** [ɔrd] *nf* horde

horizon [ɔrizɔ̃] *nm aussi Fig* horizon; **à l'h.** on the horizon; **à l'h. 2010** in the year 2010; **h. intellectuel** intellectual horizons

horizontal, -e, -aux, -ales [ɔrizɔ̃tal, -o] **1** *adj* horizontal **2** *nf* **horizontale** horizontal line; **à l'horizontale** horizontal

horizontalement [ɔrizɔ̃talmɑ̃] *adv* horizontally; *(dans les mots croisés)* across

horloge [ɔrlɔʒ] *nf* clock; **réglé comme une h.** as regular as clockwork; **h. biologique** biological clock; **l'h. parlante** the speaking clock; *Ordinat* **h. du système** system clock; *Ordinat* **h. en temps réel** real-time clock

horloger, -ère [ɔrlɔʒe, -ɛr] **1** *adj* **l'industrie horlogère** the watchmaking industry **2** *nm,f* watchmaker

horloger-bijoutier (*pl* **horlogers-bijoutiers**) [ɔrlɔ-ʒebiʒutje] *nm* jeweller and watchmaker

horlogerie [ɔrlɔʒri] *nf (industrie)* watchmaking; *(magasin)* watchmaker's (shop); **l'h.** *(ouvrages)* clocks and watches

***hormis** [ɔrmi] *prép Litt* except, save

hormonal, -e, -aux, -ales [ɔrmɔnal, -o] *adj* hormonal

hormone [ɔrmɔn] *nf* hormone

hormonothérapie [ɔrmɔnoterapi] *nf* hormone therapy

horodateur [ɔrɔdatœr] *nm* time and date stamping machine; *(de stationnement)* pay and display machine

horoscope [ɔrɔskɔp] *nm* horoscope

horreur [ɔrœr] *nf* **(a)** *(effroi)* horror **(b)** *(répugnance)* disgust; **avoir h. de qn/qch** to hate sb/sth; **avoir h. de faire qch** to hate doing sth; **avoir qn/qch en h.** to loathe sb/sth; **faire h. à qn** to disgust sb **(c)** *(caractère horrible)* horror; **quelle h.!** how horrible!, how awful! **(d)** *(chose ou personne exécrable)* **être une h.** to be a nightmare **(e)** **horreurs** *(atrocités)* horrors; *(calomnies)* horrible things

horrible [ɔribl] *adj* **(a)** *(effrayant)* horrible **(b)** *(très laid)* hideous

horriblement [ɔribləmɑ̃] *adv (brûlé, défiguré)* horribly; *(cher, froid)* terribly

horrifiant, -e [ɔrifjɑ̃, -ɑ̃t] *adj* horrifying

horrifier [66] [ɔrifje] *vt* to horrify

horripilant, -e [ɔripilɑ̃, -ɑ̃t] *adj* exasperating
horripiler [ɔripile] *vt* to exasperate
***hors** [ɔr] *prép* (a) *(dehors)* h. de outside; h. d'ici! get out (of here)!; ça l'a mise h. d'elle that infuriated her; être h. de soi to be beside oneself (b) *Litt (sauf)* except, save (c) *(en conjonction avec un nom)* h. antenne off-air; h. d'atteinte out of reach; h. de combat out of action; h. jeu offside; mettre qn/qch h. la loi to outlaw sb/sth; h. pair unrivalled; h. piste off piste; h. de prix extortionate; h. de question out of the question; h. saison off-season; numéro h. série special issue; h. service out of order; h. sujet not relevant; h. taxe net of tax; *(exempt de taxe)* tax-free; boutique h. taxe duty-free shop; h. d'usage *(vêtement)* worn out; *(machine)* beyond repair
***hors-bord** [ɔrbɔr] *nm inv* speedboat; moteur h. outboard motor
***hors-d'œuvre** [ɔrdœvr] *nm inv* (a) *(plat)* hors d'oeuvre, starter (b) *Fig* starter, taster
***hors-jeu** [ɔrʒø] *nm inv* offside
***hors-la-loi** [ɔrlalwa] *nm inv* outlaw
***hors-piste** [ɔrpist] *nm inv (en ski)* off-piste skiing; faire du h. to ski off piste
hortensia [ɔrtɑ̃sja] *nm* hydrangea
horticole [ɔrtikɔl] *adj* horticultural; exposition h. flower show
horticulteur [ɔrtikyltœr] *nm* nurseryman
horticulture [ɔrtikyltyr] *nf* horticulture
hospice [ɔspis] *nm* (a) *(asile)* home (b) *(monastère)* hospice
hospitalier¹, -ère [ɔspitalje, -ɛr] *adj (accueillant)* hospitable
hospitalier², -ère *adj (relatif aux hôpitaux)* hospital; personnel h. hospital staff
hospitalisation [ɔspitalizasjɔ̃] *nf* hospitalization; h. à domicile home care
hospitaliser [ɔspitalize] *vt* to hospitalize; faire h. qn to have sb hospitalized
hospitalité [ɔspitalite] *nf* hospitality
hospitalo-universitaire [ɔspitaloyniversiter] *adj* centre h. teaching hospital
hostie [ɔsti] *nf Rel* host
hostile [ɔstil] *adj* hostile (à towards)
hostilité [ɔstilite] *nf* hostility (contre *ou* envers towards); hostilités hostilities
hosto [ɔsto] *nm Fam* hospital
hôte [ot] *nm* (a) *(personne qui invite)* host (b) *(invité)* guest, visitor; h. payant paying guest (c) *Biol* host
hôtel [otel] *nm* (a) *(pour l'hébergement)* hotel; h. de passe = hotel used as a brothel (b) *(bâtiment)* h. des impôts tax office; l'h. de la Monnaie ≃ the Royal Mint; h. (particulier) mansion, town house; h. des ventes saleroom; h. de ville town hall
hôtelier, -ère [otalje, -ɛr] **1** *adj* l'industrie hôtelière the hotel industry
2 *nm,f* hotel keeper, hotelier
hôtellerie [otelri] *nf* (a) *(hôtel)* inn (b) *(secteur)* l'h. the hotel industry
hôtel-restaurant *(pl* hôtels-restaurants) [otelrestɔrɑ̃] *nm* hotel and restaurant
hôtesse [otes] *nf* (a) *(personne qui reçoit)* hostess (b) *(dans un avion)* hostess, stewardess; h. d'accueil flight attendant, receptionist; h. de l'air air hostess, flight attendant
***hotte** [ɔt] *nf* (a) *(panier)* basket; la h. du Père Noël

Santa Claus's sack (b) *(pour la ventilation)* hood; h. aspirante extractor hood
***hou** [u] *exclam* boo!; h.! la vilaine! tut-tut, you naughty girl!
***houblon** [ublɔ̃] *nm* hops
***houe** [u] *nf* hoe
***houille** [uj] *nf* coal; h. blanche hydroelectric power
***houiller, -ère** [uje, -ɛr] **1** *adj (terrain)* rich in coal; bassin h. coalfield; production houillère coal output
2 *nf* houillère coalmine, colliery
***houle** [ul] *nf* swell
***houlette** [ulet] *nf* (a) *(de berger)* crook; *Fig* sous la h. de under the leadership of (b) *(petite bêche)* trowel
***houleux, -euse** [ulø, -øz] *adj (mer)* choppy; *Fig (réunion)* stormy
***houppette** [upet] *nf (de plumes)* small tuft; *(de cheveux)* quiff; *(à poudre)* powder puff
***hourra** [ura] **1** *exclam* hurrah!; hip, hip, hip, h.! hip, hip, hooray!
2 *nm* hurrah; pousser des hourras to cheer
***houspiller** [uspije] *vt* to tell off
***housse** [us] *nf* cover; *(contre la poussière)* dust sheet; *(dans une voiture)* seat cover
***houx** [u] *nm* holly
hovercraft [ɔverkraft] *nm* hovercraft
HT (a) *(abrév* haute tension) HT (b) *(abrév* hors taxe) exclusive of tax
ᴬhublot [yblo] *nm (de bateau)* porthole; *(dans un avion, une machine à laver)* window
***huche** [yʃ] *nf* chest; h. à pain bread bin
***hue** [y, hy] *exclam (à un cheval)* gee up!; tirer à h. et à dia to pull in opposite directions
***huées** [ɥe] *nfpl* booing; quitter la scène sous les h. to be booed off the stage
***huer** [ɥe] **1** *vt* to boo
2 *vi (hibou, chouette)* to hoot
huile [ɥil] *nf* (a) *(liquide)* oil; *Fig* jeter de l'h. sur le feu to add fuel to the fire; une mer d'h. a glassy sea; h. d'amandes douces almond oil; h. d'arachide groundnut oil; *Can* h. de chauffage heating oil; *Fig* h. de coude elbow grease; h. essentielle essential oil; h. de foie de morue cod liver oil; h. de moteur engine oil; h. d'olive olive oil; h. de ricin castor oil; h. solaire suntan oil; h. de tournesol sunflower oil; h. végétale vegetable oil; h de vidange sump oil (b) *(peinture)* oil painting (c) *Fam (personne importante)* big shot
huiler [ɥile] *vt* to oil
huileux, -euse [ɥilø, -øz] *adj* oily
huis [ɥi] *nm* à h. clos behind closed doors; *Jur* in camera
huissier [ɥisje] *nm* (a) *Jur* bailiff (b) *(portier)* usher
***huit** [ɥi(t)] *adj & nm inv* eight; h. jours a week; aujourd'hui/demain en h. a week today/tomorrow; donner ses h. jours à qn to give sb a week's notice; *voir aussi* trois
***huitaine** [ɥiten] *nf* (a) *(environ huit)* (about) eight (b) *(semaine)* week; dans une h. de jours in a week or so
***huitante** [ɥitɑ̃t] *adj inv Suisse* eighty
***huitième** [ɥitjem] *adj, nm & nmf* eighth; *voir aussi* cinquième
huître [ɥitr] *nf* oyster; h. perlière pearl oyster
***hulotte** [ylɔt] *nf* tawny owl

The symbol * indicates that the initial h is aspirate and that hence there is no liaison, eg les haricots [leariko] and not [lezariko], or contraction in spelling, eg la haine and not l'haine.

*hululement [ylylmɑ̃] *nm* hoot; **des hululements** hooting
*hululer [ylyle] *vi* to hoot
*hum [œm] *exclam* hm!
humain, -e [ymɛ̃, -ɛn] **1** *adj* **(a)** *(relatif à l'homme)* human; c'est h. it's only human; **des pertes humaines énormes** a huge loss of life **(b)** *(compatissant)* humane **2** *nm* human (being)
humainement [ymɛnmɑ̃] *adv* **(a)** *(relatif à l'homme)* in human terms; **h. possible** humanly possible **(b)** *(avec bonté)* humanely
humaniser [ymanize] *vt* to make more human
humanisme [ymanism] *nm* humanism
humaniste [ymanist] *adj & nmf* humanist
humanitaire [ymanitɛr] *adj* humanitarian
humanité [ymanite] *nf* **(a)** *(genre humain)* humanity, mankind **(b)** *(bonté)* humanity; **avec h.** humanely
humanoïde [ymanɔid] *nm* humanoid
humble [œ̃bl] *adj* humble; **à mon h. avis** in my humble opinion
humblement [œ̃bləmɑ̃] *adv* humbly
humecter [ymɛkte] *vt* to moisten
*humer [yme] *vt (air)* to breathe in; *(parfum)* to smell
humérus [ymerys] *nm* humerus
humeur [ymœr] *nf* **(a)** *(disposition)* mood; **être de bonne/mauvaise h.** to be in a good/bad mood; **mettre qn de bonne/mauvaise h.** to put sb in a good/bad mood; **être d'une h.** massacrante to be in a foul mood; **plein de bonne h.** good-humoured; **être/ne pas être d'h. à faire qch** to be/not be in the mood to do sth **(b)** *(caractère)* temper, temperament; **d'h. égale** even-tempered; **d'humeur inégale** *ou* **changeante** temperamental **(c)** *Litt (mauvaise humeur)* bad mood; **geste d'h.** ill-tempered gesture; **avec h.** irritably **(d)** *Anat* **h. aqueuse** aqueous humour; **h. vitrée** vitreous humour
humide [ymid] *adj (maison, linge)* damp, wet; *(climat)* humid; **les yeux humides (de larmes)** eyes moist with tears
humidificateur [ymidifikatœr] *nm* humidifier
humidifier [66] [ymidifje] *vt* to dampen; *(air)* to humidify
humidité [ymidite] *nf (d'une maison)* dampness; *(du climat, d'une région)* humidity; **il faut beaucoup d'h. à cette plante** this plant needs a lot of moisture; **craint l'h.** *(sur un paquet)* store in a dry place
humiliant, -e [ymiljɑ̃, -ɑ̃t] *adj* humiliating
humiliation [ymiljasjɔ̃] *nf* humiliation
humilier [66] [ymilje] **1** *vt* to humiliate **2 s'humilier** *vpr* to humiliate oneself
humilité [ymilite] *nf* humility
humoriste [ymɔrist] *nmf* humorist
humoristique [ymɔristik] *adj* humorous; **dessin h.** cartoon
humour [ymur] *nm* humour; **avoir (le sens) de l'h.** to have a (good) sense of humour; **h. noir** black humour
*huppe¹ [yp] *nf (oiseau)* hoopoe
*huppe² *nf (d'un oiseau)* crest
*huppé, -e [ype] *adj* **(a)** *Fam (gens, endroit, quartier)* smart **(b)** *(oiseau)* crested
*hurlement [yrləmɑ̃] *nm (d'un loup, d'un chien)* howl; *(d'une personne)* scream; *(du vent)* roaring; *(d'une sirène)* wail
*hurler [yrle] **1** *vi (loup, chien)* to howl; *(personne)* to howl,

to scream; *(vent, tempête)* to roar; *(sirène)* to wail; *(radio)* to blare; **h. de douleur/rage** to howl with pain/rage; **c'est à h. de rire** it's screamingly funny; **h. à la lune** to bay at the moon; **il faut h. avec les loups** if you can't beat them join them **2** *vt (insultes, instructions)* to yell
hurluberlu [yrlybɛrly] *nm* oddball
*Huron [yrɔ̃] *n voir* lac
*husky *(pl* huskies) [œski] *nm* husky
*hussard [ysar] *nm* hussar
*hussarde [ysard] *nf* **à la h.** roughly
*hutte [yt] *nf* hut
hybride [ibrid] *adj & nm* hybrid
hydratant, -e [idratɑ̃, -ɑ̃t] *adj* moisturizing
hydratation [idratasjɔ̃] *nf (de la peau)* moisturizing
hydrate [idrat] *nm* hydrate; **h. de carbone** carbohydrate
hydrater [idrate] **1** *vt (peau)* to moisturize; *(organisme)* to hydrate **2 s'hydrater** *vpr* to take in water
hydraulique [idrolik] **1** *adj* hydraulic **2** *nf (science)* hydraulics *(singulier)*
hydravion [idravjɔ̃] *nm* seaplane
hydre [idr] *nf* hydra
hydrocarbure [idrɔkarbyr] *nm* hydrocarbon
hydrocution [idrɔkysjɔ̃] *nf* drowning *(after syncope caused by cold water)*
hydroélectricité [idrɔelɛktrisite] *nf* hydroelectricity
hydroélectrique [idrɔelɛktrik] *adj* hydroelectric
hydrogène [idrɔʒɛn] *nm* hydrogen
hydroglisseur [idrɔglisœr] *nm* jetfoil
hydrographie [idrɔgrafi] *nf* hydrography
hydrolyse [idrɔliz] *nf* hydrolysis
hydromel [idrɔmɛl] *nm* mead
hydrophile [idrɔfil] *adj (coton)* absorbent
hydrothérapie [idrɔterapi] *nf* hydrotherapy
hydroxyde [idrɔksid] *nm* hydroxide
hyène [jɛn] *nf* hyena
Hygiaphone® [iʒjafɔn] *nm (au guichet)* grille; **parlez dans l'H.** speak into the grille
hygiène [iʒjɛn] *nf* hygiene; **par mesure d'h.** for hygiene reasons; **h. alimentaire** diet; **h. mentale** mental health
hygiénique [iʒjenik] *adj* **(a)** *(propre)* hygienic; **peu h.** unhygienic **(b)** *(bon pour la santé)* healthy; **une promenade h.** a bracing walk
hymne [imn] *nm* hymn; **h. national** national anthem
hyper- [iper] *préf Fam* very, *Am* real
hyperbole [ipɛrbɔl] *nf* **(a)** *(figure de style)* hyperbole **(b)** *Math* hyperbola
hyperbolique [ipɛrbɔlik] *adj* hyperbolic
hyperglycémie [ipɛrglisemi] *nf* hyperglycemia
hypermarché [ipɛrmarʃe] *nm* hypermarket, superstore
hypermétrope [ipɛrmetrɔp] *adj* longsighted
hypernerveux, -euse [ipɛrnɛrvø, -øz] **1** *adj* highly-strung **2** *nm,f* highly-strung person
hypersensibilité [ipɛrsɑ̃sibilite] *nf* hypersensitivity
hypersensible [ipɛrsɑ̃sibl] *adj* hypersensitive
hypertendu, -e [ipɛrtɑ̃dy] *adj* **être h.** to have high blood pressure

---

The symbol ***** indicates that the initial **h** is aspirate and that hence there is no liaison, eg **les haricots** [leariko] and not [lezariko], or contraction in spelling, eg **la haine** and not **l'haine**.

hypertension [ipɛrtɑ̃sjɔ̃] *nf* high blood pressure, *Spéc* hypertension

hypertexte [ipɛrtɛkst] *nm Ordinat* hypertext

hypertrophie [ipɛrtrɔfi] *nf* enlargement, *Spéc* hypertrophy

hypertrophié, -e [ipɛrtrɔfje] *adj* enlarged, *Spéc* hypertrophied

hypnose [ipnoz] *nf* hypnosis; **être en état d'h.** to be in a trance

hypnotique [ipnɔtik] *adj* hypnotic

hypnotiser [ipnɔtize] *vt* to hypnotize

hypnotisme [ipnɔtism] *nm* hypnotism

hypoallergénique [ipɔalɛrʒenik] *adj* hypoallergenic

hypocalorique [ipɔkalɔrik] *adj (régime, aliment)* low-calorie

hypocondriaque [ipɔkɔ̃drijak] *adj & nmf* hypochondriac

hypocrisie [ipɔkrizi] *nf* hypocrisy

hypocrite [ipɔkrit] **1** *adj* hypocritical **2** *nmf* hypocrite

hypocritement [ipɔkritmɑ̃] *adv* hypocritically

hypodermique [ipɔdɛrmik] *adj* hypodermic

hypoglycémie [ipɔglisemi] *nf* hypoglycemia

hypokhâgne [ipɔkaɲ] *nf* = first-year arts class preparing students for the entrance examination for the "École normale supérieure"

hypophyse [ipɔfiz] *nf* pituitary gland

hypotendu, -e [ipɔtɑ̃dy] *adj* **être h.** to have low blood pressure

hypotension [ipɔtɑ̃sjɔ̃] *nf* low blood pressure, *Spéc* hypotension

hypoténuse [ipɔtenyz] *nf* hypotenuse

hypothalamus [ipɔtalamys] *nm* hypothalamus

hypothécaire [ipɔtekɛr] *adj* **contrat h.** mortgage deed; **prêt h.** mortgage (loan)

hypothèque [ipɔtek] *nf* mortgage

hypothéquer [34] [ipɔteke] *vt (propriété)* to mortgage; *Fig* **h. son avenir** to sign away one's future

hypothermie [ipɔtɛrmi] *nf* hypothermia

hypothèse [ipɔtɛz] *nf* hypothesis; **dans l'h. où nous échouerions** should we fail; **ils ont écarté l'h. du suicide** they have ruled out the possibility of suicide

hypothétique [ipɔtetik] *adj* hypothetical

hystérectomie [istɛrɛktɔmi] *nf* hysterectomy

hystérie [isteri] *nf* hysteria; **h. collective** mass hysteria

hystérique [isterik] **1** *adj* hysterical **2** *nmf* hysterical person

---

The symbol * indicates that the initial **h** is aspirate and that hence there is no liaison, eg **les haricots** [leariko] and not [lezariko], or contraction in spelling, eg **la haine** and not **l'haine**.

I, i [i] *nm inv* I, i

ibère [ibɛr] **1** *adj* Iberian
2 *nmf* **I.** Iberian

ibérique [iberik] *adj* Iberian

ibis [ibis] *nm* ibis

iceberg [ajsbɛrg, isbɛrg] *nm* iceberg; *Fig* **la partie visible de l'i.** the tip of the iceberg

ichtyologie [iktjɔlɔʒi] *nf* ichthyology

ici [isi] *adv* **(a)** *(dans l'espace)* here; **i. et là** here and there; **i. même** on this very spot; **les gens d'i.** the people from round here, the locals; **c'est i.** this is the place; **c'est i. que ça s'est passé** this is where it happened; *Fig* **je reprends i. ses propres paroles** and here I'm using her own words; **i. Thomas** *(au téléphone)* this is Thomas **(b)** *(dans le temps)* **jusqu'i.** until now, up to now; **d'i. vendredi/demain** by Friday/tomorrow; **d'i. là** by that time, by then; **d'i. peu** before long; **d'i. à ce que vous ayez fini, je serai parti** by the time you've finished, I'll have gone; **d'i. à ce qu'il la quitte, il n'y a pas loin** he will have left her before long

icône [ikon] *nf Rel & Ordinat* icon; *Ordinat* **i. de la corbeille** wastebasket icon, *Am* trash icon

iconoclaste [ikɔnɔklast] **1** *adj* iconoclastic
2 *nmf* iconoclast

iconographie [ikɔnɔgrafi] *nf* **(a)** *(dans un domaine particulier)* iconography **(b)** *(dans l'édition)* illustrations, art work

iconographique [ikɔnɔgrafik] *adj* iconographic

idéal, -e, -als *ou* **-aux, -ales** [ideal, -o] **1** *adj* ideal
2 *nm* ideal; **l'i.** the ideal thing; **dans l'i.** ideally; **l'i. serait que tu y ailles tout seul** it would be best if you went alone

idéalement [idealmɑ̃] *adv* ideally

idéalisation [idealizasjɔ̃] *nf* idealization

idéaliser [idealize] *vt* to idealize

idéalisme [idealism] *nm* idealism

idéaliste [idealist] **1** *adj* idealistic
2 *nmf* idealist

idée [ide] *nf* **(a)** *(inspiration)* idea; **i. de génie, i. lumineuse** brilliant idea; **avoir la bonne i. de faire qch** to have the bright idea of doing sth; **avoir une i. derrière la tête** to be up to something; **donner des idées à qn** to put ideas into sb's head; **quelle drôle d'i.!, en voilà une i.!** the very idea!; **se faire des idées** to imagine things; **i. fixe** obsession; **idées noires** black thoughts; **i. reçue** generally accepted idea **(b)** *(notion)* idea; **pour vous donner une i.** to give you an idea; **as-tu une i. du prix que ça coûte?** have you any idea how much it costs?; **je n'en ai pas la moindre i.** I haven't got the faintest idea; *Fam* **on n'a pas i. de faire des choses pareilles!** whoever heard of such a thing! **(c)**

(opinion) view, opinion; **avoir une haute i. de qn/qch** to have a high opinion of sb/sth; **se faire une i. de qn/qch** to get an idea of sb/sth; **avoir sa petite i. sur qch** to have one's pet theory about sth; **avoir les idées larges** to be broadminded; **fais à ton i.** do as you like; **changer d'i.** to change one's mind **(d)** *(esprit)* **ça ne m'est jamais venu à l'i.** it's never occurred to me; **je ne peux pas lui ôter cela de l'i.** I can't get her to change her mind about it; **se mettre dans l'i. que/de faire qch** to get it into one's head that/to do sth; **cela m'était sorti de l'i.** it had slipped my mind

idem [idɛm] *adv* ditto

identification [idɑ̃tifikasjɔ̃] *nf* identification **(avec** *ou* **à** with); *Ordinat* **i. de l'utilisateur** user identification

identifier [66] [idɑ̃tifje] **1** *vt* to identify
2 s'identifier *vpr* to identify **(avec** *ou* **à** with)

identique [idɑ̃tik] *adj* identical **(à** to)

identité [idɑ̃tite] *nf* identity; **papiers** *ou* **pièces d'i.** identity papers

idéogramme [ideɔgram] *nm* ideogram

idéologie [ideɔlɔʒi] *nf* ideology

idéologique [ideɔlɔʒik] *adj* ideological

idiomatique [idjɔmatik] *adj* idiomatic; **expression i.** idiom

idiome [idjom] *nm* idiom

idiot, -e [idjo, -ɔt] **1** *adj* *(stupide)* idiotic, stupid; *(regrettable)* stupid, silly; **ce système n'est pas i.** this system is pretty smart
2 *nm,f* idiot; *Fam* **l'i. du village** the village idiot; **faire l'i.** *(faire des bêtises)* to act the fool; *(feindre de ne pas comprendre)* to act dumb

idiotie [idjɔsi] *nf* *(chose, parole idiote)* stupid thing; *(caractère stupide)* stupidity; **ne dites pas d'idioties!** don't talk rubbish!

idolâtrer [idɔlɑtre] *vt* to idolize

idolâtrie [idɔlɑtri] *nf* idolatry

idole [idɔl] *nf* idol; **i. des jeunes** teenage idol

idylle [idil] *nf* **(a)** *(aventure)* romance **(b)** *(poème)* idyll

idyllique [idilik] *adj* idyllic

IEP [iəpe] *nm (abrév* **Institut d'études politiques)** = higher education establishment for political science students

if [if] *nm* yew

IGF [iʒeɛf] *nm inv (abrév* **impôt sur les grandes fortunes)** wealth tax

igloo, iglou [iglu] *nm* igloo

IGN [iʒeɛn] *nm (abrév* **Institut géographique national)** *Br* ≃ Ordnance Survey, *Am* ≃ United States Geological Survey

ignare [iɲar] **1** *adj* ignorant
2 *nmf* ignoramus
ignifuge [iɲnifyʒ] **1** *adj* fireproof
2 *nm* fireproofing material
ignifugé, -e [iɲifyʒe] *adj* fireproofed
ignoble [iɲɔbl] *adj* **(a)** *(personne, conduite)* vile **(b)** *(habitation, quartier)* filthy; *(nourriture)* disgusting
ignominie [iɲɔmini] *nf* **(a)** *(caractère)* ignominy; **se couvrir d'i.** to bring shame upon oneself **(b)** *(action)* shameful thing; **c'est une i.!** it's a disgrace!
ignorance [iɲɔrɑ̃s] *nf* ignorance; **être/tenir qn dans l'i.** to be/keep sb in the dark
ignorant, -e [iɲɔrɑ̃, -ɑ̃t] **1** *adj* ignorant **(de** of) **2** *nm,f* ignoramus; **faire l'i.** to pretend one doesn't know
ignoré, -e [iɲɔre] *adj* unknown; *(négligé)* ignored; **vivre i.** to live in obscurity
ignorer [iɲɔre] **1** *vt* **(a)** *(ne pas savoir)* not to know (about); **il en ignore tout de cela** he knows nothing about it; **ne rien l. de qch** to know all about sth. **personne n'ignore que...** everybody knows that...; **i. la peur/la jalousie** to feel no fear/jealousy **(b)** *(mépriser)* *(personne, conseil, interdiction)* to ignore
2 s'ignorer *vpr* **(a)** *(se mépriser l'un l'autre)* to ignore each other **(b)** *(se méconnaître)* **c'est un artiste qui s'ignore** he's an artist but he doesn't know it
iguane [igwan] *nm* iguana
il [il] *pron personnel* **(a)** *(personne)* he; *(chose, animal)* it; **ton père est-il toujours à l'hôpital?** is your father still in hospital?
  (b) *(impersonnel)* it; **il est cinq heures** it's five o'clock; **il pleut** it's raining; **il existe de nombreuses possibilités** there are many possibilities
île [il] *nf* island; **dans une î.** on an island; **i. déserte** desert island; **les îles Anglo-Normandes** the Channel Islands; **Culin i.** flottante floating island *(beaten egg whites served on custard)*; **les îles Salomon** the Solomon Islands; **les îles de la Société** the Society Islands; **les îles Sous-le-Vent** the Leeward Islands
Île-de-France [ildəfrɑ̃s] *nf* l'Î. – administrative region including Paris
iliaque [iljak] *adj Anat* iliac; **os i.** ilium
illégal, -e, -aux, -ales [ilegal, -o] *adj* illegal
illégalement [ilegalmɑ̃] *adv* illegally
illégalité [ilegalite] *nf* illegality; **vivre dans l'i.** to live outside the law; **être dans l'i.** to break the law
illégitime [ileʒitim] *adj* *(enfant)* illegitimate; *(union)* unlawful; *(demande)* unwarranted
illettré, -e [iletre] *adj & nm,f* illiterate
illettrisme [iletrism] *nm* illiteracy
illicite [ilisit] *adj* illicit, unlawful
illico [iliko] *adv Fam* **i. (presto)** pronto
illimité, -e [ilimite] *adj* *(pouvoirs, moyens, crédit)* unlimited; *(confiance)* boundless
illisible [ilizibl] *adj* **(a)** *(indéchiffrable)* illegible; *Ordinat (fichier, disquette)* unreadable **(b)** *(incompréhensible)* unreadable
illogique [ilɔʒik] *adj* illogical
illumination [ilyminasjɔ̃] *nf* **(a)** *(action d'illuminer)* illumination; *(par projecteurs)* floodlighting **(b)** *(lumière)* **illuminations** *(c)* *(inspiration)* flash of inspiration
illuminé, -e [ilymine] **1** *adj* *(éclairé)* lit up, illuminated; *(par projecteurs)* floodlit
2 *nm,f Péj* fanatic
illuminer [ilymine] **1** *vt* *(éclairer)* to light up, to illuminate;

(par projecteurs) to floodlight; *Fig (visage, yeux)* to light up
2 s'illuminer *vpr aussi Fig* to light up **(de** with)
illusion [ilyzjɔ̃] *nf* illusion; **se faire des illusions** to delude oneself; **je ne me fais aucune i. sur ses intentions** I have no illusions about her intentions; **perdre ses illusions** to become disillusioned; **enlever** *ou* **faire perdre ses illusions à qn** to disillusion sb; **faire i.** to take people in, **i. d'optique** optical illusion
illusionner [ilyzjɔne] **s'illusionner** *vpr* to delude oneself **(sur** about)
illusionniste [ilyzjɔnist] *nmf* conjurer
illusoire [ilyzwar] *adj* illusory
illustrateur, -trice [ilystratœr, -tris] *nm,f* illustrator
illustration [ilystrasjɔ̃] *nf* illustration
illustre [ilystr] *adj* illustrious; *Hum* **un i. inconnu** a famous person no one has ever heard of
illustré, -e [ilystre] **1** *adj* illustrated **2** *nm Vieilli (pour enfants)* comic
illustrer [ilystre] **1** *vt (livre, récit)* to illustrate **(de** with)
2 s'illustrer *vpr* to distinguish oneself **(par** by)
îlot [ilo] *nm (île)* small island; *(groupe d'immeubles)* block; *Fig* **î. de verdure** island of greenery
îlotage [ilɔtaʒ] *nm* community policing
ils [il] *pron personnel* they; **les magasins sont-i. ouverts le dimanche?** are the shops open on Sunday?
image [imaʒ] *nf* **(a)** *(dans un miroir)* reflection, image; *(à la télévision)* picture; **vingt-quatre images par seconde** twenty-four frames a second; **être à l'i.** to be on camera; **nous n'avons plus d'i.** the picture's gone; **i. d'archives** stock shot; *Ordinat* **i. bitmap** bitmap image; **images de synthèse** computer-generated images; *Ordinat* **i. vectorielle** outline image; **(b)** *Fig* image, soigner son i. to cultivate one's image; **donner une bonne/mauvaise i. de** to present a good/bad image of; **i. de marque** *(d'un produit)* brand image; *(d'un homme politique, d'une entreprise)* public image **(c)** *(dessin)* picture; *(récompense scolaire)* ≃ gold star
imagé, -e [imaʒe] *adj* vivid
imagerie [imaʒri] *nf* imagery; *Méd* **i. médicale** medical imaging; *Méd* **i. par résonance magnétique** magnetic resonance imaging
imaginable [imaʒinabl] *adj* imaginable
imaginaire [imaʒiner] **1** *adj* *(personnage, pays, animal)* imaginary
2 *nm* **l'i.** the imagination
imaginatif, -ive [imaʒinatif, -iv] *adj* imaginative
imagination [imaʒinasjɔ̃] *nf* imagination; **avoir de l'i.** to be imaginative
imaginer [imaʒine] **1** *vt* **(a)** *(inventer)* to devise **(b)** *(se figurer)* to imagine; **tu l'imagines avec des enfants!** just imagine him with children!; **j'imagine qu'elle viendra vers neuf heures** she'll arrive about nine o'clock, I should imagine
2 s'imaginer *vpr* **(a)** *(croire)* **s'i. que** to think that; **il s'imagine tout savoir** he thinks he knows it all **(b)** *(se figurer)* to imagine; *(soi-même)* to picture oneself; **tu t'imagines la tête qu'a faire** you can imagine how she'll take it; **je me l'imaginais bien plus jeune** I imagined him much younger
imam [imam] *nm* imam
imbattable [ɛ̃batabl] *adj* unbeatable
imbécile [ɛ̃besil] **1** *adj* idiotic, stupid
2 *nmf* idiot, fool; **c'est un i. heureux** he's living in blissful ignorance; **faire l'i.** *(faire des bêtises)* to play or act the fool; *(feindre de ne pas comprendre)* to act stupid
imbécillité [ɛ̃besilite] *nf* **(a)** *(caractère stupide)* idiocy,

stupidity (**b**) *(parole, chose stupide)* idiotic thing; **dire des imbécillités** to talk nonsense

imberbe [ɛ̃bɛrb] *adj* beardless

imbiber [ɛ̃bibe] **1** *vt* **i. qch de qch** to soak sth in sth; **imbibé d'eau** *(coton, éponge)* saturated (with water); *(terrain)* waterlogged
2 s'imbiber *vpr* **s'i. de qch** to become soaked with sth

imbrication [ɛ̃brikasjɔ̃] *nf* overlapping; *Fig (ensemble complexe)* web; *Ordinat* embedding; *(de commandes)* nesting

imbriquer [ɛ̃brike] **1** *vt* to overlap; *Ordinat* to embed; *(commandes)* to nest
2 s'imbriquer *vpr (s'emboîter)* to overlap; *Fig (problèmes, situations)* to be interwoven

imbroglio [ɛ̃brɔljo] *nm* imbroglio

imbu, -e [ɛ̃by] *adj* **i. de sa personne** *ou* **de soi-même** full of oneself

imbuvable [ɛ̃byvabl] *adj* undrinkable; *Fig (personne)* insufferable

imitateur, -trice [imitatœr, -tris] *nm,f (amateur)* mimic; *(professionnel)* impersonator, impressionist

imitation [imitasjɔ̃] *nf* (**a**) *(d'une personne)* impersonation, impression; *(d'un produit, d'un style)* imitation; *(d'une signature, d'un billet)* forgery (**b**) *(copie)* imitation; **bijoux en i. argent** imitation silver jewellery

imiter [imite] *vt (personne) (singer)* to imitate; *(faire une imitation de)* to impersonate; *(produit, style)* to imitate; *(signature)* to forge; *(billet, pièce de monnaie)* to counterfeit; **il leva son verre et tout le monde l'imita** he raised his glass and everyone did the same

immaculé, -e [imakyle] *adj (draps, linge, réputation)* spotless; **d'un blanc i.** spotlessly white; *Rel* **l'Immaculée Conception** the Immaculate Conception

immangeable [ɛ̃mɑ̃ʒabl] *adj* inedible

immanquablement [ɛ̃mɑ̃kabləmɑ̃] *adv* inevitably

immatériel, -elle [imaterjɛl] *adj Phil* immaterial; *Fin (actif)* intangible; *Litt (pâleur, minceur)* ethereal

immatriculation [imatrikylasjɔ̃] *nf* registration (**à** with); (**numéro d')i.** *Br* registration number, *Am* license number

immatriculer [imatrikyle] *vt* to register (**à** with); **la voiture est immatriculée en Dordogne** the car has a Dordogne *Br* number plate *or Am* license plate

immature [imatyr] *adj* immature

immaturité [imatyrite] *nf* immaturity

immédiat, -e [imedja, -at] **1** *adj* immediate; *(contact)* direct; *(mort)* instantaneous
2 *nm* **dans l'i.** for the time being

immédiatement [imedjatmɑ̃] *adv* immediately

immémorial, -e, -aux, -ales [imemɔrjal, -o] *adj Litt* age-old; **en des temps immémoriaux** in ancient times

immense [imɑ̃s] *adj* immense

immensément [imɑ̃semɑ̃] *adv* immensely

immensité [imɑ̃site] *nf* immensity

immerger [45] [imɛrʒe] *vt* to immerse (**dans** in)

immérité, -e [imerite] *adj* unmerited, undeserved

immersion [imɛrsjɔ̃] *nf* immersion (**dans** in)

immettable [ɛ̃metabl] *adj* unwearable

immeuble [imœbl] **1** *nm (bâtiment)* building; *(d'appartements) Br* block of flats, *Am* apartment block
2 *adj voir* **bien**

immigrant, -e [imigrɑ̃, -ɑ̃t] *adj & nm,f* immigrant

immigration [imigrasjɔ̃] *nf* immigration

immigré, -e [imigre] *adj & nm,f* immigrant

immigrer [imigre] *vi* to immigrate

imminence [iminɑ̃s] *nf* imminence

imminent, -e [iminɑ̃, -ɑ̃t] *adj* imminent

immiscer [16] [imise] **s'immiscer** *vpr* to interfere (**dans** in)

immobile [imɔbil] *adj* motionless, still; *Fig (figé)* unchanging

immobilier, -ère [imɔbilje, -ɛr] **1** *adj Br* property, *Am* real-estate
2 *nm* **l'i.** *Br* property, *Am* real estate

immobilisation [imɔbilizasjɔ̃] *nf* (**a**) *(fait de ne plus bouger)* immobilization (**b**) *Fin* **immobilisations** fixed assets

immobiliser [imɔbilize] **1** *vt* (**a**) *(blessé)* to immobilize; *(train)* to bring to a standstill; *(véhicule) (avec un sabot)* to clamp (**b**) *(capital)* to tie up
2 s'immobiliser *vpr* to come to a stop

immobilisme [imɔbilism] *nm* opposition to change

immobilité [imɔbilite] *nf* stillness; *(d'un visage)* immobility

immodéré, -e [imɔdere] *adj* immoderate

immodérément [imɔderemɑ̃] *adv* immoderately

immoler [imɔle] *Litt* **1** *vt aussi Fig* to sacrifice (**à** to)
2 s'immoler *vpr* to sacrifice oneself; **s'i. par le feu** to die by setting fire to oneself

immonde [imɔ̃d] *adj (sale)* foul; *(ignoble, laid)* vile

immondices [imɔ̃dis] *nfpl* refuse

immoral, -e, -aux, -ales [imɔral, -o] *adj* immoral

immoralité [imɔralite] *nf* immorality

immortaliser [imɔrtalize] *vt* to immortalize

immortalité [imɔrtalite] *nf* immortality

immortel, -elle [imɔrtɛl] **1** *adj (dieu, être)* immortal; *(amour)* everlasting
2 *nm,f (membre de l'Académie française)* member of the "Académie Française"
3 *nf* **immortelle** *(plante)* everlasting flower

immuable [imɥabl] *adj (vérité)* unchanging, immutable; *(opinion, sourire)* fixed

immunisation [imynizasjɔ̃] *nf* immunization (**contre** against)

immuniser [imynize] *vt* to immunize (**contre** against)

immunitaire [imyniter] *adj (système, réactions, défenses)* immune

immunité [imynite] *nf* immunity; **i. parlementaire/diplomatique** parliamentary/diplomatic immunity

immunodéficitaire [imynɔdefisiter] *adj Méd* immunodeficient

immunodépresseur [imynɔdepresœr] *adj m & nm Méd* immunosuppressive

immunologie [imynɔlɔʒi] *nf* immunology

immunologique [imynɔlɔʒik] *adj* immunological

immunosuppresseur [imynɔsypresœr] *adj m & nm Méd* immunosuppressive

impact [ɛ̃pakt] *nm* impact; **avoir un i. sur qch** to have an impact on sth

impair, -e [ɛ̃pɛr] **1** *adj (nombre, jours)* odd; *(côté d'une rue)* odd-numbered
2 *nm* (**a**) *(à la roulette)* odd numbers (**b**) *(maladresse)* blunder; **faire** *ou* **commettre un i.** to make a blunder

impalpable [ɛ̃palpabl] *adj* impalpable

imparable [ɛ̃parabl] *adj (coup)* unstoppable; *Fig (argument, logique)* irrefutable

impardonnable [ɛ̃pardɔnabl] *adj* unforgivable; **j'ai encore pris votre parapluie, je suis i.** I've taken your umbrella again, how unforgivable of me!

imparfait, -e [ɛ̃parfɛ, -ɛt] **1** adj **(a)** (qui a des défauts) imperfect **(b)** (inachevé) unfinished **2** nm Gram imperfect (tense); **à l'i.** in the imperfect (tense)
impartial, -e, -aux, -ales [ɛ̃parsjal, -o] adj impartial, unbiased
impartialité [ɛ̃parsjalite] nf impartiality
impartir [ɛ̃partir] vt Litt **i. qch à qn** (droit) to grant sth to sb; (tâche) to assign sth to sb; **dans le délai imparti** within the time allowed; **le temps qui vous est imparti** the time allotted to you
impasse [ɛ̃pas] nf **(a)** (cul-de-sac) dead end, cul de sac; Fig impasse, deadlock; Fig **être dans une i.** to be deadlocked; Fig **sortir de l'i.** to break the deadlock **(b) faire une i.** (en révisant) = to miss out part of a subject when revising
impassibilité [ɛ̃pasibilite] nf impassiveness
impassible [ɛ̃pasibl] adj impassive
impatiemment [ɛ̃pasjamɑ̃] adv impatiently
impatience [ɛ̃pasjɑ̃s] nf impatience; **avec i.** impatiently
impatient, -e [ɛ̃pasjɑ̃, -ɑ̃t] **1** adj impatient; **d'un air i.** impatiently; **être i. de faire qch** to be impatient to do sth **2** nf **impatiente** (plante) Busy Lizzie
impatienter [ɛ̃pasjɑ̃te] **1** vt to annoy, to irritate **2 s'impatienter** vpr to get impatient **(de/contre** at/with)
impavide [ɛ̃pavid] adj Litt impassive
impayable [ɛ̃pɛjabl] adj Fam (histoire, personne) priceless
impayé, -e [ɛ̃peje] **1** adj unpaid **2** nm outstanding payment
impec [ɛ̃pɛk] adj Fam spotless; **i.!** (parfait) great!
impeccable [ɛ̃pɛkabl] adj impeccable; **d'une propreté i.** impeccably clean; **i.!** (parfait) great!
impeccablement [ɛ̃pɛkabləmɑ̃] adv impeccably
impénétrable [ɛ̃penetrabl] adj **(a)** (forêt, citadelle) impenetrable **(b)** (visage, caractère, air) inscrutable; (mystère, texte) impenetrable; **les voies du Seigneur sont impénétrables** God works in mysterious ways
impénitent, -e [ɛ̃penitɑ̃, -ɑ̃t] adj unrepentant
impensable [ɛ̃pɑ̃sabl] adj unthinkable; **il est i. que vous ne soyez pas remplacé** it's unthinkable that they're not going to replace you
imper [ɛ̃pɛr] nm Fam raincoat, Br mac
impératif, -ive [ɛ̃peratif, -iv] **1** adj **(a)** (ton, geste) imperious **(b)** (nécessité, besoin) imperative; **il est i. de connaître le francais** it is imperative to know French **2** nm **(a)** (exigence) requirement; **savoir nager est un i.** it is essential to be able to swim; **les impératifs de la mode** the dictates of fashion **(b)** Gram imperative (mood); **à l'i.** in the imperative (mood)
impérativement [ɛ̃perativmɑ̃] adv **il faut i. que je la voie** it is imperative that I see her
impératrice [ɛ̃peratris] nf empress
imperceptible [ɛ̃pɛrsɛptibl] adj imperceptible (à to)
imperceptiblement [ɛ̃pɛrsɛptibləmɑ̃] adv imperceptibly
imperdable [ɛ̃pɛrdabl] adj **le match/le procès est i.** the match/the case can't be lost
imperfectible [ɛ̃pɛrfɛktibl] adj imperfectible
imperfection [ɛ̃pɛrfɛksjɔ̃] nf imperfection
impérial, -e, -aux, -ales [ɛ̃perjal, -o] **1** adj aussi Fig imperial **2** nf **impériale** (d'un bus) top deck
impérialisme [ɛ̃perjalism] nm imperialism
impérialiste [ɛ̃perjalist] adj & nmf imperialist
impérieux, -euse [ɛ̃perjø, -øz] adj **(a)** (autoritaire) imperious **(b)** (nécessité, désir, besoin) urgent, pressing

impérissable [ɛ̃perisabl] adj (œuvre, souvenir) enduring; **ça ne m'a pas laissé un souvenir i.** it didn't make a lasting impression on me
imperméabilisant, -e [ɛ̃pɛrmeabilizɑ̃, -ɑ̃t] **1** adj waterproofing **2** nm waterproofing agent
imperméabiliser [ɛ̃pɛrmeabilize] vt to waterproof
imperméable [ɛ̃pɛrmeabl] **1** adj impermeable; (à l'eau) waterproof; Fig **être i. à qch** to be impervious to sth **2** nm raincoat, Br mackintosh
impersonnel, -elle [ɛ̃pɛrsɔnɛl] adj impersonal
impertinemment [ɛ̃pɛrtinamɑ̃] adv impertinently
impertinence [ɛ̃pɛrtinɑ̃s] nf impertinence; **avec i.** impertinently
impertinent, -e [ɛ̃pɛrtinɑ̃, -ɑ̃t] **1** adj impertinent **2** nm,f impertinent person; **un petit i.** an impertinent little boy
imperturbable [ɛ̃pɛrtyrbabl] adj (personne) imperturbable; (optimisme) unshakeable
imperturbablement [ɛ̃pɛrtyrbabləmɑ̃] adv imperturbably
impétigo [ɛ̃petigo] nm impetigo
impétueusement [ɛ̃petɥøzmɑ̃] adv impetuously
impétueux, -euse [ɛ̃petɥø, -øz] adj **(a)** (personne) impetuous; (tempérament) fiery **(b)** Litt (torrent) raging
impétuosité [ɛ̃petɥozite] nf (fougue) impetuosity
impie [ɛ̃pi] Litt **1** adj impious **2** nmf impious person
impitoyable [ɛ̃pitwajabl] adj merciless
impitoyablement [ɛ̃pitwajabləmɑ̃] adv mercilessly
implacable [ɛ̃plakabl] adj (personne, vengeance, logique) implacable; (avancée) relentless
implant [ɛ̃plɑ̃] nm implant; **i. mammaire** breast implant; **implants (capillaires)** hair graft
implantation [ɛ̃plɑ̃tasjɔ̃] nf **(a)** (installation) establishment **(b)** (des cheveux) line, (des dents) arch
implanter [ɛ̃plɑ̃te] **1** vt **(a)** (installer) to establish **(b)** (chirurgicalement) to implant **2 s'implanter** vpr to become established
implication [ɛ̃plikasjɔ̃] nf **(a)** (engagement) involvement **(b)** implications (conséquences) implications
implicite [ɛ̃plisit] adj implicit
implicitement [ɛ̃plisitmɑ̃] adv implicitly
impliquer [ɛ̃plike] **1** vt **(a)** (compromettre) to implicate (dans in) **(b)** (supposer) to imply; **i. que** to imply that **2 s'impliquer** vpr to get involved (dans in)
implorer [ɛ̃plɔre] vt to implore, to beseech; **i. le pardon de qn** to beg sb's forgiveness; **i. qn de faire qch** to implore or beseech sb to do sth
imploser [ɛ̃ploze] vi to implode
implosion [ɛ̃plozjɔ̃] nf implosion
impoli, -e [ɛ̃pɔli] adj impolite, rude
impoliment [ɛ̃pɔlimɑ̃] adv impolitely, rudely
impolitesse [ɛ̃pɔlitɛs] nf **(a)** (d'une personne, d'une remarque) impoliteness, rudeness **(b)** (acte) impolite act; (remarque) rude remark
impondérable [ɛ̃pɔ̃derabl] adj & nm imponderable
impopulaire [ɛ̃pɔpylɛr] adj unpopular
import [ɛ̃pɔr] nm import; Ordinat **i. de données** data import
importable [ɛ̃pɔrtabl] adj (vêtement) unwearable
importance [ɛ̃pɔrtɑ̃s] nf **(a)** (d'un événement, d'un acte, d'une personne) importance; **avoir de l'i. (pour)** to be

important (to); **sans i.** unimportant; **cela n'a aucune i.** it's of no importance; **cela n'a aucune i.** it's capitale it's extremely important; **de la première** ou **de la plus haute i.** extremely important; **attacher** ou **donner de l'i. à qch** to attach importance to sth; **et alors, quelle i.?** well, so what? **(b)** *(d'une ville, d'une somme, d'un projet)* size; *(de dégâts, d'une catastrophe)* extent; **prendre de l'i.** *(société)* to expand; *(mouvement, parti)* to gain ground

important, -e [ɛ̃pɔrtɑ̃, -ɑ̃t] **1** *adj* **(a)** *(événement, acte, personne)* important **(pour** to); **il est i. que vous le sachiez** it's important for you to know; **peu i.** unimportant; **se donner des airs importants** to give oneself airs **(b)** *(ville, projet)* large; *(somme d'argent, dégâts, retard)* considerable; *(chiffre)* high
2 *nm,f Péj* **faire l'i.** to act important
3 *nm* **l'i.,** c'est que tu sois satisfait the important thing is that you're satisfied

importateur, -trice [ɛ̃pɔrtatœr, -tris] **1** *nm,f* importer **2** *adj* importing; **les pays importateurs de pétrole** oil-importing countries

importation [ɛ̃pɔrtasjɔ̃] *nf* **(a)** *(de marchandises)* importing; **articles** ou **produits d'i.** imports; **licence d'i.** import licence **(b)** *(produit)* import

importer¹ [ɛ̃pɔrte] *vt* **(a)** *(marchandises)* to import **(b)** *Ordinat* to download

importer² **1** *vi (compter)* to matter **(à** to); **ce qui importe, c'est que tu viennes** the important thing is that you come **2** *v impersonnel* **(a)** *(être important)* **il importe que vous y soyez** it's important that you're there; **peu importe** it doesn't matter; **peu m'importe** I don't mind; **qu'importe?** what does it matter? **(b)** **faire qch n'importe où/quand/comment** to do sth anywhere/any time/anyhow; *Fam* **n'importe comment,** c'est trop tard anyway, it's too late; **n'importe** never mind; **n'importe quel homme** any man; **n'importe qui** anyone, anybody; **n'importe qui d'autre** anyone else; **n'importe quoi** anything; *Péj* **dire/écrire n'importe quoi** to talk/write nonsense; *Fam* **n'importe quoi!** rubbish!

import-export [ɛ̃pɔrɛkspɔr] *nm* import-export business

importun, -e [ɛ̃pɔrtœ̃, -yn] **1** *adj (personne, visiteur, question)* importunate; *(arrivée, remarque)* ill-timed **2** *nm,f (personne)* nuisance

importuner [ɛ̃pɔrtyne] *vt Formel* to bother

imposable [ɛ̃pozabl] *adj* taxable

imposant, -e [ɛ̃pozɑ̃, -ɑ̃t] *adj* imposing

imposé, -e [ɛ̃poze] *adj (taxé)* taxed; **être i. à la source** to be taxed at source

imposer [ɛ̃poze] **1** *vt* **(a)** *(une condition)* to impose **(à** on); **i. une tâche à qn** to set sb a task; **i. le respect** to command respect; **i. sa loi** to lay down the law; **i. le silence à qn** to make sb keep quiet; **i. sa présence à qn** to impose on sb **(b)** *(soumettre à l'impôt)* to tax **2** *vi* **en i.** to be impressive; **en i. à qn** to impress sb **3** **s'imposer** *vpr* **(a)** *(faire reconnaître sa valeur)* to assert oneself; *(gagner)* to win **(b)** *(déranger)* **je ne voulais pas m'i.** I didn't want to impose **(c)** *(être nécessaire)* to be essential; **prendre les mesures qui s'imposent** to take the necessary steps **(d)** *(se contraindre)* **s'i. un sacrifice** to force oneself to make a sacrifice; **s'i. de faire qch** to make it a rule to do sth

imposition [ɛ̃pozisjɔ̃] *nf (taxation)* taxation

impossibilité [ɛ̃posibilite] *nf* impossibility; **être** ou **se trouver dans l'i. de faire qch** to find it impossible to do sth

impossible [ɛ̃posibl] **1** *adj* impossible; **i. à lire** impossible to read; **il est i. qu'il revienne avant lundi** he can't possibly be back before Monday; **il m'est i. de le faire** it's impossible for me to do it; **i. n'est pas français** there's no such word as can't; **rendre la vie i. à qn** to make life impossible for sb; **tu es i.!** you're impossible! **2** *nm* **tenter/demander l'i.** to attempt/to ask the impossible; **faire l'i. pour faire qch** to do everything possible to do sth

imposteur [ɛ̃pɔstœr] *nm* impostor

imposture [ɛ̃pɔstyr] *nf* deception

impôt [ɛ̃po] *nm* tax; **payer 200 euros d'impôts** to pay 200 euros in tax; *Fam* **les impôts m'ont envoyé une lettre** the tax man has sent me a letter; **i. direct/indirect** direct/indirect tax; **i. foncier** land tax; **i. sur les grandes fortunes** wealth tax; **impôts locaux** local taxes; **i. sur le revenu** income tax; **i. sur les sociétés** corporation tax

impotence [ɛ̃pɔtɑ̃s] *nf (infirmité)* disability; *(due à la vieillesse)* infirmity

impotent, -e [ɛ̃pɔtɑ̃, -ɑ̃t] **1** *adj (infirme)* disabled; *(à cause de la vieillesse)* infirm **2** *nm,f (infirme)* disabled person; *(vieillard)* infirm person

impraticable [ɛ̃pratikabl] *adj* **(a)** *(où l'on ne peut pas passer)* impassable **(b)** *(terrain de sport)* unfit for play **(c)** *(irréalisable)* impracticable

imprécation [ɛ̃prekasjɔ̃] *nf Litt* imprecation

imprécis, -e [ɛ̃presi, -iz] *adj* imprecise

imprécision [ɛ̃presizjɔ̃] *nf* imprecision

imprégner [34] [ɛ̃preɲe] **1** *vt* **(a)** *(sujet: eau, odeur)* to impregnate **(b)** *Fig (influencer)* **être imprégné de qch** to be full of sth **2** **s'imprégner** *vpr* **(a)** *(s'imbiber)* to become impregnated *(de* with); **s'i. d'eau** to become soaked with water **(b)** *Fig* **s'i. d'un auteur** to immerse oneself in an author

imprenable [ɛ̃prɔnabl] *adj* **(a)** *(forteresse, ville)* impregnable **(b)** *(vue)* unobstructed

imprésario [ɛ̃presarjo] *nm* manager

imprescriptible [ɛ̃prɛskriptibl] *adj Jur* imprescriptible

impression [ɛ̃presjɔ̃] *nf* **(a)** *(sensation)* impression; **donner à qn l'i. que** to give sb the impression that; **faire bonne/mauvaise/forte i. (à** qn) to make a good/bad/strong impression (on sb); **ça m'a fait une drôle d'i.** it gave me a funny feeling; **j'ai l'i. de l'avoir déjà vue** I've a feeling that I've seen her before; **j'ai l'i. qu'elle est jalouse** I have the impression that she's jealous **(b)** *(action d'imprimer)* printing; *(copie)* printout; *Ordinat* **i. écran** screen dump; **i. laser** laser printing; *(copie)* laser printout **(c)** *(motif)* **tissu à impressions florales** material with a floral pattern

impressionnable [ɛ̃presjɔnabl] *adj (personne)* impressionable

impressionnant, -e [ɛ̃presjɔnɑ̃, -ɑ̃t] *adj (imposant)* impressive; *(bouleversant)* upsetting

impressionner [ɛ̃presjɔne] *vt* **(a)** *(frapper)* to impress; *(bouleverser)* to upset; **se laisser i.** to let oneself be overawed **(b)** *Phot (pellicule)* to expose

impressionnisme [ɛ̃presjɔnism] *nm* impressionism

impressionniste [ɛ̃presjɔnist] *adj & nmf* impressionist

imprévisible [ɛ̃previzibl] *adj (temps, réaction, personne)* unpredictable; *(événement)* unforeseeable

imprévoyance [ɛ̃prevwajɑ̃s] *nf* lack of foresight

imprévoyant, -e [ɛ̃prevwajɑ̃, -ɑ̃t] *adj* lacking in foresight

imprévu, -e [ɛ̃prevy] **1** *adj* unexpected, unforeseen **2** *nm* **(a)** *(surprise)* **aimer l'i.** to like the unexpected; **un voyage plein d'i.** a journey full of surprises **(b)** *(incident)* unexpected or unforeseen event; **sauf i., à moins d'un i.** unless something unexpected happens

imprimable [ɛ̃primabl] *adj* printable

imprimante [ɛ̃primɑ̃t] *nf* printer; **i. à aiguilles** 24 pin printer; **i. feuille à feuille** sheet-fed printer; **i. graphique** graphics printer; **i. à jet d'encre** ink-jet printer; **i. (à) laser** laser printer

imprimé, -e [ɛ̃prime] **1** *adj* printed
2 *nm* (**a**) *(formulaire)* form; **imprimés** *(journaux, prospectus)* printed matter (**b**) *(sur un tissu)* print; **un i. à fleurs/à motifs géométriques** a floral/geometric print

imprimer [ɛ̃prime] *vt* (**a**) *(livre)* to print; *Ordinat* to print (out); *Ordinat* **i. un écran** to do a print screen (**b**) *(motif, empreinte, tissu)* to print (**c**) *(mouvement)* to impart (**à** to)

imprimerie [ɛ̃primri] *nf* (**a**) *(technique)* printing (**b**) *(atelier, usine)* printing works; **l'I. nationale** = French government printing office

imprimeur [ɛ̃primœr] *nm* printer

improbable [ɛ̃prɔbabl] *adj* improbable, unlikely

improductif, -ive [ɛ̃prɔdyktif, -iv] *adj* unproductive

impromptu, -e [ɛ̃prɔ̃pty] *adj* & *nm* impromptu

imprononçable [ɛ̃prɔnɔ̃sabl] *adj* unpronounceable

impropre [ɛ̃prɔpr] *adj* (**a**) *(incorrect)* incorrect (**b**) *(inadapté)* **i. à qch** unfit for sth; **i. à la consommation** unfit for human consumption

improprement [ɛ̃prɔprəmɑ̃] *adv* incorrectly

improvisation [ɛ̃prɔvizasjɔ̃] *nf* improvisation; **faire une i.** to improvise

improvisé, -e [ɛ̃prɔvize] *adj* improvised

improviser [ɛ̃prɔvize] **1** *vt* & *vi* to improvise
2 s'improviser *vpr* **un départ en vacances, ça ne s'improvise pas** going on holiday isn't something you can do just like that

improviste [ɛ̃prɔvist] **à l'improviste** *adv* unexpectedly

imprudemment [ɛ̃prydamɑ̃] *adv* *(parler, agir)* rashly; *(conduire)* recklessly

imprudence [ɛ̃prydɑ̃s] *nf* (**a**) *(d'un acte, d'une personne)* rashness (**b**) *(acte)* **commettre une i.** to act rashly

imprudent, -e [ɛ̃prydɑ̃, -ɑ̃t] **1** *adj* rash; *(conducteur)* reckless
2 *nm,f* rash person

impubliable [ɛ̃pyblijabl] *adj* unpublishable

impudence [ɛ̃pydɑ̃s] *nf* impudence

impudent, -e [ɛ̃pydɑ̃, -ɑ̃t] *adj* impudent

impudeur [ɛ̃pydœr] *nf* shamelessness

impudique [ɛ̃pydik] *adj* shameless

impuissance [ɛ̃pɥisɑ̃s] *nf* (**a**) *(incapacité)* powerlessness (**à faire qch** to do sth) (**b**) *(sexuelle)* impotence

impuissant, -e [ɛ̃pɥisɑ̃, -ɑ̃t] **1** *adj* (**a**) *(désarmé)* powerless (**b**) *(sexuellement)* impotent
2 *nm* impotent man

impulsif, -ive [ɛ̃pylsif, -iv] **1** *adj* impulsive
2 *nm,f* impulsive person

impulsion [ɛ̃pylsjɔ̃] *nf* (**a**) *Tech* impulse (**b**) *Fig (élan)* impulse; **faire qch sous l'i. de la colère** to do sth in a fit of anger (**c**) *(essor)* impetus

impulsivité [ɛ̃pylsivite] *nf* impulsiveness

impunément [ɛ̃pynemɑ̃] *adv* with impunity

impuni, -e [ɛ̃pyni] *adj* unpunished

impunité [ɛ̃pynite] *nf* impunity; **agir en toute i.** to act with impunity

impur, -e [ɛ̃pyr] *adj* impure

imputable [ɛ̃pytabl] *adj* (**a**) *(erreur)* attributable (**à** to) (**b**) *Fin* chargeable (**sur** to)

imputer [ɛ̃pyte] *vt* (**a**) *(crime, erreur)* **i. qch à qn** to attribute sth to sb (**b**) *Fin* **i. des frais sur un compte** to charge expenses to an account

inabordable [inabɔrdabl] *adj (endroit)* inaccessible; *(prix, marchandises)* unaffordable; *(personne)* unapproachable

inacceptable [inaksɛptabl] *adj* unacceptable

inaccessible [inaksesibl] *adj* (**a**) *(lieu)* inaccessible; *(objectif)* unattainable (**b**) *(personne)* unapproachable (**c**) *(insensible)* **i. à la pitié** incapable of pity; **i. à la flatterie** impervious to flattery

inachevé, -e [inaʃəve] *adj* unfinished

inactif, -ive [inaktif, -iv] **1** *adj* (**a**) *(personne)* inactive; *Écon* **la population inactive** the non-working population (**b**) *(remède)* ineffective
2 *nm,f* **un i.** a person without paid employment; **les inactifs** the non-working population

inaction [inaksjɔ̃] *nf* inaction

inactivité [inaktivite] *nf* inactivity

inadapté, -e [inadapte] **1** *adj (personne) (socialement)* maladjusted; *(physiquement, mentalement)* handicapped; *(matériel)* unsuitable (**à** for)
2 *nm,f (socialement)* maladjusted person; *(physiquement, mentalement)* handicapped person; **les inadaptés** the maladjusted/handicapped

inadéquation [inadekwasjɔ̃] *nf* inadequacy

inadmissible [inadmisibl] *adj* inadmissible

inadvertance [inadvɛrtɑ̃s] **par inadvertance** *adv* inadvertently

inaliénable [inaljenabl] *adj* *Jur (droit)* inalienable

inaltérable [inalterabl] *adj* (**a**) *(métal, revêtement)* stable (**b**) *Fig (constant)* unwavering

inamical, -e, -aux, -ales [inamikal, -o] *adj* unfriendly

inamovible [inamɔvibl] *adj* (**a**) *(four, autoradio)* built-in (**b**) *(juge, magistrat)* permanent

inanimé, -e [inanime] *adj* (**a**) *(mort)* lifeless; *(inconscient)* unconscious; **tomber i.** to fall down in a faint (**b**) *(objet)* inanimate

inanité [inanite] *nf (d'un effort)* futility; *(d'une conversation)* inanity

inanition [inanisjɔ̃] *nf* starvation; **mourir d'i.** to die of starvation

inaperçu, -e [inapɛrsy] *adj* **passer i.** to go unnoticed

inapplicable [inaplikabl] *adj (réforme, loi)* unenforceable; *(théorie)* inapplicable

inappréciable [inapresjabl] *adj (précieux)* invaluable

inapte [inapt] *adj (pour raisons médicales)* unfit; *(intellectuellement)* unsuited; **être i. à qch/à faire qch** *(pour raisons médicales)* to be unfit for sth/to do sth; *(intellectuellement)* to be unsuited for sth/to do sth; **être i.** *(au service) (appelé)* to be unfit (for service)

inarticulé, -e [inartikyle] *adj (son, cris)* inarticulate

inassouvi, -e [inasuvi] *adj (faim, désir, vengeance)* unsatisfied; *(soif)* unquenched

inattaquable [inatakabl] *adj* unassailable

inattendu, -e [inatɑ̃dy] *adj* unexpected

inattentif, -ive [inatɑ̃tif, -iv] *adj (distrait)* inattentive; **i. à qch** *(indifférent)* heedless of sth

inattention [inatɑ̃sjɔ̃] *nf* lack of attention; **un moment d'i.** a lapse of concentration

inaudible [inodibl] *adj* inaudible

inaugural, -e, -aux, -ales [inogyral, -o] *adj (discours, séance)* inaugural

inauguration [inogyrasjɔ̃] *nf (d'un bâtiment, d'une route)* (official) opening, inauguration; *(d'une statue, d'un monument)* unveiling

inaugurer [inogyʀe] *vt(bâtiment, route)* to officially open, to inaugurate; *(statue, monument)* to unveil; *Fig (politique, méthode)* to implement; *(époque)* to usher in

inavouable [inavwabl] *adj* shameful

inavoué, -e [inavwe] *adj* unconfessed

INC [iɛnse] *nm (abrév* **Institut national de la consommation)** = national institute for consumer advice

inca [ɛ̃ka] **1** *adj* Inca
2 *nmf* I. Inca

incalculable [ɛ̃kalkylabl] *adj* incalculable; **un nombre i. de fois** countless times

incandescence [ɛ̃kɑ̃desɑ̃s] *nf* incandescence

incandescent, -e [ɛ̃kɑ̃desɑ̃, -ɑ̃t] *adj* incandescent

incantation [ɛ̃kɑ̃tasjɔ̃] *nf* incantation

incantatoire [ɛ̃kɑ̃tatwar] *adj* incantatory

incapable [ɛ̃kapabl] **1** *adj* **(a)** *(personne)* incapable, incompetent; *Jur* incompetent **(b)** **être i. de faire qch** to be incapable of doing sth; **i. de lâcheté** incapable of cowardice
2 *nmf* **(a)** *(incompétent)* incompetent **(b)** *Jur* incompetent person

incapacité [ɛ̃kapasite] *nf* **(a)** *(impossibilité)* **i. à faire qch** inability to do sth; **être dans l'i. de faire qch** to be unable to do sth **(b)** *(incompétence)* incompetence **(c)** *(invalidité)* disability; **i. de travail** unfitness for work **(d)** *Jur* incompetence

incarcération [ɛ̃karserasjɔ̃] *nf* incarceration

incarcérer [34] [ɛ̃karsere] *vt* to incarcerate

incarnation [ɛ̃karnasjɔ̃] *nf aussi Fig* incarnation

incarné, -e [ɛ̃karne] *adj* **(a)** *Rel & Fig* incarnate **(b)** *(ongle)* ingrowing

incarner [ɛ̃karne] **1** *vt* **(a)** *(représenter)* to embody **(b)** *Th & Cin* **i.** **(le rôle de) qn** to play (the part of) sb
2 s'incarner *vpr* **(a)** *Rel* to become incarnate **(b)** *(ongle)* to become ingrown

incartade [ɛ̃kartad] *nf* indiscretion

incassable [ɛ̃kasabl] *adj* unbreakable

incendiaire [ɛ̃sɑ̃djɛr] **1** *adj (bombe)* incendiary; *Fig (discours)* inflammatory
2 *nmf (personne)* arsonist, fire-raiser

incendie [ɛ̃sɑ̃di] *nm* fire; **i. de forêt** forest fire; **un i. criminel** arson

incendier [66] [ɛ̃sɑ̃dje] *vt* **(a)** *(mettre le feu à)* to set on fire **(b)** *Fam (accabler de reproches)* **i. qn** to haul sb over the coals; **se faire i.** to get hauled over the coals

incertain, -e [ɛ̃sɛrtɛ̃, -ɛn] *adj (fait, donnée, résultat)* uncertain; *(temps)* unsettled; *(mémoire)* unreliable; *(personne)* indecisive; *(démarche, pas)* unsteady; *(couleur)* vague

incertitude [ɛ̃sɛrtityd] *nf* uncertainty; **être dans l'i. (quant à)** to be uncertain (about)

incessamment [ɛ̃sesamɑ̃] *adv* very soon

incessant, -e [ɛ̃sesɑ̃, -ɑ̃t] *adj* incessant, constant

incessible [ɛ̃sesibl] *adj (pension, titre de propriété)* non-transferable; *(droit)* inalienable

inceste [ɛ̃sɛst] *nm* incest

incestueux, -euse [ɛ̃sɛstɥø, -øz] *adj* incestuous; **enfant i.** child of an incestuous relationship

inchangé, -e [ɛ̃ʃɑ̃ʒe] *adj* unchanged

incidemment [ɛ̃sidamɑ̃] *adv* in passing

incidence [ɛ̃sidɑ̃s] *nf* **(a)** *(répercussion)* impact **(sur** on) **(b)** *Méd & Phys* incidence

incident, -e [ɛ̃sidɑ̃, -ɑ̃t] **1** *nm* **(a)** *(événement sans conséquence)* hitch; **se dérouler sans i.** to go off without

incident; **i. de parcours** minor setback; **i. technique** technical hitch **(b)** *(événement plus grave)* incident; **i. diplomatique** diplomatic incident
2 *adj (question, remarque)* incidental

incinérateur [ɛ̃sineratœr] *nm* incinerator

incinération [ɛ̃sinerasjɔ̃] *nf (de déchets)* incineration; *(d'une personne)* cremation

incinérer [34] [ɛ̃sinere] *vt (déchets)* to incinerate; *(personne)* to cremate

inciser [ɛ̃size] *vt (peau)* to make an incision in; *(abcès)* to lance

incisif, -ive [ɛ̃sizif, -iv] **1** *adj (remarque, personne, style)* incisive
2 *nf* **incisive** incisor

incision [ɛ̃sizjɔ̃] *nf* incision

incitation [ɛ̃sitasjɔ̃] *nf (à la violence, l'émeute)* incitement; *(encouragement)* incentive; **i. fiscale** tax incentive; **i. à l'achat** incentive to buy; **i. de mineurs à la débauche** corruption of minors

inciter [ɛ̃site] *vt* **i. qn à faire qch** to encourage sb to do sth; **i. qn à la prudence/la clémence** *(sujet : événement)* to incline sb to be cautious/merciful

inclassable [ɛ̃klasabl] *adj* unclassifiable; **un roman/ peintre i.** a novel/painter that cannot be pigeonholed

inclinable [ɛ̃klinabl] *adj (siège, dossier)* reclining

inclinaison [ɛ̃klinɛzɔ̃] *nf (d'un toit)* slope; *(d'une pente)* incline; *(de la tête, d'un chapeau)* tilt

inclination [ɛ̃klinasjɔ̃] *nf* **(a)** **i. de la tête** *(pour saluer)* nod **(b)** *(tendance)* inclination **(pour** for)

incliné, -e [ɛ̃kline] *adj (mât, toit)* sloping; *(table à dessin, dossier)* tilted

incliner [ɛ̃kline] **1** *vt* **(a)** *(pencher)* to tilt; **i. la tête** *(en avant)* to bow one's head; *(en signe de salut)* to nod; *(sur le côté)* to tilt one's head to one side **(b)** *(pousser)* **i. qn à faire qch** to incline sb to do sth; **i. qn à la prudence/la clémence** to incline sb to be cautious/merciful
2 s'incliner *vpr* **(a)** *(terrain)* to slant, to slope; *(bateau)* to heel *or* keel over; *(avion)* to bank **(b)** *(se pencher)* *(en avant)* to lean forward; *(sur le côté)* to lean to one side; *(pour saluer)* to bow; *Fig* **s'i. devant qch** to bow to sth **(c)** *(se soumettre)* to give in **(devant** to) **(d)** *(être battu)* to lose **(devant** to)

inclure [17] [ɛ̃klyr] *vt* **(a)** *(dans un courrier)* to enclose **(dans** with) **(b)** *(englober, insérer) & Math* to include

inclus, -e [ɛ̃kly, -yz] *adj* **(a)** *(compris)* **jusqu'à la page 5 incluse** up to and including page 5; **jusqu'au mardi i.** *Br* up to and including Tuesday, *Am* through Tuesday; **du 7 au 18 i.** from the 7th to the 18th inclusive; **ils seront 35, enfants i.** there will be 35 of them, including the children **(b)** *(dent)* impacted

inclusion [ɛ̃klyzjɔ̃] *nf* **(a)** *(dans un courrier)* enclosure **(dans** with) **(b)** *(insertion)* insertion **(c)** *(objet décoratif)* = flower, shell etc set into plastic and used as a paperweight, an ornament, jewellery etc **(d)** *(d'une dent)* impacting **(e)** *Ordinat (de fichier)* insertion

incognito [ɛ̃kɔɲito] **1** *adv* incognito
2 *nm* **garder l'i.** to remain incognito

incohérence [ɛ̃kɔerɑ̃s] *nf (d'une personne, dans un film, une histoire)* inconsistency; *(d'un discours, d'idées)* incoherence

incohérent, -e [ɛ̃kɔerɑ̃, -ɑ̃t] *adj (personne, histoire, attitude)* inconsistent; *(idées, argumentation, discours)* incoherent; **tenir des propos incohérents** to talk incoherently

incollable [ɛ̃kɔlabl] *adj* **(a)** *(riz)* non-stick **(b)** *Fam (personne)* **elle est i. sur la question/en histoire** you can't catch her out on the subject/on history

incolore [ɛ̃kɔlɔr] *adj* colourless

incomber [ɛ̃kɔ̃be] **incomber à** *vt ind (responsabilité)* to lie with; *(devoirs)* to fall to; **il m'incombe/il lui incombe de…** it falls to me/to him to…

incombustible [ɛ̃kɔ̃bystibl] *adj* incombustible

incommensurable [ɛ̃kɔmɑ̃syrabl] *adj (richesse)* immeasurable; *(espace)* boundless; *Hum* **être d'une bêtise i.** to be incredibly stupid

incommodant, -e [ɛ̃kɔmɔdɑ̃, -ɑ̃t] *adj* discomforting

incommode [ɛ̃kɔmɔd] *adj (horaire, arrangement)* inconvenient; *(situation)* awkward

incommoder [ɛ̃kɔmɔde] *vt* to bother

incomparable [ɛ̃kɔ̃parabl] *adj (sans pareil)* beyond compare, matchless

incomparablement [ɛ̃kɔ̃parablomɑ̃] *adv* incomparably

incompatibilité [ɛ̃kɔ̃patibilite] *nf* incompatibility; **i. d'humeur** *ou* **de caractère** mutual incompatibility

incompatible [ɛ̃kɔ̃patibl] *adj* incompatible **(avec** with)

incompétence [ɛ̃kɔ̃petɑ̃s] *nf* incompetence

incompétent, -e [ɛ̃kɔ̃petɑ̃, -ɑ̃t] *adj* incompetent

incomplet, -ète [ɛ̃kɔ̃plɛ, -ɛt] *adj* incomplete

incompréhensible [ɛ̃kɔ̃preɑ̃sibl] *adj* incomprehensible

incompréhension [ɛ̃kɔ̃preɑ̃sjɔ̃] *nf* incomprehension

incompressible [ɛ̃kɔ̃prɛsibl] *adj* **(a)** *(matériau)* incompressible **(b)** *Jur (peine)* to be served in full **(c)** *(dépenses)* which cannot be reduced

incompris, -e [ɛ̃kɔ̃pri, -iz] **1** *adj* misunderstood **2** *nm,f* **être un i.** to be misunderstood

inconcevable [ɛ̃kɔ̃səvabl] *adj* inconceivable

inconciliable [ɛ̃kɔ̃siljabl] *adj (théorie)* irreconcilable **(avec** with); *(mode de vie, activité)* incompatible **(avec** with)

inconditionnel, -elle [ɛ̃kɔ̃disjɔnɛl] **1** *adj (soutien, retrait)* unconditional; *(obéissance)* unquestioning, unconditional; *(supporter)* staunch **2** *nm,f* fan; **c'est un i. de la pêche/du hard rock** he's absolutely mad about fishing/hard rock

inconfort [ɛ̃kɔ̃fɔr] *nm (matériel)* discomfort; *(moral)* awkwardness

inconfortable [ɛ̃kɔ̃fɔrtabl] *adj aussi Fig* uncomfortable

incongru, -e [ɛ̃kɔ̃gry] *adj* inappropriate; *(bruit)* rude

incongruité [ɛ̃kɔ̃grɥite] *nf* **(a)** *(manque d'à-propos)* inappropriateness **(b)** *(remarque déplacée)* inappropriate remark

inconnu, -e [ɛ̃kɔny] **1** *adj (auteur, civilisation, destination)* unknown **(de** to); *(lieu, visage)* strange; **il m'est i.** I've never heard of him/it; **né de père i.** *(sur document administratif)* father unknown; **i. à cette adresse** not known at this address; *Fam* **Durand? i. au bataillon!** Durand? never heard of him! **2** *nm,f (étranger)* stranger; *(personne non célèbre)* unknown **3** *nm* **la peur de l'i.** the fear of the unknown **4** *nf* **inconnue** *Math & Fig* unknown (quantity)

inconsciemment [ɛ̃kɔ̃sjamɑ̃] *adv* **(a)** *(sans réfléchir)* without thinking **(b)** *(dans l'inconscient)* subconsciously

inconscience [ɛ̃kɔ̃sjɑ̃s] *nf* **(a)** *(perte de connaissance)* unconsciousness; **sombrer** *ou* **tomber dans l'i.** to lose consciousness **(b)** *(manque de jugement)* recklessness; **c'est de l'i.!** it's sheer madness!

inconscient, -e [ɛ̃kɔ̃sjɑ̃, -ɑ̃t] **1** *adj* **(a)** *(évanoui)* unconscious **(b)** *(acte)* unconscious; **i. du danger** oblivious to the danger **(c)** *(irréfléchi) (personne)* reckless **2** *nm* **l'i.** the unconscious, the subconscious; **l'i. collectif** the collective unconscious

inconséquence [ɛ̃kɔ̃sekɑ̃s] *nf (caractère)* recklessness; *(acte)* reckless act

inconséquent, -e [ɛ̃kɔ̃sekɑ̃, -ɑ̃t] *adj* **(a)** *(irréfléchi)* reckless **(b)** *(illogique)* inconsistent

inconsidéré, -e [ɛ̃kɔ̃sidere] *adj (acte, remarque)* ill-considered; *(dépenses)* reckless

inconsistance [ɛ̃kɔ̃sistɑ̃s] *nf* **(a)** *(d'une pâte, d'une soupe)* thinness **(b)** *(d'une personne, d'une conduite)* inconsistency **(c)** *(d'une intrigue, d'un film, d'un roman)* thinness

inconsistant, -e [ɛ̃kɔ̃sistɑ̃, -ɑ̃t] *adj* **(a)** *(pâte, crème, soupe)* thin **(b)** *(conduite, personne)* inconsistent **(c)** *(intrigue, film, roman)* thin

inconsolable [ɛ̃kɔ̃sɔlabl] *adj* inconsolable

inconstance [ɛ̃kɔ̃stɑ̃s] *nf (instabilité)* changeableness; *(infidélité)* fickleness

inconstant, -e [ɛ̃kɔ̃stɑ̃, -ɑ̃t] *adj (instable)* changeable; *(infidèle)* fickle

inconstitutionnel, -elle [ɛ̃kɔ̃stitysjɔnɛl] *adj* unconstitutional

incontestable [ɛ̃kɔ̃tɛstabl] *adj* indisputable

incontestablement [ɛ̃kɔ̃tɛstabləmɑ̃] *adv* indisputably

incontesté, -e [ɛ̃kɔ̃tɛste] *adj* undisputed

incontinence [ɛ̃kɔ̃tinɑ̃s] *nf Méd* incontinence; **i. verbale** verbal diarrhoea

incontinent, -e [ɛ̃kɔ̃tinɑ̃, -ɑ̃t] *adj Méd* incontinent

incontournable [ɛ̃kɔ̃turnabl] *adj (film, artiste)* that cannot be ignored; **son argument était i.** there was no getting away from her argument

incontrôlable [ɛ̃kɔ̃trolabl] *adj* **(a)** *(incendie, bâillements)* uncontrollable; **des éléments incontrôlables** rowdy elements **(b)** *(affirmation)* unverifiable

incontrôlé, -e [ɛ̃kɔ̃trole] *adj (éléments, bande)* uncontrolled

inconvenance [ɛ̃kɔ̃vənɑ̃s] *nf (indécence)* impropriety; **dire/commettre une i.** to say/to do something improper

inconvenant, -e [ɛ̃kɔ̃vənɑ̃, -ɑ̃t] *adj (propos, remarque, acte)* improper

inconvénient [ɛ̃kɔ̃venjɑ̃] *nm* drawback, disadvantage; **je n'y vois pas d'i.** I have no objection

inconvertible [ɛ̃kɔ̃vɛrtibl] *adj (monnaie)* non-convertible

incorporation [ɛ̃kɔrpɔrasjɔ̃] *nf* **(a)** *(mélange)* blending, mixing **(de qch dans qch** of sth into sth) **(b)** *Mil* conscription

incorporé, -e [ɛ̃kɔrpɔre] *adj (flash, micro)* built-in

incorporer [ɛ̃kɔrpɔre] **1** *vt* **(a)** *(mélanger)* **i. qch à qch** to blend *or* mix sth into sth **(b)** *(insérer)* to insert **(à** in) **(c)** *(troupes)* to draft **2 s'incorporer** *vpr* **s'i. dans un groupe** to join a group

incorrect, -e [ɛ̃kɔrɛkt] *adj* **(a)** *(erroné)* incorrect, wrong **(b)** *(personne)* impolite; *(attitude)* improper **(c)** *(tenue, déplacée)* unsuitable; *(indécente)* improper

incorrectement [ɛ̃kɔrɛktəmɑ̃] *adv* **(a)** *(en faisant des erreurs)* incorrectly, wrongly **(b)** *(impoliment)* impolitely **(c)** *(habillé)* unsuitably; *(de façon déplacée)* unsuitably; *(de façon indécente)* improperly

incorrection [ɛ̃kɔrɛksjɔ̃] *nf* **(a)** *(impolitesse)* impoliteness **(b)** *(action)* impolite action; *(propos)* impolite remark **(c)** *(grammaticale)* mistake

incorrigible [ɛ̃kɔriʒibl] *adj* incorrigible

incorruptible [ɛ̃kɔryptibl] **1** *adj* incorruptible **2** *nmf* incorruptible person

incrédule [ɛ̃kredyl] *adj (sceptique)* incredulous; **d'un air i.** with a look of disbelief

incrédulité [ɛ̃kredylite] *nf* incredulity

increvable [ɛ̃krəvabl] *adj* **(a)** *(pneu)* puncture-proof **(b)** *Fam (personne)* tireless; *(voiture, moteur)* indestructible

incriminer [ɛ̃krimine] *vt (personne)* to accuse; *(sujet: événement)* to condemn; *(comportement, décision)* to condemn

incrochetable [ɛ̃krɔʃtabl] *adj* unpickable

incroyable [ɛ̃krwajabl] *adj* incredible; **c'est i., ça!** I don't believe it!

incroyablement [ɛ̃krwajabləmã] *adv* incredibly

incroyance [ɛ̃krwajãs] *nf* unbelief

incroyant, -e [ɛ̃krwajã, -ãt] **1** *adj* unbelieving **2** *nm,f* unbeliever

incrustation [ɛ̃krystasjɔ̃] *nf* **(a)** *(ornement)* inlay **(b)** *(dépôt calcaire)* fur, scale **(c)** *TV (image)* inset

incruster [ɛ̃kryste] **1** *vt* **(a)** *(bois, métal)* to inlay **(de** with) **(b)** *(entartrer)* to scale, to fur up **2 s'incruster** *vpr* **(a)** *(adhérer)* to become encrusted **(b)** *(chaudière, bouilloire)* to fur up **(c)** *Fam (s'imposer)* **quand on l'invite, il s'incruste** once you invite him you can't get rid of him

incubateur [ɛ̃kybatœr] *nm* incubator

incubation [ɛ̃kybasjɔ̃] *nf* incubation; **période d'i.** incubation period

incuber [ɛ̃kybe] *vt* to incubate, to hatch

inculpation [ɛ̃kylpasjɔ̃] *nf* indictment; **sous l'i. d'assassinat** charged with murder

inculpé, -e [ɛ̃kylpe] *nm,f* **l'i.** the accused

inculper [ɛ̃kylpe] *vt* to indict, to charge **(de** with)

inculquer [ɛ̃kylke] *vt* to instil **(à qn** in sb)

inculte [ɛ̃kylt] *adj (terre, personne)* uncultivated

incultivable [ɛ̃kyltivabl] *adj* untillable

inculture [ɛ̃kyltyr] *nf* lack of culture

incurable [ɛ̃kyrabl] **1** *adj* incurable; **d'une paresse i.** incurably lazy **2** *nmf* person with an incurable disease

incurie [ɛ̃kyri] *nf Formel* negligence

incursion [ɛ̃kyrsjɔ̃] *nf* **(a)** *(invasion)* raid, incursion **(b)** *Fig (entrée soudaine)* intrusion; **faire une i. dans une pièce/une réunion** to burst into a room/a meeting

incurvé, -e [ɛ̃kyrve] *adj* bent, curved

indatable [ɛ̃databl] *adj* that cannot be dated

Inde [ɛ̃d] *nf* **l'I.** India

indécence [ɛ̃desãs] *nf* indecency

indécent, -e [ɛ̃desã, -ãt] *adj* indecent

indéchiffrable [ɛ̃deʃifrabl] *adj* **(a)** *(illisible)* indecipherable **(b)** *(incompréhensible)* impenetrable

indéchirable [ɛ̃deʃirabl] *adj* tearproof

indécis, -e [ɛ̃desi, -iz] *adj* **(a)** *(personne) (de caractère)* indecisive; *(ponctuellement)* undecided; **je suis encore indécise** I haven't made my mind up yet **(b)** *(peu net) (victoire, bataille)* inconclusive; *(contour)* vague **2** *nm,f* indecisive person; *Pol* **les i.** the floating voters

indécision [ɛ̃desizjɔ̃] *nf (de caractère)* indecisiveness; *(ponctuelle)* indecision

indécrottable [ɛ̃dekrɔtabl] *adj Fam (incorrigible)* hopeless; **être d'une bêtise i.** to be hopelessly stupid

indéfendable [ɛ̃defɑ̃dabl] *adj* indefensible

indéfini, -e [ɛ̃defini] *adj* **(a)** *(illimité)* indefinite **(b)** *(imprécis) (tristesse, malaise)* vague, undefined **(c)** *Gram (pronom, article)* indefinite

indéfiniment [ɛ̃definimã] *adv* indefinitely

indéfinissable [ɛ̃definisabl] *adj* indefinable

indéformable [ɛ̃defɔrmabl] *adj* that keeps its shape

indélébile [ɛ̃delebil] *adj* indelible

indélicat, -e [ɛ̃delika, -at] *adj* **(a)** *(sans tact)* tactless, insensitive **(b)** *(malhonnête)* dishonest

indélicatesse [ɛ̃delikatɛs] *nf* **(a)** *(manque de tact)* tactlessness **(b)** *(malhonnêteté)* dishonesty; *(acte malhonnête)* dishonest act; **commettre une i.** to behave dishonestly

indemne [ɛ̃dɛmn] *adj* unharmed, unscathed

indemnisation [ɛ̃dɛmnizasjɔ̃] *nf* compensation

indemniser [ɛ̃dɛmnize] *vt* to compensate **(de** for)

indemnité [ɛ̃dɛmnite] *nf* **(a)** *(pour perte encourue)* compensation; *(pour délai, non-livraison)* penalty **(b)** *(allocation)* allowance; **i. journalière** daily allowance; **i. de licenciement** severance pay, redundancy payment; **i. parlementaire** = salary paid to member of French parliament; **i. de transport** travel allowance

indémodable [ɛ̃demɔdabl] *adj* perennially fashionable

indémontrable [ɛ̃demɔ̃trabl] *adj* unprovable

indéniable [ɛ̃denjabl] *adj* undeniable

indéniablement [ɛ̃denjabləmã] *adv* undeniably

indépendamment [ɛ̃depɑ̃damã] *adv* independently; **i. de** apart from

indépendance [ɛ̃depɑ̃dãs] *nf* independence; **accéder à l'i.** to gain independence

indépendant, -e [ɛ̃depɑ̃dã, -ãt] **1** *adj* **(a)** *(personne, pays, vie)* independent **(de** of); *(travailleur)* self-employed, freelance; *(appartement)* self-contained; **i. de ma volonté** beyond my control **(b)** *Gram* **proposition indépendante** main clause **2** *nm,f (travailleur)* self-employed person, freelancer

indépendantisme [ɛ̃depɑ̃dãtism] *nm* independence movement

indépendantiste [ɛ̃depɑ̃dãtist] *nmf Pol (partisan de l'indépendance)* supporter of independence; *(activiste)* freedom fighter

indéracinable [ɛ̃derasinabl] *adj (préjugés)* deep-rooted

indescriptible [ɛ̃dɛskriptibl] *adj* indescribable

indésirable [ɛ̃dezirabl] *adj & nmf* undesirable

indestructible [ɛ̃dɛstryktibl] *adj* indestructible

indétectable [ɛ̃detɛktabl] *adj* undetectable

indéterminé, -e [ɛ̃detɛrmine] *adj* **(a)** *(date, heure)* unspecified; *(raison)* unknown **(b)** *(personne)* undecided

index [ɛ̃dɛks] *nm* **(a)** *(doigt)* forefinger, index finger **(b)** *(de livre)* index; *Fig* **mettre qn/qch à l'i.** to blacklist sb/sth **(c)** *Ordinat* index

indexation [ɛ̃dɛksasjɔ̃] *nf Écon* index-linking; *Ordinat* indexing

indexer [ɛ̃dɛkse] *vt* **(a)** *Écon* to index-link **(sur** to) **(b)** *aussi Ordinat (ajouter un index à)* to index

indic [ɛ̃dik] *nm Fam* grass, informer

indicateur, -trice [ɛ̃dikatœr, -tris] **1** *adj voir* **panneau, poteau 2** *nm* **(a)** *(livre)* **i. des rues de Paris** Paris street finder; **i. des chemins de fer** railway timetable **(b)** *(instrument)* indicator, gauge; *Av* **i. d'altitude** altimeter; **i. de niveau de carburant** fuel gauge **(c)** *(informateur)* informer **(d)** *Écon* indicator

indicatif, -ive [ɛ̃dikatif, -iv] **1** *adj* indicative **(de** of); **à titre i.** as a guide **2** *nm* **(a)** *Gram* indicative (mood); **à l'i.** in the indicative **(b)** *Tél* dialling code; *TV & Rad* theme tune

indication [ɛ̃dikasjɔ̃] *nf* **(a)** *(action)* indication **(b)** *(renseignement)* (piece of) information **(c)** *(directive)* instruction, direction; **sauf i. contraire** unless otherwise specified; *Th* **indications scéniques** stage directions (**d**) *(sur notice pharmaceutique)* **indications:**... suitable for...

indice [ɛ̃dis] *nm* (**a**) *(signe)* sign, indication (**de** of); *(dans une enquête)* clue (**de** to) (**b**) *(chiffre indicateur) & Math* index; *Typ* subscript; *Aut* **i. d'octane** octane rating; **i. des prix** price index; **i. de protection** *(d'une crème solaire)* protection factor

indicible [ɛ̃disibl] *adj Litt* indescribable

indien, -enne [ɛ̃djɛ̃, -ɛn] **1** *adj* Indian **2** *nm,f* **I.** *(d'Inde, d'Amérique)* Indian

indifféremment [ɛ̃diferamɑ̃] *adv (sans distinction)* equally

indifférence [ɛ̃diferɑ̃s] *nf* indifference

indifférencié, -e [ɛ̃diferɑ̃sje] *adj* undifferentiated

indifférent, -e [ɛ̃diferɑ̃, -ɑ̃t] *adj* (**a**) *(peu ou pas intéressé)* indifferent (**à** to); **laisser qn i.** to leave sb cold; **il m'est i.** I'm indifferent to him (**b**) *(sans importance)* irrelevant; **cela m'est i.** it makes no difference to me; **parler de choses indifférentes** to chat about nothing in particular

indifférer [34] [ɛ̃difere] *vt* **cela m'indiffère** it's a matter of complete indifference to me

indigence [ɛ̃diʒɑ̃s] *nf* destitution

indigène [ɛ̃diʒɛn] *adj & nmf* native

indigent, -e [ɛ̃diʒɑ̃, -ɑ̃t] **1** *adj* destitute **2** *nm,f* pauper; **les indigents** the poor

indigeste [ɛ̃diʒɛst] *adj aussi Fig* indigestible

indigestion [ɛ̃diʒɛstjɔ̃] *nf* **avoir une i.** to have a stomach upset; **faire une i. de chocolat** to make oneself sick from eating chocolate; *Fig* **j'en ai une i.** I'm fed up with it

indignation [ɛ̃di ɲasjɔ̃] *nf* indignation

indigne [ɛ̃diɲ] *adj (personne)* unworthy (**de** of); *(action, conduite)* shameful

indigner [ɛ̃diɲe] **1** *vt* to outrage **2 s'indigner** *vpr* to be indignant (**de** at)

indignité [ɛ̃diɲite] *nf* (**a**) *(d'une personne)* unworthiness; *(d'une action)* shamefulness (**b**) *(action)* shameful act

indigo [ɛ̃digo] *nm & adj inv* indigo

indiqué, -e [ɛ̃dike] *adj (recommandé)* advisable; **il est tout à fait i. pour ce poste** he's the right person for the job

indiquer [ɛ̃dike] *vt* (**a**) *(montrer) (sujet: personne)* to point out; **i. qch du doigt** to point to or at sth; **i. le chemin à qn** to tell sb the way, to direct sb (**b**) *(marquer) (sujet: panneau, étiquette, carte)* to show, to indicate; *(sujet: compteur)* to read (**c**) *(donner) (date, adresse)* to give, **à l'heure indiquée** at the agreed time; **pourriez-vous m'i. le prix de ce vase?** could you tell me how much this vase costs? (**d**) *(recommander)* to recommend; **elle m'a indiqué un excellent dentiste/restaurant** she recommended me an excellent dentist/restaurant to me (**e**) *(dénoter)* to point to, to indicate

indirect, -e [ɛ̃dirɛkt] *adj aussi Gram* indirect

indirectement [ɛ̃dirɛktəmɑ̃] *adv* indirectly

indiscipline [ɛ̃disiplin] *nf* indiscipline

indiscipliné, -e [ɛ̃disipline] *adj* undisciplined; *(cheveux)* unmanageable

indiscret, -ète [ɛ̃diskrɛ, -ɛt] **1** *adj* (**a**) *(qui parle trop)* indiscreet (**b**) *(curieux)* inquisitive; **à l'abri des regards indiscrets** safe from prying eyes **2** *nm,f* (**a**) *(qui parle trop)* indiscreet person (**b**) *(curieux)* inquisitive person

indiscrétion [ɛ̃diskresjɔ̃] *nf* (**a**) *(manque de discrétion)* indiscretion (**b**) *(curiosité)* inquisitiveness; **sans i., combien l'avez-vous payé?** if you don't mind me asking, how much did you pay for it? (**c**) *(remarque)* indiscreet remark

indiscutable [ɛ̃diskytabl] *adj* indisputable

indiscutablement [ɛ̃diskytabləmɑ̃] *adv* indisputably

indispensable [ɛ̃dispɑ̃sabl] **1** *adj* indispensable, essential (**à qch** for sth); **i. à qn** indispensable to sb; **il est i. que tu y ailles** it is essential that you go **2** *nm* **l'i.** the essentials

indisponibilité [ɛ̃dispɔnibilite] *nf* unavailability

indisponible [ɛ̃dispɔnibl] *adj* unavailable

indisposé, -e [ɛ̃dispoze] *adj* indisposed, unwell; *Euph* **elle est indisposée** it's her time of the month

indisposer [ɛ̃dispoze] *vt* (**a**) *(rendre malade)* **i. qn** *(odeur, climat)* to make sb feel ill, *(nourriture)* to disagree with sb (**b**) *(contrarier)* to annoy

indisposition [ɛ̃dispozisjɔ̃] *nf* indisposition, slight illness

indissociable [ɛ̃disɔsjabl] *adj* indissociable

indissoluble [ɛ̃disɔlybl] *adj* indissoluble

indistinct, -e [ɛ̃distɛ̃, -ɛkt] *adj* indistinct

indistinctement [ɛ̃distɛ̃ktəmɑ̃] *adv* (**a**) *(voir, parler)* indistinctly (**b**) *(indifféremment)* equally

individu [ɛ̃dividy] *nm* (**a**) *(être humain)* individual (**b**) *Péj (homme)* individual, character; **un drôle d'i.** a strange individual or character

individualiser [ɛ̃dividɥalize] *vt* (**a**) *(différencier)* to make individual (**b**) *(adapter)* to adapt to individual circumstances

individualisme [ɛ̃dividɥalism] *nm* individualism

individualiste [ɛ̃dividɥalist] **1** *adj* individualistic **2** *nmf* individualist

individualité [ɛ̃dividɥalite] *nf* individuality

individuel, -elle [ɛ̃dividɥɛl] *adj* individual; *(liberté, responsabilité)* personal; *(maison)* detached; *(chambre)* single

individuellement [ɛ̃dividɥɛlmɑ̃] *adv* individually

indivisible [ɛ̃divizibl] *adj* indivisible

Indochine [ɛ̃dɔʃin] *nf* **l'I.** Indochina

indocile [ɛ̃dɔsil] *adj* disobedient

indo-européen, -enne (*mpl* **indo-européens**, *fpl* **indo-européennes**) [ɛ̃dɔørɔpeɛ̃, -ɛn] **1** *adj* Indo-European **2** *nm,f* **I.** Indo-European **3** *nm (langue)* Indo-European

indolence [ɛ̃dɔlɑ̃s] *nf* laziness

indolent, -e [ɛ̃dɔlɑ̃, -ɑ̃t] *adj* lazy

indolore [ɛ̃dɔlɔr] *adj* painless

indomptable [ɛ̃dɔ̃tabl] *adj* (**a**) *(animal)* untamable (**b**) *Fig (orgueil, caractère)* indomitable; *(passion)* uncontrollable

indompté, -e [ɛ̃dɔ̃te] *adj* (**a**) *(animal)* untamed (**b**) *Fig (passion, orgueil)* uncontrolled

Indonésie [ɛ̃dɔnezi] *nf* **l'I.** Indonesia

indonésien, -enne [ɛ̃dɔnezjɛ̃, -ɛn] **1** *adj* Indonesian **2** *nm,f* **I.** Indonesian

indu, -e [ɛ̃dy] *adj* **à une heure indue** at an ungodly hour; **il rentre à des heures indues** he comes home at all hours of the night

indubitable [ɛ̃dybitabl] *adj* indubitable, indubitable; **c'est i.** there's no doubt about it

indubitablement [ɛ̃dybitabləmɑ̃] *adv* undoubtedly

induire [18] [ɛ̃dɥir] *vt* (**a**) *(entraîner)* **i. qn à faire qch** to induce sb to do sth; **i. qn en erreur** to mislead sb (**b**) *(conclure)* to infer (**de** from)

indulgence [ɛ̃dylʒɑ̃s] *nf* (**a**) *(bienveillance)* indulgence, leniency; **faire preuve d'i. envers qn** to be indulgent towards sb; **rires sans i.** merciless laughter; **faire de qn un portrait sans i.** to describe sb warts and all (**b**) *Rel* indulgence

indulgent, -e [ɛ̃dylʒɑ̃, -ɑ̃t] *adj* indulgent

indûment [ɛ̃dymɑ̃] *adv* unduly

industrialisation [ɛ̃dystrijalizasjɔ̃] *nf* industrialization

industrialiser [ɛ̃dystrijalize] **1** *vt* to industrialize **2** *s'industrialiser* *vpr* to become industrialized

industrie [ɛ̃dystri] *nf* industry; **travailler dans l'i.** to work in industry; **l'i. alimentaire** the food industry; **l'i. automobile** the car industry; **l'i. lourde** heavy industry; **l'i. pharmaceutique** the pharmaceutical industry

industriel, -elle [ɛ̃dystrijɛl] **1** *adj* industrial; *Fam* **des magazines en quantité industrielle** vast quantities of magazines **2** *nm* manufacturer, industrialist

industriellement [ɛ̃dystrijɛlmɑ̃] *adv* industrially

industrieux, -euse [ɛ̃dystrijø, -øz] *adj Litt (habile)* skilful, ingenious; *(travailleur)* industrious

inébranlable [inebrɑ̃labl] *adj (mur, rocher)* immovable; *Fig* unshakeable

inédit, -e [inedi, -it] **1** *adj* **(a)** *(livre)* previously unpublished; *(disque)* previously unreleased **(b)** *(spectacle, projet, idée)* new, original **2** *nm (texte)* previously unpublished work; *(disque)* previously unreleased record

ineffable [inefabl] *adj* ineffable, unutterable

ineffaçable [inefasabl] *adj aussi Fig* indelible

inefficace [inefikas] *adj (personne)* inefficient; *(remède, méthode, loi)* ineffective

inefficacité [inefikasite] *nf (de personne)* inefficiency; *(d'un remède, d'une méthode, d'une loi)* ineffectiveness

inégal, -e, -aux, -ales [inegal, -o] *adj* **(a)** *(non égal) (parts, partage, force, lutte)* unequal **(b)** *(irrégulier) (sol)* uneven; *(pouls)* irregular; *Fig (travail, écrivain, style, qualité)* inconsistent; *(humeur)* changeable

inégalable [inegalabl] *adj* incomparable, matchless

inégalé, -e [inegale] *adj (qualité, personne)* unequalled; *(record)* unbeaten

inégalement [inegalmɑ̃] *adv* **(a)** *(injustement)* unequally **(b)** *(irrégulièrement)* unevenly

inégalité [inegalite] *nf* **(a)** *(injustice)* inequality **(entre** between) **(b)** *(différence)* disparity **(de** in) **(c)** *(du sol)* unevenness; *Fig* **i. d'humeur** moodiness

inélégant, -e [inelegɑ̃, -ɑ̃t] *adj Litt (mal habillé)* inelegant; *(discourtois)* discourteous

inéligible [ineliʒibl] *adj* ineligible

inéluctable [inelyktabl] *adj* inescapable

inemployable [inɑ̃plwajabl] *adj* unusable

inemployé, -e [inɑ̃plwaje] *adj (objet, machine, talent)* unused; *(ressources)* untapped; *(forces)* unchannelled

inénarrable [inenarabl] *adj* comical

inepte [inɛpt] *adj (remarque, réponse, histoire)* inane; *(personne)* inept

ineptie [inɛpsi] *nf* **(a)** *(d'un comportement, d'un film)* inanity **(b)** *(action)* stupid thing; *(remarque)* stupid comment

inépuisable [inepɥizabl] *adj (réserves, sujet, curiosité)* inexhaustible; *(imagination)* limitless; **sur ce sujet-là, elle est i.** you can never get her off the subject

inerte [inɛrt] *adj* **(a)** *(masse, corps, matière)* inert **(b)** *(personne) (inanimé)* lifeless; *(passif)* apathetic

inertie [inɛrsi] *nf* **(a)** *Phys* inertia **(b)** *(manque de réaction)* apathy

inespéré, -e [inɛspere] *adj* unexpected, unhoped-for

inesthétique [inɛstetik] *adj* unaesthetic

inestimable [inɛstimabl] *adj (dégâts, coût, richesse)*

incalculable; *(aide, chance)* invaluable; *(œuvre d'art)* priceless; **d'une valeur i.** priceless

inévitable [inevitabl] *adj* inevitable, unavoidable

inévitablement [inevitabləmɑ̃] *adv* inevitably, unavoidably

inexact, -e [inɛgzakt] *adj* **(a)** *(incorrect) (réponse, description, détail)* inaccurate; *(somme, calcul)* wrong, incorrect **(b)** *(manquant de ponctualité)* unpunctual

inexactitude [inɛgzaktityd] *nf* **(a)** *(caractère erroné, erreur)* inaccuracy **(b)** *(manque de ponctualité)* unpunctuality

inexcusable [inɛkskyzabl] *adj* inexcusable, unforgivable

inexhaustible [inɛgzostibl] *adj Litt* inexhaustible

inexistant, -e [inɛgzistɑ̃, -ɑ̃t] *adj* non-existent; *Hum* **il est totalement i.** he's a complete nonentity

inexistence [inɛgzistɑ̃s] *nf* non-existence

inexorable [inɛgzɔrabl] *adj (destin)* inexorable; *(juge)* pitiless; *(volonté)* inflexible

inexorablement [inɛgzɔrabləmɑ̃] *adv* inexorably

inexpérience [inɛksperjɑ̃s] *nf* inexperience

inexpérimenté, -e [inɛksperimɑ̃te] *adj* inexperienced

inexplicable [inɛksplikabl] *adj* inexplicable

inexpliqué, -e [inɛksplike] *adj* unexplained

inexploité, -e [inɛksplwate] *adj (mine)* unworked; *(terre)* undeveloped; *(ressources)* untapped

inexploré, -e [inɛksplɔre] *adj* unexplored

inexpressif, -ive [inɛkspresif, -iv] *adj (a)* inexpressive, expressionless

inexprimable [inɛksprimabl] *adj* inexpressible

inexprimé, -e [inɛksprime] *adj* unexpressed

in extenso [inɛkstɛ̃so] *adv* in full

in extremis [inɛkstremis] *adv* at the last minute

inextricable [inɛkstrikabl] *adj* inextricable

inextricablement [inɛkstrikabləmɑ̃] *adv* inextricably

infaillibilité [ɛ̃fajibilite] *nf* infallibility

infaillible [ɛ̃fajibl] *adj* infallible

infailliblement [ɛ̃fajibləmɑ̃] *adv* infallibly

infaisable [ɛ̃fəzabl] *adj* not feasible, impossible

infamant, -e [ɛ̃famɑ̃, -ɑ̃t] *adj (a)* *(déclaration, accusation)* defamatory, slanderous **(b)** *Jur (peine)* involving loss of civil rights

infâme [ɛ̃fɑm] *adj (mensonge, personne)* despicable; *(acte, crime)* unspeakable; *(taudis)* squalid; *(odeur, nourriture)* revolting

infamie [ɛ̃fami] *nf* **(a)** *(caractère infâme)* infamy **(b)** *(action)* unspeakable act; *(remarque)* slanderous remark

infant, -e [ɛ̃fɑ̃, -ɑ̃t] *nm,f* infante, *f* infanta

infanterie [ɛ̃fɑ̃tri] *nf* infantry; **i. de marine** marine corps, marines

infanticide [ɛ̃fɑ̃tisid] **1** *adj* infanticidal **2** *nmf (personne)* child-killer, infanticide **3** *nm (crime)* infanticide

infantile [ɛ̃fɑ̃til] *adj* **(a)** *(maladie)* childhood **(b)** *Péj (comportement, personne)* childish, infantile

infantiliser [ɛ̃fɑ̃tilize] *vt Péj* **la télévision infantilise les gens** television makes people behave like children

infarctus [ɛ̃farktys] *nm* heart attack; **i. du myocarde** myocardial infarction, coronary thrombosis

infatigable [ɛ̃fatigabl] *adj* tireless

infatué, -e [ɛ̃fatɥe] *adj* conceited; **i. de soi-même** full of oneself

infécond, -e [ɛ̃fekɔ̃, -ɔ̃d] *adj* infertile

infect, -e [ɛ̃fɛkt] *adj* foul

infecter [ɛ̃fɛkte] **1** *vt* (**a**) *(plaie, blessure)* to infect (**b**) *(atmosphère, eau, sol)* to contaminate **2 s'infecter** *vpr* to become infected, to go septic

infectieux, -euse [ɛ̃fɛksjø, -øz] *adj* infectious

infection [ɛ̃fɛksjɔ̃] *nf* (**a**) *Méd & Ordinat* infection (**b**) *(puanteur)* stench, stink; **quelle i. dans cette pièce!** this room stinks!

inférieur, -e [ɛ̃terjœr] **1** *adj* (**a**) *(qui est en bas) (étagère, niveau)* bottom; *(étages, lèvre, paupière, membres, mâchoire)* lower; **partie inférieure** bottom (part); **allez voir à l'étage i.** go and look on the floor below (**b**) *(dans une hiérarchie) (qualité, marchandises, intelligence)* inferior; **d'un rang i.** of a lower rank; **être rétrogradé à l'échelon i.** to be demoted to the grade below (**c**) *(dans une comparaison)* **i. à** *(qualité)* inferior to; *(quantité)* less than; **i. ou égal à** less than or equal to; **note inférieure à douze** mark below twelve; **i. en nombre** fewer in number; **i. à la moyenne** below average **2** *nmf* inferior

infériorité [ɛ̃ferjɔrite] *nf* inferiority

infernal, -e, -aux, -ales [ɛ̃fɛrnal, -o] *adj* (**a**) *(de l'enfer)* infernal; *Fig (cruauté, méchanceté)* diabolical (**b**) *Fam (insupportable) (chaleur, bruit)* infernal; **à une vitesse infernale** at breakneck speed; **des cadences infernales** an impossible rate of work; **cet enfant est i.** this child's a little devil

infertile [ɛ̃fɛrtil] *adj* infertile

infertilité [ɛ̃fɛrtilite] *nf* infertility

infester [ɛ̃fɛste] *vt (sujet: vermine)* to infest, *Fig (sujet: personnes)* to overrun; **infesté de** infested/overrun with

infidèle [ɛ̃fidɛl] **1** *adj* (**a**) *(déloyal)* unfaithful (**à** to) (**b**) *(inexact) (traduction, rapport)* inaccurate (**c**) *Rel* infidel **2** *nmf Rel* infidel

infidélité [ɛ̃fidelite] *nf* (**a**) *(déloyauté)* unfaithfulness (**à** to); **faire des infidélités à** to be unfaithful to (**b**) *(manque d'exactitude) (dans une traduction, un compte rendu)* inaccuracy

infiltration [ɛ̃filtrasjɔ̃] *nf* (**a**) *(d'un liquide)* infiltration; **il y a des infiltrations dans le plafond** there are some leaks in the ceiling (**b**) *(d'espions)* infiltration (**c**) *(piqûre)* **faire des infiltrations à qn** to give sb injections

infiltrer [ɛ̃filtre] **1** *vt (noyauter) (parti, pays)* to infiltrate **2 s'infiltrer** *vpr* (**a**) *(fluide)* to infiltrate; **s'i. dans** to seep into (**b**) *(espion)* **s'i. dans** to infiltrate

infime [ɛ̃fim] *adj* tiny

infini, -e [ɛ̃fini] **1** *adj* infinite; **ça prend un temps i.** it takes an eternity **2** *nm* **l'i.** infinity; **à l'i.** *(s'étendre, se refléter)* to infinity; *(discutailler)* ad infinitum

infiniment [ɛ̃finimɑ̃] *adv (énormément)* infinitely; **i. petit** infinitesimal; **i. reconnaissant** extremely grateful; **je regrette i.** I'm extremely sorry; **je vous remercie infiniment** thank you so much

infinité [ɛ̃finite] *nf* infinity; **une i. de** an infinite number of

infinitésimal, -e, -aux, -ales [ɛ̃finitezimal, -o] *adj* infinitesimal

infinitif, -ive [ɛ̃finitif, -iv] **1** *adj* infinitive **2** *nm* infinitive; **à l'i.** in the infinitive

infirmation [ɛ̃firmasjɔ̃] *nf Jur* invalidation

infirme [ɛ̃firm] **1** *adj* disabled **2** *nmf* disabled person; **les infirmes** the disabled

infirmer [ɛ̃firme] *vt* to invalidate

infirmerie [ɛ̃firməri] *nf (d'une prison, d'une caserne)* infirmary; *(à l'école, dans un bateau)* sick bay

infirmier [ɛ̃firmje] *nm* (male) nurse

infirmière [ɛ̃firmjɛr] *nf* nurse; **i. de jour/nuit** day/night nurse

infirmité [ɛ̃firmite] *nf* disability

inflammable [ɛ̃flamabl] *adj* inflammable, flammable

inflammation [ɛ̃flamasjɔ̃] *nf Méd* inflammation

inflation [ɛ̃flasjɔ̃] *nf* inflation

inflationniste [ɛ̃flasjɔnist] *adj* inflationary

infléchir [ɛ̃fleʃir] **1** *vt* (**a**) *(rayon)* to bend (**b**) *(politique)* to change the direction of; **i. le cours des événements** to change the course of events **2 s'infléchir** *vpr* (**a**) *(dévier) (route, ligne)* to bend (**b**) *(changer) (politique)* to change direction

inflexibilité [ɛ̃flɛksibilite] *nf* inflexibility

inflexible [ɛ̃flɛksibl] *adj* inflexible

inflexion [ɛ̃flɛksjɔ̃] *nf* (**a**) *(mouvement)* **i. du corps** bend of the body; *(pour saluer)* bow; **i. de (la) tete** tilt of the head; *(pour saluer, acquiescer)* nod (**b**) *(de la voix)* inflection (**c**) *(de courbe, rayon)* inflection

infliger [45] [ɛ̃fliʒe] *vt* **i. qch à qn** *(correction, punition)* to inflict sth on sb; *(peine, amende)* to impose sth on sb

influençable [ɛ̃flyɑ̃sabl] *adj* easily influenced

influence [ɛ̃flyɑ̃s] *nf* influence (**sur** on); **trafic d'i.** corruption (involving a public official)

influencer [16] [ɛ̃flyɑ̃se] *vt* to influence; **il ne faut pas te laisser i.** you mustn't let yourself be influenced; **il se laisse facilement i.** he's easily influenced

influent, -e [ɛ̃flyɑ̃, -ɑ̃t] *adj* influential

influer [ɛ̃flye] *vi* **i. sur** to influence

influx [ɛ̃fly] *nm* **i. nerveux** nerve impulse

info [ɛ̃fo] *nf Fam (nouvelle)* news item; **les infos** the news *(singulier)*

Infographie® [ɛ̃fografi] *nf* computer graphics

informateur, -trice [ɛ̃fɔrmatœr, -tris] *nm,f* informant; *(de police)* informer

informaticien, -enne [ɛ̃fɔrmatisjɛ̃, -ɛn] **1** *nm,f* computer scientist **2** *adj* **ingénieur i.** computer engineer

information [ɛ̃fɔrmasjɔ̃] *nf* (**a**) *(renseignement)* (piece of) information; **informations** information; **pour votre i.** for your information; **à titre d'i.** for information; **assurer l'i. du public en matière de santé** to ensure that the public is kept informed about health matters; **le droit à l'i.** freedom of information (**b**) *(nouvelle)* news item; **une i. de dernière minute** some late news; **les informations** the news *(singulier)* (**c**) *(médias)* **l'i.** the media (**d**) *Ordinat* data, information; **traitement de l'i.** data processing; **théorie de l'i.** information theory (**e**) *Jur (enquête)* inquiry; *(instruction préparatoire)* preliminary investigation; **ouvrir une i.** to begin legal proceedings

informatique [ɛ̃fɔrmatik] *nf (traitement de l'information)* data processing; *(science)* computer science, computing; **travailler dans l'i.** to work in computers; **société/magazine/cours d'i.** computer company/magazine/course

informatisation [ɛ̃fɔrmatizasjɔ̃] *nf* computerization

informatiser [ɛ̃fɔrmatize] *vt* to computerize

informe [ɛ̃fɔrm] *adj (masse, objet, vêtement)* shapeless; *(monstre, être)* misshapen

informé, -e [ɛ̃fɔrme] **1** *adj* informed; **bien i.** well-informed; **mal i.** ill-informed; **dans les milieux informés** in informed circles **2** *nm Jur* inquiry; **jusqu'à plus ample i.** until we have further information

informel, -elle [ɛ̃fɔrmɛl] *adj* informal

informer [ɛ̃fɔrme] **1** *vt* to inform (**de** of); **i. qn que...** to inform sb that...; **nous informons les voyageurs que...** we would like to inform passengers that...
2 s'informer *vpr (se renseigner)* to inquire, to ask (**de/au sujet de** about); *(se tenir au courant)* to keep oneself informed

infortune [ɛ̃fɔrtyn] *nf* misfortune; **compagnons d'i.** companions in adversity

infortuné, -e [ɛ̃fɔrtyne] **1** *adj* unfortunate
2 *nm,f* unfortunate wretch

infoutu, -e [ɛ̃futy] *adj Fam* downright incapable (**de** of)

infraction [ɛ̃fraksjɔ̃] *nf (à un règlement, à la loi)* infringement; *(délit)* offence; **être en i.** to be committing an offence

infranchissable [ɛ̃frɑ̃ʃisabl] *adj (rivière, col, gouffre)* impassable; *(obstacle, difficulté)* insurmountable

infrarouge [ɛ̃fraruʒ] *adj & nm* infrared

infrastructure [ɛ̃frastryktyr] *nf* (**a**) *Constr* substructure (**b**) *(d'équipements)* infrastructure; **i. routière/touristique** road/tourist infrastructure

infructueux, -euse [ɛ̃fryktɥø, -øz] *adj* fruitless

infumable [ɛ̃fymabl] *adj* unsmokable

infuse [ɛ̃fyz] *adj f voir* **science**

infuser [ɛ̃fyze] **1** *vi (thé)* to brew; *(tisane)* to infuse
2 *vt* (**a**) *(faire pénétrer)* to instil (**dans** into) (**b**) *(herbes)* to infuse; *(thé)* to brew

infusion [ɛ̃fyzjɔ̃] *nf* (**a**) *(boisson)* herb tea; **une i. de camomille** some camomile tea (**b**) *(processus)* infusion; *(de thé)* brewing

ingénier [66] [ɛ̃ʒenje] **s'ingénier** *vpr* **s'i. à faire qch** to strive to do sth; **il s'ingénie à me contredire** he goes out of his way to contradict me

ingénierie [ɛ̃ʒeniri] *nf* engineering

ingénieur [ɛ̃ʒenjœr] *nm* engineer; **i. agronome** agricultural engineer; **i. électronicien** electronics engineer; **i. des mines** mining engineer; **i. du son** sound engineer; **i. des travaux publics** civil engineer

ingénieur-conseil (*pl* **ingénieurs-conseils**) [ɛ̃ʒenjœrkɔ̃sɛj] *nm* consultant engineer

ingénieusement [ɛ̃ʒenjøzmɑ̃] *adv* ingeniously

ingénieux, -euse [ɛ̃ʒenjø, -øz] *adj* ingenious

ingéniosité [ɛ̃ʒenjozite] *nf* ingenuity

ingénu, -e [ɛ̃ʒeny] **1** *adj* ingenuous
2 *nm,f* ingenuous person

ingénuité [ɛ̃ʒenɥite] *nf* ingenuousness

ingérence [ɛ̃ʒerɑ̃s] *nf* interference (**dans** in)

ingérer [34] [ɛ̃ʒere] *vt* to ingest

ingestion [ɛ̃ʒɛstjɔ̃] *nf* ingestion

ingrat, -e [ɛ̃gra, -at] **1** *adj (personne)* ungrateful (**envers** to); *(sol, terre)* barren; *(tâche)* thankless; *(travail, sujet)* unrewarding; *(physique, visage)* unattractive
2 *nm,f* ungrateful person

ingratitude [ɛ̃gratityd] *nf* ingratitude

ingrédient [ɛ̃gredjɑ̃] *nm* ingredient

inguérissable [ɛ̃gerisabl] *adj* incurable

ingurgiter [ɛ̃gyrʒite] *vt (aliment, boisson)* to gulp down; *Fam Fig (connaissances)* to cram into one's head

inhabitable [inabitabl] *adj* uninhabitable

inhabité, -e [inabite] *adj* uninhabited

inhabituel, -elle [inabitɥel] *adj* unusual

inhalation [inalasjɔ̃] *nf* inhalation; *Méd* **faire des inhalations** to inhale

inhaler [inale] *vt* to inhale

inhérent, -e [inerɑ̃, -ɑ̃t] *adj* inherent (**à** in)

inhiber [inibe] *vt* to inhibit

inhibition [inibisjɔ̃] *nf* inhibition

inhospitalier, -ère [inɔspitalje, -ɛr] *adj* inhospitable

inhumain, -e [inymɛ̃, -ɛn] *adj* inhuman

inhumanité [inymanite] *nf* inhumanity

inhumation [inymasjɔ̃] *nf* burial

inhumer [inyme] *vt* to bury

inimaginable [inimaʒinabl] *adj* unimaginable

inimitable [inimitabl] *adj* inimitable

inimitié [inimitje] *nf* enmity

ininflammable [inɛ̃flamabl] *adj* non-flammable

inintelligent, -e [inɛ̃teliʒɑ̃, -ɑ̃t] *adj* unintelligent

inintelligible [inɛ̃teliʒibl] *adj* unintelligible

inintéressant, -e [inɛ̃teresɑ̃, -ɑ̃t] *adj* uninteresting

ininterrompu, -e [inɛ̃terɔ̃py] *adj* continuous

inique [inik] *adj* iniquitous

iniquité [inikite] *nf* iniquity

initial, -e, -aux, -ales [inisjal, -o] **1** *adj* initial
2 *nf* **initiale** initial

initialement [inisjalmɑ̃] *adv* initially

initialisation [inisjalizasjɔ̃] *nf Ordinat* initialization

initialiser [inisjalize] *vt Ordinat (disque)* to initialize; *(ordinateur)* to boot (up)

initiateur, -trice [inisjatœr, -tris] **1** *nm,f (d'un projet, d'une réforme)* initiator
2 *adj* initiatory

initiation [inisjasjɔ̃] *nf* (**a**) *(formation)* introduction (**à** to) (**b**) *(rituels)* initiation (**à** into)

initiatique [inisjatik] *adj* initiatory

initiative [inisjativ] *nf* initiative; **à l'i. de qn** on sb's initiative; **prendre l'i. de faire qch** to take the initiative in doing sth; **faire qch de sa propre i.** to do sth on one's own initiative; **il n'a aucune i.** he's got no initiative

initié, -e [inisje] *nm,f* initiate

initier [66] [inisje] **1** *vt* (**a**) *(former)* to introduce (**à** to) (**b**) *(rituellement)* to initiate (**à** into)
2 s'initier *vpr* **s'i. à qch** to start learning sth

injectable [ɛ̃ʒɛktabl] *adj* injectable

injecté, -e [ɛ̃ʒɛkte] *adj* **yeux injectés de sang** bloodshot eyes

injecter [ɛ̃ʒɛkte] *vt (substance, capitaux)* to inject (**dans** into)

injection [ɛ̃ʒɛksjɔ̃] *nf (de substance, de capital)* injection; **moteur à i.** fuel-injection engine

injonction [ɛ̃ʒɔ̃ksjɔ̃] *nf* injunction; **recevoir l'i. de faire qch** to get the order to do sth

injure [ɛ̃ʒyr] *nf* insult; **injures** abuse, insults; **faire i. à qn** to insult sb

injurier [66] [ɛ̃ʒyrje] *vt* to insult, to abuse

injurieux, -euse [ɛ̃ʒyrjø, -øz] *adj* insulting, abusive

injuste [ɛ̃ʒyst] *adj* unfair (**envers** *ou* **avec** to *or* towards)

injustement [ɛ̃ʒystəmɑ̃] *adv* unjustly, unfairly

injustice [ɛ̃ʒystis] *nf* (**a**) *(iniquité)* injustice, unfairness (**envers** towards); **i. sociale** social injustice (**b**) *(acte, parole)* injustice

injustifiable [ɛ̃ʒystifjabl] *adj* unjustifiable

injustifié, -e [ɛ̃ʒystifje] *adj* unjustified

inlassable [ɛ̃lɑsabl] *adj* untiring

inlassablement [ɛ̃lɑsabləmɑ̃] *adv* untiringly; *(répéter)* ceaselessly

inné, -e [ine] *adj* innate, inborn

innocemment [inɔsamã] *adv* innocently

innocence [inɔsɑ̃s] *nf* innocence; **en toute i.** in all innocence

innocent, -e [inɔsɑ̃, -ɑ̃t] **1** *adj* innocent (**de** of) **2** *nm,f (non coupable)* innocent person; *(idiot)* simpleton; **ne fais pas l'i.!** don't act the innocent!; *Prov* **aux innocents les mains pleines** fortune favours fools

innocenter [inɔsɑ̃te] *vt* to clear (**de** of)

innocuité [inɔkɥite] *nf* harmlessness

innombrable [inɔ̃brabl] *adj* innumerable, countless; *(foule)* huge

innommable [inɔmabl] *adj Péj (conduite, actes)* unspeakable; *(nourriture, odeur)* vile

innovateur, -trice [inɔvatœr, -tris] **1** *adj* innovative **2** *nm,f* innovator

innovation [inɔvasjɔ̃] *nf* innovation

innover [inɔve] *vi* to innovate

inoccupé, -e [inɔkype] *adj* unoccupied

inoculation [inɔkylasjɔ̃] *nf Méd* inoculation

inoculer [inɔkyle] *vt* (**a**) **i. un virus/un vaccin à qn** to inoculate sb with a virus/a vaccine; **i. une maladie à qn** to infect sb with a disease; *Fig* **elle nous a inoculé sa gaieté** she infected us with her cheerfulness (**b**) **i. qn (contre une maladie)** to inoculate sb (against a disease)

inodore [inɔdɔr] *adj* odourless

inoffensif, -ive [inɔfɑ̃sif, -iv] *adj* harmless

inondation [inɔ̃dasjɔ̃] *nf* flood; *(action)* flooding

inondé, -e [inɔ̃de] *adj (lieu)* flooded; **populations inondées** flood victims; **visage i. de larmes** face streaming with tears; **i. de lumière** flooded with light

inonder [inɔ̃de] *vt (lieu)* to flood; *Fig (marché)* to flood, to inundate (**de** with); **être inondé de réclamations** to be inundated with complaints

inopérable [inɔperabl] *adj* inoperable

inopérant, -e [inɔperɑ̃, -ɑ̃t] *adj* ineffective

inopiné, -e [inɔpine] *adj* unexpected

inopportun, -e [inɔpɔrtœ̃, -yn] *adj* inopportune

inoubliable [inublijabl] *adj* unforgettable

inouï, -e [inwi] *adj* (**a**) *(ahurissant)* incredible; **il leur est arrivé une histoire inouïe** something incredible happened to them; **c'est/vous êtes i.!** it's/you're incredible! (**b**) *(nouveau)* unheard-of

Inox® [inɔks] *nm* stainless steel

inoxydable [inɔksidabl] *adj (métal)* rustproof; **acier i.** stainless steel

inqualifiable [ɛ̃kalifjabl] *adj* unspeakable

inquiet, -ète [ɛ̃kjɛ, -ɛt] **1** *adj (anxieux) (personne, air, voix)* worried, anxious (**au sujet de** about); *(attente)* anxious **2** *nm,f* worrier

inquiétant, -e [ɛ̃kjetɑ̃, -ɑ̃t] *adj* (**a**) *(alarmant)* worrying (**b**) *(qui effraie) (air, sourire)* frightening

inquiéter [34] [ɛ̃kjete] **1** *vt* to worry; **être inquiété par la police** to be bothered by the police **2 s'inquiéter** *vpr* (**a**) *(se faire du souci)* to worry; **il n'y a pas de quoi s'i.** there's nothing to worry about; **s'i. pour qn** to be worried about sb (**b**) **s'i. de** *(se faire du souci pour)* to be worried about; *(s'informer de)* to inquire about; **sans s'i. de rien** without a care in the world

inquiétude [ɛ̃kjetyd] *nf* anxiety, worry; **sujet d'i.** cause for anxiety; **éprouver quelques inquiétudes** to feel a bit worried

inquisiteur, -trice [ɛ̃kizitœr, -tris] **1** *adj (regard)* inquisitive **2** *nm* inquisitor

inquisition [ɛ̃kizisjɔ̃] *nf* inquisition; **l'I.** the Inquisition

insaisissable [ɛ̃sezizabl] *adj* (**a**) *(personne)* elusive (**b**) *(son, différence, nuance)* imperceptible

insalubre [ɛ̃salybr] *adj (climat, habitation, pays)* insalubrious; *(occupation)* unhealthy

insanité [ɛ̃sanite] *nf (de raisonnement, de propos)* insanity; **des insanités** complete nonsense

insatiable [ɛ̃sasjabl] *adj* insatiable

insatisfait, -e [ɛ̃satisfɛ, -ɛt] **1** *adj (personne)* dissatisfied; *(désir)* unsatisfied **2** *nm,f* **c'est un éternel i.** he's never satisfied

inscription [ɛ̃skripsjɔ̃] *nf* (**a**) *(action) (dans un journal, un registre)* entering; *(immatriculation)* registration (**b**) *(sur une tombe, un mur)* inscription; *(dans un livre de comptes)* entry

inscrire [30] [ɛ̃skrir] **1** *vt* (**a**) *(renseignements, date)* to write down; *(dans un journal, dans un registre)* to enter (**b**) *(pour participer)* **i. qn à un club/à une activité** to enrol sb in a club/for an activity; **i. un enfant dans une école** to enrol a child at a school (**c**) *(dans la pierre)* to inscribe **2 s'inscrire** [ɛ̃skrir] *Br* to matriculate, *Am* to register (**à** at); *(à un tournoi, à un concours)* to enter (**à** for); *(à une activité)* to enrol (**à** for); *(dans une école)* to enrol (**dans** at); **s'i. dans un club/à un club/party** to join a club/party; **s'i. sur les listes électorales** to register to vote, **s'i. en faux contre** qch to deny sth; **s'i. dans le cadre de** to come within the framework of

inscrit, -e [ɛ̃skri, -it] **1** *adj (électeur, candidat)* registered **2** *nm,f (à l'université)* registered student; *(à un concours)* registered entrant; *(électeur)* registered voter

insecable [ɛ̃sekabl] *adj* indivisible

insecte [ɛ̃sɛkt] *nm* insect

insecticide [ɛ̃sɛktisid] **1** *adj* insecticidal **2** *nm* insecticide

insectivore [ɛ̃sɛktivɔr] **1** *adj* insectivorous **2** *nm* insectivore

insécurité [ɛ̃sekyrite] *nf* insecurity

insémination [ɛ̃seminasjɔ̃] *nf* insemination; **i. artificielle** artificial insemination

inséminer [ɛ̃semine] *vt* to inseminate

insensé, -e [ɛ̃sɑ̃se] **1** *adj (projet, idée)* crazy; *(action, espoir, dépenses)* wild; **c'est i.!** it's crazy! **2** *nm,f* madman, *f* madwoman

insensibilité [ɛ̃sɑ̃sibilite] *nf* insensitivity (**à** to)

insensible [ɛ̃sɑ̃sibl] *adj (à la douleur, au froid)* insensitive (**à** to); **i. à la critique** impervious to criticism; **elle demeura i. à leurs larmes** she remained unmoved by their tears

insensiblement [ɛ̃sɑ̃sibləmɑ̃] *adv* imperceptibly

inséparable [ɛ̃separabl] *adj* inseparable

insérer [34] [ɛ̃sere] **1** *vt* to insert (**dans** in); **i. une annonce dans un journal** to put an advertisement in a paper **2 s'insérer** *vpr* (**a**) *(s'attacher)* to be attached (**sur** to) (**b**) **s'i. dans** *(réformes, politique)* to fit into

insertion [ɛ̃sersjɔ̃] *nf* insertion; **i. sociale** *(social)* integration; **i. professionnelle** integration into the job market, *(introduction)* insertion; **i. mode d'i.** insert mode; *Ordinat* **i. de ligne** line insert; **i. publicitaire** advertisement

insidieusement [ɛ̃sidjøzmɑ̃] *adv* insidiously

insidieux, -euse [ɛ̃sidjø, -øz] *adj* insidious

insigne[1] [ɛ̃siɲ] *nm* badge; **insignes de la royauté** insignia of royalty

insigne[2] [ɛ̃siɲ] *adj Formal (remarquable)* signal (**b**) *Hum (indiscrétion, maladresse)* remarkable

insignifiant, -e [ɛ̃siɲifjɑ̃, -ɑ̃t] *adj* insignificant

insinuation [ɛ̃sinɥasjɔ̃] *nf* insinuation

insinuer [ɛ̃sinɥe] **1** *vt* to insinuate; **que voulez-vous i.?** what are you insinuating? **2 s'insinuer** *vpr* **s'i. dans** *(froid, odeur)* to creep into; *(personne)* to worm one's way into; **le doute/l'idée qui s'insinue dans mon esprit** the doubt/the idea that is creeping into my mind

insipide [ɛ̃sipid] *adj* insipid

insistance [ɛ̃sistɑ̃s] *nf* insistence; **avec i.** insistently

insistant, -e [ɛ̃sistɑ̃, -ɑ̃t] *adj* insistent

insister [ɛ̃siste] *vi* **(a)** *(persévérer)* to insist; **elle a beaucoup insisté** she was very insistent; **i. pour faire qch** to insist on doing sth; **elle a essayé la dance classique mais elle n'a pas insisté** she tried ballet but soon gave it up; **j'ai dit non, n'insistez pas!** *ou* **inutile d'i.!** I said no, don't go on about it!; **ça ne répond pas – insiste encore un peu** there's no answer – hang on a bit **(b)** *(mettre l'accent sur)* **i. sur qch** to stress sth; **nous insistons particulièrement sur la ponctualité** we lay particular stress on punctuality

insolation [ɛ̃sɔlasjɔ̃] *nf* **(a)** *Méd* sunstroke; **attraper une i.** to get sunstroke **(b)** *(ensoleillement)* sunshine

insolence [ɛ̃sɔlɑ̃s] *nf* **(a)** *(impertinence)* insolence **(b)** *(remarque, action)* impertinence

insolent, -e [ɛ̃sɔlɑ̃, -ɑ̃t] **1** *adj* **(a)** *(impertinent)* insolent **(envers** *ou* **avec** to) **(b)** *(dans la victoire)* haughty **(c)** *(succès)* outrageous; *(luxe)* unashamed **2** *nm,f* insolent person

insolite [ɛ̃sɔlit] **1** *adj* unusual, strange **2** *nm* **l'i.** the unusual

insoluble [ɛ̃sɔlybl] *adj* insoluble

insolvable [ɛ̃sɔlvabl] *adj* insolvent

insomniaque [ɛ̃sɔmnjak] *adj & nmf* insomniac

insomnie [ɛ̃sɔmni] *nf* insomnia

insondable [ɛ̃sɔ̃dabl] *adj* *(océan, gouffre, mystère)* unfathomable; *(bêtise)* immense

insonorisation [ɛ̃sɔnɔrizasjɔ̃] *nf* soundproofing

insonoriser [ɛ̃sɔnɔrize] *vt* to soundproof

insouciance [ɛ̃susjɑ̃s] *nf* carefree attitude; **vivre dans l'i.** to live a carefree life

insouciant, -e [ɛ̃susjɑ̃, -ɑ̃t] *adj* carefree; **i. de son avenir** unconcerned about his future

insoumis, -e [ɛ̃sumi, -iz] **1** *adj* **(a)** *(peuple, tribus)* unsubdued **(b)** *(personne)* rebellious **(c)** *Mil (soldat)* absentee **2** *nm Mil* absentee

insoupçonnable [ɛ̃supsɔnabl] *adj* *(personne)* beyond suspicion

insoupçonné, -e [ɛ̃supsɔne] *adj* unsuspected **(de** by)

insoutenable [ɛ̃sutnabl] *adj* **(a)** *(spectacle, odeur)* unbearable **(b)** *(opinion, position)* untenable

inspecter [ɛ̃spɛkte] *vt* to inspect

inspecteur, -trice [ɛ̃spɛktœr, -tris] *nm,f* inspector; **i. d'Académie** school inspector; **i. de police** police inspector; **i. du travail** factory inspector; **i. des travaux finis** idler *(who arrives after the work has been done)*

inspection [ɛ̃spɛksjɔ̃] *nf* **(a)** *(examen)* inspection; **faire l'i. de** to inspect **(b)** *(service)* inspectorate; **i. académique** school inspectorate; **i. du travail** factory inspectorate

inspiration [ɛ̃spirasjɔ̃] *nf* **(a)** *(créatrice)* inspiration; **avoir de l'i.** to be inspired; **un poème d'i. romantique** a poem in the romantic style **(b)** *(idée)* inspiration **(c)** *(d'air)* breathing in

inspiré, -e [ɛ̃spire] *adj* *(style, poète, artiste, air)* inspired **(de** by); **être bien/mal i. de faire qch** to do the right/wrong thing in doing sth

inspirer [ɛ̃spire] **1** *vt* **(a)** *(donner de l'inspiration à)* to inspire; **ça m'a inspiré une chanson** it inspired me to write a song; **Hum ça ne m'inspire pas** it doesn't exactly inspire me **(b)** *(susciter)* **i. confiance à qn** to inspire confidence in sb; **ça m'inspire la plus grande inquiétude** it gives me great cause for concern **(c)** *(air)* to breathe in **2** *vi* to breathe in **3 s'inspirer** *vpr* **s'i. de** to be inspired by

instabilité [ɛ̃stabilite] *nf* instability; *(du temps)* changeability

instable [ɛ̃stabl] *adj* unstable; *(temps)* changeable

installateur, -trice [ɛ̃stalatœr, -tris] *nm,f* fitter

installation [ɛ̃stalasjɔ̃] *nf* **(a)** *(fait d'installer)* *(d'une machine, du chauffage, d'un ascenseur)* installation; *(d'une cuisine)* fitting out; *(de rideaux)* putting up **(b)** *(emménagement)* move; **prévoir son i. dans une région** to plan to settle in an area **(c)** *(d'un ecclésiastique, d'un magistrat)* installation **(d)** *Ordinat* **programme d'i.** installation program; **i. en réseau** network installation **(e) installations** *(d'une maison, d'un atelier)* fittings; **l'i. électrique** the wiring; **installations sanitaires** sanitary fittings; **installations touristiques** tourist facilities

installer [ɛ̃stale] **1** *vt* **(a)** *(mettre en place)* *(machine, chauffage, ascenseur)* to install, to put in; *(cuisine)* to fit out; *(rideaux)* to put up **(b)** *(placer)* **i. qn dans un fauteuil/devant la télévision** to settle sb down in an armchair/in front of the television; **je les ai installés dans la chambre bleue** I've put them in the blue room **(c)** *(aménager)* **les nouveaux bureaux sont très bien installés** the new offices are very well fitted out; **il a installé son bureau au grenier** he set up his office in the attic **(d)** *(dans une fonction)* *(ecclésiastique, magistrat)* to install **2 s'installer** *vpr* **(a)** *(supermarché, cirque)* to be set up; *(personne)* *(dans un fauteuil)* to settle down; *(dans un bureau)* to install oneself; **confortablement installé dans un fauteuil** comfortably installed in an armchair; **s'i. à Paris** to settle in Paris; **des bourgeois bien installés** comfortably-off middle-class people; **s'i. comme médecin** to set up as a doctor; **un climat d'insécurité s'est installé dans le pays** a climate of insecurity has taken hold of the country

instamment [ɛ̃stamɑ̃] *adv* earnestly

instance [ɛ̃stɑ̃s] *nf* **(a)** *(insistance)* plea; **demander à qn de faire qch avec i.** to plead with sb to do sth **(b)** *Jur* proceedings; **en seconde i.** on appeal **(c)** *(autorité)* authority; **les instances internationales** the international authorities; **l'i. compétente** the relevant authority **(d)** *(cours)* **être en i. de divorce** to be waiting for a divorce; **courrier en i.** mail waiting to go out; **être en i.** *(affaire)* to be pending

instant [ɛ̃stɑ̃] *nm* moment, instant; **à chaque** *ou* **tout i.** all the time; **pendant un i.** for a moment; **un i.!** one moment!; **sans perdre un i.** without wasting a second; **d'un i. à l'autre** at any moment; **à l'i.** *(just)* a moment ago; **à l'i. même où** at the very moment that; **j'en reviens à l'i.** I've just come back from there; **pour l'i.** for the moment; **dans un i.** in a moment; **en un i.** in no time at all

instantané, -e [ɛ̃stɑ̃tane] **1** *adj* *(mort, riposte)* instantaneous; *(café, soupe)* instant **2** *nm* *(photo)* snap

instantanément [ɛ̃stɑ̃tanemɑ̃] *adv* instantaneously

instar [ɛ̃star] **à l'instar de** *prép* following the example of

instauration [ɛ̃stɔrasjɔ̃] *nf* establishment

instaurer [ɛ̃stɔre] **1** *vt* to establish **2 s'instaurer** *vpr* to be established

instigateur, -trice [ɛ̃stigatœr, -tris] *nm,f* instigator

instigation [ɛ̃stigasjɔ̃] nf instigation; à l'i. de qn at sb's instigation

instinct [ɛ̃stɛ̃] nm instinct; **faire qch d'i.** to do sth by instinct

instinctif, -ive [ɛ̃stɛ̃ktif, -iv] adj instinctive

instinctivement [ɛ̃stɛ̃ktivmɑ̃] adv instinctively

instit [ɛ̃stit] nmf Fam (primary school) teacher

instituer [ɛ̃stitɥe] vt to establish

institut [ɛ̃stity] nm institute; **i. de beauté** beauty salon; **i. médico-légal** mortuary

instituteur, -trice [ɛ̃stitytœr, -tris] nm,f (primary school) teacher

institution [ɛ̃stitysjɔ̃] nf (**a**) (création) establishment (**b**) (école) private school (**c**) (coutume) institution (**d**) Pol institutions institutions

institutionnaliser [ɛ̃stitysjɔnalize] vt to institutionalize

institutionnel, -elle [ɛ̃stitysjɔnɛl] adj institutional

instructeur [ɛ̃stryktœr] **1** nm instructor **2** adj m Jur juge I. examining magistrate

instructif, -ive [ɛ̃stryktif, -iv] adj instructive

instruction [ɛ̃stryksjɔ̃] nf (**a**) (éducation) education; Mil training; **avoir de l'i.** to be well educated; **sans i.** uneducated; **i. civique** civics (**b**) (cours) lesson; **i. musicale** musical training; **i. religieuse** religious instruction (**b**) Ordinat instruction (**c**) (circulaire) memo (**d**) Jur (d'une affaire) preliminary investigation (**e**) **instructions** instructions

instruire [18] [ɛ̃strɥir] **1** vt (**a**) (enseigner à) to teach, to educate; **i. par le jeu** to teach through play (**b**) (soldats) to train (**c**) (informer) **i. qn de qch** to inform sb of sth (**d**) Jur (affaire) to investigate **2 s'instruire** vpr to educate oneself; **s i. de** to find out about

instruit, -e [ɛ̃strɥi, -it] adj educated

instrument [ɛ̃strymɑ̃] nm (**a**) (outil) instrument; **i. de mesure/de précision** measuring/precision instrument; Fig **il n'a été qu'un i.** he was merely a tool (**b**) **i. (de musique)** (musical) instrument; **i. à vent/cordes** wind/string instrument

instrumental, -e, -aux, -ales [ɛ̃strymɑ̃tal, -o] adj instrumental

instrumentiste [ɛ̃strymɑ̃tist] nmf instrumentalist

insu [ɛ̃sy] à l'insu de prép without the knowledge of; à leur i. without their knowing; je l'ai fait à mon i. I did it without realizing

insubmersible [ɛ̃sybmɛrsibl] adj unsinkable

insubordination [ɛ̃sybɔrdinasjɔ̃] nf insubordination

insuccès [ɛ̃syksɛ] nm failure

insuffisamment [ɛ̃syfizamɑ̃] adv insufficiently, inadequately

insuffisance [ɛ̃syfizɑ̃s] nf (**a**) (manque) insufficiency; (de personnel, de réserves) shortage; (de moyens) inadequacy (**b**) Méd (d'un organe) insufficiency; **i. respiratoire/cardiaque** respiratory/cardiac insufficiency (**c**) **insuffisances** (faiblesses) shortcomings

insuffisant, -e [ɛ̃syfizɑ̃, -ɑ̃t] adj (quantité) insufficient; (moyens, mesures) inadequate; **tes résultats sont insuffisants** your results are not good enough

insuffler [ɛ̃syfle] vt Méd to insufflate (**dans** into); **ce succès a insufflé un nouvel élan à l'entreprise** this success breathed new life into the company

insulaire [ɛ̃sylɛr] **1** adj island; Péj (mentalité) insular **2** nmf islander

insuline [ɛ̃sylin] nf insulin

insulte [ɛ̃sylt] nf insult; **faire i. à qn** to insult sb

insulter [ɛ̃sylte] vt to insult

insupportable [ɛ̃sypɔrtabl] adj unbearable

insurgé, -e [ɛ̃syrʒe] adj & nm,f insurgent

insurger [45] [ɛ̃syrʒe] **s'insurger** vpr to rise up (**contre** against)

insurmontable [ɛ̃syrmɔ̃tabl] adj (difficulté, obstacle) insurmountable; (aversion, dégoût) unconquerable

insurrection [ɛ̃syreksjɔ̃] nf uprising, rebellion; **en état d'i.** in a state of rebellion

insurrectionnel, -elle [ɛ̃syreksjɔnɛl] adj insurrectionary

intact, -e [ɛ̃takt] adj intact

intangible [ɛ̃tɑ̃ʒibl] adj (loi, institution) sacred

intarissable [ɛ̃tarisabl] adj inexhaustible

intégral, -e, -aux, -ales [ɛ̃tegral, -o] **1** adj (**a**) (paiement, remboursement) full; (texte) unabridged; Fam un fumiste/crétin/menteur i. a complete clown/idiot/liar (**b**) Math calcul i. integral calculus **2** nf intégrale (**a**) Math integral (**b**) (totalité) l'intégrale des symphonies de Beethoven/des œuvres de Shakespeare the complete Beethoven symphonies/works of Shakespeare

intégralement [ɛ̃tegralmɑ̃] adv (citer, rembourser) fully, in full

intégralité [ɛ̃tegralite] nf l'i. the whole (**de** of); dans son i. in its entirety

intégrante [ɛ̃tegrɑ̃t] adj f une partie i. de an integral part of; **faire partie i.** de to be an integral part of

intégration [ɛ̃tegrasjɔ̃] nf (au sein d'un groupe) & Math integration; (dans une grande école) admission

intègre [ɛ̃tegr] adj upright, honest

intégrer [34] [ɛ̃tegre] **1** vt (incorporer) to integrate (à/dans into) **2 s'intégrer** vpr to become integrated (**à/dans** into); **cette sculpture s'intègre bien au paysage** this sculpture blends in well with the countryside

intégrisme [ɛ̃tegrism] nm fundamentalism

intégriste [ɛ̃tegrist] adj & nmf fundamentalist

intégrité [ɛ̃tegrite] nf integrity; Ordinat **i. des données** data integrity

intellect [ɛ̃telɛkt] nm intellect

intellectuel, -elle [ɛ̃telɛktɥel] **1** adj intellectual; (fatigue) mental; (travail) non-manual **2** nm,f intellectual

intelligemment [ɛ̃teliʒamɑ̃] adv intelligently

intelligence [ɛ̃teliʒɑ̃s] nf (**a**) (intellect) intelligence; **avoir l'i. de faire qch** to have the intelligence to do sth; **i. artificielle** artificial intelligence (**b**) (compréhension) understanding (**c**) (entente) vivre en bonne/mauvaise i. avec qn to be on good/bad terms with sb (**d**) (connivence) un regard/sourire d'i. a knowing look/smile; faire des signes d'i. à qn to signal to sb

intelligent, -e [ɛ̃teliʒɑ̃, -ɑ̃t] adj intelligent, clever; Ordinat smart, intelligent

intelligentsia [ɛ̃teliʒɛnsja] nf l'i. the intelligentsia

intelligible [ɛ̃teliʒibl] adj (compréhensible) intelligible; (clair) clear; à haute et i. voix in a loud, clear voice

intello [ɛ̃telo] nmf Fam souvent Péj intellectual, highbrow

intempéries [ɛ̃tɑ̃peri] nfpl bad weather; **exposé aux i.** exposed to the elements

intempestif, -ive [ɛ̃tɑ̃pɛstif, -iv] adj untimely, ill-timed

intemporel, -elle [ɛ̃tɑ̃pɔrɛl] adj (hors du temps) timeless

intenable [ɛ̃tənabl] adj (chaleur, situation) intolerable, unbearable; (position) untenable; Fam (enfant) uncontrollable

intendance [ɛ̃tɑ̃dɑ̃s] *nf* (a) *Scol* bursary; *(bureau)* bursar's office (b) *Mil* commissariat (c) *(d'un domaine)* stewardship (d) *Fig (questions matérielles)* practical matters

intendant [ɛ̃tɑ̃dɑ̃] *nm* (a) *Scol* bursar (b) *Mil* quartermaster (c) *(d'un domaine)* steward

intendante [ɛ̃tɑ̃dɑ̃t] *nf* (a) *Scol* (woman) bursar (b) *(d'une maison)* housekeeper

intense [ɛ̃tɑ̃s] *adj* intense

intensément [ɛ̃tɑ̃semɑ̃] *adv* intensely

intensif, -ive [ɛ̃tɑ̃sif, -iv] *adj* intensive

intensification [ɛ̃tɑ̃sifikasjɔ̃] *nf* intensification

intensifier [66] [ɛ̃tɑ̃sifje] **1** *vt* to intensify
2 s'intensifier *vpr* to intensify

intensité [ɛ̃tɑ̃site] *nf* intensity

intenter [ɛ̃tɑ̃te] *vt Jur* **i. une action contre qn** to bring an action against sb; **i. un procès à** *ou* **contre qn** to institute proceedings against sb

intention [ɛ̃tɑ̃sjɔ̃] *nf (projet)* intention; *Jur* intent; **avoir l'i. de faire qch** to intend to do sth; **dans l'i. de faire qch** with a view to *or* with the intention of doing sth; **elle a de bonnes intentions** she means well; **c'est l'i. qui compte** it's the thought that counts; **à l'i. de... (pour)** for...; *(en l'honneur de)* in honour of...; *(sur une lettre)* for the attention of...

intentionné, -e [ɛ̃tɑ̃sjɔne] *adj* **bien/mal i.** well-/ill-intentioned; **bien/mal i. envers qn** well-/ill-disposed towards sb

intentionnel, -elle [ɛ̃tɑ̃sjɔnɛl] *adj* intentional, deliberate

intentionnellement [ɛ̃tɑ̃sjɔnɛlmɑ̃] *adv* intentionally, deliberately

interactif, -ive [ɛ̃tɛraktif, -iv] *adj Ordinat* interactive

interaction [ɛ̃tɛraksjɔ̃] *nf* interaction

interallié, -e [ɛ̃tɛralje] *adj* allied

interbancaire [ɛ̃tɛrbɑ̃kɛr] *adj* interbank

intercalaire [ɛ̃tɛrkalɛr] **1** *adj (jour)* intercalary; **feuillet i.** insert
2 *nm (feuillet)* insert; *(dans un classeur)* divider

intercaler [ɛ̃tɛrkale] **1** *vt (dans un texte, un film)* to insert, to include; *(dans un programme, entre deux événements)* to slot in
2 s'intercaler *vpr* to come in between

intercéder [34] [ɛ̃tɛrsede] *vi* to intercede **(en faveur de/auprès de** on behalf of/with)

intercepter [ɛ̃tɛrsɛpte] *vt (lettre, avion, ballon, personne)* to intercept; *(bruit, lumière)* to shut out

interchangeable [ɛ̃tɛrʃɑ̃ʒabl] *adj* interchangeable

interclasse [ɛ̃tɛrklas] *nm* = short break between classes

intercontinental, -e, -aux, -ales [ɛ̃tɛrkɔ̃tinɑ̃tal, -o] *adj* intercontinental

interdépartemental, -e, -aux, -ales [ɛ̃tɛrdepartəmɑ̃tal, -o] *adj* = shared by several French "départements"

interdépendant, -e [ɛ̃tɛrdepɑ̃dɑ̃, -ɑ̃t] *adj* interdependent

interdiction [ɛ̃tɛrdiksjɔ̃] *nf* (a) *(défense)* ban, banning; **i. de fumer/stationner** *(sur panneau)* no smoking/parking (b) *(suspension)* banning; **i. de séjour** = order banning former prisoner from certain areas

interdire [27b] [ɛ̃tɛrdir] **1** *vt* (a) *(défendre) (stationnement, port d'armes)* to ban; **i. qch à qn** to forbid sb sth; **le centre-ville est interdit aux camions** lorries are not allowed in the town centre; **i. à qn de faire qch** to forbid sb to do sth, to ban sb from doing sth; **il nous est interdit de révéler...** we are not allowed to reveal... (b) *(empêcher)* to prevent, to stop **(de faire qch** from doing sth)

2 s'interdire *vpr* **s'i. le tabac** to abstain from smoking; **il s'interdit d'y penser** he doesn't let himself think about it

interdit, -e [ɛ̃tɛrdi, -it] **1** *adj* (a) *(défendu)* forbidden; **il est i. de fumer** smoking is not allowed; **i. au public** *(sur un écriteau)* no unauthorized entry; **un film i. aux moins de 18 ans** an 18 film; **i. de séjour** = banned from living in certain areas; **être i. de chéquier** to have (had) one's chequebook facilities withdrawn; *Ordinat* **i. d'écriture** *(disquette)* write-protected (b) *(déconcerté)* disconcerted, taken aback
2 *nm,f Jur* **i. de séjour** = former prisoner banned from certain areas
3 *nm (social)* taboo; *(religieux)* interdict; **frapper qn/qch d'i.** to impose a ban on sb/sth

intéressant, -e [ɛ̃teresɑ̃, -ɑ̃t] **1** *adj* (a) *(attirant)* interesting (b) *(avantageux)* worthwhile; *(prix)* attractive; *(lucratif)* profitable
2 *nm,f Fam* **faire l'i.** to show off

intéressé, -e [ɛ̃terese] **1** *adj* (a) *(concerné)* **les parties intéressées** the interested parties, the persons concerned (b) *(égoïste) (personne)* self-seeking; *(sentiment)* self-interested; *(conseil)* biased; **agir dans un but i.** to have an axe to grind
2 *nm,f* **l'i.** the person concerned

intéresser [ɛ̃terese] **1** *vt* (a) *(captiver)* to interest; **l'art m'intéresse beaucoup** I'm very interested in art; **est-ce que ça t'intéresse d'aller au théâtre?** would you like to go to the theatre? (b) *Ind & Com* **i. les employés (aux bénéfices)** to operate a profit-sharing scheme; **être intéressé dans une affaire** to have a financial interest in a business (c) *(concerner)* to concern, to affect
2 s'intéresser *vpr* **s'i. à qn/qch** to take an interest in sb/sth, to be interested in sb/sth

intérêt [ɛ̃terɛ] *nm* (a) *(avantage)* interest; **c'est dans mon i. de le faire** it's in my interest to do it; **on a i. à réserver** on vout ajoute des places we'd better book if we want seats; *Fam* **tu n'as pas i. à recommencer!** you'd better not do it again!; **agir dans/contre l'i. de qn** to act in/against sb's interest(s); **agir par i. personnel** to act out of self-interest; **faire un mariage d'i.** to marry for money; **l'i. des vacances en groupe, c'est de faire des rencontres** the advantage of group holidays is that you meet people; *Fam* **tu viens à la réunion du syndicat? – y a il!** are you coming to the union meeting? – **you bet (I am)!** (b) *(attrait)* interest; **sans i.** uninteresting (c) *(curiosité)* interest **(pour** in) (d) *Fin* interest; **i. fixe** fixed interest; **i. variable** variable-rate interest

interface [ɛ̃tɛrfas] *nf Ordinat* interface; **i. graphique** graphic interface; **i. d'imprimante** printer interface; **i. numérique** digital interface; **i. parallèle** parallel interface; **i. utilisateur** user interface; **i. vidéo numérique** digital video interface

interférence [ɛ̃tɛrferɑ̃s] *nf (d'ondes)* interference; *Fig (d'événements)* combination

interférer [34] [ɛ̃tɛrfere] *vi aussi Fig* to interfere

intergouvernemental, -e, -aux, -ales [ɛ̃tɛrguvɛrnəmɑ̃tal, -o] *adj* intergovernmental

intérieur, -e [ɛ̃terjœr] **1** *adj* (a) *(dans l'espace) (escalier)* interior, inside; *(cour)* inner; *(poche)* inside; *(partie)* inside, internal; *(mer)* inland (b) *(national)* domestic (c) *(vie, sentiments, force)* inner
2 *nm* (a) *(dedans)* inside, interior; **à l'i.** inside; **à l'i. de la gare** inside the station; **fermé de l'i.** locked from the inside; **tourné en i.** *(film)* shot indoors (b) *(d'un pays)* interior; **dans l'i. du pays** inland (c) *(maison)* home; **femme,f d'i.** houseproud housewife

intérieurement [ɛ̃terjœrmɑ̃] *adv* inwardly

intérim [ɛ̃terim] *nm (travail intérimaire)* temporary work,

temping; **faire de l'i.** to to temp; **par i.** acting; **assurer l'i.** (de qn) to stand in (for sb) **intérimaire** [ɛ̃terimɛr] **1** adj (fonction, employé) temporary; (directeur, ministre) acting; (cabinet, gouvernement) caretaker **2** nmf (travailleur) temporary worker; (secrétaire) temp
intérioriser [ɛ̃terjɔrize] vt to internalize
interjection [ɛ̃terʒɛksjɔ̃] nf interjection
interligne [ɛ̃terliɲ] nm line spacing; **dans l'i.** in the space between the lines; **simple/double i.** single/double spacing
interlocuteur, -trice [ɛ̃terlɔkytœr, -tris] nm,f (a) (dans une conversation) speaker; **mon i.** the person I was/am speaking to (b) (dans une négociation) discussion partner
interloqué, -e [ɛ̃terlɔke] adj taken aback
interlude [ɛ̃terlyd] nm interlude
intermède [ɛ̃termɛd] nm aussi Fig interlude
intermédiaire [ɛ̃termedjɛr] **1** adj intermediate; **i. entre** halfway between; **trouver une solution i.** to find a compromise solution; **pointure i.** size in between **2** nmf (personne) intermediary, go-between; Com middleman; **sans i.** directly **3** nm **par l'i. de** through; **sans l'i. de** without
interminable [ɛ̃terminabl] adj interminable
interministériel, -elle [ɛ̃terministerjɛl] adj interministerial
intermittence [ɛ̃termitɑ̃s] nf **par i.** intermittently, on and off
intermittent, -e [ɛ̃termitɑ̃, -ɑ̃t] **1** adj (lumière, bruit, tir) intermittent, sporadic; (travail) casual **2** nm,f casual worker
internat [ɛ̃terna] nm (a) Scol (système) boarding; (pensionnat) boarding school (b) Méd (concours) entrance examination for Br a housemanship or Am an internship; (formation) Br clinicals, Am internship
international, -e, -aux, -ales [ɛ̃ternasjɔnal, -o] **1** adj & nm,f international
2 nf **l'Internationale** (groupement) the International; (chant) the Internationale
internationalisation [ɛ̃ternasjɔnalizasjɔ̃] nf internationalization
internationaliser [ɛ̃ternasjɔnalize] **1** vt to internationalize **2** s'internationaliser vpr to become international
internaute [ɛ̃ternot] nmf Internet surfer
interne [ɛ̃tern] **1** adj (structure, paroi, hémorragie) internal; (côté) inner; (de l'entreprise) in-house **2** nmf (élève) boarder; **i. (des hôpitaux)** Br house doctor, Am intern
internement [ɛ̃ternəmɑ̃] nm (emprisonnement) internment; (hospitalisation) confinement
interner [ɛ̃terne] vt (emprisonner) to intern; (hospitaliser) to commit
Internet [ɛ̃ternɛt] nm **l'I.** the Internet; **sur I.** on the Internet
interparlementaire [ɛ̃terparləmɑ̃tɛr] adj (réunion) interparliamentary; (commission) joint
interpellation [ɛ̃terpelasjɔ̃] nf (appel) calling out; (au Parlement) question; **la police a procédé à plusieurs interpellations** the police took several people in for questioning
interpeller [ɛ̃terpele] **1** vt (a) (appeler) to call (out) to; (sujet: police) to take in for questioning; (ministre) to heckle; (sujet: sentinelle) to challenge (b) (toucher) **ce roman m'a interpellé** I can really relate to this novel

2 s'interpeller vpr (s'appeler) to call (out) to each other; (s'insulter) to shout insults at each other
Interphone® [ɛ̃terfɔn] nm (de bureau) intercom; (d'immeuble) Entryphone®; **à l'i.** on the intercom/Entryphone®
interplanétaire [ɛ̃terplanetɛr] adj interplanetary
interpolation [ɛ̃terpɔlasjɔ̃] nf interpolation
interpoler [ɛ̃terpɔle] vt to interpolate
interposé, -e [ɛ̃terpoze] adj **par personne interposée** through an intermediary
interposer [ɛ̃terpoze] **1** vt to interpose (**entre** between) **2 s'interposer** vpr (intervenir) to intervene
interprétariat [ɛ̃terpretarja] nm interpreting
interprétation [ɛ̃terpretasjɔ̃] nf (a) (d'un texte, d'un rôle, d'un rêve, d'un rôle) interpretation (b) (traduction) interpreting
interprète [ɛ̃terprɛt] nmf (dans une autre langue) interpreter; (d'un rôle, d'une œuvre musicale) performer; (porte-parole) spokesman, f spokeswoman; **i. de conférence** conference interpreter
interpréter [34] [ɛ̃terprete] vt (a) (rôle, œuvre musicale) to perform, to interpret (b) (texte, paroles, geste, rêve) to interpret; **mal i. les paroles de qn** to misinterpret sb's words
interrogateur, -trice [ɛ̃terɔgatœr, -tris] **1** adj questioning **2** nm,f (examinateur) (oral) examiner
interrogatif, -ive [ɛ̃terɔgatif, -iv] **1** adj (a) (air, ton) inquiring, questioning (b) (pronom, phrase) interrogative **2** nm interrogative **3** nf **interrogative** interrogative (clause)
interrogation [ɛ̃terɔgasjɔ̃] nf (a) (question) question; **i. directe/indirecte** direct/indirect question; **i. écrite/orale** written/oral test (b) (d'un prisonnier, d'un suspect) questioning, interrogation (c) Ordinat (d'une base de données) inquiry, query; (activité) interrogation; **i. à distance** remote interrogation
interrogatoire [ɛ̃terɔgatwar] nm questioning
interroger [45] [ɛ̃terɔʒe] **1** vt (a) (personne) to question; (candidat, élève) to test; **i. qn du regard** to look at sb questioningly (b) Ordinat (base de données) to query, to interrogate **2 s'interroger** vpr to ask oneself, to wonder (**sur** about)
interrompre [ɛ̃terɔ̃pr] **1** vt to interrupt; (trafic) to hold up; (grossesse) to terminate **2 s'interrompre** vpr to break off
interrupteur [ɛ̃teryptœr] nm switch; **i. à bascule** toggle switch; Ordinat **i. DIP** ou **à plusieurs positions** DIP switch
interruption [ɛ̃terypsjɔ̃] nf (arrêt) interruption; (de négociations) breaking off; **sans i.** non-stop, continuously; Ordinat **fonction d'i.** interrupt function; **i. volontaire de grossesse** termination (of pregnancy)
intersection [ɛ̃terseksjɔ̃] nf intersection, junction
intersidéral, -e, -aux, -ales [ɛ̃tersideral, -o] adj interstellar
Interstice [ɛ̃terstis] nm chink, crack
intersyndical, -e, -aux, -ales [ɛ̃tersɛ̃dikal, -o] **1** adj interunion **2** nf **intersyndicale** (association) interunion group
intertitre [ɛ̃tertitr] nm Journ subheading; Cin subtitle
interurbain, -e [ɛ̃teryrbɛ̃, -ɛn] **1** adj interurban; Vieilli Tél **appel i.** trunk call **2** nm Vieilli Tél long-distance service
intervalle [ɛ̃terval] nm (a) (dans le temps, en musique) interval; **un i. d'une heure** a one-hour interval; **à deux mois d'i.** two months apart; **par intervalles** at intervals,

now and then; **dans l'i.** in the meantime, meanwhile (**b**) *(dans l'espace)* gap, space; **à 2 mètres d'i.** 2 metres apart (**c**) *Math* interval

intervenant, -e [ɛ̃tɛrvənɑ̃, -ɑ̃t] *nm,f (dans une conférence, un débat)* speaker, contributor

intervenir [70] [ɛ̃tɛrvənir] *vi* (**a**) *(agir, prendre la parole)* to intervene (**dans** in); **i. pour faire qch** to intervene or step in to do sth; **i. en faveur de qn** to intervene on sb's behalf; **i. auprès de qn** to intercede with sb; **faire i. qn** to bring sb in (**b**) *(arriver) (événement, changement)* to occur; *(accord)* to be reached (**c**) *(jouer un rôle)* to play a part (**dans** in)

intervention [ɛ̃tɛrvɑ̃sjɔ̃] *nf* (**a**) *(intercession, ingérence)* intervention (**en faveur de/auprès de** on behalf of/with) (**b**) *(prise de parole)* intervention; *(discours)* speech (**c**) *(opération)* **i.** (**chirurgicale**) operation

interventionniste [ɛ̃tɛrvɑ̃sjɔnist] *adj & nmf* interventionist

interversion [ɛ̃tɛrvɛrsjɔ̃] *nf* inversion, reversal

intervertir [ɛ̃tɛrvɛrtir] *vt (l'ordre de qch)* to invert, to reverse; *(objets, éléments)* to switch (round); *(rôles)* to reverse

intervienne *voir* **intervenir**

interview [ɛ̃tɛrvju] *nm ou nf* interview

interviewer [ɛ̃tɛrvjuve] *vt* to interview

intestin¹, -e [ɛ̃tɛstɛ̃, -in] *adj Litt* internal

intestin² *nm* intestine; **intestins** intestines, bowels; **gros i.** large intestine; **i. grêle** small intestine

intestinal, -e, -aux, -ales [ɛ̃tɛstinal, -o] *adj* intestinal

intime [ɛ̃tim] **1** *adj* intimate; *(hygiène, toilette)* personal; **être i. avec qn** to be close to sb; **avoir l'i. conviction que...** to be thoroughly convinced that...
2 *nmf* close friend; **pour les intimes** to my/her/*etc* friends

intimement [ɛ̃timmɑ̃] *adv* intimately; **i. liés** *(amis)* very close; *(phénomènes)* closely linked; **être i. persuadé que...** to be thoroughly convinced that...

intimer [ɛ̃time] *vt* (**a**) *(ordonner)* **i. à qn l'ordre de faire qch** to order sb to do sth (**b**) *Jur* to summon before the Court of Appeal

intimidant, -e [ɛ̃timidɑ̃, -ɑ̃t] *adj* intimidating

intimidation [ɛ̃timidasjɔ̃] *nf* intimidation

intimider [ɛ̃timide] *vt* to intimidate

intimité [ɛ̃timite] *nf (vie privée)* privacy; *(familiarité)* intimacy, closeness; **dans l'i.** in private; **le mariage a eu lieu dans la plus stricte i.** only close family and friends attended the wedding

intitulé [ɛ̃tityle] *nm (de livre)* title; *(de chapitre)* heading, title

intituler [ɛ̃tityle] **1** *vt (livre, chanson)* to give a title to; **un livre intitulé...** a book entitled or called...
2 s'intituler *vpr (livre, chanson)* to be entitled, to be called; *(personne)* to call oneself

intolérable [ɛ̃tɔlerabl] *adj* intolerable

intolérance [ɛ̃tɔlerɑ̃s] *nf* intolerance; *Méd* **i. à qch** intolerance to sth

intolérant, -e [ɛ̃tɔlerɑ̃, -ɑ̃t] *adj* intolerant

intonation [ɛ̃tɔnasjɔ̃] *nf* intonation

intouchable [ɛ̃tuʃabl] *adj & nmf* untouchable

intox [ɛ̃tɔks] *nf Fam* brainwashing

intoxication [ɛ̃tɔksikasjɔ̃] *nf (empoisonnement)* poisoning; *Fig* brainwashing; **i. alimentaire** food poisoning

intoxiquer [ɛ̃tɔksike] **1** *vt (empoisonner)* to poison; *Fig* to brainwash
2 s'intoxiquer *vpr* to poison oneself

intradermique [ɛ̃tradɛrmik] *Méd* **1** *adj* intradermal
2 *nf* intradermal injection

intraduisible [ɛ̃traduizibl] *adj* untranslatable

intraitable [ɛ̃trɛtabl] *adj* uncompromising, inflexible (**sur** about)

intra-muros [ɛ̃tramyros] **1** *adj inv* **Londres/Paris i.** inner London/Paris
2 *adv* within the city

intramusculaire [ɛ̃tramyskylɛr] **1** *adj* intramuscular
2 *nf* intramuscular injection

intransigeance [ɛ̃trɑ̃ziʒɑ̃s] *nf* intransigence

intransigeant, -e [ɛ̃trɑ̃ziʒɑ̃, -ɑ̃t] *adj (personne)* intransigent, uncompromising (**envers/sur** with/about); *(morale)* uncompromising

intransitif, -ive [ɛ̃trɑ̃zitif, -iv] *adj & nm Gram* intransitive

intransmissible [ɛ̃trɑ̃smisibl] *adj* untransferable

intransportable [ɛ̃trɑ̃spɔrtabl] *adj (objet)* untransportable; *(blessé)* unfit to travel

intraveineux, -euse [ɛ̃travɛnø, -øz] **1** *adj* intravenous
2 *nf* intraveineuse intravenous injection

intrépide [ɛ̃trepid] *adj* intrepid, fearless

intrépidité [ɛ̃trepidite] *nf* fearlessness

intrigant, -e [ɛ̃trigɑ̃, -ɑ̃t] **1** *adj* scheming, plotting
2 *nm,f* schemer

intrigue [ɛ̃trig] *nf (machination)* intrigue; *(liaison amoureuse)* (love) affair; *(d'un roman, d'un film)* plot

intriguer [ɛ̃trige] **1** *vt* to intrigue
2 *vi* to scheme, to intrigue

intrinsèque [ɛ̃trɛ̃sɛk] *adj* intrinsic

intrinsèquement [ɛ̃trɛ̃sɛkmɑ̃] *adv* intrinsically

intro [ɛ̃tro] *nf Fam* intro; *(musicale)* theme tune

introductif, -ive [ɛ̃trodyktif, -iv] *adj* (**a**) *(discours, exposé)* introductory, opening (**b**) *Jur* introductory

introduction [ɛ̃trodyksjɔ̃] *nf* introduction; *(insertion)* insertion, introduction (**dans** into); *(au rugby)* put-in; **i. en Bourse** listing on the stock market

introduire [18] [ɛ̃trodɥir] **1** *vt (dans une serrure, dans un trou)* to insert (**dans** into); *(marchandises)* to bring in; *(coutume, réforme, mesures, mode)* to introduce; *(étranger, visiteur)* to show in; **i. qn auprès de qn** *(faire entrer)* to show sb in to see sb; *(présenter)* to introduce sb to sb; **i. en Bourse** to list on the stock market; **i. sur le marché** to launch onto the market
2 s'introduire *vpr* **s'i. dans une maison** to get into a house; **l'eau s'introduit partout** there's water coming in everywhere

intronisation [ɛ̃tronizasjɔ̃] *nf* enthronement; *Fig* establishment

introniser [ɛ̃tronize] *vt* to enthrone; *Fig* to establish

introspection [ɛ̃trospɛksjɔ̃] *nf* introspection

introuvable [ɛ̃truvabl] *adj (produit, denrées)* unobtainable; *(personne)* nowhere to be found

introversion [ɛ̃trovɛrsjɔ̃] *nf* introversion

introverti, -e [ɛ̃trovɛrti] **1** *adj* introverted
2 *nm,f* introvert

intrus, -e [ɛ̃try, -yz] *nm,f aussi Ordinat* intruder

intrusion [ɛ̃tryzjɔ̃] *nf* intrusion (**dans** into)

intuitif, -ive [ɛ̃tɥitif, -iv] **1** *adj* intuitive
2 *nm,f* **c'est un i.** he's an intuitive sort

intuition [ɛ̃tɥisjɔ̃] *nf* intuition; **avoir l'i. de qch/que** to sense sth/that

intuitivement [ɛ̃tɥitivmɑ̃] *adv* intuitively

inusable [inyzabl] *adj aussi Fig* hard-wearing

inusité, -e [inyzite] *adj (mot)* uncommon
inutile [inytil] *adj (qui ne sert à rien)* useless; *(effort)* vain, pointless; *(précautions, démarche, bagages)* unnecessary; **c'est i.!** *(ça ne sert à rien)* it's pointless!; *(ce n'est pas nécessaire)* you/he/*etc* needn't bother!; **i. de dire que...** needless to say,...; **c'est i. d'attendre** there's no point in waiting; **i. d'insister, je ne viens pas** don't go on about it, I'm not coming
inutilement [inytilmɑ̃] *adv* needlessly, unnecessarily
inutilisable [inytilizabl] *adj* unusable
inutilisé, -e [inytilize] *adj* unused
inutilité [inytilite] *nf (d'un objet)* uselessness; *(d'un effort, d'un argument)* pointlessness
invaincu, -e [ɛ̃vɛ̃ky] *adj* undefeated
invalidant, -e [ɛ̃validɑ̃, -ɑ̃t] *adj* disabling
invalidation [ɛ̃validasjɔ̃] *nf Jur* invalidation
invalide [ɛ̃valid] **1** *adj* disabled
2 *nmf* disabled person, invalid; **i. de guerre** disabled ex-serviceman/cx-servicewoman
invalider [ɛ̃valide] *vt Jur* to invalidate
invalidité [ɛ̃validite] *nf* disability
invariable [ɛ̃varjabl] *adj* invariable
invariablement [ɛ̃varjabləmɑ̃] *adv* invariably
invasion [ɛ̃vazjɔ̃] *nf aussi Fig* invasion
invective [ɛ̃vɛktiv] *nf* invective; **invectives** abuse
invectiver [ɛ̃vɛktive] **1** *vt* to hurl abuse at
2 s'invectiver *vpr* to hurl abuse at each other
invendable [ɛ̃vɑ̃dabl] *adj* unsellable
invendu, -e [ɛ̃vɑ̃dy] **1** *adj* unsold
2 *nm* **invendus** unsold goods; *(journaux, livres)* unsold copies; *(revendus moins cher)* remainders
inventaire [ɛ̃vɑ̃tɛr] *nm* **(a)** *(liste)* inventory **(b)** *(de marchandises)* stocklist; **faire** *ou* **dresser l'i. (des stocks)** to stocktake, **fermé pour cause d'i.** *(sur un écriteau)* closed for stocktaking **(c)** *Fig (de peintures, de richesses artistiques)* survey
inventer [ɛ̃vɑ̃te] **1** *vt (machine)* to invent; *(concept, moyen)* to think up; *(histoire, excuse)* to make up; *(expression)* to coin; **qu'est-ce qu'il va encore i.?** what's he going to come out with next?; *Fam* **il n'a pas inventé la poudre** *ou* **le fil à couper le beurre** he'll never set the Thames on fire
2 s'inventer *vpr* **ça ne s'invente pas** you can't make something like that up; **s'i. un passé** to invent a past for oneself
inventeur, -trice [ɛ̃vɑ̃tœr, -tris] *nm,f* **(a)** *(d'une machine, d'un procédé)* inventor **(b)** *Jur (d'un trésor)* finder
inventif, -ive [ɛ̃vɑ̃tif, -iv] *adj* inventive
invention [ɛ̃vɑ̃sjɔ̃] *nf* **(a)** *(action)* invention; *(faculté)* inventiveness **(b)** *(chose découverte, mensonge)* invention **(c)** *Jur (d'un trésor)* finding
inventorier [66] [ɛ̃vɑ̃tɔrje] *vt* to make an inventory of; *(marchandises)* to make a stocklist of
invérifiable [ɛ̃verifjabl] *adj* unverifiable
inverse [ɛ̃vɛrs] **1** *adj aussi Math* inverse; **en sens i. (de)** in the opposite direction (to); **dans l'ordre i.** in reverse order; **dans le sens i. des aiguilles d'une montre** *Br* anti-clockwise, *Am* counterclockwise
2 *nm* **l'i.** the opposite, the reverse; **faire l'i. (de)** to do the opposite (of); **à l'i.** on the contrary
inversement [ɛ̃vɛrsəmɑ̃] *adv* **et i.** and vice versa; **i., on peut dire que...** conversely, one can say that...; **i. proportionnel (à)** inversely proportional (to)
inverser [ɛ̃vɛrse] *vt (ordre, tendance)* to reverse; *(deux mots)* to invert
inversion [ɛ̃vɛrsjɔ̃] *nf (d'ordre, de mots)* inversion; *Ordinat* **i. vidéo** reverse video

invertébré, -e [ɛ̃vɛrtebre] *adj & nm* invertebrate
inverti, -e [ɛ̃vɛrti] *adj (sucre)* invert
investigateur, -trice [ɛ̃vɛstigatœr, -tris] **1** *adj (regard)* searching
2 *nm,f* investigator
investigation [ɛ̃vɛstigasjɔ̃] *nf* investigation
investir [ɛ̃vɛstir] **1** *vt* **(a)** *(argent, temps, énergie)* to invest **(dans** in) **(b)** *(ville, édifice)* to besiege **(c)** *(charger)* **i. qn d'une mission** to entrust sb with a mission
2 *vi* to invest **(dans** in)
3 s'investir *vpr* **s'i. dans qch** to put a lot into sth
investissement [ɛ̃vɛstismɑ̃] *nm* investment; **i. à court/ long terme** short-/long-term investment
investisseur [ɛ̃vɛstisœr] *nm* investor
investiture [ɛ̃vɛstityr] *nf (d'un candidat)* nomination; *(d'un gouvernement)* voting in; *(d'un évêque)* investiture
invétéré, -e [ɛ̃vetere] *adj* inveterate
invincible [ɛ̃vɛ̃sibl] *adj (armée, adversaire)* invincible; *(peur)* unconquerable
inviolabilité [ɛ̃vjɔlabilite] *nf Jur* inviolability, *(d'un parlementaire)* immunity; **i. diplomatique** diplomatic immunity
inviolable [ɛ̃vjɔlabl] *adj (coffre)* burglarproof; *(droit, asile)* inviolable; *(parlementaire)* immune
invisibilité [ɛ̃vizibilite] *nf* invisibility
invisible [ɛ̃vizibl] *adj* invisible
invitation [ɛ̃vitasjɔ̃] *nf* invitation; **venir à** *ou* **sur l'i. de qn** to come at sb's invitation; **sur i.** by invitation
invite [ɛ̃vit] *nf* **(a)** *(invitation)* invitation **(b)** *Ordinat* prompt; **i. du DOS** DOS prompt; **i. du système** system prompt
invité, -e [ɛ̃vite] *nm,f* guest
inviter [ɛ̃vite] **1** *vt* **(a)** *(convier)* to invite; **i. qn à dîner** to invite *ou* ask sb to dinner **(b)** **i. qn à faire qch** *(inciter)* to urge sb to do sth; *(prier)* to request sb to do sth; **je vous invite à me suivre** would you be so kind as to follow me
2 *vi (payer)* **c'est moi qui invite!** it's my treat!
3 s'inviter *vpr* to invite oneself
in vitro [invitro] *adj inv & adv* in vitro
invivable [ɛ̃vivabl] *adj* unbearable
in vivo [invivo] *adj inv & adv* in vivo
invocation [ɛ̃vɔkasjɔ̃] *nf* invocation
involontaire [ɛ̃vɔlɔ̃tɛr] *adj (mouvement, geste)* involuntary; *(erreur, réaction)* unintentional; *(témoin)* unwilling
involontairement [ɛ̃vɔlɔ̃tɛrmɑ̃] *adv* involuntarily, unintentionally
invoquer [ɛ̃vɔke] *vt* **(a)** *(raison, argument)* to put forward; *(prétexte, excuse)* to plead; *(loi, texte)* to refer to **(b)** *(Dieu, divinité, esprit)* to invoke; **i. l'aide de qn** to call upon sb's help
invraisemblable [ɛ̃vrɛsɑ̃blabl] *adj* **(a)** *(hypothèse)* unlikely **(b)** *(excuses, alibi)* implausible **(c)** *(extraordinaire)* incredible
invraisemblance [ɛ̃vrɛsɑ̃blɑ̃s] *nf (improbabilité)* unlikelihood; *(d'un récit, d'une excuse)* implausibility; **des invraisemblances** implausibilities
invulnérabilité [ɛ̃vylnerabilite] *nf* invulnerability
invulnérable [ɛ̃vylnerabl] *adj* invulnerable
iode [jɔd] *nm* iodine
iodé, -e [jɔde] *adj (eau, air)* iodized
ion [jɔ̃] *nm* ion
iota [jɔta] *nm inv* iota; **ça n'a pas changé d'un i.** it hasn't changed one iota; **ne pas bouger d'un i.** not to budge an inch

ipso facto [ipsofakto] *adv* ipso facto
ira, irai *etc voir* **aller**
Irak [irak] *nm* **l'I.** Iraq
irakien, -enne [irakjɛ̃, -ɛn] **1** *adj* Iraqi
2 *nm,f* **I.** Iraqi
Iran [irɑ̃] *nm* **l'I.** Iran
iranien, -enne [iranjɛ̃, -ɛn] **1** *adj* Iranian
2 *nm,f* **I.** Iranian
3 *nm (langue)* Iranian
Iraq [irak] = **Irak**
iraquien, -enne [irakjɛ̃, -ɛn] = **irakien**
irascible [irasibl] *adj Litt* irascible
iriez *etc voir* **aller**
iris [iris] *nm* **(a)** *(de l'œil)* iris **(b)** *(fleur)* iris
irisé, -e [irize] *adj* iridescent
irlandais, -e [irlɑ̃dɛ, -ɛz] **1** *adj* Irish
2 *nm,f* **I.** Irishman, *f* Irishwoman; **I. du Nord** person from Northern Ireland; **les I.** the Irish
3 *nm (langue)* Irish
Irlande [irlɑ̃d] *nf* **l'I.** Ireland, Eire; **l'I. du Nord** Northern Ireland, Ulster
IRM [iɛrɛm] *nf Méd (abrév* **imagerie par résonance magnétique**) MRI
ironie [irɔni] *nf* irony; **l'i. du sort a voulu que...** as fate would have it,...
ironique [irɔnik] *adj* ironic(al)
ironiquement [irɔnikmɑ̃] *adv* ironically
ironiser [irɔnize] *vi* to be ironical (**sur** about)
irradiation [iradjasjɔ̃] *nf Phys & Méd* irradiation
irradier [66] [iradje] **1** *vi (rayons)* to radiate; *(douleur)* to spread
2 *vt* to irradiate
irraisonné, -e [irɛzɔne] *adj* irrational
irrationnel, -elle [irasjɔnɛl] *adj* irrational
irrattrapable [iratrapabl] *adj (retard)* that cannot be made up; *(erreur)* irredeemable
irréalisable [irealizabl] *adj (rêve)* unrealizable; *(projet)* impracticable
irréaliste [irealist] *adj* unrealistic
irréalité [irealite] *nf* unreality
irrecevable [irəsəvabl] *adj (inacceptable)* unacceptable; *Jur (preuve, demande)* inadmissible
irrécupérable [irekyperabl] *adj (argent)* irrecoverable; *(personne)* irredeemable; *(appareil, voiture)* beyond repair
irrécusable [irekyzabl] *adj* **(a)** *(indéniable) (preuve, signe)* indisputable **(b)** *Jur (témoignage, juge)* unimpeachable
irréductible [iredyktibl] **1** *adj* **(a)** *(volonté, optimisme)* indomitable, invincible; *(attachement, fidélité)* unshakeable; *(opposition, ennemi)* implacable **(b)** *(fracture, fraction)* irreducible
2 *nmf* diehard
irréel, -elle [ireɛl] **1** *adj* unreal
2 *nm* **l'i.** the unreal; *Gram* **l'i. du présent/passé** the hypothetical present/past
irréfléchi, -e [irefleʃi] *adj* rash
irréfutable [irefytabl] *adj* irrefutable
irrégularité [iregylarite] *nf* **(a)** *(du sol, d'un terrain)* unevenness; *(du pouls, de traits, d'horaires)* irregularity **(b)** *(acte)* irregularity
irrégulier, -ère [iregylje, -ɛr] *adj* **(a)** *(sol, terrain)* uneven; *(rythme, respiration, traits, verbe)* irregular; *(résultats, athlète)* inconsistent **(b)** *(malhonnête) (procédure, situation)* irregular; **être en situation irrégulière** *(étranger)*

not to have one's residence papers in order; *(voyageur)* not to hold a valid ticket
irrégulièrement [iregyljɛrmɑ̃] *adv* irregularly
irréligieux, -euse [ireliʒjø, -øz] *adj* irreligious
irrémédiable [iremedjabl] *adj (préjudice, perte, problème)* irreparable; *(désastre)* irreversible
irrémissible [iremisibl] *adj Litt* **(a)** *(impardonnable)* unpardonable **(b)** *(irrémédiable)* irreversible
irremplaçable [irɑ̃plasabl] *adj* irreplaceable
irréparable [ireparabl] **1** *adj (tort, perte, erreur)* irreparable; *(affront)* unpardonable; *(vêtement, voiture, télévision)* beyond repair
2 *nm* commettre **l'i.** to go beyond the point of no return
irrépressible [irepresibl] *adj* irrepressible
irréprochable [ireprɔʃabl] *adj (personne, conduite)* irreproachable; *(tenue, travail)* impeccable; **d'une propreté** **i.** impeccably clean
irrésistible [irezistibl] *adj (personne, charme)* irresistible; *(envie, besoin)* compelling
irrésolu, -e [irezɔly] *adj* **(a)** *(personne)* indecisive; *(pas)* uncertain **(b)** *(problème)* unresolved
irrespect [irɛspɛ] *nm* disrespect (**envers** towards)
irrespectueux, -euse [irɛspɛktɥø, -øz] *adj* disrespectful (**envers** towards)
irrespirable [irɛspirabl] *adj (air)* unbreathable; *Fig (atmosphère)* unbearable
irresponsable [irɛspɔ̃sabl] **1** *adj* irresponsible
2 *nmf* irresponsible person
irrévérence [ireverɑ̃s] *nf* irreverence
irrévérencieux, -euse [ireverɑ̃sjø, -øz] *adj* irreverent
irréversible [ireversibl] *adj* irreversible
irrévocabilité [irevɔkabilite] *nf* irrevocability
irrévocable [irevɔkabl] *adj* irrevocable
irrévocablement [irevɔkabləmɑ̃] *adv* irrevocably
irrigation [irigasjɔ̃] *nf* irrigation; **l'i. du cerveau** the blood supply to the brain
irriguer [irige] *vt* to irrigate; **le cerveau n'est plus irrigué** the brain is no longer being supplied with blood
irritable [iritabl] *adj* irritable
irritant, -e [iritɑ̃, -ɑ̃t] *adj* **(a)** *(personne, comportement)* irritating **(b)** *(substance)* irritant (**pour** to)
irritation [iritasjɔ̃] *nf aussi Méd* irritation
irrité, -e [irite] *adj* **(a)** *(énervé)* irritated (**contre** with) **(b)** *(enflammé)* irritated, inflamed
irriter [irite] **1** *vt (énerver, enflammer)* to irritate
2 s'irriter *vpr (s'énerver)* **s'i. contre qn/de qch** to get irritated with sb/at sth **(b)** *(s'enflammer)* to become irritated *or* inflamed
irruption [irypsjɔ̃] *nf* **(a)** *(entrée)* irruption; **faire i. dans** *(lieu)* to burst into **(b)** *(invasion)* invasion **(c)** *(émergence)* upsurge
islam [islam] *nm* **l'I.** Islam
islamique [islamik] *adj* Islamic
islamiste [islamist] *nmf* Islamic fundamentalist
islandais, -e [islɑ̃dɛ, -ɛz] **1** *adj* Icelandic
2 *nm,f* **I.** Icelander
3 *nm (langue)* Icelandic
Islande [islɑ̃d] *nf* **l'I.** Iceland
isobare [izɔbar] **1** *adj* isobaric
2 *nf* isobar
isocèle [izɔsɛl] *adj* isosceles
isolant, -e [izɔlɑ̃, -ɑ̃t] **1** *adj (contre le froid, en électricité)* insulating; *(contre le bruit)* soundproofing

2 *nm (contre le froid, en électricité)* insulating material; *(contre le bruit)* soundproofing (material)

isolation [izɔlasjɔ̃] *nf (électrique)* insulation; **i. acoustique** *ou* **phonique** soundproofing; **i. thermique** (thermal) insulation

isolationniste [izɔlasjɔnist] *adj & nmf* isolationist

isolé, -e [izɔle] *adj* **(a)** *(personne, cas, endroit, maison)* isolated **(b)** *(protégé) (en électricité, du froid)* insulated; *(du bruit)* soundproofed

isolement [izɔlmɑ̃] *nm* **(a)** *(d'une personne, d'une maison)* isolation **(b)** *(isolation)* insulation

isolément [izɔlemɑ̃] *adv (agir)* in isolation; *(interroger des gens)* individually

isoler [izɔle] **1** *vt* **(a)** *(séparer)* to isolate (**de** from) **(b)** *(protéger) (du froid, d'un courant électrique)* to insulate; *(du bruit)* to soundproof
2 s'isoler *vpr* to isolate oneself

isoloir [izɔlwar] *nm* polling booth

isotherme [izɔtɛrm] **1** *adj* maintained at a constant temperature; **boîte/sac i.** cool box/bag; **bouteille i.** vacuum flask
2 *nf* isotherm

Israël [israɛl] *n* Israel

israélien, -enne [israeljɛ̃, -ɛn] **1** *adj* Israeli
2 *nm,f* I. Israeli

israélite [israelit] **1** *adj* Jewish
2 *nmf* Jew

issu, -e [isy] *adj* **être i. de** *(être originaire de)* to come from; *(résulter de)* to stem from

issue [isy] *nf* **(a)** *(sortie)* exit; *Fig (solution)* way out; **i. de secours** emergency exit **(b)** *(fin)* outcome; **à l'i. de** at the end of

Istanbul [istɑ̃bul] *n* Istanbul

isthme [ism] *nm* isthmus

Italie [itali] *nf* l'l. Italy

italien, -enne [italjɛ̃, -ɛn] **1** *adj* Italian
2 *nm,f* I. Italian
3 *nm (langue)* Italian
4 *nf* **italienne** *Ordinat* **imprimer à l'italienne** to print landscape

italique [italik] **1** *adj* italic
2 *nm* **en italique(s)** in italics

Ithaque [itak] *nf* Ithaca

itinéraire [itinerɛr] *nm* route, itinerary; **i. bis** = alternative route recommended when roads are highly congested, especially at peak holiday times; **i. touristique** tourist route

itinérant, -e [itinerɑ̃, -ɑ̃t] *adj (comédiens, exposition)* travelling; *(ambassadeur)* roving

itou [itu] *adv Fam Vieilli* likewise, too; **et moi i.!** me too!

IUFM [iyɛfɛm] *nm (abrév* **Institut universitaire de formation des maîtres)** ≃ teacher training college

IUT [iyte] *nm (abrév* **Institut universitaire de technologie)** = vocational higher education college

IVG [iveʒe] *nf (abrév* **interruption volontaire de grossesse)** termination (of pregnancy)

ivoire [ivwar] *nm* ivory

ivoirien, -enne [ivwarjɛ̃, -ɛn] **1** *adj* of the Ivory Coast
2 *nm, f* I. person from the Ivory Coast

ivre [ivr] *adj* drunk; **i. mort** blind drunk; **i. de joie** beside oneself with joy

ivresse [ivrɛs] *nf (ébriété)* drunkenness; *(extase)* exhilaration; **conduite en état d'i.** drink-driving

ivrogne [ivrɔɲ] *nmf* drunkard

ivrognerie [ivrɔɲri] *nf* drunkenness

J, j [ʒi] *nm inv* J, j

j' [ʒ] *voir* je

jabot [ʒabo] *nm* (a) *(d'oiseau)* crop (b) *(de chemise)* frill, ruffle

jacassements [ʒakasmɑ̃] *nmpl (d'une pie, d'une personne)* chattering

jacasser [ʒakase] *vi (pie, personne)* to chatter

jachère [ʒaʃɛr] *nf* leaving land fallow; **laisser en j.** *(champ)* to leave fallow; *Fig (talent)* to leave undeveloped

jacinthe [ʒasɛ̃t] *nf* hyacinth

jacquard [ʒakar] *adj (pull)* argyle

jacquet [ʒakɛ] *nm* backgammon

jacter [ʒakte] *vi Fam* to gab

Jacuzzi® [ʒakyzi] *nm* Jacuzzi®

jade [ʒad] *nm* (a) *(pierre)* jade (b) *(objet)* jade object

jadis [ʒadis] *Litt* **1** *adv* in times past, formerly; **les chevaliers de j.** the knights of old **2** *adj* **au temps j.** in the olden days

jaguar [ʒagwar] *nm* jaguar

jaillir [ʒajir] *vi* (a) *(source, liquide)* to gush out; *(étincelles, flammes, foule)* to shoot out; *(lumière)* to flash (b) *(rires, cris)* to burst out

jais [ʒɛ] *nm* jet; **(d'un noir) de j.** jet-black

Jakarta [dʒakarta] *n* Jakarta

jalon [ʒalɔ̃] *nm* ranging pole; *Fig* **poser des jalons** to prepare the ground

jalonner [ʒalɔne] *vt (marquer) (parcelle, piste d'atterrissage)* to mark out; *(ponctuer) (route, côte)* to line (**de** with); *Fig* to punctuate

jalousement [ʒaluzmɑ̃] *adv* jealously

jalouser [ʒaluze] *vt* to be jealous of

jalousie [ʒaluzi] *nf* (a) *(sentiment)* jealousy; **éprouver de la j. envers qn** to feel jealous of sb; **être malade de j.** to be green with envy (b) *(store)* Venetian blind

jaloux, -ouse [ʒalu, -uz] **1** *adj* jealous (**de** of); **j. comme un tigre** wildly jealous **2** *nm,f* **c'est un j.** he's a jealous man; **faire des j.** to make people jealous

jamaïcain, -e, jamaïquain, -e [ʒamaikɛ̃, -ɛn] **1** *adj* Jamaican **2** *nm,f* **J.** Jamaican

Jamaïque [ʒamaik] *nf* **la J.** Jamaica

jamais [ʒamɛ] *adv* (a) *(positif)* ever; **plus que j.** more than ever; **à (tout) j.** for good, for ever; **si j. elle revenait** if she ever came back; **le film le plus triste que j'aie j. vu** the saddest film I've ever seen (b) *(négatif)* never; **je ne l'ai j. vu** I've never seen him; **il a passé toute sa vie sans j. boire un verre d'alcool** he's spent all his life without ever touching a drop of alcohol; **j. plus** never again; **j., au grand j., je ne le dirai** I shall never ever tell; **elle n'a j. que dix minutes de retard** she's only ten minutes late; *Fam* **j. de la vie!** not on your life!; *Prov* **j. deux sans trois** things come in threes

jambe [ʒɑ̃b] *nf* leg; **jambes nues** bare-legged; **traîner la j.** *(de fatigue)* to drag one's feet; *(en boitant)* to drag one foot behind one; **à toutes jambes** as fast as one can; **prendre ses jambes à son cou** to take to one's heels; **être dans les jambes de qn** to be under sb's feet; **traiter qn par-dessous** *ou* **par-dessus la j.** to treat sb in an offhand manner; *Fam* **ça me fait une belle j.!** a fat lot of good that does me!; *Fam* **tenir la j. à qn** to drone on and on at sb; **j. de bois** wooden leg

jambière [ʒɑ̃bjɛr] *nf* (a) *(de sport)* (shin) pad (b) *(pour tenir chaud)* legwarmer

jambon [ʒɑ̃bɔ̃] *nm* ham; **j. blanc** boiled ham; **j. cru** raw ham; **j. fumé** smoked ham; **j. de Parme** Parma ham

jambonneau, -x [ʒɑ̃bɔno] *nm* knuckle of ham

jante [ʒɑ̃t] *nf* rim

janvier [ʒɑ̃vje] *nm* January; **en j., au mois de j.** in January; **nous sommes le 7 j.** it's the 7th of January, it's January the 7th; **j'y vais le 7 j.** I'm going on the 7th of January *or* January the 7th

Japon [ʒapɔ̃] *nm* **le J.** Japan

japonais, -e [ʒapɔnɛ, -ɛz] **1** *adj* Japanese **2** *nm,f* **J.** Japanese; **les J.** the Japanese **3** *nm (langue)* Japanese

jappement [ʒapmɑ̃] *nm* yap, yelp; **jappements** yapping, yelping

japper [ʒape] *vi* to yap, to yelp

jaquette [ʒakɛt] *nf* (a) *(d'homme)* morning coat; *(de femme)* jacket; *Can (chemise de nuit)* nightdress (b) *(de livre)* (dust) jacket, (dust) cover

jardin [ʒardɛ̃] *nm* garden; *Fig* **c'est mon j. secret** I keep it very much to myself; **j. botanique** botanical garden(s); **j. d'enfants** kindergarten; **j. potager** vegetable garden; **j. public** gardens; **j. zoologique** zoological gardens

jardinage [ʒardinaʒ] *nm* gardening

jardiner [ʒardine] *vi* to do some gardening

jardinet [ʒardinɛ] *nm* small garden

jardinier, -ère [ʒardinje, -ɛr] **1** *nm,f* gardener **2** *nf* **jardinière** (a) *(pour balcon)* window box; *(intérieure)* jardinière (b) *Culin* **jardinière (de légumes)** mixed vegetables

jargon [ʒargɔ̃] *nm* (a) *(argot, de métier)* jargon (b) *(langage incompréhensible)* gibberish

jarre [ʒar] *nf* (earthenware) jar

jarret [ʒarɛ] *nm* (**a**) *(de personne)* back of the knee; *(de cheval)* hock (**b**) *(pièce de viande) (de veau)* knuckle; *(de bœuf)* shin

jarretelle [ʒartɛl] *nf Br* suspender, *Am* garter

jarretière [ʒartjɛr] *nf* garter

jaser [ʒaze] *vi* (**a**) *(médire)* to gossip; **cela va faire j.** that'll set tongues wagging (**b**) *Can (bavarder)* to chatter (**de** about)

jasmin [ʒasmɛ̃] *nm* jasmine

jatte [ʒat] *nf* bowl

jauge [ʒoʒ] *nf* (**a**) *(instrument de mesure)* gauge, **j. d'essence** *Br* petrol *or Am* gas gauge; **j. de niveau d'huile** oil-level indicator; *(manuelle)* dipstick (**b**) *(de navire)* tonnage

jauger [45] [ʒoʒe] **1** *vt* (**a**) *(mesurer) (tonneau, réservoir)* to measure the capacity of; *(navire)* to measure the tonnage of (**b**) *Fig (personne, situation)* to size up
2 *vi* **j. 300 tonneaux** to be of 300 tons burden

jaunâtre [ʒonɑtr] *adj* yellowish

jaune [ʒon] **1** *adj (couleur, objet)* yellow; *(teint)* sallow; **j. canari** canary yellow; **j. citron** lemon yellow; **j. moutarde** mustard yellow, **j. d'or** golden yellow, **j. paille** straw-coloured
2 *nm* (**a**) *(couleur)* yellow (**b**) **j. d'œuf** (egg) yolk (**c**) *Can (lâche)* yellowbelly
3 *adv* **rire j.** to give a forced laugh

jauni, -e [ʒoni] *adj* yellowed

jaunir [ʒonir] *vt & vi* to turn yellow

jaunisse [ʒonis] *nf* jaundice; *Fam Fig* **en faire une j.** to get into a state about it

java [ʒava] *nf* (**a**) *(danse)* = type of popular waltz (**b**) *Fam (fête)* **faire la j.** to live it up

Javel [ʒavɛl] *n voir* eau

javelot [ʒavlo] *nm* javelin

jazz [dʒaz] *nm* jazz

J.-C. *(abrév* Jésus-Christ) JC, **av. J.-C.** BC, **ap. J.-C.** AD

je [ʒə]

> **j'** is used before a word beginning with a vowel or h mute.

pron personnel I

jean [dʒin] *nm (pantalon)* jeans; *(tissu)* denim; **un j.** a pair of jeans; **veste en j.** denim jacket

Jeanne [ʒan] *npr* **J. d'Arc** Joan of Arc

Jeep® [dʒip] *nf* Jeep®

Jéhovah [ʒeova] *npr* Jehovah

je-m'en-foutisme [ʒmɑ̃futism] *nm très Fam* couldn't-care-less attitude

je-m'en-foutiste (*pl* je-m'en-foutistes) [ʒmɑ̃futist] *nmf très Fam* couldn't-care-less type

je-ne-sais-quoi [ʒənsɛkwa] *nm inv* **un j.** a certain something

Jérémiades [ʒeremjad] *nfpl* whining

jerrican(e), jerrycan [dʒerikan, ʒerikan] *nm* jerry can

Jérusalem [ʒeryzalɛm] *n* Jerusalem

jésuite [ʒezɥit] **1** *adj* Jesuit; *Fig & Péj* jesuitical
2 *nm* Jesuit

Jésus(-Christ) [ʒezy(kri)] *npr* Jesus (Christ)

jet¹ [ʒɛ] *nm* (**a**) *(lancer) (de pierre)* throwing; *Fig* **faire qch d'un seul j.** to do sth in one go (**b**) *(de liquide, de vapeur)* jet; **premier j.** *(d'un roman)* first draft; **j. d'eau** *(fontaine)* fountain

jet² [dʒɛt] *nm (avion)* jet

jetable [ʒətablə] *adj* disposable

jeté, -e [ʒəte] **1** *nm* (**a**) *(en danse)* jeté (**b**) **j. de lit** bedspread
2 *adj très Fam* barking (mad)

jetée [ʒəte] *nf* jetty, pier

jeter [42] [ʒəte] **1** *vt* (**a**) *(lancer)* to throw; *(plus fort)* to fling, to hurl; *(filets)* to cast; **j. qch à qn** to throw sb sth, to throw sth to sb; **j. qn à terre** to throw sb to the ground; **j. qch à terre** *ou* **par terre** to throw sth on the ground; **j. qn en prison** to throw sb in prison; **j. les bras autour de qn** to throw one's arms around sb; **j. quelques idées sur le papier** to jot down a few ideas; **j. le trouble dans l'esprit de qn** to trouble sb; **ça a jeté un froid** it cast a chill (**b**) *(se défaire de)* to throw away *or* out; **j. son argent par les fenêtres** to throw one's money down the drain, *Fam* **se faire j.** (**de**) to get chucked out (of)
(**c**) *(émettre) (cri)* to utter; **j. un regard à qn** to glance at sb; **j. un coup d'œil (sur qch)** to have a quick glance (at sth)
(**d**) *(établir)* **j. les fondements de qch** to lay the foundations for sth
(**e**) *Fam* **ça (en) jette!** it's really something!
3 se jeter *vpr* (**a**) *(fleuve, rivière)* **se j. dans** to flow into (**b**) *(personne)* to throw oneself; **se j. sur qn** to throw oneself at sb; *Fig* to pounce on sb; **se j. sur** *(nourriture)* to pounce on; *(occasion)* to jump at; **se j. à l'eau** to plunge into the water, *Fig* to take the plunge; **se j. par la fenêtre** to throw oneself out of the window; **se j. aux pieds de qn** to throw oneself at sb's feet; *Fig* **se j. à la tête de qn** *(le draguer)* to throw oneself at sb

jeton [ʒətɔ̃] *nm* (**a**) *(au jeu)* chip; *(pour téléphone, machine)* token; **j. de présence** *(objet)* token *(issued as voucher for attendance at meeting)*; *(honoraires)* director's fees (**b**) *Fam* **avoir les jetons** to have the jitters

jeu, -x [ʒø] *nm* (**a**) *(amusement)* play; **faire qch par j.** to do sth for fun; *Fig* **entrer en j.** to come into play; *Fig* **c'est un j. d'enfant** it's child's play; *Prov* **jeux de mains, jeux de vilains** all this fooling around is going to end in tears; **j. de mots** play on words, pun; **j. de rôles** role-playing (**b**) *(activité)* game, **mettre la balle en j.** to bring the ball into play; *Fig* **jouer le j.** to play the game; *Fig* **jouer franc j. (avec qn)** to play fair (with sb); *Fig* **se prendre au j.** to get caught up in it; *Fig* **faire le j. de qn** to play sb's hands; **on aurait beau j. de répondre** it would be quite easy to answer; **j. d'adresse** game of skill; **j. de cartes** card game; **j. électronique** computer game; **le j. de l'oie** = board game similar to snakes and ladders; **les jeux Olympiques** the Olympic Games, the Olympics; **jeux de société** *(charades, devinettes)* parlour games; *(petits chevaux, jeu de l'oie)* board games; **j. télévisé** (television) game show; *(avec questions)* (television) quiz show; **j. vidéo** video game (**c**) *(au casino)* **le j.** gambling; **se ruiner au j.** to bankrupt oneself gambling; **mettre qch en j.** *(argent, voiture, carrière)* to stake sth; *Fig* **être en j.** to be at stake; **les jeux sont faits** *(à la roulette)* no more bets!; **faites vos jeux!** place your bets!; **jeux de hasard** games of chance
(**d**) *(cartes en main)* hand; **avoir du j.** to have a good hand; **cacher son j.** to hide one's hand; *Fig* to keep one's cards close to one's chest; *Fig* **sortir le grand j.** to pull out all the stops
(**e**) *(au tennis)* game; **j., set et match** game, set and match; **j. Ferreira** game (to) Ferreira; **j. blanc** love game
(**f**) *(d'un acteur)* acting; *(d'un musicien)* playing; **j. de jambes** *(d'un boxeur, d'un tennisman)* footwork
(**g**) *(d'outils, de clefs)* set; **j. de boules/quilles** set of bowls/skittles; **j. de cartes** *Br* pack *or Am* deck of cards; **j. d'échecs** chess set
(**h**) **il y a du j.** *(ça bouge)* there's a bit of play
(**i**) *(mécanisme)* **le j. de l'offre et de la demande** the system of supply and demand

jeu-concours (*pl* **jeux-concours**) [ʒøkɔ̃kur] *nm* competition

jeudi [ʒødi] *nm* Thursday; **le j.** saint Maundy Thursday; *Fam* **la semaine des quatre jeudis** when pigs fly; *voir aussi* **samedi**

jeun [ʒœ̃] **à jeun 1** *adj* **être à j.** *(sans avoir mangé ni bu)* not to have eaten or drunk anything; *(pas ivre)* to be sober **2** *adv* **prendre qch à j.** to take sth on an empty stomach

jeune [ʒœn] **1** *adj (personne, vin, pays)* young; *(apparence, allure)* youthful; *(coiffure, vêtement)* that makes one look young; **être j. d'esprit** to have a youthful outlook; **faire plus j. que son âge** to look younger than one's age; **elle n'est plus toute j.** she's not as young as she was **2** *nmf* **un j.** a youngster; **une j.** a girl; *Fam* **un petit j.** a young guy; **les jeunes** young people **3** *adv* **s'habiller j.** to dress in a youthful style; **ça fait j.** it makes you/her/*etc* look young

jeûne [ʒøn] *nm* **(a)** *(période)* fast; **rompre le j.** to break one's fast **(b)** *(pratique)* fasting

jeûner [ʒøne] *vi* to fast

jeunesse [ʒœnɛs] *nf* **(a)** *(période)* youth **(b)** *(d'apparence, d'esprit)* youthfulness **(c)** *(jeunes gens)* young people

jeunot, -otte [ʒœno, -ɔt] *Fam* **1** *adj* youngish **2** *nm,f Péj* youngster; **un petit j.** a young little fellow

JF (a) *(abrév* **jeune fille)** girl **(b)** *(abrév* **jeune femme)** young woman

JH *(abrév* **jeune homme)** young man

jingle [dʒingəl] *nm* jingle

JO [ʒio] **1** *nm (abrév* **Journal officiel)** = French government publication giving information to the public about new laws, government business, new companies etc **2** *nmpl (abrév* **jeux Olympiques)** Olympic Games

joaillerie [ʒɔajri] *nf* **(a)** *(magasin)* jeweller's shop **(b)** *(bijoux)* jewellery

joaillier, -ère [ʒɔaje, -ɛr] *nm,f* jeweller

job [dʒɔb] *nm Fam* job

jockey [ʒɔkɛ] *nm* jockey

Joconde [ʒɔkɔ̃d] *nf* **la J.** the Mona Lisa

joggeur, -euse [dʒɔgœr, -øz] *nm,f* jogger

jogging [dʒɔgiŋ] *nm* **(a)** *(vêtement)* jogging suit **(b)** *(activité)* jogging; **faire du j.** to go jogging, to jog

Johannesburg [ʒɔanɛsbur] *n* Johannesburg

joie [ʒwa] *nf* joy, delight; **avec j.** with pleasure, gladly; *Fam* **c'est pas la j.!** it's no fun!; **faire la j. de qn** to make sb happy; **se faire une j. de faire qch** *(envisager)* to look forward to doing sth; *(faire avec plaisir)* to be delighted to do sth; **faire une fausse j. à qn** to falsely raise sb's hopes; **j. de vivre** joie de vivre

joignable [ʒwaɲabl] *adj* contactable

joignais etc *voir* **joindre**

joindre [43] [ʒwɛ̃dr] **1** *vt* **(a)** *(réunir)* to join; **j. les mains** to put one's hands together; *Fam Fig* **j. les deux bouts** to make ends meet **(b)** *(ajouter)* to add (**à** to); *(dans une lettre, un colis)* to enclose (**à** with); **j. le geste à la parole** to suit the action to the word; **j. l'utile à l'agréable** to combine business with pleasure **(c)** *(contacter)* to contact **2 se joindre** *vpr* **se j. à qn** to join sb; **se j. à qch** to join in sth

joint, -e [ʒwɛ̃, -ɛt] **1** *pp de* **joindre 2** *adj* **sauter à pieds joints** to jump from a standing position; **les mains jointes** with hands together; **pièces jointes** *(dans une lettre)* enclosures **3** *nm* **(a)** *(d'étanchéité)* seal; *(articulation)* joint; **j. de culasse** cylinder head gasket; **j. de dilatation** expansion joint **(b)** *Fam (à fumer)* joint

jointure [ʒwɛ̃tyr] *nf (articulation)* joint

jojo [ʒoʒo] *Fam* **1** *nm voir* **affreux 2** *adj inv* **ne pas être j.** *(physiquement)* not to look very nice; *(moralement)* not to be very nice

jojoba [ʒoʒoba] *nm* jojoba

joker [ʒɔkɛr] *nm (aux cartes)* joker; *Ordinat* wild-card

joli, -e [ʒɔli] **1** *adj* **(a)** *(personne, ville, voix)* pretty, attractive; **il est j. garçon** he's good-looking; **j. comme un cœur** pretty as a picture; **faire le j. cœur** to flirt **(b)** *(situation, somme)* nice; **c'est bien j. tout ça mais...** all well and good but...; *Fam* **c'est pas j. j.** *(blâmable)* that's not very nice; *(laid)* it's not a pretty sight **2** *nm Ironique* **c'est du j.!** marvellous!

joliment [ʒɔlimɑ̃] *adv* **(a)** *(bien)* nicely; **c'est j. dit** that's nicely put; *Ironique* **te voilà j. arrangé!** you're in a right mess! **(b)** *Fam (extrêmement)* really; **elle s'est j. fait engueuler** she got a good telling-off

jonc [ʒɔ̃] *nm (plante)* rush

joncher [ʒɔ̃ʃe] *vt* to strew (**de** with)

jonction [ʒɔ̃ksjɔ̃] *nf* junction

jongler [ʒɔ̃gle] *vi* to juggle (**avec** with)

jongleur, -euse [ʒɔ̃glœr, -øz] *nm,f* juggler

jonquille [ʒɔ̃kij] *nf* daffodil

Jordanie [ʒɔrdani] *nf* **la J.** Jordan

jordanien, -enne [ʒɔrdanjɛ̃, -ɛn] **1** *adj* Jordanian **2** *nm,f* **J.** Jordanian

jouable [ʒwabl] *adj* playable

joual, -e [ʒwal] *Can* **1** *nm* joual *(French-Canadian dialect)* **2** *adj* **langue jouale** joual

joue [ʒu] *nf (de personne, d'animal)* cheek; **mettre qn en j.** to take aim at sb; **tenir qn en j.** to keep sb in one's sights

jouer [ʒwe] **1** *vt* **(a)** *(parier)* to stake (**sur** on); *(cheval)* to back, to bet on **(b)** *(participer à)* **j. la finale** to play in the final **(c)** *(carte)* to play; *(pion, pièce)* to move **(d)** *(rôle)* to act, to play; **j. la surprise** to pretend to be surprised; **j. les héros** to play the hero; *Hum* **j. la fille de l'air** to vanish into thin air **(e)** *(air)* to play; **j. du Bach** to play (some) Bach **2** *vi* **(a)** *(s'amuser)* to play; *Fig* **j. sur les mots** to play with words; *Fig* **j. avec les sentiments de qn** to play with sb's feelings; *Fig* **j. avec son avenir** to risk one's future; *Fig* **j. avec le feu** to play with fire; **c'est à qui de j.?** whose turn is it?; *(aux échecs, aux dames)* whose move is it?; *Fig* **maintenant à vous de j.** now it's your turn **(b)** *(acteur)* to act; *(troupe)* to perform; **il joue très mal** he's a very bad actor **(c)** *(parier)* to gamble; **j. en Bourse** to speculate on the stock market **(d)** *(fonctionner)* **j. en faveur/défaveur de qn** to work in sb's favour/against sb; **faire j. un ressort** to release a spring; *Fig* **faire j. ses relations pour obtenir qch** to pull a few strings to get sth **(e)** *(bois)* to warp; *(pièce)* to work loose **3 jouer à** *vt ind* **(a)** *(pratiquer)* to play; **j. au squash/aux cartes** to play squash/cards; **j. aux gendarmes et aux voleurs** to play cops and robbers; **j. à la marchande** to play shops; *Fig* **j. au plus fin** to try to outwit each other **(b)** *(parier sur)* **j. aux courses** to bet on or back horses **4 jouer de** *vt ind* **j. du piano/de la harpe** to play the piano/the harp; *Fig* **j. des coudes** to elbow one's way through **5 se jouer** *vpr* **(a)** *(match)* to be played **(b)** *(se décider)* **son sort est en train de se j.** his/her fate is hanging in the balance **(c)** **se j. de qn** to trifle with sb; **se j. des lois** to make a mockery of the law; **se j. des difficultés** to make light of difficulties **(d)** *(pièce de théâtre, film)* to be on

jouet [ʒwɛ] *nm* toy; *Fig* **être le j.** de to be the victim of

joueur, -euse [ʒwœr, -øz] **1** *nm,f* (**a**) *(d'un jeu, d'un sport, d'un instrument de musique)* player; **j.** **de tennis/cartes** tennis/card player; **être beau/mauvais j.** to be a good/bad loser (**b**) *(au casino)* gambler **2** *adj (enfant, chien)* playful

joufflu, -e [ʒufly] *adj (bébé, angelot)* chubby-cheeked; *(visage)* chubby

joug [ʒu] *nm aussi Fig* yoke

jouir [ʒwir] *vi* (**a**) *(profiter)* **j.** **de qch** to enjoy sth (**b**) *(sexuellement)* to come (**c**) *(être en possession)* **j.** **d'une bonne réputation** to have a good reputation; **j.** **d'une bonne santé** to enjoy good health

jouissance [ʒwisɑ̃s] *nf* (**a**) *(plaisir)* enjoyment; *(sexuel)* orgasm (**b**) *Jur (usage)* use

jouisseur, -euse [ʒwisœr, øz] *nm,f* sensualist

jouissif, -ive [ʒwisif, -iv] *adj très Fam* orgasmic

joujou, -x [ʒuʒu] *nm (langage enfantin)* toy; **faire j.** to play joule [ʒul] *nm* joule

jour [ʒur] *nm* (**a**) *(clarté)* daylight; **au petit j.** at daybreak; **en plein j.** in broad daylight; *Fig* **au grand j.** publicly; **travailler le** *ou* **de j.** to work days; **j.** **et nuit** day and night, *Fig* **elle et son frère, c'est le j.** **et la nuit** she and her brother are like chalk and cheese; **elle est belle comme le j.** she's a real beauty; **il fait j.** it's light
(**b**) *(journée)* day; **huit jours** a week; **quinze jours** two weeks, *Br* a fortnight; **un j.** **ou l'autre** one day; **de j.** **en j.** day by day; **du j.** **au lendemain** overnight; **nous l'attendons d'un j.** **à l'autre** we're expecting him any day (now); **un de ces jours** one of these days; **un beau j.**, **elle décida de...** one day, she decided to...; **vivre au j.** **le j.** *(sans faire de projets)* to live from day to day; *(financièrement)* to live from hand to mouth; **mettre qch à j.** to update sth, to bring sth up to date; **tenir qch à j.** to keep sth up to date; **décidément, ce n'est pas mon j.!** it just isn't my day today! **il y a des jours avec et les jours sans** there are good days and bad days; **le j.** **de l'an** New Year's Day; **j.** **de congé** day off; **j.** **férié** public holiday, *Br* bank holiday; **le jour J** D-day, **le j.** **de Noël** Christmas Day, **j.** **ouvrable** working day; **j.** **de repos** day off (**c**) *(date)* day; **quel j.** **sommes-nous?** what's the date (today)?; **le j.** **de mes vingt ans** my twentieth birthday; **il y a six ans j.** **pour j.** six years ago to the day; **à ce j.**, **nous n'avons toujours pas reçu votre lettre** to date we still have not received your letter (**d**) *(époque)* **de nos jours** these days, nowadays; **les beaux jours** the fine days of summer; **pour mes vieux jours** for my old age (**e**) *(vie)* **donner le j.** **à un enfant** to give birth to a child; **mettre fin à ses jours** to put an end to one's life; **il vit le j.** **à Paris** he was born in Paris; **jusqu'à mon dernier j.** to my dying day (**f**) *(éclairage)* light; *Fig* **voir qch sous un j.** **nouveau/sous son vrai j.** to see sth in a new light/in its true light; *Fig* **présenter qch sous un j.** **favorable** to present sth in a favourable light (**g**) *(ouverture)* gap

Jourdain [ʒurdɛ̃] *nm* **le J.** the River Jordan

journal, -aux [ʒurnal, -o] *nm* (**a**) *(publication)* paper, newspaper; **j.** **(télévisé)** (television) news (**b**) *(récit d'événements, d'expériences)* journal; *Ordinat* log; **tenir un j.** to keep a journal; **j.** **de bord** log (book); **j.** **intime** diary; **J.** **officiel** = French government publication giving information to the public about new laws, government business, new companies etc

journalier, -ère [ʒurnalje, -er] **1** *adj* daily **2** *nm,f (ouvrier agricole)* day labourer

journalisme [ʒurnalism] *nm* journalism

journaliste [ʒurnalist] *nmf* journalist; **elle est j.** **au Monde** she's a journalist with Le Monde; **j.** **d'investigation** investigative journalist; **j.** **sportif** sports journalist

journalistique [ʒurnalistik] *adj* journalistic

journée [ʒurne] *nf* (**a**) *(par opposition à nuit)* day(time); **pendant la j.** in the daytime, during the day; **dans la j.** in the course of the day; **toute la j.** all day (**b**) *(unité de temps)* day; **j.** **de travail** *(jour non chômé)* working day; *(quantité de travail)* day's work; **faire la j.** **continue** *(personne)* to work through lunch; **j.** **portes ouvertes** *Br* open day, *Am* open house

journellement [ʒurnɛlmɑ̃] *adv* daily

joute [ʒut] *nf (combat médiéval)* joust; *Fig* **joutes oratoires** verbal jousting

jouvence [ʒuvɑ̃s] *nf Litt* **cela a été un bain** *ou* **une cure de j.** it has rejuvenated me

jouvenceau, -x [ʒuvɑ̃so] *nm Hum* stripling

jouvencelle [ʒuvɑ̃sɛl] *nf Hum* maiden

jouxter [ʒukste] *vt* to adjoin

jovial, -e, -als *ou* **-aux, -ales** [ʒɔvjal, -o] *adj* jovial, jolly

jovialité [ʒɔvjalite] *nf* joviality, jolliness

joyau, -x [ʒwajo] *nm aussi Fig* jewel

joyeusement [ʒwajøzmɑ̃] *adv* joyfully

joyeux, -euse [ʒwajø, -øz] *adj* joyful; **j.** **anniversaire!** happy birthday!; **j.** **Noël!** Happy *or* Merry Christmas!

JT [ʒite] *nm (abrév* **journal télévisé)** TV news

jubilation [ʒybilasjɔ̃] *nf* jubilation

jubilé [ʒybile] *nm* jubilee

jubiler [ʒybile] *vi* to be jubilant; *(méchamment)* to gloat

jucher [ʒyʃe] **1** *vt* to perch (**sur** on) **2 se jucher** *vpr* to perch (**sur** on)

judaïque [ʒydaik] *adj* Jewish; *(loi)* Judaic

judaïsme [ʒydaism] *nm* Judaism

judas [ʒyda] *nm (ouverture)* peephole

judéo-chrétien, -enne (*mpl* **judéo-chrétiens** *fpl* **judéo-chrétiennes)** [ʒydeokretjɛ̃, -ɛn] *adj* Judaeo-Christian

judiciaire [ʒydisjer] *adj (pouvoir, enquête, acte)* judicial; *(aide, autorité)* legal

judicieusement [ʒydisjøzmɑ̃] *adv* judiciously

judicieux, -euse [ʒydisjø, -øz] *adj* judicious; **peu j.** injudicious

judo [ʒydo] *nm* judo

judoka [ʒydoka] *nmf Sp* judoka

juge [ʒyʒ] *nm* judge; **Monsieur le J.** Your Honour; **les juges** the bench; **je vous laisse j.** I'll let you be the judge; *Fig* **être à la fois j.** **et partie** to sit in judgement on oneself; **j.** **d'instruction** examining magistrate; **j.** **de ligne** line judge; **j.** **de touche** *(au football)* linesman; *(au rugby)* touch judge

jugé [ʒyʒe] **au jugé** *adv (tirer)* blind; *(calculer)* roughly

jugement [ʒyʒmɑ̃] *nm* (**a**) *Jur (d'une affaire)* trial; **passer en j.** to stand trial (**b**) *Jur (décision)* decision; *(dans des affaires criminelles)* sentence (**c**) *(opinion)* judgement; **porter un j.** **sur qch** to pass judgement on sth; **j.** **de valeur** value judgement (**d**) *(discernement)* judgement

jugeote [ʒyʒɔt] *nf Fam* common sense

juger[1] [ʒyʒe] **1** *vt* (**a**) *(affaire, prévenu)* to try; *(demande, litige)* to adjudicate (**b**) *(évaluer, condamner)* to judge (**sur** by); **à toi de j.** it's for you to judge (**c**) *(croire)* **j.** **que** to consider that; **on le jugeait fou** people considered him mad; **j.** **superflu de faire qch** to consider it superfluous to do sth

2 juger de *vt ind* to judge; **jugez de ma surprise!** imagine my surprise!; **à en j. par...** judging by...

juger² = jugé

jugulaire [ʒygylɛr] *nf* **(a)** *(veine)* jugular (vein) **(b)** *(de casque)* chin strap

juguler [ʒygyle] *vt (rébellion)* to quell; *(inflation, épidémie)* to check

juif, -ive [ʒɥif, -iv] **1** *adj* Jewish **2** *nm,f* J. Jew

juillet [ʒɥijɛ] *nm* July; **le 14-J.** Bastille Day *(day of national celebration in France)*; *voir aussi* **janvier**

juin [ʒɥɛ̃] *nm* June; *voir aussi* **janvier**

juke-box [dʒykbɔks, ʒykbɔks] *nm inv* jukebox

Jules [ʒyl] *npr* J. César Julius Caesar

jules [ʒyl] *nm Fam (mari, petit ami)* guy

julienne [ʒyljɛn] *nf* j. de légumes vegetables julienne *(cut into thin strips)*

jumbo [dʒœmbo], **jumbo-jet** *(pl* jumbo-jets) [dʒœmbodʒɛt] *nm* jumbo (jet)

jumeau, -elle, -x, -elles [ʒymo, -ɛl] **1** *adj (frère, sœur)* twin **2** *nm,f* twin; *(sosie)* double; **vrais/faux jumeaux** identical/fraternal twins

jumelage [ʒymlaʒ] *nm (de villes)* twinning

jumelé, -e [ʒymle] *adj (villes)* twinned; *(maisons)* semidetached

jumelles [ʒymɛl] *nfpl* **(paire de) j.** (pair of) binoculars; **j. de théâtre** opera glasses

jument [ʒymã] *nf* mare

jungle [ʒɔ̃gl, ʒœ̃gl] *nf aussi Fig* jungle

junior [ʒynjɔr] **1** *adj (mode, taille)* junior **2** *nmf Sp* junior *(19 to 20 years old)*

junte [ʒœ̃t] *nf* junta

jupe [ʒyp] *nf* skirt; *Fam* **être dans les** *ou* **pendu aux jupes de sa mère** to be clinging to one's mother's skirts; **j. droite** straight skirt

jupe-culotte *(pl* jupes-culottes) [ʒypkylɔt] *nf* culottes

jupette [ʒypɛt] *nf* skirt

Jupiter [ʒypitɛr] *npr (dieu, planète)* Jupiter

jupon [ʒypɔ̃] *nm* underskirt, petticoat

Jura [ʒyra] *nm* le J. the Jura (Mountains)

jurassique [ʒyrasik] *Géol* **1** *adj* Jurassic **2** *nm* le J. the Jurassic period

juré, -e [ʒyre] **1** *adj* ennemi j. sworn enemy **2** *nm,f* juror; **les jurés** the jury

jurer [ʒyre] **1** *vt* to swear; **je le jure** I swear; **j. qch sur la tête de qn** to swear sth on sb's grave; **j'aurais juré qu'il était là** I could have sworn that it was there; **j. de faire qch** to swear to do sth; **ne j. que par** to swear by; *Prov* **il ne faut j. de rien** you never can tell **2** *vi* **(a)** *(dire des gros mots)* to swear **(b)** *(couleurs, vêtements)* to clash **(avec** with) **3 se jurer** *vpr* **(a)** *(l'un à l'autre)* **se j.** fidélité to swear to be faithful to each other **(b)** *(à soi-même)* **se j.** que to swear (to oneself) that; **se j. de faire qch** to swear to do sth

juridiction [ʒyridiksjɔ̃] *nf (compétence)* jurisdiction; *(tribunaux)* courts

juridique [ʒyridik] *adj* legal

jurisprudence [ʒyrisprydãs] *nf* case law; **faire j.** to set a precedent

juriste [ʒyrist] *nmf* legal expert

juron [ʒyrɔ̃] *nm* swearword

jury [ʒyri] *nm* **(a)** *(d'un tribunal)* jury **(b)** *(pour l'attribution d'un prix)* (panel of) judges; *(d'examen)* board of examiners

jus [ʒy] *nm* **(a)** *(de fruits, de légumes)* juice; *(de viande)* juices; **j. d'orange/de fruit** orange/fruit juice; *Fam Hum* **j. de chaussettes** *(café)* dishwater **(b)** *Fam (courant électrique)* juice; **prendre le j.** to get an electric shock

jusant [ʒyzã] *nm* ebb tide

jusque [ʒysk, ʒyskə] *prép* **(a)** **jusqu'à** *(délimite un espace)* as far as; *(délimite une mesure)* up to; **jusqu'ici** as far as here; **j.-là** as far as there; *Fam* **s'en mettre j.-là** to stuff oneself; **jusqu'où?** how far?; **avoir de l'eau jusqu'à la taille** to have water right up to one's waist; **compter jusqu'à dix** to count (up) to ten; **jusqu'au bout (de la rue)** to the end (of the street); **j. dans les campagnes** right into the countryside; *Fig* **aller jusqu'au bout d'un raisonnement** to follow an argument through; **aller jusqu'à faire qch** to go so far as to do sth **(b)** *(indique le temps)* until, till; **jusqu'ici, jusqu'à maintenant, jusqu'à présent** until now, up to now; **j.-là, jusqu'alors** until then, up to then; **jusqu'à ce que** + *subjunctive* until, till; **jusqu'à (l'âge de) douze ans** up to the age of twelve; **jusqu'à nouvel ordre** until further notice; **jusqu'au jour** *ou* **moment où...** until the time when...; **si nous remontons jusqu'en** *ou* **jusqu'à 1800** if we go right back to 1800 **(c)** *(également)* **jusqu'à** even

justaucorps [ʒystokɔr] *nm (de sport)* leotard

juste [ʒyst] **1** *adj* **(a)** *(équitable)* fair **(avec** *ou* **envers** to); à **j. titre** rightly **(b)** *(exact) (calcul, réponse)* right, correct; *(raisonnement)* sound; *(note)* right; **arriver à l'heure j.** to arrive right on time; **avez-vous l'heure j.?** do you have the right time? **(c)** *(trop petit) (chaussures, vêtement)* tight; **une bouteille pour six, c'est un peu j.** one bottle isn't quite enough for six people **(d)** *Fam (financièrement)* **être (un peu) j.** to be (a bit) strapped for cash **2** *adv* **(a)** *(avec exactitude) (viser, parler)* accurately; *(chanter)* in tune; *Fam* **tomber j.** to guess right; **tout j.!** that's right! **(b)** *(précisément)* just; **à dix heures j.** on the stroke of ten; **j. au coin/en face/à côté** just *or* right on the corner/opposite/next door; **arriver j. à temps** to arrive just in time; **ça fait cinq euros tout j.** that's five euros exactly **(c)** *(à peine)* just; **c'est tout j. s'il sait lire** he can barely read; **avoir j. le temps (de faire qch)** to have just enough time (to do sth); **ils ont tout j. fini de manger** they've only just finished eating **(d)** *(trop peu)* **calculer trop j. (pour)** not to allow enough (for) **(e)** **au j.** *(exactement)* exactly

justement [ʒystəmã] *adv* **(a)** *(précisément)* exactly; **j'allais t. t'appeler** I was just going to ring you **(b)** *(avec justesse)* rightly **(c)** *(avec justice)* justly

justesse [ʒystɛs] *nf* **(a)** *(précision) (d'une expression, d'une remarque)* aptness **(b)** **de j.** only just; **j'ai eu mon train de j.** I (only) just caught my train

justice [ʒystis] *nf* **(a)** *(équité)* justice; **faire** *ou* **rendre j. à qn** to do justice to sb; **se venger** *ou* **se faire j.** to take the law into one's own hands; *(se tuer)* to take one's own life **(b)** *Jur* **la j.** the law; **aller en j.** to go to law

justicier, -ère [ʒystisje, -ɛr] *nm,f* righter of wrongs

justifiable [ʒystifjabl] *adj* justifiable

justificatif, -ive [ʒystifikatif, -iv] **1** *adj* justificatory; **pièces justificatives** *(d'un dossier)* supporting documents **2** *nm* written proof

justification [ʒystifikasjɔ̃] *nf* **(a)** *(explication)* justification **(de** for *or* of) **(b)** *(preuve)* proof **(c)** *Typ & Ordinat* justification

justifié, -e [ʒystifje] *adj* (**a**) *(légitime)* justified; **peu j.**
unjustified (**b**) *Typ & Ordinat* justified; **j. à droite/à gauche**
right-/left-justified
justifier [66] [ʒystifje] **1** *vt* (**a**) *(légitimer, démontrer)* to
justify (**b**) *Typ & Ordinat* to justify; **j. à droite/gauche** to
right-/left-justify
2 se justifier *vpr* to justify oneself

jute [ʒyt] *nm* jute; (**toile de) j.** hessian
juter [ʒyte] *vi* to be juicy
juteux, -euse [ʒytø, -øz] *adj aussi Fam Fig* juicy
juvénile [ʒyvenil] *adj* youthful
juxtaposer [ʒykstapoze] *vt* to juxtapose
juxtaposition [ʒykstapozisjɔ̃] *nf* juxtaposition

K

K, k [kɑ] *nm inv* K, k
k *(abrév* **kilo(s))** k
K7 [kaset] *nf (abrév* **cassette)** tape
Kaboul [kabul] *n* Kabul
kaki[1] [kaki] *adj inv & nm inv (couleur)* khaki
kaki[2] *nm (arbre, fruit)* persimmon
kaléidoscope [kaleidɔskɔp] *nm aussi Fig* kaleidoscope
kamikaze [kamikaz] *nm* kamikaze; *Fig* **être k.** to have a death wish
kanak, -e [kanak] = **canaque**
kangourou [kɑ̃guru] *nm* kangaroo
kapok [kapɔk] *nm* kapok
karaoké [karaɔke] *nm* karaoke
karaté [karate] *nm* karate
karatéka [karateka] *nmf* karate expert
karma [karma] *nm* karma
kart [kart] *nm* (go-)kart
karting [kartiŋ] *nm* karting, go-kart racing; **faire du k.** to go karting
kasher [kaʃɛr] *adj inv Rel* kosher
Katmandou [katmɑ̃du] *n* Katmandu
kayak [kajak] *nm* (a) *(embarcation de sport)* canoe, kayak; **faire du k.** to go canoeing (b) *(esquimau)* kayak
kayakiste [kajakist] *nmf* canoeist
kazakh, -e [kazak] **1** *adj* Kazakh
2 *nm,f* **K.** Kazakh
Kazakhstan [kazakstɑ̃] *nm* **le K.** Kazakhstan
keffieh [kefje] *nm* kaffiyeh
kendo [kɛndo] *nm* kendo
Kenya [kenja] *nm* **le K.** Kenya
kenyan, -e [kenjɑ̃, -an] **1** *adj* Kenyan
2 *nm,f* **K.** Kenyan
képi [kepi] *nm* kepi
kératine [keratin] *nf* keratin
kermesse [kɛrmɛs] *nf* (a) *(dans les Flandres)* village fair (b) *(fête de bienfaisance)* (charity) fête
kérosène [kerozɛn] *nm* kerosine
ketchup [kɛtʃœp] *nm* (tomato) ketchup
keuf [kœf] *nm très Fam* cop
kF [kaɛf] *nm (abrév* **kilofranc(s))** thousand francs
kg *(abrév* **kilogramme(s))** kg
KGB [kɑɡebe] *nm* **le K.** the KGB
khâgne [kɑɲ] *nf* = second-year arts class preparing students for the entrance examination for the "École normale supérieure"

khâgneux, -euse [kaɲø, -øz] *nm,f* = student in the "khâgne"
Khartoum [kartum] *n* Khartoum
khmer, -ère [kmɛr] **1** *adj* Khmer
2 *nm,f* **K.** Khmer; **les Khmers rouges** the Khmer Rouge
khôl [kol] *nm* kohl
kibboutz [kibuts] *nm inv* kibbutz
kidnapper [kidnape] *vt* to kidnap
kidnappeur, -euse [kidnapœr, -øz] *nm,f* kidnapper
kidnapping [kidnapiŋ] *nm* kidnapping
kif-kif [kifkif] *adj inv Fam* **c'est k. (bourricot)** it's six and half a dozen
kiki [kiki] *nm Fam* **(a)** *(cou)* **serrer le k. à qn** to wring sb's neck **(b)** *(langage enfantin) (pénis)* peter **(c)** **c'est parti mon k.!** here we go!
kilo [kilo] *nm* kilo
kilobaud [kilobo] *nm Ordinat* kilobaud
kilocalorie [kilɔkalɔri] *nf* kilocalorie
kilofranc [kilɔfrɑ̃] *nm* thousand francs
kilogramme [kilɔgram] *nm* kilogram(me)
kilohertz [kilɔɛrts] *nm* kilohertz
kilojoule [kilɔʒul] *nm* kilojoule
kilométrage [kilɔmetraʒ] *nm (distance)* ≃ mileage; **k. illimité** *(de voiture de location)* unlimited mileage
kilomètre [kilɔmɛtr] *nm* kilometre; **100 kilomètres à l'heure, 100 kilomètres-heure** 100 kilometres per *or* an hour; **taper du texte au k.** to type text straight in *(and leave the formatting etc until later)*
kilométrique [kilɔmetrik] *adj voir* **borne**
kilo-octet (*pl* **kilo-octets)** [kilɔɔktɛ] *nm Ordinat* kilobyte
kilovolt [kilɔvɔlt] *nm* kilovolt
kilowatt [kilɔwat] *nm* kilowatt
kilowattheure [kilɔwatœr] *nm Phys* kilowatt-hour
kilt [kilt] *nm* kilt
kimono [kimɔno] *nm* kimono
kiné [kine] *Fam* **1** *nmf (médecin)* physio
2 *nf (discipline)* physio
kinésithérapeute [kineziterapøt] *nmf Br* physiotherapist, *Am* physical therapist
kinésithérapie [kineziterapi] *nf Br* physiotherapy, *Am* physical therapy
Kinshasa [kinʃasa] *n* Kinshasa
kiosque [kjɔsk] *nm* **(a)** *(pavillon)* pavilion; *(point de vente)* kiosk; **k. à journaux** newspaper kiosk, newsstand; **k. à musique** bandstand **(b)** *(sur Minitel®)* **K.®** = service accessible on the Minitel® information network

kippa [kipa] *nf* kippa
kir [kir] *nm* kir
kirghiz, -e [kirgiz] **1** *adj* Kirg(h)iz
2 *nm,f* K. Kirg(h)iz
3 *nm (langue)* Kirg(h)iz
Kirghizistan [kirgizistɑ̃] *nm* **le** K. Kirg(h)izia,
Kirg(h)izstan
kirsch [kirʃ] *nm* kirsch
kit [kit] *nm* (self-assembly) kit; **en k.** in kit form; *Ordinat* **k.**
d'extension *ou* **d'évolution** upgrade kit
kitch [kitʃ] = **kitsch**
kitchenette [kitʃənɛt] *nf* kitchenette
kitsch [kitʃ] *adj inv & nm inv* kitsch
kiwi [kiwi] *nm* **(a)** *(fruit)* kiwi fruit **(b)** *(oiseau)* kiwi
Klaxon® [klaksɔn] *nm* horn; **donner un coup de K.** to
sound one's horn
klaxonner [klaksɔne] **1** *vi* to sound one's horn
2 *vt* to sound one's horn at
klebs [klɛps] = **clebs**
Kleenex® [klineks] *nm inv* tissue, Kleenex®
kleptomane [klɛptɔman] *adj & nmf* kleptomaniac
kleptomanie [klɛptɔmani] *nf* kleptomania
km *(abrév* **kilomètre(s))** km
km/h *(abrév* **kilomètres à l'heure, kilomètres-heure)**
kph
Ko *nm (abrév* **kilo-octet(s))** K, KB

K-O [kao] **1** *nm inv* knockout
2 *adj inv* **(a)** *(assommé)* knocked out; **mettre qn K.** to
knock sb out **(b)** *Fam (fatigué)* shattered
koala [kɔala] *nm* koala (bear)
kopeck [kɔpɛk] *nm* kopeck; *Fam* **ça ne vaut pas un k.** it's
not worth a bean
kouglof [kuglɔf] *nm* kugelhopf
Koweït [kɔwɛjt, kɔwɛt] *nm* **le K.** Kuwait
koweïtien, -enne [kɔwɛjtjɛ̃, kɔwɛtjɛ̃, -ɛn] **1** *adj* Kuwaiti
2 *nm,f* K. Kuwaiti
krach [krak] *nm* **k.** (boursier) (stock market) crash
kraft [kraft] *nm voir* **papier**
Kremlin [krɛmlɛ̃] *nm* **le K.** the Kremlin
kumquat [kɔmkwat, kumkwat] *nm (fruit)* kumquat
kung-fu [kuŋfu] *nm inv* kung fu
kurde [kyrd] **1** *adj* Kurdish
2 *nmf* K. Kurd
3 *nm (langue)* Kurdish
Kurdistan [kyrdistɑ̃] *nm* **le K.** Kurdistan
kW *(abrév* **kilowatt(s))** kW
K-way® [kawe] *nm inv* cagoule
kWh *(abrev* **kilowattheure(s))** kWh
kyrielle [kirjɛl] *nf (de mots, de fautes)* string; *(d'insultes)*
stream; *(d'enfants)* crowd; **elle a toute une k. d'amis** she
has masses of friends
kyste [kist] *nm* cyst

L, l [ɛl] *nm inv* L, l
l *(abrév* **litre(s))** l
l' [l] **1** *art défini voir* **le¹**
  2 *pron personnel voir* **la²**, **le²**
la¹ [la] *art défini voir* **le¹**
la² [la]

> **l'** is used before a word beginning with a vowel or h mute.

pron personnel (femme, fille) her; *(chose, idée)* it; *(animal)* it, her; **je la connais bien** I know her well; **il te la rendra demain** he'll give it back to you tomorrow; **et ta cousine, tu l'as vue?** have you seen your cousin?; **la voilà** here she/it is
la³ *nm inv (note)* A; *(chantée)* la
là [la] **1** *adv* (**a**) *(là-bas)* there; *(ici)* here; **il est là** *(présent)* he's in; *(près d'ici)* he's here; *(là-bas)* he's there; **est-ce que Paul est là?** *(au téléphone)* is Paul there?; **je suis là pour ça** that's what I'm here for; **à quelques mètres de là** a few metres away; **de là à New York, il n'y a que quelques kilomètres** it's only a few kilometres (away) from New York; **là en bas/haut** down/up there; **qui va là?** who goes there?
  (**b**) *(à ce point)* **restons-en là** let's leave it at that; **la question n'est pas là** that's not the point; **c'est bien là le problème** that's the problem; **je sais bien qu'il est bizarre mais de là à dire qu'il est fou...** I know he's strange, but to say he's mad...; **je ne vois là aucune raison de s'inquiéter** I can't see any cause for concern; **de là sa réaction** hence his/her reaction
  (**c**) *(avec un relatif)* **c'est là que j'habite** that's where I live; **c'est là que j'ai compris** that's when I understood
  (**d**) **ce livre-là** that book; **ces vins-là** those wines
  2 *exclam* **oh là là!** my goodness!; **alors là, je n'aurais jamais cru!** I'd never have expected THAT!
là-bas [laba] *adv* over there; *(dans cette région, dans ce pays)* there
label [labɛl] *nm* (**a**) *Com* quality label (**b**) *Ordinat* **l. de volume** volume label
labeur [labœr] *nm Litt* labour
labo [labo] *nm Fam* lab; **l. photo** darkroom
laborantin, -e [labɔrɑ̃tɛ̃, -in] *nm,f* laboratory assistant
laboratoire [labɔratwar] *nm* laboratory; **l. d'analyses (médicales)** pathology laboratory
laborieusement [labɔrjøzmɑ̃] *adv* laboriously
laborieux, -euse [labɔrjø, -øz] *adj* (**a**) *(difficile)* laborious; *Péj (style)* laboured; *Fam* **il n'a pas encore fini? c'est l.!** hasn't he finished yet? he's making heavy weather of it! (**b**) *Litt* **les masses laborieuses** the toiling masses
labour [labur] *nm* (**a**) *(labourage)* ploughing (**b**) **labours** *(champs)* ploughed land

labourage [laburaʒ] *nm* ploughing
labourer [labure] *vt* (**a**) *(terre)* to plough (**b**) *Fig (griffer)* to claw; **visage labouré de rides** face furrowed with wrinkles
laboureur [laburœr] *nm* ploughman
labrador [labradɔr] *nm* labrador
labyrinthe [labirɛ̃t] *nm* maze, labyrinth
lac [lak] *nm* lake; **les Grands Lacs** the Great Lakes; **le l. Baïkal** Lake Baikal; **le l. Érié** Lake Erie; **le l. Huron** Lake Huron; **le l. Léman** *ou* **de Genève** Lake Geneva; **le l. Michigan** Lake Michigan; **le l. Ontario** Lake Ontario; **le l. Supérieur** Lake Superior
lacer [16] [lase] **1** *vt (chaussures)* to tie (up); *(corset)* to lace up
  2 se lacer *vpr (chaussures)* to tie (up); *(corset)* to lace up
lacérer [34] [lasere] *vt (déchirer)* to tear to shreds;*(blesser)* to lacerate
lacet [lase] *nm* (**a**) *(de chaussure, de corset)* lace; **faire ses lacets** to tie one's laces (**b**) *(tournant)* sharp bend; **faire des lacets** to twist and turn (**c**) *(collet)* snare
lâche [lɑʃ] **1** *adj* (**a**) *(ressort, nœud)* loose; *(vêtement)* loose-fitting; *(discipline)* lax (**b**) *Péj (personne, acte, attitude)* cowardly
  2 *nmf* coward
lâchement [lɑʃmɑ̃] *adv (sans courage)* in a cowardly way
lâcher [lɑʃe] **1** *vt* (**a**) *(desserrer) (corde, ceinture)* to loosen (**b**) *(ne plus tenir)* to let go of; *(laisser tomber)* to drop; *Fam Fig (cesser d'importuner)* to leave alone; **l. prise** to let go; *Fam* **il ne m'a pas lâché d'une semelle** he stuck to me like a leech; *Fam* **lâche-moi les baskets** *ou* **la grappe!** get off my back! (**c**) *Fam (abandonner) (associé)* to walk out on; *(ami)* to let down; *(amant)* to chuck, to dump; *(emploi)* to chuck in; **la voiture nous a lâchés** the car died on us (**d**) *(distancer) (poursuivant)* to shake off; *(dans une course)* to leave behind (**e**) *(libérer)* to release; **l. un chien sur qn** to set a dog on sb (**f**) *(laisser échapper) (juron, cri, pet)* to let out; *(sottise, plaisanterie)* to come out with; *Fam* **l. le morceau** to spill the beans
  2 *vi (corde, câble)* to break; *(mécanisme, pièce)* to go; *(moteur)* to die; *(freins)* to fail; *Fig* **ses nerfs ont lâché** he/she broke down
  3 *nm (de colombes, de ballons)* release
lâcheté [lɑʃte] *nf* cowardice
lâcheur, -euse [lɑʃœr, -øz] *nm,f Fam* unreliable person
lacis [lasi] *nm (de nerfs, de fils)* network; *(de ruelles)* maze
laconique [lakɔnik] *adj* laconic
laconiquement [lakɔnikmɑ̃] *adv* laconically
lacrymal, -e, -aux, -ales [lakrimal, -o] *adj* tear, *Spéc* lachrymal

lacrymogène [lakrimɔʒɛn] *adj voir* **gaz, grenade**

lacté, -e [lakte] *adj (produit)* which contains milk; *(régime)* milk

lactique [laktik] *adj Chim* lactic

lactose [laktoz] *nm Chim* lactose

lacune [lakyn] *nf (dans une liste, ses connaissances, ses souvenirs)* gap; **avoir des lacunes en qch** to have a patchy knowledge of sth

lacustre [lakystr] *adj* lakeside

lad [lad] *nm* stable lad

là-dedans [ladədã] *adv* inside, in there; **il y a l. quelque chose que je ne comprends pas** there's something here I don't understand; **elle n'a rien à voir l.!** she's got nothing to do with it!

là-dessous [latsu] *adv* underneath, under there; *Fig* **il y a quelque chose l.** there's something behind it

là-dessus [latsy] *adv* on there; *(sur ces mots)* with that; **tout le monde est d'accord l.** everybody agrees about it; **c'est l. que tu dois te concentrer** that's what you have to concentrate on

lagon [lagɔ̃] *nm* lagoon

lagopède [lagɔpɛd] *nm* l. d'Écosse grouse

lagune [lagyn] *nf* lagoon

là-haut [lao] *adv* up there; *(à un étage supérieur)* upstairs

La Havane [laavan] *n* Havana

La Haye [laɛ] *n* The Hague

laïc [laik] = **laïque**

laïciser [laisize] *vt* to secularize

laïcité [laisite] *nf (des écoles)* secularity; *Pol* secularism

laid, -e [lɛ, lɛd] **(a)** *adj (personne, visage, bâtiment)* ugly; **l. comme un pou** *ou* **à faire peur** as ugly as sin **(b)** *(langage enfantin) (méprisable)* not nice

laideron [lɛdrɔ̃] *nm l'éj (fille)* ugly girl; *(femme)* ugly woman

laideur [lɛdœr] *nf* **(a)** *(d'une personne, d'un visage, d'un bâtiment)* ugliness **(b)** *(bassesse)* meanness

laie [lɛ] *nf (animal)* wild sow

lainage [lɛnaʒ] *nm* **(a)** *(étoffe)* woollen fabric **(b)** *(vêtement en laine)* jumper; **lainages** woollens

laine [lɛn] *nf* **(a)** *(tissu)* wool; **en l.** woollen; **l. d'agneau** lambswool; **l. vierge** new wool; **(en) pure l.** pure wool **(b)** *(vêtement)* **mettre une petite l.** to put a woolly on **(c)** **l. de verre** glass wool

laineux, -euse [lɛnø, -øz] *adj (tissu)* fleecy; *(mouton, cheveux)* woolly

lainier, -ère [lɛnje, -ɛr] *adj* wool

laïque [laik] **1** *adj (État)* secular; *(école, enseignement)* non-religious **2** *nmf* layman, *f* laywoman

laisse [lɛs] *nf (pour chien)* lead, leash; **tenir un chien en l.** to keep a dog on a lead

laissé-pour-compte, laissée-pour-compte *(mpl* **laissés-pour-compte**, *fpl* **laissées-pour-compte)** [lesepurkɔ̃t] *nm,f* reject

laisser [lese] **1** *vt* **(a)** *(permettre à)* **l. qn faire qch** to let sb do sth; **laissez-le faire!** leave him alone!; **le toit laissait passer la pluie** the roof let the rain in; **l. sécher la peinture** to let the paint dry; *Fig* **laissez-moi rire!** don't make me laugh!; *aussi Fig* **l. tomber qn/qch** to drop sb/sth; *Fam* **l. courir** to leave things alone; **l. dire** to let people talk; **laisse faire!** never mind!
(b) *(quitter) (mari, femme)* to leave; **l. qn tout seul** to leave sb all on their own; **bon, je vous laisse!** well, I'll be off!; **il a laissé une veuve et trois enfants** he left a widow and three children

(c) *(ne pas prendre)* to leave; **l. qch à qn** *(le lui réserver)* to leave sth for sb
(d) *(maintenir)* **l. qch ouvert/fermé** to leave sth open/closed
(e) *(oublier)* to leave
(f) *(traces, impression, souvenir)* to leave
(g) *(ne pas s'occuper de) (personne)* to leave; **laisse, je m'en occupe** don't bother about that, I'll see to it
(h) *(donner)* **l. qch à qn** *(en héritage)* to leave sb sth; *(pour qu'il s'en occupe)* to leave sth to sb; **l. le choix à qn** to give sb a choice; **cela nous laisse le temps de...** that leaves us time to...; **ils ont laissé les enfants à la grand-mère** they left the children with their grandmother; **je vous la laisse pour 40 euros** I'll let you have it for 40 euros
(i) *(perdre) (fortune, vie, membre)* to lose
(j) *Formel* **cela n'a pas laissé de me surprendre** it could not fail to surprise him
2 se laisser *vpr* **se l. décourager/embrasser** to let oneself be discouraged/kissed; **ne te laisse p as faire!** don't let him/her walk all over you; **se l. aller** to let oneself go; **se l. aller au découragement** to let oneself get discouraged; **ce vin se laisse boire** this wine is very drinkable; **je me suis laissé dire que...** I hear that...; **se l. vivre** to take life as it comes

laisser-aller [leseale] *nm inv (relâchement)* carelessness

laissez-passer [lesepase] *nm inv* pass

lait [lɛ] *nm* **(a)** *(aliment)* milk; **petit l.** whey; *Fig* **boire du petit l.** to lap it up; **l. de brebis/de chèvre/de vache** sheep's/goat's/cow's milk; **l. caillé** curd; **l. condensé** condensed milk; **l. cru** unpasteurized milk; **l. demi-écrémé** *Br* semi-skimmed *or Am* part-skim milk; **l. écrémé** *Br* skimmed *or Am* skim milk; **l. entier** whole milk; **l. longue conservation** long-life milk; **l. maternel** mother's milk; **l. en poudre** powdered milk; **l. de soja** soya milk **(b)** *(cosmétique)* **l. après-soleil** after-sun (lotion); **l. bronzant** suntan lotion; **l. démaquillant** *ou* **de toilette** cleansing lotion

laitage [lɛtaʒ] *nm* dairy product

laitance [lɛtɑ̃s] *nf (de poisson)* milt; *Culin* soft roe

laiterie [lɛtri] *nf* dairy

laiteux, -euse [lɛtø, -øz] *adj (teint)* creamy; *(couleur, lumière)* milky

laitier¹, -ère [lɛtje, -ɛr] **1** *adj* dairy **2** *nm,f (livreur)* milkman, *f* milkwoman **3** *nf* **laitière** *(vache)* dairy cow

laitier² *nm Ind* slag

laiton [lɛtɔ̃] *nm* brass

laitue [lɛty] *nf* lettuce

laïus [lajys] *nm (discours)* speech

lama¹ [lama] *nm Rel* lama; **le Grand l.** the dalai lama

lama² *nm (animal)* llama

lambda [lɑ̃bda] *adj inv (moyen)* average

lambeau, -x [lɑ̃bo] *nm (de tissu, de papier, de viande)* scrap; **vêtements en lambeaux** clothes in tatters; **tomber en lambeaux** to fall to pieces

lambin, -e [lɑ̃bɛ̃, -in] *Fam* **1** *adj* slow **2** *nm,f Br* slowcoach, *Am* slowpoke

lambiner [lɑ̃bine] *vi Fam* to dawdle

lambris [lɑ̃bri] *nm (en bois)* panelling; *(en marbre, en stuc)* lining

lambrissé, -e [lɑ̃brise] *adj (de bois)* panelled; *(de marbre, de stuc)* lined

lambswool [lɑ̃bswul] *nm* lambswool; **en l.** lambswool

lame [lam] *nf* **(a)** *(d'épée, de couteau)* blade; *(épée)* sword; *Fig* **une fine l.** a fine swordsman; **visage en l. de couteau** hatchet face; **l. de rasoir** razor blade **(b)** *(bande) (de métal,* *de verre, de parquet)* strip; *(de store)* slat **(c)** *(vague)* wave; **l. de fond** groundswell

lamé, -e [lame] **1** *adj* lamé; **l. or** gold lamé **2** *nm* lamé; **en l.** lamé

La Mecque [lamɛk] *n* Mecca

lamelle [lamɛl] *nf* **(a)** *(de métal, de verre)* thin strip; *Bot (de champignon)* gill; *Culin* **couper en (fines) lamelles** to cut into (wafer-)thin slices **(b)** *(de microscope)* cover glass

lamentable [lamãtabl] *adj* appalling, awful; *(personne)* hopeless, pathetic

lamentablement [lamãtabləmã] *adv* *(échouer)* miserably

lamentations [lamãtasjɔ̃] *nfpl* **(a)** *(cris, pleurs)* wailing **(b)** *Péj (plaintes)* moaning, complaining

lamenter [lamãte] **se lamenter** *vpr* to moan; **se l. sur qch** to bemoan sth

laminage [laminaʒ] *nm (du métal)* rolling; **l. à chaud/à froid** hot-/cold-rolling

laminer [lamine] *vt* **(a)** *(métal)* to roll **(b)** *Fig (revenus)* to erode; *(parti politique)* to annihilate

laminoir [laminwar] *nm Ind* rolling mill

lampadaire [lãpadɛr] *nm* **(a)** *(d'intérieur) Br* standard lamp, *Am* floor lamp **(b)** *(réverbère)* lamppost

lampe [lãp] *nf* **(a)** *(appareil d'éclairage)* lamp; **l. à alcool** spirit lamp; **l. de bureau** desk lamp; **l. de chevet** bedside lamp; **l. à pétrole** oil lamp; **l. de poche** *Br* torch, *Am* flashlight **(b)** *Fam* **s'en mettre plein la l.** to have a good blowout

lampée [lãpe] *nf Fam* gulp

lampe-tempête *(pl* **lampes-tempête)** [lãptãpɛt] *nf* hurricane lamp

lampion [lãpjɔ̃] *nm* paper lantern

lampiste [lãpist] *nm (subalterne)* underling

lamproie [lãprwa] *nf* lamprey

lance [lãs] *nf* **(a)** *(pique)* spear **(b)** *(tuyau)* **l. d'incendie** fire hose

lancée [lãse] *nf* **continuer sur sa l.** to keep going; **j'ai fait les exercices 5 et 6, et sur ma l. j'ai aussi fait le 7** I did exercises 5 and 6, and while I was at it I did 7 as well

lance-flammes [lãsflam] *nm inv* flamethrower

lancement [lãsmã] *nm* **(a)** *(d'une fusée, d'un projet, d'un produit)* launch(ing) **(b)** *Ordinat (d'impression)* start; *(de programme)* running

lance-missiles [lãsmisil] *nm inv* missile launcher

lance-pierre *(pl* **lance-pierres)** [lãspjer] *nm Br* catapult, *Am* slingshot; *Fam Fig* **manger avec un l.** to wolf one's food down

lancer [16] [lãse] **1** *vt* **(a)** *(projeter)* to throw **(à** to); *(flèche)* to shoot; *(fusée)* to launch; *(bombe)* to drop; *(étincelles)* to shoot out; *Fig (idée, proposition)* to throw out; *(remarque)* to come out with; *(plaisanterie)* to crack; *(juron)* to let out; **l. un coup d'œil à qn** to dart *or* shoot a glance at sb; **l. le poids** to put the shot

(b) *(envoyer) (signaux de détresse, SOS)* to send out **(c)** *(projet, produit, artiste)* to launch; *(mode)* to start; *Fin* **l. un emprunt** to issue a bond

(d) *(faire démarrer) (moteur)* to start (up); **être lancé** *(dans une course, dans un travail)* to have got going; **l. qn sur un sujet** to start sb (off) on a subject

(e) *Ordinat (impression)* to start; *(programme)* to run, to start (up)

2 *nm* **(a)** **(pêche au) l.** rod-and-reel fishing **(b)** *Sp* **l. du javelot/du disque/du marteau** throwing the javelin/the discus/the hammer; **l. du poids** putting the shot; **l. franc** *(au basket)* free throw

3 se lancer *vpr* **(a)** *(se jeter)* **se l. dans le vide** to throw

oneself off; **se l. en avant** to rush forward; **se l. à la poursuite de qn** to rush off in pursuit of sb

(b) *(s'engager)* **se l. dans** *(affaire, discussion, aventure)* to embark on; *(dépenses)* to get involved in; *(domaine)* to launch out into

(c) *(se faire connaître)* to make a name for oneself

lance-roquettes [lãsrɔket] *nm inv* rocket launcher

lance-torpilles [lãstɔrpij] *nm inv* torpedo tube

lanceur, -euse [lãsœr, -øz] *nm,f (au cricket)* bowler; *(au base-ball)* pitcher; **l. de javelot/disque/marteau** javelin/discus/hammer thrower; **l. de poids** shot putter

lancinant, -e [lãsinã, -ãt] *adj (douleur)* shooting; *(souvenir, air, musique)* haunting; *(regret)* nagging

landau [lãdo] *nm (voiture d'enfant) Br* pram, *Am* baby carriage

lande [lãd] *nf* moor, heath

langage [lãgaʒ] *nm* **(a)** *(langue, vocabulaire)* language; *Fig* **changer de l.** to change one's tune; **l. chiffré** cipher, code **(b)** *Ordinat* language; **l. de description de page** page description language; **l. d'imprimante par pages** page printer language; **l. d'interrogation** query language; **l. machine** machine language; **l. naturel** natural language; **l. à objets** object-oriented language; **l. de programmation** programming language; **l. utilisateur** user language

lange [lãʒ] *nm (couche) Br* nappy, *Am* diaper; *Vieilli* **langes** swaddling clothes

langer [45] [lãʒe] *vt (mettre une couche à)* to put a *Br* nappy *or Am* diaper on; *Vieilli* to wrap in swaddling clothes

langoureusement [lãgurøzmã] *adv* languorously

langoureux, -euse [lãgurø, -øz] *adj* languorous

langouste [lãgust] *nf* crayfish

langoustine [lãgustin] *nf* langoustine

langue [lãg] *nf* **(a)** *(organe)* tongue; **tirer la l. à qn** to stick one's tongue out at sb; *Fig* **j'ai tiré la l.** *(peiné)* it was hard going; **avoir la l. bien pendue** to have the gift of the gab; **ne pas avoir la l. dans sa poche** never to be at a loss for words; **donner sa l. au chat** to give up; **tu as avalé** *ou* **perdu ta l.?** has the cat got your tongue?; *Culin* **l. de bœuf** ox tongue

(b) *(langage, style, jargon)* language; **peuples/pays de l. française** French-speaking people/countries; **parler la l. de bois** to come out with clichés; **l. étrangère** foreign language; **l. maternelle** native language, mother tongue; **l. morte** dead language; **l. d'oc** = medieval French dialect spoken in Southern France; **l. d'oïl** = medieval French dialect spoken in Northern France; **langues vivantes** *(matière)* modern languages

(c) *(personne)* **une mauvaise l.** a backbiter; **une l. de vipère** a spiteful gossip

(d) *(bande)* **l. de terre** strip of land

langue-de-chat *(pl* **langues-de-chat)** [lãgdəʃa] *nf* finger biscuit

languedocien, -enne [lãgdɔsjɛ̃, -ɛn] **1** *adj* of the Languedoc **2** *nm,f* **L.** person from the Languedoc

languette [lãgɛt] *nf (de bois, de métal, de chaussure)* tongue

langueur [lãgœr] *nf* **(a)** *(apathie)* listlessness **(b)** *(mélancolie, rêverie)* languor

languir [lãgir] *vi (Litt ou Hum (dépérir)* to languish **(b)** *(attendre avec impatience)* **ne nous faites pas l.** don't keep us in suspense; *Litt* **l. de faire qch** to long to do sth **(c)** *(conversation)* to be flagging

lanière [lanjer] *nf (de sac, de sandale)* strap; *(de fouet)* lash; **découper qch en lanières** to cut sth into strips

lanoline [lanɔlin] *nf* lanolin

La Nouvelle-Orléans [lanuvɛlɔrleɑ̃] *n* New Orleans

lanterne [lɑ̃tɛrn] *nf* (a) *(lampe)* lantern; *Fig* **éclairer la l. de qn** to enlighten sb; **l. chinoise** Chinese lantern (b) *(de véhicule) Br* sidelight, *Am* parking light

lanterner [lɑ̃tɛrne] *vi Fam* to dawdle; **faire l. qn** to keep sb hanging about

Laos [laɔs] *nm* **le L.** Laos

laotien, -enne [laɔsjɛ̃, -ɛn] **1** *adj* Laotian **2** *nm,f* **L.** Laotian

lapalissade [lapalisad] *nf* statement of the obvious

laper [lape] *vt* to lap up

lapidaire [lapidɛr] *adj (style, formule)* concise, succinct

lapidation [lapidasjɔ̃] *nf* stoning

lapider [lapide] *vt (mettre à mort)* to stone (to death); *Fig (critiquer)* to lambast

lapin [lapɛ̃] *nm* rabbit; **manteau en (peau de) l.** rabbitskin coat; **poser un l. à qn** to stand sb up; **mon petit l.** sweetheart; **l. de garenne** wild rabbit; *Fam* **un chaud l.** a randy devil

lapine [lapin] *nf* doe (rabbit)

lapis [lapis], **lapis-lazuli** [lapislazyli] *nm inv* lapis lazuli

lapon, -one *ou* **-onne** [lapɔ̃, -ɔn] **1** *adj* Lapp **2** *nm,f* **L.** Lapp, Laplander

Laponie [lapɔni] *nf* **la L.** Lapland

laps [laps] *nm* **un l. de temps** a period of time; **un l. de temps de trois heures** a period of three hours

lapsus [lapsys] *nm (oral)* slip of the tongue; *(écrit)* slip of the pen; **faire un l.** to make a slip (of the tongue/pen); **un l. révélateur** a Freudian slip

laquais [lakɛ] *nm* footman; *Fig & Péj* lackey

laque [lak] *nf* (a) *(vernis)* lacquer (b) *(pour les cheveux)* hair spray, lacquer (c) *(peinture)* gloss (paint)

laquelle [lakɛl] *voir* **lequel**

laquer [lake] *vt* (a) *(vernir)* to lacquer (b) *(cheveux)* to lacquer (c) *(peindre)* to paint with gloss

larbin [larbɛ̃] *nm Fam* flunkey

larcin [larsɛ̃] *nm (vol)* petty theft

lard [lar] *nm* (a) *(du porc) (viande)* bacon; *(gras)* fat; *Fig* **se demander si c'est du l. ou du cochon** to wonder what to make of it; **l. fumé** smoked bacon; **l. maigre** streaky bacon (b) *Fam (graisse)* **faire du l.** to sit around and get fat; **rentrer dans le l. à qn** to lay into sb

larder [larde] *vt Culin* to lard; *Fig* **l. qn de coups de couteau** to hack at sb with a knife; **l. un texte de citations** to pepper a text with quotations

lardon [lardɔ̃] *nm* (a) *Culin* lardon, piece of chopped bacon (b) *très Fam (enfant)* kid

large [larʒ] **1** *adj* (a) *(route, porte, chaussures)* wide; *(vêtement)* loose-fitting; *(visage, nez, geste)* broad; **l. d'épaules** broad-shouldered; **l. de 20 mètres** 20 metres wide; **terme employé dans son sens l.** term used in its broad sense; **avoir l'esprit l., être l. d'esprit** to be broadminded (b) *(considérable)* large; *(ressources)* ample; **dans une l. mesure** to a large extent (c) *(généreux)* generous **2** *nm* (a) *(espace)* **être au l.** to have plenty of room (b) *(haute mer)* open sea; **au l. de** off; **prendre le l.** to take to the open sea; *Fig (s'enfuir)* to beat it (c) *(largeur)* **faire 20 mètres de l.** to be 20 metres wide **3** *adv* **compter l.** to allow for more

largement [larʒəmɑ̃] *adv* (a) *(répandu, critiqué)* widely (b) *(abondamment) (récompenser, payer, servir)* generously; *(dépasser)* by a long way; **avoir l. de quoi vivre** to have plenty to live on; **avoir l. le temps** to have plenty of time; **c'est l. suffisant, ça suffit l.** it's more than enough

largesse [larʒɛs] *nf* (a) *(générosité)* generosity (**envers towards**) (b) **largesses** *(dons)* generous gifts

largeur [larʒœr] *nf* (a) *(dimension)* width, breadth; *(de voie ferrée)* gauge; **en l., dans la l.** widthwise; **les policiers barraient la rue sur toute sa l.** the policemen blocked off the whole width of the street; *Rad* **l. de bande** bandwidth; *Ordinat* **l. de papier** paper width (b) *Fig* **l. d'esprit** *ou* **de vues** broadmindedness

largué, -e [large] *adj Fam (qui ne comprend plus)* lost

larguer [large] *vt* (a) *(amarres)* to cast off; *(cordage)* to loose; *(voile)* to unfurl (b) *(par avion) (parachutiste, vivres, bombe)* to drop (c) *Fam (abandonner) (personne)* to chuck; **il a tout largué pour partir vivre aux Caraïbes** he chucked everything in and went to live in the Caribbean

larme [larm] *nf* (a) *(pleur)* tear; **larmes de joie** tears of joy; **avoir facilement la l. à l'œil** to be easily moved to tears; **avoir les larmes aux yeux** to have tears in one's eyes; **en larmes** in tears; **larmes de crocodile** crocodile tears (b) *(petite quantité)* drop

larmoyant, -e [larmwajɑ̃, -ɑ̃t] *adj* (a) *(pleurnicheur) (voix, ton)* tearful (b) *Péj (histoire, film, sentimentalité)* mawkish

larmoyer [32] [larmwaje] *vi* (a) *(yeux)* to water (b) *Péj (personne)* to snivel

larron [larɔ̃] *nm* **s'entendre comme larrons en foire** to be as thick as thieves

larve [larv] *nf* (a) *(de batracien, de poisson)* larva; *(d'insecte)* grub (b) *Fam (personne apathique)* wimp

larvé, -e [larve] *adj (guerre, conflit)* latent

laryngite [larɛ̃ʒit] *nf Méd* laryngitis

laryngologie [larɛ̃gɔlɔʒi] *nf Méd* laryngology

laryngologiste [larɛ̃gɔlɔʒist], **laryngologue** [larɛ̃gɔlɔg] *nmf Méd* throat specialist, *Spéc* laryngologist

larynx [larɛ̃ks] *nm Anat* larynx

las, lasse [lɑ, lɑs] *adj Litt* weary; **être l. de qch/de faire qch** to be weary of sth/of doing sth

lasagnes [lazaɲ] *nfpl* lasagne

lascar [laskar] *nm Fam* rascal

lascif, -ive [lasif, -iv] *adj* lascivious

lascivement [lasivmɑ̃] *adv* lasciviously

laser [lazɛr] *nm* laser

lassant, -e [lɑsɑ̃, -ɑ̃t] *adj* tiresome

lasser [lɑse] **1** *vt* to tire **2 se lasser** *vpr* **se l. (de qch/de faire qch)** to get tired (of sth/of doing sth)

lassitude [lɑsityd] *nf* weariness

lasso [laso] *nm* lasso; **prendre un animal au l.** to lasso an animal

latent, -e [latɑ̃, -ɑ̃t] *adj* latent; **à l'état l.** latent

latéral, -e, -aux, -ales [lateral, -o] *adj (entrée, rue, vent, choc)* side

latéralement [lateralmɑ̃] *adv (se déplacer)* sideways; *(être situé)* at the side

latex [lateks] *nm* latex

latin, -e [latɛ̃, -in] **1** *adj* Latin; *(langue)* Romance **2** *nm* Latin; **l. de cuisine** dog Latin; *Fig* **j'y perds mon l.** I can't make head or tail of it

latiniste [latinist] *nmf (spécialiste)* Latinist; *(étudiant)* Latin student

latino [latino] *nmf Fam* Latino

latino-américain, -e *(mpl* latino-américains, *fpl* latino-américaines) [latinoamerikɛ̃, -ɛn] **1** *adj* Latin-American **2** *nm,f* **L.-A.** Latin-American

latitude [latityd] *nf* (**a**) *Géog* latitude; **à 25° de l. nord** at latitude 25° north; **sous ces latitudes** in these latitudes (**b**) *(liberté)* latitude, scope; **avoir/donner à qn toute l. pour agir** to have/to give sb total freedom of action

latrines [latrin] *nfpl* latrines

latte [lat] *nf* lath; *Fam* **donner un coup de l. à qn** to give sb a kick

lattis [lati] *nm* lathing

laudanum [lodanɔm] *nm* laudanum

lauréat, -e [lɔrea, -at] **1** *adj* (prize)winning **2** *nm,f* (prize)winner

laurier [lɔrje] *nm* (**a**) *(plante)* laurel; *Culin* bay leaves (**b**) *Fig (gloire)* **lauriers** laurels; **se reposer** *ou* **s'endormir sur ses lauriers** to rest on one's laurels; **être couvert de lauriers** to be covered with glory

laurier-rose (*pl* **lauriers-roses**) [lɔrjeroz] *nm* oleander

lavable [lavabl] *adj* washable; **l. en machine/à la main** machine-/hand-washable

lavabo [lavabo] *nm* (**a**) *(cuvette)* washbasin (**b**) **lavabos** *(toilettes)* toilets

lavage [lavaʒ] *nm* washing; **l. de cerveau** brainwashing; **faire subir un l. de cerveau à qn** to brainwash sb; **faire un l. d'estomac à qn** to pump sb's stomach (out)

lavande [lavɑ̃d] **1** *nf (fleur)* lavender; **(eau de) l.** lavender water **2** *adj inv* **(bleu) l.** lavender blue

lavandière [lavɑ̃djer] *nf* (**a**) *(blanchisseuse)* washerwoman (**b**) *(oiseau)* wagtail

lave [lav] *nf* lava

lave-autos [lavoto] *nm inv Can* carwash

lave-glace (*pl* **lave-glaces**) [lavglas] *nm Br* windscreen *or Am* windshield washer

lave-linge [lavlɛ̃ʒ] *nm inv* washing machine

lave-mains [lavmɛ̃] *nm inv* handbasin

lavement [lavmɑ̃] *nm* enema

laver [lave] **1** *vt* (**a**) *(nettoyer)* to wash; *(plaie)* to bathe; **l. qch à l'eau froide** to wash sth in cold water; **il faut l. son linge sale en famille** one shouldn't wash one's dirty linen in public (**b**) *(disculper)* **l. qn d'une accusation/de tout soupçon** to clear sb of an accusation/of all suspicion (**c**) *(venger)* **l'affront a été lavé dans le sang** the insult was paid for in blood **2 se laver** *vpr* (**a**) *(se nettoyer)* to wash (oneself), to have a wash; **se l. les dents** to clean *or* brush one's teeth; **se l. les cheveux/les mains** to wash one's hair/one's hands; *Fig* **je m'en lave les mains** I wash my hands of it (**b**) *(pouvoir être lavé)* **se l. à la main/à la machine** to be hand-/machine-washable

laverie [lavri] *nf* **l. automatique** *Br* launderette, *Am* Laundromat®

lavette [lavɛt] *nf* (**a**) *(de vaisselle)* dishcloth (**b**) *Belg & Suisse (gant de toilette) Br* face cloth, *Am* washcloth (**c**) *Fam Fig (homme)* drip

laveur, -euse [lavœr, -øz] *nm,f* washer; **l. de vitres** window cleaner

lave-vaisselle [lavvɛsɛl] *nm inv* dishwasher

lave-vitre (*pl* **lave-vitres**) [lavvitr] *nm Br* windscreen *or Am* windshield washer

lavis [lavi] *nm* (**a**) *(procédé)* washing (**b**) *(dessin)* wash drawing

lavoir [lavwar] *nm* (**a**) *(établissement)* **l. (public)** (public) washhouse (**b**) *(bassin)* washtub

lavomatic [lavomatik] *nm Br* launderette, *Am* Laundromat®

laxatif, -ive [laksatif, -iv] *adj & nm* laxative

laxisme [laksism] *nm* laxness

laxiste [laksist] **1** *adj* lax **2** *nmf* lax person

layette [lɛjɛt] *nf* baby clothes

le¹, la, les [lə, la, le]

> **l'** is used instead of **le** or **la** before a word beginning with a vowel or h mute.

article défini (**a**) *(pour définir les noms)* the; **le soleil** the sun; **la lune** the moon; **l'étoile** the star; **les planètes** the planets; **le pull que je me suis acheté** the jumper I bought myself; **le Paris de 1900** Paris in 1900, the Paris of 1900; **oh, la jolie robe!** what a lovely dress!; **debout, les enfants!** get up, children!
(**b**) *(avec des notions ou des généralités)* **le français** French; **la biologie** biology; **l'amour** love; **l'homme et la femme** man and woman; **the chien est l'ami de l'homme** a dog is a man's best friend; **aider les pauvres** to help the poor; **fumer la pipe** to smoke a pipe
(**c**) *(avec les noms de lieux)* **la France** France; **les États-Unis** the United States; **le mont Blanc** Mont Blanc; **les Alpes** the Alps; **la Seine** the Seine
(**d**) *(avec les noms de personnes)* **la reine d'Angleterre** the Queen of England; **le roi Henri IV** King Henry IV; **le Docteur Dupont** Doctor Dupont
le (**e**) *(avec les parties du corps)* **avoir les yeux verts** to have green eyes; **avoir mal à la gorge** to have a sore throat; **hausser les épaules** to shrug one's shoulders; **se laver les pieds** to wash one's feet
(**f**) *(avec un adjectif)* **je préfère le rouge** I prefer the red one
(**g**) *(distributif)* **50 francs le mètre** 50 francs a metre; **35 francs de l'heure** 35 francs an hour
(**h**) *(dans un complément de temps)* **le dimanche, il ne travaille pas** he doesn't work on Sundays; **il va à l'école le matin** he goes to school in the mornings; **il y fait vraiment froid l'hiver** it's really cold there in the winter; **je n'ai rien mangé de la journée** I haven't eaten all day; **Londres, le 9 novembre 2004** *(dans une lettre)* 9 November 2004; **je suis arrivé le 28** I arrived on the 28th

le²

> **l'** is used before a word beginning with a vowel or h mute.

pron personnel (**a**) *(homme, garçon)* him; *(chose, idée)* it; *(animal)* it, him; **elle l'admire** she admires him; **je te le rendrai demain** I'll give it back to you tomorrow; **et lui, tu le connais?** do you know him?; **le voici** here it/he is
(**b**) *(remplace une proposition)* **elle me l'a dit** she told me; **il me l'a confirmé** he confirmed it
(**c**) *(remplace un adjectif, un nom)* **est-ce qu'elle est disponible? – oui, je crois qu'elle l'est** is she available? – yes, I think she is; **jaloux, il l'est sans aucun doute** he's undoubtedly jealous; **son frère est avocat, il voudrait l'être aussi** his brother is a lawyer and he'd like to be one too

leader [lidœr] *nm* leader

leasing [liziŋ] *nm* leasing; **acheter une auto en l.** to buy a car on a leasing basis

Le Caire [ləkɛr] *n* Cairo

Le Cap [ləkap] *n* Cape Town

lèche [lɛʃ] *nf très Fam* bootlicking; **faire de la l.** to be a bootlicker

lèche-bottes [lɛʃbɔt] *Fam* **1** *adj inv* **elle est l.** she's a bootlicker **2** *nmf inv* bootlicker

lèche-cul [lɛʃky] *nm inv Vulg Br* arse-licker, *Am* brown-nose

lécher [34] [leʃe] **1** vt (a) *(avec la langue)* to lick; *Fam* **l. les bottes à qn** to lick sb's boots (b) *(fignoler) (travail, style)* to polish (c) *(effleurer) (sujet: vagues)* to lap against; *(sujet: flammes)* to lick **2 se lécher** vpr **se l. les doigts** to lick one's fingers

lèche-vitrines [leʃvitrin] *nm Fam* window-shopping; **faire du l.** to go window-shopping

leçon [ləsɔ̃] *nf* (a) *(cours, contenu)* lesson; **leçons de chant** singing lessons; **l. de choses** general science *(in primary school)*; **l. particulière** private lesson; **la couture en dix leçons** needlework in ten easy lessons (b) *(conseil)* **faire la l. à qn** to give sb a lecture; **donner une l. à qn** to teach sb a lesson; **je n'ai pas de l. à recevoir de toi** I don't need your advice; **que cela te serve de l.!** let that be a lesson to you!

lecteur, -trice [lektœr, -tris] **1** *nm,f* (a) *(personne qui lit)* reader (b) *(dans l'édition)* (publisher's) reader (c) *Univ* foreign language assistant **2** *nm* (a) *(dispositif)* **l. de cassettes** cassette player; **l. de disques compacts** CD player; **l. de DVD** DVD player; **l. optique** optical reader (b) *Ordinat* **l. (de disquettes)** (disk) drive, floppy (disk) drive; **l. de bandes** tape drive or reader; **l. de CD-ROM** ou **de disque optique** CD-ROM drive; **l. de disque dur** hard disk drive

lecteur-encodeur (*pl* lecteurs-encodeurs) [lektœrɑ̃kɔdœr] *nm Ordinat* reader-encoder

lectorat [lektɔra] *nm* (a) *Univ* assistantship (b) *(lecteurs)* readership

lecture [lektyr] *nf* (a) *(action de lire)* reading; **faire la l. à qn** to read aloud to sb; *Pol* **en deuxième l.** at the second reading (b) *(ce qu'on lit)* reading; **elle m'a apporté de là l.** she brought me something to read; **avoir de mauvaises lectures** to read the wrong things; **livre de l.** reading book (c) *(interprétation)* reading (d) *Ordinat* read(ing); **l. optique** optical reading; **l. au scanneur** scan; **en l. seule** in read-only mode, **l. sur disque** reading to disk

ledit, ladite [lədi, ladit] (*mpl* lesdits [ledi], *fpl* lesdites [ledit]) *adj* the aforementioned

légal, -e, -aux, -ales [legal, -o] *adj* legal

légalement [legalmɑ̃] *adv* legally

légalisation [legalizasjɔ̃] *nf* legalization; *(de signature)* authentication

légaliser [legalize] *vt (rendre légal)* to legalize; *(authentifier)* to authenticate

légalité [legalite] *nf* (a) *(de mesure, décision)* legality (b) *(situation légale)* **la l.** the law, **agir en toute l.** to act within the law

légataire [legater] *nmf* legatee; **l. universel** sole legatee

légendaire [leʒɑ̃der] *adj* legendary

légende [leʒɑ̃d] *nf* (a) *(histoire, fable)* legend; *Fig (mensonge)* fairy tale; **entrer dans la l.** to become a legend (b) *(d'un dessin, d'une photo)* caption; *(d'une carte)* key

léger, -ère [leʒe, -ɛr] **1** *adj* (a) *(de peu de poids)* light; **l. comme une plume** as light as a feather; **avoir le cœur l.** to be light-hearted (b) *(blessure, amélioration, nuance)* slight; *(brise, vin, parfum)* light; *(tabac)* mild; *(thé, café)* weak; **il y a eu quelques blessés légers** some people were slightly injured (c) *(insuffisant) (preuves, arguments)* lightweight; *Fam* **ses résultats sont un peu légers** his/her marks are a bit on the low side (d) *(désinvolte) (personne)* thoughtless; *(en amour)* fickle; **femme légère** ou **de mœurs légères** loose woman **2** *nf* **à la légère** *(agir, parler)* thoughtlessly; **prendre qch à la légère** to make light of sth **3** *adv* **je vais manger l.** I'll have a light meal; **s'habiller l.** to wear light clothes

légèrement [leʒɛrmɑ̃] *adv* (a) *(habillé)* lightly (b) *(un peu)* slightly; **ça sent l. le moisi** there's a slight smell of

mildew; **pourrais-tu l. baisser le volume?** could you turn the volume down a bit? (c) *(avec désinvolture) (agir)* thoughtlessly

légèreté [leʒɛrte] *nf* (a) *(d'un objet, d'un danseur, d'une démarche)* lightness (b) *(faiblesse) (d'une blessure, d'une nuance)* slightness; *(d'un vin)* lightness (c) *(désinvolture)* thoughtlessness; **avec l.** *(agir, parler)* thoughtlessly (d) *(en amour)* fickleness; *(des mœurs)* looseness

légiférer [34] [leʒifere] vi to legislate (**sur** on)

légion [leʒjɔ̃] *nf* legion; *Fig (multitude)* huge number; **ils sont l.** they are legion; **la L. (étrangère)** the Foreign Legion; **la L. d'honneur** the Legion of Honour

légionnaire [leʒjɔner] *nm* (a) *Hist* legionary (b) *(à la Légion étrangère)* legionnaire

législateur, -trice [leʒislatœr, -tris] *Jur* **1** *nm,f* legislator **2** *nm (corps législatif)* legislature **3** *adj* legislative

législatif, -ive [leʒislatif, -iv] **1** *adj* legislative; **le pouvoir l.** the legislature **2** *nm* **l.** legislative power **3** *nfpl* **les législatives** the parliamentary elections

législation [leʒislasjɔ̃] *nf* legislation

législature [leʒislatyr] *nf* (a) *(durée)* term of office (b) *(corps)* legislature

légiste [leʒist] *nm* jurist

légitime [leʒitim] *adj* (a) *(légal) (pouvoir, enfant)* legitimate; *(action)* lawful; *(propriétaire)* legal; *(héritier)* rightful (b) *(juste) (récompense, motif, désir)* legitimate (c) *(justifié) (colère, action)* justified; **l. défense** self-defence; **elle était en état de l. défense** she was acting in self-defence

légitimement [leʒitimmɑ̃] *adv* legitimately; *Jur* lawfully

légitimer [leʒitime] vt (a) *(enfant, union)* to legitimize (b) *(action, demande)* to justify (c) *(titre, pouvoir)* to recognize

légitimité [leʒitimite] *nf* legitimacy

legs [lɛ, lɛg] *nm Jur* legacy, bequest; **faire un l. à qn** to leave sb a legacy (b) *Fig (héritage)* legacy

léguer [34] [lege] vt (a) *Jur* to bequeath (**à** to) (b) *(tradition, qualité)* to pass on (**à** to)

légume [legym] **1** *nm* (a) *(pour manger)* vegetable; **légumes verts** green vegetables, greens; **légumes secs** pulses (b) *Fam Fig (personne végétative)* vegetable **2** *nf Fam* **grosse l.** bigwig

leitmotiv [lajtmotif, lɛtmotif] *nm* leitmotiv

Léman [lemɑ̃] *nm* **le lac L.** Lake Geneva

lendemain [lɑ̃dmɛ̃] *nm* (a) *(jour suivant)* **le l.** the next day; **le l. matin/soir** the next morning/evening; **le l. de la bataille** the day after the battle (b) *(avenir)* **penser au l.** to think of the future; **des lendemains prometteurs** a promising future; **sans l.** *(succès, aventures)* short-lived (c) *(période qui suit)* **au l. de la guerre/de ce scandale** soon after the war/this scandal

lent, -e [lɑ̃, lɑ̃t] *adj* slow; **être l. à comprendre** to be slow to understand; **avoir l'esprit l.** to be slow-witted

lente [lɑ̃t] *nf* nit

lentement [lɑ̃tmɑ̃] *adv* slowly; **l. mais sûrement** slowly but surely

lenteur [lɑ̃tœr] *nf* slowness; **avec l.** slowly; **les lenteurs de la justice** the slowness of the law

lentille [lɑ̃tij] *nf* (a) *(plante)* lentil; **l. d'eau** duckweed (b) *(en optique)* lens; **lentilles de contact** contact lenses

léopard [leɔpar] *nm (animal)* leopard; *(fourrure)* leopard skin

LEP [ɛløpe, lɛp] *nm Anciennement (abrév* **lycée d'enseignement professionnel)** ≃ technical college

lèpre [lɛpr] *nf* leprosy

lépreux, -euse [leprø, -øz] **1** *adj* leprous
2 *nm,f* leper

lequel, laquelle [ləkɛl, lakɛl] *(mpl* **lesquels** [lekɛl], *fpl* **lesquelles** [lekɛl])

> **lequel** and **lesquel(le)s** contract with **à** to form **auquel** and **auxquel(le)s**, and with **de** to form **duquel** and **desquel(le)s**.

1 *pron relatif (personne)* who; *(après une préposition)* whom; *(chose)* which; **l'actrice à laquelle je pense** the actress (that) I'm thinking of *or* of whom I'm thinking; **le stylo avec l. j'écris** the pen I'm writing with *or* with which I'm writing
2 *adj relatif* **j'ai vu son adversaire, l. adversaire est impressionnant** I've seen his opponent, he's/she's impressive; **auquel cas** in which case
3 *pron interrogatif* which (one)

les [le] **1** *art défini voir* **le**[1]
2 *pron personnel* them; **l. voilà** here they are

lesbienne [lesbjɛn] *nf* lesbian

lèse-majesté [lɛzmaʒɛste] *nf inv* high treason, lese-majesty

léser [34] [leze] *vt* **(a)** *(désavantager) (personne)* to wrong; *(intérêts)* to harm; **la partie lésée** the injured party **(b)** *Méd* to injure

lésiner [lezine] *vi* to skimp **(sur** on); **ne pas l. sur les moyens** not to spare any expense

lésion [lezjɔ̃] *nf* lesion

lesquels, lesquelles [lekɛl] *voir* **lequel**

lessivable [lesivabl] *adj* washable

lessivage [lesivaʒ] *nm* washing

lessive [lesiv] *nf* **(a)** *(produit) (en poudre)* washing powder; *(liquide)* liquid detergent **(b)** *(action de laver)* wash(ing); **faire la l.** to do the washing; **j'ai fait trois lessives ce matin** I've done three washes this morning **(c)** *(linge propre)* washing

lessivé, -e [lesive] *adj Fam* washed out

lessiver [lesive] *vt* **(a)** *(nettoyer)* to wash **(b)** *Fam (fatiguer)* to wear out

lessiveuse [lesivøz] *nf* boiler; *Fam Fig* **en faire une l.** to make a song and dance about it

lest [lɛst] *nm (de bateau, ballon)* ballast; **lâcher du l.** to discharge ballast; *Fig (faire des concessions)* to make concessions

leste [lɛst] *adj* **(a)** *(agile)* nimble **(b)** *(grivois)* risqué

lestement [lɛstəmɑ̃] *adv (avec agilité)* nimbly

lester [lɛste] *vt* **(a)** *(bateau, ballon)* to ballast **(b)** *Fam (poche, portefeuille)* to stuff

letchi [lɛtʃi] *nm* lychee

léthargie [letarʒi] *nf* lethargy

léthargique [letarʒik] *adj* lethargic

letton, -onne *ou* **-one** [lɛtɔ̃, -ɔn] **1** *adj* Latvian
2 *nm,f* **L.** Latvian
3 *nm (langue)* Latvian

Lettonie [lɛtɔni] *nf* **la L.** Latvia

lettre [lɛtr] *nf* **(a)** *(de l'alphabet)* letter; **l. majuscule/minuscule** capital/small letter; **écrire qch en toutes lettres** to write sth out in full; **au pied de la l.** literally; **à la l.** *(suivre, exécuter)* to the letter; **il fait surréaliste avant la l.** he was a surrealist before the word had been invented; **rester l. morte** to remain a dead letter; **gagner ses lettres de noblesse** to prove one's/its worth
(b) *(missive)* letter; **l. de change** bill of exchange; **l. ouverte** (à) open letter (to); **l. recommandée** registered letter; *Fam* **c'est passé comme une l. à la poste** it went off

without a hitch; *Fam* **la nouvelle est passée comme une l. à la poste** the news was received without any fuss
(c) **lettres** *(littérature)* literature; *(à l'université)* arts subjects; **homme/femme de lettres** man/woman of letters; **avoir des lettres** to be well-read; **faculté de lettres** faculty of arts; **lettres classiques** classics; **lettres modernes** *(à l'université)* French

lettré, -e [letre] **1** *adj* well-read
2 *nm,f* well-read person

leu [lø] *nm* **à la queue l. l.** in single file

leucémie [løsemi] *nf* leukaemia

leucocyte [løkosit] *nm* leucocyte

leur[1], **leurs** [lœr] **1** *adj possessif* their; **l. chien** *(il y a un chien)* their dog; *(chacun a son chien)* their dogs; **leurs enfants** their children; **l. père et l. mère** their mother and father; **un de leurs amis** one of their friends, a friend of theirs; *Fam* **ils ont eu l. vendredi** they got Friday off
2 *pron possessif* **le l., la l., les leurs** theirs; *(en insistant)* their own; **ils le prêtent le l.** you can borrow theirs; **ils n'en ont pas besoin, ils ont le l.** they don't need it, they've got their own
3 *nm* **il faut qu'ils y mettent du l.** they have to do their share
4 *nmpl* **les leurs** *(leur famille)* their family; **nous serons des leurs ce soir** we'll be joining them tonight

leur[2] *pron personnel* to them; **donne-l. ta carte de visite** give them your business card; **je le l. ai montré** I showed it to them

leurre [lœr] *nm* **(a)** *(à la chasse)* decoy **(b)** *(illusion)* illusion

leurrer [lœre] **1** *vt (tromper)* to delude
2 se leurrer *vpr* to delude oneself **(sur** about)

levage [ləvaʒ] *nm* lifting; **appareil de l.** lifting apparatus

levain [ləvɛ̃] *nm* leaven; **pain au/sans l.** leavened/unleavened bread

levant [ləvɑ̃] **1** *adj m* **soleil l.** rising sun; **au soleil l.** at sunrise
2 *nm* **(a)** *Litt* **le l.** the east **(b)** **le L.** the Levant

levé, -e [ləve] **1** *adj* **(a)** *(en l'air) (main, poing)* raised **(b)** *(personne, soleil)* up
2 *nm (de terrain)* survey

levée [ləve] *nf* **(a)** *(d'une interdiction, de sanctions)* lifting; *(d'une séance)* close; *(d'un siège)* raising; *(de scellés)* breaking **(b)** *(de troupes)* levying **(c)** *(de lettres)* collection **(d)** *(aux cartes)* trick; **faire une l.** to take a trick **(e)** *(remblai)* levee **(f)** **l. de boucliers** general outcry; **l. du corps** = removal of the coffin; **l. d'écrou** release from prison

lever[1] [46] [ləve] **1** *vt* **(a)** *(objet)* to lift, to raise; **l. son verre (à qn/qch)** to raise one's glass (to sb/sth) **(b)** *(bras, main, jambe)* to raise, to lift; **l. la tête** to look up; **l. les yeux au ciel** to raise one's eyes to heaven; **l. les bras au ciel** to throw up one's hands; **l. la main sur qn** to raise one's hand to sb; **l. le doigt** to put one's hand up; **il n'a pas levé le petit doigt** he didn't lift a finger; *Fam* **l. le pied** *(ralentir)* to slow down
(c) *(faire cesser) (embargo, peine, interdiction)* to lift; *(difficulté, doute, ambiguïté)* to remove; *(siège)* to raise; *(séance)* to close
(d) *(débusquer) (perdrix)* to flush; *très Fam (femme)* to pull; **l. un lièvre** to start a hare; *Fig* to open a can of worms
(e) *(faire sortir du lit) (enfant, malade)* to get up
(f) *(collecter) (courrier, impôts)* to collect
(g) *(enrôler) (troupes, armée)* to raise, to levy
(h) *(plan)* to draw
2 *vi* **(a)** *(blé, grain)* to shoot
(b) *(pâte)* to rise
3 se lever *vpr (se mettre debout)* to stand up, to get up; **se l. de sa chaise** to get up from one's chair; **se l. de table** to leave the table

(b) *(quitter le lit)* to get up; *Fam* **se l.** du pied gauche to get out of bed on the wrong side **(c)** *(apparaître) (soleil, lune)* to rise; *(vent)* to get up; *(jour)* to break **(d)** *(s'éclaircir) (brouillard, brume)* to lift, to clear **(e)** *(monter) (rideau de théâtre)* to go up, to rise

lever² *nm* **(a)** *(du lit)* getting up; **demain, l. six heures** tomorrow, get up six thirty; **au l., buvez un jus d'orange** first thing in the morning, have a drink of orange juice **(b)** *(apparition)* **le l. du jour** daybreak; **le l. du soleil** sunrise **(c) l. de rideau** *(début du spectacle)* curtain up; *(première partie)* curtain raiser **(d)** *(de terrain)* survey

lève-tard [lɛvtar] *nmf inv Fam* late riser

lève-tôt [lɛvto] *nmf inv Fam* early riser

lève-vitre *(pl* **lève-vitres)** [lɛvvitr] *nm* window winder

levier [ləvje] *nm aussi Fig* lever; **faire l.** to act as a lever; **l. de commande** control lever; *Fig* **être aux leviers de commande** to be in control; **l. (de changement) de vitesse** *Br* gear lever, *Am* gearshift

lévitation [levitasjɔ̃] *nf* levitation; **être en l.** to be levitating

lèvre [lɛvr] *nf* **(a)** *(de la bouche)* lip; **un cigare aux lèvres** with a cigar in his mouth; **le sourire aux lèvres** with a smile on her lips; **manger du bout des lèvres** to pick at one's food; **rire du bout des lèvres** to force a laugh; **accepter du bout des lèvres** to accept grudgingly; *Fig* **nous étions tous suspendus à ses lèvres** we were all hanging on her every word **(b)** *(de la vulve)* **lèvres** labia; **les grandes/petites lèvres** the labia majora/minora **(c)** *(bord) (de plaie)* lip; *(de cratère)* rim

lévrette [levrɛt] *nf* greyhound bitch

lévrier [levrije] *nm* greyhound; **l. afghan** Afghan hound

levure [ləvyr] *nf* yeast; **l. chimique** baking powder

lexical, -e, -aux, -ales [lɛksikal, -o] *adj* lexical

lexicographe [lɛksikɔgraf] *nmf* lexicographer

lexicographie [lɛksikɔgrafi] *nf* lexicography

lexique [lɛksik] *nm* **(a)** *(dictionnaire)* lexicon; *(glossaire)* glossary **(b)** *(mots d'un auteur)* vocabulary

lézard [lezar] *nm (animal)* lizard; *(cuir)* lizard skin

lézarde [lezard] *nf* crack

lézarder [lezarde] **1** *vt* to crack
2 *vi Fam* to lounge in the sun
3 se lézarder *vpr* to crack

liaison [ljɛzɔ̃] *nf* **(a)** *(dans les transports)* **l. aérienne/maritime/ferroviaire/routière** air/sea/rail/road link, **toutes les liaisons Paris-Téhéran sont suspendues** all services between Paris and Teheran have been suspended **(b)** *Tél* link; **l. radio/téléphonique** radio/telephone link; **l. par satellite** satellite link; **établir une l. radio** to establish radio contact; *Ordinat* **l. par modem** modem link; *Ordinat* **l. spécialisée** dedicated line **(c)** *(entre des personnes)* contact; **assurer la l.** entre deux personnes/services to liaise between two people/departments; **être en l. avec qn** to be in contact with sb; **travailler en l.** (étroite) **avec qn** to work (closely) with sb **(d)** *(relation amoureuse)* (love) affair **(e)** *(enchaînement logique)* connection **(f)** *Ling* liaison *(sounding of final consonant before initial vowel sound)* **faire la l.** to make the liaison

liane [ljan] *nf* creeper

liant, -e [ljɑ̃, -ɑ̃t] **1** *adj* sociable
2 *nm Tech* binder

liasse [ljas] *nf (de lettres, papiers)* bundle; *(de billets)* wad

Liban [libɑ̃] *nm* **le L.** (the) Lebanon

libanais, -e [libanɛ, -ɛz] **1** *adj* Lebanese
2 *nmf* **L.** Lebanese; **les L.** the Lebanese

libations [libasjɔ̃] *nfpl* libations

libellé [libele] *nm* wording

libeller [libele] *vt (document, acte, contrat)* to word; **l. un chèque à l'ordre de** to make out a cheque to

libellule [libelyl] *nf* dragonfly

libéral, -e, -aux, -ales [liberal, -o] *adj & nm,f* liberal

libéralisation [liberalizasjɔ̃] *nf* liberalization

libéraliser [liberalize] *vt* to liberalize

libéralisme [liberalism] *nm* liberalism

libéralité [liberalite] *nf* **(a)** *(générosité)* generosity **(b)** *(cadeau)* generous gift; **vivre des libéralités de ses amis** to live off the generosity of one's friends

libérateur, -trice [liberatœr, -tris] **1** *adj* liberating
2 *nm,f* liberator

libération [liberasjɔ̃] *nf* **(a)** *(mise en liberté)* *(d'un prisonnier)* release; *(d'un soldat)* discharge; **l. conditionnelle** (release on) parole **(b)** *(affranchissement)* liberation **(c)** *(fin de l'Occupation)* **la L.** the Liberation *(from the Germans in 1944-45)* **(d)** *(d'énergie, d'une substance)* release

libéré, -e [libere] **1** *adj* liberated; **jeune homme l. des obligations militaires** young man who has carried out his national service duties
2 *nm,f* released prisoner

libérer [libere] [34] **1** *vt* **(a)** *(rendre sa liberté à) (otage, prisonnier)* to free, to release; *(pays, peuple)* to liberate **(b)** *(laisser partir) (élèves, étudiants)* to let go; *(soldat)* to discharge **(c)** *(soulager)* **l. qn d'un souci** *ou* **d'un poids** to take a weight off sb's mind **(d)** *(rendre disponible) (appartement, chambre d'hôtel)* to vacate **(e)** *(débloquer) (prix)* to free; *(cran de sûreté)* to release; *(instincts, passions)* to unleash; **l. le passage** to clear the way **(f)** *(décharger)* **l. qn de qch** *(dette)* to free sb from sth; *(engagement)* to release sb from sth **(g)** *(émettre) (substance, énergie)* to release
2 se libérer *vpr* **(a)** *(s'affranchir)* to free oneself *(de* from) **(b)** *(se rendre disponible)* **je suis tâché de me libérer demain, je ne pas pu me l.** plus tôt I couldn't get away any earlier; **il y a un poste qui vient de se l.** a job vacancy has just come up

Liberia [liberja] *nm* **le L.** Liberia

libérien, -enne [liberjɛ̃, -ɛn] **1** *adj* Liberian
2 *nm,f* **L.** Liberian

libertaire [liberter] *adj & nmf* libertarian

liberté [liberte] *nf* **(a)** *(condition)* freedom, liberty; **en l.** *(fugitif)* at large; *(animal)* in the wild; **rendre sa l. à qn/un animal** to let sb/an animal go; **reprendre sa l.** to regain one's freedom; **mettre qn en l.** to set sb free; **(mise en) l. conditionnelle** parole; **l. surveillée** probation; **mettre qn en l. provisoire/conditionnelle/surveillée** to release sb on bail/parole/probation **(b)** *(droit de l'individu)* freedom, liberty; **l., égalité, fraternité** liberty, equality, fraternity; **l. d'expression** freedom of expression or speech; **l. d'opinion** freedom of opinion; **l. de la presse** freedom of the press **(c)** *(absence de contrainte)* freedom; **l. d'entreprise** free enterprise; **avoir toute l. d'action** to have complete freedom of action; **avoir toute l. pour faire qch** to have complete freedom to do sth; **en toute l.** *(s'exprimer, agir)* freely; **prendre la l. de faire qch** to take the liberty of doing sth **(d)** *(familiarités)* **prendre** *ou* **se permettre des libertés avec qn** to take liberties with sb

libertin, -e [libertɛ̃, -in] **1** *adj (personne)* dissolute; *(livre, propos)* licentious

libertinage [libertinaʒ] *nm* licentiousness

libidineux, -euse [libidinø, -øz] *adj* lustful

libido [libido] *nf* libido

libraire [librɛr] *nmf* bookseller

librairie [librɛri] *nf (magasin)* bookshop; *(activité)* bookselling

librairie-papeterie *(pl* librairies-papeteries) [librɛripapetri] *nf* bookshop and stationer's

libre [libr] *adj* **(a)** *(non soumis)(personne, pays)* free; **être l. de faire qch** to be free to do sth; **l. à vous de le faire** you're quite at liberty to do it; **donner l. cours à son enthousiasme/son imagination** to give one's enthusiasm/imagination free rein; **l. de** *(souci, contrainte, préjugé)* free from; **l. arbitre** free will; **l. pensée** free thinking; **l. penseur** free thinker **(b)** *(disponible) (personne, siège)* free; *(appartement, chambre)* available; *(toilettes)* vacant; **je n'ai pas eu une minute de l.** aujourd'hui I haven't had a spare minute today; **être l. comme l'air** to be as free as a bird; **avoir les mains libres** to have one's hands free; *Fig* to have a free hand; **l. de suite** *(dans une annonce)* available immediately; **la ligne n'est pas l.** the line's *Br* engaged *or Am* busy **(c)** *(non bloqué) (route)* clear; *Fig* **la voie est l.** the coast is clear **(d)** *(privé)* **enseignement/école l.** independent Catholic education/school; **radio l.** independent radio **(e)** *(non réglementé) (prix)* free; *(honoraires)* unrestricted; **la l. entreprise** free enterprise; **il pratique les honoraires libres** there are no restrictions on his fees

libre-échange [librɛʃɑʒ] *nm* free trade

librement [librəmɑ̃] *adv* freely

libre-service *(pl* libres-services) [librəsɛrvis] *nm* **(a)** *(principe)* self-service; **station-service en l.** self-service *Br* petrol *or Am* gas station **(b)** *(magasin)* self-service shop; *(restaurant)* self-service restaurant

Libreville [librəvil] *n* Libreville

Libye [libi] *nf* **la L.** Libya

libyen, -enne [libjɛ̃, -ɛn] **1** *adj* Libyan **2** *nm,f* **L.** Libyan

lice [lis] *nf* **entrer en l.** to enter the fray

licence [lisɑ̃s] *nf* **(a)** *Univ* (bachelor's) degree; **l. ès** *ou* **de lettres/ès** *ou* **de sciences/en droit** arts/science/law degree; **faire une l.** to do a degree **(b)** *(dans le commerce)* licence **(c)** *Sp* permit *(giving right of entry into competition)* **(d)** *(liberté)* licence; **l. poétique** poetic licence **(e)** *(dérèglement)* licentiousness

licencié, -e [lisɑ̃sje] *nm,f* **(a)** *Univ* **l. ès lettres/ès** *ou* **en sciences/en droit** arts/science/law graduate **(b)** *Sp* permit holder

licenciement [lisɑ̃simɑ̃] *nm (pour raisons économiques)* redundancy; *(pour faute professionnelle)* dismissal; **l. collectif** mass redundancies; **l. économique** redundancy

licencier [66] [lisɑ̃sje] *vt (pour raisons économiques)* to make redundant; *(pour faute professionnelle)* to dismiss

lichen [likɛn] *nm* lichen

lichette [liʃɛt] *nf Fam (de pain, fromage)* tiny bit

licol [likɔl] *nm* halter

licorne [likɔrn] *nf* unicorn

licou [liku] *nm* halter

LICRA [likra] *nf (abrév* **Ligue internationale contre le racisme et l'antisémitisme)** = anti-racist movement

lie [li] *nf* dregs; *Fig* **la l. de la société** the dregs of society

lié, -e [lje] *adj* **(a)** *(attaché)* bound; **avoir les mains liées** to have one's hands tied; *Fig* **j'ai les mains liées** my hands are tied; *Fig* **être pieds et poings liés** to be bound hand and foot **(b)** *(en relation étroite)* **être (très) l. avec qn** to be (great) friends with sb

liège [ljɛʒ] *nm* cork; **bouchon de l.** cork

liégeois, -e [ljeʒwa, -az] **1** *adj* **(a)** *(personne)* of Liège **(b)** *Culin* **café/chocolat l.** = coffee/chocolate ice cream topped with crème Chantilly **2** *nm,f* **L.** person from Liège

lien [ljɛ̃] *nm* **(a)** *(attache)* bond; *aussi Fig* **se libérer de ses liens** to free oneself from one's bonds **(b)** *(relation)* link, connection; **l. de parenté** *ou* **de famille** family relationship; **il y a un l. de parenté entre ces deux familles** the two families are related; **les liens du mariage** the bonds of marriage; **l. d'amitié** bond of friendship **(c)** *Ordinat* **l. hypertexte** hypertext link

lier [66] [lje] **1** *vt* **(a)** *(attacher)* to tie up; *(sujet: contrat, serment)* to be binding on **(b)** *(unir) (personnes)* to bind together **(c)** *(établir un rapport entre) (événements, paragraphes)* to connect, to link; **tout est lié** everything's connected **(d)** *Culin (sauce)* to thicken **(e)** **l. amitié/conversation avec qn** to strike up a friendship/conversation with sb **2** **se lier** *vpr* **se l. (d'amitié) avec qn** to strike up a friendship with sb

lierre [ljɛr] *nm* ivy

liesse [ljɛs] *nf* jubilation; **en l.** jubilant

lieu¹, -x [ljø] *nm* **(a)** *(endroit)* place; **en l. sûr** in a safe place; **un l. de passage** a busy place; **les lieux** *(local)* the premises; *(d'un accident, d'un crime)* the scene; **quitter les lieux** to vacate the premises; **un haut l. de** a mecca for; **en haut l.** in high places; **l. de naissance** place of birth; **l. de perdition** den of vice; **l. public** public place; **l. de rendez-vous** meeting place; **l. saint** holy place **(b)** *(pour indiquer un ordre)* **en premier l.** in the first place; **en dernier l.** last(ly) **(c)** **l. commun** commonplace **(d)** *(locutions)* **avoir l.** to take place; **il y a l. de supposer que...** there is reason to suppose that...; **il n'y a pas l. de s'inquiéter** there's no need to worry; **s'il y a l.** if necessary; **donner l. à qch** to give rise to sth; **tenir l. de qch** to take the place of sth; **au l. de** instead of; **au l. de te plaindre** instead of complaining; **au l. de cela** instead

lieu² *(pl* lieus) *nm (poisson)* **l. jaune** pollack; **l. noir** coalfish

lieu-dit *(pl* lieux-dits) [ljødi] *nm* locality

lieue [ljø] *nf* league; *Naut* **l. marine** marine league; **j'étais à cent** *ou* **mille lieues de penser que...** I never dreamt for a single moment that...

lieutenant [ljøtnɑ̃] *nm (dans l'armée de terre)* lieutenant; *(dans l'armée de l'air) Br* flying officer, *Am* first lieutenant; *(dans la marine marchande)* mate

lieutenant-colonel *(pl* lieutenants-colonels) [ljøtnɑ̃kɔlɔnɛl] *nm (dans l'armée de terre)* lieutenant-colonel; *(dans l'armée de l'air) Br* wing commander, *Am* lieutenant-colonel

lièvre [ljɛvr] *nm* hare; **courir deux lièvres à la fois** to try to do two things at once

lifter [lifte] *vt (balle)* to put topspin on

liftier, -ère [liftje, -ɛr] *nm,f Br* lift attendant, *Am* elevator operator

lifting [liftiŋ] *nm* face lift

ligament [ligamɑ̃] *nm* ligament

ligature [ligatyr] *nf Méd* ligature; **l. des trompes** tying of tubes

ligaturer [ligatyre] *vt Méd* to ligature

ligne [liɲ] *nf* **(a)** *(trait)* line; **l. droite** straight line; **lire les lignes de la main à qn** to read sb's palm; **l. d'arrivée** finishing line; **l. blanche** *(sur la route) Br* white line, *Am* yellow line; **l. continue** *(sur la route)* continuous line; **l. de démarcation** demarcation line; **l. de départ** starting line; **l. discontinue** *(sur la route)* broken line; **l. de flottaison** waterline; **l. d'horizon** horizon; **l. jaune** *(sur la route) Br* white line, *Am* yellow line; **l. de mire** line of sight; *Fig* **avoir qn dans sa l. de mire** to have sb in one's sights; **l. de touche** touchline (**b**) *(d'écriture)* line; **lire entre les lignes** to read between the lines; **aller à la l.** to begin a new paragraph; **à la l.** *(en dictant)* new paragraph; *Fig* **entrer en l.** **de compte** to be taken into consideration (**c**) *(contour, silhouette) (de voiture, d'objet)* line; *(de personne)* figure; **avoir la l.** to have a good figure (**d**) *(rangée)* line; **se mettre en l.** to line up; *Mil & Fig* **en première l.** in the front line; *Mil* **les lignes ennemies** the enemy lines; *Fig* **sur toute la l.** completely (**e**) *(orientation)* line; **l. d'action/de conduite** line of action/conduct; **la l. du parti** the party line; **l. directrice** guideline (**f**) *(dans les transports)* **l. de chemin de fer** *Br* railway *or Am* railroad line; **grandes lignes** main lines; **l. maritime/ aérienne** shipping/air route; **l. d'autobus** bus service; *(parcours)* bus route; **lignes de banlieue** suburban lines; **l. de métro** *Br* underground *or Am* subway line (**g**) *Él* **l. électrique** power line; **l. à haute tension** high tension line (**h**) *Tél* **l. (téléphonique)** (telephone) line; **rappelez plus tard, elle est en l.** call back later, her line's *Br* engaged *or Am* busy; **vous êtes en l.** you're through; **l. extérieure** outside line (**i**) *(fil)* line; *(de pêche)* (fishing) line (**j**) *(de produits)* line, range (**k**) *(filiation)* **descendre en l. directe** *ou* **en droite l. de…** to be directly descended from… (**l**) *Ordinat* line; on line; **hors l.** off line; **changer de l.** to do a line feed; **l. d'état** status line

lignée [liɲe] *nf* descendants; *Fig* **dans la l. de** in the tradition of

lignite [liɲit] *nm* lignite

ligoter [ligɔte] *vt* to tie up (**à** to)

ligue [lig] *nf* league

liguer [lige] **1** *vt* **être ligués contre** to be lined up against **2 se liguer** *vpr (États)* to form a league (**avec /contre** with/against); *(personnes)* to gang up (**avec/contre** with/against)

lilas [lila] *nm & adj inv* lilac

Lilliputien, -enne [lilipysjɛ̃, ɛn] *adj (minuscule)* Lilliputian

Lima [lima] *n* Lima

limace [limas] *nf* slug; *Fam (personne lente) Br* slowcoach, *Am* slowpoke

limaille [limaj] *nf* filings

limande [limɑ̃d] *nf* dab; **l.-sole** lemon sole

lime [lim] *nf (outil)* file; **l. à ongles** nail file

limer [lime] **1** *vt* to file; *(barreaux de cellule)* to file through **2 se limer** *vpr* **se l. les ongles** to file one's nails

limier [limje] *nm (chien)* bloodhound; *Fig* sleuth; **un fin l.** a supersleuth

limitatif, -ive [limitatif, -iv] *adj* restrictive

limitation [limitasjɔ̃] *nf* limitation; **l. des naissances** birth control; **l. de vitesse** speed limit

limite [limit] **1** *nf* (**a**) *(frontière)* boundary (**b**) *(maximum)* limit; **ma patience a des limites!** there are limits to my patience!; **mettre une l./des limites à qch** to set a limit/ limits to sth; **c'est à la l. de la vulgarité/du supportable** it's bordering on vulgarity/the unacceptable; **dans la l. des stocks disponibles** while stocks last; **à la l., on pourrait changer d'hôtel** if it came to it, we could change hotels; **sans limites** unbounded, limitless **2** *adj* **cas l.** borderline case; **vitesse l.** maximum speed; *Fam* **je ne lui ai pas mis une claque, mais c'était l.** I didn't slap him, but it was a near thing; *Fam* **je suis un peu l. financièrement** I'm a bit short of cash

limité, -e [limite] *adj (réduit)* limited; *Fam Péj (obtus)* thick

limiter [limite] **1** *vt* (**a**) *(délimiter) (pays, territoire)* to bound (**b**) *(restreindre)* to limit, to restrict (**à** to); *Fam* **l. les dégâts** to limit the damage **2 se limiter** *vpr (personne)* to limit oneself; **se l. à qch/à faire qch** *(personne)* to limit *or* restrict oneself to sth/to doing sth; **son œuvre se limite à quelques essais** his works amount to no more than a few essays

limitrophe [limitrɔf] *adj* neighbouring; **être l. de** *(pays)* to border on; *(région)* to adjoin

limogeage [limɔʒaʒ] *nm* dismissal

limoger [45] [limɔʒe] *vt* to dismiss

limon [limɔ̃] *nm (alluvions)* silt

limonade [limɔnad] *nf (boisson gazeuse)* lemonade

limousine [limuzin] *nf* limousine

limpide [lɛ̃pid] *adj (eau, diamant, regard)* limpid; *(explication)* lucid

limpidité [lɛ̃pidite] *nf (de l'eau, d'un diamant, d'un regard)* limpidity; *(d'une explication)* lucidity

lin [lɛ̃] *nm* (**a**) *(tissu)* linen (**b**) *(plante)* flax

linceul [lɛ̃sœl] *nm* shroud

linéaire [lineɛr] *adj* **1** (**a**) *(récit)* & *Math* linear (**b**) *(dessin)* line **2** *nm (dans un magasin)* shelf space

linge [lɛ̃ʒ] *nm* (**a**) *(draps, serviettes, nappes)* linen; **l. de maison** household linen; **l. de table** table linen (**b**) *(lessive)* washing (**c**) *(dessous)* **l. (de corps)** underwear; *Fam Fig* **du beau l.** top-drawer people (**d**) *(morceau de tissu)* cloth

lingerie [lɛ̃ʒri] *nf* (**a**) *(dessous)* underwear, lingerie (**b**) *(pièce)* linen room

lingot [lɛ̃go] *nm (de métal)* ingot; **l. (d'or)** gold bar *or* ingot

linguiste [lɛ̃gɥist] *nmf* linguist

linguistique [lɛ̃gɥistik] **1** *adj* linguistic **2** *nf* linguistics *(singulier)*

lino [lino] *nm Fam* lino

linoléum [linɔleɔm] *nm* linoleum

linotte [linɔt] *nf voir* **tête**

linteau, -x [lɛ̃to] *nm Constr* lintel

lion [ljɔ̃] *nm* (**a**) *(animal)* lion; **tourner comme un l. en cage** to prowl around (**b**) *Astron & Astrol* **le L.** Leo; **être L.** to be (a) Leo

lionceau, -x [ljɔ̃so] *nm* lion cub

lionne [ljɔn] *nf* lioness

lipide [lipid] *nm* lipid

liposome [lipozom] *nm Chim* liposome

liposuccion [liposysjɔ̃] *nf* liposuction

liquéfaction [likefaksjɔ̃] *nf* liquefaction

liquéfier [66] [likefje] **1** *vt* to liquefy **2 se liquéfier** *vpr* to liquefy

liquette [likɛt] *nf* grandad shirt

liqueur [likœr] *nf* (**a**) *(spiritueux)* liqueur (**b**) *Can* **l. (douce)** soft drink

liquidation [likidasjɔ̃] *nf Jur* liquidation; **l. judiciaire** official receivership (**b**) *(d'une dette, en Bourse)* settlement (**c**) *Com (de stocks)* selling off; **l. totale** *(sur une vitrine)* stock clearance (**d**) *Fam (meurtre)* liquidation

liquide [likid] **1** *adj (non solide)* liquid; *(trop fluide)* thin **2** *nm* (**a**) *(substance)* liquid, fluid; **l. correcteur** correction fluid; **l. de frein** brake fluid; **l. vaisselle** washing-up liquid (**b**) *(espèces)* cash; **payer en l.** to pay cash

liquider [likide] *vt* (**a**) *Jur (affaire)* to liquidate (**b**) *Fin (dette)* to settle (**c**) *Fam (tuer)* to liquidate (**d**) *Fam (travail, restes, bouteille)* to finish off (**e**) *(stocks)* to sell off; **on liquide** *(sur une vitrine)* stock clearance

liquidités [likidite] *nfpl Fin* liquid assets

liquoreux, -euse [likɔrø, -øz] *adj (vin)* syrupy

lire¹ [44] [lir] **1** *vt* (**a**) *(déchiffrer, interpréter)* to read; **l. qch à qn** to read sth to sb; **lu et approuvé** read and approved; **l. dans les pensées de qn** to read sb's thoughts (**b**) *Fig (deviner) (sur un visage, dans un regard)* to read **2 se lire** *vpr (se deviner)* to show

lire² *nf (monnaie)* lira

lis [lis] *nm* lily; **l. blanc** white lily

lisais *etc voir* **lire**

Lisbonne [lizbɔn] *n* Lisbon

lise *etc voir* **lire**

liseré [lizre], **liséré** [lizere] *nm* border, edging

liseron [lizrɔ̃] *nm* bindweed, convolvulus

lisibilité [lizibilite] *nf (d'une écriture)* legibility; *(d'un roman, d'un fichier informatique)* readability

lisible [lizibl] *adj (écriture)* legible; *(roman, fichier informatique)* readable

lisiblement [liziblǝmã] *adv* legibly

lisière [lizjer] *nf (d'un champ, d'une forêt)* edge

lisiez *etc voir* **lire**

lissage [lisaʒ] *nm Ordinat* **l. de courbes/des caractères** curve/character smoothing

lisse [lis] *adj (surface, peau, eau)* smooth; *(pneu)* bald; *(cheveux)* sleek

lisser [lise] *vt (cheveux)* to smooth down; *(vêtement)* to smooth out; *(sujet: oiseau) (plumes)* to preen

liste [list] *nf* list; **l. d'attente** waiting list; **l. électorale** electoral roll; *Ordinat* **l. de fichiers à imprimer** print list, print queue; **l. de mariage** wedding list; **l. noire** blacklist; **être sur (la) l. rouge** *(du téléphone) Br* to be ex-directory, *Am* to be unlisted

listing [listiŋ] *nm Ordinat* listing, printout

lit [li] *nm* (**a**) *(meuble)* bed; **être au l.** to be in bed; **aller au l.** to go to bed; **mettre qn au lit** to put sb to bed; **au l., les enfants!** bedtime, children!; **faire son l.** to make one's bed; **faire l. à part** to sleep in separate beds; **enfant d'un premier l.** child from a first marriage; **l. à baldaquin** four-poster (bed); **l. de camp** *Br* camp bed, *Am* cot; **l. conjugal** marital bed; **grand l.** double bed; **l. d'enfant** *Br* cot, *Am* crib; **lits jumeaux** twin beds; **être sur son l. de mort** to be on one's death bed; **l. une place/deux places** single/double bed; **lits superposés** bunk beds (**b**) *(couche) (d'argile, de pierres)* bed, layer; *Culin* bed (**c**) *(de rivière)* bed; **sortir de son l.** to burst its banks

litanie [litani] *nf aussi Fig* litany

litchi [litʃi] *nm* lychee

literie [litri] *nf* bedding

lithium [litjɔm] *nm Chim* lithium

lithographie [litografi] *nf* (**a**) *(technique)* lithography (**b**) *(œuvre)* lithograph

litière [litjer] *nf* (**a**) *(pour cheval, pour chat)* litter (**b**) *(palanquin)* litter

litige [litiʒ] *nm (conflit)* dispute; *(procès)* lawsuit

litigieux, -euse [litiʒjø, -øz] *adj (question, cas)* contentious

litote [litɔt] *nf* understatement, *Spéc* litotes

litre [litr] *nm* litre

litron [litrɔ̃] *nm Fam* bottle of wine

littéraire [literer] **1** *adj* literary **2** *nmf* (**a**) *(doué pour la littérature)* literary person (**b**) *(étudiant)* student of literature

littéral, -e, -aux, -ales [literal, -o] *adj (traduction, sens)* literal

littéralement [literalmã] *adv* literally

littérature [literatyr] *nf (œuvres, documentation)* literature; *(métier)* writing

littoral, -e, -aux, -ales [litɔral, -o] **1** *adj* coastal **2** *nm* coast(line)

Lituanie [litɥani] *nf* la L. Lithuania

lituanien, -enne [litɥanjɛ̃, -ɛn] **1** *adj* Lithuanian **2** *nm,f* L. Lithuanian **3** *nm (langue)* Lithuanian

liturgie [lityrʒi] *nf* liturgy

liturgique [lityrʒik] *adj* liturgical

livide [livid] *adj (pâle)* pallid

living [liviŋ], **living-room** (*pl* living-rooms) [liviŋrum] *nm Vieilli* living room

livraison [livrɛzɔ̃] *nf* (**a**) *(de marchandises)* delivery; **payable à la l.** payable on delivery; **faire la l. de pain/journaux** to deliver the bread/the newspapers; **prendre l. de qch** to take delivery of sth; **l. à domicile** home delivery (**b**) *(d'ouvrage publié en fascicules)* part

livre¹ [livr] *nm* (**a**) *(ouvrage, partie d'un ouvrage)* book; **l. d'histoire/d'allemand** history/German book; **l. de chevet** bedside book; **l. de classe** *ou* scolaire schoolbook; **l. de cuisine** *ou* **de recettes** cookery book, cookbook; **l. pour enfants** children's book; **l. d'images** picture book (**b**) *(édition)* **l'industrie du l., le l.** the book trade (**c**) *(registre)* **l. de bord** *Naut* log(book); *Scol* (teacher's) record book; **l. de comptes** account book; **l. d'or** visitors' book; **grand l.** ledger

livre² *nf* (**a**) *(unité de poids)* half kilo, ≃ pound; *Can* pound (**b**) *(monnaie)* **l. (sterling)** pound (sterling); *Anciennement* **l. irlandaise** Irish pound, punt

livre-cassette (*pl* livres-cassettes) [livrǝkasɛt] *nm* audio book

livrée [livre] *nf (de domestique)* livery

livrer [livre] **1** *vt* (**a**) *(marchandises)* to deliver; **nous livrons à domicile** we deliver; **vous serez livré dès demain** you'll receive delivery tomorrow (**b**) *(abandonner)* **l. un village au pillage/un pays à l'anarchie** to abandon a village to pillage/a country to anarchy; **livré à soi-même** left to oneself (**c**) *(remettre)* **l. qn à qn** *(coupable, complice)* to hand sb over to sb; **l. un secret à qn** to reveal a secret to sb (**d**) *(locutions)* **l. bataille** to join battle; **l. passage à qn** to let sb pass **2 se livrer** *vpr* (**a**) *(se rendre)* to give oneself up (**à** to) (**b**) *(se confier)* to open up; **se l. à qn** to confide in sb (**c**) *(s'abandonner)* **se l. à qch** *(vice, spéculations)* to indulge in sth; *(désespoir)* to give way to sth (**d**) *(s'occuper)* **se l. à qch** *(occupations, recherches)* to be engaged in sth; *(étude, lecture)* to devote oneself to sth

livret [livrɛ] *nm* (**a**) *(petit livre)* booklet; **l. (de caisse) d'épargne** bankbook, passbook; **l. de famille** family record book *(for registration of births and deaths)*; **l. militaire** service record; **l. scolaire** (school) report book (**b**) *Mus (d'opéra)* libretto

livreur, -euse [livrœr, -øz] *nm,f* delivery man, *f* delivery woman

lob [lɔb] *nm* lob; **faire un l.** to hit a lob

lobe [lɔb] *nm* (**a**) *Anat & Bot* lobe (**b**) *Archit* foil

lober [lɔbe] *vt & vi* to lob

lobotomie [lɔbɔtɔmi] *nf Méd* lobotomy

local, -e, -aux, -ales [lɔkal, -o] **1** *adj aussi Méd* local; *(averses)* scattered **2** *nm* (**a**) *(lieu) (de société, d'organisation)* premises; *(sans usage précis)* place; **locaux commerciaux** business premises (**b**) *Can Tél* extension

localement [lɔkalmã] *adv* locally

localisation [lɔkalizasjɔ̃] *nf (repérage)* location; *(d'un appel téléphonique)* tracing

localisé, -e [lɔkalize] *adj (circonscrit)* localized

localiser [lɔkalize] *vt (repérer) (bruit, gène, personne)* to locate; *(appel téléphonique)* to trace

localité [lɔkalite] *nf (ville)* town; *(village)* village

locataire [lɔkatɛr] *nmf* tenant; *(chez le propriétaire)* lodger

locatif, -ive [lɔkatif, -iv] *adj voir* charge

location [lɔkasjɔ̃] *nf* (a) *(de voiture, d'équipement, de costume) (par le locataire)* renting, *Br* hiring; *(par le propriétaire)* renting out, *Br* hiring out; **prendre qch en l.** to rent sth, *Br* to hire sth; **donner qch en l.** to rent sth out, *Br* to hire sth out; **l. de voitures** car rental, *Br* car hire (b) *(de logement) (par le locataire)* renting; *(par le propriétaire)* renting out, *Br* letting (out) (c) *(appartement, maison)* rented accommodation (d) *(de places de spectacle)* booking

location-vente *(pl* locations-ventes) [lɔkasjɔ̃vɑ̃t] *nf Br* hire purchase, *Am* installment plan

loche [lɔʃ] *nf (poisson)* loach

locomoteur, -trice [lɔkɔmɔtœr, -tris] *adj* locomotor

locomotion [lɔkɔmɔsjɔ̃] *nf* locomotion, **moyen de l.** means of transport

locomotive [lɔkɔmɔtiv] *nf* (a) *(de train)* locomotive, engine; **l. à vapeur** steam engine (b) *Fig (leader)* pacemaker

locuteur, -trice [lɔkytœr, -tris] *nm,f Ling* speaker

locution [lɔkysjɔ̃] *nf* expression, phrase

loft [lɔft] *nm* converted loft

logarithme [lɔgaritm] *nm* logarithm

loge [lɔʒ] *nf* (a) *(d'artiste)* dressing room (b) *(sièges)* box; *Fig* **être aux premières loges** to have a ringside seat (c) *(maçonnique, de concierge)* lodge

logement [lɔʒmɑ̃] *nm* (a) *(habitation)* accommodation; *(maison)* house; *(appartement) Br* flat, *Am* apartment; **l. de fonction** accommodation that goes with the job; **logements sociaux** *Br* ~ council flats, *Am* ≃ low rent housing (b) *(action)* housing; **la crise du l.** the housing shortage

loger [45] [lɔʒe] **1** *vi (en permanence)* to live; *(temporairement)* to stay; **l. chez l'habitant** *(en vacances)* to stay in a private house
2 *vt* (a) *(héberger)* to put up; **être logé et nourri** to have board and lodging (b) *(contenir) (sujet: hôtel, maison)* to accommodate (c) *(placer)* to put
3 se loger *vpr* (a) **(trouver à) se l.** *(permanent)* to find somewhere to live; *(temporaire)* to find accommodation (b) *(se placer)* to lodge itself

logeur, -euse [lɔʒœr, -øz] *nm,f* landlord, *f* landlady *(of furnished apartments)*

loggia [lɔdʒja] *nf Archit* loggia

logiciel [lɔʒisjɛl] *nm Ordinat* software; **un l.** a software package, a software; **l. d'application** application software; **l. bureautique** business software (package); **l. de communication** communications package, comms package, communications software; **l. de compression de données** data compression software; **l. de comptabilité** accounts package, accounts software; **l. de décompression** decompression software, decompressor; **l. de dessin** art package, drawing program; **l. d'exploitation** operating system software; **l. grapheur** graphics package, graphics software; **l. de jeu** games software; **l. de mise en page** desktop publishing package; **l. public** freeware; **l. de reconnaissance de caractères** OCR software, character recognition software; **l. de reconnaissance vocale** voice recognition software; **l. de réseau** network software; **l. de SGBD**

DBMS software; **l. de télémaintenance** remote access software; **logiciels de traitement de texte** word-processing software, word-processing software packages

logique [lɔʒik] **1** *adj* logical
2 *nf* logic; **en toute l.,...** logically,...; *Ordinat* **l. câblée** wired logic; **l. floue** fuzzy logic

logiquement [lɔʒikmɑ̃] *adv* logically

logis [lɔʒi] *nm Litt (maison)* dwelling, abode

logistique [lɔʒistik] **1** *adj* logistic
2 *nf* logistics *(singulier)*

logo [lɔgo] *nm* logo

loi [lwa] *nf* law; **nul n'est censé ignorer la l.** ignorance of the law is no excuse; **faire** *ou* **sa l.** to lay down the law; *Pol* **l. de finances** Finance Act; **la l. de la jungle** the law of the jungle; **la l. martiale** martial law; **la l. de l'offre et de la demande** the law of supply and demand; **la l. du plus fort** the law of the strongest; **la l. du talion** an eye for an eye

loi-cadre *(pl* lois-cadres) [lwakadr] *nf* outline law

loin [lwɛ̃] **1** *adv* (a) *(dans l'espace)* far (de from); **la poste est l.** the post office is a long way away; **c'est encore l., le théâtre/Angers?** is it far to the theatre/Angers?; **il y a l. d'ici à Paris** it's a long way to Paris; **plus l.** further (on); **voir plus l.** *(dans un texte)* see below; **de l.** *(reconnaître, admirer)* from a distance; *Prov* **l. des yeux, l. du cœur** out of sight, out of mind
(b) *(dans le temps)* far away *(de* from); **comme c'est l., tout ça!** that all happened such a long time ago!; **ce jour est encore l.** that day is still a long way off; **d'aussi l.** *ou* du plus **l. qu'elle se souvienne** for as long as she can remember (c) *Fig* de là to **l'accuser de mensonge il n'y a pas l.** it's practically calling him/her a liar; **aller l.** *(réussir)* to go far; **aller trop l.** *(exagérer)* to go too far; **nous étions l. de penser que...** we never thought for a moment that...; **elle est l. d'être bête** she's far from stupid; **je ne suis pas fâché, l. de là!** I'm not angry, far from it!; **l. de moi l'idée d'insinuer que...** far be it from me to insinuate that...; **l. de moi cette idée!** I wouldn't dream of it!, perish the thought!; **par l. de** *(presque)* not far off; **de l.** *(de beaucoup)* by far; **de l. en l.** *(de temps en temps)* every now and then
2 *nm* au **l.** in the distance

lointain, -e [lwɛ̃tɛ̃, -ɛn] **1** *adj (dans l'espace, dans le temps)* distant; *(ressemblance)* vague; *(air, regard)* faraway; **dans un avenir l.** in the distant future
2 *nm* **dans le l., au l.** in the distance

loir [lwar] *nm* dormouse

Loire [lwar] *nf* **la L.** the Loire

loisir [lwazir] *nm* (a) *(temps libre)* leisure; **activités de l.** leisure *or* spare-time activities; **loisirs** spare time; **avoir des loisirs** to have some spare time (b) *(activité)* pastime; **les loisirs** leisure *or* spare-time activities (c) *Formel (possibilité, temps nécessaire)* **avoir le l. de faire qch** to have time to do sth; **donner** *ou* **laisser à qn le l. de faire qch** to give sb the opportunity to do sth; *Litt* **à l.** at one's leisure

lolo [lolo] *nm Fam* (a) *(langage enfantin) (lait)* milk (b) *(sein)* boob

lombaire [lɔ̃bɛr] *Anat* **1** *adj* lumbar
2 *nf* lumbar vertebra

lombalgie [lɔ̃balʒi] *nf Méd* lumbago

lombric [lɔ̃brik] *nm* earthworm

Lomé [lɔme] *n* Lomé

londonien, -enne [lɔ̃dɔnjɛ̃, -ɛn] **1** *adj* London
2 *nm,f* **L.** Londoner

Londres [lɔ̃dr] *n* London

long, longue [lɔ̃, lɔ̃g] **1** *adj* (a) *(dans l'espace)* long; *(personne)* tall; **l. de cinq mètres** five metres long (b) *(dans*

le temps) long; **dix jours, c'est l.** ten days is a long time; **ce ne sera pas l.** it won't take long; **pendant de longues années** for many years; **longue durée** *(pile)* long-life; *(cassette)* extended play; **de longue durée** *(chômage, chômeur)* long-term **(c)** *(lent)* slow; **être l. à faire qch** to be slow to do sth
2 *nm* **(a)** *(dans l'espace)* **faire trois mètres de l.** to be three metres long; **(tout) le l. de** (all) along; **de tout son l.** *(être étendu)* at full length; *(tomber)* flat on one's face; **de l. en large** up and down, to and fro; **en l.** *(couper, fendre)* lengthwise; *Fam* **expliquer qch en l. et en large** *ou* **en l., en large et en travers** to explain sth in great detail **(b)** *(dans le temps)* **tout au l. de** throughout
3 *adv* **(a)** *(beaucoup)* **en dire l.** *(être révélateur)* to speak volumes; **en savoir l. (sur)** to know a lot (about) **(b)** **s'habiller l.** to wear long clothes

long-courrier *(pl* **long-courriers)** [lɔ̃kurje] **1** *adj* *(navire)* ocean-going; *(avion)* long-haul
2 *nm* *(navire)* ocean-going ship; *(avion)* long-haul aircraft

longe¹ [lɔ̃ʒ] *nf (pour guider)* leading rein; *(pour attacher)* tether

longe² *nf Culin (de veau, de porc)* loin

longer [45] [lɔ̃ʒe] *vt* **(a)** *(sujet: personne, voiture) (route, rivière)* to go along; *(mur, côte)* to hug **(b)** *(sujet: sentier, canal, voie ferrée)* to run alongside

longévité [lɔ̃ʒevite] *nf (longue vie)* longevity; *(espérance de vie)* life expectancy

longiligne [lɔ̃ʒiliɲ] *adj* willowy

longitude [lɔ̃ʒityd] *nf Géog* longitude; **à 10° de l. ouest** at longitude 10° west

longitudinal, -e, -aux, -ales [lɔ̃ʒitydinal, -o] *adj* longitudinal, lengthwise

longtemps [lɔ̃tɑ̃] *adv* **(a)** *(attendre, rester)* (for) a long time; **ça ne durera pas l.** it won't last (for) long; *Fig* **tu peux attendre l.** you'll have a long wait **(b)** *(avec une préposition, avec "il y a")* **avant l.** before long; **pas avant l.** not for a long time; **cela existe depuis l.** it has existed for a long time; **pendant l.** for a long time; **je n'en ai pas pour l.** I won't be long; **il n'en a plus pour l.** *(il va bientôt mourir)* he doesn't have much longer to live; **il y a l.** a long time ago; **il y a l. qu'il est mort** he's been dead for a long time; **il y a l. que je ne l'ai pas vue** it's a long time since I saw her; **l. avant/ après** long before/after

longue [lɔ̃g] **1** *adj voir* **long**
2 *nf* **à la l.** in the end

longuement [lɔ̃gmɑ̃] *adv (attendre, réfléchir, s'attarder)* for a long time; *(parler, expliquer)* at length; **il a l. insisté pour que je vienne** he kept on insisting I should come

longuet, -ette [lɔ̃gɛ, -ɛt] *adj Fam* longish

longueur [lɔ̃gœr] *nf* **(a)** *(dimension, durée) & Sp* length; **jardin de 50 mètres de l.** *ou* **d'une l. de 100 mètres** garden 50 metres long; **en l., dans le sens de la l.** *(couper, fendre)* lengthwise; **avoir une l. d'avance sur** *Sp* to be one length ahead of; *Fig* to have a clear lead over; **à l. de journée/de semaine/d'année** all day/week/year long **(b)** *Péj (développement trop long)* **longueurs** drawn-out passages **(c)** *Rad* **l. d'ondes** wavelength; *Fig* **être sur la même l. d'ondes** to be on the same wavelength

longue-vue *(pl* **longues-vues)** [lɔ̃gvy] *nf* telescope

look [luk] *nm Fam* look; **avoir un l. d'enfer** to look out of this world

looping [lupiŋ] *nm Av* loop; **faire un l./des loopings** to loop the loop

lopin [lɔpɛ̃] *nm* **l. de terre** patch *or* plot of land

loquace [lɔkas] *adj* talkative

loque [lɔk] *nf* **(a)** *(vêtement)* rag; **être en loques** to be in

rags; **tomber en loques** to fall to pieces **(b)** *Fig (personne)* wreck

loquet [lɔkɛ] *nm* latch

lordose [lɔrdoz] *nf Méd* hollow-back, *Spéc* lordosis

lorgner [lɔrɲe] *vt* **(a)** *(regarder indiscrètement)* to eye; *(avec concupiscence)* to eye up **(b)** *(convoiter)* to have one's eye on

lorgnette [lɔrɲɛt] *nf* opera glasses; *Fig* **regarder** *ou* **voir les choses par le petit bout de la l.** to take a narrow-minded view of things

lorgnon [lɔrɲɔ̃] *nm (avec tige)* lorgnette; *(avec ressort)* pince-nez

lorrain, -e [lɔrɛ̃, -ɛn] **1** *adj* of Lorraine
2 *nm,f* **L.** person from Lorraine

lors [lɔr] *adv* **l. de** *(pendant)* during; *(au moment de)* at the time of; *Litt* **depuis l.** from that time

lorsque [lɔrsk] *conj* when

losange [lɔzɑ̃ʒ] *nm (forme)* diamond; *(en géométrie)* rhombus

Los Angeles [lɔsɑ̃dʒəlɛs] *n* Los Angeles

lot [lo] *nm* **(a)** *(dans une loterie)* prize; **gros l.** jackpot; *Fam Fig* **tirer le gros l.** to hit the jackpot; **l. de consolation** consolation prize **(b)** *Com (de marchandises)* batch; *(de serviettes, de casseroles)* set; *(de chaussettes, de savonnettes)* pack; *Fig* **dans le l., il y en aura bien un de bon** *(choses, personnes)* at least one out of this lot should be some good; **se détacher** *ou* **être au-dessus du l.** to stand out from the crowd **(c)** *(de terrain)* plot **(d)** *Litt (sort)* lot **(e)** *Ordinat* **traitement par lots** batch processing

loterie [lɔtri] *nf* lottery; **gagner à la l.** to win on the lottery; **l. nationale** national lottery

loti, -e [lɔti] *adj* **être bien/mal l.** to be well/badly off

lotion [losjɔ̃] *nf* lotion; **l. après-rasage** aftershave (lotion); **l. capillaire** hair lotion; **l. tonique** toner

lotissement [lɔtismɑ̃] *nm (ensemble résidentiel)* housing estate

loto [lɔto] *nm* **(a)** *(jeu de hasard)* lotto **(b)** *(jeu national)* national lottery; **jouer au l.** to do the lottery

lotte [lɔt] *nf (de rivière)* burbot; *(de mer)* monkfish

lotus [lɔtys] *nm* lotus; **fleur de l.** lotus; **position du l.** lotus position

louable [lwabl] *adj (admirable)* praiseworthy, laudable

louage [lwaʒ] *nm* **contrat de l.** rental agreement; **voiture de l.** hired carriage

louange [lwɑ̃ʒ] *nf* praise; **digne de louange(s)** praiseworthy; **chanter les louanges de qn** to sing sb's praises

loubard [lubar] *nm Fam* hooligan

louche¹ [luʃ] *adj* shady

louche² *nf* ladle

loucher [luʃe] *vi (volontairement)* to squint; *(être atteint de strabisme)* to have a squint; **l. de l'œil gauche** to have a squint in one's left eye; *Fig* **l. sur qch** *(regarder)* to eye sth; *(convoiter)* to have one's eye on sth

louer¹ [lwe] *vt* **(a)** *(donner en location) (logement)* to rent out, *Br* to let (out) **(à** to); *(équipement, véhicule, costume)* to rent out, *Br* to hire out **(à** to); **maison à l.** house *Br* to let *or Am* for rent **(b)** *(prendre en location) (logement)* to rent **(à** from); *(équipement, véhicule, costume)* to rent, *Br* to hire; *(place de spectacle)* to book

louer² [lwe] *vt (exalter)* to praise; **l. qn de** *ou* **pour qch** to praise sb for sth; **louons le Seigneur!** praise the Lord!
2 se louer *vpr* **se l. de qch** to be very satisfied with sth; **je n'ai qu'à me l. de lui/de ses services** I have nothing but praise for him/for his/her work; **se l. d'avoir fait qch** to congratulate oneself on having done sth

loufdingue [lufdɛg] *adj Fam* bonkers
loufoque [lufɔk] *adj Fam* crazy
louis [lwi] *nm* l. (d'or) louis(-d'or)
Louisiane [lwizjan] *nf* **la L.** Louisiana
loukoum [lukum] *nm* piece of Turkish delight; **des loukoums** Turkish delight
loup [lu] *nm* (a) (mammifère) wolf; *Fig* **il est connu comme le l.** blanc everybody knows him; **quand on parle du l.** on en voit la queue talk of the devil; *Fig* **jeune l.** young go-getter; *(en politique)* Young Turk; *Fam* **mon petit l., mon gros l.** darling, pet (b) (poisson) bass (c) (demi-masque) eye mask (d) (vieux) l. de mer (marin) old salt, sea dog
loupe [lup] *nf* (instrument d'optique) magnifying glass; **regarder qch à la l.** to look at sth through a magnifying glass; *Fig* to put sth under the microscope
louper [lupe] *Fam* **1** *vt* (a) (ne pas réussir) (travail, plat) to botch, to bungle; (examen) to flunk; **l. son entrée** *(au théâtre)* to fluff one's entrance; **loupe!** missed!; **la soirée est loupée** the party's a flop (b) (ne pas prendre) (son tour, occasion, train) to miss; **il n'en loupe pas une!** (en actions) it's one stupid thing after another!; (en paroles) he's always opening his big mouth!; **je ne vais pas le l.!** I won't let him get away with it! **2** *vi* **je lui ai dit qu'il attraperait froid et ça n'a pas loupé** I told him he'd catch cold and sure enough he did **3** se louper *vpr* (manquer son suicide) to bungle it; *Ironique* **il ne s'est pas loupé!** he made a proper job of it!
loup-garou [lugaru] *nm* werewolf, (pour faire peur aux enfants) bogeyman
loupiote [lupjɔt] *nf Fam* (lampe) small light
lourd, -e [lur, lurd] **1** *adj* (a) (pesant) heavy; **j'ai la tête lourde** I've got a thick head, **avoir l'estomac l.** to feel bloated; **yeux lourds de fatigue** eyes heavy with tiredness (b) (à l'aspect pesant) (personne) heavily built; (tentures) heavy (c) (peu subtil) (personne, plaisanterie) unsubtle; (mouvement, style) heavy (d) (perte, dépenses, responsabilité) heavy (e) (temps) close; (parfum) heavy (f) (plein) **l. de conséquences** fraught with consequences; **l. de menaces** ominous **2** *adv* **peser l.** to weigh a lot, to be heavy; *Fam* **pas l.** not much
lourdaud, -e [lurdo, -od] **1** *adj* oafish **2** *nm,f* oaf
lourdement [lurdəmɑ̃] *adv* heavily; **se tromper l.** to be greatly mistaken; **insister l.** to keep on insisting
lourder [lurde] *vt Fam* **l. qn** to give sb the boot; **se faire l.** (par qn) to get the boot (from sb)
lourdeur [lurdœr] *nf* (poids, manque de subtilité) heaviness; (de la bureaucratie) unwieldiness; (d'une responsabilité, d'une tâche) weight; (du temps) closeness; **l. d'esprit** slow-wittedness; **j'ai des lourdeurs d'estomac** I feel bloated
lourdingue [lurdɛg] *adj Fam* (style) heavy; (personne, plaisanterie) unsubtle
loustic [lustik] *nm Fam* **un drôle de l.** (louche) a dodgy character
loutre [lutr] *nf* otter; (fourrure) otter skin
louve [luv] *nf* she-wolf
louveteau, -x [luvto] *nm* (a) (animal) wolf cub (b) (jeune scout) Cub (Scout)
louvoyer [32] [luvwaje] *vi Naut* to tack; *Fig* to hedge
lover [lɔve] **se lover** *vpr* (serpent) to coil up; (personne) to curl up
loyal, -e, -aux, -ales [lwajal, -o] **1** *adj* (a) (honnête) fair (b) (fidèle) (serviteur, ami) loyal; **après 20 ans de bons et**

---

loyaux services after 20 years of good and faithful service **2** *nf* **loyale** *Fam* **se battre à la loyale** to fight cleanly
loyalement [lwajalmɑ̃] *adv* (a) (honnêtement) fairly (b) (fidèlement) loyally
loyaliste [lwajalist] *adj & nmf Pol* loyalist
loyauté [lwajote] *nf* (a) (honnêteté) fairness (b) (fidélité) loyalty (envers to)
loyer [lwaje] *nm* rent; **j'ai deux loyers de retard** I'm two months behind with the rent
LP [ɛlpe] *nm* (abrév **lycée professionnel**) technical college
LSD [ɛlɛsde] *nm* LSD
lu, -e *voir* **lire**
lubie [lybi] *nf* whim, fad
lubrifiant, -e [lybrifjɑ̃, -ɑ̃t] **1** *adj* lubricating **2** *nm* lubricant
lubrifier [66] [lybrifje] *vt* to lubricate
lubrique [lybrik] *adj* lustful, lecherous
lucarne [lykarn] *nf* (a) (dans un toit) skylight; (en saillie) dormer (window) (b) (au football) top corner
lucide [lysid] *adj* lucid
lucidement [lysidmɑ̃] *adv* lucidly
lucidité [lysidite] *nf* lucidity
Lucifer [lysifɛr] *npr* Lucifer
luciole [lysjɔl] *nf* firefly
lucratif, -ive [lykratif, -iv] *adj* lucrative; **à but l.** profit-making; **sans but l.** *Br* non-profit-making, *Am* not-for-profit
lucre [lykr] *nm Litt* lucre
ludique [lydik] *adj* play
ludothèque [lydɔtɛk] *nf* toy and game library
luette [lɥɛt] *nf* *Anat* uvula
lueur [lɥœr] *nf* (a) (lumière faible) glow; **à la l. d'une bougie/des étoiles** by candlelight/starlight; **à la l. des derniers événements** in the light of recent events (b) *Fig* (de lucidité, de colère) flash; (d'intelligence, d'espoir) glimmer
luge [lyʒ] *nf* toboggan, *Br* sledge, *Am* sled; **faire de la l.** to go tobogganing or *Br* sledging or *Am* sledding
lugubre [lygybr] *adj* gloomy; (son, cri) mournful
lui [lɥi] *pron personnel* (a) (sujet) (personne) he; (chose, animal) it; **l., il aurait fait un effort** HE would have made an effort; **mon frère, l., n'est pas venu** as for my brother, he didn't come; **si j'étais l., je me méfierais** if I were him I'd be careful
(b) (objet direct) (personne) him; (chose, animal) it; **et l., tu le connais?** and what about him, do you know him?
(c) (objet indirect) (homme) to him; (femme) to her; (chose, animal) to it; **donnez-le-l.** give it to him/her/it, give him/her/it it; **je l. ai serré la main** I shook his/her hand; **il l. jeta une pierre** he threw a stone at him/her/it
(d) (avec préposition) (personne) him; (chose, animal) it; **elle pense encore à l.** she still thinks about him; **dis-le-lui, à l.** tell HIM; **ce livre est à l.** this book is his
(e) (réfléchi) (personne) himself; (chose, animal) itself; **il ne pense qu'à** l. he thinks only of himself; **il a un appartement à l.** he's got his own flat; **un ami à l.** a friend of his
(f) (dans les comparaisons) him; **elle gagne plus que l.** she earns more than him or she does
lui-même [lɥimɛm] *pron personnel* (personne) himself; (chose, animal) itself
luire [18] [lɥir] *vi* (métal, astre, yeux) to shine; (surface de l'eau, trottoir mouillé) to glisten; (flamme, braises) to glow
luisais *etc voir* **luire**
luisant, -e [lɥizɑ̃, -ɑ̃t] **1** *adj* (étoile, métal, yeux) shining;

(surface, pelage, peau) shiny; *(braise)* glowing; **front l.** de
sueur forehead glistening with sweat
  2 *nm* sheen
lumbago [lɔ̃bago] *nm* lumbago
lumière [lymjɛr] *nf* **(a)** *(clarté)* light; **à la l.** de la lune by
moonlight; **il y a de la l.** chez lui there's a light on/there are
lights on at his place; *Fig* **j'ai besoin de tes lumières** I need
the benefit of your knowledge; **l. d'ambiance** subdued
lighting **(b)** *(locutions)* **à la l.** de son exposé,... in the light
of his account,...; **faire (toute) la l.** sur qch to get (right) to
the bottom of sth; **mettre qch en l.** to bring sth out; *Fam* **ce
n'est pas une l.** he's/she's not very bright
lumignon [lymiɲɔ̃] *nm* small light
luminaire [lyminɛr] *nm* **magasin de luminaires** lighting
shop
luminescent, -e [lyminɛsɑ̃, -ɑ̃t] *adj* luminescent
lumineux, -euse [lyminø, -øz] *adj* **(a)** *(corps, cadran)*
luminous; *(pièce, ciel)* bright **(b)** *(radieux) (regard)* radiant;
(teint) glowing **(c)** *(explication, propos)* lucid; *(idée)* brilliant
luminosité [lyminozite] *nf* **(a)** *(du ciel)* brightness; *(d'un
regard)* radiance; *Phot* **la l.** the amount of light available **(b)**
(d'un écran) brightness
lump [lœp] *nm* **œufs de l.** lumpfish roe
lunaire [lynɛr] *adj* lunar; *Fig* **un visage l.** a moon face
lunatique [lynatik] *adj* quirky
lunch [*pl* **lunchs** *ou* **lunches**) [lœntʃ] *nm* buffet lunch
lundi [lœdi] *nm* Monday; **le l.** de Pâques/de la Pentecôte
Easter/Whit Monday; *voir aussi* **samedi**
lune [lyn] *nf* **(a)** *(astre)* moon; *Fig* **je ne te demande pas
la l.** I'm not asking for the moon; **être dans la l.** to be miles
away; **la nouvelle/pleine l.** the new/full moon; **l. de miel**
honeymoon **(b)** *Fam (derrière)* bottom
luné, -e [lyne] *adj Fam* **être bien/mal l.** to be in a good/
bad mood
lunette [lynɛt] *nf* **(a)** *(pour la vue)* **lunettes** glasses,
spectacles; **lunettes noires** dark glasses; **lunettes de
soleil** sunglasses; **lunettes de vue** corrective glasses **(b)**
(instrument d'optique) telescope **(c)** *(siège des W.-C.)* seat **(d)**
(de voiture) **l. arrière** rear window
lupin [lypɛ̃] *nm* lupin
lurette [lyrɛt] *nf* **il y a belle l.** ages ago; **il y a belle l.** que
je ne l'ai pas vu I haven't seen him for ages
luron [lyrɔ̃] *nm* **c'est un gai** *ou* **joyeux l.** he's a bit of a lad
lustre[1] [lystr] *nm* **(a)** *(lampe)* chandelier **(b)** *(brillant)*
lustre **(c)** *(prestige)* lustre
lustre[2] *nm* **ça dure depuis des lustres** it's been going on
for ages
lustrer [lystre] *vt (glace, meuble, voiture)* to polish; **lustré
par l'usure** shiny with wear
lustrine [lystrin] *nf* cotton lustre
luth [lyt] *nm* lute
luthier [lytje] *nm* stringed-instrument maker
lutin [lytɛ̃] *nm* imp, elf
lutrin [lytrɛ̃] *nm (à la messe)* lectern; *(pour soutenir un livre,
des feuilles)* reading stand
lutte [lyt] *nf* **(a)** *(combat)* fight, struggle; *(antagonisme)*
conflict; *(contre une maladie, contre la pollution)* fight;

entrer/être en l. contre qn to enter into/to be in conflict
with sb; **gagner de haute l.** to win after a hard struggle; **l.
armée** armed struggle; **la l. des classes** the class struggle
(b) *Sp* wrestling; **faire de la l.** to wrestle
lutter [lyte] *vi* **(a)** *(se battre)* to struggle, to fight; **l. contre**
(adversaire, oppresseur) to fight against; *(maladie, incendie,
tentation)* to fight; *(sommeil)* to fight off **(b)** *(rivaliser)* **l. de
vitesse avec qn** to race sb **(c)** *Sp* to wrestle (**avec** *ou* **contre**
with)
lutteur, -euse [lytœr, -øz] *nm,f Sp* wrestler
luxation [lyksasjɔ̃] *nf Méd* dislocation
luxe [lyks] *nm* **(a)** *(abondance, richesse)* luxury; *(d'une
maison, de l'ameublement)* luxuriousness **(b)** *(qualité)* **de l.**
(produits) luxury; *(voiture, édition)* de luxe; **boutique de l.**
luxury goods shop *ou Am* store **(c)** *(bien superflu)* luxury;
Fig **s'offrir** *ou* **se payer le l.** de faire qch to give oneself the
luxury of doing sth; **je vais faire nettoyer ce vieil
imperméable, ce ne sera pas du l.** I'm going to have this
old raincoat cleaned, and not before time **(d)** *(profusion)* **un
l. de précautions/de détails** a wealth of precautions/
details
Luxembourg [lyksãbur] **1** *n (ville)* Luxembourg
  2 *nm* **le L.** Luxembourg
luxembourgeois, -e [lyksãburʒwa, -az] **1** *adj* of
Luxembourg
  2 *nm,f* **L.** Luxembourger
luxer [lykse] *se* **luxer** *vpr* **se l. l'épaule/le poignet** to
dislocate one's shoulder/one's wrist
luxueux, -euse [lyksɥø, -øz] *adj* luxurious
luxure [lyksyr] *nf Litt* lust
luxuriant, -e [lyksyrjã, -ãt] *adj (végétation, forêt,
chevelure)* luxuriant; *(imagination)* fertile
luzerne [lyzɛrn] *nf Br* lucerne, *Am* alfalfa
lycée [lise] *nm Br* ≃ secondary school, *Am* ≃ high school
(for pupils aged fifteen to eighteen); **l. professionnel**
vocational school; **l. technique** technical school
lycéen, -enne [liseɛ̃, -ɛn] *nm,f Br* ≃ secondary school
pupil, *Am* ≃ high school pupil
Lycra® [likra] *nm* Lycra®
lymphatique [lɛ̃fatik] *adj* **(a)** *Biol* lymphatic **(b)**
(personne) lethargic
lymphe [lɛ̃f] *nf* lymph
lymphocyte [lɛ̃fɔsit] *nm Biol* lymphocyte
lyncher [lɛ̃ʃe] *vt* to lynch
lynx [lɛ̃ks] *nm* lynx; *Fig* **avoir des yeux de l.** to have eyes
like a hawk
Lyon [ljɔ̃] *n* Lyons
lyonnais, -e [ljɔnɛ, -ɛz] **1** *adj* of Lyons
  2 *nm,f* **L.** person from Lyons
lyophilisé, -e [ljɔfilize] *adj* freeze-dried
lyre [lir] *nf* lyre
lyrique [lirik] *adj* **(a)** *(poème, poète)* lyric **(b)** *(passionné)*
lyrical
lyrisme [lirism] *nm* lyricism; **parler de qch avec l.** to wax
lyrical about sth
lys [lis] = **lis**

M

M, m [ɛm] *nm inv* M, m

m (a) M. *(abrév* **Monsieur)** Mr **(b)** *(abrév* **mètre(s))** m; **1 m 50** 1.5 m **(c)** *Gram (abrév* **masculin)** m

m' [m] *voir* **me**

ma [ma] *voir* **mon**

MA [ɛma] *nm (abrév* **maitre auxiliaire)** *Br* supply *or Am* substitute teacher

maboule, -e [mabul] *Fam* **1** *adj (fou)* crazy **2** *nm,f* nutcase

mac [mak] *nm très Fam (maquereau)* pimp

macabre [makabr] *adj (découverte, histoire)* macabre, gruesome; *(humour)* macabre

macadam [makadam] *nm* **(a)** *(revêtement)* macadam; **m. goudronné** tarmac(adam) **(b)** *(route)* road

macaque [makak] **1** *nm (singe)* macaque; **m. rhésus** rhésus monkey **2** *nmf Fam (personne laide)* pig

macareux [makarø] *nm* puffin

macaron [makarɔ̃] *nm* **(a)** *Culin* macaroon **(b)** **macarons** *(coiffure)* coils *(over the ears)* **(c)** *(badge)* badge; *(décoration)* rosette; *(autocollant)* sticker; *Journ* **m. de presse** press badge

macaroni [makarɔni] *nm* **(a)** *(pâte)* piece of macaroni; **des macaronis** macaroni **(b)** *(Italien)* wop, = racist term used to refer to an Italian

Macédoine [masedwan] *nf* **la M.** Macedonia

macédoine [masedwan] *nf* **m. de fruits** fruit salad; **m. de légumes** mixed vegetables

macédonien, -enne [masedɔnjɛ̃, -ɛn] **1** *adj* Macedonian **2** *nm,f* **M.** Macedonian

macération [maserasjɔ̃] *nf* steeping

macérer [34] [masere] **1** *vt* to steep **2** *vi* to steep; **faire m. qch** to steep sth; *Fig* **laisser m. qn** to leave sb to stew

mâche [maʃ] *nf* lamb's lettuce

mâcher [maʃe] *vt (nourriture)* to chew; **ne pas m. ses mots** not to mince one's words

machette [maʃɛt] *nf* machete

machiavélique [makjavelik] *adj* Machiavellian

machin [maʃɛ̃] *nm Fam* **(a)** *(objet)* thingy, thingummy **(b)** *(personne)* what's-his-name, *f* what's-her-name; **monsieur M.** Mr What's-his-name; **madame M.** Mrs What's-her-name

machinal, -e, -aux, -ales [maʃinal, -o] *adj (action, geste, travail)* mechanical; *(réaction)* automatic

machinalement [maʃinalmɑ̃] *adv (agir)* mechanically; *(réagir, répondre)* automatically

machination [maʃinasjɔ̃] *nf* conspiracy

machine [maʃin] *nf* **(a)** *(appareil)* machine; **m. à café** coffee machine; **m. à calculer** calculator; *(plus grande)* calculating machine; **m. à coudre** sewing machine; **m. à écrire** typewriter; **écrire qch à la m.** to type sth; **m. à laver** washing machine; **m. à sous** slot machine, *Br* fruit machine; **m. à tricoter** knitting machine **(b)** *(dans un bateau)* **stopper les machines** to stop engines; **faire m. arrière** to reverse engines; *Fig* to backtrack **(c)** *(locomotive)* engine; *Fam (moto)* machine **(d)** *(organisation)* machinery

machine-outil *(pl* **machines-outils)** [maʃinuti] *nf* machine tool

machiner [maʃine] *vt* to plot

machinisme [maʃinism] *nm* mechanization

machiniste [maʃinist] *nmf* **(a)** *(dans un théâtre)* sceneshifter, stagehand; *(au cinéma, à la télévision)* grip **(b)** *(conducteur d'autobus)* driver

machisme [matʃism, maʃism] *nm* machismo

macho [matʃo] *adj & nm Fam* macho

mâchoire [mɑʃwar] *nf* **(a)** *(d'une personne, d'un animal)* jaw **(b)** *(d'une poulie)* flange **(c)** **mâchoires** *(d'un étau, d'une tenaille)* jaws; *(de frein)* shoes

mâchonner [maʃɔne] *vt* **(a)** *(mâcher)* to chew **(b)** *(marmonner)* to mutter

mâchouiller [maʃuje] *vt Fam* to chew away at

maçon [masɔ̃] *nm* **(a)** *(d'ouvrage en briques)* bricklayer; *(d'ouvrage en pierre)* (stone)mason **(b)** *(franc-maçon)* mason

maçonnerie [masɔnri] *nf* **(a)** *(de briques)* brickwork; *(de pierres)* masonry, stonework **(b)** *(franc-maçonnerie)* masonry

maçonnique [masɔnik] *adj* masonic

macramé [makrame] *nm* macramé

macrobiotique [makrɔbjɔtik] **1** *adj* macrobiotic **2** *nf* macrobiotics *(singulier)*

macro-commande *(pl* **macro-commandes)** [makrokɔmɑ̃d] *nf Ordinat* macro(-command)

macroéconomie [makroekɔnɔmi] *nf* macroeconomics *(singulier)*

macrolangage [makrolɑ̃gaʒ] *nm Ordinat* macrolanguage

maculer [makyle] *vt* to stain **(de** with)

Madagascar [madagaskar] *n* Madagascar

madame [madam] *(pl* **mesdames** [medam]) *nf* **(a)** *(titre)* Mrs; **M. Guérin** Mrs Guérin; **M. le Ministre** the Minister **(b)** *(en apostrophe)* madam; **M. le Ministre** Madam Minister; **au revoir, m.** goodbye; **M.,** *(dans une lettre)* Dear Madam,; **par ici, mesdames** this way, ladies; **mesdames, messieurs** ladies and gentlemen

madeleine [madlɛn] *nf (gâteau)* madeleine

mademoiselle [madmwazɛl] (*pl* **mesdemoiselles** [medmwazɛl]) *nf* (**a**) *(suivi d'un nom)* Miss; **M.** Duval Miss Duval; **Mesdemoiselles Duval et Morin** the Misses Duval and Morin (**b**) *(en apostrophe)* **merci m.** thank you; **mesdemoiselles, un peu de silence je vous prie!** *(dans une classe)* let's have some quiet, girls, please! (**c**) *(dans une lettre)* **M.** Dear Madam (**d**) *(utilisé seul)* **M. se plaint que...** *(dans un magasin)* this young lady is complaining that...

Madère [madɛr] *n* Madeira

madère [madɛr] *nm* Madeira (wine)

madone [madɔn] *nf* Madonna

madras [madrɑs] *nm (tissu)* madras (cotton)

Madrid [madrid] *n* Madrid

madrier [madrije] *nm* beam

madrilène [madrilɛn] **1** *adj* of Madrid **2** *nmf* **M.** person from Madrid

maestria [maɛstrija] *nf* mastery

maf(f)ia [mafja] *nf* Mafia; **la M.** the Mafia

maf(f)ieux, -euse [mafjø, -øz] **1** *adj* Mafia **2** *nm,f* Mafioso

maf(f)ioso [mafjozo] (*pl* **maf(f)iosi** [mafjozi]) *nm* Mafioso

maganer [magane] *vt Can (chose)* to spoil, to waste; *(personne)* to manhandle

magasin [magazɛ̃] *nm* (**a**) *(boutique)* Br shop, Am store; **avoir qch en m.** to have sth in stock; **courir** *ou* **faire les magasins** to go shopping; **grand m.** department store (**b**) *(entrepôt)* warehouse (**c**) *(d'un appareil photo, d'une arme)* magazine

magasinage [magazinaʒ] *nm* (**a**) *(mise en dépôt)* warehousing (**b**) *(droits)* warehouse charges (**c**) *Can* **faire du m.** to go shopping

magasiner [magazine] *vi Can* to go shopping

magasinier [magazinje] *nm* warehouseman

magazine [magazin] *nm* (**a**) *(journal)* magazine (**b**) *(émission à la radio ou à la télévision)* magazine programme

mage [maʒ] *nm* magus

Maghreb [magrɛb] *nm* **le M.** the Maghreb

maghrébin, -e [magrebɛ̃, -in] **1** *adj* of the Maghreb **2** *nm,f* **M.** person from the Maghreb

magicien, -enne [maʒisjɛ̃, -ɛn] *nm,f* magician

magie [maʒi] *nf* magic; **m. blanche/noire** white/black magic

magique [maʒik] *adj* (**a**) *(surnaturel)* magic (**b**) *(extraordinaire)* magical

magiquement [maʒikmɑ̃] *adv* magically

magistère [maʒistɛr] *nm* (**a**) *(diplôme)* = post-graduate vocational qualification (**b**) *(autorité)* authority

magistral, -e, -aux, -ales [maʒistral, -o] *adj* (**a**) *(admirable) (interprétation, démonstration)* masterly; *(réussite)* brilliant (**b**) *(énorme) (correction, dispute)* proper; *(erreur)* colossal (**c**) *(docte) (ton)* magisterial

magistralement [maʒistralmɑ̃] *adv* authoritatively

magistrat [maʒistra] *nm* magistrate

magistrature [maʒistratyr] *nf* magistrature

magma [magma] *nm* (**a**) *Géol* magma (**b**) *(ensemble confus)* jumble

magnanime [maɲanim] *adj* magnanimous

magnanimité [maɲanimite] *nf* magnanimity

magnat [magna] *nm* magnate, tycoon; **m. de la presse** press baron

magner [maɲe] **se magner** *vpr Fam* to get a move on

magnésium [maɲezjɔm] *nm* magnesium

magnétique [maɲetik] *adj* magnetic

magnétiser [maɲetize] *vt* (**a**) *(matériau, corps)* to magnetize (**b**) *(personne, foule)* to hypnotize

magnétisme [maɲetism] *nm (d'un matériau, de la terre, d'une personne)* magnetism

magnéto [maɲeto] *nm Fam* tape recorder

magnétophone [maɲetɔfɔn] *nm* tape recorder

magnétoscope [maɲetɔskɔp] *nm Br* video(recorder), *Am* VCR

magnificence [maɲifisɑ̃s] *nf* magnificence

magnifier [66] [maɲifje] *vt* to magnify, to glorify

magnifique [maɲifik] *adj* magnificent

magnifiquement [maɲifikmɑ̃] *adv* magnificently

magnitude [maɲityd] *nf* magnitude

magnolia [maɲɔlja] *nm* magnolia (tree)

magnum [magnɔm] *nm* magnum

magot [mago] *nm Fam* hoard

magouille [maguj] *nf Fam* scheming; **faire des magouilles** to scheme

magouiller [maguje] *vt & vi Fam* to scheme

magouilleur, -euse [magujœr, -øz] *nm,f Fam* schemer

magret [magrɛ] *nm (de canard)* fillet

Mahomet [maɔmɛ] *npr* Mohammed

mai [mɛ] *nm* May; **le premier m.** *(fête)* May Day; **le huit m.** *(fête)* VE day; *voir aussi* **janvier**

maigre [mɛgr] **1** *adj* (**a**) *(très mince) (personne, partie du corps)* thin (**b**) *(sans gras) (viande)* lean; *(fromage, yaourt)* low-fat (**c**) *(peu abondant) (filet d'eau)* thin; *(repas, salaire)* meagre; *(végétation, barbe)* sparse (**d**) *(peu conséquent) (conclusions, explication)* thin; *(succès)* very limited **2** *nm (de viande)* lean part **3** *nmf* thin person **4** *adv* **faire m.** not to eat meat

maigrelet, -ette [mɛgrəlɛ, -ɛt] *adj* skinny

maigreur [mɛgrœr] *nf (d'une personne)* thinness

maigrichon, -onne [megriʃɔ̃, -ɔn] *adj* skinny

maigrir [mɛgrir] *vi* to get thinner

mailing [mɛliŋ] *nm* mailshot

maillage [majaʒ] *nm* networking

maille [maj] *nf* (**a**) *(de tricot)* stitch; **m. à l'endroit/à l'envers** plain/purl stitch (**b**) *(de filet)* mesh; *Fig* **passer entre les mailles du filet** to slip through the net (**c**) *(tissu)* knitted fabric (**d**) *(de chaîne)* link (**e**) **avoir m. à partir avec qn** to have a set-to with sb

maillet [majɛ] *nm* mallet

maillon [majɔ̃] *nm* link

maillot [majo] *nm (de footballeur, de coureur cycliste)* shirt, jersey; **m. de bain** *(pour femmes)* swimsuit; *(pour hommes)* (swimming) trunks; **m. de corps** *Br* vest, *Am* undershirt; **m. jaune** yellow jersey *(in the Tour de France)*

main [mɛ̃] **1** *nf* hand; **avoir qch en m.** *(situation)* to have sth in hand; *(voiture)* to have the feel of sth; **avoir la m. heureuse** to be lucky; **avoir la m. leste** to be quick to raise one's hand; **avoir la m. lourde** *(être brutal)* to be heavy-handed; **il a eu la m. lourde avec le sel** he was a bit heavy-handed with the salt; **donner la m. à qn** to hold sb's hand; **faire m. basse sur qch** to get one's hands on sth; **mettre la m. sur qch** *(trouver ce que l'on cherchait)* to lay one's hands on sth; **mettre la m. à la pâte** *ou* **à l'ouvrage** to lend a hand; **mettre la dernière m. à qch** to put the finishing touches to sth; **en mettre sa m. au feu** *ou* **à couper** to stake one's life on it; **ne pas y aller de m. morte** *(en frappant, en insultant)* not to pull one's punches; *(forcer une description, une action)*

to overdo it; **prendre qn par la m.** to take sb's hand; *Fig* **se prendre par la m.** to take oneself in hand; **prendre qn/ qch en m.** to take sb/sth in hand, **prendre qn à m. dans le sac** to catch sb red-handed; **à la m.** *(faire, fabriquer)* by hand; *(tenir, avoir)* in one's hand; **écrit à la m.** handwritten; **fait à la m.** *(pull, poterie)* handmade; **à deux mains** in both hands; **à quatre mains** *(morceau)* for four hands; *(jouer)* four-handed; **à m.** armée *(vol, attaque)* armed; **à main(s) nue(s)** with bare hands; **à pleines mains** by the handful; **de m. en m.** from hand to hand; **de la m. à la m.** cash in hand; **de m. de maître** with a master's hand; **de première m.** firsthand; **de seconde m.** secondhand; **en mains propres** in person; **haut les mains!, les mains en l'air!** hands up!; **les mains vides** empty-handed; *Fig* **les mains dans les poches** unprepared; **sous la m.** handy; m. **courante** handrail
2 *adv* **tricoté/fait/cousu m.** hand-knitted/-made/-sewn

main-d'œuvre [mɛ̃dœvr] *nf* labour

main-forte [mɛ̃fɔrt] *voir* prêter

mainmise [mɛ̃miz] *nf* seizure (**sur** of)

maint, -e [mɛ̃, mɛ̃t] *adj indéfini Litt* many a; **maintes et maintes fois, en maintes et maintes occasions** time and (time) again

maintenance [mɛ̃tnɑ̃s] *nf* maintenance

maintenant [mɛ̃tnɑ̃] *adv* now

maintenir [70] [mɛ̃tnir] **1** *vt* **(a)** *(soutenir)* to hold in position **(b)** *(empêcher d'avancer)* *(foule)* to hold back; m. qn à distance to keep sb at a distance **(c)** *(conserver) (tradition, paix)* to maintain, to keep; *(décision)* to abide by; m. qn en vie to keep sb alive **(d)** *(affirmer)* to maintain **(que** that)
2 se maintenir *vpr* to hold up

maintien [mɛ̃tjɛ̃] *nm* **(a)** *(conservation)* maintenance; *(de la loi)* upholding; **m. de l'ordre** maintenance of law and order **(b)** *(allure, posture)* bearing

maintiendrai *etc voir* maintenir

maire [mɛr] *nm* mayor

mairie [mɛri] *nf (lieu) Br* town hall, *Am* city hall; *(administration) Br* town council, *Am* city hall

mais [mɛ] **1** *conj* **(a)** *(marque l'opposition ou la transition)* but; non seulement..., **m. aussi ou encore...** not only... but also...; m. qu'est-ce qui t'arrive? whatever's the matter with you?; **m. j'y pense, je ne l'ai pas encore appelée!** I've just thought, I haven't rung her yet! **(b)** *(emphatique)* m. oui! of course!; m. non! of course not!; **m. enfin** well really; **elle ne fait rien, m.** vraiment rien she does nothing all day, and I mean nothing; **on a ri, m. ri!** we laughed, and I mean laughed!
2 *nm* il y a un m. there's a but

maïs [mais] *nm Br* maize, *Am* corn; *Culin* sweetcorn

maison [mɛzɔ̃] **1** *nf* **(a)** *(habitation)* house; m. de campagne *(résidence secondaire)* house in the country; m. individuelle detached house; m. de poupée doll's house **(b)** *(foyer)* home; **à la m.** at home; **toute la m. dort** the whole house is asleep **(c)** *(entreprise)* company; m. de couture fashion house; m. d'édition publishing house; m. mère parent company **(d)** *(lignée)* house **(e)** *(institution)* m. d'arrêt remand centre; m. close ou de passe brothel; m. de correction ou de redressement detention centre; m. de la culture arts centre; m. des jeunes et de la culture = youth club and arts centre; m. de retraite old people's home
2 *adj inv* **(a)** *(artisanal)* home-made **(b)** *(au sein de l'entreprise)* in-house **(c)** *Fam (énorme)* colossal

Maison-Blanche [mɛzɔ̃blɑ̃ʃ] *nf* la M. the White House

maisonnée [mɛzɔne] *nf* household

maisonnette [mɛzɔnɛt] *nf* small house

maître [mɛtr] **1** *nm* **(a)** *(de situation, de chien)* master; **m. de maison** host; **en m.** authoritatively; **être m. de son destin** to be master of one's own destiny; **être m. de soi** to have self-control; **il n'était plus m. de ses actes** he didn't know what he was doing **(b)** *(dans des fonctions)* m. **(d'école)** *(Br* primary school *or Am* elementary school) teacher; m. **assistant** = assistant lecturer; m. **auxiliaire** *Br* supply *or Am* substitute teacher; m. **de conférence** *Br* (senior) lecturer, *Am* assistant professor; m. **d'hôtel** *(dans une maison)* butler; *(dans un restaurant)* head waiter; m. **nageur** swimming instructor; m. **d'œuvre** project manager **(c)** *(titre octroyé à un peintre, à un musicien)* maestro; **les grands maîtres** the great masters, **être passé m. dans l'art de qch/de faire qch** to be a past master at sth/at doing sth **(d)** *(titre donné à un avocat)* = form of address for lawyer **(e)** m. **chanteur** blackmailer
2 *adj* m. **mot** key word

maîtresse [mɛtrɛs] **1** *nf* mistress; **être m. de son destin** to be mistress of one's own destiny; **être m. de soi** to have self-control; m. **(d'école)** *(Br* primary school *or Am* elementary school) teacher; m. **de maison** hostess
2 *adj* main, principal; m. **femme** capable woman

maîtrise [mɛtriz] *nf* **(a)** *(diplôme universitaire)* ≃ master's degree **(de** in) **(b)** *(contrôle) (de ses passions)* mastery; m. **de soi** self-control **(c)** *(connaissance)* mastery **(d)** *(école de chant)* choir school

maîtriser [mɛtrize] **1** *vt* **(a)** *(soumettre) (agresseur)* to overpower; *(élèves, animal)* to control; *(flammes, opposition)* to subdue; *(incendie, épidémie)* to control **(b)** *(contrôler) (passion)* to control; *(peur)* to overcome **(c)** *(connaître parfaitement) (sujet, langue)* to master; **il ne maîtrise pas la langue** he hasn't mastered the language **(d)** *(rester maître de) (véhicule)* to have under control
2 se maîtriser *vpr* to control oneself

Maïzena® [maizena] *nf Br* cornflour, *Am* cornstarch

majesté [maʒɛste] *nf* **(a)** *(noblesse)* majesty **(b)** **Sa M. (le Roi)** His Majesty (the King); **Sa M. (la Reine)** Her Majesty (the Queen)

majestueux, -euse [maʒɛstɥø, -øz] *adj* majestic

majeur, -e [maʒœr] **1** *adj* **(a)** *(principal)* major **(b)** *(personne)* of age **(c)** *Mus (mode, intervalle)* major
2 *nm (doigt)* middle finger

major [maʒɔr] *nm* **(a)** *(d'une promotion)* top student **(b)** *(officier)* regimental adjutant *(with administrative duties)*

majoration [maʒɔrasjɔ̃] *nf (d'une facture)* surcharge *(de* on); *(d'un prix)* increase **(de** in)

majordome [maʒɔrdɔm] *nm* major-domo

majorer [maʒɔre] *vt (facture)* to put a surcharge on; *(prix)* to increase

majorette [maʒɔrɛt] *nf (drum)* majorette

majoritaire [maʒɔritɛr] *adj* majority; **être m.** to be in the majority

majorité [maʒɔrite] *nf* **(a)** *(supériorité en nombre)* majority; **en m.** for the most part; **avoir la m.** to be in the majority **(b)** *(dans des élections)* majority; m. **relative/ absolue** relative/absolute majority **(c)** *(parti politique)* majority party **(d)** *(âge)* majority, coming of age

Majorque [maʒɔrk] *n* Majorca

majorquin, -e [maʒɔrkɛ̃, -in] **1** *adj* Majorcan
2 *nm,f* M. Majorcan

majuscule [maʒyskyl] **1** *adj (lettre)* capital
2 *nf* capital letter

mal¹, maux [mal, mo] *nm (douleur)* pain, ache; **avoir m. à l'estomac/à la tête/au dos** to have stomach ache/a headache/backache; **avoir m. à la gorge** to have a sore throat; **j'ai m. au bras** my arm hurts, I have a sore arm; **avoir m. aux dents** to have toothache; **avoir des maux d'estomac/de tête** to get stomach ache/headaches; **où avez-vous m.?** where does it hurt?; **faire m. à qn** to hurt sb; **mon genou/œil me fait m.** my knee/eye hurts; **se faire m.** to hurt oneself; *Fam* **attraper du m.** to catch cold; **ça fait m. au cœur de voir ça!** it's sickening to see things like that!; *Fam* **ça me ferait m.!** I'm not having it!; **être en m. de qch** to crave sth; **être en m. d'enfants** to be broody; **m. de cœur** sickness; **m. de dents** toothache; **m. de gorge** sore throat; **m. de mer** seasickness; **avoir le m. de mer** to be seasick; **m. du pays** homesickness; **avoir le m. du pays** to be homesick; *Litt* **m. du siècle** world-weariness; **m. de tête** headache; **m. des transports** travel-sickness; *Prov* **aux grands maux les grands remèdes** desperate situations call for desperate remedies

(b) *(préjudice)* harm; **faire du m. à qn** to harm sb; **ça n'a jamais fait de m. à personne!** it never did anyone any harm!; **vouloir du m. à qn** to mean to harm sb; **cela fera plus de m. que de bien** it will do more harm than good; **le m. est fait** the damage has been done; **un m. nécessaire** a necessary evil; **il n'y a pas de m. à cela** there's no harm in that; *Fam* **il n'y a pas de m.** there's no harm done; **dire du m. de qn** to speak ill of sb; **ne pas penser à m.** to mean well

(c) *(contraire du bien)* wrong; **le bien et le m.** right and wrong, good and evil; **voir le m. partout** to always see the bad side

(d) *(difficulté)* **avoir du m. à faire qch** to have difficulty *or* trouble doing sth; *Fam* **avoir un m. de chien à faire qch** to have a hell of a job doing sth; **non sans m.** not without difficulty; **se donner du m. pour faire qch** to take pains to do sth; **donner du m. à qn** to give sb trouble

mal² **1** *adv* **(a)** *(médiocrement)* badly; *(incorrectement)* wrongly; **elle chante m.** she's a bad singer; **la porte est m. fermée** the door isn't closed properly; **il travaille m. à l'école** he's a poor student; **cette lampe éclaire m.** this lamp doesn't give much light; **m. comprendre** to misunderstand; **m. interpréter** to misinterpret; **m. choisir** to make the wrong choice; **ça va m. finir** it'll end in tears; **on y mange m.** the food's not very good there; **je ne pensais pas m. faire** I didn't think I was doing anything wrong; **aller de m. en pis** to go from bad to worse; **on voit m. d'ici** you can't see very well from here; *Fam* **se mettre m. avec qn** to fall out with sb; *Fam* **être m. avec qn** to be on bad terms with sb; **vous ne feriez pas m. de…** you would be wise to…

(b) *(en mauvaise santé)* **se sentir m.** to feel ill; **se trouver m.** to faint; **aller m.** to be ill; **être au plus m.** to be at death's door; **être m. en point** to be in a bad way

(c) *(une certaine quantité)* **pas m. de** quite a lot of; **il y en a pas m.** there is/are quite a lot; **cela m'a pris pas m. de temps** it took me quite a while

2 *adj inv (contraire à la morale)* bad; **c'est très m. de faire ça** it's very naughty to do that; **c'est pas m.** it's not bad, it's quite good; **elle n'est pas m.** she's not bad; **on n'est pas m. ici** we've found a nice place here

malabar [malabar] *nm Fam* hulk

malade [malad] **1** *adj* **(a)** *(souffrant)* ill, sick; **tomber m.** to fall or be taken ill; **être m. du cœur/du foie** to have heart/liver trouble; **être m. d'inquiétude/de jalousie** to be sick with worry/jealousy **(b)** *(qui fonctionne mal) (organe, dent)* bad; *Fig (industrie)* ailing **(c)** *(dérangé intellectuellement)* mad **2** *nmf* sick person; *(dans un hôpital)* patient; **un m. mental** a mentally ill person; *(dans un hôpital)* a mental patient; **un m. imaginaire** a hypochondriac

maladie [maladi] *nf* illness, disease; *Fig* **en faire une m.** to make a song and dance about it; **m. bleue** cyanosis; **m. sexuellement transmissible** sexually transmitted disease; **m. de la vache folle** mad cow disease

maladif, -ive [maladif, -iv] *adj* **(a)** *(personne, teint)* sickly **(b)** *(curiosité, pensées)* morbid **(c)** *(susceptibilité, jalousie)* pathological

maladresse [maladrɛs] *nf* **(a)** *(manque d'habileté physique)* clumsiness, awkwardness **(b)** *(manque de tact)* tactlessness; *(bévue)* blunder

maladroit, -e [maladrwa, -at] **1** *adj* **(a)** *(inhabile)* clumsy, awkward **(b)** *(manquant de tact)* tactless **2** *nmf* **(a)** *(personne inhabile)* clumsy *or* awkward person **(b)** *(personne sans tact)* tactless person

maladroitement [maladrwatmã] *adv* **(a)** *(de façon gauche)* clumsily **(b)** *(sans tact)* tactlessly

malais, -e [malɛ, -ɛz] **1** *adj* Malaysian **2** *nm,f* **M.** Malaysian **3** *nm (langue)* Malay

malaise [malɛz] *nm* **(a)** *(trouble physique)* feeling of sickness; *(étourdissement)* dizzy spell; **avoir un m.** to feel faint **(b)** *(inconfort moral)* uneasiness **(c)** *(état de crise)* unrest

malaisé, -e [malɛze] *adj* difficult

Malaisie [malɛzi] *nf* **la M.** Malaysia

malaria [malarja] *nf* malaria; **avoir la m.** to have malaria

malavisé, -e [malavize] *adj Litt* unwise **(de faire qch to do sth)**

Malawi [malawi] *nm* **le M.** Malawi

malaxer [malakse] *vt* to knead

malchance [malʃãs] *nf* bad luck; **par m.** as bad luck would have it

malchanceux, -euse [malʃãsø, -øz] **1** *adj* unlucky **2** *nm,f* unlucky person

malcommode [malkɔmɔd] *adj (appareil)* impractical; *(vêtement)* unsuitable

Maldives [maldiv] *nfpl* **les (îles) M.** the Maldives

maldonne [maldɔn] *nf* misdeal; *Fig* **il y a m.** something's gone wrong somewhere

mâle [mɑl] **1** *adj* **(a)** *(du sexe masculin)* male **(b)** *(viril) (courage, assurance)* manly; *(style)* virile **(c)** **prise m.** plug **2** *nm* male

malédiction [malediksjõ] *nf* curse

maléfice [malefis] *nm* evil spell

maléfique [malefik] *adj* evil

malencontreusement [malãkõtrøzmã] *adv* unfortunately

malencontreux, -euse [malãkõtrø, -øz] *adj* unfortunate

malentendant, -e [malãtãdã, -ãt] **1** *adj* hard of hearing **2** *nm,f* person who is hard of hearing

malentendu [malãtãdy] *nm* misunderstanding

malfaçon [malfasõ] *nf* defect

malfaisant, -e [malfəzã, -ãt] *adj* harmful

malfaiteur [malfɛtœr] *nm* criminal

malfamé, -e [malfame] *adj* disreputable

malformation [malfɔrmasjõ] *nf* malformation

malfrat [malfra] *nm Fam* crook

malgache [malgaʃ] **1** *adj* Madagascan **2** *nmf* **M.** Madagascan **3** *nm (langue)* Malagasy

malgré [malgre] *prép (en dépit de)* in spite of, despite; **m. tout** *(en dépit de tout)* in spite of *or* despite everything; *(pourtant)* all the same

malhabile [malabil] *adj* clumsy, awkward

malheur [malœr] **1** *nm* **(a)** *(drame, catastrophe)* misfortune; **le m., c'est que…** the unfortunate thing is that…; **faire un m.** to be a big hit; **un m. n'arrive jamais**

seul it never rains but it pours (**b**) *(chagrin, infortune)* misfortune; **faire le m.** de qn to cause sb a lot of unhappiness (**c**) *(malchance)* bad luck; **par m.** unfortunately; **porter m.** à qn to bring sb bad luck; **avoir le m.** de faire qch to make the big mistake of doing sth **2** *exclam* hell!

malheureusement [malørøzmã] *adv* unfortunately
malheureux, -euse [malørø, -øz] **1** *adj* (**a**) *(triste)* unhappy, miserable (**b**) *(malchanceux) (personne)* unlucky; *(candidat, tentative)* unsuccessful; *(amour)* unrequited; **m. au jeu/en amour** unlucky at gambling/in love (**c**) *(regrettable)* unfortunate (**d**) *(négligeable)* miserable, wretched
2 *nm,f* (**a**) *(personne infortunée)* poor wretch (**b**) *(indigent)* poor or needy person; **les m.** the poor, the needy

malhonnête [malɔnɛt] *adj* (**a**) *(personne, pratique)* dishonest (**b**) *(indécent) (proposition)* indecent
malhonnêteté [malɔnɛtte] *nf* dishonesty

Mali [mali] *nm* **le M.** Mali

mallce [malis] *nf* (**a**) *(espièglerie)* mischief (**b**) *(méchanceté)* malice; **sans m.** without malice

malicieusement [malisjøzmã] *adv* mischievously
malicieux, -euse [malisjø, -øz] *adj (espiègle)* mischievous

malien, -enne [maljɛ̃, -ɛn] **1** *adj* Malian
2 *nm,f* **M.** Malian

malignité [malinite] *nf* (**a**) *(méchanceté)* malice (**b**) *(d'une tumeur)* malignancy

malin, -igne [malɛ̃, -iɲ] *adj* (**a**) *(rusé) (personne)* crafty; *(regard)* knowing; *Ironique* **c'est m.!** that's clever! (**b**) *(méchant) (plaisir)* perverse, malicious; **prendre un m. plaisir à faire qch** to take a perverse or malicious pleasure in doing sth (**c**) *(tumeur)* malignant
2 *nm,f* crafty person; **faire le m.** to show off

malingre [malɛ̃gr] *adj* puny
malintentionné, -e [malɛ̃tãsjɔne] *adj* ill-intentioned
malle [mal] *nf* (**a**) *(valise)* trunk; *Fam* **se faire la m.** to clear off (**b**) *(de voiture) Br* boot, *Am* trunk (**c**) *Can* **mettre une lettre à la m.** to mail or *Br* post a letter
malléable [maleabl] *adj* malleable
mallette [malɛt] *nf (porte-documents)* briefcase
malmener [46] [malmøne] *vt* (**a**) *(brutaliser) (personne)* to manhandle, to treat roughly; *(verbalement)* to attack; *(matériel, véhicule)* to mistreat (**b**) *(dominer)* **m. qn** to give sb a hard time
malnutrition [malnytrisjɔ̃] *nf* malnutrition
malodorant, -e [malɔdɔrã, -ãt] *adj* smelly
malotru, -e [malɔtry] *nm,f* lout
Malouines [malwin] *nfpl* **les (îles) M.** the Falkland Islands, the Falklands
malpoli, -e [malpɔli] *Fam* **1** *adj* rude
2 *nm,f* rude person
malpropre [malprɔpr] *adj* (**a**) *(sale) (mains)* dirty; *(apparence, travail)* slovenly (**b**) *(inconvenant)* smutty (**c**) *(malhonnête)* despicable
malsain, -e [malsɛ̃, -ɛn] *adj* (**a**) *(dangereux pour la santé)* unhealthy (**b**) *(pernicieux)* unhealthy; *(personne)* unwholesome
malséant, -e [malseã, -ãt] *adj Litt* unseemly
malt [malt] *nm* malt
maltais, -e [maltɛ, -ɛz] **1** *adj* Maltese
2 *nm,f* **M.** Maltese; **les M.** the Maltese
3 *nm (langue)* Maltese
Malte [malt] *n* Malta
maltraitance [maltrɛtãs] *nf* ill-treatment

maltraiter [maltrɛte] *vt* (**a**) *(brutaliser)* to ill-treat (**b**) *(verbalement)* to attack
malus [malys] *nm* partial loss of no-claims bonus *(due to insurance claim)*
malveillance [malvɛjãs] *nf* spite
malveillant, -e [malvɛjã, -ãt] *adj* spiteful
malvenu, -e [malvəny] *adj* out of place, inappropriate
malversation [malvɛrsasjɔ̃] *nf* embezzlement
maman [mamã] *nf Br* mum, *Am* mom; *(langage enfantin) Br* mummy, *Am* mommy
mamelle [mamɛl] *nf (de vache)* udder; *(de chienne, de truie)* teat
mamelon [mamlɔ̃] *nm* (**a**) *(du sein)* nipple (**b**) *(colline)* hillock
mamie [mami] *nf* grandma, gran(ny)
mammaire [mamɛr] *adj* mammary
mammifère [mamifɛr] **1** *adj* mammalian
2 *nm* mammal
mammographie [mamɔgrafi] *nf* mammography
mammouth [mamut] *nm* mammoth
mamours [mamur] *nmpl Fam* kissing and cuddling; **faire des m.** à qn to kiss and cuddle sb
manager[1] [manadʒɛr] *nm* manager
manager[2] [45] [manadʒe] *vt* to manage
manant [manã] *nm* (**a**) *Hist (villageois)* villager; *(paysan)* peasant (**b**) *Litt (mufle)* churl, boor
Manche [mãʃ] *nf* **la M.** the (English) Channel
manche[1] [mãʃ] *nf* (**a**) *(de vêtement)* sleeve; **en manches de chemise** in one's shirtsleeves; **manches longues/courtes** long/short sleeves; **manches ballon/kimono/ raglan** puff/kimono/raglan sleeves (**b**) *(de jeu, de compétition)* round; *(au tennis)* set (**c**) *Fam* **faire la m.** to beg
manche[2] *nm* (**a**) *(d'outil)* handle; **m. à balai** broomstick; *(d'avion)* joystick (**b**) *(de guitare)* neck
manchette [mãʃɛt] *nf* (**a**) *(extrémité de la manche)* cuff (**b**) *(de journal)* headline (**c**) *(au catch)* forearm smash; *(au volley-ball)* dig
manchon [mãʃɔ̃] *nm* (**a**) *(vêtement)* muff (**b**) *Tech* sleeve
manchot[1], **-e** [mãʃo, -ɔt] **1** *adj (privé d'un bras)* one-armed; *Fam* **il n'est pas m.** *(adroit)* he's clever with his hands; *(il peut le faire lui-même)* he's got hands, hasn't he?
2 *nm,f* one-armed person
manchot[2] *nm (oiseau)* penguin
mandale [mãdal] *nf très Fam* clout, slap
mandarin [mãdarɛ̃] *nm* (**a**) *(de Chine)* mandarin (**b**) *Fig & Péj (personnage influent)* mandarin (**c**) *(langue)* Mandarin (Chinese)
mandarine [mãdarin] *nf (fruit)* mandarin (orange)
mandat [mãda] *nm* (**a**) *(mission) (de député)* mandate; *(de président)* term of office (**b**) *(ordre)* warrant; **m. d'amener** = summons; **m. d'arrêt** arrest warrant; **m. de dépôt** committal order; **m. de perquisition** search warrant (**c**) *(mode de paiement)* order; **m. postal** *Br* postal order, *Am* money order (**d**) *(autorité)* mandate (**e**) *(procuration)* power of attorney
mandataire [mãdatɛr] *nmf (d'électeurs)* representative; *(dans une réunion)* proxy
mandat-carte (*pl* mandats-cartes) [mãdakart] *nm Br* postal order, *Am* money order *(in postcard form)*
mandater [mãdate] *vt* (**a**) *(représentant)* to commission; *(membre parlementaire)* to give a mandate to (**b**) *(frais)* to pay by order
mandat-lettre (*pl* mandats-lettres) [mãdalɛtr] *nm Br* postal order, *Am* money order *(in letter-card form)*

mandibule [mãdibyl] *nf* mandible

mandoline [mãdɔlin] *nf* mandolin

mandrin [mãdrɛ̃] *nm (pour percer)* punch; *(pour élargir un trou)* drift

manège [manɛʒ] *nm* **(a)** *(attraction foraine) Br* roundabout, merry-go-round, *Am* carousel **(b)** *(en équitation)* riding school **(c)** *(manigances)* game

manette [manɛt] *nf* lever

manganèse [mãganɛz] *nm* manganese

mangeable [mãʒabl] *adj* **(a)** *(comestible)* edible **(b)** *(médiocre)* eatable

mangeoire [mãʒwar] *nf* manger

manger [45] [mãʒe] **1** *vt* **(a)** *(aliments)* to eat; **m. qn/qch des yeux** to look at sb/sth longingly; **m. ses mots** to mumble; **ça ne mange pas de pain** it doesn't cost anything; **je ne mange pas de ce pain-là** I don't go in for that sort of thing **(b)** *(attaquer)* to eat away **(c)** *(consommer)* to get through **(d)** *(dépenser)* to get through
2 *vi* to eat; **donner à m. à qn** to give sb something to eat; **m. comme quatre** *ou* **comme un ogre** to eat like a horse; **m. comme un oiseau** to eat like a sparrow; **m. à sa faim** to eat one's fill
3 se manger *vpr* to be eaten

mange-tout [mãʒtu] *nm inv (pois) Br* mangetout, *Am* snow pea; *(haricot) Br* runner bean, *Am* string bean

mangeur, -euse [mãʒœr, -øz] *nm,f* **gros m.** big eater; **tigre/requin m.** d'hommes man-eating tiger/shark

mangue [mãg] *nf* mango

maniable [manjabl] *adj (outil)* handy; *(véhicule)* easy to handle

maniaque [manjak] **1** *adj* **(a)** *(pointilleux)* fussy **(b)** *(fou)* manic
2 *nmf* **(a)** *(pointilleux) Br* fusspot, *Am* fussbudget; **être un m. de qch** to be fanatical about *or* obsessed with sth **(b)** *(fou)* maniac

manichéen, -enne [manikeɛ̃, -ɛn] *adj* Manichean

manichéisme [manikeism] *nm* Manicheism

manie [mani] *nf* **(a)** *(habitude)* odd habit **(b)** *(idée fixe)* mania, obsession **(c)** *Méd* mania

maniement [manimã] *nm* handling

manier [66] [manje] *vt* **(a)** *(manipuler) (objet)* to handle **(b)** *(utiliser) (véhicule)* to handle; *(outil, ironie)* to use

manière [manjɛr] *nf* **(a)** *(façon)* way, manner; **faire qch à sa m.** to do sth one's (own) way; **de m. à faire qch** so as to do sth; **de m. que** + *subjunctive* so that, in such a way that; **d'une** *ou* **de m. générale** generally speaking; **en aucune m.** under no circumstances; **de toute m.** in any case; **d'une certaine m.** in a manner of speaking, in a sense; **c'est sa m. d'être** that's the way he is; **la m. forte** strong-arm tactics **(b)** *(conduite)* **manières** manners; **faire des manières** *(agir de façon pompeuse)* to put on airs and graces; *(se faire prier)* to make a fuss **(c)** *(d'une œuvre)* **à la m. de** in the style of

maniéré, -e [manjere] *adj* affected

maniérisme [manjerism] *nm* mannerism

manif [manif] *nf Fam* demo

manifestant, -e [manifɛstã, -ãt] *nm,f* demonstrator

manifestation [manifɛstasjõ] *nf* **(a)** *(de sentiments)* display **(b)** *(rassemblement politique)* demonstration **(c)** *(événement organisé)* event

manifeste¹ [manifɛst] *adj* obvious, manifest

manifeste² *nm* manifesto

manifestement [manifɛstəmã] *adv* obviously, manifestly

manifester [manifɛste] **1** *vt (exprimer)* to show

2 *vi* to demonstrate
3 se manifester *vpr* **(a)** *(personne)* to make oneself known **(b)** *(maladie)* to show *or* manifest itself **(par** in)

manigancer [16] [manigãse] *vt* to scheme

manigances [manigãs] *nfpl* scheming

Manille [manij] *n* Manila

manioc [manjɔk] *nm* manioc, cassava

manipulateur, -trice [manipylatœr, -tris] **1** *nm,f* **(a)** *(de machines)* operator **(b)** *Péj (de personnes)* manipulator
2 *nm (appareil de transmission)* (sending) key

manipulation [manipylasjõ] *nf* **(a)** *(d'appareils, de produits)* handling; **m. génétique** genetic engineering **(b)** **manipulations** *(en science)* experiments, practical work **(c)** *Péj (de personnes)* manipulation **(d)** *Ordinat* **m. de colonnes** column handling

manipuler [manipyle] *vt* **(a)** *(appareils, produits)* to handle **(b)** *Péj (personnes)* to manipulate **(c)** *(statistiques)* to massage

manivelle [manivɛl] *nf* crank

manne [man] *nf (dans la Bible)* manna; *Fig (don inespéré)* godsend

mannequin [mankɛ̃] *nm* **(a)** *(personne)* model **(b)** *(de magasin, de couturier)* dummy

manœuvre¹ [manœvr] *nf* **(a)** *(conduite, direction) (de machines)* operation; *(de véhicules)* manoeuvring; **faire une m.** to (do a) manoeuvre; **faire une fausse m.** *(en voiture)* to manoeuvre badly; *Fig* to get it wrong **(b)** *(intrigue)* manoeuvre; **manœuvres** manoeuvring **(c)** *Mil (dans une bataille)* manoeuvre; **être en manœuvres** to be on manoeuvres **(d)** *(d'un bateau)* manoeuvre

manœuvre² *nm (ouvrier)* unskilled worker

manœuvrer [manœvre] **1** *vt* **(a)** *(faire fonctionner) (machine)* to operate; *(véhicule)* to manoeuvre **(b)** *(influencer)* to influence
2 *vi aussi Fig* to manoeuvre

manoir [manwar] *nm* manor house

manomètre [manɔmɛtr] *nm* pressure gauge, manometer

manquant, -e [mãkã, -ãt] *adj* missing

manque [mãk] **1** *nm* **(a)** *(insuffisance)* lack; **par m. de** through lack of; **m. de chance!** bad luck!; **m. à gagner** loss of earnings **(b)** *(lacune)* gap **(c)** *(d'un drogué)* withdrawal symptoms; **être en (état de) m.** to have withdrawal symptoms
2 *nf Fam* **à la m.** useless, pathetic

manqué, -e [mãke] **1** *adj* **(a)** *(occasion, rendez-vous)* missed **(b)** *(tentative, expérience)* unsuccessful **(c)** *(personne)* **c'est un poète/un médecin m.** he should have been a poet/doctor
2 *nm (gâteau)* = sponge cake with almond-flavoured or fruit-flavoured icing

manquement [mãkmã] *nm* breach **(à** of)

manquer [mãke] **1** *vt* **(a)** *(cible, train, occasion)* to miss **(b)** *(échouer à)* to fail
2 *vi* **(a)** *(faire défaut)* to be lacking; **le temps/la place me manque** I don't have enough time/room; **elle me manque** I miss her **(b)** *(échouer)* to fail; **ça n'a pas manqué, il est arrivé en retard** sure enough, he was late **(c)** *(être absent)* to be missing **(à** from)
3 *v impersonnel* **il ne manque personne** there's no one missing; **il manque quelques pages** there are a few pages missing; **il manque un bouton à ta veste** there's a button missing from your jacket; **il me manque cinq euros!** I'm five euros short; **il ne manquait plus que cela!** that's all I/he/*etc* needed!
4 manquer à *vt ind (devoir, honneur)* to fail in; *(parole, promesses)* to break

5 manquer de *vt ind* (**a**) *(argent, main-d'œuvre)* to be short of, to lack; *(temps)* to be short of; *(courage, bon sens, charme)* to lack; **ne m.** de rien to have all that one needs; **m. de respect à qn** to show a lack of respect towards sb; **on manque d'air ici** there isn't enough air in here (**b**) *(faillir)* **m.** (**de**) **faire qch** to almost do sth (**c**) *(à la forme négative)* **ne pas m. de faire qch** to be sure to do sth; **je n'y manquerai pas** I certainly will

6 se manquer *vpr* to miss each other *(by not being in the same place at the same time)*

mansarde [mɑ̃sard] *nf* attic

mansardé, -e [mɑ̃sarde] *adj (chambre)* attic

mante [mɑ̃t] *nf* mantis; **m. religieuse** praying mantis

manteau, -x [mɑ̃to] *nm* coat; **m. de fourrure** fur coat; *Fig* **sous le m.** secretly

mantille [mɑ̃tij] *nf* mantilla

manucure [manykyr] **1** *nmf (personne)* manicurist **2** *nf (soin)* manicure

manuel¹, -elle [manɥɛl] **1** *adj (travail, activité)* manual; **être m.** *(personne)* to be good with one's hands **2** *nm,f (travailleur)* manual worker (**b**) *(personne adroite de ses mains)* **c'est un m.** he's good with his hands

manuel² *nm (d'utilisation, d'entretien)* manual, handbook; *(scolaire)* textbook

manuellement [manɥɛlmɑ̃] *adv* manually

manufacture [manyfaktyr] *nf (usine)* factory

manufacturer [manyfaktyre] *vt* to manufacture

manu militari [manymilitari] *adv* by force

manuscrit, -e [manyskri, -it] **1** *adj* handwritten **2** *nm* manuscript

manutention [manytɑ̃sjɔ̃] *nf* handling

manutentionnaire [manytɑ̃sjɔnɛr] *nmf* warehouseman, *f* warehousewoman

maous, -ousse [maus] *adj Fam* enormous

mappemonde [mapmɔ̃d] *nf* (**a**) *(carte)* map of the world *(in two hemispheres)* (**b**) *(globe)* globe

maquereau¹, -x [makro] *nm (poisson)* mackerel

maquereau², -x *nm très Fam (souteneur)* pimp

maquerelle [makrɛl] *nf très Fam* madam

maquette [makɛt] *nf* (**a**) *(de livre)* dummy (**b**) *(d'une construction architecturale)* (scale) model; *(de mise en page)* paste-up (**c**) *(jouet)* model; **m. d'avion/de bateau** model plane/boat

maquettiste [maketist] *nmf* (**a**) *(dans une entreprise)* model maker (**b**) *(graphiste)* graphic designer

maquignon [makiɲɔ̃] *nm* (**a**) *(marchand de chevaux)* horse dealer (**b**) *Fig (entremetteur malhonnête)* crooked dealer

maquillage [makijaʒ] *nm* (**a**) *(de visage) (action)* making up; *(produits)* make-up (**b**) *(de documents)* forging; *(de photos)* faking; *(de comptes)* falsification

maquiller [makije] **1** *vt* (**a**) *(personne, visage)* to make up (**b**) *(documents)* to forge; *(photos)* to fake; *(comptes)* to falsify **2 se maquiller** *vpr* to put one's make-up on

maquilleur, -euse [makijœr, -øz] *nm,f* make-up artist

maquis [maki] *nm* (**a**) *(végétation)* maquis (**b**) *Fig (d'une procédure, de l'administration)* jungle (**c**) *Hist* maquis *(Resistance movement in World War II)*; **prendre le m.** to take to the hills

maquisard [makizar] *nm Hist* member of the maquis, Resistance fighter *(in World War II)*

marabout [marabu] *nm* (**a**) *(sorcier)* witchdoctor (**b**) *(oiseau)* marabou

maracas [maraka] *nfpl* maracas

maraîcher, -ère [mareʃe, -ɛr] **1** *adj* **culture maraîchère** *Br* market gardening, *Am* truck farming; **produits maraîchers** *Br* market garden produce, *Am* truck **2** *nm,f Br* market gardener, *Am* truck farmer

marais [marɛ] *nm* marsh; **m. salant** saltern

marasme [marasm] *nm* (**a**) *(ralentissement)* stagnation (**b**) *(découragement)* depression

marathon [maratɔ̃] *nm* marathon

marathonien, -enne [maratɔnjɛ̃, -ɛn] *nm,f* marathon runner

marâtre [marɑtr] *nf* (**a**) *(belle-mère)* stepmother (**b**) *(mère cruelle)* cruel mother

maraude [marod] *nf* pilfering

marauder [marode] *vi* (**a**) *(voler)* to pilfer (**b**) *(taxi)* to cruise for fares (**c**) *(rôdeur)* to prowl around

maraudeur, -euse [marodœr, -øz] *nm,f* pilferer

marbre [marbr] *nm* (**a**) *(roche)* marble; **en ou de m.** marble; *Fig* **rester de m.** to remain impassive (**b**) *(statue)* marble (statue) (**c**) *(table de traçage)* faceplate (**d**) *(de presse)* bed

marbré, -e [marbre] *adj* (**a**) *(surface, couverture de livre)* marbled; *(pierre)* veined (**b**) *(peau)* blotchy (**c**) **gâteau m.** marble cake

marbrier [marbrije] *nm* monumental mason

marbrière [marbrijɛr] *nf* marble quarry

marbrure [marbryr] *nf* (**a**) *(sur un livre)* marbling (**b**) *(sur la peau)* mottling

marc [mar] *nm* (**a**) *(de raisins, d'olives)* marc (**b**) *(eau-de-vie)* marc (brandy) (**c**) *(de café)* grounds

marcassin [markasɛ̃] *nm* young wild boar

marchand, -e [marʃɑ̃, -ɑ̃d] **1** *adj (prix)* trade **2** *nm,f (dans un magasin) Br* shopkeeper, *Am* storekeeper; *(de vin)* merchant; *(de meubles, de chevaux)* dealer; **m. ambulant** street vendor; **m. forain** travelling stallholder; **m. de glaces** ice cream seller; **m. de journaux** *Br* newsagent, *Am* newsdealer; **m. de légumes** greengrocer; **m. de tableaux** art dealer; **m. de tapis** carpet dealer

marchandage [marʃɑ̃daʒ] *nm* haggling

marchander [marʃɑ̃de] **1** *vt* to haggle over **2** *vi* to haggle

marchandisage [marʃɑ̃dizaʒ] *nm* merchandizing

marchandise [marʃɑ̃diz] *nf* commodity; **marchandises** goods, merchandise

marche [marʃ] *nf* (**a**) *(d'escalier)* step, stair (**b**) *(action de marcher)* walking; *(promenade)* walk; *(allure)* pace; **faire une m.** to go for a walk; **à une heure de m.** one hour's walk away; **m. à pied** walking (**c**) *(défilé, manifestation)* march; **ouvrir la m.** to lead the way; **fermer la m.** to bring up the rear (**d**) *(morceau de musique)* march; **m. funèbre** funeral march (**e**) *(déplacement)* **être en m.** *(véhicule)* to be moving; *(mouvement, progrès)* to be on the march; **se mettre en m.** *(véhicule)* to move off; *(personne)* to set off *or* out; **dans le sens de la m.** *(en voyage)* facing forward; **dans le sens contraire de la m.** facing backwards; **m. avant/arrière** *(vitesse)* forward/reverse gear; **faire m. arrière** *(véhicule)* to reverse; *Fig* to backtrack (**f**) *(fonctionnement)* running, working; **mettre qch en m.** to start sth; **se mettre en m.** to start (**g**) *(des événements, de l'histoire)* course; *(du temps)* march; **m. à suivre** procedure

marché [marʃe] *nm* (**a**) *(accord)* deal, bargain; *(plus officiel)* contract; **m. conclu!** it's a deal!; **par-dessus le m.** into the bargain; **bon m.** cheap (**b**) *(lieu public de vente)* market; **faire son m.** to go shopping; **M. commun**

Common Market; **m. noir** black market; **m. aux puces** flea market; **M. unique (européen)** Single (European) Market (**c**) *(débouché économique)* market (**d**) *Fin* market; **m. des changes** foreign exchange market; **m. haussier/baissier** bull/bear market; **m. à terme** futures market

marchepied [marʃəpje] *nm* (**a**) *(de train)* step (**b**) *(escabeau)* steps (**c**) *Fig* stepping-stone

marcher [marʃe] *vi* (**a**) *(se déplacer à pied)* to walk; *(mettre le pied)* to step (**dans/sur** in/on); *aussi Fig* **m. sur les pieds de qn** to tread on sb's toes; *Fig* **m. droit** to keep on the straight and narrow (**b**) *(fonctionner)* (machine) to work, to run; *(plans)* to work; **faire m. qch** to work *or* operate sth; **comment ça marche?** how does it work?; *Fig* **les affaires marchent (bien)** business is doing well; **ça marche!** *(d'accord)* sure! (**c**) *(avancer)* to march (**vers/sur** towards/ on) (**d**) *Fam (croire sans réserve)* to fall for it; **faire m. qn** to pull sb's leg (**e**) *Fam (accepter)* to go along with it

marcheur, -euse [marʃœr, -øz] *nm,f* walker

mardi [mardi] *nm* Tuesday; **M. gras** Shrove Tuesday; *voir aussi* **samedi**

mare [mar] *nf* (**a**) *(étendue d'eau)* pond (**b**) *(grande quantité)* pool

marécage [mareka3] *nm* marsh, bog

marécageux, -euse [mareka3ø, -øz] *adj* (**a**) *(terrain)* marshy, boggy (**b**) *(plante)* marsh

maréchal, -aux [mareʃal, -o] *nm* **m. (de France)** *(officier général)* field marshal; *(d'un roi)* marshal; **m. des logis** sergeant

maréchal-ferrant [mareʃalferɑ̃] (*pl* **maréchaux-ferrants** [mareʃoferɑ̃]) *nm* blacksmith

marée [mare] *nf* (**a**) *(de la mer)* tide; **à m. haute/basse** at high/low tide; **à la m. montante/descendante** when the tide comes in/goes out; **m. noire** oil slick (**b**) *Fig (de personnes)* surging mass (**c**) *(fruits de la pêche)* fresh seafood

marelle [marɛl] *nf* hopscotch

marémoteur, -trice [maremɔtœr, -tris] *adj (énergie)* tidal; **usine marémotrice** tidal power station

mareyeur, -euse [marɛjœr, -øz] *nm,f* fish wholesaler

margarine [margarin] *nf* margarine

marge [mar3] *nf* (**a**) *(de page)* margin; **en m. de** on the fringes of; **vivre en m. (de la société)** to live on the fringes of society (**b**) *(liberté d'action)* leeway; **avoir de la m.** to have some leeway; *(temps)* to have time to spare; **m. d'erreur** margin of error; **m. de négociation/manœuvre** room for negotiation/manoeuvre; **m. de sécurité** safety margin (**c**) *(commerciale)* **m. (bénéficiaire)** profit margin

margelle [mar3ɛl] *nf (de puits)* coping, curb

marger [45] [mar3e] *vt (page)* to feed in; *Ordinat* to set the margins for

marginal, -e, -aux, -ales [mar3inal, -o] **1** *adj* (**a**) *(personne, mode de vie)* on the fringes of society (**b**) *(secondaire) (occupations, importance)* marginal
2 *nm,f* dropout

marginalisation [mar3inalizasjɔ̃] *nf* marginalization

marginaliser [mar3inalize] **1** *vt* to marginalize
2 se marginaliser *vpr* to become marginalized

marguerite [margərit] *nf* (**a**) *(fleur)* daisy (**b**) *(de machine à écrire)* daisy wheel

mari [mari] *nm* husband

mariage [marja3] *nm* (**a**) *(cérémonie)* wedding; *(union)* marriage; **m. d'amour** love match; **m. blanc** marriage in name only *(primarily in order to acquire nationality)*; **m. civil** ≃ civil wedding, *Br* registry office wedding; **m. de raison** marriage of convenience (**b**) *(de choses)* combination, marriage; *(de couleurs)* blend(ing)

Marianne [marjan] *nf* = young woman symbolizing the French Republic

marié, -e [marje] **1** *adj* married; **non m.** unmarried, single
2 *nm,f* groom, *f* bride; **les mariés** the bride and groom; **les jeunes mariés** the newly-weds

marier [66] [marje] **1** *vt* (**a**) *(sujet: prêtre)* to marry; *(sujet: père)* to marry off (**b**) *(qualités)* to combine; *(sociétés)* to merge; *(couleurs)* to blend; *(styles)* to harmonize
2 se marier *vpr* (**a**) *(personnes)* to get married, to marry; **se m. avec qn** to marry sb (**b**) *(couleurs)* to blend (**avec** with); *(styles)* to go together (**avec** with)

marieur, -euse [marjœr, -øz] *nm,f* *Fam* matchmaker

marihuana [marirwana], **marijuana** [mari3ɥana] *nf* marijuana

marin, -e [marɛ̃, -in] **1** *adj* (**a**) *(air, brise)* sea; *(plante, animal)* marine (**b**) *(carte)* sea; *(mille)* nautical
2 *nm* seaman, sailor; **m. pêcheur** (deep-sea) fisherman; **m. d'eau douce** landlubber

marina [marina] *nf* marina

marinade [marinad] *nf (mélange aromatique)* marinade; **m. de poissons/de gibier** marinated fish/game

marine [marin] **1** *nf* (**a**) *(flotte)* navy; **la m. de guerre** the navy; **la m. marchande** the merchant navy; **la M. nationale** the French navy (**b**) *(navigation)* seamanship (**c**) *(tableau)* seascape
2 *adj inv* navy (blue)
3 *nm (fusilier) Br* (Royal) Marine, *Am* marine

mariner [marine] **1** *vt* to marinate
2 *vi* (**a**) *(aliment)* to marinate; **faire m. qch** to marinate sth; **harengs marinés** pickled herrings (**b**) *Fam Fig (personne)* to hang around; **faire** *ou* **laisser m. qn** *(dans un lieu)* to keep sb hanging around; *(dans une situation)* to leave sb to stew

maringouin [marɛ̃gwɛ̃] *nm Can* mosquito

marinier [marinje] *nm Br* bargee, *Am* bargeman

marinière [marinjer] *nf* (sailor's) smock

mariole [marjɔl] *nm Fam* sly devil; **faire le m.** to try to be clever

marionnette [marjɔnɛt] *nf* puppet

marionnettiste [marjɔnetist] *nmf* puppeteer

marital, -e, -aux, -ales [marital, -o] *adj* marital

maritalement [maritalmɑ̃] *adv* **vivre m.** to cohabit

maritime [maritim] *adj* (**a**) *(navigation, plante, trafic)* maritime; *(ville)* seaside (**b**) *Can* **les Maritimes** the Maritimes

marivaudage [marivoda3] *nm Litt* light-hearted banter

marjolaine [mar3ɔlɛn] *nf* marjoram

mark [mark] *nm* (German) mark

marketing [marketiŋ] *nm* marketing

marmaille [marmaj] *nf Fam* brood, kids

marmelade [marməlad] *nf* compote; **m. (d'oranges)** (orange) marmalade; *Fig* **en m.** reduced to a pulp

marmite [marmit] *nf* (cooking) pot; *Fig* **faire bouillir la m.** to bring home the bacon

marmonner [marmɔne] *vt & vi* to mumble, to mutter

marmot [marmo] *nm Fam* kid

marmotte [marmɔt] *nf* marmot

marmotter [marmɔte] *vt* to mumble, to mutter

marner [marne] *vi Fam* to slog

Maroc [marɔk] *nm* **le M.** Morocco

marocain, -e [marɔkɛ̃, -ɛn] **1** *adj* Moroccan
2 *nm,f* **M.** Moroccan

maronite [marɔnit] *adj & nmf* Maronite

maroquin [marɔkɛ̃] *nm* morocco (leather)

maroquinerie [marɔkinri] *nf* (a) *(fabrication)* leather tanning (b) *(magasin)* leather goods *Br* shop *or Am* store (c) *(articles)* leather goods

maroquinier [marɔkinje] *nm* (a) *(fabricant)* leather worker (b) *(commerçant)* dealer in leather goods

marotte [marɔt] *nf (idée fixe)* craze

marquant, -e [markɑ̃, -ɑ̃t] *adj (incident, personne, journée)* remarkable; *(épisode)* significant

marque [mark] *nf* (a) *(signe, trace)* mark (b) *(de produits, d'appareils)* brand; *(de voiture)* make; **de m.** *(produits)* branded; *(vêtements)* designer; **m. déposée** registered trademark (c) *(preuve) (d'amitié)* token; *(de confiance)* sign (d) *(cachet)* stamp; **porter la m. du génie** to bear the stamp of genius (e) *Ordinat* marker; **m. d'insertion** insertion marker (f) **de m.** *(important)* distinguished, prominent (g) **marques** *(repères)* marks; **à vos marques! prêts? partez!** on your marks! get set! go!

marqué, -e [marke] *adj* (a) *(visage)* lined; **il est très m.** his face is very lined (b) *(différence, penchant)* marked

marque-page *(pl* **marque-pages)** [markpaʒ] *nm* bookmark

marquer [marke] **1** *vt* (a) *(faire un signe sur)* to mark (b) *(écrire)* to write (c) *(délimiter)* to mark (d) *(adversaire)* to mark; *(but, essai)* to score (e) *(indiquer)* to show (f) *(accentuer)* to mark; **m. le pas** to mark time; *Fig* **m. le coup** to mark the occasion (g) *(impressionner)* to make an impression on (h) *Ordinat* to mark
2 *vi (laisser une trace)* to leave a mark

marqueterie [markətri] *nf* marquetry

marqueur [markœr] *nm* (a) *(stylo)* (felt-tip) marker (b) *(biologique, génétique)* marker

marquis [marki] *nm* marquis

marquise [markiz] *nf* (a) *(auvent)* canopy (b) *(canapé)* (two-seater) sofa (c) *(personne)* marchioness

Marquises [markiz] *nfpl* **les (îles) M.** the Marquesas Islands

marraine [marɛn] *nf* (a) *(d'un enfant)* godmother (b) *(d'un bateau)* = woman who launches a new ship

Marrakech [marakeʃ] *n* Marrakech

marrant, -e [marɑ̃, -ɑ̃t] *adj Fam* funny

marre [mar] *adv Fam* **en avoir m. (de qn/qch)** to be fed up (with sb/sth); **en avoir m. de faire qch** to be fed up with doing sth

marrer [mare] **se marrer** *vpr Fam* to have a good laugh

marron¹ [marɔ̃] **1** *adj inv (couleur)* brown
2 *nm* (a) *(fruit)* chestnut; **marrons chauds** roast chestnuts; **marrons glacés** marrons glacés; **m. d'Inde** horse chestnut (b) *(couleur)* brown (c) *Fam (coup de poing)* thump

marron², -onne [marɔ̃, -ɔn] *adj (médecin, homme de loi)* quack

marronnier [marɔnje] *nm* horse chestnut (tree)

Mars [mars] *npr (dieu, planète)* Mars

mars [mars] *nm* March; *voir aussi* **janvier**

marseillais, -e [marsɛjɛ, -ɛz] **1** *adj* of Marseilles
2 *nmf* **M.** person from Marseilles
3 *nf* **la Marseillaise** the Marseillaise

Marseille [marsɛj] *n* Marseilles

marsouin [marswɛ̃] *nm* porpoise

marsupial, -e, -aux, -ales [marsypjal, -o] *adj & nm* marsupial

marteau, -x [marto] **1** *adj Fam* crazy
2 *nm* (a) *(outil)* hammer; **m. piqueur** pneumatic drill; *Fig* **être entre le m. et l'enclume** to be between the devil and the deep blue sea (b) *(de porte)* (door) knocker (c) *(de piano)* hammer

martel [martɛl] *nm* **se mettre m. en tête** to worry oneself sick

martèlement [martɛlmɑ̃] *nm* hammering

marteler [39] [martəle] *vt* (a) *(métal, pieu)* to hammer; **m. la table à coups de poing** to hammer on the table (b) *(mot, phrase)* to hammer out

martial, -e, -aux, -ales [marsjal, -o] *adj* martial

martien, -enne [marsjɛ̃, -ɛn] *adj & nmf* Martian

martinet¹ [martinɛ] *nm (fouet)* strap

martinet² *nm (oiseau)* swift

martingale [martɛ̃gal] *nf (sur un vêtement)* half belt

martiniquais, -e [martinikɛ, ɛz] **1** *adj* Martinican
2 *nmf* **M.** Martinican

Martinique [martinik] *nf* **la M.** Martinique

martin-pêcheur *(pl* **martins-pêcheurs)** [martɛ̃-pɛʃœr] *nm* kingfisher

martyr, -e [martir] **1** *adj (enfant)* battered; *(peuple)* martyred
2 *nm,f* martyr

martyre [martir] *nm* martyrdom

martyriser [martirize] *vt (maltraiter)* to batter; *(harceler)* to bully

marxisme [marksism] *nm* Marxism

marxiste [marksist] *adj & nmf* Marxist

mas [mɑ, mɑs] *nm (en Provence) (ferme)* farm; *(maison)* farmhouse

mascara [maskara] *nm* mascara

mascarade [maskarad] *nf* masquerade; *Fig* sham

mascotte [maskɔt] *nf* mascot

masculin, -e [maskylɛ̃, in] **1** *adj* (a) *(sexe, mode, métier)* male; *(trait de caractère, prénom)* masculine (b) *(nom, genre)* masculine (c) *(rime)* masculine
2 *nm* masculine; **au m.** in the masculine

masculinité [maskylinite] *nf* masculinity

maskinongé [maskinɔ̃ʒe] *nm Can* muskellunge

maso [mazo] *Fam* **1** *adj* masochistic
2 *nmf* masochist

masochisme [mazɔfism] *nm* masochism

masochiste [mazɔfist] **1** *adj* masochistic
2 *nmf* masochist

masquage [maskaʒ] *nm Ordinat* masking

masque [mask] *nm* (a) *(déguisement)* mask; **m. à gaz/oxygène** gas/oxygen mask; **m. de plongée** diving mask (b) *(apparence)* façade; **lever le m.** to remove one's mask (c) *(soin cosmétique)* mask; **(de beauté)** face mask *or* pack (d) *Ordinat* mask; **m. d'entrée, m. de saisie** input mask

masqué, -e [maske] *adj (personne)* masked

masquer [maske] *vt* to mask

massacrante [masakrɑ̃t] *adj f voir* **humeur**

massacre [masakr] *nm* (a) *(tuerie)* massacre (b) *Fig (travail mal fait)* mess; **faire un m.** *(travailler mal)* to make a complete mess; *(remporter un grand succès)* to be a runaway success

massacrer [masakre] *vt* (a) *(tuer, exterminer)* to massacre (b) *Fam (abîmer) (travail)* to make a mess of; *(mal interpréter) (morceau de musique, texte)* to murder

massage [masaʒ] *nm* massage; **faire un m. à qn** to give sb a massage

masse¹ [mas] *nf* (a) *(volume)* mass; **m. d'air** air mass; **taillé/sculpté dans la m.** carved/sculpted from the block; **tomber comme une m.** to fall in a heap (b) *(grande quantité)* mass; **de m.** *(culture, communication)* mass; **en m.** en masse; **une m. de** masses of; *Fam* **pas des masses** not much; *(nombre)* not many; **m. monétaire** money supply; *m.*

salariale wage bill (**c**) **les masses** *(le peuple)* the masses; **masses laborieuses** working masses (**d**) *Phys* mass (**e**) *Él Br* earth, *Am* ground; **mettre qch à la m.** *Br* to earth sth, *Am* to ground sth; *Fam Fig* **être à la m.** to be off one's head

masse² *nf (marteau)* sledgehammer

massepain [maspɛ̃] *nm* marzipan

masser¹ [mase] **1** *vt (rassembler)* to assemble; *(troupes)* to mass
2 se masser *vpr* to assemble

masser² **1** *vt (faire un massage à)* to massage; **se faire m.** to have a massage
2 se masser *vpr* to massage oneself; **se m. le pied** to massage one's foot

masseur, -euse [mascœr, -øz] *nm,f* masseur, *f* masseuse

massicot [masiko] *nm* guillotine

massif, -ive [masif, -iv] **1** *adj* (**a**) *(formes, meuble, porte)* massive; *(personne)* heavily built (**b**) *(argent, or, bois)* solid (**c**) *(dose)* massive
2 *nm* (**a**) *(de plantes, d'arbres)* clump; **m. de fleurs** flower bed (**b**) *(ensemble de montagnes)* massif; **le M. central** the Massif Central *(mountains in central France)*

massivement [masivmɑ̃] *adv (répondre, voter)* en masse

mass media [masmedja] *nmpl* mass media

massue [masy] **1** *adj inv (argument)* sledgehammer
2 *nf* club

mastectomie [mastɛktɔmi] *nf* mastectomy

mastic [mastik] *nm (pour fenêtres)* putty; *(pour bois)* mastic

mastication [mastikasjɔ̃] *nf* chewing

mastiquer¹ [mastike] *vt (mâcher)* to chew

mastiquer² *vt (fissures)* to fill (in); *(vitre)* to put putty round

mastoc [mastɔk] *adj inv Fam (personne)* hulking; *(construction)* clumsy

mastodonte [mastɔdɔ̃t] *nm* (**a**) *Fam (personne)* colossus; *(objet)* hulking great thing (**b**) *(animal)* mastodon

masturbation [mastyrbasjɔ̃] *nf* masturbation

masturber [mastyrbe] **1** *vt* to masturbate
2 se masturber *vpr* to masturbate

m'as-tu-vu [matyvy] *nmf inv Fam* show-off

masure [mazyr] *nf* hovel

mat¹, -e [mat] *adj (métal, couleur)* matt; *(teint)* darkish; *(son)* dull

mat² **1** *adj inv (aux échecs)* checkmated
2 *nm* checkmate

mât [mɑ] *nm* (**a**) *(d'un voilier)* mast (**b**) *(poteau)* pole; **m. de cocagne** greasy pole

matador [matadɔr] *nm* matador

match *(pl* **matchs** *ou* **matches)** [matʃ] *nm Br* match, *Am* game; **m. aller/retour** first/return leg; **un m. amical** a friendly; **m. nul** draw; **faire m. nul** to draw

matelas [matlɑ] *nm* mattress; **m. pneumatique** air bed

matelassé, -e [matlase] *adj (tissu, blouson)* quilted; *(enveloppe)* padded

matelot [matlo] *nm* sailor

mater¹ [mate] *vt (se rendre maître de) (personne)* to bring to heel; *(rébellion)* to put down

mater² *vt Fam (regarder)* to ogle

matérialisation [materjalizasjɔ̃] *nf* materialization

matérialiser [materjalize] **se matérialiser** *vpr* to materialize

matérialisme [materjalism] *nm* materialism

matérialiste [materjalist] **1** *adj* materialistic
2 *nmf* materialist

matériau, -x [materjo] *nm* (**a**) *(substance)* material (**b**) **matériaux** *(de construction)* material(s); *(documents)* material

matériel¹, -elle [materjɛl] *adj (confort, besoins, dégâts)* material; *(organisation, problème)* practical

matériel² *nm* (**a**) *(pour une activité, un sport)* equipment; **m. de bureau** office equipment; **m. pédagogique** teaching material; **m. agricole** farm equipment (**b**) *(d'une entreprise)* plant; **m. d'exploitation** working plant (**c**) *Ordinat* **m. (informatique)** (computer) hardware

matériellement [materjɛlmɑ̃] *adv* (**a**) *(sur le plan matériel)* materially (**b**) **c'est m. impossible** it's physically impossible

maternel, -elle [matɛrnɛl] *adj* (**a**) *(personne, attitude, gestes)* maternal (**b**) *(langue)* native

maternelle [matɛrnɛl] *nf* nursery (school), kindergarten

materner [matɛrne] *vt* to mother

maternisé, -e [matɛrnize] *adj* **lait m.** milk suitable for infants

maternité [matɛrnite] *nf* (**a**) *(fait d'être mère)* motherhood (**b**) *(hôpital)* maternity hospital (**c**) *(tableau)* Madonna and Child

mathématicien, -enne [matematisjɛ̃, -ɛn] *nm,f* mathematician

mathématique [matematik] **1** *adj* (**a**) *(science)* mathematical (**b**) *(esprit)* logical; *(rigueur)* mathematical
2 *nfpl* **les mathématiques** mathematics *(singulier)*

mathématiquement [matematikmɑ̃] *adv* mathematically

matheux, -euse [matø, -øz] *nm,f Fam* mathematician

maths [mat] *nfpl Fam Br* maths, *Am* math; **M. Sup/Spé** = first/second year of classes preparing students for entrance to science-oriented "grandes écoles"

matière [matjer] *nf* (**a**) *(substance)* material; **matières grasses** fat; **m. grise** grey matter; *Fam* **faire fonctionner sa m. grise** to exercise one's grey matter; **m. plastique** plastic; **matières premières** raw materials (**b**) *(sujet)* *(scolaire)* subject; *(pour en faire un film, un livre, une étude)* material; **il n'y a pas m. à rire** it's no laughing matter; **donner m. à qch** to give cause for sth; **en m. de** as regards (**c**) *(d'un corps physique)* matter

Matignon [matiɲɔ̃] *n* **(l'hôtel) M.** = French Prime Minister's offices

matin [matɛ̃] *nm* morning; **ce m.** this morning; **quatre heures du m.** four o'clock in the morning, 4 am; **le jeudi 2 au m.** on the morning of Thursday the 2nd; **faire qch le m.** to do sth in the morning; **être du m.** to be a morning person; **tous les mardis m.** every Tuesday morning; **de grand** *ou* **bon m.** early in the morning, in the early morning; **au petit m.** in the small *or* early hours; **du m. au soir** from morning till night

matinal, -e, -aux, -ales [matinal, -o] *adj* (**a**) *(heure)* early; *(excursion, activité)* morning (**b**) *(personne)* **être m.** to be an early riser

mâtiné, -e [matine] *adj* crossbred; **m. de** crossed with; *Fig* mixed with

matinée [matine] *nf* (**a**) *(matin)* morning; **dans la m.** in (the course of) the morning; **en fin de m.** towards the end of the morning (**b**) *(au théâtre, cinéma)* matinée

maton, -onne [matɔ̃, -ɔn] *nm,f Fam* hack, bull *(prison guard)*

matos [matos] *nm Fam* gear

matou [matu] *nm* tom (cat)

matraquage [matrakaʒ] *nm* (**a**) *(avec une matraque)* bludgeoning (**b**) *(insistance)* **m. publicitaire** hype

matraque [matrak] *nf* bludgeon; *(d'agent de police) Br* truncheon, *Am* nightstick

matraquer [matrake] *vt* (**a**) *(frapper)* to club (**b**) *Fig (harceler)* to bombard (**c**) *Fam (faire payer très cher)* to rip off, to fleece

matriarcal, -e, -aux, -ales [matrijarkal, -o] *adj* matriarchal

matrice [matris] *nf* (**a**) *(moule)* matrix, die; *(de disque)* matrix (**b**) *Math* matrix (**c**) *Ordinat* array; **m. d'aiguilles** dot matrix

matricide [matrisid] *nm* matricide

matriciel, -elle [matrisjɛl] *Ordinat* **1** *adj* **imprimante matricielle** dot matrix printer **2** *nf* **matricielle** dot matrix

matricule [matrikyl] **1** *nm (numéro)* number **2** *nf (registre)* register

matrimonial, -e, -aux, -ales [matrimɔnjal, -o] *adj* matrimonial

matrone [matron] *nf Péj* stout woman

mature [matyr] *adj* mature

mâture [matyr] *nf* masts

maturité [matyrite] *nf (de personne)* maturity; *(de fruit)* ripeness; **arriver** *ou* **venir à m.** *(fromage, vin)* to mature; *(fruit)* to ripen

maudire [modir] *vt* to curse

maudit, -e [modi, -it] *adj* (**a**) *(damné)* cursed (**b**) *(avant le nom) (insupportable)* damn(ed)

maugréer [24] [mogree] *vi* to grumble (**contre** about *or* at)

maure [mɔr] **1** *adj* Moorish **2** *nm* **M.** Moor

mauresque [mɔrɛsk] **1** *adj* Moorish **2** *nf* **M.** Moorish woman

Maurice [mɔris] *n* **l'île M.** Mauritius

mauricien, -enne [mɔrisjɛ̃, -ɛn] **1** *adj* Mauritian **2** *nmf* **M.** Mauritian

Mauritanie [mɔritani] *nf* **la M.** Mauritania

mauritanien, -enne [mɔritanjɛ̃, -ɛn] **1** *adj* Mauritanian **2** *nmf* **M.** Mauritanian

mausolée [mozole] *nm* mausoleum

maussade [mosad] *adj* (**a**) *(de mauvaise humeur)* sullen (**b**) *(temps, paysage)* gloomy

mauvais, -e [mɔvɛ, -ɛz] **1** *adj* (**a**) *(défectueux) (santé, vue, excuse)* poor (**b**) *(incompétent) (élève, professeur, mère)* bad (**en** at) (**c**) *(nuisible)* bad (**pour** for) (**d**) *(inapproprié) (clef, numéro, moment)* wrong (**e**) *(méchant) (personne)* bad, nasty; *(chien)* vicious (**f**) *(mer)* rough (**g**) *Fam* **je l'ai trouvée mauvaise** I didn't find it at all funny **2** *adv* (**a**) **sentir m.** to smell (bad) (**b**) **il fait m.** the weather's bad

mauve [mov] **1** *adj* mauve **2** *nm (couleur)* mauve

mauviette [movjɛt] *nf Fam* wimp

max [maks] *nm Fam* **un m. de gens** *(le plus possible)* as many people as possible; *(énormément)* loads of people

max. *(abrév* **maximum**) max

maxillaire [maksilɛr] *nm* jawbone, *Spéc* maxilla

maxima [maksima] *voir* **maximum**

maximal, -e, -aux, -ales [maksimal, -o] *adj* maximum

maxime [maksim] *nf* maxim

maximiser [maksimize] *vt* to maximize

maximum [maksimɔm] (*pl* **maximums** *ou* **maxima** [maksima]) **1** *adj* maximum **2** *nm* maximum; **faire le m. (pour faire qch)** to do one's

very best (to do sth); **au m.** at the most; *Fam* **un m.** *(beaucoup)* loads; *Fam* **un m. de gens** *(le plus possible)* as many people as possible; *(énormément)* loads of people

maya [maja] **1** *adj* Maya, Mayan **2** *nmf* **M.** Maya, Mayan **3** *nm (langue)* Mayan

mayonnaise [majɔnɛz] *nf* mayonnaise

mazout [mazut] *nm (fuel)* oil

mazouté, -e [mazute] *adj (plage)* oil-polluted; *(oiseau)* covered in oil

Mbps *Ordinat (abrév* **mégabits par seconde**) mbps

me [mə]

> **m'** is used before a word beginning with a vowel or h mute.

pron personnel (**a**) *(objet direct)* me; **me voici** here I am (**b**) *(objet indirect)* to me; **elle m'a serré la main** she shook my hand; **ils m'ont lancé des cailloux** they threw stones at me (**c**) *(dans les réfléchis)* myself; **je vais me doucher** I'm going to have a shower (**d**) *(dans les pronominaux)* **je me suis trompé** I made a mistake

mea culpa [meakylpa] *nm inv* **faire son m.** to own up

méandre [meɑ̃dr] *nm (de rivière)* meander; *(de route)* bend; *Fig* **méandres** *(d'un raisonnement)* intricacies

mec [mɛk] *nm Fam (homme quelconque)* guy; *(amoureux)* man

mécanicien, -enne [mekanisjɛ̃, -ɛn] *nm,f* (**a**) (garage *or* motor) mechanic (**b**) *(conducteur de train) Br* train driver, *Am* engineer

mécanique [mekanik] **1** *adj* mechanical **2** *nf* (**a**) *(science du mouvement)* mechanics *(singulier)* (**b**) *(des moteurs, des machines)* mechanical engineering (**c**) *(mécanisme)* mechanism

mécaniquement [mekanikmɑ̃] *adv* mechanically

mécanisation [mekanizasjɔ̃] *nf* mechanization

mécanisme [mekanism] *nm* (**a**) *(d'une machine, d'une montre, d'un moteur)* mechanism (**b**) *(de la pensée, de la parole)* mechanics

mécénat [mesena] *nm* sponsorship; **m. d'entreprise** corporate sponsorship

mécène [mesɛn] *nm* sponsor

méchamment [meʃamɑ̃] *adv* (**a**) *(avec méchanceté)* nastily (**b**) *Fam (en intensif)* être m. déçu/embêté to be terribly disappointed/annoyed

méchanceté [meʃɑ̃te] *nf* (**a**) *(d'une personne, d'une remarque)* nastiness; *(d'un enfant)* naughtiness (**b**) *(action)* nasty action; *(parole)* nasty remark

méchant, -e [meʃɑ̃, -ɑ̃t] **1** *adj* (**a**) *(personne, remarque)* nasty; *(enfant)* naughty; *(animal)* vicious; **attention chien m.** *(sur panneau)* beware of the dog (**b**) *(désagréable) (affaire)* unpleasant; *(blessure, grippe)* nasty; *(humeur)* foul **2** *nm,f Fam* baddie, baddy

mèche¹ [mɛʃ] *nf* (**a**) *(de bougie, de lampe)* wick; *(de charge explosive)* fuse (**b**) *(de perceuse)* bit (**c**) *(de cheveux)* strand; *(boucle)* lock; **se faire des mèches** to get highlights (in one's hair)

mèche² *nf* être de m. avec qn to be in cahoots with sb

méchoui [meʃwi] *nm* spit-roasted lamb

méconnaissable [mekɔnɛsabl] *adj* unrecognizable

méconnaître [20] [mekɔnɛtr] *vt* (**a**) *(faits)* to fail to take account of (**b**) *(talent, artiste)* to fail to recognize

méconnu, -e [mekɔny] *adj (talent, artiste)* unrecognized

mécontent, -e [mekɔ̃tɑ̃, -ɑ̃t] **1** *adj (insatisfait)* displeased (**de** with); *(contrarié)* annoyed **2** *nm,f* grumbler; *(électeur)* malcontent

mécontentement [mekɔ̃tɑ̃tmɑ̃] *nm (insatisfaction)* displeasure; *(contrariété)* annoyance

mécontenter [mekɔ̃tɑ̃te] *vt (ne pas satisfaire)* to displease; *(contrarier)* to annoy

Mecque [mɛk] *n voir* **La Mecque**

médaille [medaj] *nf* **(a)** *(prix, décoration)* medal; **la m. d'or/d'argent/de bronze** the gold/silver/bronze medal **(b)** *(bijou) (avec le nom)* pendant *(with name engraved on it)*; *(à l'effigie d'un saint)* medal **(c)** *(de chat, de chien)* identity disc

médaillé, -e [medaje] **1** *adj (sportif)* holding a medal; *(soldat)* decorated
2 *nm,f (sportif)* medallist; *(soldat)* medal-holder

médaillon [medajɔ̃] *nm* **(a)** *(bijou)* locket **(b)** *(de poisson, de viande)* medallion

médecin [medsɛ̃] *nm* doctor; **m. généraliste** *Br* general practitioner, GP, *Am* family practitioner; **m. légiste** *Br* forensic scientist, *Am* medical examiner; **m. traitant** consulting physician; **m. du travail** = doctor who carries out the annual medical examination, required by law, of a company's employees

médecine [medsin] *nf* medicine; **exercer la m.** to practise medicine; **m. douce** *ou* **parallèle** alternative medicine; **m. générale** general medicine; **m. du travail** industrial medicine

média [medja] *nm* medium; **les médias** the media

médian, -e [medjɑ̃, -an] **1** *adj* median
2 *nf* **médiane** median

médiateur, -trice [medjatœr, -tris] **1** *adj* mediating
2 *nm,f* mediator
3 *nm* **le M. (de la République)** ≃ Ombudsman, Parliamentary Commissioner for Administration

médiathèque [medjatɛk] *nf* media library

médiation [medjasjɔ̃] *nf* mediation

médiatique [medjatik] *adj* media

médiatisation [medjatizasjɔ̃] *nf* media coverage

médiatiser [medjatize] *vt* to give media coverage to

médiator [medjatɔr] *nm Mus* plectrum

médiatrice [medjatris] *nf* median

médical, -e, -aux, -ales [medikal, -o] *adj* medical

médicalisé, -e [medikalize] *adj* **logement m.** nursing home

médicaliser [medikalize] *vt* **(a)** *(région, pays, population)* to make medical care available to **(b)** *(grossesse)* to treat as a medical matter

médicament [medikamɑ̃] *nm* medicine; **m. de confort** = medication prescribed to relieve pain and symptoms rather than as a cure for a particular illness

médicinal, -e, -aux, -ales [medisinal, -o] *adj* medicinal

médico-légal, -e *(mpl* **médico-légaux,** *fpl* **médico-légales)** [medikolegal, -o] *adj* forensic

médico-social, -e *(mpl* **médico-sociaux,** *fpl* **médico-sociales)** [medikosɔsjal, -o] *adj* **centre m.** health centre

médiéval, -e, -aux, -ales [medjeval, -o] *adj* medieval

médiocre [medjɔkr] *adj* mediocre

médiocrement [medjɔkrəmɑ̃] *adv* indifferently

médiocrité [medjɔkrite] *nf* mediocrity

médire [27b] [medir] **médire de** *vt ind* to speak ill of

médisance [medizɑ̃s] *nf* **(a)** *(action)* scandalmongering, gossiping **(b)** *(propos)* piece of scandal *or* gossip; **médisances** scandal, gossip

médisant, -e [medizɑ̃, -ɑ̃t] *adj (paroles)* slanderous; *(personne)* scandalmongering

méditation [meditasjɔ̃] *nf* meditation

méditer [medite] **1** *vt* **(a)** *(considérer par une profonde réflexion)* to contemplate **(b)** *(préparer)* to mull over
2 *vi* to meditate
3 **méditer sur** *vt ind* to meditate on

Méditerranée [mediterane] *nf* **la (mer) M.** the Mediterranean (Sea)

méditerranéen, -enne [mediteraneɛ̃, -ɛn] **1** *adj* Mediterranean
2 *nm,f* **M.** person from a Mediterranean country

médium [medjɔm] *nmf (voyant)* medium

médius [medjys] *nm* middle finger

méduse [medyz] *nf* jellyfish

méduser [medyze] *vt* to dumbfound

meeting [mitiŋ] *nm* meeting; **m. aérien** air show

méfait [mefɛ] *nm* misdemeanour; **les méfaits du tabac** the damage caused by smoking

méfiance [mefjɑ̃s] *nf (manque de confiance)* distrust; *(suspicion)* mistrust, suspicion

méfiant, -e [mefjɑ̃, -ɑ̃t] *adj (n'ayant pas confiance)* distrustful; *(suspicieux)* suspicious **(à l'égard de** *ou* **avec of**)

méfier [66] [mefje] **se méfier** *vpr* to be careful; **se m. de qn** not to trust sb; **se m. de qch** to watch out for sth

méga¹ [mega] *nm Ordinat* megabyte, meg

méga² *adj inv Fam* mega

mégalo [megalo] *adj & nmf Fam* megalomaniac

mégalomane [megaloman] *adj & nmf* megalomaniac

mégalomanie [megalomani] *nf* megalomania

mégalopole [megalopol] *nf* megalopolis

méga-octet *(pl* **méga-octets)** [megaɔktɛ] *nm Ordinat* megabyte

mégaphone [megafɔn] *nm Br* megaphone, *Am* bullhorn

mégarde [megard] **par mégarde** *adv* inadvertently, accidentally

mégère [meʒɛr] *nf (femme)* shrew

mégot [mego] *nm* cigarette butt *or* end

mégoter [megote] *vi Fam* to skimp **(sur** on)

meilleur, -e [mɛjœr] **1** *adj* **(a)** *(comparatif de* **bon)** better **(que** than) **(b)** *(superlatif de* **bon)** **le m. élève** *(de la classe)* the best pupil; *(parmi deux élèves)* the better pupil
2 *nm,f (personne)* **le m.** *(de tous)* the best; *(des deux)* the better; *Fam* **alors ça, c'est la meilleure!** that's just great!
3 *nm (ce qu'il y a de mieux)* **le m.** the best; **pour le m. et pour le pire** for better and for worse
4 *adv* **il fait m.** it's warmer

méjuger [45] [meʒyʒe] **1** *vt Litt (mal juger)* to misjudge; *(sous-estimer)* to underestimate
2 **méjuger de** *vt ind (mal juger)* to misjudge; *(sous-estimer)* to underestimate

mélancolie [melɑ̃kɔli] *nf* melancholy

mélancolique [melɑ̃kɔlik] *adj* melancholy

Mélanésie [melanezi] *nf* **la M.** Melanesia

mélanésien, -enne [melanezjɛ̃, -ɛn] **1** *adj* Melanesian
2 *nm,f* **M.** Melanesian
3 *nm (langue)* Melanesian

mélange [melɑ̃ʒ] *nm* **(a)** *(action)* mixing **(b)** *(résultat)* mixture; **je ne fais jamais de mélanges** I never mix my drinks

mélanger [45] [melɑ̃ʒe] **1** *vt* **(a)** *(mettre ensemble)* to mix **(b)** *(confondre, déranger)* to mix up; **je mélange tout en espagnol** I get everything in Spanish mixed up **(c)** *(cartes)* to shuffle
2 **se mélanger** *vpr* **(a)** *(s'incorporer)* to mix **(b)** *(se confondre)* to get mixed up **(c)** *Fam* **se m. les pédales** *ou* **les pinceaux** to get into a muddle

mélangeur [melãʒœr] *nm* **(robinet) m.** *Br* mixer tap, *Am* mixing faucet

mélanome [melanom] *nm Méd* melanoma

mêlant [mɛlã] *adj m Can* **c'est pas m.** there's no doubt about it

mélasse [melas] *nf Br* (black) treacle, *Am* molasses *(singulier)*; *Fam* **être dans la m.** to be in a mess

Melba [mɛlba] *adj inv* **pêche M.** peach Melba

mêlé, -e [mele] *adj* mixed **(de** with)

mêlée [mele] *nf* **(a)** *(conflit)* fray, mêlée **(b)** *(au rugby)* scrum, scrummage

mêler [mele] **1** *vt* **(a)** *(mettre ensemble)* to mix **(à** ou **avec** with) **(b)** *(impliquer)* **m. qn à qch** *(affaire, conversation)* to involve sb in sth

2 se mêler *vpr* **(a)** *(substances)* to combine **(b)** *(se joindre)* **se m. à qch** *(foule)* to mingle with sth; *(cortège)* to join sth; *(conversation)* to join in sth **(c)** *(s'occuper)* **se m. de qch** to get involved in sth; **mêle-toi de tes affaires!** mind your own business!

mélèze [melɛz] *nm* larch (tree)

méli-mélo *(pl* **mélis-mélos)** [melimelo] *nm Fam* jumble

mélo [melo] *Fam* **1** *adj* melodramatic

2 *nm* melodrama

mélodie [melɔdi] *nf* **(a)** *(composition musicale)* melody, tune **(b)** *(de vers, d'une langue)* melodiousness, tunefulness

mélodieusement [melɔdjøzmã] *adv* melodiously, tunefully

mélodieux, -euse [melɔdjø, -øz] *adj* melodious, tuneful

mélodique [melɔdik] *adj* melodic

mélodiste [melɔdist] *nmf* melody writer

mélodrame [melɔdram] *nm* melodrama

mélomane [melɔman] **1** *adj* music-loving

2 *nmf* music lover

melon [məlɔ̃] *nm* **(a)** *(fruit)* melon **(b)** *(chapeau) Br* bowler (hat), *Am* derby

membrane [mãbran] *nf* membrane

membre [mãbr] **1** *adj (État, pays)* member

2 *nm* **(a)** *(partie du corps)* limb; **m. supérieur/inférieur** upper/lower limb; **m. viril** male member **(b)** *(d'une association, d'un groupe)* member

mémé [meme] *nf (grand-mère)* gran(ny), grandma; *Fam (vieille femme)* old dear

même [mɛm] **1** *adj indéfini* **(a)** *(avant le nom) (identique)* same; **j'ai la m. voiture que toi** I have the same car as you (do)

(b) *(après le nom, pour insister)* **je l'ai fait le jour m.** I did it that (very) same day; **c'est cela m.** that's it exactly; **c'est la gentillesse m.** she's kindness itself *or* personified

2 *pron indéfini* **le/la m.** the same (one); **j'ai les mêmes que lui** I have the same (ones) as him; **cela revient au m.** it comes *or* amounts to the same thing

3 *adv* **(a)** *(pour insister)* even; **il n'est m. pas beau** he's not even good-looking; **m. moi, je le sais!** even I know that!; **elle habite ici m.** she lives in this very place; **aujourd'hui m.** this very day; **je pense m. qu'il sera d'accord** I think he'll actually agree

(b) **être à m. de faire qch** to be able *or* in a position to do sth; **dormir à m. le sol** to sleep on the bare ground; **porter un pull-over à m. la peau** to wear a jumper next to one's bare skin; **de m.** likewise; **Joyeux Noël – vous de m.** Merry Christmas – same to you; **il en est de m. des autres** the same goes for the others; **faire de m.** to follow suit; **de m. que** just like sb; **de m. que** just like sth; *(aussi bien que qch)* as well as sth; **m. si je l'avais, je ne te le donnerais pas** even if I had it, I wouldn't give it to you; **tout**

de m., *Fam* **quand m.** all the same; *Fam* **enfin, quand m.!** honestly!; *Fam* **m. que je te l'avais déjà dit!** but I already TOLD you!

mémento [memɛ̃to] *nm* **(a)** *(pour réviser)* revision notes; **m. de chimie** chemistry revision notes **(b)** *(carnet)* diary

mémère [memɛr] *nf Fam Péj* **une grosse m.** a fat old bag

mémo [memo] *nm* memo

mémoire[1] [mɛmwar] *nf* **(a)** *(faculté)* memory; **avoir de la m.** to have a good memory; **avoir la m. des noms/dates** to have a good memory for names/dates; **avoir la m. courte** to have a short memory; **se rafraîchir la m.** to refresh one's memory; **à la m. de qn** *(monument)* in memory of sb; **de m.** *(citer)* from memory; **de m. d'homme** within living memory; **pour m.** for the record; **si j'ai bonne m.** if I remember correctly; **avoir une m. d'éléphant** to have a memory like an elephant; **la m. collective** collective memory

(b) *Ordinat* memory; **mettre un dossier en m.** to write a file to memory; **carte d'extension de m.** memory expansion card; **m. cache** cache memory; **m. centrale** main memory; **m. à disque** disk memory, RAM disc; **m. etendue** extended memory; **m. expansee** expanded memory; **m. haute** high memory; **m. de masse** mass storage; **m. morte** read only memory; **m. non effaçable** non-erasable memory; **m. paginée** expanded memory; **m. permanente** permanent memory; **m. tampon** buffer (store *or* memory); **m. vidéo** video memory; **m. vive** random access memory, RAM; **m. vive dynamique** DRAM, dynamic random access memory; **m. vive statique** static RAM, static random access memory

mémoire[2] *nm* **(a)** *(thèse)* thesis, dissertation **(b)** *(rapport)* report **(c) Mémoires** *(chronique)* memoirs

mémorable [memɔrabl] *adj* memorable

mémorandum [memɔrãdɔm] *nm* **(a)** *(note)* memorandum **(b)** *(carnet)* notebook

mémorial, -aux [memɔrjal, -o] *nm (monument)* memorial

mémoriser [memɔrize] *vt* to memorize

menaçant, -e [mənasã, -ãt] *adj* threatening, menacing

menace [mənas] *nf* threat **(de** of); **menaces de mort** death threats

menacer [16] [mənase] **1** *vt* to threaten **(de** with); **m. qn du poing** to shake one's fist at sb; **m. de faire qch** to threaten to do sth

2 *vi (tempête, orage, révolution)* to be brewing; **la pluie menace** it's threatening to rain

ménage [menaʒ] *nm* **(a)** *(nettoyage)* **faire le m.** *(à la maison)* to do the housework; *Fig* to have a shake-up; **faire des ménages** to go out cleaning **(b)** *(couple)* couple; **se mettre en m.** to move in together; **se mettre en m. avec qn** to move in with sb); **faire bon/mauvais m. (avec qn)** to get on well/badly with sb); **m. à trois** ménage à trois **(c)** *Écon* household

ménagement [menaʒmã] *nm* care, caution; *(tact)* consideration; **sans m.** *(annoncer)* bluntly

ménager[1], **-ère** [menaʒe, -ɛr] **1** *adj (équipement, appareils)* household

2 *nf* **ménagère** *(femme)* housewife

ménager[2] [45] [menaʒe] **1** *vt* **(a)** *(utiliser avec parcimonie) (argent)* to use sparingly; *(forces)* to conserve, to save; *(santé)* to take care of; **ne pas m. sa peine** to put in a lot of effort **(b)** *(traiter avec soin)* to treat carefully; *Fig* **m. la chèvre et le chou** to keep everyone happy **(c)** *(arranger) (entrevue, réunion)* to arrange, to organize; *(sortie)* to provide; *(réconciliation)* to bring about

2 se ménager *vpr* **(a)** *(prendre soin de soi)* to take care of oneself, to look after oneself **(b)** *(se réserver)* to set aside

ménagerie [menaʒri] *nf* menagerie
mendiant, -e [mɑ̃djɑ̃, -ɑ̃t] **1** *adj (moine, ordre)* mendicant
2 *nm,f* beggar
mendicité [mɑ̃disite] *nf* begging
mendier [66] [mɑ̃dje] **1** *vt* to beg for
2 *vi* to beg
mener [46] [məne] **1** *vt* (**a**) *(accompagner)* to take (**à** to) (**b**) *(cortège, course)* to lead; **m. qch à bien** to bring sth to a successful conclusion; *Fig* **m. la danse** to call the tune (**c**) *(vie)* to lead; **m. la vie dure à qn** to give sb a hard time (**d**) *(débat, enquête)* to lead (**e**) *(contrôler) (personne)* **m. qn à la baguette** to have sb under one's thumb; **m. qn par le bout du nez** to lead sb by the nose
2 *vi* (**a**) *(dans un match, une compétition)* to lead; **m. par 2 buts à 1** to lead by 2 goals to 1 (**b**) **m. à un lieu** to lead to a place; *Fig* **cela ne mène à rien** this is getting us nowhere (**c**) *Fam* **elle n'en menait pas large** her heart was in her mouth
meneur, -euse [mənœr, -øz] **1** *nm,f (de parti politique)* leader; *(agitateur)* ringleader; **m. d'hommes** born leader; **m. de jeu** question master, quiz master; *Sp* play maker
2 *nf* **meneuse de revue** principal chorus girl
menhir [menir] *nm* menhir
méninges [menɛ̃ʒ] *nfpl Fam* brains
méningite [menɛ̃ʒit] *nf* meningitis; **avoir une m.** to have meningitis
ménisque [menisk] *nm* meniscus
ménopause [menɔpoz] *nf* menopause
menotte [mənɔt] *nf* (**a**) *Fam (petite main)* little hand (**b**) **menottes** *(bracelets métalliques)* handcuffs; **mettre** *ou* **passer les menottes à qn** to handcuff sb, to put handcuffs on sb
mensonge [mɑ̃sɔ̃ʒ] *nm* (**a**) *(propos)* lie; **petit m., pieux m.** white lie (**b**) *(acte)* lying
mensonger, -ère [mɑ̃sɔ̃ʒe, -ɛr] *adj (propos)* untrue; *(publicité)* misleading
menstruation [mɑ̃stryasjɔ̃] *nf* menstruation
menstruel, -elle [mɑ̃stryɛl] *adj* menstrual
mensualiser [mɑ̃syalize] *vt* to pay monthly; **être mensualisé** *(pour les impôts)* = to pay one's income tax in advance monthly instalments, the amount paid being an estimation based on previous years
mensualité [mɑ̃syalite] *nf* monthly payment
mensuel, -elle [mɑ̃syɛl] **1** *adj* monthly
2 *nm (publication)* monthly (magazine)
mensuellement [mɑ̃syɛlmɑ̃] *adv* monthly, every month
mensuration [mɑ̃syrasjɔ̃] *nf* (**a**) *(action)* measurement, measuring (**b**) **mensurations** *(dimensions)* measurements
mental, -e, -aux, -ales [mɑ̃tal, -o] **1** *adj* mental
2 *nm* mental attitude
mentalement [mɑ̃talmɑ̃] *adv* mentally
mentalité [mɑ̃talite] *nf* mentality
menteur, -euse [mɑ̃tœr, -øz] **1** *adj (personne)* untruthful, lying
2 *nm,f* liar
menthe [mɑ̃t] *nf (plante)* mint; **m. à l'eau** peppermint cordial
menthol [mɑ̃tɔl] *nm* menthol
mentholé, -e [mɑ̃tɔle] *adj* menthol, mentholated
mention [mɑ̃sjɔ̃] *nf* (**a**) *(fait de citer)* mention; **faire de qn/qch** to mention sb/sth (**b**) **rayer la m. inutile** *(sur formulaire)* delete where applicable (**c**) *(à un examen)* **m. passable** ≃ C; **m. assez bien** ≃ B; **m. bien/très bien** ≃ A

mentionner [mɑ̃sjɔne] *vt* to mention
mentir [64b] [mɑ̃tir] *vi* to lie (**à** to); **sans m.** honestly
menton [mɑ̃tɔ̃] *nm* chin; **m. en galoche** jutting-out chin; **m. fuyant** receding chin; **double m.** double chin
mentor [mɑ̃tɔr] *nm* mentor
menu¹, -e [məny] **1** *adj* (**a**) *(détail, monnaie)* small (**b**) *(taille)* slim; *(personne)* petite
2 *adv* small, fine
menu² *nm* (**a**) *(au restaurant)* set menu, fixed-price menu (**b**) *Ordinat* menu; **contrôlé par m.** menu-driven; **m. d'aide** help menu; **m. déroulant** pull-down menu; **m. fichier** file menu; **m. primaire/secondaire/principal** primary/ secondary/main menu
menuet [mənɥɛ] *nm* minuet
menuiserie [mənɥizri] *nf* (**a**) *(atelier)* (joiner's) workshop (**b**) *(travail du bois, résultat)* joinery, woodwork
menuisier [mənɥizje] *nm* joiner, carpenter
méprendre [58] [meprɑ̃dr] **se méprendre** *vpr* to be mistaken (**sur** about); **elle te ressemble à s'y m.** she looks exactly like you
mépris¹, -e *voir* **méprendre**
mépris² [mepri] *nm* contempt, scorn; **avec m.** scornfully, contemptuously; **avoir du m. pour qn** to despise sb; **au m. de qch** regardless of sth
méprisable [meprizabl] *adj* contemptible, despicable
méprisant, -e [meprizɑ̃, -ɑ̃t] *adj* scornful, contemptuous
méprise [mepriz] *nf* mistake
mépriser [meprize] *vt* (**a**) *(dédaigner) (personne, argent)* to despise (**b**) *(ignorer) (conseil, offre, danger)* to disregard
mer [mɛr] *nf* (**a**) *(étendue d'eau)* sea; **en haute** *ou* **pleine m.** (out) at sea; **au bord de la m.** at the seaside; **aller à la m.** to go to the seaside; **prendre la m.** to set sail, to put (out) to sea; *Fam* **ce n'est pas la m. à boire** it's no big deal; **une m. d'huile** a sea as calm as a millpond; **la m. Adriatique** the Adriatic Sea; **la m. d'Aral** the Aral Sea; **la m. Caspienne** the Caspian Sea; **la m. de Chine** the China Sea; **la m. de Corail** the Coral Sea; **la m. Égée** the Aegean Sea; **la m. d'Irlande** the Irish Sea; **la m. Morte** the Dead Sea; **la m. Noire** the Black Sea; **la m. du Nord** the North Sea; **la m. Rouge** the Red Sea; **la m. des Sargasses** the Sargasso Sea (**b**) *(marée)* tide
mercantile [mɛrkɑ̃til] *adj* mercenary
mercatique [mɛrkatik] *nf* marketing
mercenaire [mɛrsənɛr] *adj & nm* mercenary
mercerie [mɛrsəri] *nf* (**a**) *(magasin)* *Br* haberdasher's (shop), *Am* notions store (**b**) *(articles)* *Br* haberdashery, *Am* notions
merchandising [mɛrʃɑ̃dajziŋ] *nm* merchandizing
merci [mɛrsi] **1** *exclam* thank you, thanks (**de** *ou* **pour** for); **(non) m.** no thank you, no thanks; **dire m. (à qn)** to say thank you *or* thanks (to sb); **m. bien, m. beaucoup** thank you *or* thanks very much
2 *nm* thank you
3 *nf* **être à la m. de qn/qch** to be at the mercy of sb/sth; **sans m.** merciless
mercier, -ère [mɛrsje, -ɛr] *nm,f Br* haberdasher, *Am* notions dealer
mercredi [mɛrkrədi] *nm* Wednesday; **le m. des Cendres** Ash Wednesday; *voir aussi* **samedi**
Mercure [mɛrkyr] *npr (dieu, planète)* Mercury
mercure [mɛrkyr] *nm* mercury
Mercurochrome® [mɛrkyrɔkrom] *nm* Mercurochrome®
merde [mɛrd] *Vulg* **1** *nf* shit; *Fig* **être dans la m.** to be in

the shit; **ne pas se prendre pour de la m.** to think the sun shines out of one's arse; **c'est de la m.** *(c'est de la mauvaise qualité)* it's shit; **de m.** *(voiture, idée)* shitty **2** *exclam* shit!; *Fig* **dire m. à qn** *(l'envoyer au diable)* to tell sb to bugger off; **je te dis m.!** *(bonne chance)* break a leg!; **m. alors!** oh shit!

merder [mɛrde] *vi très Fam (ne pas fonctionner) (projet)* to go down the pan; **ça merde entre eux** things between them are really screwed up; **j'ai merdé à l'examen** I really screwed up in the exam

merdeux, -euse [mɛrdø, -øz] *très Fam* **1** *adj* **se sentir m.** to feel shitty **2** *nm,f (enfant)* **un petit m.** a little shit

merdier [mɛrdje] *nm Vulg* **être dans le m.** to be in the shit

merdique [mɛrdik] *adj très Fam* shitty

mère [mɛr] **1** *adj voir* **maison 2** *nf* **(a)** *(parent)* mother; **elle est m. de trois enfants** she is the mother of three children; **m. célibataire** single mother; **être m. de famille** to be a wife and mother; **m. nourricière** foster mother; **m. patrie** mother country; **motherland; m. porteuse** surrogate mother; **m. poule** mother hen **(b)** *Fam (femme)* **la m. Duval** old Mrs Duval

merguez [mɛrgɛz] *nf* merguez *(spicy North African sausage)*

méridien, -enne [meridjɛ̃, -ɛn] **1** *adj (ligne)* meridian, meridional **2** *nm Géog* meridian **3** *nf* **méridienne** *(canapé)* day bed

méridional, -e, -aux, -ales [meridjɔnal, -o] **1** *adj (du Sud)* southern; *(du sud de la France)* from the South of France **2** *nm,f (du Sud)* southerner; *(du sud de la France)* person from the South of France

meringue [mərɛ̃g] *nf* meringue

mérinos [merinos] *nm* merino

merisier [mərizje] *nm (arbre)* wild cherry (tree); *(bois)* cherry (wood)

méritant, -e [meritɑ̃, -ɑ̃t] *adj* deserving

mérite [merit] *nm* merit; *(honneur)* credit; **avoir du m.** (à **faire qch)** to deserve credit (for doing sth); **au moins, son livre a le m. de la clarté** at least her book has the merit of being clearly written; **tout le m. lui revient** he deserves all the credit

mériter [merite] *vt* **(a)** *(après une action)* to deserve; **m. d'être puni/récompensé** to deserve to be punished/ rewarded; **elle mérite qu'on le lui dise** she deserves to be told **(b)** *(demander)* to be worth; **m. réflexion** to be worth thinking about; **ce livre mérite d'être lu** this book is worth reading

méritoire [meritwar] *adj* commendable, praiseworthy

merlan [mɛrlɑ̃] *nm* **(a)** *(poisson)* whiting **(b)** *très Fam (coiffeur)* hairdresser

merle [mɛrl] *nm* blackbird

merlu [mɛrly] *nm* hake

mérou [meru] *nm* grouper

mérovingien, -enne [merɔvɛ̃ʒjɛ̃, -ɛn] **1** *adj* Merovingian **2** *nmpl* **les Mérovingiens** the Merovingians

merveille [mɛrvɛj] *nf* **(a)** *(chose remarquable)* marvel, wonder; **à m.** wonderfully (well); **se porter à m.** to be in the best of health; *Fig* **faire des merveilles** to work wonders; **les Sept Merveilles du monde** the Seven Wonders of the World **(b)** *(gâteau)* = sweet fritter

merveilleusement [mɛrvɛjøzmɑ̃] *adv* marvellously, wonderfully

merveilleux, -euse [mɛrvɛjø, -øz] **1** *adj* marvellous, wonderful **2** *nm* **le m.** the supernatural

mes [me] *voir* **mon**

mésalliance [mezaljɑ̃s] *nf* unsuitable marriage; **faire une m.** to marry beneath oneself

mésallier [66] [mezalje] **se mésallier** *vpr* to marry beneath oneself

mésange [mezɑ̃ʒ] *nf* tit; **m. bleue** blue tit; **m. charbonnière** coal tit

mésaventure [mezavɑ̃tyr] *nf* misadventure

mesdames [medam] *nfpl voir* **madame**

mésentente [mezɑ̃tɑ̃t] *nf* disagreement

mésestimer [mezɛstime] *vt* to underestimate

mésothérapie [mezɔterapi] *nf* mesotherapy

mesquin, -e [mɛskɛ̃, -in] *adj* mean, petty

mesquinement [mɛskinmɑ̃] *adv* meanly

mesquinerie [mɛskinri] *nf* **(a)** *(d'un caractère, d'un procédé)* meanness, pettiness **(b)** *(action)* mean or petty thing (to do)

mess [mɛs] *nm* mess

message [mesaʒ] *nm* message; *Ordinat* **m. d'accueil** welcome message; *Ordinat* **m. d'alerte** warning message, alert box; *Ordinat* **m. d'erreur** error message; *Ordinat* **m. publicitaire** advertisement; **m. d'invite** *(du système)* prompt; **m. publicitaire** advertisement

messager, -ère [mesaʒe, -ɛr] *nm,f* messenger

messagerie [mesaʒri] *nf* **(a)** *(service de transports)* courier company; **messageries aériennes** air freight company **(b)** *(service télématique)* **m. électronique** e-mail **(c)** *(entreprise de routage)* **m. de presse** newspaper distributing service

messe [mɛs] *nf (office religieux, composition musicale)* mass; **aller à la m.** to go to mass; *Fig* **faire des messes basses** to whisper; **m. de minuit** midnight mass

messeigneurs [mesɛɲœr] *nmpl voir* **monseigneur**

Messie [mesi] *nm* **le M.** the Messiah

messieurs [mesjø] *nmpl voir* **monsieur**

mesurable [məzyrabl] *adj* measurable

mesure [məzyr] *nf* **(a)** *(dimension)* measurement; *(action)* measurement, measuring; **prendre les mesures de qn/ qch** to measure sb/sth; *Fig* **prendre la m. de qn/qch** to size sb/sth up; **sur m.** *(costume)* made to measure; *(rôle, emploi)* ideal; **donner toute sa m.** to show what one is capable of; **être à la m. de qn/qch** to measure up to sb/sth; **être sans commune m. avec qch** to be out of proportion to sth; **elle a trouvé quelqu'un/un homme à sa m.** she met her match **(b)** *(moyen)* measure; **prendre des mesures** to take measures; **m. de sécurité** safety measure or precaution; **par m. d'économie** as a way to save money **(c)** *(quantité, unité)* measure; **sans commune m.** unrivalled **(d)** *(modération)* moderation; **sans m.** *(ambition, jalousie)* limitless **(e)** *Mus (temps)* time; *(division)* bar; **m. à quatre temps** four-four time, common time; **battre la m.** to beat time; **en m.** in time **(f)** *(locutions)* **à m. que** as; **(au fur et) à m.** as one goes along; **dans une certaine m.** to some or a certain extent; **dans la m. où** in so far as; **dans la m. du possible** as far as is possible; **être en m. de faire qch** to be in a position to do sth

mesuré, -e [məzyre] *adj (pas)* measured; *(langage, personne)* restrained

mesurer [məzyre] **1** *vt* **(a)** *(dimensions, taille)* to measure; *(tissu)* to measure off **(b)** *(déterminer)* to assess **(c)** *(limiter)* to

limit; **m. l'argent à qn** to ration out money to sb **(d)**. **ses paroles** to moderate one's language
2 *vi* to measure; **m. 2 mètres *(personne)*** to be 2 metres tall; *(tour, colonne)* to be 2 metres high
3 se mesurer *vpr* **se m. à qn** to pit oneself against sb

met *voir* **mettre**

métabolique [metabɔlik] *adj* metabolic
métabolisme [metabɔlism] *nm* metabolism
métairie [metɛri] *nf* small farm *(worked by share-cropper)*
métal, -aux [metal, -o] *nm* metal
métallique [metalik] *adj* metallic
métallisé, -e [metalize] *adj (peinture, couleur)* metallic
métallo [metalo] *nm Fam* metalworker
métallurgie [metalyrʒi] *nf* **(a)** *(industrie)* metallurgical industry **(b)** *(procédé)* metallurgy
métallurgique [metalyrʒik] *adj* metallurgical
métallurgiste [metalyrʒist] *nm* **(a)** *(ouvrier)* metalworker **(b)** *(chef d'entreprise)* metallurgist
métamorphose [metamɔrfoz] *nf aussi Fig* metamorphosis
métamorphoser [metamɔrfoze] **1** *vt* to transform **(en** into)
2 se métamorphoser *vpr Biol* to metamorphose; *Fig* to be transformed **(en** into)
métaphore [metafɔr] *nf* metaphor
métaphorique [metafɔrik] *adj* metaphorical
métaphoriquement [metafɔrikmã] *adv* metaphorically
métaphysique [metafizik] **1** *adj* metaphysical
2 *nf* metaphysics *(singulier)*
métastase [metastaz] *nf* metastasis
métayer, -ère [metɛje, -ɛr] *nm,f* sharecropper
météo [meteo] *Fam* **1** *adj* weather
2 *nf (bulletin)* weather forecast; *(organisme) Br* weather centre, *Am* weather bureau
météore [meteɔr] *nm* meteor
météorite [meteɔrit] *nf* meteorite
météorologie [meteɔrɔlɔʒi] *nf* meteorology
météorologique [meteɔrɔlɔʒik] *adj (bulletin, prévisions)* weather
météorologiste [meteɔrɔlɔʒist], **météorologue** [meteɔrɔlɔg] *nmf* meteorologist
métèque [metɛk] *nm* = racist term used to refer to any dark-skinned foreigner living in France, especially one from the Mediterranean
méthane [metan] *nm* methane
méthanol [metanɔl] *nm* methanol
méthode [metɔd] *nf* **(a)** *(démarche)* method; **m. pour faire qch** method of doing sth **(b)** *(ordre)* method; **avec m.** methodically **(c)** *(livre)* **m. d'anglais** English course book; **m. de piano** piano tutor
méthodique [metɔdik] *adj* methodical
méthodiquement [metɔdikmã] *adv* methodically
méthodiste [metɔdist] *adj & nmf* Methodist
méthodologie [metɔdɔlɔʒi] *nf* methodology
méthodologique [metɔdɔlɔʒik] *adj* methodological
méthylène [metilɛn] *nm* methylene
méticuleusement [metikyløzmã] *adv* meticulously
méticuleux, -euse [metikylø, -øz] *adj* meticulous
méticulosité [metikylozite] *nf* meticulousness
métier [metje] *nm* **(a)** *(manuel, commercial)* trade; *(intellectuel)* profession; **exercer un m.** to have a job; **j'exerce le m. de chimiste** I'm a chemist by profession;

quel m. veux-tu faire plus tard? what do you want to be when you grow up?; **il n'est pas *ou* il n'y a pas de sot m. a** job's a job; **être du m.** to be in the business; **connaître son m.** to know what one is doing **(b)** *(savoir-faire, expérience)* experience; **avoir du m.** to have experience; **elle a plusieurs années de m.** she has several years' experience **(c)** *(machine)* **m. à tisser** loom
métis, -isse [metis] **1** *adj (personne)* mixed-race **2** *nm,f (personne)* mixed-race **3** *nm (tissu)* linen and cotton mixture
métissage [metisaʒ] *nm* crossbreeding
métisser [metise] *vt* to cross(breed)
métrage [metraʒ] *nm* **(a)** *(action)* measuring **(b)** *(coupon de tissu)* length **(c)** *(longueur d'un film)* footage, length; **long/moyen/court m.** feature/medium-length/short movie *or Br* film
mètre¹ [mɛtr] *nm* **(a)** *(unité de longueur)* metre; **m. carré/cube** square/cubic metre **(b)** *(pour mesurer)* tape measure; *(en bois, en métal)* rule; **m. à ruban** tape measure
mètre² *nm (en poésie)* metre
métreur [metrœr] *nm* quantity surveyor
métrique¹ [metrik] *adj (système)* metric
métrique² **1** *adj (en poésie)* metrical
2 *nf* metrics *(singulier)*
métro [metro] *nm Br* underground, *Am* subway
métronome [metrɔnɔm] *nm* metronome
métropole [metrɔpɔl] *nf* **(a)** *(grande ville)* metropolis **(b)** *(pays)* mother country
métropolitain, -e [metrɔpɔlitɛ̃, -ɛn] **1** *adj (non insulaire)* metropolitan
2 *nm Vieilli (métro) Br* underground, *Am* subway
mets¹ [mɛ] *voir* **mettre**
mets² *nm* dish
mettable [mɛtabl] *adj* wearable
mette *etc voir* **mettre**
metteur [mɛtœr] *nm* **m. en scène** director
mettre [47] [mɛtr] **1** *vt* **(a)** *(placer)* to put; **m. qch sur/dans qch** to put sth on/in sth; **m. qn à mal** *(verbalement)* to berate sb; *(physiquement)* to beat sb up **(b)** *(vêtement, chaussures, lunettes, pansement)* to put on **(c)** *(moquette)* to lay; *(papier peint, étagères)* to put up **(d)** *(allumer)* to put on, to switch on; **m. qch en marche** to turn sth on; **m. qch plus fort** to turn sth up; **m. de la musique** to put some music on; **m. le réveil (à huit heures)** to set the alarm (for eight o'clock); **faire m. le téléphone** to get the phone put in
(e) **elle y a mis beaucoup d'argent** she's spent a lot of money on it
(f) **elle a mis du temps/deux ans à le faire** it took her a while/two years to do it; **combien de temps met-on pour y aller?** how long does it take to get there?
(g) **ça va prendre, mettons, trois mois** it will take, (let's) say, three months; **mettons que je n'ai rien dit** pretend I didn't say anything
(h) *(écrire)* to put
(i) *Fam* **qu'est-ce qu'on leur a mis!** we really thrashed them!; **m. les bouts** *ou* **les voiles** to make a move **2** *vi* **(a) m. bas** to give birth
(b) *Vulg* **va te faire m.!** go fuck yourself!
3 se mettre *vpr* **(a)** *(se placer)* **mets-toi là!** *(va là-bas)* stand there!; *(assieds-toi là-bas)* sit there!; **se m. au soleil** *(s'asseoir)* to sit in the sun; *(s'allonger)* to lie in the sun; **se m. au lit** to get into bed; **se m. sur le dos/ventre** to lie on one's back/stomach; *(en se tournant)* to turn (over) onto one's back/stomach; *Fig* **se m. en avant** to push oneself forward; *Fig* **je ne savais plus où me m.** I didn't know where to put myself

(b) *(maquillage, vêtement)* to put on; **je n'ai plus rien à me m.** I haven't a thing to wear **(c)** *(commencer)* **se m. à qch** *(activité)* to take sth up; **se m. au travail** to get (down) to work; **se m. à faire qch** to begin *or* to start doing sth; **le temps s'est mis à la pluie** it turned to rain; *Fam* **si tu t'y mets aussi!** don't **YOU** start! **(d) il a fallu se m. à trois pour la déplacer** it took three of us to move it **(e)** *Fam* **qu'est-ce qu'ils se sont mis!** they really laid into each other!

meuble [mœbl] **1** *adj* **(a)** *(sol, terre, roche)* soft **(b)** *(biens)* movable **2** *nm* piece of furniture; **meubles** furniture; **être dans ses meubles** to have a place of one's own; *Fam* **faire partie des meubles** to be part of the furniture

meublé, -e [mœble] **1** *adj* furnished; **non m.** unfurnished **2** *nm (chambre)* furnished room; *(appartement)* furnished *Br* flat *or Am* apartment

meubler [mœble] **1** *vt* **(a)** *(pièce, maison)* to furnish (**de** with) **(b)** *(remplir)* to fill (**de** with); **m. la conversation** to make conversation **2 se meubler** *vpr* to furnish one's home

meuf [mœf] *nf très Fam Br* bird, *Am* chick

meuglement [møgləmã] *nm* moo, des meuglements mooing

meugler [møgle] *vi* to moo

meule [møl] *nf* **(a)** *(d'herbe, de céréales)* stack; **m. de foin** haystack **(b)** *(de moulin)* millstone **(c)** *(de fromage)* round

meunier, -ère [mønje, -ɛr] **1** *adj* **(a)** *(industrie)* flour-milling **(b)** **(à la) meunière** *(poisson)* = coated with flour and fried in butter **2** *nmf* miller, *f* miller's wife

meurs, meurt *voir* **mourir**

meurtre [mœrtr] *nm* murder

meurtri, -e [mœrtri] *adj* bruised

meurtrier, -ère [mœrtrije, -ɛr] **1** *adj (guerre, attentat, colère)* murderous; *(arme, épidémie)* deadly **2** *nmf* murderer **3** *nf* **meurtrière** *Archit* loophole

meurtrir [mœrtrir] *vt* to bruise

meurtrissure [mœrtrisyr] *nf* bruise

meute [møt] *nf aussi Fig* pack

MEV [mɛv] *nf Ordinat (abrév* **mémoire vive)** RAM

mexicain, -e [mɛksikɛ̃, -ɛn] **1** *adj* Mexican **2** *nmf* **M.** Mexican

Mexico [mɛksiko] *n* Mexico City

Mexique [mɛksik] *nm* **le M.** Mexico

mézigue [mezig] *pron personnel Fam* yours truly

mezzanine [mɛdzanin] *nf* **(a)** *(entre deux étages)* mezzanine (floor) **(b)** *(au théâtre) Br* dress circle, *Am* mezzanine

mezzo-soprano *(pl* **mezzo-sopranos)** [mɛdzosoprano] **1** *nm (voix)* mezzo-soprano **2** *nf (cantatrice)* mezzo-soprano

MF [ɛmɛf] *nf Rad (abrév* **modulation de fréquence)** FM

mg *(abrév* **milligramme(s))** mg

Mgr *Rel (abrév* **Monseigneur)** Mgr

mi [mi] *nm inv (note)* E; *(chantée)* mi

mi- [mi] *adv* **la mi-avril** mid-April; **à mi-hauteur** *(en montant)* halfway up; *(en descendant)* halfway down; **elle avait de l'eau jusqu'à mi-jambe** the water was halfway up her legs; **mi-amusé, mi-intrigué** half-amused, half-puzzled; **mi-figue, mi-raisin** *(sourire)* half-hearted; *(plaisanterie)* half-serious

miam-miam [mjammjam] *exclam* yum yum!

miaou [mjau] *exclam* miaow!

miasme [mjasm] *nm* miasma

miaulement [mjolmã] *nm* miaowing

miauler [mjole] *vi* to miaow

mi-bas [miba] *nm inv (en laine)* knee sock; *(en voile)* knee-high

mica [mika] *nm* mica

mi-carême *(pl* **mi-carêmes)** [mikarɛm] *nf* = third Thursday in Lent

miche [miʃ] *nf* **(a)** *(pain)* round loaf **(b)** *Fam* **miches** *(fesses) Br* bum, *Am* butt

Michel-Ange [mikɛlãʒ] *npr* Michelangelo

micheline [miʃlin] *nf* railcar

mi-chemin [miʃmɛ̃] **à mi-chemin** *adv* halfway

Michigan [miʃigã] *n voir* **lac**

mi-clos, -e *(mpl* **mi-clos,** *fpl* **mi-closes)** [miklo, mikloz] *adj* half-closed

micmac [mikmak] *nm Fam* muddle

mi-côte [mikot] **à mi-côte** *adv (en partant du bas)* halfway up the hill; *(en partant du haut)* halfway down the hill

mi-course [mikurs] **à mi-course** *adv* at the halfway mark

micro [mikro] **1** *nm* **(a)** *(microphone)* mike **(b)** *Ordinat* micro(computer) **2** *nf Ordinat* microcomputing

microbe [mikrob] *nm* **(a)** *(germe)* microbe, germ **(b)** *Fam (personne chétive)* little squirt

microbien, -enne [mikrobjɛ̃, ɛn] *adj* microbial

microbiologie [mikrobjolɔʒi] *nf* microbiology

microchirurgie [mikroʃiryrʒi] *nf* microsurgery

microcircuit [mikrosirkɥi] *nm Ordinat* microcircuit; **microcircuits** microcircuitry

microclimat [mikroklima] *nm* microclimate

microcosme [mikrokosm] *nm* microcosm

microéconomie [mikroekonomi] *nf* microeconomics *(singulier)*

microéconomique [mikroekonomik] *adj* microeconomic

microédition [mikroedisjɔ̃] *nf Ordinat* desktop publishing, DTP

microfiche [mikrofiʃ] *nf* microfiche

microfilm [mikrofilm] *nm* microfilm

micro-informatique [mikroɛ̃formatik] *nf Ordinat* microcomputing

micron [mikrɔ̃] *nm* micron

Micronésie [mikronezi] *nf* **la M.** Micronesia

micro-ondes [mikroɔ̃d] *nm inv* microwave

micro-ordinateur *(pl* **micro-ordinateurs)** [mikroordinatœr] *nm Ordinat* microcomputer

micro-organisme *(pl* **micro-organismes)** [mikroorganism] *nm* micro-organism

microphone [mikrofɔn] *nm* microphone

micropilule [mikropilyl] *nf* mini pill

microprocesseur [mikroprosɛsœr] *nm Ordinat* microprocessor

microscope [mikroskɔp] *nm* microscope; **au m.** under a microscope; **m. électronique** electron microscope

microscopique [mikroskɔpik] *adj* microscopic

microsillon [mikrosijɔ̃] *nm (de disque)* groove

midi [midi] *nm* **(a)** *(heure)* twelve o'clock, midday; **m. et demie** half past twelve; **entre m. et deux** at lunchtime **(b)**

(moment du déjeuner) lunchtime **(c)** *(partie sud)* south; **le M. (de la France)** the South of France

midinette [midinɛt] *nf* silly young girl

mi-distance [midistɑ̃s] **à mi-distance** *adv* halfway **(de in)**

mie [mi] *nf (de pain)* soft part

miel [mjɛl] *nm* honey

mielleusement [mjɛløzmɑ̃] *adv (parler)* in honeyed tones

mielleux, -euse [mjɛlø, -øz] *adj (discours, sourire)* sugary; *(personne)* smooth

mien, mienne [mjɛ̃, mjɛn] **1** *pron possessif* **le m., la mienne, les miens, les miennes** mine; *(en insistant)* my own; **je te prête le m.** you can borrow mine; **je n'en ai pas besoin, j'ai le m.** I don't need it, I've got my own
2 *nm* **j'y ai mis du m.** I did my share
3 *nmpl* **les miens** *(ma famille)* my family

miette [mjɛt] *nf (de pain)* crumb; *Fig* **en miettes** in pieces; **mettre qch en miettes** *(briser)* to smash sth to pieces; **ne pas perdre une m. de qch** *(conversation)* not to miss a word of sth

mieux [mjø] **1** *adv* **(a)** *(comparatif)* better; **m. que** better than; **il vaut m. les surveiller** it's best to watch them; **vous feriez m. de m'écouter** you'd do better to listen to me; **elle va m.** she's (feeling) better; **c'est on ne peut m.** it couldn't be better; **j'espérais m. de votre part** I expected better of you; **plus on se voit et m. on s'apprécie** the more we see each other, the more we like each other; **de m. en m.** better and better; **faire qch à qui m. m.** to try to outdo each other in doing sth **(b)** *(superlatif)* **c'est elle qui s'exprime le m.** she expresses herself (the) best; **le plus tôt sera le m.** the sooner the better; **le m. serait de...** the best thing would be to...; **ils s'entendent le m. du monde** they get on extremely well; **être au m. avec qn** to be on the best of terms with sb; **un service des m. organisés** an extremely well-organized department
2 *adj* better; *(plus beau)* better-looking; **si tu n'as rien de m. à faire** if you've nothing better to do; **c'est le m. (de tous)** *(le plus beau)* he's the best-looking (of all)
3 *nm* **espérer m.** to hope for better things; **il y a un m.** *ou* **du m.** there's been a change for the better; **faire** *ou* **agir pour le m.** to act for the best; **faire de son m.** to do one's best; **fais du m. que tu peux** do the best you can

mièvre [mjɛvr] *adj* insipid

mièvrerie [mjɛvrəri] *nf* insipidness

mignon, -onne [miɲɔ̃, -ɔn] **1** *adj* **(a)** *(joli, charmant)* cute **(b)** *(gentil)* nice
2 *nm (favori)* minion
3 *nm,f* **mon m.** darling

migraine [migrɛn] *nf (douleur violente)* migraine; *(mal de tête)* headache

migraineux, -euse [migrɛnø, -øz] *nm,f* migraine sufferer

migrant, -e [migrɑ̃, -ɑ̃t] *adj & nm,f* migrant

migrateur, -trice [migratœr, -tris] *adj (animaux)* migratory

migration [migrasjɔ̃] *nf* migration

migratoire [migratwar] *adj* migratory

migrer [migre] *vi (aussi Ordinat* to migrate **(vers** to)

mijaurée [miʒɔre] *nf (jeune fille)* affected girl; **faire la** *ou* **sa m.** to give oneself airs

mijoter [miʒɔte] **1** *vt* **(a)** *(faire cuire)* to simmer; *(préparer avec soin)* to cook up **(b)** *(tramer)* to cook up
2 *vi* to simmer

mikado [mikado] *nm (jeu)* jack-straws, spillikins

mil¹ [mil] *adj inv* **l'an m.** the year one thousand

mil² [mij, mil] *nm (céréale)* millet

Milan [milɑ̃] *n* Milan

mildiou [mildju] *nm (des céréales)* mildew; *(de la vigne)* brown rot

mile [majl] *nm* mile

milice [milis] *nf* militia

milicien, -enne [milisjɛ̃, -ɛn] *nm,f* militiaman, *f* militiawoman

milieu, -x [miljø] *nm* **(a)** *(centre)* middle; **au m. de** in the middle of; **en plein** *ou* **au beau m. de** right in the middle of sth; **la table du m.** the middle table **(b)** *(environnement)* environment; *(social)* background; *Phys* medium; **le m. familial** the home environment; **dans les milieux autorisés** in official circles **(c)** *(position intermédiaire)* middle course; **le juste m.** the happy medium **(d)** *(pègre)* **le m.** the underworld

militaire [militɛr] **1** *adj* military; *(port)* naval
2 *nm* serviceman; **m. de carrière** professional soldier

militant, -e [militɑ̃, -ɑ̃t] *adj & nm,f* militant

militantisme [militɑ̃tism] *nm* militancy

militarisation [militarizasjɔ̃] *nf* militarization

militariser [militarize] *vt* to militarize

militariste [militarist] **1** *adj* militaristic
2 *nmf* militarist

militer [milite] *vi* to campaign **(pour** *ou* **en faveur de/contre** for/against)

milk-shake *(pl* **milk-shakes)** [milkʃɛk] *nm* milk shake

mille¹ [mil] **1** *adj inv* **(a)** *(cardinal)* a or one thousand; **deux m.** two thousand; **l'an m.** the year one thousand **(b)** *Fig (nombreux) (exemples, occasions)* countless; **je vous l'ai dit m. fois** I've told you a thousand times; **vous avez m. fois raison** you're absolutely right; **c'est m. fois trop grand** it's far too big
2 *nm inv* **(a)** *(nombre)* a or one thousand; **plusieurs centaines de m.** several hundred thousand; **cinq pour m.** five per thousand **(b)** *(locutions)* **mettre (en plein) dans le m.** to hit the bull's-eye; **gagner des m. et des cents** to make a mint; *voir aussi* **trois**

mille² *nm* **m. (marin** *ou* **nautique)** nautical mile

mille-feuille *(pl* **mille-feuilles)** [milfœj] *nm Br* ≃ vanilla slice, millefeuille, *Am* ≃ napoleon

millénaire [milenɛr] **1** *adj* thousand-year-old
2 *nm* millennium

mille-pattes [milpat] *nm inv* centipede, millipede

millepertuis [milpɛrtɥi] *nm* St John's wort

millésime [milezim] *nm (de vin, de voiture)* year; *(sur pièce de monnaie)* date

millésimé, -e [milezime] *adj (vin)* vintage; *(pièce de monnaie)* dated

millet [mijɛ] *nm* millet

milliard [miljar] *nm* billion

milliardaire [miljardɛr] *adj & nmf* billionaire

millibar [milibar] *nm* millibar

millième [miljɛm] *nmf, nm & adj* thousandth; *voir aussi* **cinquième**

millier [milje] *nm* thousand; **un m. de personnes** a thousand people; **des milliers de personnes** thousands of people; **par milliers** in thousands

milligramme [miligram] *nm* milligram(me)

millilitre [mililitr] *nm* millilitre

millimètre [milimɛtr] *nm* millimetre

millimétré, -e [milimetre] *adj* **papier m.** *(millimetre)*, **millimétrique** [milimetrik] *adj voir* **papier**

million [miljɔ̃] *nm* million; **un m. de francs** a million francs; **trois millions d'hommes** three million men; **par millions** in millions

millionnaire [miljɔnɛr] *adj & nmf* millionaire

millivolt [milivɔlt] *nm* millivolt

mime [mim] **1** *nm (art)* mime
2 *nmf (artiste)* mime (artist)

mimer [mime] *vt* (**a**) *(exprimer)* to mime (**b**) *(imiter)* to mimic

mimétisme [mimetism] *nm* mimicry

mimi [mimi] **1** *nm (langage enfantin)* kiss; **faire un m. à qn** to give sb a kiss
2 *adj inv Fam (mignon)* sweet

mimique [mimik] *nf* expression

mimolette [mimɔlɛt] *nf* = type of Dutch hard cheese

mimosa [mimoza] *nm* mimosa

min *(abrév* **minute(s))** min

min. *(abrév* **minimum)** min

minable [minabl] **1** *adj* (**a**) *(mesquin, pauvre)* shabby (**b**) *(incompétent, insuffisant)* pathetic
2 *nmf* failure, loser

minaret [minarɛ] *nm* minaret

minauder [minode] *vi* to simper

minauderie [minodri] *nf* simpering; **faire des minauderies** to simper

mince [mɛ̃s] **1** *adj* (**a**) *(fin) (tranche, mur)* thin; *(taille, personne)* slim (**b**) *(insuffisant)* slight; **c'est un peu m., comme excuse!** it's a bit of a poor excuse!
2 *exclam Fam* **m. (alors)!** *(surprise)* well, blow me!; *(déception)* blast!

minceur [mɛ̃sœr] *nf* (**a**) *(d'une tranche, d'un tissu)* thinness; *(de la taille, d'une personne)* slimness (**b**) *(insuffisance)* slightness

mincir [mɛ̃sir] *vi* to get slimmer

mine¹ [min] *nf* (**a**) *(gisement)* mine *Fig* **une m. de renseignements** a mine of information; **m. de charbon** coalmine; *aussi Fig* **m. d'or** goldmine (**b**) *(de crayon)* lead (**c**) *(explosif)* mine (**d**) **les Mines** = government department responsible for supervising all construction projects involving tunnelling; **Ecole des Mines,** *Fam* **les Mines** = university-level institute for geological engineers

mine² *nf (a) (expression)* look; **avoir bonne/mauvaise m.** to look well/ill; **avoir une m. de papier mâché** to look like death warmed up; **faire** *ou* **avoir triste m.** to look down in the dumps; **faire grise m.** not to look pleased; **faire m. de faire qch** to make as if to do sth (**b**) *(allure)* appearance; **juger les gens sur la m.** to judge people by appearances; *Fam* **ne pas payer de m.** not to be much to look at; *Fam* **m. de rien, il n'est pas bête** you wouldn't think it to look at him, but he's not stupid (**c**) *Péj* **mines** *(simagrées)* faces

miner¹ [mine] *vt* (**a**) *(creuser)* to eat away (**b**) *(ruiner moralement)* to wear down

miner² *vt (poser des explosifs dans)* to mine

minerai [minrɛ] *nm* ore; **m. de fer** iron ore

minéral, -e, -aux, -ales [mineral, -o] *adj & nm* mineral

minéralogique [mineralɔʒik] *adj* (**a**) **plaque m.** *Br* number *or Am* license plate (**b**) *Géol* mineralogical

minerve [minɛrv] *nf* (surgical) collar

minestrone [minɛstron] *nm* minestrone

minet, -ette [minɛ, -ɛt] *nm,f Fam* (**a**) *(chat)* pussy cat (**b**) *(personne coquette)* trendy

mineur¹ [minœr] *nm (ouvrier)* miner; **m. de fond** underground worker

mineur², -e 1 *adj* (**a**) *(secondaire)* minor (**b**) *(qui n'a pas la majorité légale)* underage (**c**) *Mus* minor
2 *nm,f* minor

mini [mini] *Fam* **1** *adj inv (jupe, robe)* mini
2 *nm* (**a**) *(mode)* **le m.** miniskirts (**b**) *(mini-ordinateur)* mini

miniature [minjatyr] **1** *nf* miniature; **en m.** in miniature
2 *adj* miniature

miniaturiser [minjatyrize] *vt* to miniaturize

minibus [minibys] *nm* minibus

minichaîne [miniʃɛn] *nf* mini-hifi

minier, -ère [minje, -ɛr] *adj* mining

minigolf [minigɔlf] *nm* crazy golf

minijupe [miniʒyp] *nf* miniskirt

minima [minima] *voir* **minimum**

minimal, -e, -aux, -ales [minimal, -o] *adj* minimum; *(art)* minimal

minimaliste [minimalist] *adj & nmf* minimalist

minime [minim] **1** *adj* minimal
2 *nmf Sp* junior *(13 to 15 years old)*

minimiser [minimize] *vt* to minimize

minimum [minimɔm] *(pl* **minimums** *ou* **minima** [minima]) **1** *adj* minimum
2 *nm* minimum; **avec un m. d'efforts** with a minimum of effort; **en un m. de temps** in as short a time as possible; **réduire qch au m.** to minimize sth; **faire le m. (pour faire qch)** to do the bare minimum (to do sth); **c'est vraiment le m. que tu puisses faire pour elle** it's the very least you can do for her; **au m.** at the very least, **le m. vital** a minimum to live on; **le strict m.** the absolute minimum

mini-ordinateur *(pl* **mini-ordinateurs)** [mini-ordinatœr] *nm* minicomputer

minipilule [minipilyl] *nf* mini pill

ministère [ministɛr] *nm (a) (département)* government department, *Br* ministry; **m. des Affaires étrangères** *Br* ≃ Foreign Office, *Am* ≃ State Department; **m. de la Défense (nationale)** *Br* ≃ Ministry of Defence, *Am* ≃ Department of Defense; **m. de l'Éducation nationale** *Br* ≃ Department of Education (**b**) *(gouvernement)* government (**c**) *Jur* **le m. public** *Br* ≃ the Crown Prosecution Service, *Am* ≃ the District Attorney's Office (**d**) *Rel* ministry

ministériel, -elle [ministerjɛl] *adj (arrêté, décret, entourage)* ministerial; *(crise, remaniement)* cabinet

ministre [ministr] *nm* (**a**) *(homme d'État)* secretary, *Br* minister; **m. des Affaires étrangères** *Br* ≃ Foreign Secretary, *Am* ≃ Secretary of State; **m. de la Défense (nationale)** ≃ Secretary of State for Defence; **m. de l'Éducation nationale** ≃ Secretary of State for Education; **m. d'État** ≃ secretary of state, *Br* ≃ cabinet minister; **Premier m.** Prime Minister; *Can (d'une province)* Premier (**b**) *(pasteur)* minister

Minitel® [minitɛl] *nm* = consumer information network accessible via home computer terminal; **le M. rose** = dating and erotic entertainment service available on Minitel®

minitéliste [minitelist] *nmf* Minitel® user

minois [minwa] *nm* pretty face

minorer [minɔre] *vt* (**a**) *(minimiser)* to downplay (**b**) *(faire baisser)* to reduce

minoritaire [minɔritɛr] *adj* minority; **être m.** to be in the minority

minorité [minɔrite] *nf* (**a**) *(de choses, de personnes)* minority; **être en m.** to be in the minority; **m. ethnique** ethnic minority (**b**) *(avant la majorité légale)* minority

Minorque [minɔrk] *n* Minorca

minorquin, -e [minɔrkɛ̃, -in] **1** *adj* Minorcan
2 *nm,f* **M.** Minorcan

minoterie [minɔtri] *nf (moulin)* flour mill; *(activité)* flour-milling

minou [minu] *nm Fam (chat)* pussy cat

Minsk [minsk] *n* Minsk

minuit [minɥi] *nm* midnight

minuscule [minyskyl] **1** *adj* **(a)** *(très petit)* tiny, minute **(b)** *(lettre)* small
2 *nf* small letter

minute [minyt] **1** *nf* **(a)** *(unité de temps)* minute; **une m. de silence** a minute's silence; **de dernière m.** last-minute; **faire qch à la m.** to do sth this very minute; **d'une m. à l'autre** any minute **(b)** *(court moment)* minute, moment; **la m. de vérité** the moment of truth; **m.!** hold on a minute! **(c)** *(de contrat)* minute; *(d'acte notarié, de jugement)* record
2 *adj (sur panneau)* **nettoyage m.** dry-cleaning while you wait; **talons m.** heel bar

minuter [minyte] *vt* to time

minuterie [minytri] *nf (pour l'éclairage)* time switch; *(d'un four)* timer

minuteur [minytœr] *nm* timer

minutie [minysi] *nf* meticulousness; **avec m.** meticulously

minutieusement [minysjøzmã] *adv* meticulously

minutieux, -euse [minysjø, -øz] *adj* meticulous

mioche [mjɔʃ] *nmf Fam* kid

MIPS [mips] *nm Ordinat (abrév* **million d'instructions par seconde)** MIPS

mirabelle [mirabɛl] *nf* mirabelle plum

miracle [mirakl] **1** *nm* miracle; **faire un m.** to perform a miracle; *Fig* **faire des miracles** to work miracles; **par m.** by a miracle
2 *adj inv* miracle

miraculé, -e [mirakyle] **1** *adj (malade)* miraculously cured; *(rescapé)* miraculously saved
2 *nm,f (malade)* miraculously cured person; *(rescapé)* miraculous survivor

miraculeusement [mirakyløzmã] *adv* miraculously

miraculeux, -euse [mirakylø, -øz] *adj* miraculous

mirador [miradɔr] *nm* watchtower

mirage [miraʒ] *nm* mirage

mire [mir] *nf* test card

mirer [mire] **se mirer** *vpr Litt* **(a)** *(se regarder)* to gaze at oneself **(b)** *(se refléter)* to be reflected

mirettes [mirɛt] *nfpl Fam* eyes

mirifique [mirifik] *adj* wonderful

mirobolant, -e [mirɔbɔlã, -ãt] *adj* fabulous

miroir [mirwar] *nm* mirror; *Fig* **m. aux alouettes** lure; **m. de courtoisie** vanity mirror; **m. grossissant** magnifying mirror; **m. de poche** pocket mirror

miroiter [mirwate] *vi* to shimmer; *Fig* **faire m. qch à qn** to lure sb with the prospect of sth

miroton [mirɔtɔ̃] *nm* = sliced beef and onions stewed in white wine

mis, -e *pp voir* **mettre**

misanthrope [mizãtrɔp] **1** *adj* misanthropic
2 *nmf* misanthropist, misanthrope

mise [miz] *nf* **(a)** *(placement)* putting; **m. en accusation** committal (for trial); **m. en application** implementation; **m. en demeure** formal demand; **m. en disponibilité** leave of absence; *Can* layoff; **m. en examen** indictment; **m. à feu** *(d'une fusée)* launch; **m. de fonds** investment; **m. en garde** warning; **m. à jour** updating; **m. en liberté provisoire** release on bail; **m. à mort** killing; **m. en page(s)** page make-up; **m. à pied** suspension; *Can* layoff; **m. en place** putting into place; **m. en plis** set *(hairstyle)*; **m. au point** *(d'un objectif)* focusing; *(d'une technique)* perfecting; *(d'un*

moteur) tuning; *(d'un document, d'un rapport)* finalization; *Fig* **faire une m. au point** to make things clear; **m. en route** start-up; **m. en scène** *(d'une pièce de théâtre)* production; *(d'un film)* direction; **m. en service** *(d'une machine)* commissioning; **m. en vigueur** implementation **(b)** *(habillement)* attire **(c)** *(au jeu)* stake; *(à une vente aux enchères)* bid; *Fig* **sauver la m. à qn** to get sb out of a tight spot **(d)** **être de m.** to be acceptable **(e)** *Ordinat* **m. en attente des fichiers à imprimer** printer spooling; **m. en forme** formatting; **m. en mémoire** saving; **m. à niveau** upgrade; **m. en relation** *(avec un service)* logon; **m. en réseau** networking; **m. sous tension** power-up

miser [mize] *vt* to stake **(sur** on); **m. sur qn/qch** *(parier)* to bet on sb/sth; *(compter sur)* to count on sb/sth; **m. sur tous les tableaux** to hedge one's bets

misérabilisme [mizerabilism] *nm* sordid realism

misérable [mizerabl] **1** *adj* **(a)** *(indigent) (personne)* poor; *(condition, existence)* wretched **(b)** *(pitoyable, insignifiant)* miserable
2 *nmf* **(a)** *(personne indigente)* poor wretch **(b)** *(coquin, fripouille)* scoundrel

misérablement [mizerabləmã] *adv* **(a)** *(pauvrement)* wretchedly **(b)** *(pitoyablement)* miserably

misère [mizɛr] *nf* **(a)** *(indigence)* extreme poverty; **être dans la m.** to be poverty-stricken; **être dans une m. noire** to be destitute; **salaire de m.** starvation wage **(b)** *(ennui)* trouble; **faire des misères à qn** to give sb trouble **(c)** *(vétille)* **payer qch une m.** to pay next to nothing for sth

miséreux, -euse [mizerø, -øz] *adj* poverty-stricken

miséricorde [mizerikɔrd] **1** *nf* mercy
2 *exclam Vieilli* mercy!

miséricordieux, -euse [mizerikɔrdjø, -øz] *adj* merciful **(envers** to)

misogyne [mizɔʒin] **1** *adj* misogynous
2 *nmf* misogynist

misogynie [mizɔʒini] *nf* misogyny

miss *(pl* miss *ou* misses) [mis] *nf (reine de beauté)* beauty queen; **M. Monde/France** Miss World/France

missel [misɛl] *nm* missal

missile [misil] *nm* missile

mission [misjɔ̃] *nf* **(a)** *(tâche)* mission; *(d'un employé)* task; **partir en m.** *(cadre)* to go away on business; *(diplomate)* to go off on a mission **(b)** *(groupe)* delegation; **m. scientifique** scientific expedition **(c)** *Rel (vocation, organisation)* mission; *(bâtiment)* mission (station)

missionnaire [misjɔnɛr] *adj & nmf* missionary

Mississippi [misisipi] *nm (fleuve)* **le M.** the Mississippi

missive [misiv] *nf Litt* missive

mistral [mistral] *nm* mistral

mitaine [mitɛn] *nf* fingerless glove; *Can (moufle)* mitten

mite [mit] *nf* moth

mité, -e [mite] *adj* moth-eaten

mi-temps [mitã] **1** *nf inv (moitié)* half; *(pause)* half-time
2 *nm inv* part-time job; **travailler** *ou* **être à m.** to work part-time

miteux, -euse [mitø, -øz] *adj* shabby

mitigé, -e [mitiʒe] *adj (enthousiasme, accueil)* lukewarm; *(sentiments, impressions)* mixed

mitigeur [mitiʒœr] *nm Br* mixer tap, *Am* mixing faucet

mitonner [mitɔne] **1** *vt* **(a)** *(cuire à feu doux)* to simmer **(b)** *Fig (projet)* to concoct
2 *vi* to simmer

mitoyen, -enne [mitwajɛ̃, -ɛn] *adj (mur)* party

mitrailler [mitraje] *vt* to machine-gun; *Fig* **m. qn de questions** to bombard sb with questions

mitraillette [mitrajɛt] *nf* submachine gun

mitrailleuse [mitrajøz] *nf* machine gun

mitre [mitr] *nf* (**a**) *(d'évêque)* mitre (**b**) *(de cheminée)* cowl

mi-voix [mivwa] **à mi-voix** *adv* in a low voice

mixage [miksaʒ] *nm* mixing

mixer¹ [mikse] *vt* (**a**) *(film)* to mix (**b**) *(ingrédients) (mélanger)* to mix; *(réduire à l'état liquide)* to blend

mixer², **mixeur** [miksœr] *nm (pour mélanger)* mixer; *(pour réduire à l'état liquide)* blender

mixité [miksite] *nf* coeducation

mixte [mikst] *adj* (**a**) *(des deux sexes)* mixed; **double m.** *(au tennis)* mixed doubles (**b**) *(combiné) (commission)* joint; *(mariage)* mixed; *(cuisinière)* gas- and-electric

mixture [mikstyr] *nf* (**a**) *(pharmaceutique)* mixture (**b**) *Fig* concoction

MJC [ɛmʒise] *nf (abrév* **maison des jeunes et de la culture)** community centre

ml *(abrév* **millilitre(s))** ml

MLF [ɛmɛlɛf] *nm (abrév* **Mouvement de libération des femmes)** ≃ Women's Liberation Movement

Mlle *(abrév* **Mademoiselle)** Miss

MM *(abrév* **Messieurs)** Messrs

mm *(abrév* **millimètre(s))** mm

Mme *(abrév* **Madame)** Mrs

Mmes *(abrév* **Mesdames)** M. Leclerc et Mathieu Mrs Leclerc and Mrs Mathieu

Mo *nm Ordinat (abrév* **méga-octet(s))** Mb

mobile [mɔbil] **1** *adj* (**a**) *(cloison)* movable; *(feuillets)* loose; *(cible)* moving (**b**) *(expression, regard)* shifting; *(visage)* lively (**c**) *(personne âgée, main d'œuvre, population)* mobile
2 *nm* (**a**) *(motif)* motive (**de** for) (**b**) *(objet décoratif)* mobile (**c**) *(objet en mouvement)* moving body

mobilier, -ère [mɔbilje, -ɛr] **1** *adj Jur* movable
2 *nm* furniture

mobilisation [mɔbilizasjɔ̃] *nf* mobilization; **m. générale** general mobilization

mobiliser [mɔbilize] **1** *vt* to mobilize; *Fig (énergie, courage)* to summon up
2 **se mobiliser** *vpr* to mobilize (**contre/en faveur de** against/in support of)

mobilité [mɔbilite] *nf* mobility

Mobylette® [mɔbilɛt] *nf* moped, motor scooter

mocassin [mɔkasɛ̃] *nm* moccasin

moche [mɔʃ] *adj Fam* (**a**) *(laid)* ugly (**b**) *(moralement)* rotten

modal, -e, -aux, -ales [mɔdal, -o] *adj* modal

modalité [mɔdalite] *nf* (**a**) *(manière)* mode; **modalités de paiement** conditions of payment (**b**) *(d'un acte juridique)* clause

mode¹ [mɔd] **1** *adj inv* **c'est très m.** it's very fashionable
2 *nf* (**a**) *(vestimentaire, de consommation) fashion*; **à la m.** fashionable; **revenir à la m.** to come back into fashion (**b**) *(manière)* **à la m. de Toulouse/Provence** Toulouse/Provence style

mode² *nm* (**a**) *(manière)* **m. de** means of; **m. de cuisson** cooking instructions; **m. d'emploi** instructions; **m. de paiement** means of payment; **m. de transport** mode of transport; **m. de vie** way of life (**b**) *Gram* mood (**c**) *Mus* mode (**d**) *Ordinat* mode

modèle [mɔdɛl] **1** *adj (parfait)* model; *(appartement, maison)* show

2 *nm* (**a**) *(exemple)* model; **prendre qn pour m.** to take sb as one's model; **m. de lettre** standard letter (**b**) *(personne)* **m. de générosité/fidélité** model of generosity/fidelity; **m. de vertu** paragon of virtue (**c**) *(exemplaire) (de voiture, d'appareil)* model; *(de robe)* style; *(de tricot)* pattern; **vous n'auriez pas un plus grand m.?** do you have it in a larger size?; **m. déposé** registered design (**d**) *(d'un peintre, d'un sculpteur)* model (**e**) *(maquette)* **m. réduit** small-scale model

modeler [39] [mɔdle] **1** *vt (argile, pot)* to model; *Fig (relief, caractère, destinée)* to shape; **m. sa personnalité sur celle de qn** to model oneself on sb
2 se modeler *vpr* **se m. sur qn** to model oneself on sb

modélisme [mɔdelism] *nm* model-making

modem [mɔdɛm] *nm Ordinat* modem; **carte m.** modem card

modérateur, -trice [mɔderatœr, -tris] **1** *adj* moderating
2 *nm* (**a**) *(personne)* moderator (**b**) *(de moteur)* regulator

modération [mɔderasjɔ̃] *nf* (**a**) *(retenue)* moderation; **avec m.** in moderation; **à consommer avec m.** *(dans les publicités)* drink in moderation *(health warning on all products advertising alcoholic drinks)* (**b**) *(réduction)* reduction

modéré, -e [mɔdere] *adj & nm,f* moderate

modérément [mɔderemã] *adv* moderately; *Euph* **j'ai m. apprécié sa remarque** I didn't much appreciate her remark

modérer [34] [mɔdere] **1** *vt* (**a**) *(passions, désirs, envies)* to moderate, to restrain; *Hum* **modère tes ardeurs!** control yourself!; **je te prie de m. ton langage!** please mind your language! (**b**) *(prix, vitesse)* to reduce
2 se modérer *vpr (personne)* to calm down

moderne [mɔdɛrn] **1** *adj* modern
2 *nm* **le m.** the modern style

modernisation [mɔdɛrnizasjɔ̃] *nf* modernization

moderniser [mɔdɛrnize] *vt* to modernize

modernisme [mɔdɛrnism] *nm* modernism

moderniste [mɔdɛrnist] *adj & nmf* modernist

modernité [mɔdɛrnite] *nf* modernity

modeste [mɔdɛst] **1** *adj* modest
2 *nmf* **faire le m.** to be modest

modestement [mɔdɛstəmã] *adv* modestly; **être m. logé** to live in modest surroundings

modestie [mɔdɛsti] *nf* modesty; **fausse m.** false modesty

modicité [mɔdisite] *nf* lowness

modifiable [mɔdifjabl] *adj* modifiable

modification [mɔdifikasjɔ̃] *nf* alteration, modification; **apporter *ou* faire une m. à qch** to make an alteration to sth

modifier [66] [mɔdifje] **1** *vt* to alter, to modify; *Gram* to modify
2 se modifier *vpr* to alter

modique [mɔdik] *adj* modest

modiste [mɔdist] *nmf* milliner

modulable [mɔdylabl] *adj (horaires)* flexible; *(éclairage, chauffage)* adjustable

modulaire [mɔdylɛr] *adj* modular

modulation [mɔdylasjɔ̃] *nf* (**a**) *(des sons, de la voix)* modulation (**b**) *(adaptation)* adjustment (**en fonction de** in relation to) (**c**) *Rad* modulation; **m. de fréquence** frequency modulation

module [mɔdyl] *nm* (**a**) *(élément d'un tout)* unit; **m. (d'enseignement)** module (**b**) *(d'un vaisseau spatial)* module; **m. lunaire/de commande** lunar/command module

moduler [mɔdyle] **1** vt **(a)** (sons, amplitude, voix) to modulate **(b)** (adapter) to adjust (**en fonction de** in relation to) **2** vi to modulate

modus vivendi [mɔdysvivɛ̃di] nm inv modus vivendi

moelle [mwal] nf marrow; Fig **jusqu'à la m.** to the core; **m. épinière** spinal cord; **m. osseuse** bone marrow

moelleusement [mwaløzmɑ̃] adv snugly

moelleux, -euse [mwalø, -øz] adj **(a)** (au toucher) soft **(b)** (fromage, vin) smooth; (gâteau) spongy

moellon [mwalɔ̃] nm quarry stone

mœurs [mœr, mœrs] nfpl **(a)** (coutumes) customs; **entrer ou passer dans les m.** to become part of everyday life **(b)** (d'animaux) habits **(c)** (sens moral) morals; **bonnes m.** morality; **contraire aux bonnes m.** contrary to accepted standards of behaviour; **femme de m. légères ou faciles** woman of easy virtue

mohair [mɔɛr] nm mohair

moi [mwa] **1** pron personnel **(a)** (sujet) I; **qui vient avec nous?** – **m.** who's coming with us? – I am or me; **m., quand je serai grand...** when I grow up,...; **m., je n'aurais pas fait comme ça** I wouldn't have done it like that **(b)** (objet direct) me; **et m., tu m'oublies?** and what about me, have you forgotten me?
(c) (avec préposition) me; **fais-m. voir, à m.** show ME; **ce livre est à m.** this book is mine; **j'ai mes petits secrets à m.** I've got my own little secrets; Fam **un ami à m.** a friend of mine; **à m.! help!; je ne le fais pas que pour m.** I'm not doing it just for myself
(d) (dans les comparaisons) me; **elle boit plus que m.** she drinks more than me or than I do
2 nm ego, self

moignon [mwaɲɔ̃] nm stump

moi-même [mwamɛm] pron personnel myself

moindre [mwɛ̃dr] adj **(a)** (comparatif) lesser; (prix) lower; (quantité) smaller; (vitesse) slower; **c'est un m.** mal it's not as bad as it might have been **(b)** (superlatif) **le/la m.** the least; **pas la m. chance/idée** not the slightest chance/idea; **au m. reproche** at the slightest reproach; **dans les moindres détails** in the smallest detail; **c'est la m. des choses** it's the least I/he/etc can do; **on a fait venir un expert, et non des moindres** we called in an expert, and not just any old one

moine [mwan] nm monk

moineau, -x [mwano] nm sparrow

moins [mwɛ̃] **1** adv **(a)** (comparatif) less; **je gagne m. que vous** I earn less than you (do); **elle est m. intelligente que sa sœur** she's not as intelligent as her sister; **il n'est pas m. nerveux que toi** he's no less nervous than you (are); **m. de** (argent, patience) less; (hommes, occasions) fewer; (avec un nombre) less than; **elle a m. de vingt ans** she's under twenty; **m. tu feras d'exercice, plus tu grossiras** the less exercise you do, the faster you'll get; **de m. en m.** less and less; **celui-ci coûte 10 euros de m. que l'autre** this one costs 10 euros less than the other one; **il y a eu 20% de visiteurs de m. ou en m.** there have been 20% fewer visitors; **il n'en est pas m. vrai que...** the fact remains that...
(b) (superlatif) **le m.** the least; **c'est celui qui me plaît le m.** that's the one I like (the) least; **les élèves les m. appliqués** the least industrious pupils; **pas le m. du monde** not in the least or slightest
(c) (locutions) **à m. d'un imprévu/d'un miracle** barring unforeseen circumstances/a miracle; **à m. de partir tout de suite** unless I/you/etc leave at once; **à m. que...** + subjunctive unless...; **au m.** at least; Fam **tu as fait ton travail, au m.?** you've done your work, I hope?; **du m.** at least; **c'est pour le m. surprenant** it's surprising, to say the least; Fam **un m. que rien** a nobody

2 prép (dans les calculs, les températures) minus; **une heure m. cinq** five (minutes) to one; **il est m. vingt** it's twenty to; Fam **il était m. une** it was a close shave or a near thing **3** nm (signe) minus (sign)

moins-value (pl **moins-values**) [mwɛ̃valy] nf Fin depreciation; (après une vente) capital loss

moire [mwar] nf moire

moiré, -e [mware] adj **(a)** (tissu) watered, moiré **(b)** (aux reflets changeants) shimmering

mois [mwa] nm **(a)** (période) month; **au m. d'août** in August; **un m. de vacances/salaire** a month's holiday/wages **(b)** (paie mensuelle) monthly salary; **treizième m.** extra month's salary (paid as an annual bonus)

Moïse [mɔiz] npr Moses

moisi, -e [mwazi] **1** adj (aliment) mouldy; (mur, livre) mildewed **2** nm (sur un aliment) mould; (sur un mur, un tissu) mildew

moisir [mwazir] vi **(a)** (aliment) to go mouldy; (mur, livre) to go mildewed **(b)** (personne) (stagner) to moulder away; (attendre longtemps) to hang about

moisissure [mwazisyr] nf mould

moisson [mwasɔ̃] nf **(a)** (récolte, époque) harvest; **faire la m. ou les moissons** to harvest **(b)** Fig (de documents, d'idées) wealth

moissonner [mwasɔne] vt **(a)** (céréales) to harvest; (champ) to reap **(b)** Fig (informations, idées) to collect, to gather

moissonneur, -euse [mwasɔnœr, -øz] **1** nm,f harvester **2** nf **moissonneuse** (machine) harvester

moissonneuse-batteuse (pl **moissonneuses-batteuses**) [mwasɔnøzbatøz] nf combine harvester

moite [mwat] adj (mains, front, chaleur) sticky; (atmosphère, air) muggy

moiteur [mwatœr] nf (des mains, du front) stickiness; (d'atmosphère, d'air) mugginess

moitié [mwatje] nf **(a)** (d'un tout) half; **la m. des livres/de la journée** half (of) the books/the day; **m. anglais, m. irlandais** half English, half Irish; **c'est m. moins cher** it's half the price; Fam **m.-m.** fifty-fifty; **faire m.-m.** to go halves; **à m. plein/vide** half-full/-empty; **à m. mort** half-dead; **vendre qch à m. prix** to sell sth (at) half-price; **ne pas faire les choses à m.** not to do things by halves **(b)** Fam (époux, épouse) **ma m.** my better half

moka [mɔka] nm **(a)** (café) mocha **(b)** (gâteau) coffee cake

molaire [mɔlɛr] nf molar

moldave [mɔldav] **1** adj Moldavian **2** nmf **M.** Moldavian

Moldavie [mɔldavi] nf **la M.** Moldavia

mole [mɔl] nf Phys mole

moléculaire [mɔlekyler] adj molecular

molécule [mɔlekyl] nf molecule

moleskine [mɔlɛskin] nf imitation leather

molester [mɔlɛste] vt to manhandle

molette [mɔlɛt] nf **(a)** (de briquet, de clé) wheel; (de jumelles) focus wheel **(b)** (pour couper le verre) cutting wheel

Molières [mɔljɛr] nmpl **les M.** (cérémonie) ≃ French theatre awards ceremony

mollard [mɔlar] nm très Fam gob of spit

mollasson, -onne [mɔlasɔ̃, -ɔn] Fam **1** adj (personne) lethargic **2** nm,f lazy lump

molle [mɔl] voir **mou**¹

mollement [mɔlmɑ̃] adv **(a)** (avec abandon) languidly; (avec lenteur) gently **(b)** (sans énergie) feebly

mollesse [mɔlɛs] *nf* **(a)** *(d'un coussin, d'un matelas)* softness; *(de tissus, de muscles)* flabbiness **(b)** *(d'une personne)* lethargy; *(d'un gouvernement)* laxness; *(du style)* limpness

mollet¹ [mɔlɛ] *adj (œuf)* soft-boiled

mollet² *nm* calf; **avoir des mollets de coq** to have spindly legs

molleton [mɔltɔ̃] *nm* **(a)** *(tissu) (en coton)* flannelette; *(en laine)* flannel **(b)** *(sous-nappe)* table felt

molletonné, -e [mɔltɔne] *adj* fleece-lined

mollir [mɔlir] *vi* **(a)** *(faiblir) (vent)* to die down; *(courage, enthousiasme)* to flag; **sentir ses jambes m.** to feel one's legs give way **(b)** *(devenir moins ferme) (matière)* to soften; *(sol)* to give way **(sous** beneath)

mollo [mɔlo] *adv Fam* **y aller m.** to take it easy

mollusque [mɔlysk] *nm* **(a)** *(animal)* mollusc **(b)** *Fam (personne)* lazy lump

molosse [mɔlɔs] *nm* big dog

môme [mom] *nmf Fam (enfant)* kid

moment [mɔmɑ̃] *nm* **(a)** *(point précis dans le temps)* moment; **arriver au bon m.** to arrive at just the right time; **le m. venu** *(dans le passé)* when the time came; *(dans l'avenir)* when the time comes; **c'est le m. ou jamais** it's now or never; **c'est le m. ou jamais de le faire** now's the time to do it; **au m. de qch** at the time of sth; **au m. où j'allais me coucher, le téléphone a sonné** just as I was going to bed, the phone rang; **à quel m. de sa vie?** at what point in his life?; **à un m. donné** at one point; **dans ces moments-là** at times like that; **d'un m. à l'autre** (at) any moment; **en ce m.** at the moment, just now; **jusqu'au m. où... until...; par moments** at times, now and again; **pour le m.** for the moment, for the time being; **sur le m.** at the time, à tout m., à tous moments** *(sans cesse)* constantly; *(n'importe quand)* (at) any moment; **à ce m.-là** then; *(dans ces conditions)* in that case

   (b) *(durée)* moment; **un m.!** just a moment!; **je suis à vous dans un m.** I'll be with you in a moment; **passer un bon m.** to have a good time; **ce n'est qu'un mauvais m. à passer** it'll soon be over with; **j'en ai pour un m.** I'll be a while; **ne pas avoir un m. à soi** not to have a moment to oneself; **dans un m. de bonté** in a moment of kindness

   (c) *(temps présent)* **du m.** *(disque, star)* of the moment **(d)** *(locutions)* **du m. que...** seeing that...

momentané, -e [mɔmɑ̃tane] *adj (bref)* brief; *(temporaire)* temporary

momentanément [mɔmɑ̃tanemɑ̃] *adv (brièvement)* briefly; *(temporairement)* temporarily

momie [mɔmi] *nf* mummy

momifier [66] [mɔmifje] **1** *vt* to mummify **2 se momifier** *vpr* to become fossilized

mon, ma, mes [mɔ̃, ma, me]

> ma becomes **mon** before a word beginning with a vowel or mute h.

adj possessif **(a)** *(marquant la possession)* my; **m. chien** my dog; **ma voiture** my car; **m. ami/amie** my friend; **mes enfants** my children; **mon père et ma mère** my mother and father; **un de mes amis** one of my friends, a friend of mine; *Fam* **j'ai eu m. vendredi** I got Friday off **(b)** *(en s'adressant à quelqu'un)* **non, m. général** no, General

monacal, -e, -aux, -ales [mɔnakal, -o] *adj* monastic

Monaco [mɔnako] *n* Monaco

monarchie [mɔnarʃi] *nf* monarchy

monarchique [mɔnarʃik] *adj* monarchical

monarchiste [mɔnarʃist] *adj & nmf* monarchist

monarque [mɔnark] *nm* monarch

monastère [mɔnastɛr] *nm (d'hommes)* monastery; *(de femmes)* convent

monastique [mɔnastik] *adj* monastic

monceau, -x [mɔ̃so] *nm* heap, pile

mondain, -e [mɔ̃dɛ̃, -ɛn] **1** *adj* **(a)** *(soirée, journaliste)* society **(b)** *Péj (personne)* être très m.** to be a great socialite **2** *nmf* socialite **3** *nf Fam Vieilli* **la mondaine** the drugs squad

mondanités [mɔ̃danite] *nfpl* **(a)** *(événements)* society life **(b)** *(politesses)* social niceties; *(conversations superficielles)* social chitchat

monde [mɔ̃d] *nm* **(a)** *(univers, humanité)* world; **l'autre m.** the next world; **dans le m. entier** *(connu, en vente)* worldwide, all over the world; **personne au m.** no one in the world; **pour rien au m.** not for anything in the world; **mettre un enfant au m.** to bring a child into the world; **venir au m.** to come into the world; *Litt* **il n'est plus de ce m.** he is no longer of this world; **les meilleurs amis du m.** the best friends in the world; **en ce bas m.** here on earth; *Fam* **c'est (quand même) un m.!** that's a bit much!; *Fam* **se faire un m. de qch** to get worked up about sth; **comme le m. est petit!** it's a small world!; **c'est le m. à l'envers** the world's gone mad

   (b) *(milieu)* world; **être du même m.** to belong to the same crowd; **le (beau) m.** fashionable) society **(c)** *(gens)* people; **tout le m.** everyone, everybody; **il y a du m.** *(beaucoup de gens)* there are a lot of people; **peu de m., pas grand m.** not many people; **avoir du m. à dîner** to have people to dinner **(d)** *(vie séculière)* world

mondial, -e, -aux, -ales [mɔ̃djal, -o] *adj* world, global; **guerre mondiale** world war

mondialement [mɔ̃djalmɑ̃] *adv* throughout the world

mondialisation [mɔ̃djalizasjɔ̃] *nf* globalization

mondialiser [mɔ̃djalize] **1** *vt* to globalize **2 se mondialiser** *vpr* to become globalized

monégasque [mɔnegask] **1** *adj* Monegasque **2** *nmf* **M.** Monegasque

monétaire [mɔnetɛr] *adj (unité, système, questions)* monetary; *(marché)* money

monétarisme [mɔnetarism] *nm* monetarism

monétariste [mɔnetarist] *adj & nmf* monetarist

mongol, -e [mɔ̃gɔl] **1** *adj* Mongolian **2** *nm/f* **M.** Mongolian **3** *nm (langue)* Mongolian

Mongolie [mɔ̃gɔli] *nf* la M. Mongolia

mongolien, -enne [mɔ̃gɔljɛ̃, -ɛn] **1** *adj* être m.** to have Down's syndrome **2** *nm,f (bébé)* Down's syndrome baby; *(personne)* person with Down's syndrome

mongolisme [mɔ̃gɔlism] *nm* Down's syndrome

moniteur, -trice [mɔnitœr, -tris] **1** *nm,f* **(a)** *(d'activités sportives, d'auto-école)* instructor **(b)** *(dans une colonie de vacances) Br* assistant, *Am* (camp) counselor **2** *nm aussi Ordinat* monitor; **m. cardiaque** heart monitor

monitoring [mɔnitoriŋ] *nm* monitoring

monnaie [mɔnɛ] *nf* **(a)** *(argent)* money; *(d'un pays)* currency; **m. électronique** plastic money; **fausse m.** counterfeit money; **c'est m. courante** to be common in these circles; *Fam* **payer qn en m. de singe** to fob sb off **(b)** *(pièces)* change; **avoir la m. de 50 euros** to have change of 50 euros; **faire (de) la m.** to get some change; **faire la m. de 50 euros** to get change for 50 euros; **petite** *ou* **menue m.** small change

monnayable [mɔnɛjabl] *adj* convertible into cash; *Fig* **être m.** *(expérience, information)* to be worth money

monnayer [53] [mɔneʒe] **1** vt (a) (terrains, biens) to convert into cash (b) (expérience, information) to cash in on **2 se monnayer** vpr **ici tout se monnaye** money can buy you anything here

monnayeur [mɔnɛʒœr] nm (appareil) change machine

monochrome [mɔnokrom] adj monochrome

monocle [mɔnɔkl] nm monocle

monocoque [mɔnokɔk] nm monohull

monocorde [mɔnokɔrd] adj monotonous

monoculture [mɔnokyltyr] nf monoculture

monogame [mɔnɔgam] adj monogamous

monogamie [mɔnɔgami] nf monogamy

monogramme [mɔnɔgram] nm monogram

monoï [mɔnɔj] nm inv scented coconut oil

monokini [mɔnokini] nm monokini; **faire du m.** to go topless

monolingue [mɔnolɛ̃g] adj monolingual

monolithe [mɔnɔlit] nm monolith

monolithique [mɔnɔlitik] adj aussi Fig monolithic

monologue [mɔnɔlɔg] nm monologue; **m. intérieur** interior monologue

monologuer [mɔnɔlɔge] vi (a) (monopoliser la parole) to carry on a monologue (b) (au théâtre) to soliloquize

monôme [mɔnom] nm Math monomial

mononucléose [mɔnonykleoz] nf **m. (infectieuse)** Br glandular fever, Am mono

monoparental, -e, -aux, -ales [mɔnoparɑ̃tal, -o] adj (famille) single-parent, one-parent

monoplace [mɔnoplas] adj & nm single-seater

monopole [mɔnopɔl] nm monopoly; **avoir le m. de qch** to have a monopoly on sth; **m. d'État** state monopoly

monopoliser [mɔnopɔlize] vt to monopolize

monoposte [mɔnopɔst] nm Ordinat stand-alone

monoski [mɔnoski] nm mono-ski; **faire du m.** to mono-ski

monosyllabe [mɔnosilab] **1** adj monosyllabic **2** nm monosyllable

monosyllabique [mɔnosilabik] adj monosyllabic

mono-tâche [mɔnotaʃ] adj inv Ordinat single-tasking

monothéisme [mɔnoteism] nm monotheism

monotone [mɔnɔtɔn] adj monotonous

monotonie [mɔnɔtɔni] nf monotony

monoxyde [mɔnɔksid] nm **m. de carbone** carbon monoxide

monseigneur [mɔ̃sɛɲœr] (pl **messeigneurs** [mesɛɲœr]) nm (a) (titre) (d'un prince) His Royal Highness; (d'un cardinal) His Eminence; (d'un évêque) His Lordship (b) (en s'adressant au prince) Your Royal Highness; (au cardinal) Your Eminence; (à l'évêque) Your Lordship

monsieur [məsjø] (pl **messieurs** [mesjø]) nm (a) (titre) M. Olivier Petit Mr Olivier Petit; **M. le Ministre** the Minister; Fam **m. je-sais-tout** Mr Know-it-all; **m. météo** the weatherman; **m. tout-le-monde** the man in the street (b) (en apostrophe) sir; **M. le Ministre** Minister; **au revoir, m.** goodbye; **M.,** (dans une lettre) Dear Sir,; **que prendront ces messieurs?** what will you have, gentlemen?; **bonsoir, messieurs; messieurs-dames!** good evening! (c) (homme quelconque) gentleman

monstre [mɔ̃str] **1** adj Fam huge **2** nm monster; **m. d'ingratitude/d'égoïsme** ungrateful/ selfish monster; **petit m.!** you little monster!; **m. sacré** giant

monstrueusement [mɔ̃stryøzmɑ̃] adv monstrously

monstrueux, -euse [mɔ̃stryø, -øz] adj (a) (malformé) monstrous (b) (énorme) huge; **être d'un égoïsme m.** to be extremely selfish (c) (scandaleux) monstrous

monstruosité [mɔ̃stryozite] nf monstrosity

mont [mɔ̃] nm mountain; Fig **être toujours par monts et par vaux** to be always on the move; **le m. Blanc** Mont Blanc

montage [mɔ̃taʒ] nm (a) (pose) (de bijou) mounting; (d'appareils) assembling (b) (d'un film) editing; (image truquée) montage; **m. vidéo** video(tape) editing (c) Écon **m. financier** financial arrangement (d) (d'installation électrique) wiring (up)

montagnard, -e [mɔ̃taɲar, -ard] **1** adj mountain **2** nm,f mountain dweller

montagne [mɔ̃taɲ] nf (a) (élévation) mountain; (région) mountains; **à la m.** in the mountains; Fig **se faire une m. de qch** to make a great song and dance about sth; **en haute m.** in the high mountains (b) **faire de la m.** (alpinisme) to go mountain climbing; (randonnée) to go hill walking (c) Fig (grande quantité) **une m. de** a mountain of (d) **montagnes russes** (attraction foraine) big dipper, rollercoaster

montagneux, -euse [mɔ̃taɲø, -øz] adj mountainous

montant [mɔ̃tɑ̃] nm (a) (somme) amount; **versement d'un m. de 500 euros** payment of 500 euros; **montants compensatoires** subsidies (b) (d'échelle) upright; (de lit) post; (de fenêtre) jamb

mont-de-piété (pl **monts-de-piété**) [mɔ̃dpjete] nm pawnshop

monté, -e [mɔ̃te] adj (équipé) **être bien m. (en qch)** to be well stocked (with sth)

monte-charge (pl **monte-charges**) [mɔ̃tʃarʒ] nm goods Br lift or Am elevator

montée [mɔ̃te] nf (a) (côte) slope, hill (b) (d'une côte) climb; (d'un avion) ascent; **la m. des eaux** the rise in the water level (c) (des prix) rise (de in) (d) (apparition) (du nationalisme, du fascisme) rise, growth

monte-plats [mɔ̃tpla] nm inv dumb waiter

monter [mɔ̃te] **1** vt (aux avoir) (a) (colline, escalier) (en s'éloignant) to go up, to climb (up); (en s'approchant) to come up, to climb (up); **m. la rue en courant** to run up the street (b) (porter en haut) (en s'éloignant) to take up; (en s'approchant) to bring up (c) (son, chauffage) to turn up (d) (assembler) (meuble) to assemble; (tente) to put up; (bijou, photo) to mount (e) (pièce de théâtre) to put on, to stage (f) (film) to edit (g) (créer) (entreprise, magasin) to set up; (complot) to hatch; **m. un coup** to plan a job (h) (trousseau) to put together (i) (en tricot) **m. les mailles** to cast on (j) (cheval) to ride (k) (locutions) **m. la garde** to mount guard; **m. (la tête à) qn contre qn** to set sb against sb **2** vi (aux être) (a) (aller vers le haut) to go up; (venir vers le haut) to come up; (oiseau) to fly up; (avion) to climb; **m. se coucher** to go (up) to bed; **faire m. qn** to show sb up; **m. sur qch** to climb onto sth; **m. à qch** to climb (up) sth; **m. à Paris** (y déménager) to move up to Paris; (en visite) to go up to Paris; **m. à la tête de qn** (sang) to rush to sb's head; Fig to go to sb's head; **les larmes lui sont montées aux yeux** his eyes filled with tears (b) (prendre place) **m. dans qch** (voiture, barque) to get in sth; (train, autobus, avion) to get on sth; **m. sur qch** to get on sth; **m. à bord** to go on board; **m. à bicyclette** to ride a bicycle; **m. à cheval** to ride, to go riding; **m. en voiture** to get into a car

(c) *(route)* to climb
(d) *(prix, baromètre, marée)* to rise; **m. en flèche** *(prix)* to soar; **faire m. les prix** to put up prices; **m. à** *(s'élever à)* to amount to, to come to
3 se monter *vpr* **(a)** *(s'élever)* **se m. à** to come to, to amount to
(b) *(s'équiper)* **se m. en qch** to provide oneself with sth
(c) *Fam* **se m. la tête** *(s'exalter)* to get carried away with oneself
monteur, -euse [mɔ̃tœr, -øz] *nm,f* Cin editor
Montevideo [mɔ̃tevideo] *n* Montevideo
montgolfière [mɔ̃gɔlfjɛr] *nf* hot-air balloon
monticule [mɔ̃tikyl] *nm* hillock, mound
montre [mɔ̃tr] *nf* **(a)** *(instrument)* watch; **à ma m.** il est midi by my watch it's twelve o'clock; **m. en main** exactly; **m. de plongée** diver's watch; **m. à quartz** quartz watch **(b)** *(preuve)* **faire m. de qch** to show sth
Montréal [mɔ̃real] *n* Montreal
montréalais, -e [mɔ̃reale, -ɛz] **1** *adj* of Montreal **2** *nm,f* **M.** Montrealer
montre-bracelet *(pl* **montres-bracelets)** [mɔ̃trəbraslɛ] *nf* wristwatch
montrer [mɔ̃tre] **1** *vt* **(a)** *(révéler)* to show (à to); **tu devrais m. ça au médecin** you should let the doctor take a look at it; **m. le chemin à qn** to show sb the way; **m. les dents** to bare one's teeth **(b)** *(désigner)* to point out; **m. qn/qch du doigt** to point at sb/sth; *Fig* to point the finger at sb/sth **(c)** *(faire preuve de)* to show **2 se montrer** *vpr* **(a)** *(se présenter) (personne)* to show oneself **(b)** *(s'avérer)* **se m. gentil/courageux** to be kind/courageous
montreur, -euse [mɔ̃trœr, -øz] *nm,f* **m. d'ours** bear leader
monture [mɔ̃tyr] *nf* **(a)** *(de lunettes)* frame; *(de bijou)* setting **(b)** *(cheval)* mount
monument [mɔnymɑ̃] *nm* **(a)** *(statue)* monument; **m. funéraire** monument *(over a tomb)*; **m. aux morts** war memorial **(b)** *(édifice public)* monument; **m. classé** listed building; **être classé m.** historique to be a listed building **(c)** *Fig (livre, film)* masterpiece
monumental, -e, -aux, -ales [mɔnymɑ̃tal, -o] *adj* monumental
moquer [mɔke] **se moquer** *vpr* **(a)** *(rire)* **se m. de qn/qch** to make fun of sb/sth; *Fig* **il se moque du monde** who does he think he is? **(b)** *(ignorer)* **se m. de qch** not to care about sth; *Fam* **se m. de qch comme de l'an quarante** *ou* **comme de sa première chemise** not to give two hoots about sth
moquerie [mɔkri] *nf* mockery
moquette [mɔkɛt] *nf* (fitted) carpet; **poser de la m.** to fit a carpet
moqueur, -euse [mɔkœr, -øz] *adj (remarque, rires)* mocking; *(personne)* given to mockery
moraine [mɔrɛn] *nf* moraine
moral, -e, -aux, -ales [mɔral, -o] **1** *adj* moral **2** *nm* morale; **avoir le m.** to be in good spirits; **avoir le m. au beau fixe** to be in fine spirits; **avoir un m. d'acier** to be very resilient; *Fam* **avoir le m. à zéro** to feel really down; **remonter le m. à qn** to cheer sb up
morale [mɔral] *nf* **(a)** *(bien)* morals; **contraire à la m.** immoral **(b)** *(règles)* morality; **faire une leçon de m. à qn, faire la m. à qn** to lecture sb **(c)** *(d'une histoire)* moral
moralement [mɔralmɑ̃] *adv* morally
moralisateur, -trice [mɔralizatœr, -tris] **1** *adj (discours, personne)* moralizing **2** *nm,f* moralizer

moraliste [mɔralist] **1** *adj* moralistic **2** *nmf* moralist
moralité [mɔralite] *nf* **(a)** *(conduite, attitude)* morality; **être d'une m. irréprochable** to have impeccable moral standards **(b)** *(d'une histoire)* moral; **m.: quand on veut, on peut** the moral of the story is, you can do anything if you put your mind to it
moratoire [mɔratwar] *nm* Jur moratorium
morbide [mɔrbid] *adj* morbid
morbidité [mɔrbidite] *nf* morbidness
morceau, -x [mɔrso] *nm* **(a)** *(de nourriture)* piece, bit; *Fam* **le gros m.** *(le plus difficile)* the big one; *Fam* **manger un m.** to have a bite to eat; *Fam Fig* **lâcher** *ou* **cracher le m.** to spill the beans; **m. de choix** choice morsel; **bas morceaux** *(de viande)* cheap cuts **(b)** *(de savon, de tissu, de papier)* piece, bit; *(de sucre)* lump; *(de terre)* piece; **en morceaux** in pieces; **mettre qch en morceaux** to tear sth to pieces; **tomber en morceaux** to fall to pieces **(c)** *(de musique)* piece **(d)** *(extrait)* **m. d'anthologie** anthology piece; **m. de bravoure** purple passage; **morceaux choisis** selected passages *or* extracts
morceler [42] [mɔrsəle] *vt* to divide up
morcellement [mɔrsɛlmɑ̃] *nm* dividing up
mordant, -e [mɔrdɑ̃, -ɑ̃t] **1** *adj* **(a)** *(esprit, remarque, ton)* biting, caustic **(b)** *(froid)* biting **2** *nm (causticité)* bite
mordicus [mɔrdikys] *adv Fam* stubbornly
mordiller [mɔrdije] *vt* to nibble
mordoré, -e [mɔrdore] *adj (couleur)* bronze
mordre [mɔrdr] **1** *vt* **(a)** *(sujet: personne, animal)* to bite; **m. qn au bras** to bite sb's arm, to bite sb on the arm; **se faire m. par un chien** to be bitten by a dog **(b)** *(entamer) (sujet: lime)* to bite into; *(sujet: acide)* to eat into **2** *vi (personne, chien)* to bite; **m. dans une pomme** to bite into an apple; **ça mord?** *(poissons)* are the fish biting?
3 mordre à *vt* **(a)** *(poisson)* **m. à l'appât** *ou* à **l'hameçon** to rise to the bait **(b)** *Fam (prendre goût à)* to take to
4 mordre sur *vt* ind *(déborder)* **m. sur qch** to encroach (up)on sth; **m. sur la ligne** *(sportif)* to have one's foot over the line
5 se mordre *vpr* **se m. la langue** to bite one's tongue; *Fig* **se m. les doigts d'avoir fait qch** to kick oneself for doing sth; **vous vous en mordrez les doigts** you'll be sorry
mordu, -e [mɔrdy] *Fam* **1** *adj* **(a)** *(amoureux)* madly in love **(b)** *(passionné)* **être m. de qch** to be mad on sth **2** *nm,f* fanatic; **un m. d'opéra/de cinéma** an opera/a movie fan
morfal, -e, -als, -ales [mɔrfal] *nm,f Fam* greedy-guts
morfondre [mɔrfɔ̃dr] **se morfondre** *vpr* to mope
morgue¹ [mɔrg] *nf (arrogance)* haughtiness; **plein de m.** haughty
morgue² [mɔrg] *nf (dans un hôpital)* mortuary; *(pour les corps non identifiés)* morgue
moribond, -e [mɔribɔ̃, -ɔ̃d] **1** *adj* dying **2** *nm,f* dying man, *f* dying woman
morille [mɔrij] *nf* morel
mormon, -e [mɔrmɔ̃, -ɔn] *adj & nm,f* Mormon
morne [mɔrn] *adj (personne, regard)* glum; *(silence)* gloomy; *(temps)* dismal, dreary
morose [mɔroz] *adj (personne, humeur)* morose; *(temps)* miserable
morosité [mɔrozite] *nf (d'une personne, de l'humeur)* moroseness; *(du temps)* miserable nature
morphine [mɔrfin] *nf* morphine
morphologie [mɔrfɔlɔʒi] *nf* morphology

morphologique [mɔrfɔlɔʒik] adj morphological
morpion [mɔrpjɔ̃] nm (a) très Fam (pou) crab (b) Fam (enfant) kid (c) (jeu) Br noughts and crosses, Am tic-tac-toe
mors [mɔr] nm bit; Fig **prendre le m.** aux dents to take the bit between one's teeth
morse¹ [mɔrs] nm (animal) walrus
morse² nm (code) Morse (code)
morsure [mɔrsyr] nf bite
mort¹, -e [mɔr, mɔrt] **1** pp voir **mourir**
2 adj (a) (personne, feuille, langue) dead; plus m. que vif more dead than alive; **m. de peur/d'inquiétude/de froid** frightened/worried/frozen to death; Fam **être m. de rire** to fall about laughing; Fam **être m. (de fatigue)** to be dead tired (b) (hors d'usage) (pile) dead; Fam **être m.** (voiture, chaussures) to have had it
3 nm,f dead man, f dead woman; **les morts** the dead; Rel **le jour** ou **la fête des morts** All Souls' Day; **faire le m.** to pretend to be dead; Fig to lie low; **l'accident a fait deux morts** two people were killed in the accident
4 nm (aux cartes) dummy
mort² nf death; **trouver la m.** dans un accident to die in an accident; **se donner la m.** to take one's own life; **mettre qn à m.** to put sb to death; **en vouloir à qn à m.** to have a huge grudge against sb; **la m.** dans **l'âme** with a heavy heart; Fam **c'est pas la m.!** it won't kill you/him/etc!
mortadelle [mɔrtadɛl] nf mortadella
mortaise [mɔrtez] nf mortise
mortalité [mɔrtalite] nf mortality, death rate; **m. infantile** infant mortality
mort-aux-rats [mɔrora] nf inv rat poison
mortel, -elle [mɔrtɛl] **1** adj (a) (éphémère) mortal (b) (fatal) (maladie, accident) fatal; (dose) lethal; (champignon, poison) deadly (c) (péché, ennemi) deadly; (silence) deathly; **d'une pâleur mortelle** deathly pale (d) Fam (ennuyeux) deadly boring
2 nm,f mortal
mortellement [mɔrtɛlmɑ̃] adv (blessé) fatally; (ennuyeux) deadly
morte-saison (pl **mortes-saisons**) [mɔrtsɛzɔ̃] nf off-season
mortier [mɔrtje] nm mortar; **tirs de m.** mortar fire
mortifiant, -e [mɔrtifjɑ̃, -ɑ̃t] adj mortifying
mortification [mɔrtifikasjɔ̃] nf mortification
mortifié, -e [mɔrtifje] adj mortified
mortifier [66] [mɔrtifje] **1** vt to mortify
2 se mortifier vpr to mortify oneself
mort-né, -e (mpl **mort-nés**, fpl **mort-nées**) [mɔrne] **1** adj aussi Fig stillborn
2 nm,f stillborn child
mortuaire [mɔrtɥer] adj death
morue [mɔry] nf (a) (poisson) cod (b) très Fam (prostituée) tart
morve [mɔrv] nf snot
morveux, -euse [mɔrvø, -øz] **1** adj (enfant) runny-nosed; (nez) runny
2 nm,f Fam Péj (gamin) brat; (jeune prétentieux) upstart
mosaïque [mɔzaik] nf (a) (en décoration) mosaic (b) Fig (de couleurs) kaleidoscope; (de populations) medley
Moscou [mɔsku] n Moscow
moscovite [mɔskɔvit] **1** adj Muscovite
2 nmf M. Muscovite
mosquée [mɔske] nf mosque
mot [mo] nm (a) (parole) word; **avoir son m. à dire** to have one's say; **avoir toujours le m. pour rire** to be always ready with a joke; **avoir des mots avec qn** to have words

with sb; **avoir le dernier m.** to have the last word; **je n'ai pas dit mon dernier m.** I'm not finished yet; **dire un m.** ou **deux mots à qn** to have a word with sb; **se donner le m.** to pass the word around; **prendre qn au m.** to take sb at his/her word; **traduire m. à m., faire du m. à m.** to translate word for word; **répéter qch m. pour m.** to repeat sth word for word; **sans m. dire** without (saying) a word; **sur ces mots** and with these words; **en un m.** in a word; **au bas m.** at least; **à mots couverts** in veiled terms; **mots doux,** **mots d'amour** sweet nothings; **mots croisés** crossword; **faire des mots croisés** to do crosswords; **m. d'ordre** watchword, slogan; **m. de passe** password; **bon m.** witty remark; **gros m.** swear word; **dire des gros mots** to swear (b) (message écrit) note; **envoyer un m.** à qn to drop sb a line; **m. d'excuse** note (explaining absence)
(c) Ordinat **m. de 6 bits** 6-bit byte; **m. binaire** binary word
motard, -e [mɔtar, -ard] **1** nm,f Fam (conducteur de moto) biker
2 nm (policier) motorcycle policeman
mot-clef (pl **mots-clefs**) [mɔkle] nm keyword
motel [mɔtɛl] nm motel
moteur, -trice [mɔtœr, -tris] **1** adj (a) (force, roue) driving; **à deux/quatre roues motrices** two-/four-wheel drive (b) (nerf, trouble) motor
2 nm engine; (électrique) motor; Fig driving force; Cin **m.!** camera!; **à m.** motor(-driven); **m. à deux/quatre temps** two-/four-stroke engine; **m. à explosion** internal combustion engine; **m. à injection** fuel-injected engine; **m. à réaction** jet engine; Ordinat **m. de recherche** search engine
3 nf Rail **motrice** engine
motif [mɔtif] nm (a) (raison) reason (de for); **elle n'a aucun m. de mécontentement** she has no reason to be unhappy (b) (dessin) pattern, motif (c) (dans un morceau de musique) motif
motion [mɔsjɔ̃] nf motion; **m. de censure** motion of censure
motivant, -e [mɔtivɑ̃, -ɑ̃t] adj (travail) motivating; (salaire, rémunération) attractive
motivation [mɔtivasjɔ̃] nf motivation
motivé, -e [mɔtive] adj (a) (personne) motivated (b) (action) justified
motiver [mɔtive] vt (a) (provoquer, stimuler) to motivate (b) (justifier) to justify
moto [mɔto] nf motorbike; **faire de la m.** to ride a motorbike; **m. tout terrain** trial bike
motocross [mɔtokrɔs] nm motocross
motoculteur [mɔtokyltœr] nm motor cultivator
motocyclette [mɔtosiklɛt] nf motorcycle
motocycliste [mɔtosiklist] nmf motorcyclist; Mil dispatch rider
motomarine [mɔtomarin] nf Can jet ski
motoneige [mɔtonɛʒ] nf Can snowmobile
motorisé, -e [mɔtɔrize] adj motorized; **être m.** (personne) to have transport
motrice [mɔtris] voir **moteur**
motricité [mɔtrisite] nf motor function
motte [mɔt] nf (a) (de terre) clod, clump (b) (de beurre) block
motus [mɔtys] exclam **m. (et bouche cousue)!** not a word!
mou¹, molle [mu, mɔl] **1** adj (a) (matelas, substance) soft; (chair, ventre) flabby; **j'ai les jambes molles** my legs are like jelly (b) (personne, gouvernement) spineless; (protestation) feeble; (poignée de main) limp
2 nm,f Fam wimp
3 nm (d'un cordage, d'un câble) slack

mou² nm (abats) lights, lungs

mouchard, -e [muʃar, -ard] Fam **1** nm f (informateur) Br grass, Am fink; (à l'école) sneak **2** nm (de camion) tachograph

moucharder [muʃarde] Fam **1** vt (personne) to squeal or Br grass on; (élève) to sneak on **2** vi (élève) to sneak on people

mouche [muʃ] nf (a) (insecte) fly; **prendre la m.** to fly off the handle; **elle ne ferait pas de mal à une m.** she wouldn't hurt a fly; **quelle m. te pique?** what's got into you?; **m. tsé-tsé** tsetse fly; **fine m.** sharp customer (b) (de cible) bull's-eye; **faire m.** to hit the bull's-eye; Fig to hit home (c) (accessoire cosmétique) beauty spot

moucher [muʃe] **1** vt (a) (nez) to blow; **m. un enfant** to blow a child's nose (b) Fig **m. qn** to put sb in his/her place (c) (chandelle) to snuff out **2 se moucher** vpr to blow one's nose; Fam **ne pas se m. du coude** ou **du pied** to think one is the bee's knees

moucheron [muʃrɔ̃] nm midge

moucheté, -e [muʃte] adj (cheval) dappled; (tissu) speckled

mouchoir [muʃwar] nm handkerchief; **arriver dans un m.** to come in neck and neck; **grand comme un m. de poche** no bigger than a pocket handkerchief; **m. en papier** tissue; **m. en tissu** handkerchief

moudre [48] [mudr] vt to grind

moue [mu] nf pout; **faire la m.** to pout

mouette [mwɛt] nf (sea)gull

moufle [mufl] nf mitten, mitt

mouflet, -ette [muflɛ, -ɛt] nm f Fam kid

mouflon [muflɔ̃] nm mouflon

mouillage [muja3] nm (a) (de bateau) (manœuvre) anchoring; (emplacement) anchorage; **être au m.** to be riding at anchor (b) (du vin) watering down

mouillé, -e [muje] adj (a) (vêtement, personne, pieds) wet; **tout m.** soaking wet (b) (consonne) palatalized

mouiller [muje] **1** vt (a) (rendre humide) to wet; **se faire m.** to get wet; Fig **m. sa chemise** to work up a sweat (b) (vin, lait) to water down (c) (ancre) to drop (d) Fam (compromettre) to involve **2** vi (bateau) to anchor **3 se mouiller** vpr (a) (personne) to get wet; **se m. les pieds** to get one's feet wet (b) Fam (prendre position) to stick one's neck out

mouillette [mujet] nf finger (of bread)

mouise [mwiz] nf très Fam **être dans la m.** to be hard up

moulage [mula3] nm (a) (action) casting (b) (objet) plaster cast

moule¹ [mul] nm aussi Fig mould; Fig **être coulé dans le même m.** to be cast in the same mould; **m. à gâteaux** Br cake tin, Am cake pan; **m. à gaufres** waffle iron; **m. à tarte** flan dish

moule² nf mussel; **moules marinières** moules marinières, = mussels in white wine

mouler [mule] vt (a) (statue) to mould (b) (sujet: vêtement) to fit closely

moulin [mulɛ̃] nm (a) (bâtiment) mill; **on y entre comme dans un m.** anyone can just walk in; **m. à eau** watermill; Can **m. à scie** sawmill; **m. à vent** windmill (b) (appareil) **m. à café** coffee grinder; **m. à légumes** vegetable mill; Fig **m. à paroles** chatterbox; **m. à poivre** pepper mill

mouliner [muline] vt (aliment) to pass through a food mill

moulinet [mulinɛ] nm (a) (de canne à pêche) reel (b) (rotation) **faire des moulinets (avec les bras)** to circle one's arms

Moulinette® [mulinɛt] nf food mill

moult [mult] adv Hum ou Vieilli many

moulu, -e [muly] **1** pp voir **moudre** **2** adj (a) (café, poivre) ground (b) Fig **être m. (de fatigue)** to be shattered

moulure [mulyr] nf (ornamental) moulding

mourant, -e [murā, -āt] **1** adj dying **2** nm f dying man, f dying woman

mourir [49] [murir] (aux être) **1** vi (a) (personne, animal, plante) to die; **m. de sa belle mort** ou **de mort naturelle** to die a natural death; **m. de vieillesse** to die of old age; **m. assassiné** to be murdered; **m. d'inquiétude/de peur** to be worried/frightened to death; **m. de faim** to starve to death; Fam (avoir très faim) to be starving; **m. de soif/ d'ennui** to die of thirst/boredom; **s'ennuyer à m.** to be bored to death; **aimer qn à en m.** to be desperately in love with sb; **à m. d'ennui** deadly boring; **à m. de rire** hilarious, hysterical; **m. d'envie de faire qch** to be dying to do sth; Fig **tu ne vas pas en m.!** it won't kill you! (b) (coutume, industrie, civilisation) to die out; (feu, région) to die **2** v impersonnel **il meurt des milliers d'enfants chaque jour** thousands of children die every day **3 se mourir** vpr Litt (personne) to be dying

mouroir [murwar] nm Fam Péj old people's home

mouron [murɔ̃] nm Fam **se faire du m.** to worry

mousquetaire [muskətɛr] nm musketeer

mousqueton [muskətɔ̃] nm (a) (anneau) snap clasp; (d'alpiniste) karabiner (b) (arme) carbine

moussaka [musaka] nf moussaka

moussant, -e [musã, -ãt] adj **être très m.** to produce a lot of lather; **bain m.** bubble bath

mousse¹ [mus] nf (a) (végétation) moss (b) (écume) foam; (sur verre de bière) head; (de savon) lather; Fam **une m.** (bière) a beer; **m. à raser** shaving foam (c) (plat, dessert) mousse; **m. au chocolat/de saumon** chocolate/salmon mousse (d) (matériau synthétique) foam rubber

mousse² nm ship's boy

mousseline [muslin] nf (tissu) muslin; **m. de soie** chiffon

mousser [muse] vi (bière) to froth; (savon, lessive) to lather; (vin, eau gazeuse) to fizz; Fam Fig **se faire m.** to show off

mousseux, -euse [musø, -øz] **1** adj (a) (vin, cidre) sparkling (b) (lait, bière) frothy **2** nm sparkling wine

mousson [musɔ̃] nf monsoon

moussu, -e [musy] adj mossy

moustache [mustaʃ] nf (a) (d'un homme) moustache; **porter la m.** to have a moustache (b) (de chat, de rongeur) whiskers

moustachu, -e [mustaʃy] **1** adj with a moustache; **être m.** to have a moustache **2** nm man with a moustache

moustiquaire [mustikɛr] nf mosquito net

moustique [mustik] nm mosquito

moût [mu] nm (de raisins) must; (de bière) wort

moutard [mutar] nm Fam kid

moutarde [mutard] **1** adj inv (jaune) m. mustard (yellow) **2** nf mustard; Fig **la m. me monte au nez** I'm beginning to lose my temper; **m. forte/de Dijon** strong/Dijon mustard

moutardier [mutardje] nm (pot) mustard pot

mouton [mutɔ̃] nm (a) (animal) sheep; (peau de) m. sheepskin; **être frisé comme un m.** to have curly hair; Fig **revenons à nos moutons** let's get back to the subject;

compter les moutons *(pour s'endormir)* to count sheep; *Fig* **m. à cinq pattes** rare bird (**b**) *(viande)* mutton (**c**) **moutons** *(écume)* white horses; *(poussière)* fluff

moutonner [mutɔne] *vi (mer)* to be flecked with foam

moutonneux, -euse [mutɔnø, -øz] *adj* (**a**) *(mer)* foam-flecked (**b**) *(ciel)* dotted with fleecy clouds

mouture [mutyr] *nf* (**a**) *(action de moudre)* grinding (**b**) *(d'un ouvrage, d'un livre)* version

mouvance [muvɑ̃s] *nf* **il faisait partie de la m.** surréaliste he moved in surrealist circles

mouvant, -e [muvɑ̃, ɑ̃t] *adj (terrain)* unstable; *(cible)* moving; *Fig (situation)* uncertain

mouvement [muvmɑ̃] *nm* (**a**) *(déplacement)* movement, motion; *(des marchandises, des capitaux)* movement; *(geste)* gesture; **faire un m.** to make a movement; **faire un faux m.** *(se faire mal)* to move the wrong way; **en m.** in motion; **ralentir le m.** to slow down; **suivre le m.** to go with the flow; **il y eut un m. de foule** a ripple ran through the crowd; **m. de tête** *(pour acquiescer)* nod; *(pour nier)* shake of the head (**b**) *(de gymnastique)* exercise (**c**) *(élan)* impulse; **m. d'humeur** outburst (of temper); **m. de colère** fit of anger (**d**) *(politique, artistique)* movement; **m. de grève** strike action (**e**) *(d'un concerto, d'une symphonie)* movement

mouvementé, -e [muvmɑ̃te] *adj (discussion, débat)* animated, lively; *(journée, voyage, vie)* eventful

mouvoir [31b] [muvwar] **1** *vt Litt* (**a**) *(machine)* to drive; *(bateau)* to propel; **mû par la vapeur** steam-driven (**b**) *(pousser)* **mû par l'intérêt** prompted by self-interest **2 se mouvoir** *vpr* to move

moyen¹, -enne [mwajɛ̃, -ɛn] *adj* (**a**) *(du milieu)* middle; **trouver un m. terme** to find a happy medium (**b**) *(coût, taille, vitesse)* average; **de taille moyenne** medium-sized; *(personne)* of average height (**c**) *(quelconque, médiocre)* average; **le Français m.** the average Frenchman

moyen² *nm* (**a**) *(façon, possibilité)* means, way; *aussi Hum* **trouver le m. de faire qch** to manage to do sth; **se donner les moyens de faire qch** to provide oneself with the means to do sth; **faire qch par ses propres moyens** to do sth on one's own; **employer les grands moyens** to take extreme measures; **au m. de qch** by means of sth; **par tous les moyens** any way I/you/*etc* can; **il n'y a pas m. de le lui faire comprendre** it's impossible to make him understand; **faire avec les moyens du bord** to make do with what one has; **moyens de communication/ production/transport** means of communication/production/transport (**b**) **avoir des moyens** *(capacité mentale)* to be bright; **perdre tous ses moyens** to go to pieces (**c**) **moyens** *(financiers)* means; **j'en ai/je n'en ai pas les moyens** I can/can't afford it

Moyen Âge [mwajɛnɑʒ] *nm* **le M.** the Middle Ages

moyenâgeux, -euse [mwajɛnɑʒø, -øz] *adj* medieval

moyen-courrier *(pl* **moyen-courriers)** [mwajɛ̃kurje] *nm (avion)* **m.** medium-haul aircraft

moyennant [mwajɛnɑ̃] *prép* (in return) for; **faire qch m. finance** to do sth in return for payment; **m. quoi** in return for which

moyenne [mwajɛn] **1** *adj voir* **moyen¹** **2** *nf* (**a**) *(niveau le plus courant)* average; **en m.** on average (**b**) *(à un examen)* pass mark; *(sur une période)* average (mark); **avoir 12 sur 20 de m.** to average 12 out of 20

moyennement [mwajɛnmɑ̃] *adv* moderately, fairly

Moyen-Orient [mwajɛnɔrjɑ̃] *nm* **le M.** the Middle East

moyeu [mwajø] *nm* hub

mozambicain, -e [mɔzɑ̃bikɛ̃, -ɛn] **1** *adj* Mozambican **2** *nm,f* **M.** Mozambican

Mozambique [mɔzɑ̃bik] *nm* **le M.** Mozambique

mozzarella [mɔdzarɛla], **mozzarelle** [mɔdzarɛl] *nf* mozzarella

MRAP [mrap] *nm (abrév* **Mouvement contre le racisme, l'antisémitisme et pour la paix)** = French anti-racist pacifist movement

MRG [ɛmɛrʒe] *nm (abrév* **Mouvement des radicaux de gauche)** = French left-wing political grouping of local councillors

MST¹ [ɛmɛste] *nf (abrév* **maladie sexuellement transmissible)** STD

MST² *nf (abrév* **maîtrise de sciences et techniques)** = Master's degree in science and technology

mû [my] *voir* **mouvoir**

mucoviscidose [mykovisidoz] *nf* cystic fibrosis

mucus [mykys] *nm* mucus

mue [my] **1** *pp voir* **mouvoir** **2** *nf* (**a**) *(d'oiseaux, de mammifères)* moulting; *(de reptiles)* sloughing (**b**) *(à la puberté)* breaking of the voice

muer [mɥe] **1** *vi* (**a**) *(mammifère)* to moult; *(serpent)* to slough (**b**) *(voix)* to break; **il commence à m.** his voice is breaking **2 se muer** *vpr* **se m. en** to change into

muesli [mysli] *nm* muesli

muet, -ette [mɥɛ, -ɛt] **1** *adj* (**a**) *(personne)* dumb; *Fig (silencieux)* silent; **m. d'étonnement/de colère** speechless with astonishment/anger; **m. comme la tombe** as quiet as the grave; **il est resté m. comme une carpe** he didn't open his mouth (**b**) *(film, réprobation)* silent; *(rôle)* non-speaking (**c**) *Ling* silent **2** *nm,f* mute **3** *nm Cin* **le m.** silent films

muezzin [mɥɛdzin] *nm* muezzin

mufle [myfl] *nm* (**a**) *Fam (homme)* lout (**b**) *(du bœuf, du bison)* muffle; *(du lion, du taureau)* muzzle

muge [myʒ] *nm* mullet

mugir [myʒir] *vi (vache)* to moo; *(taureau)* to bellow (**b**) *(vent)* to howl

mugissement [myʒismɑ̃] *nm* (**a**) *(de vache)* moo; *(de taureau)* bellow; **des mugissements** *(de vache)* mooing; *(de vent)* bellowing (**b**) *(du vent)* howling

muguet [mygɛ] *nm (plante)* lily of the valley

mulâtre [mylɑtr] *adj & nm* mulatto

mulâtresse [mylɑtrɛs] *nf* mulatto

mule¹ [myl] *nf (animal)* mule

mule² *nf (chaussure)* mule

mulet¹ [mylɛ] *nm (équidé)* mule

mulet² *nm (poisson)* grey mullet

muletier, -ère [myltje, -ɛr] *nm,f* mule driver

mulot [mylo] *nm* field mouse

multicarte [myltikart] *adj (représentant)* for several companies

multicolore [myltikɔlɔr] *adj* multicoloured

multicoque [myltikɔk] *nm* multihull

multicritère [myltikritɛr] *nm Ordinat* multicriterion

multiculturel, -elle [myltikyltyrɛl] *adj* multicultural

multidisciplinaire [myltidisiplinɛr] *adj* multidisciplinary

multi-écran *(pl* **multi-écrans)** [myltiekrɑ̃] *nm* split screen

multifonctions [myltifɔ̃ksjɔ̃] *adj* multi-functional

multiforme [myltifɔrm] *adj* multifaceted

multilatéral, -e, -aux, -ales [myltilateral, -o] *adj* multilateral

multimédia [myltimedja] *adj & nm* multimedia
multimilliardaire [myltimiljardɛr] *adj & nmf* multimillionaire
multimillionnaire [myltimiljɔnɛr] *adj & nmf* multimillionaire
multinational, -e, -aux, -ales [myltinasjɔnal, -o] **1** *adj* multinational **2** *nf* **multinationale** multinational (company)
multiple [myltipl] **1** *adj* (**a**) *(nombreux)* many, numerous; **à usages multiples** multipurpose; **à de multiples reprises** repeatedly; *Ordinat* **à accès m.** multi-access (**b**) *(divers)* many, multiple **2** *nm Math* multiple; **le plus petit commun m.** the lowest common multiple
multiplex [myltiplɛks] *adj inv & nm inv* multiplex
multiplicateur, -trice [myltiplikatœr, -tris] **1** *adj* multiplying **2** *nm* multiplier
multiplication [myltiplikasjɔ̃] *nf* (**a**) *(calcul)* multiplication (**b**) *(augmentation)* increase (**de** in)
multiplicite [myltiplisite] *nf* multiplicity
multiplier [66] [myltiplije] **1** *vt* (**a**) *(somme, chiffre)* to multiply (**par** by) (**b**) *(répéter)* **m. les mises en garde** to issue repeated warnings; **m. les erreurs** to make mistake after mistake **2 se multiplier** *vpr* (**a**) *(augmenter)* to increase (**b**) *(se reproduire)* to multiply
multiposte [myltipɔst] *adj Ordinat* multi-station
multiprocesseur [myltiprɔsesœr] *nm Ordinat* multiprocessor
multiprogrammation [myltiprɔgramasjɔ̃] *nf Ordinat* multiprogramming
multipropriété [myltiprɔprijete] *nf* time-share; **acheter un appartement en m.** to buy a time-share *Br* flat *or Am* apartment
multiracial, -e, -aux, -ales [myltirasjal, -o] *adj* multiracial
multirisque [myltirisk] *adj* comprehensive
multisalles [myltisal] *adj* **complexe m.** multiplex (*Br* cinema *or Am* movie theater)
multitâche [myltitaʃ] *adj Ordinat* multitasking
multitraitement [myltitretmɑ̃] *nm Ordinat* multiprocessing
multitude [myltityd] *nf* multitude (**de** of)
multi-utilisateurs [myltiytilizatœr] *adj inv Ordinat* multiuser
municipal, -e, -aux, -ales [mynisipal, -o] **1** *adj* municipal **2** *nfpl* **les municipales** municipal *or* local (government) elections
municipalité [mynisipalite] *nf* (**a**) *(commune)* municipality (**b**) *(maire et conseillers)* (local) council
munir [mynir] **1** *vt (personne)* to supply, to provide (**de** with); *(voiture, chambre)* to fit, to equip (**de** with) **2 se munir** *vpr* **se m. de qch** to take sth
munitions [mynisjɔ̃] *nfpl* ammunition, munitions
munster [mœ̃stɛr] *nm* Munster (cheese)
muqueuse [mykøz] *nf* mucous membrane
mur [myr] *nm* (**a**) *(construction)* wall; **l'ennemi est dans nos murs** the enemy is within the gates; **le m. de Berlin** the Berlin Wall; **le M. des lamentations** the Wailing Wall; **m. porteur** load-bearing wall; **m. du son** sound barrier; **franchir le m. du son** to break the sound barrier; **m. de soutènement** retaining wall (**b**) *Fig (résistance)* brick wall
mûr, -e [myr] *adj* (**a**) *(fruit)* ripe; *Fig* **être m. pour qch** to

be ripe for sth (**b**) *(personne, esprit)* mature (**c**) *(intense)* **après mûre réflexion** after careful consideration
muraille [myraj] *nf* wall; **la Grande M.** de Chine the Great Wall of China
mural, -e, -aux, -ales [myral, -o] *adj* wall
mûre [myr] *nf* mulberry; *(fruit de la ronce)* blackberry
mûrement [myrmɑ̃] *adv* **après avoir m. réfléchi** after careful consideration; **un projet m. réfléchi** a carefully thought-out plan
murène [myrɛn] *nf* moray (eel)
murer [myre] **1** *vt* (**a**) *(ville, jardin)* to wall in (**b**) *(porte, fenêtre, personne)* to wall up **2 se murer** *vpr* to shut oneself away; **se m. dans le silence/la solitude** to retreat into silence/solitude
muret [myrɛ] *nm*, **murette** [myrɛt] *nf (mur bas)* low wall; *(de pierres sèches)* dry-stone wall
mûrier [myrje] *nm* (**a**) *(arbre)* mulberry tree (**b**) *(roncier)* blackberry bush
mûrir [myrir] *vi* (**a**) *(fruit)* to ripen (**b**) *(projet, sentiment)* to evolve, to develop (**c**) *(personne)* to mature
murmure [myrmyr] *nm* murmur
murmurer [myrmyre] *vt & vi* to murmur
musaraigne [myzarɛɲ] *nf* shrew
musarder [myzarde] *vi (flâner)* to wander around; *(faineanter)* to lounge around
musc [mysk] *nm* musk
muscade [myskad] *nf* **m., noix (de) m.** nutmeg
muscat [myska] *nm* (**a**) *(raisin)* muscat grape (**b**) *(vin)* muscatel (wine)
muscle [myskl] *nm* muscle; **être tout en m.** to be all muscle
musclé, -e [myskle] *adj* (**a**) *(personne, bras, jambes)* muscular (**b**) *Fig (campagne électorale, discours)* punchy; *(intervention)* forceful; *(politique, mesure)* tough
muscler [myskle] **1** *vt* to develop the muscles of **2 se muscler** *vpr* to develop one's muscles
muscu [mysky] *Fam* = musculation
musculaire [myskyler] *adj (système, tissu, force)* muscular; *(fibre)* muscle
musculation [myskylasjɔ̃] *nf* body-building; **faire de la m.** to do body-building
musculature [myskylatyr] *nf* musculature
muse [myz] *nf* muse
museau, -x [myzo] *nm* (**a**) *(d'animal)* muzzle, snout (**b**) *Fam (visage)* face
musée [myze] *nm* museum; **m. (de peinture)** art gallery; **m. des horreurs** chamber of horrors
museler [42] [myzle] *vt aussi Fig* to muzzle
muselière [myzəljer] *nf* muzzle
musette [myzɛt] **1** *nf* (**a**) *(instrument de musique)* musette (**b**) *(sac)* bag; *(de soldat)* haversack; *(d'écolier)* satchel **2** *nm Fam* **le m.** accordion music
muséum [myzeɔm] *nm* natural history museum
musical, -e, -aux, -ales [myzikal, -o] *adj* musical
musicalement [myzikalmɑ̃] *adv* musically
music-hall [pl **music-halls**] [myzikol] *nm (genre, salle)* music hall
musicien, -enne [myzisjɛ̃, -ɛn] **1** *adj* musical **2** *nm,f* musician
musicologie [myzikɔlɔʒi] *nf* musicology
musicologue [myzikɔlɔg] *nmf* musicologist
musique [myzik] *nf* music; **mettre qch en m.** to set sth to music; **faire de la m.** to make music; *Fig* **connaître la m.**

to have heard it all before; **Can faire face à la m.** to face the music; **m. d'ambiance** *ou* **de fond** background music; **m. de chambre** chamber music; **m. classique** classical music; **m. folklorique** folk music; **m. religieuse** religious music; **m. sacrée** sacred music

musqué, -e [myske] *adj (odeur)* musky

must [mœst] *nm Fam* must

mustang [mystɑ̃g] *nm* mustang

musulman, -e [myzylmɑ̃, -an] *adj & nm,f* Moslem, Muslim

mutant, -e [mytɑ̃, ɑ̃t] *adj & nm,f* mutant

mutation [mytasjɔ̃] *nf* (**a**) *(de personnel)* transfer (**b**) *(changement)* change, alteration

muter [myte] *vt* to transfer

mutilation [mytilasjɔ̃] *nf* mutilation

mutilé, -e [mytile] *nm,f* **mutilés de guerre** disabled ex-servicemen

mutiler [mytile] **1** *vt (personne)* to mutilate, to maim; *(partie du corps)* to badly injure; *(paysage)* to disfigure
 2 se mutiler *vpr* to mutilate oneself

mutin¹ [mytɛ̃] *nm* mutineer

mutin², -e [mytɛ̃, -in] *adj (espiègle)* mischievous

mutiner [mytine] **se mutiner** *vpr* to mutiny (**contre** against)

mutinerie [mytinri] *nf* mutiny

mutisme [mytism] *nm* silence; **observer un m. absolu** to maintain total silence

mutualité [mytɥalite] *nf* mutual insurance

mutuel, -elle [mytɥɛl] **1** *adj* mutual
 2 *nf* mutual insurance company

mutuellement [mytɥɛlmɑ̃] *adv* each other, one another

Myanmar [mjanmar] *nm* **le M.** Myanmar

mycose [mikoz] *nf* fungal infection, *Spéc* mycosis

mygale [migal] *nf* trapdoor spider

myocarde [mjɔkard] *nm* myocardium

myopathe [mjɔpat] *nmf* person with muscular dystrophy

myopathie [mjɔpati] *nf* muscular dystrophy

myope [mjɔp] **1** *adj* shortsighted, *Spéc* myopic; *Fig* **m. comme une taupe** as blind as a bat
 2 *nmf* shortsighted person

myopie [mjɔpi] *nf* shortsightedness, *Spéc* myopia

myosotis [mjɔzɔtis] *nm* forget-me-not

myriade [mirjad] *nf* myriad (**de** of)

myrrhe [mir] *nf* myrrh

myrtille [mirtij] *nf Br* bilberry, *Am* blueberry

mystère [mister] *nm* (**a**) *(énigme)* mystery; **faire des mystères** to be mysterious; **faire m. de qch** to make a secret of sth; **il n'y a pas de m.** it's quite simple; *Fam* **m. et boule de gomme!** search me! (**b**) *(pièce de théâtre)* mystery (play) (**c**) **Mystère®** *(dessert glacé)* = vanilla ice cream filled with meringue and coated with chopped nuts

mystérieusement [misterjøzmɑ̃] *adv* mysteriously

mystérieux, -euse [misterjø, -øz] *adj* mysterious; *(secret)* secret

mysticisme [mistisism] *nm* mysticism

mystification [mistifikasjɔ̃] *nf* hoax

mystifier [66] [mistifje] *vt* to take in

mystique [mistik] **1** *adj* mystical
 2 *nmf* mystic

mythe [mit] *nm* myth

mythique [mitik] *adj* mythical

mythologie [mitɔlɔʒi] *nf* mythology

mythologique [mitɔlɔʒik] *adj* mythological

mythomane [mitɔman] **1** *adj* **être m.** to be a pathological liar
 2 *nmf* pathological liar, *Spéc* mythomaniac

mythomanie [mitɔmani] *nf* mythomania

myxomatose [miksɔmatoz] *nf* myxomatosis

N, n [ɛn] *nm inv* N, n
N [ɛn] **1** *(abrév* **Nord**) N
2 *nf (abrév* **route nationale)** = designation of major
road
nabot, -e [nabo, -ɔt] *nm,f Péj* midget
nacelle [nasɛl] *nf* **(a)** *(de montgolfière)* basket; *(de
dirigeable)* gondola **(b)** *(de landau) (détachable)* carrycot;
(fixe) carriage
nacre [nakr] *nf* mother-of-pearl; **un collier de** *ou* **en n.** a
mother-of-pearl necklace
nacré, -e [nakre] *adj* pearly
nage [naʒ] *nf* **(a)** *(activité)* swimming; *(manière)* stroke;
traverser une rivière à la n. to swim across a river; **le 100
mètres quatre nages** the 4 x 100 metres relay; **n. indienne**
sidestroke; **n. libre** freestyle **(b) être en n.** to be dripping
with sweat
nageoire [naʒwar] *nf (de poisson)* fin; *(de dauphin, de
cétacé)* flipper
nager [45] [naʒe] **1** *vt* to swim; **aller n.** to go for a swim; **n.
vers la côte** to swim for the shore; *Fig* **n. entre deux eaux**
to sit on the fence; *Fig* **n. dans son sang** to be bathed in
blood; *Fig* **n. dans le bonheur** to be on cloud nine; *Fam* **il
nage dans ses vêtements** his clothes are far too baggy on
him; *Fam* **je nage complètement!** I'm totally at sea!
2 *vt* **(a)** *(la brasse, le crawl)* to do, to swim **(b)** *(disputer)* **n. le
100 mètres** to swim (in) the 100 metres
nageur, -euse [naʒœr, -øz] *nm,f* swimmer
naguère [nagɛr] *adv Litt* not long ago; *(autrefois)* formerly
naïf, -ïve [naif, -iv] **1** *adj* naive
2 *nm,f* **(a)** *(personne)* fool **(b)** *(peintre)* naive painter
nain, -e [nɛ̃, nɛn] **1** *adj (personne)* dwarf
2 *nm,f* dwarf
Nairobi [nerobi] *n* Nairobi
naissance [nɛsɑ̃s] *nf* **(a)** *aussi Fig* birth; **sourd/aveugle
de n.** deaf/blind from birth, born deaf/blind; **français de
n.** French by birth; **donner n. à un enfant** to give birth to a
child; **donner n. à une rumeur** to give rise to a rumour; **il
était blond à la n.** his hair was blond when he was born **(b)**
(d'ongle) root; *(du cou)* base; **prendre n.** to originate; *(rivière)*
to rise
naissant, -e [nɛsɑ̃, -ɑ̃t] *adj (jour)* dawning; *(beauté)*
nascent; **une barbe naissante** stubble
naître [50a] [nɛtr] *vi (aux* **être) (a)** *(personne, animal)* to be
born; **enfant à n.** unborn child; **il naît plus de filles que
de garçons** more girls are born than boys; **elle est née en
1970** she was born in 1970; *Fam* **je ne suis pas né d'hier** *ou*
de la dernière pluie I wasn't born yesterday **(b)** *(espoir)* to
arise; *(projet, idée)* to originate **(de** in); **faire n.** *(espoir, doute,
soupçons)* to give rise to; *(sourire)* to raise

naïvement [naivmɑ̃] *adv* naively
naïveté [naivte] *nf* naivety; **avoir la n. de croire qch** to
be naive enough to believe sth
Namibie [namibi] *nf* la **N.** Namibia
namibien, -enne [namibjɛ̃, -ɛn] **1** *adj* Namibian
2 *nm,f* **N.** Namibian
nana [nana] *nf Fam* girl
nanisme [nanism] *nm* dwarfism
nano- [nano] *préf* nano-
nanti, -e [nɑ̃ti] **1** *adj* well-to-do
2 *nm,f* well-to-do person; **les nantis** the well-to-do
nantir [nɑ̃tir] *vt* **n. qn de qch** to provide sb with sth
napalm [napalm] *nm* napalm
naphtaline [naftalin] *nf* naphthalene; **boules de n.**
mothballs; *Can Fig* **sortir qch de la n.** to take sth out of
mothballs
Napoléon [napɔleɔ̃] **1** *npr* Napoleon
2 *nm Anciennement* n. *(pièce)* 20-franc piece *(bearing the
effigy of Napoleon)*
nappage [napaʒ] *nm* coating
nappe [nap] *nf* **(a)** *(de table)* tablecloth; **mettre la n.** to put
the tablecloth on; **ôter la n.** to take the tablecloth off **(b)** *Fig*
n. de brouillard fog patch; **n. d'eau** expanse of water; **n.
de pétrole** *(souterraine)* layer of oil; *(de marée noire)* oil slick;
n. phréatique water table
napper [nape] *vt* to coat **(de** with)
napperon [naprɔ̃] *nm* mat
narcisse [narsis] *nm* **(a)** *(fleur)* narcissus **(b)** *(personne)*
narcissist
narcissique [narsisik] *adj* narcissistic
narcissisme [narsisism] *nm* narcissism
narcodollars [narkodɔlar] *nmpl* drug money
narcotique [narkɔtik] *adj & nm* narcotic
narcotrafiquant, -e [narkotrafikɑ̃, -ɑ̃t] *nm,f* drug
trafficker
narguer [narge] *vt* to taunt
narine [narin] *nf* nostril
narquois, -e [narkwa, -az] *adj* taunting
narquoisement [narkwazmɑ̃] *adv* tauntingly
narrateur, -trice [naratœr, -tris] *nm,f* narrator
narratif, -ive [naratif, -iv] *adj* narrative
narration [narasjɔ̃] *nf* **(a)** *(genre)* narration **(b)** *(récit)*
narrative
narrer [nare] *vt Litt* to narrate
narval, -als [narval] *nm* narwhal
nasal, -e, -aux, -ales [nazal, -o] *adj* nasal

nase [naz] *adj Fam (personne)* shattered; *(machine, voiture)* kaput

naseau, -x [nazo] *nm* nostril

nasillard, -e [nazijar, -ard] *adj* nasal; *(vieux disque)* tinny

nasse [nas] *nf* pot

natal, -e, -als, -ales [natal] *adj* native

nataliste [natalist] *adj* politique n. pro-birth policy

natalité [natalite] *nf* **(taux de) n.** birth rate

natation [natasjɔ̃] *nf* swimming; **faire de la n.** to swim; **n. synchronisée** synchronized swimming

natif, -ive [natif, -iv] **1** *adj* native; **être n. de** to be a native of
2 *nm,f* native

nation [nasjɔ̃] *nf* nation; **les Nations unies** the United Nations

national, -e, -aux, -ales [nasjɔnal, -o] **1** *adj* national
2 *nmpl* **nationaux** nationals
3 *nf* **nationale** *(route) Br* ≃ A road, *Am* ≃ highway

nationalisation [nasjɔnalizasjɔ̃] *nf* nationalization

nationaliser [nasjɔnalize] *vt* to nationalize

nationalisme [nasjɔnalism] *nm* nationalism

nationaliste [nasjɔnalist] *adj & nmf* nationalist

nationalité [nasjɔnalite] *nf* nationality; **être de n. française** to be a French national

national-socialisme [nasjɔnalsɔsjalism] *nm Hist* National Socialism

nativité [nativite] *nf (Noël, peinture)* Nativity

natte [nat] *nf* **(a)** *(de cheveux) Br* plait, *Am* braid **(b)** *(de paille)* mat

natter [nate] *vt (cheveux, paille) Br* to plait, *Am* to braid

naturalisation [natyralizasjɔ̃] *nf* naturalization

naturaliser [natyralize] *vt* to naturalize; **se faire n.** to become naturalized

naturalisme [natyralism] *nm* naturalism

nature [natyr] **1** *nf* **(a)** *(univers)* nature; **contre n.** unnatural; **plus grand que n.** larger than life; **laisser faire la n.** to let nature take its course; *Fam* **elle n'est pas gâtée par la n.** nature hasn't been kind to her **(b)** *(campagne)* country; **en pleine n.** in the middle of the country; *Fig* **disparaître dans la n.** to vanish into thin air **(c)** *(caractère)* nature; **être timide de** *ou* **par n.** to be shy by nature; **être de n. à faire qch** to be likely to do sth; **chez elle, c'est une seconde n.** it's second nature to her; *Fam* **c'est une petite n.** he's a bit fragile **(d)** **payer en n.** to pay in kind **(e) n. morte** still life
2 *adj inv* **(a)** *(yaourt, omelette)* plain; **thé n.** black tea **(b)** *Fam (personne)* natural

naturel, -elle [natyrɛl] **1** *adj* natural; *(besoin)* bodily; **mort naturelle** death from natural causes; **mais c'est tout n.** don't mention it
2 *nm* **(a)** *(caractère)* nature; **être d'un n. peureux** to be timid by nature; *Prov* **chassez le n., il revient au galop** what's bred in the bone will come out in the flesh **(b)** *(simplicité)* naturalness; **avec (beaucoup de) n.** (very) naturally **(c)** **thon au n.** tuna in brine

naturellement [natyrɛlmɑ̃] *adv* naturally

naturisme [natyrism] *nm* naturism

naturiste [natyrist] *nmf & adj* naturist

naufrage [nofraʒ] *nm* (ship)wreck; *Fig (d'entreprise)* failure; **faire n.** *(bateau)* to be wrecked; *(marin)* to be shipwrecked; *Fig (entreprise)* to founder

naufragé, -e [nofraʒe] **1** *adj (bateau)* wrecked; *(marin)* shipwrecked
2 *nm,f* shipwrecked person

nauséabond, -e [nozeabɔ̃, -ɔ̃d] *adj (odeur)* nauseating; *(personne, pièce)* foul-smelling; *Fig (thèses)* sickening

nausée [noze] *nf* **(a)** *(envie de vomir)* nausea, sickness; **avoir la n., avoir des nausées** to feel sick **(b)** *Fig* disgust

nauséeux, -euse [nozeø, -øz] *adj* **se sentir n.** to feel sick *or* nauseous

nautique [notik] *adj* nautical

nautisme [notism] *nm* water sports

naval, -e, -als, -ales [naval] *adj* naval

navet [navɛ] *nm* turnip; *Fam* **c'est un n.** *(film, pièce)* it's a load of rubbish

navette [navɛt] *nf* **(a)** *(véhicule)* shuttle; **faire la n. entre deux endroits/services** to shuttle back and forth between two places/departments; **n. gratuite** courtesy bus **(b)** *(fusée)* **n. (spatiale)** (space) shuttle

navigable [navigabl] *adj* navigable

navigant, -e [naviɡɑ̃, -ɑ̃t] *adj voir* **personnel**

navigateur, -trice [navigatœr, -tris] **1** *nm,f (marin)* navigator; **n. solitaire** lone yachtsman
2 *nm Ordinat* browser

navigation [navigasjɔ̃] *nf* navigation; **après un mois de n.** after a month at sea

naviguer [navige] *vi* to sail **(vers** to); **n. sur l'Internet** to surf the Net

navire [navir] *nm* ship; **n.-école** training ship; **n. de guerre** warship

navrant, -e [navrɑ̃, -ɑ̃t] *adj* appalling; **un film n. de bêtise** an appallingly stupid film

navré, -e [navre] *adj (personne, expression, ton)* distressed; **être n. (de qch)** to be terribly sorry (about sth)

navrer [navre] *vt* to appal

naze [naz] = **nase**

nazi, -e [nazi] *adj & nm,f Hist* Nazi

nazisme [nazism] *nm Hist* Nazism

NB *(abrév* nota bene) NB

NDLR *(abrév* note de la rédaction) Ed

NdT *(abrév* note du traducteur) translator's note

ne [nə] *adv* **(a)** *voir* **aucun, guère, jamais, pas, personne, plus, que, rien (b)** *(utilisé seul)* **je n'ai que faire de vos conseils** I have no need of your advice; **elle est plus intelligente qu'elle n'y paraît** she's more intelligent than she seems; **qui ne connaît cette œuvre?** who doesn't know this work?

né, -e [ne] **1** *pp voir* **naître**
2 *adj* born; **Mme Martin, née Dupond** Mrs Martin, née Dupond; **né de parents anglais/inconnus** of English/unknown parentage; **être bien né** to be of noble birth; *Fig* **être né coiffé** to be born with a silver spoon in one's mouth; **c'est un conteur né** he's a born storyteller

néanmoins [neɑ̃mwɛ] *adv* nevertheless

néant [neɑ̃] *nm* **(a)** *(ce qui n'existe pas)* nothingness; **réduire qch à n.** to reduce sth to nothing **(b)** *(sur formulaire)* none

nébuleux, -euse [nebylø, -øz] **1** *adj aussi Fig* hazy
2 *nf* **nébuleuse** *Astron* nebula

nécessaire [nesesɛr] **1** *adj* necessary (à for); **n. pour faire qch** necessary to do sth; **il est n. que vous y alliez** you must go; **elles n'ont pas jugé n. de me le dire** they didn't think it necessary to tell me
2 *nm* **le n.** the necessities; **faire le n.** to do what's necessary; **n. de couture** sewing kit; **n. de toilette** toilet bag; **n. de voyage** overnight bag

nécessairement [nesesɛrmɑ̃] *adv* necessarily

nécessité [nesesite] *nf* necessity; **être dans la n. de faire**

qch to have no choice but to do sth; **quelle** n. **y avait-il de le faire?** why did it need to be done?; **faire de** n. **vertu** to make a virtue out of necessity; **produits de première** n. basic essentials; *Prov* n. **fait loi** needs must

nécessiter [nesesite] *vt* to require, to necessitate

nécessiteux, -euse [nesesitø, -øz] **1** *adj* needy **2** *nm,f* person in need; **les n.** the needy

nec plus ultra [nɛkplyzyltra] *nm inv* **le n.** the best there is

nécrologie [nekrɔlɔʒi] *nf (notice)* obituary; *(liste)* obituary column

nécrologique [nekrɔlɔʒik] *adj voir* rubrique

nécropole [nekrɔpɔl] *nf* necropolis

nécrose [nekroz] *nf* necrosis

nécroser [nekroze] **1** *vt* to necrose **2 se nécroser** *vpr* to necrose

nectar [nɛktar] *nm* nectar

nectarine [nɛktarin] *nf* nectarine

néerlandais, -e [neerlɑ̃dɛ, -ɛz] **1** *adj* Dutch **2** *nm,f* **N.** Dutchman, *f* Dutchwoman; **les N.** the Dutch **3** *nm (langue)* Dutch

nef [nɛf] *nf (d'église)* n. **(centrale)** nave; **n. latérale** aisle

néfaste [nefast] *adj* harmful

nèfle [nɛfl] *nf* medlar; *Fam* **des nèfles!** no way!

négatif, -ive [negatif, -iv] **1** *adj* negative **2** *nm Phot* negative

négation [negasjɔ̃] *nf* **(a)** *(fait de nier)* negation **(b)** *Gram* negative

négationniste [negasjɔnist] *adj & nmf* revisionist

négativement [negativmɑ̃] *adv (réagir)* negatively; *(répondre)* in the negative

négligé, -e [negliʒe] **1** *adj* **(a)** *(peu soigné)* slovenly **(b)** *(délaissé)* neglected **2** *nm (vêtement)* negligée

négligeable [negliʒabl] *adj* negligible; **un avantage non** n. a not inconsiderable advantage; **une quantité non n. de** a significant quantity of

négligemment [negliʒamɑ̃] *adv* **(a)** *(habillé)* carelessly **(b)** *(répondre, lire)* casually

négligence [negliʒɑ̃s] *nf* **(a)** *(manque de soin)* carelessness, negligence; *(abandon)* neglect; **avec n.** carelessly **(b)** *(acte négligent)* act of carelessness; *(oubli)* oversight; **par n.** through carelessness

négligent, -e [negliʒɑ̃, -ɑ̃t] *adj* careless, negligent

négliger [45] [negliʒe] **1** *vt* **(a)** *(délaisser)* to neglect **(b)** *(omettre)* to disregard; **n. de faire qch** to neglect to do sth **2 se négliger** *vpr* to neglect oneself

négoce [negɔs] *nm* trade

négociable [negɔsjabl] *adj* negotiable

négociant, -e [negɔsjɑ̃, -ɑ̃t] *nm,f* merchant, dealer

négociation [negɔsjasjɔ̃] *nf* negotiation; **entamer des négociations sur qch** to enter into negotiations on sth; **être en n. avec qn** to be in negotiation with sb

négocier [66] [negɔsje] **1** *vt* **(a)** *(prêt, salaire, paix)* to negotiate; **prix à n.** price negotiable **(b)** *(virage)* to negotiate **2** *vi (discuter)* to negotiate **(avec** with)

nègre [nɛgr] **1** *nm* **(a)** *Injurieux* Negro **(b)** *Fig (écrivain)* ghost writer; **être le n. de qn** to ghost for sb **2** *adj (a)* **l'art n.** Negro art **(b)** *Injurieux (personne)* Negro

négresse [negrɛs] *nf Injurieux* Negress

neige [nɛʒ] *nf (a) (flocons)* snow; *Can* **banc de n.** snow bank; **être bloqué par la n.** to be snowbound; **aller à la n.** to go on a skiing holiday; **fondre comme n. au soleil** to melt away; **être blanc comme n.** to be as white as snow;

Fig to be as pure as the driven snow; **n. artificielle** artificial snow; **n. carbonique** dry ice; **neiges éternelles** perpetual snow; **n. fondue** *(qui tombe)* sleet; *(par terre)* slush **(b)** *très Fam (cocaïne)* snow

neiger [45] [neʒe] *v impersonnel* to snow

neigeux, -euse [neʒø, -øz] *adj (temps, blanc)* snowy; *(pic, pente)* snow-covered

nem [nɛm] *nm* spring roll

néné [nene] *nm Fam* tit, boob

nénette [nenɛt] *nf Fam* **(a)** *(jeune fille)* chick **(b)** *(petite amie)* girl **(c)** *(tête)* **se casser la n.** to rack one's brains

nénuphar [nenyfar] *nm* water lily

néo- [neo] *préf* neo-

néo-calédonien, -enne *(mpl* néo-calédoniens, *fpl* **néo-calédoniennes)** [neokaledɔnjɛ̃, -ɛn] **1** *adj* New Caledonian **2** *nm,f* **N.-C.** New Caledonian

néoclassique [neoklasik] *adj* neoclassical

néocolonialisme [neokɔlɔnjalism] *nm* neocolonialism

néolithique [neolitik] *Géol* **1** *adj* Neolithic **2** *nm* **le N.** the Neolithic period

néologisme [neolɔʒism] *nm* neologism

néon [neɔ̃] *nm (gaz)* neon; *(tube)* neon tube; *(enseigne)* neon sign

néonazi, -e [neonazi] *adj & nm,f* neo-Nazi

néonazisme [neonazism] *nm* neo-Nazism

néophyte [neofit] *nmf (nouvel adepte)* novice

néo-zélandais, -e *(mpl* néo-zélandais, *fpl* néo-**zélandaises)** [neozelɑ̃dɛ, -ɛz] **1** *adj* New Zealand **2** *nm,f* **N.-Z.** New Zealander

Népal [nepal] *nm* **le N.** Nepal

népalais, -e [nepalɛ, -ɛz] **1** *adj* Nepalese **2** *nm,f* **N.** Nepalese; **les N.** the Nepalese **3** *nm (langue)* Nepali

néphrétique [nefretik] *adj voir* colique

népotisme [nepɔtism] *nm* nepotism

Neptune [nɛptyn] *npr (dieu, planète)* Neptune

nerf [nɛr] *nm* **(a)** *(optique, spinal)* nerve; **viande pleine de nerfs** meat full of gristle; **avoir les nerfs solides** to have strong nerves; **être malade des nerfs** to suffer from nerves; **être sur les nerfs** to live on one's nerves; **être à bout de nerfs** to be at the end of one's tether; **passer ses nerfs sur qn/qch** to take it out on sb/sth; *Fam* **avoir les nerfs en pelote** *ou* **en boule** to be on edge; *Fam* **porter** *ou* **taper** *ou Can* **tomber sur les nerfs à qn** to get on sb's nerves; *Fam* **c'est un paquet** *ou* **une boule de nerfs** he's a bag of nerves **(b)** *(force)* **un peu de n.!, du n.!** get stuck in!; **l'argent est le n. de la guerre** money is the sinews of war

nerveusement [nɛrvøzmɑ̃] *adv* nervously

nerveux, -euse [nɛrvø, -øz] *adj* **(a)** *(système, maladie)* nervous **(b)** *(émotif) (personne, rire, toux)* nervous **(c)** *(dynamique) (personne, style)* dynamic; **une conduite nerveuse** jerky driving **(d)** *(corps, main)* sinewy; *(viande)* stringy **2** *nm,f* nervous person

nervosité [nɛrvozite] *nf (excitation)* nervousness; *(irritabilité)* irritability

nervure [nɛrvyr] *nf (de feuille, d'aile d'insecte)* rib *(de voûte)* rib

n'est-ce pas [nɛspɑ] *adv* **tu viendras, n.?** you'll come, won't you?; **tu l'as, n.?** you've got it, haven't you?; **n. qu'elle est mignonne?** she's cute, isn't she?; **le problème, n., c'est qu'il est déjà tard** the problem is that it's already late, you think?

net, nette [nɛt] **1** *adj (a) (propre)* clean; *Fig (conscience)* clear; **faire place nette** to clear everything out **(b)** *(précis) (contour)* sharp; *(différence, souvenir)* clear; *(écriture)* neat; *(cassure)* clean; **il fait plus froid, c'est très n.** it's noticeably colder **(c)** *(prix, salaire, profit)* net; **n. d'impôt** net of tax **(d)** *Fam* **il n'est pas n.** *(fou)* he's not all there; *(louche)* he's a bit dodgy

2 *adv* **(a)** *(brutalement)* **refuser (tout) n.** to refuse point-blank; **s'arrêter n.** to stop dead; **se casser n.** to break clean through; **tué n.** killed outright **(b)** *Com* **100 euros n.** 100 euros net; **n. à payer** net payable

nettement [nɛtmɑ̃] *adv* **(a)** *(avec précision)* clearly **(b)** *(incontestablement)* distinctly **(c)** *(beaucoup)* much; **il va n. mieux** he's much better; **il est n. moins bon qu'elle** he's not nearly as good as her

netteté [nɛtte] *nf* **(a)** *(propreté)* cleanness **(b)** *(précision) (de cassure)* cleanness **(c)** *(clarté) (de vision, d'objet)* distinctness; *(d'image)* sharpness; *(de refus)* flatness

nettoiement [nɛtwamɑ̃] *nm* cleaning; **service du n.** refuse collection service

nettoyage [nɛtwajaʒ] *nm* cleaning; **faire du n.** to do the cleaning; **faire le n. par le vide** to throw everything out; **grand n. de printemps** spring cleaning; **n. à sec** dry-cleaning

nettoyant, -e [nɛtwajɑ̃, -ɑ̃t] **1** *adj* cleaning
2 *nm* cleaning product

nettoyer [32] [nɛtwaje] **1** *vt* **(a)** *(rendre propre)* to clean; **n. à sec** to dry-clean **(b)** *Fam (sujet: cambrioleur) (maison)* to clean out; **se faire n. au jeu** to be cleaned out gambling
2 se nettoyer *vpr* **(a) se n. les oreilles/les mains** to clean one's ears/hands **(b) le four se nettoie automatiquement** the oven is self-cleaning

neuf¹ [nœf] *adj & nm inv* nine; *voir aussi* **trois**

neuf², neuve [nœf, nœv] **1** *adj* new; **tout n.** brand new; **comme n.** as good as new; **quoi de n.?** what's new?
2 *nm* **habillé de n.** wearing new clothes; **acheter du n.** *(dans l'immobilier)* to buy new; **remettre qch à n.** to make sth as good as new; *(machine)* to recondition sth

neurasthénie [nørasteni] *nf* depression

neurasthénique [nørastenik] *adj & nmf* depressive

neurochirurgie [nøroʃiryrʒi] *nf* neurosurgery

neurochirurgien, -enne [nøroʃiryrʒjɛ̃, -ɛn] *nm,f* neurosurgeon

neuroleptique [nørolɛptik] *adj & nm* neuroleptic

neurologie [nørolɔʒi] *nf* neurology

neurologue [nørolɔg] *nmf* neurologist

neurone [nørɔn, nøron] *nm* neuron

neutraliser [nøtralize] **1** *vt* to neutralize
2 se neutraliser *vpr* to neutralize each other

neutralité [nøtralite] *nf* neutrality; **sortir de sa n.** to abandon one's neutral position

neutre [nøtr] **1** *adj* **(a)** *(ni masculin ni féminin)* neuter **(b)** *(impartial)* neutral **(c)** *(ton de voix, couleur)* neutral **(d)** *Chim & Él* neutral
2 *nm* **(a)** *Gram* neuter **(b)** *Can Aut* neutral; **se mettre sur le n.** to go into neutral

neutron [nøtrɔ̃] *nm* neutron

neuvième [nœvjɛm] *nmf, nm & adj* ninth; *voir aussi* **cinquième**

névé [neve] *nm* névé, firn

neveu, -x [nəvø] *nm* nephew; *Fam* **un peu, mon n.!** absolutely!

névralgie [nevralʒi] *nf* neuralgia; **avoir des névralgies** to suffer from neuralgia

névralgique [nevralʒik] *adj* neuralgic

névrose [nevroz] *nf* neurosis; **n. post-traumatique** post-traumatic stress disorder

névrosé, -e [nevroze] *adj & nm,f* neurotic

New York [nujɔrk] *n* New York

new-yorkais, -e *(mpl* new-yorkais, *fpl* new-yorkaises) [njujɔrkɛ, -ɛz] **1** *adj* of New York
2 *nm,f* **N.-Y.** New Yorker

nez [ne] *nm* **(a)** *(organe)* nose; **n. en trompette** turned-up nose; **avoir le n. bouché** to have a blocked nose; **parler du n.** to speak through one's nose; **sentir qch à plein n.** to smell strongly of sth; **rire au n. de qn** to laugh in sb's face; **faire qch au n. et à la barbe de qn** to do sth right under sb's nose; **fermer** *ou* **claquer la porte au n. de qn** to shut the door in sb's face; **se trouver n. à n. avec qn** to find oneself face to face with sb; **avoir le n. dans son journal** to have one's nose in one's newspaper; **avoir le n. en l'air** to be looking up in the air; *Fig (rêvasser)* to have one's head in the clouds; *Fig* **mener qn par le bout du n.** to lead sb by the nose; *Fam* **fourrer** *ou* **mettre son n. dans les affaires de qn** to poke one's nose into sb's affairs; *Fam* **avoir un verre** *ou* **un coup dans le n.** to have had one too many; **je n'ai pas mis le n. dehors de toute la journée** I didn't set foot outside all day; **tu ne vois pas plus loin que le bout de ton n.** you can't see past the end of your nose; *Fam* **elle nous a dans le n.** she can't stand us; **ça lui pend au n.** she's got it coming to her; **ça se voit comme le n. au milieu de la figure** it's as plain as the nose on your face; **où est-il? – il est sous ton n.** *ou* **tu as le n. dessus** where is it? – it's right under your nose **(b)** *(odorat)* sense of smell; **avoir le n. fin** to have a good nose; *Fig* **avoir du n.** to be shrewd **(c)** *(de bateau, d'avion)* nose **(d)** *(parfumeur)* nose

ni [ni] *conj* **ni... ni...** neither... nor...; **ni Pierre ni Paul ne sont venus** neither Pierre nor Paul came; **sans argent ni bagages** without money or luggage; **il est parti sans manger ni boire** he left without eating or drinking; **ni l'un ni l'autre** neither (of them); **ni plus ni moins** neither more nor less

niais, -e [njɛ, -njɛz] **1** *adj* silly
2 *nm,f* fool

niaisage [njɛzaʒ] *nm Can* idleness

niaisement [njɛzmɑ̃] *adv* foolishly

niaiser [njɛze] *Can* **1** *vt* **n. qn** *(faire tourner en bourrique)* to drive sb crazy; *(se moquer de)* to laugh at sb; *(raconter des histoires à)* to pull sb's leg
2 *vi (ne rien faire)* to hang around doing nothing

niaiserie [njɛzri] *nf* **(a)** *(caractère stupide)* silliness **(b)** *(acte, remarque)* silly thing

niaiseux, -euse [njɛzø, -øz] *Can Fam* **1** *adj* silly
2 *nm,f* fool

Nicaragua [nikaragwa] *nm* **le N.** Nicaragua

nicaraguayen, -enne [nikaragwajɛ̃, -ɛn] **1** *adj* Nicaraguan
2 *nm,f* **N.** Nicaraguan

niche [niʃ] *nf* **(a)** *(renfoncement)* niche, recess **(b)** *(de chien)* kennel

nichée [niʃe] *nf (d'oisillons)* brood; *(de souris, de chiots)* litter

nicher [niʃe] **1** *vi (oiseau)* to nest **(dans** in)
2 *vt* **n. sa tête au creux de l'épaule de qn** to nestle one's head against sb's shoulder
3 se nicher *vpr (a) (oiseau)* to nest **(b)** *Fam (se cacher)* **où est-elle allée se n.?** where's she hiding (herself)?

nichon [niʃɔ̃] *nm Fam* boob, tit

nickel [nikɛl] **1** *nm* nickel
2 *adj inv Fam (propre)* spotlessly clean

nicotine [nikɔtin] *nf* nicotine

nid [ni] *nm aussi Fig* nest; *Fig* **n. à poussière** dust trap; *Prov* **petit à petit, l'oiseau fait son n.** slow and steady wins the race
nid-de-poule (*pl* **nids-de-poule**) [nidpul] *nm* pothole
nièce [njɛs] *nf* niece
nier [66] [nje] **1** *vt* to deny; **je nie l'avoir vue** I deny having seen her; **on ne peut pas n. que...** there's no denying that ; **n. l'évidence** to deny the obvious **2** *vi (accusé)* to deny the charge
nigaud, -e [nigo, -od] *nm,f* ninny; **gros n.!** you big ninny!
Niger [niʒer] *nm* **le N.** *(pays)* Niger; *(fleuve)* the Niger
Nigeria [niʒerja] *nm* **le N.** Nigeria
nigérian, -e [niʒerjɑ̃, -an] **1** *adj* Nigerian **2** *nm,f* **N.** Nigerian
nigérien, -enne [niʒerjɛ̃, -ɛn] **1** *adj* Nigerien **2** *nm,f* **N.** Nigerien
nihilisme [niilism] *nm* nihilism
nihiliste [niilist] **1** *adj* nihilistic **2** *nmf* nihilist
Nil [nil] *nm* **le N.** the Nile
n'importe [nɛ̃pɔrt] *voir* **Importer**
nipper [nipe] *Fam* **1** *vt* to dress; **bien nippé** dolled up **2 se nipper** *vpr* to dress
nippes [nip] *nfpl Fam (vêtements)* gear, togs
nippon, -onne *ou* **-one** [nipɔ̃, -ɔn] **1** *adj* Japanese **2** *nm,f* **N.** Japanese; **les Nippons** the Japanese
nique [nik] *nf Fam* **faire la n. à qn** to cock a snook at sb
niquer [nike] *vt* **(a)** *très Fam (abîmer)* to knacker **(b)** *Vulg (sexuellement)* to shag. In screw **(c)** *très Fam (escroquer)* **se faire n.** to get shafted
nitrate [nitrat] *nm* nitrate
nitreux, -euse [nitrø, -øz] *adj* nitrous
nitrique [nitrik] *adj* nitric
nitroglycérine [nitrogliserin] *nf* nitroglycerine
niveau, -x [nivo] *nm* **(a)** *(hauteur, étage)* level; **n. de l'eau/de la mer** water/sea level; **au n. de la mer** at sea level; **au n. régional/local** at regional/local level; *Fam* **au n. sentimental** as far as one's love life is concerned; *aussi Fig* **se mettre au n. de qn** to put oneself on sb's level; **l'eau nous arrivait au n. de la taille** the water came up to our waists **(b)** *(degré)* level; *Scol* standard; **avoir le n. (requis), être au n.** to be up to standard; **ne pas avoir le n. pour passer un concours** not to be of a high enough standard to take an examination; **elle a un très bon n. en anglais** she's reached a very high standard in English; **ils sont d'un n. social différent** they are from different social backgrounds; *Ordinat* **n. d'accès** *(dans un réseau)* access level; *Ordinat* **n. de gris** grey scale; **n. de langue** register; **n. de vie** standard of living
niveler [42] [nivle] *vt* **(a)** *(sol)* to level **(b)** *(fortunes)* to even out
nivellement [nivɛlmɑ̃] *nm (de terrain, des classes sociales)* levelling; **n. par le bas** levelling down
nobiliaire [nɔbiljɛr] *adj* **titre n.** title, **particule n.** nobiliary particle
noble [nɔbl] **1** *adj* noble; **le n. art** *(boxe)* the noble art **2** *nmf* nobleman, *f* noblewoman; **les nobles** the nobility
noblement [nɔbləmɑ̃] *adv* nobly
noblesse [nɔblɛs] *nf* nobility; **la haute et la petite n.** the nobility and the gentry; **n. oblige** noblesse oblige
noce [nɔs] *nf* **(a)** *(cérémonie du mariage)* wedding; *(ensemble des invités)* wedding party; **noces d'argent/d'or/ de diamant** silver/golden/diamond wedding; **il l'a épousée en secondes noces** she's his second wife **(b)**

Fam **faire la n.** to live it up **(c)** *Fam* **je n'étais pas à la n.** it was no picnic
noceur, -euse [nɔsœr, -øz] *nm,f Fam* party animal, raver
nocif, -ive [nɔsif, -iv] *adj* harmful
nocivité [nɔsivite] *nf* harmfulness
noctambule [nɔktɑ̃byl] *nmf* night owl
nocturne [nɔktyrn] **1** *adj (animal)* nocturnal; *(attaque, visite)* night; **évasion n.** escape by night **2** *nm (musique)* nocturne **3** *nf* **(a)** *(de magasin)* late-night opening **(b)** *(disputé)* **en n.** evening game
nodal, -e, -aux, -ales [nɔdal, -o] *adj* nodal
nodule [nɔdyl] *nm Géol & Méd* nodule
Noé [nɔe] *n* Noah
Noël [nɔɛl] *nm* **(a)** *(fête)* Christmas; **à N.** at Christmas (time); **le jour de N.** Christmas Day; **arbre** *ou* **sapin de N.** Christmas tree; **joyeux N.!** Happy *or* Merry Christmas! **(b)** *(chanson)* **n.** (Christmas) carol **(c)** *(cadeau)* **(petit) n.** Christmas present
nœud [nø] *nm* **(a)** *(entrecroisement)* knot, **faire un n.** (à **qch**) to make *or* tie a knot (in sth); **n. coulant** *(pour serrer)* slipknot; *(pour étrangler)* noose; **n. de vipères** nest of vipers **(b)** *(ornement)* bow, **n. de cravate** tie knot; **faire un n. de cravate** to knot a tie; *Fam* **n. pap** bow tie; **n. papillon** bow tie **(c)** *(de courbe) & Ordinat* node **(d)** *(sur bois)* knot **(e)** *Naut (vitesse)* knot; **filer** *ou* **faire 20 nœuds** to do *or* make 20 knots **(f)** *Vulg (pénis)* cock
noie *etc voir* **noyer**
noir, -e [nwar] **1** *adj (couleur)* black; **la place était noire de monde** the square was swarming with people **(b)** *(très sombre)* dark; **il fait tout n.** it's pitch-black **(c)** *(sale)* black **(d)** *Fig (pensées, dessein, regard)* black; **être d'une humeur noire** to be in a black mood **2** *nm,f* **N.** Black (man), *f* Black (woman) **3** *nm* **(a)** *(couleur)* black; **en n. et blanc** *(film, photo)* black and white; **être en n.** to be dressed in black; **c'était écrit n. sur blanc** it was there in black and white **(b)** *(obscurité)* dark; **avoir peur du n.** to be afraid of the dark **(c)** *(salissure)* **avoir du n. sur le visage** to have a black mark on one's face **(d)** *(d'une cible)* bull's-eye **(e)** *(café)* **un (petit) n.** a (small) black coffee **(f)** *Fig* **voir tout en n.** to look on the dark side of everything **(g)** *Fam* **le travail au n.** moonlighting; **travailler au n.** to moonlight **4** *nf* **noire** *(note de musique) Br* crotchet, *Am* quarter note
noirâtre [nwaratr] *adj* blackish
noirceur [nwarsœr] *nf* **(a)** *(couleur)* blackness; *Litt (d'un crime)* heinousness **(b)** *Can (obscurité)* dark, darkness; **dans la n.** in the dark *or* darkness; **avoir peur dans la n.** to be afraid of the dark
noircir [nwarsir] **1** *vt* to blacken; *Fig* **n. du papier** to write pages and pages; *Fig* **n. (la réputation de) qn** to blacken sb's reputation; *Fig* **n. le tableau** *ou* **la situation** to paint things blacker than they are **2** *vi* to turn *or* go black **3** *nm noircir vpr* **(a)** *(ciel)* to darken **(b)** **se n. le visage** to black one's face; *Th* to black up
noise [nwaz] *nf* **chercher n.** *ou* **des noises à qn** to try to pick a quarrel with sb
noisetier [nwaztje] *nm (arbre)* hazel tree; *(bois)* hazel (wood)
noisette [nwazɛt] **1** *nf* **(a)** *(fruit)* hazelnut **(b)** *(petite quantité) (de beurre)* small knob; *(de gel)* small amount **2** *adj inv* **yeux n.** hazel eyes

noix [nwa] *nf* (**a**) *(fruit)* walnut; **n. de cajou** cashew nut; **n. de coco** coconut; **n. de pécan** pecan (**b**) *(petite quantité) (de beurre)* knob (**c**) **n. de veau** cushion of veal (**d**) *Fam* **à la n.** lousy

nom [nɔ̃] *nm* (**a**) *(de personne, de chose)* name; **un homme du n.** de Michel a man by the name of Michel; **n....** prénom... *(sur formulaire)* surname... first name...; **vos n.**, **prénoms et adresse** your full name and address; **porter le n. de sa mère** to be named after one's mother; **sous le n. de Leduc** under the name of Leduc; **se faire un n.** to make a name for oneself; **appeler les choses par leur n.** to call a spade a spade; **traiter qn de tous les noms** to call sb everything under the sun; **quelqu'un dont je tairai le n.** someone who shall remain nameless; **une impolitesse sans n.** unspeakable rudeness; **un grand n. de la musique** one of the great names in music; **au n. de la loi/de l'amitié** in the name of the law/of friendship; *Fam* **avoir un n. à coucher dehors** to have a totally unpronounceable name; **n. de baptème** Christian name; *Ordinat* **n. de champ** field name; **n. d'emprunt** assumed name; **n. de famille** surname; *Ordinat* **n. de fichier** file name; **n. de jeune fille** maiden name; **n. à particule** aristocratic name *(with a nobiliary particle)*; **n. de plume** nom de plume, pen name; *Fam* **n. à rallonges** *ou* **à tiroirs** long aristocratic name; **n. de scène** *ou* **de théâtre** stage name (**b**) *Gram* noun; **n. commun** common noun; **n. composé** compound (noun); **n. propre** proper noun (**c**) *Fam* **n. d'une pipe!, n. d'un chien!** hell!; **n. de Dieu!** for Christ's sake!

nomade [nɔmad] **1** *adj* nomadic
2 *nmf* nomad

nomadisme [nɔmadism] *nm* nomadism

nombre [nɔ̃br] *nm aussi Gram* number; **un grand/petit n. d'entre nous** many/a few of us; **le plus grand n.** the majority; (**bon**) **n. de** a good many; **supérieur en n.** superior in number(s); **nous sommes en n. suffisant** there are enough of us; **venir en n.** to come in large numbers; **ils sont au n. de dix** there are ten of them; **être au n. ou du n. de** to be among; **faire n.** to make up the numbers; *Phys* **n. atomique** atomic number; *Math* **n. décimal** decimal (number); *Math* **n. entier** whole number, integer; *Math* **n. premier** prime number

nombreux, -euse [nɔ̃brø, -øz] *adj (membres, objets)* numerous, many; *(famille, armée, groupe)* large; **nous sommes peu n.** there aren't many of us; **venir (très) n.** to come in (very) large numbers

nombril [nɔ̃bri, nɔ̃bril] *nm* navel; **une chemise ouverte jusqu'au n.** a shirt open to the waist; **il se prend pour le n. du monde** he thinks the whole world revolves around him; *Fig* **se regarder le n.** to contemplate one's navel

nombrilisme [nɔ̃brilism] *nm* navel-gazing
nombriliste [nɔ̃brilist] *adj* self-absorbed

nomenclature [nɔmɑ̃klatyr] *nf (de termes techniques)* nomenclature; *(d'un dictionnaire)* word list

nominal, -e, -aux, -ales [nɔminal, -o] *adj* (**a**) *(prix, autorité) & Fin* nominal (**b**) *(par noms de famille)* **appel n.** roll call; **liste nominale** list of names (**c**) *Gram* noun

nominalement [nɔminalmɑ̃] *adv* (**a**) *(de nom seulement)* in name only (**b**) *Gram (employé)* as a noun

nominatif, -ive [nɔminatif, -iv] *adj (carte d'adhérent, billet)* nontransferable; *Fin (titre)* registered

nomination [nɔminasjɔ̃] *nf* (**a**) *(à un poste)* appointment (à to) (**b**) *(pour une remise de récompense)* nomination (à for)

nominativement [nɔminativmɑ̃] *adv* by name

nominé, -e [nɔmine] *adj* nominated (à for)

nommé, -e [nɔme] **1** *adj (personne, objet)* named

2 *nm,f* **un n.** Bertrand a appelé someone called Bertrand called

nommément [nɔmemɑ̃] *adv* (**a**) *(par son nom)* by name (**b**) *(spécialement)* especially, in particular

nommer [nɔme] **1** *vt* (**a**) *(donner un prénom à)* to name, to call (**b**) *(donner un nom à)* **on nomme aumôniers les prêtres attachés à un régiment** priests attached to a regiment are called chaplains (**c**) *(désigner)* to name; *Hum* **M. Boivin, pour ne pas le n.** without mentioning any names, Mr Boivin (**d**) *(à un poste)* to appoint (à to); **être nommé à Lille** to be posted to Lille

2 se nommer *vpr* (**a**) *(avoir pour nom)* to be called (**b**) *(s'identifier)* to give one's name

non [nɔ̃] **1** *adv* (**a**) *(en réponse, exprime la surprise, l'indignation)* no; **je pense que n.** I don't think so; **faire signe que n.** *(de la tête)* to shake one's head; **n. mais!** honestly! (**b**) *(n'est-ce pas?)* **c'est dégoûtant, n.?** it's disgusting, isn't it?; **il est pas mal, n.?** he's not bad-looking, is he? (**c**) *(pas)* not; **n. loin** not far; **qu'elle vienne ou n.** whether she comes or not; **elle veut déménager, lui n.** she wants to move house but he doesn't; *Littr* **n. (pas) que je le craigne** not that I fear him

2 *nm inv* no

nonagénaire [nɔnaʒenɛr] *adj & nmf* nonagenarian

non-agression [nɔnagresjɔ̃] *nf voir* **pacte**

non-alcoolisé, -e [nɔnalkɔlize] *adj* non-alcoholic

non-aligné, -e [nɔnaliɲe] *adj Pol* non-aligned

nonante [nɔnɑ̃t] *adj & nm inv Belg & Suisse* ninety; *voir aussi* **trois**

non-assistance [nɔnasistɑ̃s] *nf Jur* **n. à personne en danger** = failure to assist injured people, for example at the scene of an accident

non-autorisé, -e [nɔnɔtɔrize] *adj Ordinat (nom de fichier)* illegal

non-belligérant, -e [nɔ̃beliʒerɑ̃, -ɑ̃t] *adj* non-belligerent

nonchalamment [nɔ̃ʃalamɑ̃] *adv* nonchalantly

nonchalance [nɔ̃ʃalɑ̃s] *nf* nonchalance

nonchalant, -e [nɔ̃ʃalɑ̃, -ɑ̃t] *adj* nonchalant

non-conformisme [nɔ̃kɔ̃fɔrmism] *nm* non-conformism

non-conformiste [nɔ̃kɔ̃fɔrmist] *adj & nmf* non-conformist

non-conformité [nɔ̃kɔ̃fɔrmite] *nf* nonconformity

non-connecté, -e [nɔ̃kɔnɛkte] *adj Ordinat* off-line

non-dit [nɔ̃di] *nm* **le n.** what is unspoken; **un film riche en non-dits** a film full of meaningful silences

non-formaté, -e [nɔ̃fɔrmate] *adj Ordinat* unformatted

non-fumeur, -euse [nɔ̃fymœr, -øz] **1** *adj* non-smoking
2 *nm,f* non-smoker

non-ingérence [nɔnɛ̃ʒerɑ̃s] *nf* noninterference

non-initialisé, -e [nɔninisjalize] *adj Ordinat* uninitialized

non-initié, -e [nɔninisje] *nm,f* uninitiated person; **les non-initiés** the uninitiated

non-inscrit, -e [nɔnɛ̃skri, -it] *nm,f Pol* independent

non-intervention [nɔnɛ̃tɛrvɑ̃sjɔ̃] *nf* non-intervention

non-interventionniste [nɔnɛ̃tɛrvɑ̃sjɔnist] *adj* non-interventionist

non-lieu, -x [nɔ̃ljø] *nm Jur* **bénéficier d'un n.** to be discharged through lack of evidence

nonne [nɔn] *nf* nun

nono, -ote [nɔno, -ɔt] *nm,f Can Fam* idiot

non-paiement [nɔ̃pɛmɑ̃] *nm* non-payment

non-polluant, -e [nɔ̃pɔlɥɑ̃, -ɑ̃t] *adj* environmentally friendly

non-prolifération [nɔ̃prɔliferajɔ̃] *nf* nonproliferation

non-remboursable [nɔ̃rɑ̃bursabl] *adj* non-refundable

non-respect [nɔ̃rɛspɛ] *nm (d'une loi)* non-observance

non-retour [nɔ̃rətur] *nm* point de n. point of no return

non-salarié, -e [nɔ̃salarje] *nm,f* self-employed person

non-sens [nɔ̃sɑ̃s] *nm inv* **(a)** *(dans une traduction)* meaningless phrase **(b)** *(absurdité)* **un n.** a nonsense

non-stop [nɔnstɔp] *adj inv & adv Fam* non-stop

non-syndiqué, -e [nɔ̃sɛ̃dike] **1** *adj* non-union **2** *nm,f* non-union worker

non-violence [nɔ̃vjɔlɑ̃s] *nf* non-violence

non-violent, -e [nɔ̃vjɔlɑ̃, -ɑ̃t] *adj* non-violent

non-voyant, -e *(mpl* **non-voyants,** *fpl* **non-voyantes)** [nɔ̃vwajɑ̃, -ɑ̃t] *nm,f* unsighted person; **les non-voyants** the unsighted

nord [nɔr] **1** *nm* north; **un vent du n.** a northerly *or* north wind; **le vent du n.** the north wind; **au n.** in the north; **au n. de** (to the) north of; *Fig* **il ne perd pas le n.** he's keeping a cool head; **le grand N.** the Frozen North **2** *adj inv (côte, face)* north; *(régions)* northern

nord-africain, -e *(mpl* **nord-africains,** *fpl* **nord-africaines)** [nɔrafrikɛ̃, -ɛn] **1** *adj* North African **2** *nm,f* **N.-A.** North African

nord-américain, -e *(mpl* **nord-américains,** *fpl* **nord-américaines)** [nɔramerikɛ̃, -ɛn] **1** *adj* North American **2** *nm,f* **N.-A.** North American

nord-coréen, -enne *(mpl* **nord-coréens,** *fpl* **nord-coréennes)** [nɔrkɔreɛ̃, -ɛn] **1** *adj* North Korean **2** *nm,f* **N.-C.** North Korean

nord-est [nɔrɛst] *nm & adj inv* north-east

nordique [nɔrdik] **1** *adj* Nordic, Scandinavian **2** *nmf* N. Scandinavian

nordiste [nɔrdist] *adj & nmf* Unionist

nord-nord-est [nɔrnɔrɛst] *nm & adj inv* north-north-east

nord-nord-ouest [nɔrnɔrwɛst] *nm & adj inv* north-northwest

nord-ouest [nɔrwɛst] *nm & adj inv* northwest

nord-vietnamien, -enne *(mpl* **nord-vietnamiens,** *fpl* **nord-vietnamiennes)** [nɔrvjɛtnamjɛ̃, -ɛn] **1** *adj* North Vietnamese **2** *nm,f* **N.-V.** North Vietnamese

noria [nɔrja] *nf* noria

normal, -e, -aux, -ales [nɔrmal, -o] **1** *adj (dans la norme, naturel)* normal; **c'est tout à fait n. que la jeunesse se rebelle** it's perfectly normal for young people to rebel; **ce n'est pas n. (que** + *subjunctive)* it's not right (that); **en temps n.** in normal circumstances **(b)** *(moyen) (poids, taille)* standard **2** *nf* **normale (a) la normale** normal, the norm; **au-dessus/au-dessous de la normale** above/below average; **température au-dessous des normales saisonnières** temperature below the seasonal average **(b)** *Fam Univ* **Normale Sup** = university-level college preparing students for senior posts in teaching

normalement [nɔrmalmɑ̃] *adv* normally

normalien, -enne [nɔrmaljɛ̃, -ɛn] *nm,f Univ* = student or former student of the "École normale supérieure"

normalisation [nɔrmalizasjɔ̃] *nf* **(a)** *(des relations diplomatiques)* normalization **(b)** *Ind* standardization

normaliser [nɔrmalize] *vt* **(a)** *(relations diplomatiques)* to normalize **(b)** *Ind* to standardize

normalité [nɔrmalite] *nf* normality

normand, -e [nɔrmɑ̃, -ɑ̃d] *aussi Hist* **1** *adj* Norman **2** *nm,f* **N.** Norman

Normandie [nɔrmɑ̃di] *nf* **la N.** Normandy

norme [nɔrm] *nf* **(a)** *(règle)* norm; **dans la n.** within the norm **(b)** *Ind & Com* standard

noroît [nɔrwa] *nm* north-wester

Norvège [nɔrvɛʒ] *nf* **la N.** Norway

norvégien, -enne [nɔrveʒjɛ̃, -ɛn] **1** *adj* Norwegian **2** *nm,f* **N.** Norwegian **3** *nm (langue)* Norwegian

nos [no] *voir* **notre**

nostalgie [nɔstalʒi] *nf* nostalgia; *(mal du pays)* homesickness; **avoir la n. de qch** to feel nostalgic for sth; **avoir la n. du pays** to be homesick

nostalgique [nɔstalʒik] *adj* nostalgic

nota bene [nɔtabene] *nm inv* nota bene

notable [nɔtabl] *adj & nm* notable

notablement [nɔtabləmɑ̃] *adv* notably

notaire [nɔtɛr] *nm* notary (public)

notamment [nɔtamɑ̃] *adv* notably

notarié, -e [nɔtarje] *adj* **(acte n.** notarized deed

notation [nɔtasjɔ̃] *nf* **(a)** *(d'un travail scolaire)* marking **(b)** *(pour des symboles)* notation; *Ordinat* **n. hexadécimale** hexor hexadecimal code

note [nɔt] *nf* **(a)** *(annotation, communication écrite)* note; **prendre des notes** to take (down) notes; **prendre bonne n. de qch** to take due note of sth; *Typ & Ordinat* **n. de** *ou* **en bas de page** footnote, *n. de service memo **(b)** *(appréciation) Br* mark, *Am* grade **(c)** *Mus* note **(d)** *(facture)* bill; *(dans un hôtel) Br* bill, *Am* check; **n. de frais** expenses; **n. de téléphone** phone bill **(e)** *(nuance)* touch, note

notebook [nɔtbuk] *nm Ordinat* notebook

noter [nɔte] *vt* **(a)** *(mettre par écrit)* to note down, to make a note of **(b)** *(remarquer)* to note; **note bien que...** mind you,...; *Fig* **c'est noté, je note** got it **(c)** *(travail scolaire, élève) Br* to mark, *Am* to grade

notice [nɔtis] *nf* *(mode d'emploi)* instructions; *(d'un médicament)* directions

notification [nɔtifikasjɔ̃] *nf Jur* notification

notifier [66] [nɔtifje] *vt* **n. qch à qn** to notify sb of sth

notion [nɔsjɔ̃] *nf* **(a)** *(concept)* notion, concept; **perdre la n. du temps/de la réalité** to lose track of time/all sense of reality **(b)** **notions** *(connaissances sommaires)* basics; **avoir des notions de qch** to know the basics of sth

notoire [nɔtwar] *adj (fait)* well-known; *(criminel, mesquinerie)* notorious

notoriété [nɔtɔrjete] *nf (d'une personne)* fame; **il est de n. publique que...** it's common knowledge that...

notre, nos [nɔtr, no] *adj possessif* our; **n. chien** *(il y a un chien)* our dog; *(chacun a son chien)* our dogs; **nos enfants** our children; **n. père et n. mère** our mother and father; **un de nos amis** one of our friends, a friend of ours; *Fam* **nous avons n. vendredi** we've got Friday off

nôtre [notr] **1** *pron possessif* **le n., la n., les nôtres** ours; *(en insistant)* our own; **nous te prêtons le n.** you can borrow ours; **nous n'en avons pas besoin, nous avons le n.** we don't need it, we've got our own; *Fam* **à la n.!** here's to us!

2 *nm* **il faut y mettre du n.** we have to do our share **3** *nmpl* **les nôtres** *(notre famille)* our family; **serez-vous des nôtres ce soir?** will you be joining us this evening?

nouba [nuba] *nf Fam* party; **faire la n.** to party

noué, -e [nwe] *adj* **avoir l'estomac n.** to have a knot in one's stomach; **avoir la gorge nouée** to have a lump in one's throat

nouer [nwe] **1** vt (**a**) (ficelle, ruban, lacets) to tie; (cheveux) to tie up; (cravate) to knot (**b**) (relations) to establish (**avec with**) **2 se nouer** vpr (**a**) (amitié) to be formed (**b**) (intrigue) to take shape

noueux, -euse [nwø, -øz] adj (bois) knotty; (tronc d'arbre, mains, doigts) gnarled

nougat [nuga] nm nougat

nougatine [nugatin] nf nougatine

nouille [nuj] nf (**a**) Culin nouilles noodles (**b**) Fam (personne) (molle) drip; (niaise) dimwit

nounou [nunu] nf (langage enfantin) nanny

nounours [nunurs] nm (langage enfantin) teddy (bear)

nourri, -e [nuri] adj (applaudissements) prolonged; (feu) heavy

nourrice [nuris] nf (**a**) (assistante maternelle) child minder; **n. agréée** registered child minder (**b**) Vieilli (qui allaite) wet nurse

nourricier, -ère [nurisje, -ɛr] adj Litt (terre) nourishing

nourrir [nurir] **1** vt (**a**) (personnes, animaux) to feed (**de** with); **le lait nourrit** milk is nourishing (**b**) (peau, visage, cuir) to nourish; (feu) to feed (**c**) Litt (entretenir) (idées de vengeance, illusion) to harbour; (espoir) to cherish; (projet) to nurse **2 se nourrir** vpr (manger) to eat; **se n. de qch** to live on sth; Fig & Litt to feed on sth

nourrissant, -e [nurisɑ̃, -ɑ̃t] adj nourishing

nourrisson [nurisɔ̃] nm infant

nourriture [nurityr] nf food

nous [nu] **1** pron personnel (**a**) (sujet) we; **n. deux/tous** both/all of us; **n. autres Français** we French; **n., n. n'aurions pas fait comme ça** WE wouldn't have done it like that (**b**) (objet direct) us; **et n., tu n. oublies?** and what about us, have you forgotten us? (**c**) (objet indirect) to us; **lisez-le-n.** read it to us; **il n. a serré la main** he shook our hands; **les enfants n. ont jeté des pierres** the children threw stones at us (**d**) (avec préposition) us; **n. ne pensons pas qu'à n.** we're not just thinking of ourselves; **tu n. le montres, à n.?** can you show US?; **ce livre est à n.** this book is ours; **n. avons nos règles à n.** we have our own rules; Fam **un ami à n.** a friend of ours; **à n. deux** (sur un ton menaçant) I want a word with you; Hum I'm all yours (**e**) (dans les réfléchis) ourselves; **n. n. sommes amusés** we enjoyed ourselves (**f**) (dans les pronominaux) **n. n. déciderons demain** we'll decide tomorrow (**g**) (réciproque) each other; **n. n. aimons** we love each other (**h**) (dans les comparaisons) us; **vous buvez plus que n.** you drink more than us or than we do **2** nm **le n. de majesté** the royal we

nous-mêmes [numɛm] pron personnel ourselves

nouveau, -elle, -x, -elles [nuvo, -ɛl] **1** adj

> **nouvel** is used before masculine singular nouns beginning with a vowel or h mute.

(**a**) (récent, moderne, autre) new; (mode) latest; **les nouveaux pères** modern fathers; Fam **tout n. tout beau** it's all new and exciting; **le nouvel an** the New Year; **nouvelle cuisine** nouvelle cuisine; Péj **n. riche** nouveau riche (**b**) (avec une fonction adverbiale) **les nouveaux arrivants** the newcomers; **les nouveaux élus** those newly elected; **n. pays industrialisé** newly industrialized country (**c**) **à n., de n.** again

2 nm **il y a du n.** there's been a new development **3** nm,f (personne) new person; (à l'école) new pupil

Nouveau-Brunswick [nuvobrœ̃zvik] nm **le N.** New Brunswick

Nouveau-Mexique [nuvomɛksik] nm **le N.** New Mexico

nouveau-né, -e (mpl nouveau-nés, fpl nouveau-nées) [nuvone] **1** adj newborn **2** nm,f newborn baby

nouveauté [nuvote] nf (**a**) (caractère nouveau) novelty (**b**) (produit récent) (livre) new publication; (disque) new release; Fam **ce n'est pas une n.!** that's nothing new!

nouvel [nuvɛl] voir nouveau

nouvelle [nuvɛl] nf (**a**) (annonce d'un événement) **une n.** a piece of news; **je viens d'apprendre la n.** I've just heard the news; Fam **première n.!** that's news to me! (**b**) (information) **avoir des nouvelles de qn** (directement) to have heard news of sb; (indirectement) to have had news about sb; Fig **vous aurez de mes nouvelles!** you'll be hearing from me!; **demander ou prendre des nouvelles de qn** to inquire or ask about sb; **être sans nouvelles de qn** to have no news from sb; **aux dernières nouvelles,...** the last I/we/ etc heard,...; **les nouvelles vont vite!** (good) news travels fast!; **goûtez cela, vous m'en direz des nouvelles** taste this, you'll love it; **pas de nouvelles, bonnes nouvelles** no news is good news (**c**) Journ news item; **les nouvelles** the news (**d**) (roman court) short story

Nouvelle-Angleterre [nuvɛlɑ̃glətɛr] nf **la N.** New England

Nouvelle-Calédonie [nuvɛlkaledɔni] nf **la N.** New Caledonia

Nouvelle-Écosse [nuvɛlekɔs] nf **la N.** Nova Scotia

nouvellement [nuvɛlmɑ̃] adv newly, recently

Nouvelle-Orléans [nuvɛlɔrleɑ̃] voir La Nouvelle-Orléans

Nouvelles-Hébrides [nuvɛlzebrid] nfpl **les N.** the New Hebrides

Nouvelle-Zélande [nuvɛlzelɑ̃d] nf **la N.** New Zealand

novateur, -trice [nɔvatœr, -tris] **1** adj innovative **2** nm,f innovator

novembre [nɔvɑ̃br] nm November; **le onze n.** (fête) Br Armistice Day, Am Veterans Day; voir aussi janvier

novice [nɔvis] nmf aussi Rel novice

noyade [nwajad] nf drowning

noyau, -x [nwajo] nm (**a**) (de fruit) stone, Am pit (**b**) (centre) (d'atome, de cellule) nucleus; (de la terre) core (**c**) (petit groupe) small group; **le n. dur** the hard core (**d**) Ordinat node

noyauter [nwajote] vt to infiltrate

noyé, -e [nwaje] **1** adj (**a**) (dans l'eau) **mourir n.** to die by drowning; Fig **être n.** (perdu) to be out of one's depth (**b**) (plein) **yeux noyés de larmes** eyes brimming with tears (**c**) (perdu) **le village était n. dans la brume** the village was shrouded in mist; **les points essentiels sont noyés dans le détail** the essential points are buried in too many details **2** nm,f drowned person

noyer¹ [nwaje] nm (arbre) walnut (tree); (bois) walnut

noyer² [32] **1** vt (**a**) (personne, animal) to drown; (terres, champs) to swamp; Fig **n. une rébellion dans le sang** to bloodily quash a rebellion; Fig **n. son chagrin (dans l'alcool)** to drown one's sorrows (in drink); **n. le poisson** to confuse the issue deliberately (**b**) (moteur) to flood (**c**) (diluer) (vin) to drown **2 se noyer** vpr (accidentellement) to drown; (volontairement) to drown oneself; Fig **se n. dans les détails** to get bogged down in details; **se n.** dans un verre d'eau to make a mountain out of a molehill

NPI [ɛnpei] *nm* (*abrév* **nouveau pays industrialisé**) NIC

nu, -e [ny] **1** *adj* (**a**) *(dévêtu) (personne)* naked; *(partie du corps)* bare; *Art* nude; **être tout nu** to be naked *or* in the nude; **se baigner tout nu** to go swimming in the nude; **nu comme un ver** stark naked; **aller pieds nus** to go barefoot; **se battre à mains nues** to fight with bare fists; **visible à l'œil n.** visible to the naked eye (**b**) *Fig (paysage, arbre, pièce)* bare; *(style)* plain
2 *nm Art* nude; **mettre qch à nu** *(surface)* to expose sth; *(fil électrique)* to strip sth

nuage [nɥaʒ] *nm* (**a**) *(dans le ciel)* cloud; **sans nuages** *(ciel)* cloudless; *Fig (vie, avenir)* unclouded; *(bonheur)* perfect; *Fig* **être dans les nuages** to have one's head in the clouds; **n. radioactif** cloud of radioactive dust (**b**) *(de lait)* drop

nuageux, -euse [nɥaʒø, -øz] *adj* cloudy

nuance [nɥɑ̃s] *nf* (**a**) *(de couleur)* shade (**b**) *(légère trace)* touch, hint (**c**) *(subtilité)* nuance; *(légère différence)* slight difference; **tout en nuances** full of nuances; **j'ai dit peut-être, pas oui, n.!** I said perhaps, not yes, there's a slight difference!; **être sans nuances** *(personne)* to see everything in black and white

nuancé, -e [nɥɑ̃se] *adj* full of nuances

nuancer [16] [nɥɑ̃se] *vt* to qualify

nucléaire [nykleɛr] **1** *adj* nuclear
2 *nm* **le n.** nuclear power

nucléon [nykleɔ̃] *nm Phys* nucleon

nudisme [nydism] *nm* nudism

nudiste [nydist] *nmf* nudist

nudité [nydite] *nf (d'une personne)* nudity, nakedness; *(d'un mur, d'un paysage)* bareness; *(d'un style)* plainness

nue [ny] *nf* **porter qn/qch aux nues** to praise sb/sth to the skies; **tomber des nues** to be taken aback

nuée [nɥe] *nf* (**a**) *(d'insectes, de criquets)* cloud, swarm; *(de personnes)* horde (**b**) *Litt (dans le ciel)* cloud

nui *voir* **nuire**

nuire [18] [nɥir] **1 nuire à** *vt ind* to harm; **nuit gravement à la santé** *(sur paquet de cigarettes)* tobacco seriously damages health; **mettre qn hors d'état de n.** *(en lieu sûr)* to put sb out of harm's way
2 se nuire *vpr* **se n.** (à soi-même) to do oneself harm

nuisais *etc voir* **nuire**

nuisance [nɥizɑ̃s] *nf* nuisance; **nuisances acous-tiques** noise pollution

nuise *voir* **nuire**

nuisette [nɥizɛt] *nf* baby doll nightie

nuisible [nɥizibl] *adj* harmful (à to); **animaux nuisibles** vermin, pests

nuit [nɥi] *nf* night; **cette n.** *(ce soir)* tonight; *(passée)* last night; **bonne n.!** good night!; **le train/bateau de n.** the night train/boat; **voyager de n.** to travel by *or* at night; **il commence à faire n.** it's getting dark; **il fait n.** it's dark; **il fait n. noire** it's pitch-black; **à la n. tombante** at nightfall; *Fig* **perdu dans la n. des temps** lost in the mists of time; *Prov* **la n. porte conseil** it would be best to sleep on it; *Prov* **la n., tous les chats sont gris** all cats are grey in the dark; **passer une n. blanche** *(avoir une insomnie)* to have a sleepless night; *(volontairement)* to stay up all night; **n. de noces** wedding night

nuitée [nɥite] *nf* overnight stay

nul, nulle [nyl] **1** *adj* (**a**) *(inexistant) (différence, risques, écart)* nil (**b**) *(non valable) (bulletin de vote)* spoilt; *Jur* **n. et non avenu** null and void (**c**) *Fam (qui ne vaut rien) (réponse, personne)* useless; *(film, livre, chanson, blague)* rubbish; **être n. en qch** to be useless at sth; *Vulg* **c'est n. à chier!** it's a load of crap!
2 *nm, f Fam* useless idiot
3 *adj indéfini Litt* no
4 *pron indéfini Litt* no one, nobody

nullard, -e [nylar, -ard] *nm, f très Fam* useless idiot

nullement [nylmɑ̃] *adv* not at all

nulle part [nylpar] *adv* nowhere; **je ne les vois n.** I can't see them anywhere; **n. ailleurs** nowhere else

nullité [nylite] *nf (d'un contrat, d'un mariage)* nullity, invalidity

numéraire [nymerɛr] *nm* cash

numéral, -e, -aux, -ales [nymeral, -o] *adj & nm* numeral

numérateur [nymeratœr] *nm Math* numerator

numération [nymerasjɔ̃] *nf Math* numeration

numérique [nymerik] *adj* (**a**) *(valeur, supériorité)* numerical (**b**) *Ordinat (ordinateur, donnée)* digital; **balance à affichage n.** digital scales

numérisation [nymerizasjɔ̃] *nf Ordinat* digitization

numériser [nymerize] *vt Ordinat* to digitize

numériseur [nymerizœr] *nm Ordinat* digitizer; **n. d'image** image digitizer

numéro [nymero] *nm* (**a**) *(chiffre)* number; *Fig* **tirer le bon n.** to strike (it) lucky; **n. azur** = special telephone number for which users are charged at local rate irrespective of distance; **n. de compte** account number; **n. de fax** fax number; **n. d'immatriculation** *Br* registration number, *Am* license number; **n. de téléphone** telephone number; **n. vert** *Br* Freefone® number, *Am* toll-free number; **n. de vol** flight number (**b**) *(de périodique)* issue, number; **la suite au prochain n.** (to be) continued in the next issue; *Fig* **watch this space; n. spécial** special issue (**c**) *(spectacle)* act, number; *Fam Fig* **faire son petit n.** to do one's little act (**d**) *Fam (personne)* character

numérotation [nymerɔtasjɔ̃] *nf* numbering

numéroter [nymerɔte] *vt* to number

numismate [nymismat] *nmf* numismatist

numismatique [nymismatik] **1** *adj* numismatic
2 *nf numismatics (singulier)*

nunuche [nynyʃ] *adj Fam* twee

nu-pieds [nypje] **1** *nm inv* sandal
2 *adv* barefoot

nuptial, -e, -aux, -ales [nypsjal, -o] *adj (anneau, marche)* wedding; *(chambre, cortège)* bridal

nuque [nyk] *nf* nape, back of the neck

nurse [nœrs] *nf Vieilli* nanny

nu-tête [nytɛt] *adv* bareheaded

nutritif, -ive [nytritif, -iv] *adj* nutritious

nutrition [nytrisjɔ̃] *nf* nutrition

nutritionniste [nytrisjɔnist] *nmf* nutritionist

Nylon® [nilɔ̃] *nm* nylon

nymphe [nɛ̃f] *nf (déesse)* nymph

nymphette [nɛ̃fɛt] *nf* nymphet

nymphomane [nɛ̃fɔman] *adj & nf* nymphomaniac

nymphomanie [nɛ̃fɔmani] *nf* nymphomania

O

O, o [o] *nm inv* O, o
O *(abrév* **ouest)** W
ô [o] *exclam Litt* O!

OAS [oaɛs] *nf (abrév* **Organisation de l'armée secrète)** OAS *(terrorist group opposed to Algerian independence)*

oasis [ɔazis] *nf* oasis; *Fig* haven

obédience [ɔbedjɑ̃s] *nf* d'o. communiste/musulmane of the Communist/Muslim persuasion

obéir [ɔbeir] *vi* (a) *(personne)* to obey; **o. à qn/qch** to obey sb/sth; **o. à une impulsion** to act on an impulse; **o. à qn au doigt et à l'œil** to be at sb's beck and call; **se faire o.** to command obedience **(b)** *(freins, mécanisme)* to respond (**à** to)

obéissance [ɔbeisɑ̃s] *nf* obedience (**à** to); **jurer o. à qn** to swear allegiance to sb

obéissant, -e [ɔbeisɑ̃, -ɑ̃t] *adj* obedient

obélisque [ɔbelisk] *nm* obelisk

obèse [ɔbɛz] **1** *adj* obese
2 *nmf* obese person

obésité [ɔbezite] *nf* obesity

objecter [ɔbʒɛkte] *vt* (a) *(rétorquer)* **n'avoir rien à o. à qch** to have no objection to sth; **o. que...** to object that... **(b)** *(invoquer)* **on lui objecta sa jeunesse** his youth was held against him

objecteur [ɔbʒɛktœr] *nm* **o. de conscience** conscientious objector

objectif, -ive [ɔbʒɛktif, -iv] **1** *adj* objective
2 *nm* **(a)** *(but, cible)* objective **(b)** *(d'un appareil photo)* lens; *(d'un microscope)* objective; *Fig* **devant l'o.** in front of the camera

objection [ɔbʒɛksjɔ̃] *nf aussi Jur* objection

objectivement [ɔbʒɛktivmɑ̃] *adv* objectively

objectivité [ɔbʒɛktivite] *nf* objectivity; **en toute o.** quite objectively

objet [ɔbʒɛ] *nm* **(a)** *(chose)* object; **(bureau des) objets trouvés** *Br* lost-property office, *Am* lost and found; **femme-o.** sex object; **o. d'art** objet d'art; **objets de valeur** valuables; **o. volant non identifié** unidentified flying object
(b) *Gram* object; **o. direct/indirect** direct/indirect object
(c) *(sujet)* *(d'une dispute, d'une conversation)* subject; **être** *ou* **faire l'o. de qch** to be the object of sth; *Hum* **l'o. de ses désirs** the object of her desires
(d) *(but)* object, aim; **ma visite a pour o. de...** the object of my visit is to...; **sans o.** *(remarque, réclamation)* unjustified
(e) *Ordinat* object

obligataire [ɔbligatɛr] *Fin* **1** *nmf* bondholder, debenture holder
2 *adj (emprunt, marché)* debenture

obligation [ɔbligasjɔ̃] *nf* **(a)** *(contrainte)* obligation; **tu viens si tu veux, mais ce n'est pas une o.** you can come if you want, but you don't have to; **avoir l'o. de faire qch** to be under an obligation to do sth; **être** *ou* **se voir dans l'o. de faire qch** to be obliged to do sth; **sans o. d'achat** no purchase necessary; **être dégagé des obligations militaires** to have done one's military service **(b)** *Fin* bond, debenture; **o. au porteur** bearer bond

obligatoire [ɔbligatwar] *adj* obligatory, compulsory; *Fam (inévitable)* inevitable

obligatoirement [ɔbligatwarmɑ̃] *adv* **vous devez o. montrer votre passeport** you are required to show your passport; **pas o.** not necessarily

obligé, -e [ɔbliʒe] *adj* **(a)** *Fam (inévitable)* inevitable **(b)** *Formel (reconnaissant)* **être o. à qn de qch** to be obliged to sb for sth

obligeance [ɔbliʒɑ̃s] *nf Formel* **avoir l'o. de faire qch** to be so kind as to do sth

obligeant, -e [ɔbliʒɑ̃, -ɑ̃t] *adj* obliging, kind

obliger [45] [ɔbliʒe] **1** *vt* (a) *(contraindre)* **o. qn à faire qch** to force sb to do sth; **son état de santé l'oblige au repos** the state of his health means he has to rest; **être obligé de faire qch** to be obliged to do sth; **ne te crois pas obligé de tout manger** don't feel you have to eat everything; **tu y es allé? – bien obligé!** did you go? – I had to! **(b)** *Formel (rendre service à)* **vous m'obligeriez en fermant la fenêtre** I'd be obliged if you would close the window
2 s'obliger *vpr* **s'o. à faire qch** to force oneself to do sth

oblique [ɔblik] **1** *adj (ligne)* oblique; *(regard)* sidelong
2 *nf* oblique (line)

obliquement [ɔblikmɑ̃] *adv* obliquely

obliquer [ɔblike] *vi* **o. à gauche/à droite** to bear left/right

oblitérer [34] [ɔblitere] *vt* (a) *(timbre)* to cancel **(b)** *Litt (souvenirs, passé)* to obliterate

oblong, -ongue [ɔblɔ̃, -ɔ̃g] *adj* oblong

obnubiler [ɔbnybile] *vt* to obsess

obole [ɔbɔl] *nf* small contribution; **apporter** *ou* **verser son o. à qch** to make a small contribution to sth

obscène [ɔpsɛn] *adj* obscene

obscénité [ɔpsenite] *nf* obscenity

obscur, -e [ɔpskyr] *adj* **(a)** *(sombre)* dark **(b)** *(difficile à comprendre)* obscure **(c)** *(pressentiment, impression)* vague **(d)** *(écrivain, peintre)* obscure

obscurantisme [ɔpskyrɑ̃tism] *nm* obscurantism

obscurcir [ɔpskyrsir] **1** vt (a) (assombrir) to darken (b) (rendre confus) (faits, sens) to obscure; (jugement) to cloud **2** s'obscurcir vpr (pièce, ciel) to darken, to grow dark; (esprit, vue) to grow dim

obscurément [ɔpskyremã] adv vaguely

obscurité [ɔpskyrite] nf (a) (noirceur) darkness; **dans l'o.** in the dark (b) (anonymat) obscurity

obsédant, -e [ɔpsedã, -ãt] adj (souvenir, musique) haunting; (pensée) obsessive

obsédé, -e [ɔpsede] nm,f fanatic; **o. (sexuel)** sex maniac; **un o. du cinéma/du rangement** a film/tidiness fanatic

obséder [34] [ɔpsede] vt to obsess; **être obsédé par qch** to be obsessed by or with sth

obsèques [ɔpsɛk] nfpl funeral; **o. nationales** state funeral

obséquieux, -euse [ɔpsekjø, -øz] adj obsequious

observateur, -trice [ɔpsɛrvatœr, -tris] **1** adj observant **2** nm,f observer

observation [ɔpsɛrvasjõ] nf (a) (étude, surveillance) observation; **être en o.** (à l'hôpital) to be under observation; **avoir l'esprit d'o.** to be very observant (b) (remarque) observation; (critique) remark (c) (respect) observance

observatoire [ɔpsɛrvatwar] nm (astronomique, météorologique) observatory; Mil observation post

observer [ɔpsɛrve] **1** vt (a) (regarder) to watch, to observe; **se sentir observé** to feel one is being watched (b) (remarquer) to notice; **faire o. qch à qn** to point sth out to sb; **faire o. à qn que...** to point out to sb that... (c) (étudier) to observe (d) (respecter) to observe; **o. une minute de silence** to observe a minute's silence **2** s'observer vpr (a) (l'un l'autre) to watch or observe each other (b) (phénomène, attitude) to be seen

obsession [ɔpsesjõ] nf obsession; **mais c'est une o. ou de l'o.!** you're/he's/etc obsessed!

obsessionnel, -elle [ɔpsesjɔnɛl] adj Psy obsessional

obsidienne [ɔpsidjɛn] nf obsidian

obsolète [ɔpsɔlɛt] adj obsolete

obstacle [ɔpstakl] nm aussi Fig obstacle; (aux courses) fence, jump; **faire o. à qch** to stand in the way of sth

obstétricien, -enne [ɔpstetrisjẽ, -ɛn] nm,f obstetrician

obstétrique [ɔpstetrik] nf obstetrics (singulier)

obstination [ɔpstinasjõ] nf obstinacy, stubbornness

obstiné, -e [ɔpstine] adj (personne, caractère) obstinate, stubborn; (résistance, efforts) dogged; (refus) stubborn

obstinément [ɔpstinemã] adv (travailler, avancer) doggedly; (refuser) stubbornly

obstiner [ɔpstine] s'obstiner vpr to persist; **s'o. à faire qch** (continuer) to persist in doing sth; (vouloir) to be set on doing sth; **s'o. dans ses convictions** to cling stubbornly to one's convictions

obstruction [ɔpstryksjõ] nf obstruction; **faire de l'o.** Pol to be obstructive; Sp to obstruct

obstructionnisme [ɔpstryksjɔnism] nm Pol obstructionism

obstruer [ɔpstrye] vt to obstruct

obtempérer [34] [ɔptãpere] **obtempérer à** vt ind to comply with; Jur **refus d'o.** obstruction

obtenir [70] [ɔptənir] vt to get, to obtain; **o. qch de qn** to get sth from sb; **faire o. qch à qn** to get sth for sb; **o. de faire qch** to get permission to do sth; **j'ai obtenu qu'elle revienne** I got her to come back

obtention [ɔptãsjõ] nf obtaining; **depuis l'o. de son diplôme** since obtaining her diploma

obtenu, -e voir obtenir

obtiendrai etc voir obtenir

obtienne voir obtenir

obturateur [ɔptyratœr] nm Phot shutter

obtus, -e [ɔpty, yz] adj (angle, personne) obtuse

obus [ɔby] nm shell

OC nfpl (abrév ondes courtes) SW

oc [ɔk] voir langue

ocarina [ɔkarina] nm ocarina

occase [ɔkaz] nf Fam (a) (affaire) bargain (b) (article de seconde main) second-hand item; **d'o.** second-hand

occasion [ɔkazjõ] nf (a) (circonstance favorable) opportunity, chance; **avoir l'o. de faire qch** to have the opportunity or chance to do sth; Hum **tu as encore perdu l'o. de te taire** why can't you keep your big mouth shut?; **c'est l'o. ou jamais** it's now or never; **c'est l'o. ou jamais d'essayer** now's the time to try; **venez boire un coup à l'o.** come for a drink when you get the chance; **à la première o.** at the first opportunity; Prov **l'o. fait le larron** opportunity makes the thief (b) (moment) occasion; **à plusieurs occasions** on several occasions; **à l'o. de** (pour fêter) on the occasion of, **à l'o. d'une visite de routine** during a routine visit; **dans/pour les grandes occasions** on/for special occasions; **être l'o. de qch** to be the occasion of sth (c) (affaire) bargain (d) (article de seconde main) second-hand item; **le marché de l'o.** the second-hand market; **d'o.** second-hand

occasionnel, -elle [ɔkazjɔnɛl] adj occasional; (rencontre) chance; (aide) casual

occasionnellement [ɔkazjɔnɛlmã] adv occasionally

occasionner [ɔkazjɔne] vt to cause

occident [ɔksidã] nm west; Pol **l'O.** the West

occidental, -e, -aux, -ales [ɔksidãtal, -o] **1** adj western; **l'Europe occidentale** Western Europe **2** nm,f **O.** Westerner

occidentaliser [ɔksidãtalize] **1** vt to westernize **2** s'occidentaliser vpr to become westernized

occiput [ɔksipyt] nm back of the head

occire [ɔksir] vt to slay

occitan, -e [ɔksitã, -an] **1** adj of the langue d'oc **2** nm (langue) = language spoken in some parts of southern France

occlusion [ɔklyzjõ] nf occlusion; **o. intestinale** intestinal obstruction

occulte [ɔkylt] adj (surnaturel) occult; (secret) secret; (cause) hidden; (rôle) clandestine

occulter [ɔkylte] vt Astron to occult; (signal lumineux) to block out; Fig (informations, intentions) to conceal

occupant, -e [ɔkypã, -ãt] **1** adj (armée) occupying **2** nm,f (d'une maison) occupier, occupant; Mil **l'o.** the occupying forces

occupation [ɔkypasjõ] nf (a) (d'un lieu) & Mil occupation; Hist **l'O.** the Occupation; **grève avec o. des locaux** sit-down strike (b) (activité) occupation; **vaquer à ses occupations** to go about one's business

occupé, -e [ɔkype] adj (personne) busy; (place) taken; (ligne téléphonique) Br engaged, Am busy; (toilettes) engaged; **en territoire o.** in occupied territory

occuper [ɔkype] **1** vt (a) (maison, lieu) to occupy; (place) to take up, to occupy; **le magasin occupe le rez-de-chaussée** the shop takes up or occupies the ground floor (b) (par la force) (pays) to occupy (c) (temps) to fill, to occupy (d) (poste, fonction) to have, to hold (e) (employé) to employ sb; (ouvrier) to keep sb busy, to occupy sb **2** s'occuper vpr (a) (avoir une activité) to keep oneself busy *or* occupied, to occupy oneself; **s'o. en lisant** to spend one's time reading; **on a toujours de quoi s'o.** there's always something to keep you busy **(b) s'o. de** *(s'intéresser à)* to be interested in; *(se charger de)* to take care of; **s'o. de faire qch** to see about doing sth; **je m'en occuperai** I'll see to it; *Fam* **occupe-toi de ce qui te regarde** *ou* **de tes affaires** *ou* **de tes oignons!** mind your own business!; *Fam* **t'occupe (pas)!** keep your nose out!; *Ironique* **je vais m'o. de lui** I'll take care of him; **est-ce qu'on s'occupe de vous?** *(dans un magasin)* are you being attended to?

occurrence [ɔkyrɑ̃s] *nf* **(a)** *(circonstance)* **en l'o.** in this case **(b)** *Ling* occurrence

OCDE [osedeə] *nf* *(abrév* **Organisation de coopération et de développement économiques)** OECD

océan [ɔseɑ̃] *nm* ocean; **l'O.** *(l'Atlantique)* the Atlantic; **l'O. Atlantique/Pacifique/Indien** the Atlantic/Pacific/Indian Ocean; **l'o. (Glacial) Arctique** the Arctic Ocean; *Fig* **un o. de fleurs/couleurs** a sea of flowers/colour

Océanie [ɔseani] *nf* **l'O.** Oceania

océanique [ɔseanik] *adj* oceanic

océanographie [ɔseanɔgrafi] *nf* oceanography

ocelot [ɔslo] *nm* ocelot

ocre [ɔkr] *nm & adj inv* ochre

octane [ɔktan] *nm* octane

octante [ɔktɑ̃t] *adj & nm inv* *Belg & Suisse* eighty; *voir aussi* **trois**

octave [ɔktav] *nf* octave

octet [ɔktɛ] *nm Ordinat* byte; **milliard d'octets** gigabyte

octobre [ɔktɔbr] *nm* October; *voir aussi* **janvier**

octogénaire [ɔktɔʒenɛr] *adj & nmf* octogenarian

octogonal, -e, -aux, -ales [ɔktɔgɔnal, -o] *adj* octagonal

octogone [ɔktɔgɔn] *nm* octagon

octroyer [32] [ɔktrwaje] **1** *vt* **o. qch à qn** to grant sb sth **2 s'octroyer** *vpr* **s'o. qch** to grant oneself sth

oculaire [ɔkylɛr] **1** *adj* **hygiène o.** eye care; **témoin o.** eyewitness **2** *nm* eyepiece

oculiste [ɔkylist] *nmf* eye specialist

ode [ɔd] *nf* ode

odeur [ɔdœr] *nf* smell; **une o. de brûlé** a smell of burning; **sans o.** odourless; **bonne/mauvaise o.** pleasant/unpleasant smell; *Fig* **ne pas être en o. de sainteté auprès de qn** to be in sb's bad books; *Prov* **l'argent n'a pas d'o.** money has no smell

odieux, -euse [ɔdjø, -øz] *adj* odious

odorant, -e [ɔdɔrɑ̃, -ɑ̃t] *adj* *(agréable)* sweet-smelling, fragrant; *(désagréable)* strong-smelling

odorat [ɔdɔra] *nm* (sense of) smell

odyssée [ɔdise] *nf* odyssey; **l'O.** the Odyssey

œcuménique [ekymenik, økymenik] *adj* ecumenical

œdème [edɛm, ødɛm] *nm* oedema; **avoir un o. aux poumons** to have pulmonary oedema

œil [œj] *(pl* **yeux** [jø]) *nm* **(a)** *(organe)* eye; **avoir les yeux bleus** to have blue eyes; **o. de verre** glass eye; **un o. au beurre noir, un o. poché** a black eye; **j'ai le soleil dans les yeux** *ou* **dans l'o.** the sun's in my eyes; **visible à l'o. nu** visible to the naked eye; **voir qch de ses (propres) yeux** to see sth with one's own eyes; **je n'ai pas fermé l'o. de la nuit** I didn't sleep a wink all night; **faire qch les yeux fermés** to do sth with one's eyes closed; **ouvrir de grands yeux** to look surprised; **faire les gros yeux (à qn)** to glare (at sb); *Fam* **avoir de petits yeux** to look tired; **ouvrir l'o. tout ronds** to gape in amazement; *Fam* **entre quat'z'yeux** in private; **les yeux dans les yeux** gazing into each other's

eyes; **o. pour o., dent pour dent** an eye for an eye, a tooth for a tooth; **je ne le fais pas pour ses beaux yeux** I'm not doing it just to please him; **tu as les yeux plus gros** *ou* **grands que le ventre** your eyes are bigger than your belly; **n'avoir plus que les** *ou* **ses yeux pour pleurer** to have nothing left but the clothes on one's back; *Fam* **mon o.!** my foot!; *Fam* **à l'o.** free; **faire les yeux doux à qn** to make eyes at sb; *Fam* **faire de l'o. à qn** to give sb the eye; **le mauvais o.** the evil eye; **sous mes/leurs yeux** right before my/their eyes; **avoir qch sous les yeux** to have sth right in front of one **(b)** *(vue)* **yeux** (eye)sight, eyes; **avoir de bons/mauvais yeux** to have good/bad (eye)sight; **avoir des yeux de lynx** to be eagle-eyed **(c)** *(attention)* **avoir l'o. sur qch** to keep an eye on sth; **avoir qn à l'o.** to keep an eye on sb; **avoir l'o. à tout** to keep an eye on everything; *Fam* **ouvrir l'o. (et le bon)** to keep one's eyes open *or* peeled; **ne pas avoir les yeux en face des trous** to be half-asleep; *Fam* **ne pas avoir les yeux dans sa poche** to have sharp eyes; **fermer les yeux sur qch** to turn a blind eye to sth; **coup d'o.** glance; **au** *ou* **du premier coup d'o.** at a glance; **jeter un coup d'o. sur qch** to have a glance at sth; **avoir le coup d'o., avoir l'o.** to have a good eye; **ça vaut** *ou* **ça mérite le coup d'o.** it's worth a look **(d)** *(point de vue)* **voir qch d'un autre o.** to look at sth differently; **voir qch d'un bon/mauvais o.** to look favourably/unfavourably on sth; **aux yeux de la loi** in the eyes of the law; **à mes yeux** in my eyes **(e)** *(dans la soupe)* speck of fat **(f)** *(d'un cyclone)* eye

œil-de-bœuf *(pl* **œils-de-bœuf** *)* [œjdəbœf] *nm* bull's-eye (window)

œillade [œjad] *nf* wink; **lancer une o. à qn** to wink at sb

œillère [œjɛr] *nf* *Br* blinker, *Am* blinder; *Fig* **avoir des œillères** to wear *Br* blinkers *or Am* blinders

œillet [œjɛ] *nm* **(a)** *(fleur)* carnation **(b)** *(trou) (de vêtement, de chaussure)* eyelet **(c)** *(en papeterie)* reinforcement ring

œnologie [enɔlɔʒi, ønɔlɔʒi] *nf* oenology

œnologue [enɔlɔg, ønɔlɔg] *nmf* oenologist

œsophage [ezɔfaʒ, øzɔfaʒ] *nm* oesophagus

œstrogène [ɛstrɔʒɛn, østrɔʒɛn] *adj & nm* oestrogen

œuf [œf, *pl* ø] *nm* egg; **œufs** *(de poisson)* spawn, hard roe; *Fig* **mettre tous ses œufs dans le même panier** to put all one's eggs in one basket; *Fam Fig* **marcher sur des œufs** *(avancer)* to walk carefully; *(être prudent)* to be walking on eggs; *Fam* **va te faire cuire un o.!** take a running jump!; **étouffer** *ou* **tuer qch dans l'o.** to nip sth in the bud; **œufs brouillés** scrambled eggs; **o. en chocolat** chocolate egg; **o. à la coque** boiled egg; **o. dur** hard-boiled egg; **o. mollet** soft-boiled egg; **œufs à la neige** floating islands *(beaten egg whites served on custard)*; **œufs en neige** beaten egg whites; **o. de Pâques** Easter egg; **o. au plat** *ou* **sur le plat** fried egg; **o. poché** poached egg; **o. à repasser** darning egg

œuvre [œvr] **1** *nf* **(a)** *(travail)* work; **être à l'o.** to be at work; **se mettre à l'o.** to get down to work; **mettre qch en o.** *(traité, loi, système)* to implement sth; **mettre tout en o. pour faire qch** to do everything possible; **les bonnes œuvres** charitable work **(b)** *(création)* work; *(ensemble de créations)* works; **o. d'art** work of art; **œuvres complètes/choisies** complete/ selected works **2** *nm Constr* **gros o.** fabric; **à pied d'o.** on site; *Fig* **ready to start work**

œuvrer [œvre] *vi* to work **(pour** for)

offensant, -e [ɔfɑ̃sɑ̃, -ɑ̃t] *adj* offensive

offense [ɔfɑ̃s] *nf* **(a)** *(affront)* insult **(b)** *Rel* transgression

offenser [ɔfɑ̃se] **1** *vt* **(a)** *(insulter)* to offend; **sans vouloir**

vous o.... with all due respect... **(b)** *Litt (bon goût, délicatesse)* to offend against
2 s'offenser *vpr* to take offence **(de** at)
offensif, -ive [ɔfɑ̃sif, -iv] *adj* offensive
offensive [ɔfɑ̃siv] *nf* offensive; **passer à l'o.** to go on the offensive
offert, -e *voir* **offrir**
office [ɔfis] *nm* **(a)** *(charge)* office; **faire o. de secrétaire/ témoin** to act as secretary/witness; **d'o.** without having any say in the matter, **être commis d'o.** to be appointed by the court **(b)** *(assistance)* **recourir aux bons offices de qn** to turn to sb for assistance **(c)** *Rel* service **(d)** *(pièce)* pantry **(e) o. du tourisme** tourist information centre
officialiser [ɔfisjalize] *vt* to make official
officiel, -elle [ɔfisjɛl] *adj & nm* official
officiellement [ɔfisjɛlmɑ̃] *adv* officially
officier¹ [ɔfisje] *nm* officer; **o. de réserve** reserve officer
officier² [66] *vi* to officiate
officieusement [ɔfisjøzmɑ̃] *adv* unofficially; *(en confidence)* off-the-record
officieux, -euse [ɔfisjø, -øz] *adj* unofficial; *(confidentiel)* off-the-record
off-line [ɔflajn] *adj Ordinat* off-line
offrande [ɔfrɑ̃d] *nf* offering; **en o.** as an offering
offrant [ɔfrɑ̃] *nm* **vendre au plus o.** to sell to the highest bidder
offre [ɔfr] *nf* offer, *(dans un appel d'offres)* tender; *(dans une vente aux enchères)* bid; **o. d'emploi** job offer; **o. spéciale** special offer; **o. publique d'achat** takeover bid; **faire ou lancer une o. publique d'achat (sur)** to make a takeover bid (for); **l'o. et la demande** supply and demand
offrir [52] [ɔfrir] **1** *vt* **(a)** *(cadeau)* to give (à to); **c'est pour o.,** it's a gift; **je t'offre un verre** I'll buy you a drink, **o. la main de sa fille à qn** to offer one's daughter's hand in marriage to sb **(b)** *(proposer)* to offer; **o. de faire qch** to offer to do sth, **combien t'en a t elle offert?** how much did she offer you for it? **(c)** *(présenter)* *(avantage, garantie)* to offer; **o. une résistance acharnée** to put up stiff resistance **2 s'offrir** *vpr* **(a)** *(se proposer)* **s'o. pour faire qch** to offer to do sth; **s'o. aux regards** *(spectacle, vue)* to meet our/your/etc eyes **(b)** *(se présenter)* *(occasion, possibilité)* to present itself **(c)** *(s'acheter)* **s'o. un bon cigare/une semaine de vacances** to treat oneself to a good cigar/a week's *Br* holiday *or Am* vacation; **je ne peux pas m'o. de vacances** I can't afford a *Br* holiday *or Am* vacation
offset [ɔfsɛt] *nm inv* offset
offusquer [ɔfyske] **1** *vt* to offend
2 s'offusquer *vpr* to take offence **(de** at)
ogive [ɔʒiv] *nf* **(a)** *Archit (diagonal)* rib **(b)** *Mil (d'un obus)* head; *(d'une roquette)* nose cone; **o. nucléaire** nuclear warhead
ogre [ɔgr] *nm* ogre
ogresse [ɔgrɛs] *nf* ogress
oh [o] *exclam* oh!; **oh! hisse!** heave-ho!
ohé [ɔe] *exclam* hey!
ohm [om] *nm* ohm
oie [wa] *nf* goose; **o. sauvage** wild goose; *Fig* **une o. blanche** an innocent young thing
oignon [ɔɲɔ̃] *nm* **(a)** *(légume)* onion; **petits oignons** *(pour les salades)* spring onions; *Fam Fig* **aux petits oignons** first-rate; *Fam* **mêle-toi de tes oignons** mind your own business; *Fam* **ce ne sont pas tes oignons** it's none of your business **(b)** *Bot* bulb **(c)** *Méd* bunion
oindre [43] [wɛ̃dr] *vt* **(a)** *(enduire)* to oil **(b)** *Rel* to anoint
oiseau, -x [wazo] *nm* bird; *Fam Fig* **c'est un drôle d'o.** he's

an odd character; **o. de malheur, o. de mauvais augure** bird of ill omen; **o. marin** sea bird; **o. nocturne** nocturnal bird; *Fig* **o. de nuit** night owl; **o. de proie** bird of prey; **l'o. rare** the ideal person
oiseau-lyre *(pl* **oiseaux-lyres)** [wazolir] *nm* lyrebird
oiseau-mouche *(pl* **oiseaux-mouches)** [wazomuʃ] *nm* hummingbird
oiseleur [wazlœr] *nm* bird catcher
oiseux, -euse [wazø, -øz] *adj (conversation)* idle; *(débat)* pointless; *(explication)* unsatisfactory
oisif, -ive [wazif, -iv] **1** *adj* idle
2 *nm,f* person of leisure
oisillon [wazijɔ̃] *nm* fledgling
oisiveté [wazivte] *nf* idleness; *Prov* **l'o. est (la) mère de tous les vices** the Devil finds work for idle hands
OIT [oite] *nf (abrév* **Organisation internationale du travail)** ILO
okapi [ɔkapi] *nm* okapi
oléagineux, -euse [ɔleaʒinø, -øz] **1** *adj* oil-yielding
2 *nmpl* oil-yielding plants
oléoduc [ɔleɔdyk] *nm* pipeline
olé olé [ɔleɔle] *adj inv Fam (propos, spectacle)* risqué; *(gens)* wild
olfactif, -ive [ɔlfaktif, -iv] *adj* olfactory
olibrius [ɔlibrijys] *nm Fam* oddball
oligarchie [ɔligarʃi] *nf* oligarchy
oligarchique [ɔligarʃik] *adj* oligarchic
oligoélément [ɔligoelemɑ̃] *nm* trace element
olivâtre [ɔlivɑtr] *adj* olive greenish; *(teint)* sallow
olive [ɔliv] **1** *nf* olive
2 *adj inv* olive (green)
oliveraie [ɔlivrɛ] *nf* olive grove
olivier [ɔlivje] *nm (arbre)* olive tree; *(bois)* olive (wood)
OLP [oɛlpe] *nf (abrév* **Organisation de libération de la Palestine)** PLO
olympiade [ɔlɛ̃pjad] *nf* Olympiad
olympique [ɔlɛ̃pik] *adj* Olympic
ombilical, -e, -aux, -ales [ɔ̃bilikal, -o] *adj* umbilical
omble [ɔ̃bl] *nm* **o.(-chevalier)** char
ombrage [ɔ̃braʒ] *nm* shade; **prendre o. de qch** to take umbrage at sth; **porter o. à qn** to give offence to sb
ombragé, -e [ɔ̃braʒe] *adj* shady
ombrageux, -euse [ɔ̃braʒø, -øz] *adj (personne)* touchy
ombre¹ [ɔ̃br] *nf* **(a)** *(forme)* shade; **ombres chinoises** shadow play; **jeter une o. sur qch** to cast a shadow over sth **(b)** *(zone sombre)* shade; **40 degrés à l'o.** 40 degrees in the shade; **faire de l'o. à qn** to be in sb's light; *Fig* to put sb in the shade; *Fig* **il y a une o. au tableau** there's a fly in the ointment **(c)** *(obscurité)* darkness; *Fig (anonymat)* obscurity; *Fig* **rester dans/sortir de l'o.** to remain in/emerge from obscurity; *Fig* **laisser qch dans l'o.** to keep sth dark; *Fig* **travailler dans l'o.** to work behind the scenes; *Fam* **mettre qn à l'o.** to put sb inside **(d)** *Litt (fantôme)* shade; *Fig* **n'être plus que l'o. de soi-même** to be a mere shadow of one's former self **(e)** *(trace)* hint; **vous n'avez pas l'o. d'une chance** you haven't the ghost of a chance; **il n'y a pas l'o. d'un doute** there isn't the shadow of a doubt; **pas l'o. d'un** not a single one **(f) o. à paupières** eye shadow
ombre² *nm (poisson)* char; **o. de rivière** grayling
ombré, -e [ɔ̃bre] *adj Ordinat* shading
ombrelle [ɔ̃brɛl] *nf* sunshade, parasol
omelette [ɔmlɛt] *nf* omelette; *Fig* **on ne fait pas d'o. sans casser des œufs** you can't make an omelette without breaking eggs; **o. norvégienne** ≃ baked Alaska

omettre [47] [ɔmɛtr] *vt* to omit; **o. de faire qch** to omit to do sth

omis, -e *voir* omettre

omission [ɔmisjɔ̃] *nf (d'un mot, d'un détail)* omission; *(oubli)* oversight

omnibus [ɔmnibys] *nm* slow train

omnipotence [ɔmnipɔtɑ̃s] *nf* omnipotence

omnipotent, -e [ɔmnipɔtɑ̃, -ɑ̃t] *adj* omnipotent

omniprésence [ɔmniprezɑ̃s] *nf* omnipresence

omniprésent, -e [ɔmniprezɑ̃, -ɑ̃t] *adj* omnipresent

omniscience [ɔmnisjɑ̃s] *nf* omniscience

omniscient, -e [ɔmnisjɑ̃, -ɑ̃t] *adj* omniscient

omnisports [ɔmnispɔr] *adj inv* **stade/centre o.** sports stadium/centre

omnivore [ɔmnivɔr] **1** *adj* omnivorous
2 *nm* omnivore

omoplate [ɔmɔplat] *nf* shoulder blade, *Spéc* scapula

OMS [oɛmɛs] *nf (abrév* **Organisation mondiale de la santé)** WHO

on [ɔ̃] *pron indéfini* **(a)** *(indéterminé)* you, people; *(quelqu'un)* somebody, someone; **on ne sait jamais** you never know; **on nous prend parfois pour deux sœurs** people sometimes take us for sisters; **on dit qu'il est malade, on le dit malade** they say he's ill; **on sonne** there's somebody at the door; **dans tous les pays où l'on parle français** in every country where French is spoken; **on m'a volé mon sac** my bag's been stolen, someone's stolen my bag **(b)** *Fam (nous)* we; **on ne s'est plus jamais quittés** we've been together ever since

onanisme [ɔnanism] *nm* onanism

once [ɔ̃s] *nf aussi Fig* ounce

oncle [ɔ̃kl] *nm* uncle; **o. d'Amérique** rich uncle

onctueux, -euse [ɔ̃ktɥø, -øz] *adj aussi Fig & Péj* smooth

onctuosité [ɔ̃ktɥozite] *nf* smoothness

onde [ɔ̃d] *nf* **(a)** *Phys* wave; *Rad* **grandes ondes** long wave; *Rad* **ondes courtes/moyennes** short/medium wave; **o. de choc** shock wave; **sur les ondes** on the radio; **passer sur les ondes** to be on the radio; **o. sonore** sound wave **(b)** *Litt (eau)* waters

ondée [ɔ̃de] *nf* sudden downpour

on-dit [ɔdi] *nm inv* rumour, hearsay; **ce ne sont que des o.** it's only hearsay

ondoyant, -e [ɔ̃dwajɑ̃, -ɑ̃t] *adj Litt* undulating

ondoyer [32] [ɔ̃dwaje] *vi (blés)* to sway; *(drapeau)* to wave; *(surface de l'eau)* to ripple; *(flamme)* to flicker

ondulant, -e [ɔ̃dylɑ̃, -ɑ̃t] *adj (plaine)* rolling, undulating; *(vagues)* rippling; *(chevelure)* wavy; *(démarche)* swaying

ondulation [ɔ̃dylasjɔ̃] *nf (des vagues)* ripple; **les ondulations de la plaine** the rolling or undulating plain; **les ondulations de sa chevelure** her wavy hair

ondulé, -e [ɔ̃dyle] *adj (sol)* undulating; *(cheveux)* wavy; *(tôle, carton)* corrugated

onduler [ɔ̃dyle] *vi* to undulate; *(cheveux)* to be wavy

onduleur [ɔ̃dylœr] *nm Ordinat* uninterruptible power supply, UPS

onéreux, -euse [ɔnerø, -øz] *adj* costly

ONF [oɛnɛf] *nm (abrév* **Office national des forêts)** *Br* ≃ Forestry Commission, *Am* ≃ National Forestry Service

ONG [oɛnʒe] *nf (abrév* **organisation non gouvernementale)** NGO

ongle [ɔ̃gl] *nm* (finger)nail; *(des orteils)* (toe)nail; *(d'un animal)* claw; *(d'un oiseau de proie)* talon; **se faire les ongles** to do one's nails; **o. incarné** ingrowing nail; *Fig* **jusqu'au bout des ongles** to one's fingertips

onglée [ɔ̃gle] *nf* **j'ai l'o.** my fingers are numb with cold

onglet [ɔ̃glɛ] *nm* **(a)** *(d'un répertoire)* tab; *(d'un canif)* thumbnail groove; **dictionnaire à onglets** thumb-indexed dictionary **(b)** *Culin* flank of beef

onguent [ɔ̃gɑ̃] *nm Litt* ointment

onirique [ɔnirik] *adj* dreamlike

onomatopée [ɔnɔmatɔpe] *nf* onomatopoeia

ont *voir* avoir

Ontario [ɔ̃tarjo] *n voir* lac

ONU [ɔny, oɛny] *nf (abrév* **Organisation des Nations unies)** UN

onyx [ɔniks] *nm* onyx

onze [ɔ̃z] *adj & nm inv* eleven; *voir aussi* **trois**

onzième [ɔ̃zjɛm] *nmf, nm & adj* eleventh; *voir aussi* **cinquième**

OPA [opea] *nf (abrév* **offre publique d'achat)** takeover bid; **lancer une O. (sur)** to make a takeover bid (for)

opacité [ɔpasite] *nf* opacity

opale [ɔpal] *nf* opal

opaque [ɔpak] *adj aussi Fig* opaque

OPEP [ɔpɛp] *nf (abrév* **Organisation des pays exportateurs de pétrole)** OPEC

opéra [ɔpera] *nm* **(a)** *(genre, œuvre)* opera **(b)** *(lieu)* opera house; **aller à l'o.** to go to the opera; **l'O. (de Paris)** the Paris Opera House; **o. bouffe** comic opera

opérable [ɔperabl] *adj* operable

opérateur, -trice [ɔperatœr, -tris] **1** *nm,f (personne)* operator; *Cin* cameraman
2 *nm* **(a)** *Math* operator **(b)** *Ordinat* **o. logique** logical operator; **o. de saisie** keyboarder

opération [ɔperasjɔ̃] *nf* **(a)** **o. (chirurgicale)** operation; **o. à cœur ouvert** open-heart surgery **(b)** *Math* operation; **faire des opérations** to do some calculations **(c)** *(transaction)* deal, transaction; **o. financière** financial transaction **(d)** *(action)* operation; **o. de police** police operation

opérationnel, -elle [ɔperasjɔnɛl] *adj* operational

opératoire [ɔperatwar] *adj (procédure)* operating

opérer [34] [ɔpere] **1** *vt* **(a)** *(réforme, restructuration)* to carry out; *(changement, distinction)* to make **(b)** *(patient)* to operate on; **se faire o.** to have an operation; **se faire o. des amygdales** to have one's tonsils (taken) out; **se faire o. du cœur/de la hanche** to have a heart/hip operation; **se faire o. d'une tumeur** to have an operation to remove a tumour
2 *vi* **(a)** *(être efficace)* to work **(b)** *(procéder)* to operate
3 s'opérer *vpr (changement, transformation)* to take place

opérette [ɔperɛt] *nf* operetta

ophtalmo [ɔftalmo] *nmf Fam* ophthalmologist

ophtalmologie [ɔftalmɔlɔʒi] *nf Méd* ophthalmology

ophtalmologiste [ɔftalmɔlɔʒist], **ophtalmologue** [ɔftalmɔlɔg] *nmf Méd* ophthalmologist

opiner [ɔpine] *vi* **o. du chef** *ou* **du bonnet** to nod one's assent

opiniâtre [ɔpinjɑtr] *adj* stubborn

opinion [ɔpinjɔ̃] *nf* opinion **(de/sur** of/about); **se faire une o. sur qch** to make up one's mind about sth, to form an opinion about sth; **sans o.** *(dans un sondage)* don't know; **avoir une bonne/mauvaise o. de qn/qch** to have a good/bad opinion of sb/sth; **o. publique** public opinion

opiomane [ɔpjɔman] *nmf* opium addict

opium [ɔpjɔm] *nm* opium

opossum [ɔpɔsɔm] *nm* opossum

opportun, -e [ɔpɔrtœ̃, -yn] *adj (arrivée)* timely, opportune; *(moment, jour)* right

opportunément [ɔpɔrtynemā] *adv* opportunely

opportunisme [ɔpɔrtynism] *nm* opportunism

opportuniste [ɔpɔrtynist] *adj & nmf* opportunist

opportunité [ɔpɔrtynite] *nf (d'une arrivée)* timeliness; *(d'un projet, d'une décision)* advisability

opposant, -e [ɔpozā, -āt] **1** *adj* opposing **2** *nm,f* opponent **(à** of)

opposé, -e [ɔpoze] **1** *adj* **(a)** *(en contradiction) (armées, caractères, équipe)* opposing; *(intérêts)* conflicting **(b)** *(dans l'espace) (côtés, rivage, direction)* opposite **(c)** *(contre)* **être o. à qch** to be opposed to sth **2** *nm (contraire)* **l'o.** the opposite; **à l'o.** *(côté)* on the opposite side; *(direction)* in the opposite direction; *Fig* on the other hand; **à l'o. de** *(côté)* on the opposite side to; *(contrairement à)* unlike; **à l'o. de ce qu'elle dit** contrary to what she says

opposer [ɔpoze] **1** *vt* **(a)** *(mettre en conflit) (armées, pays)* to bring into conflict (with each other); *(équipes)* to pit against each other; **o. à** *(armée, pays)* to bring into conflict with; *(équipe)* to pit against **(b)** *(objecter) (argument)* to put forward **(à** against); **o. une résistance vigoureuse** to put up stiff resistance **(c)** *(mettre en contraste) (théories, styles, conceptions)* to contrast **2 s'opposer** *vpr* **(a)** *(théories, styles, conceptions)* to contrast; *(équipes, adversaires)* to confront each other **(b) s'o. à qch** to be opposed to sth

opposition [ɔpozisjō] *nf* **(a)** *(résistance)* opposition; *Pol* **l'o.** the Opposition; **faire o. à un chèque** to stop a cheque **(b)** *(contraste)* contrast; **tout cela est en o. totale avec ce que je pense** all that is the complete opposite of what I think; **par o. à qch** as opposed to sth

oppressant, -e [ɔpresā, -āt] *adj* oppressive

oppresser [ɔprese] *vt* **(a)** *(sujet: situation, atmosphère)* to oppress **(b)** *Litt (peuple, nation)* to oppress

oppresseur [ɔprescœr] **1** *nm* oppressor **2** *adj* oppressive

oppression [ɔpresjō] *nf* **(a)** *(asservissement)* oppression **(b)** *Méd* tightness of the chest

opprimé, -e [ɔprime] **1** *adj* oppressed **2** *nm,f* **les opprimés** the oppressed

opprimer [ɔprime] *vt (peuple, nation)* to oppress

opprobre [ɔprɔbr] *nm Litt* opprobrium; **jeter l'o. sur qn** to cast opprobrium on sb

opter [ɔpte] *vi* **o. pour qch** to opt for sth; **o. entre deux choses** to choose between two things

opticien, -enne [ɔptisjē, -ɛn] *nm,f* optician

optimal, -e, -aux, -ales [ɔptimal, -o] *adj* optimum, optimal

optimiser [ɔptimize] *vt* to optimize

optimisme [ɔptimism] *nm* optimism; **avec o.** optimistically

optimiste [ɔptimist] **1** *adj* optimistic **2** *nmf* optimist

option [ɔpsjō] *nf* **(a)** *(choix)* option **(b)** *(chose facultative)* optional extra; *Scol (matière)* option; **le flash est en o.** the flash is an optional extra; *Scol* **matières à o.** optional subjects **(c)** *(d'achat)* **prendre une o. sur qch** to take (out) an option on sth **(d)** *Ordinat* **o. d'impression** print option; **o. de menu** menu option

optionnel, -elle [ɔpsjɔnɛl] *adj* optional

optique [ɔptik] **1** *adj (nerf)* optic; *(verre)* optical **2** *nf* **(a)** *(science)* optics *(singulier)*; **instruments d'o.** optical instruments **(b)** *(perspective)* perspective; **dans cette o.** from this perspective **(c)** *(d'un projecteur)* optical system

opulence [ɔpylās] *nf* **(a)** *(richesse)* opulence **(b)** *(des formes)* fullness

opulent, -e [ɔpylā, -āt] *adj (pays, personne)* opulent; *(pâturage)* abundant; *(poitrine)* full

opuscule [ɔpyskyl] *nm* opuscule

or¹ [ɔr] *nm* **(a)** *(métal)* gold; **montre/dent en or** gold watch/tooth; *Fam* **j'ai une femme en or** my wife is worth her weight in gold; **pour tout l'or du monde** for all the money in the world; *Fig* **c'est de l'or en barre** it's a safe investment; **le silence est d'or** silence is golden; **or fin** fine gold; **or massif** solid gold; **or noir** black gold; **or pur** pure gold **(b)** *(couleur)* gold; **cheveux d'or** golden hair

or² *conj (pour introduire une précision)* now; *(pour introduire une opposition)* well

oracle [ɔrakl] *nm* oracle

orage [ɔraʒ] *nm* (thunder)storm; *aussi Fig* **il y a de l'o. dans l'air** there's a storm brewing

orageux, -euse [ɔraʒø, -øz] *adj aussi Fig* stormy

oraison [ɔrezō] *nf* prayer; **o. funèbre** funeral oration

oral, -e, -aux, -ales [ɔral, -o] **1** *adj* oral; **par voie orale** orally **2** *nm* oral

oralement [ɔralmā] *adv* orally

orange [ɔrāʒ] **1** *nf* orange; **o. givrée** – orange sorbet served inside the skin of a whole orange; **o. pressée** freshly squeezed orange juice served with water and sugar; **o. sanguine** blood orange **2** *nm (couleur)* orange; **passer à l'o.** *(automobiliste)* to go through (the lights) on amber **3** *adj inv* orange

orangé, -e [ɔrāʒe] *adj* orange-coloured

orangeade [ɔrāʒad] *nf Br* orange squash, *Am* orangeade

oranger [ɔrāʒe] *nm* orange tree

orangeraie [ɔrāʒrɛ] *nf* orange grove

orangerie [ɔrāʒri] *nf* orangery

orang-outan *(pl* **orangs-outans)**, **orang-outang** *(pl* **orangs-outangs)** [ɔrāutā] *nm* orang-outang, orang-utan

orateur, -trice [ɔratœr, -tris] *nm,f (personne éloquente)* orator; *(personne qui prend la parole)* speaker

oratoire¹ [ɔratwar] *adj* oratorical

oratoire² *nm (chapelle)* oratory

oratorio [ɔratɔrjo] *nm* oratorio

orbite [ɔrbit] *nf* **(a)** *Astron & Fig* orbit; **en o.** in orbit; **mettre** *ou* **placer un satellite en o.** *ou* **sur o.** to put a satellite into orbit **(b)** *(de l'œil)* socket

Orcades [ɔrkad] *nfpl* **les (îles) O.** the Orkneys, Orkney Islands

orchestral, -e, -aux, -ales [ɔrkɛstral, -o] *adj* orchestral

orchestration [ɔrkɛstrasjō] *nf aussi Fig* orchestration

orchestre [ɔrkɛstr] *nm* **(a)** *(de musiciens)* orchestra; **o. de chambre** chamber orchestra; **o. de jazz** jazz band **(b)** *(partie de la salle) Br* stalls, *Am* orchestra

orchestrer [ɔrkɛstre] *vt aussi Fig* to orchestrate

orchidée [ɔrkide] *nf* orchid

ordinaire [ɔrdinɛr] **1** *adj* **(a)** *(habituel)* ordinary, usual; **peu** *ou* **pas o.** unusual **(b)** *(commun)* ordinary **2** *nm* **(a)** *(habitude)* **d'o.** usually; **comme à l'o.** as usual; **moins/plus que d'o.** less/more than usual **(b)** *(moyenne)* ça **sort de l'o.** it's out of the ordinary **(c)** *(régime habituel)* standard fare; *Mil* (company) mess **(d)** *(essence) Br* two-star, *Am* regular

ordinal, -e, -aux, -ales [ɔrdinal, -o] *adj* ordinal

ordinateur [ɔrdinatœr] *nm* computer; **o. autonome** stand-alone (computer); **o. bloc-notes** notebook (computer); **o. central** mainframe (computer); **o. domestique** home computer; **o. individuel** personal computer; **o. portable** laptop (computer)

ordination [ɔrdinasjɔ̃] *nf* ordination

ordonnance [ɔrdɔnɑ̃s] *nf* (**a**) *(document)* prescription; **délivré seulement sur o.** available only on prescription (**b**) *(disposition)* arrangement (**c**) *Jur* order, ruling (**d**) *Mil* orderly

ordonné, -e [ɔrdɔne] **1** *adj* (**a**) *(vie)* orderly (**b**) *(personne, armoire, bureau)* tidy
2 *nf* **ordonnée** *Math* ordinate; **axe des ordonnées** Y-axis

ordonner [ɔrdɔne] *vt* (**a**) *(mettre de l'ordre dans)* to organize (**b**) *(commander)* to order; **o. à qn de faire qch** to order sb to do sth (**c**) *Rel* to ordain

ordre [ɔrdr] *nm* (**a**) *(organisation)* order; **par o. alphabétique/chronologique** in alphabetical/chronological order; **procéder par o.** to do things in order; **par o. d'apparition à l'écran** in order of appearance; *Fig* **c'est dans l'o. des choses** it's in the nature of things (**b**) *(de pièce, de personne)* tidiness; **en o.** *(bureau, maison)* tidy; *(comptes)* in order; **mettre de l'o.** to tidy up (**c**) *(discipline)* order; **maintenir/rétablir l'o.** to maintain/restore order; **tout est rentré dans l'o.** everything has returned to normal; **l'o. établi** the established order; **l'o. public** law and order; **troubler l'o. public** to cause a breach of the peace (**d**) *(catégorie)* order; **de premier/second/troisième o.** first-/second-/third-rate; **renseignements/idées d'o. général** general information/ideas; **d'o. privé/pratique** of a private/practical nature; **du même o.** of the same order; **de l'o. de** in the order of (**e**) *(communauté)* order; **religieux** religious order; **entrer dans les ordres** to take holy orders; **l'o. des médecins** *Br* ≃ the British Medical Association, *Am* ≃ the American Medical Association (**f**) *(commandement)* order; **donner l'o. à qn de faire qch** to give sb the order to do sth; **je ne suis pas à tes ordres!** I don't take orders from you!; **à vos ordres, mon général!** yes sir!; **sur l'o. de qn** on the order of sb; **jusqu'à nouvel o.** until further notice (**g**) *Fin* order; **à l'o. de…** payable to (the order of)… (**h**) **o. du jour** *(d'un comité)* agenda; *Mil* order of the day

ordure [ɔrdyr] *nf* (**a**) *(saleté)* dirt, filth (**b**) **ordures** *(déchets)* *Br* rubbish, *Am* garbage; **ordures ménagères** household *Br* rubbish *or* *Am* garbage; **jeter** *ou* **mettre qch aux ordures** to throw sth in the *Br* dustbin *or* *Am* garbage can (**c**) *Fam (personne méprisable)* bastard

ordurier, -ère [ɔrdyrje, -ɛr] *adj* filthy

orée [ɔre] *nf* **à l'o. de la forêt/du bois** on the edge of the forest/wood

oreille [ɔrɛj] *nf* (**a**) *(d'une personne, d'un animal)* ear; **o. externe/interne** outer/inner ear; *Fam* **avoir les oreilles en feuilles de chou** to have sticky-out ears; **il partit l'o. basse** he went off with his tail between his legs; **tirer les oreilles à qn** to pull sb's ears; *Fig* **o.** to give sb a telling-off; **n'écouter que d'une o., écouter d'une o. distraite** to listen with half an ear; **dire qch à l'o. de qn** to whisper sth in sb's ear; **dresser** *ou* **tendre l'o.** to prick up one's ears; **je n'en crois pas mes oreilles** I can't believe my ears; **faire la sourde o.** to turn a deaf ear; **ce n'est pas tombé dans l'o. d'un sourd** it didn't fall on deaf ears; *Fig* **elle ne l'entend pas de cette o.** she won't hear of it; **être dur d'o.** to be hard of hearing; **avoir de l'o.** to have a good ear (**b**) *(d'un fauteuil)* wing; *(d'un plat, d'un vase)* handle; *(d'une casquette)* ear flap; **écrou à oreilles** wing nut

oreiller [ɔreje] *nm* pillow; **sur l'o.** in bed; **confidences sur l'o.** pillow talk

oreillette [ɔrejet] *nf* (**a**) *(du cœur)* auricle (**b**) *(d'une casquette)* ear flap

oreillons [ɔrejɔ̃] *nmpl* mumps; **avoir les o.** to have mumps

Orénoque [ɔrenɔk] *nm* **l'O.** the Orinoco

ores [ɔr] **d'ores et déjà** *adv* already

orfèvre [ɔrfɛvr] *nm* *(d'or)* goldsmith; *(d'argent)* silversmith; *Fig* **être o. en la matière** to be an expert in the matter

orfèvrerie [ɔrfɛvrəri] *nf* *(travail de l'or)* goldsmith's trade; *(travail de l'argent)* silversmith's trade; *(objets)* plate

organe [ɔrgan] *nm* (**a**) *Anat* organ; **organes génitaux** genitals; **organes des sens** sense organs (**b**) *(d'une machine)* part; **organes de transmission** transmission system (**c**) *Fig (instrument)* organ; **o. de publicité** advertising agency; **l'o. officiel du parti** the official organ of the party (**d**) *Hum (voix)* voice

organigramme [ɔrganigram] *nm* organization chart; *Ordinat* (data) flow chart

organique [ɔrganik] *adj* organic

organisateur, -trice [ɔrganizatœr, -tris] **1** *adj* organizing
2 *nm,f* organizer; **o. de conférences/de congrès** conference organizer; **o. de voyages** tour operator

organisation [ɔrganizasjɔ̃] *nf* (**a**) *(action, résultat)* organization (**b**) *(groupement)* organization; **o. à but non lucratif** *Br* non-profit-making *or* *Am* not-for-profit organization; **o. politique/syndicale** political/*Br* trade-union *or* *Am* labor-union organization; **O. mondiale de la santé** World Health Organization; **O. des Nations unies** United Nations Organization; **O. du Traité de l'Atlantique Nord** North Atlantic Treaty Organization

organisé, -e [ɔrganize] *adj* organized

organiser [ɔrganize] **1** *vt* to organize
2 **s'organiser** *vpr* to get organized

organisme [ɔrganism] *nm* (**a**) *Biol & Zool* organism; *Anat* system (**b**) *(organisation)* organization, body; **o. de crédit** credit institution; **o. international** international organization

organiste [ɔrganist] *nmf* organist

orgasme [ɔrgasm] *nm* orgasm

orge [ɔrʒ] *nf* barley

orgeat [ɔrʒa] *nm* **sirop d'o.** barley water

orgelet [ɔrʒəle] *nm* sty

orgie [ɔrʒi] *nf* orgy

orgue [ɔrg] **1** *nm* organ; **o. de Barbarie** barrel organ
2 *nfpl* (**a**) *Mus* **orgues** organ (**b**) *Géol* **orgues de basalte** basalt columns

orgueil [ɔrgœj] *nm* pride

orgueilleux, -euse [ɔrgœjø, -øz] *Péj* **1** *adj* proud
2 *nm,f* proud person

orient [ɔrjɑ̃] *nm* east; **l'O.** the East, the Orient; **en O.** in the East

orientable [ɔrjɑ̃tabl] *adj* *(grue)* swivelling; *(lampe, antenne)* adjustable

oriental, -e, -aux, -ales [ɔrjɑ̃tal, -o] **1** *adj (région, côte)* eastern; *(langue)* oriental
2 *nm,f* **O.** Oriental

orientateur, -trice [ɔrjɑ̃tatœr, -tris] = **orienteur**

orientation [ɔrjɑ̃tasjɔ̃] *nf* (**a**) *(détermination de position)* orientation; **avoir le sens de l'o.** to have a good sense of direction (**b**) *Scol* careers guidance; **choisir une o.** to choose a course of study (**c**) *(d'une grue, d'une antenne)* positioning (**d**) *(d'une maison)* aspect (**e**) *(d'une politique, de recherches)* direction

orienté, -e [ɔrjɑ̃te] *adj* (**a**) *(disposé)* **maison/pièce orientée au sud** south-facing house/room (**b**) *(peu*

objectif) biased (**c**) *Ordinat* **o. ligne** line-orientated; **o.**
objet object-orientated

orienter [ɔrjɑ̃te] **1** *vt* (**a**) *(bâtiment)* to orientate; *(canon,*
fusil, télescope) to point (**vers** *ou* **sur** at) (**b**) *(voyageur)* to
direct, to guide; *Scol* **on l'a bien/mal orientée** she was
given good/bad careers advice; **o. la conversation sur** to
steer the conversation to; **o. ses recherches vers** to direct
one's research towards **2 s'orienter** *vpr* (**a**) *(trouver sa route)* to get one's bearings
(**b**) *Fig* **s'o. vers** *(sujet: étudiant)* to specialize in; *(sujet:*
recherches) to be directed towards

orienteur, -euse [ɔrjɑ̃tœr, -øz] *nm,f Scol* careers
adviser

orifice [ɔrifis] *nm* opening; *(du corps)* orifice; *Tech* port

oriflamme [ɔriflam] *nf* (**a**) *Hist* oriflamme (**b**) *(bannière)*
banner

origan [ɔrigɑ̃] *nm* oregano

originaire [ɔriʒinɛr] *adj* **être o. de** *(sujet: personne)* to be
a native of; *(sujet: coutume, plat)* to originate from

original, -e, -aux, -ales [ɔriʒinal, -o] **1** *adj* (**a**) *(premier,*
nouveau) original (**b**) *(excentrique)* eccentric
2 *nm,f (excentrique)* eccentric
3 *nm (œuvre, document)* original; *(d'un fichier, d'une*
disquette) master copy

originalite [ɔriʒinalite] *nf* (**a**) *(nouveauté)* originality (**b**)
(excentricité) eccentricity (**c**) *(trait original)* original feature

origine [ɔriʒin] *nf* origin; **des origines à nos jours** from
the earliest times to the present day; **à l'o.** originally; **être à**
l'o. de qch to be at the origin of sth; **être d'o. modeste** to
be of humble origin; **être d'o. anglaise, être anglais d'o.**
to be of English origin

originel, -elle [ɔriʒinɛl] *adj* original

orignal, -aux [ɔriɲal, -o] *nm* moose

oripeaux [ɔripo] *nmpl* rags, tatters

ORL [ɔɛrɛl] *nmf Méd (abrév* **oto rhino laryngologiste)**
ENT specialist

orme [ɔrm] *nm* elm

ormeau, -x [ɔrmo] *nm* (**a**) *(arbre)* young elm (**b**)
(mollusque) abalone

ornement [ɔrnəmɑ̃] *nm aussi Mus* ornament

ornemental, -e, -aux, -ales [ɔrnəmɑ̃tal, -o] *adj*
ornamental

orner [ɔrne] *vt* to decorate (**de** with); *(vêtement)* to trim
(**de** with)

ornière [ɔrnjɛr] *nf* rut; *Fig* **sortir de l'o.** to get out of
trouble

ornithologie [ɔrnitɔlɔʒi] *nf* ornithology
ornithologiste [ɔrnitɔlɔʒist], **ornithologue** [ɔrnitɔ-
lɔg] *nmf* ornithologist

oronge [ɔrɔ̃ʒ] *nf* agaric

orphelin, -e [ɔrfəlɛ̃, -in] **1** *adj* orphan(ed); **o. de père**
fatherless; **o. de mère** motherless
2 *nm,f* orphan

orphelinat [ɔrfəlina] *nm* orphanage

orque [ɔrk] *nf* killer whale

Orsay [ɔrsɛ] *n voir* quai

ORSEC [ɔrsɛk] (*abrév* **organisation des secours**) **le plan**
O. = disaster contingency plan

orteil [ɔrtɛj] *nm* toe; **gros/petit o.** big/little toe

orthodontiste [ɔrtɔdɔ̃tist] *nmf* orthodontist

orthodoxe [ɔrtɔdɔks] **1** *adj aussi Rel* orthodox; **peu o.**
unorthodox
2 *nmf Rel (de stricte obédience)* person of orthodox beliefs;
(de l'Église orthodoxe) member of the Orthodox Church

orthodoxie [ɔrtɔdɔksi] *nf* orthodoxy

orthogonal, -e, -aux, -ales [ɔrtɔgɔnal, -o] *adj*
orthogonal

orthographe [ɔrtɔgraf] *nf* spelling; **avoir une bonne o.**
to be good at spelling

orthographier [66] [ɔrtɔgrafje] *vt* to spell; **mal o. un**
mot to misspell a word

orthographique [ɔrtɔgrafik] *adj* orthographic

orthopédie [ɔrtɔpedi] *nf* orthopaedics *(singulier)*

orthopédique [ɔrtɔpedik] *adj* orthopaedic

orthopédiste [ɔrtɔpedist] *nmf* (**a**) *(médecin)*
orthopaedist (**b**) *(fabricant)* maker of orthopaedic apparatus

orthophonie [ɔrtɔfɔni] *nf* speech therapy

orthophoniste [ɔrtɔfɔnist] *nmf* speech therapist

ortie [ɔrti] *nf* nettle

ortolan [ɔrtɔlɑ̃] *nm* ortolan (bunting)

OS [ɔɛs] *nm (abrév* **ouvrier spécialisé)** semi-skilled worker

os [ɔs, *pl* o] *nm* bone; *Fam Fig (obstacle)* snag, **mouillé** *ou*
trempé jusqu'aux os soaked to the skin; **il ne fera pas de**
vieux os he won't make old bones; *Fam* **tomber sur un os**
to hit a snag, *très Fam* **je l'ai dans l'os** I've had it, **os à**
moelle marrowbone

oscar [ɔskar] *nm (récompense)* Oscar

oscillateur [ɔsilatœr] *nm Phys* oscillator

oscillation [ɔsilasjɔ̃] *nf* (**a**) *(d'un pendule)* swing; *(d'une*
aiguille) flickering; *(d'un bateau)* rocking; *Phys* oscillation (**b**)
Fig (du marché, de l'opinion) fluctuation

osciller [ɔsile] *vi* (**a**) *(pendule)* to swing; *(aiguille)* to flicker;
(bateau) to rock; *Phys* to oscillate (**b**) *(hésiter)* **o. entre** to
waver between

osé, -e [ɔze] *adj* daring

oseille [ozɛj] *nf* (**a**) *(plante)* sorrel (**b**) *Fam (argent)* dosh

oser [oze] *vt* **o. faire qch** to dare (to) do sth; **j'ose croire**
que... I dare say that...; **si j'ose dire** if I may say so;
comment oser vous! how dare you!

osier [ozje] *nm* (**a**) *(arbre)* osier (**b**) *(en vannerie)* wicker

Oslo [ɔslo] *n* Oslo

osmose [ɔsmoz] *nf aussi Fig* osmosis

ossature [ɔsatyr] *nf* (**a**) *(d'un homme, d'un animal)* frame
(**b**) *Fig (d'un bâtiment, d'un texte)* framework

osselets [ɔslɛ] *nmpl* **jouer aux o.** to play at knucklebones

ossements [ɔsmɑ̃] *nmpl* bones

osseux, -euse [ɔsø, -øz] *adj (visage, main)* bony; *(tissu,*
greffe) bone

ossuaire [ɔsɥɛr] *nm* ossuary

ostensible [ɔstɑ̃sibl] *adj* open

ostensiblement [ɔstɑ̃sibləmɑ̃] *adv* openly

ostensoir [ɔstɑ̃swar] *nm Rel* monstrance

ostentation [ɔstɑ̃tasjɔ̃] *nf* ostentation; **sans o.**
unostentatiously

ostéopathe [ɔsteɔpat] *nmf* osteopath

ostéoporose [ɔsteɔpɔroz] *nf Méd* osteoporosis

ostracisme [ɔstrasism] *nm* ostracism

ostréiculteur, -trice [ɔstreikyltœr, -tris] *nm,f* oyster
farmer

ostréiculture [ɔstreikyltyr] *nf* oyster farming

otage [ɔtaʒ] *nm* hostage; **prendre qn en o.** to take sb
hostage

otalgie [ɔtalʒi] *nf Méd* earache, *Spéc* otalgia

OTAN [ɔtɑ̃] *nf (abrév* **Organisation du traité de**
l'Atlantique Nord) l'O. NATO

otarie [ɔtari] *nf* sea lion

OTASE [ɔtaz] *nf* (*abrév* **Organisation du traité de l'Asie du Sud-Est**) **l'O.** SEATO

ôter [ote] **1** *vt* (**a**) *(enlever)* to take away, to remove; *(vêtement)* to take off; *(tache)* to remove; *(assiettes)* to clear away; **ô. qch à qn** to take sth away from sb; *(illusions)* to rid sb of sth; **cela lui a ôté l'appétit** it's made him lose his appetite; **je vais t'ô. l'envie de recommencer!** I'll teach you not to start that again!; **tu ne m'ôteras pas de l'idée que…** I'm quite convinced that… (**b**) *Math* **10 ôté de 30 égale 20** 10 from 30 leaves 20
2 s'ôter *vpr* **ôtez-vous de là!** move yourself!; **s'ô. une idée de la tête** to get an idea out of one's head

otite [ɔtit] *nf Méd* ear infection, *Spéc* otitis

oto-rhino (*pl* **oto-rhinos**) [ɔtorino] *nmf Fam* ENT specialist

oto-rhino-laryngologiste (*pl* **oto-rhino-laryngologistes**) [ɔtorinolarɛ̃gɔlɔʒist] *nmf* ear, nose and throat specialist

Ottawa [ɔtawa] *n* Ottawa

ou [u] *conj* or; **ou… ou (bien)…** either… or (else)…

où [u] **1** *adv* (**a**) *(interrogatif, relatif)* where; **d'où vient ce mot?** where does this word come from?; **par où est-il passé?** which way did he go?; **je ne sais pas où aller** I don't know where to go (**b**) *(indéfini)* **où que vous soyez** wherever you may be (**c**) *(exprime la conséquence)* **d'où sa tristesse** hence his sadness
2 *pron relatif* (**a**) *(dans l'espace)* where; **là où** where; **partout où** wherever (**b**) *(dans le temps)* when (**c**) *(dans lequel, auquel)* **dans l'état où elle est** in the state she's in; **au prix où est le champagne** with champagne the price it is

OUA [oya] *nf* (*abrév* **Organisation de l'unité africaine**) **l'O.** the OAU

ouache [waʃ] *nf Can* bear's den

ouah [wa] *exclam* (**a**) *(aboiement)* woof! (**b**) *(exprime l'admiration)* wow!

ouailles [wɑj] *nfpl Litt ou Hum* flock

ouais [wɛ] *exclam Fam* yeah!

ouananiche [wananiʃ] *nf Can* freshwater salmon

ouaouaron [wawarɔ̃] *nm Can* bullfrog

ouate [wat] *nf* (**a**) *(pour soins) Br* cotton wool, *Am* absorbent cotton (**b**) *(pour rembourrage)* padding

ouatine [watin] *nf* quilting (material)

ouatiné, -e [watine] *adj* quilted

oubli [ubli] *nm* (**a**) *(trou de mémoire)* oversight; *(lacune)* omission (**b**) *(général)* oblivion; **tomber dans l'o.** to sink into oblivion (**c**) *(acte d'oublier)* forgetting

oublier [66] [ublije] **1** *vt* to forget; *(omettre)* to leave out; **o. de faire qch** to forget to do sth
2 s'oublier *vpr* (**a**) *(se relâcher)* to forget oneself; *Euph (chien)* to make a mess (**b**) *(sortir de la mémoire)* to be forgotten; **c'est comme le vélo, ça ne s'oublie pas** it's like riding a bike, once you learn you never forget

oubliettes [ublijɛt] *nfpl* dungeon; *Fig* **mettre qch aux o.** to shelve sth

ouest [wɛst] **1** *nm* west; **un vent d'o.** a westerly wind; **le vent d'o.** the west wind; **à l'o.** in the west; **à l'o. de** (to the) west of; *Géog & Pol* **l'O.** the West
2 *adj inv* *(côte, face)* west; *(régions)* western

ouf [uf] *exclam* phew!; *Fam* **elle n'a pas eu le temps de dire o.** she didn't even have time to catch her breath

Ouganda [ugɑ̃da] *nm* **l'O.** Uganda

ougandais, -e [ugɑ̃dɛ, -ɛz] **1** *adj* Ugandan
2 *nm,f* **O.** Ugandan

oui [wi] **1** *adv* yes; **répondre par o. ou par non** to answer

yes or no; **je crois que o.** I think so; **faire signe que o.** to nod (one's head); **ah, o.?** really?; *Fam* **tu viens, o.?** are you coming?; *Fam* **tu viens, o. ou non?** are you coming or aren't you?
2 *nm inv Pol* aye; *Fam* **se quereller/pleurer pour un o., pour un non** to quarrel/cry over the slightest thing

ouï-dire [widir] *nm* hearsay; **par o.** by hearsay

ouïe [wi] *nf* (**a**) *(sens)* hearing; **avoir l'o. fine** to have sharp ears; *Hum* **être tout o.** to be all ears (**b**) *(de poisson)* **ouïes** gills (**c**) *Mus* **ouïes** sound holes

ouille [uj] *exclam* ouch!, ow!

ouistiti [wistiti] *nm* marmoset; *Fam Fig* **un drôle de o.** an odd character

ouragan [uragɑ̃] *nm* hurricane; *Fig (de protestations)* storm; **entrer comme un o. dans une pièce** to burst into a room

Oural [ural] *nm* **l'O.** *(montagnes)* the Urals

ourler [urle] *vt* (**a**) *(faire un ourlet à)* to hem (**b**) *(border)* to edge (**de** with)

ourlet [urlɛ] *nm* (**a**) *(d'un vêtement)* hem; **faire un o. à** to put a hem on (**b**) *(de l'oreille)* rim

ours [urs] *nm aussi Fig* bear; *Prov* **il ne faut pas vendre la peau de l'o. avant de l'avoir tué** don't count your chickens before they're hatched; **o. blanc** polar bear; **o. brun** brown bear; *Fig* **o. mal léché** boor; **o. en peluche** teddy bear; **o. polaire** polar bear

ourse [urs] *nf* she-bear; *Astron* **la Grande O.** the Great Bear; **la Petite O.** the Little Bear

oursin [ursɛ̃] *nm* sea urchin

ourson [ursɔ̃] *nm* bear cub

oust(e) [ust] *exclam (pour presser)* get a move on!; *(pour chasser)* scram!

outarde [utard] *nf Can* Canada goose

outil [uti] *nm aussi Fig* tool; **outils pédagogiques** teaching aids; **o. de travail** tool

outillage [utijaʒ] *nm* (**a**) *(ensemble d'outils)* (set of) tools (**b**) *(industriel, agricole)* equipment

outiller [utije] **1** *vt* to equip
2 s'outiller *vpr (bricoleur)* to equip oneself; *(usine)* to equip itself

outrage [utraʒ] *nm (au bon goût, au bon sens)* insult (**à** to); *Euph & Litt* **faire subir les derniers outrages à une femme** to violate a woman; *Jur* **o. aux bonnes mœurs** affront to public decency; **o. à magistrat** contempt of court; **o. à la pudeur** public indecency

outrageant, -e [utraʒɑ̃, -ɑ̃t] *adj (proposition, refus)* insulting; *(plaisanterie, propos)* offensive; *(accusation)* outrageous

outrageusement [utraʒøzmɑ̃] *adv (excessivement)* outrageously

outrance [utrɑ̃s] *nf (d'une tenue, d'une attitude, de propos)* extravagance; **à o.** excessively

outre¹ [utr] *nf* wine skin

outre² [utr] **1** *prép* (**a**) *(en plus de)* besides (**b**) **o. mesure** unduly
2 *adv* **en o.** besides; **passer o.** *(malgré une interdiction)* to carry on regardless; **passer o. à qch** to disregard sth
3 *conj* **o. (le fait) que…** apart from the fact that…

outré, -e [utre] *adj* (**a**) *(indigné)* outraged (**de** *ou* **par** by) (**b**) *(excessif)* overdone

outre-Atlantique [utratlɑ̃tik] *adv* across the Atlantic

outrecuidance [utrəkɥidɑ̃s] *nf Litt* (**a**) *(insolence)* impertinence; **avoir l'o. de faire qch** to have the impertinence to do sth (**b**) *(orgueil)* presumptuousness

outrecuidant, -e [utrəkɥidɑ̃, -ɑ̃t] *adj* (**a**) *(insolent)* impertinent (**b**) *(orgueilleux)* presumptuous

outre-Manche [utrəmɑ̃ʃ] *adv* across the Channel
outre-mer [utrəmɛr] *adv* overseas
outrepasser [utrəpase] *vt* to exceed, to go beyond
outre-Rhin [utrərɛ̃] *adv* across the Rhine
outre-tombe [utrətɔ̃b] *d'outre-tombe adj (voix)* sepulchral
ouvert, -e [uvɛr, -ɛrt] **1** *pp voir* ouvrir
2 *adj* (a) *(porte, yeux, plate, vêtement, magasin)* open, **grand** o. wide open; être o. à qn *(lieu, concours)* to be open to sb (b) *(gaz, robinet)* on (c) *Fig (franc, sans préjugés)* open; **avoir l'esprit o.** to be open-minded; **être o. à toute proposition** to be open to suggestions
ouvertement [uvɛrtəmɑ̃] *adv* openly
ouverture [uvɛrtyr] *nf* (a) *(d'une porte, d'une séance, d'un compte)* opening; *(des hostilités)* outbreak; **l'o. de la chasse/de la pêche** the start of the hunting season/fishing season; **à l'o.** *(de la Bourse)* at the start of trading; *Fig* **o. d'esprit** open-mindedness; *Ordinat* **o. de session** log-on (b) *(orifice)* opening (c) **ouvertures** *(avances)* overtures; **faire des ouvertures à qn** to make overtures to sb (d) *Mus* overture (e) *Phot* aperture (f) *Pol* **politique d'o.** policy of conciliation (g) *(aux échecs, aux cartes)* opening
ouvrable [uvrabl] *adj voir* jour
ouvrage [uvraʒ] **1** *nm* (a) *(travail)* work; **se mettre à l'o.** to get down to work (b) *Constr* work; **ouvrages d'art civil** engineering works (c) *(livre)* work; **o. de référence** reference work (d) *(résultat d'un travail)* piece of work; *(tricot, broderie)* work
2 *nf Fam* **c'est de la belle o.** that's a nice piece of work
ouvragé, -e [uvraʒe] *adj* elaborate
ouvrant, -e [uvrɑ̃, -ɑ̃t] *adj voir* toit
ouvre-boîtes [uvrəbwat] *nm inv* can opener
ouvre-bouteilles [uvrəbutɛj] *nm inv* bottle opener
ouvreur, -euse [uvrœr, -øz] *nm,f* usher, *f* usherette
ouvrier, -ère [uvrije, -er] **1** *adj (quartier, tradition)* working-class; *(agitation)* industrial
2 *nm,f* worker; **une famille d'ouvriers** a working-class family; **o. agricole** farm worker; **o. qualifié** skilled worker; **o. spécialisé** semi-skilled worker
3 *nm (dans les travaux publics, le bâtiment)* workman
4 *nf* **ouvrière** *(abeille, fourmi)* worker
ouvrir [52] [uvrir] **1** *vt* (a) *(porte, boîte, bouteille, rideaux)* to open; *(verrou)* to draw; *(avec une clef)* to unlock; *(robinet, gaz)* to turn on; *(électricité)* to switch on; (b) *Méd (abcès)* to lance; *(pour opérer)* to open up (c) *(lancer) (boutique, compte, débat)* to open; **o. la marche** to lead the way; *Ordinat* **o. une session** to log in, to log on (d) *Fig* **cela ouvre l'appétit** it

whets the appetite; **o. son cœur à qn** to open one's heart to sb; **o. l'esprit à qn** to broaden sb's mind; **o. qch à qn** *(domaine, profession, perspectives)* to open up sth to sb
2 *vi (magasin, porte)* to open
3 *s'ouvrir vpr* (a) *(porte, yeux, séance, fleur)* to open; *Fig* **s'o. à qn** *(perspectives, domaine)* to open up for sb (b) *(se couper)* **s'o. la main/le menton** to cut open one's hand/chin; **s'o. les veines** to slash one's wrists
ouzbek [uzbɛk] **1** *adj* Uzbek
2 *nmf* O. Uzbek
Ouzbékistan [uzbekistɑ̃] *nm* l'O. Uzbekistan
ovaire [ɔvɛr] *nm* ovary
ovale [ɔval] *adj & nm* oval
ovariectomie [ɔvarjɛktɔmi] *nf Méd* ovariectomy
ovarien, -enne [ɔvarjɛ̃, -ɛn] *adj* ovarian
ovation [ɔvasjɔ̃] *nf* ovation; **faire une o. à qn** to give sb an ovation
ovationner [ɔvasjɔne] *vt* **o. qn** to give sb an ovation
overdose [ɔvœrdoz] *nf aussi Fig* overdose; **faire une o.** *(de qch) (drogue)* to take an overdose (of sth); *Fig* to overdose (on sth)
ovin, -e [ɔvɛ̃, -in] *Zool* **1** *adj* ovine
2 *nm* sheep
ovni [ɔvni] *nm (abrév* objet volant non identifié) UFO
ovulation [ɔvylasjɔ̃] *nf* ovulation
ovule [ɔvyl] *nm* ovum
ovuler [ɔvyle] *vi* to ovulate
oxhydrique [ɔksidrik] *adj* oxyhydrogen
oxydant, -e [ɔksidɑ̃, ɑ̃t] **1** *adj* oxidizing
2 *nm* oxidizer
oxydation [ɔksidasjɔ̃] *nf* oxidization
oxyde [ɔksid] *nm Chim* oxide; **o. de carbone** carbon monoxide
oxyder [ɔkside] **1** *vt* to oxidize
2 *s'oxyder vpr* to oxidize
oxygéné, -e [ɔksiʒene] *adj Chim* oxygenated; *(cheveux)* peroxide blonde, bleached
oxygène [ɔksiʒɛn] *nm* oxygen; *Fig* **j'ai besoin d'o.** I need some fresh air
oxygéner [34] [ɔksiʒene] **1** *vt* (a) *Chim (liquide, tissu vivant)* to oxygenate; *(élément, produit chimique)* to oxidize (b) *(cheveux)* to bleach, to peroxide
2 *s'oxygéner vpr (respirer)* to get some fresh air
oyat [ɔja] *nm* marram grass
ozone [ozon] *nm* ozone

P, p [pe] *nm inv* P, p

PAC [pak] *nf* (*abrév* **politique agricole commune**) CAP

PACA [paka] *nf* (*abrév* **Provence-Alpes-Côte d'Azur**) = region of south-eastern France

pacage [paka3] *nm* (*champ*) pasture

pacemaker [pɛsmɛkœr] *nm* pacemaker

pacha [paʃa] *nm* pasha; *Fig* **mener une vie de p.** to live like a lord

pachyderme [paʃidɛrm] *nm* pachyderm; *Fig* (*personne*) lumbering oaf

pacification [pasifikasjɔ̃] *nf* pacification

pacifier [66] [pasifje] *vt* to pacify

pacifique [pasifik] **1** *adj* (*sans violence, calme*) peaceful; (*qui aime la paix*) peace-loving
2 *nm* **le P.** (*océan*) the Pacific; **le P. sud** the South Pacific

pacifisme [pasifism] *nm* pacifism

pacifiste [pasifist] *adj & nmf* pacifist

pack [pak] *nm* (*lot*) & *Sp* pack; **vendu en p.** sold in packs

pacotille [pakɔtij] *nf* junk; **de p.** (*marchandise*) shoddy; (*bijoux*) paste; *Fig* third-rate

pacson [paksɔ̃] *nm Fam* (*argent*) packet

pacte [pakt] *nm* pact; **p. de non-agression** non-aggression pact; **le p. de Varsovie** the Warsaw Pact

pactiser [paktize] *vi* **p. avec l'ennemi** to make a pact with the enemy

pactole [paktɔl] *nm Fam* (*au loto*) jackpot; **un joli p.** a nice little sum

paddock [padɔk] *nm* paddock; *Fam* (*lit*) bed

paella [paɛla] *nf* paella

PAF [paf] *nm* (*abrév* **paysage audiovisuel français**) = French broadcasting

paf [paf] **1** *exclam* (*chute*) bang!; (*claque*) slap!; (*coup de poing*) wham!
2 *adj inv Fam* (*ivre*) wasted

pagaie [pagɛ] *nf* paddle

pagaïe, pagaille [pagaj] *nf Fam* (**a**) (*désordre*) mess; **en p.** in a mess (**b**) (*confusion*) chaos; **semer la p.** to cause chaos (**c**) **des cadeaux/des jouets en p.** loads of presents/toys

pagayer [53] [pageje] *vi* to paddle

page¹ [pa3] *nf* (**a**) (*d'un livre, d'un cahier, sur l'Internet*) page; *Fig* (*extrait*) passage; (*de l'histoire, d'une vie*) chapter; **en première p.** (*des journaux*) on the front page (of the newspapers); *Typ* **mettre qch en page(s)** to make sth up; **perdre la p.** to lose one's place; *Fig* **tourner la p.** to make a fresh start; **p. centrale** (*d'un magazine*) centre pages; **p. de garde** flyleaf; **les pages jaunes** (*de l'annuaire*) the Yellow

Pages®; *Ordinat* **p. précédente** page up; *Rad & TV* **p. de publicité** commercial break; *Ordinat* **p. suivante** page down (**b**) **être à la p.** (*à la mode*) to be up to date

page² *nm* page(boy)

pagination [paʒinasjɔ̃] *nf* pagination

paginer [paʒine] *vt* to paginate

pagne [paɲ] *nm* loincloth; (*en paille*) grass skirt

pagode [pagɔd] *nf* pagoda

paie [pɛ] **1** *voir* **payer**
2 *nf* (**a**) (*salaire*) pay, wages (**b**) *Fam* **ça fait une p.** it's ages ago; **ça fait une p. que je ne l'ai pas vue** I haven't seen her for ages

paiement [pɛmɑ̃] *nm* payment; *aussi Fig* **en p. de qch** as payment for sth; **p. à la commande** cash with order; **p. à la livraison** cash on delivery

païen, -enne [pajɛ̃, -ɛn] *adj & nm,f* pagan, heathen

paiera *etc voir* **payer**

paillard, -e [pajar, -ard] *adj* bawdy

paillasse [pajas] *nf* (**a**) (*matelas*) straw mattress (**b**) (*de l'évier*) draining board; (*de laboratoire*) bench

paillasson [pajasɔ̃] *nm aussi Fig* doormat

paille [paj] **1** *nf* (**a**) (*de céréales*) straw; *Fig* **être sur la p.** to be down and out; **tirer à la courte p.** to draw lots; **p. de fer** steel wool (**b**) (*pour boire*) straw
2 *adj inv* (*jaune*) straw-coloured

paillé, -e [paje] *adj* (*chaise*) straw-bottomed

pailleté, -e [pajte] *adj* sequined

paillette [pajɛt] *nf* (**a**) (*sur vêtement*) sequin; **paillettes** (*pour se maquiller*) glitter; **à paillettes** sequined (**b**) (*d'or*) speck; (*de savon*) flake

paillote [pajɔt] *nf* straw hut

pain [pɛ̃] *nm* (**a**) (*aliment*) bread; (*miche*) loaf; *Fig* **avoir du p. sur la planche** to have a lot on one's plate; **gagner son p.** to earn one's living; **je ne mange pas de ce p.-là** I'm having nothing to do with that; **ça ne mange pas de p.** it won't cost you/him/*etc* anything; **ôter le p. de la bouche à qn** to take the bread out of sb's mouth; **petit p.** (bread) roll; **p. partir** *ou* **se vendre comme des petits pains** to sell like hot cakes; **p. azyme** unleavened bread; **p. bénit** consecrated bread; **p. bis** brown bread; **p. de campagne** farmhouse bread; **p. au chocolat** chocolate-filled pastry; **p. complet** wholewheat bread; **p. d'épices** ≃ gingerbread; **p. grillé** toast; **p. au lait** sweet roll; **p. de mie** sliced white bread; **p. perdu** French toast; **p. aux raisins** = circular pastry made from sweetened dough and raisins; **p. de seigle** rye bread; **p. au** *ou* **de son** bran bread; **p. de sucre** sugarloaf (**b**) (*de savon*) bar (**c**) *Fam* (*coup de poing*) punch

pair, -e [pɛr] **1** *adj* (*nombre, jours*) even

2 nm (a) (égal) être jugé par ses pairs to be judged by one's peers; **aller de p.** avec qch to go hand in hand with sth (b) (noble) peer (c) **jeune fille au p.** au pair; **être** ou **travailler au p.** to work as an au pair (d) (au jeu) even numbers

paire [pɛr] nf pair; (de gibier à plumes, de pistolets) brace; **il a reçu une p. de claques** he got his face slapped; Fam Fig **ça, c'est une autre p. de manches** that's a different kettle of fish

paisible [pɛzibl] adj peaceful; (personne) quiet

paisiblement [pɛziblǝmā] adv peacefully

paître [50b] [pɛtr] **1** vt (herbe) to crop; (feuilles) to feed on **2** vi to feed; (manger de l'herbe) to graze; (manger des feuilles) to browse; Fam Fig **envoyer p. qn** to send sb packing

paix [pɛ] nf (a) (entre États) peace; **faire la p.** (avec qn) to make peace (with sb); Fig to make it up (with sb); **vivre en p. avec sa conscience** to have a clear conscience (b) Rel **p. à son âme** may his soul rest in peace; **allez en p.** go in peace (c) (tranquillité) peace; **avoir la p.** to have some peace (and quiet); **faire qch en p.** to do sth in peace (and quiet); **laisser qn en p.** to leave sb in peace; Fam **fiche-moi** ou **fous-moi la p.!** get off my back!; Fam **la p.!** quiet!

Pakistan [pakistã] nm **le P.** Pakistan

pakistanais, -e [pakistanɛ, -ɛz] **1** adj Pakistani **2** nmf **P.** Pakistani

Pal [pal] adj inv TV (abrév **phase alternation line**) PAL

palabres [palabr] nfpl endless discussion

palace [palas] nm luxury hotel

palais¹ [palɛ] nm (a) (d'un roi, d'un noble) palace; **le p. Bourbon** = home of the French parliament; **p. des congrès** conference centre; **le p. de l'Élysée** the Élysée (Palace) (official residence of the French President); **le p. Garnier** = the former Paris Opera House; **le p. du Luxembourg** = home of the French Senate; **p. des sports** sports centre (b) (tribunal) **le P. (de justice)** the law courts

palais² nm (partie de la bouche, goût) palate

palan [palã] nm hoist

pale [pal] nf blade

pâle [pɑl] adj (a) pale; **p. comme un linge** as white as a sheet; **p. comme la mort** deathly pale; Fam Mil **se faire porter p.** to report sick (b) Fig (sourire) faint; (style) colourless; **une p. imitation de qch** a pale imitation of sth

palefrenier [palfrǝnje] nm groom

paléolithique [paleolitik] Géol **1** adj Palaeolithic **2** nm **le p.** the Palaeolithic period

paléontologie [paleɔ̃tolɔʒi] nf palaeontology

paléontologiste [paleɔ̃tolɔʒist], **paléontologue** [paleɔ̃tolɔg] nmf palaeontologist

Palerme [palɛrm] n Palermo

Palestine [palɛstin] nf **la P.** Palestine

palestinien, -enne [palɛstinjɛ̃, -ɛn] **1** adj Palestinian **2** nmf **P.** Palestinian

palet [palɛ] nm (a) (pour hockey) puck (b) (gâteau sec) round butter Br biscuit or Am cookie

paletot [palto] nm (short) overcoat; Fam Fig **tomber sur le p. à qn** (l'attaquer) to jump on sb; (pour lui parler) to buttonhole sb

palette [palɛt] nf (a) (de peintre) palette; Fig (éventail) range; Ordinat **p. graphique** graphics palette; Ordinat **p. d'outils** tool palette (b) (pour la manutention) pallet (c) Culin (de mouton, de porc) shoulder

palétuvier [paletyvje] nm mangrove

pâleur [pɑlœr] nf (d'une personne) pallor; (d'une couleur, de la lumière) paleness; (du style) colourlessness; **d'une p. mortelle** deathly pale

pâlichon, -onne [paliʃɔ̃, -ɔn] adj Fam a bit pale

palier [palje] nm (a) (d'escalier) landing (b) (dans une évolution) plateau; **par paliers** in stages

palindrome [palɛ̃drom] nm Ling palindrome

pâlir [pɑlir] vi (personne) to turn or go pale; (lumière, couleur, souvenir) to fade; **p. de rage** to turn white with anger; Fig **faire p. qn de jalousie** to make sb green with envy

palissade [palisad] nf fence

palliatif, -ive [paljatif, -iv] **1** adj palliative **2** nm Méd palliative; Fig stopgap measure

pallier [66] [palje] **1** vt (manque) to compensate for, (erreur, problème) to lessen the impact of **2** **pallier à** vt ind (manque) to compensate for; (erreur, problème) to lessen the impact of

palmarès [palmarɛs] nm (à un concours) list of prize-winners; (d'une compétition sportive) list of winners; **le p. (de la chanson)** the charts; **être** ou **figurer au p.** (d'un concours, d'une compétition) to be among the (prize-) winners; (de la chanson) to be in the charts; **avoir** ou **compter cinquante victoires à son p.** to have fifty wins to one's credit

palme [palm] nf (a) (de palmier) palm (branch) (b) (récompense) **les palmes académiques** = decoration awarded to teachers; **la P. d'or** (du festival de Cannes) the Palme d'or (c) (pour nager) flipper

palmé, -e [palme] adj (a) (feuille) palmate (b) (pattes) webbed

palmeraie [palmǝrɛ] nf palm grove

palmier [palmje] nm (a) (arbre) palm (tree); **p. dattier** date palm (b) (gâteau sec) = sweet heart-shaped pastry

palmipède [palmiped] nm Zool web-footed bird; Spéc palmiped

palombe [palɔ̃b] nf wood pigeon

pâlot, -otte [palo, -ɔt] adj Fam a bit pale

palourde [palurd] nf clam

palpable [palpabl] adj palpable

palpation [palpasjɔ̃] nf Méd palpation

palper [palpe] vt (a) (objet) to feel (with one's hands); Méd to palpate (b) Fam (somme) to be paid, to get

palpitant, -e [palpitã, -ãt] **1** adj (a) (cœur, pouls) fluttering; (plus fort) throbbing; (personne) (d'émotion) quivering (b) (passionnant) thrilling **2** nm très Fam (cœur) ticker

palpitations [palpitasjɔ̃] nfpl palpitations

palpiter [palpite] vi (cœur, pouls) to flutter; (plus fort) to throb

paludisme [palydism] nm malaria

pâmer [pame] **se pâmer** vpr Vieilli to swoon; Fig & Hum **se p. d'aise** to be blissfully happy; Fig & Hum **se p. (devant)** to swoon (over)

pamphlet [pãflɛ] nm satirical tract

pamplemousse [pãplǝmus] nm grapefruit

pan¹ [pã] nm (a) (de chemise, de manteau) tail; (de jupe) panel (b) (morceau) section, piece; Fig (d'une époque) part; **p. de mur** section of wall

pan² exclam (coup de feu) bang!; (gifle) whack!; **et p., la voilà qui entre!** and lo and behold, in she walks!

panacée [panase] nf panacea

panachage [panaʃaʒ] nm mixing; (de liste électorale) = voting for candidates from more than one list

panache [panaʃ] nm (a) (plume) plume (b) (brio, éclat) panache

panaché, -e [panaʃe] **1** adj multicoloured; **p. de blanc**

streaked with white, with white streaks
2 *nm (boisson)* = beer mixed with lemon soda
panacher [panaʃe] *vt* to mix
panade [panad] *nf Fam* **être dans la p.** *(avoir des ennuis)* to be in a bit of a mess; *(manquer d'argent)* to be flat broke
panafricain, -e [panafrikɛ̃, -ɛn] *adj* Pan-African
panais [panɛ] *nm* parsnip
Panama [panama] *nm* **le P.** Panama
panama [panama] *nm (chapeau)* panama hat
Paname [panam] *n Fam* Paris
panaméen, -enne [panameɛ̃, -ɛn] **1** *adj* Panamanian **2** *nm,f* **P.** Panamanian
panaméricain, -e [panamerikɛ̃, -ɛn] *adj* Pan-American
panard [panar] *nm Fam* foot
panaris [panari] *nm* whitlow
pan-bagnat *(pl* **pans-bagnats)** [pãbaɲa] *nm* = large bread roll filled with salade niçoise
pancarte [pãkart] *nf (affiche)* sign, notice; *(pour manifestation)* placard
pancréas [pãkreas] *nm* pancreas
panda [pãda] *nm* panda
pané, -e [pane] *adj* coated with breadcrumbs, breaded
panégyrique [paneʒirik] *nm* eulogy; **faire le p. de qn** to eulogize sb
panel [panɛl] *nm (groupe)* panel; *(échantillon)* sample (group)
paneuropéen, -enne [panørɔpeɛ̃, -ɛn] *adj* Pan-European
panier [panje] *nm* **(a)** *(corbeille)* basket; **mettre** *ou* **jeter qch au p.** to throw sth in the wastepaper basket; *Fig* **le dessus du p.** the pick of the bunch; *Fig* **c'est un p. de crabes** they're always at each other's throats; **p. à linge** linen basket; **Fam p. percé** spendthrift; **p. à provisions** shopping basket; **p. à salade** salad shaker; *Fam (convoi cellulaire) Br* black Maria, *Am* paddy wagon **(b)** *(au basketball)* basket **(c)** *(pour diapositives)* slide magazine **(d)** *(de robe)* hoop
panier-repas *(pl* **paniers-repas)** [panjerəpa] *nm* packed lunch
panique [panik] **1** *nf* panic; **être pris de p.** to panic; **ne pas céder à la p.** not to panic; **il y a eu un début de p.** people started to panic; **il y a eu un mouvement de p.** people panicked **2** *adj* **peur p.** panic
paniqué, -e [panike] *adj Fam* in a panic
paniquer [panike] *vt & vi Fam* to panic
panislamisme [panislamism] *nm* Pan-Islamism
panne [pan] *nf* breakdown; *Ordinat* failure, crash; **être en p.** *(machine)* to be out of order; *(automobiliste)* to have broken down; **tomber en p.** to break down; **tomber en p. d'essence, tomber en p. sèche** to run out of *Br* petrol or *Am* gas; *Fam* **il m'a fait le coup de la p.** he tried to pull the old "the car won't start" trick on me; **p. (de courant** *ou* **d'électricité)** power failure *or* cut; **p. de moteur** engine failure; **p. de secteur** power failure
panneau, -x [pano] *nm* **(a)** *(pour afficher)* board; **p. d'affichage** *Br* notice board, *Am* bulletin board; **p. indicateur** road sign; **p. publicitaire** *Br* hoarding, *Am* billboard **(b)** *(sur la route)* **p. (de signalisation routière), p. indicateur** road sign **(c)** *(élément plan)* panel **(d)** *Fig* **tomber** *ou* **donner dans le p.** to fall into the trap
panonceau, -x [panɔ̃so] *nm* **(a)** *(de notaire)* plaque **(b)** *(pancarte)* sign
panoplie [panɔpli] *nf* **(a)** *(habit)* outfit **(b)** *(assortiment)* set

panorama [panɔrama] *nm* panorama; *Fig* overview
panoramique [panɔramik] *adj (vue)* panoramic; *(restaurant)* with panoramic views; *(écran)* wide
panse [pãs] *nf* **(a)** *(de ruminant)* rumen **(b)** *Fam (ventre)* belly; **s'en mettre plein la p.** to stuff oneself
pansement [pãsmã] *nm* dressing; **p. (adhésif)** *Br* (sticking) plaster, *Am* Band-aid®; **faire un p. (à qn)** to put a dressing on (sb); **refaire un p. à qn** to change sb's dressing
panser [pãse] *vt* **(a)** *(blessure)* to dress; *(membre)* to bandage; **p. qn** to dress sb's wounds; *Fig* **p. ses blessures** to lick one's wounds **(b)** *(cheval)* to groom
pantagruélique [pãtagryelik] *adj* gigantic
pantalon [pãtalɔ̃] *nm Br* trousers, *Am* pants; **un p.** a pair of *Br* trousers *or Am* pants; **p. de golf** plus-fours; **p. à pattes d'éléphant** flares; **p. à pinces** pleated *Br* trousers *or Am* pants; **p. de pyjama** pyjama *Br* trousers *or Am* pants
pantalonnade [pãtalɔnad] *nf (spectacle)* burlesque farce
pantelant, -e [pãtlɑ̃, -ɑ̃t] *adj Litt (à bout de souffle)* panting
panthère [pãtɛr] *nf* leopard; **p. noire** panther
pantin [pãtɛ̃] *nm (jouet)* jumping-jack; *Péj (fantoche)* puppet
pantois, -e [pãtwa, -az] *adj* speechless; **en rester p.** to be speechless
pantomime [pãtɔmim] *nf (art)* mime; *(spectacle)* mime show
pantouflard, -e [pãtuflar, -ard] *adj & nm,f Fam* stay-at-home
pantoufle [pãtufl] *nf* slipper
pantoufler [pãtufle] *vi Fam* to join the private sector
PAO [peao] *nf Ordinat (abrév* **publication assistée par ordinateur)** DTP
paon [pã] *nm* peacock
papa [papa] *nm* dad; *(langage enfantin)* daddy; **p. gâteau** indulgent father; **p. poule** doting father; *Fam Péj* **de p.** old-fashioned; **jouer au p. et à la maman** to play mummies and daddies
papal, -e, -aux, -ales [papal, -o] *adj* papal
paparazzi [paparadzi] *nmpl* paparazzi
papauté [papote] *nf* papacy
papaye [papaj] *nf* papaya
pape [pap] *nm* pope; *Fam* **sérieux comme un p.** deadly serious
papelard [paplar] *nm Fam* piece of paper
paperasse [papras] *nf Péj* papers, *Br* bumf
paperasserie [paprasri] *nf Péj* **(a)** *(documents)* papers, *Br* bumf; **faire de la p.** to do paperwork **(b)** *(d'un système bureaucratique)* red tape
papeterie [papɛtri] *nf (usine)* paper mill; *(magasin)* stationer's; *(articles)* stationery
papetier, -ère [papətje, -er] *nm,f* **(a)** *(industriel)* paper manufacturer **(b)** *(commerçant)* stationer
papi [papi] *nm* grandpa, granddad
papier [papje] *nm* **(a)** *(pour écrire)* paper; **un p.** a piece of paper; *Fam* **être dans les petits papiers de qn** to be in sb's good books; *Fam* **p. alu** tinfoil; **p. avion** airmail paper; *Ordinat* **p. à bandes perforées** perforated paper; **p. de bonbon** sweet wrapper; **p. cadeau** gift wrap, wrapping paper; *Ordinat* **p. continu** continuous paper *or* stationery; **p. continu plié en accordéon** fanfold paper; **p. crépon** crêpe paper; *très Fam* **p. cul** TP; **p. à dessin** drawing paper; **p. d'emballage** brown paper; **p. à entête** headed notepaper; **p. glacé** glazed paper; **papiers**

gras litter; **p. hygiénique** toilet paper; **p. journal** newspaper; **p. kraft** brown paper; **p. à lettres** writing paper; *Ordinat* **p. listing** listing paper; **p. mâché** papier-mâché; *Fig* **avoir une mine de p.** mâché to look like death warmed up; **p. machine** typing paper; **p. millimétré** graph paper; **p. à musique** manuscript paper; *Fig* **être réglé comme du p. à musique** *(événement)* to be as regular as clockwork; **elle est réglée comme du p. à musique** you can set your watch by her; **p. peint** wallpaper; **p. de soie** tissue paper; **p. toilette** toilet paper; **p. de verre** sandpaper; **passer qch au p. de verre** to sandpaper sth **(b) papiers** *(documents officiels)* papers; **papiers (d'identité)** *(identity)* papers; *(d'un automobiliste) Br* driving licence, *Am* driver's license **(c)** *Fam (article de journal)* article

papilles [papij] *nfpl* **p. gustatives** taste buds

papillon [papijɔ̃] *nm* **(a)** *(insecte)* butterfly; **p. de nuit** moth; *Fam* **minute p.!** hold on a minute! **(b)** *(écrou)* wing nut **(c)** *(sur document)* flag **(d)** *Fam (contravention)* (parking) ticket **(e)** *(nage)* butterfly

papillonner [papijɔne] *vi* **(a)** *(paupières)* to flutter **(b)** *(d'une personne à une autre)* to flit about

papillote [papijɔt] *nf* **(a)** *Culin* **cailles en papillotes** quails en papillote *(cooked in paper parcels or tinfoil)* **(b)** *(de gigot)* frill **(c)** *Fam* **tu peux en faire des papillotes** you can chuck it away

papilloter [papijɔte] *vi (yeux)* to blink, *(lumière)* to flicker

papoter [papɔte] *vi Fam* to chat

papou, -e [papu] **1** *adj* Papuan **2** *nm,f* **P.** Papuan

Papouasie-Nouvelle-Guinée [papwazinuvɛlgine] *nf* **la P.** Papua New Guinea

papouille [papuj] *nf Fam* **faire des papouilles à qn** to tickle sb

paprika [paprika] *nm* paprika

papyrus [papirys] *nm* papyrus

paqson [paksɔ̃] = **pacson**

Pâque [pɑk] *nf* **P., la P.** juive Passover

paquebot [pakbo] *nm* liner

pâquerette [pakrɛt] *nf* daisy

pâques [pɑk] **1** *nfpl* **joyeuses p.!** Happy Easter! **2** *nm* **P.** Easter; *Fam* **à P. ou à la Trinité!** never in a month of Sundays!

paquet [pakɛ] *nm* **(a)** *(sac)* packet; *(de sucre)* bag; *(de cigarettes)* packet, *Am* pack; *(postal)* parcel, package; *Fam* **toucher un joli p.** to make a packet; *Fam* **mettre le p.** to pull out all the stops; *Fam* **c'est un p. de nerfs** she's a bundle *or* a bag of nerves; **p.-cadeau** gift-wrapped parcel; **je vous fais un p.-cadeau?** would you like it gift-wrapped?

paquetage [paktaʒ] *nm (soldier's)* pack; **faire son p.** to get one's kit ready

par [par] *prép* **(a)** *(à travers)* through; **p. la porte/le trou de la serrure** through the door/the keyhole; **regarder p. la fenêtre** *(de l'intérieur)* to look out (of) the window; *(de l'extérieur)* to look through the window; **passer p.** Calais to go via Calais; **p. ici/là** this/that way; **p. où est-il passé?** which way did he go?
(b) *(position)* **p. ici** round about here; **p. là** over there; **p. 100 mètres de fond** at a depth of 100 metres; **p. endroits** in places
(c) *(pendant)* **p. une belle journée d'automne** on a beautiful autumn day; **p. cette chaleur** in this heat; **p. le passé** in the past; *Litt* **p. deux fois** twice
(d) *(introduit le complément d'agent)* by; **c'est p. eux que je l'ai appris** I found out from them; **faire faire qch p. qn** to have sth done by sb
(e) *(indique la cause)* out of; **faire qch p. amitié/pitié** to do

sth out of friendship/pity; **p. hasard/erreur** by chance/mistake; **p. malheur** unfortunately, as bad luck would have it; **p. pitié!** for pity's sake!
(f) *(au moyen de)* with, by; **retenu p. une corde** held by a rope; **fermé p. un cadenas** padlocked; **p. train/avion/voiture/bateau** by train/plane/car/boat; **conduire/prendre qn p. la main** to lead/take sb by the hand; **tenir qn p. la taille** to hold sb round the waist; **pendu p. les pieds** hanging by the feet; **envoyer qch p. la poste** to send sth by post; **répondre p. oui ou p. non** to answer yes or no; **se terminer p. un divorce/une dispute** to end in divorce/an argument; **p. tous les moyens** by every possible means; **il est monté p. l'escalier** he took the stairs up; **obtenir qch p. la force** to obtain sth by force; **appeler qn p. son nom** to call sb by his/her name
(g) *(selon)* according to; **p. ordre de grandeur** according to size
(h) *(distributif)* per, a; **deux p. deux** two by two; **p. groupes de six** in groups of six; **deux jours p. semaine** two days a week; **10 000 euros p. an** 10,000 euros a year; **un siège p. personne** one seat per person
(i) **de p.** *(à cause de)* due to; **de p. le monde** the world over

para [para] *nm Fam* para

parabole [parabɔl] *nf* **(a)** *(allégorie)* parable **(b)** *(courbe)* parabola **(c)** *(antenne)* (parabolic) dish

parabolique [parabɔlik] *adj* parabolic

paracétamol [parasetamɔl] *nm* paracetamol

parachever [46] [paraʃəve] *vt* to complete, to finish off

parachutage [paraʃytaʒ] *nm* parachuting

parachute [paraʃyt] *nm* parachute, **faire du p.** to go parachuting; **p. ascensionnel** parascending

parachuter [paraʃyte] *vt (vivres, soldats)* to parachute in; *Fam (nommer)* to draft in

parachutisme [paraʃytism] *nm* parachuting

parachutiste [paraʃytist] *nmf* **(a)** *(sportif)* parachutist **(b)** *(soldat)* paratrooper

parade¹ [parad] *nf* **(a)** *(exhibition)* show, ostentation; **faire p. de qch** to show sth off **(b)** *(défilé)* parade

parade² *nf* **(a)** *(en escrime, boxe)* parry **(b)** *(réplique)* riposte; *Fig* **je n'ai pas encore trouvé la p.** I haven't come up with a way of handling him/it/etc yet

parader [parade] *vi* to show off

paradis [paradi] *nm* heaven; *Fig* paradise; **le p. terrestre** the Garden of Eden; *Fig* heaven on earth; **aller au p.** to go to heaven; **un p. fiscal** a tax haven; *Fam* **le p.** *(d'un théâtre)* the gods; *Fam* **il ne l'emportera pas au p.** he won't get away with it, he'll be sorry

paradisiaque [paradizjak] *adj* heavenly

paradoxal, -e, -aux, -ales [paradɔksal, -o] *adj* paradoxical

paradoxalement [paradɔksalmɑ̃] *adv* paradoxically

paradoxe [paradɔks] *nm* paradox

parafe [paraf] = **paraphe**

parafer [parafe] = **parapher**

paraffine [parafin] *nf* paraffin

parafiscalité [parafiskalite] *nf* = taxes paid to the state and used for administration purposes

parages [paraʒ] *nmpl* **(a)** *Naut* waters **(b)** *(alentours)* **dans les p. de...** in the vicinity of...; *Fam* **est-ce qu'elle est dans les p.?** is she around?

paragraphe [paragraf] *nm* **(a)** paragraph **(b)** *Typ* paragraph (sign)

Paraguay [paragwɛ] *nm* **le P.** Paraguay

paraguayen, -enne [paragwɛjɛ̃, -ɛn] **1** *adj* Paraguayan **2** *nm,f* **P.** Paraguayan

paraître [20] [parɛtr] **1** *vi* (**a**) *(apparaître)* to appear; *(étoile, lune)* to come out; **laisser p. sa déception** to let one's disappointment show; **un faible sourire parut sur ses lèvres** he/she smiled weakly; **elle ne pense qu'à p.** all she thinks about is showing off (**b**) *(livre)* to come out, to be published (**c**) *(sembler)* to seem, to appear; **cette décision me paraît bizarre** it seems a strange decision to me; **elle paraissait furieuse** *(à la voir)* she looked furious; *(à l'entendre)* she sounded furious **2** *v impersonnel* (**a**) **il me paraît utile de...** *(il semble utile de...)* I think it would be useful to...; **demain, il n'y paraîtra plus** there'll be no trace of it tomorrow; **sans qu'il y paraisse** without it being apparent (**b**) **il paraît que...** *(on dit)* it seems *or* appears that...; **il paraît qu'elle s'en va, elle s'en va, paraît-il** it seems *or* appears that she's leaving, apparently she's leaving; **il paraît que ça fait maigrir** apparently it helps you lose weight; **il paraît que oui** so it would appear, apparently (so); **il paraît que non** it would appear not, apparently not; **à ce qu'il paraît** apparently **3** *nm* **le p.** appearance

parallèle [paralɛl] **1** *adj* parallel (**à** to *or* with); *(police, marché)* unofficial; **mener une vie p.** to lead a secret life; *Ordinat* **imprimante/interface p.** parallel printer/interface **2** *nf* parallel (line) **3** *nm* parallel; **mettre qch en p. avec qch** to draw a parallel between sth and sth

parallèlement [paralɛlmã] *adv* parallel (**à** to *or* with); *(simultanément)* at the same time (**à** as)

parallélépipède [paralelepipɛd] *nm* parallelepiped

parallélisme [paralelism] *nm* parallelism; **p. (des roues)** (wheel) alignment

parallélogramme [paralelɔgram] *nm* parallelogram

paralysant, -e [paralizã, -ãt] *adj* paralysing

paralysé, -e [paralize] *adj aussi Fig* paralysed

paralyser [paralize] *vt aussi Fig* to paralyse; **le froid lui paralyse les mains** his hands are numb with the cold

paralysie [paralizi] *nf aussi Fig* paralysis

paralytique [paralitik] *adj & nmf* paralytic

paramédical, -e, -aux, -ales [paramedikal, -o] **1** *adj* paramedical **2** *nm* **les emplois du p.** paramedical jobs

paramétrable [parametrabl] *adj Ordinat* configurable; **p. par l'utilisateur** user-definable

paramètre [parametr] *nm Math & Fig* parameter; *Ordinat* parameter, setting; *(du DOS)* switch

paramétrer [34] [parametre] *vt Ordinat* to configure

paramilitaire [paramilitɛr] *adj* paramilitary

parano [parano] *Fam* **1** *adj* paranoid **2** *nf* **faire de la p.** to be paranoid

paranoïa [paranɔja] *nf* paranoia

paranoïaque [paranɔjak] *adj & nmf* paranoiac

paranormal, -e, -aux, -ales [paranɔrmal, -o] *adj* paranormal

parapente [parapãt] *nm (activité)* paragliding; *(parachute)* paraglider; **faire du p.** to go paragliding

parapet [parapɛ] *nm* parapet

paraphe [paraf] *nm* initials

parapher [parafe] *vt* to initial

paraphrase [parafraz] *nf* paraphrase

paraphraser [parafraze] *vt* to paraphrase

paraplégie [papleʒi] *nf* paraplegia

paraplégique [parapleʒik] *adj & nmf* paraplegic

parapluie [paraplɥi] *nm* umbrella

parapsychologie [parapsikɔlɔʒi] *nf* parapsychology

parascolaire [paraskɔlɛr] *adj* extra-curricular

parasite [parazit] **1** *nm aussi Fig* parasite; **parasites** *(à la radio)* interference **2** *adj (insecte, plante)* parasitic

parasol [parasɔl] *nm* parasol, sunshade; *(de plage)* beach umbrella

paratonnerre [paratɔnɛr] *nm* lightning conductor

paravent [paravã] *nm aussi Fig* screen; *Fig* **servir de p. à qch** to be a screen for sth

parbleu [parblø] *exclam Vieilli* good Lord!; *(évidemment)* good Lord, yes!

parc [park] *nm* (**a**) *(jardin)* park; *(d'un château)* grounds; **p. naturel** nature reserve; **p. zoologique** zoo (**b**) *(enclos) (pour enfant)* playpen; **p. d'attractions** theme park; **p. des expositions** exhibition centre; **p. à huîtres** oyster bed; **p. de stationnement** *Br* car park, *Am* parking lot (**c**) *(ensemble)* **le p. automobile français** the number of cars in France

parcelle [parsɛl] *nf* small piece; **p. de terrain** plot; *Fig* **pas la moindre p. d'intelligence** not an ounce of intelligence

parce que [parskə] *conj* because; **ce n'est pas parce qu'il fait froid qu'on doit rester à la maison** just because it's cold doesn't mean we have to stay in; **pourquoi ne viens-tu pas? – p.** why aren't you coming? – (just) because

parchemin [parʃəmɛ̃] *nm* parchment

parcimonie [parsimɔni] *nf* thrift; **avec p.** sparingly

parcimonieux, -euse [parsimɔnjø, -øz] *adj* thrifty

parcmètre [parkmɛtr] *nm* (parking) meter

parcourir [22] [parkurir] *vt* (**a**) *(lieu)* to walk round; *(pays)* to travel through; *(rues)* to walk through; *(mer)* to sail; **p. un lieu à la recherche de qn** to scour a place for sb; **p. la terre entière pour retrouver qn** to travel the world to find sb; **p. une distance de plusieurs kilomètres** to cover a distance of several kilometres; **il reste trois kilomètres à p.** there are three kilometres to go; *Fig* **un frisson me parcourut l'échine** *ou* **le dos** a shiver ran down my spine; *Fig* **un murmure a parcouru la foule** a murmur ran through the crowd (**b**) *(regarder) (texte, journal)* to skim through; *Ordinat* to scroll through; **p. qch des yeux** *ou* **du regard** to glance at sth

parcours [parkur] *nm (de défilé, de bus)* route; *(circuit automobile)* circuit; *(d'équitation, de golf, d'un fleuve)* course; *Mil* **le p. du combattant** the assault course; **faire un p. sans faute** *(cheval)* to have a clear round; *Fig (dans une carrière)* to have a copybook career; **refaire le p. pour retrouver qch** to retrace one's steps to find sth; **elle fait plusieurs fois le p. dans la journée** she does the journey several times a day

par-delà [pardəla] *prép & adv* beyond

par-derrière [pardɛrjɛr] **1** *prép* behind **2** *adv (attaquer)* from behind; *(se boutonner)* at the back; **passer p.** to go in the back door; *Fig* **dire des choses de qn p.** to talk about sb behind his/her back

par-dessous [pardəsu] **1** *prép* under, underneath **2** *adv* underneath

pardessus [pardəsy] *nm* overcoat

par-dessus [pardəsy] **1** *prép* over; **p. tout** above all **2** *adv* over

par-devant [pardəvã] **1** *prép Jur* **acte signé p. notaire** deed signed in the presence of a lawyer **2** *adv (attaquer)* from the front; *(se boutonner)* at the front

pardi [pardi] *exclam Fam* of course!

pardon [pardɔ̃] *nm* (**a**) *(grâce)* forgiveness; **accorder son p. à qn** to forgive sb; **demander p. à qn** to apologize to sb; **(je vous demande) p.!** *(pour passer)* excuse me!; *(pour s'excuser)* (I'm) sorry!; **(je vous demande) p.?** *(je n'ai pas entendu)* pardon?; *(je suis indigné)* I beg your pardon!; *Fam* **elle est intelligente, mais sa fille, p.!** she's pretty clever but you should see her daughter! (**b**) *Rel* **le Grand P.** the Day of Atonement, Yom Kippur

pardonnable [pardɔnabl] *adj* forgivable, excusable

pardonner [pardɔne] **1** *vt* to forgive; **p. qch à qn** to forgive sb sth; **elle m'a pardonné d'avoir oublié** she forgave me for forgetting; **pour me/te/***etc* **faire p. to** make it up; **tu es tout pardonné** I'll let you off
2 *vi* (**a**) *(oublier une faute)* to forgive (**b**) **ça ne pardonne pas** it's fatal
3 se pardonner *vpr* **je ne me le pardonnerai jamais** I'll never forgive myself

paré, -e [pare] *adj* (**a**) *(prêt)* prepared (**contre** for) (**b**) *(revêtu)* adorned (**de** with)

pare-avalanches [paravalɑ̃ʃ] *nm inv* avalanche barrier

pare-balles [parbal] *adj inv* bulletproof

pare-boue [parbu] *nm inv* mudflap

pare-brise [parbriz] *nm inv Br* windscreen, *Am* windshield

pare-chocs [parʃɔk] *nm inv* bumper

pare-feu [parfø] *nm inv* (**a**) *(dans la forêt)* firebreak (**b**) *(de cheminée)* fireguard

pareil, -eille [parɛj] **1** *adj* (**a**) *(identique)* the same; **elles sont presque pareilles** they're almost the same; **ce n'est pas p.** it's not the same (thing); *Litt* **à nul autre p.** unparalleled; **p. que** *ou* **à** the same as, just like; *Fam* **si ça ne te plaît pas, c'est p.** if you don't like it, too bad (**b**) *(tel)* such; **en p. cas** in such cases; **dans des moments pareils** at times like these; **mais je n'ai jamais dit une chose pareille!** but I never said any such thing!
2 *nm,f* **elle n'a pas sa pareille** she's second to none; **sans p.** unparalleled; **mes pareils** my equals
3 *nf* **rendre la pareille à qn** *(se venger de qn)* to get one's own back on sb, to pay sb back *(rendre un service à qn)* to repay sb
4 *nm Fam* **c'est du p. au même** it's six of one and half a dozen of the other
5 *adv Fam* **faire p.** to do the same (thing)

pareillement [parɛjmɑ̃] *adv* (**a**) *(de la même manière)* in a similar manner, in the same way (**b**) *(aussi)* likewise

parement [parmɑ̃] *nm* (de manche, de col) facing

parent, -e [parɑ̃, -ɑ̃t] **1** *adj* related
2 *nm,f* (tante, oncle, cousin) relative, relation
3 *nmpl* **parents** *(père et mère)* parents; **parents adoptifs** adoptive parents; **parents biologiques** biological parents

parental, -e, -aux, -ales [parɑ̃tal, -o] *adj* parental

parenté [parɑ̃te] *nf* relationship; **avoir un lien de p. avec qn** to be related to sb

parenthèse [parɑ̃tez] *nf* bracket, parenthesis; *Fig (dans un discours)* digression; **entre parenthèses** in brackets

parer¹ [pare] **1** *vt* (**a**) *aussi Fig (éviter)* to parry (**b**) *(protéger)* to protect (**contre** against)
2 **parer à** *vt ind (accident)* to prevent; *(problème)* to avoid; **p. au plus pressé** to attend to the most urgent things first

parer² [pare] *Litt* **1** *vt (vêtir)* to adorn (**de** with); *Fig* **p. qn de toutes les vertus** to endow sb with every virtue
2 se parer *vpr* to get dressed up (**de** in)

pare-soleil [parsɔlɛj] *nm inv (de voiture)* sun visor

paresse [parɛs] *nf* (**a**) *(indolence)* laziness; **incroyable** incredibly lazy (**b**) *(lenteur)* **p. intellectuelle** laziness of mind; **p. intestinale** sluggishness of the bowels

paresser [parɛse] *vi* to laze about *or* around

paresseux, -euse [parɛsø, -øz] **1** *adj* (**a**) *(nonchalant)* lazy (**b**) *(intestin)* sluggish
2 *nm,f* lazy person
3 *nm (animal)* sloth

parfaire [36] [parfɛr] *vt (travail)* to finish off, to complete; *(technique)* to perfect

parfait, -e [parfɛ, -ɛt] **1** *adj* (**a**) *(sans fautes)* perfect (**b**) *(complet) (bonheur)* perfect, complete; *(ressemblance)* exact; *Fam* **un p. imbécile** an utter fool
2 *nm Culin* parfait; **p. au café** coffee parfait

parfaitement [parfɛtmɑ̃] *adv* (**a**) *(sans fautes)* perfectly; **parler p. le français** to speak perfect French (**b**) *(complètement)* completely, thoroughly; *(compréhensible, clair, heureux)* perfectly; **ça m'est p. égal** it makes absolutely no difference to me; **j'ai p. conscience de... I'm perfectly aware of... (**c**) *(tout à fait)* **vous affirmez que vous l'avez vu? – p.!** you say you saw it? – **I certainly did!**

parfois [parfwa] *adv* sometimes

parfum [parfœ̃] *nm* (**a**) *(essences)* perfume (**b**) *(senteur)* *(d'une fleur)* fragrance, scent; *(d'un vin)* bouquet; *Fig* **un p. de scandale** a whiff of scandal (**c**) *(de glace, de yaourt)* flavour (**d**) *Fam* **être au p.** to be in the know; **mettre qn au p.** to fill sb in

parfumer [parfyme] **1** *vt* (**a**) *(embaumer)* to scent (**b**) *(gâteau, glace)* to flavour (**à** with) (**c**) *(mouchoir)* to scent; **je vous parfume?** *(à une cliente)* would you like to try some perfume?
2 se parfumer *vpr* to put perfume on

parfumerie [parfymri] *nf (magasin)* perfumery; *(rayon)* perfume counter; *(produits)* perfumes, *(industrie)* perfume industry

parfumeur, -euse [parfymœr, -øz] *nm,f* perfumer

pari [pari] *nm* bet; **faire un p. avec qn** to make a bet with sb; **p. mutuel** *Br* tote, *Am* pari-mutuel

paria [parja] *nm Fig* pariah, (social) outcast

parier [66] [parje] **1** *vt* to bet; **il y a fort** *ou* **gros à p. que...** the odds are that...; **je te parie qu'elle viendra** I bet you she'll come; **je l'aurais parié** I thought as much
2 *vi* to bet; **p. avec qn/sur qch** to bet with sb/on sth; **je te dis qu'elle viendra on parie?** she'll come I tell you – **(do you) want a bet?**

parieur, -euse [parjœr, -øz] *nm,f* better

parigot, -e [parigo, -ɔt] *Fam* **1** *adj* Parisian
2 *nm,f* **P.** Parisian

Paris [pari] *n* Paris

parisien, -enne [parizjɛ̃, -ɛn] **1** *adj* Parisian
2 *nm,f* **P.** Parisian

parité [parite] *nf aussi Ordinat* parity

parjure [parʒyr] **1** *nm (action)* perjury
2 *nmf (personne)* perjurer
3 *adj* treacherous

parjurer [parʒyre] **se parjurer** *vpr* to perjure oneself

parka [parka] *nm ou nf* parka

parking [parkiŋ] *nm Br* car park, *Am* parking lot

parlant, -e [parlɑ̃, -ɑ̃t] *adj (geste)* eloquent, meaningful; *(description)* vivid

parlé, -e [parle] *adj* **l'anglais p.** spoken English; **journal p.** news (programme)

parlement [parləmɑ̃] *nm* **le P.** Parliament; **le P. européen** the European Parliament

parlementaire [parləmɑ̃tɛr] **1** *adj* parliamentary
2 *nmf Br* ≃ Member of Parliament, *Am* ≃ Congressman, *f* Congresswoman

parlementarisme [parləmɑ̃tarism] *nm* parliamentary government

parlementer [parləmɑ̃te] *vi* to negotiate *(avec* with)

parler¹ [parle] **1** *vi* **(a)** *(s'exprimer)* to speak, to talk; *(avouer)* to talk; **elle parle bien** *(oratrice)* she's a good speaker; **p. par signes** to use sign language; **parlez-vous sérieusement?** are you serious?; **les résultats/faits parlent d'eux-mêmes** the results/facts speak for themselves; **p. pour ne rien dire** to talk for the sake of talking; **c'est comme si je parlais à un mur** it's like talking to a brick wall; **p. de qn/qch (à qn)** to talk (to sb) about sb/ sth; **p. de** *(sujet: livre, film)* to be about; **on m'a beaucoup parlé de vous** I've heard a lot about you; **n'en parlons plus** let's drop the subject; **faire p. de soi** to be talked about; **p. de faire qch** to talk about doing sth **(b)** *(locutions)* **je sais de quoi je parle** I know what I'm talking about; **Fam tu peux p.!** YOU can talk!; **Fam parle pour toi!** speak for yourself!; **Fam tu parles!** you bet!; **Fam tu parles d'une occasion/d'un idiot!** talk about an opportunity/an idiot!; **Fam ses ambitions? parlons-en!** his ambitions? who are you kidding? *or* you've got to be joking!; **Fam ne m'en parlez pas!** you're telling me!; **sans p. de...** not to mention...; **trouver à qui p.** to get more than one bargains for
2 *vt (langue)* to speak; **p. (le) français** to speak French; **ici on parle anglais** *(dans un magasin)* English spoken; **p. chiffons/cuisine** to talk about clothes/cooking; **p. affaires/politique** to talk business/politics
3 se parler *vpr* **(a)** *(langue)* to be spoken **(b)** *(l'un à l'autre)* to talk to each other

parler² *nm* speech; *(régional)* dialect; **il a un p. très rude** he has a very abrupt way of speaking

parleur, -euse [parlœr, -øz] *nm,f Péj* **beau p.** smooth talker

parloir [parlwar] *nm* visiting room

parlot(t)e [parlɔt] *nf Fam* chat

Parme [parm] *n* Parma

parmesan [parməzɑ̃] *nm* Parmesan (cheese)

parmi [parmi] *prép* among; **choisir p. plusieurs possibilités** to choose from several possibilities; **nous espérons vous revoir p. nous** we hope to see you back with us

parodie [parɔdi] *nf* parody

parodier [66] [parɔdje] *vt* to parody

parodique [parɔdik] *adj* parodic

paroi [parwa] *nf* **(a)** *(d'une falaise, d'une montagne)* face **(b)** *(d'une pièce, d'une caverne)* wall; *(d'un tunnel, d'une estomac)* lining

paroisse [parwas] *nf* parish

paroissial, -e, -aux, -ales [parwasjal, -o] *adj* parish

paroissien, -enne [parwasjɛ̃, -ɛn] *nm,f* parishioner

parole [parɔl] *nf* **(a)** *(mot)* word; **paroles** *(de chanson)* lyrics, words; **histoire sans paroles** short silent film; **une p. blessante** a hurtful remark; *Ironique* **de belles paroles** fine words; **ce ne sont que des paroles en l'air** they're just empty threats **(b)** *Fig (engagement)* promise, word; **tenir p.** to keep one's promise *or* word; **manquer à sa p.** to break one's promise *or* word; **il n'a qu'une p.** he's a man of his word; **donner sa p. (d'honneur)** à qn que... to give sb one's word that...; **(ma) p. d'honneur!** I give you my word! **(c)** **la p.** *(faculté de parler)* speech; *(diction)* delivery; **adresser la p. à qn** to speak to sb; **couper la p. à qn** to interrupt sb; **prendre la p.** to speak; **laisser la p. à qn** to let sb speak; **la p. est à M. Petit, M. Petit a la p.** Mr Petit has the floor; **la p. est d'argent mais le silence est d'or** speech is silver, silence is golden **(d)** *(aux cartes)* **p.!** pass!; *(au bridge)* no bid!

parolier, -ère [parɔlje, -ɛr] *nm,f* lyricist

paroxysme [parɔksism] *nm* **atteindre son p.** to reach its

peak *or* climax; **être au p. de la joie** to be ecstatically happy

parpaing [parpɛ̃] *nm* breeze block

parquer [parke] *vt (bétail)* to pen in; *(prisonniers)* to confine

parquet [parke] *nm* **(a)** *(sol)* wooden floor; *(avec des motifs)* parquet floor **(b)** *Jur* public prosecutor's office

parrain [parɛ̃] *nm (pour un baptême, d'une organisation criminelle)* godfather; *(d'un sportif, d'un membre d'un club)* sponsor

parrainer [parene] *vt (sportif, nouveau membre)* to sponsor

parricide [parisid] **1** *adj* parricidal
2 *nmf & nm* parricide

pars *voir* **partir**

parsemer [46] [parsəme] *vt* to scatter **(de** with)

part¹ [par] *voir* **partir**

part² *nf* **(a)** *(partie d'un tout)* part; *(d'un marché, de bénéfices, d'un héritage)* share; *(d'un gâteau, d'une pizza)* slice; **diviser qch en parts égales** to divide sth into equal parts; **ils viennent pour une bonne p. des environs de Bordeaux** a good many of them come from the Bordeaux area; **à p. entière** fully-fledged; **pour ma p.** personally, as for me; **faire la p. du feu** to cut one's losses; **la p. du lion** the lion's share
(b) *(participation)* share, part; **prendre p. à qch** to take part in sth; *(joie, douleur)* to share sth; **faire p. de qch à qn** to inform sb of sth, to tell sb about sth; **faire la p. des choses** to get things in perspective
(c) *(côté)* **de p. et d'autre** on both sides; **de p. en p.** right through; **d'une p...., d'autre p....** on the one hand..., on the other hand...; **de toutes parts** on all sides
(d) **de la p. de qn** *(en provenance de)* from sb; *(à la place de)* on sb's behalf; **c'est de la p. de qui?** *(au téléphone)* who's calling?; **ce serait bien aimable de votre p.** that would be very kind of you; **cela m'étonne de sa p.** that surprises me, coming from him/her
(e) *(locutions)* **prendre qn à p.** to take sb aside; **à p. lui/ quelques erreurs** apart from him/a few mistakes; **c'est un cas à p.** he's a special case; *Fam* **à p. que...** apart from the fact that...

partage [partaʒ] *nm* **(a)** *(action)* *(d'une fortune, d'un domaine)* dividing up; *(de tâches, de responsabilités)* sharing out; **faire la p. de qch** to divide sth up; **sans p.** *(amour)* total; *Ordinat* **p. d'imprimantes** printer sharing **(b)** *(lot)* **recevoir qch en p.** to be left sth *(in a will)*

partagé, -e [partaʒe] *adj* **(a)** *(entre plusieurs personnes)* shared; *(amour)* mutual; *Ordinat* **travail en temps p.** timesharing **(b)** *(indécis)* **être p.** to be torn; **les avis sont partagés** opinions are divided

partager [45] [partaʒe] **1** *vt* **(a)** *(répartir)* to divide (up); **p. son temps entre** to divide one's time between; **p. qch en deux** to divide sth in two **(b)** *(avoir en commun)* to share *(avec* with); **p. l'avis de qn** to share sb's opinion; **p. la joie de qn** to share (in) sb's joy
2 *vi* to share
3 se partager *vpr* **(a)** *(se répartir)* **ils se le sont partagé** they shared it between them **(b)** *(partager son temps)* to divide one's time **(entre** between)

partageur, -euse [partaʒœr, -øz] *adj* willing to share

partance [partɑ̃s] *nf* **en p.** about to depart; **en p. pour Bordeaux** for Bordeaux

partant¹ [partɑ̃] *conj Litt* consequently, therefore

partant², -e [partɑ̃, -ɑ̃t] **1** *adj Fam* **je suis p.!** count me in!
2 *nm,f (coureur, cheval)* starter

partenaire [partənɛr] *nmf* partner; **les partenaires sociaux** workers and management

partenariat [partənarja] *nm* partnership

parterre [parter] *nm* (**a**) *(de fleurs)* flower bed; *(plate-bande)* border (**b**) *(au théâtre)* Br stalls, *Am* orchestra (**c**) *Fam (sol)* floor

parti¹ [parti] *nm* (**a**) *(camp)* side; **prendre le p. de qn** to take sb's side; **prendre p. pour qn** to side with sb; **prendre p. contre qn** to take sides against sb (**b**) **p.** (**politique**) *(political)* party; **le P.** (**communiste**) the Communist Party (**c**) *(personne)* **un beau p.** a good match (**d**) *(choix)* **prendre le p. de faire qch** to make up one's mind to do sth; **en prendre son p.** to resign oneself to the fact (**e**) *(profit)* **tirer p. de qch** to make good use of sth (**f**) **p. pris** bias

parti², **-e** *adj Fam (ivre)* tight; *(drogué)* high

partial, **-e**, **-aux**, **-ales** [parsjal, -o] *adj* biased

partialement [parsjalmɑ̃] *adv* in a biased way

partialité [parsjalite] *nf* bias (**envers/contre** in favour of/against)

participant, -e [partisipɑ̃, -ɑ̃t] **1** *adj* participating **2** *nm,f (personne présente)* participant (**à** in); *(sportif)* competitor

participation [partisipasjɔ̃] *nf* (**a**) *(collaboration, en classe)* participation (**à** in); *(argent)* contribution (**à** towards); *(nombre de votants)* turnout (**à** at); **avec la p. de Claire Roux (dans le rôle de...)** with Claire Roux (as...); **p. aux frais** contribution towards costs; **p. aux bénéfices** profit-sharing (**b**) *Fin* interest (**à** in)

participe [partisip] *nm Gram* participle

participer [partisipe] **participer à** *vt ind* (**a**) *(assister à)* to take part in, to participate in; *(spectacle)* to appear in; **p. activement à qch** to take an active part in sth (**b**) *(financièrement)* to contribute to (**c**) **p. aux bénéfices** to share in the profits

particulariser [partikylarize] *vt* to particularize

particularisme [partikylarism] *nm* particularism

particularité [partikylarite] *nf* distinctive feature

particule [partikyl] *nf* particle

particulier, -ère [partikylje, -ɛr] **1** *adj* (**a**) *(propre)* characteristic (**à** of) (**b**) *(remarquable)* unusual, exceptional; *(soin, intérêt)* particular (**c**) *Péj (bizarre)* peculiar (**d**) *(privé) (maison, voiture)* private; *(salle de bain)* **en suite** (**e**) **en p.** *(spécialement)* in particular; *(en privé)* in private **2** *nm (individu)* private individual; **un simple p.** an ordinary person

particulièrement [partikyljɛrmɑ̃] *adv* particularly; **j'attire tout p. votre attention sur...** I would particularly like to draw your attention to...

partie [parti] *nf* (**a**) *(morceau)* part; **la plus grande p. de qch** the greatest part of sth; **en p.** partly, in part; **en grande** *ou* **majeure p.** for the most part; **être en p. remboursé** to be partially refunded; **faire p. de qch** to be part of sth; *Fam* **faire p. des meubles** to be part of the furniture; **les parties communes** the communal areas; *Fam* **les parties** the private parts; **les parties génitales** the genitals (**b**) *(domaine)* field, subject; **je ne suis pas de la p.** that's not my field (**c**) *(d'un chanteur, d'un instrument)* part (**d**) *(fête)* party; **ce n'est pas une p. de plaisir!** it's not my idea of fun!; **p. de campagne** day in the country; **p. de chasse** shooting party; *Fam* **p. de jambes en l'air** roll in the hay; *Can* **p. de sucre** sugaring-off party (**e**) *(jeu)* game; **faire une p. de cartes** to have a game of cards; *Fig* **ce n'est que p. remise** we'll do it another time (**f**) *Jur* party; **la p. adverse** the other side; **être p. prenante** to be an interested party; **p. civile** plaintiff; **se constituer** *ou* **se porter p. civile** to institute proceedings *(in a civil case)* (**g**) *(locutions)* **avoir affaire à forte p.** to have a tough

opponent on one's hands; **prendre qn à p.** to take sb to task; **avoir p. liée avec qn** to be hand in glove with sb

partiel, -elle [parsjɛl] **1** *adj* partial; **élection partielle** by-election; **travailler à temps p.** to work part-time **2** *nm Univ* end-of-term exam **3** *nf* **partielle** by-election

partiellement [parsjɛlmɑ̃] *adv* partially

partir [64a] [partir] *vi (aux être)* (**a**) *(s'en aller)* to go, to leave; *(commencer un voyage)* to set off; *(sans destination particulière)* to go off; *(bateau, avion)* to leave; *(moteur)* to start; *(fusil, pétard)* to go off; *Euph (mourir)* to pass away; **p. en vacances** to go (away) on holiday; **p. en promenade** to go for a stroll; **p. faire ses courses** to go out shopping; **p. en courant** to run off; **p. de rien** to start from nothing; **p. d'un éclat de rire** to burst out laughing; **être bien/mal parti** to have got off to a good/bad start; **faire p.** *(fusil)* to fire; *(feux d'artifice)* to let off; *(moteur)* to start; *Fam* **c'est parti, mon kiki!** here we go!

(**b**) *(disparaître) (douleur, bleu)* to go, to disappear; *(tache)* to come out; *(peinture, vernis)* to come off; **faire p. une tache** to get a stain out

(**c**) *(sortir)* **p. de** *(sujet: route, chemin)* to start from; **en partant du principe que...** assuming that...; **ça partait d'un bon sentiment** the thought was there; **et, partant de là,...** on that assumption,...

(**d**) *(suivi de "à", "de")* **à p.** *(du village)* from the village; **à p. d'aujourd'hui** from today (onwards); **à p. de maintenant** from now on; **à p. de 50 euros** from 50 euros (upwards)

partisan, -e [partizɑ̃, -an] **1** *nm* (**a**) *(fidèle)* supporter (**b**) *(combattant)* partisan **2** *adj (esprit)* partisan; **querelles partisanes** sectarian quarrels; **être p. de qch/de faire qch** to be in favour of sth/of doing sth

partitif, -ive [partitif, -iv] *adj & nm Gram* partitive

partition [partisjɔ̃] *nf (musique)* score

partout [partu] *adv* (**a**) *(en tous lieux)* everywhere; **p. où je vais** everywhere I go; **un peu p.** all over the place; **j'ai mal p.** I'm aching all over (**b**) **3 buts p.** *(au football)* 3 all, **15/30 p.** *(au tennis)* 15/30 all; **40 p.** *(au tennis)* deuce

partouze [partuz] *nf très Fam* orgy

paru, -e *voir* **paraître**

parure [paryr] *nf (ensemble)* set; **p. de lit** set of bed linen

parution [parysjɔ̃] *nf* appearance, publication

parvenir [70] [parvənir] **parvenir à** *vt ind (aux être)* (**a**) *(atteindre) (endroit, personne)* to reach; **p. à ses fins** to achieve one's ends; **faire p. qch à qn** to send sth to sb (**b**) *(réussir)* **p. à faire qch** to manage to do sth

parvenu, -e [parvəny] *nm,f Péj* upstart

parvis [parvi] *nm* square *(in front of a church)*

pas¹ [pɑ] *nm* (**a**) *(enjambée, de danse)* step; *(allure)* pace; **p. à p.** step by step; **à p. de loup** stealthily; **marcher à grands p.** to stride along; **marcher à petits p.** to toddle along; **marcher d'un p. hésitant** to walk hesitantly; **faire un faux p.** to trip; *Fig* to make a faux pas; **faire un p. (vers)** to take a step (towards); **faire un** *ou* **en avant/en arrière** to (take a) step forward/back; **faire les cent p.** to pace up and down; *Fig* **faire le premier p.** to take the first step; **marcher au p.** *(soldat)* to march in step; **rouler au p.** *(en voiture)* to crawl along; **ils habitent à deux p. d'ici** they live a few yards away; **j'y vais de ce p.** I'll do it right away; **p. de deux** pas de deux; **p. de course** *ou* **gymnastique** jog trot

(**b**) *(trace)* footprint; **revenir** *ou* **retourner sur ses p.** to retrace one's steps

(**c**) *(seuil)* **p. de la porte** doorstep

(**d**) *(passage)* **le p. de Calais** the Straits of Dover

(**e**) *(de vis, d'hélice)* pitch

(**f**) *(locutions)* **prendre le p. sur qch** to take precedence over sth; **tirer qn d'un mauvais p.** to get sb out of a tight corner

pas² *adv* not; **je ne sais p.** I don't know; **je ne l'ai p. vue** I haven't seen her; **il est difficile de ne p.** le lui dire it's difficult not to tell him; **qu'elle vienne ou p.** whether she comes or not; **viendra? viendra p.?** will she come or won't she?; **p.** mal not bad; **une explication p.** claire an unclear explanation; **p. un n'a réagi** not one of them reacted; **p. de sucre/lecteurs** no sugar/readers; **p. du tout** not at all

pascal¹, -e, -als *ou* **-aux, -ales** [paskal, -o] *adj* Easter; *(agneau)* paschal

pascal², -als *nm Phys* pascal

passable [pasabl] *adj* passable, fair

passablement [pasabləmɑ̃] *adv* fairly

passade [pasad] *nf* passing whim

passage [pasaʒ] *nm* **(a)** *(d'une route, d'une rivière)* crossing; *(d'un lieu)* passing; **on sourit sur son p.** people smile as he goes by; **les soldats ont tout détruit sur leur p.** the soldiers destroyed everything in their path; **être de p. dans une ville** to be passing through a town; *Fig* **et au p., je te ferai remarquer que...** and incidentally, let me draw your attention to the fact that...; *Fam* **p. à tabac** beating up; *Ordinat* **p. automatique à la ligne suivante** wordwrap **(b)** *(chemin)* passage; *(ruelle)* alley(way); *(galerie commerciale)* (shopping) arcade; **p. clouté** *Br* pedestrian crossing, *Am* crosswalk; **p. à niveau** *Br* level crossing, *Am* grade crossing; **p. pour piétons** *Br* pedestrian crossing, *Am* crosswalk; *(souterrain)* pedestrian subway; **p. souterrain** underpass **(c)** *(extrait)* passage **(d)** *(moment)* **p. nuageux/pluvieux** cloudy/rainy spell; *Fam* **avoir un p. à vide** to go through a bad patch

passager, -ère [pasaʒe, -ɛr] **1** *adj* momentary; **des pluies passagères** occasional showers; **ils ont eu une petite brouille passagère** they fell out for a while **2** *nm,f* passenger; **p. clandestin** stowaway

passant¹ [pasɑ̃] *nm (de ceinture)* loop

passant², -e [pasɑ̃, -ɑ̃t] **1** *adj (rue)* busy **2** *nm,f* passer-by

passation [pasasjɔ̃] *nf (d'un accord)* signing; **p. de pouvoirs** transfer of power

passe¹ [pas] *nf* **(a)** *(au football)* pass; **p. en avant/en retrait** forward/back pass **(b)** *(d'une prostituée)* trick; **hôtel de p.** = hotel used by prostitutes and their clients; **maison de p.** brothel **(c)** *(à la roulette)* passe *(any number above 18)* **(d)** *Fig* **être en p. de faire qch** to be on the way to doing sth; **être dans une mauvaise p.** to be going through a bad patch

passe² *nm Fam (clef)* master key

passé, -e [pase] **1** *adj* **(a)** *(écoulé) (temps)* past; **la semaine passée** last week; **il est quatre heures passées** it's gone *or* after four; **elle a quarante ans passés** she's over forty **(b)** *(terminé)* over; **penser à son enfance passée** to think about one's childhood **(c)** *(décoloré)* faded **(d)** **p. de mode** out of fashion **2** *nm* **(a)** *(période)* **le p.** the past; **par le p.** in the past; **tout ça, c'est du p.** that's all in the past **(b)** *Gram* past (tense); **p. antérieur** past anterior; **p. composé** perfect (tense); **p. simple** preterite, past historic; **au p.** in the past (tense) **3** *prép* after

passe-droit *(pl* **passe-droits)** [pasdrwa] *nm* privilege

passéiste [paseist] *Péj* **1** *adj* living in the past **2** *nmf* person who lives in the past

passe-montagne *(pl* **passe-montagnes)** [pasmɔtaɲ] *nm* balaclava (helmet)

passe-partout [paspartu] **1** *nm inv* master key **2** *adj inv* all-purpose

passe-plat *(pl* **passe-plats)** [paspla] *nm* serving hatch

passeport [paspɔr] *nm aussi Fig* passport

passer [pase] **1** *vi (aux* être) **(a)** *(se déplacer)* to go past; **p. devant qn/qch** to go past sb/sth; **laisser p. qn** to let sb past; *(dans une queue)* to let sb in; **je ne peux pas p.** I can't get by *or* past; **p. sur les détails** to skip the details; **elle nous a fait p. dans son bureau** she showed us into her office; **mais où est-il passé?** where's he/it got to?; **dire qch en passant** to mention sth in passing; **soit dit en passant** incidentally **(b)** *(évoluer)* **p. de qch à qch** to go from sth to sth; **p. dans la classe supérieure** to move up a class; **p. en première/seconde** *(en voiture)* to change into first/second; **p. capitaine** to be promoted to captain **(c)** *(traverser)* **p. par le village/Bordeaux** to go through the village/Bordeaux; **par où est -il passé?** which way did he go?; **laisser p. qch** *(lumière, air)* to let sth in **(d)** *(apparaître)* **p. à la radio/télévision** to be on the radio/television; **p. au cinéma** to be on at the cinema **(e)** *(aller)* **je suis passé chez elle/à la boulangerie** I went round to her house/to the bakery; **le facteur est déjà passé** the postman's already been; **je ne fais que p.** I'm not staying **(f)** *(disparaître)* to go; **laisser p. qch** *(occasion)* to pass up sth; *(erreur)* to miss sth; **le plus dur est passé** the worst is over; **j'avais mal à la tête mais ça m'a passé** I had a headache but it's gone away; **il était amoureux d'elle mais ça lui a passé** he was in love with her but he's got over it **(g)** *(année, temps)* to pass, to go by **(h)** *(être considéré)* **p. pour un génie** to be considered a genius; **faire p. qn pour** to pass sb off as **(i)** *(être adopté) (loi, proposition)* to be passed, to go through **(j)** **passe!** *(aux cartes)* pass! **(k)** *Fam* **il a bien failli y p.** *(mourir)* he nearly didn't make it; **toute sa fortune y est passée** she spent her entire fortune on it

2 *vt (aux* avoir) **(a)** *(pont, rivière, frontière)* to go over; *(porte, douane)* to go through; **il a passé la soixantaine** he's in his sixties **(b)** *(donner) (ballon, témoin)* to pass; **p. qch à qn** to pass *or* give sth to sb; *Fam* **p. son rhume à qn** to give sb one's cold; **p. la parole à qn** to hand over to sb; **pourriez-vous me la p.?** *(au téléphone)* could you put me through to her? **(c)** *(mettre) (vêtement)* to slip on; **p. un coup d'éponge sur qch** to give sth a sponge; **p. la tête par la fenêtre** to lean one's head out of the window; **p. le doigt sur qch** to run one's finger over sth; **p. la seconde/troisième** *(en voiture)* to change into second/third; *Fam* **qu'est-ce qu'il va nous p.!** he's going to make us wish we'd never been born! **(d)** *(film)* to show; *(disque)* to play; *(vidéo)* to put on **(e)** *(temps, vacances)* to spend; **p. son temps à faire qch** to spend one's time doing sth; **pour p. le temps** to pass the time **(f)** *(pardonner)* **elle lui passe tout** she lets him get away with everything **(g)** *(omettre)* to leave out; **p. son tour** to miss a turn; **j'en passe et des meilleures** and that's not the half of it **(h)** *(examen)* to take *or* sit; *(visite médicale)* to have; **faire p. un examen à qn** to take sb for an exam **(i)** *(accord, contrat)* to enter into, to sign; *(commande)* to place **(à with) **(j)** *(liquide)* to strain; *(café)* to filter

3 *se passer vpr* **(a)** *(se produire)* to happen; **que se passe-t-il?, qu'est-ce qui se passe?** what's happening?; **ça s'est bien passé** it went well; **l'histoire se passe en 1812/en Bretagne** the story takes place in 1812/in Brittany; *Fam* **ça ne se passera pas comme ça!** I'm not having it! **(b)** *(mettre)* **se p. la main dans les cheveux** to run one's fingers through one's hair; **se p.** de l'eau sur la figure to splash one's face with water **4 se passer de** *vt ind (se priver de)* to do without

passereau, -x [pasro] *nm* passerine

passerelle [pasrɛl] *nf* **(a)** *(au-dessus d'une rue, d'un ruisseau)* footbridge **(b)** *(de navire)* bridge; **p.** de débarquement *ou* **d'embarquement** *(de navire)* gangway; *(d'avion) (amovible)* steps **(c)** *Fig (intermédiaire)* link **(d)** *Ordinat* **p. (de connexion) (avec)** gateway (to)

passe-temps [pastā] *nm inv* pastime

passe-thé [paste] *nm inv* tea-strainer

passeur, -euse [pasœr, -øz] *nm,f (de bac)* ferryman, *f* ferrywoman; *(de frontière)* = person who helps wanted people across the border to safety

passible [pasibl] *adj* liable **(de** to)

passif, -ive [pasif, -iv] **1** *adj* passive **2** *nm* **(a)** *Gram* passive; **au p.** in the passive **(b)** *Fin* liabilities

passion [pasjɔ̃] *nf* **(a)** *(sentiment dévorant)* passion; **avoir une p. pour qn/qch** to have a passion for sb/sth; **vivre une p.** to have a passionate love affair; **avec p.** passionately **(b)** *Rel* **la P. selon saint Jean** the St John Passion

passionnant, -e [pasjɔnɑ̃, -ɑ̃t] *adj* fascinating

passionné, -e [pasjɔne] **1** *adj* passionate; **p. de qch** extremely keen on sth **2** *nm,f* enthusiast; **un p. de flamenco** a lover of flamenco

passionnel, -elle [pasjɔnɛl] *adj* passionate

passionnément [pasjɔnemɑ̃] *adv* passionately

passionner [pasjɔne] **1** *vt (sujet: livre, film)* to fascinate; **son métier la passionne** she finds her job fascinating **2 se passionner** *vpr* **se p. pour qch** to have a passion for sth

passivement [pasivmɑ̃] *adv* passively

passivité [pasivite] *nf* passivity, passiveness

passoire [paswar] *nf (à petits trous)* sieve; *(à gros trous)* colander

pastel [pastɛl] *nm & adj inv* pastel

pastèque [pastɛk] *nf* watermelon; *Fam* **j'ai la tête comme une p.** my head's throbbing

pasteur [pastœr] *nm* **(a)** *Litt (berger)* shepherd **(b)** *(religieux)* pastor, minister

pasteurisation [pastœrizasjɔ̃] *nf* pasteurization

pasteuriser [pastœrize] *vt* to pasteurize

pastiche [pastiʃ] *nm* pastiche

pastille [pastij] *nf (bonbon mou)* pastille; *(médicament)* lozenge; **p. contre la toux** cough sweet *or* lozenge; **p. de menthe** mint

pastis [pastis] *nm* **(a)** *(boisson)* pastis **(b)** *Fam* **être dans le p.** to be in a fix

pastoral, -e, -aux, -ales [pastɔral, -o] **1** *adj* pastoral **2** *nf* **pastorale** *(musique)* pastorale

patachon [pataʃɔ̃] *nm Fam* **mener une vie de p.** to lead a wild life

Patagonie [patagɔni] *nf* **la P.** Patagonia

patapouf [patapuf] **1** *exclam* flop! **2** *nm (langage enfantin)* **gros p.** fatty

pataquès [patakɛs] *nm (faute de langage)* malapropism

patate [patat] *nf Fam (pomme de terre)* spud; *Fig (imbécile)* clot; *Fig* **en avoir gros sur la p.** to be down in the mouth

patati [patati] *exclam Fam* **et p. et patata** and so on and so forth

patatras [patatra] *exclam Fam* crash!

pataud, -e [pato, -od] *adj Fam* clumsy

Pataugas® [patogas] *nm* canvas walking boot

pataugeoire [patoʒwar] *nf* paddling pool

patauger [45] [patoʒe] *vi (s'embourber)* to squelch **(dans** in); *(barboter)* to splash about **(dans** in); *Fam (s'embrouiller)* to flounder **(dans** in)

pâte [pat] *nf* **1 (a)** *(pour une tarte)* pastry; *(pour le pain)* dough; *(pour un gâteau)* mixture; **p. brisée** shortcrust pastry; **p. à choux** choux pastry; **p. à crêpes** pancake batter; **p. feuilletée** puff *or* flaky pastry; **p. à frire** batter; **p. à pain** bread dough; **p. sablée** rich shortcrust pastry; **p. à tarte** pastry; **p. à tartiner** chocolate spread **(b)** *(mixture)* **p. d'amandes** marzipan; **p. de fruits** fruit jelly; **p. à modeler** modelling clay; **p. à papier** pulp **2** *nfpl* **pâtes (alimentaires)** pasta; **pâtes fraiches** fresh pasta

pâté [pate] *nm* **(a)** *(terrine)* pâté; **p. de campagne** pâté de campagne *(coarse pâté made with pork)*; **p. en croûte** ≃ pork pie; **p. de foie** liver pâté **(b) p. (de sable)** sandpie **(c) p. de maisons** block of houses **(d)** *(tache d'encre)* blot; **faire un p. sur qch** to get a blot on sth

pâtée [pate] *nf* **(a)** *(de chat)* cat food; *(de chien)* dog food **(b)** *Fam (défaite)* **prendre la p.** to get thrashed; **mettre la p. à qn** to thrash sb

patelin¹ [patlɛ̃] *nm Fam* village

patelin², -e [patlɛ̃, -in] *adj Litt & Péj* unctuous

patent, -e [patɑ̃, -ɑ̃t] *adj* **(a)** *(évident)* patent **(b)** *Littr* letters patent

patente [patɑ̃t] *nf (impôt)* tax *(paid by self-employed people)*

patenté, -e [patɑ̃te] *adj* licensed

patère [patɛr] *nf (coat)* peg

paternaliste [patɛrnalist] *adj* paternalistic

paternel, -elle [patɛrnɛl] **1** *adj* paternal; *(ton)* fatherly; **du côté p.** on the father's side; **ma grand-mère paternelle** my grandmother on my father's side **2** *nm Fam* **le p.** the old man

paternité [patɛrnite] *nf* paternity, fatherhood; **recherche de p.** establishment of paternity

pâteux, -euse [patø, -øz] *adj* **(a)** *(nourriture)* doughy; **avoir la langue pâteuse** to have a furry tongue **(b)** *(sauce)* thick

pathétique [patetik] *adj* pathetic, moving

pathogène [patoʒɛn] *adj* pathogenic

pathologique [patɔlɔʒik] *adj aussi Fam Fig* pathological

patibulaire [patibylɛr] *adj* **avoir une mine p.** to have a sinister look

patiemment [pasjamɑ̃] *adv* patiently

patience [pasjɑ̃s] *nf* **(a)** *(qualité)* patience; **avoir de la p. (avec qn)** to be patient (with sb); **avoir une p. d'ange** to have the patience of a saint; **prendre son mal en p.** to suffer in silence; **perdre p.** to lose patience; *Prov* **p. et longueur de temps font plus que force ni que rage** all things take their time **(b)** *(jeu de cartes) Br* patience, *Am* solitaire

patient, -e [pasjɑ̃, -ɑ̃t] **1** *adj* patient **2** *nm,f (malade)* patient

patienter [pasjɑ̃te] *vi* to wait; **faire p. qn** to ask sb to wait

patin [patɛ̃] *nm* **(a)** *(de patineur)* skate; **patins à glace/à roulettes** ice/roller skates; **faire du p. à glace/à roulettes** to go ice-/roller-skating **(b)** *(pour parquet)* cloth pad **(c)** *Tech* shoe; **p. de frein** brake shoe

patinage [patinaʒ] *nm (sport)* skating; **p. artistique** figure skating; **p. de vitesse** speed skating

patine [patin] *nf* patina

patiner¹ [patine] *vi* **(a)** *(faire du patinage)* to skate **(b)**

(glisser) (voiture) to skid; *(embrayage)* to slip; **ça patine!** it's like a skating rink!

patiner² *vt* to give a patina to

patinette [patinɛt] *nf* scooter

patineur, -euse [patinœr, -øz] *nm,f* skater

patinoire [patinwar] *nf* skating *or* ice rink

pâtir [patir] *vi* to suffer **(de** because of)

pâtisserie [patisri] *nf* **(a)** *(magasin)* cake shop; **p.-confiserie** confectioner's **(b)** *(gâteau)* pastry, cake **(c)** *(confection)* pastry-making; **faire de la p.** to make cakes

pâtissier, -ère [patisje, -ɛr] **1** *nm,f (artisan)* pastry cook; *(commerçant)* confectioner
2 *adj voir* **crème**

patois [patwa] *nm* patois

patraque [patrak] *adj Fam* out of sorts

patriarcal, -e, -aux, -ales [patriarkal, -o] *adj* patriarchal

patriarche [patrijarʃ] *nm* patriarch

patrie [patri] *nf* homeland; **ma seconde p.** my second home; *Fig* **la p. des arts** the cradle of the arts

patrimoine [patrimwan] *nm* heritage; *(biens)* property; **p. culturel** cultural heritage; *Biol* **p. génétique** genotype

patriote [patrijɔt] **1** *adj* patriotic
2 *nmf* patriot

patriotique [patrijɔtik] *adj* patriotic

patriotisme [patrijɔtism] *nm* patriotism

patron, -onne [patrɔ̃, -ɔn] **1** *nm,f* **(a)** *(dirigeant)* boss; *(propriétaire)* owner **(b)** *Rel* patron saint **(de** of)
2 *nm* **(a)** *(médecin)* senior consultant **(b)** *(pour la couture)* pattern

patronage [patrɔnaʒ] *nm* **(a)** *(parrainage)* patronage; **placé sous le p. de...** sponsored by... **(b)** *(organisation)* youth club

patronal, -e, -aux, -ales [patrɔnal, -o] *adj* employers'

patronat [patrɔna] *nm* employers

patronnesse [patrɔnɛs] *adj f* **dame p.** patroness

patronyme [patrɔnim] *nm* patronymic

patrouille [patruj] *nf* patrol

patrouiller [patruje] *vi* to patrol

patte [pat] *nf* **(a)** *(de chien, de chat)* paw; *(d'oiseau)* foot; *(d'insecte)* leg; **pattes de devant** forelegs; *(partie griffue)* front paws; **pattes de derrière** hind legs; *(partie griffue)* back paws; **court/haut sur pattes** short-/long-legged; **marcher/se mettre à quatre pattes** to walk/get down on all fours; *Fig* **tirer dans les pattes à qn** to give sb a hard time; *Fig* **retomber sur ses pattes** to land on one's feet; *Fig* **montrer p. blanche** to show one's credentials; *Fam* **bas les pattes!** hands off!; *Fam* **pattes de mouche** (b) cramped handwriting **(b)** *(de cartable, de sac)* tab **(c)** *(de poche)* flap; *(d'épaule)* epaulette **(d)** **pattes** *(favoris)* sideburns

patte-d'oie [patdwa] *nf* **(a)** *(carrefour)* crossroads *(singulier)* **(b)** *(ride)* crow's foot

pattemouille [patmuj] *nf* damp cloth *(for ironing clothes)*

pâturage [patyraʒ] *nm (endroit)* pasture; **pâturages** pasture land

paume [pom] *nf* palm

paumé, -e [pome] *Fam* **1** *adj* lost
2 *nm,f* loser

paumer [pome] *Fam* **1** *vt* to lose
2 **se paumer** *vpr* to get lost

paupérisation [poperizasjɔ̃] *nf* impoverishment

paupière [popjɛr] *nf* eyelid

paupiette [popjɛt] *nf* (meat) olive; **paupiettes de veau** veal olives

pause [poz] *nf* **(a)** *(dans une activité)* break; *(en parlant)* pause; **faire une p.** to have a break; *(en parlant)* to pause; **p. de midi** lunch break; **p.-café** coffee break **(b)** *Mus Br* semibreve rest, *Am* whole rest

pauvre [povr] **1** *adj* **(a)** *(personne, sol)* poor; **p. en vitamine C** with a low vitamin C content; **p. de moi!** poor old me! **(b)** *(misérable) (robe, meubles)* shabby; *(sourire)* weak; *(excuse)* poor **(c)** *Péj* sad, pathetic; *Fam* **p. mec!** you sad individual!
2 *nmf* poor man, *f* poor woman; **les pauvres** the poor; *Fig* **p. d'esprit** half-wit

pauvrement [povrǝmã] *adv* poorly

pauvresse [povrɛs] *nf (fille)* poor girl; *(femme)* poor woman

pauvreté [povrǝte] *nf aussi Fig* poverty

pavane [pavan] *nf Mus* pavane

pavaner [pavane] **se pavaner** *vpr* to strut about

pavé [pave] *nm (morceau de grès)* paving stone; *Fam Péj (livre)* massive tome; *Fig* **un p. dans la mare** a bombshell **(b)** *(revêtement)* paving; *Fig* **tenir le haut du p.** to be at the top; *Fig* **battre le p.** to hang about the streets; *Fig* **être sur le p.** to be on the street **(c)** *Ordinat* keypad; **p. numérique** numeric keypad

paver [pave] *vt* to pave *(with small stones)*; *Fig* **l'enfer est pavé de bonnes intentions** the road to hell is paved with good intentions

pavillon [pavijɔ̃] *nm* **(a)** *(petite maison)* detached house; **p. de chasse** hunting lodge **(b)** *(d'hôpital)* wing **(c)** *(partie évasée) (d'un Klaxon®, d'un haut-parleur)* horn; *(d'une trompette)* bell; *(d'un entonnoir)* mouth; **p. de l'oreille** external ear **(d)** *(drapeau)* flag; **p. de complaisance** flag of convenience

pavillonnaire [pavijɔnɛr] *adj* **banlieue p.** suburb

pavoiser [pavwaze] *vi Fam* to gloat

pavot [pavo] *nm* poppy

payable [pɛjabl] *adj* payable; **p. comptant** payable in cash; **p. à la livraison** payable on delivery; **p. à vue** payable at sight

payant, -e [pɛjɑ̃, -ãt] *adj (qui paie) (hôte, élève)* paying; *(où il faut payer)* with a charge for admission; **l'entrée est payante** there is a charge for admission; *Fig* **ça s'est avéré p.** it turned out to be worth it

paye [pɛj] = **paie**

payement [pɛjmã] = **paiement**

payer [53] [pɛje] **1** *vt* **(a)** *(somme, dette, loyer, personne)* to pay; *(objet, service)* to pay for; **faire p. qch** *(service)* to charge for sth; *(somme)* to charge sth; **se faire p.** to get *or* be paid; **je le lui ai payé 100 euros** I paid her 100 euros for it; *Fam* **p. qch à qn** *(le lui offrir)* to buy sth for sb; *Fig* **p. les pots cassés** to carry the can **(b)** *Fig (expier)* to pay for it; **il l'a payé de sa vie** he paid for it with his life; **tu me le paieras!** you'll pay for it!; *Fam* **je suis payé pour le savoir** I've learnt it the hard way
2 *vi* **(a)** *(verser de l'argent)* to pay; **p. en liquide/par carte (de crédit)/par chèque** to pay (in) cash/by credit card/by cheque; **p. de sa poche** to pay out of one's own pocket **(b)** *Fig* **p. de sa personne** to put oneself out; **il ne paie pas de mine,** mais il est doué he doesn't look it, but he's very clever **(c)** *(rapporter)* to pay
3 **se payer** *vpr Fam (s'offrir)* **se p. qch** to treat oneself to sth; **se p. un arbre** to crash into a tree; **se p. la tête de qn** to take the mickey out of sb; **se p. le culot de faire qch** to have the nerve to do sth

payeur, -euse [pɛjœr, -øz] *nm,f* payer

pays [pei] *nm* **(a)** *(nation)* country; **p. en voie de développement** developing country; **les p. de l'Est** Eastern European countries **(b)** *(région)* region; **voir du p.**

to travel around; **revenir au p.** to go back home; **p. de chasse/pêche** hunting/fishing country (**c**) **le P. basque** the Basque country; **le p. de Galles** Wales

paysage [peizaʒ] *nm* (**a**) *(site)* landscape; *(vue)* scenery; *Fig (ensemble)* scene; **le p. audiovisuel français** French broadcasting (**b**) *(peinture)* landscape (painting) (**c**) *Ordinat* **mode p.** landscape mode

paysager, -ère [peizaʒe, -ɛr] *adj (jardin)* landscaped; *(bureau)* open-plan

paysagiste [peizaʒist] *nmf* (**a**) *(peintre)* landscape painter (**b**) (**jardinier**) **p.** landscape gardener

paysan, -anne [peizã, -an] **1** *adj* country; *(syndicat)* farmers'; *Péj* peasant
  2 *nm,f* farmer; *Péj* peasant

paysannerie [peizanri] *nf* **la p.** the peasantry

Pays-Bas [peiba] *nmpl* **les P.** the Netherlands

PC [pese] *nm* (**a**) *(abrév* **parti communiste**) CP (**b**) *(abrév* **personal computer**) PC

PCF [peseɛf] *nm (abrév* **parti communiste français**) French Communist Party

PCV [peseve] *nm* (**appel en**) **P.** *Br* reverse-charge call, *Am* collect call; **appeler en P.** *Br* to reverse the charges, *Am* to call collect

P-DG [pedeʒe] *nm inv (abrév* **président-directeur général**) *Br* chairman and managing director, *Am* chief executive officer

péage [peaʒ] *nm* (**a**) *(droit)* toll; **pont à p.** toll bridge (**b**) *(installation)* tollbooth (**c**) **chaîne (de télévision) à p.** pay channel

peau, -x [po] *nf* (**a**) *(derme)* skin; **avoir la p. grasse** to have greasy skin; **avoir la p. blanche/noire** to be white/ black; **avoir une p. de pêche** to have velvety skin; *Fig* **faire p. neuve** *(personne)* to turn over a new leaf; *(entre prise, parti)* to get a new image; **entrer dans la p. d'un personnage** to get right inside a character; **n'avoir que la p. et les os** to be nothing but skin and bone; **diminuer comme une p. de chagrin** to dwindle away, *Fam* **être bien/mal dans sa p.** to feel/not to feel good about oneself; *Fam* **avoir qch dans la p.** to have sth in one's blood; *Fam* **avoir qn dans la p.** to be crazy about sb; *Fam* **tenir à sa p.** to value one's life; *Fam* **risquer sa p.** to risk one's neck; *Fam* **sauver sa p.** to save one's skin; *Fam* **avoir la p. de qn** to have sb's hide; *Fam* **prendre douze balles dans la p.** to be shot by a firing squad; *Fam* **p. de vache** *(homme)* bastard; *(femme)* cow
  (**b**) *(dépouille) (d'un animal)* skin; *(d'un animal à fourrure)* pelt
  (**c**) *(cuir)* hide, leather; *(d'un tambour)* skin; **p. de chamois** chamois (leather); **p. de mouton** sheepskin; **p. de serpent** snakeskin
  (**d**) *(de fruit, de légume)* skin; *(d'agrume, de pomme)* peel; **p. de banane** banana skin; **p. d'orange** orange peel; *Fig* orange-peel skin
  (**e**) *(du lait)* skin
  (**f**) *(des ongles)* hangnail

peaufiner [pofine] *vt* to polish *(with a chamois leather)*; *Fam Fig (fignoler)* to add the final touches to

Peau-Rouge [poruʒ] (*pl* **Peaux-Rouges**) [poruʒ] *nmf* Red Indian

peausserie [posri] *nf* (**a**) *(commerce)* skin trade (**b**) *(marchandise)* leatherwear

pécari [pekari] *nm* peccary

peccadille [pekadij] *nf* peccadillo

péché [peʃe] *nm* sin; **les sept péchés capitaux** the seven deadly sins; **p. de jeunesse** youthful indiscretion; **p. mignon** weakness; **le p. originel** original sin

pêche¹ [peʃ] *nf* (**a**) *(fruit)* peach; **p. blanche** white

peach; **p. jaune** yellow peach (**b**) *Fam (coup)* clout (**c**) *Fam (forme)* **avoir la p.** to be on form
  2 *adj inv* peach(-coloured)

pêche² *nf* (**a**) *(activité)* fishing; **aller à la p.** to go fishing; **p. à la ligne** angling; **p. à la mouche** fly fishing; *Can* **p. sous la glace** ice fishing (**b**) *(produits pêchés)* catch; **faire une bonne p.** to get a good catch

pécher [34] [peʃe] *vi* to sin; **il pèche par excès de timidité** he's painfully shy; **cette enquête pèche sur un point** the inquiry falls down on one point; **p. par omission** to sin by omission

pêcher¹ [peʃe] *nm* peach tree

pêcher² **1** *vt* (**a**) *(chercher à prendre)* to fish for; *(prendre)* to catch; **p. la baleine** to go whaling (**b**) *Fam (trouver)* **où avez-vous pêché cela?** where did you pick that up?
  2 *vi* to fish; **p. à la ligne** to go angling; *Fig* **p. en eau trouble** to fish in troubled waters

pécheresse [peʃrɛs] *voir* **pécheur**

pêcherie [peʃri] *nf* fishery, fishing ground

pêcheur, -eresse [peʃœr, peʃrɛs] *nm,f* sinner

pêcheur, -euse [peʃœr, -øz] *nm,f* fisherman, *f* fisherwoman; **p. à la ligne** angler; **p. de baleines** whaler; **p. de corail** coral fisher

pécore [pekɔr] *nmf Fam Péj* hick, yokel

pectoral, -e, -aux, -ales [pektɔral, -o] **1** *adj* pectoral
  2 *nm* pectoral muscle

pécule [pekyl] *nm* savings, nest egg

pécuniaire [pekynjɛr] *adj* financial

pédagogie [pedagɔʒi] *nf* (**a**) *(discipline)* pedagogy (**b**) *(qualité du pédagogue)* teaching skills

pédagogique [pedagɔʒik] *adj (voyage, sortie)* educational; *(méthode)* teaching

pédagogue [pedagɔg] *nmf* (**a**) *(spécialiste)* educationalist (**b**) *(personne qui sait enseigner)* teacher

pédale [pedal] *nf* (**a**) *(de vélo, de voiture, de piano)* pedal; **p. d'accélérateur** accelerator pedal; **p. d'embrayage** clutch pedal; **p. de frein** brake pedal; *Fam Fig* **mettre la p. douce** to go easy; *Fam Fig* **perdre les pédales** *(s'affoler)* to lose one's head (**b**) *Fam Péj (homosexuel)* fag, = offensive term used to refer to a male homosexual

pédaler [pedale] *vi* to pedal; *Fam* **p. dans la choucroute** *ou* **la semoule** to be all at sea

pédalier [pedalje] *nm* (**a**) *(de vélo)* crank gear (**b**) *(clavier d'orgue)* pedal board

Pédalo® [pedalo] *nm* pedal boat, pedalo

pédant, -e [pedã, -ãt] **1** *adj* pedantic
  2 *nm,f* pedant

pédé [pede] *nm très Fam* fag, = offensive term used to refer to a male homosexual

pédéraste [pederast] *nm* (**a**) *(homosexuel)* homosexual (**b**) *(pédophile)* pederast

pédestre [pedɛstr] *adj (voyage)* on foot; **chemin p.** footpath; **randonnée p.** hike

pédiatre [pedjatr] *nmf* paediatrician

pédiatrie [pedjatri] *nf* paediatrics *(singulier)*

pédicure [pedikyr] *nmf* chiropodist

pedigree [pedigre] *nm* pedigree

pédoncule [pedɔkyl] *nm* peduncle

pédophile [pedɔfil] *nmf* paedophile

pègre [pɛgr] *nf* underworld

peignais, peigne *etc voir* **peindre**

peigne [pɛɲ] *nm* (**a**) *(pour les cheveux)* comb; **se donner un coup de p.** to give one's hair a comb; **p. fin** fine-tooth comb; *Fig* **passer qch au p. fin** to go through sth with a fine-tooth comb (**b**) *(pour la laine)* card

peigne-cul *(pl* **peigne-culs**) [pɛɲky] *nm très Fam Péj* creep

peignée [peɲe] *nf Fam* thrashing

peigner [peɲe] **1** *vt* (**a**) *(cheveux)* to comb; **p. un enfant** to comb a child's hair; *Fam* **p. la girafe** to waste one's time (**b**) *(laine)* to card
2 se peigner *vpr* to comb one's hair

peignoir [pɛɲwar] *nm* (**a**) *(vêtement d'intérieur)* housecoat; *(robe de chambre)* dressing gown; **p. (de bain)** bathrobe (**b**) *(chez le coiffeur)* cape

peinard, -e [penar, -ard] *adj Fam (poste)* cushy; *(personne)* nice and comfortable

peindre [54] [pɛ̃dr] **1** *vt* (**a**) *(avec de la peinture)* to paint; **p. qch en vert** to paint sth green (**b**) *(décrire)* to depict
2 *vi* to paint
3 se peindre *vpr* **l'émotion/la consternation se peignit sur son visage** emotion/dismay was written on his face

peine [pen] *nf* (**a**) *(sanction)* punishment; **p. capitale** capital punishment; **p. de mort** death penalty; **p. de prison** prison sentence; **défense d'entrer sous p. d'amende** *(sur panneau)* trespassers will be prosecuted; **pour la** *ou* **ta p., tu vas descendre la poubelle** just for that, you can take the bin down
(**b**) *(chagrin)* sorrow, sadness; **avoir de la p.** to be upset; **faire de la p. à qn** to upset sb; **elle fait p. à voir** she's a pitiful sight; **p. de cœur** heartache
(**c**) *(effort)* trouble; **se donner de la p. pour faire qch** to go to a lot of trouble to do sth; **donnez-vous** *ou* **prenez la p. d'entrer** please come in; **c'est p. perdue** it's a waste of time; **elle n'est pas au bout de ses peines** her troubles aren't over yet; **en être pour sa p.** to have nothing to show for one's trouble; **ça vaut la p. d'essayer** it's worth a try; **ça ne vaut pas la p.** it's not worth it; **ce n'est pas la p. de débarrasser la table** there's no point (in) clearing the table; **est-ce que ça vaut la p. que je vienne?** do I need to come?; *Ironique* **c'était bien la p. de se donner tout ce mal!** it was really worth going to all that trouble!
(**d**) *(difficulté)* difficulty; **avoir de la p. à faire qch** to have difficulty doing sth; **j'ai (de la) p. à croire que...** I find it hard to believe that...; **elle serait bien en p. de t'expliquer comment ça marche** she'd be hard put to explain to you how it works; **cela n'a pas été sans p.** it was no easy matter
(**e**) **à p.** hardly, scarcely; **c'est à p. si je le connais** I hardly know him; **il est à p. quatre heures** it's only just four o'clock; **à p. étions-nous sortis que...** we'd only just gone out when...; **j'arrive à p.** I've only just arrived; **à p. arrivée, elle alluma une cigarette** no sooner had she arrived than she lit a cigarette

peiner [pene] **1** *vt* to upset, to sadden; **d'un ton peiné** in a sad voice
2 *vi* to labour

peint, -e *voir* **peindre**

peintre [pɛ̃tr] *nm* (**a**) *(artisan, artiste)* painter; **p. en bâtiment** painter and decorator (**b**) *Fig* portrayer

peinture [pɛ̃tyr] *nf* (**a**) *(art, action)* painting; **p. à l'eau** watercolour (painting); **p. à l'huile** oil painting (**b**) *(tableau)* painting, picture; *Fig (description)* depiction; *Fig* **je ne peux pas le voir en p.** I can't stand the sight of him; **p. murale** mural (**c**) *(matière)* paint; **fraîche** *(sur écriteau)* wet paint (**d**) *(surface peinte)* paintwork; **il faudra refaire les peintures** the paintwork will have to be done

peinturer [pɛ̃tyre] *vt Can* to paint

peinturlurer [pɛ̃tyrlyre] *vt Fam* to daub with paint; **se p. le visage** to plaster make-up on one's face

péjoratif, -ive [peʒɔratif, -iv] *adj* pejorative

Pékin [pekɛ̃] *n* Peking, Beijing

pékinois, -e [pekinwa, -az] **1** *adj* of Peking, of Beijing
2 *nm,f* **P.** person from Peking *or* Beijing
3 *nm* (**a**) *(chien)* pekin(g)ese (**b**) *(langue)* Pekingese

pelade [pəlad] *nf* alopecia

pelage [pəlaʒ] *nm* coat, fur

pelé, -e [pəle] **1** *adj (personne, fourrure)* bald; *Fig (paysage)* bare; *(tissu)* threadbare
2 *nm Fam* **il y avait trois pelés et un tondu** there was hardly a soul there

pêle-mêle [pɛlmɛl] *adv* higgledy-piggledy

peler [39] [pəle] **1** *vt* to peel
2 *vi (peau)* to peel; **j'ai le front qui pèle** my forehead is peeling; *Fam Fig* **je pèle (de froid)** I'm freezing (cold)
3 se peler *vpr Fam* **on se pèle (de froid)** it's freezing (cold)

pèlerin [pɛlrɛ̃] *nm* pilgrim

pèlerinage [pɛlrinaʒ] *nm* pilgrimage; **faire un p.** to go on a pilgrimage

pèlerine [pɛlrin] *nf* cape

pélican [pelikɑ̃] *nm* pelican

pelisse [pəlis] *nf* pelisse

pelle [pɛl] *nf* shovel; *(d'enfant)* spade; *Fig* **à la p.** by the bucketful; *Fam* **ramasser** *ou* **se prendre une p.** to fall flat on one's face; **p. mécanique** mechanical shovel; **p. à ordures** dustpan; **p. à tarte** cake slice

pelletée [pɛlte] *nf* shovelful

pelleteuse [pɛltøz] *nf* mechanical shovel

pellicule [pelikyl] *nf* (**a**) *(de glace, de peinture)* thin layer; *(sur un liquide)* film (**b**) *Cin & Phot* film (**c**) *(dans les cheveux)* **pellicules** dandruff; **avoir des pellicules** to have dandruff

pelote [pəlɔt] *nf* (**a**) *(de laine, de ficelle)* ball; *Fig* **avoir les nerfs en p.** to be on edge (**b**) *(sport)* **p. (basque)** pelota (**c**) **p. (à épingles)** pincushion

peloter [pəlɔte] *vt Fam* to pet

peloton [pəlɔtɔ̃] *nm* (**a**) *(petite pelote)* small ball (**b**) *(en cyclisme)* pack; *aussi Fig* **le p. de tête** the leaders (**c**) *Mil* platoon; **p. d'exécution** firing squad

pelotonner [pəlɔtɔne] **se pelotonner** *vpr* to curl up; *(pour avoir chaud)* to snuggle up

pelouse [pəluz] *nf* lawn

peluche [pəlyʃ] *nf* (**a**) *(tissu)* plush; **jouet en p.** soft *or* cuddly toy (**b**) *(jouet)* soft *or* cuddly toy (**c**) *(bout d'étoffe)* piece of fluff

pelucheux, -euse [pəlyʃø, -øz] *adj* fluffy

pelure [pəlyr] *nf* (**a**) *(peau) (de fruit)* peel; *(de légumes)* peelings (**b**) *Fam (vêtement)* coat

pelvis [pɛlvis] *nm* pelvis

pénal, -e, -aux, -ales [penal, -o] *adj* penal

pénaliser [penalize] *vt* to penalize

pénalité [penalite] *nf* penalty

penalty [penalti] *nm* penalty

pénates [penat] *nmpl Fam* **regagner ses p.** to return home

penaud, -e [pəno, -od] *adj* sheepish; **d'un air p.** sheepishly

penchant [pɑ̃ʃɑ̃] *nm (tendance)* propensity (**pour** for); *(préférence)* penchant (**pour** for)

penché, -e [pɑ̃ʃe] *adj* leaning; *(écriture)* sloping

pencher [pɑ̃ʃe] **1** *vt (récipient, meuble)* to tilt; **p. la tête en avant/en arrière** to lean forward/backwards; **p. la tête à droite** to lean one's head to the right
2 *vi (s'écarter de la position verticale)* to lean over; *(bateau)* to list; **p. vers la droite** to lean to the right; *Fig* **p. pour qch** to incline towards sth

3 se pencher *vpr* to lean over; **se p. en avant/en arrière/ sur le côté** to lean forward/backwards/to the side; **se p. par la fenêtre** to lean out of the window; *Fig* **se p. sur un problème** to look into a problem

pendaison [pɑ̃dɛzɔ̃] *nf* hanging; **p. de crémaillère** housewarming (party)

pendant¹, -e [pɑ̃dɑ̃, -ɑ̃t] **1** *adj* **(a)** *(qui pend)* hanging; *(jambes)* dangling; **le chien avait la langue pendante** the dog's tongue was hanging out **(b)** *(en attente)* pending **2** *nm* **(a) p. (d'oreille)** drop earring **(b)** *(d'un tableau, d'un bibelot)* matching piece **(de** to); **se faire p.** to go together

pendant² **1** *prép* **(a)** *(au cours de)* during; **p. mon séjour** during my stay **(b)** *(pour une durée de)* **p. dix minutes/deux mois** for ten minutes/two months; **p. tout le trajet** throughout the journey, for the whole journey; **p. ce temps(-là)** in the meantime **2** *conj* **p. que** while; **p. que vous y êtes** while you're at it

pendentif [pɑ̃dɑ̃tif] *nm (bijou)* pendant

penderie [pɑ̃dri] *nf Br* wardrobe, *Am* closet

pendouiller [pɑ̃duje] *vi Fam* to dangle

pendre [pɑ̃dʁ] **1** *vt* **(a)** *(accrocher)* to hang (up) **(b)** *(mettre à mort)* to hang; **p. qn haut et court** to string sb up; *Fam Fig* **qu'il aille se faire p. ailleurs** let him go hang; *Fig* **je veux bien être pendu si...** I'll be hanged if...
2 *vi* to hang; *(cheveux)* to hang down; *(langue d'un animal)* to hang out; *(bras, jambes)* to dangle; **ton pan de chemise pend** your shirt's hanging out; *Fam* **ça lui pend au nez** she's got it coming to her
3 se pendre *vpr* **(a)** *(se suicider)* to hang oneself **(b)** *(s'accrocher)* **se p. à qch** to hang from sth; **se p. au cou de qn** to throw one's arms round sb's neck

pendu, -e [pɑ̃dy] **1** *adj* **(a)** *(mort)* hanged **(b)** *(accroché)* hanging up; **p. à** hanging from; **p. aux jupes de sa mère** clinging to one's mother's skirts; *Fig* **avoir la langue bien pendue** to be a great talker; **elle est toujours pendue au téléphone** she's never off the phone **2** *nm,f* hanged man, *f* hanged woman; **le p.** *(jeu)* hangman

pendule [pɑ̃dyl] **1** *nf* clock; *Fig* **remettre les pendules à l'heure** to get things straight **2** *nm* pendulum

pendulette [pɑ̃dylɛt] *nf* small clock

pêne [pɛn] *nm* bolt

pénétrant, -e [penetʁɑ̃, -ɑ̃t] *adj (vent, froid)* piercing; *(pluie)* soaking; *(odeur, regard, esprit)* penetrating

pénétration [penetʁasjɔ̃] *nf* penetration

pénétré, -e [penetʁe] *adj (air, ton)* earnest; **p. d'un sentiment/d'une idée** imbued with a feeling/an idea; **il est p. de son importance** he's full of his own importance

pénétrer [34] [penetʁe] **1** *vi* to penetrate; **p. dans une maison** to get into a house
2 *vt* **(a)** *(sujet: balle)* to penetrate; *(sujet: liquide)* to soak into; *Fig (pensée, intentions)* to fathom; *(marché)* to penetrate **(b)** *(sexuellement)* to penetrate
3 se pénétrer *vpr* **se p. d'une idée** to become convinced of an idea

pénible [penibl] *adj* **(a)** *(tâche, voyage, vie)* hard; *(hiver, froid)* severe **(b)** *(spectacle, nouvelles)* painful **(c)** *Fam (personne)* **ce qu'il est p.!** he's such a pain!

péniblement [peniblǝmɑ̃] *adv* with difficulty; **avancer ou marcher p.** to struggle along

péniche [penif] *nf* barge

pénicilline [penisilin] *nf* penicillin

péninsule [penɛ̃syl] *nf* peninsula

pénis [penis] *nm* penis

pénitence [penitɑ̃s] *nf* **(a)** *Rel (repentir)* penitence; *(peine)*

penance (b) *(punition)* punishment; **mettre un enfant en p.** to punish a child

pénitencier [penitɑ̃sje] *nm* prison, *Am* penitentiary

pénitent, -e [penitɑ̃, -ɑ̃t] *adj & nm,f* penitent

pénitentiaire [penitɑ̃sjɛʁ] *adj* prison

Pennsylvanie [pɛnsilvani] *nf* **la P.** Pennsylvania

pénombre [penɔ̃bʁ] *nf* half-light

pensable [pɑ̃sabl] *adj* **ce n'est pas p.** it's unthinkable

pensant, -e [pɑ̃sɑ̃, -ɑ̃t] *adj* thinking; **bien p.** conformist

pense-bête *(pl* pense-bêtes) [pɑ̃sbɛt] *nm Fam* reminder

pensée¹ [pɑ̃se] *nf (fleur)* pansy

pensée² *nf (idée)* thought; *(activité)* thinking; **perdu dans ses pensées** lost in thought; **deviner les pensées de qn** to guess what sb is thinking; **dire le fond de sa p.** to say what one really thinks; **à la p. des vacances,...** at the thought of the holidays,...; **la seule p. de ce repas me met l'eau à la bouche** just thinking about this meal makes my mouth water; **la p. marxiste/bouddhiste** Marxist/ Buddhist thought *or* thinking; **je suis avec vous en p.** you're in my thoughts; **avoir une p. pour qn** to think of sb

penser [pɑ̃se] **1** *vi* **(a)** *(songer, réfléchir)* to think; **p. à qn/ qch** to think of *or* about sb/sth; **pensez vous!** what an idea!; **vous n'y pensez pas!** you're not serious!; **n'y pensons plus** let's forget (about) it; **ce n'est même pas la peine d'y p.** it's not even worth thinking about; **ah, j'y pense!** by the way!; **rien que d'y p., ça me donne des frissons** just thinking about it gives me the shivers; **elle l'a fait sans p. à mal** she didn't mean any harm by it
(b) *(se souvenir)* **p. à faire qch** to remember to do sth; **fais-moi p. à vérifier que...** remind me to check that...; **elle me fait p. à ma mère** she reminds me of my mother
2 *vt* **(a)** *(estimer)* to think; **c'est bien ce que je pensais** I thought as much; **je pense que oui/non** I think/don't think so, *Fam* **pensez si j'étais furieux** you can imagine how angry I was; **p. du bien/du mal de qn** to think a lot/ not to think much of sb
(b) p. faire qch *(espérer)* to hope to do sth; *(avoir l'intention)* to be thinking of doing sth
(c) *(croire à)* to mean; **elle ne pense pas ce qu'elle dit** she doesn't mean what she says; *(concevoir)* **c'est bien/mal pensé** it's well/badly thought out

penseur, -euse [pɑ̃sœʁ, -øz] *nm,f* thinker

pensif, -ive [pɑ̃sif, -iv] *adj* pensive, thoughtful

pension [pɑ̃sjɔ̃] *nf* **(a)** *(allocation)* pension; **p. alimentaire** maintenance, alimony; **p. de retraite** (retirement *or* old age) pension **(b)** *(pensionnat)* boarding school; **mettre un enfant en p.** to send a child to boarding school **(c)** *(hôtel)* **p. (de famille)** boarding house; **être en p. chez qn** to board with sb; **prendre qn en p.** to take sb in as a lodger; **p. complète** *Br* full board, *Am* American plan

pensionnaire [pɑ̃sjɔnɛʁ] *nmf (dans une pension de famille, à l'école)* boarder; *(dans une maison privée)* lodger; *Fam (d'une prison)* inmate

pensionnat [pɑ̃sjɔna] *nm* boarding school

pensionné, -e [pɑ̃sjɔne] *nm,f* pensioner

pensionner [pɑ̃sjɔne] *vt* to pension

pensivement [pɑ̃sivmɑ̃] *adv* thoughtfully, pensively

pensum [pɛ̃sɔm] *nm* **(a)** *(travail ennuyeux)* chore **(b)** *Vieilli Scol* imposition

pentagone [pɛ̃tagɔn] *nm* **(a)** *(figure)* pentagon **(b) le P.** *(aux États-Unis)* the Pentagon

pente [pɑ̃t] *nf* slope; **en p.** sloping; *Fig* **être sur une mauvaise p.** to be going downhill; *Fig* **remonter la p.** to get back on one's feet

Pentecôte [pɑ̃tkot] *nf Rel* Pentecost; *(jours fériés)* Whit(sun)

pentu, -e [pɑ̃ty] *adj* sloping

pénultième [penyltjɛm] *adj & nf* penultimate

pénurie [penyri] *nf* shortage, scarcity

pépé [pepe] *nm (grand-père)* grandpa, grandad; *Fam (vieux monsieur)* grandad

pépée [pepe] *nf Fam Vieilli* chick

pépère [pepɛr] *Fam* **1** *nm* **(a)** *c'est un gros p. (enfant)* he's a chubby little fellow **(b)** *(grand-père)* grandad **2** *adj (endroit)* quiet; *(travail)* easy; **un petit coin p.** a nice quiet little spot; **être p.** *(dans une situation confortable)* to have it easy

pépie [pepi] *nf Fam* **avoir la p.** to be parched

pépiement [pepimɑ̃] *nm* cheeping, chirping

pépier [66] [pepje] *vi* to cheep, to chirp

pépin [pepɛ̃] *nm* **(a)** *(de fruit)* seed, *Br* pip; **sans pépins** seedless **(b)** *Fam (ennui)* hitch **(c)** *Fam (parapluie)* umbrella

pépinière [pepinjɛr] *nf* **(a)** *(d'arbustes)* nursery **(b)** *Fig* training ground **(de** for)

pépite [pepit] *nf (d'or)* nugget; **pépites de chocolat** chocolate chips

péquenaud, -e [pekno, -od] *nm,f Fam* peasant, hick

péquiste [pekist] **1** *adj* of the Parti Québécois **2** *nmf (membre)* member of the Parti Québécois; *(partisan)* supporter of the Parti Québécois

percale [perkal] *nf* percale

perçant, -e [persɑ̃, -ɑ̃t] *adj (regard, cri)* piercing; *(voix)* penetrating; *(vue)* sharp

percée [perse] *nf* **(a)** *(ouverture)* opening **(b)** *Mil, Sp & Fig* breakthrough

percement [persəmɑ̃] *nm (d'un trou, d'un passage, d'un tunnel)* boring; *(d'une avenue)* opening; *(d'un canal)* cutting

perce-neige [persənɛʒ] *nm ou nf inv* snowdrop

perce-oreille *(pl* perce-oreilles) [persɔrɛj] *nm* earwig

percepteur [persɛptœr] *nm* tax collector

perceptible [persɛptibl] *adj* **(a)** *(que l'on peut percevoir)* perceptible **(b)** *(impôt)* collectable

perception [persɛpsjɔ̃] *nf* **(a)** *(par les sens)* perception **(b)** *(d'impôts, de droits, de loyer)* collection **(c)** *(bureau)* tax office

percer [16] [perse] **1** *vt* **(a)** *(transpercer) (corps, surface, armure)* to pierce; *(abcès)* to lance; **le soleil perce les nuages** the sun's breaking through the clouds **(b)** *(découvrir) (complot, secret)* to uncover; *(mystère, énigme)* to solve; **p. qch à jour** to see through sth **(c)** *(trouer)* to make a hole in; *(trou)* to make; *(avec une perceuse)* to drill, to bore; *(tunnel)* to bore; *(avenue)* to open; *(canal, fenêtre)* to cut; *(tonneau)* to broach; *(coffre-fort)* to crack; **se faire p. les oreilles** to have one's ears pierced **2** *vi* **(a)** *(apparaître) (soleil)* to break through; *(dents)* to come through **(b)** *(être révélé)* to get out; **rien n'a percé de leur entretien** nothing's got out about their meeting **(c)** *(devenir célèbre)* to make a name for oneself

perceuse [persøz] *nf* drill

percevable [persəvabl] *adj (impôt)* collectable

percevoir [60] [persəvwar] *vt* **(a)** *(par les sens, l'intellect)* to perceive; *(bruit)* to hear; **être bien/mal perçu** to be well/badly received **(b)** *(impôts, loyers)* to collect; *(intérêts, allocation, commission)* to receive

perchaude [perʃod] *nf Can* yellow perch

perche¹ [pɛrʃ] *nf (tige)* pole; *(pour micro)* boom; *Fam Fig* **une grande p.** *(personne)* a beanpole; *Fig* **tendre la p. à qn** to throw sb a line

perche² *nf (poisson)* perch

percher [perʃe] **1** *vi* **(a)** *(oiseaux)* to perch; *(poules)* to roost **(b)** *Fam (personne)* to live **2** *vt Fam (mettre)* to perch **3 se percher** *vpr* to perch

percheron [perʃərɔ̃] *nm* percheron

perchiste [perʃist] *nmf Sp* pole vaulter; *Cin & TV* boom operator

perchman [perʃman] *nm* ski-lift attendant; *Cin & TV* boom operator

perchoir [perʃwar] *nm aussi Fig* perch; *(pour les volailles)* roost

perclus, -e [pɛrkly, -yz] *adj* **p. de rhumatismes** crippled with rheumatism

percolateur [perkɔlatœr] *nm* percolator

perçu, -e *voir* percevoir

percussion [pɛrkysjɔ̃] *nf* percussion

percussionniste [pɛrkysjɔnist] *nmf* percussionist

percutant, -e [pɛrkytɑ̃, -ɑ̃t] *adj* forceful

percuter [pɛrkyte] **1** *vt* to crash into **2** *vi* **p. contre qch** to crash into sth **3 se percuter** *vpr* to crash into each other

percuteur [pɛrkytœr] *nm* firing pin

perdant, -e [pɛrdɑ̃, -ɑ̃t] **1** *adj* losing; **partir p.** to start out with low hopes **2** *nm,f* loser; **être bon/mauvais p.** to be a good/bad loser

perdition [pɛrdisjɔ̃] *nf* **(a)** *Rel* perdition; **lieu de p.** den of iniquity **(b)** *Naut* **navire en p.** ship in distress; *Fig* **entreprise en p.** company in difficulties

perdre [pɛrdr] **1** *vt* **(a)** *(objet)* to lose; *(habitude)* to get out of; *(occasion)* to miss; *aussi Fig* **p. qn/qch de vue** to lose sight of sb/sth; **p. de son assurance/sa souplesse** to lose some of one's confidence/suppleness; **il perd son pantalon** his trousers keep slipping down; **tu ne perds rien pour attendre!** just you wait!; **p. son temps** to waste one's time; **il n'y a pas de temps à p.** there's no time to lose; **tu n'as rien perdu en ne venant pas** you didn't miss anything by not coming; **y p.** *(dans un échange)* to lose out; *(dans une vente)* to make a loss; **p. au change** to lose out on the deal **(b)** *(ruiner)* **ta générosité/ton ambition te perdra** your generosity/ambition will be the ruin of you **2 se perdre** *vpr* **(a)** *(s'égarer)* to get lost; *Fig* **se p. de vue** to lose touch with each other; **se p. en conjectures/dans les détails** to get lost in conjecture/details; *Fam* **je m'y perds** I'm lost **(b)** *(être gâché) (nourriture, récolte)* to go to waste; **il y a des claques qui se perdent** you/they/*etc* need a good slap **(c)** *(disparaître) (usage, tradition)* to die out

perdreau, -x [pɛrdro] *nm* young partridge

perdrix [pɛrdri] *nf* partridge; **p. des neiges** ptarmigan

perdu, -e [pɛrdy] *adj* **(a)** *(égaré)* lost; *(vêtement, récolte)* ruined; *(endroit)* out-of-the-way; *(emballage)* non-returnable; **p. dans ses pensées** lost in thought; **il est p.** *(d'un malade)* there's no hope for him; **à mes moments perdus, à mes heures perdues** in my spare time; **un de p., dix de retrouvés** there are plenty more fish in the sea

perdurer [pɛrdyre] *vi Litt* to continue

père [pɛr] *nm* **(a)** *(géniteur)* father; **p. de famille** father; **de p. en fils** from father to son; *Prov* **tel p., tel fils** like father, like son; **nos pères** our forefathers, our ancestors; *Fig* **le p. de la psychanalyse** the father of psychoanalysis; *Fam* **(mon) petit p.** *Br* old chap, *Am* old buddy; **le p. Paul** old Paul; **le p. Noël** Father Christmas, Santa Claus; *aussi Fam Fig* **croire au p. Noël** to believe in Father Christmas **(b)** *Rel* father; **le (révérend) p. Martin** Father Martin; **mon p.** father

pérégrinations [peregrinasjɔ̃] *nfpl* peregrinations

péremption [perɑ̃psjɔ̃] *nf* **date de p.** use-by date

péremptoire [perɑptwar] *adj* peremptory

pérennité [perenite] *nf* permanence

péréquation [perekwasjɔ̃] *nf* equalization

perestroïka [perɛstrɔika] *nf* perestroika

perfectif, -ive [pɛrfɛktif, -iv] *adj & nm* perfective

perfection [pɛrfɛksjɔ̃] *nf* perfection; **à la p.** to perfection

perfectionné, -e [pɛrfɛksjɔne] *adj* sophisticated

perfectionnement [pɛrfɛksjɔnmɑ̃] *nm* **(a)** *(action)* perfecting, improving; *(formation)* further training; **cours de p.** proficiency course **(b)** *(résultat)* improvement

perfectionner [pɛrfɛksjɔne] **1** *vt* to perfect, to improve **2 se perfectionner** *vpr* to improve; **se p. en espagnol** to improve one's Spanish

perfectionnisme [pɛrfɛksjɔnism] *nm* perfectionism

perfectionniste [pɛrfɛksjɔnist] *nmf* perfectionist

perfide [pɛrfid] *adj* perfidious; **la p. Albion** perfidious Albion

perfidie [pɛrfidi] *nf* *Litt* **(a)** *(déloyauté)* perfidiousness **(b)** *(action)* perfidy

perforation [pɛrfɔrasjɔ̃] *nf* **(a)** *(action)* perforation; *Ordinat* punching **(b)** *(trou) & Méd* perforation; *Ordinat* punch (hole)

perforatrice [pɛrfɔratris] *nf* *(pour papier)* (hole) punch

perforer [pɛrfɔre] *vt* **(a)** *(papier, organe)* to perforate; *(cuir)* to punch; *(sujet: missile)* to pierce **(b)** *Ordinat (carte, bande)* to punch; **bande perforée** punched tape; **carte perforée** punch card

perforeuse [pɛrfɔrøz] *nf* hole punch

performance [pɛrfɔrmɑ̃s] *nf* *(en sport)* performance; *Fig (exploit)* feat, achievement; **performances** *(d'une voiture, d'un ordinateur)* performance

performant, -e [pɛrfɔrmɑ̃, -ɑ̃t] *adj (machine)* high-performance; *(personne)* highly efficient

perfusion [pɛrfyzjɔ̃] *nf Br* drip, *Am* IV; **être sous p.** to be on *Br* a drip *or Am* an IV

péricliter [periklite] *vi* to collapse

péridurale [peridyral] *nf* epidural

Périgord [perigɔr] *nm* **le P.** Périgord

périgourdin, -e [perigurdɛ̃, -in] **1** *adj* of Périgord **2** *nm,f* **P.** person from Périgord

péril [peril] *nm* peril, danger; **au p. de sa vie** at the risk of one's life; **en p.** in peril; **mettre qch en p.** to imperil *or* endanger sth; **à ses risques et périls** at one's own risk; **il n'y a pas p. en la demeure** it's not a matter of urgency

périlleux, -euse [perijø, -øz] *adj* perilous, dangerous

périmé, -e [perime] *adj (billet, passeport, coupon)* out of date; *(nourriture, article)* past its sell-by date; *(idée, conception)* outdated

périmètre [perimɛtr] *nm* perimeter; **dans un p. de 100 km** within a 100-km radius

périnée [perine] *nm* perineum

période [perjɔd] *nf* period; **p. bleue/blanche/rouge** *(de trains)* = off-peak/peak/high-peak periods of rail schedules during which ticket prices vary accordingly; **p. d'essai** trial period

périodique [perjɔdik] **1** *adj* **(a)** *(cyclique)* periodic **(b)** *(hygiénique)* **serviette p.** sanitary *Br* towel *or Am* napkin **2** *nm* periodical

périodiquement [perjɔdikmɑ̃] *adv* periodically

péripétie [peripesi] *nf Litt* event

périph [perif] *nm Fam Br* ring road, *Am* beltway

périphérie [periferi] *nf* periphery; *(banlieue)* outskirts

périphérique [periferik] **1** *adj aussi Ordinat* peripheral; **boulevard p.** *Br* ring road, *Am* beltway; **radio** *ou* **station p.** = private radio station broadcasting from outside national territory **2** *nm* **(a)** *(route) Br* ring road, *Am* beltway **(b)** *Ordinat* peripheral; **p. d'impression** printer peripheral; **p. de sortie** output device

périphrase [perifraz] *nf* circumlocution, *Spéc* periphrasis

périple [peripl] *nm (voyage)* tour, journey; *(par mer)* voyage

périr [perir] *vi* to perish

périscolaire [periskɔler] *adj* extracurricular

périscope [periskɔp] *nm* periscope

périssable [perisabl] *adj (denrées, produit)* perishable; *Fig (sentiment)* transient

péristyle [peristil] *nm* peristyle

péritonite [peritɔnit] *nf* peritonitis

perle [pɛrl] *nf* **(a)** *(naturelle)* pearl; *(de verre, de métal) & Fig (de sueur)* bead; **p. fine/de culture** real/cultured pearl; *Fig* jeter des perles aux pourceaux to cast pearls before swine; *Fam Fig* **enfiler des perles** to waste one's time on trivia **(b)** *(personne)* gem, treasure; **c'est la p. des sœurs** she's the best sister in the world; **ma bonne est une p. rare** my maid is a real gem **(c)** *Hum (erreur)* howler

perlé, -e [pɛrle] *adj (orné de perles)* set with pearls; *(de perles de verre)* beaded; **grève perlée** *Br* go-slow, *Am* slowdown

perler [pɛrle] *vi (larmes, sueur)* to form in beads

perlimpinpin [pɛrlɛ̃pɛ̃pɛ̃] *nm* **poudre de p.** magic powder

perm [pɛrm] *nf Fam* **(a)** *Mil* leave **(b)** *Scol* study room; **avoir deux heures de p.** to have two hours' private study

permanence [pɛrmanɑ̃s] *nf* **(a)** *(continuité)* permanence; **en p.** permanently **(b)** *(lieu)* duty office; **la p. est assurée le dimanche** there's someone on duty on Sundays; **être de p.** to be on duty **(c)** *Scol* study room; **avoir deux heures de p.** to have two hours' private study

permanent, -e [pɛrmanɑ̃, -ɑ̃t] **1** *adj (commission)* standing; *(spectacle)* continuous; *(tribunal)* permanent; **cinéma p.** continuous showing **2** *nm,f Pol* official **3** *nf* **permanente** perm

perméable [pɛrmeabl] *adj* permeable (**à** to); *Fig* susceptible (**à** to)

permettre [47] [pɛrmɛtr] **1** *vt* **(a)** *(autoriser)* to allow, to permit; **p. à qn de faire qch** to allow *or* permit sb to do sth; **p. qch à qn** to allow sb sth; **permettez-moi de...** allow me to...; **permettez!** excuse me!; **vous permettez?** may I?; **il se croit tout permis** he thinks he can do whatever he likes; *Fam* **il est égoïste comme ce n'est pas permis!** he's incredibly selfish! **(b)** *(rendre possible)* to allow; **p. à qn de faire qch** to allow sb to do sth; **mes moyens ne me le permettent pas** I can't afford it; **si le temps le permet** weather permitting; **si mon emploi du temps le permet** if my schedule allows it **2 se permettre** *vpr* **se p. qch** to allow oneself sth; **se p. de faire qch** to take the liberty of doing sth; **je me permets d'attirer votre attention sur...** may I draw your attention to...

permis, -e [pɛrmi, -iz] **1** *adj* allowed, permitted **2** *nm* permit, licence; **p. de chasse** hunting permit; **p. de conduire** *Br* driving licence, *Am* driver's license; *(examen)* driving test; **p. de construire** planning permission; **p. de séjour** residence permit; **p. de travail** work permit

permissif, -ive [pɛrmisif, -iv] *adj* permissive

permission [pɛrmisjɔ̃] *nf* **(a)** *(autorisation)* permission; **demander/donner la p.** à qn de faire qch to ask/give sb permission to do sth **(b)** *Mil (congé)* leave; *(certificat)* pass; **en p.** on leave

permissionnaire [pɛrmisjɔnɛr] *nmf* person on leave

permutation [pɛrmytasjɔ̃] *nf* **(a)** *(échange)* exchange of posts; *Mil* transfer **(b)** *(de lettres, de chiffres)* transposition; *Math* permutation

permuter [pɛrmyte] **1** *vt (lettres, chiffres)* to transpose; *Math* to permute **2** *vi* to exchange posts

pernicieux, -euse [pɛrnisjø, -øz] *adj* pernicious

péroné [perɔne] *nm* fibula

péroraison [perɔrezɔ̃] *nf* peroration

pérorer [perɔre] *vi Péj* to hold forth

Pérou [peru] *nm* **le P.** Peru; *Fig* **ce n'est pas le P.** *(pas extraordinaire)* it's no great shakes; *(peu d'argent)* it's not a fortune

peroxyde [perɔksid] *nm* peroxide

perpendiculaire [pɛrpɑ̃dikylɛr] *adj & nf* perpendicular **(à** to**)**

perpète [pɛrpɛt] *nf Fam* **(a)** *(perpétuité)* **condamné à p.** sentenced to life; **prendre p.** to get life; **jusqu'à p.** for ever **(b)** *(distance)* **à p.** miles away

perpétrer [34] [pɛrpetre] *vt* to perpetrate

perpette [pɛrpɛt] = **perpète**

perpétuel, -elle [pɛrpetɥɛl] *adj* perpetual; *(secrétaire, membre)* permanent

perpétuellement [pɛrpetɥɛlmɑ̃] *adv* perpetually

perpétuer [pɛrpetɥe] **1** *vt* to perpetuate **2 se perpétuer** *vpr* to be perpetuated

perpétuité [pɛrpetɥite] *nf* perpetuity; **à p.** *(concession)* in perpetuity; *(emprisonnement)* for life; **être condamné (à la réclusion) à p.** to be sentenced to life (imprisonment)

perplexe [pɛrplɛks] *adj* perplexed, puzzled; **laisser qn p.** to perplex *or* puzzle sb

perplexité [pɛrplɛksite] *nf* perplexity

perquisition [pɛrkizisjɔ̃] *nf* search; **faire une p.** to make a search

perquisitionner [pɛrkizisjɔne] **1** *vi* to make a search **2** *vt* to search

perron [perɔ̃] *nm* steps *(leading to a building)*

perroquet [perɔke] *nm* **(a)** *(oiseau)* parrot; **p. de mer** puffin **(b)** *(voile)* topgallant

perruche [peryʃ] *nf* budgerigar

perruque [peryk] *nf* wig

perruquier, -ère [perykje, -ɛr] *nm,f* wig maker

pers [pɛr] *adj m Litt* sea green, perse

persan, -e [pɛrsɑ̃, -an] **1** *adj* Persian **2** *nm,f* **P.** Persian **3** *nm (langue)* Persian

perse [pɛrs] **1** *adj* Persian **2** *nm,f* **P.** Persian **3** *nm (langue)* Persian **4** *nf* **la P.** Persia

persécuter [pɛrsekyte] *vt* to persecute

persécution [pɛrsekysjɔ̃] *nf* persecution; **manie** *ou* **délire de p.** persecution mania

persévérance [pɛrseverɑ̃s] *nf* perseverance

persévérant, -e [pɛrseverɑ̃, -ɑ̃t] *adj* persevering

persévérer [34] [pɛrsevere] *vi* to persevere **(dans** in**)**

persienne [pɛrsjɛn] *nf* shutter

persifler [pɛrsifle] *vt* to mock, to ridicule

persil [pɛrsi] *nm* parsley

persillé, -e [pɛrsije] *adj (viande)* marbled; *(assaisonné de persil)* sprinkled with chopped parsley; *(fromage)* veined

Persique [pɛrsik] *adj voir* **golfe**

persistance [pɛrsistɑ̃s] *nf* persistence **(à faire qch** in doing sth**)**; **avec p.** persistently; **p. dans le mensonge** persistent lying

persistant, -e [pɛrsistɑ̃, ɑ̃t] *adj* persistent; **à feuillage p.** evergreen

persister [pɛrsiste] *vi* **(a)** *(persévérer)* to persist **(dans** in**)**; **p. à faire qch** to persist in doing sth **(b)** *(continuer)* to persist; **il persiste un doute** there remains a doubt

personnage [pɛrsɔnaʒ] *nm* **(a)** *(de fiction)* character; *aussi Fig* **jouer un p.** to play a part *or* a role **(b)** *(individu)* character **(c)** *(image publique)* image, persona **(d)** *(personnalité)* important person; **p. célèbre** celebrity; **un p. officiel** VIP; **un grand p. de l'État** a state dignitary

personnalisation [pɛrsɔnalizasjɔ̃] *nf* personalization

personnalisé, -e [pɛrsɔnalize] *adj* personalized; *(voiture, crédit)* customized

personnaliser [pɛrsɔnalize] *vt* to personalize; *(voiture)* to customize

personnalité [pɛrsɔnalite] *nf* **(a)** *(caractère)* personality; **avoir de la p.** to have lots of personality; **manquer de p.** to have no personality **(b)** *(personnage important)* personality **(c)** *Jur* **p. juridique** legal personality

personne [pɛrsɔn] **1** *nf* **(a)** *(individu)* person; **deux personnes** two people; **les personnes intéressées** those interested; **les personnes âgées** the elderly, elderly people; **une grande p.** a grown-up; **une jeune p.** a young lady **(b)** *(soi-même)* **en p.** in person, personally; **être bien de sa p.** to be good-looking; **être satisfait de sa petite p.** to be pleased with oneself **(c)** *Jur* **p. morale** legal entity; **p. physique** natural person **(d)** *Gram* person **2** *pron indéfini* **(a)** *(quiconque)* anyone, anybody; **elle le sait mieux que p.** she knows better than anyone **(b)** *(aucune personne)* no one, nobody; **p. n'est venu** no one has come; **il n'y a p. de blessé** no one has been injured; **p. d'autre** no one else, nobody else; **je n'y suis pour p.** I'm not at home to anyone; **ne connaissez-vous p. qui puisse nous aider?** don't you know anyone who could help us?; *Fam* **dès qu'il s'agit de travailler, il n'y a plus p.** as soon as there's work to be done, you can't see anyone for dust

personnel, -elle [pɛrsɔnɛl] **1** *adj* **(a)** *(à soi)* personal **(b)** *(égoïste)* selfish; *(intérêt)* vested **2** *nm (d'une firme, d'une école)* staff; *(d'une usine)* workforce; *(dans l'armée)* personnel; **faire partie du p. de...** to be on the staff of…; **manquer de p.** to be understaffed; **un membre du p.** a member of staff; **p. de bureau** office *or* clerical staff; **p. navigant** flight personnel; **p. au sol** ground personnel

personnellement [pɛrsɔnɛlmɑ̃] *adv* personally

personnifier [66] [pɛrsɔnifje] *vt* to personify; **il est la bêtise personnifiée** he's stupidity personified

perspective [pɛrspɛktiv] *nf* **(a)** *(de dessin)* perspective **(b)** *(idée)* prospect; **à la p. de faire qch** at the prospect of doing sth; **en p.** in prospect; **des perspectives de reprise** outlook for recovery; **des perspectives d'avenir** future prospects **(c)** *(point de vue)* viewpoint, point of view

perspicace [pɛrspikas] *adj* shrewd

perspicacité [pɛrspikasite] *nf* shrewdness

persuader [pɛrsɥade] **1** *vt* **p. qn (de qch)** to persuade *or* convince sb (of sth); **p. qn de faire qch** to persuade sb to do sth; **être persuadé de qch/que…** to be convinced of sth/that… **2 se persuader** *vpr* **se p. de qch/que…** to convince oneself of sth/that…

persuasif, -ive [pεrsɥazif, -iv] *adj* persuasive
persuasion [pεrsɥazjɔ̃] *nf* persuasion
perte [pεrt] *nf* (**a**) *(d'un objet, d'une personne, d'un procès)* loss; **de lourdes pertes en hommes et en matériel** heavy losses of men and equipment; **à p. de vue** as far as the eye can see; **vendre qch à p.** to sell sth at a loss; *aussi Fig* **passer qch par pertes et profits** to write sth off; **p. sèche** dead loss; **ce n'est pas une grosse p.** it's no great loss (**b**) *(gaspillage)* **une p.** **de temps** a waste of time; **en pure p.** to no purpose (**c**) *(déperdition)* loss; **être en p. de vitesse** to be losing speed; *Fig* to be running out of steam; **pertes blanches** vaginal discharge; **p. de chaleur** heat loss; **p. de connaissance** loss of consciousness; *Ordinat* **p. de données irréparable** irretrievable data loss (**d**) *(destruction)* ruin; **jurer la p. de qn** to swear to ruin sb; **courir à sa p.** to be heading for disaster
pertinemment [pεrtinamɑ̃] *adv* **savoir qch p.** to know sth for a fact
pertinence [pεrtinɑ̃s] *nf* pertinence, relevance
pertinent, -e [pεrtinɑ̃, -ɑ̃t] *adj* pertinent, relevant
perturbant, -e [pεrtyrbɑ̃, -ɑ̃t] *adj* disturbing, upsetting
perturbateur, -trice [pεrtyrbatœr, -tris] **1** *adj* disruptive **2** *nm,f* troublemaker
perturbation [pεrtyrbasjɔ̃] *nf* disruption; **p. (atmosphérique)** (atmospheric) disturbance
perturber [pεrtyrbe] *vt* *(services publics, circulation)* to disrupt; *(personne)* to perturb, to upset
péruvien, -enne [peryvjɛ̃, -εn] **1** *adj* Peruvian **2** *nm,f* **P.** Peruvian
pervenche [pεrvɑ̃ʃ] *nf* (**a**) *(plante)* periwinkle; (**bleu**) **p.** periwinkle blue (**b**) *Fam (contractuelle) Br* (female) traffic warden, *Am* meter maid
pervers, -e [pεrvεr, -εrs] **1** *adj* perverse **2** *nm,f* pervert
perversion [pεrvεrsjɔ̃] *nf* perversion
perversité [pεrvεrsite] *nf* perversity
pervertir [pεrvεrtir] **1** *vt* to pervert **2 se pervertir** *vpr* to become perverted
pesamment [pəzamɑ̃] *adv* heavily
pesant, -e [pəzɑ̃, -ɑ̃t] **1** *adj* heavy; *(sommeil)* deep; *(ambiance)* oppressive; **marcher à pas pesants** to walk heavily **2** *nm* **valoir son p. d'or** to be worth one's/its weight in gold
pesanteur [pəzɑ̃tœr] *nf* (**a**) *(attraction terrestre)* gravity (**b**) *(lourdeur)* heaviness
pesée [pəze] *nf* (**a**) *(pour connaître le poids)* weighing; *(de boxeur, de chevaux)* weigh-in (**b**) *(pression)* force
pèse-lettre *(pl* pèse-lettres) [pεzlεtr] *nm* letter scales
pèse-personne *(pl* pèse-personnes) [pεzpεrsɔn] *nm* scales
peser [46] [pəze] **1** *vt* to weigh; *Fig* **le pour et le contre** to weigh up the pros and cons; *Fig* **p. ses mots** to weigh one's words; *Fig* **tout bien pesé** all things considered **2** *vi* *(être lourd)* to be heavy; **p. trois kilos** to weigh three kilos; **p. sur qch** to press on sth; *Fig* **p. sur la conscience** to lie heavy on one's conscience; *Fig* **p. sur l'estomac** to lie heavy on the stomach; *Fig* **p. sur ou dans une décision** to carry weight in a decision; **la solitude me pèse** the solitude is getting me down **3 se peser** *vpr* to weigh oneself
peseta [pezeta] *nf Anciennement* peseta
peso [pezo] *nm* peso
pessimisme [pesimism] *nm* pessimism
pessimiste [pesimist] **1** *adj* pessimistic **2** *nmf* pessimist

peste [pεst] *nf* (**a**) *(maladie)* plague; *Fig* **je me méfie de lui comme de la p.** I don't trust him as far as I could throw him; **la p. bubonique** the bubonic plague; *Hist* **la p. noire** the Black Death (**b**) *Fig & Péj (personne)* pest
pester [pεste] *vi* **p. contre qn/qch** to curse sb/sth
pesticide [pεstisid] **1** *adj* pesticidal **2** *nm* pesticide
pestiféré, -e [pεstifere] **1** *adj* plague-stricken **2** *nm,f* plague victim
pestilentiel, -elle [pεstilɑ̃sjεl] *adj* stinking
pet [pε] *nm Fam (gaz)* fart; **lâcher un p.** to fart; **ça ne vaut pas un p. (de lapin)** it isn't worth a monkey's fart; **il a toujours un p. de travers** there's always something up with him
pétale [petal] *nm* petal
pétanque [petɑ̃k] *nf* ≃ bowls *(played in the South of France)*
pétant, -e [petɑ̃, -ɑ̃t] *adj Fam* **à une heure pétante** at one o'clock on the dot
pétarade [petarad] *nf* (**a**) *(de feux d'artifice, d'armes à feu)* crackling (**b**) *(de véhicule)* backfiring
pétarader [petarade] *vi* (**a**) *(feux d'artifice, armes à feu)* to crackle (**b**) *(véhicule)* to backfire
pétard [petar] *nm* (**a**) *(feu d'artifice)* (fire)cracker, *Br* banger (**b**) *(pistolet)* shooter (**c**) *Fam (joint)* joint (**d**) *Fam* **être en p. (contre)** to be raging (at)
pétasse [petas] *nf Vulg* slag
pétaudière [petodjεr] *nf Fam* bedlam
pété, -e [pete] *adj Fam (ivre)* smashed
péter [34] [pete] *Fam* **1** *vi* (**a**) *(bois qui brûle)* to crackle; *(bouchon)* to pop; *(personne)* to fart; *Vulg* **il pète plus haut que son cul** he thinks he's God's gift to humanity (**b**) *(exploser)* to blow up; *Fig* **je veux que ça pète!** get your finger out! (**c**) *(casser)* to bust
2 *vt* (**a**) **p. le feu** *ou* **la forme** to be full of beans; **p. les plombs** to blow one's top (**b**) *(casser)* to bust
3 se péter *vpr (se casser)* to bust; **se p. la gueule** to get wasted
pète-sec [pεtsεk] *adj inv Fam* curt
péteux, -euse [petø, -øz] *Fam Péj* **1** *adj (honteux)* sheepish **2** *nm,f* (**a**) *(lâche)* yellowbelly (**b**) *(prétentieux)* upstart
pétillant, -e [petijɑ̃, -ɑ̃t] *adj (vin, yeux)* sparkling; *(eau)* fizzy
pétillement [petijmɑ̃] *nm (du vin, des yeux)* sparkling
pétiller [petije] *vi (vin, yeux)* to sparkle; **p. d'intelligence** *(yeux)* to sparkle with intelligence
petit, -e [pəti, -it] **1** *adj* (**a**) *(de taille réduite)* small, little; *(distance, séjour)* short; *(somme)* small; **tout p.** tiny; **un p. moment** a little while; *Fam* **une petite demi-heure** barely half an hour; *Fig* **se faire tout p.** to make oneself as inconspicuous as possible; **petites et moyennes entreprises** small and medium-sized businesses (**b**) *(peu grave)* *(problème, erreur)* small; *(accident)* minor; *(rhume)* slight (**c**) *(jeune)* little; *(ami)* little; **mon p. frère** my little brother; **p. cousin** first cousin once removed; **un p. Américain** an American boy (**d**) *(faible)* *(voix)* small; *(bruit)* little; **avoir une petite santé** to be delicate (**e**) *(de niveau inférieur) Scol* **les petites classes** the lower classes; **petite route** minor road; **p. commerçant/artisan** small trader/craftsman (**f**) *(pour insister)* little; **p. crétin/con!** little idiot/bastard!; **mon p. ange** my little angel; **je fumerais bien une petite cigarette** I'd love a cigarette; *Fam* **p. nom** first name

(g) *(mesquin)* petty
2 *nm,f* **(a)** *(enfant)* (little) boy, *f* (little) girl; **les petits** the little ones; *Fam* **mon p.** my dear; **pauvre p.!** poor little thing!

(b) *(en taille)* **les petits devant, les grands derrière** small people in front and the tall ones behind
3 *nm (d'un chien)* puppy; *(d'un chat)* kitten; **faire** *ou* **avoir des petits** to have puppies/kittens/*etc*; *Fam* **faire des petits** *(argent)* to multiply
4 *adv (écrire)* small; **p. à p.** little by little

petit-beurre *(pl* **petits-beurre)** [pətibœr] *nm* butter *Br* biscuit *or Am* cookie

petit-bourgeois, petite-bourgeoise *(mpl* **petits-bourgeois,** *fpl* **petites-bourgeoises)** [pətiburʒwa, pətiturʒwaz] *aussi Péj* **1** *adj* lower middle class
2 *nm,f* member of the lower middle class

petite-fille *(pl* **petites-filles)** [pətitfij] *nf* granddaughter
petitesse [pətites] *nf (d'un objet)* smallness; *Péj (mesquinerie)* pettiness
petit-fils *(pl* **petits-fils)** [pətifis] *nm* grandson
pétition [petisjɔ̃] *nf* petition
petit-lait *(pl* **petits-laits)** [pətile] *nm* whey; *Fam* **se boire comme du p.** to go down a treat
petit-nègre [pətinɛgr] *nm Fam (mauvais français)* pidgin French; **c'est du p.** *(mal écrit)* it's gibberish
petits-enfants [pətizɑ̃fɑ̃] *nmpl* grandchildren
petit-suisse *(pl* **petits-suisses)** [pətisɥis] *nm* = thick fromage frais sold in small individual portions
pétoche [petɔʃ] *nf Fam* jitters; **avoir la p.** to have the jitters; **flanquer la p. à qn** to give sb the jitters
pétoire [petwar] *nf Fam (fusil)* popgun
pétri, -e [petri] *adj* **p. de qch** *(orgueil)* puffed up with sth; *(contradictions)* riddled with sth
pétrifier [66] [petrifje] *vt aussi Fig* to petrify
pétrin [petrɛ̃] *nm* kneading trough; *Fam* **être dans le p.** to be in a mess
pétrir [petrir] *vt (pâte à pain, argile)* to knead
pétrochimique [petroʃimik] *adj* petrochemical
pétrodollar [petrodɔlar] *nm Fin* petrodollar
pétrole [petrɔl] *nm* oil, petroleum
pétrolette [petrɔlɛt] *nf Fam* moped
pétrolier, -ère [petrɔlje, -ɛr] **1** *adj* **l'industrie pétrolière** the oil industry
2 *nm* (oil) tanker
pétrolifère [petrɔlifɛr] *adj* oil-bearing; **gisement p.** oilfield
pétulant, -e [petylɑ̃, -ɑ̃t] *adj* exuberant
pétunia [petynja] *nm* petunia
peu [pø] **1** *adv* **(a)** *(avec un verbe)* not much; **elle mange/parle p.** she doesn't eat/talk much
(b) *(avec un adjectif ou un adverbe)* not very; **il a agi p. honorablement** he didn't behave very honourably; **très/trop p.** very/too little
(c) *(avec un nom)* **p. de** *(temps, courage, vin)* little, not much; *(amis, lettres, illusions)* few, not many; **ne te fâche pas pour si p.** don't get angry over such a small thing; **c'est p. de chose** it's nothing; *Fam* **très p. pour moi!** not for me!
(d) *(un petit nombre)* few; **p. ont compris** few (people) understood
(e) *(indique la durée)* **sous p., avant p., d'ici p.** soon, shortly; **p. après** shortly afterwards; **depuis p.** lately, recently; **c'est ouvert depuis p.** it hasn't been open long; **j'ai manqué le train de p.** I (only) just missed the train; **il y a p.** not very long ago, recently; **p. à p.** little by little, gradually

(f) **pour p. que** + *subjunctive* if by chance; **pour p. qu'il ait oublié la clé,...** if by chance he's forgotten the key,...
2 *nm* **(a)** *(petite quantité)* **le p. que je sais d'elle** the little I know about her; **le p. d'argent qu'il me reste** what little money I have left; **son p. d'instruction** what little education he/she has had
(b) **un p.** a little *or* a bit; **un peu grand/ennuyeux** a little *or* a bit big/boring; **un p. de temps/lait** a bit of *or* a little time/milk; **je le connais un p.** I know him slightly *or* a little; **un p. plus/moins** a little *or* a bit more/less; **un tout petit p.** a tiny bit; **il est un p. artiste** he's a bit of an artist; **un p. plus et elle tombait** she very nearly fell; **pour un p. je l'aurais jeté dehors** I all but *or* I very nearly threw him out; **écoutez un p.** just listen; **viens un p. ici** come here a minute; *Fam* **tu ferais ça? – un p.!** you'd do that? – **you bet!**
(c) *(de temps)* **un p.** a bit, a little while; **restez encore un p.** stay a bit longer, stay a little (while) longer

peuchère [pøʃɛr] *exclam* heavens!
peuh [pø] *exclam* pooh!
peuplade [pœplad] *nf* tribe
peuple [pœpl] *nm* **(a)** *(nation)* people; **le p. français** the French people **(b)** *(citoyens)* people; **les gens du p.** ordinary people **(c)** *Fam (foule)* crowd
peuplé, -e [pœple] *adj* inhabited **(de** by); **très/peu p.** densely/sparsely populated
peuplement [pœpləmɑ̃] *nm (d'une région)* populating
peupler [pœple] **1** *vt* **(a)** *(installer une population dans)* to populate **(b)** *(habiter)* to inhabit; *Fig* **peuplé de qch** full of sth
2 se peupler *vpr* to become populated
peuplier [pøplije] *nm* poplar
peur [pœr] *nf* fear; *(subite)* fright; **avoir p. (de)** to be afraid *or* frightened (of); *Fam* **avoir une p. bleue de qn/qch** to be frightened *or* scared to death of sb/sth; **faire p. à qn** to frighten *or* scare sb; **par p. de qch** through fear of sth; **de p. de faire qch** for fear of doing sth; **de p. qu'il ne le fasse** for fear that he would do it; **j'ai bien p. qu'il (ne) soit en retard** I'm very much afraid he's going to be late
peureux, -euse [pœrø, -øz] **1** *adj* fearful
2 *nm,f* fearful person
peut *voir* **pouvoir**
peut-être [pøtɛtr] *adv* perhaps, maybe; **p. que oui, p. que non** perhaps yes, perhaps not; **p. (bien) qu'il viendra, p. viendra-t-elle** perhaps she'll come; **je ne suis p. pas riche, mais...** I may not be rich, but...; *Ironique* **tu le sais mieux que moi, p.?** you think you'd know better, do you?
peux *voir* **pouvoir**
pèze [pɛz] *nm très Fam (argent)* cash, *Am* bucks
pH [peaʃ] *nm Chim* pH
phacochère [fakɔʃɛr] *nm* warthog
phagocyter [fagɔsite] *vt Biol* to phagocytose; *Fig* to swallow up
phalange [falɑ̃ʒ] *nf (du doigt)* phalanx
phallique [falik] *adj* phallic
phallocrate [falɔkrat] *nm Péj* male chauvinist
phalloïde [falɔid] *adj voir* **amanite**
phallus [falys] *nm* phallus
phantasme [fɑ̃tasm] *nm* = **fantasme**
pharamineux, -euse [faraminø, -øz] = **faramineux**
pharaon [faraɔ̃] *nm* Pharaoh
phare [far] **1** *nm* **(a)** *(pour navires)* lighthouse; *(pour avions)* beacon **(b)** *(de voiture)* headlight; **faire un appel de phares** to flash one's headlights; **se mettre en phares**

Br to dip or Am to dim one's headlights; **p. antibrouillard** foglight
2 adj **film-p.** seminal movie; **épreuve-p.** star event
pharmaceutique [farmasøtik] adj pharmaceutical
pharmacie [farmasi] nf **(a)** (science) pharmacy **(b)** (magasin) Br chemist's, Am drugstore **(c)** (médicaments) pharmaceuticals; **(armoire à) p.** medicine cabinet
pharmacien, -enne [farmasjɛ̃, ɛn] nm,f (vendeur) Br chemist, Am druggist; (chercheur) pharmacist, Br chemist
pharmacologie [farmakɔlɔʒi] nf pharmacology
pharyngite [farɛ̃ʒit] nf Méd pharyngitis
pharynx [farɛ̃ks] nm Anat pharynx
phase [faz] nf phase; **cancer en p. terminale** terminal cancer; **être en p.** Phys to be in phase; Fam to be on the same wavelength
phénicien, -enne [fenisjɛ̃, -ɛn] Hist **1** adj Phoenician
2 nm,f P. Phoenician
phénix [feniks] nm (animal mythologique) phoenix; Fig & Litt paragon
phénoménal, -e, -aux, -ales [fenɔmenal, o] adj Fam phénoménal
phénomène [fenɔmɛn] nm phenomenon; Fam (personne) character; **un p. de foire** a freak
Philadelphie [filadɛlfi] n Philadelphia
philanthrope [filɑ̃trɔp] nmf philanthropist
philanthropique [filɑ̃trɔpik] adj philanthropic
philatélie [filateli] nf philately, stamp collecting
philatéliste [filatelist] nmf philatelist, stamp collector
philharmonique [filarmɔnik] adj philharmonic
philippin, -e [filipɛ̃, -in] **1** adj Filipino
2 nm,f P. Filipino
Philippines [filipin] nfpl **les P.** the Philippines
philosophale [filozɔfal] adj f voir **pierre**
philosophe [filozɔf] **1** nmf philosopher
2 adj philosophical
philosopher [filozɔfe] vi to philosophize
philosophie [filozɔfi] nf philosophy; Fig **avec p.** philosophically
philosophique [filozɔfik] adj philosophical
philtre [filtr] nm philtre; **p. d'amour** love potion
phlébite [flebit] nf Méd phlebitis
phlébologue [flebɔlɔg] nmf Méd vein specialist; Spéc phlebologist
Phnom Penh [pnɔmpɛn] n Phnom Penh
phobie [fɔbi] nf phobia; **avoir la p. de qch** to have a phobia about sth
phonème [fɔnɛm] nm phoneme
phonétique [fɔnetik] **1** adj phonetic
2 nf phonetics (singulier)
phonographe [fɔnɔgraf] nm Vieilli Br gramophone, Am phonograph
phoque [fɔk] nm **(a)** (animal) seal; très Fam **il est pédé comme un p.** he's a screaming queen **(b)** (fourrure) sealskin
phosphate [fɔsfat] nm phosphate; **sans phosphates** phosphate-free
phosphore [fɔsfɔr] nm phosphorus
phosphorescent, -e [fɔsfɔresɑ̃, -ɑ̃t] adj phosphorescent
photo [foto] **1** nf **(a)** (cliché) photo; **prendre qn/qch en p.** to take a photo of sb/sth; Fam **tu veux ma p.?** who do you think you're staring at?; **p. d'identité** passport-sized photograph; **p. de mode** fashion photo; **p. souvenir** souvenir photo **(b)** (activité) **faire de la p.** (en amateur) to take photographs; (en professionnel) to be a photographer
2 adj inv voir **appareil**
photocomposition [fotokɔ̃pozisjɔ̃] nf photosetting
photocopie [fotokɔpi] nf photocopy
photocopier [66] [fotokɔpje] vt to photocopy
photocopieur [fotokɔpjœr] nm, **photocopieuse** [fotokɔpjøz] nf photocopier
photoélectrique [fotoelɛktrik] adj photoelectric
photo-finish (pl **photos-finish**) [fotofiniʃ] nf photo finish; (appareil) photo-finish camera
photogénique [fotoʒenik] adj photogenic
photographe [fotograf] nmf **(a)** (professionnel) photographer; **p. de mode** fashion photographer; **p. de presse** press photographer **(b)** (commerçant) **chez le p.** at the photo shop
photographie [fotografi] nf **(a)** (technique) photography; **faire de la p.** to take photographs **(b)** (cliché) photograph; **prendre une p. de** to take a photograph of; **p. aérienne** aerial photograph
photographier [66] [fotografje] vt to photograph; **se faire p.** to have one's photograph taken
photographique [fotografik] adj photographic
photogravure [fotogravyr] nf photogravure
Photomaton® [fotomatɔ̃] nm photo booth
photomontage [fotomɔ̃taʒ] nm photomontage
photon [fotɔ̃] nm Phys photon
photoreportage [fotorəpɔrtaʒ] nm photo report
photosensible [fotosɑ̃sibl] adj photosensitive
photostyle [fotostil] nm Ordinat light pen
photosynthèse [fotosɛ̃tɛz] nf Biol photosynthesis
phrase [fraz] nf sentence; (musicale) phrase; Fig **faire de grandes phrases** to use flowery language
phrasé [fraze] nm Mus phrasing
phraséologie [frazeɔlɔʒi] nf phraseology; Péj flowery language
phréatique [freatik] adj voir **nappe**
phrygien, -enne [friʒjɛ̃, -ɛn] adj Hist **bonnet p.** Phrygian cap (in French Revolution)
phtisie [ftizi] nf Vieilli consumption
phylloxéra, phylloxera [filɔksera] nm phylloxera
physicien, -enne [fizisjɛ̃, -ɛn] nm,f physicist
physiologie [fizjɔlɔʒi] nf physiology
physiologique [fizjɔlɔʒik] adj physiological
physionomie [fizjɔnɔmi] nf **(a)** (traits du visage) features; **juger les gens à leur p.** to judge people by appearances **(b)** (aspect) face
physionomiste [fizjɔnɔmist] adj **être p.** to have a good memory for faces
physiothérapie [fizjɔterapi] nf natural medicine
physique [fizik] **1** adj physical; Fam **je ne le supporte pas, c'est p.** he absolutely repulses me
2 nf (science) physics (singulier); **p. nucléaire** nuclear physics
3 nm (d'une personne) physique; **avoir un p. avantageux** to have a good physique; **avoir le p. de l'emploi** to look the part
physiquement [fizikmɑ̃] adv physically
phytoplancton [fitoplɑ̃ktɔ̃] nm phytoplankton
phytothérapie [fitoterapi] nf herbal medicine
piaf [pjaf] nm Fam sparrow
piaffer [pjafe] vi (cheval) to paw the ground; Fig **p. d'impatience** to fidget impatiently

piaillement [pjɑjmɑ̃] *nm (d'un oiseau)* cheeping; *Fam (d'un enfant)* squealing

piailler [pjɑje] *vi (oiseau)* to cheep; *Fam (enfant)* to squeal

pianiste [pjanist] *nmf* pianist

piano¹ [pjano] *nm* piano; **jouer** *ou* **faire du p.** to play the piano; **p. demi-queue** baby grand; **p. droit** upright piano; **p. à queue** grand piano

piano² *adv Mus* piano; *Fig* gently

pianoter [pjanɔte] *vi Fam* (a) *(mal jouer)* to tinkle away (b) *(tapoter)* **p. sur qch** *(table)* to drum one's fingers on sth; *Fam (clavier)* to tap away at sth

piastre [pjastr] *nf* piastre; *Can Fam (dollar)* buck

piaule [pjol] *nf Fam* pad

piauler [pjole] *vi (poussins)* to cheep

PIB [peibe] *nm Écon (abrév* **produit intérieur brut)** GDP

pic [pik] *nm* (a) *(pioche)* pick(axe); **p. à glace** ice pick (b) *(sommet)* peak; **couler à p.** to sink like a stone; **tomber à p.** *(falaise)* to go straight down; *Fam* to come at just the right moment

picard, -e [pikar, -ard] **1** *adj* of Picardy
2 *nmf* **P.** person from Picardy

Picardie [pikardi] *nf* **la P.** Picardy

picaresque [pikarɛsk] *adj* picaresque

pichenette [piʃnɛt] *nf* flick

pichet [piʃɛ] *nm Br* jug, *Am* pitcher

pickpocket [pikpɔkɛt] *nm* pickpocket

pick-up [pikœp] *nm inv* (a) *Vieilli (électrophone)* record player (b) *(véhicule)* pick-up (truck)

picoler [pikɔle] *vi Fam* to booze

picorer [pikɔre] **1** *vt (sujet: oiseau)* to peck (at); *(sujet: personne)* to nibble
2 *vi (oiseau)* to pick about; *(personne)* to pick at one's food

picotement [pikɔtmɑ̃] *nm (dans la gorge, dans le nez)* tickling; *(dans les yeux)* stinging; *(sur la peau)* prickling

picoter [pikɔte] *vt* **j'ai la gorge qui (me) picote** I've got a tickle in my throat; **la fumée me picotait les yeux** the smoke made my eyes sting; **j'ai la peau qui (me) picote** my skin's prickling

Pictes [pikt] *nmpl* **les P.** the Picts

pictogramme [piktɔgram] *nm* pictogram

pictural, -e, -aux, -ales [piktyral, -o] *adj* pictorial

pic-vert *(pl* **pics-verts)** [pivɛr] = **pivert**

pie [pi] **1** *nf* magpie; *Fam (personne)* chatterbox; *Fam* **être bavard comme une p.** to be a real chatterbox
2 *adj inv (cheval)* piebald; *(vache)* black-and-white

pièce [pjɛs] *nf* (a) *(salle)* room
(b) *(élément)* piece; *(d'un mécanisme)* part; **un service complet de trente-six pièces** a complete thirty-six piece service; **coûter 10 euros p.** to cost 10 euros each; **travailler à la p.** to do piecework; *Fig* **être tout d'une p.** to be straightforward; *Fig* **une histoire fabriquée de toutes pièces** a completely made-up story; **mettre qch en pièces** to tear sth to pieces; **p. de bœuf** cut *ou* piece of beef; **p. de collection** collector's item; **p. d'eau** ornamental lake; *(plus petite)* ornamental pond; **p. montée** = large pyramid of caramel-covered profiteroles often served at weddings, baptisms etc; **p. de musée** museum piece; **pièces de rechange, pièces détachées** spare parts, spares; **p. de résistance** main dish; *Fig* **p.** pièce de résistance
(c) *(argent)* **p. (de monnaie)** coin; **p. de 10 euros** 10-euro piece
(d) **p. (de théâtre)** play
(e) *(raccord)* patch; **mettre une p. à qch** to put a patch on sth
(f) *(document)* document; **juger sur pièces** to judge on the evidence; **p. à conviction** exhibit *(in criminal case)*; **p. d'identité** proof of identity; **p. jointe** *(à une lettre)* enclosure
(g) *(aux échecs)* piece; *(aux dames) Br* draught, *Am* checker

piécette [pjesɛt] *nf* small coin

pied [pje] *nm* (a) *(d'une personne)* foot; **avoir les pieds plats** to have flat feet; **avoir un p. bot** to have a club foot; **se prendre les pieds dans qch** to get one's feet caught in sth; **avoir p.** to be within one's depth; **perdre p.** to get out of one's depth; **mettre p. à terre** *(de cheval, de vélo)* to dismount; **de p. en cap** from head to toe
(b) *(de cheval)* hoof; *Culin* **p. de porc** pig's trotter
(c) *(de vigne)* stock; *(de céleri, de salade)* head
(d) *(de chaise, de table)* leg; *(de verre)* stem; *(d'appareil photo, de lampadaire)* stand
(e) *(base)* foot
(f) **à p.** on foot; **j'y suis allé à p.** I walked there, I went there on foot; **faire trois kilomètres à p.** to walk three kilometres; **tu en as pour dix minutes à p.** it'll take you ten minutes to walk (there)
(g) *(mesure)* foot; *Fig* **six pieds sous terre** six feet under
(h) *(locutions)* **mettre qch sur p.** to set sth up; **être sur p.** *(personne)* to be up and about; **être à p. d'œuvre** to be ready to get on with the job; **être sur un p. d'égalité avec qn** to be on an equal footing with sb; *Fig* **être sur le p. de guerre** to be ready for action; **avoir bon p. bon œil** to be hale and hearty; **avoir un p. dans la tombe** to have one foot in the grave; **avoir le p. marin** to be a good sailor; *Fam* **faire du p. à qn** to play footsie with sb; *Fam* **ça lui fera les pieds!** that'll teach him a lesson!; *Fam* **prendre son p.** to get one's kicks; *Fam* **c'est le p.!** it's fantastic!

pied-à-terre [pjetatɛr] *nm inv* pied-à-terre

pied-bot *(pl* **pieds-bots)** [pjebo] *nm* club-footed person

pied-de-biche *(pl* **pieds-de-biche)** [pjedbiʃ] *nm (outil)* nail claw

pied-de-poule *(pl* **pieds-de-poule)** [pjedpul] *adj inv & nm* hound's-tooth

piédestal, -aux [pjedɛstal, -o] *nm* pedestal

pied-noir *(pl* **pieds-noirs)** [pjenwar] *nmf Fam* = French settler in North Africa

piège [pjɛʒ] *nm aussi Fig* trap; **tendre un p. (à)** to set a trap (for); **prendre un animal au p.** to catch an animal in a trap; **tomber dans un p.** to fall into a trap; *très Fam* **p. à cons** con

piéger [59] [pjeʒe] *vt* (a) *aussi Fig (attraper)* to trap; **se faire p.** to be trapped; **se laisser p.** to fall into a trap (b) *(placer une bombe dans)* to booby-trap; **colis piégé** parcel bomb; **lettre piégée** letter bomb; **voiture piégée** car bomb

Piémont [pjemɔ̃] *nm* **le P.** Piedmont

piémontais, -e [pjemɔ̃tɛ, -ɛz] **1** *adj* Piedmontese
2 *nmf* **P.** Piedmontese
3 *nm (langue)* Piedmontese

pierraille [pjɛraj] *nf* loose stones

pierre [pjɛr] *nf* (a) *(matière, caillou)* stone; *(rocher)* rock; **mur de p.** stone wall; **maison en p.** stone(-built) house; **investir dans la p.** to invest in bricks and mortar; **poser la**

première p. à qch to lay the foundation stone for sth; *Fig*
jeter la p. à qn to reproach sb; *Fig* **faire d'une p.**
deux
coups to kill two birds with one stone; **c'est être**
malheureux comme les pierres to be extremely
unhappy; *Prov* **p. qui roule n'amasse pas mousse** a
rolling stone gathers no moss; **p. d'achoppement**
stumbling block; *aussi Fig* **p. angulaire** cornerstone; **p. à**
briquet flint *(for lighter)*; **p. philosophale** philosopher's
stone; **p. ponce** pumice stone; **p. de taille** dressed stone;
p. tombale tombstone; *aussi Fig* **p. de touche** touchstone
(b) *(en bijouterie)* stone; **p. précieuse** precious stone, gem;
p. fine *ou* **semi-précieuse** semi-precious stone

pierreries [pjɛrəri] *nfpl* precious stones, gems

pierreux, -euse [pjɛrø, -øz] *adj (sol, route)* stony; *(lit de*
rivière) gravelly

piétaille [pjetaj] *nf Péj* rank and file

piété [pjete] *nf* **(a)** *(ferveur religieuse)* piety **(b)** *(affection)* **p.**
filiale filial devotion

piétinement [pjetinmɑ̃] *nm (bruit)* stamping, *(marche*
sur place) standing around; *Fig (stagnation)* lack of progress

piétiner [pjetine] **1** *vt* **p. qch** *(en trépignant)* to stamp on
sth; *(en marchant)* to trample on sth; *(écraser)* to trample sth
underfoot; **ils sont morts piétinés par la foule** they were
trampled to death by the crowd

2 *vi* **(a) p. d'impatience** to stamp (one's feet) impatiently
(b) *(faire du surplace)* to stand around; *Fig* to make no
progress

piéton, -onne [pjetɔ̃, -ɔn] **1** *nm,f* pedestrian
2 *adj* **rue piétonne** pedestrianized street; **zone piétonne**
pedestrian precinct

piétonnier, -ère [pjetɔnje, -ɛr] *adj* pedestrian; **rue**
piétonnière pedestrianized street; **zone piétonnière**
pedestrian precinct

piètre [pjɛtr] *adj Litt (compagnon)* wretched; *(excuse)*
paltry; *(consolation)* small

pieu¹, -x [pjø] *nm (piquet)* stake

pieu², x *nm Fam (lit)* bed; **se mettre au p., aller au p.** to
hit the sack

pieuter [pjøte] **se pieuter** *vpr Fam* to hit the sack

pieuvre [pjœvr] *nf* octopus

pieux, -euse [pjø, -øz] *adj* pious, devout

pif [pif] *nm Fam (nez)* conk; *Fig* **faire qch au p.** to do sth by
guesswork; **répondre au p.** to hazard a guess; **au p., je**
dirais... at a rough guess, I'd say...

pif(f)er [pife] *vt Fam* **je ne peux pas le p.** I can't stomach
him

pifomètre [pifɔmɛtr] *nm Fam* **faire qch au p.** to do sth by
guesswork; **répondre au p.** to hazard a guess; **au p., je**
dirais... at a rough guess, I'd say...

pige [piʒ] *nf* **(a)** *(article)* freelance contribution; **faire des**
piges to do freelance work **(b)** *Fam (année)* **elle a 40 piges**
she's 40; **à 60 piges** at 60

pigeon [piʒɔ̃] *nm* **(a)** *(oiseau)* pigeon; **p. d'argile** clay
pigeon; **p. ramier** wood pigeon; **p. vole** – children's game
with forfeits; ≃ Simon says; **p. voyageur** carrier pigeon,
homing pigeon **(b)** *Fam Péj (personne)* sucker

pigeonnant, -e [piʒɔnɑ̃, -ɑ̃t] *adj Fam* **poitrine**
pigeonnante high bust; **soutien-gorge p.** uplift bra

pigeonnier [piʒɔnje] *nm* dovecot

piger [45] [piʒe] *Fam* **1** *vt* to get; **ne rien p.** à qch *(maths,*
anglais) not to have a clue about sth; **je n'ai rien pigé à ce**
qu'il a dit I didn't get any of what he said
2 *vi* to get it

pigiste [piʒist] *nmf* freelance journalist

pigment [pigmɑ̃] *nm* pigment

pigmentation [pigmɑ̃tasjɔ̃] *nf* pigmentation

pignon¹ [piɲɔ̃] *nm (de mur)* gable; **avoir p. sur rue** to be
of some standing

pignon² *nm (petite roue)* pinion

pignon³ *nm (graine)* pine nut

pilage [pilaʒ] *nm* crushing

pile¹ [pil] *nf* **(a)** *(tas)* pile; **en p.** in a pile **(b) p. (électrique)**
battery; **marcher avec des piles** to work off batteries; **p.**
atomique atomic pile

pile² *nf (d'une pièce)* reverse; **p. ou face?** heads or tails?;
tirer à p. ou face to toss for it
2 *adv Fam* **s'arrêter p.** to stop dead; **tomber p.** to come at
just the right time; **à sept heures p.** at seven (o'clock) on
the dot; **nous étions p. dix à table** there were exactly ten
of us at the table; **elle est arrivée p. le même jour que moi**
she arrived on exactly the same day as I did

piler [pile] **1** *vt* **(a)** *(broyer)* to crush; *(amandes)* to grind **(b)**
Fam (battre) to thrash
2 *vi Fam* to slam on the brakes

pileux, -euse [pilø, -øz] *adj* hair, **système p.** body
hair

pilier [pilje] *nm* **(a)** *(colonne)* pillar **(b)** *(au rugby)* prop
(forward) **(c)** *Fam Péj* **c'est un p. de bar** he's always
propping up the bar

pillage [pijaʒ] *nm* pillaging, looting; *(lors d'une émeute)*
looting

pillard, -e [pijar, -ard] **1** *adj* pillaging, looting; *(lors d'une*
émeute) looting
2 *nm,f* pillager; *(lors d'une émeute)* looter

piller [pije] *vt* to pillage, to loot; *(lors d'une émeute)* to loot

pilleur, -euse [pijœr, -øz] *nm,f* pillager; *(lors d'une*
émeute) looter; **p. d'épaves** looter of wrecks

pilon [pilɔ̃] *nm* **(a)** *(de pharmacien)* pestle; *Fig* **mettre un**
livre au p. to pulp a book **(b)** *(de poulet)* drumstick **(c)**
(jambe de bois) wooden leg

pilonnage [pilɔnaʒ] *nm (bombardement)* bombardment

pilonner [pilɔne] *vt (bombarder)* to bombard

pilori [pilɔri] *nm* pillory; *aussi Fig* **mettre qn au p.** to
pillory sb

pilosité [pilozite] *nf* hairiness

pilotage [pilɔtaʒ] *nm* **(a)** *(d'un navire, d'un avion)* piloting;
p. automatique automatic piloting **(b)** *Ordinat* control

pilote [pilɔt] **1** *nm* **(a)** *(de navire, d'avion)* pilot; *(de voiture de*
course) driver; *(de moto de course)* rider; *Fig* **servir de p.** à qn
to show sb round; **p. automatique** automatic pilot,
autopilot; **p. de chasse** fighter pilot; **p. d'essai** test pilot;
p. de ligne airline pilot **(b)** *Ordinat* driver; **p. d'affichage**
display driver; **p. d'imprimante** printer driver
2 *adj* **installation(-)p.** pilot plant; **université(-)p.**
experimental university

piloter [pilɔte] *vt* **(a)** *(navire)* to pilot; *(avion)* to pilot, to fly;
(voiture) to drive; *(moto)* to ride; *Fig (projet)* to be in charge
of; *(touriste)* to show round **(b)** *Ordinat* to drive; **piloté par**
menu menu-driven

pilotis [pilɔti] *nmpl* stilts

pilule [pilyl] *nf* pill, tablet; **la p.** *(contraceptif)* the pill;
prendre la p. to be on the pill; **p. abortive** abortion pill; **p.**
du lendemain morning-after pill

pimbêche [pɛ̃bɛʃ] **1** *nf (fille)* stuck-up girl; *(femme)* stuck-
up woman
2 *adj* stuck-up

piment [pimɑ̃] *nm* **(a)** *(piquant)* chilli; **p. doux** (sweet)
pepper **(b)** *Fig* spice

pimenter [pimɑ̃te] *vt aussi Fig* to spice up

pimpant, -e [pɛ̃pɑ̃, -ɑ̃t] *adj* smart

pin [pɛ̃] *nm* pine; **p. maritime** maritime pine; **p. parasol** umbrella pine; **p. sylvestre** Scots pine

pinacle [pinakl] *nm* être au p. to be at the top; **porter qn au p.** to praise sb to the skies

pinailler [pinaje] *vi Fam* to nitpick (**sur** over)

pinailleur, -euse [pinajœr, -øz] *Fam* **1** *adj* nitpicking **2** *nm,f* nitpicker

pinard [pinar] *nm Fam* wine

pince [pɛ̃s] *nf* (**a**) *(outil)* pliers; *(de forgeron)* tongs; **p. à cheveux** hair clip; **p. crocodile** crocodile clip; **p. à épiler** tweezers; **p. à linge** clothes peg; **p. à sucre** sugar tongs; **p. à vélo** bicycle clip (**b**) *(des crustacés)* pincer, claw (**c**) *(sur un vêtement)* dart (**d**) *Fam* **serrer la p. à qn** to shake hands with sb (**e**) *Fam* **à pinces** on foot

pincé, -e [pɛ̃se] *adj (air)* stiff, starchy; *(sourire)* tight-lipped; *(lèvres)* pursed

pinceau, -x [pɛ̃so] *nm (brosse)* brush, paintbrush; **avoir un bon coup de p.** to be a good painter

pincée [pɛ̃se] *nf* pinch

pincement [pɛ̃smɑ̃] *nm* (**a**) **avoir un p. au cœur** *(être ému)* to feel a pang of sadness (**b**) *(fait de pincer)* pinching; *(des cordes d'un instrument)* plucking

pince-monseigneur *(pl* pinces-monseigneur) [pɛ̃smɔ̃sɛɲœr] *nf* jemmy

pince-nez [pɛ̃sne] *nm inv* pince-nez

pincer [16] [pɛ̃se] **1** *vt* (**a**) *(serrer)* to pinch, to nip; *(lèvres)* to purse; *(cordes d'un instrument)* to pluck (**b**) *Fam (attraper)* to catch; **se faire p.** to get caught (**c**) *Fam* **en p. pour qn** to be crazy about sb (**d**) *Fam* **ça pince** it's freezing **2 se pincer** *vpr* **se p. le doigt** to catch one's finger; **se p. le nez** to hold one's nose

pince-sans-rire [pɛ̃sɑ̃rir] **1** *nmf inv* person with a dry sense of humour **2** *adj inv* dry, deadpan

pincette [pɛ̃sɛt] *nf (petite pince)* tweezers; **pincettes** *(à feu)* (fire) tongs; *Fig* **il n'est pas à prendre avec des pincettes** he's like a bear with a sore head

pinçon [pɛ̃sɔ̃] *nm* pinch mark

pinède [pinɛd] *nf* pine wood

pingouin [pɛ̃gwɛ̃] *nm* auk; *(manchot)* penguin

ping-pong [piŋpɔ̃g] *nm* table tennis, Ping-Pong®

pingre [pɛ̃gr] *adj* stingy

pingrerie [pɛ̃grəri] *nf* stinginess

pin's [pinz] *nm inv* badge

pinson [pɛ̃sɔ̃] *nm* chaffinch

pintade [pɛ̃tad] *nf* guinea fowl

pinte [pɛ̃t] *nf (ancienne mesure)* pint *(0.93 litres)*; *(au Royaume-Uni, aux États-Unis)* pint; *Can* quart

pinter [pɛ̃te] *très Fam* **1** *vi* to booze **2 se pinter** *vpr* to get wasted

pin-up [pinœp] *nf inv* pin-up

pioche [pjɔʃ] *nf* (**a**) *(outil)* pick, pickaxe (**b**) *(aux cartes, aux dominos)* stock, pile

piocher [pjɔʃe] **1** *vt (creuser)* to dig *(with a pick)* **2** *vi (aux cartes, aux dominos)* to pick up; *Fig* **p. dans qch** *(tas)* to plunge one's hand into sth; *(économies, réserves)* to dip into sth

piolet [pjɔlɛ] *nm* ice axe

pion¹ [pjɔ̃] *nm (de jeu de société)* piece; *(aux échecs)* pawn; *(aux dames) Br* draught, *Am* checker; *Fig* **n'être qu'un p.** *(sur l'échiquier)* to be only a pawn in the game

pion², pionne [pjɔ̃, pjɔn] *nm,f Fam (surveillant)* supervisor *(paid to supervise pupils outside class hours)*

pioncer [16] [pjɔ̃se] *vi Fam* to sleep

pionnier, -ère [pjɔnje, -ɛr] *nm,f aussi Fig* pioneer

pipe [pip] *nf* (**a**) *(de fumeur)* pipe; *Fam Fig* **casser sa p.** to kick the bucket (**b**) *Vulg* **faire** *ou* **tailler une p. à qn** to give sb a blowjob

pipeau, -x [pipo] *nm Mus* (reed) pipe; *Fam* **c'est du p.** it's all claptrap

pipelette [piplɛt] *nf Fam* gossip

pipeline, pipe-line *(pl* pipe-lines) [piplin, pajplajn] *nm* pipeline

piper [pipe] *vt* (**a**) *(dés)* to load; *(cartes)* to mark; *Fig* **les dés sont pipés** the dice are loaded (**b**) **ne pas p. (mot)** to keep mum

pipette [pipɛt] *nf* pipette

pipi [pipi] *nm Fam* pee; **faire p.** to pee; **faire p. au lit** to wet the bed; *Fam Péj* **c'est du p. de chat** *(boisson)* it's dishwater

piquant, -e [pikɑ̃, ɑ̃t] **1** *adj* (**a**) *(au goût)* spicy, hot; *(moutarde)* hot (**b**) *(plante)* prickly, thorny; *(barbe)* prickly; *(vent)* biting (**c**) *Fig (détail, style, situation)* piquant; *(histoire)* spicy; **une petite brune piquante** a striking little brunette **2** *nm* (**a**) *(d'une plante)* thorn; *(d'un porc-épic, d'un hérisson)* spine; *(de barbelé)* spike, barb (**b**) *(d'un style, d'une situation)* piquancy; *(d'une histoire)* spice; **avoir du p.** *(femme)* to be striking

pique¹ [pik] **1** *nf (arme)* pike; *(d'un picador)* lance **2** *nm (carte)* spade; *(couleur)* spades

pique² *nf (méchanceté)* spiteful remark; **envoyer** *ou* **lancer des piques à qn** to have a go at sb

piqué, -e [pike] **1** *adj* (**a**) *(bois)* wormeaten; *(livre)* foxed; *(miroir)* tarnished; *(métal)* pitted; *Fam* **une histoire/angine pas piquée des hannetons** *ou* **des vers** one heck of a story/sore throat (**c**) *Fam (fou)* bonkers (**d**) *Mus (note)* staccato **2** *nm* (**a**) *Av* **descente en p.** nose dive (**b**) *(tissu)* piqué

pique-assiette *(pl* pique-assiettes) [pikasjɛt] *nmf Fam* scrounger, sponger

pique-feu [pikfø] *nm inv* poker

pique-nique *(pl* pique-niques) [piknik] *nm* picnic; **faire un p.** to have a picnic

pique-niquer [piknike] *vi* to have a picnic, to picnic

piquer [pike] **1** *vt* (**a**) *(avec une pointe)* to prick; *(sujet: guêpe)* to sting; *(sujet: puce, moustique)* to bite; *(cheval)* to spur on; *(bœuf)* to goad; **la fumée me pique les yeux** the smoke is making my eyes sting; **ça me pique la gorge/le nez** it tickles my throat/nose (**b**) *Fam (faire une piqûre à)* **p. qn** to give sb an injection; **p. un chien** to put a dog down, to put a dog to sleep (**c**) *Fam (voler)* to pinch, *Br* to nick (**à** from); **je me suis fait p. mon stylo** my pen got pinched (**d**) *(coudre)* to stitch (**e**) *(enfoncer)* to stick (**dans** into) (**f**) *Fam* **p. un cent mètres** to sprint off; **p. une crise** to throw a fit; **p. une tête** to dive (**g**) *(nager)* **p. qn au vif** to cut sb to the quick (**h**) *(exciter)* **p. la curiosité de qn** to arouse *or* excite sb's curiosity (**i**) *(sujet: acide, vers)* to eat into; *(sujet: humidité)* to spot, to mark (**j**) *Culin* **p. qch d'ail** to stick garlic into sth **2** *vi* (**a**) *Av* **p. (du nez)** to nosedive; *Fig* **p. du nez** *(s'assoupir)* to nod off; *(baisser les yeux)* to look down (**b**) *(plat)* to be spicy *or* hot; *(vin)* to be sour (**c**) *(guêpe)* to sting; *(puce, moustique)* to bite; *(plante)* to be prickly; **tu piques!** *(à un homme mal rasé)* you're all bristly! **3 se piquer** *vpr* (**a**) *(se blesser)* to prick oneself; **se p. le doigt** to prick one's finger (**b**) *(se faire une piqûre)* to give oneself an injection; *Fam (se droguer)* to shoot up (**c**) *(se vexer)* to take offence (**d**) *(vin)* to (turn) sour (**e**) *(locutions)* **se p. au jeu** to get into it; *Litt* **se p. de faire qch** to pride oneself on doing sth

piquet [pikɛ] *nm* (**a**) *(pieu)* stake, post; *(de tente)* peg (**b**)

Vieilli Scol **mettre** *ou* **envoyer qn au p.** to send sb to stand in the corner **(c) p. de grève** picket

piquette [pikɛt] *nf* **(a)** *Péj (vin)* cheap wine **(b)** *Fam (défaite)* **prendre une** *ou* **la p.** to get a hammering

piqûre [pikyr] *nf* **(a)** *(de guêpe)* sting; *(de puce, de moustique)* bite; **p. d'épingle** pinprick **(b)** *Méd* injection, shot; **faire une p. à qn** to give sb an injection **(c) piqûres** *(d'un tissu, du cuir)* stitching **(d)** *(de rouille, de moisi)* spot, speck

piranha [pirana] *nm* piranha

piratage [pirataʒ] *nm* pirating; **p. informatique** hacking

pirate [pirat] **1** *nm* **(a)** *(des mers)* pirate; **p. de l'air** hijacker, skyjacker; **p. informatique** hacker **(b)** *(escroc)* crook
2 *adj (radio, enregistrement)* pirate

pirater [pirate] *vt (enregistrement, cassette)* to pirate; *Ordinat* to hack into

piraterie [piratri] *nf* **(a)** *(sur les mers)* piracy **(b)** *Fig (escroquerie)* swindling

pire [pir] **1** *adj* **(a)** *(comparatif)* worse; **c'est de p. en p.** it's getting worse and worse **(b)** *(superlatif)* worst
2 *nm* **le p., c'est que...** the worst thing about it is...; **craindre le/s'attendre au p.** to fear/to expect the worst; **au p.** if the worst comes to the worst...

pirogue [pirɔg] *nf* dugout (canoe)

pirouette [pirwɛt] *nf (tour sur soi-même)* pirouette; *(saut périlleux)* somersault; *Fig (dérobade)* flippant answer

pis¹ [pi] *nm (mamelle)* udder

pis² **1** *adv* **aller de mal en p.** to go from bad to worse
2 *adj Litt* worse
3 *nm* **(a)** *Litt (comparatif)* worse; **il y a p.** there is/are worse **(b)** *Litt (superlatif)* worst; **au p.** if the worst comes to the worst, **au p. aller** at the very worst **(c) dire p. que pendre de qn** to call sb every name under the sun

pis-aller [pizale] *nm inv* stopgap (solution)

pisciculture [pisikyltyr] *nf* fish farming

piscine [pisin] *nf* (swimming) pool; **p. couverte/en plein air** indoor/outdoor pool

Pise [piz] *n* Pisa

pisse [pis] *nf très Fam* piss, pee

pisse-froid [pisfrwa] *nm inv Fam* wet blanket

pissenlit [pisɑ̃li] *nm* dandelion; *Fam* **manger les pissenlits par la racine** to be pushing up the daisies

pisser [pise] **1** *vi* **(a)** *très Fam (uriner)* to piss; **c'est comme si je pissais dans un violon** it's like pissing in the wind; **laisse p.!** forget it!; **c'était à p. de rire** we were wetting ourselves **(b)** *Fam (fuir)* to leak
2 *vt* **(a)** *très Fam* **p. du sang** to piss blood **(b)** *Fam* **son bras pissait le sang** blood was pouring from his/her arm

pisseux, -euse [pisø, -øz] *adj Fam (couleur)* washed out

pissotière [pisɔtjɛr] *nf Fam* (public) urinal

pistache [pistaʃ] **1** *nf (graine)* pistachio (nut); **glace à la p.** pistachio ice cream
2 *adj inv (couleur)* pistachio (green)

piste [pist] *nf* **(a)** *(trace)* track, trail; *(indices)* lead; **être sur la p. de qn** to be on sb's track; **suivre une fausse p.** to be on the wrong track **(b)** *Sp* track; *(de courses de chevaux)* Br racecourse, *Am* racetrack; *(de course automobile)* racetrack; *(de ski)* run, piste; *(de cirque)* ring; **p. artificielle** *(de ski)* artificial *or* dry ski slope; **p. de danse** dance floor **(c)** *Av* runway; **p. d'atterrissage** landing strip; *(dans la brousse, dans la forêt)* airstrip **(d)** *(chemin)* track, trail; **p. cyclable** cycle path **(e)** *(de magnétophone, de disque)* track; *Ordinat* **p. d'amorçage** boot track; *Ordinat* **p. magnétique** magnetic stripe

pister [piste] *vt (animal)* to track; *(personne)* to tail

pistil [pistil] *nm Bot* pistil

pistolet [pistɔlɛ] *nm* **(a)** *(arme à feu)* pistol, gun; **p. à air comprimé** air pistol; **p. à eau** water pistol **(b)** *(à peinture)* paint gun

pistolet-mitrailleur *(pl* pistolets-mitrailleurs*)* [pistɔlɛmitrajœr] *nm* submachine-gun

piston [pistɔ̃] *nm* **(a)** *Tech* piston **(b)** *Fam Fig (recommandation)* string-pulling; **il a eu la place par p.** someone pulled some strings to get him the job **(c)** *(d'instrument à vent)* valve

pistonner [pistɔne] *vt Fam* to pull strings for; **elle s'est fait p.** she got someone to pull strings for her

pistou [pistu] *nm (sauce)* pesto; *(soupe)* vegetable soup with pesto

pitance [pitɑ̃s] *nf Vieilli (nourriture)* sustenance

pit-bull *(pl* pit-bulls*)* [pitbul] *nm* pit bull (terrier)

piteux, -euse [pitø, -øz] *adj* **(a)** *(mauvais) (résultat)* poor, pitiful; **en p. état** in a sorry state **(b)** *(honteux)* shamefaced

pithiviers [pitivje] *nm Culin* – cake made of puff pastry containing rum and almond-flavoured cream

pitié [pitje] *nf* **(a)** *(compassion)* pity; **avoir p. de qn** to pity sb; **il me faisait p.** I felt sorry for him; **faire p. (à voir)** to be a pitiful sight; **être sans p.** to be ruthless; **(par) p.!** *(pour demander grâce)* (have) mercy!; *(exprime l'agacement)* for pity's sake! **(b)** *(tristesse)* **quelle p.!** what a terrible shame!

piton [pitɔ̃] *nm* **(a)** *Tech* eye bolt; *(d'alpiniste)* piton **(b)** *(sommet)* **p. (rocheux)** (rocky) peak

pitoyable [pitwajabl] *adj* **(a)** *(digne de pitié)* pitiful **(b)** *Péj (excuse, plaisanterie)* pathetic

pitre [pitr] *nm* clown; **faire le p.** to clown around

pitrerie [pitrəri] *nf* piece of clowning; **pitreries** clowning

pittoresque [pitɔrɛsk] *adj (lieu)* picturesque; *(description, style)* vivid

pivert [pivɛr] *nm* green woodpecker

pivoine [pivwan] *nf* peony

pivot [pivo] *nm* **(a)** *(axe)* pivot; *(de levier)* fulcrum; *(de compas, de boussole)* centre pin; *(en dentisterie)* post **(b)** *Fig (d'un drame, d'une argumentation)* pivot **(c)** *(au basket)* pivot, post

pivotant, -e [pivotɑ̃, -ɑ̃t] *adj (grue, lampe)* swivelling; *(présentoir)* revolving

pivoter [pivote] *vi* to pivot, to swivel **(sur** on); **faire p. qch** to swivel sth round

pixel [piksɛl] *nm Ordinat* pixel

pixélisé, -e [pikselize] *adj Ordinat* bit-mapped

pizza [pidza] *nf* pizza

pizzeria [pidzerja] *nf* pizzeria

PJ [peʒi] *nf Fam (abrév* police judiciaire*)* Br ≃ CID, *Am* ≃ FBI

placage [plakaʒ] *nm* **(a)** *(bois)* veneer; *(métal)* plating **(b)** *(au rugby)* tackle

placard [plakar] *nm* **(a)** *(armoire)* cupboard; *Fam Fig* **mettre qn au p.** to sideline sb; *Fam Fig* **mettre qch au p.** to put sth on ice, to shelve sth **(b)** *(affiche)* poster

placarder [plakarde] *vt (affiche)* to stick up, to put up; **p. un mur d'affiches** to cover a wall with posters

place [plas] *nf* **(a)** *(endroit, rôle)* place; **changer qch de p.** to move sth; *Fig* **se mettre à la p. de qn** to put oneself in sb's position; **mettre qch en p.** to put sth in place; **être en p.** *(objet)* to be in place; *(au pouvoir)* to be in office; **les gens en p.** people in high places; *Fig* **remettre qn à sa p.** to put sb in his/her place; **il ne tient pas en p.** he can't keep still; **à la p. de qn** *(au lieu de)* instead of sb; **à votre p....** if I were you...; **sur p.** on the spot; **faire p. nette** to have a clearout; **p. de parking** parking place *or* space **(b)** *(espace)* room, space; **prendre beaucoup de p.** to take up a lot of room *or* space; **faire de la p. à qn** to make room for sb; *Fig* **faire p. à qn/qch** to make way for sb/sth **(c)** *(siège)* seat; **(voiture à) deux/cinq places** two-/five-seater (car); **prendre p.** to take a seat; **p. assise** seat; **p. debout** *(billet)* standing ticket; **la p.** du mort the passenger seat **(d)** *(poste)* job, post **(e)** *(lieu public)* square; **p. du marché** market place **(f)** *(rang)* place **(g)** *Mil* **p. forte** fortified town **(h)** *Com & Fin* market; **sur la p. de Paris** on the Paris market; **p. financière** financial market

placé, -e [plase] *adj* **être bien/mal p.** pour faire qch to be well/badly placed to do sth

placebo [plasebo] *nm* placebo

placement [plasmɑ̃] *nm* **(a)** *(d'argent)* investment; **faire des placements** to invest (money) **(b)** *(à un emploi)* placement, placing

placenta [plasɛ̃ta] *nm* placenta

placer [16] [plase] **1** *vt* **(a)** *(mettre à sa place)* to place, to put; *(faire asseoir)* to seat **(b)** *(procurer un emploi à)* to find a job for, to place; **p. qn comme apprenti chez qn** to apprentice sb to sb **(c)** *(vendre)* to sell **(d)** *(dans la conversation)* to get in; *Fam* **avec elle, on ne peut pas en p. une!** you can't get a word in edgeways with her! **(e)** *(argent)* to invest **2 se placer** *vpr* **(a)** *(debout)* to stand; *(assis)* to sit **(b)** **se p. sous la protection de qn** to place oneself under sb's protection; **il faut se p. dans son optique** you have to look at things from her point of view **(c)** *(trouver un emploi)* to find a job

placide [plasid] *adj* placid, calm

placoter [plakɔte] *vi Can Fam* to chat

plafond [plafɔ̃] *nm aussi Fig* ceiling; **être haut/bas de p.** to have a high/low ceiling; **prix/vitesse p.** maximum price/speed

plafonner [plafɔne] *vi (quantité, salaire)* to have reached a ceiling (**à** of)

plafonnier [plafɔnje] *nm* ceiling light

plage [plaʒ] *nf* **(a)** *(grève)* beach; **aller en vacances à la p.** to go on holiday to the seaside; **p. de sable/de galets** sandy/pebble beach **(b)** *(surface)* area **(c)** *(dans un emploi du temps, à la télé, à la radio)* slot; **p. horaire** time slot **(d)** *(d'un disque)* track **(e)** **p. arrière** *(d'une voiture)* back shelf

plagiaire [plaʒjɛr] *nmf* plagiarist

plagiat [plaʒja] *nm* plagiarism

plagier [66] [plaʒje] *vt* to plagiarize

plaid [plɛd] *nm* travelling rug

plaider [plede] **1** *vt* to plead; **p. coupable/non coupable** to plead guilty/not guilty; **p. la cause de qn** *Jur* to plead sb's case; *Fig* to plead sb's cause **2** *vi (avocat)* to plead; **p. pour/contre qn** to defend/prosecute sb; *Fig* **p. en faveur de qn/qch** to speak for sb/sth, to defend sb/sth

plaidoirie [pledwari] *nf Jur* speech for the defence

plaidoyer [pledwaje] *nm Jur* speech for the defence; *Fig* plea

plaie [plɛ] *nf* **(a)** *aussi Fig* wound **(b)** *(fléau)* affliction, scourge; *(personne, chose)* pest, nuisance

plaignant, -e [plɛɲɑ̃, -ɑ̃t] *nm,f Jur* plaintiff

plaindre [23] [plɛ̃dr] **1** *vt* to pity, to feel sorry for; **je vous plains de voyager dans ces conditions** I feel sorry for you having to travel in these conditions; **elle n'est pas à p.** she's got nothing to worry about **2 se plaindre** *vpr* **(a)** *(protester)* to complain; **se p. de** to complain about; *(douleur)* to complain of **(b)** *(gémir)* to moan

plaine [plɛn] *nf* plain

plain-pied [plɛ̃pje] **de plain-pied** *adv (pièce)* on the same level (**avec** as); *(maison)* single-storey

plainte [plɛ̃t] *nf* **(a)** *(protestation)* complaint **(b)** *(gémissement)* moan **(c)** *Jur* complaint; **porter p. contre qn** (**auprès de**) to lodge a complaint against sb (with); **p. contre X** complaint against person or persons unknown

plaintif, -ive [plɛ̃tif, -iv] *adj* plaintive

plaire [55a] [plɛr] **1** *vi* **(a)** *(être apprécié)* **cet homme me plaît** I like this man; **ce livre m'a plu** I liked *or* enjoyed the book; **cette offre devrait lui p.** the offer should appeal to him; **ça plaît beaucoup** it's very popular; **je fais ce qui me plaît** I do whatever I want; **que cela te plaise ou non** whether you like it or not **(b)** *(se rendre agréable)* to please; **rien à faire, elle ne plaît pas** no matter what she does, no one finds her attractive **2** *v impersonnel* **s'il te/vous plaît** please; **et pas n'importe qui, s'il vous plaît** and not just anybody, if you please; **comme il vous plaira** just as you like **3 se plaire** *vpr* **(a)** *(soi-même)* **elle se plaît dans cette robe** she likes herself in that dress **(b)** *(l'un l'autre)* to like each other **(c)** *(se trouver bien)* **je me plais beaucoup à Lille** I'm very happy in Lille; **se p. à faire qch** to enjoy *or* like doing sth

plaisance [plɛzɑ̃s] *nf* **la (navigation de) p.** boating

plaisancier, -ère [plɛzɑ̃sje, -ɛr] *nm,f* (amateur) yachtsman, *f* yachtswoman

plaisant, -e [plɛzɑ̃, -ɑ̃t] **1** *adj* **(a)** *(agréable)* pleasant, agreeable **(b)** *(drôle)* funny, amusing **2** *nm* **mauvais p.** malicious joker

plaisanter [plɛzɑ̃te] **1** *vi* to joke; **dire qch en plaisantant** to say sth as a joke; **vous plaisantez!** you're joking!; **on ne plaisante pas avec la santé** health is a serious matter **2** *vt* to tease, to poke fun at (**sur** about)

plaisanterie [plɛzɑ̃tri] *nf (acte, propos)* joke; **elle ne comprend pas la p.** she can't take a joke; **par p.** for a joke; **tourner qch en p.** to make a joke out of sth; **les plaisanteries les plus courtes sont les meilleures** brevity is the soul of wit

plaisantin [plɛzɑ̃tɛ̃] *nm* joker

plaise *etc voir* **plaire**

plaisir [plɛzir] *nm* **(a)** *(sensation agréable)* pleasure; **j'ai le p. de vous apprendre que…** I'm pleased to be able to tell you that…; **faire qch pour le p.** to do sth for fun; *Ironique* **je vous souhaite bien du p.!** the best of luck!; **ça m'a fait p. de revoir** I was pleased to see you again; **ça me ferait p. que tu viennes** I'd be pleased if you came; **fais-moi p., viens danser** do me a favour, come and dance; **si cela peut te faire p.** if it makes you happy; **il va se faire un p. de téléphoner demain** he'll be only too pleased to phone my tomorrow; **cela fait p. à voir** it's good to see; **prendre p. à qch/à faire qch** to enjoy sth/doing sth; **les plaisirs de la table** fine food and wine **(b)** *(distraction)* pleasure; **c'est son plus grand p.** it's his greatest pleasure

plan¹, -e [plɑ̃, plɑ̃] **1** *adj (terrain, surface)* flat; *Math* plane **2** *nm* **(a)** *Math* plane **(b)** *(surface)* **p. de cuisson** hob; **p. d'eau** lake; **p. incliné** inclined plane; **p. de travail** *(d'une cuisine)* worktop **(c)** *Cin, Phot & Fig* **au premier p.** in the foreground; **au second p.** in the background; **un artiste de premier p.** a leading artist; **sur le même p. (que)** on the same level (as); **sur le p. politique/économique** from a political/an economic point of view; **gros p.** close-up; **en gros p.** in close-up

plan² *nm* **(a)** *(relevé)* plan; *(carte) (de ville)* map; **p. d'occupation des sols** land-use map **(b)** *(projet)* plan; *Fam* **un bon p.** *(combine)* a good trick; **p. social** = corporate restructuring plan, usually involving job losses **(c)** *(d'un roman, d'un devoir)* plan, framework **(d)** *Fin* **p. d'épargne** savings plan; **p. d'épargne en actions** investment trust; **p. d'épargne-logement** *Br* ≃ building society account, *Am*

≈ savings and loan association account; **p. d'épargne-retraite** personal pension plan

plan³ *nm Fam* **laisser qn en p.** to leave sb in the lurch; **tout laisser en p.** to drop everything

planant, -e [plɑ̃nɑ̃, ɑ̃t] *adj Fam* mind-blowing

planche [plɑ̃ʃ] *nf* (**a**) *(pièce de bois)* plank; *(plus large)* board; **faire la p.** *(flotter)* to float on one's back; *Fam* **c'est une vraie p. à pain** she's as flat as a pancake; **p. à découper** chopping board; **p. à dessin** drawing board; **p. à repasser** ironing board; **p. de salut** last hope (**b**) *Th* **monter sur les planches** to go on the stage, to tread the boards (**c**) *(d'imprimerie, de gravure)* plate, block (**d**) *Sp* **p. (de surf)** surfboard; **p. (à voile)** windsurfer; *Can* **p. à neige** snowboard; **p. à roulettes** skateboard; **faire de la p. à roulettes** to skateboard; **faire de la p. à voile** to go windsurfing

plancher¹ [plɑ̃ʃe] *nm* (**a**) *(sol)* floor; *Fam* **le p. des vaches** dry land, terra firma; *Fig* **mettre le pied au p.** to put one's foot down (**b**) *Fig (minimum)* minimum; *prix* **p.** bottom price

plancher² **1** *vi Fam Scol* to have an exam **2 plancher sur** *vt ind* **p. sur un problème** to work on a problem

plancton [plɑ̃ktɔ̃] *nm* plankton

plané [plane] *adj m voir* **vol**

planer [plane] *vi* (**a**) *(oiseau, planeur)* to glide; *(brume, fumée)* to hang; *Fig* **p. sur qn/qch** *(danger)* to hang over sb/sth (**b**) *Fam (se sentir bien)* to be floating on air, to be on a high; *(après s'être drogué)* to be high; *(rêver)* to dream

planétaire [planeter] *adj* (**a**) *Astron* planetary (**b**) *(expansion, action)* worldwide

planétarium [planetarjɔm] *nm* planetarium

planète [planɛt] *nf* planet

planeur [plançœr] *nm (avion)* glider

planification [planifikasjɔ̃] *nf Écon* planning

planifier [66] [planifje] *vt* to plan

planisphère [planisfɛr] *nm* planisphere

planning [planiŋ] *nm* schedule; **p. familial** family planning; *(lieu)* family planning clinic

planque [plɑ̃k] *nf Fam* (**a**) *(d'un gangster)* hideout; *(pour un butin)* hiding place (**b**) *(travail facile)* cushy job

planqué, -e [plɑ̃ke] *nm,f Fam* person with an easy job; *Mil* draft dodger

planquer [plɑ̃ke] *Fam* **1** *vt* to hide **2 se planquer** *vpr* to hide

plant [plɑ̃] *nm (d'arbre)* sapling; *(de plante)* seedling

plantaire [plɑ̃tɛr] *adj Anat* plantar

plantation [plɑ̃tasjɔ̃] *nf (exploitation agricole)* plantation

plante¹ [plɑ̃t] *nf* **p. du pied** sole (of the foot)

plante² *nf (végétal)* plant; *Fam Fig* **une belle p.** *(femme)* a voluptuous woman; **p. d'appartement** house plant; **p. grasse** succulent (plant); **p. potagère** plant grown for food; **p. verte** house plant

planté, -e [plɑ̃te] *adj* (**a**) *(debout)* standing; *Fam* **rester p. (comme un piquet)** *(immobile)* to stand there doing nothing (**b**) **bien p.** *(robuste)* sturdy

planter [plɑ̃te] **1** *vt* (**a**) *(graines, fleurs, arbre)* to plant; **une colline plantée d'arbres** a hill planted with trees (**b**) *(clou)* to hammer in; *(tente)* to put up, to pitch; **p. un clou dans qch** to hammer a nail into sth; *Fig* **p. un baiser sur la joue à qn** to plant a kiss on sb's cheek (**c**) *Fam* **p. là qn** to dump sb; **il veut tout p. là** he wants to pack it all in **2 se planter** *vpr* (**a**) *(se tenir immobile)* to stand (**b**) *Fam (se tromper)* to get it wrong (**c**) *Fam (tomber)* to come a cropper (**d**) *Fam (en voiture)* to crash

planteur [plɑ̃tœr] *nm* (**a**) *(exploitant)* planter (**b**) *(cocktail)* planter's punch

plantigrade [plɑ̃tigrad] *nm Zool* plantigrade

planton [plɑ̃tɔ̃] *nm Mil* orderly

plantureux, -euse [plɑ̃tyrø, -øz] *adj (femme)* buxom; *(poitrine)* ample

plaquage [plakaʒ] = **placage** (**b**)

plaque [plak] *nf* (**a**) *(de métal)* plate, sheet, *(de marbre)* slab; *(de chocolat)* bar; *(de beurre)* pack; *(de verglas)* sheet; **p. chauffante** hotplate; **p. d'égout** manhole cover; *Fig* **p. tournante** hub, centre (**b**) *(sur une porte)* nameplate; *(commémorative)* plaque; **p. d'immatriculation** *ou* **minéralogique** *Br* number plate, *Am* license plate; **p. de rue** street sign (**c**) *(sur la peau)* patch; **p. (dentaire)** (dental) plaque (**d**) *Fam* **être à côté de la p.** to be wide of the mark

plaqué, -e [plake] **1** *adj* **p. or/argent** gold-/silver-plated **2** *nm* **p. or/argent** gold/silver plate; **montre en p. or** gold-plated watch (**b**) *(bois)* veneered wood

plaquer [plake] **1** *vt* (**a**) *(cheveux)* to plaster down; **p. qn contre un mur** to pin sb against a wall (**b**) *Fam (petit ami)* to ditch, to chuck; **tout p.** to chuck it all in (**c**) *(au rugby)* to tackle (**d**) *Mus (accord)* to play (**e**) *(bois)* to veneer; *(métal)* to plate **2 se plaquer** *vpr* **se p. au sol** to lie flat on the ground; **se p. contre un mur** to flatten oneself against a wall

plaquette [plakɛt] *nf* (**a**) *(de métal)* (small) plate; *(portant une inscription)* (small) plaque; *Ordinat* circuit board; *Aut* **p. de frein** brake pad (**b**) *(de chocolat)* bar; *(de beurre)* pack (**c**) *(petit livre)* booklet (**d**) *Méd* **plaquettes** (blood) platelets

plasma [plasma] *nm Biol & Phys* plasma

plastic [plastik] *nm* plastic explosive

plasticage [plastikaʒ] *nm* bombing (de uf)

plastifier [66] [plastifje] *vt* to laminate

plastiquage [plastikaʒ] = **plasticage**

plastique [plastik] **1** *adj & nm* plastic **2** *nf* (**a**) *(art)* art of modelling (**b**) *(du corps)* figure

plastiquer [plastike] *vt* to bomb

plastron [plastrɔ̃] *nm* (**a**) *(de chemise)* shirt front (**b**) *(d'escrimeur)* plastron

plat, -e [pla, plat] **1** *adj* (**a**) *(sans relief)* flat, level; *(chaussure)* flat; *(mer)* smooth; *(eau)* still; *Fam* **plate comme une limande** *(femme)* as flat as a pancake (**b**) *Fig (ennuyeux)* flat, dull (**c**) **à p.** *(pneu, batterie)* flat, *Fam* **être à p.** *(épuisé)* to be run down; **mettre qch à p.** to lay sth (down) flat; *Fig* **tomber à p.** *(proposition, plaisanterie)* to fall flat; **se mettre à p. ventre** to lie face down; *Fig* **se mettre à p. ventre devant qn** to grovel to sb **2** *nm* (**a**) *(assiette)* dish; *Fig* **mettre les petits plats dans les grands** to put on a marvellous spread (**b**) *(mets)* dish; *(partie du menu)* course; *Fam* **en faire tout un p.** to make a song and dance about it; **p. cuisiné** ready meal; **p. du jour** today's special, dish of the day; **p. principal** *ou* **de résistance** main course (**c**) *(de la main, d'une épée)* flat (**d**) *(en cyclisme, en hippisme)* **sur le p.** on the flat (**e**) **faire un p.** *(en plongeant)* to do a bellyflop *Fam* **faire du p. à qn** *Br* to chat sb up, *Am* to hit on sb

platane [platan] *nm* plane tree

plateau, -x [plato] *nm* (**a**) *(plat)* tray; **p. à fromages** cheeseboard; **p. de fruits de mer** seafood platter (**b**) *(d'une balance)* pan; *(d'une platine, d'un four micro-ondes)* turntable (**c**) *Géog* plateau; **haut p.** high plateau (**d**) *TV & Cin* set (**e**) *(de vélo)* chain wheel

plateau-repas [platorǝpa] *(pl* **plateaux-repas** [platorǝpa]*) nm* meal on a tray

plate-bande [platbɑ̃d] *(pl* **plates-bandes** [platbɑ̃d]*) nf* flower bed; *Fam* **marcher sur les plates-bandes de qn** to tread on sb's toes

plate-forme (*pl* **plates-formes**) [platfɔrm] *nf* (**a**) *(surface plane)* platform; **p. pétrolière** *ou* **de forage** oil rig (**b**) *Géog* **p. continentale** continental shelf (**c**) *Ordinat* platform

platement [platmɑ̃] *adv* (**a**) *(s'exprimer, écrire)* dully (**b**) *(s'excuser)* humbly

platine¹ [platin] *nf (tourne-disque)* turntable; **p. cassettes** cassette *or* tape deck; **p. laser** CD player

platine² **1** *nm* platinum **2** *adj inv* **cheveux (blonds) p.** platinum blond hair

platiné, -e [platine] *adj* (**a**) *(recouvert de platine)* platinum-plated (**b**) *(cheveux)* platinum blond; **une blonde platinée** a platinum blonde

platitude [platityd] *nf* (**a**) *(manque d'intérêt)* dullness (**b**) *(propos)* platitude

Platon [platɔ̃] *npr* Plato

platonique [platɔnik] *adj (amour)* platonic

plâtras [plɑtra] *nmpl* (plaster) rubble

plâtre [plɑtr] *nm* plaster; *(sculpture)* plaster cast; *(pour jambe cassée)* plaster (cast); **avoir la jambe dans le p.** to have one's leg in plaster; *Fig* **essuyer les plâtres** to put up with the teething problems

plâtrer [plɑtre] *vt* (**a**) *(mur, plafond)* to plaster; *(trou, fissure)* to plaster over (**b**) *(jambe, bras)* to put in plaster

plâtreux, -euse [plɑtrø, -øz] *adj (fromage)* chalky

plâtrier [plɑtrije] *nm* plasterer

plausible [plozibl] *adj* plausible

play-back [plɛbak] *nm inv* miming; **chanter en p.** to mime

play-boy (*pl* **play-boys**) [plɛbɔj] *nm* playboy

plèbe [plɛb] *nf* **la p.** the plebs

plébéien, -enne [plebejɛ̃, -ɛn] *adj & nm,f* plebeian

plébiscite [plebisit] *nm* plebiscite

plébisciter [plebisite] *vt* (**a**) *(élire)* **p. qn/qch** to vote for sb/sth by plebiscite (**b**) *Fig* to endorse

pléiade [plejad] *nf* **une p. de** a host of

plein, -e [plɛ̃, plɛn] **1** *adj* (**a**) *(rempli)* full (**de** of); **il a les doigts pleins d'encre** his fingers are covered with ink; **p. à craquer** full to bursting; **p. comme un œuf** stuffed full (**b**) *(complet)* *(accord, pouvoirs)* full; **pleine lune** full moon; **pleine mer** high tide; **p. tarif** full price; *(de transports)* full fare; **travailler à p. temps** to work full-time (**c**) *(solide)* solid (**d**) *(en intensif)* **une pleine bouteille** a whole bottle; **p. sud** due south; **en p. (milieu du) désert/village** right in the middle of the desert/village; **en p. dans/devant/sur** right in/in front of/on; **en pleine figure/poitrine** right in the face/chest; **être en p. travail** to be hard at work; **en p. hiver** in the depths of winter; **en p. soleil** in the full heat of the sun (**e**) *(animal)* pregnant (**f**) *Fam (soûl)* wasted; **p. comme une œuf** totally wasted

2 *adv* **il avait des larmes p. les yeux** his eyes were full of tears; **elle avait de la colle p. les mains** her hands were covered with glue; **à p.** *(fonctionner)* at full capacity; *Fam* **gentil tout p.** really kind; *Fam* **p. de** *(beaucoup de)* lots *or* loads of

3 *nm* (**a**) *(d'essence)* **faire le p.** *(d'essence)* to fill up (with *Br* petrol *or Am* gas); *Fig* **faire le p. d'air pur/de soleil** to get a good dose of fresh air/of sunshine (**b**) *(trait)* downstroke (**c**) **battre son p.** to be in full swing

pleinement [plɛnmɑ̃] *adv* fully; **profiter p. de qch** to take full advantage of sth

plein-emploi [plɛnɑ̃plwa] *nm* full employment

plénier, -ère [plenje, -ɛr] *adj* plenary

plénipotentiaire [plenipɔtɑ̃sjɛr] *adj & nm* plenipotentiary

plénitude [plenityd] *nf* fullness

pléonasme [pleɔnasm] *nm* pleonasm

pléthore [pletɔr] *nf* plethora (**de** of)

pleurer [plœre] **1** *vi* (**a**) *(verser des larmes)* to cry, to weep (**sur/pour** over/for); **p. sur son sort** to bewail one's fate; **p. de joie** to weep for joy; **p. de rage** to cry with rage; **p. à chaudes larmes**, *Fam* **p. comme une madeleine** *ou* **comme un veau** to cry one's eyes out; **bête/triste à p.** terribly stupid/sad; **j'ai les yeux qui pleurent** my eyes are watering (**b**) *Fig & Péj (réclamer plaintivement)* to beg; **aller p. auprès de qn** to go begging to sb

2 *vt* (**a**) *(regretter)* *(personne disparue)* to mourn (for) (**b**) **p. toutes les larmes de son corps** to cry one's eyes out

pleurésie [plœrezi] *nf* pleurisy

pleureur [plœrœr] *adj m voir* **saule**

pleureuse [plœrøz] *nf* (hired) mourner

pleurnichard, -e [plœrniʃar, -ard] = **pleurnicheur**

pleurnicher [plœrniʃe] *vi Fam* to whine

pleurnicheur, -euse [plœrniʃœr, -øz] *Fam* **1** *nm,f* whine **2** *adj* whining

pleurote [plœrɔt] *nm* oyster mushroom

pleurs [plœr] *nmpl* **en p.** in tears

pleut *voir* **pleuvoir**

pleutre [pløtr] *adj & nm Litt* craven

pleuvoir [56] [pløvwar] **1** *v impersonnel* to rain; **il pleut** it's raining; **il pleut à verse** it's pouring (down); *Fam* **il pleut des cordes** it's coming down in buckets; *Fam* **il pleut comme vache qui pisse** it's chucking it down; **des cadeaux comme s'il en pleuvait** presents galore **2** *vi (obus, coups, insultes)* to rain down (**sur** on)

plèvre [plɛvr] *nf* pleura

Plexiglas® [plɛksiglas] *nm Br* Perspex®, *Am* Plexiglass®

plexus [plɛksys] *nm* plexus; **p. solaire** solar plexus

pli [pli] *nm* (**a**) *(de rideaux, de tissu, de papier)* fold; *(en couture)* pleat; **(faux) p.** crease; *Fig* **ça ne fait pas un p.** there's no doubt about it; *Fig* **prendre le p. (de faire qch)** to get into the habit (of doing sth); *Fig* **prendre un mauvais p.** to get into a bad habit (**b**) *(de la peau)* *(du ventre, du cou, du menton)* fold; *(de la bouche, des yeux)* wrinkle; *(du front)* line (**c**) *(enveloppe)* envelope; *(lettre)* letter; **sous p. séparé** under separate cover; **p. cacheté** sealed envelope; **envoyer qch sous p. cacheté** to send sth in a sealed envelope (**d**) *(aux cartes)* trick; **faire un p.** to take a trick (**e**) *Géol* fold

pliage [plijaʒ] *nm* folding

pliant, -e [plijɑ̃, -ɑ̃t] **1** *adj (chaise, table)* folding **2** *nm* folding stool

plie [pli] *nf* plaice

plier [66] [plije] **1** *vt* (**a**) *(draps, vêtements)* to fold; *(page)* to turn down; *(voile)* to furl; *(parapluie, pliant)* to fold up; *Fig* **p. bagage** to pack one's bags (**b**) *(courber)* *(branche, genou)* to bend; *Fam Fig* **être plié de rire/de douleur** to be doubled up with laughter/with pain; **être plié en deux** *ou* **en quatre** *(de rire)* to be doubled up *or* bent double; **être plié en deux** *(de douleur)* to be doubled up *or* bent double, in pain **p. qn à la discipline/une règle** to impose discipline/a rule on sb **2** *vi* (**a**) *(se courber)* to bend (over); **p. sous le poids de qch** *(poutre, branches)* to bend under the weight of sth (**b**) *(se soumettre)* to submit, to yield; *(armée, troupes)* to give way **3** *se plier vpr* (**a**) *(pouvoir être plié)* *(parapluie, chaise)* to fold up (**b**) *(se soumettre)* **se p. à la discipline** to submit to discipline; **se p. aux lois** to obey the law; **se p. aux caprices/volontés de qn** to give in to sb's whims/wishes

plinthe [plɛ̃t] *nf* **(a)** *(de mur) Br* skirting (board), *Am* baseboard **(b)** *(de colonne)* plinth

plissé, -e [plise] **1** *adj* **(a)** *(visage, front)* wrinkled **(b)** *jupe* **plissée** pleated skirt **2** *nm* pleats

plissement [plismɑ̃] *nm* **(a)** *(des yeux)* screwing up **(b)** *Géol* fold

plisser [plise] **1** *vt* **(a)** *(front)* to wrinkle; *(lèvres)* to pucker; *(yeux)* to screw up **(b)** *(tissu, jupe)* to pleat **2** *vi* *(vêtement)* to crease **3 se plisser** *vpr* *(étoffe)* to crease; *(bouche)* to pucker; *(yeux)* to wrinkle up; **son front se plissa** she frowned

pliure [plijyr] *nf* *(d'un tissu)* fold; *(de papier)* folding; *(du genou)* bend

plomb [plɔ̃] *nm* **(a)** *(métal)* lead; **ciel de p.** leaden sky; **soleil de p.** blazing sun; *Fig* **n'avoir pas de p.** **dans la tête** to be scatterbrained; **cela lui mettra un peu de p. dans la tête** *ou* **dans la cervelle** that'll knock some sense into him **(b)** *(de chasse)* shot, *Fam Fig* **avoir du p. dans l'aile** to be in a bad way **(c)** *Él (fusible)* fuse; **faire sauter les plombs** to blow the fuses; *très Fam* **j'ai pété les plombs** I blew my top **(d)** *(pour la pêche)* sinker **(e)** *(sceau)* lead seal

plombage [plɔ̃baʒ] *nm* **(a)** *(fait de mettre des plombs)* weighting with lead **(b)** *(d'une dent)* filling

plombe [plɔ̃b] *nf Fam* hour

plombé, -e [plɔ̃be] *adj* *(toit)* lead(-covered); *Fig (teint)* livid; *(ciel)* leaden

plomber [plɔ̃be] **1** *vt* **(a)** *(couvrir de plomb)* to cover with lead **(b)** *(mettre des plombs à)* to weight with lead **(c)** *(dent)* to fill **2 se plomber** *vpr (ciel)* to become leaden

plomberie [plɔ̃bri] *nf* *(installations, métier)* plumbing

plombier [plɔ̃bje] *nm* plumber

plonge [plɔ̃ʒ] *nf Fam* dishwashing, *Br* washing up; **faire la p.** to wash dishes

plongeant, -e [plɔ̃ʒɑ̃, -ɑ̃t] *adj* *(tir, décolleté)* plunging; **vue plongeante (sur)** bird's-eye view (onto)

plongée [plɔ̃ʒe] *nf* **(a)** *(discipline)* diving; **faire de la p.** to dive; **p. sous-marine** skin *or* scuba diving **(b)** *(de sous-marin)* dive **(c)** *Cin & TV* elevated shot; *(verticale)* bird's-eye view

plongeoir [plɔ̃ʒwar] *nm* diving board

plongeon [plɔ̃ʒɔ̃] *nm* **(a)** *(fait de plonger)* dive; **faire un p.** *(nageur, gardien de but)* to dive; *Fam Fig* **faire le p.** to hit the rocks **(b)** *(oiseau) Am* loon

plonger [45] [plɔ̃ʒe] **1** *vi* **(a)** *(nageur, sous-marin)* to dive **(dans** into) **(b)** *(avion, oiseau)* to dive **(sur** onto) **2** *vt aussi Fig* to plunge **(dans** into) **3 se plonger** *vpr* **se p. dans l'étude** to immerse oneself in one's studies; **plongé dans ses pensées** lost *or* deep in thought; **être plongé dans le silence** to be plunged in silence

plongeur, -euse [plɔ̃ʒœr, -øz] **1** *nm,f* **(a)** *(dans l'eau)* diver; **p. sous-marin** skin *or* scuba diver **(b)** *Fam (dans un restaurant)* dishwasher **2** *nm (oiseau)* diver

plot [plo] *nm* **(a)** *Él* contact **(b)** **p. de départ** starting block

plouc [pluk] *nm Péj* yokel, peasant

plouf [pluf] *exclam* plop!; *(objet plus lourd)* splash!

ploutocratie [plutokrasi] *nf* plutocracy

ployer [32] [plwaje] **1** *vi* *(courber)* to bend; *(plancher, poutre)* to sag; *(sous un joug, un fardeau)* to bend **2** *vt* to bend

plu *voir* **plaire, pleuvoir**

pluie [plɥi] *nf* **(a)** *(précipitations)* rain; **pluies acides** acid

rain; **p. battante** driving rain; **p. fine** drizzle; **temps de p.** rainy *or* wet weather; **sous la p.** in the rain; **parler de la p. et du beau temps** to talk of this and that; **il n'est pas tombé** *ou* **né de la dernière p.** he wasn't born yesterday; *Fam* **faire la p. et le beau temps** to rule the roost; *Prov* **après la p.**, **le beau temps** it's a long road that has no turning **(b)** *Fig (de coups, de projectiles)* hail, shower; *(d'injures, de compliments)* stream

plumage [plymaʒ] *nm* plumage

plumard [plymar] *nm Fam* bed

plume [plym] *nf* **(a)** *(d'oiseau)* feather; *Fam Fig* **il y a laissé des plumes** he didn't come out of it unscathed; *Fam Fig* **on lui a volé dans les plumes** they laid into him; **léger comme une p.** as light as a feather; *Hum* **perdre ses plumes** to go thin on top **(b)** *(de stylo)* nib; **p. (d'oie)** quill (pen); **écrire au fil de la p.** to write just what comes into one's head; **dessin à la p.** pen (and ink) drawing; **prendre la p.** to put pen to paper; **vivre de sa p.** to live by one's pen; **avoir la p. facile** to have a gift for writing

plumeau, -x [plymo] *nm* feather duster

plumer [plyme] *vt* *(volaille)* to pluck; *Fam (personne)* to fleece

plumier [plymje] *nm* pencil box

plupart [plypar] *nf* **la p.** most; **la p. des gens/des cas** most people/cases; **la p. d'entre eux** most of them; **la p.** **du temps** most of the time; *(en général)* in most cases; **pour la p.** for the most part, mostly

pluralisme [plyralism] *nm* pluralism

pluridisciplinaire [plyridisipliner] *adj* multidisciplinary

pluriel, -elle [plyrjɛl] **1** *adj* plural **2** *nm* plural; **au p.** in the plural

plus **1** *adv* [ply] **(a)** *(comparatif)* more, je **gagne p. que vous** I earn more than you (do); **il est p. grand que moi** he's taller than I am *or* than me; **elle est p. jolie que belle** she is pretty rather than beautiful; **p. de** *(temps, hommes)* more; *(avec un nombre)* more than; **il a p. de vingt ans** he's over twenty; **p...., p....** the more... the more..., **p...., moins....** the more... the less...; **p. on va vers le sud, p. les jours allongent** the further south you go, the longer the days get; **de p. en p.** more and more; **de p. en p. froid** colder and colder; **celui-ci coûte 10 euros de p. que l'autre** this one costs 10 euros more than the other one; **cette année, il y a trois élèves de** *ou* **en p.** this year there are three more *or* extra pupils; **le vin est en p.** the wine is extra; **de p.** *(aussi)* furthermore; **en p.** *(aussi)* what's more; **en p. de** besides; **sans p. attendre** without further ado **(b)** *(superlatif)* **le p.** the most; **la p. longue rue** *ou* **la rue la p. longue de la ville** the longest street in the town; **c'est tout ce qu'il y a de p. simple** nothing could be simpler; **une soirée des p. réussies** a most successful evening; **qui peut le p. peut le moins** you've/he's/*etc* done more difficult things than that before **(c)** *(indique la négation)* **ne... p.** no more, no longer; **je ne les vois p.** I don't see them any more, I no longer see them; **je ne le ferai p.** I won't do it again; **il n'y a p. rien** there's nothing left; **p. que dix minutes!** only ten minutes left!; **non p.** neither; **je ne suis jamais allé en Australie – moi non p.** I've never been to Australia – **neither** *or* nor have I **(d)** *(locutions)* **p. ou moins** more or less; **ni p. ni moins** no more no less; **sans p.** but no more than that **2** *conj* [plys] *(dans les calculs, dans les températures)* plus **3** *nm* [plys] **(a)** *(signe)* plus (sign) **(b)** *Fig (atout)* plus

plusieurs [plyzjœr] *adj indéfini & pron indéfini* several

plus-que-parfait *(pl* **plus-que-parfaits)** [plyskəparfɛ] *nm Gram* pluperfect, past perfect

plus-value *(pl* **plus-values)** [plyvaly] *nf (bénéfice)* profit;

(augmentation de la valeur) appreciation; *(excédent) (d'impôts)* surplus; **impôt sur les plus-values** capital gains tax

Pluton [plytɔ̃] *npr (dieu, planète)* Pluto

plutonium [plytɔnjɔm] *nm* plutonium

plutôt [plyto] *adv* rather; **p. que de faire qch** rather than doing sth

pluvial, -e, -aux, -ales [plyvjal, -o] *adj* pluvial; **eau pluviale** rainwater

pluvieux, -euse [plyvjø, -øz] *adj* rainy, wet

PME [peɛmə] *nf (abrév* **petite et moyenne entreprise)** small business

PMI [peɛmi] *nf (abrév* **petite et moyenne industrie)** small industry

PMU [peɛmy] *nm (abrév* **Pari mutuel urbain)** = state-run betting system, *Br* ≃ tote, *Am* ≃ pari-mutuel

PNB [peɛnbe] *nm (abrév* **produit national brut)** GNP

pneu [pnø] *nm* **(a)** *(de véhicule)* tyre; **avoir un p. à plat/ crevé** to have a flat/a puncture; **p. à clous, p. clouté** studded tyre; *Can* **p. d'hiver** winter tyre; **p. neige** snow tyre; **p. pluie** wet-weather tyre; *Can* **p. quatre-saisons** all-season tyre **(b)** *(lettre)* express letter *(sent through a pneumatic dispatch system)*

pneumatique [pnømatik] **1** *adj (qui fonctionne à l'air)* pneumatic; *(gonflable)* inflatable
2 *nm* = **pneu**

pneumonie [pnømɔni] *nf* pneumonia

pneumothorax [pnømotɔraks] *nm* pneumothorax

poche [pɔʃ] *nf* **(a)** *(de vêtement)* pocket; **p. revolver** hip pocket; *Fam* **faire les poches à qn** to go through sb's pockets; **de p.** pocket; **en être de sa p.** to be out of pocket; **payer de sa p.** to pay out of one's own pocket; *Fig* **connaître un endroit comme sa p.** to know a place like the back of one's hand; *Fam Fig* **se remplir les poches, s'en mettre plein les poches** to make a packet; **sans un sou en p.** without a penny in one's pocket; *Fam* **c'est dans la p.** it's in the bag **(b)** *(sac)* bag; **p. de glace** ice pack **(c)** *(amas de substance)* pocket; **p. de pétrole/gaz** pocket of oil/gas **(d)** *(déformation)* **poches sous les yeux** bags under the eyes; **son pantalon fait des poches aux genoux** his trousers are baggy at the knees **(e)** *(de kangourou)* pouch **(f)** *(zone)* **p. de résistance/pauvreté** pocket of resistance/deprivation

pocher [pɔʃe] *vt* **(a)** *(œuf, poisson)* to poach **(b)** *Fam* **p. l'œil à qn** to give sb a black eye

pochette [pɔʃɛt] *nf* **(a)** *(petit sac)* (small) bag; *(d'un disque)* sleeve; *(de photos)* wallet; **p. d'allumettes** book of matches **(b)** *(mouchoir)* pocket handkerchief

pochette-surprise *(pl* **pochettes-surprises)** [pɔʃɛt-syrpriz] *nf* lucky bag; *Fam* **il a eu son permis dans une p.** it's a miracle he passed his test

pochoir [pɔʃwar] *nm* stencil

podium [pɔdjɔm] *nm* podium; **monter sur le p.** to mount the podium

poêle¹ [pwal] *nf Br* frying pan; *Am* fry pan; **passer qch à la p.** to fry sth

poêle² *nm (appareil de chauffage)* stove; **p. à mazout** oil stove

poêlon [pwalɔ̃] *nm* casserole (dish)

poème [pɔɛm] *nm* poem

poésie [pɔezi] *nf* **(a)** *(art)* poetry **(b)** *(poème)* poem

poète [pɔɛt] *nm aussi Fig* poet

poétesse [pɔetɛs] *nf* poetess

poétique [pɔetik] *adj* poetic

poétiquement [pɔetikmɑ̃] *adv* poetically

pogne [pɔɲ] *nf Fam* paw

pognon [pɔɲɔ̃] *nm Fam (argent)* cash, *Am* bucks

pogrom(e) [pɔgrɔm] *nm* pogrom

poids [pwa] *nm* **(a)** *(masse)* weight; **de tout son p.** with all one's weight; **perdre/prendre du p.** to lose/gain weight; **vendre au p.** to sell by weight; *Fam* **il ne fait pas le p.** he's not up to scratch; **p. net/brut** net/gross weight; **p. léger** *(en boxe)* lightweight; **p. lourd** *(camion) Br* lorry, *Am* truck; *(en boxe)* heavyweight; **p. mouche** flyweight; **p. plume** *(en boxe)* featherweight; *Fig* lightweight **(b)** *Fig (charge pénible)* burden; *Litt* **le p. des ans** the weight of the years; **le p. des impôts** the burden of taxation **(c)** *Fig (importance)* weight; **donner du p. à qch** to give weight to sth; **avoir du p.** to carry weight; **faire deux poids deux mesures** to apply double standards **(d)** *(sport)* shot; **lancer le p.** to put the shot

poignant, -e [pwaɲɑ̃, -ɑ̃t] *adj* poignant

poignard [pwaɲar] *nm* dagger

poignarder [pwaɲarde] *vt* to stab

poigne [pwaɲ] *nf* grip; **avoir de la p.** to have a strong grip; *Fig* to be firm

poignée [pwaɲe] *nf* **(a)** *(quantité, petit nombre)* handful **(b)** *(de porte, sac)* handle; *(d'épée)* hilt **(c)** **p. de main** handshake

poignet [pwaɲɛ] *nm* **(a)** *(du bras)* wrist; *Fig* **faire qch à la force du p.** to do sth by sheer hard work **(b)** *(de chemise)* cuff

poil [pwal] *nm* **(a)** *(d'un animal, d'une personne, d'une plante)* hair; *(pelage)* coat; *(d'une brosse, d'un pinceau)* bristle; **à p.** *long/ras* long-/short-haired; *Fam* **caresser qn dans le sens du p.** to rub sb up the right way; *Fam* **tomber sur le p. à qn** to lay into sb; *Fam* **à p.** stark naked; *Fam* **se mettre à p.** to strip off; *Fam* **avoir un p. dans la main** to be bone idle; *Fam* **reprendre du p. de la bête** to pick up again; *Fam Fig* **de tous poils** of all sorts; *Fig* **être de bon/mauvais p.** to be in a good/bad mood; *Fam* **au quart de p.** perfectly; *Fam* **à un p. près** very nearly; *Fam* **un p. plus haut/moins vite** a touch higher/slower; *Fam* **au p.** great **(b)** **à gratter** itching powder

poiler [pwale] **se poiler** *vpr Fam* to kill oneself laughing

poilu, -e [pwaly] **1** *adj* hairy
2 *nm Fam* poilu *(French soldier 1914-1918)*

poinçon [pwɛ̃sɔ̃] *nm* **(a)** *(de graveur)* style; *(de cordonnier)* awl; *(marque)* hallmark

poinçonner [pwɛ̃sɔne] *vt (perforer)* to punch; *(or, argent)* to hallmark

poinçonneur, -euse [pwɛ̃sɔnœr, -øz] **1** *nm,f (personne)* ticket puncher
2 *nf* poinçonneuse punching machine

poindre [43] [pwɛ̃dr] *vi (jour)* to dawn, to break; *(plantes, étoiles)* to appear

poing [pwɛ̃] *nm* fist; **sabre/revolver au p.** sword/ revolver in hand; **les poings sur les hanches** hands on hips, arms akimbo; **dormir à poings fermés** to sleep like a log

point¹ [pwɛ̃] *nm* **(a)** *(endroit)* point, spot; *(en géométrie)* point; **les quatre points cardinaux** the (four) points of the compass; *Ordinat* **p. de césure** breakpoint, hyphenation point; **p. chaud** *(zone de conflits)* hot spot, trouble spot; **p. de côté** *(douleur)* stitch; *aussi Fig* **p. de départ** starting point; **p. d'eau** *(dans le désert)* waterhole; **p. de mire** target; *Fig* focus; *Aut* **p. mort** neutral; *Fig* **être au p. mort** to be at a standstill; **p. noir** *(comédon)* blackhead; *(embouteillage)* blackspot; **p. de rencontre** meeting point; **p. de vente** *(magasin)* point of sale, sales outlet; **p. de vue** *(panorama)* viewpoint; *(opinion)* point of view; **du p. de vue international/économique** from an international/ economic point of view

(b) *(marque)* dot; *(en fin de ligne)* Br full stop, Am period; *Fig* **mettre les points sur les i (à qn)** to make oneself perfectly clear (to sb); *Typ & Ordinat* **points par pouce** dots per inch; **deux points** colon; **p. d'exclamation** exclamation Br mark or Am point; **p. final** Br full stop, Am period; *Fam* **un p.**, **c'est tout!**, **p. final!** and that's that!; *aussi Fig* **p. d'interrogation** question mark; **points de suspension** suspension points; *Ordinat* **p. de tabulation** tab marker **(c)** *(aspect, question)* point; **en tous points** in every way, in all respects; **p. faible/fort** weak/strong point **(d)** *(de couture, de tricot)* stitch; **p. de croix** cross-stitch; **p. mousse** garter stitch **(e)** *(phase, degré)* point, stage; **traiter un problème en trois points** to deal with a problem in three stages; **(cuit) à p.** done to a turn; *(steak)* medium-rare; **jusqu'à un certain p.** to a certain extent, up to a certain point; **au p. où j'en suis...** at the stage I've reached...; **à tel p. que...**, **au p. que...** to such an extent that..., so much so that...; **vous n'êtes pas malade à ce p.-là** you're not as ill as all that; **au plus haut p.** extremely **(f)** *(dans le temps)* point; **être sur le p. de faire qch** to be about to do sth, to be on the point of doing sth; **arriver à p. nommé** to arrive just at the right moment **(g)** *(dans un score, dans un pourcentage)* point; *(dans une notation)* mark; *Scol* **bon p.** ≃ gold star **(h)** **mettre au p.** *(objectif)* to focus; *(moteur)* to tune; *(technique)* to perfect; *(stratégie)* to finalize; **être au p.** to be up to scratch **(i)** *Naut & Av* **faire le p.** to take one's bearings; *Fig* to take stock; *Fig* **faire le p. sur qch** to take stock of sth

point² *adv Vieilli* = **pas¹**

pointage [pwɛtaʒ] *nm* **(a)** *(contrôle)* *(de noms sur une liste)* ticking off; *(de votes)* counting; *(au travail)* *(à l'arrivée)* clocking in; *(au départ)* clocking out **(b)** *(d'un télescope)* pointing, *(de fusil)* aiming

pointe [pwɛt] *nf* **(a)** *(extrémité)* *(d'aiguille, de couteau)* point; *(de flèche)* tip; *(de balle)* nose, *(de chaussure)* toe, *(de sein)* nipple; **p. d'asperge** asparagus tip; **en p.** pointed; **sur la p. des pieds** on tiptoe; **entrer sur la p. des pieds** to tiptoe in; **faire des pointes** *(en danse)* to go up on points **(b)** *(maximum)* peak; **de vitesse** burst of speed; **faire une p. de vitesse** to put on a burst of speed; **vitesse de p.** top speed **(c)** *(summum)* **être à la p. de la technique/de la recherche** to be in the forefront of technology/of research; **de p.** *(secteur, industrie, technique)* state-of-the-art **(d)** *(petite quantité)* *(d'accent, d'ironie)* hint; *(d'ail, de vanille)* dash **(e)** *(raillerie)* dig, **lancer des pointes à qn** to make digs at sb **(f)** *(clou)* nail; *(pour tapis)* tack; *(sur une chaussure de sport)* spike; **chaussures à pointes** spiked shoes

pointer¹ [pwɛte] **1** *vt* **(a)** *(vérifier)* *(noms sur une liste)* to tick off; *(votes)* to count **(b)** *(dresser)* **p. les oreilles** to prick up its ears **(c)** *(diriger)* *(télescope)* to point **(sur** at); *(fusil)* to aim **(sur** at); *Ordinat (curseur)* to position **(sur** on); **j'ai pointé le doigt vers lui** I pointed (my finger) at him **2** *vi* **(a)** *(au travail)* *(à l'arrivée)* to clock in; *(à la sortie)* to clock out **(b)** *(apparaître)* *(plante)* to come up; *(jour)* to dawn **(c)** *(se dresser)* *(clocher, tour, arbre)* to rise **(d)** *(au jeu de boules)* to get one's ball nearest to the jack **3** **se pointer** *vpr Fam* to show up

pointer² [pwɛtɛr] *nm (chien)* pointer

pointeur, -euse [pwɛtœr, -øz] **1** *nm,f (contrôleur)* timekeeper; *(en sport)* scorer **2** *nm Ordinat* pointer **3** *nf* **pointeuse** *(machine)* timeclock

pointillé [pwɛtije] *nm* **(a)** *(trait)* dotted line; *(sur une feuille détachable)* perforations; **découper suivant les pointillés** to cut along the dotted line **(b)** *(technique de dessin)* stippling

pointilleux, -euse [pwɛtijø, -øz] *adj* particular, fussy **(sur** about)

pointu, -e [pwɛty] **1** *adj* **(a)** *(en forme de pointe)* pointed; *(voix)* shrill **(b)** *Fig (susceptible)* *(ton de la voix, humeur)* touchy **(c)** *Fig (spécialisé)* specialized **2** *adv* **parler p.** to speak with a clipped Parisian accent

pointure [pwɛtyr] *nf* size; *Fam Fig* **une (grosse) p. du cinéma français** a big name in French cinema

point-virgule *(pl* **points-virgules)** [pwɛvirgyl] *nm* semicolon

poire [pwar] *nf* **(a)** *(fruit)* pear; *Fig* **couper la p. en deux** to meet each other halfway; *(faire la moyenne entre deux quantités)* to split the difference **(b)** *(objet en forme de poire)* *(d'un appareil photo)* bulb; *(interrupteur)* switch **(c)** *Fam (tête)* mug; **en pleine p.** right in the face **(d)** *Fam (idiot)* sucker; **et moi, bonne p., j'ai accepté** and like the sucker I am, I accepted

poireau, -x [pwaro] *nm* leek; *Fam* **faire le p.** to hang around

poireauter [pwarote] *vi Fam* to hang around

poirier [pwarje] *nm* **(a)** *(arbre)* pear tree; **faire le p.** to do a headstand, to stand on one's head **(b)** *(bois)* pear-tree wood

pois [pwa] *nm* **(a)** *(plante)* pea; **petit p.** (garden) pea; **p. cassés** split peas; **p. chiche** Br chickpea, Am garbanzo (bean); **p. de senteur** sweet pea **(b)** *(rond)* (polka) dot; **à p.** polka-dot

poison [pwazɔ̃] **1** *nm* poison **2** *nmf Fam (personne)* pest

poisse [pwas] *nf Fam* bad luck

poisseux, -euse [pwasø, -øz] *adj* sticky

poisson [pwasɔ̃] *nm* **(a)** *(animal)* fish; **p. d'eau douce/de mer** freshwater/saltwater fish; *Prov* **petit p. deviendra grand** great oaks from little acorns grow; **p. d'argent** silverfish; **p. d'avril** April fool; **p. rouge** goldfish; **p. volant** flying fish **(b)** *Astron & Astrol* **les Poissons** Pisces; **être Poissons** to be (a) Pisces

poisson-chat *(pl* **poissons-chats)** [pwasɔ̃ʃa] *nm* catfish

poissonnerie [pwasɔnri] *nf* fish shop

poissonneux, -euse [pwasɔnø, -øz] *adj* full of fish

poissonnier, -ère [pwasɔnje, -ɛr] *nm,f Br* fishmonger, *Am* fish merchant

poitevin, -e [pwatvɛ̃, -in] *adj (de Poitiers)* of Poitiers; *(du Poitou)* of Poitou

poitrail [pwatraj] *nm (d'animal)* breast; *Fam (poitrine)* chest

poitrinaire [pwatrinɛr] *adj & nmf Vieilli* consumptive

poitrine [pwatrin] *nf* **(a)** *(thorax)* chest; *(seins)* bust; **serrer qn contre sa p.** to hold sb to one's breast; **ne pas avoir beaucoup de p.** to have a small bust **(b)** *Culin (de veau)* breast; *(de bœuf)* brisket; *(de porc)* belly

poivre [pwavr] *nm* pepper; **p. en grains** peppercorns; **p. et sel** *(cheveux, barbe)* pepper-and-salt

poivré, -e [pwavre] *adj* **(a)** *(nourriture, odeur)* peppery **(b)** *Fig (histoire)* spicy

poivrer [pwavre] **1** *vt* to put pepper on/in **2** **se poivrer** *vpr Fam* to get wasted

poivrier [pwavrije] *nm* **(a)** *(plante)* pepper plant **(b)** *(petit pot)* pepper pot; *(moulin)* pepper mill

poivron [pwavrɔ̃] *nm* pepper

poivrot, -e [pwavro, -ɔt] *nm,f Fam* drunk

poix [pwa] *nf* pitch

poker [pɔkɛr] *nm* poker

polaire [pɔlɛr] *adj (faune, expédition)* polar; *(froid)* Arctic

polar [pɔlar] *nm Fam* thriller

polarisation [pɔlarizasjɔ̃] *nf* **(a)** *Phys* polarization **(b)** *Fig (focalisation)* focusing

polariser [pɔlarize] **1** vt Phys to polarize; Fig (attention) to focus
2 se polariser vpr **se p. sur** to focus on
Polaroid® [pɔlarɔid] nm Polaroid® (camera)
pôle [pol] nm (**a**) Géog pole; **p. Nord/Sud** North/South Pole (**b**) Fig **p. d'intérêt** focus of interest; **p. d'attraction** centre of attention
polémique [pɔlemik] **1** adj polemical **2** nf heated debate
polémiquer [pɔlemike] vi to debate
poli¹, -e [pɔli] adj (lisse) polished
poli², -e adj (courtois) polite (avec to)
police¹ [pɔlis] nf (**a**) (maintien de l'ordre) policing; **faire la p.** to keep order (**b**) (institution) **la p.** the police; **appeler p. secours** to call the police (in an emergency); **être de** ou **dans la p.** to be in the police; **p. de l'air et des frontières** airport and border police; **p. judiciaire** police investigation department; **p. mondaine** ou **des mœurs** vice squad; **p. montée** mounted police; **p. municipale** local police; **la p. nationale** the national police force; **p. secrète** secret police
police² nf (**a**) (d'assurance) policy; **p. d'assurance** insurance policy (**b**) Ordinat **p. (de caractères)** font; **p. bitmap** ou **pixélisée** bitmap font; **p. de taille variable** scalable font; **p. vectorielle** outline font
polichinelle [pɔliʃinɛl] nm (**a**) (marionnette) Punch (**b**) Fig & Péj buffoon
policier, -ère [pɔlisje, -ɛr] **1** adj (enquête, État, régime) police; (roman, film) detective **2** nm (**a**) (personne) policeman, police officer; **femme p.** policewoman, (female) police officer (**b**) (roman) detective novel; (film) detective film
policlinique [pɔliklinik] nf outpatients' clinic
poliment [pɔlimã] adv politely
polio [pɔljo] **1** nf polio **2** nmf polio victim
poliomyélite [pɔljɔmjelit] nf poliomyelitis
polir [pɔlir] vt to polish
polisson, -onne [pɔlisɔ̃, -ɔn] **1** nm,f (enfant espiègle) rascal **2** adj (**a**) (espiègle) naughty (**b**) (grivois) saucy
politesse [pɔlitɛs] nf politeness; **par p.** out of politeness; **ce serait la moindre des politesses de le prévenir** it's only polite to warn him; **rendre la p. à qn** to return sb's favour
politicien, -enne [pɔlitisjɛ̃, -ɛn] **1** nm,f politician **2** adj Péj **politique politicienne** politicking
politique [pɔlitik] **1** adj political **2** nf (**a**) (de gouvernement, d'entreprise) policy; **p. intérieure/extérieure** domestic/foreign policy; **la p. du pire** = the policy of presenting one's situation in the worst possible light in order to achieve one's objectives; **la p. agricole commune** the Common Agricultural Policy (**b**) (affaires publiques) politics; **faire de la p.** (en tant que politicien) to be in politics; (en tant que militant) to be involved in politics **3** nm (personne) politician
politiquement [pɔlitikmã] adv politically
politisation [pɔlitizasjɔ̃] nf politicization
politiser [pɔlitize] vt to politicize
politologue [pɔlitɔlɔg] nmf political scientist
polka [pɔlka] nf polka
pollen [pɔlɛn] nm pollen
polluant, -e [pɔlɥɑ̃, -ɑ̃t] **1** adj polluting; **produit p.** pollutant **2** nm pollutant

pollué, -e [pɔlɥe] adj polluted
polluer [pɔlɥe] vt to pollute
pollueur, -euse [pɔlɥœr, -øz] **1** nm,f polluter **2** adj polluting
pollution [pɔlysjɔ̃] nf pollution
polo [pɔlo] nm (**a**) (sport) polo (**b**) (chemise) polo shirt
polochon [pɔlɔʃɔ̃] nm Fam bolster; **bataille de polochons** pillow fight
Pologne [pɔlɔɲ] nf **la P.** Poland
polonais, -e [pɔlɔnɛ, -ɛz] **1** adj Polish **2** nm,f **P.** Pole **3** nm (langue) Polish **4** nf **polonaise** (danse) polonaise
poltron, -onne [pɔltrɔ̃, -ɔn] **1** adj cowardly **2** nm,f coward
polyamide [pɔljamid] nm polyamide
polychrome [pɔlikrom] adj polychrome
polyclinique [pɔliklinik] nf polyclinic
polycopie [pɔlikɔpi] nf (procédé) duplication; (document) duplicate
polycopié, -e [pɔlikɔpje] **1** adj duplicated **2** nm duplicate; Scol & Univ duplicated course material
polycopier [66] [pɔlikɔpje] vt to duplicate
polyculture [pɔlikyltyr] nf mixed farming
polyester [pɔliɛstɛr] nm polyester
polygame [pɔligam] **1** adj polygamous **2** nm polygamist
polygamie [pɔligami] nf polygamy
polyglotte [pɔliglɔt] adj & nmf polyglot
polygone [pɔligɔn, pɔligɔn] nm (**a**) (figure) polygon (**b**) Mil shooting range
polymère [pɔlimɛr] **1** adj polymeric **2** nm polymer
Polynésie [pɔlinezi] nf **la P.** Polynesia; **la P. française** French Polynesia
polynésien, -enne [pɔlinezjɛ̃, -ɛn] **1** adj Polynesian **2** nm,f **P.** Polynesian
polype [pɔlip] nm polyp
polyphonie [pɔlifɔni] nf polyphony
polysémique [pɔlisemik] adj polysemous
polystyrène [pɔlistirɛn] nm polystyrene
polytechnicien, -enne [pɔliteknisjɛ̃, -ɛn] nm,f graduate of the "École polytechnique"
Polytechnique [pɔliteknik] nf (l'École) **p., P.** = "grande école" specializing in engineering
polythéisme [pɔliteism] nm polytheism
polyvalence [pɔlivalɑ̃s] nf (en chimie) polyvalency; Fig (d'une personne) versatility
polyvalent, -e [pɔlivalɑ̃, -ɑ̃t] adj (**a**) (en chimie) polyvalent, (**b**) (salle) multi-purpose; (outil, personne) versatile **2** nm tax inspector
poméló [pɔmelo] nm pomelo
pommade [pɔmad] nf ointment; Fam **passer de la p. à qn** to butter sb up
pomme [pɔm] nf (**a**) (fruit) apple; Fam **haut comme trois pommes** knee-high to a grasshopper; Fam **tomber dans les pommes** to pass out; Fam **être dans les pommes** to be out for the count; **p. d'Adam** Adam's apple; **p. de discorde** bone of contention; **p. de pin** pine cone; (de sapin) fir cone (**b**) (partie arrondie) (de bois de lit, de canne) knob; (d'arrosoir) rose; **p. de douche** shower head (**c**) (pomme de terre) **pommes allumettes** matchstick Br chips

or Am potatoes; **pommes chips** (potato) *Br* crisps *or Am* chips; **pommes dauphine** dauphine potatoes; **p. de terre** potato; **pommes (de terre) à l'eau** boiled potatoes; **pommes (de terre) frites** *Br* chips, *Am* (French) fries; **pommes (de terre) sautées** sauté potatoes; **pommes vapeur** steamed potatoes **(d)** *Fam (personne)* **ma p.** yours truly; **ta p.** you; **sa p.** him/her **(e)** *Fam (idiot)* sucker

pommeau, -x [pɔmo] *nm (d'un sabre, d'une selle)* pommel; *(d'une canne, d'un levier de vitesse)* knob

pommelé, -e [pɔmle] *adj* dappled; **gris p.** *(cheval)* dapple-grey; **ciel p.** mackerel sky

pommer [pɔme] *vi (chou, salade)* to form a heart

pommeraie [pɔmrε] *nf* apple orchard

pommette [pɔmεt] *nf* cheekbone

pommier [pɔmje] *nm* apple tree; **p. sauvage** crab-apple tree

pompage [pɔpaʒ] *nm* pumping

pompe¹ [pɔp] *nf (cérémonie)* pomp, ceremony; **en grande p.** with great (pomp and) ceremony

pompe² *nf* **(a)** *(machine)* pump; **p. à essence** *(distributeur) Br* petrol *or Am* gas pump; *(station-service) Br* petrol *or Am* gas station; **p. à incendie** water pump *(on a fire engine)*; **p. à vélo** bicycle pump; *Fam* **à toute p.** lightning; *Fam* **faire des pompes** to do *Br* press-ups *or Am* push-ups **(b)** *Fam* **pompes** *(chaussures)* shoes; *Fig* **il est à côté de ses pompes** he's not with it **(c)** **pompes funèbres** undertaker's

pomper [pɔpe] **1** *vt* **(a)** *(puiser) (eau, air)* to pump; *(faire monter)* to pump up; *(évacuer)* to pump out; *Fam Fig* **p. qn** *(épuiser)* to do sb in; *Fam* **être pompé** to be done in; *Fam* **tu me pompes l'air** you're getting on my nerves **(b)** *Fam (boisson)* to knock back **(c)** *Fam Scol* to crib **(sur** from) **2** *vi* **(a)** *(faire marcher une pompe)* to pump **(b)** *Fam Scol* to crib **(sur** from)

pompette [pɔpεt] *adj Fam* tipsy

pompeux, -euse [pɔpø, -øz] *adj Péj* pompous

pompier¹ [pɔpje] *nm* fireman; **appeler les pompiers** to call the fire *Br* brigade *or Am* department

pompier², -ère [pɔpje, -εr] *adj (art, style)* pompous

pompiste [pɔpist] *nmf* pump attendant

pompon [pɔpɔ̃] *nm* pompom, bobble; **bonnet à p.** bobble hat; *Fam* **c'est le p.!** that's the limit!

pomponner [pɔpɔne] **se pomponner** *vpr Fam* to doll oneself up

ponce [pɔs] *adj voir* **pierre**

poncer [16] [pɔse] *vt* **(a)** *(au papier de verre, avec une ponceuse)* to sand (down) **(b)** *(passer à la pierre ponce)* to pumice

ponceuse [pɔsøz] *nf* sander

poncho [pɔtʃo] *nm* poncho

poncif [pɔsif] *nm* cliché, commonplace

ponction [pɔksjɔ̃] *nf Méd* puncture; *(de poumon)* tapping; **p. lombaire** lumbar puncture; *Fig* **faire des ponctions dans ses économies** to draw on one's savings; **p. fiscale** taxation

ponctualité [pɔktɥalite] *nf* punctuality

ponctuation [pɔktɥasjɔ̃] *nf* punctuation

ponctuel, -elle [pɔktɥεl] *adj* **(a)** *(à l'heure)* punctual **(b)** *(unique) Br* one-off, *Am* one-of-a-kind; *(isolé)* selective

ponctuellement [pɔktɥεlmɑ̃] *adv (de façon limitée)* on a *Br* one-off *or Am* one-of-a-kind basis

ponctuer [pɔktɥe] *vt aussi Fig* to punctuate **(de** with)

pondaison [pɔdεzɔ̃] *nf* egg-laying time

pondérale [pɔderal] *adj f voir* **surcharge**

pondération [pɔderasjɔ̃] *nf* **(a)** *(modération)* level-headedness **(b)** *Écon* weighting

pondéré, -e [pɔdere] *adj* **(a)** *(personne)* level-headed **(b)** *Écon* weighted

pondeuse [pɔdøz] *adj f & nf* **(poule) p.** layer

pondre [pɔdr] *vt* **(a)** *(œuf)* to lay **(b)** *Fam (produire)* to turn out

poney [pɔnε] *nm* pony

pont [pɔ] *nm* **(a)** *(sur un cours d'eau)* bridge; **les Ponts et Chaussées** the Highways Department; *Fig* **faire un p. d'or à qn** to give sb a golden hello; **p. suspendu** suspension bridge **(b)** *Fig (congés)* long weekend; **le p. du premier mai** the May Day long weekend; **faire le p.** to make a long weekend of it **(c)** *(d'un navire)* deck; **sur le p.** on deck **(d)** *(lien)* **couper les ponts (avec qn)** to break off all relations (with sb); **p. aérien** airlift; *Ordinat* **p. routeur** routing node **(e)** *Ind* **p. roulant** travelling crane

pontage [pɔtaʒ] *nm Méd* bypass (operation)

ponte¹ [pɔt] *nf (action)* (egg) laying; *(œufs)* eggs (laid)

ponte² *nm Fam* **(grand) p.** *(personnage important)* big shot

pontife [pɔtif] *nm Rel* pontiff; **le souverain p.** the Supreme Pontiff

pontifiant, -e [pɔtifjɑ̃, ɑt] *adj Péj* pontificating

pontifical, -e, -aux, -ales [pɔtifikal, -o] *adj* papal

pontifier [66] [pɔtifje] *vi* to pontificate

pont-l'évêque [pɔlevεk] *nm inv* Pont-l'Évêque (cheese)

pont-levis *(pl* **ponts-levis)** [pɔləvi] *nm* drawbridge

ponton [pɔtɔ̃] *nm* pontoon

pop [pɔp] *adj Inv & nf* pop

pop-corn [pɔpkɔrn] *nm inv* popcorn

pope [pɔp] *nm Rel* (Orthodox) priest

popeline [pɔplin] *nf* poplin

popote [pɔpɔt] **1** *nf* **(a)** *Fam (cuisine)* cooking; **faire la p.** to do the cooking **(b)** *Mil* officers' mess **2** *adj inv Fam* stay-at-home

popotin [pɔpɔtɛ̃] *nm Fam Br* bum, *Am* butt

populace [pɔpylas] *nf* rabble, mob

populaire [pɔpylεr] *adj* **(a)** *(du peuple, qui plaît)* popular **(b)** *(langue, expression)* vernacular **(c)** *(ouvrier)* working-class; **les classes populaires** the working classes

populariser [pɔpylarize] *vt* to popularize

popularité [pɔpylarite] *nf* popularity

population [pɔpylasjɔ̃] *nf* population; **p. active** working population

populeux, -euse [pɔpylø, -øz] *adj* crowded

populisme [pɔpylism] *nm* populism

populo [pɔpylo] *nm Fam (foule)* crowd (of people)

porc [pɔr] *nm* **(a)** *(animal)* pig, *Am* hog; *Fig (homme grossier)* pig **(b)** *(viande)* pork **(c)** *(cuir)* pigskin

porcelaine [pɔrsəlεn] *nf (matière)* porcelain, china; *(objet)* piece of porcelain

porcelet [pɔrsəlε] *nm* piglet

porc-épic *(pl* **porcs-épics)** [pɔrkepik] *nm* porcupine

porche [pɔrʃ] *nm* porch

porcherie [pɔrʃəri] *nf aussi Fig Br* pigsty, *Am* pigpen

porcin, -e [pɔrsɛ̃, -in] **1** *adj* pig; *Péj (visage, yeux)* piggy **2** *nmpl* **porcins** pigs, *Am* hogs

pore [pɔr] *nm* pore

poreux, -euse [pɔrø, -øz] *adj* porous

porno [pɔrno] *adj & nm Fam* porn

pornographie [pɔrnɔgrafi] *nf* pornography

pornographique [pɔrnɔgrafik] *adj* pornographic

port¹ [pɔr] *nm* (**a**) *(pour bateaux)* harbour; *(plus important)* port; *Fig* **arriver à bon p.** to arrive safe and sound; **p. d'attache** home port; *Fig* home base; **p. de commerce** commercial port; **p. de pêche** fishing port; **p. de plaisance** marina (**b**) *Ordinat* port; **p. de communication** comms port, communications port; **p. d'entrée/sortie** input/output port; **p. d'E/S** I/O port; **p. d'extension** expansion port; **p. modem** modem port; **p. parallèle** parallel port; (**a**) **p. série** serial port; **p. souris** mouse port

port² *nm* (**a**) *(fait de transporter)* carrying; **p. d'armes** carrying of firearms (**b**) *(fait de revêtir)* wearing; **le p. du casque est obligatoire** *(sur panneau)* safety helmets must be worn (**c**) *(de marchandises)* carriage; *(de paquets, de lettres, de télégrammes)* delivery; **p. et emballage** postage and packing; **p. franc** *(de marchandises)* carriage paid; **p. payé** *(de magazine)* postage paid (**d**) *(allure)* bearing; **un gracieux p. de tête** a graceful manner of holding one's head

portabilité [pɔrtabilite] *nf Ordinat* portability

portable [pɔrtabl] **1** *adj* (**a**) *(ordinateur, machine à écrire)* portable (**b**) *(vêtement)* wearable **2** *nm (ordinateur)* laptop, portable

portage [pɔrtaʒ] *nm Can* portage

portager [45] [pɔrtaʒe] *vi Can* to portage

portail [pɔrtaj] *nm* portal

portant, -e [pɔrtɑ̃, -ɑ̃t] *adj* **être bien/mal p.** to be in good/poor health

portatif, -ive [pɔrtatif, -iv] *adj* portable

Port-au-Prince [pɔropɾɛ̃s] *n* Port-au-Prince

porte [pɔrt] *nf* (**a**) *(de maison, de placard, de véhicule)* door; **à ma p.** on my doorstep; **de p. à p.** door to door; *Fig* **entre deux portes** briefly; **mettre qn à la p.** to throw sb out; *(d'un emploi)* to fire sb; **trouver p. close** to find nobody in; *Fam* **ce n'est pas la p. à côté** it's hardly just around the corner; **c'est la p. ouverte à...** it's leaving the door wide open to...; (**voiture**) **deux/quatre/cinq portes** two-/four-/five-door car; **p. cochère** carriage entrance; **p. de derrière** back door; **p. d'entrée** front door; **p. tournante, p. à tambour** revolving door; **p. vitrée** glass door (**b**) *(d'une ville)* gate; **aux portes du désert** at the gateway to the desert; **p. (d'embarquement)** *(dans un aéroport)* (boarding) gate (**c**) *(en ski)* gate

porté, -e [pɔrte] *adj (enclin)* **être p. à faire qch** to be inclined to do sth; *Fam* **être p. sur la bouteille** to be fond of the bottle; *Fam* **être p. sur la chose** to have a one-track mind

porte-à-faux [pɔrtafo] **en porte-à-faux** *adv* overhanging; *Fig* **être en p.** to be awkwardly placed

porte-à-porte [pɔrtapɔrt] *nm* door-to-door selling; **faire du p.** *(pour vendre)* to sell from door to door; *(faire des enquêtes)* to go from door to door

porte-avions [pɔrtavjɔ̃] *nm inv* aircraft carrier

porte-bagages [pɔrtbagaʒ] *nm inv (de bicyclette)* carrier; *(de train)* luggage rack

porte-bébé (*pl* **porte-bébés**) [pɔrtbebe] *nm* baby carrier

porte-bonheur [pɔrtbɔnœr] *nm inv* (lucky) charm

porte-bouteilles [pɔrtbutɛj] *nm inv (pour stocker)* wine rack; *(pour porter)* bottle-carrier

porte-cartes [pɔrtəkart] *nm inv (portefeuille)* card-holder

porte-cigarettes [pɔrtsigarɛt] *nm inv* cigarette case

porte-clefs, porte-clés [pɔrtəkle] *nm inv* key ring

porte-documents [pɔrtdɔkymɑ̃] *nm inv* briefcase

porte-drapeau (*pl* **porte-drapeaux** *ou* **porte-drapeau**) [pɔrtdrapo] *nm aussi Fig* standard bearer

portée [pɔrte] *nf* (**a**) *(petits)* litter; *(d'une truie)* farrow (**b**) *(amplitude)* *(d'un fusil, d'un émetteur, de la voix)* range; *Fig (d'un traité)* scope; **à p. de (la) main** within reach, to hand; **à p. de (la) voix** within earshot; **à la p. de toutes les bourses** within everyone's means; **c'est à ma p.** *(objet)* it's within my reach; *Fig (livre)* I can understand it; **hors de ma p.** *(objet)* beyond my reach; *Fig (livre)* beyond me; **hors de p.** out of reach (**c**) *Fig (impact) (de paroles, d'une décision)* significance (**d**) *Mus* stave

portefaix [pɔrtəfɛ] *nm* porter

porte-fenêtre (*pl* **portes-fenêtres**) [pɔrtfənɛtr] *nf* French window

portefeuille [pɔrtəfœj] *nm* (**a**) *(pour l'argent)* wallet, *Am* billfold; **faire un lit en p.** to make *Br* an apple-pie bed *or Am* a short-sheeted bed; **jupe p.** wrapover skirt (**b**) *Fin & Pol* portfolio; **p. d'actions/de titres** share/securities portfolio

porte-jarretelles [pɔrtʒartɛl] *nm inv Br* suspender *or Am* garter belt

porte-malheur [pɔrtmalœr] *nm inv* jinx

portemanteau, -x [pɔrtmɑ̃to] *nm (au mur)* coat rack; *(sur pied)* coat stand

portemine [pɔrtəmin] *nm* propelling pencil

porte-monnaie [pɔrtmɔnɛ] *nm inv Br* purse, *Am* change purse; **p. électronique** electronic purse

porte-parapluies [pɔrtparaplɥi] *nm inv* umbrella stand

porte-parole [pɔrtparɔl] *nm inv* spokesperson, spokesman, *f* spokeswoman

porte-plume [pɔrtəplym] *nm inv* penholder

porter [pɔrte] **1** *vt* (**a**) *(soutenir)* to carry; **mes jambes ne me portent plus** my legs won't carry me any further; **je ne le porte pas dans mon cœur** he's not exactly my favourite person

(**b**) *(emporter)* to take; *(amener)* to bring
(**c**) *(vêtement, chapeau, lunettes)* to wear; *(signature, date)* to bear; *(prénom, nom)* to have; **p. une moustache/la barbe** to have a moustache/a beard; **p. les cheveux courts/longs** to wear one's hair short/long, to have short/long hair; **p. le nom de qn** to be named after sb; **p. le titre de...** *(livre, film)* to be entitled...
(**d**) *(produire) (fruits)* to bear
(**e**) *(diriger)* **p. un coup à qn** to strike sb; **p. la main à son front** to hold one's hand to one's forehead; **p. son attention sur qch** to turn one's attention to sth, to give sth one's attention; **p. une affaire devant les tribunaux** to bring a matter to court; **p. qch à la connaissance de qn** to bring sth to sb's attention
(**f**) *(inscrire)* to enter; **se faire p. malade** to report sick
(**g**) *(inciter)* **tout (me) porte à croire que...** everything leads me to believe that...
(**h**) *(à un niveau plus élevé)* **p. la température à 100°** to raise the temperature to 100°; **portez le liquide à ébullition** bring the liquid to the boil; **cela portera à 75 euros le prix du billet** that will bring the price of the ticket up to 75 euros

2 *vi* (**a**) *(cogner)* **p. sur/contre qch** to hit sth
(**b**) *(atteindre son objectif) (coup)* to strike home, to hit its target; *(voix)* to carry

3 porter sur *vt ind* (**a**) *(avoir pour sujet)* to be about
(**b**) *Fam* **p. sur les nerfs à qn** to get on sb's nerves

4 se porter *vpr* (**a**) *(physiquement)* **se p. bien** to be well; **je ne m'en porte pas plus mal** I'm none the worse for it; *Hum* **moins je le vois, mieux je me porte** the less I see him, the better I feel
(**b**) *(devoir être porté)* to be worn; *(être à la mode)* to be fashionable
(**c**) *(se présenter comme)* **se p. candidat** to *Br* stand *or Am* run as a candidate; **se p. caution** to stand surety

(d) *(aller)* **se p. au secours de qn** to go to sb's assistance **(e) se p. sur** *(sujet: regard, choix)* to fall on

porte-savon *(pl* **porte-savons** *ou* **porte-savon)** [pɔrtsavɔ̃] *nm* soapdish

porte-serviettes [pɔrtsɛrvjɛt] *nm inv* towel rail

porteur, -euse [pɔrtœr, -øz] **1** *nm,f* **(a)** *(d'un message, de nouvelles)* bearer; **par p.** by messenger **(b)** *(de gare, d'aéroport)* porter; **p. d'eau** water carrier **(c)** *Méd* carrier; **p. sain** (unaffected) carrier **(d)** *(détenteur)* holder; *(d'un chèque)* bearer; **payable au p.** payable to bearer **2** *adj* **(a)** *Él* **fréquence/onde porteuse** carrier frequency/wave **(b)** *(marché, créneau)* growth

porte-voix [pɔrtəvwa] *nm inv* megaphone; *(électrique) Br* loudhailer, *Am* bullhorn; **mettre ses mains en p.** to cup one's hands round one's mouth

portier [pɔrtje] *nm* porter, doorkeeper; *(dans un hôtel)* commissionaire; **p. de nuit** night porter

portière [pɔrtjɛr] *nf (d'une voiture, d'un train)* door

portillon [pɔrtijɔ̃] *nm* gate; *(d'un passage à niveau)* side gate; **p. (automatique)** *(de gare, de métro)* gate, barrier

portion [pɔrsjɔ̃] *nf* portion; **être réduit à la p. congrue** to get the smallest share

portique [pɔrtik] *nm* **(a)** *(colonnes)* portico **(b)** *(pour agrès)* (cross)beam

Porto [pɔrto] *n* Oporto

porto [pɔrto] *nm* port

portoricain, -e [pɔrtɔrikɛ̃, -ɛn] **1** *adj* Puerto Rican **2** *nm,f* **P.** Puerto Rican

Porto Rico [pɔrtoriko] *n* Puerto Rico

portrait [pɔrtrɛ] *nm* **(a)** *(peinture, dessin, photo)* portrait; **le p.** *(genre)* portrait painting, portraiture; **faire le p. de qn** to do a portrait of sb; *Fig* **c'est le p. vivant de son père, c'est tout le p. de son père** he's the spitting image of his father; *Fam* **il s'est fait abîmer** *ou* **arranger le p.** someone's made a real mess of his face; *Fam* **se faire tirer le p.** to have one's photo taken **(b)** *(description)* description; **faire le p. de qn/qch** to paint a picture of sb/sth **(c)** *Ordinat* **mode p.** portrait mode

portraitiste [pɔrtretist] *nmf* portrait painter, portraitist

portrait-robot *(pl* **portraits-robots)** [pɔrtrɛrɔbo] *nm* Photofit® (picture), identikit picture; *Fig* profile

portuaire [pɔrtɥɛr] *adj* port, harbour

portugais, -e [pɔrtɥgɛ, -ɛz] **1** *adj* Portuguese **2** *nm,f* **P.** Portuguese **3** *nm (langue)* Portuguese **4** *nf* **portugaise (a)** *(huître)* Portuguese oyster **(b)** *Fam (oreille)* **avoir les portugaises ensablées** to be as deaf as a post

Portugal [pɔrtɥgal] *nm* **le P.** Portugal

pose [poz] *nf* **(a)** *(de rideaux, de papier peint)* putting up, hanging; *(d'une vitre)* putting in; *(de moquette, de câbles)* laying; *(d'appareils)* installation; *(d'une bombe)* planting; *Méd (d'un stérilet)* putting in; *(de ventouses)* application **(b)** *(pour photo, portrait)* pose; **prendre la p.** to pose; **garder la p.** to hold the pose; *Péj* **prendre des poses** to pose **(c)** *Phot* exposure; **pellicule de 24 poses** 24-exposure film

posé, -e [poze] *adj (réfléchi)* composed, calm

posément [pozemɑ̃] *adv* calmly

poser [poze] **1** *vt* **(a)** *(mettre)* to put down; **p. qch sur/sous qch** to put sth on/under sth; *Fig* **p. son regard sur qn/qch** to look at sb/sth **(b)** *(formuler) (question)* to ask; *(hypothèse)* to put forward; *(principe)* to lay down; **p. une question à qn** to ask sb a question; **p. un problème à qn** to pose a problem for sb; **p. sa candidature** *(aux élections)* to put oneself forward (as a candidate); *Br* to stand (as a candidate); *(à un poste)* to apply

(c) *(rideaux, papier peint)* to put up, to hang; *(vitre)* to put in; *(moquette, câble)* to lay; *(appareil)* to install; *(bombe)* to plant; *Méd* **p. qch à qn** *(stérilet)* to put sth in sb; *(ventouses)* to apply sth to sb **(d)** *Math (opération, équation)* to set out; **je pose deux et je retiens un** put down two and carry one **2** *vi (pour une photo, pour un tableau)* to pose; *Péj* **p. pour la galerie** to play to the gallery **3 se poser** *vpr* **(a)** *(oiseau, avion)* to land; *Fig* **se p. sur** *(sujet: regard)* to rest on **(b)** *(question, problème)* to arise, to come up **(c)** *(à soi-même)* **se p. des questions** to ask oneself questions; *(avoir des doutes)* to have one's doubts **(d)** *Fam* **comme cuisinier, il se pose un peu là!** he's some cook, I don't think!; **comme enquiquineur, il se pose là!** he's a real pain! **(e)** *(se prétendre)* **se p. en réformateur/redresseur de torts** to set oneself up as a reformer/a righter of wrongs

poseur, -euse [pozœr, -øz] *nm,f* **(a)** *(de câbles, de carrelage)* layer; **p. d'affiches** billsticker, billposter; **la police recherche les poseurs de bombes** the police are hunting the people who planted the bombs **(b)** *Péj (pédant)* show-off, poseur

positif, -ive [pozitif, -iv] *adj* positive; **il est p.** *(à l'Alcotest, au contrôle antidopage)* his test result is positive

position [pozisjɔ̃] *nf* **(a)** *(emplacement)* position, être en première/deuxième p.** *(dans une course)* to be in first/second place; *(sur une liste)* to be first/second; **arriver en première/deuxième p.** to come first/second **(b)** *(attitude, en danse)* position; **être/se mettre en p.** to be in/get into position; **en p. debout/assise** in a standing/sitting position **(c)** *(opinion)* position **(sur on)**; **prendre p.** to take a stand, **rester sur ses positions** to stand one's ground **(d)** *(situation)* position; **être en p. de faire qch** to be in a position to do sth; **p. sociale** social position

positionner [pozisjɔne] **1** *vt* to position **2 se positionner** *vpr* to position oneself

positivement [pozitivmɑ̃] *adv* positively

posologie [pozɔlɔʒi] *nf* *Méd* dosage

possédé, -e [posede] **1** *adj (du démon)* possessed **2** *nm,f* person possessed; **hurler comme un p.** to scream like one possessed

posséder [34] [posede] *vt* **(a)** *(biens matériels)* to possess, to own; *(talent, qualité)* to possess, to have **(b)** *(sujet)* to have a thorough knowledge of; *(langue, technique)* to have mastered **(c)** *(sujet: démon, passion)* to possess **(d)** *Fam (tromper)* to take in; **se faire p.** to be taken in **(e)** *Litt (femme)* to possess

possesseur [posesœr] *nm* owner; *(d'un titre)* holder

possessif, -ive [posesif, -iv] *adj & nm* possessive

possession [posesjɔ̃] *nf* **(a)** *(fait d'avoir)* ownership, possession; *(d'un titre)* holding; **avoir qch en sa p.** to have sth in one's possession; **être en p. de qch** to be in possession of sth; **prendre p. de qch** to take possession of sth **(b)** *(bien, territoire)* possession **(c)** *(par le démon)* possession **(d)** *(maîtrise)* **être en p. de toutes ses facultés** to be in full possession of one's faculties; **être en pleine p. de ses moyens** to be at the peak of one's powers

possibilité [posibilite] *nf* **(a)** *(éventualité)* possibility **(b)** *(moyen, occasion)* opportunity, chance; **avoir la p. de faire qch** to have the opportunity *or* the chance of doing sth **(c)** **possibilités** *(intellectuelles)* potential; *(financières)* means **(d)** *Ordinat* **possibilités d'extension** upgradeability

possible [posibl] **1** *adj* **(a)** *(faisable, vraisemblable)* possible; **il leur est p. de vous héberger** it's possible for them to put you up; **il est p. qu'il soit mort** it's possible that he's dead, he might be dead; **aussitôt que p., dès que p.** as soon as possible; *Fam* **pas p.!** I don't believe it!; **si p.** if possible (**b**) *(comme superlatif)* **elle nous en parle le moins/plus p.** she talks to us about it as little/much as possible; **le moins/plus souvent p.** as infrequently/frequently as possible; **le moins/plus de détails p.** as few/many details as possible; **la salle la plus grande p.** the largest room possible; **tous les détails possibles (et imaginables)** every possible detail (**c**) *Fam (supportable)* **pas p.** *(personne, situation)* impossible; **ça n'est plus p.!** I've had enough!

2 *nm* **faire tout son p.** (**pour faire qch**) to do everything one possibly can (to do sth)

postal, -e, -aux, -ales [pɔstal, -o] *adj (tarif, services)* postal; *(train, wagon)* mail

postdater [pɔstdate] *vt* to postdate

poste¹ [pɔst] *nf* (**a**) *(service)* mail, *Br* post; **la P.** the postal service; **mettre qch à la p.** to mail *or Br* post sth; **par la p.** by mail, *Br* by post; **p. aérienne** airmail (**b**) *(lieu)* (**bureau de**) **p.** post office; **p. restante** *Br* poste restante, *Am* general delivery

poste² *nm* (**a**) *(fonction)* position, post; **p. à pourvoir** vacancy (**b**) *(appareil)* **p.** (**de radio/télévision**) radio/television (set); *Rad* **p. émetteur** *(équipement)* transmitter (**c**) *(local)* **p.** (**de police**) (police) station; **p. d'aiguillage** signal box; **p. d'essence** *Br* petrol *or Am* gas station; *Ordinat* **p. de travail** workstation (**d**) *(d'un soldat)* post; **être à son p.** to be at one's post; **p. de pilotage** cockpit (**e**) *(d'un standard)* extension (**f**) *(comptable)* entry, item

poster¹ [pɔste] **1** *vt (sentinelle, hommes, troupes)* to post, to station

2 se poster *vpr* to take up a position, to station oneself

poster² *vt (courrier)* to mail, *Br* to post

poster³ [pɔstɛr] *nm* poster

postérieur, -e [pɔsterjœr] **1** *adj* (**a**) *(dans le temps)* later, subsequent; **p. à** after (**b**) *(de derrière) (pattes)* back, hind; *Anat* posterior

2 *nm Hum (derrière)* posterior

postérieurement [pɔsterjœrmɑ̃] *adv* later, subsequently; **p. à** after

postérité [pɔsterite] *nf* posterity; **passer à la p.** *(personne)* to go down in history; *(œuvre, mot)* to be handed down to posterity

postface [pɔstfas] *nf* postscript

posthume [pɔstym] *adj* posthumous

postiche [pɔstiʃ] **1** *adj* false

2 *nm* hairpiece

postier, -ère [pɔstje, -ɛr] *nm,f* postal worker

postillon [pɔstijɔ̃] *nm* (**a**) *Hist (cocher)* postilion (**b**) **postillons** *(salive)* shower of spit; **envoyer des postillons** to splutter

postillonner [pɔstijɔne] *vi* to splutter

postindustriel, -elle [pɔstɛ̃dystrijɛl] *adj* post-industrial

postmoderne [pɔstmɔdɛrn] *adj* post-modernist

postopératoire [pɔstɔperatwar] *adj Méd* post-operative

post-scriptum [pɔstskriptɔm] *nm inv* postscript

postsynchroniser [pɔstsɛ̃krɔnize] *vt Cin* to dub

postulant, -e [pɔstylɑ̃, -ɑ̃t] *nm,f (à un emploi)* applicant, candidate (**à** for)

postulat [pɔstyla] *nm* postulate

postuler [pɔstyle] *vi* **p. à** *ou* **pour un emploi** to apply for a job

posture [pɔstyr] *nf* (**a**) *(attitude)* posture (**b**) *(situation)* **être en fâcheuse p.** to be in an awkward situation

pot [po] *nm* (**a**) *(récipient, contenu)* pot; *(en verre)* jar; **p. à eau/à lait** water/milk jug; *Fam* **le p.** *(pour enfant)* the potty;

mettre en p. *(plante)* to pot; *Fam* **quel p. de colle!** he sticks to you like glue!; **découvrir le p. aux roses** to find out what's been going on; **petit p.** *(pour bébé)* jar of baby food; **p. de chambre** chamber pot; **p. de fleurs** *(récipient)* flowerpot; *(plante)* pot of flowers; *Fam* **c'est un vrai p. de peinture!** *(femme)* she wears make-up an inch thick! (**b**) *Fam (chance)* **avoir du p.** to be lucky; **manque de p.,...** unfortunately,... (**c**) *(tuyau)* **p.** (**d'échappement**) *Br* exhaust (pipe), *Am* tail pipe; **p. catalytique** catalytic converter

potable [pɔtabl] *adj* (**a**) *(que l'on peut boire)* drinkable; **eau p./non p.** drinking/non-drinking water (**b**) *Fam (correct)* passable

potache [pɔtaʃ] *nm Fam* schoolboy

potage [pɔtaʒ] *nm* soup; **p. aux légumes** vegetable soup

potager, -ère [pɔtaʒe, -ɛr] **1** *adj voir* **jardin, plante**

2 *nm* vegetable *or* kitchen garden

potasser [pɔtase] *vt Fam (matière)* to bone up on; *(examen)* to bone up for

potassium [pɔtasjɔm] *nm Chim* potassium

pot-au-feu [pɔtofø] *nm inv* = boiled beef with vegetables

pot-de-vin (*pl* **pots-de-vin**) [pɔdvɛ̃] *nm* bribe

pote [pɔt] *nm Fam* pal

poteau, -x [pɔto] *nm* (**a**) *(piquet)* post; *(de but)* (goal) post; *Fam* **poteaux** *(jambes)* legs like tree trunks; **p.** (**d'exécution**) execution stake; **p. électrique** electricity pylon; **p. indicateur** signpost; **p. télégraphique** telegraph pole (**b**) *Fam (ami)* pal

potée [pɔte] *nf* = boiled beef or pork with cabbage and root vegetables

potelé, -e [pɔtle] *adj* chubby, plump

potence [pɔtɑ̃s] *nf* (**a**) *(gibet)* gallows *(singulier)* (**b**) *(pièce de charpente)* bracket

potentiel, -elle [pɔtɑ̃sjɛl] *adj & nm* potential

potentiellement [pɔtɑ̃sjɛlmɑ̃] *adv* potentially

poterie [pɔtri] *nf* (**a**) *(art)* pottery; **faire de la p.** to make pottery (**b**) *(objet)* piece of pottery; *(objets)* pottery

potiche [pɔtiʃ] *nf* (**a**) *(vase)* oriental vase (**b**) *Fig* figurehead

potier, -ère [pɔtje, -ɛr] *nm,f* potter

potin [pɔtɛ̃] *nm Fam* (**a**) **potins** *(ragots)* gossip (**b**) *(bruit)* row; **faire du p.** to kick up a row

potion [posjɔ̃] *nf* potion

potiron [pɔtirɔ̃] *nm* pumpkin

pot-pourri (*pl* **pots-pourris**) [popuri] *nm (chanson)* medley; *(fleurs séchées)* potpourri

pou, -x [pu] *nm* louse; *Fam* **chercher des poux dans la tête à qn** to try and pick a quarrel with sb

poubelle [pubɛl] *nf Br* (dust)bin, *Am* garbage can; **jeter** *ou* **mettre qch à la p.** to throw sth out; **faire les poubelles** to scrounge in *Br* dustbins *or Am* garbage cans

pouce [pus] *nm* (**a**) *(doigt)* thumb; *(gros orteil)* big toe; **p.!** *(dans un jeu)* truce!; *Fig* **manger sur le p.** to grab something to eat (**b**) *(mesure)* inch; **ne pas bouger d'un p.** not to move an inch (**c**) *Can* **faire du p.** *(faire du stop)* to hitch(hike)

Poucet [pusɛ] *npr* **le Petit P.** Tom Thumb

poudre [pudr] *nf* (**a**) *(poussière)* powder; **réduire qch en p.** to reduce sth to powder; *Fig* **jeter de la p. aux yeux à qn** to try and dazzle sb; **p. compacte/libre** *(maquillage)* pressed/loose powder; **p. à éternuer** sneezing powder; **p. à laver** washing powder; **p. à récurer** scouring powder; *Vieilli* **p. de riz** face powder (**b**) *(explosif)* (gun)powder

poudrer [pudre] **1** *vt* to powder; **une femme poudrée** a woman with a powdered face

2 se poudrer *vpr* to powder one's face

poudrerie [pudrəri] *nf* (a) *(fabrique de poudre)* (gun)powder factory (b) *Can (neige)* drifting snow

poudreux, -euse [pudrø, -øz] **1** *adj* powdery; **neige poudreuse** powder snow
2 *nf* **poudreuse** powder snow

poudrier [pudrije] *nm* (powder) compact

poudrière [pudrijɛr] *nf (entrepôt)* powder magazine; *Fig* powder keg

pouf [puf] **1** *exclam (chute)* thud!
2 *nm* (a) *(meuble)* pouf (b) *Belg* à p. *(à crédit)* on credit; **taper à p.** *(deviner)* to make a wild guess

pouffer [pufe] *vi* **p. (de rire)** to burst out laughing

pouffiasse [pufjas] *nf Vulg* bitch

pouilleux, -euse [pujø, -øz] **1** *adj (personne)* filthy; *(quartier, maison)* squalid
2 *nm,f* down-and-out

poulailler [pulaje] *nm* (a) *(basse-cour)* hen house (b) *(au théâtre)* **le p.** the gods

poulain [pulɛ̃] *nm* foal; *Fig* protégé

poulamon [pulamɔ̃] *nm Can* tomcod

poularde [pulard] *nf* fattened pullet

poulbot [pulbo] *nm Vieilli* = street urchin of Montmartre

poule¹ [pul] *nf* (a) *(animal)* hen; *Culin* (boiling) fowl; *Fig* **la p. aux œufs d'or** the goose that lays the golden eggs; **quand les poules auront des dents** when pigs fly; **p. d'eau** moorhen; **p. faisane** hen pheasant; *Péj* **p. mouillée** wimp; **p. au pot** boiled chicken (b) *(terme d'affection)* **ma (petite) p.** darling (c) *Fam Péj (femme légère)* whore; *(maîtresse)* mistress

poule² *nf (compétition)* tournament; *(groupe)* group

poulet [pulɛ] *nm* (a) *(animal)* chicken; **p. d'élevage** battery-reared chicken; **p. fermier** free-range chicken; **p. de grain** corn-fed chicken; **p. rôti** roast chicken (b) *(terme d'affection)* **mon (petit) p.** darling (c) *Fam (policier)* cop

poulette [pulɛt] *nf* (a) *(jeune poule)* pullet (b) *(terme d'affection)* **ma p.** darling

pouliche [puliʃ] *nf* filly

poulie [puli] *nf* pulley

poulpe [pulp] *nm* octopus

pouls [pu] *nm* pulse; **tâter le p. à qn** to feel sb's pulse; **prendre le p. à qn** to take sb's pulse

poumon [pumɔ̃] *nm* lung; **p. d'acier** iron lung; **respirer à pleins poumons** to breathe deeply

poupe [pup] *nf Naut* stern, poop

poupée [pupe] *nf* (a) *(jouet)* doll; **jouer à la p.** to play with dolls; **p. mannequin** Barbie doll®; **poupées russes** Russian dolls (b) *Fam (jolie fille)* doll (c) *(pansement)* finger bandage

poupin, -e [pupɛ̃, -in] *adj (personne)* chubby-cheeked; **visage p.** baby face

poupon [pupɔ̃] *nm* (a) *(bébé)* tiny baby (b) *(jouet)* baby doll

pouponner [pupɔne] *vi* to play the doting mother/father

pour [pur] **1** *prép* (a) *(indique le but, la destination)* for; **tiens, c'est p. toi** look, it's for you; **livres p. enfants** children's books; **p. faire qch** (in order) to do sth; **p. ne pas être en retard** so as not to be late; **p. bien faire** to do things properly; **p. que** + *subjunctive* so that, in order that; **j'épargne p. quand je serai vieux** I'm saving for when I'm old; **p. affaires** on business; **je viens p. le lave-vaisselle** I've come about the dishwasher; **c'est p. cela qu'il est venu** that's why he came, that's the reason he came; **p. quoi faire?** what for?; **tout ça p. rien!** all that for nothing!; *Fam* **c'est fait p.** that's what it's there for
(b) *(indique la direction)* for; **partir p. la France** to leave for

France; **le train p. Paris** the Paris train, the train to *or* for Paris
(c) *(dans le temps)* for; **j'en ai p. une heure** it'll take me an hour, I'll be an hour; **il sera ici p. midi** he'll be here by midday
(d) *(contre)* for; **il me l'a vendu p. trois fois rien** he sold it to me for next to nothing; **donnez-moi p. 50 euros d'essence** give me 50 euros' worth of *Br* petrol *or Am* gas
(e) *(en faveur de)* for, in favour of; **je suis p.** I'm (all) for it, I'm in favour of it
(f) *(à la place de)* for
(g) *(comme)* for; **j'avais p. ambition de...** my ambition was to..., **laisser qn p. mort** to leave sb for dead
(h) *(quant à, par rapport à)* for; **il est grand p. son âge** he's tall for his age; **p. ce qui est de...** as regards..., with regard to...; **p. moi, c'est absurde** in my opinion it's ridiculous, I think it's ridiculous
(i) *(indique le résultat)* **être trop faible p. marcher** to be too weak to walk; **cette situation n'était pas p. lui déplaire** the situation was rather to his liking
(j) *(à cause de)* for; **on l'apprécie p. sa gentillesse** people like her because she's so kind; **p. avoir désobéi** for having disobeyed, for disobeying
(k) *Litt (indique la concession)* **p. être célèbre, il n'en est pas moins modeste** although famous, he's nonetheless modest
(l) *(locutions)* **être p. beaucoup dans qch** to have a lot to do with sth; **je n'y suis p. rien!** it's got nothing to do with me!; *Fam* **être p. faire qch** *(être sur le point de)* to be about to do sth; *Fam* **p. une surprise, c'est une surprise!** that's a surprise and a half!; **perdre p. perdre, autant que le...** if you're going to lose anyway, you might as well...
2 *nm inv* **le p. et le contre** the pros and cons

pourboire [purbwar] *nm* tip; **cinq euros/10% de p.** a five-euro/10% tip; **être payé au p.** to be paid in tips

pourceau, -x [purso] *nm Litt* swine

pourcentage [pursɑ̃taʒ] *nm* percentage; **etre payé au p.** to be paid on a commission basis

pourchasser [purʃase] *vt* to pursue

pourfendre [purfɑ̃dr] *vt Hum (injustices, hypocrisie)* to combat

pourlécher [34] [purleʃe] **se pourlécher** *vpr* **se p. (les babines)** to lick one's lips

pourparlers [purparle] *nmpl* talks, negotiations; **entrer/être en p. (avec)** to enter into/be having talks (with)

pourpre [purpr] **1** *adj & nm* crimson
2 *nf (teinte naturelle)* purple (dye)

pourquoi [purkwa] **1** *adv & conj* why; **c'est p....** that's why...; **p. pas?** why not?
2 *nm inv (raison)* **le p. de** the reason for; **le p. et le comment** the whys and wherefores

pourrais *etc voir* **pouvoir**

pourri, -e [puri] **1** *adj* (a) *(bois, dent)* rotten; *(chair)* putrid; *(fruit, œufs)* bad (b) *(corrompu)* corrupt (c) *Fam (déplaisant)* rotten (d) *Fam* **être p. de fric** to be stinking rich
2 *nm* (a) *(d'un fruit)* bad part; **sentir le p.** to smell rotten (b) *très Fam (personne)* bastard

pourrir [purir] **1** *vi (bois, dent)* to rot; *(corps)* to putrefy; *(aliments)* to go bad; *Fig* **p. en prison** to rot in prison
2 *vt* (a) *(gâter)* to rot (b) *Fam (enfant)* to spoil

pourriture [purityr] *nf* (a) *(décomposition)* rot (b) *Fam (corruption)* corruption (c) *très Fam (personne)* bastard

poursuite [pursɥit] *nf* (a) *(chasse)* pursuit; **se lancer à la p. de qn** to set off in pursuit of sb; **être à la p. de qch** *(bonheur, paix)* to be in pursuit of sth (b) *(continuation)* continuation (c) *Jur* **poursuites (judiciaires)** (legal) proceedings; *(en droit pénal)* prosecution; **engager des**

poursuites contre qn to start proceedings against sb; *(en droit pénal)* to prosecute sb **(d)** *(course cycliste)* pursuit

poursuivant, -e [pursɥivɑ̃, -ɑ̃t] *nm,f* pursuer

poursuivre [65] [pursɥivr] **1** *vt* **(a)** *(pourchasser)* to pursue; *(sujet: idée, crainte)* to haunt; *(sujet: malchance)* to dog **(b)** *(idéal, rêve, but)* to pursue **(c)** *(harceler)* to pester **(de** with**)**; *(sujet: créancier)* to hound; **p. qn de ses assiduités** to force one's attentions on sb **(d)** *Jur* **p. qn (en justice)** to bring proceedings against sb; *(en droit pénal)* to prosecute sb **(e)** *(continuer)* to continue, to go on with; **poursuivez** *(histoire, exposé)* go on
2 se poursuivre *vpr (continuer)* to continue, to go on

pourtant [purtɑ̃] *adv* yet; **tout avait p. bien commencé** yet it all started so well; **je ne peux p. pas l'empêcher de venir** still, I can't stop him from coming; **ça n'est p. pas compliqué!** it's hardly complicated!

pourtour [purtur] *nm* circumference, perimeter

pourvoi [purvwa] *nm Jur* appeal; **p. en cassation** appeal to a higher court

pourvoir [73b] [purvwar] **1** *vt* **p. qn de qch** to provide sb with sth; **p. qch de qch** to equip *or* fit sth with sth
2 pourvoir à *vt ind (besoins)* to provide *or* cater for
3 se pourvoir *vpr* **(a)** *(se munir)* **se p. de qch** to provide oneself with sth **(b)** *Jur* **se p. en cassation** to take one's case to the Court of Appeal

pourvoyeur, -euse [purvwajœr, -øz] *nm,f* supplier

pourvu¹ [purvy] **pourvu que** *conj* **(a)** *(condition)* **p. que tu y sois** provided (that) *or* so long as you're there **(b)** *(souhait)* **p. qu'il le fasse!** let's just hope he does it!

pourvu², -e *voir* **pourvoir**

pousse [pus] *nf* **(a)** *(des feuilles, des cheveux)* growth **(b)** *(bourgeon)* shoot; **p. de bambou** bamboo shoot

poussé, -e [puse] *adj (en profondeur)* thorough

pousse-café [puskafe] *nm inv* (glass of) liqueur *(after coffee)*

poussée [puse] *nf* **(a)** *(pression)* pressure; *(d'un liquide)* upthrust; **la p. de la foule** the pushing and shoving of the crowd **(b)** *(croissance)* growth; *(de boutons, d'herpès)* eruption; **p. de fièvre** sudden rise in temperature; **p. démographique** sudden population increase; **faire une p. de croissance** to shoot up **(c)** *Fig (des prix)* upsurge **(de** in**)**

pousse-pousse [puspus] *nm inv* rickshaw

pousser [puse] **1** *vt* **(a)** *(soumettre à une force)* to push; *(sujet: vent) (embarcation)* to drive; **p. qn du coude** to nudge sb with one's elbow; *Fam* **à la va comme je te pousse** slipshod; *Fam* **faut pas p. Mémé** *ou* **Mémère dans les orties!** don't push your luck!
(b) *(inciter)* **p. qn à faire qch** *(sujet: faim, jalousie)* to drive sb to do sth; *(sujet: personne)* to urge sb to do sth; **p. qn à qch** to drive sb to sth; **poussé par la curiosité** prompted by curiosity
(c) *(continuer)* **p. trop loin une plaisanterie** to take a joke too far; **il a poussé la générosité jusqu'à l'héberger** he was so generous that he even put him up
(d) *(émettre)* **p. un cri** to shout, to give a shout; **p. des cris** to shout; **p. un soupir** to sigh, to heave a sigh; **p. un gémissement** to groan; *Fam* **p. la chansonnette** to sing a song
2 *vi* **(a)** *(exercer une pression)* to push; *(aux toilettes)* to strain; *(en accouchant)* to push; *Fam* **faut pas p.!** don't push your luck!
(b) *(continuer)* **p. jusqu'au bois** to push on as far as the wood
(c) *(plante, cheveux, ongles)* to grow; *(bourgeon)* to sprout; *(dents)* to come through; *Fam (enfant)* to shoot up; **se laisser p. la barbe** to grow a beard

3 se pousser *vpr (pour faire de la place)* to move over *or* up

poussette [pusɛt] *nf (pour enfants) Br* pushchair, *Am* stroller

poussière [pusjɛr] *nf* dust; **une p.** a speck of dust; *Fam* **faire la p.** *ou* **les poussières** to do the dusting, to dust; *Fig* **tomber en p.** to crumble to dust; *Fig* **mordre la p.** to bite the dust; *Fam* **100 euros et des poussières** 100 and a bit euros

poussiéreux, -euse [pusjerø, -øz] *adj* dusty; *Fig* stuffy

poussif, -ive [pusif, -iv] *adj (moteur, personne)* wheezy

poussin [pusɛ̃, -in] **1** *nm* chick; *Fam* **mon p.** pet
2 *nm,f Sp* junior *(9 years old)*

poutre [putr] *nf (en bois)* beam; *(en métal)* girder; **p. apparente** exposed beam; **p. maîtresse** main beam/girder

poutrelle [putrɛl] *nf* girder

pouvoir¹ [puvwar] *nm* **(a)** *(puissance)* power; **prendre le p.** to assume power; **être au p.** to be in power; **p. absolu** absolute power; **p. exécutif** executive power; **p. judiciaire** judicial power; **p. législatif** legislative power; **les pouvoirs publics** the authorities **(b)** *(attributions)* power; **il n'est pas en mon p. de...** it is not within my power to... **(c)** **p. d'achat** purchasing power

pouvoir² [57] **1** *vt* **(a)** *(être capable de)* can, to be able; **p. faire qch** to be able to do sth; **si je peux** if I can, if I'm able to; **je ne peux pas** I can't, I'm unable to; **comment a-t-il pu dire cela?** how could he say that?; **on n'y peut rien** it can't be helped, there's nothing that can be done about it; **on ne peut plus/moins aimable** extremely friendly/unfriendly; **il n'en peut plus** *(de fatigue)* he's exhausted; *(d'exaspération, d'impatience)* he can't take any more; **dès que je pourrai** as soon as I can; **où peut-il bien être?** where can he be?; **nous ne pouvons rien pour vous** we can't do anything for you
(b) *(avoir le droit, la permission de)* can, to be allowed; **vous pouvez partir** you can go; **puis-je entrer?** can I come in?
(c) *(être possible)* **la porte a pu se fermer toute seule** the door might have *or* could have closed on its own; **tout le monde peut se tromper** anyone can make a mistake; **elle peut bien s'excuser, je ne lui pardonnerai pas** she can apologize all she likes, but I won't forgive her; *Fam* **qu'est-ce que ça peut te faire?** what's that got to do with you?
2 *v impersonnel* **cela se peut/se pourrait (bien)** it's quite possible; **il se peut qu'il vienne** he may *or* might come

PPCM [pepeseɛm] *nm Math (abrév* **plus petit commun multiple**) LCM

PQ [peky] *nm* **(a)** *Can Pol (abrév* **Parti Québécois)** PQ **(b)** *Fam (papier hygiénique)* toilet paper, TP

pragmatique [pragmatik] *adj* pragmatic

pragois, -e [pragwa, -az] **1** *adj* of Prague
2 *nm,f* **P.** person from Prague

Prague [prag] *n* Prague

praire [prɛr] *nf* clam

prairie [preri] *nf* meadow; *Géog* **la P.** the Prairies

praline [pralin] *nf* praline

praliné, -e [praline] *adj (chocolat)* praline-filled; *(glace)* praline-flavoured

praticable [pratikabl] *adj* **(a)** *(route)* passable, negotiable; *(terrain)* playable **(b)** *(réalisable)* practicable

praticien, -enne [pratisjɛ̃, -ɛn] *nm,f (médecin)* (medical) practitioner

pratiquant, -e [pratikɑ̃, -ɑ̃t] **1** *adj* practising
2 *nm,f* practising Christian/Jew/Muslim/*etc*

pratique [pratik] **1** *adj (méthode, personne)* practical; *(outil)* handy; *(date, heure, jour)* convenient; **avoir l'esprit p.** to have a practical turn of mind

2 *nf* (**a**) *(application)* practice; **mettre qch en p.** to put sth into practice; **dans la p.** in practice (**b**) *(expérience)* (practical) experience; **avoir une longue p. de qch** to have had a lot of (practical) experience of sth (**c**) *(d'un sport)* playing; **la p. du yoga** doing yoga (**d**) *(procédé, coutume)* practice

pratiquement [pratikmā] *adv* (**a**) *(concrètement)* in practice (**b**) *(presque)* practically

pratiquer [pratike] **1** *vt* (**a**) *(religion)* to practise; *(activité)* to take part in; *(langue)* to use; *(sport)* to play; **p. la natation** to swim; **les prix pratiqués ici** the prices being asked here (**b**) *(faire)* *(ouverture)* to make; *(opération chirurgicale)* to carry out
2 *vi* (**a**) *(médecin, avocat)* to practise (**b**) *(être religieux)* to practise one's religion; **il est catholique mais il ne pratique pas** he's a Catholic but he doesn't go to church
3 se pratiquer *vpr (sport)* to be played; *(coutume)* to be practised

pré [pre] *nm* meadow

préadolescent, -e [preadɔlesã, -ãt] *nm,f* preadolescent

préalable [prealabl] **1** *adj* previous, prior (**à** to); *(accord)* prior; *(formalités)* preliminary
2 *nm (condition)* prerequisite, precondition; **au p.** first, beforehand

préalablement [prealabləmã] *adv* first, beforehand; **p. à...** prior to...

préambule [preãbyl] *nm* preamble (**de** to); **sans p.**, **elle annonça...** without any warning, she announced...

PréAO [preao] *nf* Ordinat *(abrév* **présentation assistée par ordinateur)** computer-assisted presentation

préau, -x [preo] *nm (de cour d'école)* covered area; *(salle)* hall

préavis [preavi] *nm* (advance) notice; **un p. de trois mois** three months' notice; **p. de grève** strike notice; **déposer un p. de grève** to give notice of strike action; **p. de licenciement** notice (of dismissal)

précaire [preker] *adj (position)* precarious; *(santé)* delicate; **être en équilibre p.** to be precariously balanced

précambrien, -enne [prekãbrijẽ, -ɛn] *Géol* **1** *adj* Pre-Cambrian
2 *nm* **le P.** the Pre-Cambrian period

précarité [prekarite] *nf* precariousness

précaution [prekosjɔ̃] *nf* (**a**) *(mesure)* precaution; **par (mesure de) p.** as a precaution; **prendre des** *ou* **ses précautions** to take precautions; *Prov* **deux précautions valent mieux qu'une** better safe than sorry (**b**) *(prudence)* caution, care; **pour plus de p.** to be on the safe side

précautionneux, -euse [prekosjɔnø, -øz] *adj* careful

précédemment [presedamã] *adv* previously, before

précédent, -e [presedã, -ãt] **1** *adj* previous
2 *nm* precedent; **sans p.** unprecedented, without precedent

précéder [34] [presede] **1** *vt* to precede; **je l'ai précédé de dix minutes** I got there ten minutes before he did
2 *vi* **la page qui précède** the preceding *or* previous page; **dans les jours qui précèdent** in the preceding days; **ce qui précède** the foregoing

précepte [presɛpt] *nm* precept

précepteur, -trice [preseptœr, -tris] *nm,f* (private) tutor

préchauffage [preʃofaʒ] *nm* preheating

préchauffer [preʃofe] *vt* to preheat

prêcher [preʃe] **1** *vt* (**a**) *(enseigner)* to preach (**à** to) (**b**) *(prôner)* to advocate; *Hum* **p. la bonne parole** to spread the word
2 *vi (prononcer un sermon)* to preach; *Fig* **p. dans le désert** to be a voice crying in the wilderness; *Fig* **p. pour sa paroisse** to look after one's own interests

prêchi-prêcha [preʃipreʃa] *nm inv* Fam Péj preachifying

précieusement [presjøzmã] *adv* **garder** *ou* **conserver qch p.** to keep sth safe

précieux, -euse [presjø, -øz] *adj* (**a**) *(coûteux)* precious (**b**) *(conseil, temps)* valuable (**à** to) (**c**) *(style, personne)* precious, affected

préciosité [presjozite] *nf* Litt affectation, preciosity

précipice [presipis] *nm* chasm, abyss; *(d'une falaise, d'un ravin)* precipice; *Fig* abyss; *Fig* **être au bord du p.** to be on the edge of an abyss

précipitamment [presipitamã] *adv* hurriedly, hastily; **entrer/sortir p.** to rush or dash in/out

précipitation [presipitasjɔ̃] *nf* (**a**) *(hâte)* haste (**b**) *Chim* precipitation (**c**) **précipitations** *(pluies)* precipitation

précipité, -e [presipite] **1** *adj* hasty, hurried
2 *nm Chim* precipitate

précipiter [presipite] **1** *vt* (**a**) *(entraîner)* to throw down, to hurl down; *Fig* to plunge; **p. qn dans le vide** to hurl sb over the edge (**b**) *(hâter)* to speed up; *(événements)* to precipitate; *(la mort de quelqu'un)* to hasten; **il ne faut rien p.** we mustn't rush things (**c**) *Chim* to precipitate
3 se précipiter *vpr* (**a**) *(se hâter)* to rush, to hurry (**b**) *(s'accélérer)* **les événements se sont précipités** things started happening quickly (**c**) *(se jeter)* to rush (**sur/vers** at/towards)

précis, -e [presi, -iz] *adj* precise, exact; à six o'clock precisely *or* exactly; **penser à quelque chose de p.** to have something specific in mind
2 *nm* précis, summary; *(livre)* handbook; **p. d'histoire de France** short history of France

précisément [presizemã] *adv* precisely, exactly

préciser [presize] **1** *vt (déterminer)* *(date)* to specify (**b**) *(clarifier)* *(pensée)* to clarify; **je tiens à p. que...** I wish to make it clear that...; **pourriez-vous p.?** could you be more specific?
2 se préciser *vpr* to become clear(er); *(idée)* to take shape

précision [presizjɔ̃] *nf* (**a**) *(d'une information, d'une description)* accuracy; *(de mouvements)* preciseness, precision; **avec p.** precisely (**b**) *(détail)* **donner** *ou* **apporter des précisions sur qch** to give precise details about sth; **demander des précisions sur qch** to ask for further information about sth

précoce [prekɔs] *adj (enfant)* precocious; *(fruit, été)* early; *(sénilité, calvitie)* premature

précocité [prekɔsite] *nf* precociousness; *(d'un fruit, d'une saison)* earliness

précolombien, -enne [prekɔlɔ̃bjẽ, -ɛn] *adj* pre-Columbian

préconçu, -e [prekɔ̃sy] *adj* preconceived

préconiser [prekɔnize] *vt* to advocate; *(remède)* to recommend

précuit, -e [prekɥi, -it] *adj* precooked

précurseur [prekyrsœr] *nm* precursor, forerunner
2 *adj* **signe p.** forewarning

prédateur [predatœr] *nm* predator

prédécesseur [predesesœr] *nm* predecessor

prédécoupé, -e [predekupe] *adj* precut

prédestination [predɛstinasjɔ̃] *nf* predestination

prédestiné, -e [predɛstine] *adj* predestined (**à qch/à faire qch** for sth/to do sth)

prédestiner [predɛstine] *vt* to predestine (**à qch/à faire qch** for sth/to do sth)

prédicat [predika] *nm* Gram predicate

prédicateur, -trice [predikatœr, -tris] *nm,f* preacher

prédiction [prediksjɔ̃] *nf* prediction

prédilection [predilɛksjɔ̃] *nf* predilection, partiality; **de p.** favourite; **avoir une p. pour qch** to be partial to sth, to have a predilection for sth

prédire [27b] [predir] *vt* to predict; **p. qch à qn** to predict sth for sb

prédisposer [predispoze] *vt* to predispose (**à** to)

prédisposition [predispozisjɔ̃] *nf* predisposition (**à** to)

prédominant, -e [predɔminɑ̃, -ɑ̃t] *adj* predominant

prédominer [predɔmine] *vi* to predominate

préélectoral, -e, -aux, -ales [preelɛktɔral, -o] *adj* pre-electoral, pre-election

préemballé, -e [preɑ̃bale] *adj* prepacked

prééminence [preeminɑ̃s] *nf* pre-eminence

prééminent, -e [preeminɑ̃, -ɑ̃t] *adj* pre-eminent

préempter [preɑ̃pte] *vt Jur* to pre-empt

préemption [preɑ̃psjɔ̃] *nf Jur* pre-emption

préenregistré, -e [preɑ̃rəʒistre] *adj* prerecorded

préétablir [preetablir] *vt* to pre-establish

préexistant, -e [preɛgzistɑ̃, -ɑ̃t] *adj* pre-existing

préexister [preɛgziste] *vi* to pre-exist; **p. à qch** to pre-exist sth

préfabrication [prefabrikasjɔ̃] *nf* prefabrication

préfabriqué, -e [prefabrike] **1** *adj* prefabricated **2** *nm* prefabricated material; **c'est du p.** it's prefabricated

préface [prefas] *nf* preface, foreword (**à** *ou* **de** to)

préfacer [16] [prefase] *vt* to preface

préfectoral, -e, -aux, -ales [prefɛktɔral, -o] *adj* = relating to a "préfecture" or "préfet"

préfecture [prefɛktyr] *nf* prefecture; *(ville)* = administrative centre of a "département"; **la P. de police** police headquarters

préférable [preferabl] *adj* preferable (**à** to); **il serait p. de le revoir** *ou* **que nous le revoyions** it would be preferable to see him again

préféré, -e [prefere] *adj* & *nm,f* favourite

préférence [preferɑ̃s] *nf* preference; **de p.** preferably; **de p. à** in preference to

préférentiel, -elle [preferɑ̃sjɛl] *adj* preferential

préférer [34] [prefere] *vt* to prefer (**à** to); **je préférerais du vin** I'd prefer wine, I'd rather have wine; **je préférerais que vous veniez** I'd prefer it if you came, I'd rather you came; **p. faire qch** to prefer to do sth

préfet [prefɛ] *nm* prefect *(administrative head of a "département")*; **p. de police** = chief commissioner of police

préfigurer [prefigyre] *vt* to prefigure, to foreshadow

préfixe [prefiks] *nm* prefix

pré-formaté, -e *(mpl* **pre-formatés,** *fpl* **pré-formatées)** [prefɔrmate] *adj Ordinat* pre-formatted

préhension [preɑ̃sjɔ̃] *nf* gripping

préhistoire [preistwar] *nf* prehistory

préhistorique [preistɔrik] *adj* prehistoric

pré-impression [preɛ̃presjɔ̃] *nf Typ* pre-press

préindustriel, -elle [preɛ̃dystrijɛl] *adj* pre-industrial

préinscription [preɛ̃skripsjɔ̃] *nf* pre-registration

préjudice [preʒydis] *nm (à une cause)* prejudice, detriment; *(à une personne)* harm, wrong; *Jur* tort; **subir un p. matériel** to sustain damage; **subir un p. moral** to suffer mental distress; **porter p. à qn** to do sb harm; **au p. de qch** to the detriment of sth

préjugé [preʒyʒe] *nm* prejudice, bias **(contre** against); **avoir un p. contre qn/qch** to be prejudiced *or* biased against sb/sth

prélasser [prelase] **se prélasser** *vpr* to lounge

prélat [prela] *nm* prelate

prélavage [prelavaʒ] *nm* pre-wash

prélèvement [prelɛvmɑ̃] *nm* **(a)** *(en argent)* deduction (**sur** from); **faire un p. sur un compte** to debit an account; **p. automatique** direct debit; **prélèvements obligatoires** = tax and social security contributions **(b)** *(extraction) (d'un organe)* removal; *(de sécrétions)* taking a sample; *(d'un échantillon)* taking; **faire un p. de sang** *ou* **sanguin à qn** to take a blood sample from sb **(c)** *(partie prélevée) (de sécrétions)* swab; *(de sang)* sample

prélever [46] [prelve] *vt* **(a)** *(argent)* to deduct (**sur** from); *(impôt)* to levy **(b)** *(organe)* to remove; *(sécrétions, échantillon)* to take; **p. du sang à qn** to take a blood sample from sb

préliminaire [preliminer] **1** *adj* preliminary **2** *nmpl* **préliminaires** preliminaries

prélude [prelyd] *nm Mus & Fig* prelude (**de** *ou* **à** to)

prématuré, -e [prematyre] **1** *adj* premature; **être p. de quatre semaines** to be four weeks premature **2** *nm,f* premature baby

prématurément [prematyremɑ̃] *adv* prematurely

préméditation [premeditasjɔ̃] *nf* premeditation; **meurtre avec p.** premeditated murder

préméditer [premedite] *vt* to premeditate

prémenstruel, -elle [premɑ̃stryɛl] *adj* premenstrual

premier, -ère [prəmje, -ɛr] **1** *adj* **(a)** *(initial, dominant)* first; **les trois premières années** the first three years; **la première marche** the bottom stair; **le p. rang** the front row; **prendre la première place** *(dans une course)* to take the lead; **le p. venu** the first person who comes along; **les premiers arrivés** the first to arrive; **je suis le p. concerné** I'm the one most affected; **en p.** in the first place, firstly; **le p. de l'an** New Year's Day **(b)** *(original)* primary, original **2** *nm,f* **(a)** *(dans un classement)* first; **arriver le p.** *ou* **en p.** to arrive first; **être le p. de sa classe** to be top of one's class; **être le p. à faire qch** to be (the) first to do sth; *voir aussi* **cinquième** **(b)** *(acteur)* **jeune p.** (young) romantic lead; *Fig* **avoir des airs de jeune p.** to look like a film star **3** *nm (date)* **le p. janvier** the first of January, January the first **4** *nf* **première (a)** *(d'une pièce)* first *or* opening night; *(d'un film)* première **(b)** *(classe) Br* ≃ lower sixth, *Am* ≃ eleventh grade **(c)** *(de train, d'avion)* first class; **voyager en première** to travel first-class **(d)** *(vitesse)* first (gear) **(e)** *(de chaussure)* insole **(f)** *Fam* **de première** *(de très bonne qualité)* first-rate, first-class

premièrement [prəmjɛrmɑ̃] *adv* first, in the first place

prémisse [premis] *nf* premise

prémolaire [premɔler] *nf* premolar

prémonition [premɔnisjɔ̃] *nf* premonition

prémonitoire [premɔnitwar] *adj* premonitory

prémunir [premynir] **se prémunir** *vpr* **se p. contre qch** to be on one's guard against sth

prenant, -e [prənɑ̃, -ɑ̃t] *adj (livre, spectacle)* fascinating; *(travail)* time-consuming

prénatal, -e, -als, -ales [prenatal] *adj* antenatal, prenatal

prendre [58] [prɑ̃dr] **1** *vt* **(a)** *(saisir)* to take; **p. qch dans un tiroir** to take sth out of a drawer; **prends-le par la poignée** take hold of it by the handle; **c'est à p. ou à laisser** take it or leave it; *Fam* **il faut savoir le p.** you have to know how to handle him; *Fam* **c'est toujours ça de pris** that's something at least; *Fam* **qu'est-ce qu'on va a p.! we're in for it!**
(b) *(enlever)* to take (away); **p. qch à qn** to take sth (away) from sb; **cela m'a pris du temps/deux heures** it took me a while/two hours; **p. 25 euros de l'heure** to take 25 euros an hour
(c) *(s'emparer de) (personne, gibier)* to catch, *(ville, région)* to take, to capture; **se laisser p.** to let oneself be *or* get caught; *Fig* to let oneself be taken in; *Prov* **tel est pris qui croyait p.** it's a case of the biter bit
(d) *(aller chercher)* to collect, to pick up; **attends, je vais p. mon sac** wait till I get my bag
(e) *(acheter)* to get; *(chambre, studio)* to take; **cette robe me plaît, je la prends** I like this dress, I'll take it
(f) *(bonne, assistant)* to take on; *(pensionnaire)* to take in; *(travail)* to take; **être pris** *(élève, candidat)* to be accepted; *(acteur)* to get the part
(g) *(repas, boisson, bain)* to have; *(médicament)* to take
(h) *(moyen de transport)* to take
(i) *(apparence)* to take on, to assume; *(attitude)* to take; *(accent)* to pick up
(j) p. l'eau *(bateau)* to be leaking, to be letting in water
(k) *(personne)* **p. qn comme exemple** to take sb as an example; **p. qn/qch pour** to take sb/sth for
(l) *Fam (arriver)* **qu'est-ce qui lui prend?** what's come over him?; **ça te prend souvent?** do you get like that often?
2 *vi* **(a)** *(ciment, flan)* to set
(b) *(plante)* to take (root)
(c) *(feu)* to catch
(d) *(réussir) (vaccin)* to take effect; *(mode)* to catch on; *Fam* **avec moi, ça ne prend pas!** you can't fool me!
(e) *(tourner)* **p. à gauche/droite** to go left/right
(f) p. sur soi to restrain *or* contain oneself
3 se prendre *vpr* **(a)** *(s'accrocher)* **se p. dans une porte/à un clou** to get caught in the door/on a nail
(b) *(se considérer)* **se p. pour un héros** to consider oneself a hero; **pour qui vous prenez-vous?** who do you think you are?
(c) *(locutions)* **s'en p. à qn/qch** to take it out on sb/sth; **ne t'en prends qu'à toi-même** you've only got yourself to blame; **s'y p. bien avec qn** to know how to handle sb; **s'y p. mal avec qn** not to handle sb the right way; **vous vous y prenez mal** you're going about it the wrong way; **s'y p. à deux fois pour faire qch** to take two attempts to do sth

preneur, -euse [prənœr, -øz] *nm,f* *(acheteur)* buyer, purchaser; **trouver p.** to find a buyer; **je suis p.!** I'm interested! **(b) p. d'otages** hostage taker; **p. de son** sound engineer

prenne *etc voir* **prendre**

prénom [prenɔ̃] *nm Br* first *or Am* given name

prénommé, -e [prenɔme] *adj* **le p. Louis** the man/boy called Louis

prénommer [prenɔme] **1** *vt* to call, to name
2 se prénommer *vpr* **il se prénomme Christophe** his *Br* first *or Am* given name is Christophe

prénuptial, -e, -aux, -ales [prenypsjal, -o] *adj* premarital; **examen p.** premarital medical check-up

préoccupant, -e [preɔkypɑ̃, -ɑ̃t] *adj* worrying

préoccupation [preɔkypasjɔ̃] *nf* concern, preoccupation; **j'ai d'autres préoccupations** I have other things to worry about

préoccupé, -e [preɔkype] *adj* worried

préoccuper [preɔkype] **1** *vt* to worry; **être préoccupé**

par qch to be worried about sth; **sa santé me préoccupe** I'm worried about his health
2 se préoccuper *vpr* **se p. de qn/qch** to concern oneself with sb/sth

prépa [prepa] *nf Fam Scol* preparatory class *(for the entrance exam to the "grandes écoles")*; **faire une p., être en p.** to be studying for the entrance exam to the "grandes écoles"

préparateur, -trice [preparatœr, -tris] *nm,f* laboratory assistant; **p. en pharmacie** pharmacist's *or Br* chemist's assistant

préparatifs [preparatif] *nmpl* preparations **(de** for)

préparation [preparasjɔ̃] *nf* preparation (à for); **faire une p. militaire** = to do an officer training course in preparation for military service; **faire une p. aux grandes écoles** to prepare for the entrance exam to the "grandes écoles"

préparatoire [preparatwar] *adj* preparatory

préparer [prepare] **1** *vt* **(a)** *(discours, repas, plat)* to prepare; *(réunion, soirée, vacances)* to make preparations for, to arrange; *(ordonnance)* to make up; *(plats* **tout préparés** ready-cooked meals; *Fig* **je suis sûr qu'il nous prépare quelque chose** I'm sure he's up to something **(b)** *(personne)* **p. qn à qch** to prepare sb for sth; *(entraîner)* to train sb for sth **(c)** *(examen)* to prepare for, to study for
2 se préparer *vpr* **(a)** *(être imminent)* to be in the offing **(b)** *(s'apprêter)* **se p. à qch/à faire qch** to prepare for sth/to do sth **(c)** *(se faire)* **se p. qch** *(boisson, plat)* to make oneself sth; **tu te prépares bien des désillusions** you're in for a big disappointment

prépayé, -e [prepeje] *adj* prepaid

prépondérant, -e [prepɔ̃derɑ̃, -ɑ̃t] *adj* predominant

préposé, -e [prepoze] *nm,f (employé)* employee; *(dans un vestiaire)* attendant; **p. (des postes)** *Br* postman, *f* postwoman, *Am* mailman, *f* mailwoman

préposer [prepoze] *vt* **p. qn à qch** to appoint sb to sth

préposition [prepozisjɔ̃] *nf Gram* preposition

prépuce [prepys] *nm Anat* foreskin, *Spéc* prepuce

préraphaélite [prerafaelit] *adj & nm* Pre-Raphaelite

préretraite [preretret] *nf* early retirement; *(pension)* early retirement pension; **partir en p.** to take early retirement

prérogative [prerɔgativ] *nf* prerogative

près [prɛ] *adv* **(a)** *(dans l'espace)* near, close; *(dans le temps)* close; **de p.** closely; **voir qch de p.** to see sth close up; **à quelques détails p.** except for a few details; **la longueur, à cinq centimètres p.** the length, to within five centimetres; **à deux minutes p., je ratais le train** two minutes later and I would have missed the train; **je n'en suis pas à un euro p.** one euro more or less doesn't matter; **à peu de chose(s) p.** more or less
(b) p. de *(dans l'espace)* near (to), close to; *(dans le temps)* close to; *(environ)* nearly, almost; **p. de là** nearby, close by; **de chez eux** near (to) *or* close to where they live; *Fam* **être p. de ses sous** to be tight-fisted; *Hum* **nous ne sommes pas p. de le revoir** we won't see him again in a hurry
(c) **à peu p.** *(pas tout à fait)* nearly, almost; *(approximativement)* about, approximately; **il est à peu p. certain que…** it is fairly certain that…

présage [prezaʒ] *nm* omen, sign; **mauvais p.** bad omen

présager [prezaʒe] [45] *vt* **(a)** *(annoncer)* to presage; **cela ne présage rien de bon** it doesn't bode well **(b)** *(prévoir)* to predict; **ces gros nuages noirs laissent p. un orage** those big black clouds are a sure sign of a storm

pré-salé *(pl* **prés-salés)** [presale] *nm (mouton)* salt-meadow sheep; *(viande)* salt-meadow lamb

presbyte [prɛsbit] *adj* long-sighted

presbytère [prɛsbitɛr] *nm* presbytery

presbytérien, -enne [prɛsbiterjɛ̃, -ɛn] *adj & nm,f* Presbyterian

presbytie [prɛsbisi] *nf* long-sightedness

préscolaire [preskɔlɛr] *adj* preschool

prescription [prɛskripsjɔ̃] *nf* (**a**) *Jur* après cinquante ans, il y a p. the statute of limitations runs out after fifty years (**b**) *(ordonnance)* prescription (**c**) *(instruction)* rule, regulation

prescrire [30] [prɛskrir] *vt (médicament)* to prescribe; à la date prescrite on the date specified

préséance [preseɑ̃s] *nf* precedence, priority (**sur** over)

présélection [preselɛksjɔ̃] *nf* preselection; *(de candidats)* short-listing

présélectionner [preselɛksjɔne] *vt* to preselect; *(candidats)* to short-list

présence [prezɑ̃s] *nf* (**a**) *(dans un lieu)* presence; *(à l'école)* attendance; il ignore votre p. he doesn't know you're here; avoir de la p. *(acteur)* to have great presence; les parties en p. the parties present; en p. de toute la famille in front of the whole family; en p. du virus when the virus is present (**b**) avoir la p. d'esprit de faire qch to have the presence of mind to do sth

présent¹, -e [prezɑ̃, -ɑ̃t] **1** *adj* (**a**) *(physiquement)* present; les personnes présentes those present; Jacques Martelin, ici p., vous le dira Jacques Martelin, who is here with us, will tell you; Tardieu? – p.! Tardieu. – here! *or* present! (**b**) *(situation, moment)* present; vivre dans l'instant p. to live in the present

2 *nm* (**a**) *Gram* present (tense); le p. du subjonctif/de l'indicatif the present subjunctive/indicative; au p. in the present (**b**) *(moment présent)* present; vivre dans le p. to live in the present (**c**) à p. at present, (just) now; jusqu'à p. up to now, until now; jusqu'à p., je n'ai pas reçu de nouvelles I've not received any news as yet; dès à p. from now on; à p. que... now that...

3 *nf* par la présente *(par cette lettre)* hereby

présent² *nm Litt (cadeau)* present, gift; faire p. de qch à qn to present sth to sb

présentable [prezɑ̃tabl] *adj* presentable

présentateur, -trice [prezɑ̃tatœr, -tris] *nm,f* presenter; *(d'un spectacle télévisé)* compère; p. de journal télévisé newscaster, newsreader

présentation [prezɑ̃tasjɔ̃] *nf* (**a**) *(de faits, d'un billet)* presentation; 15% de réduction sur p. de la carte 15% discount on presentation of this card (**b**) *(apparence) (d'une personne)* appearance; *(d'un document)* presentation, layout; recherche hôtesses, excellente p. *(petite annonce)* hostesses required, must have smart appearance; *Ordinat* p. assistée par ordinateur computer-aided presentation (**c**) *(dans un groupe)* introduction (à to); faire les présentations to make the introductions (**d**) *(d'un film)* showing, presentation; p. de mode fashion show

présenter [prezɑ̃te] **1** *vt* (**a**) *(montrer)* to show, to present; *(symptôme)* to present; *(facture)* to submit

(**b**) *(par écrit)* to present

(**c**) *(oralement) (arguments)* to present, to set out; *(spectacle)* to present, to host; p. ses condoléances à qn to offer sb one's condolences

(**d**) *(projet de loi)* to bring in, to introduce; p. sa candidature à un poste to apply for a job

(**e**) *(personne)* p. qn à qn to introduce sb to sb; je vous présente Claire this is Claire

2 *vi Fam* bien/mal p. to look/not to look good

3 se présenter *vpr* (**a**) *(occasion, cas)* to arise, to present itself; ça se présente bien things are looking promising

(**b**) *(à un poste)* to apply (à for); se p. à un examen to take *or Br* sit an examination; se p. aux élections to be a candidate at *or Br* stand at the elections

(**c**) *(arriver)* to turn up; présentez-vous au commissariat à dix heures be at the police station at ten o'clock; se p. chez qn to call on sb

(**d**) *(dire son nom)* to introduce oneself (à to)

(**e**) le bébé se présente par la tête the baby is presenting normally

présentoir [prezɑ̃twar] *nm* display unit

préservatif [prezɛrvatif] *nm* condom; p. féminin female condom

préservation [prezɛrvasjɔ̃] *nf* preservation, protection

préserver [prezɛrve] **1** *vt* to preserve, to protect (**de** from); le ciel m'en préserve! heaven forbid!

2 se préserver *vpr* to protect oneself (**de** from)

présidence [prezidɑ̃s] *nf* (**a**) *(d'un état)* presidency (**b**) *(d'un club)* chairmanship

président, -e [prezidɑ̃, -ɑ̃t] *nm,f* (**a**) *(d'un état)* president; le p. de la République the President of the Republic (**b**) *(d'une assemblée, d'un club)* chairman, *f* chairwoman; P. du conseil d'administration Chairman of the Board; p.-directeur général *Br* chairman and managing director, *Am* chief executive officer (**c**) *(magistrat)* presiding judge; p. du jury foreman of the jury

présidentiel, -elle [prezidɑ̃sjɛl] **1** *adj* presidential

2 *nfpl* présidentielles presidential elections

présider [prezide] **1** *vt* (**a**) *(conseil)* to preside over; *(réunion)* to chair (**b**) *(banquet)* to be the guest of honour at

2 présider à *vt ind Litt* p. aux destinées de... to preside over the destinies of...

présomption [prezɔ̃psjɔ̃] *nf* presumption

présomptueux, -euse [prezɔ̃ptɥø, -øz] *adj* presumptuous

presque [prɛsk] *adv* (**a**) *(à peu près)* almost, nearly; p. jamais/rien scarcely *or* hardly ever/anything; je ne dors p. pas I hardly *or* scarcely get any sleep; rien ou p. scarcely anything (**b**) *(devant un nom)* la p. totalité de son œuvre nearly *or* almost all of his work

presqu'île [prɛskil] *nf* peninsula

pressant, -e [presɑ̃, -ɑ̃t] *adj (besoin)* pressing, urgent; *(demande, vendeur)* insistent; *Fam Euph* avoir un besoin p. to need to go *(to the toilet)*

presse [prɛs] *nf* (**a**) *(ensemble des journaux)* press; travailler dans la p. to work in journalism; je l'ai lu dans la p. I read it in the papers; *Fig* avoir bonne/mauvaise p. (auprès de) to be well/badly thought of (by); la p. écrite the print media, the press; la p. à scandale, la p. à sensation the popular press, the tabloids (**b**) *Tech* press (**c**) *(pour imprimer)* (printing) press; mettre qch sous p. to send sth to press

pressé, -e [prese] *adj* (**a**) *(personne)* in a hurry *or* rush; p. de faire qch in a hurry to do sth; être p. par le temps to be pushed for time; d'un pas p. hurriedly; on n'est pas p. there's no rush (**b**) *(urgent)* urgent; aller *or* parer au plus p. to deal with the most urgent thing(s) first

presse-agrumes [presagrym] *nm inv* juice extractor, juicer

presse-ail [presaj] *nm inv* garlic press

presse-citron [presitrɔ̃] *nm inv* lemon squeezer

pressentiment [presɑ̃timɑ̃] *nm* presentiment; *(d'un malheur)* foreboding; j'ai le p. que... I've a (funny) feeling that...

pressentir [64a] [presɑ̃tir] *vt* (**a**) *(deviner)* to have a premonition of, to sense; *(malheur)* to have a foreboding of (**b**) p. qn (pour qch) to sound sb out (about sth)

presse-papiers [prɛspapje] *nm inv* paperweight; *Ordinat* clipboard

presse-purée [prɛspyre] *nm inv* potato masher

presser [prese] **1** *vt* (**a**) *(agrume, éponge)* to squeeze; *(raisin, pommes)* to press; **p. qn contre son cœur** to clasp sb in one's arms, to hug sb (**b**) *(sonnette, bouton)* to press, to push (**c**) *(harceler)* **p. qn de questions** to ply *or* bombard sb with questions; **p. qn de faire qch** to urge sb to do sth (**d**) *(faire se hâter) (personne)* to hurry (up); *(travail, mouvement)* to speed up; **p. le pas** *ou* **l'allure** to speed up, to quicken one's pace
2 *vi* **le temps presse** there isn't much time (left); **rien ne presse** there's no hurry *or* rush; **allons, pressons!** come on, let's get a move on!
3 se presser *vpr* (**a**) *(se dépêcher)* to hurry (up); **se p. de faire qch** to hurry to do sth; **faire qch sans se p.** to take one's time doing sth (**b**) *(se serrer)* **se p. contre** to press (oneself) against; **se p. autour de** to crowd *or* cluster around

pressing [presiŋ] *nm* dry cleaner's

pression [presjɔ̃] *nf* (**a**) *Tech* pressure; **mettre qch sous p.** to pressurize sth; **sous p.** *(récipient)* pressurized; *Fig* **être sous p.** to be under pressure; **p. atmosphérique** atmospheric pressure; **zone de hautes/basses pressions** area of high/low pressure (**b**) *(action de presser)* pressure; **d'une simple p. du doigt** at the touch of a button (**c**) *Fig (influence)* pressure; **faire p. sur qn** to put pressure on sb, to pressurize sb; **subir des pressions** to be under pressure (**d**) *(bouton) Br* press stud, *Am* snap fastener (**e**) **bière (à la) p.** draught beer; **une p., s'il vous plaît** *Br* ≃ a half pint of lager, please, *Am* ~ a beer, please

pressoir [preswar] *nm* (**a**) *(instrument)* press (**b**) *(lieu)* press house, press room

pressurer [presyre] *vt (exploiter)* to squeeze

pressurisation [presyrizasjɔ̃] *nf* pressurization

prestance [prestɑ̃s] *nf* presence; **avoir de la p.** to have (great) presence

prestataire [prestater] **1** *nmf* (**a**) *(bénéficiaire)* person receiving benefits (**b**) *(fournisseur)* **p. de service** service provider
2 *nm Ordinat* **p. d'accès** access provider

prestation [prestasjɔ̃] *nf* (**a**) *(allocation)* benefit; **prestations familiales** family benefits; **prestations sociales** social security benefits (**b**) **prestations** *(services fournis)* services (**c**) *(fait de fournir)* provision; **p. de service** provision of a service (**d**) *(d'un comédien)* performance (**e**) **p. de serment** taking the oath

preste [prest] *adj* nimble

prestement [prestəmɑ̃] *adv* promptly

prestidigitateur, -trice [prestidiʒitatœr, -tris] *nm,f* conjurer, magician

prestidigitation [prestidiʒitasjɔ̃] *nf* conjuring, magic

prestige [prestiʒ] *nm* prestige; **de p.** *(voiture, hôtel)* luxury; *(réalisation)* prestige; **le p. de l'uniforme** the glamour of the uniform

prestigieux, -euse [prestiʒjø, -øz] *adj* prestigious

présumer [prezyme] **1** *vt (supposer)* to presume, to assume; **p. qn innocent** to presume sb (to be) innocent
2 présumer de *vt ind* **trop p. de soi** to be overconfident; **p. de ses forces** to overestimate one's strength

présupposer [presypoze] *vt* to presuppose

présure [prezyr] *nf* rennet

prêt¹, -e [prɛ, prɛt] *adj* ready; **être p. à tout** to be prepared to do anything; **être p. à faire qch** to be ready to do sth

prêt² *nm (action)* lending; *(somme)* loan

prêt-à-porter [pretaporte] *nm* (**a**) *(vêtements)* ready-to-wear clothes (**b**) *(secteur)* ready-to-wear (clothing business)

prétendant, -e [pretɑ̃dɑ̃, -ɑ̃t] **1** *nm,f (à un poste)* applicant, candidate (**à** for); *(à un bien, à un titre)* claimant (**à** to); *(au trône)* pretender (**à** to)
2 *nm (d'une femme)* suitor

prétendre [pretɑ̃dr] **1** *vt (déclarer)* to maintain, to claim; **on prétend que...** people say that..., it is said that...; **à ce qu'il prétend** according to him; **il ne prétend pas être artiste** he doesn't claim *or* pretend to be an artist; **on le prétend fou** they say he's mad
2 prétendre à *vt ind* to lay claim to; **p. à la victoire** to aim to win
3 se prétendre *vpr* to claim to be

prétendu, -e [pretɑ̃dy] *adj (coupable, voleur)* alleged; *(progrès, égalité, héros)* so-called

prétendument [pretɑ̃dymɑ̃] *adv* supposedly

prête-nom [pl **prête-noms**) [pretnɔ̃] *nm Fig* figurehead

prétentieux, -euse [pretɑ̃sjø, -øz] **1** *adj* pretentious
2 *nm,f* pretentious person

prétention [pretɑ̃sjɔ̃] *nf* (**a**) *(vanité)* pretentiousness, pretension; **sans p.** *(repas, maison, personne)* unpretentious (**b**) *(revendication, ambition)* pretension, claim (**à** to); **avoir la p. de faire qch** to claim *or* pretend to be able to do sth; **quelles sont vos prétentions?** *(salaire demandé)* what sort of salary are you looking for?

prêter [prete] **1** *vt* (**a**) *(temporairement)* to lend, *Am* to loan; **p. qch à qn** to lend sth to sb, to lend sb sth; **p. sur gages** to lend against security; *Prov* **on ne prête qu'aux riches** people don't lend money to those who really need it; *Fig* people are judged according to their reputation (**b**) *(donner)* **p. son appui** *ou* **son concours à qn** to give sb one's support; **p. assistance** *ou* **secours à qn** to lend *or* give assistance to sb; **p. main-forte à qn** to lend *or* give sb a hand; **p. l'oreille (à)** to listen *or* lend an ear (to); **p. attention à qch** to pay attention to sth; **p. serment** to take an oath; **p. le flanc à la critique** to lay oneself open to criticism (**c**) *(attribuer)* **p. qch à qn** *(propos, intentions)* to attribute *or* ascribe sth to sb
2 prêter à *vt ind* **p. à confusion** to give rise to confusion; **cela prête à rire** that's laughable
3 se prêter *vpr* (**a**) *(consentir)* **se p. à** to lend oneself to (**b**) *(convenir)* **se p. à** to lend itself to; **la situation ne s'y prête pas** the situation isn't ideal

prétérit [preterit] *nm* preterite (tense); **au p.** in the preterite

prêteur, -euse [pretœr, -øz] **1** *nm,f* lender; **p. sur gages** pawnbroker
2 *adj* ready *or* willing to lend things; **je ne suis pas p.** I don't like lending things

prétexte [pretekst] *nm* pretext, excuse; **sous p. de faire qch** on the pretext of doing sth; **sous p. que...** on the pretext that...; **sous aucun p.** on no account, under no circumstances

prétexter [pretekste] *vt* to give as a pretext *or* an excuse; **il a prétexté qu'il était malade** he gave the excuse that he was ill; **p. la fatigue** to plead tiredness

Pretoria [pretɔrja] *n* Pretoria

prêtre [pretr] *nm* priest

prêtresse [pretres] *nf* priestess

prêtrise [pretriz] *nf* priesthood

preuve [prœv] *nf* (**a**) *(pour démontrer)* piece of evidence; **il nous faut des preuves** we need proof *or* evidence; **faire la p. de qch** to prove sth; *avoir* la **p. que/de...** to have proof that/of...; **faire p. d'intelligence/de courage** to show intelligence/courage; **faire ses preuves** *(personne)* to prove oneself, to show one's ability; *(technique)* to be tried and tested; **jusqu'à p. du contraire** until there's proof to the contrary; *Fam* **elle ne m'aime pas: la p.**, **elle ne m'écrit jamais** I know she doesn't like me because she never writes to me; **j'en veux pour p....** the proof of it is...; **p. d'achat** proof of purchase **(b)** *Jur* evidence **(c)** *(témoignage)* **une p. d'amour/d'amitié** a token of love/friendship **(d)** *Math* **faire la p. d'une opération** to prove *or* test the validity of a mathematical operation; **faire la p. par neuf** to cast out nines

prévaloir [69] [prevalwar] **1** *vi* to prevail **(sur** over); **faire p. son opinion** to win acceptance for one's opinion
2 se prévaloir *vpr* **se p. de qch** *(profiter de)* to take advantage of sth; *(s'enorgueillir)* to pride oneself on sth

prévenant, -e [prevnã, -ãt] *adj (personne)* kind **(envers ou avec** to), considerate **(envers** *ou* **avec** towards); *(geste)* thoughtful **(envers** *ou* **avec** towards)

prévenir [70] [prevnir] *vt* **(a)** *(informer)* to inform, to let know **(de** about *or* of); *(mettre en garde)* to warn; **tu es prévenu!** you've been warned!; **partir sans p.** to leave without telling anyone *or* without warning **(b)** *(empêcher) (maladie)* to prevent, to guard against; *(danger, accident)* to avert; *Prov* **mieux vaut p. que guérir** prevention is better than cure **(c)** *(devancer) (désir)* to anticipate; *(objection)* to forestall

préventif, -ive [prevãtif, -iv] *adj* preventive; *Jur* **détention préventive** custody; **être en détention préventive** to be remanded in custody

prévention [prevãsjɔ̃] *nf* **(a)** *(pour empêcher)* prevention; **p. routière** road safety **(b)** *Jur* custody; **mettre qn en p.** to remand sb in custody

prévenu, -e [prevny] *nm,f Jur* defendant, accused

prévisible [previzibl] *adj* foreseeable

prévision [previzjɔ̃] *nf* forecast; *(activité)* forecasting; **en p. de qch** in expectation *or* anticipation of sth; **prévisions budgétaires** budget projections *or* forecasts; **prévisions météorologiques** weather forecast

prévisionnel, -elle [previzjɔnɛl] *adj (coûts)* estimated; *(budget)* projected; *(analyse)* preliminary

prévoir [73c] [prevwar] *vt* **(a)** *(météo)* to forecast; *(réaction, difficultés, retards)* to expect, to anticipate; **on ne peut pas tout p.** you can't think of everything **(b)** *(programmer) (sortie, vacances)* to plan; **la réunion est prévue pour demain** the meeting is scheduled for tomorrow; **il faudra p. des vêtements de pluie** we'll have to take waterproof clothes; **qu'est-ce que tu as prévu pour le dessert?** what are you planning to have for dessert?; **comme prévu** as planned; **cela s'est passé comme prévu** it went according to plan; **plus tôt/tard que prévu** sooner/later than expected; **cela n'était pas prévu au programme** that wasn't on the agenda

prévoyance [prevwajãs] *nf* foresight, forethought

prévoyant, -e [prevwajã, -ãt] *adj* far-sighted

prie-Dieu [pridjø] *nm inv* prie-dieu, prayer stool

prier [66] [prije] **1** *vi* to pray **(pour** for)
2 *vt* **(a)** *(dieu)* to pray to **(b)** *(supplier)* to beg; **il ne s'est pas fait p. pour venir** he didn't need much persuading to come; **allez, viens, arrête de te faire p.!** come on, stop being so difficult!; **sans te faire p.** without hesitation **(c)** *(demander à)* **p. qn de faire qch** to ask sb to do sth; **je te prie de te dépêcher!** please hurry up!; **taisez-vous, je vous prie!** please be quiet!; **je te prie de croire qu'elle a été surprise!** she was surprised, believe you me!; **je vous en prie!** *(faites-le)* please do!, of course!; *(taisez-vous)* stop it!; *(il n'y a pas de quoi)* you're welcome!

prière [prijer] *nf* **(a)** *Rel* prayer; **faire** *ou* **dire sa p.** to say one's prayers **(b)** *(demande)* request; **p. de ne pas fumer**

(sur écriteau) no smoking; **p. de fermer la porte** *(sur écriteau)* please close the door

prieuré [prijœre] *nm* priory

primaire [primer] **1** *adj* **(a)** *(école, couleur, secteur, ère)* primary **(b)** *Péj (personne)* simple-minded; *(réaction, racisme)* narrow-minded
2 *nm* **(a)** *Scol* primary education; **être en p.** to be at primary school **(b)** *Géol* Primary era **(c)** *Écon* primary sector

primate [primat] *nm Zool* primate

primauté [primote] *nf* primacy

prime[1] [prim] *adj* **(a) de p. abord** at first sight; *Litt* **dès sa p. jeunesse** since her early youth **(b)** *Math* **B p.** B prime

prime[2] *nf (d'assurance)* premium; *(allocation)* grant; *(sur salaire)* bonus; **et vous aurez droit à un stylo en p.** and you will receive a free pen; *Fig* **en p.** into the bargain; **p. d'ancienneté** long-service award; **p. d'assurance** insurance premium; **p. de licenciement** severance payment; **p. de transport** transport allowance

primer[1] [prime] **1** *vt (avoir la priorité sur)* to take precedence over
2 *vi* to come first; **p. sur** to take precedence over

primer[2] *vt (attribuer un prix à)* to award a prize to; **primé** *(taureau)* prize(winning); *(roman, film)* prizewinning, award-winning

primeur [primœr] *nf* **(a) primeurs** *(fruits et légumes)* (early) fruit and vegetables; **marchand de primeurs** greengrocer *(selling early produce)* **(b)** *(exclusivité)* **avoir la p. d'une nouvelle** to be the first to hear a piece of news

primevère [primver] *nf* primrose

primitif, -ive [primitif, -iv] **1** *adj* primitive; *(originel)* original
2 *nm (artiste)* primitive

primo [primo] *adv* first(ly), in the first place

primordial, -e, -aux, -ales [primɔrdjal, -o] *adj* essential, primordial

prince [prɛ̃s] *nm* prince; **comme un p.** *(traité, élevé, habillé)* like a prince; **être** *ou* **se montrer bon p.** to be very decent; **le p. charmant** Prince Charming

prince-de-galles [prɛ̃sdəgal] *adj inv* Prince of Wales check

princesse [prɛ̃sɛs] *nf* princess

princier, -ère [prɛ̃sje, -ɛr] *adj* princely

principal, -e, -aux, -ales [prɛ̃sipal, -o] **1** *adj aussi Gram* main; *(question, raison, but)* main, principal; *(rôle, acteur)* leading
2 *nm* **(a)** *(ce qui compte le plus)* **le p.** the main thing, the most important thing **(b)** *(d'une école) Br* headmaster, *f* headmistress, *Am* head

principalement [prɛ̃sipalmã] *adv* mainly, principally

principauté [prɛ̃sipote] *nf* principality

principe [prɛ̃sip] *nm* principle; **un accord de p.** an agreement in principle; **partir du p. que...** to assume that...; **c'est une question de p.** it's a matter of principle; **avoir pour p. de...** to make it a matter of principle to...; **avoir des principes** to have (high) principles; **en p.** in principle, theoretically; **par p.** on principle

printanier, -ère [prɛ̃tanje, -ɛr] *adj* spring

printemps [prɛ̃tã] *nm* spring; **au p.** in (the) spring(time); **une journée de p.** a spring day; *Fig* **ses vingt-six p.** twenty-six summers

prioritaire [prijɔriter] *adj* (that has) priority; **être p.** to have priority; *(en voiture)* to have the right of way

priorité [prijɔrite] *nf* **(a)** *(précédence)* priority; **donner la p. à qn/qch** to give sb/sth priority; **leur dossier sera traité**

en p. their file will get priority treatment; **avoir la p. sur** to have priority over **(b)** *Aut* right of way, priority; **avoir p.** to have the right of way; **accorder** *ou* **laisser la p. à une voiture** *Br* to give way *or Am* to yield to a car; **refuser la p.** to refuse to give way; **p. à droite** *(sur panneau)* = give way to vehicles coming from the right

pris, -e [pri, priz] **1** *pp voir* **prendre**
2 *adj* **(a)** *(siège)* occupied, taken; **avoir les mains prises** to have one's hands full **(b)** *(personne)* busy; **je suis déjà p. ce jour-là** I've already got something on that day **(c)** *(saisi)* **p. de peur** seized with fear; **p. de panique** panic-stricken; **p. de remords** racked with guilt **(d)** *(gelé)* frozen (over) **(e)** *(encombré)* **avoir le nez p.** to have a blocked nose; **avoir la gorge prise** to have a sore throat **(f)** **avoir la taille bien prise** to have a trim waist

prise [priz] *nf* **(a)** *(d'une ville, de prisonniers)* taking, capture; *(à la pêche)* catch; *(de drogue)* seize **(b)** *Él* **p. (de courant** *ou* **électrique)** *(femelle)* *Br* socket, *Am* outlet; *(mâle)* plug; **p. multiple** adaptor; *Ordinat* **p. péritel** scart connector; **p. de terre** *Br* earth *or Am* ground (connection)
(c) *Cin, Phot & TV* **p. de son** sound recording; **p. de vue** *(cliché)* shot, *(de tournage)* take; *(action)* shooting
(d) *Tech* **en p.** in gear, engaged; *Fig* **en p. (directe) sur** *ou* **avec qch** in touch with sth
(e) *(de judo, de lutte)* hold; *(pour se retenir)* hold; *(plus ferme)* grasp, grip; *(pour le pied)* foothold; *Fig* **avoir p. sur qn** to have a hold on *or* over sb; **lâcher p.** to lose one's grip; *Fig* to give up; **donner p. aux reproches/critiques** to lay oneself open to reproach/criticism; **être aux prises avec des difficultés** to be grappling with difficulties; **être aux prises avec qn** to be at odds with sb
(f) *(locutions)* *Fam* **p. de bec** row, squabble; **p. en charge** *(par un taxi)* (d'un passager) picking up; *(comme)* minimum charge; *(par la Sécurité sociale)* (guaranteed) reimbursement; **p. de conscience** awareness, realization; **p. de contact** initial contact *or* meeting; **p. de notes** notetaking; **p. d'otages** hostage-taking; **p. de position** stance; **p. de pouvoir** *(politique)* takeover; **faire une p. de sang à qn** to take a blood sample from sb

priser¹ [prize] **1** *vt* **p. du tabac** to take snuff
2 *vi* to take snuff

priser² *vt Litt (estimer)* to prize, to value

prisme [prism] *nm* prism

prison [prizɔ̃] *nf* **(a)** *(lieu de détention)* prison, jail; **mettre qn en prison** to put sb in prison; **faire de la p.** to serve a prison sentence **(b)** *(peine)* imprisonment; **deux ans de p.** two years' imprisonment

prisonnier, -ère [prizɔnje, -ɛr] **1** *nm,f* prisoner; **faire qn p.** to take sb prisoner; **p. de droit commun** common criminal; **p. de guerre** prisoner of war, POW; **p. politique** political prisoner
2 *adj* imprisoned, in prison; **ils sont encore prisonniers sous les décombres** they are still trapped in the rubble; **être p. de** to be a prisoner of; *Fig* to be a slave to

privation [privasjɔ̃] *nf* **(a)** *(action de priver)* deprivation **(b)** **privations** *(manque)* hardship, privation; **s'imposer des privations** to deprive oneself, to go without

privatisation [privatizasjɔ̃] *nf* privatization

privatiser [privatize] *vt* to privatize

privautés [privote] *nfpl* (undue) familiarity; **prendre** *ou* **se permettre des p. avec qn** to be over-familiar with sb

privé, -e [prive] **1** *adj* private; **à titre p.** in a private capacity
2 *nm* **(a)** *(secteur)* **le p.** the private sector; *Scol* the private education system; **mes enfants sont dans le p.** my children go to a private school **(b)** *(intimité)* **dans le p.**

privately; **connaître qn dans le p.** to know sb personally; **en p.** in private **(c)** *Fam (détective)* private eye

priver [prive] **1** *vt* **p. qn de qch** to deprive sb of sth; **p. qn de sorties** not to allow sb to go out; **être privé de dessert** to go without pudding; **ça ne le prive pas du tout de ne plus fumer** he doesn't find it a hardship not to smoke any more
2 se priver *vpr* to do *or* go without; **se p.** **de** to do *or* go without; *(plaisir)* to deprive oneself of, to deny oneself; **ne pas se p.** **de faire qch** not to hesitate to do sth

privilège [privilɛʒ] *nm* privilege

privilégié, -e [privileʒje] **1** *adj (personne, site)* privileged; *(conditions)* privileged, favourable; *(relations)* special
2 *nm,f* privileged person; **les privilégiés** the privileged

privilégier [66] [privileʒje] *vt (personne, groupe)* to privilege; *(facteur, aspect)* to prioritize

prix [pri] *nm* **(a)** *(coût)* price; **à tout p.** at all costs, at any price; **à aucun p.** not at any price, on no account; **se vendre à p. d'or** to fetch huge prices; **acheter qch à p. d'or** to pay a (small) fortune for sth; **payer qch au p. fort** to pay a high price for sth; **faire un p. à qn** to give sb a good deal; **je vous fais un p. d'ami** I'll let you have it cheap; **y mettre le p.** to pay a high price; **la santé/le bonheur, ça n'a pas de p.** you can't put a price on health/happiness; **mettre à p. la tête de qn** to put a price on sb's head; **c'est mon dernier p.** that's my final offer; **votre p. sera le mien** name your price; **au p. coûtant** at cost price; **p. de revient** cost price; **p. de vente** selling price **(b)** *(importance)* **attacher beaucoup de p.** *ou* **un grand p. à qch** to set great store by sth **(c)** *(récompense)* prize; **p. de consolation** consolation prize; **le p. Goncourt** = prestigious French literary prize; **p. Nobel** *(récompense)* Nobel Prize; *(personne)* Nobel *Br* prizewinner *or Am* laureate; **le p. Nobel de la Paix** *(récompense)* the Nobel Peace Prize

pro [pro] *nmf Fam* pro

probabilité [probabilite] *nf* probability, likelihood; **selon toute p.** in all probability *or* likelihood; *Math* **calcul des probabilités** theory of probability

probable [probabl] *adj* probable, likely; **il est p. qu'elle viendra** she'll probably come; **peu p.** improbable, unlikely; **il est peu p. qu'elle vienne** she's not likely *or* she's unlikely to come

probablement [probabləmɑ̃] *adv* probably

probant, -e [probɑ̃, -ɑ̃t] *adj* convincing, conclusive

probité [probite] *nf* probity, integrity

problématique [problematik] **1** *adj* problematic(al)
2 *nf* set of problems

problème [problɛm] *nm* problem; **c'est tout un p.!** it's such a problem!; **peau/cheveux à problèmes** problem skin/hair; **avoir des problèmes familiaux/d'argent** to have family/money problems

procédé [prosede] *nm* **(a)** *(façon de faire)* method; **échange de bons procédés** exchange of friendly services **(b)** *(technique)* process; **p. de fabrication** manufacturing process; *Péj* **ça sent le p.** it seems rather artificial

procéder [34] [prosede] **1** *vi* **(a)** *(agir)* to proceed, to act; **par ordre** to do things in order; **avec méthode** to proceed methodically; **p. par élimination** to follow a process of elimination **(b)** *Formel* **p. de** *(venir de)* to arise out of, to originate in
2 procéder à *vt ind (recherches, arrestation, vérification)* to carry out; *(élections)* to hold

procédure [prosedyr] *nf* **(a)** *(méthode)* procedure **(b)** *Jur* proceedings; **engager une p.** to take proceedings **(c)** *Ordinat* procedure; **p. de chargement** loading procedure

procédurier, -ère [prosedyrje, -ɛr] *adj* quibbling

procès [prɔsɛ] *nm Jur* (legal) proceedings; *(civil)* lawsuit; *(criminel)* (criminal) trial; **engager un p.** to take legal action; **faire** *ou* **intenter un p. à qn** to take proceedings against sb; **être en p.** **avec qn** to be involved in legal proceedings with sb; **gagner/perdre son p.** to win/lose one's case; **faire un p. d'intention à qn** to accuse sb on the basis of assumptions not facts; **faire le p.** **de qn/qch** *(critiquer)* to attack sb/sth; *Fig* **sans autre forme de p.** without (any) further ceremony, without further ado

processeur [prɔsɛsœr] *nm Ordinat* processor; **p. central** central processing unit, CPU; **p. de données** data processor

procession [prɔsesjɔ̃] *nf* procession

processus [prɔsesys] *nm* process

procès-verbal [prɔsɛvɛrbal] *(pl* **procès-verbaux** [prɔsɛvɛrbo])) *nm* **(a)** *Jur* policeman's report *(about an offence); (amende)* fine **(b)** *(rapport)* (official) report; *(d'une réunion)* minutes; *(d'un témoignage)* record

prochain, -e [prɔʃɛ̃, -ɛn] **1** *adj* **(a)** *(qui suit)* next; **ce sera pour une prochaine fois** *Br* another time, perhaps, *Am* let's take a rain check; **à la prochaine (fois)!** see you (soon)!; *Fam* **je descends à la prochaine** I'm getting off at the next stop **(b)** *(imminent)* imminent; **dans un avenir p.** in the near *or* not too distant future; **un jour p.** one day soon **2** *nm (semblable)* **aimer son p.** to love one's neighbour

prochainement [prɔʃɛnmɑ̃] *adv* shortly, soon; **p. sur vos écrans** coming soon to a *Br* cinema *or Am* movie theater near you

proche [prɔʃ] **1** *adj* **(a)** *(dans l'espace)* near, close; **p. de qch** close to *or* near sth **(b)** *(dans l'avenir)* near, imminent; **dans un avenir p.** in the near *or* not too distant future; **la fin est p.** the end is nigh **(c)** *(récent)* recent **(d)** *(semblable, intime)* close **(de** to); **ils sont proches parents** they are closely related **(e) de p. en p.** gradually, step by step **2** *nm* close relative *or* relation

Proche-Orient [prɔʃɔrjɑ̃] *nm* **le P.** the Middle East

proclamation [prɔklamasjɔ̃] *nf* proclamation

proclamer [prɔklame] *vt* to proclaim; *(résultats de scrutin)* to declare

procréation [prɔkreasjɔ̃] *nf* procreation

procréer [24] [prɔkree] *vi* to procreate

procuration [prɔkyrasjɔ̃] *nf* proxy, power of attorney; **par p.** by proxy, *Spéc* per pro(curationem); *Fig* **vivre par p.** to live by proxy

procurer [prɔkyre] **1** *vt* **p. qch à qn** *(sujet:personne)* to get sth for sb; *(sujet: chose)* to bring sb sth **2 se procurer** *vpr* to get (hold of), to obtain

procureur [prɔkyrœr] *nm Jur* procurator, proxy; **p. général/de la République** *Br* ≃ public prosecutor, *Am* ≃ district attorney

prodigalité [prɔdigalite] *nf* extravagance, prodigality

prodige [prɔdiʒ] **1** *nm* wonder, marvel; *(personne)* prodigy; **faire des prodiges** to work wonders; **tenir du p.** to be extraordinary, to be something of a miracle **2** *adj* **enfant p.** child prodigy

prodigieusement [prɔdiʒjøzmɑ̃] *adv* prodigiously

prodigieux, -euse [prɔdiʒjø, -øz] *adj* prodigious, extraordinary

prodigue [prɔdig] *adj (dépensier)* wasteful, spendthrift; *(généreux)* lavish, unsparing **(de** in *or* with)

prodiguer [prɔdige] *vt* **p. qch à qn** to lavish sth on sb; **p. des conseils à qn** to pour out advice to sb

producteur, -trice [prɔdyktœr, -tris] **1** *adj* **pays p. de blé/pétrole** wheat-growing/oil-producing country **2** *nm,f* producer

productif, -ive [prɔdyktif, -iv] *adj* productive

production [prɔdyksjɔ̃] *nf* **(a)** *Ind & Cin* production; *(d'électricité)* production, generation **(b)** *(produit)* product; *Cin* production; *(d'une usine)* output; **p. littéraire** literary output

productivité [prɔdyktivite] *nf* productivity

produire [18] [prɔdɥir] **1** *vt* **(a)** *(marchandise, émission, gaz)* to produce; *(chaleur, électricité, odeur)* to generate, to produce **(b)** *(résultat, effet)* to produce, to bring about; *(irritation, sensation)* to cause **2 se produire** *vpr* **(a)** *(événement)* to happen **(b)** *(acteur)* to appear

produit [prɔdɥi] *nm* **(a)** *(marchandise)* product; **produits agricoles** agricultural *or* farm produce; **p. de beauté** beauty product; **p. chimique** chemical; **p. de consommation** consumer product; **p. d'entretien** (household) cleaning product; **p. fini** finished product; **p. intérieur brut** gross domestic product; **p. de luxe** luxury product; **p. manufacturé** manufactured product; **produits ménagers** (household) cleaning products; **p. national brut** gross national product **(b)** *(profit)* yield; **p. d'une vente** proceeds of a sale; **le p. de six années de travail** the result of six years' work; **vivre du p. de la terre** to live off the land **(c)** *Math (d'une multiplication)* product **(d)** *(création)* **c'est le p. de son imagination** it's the product of his imagination

proéminent, -e [prɔeminɑ̃, -ɑ̃t] *adj* prominent

prof [prɔf] *nmf Fam* teacher

profanateur, -trice [prɔfanatœr, -tris] *nm,f (de tombes)* desecrator

profanation [prɔfanasjɔ̃] *nf* desecration, violation

profane [prɔfan] **1** *adj* non-religious, secular; *Fig* **être p. en la matière** to know nothing about the subject **2** *nmf (non-initié)* layman, *f* laywoman

profaner [prɔfane] *vt (église)* to desecrate; *(tombe)* to desecrate, to violate; *(souvenir, mémoire)* to defile

proférer [34] [prɔfere] *vt* to utter

professer [prɔfese] *vt* to profess

professeur [prɔfesœr] *nm* teacher; *(à l'université)* professor; **p. principal** *Br* class *or* form teacher, *Am* homeroom teacher

profession [prɔfesjɔ̃] *nf* **(a)** *(métier)* profession, occupation; *(d'artisans)* trade; **de p.** *(musicien)* professional; *(menuisier)* by trade; **p. libérale** profession; **sans p.** *(dans un questionnaire)* not working; **je suis sans p.** I don't work **(b)** *(déclaration)* **faire p. de qch** to profess sth; **p. de foi** profession of faith

professionnalisation [prɔfesjɔnalizasjɔ̃] *nf* professionalization

professionnalisme [prɔfesjɔnalism] *nm* professionalism

professionnel, -elle [prɔfesjɔnɛl] **1** *adj (attitude, sportif)* professional; *(enseignement)* vocational; *(maladie)* occupational **2** *nm,f* professional

professionnellement [prɔfesjɔnɛlmɑ̃] *adv* professionally

professoral, -e, -aux, -ales [prɔfesɔral, -o] *adj* professorial

professorat [prɔfesɔra] *nm* teaching profession *(especially in higher education)*

profil [prɔfil] *nm aussi Fig* profile; **dessiner qn de p.** to draw sb in profile; **se mettre de p.** to turn one's face *(so it is in profile); Fig* **adopter un p. bas** to adopt a low profile; **p. de poste** job description; **avoir le p. de l'emploi** to fit the job description

profilé, -e [prɔfile] *adj* streamlined

profiler [prɔfile] **se profiler** *vpr* to stand out (in profile), to be outlined (**sur** *ou* **contre** against); *(problèmes)* to emerge, to loom; *(solution)* to emerge; *(événement)* to be in the offing

profit [prɔfi] *nm* (**a**) *(avantage)* profit, benefit; **mettre qch à p.** to put sth to good use; **tirer p. de qch** to take advantage of sth; **ce manteau m'a fait du p.** this coat has served me well; **au p. des pauvres** in aid of the poor; **concert donné au p. des orphelins** benefit concert for orphans; **perdre des voix au p. de qn** to lose votes to sb (**b**) *(gain)* profit; **il n'y a pas de petits profits** every little helps

profitable [prɔfitabl] *adj* profitable

profiter [prɔfite] **1 profiter de** *vt ind* to take advantage of; **je profite d'un moment de calme pour vous dire que…** I'm using these few moments of peace and quiet to tell you that…; **p. de la vie/de sa jeunesse** to make the most of life/one's youth
2 profiter à *vt ind* to be of benefit to, to benefit; **ses vacances lui ont bien profité** his holiday has done him a lot of good
3 *vi Fam (enfant, plante)* to thrive

profiteur, -euse [prɔfitœr, -øz] *nm,f Péj* profiteer

profond, -e [prɔfɔ̃, -ɔ̃d] **1** *adj* (**a**) *(trou, lac, voix)* deep; *(décolleté)* plunging; *(forêt)* dense, thick, *(sommeil)* deep, sound (**b**) *(cause)* underlying (**c**) *(paroles)* profound; *(haine, silence, dégoût)* profound, deep; *(soupir)* heavy
2 *adv* deep
3 *nm* **au plus p. de mon cœur** in my heart of hearts, deep down; **au plus p. de la nuit** at dead of night

profondément [prɔfɔ̃demɑ̃] *adv (choqué, déçu, ému)* deeply, profoundly; *(aimer, mépriser)* deeply; *(dormir)* soundly; *(creuser)* deep; **p. endormi** sound *or* fast asleep; **j'en suis p. convaincu** I'm quite convinced of it

profondeur [prɔfɔ̃dœr] *nf* (**a**) *(de l'eau, d'un trou)* depth; **faire 10 mètres de p.** to be 10 metres deep; **en p.** *(étude, analyse)* in-depth; *Phot* **p. de champ** depth of field (**b**) *(d'un sentiment)* depth; *(d'un texte)* profoundness, profundity

profusion [prɔfyzjɔ̃] *nf* profusion, abundance; **à p.** in profusion

progéniture [prɔʒenityr] *nf* progeny, offspring

progiciel [prɔʒisjɛl] *nm Ordinat* software package; **p. de communication** comms package

prognathe [prɔɡnat] *adj (visage)* undershot, underhung, *Spéc* prognathous

programmable [prɔɡramabl] *adj* programmable

programmateur, -trice [prɔɡramatœr, -tris] **1** *nm,f Rad & TV* programme planner
2 *nm Tech* automatic control (device); *Ordinat* programmer

programmation [prɔɡramasjɔ̃] *nf* (**a**) *TV & Rad* programme planning (**b**) *Ordinat* programming

programme [prɔɡram] *nm* (**a**) *(émissions, œuvres)* programme; *(brochure) (de télévision)* TV guide; *(de cinéma)* cinema guide; *(au concert, au théâtre)* programme (**b**) *(d'activités)* programme (**c**) *Scol* curriculum; *(d'un cours)* syllabus; **les auteurs au** *ou* **du p.** the set books (**d**) *(d'un parti politique)* manifesto; **p. électoral** (election) platform; *Fig* **c'est tout un p.!** that'll be interesting! (**e**) *Ordinat* program; **p. d'amorçage** boot program; **p. d'arrière-plan** background program; **p. d'auto-test** self-test program; **p. de configuration** configuration program; **p. de conversion** conversion program; **p. détecteur de virus** virus detection program; **p. éditeur de liens** link program, linker; **p. d'évaluation de performance** benchmark program; **p. de formatage** formatter

programmer [prɔɡrame] *vt* (**a**) *Ordinat* to program (**b**) *TV & Rad* to schedule (**c**) *(vacances, changements)* to plan

programmeur, -euse [prɔɡramœr, -øz] *nm,f Ordinat* programmer

progrès [prɔɡrɛ] *nm* progress; **faire des p.** to make progress; **être en p.** to be making progress; *Fam* **il y a du** *ou* **un p.** there's been an improvement

progresser [prɔɡrɛse] *vi* (**a**) *(avancer) (armée)* to advance, to progress; *(marcheur)* to make progress (**b**) *(épidémie, incendie)* to spread; *(chômage, délinquance)* to rise, to increase (**c**) *(faire des progrès)* to make progress

progressif, -ive [prɔɡresif, -iv] *adj* progressive; *(changement)* gradual

progression [prɔɡresjɔ̃] *nf* (**a**) *(avance) (d'une armée)* advance, progress; *(de marcheurs)* progress (**b**) *(d'un incendie, d'une épidémie)* spread; *(de la délinquance, du chômage)* rise, increase; **être en p.** *(secteur économique)* to be growing *or* expanding; *(maladie)* to be spreading; *(chômage, criminalité)* to be rising, to be on the increase

progressiste [prɔɡresist] *adj & nmf* progressive

progressivement [prɔɡresivmɑ̃] *adv* progressively

prohiber [prɔibe] *vt* to prohibit, to forbid

prohibitif, -ive [prɔibitif, -iv] *adj* prohibitive

prohibition [prɔibisjɔ̃] *nf* prohibition; *Hist* **la P.** Prohibition

proie [prwa] *nf* prey; **être la p. de qn** to fall prey *or* victim to sb; **être en p. à** *(remords, doute)* to be racked *or* tormented by; *(hallucinations)* to suffer from; **lâcher la p. pour l'ombre** to go chasing after rainbows

projecteur [prɔʒɛktœr] *nm* (**a**) *Cin & Phot* projector (**b**) *(dans un stade, sur un monument)* floodlight; *Th* spotlight; *Fig* **sous les projecteurs de l'actualité** in the limelight

projectile [prɔʒɛktil] *nm* missile

projection [prɔʒɛksjɔ̃] *nf* (**a**) *(lancer)* projection; *(d'un liquide, de boue)* splashing; *(de graisse)* spattering; *(de cendres, de roches)* spewing out; **des projections de boue** splashes of mud (**b**) *Cin* projection; *(séance)* screening; showing; **p. de diapositives** slide show; **p. privée** private screening

projectionniste [prɔʒɛksjɔnist] *nmf* projectionist

projet [prɔʒɛ] *nm* *(intention)* plan; *(étude)* project; **faire des projets** to make plans; **p. de loi** bill; **en p.** at the planning stage; **c'est resté à l'état de p.** it never got off the ground

projeter [42] [prɔʒte] **1** *vt* (**a**) *(lancer)* to project; *(graisse)* to spatter; *(liquide, boue)* to splash; *(cendres, roches)* to spew out; **être projeté au sol** to be hurled to the ground (**b**) *(prévoir)* to plan; **p. de faire qch** to plan to do sth (**c**) *(film)* to show, to screen (**d**) *(faire apparaître) (ombre)* to cast, to throw; *(image)* to project (**e**) *Psy* to project (**sur** onto)
2 se projeter *vpr (ombre)* to be cast

prolétaire [prɔletɛr] *adj & nmf* proletarian

prolétariat [prɔletarja] *nm* proletariat

prolétarien, -enne [prɔletarjɛ̃, -ɛn] *adj* proletarian

prolifération [prɔliferasjɔ̃] *nf* proliferation

proliférer [34] [prɔlifere] *vi* to proliferate

prolifique [prɔlifik] *adj* prolific

prolixe [prɔliks] *adj* wordy, verbose

prolo [prɔlo] *Fam* **1** *adj* prole
2 *nmf* prole

prologue [prɔlɔɡ] *nm* prologue (**de** to)

prolongation [prɔlɔ̃ɡasjɔ̃] *nf (de discussions)* prolongation; *(d'un congé, d'un séjour)* extension; **jouer les prolongations** *(au football)* to play extra time *or Am* overtime

prolongé, -e [prɔlɔ̃ʒe] *adj (absence, séjour)* prolonged, lengthy; *(effort)* prolonged, sustained; *(week-end)* long; **pas**

d'utilisation prolongée sans avis médical *(sur un médicament)* ≃ if symptoms persist, consult your doctor

prolongement [prɔlɔ̃ʒmɑ̃] *nm* (a) *(d'une rue)* continuation; *(d'une mur, d'une voie de chemin de fer)* extension; **être dans le p. de qch** *(meuble)* to be flush with sth; *(rue)* to be a continuation of sth (b) **prolongements** *(d'une action)* repercussions

prolonger [45] [prɔlɔ̃ʒe] **1** *vt* *(vie, débat, repas)* to prolong; *(séjour, absence)* to prolong, to extend; *(mur, route, voie ferrée)* to extend
2 se prolonger *vpr* *(séjour, absence)* to be prolonged *or* extended; *(réunion)* to go on; *(rue)* to continue, to extend

promenade [prɔmnad] *nf* (a) *(marche)* walk; *(courte)* stroll; **faire une p.** to go for a walk/stroll; **faire une p. en voiture** to go for a drive; **faire une p. à bicyclette** to go for a bike ride; **faire une p. à cheval** to go (horse)riding; **l'heure de la p.** *(d'un détenu)* exercise time (b) *(avenue)* promenade

promener [46] [prɔmne] **1** *vt* (a) *(personne, chien)* to take for a walk; *Fig* **il m'a promené de bureau en bureau** he dragged me from office to office; *Fam* **cela te promènera un peu** it'll get you out a bit (b) *(passer)* **p. sa main/son regard sur qch** to run one's hand/one's eyes over sth
2 se promener *vpr* to go for a walk; **aller se p.** to go for a walk; *Ordinat* **se p. dans** *(texte)* to scroll through

promeneur, -euse [prɔmnœr, -øz] *nm,f* walker

promesse [prɔmɛs] *nf* promise; **faire une p. à qn** to make sb a promise; **p. de Gascon** empty promise; **p. d'achat/de vente** undertaking to buy/to sell

prometteur, -euse [prɔmetœr, -øz] *adj* promising

promettre [47] [prɔmɛtr] **1** *vt* (a) *(s'engager à)* to promise; **p. qch à qn** to promise sb sth; **je ne peux rien te p.** I can't promise (you) anything; **tu me le promets?** (do you) promise?; **je te promets de le faire** I promise you I'll do it; **je le ferai, c'est promis** I'll do it, I promise; **p. monts et merveilles à qn** to promise sb the earth *or* the moon (b) *(être prometteur)* **la soirée promet d'être amusante** it promises to be an amusing evening; *Fam* **ça ne promet rien de bon** it doesn't look good
2 *vi* *(projet, enfant)* to be promising; *Fam Ironique* **ça promet!** that's promising!
3 se promettre *vpr* **se p. qch** *(à soi-même)* to promise oneself sth; *(l'un l'autre)* to promise each other sth; **se p. de faire qch** *(à soi-même)* to resolve to do sth; **ils se sont promis de ne jamais se quitter** they promised each other they'd never part

promis, -e [prɔmi, -iz] **1** *adj* promised
2 *nm,f Vieilli* betrothed

promiscuité [prɔmiskɥite] *nf* overcrowding; **vivre dans la p.** to live in overcrowded conditions

promo [prɔmo] *nf Fam* promo; **en p.** on special offer

promontoire [prɔmɔ̃twar] *nm* promontory, headland

promoteur, -trice [prɔmotœr, -tris] *nm,f* (a) **p. (immobilier)** property developer (b) *(créateur)* originator (**de** of)

promotion [prɔmosjɔ̃] *nf* (a) *(avancement)* promotion; **p. à l'ancienneté** promotion by seniority; **p. interne** internal promotion; **p. sociale** upward mobility (b) *(d'une école) Br* year, *Am* class; **premier de sa p.** first in one's *Br* year *or Am* class (c) *(dans le commerce)* promotion; **faire la p. de qch** to promote sth; **la p. de la semaine** this week's special offer; **en p.** on special offer

promotionnel, -elle [prɔmosjɔnɛl] *adj (article)* promotional; *(tarif)* special; **vente promotionnelle** special offer

promouvoir [31a] [prɔmuvwar] *vt aussi Fig* to promote; **être promu directeur des ventes** to be promoted to sales director

---

prompt, -e [prɔ̃, prɔ̃t] *adj (réaction)* prompt; **p. à faire qch** quick to do sth; **p. à la riposte** quick with a riposte

promptement [prɔ̃tmɑ̃, prɔ̃ptəmɑ̃] *adv Litt* promptly

promptitude [prɔ̃tityd] *nf Litt (d'une réaction)* promptness

promu, -e *voir* **promouvoir**

promulgation [prɔmylgasjɔ̃] *nf* promulgation

promulguer [prɔmylge] *vt* to promulgate

prôner [prone] *vt* to advocate

pronom [prɔnɔ̃] *nm Gram* pronoun; **p. personnel/indéfini/interrogatif** personal/indefinite/interrogative pronoun

pronominal, -e, -aux, -ales [prɔnɔminal, -o] *adj Gram* pronominal

prononcé, -e [prɔnɔ̃se] **1** *adj* pronounced, strong
2 *nm Jur* **le p. du jugement** the verdict

prononcer [16] [prɔnɔ̃se] **1** *vt* (a) *(articuler)* to pronounce; **mal p. un mot** to mispronounce a word (b) *(dire) (mot)* to utter; *(discours)* to deliver; *(sentence, divorce)* to pronounce
2 se prononcer *vpr* (a) *(être articulé)* to be pronounced; **ça s'écrit comme** *(se prononce* it's written as it's pronounced (b) *(s'exprimer)* to give one's opinion; *(juge)* to give a verdict; **se p. pour** *ou* **en faveur de qn/qch** to express one's support for sb/sth; **se p. contre qn/qch** to express one's opposition to sb/sth; **5% ne se prononcent pas** *(dans un sondage)* 5% are undecided

prononciation [prɔnɔ̃sjasjɔ̃] *nf* pronunciation; **elle a une bonne/mauvaise p.** her pronunciation is good/bad

pronostic [prɔnɔstik] *nm* forecast; *(d'un médecin)* prognosis

propagande [prɔpagɑ̃d] *nf* propaganda; **faire de la p. pour qn/qch** to put out propaganda for sb/sth; *(pour une élection)* to campaign for sb/sth

propagation [prɔpagasjɔ̃] *nf* spreading

propager [45] [prɔpaʒe] **1** *vt* to spread
2 se propager *vpr* (a) *(épidémie, nouvelle, idée)* to spread (b) *(lumière, son)* to be propagated

propane [prɔpan] *nm Chim* propane

propension [prɔpɑ̃sjɔ̃] *nf* propensity (**à** for); **p. à faire qch** propensity to do sth

prophète [prɔfɛt] *nm* prophet; **p. de malheur** prophet of doom; *Prov* **nul n'est p. en son pays** no man is a prophet in his own country

prophétie [prɔfesi] *nf* prophecy

prophétique [prɔfetik] *adj* prophetic

prophylactique [prɔfilaktik] *adj* prophylactic

propice [prɔpis] *adj* **le moment p.** the right moment; **p. à qch** good for sth; **un endroit p. au repos** a restful spot; **un endroit p. aux rencontres** a good place to meet people

proportion [prɔpɔrsjɔ̃] *nf* proportion; **respecter les proportions** to get the proportions right; **en p. de qch** in proportion to sth; **hors de (toute) p. avec** out of (all) proportion to; **toutes proportions gardées** relatively speaking

proportionné, -e [prɔpɔrsjɔne] *adj* (a) *(bâti)* **bien/mal p.** well-/badly-proportioned (b) *(lié)* **être p. à** to be proportionate to

proportionnel, -elle [prɔpɔrsjɔnɛl] **1** *adj* proportional (**à** to); **inversement p. à qch** inversely proportional to sth
2 *nf* **proportionnelle** *Pol* proportional representation

proportionnellement [prɔpɔrsjɔnɛlmɑ̃] *adv* proportionally (**à** to)

propos [prɔpo] *nm* (a) *(sujet)* **à p. de qn/qch** about sb/sth; **à ce p.,...** talking of which...; **à tout p.** constantly; **à p., avez-vous vu ce film?** by the way, have you seen this movie?; **c'est à quel p.**? what's it about?; **arriver fort à p.** to arrive at just the right moment; **juger à p.** de faire qch to think it right to do sth; **hors de p.** *(remarque)* inappropriate **(b)** *(intention)* purpose, intention; **de p. délibéré** deliberately, on purpose **(c)** *(parole)* **des p.** talk, words; **tenir des p.** étonnants to say some surprising things

proposer [prɔpoze] **1** *vt (suggérer)* to suggest, to propose; *(offrir)* to offer; *(amendement, loi)* to table; **p. qch à qn** to suggest *or* propose sth to sb; *(argent, travail)* to offer sb sth; **je vous en propose 6000 euros/un bon prix** I'll give you 6,000 euros/a good price for it; **voilà ce que je vous propose** this is what I suggest; **le cinéma L'Odéon vous propose cette semaine…** L'Odéon will be showing the following movies this week…; **je leur ai proposé de venir avec moi** I suggested (to them) that they should come with me; **elle m'a proposé de m'aider** she offered to help me; **je propose qu'on y aille demain** I suggest going tomorrow **2 se proposer** *vpr* **(a)** *(être volontaire)* to offer one's services; **se p. pour faire qch** to offer to do sth **(b) se p. de faire qch** *(en avoir l'intention)* to propose to do sth

proposition [prɔpozisjɔ̃] *nf* **(a)** *(suggestion)* suggestion, proposal; *(offre)* offer; **faire une p.** (à qn) to make a suggestion *or* proposal (to sb); **faire des propositions à une femme** to proposition a woman; **sur la p. de qn** at sb's suggestion; **p. de loi** bill **(b)** *Phil & Math* proposition **(c)** *Gram* clause

propre [prɔpr] **1** *adj* **(a)** *(impeccable)* (personne, linge, maison)* clean; *(bébé)* potty-trained; *(copie d'élève)* neat; **n'utilise pas le peigne des autres, ce n'est pas p.!** don't use other people's combs, it's not hygienic!; **p. comme un sou neuf** spick and span; *Fam* **nous voilà propres!** now we're in a mess! **(b)** *(à soi)* own; **voir qch de ses propres yeux** to see sth with one's own eyes; **ce sont là ses propres paroles** those are his very words **(c)** *(particulier)* **être p. à qn/qch** to be characteristic of *or* peculiar to sb/sth **(d)** *(adapté)* **être p. à qch** to be suitable for sth **(e)** *(littéral)* **au sens p.** In the literal sense, literally **2** *nm* **(a)** *(caractéristique)* characteristic feature **(b) appartenir en p. à qn** to be sb's sole property **(c)** *(sens propre)* **au p.** literally **(d) recopier qch au p.** to make a clean copy of sth **(e) sentir le p.** to smell clean **(f)** *Fam* **c'est du p.!** that's a fine way to carry on!

propre-à-rien *(pl* **propres-à-rien)** [prɔprarjɛ̃] *nmf* good-for-nothing

proprement [prɔprəmɑ̃] *adv* **(a)** *(avec propreté)* cleanly; *(vêtu)* tidily; **manger p.** to eat without making a mess **(b)** *(strictement)* strictly; **c'est un problème p. urbain** it's strictly an inner-city problem **(c)** *à p. parler* strictly speaking; **voilà la bibliothèque p. dite** there's the actual library **(d)** *Fam (vraiment)* **c'est p. scandaleux!** it's an absolute disgrace!

propreté [prɔprəte] *nf* *(hygiène)* cleanliness; *(des vêtements, de la vaisselle, d'une maison)* cleanness; *(d'un travail)* neatness

propriétaire [prɔprijetɛr] *nmf* **(a)** *(d'une voiture, d'une propriété, d'un hôtel)* owner; **devenir** *ou* **se rendre p. de qch** to become the owner of sth; **être p.** to be a landowner; *(de maison)* to be a home owner; **p. foncier** landowner **(b)** *(d'une location)* landlord, *f* landlady

propriété [prɔprijete] *nf* **(a)** *(fait de posséder)* ownership; **p. littéraire** copyright; **p. foncière** property ownership **(b)** *(chose ou terre possédée)* property; **p. privée** private property **(c)** *(caractéristique)* property

proprio [prɔprijo] *nmf Fam* landlord, *f* landlady

propulser [prɔpylse] **1** *vt* to propel **2 se propulser** *vpr Fam* **se p. en tête du peloton** to shoot to the front of the pack

propulsion [prɔpylsjɔ̃] *nf* propulsion; **sous-marin à p. nucléaire** nuclear-powered submarine

prorata [prɔrata] *nm inv* proportion; **au p. de qch** in proportion to sth

prorogation [prɔrɔgasjɔ̃] *nf (de contrat, de bail)* extension

proroger [45] [prɔrɔʒe] *vt (contrat, bail)* to extend; *(échéance)* to defer

prosaïque [prɔzaik] *adj* prosaic

proscrire [30] [prɔskrir] *vt* to ban, to proscribe

proscrit, -e [prɔskri, -it] **1** *adj* banned, proscribed **2** *nm,f Litt (banni)* exile

prose [proz] *nf* prose; **en p.** *(écrire)* in prose; *(texte, poème)* prose

prosélytisme [prɔzelitism] *nm* proselytism; **faire du p.** to proselytize

prosodie [prɔzɔdi] *nf* prosody

prospecter [prɔspɛkte] *vt* **(a)** *(terrain)* to prospect **(b)** *(client)* to canvass; *(marché)* to explore

prospecteur, -trice [prɔspɛktœr, -tris] *nm,f* **(a)** *(de terrain)* prospector **(b)** *(de clients)* canvasser

prospection [prɔspɛksjɔ̃] *nf* **(a)** *(de terrain)* prospecting; **faire de la p.** to prospect **(b)** *(de clients)* canvassing; **faire de la p. to explore the market; p. téléphonique** telephone canvassing

prospectus [prɔspɛktys] *nm* leaflet

prospère [prɔspɛr] *adj* prosperous; *(santé)* glowing

prospérer [34] [prɔspere] *vi* to prosper

prospérité [prɔsperite] *nf* prosperity; **en période de p.** in times of prosperity

prostate [prɔstat] *nf Anat* prostate (gland)

prosterner [prɔstɛrne] **se prosterner** *vpr (saluer)* to prostrate oneself **(devant** before); *Fig (s'abaisser)* to grovel, to kowtow **(devant** to)

prostitué, -e [prɔstitɥe] *nm,f (homme)* male prostitute; *(femme)* prostitute

prostituer [prɔstitɥe] **1** *vt* to prostitute **2 se prostituer** *vpr* to prostitute oneself

prostitution [prɔstitysjɔ̃] *nf* prostitution

prostré, -e [prɔstre] *adj* prostrate

protagoniste [prɔtagɔnist] *nmf* protagonist

protecteur, -trice [prɔtɛktœr, -tris] **1** *adj (qui protège)* protective **(avec** towards); *Péj (ton)* patronizing **2** *nm,f* **(a)** *(d'une personne)* *(d'une prostituée)* pimp **(b)** *(des arts)* patron

protection [prɔtɛksjɔ̃] *nf* **(a)** protection **(contre** from *or* against); **de p.** *(écran, visière, vernis)* protective; **sous la p. de la police** under police protection; **p. de l'environnement** protection of the environment; **p. sociale** social welfare system; *Ordinat* **p. d'accès** logical access protection; **p. contre l'écriture** write-protection; **p. contre la copie** copy protection; **p. des fichiers** file protection; **p. par mot de passe** password protection **(b)** *Écon* protectionism

protectionnisme [prɔtɛksjɔnism] *nm Écon* protectionism

protectorat [prɔtɛktɔra] *nm* protectorate

protégé, -e [prɔteʒe] **1** *adj* protected; *Ordinat* **p. contre la copie** copy-protected **2** *nm,f* protégé, *f* protégée

protège-cahier *(pl* **protège-cahiers)** [prɔtɛʒkaje] *nm* exercise book cover

protège-dents [prɔtɛʒdɑ̃] nm inv gum shield

protéger [59] [prɔteʒe] **1** vt to protect (**contre/de** against/from); **ça protège bien** it gives good protection; **que Dieu vous protège!** God keep you!; Ordinat **p. contre l'écriture** ou **en écriture** to write-protect **2 se protéger** vpr to protect oneself (**contre/de** against/from)

protège-slip (pl **protège-slips**) [prɔtɛʒslip] nm pantyliner

protéine [prɔtein] nf protein

protestant, -e [prɔtɛstɑ̃, -ɑ̃t] adj & nm,f Protestant

protestantisme [prɔtɛstɑ̃tism] nm Protestantism

protestataire [prɔtɛstater] nmf protester

protestation [prɔtɛstasjɔ̃] nf (**a**) (plainte) protest; **émettre des protestations** to voice one's protest; **en signe de p.** as a protest (**b**) **des protestations d'amitié** protestations of friendship

protester [prɔtɛste] **1** vi to protest (**contre** against); **p. auprès de qn** to protest to sb **2 protester de** vt ind (innocence, bonne foi) to protest

prothèse [prɔtɛz] nf prosthesis; **p. auditive** hearing aid; **p. dentaire** (complète) false teeth, dentures; (partielle) bridge

protocole [prɔtɔkɔl] nm (**a**) (usages) protocol (**b**) **p. d'accord** protocol of agreement (**c**) Ordinat protocol; **p. de téléchargement** download protocol; **p. de transmission** transmission protocol

proton [prɔtɔ̃] nm proton

prototype [prɔtɔtip] nm prototype

protozoaire [prɔtɔzɔer] nm protozoan; **les protozoaires** the Protozoa

protubérance [prɔtyberɑ̃s] nf protuberance

protubérant, -e [prɔtyberɑ̃, -ɑ̃t] adj protuberant

proue [pru] nf bows, prow

prouesse [prues] nf feat; **faire des prouesses pour obtenir qch** to work wonders to get sth

prouver [pruve] **1** vt (**a**) (établir comme vrai) to prove; **p. qch à qn** to prove sth to sb; **p. qch par A plus B** to prove sth in a logical fashion; **cela reste à p.** it still has to be proved (**b**) (être la preuve de) to prove, to show (**que** that) **2 se prouver** vpr **se p. qch** (à soi-même) to prove sth to oneself

provenance [prɔvnɑ̃s] nf origin; **marchandises de p. italienne** goods of Italian origin; **en p. de Bordeaux** from Bordeaux

provençal, -e, -aux, -ales [prɔvɑ̃sal, -o] **1** adj Provençal **2** nm,f **P.** person from Provence **3** nm (langue) Provençal

Provence [prɔvɑ̃s] nf **la P.** Provence

provenir [70] [prɔvnir] vi **p. de** to come from; (difficultés) to arise from

proverbe [prɔvɛrb] nm proverb

proverbial, -e, -aux, -ales [prɔvɛrbjal, -o] adj proverbial

providence [prɔvidɑ̃s] nf (**a**) (sort) providence; **cette auberge est la p. des marcheurs** this inn is a haven for walkers (**b**) **la P.** Providence

providentiel, -elle [prɔvidɑ̃sjɛl] adj providential

province [prɔvɛ̃s] **1** nf (**a**) (région) province; Can **les Provinces Maritimes** the Maritime Provinces (**b**) **la p.** the provinces; **de p.** provincial; **en p.** in the provinces; **arriver de sa p.** to be new in town **2** adj inv Fam Péj provincial

provincial, -e, -aux, -ales [prɔvɛ̃sjal, -o] adj & nm,f provincial

proviseur [prɔvizœr] nm Br headmaster, f headmistress, Am principal

provision [prɔvizjɔ̃] nf (**a**) (réserve) stock, supply; **provisions** (nourriture) shopping; **faire des provisions** ou **faire p. de qch** to stock up on sth (**b**) (de compte bancaire) credit; (acompte) deposit

provisionnel, -elle [prɔvizjɔnɛl] adj voir **tiers**

provisoire [prɔvizwar] adj temporary; **à titre p.** temporarily

provisoirement [prɔvizwarmɑ̃] adv temporarily, provisionally

provocant, -e [prɔvɔkɑ̃, -ɑ̃t] adj provocative

provocateur, -trice [prɔvɔkatœr, -tris] **1** adj provocative; **agent p.** agent provocateur **2** nm,f troublemaker

provocation [prɔvɔkasjɔ̃] nf provocation; **il l'a dit par p.** he said it to be provocative

provoquer [prɔvɔke] vt (**a**) (personne) to provoke (**b**) (réaction) to provoke; (incendie, mort, malaise) to cause; (jalousie, colère) to arouse; **p. l'accouchement** to induce labour

proxénète [prɔksenɛt] nmf pimp

proxénétisme [prɔksenetism] nm pimping

proximité [prɔksimite] nf closeness, proximity; **à p.** close by; **à p. de qch** close to sth

prude [pryd] Péj **1** adj prudish **2** nf prude

prudemment [prydamɑ̃] adv carefully, cautiously

prudence [prydɑ̃s] nf care, caution; **par (mesure de) p.** as a precaution; Prov **p. est mère de sûreté** discretion is the better part of valour

prudent, -e [prydɑ̃, -ɑ̃t] adj (personne) careful, cautious; (décision) wise, sensible

prud'homme [prydɔm] nm Jur member of an industrial tribunal; **conseil des prud'hommes** industrial tribunal

prune [pryn] **1** nf (fruit) plum; (liqueur) plum brandy; Fam **pour des prunes** for nothing **2** adj inv plum-coloured

pruneau, -x [pryno] nm (**a**) (fruit) prune (**b**) Fam (balle) slug

prunelle [prynɛl] nf (pupille) pupil; Fig **j'y tiens comme à la p. de mes yeux** it's the apple of my eye

prunier [prynje] nm plum tree; Fam **secouer qn comme un p.** to shake sb like a rag doll

prurit [pryrit] nm Méd pruritus

Prusse [prys] nf voir **bleu**

PS [peɛs] nm (**a**) (abrév **Parti socialiste**) Socialist Party (**b**) (abrév **post-scriptum**) PS

psalmodier [66] [psalmɔdje] **1** vt to chant; Fig to drone out **2** vi to chant; Fig to drone on

psaume [psom] nm psalm

pseudo- [psødo] préf pseudo-; **un p.-intellectuel** a pseudo-intellectual

pseudonyme [psødɔnim] nm (pour un écrivain) pen name, pseudonym; (pour la scène) stage name

psy [psi] nmf Fam (médecin) shrink

psychanalyse [psikanaliz] nf psychoanalysis; **faire une p.** to be in psychoanalysis

psychanalyser [psikanalize] vt to psychoanalyse; **se faire p.** to be psychoanalysed

psychanalyste [psikanalist] nmf psychoanalyst

psyché [psiʃe] nf (miroir) cheval glass

psychédélique [psikedelik] adj psychedelic

psychiatre [psikjatr] *nmf* psychiatrist
psychiatrie [psikjatri] *nf* psychiatry
psychiatrique [psikjatrik] *adj* psychiatric
psychique [psifik] *adj* psychic
psychisme [psifism] *nm* psyche
psychodrame [psikodram] *nm* role-playing, *Spéc* psychodrama
psychologie [psikoloʒi] *nf* psychology; **comprendre la p.** de qn to understand the way sb's mind works
psychologique [psikoloʒik] *adj* psychological
psychologiquement [psikoloʒikmã] *adv* psychologically
psychologue [psikoloɡ] **1** *nmf* psychologist; *Fig* être fin **p.** to be a good psychologist **2** *adj* être **p.** to be a good psychologist
psychopathe [psikopat] *nmf* psychopath
psychose [psikoz] *nf* psychosis; **p.** maniaco-dépressive manic depression; *Fig* la **p.** de la maladie an obsessive fear of illness
psychosomatique [psikosomatik] *adj* psychosomatic
psychothérapeute [psikoterapøt] *nmf* psychotherapist
psychothérapie [psikoterapi] *nf* psychotherapy; **p.** de groupe group therapy
psychotique [psikotik] *adj & nmf* psychotic
PTT [petete] *nfpl Anciennement* (*abrév* **Postes, Télécommunications et Télédiffusion**) ≃ Post Office and Telecommunications Service
pu *voir* **pouvoir**
puant, -e [pɥɑ̃, -ɑ̃t] *adj* stinking; *Fig* **p.** (*personne*) y, arrogant
puanteur [pɥɑ̃tœr] *nf* stink, stench
pub [pyb] *nf Fam* (**a**) (*secteur*) advertising (**b**) (*message*) ad
pubère [pybɛr] *adj* pubescent
puberté [pybɛrte] *nf* puberty
pubis [pybis] *nm Anat* pubis; (*os*) pubic bone
public, -ique [pyblik] **1** *adj* public **2** *nm* (*d'un spectacle*) audience; **en p.** in public; (*émission*) before a live audience; **le grand p.** the general public
publication [pyblikasjɔ̃] *nf* (**a**) (*d'un ouvrage, d'une nouvelle*) publication; **p.** assistée par ordinateur desk-top publishing (**b**) (*ouvrage*) publication
publiciste [pyblisist] *nmf Fam* advertising executive
publicitaire [pyblisitɛr] **1** *adj* advertising **2** *nmf* advertising executive
publicité [pyblisite] *nf* (**a**) (*secteur*) advertising; **être dans la p.** to be in advertising; **faire de la p.** pour qch to advertise sth; *Fig* **faire de la p. à qn** to be publicity for sb; **p.** comparative comparative advertising; **p.** mensongère misleading advertising (**b**) (*message*) advertisement, advert; **une pleine page de p.** a full-page advertisement
publier [66] [pyblije] *vt* to publish; (*communiqué*) to issue
Publiphone® [pyblifɔn] *nm* card phone
publiquement [pyblikmã] *adv* publicly
puce [pys] *nf* (**a**) (*insecte*) flea; **le marché aux puces, les puces** the flea market; *Fig* **mettre la p. à l'oreille à qn** to make sb suspicious; *Fam* **secouer les puces à qn** to give sb a good telling-off; *Fam* **être excité comme une p.** to be jumping up and down with excitement (**b**) *Ordinat* (micro)chip; **p.** mémoire memory chip; **p.** de reconnaissance vocale voice recognition chip
puceau, -x [pyso] *nm & adj m Fam* virgin
pucelle [pysɛl] *nf & adj f* virgin
puceron [pysrɔ̃] *nm* greenfly

pudeur [pydœr] *nf* modesty; **avec p.** modestly; **sans p.** boldly; **par p.** out of a sense of decency; **avoir la p.** de faire qch to have the decency to do sth
pudibond, -e [pydibɔ̃, -ɔ̃d] *adj* prudish
pudique [pydik] *adj* modest
puer [pɥe] **1** *vi* to stink; **il pue des pieds** his feet stink **2** *vt* to stink of
puéricultrice [pɥerikyltris] *nf* nursery nurse
puériculture [pɥerikyltyr] *nf* child care
puéril, -e [pɥeril] *adj* childish, puerile
pugilat [pyʒila] *nm* brawl
pugnace [pygnas] *adj Littr* pugnacious
puis [pɥi] *adv* then; **et p.** (*ensuite*) and then; (*d'ailleurs*) and besides; **et p.** c'est tout! and that's all there is to it!; **et p.** après? (*et ensuite?*) then what?; *Fam* (*et alors?*) so what?
puisatier [pɥizatje] *nm* well digger
puiser [pɥize] *vt* (*eau, carte*) to draw (à from); *Fig* (*inspiration, idées*) to draw (dans/chez from); **p.** dans ses réserves to draw on one's reserves; **p.** dans la caisse to have one's hand in the till
puisque [pɥiskə] *conj* since, as; **p.** c'est comme ça if that's the way it is; **p.** je te dis que je l'ai vu! I'm telling you I saw him/it!; **tu en es bien sûr?** mais p. je te le dis! are you really sure? – I've said I am, haven't I?
puissamment [pɥisamã] *adv* powerfully
puissance [pɥisãs] *nf* power; **p.** de feu fire power; **les grandes puissances** the great powers; *Math* **élever un nombre à la p.** trois/quatre to raise a number to the third/fourth power; **dix (à la) p.** quatre ten to the power of four; **en p.** (*meurtrier*) potential
puissant, -e [pɥisã, -ãt] *adj* powerful
puisse *etc voir* **pouvoir**
puits [pɥi] *nm* (**a**) (*pour l'eau*) well; **p.** de pétrole oil well; *Fig* **c'est un p.** de science he's/she's a fount of knowledge (**b**) (*de mine*) shaft, pit
pull [pyl] *nm Fam* sweater
pull-over (*pl* pull-overs) [pylɔvœr] *nm* sweater
pulluler [pylyle] *vi* (**a**) (*se reproduire*) to proliferate (**b**) (*exister en profusion*) to abound
pulmonaire [pylmɔnɛr] *adj* pulmonary
pulpe [pylp] *nf* (**a**) (*de fruit*) pulp; **yaourt à la p.** de fruits yoghurt with real fruit (**b**) (*des doigts, des orteils*) pad; (*des dents*) pulp
pulpeux, -euse [pylpø, -øz] *adj* fleshy; (*femme*) curvaceous
pulsar [pylsar] *nm Astron* pulsar
pulsation [pylsasjɔ̃] *nf* (*de cœur*) beat; (*pulsations*) beating
pulsion [pylsjɔ̃] *nf* impulse; **pulsions sexuelles** sexual urges; **p.** de mort death wish
pulvérisateur [pylverizatœr] *nm* spray
pulvérisation [pylverizasjɔ̃] *nf* (*de liquides*) spraying
pulvériser [pylverize] *vt* (**a**) (*réduire en poudre*) to pulverize; *Fam* (*voiture*) to smash up (**b**) (*vaporiser*) to spray (**c**) *Fam* (*record*) to smash
puma [pyma] *nm* puma
punaise [pynɛz] *nf* (**a**) (*insecte*) bug; *Fam* **oh p.!** good grief! (**b**) (*pour accrocher*) *Br* drawing pin, *Am* thumbtack
punaiser [pyneze] *vt Fam* to pin up; **p.** qch à qch to pin sth to sth
punch¹ [pɔ̃ʃ] *nm* (*boisson*) punch
punch² [pœnʃ] *nm* punch; *Fig* (*de personne*) drive

punching-ball (*pl* **punching-balls**) [pœnʃiŋbol] *nm* punchball

punir [pynir] *vt (personne, crime)* to punish; **p. qn de mort** to punish sb with death; **p. qn d'un crime** to punish sb for a crime; **me voilà puni de ma gourmandise!** it serves me right for being greedy!

punitif, -ive [pynitif, -iv] *adj* punitive

punition [pynisjɔ̃] *nf* punishment; **p. corporelle** corporal punishment

punk [pœnk] *adj inv & nmf* punk

pupille[1] [pypij] *nmf (orphelin)* ward; **pupilles de la Nation** war orphans

pupille[2] *nf (de l'œil)* pupil

pupitre [pypitr] *nm* (**a**) *(d'écolier)* desk; *(d'orateur)* lectern; *(de musicien)* music stand (**b**) *Ordinat* **p. (de commande)** console (desk); **p. de visualisation** visual display unit

pupitreur, -euse [pypitrœr, -øz] *nm,f Ordinat* console operator

pur, -e [pyr] *adj* (**a**) *(or, air)* pure; *(ciel)* clear; *(whisky, gin)* straight, neat; **pure laine** pure wool; **biscuits p. beurre** all butter *Br* biscuits *or Am* cookies (**b**) *(recherche, mathématiques, théorie)* pure; **un communiste p. et dur** a hard-line Communist; **la vérité pure et simple** the plain and simple truth; **du vol p. et simple** sheer robbery; **c'est de la folie pure** it's sheer madness (**c**) *(lignes)* clean; *(visage)* clean-cut

purée [pyre] **1** *nf* purée; **p. (de pommes de terre)** mashed potatoes; *Fam Fig* **p. de pois** peasouper
2 *exclam Fam (colère)* hell!; *(surprise)* wow!

purement [pyrmɑ̃] *adv* purely; **p. et simplement** purely and simply

pureté [pyrte] *nf* purity; *(du ciel)* clearness; *(de lignes)* cleanness

purgatoire [pyrgatwar] *nm* purgatory

purge [pyrʒ] *nf* (**a**) *(pour raisons médicales)* purge (**b**) *(à des fins politiques)* purge (**c**) *(de freins, de radiateur)* bleeding

purger [45] [pyrʒe] *vt* (**a**) *(patient)* to purge (**b**) *(freins, radiateur)* to bleed (**c**) *(peine)* to serve

purifiant, -e [pyrifjɑ̃, -ɑ̃t] *adj* purifying

purificateur, -trice [pyrifikatœr, -tris] *adj* purifying

purification [pyrifikasjɔ̃] *nf* purification; **p. ethnique** ethnic cleansing

purifier [66] [pyrifje] **1** *vt aussi Fig* to purify; *(sang, teint)* to cleanse
2 se purifier *vpr* to be purified

purin [pyrɛ̃] *nm* liquid manure

puriste [pyrist] *nmf* purist

puritain, -e [pyritɛ̃, -ɛn] **1** *nm,f* puritan; *Hist* Puritan
2 *adj* puritanical; *Hist* Puritan

puritanisme [pyritanism] *nm* puritanism; *Hist* Puritanism

pur-sang [pyrsɑ̃] *nm inv* thoroughbred

purulent, -e [pyrylɑ̃, -ɑ̃t] *adj* suppurating

pus [py] *nm* pus

pusillanime [pyzilanim] *adj Litt* pusillanimous

pustule [pystyl] *nf* pustule

putain [pytɛ̃] *Vulg* **1** *nf* (**a**) *(prostituée)* whore (**b**) **p. de bagnole/temps!** (this) fucking car/weather!
2 *exclam* fuck!

pute [pyt] *nf Vulg* whore; **fils de p.** son of a bitch

putois [pytwa] *nm* polecat; *Fam* **crier comme un p.** to scream blue murder

putréfaction [pytrefaksjɔ̃] *nf* putrefaction; **matière en p.** putrefying matter

putréfier [66] [pytrefje] **1** *vt* to putrefy
2 se putrifier *vpr* to putrefy

putrescent, -e [pytresɑ̃, -ɑ̃t] *adj* putrescent

putride [pytrid] *adj* putrid

putsch [putʃ] *nm* putsch

putschiste [putʃist] **1** *adj* putsch
2 *nmf* putschist

puzzle [pœzl] *nm* jigsaw (puzzle); *Fig* puzzle

P.-V. [peve] *nm Fam (abrév* **procès-verbal**) (parking) ticket

PVC [pevese] *nm (abrév* **polychlorure de vinyle**) PVC; **siège en p.** PVC seat

PVD [pevede] *nm (abrév* **pays en voie de développement**) developing country

pygmée [pigme] *nmf* pygmy

pyjama [piʒama] *nm* pyjamas; **un p.** a pair of pyjamas

pylône [pilon] *nm* pylon; *(pour fils télégraphiques)* mast

pyramidal, -e, -aux, -ales [piramidal, -o] *adj* pyramid-shaped

pyramide [piramid] *nf* pyramid; **p. des âges** population pyramid; **structure en p.** pyramid-like structure

pyrénéen, -enne [pireneɛ̃, -ɛn] **1** *adj* Pyrenean
2 *nm,f* **P.** Pyrenean
3 *nm (chien)* Pyrenean mountain dog

Pyrénées [pirene] *nfpl* **les P.** the Pyrenees

Pyrex [pirɛks] *nm* Pyrex®; **plat en P.** Pyrex® dish

pyrogravure [pirogravyr] *nf* poker work, pyrography; *(gravure)* pyrograph

pyrolyse [piroliz] *nf* pyrolysis; **four à p.** self-cleaning oven

pyromane [piroman] *nmf* arsonist; *Psy* pyromaniac

pyromanie [piromani] *nf* pyromania

pyrotechnique [piroteknik] *adj* pyrotechnic

python [pitɔ̃] *nm* python

Q, q [ky] *nm inv* Q, q

Qatar [katar] *nm* le Q. Qatar

QCM [kyseɛm] *nm inv* (*abrév* **questionnaire à choix multiple**) multiple-choice questionnaire

QG [kyʒe] *nm inv* (*abrév* **quartier général**) HQ

QI [kyi] *nm inv* (*abrév* **quotient intellectuel**) IQ

quadra [kwadra] *nmf Fam* fortysomething

quadragénaire [kwadraʒenɛr] **1** *adj* être q. to be in one's forties
2 *nmf* person in his/her forties

quadrangulaire [kwadrɑ̃gylɛr] *adj* quadrangular

quadrature [kwadratyr] *nf* quadrature; **c'est la q. du cercle** it's like trying to square the circle

quadriceps [kwadriseps] *nm* quadriceps

quadrilatère [kwadrilatɛr, kadrilatɛr] *nm* quadrilateral

quadrillage [kadrijaʒ] *nm* (**a**) (*par la police*) tight surveillance (**b**) (*d'un tissu*) *Br* check *or Am* checkered pattern; (*sur une carte*) grid

quadrille [kadrij] *nm* quadrille

quadrillé, -e [kadrije] *adj* (*papier*) squared

quadriller [kadrije] *vt* (**a**) (*quartier, ville, région*) to put under tight surveillance (**b**) (*papier*) to mark into squares

quadrimoteur [kwadrimɔtœr, kadrimɔtœr] **1** *adj* four-engined
2 *nm* four-engined plane

quadriparti, -e [kwadriparti], **quadripartite** [kwadripartit] *adj* (*traité*) quadripartite; (*conférence, commission*) (*entre parties*) four-party; (*entre pays*) four-power

quadriphonie [kwadrifoni] *nf* quadraphony

quadrupède [kwadrypɛd, kadrypɛd] *adj & nm* quadruped

quadruple [kwadrypl, kadrypl] **1** *adj* quadruple, fourfold; *Mus* q. croche *Br* hemidemisemiquaver, *Am* sixty-fourth note
2 *nm* le q. (de) (*quantité, prix*) four times as much (as); (*nombre*) four times as many (as); **douze est le q. de trois** twelve is four times three

quadrupler [kwadryple, kadryple] *vt & vi* to quadruple, to increase fourfold

quadruplés, -ées [kwadryple, kadryple] *nm,fpl* quadruplets

quai [kɛ] *nm* (**a**) (*de gare, de métro*) platform (**b**) (*d'un port*) quay; **se mettre à q.** to berth (**c**) (*d'une rivière, d'un fleuve*) embankment; **le Q. des Orfèvres** Police Headquarters (*in Paris*); **le Q. d'Orsay** the French Foreign Office

qualificatif, -ive [kalifikatif, -iv] **1** *adj Gram* (*adjectif*) qualifying
2 *nm* term

qualification [kalifikasjɔ̃] *nf* (**a**) (*formation*) qualification (**b**) (*d'une équipe, d'un sportif*) qualification (**c**) (*désignation*) description

qualifié, -e [kalifje] *adj* (**a**) (*compétent*) qualified (**pour faire qch** to do sth) (**b**) (*délit, vol*) aggravated

qualifier [66] [kalifje] **1** *vt* (**a**) (*appeler*) to describe (**de** as) (**b**) (*autoriser*) q. qn pour qch/pour faire qch to qualify sb for sth/to do sth
2 se qualifier *vpr* (*sportif, équipe*) to qualify (**pour** for)

qualitatif, -ive [kalitatif, -iv] *adj* qualitative

qualité [kalite] *nf* (**a**) (*d'un produit*) quality; **de q.** quality; **de bonne/mauvaise q.** of good/poor quality; *Ordinat* q. brouillon, q. liste rapide, q. listing draft quality; *Ordinat* q. courrier (*near*) letter quality; **la q. de la vie** the quality of life (**b**) (*d'une personne*) quality; **elle n'a pas que des qualités** she isn't all good (**c**) (*occupation*) occupation; (*fonction*) capacity; **en q. de** in my/her/*etc* capacity as

quand [kɑ̃] **1** *conj* (*lorsque*) when; **je lui en parlerai q. je le verrai** I'll mention it to him when I see him; *Fam* q. je pense que le voyage devait être annulé! when I think that they were going to cancel the trip! (**b**) (*alors que*) when
2 *adv* when; **q. viendra-t-il?** when will he come?; **demande-lui q. il va partir** ask him when he's going to leave; **à q. le mariage?** when's the wedding?; **de q. est ce papier?** what's the date of this paper?; **pour q. est la réunion?** when is the meeting?

quant [kɑ̃] **quant à** *prép* as for

quant-à-soi [kɑ̃taswa] *nm inv* **rester sur** *ou* **se tenir sur son q.** to keep oneself to oneself

quantième [kɑ̃tjɛm] *nm* day of the month

quantifiable [kɑ̃tifjabl] *adj* quantifiable

quantifier [66] [kɑ̃tifje] *vt* to quantify

quantitatif, -ive [kɑ̃titatif, -iv] *adj* quantitative

quantitativement [kɑ̃titativmɑ̃] *adv* quantitatively

quantité [kɑ̃tite] *nf* quantity; **en grande/petite q.** in large/small quantities; **en q.** in abundance; **q. de gens/réponses** a great many people/replies

quarantaine [karɑ̃tɛn] *nf* (**a**) (*environ quarante*) **une q.** (**de**) about forty, forty or so (**b**) (*âge*) **avoir la q.** to be about forty; **approcher de la q.** to be getting on for forty (**c**) (*isolement*) quarantine; **mettre qn en q.** to put sb in quarantine; *Fig* to send sb to Coventry

quarante [karɑ̃t] *adj & nm inv* forty; *Fam* **se ficher de qch comme de l'an q.** not to give two hoots about sth; *voir aussi* **trois**

quarante-cinq tours [karɑ̃tsɛ̃tur] *nm inv* single, 45

quarantième [karɑ̃tjɛm] *nmf, nm & adj* fortieth; *voir aussi* **cinquième**

quart¹ [kar] *adj* **le q. monde** *(dans les pays riches)* the underclass

quart² *nm* (**a**) *(fraction)* quarter; **un q.** de siècle/de beurre a quarter (of a) century/kilo of butter; **un q. d'heure** a quarter of an hour; *Fam* **passer un mauvais q. d'heure** to have a bad time of it; **deux heures et q.** (**a**) quarter past *or Am* after two; **deux heures moins le q.** (**a**) quarter to *or Am* of two; **il est moins le q.** it's (a) quarter to; **démarrer** *ou* **partir au q. de tour** *(voiture)* to start first time; *(personne)* to fly off the handle; **q. de cercle** quadrant; **q. de finale** quarter final; **q. de soupir** *Br* semiquaver *or Am* sixteenth rest (**b**) *(bouteille, pichet)* quarter litre (**c**) *(veille sur un bateau)* watch; **être de q.** to be on watch

quarte [kart] *nf Mus* fourth

quarté [karte] *nm* = system of betting on four horses in the same race

quartette [kwartɛt] *nm* jazz quartet

quartier [kartje] *nm* (**a**) *(d'une ville)* district, area; **les beaux quartiers** the fashionable districts; **les quartiers sud de la ville** the south side of the town; **de q., du q.** local (**b**) *(morceau)* *(d'une orange)* segment; *(d'une pomme)* piece (**c**) *(de la lune)* quarter (**d**) *(de viande)* quarter (**e**) *(en héraldique)* quarter; **avoir quatre quartiers de noblesse** to belong to the established nobility (**f**) *(locutions)* **avoir q. libre** to be off duty; **ne pas faire de q.** to give no quarter

quartz [kwarts] *nm* quartz; **horloge/montre à q.** quartz clock/watch

quasi [kazi] *adv* almost, nearly

quasi- [kazi] *préf* **la q.-totalité des membres** almost all the members

quasiment [kazimɑ̃] *adv* almost, nearly; **je n'ai q. rien senti** I hardly felt a thing

quaternaire [kwatɛrnɛr] *Géol* **1** *adj* Quaternary **2** *nm* Quaternary era

quatorze [katɔrz] *adj & nm inv* fourteen; *voir aussi* **trois**

quatorzième [katɔrzjɛm] *nmf, nm & adj* fourteenth; *voir aussi* **cinquième**

quatrain [katrɛ̃] *nm* quatrain

quatre [katr] *adj & nm inv* four; **aux q. coins du monde** throughout the world; **monter l'escalier q. à q.** to rush up the stairs; *Fig* **se mettre en q. pour qn/pour faire qch** to bend over backwards for sb/to do sth; *voir aussi* **trois**

quatre-quarts [katkar, katrəkar] *nm inv* pound cake

quatre-quatre [katkatr] *nm inv ou nf inv* four-wheel drive

quatre-saisons [katsɛzɔ̃, katrəsɛzɔ̃] *nfpl* **marchand des q.** fruit-and-vegetable merchant *(with outdoor stall)*

quatre-vingt [katrəvɛ̃] *voir* **quatre-vingts**

quatre-vingt-dix [katrəvɛ̃dis] *adj & nm inv* ninety; *voir aussi* **trois**

quatre-vingt-dixième [katrəvɛ̃dizjɛm] *adj, nmf & nm* ninetieth; *voir aussi* **cinquième**

quatre-vingtième [katrəvɛ̃tjɛm] *adj, nmf & nm* eightieth; *voir aussi* **cinquième**

quatre-vingts [katrəvɛ̃] *adj & nm inv* eighty; **quatre-vingt-deux** eighty-two; **page quatre-vingt** page eighty; *voir aussi* **trois**

quatrième [katrijɛm] **1** *adj & nmf* fourth **2** *nf* (**a**) *(classe)* *Br* ≃ third form, *Am* ≃ ninth grade (**b**) *(vitesse)* fourth (gear); *voir aussi* **cinquième**

quatrièmement [katrijɛmmɑ̃] *adv* fourthly

quatuor [kwatyɔr] *nm* quartet; **q. à cordes** string quartet

que¹ [k(ə)]

En anglais, le pronom relatif objet (voir (**a**)) peut être omis.

---

pron relatif (**a**) *(objet)* *(personne)* that, whom; *(chose)* that, which; **l'homme q. vous voyez** the man (that) you see; **le gâteau q. j'ai fait cuire** the cake (that) I baked; **c'est le meilleur q. nous ayons** it is the best (that) we have (**b**) *(attribut)* **il mourut en brave soldat qu'il était** he died like the brave soldier he was (**c**) *(dans le temps)* **il y a trois mois q. j'habite Lyon** I've been living in Lyons for three months; **un jour q. j'étais de service** one day when I was on duty

que² *pron interrogatif* what; **q. voulez-vous?** what do you want?; **il ne savait q. penser** he didn't know what to think

que³ *adv exclamatif* **qu'elle est intelligente!** she's so intelligent!; **q. de monde!** what a lot of people!

que⁴

La conjonction "that" peut être omise après les verbes d'opinion, ainsi que "say", "know", etc: **je sais que c'est possible** I know (that) it's possible.

---

conj (**a**) *(complétif)* that; **je pense qu'il a raison** I think (that) he's right; **je veux qu'il vienne** I want him to come; **c'est q. je ne le savais pas** I just didn't know (**b**) *(exprime le souhait)* **qu'elle entre!** let her come in! (**c**) *(exprime l'hypothèse)* **q. la machine chauffe, et il y aura un accident** let the machine get hot and there will be an accident; **qu'il essaie encore une fois!** just let him try again! (**d**) *(dans une alternative)* **q. tu le veuilles ou non** whether you like it or not (**e**) *(relie deux conditionnels)* **il me le dirait lui-même q. je ne le croirais pas** he could tell me himself and I still wouldn't believe it (**f**) *(afin que, pour que)* **approchez qu'on vous entende** come closer so (that) we can hear you (**g**) *(pour ne pas répéter une autre conjonction)* **quand tu iras mieux et q. tu voudras sortir** when you're better and you want to go out; **si ça te plaît et que tu veux l'acheter...** if you like it and you want to buy it... (**h**) *(dans les comparaisons)* **plus/moins grand q. moi** bigger/smaller than me; **aussi grand q. moi** as big as me (**i**) **ne... q.** only; **il n'a qu'une jambe** he's only got one leg; **il ne me reste plus q. 20 euros** I've got 20 euros left (**j**) *Fam* **ah! q. non!** surely not!; **il va au cercle – qu'il dit!** he goes to the club – **so he says!**

Québec [kebɛk] **1** *nm (province)* **le Q.** Quebec **2** *n (ville)* Quebec

québécisme [kebesism] *nm* = word or expression peculiar to Quebec French

québécois, -e [kebekwa, -az] **1** *adj* of Quebec **2** *nm, f* **Q.** Quebecker **3** *nm (langue)* Quebec French

quel, quelle [kɛl] **1** *adj interrogatif* *(personne)* which; *(chose)* which, what; **q. homme?** which man?; **quelle heure est-il?** what time is it?, what's the time?; **q. genre d'homme est-ce?** what sort of a man is he?; **si tu savais à q. point il y tient** if you knew how fond he is of it; **à q. film faites-vous référence?** which or what film are you referring to?; **quelles sont ses raisons?** what are his reasons?; *Litt* **est cet homme?** who is this man? **2** *adj exclamatif* **q. homme!** what a man!; **q. dommage!** what a shame!; **quelle bêtise de sa part!** how stupid of him! **3** *adj relatif* **q. que soit le coupable** whoever the culprit may be; **q. que soit le résultat** whatever the result may be; **q. que soit l'endroit où...** no matter where... **4** *pron interrogatif* which (one)

quelconque [kɛlkɔ̃k] **1** *adj indéfini* **donne-moi un livre q.** give me any book; **sous un prétexte q.** on some pretext or other **2** *adj (insignifiant)* ordinary

quelle [kɛl] *voir* **quel**

quelque [kɛlk] **1** *adj indéfini* some; **quelques** some, a few; **il y a quelques jours** a few days ago; **et quelque(s)** or so; **cent et quelques mètres** a hundred metres plus; **q....** **que** + *subjunctive* whatever; **sous q. prétexte que ce soit** on whatever pretext; **de q.** côté que vous regardiez whichever way you look **2** *adv* some, about; **q. dix ans** some *or* about ten years; **les q. 500 euros qu'il m'a prêtés** the 500 euros or so that he lent me

quelque chose [kɛlkəʃoz] *pron indéfini* something; **avez-vous q. à dire?** do you have anything *or* something to say?; **est-ce que je peux te demander q.?** can I ask you something?; **q. d'autre/de neuf** something else/new; **cela m'a fait q.** it touched me; **ça te ferait vraiment q. si je m'en allais?** would it really matter to you if I went away?; *Fam* **ah, mais c'est q., ça!** that's a bit much!; *Fam* **un petit q.** *(cadeau)* a little something

quelquefois [kɛlkəfwa] *adv* sometimes

quelque part [kɛlkəpar] *adv* somewhere; *(dans les questions, les hypothèses)* anywhere; **q. où tu n'es jamais allé** somewhere you've never been before; *Fam* **je lui ai donné un coup de pied q.** I kicked him where it hurts

quelques-uns, quelques-unes [kɛlkəzœ̃, -yn] *pron indéfini* some, a few (**de** of)

quelqu'un [kɛlkœ̃] *pron indéfini* (**a**) *(une personne)* someone, somebody; *(dans les questions, les hypothèses)* anyone, anybody; **q. de trop** one too many; **q. d'important** someone important; **c'est q. de bien** he's a decent person (**b**) *(personne importante)* somebody

quémander [kemɑ̃de] *vt* to beg for (**à** from)

qu'en-dira-t-on [kɑ̃diratɔ̃] *nm* **le q.** gossip

quenelle [kənɛl] *nf* quenelle

quenotte [kənɔt] *nf Fam* tooth

quenouille [kənuj] *nf (pour filer)* distaff

quéquette [kekɛt] *nf Fam* peter

querelle [kərɛl] *nf* quarrel; **chercher q. à qn** to try to pick a quarrel with sb; **q. de clocher** petty dispute

quereller [kərele] **se quereller** *vpr* to quarrel (**avec** with)

querelleur, -euse [kərɛlœr, -øz] *adj* quarrelsome

quérir [kerir] *vt Litt* **aller q. qn/qch** to go and fetch sb/sth

qu'est-ce que [kɛskə] **1** *pron interrogatif* what; **q. vous voulez?** what do you want?; **q. c'est que ça?** what's that?; *Fam* **q. tu avais besoin d'aller lui dire ça?** what did you have to go and tell him that for? **2** *pron exclamatif* **qu'est-ce qu'il fait beau!** what lovely weather!; **qu'est-ce qu'il fait chaud!** it's so hot!; **qu'est-ce qu'on a rigolé!** we had such a good laugh!; **q. tu as changé!** how you've changed!; **q. j'ai mangé!** I've eaten so much!

qu'est-ce qui [kɛski] *pron interrogatif* what

question [kɛstjɔ̃] *nf* (**a**) *(interrogation)* question (**sur** about); **q. de confiance** vote of confidence; **q. piège** trick question; **q. subsidiaire** tie-break (**b**) *(affaire)* question, matter; **le dossier en q.** the file in question; **remettre qch en q.** to call sth into question; **une q. d'argent/de temps/d'habitude** a question *or* matter of money/of time/of habit; **c'est une q. de vie ou de mort** it's a matter of life or death; **il est q. qu'ils déménagent** there's some talk of them moving; **il n'en est pas q.** it's out of the question; **là n'est pas la q.** it's not a question of that; *Fam* **pas q.!** no way!, no chance!; *Fam* **q. argent, ça va** moneywise *or* as far as money goes, things are OK

questionnaire [kɛstjɔnɛr] *nm* questionnaire; **q. à choix multiple** multiple-choice questionnaire

questionner [kɛstjɔne] *vt* to question (**sur** about)

quête [kɛt] *nf* (**a**) *(recherche)* quest, search (**de** for); **se mettre en q. de qn/qch** to go in search of sb/sth (**b**) *(collecte)* collection; **faire la q.** *(à l'église)* to take the collection

quêter [kete] **1** *vt* to seek **2** *vi* to collect money (**pour** for)

quêteux, -euse [kɛtø, -øz] *nm,f Can* beggar

quetsche [kwɛtʃ] *nf* (**a**) *(prune)* dark-red plum (**b**) *(eau-de-vie)* plum brandy

queue [kø] *nf* (**a**) *(d'animal)* tail; **n'avoir ni q. ni tête** to have neither rhyme nor reason; **faire une q. de poisson à qn** to cut (in) in front of sb; **finir en q. de poisson** *(pièce de théâtre, projet)* to end up in the air (**b**) *(d'une casserole)* handle; *(d'une comète, d'un cerf-volant)* tail; *(d'un fruit, d'une fleur)* stalk; *(d'une note de musique)* stem (**c**) *(d'une procession)* rear; **de q.** *(voiture, wagon)* rear; **être en q. de peloton** to be at the back of the bunch; **être en q. de classement** to be bottom of the table (**d**) *(file) Br* queue, *Am* line; **à la q. leu leu** in single file; **faire la q.** *Br* to queue (up), *Am* to stand in line (**e**) *(pour le billard)* cue (**f**) *Vulg (pénis)* cock

queue-de-cheval *(pl* **queues-de-cheval)** [kødʃəval] *nf* ponytail

queue-de-pie *(pl* **queues-de-pie)** [kødpi] *nf Fam* tails

qui¹ [ki]

> En anglais, le pronom relatif objet peut être omis lorsque la préposition qu'il introduit est rejetée en fin de phrase: **l'amie avec qui j'ai passé mes vacances** the friend (who) I spent my holidays with.

pron relatif (**a**) *(personne)* who, that; *(animal, chose)* which, that; **vous q. êtes du pays, pourriez-vous me dire si...** you being from the country, could you tell me if...; **je le vois q. vient** I can see him coming (**b**) *(ce qui)* **q. plus est** what's more; **voilà q. me plaît** that's what I like (**c**) *(après une préposition)* who, whom; **voilà l'homme à q. je pensais** there's the man (who) I was thinking about; **il cherche quelqu'un avec q. jouer** he's looking for someone to play with; **c'est à q. finira le premier** everyone's trying to be the first to finish (**d**) **q. que vous soyez** whoever you are; **je défie q. ce soit de le prouver** I challenge anyone to prove it

qui² *pron interrogatif* who; *(complément d'objet ou après une préposition)* who, whom; **q. a dit cela?** who said that?; **savez-vous q. a dit cela?** do you know who said that?; **à q. est-ce?** whose is it?; **q. parlez-vous?** who are you talking about?; **de q. êtes-vous le fils?** whose son are you?; **q. d'autre?** who else?; *Fam* **q. ça?** who's that?; *Fam* **il est là – q. donc?** he's here – who?

quiche [kiʃ] *nf* quiche; **q. lorraine** quiche lorraine

quiconque [kikɔ̃k] *pron indéfini (sujet)* whoever, anyone who; *(complément)* anyone, anybody; **q. désobéira sera puni** anyone who disobeys will be punished; **sans l'aide de q.** without anyone's help

quidam [kidam] *nm* fellow

quiétude [kjetyd] *nf Litt* peace; **en toute q.** *(sans être dérangé)* without being disturbed; *(sans souci)* with an easy mind

quignon [kiɲɔ̃] *nm* hunk

quille¹ [kij] *nf* (**a**) **quilles** *(jeu)* skittles (**b**) *Fam* **la q.** *(fin du service militaire)* discharge (**c**) *Fam* **quilles** *(jambes)* pins

quille² *nf (d'un bateau)* keel

quilleur, -euse [kijœr, -øz] *nm,f Can* skittle player

quincaillerie [kɛ̃kajri] *nf* (**a**) *(magasin)* hardware shop, *Br* ironmonger's (**b**) *(ustensiles)* hardware (**c**) *Fam (bijoux voyants)* cheap jewellery

quincaillier, -ère [kɛ̃kaje, -ɛr] *nm,f* hardware dealer, *Br* ironmonger

quinconce [kɛ̃kɔ̃s] **en quinconce** *adv* in staggered rows

quinine [kinin] *nf* quinine

quinquagénaire [kɛ̃kaʒenɛr] **1** *adj* être q. to be in one's fifties **2** *nmf* person in his/her fifties

quinquennal, -e, -aux, -ales [kɛ̃kenal, -o] *adj (plan)* five-year; *(exposition, élection)* five-yearly

quinquennat [kɛ̃kena] *nm* five-year term

quintal, -aux [kɛ̃tal, -o] *nm* quintal *(= 100 kg)*

quinte [kɛ̃t] *nf* **(a)** *(accès)* **q. de toux** coughing fit **(b)** *Mus* fifth

quintessence [kɛ̃tesɑ̃s] *nf* quintessence

quintette [kɛ̃tɛt, kɥɛ̃tɛt] *nm* quintet

quintuple [kɛ̃typl] **1** *adj* quintuple, fivefold **2** *nm* **le q. (de)** *(quantité, prix)* five times as much (as); *(nombre)* five times as many (as); **quinze est le q. de trois** fifteen is five times three

quintupler [kɛ̃typle] *vt & vi* to quintuple, to increase fivefold

quintuplés, -ées [kɛ̃typle] *nm,fpl* quintuplets

quinzaine [kɛ̃zɛn] *nf* **(a)** *(environ quinze)* **une q. (de)** about fifteen, fifteen or so **(b)** *(deux semaines)* two weeks, *Br* fortnight; **Com** = sale lasting two weeks

quinze [kɛ̃z] **1** *adj inv* fifteen; **q. jours** two weeks, *Br* a fortnight **2** *inv* fifteen; **demain en q.** two weeks *or Br* a fortnight tomorrow; **les Quinze** *(de l'Europe)* the member countries of the EU; *voir aussi* **trois**

quinzième [kɛ̃zjɛm] *nmf, nm & adj* fifteenth; *voir aussi* **cinquième**

quiproquo [kiprɔko] *nm* mix-up

quittance [kitɑ̃s] *nf* receipt; **q. de loyer** rent receipt

quitte [kit] *adj* **(a)** *(libéré)* **nous sommes quittes** we're quits **(b)** *(locutions)* **en être q. pour qch** to get off with sth; **q. ou double** double or quits; **q. à faire qch** even if it means doing sth

quitter [kite] **1** *vt* **(a)** *(personne, lieu)* to leave; *(chambre d'hôtel)* to vacate; **q. la route** *(par accident)* to go off the road; *(délibérément)* to turn off the road; **un ami très cher vient de nous q.** we have just lost a very dear friend; *Ordinat* **q. le système** to quit (the system) **(b)** *(fonctions, poste)* to leave **(c)** *(vêtement)* to take off **(d)** *(au téléphone)* **ne quittez pas** hold the line **(e)** **ne pas q. qn/qch des yeux** to keep one's eye on sb/sth **2 se quitter** *vpr* to part; **ils ne se quittent plus** they are inseparable

qui-vive [kiviv] *nm* être *ou* **se tenir sur le q.** to be on the alert

quoi¹ [kwa] *pron relatif* **(a)** what; **ce à q.** je m'oppose what I object to; **après q.** after which; **sur q.** whereupon; **avoir de q.** vivre to have enough to live on; **avez-vous de q. écrire?** do you have something to write with?; **il n'y a pas de q.** être fier that's nothing to be proud of; **il y a de q. se mettre en colère!** it's enough to make you really angry!; **je suis en colère – il y a de q.** I'm angry – you've every right to be; **il n'y a pas de q.** *(après des remerciements)* don't mention it, not at all **(b)** **q. que tu dises** whatever you say; **q. qu'il advienne** whatever happens; **q. qu'il en soit be** that as it may

quoi² *pron interrogatif* what; **q. d'autre?** what else?; **q. de neuf?** what's new?; **q. de plus simple?** what could be simpler?; **je ne sais q. penser** I don't know what to think; **à q. pensez-vous?** what are you thinking about?; **de q. parlez-vous?** what are you talking about?; **à q. bon?** what's the use?; *Fam* **tu es sourd ou q.?** are you deaf or what?; *Fam* **q.?** *(pardon?)* what?

quoi³ *exclam* what!; **et q. encore!** whatever next!; *Fam* **enfin, c'était nul, q.!** it was crap, basically!

quoique [kwak] *conj* (al)though; **q. je le sache déjà** (al)though I already know

quolibet [kɔlibɛ] *nm* gibe, jeer

quorum [kwɔrɔm] *nm* quorum; **atteindre le q.** to have a quorum

quota [kɔta] *nm* quota

quote-part *(pl* **quotes-parts)** [kɔtpar] *nf* share

quotidien, -enne [kɔtidjɛ̃, -ɛn] **1** *adj* daily **2** *nm* **(a)** *(journal)* daily (paper); **grand q.** national daily (paper) **(b)** *(routine)* daily life; **au q.** on a day-to-day basis

quotidiennement [kɔtidjɛnmɑ̃] *adv* daily

quotient [kɔsjɑ̃] *nm* quotient; **q. intellectuel** intelligence quotient

R

R, r [ɛr] *nm inv* R, r

rab [ʁab] *nm Fam (nourriture)* extra; **faire du r.** *(au travail)* to put in a bit of overtime; **en r.** left over

rabâchage [ʁabɑʃaʒ] *nm* tedious repetition

rabâcher [ʁabɑʃe] **1** *vi* to say the same thing over and over again **2** *vt (conseils, recommandations)* to keep on repeating; *(leçon)* to repeat parrot-fashion

rabais [ʁabɛ] *nm* discount, reduction; **faire un r. à qn (sur qch)** to give sb a discount (on sth); *Fig* **au r.** *(travail)* badly paid

rabaisser [ʁabese] **1** *vt* (a) *(prétentions)* to moderate (b) *(personne, valeur, talents)* to belittle **2 se rabaisser** *vpr* to belittle oneself

Rabat [ʁaba] *n* Rabat

rabat [ʁaba] *nm* (a) *(de sac à main, d'enveloppe)* flap (b) *(de costume officiel)* bands

rabat-joie [ʁabaʒwa] **1** *adj inv* **être r.** to be a killjoy **2** *nm inv* killjoy

rabattable [ʁabatabl] *adj (siège, dossier)* fold-down

rabatteur, -euse [ʁabatœr, -øz] *nm,f* (a) *(à la chasse)* beater (b) *Fig* tout

rabattre [11] [ʁabatr] **1** *vt* (a) *(col)* to turn down (b) *(couvercle)* to close; *(strapontin) (en se levant)* to fold up; *(pour s'asseoir)* to fold down (c) *(gibier, foule)* to drive (**vers** towards) (d) *(somme)* to deduct (**de** from) (e) *(prétentions)* to moderate **2 se rabattre** *vpr* (a) *(strapontin)* to fold down (b) *(véhicule)* to pull back in (c) *(foule)* **se r. vers qch** to veer off towards sth (d) *(avoir recours)* **se r. sur qn/qch** to fall back on sb/sth

rabbin [ʁabɛ̃] *nm* rabbi

rabibocher [ʁabibɔʃe] *Fam* **1** *vt* to patch things up between **2 se rabibocher** *vpr* to patch things up (**avec** with)

rabiot [ʁabjo] = **rab**

râble [ʁabl] *nm (de lièvre, lapin)* back; **r. de lièvre** *(plat)* saddle of hare

râblé, -e [ʁable] *adj* stocky

rabot [ʁabo] *nm* plane

raboter [ʁabɔte] *vt* to plane

raboteuse [ʁabɔtøz] *nf* planing machine

raboteux, -euse [ʁabɔtø, -øz] *adj* uneven

rabougri, -e [ʁabugri] *adj (plante, personne)* stunted

rabougrir [ʁabugrir] **se rabougrir** *vpr* to shrivel up

rabrouer [ʁabrue] *vt* to snub

racaille [ʁakaj] *nf (voyous)* scum; *Vieilli (populace)* rabble

raccommodage [ʁakɔmɔdaʒ] *nm (de vêtements)* mend-ing; *(de bas, de chaussettes)* darning; **faire du r.** to do some mending/darning

raccommoder [ʁakɔmɔde] **1** *vt* (a) *(vêtement)* to mend; *(bas, chaussette)* to darn (b) *Fam (personnes)* to patch things up between **2 se raccommoder** *vpr Fam* to patch things up (**avec** with)

raccompagner [ʁakɔ̃paɲe] *vt* to take back

raccord [ʁakɔr] *nm* (a) *(de papier peint)* join; *(de peinture)* touch-up (b) *(pièce d'assemblage)* connection (c) *Cin* continuity; *(plan)* link

raccordement [ʁakɔrdəmɑ̃] *nm* (a) *(lien)* link, connec-tion (b) *Ordinat* link

raccorder [ʁakɔrde] **1** *vt* (a) *(relier) (canalisations, bâtiments, routes)* to link up, to connect (**à** to); *Ordinat* to connect (b) *(bande magnétique)* to splice **2 se raccorder** *vpr* to link up; *Ordinat* **se r. à** to link up to

raccourci [ʁakursi] *nm* short cut; **en r.** *(en bref)* in brief; *(en miniature)* in miniature; *Ordinat* **r. clavier** keyboard shortcut

raccourcir [ʁakursir] **1** *vt* to shorten (**de** by) **2** *vi* to get shorter

raccrocher [ʁakrɔʃe] **1** *vt* to hang up again; **r. l'appareil** *ou* **le téléphone** to hang up **2** *vi* (a) *(au téléphone)* to hang up, to put the phone down; **r. au nez de qn** to hang up on sb, to put the phone down on sb (b) *Fam (sportif)* to retire **3 se raccrocher** *vpr* **se r. à qch** to catch hold of sth; *Fig (espérance)* to cling to sth

race [ʁas] *nf* (a) *(ethnie)* race; **la r. blanche/noire** the white/black race; **la r. humaine** the human race (b) *(animale)* breed; **de r.** *(chien)* pedigree; *(cheval)* thorough-bred

racé, -e [ʁase] *adj (animal)* pure-bred; *(cheval, voiture)* thoroughbred; *(personne)* noble-looking

rachat [ʁaʃa] *nm* (a) *(d'une voiture, d'un appartement)* repurchase, buying back (b) *(d'une société)* buy-out (c) *(d'un péché)* atonement

racheter [39] [ʁaʃte] **1** *vt* (a) *(acheter davantage de)* to buy some more (b) *(remplacer)* to buy another (**à** for) (c) *(compagnie)* to buy out (d) *(après une vente)* to buy back (**à** from) (e) *(otage, prisonnier)* to pay a ransom for (f) *(faute, faiblesse)* to make up for; *(péché)* to atone for; *(honneur, réputation)* to retrieve **2 se racheter** *vpr* to make amends, to redeem oneself

rachitique [ʁaʃitik] *adj (malade)* suffering from rickets; *(très maigre)* scrawny

rachitisme [ʁaʃitism] *nm* rickets *(singulier)*

racial, -e, -aux, -ales [ʁasjal, -o] *adj* racial

racine [rasin] *nf* root; **prendre r.** *(plante, personne)* to take root; **r. carrée/cubique** square/cube root

racisme [rasism] *nm* racism

raciste [rasist] *adj & nmf* racist

racket [rakɛt] *nm Fam* racket

racketter [rakɛte] *vt Fam (personne)* to extort money from; **se faire r.** to pay protection money

raclage [rakla3] *nm* scraping

raclée [rakle] *nf Fam* thrashing; **prendre une r.** to get a thrashing

raclement [rakləmɑ̃] *nm* scraping (noise)

racler [rakle] **1** *vt* to scrape; *(peinture, boue)* to scrape off; *Fig* **r. les fonds de tiroirs** to scrape some money together; *Fam* **r. la gorge** *ou* **le gosier** *(vin)* to be rough on the throat **2 se racler** *vpr* **se r. la gorge** to clear one's throat

raclette [raklɛt] *nf* **(a)** *(plat)* raclette *(Swiss dish consisting of potatoes covered in melted cheese)* **(b)** *(outil)* scraper

racloir [raklwar] *nm* scraper

racolage [rakɔla3] *nm (d'une prostituée)* soliciting; *(d'un publicitaire)* touting for business; **faire du r.** *(prostituée)* to solicit; *(publicitaire)* to tout for business

racoler [rakɔle] **1** *vt (sujet: prostituée)* to solicit; *(sujet: commerçant)* to tout for **2** *vi (prostituée)* to solicit; *(commerçant)* to tout for business

racoleur, -euse [rakɔlœr, -øz] **1** *adj (publicité, affiche)* eye-catching **2** *nm,f (politicien)* = canvasser who attempts to recruit party members using unscrupulous means; *(commerçant)* tout **3** *nf* **racoleuse** streetwalker

racontable [rakɔ̃tabl] *adj* relatable

racontar [rakɔ̃tar] *nm* piece of gossip; **racontars** gossip

raconter [rakɔ̃te] **1** *vt* **(a)** *(histoire, mensonge)* to tell; *(événement)* to tell about; **r. qch à qn** *(histoire)* to tell sb sth; *(événement)* to tell sb about sth **(b)** *(dire)* to say; **qu'est-ce qu'il raconte?** what's he talking about?; **alors, qu'est-ce que tu racontes (de beau** *ou* **de neuf)?** so what's new? **2 se raconter** *vpr* **(a)** *(parler de soi)* to talk about oneself **(b)** *(être raconté)* to be talked about

racornir [rakɔrnir] **1** *vt* **(a)** *(durcir)* to harden **(b)** *(ratatiner)* to shrivel **2 se racornir** *vpr* **(a)** *(durcir)* to harden **(b)** *(se ratatiner)* to shrivel

radar [radar] *nm* radar; *Fam* **être** *ou* **avancer au r.** to be on automatic pilot

rade [rad] *nf* harbour; **en r. de Toulon** off Toulon; *Fam* **laisser en r.** *(personne)* to leave in the lurch; *(projet)* to jettison; *Fam* **être en r.** *(personne)* to be stranded

radeau, -x [rado] *nm* raft; **r. pneumatique** inflatable raft; **r. de sauvetage** life raft

radial, -e, -aux, -ales [radjal, -o] *adj voir* carcasse

radiateur [radjatœr] *nm* radiator; **r. électrique** electric heater

radiation¹ [radjasjɔ̃] *nf (sur une liste)* striking off

radiation² *nf (d'une onde)* radiation

radical, -e, -aux, -ales [radikal, -o] **1** *adj* radical; **c'est r. (contre)** *(médicament, méthode)* it works like magic (on) **2** *nm (d'un mot)* stem

radicalement [radikalmɑ̃] *adv* radically

radicaliser [radikalize] **1** *vt* to radicalize **2 se radicaliser** *vpr* to become more radical

radier [66] [radje] *vt* to strike off *(de* from)

radiesthésiste [radjɛstezist] *nmf* diviner

radieux, -euse [radjø, -øz] *adj (soleil, personne)* radiant; *(temps)* glorious

radin, -e [radɛ̃, -in] *Fam* **1** *adj* stingy **2** *nm,f* skinflint

radiner [radine] **se radiner** *vpr Fam* to roll up; **tu te radines?** are you coming or not?

radio [radjo] **1** *nf* **(a)** *(poste)* radio; *(station)* radio station; **à la r.** on the radio; **faire de la r.** to be *or* work as a radio presenter; **r. libre** independent radio station; **r. locale** local radio station **(b)** *(radiotéléphonie)* radio **(c)** *Méd* X-ray; **passer une r.** to have an X-ray **2** *nm (opérateur)* radio operator **3** *adj inv* radio

radioactif, -ive [radjoaktif, -iv] *adj* radioactive

radioactivité [radjoaktivite] *nf* radioactivity

radioamateur [radjoamatœr] *nm* radio ham

radiocassette [radjokasɛt] *nf* radio cassette player

radiodiffuser [radjodifyze] *vt* to broadcast

radiodiffusion [radjodifyzjɔ̃] *nf* broadcasting

radiographie [radjografi] *nf* **(a)** *(technique)* radiography **(b)** *(cliché)* X-ray

radiographier [66] [radjografje] *vt* to X-ray

radioguidé, -e [radjogide] *adj* radio-controlled; *(missile)* guided

radiologie [radjolɔʒi] *nf* radiology

radiologique [radjolɔʒik] *adj* radiological

radiologue [radjolɔg], **radiologiste** [radjolɔʒist] *nmf (médecin)* radiologist; *(technicien)* radiographer

radiophonique [radjofɔnik] *adj (de radio)* radio; *(bon pour la radio)* good for radio

radioreportage [radjorəpɔrta3] *nm (activité)* radio reporting; *(émission)* radio report

radioreporter [radjorəpɔrter] *nmf* radio reporter

radio-réveil *(pl* **radios-réveils**) [radjorevɛj] *nm* radio-alarm (clock)

radioscopie [radjoskɔpi] *nf* radioscopy

radioscopique [radjoskɔpik] *adj (examen)* X-ray

radio-taxi *(pl* **radio-taxis**) [radjotaksi] *nm* radio taxi

radiotélescope [radjoteleskɔp] *nm* radio telescope

radiotélévisé, -e [radjotelevize] *adj* broadcast on both radio and television

radiothérapie [radjoterapi] *nf* radiotherapy

radis [radi] *nm* radish; *Fam* **ne plus avoir un r.** not to have a bean; **r. noir** black radish

radium [radjom] *nm* radium

radius [radjys] *nm* radius

radotage [radɔta3] *nm (rabâchage)* going on and on; *(divagations)* rambling

radoter [radɔte] **1** *vi (rabâcher)* to go on and on; *(divaguer)* to ramble on **2** *vt Fam* to go on and on about

radoteur, -euse [radɔtœr, -øz] *nm,f* rambling old fool

radoub [radu] *nm* **bassin de r.** dry dock

radoucir [radusir] **1** *vt* **(a)** *(temps)* to make milder **(b)** *(personne)* to calm down; *(caractère)* to soften **2 se radoucir** *vpr* **(a)** *(temps)* to become milder **(b)** *(personne)* to calm down

radoucissement [radusismɑ̃] *nm* **(a)** *(de la température)* milder spell **(b)** *(d'une personne)* calming down

rafale [rafal] *nf* **(a)** *(de vent, de pluie)* gust; **par** *ou* **en rafales** in gusts **(b)** *(de coups de feu)* burst

raffermir [rafɛrmir] **1** *vt* **(a)** *(peau, muscles)* to firm up **(b)** *(autorité, courage)* to strengthen **2 se raffermir** *vpr* **(a)** *(muscles, peau)* to firm up **(b)** *(gouvernement)* *(devenir plus intransigeant)* to take a stronger line; *(devenir plus fort)* to become stronger; *(autorité)* to strengthen

raffermissement [rafɛrmismɑ̃] *nm* **(a)** *(des muscles, de la peau)* firming up **(b)** *(de l'autorité, du pouvoir)* strengthening

raffinage [rafinaʒ] *nm* refining

raffiné, -e [rafine] *adj* refined

raffinement [rafinmɑ̃] *nm* refinement

raffiner [rafine] **1** *vt* to refine **2 raffiner sur** *vt ind* to be overparticular about

raffinerie [rafinri] *nf* refinery

raffoler [rafɔle] **raffoler de** *vt ind Fam* **r. de qch** to be mad about sth

raffut [rafy] *nm Fam (bruit)* din, racket; **faire du r.** *(bruit)* to make a din; *(scandale)* to set tongues wagging; *(pour protester)* to kick up a fuss

rafiot [rafjo] *nm Péj* old tub

rafistolage [rafistɔlaʒ] *nm Fam* patching up

rafistoler [rafistɔle] *vt Fam* to patch up

rafle [rafl] *nf* raid

rafler [rafle] *vt Fam* to swipe

rafraîchir [rafreʃir] **1** *vt* **(a)** *(rendre frais) (aliment, boisson)* to chill; *(pièce)* to air; *(atmosphère)* to cool **(b)** *(raviver) (couleur, maquillage, peintures)* to freshen up; *(appartement)* to brighten up; *Fam* **r. la mémoire à qn** to refresh sb's memory **2** *vi* to cool down **3 se rafraîchir** *vpr* **(a)** *(temps)* to turn cooler **(b)** *(se mouiller le visage)* to freshen up **(c)** *Fam (boire)* to have a cold drink

rafraîchissant, -e [rafreʃisɑ̃, -ɑ̃t] *adj* refreshing

rafraîchissement [rafreʃismɑ̃] *nm* **(a)** *(de la température, d'une boisson)* cooling **(b)** *(boisson)* cold drink; **rafraîchissements** refreshments **(c)** *Ordinat* refresh

rafting [raftiŋ] *nm* rafting

ragaillardir [ragajardir] *Fam* **1** *vt* to buck up **2 se ragaillardir** *vpr* to buck up

rage [raʒ] *nf* **(a)** *(maladie)* rabies **(b)** *(colère)* rage; **faire r.** *(tempête)* to rage; **avoir la r. au cœur** to be seething with rage; **ivre** *ou* **fou de r.** furious; **mettre qn en r.** to enrage sb; **r. de dents** raging toothache **(c)** *(passion)* passion **(de qch** for sth); **avoir la r. du jeu** to have a passion for gambling

rageant, -e [raʒɑ̃, -ɑ̃t] *adj Fam* infuriating

rager [45] [raʒe] *vi Fam* to fume; **faire r. qn** to make sb mad

rageur, -euse [raʒœr, -øz] *adj (ton, voix)* furious

rageusement [raʒøzmɑ̃] *adv* furiously

raglan [raglɑ̃] *nm* raglan coat

ragot [rago] *nm Fam* piece of gossip; **ragots** gossip

ragoût [ragu] *nm* stew; **en r.** stewed

ragoûtant, -e [ragutɑ̃, -ɑ̃t] *adj* **peu** *ou* **pas r.** *(plat)* unappetizing; *(personne)* unsavoury

rai [rɛ] *nm (de lumière)* ray

raï [raj] *nm inv* = North African popular music influenced by rock music

raid [rɛd] *nm* raid; **r. aérien** air raid

raide [rɛd] **1** *adj* **(a)** *(membre, articulation)* stiff; *(cheveux)* straight; *(câble)* taut **(b)** *(escalier, pente)* steep **(c)** *(personne, démarche)* stiff; **r. comme un piquet** as stiff as a poker **(d)** *(caractère)* inflexible; *(manières)* stiff **(e)** *Fam (difficile à croire)* far-fetched **(f)** *Fam (osé)* risqué **(g)** *Fam (fort) (alcool)* rough **2** *adv* **(a)** *(de façon abrupte)* steeply **(b)** *(brutalement)* **tomber r.** to fall to the ground; **tomber r. mort** to drop dead

raideur [rɛdœr] *nf* **(a)** *(d'un membre, d'une articulation, d'un mouvement)* stiffness; **avoir une r. dans le cou/à l'épaule** to have a stiff neck/shoulder **(b)** *(d'une personne)* stiffness **(c)** *(de caractère)* inflexibility **(d)** *(d'une pente)* steepness

raidillon [rɛdijɔ̃] *nm (chemin)* steep path; *(partie de route)* steep rise

raidir [rɛdir] **1** *vt (bras, jambes)* to brace; *(corde, câble)* to tauten; *(tissu)* to stiffen **2 se raidir** *vpr* **(a)** *(membres, articulations)* to stiffen; *(câble)* to tauten **(b)** *(personne)* to tense up

raidissement [rɛdismɑ̃] *nm* **(a)** *(d'une matière, des muscles)* stiffening; *(d'une corde)* tautening **(b)** *(montée de la tension)* **r. des rapports internationaux** increase of tension in international relations; **le r. des ouvriers face à la direction** the tougher line taken by the workers towards the management

raie¹ [rɛ] *nf* **(a)** *(motif)* stripe **(b)** *(dans les cheveux)* *Br* parting, *Am* part **(c)** *(des fesses)* cleft

raie² *nf (poisson)* skate

raifort [rɛfɔr] *nm* horseradish

rail [raj] *nm* **(a)** *(sur une voie de chemin de fer)* rail; *Fig* **remettre qn sur les rails** to get sb back on the rails **(b)** **le r.** *(les chemins de fer)* rail **(c)** **r. de sécurité** crash barrier **(d)** *(couloir) (aérien, maritime)* lane

railler [raje] *vt* to mock

raillerie [rajri] *nf* gibe

railleur, -euse [rajœr, -øz] **1** *adj* mocking **2** *nm,f* scoffer

rainette [rɛnɛt] *nf* **(a)** *(grenouille)* tree frog **(b)** *(pomme)* pippin

rainure [renyr] *nf* groove

raisin [rɛzɛ̃] *nm* grapes; **raisins de Corinthe** currants; **raisins secs** raisins; **raisins de Smyrne** sultanas

raison [rɛzɔ̃] *nf* **(a)** *(motif)* reason **(de** for); **en r. de qch** because of sth; **être absent pour r. de santé** to be absent for health reasons; **à plus forte r.** all the more so; **r. de plus (pour faire qch)** all the more reason (to do sth); **la r. pour laquelle il est parti** the reason (why) he left; **la r. d'État** reasons of State, **r. d'être** raison d'être, **r. de vivre** reason for living **(b)** *(entendement)* reason; **recouvrer la r.** to come to one's senses; **perdre la r.** to take leave of one's senses; **entendre r.** to listen to reason; **de r.** *(âge)* of reason; *(mariage)* of convenience **(c)** *(satisfaction)* satisfaction; **avoir r. de qn/qch** to get the better of sb/sth **(d)** *(proportion)* **à r. de** at the rate of **(e)** *(désignation)* **r. sociale** company name **(f)** *(locutions)* **avoir r. (de faire qch)** to be right (to do sth); **donner r. à qn** *(personne)* to admit that sb is right; *(événement)* to prove sb right; **se faire une r.** to accept the inevitable; **se ranger à la r.** to see reason; **comme de r.** as one might expect; **plus que de r.** more than is reasonable

raisonnable [rɛzɔnabl] *adj* reasonable

raisonnablement [rɛzɔnabləmɑ̃] *adv* **(a)** *(avec bon sens)* reasonably **(b)** *(modérément)* in moderation

raisonné, -e [rɛzɔne] *adj (argumentation, choix)* reasoned

raisonnement [rɛzɔnmɑ̃] *nm (argumentation)* argument; *(faculté)* reasoning; **tenir un r.** to use an argument; **r. par l'absurde** reductio ad absurdum

raisonner [rɛzɔne] **1** *vt (personne)* to reason with **2** *vi* **(a)** *(penser)* to reason **(sur** about); *Fam* **r. comme une pantoufle** to talk through one's hat **(b)** *(discuter)* to argue **(avec** with) **3 se raisonner** *vpr (personne)* to see reason

raisonneur, -euse [rɛzɔnœr, -øz] **1** adj reasoning; Péj argumentative
2 nm,f Péj arguer

rajeunir [raʒœnir] **1** vt (a) r. qn (faire paraître plus jeune) to make sb look younger; (faire se sentir plus jeune) to make sb feel younger (b) (donner un âge moins élevé à) r. qn to underestimate how old sb is; r. qn de cinq ans to take five years off sb's age (c) (robe, veste) to update (d) (organisation, bureau) to modernize; (équipe) to bring new blood into
2 vi (physiquement) to look younger; (moralement) to seem younger; il a rajeuni de dix ans he looks ten years younger; ça ne nous rajeunit pas! we're showing our age!
3 se rajeunir vpr (se prétendre plus jeune) to make oneself out to be younger than one is

rajeunissant, -e [raʒœnisɑ̃, -ɑ̃t] adj rejuvenating

rajeunissement [raʒœnismɑ̃] nm (a) (après un traitement) rejuvenation (b) (de la population, d'un secteur professionnel) decrease in age

rajout [raʒu] nm addition

rajouter [raʒute] vt to add; Fam en r. to exaggerate

rajuster [raʒyste] **1** vt (vêtement) to adjust, to straighten
2 se rajuster· vpr to tidy oneself up

râle [rɑl] nm (bruit aux poumons) rale; (d'un agonisant) death rattle

ralenti, -e [ralɑ̃ti] **1** adj slow
2 nm (a) (régime du moteur) idling speed; au r. (vivre, fonctionner) at a slower pace; tourner au r. (moteur, usine) Br to tick over, Am to turn over (b) Cin slow motion; au r. in slow motion

ralentir [ralɑ̃tir] vt & vi to slow down

ralentissement [ralɑ̃tismɑ̃] nm slowing down; (embouteillage) hold-up

ralentisseur [ralɑ̃tisœr] nm (dos d'âne) speed bump

râler [rɑle] vi (a) Fam (protester) to moan (b) (mourant) to give a death rattle

râleur, -euse [rɑlœr, -øz] Fam **1** adj moaning
2 nm,f moaner

ralliement [ralimɑ̃] nm rallying

rallier [66] [ralje] **1** vt (a) (regagner) (lieu) to return to (b) (gagner à sa cause) to win over (à to) (c) (réunir) (adhérents) to rally; r. tous les suffrages to win general approval (d) (regrouper) (troupes) to rally
2 se rallier vpr se r. à (avis) to come round to; (parti) to join; (cause) to rally to

rallonge [ralɔ̃ʒ] nf (a) (de table) extension (b) (électrique) extension (lead) (c) Fam (d'argent) extra money; (de temps) extra time

rallonger [45] [ralɔ̃ʒe] **1** vt (vêtement) to lengthen; (période, route) to extend (de by)
2 vi to get longer

rallumer [ralyme] **1** vt (a) (appareil électrique, lumière) to switch on again (b) (feu, cigarette) to light again; (querelle, colère, espoir) to rekindle
2 se rallumer vpr (a) (lumière, appareil électrique) to come back on (b) (feu, guerre, dispute) to flare up again; (espoir) to rekindle

rallye [rali] nm (a) (épreuve sportive) (car) rally (b) (soirée) = dance attended by young people from rich families looking for a husband or wife

RAM [ram] nf Ordinat RAM

ramadan [ramadɑ̃] nm Ramadan; faire le r. to observe Ramadan

ramage [ramaʒ] nm (a) (chant des oiseaux) song (b) ramages (motif) leafy design

ramassage [ramasaʒ] nm (a) (de fruits, de noix) gathering

(b) (d'ordures, de vêtements, de vieux journaux) collection; car de r. scolaire school bus

ramassé, -e [ramase] adj (a) (trapu) (personne) stocky (b) (style) compact

ramasse-miettes [ramasmjɛt] nm inv table tidy (small brush and pan for clearing crumbs off the table)

ramasser [ramase] **1** vt (a) (prendre par terre) (objet, personne) to pick up; (fruits, noix, coquillages) to gather; (champignons) to pick; (pommes de terre) to dig up; Fam se faire r. par la police to get picked up by the police (b) (copies, affaires, informations) to collect; (cartes) to pick up; r. ses forces to gather one's strength (c) (enfants, ouvriers, courrier) to pick up, to collect (d) Fam (gifle) to get; (procès-verbal) to pick up
2 se ramasser vpr (a) (après une chute) to pick oneself up (b) (se pelotonner) to curl up (c) Fam (échouer) to come a cropper

ramassette [ramasɛt] nf Belg dustpan

ramasseur, -euse [ramasœr, -øz] nm,f (a) (de champignons) picker; (de fruits) gatherer (b) (au tennis) r. de balles ball boy, f ball girl

ramassis [ramasi] nm Péj (de choses) jumble; (de gens) bunch; (d'idées) hotchpotch; un r. de mensonges a tissue of lies

rambarde [rɑ̃bard] nf (guard)rail

ramdam [ramdam] nm Fam racket; faire du r. to make a heck of a racket

rame¹ [ram] nf (pour plantes grimpantes) stick

rame² nf (aviron) oar

rame³ nf (a) (de papier) ream (b) (de wagons) train; r. (de métro) (Br underground or Am subway) train

rameau, -x [ramo] nm (a) (d'arbre) branch (b) les Rameaux Palm Sunday

ramener [46] [ramne] **1** vt (a) (amener) to bring back; (raccompagner) to take back; r. qn en voiture to give sb a lift back; r. qn à la vie to bring sb back to life; r. qn à la raison to bring sb back to his/her senses (b) Fam (rapporter, revenir avec) to bring back; r. tout à soi to bring everything back to oneself (c) (remettre) (couverture, châle) to pull up (sur over); (d) (rétablir) (ordre, paix) to restore (e) (réduire) r. qch à qch to reduce sth to sth (f) Fam r. sa fraise, la r. to show off
2 se ramener vpr (a) (se réduire) se r. à to boil down to (b) Fam (arriver) to roll up

ramequin [ramkɛ̃] nm ramekin

ramer [rame] vi (a) (pagayer) to row (b) Fam (peiner) to sweat blood

rameur, -euse [ramœr, -øz] nm,f rower

ramier [ramje] adj m voir pigeon

ramification [ramifikasjɔ̃] nf (d'une plante) ramification; (d'une famille, d'une science) branch; ramifications (d'une société, d'une affaire) ramifications

ramifier [66] [ramifje] se ramifier vpr to branch out (en into)

ramolli, -e [ramɔli] adj Fam (mentalement) soft-headed

ramollir [ramɔlir] **1** vt (substance) to soften; Fam r. qn (intellectuellement) to make sb soft in the head
2 se ramollir vpr (substance) to soften; Fam (personne) (moralement) to have no get-up-and-go

ramollissement [ramɔlismɑ̃] nm softening

ramonage [ramɔnaʒ] nm chimney sweeping

ramoner [ramɔne] vt (cheminée) to sweep

ramoneur [ramɔnœr] nm chimney sweep

rampant, -e [rɑ̃pɑ̃, -ɑ̃t] adj (a) (plante) creeping; (animal) crawling; Péj (personne, caractère) grovelling (b)

personnel r. *(de l'aviation)* ground crew **(c)** *(inflation)* rampant

rampe [rɑ̃p] *nf* **(a)** *(d'escalier)* banister, handrail **(b)** *(plan incliné)* slope, incline; **r. d'accès** *(d'un pont)* access ramp; *(d'une autoroute)* Br slip road, Am ramp; **r. de lancement** launching ramp **(c)** *(rebord d'une scène de théâtre)* footlights

ramper [rɑ̃pe] *vi (animal, enfant, soldat)* to crawl; *Péj* **r. devant qn** to grovel to sb

ramure [ramyr] *nf* **(a)** *(d'un arbre)* branches **(b)** *(d'un cerf)* antlers

rancard [rɑ̃kar] *nm Fam (rendez-vous)* meeting; *(amoureux)* date

rancarder [rɑ̃karde] *très Fam* **1** *vt* **r. qn sur qch** to tip sb off about sth
2 se rancarder *vpr* to find out **(sur** about**)**

rancart [rɑ̃kar] *nm Fam* **mettre qch au r.** to chuck sth out; **mettre qn au r.** to put sb on the rubbish heap

rance [rɑ̃s] **1** *adj* rancid
2 *nm* **goût de r.** rancid taste

ranch [rɑ̃tʃ] *nm* ranch

rancir [rɑ̃sir] *vi* to go rancid

rancœur [rɑ̃kœr] *nf* resentment, rancour; **avoir de la r. pour** *ou* **contre qn** to feel resentment towards sb

rançon [rɑ̃sɔ̃] *nf* ransom; *Fig* **la r. de la gloire** the price of fame

rançonner [rɑ̃sɔne] *vt* **r. qn** to hold sb to ransom

rancune [rɑ̃kyn] *nf* spite; **garder r. à qn, avoir de la r. contre qn** to have a grudge against sb, to bear sb a grudge; **sans r.!** no hard feelings!

rancunier, -ère [rɑ̃kynje, -ɛr] **1** *adj* spiteful
2 *nm,f* spiteful person

randonnée [rɑ̃dɔne] *nf* **(a)** *(marche à pied)* **r. (pédestre)** hike; *(activité)* hiking, rambling; *(en montagne)* hill-walking **(b)** *(en voiture)* drive; *(à vélo)* ride **(c)** *(excursion à ski)* ski-mountaineering

randonneur, -euse [rɑ̃dɔnœr, -øz] *nm,f (à pied)* hiker, rambler

rang [rɑ̃] *nm* **(a)** *(d'arbres, de sièges)* row; **se mettre en r. (par deux/trois)** to line up (in twos/threes); *Hum* **en r. d'oignons** in a neat row; **en rangs serrés** in serried ranks; *Fig* **se mettre sur les rangs** to put oneself in the running **(b)** *(position sociale)* station; *(de militaire)* rank; **de haut r.** high-ranking **(c)** *(classement)* rank; **par r. de taille** in order of size **(d)** *Can (chemin)* concession road

rangé, -e [rɑ̃ʒe] *adj* **(a)** *(maison, chambre)* tidy **(b)** *(personne)* steady

rangée [rɑ̃ʒe] *nf* row

rangement [rɑ̃ʒmɑ̃] *nm* **(a)** *(action)* tidying up; **faire du r.** to do some tidying up; **faire du r. dans ses affaires** to tidy up one's things **(b)** *(placard)* **rangements** storage space **(c)** *Ordinat* storage

ranger [45] [rɑ̃ʒe] **1** *vt* **(a)** *(pièce, maison)* to tidy (up) **(b)** *(affaires, vêtements)* to put away **(c)** *(mettre)* to put **(d)** *(classer)* to rank *(parmi* among**)**; **r. par** *(ordre alphabétique, taille)* to arrange by **(e)** *(véhicule, vélo)* to park **(f)** *(soldats, élèves)* to line up **(g)** *Ordinat* **r. en mémoire** to store
2 se ranger *vpr* **(a)** *(se disposer)* to line up **(b)** *(s'écarter)* *(piéton)* to stand aside; *(véhicule)* to pull over **(c)** *(prendre position pour)* **se r. du côté de qn** to side with sb, to take sb's side; **se r. à l'opinion de qn** to come round to sb's opinion **(d)** *(se mettre)* to go **(e)** *Fam (s'assagir)* to settle down; **se r. des voitures** to settle down

ranimer [rɑ̃nime] **1** *vt* **(a)** *(personne)* *(après un évanouissement)* to bring round; *(après un arrêt cardiaque)* to resuscitate **(b)** *(feu)* to rekindle **(c)** *(sentiment, souvenir, espoir)* to reawaken; *(débat)* to revive

2 se ranimer *vpr* **(a)** *(personne)* to come round **(b)** *(feu)* flicker into life

rap [rap] *nm* **le r.** rap

rapace [rapas] *nm* bird of prey
2 *adj* **(a)** *(oiseau)* predatory **(b)** *(personne)* grasping

rapacité [rapasite] *nf* rapaciousness

rapatrié, -e [rapatrije] **1** *adj* repatriated
2 *nm,f* repatriate

rapatriement [rapatrimɑ̃] *nm* repatriation

rapatrier [66] [rapatrije] *vt* to repatriate

râpe [rɑp] *nf* **(a)** *(de cuisine)* grater; **r. à fromage** cheese grater **(b)** *(lime)* rasp

râpé, -e [rɑpe] **1** *adj* **(a)** *(fromage, carotte)* grated **(b)** *(vêtement)* threadbare **(c)** *Fam (raté)* **c'est r.!** we've had it!
2 *nm (fromage)* grated cheese

râper [rɑpe] *vt* **(a)** *(carotte, fromage)* to grate **(b)** *(racler)* **ce vin râpe la gorge** this wine's rough on the throat **(c)** *(limer)* to rasp

rapetasser [raptase] *vt Fam ('vêtement)* to patch up

rapetisser [raptise] **1** *vt* **(a)** *(rendre plus petit)* to make smaller **(b)** *(dévaluer)* to belittle **(c)** *(faire paraître plus petit)* to make look smaller
2 *vi (vêtement, personne)* to shrink

râpeux, -euse [rɑpø, -øz] *adj (langue)* rough; *(vin)* harsh

raphia [rafja] *nm* raffia

rapiat, -e [rapja, -at] *Fam* **1** *adj (avare)* stingy
2 *nm,f* skinflint

rapide [rapid] **1** *adj (coureur, voiture, itinéraire)* fast; *(pouls, progrès)* rapid; **r. comme l'éclair** as quick as lightning; **r. comme une flèche** as swift as an arrow **(b)** *(courant)* swift-flowing **(c)** *(prompt)* *(personne, esprit, intelligence)* quick **(d)** *(fait en peu de temps)* *(lecture, décision)* quick **(e)** *(pente)* steep
2 *nm* **(a)** *(train)* express (train) **(b)** *(dans un fleuve)* rapid

rapidement [rapidmɑ̃] *adv* quickly, rapidly

rapidité [rapidite] *nf* **(a)** *(d'actions, d'une décision, d'une réponse)* speed; **r. d'esprit** quickness of mind **(b)** *Ordinat* **r. d'impression** print speed; **r. de traitement** processing speed

rapiécer [16/34] [rapjese] *vt* to patch

rapine [rapin] *nf Litt* pillage

raplapla [raplapla] *adj inv Fam (pneu, coussin)* flat as a pancake **(b)** *(personne)* washed out

rappel [rapel] *nm* **(a)** *(d'un événement, d'une promesse)* reminder; **r. de couleurs** repeat of colours; **r. à l'ordre** *(à un membre d'une assemblée)* call to order; *(d'un employé)* warning; **le r. des titres** *(de* l'actualité**)** the headlines; **dernier r.** *(de facture)* final demand **(b)** *(d'un ambassadeur, de réservistes)* recall **(c)** *(d'un salaire)* back pay **(d)** *(de vaccin)* booster; **r. avoir a booster** *(c)** *Fam (raté)* **(au théâtre)** curtain call; *(à un concert)* encore **(f)** *(en alpinisme)* abseiling; **faire une descente** *ou* **descendre en r., faire du r.** to abseil down **(g)** *Ordinat (de texte)* restore

rappeler [42] [raple, raple] **1** *vt* **(a)** *(appeler)* (personne) to call back; *(chien)* to call off
(b) *(au téléphone)* *(sujet: personne appelée)* to call back; *(sujet: personne qui appelle)* to call again; **r. dix fois** to call ten times
(c) *(faire revenir)* (personne) to call back; *(ambassadeur)* to recall; **r. qn à l'ordre** *(membre d'une association)* to call sb to order; *(employé)* to warn sb
(d) *(acteur, chanteur)* to call back
(e) *(faire penser à)* **r. qn/qch à qn** to remind sb of sb/sth; **cela ne me rappelle rien** it doesn't ring a bell
(f) *(remettre en mémoire)* **r. qch à qn** to remind sb of sth; **rappelez-moi votre nom** what was your name again?; **r.**

qn au bon souvenir de qn to remember sb to sb
2 se rappeler vpr (**a**) **se r.** qn/qch (se souvenir de) to remember sb/sth; **rappelle-toi que...** don't forget that... (**b**) Fam (au téléphone) **on se rappelle la semaine prochaine** we'll talk again next week

rappeur, -euse [rapœr, -øz] nm,f rapper

rappliquer [raplike] vi Fam to roll up

rapport [rapɔr] nm (**a**) (relation) **rapports** relations, relationship; **avoir de bons/mauvais rapports avec qn** to be on good/bad terms with sb; **entretenir des rapports amicaux avec qn** to stay on friendly terms with sb; **mettre qn en r. avec qn** to put sb in touch with sb; **être en r. avec qn** to be in touch with sb; **r. de forces** battle of wills (**b**) (lien) connection, link (**avec** with); **avoir un r. avec qch** to have something to do with sth; **n'avoir aucun r. avec qch** to have nothing to do with sth; **faire le r.** to make the connection; **être sans r. avec qch** to be unconnected with sth; **en r. avec** (lié à) in keeping with; **par r. à qch** (en comparaison) compared with sth (**c**) (aspect) **sous ce r.** in this respect; **bien sous tous rapports** nice in every respect (**d**) (proportion) ratio, proportion; **en r. avec** in proportion to; **d'un bon r. qualité-prix** good value for money (**e**) (compte rendu) report; **faire** ou **rédiger un r. sur qch** to draw up a report on sth; **r. annuel** annual report; **r. commercial** market report (**f**) (profit) return, yield; **d'un bon r.** profitable; **d'un mauvais r.** unprofitable (**g**) **rapports** (relations sexuelles) (sexual) intercourse; **avoir des rapports avec qn** to have sex with sb

rapporter [rapɔrte] **1** vt (**a**) (apporter avec soi) to bring back; **r. qch à qn** to bring sb sth back (**b**) (rendre) to bring back (**à** to); (remporter) to take back (**à** to) (**c**) (ajouter) (poche, pièce) to sew on (**d**) (raconter) to report; **on rapporte que...** it is reported that... (**e**) (produire) (bénéfice, intérêt) to yield; **r. de l'argent** to be profitable; **r. qch à qn** (financièrement) to bring sb in sth; Fig (moralement) to bring sb sth (**f**) Péj (répéter) to report (**à** to) (**g**) (sujet: chien) to retrieve; **rapporte!** fetch! **2 se rapporter** vpr (**a**) **se r. à qch** (concerner) to relate to sth (**b**) (se remettre) **s'en r. à qn/qch** to rely on sb/sth

rapporteur, -euse [rapɔrtœr, -øz] **1** adj Péj sneaky **2** nm,f Péj telltale, sneak **3** nm (**a**) (d'une commission) reporter (**b**) (instrument) protractor

rapproché, -e [raprɔʃe] adj (dans l'espace, dans le temps) close; (yeux) close-set; **des maisons très rapprochées** houses very close together; **des rendez-vous très rapprochés (dans le temps)** appointments very close to each other

rapprochement [raprɔʃmɑ̃] nm (**a**) (rapport) (de faits, d'idées) connection; **faire le r. (entre deux choses)** to make a connection (between two things) (**b**) (de deux objets) bringing together (**c**) (réconciliation) (entre personnes) reconciliation; (entre pays) rapprochement

rapprocher [raprɔʃe] **1** vt (**a**) (mettre plus près) (deux ou plusieurs objets) to move closer together; (objet) to move closer (**de** to); **ça te rapprochera (de chez toi)** that'll get you a bit closer (to home) (**b**) (réunir) to join (**c**) (séances) to group closer together (**d**) (unir) (personnes) to bring together (**e**) (lier) (idées, textes) to compare (**de** with) **2 se rapprocher** vpr (**a**) (aller plus près) to get closer (**de** to); **se r. de la vérité** to get close to the truth (**b**) (devenir proche) to get closer (**de** to); (après une brouille) to become reconciled (**de** with) (**c**) **se r. de qn/qch** (ressembler à) to be similar to sb/sth

rapsodie [rapsɔdi] nf rhapsody

rapt [rapt] nm abduction

raquer [rake] vt très Fam to fork out

raquette [rakɛt] nf (**a**) (de tennis, de badminton, de squash) racket (**b**) (de ping-pong) bat (**c**) (pour marcher dans la neige) snowshoe

rare [rar] adj (**a**) (peu commun, peu fréquent) rare; **c'est r. qu'il pleuve ici** it rarely rains here; **cela n'a rien de r.** it's quite common (**b**) (peu nombreux, peu abondant) **être r.** to be scarce; **c'est une des rares personnes que je connaisse à...** he's one of the few people I know to... (**c**) (exceptionnel) rare (**d**) (clairsemé) (végétation) sparse; **avoir le cheveu r.** to have thinning hair (**e**) **tu te fais r.** we've hardly seen you lately

raréfaction [rarefaksjɔ̃] nf (**a**) (d'une denrée, de l'argent) growing scarcity (**b**) (de l'air) rarefaction

raréfier [66] [rarefje] se raréfier vpr (**a**) (denrée, argent) to become scarce (**b**) (air) to become rarefied

rarement [rarmɑ̃] adv rarely, seldom

rareté [rarte] nf (**a**) (de denrées, de main-d'œuvre) scarcity; (de visites) infrequency; (d'un phénomène, d'un mot, d'une maladie) rareness (**b**) (objet rare) rarity

RAS [ɛraɛs] nm (abrév **rien à signaler**) everything OK

ras, -e [ra, raz] **1** adj (**a**) (cheveux) close-cropped; (barbe) short; (tapis) short-pile (**b**) (entier) (mesure) full; **deux cuillerées rases** two level spoonfuls (**c**) (locutions) **à r. bord** to the brim; **en rase campagne** in the open country **2** nm (**a**) (bord) **à** ou **au r.** de level with; **voler au r. du sol/ de l'eau** to fly close to the ground/water; Fam Fig **aux r. des pâquerettes** lowbrow (**b**) **r. du cou** (pull-over) crewneck sweater **3** adv short; Fam **en avoir r. le bol** to have had it up to here

rasade [razad] nf glassful

rasage [razaʒ] nm shaving

rasant, -e [razɑ̃, -ɑ̃t] adj (**a**) Fam (personne, discours, film) boring (**b**) (lumière) low-angled; (tir) grazing

rascasse [raskas] nf scorpion fish

rasé, -e [raze] adj shaven; **r. de près** close-shaven

rase-mottes [razmɔt] nm inv Fam **faire du** ou **voler en r.** to hedgehop

raser [raze] vt (**a**) (visage, personne) to shave; (moustache, barbe, cheveux) to shave off (**b**) (passer très près de) (sol, eau) to skim; (filet, trottoir) to graze; **r. les murs** to hug the walls (**c**) (détruire) (bâtiment, ville) to raze to the ground (**d**) Fam (ennuyer) to bore **2 se raser** vpr (**a**) (se couper la barbe) to shave, to have a shave; **se r. les jambes** to shave one's legs (**b**) Fam (s'ennuyer) to be bored

raseur, -euse [razœr, -øz] nm,f Fam bore

rasibus [razibys] adv Fam **la balle est passée r.** the bullet whizzed past really close

ras-le-bol [ralbɔl] nm **1** nm inv discontent; Fam **en avoir r. (de)** to be fed up (with) **2** exclam enough's enough!

rasoir [razwar] **1** nm razor; **r. électrique** electric razor or shaver **2** adj inv Fam boring

rassasier [66] [rasazje] **1** vt (faim, curiosité) to satisfy; **r. qn** to satisfy sb's hunger **2 se rassasier** vpr **se r. de qch** to get one's fill of sth

rassemblement [rasɑ̃bləmɑ̃] nm (**a**) (attroupement) gathering (**b**) (de documents, d'objets) collecting, gathering (**c**) (union politique) union (**d**) Mil fall in, parade; **sonner le r.** to sound the assembly

rassembler [rasɑ̃ble] **1** vt (**a**) (personnes, choses, documents) to gather (together) (**b**) (courage, forces) to muster, to summon up; **r. ses idées** to collect one's thoughts; **r. ses esprits** to collect oneself

2 se rassembler vpr (manifestants) to gather, to assemble; (famille) to get together

rasseoir [10a] [raswar] **se rasseoir** vpr to sit down again

rasséréner [34] [raserene] **1** vt r. **qn** to put sb's mind at rest
2 se rasséréner vpr to calm down

rassir [rasir] vi to go stale

rassis, -e [rasi, -iz] adj (a) (pain) stale (b) Litt (personne, esprit) calm

rassurant, -e [rasyrã, -ãt] adj reassuring

rassuré, -e [rasyre] adj at ease; **me voilà r.!** that's a relief!

rassurer [rasyre] **1** vt to reassure; **ah, tu me rassures!** well, that's a relief!
2 se rassurer vpr to reassure oneself; **rassurez-vous** rest assured

rasta [rasta] adj inv & nmf Rasta

rat [ra] **1** nm (a) (animal) rat; r. **d'égout** sewer rat; Fam être fait comme un r. to be caught like a rat in a trap; **petit r.** (de l'Opéra) ballet pupil; **mon petit r.** darling; Fam r. **de bibliothèque** bookworm; r. **d'hôtel** hotel thief (b) Can (sournois) tricky customer
2 adj Fam (a) (avare) stingy (b) Can (sournois) wily, sly

ratage [rataʒ] nm Fam botch-up

ratatiné, -e [ratatine] adj (a) (fruit) shrivelled (b) Fam (vieillard) wizened (c) Fam (véhicule) smashed up

ratatiner [ratatine] **1** vt Fam (a) (voiture) to smash up (b) (équipe) to thrash
2 se ratatiner vpr (a) (fruit) to shrivel up (b) (vieillard) to become wizened

ratatouille [ratatuj] nf ratatouille

rate¹ [rat] nf (organe) spleen

rate³ nf (animal) female rat

raté, -e [rate] **1** nm,f Fam loser
2 nm misfiring; Fig hitch; **avoir des ratés** to misfire

râteau, -x [rato] nm rake

râtelier [rɑtəlje] nm (a) (pour le fourrage) rack; Fig manger à tous les râteliers to have a finger in every pie (b) (à outils, à armes) rack (c) Fam (dentier) (set of) false teeth

rater [rate] **1** vt (a) (examen) to fail; (vie, plat) to make a mess of; **c'est raté** it hasn't worked; Fig r. **son coup** to make a mess of things (b) (train, avion, personne, occasion) to miss; **tu n'as pas raté grand-chose** you didn't miss much (c) Fam (locutions) **ne pas r. qn** to let sb have it; **elle n'en rate pas une** she's always putting her foot in it
2 vi Fam to fail; **faire r. qch** to ruin sth; **j'étais sûr qu'elle allait oublier, et ça n'a pas raté** I was sure she was going to forget, and sure enough she did
3 se rater vpr Fam (ne pas se rencontrer) to miss each other

ratiboiser [ratibwaze] vt Fam to clean out

ratier [ratje] nm (chien) ratter

ratière [ratjer] nf rat trap

ratification [ratifikasjõ] nf ratification

ratifier [66] [ratifje] vt (traité, acte) to ratify; (décision) to confirm

ratio [rasjo] nm ratio

ration [rasjõ] nf (de pain, de nourriture) ration; Fig (de critiques, de difficultés) share; r. **alimentaire** food ration

rationaliser [rasjonalize] vt to rationalize

rationnel, -elle [rasjonel] adj rational

rationnellement [rasjonelmã] adv rationally

rationnement [rasjonmã] nm rationing

rationner [rasjone] **1** vt to ration
2 se rationner vpr to ration oneself

ratissage [ratisaʒ] nm (a) (allée, sol) raking (b) Fam (par la police) combing

ratisser [ratise] **1** vt (a) (allée, sol) to rake; (feuilles) to rake up (b) Fam (quartier) to comb (c) Fam (personne) to clean out; **se faire r.** (au jeu) to be cleaned out
2 vi r. **large** to cast one's net wide

raton [ratõ] nm (a) (animal) young rat; r. **laveur** raccoon (b) Fam (Maghrébin) = racist term used to refer to a North African Arab

ratonnade [ratonad] nf = racist attack on North African Arabs

ratoureux, -euse [raturø, -øz] Can **1** adj wily, devious
2 nm,f shady customer

RATP [eratepe] nf (abrév Régie autonome des transports parisiens) = Parisian transport authority

rattachement [ratafmã] nm (d'une région) uniting (à with)

rattacher [ratafe] **1** vt (a) (attacher de nouveau) (lacets, chien, objet) to tie up again (à to); (cheveux) to put up again; r. **qch sur qch** to tie sth onto sth again (b) (région) to unite (à with) (c) être **rattaché à** (faire partie de) to be attached to (d) (lier) c'était la seule chose qui nous rattachait l'un à l'autre it was the only thing that bound us together; **c'est tout ce qui le rattache à la vie** it's the only thing keeping him alive
2 se rattacher vpr se r. **à qch** to be linked to sth

rattrapage [ratrapaʒ] nm être admis au r., être admis à passer les épreuves de r. = to be allowed to sit further oral examinations to gain a pass mark in the "baccalauréat"; **cours de r.** remedial class

rattraper [ratrape] **1** vt (a) (prisonnier, chien) to recapture; **se faire r. par la police** to get caught by the police (b) (objet ou personne qui tombe) to catch (c) (rejoindre) (personne, voiture) to catch up with (d) (regagner) r. **le temps perdu** to make up for lost time; r. **son retard** to catch up; **avoir du sommeil à r.** to have to catch up on some sleep (e) (rétablir) (erreur) to correct; (situation) to salvage
2 se rattraper vpr (a) (se rivenir) to catch oneself in time; **se r. à qch** to catch hold of sth (b) (se reprendre) to stop oneself (c) (se faire pardonner) to make up for it (d) (compenser son retard) to catch up

rature [ratyr] nf crossing-out, deletion; **faire une r.** to make a deletion

raturer [ratyre] vt (mot) to cross out, to delete

rauque [rok] adj (cri) raucous; (voix) (enrouée) hoarse; (voilée) husky

ravagé, -e [ravaʒe] adj (a) (visage) ravaged, haggard (b) Fam (fou) nuts

ravager [45] [ravaʒe] vt to ravage, to devastate

ravages [ravaʒ] nmpl (du feu, de la tempête) devastation; (d'une guerre, d'une maladie) ravages; **faire des r.** to wreak havoc; Fig (mode) to be all the rage; (jeune femme) to break hearts

ravageur, -euse [ravaʒœr, -øz] adj devastating

ravalement [ravalmã] nm cleaning

ravaler [ravale] **1** vt (a) (façade) to clean (b) (avaler de nouveau) (salive) to swallow; Fig **faire r. ses paroles à qn** to make sb eat his/her words (c) (cacher) (sanglot, larmes) to choke back; (colère, indignation, reproches) to stifle (d) (abaisser) r. **qn à** to lower sb to
2 se ravaler vpr to lower oneself; Fam **se r. la façade** to put on the war paint

ravaudage [ravodaʒ] nm (de vêtements) mending, repairing

ravauder [ravode] vt (vêtements) to mend, to repair

rave¹ [rav] nf (radis) radish; (navet) turnip

rave² [rev] nf Fam (soirée) rave

ravi, -e [ravi] adj delighted (de with); **je suis r. de vous**

voir I'm delighted to see you; **je suis r. que ça te plaise** I'm so glad you like it; **r. de vous connaître** pleased to meet you

ravier [ravje] *nm* hors d'oeuvres dish

ravigotant, -e [ravigɔtɑ̃, -ɑ̃t] *adj Fam* invigorating

ravigote [ravigɔt] *nf* = highly seasoned oil-and-vinegar dressing with herbs and capers

ravigoter [ravigɔte] *vt Fam* **r. qn** to put new life into sb

ravin [ravɛ̃] *nm* ravine

ravine [ravin] *nf* gully

raviné, -e [ravine] *adj (visage)* deeply lined

ravinement [ravinmɑ̃] *nm* gullying

raviner [ravine] *vt* to gully

ravioli [ravjɔli] *nm* piece of ravioli; **des raviolis** ravioli

ravir [ravir] *vt* **(a)** *(plaire)* to delight; **à r.** *(jouer, chanter)* delightfully; **belle à r.** ravishingly beautiful; **aller à r. à qn** to suit sb beautifully **(b)** *Litt* **r. qch à qn** to rob sb of sth

raviser [ravize] **se raviser** *vpr* to change one's mind

ravissant, -e [ravisɑ̃, -ɑ̃t] *adj* delightful

ravissement [ravismɑ̃] *nm* **(a)** *(enchantement)* rapture, ecstasy; **avec r.** *(écouter, contempler)* with great delight **(b)** *Litt (d'une femme)* ravishing

ravisseur, -euse [ravisœr, -øz] *nm,f* abductor

ravitaillement [ravitajmɑ̃] *nm (action)* supplying **(en** with); *(marchandises)* supplies; **r. (en carburant)** refuelling

ravitailler [ravitaje] **1** *vt (personne, groupe)* to supply; *(véhicule)* to refuel
2 se ravitailler *vpr* to get in supplies; **se r. (en carburant)** to refuel

raviver [ravive] *vt* **(a)** *(feu)* to rekindle **(b)** *(couleur)* to brighten up **(c)** *(colère, souvenir, querelle)* to rekindle; *(douleur)* to revive

ravoir [ravwar] *vt* **(a)** *(avoir de nouveau)* to have back **(b)** *Fam (nettoyer)* to get clean

rayé, -e [reje] *adj* **(a)** *(tissu)* striped **(b)** *(disque, parquet, carrosserie de voiture)* scratched **(c)** *(canon de fusil)* rifled

rayer [53] [reje] *vt* **(a)** *(verre, carrosserie de voiture, disque)* to scratch **(b)** *(mention, mot)* to cross out; *(médecin)* to strike off; *(avocat)* to debar; **r. qn/le nom de qn d'une liste** to cross sb/sb's name off a list

rayon¹ [rɛjɔ̃] *nm* **(a)** *(faisceau) (de lumière)* ray, beam; **r. laser** laser beam; **r. de soleil** sunbeam; *Fig* **être le r. de soleil de qn** to be sb's ray of sunshine; **rayons X** X-rays **(b)** *(d'un cercle)* radius; **dans un r. de 2 kilomètres (autour de)** within a radius of 2 kilometres (of); **r. d'action** range **(c)** *(de roue)* spoke

rayon² *nm* **(a)** *(dans un magasin)* department; *Fig* **c'est mon r.** that's my department **(b)** *(d'une étagère)* shelf; *Fam Fig* **en connaître un r.** *(sur qch)* to be well clued up (about sth) **(c)** **r. de miel** honeycomb

rayonnage [rɛjɔnaʒ] *nm* shelving, shelves

rayonnant, -e [rɛjɔnɑ̃, -ɑ̃t] *adj (chaleur, lumière)* radiant; *Fig (visage)* beaming; **r. de bonheur** radiant with happiness; **r. de santé** glowing with health

rayonne [rɛjɔn] *nf* rayon

rayonnement [rɛjɔnmɑ̃] *nm* **(a)** *(du soleil)* radiance **(b)** *(influence)* influence

rayonner [rɛjɔne] *vi* **(a)** *(soleil, visage)* to beam; **r. de joie** to beam with joy **(b)** *(voyager)* to travel around *(from a central base)* **(c)** *(se propager)* to spread its influence **(d)** *(avenues, douleur)* to radiate

rayure [rɛjyr] *nf* **(a)** *(motif)* stripe; **tissu à rayures** striped material **(b)** *(sur miroir, sur carrosserie)* scratch **(c)** *(d'un canon de fusil)* groove

raz de marée [radmare] *nm inv* tidal wave; *Fig* **r. électoral** landslide

razzia [razja] *nf* raid; *Fam* **faire une r. sur qch** to raid sth

RD [ɛrde] *nf (abrév* **route départementale)** secondary road

RDA [ɛrdea] *nf Anciennement (abrév* **République démocratique allemande)** GDR

rdc *(abrév* **rez-de-chaussée)** *Br* ground *or Am* first floor

RDS [ɛrdeɛs] *nm (abrév* **Remboursement de la Dette Sociale)** = contribution paid by every taxpayer towards the social security deficit

ré [re] *nm inv (note)* D; *(chantée)* re

réabonnement [reabɔnmɑ̃] *nm* subscription renewal

réabonner [reabɔne] **1** *vt* **r. qn** to renew sb's subscription **(à to)**
2 se réabonner *vpr* to renew one's subscription (à to)

réac [reak] *adj & nmf Fam Péj* reactionary

réaccoutumer [reakutyme] **1** *vt* to reaccustom (à to)
2 se réaccoutumer *vpr* **se r. à qch** to become reaccustomed to sth

réacteur [reaktœr] *nm* **(a)** *(moteur)* jet engine **(b)** **r. nucléaire** nuclear reactor

réaction [reaksjɔ̃] *nf* **(a)** *(attitude)* reaction; **n'avoir aucune r.** not to react; **il eut une r. de peur/de colère** his reaction was one of fear/anger; **faire qch par r.** to do sth as a reaction; **en r. à qch** in reaction to sth; **rester sans r.** not to react; **r. en chaîne** chain reaction **(b)** *(d'un organe, du corps)* reaction; **r. cutanée** skin reaction

réactionnaire [reaksjɔnɛr] *adj & nmf Péj* reactionary

réactiver [reaktive] *vt (feu, négociations, sentiments)* to revive

réactualisation [reaktɥalizasjɔ̃] *nf* updating

réactualiser [reaktɥalize] *vt* to update

réadaptation [readaptasjɔ̃] *nf* rehabilitation

réadapter [readapte] **1** *vt* to rehabilitate
2 se réadapter *vpr* to readjust

réaffirmer [reafirme] *vt* to reaffirm

réagir [reaʒir] *vi* to react (à/contre to/against); **r. sur qch** to affect sth

réajuster [reaʒyste] = **rajuster**

réalisable [realizabl] *adj* **(a)** *(projet, proposition)* feasible; *(rêve)* attainable **(b)** *(avoirs)* realizable

réalisateur, -trice [realizatœr, -tris] *nm,f (d'un film, d'un feuilleton)* director; *(d'une émission de radio ou de télévision)* producer

réalisation [realizasjɔ̃] *nf* **(a)** *(d'un projet)* realization; *(d'un rêve)* fulfilment **(b)** *(d'un film, d'un feuilleton)* direction; *(d'une émission de radio ou de télévision)* production **(c)** *(d'une œuvre d'art)* creation

réaliser [realize] **1** *vt* **(a)** *(comprendre)* to realize **(que** that) **(b)** *(ambition, projet)* to realize; *(rêve)* to fulfil **(c)** *(œuvre d'art)* to create **(d)** *(film, feuilleton)* to direct; *(émission de radio ou de télévision)* to produce **(e)** *(bénéfices)* to make; **r. un chiffre d'affaires de 2 millions d'euros** to have a turnover of 2 million euros
2 se réaliser *vpr* **(a)** *(prédiction, rêve)* to come true **(b)** *(personne)* to fulfil oneself

réalisme [realism] *nm* realism; **faire preuve de r.** to be realistic; **avec r.** realistically

réaliste [realist] **1** *adj (personne, description, portrait)* realistic
2 *nmf* realist

réalité [realite] *nf* reality; **c'est une r.** it's a reality; **en r.** in reality; *Ordinat* **r. virtuelle** virtual reality

réamorcer [16] [reamɔrse] *Ordinat* **1** *vt* to reboot
2 se réamorcer *vpr* to reboot

réanimation [reanimasjɔ̃] *nf* resuscitation; **service de r.** intensive care unit; **en r.** in intensive care

réanimer [reanime] *vt* to resuscitate

réapparaître [20] [reaparɛtr] *vi* to reappear; *(douleur)* to come back, to recur

réapparition [reaparisjɔ̃] *nf* reappearance; *(d'une douleur)* recurrence

réapprovisionner [reaprɔvizjɔne] **1** *vt (magasin)* to restock **(en** with); *(personne)* to resupply **(en** with) **2 se réapprovisionner** *vpr* to stock up again **(en** with)

réargenter [rearʒɑ̃te] *vt* to resilver

réarmement [rearmǝmɑ̃] *nm* rearmament

réarmer [rearme] **1** *vt* **(a)** *(région, pays)* to rearm **(b)** *(arme à feu)* to recock; *(appareil photo)* to reset **2** *vi (pays, région)* to rearm

réassortir [reasɔrtir] **1** *vt (magasin)* to restock **2 se réassortir** *vpr* to restock

rebaptiser [rǝbatize] *vt (rue)* to rename

rébarbatif, -ive [rebarbatif, -iv] *adj* **(a)** *(sujet, tâche)* daunting; *(style)* off putting **(b)** *(visage, mine)* forbidding

rebâtir [rǝbatir] *vt* to rebuild

rebattre [11] [rǝbatr] *vt* **r. les oreilles à qn de qch** to go on to sb about sth

rebattu, -e [rǝbaty] *adj (histoire, sujet)* hackneyed

rebelle [rǝbɛl] **1** *adj* **(a)** *(personne, esprit)* rebellious; *(camp, armée, troupes)* rebel; **r. à toute discipline** unamenable to discipline **(b)** *(mèches, boucle)* unruly **(c)** *(fièvre)* stubborn; **r. aux antibiotiques** resistant to antibiotics **2** *nmf* rebel

rebeller [rǝbɛle] **se rebeller** *vpr* to rebel **(contre** against)

rébellion [rebɛljɔ̃] *nf* rebellion

rebelote [rǝbǝlɔt] *exclam Fam* not again!

rebiffer [rǝbife] **se rebiffer** *vpr Fam* to hit back **(contre** at)

rebiquer [rǝbike] *vi Fam (mèche)* to stick up

reblochon [rǝblɔʃɔ̃] *nm* Reblochon *(type of cheese from Savoie)*

reboisement [rǝbwazmɑ̃] *nm* reafforestation

reboiser [rǝbwaze] *vt* to reafforest

rebond [rǝbɔ̃] *nm (d'un ballon)* bounce

rebondi, -e [rǝbɔ̃di] *adj (joues, personne)* chubby

rebondir [rǝbɔ̃dir] *vi* **(a)** *(ballon)* to bounce; **r. contre** *ou* **sur qch** to bounce off sth **(b)** *Fig (affaire, crise)* to be revived; **faire r. la discussion** to get the discussion going again **(c)** *Can (chèque)* to bounce

rebondissement [rǝbɔ̃dismɑ̃] *nm* **(a)** *(d'un ballon)* bounce **(b)** *Fig (d'une affaire)* revival

rebord [rǝbɔr] *nm (d'une table, d'un puits)* edge; *(de fenêtre)* sill

reboucher [rǝbuʃe] *vt* **(a)** *(bouteille)* to recork; *(tube)* to put the top back on **(b)** *(trou)* to fill in again

rebours [rǝbur] **à rebours** *adv* the wrong way; *Fig* the wrong way round

rebouteux, -euse [rǝbutø, -øz] *nmf Fam* bonesetter

reboutonner [rǝbutɔne] **1** *vt* to button up again **2 se reboutonner** *vpr* to do oneself up again

rebrousse-poil [rǝbruspwal] **à rebrousse-poil** *adv* the wrong way; **prendre qn à r.** to rub sb up the wrong way

rebrousser [rǝbruse] *vt* **r. chemin** to turn back

rebuffade [rǝbyfad] *nf* rebuff; **essuyer une r.** to meet with a rebuff

rébus [rebys] *nm* rebus

rebut [rǝby] *nm* **(article de) r.** reject; **mettre qch au r.** to throw sth out

rebutant, -e [rǝbytɑ̃, -ɑ̃t] *adj (tâche, manière, personne)* off-putting

rebuter [rǝbyte] *vt* **(a)** *(décourager)* to put off **(b)** *(déplaire)* to disgust

récalcitrant, -e [rekalsitrɑ̃, -ɑ̃t] *adj & nm,f* recalcitrant

recaler [rǝkale] *vt Fam* to fail; **être recalé, se faire r.** to fail

récapitulatif, -ive [rekapitylatif, -iv] **1** *adj* recapitulatory **2** *nm* recapitulation

récapitulation [rekapitylasjɔ̃] *nf* recapitulation; **faire la r. de qch** to recapitulate sth

récapituler [rekapityle] *vt & vi* to recapitulate

recaser [rǝkaze] *Fam* **1** *vt* **(a)** *(retrouver un emploi à)* to find a new job for **(b)** *(retrouver un logement à)* to rehouse **2 se recaser** *vpr* **(a)** *(retrouver un emploi)* to find a new job **(b)** *(se remarier)* to get hitched again

recel [rǝsɛl] *nm* receiving stolen goods

receler [39] [rǝsǝle] *vt* **(a)** *(biens volés)* to receive; *(criminel)* to harbour **(b)** *Litt (renfermer) (secret, trésor)* to conceal

receleur, -euse [rǝsǝlœr, -øz] *nm,f* receiver

récemment [resamɑ̃] *adv* recently

recensement [rǝsɑ̃smɑ̃] *nm (d'objets)* inventory; *(de la population)* census

recenser [rǝsɑ̃se] *vt (objets)* to make an inventory of; *(habitants)* to take a census of

récent, -e [resɑ̃, -ɑ̃t] *adj* recent

recentrer [rǝsɑ̃tre] *vt* **(a)** *(parti politique)* to reorientate **(b)** *(balle)* to centre again

récépissé [resepise] *nm* receipt

réceptacle [resɛptakl] *nm* **(a)** *(d'objets)* receptacle; *(de personnes)* gathering place **(b)** *Ordinat* **r. pour extension** extension slot

récepteur, -trice [resɛptœr, -tris] **1** *adj* receiving **2** *nm* **(a)** *(de téléphone)* receiver **(b)** *Ordinat* **r. de données** data receiver

réceptif, -ive [resɛptif, -iv] *adj* receptive **(à** to)

réception [resɛpsjɔ̃] *nf* **(a)** *(accueil)* reception; **faire une bonne/mauvaise r. à qn** to give sb a good/poor reception **(b)** *(d'une lettre, d'une commande, de biens)* receipt; **à payer à la r.** cash on delivery; **r. des travaux** acceptance of work **(c)** *(soirée)* reception **(d)** *(dans un hôtel)* reception (desk) **(e)** *(d'une radio)* reception **(f)** *(d'un gymnaste)* landing; *(d'un joueur de football)* control

réceptionner [resɛpsjɔne] *vt* **(a)** *(marchandises livrées)* to take delivery of **(b)** *(ballon)* to take

réceptionniste [resɛpsjɔnist] *nmf* receptionist

récessif, -ive [resesif, -iv] *adj* recessive

récession [resesjɔ̃] *nf* recession

recette [rǝsɛt] *nf* **(a)** *(pour plat)* & *Fig* recipe **(de** for) **(b)** *(bureau)* tax office **(c)** *(gain)* **recettes** takings; **recettes fiscales** tax revenue; **faire r.** to be a success

recevable [rǝsǝvabl] *adj (excuse, témoignage)* admissible

receveur, -euse [rǝsǝvœr, -øz] *nm,f* **(a)** *(fonctionnaire)* **r. des contributions** tax collector; **r. des Postes** postmaster; *f* postmistress **(b)** *(de bus)* (bus) conductor; *f* (bus) conductress

recevoir [60] [rǝsǝvwar] *vt* **(a)** *(lettre, coup de téléphone, fleurs)* to receive, to get **(de** from); **r. la visite de qn** to have a visit from sb; **r. des nouvelles de qn** to hear from sb; **je n'ai pas de conseils à r. de personne!** I don't need advice from anybody!; **nous avons bien reçu votre lettre** we are in receipt of your letter

(**b**) *(blâme, gifle, coup, balle)* to get; *Fam* **qu'est-ce que j'ai reçu!** I really got it!
(**c**) *(amis, invités)* to receive, to welcome; **être mal/bien reçu** to get a poor/good reception; **r. qn à dîner** to have sb (round) to dinner; **aimer r.** to enjoy entertaining; **savoir r.** to be a good host/hostess; **ils reçoivent très peu** they don't do much entertaining
(**d**) *(clients)* to see; **le docteur ne reçoit que sur rendez-vous** the doctor will see patients by appointment only
(**e**) *(proposition, projet)* to receive
(**f**) *(élève, candidat)* to admit; **être reçu à l'Académie française** to be admitted to the "Académie française"; **être reçu à un examen** to pass an exam
(**g**) *(pluie, soleil, lumière)* to get; **r. des radiations** to be exposed to radiation, to receive a dose of radiation
(**h**) *(chaîne)* to get; *(station de radio)* to pick up, to receive
(**i**) *(communion, absolution)* to receive
2 se recevoir *vpr (gymnaste)* to land

rechange [rəʃɑ̃ʒ] **de rechange** *adj* spare; *Fig* alternative

rechaper [rəʃape] *vt (pneu)* to retread; **pneu rechapé** retread

réchapper [reʃape] *vi* **r. de qch** to survive sth

recharge [rəʃarʒ] *nf* (**a**) *(de stylo, de briquet)* refill; **r. d'encre** ink refill (**b**) *(action) (d'une batterie)* recharging

rechargeable [rəʃarʒabl] *adj (briquet, vaporisateur)* refillable; *(pile)* rechargeable

recharger [45] [rəʃarʒe] **1** *vt* (**a**) *(batterie, pile)* to recharge; **r. ses batteries** to recharge one's batteries (**b**) *(camion, arme, appareil photo)* to reload (**c**) *(stylo, briquet, vaporisateur)* to refill
2 se recharger *vpr Ordinat* to reload

réchaud [reʃo] *nm* (portable) stove; **r. à gaz** gas ring

réchauffé, -e [reʃofe] **1** *adj* (**a**) *(plat)* reheated, warmed-up (**b**) *(plaisanterie)* stale
2 *nm* **c'est du r.** *(plaisanterie)* that's a stale joke; *(nouvelles, politique)* that's old hat

réchauffement [reʃofmɑ̃] *nm* warming up; **le r. de la planète** *ou* **de l'atmosphère** global warming

réchauffer [reʃofe] **1** *vt* (**a**) *(plat)* to reheat, to warm up (**b**) *(personne)* to warm up (**c**) *Fig* to rekindle; *(cœur)* to warm
2 se réchauffer *vpr* (**a**) *(temps)* to get warmer (**b**) *(personne)* to get warm; **se r. les pieds/les mains** to warm one's feet/one's hands

rechausser [rəʃose] **se rechausser** *vpr* to put one's shoes on again

rêche [rɛʃ] *adj* rough

recherche [rəʃɛrʃ] *nf* (**a**) *(prospection, quête)* search (**de** for); *(de la célébrité, du pouvoir)* quest (**de** for), pursuit (**de** of); **être à la r. de** to be in search of (**b**) **recherches** *(par la police) (pour retrouver une personne disparue)* search, hunt; **faire des recherches** to make inquiries (**c**) *(scientifique)* research (**sur** into); **faire de la r.** to do research; **faire des recherches pour qch** to do research into sth (**d**) *(raffinement)* elegance; **avec r.** elegantly; **sans r.** *(style)* straightforward (**e**) *Ordinat* find, search; **r. et remplacement** search and replace; **r. et remplacement global** global search and replace

recherché, -e [rəʃɛrʃe] *adj* (**a**) *(demandé) (objet)* sought-after (**b**) *(apprécié) (personne)* in demand (**c**) *(raffiné)* elegant; *(plat)* exquisite (**d**) *(criminel)* wanted

rechercher [rəʃɛrʃe] *vt* (**a**) *(chercher) (personne, objet, solution)* to look for, to search for; *(emploi)* to look for; *(sens, mot)* to look up; *(faveurs, honneurs)* to seek (**b**) *Ordinat* **r. qch** to search *or* do a search for sth; **r. et remplacer** to search and replace; **r. vers le bas/haut** to search forwards/backwards

rechigner [rəʃiɲe] *vi Fam* **r. à qch** to balk at sth; **faire**

qch en rechignant to do sth with bad grace; **faire qch sans r.** to do sth without (making) a fuss

rechute [rəʃyt] *nf* relapse; **faire une r.** to have a relapse

rechuter [rəʃyte] *vi* to have a relapse

récidive [residiv] *nf* (**a**) *(d'un délinquant)* repeat offence (**b**) *(d'une maladie)* recurrence

récidiver [residive] *vi* (**a**) *(délinquant)* to reoffend; *Fig* to do it again (**b**) *(maladie)* to recur

récidiviste [residivist] *nmf* repeat offender

récif [resif] *nm* reef; **r. de corail** *ou* **corallien** coral reef

récipient [resipjɑ̃] *nm* container

réciproque [resiprɔk] **1** *adj (sentiments)* mutual; *(bénéfices, accord, concessions)* reciprocal; **elle ne veut plus me voir, et c'est r.** she doesn't want to see me again, and the feeling's mutual
2 *nf* **la r.** the reverse

réciproquement [resiprɔkmɑ̃] *adv* mutually; **et r.** and vice versa

récit [resi] *nm* story; **faire le r. de qch** to give an account of sth

récital, -als [resital] *nm* recital

récitant, -e [resitɑ̃, -ɑ̃t] *nm,f* narrator

récitation [resitasjɔ̃] *nf* recitation

réciter [resite] *vt* to recite

réclamation [reklamasjɔ̃] *nf* complaint; **faire une r.** to make a complaint; **le service des réclamations, les réclamations** the complaints department

réclame [reklam] *nf* (**a**) *(publicité)* advertising; **faire de la r.** **pour qch** to advertise sth (**b**) *(annonce)* advertisement (**c**) *(promotion)* **en r.** on special offer

réclamer [reklame] **1** *vt* (**a**) *(demander)* to ask for; *(droit, allocation)* to claim; **la fillette réclame ses parents** the little girl is calling for her parents (**b**) *(exiger)* to demand; **r. des dommages et intérêts** to claim damages (**c**) *(nécessiter)* to require
2 se réclamer *vpr* **se r. de qn** *(se recommander)* to mention sb's name; **se r. de qch** *(d'un parti, d'une idéologie)* to identify with sth

reclasser [rəklase] *vt* (**a**) *(fichiers)* to reclassify (**b**) *(chômeur)* to find a new job for (**c**) *(personnel, salaires)* to regrade

reclus, -e [rəkly, -yz] **1** *adj* cloistered
2 *nm,f* recluse

réclusion [reklyzjɔ̃] *nf* *(peine)* imprisonment; **r. à perpétuité** life imprisonment

recoiffer [rəkwafe] **se recoiffer** *vpr* (**a**) *(arranger ses cheveux)* to redo one's hair (**b**) *(remettre son chapeau)* to put one's hat back on

recoin [rəkwɛ̃] *nm (d'un lieu)* nook; *(de la mémoire)* recess

reçois, reçoit, reçoive *etc voir* **recevoir**

recoller [rəkɔle] *vt (objet cassé)* to stick back together; *(timbre)* to stick back on; *(enveloppe)* to stick back down; *Fam* **r. les morceaux** to patch things up

récoltant, -e [rekɔltɑ̃, -ɑ̃t] **1** *adj* apiculteur **r.** honey producer; **viticulteur r.** = winegrower who harvests his own grapes
2 *nm,f* **mis en bouteille chez le r.** estate-bottled

récolte [rekɔlt] *nf* (**a**) *(action)* harvesting; **faire la r.** to harvest the crops (**b**) *(résultat)* harvest (**c**) *(d'informations)* crop

récolter [rekɔlte] *vt (cultures)* to harvest; *Fig (renseignements, documents)* to collect

recommandable [rəkɔmɑ̃dabl] *adj (personne, lieu)* reputable; **peu r.** *(personne, lieu)* disreputable

recommandation [rəkɔmɑ̃dasjɔ̃] *nf (appui, conseil)* recommendation

recommandé, -e [rəkɔmɑ̃de] **1** *adj* (**a**) *(lettre)* registered (**b**) *(conseillé)* recommended; **ce n'est pas très r.** it's not very advisable
2 *nm* **en r.** registered

recommander [rəkɔmɑ̃de] **1** *vt* (**a**) *(lieu, produit, personne)* to recommend (**à** to) (**b**) *(conseiller)* to advise; **r. à qn de faire qch** to advise sb to do sth; **r. la prudence à qn** to advise sb to be cautious (**c**) *(lettre, paquet)* to register **2 se recommander** *vpr* (**a**) *(demander de l'aide)* **se r. à qn** to commend oneself to sb (**b**) **se r. de qn** *(pour un emploi)* to give sb's name as a reference

recommencement [rəkɔmɑ̃smɑ̃] *nm* renewal; **la vie est un éternel** *ou* **perpétuel r.** life is a constant succession of new beginnings

recommencer [16] [rəkɔmɑ̃se] **1** *vt* to start *or* begin again **2** *vi* to start *or* begin again; **ne recommencez pas!** don't do it again! **3 recommencer à** *vt ind* **r. à faire qch** to start *or* begin to do sth again

récompense [rekɔ̃pɑ̃s] *nf* reward; *(prix)* award; **500 euros de r.** 500 euros reward; **en r. (de)** as a reward (for)

récompenser [rekɔ̃pɑ̃se] *vt* to reward (**de** for); **ce film a été récompensé à Cannes** this film won an award at Cannes

recomposer [rəkɔ̃poze] *vt (numéro de téléphone)* to redial

recompter [rəkɔ̃te] *vt* to count again

réconciliation [rekɔ̃siljasjɔ̃] *nf* reconciliation

réconcilier [66] [rekɔ̃silje] **1** *vt* to reconcile (**avec** with); **r. qn avec la vie** to renew sb's appetite for life **2 se réconcilier** *vpr* to make it up (**avec** with)

reconductible [rəkɔ̃dyktibl] *adj (contrat, bail)* renewable

reconduction [rəkɔ̃dyksjɔ̃] *nf* (**a**) *(d'un bail, d'un contrat)* renewal; **r. tacite** *(d'un accord)* tacit renewal (**b**) *(d'un budget, d'une politique, d'une grève)* continuation

reconduire [18] [rəkɔ̃dɥir] *vt* (**a**) *(personne)* to take sb back; **r. qn (à la porte)** to show sb out; **r. qn à la frontière** to escort sb back to the border (**b**) *(bail, contrat)* to renew (**c**) *(budget, politique, grève)* to continue

réconfort [rekɔ̃fɔr] *nm* comfort

réconfortant, -e [rekɔ̃fɔrtɑ̃, -ɑ̃t] *adj* comforting

réconforter [rekɔ̃fɔrte] *vt* to comfort; **cela me réconforte de le savoir** that's good to know

reconnaissable [rəkɔnɛsabl] *adj* recognizable (**à** by *or* from); **r. entre tous** unmistakable

reconnaissance [rəkɔnɛsɑ̃s] *nf* (**a**) *(action de reconnaître)* recognition; **en r. de qch** in recognition of sth (**b**) *(d'un droit, d'un gouvernement)* recognition; **r. de dette** IOU (**c**) *(gratitude)* gratitude (**pour** for); **avec r.** gratefully (**d**) *Mil* reconnaissance; **partir en r.** to go off on reconnaissance; *Fam Fig* to go and reconnoitre (**e**) *Ordinat* **r. de l'écriture manuscrite** handwriting recognition; **r. optique des caractères** optical character recognition, OCR; **r. de la parole, r. vocale** speech recognition

reconnaissant, -e [rəkɔnɛsɑ̃, -ɑ̃t] *adj* grateful; **être r. à qn de qch** to be grateful to sb for sth; **je vous serais r. de ne plus en parler** I'd be grateful if you didn't mention it again

reconnaître [20] [rəkɔnɛtr] **1** *vt* (**a**) *(identifier)* to recognize (**à** by *or* from); **je te reconnais bien là!** that's just like you! (**b**) *(admettre) (vérité, droit, gouvernement)* to recognize; *(enfant)* to acknowledge; **r. qn pour chef** to recognize sb as leader (**c**) *(avouer) (erreur, faute)* to acknowledge (**d**) *(accorder)* **je lui reconnais des qualités** I recognize her qualities (**e**) *(position, terrain)* to reconnoitre **2 se reconnaître** *vpr* (**a**) *(soi-même)* to recognize oneself

(**b**) *(l'un l'autre)* to recognize each other (**c**) *(s'avouer)* **se r. vaincu/coupable** to acknowledge defeat/one's guilt (**d**) *(se retrouver)* to find one's way around; **je ne me reconnais plus** I can't find my way around any more (**e**) *(être identifiable)* **le mâle se reconnaît à...** the male can be recognized by...

reconnu, -e [rəkɔny] *adj* recognized

reconquérir [7] [rəkɔ̃kerir] *vt (estime, amitié)* to win back; *(territoire)* to reconquer

reconquête [rəkɔ̃kɛt] *nf* reconquest

reconsidérer [34] [rəkɔ̃sidere] *vt* to reconsider

reconstituant, -e [rəkɔ̃stitɥɑ̃, -ɑ̃t] *adj & nm* tonic

reconstituer [rəkɔ̃stitɥe] *vt* (**a**) *(reformer) (armée, gouvernement)* to reconstitute; *(société, parti)* to revive; *(fortune, forces)* to build up again (**b**) *(rétablir) (objet archéologique, faits)* to piece together; *(bâtiment, quartier)* to restore (**c**) *(avec simulation) (crime)* to reconstruct

reconstitution [rəkɔ̃stitysjɔ̃] *nf (d'un crime, d'une bataille)* reconstruction; **r. historique** historical reconstruction

reconstruction [rəkɔ̃stryksjɔ̃] *nf* reconstruction, rebuilding

reconstruire [rəkɔ̃strɥir] *vt* to reconstruct, to rebuild

reconversion [rəkɔ̃vɛrsjɔ̃] *nf* (**a**) *(d'une usine)* conversion; **r. économique** economic restructuring (**b**) *(d'une personne)* retraining

reconvertir [rəkɔ̃vɛrtir] **1** *vt* (**a**) *(entreprise)* to convert (**b**) *(personne)* to retrain **2 se reconvertir** *vpr (personne)* to retrain; **se r. dans qch** to retrain for a new career in sth

recopier [66] [rəkɔpje] *vt* (**a**) *(faire un double de)* to recopy (**b**) *(mettre au propre)* to copy out

record [rəkɔr] **1** *adj inv (chiffre, vitesse)* record; **en un temps r.** in record time **2** *nm* record; **détenir le r. (de qch)** to hold the record (for sth); **battre le r. (de qch)** to break the record (for sth)

recordman [rəkɔrdman] *(pl* **recordmen** [rəkɔrdmɛn]*) nm* (men's) record holder

recordwoman [rəkɔrdwuman] *(pl* **recordwomen** [rəkɔrdwumɛn]*) nf* (women's) record holder

recoucher [rəkuʃe] **1** *vt (personne)* to put to bed again **2 se recoucher** *vpr* to go back to bed

recoudre [21] [rəkudr] *vt (bouton)* to sew back on; *(déchirure, plaie)* to sew *or* stitch up; *Fam (personne)* to stitch up

recoupement [rəkupmɑ̃] *nm* crosscheck; **faire le r.** to crosscheck; **par r.** by crosschecking

recouper [rəkupe] **1** *vt (couper à nouveau) (vêtement)* to recut; **r. du pain** to cut some more bread; **r. une tranche de gâteau** to cut another slice of cake (**b**) *(faire coïncider)* to confirm; **r. des témoignages** to crosscheck testimonies **2 se recouper** *vpr (témoignages)* to tally

recourbé, -e [rəkurbe] *adj (bec)* curved; *(nez)* hooked

recourber [rəkurbe] **1** *vt* to bend **2 se recourber** *vpr* to bend

recourir [22] [rəkurir] **1** *vt (épreuve sportive)* to run again **2** *vi (courir de nouveau)* to run again **3 recourir à** *vt ind* (**a**) *(personne)* to turn to (**b**) *(moyen, violence)* to resort to

recours [rəkur] *nm* (**a**) *(personne, chose)* recourse; **en dernier r.** as a last resort; **avoir r. à qn** to turn to sb; **avoir r. à qch** to resort to sth (**b**) *Jur* **r. en cassation** appeal; *Can* **r. collectif** class action; **r. en grâce** petition for reprieve

recouvrement [rəkuvrəmɑ̃] *nm (de dettes, d'une facture)* recovery; *(de l'impôt)* collection

recouvrer [rəkuvre] *vt (a) (biens, argent, santé)* to recover; *(forces, liberté, vue)* to regain; *(courage, enthousiasme)* to get back **(b)** *(percevoir) (dettes)* to recover; *(impôts)* to collect

recouvrir [52] [rəkuvrir] *vt (a) (couvrir de nouveau) (cahier, toit)* to re-cover; *(enfant)* to cover up again **(b)** *(couvrir complètement)* to cover **(de** with) **(c)** *(tapisser)* to cover **(de** with) **(d)** *(inclure)* to cover

recracher [rəkraʃe] *vt* to spit out

récré [rekre] *nf Fam Br* break, *Am* recess

récréatif, -ive [rekreatif, -iv] *adj (activité)* entertaining; *(lecture)* light

récréation [rekreasjɔ̃] *nf* **(a)** *(à l'école) Br* break, *Am* recess **(b)** *(détente)* recreation

recréer [24] [rəkree] *vt* to re-create

récrier [66] [rekrije] **se récrier** *vpr (mécontents)* to protest **(contre** about)

récrimination [rekriminasjɔ̃] *nf* recrimination

récriminer [rekrimine] *vi* to make recriminations **(contre** against)

récrire [30] [rekrir] = **réécrire**

récriture [rekrityr] = **réécriture**

recroquevillé, -e [rəkrɔkvije] *adj* huddled up

recroqueviller [rəkrɔkvije] **se recroqueviller** *vpr (personne)* to huddle up; *(papier, feuille morte)* to shrivel up

recru, -e [rəkry] *adj Litt* **r. (de fatigue)** exhausted

recrudescence [rəkrydesɑ̃s] *nf* renewed outbreak

recrue [rəkry] *nf* recruit; **faire une nouvelle r.** to gain a new recruit

recrutement [rəkrytmɑ̃] *nm* recruitment

recruter [rəkryte] **1** *vt* to recruit; **r. par concours** to recruit by competition
2 se recruter *vpr* to be recruited **(parmi** from)

rectal, -e, -aux, -ales [rektal, -o] *adj* rectal

rectangle [rektɑ̃gl] *nm* rectangle

rectangulaire [rektɑ̃gyler] *adj* rectangular

recteur [rektœr] *nm (d'une académie) Br* director *or Am* commissioner of education

rectificatif, -ive [rektifikatif, -iv] **1** *adj (lettre)* of amendment; *(texte, facture)* amended
2 *nm* correction

rectification [rektifikasjɔ̃] *nf (d'un texte, d'un calcul, d'une erreur)* correction; *(d'un compte, d'une courbe)* adjustment; *(d'un alignement)* straightening; **faire** *ou* **apporter une r.** to make a correction

rectifier [66] [rektifje] *vt* **(a)** *(texte, calcul, erreur)* to correct; *(prix, compte, courbe)* to adjust; *(alignement)* to straighten; **r. le tir** to adjust the range; *Fig* to take a slightly different tack **(b)** *Fam (tuer)* to bump off

rectiligne [rektiliɲ] *adj (mouvement, figure)* rectilinear; *(avenue)* straight

rectitude [rektityd] *nf (d'un jugement, d'un raisonnement)* soundness

recto [rekto] *nm* front, *Spéc* recto; **r. verso** on both sides

rectorat [rektora] *nm* ≃ board of education

rectum [rektɔm] *nm* rectum

reçu¹, -e *voir* **recevoir**

reçu², -e [rəsy] **1** *nm* receipt
2 *nm,f (à un examen)* successful candidate

recueil [rəkœj] *nm (de poèmes, de chansons, de recettes)* collection; *(de lois)* body; **r. de morceaux choisis** anthology

recueillement [rəkœjmɑ̃] *nm* meditation; **avec r.** meditatively

recueilli, -e [rəkœji] *adj* meditative

recueillir [5] [rəkœjir] **1** *vt* **(a)** *(argent, renseignements)* to collect **(b)** *(votes)* to win; *Fig* **r. le fruit de qch** to reap the fruit of sth **(c)** *(personne, animal)* to take in **(d)** *(miel)* to gather **(e)** *Jur* **r. un héritage** to inherit
2 se recueillir *vpr* to meditate; **se r. pour prier** to gather one's thoughts before praying

recuire [18] [rəkɥir] *vt (plat)* to cook longer

recul [rəkyl] *nm* **(a)** *(mouvement) (d'un glacier, d'une armée)* retreat; *(d'un canon)* recoil; **avoir un mouvement de r.** to recoil **(b)** *(déclin)* decline **(c)** *(baisse)* decline **(de** in) **(d)** *(espace nécessaire)* room to move back **(e)** *Fig (distance)* **considérer qch avec du r.** to consider sth with detachment; **manquer de r.** to be too closely involved; **prendre du r.** to take a step back from things

reculade [rəkylad] *nf (d'une armée)* retreat; *Fig & Péj* climbdown

reculé, -e [rəkyle] *adj (endroit, époque)* remote

reculer [rəkyle] **1** *vi* **(a)** *(aller en arrière) (personne)* to move back; *(automobiliste, voiture)* to reverse; *(troupes)* to retreat; *(glacier, eaux)* to recede; **faire r. la foule** to move the crowd back **(b)** *(régresser) (épidémie)* to lose ground; *(chômage)* to decline; *Fig* **faire r. la maladie** to bring the disease under control **(c)** *(renoncer)* to retreat **(devant** in the face of); **il ne recule devant rien** nothing daunts him; **faire r. qn** to put sb off; **il est trop tard pour r.** it's too late to pull out; **c'est r. pour mieux sauter** it's just putting off the evil day
2 *vt* **(a)** *(meuble)* to move back; *(voiture)* to reverse **(b)** *(paiement, décision)* to postpone

reculons [rəkylɔ̃] **à reculons** *adv* backwards

récupérable [rekyperabl] *adj (déchets)* salvageable; **les heures supplémentaires sont récupérables** additional time off may be taken in lieu

récupération [rekyperasjɔ̃] *nf* **(a)** *(d'une somme d'argent, d'un objet)* recovery; **la r. des heures supplémentaires** time off in lieu; **temps de r.** *(d'un sportif)* recovery time **(b)** *(de déchets)* salvage **(c)** *(d'un parti, d'une pensée)* exploitation

récupérer [34] [rekypere] *vt* **(a)** *(objet prêté ou perdu)* to get back, to recover; *Ordinat (fichier, données)* to retrieve **(b)** *(passer prendre) (personne, affaires, objet)* to collect; *(bagages)* to retrieve, to reclaim **(c)** *(retrouver) (forces)* to recover **(d)** *(recycler)* to salvage **(e)** *(détourner à son profit) (mouvement, idée)* to exploit **(f)** **r. des heures supplémentaires** to take time off in lieu

récurer [rekyre] *vt* to scour; **poudre/tampon à r.** scouring powder/pad

récurrent, -e [rekyrɑ̃, -ɑ̃t] *adj* recurring; *Ordinat* **processus r.** recursive process

récusable [rekyzabl] *adj (témoignage)* impugnable

récuser [rekyze] **1** *vt* to challenge
2 se récuser *vpr* to decline to give an opinion

recyclable [rəsiklabl] *adj* recyclable

recyclage [rəsiklaʒ] *nm* **(a)** *(de matériaux)* recycling **(b)** *(d'une personne)* retraining

recycler [rəsikle] **1** *vt* **(a)** *(matériaux)* to recycle **(b)** *(personne)* to retrain
2 se recycler *vpr (personne)* to retrain

rédacteur, -trice [redaktœr, -tris] *nm,f (d'un journal, d'un dictionnaire)* editor; **r. en chef** editor in chief

rédaction [redaksjɔ̃] *nf* **(a)** *(d'un texte)* writing **(b)** *(poste)* editorship; *(personnel)* editorial staff; *(département)* editorial department; **(salle de) r.** editorial office **(c)** *Scol* essay, composition

rédactionnel, -elle [redaksjɔnel] *adj* editorial

reddition [redisjɔ̃] *nf* surrender

redécouvrir [52] [rədekuvrir] *vt (auteur, œuvre)* to rediscover

redéfinir [rədefinir] *vt Ordinat (touche)* to redefine

redemander [rədəmãde] *vt* (**a**) *(en reposant une question)* to ask again; **r. de l'aide à qn** to ask sb for help again (**b**) *(pour en avoir plus)* **r. du vin/des timbres** to ask for more wine/stamps; **r. un litre/un kilo de qch** to ask for another litre/kilo of sth; **des gens comme ça, on en redemande** there aren't enough people like that in the world; *Ironique* **il en redemande** he's still asking for it (**c**) *(pour récupérer)* **r. qch** to ask for sth back

redémarrer [rədemare] *vi (voiture)* to start again; *(économie, ventes)* to take off again; *Ordinat* to reboot; **faire r. une voiture** to start a car again

rédemption [redãpsjã] *nf* redemption

redéploiement [rədeplwamã] *nm* redeployment

redescendre [rədesãdr, rədɛsãdr] **1** *vi (en s'approchant)* to come back down; *(en s'éloignant)* to go back down; **r. de voiture** to get back out of the car
2 *vt* (**a**) *(apporter)* to bring back down; *(emporter)* to take back down (**b**) *(escalier, rivière)* to go/come back down

redevable [rədəvabl] *adj* **être r. de qch à qn** to be indebted to sb for sth; **je vous suis r. de 20 euros** I owe you 20 euros

redevance [rədəvãs] *nf (pour la télévision)* licence fee

redevenir [70] [rədəvənir] *vi* to become again; **r. silencieux** to fall silent again; **r. normal** to get back to normal

rédhibitoire [redibitwar] *adj (prix)* prohibitive; *(conditions, salaire)* unacceptable

rediffuser [rədifyze] *vt (émission)* to repeat; *(film)* to show again

rediffusion [rədifyzjã] *nf (d'une émission)* repeat; *(d'un film)* rerun

rédiger [45] [rediʒe] *vt (contrat)* to draw up; *(article, lettre)* to write; *(ordonnance)* to write out; **savoir r.** to write well; **être bien/mal rédigé** to be well/badly written

redingote [rədɛ̃gɔt] *nf* (**a**) *(manteau cintré)* fitted coat (**b**) *(manteau à basques)* frock coat

redire [27a] [rədir] **1** *vt* (**a**) *(répéter)* to say again, to repeat; **pourrais-tu lui r. que...?** could you tell him again that...?; **on ne le redira jamais assez** it can never be said often enough (**b**) *(révéler)* to repeat (**à** to)
2 redire à *vt ind* **avoir** *ou* **trouver à r. à qch** to find fault with sth; **il n'y a rien à r. à cela** there's nothing wrong with that

redite [rədit] *nf (useless)* repetition

redondance [rədãdãs] *nf aussi Ordinat* redundancy; **redondances** redundancy

redondant, -e [rədãdã, -ãt] *adj* redundant

redonner [rədɔne] *vt* (**a**) *(donner davantage de)* **redonne-lui du café** give him some more coffee (**b**) *(rendre)* to give back; **r. de l'appétit/du courage à qn** to restore sb's appetite/courage; **r. envie à qn de faire qch** to make sb want to do sth again; **r. des forces à qn** to give sb back his/her strength (**c**) *(donner de nouveau)* to give again

redorer [rədɔre] *vt* to regild; *Fig* **r. son blason** to restore one's reputation

redoublant, -e [rədublã, -ãt] *nm,f (élève)* pupil repeating a year

redoublé, -e [rəduble] *adj* **frapper à coups redoublés** to knock harder

redoublement [rədubləmã] *nm* (**a**) *(de douleur, de joie, de prudence)* increase (**b**) *(d'une syllabe)* reduplication (**c**) *Scol =* repeating of a year; **le professeur principal décidera des redoublements** the *Br* head teacher *or Am* principal will decide who will have to repeat the year

redoubler [rəduble] **1** *vt* (**a**) *(douleur, joie, prudence)* to increase; *(efforts)* to redouble (**b**) *Scol* **r. une classe** to repeat a year
2 *vi* (**a**) *Scol* to repeat a year (**b**) *(sentiment)* to intensify **3 redoubler de** *vt ind* **r. de violence** *(orage, vent)* to become more and more severe; **r. d'efforts** to redouble one's efforts; **r. de prudence/d'attention/de douceur** to be twice as cautious/attentive/gentle

redoutable [rədutabl] *adj (adversaire, arme)* formidable; *(maladie)* dreadful

redouter [rədute] *vt* to dread; **r. de faire qch** to dread doing sth; **je redoute qu'il ne soit déjà trop tard** I'm afraid it's already too late

redoux [rədu] *nm* milder weather

redressement [rədrɛsmã] *nm* (**a**) *(économique, financier)* recovery (**b**) *(correction)* **r. fiscal** tax adjustment

redresser [rədrɛse] **1** *vt* (**a**) *(objet penché)* to put up straight; **r. la tête** to hold up one's head; *(la lever)* to raise one's head (**b**) *(rectifier) (erreur, situation)* to rectify; *(économie, entreprise)* to put back on its feet (**c**) *(bois courbé, tôle cabossée)* to straighten (out)
2 *vi (automobiliste)* to straighten up
3 se redresser *vpr* (**a**) *(personne)* to straighten up (**b**) *(économie, pays, ventes)* to recover

redresseur [rədrɛsœr] *nm* **r. de torts** righter of wrongs

réducteur, -trice [redyktœr, -tris] *adj (simpliste)* simplistic

réduction [redyksjã] *nf* (**a**) *(des prix, des dépenses, de la production)* reduction (**de** in) (**b**) *(rabais)* reduction; **faire une r. de 50 euros (à qn)** to give (sb) a reduction of 50 euros (**c**) *(reproduction)* small reproduction (**d**) *(d'une fracture)* setting

réduire [10] [redɥir] **1** *vt* (**a**) *(diminuer)* to reduce (**de** by); *(texte)* to shorten, to cut; **réduit de moitié** half size (**b**) *(transformer)* **r. qch en qch** to reduce sth to sth (**c**) *(contraindre)* **r. qn à qch** *(misère, désespoir)* to reduce sb to sth; **en être réduit à faire qch** to be reduced to doing sth (**d**) *(fracture)* to set (**e**) *(photographie, dessin)* to reduce
2 *vi (sauce)* to reduce; **faire r. qch** to reduce sth
3 se réduire *vpr* (**a**) **se r. à** *(se ramener à)* to come down to (**b**) **se r. en** *(se transformer en)* to be reduced to

réduit [redɥi] *nm (pièce)* small room

rééchelonnement [reeʃəlɔnmã] *nm* rescheduling

rééchelonner [reeʃəlɔne] *vt* to reschedule

réécrire [30] [reekrir] *vt* to rewrite

réécriture [reekrityr] *nf* rewriting

rééditer [reedite] *vt* (**a**) *(ouvrage)* to reissue (**b**) *(fait)* to repeat

réédition [reedisjã] *nf* (**a**) *(d'un ouvrage)* reissue (**b**) *(d'un fait)* repeat

rééducation [reedykasjã] *nf* (**a**) *(d'une partie du corps)* re-education; *(d'un handicapé, d'un accidenté)* rehabilitation; **faire de la r.** *(chez un kinésithérapeute)* to have physical therapy (**b**) *(de délinquants)* rehabilitation

rééduquer [reedyke] *vt (handicapé, accidenté, délinquant)* to rehabilitate; *(partie du corps)* to re-educate

réel, -elle [reɛl] **1** *adj* real
2 *nm* (**a**) *(nombre)* real number (**b**) **le r.** *(la réalité)* reality

réélection [reelɛksjã] *nf* re-election

réélire [44] [reelir] *vt* to re-elect

réellement [reɛlmã] *adv* really

réembaucher [reãboʃe] *vt* to take on again

rééquilibrage [reekilibraʒ] *nm (de pneus)* balancing; *Fig* **le r. du budget** balancing the budget again

rééquilibrer [reekilibre] *vt (pneus)* to balance; *Fig (budget)* to balance again

réessayer [53] [reɛseje] **1** *vt* to try again; *(vêtement)* to try on again **2** *vi* to try again

réévaluer [reevalɥe] *vt (monnaie)* to revalue; *(prix)* to reassess

réexamen [reɛgzamɛ̃] *nm* re-examination; *(d'une décision)* reconsideration

réexaminer [reɛgzamine] *vt* to re-examine; *(décision)* to reconsider

réexpédier [66] [reɛkspedje] *vt* **(a)** *(à une autre adresse)* to send on, to forward **(b)** *(à l'expéditeur)* to send back, to return

réexpédition [reɛkspedisjɔ̃] *nf* **(a)** *(à une autre adresse)* forwarding **(b)** *(à l'expéditeur)* return

refaire [36] [rəfɛr] **1** *vt* **(a)** *(faire à nouveau) (travail)* to do again, to redo; *(voyage)* to make again; **r. du riz** to make some more rice; **r. ses lacets** to tie one's laces again; *Hum* **ton éducation est à r.** where were you brought up?; **et si c'était à r.?** and if you had to do it again?; **r. le monde** to put the world to rights; **r. sa vie** to make a new life for oneself **(b)** *(remettre en état) (pièce, appartement)* to do up; **r. la peinture de qch** to repaint sth; **r. la moquette de qch** to recarpet sth; **r. qch à neuf** *(moteur)* to recondition sth; *(appartement)* to renovate sth completely **(c)** *Fam (duper)* to take in; **je me suis fait r. de 20 euros** I was done out of 20 euros **2 se refaire** *vpr* **(a)** *(se changer)* to change the way one is; **on ne se refait pas** you can't change the way you are *(se rétablir)* **se r. une santé** to recover **(c)** *Fam (financièrement)* to recoup one's losses **(d)** *(s'habituer)* **se r. à qch** to get used to sth again

réfection [refɛksjɔ̃] *nf* repair

réfectoire [refɛktwar] *nm* refectory, dining hall

référence [referɑ̃s] *nf* **(a)** *(renvoi)* reference (à to); **faire r. à qch** to refer to sth; **en r. à** with reference to **(b)** *(sur une lettre, sur un document)* reference; **r. à rappeler** please quote reference **(c)** *(d'employeur)* **références** references

référencer [16] [referɑ̃se] *vt Ordinat* to reference

référendum [referɛ̃dɔm] *nm* referendum; **faire un r.** to hold a referendum

référer [34] [refere] **1 référer à** *vt ind* **en r. à qn** to refer the matter to sb **2 se référer** *vpr* **se r. à qch** to refer to sth; **se r. à un auteur** to refer to an author

refermer [rəfɛrme] **1** *vt* to shut or close again **2 se refermer** *vpr (porte)* to close or shut again; *(fleur, blessure)* to close up

refiler [rəfile] *vt Fam* **r. qch à qn** *(pour s'en débarrasser)* to palm sth off on sb; *(maladie)* to give sb sth

réfléchi, -e [reflefi] *adj* **(a)** *(personne)* thoughtful **(b)** *(action, opinion)* considered; **c'est tout r.** I've made up my mind; **tout bien r.** all things considered **(c)** *(verbe, pronom)* reflexive

réfléchir [reflefir] **1** *vt* **(a)** *(image, lumière, son)* to reflect **(b)** **r. que** to realize that **2** *vi* to think (**à** ou **sur** about); **je réfléchis** I'm thinking; *(avant de décider)* I'm thinking about it; **sans r.** without thinking **3 se réfléchir** *vpr* to be reflected

réfléchissant, -e [reflefisɑ̃, -ɑ̃t] *adj* reflective

réflecteur, -trice [reflɛktœr, -tris] *adj* reflecting

reflet [rəflɛ] *nm* **(a)** *(dans un miroir, dans l'eau)* reflection; *(d'un tissu)* sheen; *(de la lune)* glint; **reflets** *(de cheveux)* highlights **(b)** *Fig (image)* reflection; **être le r. de qn** to be exactly like sb; **être le r. d'une époque** to symbolize an era

refléter [34] [rəflete] **1** *vt aussi Fig* to reflect **2 se refléter** *vpr aussi Fig* to be reflected

refleurir [rəflœrir] **1** *vi* to flower again; *Fig* to flourish again **2** *vt (tombe)* to put fresh flowers on

réflexe [reflɛks] **1** *adj* reflex **2** *nm* reflex; **avoir de bons réflexes** to have good reflexes; **devenir un r.** to become automatic; **avoir le r. de faire qch** to do sth instinctively; **r. conditionné** conditioned reflex

réflexion [reflɛksjɔ̃] *nf* **(a)** *(d'une image, de la lumière, du son)* reflection **(b)** *(pensée)* reflection, thought; **r. faite, à la r.** on reflection, on second thoughts **(c)** *(remarque)* remark; **faire une r. à qn** to make a remark to sb

refluer [rəflye] *vi (liquide)* to flow back; *(marée)* to ebb; *(foule)* to surge back

reflux [rəfly] *nm (de la marée)* ebb; *(d'une foule)* backward surge

refondre [rəfɔ̃dr] *vt (ouvrage)* to revise

refonte [rəfɔ̃t] *nf (d'un ouvrage)* revision

reformater [rəfɔrmate] *vt Ordinat (page, disque)* to reformat

réformateur, -trice [refɔrmatœr, -tris] **1** *adj* reforming **2** *nm,f* reformer

réforme [refɔrm] *nf* reform; *Hist* **la R.** the Reformation

réformé, -e [refɔrme] **1** *adj (protestant)* Protestant **2** *nm,f (recrue)* recruit rejected as unfit; *(soldat)* soldier discharged as unfit

reformer [rəfɔrme] **1** *vt* to re-form; **r. les rangs** to fall into line again **2 se reformer** *vpr* to re-form

réformer [refɔrme] *vt* **(a)** *(abus, loi)* to reform **(b)** *(recrue)* to reject as unfit; *(soldat)* to discharge as unfit

réformisme [refɔrmism] *nm* reformism

réformiste [refɔrmist] *adj & nmf* reformist

reformuler [rəfɔrmyle] *vt* to reformulate

refoulé, -e [rəfule] *adj* repressed

refouler [rəfule] **1** *vt* **(a)** *(faire reculer) (foule)* to drive or force back; *(étranger)* to turn away **(b)** *(sentiments, colère, souvenir)* to repress; *(larmes)* to hold back **2** *vi* **l'évier refoule** the water's coming up through the plughole in the sink

réfractaire [refrakter] *adj* **(a)** *(rebelle)* insubordinate; **r. à** *(loi, conseils, proposition)* unwilling to accept **(b)** *(brique, argile)* fireproof **(c)** *(prêtre)* non-juring

réfraction [refraksjɔ̃] *nf* refraction

refrain [rəfrɛ̃] *nm (d'une chanson)* chorus, refrain; *Fam* **c'est toujours le même r.** it's always the same old story

refréner [rəfrene] **, réfréner** [refrene] [34] *vt* to curb

réfrigérant, -e [refriʒerɑ̃, -ɑ̃t] *adj* **(a)** *(appareil, produit)* refrigerating **(b)** *Fam (accueil, personne)* frosty

réfrigérateur [refriʒeratœr] *nm* refrigerator

réfrigération [refriʒerasjɔ̃] *nf* refrigeration

réfrigéré, -e [refriʒere] *adj* **(a)** *(wagon)* refrigerated **(b)** *Fam (personne)* frozen

réfrigérer [34] [refriʒere] *vt (aliment, boisson)* to refrigerate

refroidir [rəfrwadir] **1** *vt* **(a)** *(eau)* to cool (down) **(b)** *Fig (amitié)* to cool; *(enthousiasme)* to dampen; *Fam* **sa réaction m'a refroidi** her reaction dampened my enthusiasm **(c)** *très Fam (tuer)* to bump off **2** *vi* **(a)** *(devenir froid)* to get cold; *(devenir moins chaud)* to cool down; **laisser r. qch** *(volontairement)* to let sth cool down; *(par négligence)* to let sth get cold **(b)** *(temps)* to get colder

3 se refroidir vpr (**a**) (temps) to get colder (**b**) Fig (amitié, relations) to cool (**c**) (prendre froid) to catch a chill

refroidissement [rəfrwadismā] nm (**a**) (de la température) drop in temperature; (de l'eau) cooling (**b**) (indisposition) chill (**c**) Fig (dans une amitié, dans des relations) cooling off

refuge [rəfyʒ] **1** nm (**a**) (lieu) & Fig refuge; **trouver/ chercher r.** (auprès de qn) to find/seek refuge (with sb) (**b**) (en montagne) (mountain) hut (**c**) (sur la route) traffic island
2 adj **valeur r.** safe investment

réfugié, -e [refyʒje] nm,f refugee

réfugier [66] [refyʒje] **se réfugier** vpr to take refuge (**dans in**)

refus [rəfy] nm (d'une invitation, d'une offre) refusal; (d'une proposition, d'un candidat, d'un manuscrit) rejection; **essuyer un r.** to meet with a refusal; **opposer un r. à qn/qch** to turn sb/sth down; Fam **ce n'est pas de r.** I won't say no; **r. de priorité** (infraction) failure to yield

refuser [rəfyze] **1** vt (**a**) (offre, invitation, demande) to refuse, to turn down; (proposition, marchandises, manuscrit) to reject; **r. qch à qn** to refuse sb sth (**b**) (clients, spectateurs) to turn away (**c**) (candidat) **être refusé** to fail
2 vi to refuse; **r. de faire qch** to refuse to do sth
3 se refuser vpr (**a**) (être rejeté) **une offre pareille, ça ne se refuse pas** you can't refuse an offer like that (**b**) **se r. qch** (se priver de) to deny oneself sth; **ne rien se r.** not to deprive oneself (**c**) (résister) **se r. à l'évidence** to shut one's eyes to the facts; **se r. à tout commentaire** to refuse to comment; **se r. à faire qch** to refuse to do sth

réfuter [refyte] vt to refute

regagner [rəgaɲe] vt (**a**) (confiance, affection, estime) to regain, to get back (**b**) (argent perdu) to win back; **r. le temps perdu** to make up for lost time (**c**) **r. du terrain** (reprendre l'avantage) to make up lost ground (**d**) (endroit) to get back to; **r. son foyer** to get back home

regain [rəgē] nm (d'intérêt, d'activité) renewal; **un r. d'espoir** renewed hope

régal, -als [regal] nm treat

régalade [regalad] nf **boire à la r.** to drink without letting the bottle touch one's lips

régaler [regale] **1** vt **r. qn** to give sb a delicious meal
2 vi Fam **c'est moi qui régale** (it's) my treat
3 se régaler vpr **je me régale** (en mangeant) I'm really enjoying it; (je m'amuse) I'm having a great time

regard [rəgar] nm (**a**) (coup d'œil) look; **porter son r. sur qn/qch** to look at sb/sth; **jeter** ou **lancer un r. à qn** to glance at sb; **jeter un r. à** ou **sur qch** to glance at sth; **lancer un r. furieux à qn** to glare at sb; **chercher qn/qch du r.** to look round for sb/sth; **interroger qn du r.** to give sb a questioning look; **soustraire qn/qch aux regards (de qn)** to keep sb/sth hidden (from sb); **attirer le r.** to attract attention; **sous les regards de la foule** while the crowd looked on; Fig **porter un nouveau r./un r. critique sur qch** to take a fresh look/a critical look at sth (**b**) (expression) look (**c**) (ouverture) (d'une porte) peephole; (d'un égout) manhole (**d**) (locutions) **au r. de la loi** in the eyes of the law; **en r.** (en face) opposite

regardant, -e [rəgardā, -āt] adj (**a**) Fam (avare) careful with money (**b**) (exigeant) particular (**sur** about)

regarder [rəgarde] **1** vt (**a**) (personne, objet) to look at; (émission, film) to watch; **r. qn droit dans les yeux** to look sb in the eye; **r. qn fixement** to stare at sb; **r. qn faire qch** to watch sb do sth; **regarde où tu marches!** watch where you're going!; Fam **non, mais tu ne m'as pas regardé!** what do you take me for? (**b**) (considérer) to regard, to consider (**comme** as); **r. qch en face** to face up to sth; **r.**

les choses telles qu'elles sont to see things as they are (**c**) (concerner) to concern; **cela ne regarde que moi** that's nobody's business but mine; **cela ne vous regarde pas** that's none of your business
2 vi (**a**) (observer) to look; **r. autour de soi/en bas/en arrière** to look round/down/back; **r. par** ou **à la fenêtre** (du dedans) to look out of the window; (du dehors) to look in through the window (**b**) (être orienté) **r. sur** ou **vers** (jardin, rue) to look onto
3 regarder à vt ind to pay attention to; **r. à la dépense** to be careful with one's money; **y r. à deux fois avant de faire qch** to think twice before doing sth; **y r. de près** to look at it closely
4 se regarder vpr (**a**) (soi-même) to look at oneself; Fam **elle ne s'est pas regardée!** she can talk! (**b**) (l'un l'autre) to look at each other; **se r. dans les yeux** to look into each other's eyes (**c**) (se faire face) to face each other

regarnir [rəgarnir] vt (garde-manger, étagères) to restock

régate [regat] nf regatta

régence [reʒās] **1** adj inv **style R.** Regency style
2 nf regency; **l'Hist la R.** the Regency

régénération [reʒenerasjɔ̃] nf (**a**) (d'une cellule, de la peau) regeneration (**b**) Ordinat **r. de l'écran** screen refresh

régénérer [34] [reʒenere] **1** vt to regenerate
2 se régénérer vpr to regenerate

régent, -e [reʒā, -āt] nm,f (**a**) (chef du gouvernement) regent (**b**) Belg Scol (secondary) schoolteacher

régenter [reʒāte] vt **vouloir tout r.** to want to run the whole show

reggae [rege] **1** adj inv reggae **2** nm **le r.** reggae

régie [reʒi] nf (**a**) (entreprise publique) state controlled company (**b**) Cin & TV (organisation) production management (**c**) TV (lieu) control room

regimber [rəʒēbe] vi (personne) to balk (**contre** at); **il est inutile de r.** it's no use protesting

régime [reʒim] nm (**a**) **r. (alimentaire)** diet; **être au r.** to be on a diet; **faire** ou **suivre un r.** to diet; **se mettre au r.** to go on a diet; **r. amincissant** slimming diet (**b**) (forme de gouvernement) government, regime (**c**) (pénitentiaire, hospitalier) system; (de retraite) scheme; **r. matrimonial** marriage settlement; **r. de Sécurité sociale** = division of social security system applying to some professional groups (**d**) (d'un moteur) speed; **r. de croisière** cruising speed; Fig **à ce r.** at this rate (**e**) (d'une rivière, d'un fleuve) rate of flow (**f**) (de bananes, de dattes) bunch

régiment [reʒimā] nm (**a**) (unité militaire) regiment; Fig (d'admirateurs, de créanciers) host; Fam **il y en a pour un r.** there's enough for a whole army

région [reʒjɔ̃] nf area, region; **la r. parisienne** the Paris area ou region; **la R.** = administrative area comprising several "départements"

régional, -e, -aux, -ales [reʒjonal, -o] adj regional

régionalisme [reʒjonalism] nm regionalism

régir [reʒir] vt (**a**) (déterminer) to govern (**b**) (domaine) to manage

régisseur [reʒisœr] nm (**a**) (d'un domaine) manager (**b**) Cin & TV assistant production manager; Th stage manager

registre [rəʒistr] nm (**a**) (livre) register; (de comptabilité) account book; **r. du commerce** trade register; **r. de l'état civil** register of births, marriages and deaths (**b**) (d'une voix, d'un instrument) register (**c**) Ordinat register; **r. d'accès mémoire** memory access register (**d**) (d'une œuvre) style

réglable [reglabl] adj adjustable

réglage [reglaʒ] nm (**a**) (d'un siège, d'un appareil) adjustment; **r. automatique** automatic control (**b**) (d'une radio, d'une télévision) tuning; **r. du contraste** contrast control

règle [rɛgl] *nf* (**a**) *(de conduite, de grammaire)* rule; *Fig* **la r. du jeu** the rules of the game; **en r.** *(passeport, papiers)* in order; **en r. générale** as a general rule; **dans** *ou* **selon les règles de l'art** according to the book; **r. d'or** golden rule; **r. de trois** rule of three (**b**) *(pour tracer des lignes)* ruler (**c**) *Ordinat (sur écran)* ruler line (**d**) **règles** *(menstruation)* period; **avoir ses règles** to have one's period

réglé, -e [regle] *adj* (**a**) *(papier)* ruled (**b**) *(organisé)* well-ordered (**c**) *(résolu)* **c'est r.** it's settled (**d**) *(jeune fille)* who has started having periods

règlement [rɛgləmɑ̃] *nm* (**a**) *(résolution)* settlement; **en cours de r.** being settled; **r. à l'amiable** amicable settlement; **r. de comptes** settling of scores (**b**) *(paiement)* payment; **pour r. de tout compte** in full settlement (**c**) *(règle)* regulations; **r. intérieur** *(d'une école)* school rules; *(d'un bureau)* company rules; **c'est le r.** that's the rule

réglementaire [rɛgləmɑ̃tɛr] *adj (tenue)* regulation; **faire qch dans le temps r.** to do sth in the time allowed

réglementation [rɛgləmɑ̃tasjɔ̃] *nf* (**a**) *(action)* regulation (**b**) *(ensemble de lois)* regulations; **la r. du travail** labour legislation

réglementer [rɛgləmɑ̃te] *vt* to regulate

régler [34] [regle] **1** *vt* (**a**) *(mécanisme, appareil, image)* to adjust; *(radio, moteur)* to tune (**b**) *(journée, emploi du temps)* to plan (**c**) **r. qch sur qch** *(conduite)* to model sth on sth; *(pas)* to adjust sth to sth (**d**) *(résoudre) (question, dispute)* to settle; **r. ses affaires** to put one's affairs in order; **r. qch à l'amiable** to settle sth out of court (**e**) *(payer) (facture)* to settle, to pay; *(employé, commerçant, loyer)* to pay; *(achats)* to pay for
2 *vi* to pay
3 se régler *vpr* (**a**) **se r. sur qn** to model oneself on sb (**b**) *(se conclure)* to be settled

réglette [reglɛt] *nf* small ruler; *Ordinat* **r. de clavier** key strip

réglisse [reglis] *nf* liquorice

réglo [reglo] *adj inv Fam* on the level

régnant, -e [reɲɑ̃, -ɑ̃t] *adj (prince, famille)* reigning; *(idéologie, opinion)* prevailing

règne [rɛɲ] *nm* (**a**) *(d'un souverain)* reign; *Fig (de l'argent, de la technologie)* rule (**b**) *(végétal, animal)* kingdom

régner [34] [reɲe] *vi* (**a**) *(souverain)* to reign, to rule (**sur** over); **r. en maître sur qch** to reign supreme over sth (**b**) *(exister)* to prevail; *(silence, atmosphère)* to reign; **faire r. la paix / l'ordre** to keep the peace/law and order; *Ironique* **la confiance règne!** there's confidence for you!

regonfler [rəgɔ̃fle] *vt (ballon, pneu)* to blow up again, to reinflate

regorger [45] [rəgɔrʒe] *vi* **r. de qch** to be overflowing with sth; **r. de monde** to be packed with people

régresser [regrese] *vi* (**a**) *(criminalité, idéologie, production)* to decline (**b**) *(personne)* to regress

régression [regresjɔ̃] *nf* (**a**) *(de la criminalité, d'une idéologie, de la production)* decline; **être en r.** to be on the decline (**b**) *(d'une personne)* regression; **être en r.** to be regressing

regret [rəgrɛ] *nm* regret (**de** for); **avoir des regrets** to have regrets; **à r.** with regret; **j'ai le r.** *ou* **je suis au r. de vous annoncer que...** I regret to tell you that...; **à mon (grand) r.** (much) to my regret

regrettable [rəgrɛtabl] *adj* regrettable

regretter [rəgrɛte] *vt* (**a**) *(avoir des remords sur)* to regret; **je ne regrette rien** I have no regrets; **il me ferait presque r. ma gentillesse** I almost regret being so kind to him; **r. de faire qch** to regret to do sth; **r. d'avoir fait qch** to regret having done sth; **r. que** + *subjunctive* to be sorry that; **il est à r. que...** it is to be regretted that...; **je regrette!** I'm sorry!

(**b**) *(personne, endroit)* to miss; **r. sa jeunesse / son enfance** to wish one was young / a child again

regroupement [rəgrupmɑ̃] *nm* (**a**) *(action)* grouping; *(d'animaux, d'enfants)* round-up; *(de sociétés)* amalgamation; *Mil* regrouping; **le r. familial** keeping immigrant families together (**b**) *(groupe)* grouping

regrouper [rəgrupe] **1** *vt* (**a**) *(personnes, objets)* to gather together; *(animaux, enfants)* to round up (**b**) *(sociétés)* to amalgamate
2 se regrouper *vpr* (**a**) *(personnes)* to gather together (**b**) *(sociétés)* to amalgamate

régularisation [regylarizasjɔ̃] *nf* (**a**) *(d'une situation)* regularization; *(d'un compte)* adjustment (**b**) *(d'un fleuve, d'un fonctionnement, de la circulation)* regulation

régulariser [regylarize] *vt* (**a**) *(situation)* to regularize; *(compte)* to adjust; **ils ont régularisé la situation** *(ils se sont mariés)* they made it official (**b**) *(fleuve, fonctionnement, circulation)* to regulate

régularité [regylarite] *nf* (**a**) *(exactitude)* regularity (**b**) *(constance)* steadiness (**c**) *(d'une décision, d'une situation)* legality

régulateur, -trice [regylatœr, -tris] **1** *adj* regulating
2 *nm* regulator

régulation [regylasjɔ̃] *nf* control; **r. des naissances** birth control

régulier, -ère [regylje, -ɛr] **1** *adj* (**a**) *(à intervalles fixes)* regular (**b**) *(constant)* steady; *(travail, résultats)* consistent (**c**) *(écriture, ligne, couche)* even; *(traits du visage)* regular (**d**) *(légal) (situation)* legitimate; **être en situation régulière** to have one's papers in order (**e**) *Gram* regular (**f**) *Fam (honnête)* on the level (**g**) *(clergé)* regular
2 *nf* **régulière** *Fam Hum (femme)* steady

régulièrement [regyljɛrmɑ̃] *adv* (**a**) *(à intervalles fixes)* regularly (**b**) *(avec constance)* steadily (**c**) *(réparti, étalé)* evenly (**d**) *(selon la loi)* legitimately

régurgiter [regyrʒite] *vt (nourriture)* to regurgitate

réhabilitation [reabilitasjɔ̃] *nf* rehabilitation

réhabiliter [reabilite] **1** *vt* (**a**) *(délinquant)* to rehabilitate (**b**) *(personne accusée)* to clear (**c**) *(bâtiment, quartier)* to renovate
2 se réhabiliter *vpr* to rehabilitate oneself

réhabituer [reabitɥe] **1** *vt* **r. qn à qch / à faire qch** to get sb used to sth/to doing sth again
2 se réhabituer *vpr* **se r. à qch / à faire qch** to get used to sth/to doing sth again

rehausser [rəose] *vt* (**a**) *(mur, bâtiment)* to make higher (**b**) *(couleur, teint)* to set off; *(détail)* to accentuate

réimplanter [reɛ̃plɑ̃te] **1** *vt* to relocate
2 se réimplanter *vpr* to relocate

réimpression [reɛ̃presjɔ̃] *nf* reprinting; **en cours de r.** *(ouvrage)* being reprinted

réimprimer [reɛ̃prime] *vt* to reprint

rein [rɛ̃] *nm* (**a**) *(organe)* kidney; **r. artificiel** kidney *or* dialysis machine (**b**) **reins** *(bas du dos)* lower back; **la chute** *ou* **le creux des reins** the small of the back; **avoir mal aux reins** to have a pain in the small of one's back; *Fig* **avoir les reins solides** to be tough; *(financièrement)* to have money behind one

réincarnation [reɛ̃karnasjɔ̃] *nf* reincarnation

réincarner [reɛ̃karne] **se réincarner** *vpr* to be reincarnated (**en** as)

reine [rɛn] *nf* (**a**) *(souveraine, épouse d'un roi)* queen; **un port** *ou* **un maintien de r.** a queenly bearing; **la r. Victoria** Queen Victoria; **la r. mère** the Queen Mother (**b**) *(femme)* **r. de beauté** beauty queen; **la r. du bal** the belle of the ball (**c**) *(abeille)* queen (bee) (**d**) **la petite r.** *(cyclisme)* cycling

reine-claude (*pl* **reines-claudes**) [rɛnklod] *nf* greengage

reinette [rɛnɛt] *nf* pippin; **r. grise** russet

réinitialiser [reinisjalize] *vt Ordinat* to reset; *(mémoire)* to reinitialize

réinscription [reɛ̃skripsjɔ̃] *nf* reregistration

réinscrire [30] [reɛ̃skrir] **1** *vt* to reregister (à for) **2 se réinscrire** *vpr* to reregister (à for)

réinsérer [34] [reɛ̃sere] **1** *vt* (**a**) *(personne)* to reintegrate (**dans** into) (**b**) *Ordinat (bloc)* to reinsert **2 se réinsérer** *vpr* to reintegrate (**dans** into)

réinsertion [reɛ̃sɛrsjɔ̃] *nf* reintegration; **r. sociale** rehabilitation

réintégrer [34] [reɛ̃tegre] *vt* (**a**) *(fonctionnaire)* **r. qn (dans ses fonctions)** to reinstate sb (**b**) *(lieu)* **r. son domicile** to return to one's home

réintroduire [18] [reɛ̃trɔdɥir] *vt* to reintroduce

réitérer [34] [reitere] *vt (demande, promesse, question)* to repeat, to reiterate; *(démarche)* to repeat

rejaillir [rəʒajir] *vi* to spurt out; *Fig* **r. sur qn** *(scandale)* to reflect on sb

rejet [rəʒɛ] *nm* (**a**) *(de produits chimiques)* discharge (**b**) *(d'une proposition, d'une personne, d'une greffe)* rejection (**c**) *(en poésie)* enjambment

rejeter [42] [rəʒte] *vt* (**a**) *(relancer)* to throw back (**b**) *(candidature, offre, greffe)* to reject; *(témoignage)* to disallow; *(réclamation, accusation)* to dismiss; *(projet de loi)* to throw out (**c**) *(personne)* to reject (**d**) *(repousser)* **r. ses cheveux en arrière** to toss one's hair back; **r. la tête en arrière** to throw one's head back; **r. un mot en fin de phrase** to put a word at the end of a sentence (**e**) *(déchets, gaz toxiques)* to discharge; *(nourriture)* to regurgitate; *(épaves)* to cast up (**f**) *(blâme, responsabilité)* to shift (**sur** on)

rejeton [rəʒtɔ̃] *nm Fam Hum (enfant)* kid

rejoindre [43] [rəʒwɛ̃dr] **1** *vt* (**a**) *(personne) (pour un rendez-vous)* to meet; *(rattraper)* to catch up (with) (**b**) *(aboutir sur) (rue, rivière)* to join (up with) (**c**) *(atteindre) (lieu)* to reach; *(règlement, poste)* to return to (**d**) *(concorder avec)* to coincide with **2 se rejoindre** *vpr* (**a**) *(amis)* to meet up (**b**) *(rivières, routes, lignes)* to join up (**c**) *(propos, idées)* to coincide

rejouer [rəʒwe] *vt (match, point)* to replay; *(morceau de musique)* to play again; *(pièce de théâtre)* to do again

réjoui, -e [reʒwi] *adj* joyful

réjouir [reʒwir] **1** *vt (personne)* to delight **2 se réjouir** *vpr* to be delighted (**de** at); **se r. que** + *subjunctive* to be delighted that; **se r. de faire qch** to be delighted to be doing sth

réjouissance [reʒwisɑ̃s] *nf* rejoicing; **en signe de r.** to mark the occasion; **réjouissances** festivities

réjouissant, -e [reʒwisɑ̃, -ɑ̃t] *adj* delightful

relâche [rəlɑʃ] *nf* (**a**) *(arrêt)* **sans r.** without a break (**b**) *(au théâtre)* **il y a r.** *(ce soir)* there is no performance this evening; **faire r.** to be closed; **r.** *(sur panneau)* closed

relâché, -e [rəlɑʃe] *adj (mœurs, conduite)* lax

relâchement [rəlɑʃmɑ̃] *nm* (**a**) *(des muscles)* relaxing; *(d'une corde)* slackening (**b**) *(de la discipline)* relaxation; *(des mœurs)* laxness; *(des efforts)* let-up; *(de l'attention)* wavering

relâcher [rəlɑʃe] **1** *vt* (**a**) *(muscles)* to relax; *(corde, étreinte)* to loosen (**b**) *(discipline)* to relax; *(efforts)* to let up; **r. son attention** to let one's attention waver (**c**) *(prisonnier)* to release, to let go **2 se relâcher** *vpr* (**a**) *(muscles)* to relax; *(corde)* to slacken (**b**) *(attention)* to loosen (**b**) *(discipline, mœurs)* to become lax; *(élève, employé)* to slack off; *(attention)* to waver

relais [rəlɛ] *nm* (**a**) *(épreuve sportive)* **(course de) r.** relay

(race); **r. 4 x 100 mètres** 4 x 100-metre relay (**b**) *(relève)* passer le **r. à qn** to hand over to sb; **prendre le r. (de)** to take over (from) (**c**) *(intermédiaire)* intermediary (**d**) *(auberge)* coaching inn; **r. gastronomique** gourmet restaurant (**e**) *(dispositif émetteur)* relay

relance [rəlɑ̃s] *nf* (**a**) *(de l'économie, de la production)* revival (**b**) *(au jeu)* raise

relancer [16] [rəlɑ̃se] *vt (lancer de nouveau)* to throw again; *(rendre)* to throw back (**b**) *(économie, ventes, production)* to boost (**c**) *(moteur)* to restart; *Ordinat (programme)* to rerun; *(logiciel)* to restart (**d**) *(client)* to follow up

relater [rəlate] *vt Litt (raconter)* to relate

relatif, -ive [rəlatif, -iv] **1** *adj* relative; **r. à** relating to **2** *nm (pronom)* relative pronoun **3** *nf* **relative** *(proposition)* relative clause

relation [rəlasjɔ̃] *nf* (**a**) *(rapports entre personnes)* relationship; **être en r. avec qn** to be in touch with sb; **mettre qn en r. (avec qn)** to put sb in touch (with sb); **avoir de bonnes/mauvaises relations avec qn** to be on good/ bad terms with sb; **r. (amoureuse)** (love) affair; **relations extérieures** foreign affairs; **relations publiques** public relations; **relations sexuelles** (sexual) intercourse (**b**) *(lien)* *(entre des phénomènes, des faits)* relationship, connection; **être sans r. avec qch** to bear no relation to sth; **en r. avec...** in relation to...; **r. de cause à effet** cause-and-effect relationship (**c**) *(connaissance)* acquaintance; **avoir des relations** to have contacts; **une r. de travail** a colleague (**d**) *(récit)* account

relationnel, -elle [rəlasjɔnɛl] *adj* relational; *Ordinat* **base de données relationnelles** relational database

relativement [rəlativmɑ̃] *adv* (**a**) *(assez)* relatively (**b**) **r. à** *(par rapport à)* compared to

relativiser [rəlativize] *vt* to put into perspective; **il faut r. you have to** put things into perspective

relativisme [rəlativism] *nm* relativism

relativité [rəlativite] *nf* relativity

relax [rəlaks] *adj Fam* laid-back

relaxant, -e [rəlaksɑ̃, -ɑ̃t] *adj* relaxing

relaxation [rəlaksasjɔ̃] *nf* relaxation; **faire de la r.** to do relaxation exercises

relaxer [rəlakse] **1** *vt* (**a**) *(détendre)* to relax (**b**) *(prisonnier)* to release **2 se relaxer** *vpr* to relax

relayer [53] [rəleje] **1** *vt (personne)* to take over from **2 se relayer** *vpr* (**a**) *(se remplacer)* to take turns; **se r. pour faire qch** to take turns doing sth; **on se relaie toutes les trois heures** we change over every three hours (**b**) *(coureurs)* to take over from each other

relecture [rələktyr] *nf* (**a**) *(d'épreuves)* proofreading (**b**) *(d'un livre, d'un texte)* rereading

reléguer [34] [rəlege] *vt* to relegate (à/en to); *Fig* **r. qch au second plan** to push sth into the background

relent [rəlɑ̃] *nm* (**a**) *(odeur)* stench (**b**) *(de scandale)* whiff

relevable [rələvabl] *adj (dossier, appuie-tête)* adjustable; *(accoudoir)* folding

relevé, -e [rəlve] **1** *adj (style)* lofty (**b**) *(sauce, plat)* spicy **2** *nm (d'un compteur)* reading; **r. de compte** bank statement; **r. d'identité bancaire** = document giving details of one's bank account

relève [rəlɛv] *nf* relief; **assurer** *ou* **prendre la r. (de qn)** to take over (from sb)

relèvement [rələvmɑ̃] *nm* (**a**) *(d'une économie, d'un pays)* recovery (**b**) *(des salaires, des tarifs, d'un impôt)* raising

relever [46] [rəlve] **1** *vt* (**a**) *(objet renversé)* to pick up; *(personne)* to help back up; **r. la tête** to look up; *Fig* to stand up for oneself (**b**) *(économie, pays)* to revive (**c**) *(col)* to turn up; *(manches, bas de pantalon)* to roll up, to turn up; *(voilette, jupe)* to lift (up); *(cheveux)* to put up (**d**) *(augmenter)* to raise (**e**) *(contradiction, erreur)* to pick out; *(traces, empreinte)* to find (**f**) *(prêter attention à)* **r. l'allusion** to pick up on the hint; **je n'ai pas relevé** I let it go (**g**) *(adresse, coordonnées)* to take down; *(compteur)* to read; *(copies)* to collect; **r. le gaz** to read the gas meter (**h**) *(défi)* to accept (**i**) *(sauce, plat)* to spice up (**j**) *(remplacer) (troupes, sentinelle)* to relieve (**k**) *(libérer)* **r. qn de ses fonctions** to relieve sb of his/her duties **2 relever de** *vt ind* (**a**) *(dépendre de) (personne, autorité)* to be answerable to; **r. de l'article 3** to come under article 3; **cette affaire relève de la justice** this is a matter for the courts; **son cas relève de la folie** he's well and truly insane (**b**) *(se remettre de)* to be recovering from **3 se relever** *vpr* (**a**) *(après une chute)* to get up (**b**) *(accoudoir, siège)* to lift up (**c**) *(se remettre)* **se r. de qch** to get over sth, to recover from sth

relief [rəljɛf] *nm* (**a**) *(d'un paysage, d'une médaille)* relief; **en r.** in relief; *Fig* **mettre qch en r.** *(idées, qualité)* to bring sth out; *(beauté)* to set sth off; *(avantage)* to highlight; **sans r.** *(paysage, style)* flat (**b**) *Litt* **reliefs** *(d'un repas)* remains; *Fig (de la gloire)* shreds (**c**) *Ordinat* highlight; **mettre qch en r.** to highlight sth

relier [66] [rəlje] **1** *vt* (**a**) *(mettre en contact)* to connect, to link (**à** to) (**b**) *(idées, faits)* to link together (**c**) *(livre)* to bind **2 se relier** *vpr Ordinat* to link up

relieur, -euse [rəljœr, -øz] *nm,f* (book)binder

religieusement [rəliʒjøzmɑ̃] *adv* (**a**) *(selon la religion)* religiously; **se marier r.** to get married in church (**b**) *(avec révérence)* reverently (**c**) *(scrupuleusement)* religiously

religieux, -euse [rəliʒjø, -øz] **1** *adj* religious; *(mariage)* church; *Fig (silence)* respectful **2** *nm (moine)* monk **3** *nf* **religieuse** (**a**) *(sœur)* nun (**b**) *(gâteau)* cream puff

religion [rəliʒjɔ̃] *nf* religion; **entrer en r.** to join a religious order

reliquaire [rəlikɛr] *nm* reliquary

reliquat [rəlika] *nm (d'argent)* remainder; **r. de caisse** cash balance; **r. de compte** account balance

relique [rəlik] *nf* relic

relire [44] [rəlir] **1** *vt* (**a**) *(livre, auteur, notes)* to reread (**b**) *(épreuves)* to proofread **2 se relire** *vpr* to read (over) what one has written

reliure [rəljyr] *nf* (**a**) *(activité, art)* bookbinding (**b**) *(couverture)* binding

reloger [45] [rələʒe] *vt* to rehouse

reluire [18] [rəlɥir] *vi (parquet, meuble, métal)* to shine, to gleam; **faire r. qch** to polish sth (up)

reluisant, -e [rəlɥizɑ̃, -ɑ̃t] *adj (parquet, meuble, métal)* shining, gleaming (**b**) *Fig* **ce qu'il a fait n'est pas très r.** what he did doesn't reflect very well on him

reluquer [rəlyke] *vt Fam* to eye up

remâcher [rəmɑʃe] *vt (colère, échec)* to brood over

remake [rimɛk] *nm* remake

remaniement [rəmanimɑ̃] *nm* (**a**) *(d'un texte)* revision (**b**). **r. ministériel** cabinet reshuffle

remanier [66] [rəmanje] *vt* (**a**) *(texte)* to revise (**b**) *(ministère)* to reshuffle

remariage [rəmarjaʒ] *nm* remarriage

remarier [66] [rəmarje] **se remarier** *vpr* to remarry; **se r. avec qn** to remarry sb

remarquable [rəmarkabl] *adj* remarkable (**par** for)

remarquablement [rəmarkabləmɑ̃] *adv* remarkably

remarque [rəmark] *nf* (**a**) *(orale)* remark; **faire une r.** to make a remark (**b**) *(écrite)* comment

remarqué, -e [rəmarke] *adj (entrée, absence)* conspicuous; *(intervention)* that attracted attention

remarquer [rəmarke] **1** *vt* (**a**) *(observer)* to notice; **faire r. qch à qn** to point sth out to sb; **je vous ferai r. que...** I'd like to point out that...; **se faire r.** to attract attention; *Fam* **remarque, il n'est pas le seul** he's not the only one, mind you (**b**) *(dire)* to remark, to observe **2 se remarquer** *vpr (tache, cicatrice)* to show

remballer [rɑ̃bale] *vt (marchandises)* to repack; *Fig (compliment)* to keep to oneself

rembarrer [rɑ̃bare] *vt Fam* to snub

remblai [rɑ̃blɛ] *nm* embankment

remblayer [53] [rɑ̃bleje] *vt (route, voie ferrée)* to bank (up)

remboîter [rɑ̃bɔite] **1** *vt* to rewind **2 se remboîter** *vpr* to rewind

rembourrage [rɑ̃buraʒ] *nm (action, matériau)* stuffing

rembourrer [rɑ̃bure] *vt* to stuff

remboursable [rɑ̃bursabl] *adj (emprunt)* repayable; *(frais)* refundable

remboursement [rɑ̃bursəmɑ̃] *nm (d'un emprunt)* repayment; *(de frais)* refund

rembourser [rɑ̃burse] *vt* (**a**) *(frais, achat)* to refund; *(emprunt, dettes)* to pay back; **ce médicament est remboursé à 70%** 70% of the cost of this medicine will be refunded (**b**) *(personne)* to pay back; **se faire r.** to get a refund; *Fam* **remboursez!** *(au théâtre)* give us our money back!

rembrunir [rɑ̃brynir] **se rembrunir** *vpr (visage, personne)* to become sullen

remède [rəmɛd] *nm* remedy, cure (**contre** for); **r. de bonne femme** old wives' remedy; **r. de cheval** kill-or-cure remedy

remédier [66] [rəmedje] **remédier à** *vt ind (erreur, situation)* to remedy; *(inconvénient)* to make up for

remembrement [rəmɑ̃brəmɑ̃] *nm (de terres)* grouping of land

remémorer [rəmemɔre] **se remémorer** *vpr* to remember

remerciement [rəmɛrsimɑ̃] *nm* **lettre de r.** thank-you letter; **remerciements** thanks; *(dans un livre)* acknowledgements

remercier [66] [rəmɛrsje] *vt* (**a**) *(dire merci à)* to thank (**de ou pour** for); **r. qn d'avoir fait qch** to thank sb for doing sth; **(non,) je vous remercie** no, thank you (**b**) *Euph (congédier)* to ask to leave

remettre [47] [rəmɛtr] **1** *vt* (**a**) **r. qch à qn** *(lettre, télégramme, colis)* to deliver sth to sb; *(rapport)* to submit sth to sb; *(démission)* to hand sth in to sb; *(rançon)* to hand sth over to sb; **r. qn à la justice** to turn sb over to the police; **r. son sort entre les mains de qn** to put one's fate in sb's hands

(**b**) *(retarder)* to postpone (**à** *to or* till); **r. qch à plus tard** to put sth off till later

(**c**) *(replacer)* to put back; **r. qch à sa place** *ou* **en place** to put sth back in its place; **r. qch en cause** *ou* **en question** to call sth into question; **r. qn en liberté** to set sb free

(**d**) *(reconnaître)* **je ne vous remets pas** I can't place you

(**e**) *(dans un état antérieur)* **r. une montre à l'heure** to set a watch to the right time; **r. qch à zéro** to reset sth to zero; **r. qch en marche** *(moteur, machine)* to restart sth; **r. qch en ordre** *(dossiers, maison)* to tidy sth (up)

(**f**) *(rétablir la santé de)* to make better

(**g**) *(manteau, chapeau)* to put back on

(**h**) *(chauffage, télévision)* to turn on again; *(disque, chanson)* to put on again

(**i**) *(ajouter)* *(sel, eau)* to add (**dans** to)

(**j**) *Fam (recommencer)* **on remet ça?** how when another

(one)?; tu ne vas pas r. ça! you're not going to start that again, are you?
2 se remettre *vpr* (**a**) *(dans un endroit, dans un état)* **se r. debout** to get up again; **se r. au lit** to go back to bed; **se r. en cause** *ou* **en question** to question oneself; **le temps s'est remis au beau** the weather has brightened up again (**b**) *(recommencer)* **se r. à qch/à faire qch** to start sth/ doing sth again; **se r. au français/au squash** to take up French/squash again (**c**) *(après une maladie, un choc)* to recover (**de** from); *Fig* **voyons, remettez-vous!** come on, pull yourself together! (**d**) *(faire confiance)* **je m'en remets à vous** I'll leave it to you, it's up to you (**e**) *(se placer)* **se r. entre les mains de qn** to place oneself in sb's hands (**f**) *Fam (renouer)* **se r. ensemble** to get back together again

réminiscence [reminisãs] *nf (souvenir imprécis)* vague recollection

remise [rəmiz] *nf* (**a**) *(dans son lieu ou son état d'origine)* **r. en état** *(d'une maison)* restoration; **r. à neuf** *(d'une machine)* reconditioning; **r. en question** *ou* **cause** calling into question (**b**) *(d'une lettre)* delivery (**à** to), *(d'une rançon)* handing over (**à** to); **r. des prix** prizegiving (**c**) *(réduction)* **r. de peine** reduction of sentence (**d**) *(rabais)* discount; **faire une r. à qn** to give sb a discount (**e**) *(appentis)* shed (**f**) *Ordinat.* **à blanc** *(d'une disquette)* reformatting; **r. en forme** *(de texte)* reformatting

remiser [rəmize] *vt* to put away

rémission [remisjɔ̃] *nf* (**a**) *(d'un péché)* remission; *Fig* **sans r.** *(travailler)* unremittingly; *(punir)* mercilessly (**b**) *(d'une maladie)* remission

remmener [46] [rɑ̃mne] *vt* to take back; **r. qn en voiture** to drive sb back

remodeler [39] [rəmɔdle] *vt* (**a**) *(refaçonner)* to remodel (**b**) *(réorganiser)* to restructure

remontant [rəmɔ̃tɑ̃] *nm* tonic

remontée [rəmɔ̃te] *nf* (**a**) *(d'une pente)* ascent (**b**) *(dans un classement sportif)* recovery (**c**) *(des eaux)* rising (**d**) *(pour skieurs)* **r. mécanique** ski lift

remonte-pente *(pl* **remonte-pentes)** [rəmɔ̃tpɑ̃t] *nm* ski-tow

remonter [rəmɔ̃te] **1** *vt* (**a**) *(pente, escalier)* (en s'éloignant) to go up again, to climb back up; *(en s'approchant)* to come up again, to climb back up; **r. la rue** to go/come up the street; **r. la rivière** to go upstream (**b**) *(hausser)* *(étagère, poster)* to move up; *(pantalon, jupe)* to hitch up; *(manche, chaussettes)* to pull up; *(fermeture éclair)* to do up; *(vitre de voiture)* to wind up (**c**) *(porter en haut)* to take/bring up (**d**) *(horloge, montre)* to wind (up) (**e**) *(revigorer)* *(personne)* to cheer up (**f**) *(pièces d'une machine)* to reassemble
2 *vi* (**a**) *(dans l'espace)* *(personne)* to go/come back up; *(marée)* to flow; *(baromètre)* to rise again; *(route, ruelle)* to climb again; *(jupe)* to ride up; **r. en voiture** to get back in one's car; *Fig* **r. dans les sondages** to improve one's position in the polls (**b**) *(dans le temps)* to go back (**à** to); **ça remonte à loin** *(tradition)* it goes back a long way; *(épisode)* it was a long time ago (**c**) *(actions, monnaie, température)* to go up again, to rise again
3 se remonter *vpr (moralement)* to cheer up; *(physiquement)* to recover one's strength

remontoir [rəmɔ̃twar] *nm* winder

remontrance [rəmɔ̃trɑ̃s] *nf* remonstrance; **faire des remontrances à qn** to remonstrate with sb

remontrer [rəmɔ̃tre] **1** *vt* **en r. à qn** to show one knows better than sb
2 se remontrer *vpr* to show oneself again

remords [rəmɔr] *nm* remorse; **avoir du** *ou* **des r.** to feel remorse; **je n'ai aucun r.!** I'm not the slightest bit sorry!

remorque [rəmɔrk] *nf* (**a**) *(véhicule)* trailer (**b**) **prendre qch en r.** to take sth in tow; *Fig* **être à la r.** to lag behind

remorquer [rəmɔrke] *vt (voiture, bateau)* to tow; *(train)* to pull

remorqueur [rəmɔrkœr] *nm* tug(boat)

rémoulade [remulad] *nf* *Culin* **(sauce) r.** remoulade (sauce) *(mayonnaise sauce with mustard and herbs)*

rémouleur [remulœr] *nm* knife grinder

remous [rəmu] *nm (d'une rivière)* eddy; *(d'un bateau)* wash; *Fig (de la foule)* ripple; *Fig* **provoquer** *ou* **faire des r.** to cause a stir

rempailler [rɑ̃paje] *vt* to reseat

rempart [rɑ̃par] *nm* rampart; **remparts** walls; **faire un r. de son corps à qn** to shield sb with one's body

rempiler [rɑ̃pile] *vi Fam Hum* to sign up again

remplaçable [rɑ̃plasabl] *adj* replaceable

remplaçant, -e [rɑ̃plasɑ̃, -ɑ̃t] *nm,f (personne)* replacement; *(d'un médecin)* locum *(tenens)*; *(d'un enseignant)* Br supply teacher, Am substitute teacher

remplacement [rɑ̃plasmɑ̃] *nm* replacement; **en r. de qn/qch** in place of sb/sth; **faire des remplacements** *(professeur)* to work as Br a supply teacher or Am a substitute teacher

remplacer [16] [rɑ̃plase] *vt* (**a**) *(être à la place de)* to take the place of, to replace; *(professionnellement)* to stand in for; **se faire r.** to get somebody to stand in or cover for one (**b**) *(substituer)* to replace (**par** with)

remplir [rɑ̃plir] **1** *vt* (**a**) *(récipient)* to fill (**de** with); *(espace, trou)* to fill (in); *Fig (journée, vie)* to take up; **r. qn de joie/colère** to fill sb with joy/anger (**b**) *(formulaire)* to fill in or out; *(chèque)* to write, to make out; *(page)* to fill (**c**) *(promesse, rôle, contrat)* to fulfil; *(devoirs, tâche)* to carry out
2 se remplir *vpr* to fill up (**de** with); *Fig* **se r. les poches** to line one's pockets

remplissage [rɑ̃plisaʒ] *nm* (**a**) *(d'un tonneau, d'un réservoir)* filling (up); *(d'un trou, d'un espace)* filling (in) (**b**) *Péj* **faire du r.** *(dans un texte)* to pad

remplumer [rɑ̃plyme] **se remplumer** *vpr Fam* (**a**) *(financièrement)* to be in funds again (**b**) *(grossir)* to put some weight back on

rempocher [rɑ̃pɔʃe] *vt* to put back in one's pocket

remporter [rɑ̃pɔrte] *vt* (**a**) *(reprendre)* to take back or away (**b**) *(gagner)* *(prix, victoire)* to win; *(succès)* to achieve; *Fig* **r. tous les suffrages** to meet with universal approval

rempoter [rɑ̃pɔte] *vt* to repot

remuant, -e [rəmyɑ̃, -ɑ̃t] *adj* hyperactive

remue-ménage [rəmymenaʒ] *nm inv* commotion

remuer [rəmye] **1** *vt* (**a**) *(partie du corps)* to move around; *(lèvres)* to move (**b**) **r. la queue** *(chien)* to wag its tail; **r. les oreilles** *(chien)* to waggle its ears (**c**) *(mobilier, objets)* to move, to shift (**c**) *(sauce, café)* to stir; *(salade)* to toss; *(terre)* to turn over; *Fig (vieux souvenirs, passé)* to rake up; **r. ciel et terre pour faire qch** to move heaven and earth to do sth (**d**) *(émouvoir)* to move
2 *vi (personne)* to move; *(queue)* to wag; **arrête de r.!** don't fidget!, keep still!
3 se remuer *vpr* (**a**) *(bouger)* to move (**b**) *Fam (être actif)* to have plenty of get-up-and-go; **remue-toi un peu!** get up off your backside!

rémunérateur, -trice [remyneratœr, -tris] *adj (travail)* remunerative; *(placement)* interest-bearing

rémunération [remynerasjɔ̃] *nf* remuneration (**de** for); *(salaire)* pay

rémunérer [34] [remynere] *vt (personne)* to pay; *(travail, services)* to pay for

renâcler [rənɑkle] *vi (personne)* to balk (**à faire** at doing); **il a accepté en renâclant** he accepted grudgingly

renaissance [rənɛsɑ̃s] *nf* (**a**) *(d'une personne)* rebirth (**b**) *(des lettres, des arts)* renaissance; **la R.** the Renaissance

renaître [50a] [rənɛtr] *vi* (**a**) *(personne)* to be born again; **r. de ses cendres** to rise again from its ashes (**b**) *(industrie, arts, espoir)* to revive; *Litt (printemps, plantes)* to return; *(nature)* to reawaken; **faire r. la confiance** to restore confidence

rénal, -e, -aux, -ales [renal, -o] *adj* renal

renard [rənar] *nm* (**a**) *(animal)* fox; *Fig* **c'est un vieux r.** he's a sly old fox (**b**) *(fourrure)* fox (fur)

renardeau, -x [rənardo] *nm* fox cub

rencard, rencart [rɑ̃kar] = **rancard**

renchérir [rɑ̃ʃerir] *vi* (**a**) *(prix, loyers, marchandises)* to go up (**b**) *(dire ou faire plus)* to go one better (**sur** than)

rencontre [rɑ̃kɔ̃tr] *nf* (**a**) *(de personnes)* meeting; *(de routes, de cours d'eau)* junction; **faire la r. de qn** to meet sb; **faire de mauvaises rencontres** to meet the wrong kind of people; **aller à la r. de qn** to go to meet sb (**b**) *(d'athlétisme)* meeting; *(match)* game

rencontrer [rɑ̃kɔ̃tre] **1** *vt* (**a**) *(personne)* to meet; **r. qn par hasard** to bump into *or* run into sb (**b**) *(trouver)* to come across; *(opposition, difficulté)* to encounter, to come up against

2 se rencontrer *vpr* (**a**) *(gens, rivières)* to meet (**b**) *Hum (être d'accord)* **les grands esprits se rencontrent** great minds think alike

rendement [rɑ̃dmɑ̃] *nm* (**a**) *(d'une terre, d'un impôt)* yield; *(d'un investissement)* return, yield (**b**) *(de travailleurs, d'une usine, d'une machine)* output; *(d'un ordinateur)* throughput; **travailler à plein r.** *(usine)* to work at full capacity

rendez-vous [rɑ̃devu] *nm inv* (**a**) *(rencontre)* appointment; *(amoureux)* date; **donner r. à qn** to arrange to meet sb; **prendre r. avec qn/chez le coiffeur** to make an appointment with sb/at the hairdresser's; **j'ai un r. chez le médecin** I have a doctor's appointment (**b**) *(endroit)* meeting place

rendormir [29] [rɑ̃dɔrmir] **se rendormir** *vpr* to fall asleep again

rendre [rɑ̃dr] **1** *vt* (**a**) *(objet emprunté)* to give back, to return (**à** to); *(achat)* to take back (**à** to); *(copies, cadeau)* to give back (**à** to); *(otages)* to hand back (**à** to); **r. sa liberté à qn** to set sb free

(**b**) *(rembourser)* to pay back

(**c**) *(en retour)* **je lui ai rendu son compliment/son invitation** I returned his compliment/his invitation; **r. la monnaie à qn** to give sb his/her change; *Fig* **r. à qn la monnaie de sa pièce** to get even with sb; **r. les armes** *(soldats)* to surrender; *Fig* to give up; *Fig* **elle l'aime, mais il ne le lui rend pas** she loves him, but the feeling isn't mutual

(**d**) *(vomir)* to bring up

(**e**) *(son)* to make; *(jus, eau)* to release

(**f**) *Jur (jugement, verdict)* to deliver; **r. la justice** to dispense justice

(**g**) *(sens, nuance)* to render, to express

(**h**) *(faire devenir)* to make; **r. qn triste** to make sb sad; **r. qn fou** to drive sb mad; **r. qn aveugle/sourd** to make sb go blind/deaf; *Fig* **l'amour l'a rendu aveugle** he was blinded by love

2 *vi* (**a**) *(terre)* to be productive; *(placement)* to yield (**b**) *(vomir)* to vomit

3 se rendre *vpr* (**a**) *(aller)* **se r. à** to go to; **se r. chez qn** to call on sb

(**b**) *(se soumettre)* to give oneself up

(**c**) *(devenir)* **se r. malade/utile** to make oneself ill/useful

(**d**) *(locutions)* **se r. compte de qch/que...** to realize sth/

that...; *Fam* **tu te rends compte!** who'd have believed it!; **se r. à la raison** to see reason

rendu, -e [rɑ̃dy] *adj* (**a**) *(arrivé)* **être r.** to have arrived (**b**) *Vieilli (fatigué)* tired out

rêne [rɛn] *nf* rein

renégat, -e [rənega, -at] *nm,f* renegade

renfermé, -e [rɑ̃fɛrme] **1** *adj (personne)* withdrawn **2** *nm* **odeur de r.** musty smell; **sentir le r.** to smell musty

renfermer [rɑ̃fɛrme] **1** *vt (contenir)* to contain **2 se renfermer** *vpr* to withdraw into oneself

renflé, -e [rɑ̃fle] *adj* bulging

renflement [rɑ̃fləmɑ̃] *nm* bulge

renflouer [rɑ̃flue] *vt* (**a**) *(bateau échoué)* to refloat (**b**) *(entreprise, personne)* to bail out

renfoncement [rɑ̃fɔ̃smɑ̃] *nm* recess

renforcement [rɑ̃fɔrsəmɑ̃] *nm (d'une poutre, d'une armée, d'une équipe)* strengthening, reinforcement; *(de la sécurité)* tightening up

renforcer [16] [rɑ̃fɔrse] **1** *vt* (**a**) *(poutre, armée, équipe)* to strengthen, to reinforce; *(sécurité)* to tighten up (**b**) *(couleur, éclairage)* to intensify (**c**) *(crainte)* to heighten; *(impression, convictions)* to strengthen; **r. qn dans une opinion** to confirm sb in an opinion

2 se renforcer *vpr (tendance, impression, convictions)* to grow

renfort [rɑ̃fɔr] *nm* **renforts** reinforcements; *Fig* **demander du r.** to ask for help; **à grand r. de qch** with the help of lots of sth

renfrogné, -e [rɑ̃frɔɲe] *adj* scowling

renfrogner [rɑ̃frɔɲe] **se renfrogner** *vpr* to scowl

rengager [45] [rɑ̃gaʒe] **1** *vt (personnel)* to take on again; *(combat)* to renew; *(conversation, partie, débat)* to pick up again

2 se rengager *vpr Mil* to re-enlist

rengaine [rɑ̃gɛn] *nf* tune; *Fam Fig* **c'est toujours la même r.** it's (always) the same old story

rengainer [rɑ̃gɛne] *vt (épée)* to sheathe; *Fig (compliment)* to keep to oneself

rengorger [45] [rɑ̃gɔrʒe] **se rengorger** *vpr* to strut

reniement [rənimɑ̃] *nm (d'une foi)* denial; *(d'idées, d'une action)* repudiation

renier [66] [rənje] **1** *vt (fils, racines)* to disown; *(foi)* to deny; *(action, idées)* to repudiate

2 se renier *vpr* to repudiate one's opinions

reniflement [rənifləmɑ̃] *nm* (**a**) *(action)* sniffing (**b**) *(bruit)* sniff

renifler [rənifle] **1** *vi* to sniff

2 *vt (fleur)* to sniff (at); *(tabac à priser)* to sniff (up); *Fig (bonne affaire, embrouille)* to sniff out

renne [rɛn] *nm* reindeer

renom [rənɔ̃] *nm* renown; **de r.** famous, renowned; **de grand r.** extremely famous

renommé, -e [rənɔme] *adj* renowned, famous (**pour** for)

renommée [rənɔme] *nf* fame, renown

renommer [rənɔme] *vt Ordinat (fichier)* to rename

renoncement [rənɔ̃smɑ̃] *nm* renunciation (**à** of)

renoncer [16] [rənɔ̃se] **renoncer à** *vt ind (droit, projet, activité)* to give up, to abandon; *(vacances, voyage)* to sacrifice, to forego; **r. à faire qch** to give up doing sth; *(avant d'avoir commencé)* to give up the idea of doing sth

renonciation [rənɔ̃sjasjɔ̃] *nf* renunciation (**à** of)

renoncule [rənɔ̃kyl] *nf* buttercup

renouer [rənwe] **1** *vt* (**a**) *(ruban, lacet)* to tie (up) again;

(cravate) to do up again (**b**) *(conversation, relations)* to resume; *(amitié)* to renew
2 renouer avec *vt ind* **r. avec qn** to take up with sb again; **r. avec qch** *(tradition)* to revive sth; *(habitude)* to go back to sth

renouveau, -x [rənuvo] *nm* revival

renouvelable [rənuvlabl] *adj (contrat, énergie)* renewable; *(expérience)* repeatable

renouveler [42] [rənuvle] **1** *vt* (**a**) *(stock, équipement)* to renew, to replace; *(eau)* to change (**b**) *(passeport, abonnement, demande)* to renew; *(expérience)* to repeat (**c**) *(style)* to change
2 se renouveler *vpr* (**a**) *(cellule)* to be renewed (**b**) *(se produire de nouveau)* to recur, to happen again (**c**) *(changer)* to change, **un artiste/auteur qui ne se renouvelle pas** an artist/author whose style never changes

renouvellement [rənuvɛlmɑ̃] *nm* (**a**) *(de stock, d'équipement)* replacement, renewal (**b**) *(d'un style)* change (**c**) *(d'un traité, d'un contrat)* renewal

rénovateur, -trice [renɔvatœr, -tris] **1** *adj* reforming
2 *nm,f* reformer

rénovation [renɔvasjɔ̃] *nf* (**a**) *(d'un bâtiment, du mobilier)* renovation; **en (cours de) r.** undergoing renovation (**b**) *(d'une institution)* updating, reform

rénover [renɔve] *vt* (**a**) *(bâtiment, mobilier)* to renovate (**b**) *(institution)* to update, to reform

renseigné, -e [rɑ̃seɲe] *adj* **bien/mal r.** well-/ill-informed

renseignement [rɑ̃seɲmɑ̃] *nm* (**a**) *(précision)* piece of information; **renseignements** information; **pour tout r....** for information...; **prendre des renseignements sur qn/qch** to make enquiries about sb/sth; **aller aux renseignements** to go and make enquiries (**b**) *Tél* **les renseignements (téléphoniques)** *Br* directory enquiries, *Am* directory assistance (**c**) **les renseignements généraux** = police branch concerned with political security

renseigner [rɑ̃seɲe] **1** *vt* **r. qn (sur qch)** to give sb some information (about sth), to inform sb (about sth)
2 se renseigner *vpr* to make enquiries; *(sur un point précis)* to find out (**sur** about)

rentabiliser [rɑ̃tabilize] *vt* to make profitable

rentabilité [rɑ̃tabilite] *nf* profitability

rentable [rɑ̃tabl] *adj* profitable

rente [rɑ̃t] *nf* (**a**) *(revenu)* **rentes** private income (**b**) *(pension)* annuity, pension; **r. viagère** life annuity (**c**) *(emprunt d'État)* (government) loan

rentier, -ère [rɑ̃tje, -ɛr] *nm,f* person of private means

rentré, -e [rɑ̃tre] *adj* (**a**) *(yeux)* sunken (**b**) *(colère)* suppressed

rentrée [rɑ̃tre] *nf* (**a**) *(retour)* return; **la r. (des classes)** the start of the new school year; **r. parlementaire** reopening of Parliament; **la r. sociale** the return to work (**b**) *(d'argent)* **attendre une r. d'argent** to expect some money

rentrer [rɑ̃tre] **1** *vi* (aux **être**) (**a**) *(entrer de nouveau)* (en s'éloignant) to go in again; (en s'approchant) to come in again; (entrer) to go/come in, to enter; **rentre!** come in! (**b**) *(à la maison)* to go/come back home, to return home; **r. de vacances/de Paris** to come back from holiday/from Paris; **r. en France/à Paris** to return to France/to Paris; **r. dans son pays** to go back to one's own country; **r. tard/tôt** to go or get home late/early; **en rentrant chez moi** on my way home; **en rentrant de l'école** on my/his/*etc* way home from school (**c**) *(reprendre ses occupations)* (école) to re-open; *(élève, professeur)* to go back to (**d**) *(tenir)* (objets) to go in, to fit (in); **je ne rentre plus dans mon pantalon!** I can't get into my trousers! (**e**) *(pénétrer)* to get in; **r. dans qch** to get into

sth (**f**) *(être inclus)* **r. dans une catégorie** to fall into a category (**g**) *(argent)* to come in (**h**) *(recouvrer)* **r. dans ses frais** to recover one's expenses (**i**) **r. dans** *(sujet: voiture)* to crash into; *(sujet: piéton)* to bang into; *Fam Fig* **elle m'est rentrée dedans** *ou* **dans le chou** she laid into me
2 *vt* (aux **avoir**) (**a**) *(linge, troupeau) (en venant)* to bring in; *(en allant)* to take in (**b**) *(introduire, mettre)* to put in; **r. qch dans qch** to put sth into sth (**c**) *(train d'atterrissage)* to retract, to raise; **r. ses griffes** *(chat)* to retract its claws; *Fig* to draw in one's claws; **r. le ventre** to pull one's stomach in (**d**) *(colère, larmes)* to stifle

renversant, -e [rɑ̃versɑ̃, -ɑ̃t] *adj Fam* astounding

renverse [rɑ̃vers] **à la renverse** *adv* **partir** *ou* **tomber à la r.** to fall backwards; *Fig* **j'ai failli tomber à la r.** you could have knocked me over with a feather

renversé, -e [rɑ̃verse] *adj* (**a**) *(à l'envers) (image)* reversed (**b**) *(tombé)* overturned (**c**) *Fam (stupéfait)* staggered

renversement [rɑ̃versəmɑ̃] *nm* (**a**) *(d'une tendance, des rôles)* reversal; *(d'opinions)* (dramatic) shift; **r. de situation** reversal of the situation (**b**) *(d'un gouvernement)* overthrow

renverser [rɑ̃verse] **1** *vt* (**a**) *(tendance, rôles)* to reverse; *(ordre)* to invert; *Fig* **r. la vapeur** to do a U-turn; **r. la situation** to reverse the situation (**b**) *(pencher en arrière)* **r. la tête** to tilt one's head back (**c**) *(faire tomber)* to knock over; *(liquide)* to spill; **se faire r. par une voiture** to be knocked down by a car (**d**) *(gouvernement)* to overthrow (**e**) *Fam (stupéfier)* to stagger
2 se renverser *vpr* (**a**) *(récipient)* to fall over; *(véhicule)* to overturn (**b**) *(personne)* **se r. en arrière** to lean back

renvoi [rɑ̃vwa] *nm* (**a**) *(de lettres, de marchandises, de colis)* return, sending back (**b**) *(d'employés)* dismissal, *Br* sacking; *(d'un élève)* expulsion (**c**) *(ajournement)* postponement; *Jur* adjournment (**d**) *(dans un texte)* cross-reference (**e**) *Jur (devant une autre juridiction)* transfer (**devant** to) (**f**) *(éructation)* burp, belch; **avoir des renvois** to burp, to belch

renvoyer [33] [rɑ̃vwaje] *vt* (**a**) *(au point de départ) (personne)* to send back; *(cadeau, lettre)* to send back, to return; *(ballon)* to throw back; *(balle de tennis)* to return (**b**) *(employé)* to dismiss, *Br* to sack; *(élève)* to expel; *(visiteur)* to send away (**c**) *(son)* to echo; *(chaleur, lumière)* to reflect (**d**) *(ajourner)* to postpone; *Jur* to adjourn (**e**) *(lecteur)* to refer (**à** to); *Ordinat* to cross-refer (**f**) *Jur (devant une autre juridiction)* to transfer (**devant** to)

réorganisation [reɔrganizasjɔ̃] *nf* reorganization

réorganiser [reɔrganize] **1** *vt* to reorganize
2 se réorganiser *vpr* to get reorganized

réorienter [reɔrjɑ̃te] *vt* to reorientate

réouverture [reuvɛrtyr] *nf* reopening

repaire [rəpɛr] *nm (d'animaux)* den, lair; *(de malfrats)* haunt

repaître [50c] [rəpɛtr] *Litt* **1** *vt* **r. ses yeux de qch** to feast one's eyes on sth
2 se repaître *vpr* (**a**) *(manger à satiété)* to eat one's fill (**b**) *Fig* **se r. de qch** to revel in sth

répandre [rəpɑ̃dr] **1** *vt* (**a**) *(renverser) (accidentellement)* to spill; *(volontairement)* to spread (**b**) *(émettre) (lumière)* to shed; *(odeur, chaleur)* to give off (**c**) *(larmes, sang)* to shed (**d**) *(rumeur, terreur, doctrine)* to spread
2 se répandre *vpr* (**a**) *(liquide)* to spill (**b**) *(odeur, chaleur)* to spread (**c**) *(rumeur, opinion, pratique)* to become widespread (**d**) *(foule, touristes)* to spill (**dans** into) (**e**) **se r. en excuses** to apologize profusely

répandu, -e [rəpɑ̃dy] *adj (commun)* widespread

réparable [reparabl] *adj* (**a**) *(chaussure, machine)* repairable (**b**) *(erreur)* which can be put right; *(perte financière)* which can be made up

reparaître [20] [rəparɛtr] *vi* to reappear

réparateur, -trice [reparatœr, -tris] **1** *adj (sommeil)* refreshing **2** *nm,f* repairman, *f* repairwoman

réparation [reparasjɔ̃] *nf* **(a)** *(action)* repairing, mending; *(résultat)* repair; **faire des réparations** to do repairs **(b)** *(dédommagement)* reparation; **demander r. (de qch)** to seek redress (for sth)

réparer [repare] *vt* **(a)** *(toit, appareil, chaussures)* to repair, to mend; *(déchirure, accroc)* to mend **(b)** *(faute)* to make amends for; *(erreur)* to put right, to rectify; *(dommage)* to make good

reparler [rǝparle] *vi* to speak again; **r. à qn** to speak to sb again; **elle ne lui a pas reparlé depuis** she hasn't spoken to him since; **r. de qch** to talk about sth again; **on en reparlera** we'll talk about it later

repartie, répartie [reparti] *nf* retort; **avoir l'esprit de r., avoir de la r.** to be good at repartee

repartir [64a] [rǝpartir] *vi (voyageur, train)* to set off again **(pour** to); *(machine)* to start (up) again; *Fam* **c'est reparti, ils ont encore mis la musique à fond!** they're at it again, they've put their music on full blast!; *Fam* **c'est reparti comme en quarante!** here we go!

répartir [repartir] **1** *vt* **(a)** *(tâches, argent, vivres)* to divide **(entre** between); *(responsabilités)* to allocate **(entre** between); *(frais)* to share **(entre** between) **(b)** *(dans le temps)* to spread (out) **(sur** over) **(c)** *(classifier)* to divide **(en** into) **(d)** *(poids, charge)* to distribute **2 se répartir** *vpr* **(a)** *(se diviser)* to split up **(en** into) **(b)** *(se classer)* to be divided **(en** into) **(c) se r. qch** to divide sth up

répartition [repartisjɔ̃] *nf* **(a)** *(de la population, du poids)* distribution **(b)** *(des tâches, d'argent, de vivres)* distribution **(entre** between); *(des dépenses, des responsabilités)* allocation **(entre** to) **(c)** *(dans le temps)* spreading **(sur** over)

repas [rǝpɑ] *nm* meal; **prendre un r.** to have a meal; **r. d'affaires** business lunch/dinner; **r. chaud/froid** hot/cold meal; **r. de noce** wedding breakfast

repassage [rǝpasaʒ] *nm* ironing; **faire du r.** to do some ironing

repasser [rǝpase] **1** *vi* **(a)** *(passer à nouveau) (aller)* to go by again, to pass by again; *(venir)* to come by again, to pass by again; *(retourner)* to go/come back; **r. chez qn** to drop in on sb again **(b)** *(film)* to be on again **2** *vt* **(a)** *(vêtement)* to iron **(b)** *(montagne, frontière)* to go across again **(c)** *(cassette, disque)* to play again; *(film)* to show again **(d)** *(leçon)* to go over; **r. qch dans son esprit** to go over sth in one's mind; *(examen)* to resit **(f) r. qch à qn** *(donner à nouveau)* to give sb sth again **(g)** *(au téléphone)* **je vous le repasse** I'll put you through to him again

repêchage [rǝpeʃaʒ] *nm* **(a)** *(d'un véhicule, d'un noyé)* fishing out **(b)** *(d'un candidat)* **épreuve de r.** resit; **être reçu au r.** to pass on the resit

repêcher [rǝpeʃe] *vt* **(a)** *(retirer de l'eau)* to fish out **(b)** *(candidat)* to let through

repeindre [54] [rǝpɛ̃dr] *vt* to repaint

repenser [rǝpɑ̃se] **1** *vt (concept)* to rethink **2 repenser à** *vt ind* to think again about; **quand j'y repense** thinking back, when I think back

repenti, -e [rǝpɑ̃ti] *adj* repentant, penitent

repentir¹ [rǝpɑ̃tir] *nm (remords)* regret

repentir² [64a] **se repentir** *vpr* to repent; **se r. de qch/d'avoir fait qch** to repent sth/doing sth; *Fig* to regret sth/doing sth

repérage [rǝperaʒ] *nm* **(a)** *Ordinat* marking, flagging **(b)** *(d'un lieu de tournage)* recce

répercussion [reperkysjɔ̃] *nf* **(a)** *(du son)* reverberation **(b)** *(conséquence)* repercussion **(sur** on)

répercuter [reperkyte] **1** *vt* **(a)** *(son, lumière)* to reflect **(b)** *(ordre, augmentation)* to pass **(sur** on to) **2 se répercuter** *vpr* **(a)** *(son, lumière)* to be reflected **(b)** *(avoir des conséquences)* **se r. sur** to have repercussions on

repère [rǝpɛr] *nm* **(a)** *(point de référence)* mark; *(pour s'orienter)* landmark; *aussi Fig* **point de r.** reference point **(b)** *(dans le temps)* reference point **(c)** *Ordinat* marker, flag

repérer [34] [rǝpere] **1** *vt* **(a)** *(marquer) (terrain)* to mark out **(b)** *(trouver) (défaut, endroit)* to locate; *(lieu de tournage)* to recce **(c)** *Fam (apercevoir)* to spot; **se faire r.** to attract attention **2 se repérer** *vpr* to get one's bearings, to find one's way about

répertoire [repɛrtwar] *nm* **(a)** *(liste)* index, list **(b)** *(carnet)* notebook with alphabetical index; **r. à onglets** thumb index **(c)** *Ordinat* directory; **r. central** *ou* **principal** main directory; **r. racine** root directory **(d)** *(d'un théâtre, d'un artiste)* repertoire

répertorier [repɛrtɔrje] *vt* to list

répéter [34] [repete] **1** *vt* **(a)** *(redire, refaire)* to repeat **(b)** *(pièce de théâtre, rôle)* to rehearse **2** *vi (acteur)* to rehearse **3 se répéter** *vpr (personne)* to repeat oneself; *(événement)* to recur, to happen again; **l'histoire se répète** history repeats itself

répétitif, -ive [repetitif, -iv] *adj* repetitive

répétition [repetisjɔ̃] *nf* **(a)** *(d'un mot, d'une action, d'un événement)* repetition; **fusil à r.** repeating rifle; **avoir des rhumes à r.** to have one cold after another **(b)** *(d'une pièce de théâtre)* rehearsal; **r. générale** dress rehearsal **(c)** *Ordinat* **fonction de r.** repeat function

repeuplement [rǝpœplǝmɑ̃] *nm (d'un pays)* repopulation; *(d'un étang)* restocking; *(d'une forêt)* replanting

repeupler [rǝpœple] **1** *vt (pays)* to repopulate; *(étang)* to restock; *(forêt)* to replant **2 se repeupler** *vpr (pays)* to be repopulated; *(étang)* to be restocked; *(forêt)* to be replanted

repiquage [rǝpikaʒ] *nm* **(a)** *(de plants)* pricking out, planting out **(b)** *(d'un disque, d'une cassette)* taping

repiquer [rǝpike] **1** *vt* **(a)** *(plants)* to prick out, to plant out **(b)** *(disque, cassette)* to record **(c)** *Fam (reprendre)* to catch again **2** *vi Fam* **il y a repiqué** he's been at it again

répit [repi] *nm* respite, breathing space; **sans r.** *(travailler)* without a break, continuously

replacer [16] [rǝplase] **1** *vt (remettre à sa place)* to put back **2 se replacer** *vpr (trouver un emploi)* to find (oneself) a new job

replanter [rǝplɑ̃te] *vt* to replant

replâtrer [rǝplɑtre] *vt* **(a)** *(mur)* to replaster **(b)** *Péj* to patch up

replet, -ète [rǝplɛ, -ɛt] *adj* chubby; **un enfant au visage r.** a chubby-faced child

repli [rǝpli] *nm* **(a)** *(d'une armée)* retreat, withdrawal **(b)** *(de la monnaie, des prix)* fall **(c)** *(d'un vêtement, de la peau, d'un terrain)* fold; *(d'une rivière)* bend

replier [66] [rǝplije] **1** *vt* **(a)** *(objet)* to fold up; *(lame de couteau)* to fold away; *(jambes)* to tuck up; *(ailes)* to fold **(b)** *(troupes)* to withdraw **2 se replier** *vpr* **(a)** *(objet)* to fold up; *Fig* **se r. sur soi-même** to withdraw into oneself **(b)** *(troupes)* to retreat, to withdraw

réplique [replik] *nf* **(a)** *(réponse)* retort, rejoinder; **sans r.** unanswerable **(b)** *(d'un acteur)* line(s); **donner la r. à qn** to play opposite sb **(c)** *(copie)* replica; *(sosie)* double

répliquer [replike] **1** *vt* **r. que** to reply that; **je lui ai**

répliqué que… I replied that…
2 *vi* to reply; *(avec impertinence)* to answer back; **r. à qn** to answer sb back
replonger [45] [rəplɔ̃ʒe] **1** *vt aussi Fig* to plunge back **(dans** into)
2 *vi* **(a)** *(plonger à nouveau)* to dive in again; *Fig* **r. dans l'alcoolisme** to fall back into alcoholism **(b)** *Fam (délinquant)* to reoffend
3 se replonger *vpr* **se r. dans qch** to immerse oneself in sth again
répondant [repɔ̃dɑ̃] *nm Fam* **avoir du r.** to have plenty of money stashed away
répondeur [repɔ̃dœr] *nm* **r. (automatique** *ou* **téléphonique)** (telephone) answering machine, answerphone
répondre [repɔ̃dr] **1** *vt* to answer, to reply; **je n'ai rien répondu** I made no reply
2 répondre à *vt ind* **(a)** *(personne, lettre, question)* to answer, to reply to; *(salut)* to return; *(accusation)* to answer; **elle n'a pas encore répondu** she hasn't answered yet; **r. par un sourire** to answer with a smile; *Mil* **r. à l'appel** to answer the roll **(b)** *(téléphone, porte)* to answer; **laisse, je vais r.!** leave it, I'll get it!; **ça ne répond pas** there's no answer **(c)** *(amour)* to return **(d)** *(besoin, critères)* to meet; **ne pas r. à l'attente de qn** to fall short of sb's expectations **(e)** **les freins ne répondent plus** the brakes aren't responding any more
3 répondre de *vt ind* to answer for; **j'en réponds** I guarantee it; **je ne réponds de rien** I'm promising nothing
4 se répondre *vpr (personnes)* to answer each other
réponse [repɔ̃s] *nf* **(a)** *(à une question, à une lettre)* answer, reply **(a** to); *(à une offre d'emploi)* reply **(à** to); *Fig (solution)* answer **(à** to); **avoir r. à tout** to have an answer for everything **(b)** *(réaction)* response **(c)** *Ordinat* answering; **r. automatique** unattended answering; **temps de r.** response time
report [rəpɔr] *nm* **(a)** *(de notes, de corrections)* transfer **(sur** to) **(b)** *(d'un rendez-vous)* postponement **(c)** *(en comptabilité)* carrying forward **(d)** *(dans une élection)* **r. de voix (sur)** transfer to
reportage [rəpɔrtaʒ] *nm* **(a)** *(article, émission)* report **(b)** *(activité)* reporting
reporter¹ [rəpɔrter] *nm* reporter; **r.-cameraman** film reporter; **r.-photographe** photojournalist
reporter² [rəpɔrte] **1** *vt* **(a)** *(objet)* to take back, to return **(b)** *(affection)* to transfer **(sur** to) **(c)** *(différer)* **r. qch à plus tard** to postpone sth *or* put sth off until later **(d)** *(en comptabilité)* to carry forward **(e)** *(notes, corrections)* to transfer **(sur** to) **(f)** *(dans une élection)* **r. sa voix sur qn** to transfer one's vote to sb
2 se reporter *vpr* **(a)** *(se référer)* **se r. à** *(document)* to refer to **(b)** **se r. sur** *(sujet: colère, affection)* to be transferred to
repos [rəpo] *nm* **(a)** *(détente)* rest; **un mois de r.** a month's rest; **prendre du r.** to rest; **le r. éternel** eternal rest **(b)** *(tranquillité)* peace; **ce n'est pas de tout r.!** it's not exactly restful! **(c)** *Mil* **r.!** (stand) at ease!
reposant, -e [rəpozɑ̃, -ɑ̃t] *adj* restful, relaxing
reposé, -e [rəpoze] *adj* rested, refreshed
repose-pied [rəpozpje] *nm inv* footrest
reposer [rəpoze] **1** *vt* **(a)** *(remettre)* to put back (down), to replace **(b)** *(appuyer)* **r. sa tête contre** *ou* **sur qch** to lean one's head against *or* on sth **(c)** *(détendre)* **(jambes, esprit)** to rest; **ça le reposera** it'll be a rest for him; **une couleur qui repose les yeux** a colour that is restful to the eyes **(d)** *(question)* to ask again; *(problème)* to bring up again; **r. une question à qn** to ask sb a question again **(e)** *Mil* **reposez arme!** order arms!
2 *vi* **(a)** *(s'appuyer)* **r. sur** to rest on; *Fig (être basé sur)* to be based on; *(dépendre de)* to depend on **(b)** *(liquide)* to settle;

(pâte à tarte) to rest **(c)** *(personne décédée)* to lie; **qu'il repose en paix** may he rest in peace
3 se reposer *vpr* **(a)** *(se relaxer)* to rest; **se r. les yeux/les jambes** to rest one's eyes/legs **(b)** *(question, problème)* to crop up again **(c)** **se r. sur qn/qch** *(s'en remettre à)* to rely on sb/sth
repose-tête [rəpoztɛt] *nm inv* headrest
repoussant, -e [rəpusɑ̃, -ɑ̃t] *adj* repulsive
repousser [rəpuse] **1** *vt* **(a)** *(écarter)* to push aside *or* away; *(en arrière)* to push back **(b)** *(ennemi, attaque, avances)* to repel; *(offre, idée)* to reject, to turn down; *(prétendant)* to rebuff **(c)** *(rendez-vous, réunion)* to postpone, to put off **(à** until)
2 *vi* **(arbre, plante)** to shoot up again; *(cheveux, herbe, feuilles)* to grow again
repoussoir [rəpuswar] *nm (femme)* ugly woman; **servir de r. à qn** to serve as a foil to sb
répréhensible [repreɑ̃sibl] *adj* reprehensible
reprendre [58] [rəprɑ̃dr] **1** *vt* **(a)** *(ville, territoire, fugitif)* to recapture (**à** from) **(b)** *(se resservir de)* **r. du pain/vin** to take *or* have some more bread/wine; **vous reprendrez bien un peu de café?** would you like some more coffee? **(c)** *(rechercher)* *(personne)* to pick up (again) **(d)** *(récupérer)* *(objet)* to take back; **r. sa place** *(s'asseoir)* to return to one's seat; *Com* **les articles en solde ne sont ni repris ni échangés** ≃ sale goods are not returnable **(e)** *(surprendre)* **r. qn à faire qch** to catch sb doing sth again; **on ne m'y reprendra plus!** I won't be caught again! **(f)** *(conversation, fonctions, lutte)* to resume, to take up again; *(négociations, relations)* to re-open, to resume; **r. le travail** to return *or* go back to work; **r. connaissance** to regain consciousness; **r. la parole** to speak again; **"oui, mais…", reprit-il** "yes, but…", he continued; *Fam* **ça le reprend!** he's off again! **(g)** *(répéter)* to repeat; *(refrain)* to take up **(h)** *(retoucher)* *(vêtement)* to alter **(i)** *(corriger)* to correct
2 *vi* **(a)** *(recommencer)* *(cours)* to start again; *(pourparlers, hostilités)* to resume, to re-open **(b)** *(prendre de la vigueur)* *(affaires)* to recover, to pick up; *(plante)* to pick up
3 se reprendre *vpr* **(a)** *(se ressaisir)* to pull oneself together **(b)** *(se corriger)* to correct oneself **(c)** *(recommencer)* **s'y r. à plusieurs fois pour faire qch** to make several attempts at doing sth
repreneur [rəprənœr] *nm* purchaser, buyer
représailles [reprezaj] *nfpl* reprisals, retaliation; **en r.** in retaliation, as a reprisal
représentant, -e [reprezɑ̃tɑ̃, -ɑ̃t] *nm,f* representative; **r. de commerce** sales representative
représentatif, -ive [reprezɑ̃tatif, -iv] *adj* representative **(de** of)
représentation [reprezɑ̃tasjɔ̃] *nf* **(a)** *(de la réalité, d'un concept)* representation **(b)** *(spectacle)* performance **(c)** *(métier)* commercial travelling **(d)** *Pol* **r. proportionnelle** proportional representation
représentativité [reprezɑ̃tativite] *nf* representativeness
représenter [reprezɑ̃te] **1** *vt* **(a)** *(candidat, papiers)* to present again **(b)** *(figurer)* to depict; **r. qn sous les traits de** to depict sb as **(c)** *(être le porte-parole de)* to represent **(d)** *(constituer, équivaloir à)* to represent; **r. qch pour qn** to represent sth for sb
2 se représenter *vpr* **(a)** *(occasion)* to arise again **(b)** *(s'imaginer)* to imagine **(c)** **se r. à** *(examen)* to retake *or Br* resit; *(poste)* to stand again; **se r. aux élections** to run for election again
répressif, -ive [represif, -iv] *adj* repressive
répression [represjɔ̃] *nf* repression; *(d'une émeute, abus)* suppression

réprimande [reprimɑ̃d] *nf* reprimand, rebuke; **faire des réprimandes à qn** to reprimand *or* rebuke sb
réprimander [reprimɑ̃de] *vt* to reprimand, to rebuke
réprimer [reprime] *vt* (a) *(retenir)* to repress, to suppress (b) *(crime, révolte)* to suppress
repris [rəpri] *nm* **r. de justice** ex-prisoner
reprise [rəpriz] *nf* (a) *(d'un débat, des hostilités)* resumption; *(des négociations)* re-opening, resumption (b) *(des affaires)* upturn, recovery; **les grévistes ont voté la r. du travail** the strikers have voted to go back to work; **r. économique** economic recovery (c) *(d'une émission télévisée)* repeat (d) *(d'un moteur)* pick-up, acceleration (e) à **plusieurs/trois reprises** several/three times (f) *(raccommodage)* **faire une r. à qch** to mend sth (g) *(somme payée à un locataire)* = money paid for fixtures and fittings *(paid to outgoing tenant)*; *(rachat d'un objet d'occasion)* part exchange, trade-in
repriser [rəprize] *vt* to mend
réprobateur, -trice [reprɔbatœr, -tris] *adj* reproving
réprobation [reprɔbasjɔ̃] *nf* reproof
reproche [rəprɔʃ] *nm* (a) *(remontrance)* reproach; **faire des reproches à qn (sur qch)** to reproach sb (for sth); **sans r.** *(vie, personne)* above reproach, blameless (b) *(critique)* criticism
reprocher [rəprɔʃe] **1** *vt* **r. qch à qn** to blame *or* reproach sb for sth; **r. à qn de faire qch** to blame *or* reproach sb for doing sth; **je ne vous reproche rien** I'm not blaming you for anything; **qu'est-ce que vous reprochez à ce livre?** what have you got against the book?
2 se reprocher *vpr* **se r. qch** to blame *or* reproach oneself for sth; **tu n'as rien à te r.** you've nothing to blame yourself for
reproducteur, -trice [rəprɔdyktœr, -tris] *adj* reproductive
reproduction [rəprɔdyksjɔ̃] *nf* (a) *(sexuelle)* reproduction (b) *(d'un document, d'une image, du son)* reproduction, reproducing; *(copie)* reproduction
reproduire [18] [rəprɔdɥir] **1** *vt* (a) *(son, image, document)* to reproduce; **nous reproduisons ici l'article du Monde** we reprint here the article from Le Monde (b) *(acte)* to repeat
2 se reproduire *vpr* (a) *(sexuellement)* to reproduce (b) *(événement)* to recur, to happen again
reprogrammable [rəprɔgramabl] *adj Ordinat (touche)* reprogrammable
reprogrammer [rəprɔgrame] *vt Ordinat* to reprogram
réprouver [repruve] *vt* to condemn
reptation [reptasjɔ̃] *nf* crawling
reptile [reptil] *nm* reptile
repu, -e [rəpy] **1** *pp voir* **repaître**
2 *adj* pleasantly full
républicain, -e [repyblikɛ̃, -ɛn] *adj & nm,f* republican
république [repyblik] *nf* republic; **r. bananière** banana republic; **la R. centrafricaine** the Central African Republic; *Anciennement* **la R. démocratique allemande** the German Democratic Republic; **la R. dominicaine** the Dominican Republic; *Anciennement* **la R. fédérale d'Allemagne** the Federal Republic of Germany; **la R. d'Irlande** the Republic of Ireland; **la R. Tchèque** the Czech Republic
répudiation [repydjasjɔ̃] *nf* repudiation
répudier [66] [repydje] *vt* to repudiate
répugnance [repyɲɑ̃s] *nf* (a) *(aversion)* repugnance, loathing (**pour** for); **avoir de la r. pour qn/qch** to loathe sb/sth (b) *(appréhension)* reluctance (à **faire qch** to do sth)
répugnant, -e [repyɲɑ̃, -ɑ̃t] *adj* repulsive

répugner [repyɲe] *vi* (a) *(appréhender)* **r. à faire qch** to be reluctant to do sth (b) *(être répugnant)* **r. à qn** to be repugnant to sb, to repel sb
répulsion [repylsjɔ̃] *nf* repulsion
réputation [repytasjɔ̃] *nf* reputation; **avoir (une) bonne/mauvaise r.** to have a good/bad reputation; **sa r. de chirurgien** his reputation as a surgeon; **connaître qn de r.** to know sb by reputation; **avoir la r. d'être franc** to have a reputation for being frank
réputé, -e [repyte] *adj* well-known, renowned (**pour** for); **être r.** to be reputed to be intelligent
requérir [7] [rəkerir] *vt* (a) *(solliciter)* *(faveur)* to ask for, to seek; *(présence, aide)* to request (b) *(nécessiter)* *(explication, soin, patience)* to require, to call for (c) *Jur (sentence)* to demand, to call for
requête [rəkɛt] *nf* (a) *(demande)* request; *Ordinat* query; **adresser une r. à qn** to make a request to sb (b) *Jur* petition
requiem [rekɥijɛm] *nm inv* requiem
requiers, requiert *voir* **requérir**
requin [rəkɛ̃] *nm* shark
requinquer [rəkɛ̃ke] *Fam* **1** *vt* to perk up
2 se requinquer *vpr* to perk up
requis, -e [rəki, -iz] **1** *pp voir* **requérir**
2 *adj* requisite, required; **les conditions requises** the requirements
réquisition [rekizisjɔ̃] *nf* (a) *(de vivres, de véhicules)* requisitioning, commandeering (b) *Jur (plaidoirie)* prosecution address
réquisitionner [rekizisjɔne] *vt* to requisition, to commandeer
réquisitoire [rekizitwar] *nm Jur* prosecution address; *Fig* indictment (**contre** of)
RER [ɛrəɛr] *nm (abrév* **Réseau express régional)** = express rail network serving Paris and its suburbs
RESA [reza] *nf (abrév* **réservation)** = TGV seat reservation ticket
rescapé, -e [rɛskape] **1** *adj* surviving
2 *nm,f* survivor
rescousse [rɛskus] *nf* **aller/venir à la r. de qn** to go/come to sb's rescue; **appeler qn à la r.** to call on sb for help
réseau, -x [rezo] *nm* (a) *(de routes, de voies ferrées, de rivières)* network, system; **r. autoroutier** *Br* motorway *or Am* freeway network; **r. ferroviaire** rail network (b) *Fig (de relations)* network, circle (c) *Ordinat* network; **mise en r.** networking; **r. de télématique** *ou* **de communication de données** datacomms network; **r. de données** data network; **r. local** local area network, LAN; **grand r.** wide area network, WAN; **r. numérique à intégration de services** integrated services digital network; **r. à valeur ajoutée** value-added network, VAN
réséda [rezeda] *nm* reseda
réservation [rezɛrvasjɔ̃] *nf* reservation, booking; **faire une r.** to make a reservation
réserve [rezɛrv] *nf* (a) *(restriction)* reservation; **émettre des réserves (sur qch)** to have reservations (about sth); **sous r. de qch** subject to sth; **sans r.** *(éloges, admiration)* unqualified (b) *(discrétion)* reserve; **sortir de sa r.** to come out of one's shell (c) *(de vivres, d'équipement, d'argent)* reserve; **en r.** in reserve (d) *Mil* reserve (e) *(de chasse, de pêche)* reserve; *Can* **r. faunique** wildlife reserve; **r. indienne** (Native American) reservation; **r. naturelle** nature reserve (f) *(de magasin)* storeroom; *(de bibliothèque, de musée)* reserve collection
réservé, -e [rezɛrve] *adj* (a) *(chambre, siège)* reserved,

booked (**b**) *(consacré)* **être r.** **à qn/qch** to be reserved for sb/sth (**c**) *(personne, attitude)* reserved
réserver [rezɛrve] **1** *vt* (**a**) *(chambre, place)* to reserve, to book; **vous avez réservé?** do you have a reservation? (**b**) *(mettre de côté)* to set aside, to put by (**à/pour** for); **r. le meilleur pour la fin** to save the best till last (**c**) *Fig* **r. son jugement** to reserve judgement; **r. une surprise à qn** to have a surprise in store for sb; **r. un bon accueil à qn** to welcome sb with open arms; **ce que le sort nous réserve** what fate has in store for us
2 se réserver *vpr* (**a**) *(garder pour soi)* **se r. qch** to keep sth for oneself; **se r. le droit de faire qch** to reserve the right to do sth (**b**) **se r. pour qch** to save oneself for sth
réserviste [rezɛrvist] *nm Mil* reservist
réservoir [rezɛrvwar] *nm* (**a**) *(bassin)* reservoir (**b**) *(cuve)* tank; **r. d'essence** *Br* petrol *or Am* gas tank
résidence [rezidɑ̃s] *nf* (**a**) *(demeure)* residence; **r. principale** main residence; **r. secondaire** second home; *Univ* **r. universitaire** *Br* hall of residence, *Am* dormitory (**b**) *(habitations de standing) Br* block of luxury flats, *Am* luxury apartment building (**c**) *Jur* **en r. surveillée** under house arrest (**d**) *(séjour)* residence
résident, -e [rezidɑ̃, -ɑ̃t] **1** *adj* (**a**) *(personne)* resident (**b**) *Ordinat* **r. en mémoire** memory-resident
2 *nm,f* (**a**) *(habitant)* resident (**b**) *(étranger)* foreign resident; **les résidents français en Grande-Bretagne** French nationals resident in Great Britain
résidentiel, -elle [rezidɑ̃sjɛl] *adj* residential
résider [rezide] *vi* (**a**) *(personne)* to reside (**b**) *(consister)* to lie (**dans** in)
résidu [rezidy] *nm (reste)* residue; **résidus** *(déchets)* waste
résiduel, -elle [reziduɛl] *adj* residual
résignation [rezinasjɔ̃] *nf* resignation
résigné, -e [rezine] *adj* resigned (**à** to)
résigner [rezine] **se résigner** *vpr* to resign oneself (**à** to); **se r. à faire qch** to resign oneself to doing sth
résiliable [reziljabl] *adj (contrat)* which may be terminated
résiliation [reziljasjɔ̃] *nf (d'un contrat)* termination
résilier [rezilje] *vt (accord, contrat)* to terminate
résille [rezij] *nf* hairnet
résine [rezin] *nf* resin
résiné [rezine] *adj m & nm* (**vin**) **r.** retsina
résineux, -euse [rezinø, -øz] **1** *adj* (**a**) *(bois, odeur)* resinous (**b**) *(arbre, forêt)* coniferous
2 *nm* conifer
résistance [rezistɑ̃s] *nf* (**a**) *(action)* resistance (**à** to); **n'offrir aucune r.** to put up *or* offer no resistance; **opposer une r. à qn/qch** to resist sb/sth; **r. passive** passive resistance (**b**) *Hist* **la R.** the Resistance (**c**) *(endurance)* stamina (**d**) *Él* resistance (**e**) *(conducteur) (d'un appareil)* element (**f**) *(d'un matériau)* resistance
résistant, -e [rezistɑ̃, -ɑ̃t] **1** *adj (matériau)* tough; *(plante)* hardy; **c'est quelqu'un de très r.** he has a lot of stamina
2 *nm,f (combattant)* freedom fighter; *(pendant la Résistance)* member of the Resistance
résister [reziste] **résister à** *vt ind* (**a**) *(attaque, agresseur)* to resist (**b**) *(tentation, influence, personne)* to resist; **je n'ai pas pu r., je les ai achetées** I couldn't resist, I bought them (**c**) *(supporter) (douleur, pression, froid)* to withstand; *(mauvais traitement)* to stand up to; *(maladie, épidémie, fatigue)* to overcome (**d**) *(s'opposer à)* to stand up to
résolu, -e [rezɔly] **1** *pp voir* **résoudre**
2 *adj (personne)* determined, resolute; **être r. à faire qch** to be determined to do sth
résolument [rezɔlymɑ̃] *adv* resolutely

résolution [rezɔlysjɔ̃] *nf* (**a**) *(décision)* resolution; **prendre la r. de faire qch** to make a resolution to do sth; **prendre des résolutions** to make resolutions (**b**) *(d'un problème)* solving (**c**) *(détermination)* determination, resolve (**d**) *(d'un écran)* resolution
résolvais *etc voir* **résoudre**
résonance [rezɔnɑ̃s] *nf aussi Tech* resonance; *Fig (écho)* echo
résonner [rezɔne] *vi* (**a**) *(retentir)* to resound (**b**) *(faire un écho)* to echo
résorber [rezɔrbe] **1** *vt* (**a**) *(surplus, déficit)* to absorb; *(chômage)* to bring down; *(dettes)* to clear (**b**) *(sang, pus)* to resorb
2 se résorber *vpr* (**a**) *(surplus, déficit)* to be absorbed; *(chômage)* to be brought down (**b**) *(sang, pus)* to be resorbed
résorption [rezɔrpsjɔ̃] *nf (d'un surplus, d'un déficit)* absorption; *(du chômage)* bringing down
résoudre [3b] [rezudr] **1** *vt* (**a**) *(difficulté, conflit, crise)* to resolve; *(équation, énigme, problème)* to solve (**b**) *(décider)* **r. de faire qch** to resolve to do sth (**c**) *(décomposer)* **r. qch en qch** to resolve sth into sth
2 se résoudre *vpr* **se r. à faire qch** to resolve to do sth; **je ne peux pas me r. à la quitter** I can't bring myself to leave her
respect [rɛspɛ] *nm* respect *(pour* for); **avoir du r. pour qn** to have respect for sb; **manquer de r. envers qn** to show sb a lack of respect; **tenir qn en r.** to keep sb at a distance; **sauf le r. que je vous dois, sauf votre r.** with all due respect; **respects** *(hommages)* respects
respectabilité [rɛspɛktabilite] *nf* respectability
respectable [rɛspɛktabl] *adj* respectable
respecter [rɛspɛkte] *vt* to respect; **faire r. la loi** to enforce the law; **se faire r.** to command respect; **r. la priorité** *(en voiture)* to give way
2 se respecter *vpr* (**a**) *(soi-même)* to respect oneself; **comme tout homme qui se respecte** like any self-respecting man (**b**) *(l'un l'autre)* to respect each other
respectif, -ive [rɛspɛktif, -iv] *adj* respective
respectivement [rɛspɛktivmɑ̃] *adv* respectively
respectueusement [rɛspɛktyøzmɑ̃] *adv* respectfully
respectueux, -euse [rɛspɛktyø, -øz] *adj* respectful (**de/envers** of/to)
respirable [rɛspirabl] *adj* breathable; *Fig* **l'atmosphère n'était plus r.** the atmosphere had become oppressive
respirateur [rɛspiratœr] *nm* respirator
respiration [rɛspirasjɔ̃] *nf* breathing; **reprendre sa r.** to pause for breath; **retenir sa r.** to hold one's breath; **r. artificielle** artificial respiration
respiratoire [rɛspiratwar] *adj (organe)* respiratory; *(appareil, exercice, problème)* breathing
respirer [rɛspire] **1** *vi* (**a**) *(personne, plante)* to breathe (**b**) *Fig (être soulagé)* **je respire!** I can breathe again! (**c**) *Fig (se reposer)* to have a break
2 *vt* (**a**) *(inhaler)* to breathe (in) (**b**) *(exprimer)* **r. la santé** to be glowing with health; **il ne respire pas l'intelligence** he doesn't exactly radiate intelligence
resplendir [rɛsplɑ̃dir] *vi* (**a**) *(briller)* to shine (**b**) *(personne)* to be radiant; **r. de joie/santé** to radiate joy/health
resplendissant, -e [rɛsplɑ̃disɑ̃, -ɑ̃t] *adj (personne, beauté)* radiant; **r. de joie/santé** radiant with joy/health; **il a une mine resplendissante** he looks wonderfully well
responsabiliser [rɛspɔ̃sabilize] *vt* **r. qn** to give sb a sense of responsibility
responsabilité [rɛspɔ̃sabilite] *nf (morale)* responsibility; *(légale)* liability (**de** for); **accepter une r.** to take on *or* accept

a responsibility; **avoir la r. de qn/qch** to be responsible for sb/sth; **décliner toute r.** to accept no liability; **avoir un poste à responsabilités** to have a responsible job; **r. civile** public liability; **r. limitée** limited liability; **r. au tiers** third-party liability

responsable [rɛspɔ̃sabl] **1** *adj* (**a**) *(moralement)* responsible (**de** for); *(légalement)* liable (**de** for) (**b**) *(mûr)* responsible
2 *nmf* (**a**) *(auteur, coupable)* person responsible (**de** for); **qui est le r. de cette plaisanterie?** who's responsible for this prank? (**b**) *(personne qui a la responsabilité)* person in charge (**c**) *(dirigeant élu)* official

resquiller [rɛskije] *vi (au théâtre, au concert)* to sneak in without paying; *(dans un bus, dans le métro)* to dodge paying one's fare

resquilleur, -euse [rɛskijœr, -øz] *nm,f (au théâtre, au cinéma)* = person who sneaks in without paying; *(dans un bus, dans le métro)* fare-dodger

ressac [rəsak] *nm* undertow

ressaisir [rəsezir] **se ressaisir** *vpr* to pull oneself together

ressasser [rəsase] *vt* (**a**) *(mentalement)* to brood over (**b**) *(répéter)* to keep coming out with

ressemblance [rəsɑ̃blɑ̃s] *nf (entre personnes)* resemblance, likeness; *(entre choses)* similarity

ressemblant, -e [rəsɑ̃blɑ̃, -ɑ̃t] *adj (portrait)* lifelike

ressembler [rəsɑ̃ble] **1 ressembler à** *vt ind* (**a**) *(personne)* to resemble, to be like; **à quoi ressemble-t-il?** what does he look like? (**b**) *Fig (chose)* **cela ne ressemble à rien** it doesn't look like anything; **cela ne lui ressemble pas** that's not like her
2 se ressembler *vpr* to be alike, to resemble each other; **ils se ressemblent comme des frères** you'd think they were brothers; **se r. comme deux gouttes d'eau** to be as like as two peas in a pod; **les jours se suivent et ne se ressemblent pas** day follows day and you never know what to expect; *Prov* **qui se ressemble s'assemble** birds of a feather flock together

ressemeler [42] [rəsəmle] *vt* to resole

ressentiment [rəsɑ̃timɑ̃] *nm* resentment (**de/contre** at/against)

ressentir [64a] [rəsɑ̃tir] **1** *vt* to feel
2 se ressentir *vpr* **se r. de qch** *(personne, pays)* to feel the effects of sth; *(travail)* to show the effects of sth

resserrement [rəsɛrmɑ̃] *nm (d'une amitié, de liens)* strengthening

resserrer [rəsere] **1** *vt* (**a**) *(nœud, ceinture, écrou)* to tighten (**b**) *Fig (amitié, liens)* to strengthen
2 se resserrer *vpr* (**a**) *(vallée, route)* to narrow (**b**) *(nœud)* to tighten (**c**) *Fig (liens)* to strengthen

resservir [63] [rəsɛrvir] **1** *vt (plat)* to serve up again; **r. qn** to give sb another helping
2 *vi* to be used again (**à** for)
3 se resservir *vpr* **se r. de qch** *(plat)* to take another helping of sth; *(objet)* to use sth again

ressort [rəsɔr] *nm* (**a**) *(pièce)* spring (**b**) *(force morale)* resilience; **avoir du r.** to be resilient (**c**) *(motivation)* motive (**d**) **être du r. de qn** to be sb's responsibility (**e**) **en dernier r.** *Jur* without appeal; *Fig* as a last resort

ressortir¹ [rəsɔrtir] **1** *vi (aux être)* (**a**) *(personne) (en s'éloignant)* to go back out; *(en s'approchant)* to come back out (**b**) *(se détacher)* to stand out; **faire r.** *(couleur)* to bring out; *(regard, yeux, fait)* to highlight
2 *vt (aux avoir)* (**a**) *(parapluie, vêtements)* to get out again (**b**) *Fig (histoire)* to trot out again
3 *v impersonnel (aux être)* **il ressort de ceci que...** it emerges from this that...

ressortir² ressortir à *vt ind* (**a**) *(être de la compétence de)* to come under the jurisdiction of (**b**) *Litt (dépendre de)* to come within the province of

ressortissant, -e [rəsɔrtisɑ̃, -ɑ̃t] *nm,f* national

ressouder [rəsude] **1** *vt* to resolder; *Fig* to reestablish
2 se ressouder *vpr (os, fracture)* to knit

ressource [rəsurs] *nf* (**a**) *(moyen)* possibility; **je n'ai d'autre r. que de...** the only course of action open to me is to...; **avoir de la r.** to be resourceful; **en dernière r.** as a last resort (**b**) **ressources** *(argent, moyens d'action)* resources; **être sans ressources** to be without means; **ressources humaines** human resources (**c**) *(d'une nation)* **ressources** resources

ressourcer [16] [rəsurse] **se ressourcer** *vpr Fam* to get back in touch with one's roots

ressusciter [resysite] **1** *vt* (**a**) *(un mort)* to raise from the dead; *Fig* **ça ne va pas le r.** it won't bring him back (**b**) *Fig (querelle, mode)* to revive
2 *vi* to rise from the dead; **j'ai l'impression de r.** I feel like a new person

restant, -e [rɛstɑ̃, -ɑ̃t] **1** *adj* remaining
2 *nm* remainder, rest

restaurant [rɛstɔrɑ̃] *nm* restaurant; **aller au r.** to eat out; **r. d'entreprise** staff canteen; **r. universitaire** university canteen or cafeteria

restaurateur, -trice [rɛstɔratœr, -tris] *nm,f* (**a**) *(de tableaux)* restorer (**b**) *(de restaurant)* restaurateur, restaurant owner

restauration [rɛstɔrasjɔ̃] *nf* (**a**) *(de tableaux, de bâtiments)* restoration (**b**) *(métier)* catering; **r. rapide** fast food (**c**) *Hist* **la R.** the Restoration *(return to power of the Bourbon dynasty 1814–1830)* (**d**) *Ordinat* restore (**e**) *Suisse (restaurant)* restaurant

restaurer [rɛstɔre] **1** *vt* (**a**) *(rétablir, réparer)* to restore (**b**) *Ordinat* to restore (**c**) *Litt (faire manger)* **r. qn** to give sb something to eat
2 se restaurer *vpr* to have something to eat

reste [rɛst] *nm* (**a**) *(de travail, d'argent, de vin)* rest, remainder; **le r. du temps** the rest of the time; **le r. (des gens)** the rest; **il y avait un r. de soupe/lait** there was a bit of soup/milk left (over) (**b**) **restes** *(d'un repas)* leftovers (**c**) *(ossements)* **restes** remains (**d**) *(locutions)* **du** *ou* **au r.** besides; **pour le r.** as for the rest; **avoir qch de r.** to have sth to spare; **pour ne pas être en r.** *(pour ne pas avoir de dette)* so as not to be indebted; *(pour ne pas être surpassé)* so as not to be outdone; **partir sans demander son r.** to leave without further ado; *Fam* **avoir de beaux restes** to still have one's looks

rester [rɛste] *(aux* **être)** **1** *vi* (**a**) *(subsister)* to remain, to be left; **les 2 euros qui restent** the remaining 2 euros, the 2 euros left; **c'est tout ce qui me reste** that's all I have left; **le nom lui est resté** the name stayed with him (**b**) *(demeurer)* to stay, to remain; **restez où vous êtes** stay where you are; **r. assis** to stay seated; **r. au lit** to stay in bed; **r. (à) dîner** to stay to dinner; **r. sur place** to stay put; *Fam* **j'y suis, j'y reste** here I am and here I stay; *Fam* **y r.** *(mourir)* to kick the bucket; **que cela reste entre nous** this is strictly between ourselves; **r. sur une impression** to be left with an impression; **cela m'est resté sur l'estomac** *(plat)* it's lying heavy on my stomach; *Fig* it still rankles with me; **en r. là** to stop there; **r. dans les mémoires** to live on in people's memories; **le plus dur reste à faire** the hardest part is still to be done
2 *v impersonnel* **il me reste 5 euros** I've got 5 euros left; **il ne me reste qu'à vous remercier** it only remains for me to thank you; **il reste beaucoup de choses à faire** there are still a lot of things to be done; **il reste que...** the fact remains that...; **il n'en reste pas moins que...** it is

restituer nevertheless the case that...; **(ii) reste à savoir si c'est vrai** it remains to be seen whether it's true

restituer [rɛstitɥe] *vt* **(a)** *(reconstituer) (inscription, texte)* to restore; *(passé, ambiance)* to recreate **(b)** *(rendre) (objets volés)* to restore, to return; *(argent, prêt)* to repay, to pay back **(c)** *(son)* to reproduce

restitution [rɛstitysjɔ̃] *nf* **(a)** *(reconstitution) (d'un texte)* restoration; *(d'une ambiance, du passé)* recreation **(b)** *(d'objets volés)* return; *(d'argent, d'un prêt)* repayment **(c)** *(du son)* reproduction

Restoroute® [rɛstorut] *nm Br* motorway *or Am* freeway restaurant

restreindre [54] [rɛstrɛ̃dr] **1** *vt* to restrict (**à** to) **2 se restreindre** *vpr* **(a)** *(réduire ses dépenses)* to cut down **(b)** *(domaine, recherche)* to become more restricted

restreint, -e [rɛstrɛ̃, -ɛ̃t] *adj (production, vocabulaire)* restricted (**à** to); *(espace, service)* limited

restrictif, -ive [rɛstriktif, -iv] *adj* restrictive

restriction [rɛstriksjɔ̃] *nf (diminution)* restriction **(b)** *(réserve)* reservation; **faire des restrictions** to express some reservations; **sans r.** *(accord)* unconditional; *(approuver)* unreservedly **(c)** *Ordinat* **r. d'accès** access restriction **(d) restrictions** *(mesures de rationnement)* restrictions

restructuration [rɔstryktyrasjɔ̃] *nf* restructuring

restructurer [rastryktyre] *vt* to restructure

résultant, -e [rezyltɑ̃, -ɑ̃t] **1** *adj* resulting **2** *nf* **résultante** consequence, result

résultat [rezylta] *nm* result; **sans r.** to no effect; *Fam* **r.: il a été licencié** the upshot was he was dismissed; **donner des résultats** to produce results; **résultats d'exercice** *ou* **d'exploitation** trading results

résulter [rezylte] **1** *v i* **r. de qch** to result from sth **2** *v impersonnel* **il en résulte que...** the result of this is that...

résumé [rezyme] *nm* **(a)** *(d'un texte)* summary, résumé; **faire le r.** *(d'un texte)* to give a summary of sth; *(d'une histoire, d'une situation)* to sum up sth; **en r.** *(en bref)* in short **(b)** *(livre)* study guide

résumer [rezyme] **1** *vt (article, idées)* to summarize, *(situation, histoire)* to sum up **2 se résumer** *vpr* **(a)** *(personne)* to sum up **(b)** *(se réduire)* **se r. à qch** to come down to sth

résurgence [rezyrʒɑ̃s] *nf* resurgence

resurgir [rəsyrʒir] *vi* to reappear suddenly

résurrection [rezyrɛksjɔ̃] *nf aussi Fig* resurrection

rétabli, -e [retabli] *adj (après une maladie)* recovered

rétablir [retablir] **1** *vt* **(a)** *(téléphone, eau, gaz)* to restore **(b)** *(guérir)* to restore to health **(c)** *(faits, vérité)* to re-establish **(d)** *(ordre, relations, réputation)* to restore **(e)** *(réhabiliter)* **r. qn (dans ses fonctions)** to reinstate sb; **r. qn dans ses droits** to restore sb's rights **2 se rétablir** *vpr* **(a)** *(malade)* to recover **(b)** *(silence, calme)* to return; *(situation)* to return to normal

rétablissement [retablismɑ̃] *nm* **(a)** *(de l'ordre, de la paix, d'une dynastie)* restoration **(b)** *(des communications, des relations)* restoration **(c)** *(d'un employé)* reinstatement **(d)** *(d'un malade)* recovery

rétamé, -e [retame] *adj Fam (fatigué)* whacked; *(ivre)* wasted

rétamer [retame] *vt* **(a)** *(casserole)* to retin; *(miroir)* to resilver **(b)** *Fam (épuiser)* to wear out; *(enivrer)* to knock out; **un verre de vin suffit à me r.** one glass of wine is enough to knock me out **(c)** *Fam (au jeu)* to clean out; **se faire r.** *(se faire battre)* to get hammered

retaper [rətape] **1** *vt* **(a)** *Fam (vieille maison, voiture)* to do

up **(b)** *Fam (lit)* to straighten **(c)** *Fam* **r. qn** to buck sb up **2 se retaper** *vpr Fam (convalescent)* to get back on one's feet

retard [rətar] *nm* **(a)** *(dans le temps)* delay; *(d'une personne attendue)* lateness; **je vous prie d'excuser mon r.** please excuse me for being late; **être en r.** to be late; *(sur un programme)* to be behind; **sans r.** without delay; **avoir du r.** to be late; **avoir une heure de r.** to be an hour late; **prendre du r.** *(personne)* to fall behind, *(train)* to be running late; **r. de paiement** late payment **(b)** *(dans un développement)* backwardness; **pays en r. sur les autres** country lagging behind the others; **être en r. pour son âge** to be backward for one's age; **en r. sur son temps** behind the times; **r. mental** backwardness **(c)** *(d'un véhicule)* **r. à l'allumage** retarded ignition

retardataire [rətardatɛr] **1** *nmf* latecomer **2** *adj* **un élève r.** a pupil who arrives late

retardé, -e [rətarde] *adj* **(a)** *(départ, arrivée)* late **(b)** *(mentalement) (enfant)* backward

retardement [rətardəmɑ̃] *nm* **à r.** *(bombe)* time; *(long-temps après)* belatedly

retarder [rətarde] **1** *vt* **(a)** *(faire arriver en retard)* to delay; **r. qn dans ses études** to hold sb back in his/her studies **(b)** *(différer)* to delay; **r. qch d'une heure/d'une semaine** to put sth back an hour/a week **(c)** *(montre, horloge)* to put back **(de** by) **2** *vi* **(a)** *(horloge)* to be slow; **ma montre retarde/je retarde de dix minutes** my watch is/I'm ten minutes slow **(b)** **r. sur son temps** *ou* **son époque** to be behind the times **(c)** *Fam (ne pas être au courant)* to be behind the times

retendre [rətɑ̃dr] *vt (cordes)* to retighten

retenir [70] [rətənir] **1** *vt* **(a)** *(faire rester) (personne)* to keep, to detain; **r. qn prisonnier/en otage** to keep *or* hold sb prisoner/hostage; **je ne vous retiens pas** I won't hold you back; **r. qn à dîner** to have sb stay for dinner; **r. qn par le bras** to hold sb back by the arm; **r. l'attention de qn** *(candidature, proposition)* to catch sb's attention **(b)** *(conserver) (eau, chaleur)* to retain **(c)** *(retirer) (argent)* to withhold; *(cotisation, impôt)* to deduct **(sur** from); **retenu à la source** deducted at source **(d)** *(se souvenir de) (leçon, nom)* to remember; **je le retiens, ton ami!** I won't forget your friend in a hurry! **(e)** *(réserver) (place, chambre, table)* to reserve, to book **(f)** *(accepter) (projet, suggestion)* to adopt; **votre candidature n'a pas été retenue** your application was unsuccessful **(g)** *(contenir) (colère)* to contain; *(larmes)* to hold back; *(cri)* to stifle; *(respiration, souffle)* to hold **(h)** *(garder en arrière) (personne, foule, chien)* to hold back, to restrain **(i)** *(empêcher)* **r. qn de faire qch** to restrain sb from doing sth, to hold sb back from doing sth; **qu'est-ce qui te retient de le lui dire?** what's stopping you telling her?; **qu'est-ce qui vous retient?** what's holding you back? **2 se retenir** *vpr* **(a)** *(s'accrocher)* to hold on **(à** to) **(b)** *(se contenir)* to restrain oneself; **se r. de faire qch** to stop oneself (from) doing sth

rétention [retɑ̃sjɔ̃] *nf* retention; **faire de la r. d'information** to withhold information

retentir [rətɑ̃tir] *vi* **(a)** *(Klaxon®, alarme)* to sound; *(tonnerre, canon)* to rumble; *(coup de feu, cri)* to ring out; **l'explosion retentit dans toute la ville** the explosion was heard right across the city **(b)** *(lieu)* **r. de** to resound *or* echo with **(c)** *Fig* **r. sur** to have an impact on

retentissant, -e [rətɑ̃tisɑ̃, -ɑ̃t] *adj* **(a)** *(voix)* ringing **(b)** *(succès, échec)* resounding; *(scandale)* sensational

retentissement [rətɑ̃tismɑ̃] *nm (d'un événement)* impact; **avoir un r. sur qch** to have an impact on sth

retenue [rətəny] *nf* **(a)** *(d'une somme)* deduction; **r. sur salaire** wage deduction; *(mensuel)* salary deduction **(b)** *(dans un calcul)* carry over; **n'oublie pas la r.** don't forget to carry over (**c**) *Scol* detention (**d**) *(discrétion)* restraint (**e**) *(barrage)* dam

réticence [retisãs] *nf* hesitation, unwillingness; **sans r.** unhesitatingly

réticent, -e [retisã, -ãt] *adj (hésitant)* hesitant, unwilling

rétif, -ive [retif, -iv] *adj (cheval)* stubborn; *(personne)* recalcitrant

rétine [retin] *nf* retina

retiré, -e [rətire] *adj* (**a**) *(lieu, vie)* secluded; **vivre r. du monde** to lead a secluded life (**b**) **être r. des affaires** to be retired from business

retirer [rətire] **1** *vt* (**a**) *(faire sortir)* to take out; *(objet coincé)* to get out; *(bouchon, épine)* to pull out (**de** of); **r. un enfant d'une école** to remove a child from a school; **r. qch de la circulation** to withdraw sth from circulation; **r. qch du marché** to take sth off the market; **r. les mains de ses poches** to take one's hands out of one's pockets (**b**) *(argent)* to withdraw (**de** from), to take out (**de** of); *(bagages, billet)* to collect (**de** from), to pick up (**de** from) (**c**) *(obtenir)* **r. un profit de qch** to make a profit out of sth; **r. du plaisir de qch** to get pleasure from sth (**d**) *(ôter) (gants, lunettes, vêtement)* to take off, to remove (**e**) *(confisquer)* to take away (**à** from); **r. son permis de conduire à qn** to ban sb from driving (**f**) *(ramener en arrière) (main)* to remove (**g**) *(ne pas maintenir) (offre, plainte, candidature)* to withdraw; **je retire ce que j'ai dit** I take back what I said

2 se retirer *vpr* (**a**) *(s'en aller) (personne)* to withdraw; *(foule)* to move back; **vous pouvez vous r.** you may go (**b**) *(eaux, mer)* to recede; *(marée)* to ebb (**c**) **se r. d'une association/élection** to withdraw from a partnership/an election; **se r. des affaires** to retire from business

retombées [rətɔ̃be] *nfpl* (**a**) *(répercussions)* repercussions; **avoir des retombées sur qch** to have repercussions on sth (**b**) *(déchets)* **retombées radioactives** radioactive fallout

retomber [rətɔ̃be] *vi (aux être)* (**a**) *(tomber de nouveau)* to fall again; **r. dans son fauteuil** to fall back into one's armchair; **laisser r. ses bras** to drop one's arms (**b**) *(après un saut, après avoir été en l'air) (personne, ballon)* to land; **r. sur ses pattes** *(chat)* to land on its feet; *Fig* **r. sur ses pieds** *ou Fam* **ses pattes** to land on one's feet (**c**) *(retourner)* **r. dans l'oubli** to sink back into obscurity; **r. dans le désespoir/le chaos** to fall back into despair/chaos; **r. en enfance** to lapse into one's second childhood (**d**) *(redevenir)* **r. malade** to fall ill again (**e**) *(rencontrer)* **r. sur qch** to come across sth again; *Fam* **r. sur qn** to bump into sb again (**f**) *(se répercuter)* **r. sur qn** *(blâme, responsabilité)* to fall on sb; *Fam* **ça va me r. dessus** I'm going to take the rap for it (**g**) *(baisser) (enthousiasme, intérêt, attention)* to fall off (**h**) *(cheveux, rideaux)* to hang (down) (**sur** over)

rétorquer [retɔrke] *vt* to retort

retors, -e [rətɔr, -ɔrs] *adj (personne)* crafty, wily

rétorsion [retɔrsjɔ̃] *nf* retaliation

retouche [rətuʃ] *nf* (**a**) *(sur photo)* touching up; *TV, Cin & Ordinat* **r. d'image(s)** image editing *or* retouching (**b**) *(d'un texte, d'un vêtement)* alteration

retoucher [rətuʃe] *vt* (**a**) *(photo)* to touch up (**b**) *(texte, vêtement)* to alter

retour [rətur] **1** *nm* (**a**) *(d'une personne, d'une saison)* return (**à** to); **être de r. (de)** to be back (again) (from); **de r. chez moi** back home; **à mon r.** on my return; **en r. (de)** in return (for); **payer qn de r.** to repay sb in kind; **par r. (du courrier)** by return (of post); **par un juste r. des choses** as is/was only right and proper; *Fam* **être sur le r.** to be past one's prime; **à l'envoyeur** return to sender; **r. de manivelle** backfire kick; *Fig* **il y a eu un r. de manivelle** it backfired (**b**) *(trajet)* return journey (**c**) *(changement) (de fortune)* reversal; **r. d'âge** change of life (**d**) *Ordinat* **r. d'infor-**

mation feedback; **r. ligne** line feed; **r. chariot obligatoire** hard carriage return (**e**) *(sur clavier)* return; **r. arrière** backspace; **r. de chariot** carriage return

2 *adj inv (match, touche)* return

retournement [rəturnəmã] *nm (de situation)* turnaround (**de** in), reversal (**de** of)

retourner [rəturne] **1** *vt (aux avoir)* (**a**) *(gant, vêtement)* to turn inside out; *(poche)* to turn out; *Fam* **r. sa veste** to change sides; *Fig* **r. le couteau dans la plaie** to twist the knife, to rub it in (**b**) *(terre, matelas, crêpe)* to turn (over); *(carte)* to turn over *or* up; *Fig (idée, projet)* to turn over (**c**) *Fam (bouleverser) (personne)* to shake (**d**) *(renverser) (situation)* to reverse (**e**) *(rendre) (livre, lettre, compliment)* to return (**à** to) (**f**) *Fig (utiliser)* **r. un argument contre qn** to turn an argument against sb

2 *vi (aux être)* to go back, to return (**à** to)

3 *v impersonnel Fam* **voilà de quoi il retourne** that's what it's all about

4 se retourner *vpr* (**a**) *(dormeur, voiture)* to turn over; **il doit se r. dans sa tombe** he must be turning in his grave (**b**) *Fig (s'organiser)* to get one's head together (**c**) *(tourner la tête)* to turn round; **partir sans se r.** to leave without looking back (**d**) **se r. contre qn** *(personne)* to turn against sb; *(action, ambition)* to backfire on sb (**e**) *(aller)* **s'en r. quelque part** to return somewhere

retracer [16] [rətrase] *vt (événement, vie)* to recount

rétractation [retraktasjɔ̃] *nf* retraction

rétracter¹ [retrakte] **1** *vt (griffes, antennes)* to retract

2 se rétracter *vpr (muscle)* to retract

rétracter² **1** *vt (paroles)* to retract, to withdraw

2 se rétracter *vpr (se dédire)* to retract

rétraction [retraksjɔ̃] *nf* retraction

retrait [rətrɛ] *nm* (**a**) *(d'un permis)* withdrawal; **r. du permis de conduire** driving ban (**b**) *(d'une candidature)* withdrawal (**c**) *(fait de récupérer)* **r. des bagages** baggage reclaim (**d**) *(d'argent)* withdrawal; **r. d'espèces** cash withdrawal (**e**) *(des eaux)* receding (**f**) *(en typographie)* indent; **mettre en r.** to indent (**g**) **en r.** *(étagère)* recessed; *(maison)* set back; *Fig* **être/rester en r.** *(personne)* to be/stay in the background

retraite [rətrɛt] *nf* (**a**) *(de la vie active)* retirement; **être à la r.** to be retired; **prendre sa r.** to retire; **être mis à la r.** to be retired; **r. anticipée** early retirement (**b**) *(pension)* (retirement) pension; **r. complémentaire** supplementary pension (**c**) *(procession)* **r. aux flambeaux** torchlight procession (**d**) *(refuge)* retreat; *(de voleurs)* hideout (**e**) *(expérience religieuse)* retreat; **faire une r.** to go into retreat (**f**) *Mil* retreat

retraité, -e [rətrete] **1** *adj* retired

2 *nm,f* pensioner

retraitement [rətretmã] *nm* reprocessing

retraiter [rətrete] *vt* to reprocess

retranchement [rətrãʃmã] *nm* entrenchment; *Fig* **forcer qn dans ses (derniers) retranchements** to drive sb to the wall

retrancher [rətrãʃe] **1** *vt* (**a**) *(soustraire) (chiffre)* to take away *(de* from); **r. qch sur une somme** to deduct sth from a sum of money (**b**) *(ôter) (passage, nom)* to remove (**de** from)

2 se retrancher *vpr (troupes)* to dig in; *Fig* **se r. dans le silence** to take refuge in silence; **se r. derrière qn/qch** to hide behind sb/sth

retransmettre [47] [rətrãsmɛtr] *vt* to broadcast

retransmission [rətrãsmisjɔ̃] *nf* broadcast

retravailler [rətravaje] **1** *vt (discours, texte, pas de danse)* to work on again

2 *vi* (**a**) *(reprendre le travail)* to go back to work (**b**) *(retrouver du travail)* to work again

rétréci, -e [retresi] *adj* (**a**) **un pull r.** a sweater that has shrunk (**b**) *(route)* narrow

rétrécir [retresir] **1** *vt (vêtement)* to take in **2** *vi (vêtement, tissu)* to shrink **3 se rétrécir** *vpr (route)* to narrow

rétrécissement [retresismɑ̃] *nm* (**a**) *(action) (de route)* narrowing; *(de vêtement, de tissu)* shrinking (**b**) *(partie étroite) (de tuyau,* **de route***)* narrowing

rétribuer [retribɥe] *vt (employé)* to pay; *(travail)* to pay for

rétribution [retribysjɔ̃] *nf* payment, remuneration

rétro [retro] **1** *adv* **s'habiller r.** to wear retro clothes; **meublé r.** furnished in retro style **2** *adj inv* retro **3** *nm* (**a**) *(style)* retro (**b**) *Fam (rétroviseur)* rear-view mirror

rétroactif, -ive [retroaktif, -iv] *adj* retroactive

rétroactivement [retroaktivmɑ̃] *adv* retroactively

rétroactivité [retroaktivite] *nf* retroactivity

rétrocéder [34] [retrosede] *vt (revendre)* to resell

rétrograde [retrograd] *adj (idée, mesure, politique)* reactionary

rétrograder [retrograde] **1** *vt (fonctionnaire)* to demote **2** *vi (conducteur)* to change down; **r. de troisième en seconde** to change down from third to second

retroprojecteur [retroprɔʒɛktœr] *nm* overhead projector

rétrospectif, -ive [retrɔspɛktif, -iv] **1** *adj* retrospective **2** *nf* **rétrospective** retrospective

rétrospectivement [retrɔspɛktivmɑ̃] *adv* retrospectively, in retrospect

retroussé, -e [retruse] *adj (manches)* rolled-up; *(nez)* snub, turned-up

retrousser [retruse] *vt* (**a**) *(manches, pantalon)* to roll up; *(babines)* to curl up (**b**) *(jupe)* to tuck up

retrouvailles [retruvaj] *nfpl* reunion

retrouver [retruve] **1** *vt* (**a**) *(personne disparue, objet perdu)* to find again; *(adresse, nom)* to find; **r. son chemin** to find one's way again; **je ne retrouverai jamais une occasion pareille** I'll never have another opportunity like it (**b**) *(recouvrer) (santé, forces, enthousiasme)* to recover; *(voix, appétit)* to get back (**c**) *(reconnaître)* **r. qch chez qn** to recognize sth in sb; **r. qn dans qch** to recognize sb in sth (**d**) *(rencontrer) (thème, image, motif)* to come across (**dans** in) (**e**) *(rejoindre) (amis, parents)* to meet, to see; *(lieu)* to get back to **2 se retrouver** *vpr* (**a**) *(être)* to find oneself; **se r. à la rue/sans un sou** to find oneself homeless/penniless (**b**) *(trouver son chemin)* to find one's way (**dans** round); *Fig* **je ne m'y retrouve plus!** I'm completely lost! (**c**) *Fam (financièrement)* **s'y r.** to get one's money back (**d**) *(se rencontrer)* to meet; *Fig* **on se retrouvera!** I'll get even with you!; **comme on se retrouve!** fancy meeting you! (**e**) *(soi-même)* to find oneself again (**f**) *(se reconnaître)* **se r. en qn** to recognize oneself in sb

rétroviseur [retrovizœr] *nm* rear-view mirror

réunification [reynifikasjɔ̃] *nf* reunification

réunifier [66] [reynifje] *vt* to reunify

Réunion [reynjɔ̃] *nf* **la R.** Réunion

réunion [reynjɔ̃] *nf* (**a**) *(de faits)* gathering (together); *(d'ensembles mathématiques, de pays)* union; *(d'entreprises)* merging (**b**) *(assemblée)* meeting; **être en r.** to be in a meeting; **r. de famille** family gathering

réunionnais, -e [reynjɔnɛ, -ɛz] **1** *adj* of Réunion **2** *nm,f* **R.** = person from Réunion

réunir [reynir] **1** *vt* (**a**) *(rassembler) (objets)* to put together; *(faits, documents)* to gather together; *(fonds)* to get together,

to raise (**b**) *(amis, famille)* to get together; *(après une rupture, une séparation)* to reunite (**c**) *(qualités, avantages)* to have, to possess (**d**) **r. qch à qch** to join sth to sth **2 se réunir** *vpr* (**a**) *(personnes)* to meet, to get together; **se r. autour de qn/qch** to gather round sb/sth (**b**) *(routes)* to meet (**c**) *(entreprises)* to merge; *(États)* to unite

réussi, -e [reysi] *adj* successful; *Ironique* **c'est r.!** well done!

réussir [reysir] **1** *vt* (**a**) *(bien faire)* to make a success of; *(au rugby)* *(essai)* to score; **son soufflé était très réussi** her soufflé was a great success (**b**) *(examen)* to pass **2** *vi* (**a**) *(démarche, projet)* to be successful (**b**) *(personne)* to do well, to be successful **3 réussir à** *vt ind* (**a**) **r.** à **un examen** to pass an exam; **r. à faire qch** to manage to do sth (**b**) **r. à qn** *(climat, plat)* to agree with sb; **tout lui réussit** he's successful in everything he does; **les réunions de famille ne me réussissent pas** family gatherings aren't for me

réussite [reysit] *nf* (**a**) *(succès)* success; **fêter sa r. à un examen** to celebrate passing an exam; **la r. sociale** social success (**b**) *(aux cartes) Br* patience, *Am* solitaire; **faire une r.** to play patience

réutiliser [reytilize] *vt* to reuse

revaloir [69] [rəvalwar] *vt* **je te revaudrai ça** *(je me vengerai)* I'll get you back for this!; *(je te rendrai service)* I'll do the same for you some time

revalorisation [rəvalorizasjɔ̃] *nf* (**a**) *(d'une monnaie)* revaluation; *(des salaires, des retraites)* upgrading (**b**) *(d'une image, d'une profession)* upgrading

revaloriser [rəvalorize] *vt* (**a**) *(monnaie)* to revalue; *(salaire, retraite)* to upgrade (**b**) *(image, profession)* to upgrade

revanchard, -e [rəvɑ̃ʃar, -ard] *adj & nm,f Péj* revanchist

revanche [rəvɑ̃ʃ] *nf* (**a**) *(vengeance)* revenge; **prendre sa r. (sur qn)** to get one's revenge (on sb) (**b**) *(d'un match, d'un jeu)* return game (**c**) *(locutions)* **en r.** on the other hand; à **charge de r.** on condition that I do the same for you

rêvasser [rɛvase] *vi* to daydream

rêve [rɛv] *nm* (**a**) *(de dormeur)* dream; **faire un r.** to (have a) dream; **faites de beaux rêves!** sweet dreams! (**b**) *(idéal)* dream; **de r.** *(voiture, maison)* dream; *(silhouette)* gorgeous dream!

rêvé, -e [reve] *adj* perfect, ideal

revêche [rəvɛʃ] *adj* bad-tempered

réveil [revɛj] *nm* (**a**) *(d'une personne)* waking, awakening; à **mon r., au r.** on waking (**b**) *(d'un volcan)* renewed rumblings; *(de la nature, des nationalismes)* reawakening (**c**) *(pendule)* alarm (clock)

réveille-matin [revɛjmatɛ̃] *nm inv* alarm clock

réveiller [reveje] **1** *vt* (**a**) *(personne endormie)* to wake (up), to awaken; *Fig* **r. les consciences** to stir people's consciences (**b**) *(raviver) (douleur)* to revive **2 se réveiller** *vpr* (**a**) *(personne endormie)* to wake (up), to awake; *(personne dans le coma)* to regain consciousness; *Fig (peuple)* to wake up (**b**) *(douleur)* to come back (**c**) *(nature)* to reawaken

réveillon [revɛjɔ̃] *nm* *(repas)* midnight supper; *(soirée)* midnight party *(after midnight mass on Christmas Eve or New Year's Eve)*

réveillonner [revɛjɔne] *vi* to see in Christmas/the New Year *(with a midnight supper and party)*

révélateur, -trice [revelatœr, -tris] **1** *adj (signe, attitude, remarque)* revealing **2** *nm* (**a**) *(indice)* sign (**b**) *Phot* developer

révélation [revelasjɔ̃] *nf* (**a**) *(action) (d'un secret, d'intentions)* revelation, disclosure; **faire des révélations** to disclose important information (**b**) *(découverte)* *fondamentale)* revelation **(c)** *(personne)* discovery **(d)** *(divine)* revelation

révéler [34] [revele] **1** *vt* **(a)** *(dévoiler)* to reveal **(b)** *(témoigner de)* to show
2 se révéler *vpr* **(a)** *(personne)* to reveal oneself *or* one's character; *(talent, génie)* to be revealed, to reveal itself **(b) se r. intelligent/exact** to turn out to be intelligent/correct; **il s'est révélé un bon ami** he proved to be a good friend

revenant, -e [rəvnā, -āt] *nm,f* **(a)** *(fantôme)* ghost **(b)** *Fam* **tiens, un r.!** hello, stranger!

revendeur, -euse [rəvādœr, -øz] *nm,f* retailer; *(d'articles d'occasion)* secondhand dealer

revendicatif, -ive [rəvādikatif, -iv] *adj (mouvement)* protest

revendication [rəvādikasjɔ̃] *nf* demand, claim

revendiquer [rəvādike] *vt* **(a)** *(demander)* to claim, to demand; *(droits)* to assert; *(territoire, succession)* to lay claim to; **r. le droit de faire qch** to claim the right to do sth **(b)** *(assumer) (responsabilité)* to claim; *(attentat)* to claim responsibility for

revendre [rəvādr] *vt* **(a)** *(après achat)* to resell; *Fig* **avoir du temps/de l'énergie à r.** to have time/energy to spare **(b)** *(vendre de nouveau)* to sell again

revenez-y [rəvnezi] *nm inv Fam* **avoir un goût de r.** to be very moreish

revenir [70] [rəvənir, rəvnir] *(aux* **être)** **1** *vi* **(a)** *(retourner, rentrer)* to come back, to return; **r. à Paris/en France** to come back to Paris/France; **r. de Paris** to come back from Paris; *Fig* **r. de loin** *(avoir failli mourir)* to have been at death's door; **je reviens tout de suite** I'll be back in a minute; **quand l'été reviendra** when it's summer again **(b) r. dans qch** *(refrain, image)* to crop up in sth **(c) ses propos me sont revenus** what he said got back to me **(d) r. à la mémoire** to come back to sb; **ça me revient maintenant!** it's coming back to me!; **les forces me sont revenues** I got my strength back **(e)** *Fam* **j'en suis revenu, de l'informatique!** I'm finished with computers!; **je n'en reviens pas!** I can't get over it! **(f)** *Fam* **il a une tête qui ne me revient pas** I don't like the look of him **(g) faire r. qch** to brown sth **(h) r. cher** to work out expensive
2 revenir à *vt ind* **(a)** *(coûter)* **r. à 30 euros par personne** to work out at 30 euros each; **ça me revient à 100 euros par mois** it costs me 100 euros a month **(b)** *(équivaloir à)* **cela revient à dire que...** that amounts to saying that...
3 revenir sur *vt ind* **(a)** *(sujet)* to get back to **(b)** *(aveux)* to retract; *(promesse, décision)* to go back on
4 *v impersonnel* **il me revient encore 100 euros** I still have 100 euros owing to me; **il lui revient de le faire** it's up to him/her to do it
5 s'en revenir *vpr Litt* to return, to make one's way back

revente [rəvāt] *nf* resale

revenu [rəvəny, rəvny] *nm (d'une personne)* income; *(de l'État)* revenue

rêver [rɛve] **1** *vt* to dream of; **r. que...** to dream (that)...
2 *vi* **(a)** *(dormeur)* to dream; *Fig* **on croit r.!** we must be dreaming! **(b)** *(rêvasser)* to daydream
3 rêver à *vt ind* to dream of
4 rêver de *vt ind* **(a)** *(voir en rêve)* to dream of; *Fig* **j'en rêve la nuit** I dream about it at it night **(b)** *(souhaiter)* to dream of; **r. de faire qch** to dream of doing sth

réverbération [reverberasjɔ̃] *nf (de la lumière, de la chaleur)* reflection; *(du son)* reverberation, echo

réverbère [reverber] *nm* street lamp

réverbérer [34] [reverbere] *vt (chaleur, lumière)* to reflect, to throw back; *(son)* to reverberate

reverdir [rəverdir] *vi* to grow green again

révérence [reverās] *nf* **(a)** *(salut) (d'une femme)* curtsey;

faire la r. à qn to curtsey to sb; *Fig* **tirer sa r.** to leave **(b)** *(respect)* reverence **(envers** *ou* **pour** for)

révérend, -e [reverā, -ād] **1** *adj* reverend
2 *nm* reverend

révérer [34] [revere] *vt* to revere

rêverie [rɛvri] *nf (activité, moment)* daydream, reverie

revers [rəver] *nm* **(a)** *(de pièce)* reverse side, back; *(de la main)* back; **prendre l'ennemi à r.** *(par l'arrière)* to attack the enemy from the rear; *(par le côté)* to attack the enemy from the side; *Fig* **c'est le r. de la médaille** that's the other side of the coin **(b)** *(de veste)* lapel; *(de pantalon) Br* turn-up *or Am* cuff; *(de manche)* (turned-up) cuff **(c)** *(échec)* **r. de fortune** reversal of fortune, setback **(d)** *(au tennis)* backhand (stroke)

reverser [rəverse] *vt* **(a)** *(somme)* to transfer **(à** *ou* **sur** to) **(b)** *(liquide)* to pour out again

réversible [reversibl] *adj* reversible

revêtement [rəvɛtmā] *nm (enduit)* coating; *(de sol, d'un mur intérieur)* covering; *(d'un mur extérieur)* facing; *(pour canalisation, pour câble)* sheathing; *(de la chaussée)* surface (material)

revêtir [71] [rəvɛtir] *vt* **(a)** *(habiller)* **r. qn de qch** to dress sb in sth **(b)** *(endosser) (vêtement)* to don **(c)** *(enduire)* *(sol)* to cover; *(mur extérieur)* to face; *(chaussée)* to surface **(d)** *Fig (caractère, aspect, forme)* to assume, to take on **(e) pièce revêtue d'une signature** document bearing a signature

rêveur, -euse [rɛvœr, -øz] **1** *adj* dreamy; **laisser qn r.** to leave sb baffled
2 *nm,f* dreamer

rêveusement [rɛvøzmā] *adv* dreamily

revient [rəvjɛ̃] *nm voir* **prix**

revigorant, -e [rəvigorā, -āt] *adj (vent, bain)* invigorating; *(boisson)* reviving

revigorer [rəvigore] *vt (vent, bain)* to invigorate; *(boisson)* to revive

revirement [rəvirmā] *nm (de sentiments, d'opinion)* complete change, about-turn

réviser [revize] *vt* **(a)** *(texte, loi)* to revise; *(contrat, procès, politique)* to review **(b)** *(leçon, programme)* to revise **(c)** *(voiture, moteur)* to service **(d)** *Ordinat (texte, document)* to edit

révision [revizjɔ̃] *nf* **(a)** *(d'un texte, d'une loi)* revision; *(d'un contrat, d'un procès, d'une politique)* review; **r. des salaires** salary review **(b)** *(d'une leçon, d'un programme) Br* revision, *Am* review; **faire des révisions** to revise **(c)** *(d'une voiture, d'un moteur)* service **(d)** *Ordinat* edit

révisionnisme [revizjonism] *nm* revisionism

revisser [rəvise] *vt* to screw back again

revitalisant, -e [rəvitalizā, -āt] *adj* revitalizing

revitaliser [rəvitalize] *vt* to revitalize

revivre [72] [rəvivr] **1** *vt (passé, expérience)* to relive
2 *vi* **(a)** *(recouvrer son énergie)* to come alive again; **se sentir r.** to feel alive again; **faire r. qn** to bring sb back to life **(b) r. dans qn/qch** to live on in sb/sth; **faire r. qch** *(coutume, tradition)* to revive sth; *(village)* to bring sb back to life

révocable [revokabl] *adj (fonctionnaire)* removable; *(testament)* revocable

révocation [revokasjɔ̃] *nf (d'un fonctionnaire)* removal; *(d'un testament)* revocation

revoici [rəvwasi] *prép Fam* **me r.!** here I am again!; **le r. au travail** he's back at work

revoilà [rəvwala] = **revoici**

revoir¹ [rəvwar] **au revoir 1** *exclam* goodbye
2 *nm inv* goodbye

revoir² [ʀəvwaʀ] [73a] **1** vt (a) (rencontrer) (personne) to see or meet again (b) (leçon) to revise; (comptes, texte) to go over again (c) (se représenter mentalement) to see again **2 se revoir** vpr (a) (se rencontrer) to see each other again, to meet again (b) (soi-même) to see oneself again

révoltant, -e [ʀevɔltɑ̃, -ɑ̃t] adj appalling, revolting

révolte [ʀevɔlt] nf revolt; **en r. (contre)** in revolt (against)

révolté, -e [ʀevɔlte] adj (a) (indigné) outraged, appalled (de by) (b) (en révolte) rebellious

révolter [ʀevɔlte] **1** vt to outrage, to appal; **ça me révolte d'entendre ça!** I'm appalled to hear that! **2 se révolter** vpr to revolt, to rebel (**contre** ou **devant** against)

révolu, -e [ʀevɔly] adj (jours. époque) past. bygone; **avoir quarante ans révolus** to be over forty years of age

révolution [ʀevɔlysjɔ̃] nf revolution; **faire la r.** to cause a revolution; Fig **être en r.** to be up in arms; Hist **la R.** the French Revolution

révolutionnaire [ʀevɔlysjɔnɛʀ] adj & nmf revolutionary

révolutionner [ʀevɔlysjɔne] vt (a) (transformer) (industrie, théorie) to revolutionize (b) Fam (mettre en émoi) (village) to cause a stir in

revolver [ʀevɔlvɛʀ] nm revolver

révoquer [ʀevɔke] vt (a) (fonctionnaire) to remove from office (b) (décret, contrat, testament) to revoke

revue [ʀəvy] nf (a) (examen) review; **passer qch en r.** (problèmes, possibilités) to review sth; **r. de presse** (de l'actualité) review of the papers; (sur un sujet particulier) press review (b) (magazine) magazine; (scientifique, littéraire) review, journal (c) (spectacle) revue

révulsé, e [ʀevylse] adj (yeux) rolled back; (personne) disgusted

révulser [ʀevylse] **1** vt (dégoûter) to disgust **2 se révulser** vpr (yeux) to roll back

Reykjavik [ʀekjavik] n Reykjavik

rez-de-chaussée [ʀedʃose] nm inv Br ground floor, Am first floor; **au r.** on the Br ground or Am first floor

rez-de-jardin [ʀedʒaʀdɛ̃] nm inv garden level

RF [ɛʀɛf] nf (abrév **République française**) = written abbreviation seen on official documents, government buildings etc

RFA [ɛʀɛfa] nf Anciennement (abrév **République fédérale d'Allemagne**) FRG

RG nmpl (abrév **Renseignements généraux**) = police branch concerned with political security

rhabiller [ʀabije] **1** vt (personne) to dress sb again **2 se rhabiller** vpr (mettre ses vêtements) to get dressed again; Fam **il peut aller se r.** he might as well give up and go home

rhapsodie [ʀapsɔdi] nf rhapsody

Rhénanie [ʀenani] nf **la R.** the Rhineland

Rhésus [ʀezys] nm Rhesus factor; **R. positif/négatif** Rhesus positive/negative

rhétorique [ʀetɔʀik] **1** adj (effet) rhetorical **2** nf rhetoric

Rhin [ʀɛ̃] nm **le R.** the Rhine

rhinocéros [ʀinɔseʀɔs] nm rhinoceros

rhino-pharyngite (pl **rhino-pharyngites**) [ʀinofaʀɛ̃ʒit] nf inflammation of the nose and throat, Spéc rhino-pharyngitis

Rhodes [ʀɔd] n Rhodes

rhododendron [ʀɔdɔdɛdʀɔ̃] nm rhododendron

Rhône [ʀon] nm **le R.** the Rhone

rhubarbe [ʀybaʀb] nf rhubarb

rhum [ʀɔm] nm rum

rhumatisant, -e [ʀymatizɑ̃, -ɑ̃t] adj & nm,f rheumatic

rhumatismal, -e, -aux, -ales [ʀymatismal, -o] adj rheumatic

rhumatisme [ʀymatism] nm rheumatism; **avoir des rhumatismes** to have rheumatism; **r. articulaire** rheumatoid arthritis; **r. articulaire aigu** rheumatic fever

rhumatologie [ʀymatɔlɔʒi] nf rheumatology

rhumatologue [ʀymatɔlɔg] nmf rheumatologist

rhume [ʀym] nm cold; **attraper un r.** to catch a cold; **r. de cerveau** head cold; **r. des foins** hay fever

riant, -e [ʀijɑ̃, -ɑ̃t] adj (a) (visage) smiling, cheerful; (yeux) laughing, merry (b) (paysage, campagne) cheerful, sunny

RIB [ʀib] nm (abrév **relevé d'identité bancaire**) = document showing details of one's bank account

ribambelle [ʀibɑ̃bɛl] nf (de personnes) string, crowd

ricanement [ʀikanmɑ̃] nm sneer, snigger

ricaner [ʀikane] vi to sneer, to snigger

richard, -e [ʀiʃaʀ, -aʀd] nm,f Péj moneybags

riche [ʀiʃ] **1** adj (a) (personne, pays) rich, wealthy (b) (cuisine, aliment) rich (c) (vocabulaire) extensive; (style) elaborate; (description) detailed (d) (luxueux) (demeure) luxurious; (étoffe) rich; (vêtement) sumptuous (e) Fam **c'est une r. idée** that's a fabulous idea (f) **r. en qch** rich in sth; **la journée a été r. en événements** it's been an action-packed day (g) **r. de** (espérances) full of; **livre/expérience r. d'enseignements** very instructive book/experience **2** nmf rich person; **les riches** the rich

richement [ʀiʃmɑ̃] adv richly

richesse [ʀiʃɛs] nf (a) (d'une personne, d'un pays) wealth; **c'est le tableau qui fait la r. de notre musée** this painting is the prize item in our museum's collection; **richesses** (biens) riches, wealth; Fam **voilà toutes mes richesses** this is everything I've got (b) (luxe) (d'une demeure) luxuriousness; (de vêtements) sumptuousness (c) **richesses** (ressources) resources (d) (du sol, d'un gisement) richness; (de la végétation) lushness (e) (de l'imagination) vividness, liveliness; (d'un style) elaborateness; (du vocabulaire) richness; (d'une description) detailed nature

richissime [ʀiʃisim] adj extremely wealthy

ricin [ʀisɛ̃] nm voir huile

ricocher [ʀikɔʃe] vi (projectile) to ricochet (**sur** off); (sur l'eau) to bounce (**sur** off)

ricochet [ʀikɔʃe] nm (projectile) ricochet; (sur l'eau) bounce; **faire des ricochets** (pour s'amuser) to skim pebbles; Fig **par r.** indirectly

ric-rac [ʀikʀak] adv Fam (a) (de justesse) **réussir un examen r.** to scrape through an exam (b) **être r.** (financièrement) to be a bit strapped for cash

rictus [ʀiktys] nm grimace

ride [ʀid] nf (a) (sur le visage) wrinkle, line; Fam **ne pas prendre une r.** not to age (b) (sur l'eau) ripple

ridé, -e [ʀide] adj wrinkled

rideau, -x [ʀido] nm (a) (dans une pièce) Br curtain, Am drape; **r. de fer** (de boutique) metal shutter; (en Europe) Iron Curtain (b) (de théâtre) curtain (c) (écran) (d'arbres) screen; (de feu, de fumée) wall; (de pluie) curtain

rider [ʀide] **1** vt (a) (front) to wrinkle, to line; (peau) to wrinkle, to shrivel (b) (eau, sable) to ripple **2 se rider** vpr (a) (front, peau) to become wrinkled or lined (b) (eau) to ripple

ridicule [ʀidikyl] **1** adj ridiculous, ludicrous; (prix) ridiculously low; **se rendre r.** to make a fool of oneself **2** nm (a) (absurdité) ridiculousness (b) (dérision) ridicule;

tourner qn/qch en r. to ridicule sb/sth; **se couvrir de r.** to make a complete fool of oneself

ridiculement [ridikylmã] *adv* ridiculously, ludicrously

ridiculiser [ridikylize] **1** *vt* to ridicule, to make fun of **2 se ridiculiser** *vpr* to make oneself look ridiculous, to make a fool of oneself

rien [rjɛ̃] **1** *pron indéfini* **(a)** *(avec ne)* nothing; **r.** ne **l'affecte** nothing affects him; **r. de ce que j'ai proposé ne leur a plu** they didn't like anything I suggested; **r. ne va plus!** *(au casino)* no more bets!; **ne... r.** nothing, not anything; **je n'ai r. à faire** I've got nothing to do; **il n'a r. mangé du tout** he hasn't eaten a thing; **personne n'osa r. dire** nobody dared say anything; **il n'y a r. de nouveau** there's nothing new, there isn't anything new; **ce n'est r.** it's nothing; **comme si de r. n'était** as if nothing had happened; **elle ne ressemble en r. à sa sœur** she's nothing like her sister; *Litt* **il n'en est r.** such is not the case; **il n'a r. d'un don Juan** he's no Casanova; *Fam* **r. de r.** nothing at all **(b)** *(sans ne)* **qu'avez-vous fait? – r. /presque r.** what did you do? – nothing/hardly anything; **de r.** *(je vous en prie)* you're welcome, don't mention it; **pour r.** *(gratuitement)* for nothing; **pourquoi demandez-vous cela? – pour r.** why do you ask? – no reason; **un petit problème de r.** a trivial little problem; **quinze à r.** *(au tennis)* fifteen love **(c)** *(quelque chose)* anything; **y a-t-il r. de plus triste?** is there anything more depressing?; **sans r. faire** without doing anything; **sans nous gêner en r.** without troubling us at all *or* in the slightest **(d)** *(locutions)* **r. que** just, only; **je frémis r. que d'y songer** just thinking about it makes me shudder; **r. que la vérité** nothing but the truth; **élever quatre enfants, ce n'est pas r.!** raising four children is quite an achievement! **2** *nm* **(a)** *(bagatelle)* **un r. l'habille** she looks good in anything; **s'énerver pour un r.** to get annoyed over nothing; **il court un kilomètre comme un r.** he can run a kilometre just like that **(b)** **un r. long/bête** *(un peu)* a bit long/stupid; **un r. de** *(un petit peu de)* a little; **en un r. de temps** in no time at all

rieur, -euse [rijœr, -øz] *adj (air, visage)* cheerful, bright; *(yeux)* laughing, merry

Riga [riga] *n* Riga

rigide [riʒid] *adj* **(a)** *(matériau)* rigid; *(couverture de livre)* hard **(b)** *Fig (personne, règlement, système)* rigid, inflexible

rigidité [riʒidite] *nf (d'un matériau)* rigidity; *Fig (d'une personne, d'un règlement, d'un système)* rigidity, inflexibility; **r. cadavérique** rigor mortis

rigolade [rigolad] *nf Fam* **(a)** *(amusement)* fun **(b)** **c'était de la r.** *(c'était facile)* it was a walkover; **ça n'est pas de la r.** *(c'est sérieux)* it's no joke; **prendre qch à la r.** to treat sth as a joke

rigolard, -e [rigolar, -ard] *adj Fam (air)* grinning

rigole [rigol] *nf (petit fossé)* channel; *(filet d'eau)* rivulet

rigoler [rigole] *vi Fam* **(a)** *(rire)* to laugh **(b)** *(s'amuser)* to have a laugh **(c)** *(plaisanter)* to joke **(avec** about); *Fig* **il ne faut pas r. avec le fisc** you shouldn't mess with the IRS

rigolo, -ote [rigolo, -ɔt] *Fam* **1** *adj* funny **2** *nm,f (plaisantin)* scream, hoot; *Péj (fumiste)* clown

rigorisme [rigorism] *nm* strictness

rigoriste [rigorist] **1** *adj* strict, rigorous **2** *nmf* strict moralist

rigoureusement [rigurøzmã] *adv* **(a)** *(strictement) (interdit)* strictly; *(exact)* absolutely; *(contraire)* rigorously **(b)** *(scrupuleusement)* **suivre r. les consignes** to follow the instructions to the letter **(c)** *(sévèrement)* severely

rigoureux, -euse [rigurø, -øz] *adj* **(a)** *(dur) (punition, mesures, conditions)* severe, harsh; *(hiver)* hard; *(climat)*

harsh **(b)** *(strict) (neutralité)* strict; *(analyse)* rigorous; **être r. dans qch** *(personne)* to be rigorous in sth

rigueur [rigœr] *nf* **(a)** *(dureté)* harshness, severity; *(de la loi)* rigour **(b)** *(austérité)* austerity **(c)** *(exactitude) (d'une analyse)* rigour; **manquer de r.** *(style, personne)* to be sloppy **(d)** *(locutions)* **à la r.** *(si nécessaire)* if need be; **être de r.** to be compulsory; **tenir r. à qn de qch** to hold sth against sb

rillettes [rijɛt] *nfpl* potted meat *(made from pork, rabbit, goose etc)*

rime [rim] *nf* rhyme; **sans r. ni raison** without rhyme or reason

rimer [rime] *vi* **(a)** *(mot)* to rhyme **(avec** with) **(b)** *Fig* **ne r. à rien** not to make any sense

Rimmel® [rimɛl] *nm* mascara

rinçage [rɛ̃saʒ] *nm* **(a)** *(action)* rinsing **(b)** *(pour les cheveux)* tint, rinse

rince-doigts [rɛ̃sdwa] *nm inv* finger bowl

rincée [rɛ̃se] *nf* **(a)** *Fam (averse)* downpour **(b)** *Fam (volée de coups)* walloping

rincer [16] [rɛ̃se] **1** *vt (vêtements, vaisselle, cheveux)* to rinse; *(verre, tasse)* to rinse (out) **2 se rincer** *vpr (à l'eau douce)* to rinse oneself; **se r. la bouche** to rinse out one's mouth; *Fam* **se r. l'œil** to get an eyeful

ring [riŋ] *nm* ring; **le r.** *(la boxe)* boxing

ringard, -e [rɛ̃gar, -ard] *Fam* **1** *adj* **(a)** *(démodé)* uncool, unhip **(b)** *(de mauvais goût)* tacky **2** *nm,f* square

Rio de Janeiro [rijodədʒanero] *n* Rio de Janeiro

ripaille [ripaj] *nf Fam* **faire r.** to have a blow-out

riposte [ripost] *nf* **(a)** *(en boxe, en escrime)* riposte **(b)** *(réponse)* riposte, retort **(c)** *(représailles)* counterattack

riposter [riposte] **1** *vt* **il m'a riposté que...** he retorted that... **2** *vi* **(a)** *(en boxe, en escrime)* to riposte **(b)** *(user de représailles)* to counterattack **3 riposter à** *vt ind (attaque, injures)* to counter

ripou *(pl* **ripoux** *ou* **ripous)** [ripu] *Fam* **1** *adj (policier)* bent **2** *nm* bent cop

riquiqui [rikiki] *adj inv (tout petit)* teeny-weeny; *(portion, cadeau)* stingy, mean; *(maillot de bain)* skimpy

rire¹ [rir] *nm* laughter, laughing

rire² [61] [rir] **1** *vi* **(a)** *(personne)* to laugh; **r. comme un bossu,** *Fam* **r. comme une baleine** to laugh like a drain; **r. jaune** to force a laugh; **manquer de r.** to miss; **r. aux éclats** to roar with laughter; **r. aux larmes** to cry with laughter; **r. tout bas** to laugh to oneself **(b)** *(s'amuser)* to have fun, to have a laugh; **pour r.** for a joke; **vous voulez r.!** you're joking!; **laissez-moi r.!** don't make me laugh! **2 rire de** *vt ind (se moquer de) (personne, remarques, situation)* to laugh at; *Litt* **je ris de leurs insultes** I'm impervious to their insults; **il vaut mieux en r.** you have to laugh **3 se rire** *vpr Litt* **se r. de** *(se moquer de)* to laugh at; *(se jouer de)* to make light of

ris¹ [ri] *nm (sur une voile)* reef

ris² *nm* **r. de veau** calf's sweetbread

risée [rize] *nf* **(a)** *(moquerie)* mockery, derision; **s'exposer à la r. publique** to expose oneself to public scorn **(b)** **être la r. de** to be the laughing stock of

risette [rizɛt] *nf Fam* little smile; **fais des risettes à ton papa!** smile for daddy!, give daddy a smile!

risible [rizibl] *adj* laughable, ridiculous

risque [risk] *nm* risk; **prendre un r./des risques** to take a risk/risks; **courir le r.** de faire qch to run the risk of doing sth; **c'est un r.** à courir it's a risk I/we/*etc* have to take; **avoir le goût du r.** to like taking risks; **les risques du métier** occupational hazards; **faire qch à ses risques et périls** to do sth at one's own risk; **au r.** de sa vie at the risk of her life; **au r.** de faire qch at the risk of doing sth

risqué, -e [riske] *adj* **(a)** *(dangereux)* risky **(b)** *(osé)* risqué

risquer [riske] **1** *vt* **(a)** *(mettre en danger) (vie, réputation)* to risk; **qu'est-ce que tu risques?** what have you got to lose?; **r.** sa tête to put one's head on the block; **r.** le tout pour le tout to go for broke **(b)** **r.** un œil to peep out; **r.** une question to venture a question
2 risquer de *vt ind* **il risque de se faire renvoyer** he's in danger of being sacked; **ça risque de durer longtemps** that may well last for a long time; *Fam* **il risque de gagner** he stands a good chance of winning; *Fam* **il ne risque pas de te le dire** fat chance of him telling you
3 se risquer *vpr* to take risks/a risk; **se r.** à **faire qch** to venture to do sth; **je ne m'y risquerais pas** I wouldn't risk it

risque-tout [riskətu] *nmf inv* daredevil

rissoler [risɔle] *vt & vi* to brown

ristourne [risturn] *nf* discount; **faire une r.** à **qn** to give sb a discount

rital, -e, -als, -ales [rital] *nm,f Fam (Italien)* wop, = racist term used to refer to an Italian

rite [rit] *nm* **(a)** *(religieux)* rite; **r.** de passage *ou* **initiatique** rite of passage **(b)** *Fig (cérémonie, habitude)* ritual

ritournelle [riturnɛl] *nf (phrase musicale)* ritornello; *Fam* **c'est toujours la même r.** it's always the same old story

rituel, -elle [rituɛl] **1** *adj* ritual
2 *nm* ritual; **r.** d'initiation initiation rites

rituellement [rituɛlmã] *adv* invariably

rivage [rivaʒ] *nm* shore

rival, -e, -aux, -ales [rival, -o] **1** *adj* rival
2 *nm,f* rival; **sans r.** unrivalled

rivaliser [rivalize] *vi* **r.** avec qn to compete with sb; **r.** de qch avec qn to try to outdo sb in sth

rivalité [rivalite] *nf* rivalry

rive [riv] *nf* **(a)** *(de rivière)* bank; *(de lac, de mer)* shore **(b)** la **r.** gauche/droite *(à Paris)* the Left/Right Bank

river [rive] *vt* **(a)** *(fixer)* to rivet; *Fig* **être rivé à qch** to be glued to sth; **avoir les yeux rivés sur qn/qch** not to be able to take one's eyes off sb/sth **(b)** *(goupille, clou)* to clinch; *Fam* **r.** son clou à qn to shut sb up

riverain, -e [rivrɛ̃, -ɛn] **1** *adj (propriété) (le long d'une rivière)* riverside, waterside; *(autour d'un lac)* lakeside, waterside
2 *nm,f* **(a)** *(près d'une rivière)* owner of a riverside property; *(près d'un lac)* owner of a lakeside property **(b)** *(d'une rue)* resident; **interdit sauf aux riverains** *(sur panneau)* ≃ no entry except for access

rivet [rivɛ] *nm* rivet

rivetage [rivtaʒ] *nm* riveting

riveter [42] [rivte] *vt* to rivet

riveteuse [rivtøz] *nf* riveting machine

rivière [rivjɛr] *nf* **(a)** *(cours d'eau)* river **(b)** *(de lave, de boue)* river **(c)** **r.** de diamants diamond necklace, *Spéc* diamond rivière

rixe [riks] *nf* brawl

riz [ri] *nm* rice; **r.** cantonais Cantonese rice; **r.** créole boiled rice; **r.** au lait rice pudding; **r.** pilaf pilaf *or* pilau rice

riziculture [rizikyltyr] *nf* rice growing

rizière [rizjɛr] *nf* rice field, paddy field

RMI [ɛrɛmi] *nm (abrév* revenu minimum d'insertion*)* *Br* ≃ income support, *Am* ≃ Welfare

RMiste [ɛrɛmist] *nmf Br* ≃ person on income support, *Am* ≃ person on Welfare

RN [ɛrɛn] *nf (abrév* route nationale*)* = designation of major road

RNIS [ɛrɛnis] *nm Ordinat (abrév* réseau numérique à intégration de services*)* ISDN

robe [rɔb] *nf* **(a)** *(de femme)* dress; **r.** de grossesse maternity dress; **r.** d'intérieur housecoat; **r.** de mariée wedding dress; **r.** du soir evening gown **(b)** **r.** de chambre *Br* dressing gown, *Am* robe; **pommes de terre en r.** de chambre *ou* des champs jacket potatoes **(c)** *(d'avocat, de juge)* robe, gown **(d)** *(habit religieux)* robe **(e)** *(pelage) (de cheval)* coat **(f)** *(du vin)* colour

robinet [rɔbinɛ] *nm Br* tap, *Am* faucet

robinetterie [rɔbinɛtri] *nf* plumbing

robineux [rɔbinø] *nm Can Fam Br* tramp, *Am* hobo

robot [rɔbo] *nm* robot; **r.** ménager food processor

robotique [rɔbɔtik] **1** *adj* robotic
2 *nf* robotics *(singulier)*

robotisation [rɔbɔtizasjɔ̃] *nf* automation, robotization

robotiser [rɔbɔtize] *vt* to automate, to robotize

robuste [rɔbyst] *adj (personne)* robust; *(bras, jambe)* sturdy; *(appétit)* healthy; *(plante)* hardy; **être d'une santé r.** to have a healthy constitution

robustesse [rɔbystɛs] *nf (d'une personne)* robustness; *(d'une plante)* hardiness; *(d'un véhicule)* sturdiness

roc [rɔk] *nm* rock

rocade [rɔkad] *nf (route)* bypass

rocaille [rɔkaj] **1** *nf* **(a)** *(terrain)* stony ground **(b)** *(jardin)* rockery
2 *adj inv (style)* rocaille

rocailleux, -euse [rɔkajø, -øz] *adj* **(a)** *(pierreux)* stony, rocky **(b)** *Fig (voix)* harsh, rough

rocambolesque [rɔkɑ̃bɔlɛsk] *adj* fantastic, incredible

roche [rɔʃ] *nf* rock

rocher [rɔʃe] *nm* **(a)** *(masse de pierre)* rock; *(escarpé)* crag; **le R.** Monaco; **le r.** de Gibraltar the Rock of Gibraltar **(b)** *(paroi)* rock face **(c)** **r.** (au chocolat) chocolate *(containing nuts)*

rocheux, -euse [rɔʃø, -øz] *adj (paysage, région)* rocky; **la paroi rocheuse** the rock face; **les (montagnes) Rocheuses** the Rocky Mountains

rock [rɔk] **1** *adj inv (concert, groupe, chanteur)* rock
2 *nm inv* **le r.** rock; **danser le r.** to jive

rocker [rɔkœr] *nm*, **rockeur, -euse** [rɔkœr, -øz] *nm,f (musicien)* rock musician; *(fan)* rock fan

rocking-chair *(pl* rocking-chairs*)* [rɔkiŋtʃɛr] *nm* rocking chair

rock'n roll [rɔkɛnrɔl] *nm* **le r.** rock and roll

rococo [rɔkoko] **1** *adj inv* **(a)** *(meuble, style)* rococo **(b)** *(démodé)* old-fashioned
2 *nm* rococo

rodage [rɔdaʒ] *nm (d'une voiture)* running in; **en r.** *(sur panneau)* running in

rodéo [rɔdeo] *nm (avec des chevaux)* rodeo; *Fig (bagarre)* free-for-all

roder [rɔde] *vt (moteur, voiture)* to run in; *Fig (entreprise, spectacle)* to get into its stride; *(équipe, structure)* to break in; **être rodé** *(entreprise, spectacle)* to be into its stride; *(employé)* to have got the hang of things

rôder [rode] *vi* to be on the prowl

rôdeur, -euse [rodœr, -øz] *nm,f* prowler

rogne [rɔɲ] *nf Fam* bad temper; **être en r. (contre)** to be cross (with); **mettre qn en r.** to make sb cross; **se mettre ou Fam se ficher en r.** to get mad

rogner [rɔɲe] **1** vt (a) (griffes, ongles) to clip, to trim; Fig (économies) to eat away at; Fig **r. les ailes à qn** to clip sb's wings (b) (retrancher) **r. qch à qn** to gradually take sth away from sb (c) Ordinat (image) to crop
2 rogner sur vt ind **r. sur qch** to cut down on sth

rognon [rɔɲɔ̃] nm kidney

rognures [rɔɲyr] nfpl (de cuir, de métal) trimmings, parings

rogue [rɔg] adj arrogant, haughty

roi [rwa] **1** nm (a) (souverain) king; **tirer les rois** = to celebrate Twelfth Night by eating a cake containing a small charm. The person finding the charm in their piece of cake is given a paper crown to wear; **les Rois mages** the Three Wise Men; **le R.-Soleil** the Sun King (b) Fig (le plus grand) (des animaux) king; **c'est le r. des imbéciles** he's a prize idiot; **très Fam c'est le r. des cons** he's a complete dickhead (c) (aux cartes, aux échecs) king
2 adj inv **bleu r.** royal blue

roitelet [rwatlɛ] nm (oiseau) wren

rôle [rol] nm (a) (d'une pièce de théâtre) part, role; Fig **avoir le beau r.** to have the easy job; **premier r.** leading role; **r.-titre** title role (b) (fonction) (du médecin, d'un organe, d'une activité) role, function (**dans** in); **jouer un r. de premier plan** to play a key role; **jouer un r. secondaire** to play second fiddle

ROM [rɔm] nf Ordinat ROM

romain, -e¹ [rɔmɛ̃, -ɛn] **1** adj Roman
2 nm,f **R.** Roman
3 nm (caractère d'imprimerie) roman

romaine² [rɔmɛn] nf (salade) Br cos lettuce, Am romaine; Fig **être bon comme la r.** to be extremely kind

roman¹ [rɔmɑ̃] nm (a) (en prose) novel; **le nouveau r.** the anti-novel, the nouveau roman; **r. d'amour** love story, romance; Fam **r. à l'eau de rose** schmaltzy love story, schmaltzy romance; **r. noir** thriller; **r. policier** detective novel (b) (poème) romance (c) Fig **c'est du r.** (c'est invraisemblable) it's just a fairy tale; Fig **c'est tout un r.** (c'est incroyable) it's quite a tale

roman², -e [rɔmɑ̃, -an] **1** adj (a) (langue) Romance (b) Archit Romanesque
2 nm (a) (langue) Romance (b) Archit Romanesque style

romance [rɔmɑ̃s] nf (chanson) sentimental song or ballad

romancer [16] [rɔmɑ̃se] vt (événement, histoire) to romanticize; (biographie) to fictionalize

romanche [rɔmɑ̃ʃ] adj & nm Romansch

romancier, -ère [rɔmɑ̃sje, -er] nm,f novelist

romand, -e [rɔmɑ̃, -ɑ̃d] **1** adj (Suisse) French-speaking
2 nm,f **R.** French-speaking Swiss person

romanesque [rɔmanɛsk] adj (a) (personne, aventure) romantic (b) (technique) novelistic

roman-feuilleton (pl **romans-feuilletons**) [rɔmɑ̃fœjtɔ̃] nm serial

roman-fleuve (pl **romans-fleuves**) [rɔmɑ̃flœv] nm saga

romanichel, -elle [rɔmaniʃɛl] nm,f (Tsigane) gypsy

roman-photo (pl **romans-photos**) [rɔmɑ̃fɔto] nm photo-story

romantique [rɔmɑ̃tik] **1** adj (a) (peinture, littérature, artiste) Romantic (b) (personne, idées, film) romantic
2 nmf (a) (artiste, auteur) Romantic(ist) (b) (personne) romantic

romantisme [rɔmɑ̃tism] nm (a) (courant artistique) Romanticism (b) (attitude, sensibilité) romanticism

romarin [rɔmarɛ̃] nm rosemary

rombière [rɔ̃bjɛr] nf Fam old biddy

Rome [rɔm] n Rome

rompre [rɔ̃pr] **1** vt (a) (casser) to break; **r. ses digues** (fleuve) to burst its banks (b) (négociations, fiançailles, relations) to break off; (contrat, charme, monotonie) to break; (équilibre) to upset (c) (locutions) **applaudir à tout r.** to applaud wildly; **r. les rangs** to fall out
2 vi (a) (casser) to break (b) (se séparer) to break up (**avec** with); **r. avec sa famille** to break off relations with one's family (c) **r. avec la tradition** to break with tradition
3 se rompre vpr (se casser) to break; **son cœur battait à se r.** his heart was pounding; Fig **se r. le cou** to break one's neck

rompu, -e [rɔ̃py] adj (a) (exténué) **être r. (de fatigue)** to be worn out (b) (expérimenté) **r. à qch** used to sth

romsteck [rɔmstɛk] nm rump steak

ronce [rɔ̃s] nf (a) (arbuste) bramble (bush), blackberry bush (b) (dans le bois) **r. de noyer** burr walnut

ronchon, -onne [rɔ̃ʃɔ̃, -ɔn] Fam **1** adj grouchy, grumpy
2 nm,f grumbler, grouser

ronchonnement [rɔ̃ʃɔnmɑ̃] nm Fam grumbling, grousing

ronchonner [rɔ̃ʃɔne] vi Fam to grumble, to grouse

roncier [rɔ̃sje] nm, **roncière** [rɔ̃sjɛr] nf thick bramble bush

rond, -e [rɔ̃, rɔ̃d] **1** adj (a) (balle, table, nappe) round; (ventre) rounded; (poitrine) full; (personne, joues, silhouette) plump; **avoir le dos r.** to be round-shouldered (b) (plein) (voix) full (c) (chiffre, compte) round (d) être **r. en affaires** to be straightforward where business is concerned (e) Fam (ivre) wasted; **r. comme une queue de pelle** totally out of it
2 adv **tout r.** (exactement) exactly
3 nm (a) (figure) circle; **en r.** in a circle; Fam **faire des ronds de jambe** to bow and scrape; Fam **en rester comme deux ronds de flan** to be absolutely staggered; **r. de serviette** napkin ring (b) Fam (sou) **il n'a pas un r.** he hasn't got a penny

rond-de-cuir (pl **ronds-de-cuir**) [rɔ̃dkɥir] nm Fam Péj pen-pusher

ronde [rɔ̃d] nf (a) (danse) round (dance); (chanson) round, roundelay (b) (de gardien, de vigile) round(s); (de policier) beat; **faire une/sa r.** (gardien, vigile) to patrol; (policier) to be on the beat (c) Mus (note) Br semibreve, Am whole note (d) **à la r.** (autour) around; **à 10 kilomètres à la r.** within a radius of 10 kilometres

rondeau, -x [rɔ̃do] nm rondo

rondelet, -ette [rɔ̃dlɛ, -ɛt] adj (a) (personne) plump, chubby (b) (somme) tidy

rondelle [rɔ̃dɛl] nf (a) (de citron, de saucisson) slice; **couper qch en rondelles** to slice sth (b) Can **r. (de hockey)** puck (c) (d'écrou) washer

rondement [rɔ̃dmɑ̃] adv (a) (avec entrain) briskly, promptly; **mener qch r.** to make short work of sth (b) (franchement) bluntly, frankly

rondeur [rɔ̃dœr] nf (a) (d'un corps) roundness; (des joues) plumpness (b) **rondeurs** (d'une femme) curves (c) (amabilité) **avec r.** bluntly, frankly

rondin [rɔ̃dɛ̃] nm log

rondo [rɔ̃do] nm rondo

rondouillard, -e [rɔ̃dujar, -ard] adj Fam (personne) plump, chubby

rond-point (pl **ronds-points**) [rɔ̃pwɛ̃] nm (sens giratoire) Br roundabout, Am traffic circle

ronéotyper [rɔneɔtipe] vt to roneo

ronflant, -e [rɔ̃flɑ̃, -ɑ̃t] adj Péj high-flown, high-sounding

ronflement [rɔ̃fləmɑ̃] *nm* (**a**) *(d'une personne)* snoring (**b**) *(d'un moteur, d'une machine)* whirring, purring
ronfler [rɔ̃fle] *vi* (**a**) *(dormeur)* to snore (**b**) *(moteur)* to whirr, to purr; *(poêle)* to purr
ronfleur, -euse [rɔ̃flœr, -øz] *nm,f (personne)* snorer
ronger [45] [rɔ̃ʒe] **1** *vt* (**a**) *(bois)* to gnaw (at), to nibble (at); *(os)* to gnaw (on); **rongé par les vers** worm-eaten (**b**) *(acide, rouille)* to eat away *or* into; *(falaise)* to erode (**c**) *(tourmenter)* **être rongé de chagrin** to be tormented with grief; **être rongé de remords/par la jalousie/par l'anxiété** to be eaten up with remorse/jealousy/anxiety; **être rongé par la maladie** to be wasted by illness (**d**) *Fig* **r. son frein** to champ at the bit
  2 se ronger *vpr* **se r. les ongles** to bite one's nails
rongeur, -euse [rɔ̃ʒœr, -øz] **1** *adj (mammifère)* rodent-like
  2 *nm* rodent
ronron [rɔ̃rɔ̃], **ronronnement** [rɔ̃rɔnmɑ̃] *nm* (**a**) *(d'un chat)* purr (**b**) *(d'un moteur)* purr, whirr; *(d'un avion, d'une voix)* drone; *(d'une machine)* whirr (**c**) *(routine)* humdrum routine
ronronner [rɔ̃rɔne] *vi* (**a**) *(chat)* to purr (**b**) *(moteur)* to purr, to whirr; *(avion)* to drone; *(machine)* to whirr
roquefort [rɔkfɔr] *nm* Roquefort
roquet [rɔkɛ] *nm Péj (chien)* yap
roquette¹ [rɔkɛt] *nf (salade) Br* rocket, *Am* arugula
roquette² *nf (projectile)* rocket; **r. antichar** anti-tank rocket
rorqual, -als [rɔrkwal] *nm* rorqual, finback whale
rosace [rozas] *nf* (**a**) *(vitrail)* rose window (**b**) *(au plafond)* ceiling rose (**c**) *(de guitare)* rose
rosaire [rozɛr] *nm* rosary; **dire** *ou* **réciter son r.** to say the rosary
rosâtre [rozatr] *adj* pinkish
rosbif [rɔsbif] *nm* (**a**) *(viande) (rôtie)* roast beef; *(à rôtir)* roasting beef (**b**) *Fam (Britannique)* Brit, = racist term used to refer to a British person
rose [roz] **1** *adj* pink; *Fig* **tout n'est pas r.** it's not all rosy; **r. bonbon** candy pink; **r. thé** tea rose; **vieux r.** old rose
  2 *nf (fleur)* rose; **frais comme une r.** fresh as a daisy; *Fam* **ne pas sentir la r.** to be a bit stinky; **r. trémière** hollyhock (**b**) **r. des sables** desert rose; **r. des vents** compass card
  3 *nm* pink; **voir la vie** *ou* **tout en r.** to see everything through rose-tinted glasses
rosé, -e [roze] **1** *adj* pinkish
  2 *nm (vin)* rosé
roseau, -x [rozo] *nm* reed
rosée [roze] *nf* dew
roseraie [rozrɛ] *nf* rose garden
rosette [rozɛt] *nf* (**a**) *(nœud)* bow; *(ornement)* rosette (**b**) *(insigne)* rosette *(especially of the Legion of Honour)*
rosier [rozje] *nm* rose-tree, rosebush
rosière [rozjɛr] *nf Vieilli* = village maiden awarded a wreath of roses for her virtuous conduct
rosir [rozir] **1** *vt* to turn pink
  2 *vi* to go *or* turn pink
rosse [rɔs] *Péj* **1** *adj Fam (personne, conduite, remarque)* rotten
  2 *nf* (**a**) *(cheval)* hack (**b**) *Fam (homme)* swine; *(femme)* bitch
rossée [rɔse] *nf Fam* beating, thrashing
rosser [rɔse] *vt Fam* **r. qn** to beat sb up, to give sb a good hiding; **se faire r.** to get a hiding
rossignol [rɔsiɲɔl] *nm* (**a**) *(oiseau)* nightingale (**b**) *Fam (objet)* white elephant

rot [ro] *nm Fam* belch, burp; *(de bébé)* burp; **faire un r.** *(adulte)* to belch, to burp; *(bébé)* to burp
rotatif, -ive [rɔtatif, -iv] **1** *adj (pompe, moteur)* rotary
  2 *nf* rotative rotary press
rotation [rɔtasjɔ̃] *nf* rotation; *(du stock, de fonds)* turnover
roter [rɔte] *vi Fam* to belch, to burp
rôti, -e [roti] **1** *adj* roast
  2 *nm (viande)* joint, roast; **r. de porc** *(cuit)* roast pork; *(non cuit)* joint of pork
rotin¹ [rɔtɛ̃] *nm* rattan; **chaise en r.** cane *or* rattan chair
rotin² *nm Fam Vieilli (sou)* **il n'a plus un r.** he's stone-broke
rôtir [rotir] **1** *vt (viande)* to roast
  2 *vi* (**a**) *(viande)* to roast (**b**) **r. au soleil** to bask in the sun
  3 se rôtir *vpr* **se r. au soleil** to bask in the sun
rôtisserie [rotisri] *nf* (**a**) *(boutique du rôtisseur)* = shop selling roast meat (**b**) *(restaurant)* grillroom, steakhouse
rôtissoire [rotiswar] *nf* (rotating) spit, rotisserie
rotonde [rɔtɔ̃d] *nf* rotunda
rotor [rɔtɔr] *nm* rotor
rotule [rɔtyl] *nf* kneecap; *Fam* **etre sur les rotules** to be dead beat
roturier, -ère [rɔtyrje, -ɛr] **1** *adj* common
  2 *nm,f* commoner
rouage [rwaʒ] *nm* (**a**) *(d'un mécanisme)* works (**b**) *Fig (d'une administration, d'une organisation)* workings
roublard, -e [rublar, -ard] *Fam* **1** *adj (personne, air)* wily, cunning
  2 *nm,f* wily *or* cunning devil
roublardise [rublardiz] *nf Fam* (**a**) *(caractère)* cunning, wiliness (**b**) *(action)* crafty *or* cunning trick
rouble [rubl] *nm* rouble
roucoulade [rukulad] *nf (d'oiseaux)* cooing, *Fam* roucoulades *(d'amoureux)* billing and cooing
roucoulement [rukulmɑ̃] *nm (d'un pigeon)* cooing; *Fig (d'amoureux)* billing and cooing
roucouler [rukule] *vi (pigeon)* to coo; *Fig (amoureux)* to bill and coo
  2 *vt (mots doux, promesses)* to coo
roue [ru] *nf* (**a**) *(d'un véhicule)* wheel; **être la cinquième r. du carrosse** *Br* to be a spare part, *Am* to be the fifth wheel; **faire la r.** *(oiseau)* to spread its tail; *Fig & Péj* to strut, to swagger; **un deux roues** a two-wheeled vehicle; **r. libre** freewheel; **descendre en r. libre** to freewheel downhill; **r. de secours** spare wheel (**b**) *(figure de gymnastique)* cartwheel
roué, -e [rwe] *Litt* **1** *adj* cunning, sly
  2 *nm,f* cunning person
rouer [rwe] *vt* **r. qn de coups** to beat sb black and blue
rouerie [ruri] *nf (acte)* cunning *or* sly trick (**envers** played on)
rouet [rwɛ] *nm* spinning wheel
rouge [ruʒ] **1** *adj* (**a**) *(tissu, objet, joue, vin)* red; **r. cerise** cherry-red; **r. sang** blood-red (**b**) *(personne)* **de colère/d'émotion** red *in the face with* anger/emotion; **être r. de honte** to blush with shame; **être r. comme une écrevisse** to be as red as a lobster; **être r. comme une tomate** *ou* **une pivoine** to be as red as a beetroot (**c**) *(chauffé) (fer)* red-hot
  2 *adv* **se fâcher tout r.** to lose one's temper completely; **voir r.** to see red
  3 *nm* (**a**) *(couleur)* red; **peindre/teindre qch en r.** to paint/dye sth red; **le r. lui monte aux joues** he's/she's going red (**b**) *(chaleur extrême)* **porter** *ou* **chauffer qch au r.** to heat sth red-hot (**c**) *(cosmétique)* **r. à lèvres** lipstick; **se mettre du r.** to put some of one's lipstick on (**d**) *Fam* passer **au r.** *(signal d'arrêt)* to turn *or* go red (**e**) *(vin)* red wine; *Fam*

gros r. plonk (**f**) *Fam Fig* être dans le **r.** *(financièrement)* to be in the red
4 *nmf (communiste)* Red
rougeâtre [ruʒɑtr] *adj* reddish
rougeaud, -e [ruʒo, -od] **1** *adj* red-faced
2 *nm,f* red-faced person
rouge-gorge *(pl* rouges-gorges) [ruʒgɔrʒ] *nm* robin
rougeoiement [ruʒwamɑ̃] *nm* red glow
rougeole [ruʒɔl] *nf* measles *(singulier)*; avoir la **r.** to have measles
rougeoyant, -e [ruʒwajɑ̃, -ɑ̃t] *adj* glowing (red)
rougeoyer [32] [ruʒwaje] *vi* to turn red
rouget [ruʒɛ] *nm* red mullet
rougeur [ruʒœr] *nf* (**a**) *(due à la chaleur, à l'émotion)* flush; *(due à la honte, à la gêne)* blush (**b**) *(tache)* blotch (**c**) *(couleur)* redness
rougir [ruʒir] **1** *vt* (**a**) *(ciel, feuilles)* to turn red (**b**) *(visage)* to redden
2 *vi* (**a**) *(ciel, feuilles)* to turn red (**b**) *(personne)* to turn red; *(de honte, gêne)* to blush, to go red; *Fig (avoir honte)* to be ashamed; **r.** jusqu'aux oreilles to blush to the roots of one's hair; **r.** de colère/d'émotion to flush with anger/emotion
rougissant, -e [ruʒisɑ̃, -ɑ̃t] *adj (personne, visage)* blushing
rouille [ruj] **1** *adj inv* rust(-coloured)
2 *nf* (**a**) *(sur le fer)* rust (**b**) *(sauce)* = spicy sauce made with garlic and chillis, traditionally served with fish soup
rouillé, -e [ruje] *adj* (**a**) *(métal, clef)* rusty, rusted (**b**) *Fig (personne)* rusty
rouiller [ruje] **1** *vt (métal, clef)* to rust, to make rusty
2 *vi (métal, clef)* to rust, to go rusty
3 se rouiller *vpr* (**a**) *(métal, clef)* to get rusty (**b**) *Fig (personne) (physiquement)* to get stiff; *(intellectuellement) (langue, connaissances)* to get rusty
roulade [rulad] *nf* (**a**) *(en gymnastique)* **r.** avant/arrière forward/backward roll; faire des roulades to do rolls (**b**) *(vocalise)* roulade (**c**) *(charcuterie)* rolled and stuffed meat
roulant, -e [rulɑ̃, -ɑ̃t] *adj* (**a**) *(porte)* sliding; *(pont)* travelling (**b**) *(capital)* working (**c**) *Fam (drôle) (personne, blague, histoire)* comical
roulé, -e [rule] **1** *adj* (**a**) *(journal, carte, tapis)* rolled(-up); *(charcuterie)* rolled (**b**) *Fam (femme)* être bien roulée to be curvy
2 *nm (gâteau)* Swiss roll
rouleau, -x [rulo] *nm* (**a**) *(bande) (de papier, de Scotch®, de pellicule)* roll; *Fam* être au bout du **r.** to be at the end of one's tether (**b**) *(objet circulaire) (pour peindre)* roller; **r.** compresseur steamroller; **r.** à pâtisserie rolling pin; **r.** de printemps spring roll (**c**) *(vague)* billow, roller (**d**) *(bigoudi)* roller (**e**) *(saut en hauteur)* **r.** dorsal Fosbury flop; **r.** ventral western roll
roulé-boulé *(pl* roulés-boulés) [rulebule] *nm* roll *(executed tucked up in a ball)*
roulement [rulmɑ̃] *nm* (**a**) *(d'une balle)* rolling (**b**) *(bruit)* un **r.** de tonnerre a roll *or* rumble of thunder; des roulements de tambour drum rolls (**c**) *(alternance)* rotation; par **r.** in rotation (**d**) *(pièce)* bearing; **r.** à billes ball bearing (**e**) *Fin (de fonds)* circulation; *(de capitaux)* turnover
rouler [rule] **1** *vt* (**a**) *(pierre, tonneau)* to roll (along) (**b**) *(tapis, papier, manches)* to roll up; *(cigarette)* to roll (**c**) *(yeux)* to roll (**d**) *(balancer)* **r.** les épaules to roll one's shoulders; **r.** les hanches to swing one's hips (**e**) *Fam (duper)* to do (**de** out of); se faire **r.** to be done (**f**) *(locutions)* **r.** les r to roll one's r's; *très Fam* **r.** une pelle *ou* un palot *ou* un patin à qn to French kiss sb

2 *vi* (**a**) *(balle)* to roll; faire **r.** qch sur le sol to roll sth along the ground (**b**) *(dégringoler) (personne)* to roll, to tumble (**c**) *(dans une voiture, dans un train)* to go, to travel; on a beaucoup roulé we drove for a long time; ça roule bien ce matin there are no traffic problems this morning; à quelle vitesse rouliez-vous? what speed were you doing? (**d**) *Fam* ça roule everything's fine (**e**) *Fig* **r.** sur l'or to be rolling in money (**f**) *(conversation)* **r.** sur qch to be about sth (**g**) *(tonnerre)* to roll, to rumble; *(tambour)* to roll (**h**) *(navire)* to roll
3 se rouler *vpr* (**a**) *(sur soi-même)* se **r.** par terre to roll about on the floor; *(dehors)* to roll about on the ground (**b**) se **r.** une cigarette to roll a cigarette; *Fam* se **r.** les pouces, se les **r.** to twiddle one's thumbs
roulette [rulɛt] *nf* (**a**) *(de meuble)* castor; à roulettes *(meuble)* on castors; *Fam* marcher *ou* aller comme sur des roulettes to go like clockwork (**b**) *Fam (de dentiste)* drill (**c**) *(au jeu)* roulette; **r.** russe Russian roulette
roulis [ruli] *nm* roll
roulotte [rulɔt] *nf (de bohémiens)* caravan
roulure [rulyr] *nf très Fam* whore
roumain, -e [rumɛ̃, -ɛn] **1** *adj* Romanian
2 *nm,f* **R.** Romanian
3 *nm (langue)* Romanian
Roumanie [rumani] *nf* la **R.** Romania
round [rawnd, rund] *nm* round
roupie [rupi] *nf* rupee
roupiller [rupije] *vi Fam* to sleep, to snooze
roupillon [rupijɔ̃] *nm Fam* snooze; piquer un **r.** to have a snooze
rouquin, -e [rukɛ̃, -in] *Fam* **1** *adj (personne)* red-haired
2 *nm,f* redhead
rouspéter [34] [ruspete] *vi Fam* to moan and groan, to grumble (**contre** about)
rouspéteur, -euse [ruspetœr, -øz] *Fam* **1** *adj* grumpy
2 *nm,f* moan, grouch
rousse [rus] *voir* roux
roussette [rusɛt] *nf* (**a**) *(poisson)* spotted dogfish (**b**) *(chauve-souris)* flying fox (**c**) *(grenouille)* common frog
rousseur [rusœr] *nf (couleur)* redness
roussi [rusi] *nm* ça sent le **r.** there's a smell of burning; *Fig* I smell trouble
roussir [rusir] **1** *vt* (**a**) *(rendre roux)* to turn brown (**b**) *(brûler)* to scorch, to singe
2 *vi (feuilles, arbres)* to turn brown
routage [rutaʒ] *nm (d'imprimés)* sorting and mailing
routard, -e [rutar, -ard] *nm,f Fam* backpacker
route [rut] *nf* (**a**) *(voie)* road; prendre la **r.** de Paris to take the Paris road; **r.** à double voie *ou* à deux voies *Br* dual carriageway, *Am* divided highway; par la **r.** by road; **r.** départementale secondary road, *Br* B-road; **r.** nationale main road, *Br* A-road, *Am* highway (**b**) *(itinéraire)* route, way; montrer la **r.** à qn to show sb the way; c'est sur ma **r.** it's on my way; **r.** des vins wine trail (**c**) *(trajet)* après trois heures de **r.** after three hours on the road; se mettre en **r.** *(personne)* to set off; en **r.**! let's be off!; *Fam Hum* en **r.**, mauvaise troupe! come on, you lot!; bonne **r.**! have a good trip! (**d**) *Fig (chemin)* path (**e**) *(marche)* mettre qch en **r.** *(moteur)* to start sth up; *(projet, travaux)* to get sth under way; avoir qch en **r.** to be working on sth; *Fam* ils ont un bébé en **r.** they've got a baby on the way
routeur [rutœr] *nm Ordinat* router
routier, -ère [rutje, -ɛr] **1** *adj* road
2 *nm* (**a**) *(conducteur)* *Br* long-distance lorry driver, *Am* truck driver (**b**) *(restaurant)* *Br* transport café, *Am* truck stop

routine [rutin] *nf* **(a)** *(habitude)* routine; **s'enliser dans/ sortir de la r.** to get into/out of a rut **(b)** *Ordinat* **r.**
d'édition/de logiciel edit/software routine
routinier, -ère [rutinje, -ɛr] *adj (tâches, travail)* routine; **être r.** to be set in one's ways
rouvrir [52] [ruvrir] **1** *vt* to reopen
  2 se rouvrir *vpr* to reopen, to open again
roux, rousse [ru, rus] **1** *adj (feuilles)* russet, reddish-brown; *(cheveux)* red; *(personne)* red-haired; *(sucre)* brown
  2 *nm,f (personne)* red-haired person, redhead
  3 *nm* **(a)** *(couleur)* russet, reddish-brown **(b)** *(préparation culinaire)* roux
royal, -e, -aux, -ales [rwajal, -o] *adj* **(a)** *(palais, visite)* royal **(b)** *(cadeau)* magnificent; *(pourboire)* huge **(c)** *(indifférence)* utter; *Fam* **ficher une paix royale à qn** to leave sb in complete peace
royalement [rwajalmɑ̃] *adv* **(a)** *(payé)* royally **(b)** *Fam* **je m'en fiche** *ou* **moque r.** I couldn't care less
royalisme [rwajalism] *nm* royalism
royaliste [rwajalist] **1** *adj* royalist; *Fig* **être plus r. que le roi** to overdo it
  2 *nmf* royalist
royalties [rwajalti] *nfpl* royalties
royaume [rwajom] *nm* kingdom; *Fig* realm
Royaume-Uni [rwajomyni] *nm* **le R.** the United Kingdom
royauté [rwajote] *nf (monarchie)* monarchy; *(dignité)* kingship
RPR [ɛrpeɛr] *nm* *Pol (abrév* **Rassemblement pour la République)** = right-wing political party
RSVP *(abrév* **répondez s'il vous plaît)** RSVP
ruade [rɥad] *nf (d'un cheval)* lashing out, kick
Ruanda [rwɑ̃da] = **Rwanda**
ruandais, -e [rwɑ̃dɛ, -ɛz] = **rwandais**
ruban [rybɑ̃] *nm* ribbon; **r. adhésif** adhesive *or* sticky tape; **r. encreur** *(de machine à écrire)* typewriter ribbon; *Ordinat* **r. perforé** punchtape
rubéole [rybeɔl] *nf* German measles *(singulier)*, rubella
rubicond, -e [rybikɔ̃, -ɔ̃d] *adj (teint)* florid, rubicund
rubis [rybi] *nm* **(a)** *(pierre précieuse)* ruby; *Fig* **payer r. sur l'ongle** to pay cash on the nail **(b)** *(de montre, d'horloge)* jewel
rubrique [rybrik] *nf* **(a)** *(articles)* column **(b)** *(catégorie)* heading; **r. nécrologique** obituary section
ruche [ryʃ] *nf* **(a)** *(abri)* beehive **(b)** *(essaim)* hive; *Fig (ville, école)* hive of activity
rucher [ryʃe] *nm* apiary
rude [ryd] *adj* **(a)** *(fruste)* rough, uncouth **(b)** *(sévère) (personne, voix)* harsh **(c)** *(peau, tissu)* rough **(d)** *(hiver, climat)* severe, harsh **(e)** *(tâche, métier)* tough
rudement [rydmɑ̃] *adv* **(a)** *(répondre)* harshly; **être r. éprouvé** to be severely tested **(b)** *(frapper, heurter)* hard **(c)** *Fam (très)* really
rudesse [rydɛs] *nf* harshness; **avec r.** harshly
rudimentaire [rydimɑ̃tɛr] *adj* rudimentary
rudiments [rydimɑ̃] *nmpl (d'une matière)* rudiments; **avoir des r. de chinois** to speak basic Chinese
rudoyer [32] [rydwaje] *vt* to treat harshly
rue [ry] *nf* street; **être/se retrouver à la r.** to be/find oneself out on the street; **mettre/jeter qn à la r.** to put/ throw sb out on the street; **r. piétonnière** *ou* **piétonne** pedestrian precinct; **r. principale** main street; **la grande r.** the main street
ruée [rɥe] *nf* rush; **la r. vers l'or** the gold rush
ruelle [rɥɛl] *nf* lane, alley(way)

ruer [rɥe] **1** *vi (cheval)* to kick; *Fig* **r. dans les brancards** to rebel
  2 se ruer *vpr* **se r. sur qn** to rush at sb; **se r. sur qch** to make a rush for sth; **les invités se sont rués sur le buffet** the guests made a dash for the buffet
rugby [rygbi] *nm* rugby; **r. à treize/quinze** rugby league/ union
rugbyman [rygbiman] *(pl* **rugbymen** [rygbimɛn]) *nm* rugby player
rugir [ryʒir] **1** *vi* **(a)** *(fauve)* to roar **(b)** *(personne)* to roar **(de** with) **(c)** *(vent, tempête)* to howl
  2 *vt* to roar
rugissement [ryʒismɑ̃] *nm* **(a)** *(d'un fauve)* roar; **des rugissements** roaring **(b)** *(d'une personne)* roar; **pousser des rugissements de colère** to roar with anger **(c)** *(du vent, d'une tempête)* howling
rugosité [rygozite] *nf* roughness; **rugosités** rough patches
rugueux, -euse [rygø, -øz] *adj* rough
ruine [rɥin] *nf* **(a)** *(écroulement) (d'un édifice)* **en r.** in ruins, ruined; **tomber en ruine(s)** to go to ruin **(b)** **ruines** *(décombres)* ruins **(c)** *Fig (d'une personne, d'une société)* ruin, downfall; **aller** *ou* **courir à la r.** to be on the road to ruin **(d)** *(vieille maison)* ruin **(e)** *Fam* **c'est la r.!** *(c'est coûteux)* it's ridiculously expensive!
ruiner [rɥine] **1** *vt* to ruin; *(espoirs)* to ruin, to dash
  2 se ruiner *vpr (perdre son argent)* to ruin *or* bankrupt oneself; *(dépenser beaucoup d'argent)* to spend a fortune
ruineux, -euse [rɥinø, -øz] *adj* ruinously expensive; **ce n'est pas r.** it won't ruin you/us/etc
ruisseau, -x [rɥiso] *nm* **(a)** *(cours d'eau)* brook, stream **(b)** *Fig (d'eau, de sang, de larmes)* stream; *(de larmes)* flood **(c)** *(caniveau)* gutter
ruisselant, -e [rɥislɑ̃, -ɑ̃t] *adj* dripping **(de** with)
ruisseler [42] [rɥisle] *vi* **(a)** *(liquide)* to stream, to run **(b)** *(surface)* to drip, to stream **(de** with); **le front ruisselant de sueur** with one's forehead dripping with sweat; **ses joues ruisselaient de larmes** tears were streaming down his cheeks
ruissellement [rɥislmɑ̃] *nm* streaming, running
rumba [rumba] *nf* rumba
rumeur [rymœr] *nf* **(a)** *(bruit confus)* distant murmur; *(de la circulation, d'une ville)* hum; *(de voix)* murmur **(b)** *(nouvelle)* rumour
ruminant [ryminɑ̃] *nm* ruminant
rumination [ryminasjɔ̃] *nf* rumination, ruminating
ruminer [rymine] **1** *vt (herbe)* to chew; *Fig (idée, projet)* to mull over
  2 *vi* to ruminate, to chew the cud; *Fig* to brood
rumsteck [rɔmstɛk] *nm* rump steak
rupestre [rypɛstr] *adj (peinture* **r.** rock painting; *(dans une caverne)* cave painting **(b)** *(plante)* rock
rupin, -e [rypɛ̃, -in] *Fam* **1** *adj (riche) (personne)* loaded
  2 *nm,f* **c'est un r.** he's loaded; **les rupins** the rich
rupture [ryptyr] *nf* **(a)** *(d'une corde, d'une poutre)* breaking; *(d'un barrage)* bursting; *(d'un tendon)* rupture **(b)** *(interruption) (de négociations)* breaking off **(de** of); breakdown *(de* in); **être en r.** to be at odds with sb/sth; **en r. avec la tradition** in a break with tradition; **être en r. de stock** to be out of stock **(c)** *(annulation) (de fiançailles)* breaking off; *(de contrat)* breach **(d)** *(entre amoureux)* break-up
rural, -e, -aux, -ales [ryral, -o] **1** *adj (région, vie)* rural; *(chemin)* country
  2 *nm,f* country person
ruse [ryz] *nf* **(a)** *(procédé)* ruse, trick; **r. de guerre**

stratagem (of war); *Fig* dodge (**b**) *(calcul)* **faire qch par la r.**
to do sth by trickery
rusé, -e [ryze] *adj* cunning, crafty
ruser [ryze] *vi* to use trickery *or* cunning
russe [rys] **1** *adj* Russian
2 *nmf* **R.** Russian
3 *nm (langue)* Russian
Russie [rysi] *nf* **la R.** Russia
rustaud, -e [rysto, -od] **1** *adj* uncouth
2 *nm,f* yokel, hick
Rustine® [rystin] *nf* repair patch *(for mending inner tube of bicycle)*
rustique [rystik] *adj* (**a**) *(manières, vie)* rustic; *(meuble)* rustic-style (**b**) *(plante)* hardy
rustre [rystr] **1** *adj* uncouth
2 *nm* boor
rut [ryt] *nm (de mâle)* rut(ting); *(de femelle)* heat; **en r.** *(mâle)* rutting; *(femelle)* in heat

rutabaga [rytabaga] *nm Br* swede, *Am* rutabaga
rutilant, -e [rytilɑ̃, -ɑ̃t] *adj* gleaming
rutiler [rytile] *vi* to gleam
Rwanda [rwɑ̃da] *nm* **le R.** Rwanda
rwandais, -e [rwɑ̃dɛ, -ɛz] **1** *adj* Rwandan
2 *nm,f* **R.** Rwandan
rythme [ritm] *nm* (**a**) *(succession)* rhythm; *(allure)* pace; **manquer de r.** *(film)* to be a bit slow; **au r. de** at the rate of; **r. cardiaque/respiratoire** heart/breathing rate (**b**) *(en musique)* rhythm; **en r.** in time; **marquer le r.** to beat time; **suivre le r.** to follow the beat; *Fig* to keep up; **avoir le sens du r.** to have a sense of rhythm; **avoir le r. dans la peau** to have rhythm in one's blood (**c**) *(d'une phrase)* rhythm
rythmé, -e [ritme] *adj* rhythmic(al)
rythmer [ritme] *vt* to give rhythm to
rythmique [ritmik] **1** *adj* rhythmic(al)
2 *nf (en poésie)* rhythmics *(singulier)*

S

S, s [ɛs] *nm inv* S, s; **faire des s** to zigzag; **en S** *(crochet)* S-shaped; *(route)* zigzagging

S (**a**) *(abrév* **sud**) S (**b**) *(abrév* **seconde(s)**) sec

s' [s] *voir* **se**

SA [ɛsa] *nf (abrév* **société anonyme)** plc

sa [sa] *voir* **son¹**

sabbat [saba] *nm* Sabbath

sabbatique [sabatik] *adj (repos, année, congé)* sabbatical; **prendre un an de congé s.** to take a year's sabbatical

sable [sabl] **1** *nm* sand; *Fam* **être sur le s.** *(sans travail)* to be out of work; *(sans argent)* to be down and out; *Fam* **mettre qn sur le s.** to ruin sb; **sables mouvants** quicksands
  2 *adj inv* sand-coloured

sablé, -e [sable] **1** *adj voir* **pâte**
  2 *nm* shortbread *Br* biscuit *or Am* cookie

sabler [sable] *vt* (**a**) *(chemin)* to sand; *(route)* to grit (**b**) *(bâtiment)* to sandblast (**c**) *Fam* **s. le champagne** to break open a bottle of champagne

sableuse [sabløz] *nf* sandblaster

sableux, -euse [sablø, -øz] *adj* sandy

sablier [sablije] *nm* hourglass

sablonneux, -euse [sablɔnø, -øz] *adj* sandy

sabord [sabɔr] *nm* = type of square porthole

saborder [sabɔrde] **1** *vt (navire)* to scuttle; *Fig (entreprise)* to scupper
  2 se saborder *vpr* to scuttle one's ship

sabot [sabo] *nm* (**a**) *(de cheval)* hoof; *Fam* **ça ne se trouve pas sous le s. d'un cheval** it doesn't grow on trees (**b**) *(chaussure)* clog; *Fam* **je te vois venir avec tes gros sabots** I can see what you're after (**c**) **s. de Denver** *Br* wheel clamp, *Am* Denver boot; **mettre un s. de Denver à une voiture** to *Br* (wheel-)clamp *or Am* (Denver) boot a car

sabotage [sabotaʒ] *nm* sabotage; *(acte)* act of sabotage

saboter [sabote] *vt (voiture, entreprise, plan de paix)* to sabotage; *(travail)* to make a mess of

saboteur, -euse [sabotœr, -øz] *nm,f* saboteur

sabre [sabr] *nm* sabre; **s. au clair** with drawn sword

sabrer [sabre] *vt* (**a**) **une cicatrice lui sabrait la joue** there was the gash of a scar on his cheek (**b**) *Fam (raccourcir)* to slash (**c**) *Fam (critiquer)* to slate (**d**) *Fam* **se faire s.** *(étudiant)* to flunk; **il s'est fait s. par le prof** the teacher flunked him

sac¹ [sak] *nm (contenant, contenu)* bag (**de** of); *(grand et en toile)* sack (**de** of); **s. de sable** sandbag; *Fam* **un s. de nœuds** a muddle; **partir s. au dos** to set off with one's rucksack on one's back; *Fam* **vider son s.** to get it off one's chest; *Fam* **je les mets dans le même s.** they're as bad as each other; *Fam* **l'affaire est dans le s.** it's in the bag; **s. de couchage** sleeping bag; **s. à dos** rucksack, backpack; **s. à main** handbag; *Fam* **s. d'os** bag of bones; **s. à ouvrage** work bag; **s. poubelle** *Br* bin liner, *Am* garbage bag; **s. à provisions** shopping bag; *Fam* **s. à vin** drunk; **s. de voyage** travel *or* overnight bag

sac² *nm (pillage)* sacking; **mettre une ville à s.** to sack a town

saccade [sakad] *nf* jerk, jolt; **par saccades** in fits and starts

saccadé, -e [sakade] *adj* jerky

saccage [sakaʒ] *nm* havoc; **se livrer à un s. de** to wreak havoc in

saccager [sakaʒe] *vt* (**a**) *(piller) (ville)* to sack; *(maison)* to ransack (**b**) *(dévaster) (ville, maison)* to wreak havoc in; **la récolte fut saccagée par l'orage** the crops were devastated by the storm

saccharose [sakaroz] *nm Chim* saccharose

sacerdoce [saserdɔs] *nm* priesthood; *Fig* vocation

sacerdotal, -e, -aux, -ales [saserdɔtal, -o] *adj* priestly

sachant, sache *etc voir* **savoir**

sachet [saʃɛ] *nm* sachet; **s. de thé** teabag; **thé en sachets** teabags

sacoche [sakɔʃ] *nf* (**a**) *(de vélo)* saddlebag (**b**) *(besace)* bag (**c**) *Belg & Can Br* handbag, *Am* purse

sacquer [sake] *Fam* **1** *vt* (**a**) *(renvoyer)* to fire, *Br* to sack; **se faire s.** to be fired (**b**) *(noter sévèrement)* to give a bad mark to; **se faire s. par un prof** to get a bad mark from a teacher (**c**) *(supporter)* **je ne peux pas le s.** I can't stand him
  2 *vi (professeur)* to be a tough marker

sacre [sakr] *nm (d'un roi)* coronation; *(d'un évêque)* consecration; *Fig* rite

sacré, -e [sakre] **1** *adj* (**a**) *Rel & Fig* sacred (**b**) *Fam (maudit)* damn, **s. Marcel, qu'est-ce qu'on ferait sans lui?** good old Marcel, what would we do without him?
  2 *nm* **le s.** the sacred

sacrement [sakrəmã] *nm* sacrament; **le saint S.** the Blessed Sacrament; **recevoir les derniers sacrements** to receive the last rites

sacrément [sakremã] *adv Fam* damn

sacrer [sakre] **1** *vt (roi)* to crown; *(évêque)* to consecrate; **s. qn roi** to crown sb king; *Fig* **il a été sacré champion de France en 2003** he won the French championship in 2003
  2 *vi Can* to swear

sacrifice [sakrifis] *nm* sacrifice; **offrir qn/qch en s.** to offer sb/sth up as a sacrifice; **faire le s. de sa vie** to sacrifice one's life; *Fig* **faire des sacrifices (pour)** to make sacrifices (for)

sacrifier [66] [sakrifje] **1** *vt aussi Fig* to sacrifice **(à** to); **sacrifié** *(prix)* rock-bottom; *(article)* at a rock-bottom price **2** *vi* **s. à la mode** to be a slave to fashion **3 se sacrifier** *vpr* to sacrifice oneself **(pour** for); *Fam* **allez, je me sacrifie, je vais les chercher à l'aéroport!** right, I'll be the martyr and pick them up from the airport!

sacrilège [sakrilɛʒ] **1** *adj* sacrilegious **2** *nmf (personne)* sacrilegious person **3** *nm (acte)* sacrilege

sacristie [sakristi] *nf* sacristy, vestry

sacro-saint, -e (*mpl* **sacro-saints**, *fpl* **sacro-saintes**) [sakrɔsɛ̃, -ɛ̃t] *adj aussi Ironique* sacrosanct

sadique [sadik] **1** *adj* sadistic **2** *nmf* sadist

sadisme [sadism] *nm* sadism

sadomaso [sadɔmazɔ] *adj inv Fam* SM

sadomasochisme [sadɔmazɔʃism] *nm* sadomasochism

sadomasochiste [sadɔmazɔʃist] **1** *adj* sadomasochistic **2** *nmf* sadomasochist

safari [safari] *nm* safari; **en s.** on safari; **s.-photo** photographic safari

safran [safrɑ̃] **1** *nm (plante, épice)* saffron **2** *adj inv* **(jaune) s.** saffron (yellow)

saga [saga] *nf aussi Fig* saga

sagace [sagas] *adj* shrewd, astute

sagacité [sagasite] *nf* shrewdness, astuteness; **avec s.** shrewdly, astutely

sage [saʒ] **1** *adj* **(a)** *(avisé) (personne, décision)* wise, sensible **(b)** *(calme) (enfant, animal)* good, well-behaved; **s. comme une image** as good as gold **(c)** *(chaste) (personne)* good; *(tenue, robe)* sober **2** *nm* wise man; **un vieux s.** a wise old man

sage-femme (*pl* **sages-femmes**) [saʒfam] *nf* midwife

sagement [saʒmɑ̃] *adv* **(a)** *(raisonnablement)* wisely, sensibly **(b)** *(tranquillement)* quietly

sagesse [saʒɛs] *nf* **(a)** *(intelligence)* wisdom, good sense; **avoir la s. de faire qch** to be wise *or* sensible enough to do sth; **plein de s.** very sensible; *Fig* **la voix de la s.** the voice of reason **(b)** *(calme)* good behaviour

Sagittaire [saʒiter] *nm Astron & Astrol* **le S.** Sagittarius; **être S.** to be (a) Sagittarius

sagouin [sagwɛ̃] *nm Fam (personne)* slob

Sahara [saara] *nm* **le S.** the Sahara (Desert)

saharienne [saarjen] *nf* safari jacket

Sahel [sael] *nm* **le S.** the Sahel

saignant, -e [sɛɲɑ̃, -ɑ̃t] *adj* **(a)** *(blessure)* bleeding **(b)** *(viande)* rare

saignée [seɲe] *nf* blood-letting; *Fig* drain; **faire une s. à qn** to bleed sb

saignement [sɛɲəmɑ̃] *nm* bleeding; **s. de nez** nosebleed

saigner [seɲe] **1** *vi (personne, blessure)* to bleed; **je saigne du nez** my nose is bleeding, I've got a nosebleed; *Fig & Litt* **mon cœur saigne** my heart bleeds **2** *vt (poulet, personne)* to bleed; *Fig* **s. qn à blanc** to bleed sb dry **3 se saigner** *vpr Fig* **se s. aux quatre veines** to bleed oneself dry

saillant, -e [sajɑ̃, -ɑ̃t] *adj (qui dépasse)* projecting; *(pommettes)* prominent; *(muscles)* bulging; *Fig (trait)* salient

saillie [saji] *nf* **(a)** *(partie en avant)* projection; **faire to project, to jut out **(b)** *(par un mâle)* covering

saillir [67] [sajir] **1** *vt (femelle)* to cover **2** *vi (s'avancer)* to project, to jut out **(sur** over)

sain, -e [sɛ̃, sɛn] *adj* healthy; *(fruit, gestion)* sound; *(lectures)* wholesome; **s. de corps et d'esprit** sound in body and mind; **s. et sauf** safe and sound

sainement [sɛnmɑ̃] *adv* **(a)** *(vivre)* healthily **(b)** *(juger)* sensibly

saint, -e [sɛ̃, sɛ̃t] **1** *adj (lieu)* holy; *(personne, vie)* saintly; **s. patron** patron saint; **s. Pierre** St Peter; **sainte Catherine** St Catherine; *Fam* **avoir une sainte horreur de qch** to have a holy horror of sth; *Fam* **ne rien faire de toute la sainte journée** to do nothing the whole blessed day **2** *nm,f aussi Fig* saint; **ne savoir plus à quel s. se vouer** not to know which way to turn; *Hum* **il vaut mieux s'adresser à Dieu qu'à ses saints** it's best to go right to the top **3** *nm* **le S. des Saints** the Holy of Holies

saint-bernard [sɛ̃bernar] *nm inv (chien)* St Bernard

Saint-Cyr [sɛ̃sir] *n* Saint-Cyr military academy

Sainte-Lucie [sɛ̃tlysi] *n* St Lucia

sainte-nitouche (*pl* **saintes-nitouches**) [sɛ̃tnituʃ] *nf* little hypocrite; **avec ses airs de s.** looking as if butter wouldn't melt in her mouth

Saint-Esprit [sɛ̃tɛspri] *nm* **le S.** the Holy Ghost *or* Spirit; *Hum* **par l'opération du S.** by magic

sainteté [sɛ̃təte] *nf (d'une personne)* saintliness; *(de la loi, d'un serment)* sanctity; *(d'un lieu)* holiness; **sa S. (le pape)** His Holiness (the Pope)

saint-frusquin [sɛ̃fryskɛ̃] *nm Fam* **tout le s.** the whole caboodle; **il s'est pointé avec tout son s.** he turned up with all his gear

saint-glinglin [sɛ̃glɛ̃glɛ̃] **à la saint-glinglin** *adv Fam* **on sera payés à la s.** we'll be paid when pigs fly; **repoussé à la s.** postponed till whenever

saint-honoré [sɛ̃tɔnɔre] *nm inv* Saint-Honoré *(choux pastry ring filled with confectioner's custard)*

Saint-Jean [sɛ̃ʒɑ̃] *nf* **(a) la S.** Midsummer Day **(b)** *Can* **la Saint-Jean-Baptiste** Saint-Jean-Baptiste Day *(24 July)*

Saint-Laurent [sɛ̃lɔrɑ̃] *nm* **le S.** the St Lawrence (River); **la Voie maritime du S.** the St Lawrence Seaway

Saint-Marin [sɛ̃marɛ̃] *n* San Marino

saint-nectaire [sɛ̃nɛktɛr] *nm inv* = type of firm cheese

Saint-Père [sɛ̃pɛr] *nm* **le S.** the Holy Father

Saint-Pétersbourg [sɛ̃petɛrsbur] *n* St Petersburg

Saint-Pierre-et-Miquelon [sɛ̃pjeremiklɔ̃] *n* St Pierre and Miquelon

Saint-Siège [sɛ̃sjɛʒ] *nm* **le S.** the Holy See

Saint-Sylvestre [sɛ̃silvɛstr] *nf* **la S.** New Year's Eve

sais *voir* savoir

saisie [sezi] *nf (de biens)* seizure; *Ordinat* **s. de données** data capture, keyboarding; *Ordinat* **s. automatique/ manuelle** automatic/manual input

saisine [sezin] *nf Jur* referral to a court

saisir [sezir] **1** *vt* **(a)** *(attraper) (personne, objet)* to take hold of; *(brusquement)* to grab; **s. l'occasion (de faire qch)** to seize *or* grasp the opportunity (to do sth); **j'ai été saisi par le froid** the cold really hit me **(b)** *(comprendre) (signification, nuance)* to grasp, to get; *(nom)* to catch, to get **(c)** *Ordinat (données)* to key **(d)** *Jur (bien)* to seize **(e)** *Jur* **s. un tribunal d'une affaire** to refer a matter to a court **(f)** *(viande)* to seal **2** *vi (comprendre)* to get it **3 se saisir** *vpr* **se s. de qn/qch** to take hold of sb/sth; *(brusquement)* to grab sb/sth

saisissant, -e [sezisɑ̃, -ɑ̃t] *adj (froid)* biting; *(ressemblance)* striking; *(scène)* gripping

saisissement [sezismã] *nm* (a) *(sensation de froid)* sudden chill (b) *(émotion)* shock
saison [sɛzɔ̃] *nf* season; **en cette s.** at this time of year; **en toute s.** all (the) year round; **faire une bonne/ mauvaise s.** *(équipe)* to have a good/bad season; **être de s.** *(fruits)* to be in season; **des pêches! mais ce n'est pas la s.!** peaches! but it isn't the season for them!; **un temps de s.** seasonal weather; **la belle s.** the summer months; **la haute/basse s.** the high/low season; **la morte s.** the off season; **la s. des amours** the mating season; **la s. des pluies** the rainy season
saisonnier, -ère [sezɔnje, -ɛr] **1** *adj* seasonal **2** *nm,f* seasonal worker
sait *voir* **savoir**
saké [sake] *nm* sake
salade [salad] *nf* (a) *(plante)* lettuce (b) *(plat)* salad; **s. composée** mixed salad; **s. de fruits** fruit salad; **s. niçoise** salade niçoise; **s. de tomates/de riz** tomato/rice salad; **s. verte** green salad; **champignons en s.** mushroom salad (c) *Fam (désordre)* mess (d) *Fam* **salades** *(mensonges)* whoppers
saladier [saladje] *nm* salad bowl
salaire [salɛr] *nm* (a) *(mensuel)* salary; *(hebdomadaire, journalier)* wages; *Prov* **toute peine mérite s.** the labourer is worthy of his hire; **s. minimum interprofessionnel de croissance** guaranteed minimum wage (b) *(récompense)* reward (**de** for), **le s. de la peur** the wages of fear
salaison [salɛzɔ̃] *nf (action)* salting; **des salaisons** salted meats
salamalecs [salamalɛk] *nmpl Fam* bowing and scraping
salamandre [salamɑ̃dr] *nf* salamander
salami [salami] *nm* salami
salant [salɑ̃] *adj m voir* **marais**
salarial, -e, -aux, -ales [salarjal, -o] *adj* wage; *(mensuel)* salary
salarié, -e [salarje] **1** *adj* (a) *(travailleur)* *(payé mensuellement)* salaried; *(payé hebdomadairement)* wage-earning (b) *(travail)* paid **2** *nm,f* *(payé mensuellement)* salaried employee; *(payé hebdomadairement)* wage-earner; **salariés** *(d'une société)* employees
salaud [salo] *Vulg* **1** *nm* bastard **2** *adj* **c'était vraiment s. de faire ça** that was a really shitty thing to do; **t'as vraiment été s.!** you were a real shit!
sale [sal] **1** *adj* (a) *(peu soigné)* dirty (b) *Fam (grave) (maladie, situation)* nasty; *(affaire)* dirty; **avoir une s. tête** *ou* **gueule** *(antipathique)* to look really nasty; *(malade)* to look awful; **faire un s. coup à qn** to play a dirty trick on sb; **s. bête** horrible beast; **s. boulot** rotten job; **faire le s. boulot** to do the dirty work; **s. gosse** little brat; **s. temps** filthy weather; **s. type** nasty character **2** *nm Fam* **mettre une chemise au s.** to put a dirty shirt in the wash
salé, -e [sale] **1** *adj* (a) *(non sucré)* savoury; *(conservé dans le sel)* salt; *(additionné de sel)* salted; *(au goût)* salty (b) *Fig (histoire, plaisanterie)* spicy (c) *Fam (condamnation)* stiff; *(addition)* steep **2** *nm* **le s.** savoury food; **petit s.** salt pork
salement [salmɑ̃] *adv* (a) *(manger, boire)* in a disgusting manner (b) *Fam (blessé, touché)* really badly; **je suis s. emmerdé** I'm in a real mess
saler [sale] *vt* to salt
saleté [salte] *nf* (a) *(manque de soin)* dirtiness; *(crasse)* dirt; **faire des saletés** to make a mess (b) *(objet)* trash, junk; **manger des saletés** to eat junk food (c) *(acte obscène, remarque)* obscenity (d) *Fam (personne)* bastard

salière [saljer] *nf* salt cellar
saligaud [saligo] *nm Fam (ignoble individu)* bastard
salin, -e [salɛ̃, -in] *adj* saline **2** *nm (marais salant)* salt marsh
salir [salir] **1** *vt* to make dirty, to dirty; *Fig* **s. le nom/la mémoire de qn** to sully sb's name/memory **2 se salir** *vpr* to get dirty; *Fig* **se s. les mains** to get one's hands dirty
salissant, -e [salisɑ̃, -ɑ̃t] *adj* (a) *(travail)* dirty, messy (b) *(tissu, vêtement)* easily soiled; *(couleur)* that shows the dirt
salissure [salisyr] *nf* dirty mark
salivaire [salivɛr] *adj (glande)* salivary
salive [saliv] *nf* saliva
saliver [salive] *vi* to salivate; *Fig* **s. devant qch** to drool at the sight of sth
salle [sal] *nf* (a) *(pièce)* room; **s. d'armes** *(pour l'escrime)* fencing hall; *(pour les armes)* armoury; **s. d'attente** waiting room; **s. de bain(s)** bathroom; *Ordinat* **s. blanche** clean room; **s. des coffres** vaults; **s. commune** common room; **s. d'embarquement** *(d'un aéroport)* departure lounge; **s. d'exposition** showroom; *(pour une foire)* exhibition hall; **s. des fêtes** community hall; *(d'un village)* village hall; **s. de garde** *(d'hôpital)* staff room; *(de caserne)* guardroom; **s. des machines** *(d'un navire)* engine-room; **s. à manger** dining room; *(meubles)* dining-room suite; **s. d'opération** operating *Br* theatre *or Am* room; **s. des pas perdus** *(dans une gare)* concourse; **s. des professeurs** *Br* staff room, *Am* teachers' lounge; **s. de réunion** meeting room; **s. du trône** throneroom; **s. des ventes** saleroom (b) *(pour le cinéma, pour le théâtre)* **s.** *(de spectacle)* auditorium; **toute la s. applaudit** the whole audience applauded; **les salles obscures** *Br* the cinema, *Am* the movies
salmonelle [salmɔnɛl] *nf* salmonella
salmonellose [salmɔneloz] *nf* salmonella poisoning
Salomon [salɔmɔ̃] *voir* **île**
salon [salɔ̃] *nm* (a) *(pièce)* living room; *(dans un bateau)* saloon; *(dans un train)* saloon car; *Can* **s. de barbier** barber's; **s. de coiffure** hairdressing salon; **s. d'essayage** fitting room; **s. de thé** tea room (b) *(meubles)* suite (c) *(exposition)* exhibition; **le S. des Arts ménagers** ≃ the Ideal Home Exhibition; **le S. de l'Automobile** *ou* **de l'Auto** the Motor Show; **le S. du Livre** the Book Fair; **le S. nautique** the Boat Show (d) *(littéraire)* salon; **tenir s.** to hold a salon
salopard [salɔpar] *nm Vulg* bastard
salope [salɔp] *nf Vulg (femme méprisable)* bitch; *(homme méprisable)* bastard
saloperie [salɔpri] *nf Fam* (a) *(camelote)* trash, junk (b) *(coup bas)* dirty trick (c) **dire des saloperies sur qn** to bitch about sb
salopette [salɔpɛt] *nf Br* dungarees, *Am* overalls
salpêtre [salpɛtr] *nm* saltpetre
salsa [salsa] *nf* salsa
salsifis [salsifi] *nm* salsify
saltimbanque [saltɛ̃bɑ̃k] *nmf* travelling acrobat
salto [salto] *nm* somersault
salubre [salybr] *adj* healthy
salubrité [salybrite] *nf* healthiness; **la s. publique** public health
saluer [salɥe] **1** *vt (en arrivant)* to greet; *(en partant)* to take one's leave of; *(s'incliner devant)* to bow to; *(sujet:soldat)* to salute; **s. qn d'une inclination de la tête** to nod to sb; **il est passé sans me s.** he walked past me without saying hello; **saluez-le de ma part** give him my regards; *Rel* **je vous salue, Marie** hail Mary

2 se saluer *vpr (en arrivant)* to greet each other; *(en partant)* to take leave of each other
salut [saly] **1** *nm* (a) *(salutation)* greeting; **faire un s.** à qn *(en se découvrant)* to raise one's hat to sb; *(en inclinant la tête)* to nod to sb (**b**) *(de soldat)* salute; **faire le s. militaire** to give a salute (**c**) *(sauvegarde)* rescue; *Rel* salvation **2** *exclam Fam* **s.!** *(en arrivant)* hi!; *(en partant)* bye!
salutaire [salytɛr] *adj (décision, mesure)* salutary; *(remède)* beneficial; **être s. à qn** to do sb good
salutation [salytasjɔ̃] *nf* greeting
Salvador [salvadɔr] *nm* **le S.** El Salvador
salvadorien, -enne [salvadɔrjɛ̃, -ɛn] **1** *adj* Salvadorean **2** *nm,f* **S.** Salvadorean
salve [salv] *nf* salvo, volley
Samaritain [samaritɛ̃] *nm* **le bon S.** the good Samaritan
samba [sɑ̃mba] *nf* samba
samedi [samdi] *nm* Saturday; **le S. saint** Easter Saturday; **s. prochain/dernier** next/last Saturday; **s. matin** Saturday morning; **s. soir** Saturday night *or* evening; **dans la nuit de s. à dimanche** on Saturday night; **s. 8 mai 2004** *Br* Saturday 8 May 2004, *Am* Saturday May 8 2004; **nous sommes s.** aujourd'hui today's Saturday; **je commence s.** I'm starting on Saturday; **il vient le s./tous les samedis** he comes on Saturdays/every Saturday; **un s. sur deux** every second *or* other Saturday; **s. en huit/quinze** a week/fortnight on Saturday; **passer tout son s. à faire qch** to spend one's whole Saturday doing sth
Samoa [samoa] *nfpl* **les S. occidentales** Western Samoa
samouraï [samuraj] *nm* samurai
samovar [samɔvar] *nm* samovar
SAMU [samy] *nm (abrév* **Service d'aide médicale d'urgence)** *Br* ≃ ambulance service, *Am* ≃ Paramedics; **appeler le S.** to call an ambulance
sanatorium [sanatɔrjɔm] *nm* sanatorium
sanctifier [66] [sɑ̃ktifje] *vt* (a) *(rendre saint)* to sanctify (**b**) *(révérer)* **que Ton nom soit sanctifié** hallowed be Thy name
sanction [sɑ̃ksjɔ̃] *nf (punition)* sanction; *Fig (désavantage)* price; **s. pénale** penalty; **sanctions économiques** economic sanctions; **prendre une s. contre qn** to take action against sb
sanctionner [sɑ̃ksjɔne] *vt* (a) *(punir)* to punish (**b**) *(approuver)* to sanction; **sanctionné par l'usage** sanctioned by custom
sanctuaire [sɑ̃ktɥɛr] *nm aussi Fig* sanctuary
sandale [sɑ̃dal] *nf* sandal
sandalette [sɑ̃dalɛt] *nf* (light) sandal
sandre [sɑ̃dr] *nm* pikeperch
sandwich *(pl* **sandwichs** *ou* **sandwiches)** [sɑ̃dwitʃ] *nm* sandwich; **s. au jambon** ham sandwich; *Fam* **pris en s.** (entre) sandwiched (between)
San Francisco [sɑ̃frɑ̃sisko] *n* San Francisco
sang [sɑ̃] *nm* blood; **animaux à s. chaud/froid** warm-/cold-blooded animals; *Fig* **avoir le s. bleu** to have blue blood; *Fig* **avoir le s. chaud** to be hot-blooded; *Fig* **avoir qch dans le s.** to have sth in one's blood; *Fam* **avoir du s. de navet** to be spineless; *Fam* **se faire du mauvais s.** to get all worked up; *Fam* **se ronger les sangs, se faire un s. d'encre** to worry oneself sick; **le s. lui monta au visage** the blood rushed to his face; **mon s. n'a fait qu'un tour** *(de peur)* my heart missed a beat; *(de colère)* I saw red; *très Fam* **bon s. (de bonsoir)!, bon s. de bon Dieu!** damn and blast it!
sang-froid [sɑ̃frwa] *nm inv* composure, calm; **garder**

son s. to keep calm, to keep one's head; **perdre son s.** to lose one's head, to lose one's composure; **tuer qn de s.** to kill sb in cold blood
sanglant, -e [sɑ̃glɑ̃, -ɑ̃t] *adj* bloody; *Fig (offensant)* scathing
sangle [sɑ̃gl] *nf* strap; *(de selle)* girth
sangler [sɑ̃gle] *vt* to put straps on; *(cheval)* to girth
sanglier [sɑ̃glije] *nm* (wild) boar
sanglot [sɑ̃glo] *nm* sob
sangloter [sɑ̃glɔte] *vi* to sob
sangria [sɑ̃grija] *nf* sangria
sangsue [sɑ̃sy] *nf (animal, personne)* leech
sanguin, -e [sɑ̃gɛ̃, -in] *adj (tempérament)* fiery; *(teint, visage)* ruddy
sanguinaire [sɑ̃ginɛr] *adj* (a) *(homme)* bloodthirsty (**b**) *(combat)* bloody
sanitaire [sanitɛr] **1** *adj* (a) *(personnel)* medical; *(mesures)* health (**b**) *(installation)* sanitary **2** *nmpl* **les sanitaires** *(toilettes)* the toilet; *(salle de bains et W.-C.)* the bathroom and toilet
sans [sɑ̃] **1** *prép* (a) *(indique l'absence, la privation, l'exclusion)* without; **s. travailler** without working; **non s. difficulté** not without difficulty (**b**) *(indique la condition)* but for; **s. vous, je ne l'aurais jamais fait** but for you, I'd never have done it; **s. cela, s. quoi** otherwise; *Fam* **sois sage, s. ça tu seras puni!** be good or else you'll be punished!
2 *adv Fam* without it/them; **faire s.** to do without
3 *conj* **s. que nous le sachions** without our knowing
sans-abri [sɑ̃zabri] *nmf inv* homeless person; **les s.** homeless
San Salvador [sɑ̃salvadɔr] *n* San Salvador
sans-cœur [sɑ̃kœr] *nmf inv Fam* heartless person
sans-culotte *(pl* **sans-culottes)** [sɑ̃kylɔt] *nm Hist* sansculotte *(person with extreme republican sympathies during the French Revolution)*
sans-emploi [sɑ̃zɑ̃plwa] *nmf inv* unemployed person; **les s.** the unemployed
sans-faute [sɑ̃fot] *nm inv (de compétition hippique)* clear round; **faire un s.** *(cheval)* to have a clear round; *Fig (personne)* not to put a foot wrong
sans-gêne [sɑ̃ʒɛn] **1** *adj inv* ill-mannered **2** *nm* lack of manners
sans-le-sou [sɑ̃ləsu] *nmf inv Fam* penniless person
sans-logis [sɑ̃lɔʒi] *nmf* homeless person; **les s.** the homeless
sans-papiers [sɑ̃papje] *nmf* illegal immigrant
sans-patrie [sɑ̃patri] *nmf inv* stateless person
santé [sɑ̃te] *nf* health; **être en bonne s.** to be in good health; **avoir une bonne/mauvaise s.** to be healthy/unhealthy; **c'est bon/mauvais pour la s.** it's good/bad for your health; **boire à la s. de qn** to drink sb's health; **(à votre) s.!** cheers!, good health!; *Suisse Fam* **s.!** *(quand on éternue)* bless you!; **la s. publique** public health
santiag [sɑ̃tjag] *nf Fam* cowboy boot
santon [sɑ̃tɔ̃] *nm* Christmas crib figure
São Tomé et Príncipe [saɔtɔmeeprɛ̃sip] *n* São Tomé e Príncipe
saoudien, -enne [saudjɛ̃, -ɛn] **1** *adj* Saudi (Arabian) **2** *nm,f* **S.** Saudi (Arabian)
saoul [su], **saouler** [sule] = **soûl, soûler**
sape [sap] *nf* (a) *(tranchée)* sap; *Fig* **travail de s. undermining** (**b**) *Fam* **sapes** *(vêtements)* gear
saper [sape] **1** *vt* (a) *aussi Fig* to undermine; **s. le moral à**

qn to sap sb's morale (**b**) *Fam (habiller)* to dress; **être bien sapé** to be all dolled up

2 se saper *vpr Fam* to dress

sapeur-pompier (*pl* sapeurs-pompiers) [sapœr-pɔ̃pje] *nm* fireman; **les sapeurs-pompiers** *(service)* the fire *Br* brigade *or Am* department

saphir [safir] *nm* sapphire

sapin [sapɛ̃] *nm* (**a**) *(arbre)* fir (tree) (**b**) *Fam* **ça sent le s.** that sounds as if you're heading for an early grave; **il sent le s.** he's done for (**c**) *Can* **se faire passer un s.** *(se faire avoir)* to be taken for a ride

sapristi [sapristi] *exclam Fam Vieilli ou Hum* good heavens!

saquer [sake] = **sacquer**

sarabande [sarabɑ̃d] *nf (danse, air)* saraband; *Fam (tapage)* racket

Sarajevo [saraʒevo] *n* Sarajevo

sarbacane [sarbakan] *nf* blowpipe; *(jouet)* peashooter

sarcasme [sarkasm] *nm* sarcasm; *(remarque)* sarcastic remark

sarcastique [sarkastik] *adj* sarcastic

sarcler [sarkle] *vt (jardin)* to weed; *(sol)* to hoe; *(champ)* to clean

sarclette [sarklɛt] *nf* hoe

sarcloir [sarklwar] *nm* hoe

sarcome [sarkom] *nm Méd* sarcoma; **s. de Kaposi** Kaposi's sarcoma

sarcophage [sarkɔfaʒ] *nm* sarcophagus

Sardaigne [sardɛɲ] *nf* **la S.** Sardinia

sarde [sard] **1** *adj* Sardinian

2 *nmf* **S.** Sardinian

3 *nm (langue)* Sardinian

sardine [sardin] *nf* sardine; **sardines à l'huile/à la tomate** sardines in oil/in tomato sauce; *Fam* **serrés comme des sardines** packed together like sardines

sardonique [sardɔnik] *adj* sardonic

Sargasses [sargas] *voir* **mer**

SARL [esaɛrɛl] *nf (abrév* société à responsabilité limitée) limited (liability) company; **Balacor S.** *Br* ≃ Balacor Ltd, *Am* ≃ Balacor Inc

sarment [sarmɑ̃] *nm (tige)* bine; *(de vigne)* vine shoot

saroual, -als [sarwal], **sarouel** [sarwɛl] *nm* = baggy trousers worn by North Africans

sarrasin, -e [sarazɛ̃, -in] **1** *adj Hist* Saracen

2 *nm,f Hist* **S.** Saracen

3 *nm (plante)* buckwheat

sarriette [sarjɛt] *nf* savory

sas [sɑs] *nm (pièce étanche)* airlock

Satan [satɑ̃] *npr* Satan

satané, -e [satane] *adj Fam* confounded

satanique [satanik] *adj* satanic; *Fig (cruauté, sourire)* fiendish

satellite [satelit] **1** *nm* (**a**) *(corps céleste, engin)* satellite; **émission retransmise par s.** satellite broadcast, **télévision par s.** satellite television; **s.-espion** spy satellite; **s. géostationnaire** geostationary satellite; **s. de télécommunications** telecommunications satellite; **s. de télédiffusion** broadcast satellite (**b**) *Pol* satellite

2 *adj* **pays s.** satellite state

satiété [sasjete] *nf* **manger/boire à s.** to eat/drink one's fill

satin [satɛ̃] *nm* satin

satiné, -e [satine] **1** *adj (tissu)* satiny; *(papier)* glazed; *(peau)* satin-smooth; **peinture satinée** silk-finish paint

2 *nm* satin finish; *(de la peau)* satin smoothness

satire [satir] *nf* satire; **faire la s. de qch** to satirize sth

satirique [satirik] *adj* satirical

satiriste [satirist] *nmf* satirist

satisfaction [satisfaksjɔ̃] *nf* satisfaction; **à la s. générale** to everyone's satisfaction; **donner s. à qn** to give sb satisfaction; **obtenir s.** to obtain satisfaction

satisfaire [36] [satisfɛr] **1** *vt* to satisfy

2 satisfaire à *vt ind (demande, condition, besoins)* to satisfy; *(règlement, normes de sécurité)* to comply with; *(obligation)* to fulfil

3 se satisfaire *vpr* **se s. de qch** to be satisfied with sth; **se s. de peu** to be content with very little; *Péj* to be easily satisfied

satisfaisant, -e [satisfəzɑ̃, -ɑ̃t] *adj (acceptable)* satisfactory; *(qui contente)* satisfying

satisfait, -e [satisfɛ, -ɛt] *adj* (**a**) *(heureux)* satisfied (**de** with); *Ironique* **vous voilà s.!** well, you asked for it!, **s. ou remboursé** *(dans une publicité)* satisfaction or your money back (**b**) *(suffisant)* satisfied

satisfecit [satisfesit] *nm inv Litt* **décerner un s. à qn** to congratulate sb on a job well done

saturation [satyrasjɔ̃] *nf aussi Fig* saturation; *(du réseau routier)* gridlock; *aussi Fig* **arriver à s.** to reach saturation point; *Ordinat (disquette)* to become full

saturer [satyre] **1** *vt* to saturate (**de** with); **les appels ont saturé le standard** the calls have jammed the switchboard

2 *vi Fam* **je sature!** I've had as much as I can take!

Saturne [satyrn] *npr (dieu, planète)* Saturn

satyre [satir] *nm* (**a**) *(demi-dieu)* satyr (**b**) *Fam (obsédé sexuel)* sex maniac

sauce [sos] *nf* (**a**) *(accompagnement)* sauce; **s. à la moutarde** mustard sauce; **s. de soja** soy sauce; **s. tomate** tomato sauce; *Fam Fig* **allonger la s.** to pad it out; *Fam* **mettre qch à toutes les sauces** to use sth in every way imaginable; *Fam* **à quelle s. sera-t-il mangé?** what'll be in store for him? (**b**) *Fam (pluie)* **prendre la s.** to get soaked

saucée [sose] *nf Fam (pluie)* downpour; **recevoir une s.** to get soaked

saucer [16] [sose] *vt* (**a**) *(assiette)* to mop up the sauce from (**b**) *Fam* **se faire s.** to get soaked

saucier [sosje] *nm* sauce cook

saucière [sosjɛr] *nf* sauce boat

sauciflard [sosiflar] *nm Fam* (slicing) sausage

saucisse [sosis] *nf* sausage; **s. de Francfort** frankfurter; **s. sèche** thin salami-type sausages; **s. de Strasbourg** knackwurst; **s. de Toulouse** = type of pork sausage

saucisson [sosisɔ̃] *nm* (slicing) sausage; **s. à l'ail** garlic sausage; *Hum* **s. à pattes** sausage dog; **s. pur porc** 100% pork sausage

saucissonné, -e [sosisɔne] *adj Fam* trussed up

sauf¹, sauve [sof, sov] *adj (personne)* safe, unharmed; **avoir la vie sauve** to escape with one's life; **laisser la vie sauve à qn** to spare sb's life; **l'honneur est s.** honour is saved

sauf² *prép* except (for), apart from; **s. imprévu** unless anything unforeseen happens; **s. erreur de ma part** if I'm not mistaken; **s. votre respect** with all due respect; **s. s'il pleut** unless it rains; *Fam* **s. que** except that

sauf-conduit (*pl* sauf-conduits) [sofkɔ̃dɥi] *nm* safe conduct

sauge [soʒ] *nf* sage

saugrenu, -e [sogrəny] *adj* preposterous

saule [sol] *nm* willow; **s. pleureur** weeping willow

saumâtre [somɑtr] *adj (goût, eau)* brackish; *Fig* bitter

saumon [somɔ̃] **1** *nm* salmon; **s. fumé** smoked salmon **2** *adj inv* **(rose) s.** salmon-pink

saumoné, -e [somɔne] *adj voir* **truite**

saumure [somyr] *nf* brine

sauna [sona] *nm* sauna

saupoudrer [supudre] *vt* to sprinkle (**de** with)

saupoudreuse [supudrøz] *nf* dredger

saur [sɔr] *adj m voir* **hareng**

saurai, saurais *etc voir* **savoir**

saurien [sɔrjɛ̃] *nm* saurian

saut [so] *nm (bond)* jump, leap; **faire un s.** to jump, to leap; *Fig* **faire un s. à Caen/chez le boucher/en ville** to pop over to Caen/round to the butcher's/into town; *Fig* **faire un s. de plusieurs années** to skip several years; **au s. du lit** first thing in the morning; **s. de l'ange** *Br* swallow dive, *Am* swan dive; **s. à l'élastique** bungee jumping; **s. en hauteur** high jump; **s. en longueur** long jump; **s. en parachute** parachute jump; *(activité)* parachute jumping; **faire du s. en parachute** to go parachute jumping; **s. à la perche** pole vaulting; **s. périlleux** somersault; **s. en** *ou* **à skis** ski jump; *(activité)* ski jumping; **faire du s. à skis** to go ski jumping

saute [sot] *nf* **sautes de température** sudden changes in temperature; **sautes d'humeur** mood swings

sauté, -e [sote] **1** *adj* sautéed, sauté **2** *nm* **s. de lapin** sauté of rabbit

saute-mouton [sotmutɔ̃] *nm inv* leapfrog; **jouer à s.** to play leapfrog

sauter [sote] **1** *vt* (**a**) *(fossé, barrière)* to jump (over), to leap over; *Fig* **s. le pas** to take the plunge (**b**) *(omettre) (page, ligne, repas)* to skip; *(maille)* to drop; **s. une classe** to skip a year (**c**) *Vulg (coucher avec)* to screw; **se faire s. par qn** to screw sb **2** *vi* (**a**) *(bondir)* to jump, to leap; **s. sur un pied** to hop; **s. à pieds joints** to jump with one's feet together; **s. à la perche** to pole-vault; **s. à la corde** *Br* to skip, *Am* to jump rope; **s. en parachute** to do a parachute jump; **s. à la gorge de qn** to go for sb; *(chien)* to fly at sb's throat; **s. au cou de qn** to fling one's arms round sb's neck; **s. aux yeux** to be obvious; **s. au plafond** *(bouchon)* to hit the ceiling; *Fig (de surprise)* to jump out of one's skin; *(d'indignation)* to hit the roof; **s. de joie** to jump for joy; *aussi Fam Fig* **s. sur qn** to pounce on sb; **faire s. un enfant sur ses genoux** to bounce a child on one's knees; **s. sur l'occasion** to jump at the opportunity; **s. du coq à l'âne** to jump from one subject to another; **nous allons s. directement à la page 5** we're going to jump straight to page 5; *Fam* **et que ça saute!** and make it snappy! (**b**) *(exploser)* to blow up; *(bouton)* to come off; *(fusible)* to blow; *Fig (gouvernement)* to fall; **faire s.** *(rocher)* to blast; *(pont, mine)* to blow up; *(serrure)* to force; *Fig (gouvernement)* to bring down; *(personne)* to fire, *Br* to sack; *Fam* **faire s. la banque** to break the bank (**c**) *Culin* **faire s.** to sauté

sauterelle [sotrɛl] *nf* grasshopper; *(nuisible)* locust

sauterie [sotri] *nf Vieilli ou Hum* hop

sauteur, -euse [sotœr, -øz] **1** *adj* jumping **2** *nm,f* jumper; **s. en hauteur** high-jumper; **s. en longueur** long-jumper; **s. à la perche** pole-vaulter

sautillement [sotijmɑ̃] *nm* hopping about

sautiller [sotije] *vi* to hop about; **s. d'un pied sur l'autre** to hop from one foot to the other; **avancer en sautillant** to hop along

sautoir [sotwar] *nm* (**a**) *(collier)* chain; **s. de perles** string of pearls (**b**) *(de stade)* jumping area

sauvage [sovaʒ] **1** *adj* (**a**) *(plante, animal)* wild; **redevenir s.** *(animal apprivoisé)* to go back to the wild; **à l'état s.** wild (**b**) *(peuple, tribu)* savage, primitive (**c**) *(violent) (personne,*

agression) savage (**d**) *(peu sociable)* unsociable (**e**) *(non autorisé)* unauthorized; **immigration s.** illegal immigration **2** *nmf* (**a**) *Vieilli (indigène)* savage; *Fam Hum* **on n'est pas des sauvages!** we're not savages!; *Fam Hum* **bande de sauvages!** you bunch of savages! (**b**) *(brute)* savage (**c**) *(solitaire)* recluse

sauvagement [sovaʒmɑ̃] *adv* savagely

sauvageon, -onne [sovaʒɔ̃, -ɔn] *nm,f (enfant)* little savage

sauvagerie [sovaʒri] *nf* (**a**) *(cruauté)* savagery (**b**) *(insociabilité)* unsociability

sauvegarde [sovgard] *nf* (**a**) *(protection)* safeguard (contre against) (**b**) *Ordinat* saving, backup; **faire la s. d'un fichier** to save a file; **s. externe** off-line backup; **s. en ligne** on-line backup; **copie de s.** backup (copy)

sauvegarder [sovgarde] *vt* (**a**) *(protéger)* to safeguard (contre against) (**b**) *Ordinat (fichier)* to save, to back up; **s. un fichier sur disque** to save a file to disk

sauver [sove] **1** *vt* (**a**) *(personne)* to save, to rescue (**de** from); *(âme)* to save; **s. la vie à qn** to save sb's life; **le malade est sauvé** the patient is out of danger (**b**) *(navire, marchandises)* to salvage; **s. les apparences** to keep up appearances; *Fam Fig* **s. les meubles** to salvage something from the wreckage **2** *vi* **sauve qui peut!** every man for himself! **3 se sauver** *vpr* (**a**) *(s'échapper)* to escape (**de** from) (**b**) *(s'enfuir)* to run away; *Fam* **sauve-toi, tu vas être en retard** be off, you'll be late (**c**) *(lait)* to boil over

sauvetage [sovtaʒ] *nm* (**a**) *(d'un accidenté)* rescue (**b**) *(d'un navire, de marchandises)* salvage; *(d'une entreprise)* rescue

sauveteur [sovtœr] *nm* rescuer

sauvette [sovɛt] **à la sauvette** *adv (pour ne pas être vu)* on the sly; *(à la hâte)* in a hurry; **vendre à la s.** *(illégalement)* to peddle illegally on the streets; **marchand à la s.** illegal street vendor

sauveur [sovœr] *nm* saviour

savamment [savamɑ̃] *adv* (**a**) *(avec érudition)* learnedly (**b**) *(habilement)* cleverly, skilfully

savane [savan] *nf* savanna

savant, -e [savɑ̃, -ɑ̃t] **1** *adj* (**a**) *(érudit)* learned (**b**) *(habile)* clever, skilful (**c**) *(animal)* performing **2** *nm (scientifique)* scientist; *(érudit)* scholar

savate [savat] *nf* (**a**) *Fam (pantoufle)* slipper; **traîner la s.** *(être pauvre)* to be down at heel (**b**) *Fam* **comme une s.** atrociously (**c**) *Sp* kick boxing

saveur [savœr] *nf* (**a**) *(d'un vin, d'un aliment)* flavour (**b**) *Fig (d'une remarque, d'un récit)* savour

Savoie [savwa] *nf* la S. Savoy

savoir¹ [savwar] *nm* knowledge, learning

savoir² [62] **1** *vt* (**a**) *(avoir connaissance de)* to know; **s. qch par cœur** to know sth by heart; **je n'en sais rien** I don't know; **je n'en sais trop rien** I'm not very sure; **en s. trop** to know too much; **qu'est-ce je en sais?** what do I know?; **va s.!** who knows?; **je ne veux pas le s.** I don't want to know; **n'a rien voulu s.** he didn't want to know; **reste à s. si...** it remains to be seen whether...; **je crois s. qu'il est ici** I understand he's here; **faire s. qch à qn** to tell sb sth, to let sb know about sth; **je le sais par mon frère** I heard about it from my brother; **à s.** that is (to say), namely; **pas que je sache** not that I know of; **à ce que je sache, pour autant que je sache** as far as I know; **on ne sait jamais** you never know

(**b**) *(être conscient de)* to know; **sans le s.** without realizing; **sachez que...** be advised that..., please note that...

(**c**) *(connaître)* **qui tu sais** you know who; **je ne le savais pas si susceptible** I didn't know he was so touchy

(**d**) *(être capable de)* **s. faire qch** to be able to do sth, to know how to do sth; **savez-vous nager/conduire?** can you swim/drive?; **je ne saurais vous le dire** I really couldn't tell you **2 se savoir** *vpr* (**a**) *(se répandre)* **ça se saura vite** it'll soon get out (**b**) *(avoir conscience d'être)* **il se savait perdu/surveillé** he knew he was doomed/being watched

savoir-faire [savwarfɛr] *nm* expertise, know-how

savoir-vivre [savwarvivr] *nm* good manners; **manquer de s.** to have no manners

savon [savɔ̃] *nm* soap; **s. à barbe** shaving soap; **s. de Marseille** household soap; *Fam* **passer un s. à qn** to give sb a telling-off

savonner [savɔne] **1** *vt (mains, vêtement)* to soap; *(en faisant mousser)* to lather **2 se savonner** *vpr* to soap oneself; **se s. les mains** to soap one's hands

savonnette [savɔnɛt] *nf* bar of soap

savonneux, -euse [savɔnø, -øz] *adj* soapy

savourer [savure] *vt aussi Fig* to savour

savoureux, -euse [savurø, -øz] *adj (plat)* tasty, *(vin)* full-flavoured; *Fig (récit, détails)* spicy

savoyard, -e [savwajar, -ard] **1** *adj* Savoyard **2** *nm,f* **S.** Savoyard

saxo [sakso] *nm Fam (instrument)* sax; *(musicien)* sax player

saxon, -onne [saksɔ̃, -ɔn] **1** *adj* Saxon **2** *nm,f* **S.** Saxon

saxophone [saksofɔn] *nm* saxophone

saxophoniste [saksɔfɔnist] *nmf* saxophonist

saynète [sɛnɛt] *nf (petite pièce)* sketch

sbire [sbir] *nm Péj* henchman

scabreux, -euse [skabrø, -øz] *adj* obscene

scalp [skalp] *nm (chevelure)* scalp

scalpel [skalpɛl] *nm* scalpel

scalper [skalpe] *vt* to scalp

scandale [skɑ̃dal] *nm* scandal, **faire s.** *(affaire)* to cause a scandal; **faire un s.** *(personne)* to make a scene; **au grand s. de** much to the indignation of; **c'est un s.!** it's a scandal!

scandaleux, -euse [skɑ̃dalø, -øz] *adj* scandalous, outrageous

scandaliser [skɑ̃dalize] **1** *vt* to scandalize, to shock **2 se scandaliser** *vpr* to be scandalized *or* shocked (**de** by)

scander [skɑ̃de] *vt (slogan)* to chant; *(vers)* to scan

scandinave [skɑ̃dinav] **1** *adj* Scandinavian **2** *nmf* **S.** Scandinavian

Scandinavie [skɑ̃dinavi] *nf* **la S.** Scandinavia

scanner[1] [skanɛr] *nm* scanner; **on lui a fait un s.** he was given a scan

scanner[2] [skane] *vt Ordinat* to scan

scanneur [skanœr] *nm Ordinat & TV* scanner; **s. à main** handheld scanner; **s. à plat** flatbed scanner

scaphandre [skafɑ̃dr] *nm* (**a**) *(de plongeur)* diving suit (**b**) *(d'astronaute)* space suit

scaphandrier [skafɑ̃drije] *nm* diver

scarabée [skarabe] *nm* beetle

scarlatine [skarlatin] *nf* scarlet fever; **avoir la s.** to have scarlet fever

scarole [skarɔl] *nf* endive

scatologique [skatɔlɔʒik] *adj* scatological

sceau, -x [so] *nm* seal; *Fig* **le s. du génie** the mark of genius; **sous le s. du secret** under the seal of secrecy

scélérat, -e [selera, -at] *Litt* **1** *adj* villainous **2** *nm,f* villain

scellé, -e [sele] **1** *adj* sealed **2** *nm* seal; **apposer/lever les scellés** to put on/remove the seals

sceller [sele] *vt* (**a**) *(apposer un sceau sur)* & *Fig* to seal (**b**) *Constr* to embed

scénario [senarjo] *nm* script, screenplay

scénariste [senarist] *nmf* scriptwriter

scène [sɛn] *nf* (**a**) *(plateau)* stage; **la s.** *(le métier d'acteur)* the stage; **mettre en s.** *(pièce de théâtre)* to stage; *(film)* to direct; **entrer en s.** *(acteur)* to come on; *Fig* to appear on the scene; **sortir de s.** to go off; **quitter la s.** to retire from the stage; *Fig* **la s. politique/internationale** the political/international scene; **occuper le devant de la s.** to hold centre stage (**b**) *(d'une pièce de théâtre, d'un film)* scene (**c**) *(action)* action; **la s. se passe au Moyen Âge** the action takes place in the Middle Ages (**d**) *(événement)* scene; **des scènes de panique** scenes of panic (**e**) *Fam (dispute)* scene; **il m'a fait une s.** he made a scene; **s. de ménage** domestic squabble (**f**) *(peinture)* **une s. de chasse** a hunting scene

scénique [senik] *adj* theatrical

scepticisme [sɛptisism] *nm* scepticism

sceptique [sɛptik] **1** *adj* sceptical **2** *nmf* sceptic

sceptre [sɛptr] *nm* sceptre

schema [ʃema] *nm* (**a**) *(dessin)* diagram (**b**) *(résumé)* outline (**c**) *Ordinat* **s. de clavier** keyboard map

schématique [ʃematik] *adj* schematic; *Péj* oversimplified

schématiquement [ʃematikmɑ̃] *adv (à l'aide d'un schéma)* schematically; *(en gros)* in outline

schématiser [ʃematize] *vt* to schematize; *Péj* to oversimplify

schisme [ʃism] *nm* schism

schiste [ʃist] *nm* schist, shale

schizophrène [skizɔfrɛn] *adj & nmf* schizophrenic

schizophrénie [skizɔfreni] *nf* schizophrenia

schlinguer [ʃlɛ̃ge] *vi très Fam* to stink

schnaps [ʃnaps] *nm* schnapps

schnock, schnoque [ʃnɔk] *nm Fam* **un vieux s.** an old git

schuss [ʃus] *nm* schuss; **descendre la piste en s.** *ou* **tout s.** to schuss down the slope

sciatique [sjatik] **1** *adj* sciatic **2** *nf* sciatica

scie [si] *nf* (**a**) *(outil)* saw; **s. circulaire** circular saw; **s. mécanique** *ou* **à main** hand saw; **s. à métaux** hacksaw (**b**) **s. musicale** musical saw

sciemment [sjamɑ̃] *adv* knowingly

science [sjɑ̃s] *nf* (**a**) *(savoir)* science; *Fig* **je n'ai pas la s. infuse** I can't be expected to know everything (**b**) *(domaine spécifique)* science; **sciences économiques** economics; **sciences exactes** exact sciences; **sciences expérimentales** experimental science; **sciences humaines** ≃ social sciences; **sciences naturelles** natural science; **Sciences Po** ≃ "grande école" for political science

science-fiction [sjɑ̃sfiksjɔ̃] *nf* science fiction; *Fig & Hum* **c'est de la s.!** it's unreal!

scientifique [sjɑ̃tifik] **1** *adj* scientific **2** *nmf* scientist

scientifiquement [sjɑ̃tifikmɑ̃] *adv* scientifically

scier [66] [sje] *vt* (**a**) *(bois, métal)* to saw; *(pour enlever)* *(branche)* to saw off (**b**) *Fam (étonner)* to dumbfound

scierie [siri] *nf* sawmill

scieur [sjœr] *nm* sawyer

scinder [sɛ̃de] **1** vt to split up (**en** into)
2 se scinder vpr to split up (**en** into)

scintillement [sɛ̃tijmɑ̃] nm (de bijou, de lumière, des yeux) sparkling; (d'étoile) twinkling

scintiller [sɛ̃tije] vi (bijou, lumière, yeux) to sparkle; (étoile) to twinkle

scission [sisjɔ̃] nf split; **faire s.** to split away

sciure [sjyr] nf sawdust

sclérose [skleroz] nf sclerosis; Fig ossification; **s. en plaques** multiple sclerosis

scléroser [skleroze] **1** vt Méd to sclerose
2 se scléroser vpr Méd to sclerose; Fig to become fossilized

scolaire [skɔlɛr] adj (**a**) (résultats, réussite) academic; (réforme, organisation, vie) school (**b**) Péj (esprit, mentalité) bookish

scolarisation [skɔlarizasjɔ̃] nf education

scolariser [skɔlarize] vt to send to school; **enfant scolarisé** child attending school

scolarité [skɔlarite] nf schooling; **prolonger la s.** to raise the school-leaving age

scoliose [skɔljoz] nf curvature of the spine

scoop [skup] nm scoop

scooter [skuter] nm (motor) scooter; **s. des mers** jet ski

scorbut [skɔrbyt] nm scurvy

score [skɔr] nm score; (en politique) result

scories [skɔri] nfpl (dans l'industrie) slag; (d'éruption volcanique) scoria

scorpion [skɔrpjɔ̃] nm (**a**) (animal) scorpion (**b**) Astron & Astrol **le S.** Scorpio; **être S.** to be (a) Scorpio

Scotch® [skɔtʃ] nm (ruban adhésif) Br sellotape®, Am scotch tape®

scotch [skɔtʃ] nm (boisson) scotch

scotcher [skɔtʃe] vt Br to sellotape, Am to scotch-tape

scout [skut] nm Scout

scoutisme [skutism] nm (activité) scouting; (mouvement) scout movement

scribe [skrib] nm (**a**) Péj pen-pusher (**b**) Hist scribe

scribouillard, -e [skribujar, -ard] nm,f Fam Péj pen-pusher

script [skript] nm (**a**) (écriture) printing; **écrire en s.** to print (**b**) Cin (film) script

scripte [skript] nmf Cin (homme) continuity man; (femme) continuity girl

scrupule [skrypyl] nm scruple; **sans scrupules** (personne) unscrupulous; (agir) unscrupulously

scrupuleusement [skrypyløzmɑ̃] adv scrupulously

scrupuleux, -euse [skrypylø, -øz] adj scrupulous; **peu s.** unscrupulous

scrutateur, -trice [skrytatœr, -tris] **1** adj Litt (esprit, regard) searching
2 nm,f (d'un scrutin) teller

scruter [skryte] vt to scrutinize; (horizon, paysage) to scan

scrutin [skrytɛ̃] nm (**a**) (élection) poll; **s. secret** secret vote (**b**) (vote) ballot (**c**) (système) voting system; **s. majoritaire** first-past-the-post system; **s. proportionnel** voting by proportional representation; **s. uninominal** voting for a single candidate

sculpter [skylte] vt to sculpt; (dans du bois) to carve (**dans** out of)

sculpteur [skyltœr] nm sculptor; **s. sur bois** woodcarver

sculptural, -e, -aux, -ales [skyltyral, -o] adj (art) sculptural; (silhouette, beauté) statuesque

sculpture [skyltyr] nf (œuvre, art) sculpture; **s. sur bois** woodcarving; **faire de la s.** to sculpt

SDF [ɛsdeɛf] nmf (abrév **sans domicile fixe**) person of no fixed abode; (sans abri) homeless person; **les S.** (sans abri) the homeless

SDN [ɛsdeɛn] nf (abrév **Société des Nations**) **la S.** the League of Nations

se [sə]

s' is used before a word beginning with a vowel or h mute.

pron personnel (**a**) (soi) (homme) himself; (femme) herself; (chose) itself; (indéfini) oneself; (pluriel) themselves; **se flatter** to flatter oneself; **il se rase** he is shaving; Fam **on s'est blessés** we hurt ourselves
(**b**) (à soi) (homme) to himself; (femme) to herself; (chose) to itself; (indéfini) to oneself; (pluriel) to themselves; **elle s'est coupé le doigt** she has cut her finger; Fam **on va s'acheter un ordinateur** we're going to buy (ourselves) a computer
(**c**) (réciproque) (objet direct) each other; (objet indirect) to each other; **se nuire (l'un à l'autre)** to hurt each other; **ils se sont quittés en bons termes** they parted on good terms
(**d**) (passif) **ça se mange froid** you eat it cold; **les couteaux se rangent dans ce tiroir** the knives go in this drawer

séance [seɑ̃s] nf (**a**) (réunion) session, meeting; **tenir s.** to be in session (**b**) (de travail, d'entraînement) session; **s. de photo** photo session; **s. de pose** sitting (**c**) Cin & Th performance; Cin **s. privée** private showing (**d**) **s. tenante** straight away, at once

séant, -e [seɑ̃, -ɑ̃t] **1** adj Litt (convenable) fitting
2 nm Litt ou Hum **se mettre sur son s.** to sit up

seau, -x [so] nm bucket; (contenu) bucket(ful); Fam **il pleut à seaux** it's pouring down; **s. à champagne** champagne bucket; **s. à charbon** coal scuttle; **s. à glace** ice bucket

sébacé, -e [sebase] adj sebaceous

sébum [sebɔm] nm sebum

sec, sèche [sɛk, sɛʃ] **1** adj (**a**) (temps, saison, sol, peau, bois) dry; (morue, fruit) dried; **à pied s.** without getting one's feet wet; **avoir la gorge sèche** (avoir soif) to be dry (**b**) (vin, cidre) dry (**c**) (maigre) (personne) lean; **être s. comme un coup de trique** to be wiry (**d**) (austère) (personne) hard; (réponse, ton, voix) sharp; **avoir le cœur s.** to be hard-hearted (**e**) (non appuyé) (coup) sharp (**f**) (sans rien ajouter) **boire qch s.** to drink sth neat
2 adv (**a**) (beaucoup) (frapper, pleuvoir) hard; (boire) heavily; **démarrer s.** to shoot off (**b**) Fam aussi **s.** right away
3 nm (**a**) **tenir au s.** (sur une étiquette) keep in a dry place (**b**) **être à s.** (source, puits, rivière) to be dry; Fam (sans argent) to be broke

sécable [sekabl] adj divisible

sécateur [sekatœr] nm pruning shears, Br secateurs

sécession [sesesjɔ̃] nf secession; **faire s. (de)** to secede (from)

séchage [seʃaʒ] nm drying

sèche [sɛʃ] **1** nf Fam Br fag, Am butt
2 adj voir **sec**

sèche-cheveux [sɛʃʃəvø] nm inv hairdryer

sèche-linge [sɛʃlɛ̃ʒ] nm inv (appareil) tumble-drier; (armoire) airing cupboard

sèche-mains [sɛʃmɛ̃] nm inv hand-drier

sèchement [sɛʃmɑ̃] adv (parler, répondre) curtly

sécher [34] [seʃe] **1** vt to dry; Fam **s. un cours** to skip a class

2 *vi* (**a**) *(vêtement, cheveux)* to dry; **mettre du linge à s.** to put clothes out to dry (**b**) *Fam (ne pouvoir répondre)* to be stumped
3 se sécher *vpr* to dry oneself; **se s. les cheveux/les mains** to dry one's hair/hands

sécheresse [seʃʀɛs, seʃʀɛs] *nf* (**a**) *(absence de pluie)* drought (**b**) *(de l'air, du sol, de la peau)* dryness (**c**) *(des manières, du ton)* curtness; *(du cœur)* hardness; *(du style)* dryness

séchoir [seʃwaʀ] *nm* (**a**) *(appareil)* drier; **s. (à cheveux)** hairdryer (**b**) *(dispositif pliant)* **s. (à linge)** clothes-horse

second, -e [səgɔ̃, -ɔ̃d] **1** *adj* second; *(rôle)* supporting, minor
2 *nm* (**a**) *(assistant)* assistant; *Mil* second-in-command; *Naut* first mate; *(de duelliste)* second (**b**) *(étage) Br* second *or Am* third floor
3 *nm,f* second; **je préfère le s.** I prefer the second one; *voir aussi* **cinquième**

secondaire [səgɔ̃dɛʀ] **1** *adj* (**a**) *Scol* secondary; **établissement d'enseignement s.** secondary school (**b**) *(pas essentiel)* secondary; *(personnage, rôle) Th* minor; *Fig* secondary; **c'est s.** it's of secondary importance (**c**) *Écon & Géol* secondary
2 *nm Géol* secondary era; *Écon* secondary sector

seconde [səgɔ̃d] *nf* (**a**) *(unité de temps)* second; **(attendez) une s.!** just a second!; **pendant une fraction de s.** for a fraction of a second (**b**) *(vitesse)* second (gear) (**c**) *(dans les transports)* second class; **voyager en s.** to travel second-class (**d**) *(classe) Br* ≃ fifth form, *Am* ≃ tenth grade (**e**) *Mus* second

seconder [səgɔ̃de] *vt* to assist

secouer [səkwe] **1** *vt* (**a**) *(arbre, tête, bouteille)* to shake; *(coussin, oreiller)* to plump up; *(vêtements, tapis)* to shake out; *(sujet: vent, vagues)* to buffet; **nous avons été secoués pendant la traversée** we were shaken about during the crossing; *Fam* **s. les puces à qn** *(réprimander)* to tell sb off (**b**) *(sujet: choc, maladie, nouvelles)* to shake (up) (**c**) *(se débarrasser de) (poussière, joug)* to shake off
2 se secouer *vpr* (**a**) *(s'agiter)* to shake oneself (**b**) *(agir)* to snap out of it

secourable [səkuʀabl] *adj* helpful

secourir [22] [səkuʀiʀ] *vt* to help, to assist

secourisme [səkuʀism] *nm* first aid

secouriste [səkuʀist] *nmf* first-aid worker

secours [səkuʀ] *nm* (**a**) *(aide)* help; *(financier, matériel)* aid; *Mil (renforts)* relief; **appel au s.** call for help; **au s.!** help!; **premiers s.** first aid; **porter s. à qn** to give sb help; **demander du s.** to ask for help; **aller au s. de qn** to go to sb's assistance; **cela m'a été d'un grand s.** it's been a great help to me (**b**) **de s.** *(trousse, poste)* first-aid; *(sortie, éclairage)* emergency; *(roue)* spare; *Ordinat (copie, fichier)* backup

secousse [səkus] *nf* jolt, jerk; **par secousses** *(avancer)* jerkily; **s. (sismique)** (earth) tremor

secret¹, -ète [səkʀɛ, -ɛt] *adj* (**a**) *(non divulgué)* secret (**b**) *(personne)* reticent

secret² *nm* (**a**) *(confidence, mystère)* secret; **garder un s.** to keep a secret; **mettre qn dans le s.** to let sb in on the secret; **être dans le s.** to be in on the secret; **ne pas avoir de secrets pour qn** *(discipline)* to hold no secrets for sb; **ce n'est un s. pour personne** it's no secret; **le s. du bonheur/de la réussite** the secret of happiness/of success; **secrets d'alcôve** pillow talk; **s. d'État** state secret; **s. de fabrication** trade secret; **s. de Polichinelle** open secret; **emporter un s. dans la tombe** to take a secret to the grave (**b**) *(discrétion)* secrecy; **dans le plus grand s.** in the strictest secrecy; **en s.** *(en cachette)* in secret; **s. bancaire** banking secrecy; **s. professionnel** professional secrecy (**c**) **mettre qn au s.** *(l'enfermer)* to put sb in solitary confinement

secrétaire [səkʀetɛʀ] **1** *nmf* secretary; **s. d'ambassade** secretary; **s. de direction** personal assistant; **s. d'État** Secretary of State; **s. général** secretary general; *Com* company secretary; **s. médicale** medical secretary; **s. particulier** private secretary; **s. de rédaction** sub-editor
2 *nm (meuble)* writing desk

secrétariat [səkʀetaʀja] *nm* (**a**) *(fonction)* secretaryship (**b**) *(bureau)* secretary's office; *(d'un organisme international)* secretariat (**c**) *(métier)* secretarial work (**d**) *Pol* s. d'État ministry

secrètement [səkʀɛtmɑ̃] *adv* secretly

sécréter [34] [sekʀete] *vt* to secrete; *Fig (ennui)* to exude

sécrétion [sekʀesjɔ̃] *nf* secretion

sectaire [sɛktɛʀ] *adj & nmf* sectarian

sectarisme [sɛktaʀism] *nm* sectarianism

secte [sɛkt] *nf* sect

secteur [sɛktœʀ] *nm* (**a**) *(zone)* area, district; *Fam* **changer de s.** to move somewhere else (**b**) *Él* mains; **branché sur le s.** plugged into the mains (**c**) *Écon* sector; **le s. privé/public** the private/public sector; **s. primaire/secondaire/tertiaire** primary/secondary/tertiary sector; *Fam* **ce n'est pas mon s.** that's not my line (**d**) *Math & Ordinat* sector; *Ordinat* **s. d'initialisation** boot sector

section [sɛksjɔ̃] *nf* (**a**) *(division) (d'un livre, d'un bâtiment, d'une autoroute)* section; *(d'une ligne d'autobus)* stage; *(d'un parti politique, d'un syndicat)* branch (**b**) *(de l'infanterie)* platoon; *(de l'artillerie)* section (**c**) *(coupe)* section; **ça fait 5 centimètres de s.** the diameter of the section is 5 centimetres (**d**) *Scol* = one of the groups into which "baccalauréat" students are divided, depending on their chosen kind of specialization

sectionner [sɛksjɔne] *vt* (**a**) *(couper)* to sever (**b**) *(fractionner) (service, circonscription)* to divide into sections

sectoriel, -elle [sɛktɔʀjɛl] *adj* sectorial

sécu [seky] *nf Fam (abrév* **Sécurité sociale**) *Br* ≃ Social Security, *Am* ≃ Welfare

séculaire [sekylɛʀ] *adj* (**a**) *(très ancien)* centuries-old (**b**) *(qui existe depuis un siècle)* a hundred years old (**c**) *(qui a lieu tous les cent ans)* centennial

séculier, -ère [sekylje, -ɛʀ] *adj* secular

secundo [səgɔ̃do] *adv* secondly

sécurisant, -e [sekyʀizɑ̃, -ɑ̃t] *adj* reassuring

sécuriser [sekyʀize] *vt* to reassure

sécurité [sekyʀite] *nf* (**a**) *(ordre, stabilité)* security; **être/se sentir en s.** to be/feel secure; **s. de l'emploi** job security; **s. nationale/internationale** national/international security (**b**) *(absence de danger)* safety; **s. routière** road safety; **S. Routière** = French road safety organization (**c**) *(dispositif)* safety catch; **porte munie d'une s.-enfants** door with a childproof lock (**d**) **s. sociale** *Br* Social Security, *Am* Welfare

sédatif, -ive [sedatif, -iv] *adj & nm* sedative

sédentaire [sedɑ̃tɛʀ] *adj* (**a**) *(vie, travail, travailleur)* sedentary; *(population)* settled (**b**) *(casanier)* stay-at-home

sédentariser [sedɑ̃taʀize] **1** *vt (population)* to settle
2 se sédentariser *vpr* to settle

sédiment [sedimɑ̃] *nm* sediment

sédimentaire [sedimɑ̃tɛʀ] *adj* sedimentary

sédimentation [sedimɑ̃tasjɔ̃] *nf* sedimentation

séditieux, -euse [sedisjø, -øz] **1** *adj* seditious
2 *nm,f* insurgent

sédition [sedisjɔ̃] *nf* sedition

séducteur, -trice [sedyktœr, -tris] **1** *nm,f* seducer, *f* seductress
2 *adj* seductive
séduction [sedyksjɔ̃] *nf* (**a**) *(physique)* seduction; *(par le charme)* charming (**b**) *(moyen de séduire)* attraction; **pouvoir de s.** power of attraction
séduire [18] [sedɥir] *vt* (**a**) *(charmer) (sujet: personne)* to charm; *(sujet: projet, proposition)* to appeal to (**b**) *(sexuellement)* to seduce
séduisant, -e [sedɥizɑ̃, -ɑ̃t] *adj* attractive
séfarade [sefarad] **1** *adj* Sephardic
2 *nmf* Sephardic Jew
segment [sɛgmɑ̃] *nm* segment
segmenter [sɛgmɑ̃te] *vt aussi Ordinat* to segment
ségrégation [segregasjɔ̃] *nf* segregation
ségrégationniste [segregasjɔnist] *adj & nmf* segregationist
seiche [sɛʃ] *nf* cuttlefish; **os de s.** cuttlebone
seigle [sɛgl] *nm* rye
seigneur [sɛɲœr] *nm* (**a**) *Hist* lord; **à tout s.** tout honneur honour where honour is due; **en grand s.** in grand style (**b**) *Rel* **le S.** the Lord
seigneurial, -aux, -ales [sɛɲœrjal, -o] *adj (droits, domaine)* seigniorial
sein [sɛ̃] *nm (de femme)* breast; *Litt (poitrine)* bosom; **serrer** *ou* **presser qn sur son s.** to press sb to one's bosom; **donner le s. à un enfant, nourrir un enfant au s.** to breast-feed a child; **au s. de** within
Seine [sɛn] *nf* **la S.** the Seine
séisme [seism] *nm* earthquake; *Fig & Litt* upheaval
seize [sɛz] *adj & nm inv* sixteen; *voir aussi* **trois**
seizième [sɛzjɛm] *nmf, nm & adj* sixteenth; *voir aussi* **cinquième**
séjour [seʒur] *nm* (**a**) *(période)* stay; **s. linguistique** language-learning trip (**b**) *(pièce)* **(salle de) s.** living room (**c**) *Litt (lieu)* abode
séjourner [seʒurne] *vi* to stay
sel [sɛl] *nm* (**a**) *(substance)* salt; **gros s.** coarse salt; **s. fin** fine salt; **sels de bain** bath salts; **sels** *(à respirer)* (smelling) salts (**b**) *Fig (esprit)* piquancy
sélect, -e [selɛkt] *adj Fam (soirée, clientèle)* select
sélectif, -ive [selɛktif, -iv] *adj* selective; *Ordinat* **en mode s.** in veto mode
sélection [selɛksjɔ̃] *nf* selection
sélectionné, -e [selɛksjɔne] **1** *adj* selected
2 *nm,f (sportif)* selected competitor; *(d'une équipe)* selected player
sélectionner [selɛksjɔne] *vt* to select
sélectionneur, -euse [selɛksjɔnœr, -øz] *nm,f* selector
self [sɛlf] *nm Fam* self-service restaurant
self-service *(pl* self-services) [sɛlfsɛrvis] *nm (restaurant)* self-service restaurant; *(magasin)* self-service shop
selle [sɛl] *nf* (**a**) *(de cheval, bicyclette, moto)* saddle; **se mettre en s.** to mount; **monter sans s.** to ride bareback (**b**) *(matières fécales)* stools; **aller à la s.** to have a bowel movement (**c**) *Culin* **s. de mouton/d'agneau** saddle of mutton/lamb
seller [sele] *vt* to saddle
sellette [selɛt] *nf Fam* **mettre qn/être sur la s.** to put sb/ to be in the hot seat
selon [səlɔ̃] *prép* (**a**) *(d'après)* according to; **s. moi** in my opinion (**b**) *(conformément à)* in accordance with; **s. toute vraisemblance** in all probability (**c**) *(en fonction de)* varier s. **les cas/les saisons** to vary from case to case/season to

season; *Fam* **c'est s.** it all depends; **s. que** depending on whether
semailles [səmɑj] *nfpl* (**a**) *(action)* sowing; **(temps des) s.** sowing time (**b**) *(graines)* seeds
semaine [səmɛn] *nf* (**a**) *(sept jours)* week; **vivre à la petite s.** to live from day to day; **jour de s.** weekday; **en s.** during the week, on weekdays; **la s. sainte** Holy Week (**b**) *(salaire)* week's pay; *(argent de poche)* week's *Br* pocket money *or Am* allowance (**c**) *Mil (tour de service)* week's duty; **être de s.** to be on duty for the week; **officier de s.** duty officer for the week
semainier [səmɛnje] *nm (agenda)* desk diary
sémantique [semɑ̃tik] **1** *adj* semantic
2 *nf* semantics *(singulier)*
sémaphore [semafɔr] *nm Rail* semaphore signal; *Naut* signal station
semblable [sɑ̃blabl] **1** *adj* (**a**) *(pareil)* similar; **s. à qch** similar to sth, like sth; **je n'ai rien dit de s.** I said nothing of the sort (**b**) *(tel)* **de semblables projets/propos** such plans/remarks, plans/remarks like that
2 *nm (être humain)* fellow man; **vous et vos semblables** you and your kind
semblant [sɑ̃blɑ̃] *nm* (**a**) *(apparence)* **un s. de** a semblance of (**b**) **faire s.** to pretend; **faire s. de faire qch** to pretend to do sth; **en faisant s. de rien** without making it obvious
sembler [sɑ̃ble] **1** *vi* to seem
2 *v impersonnel* **il semble que...** it seems that...; **il me/leur semble que...** it seems to me/them that...; **me semble-t-il** it seems to me; **il me semble avoir entendu son nom** I've a feeling I've heard his name; **il me semble idiot d'attendre encore plus longtemps** it seems stupid to me to wait any longer; **faites comme bon vous semble** *ou* **semblera** do as you think best; **il le fera si bon lui semble** he'll do it if he thinks fit
semé, -e [səme] *adj* **s. de** strewn with; *(fleurs)* dotted with; *(étoiles)* studded with; *(citations)* sprinkled with; **s. d'embûches** full of traps
semelle [səmɛl] *nf* sole; **s. (intérieure)** insole; **s. de caoutchouc/de cuir** rubber/leather sole; **ne pas avancer d'une s.** to make no progress whatsoever; **il ne reculera pas d'une s.** he won't give an inch; **ne pas quitter qn d'une s.** to be always at sb's heels; **c'est de la s.!** it's like shoe leather!
semence [səmɑ̃s] *nf (graine)* seed; *(sperme)* semen
semer [46] [səme] *vt* (**a**) *(graines)* to sow (**b**) *(discorde, confusion, panique, doute)* to sow, to spread; *Prov* **qui sème le vent récolte la tempête** he who sows the wind shall reap the whirlwind (**c**) *Fam (distancer)* to shake off (**d**) *Fam (perdre)* to lose
semestre [səmɛstr] *nm* half-year, six-month period; *Scol & Univ* term
semestriel, -elle [səmɛstrijɛl] *adj* half-yearly, six-monthly
semi-automatique [səmiɔtɔmatik] *adj* semi-automatic
semi-liberté [səmilibɛrte] *nf Jur* partial release
semillant, -e [semijɑ̃, -ɑ̃t] *adj (personne)* spirited; *(regard)* bright
séminaire [seminɛr] *nm* (**a**) *(colloque)* seminar (**b**) *Rel* seminary
séminariste [seminarist] *nm Rel* seminarist
sémiologie [semjɔlɔʒi] *nf* semiology
sémiotique [semjɔtik] **1** *adj* semiotic
2 *nf* semiotics *(singulier)*
semi-précieux, -euse *(mpl* semi-précieux, *fpl* semi-précieuses) [səmipresjø, -øz] *adj* semi-precious

semi-remorque *(pl* **semi-remorques)** [səmirəmɔrk] *nm (poids lourd) Br* articulated lorry, *Am* trailer truck

semis [səmi] *nm* **(a)** *(action)* sowing **(b)** *(terrain)* seedbed **(c)** *(jeune plante)* seedling

sémite [semit] **1** *adj* Semitic **2** *nmf* **S.** Semite

sémitique [semitik] *adj* Semitic

semoir [səmwar] *nm* **(a)** *(sac)* seed bag **(b)** *(machine)* seeder

semonce [səmɔ̃s] *nf (remontrance)* reprimand; *aussi Fig* **coup de s.** warning shot

semoule [səmul] *nf* semolina

sempiternel, -elle [sɑ̃pitɛrnɛl] *adj* never-ending, endless

sénat [sena] *nm* senate

sénateur [senatœr] *nm* senator

sénatorial, -e, -aux, -ales [senatɔrjal, -o] *adj* senatorial

Sénégal [senegal] *nm* **le S.** Senegal

sénégalais, -e [senegalɛ, -ɛz] **1** *adj* Senegalese **2** *nmf* **S.** Senegalese; **les S.** the Senegalese

sénile [senil] *adj* senile

sénilité [senilite] *nf* senility

senior [senjɔr] *adj & nmf Sp* senior *(above the age of 20)*

sens¹ *voir* **sentir**

sens² [sɑ̃s] *nm* **(a)** *(de la perception)* sense; **les cinq s.** the five senses; **le sixième s.** the sixth sense **(b)** **les s.** *(sensualité)* the senses; **plaisir des s.** sensual pleasure **(c)** *(jugement)* sense; **avoir le s. de l'humour/du ridicule** to have a sense of humour/of the ridiculous; **avoir le s. des affaires/de l'orientation** to have good business sense/a good sense of direction; **s. commun** common sense; **s. moral** moral sense; **s. pratique** practical sense; **bon s.** common sense; **un homme de bon s.** a sensible man **(d)** *(avis)* **à mon s.** to my mind **(e)** *(signification) (d'un mot)* meaning, sense; **au s. propre/figuré** in the literal/figurative sense, literally/figuratively; **cela n'a aucun s.** it doesn't make (any) sense; **en ce s. que...** in the sense that... **(f)** *(direction)* direction; **tenir qch dans le mauvais s.** to hold sth the wrong way round; **en s. inverse** in the opposite direction; **dans le s. des aiguilles d'une montre** clockwise; **dans le s. inverse des aiguilles d'une montre** *Br* anticlockwise, *Am* counterclockwise; **dans le s. du courant** with the current; **dans le s. de la longueur** lengthwise, lengthways; **dans le s. de la largeur** widthwise, across; **s. dessus dessous** *(en désordre)* upside down; **s. devant derrière** back to front, the wrong way round; **dans les deux s.** both ways; *Fig* **ces mesures vont dans le bon s.** these measures are heading the right way; *Ordinat* **s. de déroulement** flow direction; **s. giratoire** *Br* roundabout, *Am* traffic circle; **s. interdit** *(sur panneau)* no entry; **s. unique** *(sur panneau)* one way

sensas(s) [sɑ̃sas] *adj Fam* fantastic, great

sensation [sɑ̃sasjɔ̃] *nf* **(a)** *(perception physique)* sensation **(b)** *(impression)* feeling; **avoir la s. que...** to have a or the feeling that... **(c)** *(scandale)* **faire s.** to create a sensation

sensationnel, -elle [sɑ̃sasjɔnɛl] *adj* **(a)** *(à sensation)* sensational **(b)** *Fam (fantastique)* fantastic, great

sensé, -e [sɑ̃se] *adj* sensible

sensibilisation [sɑ̃sibilizasjɔ̃] *nf* **(a)** **s. de l'opinion (à qch)** increasing public awareness (of sth) **(b)** *Phot & Méd* sensitization

sensibiliser [sɑ̃sibilize] *vt* **(a)** *(rendre conscient)* **s. qn à qch** to increase sb's awareness of sth; **s. l'opinion (à qch)** to

increase public awareness (of sth) **(b)** *Phot & Méd* to sensitize

sensibilité [sɑ̃sibilite] *nf* sensitivity; **avoir une s. à fleur de peau** to be hypersensitive

sensible [sɑ̃sibl] *adj* **(a)** *(émotif)* sensitive **(b)** *(réceptif)* être **s. à qch** to be sensitive to sth; *(influence)* to be susceptible to sth **(c)** *(douloureux)* sensitive **(d)** *(appréciable)* noticeable, appreciable; **de manière s.** noticeably **(e)** *(balance, thermomètre, plaque)* sensitive; **s. à la lumière** light-sensitive

sensiblement [sɑ̃sibləmɑ̃] *adv* **(a)** *(notablement)* noticeably, appreciably **(b)** *(à peu près)* roughly, more or less

sensiblerie [sɑ̃sibləri] *nf* sentimentality

sensoriel, -elle [sɑ̃sɔrjɛl] *adj* sensory

sensualité [sɑ̃sɥalite] *nf* sensuality

sensuel, -elle [sɑ̃sɥɛl] *adj* sensual

sent *voir* **sentir**

sentence [sɑ̃tɑ̃s] *nf* **(a)** *(jugement)* sentence **(b)** *(maxime)* maxim

sentencieux, -euse [sɑ̃tɑ̃sjø, -øz] *adj* sententious

senteur [sɑ̃tœr] *nf* scent; *(dans un parfum)* note

senti, -e [sɑ̃ti] *adj* **bien s.** appropriate

sentier [sɑ̃tje] *nm* path; *Fig* **sortir des sentiers battus** to go off the beaten track; **sur le s. de la guerre** on the warpath

sentiment [sɑ̃timɑ̃] *nm* feeling; **prendre qn par les sentiments** to appeal to sb's feelings; *Fam* **ça partait d'un bon s.** it was well meant; **en affaires, je ne fais pas de s.** I don't let sentiment interfere with business; **avoir le s. que...** to have a or the feeling that...; **j'avais le s. de m'être trompé** I had the feeling I'd made a mistake

sentimental, -e, -aux, -ales [sɑ̃timɑ̃tal, -o] **1** *adj (personne, chanson, valeur)* sentimental; **vie sentimentale** love life **2** *nmf* sentimental person

sentimentalisme [sɑ̃timɑ̃talism] *nm* sentimentalism; **faire du s.** to be sentimental

sentinelle [sɑ̃tinɛl] *nf* sentry

sentir [64a] [sɑ̃tir] **1** *vt* **(a)** *(douleur, sensation tactile)* to feel; *Fam Fig* **je ne sens plus mes jambes/mes pieds** *(de froid)* I can't feel my legs/my feet; *(de fatigue)* my legs/my feet are killing me **(b)** *(être conscient de) (danger)* to sense; **s. que...** to have a or the feeling that...; **faire s. à qn que...** to make sb feel that...; **se faire s.** to make itself felt; *Fig* **on sent l'influence de Wagner** one can detect Wagner's influence **(c)** *(parfum, fleur)* to smell; **faire s. qch à qn** to let sb smell sth **(d)** *(avoir l'odeur de)* to smell of; **ça sent le brûlé** there's a smell of burning; **ça sent bon le pain frais** there's a delicious smell of fresh bread; *Fig & Péj* **ce livre sent l'effort** this book is very laboured; **s. le soufre** to smack of subversiveness **(e)** *Fam (supporter)* **je ne peux pas le s.** I can't stand him **2** *vi* **(a)** *(avoir comme odeur)* **s. bon/mauvais** to smell good/bad; **s. fort** to have a strong smell **(b)** *Fam (puer)* to smell; **s. des pieds** to have smelly feet **3** **se sentir** *vpr* **(a)** *(être perceptible)* **cela se sent** you can tell **(b)** *(suivi d'un adjectif ou d'un infinitif)* **se s. revivre** to feel oneself coming alive again; **se s. bien/fatigué** to feel well/tired; *Fam* **tu ne te sens pas bien, non?** have you taken leave of your senses?; **se s. capable de faire qch** to feel capable of doing sth **(c)** *(avoir)* **se s. le courage de faire qch** to feel up to doing sth **(d)** *Fam (se contrôler)* **il ne se sent plus!** he's too big for his boots!

(e) *Fam (se supporter)* **ils ne peuvent pas se s.** they can't stand each other

seoir [10a] [swar] *Litt* **1** *vi* **s. à** to suit
2 *v impersonnel* **il lui sied mal de…** it ill becomes him to…

Séoul [seul] *n* Seoul

séparable [separabl] *adj* separable **(de** from)

séparation [separasjɔ̃] *nf* **(a)** *(de personnes, d'objets)* separation **(de** from); *Ordinat* **s. automatique des pages** automatic pagination **(b)** *(cloison)* partition, division **(c)** *Jur* **s. de biens** = marriage settlement under which husband and wife administer their separate properties

séparatisme [separatism] *nm* separatism

séparatiste [separatist] *adj & nmf* separatist

séparé, -e [separe] *adj* **(a)** *(notions, chambres)* separate **(b)** *(personnes)* separated **(de** from); **nous vivons séparés** we live apart

séparément [separemɑ̃] *adv* separately

séparer [separe] **1** *vt* **(a)** *(éloigner)* to separate **(de** from) **(b)** *(partager)* to divide **(en** into) **(c)** *(opposer)* to divide; **tout les sépare** they are poles apart
2 se séparer *vpr* **(a)** *(époux)* to separate **(de** from), to split up **(de** with) **(b)** *(foule, assemblée)* to break up **(c)** *(se défaire)* **se s. de qch** to part with sth; **se s. de qn** *(employé)* to let sb go **(d)** *(rivière, route)* to divide **(en** into); **c'est ici que nos chemins se séparent** this is where we go our separate ways

sept [sɛt] *adj & nm inv* seven; *voir aussi* **trois**

septante [sɛptɑ̃t] *adj inv* Belg & Suisse seventy; *voir aussi* **trois**

septembre [sɛptɑ̃br] *nm* September; *voir aussi* **janvier**

septennat [sɛptena] *nm* (seven-year) term

septentrional, -e, -aux, -ales [sɛptɑ̃trijɔnal, -o] *adj* northern

septicémie [sɛptisemi] *nf* blood poisoning, septicaemia

septième [sɛtjɛm] *nmf, nm & adj* seventh; *voir aussi* **cinquième**

septique [sɛptik] *adj* septic

septuagénaire [sɛptɥaʒenɛr] *adj & nmf* septuagenarian

sépulcre [sepylkr] *nm* sepulchre

sépulture [sepyltyr] *nf Litt* **(a)** *(inhumation)* burial **(b)** *(lieu)* burial place

séquelles [sekɛl] *nfpl (d'une maladie, d'un accident)* aftereffects; *(d'une guerre, d'une catastrophe)* aftermath

séquence [sekɑ̃s] *nf* **(a)** *(d'objets, de mots)* sequence; *Ordinat* **s. de caractères** character string, sequence of characters **(b)** *(de film)* sequence **(c)** *(de cartes)* run

séquestre [sekɛstr] *nm (action)* sequestration; **mettre qch sous s.** to sequester sth

séquestrer [sekɛstre] *vt* **(a)** *(personne)* **s. qn** to keep sb locked up **(b)** *(biens)* to sequester

séquoia [sekɔja] *nm* sequoia

sera, serai, serais *etc voir* **être**

sérail [seraj] *nm* seraglio; *Fig* inner circle

serbe [sɛrb] **1** *adj* Serb, Serbian
2 *nmf* **S.** Serb, Serbian

Serbie [sɛrbi] *nf* **la S.** Serbia

serbo-croate *(pl* **serbo-croates**) [sɛrbɔkrɔat] **1** *adj* Serbo-Croat, Serbo-Croatian
2 *nm (langue)* Serbo-Croat

Sercq [sɛrk] *n* Sark

serein, -e [sərɛ̃, -ɛn] *adj (personne, visage, esprit)* serene; *(ciel, nuit)* clear

sereinement [sərɛnmɑ̃] *adv* calmly

sérénade [serenad] *nf* **(a)** *Mus* serenade; **donner la s. à qn** to serenade sb **(b)** *Fam (tapage)* racket

sérénité [serenite] *nf* serenity; **avec s.** serenely

serf, serve [sɛrf, sɛrv] *nm,f Hist* serf

sergent [sɛrʒɑ̃] *nm* sergeant

sergent-chef *(pl* **sergents-chefs**) [sɛrʒɑ̃ʃɛf] *nm* staff sergeant

série [seri] *nf* **(a)** *(suite, collection)* series; *(d'échantillons)* range; *(de casseroles)* set; **des démissions en s.** a series of resignations **(b)** *Rad & TV* series **(c)** *Ind* **production en s.** mass production; **voiture de s.** standard car **(d)** *(dans un classement)* group; *Sp* heat; **(film de) s. B** B movie **(e)** *(locutions)* **s. noire** *(suite de catastrophes)* series or catalogue of disasters; **(roman de) s. noire** crime thriller

sérieusement [serjøzmɑ̃] *adv* seriously; **parlez-vous s.?** are you serious?

sérieux, -euse [serjø, -øz] **1** *adj* **(a)** *(personne, lecture)* serious; **d'un air s.** seriously; **ce n'est pas s.!** you're not serious!; *Fam* **s. comme un pape** as solemn as a judge **(b)** *(offre, acheteur)* serious, genuine; *(information, entreprise)* reliable; *(employé)* conscientious **(c)** *(important) (problèmes, ennuis)* serious; *(progrès)* good
2 *nm* **(a)** *(application)* conscientiousness; **avec s.** conscientiously **(b)** *(gravité)* **garder son s.** to keep a straight face; **prendre qn/qch au s.** to take sb/sth seriously; **se prendre au s.** to take oneself seriously

sérigraphie [serigrafi] *nf* silk-screen printing

serin [sərɛ̃] *nm (oiseau)* canary

seriner [sərine] *vt Fam* **s. qch à qn** to go on and on at sb about sth; **s. à qn que…** to keep telling sb that…

seringue [sərɛ̃g] *nf* syringe

serment [sɛrmɑ̃] *nm* **(a)** *(parole solennelle)* oath; **prêter s.** to take an oath; **sous s.** on oath **(b)** *(promesse)* pledge; *(d'amoureux)* vow; **faire le s. de faire qch** to swear or vow to do sth

sermon [sɛrmɔ̃] *nm* **(a)** *Rel* sermon **(b)** *Fam (remontrance)* lecture, sermon

sermonner [sɛrmɔne] *vt Fam* to lecture

séronégatif, -ive [serɔnegatif, -iv] **1** *adj* HIV negative
2 *nm,f* person who is HIV negative

séropositif, -ive [serɔpozitif, -iv] **1** *adj* HIV positive
2 *nm,f* person who is HIV positive

serpe [sɛrp] *nf* billhook

serpent [sɛrpɑ̃] *nm* **(a)** *(reptile)* snake; **s. à sonnette** rattlesnake **(b)** *Écon* **le s. monétaire européen** the European currency snake

serpenter [sɛrpɑ̃te] *vi* to wind

serpentin [sɛrpɑ̃tɛ̃] *nm (cotillon)* streamer

serpillière [sɛrpijɛr] *nf* floorcloth; **passer la s. dans la cuisine** to clean the kitchen floor

serpolet [sɛrpɔlɛ] *nm* wild thyme

serre [sɛr] *nf* **(a)** *(local)* greenhouse **(b)** **serres** *(d'oiseau de proie)* claws, talons

serré, -e [sere] **1** *adj* **(a)** *(chaussures, vêtement)* tight; *(personnes)* packed together; *(écriture)* cramped; *(rangs)* serried; *(dents)* clenched; *(lèvres)* pressed tightly together **(b)** *(emploi du temps, budget)* tight; *(surveillance, lutte, score)* close **(c)** *(café)* strong
2 *adv* **écrire s.** to have cramped handwriting; *Fig* **jouer s.** to play a tight game

serre-livres [sɛrlivr] *nm inv* book-end

serrement [sɛrmɑ̃] *nm* **avoir un s. de cœur** to feel a pang

serrer [sere] **1** *vt* **(a)** *(tenir)* to grip; **s. la main à qn** to shake hands with sb, to shake sb's hand; **s. qn dans ses bras** to

hug sb; **s. qn/qch contre soi** to hold sb/sth tightly to one; *Fig* **s. le cœur à qn** to wring sb's heart **(b)** *(sujet: vêtement, chaussures)* to be too tight for **(c)** *(nœud, écrou, ceinture)* to tighten; *(joint)* to clamp; *(poings)* to clench; **s. les dents** to clench one's teeth; *Fig* to grit one's teeth; *Fam Fig* **s. les fesses** to be scared stiff **(d)** *(rapprocher)* to put close together; **s. les rangs** to close ranks **(e)** *(ranger)* to put away **(f)** *(raser) (trottoir)* to hug; **s. qn de près** to follow sb closely; **évite de s. la voiture de devant** keep your distance from the car in front
  2 *vi* **serrez à droite/gauche** *(sur panneau)* keep to the right/left
  3 se serrer *vpr* **(a)** *(se rapprocher)* to squeeze up; **se s. contre qn** to snuggle up to sb **(b)** *Fig* **ma gorge se serra** I had a lump in my throat **(c)** *(pour se saluer)* **se s. la main** to shake hands

serre-tête [sɛrtɛt] *nm inv* headband

serrure [seryr] *nf* lock

serrurerie [seryrri] *nf (métier)* locksmith's trade

serrurier [seryrje] *nm* locksmith

sers, sert *etc voir* **servir**

sertir [sertir] *vt (pierre précieuse)* to set

sérum [serɔm] *nm* serum; **s. physiologique** saline solution

servage [sɛrvaʒ] *nm* serfdom; *Fig* bondage

servante [sɛrvɑ̃t] *nf* (maid)servant

serve [sɛrv] *voir* **serf**

serveur, -euse [sɛrvœr, -øz] **1** *nm,f* **(a)** *(dans un bar)* barman, *f* barmaid; *(dans un restaurant)* waiter, *f* waitress **(b)** *(au tennis)* server
  2 *nm Ordinat* server; **s. de fichiers** file server; **s. de réseau** network server; **s. télématique** bulletin board (system)

serviable [sɛrvjabl] *adj* obliging, helpful

service [sɛrvis] *nm* **(a)** *(pour un client, pour un maître)* service; *Écon* **services** services; **faire le s.** *(à table)* to serve; **être au s. de qn** to be in sb's service; **à votre s.** at your service; **s. compris/non compris** service included/not included; **premier/deuxième s.** *(au restaurant)* first/second sitting; **s. après-vente** *(dépannage)* after-sales service
  (b) *Mil* **s. militaire** *ou* **national** military service; **faire son s.** to do one's military service; **bon pour le s.** fit for service **(c)** *(au tennis)* service; **au s., Roddick** Roddick to serve **(d)** *(travail)* duty; **être de s.** to be on duty; **prendre/quitter s.** to go on/off duty; *Fam* **le crétin de s.** the inevitable *or* obligatory idiot
  (e) *(département)* department; **s. d'ordre** *(surveillance)* crowd control; *(personnes)* = police, security staff etc in charge of crowd control; **s. du personnel** personnel department; **s. public** public utility; **s. de renseignements** military intelligence department; *Ordinat* **s. télématique** bulletin board service
  (f) *(d'une machine)* **en s.** in service; **mettre qch en s.** to bring sth into service
  (g) *(de transports en commun)* service; **assurer la s. entre** to provide a service between
  (h) *(aide)* favour; **rendre (un) s. à qn** *(personne)* to do sb a favour; *(objet)* to be of use to sb; **rendre un mauvais s. à qn** to do sb a bad turn
  (i) *(de vaisselle)* set

serviette [sɛrvjɛt] *nf* **(a)** *(en tissu)* **s. (de table)** serviette, napkin; **s. (de toilette)** towel; **s. de plage** beach towel **(b)** *(sac)* briefcase **(c)** **s. hygiénique** sanitary *Br* towel *or* *Am* napkin

serviette-éponge *(pl* **serviettes-éponges)** [sɛrvjɛtepɔ̃ʒ] *nf* terry towel

servile [sɛrvil] *adj* servile; *(imitation, traduction)* slavish

servilement [sɛrvilmɑ̃] *adv* servilely; *(imiter, traduire)* slavishly

servir [63] [sɛrvir] **1** *vt* **(a)** *(client, convive, nourriture)* to serve; **tout le monde est servi?** *(à table)* has everybody been served?; **s. frais** *(sur étiquette)* serve chilled; **s. à boire à qn** to give sb a drink; *Ironique* **côté ennuis, je suis servi!** I've got more than my share of worries! **(b)** *(favoriser) (personne)* to serve; *(intérêts)* to further **(c)** *(au tennis)* to serve **(d)** *(aux cartes)* **à vous de s.** it's your deal
  2 *vi* *(dans une administration)* to serve **(sous** under)
  3 servir à *vt ind* **(a)** *(être utile à)* to be of use to; **ça peut toujours s.** it might still come in useful **(b)** *(être utilisé pour)* **s. à qch/à faire qch** to be used for sth/for doing sth; **ne s. à rien** to be useless; **ne pas s. à grand-chose** not to be much use; **à quoi ça sert?** *(objet)* what's that used for?; *(démarche)* what's the use of that?
  4 servir de *vt ind (faire fonction de) (objet)* to serve as, to be used as; *(personne)* to act as; **ça me sert de table** I use it as a table
  5 *v impersonnel Litt* **il ne sert à rien de pleurer** there's no point in crying
  6 se servir *vpr* **(a)** *(prendre)* to help oneself; **je me suis déjà servie deux fois** I've already had two helpings; **se s. des pâtes/du café** to help oneself to pasta/to coffee **(b)** *(plat, vin)* to be served, **le champagne se sert frappé** champagne should be served chilled **(c)** **se s. de qn/qch** *(utiliser)* to use sb/sth **(d)** *(s'approvisionner)* **se s. chez...** to shop at...

serviteur [sɛrvitœr] *nm* servant

servitude [sɛrvityd] *nf* **(a)** *(asservissement)* servitude **(b)** *(contrainte)* constraint

ses [se] *voir* **son**[1]

sésame [sezam] *nm* **(a)** *(plante)* sesame **(b)** *Fig* **s., ouvre-toi!** open sesame!

session [sesjɔ̃] *nf* **(a)** *(d'une assemblée, d'un tribunal)* session, sitting **(b)** *(période d'examens)* (exam) session; **s. de rattrapage** repeat exams, *Br* resits

set [sɛt] *nm* **(a)** *(au tennis)* set **(b)** **s. de table** *(napperon)* table mat

setter [seter] *nm* setter; **s. irlandais** Irish setter

seuil [sœj] *nm* **(a)** *(entrée)* doorway, threshold; **sur le s.** in the doorway **(b)** *Fig* threshold; *Litt* **au s. de...** on the threshold of...; **s. de rentabilité** break-even point

seul, -e [sœl] **1** *adj* **(a)** *(unique)* only; **une seule personne** *(et pas plus)* a single person; *(parmi d'autres)* only one person; **comme un s. homme** as one man; **il suffit d'une seule fois** once is enough; **la seule pensée de sa venue** the mere thought of him coming **(b)** *(isolé)* alone; **se sentir s.** to feel lonely *or* alone; **être s. au monde** to be alone in the world; **parler s. à s. à qn** to speak to sb in private; **faire qch tout s.** to do sth (by) oneself *or* on one's own; **parler tout s.** to talk to oneself; **cela va tout s.** it's plain sailing, it's straightforward; **ça descend tout s.** *(boisson)* it just slides down **(c)** *(seulement)* only, alone; **s. un miracle...** only a miracle...
  2 *nm,f* **le s.** the only one; **un s.** *(personne, objet)* only one

seulement [sœlmɑ̃] *adv* only; **je te demande s. un peu de patience** I'm just asking you to be a bit patient; **non s...., mais en plus...** not only..., but also...; *Fam* **essaie s.!** just you try!

sève [sɛv] *nf* **(a)** *(d'une plante)* sap **(b)** *Fig (de la jeunesse)* vitality

sévère [sevɛr] *adj* severe; *(principe, règle)* strict; **être s. envers** *ou* **avec qn** to be hard on sb

sévèrement [sevɛrmɑ̃] *adv* severely; *(de façon stricte)* strictly

sévérité [severite] *nf* severity; *(d'une discipline, d'une éducation)* strictness

sévices [sevis] *nmpl* ill-treatment

Séville [sevij] *n* Seville

sévir [sevir] *vi (agir avec rigueur)* to act ruthlessly; **s. contre qn/qch** to deal ruthlessly with sb/sth (**b**) *(épidémie, guerre)* to rage; *(malfaiteurs)* to operate; **la crise qui sévit actuellement** the present crisis

sevrage [səvraʒ] *nm (d'un enfant)* weaning; *(d'un drogué, d'un alcoolique)* withdrawal

sevrer [səvre] *vt* (**a**) *(enfant)* to wean; *(drogué)* to get off drugs; *(alcoolique)* to get off drink (**b**) *Litt (priver)* **s. qn de qch** to deprive sb of sth

sexagénaire [sɛgzaʒenɛr, sɛksaʒenɛr] *nmf* person in his/her sixties

sex-appeal [sɛksapil] *nm Fam* sex appeal

sexe [sɛks] *nm* (**a**) *(genre)* sex; *Hum* **le beau s.** the fair sex; **le s. faible** the weaker sex; **le s. fort** the stronger sex (**b**) *(organes sexuels)* genitals (**c**) *(sexualité)* sex

sexisme [sɛksism] *nm* sexism

sexiste [sɛksist] *adj & nmf* sexist

sexologue [sɛksɔlɔg] *nmf* sexologist

sex-shop (*pl* **sex-shops**) [sɛksʃɔp] *nm* sex shop

sextant [sɛkstɑ̃] *nm* sextant

sextuor [sɛkstɥɔr] *nm* sextet

sextuplé, -e [sɛkstyple] *nm,f* sextuplet

sexualité [sɛksɥalite] *nf* sexuality

sexué, -e [sɛksɥe] *adj (plante, animal)* sexed; *(reproduction)* sexual

sexuel, -elle [sɛksɥɛl] *adj (rapport)* sexual; *(vie, acte, organe)* sex

sexuellement [sɛksɥɛlmɑ̃] *adv* sexually

sexy [sɛksi] *adj inv Fam* sexy

seyant, -e [sejɑ̃, -ɑ̃t] *adj* becoming

Seychelles [seʃɛl] *nfpl* **les S.** the Seychelles

SFIO [ɛsɛfio] *nf (abrév* **Section française de l'Internationale ouvrière**) = French Socialist Party 1905–1969

shaker [ʃɛkœr] *nm* cocktail shaker

shakespearien, -enne [ʃɛkspirjɛ̃, -ɛn] *adj* Shakespearean

shampoing [ʃɑ̃pwɛ̃] *nm* shampoo; **faire un s. à qn** to shampoo sb's hair, to give sb a shampoo

shampouiner [ʃɑ̃pwine] *vt* to shampoo

shampouineur, -euse [ʃɑ̃pwinœr, -øz] **1** *nm,f* shampooer
2 *nf* shampouineuse (à moquettes) *(machine)* carpet shampooer

shérif [ʃerif] *nm* sheriff

shetland [ʃɛtlɑ̃d] **1** *nfpl* **les (îles) S.** the Shetland Islands, the Shetlands
2 *nm* (**a**) *(laine)* Shetland wool; *(pull)* Shetland jumper (**b**) *(poney)* Shetland pony

shinto [ʃinto], **shintoïsme** [ʃintɔism] *nm* Shinto, Shintoism

shoot [ʃut] *nm* shot

shooter [ʃute] **1** *vi (au football)* to shoot
2 se shooter *vpr Fam (se droguer)* to shoot up; **se s. à l'héroïne** to shoot (up) heroin

shopping [ʃɔpiŋ] *nm* shopping; **faire du s.** to go shopping

short [ʃɔrt] *nm* (pair of) shorts

show [ʃo] *nm* show

show-business [ʃobiznɛs] *nm* show business

si¹ [si] *adv* (**a**) *(tellement)* so; **un si bon dîner** such a good dinner; **il n'est pas si bête (que ça)** he's not that stupid; **il était si nerveux qu'il a tout oublié** he was so nervous (that) he forgot everything (**b**) *(indique la concession)* **si... que** + *subjunctive* however...; **si jeune qu'il soit** however young he may be; **si habile soit-il** however capable (he may be) (**c**) *(oui)* yes; **je crois que si** I think so; **mais si, je l'ai vue** I DID see her; **tu ne sais pas? – si, si** you don't know? – yes, I do (**d**) **si bien que...** *(indique le résultat)* so that...

si² **1** *conj* (**a**) *(exprime l'hypothèse, la condition)* if; **qui le fera si ce n'est moi?** who'll do it if I don't?; **un des plus grands, si ce n'est le plus grand** one of the biggest, if not the biggest; **si ce n'est que...** *(sauf que)* apart from the fact that...; **et si elle l'apprend?** and what if she finds out?; **si on faisait une partie de backgammon?** what about a game of backgammon?; **oui, si on veut** yes, if you like; **si seulement...** if only...; **si tant est que...** + *subjunctive* if... (**b**) *(combien)* how; **pensez si j'étais furieux!** imagine how angry I was! (**c**) *(dans les questions indirectes)* if, whether; *Fam* **si je connais Madrid?** do I know Madrid?; *Fam* **si c'est pas malheureux (de voir ça)!** isn't it just dreadful (to see that)!
2 *nm inv* **tes si et tes mais** your ifs and buts

si³ *nm inv (note)* B; *(chantée)* ti

siamois, -e [sjamwa, -az] **1** *adj* **frères s.** Siamese twins; **sœurs siamoises** Siamese twins
2 *nm (chat)* Siamese (cat)

Sibérie [siberi] *nf* **la S.** Siberia

sibérien, -enne [siberjɛ̃, -ɛn] **1** *adj* Siberian
2 *nm,f* **S.** Siberian

sibyllin, -e [sibilɛ̃, -in] *adj (énigmatique)* cryptic, enigmatic

SICAV [sikav] *nf inv Fin (abrév* **société d'investissement à capital variable**) (**a**) *(organisme) Br* ≃ unit trust, *Am* ≃ mutual fund (**b**) *(titre)* ≃ share in a *Br* unit trust *or Am* mutual fund

Sicile [sisil] *nf* **la S.** Sicily

sicilien, -enne [sisiljɛ̃, -ɛn] **1** *adj* Sicilian
2 *nm,f* **S.** Sicilian

sida [sida] *nm (abrév* **syndrome immunodéficitaire acquis**) AIDS; **avoir le s.** to have AIDS

side-car (*pl* **side-cars**) [sajdkar, sidkar] *nm* sidecar

sidéen, -enne [sideɛ̃, -ɛn] **1** *adj* suffering from AIDS
2 *nm,f* AIDS sufferer

sidéral, -e, -aux, -ales [sideral, -o] *adj* sidereal

sidérant, -e [siderɑ̃, -ɑ̃t] *adj Fam* staggering

sidérer [34] [sidere] *vt Fam* to stagger

sidérurgie [sideryrʒi] *nf* (**a**) *(technique)* iron and steel metallurgy (**b**) *(industrie)* iron and steel industry

sidérurgique [sideryrʒik] *adj (industrie, usine)* iron and steel

sidérurgiste [sideryrʒist] *nmf* iron and steel worker

siècle [sjɛkl] *nm* (**a**) *(cent ans)* century; **au vingtième s.** in the twentieth century; **avoir un s.** to be a hundred years old; *Fam* **ça fait des siècles que j'attends** I've been waiting for ages (**b**) *(époque)* age; **le s. des Lumières** the Age of Enlightenment; **il est de son s.** he's a man of his times

sied *voir* **seoir**

siège [sjɛʒ] *nm* (**a**) *(meuble)* seat; **s. avant/arrière** front/back seat; **s. pliant** folding chair; **s. pour enfant** *(en voiture)* child seat (**b**) *(d'une société, d'un organisme)* head office; **s. administratif** administrative headquarters; **s. social** head office (**c**) *(lieu d'origine)* seat (**d**) *Mil* siege; **faire le s. de** to lay siege to; **lever le s.** to raise the siege; *Fam (partir)* to make tracks (**e**) *Pol* seat (**f**) *Méd* **accouchement par le s.** breech delivery; **se présenter par le s.** to be in the breech position

siéger [59] [sjeʒe] *vi* (a) *(tribunal, assemblée)* to sit (b) *(se trouver)* **c'est là que siège le mal** that's the root of the problem

sien, -enne [sjɛ̃, sjɛn] **1** *pron possessif* **le sien, la sienne, les siens, les siennes** *(possesseur masculin)* his; *(possesseur féminin)* hers; *(en insistant)* his/her own; **il te prête le s.** you can borrow his; **elle n'en a pas besoin, elle a le s.** she doesn't need it, she has her own; **on doit acheter la sienne** you must buy your own; **chacun doit apporter le s.** everyone must bring their own; **chaque pays a le s.** each country has its own
  2 *nm* **il faut qu'il y mette du s.** he should do his share
  3 *nmpl* **les siens** *(sa famille)* his/her family
  4 *nfpl Fam* **il a encore fait des siennes** he's been up to his old tricks again

Sierra Leone [sjeraleɔn] *nf* **la S.** Sierra Leone

sieste [sjɛst] *nf* siesta, nap; **faire la s.** to have a nap

sifflant, -e [siflɑ̃, -ɑ̃t] *adj (respiration, toux)* wheezing

sifflement [sifləmɑ̃] *nm (d'une personne, du vent)* whistling; *(d'un serpent, de la vapeur)* hissing; *(d'un asthmatique)* wheezing; **sifflements d'oreilles** ringing in the ears

siffler [sifle] **1** *vt* (a) *(air)* to whistle (b) *(chien, personne)* to whistle at (c) *(acteur, pièce)* to boo (d) *Fam (verre, bouteille)* to knock back
  2 *vi* (a) *(personne, merle, bouilloire)* to whistle; *(serpent)* to hiss (b) *(avec un sifflet)* to blow one's whistle

sifflet [siflɛ] *nm* (a) *(instrument)* whistle; *Fam* **couper le s. à qn** to shut sb up (b) *(au théâtre)* **sifflets** booing, boos

siffleux [siflø] *nm Can* groundhog, woodchuck

siffloter [siflote] *vt & vi* to whistle to oneself

sigle [sigl] *nm (acronyme)* acronym; *(suite d'initiales)* abbreviation

signal, -aux [siɲal, -o] *nm* (a) *(signe)* signal; **faire un s.** to signal; **envoyer ou lancer un s.** to send a signal; **au s.,** **levez-vous** when the signal is given, stand up; **s. lumineux** indicator light, warning light (b) *(panneau)* sign (c) *(dispositif sonore)* **s. d'alarme** alarm (signal); **s. d'alerte** warning (signal); *Tél* **s. d'appel** call(ing) signal; **s. de détresse** distress signal; **s. sonore** warning sound (d) *Ordinat* **s. d'avertissement de réception** acknowledge; **s. d'invitation à transmettre** proceed-to-send signal

signalement [siɲalmɑ̃] *nm* description, particulars

signaler [siɲale] **1** *vt* (a) *(faire remarquer)* to point out (à to); **s. à qn que...** to point out to sb that... (b) *(rapporter)* to report (à to); **rien à s.** nothing to report (c) *(par un panneau)* to signpost (d) *Ordinat (marquer)* to flag up
  2 se signaler *vpr* to distinguish oneself (par by); **se s. à l'attention de qn** to catch sb's eye

signalétique [siɲaletik] *adj* **fiche s.** personal details card; **plaque s.** identification plate

signalisation [siɲalizasjɔ̃] *nf (signaux routiers)* signs and markings; *(signaux ferroviaires)* signals; *(de piste d'atterrissage)* lights and markings; **s. routière** road signs

signaliser [siɲalize] *vt (route)* to signpost and mark; *(voie ferrée)* to install signals on; *(piste d'atterrissage)* to install lights and markings on

signataire [siɲater] *nmf* signatory

signature [siɲatyr] *nf* (a) *(griffe)* signature; **présenter qch à la s.** to present sth for signature (b) *(acte)* signing

signe [siɲ] *nm* (a) *(indice)* sign; **il n'a pas donné s. de vie** there's been no sign of him; **il n'y a aucun s. de vie dans la maison** there's no sign of life at the house; **en s. de désapprobation/solidarité** as a sign of disapproval/solidarity; **s. avant-coureur** forerunner; **donner des signes d'usure** to show signs of wear (b) *(symbole)* sign,

symbol; **s. moins/plus/égale** minus/plus/equals sign; **signes de ponctuation** punctuation marks (c) *Astrol* **s. du zodiaque** sign of the zodiac; **être né sous le s. du Capricorne** to be born under the sign of Capricorn; *Fig* **le sommet a eu lieu sous le s. de la réconciliation** the summit was held in a spirit of reconciliation (d) *(trait distinctif)* mark; **signes particuliers** distinguishing marks (e) *(geste)* sign, gesture; **faire un s. à qn** to gesture to sb; **parler par signes** to use sign language; **faire s. à qn** *(de la main)* to signal to sb; *(le contacter)* to get in touch with sb; **faire s. à qn de faire qch** to signal to sb to do sth; **faire s. que oui** *(de la tête)* to nod (one's head); **faire s. que non** *(de la tête)* to shake one's head; *(du doigt)* to shake one's finger; **faire un s. de la main (à qn)** to wave (at sb); **faire un s. de tête (à qn)** to nod (to sb) (f) *Rel* **s. de croix** sign of the cross; **faire le s. de croix** to make the sign of the cross

signer [siɲe] *vt (contrat, lettre, tableau)* to sign; *Fam Fig* **ça c'est signé!** no prizes for guessing who did that!
  2 *vi* to sign; **s. de son nom** to sign one's name
  3 se signer *vpr* to cross oneself

signet [siɲɛ] *nm* bookmark

significatif, -ive [siɲifikatif, -iv] *adj* significant; **s. de qch** indicative of sth

signification [siɲifikasjɔ̃] *nf* (a) *(d'un mot, d'un symbole)* meaning, sense; *(d'un fait)* significance (b) *Jur (d'un jugement)* notification

signifier [66] [siɲifje] *vt* (a) *(vouloir dire)* to mean; **qu'est-ce que ça signifie?** *(indignation)* what's the meaning of this? (b) *(notifier) (intention)* to make known (à to); **s. son congé à qn** *(sujet: propriétaire, employeur)* to give sb notice; **s. qch à qn** to inform or notify sb of sth

silence [silɑ̃s] *nm* (a) *(absence de bruit)* silence; **un s. de mort** a deadly silence; **rompre le s.** to break the silence; **garder le s. (sur)** to keep silent (about); **faire qch en s.** to do sth in silence; **passer qch sous s.** not to mention sth (b) *Mus* rest

silencieusement [silɑ̃sjøzmɑ̃] *adv* silently

silencieux, -euse [silɑ̃sjø, -øz] **1** *adj* silent; *(qui ne fait pas beaucoup de bruit)* quiet
  2 *nm (d'un véhicule) Br* silencer, *Am* muffler; *(d'une arme)* silencer

silex [silɛks] *nm* flint

silhouette [silwɛt] *nf* (a) *(du corps)* figure (b) *(d'un objet)* silhouette, outline

silice [silis] *nf* silica

silicium [silisjɔm] *nm Chim* silicon

silicone [silikɔn] *nf* silicone

sillage [sijaʒ] *nm (d'un navire)* wake; *Fig* **marcher dans le s. de qn** to follow in sb's wake

sillon [sijɔ̃] *nm* (a) *(d'un champ)* furrow (b) *(de disque)* groove

sillonner [sijɔne] *vt (parcourir)* to criss-cross

silo [silo] *nm* silo

simagrées [simagre] *nfpl* airs and graces; **faire des s.** to make a fuss

simiesque [simjɛsk] *adj* monkey-like, ape-like

similaire [similɛr] *adj* similar (à to)

similarité [similarite] *nf* similarity

simili [simili] *nm Fam (imitation)* imitation

similicuir [similikɥir] *nm* imitation leather

similitude [similityd] *nf* similarity

simple [sɛ̃pl] **1** *adj* (a) *(sans prétentions)* simple (b) *(facile)* simple, easy; **c'est s. comme bonjour** it's as easy as pie (c) *(crédule)* simple; **s. d'esprit** simple-minded (d) *(pur)* **c'est**

une s. question de temps it's simply a matter of time (**e**) *(ordinaire)* ordinary; **s. soldat** private (soldier) (**f**) *(composé d'un élément) (nœud)* single; **cornet s.** *(de glace)* cone with one scoop; *Ordinat* **s. densité** single density
  2 *nm* (**a**) *(au tennis)* singles (match) (**b**) *(somme, quantité)* **varier du s. au double** to vary by twice as much (**c**) *(personne)* **un s. d'esprit** a simpleton

simplement [sɛpləmɑ̃] *adv* simply; **le plus s. du monde** as if it was the most natural thing in the world; **prendre les choses s.** to take things as they come

simplet, -ette [sɛplɛ, -ɛt] *adj (personne)* simple; *(idée, explication)* simplistic

simplicité [sɛplisite] *nf* simplicity; **recevoir qn en toute s.** to entertain sb very simply; **d'une s. enfantine** childishly simple

simplificateur, -trice [sɛplifikatœr, -tris] *adj* simplifying

simplification [sɛplifikasjɔ̃] *nf* simplification

simplifier [66] [sɛplifje] *vt aussi Math* to simplify; **ça me simplifiera l'existence** it'll make my life easier

simpliste [sɛplist] *adj Péj* simplistic

simulacre [simylakr] *nm* (**a**) *(représentation)* reconstruction (**b**) *(parodie)* **s. de négociations** sham negotiations; **ce fut un s. de procès** the trial was a farce

simulateur, -trice [simylatœr, -tris] **1** *nm,f (d'un sentiment)* pretender; *(d'une maladie)* malingerer
  2 *nm Tech* simulator

simulation [simylasjɔ̃] *nf* (**a**) *(action)* feigning (**b**) *(d'un vol, d'un phénomène)* & *Ordinat* simulation

simulé, -e [simyle] *adj* (**a**) *(sentiment, maladie)* feigned; *(combat)* sham (**b**) *(vol, phénomène)* simulated

simuler [simyle] *vt* (**a**) *(sentiment, maladie, folie)* to feign (**b**) *(vol, phénomène)* to simulate

simultané, -e [simyltane] *adj* simultaneous

simultanéité [simyltaneite] *nf* simultaneousness, simultaneity

simultanément [simyltanemɑ̃] *adv* simultaneously

sincère [sɛ̃sɛr] *adj* sincere

sincèrement [sɛ̃sɛrmɑ̃] *adv* sincerely; **s., je trouve que...** frankly, I think...

sincérité [sɛ̃serite] *nf* sincerity; **en toute s.** in all sincerity

sinécure [sinekyr] *nf* sinecure; *Fam* **ce n'est pas une s.** it's not exactly a rest cure

sine die [sinedje] *adv* sine die

sine qua non [sinekwanɔn] *adj inv* **une condition s.** a prerequisite

Singapour [sɛ̃gapur] *n* Singapore

singapourien, -enne [sɛ̃gapurjɛ̃, -ɛn] **1** *adj* Singaporean
  2 *nm,f* **S.** Singaporean

singe [sɛ̃ʒ] *nm* monkey; **grand s.** ape; **malin/adroit comme un s.** as crafty/clever as a monkey; **faire le s.** to clown around

singer [45] [sɛ̃ʒe] *vt (personne)* to ape, to mimic; *(sentiment)* to feign

singeries [sɛ̃ʒri] *nfpl (grimaces, gestes)* antics; **faire des singeries** to clown around

singulariser [sɛ̃gylarize] **1** *vt* **s. qn (de)** to set sb apart (from), to make sb stand out (from)
  2 se singulariser *vpr* to draw attention to oneself; **il se singularise par sa façon de parler** the way he speaks makes him stand out

singularité [sɛ̃gylarite] *nf* peculiarity

singulier, -ère [sɛ̃gylje, -ɛr] **1** *adj* (**a**) *Gram* singular (**b**)

(combat) single (**c**) *(remarquable)* remarkable; *(étrange)* peculiar, odd
  2 *nm Gram* singular; **au s.** in the singular

singulièrement [sɛ̃gyljɛrmɑ̃] *adv* (**a**) *(étrangement)* oddly (**b**) *(en particulier)* especially, particularly (**c**) *(beaucoup)* remarkably, extremely

sinistre [sinistr] **1** *adj* (**a**) *(effrayant)* sinister; *(à faire froid dans le dos)* spooky (**b**) *(déprimant) (paysage)* bleak; *(soirée, repas)* dismal, grim (**c**) **un s. imbécile** a total idiot
  2 *nm* (**a**) *(catastrophe)* disaster (**b**) *Jur (dommage)* damage

sinistré, -e [sinistre] **1** *adj (population)* stricken; *(bâtiment)* damaged; *(région, zone)* disaster
  2 *nm,f* disaster victim

sinistrose [sinistroz] *nf Fam* pessimism, gloom

sinologue [sinɔlɔg] *nmf* sinologist

sinon [sinɔ̃] *conj* (**a**) *(autrement)* otherwise, or else (**b**) *(excepté)* except (**c**) *(si ce n'est)* if not

sinueux, -euse [sinɥø, -øz] *adj (ligne)* sinuous; *(chemin, courant)* winding, meandering; *Fig (raisonnement)* tortuous

sinuosité [sinɥozite] *nf (d'un chemin, d'une rivière)* bend; *Fig* **les sinuosités d'un raisonnement** the twists and turns of an argument

sinus¹ [sinys] *nm Anat* sinus

sinus² *nm Math* sine

sinusite [sinyzit] *nf* sinusitis

sionisme [sjɔnism] *nm* Zionism

sioniste [sjɔnist] *adj & nmf* Zionist

sioux [sju] **1** *adj* Sioux
  2 *nmf* **S.** Sioux

siphon [sifɔ̃] *nm* (**a**) *(tube)* siphon (**b**) *(bouteille)* (soda) siphon (**c**) *(d'un évier, d'une canalisation)* U-bend, trap

siphonné, -e [sifɔne] *adj Fam (fou)* crackers, crazy

siphonner [sifɔne] *vt* to siphon

sire [sir] *nm* **S.** *(à un souverain)* Sire; *Péj* **un triste s.** an unsavoury character

sirène [sirɛn] *nf* (**a**) *(personnage fantastique)* mermaid, siren; *Fig (femme)* siren (**b**) *(dispositif sonore)* siren

sirop [siro] *nm* syrup; **s. de fraise/menthe** strawberry/mint cordial; **s. d'érable** maple syrup; **s. contre la toux** cough mixture or syrup

siroter [sirɔte] *vt Fam* to sip

sirupeux, -euse [sirypø, -øz] *adj* syrupy; *(musique)* slushy

sismique [sismik] *adj* seismic

sismographe [sismɔgraf] *nm* seismograph

sismologie [sismɔlɔʒi] *nf* seismology

sitar [sitar] *nm* sitar

sitcom [sitkɔm] *nm ou nf* sitcom

site [sit] *nm* (**a**) *(emplacement)* site (**b**) *(pittoresque)* beauty spot; **s. classé** conservation area; **s. historique/archéologique** historic/archaeological site; **s. touristique** place of interest, tourist attraction

sitôt [sito] *adv* **elle le fera s. ses devoirs finis** she'll do it as soon as she's finished her homework; **s. dit, s. fait** no sooner said than done; **s. que** as soon as; **s. après** immediately after; **on ne le reverra pas de s.** we won't see him again in a hurry

situation [sitɥasjɔ̃] *nf* (**a**) *(d'une ville, d'un bâtiment)* position, location (**b**) *(circonstances)* situation; **être en s. de faire qch** to be in a position to do sth; **mettre qn en s.** to give sb experience of a real-life situation; **l'homme de la s.** the right man for the job; **s. de famille** marital status (**c**) *(emploi)* job, position (**d**) *Fin (de compte)* balance

situé, -e [sitɥe] *adj* situated

situer [sitɥe] **1** vt (a) (placer) to situate (b) (trouver) to locate (c) (dans le temps) to set; **je situe l'action au milieu du XIXᵉ siècle** I'd say the action takes place in the middle of the 19th century (d) Fig (catégoriser) to categorize **2 se situer** vpr (a) (être) to be; **se s. à droite** to be right-wing (b) (avoir lieu) to take place

six [sis] adj & nm inv six; voir aussi **trois**

sixième [sizjɛm] **1** adj, nmf & nm sixth; voir aussi **cinquième 2** nf Scol (enseignement secondaire) Br ≃ first form, Am ≃ sixth grade

sixièmement [sizjɛmmɑ] adv in the sixth place, sixthly

six-quatre-deux [siskatdø] **à la six-quatre-deux** adv Fam in a slapdash way

sixte [sikst] nf Mus sixth

Skaï® [skaj] nm imitation leather

skate [skɛt], **skateboard** [skɛtbɔrd] nm skateboard; **faire du s.** to skateboard

sketch (pl **sketches**) [skɛtʃ] nm sketch

ski [ski] nm (a) (matériel) ski (b) (activité) skiing; **faire du s.** to ski; **s. alpin/de fond** downhill/cross-country skiing; **s. nautique** water skiing

skiable [skjabl] adj voir **domaine**

skier [66] [skje] vi to ski

skieur, -euse [skjœr, -øz] nm,f skier

skin [skin], **skinhead** [skinɛd] nm skinhead

skipper [skipœr] nm skipper

slalom [slalɔm] nm slalom; Fig **faire du s. (entre)** to dodge in and out (between); **s. géant** giant slalom; **s. spécial** special slalom

slalomer [slalɔme] vi to slalom; Fig to dodge in and out (entre between)

slalomeur, -euse [slalɔmœr, -øz] nm,f slalom skier

slave [slav] **1** adj Slav, Slavonic **2** nmf **S.** Slav **3** nm (langue) Slavonic

slip [slip] nm (d'homme) briefs, underpants; (de femme) pants, briefs; **s. de bain** (d'homme) swimming trunks; (de femme) bikini bottom

slogan [slɔgɑ] nm slogan

slovaque [slɔvak] **1** adj Slovak **2** nmf **S.** Slovak **3** nm (langue) Slovak

Slovaquie [slɔvaki] nf **la S.** Slovakia

slovène [slɔvɛn] **1** adj Slovene **2** nmf **S.** Slovene **3** nm (langue) Slovene

Slovénie [slɔveni] nf **la S.** Slovenia

slow [slo] nm slow dance

smala(h) [smala] nf Fam (famille) tribe

smash [smaʃ] nm smash; **faire un s.** to smash the ball

smasher [smaʃe] **1** vt to smash **2** vi to smash the ball

SME [ɛsɛmə] nm (abrév Système monétaire européen) EMS

SMIC [smik] nm (abrév salaire minimum interprofessionnel de croissance) guaranteed minimum wage

smicard, -e [smikar, -ard] nm,f Fam minimum wage earner

smoking [smɔkiŋ] nm dinner or evening suit

snack [snak], **snack-bar** (pl **snack-bars**) [snakbar] nm snack bar

SNCF [ɛsɛnseɛf] nf (abrév Société nationale des chemins de fer français) = French national railway company

sniffer [snife] vt Fam (drogue) to sniff

snob [snɔb] **1** adj snobbish **2** nmf snob

snober [snɔbe] vt to snub

snobinard, -e [snɔbinar, -ard] Fam Péj **1** adj stuck-up **2** nm,f snob

snobisme [snɔbism] nm snobbery, snobbishness

sobre [sɔbr] adj (a) (personne) (qui n'a pas bu) sober; (qui boit ou mange peu) abstemious (b) (repas, vie) simple (c) (style, lignes, discours) sober

sobrement [sɔbrəmɑ] adv (s'exprimer, s'habiller) soberly

sobriété [sɔbrijete] nf (a) (tempérance) temperance, sobriety (b) (d'un repas, d'une vie) simplicity (c) (d'un style, de lignes, d'un discours) sobriety; **s'exprimer avec s.** to speak soberly

sobriquet [sɔbrike] nm nickname

sociabilité [sɔsjabilite] nf sociability

sociable [sɔsjabl] adj sociable

social, -e, -aux, -ales [sɔsjal, -o] **1** adj (ordre, politique, réforme) social **2** nm **le s.** social issues

social-démocrate, sociale-démocrate (mpl **sociaux-démocrates**, fpl **sociales-démocrates**) [sɔsjaldemɔkrat, sɔsjodemɔkrat] adj & nmf social democrat

social-démocratie (pl **social-démocraties**) [sɔsjaldemɔkrasi] nf social democracy

socialement [sɔsjalmɑ] adv socially

socialisation [sɔsjalizasjɔ] nf socialization

socialiser [sɔsjalize] vt to socialize

socialisme [sɔsjalism] nm socialism

socialiste [sɔsjalist] adj & nmf socialist

sociétaire [sɔsjetɛr] nmf (a) (membre) member (b) (actionnaire) shareholder

société [sɔsjete] nf (a) (communauté) society; **en s.** in society; **s. de consommation** consumer society; **la haute s.** high society (b) (association) society, association; (sportive) club; Hist **la S. des Nations** the League of Nations; **la S. protectrice des animaux** Br ≃ the RSPCA, Am ≃ the ASPCA (c) (compagnie) company, firm; **s. par actions** Br joint-stock company, Am incorporated company; **s. anonyme** Br public limited company, Am corporation; **s. en participation** joint venture; **s. à responsabilité limitée** limited (liability) company (d) (présence) company

socioculturel, -elle [sɔsjɔkyltyrɛl] adj social and cultural

socio-économique (pl **socio-économiques**) [sɔsjoekɔnɔmik] adj socioeconomic

sociolinguistique [sɔsjɔlɛ̃gɥistik] **1** adj sociolinguistic **2** nf sociolinguistics (singulier)

sociologie [sɔsjɔlɔʒi] nf sociology

sociologique [sɔsjɔlɔʒik] adj sociological

sociologiquement [sɔsjɔlɔʒikmɑ] adv sociologically

sociologue [sɔsjɔlɔg] nmf sociologist

socioprofessionnel, -elle [sɔsjɔprɔfɛsjɔnɛl] adj socio-professional

socle [sɔkl] nm (de statue, de colonne) plinth, pedestal; (de vase, de pendule, d'appareil) base; Ordinat **s. orientable** ou **pivotant** (d'un moniteur) swivel base

socquette [sɔkɛt] nf ankle sock

Socrate [sɔkrat] npr Socrates

soda [sɔda] nm Br fizzy drink, Am soda

sodium [sɔdjɔm] nm sodium

sodomie [sɔdɔmi] nf sodomy, buggery

sodomiser [sɔdɔmize] *vt* to sodomize, to bugger

sœur [sœr] *nf* (**a**) *(parente)* sister; *Fam* **et ta s.!** get lost!; **s. de lait** foster sister (**b**) *Rel* nun, sister

sœurette [sœrɛt] *nf Fam* little sister

sofa [sɔfa] *nm* sofa, settee

Sofia [sɔfja] *n* Sofia

SOFRES [sɔfrɛs] *nf (abrév* **Société française d'enquêtes par sondage)** = French opinion poll company

software [sɔftwɛr] *nm Ordinat* software

soi [swa] *pron personnel* (**a**) *(personne indéfinie)* oneself; *(homme)* himself; *(femme)* herself; **chez s.** at home; **il faut regarder devant s.** you must keep looking in front of you; **revenir à soi** to regain consciousness (**b**) *(chose, concept)* **en s.** in itself, per se

soi-disant [swadizɑ̃] **1** *adv* supposedly **2** *adj inv* so-called

soie [swa] *nf* (**a**) *(étoffe)* silk; **s. grège/naturelle** raw/ natural silk (**b**) *(de sanglier, de porc)* bristle

soierie [swari] *nf* (**a**) *(tissu)* silk (**b**) *(commerce)* silk trade

soif [swaf] *nf aussi Fig* thirst; **avoir s.** to be thirsty; **donner s. à qn** to make sb thirsty; **boire jusqu'à plus s.** to drink one's fill; *Fig* **s. de qch/de faire qch** thirst for sth/to do sth

soignant, -e [swaɲɑ̃, -ɑ̃t] *adj* **personnel s.** nursing staff; **équipe soignante** team of nursing staff

soigné, -e [swaɲe] *adj* (**a**) *(travail)* careful; *(style)* polished (**b**) *(personne, apparence)* neat, tidy; *(mains, ongles, jardin)* well-kept (**c**) *Fam (addition)* shockingly high

soigner [swaɲe] **1** *vt* (**a**) *(maladie)* to treat (**b**) *(malade) (sujet: médecin)* to treat; *(sujet: parent, infirmière)* to look after, to take care of; *Fam Fig* **il faut te faire s.!** you need your head examined! (**c**) *(apparence, invités, image)* to look after, to take care of; *(travail, présentation)* to take care over **2 se soigner** *vpr* (**a**) *(personne) (médicalement)* to treat oneself; *(faire attention à soi)* to take care of oneself, to look after oneself (**b**) *(maladie)* **ça se soigne très bien** it's easily treated

soigneur [swaɲœr] *nm* trainer; *(en boxe)* second

soigneusement [swaɲøzmɑ̃] *adv* carefully

soigneux, -euse [swaɲø, -øz] *adj* (**a**) *(attentif)* careful (**de** with) (**b**) *(méticuleux)* tidy, neat

soi-même [swamɛm] *pron personnel* oneself; *Prov* **on n'est jamais si bien servi que par s.** if you want something done, do it yourself

soin [swɛ̃] *nm* (**a**) *(attention)* care; **avec s.** carefully, with care; **sans s.** *(travail, exécution)* careless; *(travailler, exécuter)* carelessly; **aux bons soins de** *(sur une lettre)* care of..., c/o...; **avoir** *ou* **prendre s. de qn/qch** to look after *or* take care of sb/sth; **prendre s. de faire qch** to take care to do sth; **confier à qn le s. de faire qch** to entrust sb with the task of doing sth; **laisser à qn le s. de faire qch** to leave it to sb to do sth; **les soins du ménage** housekeeping (**b**) *(traitement)* **soins** care, attention; **soins de beauté** beauty care; **être aux petits soins pour** *ou* **avec qn** to wait on sb hand and foot (**c**) *(traitement médical)* **premiers soins, soins d'urgence** first aid; **soins à domicile** home care *or* nursing; **soins intensifs** intensive care; **soins médicaux** medical care; **soins palliatifs** palliative care

soir [swar] *nm* evening; **ce s.** this evening, tonight; **à ce s.!** see you tonight!; **à dix heures du s.** at ten o'clock in the evening *or* at night; **le Mardi 25 au s.** on the evening of Tuesday 25th; **tous les lundis s.** every Monday evening; **faire qch le s.** to do sth in the evening; **être du s.** to be a night owl

soirée [sware] *nf* (**a**) *(soir)* evening; **dans la s.** in (the course of) the evening; **en fin de s.** towards the end of the evening (**b**) *(fête)* party; **s. dansante** dance (**c**) *Th & Cin*

evening performance; **le film passe en s.** there is an evening performance of the film

sois, soit[1] *etc voir* **être**

soit[2] **1** [swat] *adv* all right **2** [swa] *conj* (**a**) *(supposons)* **s. un point P** given a point P (**b**) *(c'est-à-dire)* that is to say; (**c**) **s...., s....** either... or...; **s. l'un, s. l'autre** (either) one or the other

soixantaine [swasɑ̃tɛn] *nf* (**a**) *(environ soixante)* **une s.** **(de)** about sixty, sixty or so (**b**) *(âge)* **avoir la s.** to be around sixty; **approcher de la s.** to be getting on for sixty

soixante [swasɑ̃t] *adj & nm inv* sixty; **s. et onze** seventy-one; *voir aussi* **trois**

soixante-dix [swasɑ̃tdis] *adj inv & nm* seventy; *voir aussi* **trois**

soixante-dixième [swasɑ̃tdizjɛm] *nmf, nm & adj* seventieth; *voir aussi* **cinquième**

soixante-huitard, -e [mpl soixante-huitards, fpl soixante-huitardes] [swasɑ̃tɥitar, -ard] *nm,f* = person involved in the events of May 1968

soixantième [swasɑ̃tjɛm] *nmf, nm & adj* sixtieth; *voir aussi* **cinquième**

soja [sɔʒa] *nm* soya

sol[1] [sɔl] *nm* (**a**) *(surface) (dehors)* ground; *(à l'intérieur)* floor; **au s.** at ground level (**b**) *(territoire)* soil (**c**) *(matière)* soil

sol[2] *nm inv (note)* G; *(chantée)* sol

sol-air [sɔlɛr] *adj inv (missile)* ground-to-air

solaire [sɔlɛr] *adj (système, chauffage, four)* solar; *(lotion, crème)* sun

solarium [sɔlarjɔm] *nm* (**a**) *(établissement)* solarium (**b**) *(terrasse)* sun terrace

soldat [sɔlda] *nm* (**a**) *(personne)* soldier; **s. de deuxième classe** private; **s. de première classe** *Br* lance-corporal, *Am* private first class; **le S. inconnu** the Unknown Soldier (**b**) *(jouet)* (toy) soldier; **s. de plomb** tin soldier

solde[1] [sɔld] *nf (rémunération)* pay; *Péj* **à la s. de qn** in sb's pay

solde[2] *nm* (**a**) *(de compte)* balance; **pour s. (de tout compte)** in (full *or* final) settlement (**b**) *(rabais)* **acheter qch en s.** to buy sth in the sale; **vendre qch en s.** to sell sth off; **c'était en s.** it was in the sale; **des soldes** *(articles)* sale goods; **faire les soldes** *(acheteur)* to go round the sales; **faire des soldes** *(magasin)* to have a sale

solder [sɔlde] **1** *vt* (**a**) *(compte)* to close (**b**) *(article)* to sell off, to clear **2 se solder** *vpr* **se s. par qch** *Fin* to show sth; *Fig (résultat, échec)* to end in sth

soldeur, -euse [sɔldœr, -øz] *nm,f* discount trader

sole [sɔl] *nf (poisson)* sole

soleil [sɔlɛj] *nm* (**a**) *(astre)* sun; **s. de minuit** midnight sun (**b**) *(lumière, chaleur)* sun, sunshine; **il y a** *ou* **il fait du s.** the sun's shining, it's sunny; *Fig* **se faire une place au s.** to find a place in the sun; *Fig* **avoir des biens au s.** to own property

solennel, -elle [sɔlanɛl] *adj* (**a**) *(occasion, cérémonie)* formal; *(serment, déclaration)* solemn (**b**) *Péj* pompous

solennellement [sɔlanɛlmɑ̃] *adv (officiellement)* formally; *(gravement)* solemnly

solennité [sɔlanite] *nf* (**a**) *(d'une occasion, d'une cérémonie)* formality; *(d'un serment, d'une déclaration)* solemnity (**b**) *Péj* pomposity

Solex® [sɔlɛks] *nm* moped, motor scooter

solfège [sɔlfɛʒ] *nm* (**a**) *(théorie)* music theory (**b**) *(recueil)* music primer

solfier [66] [sɔlfje] *vt* to sol-fa

solidaire [sɔlidɛr] adj **(a)** (personne) être s. de qn to stand by sb, to support sb; se sentir s. de qn to feel a sense of solidarity with sb **(b)** (pièces) interdependent; roue s. d'une autre wheel integral with another

solidairement [sɔlidɛrmɑ̃] adv jointly

solidariser [sɔlidarize] se solidariser vpr to show solidarity (avec with)

solidarité [sɔlidarite] nf (entre personnes) solidarity

solide [sɔlid] **1** adj **(a)** (résistant) (mur, meuble) solid; (tissu) strong; (personne) sturdy; s. sur ses jambes steady on one's feet; être s. comme un chêne ou un roc to be hale and hearty **(b)** (amitié, relation, liens) strong **(c)** (éducation, argumentation) sound; Fig ça ne repose sur rien de s. there's no sound basis for that **(d)** (repas) solid; (appétit) healthy **(e)** (position, affaire) sound, strong **(f)** (non liquide) solid
2 nm **(a)** (corps) solid **(b)** Fam c'est du s.! (meuble) that's pretty solid!; (vêtement) it's indestructible!

solidement [sɔlidmɑ̃] adv (construit) solidly; (attaché, implanté) firmly

solidifier [66] [sɔlidifje] **1** vt to solidify
2 se solidifier vpr to solidify

solidité [sɔlidite] nf **(a)** (d'un objet) solidity; (d'un matériau) strength; être d'une s. à toute épreuve to be able to stand up to anything **(b)** (d'un jugement) soundness **(c)** (d'une amitié) strength

soliloque [sɔlilɔk] nm soliloquy

soliste [sɔlist] nmf soloist

solitaire [sɔliter] **1** adj **(a)** (personne) (par choix) solitary; (involontairement) lonely; passer des vacances solitaires to spend one's holidays on one's own **(b)** (arbre, maison) solitary, lone
2 nmf (personne) loner; en s. on one's own, alone
3 nm (a) (jeu) solitaire **(b)** (diamant) solitaire

solitairement [sɔlitɛrmɑ̃] adv on one's own, alone

solitude [sɔlityd] nf **(a)** (retraite) solitude; (involontaire) loneliness; aimer la s. to like being alone **(b)** (d'un lieu) loneliness

solive [sɔliv] nf Constr joist

sollicitation [sɔlisitasjɔ̃] nf request

solliciter [sɔlisite] vt **(a)** (entretien, audience) to request; (emploi) to apply for **(b)** (personne) s. qn (pour faire qch) to appeal to sb (to do sth); être sollicité de toutes parts to be very much in demand **(c)** (attention, regards) to attract; (curiosité) to arouse

sollicitude [sɔlisityd] nf solicitude, concern (pour for)

solo [sɔlo] **1** adj inv solo
2 nm solo; jouer en s. to play solo

sol-sol [sɔlsɔl] adj inv (missile) ground-to-ground

solstice [sɔlstis] nm solstice; s. d'été/d'hiver summer/winter solstice

soluble [sɔlybl] adj **(a)** (produit) soluble; (café) instant **(b)** (problème) solvable

solution [sɔlysjɔ̃] nf **(a)** (de problème, de situation, d'équation) solution, answer (de to); s. de facilité easy way out **(b)** (liquide) solution

solutionner [sɔlysjɔne] vt Fam to solve

solvabilité [sɔlvabilite] nf solvency

solvable [sɔlvabl] adj solvent

solvant [sɔlvɑ̃] nm solvent

somali, -e [sɔmali] **1** adj Somali
2 nmf S. Somali
3 nm (langue) Somali

Somalie [sɔmali] nf la S. Somalia

somalien, -enne [sɔmaljɛ̃, -ɛn] **1** adj Somalian
2 nmf S. Somalian

somatique [sɔmatik] adj somatic

somatiser [sɔmatize] vt to react psychosomatically to

sombre [sɔ̃br] adj **(a)** (couleur) dark **(b)** (forêt, pièce) dark; (ciel) dull; il fait s. (temps) it's dull; (dans une pièce) it's dark **(c)** (visage, pensées, caractère) gloomy, sombre **(d)** (sinistre) une s. histoire de... a sordid tale of... **(e)** Fam un s. imbécile a total fool

sombrement [sɔ̃brəmɑ̃] adv (tristement) gloomily, sombrely

sombrer [sɔ̃bre] vi **(a)** (navire) to sink; (empire) to founder; (affaire) to fail **(b)** (personne) s. dans la déprime/la misère to sink into depression/destitution

sombrero [sɔ̃brero] nm sombrero

sommaire [sɔmɛr] **1** adj **(a)** (récit) brief **(b)** (rudimentaire) (examen) hasty; (connaissances, repas, étude) basic; (jugement, exécution) summary; faire une toilette s. to have a quick wash
2 nm (table des matières) contents; et au s. de l'émission de ce soir... coming up in tonight's programme...

sommairement [sɔmɛrmɑ̃] adv (a) (expliquer, raconter) briefly **(b)** (de façon rudimentaire) (meublé) basically; (juger) summarily

sommation [sɔmasjɔ̃] nf (a) Jur (injonction) demand **(b)** Mil warning

somme¹ [sɔm] nf voir bête

somme² nf **(a)** (d'une addition) sum, total; faire la s. de to add up **(b)** (quantité) (d'objets) number; (de travail, d'efforts) amount **(c)** (argent) s. (d'argent) sum (of money); pour la s. de 200 euros for 200 euros; dépenser des sommes folles to spend vast sums of money; c'est une s.! that's a lot of money! **(d)** (locutions) en s. (tout compte fait) on the whole; (en bref) in short; s. toute when all's said and done

somme³ nm nap, snooze; faire un (petit) s. to have or take a nap or a snooze

sommeil [sɔmɛj] nm **(a)** (repos) sleep; avoir s. to be or feel sleepy; dormir d'un s. de plomb to sleep like a log; avoir le s. léger/profond to be a light/heavy sleeper; chercher le s. to try to sleep; tomber de s. to be dead on one's feet; Fig le s. éternel eternal rest **(b)** en s. (projet) (lying) dormant; Fig laisser qch en s. to put sth on hold

sommeiller [sɔmeje] vi **(a)** (personne) to doze **(b)** Fig to lie dormant

sommelier [sɔməlje] nm wine waiter

sommer [sɔme] vt s. qn de faire qch to charge sb to do sth

sommes voir être

sommet [sɔmɛ] nm **(a)** (de montagne) top, summit; (d'arbre, de toit) top; (de vague) crest; (de la tête) crown **(b)** Fig (de hiérarchie) top; (du pouvoir, de la gloire) height **(c)** (rencontre politique) summit; conférence/rencontre au s. summit conference/meeting **(d)** (d'angle) vertex

sommier [sɔmje] nm base; s. à ressorts/lattes sprung/slatted base

sommité [sɔmite] nf leading figure or light

somnambule [sɔmnɑ̃byl] **1** adj être s. to be a sleepwalker, to walk in one's sleep
2 nmf sleepwalker

somnambulisme [sɔmnɑ̃bylism] nm sleepwalking

somnifère [sɔmnifɛr] nm (substance) sedative; (cachet) sleeping pill

somnolence [sɔmnɔlɑ̃s] nf sleepiness, drowsiness; peut provoquer un état de s. (sur notice) may cause drowsiness

somnolent, -e [sɔmnɔlɑ̃, -ɑ̃t] adj sleepy, drowsy

somnoler [sɔmnɔle] vi to doze

somptuaire [sɔ̃ptɥer] adj extravagant

somptueusement [sɔ̃ptɥøzmɑ̃] *adv* sumptuously

somptueux, -euse [sɔ̃ptɥø, -øz] *adj* sumptuous

somptuosité [sɔ̃ptɥozite] *nf* sumptuousness

son¹, sa, ses [sɔ̃, sa, se]

> sa becomes son before a word beginning with a vowel or mute h.

adj possessif (possesseur masculin) his; *(possesseur féminin)* her; *(d'animal, de chose, de pays)* its; *(possesseur indéfini)* one's; **un de ses amis** one of his/her friends, a friend of his/hers; **chacun a pris s. sac** everyone took their bag; **perdre s. temps** to waste one's time; *Fam* **elle a eu s. vendredi** she got Friday off

son² *nm (de voix, d'instrument) & Cin* sound; *Fig* **n'entendre qu'un s. de cloche** to hear only one side of the story; **(spectacle) s. et lumière** son et lumière

son³ *nm (de grains)* bran

sonar [sɔnar] *nm* sonar

sonate [sɔnat] *nf* sonata; **s. pour violon** violin sonata

sondage [sɔ̃daʒ] *nm* **(a)** *(de population)* poll, survey; **faire un s.** to carry out a poll *or* a survey; **s. d'opinion** opinion poll; **s. par téléphone** telephone poll *or* survey **(b)** *(de terrain)* boring, drilling

sonde [sɔ̃d] *nf* **(a)** *(de bateau)* sounding line **(b)** *(de pompe, de puits)* sounding rod **(c)** *Météo & Av* **s. aérienne** sounding balloon; **s. spatiale** space probe **(d)** *Méd (pour examiner)* probe; *(pour intervenir)* tube **(e)** *(de terrain)* borer, drill

sondé, -e [sɔ̃de] *nm,f* respondent

sonder [sɔ̃de] *vt* **(a)** *(fond)* to sound; *Fig (mystère)* to fathom **(b)** *Météo (atmosphère)* to probe **(c)** *(terrain)* to bore, to drill; *Fig* **s. le terrain** to see how the land lies **(d)** *(personne, opinion, intentions)* to sound out **(e)** *Méd (blessure)* to probe; *(patient)* to sound

sondeur, -euse [sɔ̃dœr, -øz] **1** *nm (appareil)* sounder **2** *nm,f (d'opinions)* pollster

songe [sɔ̃ʒ] *nm Litt* dream; **en s.** in a dream; **faire un s.** to have a dream

songer [45] [sɔ̃ʒe] **1 songer à** *vt ind* **(a)** *(penser à, se souvenir de)* to think about **(b)** *(envisager)* to consider; **il ne faut pas y s.** that's quite out of the question; **s. à faire qch** to think of doing sth **2** *vt* **s. que** to think that

songerie [sɔ̃ʒri] *nf Litt* reverie

songeur, -euse [sɔ̃ʒœr, -øz] *adj* **(a)** *(rêveur)* dreamy **(b)** *(pensif)* pensive, thoughtful

sonnant, -e [sɔnɑ̃, -ɑ̃t] *adj* **arriver à deux heures sonnantes** to arrive on the stroke of two *or* at two o'clock sharp

sonné, -e [sɔne] *adj* **(a)** *(accompli)* **avoir cinquante ans bien sonnés** to be well over fifty **(b)** *Fam (étourdi)* groggy **(c)** *Fam (fou)* mad

sonner [sɔne] **1** *vi* **(a)** *(horloge)* to strike; *(cloches, téléphone)* to ring; *(réveil)* to go off; **faire s. son réveil (à six heures)** to set one's alarm (for six o'clock); **s. creux** *(mur)* to sound hollow; *Fig* to ring hollow; *Fig* **s. faux** not to ring true; *Fig* **s. bien/mal** to sound good/bad **(b)** *(heure)* **six heures sonnèrent** the clock struck six; *Fig* **son heure** *ou* **sa dernière heure a sonné** his/her last hour has come **(c)** *(à la porte)* **on a sonné** that was the bell, there's someone at the door; **s. chez qn** to ring sb's bell; **s. avant d'entrer** *(sur panneau)* ring before entering **(d)** *(jouer)* **s. du clairon/de la trompette** to sound the bugle/the trumpet **2** *vt* **(a)** *(cloche)* to ring; *Fam* **s. les cloches à qn** to tell sb off; **se faire s. les cloches** to get a good telling-off **(b)** *(heure)* to strike; *(messe, repas)* to ring the bell for **(c)**

(domestique, infirmière) to ring for; *Fam* **on ne t'a pas sonné!** nobody asked you! **(c)** *Fam (assommer)* to knock out

sonnerie [sɔnri] *nf* **(a)** *(son) (de cloches, du téléphone)* ringing; *(de clairon, de trompette)* call **(b)** *(sonnette)* bell

sonnet [sɔnɛ] *nm* sonnet

sonnette [sɔnɛt] *nf* bell; **s. d'alarme** alarm bell; *aussi Fig* **tirer la s. d'alarme** to sound the alarm

sono [sɔno] *nf Fam* PA system

sonore [sɔnɔr] **1** *adj* **(a)** *(effet)* sound; *(pollution)* noise **(b)** *(voix)* ringing; *(rire)* resounding; *(salle)* echoing **(c)** *Ling (consonne)* voiced **2** *nf Ling* voiced consonant

sonorisation [sɔnɔrizasjɔ̃] *nf* **(a)** *(de film)* addition of the soundtrack **(de to) (b)** *(de salle)* fitting of a PA system **(de to) (c)** *(équipement)* PA system, public address system

sonoriser [sɔnɔrize] *vt* **(a)** *(film)* to add the soundtrack to **(b)** *(salle)* to fit with a PA system

sonorité [sɔnɔrite] *nf* tone

sont *voir* être

sophisme [sɔfism] *nm* sophism

sophistication [sɔfistikasjɔ̃] *nf* sophistication

sophistiqué, -e [sɔfistike] *adj* sophisticated

soporifique [sɔpɔrifik] *adj aussi Fig* soporific

soprano [sɔprano] **1** *adj (saxophone)* soprano **2** *nmf (personne)* soprano **3** *nm* soprano (voice)

sorbet [sɔrbɛ] *nm* sorbet

sorbetière [sɔrbətjɛr] *nf* ice-cream maker

sorbier [sɔrbje] *nm* sorb (tree), service (tree)

sorcellerie [sɔrsɛlri] *nf* witchcraft, sorcery

sorcier [sɔrsje] **1** *adj Fam* **ce n'est pas s.** it's simple enough **2** *nm* sorcerer, wizard

sorcière [sɔrsjɛr] *nf* sorceress, witch; *Fam Péj* **vieille s.** old witch

sordide [sɔrdid] *adj* **(a)** *(pièce, quartier)* squalid **(b)** *(crime, détails, avarice)* sordid

sorgho [sɔrgo] *nm* sorghum

Sorlingues [sɔrlɛ̃g] *nfpl* **les S.** the Scilly Isles

sornettes [sɔrnɛt] *nfpl* twaddle, rubbish

sors, sort¹ *etc voir* sortir

sort² [sɔr] *nm* **(a)** *(condition)* lot; *Fam* **faire un s. à qch** *(bouteille, plat)* to polish sth off **(b)** *(destin)* fate **(c)** *(hasard)* chance; **tirer au s.** to draw lots; **le s. en est jeté** the die is cast **(d)** *(magique)* spell; **jeter un s. à qn** to cast a spell on sb; **conjurer le mauvais s.** to ward off bad luck

sortable [sɔrtabl] *adj Fam* **tu n'es pas s.!** I can't take you anywhere!

sortant, -e [sɔrtɑ̃, -ɑ̃t] *adj (numéro de loterie)* winning; *(élu)* outgoing

sorte [sɔrt] *nf* **(a)** *(genre)* sort, kind; **toutes sortes de choses/gens, des choses/gens de toutes sortes** all sorts *or* kinds of things/people; **un homme de la s.** a man of that kind; **une s. de...** a sort *or* kind of...; **je n'ai rien dit/fait de la s.** I said/did no such thing, I said/did nothing of the sort **(b)** *(manière)* **de la s.** in that way; **en quelque s.** as it were, in a way; **de s. que je puisse...** so that I can...; **de s. qu'il est arrivé en retard** with the result that he arrived late; **de s. à faire qch** so as to do sth; **faire en s. que** + *subjunctive* to see to it that; **fais en s. d'être à l'heure** see to it that you're on time

sortie [sɔrti] *nf* **(a)** *(fait de sortir d'un lieu)* **c'était ma première s. depuis...** it was my first time out since...; **à sa s. de l'hôpital** when he/she came out of the hospital; **à la s.**

de l'**école/du travail** after school/work; **à la s. des bureaux** when the offices come out (**b**) *(issue)* exit, way out; **à la s. de la gare** at the station exit; **s. d'autoroute** motorway exit; **s. de secours** emergency exit
(**c**) *(d'un livre, d'un journal)* publication; *(d'un film, d'un disque)* release; *(d'un modèle)* launch
(**d**) *(de liquide, d'air)* outflow
(**e**) *(dispositif)* outlet
(**f**) *(de marchandises)* export
(**g**) *(dépense)* **sorties** outgoings
(**h**) *(excursion)* trip, outing; **priver qn de s.** to stop sb from going out; **s. en mer** short sea trip; **jour de s.** day out; **ce soir je suis de s.** I'm going out tonight; **désolé, mais elle est de s.** sorry, but she's out
(**i**) *Mil* sortie
(**j**) *Fam (emportement)* outburst
(**k**) *Ordinat* exit; *(information)* output; **s. d'imprimante** printer output; **dispositif de s.** output device; **signal de s.** output signal; **s. écran** screen output; **s. imprimante** printout; **s. imprimée** printed output; **s. parallèle** parallel output; **s. série** serial output

sortie-de-bain *(pl* **sorties-de-bain)** [sɔrtidbɛ̃] *nf* bathrobe

sortilège [sɔrtilɛʒ] *nm* spell

sortir[1] [64a] [sɔrtir] **1** *vt (aux* **avoir**) (**a**) *(enfant, chien)* to take out; *(voiture)* to get out; **s. qn de** *(situation)* to get sb out of
(**b**) *(objet)* to take out (**de** of); **et si tu sortais ton bon whisky?** how about getting out your good whisky?
(**c**) *(mettre sur le marché) (livre, journal)* to bring out, to publish; *(film, disque)* to bring out, to release
(**d**) *Fam (dire)* to come out with
(**e**) *Fam (expulser)* to throw out; *(vaincre)* to knock out
2 *vi (aux* **être**) (**a**) *(aller)* to go out (**de** of), *(venir)* to come out (**de** of); *(partir)* to leave; *(s'extraire finir de travailler)* to get out (**de** of); **s. en courant/en boitant** to run/limp out; **est-ce que je peux s.?** *(en classe)* may I be excused?; **sortez (d'ici)!** get out (of here)!; **s. de table** to leave the table; **je sors d'une mauvaise grippe** I'm just getting over a bad dose of flu; **il est sorti discrédité de ce scandale** he came out of this scandal with his reputation in ruins; **cela ne doit pas s. d'ici** *(secret)* it mustn't go any further; *Fam* **d'où sors-tu?** *(d'où viens-tu?)* where did you spring from?; *(tu n'es pas au courant)* what planet have you been on?; **cela m'est sorti de la tête** it's gone right out of my head; **il ne sortira pas grand-chose de tout cela** nothing much will come of all this
(**b**) *(pour s'amuser)* to go out; **s. avec qn** to go out with sb; *Fig* **il faut s. un peu!** *(pour être au courant)* what planet have you been on?
(**c**) *(livre, journal)* to come out, to be published; *(film, disque)* to come out, to be released
(**d**) *(être issu)* **s. de** *(famille, milieu)* to come from; **elle sort de Yale** she was at Yale
(**e**) *(numéro de loto, sujet d'examen)* to come up
(**f**) *(apparaître) (fleur)* to come out; *(dent)* to come through; **les yeux lui sortaient de la tête** his eyes were popping out of his head
(**g**) *Ordinat (d'un système)* to exit
3 *se sortir vpr* **se s. de** *(situation)* to get out of; **s'en s.** *(d'un travail)* to manage; *(d'une difficulté)* to get through it; *(malade)* to pull through

sortir[2] *nm* **au s. du cinéma** on coming out of the cinema; **au s. de l'école** after school; **au s. de l'hiver** at the end of winter

SOS [ɛsoɛs] *nm* SOS; **lancer un S. (à)** to send (out) an SOS (to); **S. Amitié** = helpline for people in need of emotional support; **S. femmes battues** = helpline for female victims

of domestic violence; **S. médecins** emergency medical service; **S.-Racisme** = voluntary organization set up to combat racism in French society

sosie [sɔzi] *nm* lookalike, double; **c'est un s. de Brando** he's a Brando lookalike; **c'est le s. de mon frère** he's my brother's double

sot, sotte [so, sɔt] **1** *adj* stupid, foolish; **il n'y a pas de sot métier** there's no such thing as a worthless profession
2 *nm,f* fool

sottement [sɔtmɑ̃] *adv* stupidly, foolishly

sottise [sɔtiz] *nf* (**a**) *(stupidité)* stupidity, foolishness (**b**) *(action)* stupid act; **faire des sottises** to do stupid things; **faire une s.** to do something stupid (**c**) *(parole)* stupid remark; **dire des sottises** to say stupid things; **dire une s.** to say something stupid

sottisier [sɔtizje] *nm* collection of howlers

sou [su] *nm* (**a**) *(argent)* **être sans le s.** to be penniless; **il est toujours en train de compter ses sous** he's always counting every penny; **avoir des sous** to have money; **c'est une affaire de gros sous** there's big money involved; **être près de ses sous** to be a penny-pincher; *Fig* **n'avoir pas (pour) un s. de courage/bon sens** not to have an ounce of courage/common sense (**b**) *(pièce)* **un s. est un s.** every penny counts (**c**) *(ancienne monnaie)* sou (**d**) *Can (cent)* cent

soubassement [subasmɑ̃] *nm (de construction)* base

soubresaut [subrəso] *nm (de véhicule)* jolt; *(de personne)* jerk

soubrette [subrɛt] *nf* maid

souche [suʃ] *nf* (**a**) *(d'arbre)* stump; *Fam* **rester (planté) comme une s.** to be rooted to the spot; **dormir comme une s.** to sleep like a log (**b**) *(de famille)* founder; **faire s.** to found a line (**c**) *(de virus)* strain (**d**) *(de chèques, de tickets)* counterfoil, stub (**e**) *(de langue)* root

souci[1] [susi] *nm* (**a**) *(inquiétude)* worry, anxiety; **avoir des soucis** to have worries; **se faire du s. (pour)** to worry (about); **donner du s. à qn** to worry sb; **c'est le dernier** *ou* **le cadet de mes soucis** that's the least of my worries (**b**) *(soin)* concern (**de** for); **avoir le s. de plaire** to be anxious to please

souci[2] *nm (fleur)* marigold

soucier [66] [susje] **se soucier** *vpr* **se s. de** to worry about; **ne se s. de rien** not to worry about anything; *Fam* **se s. de qch comme de l'an quarante** *ou* **de sa première chemise** to give a damn about sth

soucieux, -euse [susjø, -øz] *adj* (**a**) *(attentif)* anxious, concerned (**de** about); **être s. de faire qch** to be anxious to do sth; **peu s. de qch** unconcerned about sth (**b**) *(inquiet)* worried

soucoupe [sukup] *nf* saucer; **s. volante** flying saucer

soudain, -e [sudɛ̃, -ɛn] **1** *adv* suddenly, all of a sudden
2 *adj* sudden

soudainement [sudɛnmɑ̃] *adv* suddenly

soudaineté [sudɛnte] *nf* suddenness

Soudan [sudɑ̃] *nm* **le S.** the Sudan

soudanais, -e [sudanɛ, -ɛz] **1** *adj* Sudanese
2 *nm,f* **S.** Sudanese; **les S.** the Sudanese

soudard [sudar] *nm Fam* brutish soldier

soude [sud] *nf* soda; **s. caustique** caustic soda

souder [sude] **1** *vt* (**a**) *(par alliage)* to solder; *(par soudure autogène)* to weld (**b**) *(os fracturé)* to knit (**c**) *Fig (groupes, personnes)* to unite
2 *se souder vpr* (**a**) *(os)* to knit (together) (**b**) *Fig (groupe)* to unite

soudeur, -euse [sudœr, -øz] *nm,f (avec soudure par alliage)* solderer; *(avec soudure autogène)* welder

soudoyer [32] [sudwaje] *vt* to bribe

soudure [sudyr] *nf* (**a**) *(opération) (par alliage)* soldering; *(autogène)* welding (**b**) *(résultat) (par alliage)* soldered joint; *(autogène)* weld (**c**) *(d'os)* knitting (**d**) *Fig* **faire la s.** to make ends meet

soufflage [sufla3] *nm (du verre)* blowing

souffle [sufl] *nm* (**a**) *(d'air, de vent)* breath, puff (**b**) *(respiration)* breathing; **avoir du s.** to have stamina; **retenir son s.** to hold one's breath; **manquer de s.** to be short-winded; **avoir le s. court** to be short of breath; **à bout de s.** out of breath; *Fig* **couper le s. à qn** to take sb's breath away (**c**) *(d'une explosion)* blast (**d**) *(d'hélices)* slipstream, wash (**e**) *Méd* murmur; **s. au cœur** heart murmur (**f**) *(force créatrice)* inspiration (**g**) *(impulsion)* **donner un nouveau s. à qch** to give sth a new lease of life

soufflé, -e [sufle] **1** *adj* (**a**) *Culin* soufflé (**b**) *Fam (ahuri)* flabbergasted, staggered
2 *nm* soufflé; **s. au fromage** cheese soufflé

souffler [sufle] **1** *vt* (**a**) *(fumée, poussière)* to blow; *(bougie)* to blow out (**b**) *(dire)* to whisper (**à** to); **s. une réplique à un acteur** to prompt an actor; **quelqu'un a dû lui s. l'idée** someone must have given him the idea; **ne pas s. mot (de qch)** not to breathe a word (about sth); **on ne souffle pas!** no prompting! (**c**) *Fam (prendre)* to pinch (**à** from); **se faire s. qch** to have sth pinched (**d**) *(détruire)* to blast (**e**) *Fam (ahurir)* to stagger (**f**) *(verre)* to blow (**g**) *(aux dames)* to huff; **s. n'est pas jouer** huffing doesn't count as a go
2 *vi* (**a**) *(expirer)* to blow; **s. dans ses doigts** to blow on one's fingers; **s. dans une trompette** to blow a trumpet (**b**) *(se reposer)* **laisser s. qn** to give sb time to catch his/her breath (**c**) *(haleter)* to pant, to puff; *Fam* **s. comme un bœuf** to puff and pant (**d**) *(vent)* to blow; *Fig* **un vent de révolte soufflait sur le pays** there was a spirit of revolt in the country

soufflerie [sufləri] *nf* (**a**) *(d'orgue, de forge)* bellows (**b**) *(de climatiseur)* blower

soufflet [sufle] *nm* (**a**) *(de forge)* bellows (**b**) *Rail (couloir)* concertina vestibule (**c**) *(en couture)* gusset (**d**) *(d'orgue)* swell (**e**) *Litt (gifle)* slap (in the face)

souffleter [42] [suflǝte] *vt Litt* **s. qn** to slap sb's face

souffleur, -euse [suflœr, -øz] **1** *nm* **s. de verre** glass blower
2 *nm,f (au théâtre)* prompter
3 *nf* **souffleuse** *Can* snowblower

souffrance [sufrɑ̃s] *nf* (**a**) *(douleur)* suffering (**b**) **en s.** *(travail)* pending

souffrant, -e [sufrɑ̃, -ɑ̃t] *adj (indisposé)* unwell, poorly

souffre-douleur [sufrǝdulœr] *nm inv* object of abuse

souffreteux, -euse [sufrǝtø, -øz] *adj* sickly

souffrir [52] [sufrir] **1** *vi* to suffer (**de** from); **faire s. qn** *(physiquement)* to hurt sb; *(moralement)* to make sb suffer; **je souffre de la voir malade** it upsets me to see her ill
2 *vt* (**a**) *(physiquement)* **s. le martyre** to go through agony; **faire s. le martyre à qn** to put sb through agony (**b**) *(supporter)* **je ne peux pas la s.** I can't stand her; **je ne peux pas s. qu'on vienne me déranger** I can't stand being disturbed; **il ne souffre pas la contradiction** he can't stand being contradicted; *Litt* **souffrez que je fasse une critique** permit me to make a criticism (**c**) *Litt (admettre)* **situation qui ne souffre aucun retard** situation that admits of no delay
3 *se souffrir* *vpr Fam* **ils ne peuvent pas se s.** they can't stand each other

soufre [sufr] *nm* sulphur

souhait [swɛ] *nm* wish; **faire un s.** to make a wish; **à s.** *(à merveille)* perfectly; **doré/ensoleillé à s.** beautifully golden/sunny; **à vos souhaits!** bless you!

souhaitable [swɛtabl] *adj* desirable; **il serait s. que tu lui parles** it is desirable that you should talk to him

souhaiter [swete] *vt* to wish for; **s. qch à qn** to wish sb sth; **s. faire qch** to hope to do sth; **s. à qn de faire qch** to hope that sb does sth; **s. que** + *subjunctive* to hope that; **je vous souhaite une bonne année/un joyeux anniversaire** best wishes for a happy New Year/a happy birthday; *Ironique* **je te souhaite bien du plaisir!** have fun!

souiller [suje] *vt Litt* (**a**) *(vêtements)* to soil, to dirty (**de** with) (**b**) *(réputation, mémoire)* to tarnish

souillon [sujɔ̃] *nf Litt* slut, sloven

souillure [sujyr] *nf Litt* (**a**) *(sur un vêtement)* stain (**b**) *Fig (morale)* blot, blemish

souk [suk] *nm* (**a**) *(marché)* souk (**b**) *Fam (lieu en désordre)* shambles *(singulier)*

soul [sul] *adj inv & nf* soul

soûl, -e [su, sul] **1** *adj* drunk
2 *nm* **tout son s.** to one's heart's content

soulagement [sula3mɑ̃] *nm* relief (**pour** to)

soulager [45] [sula3e] **1** *vt (douleur)* to ease, to relieve; *(esprit, chagrin)* to soothe; *(personne)* to relieve; **ce médicament vous soulagera** this medicine will make you feel better; **donne-moi un de tes sacs, ça te soulagera** give me one of your bags, that will take some of the weight off you; *Fam* **s. qn de son portefeuille** to relieve sb of his/her wallet
2 *se soulager* *vpr* (**a**) *(en parlant)* to ease one's mind (**b**) *Fam (satisfaire un besoin naturel)* to relieve oneself

soûlant, -e [sulɑ̃, -ɑ̃t] *adj Fam* exhausting

soûlard, -e [sular, -ard], **soûlaud, -e** [sulo, -od] *nm,f Fam* drunkard

soûler [sule] *Fam* **1** *vt* (**a**) *(enivrer)* **s. qn** to make sb drunk; *Fig (sujet: parfum, succès, idées)* to go to sb's head (**b**) *(ennuyer)* **arrête, tu me soûles!** stop, you're giving me a headache!
2 *se soûler* *vpr* to get drunk; *Fig* **se s. de paroles** to like the sound of one's own voice

soulèvement [sulɛvmɑ̃] *nm* (**a**) *(de terrain)* rising (**b**) *(révolte)* uprising

soulever [46] [sulve] **1** *vt* (**a**) *(charge, personne, couvercle)* to lift (up); *(rideau)* to raise (**b**) *(agiter) (poussière)* to raise, to throw up; *Fig* **s. le cœur à qn** to make sb feel sick (**c**) *(doutes, question, objection)* to raise (**d**) *(population)* to rouse, to stir up (**e**) *(passion, enthousiasme, indignation)* to excite, to arouse; **s. un tollé** to raise an outcry
2 *se soulever* *vpr* (**a**) *(s'élever)* to rise (**b**) *(se lever) (personne)* to raise oneself, to lift oneself up (**c**) *(se révolter)* to rise up

soulier [sulje] *nm* shoe; *Fam Fig* **être dans ses petits souliers** to feel awkward

souligner [suliɲe] *vt* (**a**) *(mot, passage)* to underline (**b**) *(yeux, taille)* to emphasize (**c**) *Fig (mettre en valeur)* to emphasize

soumettre [47] [sumetr] **1** *vt* (**a**) *(population, pays, passions)* to subdue (**b**) *(rapport, demande, projet)* to submit (**à** to) (**c**) **s. qn à** *(examen)* to subject sb to; *(épreuve)* to put sb through; *(traitement)* to put sb on; **être soumis à des règles strictes** to be bound by strict rules; **s. les revenus à l'impôt** to make income liable to tax
2 *se soumettre* *vpr (obéir)* to submit; **se s. à** *(autorité)* to submit to; *(volonté)* to comply with; *(loi, décision)* to abide by

soumis, -e [sumi, -iz] *adj (docile)* submissive, obedient (**à** to)

soumission [sumisjɔ̃] *nf* (**a**) *(à une loi, à une autorité)* submission (**à** to) (**b**) *(docilité)* submissiveness, obedience (**à** to)

soupape [supap] *nf* valve; **s. de sécurité** safety valve

soupçon [supsɔ̃] *nm* (**a**) *(suspicion)* suspicion; **avoir des soupçons sur qn** to have (one's) suspicions about sb; **être au-dessus** *ou* **à l'abri de tout s.** to be above all suspicion (**b**) *(faible quantité) (de vinaigre, d'ail)* dash, hint; *(de fièvre, de fard, d'ironie)* touch; *(de vin)* drop

soupçonner [supsɔne] *vt* to suspect; **s. qn de qch/de faire qch** to suspect sb of sth/of doing sth; **je soupçonne qu'il le sait** I suspect that he knows

soupçonneux, -euse [supsɔnø, -øz] *adj* suspicious

soupe [sup] *nf* (**a**) *(plat)* soup; *Fam* **à la s.!** grub's up!; *Fam* **être s. au lait** to flare up easily (**b**) **s. populaire** soup kitchen

soupente [supɑ̃t] *nf (sous un toit)* loft; *(sous un escalier) Br* cupboard, *Am* closet

souper[1] [supe] *nm* (**a**) *(dîner)* dinner (**b**) *(après le spectacle)* supper

souper[2] *vi* (**a**) *(dîner)* to have dinner (**b**) *(après le spectacle)* to have supper (**c**) *Fam Fig (être excédé)* **avoir soupé de qn/qch** to be fed up with sb/sth

soupeser [46] [supəze] *vt (objet)* to feel the weight of, to weigh in one's hand; *Fig (problème, argument)* to weigh up

soupière [supjɛr] *nf* soup tureen

soupir [supir] *nm* (**a**) *(souffle)* sigh; **pousser un s.** to let out *or* give a sigh; **rendre le dernier s.** to breathe one's last; **un gros s.** a heavy *or* deep sigh (**b**) *Mus Br* crotchet *or Am* quarter rest

soupirail, -aux [supiraj, -o] *nm* cellar window

soupirant [supirɑ̃] *nm Hum* suitor, admirer

soupirer [supire] **1** *vt* to sigh **2** *vi* to sigh; **en soupirant** with a sigh **3** **soupirer après** *vt ind Litt* to long for, to yearn for

souple [supl] *adj* (**a**) *(branche)* flexible; *(corps, danseur)* supple; *(reliure)* limp; *(cuir)* soft, supple (**b**) *Fig (système, loi, personne)* flexible; *(esprit)* adaptable

souplesse [suples] *nf* (**a**) *(de branche)* flexibility; *(de corps, de danseur)* suppleness; **en s.** *(démarrer)* smoothly (**b**) *Fig (de système, de loi, de personne)* flexibility

source [surs] *nf* (**a**) *(d'eau)* spring; **s. d'eau minérale** mineral spring; **s. thermale** hot spring (**b**) *(de rivière)* source; **prendre sa s.** to rise (**c**) *(de chaleur, d'énergie)* source (**d**) *Fig (du mal, de richesse, d'informations)* source; **tenir qch de bonne s.** to have sth on good authority *or* from a reliable source; **apprendre qch de s. sûre** to learn sth from a reliable source; **s. de revenus** source of revenue (**e**) *Ordinat* **s. de données** data source; **code s.** source code

sourcier [sursje] *nm* water diviner

sourcil [sursil] *nm* eyebrow

sourciller [sursije] *vi* **ne pas s.** not to bat an eyelid *or* turn a hair; **sans s.** without batting an eyelid, without turning a hair

sourcilleux, -euse [sursijø, -øz] *adj* fussy, finicky

sourd, -e [sur, surd] **1** *adj* (**a**) *(personne)* deaf; **devenir s.** to go deaf, *Fig* **rester s. à qch** to turn a deaf ear to sth, to be deaf to sth; **s. de naissance** deaf from birth; **s. d'une oreille** deaf in one ear; *Fam* **s. comme un pot** deaf as a post (**b**) *(douleur, bruit)* dull; *(voix)* hollow; *(désir, lutte)* secret; *(hostilité)* veiled; *(consonne)* voiceless **2** *nmf (personne)* deaf person; **les sourds** the deaf, deaf people; **comme un s.** *(crier)* at the top of one's voice; *(frapper, taper)* wildly **3** *nf* **sourde** *Ling* voiceless consonant

sourdine [surdin] *nf* mute; *(d'un piano)* practice pedal; **en s.** *(violons)* muted; *(en secret)* on the quiet; *Fam Fig* **mets-la en s.!** put a sock in it!

sourdingue [surdɛ̃g] *Fam* **1** *adj* cloth-eared **2** *nmf* cloth-ears

sourd-muet, sourde-muette *(mpl* **sourds-muets,** *fpl* **sourdes-muettes)** [surmɥe, surdmɥet] **1** *adj* deaf-mute **2** *nm,f* deaf mute

souriant, -e [surjɑ̃, -ɑ̃t] *adj* smiling

souriceau, -x [suriso] *nm* young mouse

souricière [surisjɛr] *nf* mousetrap; *Fig* trap

sourire [61] [surir] **1** *vi* (**a**) *(personne)* to smile (**à** at); *Ironique* **ça fait s.** it makes you laugh (**b**) *(être favorable)* **la chance lui sourit** fortune smiles on him; **tout lui sourit** everything goes right for her **2** *nm* smile; **le s. aux lèvres** with a smile on one's lips; **faire un s. à qn** to give sb a smile; **avoir le s.** to have a smile on one's face; **garder le s.** to keep smiling; **retrouver le s.** to be smiling again

souris [suri] *nf* (**a**) *(animal)* mouse; **s. blanche** white mouse (**b**) *Ordinat* mouse; **s. à trois boutons** three-button mouse; **s. à infrarouge** infrared mouse; **s. optique** optical mouse; **s. sans fil** cordless mouse; **s. tactile** touchpad mouse (**c**) *Fam (femme) Br* bird, *Am* dame (**d**) *(de gigot)* knuckle end

sournois, -e [surnwa, -az] **1** *adj* sly **2** *nm,f* sly person

sournoisement [surnwazmɑ̃] *adv* slyly

sournoiserie [surnwazri] *nf* slyness

sous [su] *prép* (**a**) *(position)* under(neath); **s. terre** underground; **nager s. l'eau** to swim underwater; **lettre s. enveloppe** letter in an envelope; **s. la pluie** in the rain; **s. les tropiques** in the tropics; **s. les yeux de qn** before sb's eyes; **s. cet angle** from that angle; **chercher un mot s. la lettre S** to look up a word under the letter S *(à l'époque de) (monarque, président)* under; **s. la IIIᵉ République** during the Third Republic (**c**) *(d'ici)* within; **s. peu** shortly, before long (**d**) *(locutions)* **connu s. le nom de...** known as...; **être s. antibiotiques** to be on antibiotics; **opérer s. anesthésie** to operate under anaesthetic; **s. le poids de qch** under the weight of sth; **travailler s. les ordres de qn** to work under sb; **s. certaines conditions** on certain conditions; **s. peine de mort** on *or* under pain of death

sous-alimentation [suzalimɑ̃tasjɔ̃] *nf* malnutrition, undernourishment

sous-alimenté, -e *(mpl* **sous-alimentés,** *fpl* **sous-alimentées)** [suzalimɑ̃te] *adj* malnourished, undernourished

sous-bois [subwa] *nm inv* undergrowth

sous-chef *(pl* **sous-chefs)** [suʃef] *nm* second-in-command; *(dans un restaurant)* sous-chef

sous-continent *(pl* **sous-continents)** [sukɔ̃tinɑ̃] *nm* subcontinent

sous-couche *(pl* **sous-couches)** [sukuʃ] *nf* undercoat

souscripteur, -trice [suskriptœr, -tris] *nm,f (d'un emprunt)* subscriber (**de** to); *(d'une police d'assurance)* policy holder

souscription [suskripsjɔ̃] *nf (à un emprunt)* subscription (**à** to); **la s. d'une police d'assurance** taking out an insurance policy

souscrire [30] [suskrir] **1** *vt (police d'assurance)* to take out **2** **souscrire à** *vt ind aussi Fig* to subscribe to

sous-culture *(pl* **sous-cultures)** [sukyltyr] *nf* subculture

sous-cutané, -e *(mpl* **sous-cutanés,** *fpl* **sous-cutanées)** [sukytane] *adj* subcutaneous

sous-développé, -e *(mpl* **sous-développés,** *fpl* **sous-développées)** [sudevlɔpe] *adj (pays)* under-developed

sous-développement [sudevlɔpmɑ̃] *nm* under-development

sous-directeur, -trice (*mpl* sous-directeurs, *fpl* sous-directrices) [sudirɛktœr, -tris] *nm,f* (*dans une entreprise*) assistant manager

sous-division *nf* subdivision

sous-emploi [suzɑ̃plwa] *nm* underemployment

sous-employé, -e (*mpl* sous-employés, *fpl* sous-employées) [suzɑ̃plwaje] *adj* underemployed

sous-ensemble (*pl* sous-ensembles) [suzɑ̃sɑ̃bl] *nm* subset

sous-entendre [suzɑ̃tɑ̃dr] *vt* to imply

sous-entendu (*pl* sous-entendus) [suzɑ̃tɑ̃dy] *nm* insinuation

sous-équipé, -e (*mpl* sous-équipés, *fpl* sous-équipées) [suzekipe] *adj* underequipped

sous-estimer [suzɛstime] *vt* to underestimate

sous-évaluer [suzevalɥe] *vt* to undervalue

sous-exposer [suzɛkspoze] *vt* to underexpose

sous-fifre (*pl* sous-fifres) [sufifr] *nm Fam* underling

sous-homme (*pl* sous-hommes) [suzɔm] *nm* subhuman

sous-jacent, -e (*mpl* sous-jacents, *fpl* sous-jacentes) [suʒasɑ̃, -ɑ̃t] *adj* underlying

Sous-le-Vent [sulvɑ̃] *n* **les îles S.** the Leeward Islands

sous-lieutenant (*pl* sous-lieutenants) [suljøtnɑ̃] *nm* (**a**) (*dans l'armée de terre*) second lieutenant (**b**) (*dans la marine*) sub-lieutenant (**c**) (*dans l'armée de l'air*) *Br* pilot officer, *Am* second lieutenant

sous-locataire (*pl* sous-locataires) [sulɔkater] *nmf* subtenant

sous-location (*pl* sous-locations) [sulɔkasjɔ̃] *nf* (**a**) (*par le locataire*) subletting (**b**) (*par le sous-locataire*) subrenting

sous-louer [sulwe] *vt* (**a**) (*sujet: locataire*) to sublet (**b**) (*sujet: sous-locataire*) to subrent

sous-main [sumɛ̃] *nm inv* desk blotter; *Fig* **en s.** secretly

sous-marin, -e (*mpl* sous-marins, *fpl* sous-marines) [sumarɛ̃, -in] **1** *adj* underwater **2** *nm* submarine; **s. nucléaire** nuclear(-powered) submarine

sous-marinier (*pl* sous-mariniers) [sumarinje] *nm* submariner

sous-multiple (*pl* sous-multiples) [sumyltipl] *nm Math* submultiple (**de** of)

sous-nappe (*pl* sous-nappes) [sunap] *nf* undercloth

sous-officier (*pl* sous-officiers) [suzɔfisje] *nm* non-commissioned officer

sous-payer [53] [supeje] *vt* to underpay

sous-peuplé, -e (*mpl* sous-peuplés, *fpl* sous-peuplées) [supœple] *adj* underpopulated

sous-préfecture (*pl* sous-préfectures) [supre-fɛktyr] *nf* subprefecture

sous-préfet (*pl* sous-préfets) [suprefɛ] *nm* subprefect

sous-production [suprɔdyksjɔ̃] *nf* under-production

sous-produit (*pl* sous-produits) [suprɔdɥi] *nm* by-product; *Fig* poor imitation

sous-prolétaire (*pl* sous-prolétaires) [suprɔleter] *nmf* member of the underclass

sous-prolétariat (*pl* sous-prolétariats) [suprɔ-letarja] *nm* underclass

sous-pull (*pl* sous-pulls) [supyl] *nm* thin sweater

sous-répertoire (*pl* sous-répertoires) [surepertwar] *nm Ordinat* subdirectory

sous-secrétaire (*pl* sous-secrétaires) [susəkreter] *nmf* **s. d'État** Under-Secretary of State

soussigné, -e [susiɲe] *adj & nm,f* undersigned; **je, s. Éric Poulain, donne mon autorisation à...** I, the undersigned Éric Poulain, hereby authorize...

sous-sol (*pl* sous-sols) [susɔl] *nm* (**a**) (*d'une maison*) basement (**b**) *Géol* subsoil

sous-tasse (*pl* sous-tasses) [sutas] *nf* saucer

sous-tendre [sutɑ̃dr] *vt* (*théorie*) to underlie

sous-titrage (*pl* sous-titrages) [sutitraʒ] *nm Cin* subtitling

sous-titre (*pl* sous-titres) [sutitr] *nm* (*de livre, de film*) subtitle

sous-titrer [sutitre] *vt Cin* to subtitle; **film sous-titré en anglais** movie with English subtitles

sous-total (*pl* sous-totaux) [sutɔtal, -o] *nm* subtotal

soustraction [sustraksjɔ̃] *nf* subtraction

soustraire [28] [sustrer] **1** *vt* (**a**) (*enlever*) **s. qch à qn** to take sth away *or* remove sth from sb; **s. qn au danger/à l'influence de qn** to protect *or* shield sb from danger/from sb's influence (**b**) (*chiffre, somme*) to subtract (**de** from) **2 se soustraire** *vpr* **se s. à** (*influence, regard*) to avoid, to elude; (*obligation*) to shirk

sous-traitance [sutrɛtɑ̃s] *nf* subcontracting; **travaux effectués en s.** subcontracted work

sous-traitant, -e [sutrɛtɑ̃, -ɑ̃t] **1** *adj* subcontracting **2** *nm* subcontractor

sous-traiter [sutrete] *vt* to subcontract

sous-verre [suver] *nm inv* (*cadre*) glass mount; (*photo, image*) = photograph or picture mounted under glass

sous-vêtement [suvetmɑ̃] *nm* undergarment; **sous-vêtements** underwear

soutane [sutan] *nf* cassock

soute [sut] *nf* (*de bateau*) store; (*d'avion*) hold; **s. à bagages** (*d'avion*) baggage hold

soutenable [sutnabl] *adj* (**a**) (*supportable*) bearable (**b**) (*défendable*) tenable

soutenance [sutnɑ̃s] *nf Univ* viva (voce)

soutènement [sutɛnmɑ̃] *nm voir* **mur**

souteneur [sutnœr] *nm* pimp

soutenir [70] [sutnir] **1** *vt* (**a**) (*maintenir*) to support, to hold up (**b**) (*aider*) to support (**c**) (*opinion, théorie*) to maintain, to uphold; **s. que...** to maintain that... (**d**) *Univ* (*thèse*) to defend (**e**) (*conversation, vitesse, rythme*) to keep up, to maintain (**f**) (*résister à*) (*regard*) to hold; **s. la comparaison** to bear comparison **2 se soutenir** *vpr* (*personnes*) to support each other; **se s. moralement** to give each other moral support

soutenu, -e [sutny] *adj* (**a**) (*attention, effort, intérêt*) sustained; (*rythme*) steady (**b**) (*style, langage*) formal, elevated (**c**) (*couleur*) deep

souterrain, -e [suterɛ̃, -ɛn] **1** *adj* (**a**) (*eau, explosion*) underground; (*économie*) black (**b**) *Fig* (*manœuvres*) secret **2** *nm* underground passage

soutien [sutjɛ̃] *nm* (**a**) (*aide*) support; **apporter son s. à qn/qch** to give sb/sth one's support (**b**) (*personne, groupe*) support; **s. de famille** breadwinner

soutien-gorge (*pl* soutiens-gorge) [sutjɛ̃gɔrʒ] *nm* bra; **s. à armatures/d'allaitement** underwired/nursing bra

soutirer [sutire] *vt* (**a**) (*vin*) to rack, to decant (**b**) **s. qch à qn** (*argent, information*) to extract sth from sb

souvenance [suvnɑ̃s] *nf* **avoir s. de qch** to recollect sth

souvenir [suvnir] **1** *nm* (**a**) (*réminiscence*) memory; **en s. de** in memory of; **en s. du passé** for old times' sake; **garder un bon/mauvais s. de qch** to have good/bad memories of sth; **souvenirs d'enfance** childhood memories (**b**) (*objet*) memento; (*touristique*) souvenir

2 *v impersonnel Litt* **il me souvient que...** I recall that...
3 se souvenir *vpr* **se s. de** to remember; **se s. que** to remember that; **je ne me souviens de rien** I can't remember anything

souvent [suvɑ̃] *adv* often; **le plus s.** usually, more often than not; **plus s. qu'à son tour** far too often

souverain, -e [suvʀɛ̃, -ɛn] **1** *adj (puissance, état, remède)* sovereign; *(bonheur, mépris)* supreme
2 *nm,f* sovereign

souverainement [suvʀɛnmɑ̃] *adv (intelligent, doué)* supremely; *(agacer, déplaire)* intensely

souveraineté [suvʀɛnte] *nf* sovereignty

soviétique [sɔvjetik] *Anciennement* **1** *adj* Soviet
2 *nmf* **S.** Soviet (citizen)

soyeux, -euse [swajø, -øz] **1** *adj* silky
2 *nm* silk merchant

soyez, soyons *etc voir* **être**

SPA [ɛspea] *nf (abrév* **Société protectrice des animaux)** *Br* ≃ RSPCA, *Am* ≃ ASPCA

spacieusement [spasjøzmɑ̃] *adv* **être logé s.** to have spacious accommodation

spacieux, -euse [spasjø, -øz] *adj* spacious

spaghetti [spageti] *nm* piece of spaghetti; **des spaghettis** spaghetti

sparadrap [spaʀadʀa] *nm Br* sticking plaster, *Am* adhesive tape

spartiate [spaʀsjat] **1** *adj* Spartan; *Fig* **à la s.** in a spartan way
2 *nfpl* **spartiates** Roman sandals

spasme [spasm] *nm* spasm

spasmodique [spasmɔdik] *adj* spasmodic

spasmophilie [spasmɔfili] *nf* spasmophilia

spatial, -e, -aux, -ales [spasjal, -o] *adj (a) (de l'espace)* spatial **(b)** *(de l'espace interplanétaire)* space

spatio-temporel, -elle *(mpl* **spatio-temporels,** *fpl* **spatio-temporelles)** [spasjɔtɑ̃pɔʀɛl] *adj* spatio-temporal)

spatule [spatyl] *nf* **(a)** *(de cuisinier, de peintre)* spatula **(b)** *(de ski)* tip **(c)** *(oiseau)* spoonbill

speaker, speakerine [spikœʀ, spikʀin] *nm,f* announcer

spécial, -e, -aux, -ales [spesjal, -o] *adj* **(a)** *(particulier, extraordinaire)* special **(b)** *(bizarre)* peculiar, odd

spécialement [spesjalmɑ̃] *adv (particulièrement)* especially, particularly; *(exprès)* specially

spécialisation [spesjalizasjɔ̃] *nf* specialization

spécialisé, -e [spesjalize] *adj (travail, enseignement)* specialized; *(ouvrier)* semi-skilled; *(école, hôpital)* special

spécialiser [spesjalize] **se spécialiser** *vpr* to specialize **(dans** *ou* **en** in)

spécialiste [spesjalist] *nmf* specialist **(de/en** in)

spécialité [spesjalite] *nf Br* speciality, *Am* specialty; **s. maison** speciality of the house

spécieux, -euse [spesjø, -øz] *adj Litt* specious

spécification [spesifikasjɔ̃] *nf* specification

spécificité [spesifisite] *nf* specificity

spécifier [spesifje] *vt* to specify

spécifique [spesifik] *adj* specific

spécifiquement [spesifikmɑ̃] *adv* specifically

spécimen [spesimɛn] *nm* **(a)** *(modèle)* specimen **(b)** *(livre, fascicule)* specimen copy

spectacle [spɛktakl] *nm* **(a)** *(représentation)* show; **le s.** *(industrie)* show business; **film à grand s.** epic (film); **s. de variétés** variety show **(b)** *(vue)* sight; **se donner en s.** to make an exhibition *or* a spectacle of oneself

spectaculaire [spɛktakylɛʀ] *adj* spectacular

spectateur, -trice [spɛktatœʀ, -tʀis] *nm,f* **(a)** *(d'un événement sportif)* spectator; *(d'un spectacle)* member of the audience; **spectateurs** *(au spectacle)* audience **(b)** *(témoin)* witness

spectre [spɛktʀ] *nm* **(a)** *(fantôme)* ghost, phantom; *Fig (de la guerre, de la misère)* spectre **(b)** *Phys* spectrum

spéculateur, trice [spekylatœʀ, -tʀis] *nm,f* speculator

spéculation [spekylasjɔ̃] *nf* speculation

spéculer [spekyle] *vi* **(a)** *(intellectuellement)* to speculate **(sur** on *or* about) **(b)** *(à la Bourse)* to speculate **(sur** in); *Fig* **s.**

sur qch to count *or* bank on sth

speech *(pl* **speeches)** [spitʃ] *nm Fam* speech; **faire un s. à qn sur qch** to give sb a speech about sth

speedé, -e [spide] *adj Fam (hyperactif)* hyped up, hyper

speeder [spide] *vi Fam* to get a move on

spéléologie [speleɔlɔʒi] *nf* **(a)** *(exploration) Br* potholing, *Am* spelunking **(b)** *(science)* speleology

spéléologue [speleɔlɔg] *nm,f* **(a)** *(explorateur) Br* potholer, *Am* spelunker **(b)** *(spécialiste)* speleologist

spencer [spɛnsœʀ] *nm* short jacket

spermatozoïde [spɛʀmatɔzɔid] *nm* spermatozoon

sperme [spɛʀm] *nm* sperm

sphère [sfɛʀ] *nf* **(a)** *(boule)* sphere **(b)** *(d'activité, d'influence)* sphere; **les hautes sphères de la politique** the higher realms of politics

sphérique [sferik] *adj* spherical

sphinx [sfɛks] *nm* **(a)** *(monstre fabuleux)* sphinx **(b)** *(insecte)* hawk *or* sphinx moth

spirale [spiʀal] *nf* spiral; **en s.** *(s'élever)* in a spiral; *(escalier, coquillage)* spiral

spiritisme [spiʀitism] *nm* spiritualism

spiritualité [spiʀitɥalite] *nf* spirituality

spirituel, -elle [spiʀitɥɛl] *adj* **(a)** *(pouvoir, vie)* spiritual **(b)** *(fin)* witty; *Ironique* **que c'est s.!** very witty!

spirituellement [spiʀitɥɛlmɑ̃] *adv* **(a)** *(moralement)* spiritually **(b)** *(finement)* wittily

spiritueux [spiʀitɥø] *nm* spirit

spleen [splin] *nm Litt* spleen, melancholy; **avoir le s.** to be melancholy

splendeur [splɑ̃dœʀ] *nf* splendour; **c'est une s.** it's splendid

splendide [splɑ̃did] *adj* splendid; *(soleil)* brilliant; *(œuvre d'art, personne)* magnificent

splendidement [splɑ̃didmɑ̃] *adv* splendidly

spolier [spɔlje] *vt* to despoil **(de** of)

spongieux, -euse [spɔ̃ʒjø, -øz] *adj* spongy

sponsor [spɔ̃sɔʀ] *nm* sponsor

sponsoriser [spɔ̃sɔʀize] *vt* to sponsor

spontané, -e [spɔ̃tane] *adj* spontaneous

spontanéité [spɔ̃taneite] *nf* spontaneity

spontanément [spɔ̃tanemɑ̃] *adv* spontaneously

sporadique [spɔʀadik] *adj* sporadic

spore [spɔʀ] *nf* spore

sport [spɔʀ] **1** *nm* **(a)** *(activité)* sport; **de s.** *(chaussures, terrain, voiture)* sports; **faire du s.** to do sport; **s. de combat** combat sport; **s. d'équipe/individuel** team/individual sport; **sports d'hiver** winter sports; **aller aux sports d'hiver** to go skiing; **sports nautiques** water sports **(b)** *Fam (locutions)* **il va y avoir du s.!** there's going to be some fun!; **c'est du s.** it's a tough job
2 *adj inv (vêtement)* casual

sportif, -ive [spɔʀtif, -iv] **1** *adj* **(a)** *(résultats, journal, club)*

sports (**b**) *(fair-play)* sporting (**c**) *(dynamique)* sporty
2 *nm,f* sportsman, *f* sportswoman
sportivité [spɔrtivite] *nf* sportsmanship
spot [spɔt] *nm* (**a**) *(projecteur)* spot, spotlight (**b**) *(à la télé, à la radio)* **s. publicitaire** commercial, advert
spoutnik [sputnik] *nm* sputnik
spray [sprɛ] *nm* spray, aerosol
sprint [sprint] *nm* *(accélération finale)* (final) sprint; *(course)* sprint; *Fam* **piquer un s.** to sprint
sprinter[1] [sprintœr] *nm* sprinter
sprinter[2] [sprinte] *vi* to sprint
squale [skwal] *nm* shark
square [skwar] *nm* public garden
squash [skwaʃ] *nm* squash
squat [skwat] *nm* squat
squatter[1] [skwatœr] *nm* squatter
squatter[2] [skwate] *vt* to 'squat in
squelette [skəlɛt] *nm* (**a**) *(d'être humain, d'animal)* skeleton; **c'est un vrai s.** he's/she's a bag of bones; **c'est un s. ambulant** he's/she's a walking skeleton (**b**) *Fig (de roman, de bâtiment)* skeleton, framework
squelettique [skəletik] *adj* (**a**) *(personne, partie du corps)* skeleton-like (**b**) *(personnel, armée)* skeleton
Sri Lanka [srilāka] *nm* **le S.** Sri Lanka
sri lankais, -e [srilākɛ, -ɛz] **1** *adj* Sri Lankan
2 *nm,f* **S.** Sri Lankan
SRPJ [ɛsɛrpeʒi] *nm* *(abrév* **Service régional de la police judiciaire)** = regional crime unit
stabilisateur, -trice [stabilizatœr, -tris] **1** *adj* stabilizing
2 *nm (de vélo)* stabilizer
stabilisation [stabilizasjɔ̃] *nf* stabilization
stabiliser [stabilize] **1** *vt* to stabilize
2 se stabiliser *vpr* to stabilize; *(personne)* to settle down
stabilité [stabilite] *nf* stability
stable [stabl] *adj* stable
stade [stad] *nm* (**a**) *(sportif)* stadium (**b**) *(étape)* stage; **en être au s. embryonnaire** to be at an embryonic stage
stage [staʒ] *nm (professionnel)* training course; **faire un s. de tennis/de voile** to have tennis/sailing lessons; *(vacances)* to go on a tennis/sailing holiday; **être en s.** to be on a training course; **s. de formation** training course
stagiaire [staʒjɛr] *adj & nmf* trainee
stagnant, -e [stagnā, -āt] *adj* stagnant
stagnation [stagnasjɔ̃] *nf* stagnation
stagner [stagne] *vi* to stagnate
stalactite [stalaktit] *nf* stalactite
stalagmite [stalagmit] *nf* stalagmite
stalinien, -enne [stalinjē, -ɛn] *adj & nm,f* Stalinist
stalle [stal] *nf (dans une écurie, une église)* stall
stand [stād] *nm* (**a**) *(d'exposition)* stand; *(de foire)* stall; **s. de tir** rifle range (**b**) *(de course automobile)* **s. (de ravitaillement)** pit
standard [stādar] **1** *adj inv* standard
2 *nm* (**a**) *(norme)* standard (**b**) **s. (téléphonique)** switchboard
standardisation [stādardizasjɔ̃] *nf* standardization
standardiser [stādardize] *vt* to standardize
standardiste [stādardist] *nmf* (switchboard) operator
standing [stādiŋ] *nm* (social) standing; **de grand s.** *(appartement)* luxury; *(quartier)* select
staphylocoque [stafilokɔk] *nm* staphylococcus
star [star] *nf* star

starlette [starlet] *nf* starlet
starter [starter] *nm* (**a**) *(de voiture)* choke (**b**) *(dans une course)* starter
starting-block *(pl* **starting-blocks)** [startiŋblɔk] *nm* starting block
station [stasjɔ̃] *nf* (**a**) *(de métro)* station; *(de train)* halt; *(de bus)* stop; **s. de taxis** *Br* taxi rank, *Am* taxi stand (**b**) *(ville, village)* **s. balnéaire** seaside resort; **s. de ski** ski resort; **s. de sports d'hiver** winter sports resort; **s. thermale** spa town (**c**) *(établissement)* station; **s. d'essence** *Br* petrol *or Am* gas station; **s. de lavage** car wash; **s. spatiale** space station (**d**) *(position)* **s. debout** standing position (**e**) **s. de radio** radio station (**f**) *Ordinat (d'un réseau)* station, node; **s. d'accueil** docking station; **s. individuelle** stand-alone workstation; **s. de travail** workstation
stationnaire [stasjɔner] *adj (satellite)* stationary; *(baromètre)* steady; *(état d'un malade)* stable
stationnement [stasjɔnmā] *nm* (**a**) *(de voitures)* parking; **s. interdit** *(sur panneau)* no parking; **s. gênant** *(sur panneau)* ≃ restricted parking (**b**) *Can (parking)* car park, *Am* parking lot
stationner [stasjɔne] *vi* to park; **défense de s.** *(sur panneau)* no parking
station-service *(pl* **stations-service)** [stasjɔ̃servis] *nf* service station, *Br* petrol *or Am* gas station
statique [statik] **1** *adj* static
2 *nf* statics *(singulier)*
statisticien, -enne [statistisjē, -ɛn] *nm,f* statistician
statistique [statistik] **1** *adj* statistical
2 *nf* (**a**) *(donnée)* statistic (**b**) *(science)* statistics *(singulier)*
statistiquement [statistikmā] *adv* statistically
statuaire [statɥer] *adj & nf* statuary
statue [staty] *nf* statue
statuer [statɥe] **statuer sur** *vt ind* to give a ruling on
statuette [statɥɛt] *nf* statuette
statu quo [statykwo] *nm* status quo
stature [statyr] *nf* stature
statut [staty] *nm* (**a**) *(position)* status; **s. juridique** *ou* **légal** legal status; **s. social** social status (**b**) **statuts** *(d'une société, d'une association)* statutes
statutaire [statyter] *adj* statutory
St *(abrév* **Saint)** St
Ste *(abrév* **Sainte)** St
Sté *(abrév* **Société)** Co
steak [stɛk] *nm* steak; **s. frites** steak and chips; **un s. haché** a beefburger; **du s. haché** *Br* mince, *Am* ground beef; **s. au poivre** pepper steak; **s. tartare** steak tartare *(raw minced beef served with a raw egg)*
stèle [stɛl] *nf* stele
stellaire [steler] *adj* stellar
stencil [stensil] *nm* stencil
sténo [steno] **1** *nf (abrév* **sténographie)** shorthand; **prendre qch en s.** to take sth down in shorthand
2 *nmf (abrév* **sténographe)** stenographer
sténodactylo [stenodaktilo] **1** *nf* shorthand typing
2 *nmf* shorthand typist
sténodactylographie [stenodaktilɔgrafi] *nf* shorthand typing
sténographe [stenɔgraf] *nmf* stenographer
sténographie [stenɔgrafi] *nf* shorthand
sténographier [stenɔgrafje] *vt* to take down in shorthand
sténographique [stenɔgrafik] *adj* shorthand
stentor [stātɔr] *nm voir* **voix**

steppe [stɛp] *nf* steppe
stéréo [stereo] **1** *adj inv* stereo
 2 *nf* stereo; **en s.** in stereo
stéréophonie [stereofɔni] *nf* stereophony
stéréophonique [stereofɔnik] *adj* stereophonic
stéréotype [stereotip] *nm* stereotype
stéréotypé, -e [stereotipe] *adj* stereotyped
stérile [steril] *adj* (**a**) *(personne, animal)* sterile; *(mariage)* childless; *(terre)* barren (**b**) *(discussion, efforts)* futile (**c**) *(instrument, chambre)* sterile
stérilet [sterilɛ] *nm* coil, IUD
stérilisation [sterilizasjɔ̃] *nf* sterilization
stériliser [sterilize] *vt* to sterilize
stérilité [sterilite] *nf* (**a**) *(d'une personne, d'un animal)* sterility; *(de la terre)* barrenness (**b**) *(d'une discussion, d'efforts)* futility
sterling [sterliŋ] *adj inv voir* livre²
sterne [stɛrn] *nf* tern
sternum [stɛrnɔm] *nm* breastbone, *Spéc* sternum
stéthoscope [stetoskɔp] *nm* stethoscope
steward [stjuwart, stiwart] *nm* steward
stick [stik] *nm (de colle, pour les lèvres)* stick; **déodorant en s.** stick deodorant
stigmate [stigmat] *nm* (**a**) *(trace)* mark (**b**) *Rel* stigmates stigmata
stigmatiser [stigmatize] *vt (dénoncer)* to condemn
stimulant, -e [stimylɑ̃, ɑ̃t] **1** *adj* stimulating; *(résultats)* encouraging
 2 *nm* (**a**) *(remède)* stimulant (**b**) *Fig* stimulus, incentive
stimulateur [stimylatœr] *nm* **s. cardiaque** pacemaker
stimulation [stimylasjɔ̃] *nf* stimulation
stimuler [stimyle] *vt* to stimulate
stipuler [stipyle] *vt* to stipulate
stock [stɔk] *nm* stock; **en s.** in stock
stockage [stɔkaʒ] *nm* (**a**) *(de marchandises)* stocking (**b**) *Ordinat* storage; **s. en mémoire tampon** buffering
stock-car (*pl* stock-cars) [stɔkkar] *nm (voiture)* stock car; *(sport)* stock-car racing
stocker [stɔke] *vt* (**a**) *(marchandises)* to stock (**b**) *Ordinat* to store
Stockholm [stɔkɔlm] *n* Stockholm
stoïcisme [stɔisism] *nm* (**a**) *(attitude)* stoicism (**b**) *(doctrine philosophique)* Stoicism
stoïque [stɔik] *adj* stoical
stoïquement [stɔikmɑ̃] *adv* stoically
stomatologie [stɔmatɔlɔʒi] *nf* stomatology
stop [stɔp] **1** *exclam* stop!; *(dans un télégramme)* stop; **savoir dire s.** to know when to say stop
 2 *nm* (**a**) *(panneau)* stop sign (**b**) *(d'un véhicule)* brake light (**c**) *Fam (auto-stop)* hitching, hitchhiking; **faire du s.** to hitch, to hitchhike
stopper [stɔpe] *vt & vi (arrêter)* to stop
store [stɔr] *nm* (**a**) *(de fenêtre)* blind; **s. vénitien** Venetian blind (**b**) *(de magasin)* awning
strabisme [strabism] *nm* squint
stradivarius [stradivarjys] *nm* Stradivarius
strangulation [strɑ̃gylasjɔ̃] *nf* strangulation
strapontin [strapɔ̃tɛ̃] *nm (siège)* folding seat, tip-up seat
Strasbourg [strazbur] *n* Strasbourg
strasbourgeois, -e [strazburʒwa, -waz] **1** *adj* of Strasbourg
 2 *nm,f* **S.** person from Strasbourg

strass [stras] *nm* paste; **en s.** paste
stratagème [strataʒɛm] *nm* stratagem
strate [strat] *nf* stratum
stratège [strateʒ] *nm* strategist
stratégie [strateʒi] *nf* strategy
stratégique [strateʒik] *adj* strategic
stratification [stratifikasjɔ̃] *nf* stratification
stratifié, -e [stratifje] *adj* (**a**) *(roche)* stratified (**b**) *(bois)* laminated
stratosphère [stratosfɛr] *nf* stratosphere
streptocoque [strɛptokɔk] *nm* streptococcus
stress [strɛs] *nm* stress
stressant, -e [strɛsɑ̃, -ɑ̃t] *adj* stressful
stresser [strɛse] *vt* **1** to put under stress; **être stressé** to be stressed
 2 *vi Fam* to get stressed
Stretch® [strɛtʃ] *nm* stretch material
strict, -e [strikt] *adj* (**a**) *(obligation, principes)* strict; **au sens s.** in the strict sense of the word; **le s. minimum** the bare minimum; **le s. nécessaire** the bare essentials; **c'est la stricte vérité** that's the absolute truth; **c'est son droit le plus s.** it's her absolute right (**b**) *(personne)* strict (**sur** about) (**c**) *(costume, coupe de cheveux)* severe
strictement [striktəmɑ̃] *adv* (**a**) *(rigoureusement)* strictly; **je ne comprends s. rien** I don't understand a single thing (**b**) *(habillé)* severely
stricto sensu [striktosɛsy] *adv* strictly speaking
strident, -e [stridɑ̃, -ɑ̃t] *adj* strident, shrill
strie [stri] *nf* groove
strié, -e [strije] *adj* grooved
string [striŋ] *nm* G-string
strip-tease (*pl* strip-teases) [striptiz] *nm* striptease
strip-teaseuse (*pl* strip-teaseuses) [striptizøz] *nf* stripper, striptease artist
stroboscope [strɔbɔskɔp] *nm* strobe, stroboscope
strophe [strɔf] *nf* stanza, verse
structural, -e, -aux, -ales [stryktyral, -o] *adj* structural
structuralement [stryktyralmɑ̃] *adv* structurally
structuralisme [stryktyralism] *nm* structuralism
structuraliste [stryktyralist] *adj & nmf* structuralist
structure [stryktyr] *nf* (**a**) *(disposition)* structure (**b**) *(organisation)* **s. d'accueil** reception facilities (**c**) *Ordinat* **s. en anneau** ring structure; **s. en arbre** tree structure; **s. de bloc** block structure
structuré, -e [stryktyre] *adj* (**a**) *(ensemble, langage)* structured (**b**) *Ordinat* **fichier non s.** flat file
structurel, -elle [stryktyrɛl] *adj* structural
structurer [stryktyre] *vt* to structure
strychnine [striknin] *nf* strychnine
stuc [styk] *nm* stucco
studieusement [stydjøzmɑ̃] *adv* studiously
studieux, -euse [stydjø, -øz] *adj (personne)* studious; *(vacances)* study
studio [stydjo] *nm* (**a**) *(pour travailler)* studio; **s. de cinéma** Br film studio, Am movie studio; **tourné en s.** filmed in the studio; **s. d'enregistrement** recording studio (**b**) *(logement)* Br studio flat, Am studio apartment
stupéfaction [stypefaksjɔ̃] *nf* amazement, astonishment
stupéfait, -e [stypefɛ, -ɛt] *adj* amazed, astounded
stupéfiant, -e [stypefjɑ̃, -ɑ̃t] **1** *adj* amazing, astounding
 2 *nm* drug, narcotic

stupéfier [stypefje] *vt* to amaze, to astound

stupeur [stypœr] *nf* amazement, astonishment

stupide [stypid] *adj* stupid

stupidement [stypidmɑ̃] *adv* stupidly

stupidité [stypidite] *nf* **(a)** *(caractère)* stupidity **(b)** *(remarque)* stupid remark; **dire des stupidités** to say stupid things

style [stil] *nm* style; **de s.** *(meuble)* period; **s.** Louis XIII/ Régence Louis XIII-/Regency-style; **avoir du s.** to have style, to be stylish; *Fam* **ça serait bien son s.!** that would be just his style!; **s. de vie** lifestyle; *Gram* **s. direct/indirect** direct/indirect speech

stylé, -e [stile] *adj (domestique)* trained

stylet [stilɛ] *nm* **(a)** *(poignard)* stiletto **(b)** *Ordinat* **s. lumineux** light pen

styliser [stilize] *vt* to stylize

stylisme [stilism] *nm* designing

styliste [stilist] *nmf* designer

stylistique [stilistik] **1** *adj* stylistic **2** *nf* stylistics *(singulier)*

stylo [stilo] *nm* pen; **s. à encre** *ou* **à plume** fountain pen; **s. (à) bille** ballpoint (pen)

stylo-feutre *(pl* **stylos-feutres)** [stiloføtr] *nm* felt-tip (pen)

su¹ *voir* **savoir**

su² [sy] *nm* **au vu et au su de tout le monde** quite openly

suave [sɥav] *adj* **(a)** *(parfum, mélodie)* sweet **(b)** *(ton, manières)* suave, smooth

suavité [sɥavite] *nf* **(a)** *(d'un parfum, d'une mélodie)* sweetness **(b)** *(des manières)* suavity

subalterne [sybaltɛrn] **1** *adj (officier, position)* subordinate, minor; *(employé)* junior **2** *nmf* subordinate

subconscient, -e [sybkɔ̃sjɑ̃, -ɑ̃t] *adj & nm* subconscious

subdiviser [sybdivize] **1** *vt* to subdivide **(en** into) **2** **se subdiviser** *vpr* to be subdivided **(en** into)

subdivision [sybdivizjɔ̃] *nf* subdivision

subir [sybir] *vt* **(a)** *(violence, conséquences)* to suffer; *(défaite, pertes)* to suffer, to sustain; *(influence)* to be under; **faire s. qch à qn** to subject sb to sth **(b)** *(examen, opération, changement)* to undergo **(c)** *Fam (personne)* to put up with

subit, -e [sybi, -it] *adj* sudden

subitement [sybitmɑ̃] *adv* suddenly, all of a sudden

subjectif, -ive [sybʒɛktif, -iv] *adj* subjective

subjectivement [sybʒɛktivmɑ̃] *adv* subjectively

subjectivité [sybʒɛktivite] *nf* subjectivity

subjonctif, -ive [sybʒɔ̃ktif, -iv] *Gram* **1** *adj* subjunctive **2** *nm* subjunctive; **au s.** in the subjunctive

subjuguer [sybʒyge] *vt (séduire)* to captivate

sublimation [syblimasjɔ̃] *nf* sublimation

sublime [syblim] **1** *adj* sublime **2** *nm* **le s.** the sublime

sublimement [syblimmɑ̃] *adv* sublimely

sublimer [syblime] *vt* to sublimate

subliminal, -e, -aux, -ales [sybliminal, -o] *adj* subliminal

submerger [sybmɛrʒe] *vt* to submerge; **submergé de travail** snowed under with work

submersible [sybmɛrsibl] **1** *adj* submersible **2** *nm* submarine

subodorer [sybodɔre] *vt Fam (danger, complot)* to scent

subordination [sybɔrdinasjɔ̃] *nf* subordination

subordonné, -e [sybɔrdɔne] **1** *adj Gram (proposition)* subordinate **2** *nm,f (personne)* subordinate **3** *nf* **subordonnée** *Gram* subordinate clause

subordonner [sybɔrdɔne] *vt* **(a)** *(dans une hiérarchie)* **être subordonné à qn** to be subordinate to sb **(b)** *(faire passer après)* **s. qch à qch** to accord less importance to sth than to sth **(c)** *(faire dépendre)* **être subordonné à qch** to be dependent on sth

subornation [sybɔrnasjɔ̃] *nf Jur* subornation

suborner [sybɔrne] *vt* **(a)** *Jur (témoin)* to suborn, to bribe **(b)** *Litt (séduire)* to seduce

subrepticement [sybrɛptismɑ̃] *adv* surreptitiously

subséquent, -e [sypsekɑ̃, -ɑ̃t] *adj* subsequent

subside [sybzid] *nm* subsidy, grant

subsidiaire [sybzidjɛr] *adj* subsidiary

subsistance [sybzistɑ̃s] *nf* subsistence; **pourvoir à la s. de sa famille** to keep *or* support one's family

subsistant, -e [sybzistɑ̃, -ɑ̃t] *adj* remaining

subsister [sybziste] *vi* **(a)** *(chose)* to remain **(b)** *(personne)* to subsist

substance [sypstɑ̃s] *nf* substance; **en s.** in substance

substantiel, -elle [sypstɑ̃sjɛl] *adj* substantial

substantiellement [sypstɑ̃sjɛlmɑ̃] *adv* substantially

substantif, -ive [sypstɑ̃tif, -iv] *Gram* **1** *adj* substantive **2** *nm* noun, substantive

substantiver [sypstɑ̃tive] *vt* to use as a noun *or* substantively

substituer [sypstitɥe] **1** *vt* **s. qn/qch à** to substitute sb/ sth for **2** **se substituer** *vpr* **se s. à** to substitute for, to take the place of

substitut [sypstity] *nm* **(a)** *Jur* deputy public prosecutor **(b)** *(remplacement)* substitute

substitution [sypstitysjɔ̃] *nf* substitution

substrat [sypstra] *nm Géol* substratum

subterfuge [sypterfyʒ] *nm* subterfuge; **user de subterfuges** to resort to subterfuge

subtil, -e [syptil] *adj* subtle

subtilement [syptilmɑ̃] *adv* subtly

subtiliser [syptilize] *vt* to make off with; **on lui a subtilisé son portefeuille** someone's made off with his wallet

subtilité [syptilite] *nf* subtlety

subtropical, -e, -aux, -ales [syptrɔpikal, -o] *adj* subtropical

subvenir [sybvənir] **s. à** *vt ind* to meet

subvention [sybvɑ̃sjɔ̃] *nf* subsidy, grant

subventionner [sybvɑ̃sjɔne] *vt* to subsidize

subversif, -ive [sybvɛrsif, -iv] *adj* subversive

subversion [sybvɛrsjɔ̃] *nf* subversion

suc [syk] *nm* **(a)** *(de fruit, de viande)* juice **(b)** *Fig & Litt* essence

succédané [syksedane] *nm* substitute **(de** for)

succéder [syksede] **1** **succéder à** *vt ind* **(a)** *(personne)* to succeed, to take over from **(b)** *(phénomène)* **la résignation succéda à la colère** anger gave way to resignation **2** **se succéder** *vpr* to follow one another

succès [syksɛ] *nm* **(a)** success; **avoir du s. (auprès de qn)** to be successful (with sb); **avoir un s. fou (auprès de qn)** to be a big hit (with sb); **faire le s. de qn** to make sb's name; **avec s.** successfully; **sans s.** unsuccessfully; **à s.** successful **(b)** *(pièce, chanson)* hit, success

successeur [syksesœr] *nm* successor (**de** to)

successif, -ive [syksesif, -iv] *adj* successive

succession [syksesjɔ̃] *nf* (**a**) *(suite)* succession (**b**) *(remplacement)* succession (**à** to); **prendre la s. de qn** to succeed sb, to take over from sb (**c**) *Jur (par héritage)* succession; *(biens)* inheritance

successivement [syksesivmɑ̃] *adv* successively

succinct, -e [syksɛ̃, -ɛ̃t] *adj* succinct

succinctement [syksɛ̃tmɑ̃] *adv* succinctly

succion [sysjɔ̃, syksjɔ̃] *nf* suction

succomber [sykɔ̃be] *vi* to succumb (**à** to); **s. sous le nombre** to yield to greater numbers

succulent, -e [sykylɑ̃, -ɑ̃t] *adj (nourriture)* succulent

succursale [sykyrsal] *nf* branch

sucer [syse] *vt* to suck

sucette [sysɛt] *nf* (**a**) *(confiserie)* lollipop (**b**) *(tétine) Br* dummy, *Am* pacifier

suçon [sysɔ̃] *nm Fam Br* lovebite, *Am* hickey

suçoter [sysɔte] *vt* to suck (at)

sucre [sykr] *nm* (**a**) *(aliment, morceau)* sugar; *Fig* **être tout s. tout miel** to be all sweetness and light; **s. candi** candy sugar; **s. de canne** cane sugar; **s. cristallisé** granulated sugar; **s. glace** *Br* icing *or Am* confectioner's sugar; **s. en morceaux/en poudre** lump/caster sugar; **s. roux** brown sugar; **s. semoule** caster sugar (**b**) **s. d'orge** *(substance)* barley sugar; *(bâton)* stick of barley sugar

sucré, -e [sykre] *adj* (**a**) *(naturellement)* sweet; *(additionné de sucre)* sweetened (**b**) *Fig (paroles, sourire)* sugary

sucrer [sykre] **1** *vt* (**a**) *(boisson)* to sugar; *(mets)* to sweeten; *Fam Fig* **s. les fraises** *(trembler)* to shake; *(être gâteux)* to be an old dodderer (**b**) *Fam (supprimer) (passage, émission)* to cut; **on lui a sucré sa prime** they've cancelled his bonus

2 *vi (miel, aspartame)* to sweeten

3 se sucrer *vpr Fam* (**a**) *(prendre du sucre)* to help oneself to sugar (**b**) *(s'enrichir)* to line one's pockets

sucrerie [sykrəri] *nf* (**a**) *(usine)* sugar refinery (**b**) *(friandise)* **sucreries** sweet things

Sucrette® [sykrɛt] *nf* (artificial) sweetener

sucrier, -ère [sykrije, -ɛr] **1** *adj* sugar

2 *nm* (**a**) *(récipient)* sugar bowl; *(verseur)* sugar shaker (**b**) *(fabricant)* sugar manufacturer

sud [syd] **1** *nm* south; **le vent du s.** the south wind; **dans le S. de l'Angleterre** in the South of England; **au s.** in the south; **au s. de** (to the) south of; **vers le s.** south, southward

2 *adj inv* southern

sud-africain, -e (*mpl* sud-africains, *fpl* sud-africaines) [sydafrikɛ̃, -ɛn] **1** *adj* South African

2 *nm,f* **S.** South African

sud-américain, -e (*mpl* sud-américains, *fpl* sud-américaines) [sydamerikɛ̃, -ɛn] **1** *adj* South American

2 *nm,f* **S.** South American

sud-coréen, -enne (*mpl* sud-coréens, *fpl* sud-coréennes) [sydkɔreɛ̃, -ɛn] **1** *adj* South Korean

2 *nm,f* **S.** South Korean

sud-est [sydɛst] **1** *nm* south-east; **le S. asiatique** South-east Asia

2 *adj inv* south-east

sudiste [sydist] *adj & nmf Hist* Confederate

sud-ouest [sydwɛst] *nm & adj inv* south-west

Suède [sɥɛd] *nf* **la S.** Sweden

suédine [sɥedin] *nf* suedette

suédois, -e [sɥedwa, -az] **1** *adj* Swedish

2 *nm,f* **S.** Swede

3 *nm (langue)* Swedish

suée [sɥe] *nf Fam* sweat; **prendre une s.** to work up a sweat

suer [sɥe] **1** *vi* (**a**) *(personne)* to sweat; **s. à grosses gouttes** to be pouring with sweat; *Fam* **faire s. qn** *(embêter)* to bug sb; *Fam* **se faire s.** to be bored stiff (**b**) *(mur)* to ooze (**c**) *Fig (travailler)* to labour, to sweat

2 *vt (ennui, hypocrisie)* to ooze; **s. sang et eau** to sweat blood and tears

sueur [sɥœr] *nf* sweat; **être en s.** to be sweating *or* in a sweat; **avoir des sueurs froides** to be in a cold sweat; **à la s. de son front** by the sweat of one's brow

suffire [syfir] **1** *vi* to be enough, to be sufficient (**à/pour** for); **ça suffit!** that's enough!, that'll do!

2 *v impersonnel* **il suffit d'appuyer sur le bouton** you just have to press the button; **il suffit que je sorte deux minutes pour que le téléphone sonne** I only have to go out for two minutes for the phone to start ringing; **il a suffi de quelques mots pour le persuader** a few words were enough to persuade him

3 se suffire *vpr* **se s. (à soi-même)** to be self-sufficient

suffisamment [syfizamɑ̃] *adv* sufficiently, enough; **s. de** sufficient, enough

suffisance [syfizɑ̃s] *nf* self-importance

suffisant, -e [syfizɑ̃, -ɑ̃t] *adj* (**a**) *(satisfaisant)* sufficient, enough (**b**) *(vaniteux)* self-important, conceited

suffixe [syfiks] *nm Gram & Ordinat* suffix

suffocant, -e [syfɔkɑ̃, -ɑ̃t] *adj* (**a**) *(chaleur)* suffocating, stifling (**b**) *Fig (nouvelle, réponse)* staggering, astounding

suffocation [syfɔkasjɔ̃] *nf* suffocation

suffoquer [syfɔke] **1** *vt* (**a**) *(sujet: odeur, fumée, chaleur)* to suffocate (**b**) *Fig (sujet: nouvelles)* to stagger, to astound

2 *vi* to suffocate, to choke; *Fig* **s. de colère/d'indignation** to choke with anger/indignation

suffrage [syfraʒ] *nm (voix)* vote; *(système)* suffrage; **s. direct/indirect** direct/indirect suffrage; **s. universel** universal suffrage

suffragette [syfraʒɛt] *nf* suffragette

suggérer [sygʒere] *vt* (**a**) *(proposer)* to suggest (**à** to); **s. de faire qch** to suggest doing sth; **s. à qn de faire qch** to suggest to sb that he/she should do sth (**b**) *(faire penser à)* to evoke

suggestif, -ive [sygʒestif, -iv] *adj* (**a**) *(ton, musique)* evocative (**b**) *(plaisanterie, geste)* suggestive

suggestion [sygʒestjɔ̃] *nf* suggestion

suicidaire [sɥisidɛr] **1** *adj* suicidal

2 *nmf* suicidal person

suicide [sɥisid] *nm* suicide

suicidé, -e [sɥiside] **1** *adj* who has committed suicide

2 *nm,f* suicide

suicider [sɥiside] **se suicider** *vpr* to commit suicide

suie [sɥi] *nf* soot

suif [sɥif] *nm* tallow

suintant, -e [sɥɛ̃tɑ̃, ɑ̃t-] *adj (rocher, mur)* oozing, dripping; *(plaie)* weeping

suintement [sɥɛ̃tmɑ̃] *nm (de rochers, de mur)* oozing, dripping; *(de plaie)* weeping

suinter [sɥɛ̃te] *vi* (**a**) *(rocher, mur)* to ooze, to drip; *(plaie)* to weep (**b**) *(liquide)* to ooze

suis *voir* être, suivre

Suisse [sɥis] *nf* **la S.** Switzerland; **la S. alémanique/ romande** German-speaking/French-speaking Switzerland

suisse [sɥis] **1** *adj* Swiss

2 *nmf* **S.** Swiss (person); **les Suisses** the Swiss

3 *nm (employé d'église)* verger; *Fam Fig* **manger/boire qch en s.** to eat/drink sth without sharing it

Suissesse [sɥisɛs] *nf* Swiss (woman)

suit *voir* suivre

suite [sɥit] *nf* (**a**) *(reste)* rest (**de** of); **faire s. à qch** to follow on from sth; **s. à votre lettre du ...** further to your letter of ...; **donner s.** *à (demande, lettre)* to follow up; *(commande)* to deal with; *(décision)* to give effect to; **prendre la s. de** *(personne)* to take over from; *(affaires)* to take over; **à la s.** **(les uns des autres)** one after the other; **à la s.** de cette **discussion** following this discussion (**b**) *(de roman, de film)* sequel; *(nouvel épisode)* continuation; **s. à la page 55** continued on page 55; **s. et fin** concluded; **la s.** **au prochain numéro** continued in the next issue (**c**) *(cohérence)* coherence; **sans s.** *(paroles, pensées)* incoherent; *(parler)* incoherently; **avoir de la s. dans les idées** to be very single-minded (**d**) *(escorte) (d'un président)* suite; *(d'un monarque)* retinue (**e**) *(série)* series (**f**) *Math* series (**g**) *Mus* suite (**h**) *(conséquence)* consequence; **suites** *(de maladie)* aftereffects; **mourir des suites d'une blessure** to die as the result of an injury; **par s.** consequently; **par s.** **de qch** as a result of sth (**i**) *(appartement)* suite (**j**) *(locutions)* **de s.** in a row; **et ainsi de s.** and so on; **tout de s.,** *Fam* **de s.** right away, immediately; **par la s.** afterwards

suivant¹ [sɥivɑ̃] **1** *prép* (**a**) *(direction)* along (**b**) *(selon)* according to (**c**) *(conformément à)* **s. son habitude** as is/was his habit
2 *conj* **s. que** according to whether

suivant², **-e** [sɥivɑ̃, -ɑ̃t] **1** *adj* (**a**) *(page, jour)* next, following; **voir page 6 et suivantes** see page 6 and following; **notre méthode est la suivante** our method is as follows (**b**) *(personne)* next
2 *nm,f (prochain)* **le s.,** **la suivante** the next (one); **au s.!** next!
3 *nf* **suivante** *(personnage de théâtre)* attendant

suiveur [sɥivœr] *nm* (**a**) *(personne sans initiative)* follower (**de** of) (**b**) *(dans une course cycliste)* **les suiveurs** = officials and back-up squads following a cycle race

suivi, -e [sɥivi] **1** *adj* (**a**) *(discours, raisonnement)* coherent (**b**) *(correspondance)* regular; *(travail, effort, qualité)* consistent (**c**) *(émission, feuilleton)* popular
2 *nm* follow-up; **assurer le s. de qch** to follow sth through

suivre [sɥivr] **1** *vt* (**a**) *(aller derrière)* to follow; **nous sommes suivis** we're being followed; **partez, je vous suis** you go, I'll follow (on); **s. qn des yeux** *ou* **du regard** to follow sb with one's eyes
(**b**) *(se placer après)* to follow, to come after
(**c**) *(longer)* to go along, to follow
(**d**) *(accompagner)* to go with, to accompany
(**e**) *(ligne de conduite, conseil, intuition)* to follow; **s. son idée** to do things one's own way
(**f**) *(comprendre)* to follow; **là je ne la suis plus** she's lost me there
(**g**) *(faire attention à, observer) (propos, démonstration)* to follow; *(malade, élève)* to monitor the progress of; **suivez bien ce que je vais dire** pay attention to what I'm about to say; **c'est une affaire à s.** it's worth keeping an eye on
(**h**) *(mode, traitement, régime)* to follow; **s. le mouvement** to follow the crowd; **s. l'exemple de qn** to follow sb's example; **voici la marche à s.** this is what you have to do
(**i**) *(assister à) (série de concerts, de conférences)* to attend; *(cours)* to follow
2 *vi* (**a**) *(venir après)* to follow; **le reste du repas suit** the rest of the meal is coming; **les personnes dont les noms suivent** the following people; **faire s. une lettre** to forward a letter; **(prière de) faire s.** *(sur une enveloppe)* please forward; **faire s. ses bagages** to have one's luggage sent on; **à s.** *(à la fin d'un feuilleton)* to be continued
(**b**) *(comprendre)* to follow; *(faire attention)* to pay attention
(**c**) *(élève)* to keep up

(**d**) *Fig (progresser au même rythme) (salaire)* to keep up
3 se suivre *vpr* to follow each other

sujet¹, **-ette** [syʒɛ, -ɛt] **1** *adj* **être s. à qch** *(maladie)* to be subject *or* prone to sth; **être s. à caution** to be unconfirmed; **être s. à faire qch** to be apt *or* liable to do sth
2 *nm,f (d'un monarque)* subject

sujet² *nm* (**a**) *(cause)* cause (**de** for); **s. de querelle** *ou* **dispute** cause for dispute; **avoir s. de se plaindre** to have cause for complaint (**b**) *(thème)* subject, topic; **changer de s.** to change the subject; **au s. de qn/qch** about sb/sth; **elle ne m'a rien dit à ce s.** she said nothing to me about it; **à ce s., je voulais vous dire que...** talking of which, I meant to tell you (that)... (**c**) *Gram & Ling* subject (**d**) *(individu)* individual; *Scol* **brillant s.** brilliant pupil (**e**) *(d'une expérience)* subject

sujétion [syʒesjɔ̃] *nf Litt* (**a**) *(servitude)* subjection (**à** to) (**b**) *(contrainte)* constraint

sulfate [sylfat] *nm* sulphate

sulfater [sylfate] *vt Agr & Ind* to sulphate

sulfure [sylfyr] *nm* sulphide

sulfureux, -euse [sylfyrø, -øz] *adj* (**a**) *(substance)* sulphurous; *(eau, source)* sulphur (**b**) *Fig (écrits, discours)* subversive

sulfurique [sylfyrik] *adj* sulphuric

sulfurisé, -e [sylfyrize] *adj (papier)* greaseproof

sulky [sylki] *nm* sulky

sultan [syltɑ̃] *nm* sultan

sultanat [syltana] *nm* sultanate

sultane [syltan] *nf (épouse d'un sultan)* sultana, sultaness

summum [sɔmɔm] *nm* **le s. de** the height of

sumo [symo] *nm* sumo (wrestling)

sunnite [synit] *adj & nmf* Sunni

super- [sypɛr] *préf Fam* very, *Am* real

super [sypɛr] **1** *adj inv & exclam Fam* great, terrific
2 *nm Br* four-star (petrol), *Am* premium gas; **s. sans plomb** unleaded

superbe [sypɛrb] **1** *adj* (**a**) *(lieu, temps, spectacle)* superb, magnificent (**b**) *(personne)* beautiful
2 *nf Litt* pride, haughtiness

superbement [sypɛrbəmɑ̃] *adv* superbly, magnificently

supercarburant [sypɛrkarbyrɑ̃] *nm Br* four-star petrol, *Am* premium gasoline

supercherie [sypɛrʃəri] *nf* deception, hoax

supérette [sypɛrɛt] *nf* mini-market, small supermarket

superfétatoire [sypɛrfetatwar] *adj Litt* superfluous

superficialité [sypɛrfisjalite] *nf* superficiality

superficie [sypɛrfisi] *nf* (**a**) *(étendue)* (surface) area (**b**) *(surface)* surface

superficiel, -elle [sypɛrfisjɛl] *adj* superficial

superficiellement [sypɛrfisjɛlmɑ̃] *adv* superficially

superflu, -e [sypɛrfly] **1** *adj* superfluous
2 *nm* **le s.** the superfluous

supergrand [sypɛrgrɑ̃] *nm* superpower

super-huit [sypɛrɥit] *adj inv & nm inv Cin* super-eight

supérieur, -e [syperjœr] **1** *adj* (**a**) *(plus haut)* upper; **on a dû évacuer les étages supérieurs** the upper floors had to be evacuated; **elle est à l'étage s.** she's on the floor above (**b**) *(plus grand)* superior (**à/en** to/in); **s. à la moyenne** above average (**c**) *(intelligence, esprit)* superior (**d**) *(dans la hiérarchie) (rang, grade)* higher; *(cadre)* senior; **passer dans la classe supérieure** to go up into the class above (**e**) *(manières, ton)* condescending
2 *nm,f aussi Rel* superior

supérieurement [syperjœrmɑ̃] *adv* exceptionally

supériorité [syperjɔrite] *nf* superiority

superlatif, -ive [syperlatif, -iv] *adj & nm* superlative

supermarché [sypermarʃe] *nm* supermarket

supernova [sypernɔva] (*pl* **supernovæ** [sypernɔve]) *nf* supernova

superpétrolier [syperpetrɔlje] *nm* supertanker

superposable [syperpozabl] *adj (caisses)* stacking; *(images)* superimposable

superposé, -e [syperpoze] *adj (images)* superimposed

superposer [syperpoze] **1** *vt (caisses)* to stack; *(images)* to superimpose (**à** on); *Ordinat* **s. une écriture** to overwrite **2 se superposer** *vpr (caisses, chaises)* to stack, to be stackable; *(images)* to be superimposed

superposition [syperpozisjɔ̃] *nf (de caisses, de chaises)* stacking; *(d'images)* superimposition; *Ordinat* **mode de s. d'écriture** overwrite mode

superproduction [syperprɔdyksjɔ̃] *nf* big-budget movie

superpuissance [syperpɥisɑ̃s] *nf* superpower

supersonique [sypersɔnik] *adj* supersonic

superstar [syperstar] *nf* superstar

superstitieux, -euse [syperstisjø, -øz] *adj* superstitious

superstition [syperstisjɔ̃] *nf* superstition

supertanker [sypertɑ̃kœr] *nm* supertanker

superviser [sypervize] *vt* to supervise; *Ordinat* to control

superviseur [sypervizœr] *nm* supervisor; *Ordinat* **s. d'alimentation** power supply controller

supervision [sypervizjɔ̃] *nf* supervision

supplanter [syplɑ̃te] *vt* to supplant, to supersede

suppléance [sypleɑ̃s] *nf Br* supply *or Am* substitute post

suppléant, -e [sypleɑ̃, -ɑ̃t] **1** *adj (fonctionnaire)* acting, temporary; *(juge)* surrogate **2** *nm,f* substitute, replacement (**de** for)

suppléer [syplee] **1** *vt* (**a**) *(personne)* to stand in for, to replace; **se faire s.** to be replaced (**b**) *Litt (manque)* to supply, to make up (for) **2 suppléer à** *vt ind* to make up for, to compensate for

supplément [syplemɑ̃] *nm* (**a**) *(surcroît)* un **s. de** *(information, travail)* additional, extra; **en s.** extra (**b**) *(de prix)* extra *or* additional charge; *(de billet de train)* supplement (**c**) *(livre, magazine)* supplement (**d**) *(de plat)* extra portion

supplémentaire [syplemɑ̃ter] *adj* additional, extra

suppliant, -e [sypliɑ̃, -ɑ̃t] *adj* imploring, pleading

supplication [syplikasjɔ̃] *nf* entreaty, plea

supplice [syplis] *nm* (**a**) *(torture)* torture (**b**) *(tourment, douleur)* torture, agony; **être au s.** to be in agony; **mettre qn au s.** to torture sb

supplicié, -e [syplisje] *nm,f* victim of torture

supplier [syplije] *vt* **s. qn de faire qch** to implore *or* beg sb to do sth; **je vous en supplie!** I beg you!

supplique [syplik] *nf* petition

support [sypɔr] *nm* (**a**) *(étai)* support (**b**) *(d'outils, de lampe)* stand (**c**) *Fig (de communication)* medium; **s. audiovisuel** audiovisual aid; **s. publicitaire** publicity *or* advertising medium; **s. visuel** visual aid (**d**) *Ordinat* **s. d'affichage** billboard; **s. de sortie** output medium; **s. de souris** mouse support; **s. de stockage** storage medium

supportable [sypɔrtabl] *adj* (**a**) *(douleur)* bearable; *(comportement)* tolerable (**b**) *(acceptable)* reasonable

supporter[1] [sypɔrter] *nm* supporter

supporter[2] [sypɔrte] **1** *vt* (**a**) *(résister à)* (*sujet: matériau, plante*) to withstand; **je supporte bien la chaleur** I can take

the heat; **il ne supporterait pas le voyage** the journey would kill him; **je ne supporte pas l'aspirine/l'alcool** aspirin/alcohol doesn't agree with me (**b**) *(tolérer) (personne, situation)* to put up with; **je ne la supporte pas** I can't stand her; **il ne supporte pas qu'on le contredise** he can't stand *or* bear being contradicted (**c**) *(assumer) (conséquence, coût)* to bear (**d**) *(soutenir) (plafond, structure)* to support **2 se supporter** *vpr (l'un l'autre)* to put up with each other; **ils ne se supportent plus** they can't stand each other any more

supposé, -e [sypoze] *adj (voleur)* alleged; *(auteur)* supposed

supposer [sypoze] *vt* (**a**) *(imaginer)* to suppose, to assume *(que* that); **à s. que...** + subjunctive suppose *or* supposing that...; **on suppose que...** it's thought that...; **être supposé faire qch** to be supposed to do sth (**b**) *(impliquer)* to imply *(que* that)

supposition [sypozisjɔ̃] *nf* supposition, assumption

suppositoire [sypozitwar] *nm* suppository

suppôt [sypo] *nm* henchman; **s. de Satan** fiend

suppression [sypresjɔ̃] *nf* (**a**) *(de loi, d'impôt)* abolition; *(de train)* cancellation; *(de crédits, d'emploi, de service)* axing (**b**) *(de mot, de phrase)* deletion (**c**) *Jur (de document)* suppression

supprimer [syprime] **1** *vt* (**a**) *(loi, impôt)* to abolish; *(autobus, train)* to cancel; *(financement, crédits)* to withdraw; *(emploi, service)* to axe; *(mot, phrase)* to delete (**b**) *Jur (document)* to suppress (**c**) *(sucre, sel)* to cut out (**de** from) (**d**) *(ôter)* **s. qch à qn** to take sth away from sb (**e**) *(tuer)* to do away with **2 se supprimer** *vpr* to do away with oneself

suppurer [sypyre] *vi* to suppurate

supputation [sypytasjɔ̃] *nf* calculation

supputer [sypyte] *vt* to calculate

supranational, e, aux, aloc [sypranasjɔnal, o] *adj* supranational

supranationalité [sypranasjɔnalite] *nf* supranationality

suprématie [sypremasi] *nf* supremacy

suprême [syprɛm] **1** *adj* (**a**) *(effort, bonheur)* supreme (**b**) *(dernier)* final, last **2** *nm Culin* **s. de volaille** chicken supreme

suprêmement [sypremmɑ̃] *adv* supremely

sur[1] [syr] *prép* (**a**) *(dessus)* on; *(avec mouvement)* on, onto; **s. la photo** in the picture; **regarder s. la carte** to look at the map; **la clef est s. la porte** the key's in the door; *aussi Fig* **les uns s. les autres** on top of each other (**b**) *(au-dessus de)* over, above; **un pont s. une rivière** a bridge over *or* across a river (**c**) *(vers)* towards; **fenêtre qui donne s. le jardin** window which looks onto the garden; **la police a tiré s. la foule** the police fired at the crowd; **s. la droite/gauche** to the right/left (**d**) *(à propos de)* on, about; **savoir qch s. qn** to know sth about sb (**e**) *(parmi)* out of; **7 s. 10** 7 out of 10, **une fois s. deux** every other time; **une femme s. deux** one in two women (**f**) *(mesure)* by; **10 mètres s. 2** 10 metres by 2; **virages s. 2 kilomètres** *(sur un panneau)* bends for 2 kilometres (**g**) *(avec)* vivre **s.** to live off; **s. ces économies** to live off one's savings; **s. des paroles de Prévert/une musique de Michael Nyman** to words by Prévert/music by Michael Nyman; **ne me parle pas s. ce ton!** don't talk to me in that tone of voice!

sur[2], **-e** *adj (fruit)* sour

sur- [syr] *préf* over-

sûr, -e [syr] **1** *adj* **(a)** *(lieu)* safe; **peu s.** unsafe **(b)** *(digne de confiance) (personne, mémoire)* trustworthy, reliable; *(ami)* true; *(information, entreprise, goût)* reliable **(c)** *(certain)* sure, certain **(de** of); **je suis s. de te l'avoir dit** I'm sure I told you; **s. de soi** self-assured; **être s. et certain (de qch)** to be absolutely certain (of sth) **2** *nm* **le plus s. serait de...** the safest thing would be to...

surabondance [syrabɔ̃dɑ̃s] *nf* overabundance; **une s. de richesses/de détails** a wealth of riches/details

surabondant, -e [syrabɔ̃dɑ̃, -ɑ̃t] *adj* overabundant

surabonder [syrabɔ̃de] *vi* to be overabundant

suractivé, -e [syraktive] *adj* superactivated

surajouter [syraʒute] **1** *vt* to add (on) **2 se surajouter** *vpr* to be added (on)

suralimentation [syralimɑ̃tasjɔ̃] *nf (de personne)* overfeeding; *(de malade)* feeding up

suralimenter [syralimɑ̃te] *vt (personne)* to overfeed; *(malade)* to feed up

suranné, -e [syrane] *adj* outdated, old-fashioned

surarmement [syrarmɑməmɑ̃] *nm* excessive arms build-up

surbooker [syrbuke] *vt* to overbook

surcapacité [syrkapasite] *nf* overcapacity

surcharge [syrʃarʒ] *nf* **(a)** *(poids) (de bagages)* excess weight; *(de véhicule)* excess load; **prendre des passagers en s.** to take on excess passengers; **rouler en s.** to drive an overloaded vehicle; *Méd* **s. pondérale** excess weight **(b)** *(action) (de véhicule)* overloading **(c)** *(d'accumulateur électrique)* overcharge **(d)** *Fig* **une s. de travail** excess work **(e)** *(à payer)* surcharge **(f)** *(correction)* correction

surcharger [syrʃarʒe] *vt* **(a)** *(véhicule, cheval, estomac)* to overload; **s. qn de travail** to overload sb with work **(b)** *(accumulateur électrique)* to overcharge **(c)** *(épreuves, texte)* to write over with corrections

surchauffe [syrʃof] *nf* overheating

surchauffer [syrʃofe] *vt & vi* to overheat

surchoix [syrʃwa] *adj inv* top-quality

surclasser [syrklase] *vt* to outclass

surconsommation [syrkɔ̃sɔmasjɔ̃] *nf* overconsumption

surcroît [syrkrwa] *nm* **un s. de travail/dépenses** extra work/expenditure; **par s., de s.** in addition, moreover

surdéveloppé, -e [syrdevlɔpe] *adj* overdeveloped

surdéveloppement [syrdevlɔpmɑ̃] *nm* overdevelopment

surdité [syrdite] *nf* deafness

surdose [syrdoz] *nf* overdose

surdoué, -e [syrdwe] **1** *adj* gifted **2** *nm,f* gifted child

sureau, -x [syro] *nm* elder (tree)

sureffectif [syrefɛktif] *nm* overmanning; **en s.** surplus

surélevé, -e [syrelve] *adj* **(a)** *(voie ferrée)* elevated **(b)** *(arche, rez-de-chaussée)* raised

surélever [syrelve] *vt* to heighten, to raise

sûrement [syrmɑ̃] *adv* **(a)** *(probablement)* probably **(b)** *(absolument)* **s.!** certainly!; **s. pas!** certainly not! **(c)** *(sans risque)* safely

suremploi [syrɑ̃plwa] *nm* overemployment

surenchère [syrɑ̃ʃɛr] *nf (dans une vente)* higher bid; *Fig* **faire de la s.** to try to outbid one's rivals

surenchérir [syrɑ̃ʃerir] *vi* to bid higher; **s. sur qn** to outbid sb; *Fig* to go one further than sb

surencombré, -e [syrɑ̃kɔ̃bre] *adj* congested **(de** with)

surendetté, -e [syrɑ̃dɛte] *adj* overindebted

surendettement [syrɑ̃dɛtmɑ̃] *nm* overindebtedness

surentraîner [syrɑ̃trɛne] *vt* to overtrain

suréquipement [syrekipmɑ̃] *nm* overequipment

suréquiper [syrekipe] *vt* to overequip

surestimer [syrɛstime] **1** *vt* **(a)** *(importance, capacité, personne)* to overestimate **(b)** *(œuvre d'art)* to overvalue **2 se surestimer** *vpr* to overestimate oneself

sûreté [syrte] *nf* **(a)** *(absence de danger)* safety; **être en s.** to be safe; **mettre qch en s.** to put sth in a safe place; **pour plus de s.** to be on the safe side; **de s.** *(rasoir, épingle)* safety **(b)** *(du goût, du jugement)* soundness **(c)** *(d'un pays)* security; **la s. de l'État** national security

surévaluation [syrevalɥasjɔ̃] *nf* overvaluation

surévaluer [syrevalɥe] *vt (objet, antiquité)* to overvalue; *(efficacité, capacités)* to overestimate

surexcitation [syrɛksitasjɔ̃] *nf* overexcitement

surexciter [syrɛksite] *vt* to overexcite

surexploiter [syrɛksplwate] *vt* to overexploit

surexposer [syrɛkspoze] *vt* to overexpose

surexposition [syrɛkspozisjɔ̃] *nf* overexposure

surf [sœrf] *nm* surfing; **faire du s.** to go surfing, to surf

surface [syrfas] *nf* **(a)** *(partie extérieure)* surface; **en s.** on the surface; *Fig* superficially; **remonter à la s.** to rise to the surface, to surface; **faire s.** *(remonter, se réveiller)* to surface **(b)** *(étendue)* (surface) area; **grande s.** hypermarket; **s. de réparation** *(au football)* penalty area; **s. au sol** floor area; **s. utile** floor space; **s. de vente** sales area **(c)** *Ordinat* **s. d'affichage** display area; **s. d'enregistrement** read-write surface

surfait, -e [syrfɛ, -ɛt] *adj* overrated

surfer [sœrfe] *vi* to surf

surfeur, -euse [sœrfœr, -øz] *nm,f* surfer

surfiler [syrfile] *vt (vêtement)* to overcast, to oversew

surfin, -e [syrfɛ̃, -in] *adj* superfine

surgelé, -e [syrʒəle] **1** *adj* frozen **2** *nmpl* surgelés frozen foods

surgeler [syrʒəle] *vt* to freeze

surgénérateur [syrʒeneratœr] *nm* breeder reactor

surgir [syrʒir] *vi (personne)* to appear suddenly; *(difficulté)* to crop up

surhomme [syrɔm] *nm* superman

surhumain, -e [syrymɛ̃, -ɛn] *adj* superhuman

surimposer [syrɛ̃poze] *vt* to overtax

surimposition [syrɛ̃pozisjɔ̃] *nf* overtaxation

surimpression [syrɛ̃presjɔ̃] *nf* **(a)** *(d'images)* super-imposition; **en s.** superimposed **(b)** *Ordinat* overprinting, overstrike

Surinam(e) [syrinam] *nm* **le S.** Surinam

surinfection [syrɛ̃fɛksjɔ̃] *nf* secondary infection

surinformation [syrɛ̃fɔrmasjɔ̃] *nf* overinformation

surinformé, -e [syrɛ̃fɔrme] *adj* overinformed

sur-le-champ [syrləʃɑ̃] *adv* at once, immediately

surlendemain [syrlɑ̃dmɛ̃] *nm* **le s.** two days later; **le s. de leur arrivée** two days after they arrived

surligner [syrliɲe] *vt* to highlight

surligneur [syrliɲœr] *nm* highlighter (pen)

surlouer [syrlwe] *vt* to overbook

surmenage [syrmənaʒ] *nm* overwork; **s. intellectuel** mental strain

surmené, -e [syrməne] *adj* overworked

surmener [syrməne] **1** *vt* to overwork **2 se surmener** *vpr* to overdo it

surmonter [syrmɔ̃te] **1** vt **(a)** (être placé sur) to surmount **(b)** Fig (obstacle, difficulté) to overcome **2 se surmonter** vpr to control oneself

surnager [syrnaʒe] vi to float (on the surface)

surnaturel, -elle [syrnatyrɛl] **1** adj supernatural **2** nm **le s.** the supernatural

surnom [syrnɔ̃] nm nickname

surnombre [syrnɔ̃br] nm **il y avait trois passagers en s.** there were three passengers too many; **les exemplaires/passagers en s.** the excess copies/passengers

surnommer [syrnɔme] vt to nickname

surpasser [syrpase] **1** vt (rival) to surpass, to outdo **2 se surpasser** vpr to surpass or excel oneself

surpayer [syrpeje] vt (personne) to overpay; (activité) to pay too much for

surpeuplé, -e [syrpœple] adj (pays, région) overpopulated; (plage) overcrowded

surpeuplement [syrpœpləmɑ̃] nm (de pays, de région) overpopulation; (de plage) overcrowding

surplace [syrplas] nm **faire du s.** (cycliste) to balance; Fig (automobiliste) to crawl along; (dans une carrière, dans des négociations) to make no headway

surplomb [syrplɔ̃] nm overhang; **en s.** overhanging

surplomber [syrplɔ̃be] vt to overhang

surplus [syrply] nm surplus; **le s. de marchandises** the surplus goods, the goods that are left (over)

surpopulation [syrpɔpylasjɔ̃] nf overpopulation

surprenant, -e [syrprənɑ̃, -ɑ̃t] adj surprising; **et, chose surprenante,...** and surprisingly,...

surprendre [syrprɑ̃dr] **1** vt **(a)** (prendre par surprise) to surprise; **s. qn en train de faire qch** to catch sb doing sth; **être surpris par la pluie** to be caught in the rain **(b)** (découvrir) (conversation) to overhear; (regard) to catch **(c)** (étonner) to surprise; **cela me surprendrait qu'il revienne ou s'il revenait** I'd be surprised if he came back **2 se surprendre** vpr **s. à faire qch** to find oneself doing sth

surpris, -e [syrpri, -iz] adj surprised; **être s. de qch/de faire qch** to be surprised at sth/to do sth

surprise [syrpriz] nf surprise; **à sa grande s.** to her great surprise, much to her surprise; **à la s. générale** to everyone's surprise; **sans s.** (expédition, voyage) uneventful; **prendre qn par s.** to take sb by surprise

surprise-partie (pl **surprises-parties**) [syrprizparti] nf Vieilli party

surproduction [syrprɔdyksjɔ̃] nf overproduction

surréalisme [syrrealism] nm surrealism

surréaliste [syrrealist] adj & nmf surrealist

sursaut [syrso] nm **(a)** (mouvement) start, jump; **en s. with a start (b)** (regain) (d'énergie) burst

sursauter [syrsote] vi to start, to jump; **faire s. qn** to make sb jump, to startle sb

surseoir [syrswar] **surseoir à** vt ind (jugement) to suspend; **s. à l'exécution d'un condamné** to reprieve a condemned man

sursis [syrsi] nm **(a)** (d'exécution) & Fig reprieve; **un an de prison avec s.** a one-year suspended sentence **(b)** (de conscrit) deferment of call-up

sursitaire [syrsitɛr] **1** adj (conscrit) provisionally exempted **2** nm provisionally exempted conscript

surtaxe [syrtaks] nf (de lettre) surcharge

surtout [syrtu] adv **(a)** (particulièrement) particularly, especially; **Fam s. que...** especially as... **(b)** (avant tout) above all; **s. pas!** certainly not!

surveillance [syrvejɑ̃s] nf (de travail, d'élèves) supervision; (par la police, par un gardien) surveillance, observation; (de malade, de phénomène) watch; **être sous s.** to be under surveillance; **s. médicale** medical supervision

surveillant, -e [syrvejɑ̃, -ɑ̃t] nm,f **(a)** (d'une prison) guard, Br warder **(b)** (d'un hôpital) supervisor **(c)** Scol (pendant les examens) invigilator; (chargé de la discipline) supervisor

surveiller [syrveje] **1** vt **(a)** (contrôler) (travail, élèves) to supervise; (température, cuisson) to keep a watch on; (examen) to invigilate **(b)** (prendre soin de) to watch (over) **(c)** (situation) to keep an eye on; **s. son langage** to watch or mind one's language; **s. sa ligne** to watch one's figure **2 se surveiller** vpr to keep a watch on oneself

survenir [syrvənir] vi (événements) to occur; (crise, difficulté) to arise

survêt [syrvɛt] nm Fam = **survêtement**

survêtement [syrvɛtmɑ̃] nm tracksuit

survie [syrvi] nf survival

survivance [syrvivɑ̃s] nf (vestige) survival, relic

survivant, -e [syrvivɑ̃, -ɑ̃t] **1** adj surviving **2** nm,f survivor

survivre [syrvivr] **survivre à** vt ind (personne) to survive; (période, théorie) to outlive; (accident, maladie) to survive

survol [syrvɔl] nm **(a)** **le s. d'un lieu** flying over a place **(b)** Fig (de problème, de question) cursory glance (**de** at)

survoler [syrvɔle] vt (a) (lieu) to fly over **(b)** Fig (problème, question) to skim over

survolté, -e [syrvɔlte] adj Fam (personne) overexcited; (ambiance) highly charged

sus [sys, sy] **1** exclam **s. à l'ennemi!** at them! **2** adv **en s.** in addition; **en s. de** in addition to, over and above

susceptibilité [syseptibilite] nf touchiness, sensitivity; **ménager la s. de qn** to tread carefully where sb is concerned

susceptible [syseptibl] adj **(a)** (ombrageux) touchy, sensitive **(b)** **s. de** (interprétations, critiques) open to; **être s. de faire qch** to be liable or likely to do sth

susciter [sysite] vt (ennuis, problèmes) to cause, to create; (étonnement) to cause; (hostilité, intérêt) to arouse; (admiration, commentaires) to attract

susdit, -e [sysdi, -it] adj aforesaid, above-mentioned

susmentionné, -e [sysmɑ̃sjɔne] adj above-mentioned, aforesaid

susnommé, -e [sysnɔme] adj & nm,f above-named

suspect, -e [syspɛ(kt), -ɛkt] **1** adj (personne, action) suspicious, suspect; (idées, preuve, aliment) suspect; **s. de qch** suspected of sth **2** nm,f suspect

suspecter [syspɛkte] vt (personne) to suspect (**de** of); (sincérité) to suspect, to question

suspendre [syspɑ̃dr] **1** vt **(a)** (vêtements, tableau, hamac) to hang (up), **s. qch au mur/au plafond** to hang sth on the wall/from the ceiling **(b)** (interrompre) to suspend; (séance) to adjourn **(c)** (démettre de ses fonctions) to suspend **2 se suspendre** vpr to hang (à from)

suspendu, -e [syspɑ̃dy] adj **(a)** (pendu) hanging; **s. au mur/au plafond** hanging on the wall/from the ceiling; Fig **être s. aux lèvres de qn** to be hanging on sb's every word **(b)** (interrompu) suspended; (séance) adjourned

suspens [syspɑ̃] **en suspens** adv **(a)** (en l'air) suspended **(b)** (en attente) outstanding

suspense [syspɛns] nm suspense

suspension [syspɑ̃sjɔ̃] *nf* (**a**) *(de négociations, d'un travail)* suspension; *(d'une séance)* adjournment (**b**) *(retrait)* **s. du permis de conduire** driving ban (**c**) *(mise à pied)* suspension (**d**) *(de voiture)* suspension

suspicieux, -euse [syspisjø, -øz] *adj* suspicious

suspicion [syspisjɔ̃] *nf* suspicion

sustenter [systɑ̃te] **se sustenter** *vpr Hum* to take sustenance

susurrer [sysyre] *vt & vi* to whisper, to murmur

suture [sytyr] *nf* suture; **point de s.** stitch

suzerain, -e [syzrɛ̃, -ɛn] *nm,f* suzerain

svastika [svastika] *nm* swastika

svelte [svɛlt] *adj* slender

sveltesse [svɛltɛs] *nf* slenderness

SVP [ɛsvepe] *(abrév* **s'il vous plaît**) please

swahili, -e [swaili] **1** *adj* Swahili
 2 *nm (langue)* Swahili

Swaziland [swazilɑ̃d] *nm* **le S.** Swaziland

sweat-shirt *(pl* **sweat-shirts**) [switʃœrt, swɛtʃœrt] *nm* sweatshirt

swing [swiŋ] *nm* swing

swinguer [swiŋge] *vi* to swing

sycomore [sikɔmɔr] *nm* sycamore (tree)

syllabe [silab] *nf* syllable

syllabique [silabik] *adj* syllabic

sylphide [silfid] *nf* sylph

sylvestre [silvɛstr] *adj* woodland

sylviculture [silvikyltyr] *nf* forestry

symbiose [sɛ̃bjoz] *nf* symbiosis; *Fig* **en s. avec qn/qch** in harmony with sb/sth

symbole [sɛ̃bɔl] *nm* symbol

symbolique [sɛ̃bɔlik] **1** *adj* symbolic; *(paiement, geste)* token
 2 *nf (système de symboles)* system of symbols

symboliquement [sɛ̃bɔlikmɑ̃] *adv* symbolically

symboliser [sɛ̃bɔlize] *vt* to symbolize

symbolisme [sɛ̃bɔlism] *nm* symbolism

symétrie [simetri] *nf* symmetry

symétrique [simetrik] *adj* symmetrical

symétriquement [simetrikmɑ̃] *adv* symmetrically

sympa [sɛ̃pa] *adj Fam* nice

sympathie [sɛ̃pati] *nf* (**a**) *(affinité)* liking; **avoir** *ou* **éprouver de la s. pour qn** to like sb; **inspirer la s.** to be likable (**b**) *(compassion, condoléances)* sympathy

sympathique [sɛ̃patik] *adj* (**a**) *(agréable)* nice (**b**) *Anat* sympathetic

sympathisant, -e [sɛ̃patizɑ̃, -ɑ̃t] *nm,f* sympathizer

sympathiser [sɛ̃patize] *vi* to get on well (**avec** with)

symphonie [sɛ̃fɔni] *nf* symphony

symphonique [sɛ̃fɔnik] *adj (forme, poème)* symphonic; *(orchestre)* symphony

symposium [sɛ̃pozjɔm] *nm* symposium

symptomatique [sɛ̃ptɔmatik] *adj* symptomatic (**de** of)

symptôme [sɛ̃ptom] *nm* symptom

synagogue [sinagɔg] *nf* synagogue

synchrone [sɛ̃kron] *adj* synchronous (**avec** with)

synchronisation [sɛ̃krɔnizasjɔ̃] *nf* synchronization

synchroniser [sɛ̃krɔnize] *vt* to synchronize (**avec** with)

synclinal, -e, -aux, -ales [sɛ̃klinal, -o] *adj* synclinal

syncope [sɛ̃kɔp] *nf* (**a**) *(perte de connaissance)* blackout; **tomber en s.** to black out; *Fam* **elle a failli avoir une s.** she nearly fainted (**b**) *Mus* syncopation

syncopé, -e [sɛ̃kɔpe] *adj Mus* syncopated

syndic [sɛ̃dik] *nm* **s. (de copropriété)** property manager

syndical, -e, -aux, -ales [sɛ̃dikal, -o] *adj (Br* trade *or Am* labor) union

syndicaliser [sɛ̃dikalize] = **syndiquer**

syndicalisme [sɛ̃dikalism] *nm* (**a**) *(mouvement) Br* trade *or Am* labor unionism (**b**) *(activité)* **faire du s.** to be involved in union activities

syndicaliste [sɛ̃dikalist] **1** *adj Br* (trade) union, *Am* (labor) union
 2 *nmf Br* trade *or Am* labor unionist

syndicat [sɛ̃dika] *nm* (**a**) *(de travailleurs) (Br* trade *or Am* labor) union (**b**) *(d'employeurs, de producteurs)* association; **s. patronal** employers' association (**c**) **s. d'initiative** tourist (information) office

syndiqué, -e [sɛ̃dike] **1** *adj* belonging to a *(Br* trade *or Am* labor) union; **être s.** to belong to a *(Br* trade *or Am* labor) union
 2 *nm,f (Br* trade *or Am* labor) union member

syndiquer [sɛ̃dike] **1** *vt* to unionize
 2 se syndiquer *vpr* (**a**) *(se constituer en syndicat)* to form a *(Br* trade *or Am* labor) union (**b**) *(adhérer à un syndicat)* to join a *(Br* trade *or Am* labor) union

syndrome [sɛ̃drom] *nm* syndrome

synergie [sinɛrʒi] *nf* synergy

synode [sinɔd] *nm* synod

synonyme [sinɔnim] **1** *adj* synonymous (**de** with)
 2 *nm* synonym

synopsis [sinɔpsis] *nm Cin* synopsis

synovial, -e, -aux, -ales [sinɔvjal, -o] *adj* synovial

syntagme [sɛ̃tagm] *nm* phrase

syntaxe [sɛ̃taks] *nf Gram & Ordinat* syntax

syntaxique [sɛ̃taksik] *adj* (**a**) *Gram* syntactic (**b**) *Ordinat* syntax

synthèse [sɛ̃tez] *nf* (**a**) *(exposé)* summary; **faire la s. (de qch)** to summarize (sth) (**b**) *(opération chimique)* synthesis; **de s.** synthetic

synthétique [sɛ̃tetik] **1** *adj* (**a**) *(présentation)* all-encompassing; *(bilan)* summary (**b**) *(tissu, fibres)* synthetic, man-made
 2 *nm* synthetic material

synthétiser [sɛ̃tetize] *vt* to synthesize

synthétiseur [sɛ̃tetizœr] *nm* synthesizer

syphilis [sifilis] *nf* syphilis

syphilitique [sifilitik] *adj & nmf* syphilitic

Syrie [siri] *nf* **la S.** Syria

syrien, -enne [sirjɛ̃, -ɛn] **1** *adj* Syrian
 2 *nm,f* **S.** Syrian

systématique [sistematik] **1** *adj (automatique, méthodique)* systematic; **il est toujours en retard, c'est s.** he's consistently late

systématiquement [sistematikmɑ̃] *adv* systematically

systématiser [sistematize] *vt* to systematize

système [sistɛm] *nm* system; *Fam* **il me tape** *ou* **porte sur le s.** he gets on my nerves; **s. D** resourcefulness; *Ordinat* **s. d'exploitation** operating system; *Ordinat* **s. de gestion de bases de données** database management system; **s. nerveux** nervous system; **s. solaire** solar system

T, t [te] *nm inv* T, t; **en T** T-shaped; **disposer qch en T** to arrange sth in a T-shape

t' [t] *voir* **te, tu**

ta [ta] *voir* **ton**¹

tabac¹ [taba] **1** *nm* (**a**) *(plante, produit)* tobacco; *Fig* **du même t.** of the same ilk; **t. blond** Virginia tobacco; **t. brun** dark tobacco; **t. à chiquer** chewing tobacco; **t. à priser** snuff (**b**) *(boutique)* **(bureau de) t.** *Br* tobacconist's (shop), *Am* tobacco store *(which also sells stamps, phonecards and lottery tickets)* **2** *adj inv* buff

tabac² *nm* **coup de t.** *(tempête)* squall; *Fam* **passer qn à t.** to beat sb up; *Fam* **faire un t.** to be a big hit

tabagie [tabaʒi] *nf* (**a**) *Fam* **c'est une vraie t. ici** you can't see a thing for the smoke in here (**b**) *Can (bureau de tabac) Br* tobacconist's (shop), *Am* tobacco store

tabagisme [tabaʒism] *nm* smoking

tabasser [tabase] *vt Fam* **t. qn** to beat sb up; **se faire t.** to be or get beaten up

tabatière [tabatjɛr] *nf* (**a**) *(boîte)* snuffbox (**b**) *(lucarne)* skylight

tabernacle [tabɛrnakl] *nm* tabernacle

table [tabl] *nf* (**a**) *(meuble)* table; **mettre** ou **dresser la t.** to lay or set the table; **être à t.** to be at the table; **se mettre** ou **passer à t.** to sit down at the table; *Fam Fig* **se mettre à t.** *(avouer)* to spill the beans; **à t.!** food's ready!; *Fig* **faire t. rase de qch** to make a clean sweep of sth; **t. basse** coffee table; **t. de billard** billiard table; **t. de chevet** bedside table; **t. de cuisson** hob; **t. à dessin** drawing board; **faire t. d'hôte** = to provide a meal where all paying guests eat at the same table; **t. de jeu** card table; **t. à langer** changing table; **t. de nuit** bedside table; **t. d'opération** operating table; **t. d'orientation** orientation or panoramic table; **t. à repasser** ironing board; **t. ronde** *(conférence)* round table; **t. roulante** trolley

(**b**) *(restaurant)* **les meilleures tables de Paris** the finest restaurants in Paris

(**c**) *(écrit)* table; **Tables de la Loi** Tables of the Law; **t. des matières** (table of) contents; **t. de multiplication** multiplication table

(**d**) *(console)* **mettre qn sur t. d'écoute** to tap sb's phone; **il est sur t. d'écoute** his phone is being tapped; **t. de mixage** mixing desk

(**e**) *(d'un instrument à cordes)* **t. d'harmonie** sounding board

(**f**) *Ordinat* **t. à digitaliser** digitizing pad; **t. des fichiers** file allocation table, FAT; **t. traçante** plotter

tableau, -x [tablo] *nm* (**a**) *(panneau, support)* board; **t. (noir)** (black)board; **t. d'affichage** *Br* notice or *Am* bulletin board; **t. de bord** *(d'une voiture)* dashboard; *(d'un avion)*

instrument panel; *Ordinat* control panel (**b**) *(œuvre d'art)* painting, picture; **t. de maître** old master (**c**) *Fig & Hum (scène)* scene; **faire un joli/charmant t.** to make a pretty/ charming sight or scene; *Fig* **pour compléter le t.,...** to crown it all,... (**d**) *(au théâtre)* scene; **t. vivant** tableau (vivant) (**e**) *(liste)* list, table; *(graphique)* chart; **t. de chasse** *(de chasseur, d'aviateur)* bag; *Fig (conquêtes)* list of conquests (**f**) *Ordinat* **t. de connexions** plugboard (**g**) *(locutions)* **gagner sur les deux/sur tous les tableaux** to win on both/all counts

tablée [table] *nf (personnes à table)* table

tabler [table] **tabler sur** *vt ind* to count or bank on

tablette [tablɛt] *nf* (**a**) *(d'une etagere)* shelf; *(dans un avion)* table; **t. arrière** *(d'une voiture)* back shelf (**b**) *(de chocolat)* bar; *(de chewing-gum)* stick

tableur [tablœr] *nm Ordinat* spreadsheet; **t. de graphiques** graphics spreadsheet

tablier [tablije] *nm* (**a**) *(vêtement)* apron; *(d'écolier)* smock; *Fig* **rendre son t.** to hand in one's notice (**b**) *(de cheminée)* hood (**c**) *(de pont)* roadway

tabloïd(e) [tabloid] *adj & nm* tabloid

tabou, -e [tabu] *adj & nm* taboo

taboulé [tabule] *nm* tabbouleh

tabouret [taburɛ] *nm* stool; **t. de bar/de piano** bar/ piano stool

tabulateur [tabylatœr] *nm* tab key, tabulator

tabulation [tabylasjɔ̃] *nf* tab

tac [tak] **du tac au tac** *adv* like a shot

tache [taʃ] *nf* (**a**) *(de boue, de sang, d'huile)* stain; *(de peinture, de couleur, de lumière)* splash; **tu as fait une t. à ta chemise** you've got a stain on your shirt; *Fig* **faire t.** to stick out like a sore thumb; **t. d'encre** inkstain; *Fig* **faire t. d'huile** to spread *(sur la peau)* mark; **t. de rousseur** freckle; **t. de vin** strawberry mark (**c**) *Fig (atteinte)* blot, stain; **sans t.** *(réputation)* spotless

taché, -e [taʃe] *adj* stained; **t. d'encre/de sang** ink-/ blood-stained

tâche [taʃ] *nf* task, job; **être à la t.** to be on piecework; *Ordinat* **t. d'arrière-plan** ou **de fond** background task or job

tacher [taʃe] **1** *vt* (**a**) *(vêtement)* to stain (**b**) *(réputation)* to sully, to tarnish

2 *vi* to stain

3 se tacher *vpr (personne)* to stain one's clothes; *(tissu, vêtement)* to stain

tâcher [taʃe] **1** *vt* **tâchez que cela ne se reproduise plus** make sure it doesn't happen again

2 tâcher de *vt ind* to try to

tâcheron [tɑʃrɔ̃] nm Péj drudge
tacheté, -e [taʃte] adj speckled (**de** with); **chat noir t. de blanc** black cat with white markings
tacheter [taʃte] vt to spot, to speckle
tachycardie [takikardi] nf tachycardia
tachymètre [takimɛtr] nm tachometer; Aut speedometer
tacite [tasit] adj tacit
tacitement [tasitmɑ̃] adv tacitly
taciturne [tasityrn] adj taciturn
tacot [tako] nm Fam Péj jalopy, Br banger
tact [takt] nm tact; **avoir du t.** to be tactful; **plein de t.** very tactful; **manquer de t.** to be tactless
tacticien, -enne [taktisjɛ̃, -ɛn] nm,f tactician
tactile [taktil] adj tactile
tactique [taktik] **1** adj tactical
2 nf tactics
tadjik [tadʒik] **1** adj Tadjik
2 nmf T. Tadjik
Tadjikistan [tadʒikistɑ̃] nm le T. Tadjikistan
taffetas [tafta] nm taffeta
tag [tag] nm tag (piece of graffiti)
Tage [taʒ] nm le T. the Tagus
tagliatelle [taljatɛl] nf piece or strand of tagliatelle; **des tagliatelles** tagliatelle
taguer [tage] vt to cover in graffiti
tagueur, -euse [tagœr, -øz] nm,f tagger (graffiti artist)
Tahiti [taiti] n Tahiti
tahitien, -enne [taisjɛ̃, -ɛn] **1** adj Tahitian
2 nm,f T. Tahitian
3 nm (langue) Tahitian
taie [tɛ] nf (**a**) (enveloppe) **t. (d'oreiller)** pillowcase, pillowslip (**b**) (sur l'œil) leucoma
taïga [taiga] nf taiga
taillader [tɑjade] vt to slash, to gash
taille [tɑj] nf (**a**) (dimensions) size; **une pêche de la t. du poing** a peach the size of your fist; **quelle t. faites-vous?** what size are you?, what size do you take?; **la t. en dessus/dessous** the next size up/down; **t. unique** one size (**b**) (hauteur) height; **de petite t.** short; Fig **être de t. à faire qch** to be capable of doing sth; **trouver un adversaire à sa t.** to meet one's match (**c**) (importance) **de t.** (erreur, mensonge) big (**d**) (partie du corps, sur un vêtement) waist; **avoir la t. fine** to have a slim waist; **avoir une t. de guêpe** to be wasp-waisted (**e**) (action) (de pierre) cutting; (d'un arbre) pruning; (d'une haie) trimming (**f**) Ordinat **t. de champ** field size; **t. de disque dur** hard disk size; **t. de mémoire** memory size (**g**) Hist (impôt) tallage
taillé, -e [tɑje] adj **être t. pour faire qch** to be cut out to do sth
taille-crayon (pl **taille-crayon** ou **taille-crayons**) [tɑjkrɛjɔ̃] nm pencil sharpener
tailler [tɑje] **1** vt (**a**) (pierre, diamant) to cut; (arbre, vigne) to prune; (haie, barbe) to trim; (crayon) to sharpen; **t. une armée en pièces** to cut an army to pieces (**b**) (vêtement) to cut out
2 se tailler vpr (**a**) (se couper) **se t. la barbe** to trim one's beard (**b**) (se faire) **se t. un chemin à travers qch** to carve one's way through sth (**c**) (s'attribuer) **se t. un beau succès** to be very successful; **se t. un empire** to carve out an empire for oneself (**d**) Fam (partir) to beat it
tailleur [tɑjœr] nm (**a**) (couturier) tailor (**b**) (ensemble pour femme) suit (**c**) **s'asseoir en t.** to sit cross-legged
tailleur-pantalon (pl **tailleurs-pantalons**) [tɑjœr-pɑ̃talɔ̃] nm Br trouser or Am pant suit

taillis [tɑji] nm copse, coppice
tain [tɛ̃] nm silvering; **glace** ou **miroir sans t.** two-way mirror
taire [tɛr] **1** vt (affaire, secret) to say nothing about, not to mention; (vérité) to hide; **une personne dont je tairai le nom** a person who shall remain nameless
2 se taire vpr (**a**) (être silencieux) to be quiet or silent; (cesser de parler) to stop talking, to fall silent; (décider de ne rien dire) to keep quiet or silent; **tais-toi!** be quiet!; **faire t. qn** to make sb be quiet; (adversaire, critique) to silence; **tu as perdu une occasion de te t.** you should have kept your mouth shut (**b**) (bruit) to stop
taisais, taise etc voir **taire**
Taiwan [tajwan] n Taiwan
taiwanais, -e [tajwanɛ, -ɛz] **1** adj Taiwanese
2 nm,f T. Taiwanese
tajine [taʒin] nm tajine
talc [talk] nm talcum powder, talc
talé, -e [tale] adj bruised
talent [talɑ̃] nm (**a**) (don) talent; **son t. de pianiste** his talent as a pianist; **homme/musicien de t.** talented man/musician; **avoir du t.** to be talented (**b**) (artiste) **un jeune t.** a talented newcomer
talentueusement [talɑ̃tɥøzmɑ̃] adv with talent
talentueux, -euse [talɑ̃tɥø, -øz] adj talented
talion [taljɔ̃] nm voir **loi**
talisman [talismɑ̃] nm talisman
talkie-walkie (pl **talkies-walkies**) [tɔkiwɔki] nm walkie-talkie
Tallinn [talin] n Tallin
Talmud [talmyd] nm le T. the Talmud
taloche [talɔʃ] nf Fam (gifle) clout
talon [talɔ̃] nm (**a**) (du pied, de chaussure, de bas) heel; Fig **être sur les talons de qn** to be on sb's heels; **t. d'Achille** Achilles' heel; **talons aiguilles** stiletto heels; (chaussures) stilettos; **talons hauts** high heels; **talons plats** flat heels (**b**) (de chèque) stub, counterfoil (**c**) (aux cartes) stock
talonner [talɔne] **1** vt (**a**) (suivre) **t. qn** to follow on sb's heels (**b**) (cheval) to spur on
2 vi (au rugby) to heel
talonnette [talɔnet] nf (dans une chaussure) heel pad
talonneur [talɔnœr] nm hooker
talquer [talke] vt to put talcum powder on
talus [taly] nm (**a**) (terrain en pente) slope (**b**) (d'une voie ferrée, d'un canal) embankment
tamanoir [tamanwar] nm great anteater
tamaris [tamaris] nm tamarisk
tambouille [tɑ̃buj] nf Fam (**a**) (cuisine) cooking; **faire la t.** to do the cooking (**b**) (nourriture) food, grub
tambour [tɑ̃bur] nm (**a**) (instrument de musique) drum; **sans t. ni trompette** quietly, without any fuss; **faire qch t. battant** to do sth briskly (**b**) (personne) drummer (**c**) (d'une machine à laver) drum; **t. de frein** brake drum (**d**) (à broder) (embroidery) hoop, tambour
tambourin [tɑ̃burɛ̃] nm (instrument plat) tambourine; (tambour) tambourine
tambouriner [tɑ̃burine] **1** vi to drum
2 vt to drum out
tamis [tami] nm (pour la farine) sieve; (pour le sable) sifter; **passer au t.** (farine) to sieve; (sable) to sift
Tamise [tamiz] nf la T. the Thames
tamisé, -e [tamize] adj (lumière) subdued
tamiser [tamize] vt (farine) to sieve; (sable) to sift
tamoul, -e [tamul] **1** adj Tamil

2 *nm.f* T. Tamil
3 *nm (langue)* Tamil
tampon [tɑ̃pɔ̃] **1** *nm* **(a)** *(de coton)* pad; t. hygiénique *ou* périodique tampon **(b)** *(cachet, instrument)* stamp; *(de la poste)* postmark; t. dateur date stamp; t. encreur ink pad **(c)** *(pour nettoyer)* pad; t. à récurer scourer, scouring pad **(d)** *(bouchon)* plug, stopper **(e)** *(à l'extrémité des wagons)* & *Fig* buffer **2** *adj inv* État/zone t. buffer state/zone
tamponner [tɑ̃pɔne] **1** *vt* **(a)** *(document)* to stamp; *(lettre)* to postmark **(b)** *(plaie)* to dab **(c)** *(heurter)* to crash into **2 se tamponner** *vpr* **(a)** *(se heurter)* to crash into each other **(b)** *(s'essuyer)* se t. le front to mop one's brow; se t. les yeux to dab one's eyes; *Fam* s'en t. **(le coquillard)** not to give a damn
tamponneuse [tɑ̃pɔnøz] *adj f voir* auto
tam-tam *(pl* tam-tams*)* [tamtam] *nm (tambour africain)* tom-tom
tancer [tɑ̃se] *vt Litt* to berate, to scold
tanche [tɑ̃ʃ] *nf* tench
tandem [tɑ̃dɛm] *nm* **(a)** *(bicyclette)* tandem **(b)** *(groupe de deux personnes)* duo; travailler en t. to work in tandem
tandis [tɑ̃di, tɑ̃dis] tandis que *conj* **(a)** *(marque l'opposition)* while, whereas **(b)** *(marque la simultanéité)* while
tangage [tɑ̃gaʒ] *nm (d'un bateau)* pitching
tangent, -e [tɑ̃ʒɑ̃, -ɑ̃t] **1** *adj Math* tangential (à to), *Fig* c'était t. it was touch and go, it was a near thing **2** *nf* tangente *Math* tangent (à to); *Fam* prendre la tangente *(partir)* to slip away
tangible [tɑ̃ʒibl] *adj* tangible
tango [tɑ̃go] *nm (danse, musique)* tango; danser le t. to tango, to dance the tango
tanguer [tɑ̃ge] *vi (bateau)* to pitch; tout tanguait autour de moi everything was spinning around me
tanière [tanjɛr] *nf* **(a)** *(d'animal)* den, lair **(b)** *(retraite)* retreat
tanin [tanɛ̃] *nm* tannin
tank [tɑ̃k] *nm* tank
tanker [tɑ̃kœr] *nm* tanker
tannant, -e [tanɑ̃, -ɑ̃t] *adj Fam (ennuyeux)* annoying
tanné, -e [tane] *adj (hâlé)* weather-beaten
tanner [tane] *vt* **(a)** *(peaux)* to tan **(b)** *Fam (harceler)* to pester
tannerie [tanri] *nf (établissement)* tannery; *(industrie)* tanning
tanneur [tanœr] *nm* tanner
tannin [tanɛ̃] = tanin
tant [tɑ̃] *adv* **(a)** *(tellement, à tel point)* so much; t. de *(quantité)* so much; *(nombre)* so many; j'ai t. mangé que j'ai vomi I ate so much I was sick; pas t. que ça *(quantité)* not that much; *(nombre)* not that many; t. il est vrai que... since it is the case that...
(b) *(dans des comparaisons)* t. que as much as; t. pour vous que pour moi for you as much as for me; n'aimer rien t. que... to like nothing more than
(c) *(substitué à un chiffre, à une date)* t. pour cent so much per cent; votre lettre du t. your letter of such and such a date **(d)** t. que *(aussi longtemps que)* as long as; *(pendant que)* while; t. que vous y êtes while you're at it **(e)** *(locutions)* t. bien que mal somehow or other; t. et si bien que so much so that; t. s'en faut far from it; s'il était un t. soit peu intelligent if he was at all intelligent; t. qu'à faire, autant en acheter deux you/we/*etc* might as well buy two; en t. que *(comme)* as; t. mieux! so much the better!; t. mieux pour toi! good for you!; t. pis! too bad!; t. pis pour toi! too bad (for you)!

tante [tɑ̃t] *nf* **(a)** *(parente)* aunt **(b)** *très Fam (homosexuel)* queer, = offensive term used to refer to a male homosexual
tantine [tɑ̃tin] *nf Fam* auntie, aunty
tantinet [tɑ̃tinɛ] *nm Fam* un t. a tiny bit
tantôt [tɑ̃to] *adv* **(a)** *(parfois)* t...., t.... sometimes..., sometimes... **(b)** *(cet après-midi)* this afternoon
Tanzanie [tɑ̃zani] *nf* la T. Tanzania
tanzanien, -enne [tɑ̃zanjɛ̃, -ɛn] **1** *adj* Tanzanian **2** *nm.f* T. Tanzanian
taoïsme [taoism] *nm* Taoism
taon [tɑ̃] *nm* gadfly, horsefly
tapage [tapaʒ] *nm* **(a)** *(bruit)* din, row; faire du t. to kick up a din or row; t. nocturne breach of the peace *(at night)* **(b)** *(publicité)* fuss; faire du t. autour de qch to make a fuss about sth
tapageur, -euse [tapaʒœr, -øz] *adj* **(a)** *(enfant)* rowdy **(b)** *(vêtements, couleur)* loud, flashy; *(publicité)* blatant **(c)** *(liaison)* scandalous
tapant, -e [tapɑ̃, -ɑ̃t] *adj* à sept/dix heures t. ou tapantes at seven/ten o'clock sharp
tape [tap] *nf (pour punir)* tap; *(affectueuse)* pat
tapé, -e [tape] *adj Fam (fou)* crazy
tape-à-l'œil [tapalœj] *Fam* **1** *adj inv* gaudy, flashy **2** *nm* c'est du t. it's just show
tapecul [tapky] *nm Fam (véhicule)* rattletrap
taper [tape] **1** *vt* **(a)** *(frapper)* to hit; *(affectueusement)* to pat; *(table)* to bang **(b)** *(dactylographier)* t. qch (à la machine) to type sth **(c)** *Ordinat* to key; taper entrée ou retour select enter or return **(d)** *Fam (emprunter de l'argent à)* to cadge money off; t. qn de 5 euros to cadge 5 euros off sb
2 *vi* **(a)** *(frapper)* to knock; *(avec le poing)* to bang; t. à la porte to knock on the door; t. du pied to stamp one's foot; t. du poing sur qch to bang on sth; t. dans un ballon to kick a ball around; *Fam* t. dans l'œil à qn to take sb's fancy; t. sur qn to hit sb; *Fig (critiquer)* to knock sb **(b)** *(soleil)* to beat down; *Fam* ça tape it's scorching **(c)** *(dactylographier)* t. (à la machine) to type
3 se taper *vpr Fam* **(a)** *(se cogner)* se t. la tête/le coude to bang one's head/elbow; *Fig* c'est à se t. la tête contre les murs it's enough to drive you up the wall **(b)** *Fam (repas, boisson)* to have; je me taperais bien une bière I'd die for a beer **(c)** *Fam (corvée)* to get landed with **(d)** *très Fam (coucher avec)* to screw **(e)** *Fam (se moquer)* ses histoires de fesses, je m'en tape! I couldn't care less about his sex life!
tapette [tapɛt] *nf* **(a)** *(pour tapis)* carpet beater; *(contre les mouches)* fly swatter **(b)** *(piège)* t. (à souris) mousetrap **(c)** *(petite tape)* tap **(d)** *très Fam (homosexuel)* queer, = term used to refer to a male homosexual
tapeur, -euse [tapœr, -øz] *nm.f Fam* scrounger, sponger
tapin [tapɛ̃] *nm très Fam* faire le t. *Br* to be on the game, *Am* to work the streets
tapinois [tapinwa] en tapinois *adv* stealthily
tapioca [tapjɔka] *nm* tapioca
tapir¹ [tapir] *nm* tapir
tapir² se tapir *vpr (se blottir)* to crouch; *(se cacher)* to hide
tapis [tapi] *nm* **(a)** *(de sol)* carpet; *(de petite taille)* rug; *Fig* mettre qch sur le t. to bring sth up for discussion; t. roulant *(de marchandises, pour bagages)* conveyor belt; *(pour piétons)* moving walkway, travelator; t. de salle de bain bath mat; t. de sol earth mat; *Ordinat* t. de souris mouse mat or pad **(b)** *(en boxe)* canvas; aller au t. to go down; envoyer qn au t. to floor sb
tapis-brosse *(pl* tapis-brosses*)* [tapibrɔs] *nm* doormat
tapisser [tapise] *vt* **(a)** *(pièce, appartement)* to paper, to

wallpaper; *(fauteuil, canapé)* to upholster **(b)** *(couvrir)* être **tapissé de** *(sujet: mur)* to be covered with; *(sujet: sol)* to be carpeted with **(c)** *(paroi d'un organe)* to line

tapisserie [tapisri] *nf* **(a)** *(broderie)* tapestry work; **faire de la t.** to do tapestry work **(b)** *(tenture)* tapestry; *Fig* **faire t.** to be a wallflower **(c)** *(papier peint)* wallpaper

tapissier, -ère [tapisje, -ɛr] *nm,f* **(a)** *(tisseur)* tapestry maker **(b)** *(de meubles)* upholsterer

tapotement [tapɔtmɑ̃] *nm* tapping

tapoter [tapɔte] **1** *vt* to tap; *(joue, main)* to pat **2** *vi* **t. sur qch** to tap on sth

tapuscrit [tapyskri] *nm* typescript

taquet [takɛ] *nm* **(a)** *(de machine à écrire)* stop; *Ordinat* **t. de tabulation** tab stop **(b)** *(butée)* stop

taquin, -e [takɛ̃, -in] *adj* teasing

taquiner [takine] *vt (faire enrager)* to tease

taquinerie [takinri] *nf* **ce n'est qu'une t.** I'm/he's/*etc* only teasing; **j'en ai assez de ses taquineries** I've had enough of her teasing

tarabiscoté, -e [tarabiskɔte] *adj* over-elaborate

tarabuster [tarabyste] *vt* **(a)** *(harceler)* to pester **(b)** *(préoccuper)* to bother

tarama [tarama] *nm* taramasalata

taratata [taratata] *exclam Fam* rubbish!

tarauder [tarode] *vt* **(a)** *(acier)* to tap **(b)** *(obséder)* to gnaw at

tard [tar] **1** *adv* late; **plus t.** later (on); **au plus t.** at the latest; **t. dans la nuit** late at night; **pas plus t. qu'hier** only yesterday **2** *nm* **sur le t.** late in life

tarder [tarde] **1** *vi* to delay; **pourquoi tarde-t-elle?** why is she taking so long?; **il ne devrait pas t.** he shouldn't be long; **tu vas recevoir une gifle, cela ne va pas t.** you're going to get smacked soon; **sans t.** without delay; **t. à faire qch** to take a long time to do sth **2** *v impersonnel* **il me tarde de partir/qu'elle parte** I can't wait to leave/for her to leave

tardif, -ive [tardif, -iv] *adj (regrets, excuse)* belated; *(heure, récolte)* late

tardivement [tardivmɑ̃] *adv (prendre des mesures, s'excuser)* belatedly; *(rentrer, arriver)* late; *(se marier)* late in life

tare [tar] *nf* **(a)** *(défaut)* defect; *Hum* **ça n'est pas une t.!** it's not a crime! **(b)** *(pour calculer le poids net)* tare

taré, -e [tare] *adj* **(a)** *(anormal)* retarded **(b)** *Fam (fou)* crazy

tarentule [tarɑ̃tyl] *nf* tarantula

targette [tarʒɛt] *nf* bolt

targuer [targe] **se targuer** *vpr* **se t. de qch/de faire qch** to pride oneself on sth/on doing sth

tarif [tarif] *nm* **(a)** *(tableau des prix)* price list; *Br* tariff **(b)** *(prix)* rate; *(d'un billet d'avion, de train)* fare; **quels sont vos tarifs?** how much do you charge?; **payer plein t.** *(pour passagers)* to pay full fare; *(pour marchandises)* to pay the full rate; **faire un t. réduit pour les étudiants** to offer a student discount; **t. douanier** customs rate; **tarifs postaux** postal rates

tarifaire [tarifɛr] *adj (lois)* tariff

tarifer [tarife] *vt* to price

tarification [tarifikasjɔ̃] *nf* pricing

tarin [tarɛ̃] *nm Fam (nez) Br* hooter, *Am* snoot

tarir [tarir] **1** *vt (source, rivière)* to dry up; *(larmes)* to dry; *(créativité, inspiration)* to cause to dry up **2** *vi* **(a)** *(eau, source)* to dry up **(b)** *Fig (conversation, inspiration)* to dry up; **il ne tarit pas sur le sujet** he never

stops talking *or* shuts up about it; **ne pas t. d'éloges sur qn/qch** to be forever praising sb/sth **3 se tarir** *vpr* to dry up

tarissement [tarismɑ̃] *nm* drying up

tarot [taro] *nm* tarot; **jouer aux tarots** to play tarot

tartan [tartɑ̃] *nm* tartan

tartare [tartar] **1** *adj (sauce, steak)* tartare **2** *nmf* T. Tartar **3** *nm (steak)* steak tartare

tarte [tart] **1** *nf* **(a)** *(salée ou sucrée) Br* tart, *Am* (open) pie; *Fam* **ce n'est pas de la t.** it's no easy matter; **t. à la crème** *(au cinéma)* custard pie; *Fig* cliché; **t. aux pommes** apple *Br* tart *or Am* pie; **t.** Tatin TarteTatin *(caramelized apples covered in shortcrust pastry and turned out upside down)* **(b)** *Fam (gifle)* slap **2** *adj Fam* **(a)** *(ridicule)* naff **(b)** *(stupide)* thick

tartelette [tartəlɛt] *nf* tartlet

Tartempion [tartɑ̃pjɔ̃] *nm Fam* so-and-so

tartignole [tartiɲɔl] *adj Fam* naff

tartine [tartin] *nf* **(a)** *(tranche de pain)* slice of bread and butter; **t. de confiture** slice of bread and jam; **faire des tartines** to butter (some) bread **(b)** *Fam (texte)* screed; **en mettre des tartines** to write reams

tartiner [tartine] *vt* **(a)** *(beurre, pain)* to spread **(b)** *Fam (texte)* to churn out

tartre [tartr] *nm* **(a)** *(des dents, du vin)* tartar **(b)** *(dans une chaudière, dans une bouilloire)* fur, scale

tas [ta] *nm* **(a)** *(amas)* pile, heap; **mettre qch en t.** to pile sth up **(b)** *Fam (grand nombre)* **un t. de, des t. de** loads of **(c)** *(locutions)* **apprendre qch sur le t.** to learn sth on the job; *Fam* **dans le t. il y en aura bien un qui t'ira** you'll find one to suit you out of all that lot; *Fam* **tirer dans le t.** to fire at random

Tasmanie [tasmani] *nf* la T. Tasmania

tasse [tas] *nf* cup; **t. à café/thé** coffee/tea cup; **t. de café/thé** cup of coffee/tea; *Fig* **boire la t.** *(en nageant)* to get a mouthful of water

tassé, -e [tase] *adj* **(a)** *(serré)* crammed, squashed **(b)** *Fam* **bien t.** *(fort) (café)* strong; *(alcool)* stiff; *(dans un grand verre)* large; **il a 70 ans bien tassés** he's 70 if he's a day

tasseau, -x [taso] *nm* batten

tassement [tasmɑ̃] *nm* **(a)** *(de terre, de neige)* packing down; **t. de vertèbres** spinal compression **(b)** *(de fondations)* settling **(c)** *(déclin)* slowdown **(d in)**

tasser [tase] **1** *vt* **(a)** *(objets, personnes)* to cram, to pack *(dans into)* **(b)** *(terre, neige)* to pack down **2 se tasser** *vpr* **(a)** *(fondations)* to settle **(b)** *(personne)* to shrink **(c)** **se tasser dans qch** *(se serrer dans qch)* to squeeze into sth **(d)** *Fam* **ça se tassera** *(ça s'arrangera)* things will settle down

taste-vin [tastəvɛ̃] *nm inv* wine taster

tata [tata] *nf Fam* auntie, aunty

tatami [tatami] *nm* tatami

tâter [tɑte] **1** *vt* **(a)** *(toucher)* to feel **(b)** *Fig* **t. le terrain** to see how the land lies **2 tâter de** *vt ind (métier)* to try one's hand at; *(prison)* to have a taste of **3 se tâter** *vpr (hésiter)* to be in two minds

tâte-vin [tatvɛ̃] = **taste-vin**

tatie [tati] *nf Fam* auntie, aunty

tatillon, -onne [tatijɔ̃, -ɔn] *adj* finicky

tâtonnements [tatɔnmɑ̃] *nmpl* **(a)** *(dans le noir)* groping **(b)** *Fig (essai)* trial and error; *(de la science, de la recherche)* tentative progress

tâtonner [tɑtɔne] *vi* **(a)** *(dans le noir)* to grope about **(b)** *Fig (chercher)* to proceed by trial and error

tâtons [tɑtɔ̃] **à tâtons** *adv* **entrer/sortir à t.** to feel one's way in/out

tatou [tatu] *nm* armadillo

tatouage [tatwaʒ] *nm (action)* tattooing; *(motif)* tattoo

tatouer [tatwe] *vt* to tattoo; **se faire t.** to get a tattoo

tatoueur [tatwœr] *nm* tattoo artist

taudis [todi] *nm* slum; *Fig* dump

taulard, -e [tolar, -ard] *nm,f Fam* jailbird

taule [tol] *nf Fam Br* nick, *Am* can; **faire de la t.** to do time

taulier, -ère [tolje, -ɛr] *nm,f Fam (propriétaire)* (hotel) owner; *(gérant)* (hotel) manager

taupe [top] *nf* (a) *(animal)* mole (b) *Fam (espion)* mole (c) *Fam Péj* **vieille t.** old hag

taupinière [topinjɛr] *nf* molehill

taureau, -x [tɔro] *nm* (a) *(animal)* bull; *Fam* **prendre le t. par les cornes** to take the bull by the horns (b) *Astron & Astrol* **T.** Taurus; **êtreT.** to be (a) Taurus

tauromachie [tɔrɔmaʃi] *nf* bullfighting

tautologie [totɔlɔʒi] *nf* tautology

tautologique [totɔlɔʒik] *adj* tautological

taux [to] *nm* (a) *(montant) (des salaires, des impôts)* rate (b) *(pourcentage)* rate; *(d'alcool, de cholestérol)* level; **à t. fixe** fixed-rate; **t. de change** exchange rate; **t. de croissance** growth rate; **t. d'écoute** ratings; **t. d'épargne** savings rate; **t. d'inflation** rate of inflation; **t. d'intérêt** interest rate (c) *Ordinat* ratio, rate

tavelé, -e [tavle] *adj* marked

tavelure [tavlyr] *nf* mark

taverne [tavɛrn] *nf* (a) *(restaurant)* restaurant (b) *Can* beer parlour, tavern

tavernier, -ère [tavɛrnje, -ɛr] *nm,f* innkeeper

taxation [taksasjɔ̃] *nf* taxation

taxe [taks] *nf* tax; **toutes taxes comprises** inclusive of tax; **t. d'aéroport** airport tax; **t. d'apprentissage** = tax paid by businesses to fund training programmes; **t. d'habitation** local tax; **t. professionnelle** = tax paid by companies and self-employed people; **t. sur la valeur ajoutée** value added tax

taxer [takse] *vt* (a) *(imposer)* to tax (b) *(accuser)* **t. qn de négligence** to accuse sb of negligence (c) *Fam (soutirer)* **t. qch à qn** to cadge sth off sb

taxi [taksi] *nm* (a) *(voiture)* taxi, cab; **prendre un t.** to take a taxi (b) *Fam (chauffeur)* taxi driver, cabby

taxidermiste [taksidɛrmist] *nmf* taxidermist

taximètre [taksimetr] *nm* meter

Taxiphone® [taksifɔn] *nm Vieilli* pay phone

Tbilissi [tbilisi] *n* Tbilisi

Tchad [tʃad] *nm* **leT.** Chad

tchadien, -enne [tʃadjɛ̃, -ɛn] **1** *adj* Chadian
2 *nm,f* **T.** Chadian

tchador [tʃadɔr] *nm* chador

tchécoslovaque [tʃekɔslɔvak] *Anciennement* **1** *adj* Czechoslovakian
2 *nmf* **T.** Czechoslovak

Tchécoslovaquie [tʃekɔslɔvaki] *nf Anciennement* **la T.** Czechoslovakia

tchèque [tʃɛk] **1** *adj* Czech
2 *nmf* **T.** Czech
3 *nm (langue)* Czech

tchétchène [tʃetʃɛn] **1** *adj* Chechen
2 *nmf* **T.** Chechen

Tchétchénie [tʃetʃeni] *nf* **laT.** Chechnya

tchin-tchin [tʃintʃin] *exclam Fam* cheers!

TD [tede] *nm (abrév* **travaux dirigés)** tutorial

te [tə]

t' is used before a word beginning with a vowel or h mute.

pron personnel (a) *(objet direct)* you; **te voilà** there you are (b) *(objet indirect)* to you; **j'ai vu qu'elle t'a serré la main** I saw her shake your hand; **ils t'ont lancé des cailloux?** did they throw stones at you? (c) *(dans les réfléchis)* yourself; **va te doucher** go and have a shower (d) *(dans les pronominaux)* **tu t'es trompée** you made a mistake

té [te] *nm (règle)* T-square; **en té** T-shaped

technicien, -enne [teknisjɛ̃, -ɛn] *nm,f* technician

technicité [teknisite] *nf* technical nature

technico-commercial, -e, -aux, -ales [tekniko-kɔmɛrsjal, -jo] **1** *adj (service)* technical sales; **agent t.** sales engineer
2 *nm,f* sales engineer

technicolor® [teknikɔlɔr] *nm* Technicolor®

technique [teknik] **1** *adj* technical
2 *nf* (a) *(d'un artiste, d'un spécialiste)* technique; **avec lui, j'ai ma t.** I have my own way of dealing with him; **t. de vente** sales technique
3 *nm* **le t.** *(enseignement)* technical training

techniquement [teknikmɑ̃] *adv* technically

techno [tekno] *adj inv & nf* techno

technocrate [teknɔkrat] *nmf* technocrat

technocratie [teknɔkrasi] *nf* technocracy

technologie [teknɔlɔʒi] *nf* technology; **de haute t.** high-tech

technologique [teknɔlɔʒik] *adj* technological

teck [tɛk] *nm* teak

teckel [tekɛl] *nm* dachshund

tectonique [tektɔnik] **1** *adj* tectonic
2 *nf* tectonics *(singulier)*; **t. des plaques** plate tectonics

Te Deum [tedeɔm] *nm inv* Te Deum

teenager [tinɛdʒœr] *nmf* teenager

tee-shirt *(pl* **tee-shirts)** [tiʃœrt] *nm* T-shirt, tee-shirt

Téflon® [teflɔ̃] *nm* Teflon®

tégument [tegymɑ̃] *nm* integument

Téhéran [teerɑ̃] *n* Tehran

teignais, teigne *etc voir* **teindre**

teigne [tɛɲ] *nf* (a) *(maladie)* ringworm (b) *Fam (homme)* rat; *(femme)* cow

teigneux, -euse [tɛɲø, -øz] *adj Fam (personne)* nasty

teindre [tɛ̃dr] **1** *vt (vêtement, cheveux)* to dye; **t. qch en rouge** to dye sth red
2 se teindre *vpr* (a) *(se colorer)* **se t. les cheveux (en blond)** to dye one's hair (blond) (b) *Litt* **se t. de** *(se mêler de)* to be tinged with

teint, -e *voir* **teindre**

teint [tɛ̃] *nm* (a) *(du visage)* complexion; **t. de rose** rosy complexion (b) *(d'un tissu)* colour; **tissu bon ou grand t.** colourfast material; *Fig* **bon t.** *(catholique, communiste)* staunch, dyed-in-the-wool

teinte [tɛ̃t] *nf* (a) *(couleur)* shade, tint (b) *Fig (nuance)* tinge

teinter [tɛ̃te] **1** *vt* (a) *(colorer)* to tint; *(bois, meuble)* to stain (b) *Fig (nuancer)* **teinté de** tinged with
2 se teinter *vpr* **se t. de** to become tinged with

teinture [tɛ̃tyr] *nf* (a) *(produit)* dye (b) *(action)* dyeing (c) *(préparation pharmaceutique)* tincture; **t. d'iode** tincture of iodine

teinturerie [tɛ̃tyrri] *nf (pressing)* dry cleaner's

teinturier, -ère [tɛ̃tyrje, -ɛr] *nm,f* dry cleaner

tek [tɛk] = **teck**

tel, telle [tɛl] **1** adj **(a)** (semblable) such; **un t. homme** such a man; **une telle conduite** such behaviour; **de telles choses** such things; **t. père, t. fils** like father like son; **rien de t. qu'un bon cigare** you can't beat a good cigar; **à t. ou t. endroit** in such and such a place; **il n'a rien dit de t.** he said nothing of the kind; **sa bonté est telle que...** she's so kind that...
(b) (comme) **t. que** such as, like; **voir les choses telles qu'elles sont** to see things as they are; **t. que je le connais, il ne sera pas d'accord** knowing him, he won't agree; Litt **t. une bête furieuse** like an enraged animal
(c) (locutions) **à t. point que** to such an extent that; **de telle sorte que...** so that..., in such a way that...; **elle me l'a dit t. quel** ou Fam **t. que** she told me just like that
2 pron indéfini **t. ou t. vous dira que...** some people will tell you that...
3 pron démonstratif such; **t. est mon désir** such is my wish
4 nm,f un **t., une telle** so-and-so

télé [tele] nf Fam **(a)** (appareil) TV **(b)** (organisme) **la t.** TV; **travailler à la t.** to work in TV

téléachat [teleaʃa] nm teleshopping

télécabine [telekabin] nf cable car

Télécarte® [telekart] nf phone card

télécommande [telekɔmɑ̃d] nf remote control

télécommander [telekɔmɑ̃de] vt **(a)** (appareil) to operate by remote control **(b)** Fig (complot, soulèvement) to mastermind from a distance

télécommunications [telekɔmynikasjɔ̃] nfpl **les t.** telecommunications

téléconférence [telekɔ̃ferɑ̃s] nf teleconference

télécopie [telekɔpi] nf fax

télécopieur [telekɔpjœr] nm fax (machine)

télédiffuser [teledifyze] vt to televise

télédiffusion [teledifyzjɔ̃] nf televising

télé-enseignement [teleɑ̃sɛɲəmɑ̃] nm distance learning

téléfilm [telefilm] nm TV movie

télégénique [teleʒenik] adj telegenic

télégramme [telegram] nm telegram

télégraphe [telegraf] nm telegraph

télégraphier [telegrafje] vt to cable, to wire

télégraphique [telegrafik] adj (fil, poteau) telegraph; **en style t.** in telegraphic style

télégraphiste [telegrafist] nmf **(a)** (technicien) telegraphist **(b)** (porteur) telegraph messenger

téléguidage [telegidaʒ] nm remote control

téléguidé, -e [telegide] adj remote-controlled

téléguider [telegide] vt **(a)** (voiture, missile) to operate by remote control **(b)** Fig (complot, soulèvement) to mastermind from a distance

télématique [telematik] **1** adj telematic
2 nf telematics (singulier)

téléobjectif [teleɔbʒɛktif] nm telephoto lens

télépaiement [telepɛmɑ̃] nm telepayment

télépathe [telepat] **1** adj telepathic
2 nmf telepathist

télépathie [telepati] nf telepathy

télépathique [telepatik] adj telepathic

téléphérique [teleferik] nm cable car

téléphone [telefɔn] nm **(a)** (appareil, système) phone, telephone; **avoir le t.** to be on the phone, to have a phone; **être au t.** to be on the phone; **un coup de t.** a phone call; Fam **par le t. arabe** on the grapevine; **t. cellulaire** cellular

phone; **t. mobile** Br mobile (phone), Am cell (phone); **t. public** public phone; Pol **t. rouge** hot line; **t. sans fil** cordless phone; **t. de voiture** car phone **(b)** (numéro) phone number

téléphoner [telefɔne] **1** vt **(a)** (nouvelle) to phone, to telephone (à to) **(b)** Fam **c'était téléphoné** you could see it coming
2 vi to phone, to telephone; **t. à qn** to phone sb
3 se téléphoner vpr to phone each other

téléphonique [telefɔnik] adj telephone

téléphoniste [telefɔnist] nmf (telephone) operator

téléprompteur® [teleprɔ̃ptœr] nm Teleprompter®

téléprospecteur, -trice [teleprɔspektœr, -tris] nm,f telemarketer

téléprospection [teleprɔspeksjɔ̃] nf telemarketing

téléreportage [teler(ə)pɔrtaʒ] nm (activité) television reporting; (document) television report

télescopage [teleskɔpaʒ] nm (de trains) telescoping; **télescopages en série** (de véhicules) pile-up

télescope [teleskɔp] nm telescope

télescoper [teleskɔpe] **1** vt (véhicules, trains) to crash into
2 se télescoper vpr **(a)** (véhicules, trains) to concertina **(b)** (souvenirs, images) to intermingle

télescopique [teleskɔpik] adj telescopic

téléscripteur [teleskriptœr] nm teleprinter

télésiège [telesjɛʒ] nm chair lift

téléski [teleski] nm ski tow

téléspectateur, -trice [telespɛktatœr, -tris] nm,f (television) viewer

télésurveillance [telesyrvɛjɑ̃s] nf electronic surveillance

Télétexte® [teletɛkst] nm teletext

télétravail [teletravaj] nm teleworking

télévisé, -e [televize] adj televised

téléviseur [televizœr] nm television (set)

télévision [televizjɔ̃] nf **(a)** (organisme, technique, émissions) television; **à la t.** on television; **travailler à la t.** to work in television; **t. par câble** cable television; **t. commerciale** commercial television; **t. haute définition** high-definition television **(b)** (poste) television (set); **regarder la t.** to watch television; **t. en couleur, t. couleur** colour television

télévisuel, -elle [televizɥɛl] adj television

télex [telɛks] nm telex

télexer [telɛkse] vt to telex

tellement [tɛlmɑ̃] adv **(a)** (si) so; **c'était t. intéressant que...** it was so interesting that...; **ce n'est pas t. beau** it's not all that beautiful **(b)** (tant) so much; **t. de** (nombre) so many; (quantité) so much; **elle a t. grandi** she's grown so much; **je n'ai pas t. aimé** I didn't like it that much; **je n'ai plus t. envie d'y aller** I'm no longer that keen on going; **il a t. crié que...** he shouted so much that...; Fam **je vais craquer t. il m'énerve** he annoys me so much I'm going to crack up

tellurique [telyrik] adj (courants) telluric; **secousse t.** earth tremor

téméraire [temerɛr] adj reckless

témérité [temerite] nf recklessness

témoignage [temwaɲaʒ] nm **(a)** Jur evidence, testimony; **porter t. (en faveur de/contre qn)** to give evidence (on behalf of/against sb); **faux t.** perjury **(b)** (compte rendu) report, account **(c)** (démonstration) **en t. d'amitié** as a token of friendship

témoigner [temwaɲe] **1** vt **(a)** (attester) **t. que** to testify

that (**b**) *(sentiments, gratitude)* to show (**à** to)
2 *vi* to testify, to give evidence (**en faveur de/contre** on behalf of/against)
3 témoigner de *vt ind* (**a**) *(montrer)* to show (**b**) *(se porter garant de)* to testify to
témoin [temwɛ] **1** *nm* (**a**) *(d'un événement, d'un mariage)* witness; **être t. de qch** to witness sth, to be a witness to sth; **prendre qn à t.** to call sb to witness; **Dieu m'est t. que...** as God is my witness...; **t. à charge** witness for the prosecution; **t. oculaire** eyewitness (**b**) *(dans un duel)* second (**c**) *(preuve)* **t. les coups que j'ai reçus** witness the blows I received (**d**) *(dans un relais)* baton (**e**) *Rel* **T. de Jéhovah** Jehovah's Witness
2 *adj inv (animal, plante)* control; **appartement t.** *Br* show flat, *Am* model apartment
tempe [tãp] *nf* temple
tempérament [tãperamã] *nm* (**a**) *(caractère)* disposition; *Fam* **avoir du t.** *(avoir du caractère)* to have character (**b**) **acheter qch à t.** to buy sth *Br* on hire purchase *or Am* on the installment plan
tempérance [tãperãs] *nf* moderation, temperance
température [tãperatyr] *nf* temperature; **avoir de la t.** to have a (high) temperature; *Fig* **prendre la t. de qch** to gauge the temperature of sth
tempéré, -e [tãpere] *adj (climat)* temperate
tempérer [tãpere] *vt (enthousiasme, passion)* to moderate
tempête [tãpɛt] *nf* storm; *Fig* **une t. d'applaudissements** thunderous applause; *Fig* **une t. dans un verre d'eau** a storm in a *Br* teacup *or Am* teapot; **t. de neige** snowstorm, blizzard; **t. de sable** sandstorm
tempêter [tãpete] *vi* to storm, to rage
tempetueux, -euse [tãpetɥø, -øz] *adj Litt* stormy
temple [tãpl] *nm aussi Fig* temple; *(protestant)* church
tempo [tɛpo, tempo] *nm* tempo
temporaire [tãporɛr] *adj* temporary
temporairement [tãporɛrmã] *adv* temporarily
temporel, -elle [tãporɛl] *adj* (**a**) *(qui concerne le temps)* temporal (**b**) *(terrestre)* temporal, worldly
temporellement [tãporɛlmã] *adv* temporally
temporisateur, -trice [tãporizatœr, -tris] *adj (stratégie)* delaying
temporiser [tãporize] *vi* to play for time, to stall
temps [tã] *nm* (**a**) *(durée)* time; **avoir le t. de faire qch** to have (the) time to do sth; **avoir tout le t.** to have plenty of time; **prendre le t. de faire qch** to take the time to do sth; **prendre son t.** to take one's time; **ça prend du t.** it takes time; **ça a pris un certain t.** it took quite a while; **donner** *ou* **laisser le t. à qn de faire qch** to give sb the time to do sth; *Fig* **en deux t. trois mouvements** in two ticks; **avec le t.** in *or* with time; **combien de t. faut-il pour y aller?** how long does it take to get there?; *Prov* **le t., c'est de l'argent** time is money; *Ordinat* **base de t.** time base; *Ordinat* **t. d'adressage** address speed
(**b**) *(moment)* time; **en t. de crise** in a crisis; **en t. de guerre/paix** in wartime/peacetime; **de t. en t., de t. à autre** from time to time, **en même t. (que)** at the same time (as); **pendant ce t.** meanwhile, in the meantime; **il y a peu de t.** not long ago, a little while ago; **peu de t. après** shortly after; **d'ici quelque t.** soon, shortly; **tout le t.** all the time; **les premiers t.** at the beginning; **ces t.-ci** these days; **ces derniers t.** this last while; **il y est resté quelque t.** he stayed there for a while; **ça n'a qu'un t.** it won't last forever; **les t. forts de l'actua lité** the main points of the news; **t. libre** free time; **t. mort** lull; *(au basket-ball)* time out
(**c**) *(époque)* time, days; **de mon t.** in my day *or* time; **du t. de ma jeunesse** in my younger days; **de tout t.** from time

immemorial; **dans le t.** in the old days; **en ce t.-là** at that time, then; **par les t. qui courent** these days; **être de son t.**, **vivre avec son t.** to move with the times; **être en avance sur son t.** to be ahead of one's time; **le bon vieux t.** the good old days; **les t. sont durs** times are hard
(**d**) *(heure)* **faire qch à t.** to do sth in time; **en t. voulu** *ou* **utile** in due course; **il est t.** it's time she came down; **il n'est plus t.** it's too late; **le paquet est enfin arrivé, mais il était t.!** the parcel's finally arrived and about time too!
(**e**) *(occasion)* **il y a un t. pour tout** there's a time for everything; **chaque chose en son t.** all in good time
(**f**) *(météo)* weather; **par tous les t.** in all weathers; **quel t. fait-il?** what's the weather like?
(**g**) *Gram* tense
(**h**) *Mus* beat
(**i**) *(d'un athlète)* time
tenable [tənabl] *adj (situation)* bearable
tenace [tənas] *adj* (**a**) *(personne)* stubborn, tenacious (**b**) *(préjugé, volonté)* stubborn; *(odeur, douleur, souvenir)* lingering; *(habitude)* deep-rooted (**c**) *(colle)* strong
ténacité [tenasite] *nf* (**a**) *(d'une personne)* stubbornness, tenacity; **avec t.** stubbornly; *(travailler)* doggedly (**b**) *(d'un préjugé)* stubbornness, *(d'une odeur, d'une douleur, d'un souvenir)* lingering nature; *(d'une habitude)* deep-rootedness
tenailler [tənaje] *vt Litt* to torture; **tenaillé par la faim** ravenously hungry; **tenaillé par la douleur** gripped with pain
tenailles [tənaj] *nfpl* pincers
tenancier, -ère [tənãsje, -ɛr] *nm,f (d'un bar, d'une maison de jeu)* manager
tenant, -e [tənã, -ãt] **1** *adj voir* **séance**
2 *nm* (**a**) *(partisan)* champion, defender (**b**) **le t. du titre** the title holder (**c**) *(locutions)* **d'un seul t.** in one piece; **les tenants et les aboutissants** *(d'une affaire)* the ins and outs
tendance [tãdãs] *nf* (**a**) *(d'une personne)* tendency; **avoir t. à faire qch** to have a tendency to do sth; **avoir une t. à qch** to have a tendency to sth (**b**) *(de l'économie, du marché, d'une mode)* trend
tendancieusement [tãdãsjøzmã] *adv* tendentiously
tendancieux, -euse [tãdãsjø, -øz] *adj* tendentious
tendeur [tãdœr] *nm (pour bagages)* elastic strap
tendinite [tãdinit] *nf* tendinitis
tendon [tãdɔ̃] *nm* tendon; **t. d'Achille** Achilles tendon
tendre¹ [tãdr] **1** *adj* (**a**) *(bois, pierre, métal)* soft; *(viande, légume)* tender (**b**) *(couleur)* delicate, soft (**c**) *(personne, geste, cœur)* tender; **ne pas être t. (pour** *ou* **avec qn)** to be hard (on sb) (**d**) **l'âge t.** early childhood; **depuis ma plus t. enfance** since my earliest childhood
2 *nmf (personne)* softhearted person
tendre² **1** *vt* (**a**) *(corde)* to tighten; *(toile)* to stretch; *(muscle)* to tense; *(arc)* to bend (**b**) *(voile, filet)* to spread; *(papier peint, tapisserie)* to hang; **une pièce tendue de velours rouge** a room whose walls are covered in red velvet (**c**) *(piège)* to set (à for) (**d**) *(main, bras, jambe)* to stretch out, to hold out (à to); **les bras tendus** with outstretched arms; *Fig* **t. la main à qn** *(l'aider)* to offer sb a hand; *Fig* **t. l'oreille** to prick up one's ears
2 *vi* **t. vers zéro** to tend towards zero
3 tendre à *vt ind (avoir pour but) (idéal)* to aim for (**b**) *(avoir tendance à)* **t. à faire qch** to tend to do sth (**c**) **t. à sa fin** to come to an end
4 se tendre *vpr (cordage)* to become taut; *Fig (relations, situation)* to become strained
tendrement [tãdrəmã] *adv* tenderly, lovingly
tendresse [tãdrɛs] *nf* (**a**) *(affection)* tenderness,

affection; **avoir de la t. pour qn** to feel affection for sb; **avec t.** tenderly, affectionately **(b) tendresses** *(démonstrations)* expressions of affection

tendron [tɑ̃drɔ̃] *nm* **(a)** *(de veau)* flank **(b)** *Fam (jeune fille)* slip of a girl

tendu, -e [tɑ̃dy] *adj* **(a)** *(corde, toile)* taut, tight **(b)** *(main)* outstretched **(c)** *(relations, visage)* strained; *(personne, atmosphère, situation)* tense

ténèbres [tenɛbr] *nfpl* **les t.** the darkness

ténébreux, -euse [tenebrø, -øz] **1** *adj Litt* **(a)** *(obscur)* *(forêt)* dark, gloomy **(b)** *(mystérieux)* *(affaire)* murky; *(style)* obscure **(c)** *(personne)* melancholic
2 *nm* **beau t.** tall dark handsome man

teneur [tənœr] *nf* **(a)** *(d'un document, d'un discours)* content; *(d'un contrat)* terms **(b)** *(quantité)* content; **t. en eau/or** water/gold content

tenir [70] [tənir] **1** *vt* **(a)** *(à la main, sur ses genoux)* to hold; **t. qn par le cou/les épaules** to have one's arm round sb's neck/shoulders; *Fig* **je tiens mon homme/la solution** I've got my man/the answer; *Fam* **t. un bon rhume** to have a stinking cold; *Fam* **qu'est-ce qu'il tient!** *(il est idiot)* what a fool!; **tenez!** *(c'est pour vous)* here (you are)!; **tiens, voilà Jean-Luc!** oh, there's Jean-Luc!; *Prov* **un tiens vaut mieux que deux tu l'auras** a bird in the hand is worth two in the bush
(b) *(dans une position)* to hold; *(dans un état)* to keep; **t. sa droite** *(en voiture)* to keep to the right
(c) *(boutique, hôtel)* to run; *(caisse)* to be in charge of
(d) *(rôle)* to have
(e) *(parole, promesse)* to keep
(f) *(maîtriser)* *(enfants, cheval)* to control; **t. sa langue** to hold one's tongue
(g) *(résister à)* *Fam* **t. l'alcool** to hold one's drink; **t. la route** *(voiture)* to hold the road
(h) *(avoir)* **t. qch de qn** *(caractéristique)* to get sth from sb; **je tiens la nouvelle de ma mère** I got the news from my mother
(i) *(considérer)* **t. qn pour responsable** to hold sb responsible; **t. qch pour vrai** to consider sth to be true
2 *vi* **(a)** *(nœud, corde)* to hold; *(construction)* to stay up; *(autocollant, pansement)* to stay on; *(personne)* to last; *Fam* **il ne tient plus sur ses jambes** *ou* **debout** *(fatigué)* he's ready to drop, he's dead on his feet; *(ivre)* he can hardly stand; **t. debout** *(argument)* to stand up; **t. bon** *(personne)* to hold out; **je n'y tiens plus** I can't stand it any longer **(b)** *(durer)* to last; **mon offre/le pari tient toujours** my offer/the bet still stands; **ça tient toujours pour samedi?** is it still on for Saturday?
(c) *(être contenu)* to fit; **on tient à dix autour de cette table** this table seats ten; **ma conclusion tiendra en trois mots** my conclusion can be summed up in three words
3 *v impersonnel* **il ne tient qu'à vous que cela se fasse** it depends entirely on you whether it gets done; **s'il ne tenait qu'à moi,...** if it was just up to me,...; **qu'à cela ne tienne** that's not a problem
4 tenir à *vt ind* **(a)** *(liberté, amitié)* to value; *(ami)* to care about; *(objet)* to be attached to; **t. à faire qch** to be anxious *or* keen to do sth; **je tiens à ce que tout soit rangé** I want everything to be tidy; **si vous y tenez** if you insist
(b) *(provenir de)* to be the result of, to be due to
5 tenir de *vt ind (ressembler à) (personne)* to take after; *Fam* **entre son oncle et son père, il a de qui t.!** it's not surprising when you consider his uncle and his father!; **cela tient du miracle** it's something of a miracle
6 se tenir *vpr* **(a)** *(rester)* *(debout)* to stand; *(assis)* to sit; **se t. debout** to be standing, to stand; **se t. tranquille** to keep quiet
(b) *(se comporter)* **bien se t.** to behave (oneself); *Fig* **il n'a qu'à bien se t.!** he'd better watch his step!; **se t. mal à**

table to have no table manners
(c) *(s'accrocher)* to hold on (à to); **tenez-vous bien!** hold tight!; *Fig* **et alors, tiens-toi bien,...!** and would you believe it,...!; **se t. par la main** to hold hands; **ils se tenaient par la taille** they had their arms round each other's waist
(d) *(avoir lieu)* to be held, to take place
(e) *(être plausible)* to hang together
(f) **s'en t. à** *(généralités, sujet, budget)* to keep to; *(décision, consignes)* to abide by; **il ne s'en tint pas là** he didn't stop there; **je ne sais pas à quoi m'en t.** I don't know where I stand
(g) *(locutions)* **tiens-le-toi pour dit!** I'm telling you for the last time!

tennis [tenis] **1** *nm* **(a)** *(sport)* tennis; **t. de table** table tennis **(b)** *(court)* tennis court
2 *nm ou nf (chaussure)* tennis shoe

tennisman [tenisman] *(pl* **tennismen** [tenismɛn]) *nm* tennis player

ténor [tenɔr] **1** *adj (saxophone)* tenor
2 *nm* **(a)** *(voix, chanteur)* tenor **(b)** *Fig* **un t. de la politique** an influential figure in politics

tenseur [tɑ̃sœr] **1** *adj* **muscle t.** tensor
2 *nm* tensor

tension [tɑ̃sjɔ̃] *nf* **(a)** *(raideur, désaccord)* tension; **être sous t.** to be tense; **mettre qn sous t.** to put sb under stress; **t. nerveuse** nervous tension **(b)** **t. (artérielle)** blood pressure; **avoir de la t.** to have high blood pressure; **prendre la t. de qn** to take sb's blood pressure **(c)** *(électrique)* voltage, tension; **basse/haute t.** low/high voltage *or* tension

tentaculaire [tɑ̃takylɛr] *adj (ville)* sprawling; *(société, organisme)* octopus-like

tentacule [tɑ̃takyl] *nm* tentacle

tentant, -e [tɑ̃tɑ̃, -ɑ̃t] *adj* tempting

tentateur, -trice [tɑ̃tatœr, -tris] **1** *adj* tempting
2 *nm* tempter; *Rel* **le T.** the Tempter
3 *nf* tentatrice temptress

tentation [tɑ̃tasjɔ̃] *nf* temptation

tentative [tɑ̃tativ] *nf* attempt; **t. d'assassinat** attempted murder; **t. d'évasion** attempt to escape; **t. de suicide** suicide attempt

tente [tɑ̃t] *nf* **(a)** *(de camping)* tent; **coucher sous la t.** to sleep under canvas; **t. igloo** igloo tent **(b)** *Méd* **t. à oxygène** oxygen tent

tenter [tɑ̃te] *vt* **(a)** *(mettre à l'épreuve)* **t. sa chance** to try one's luck; *Fam* **t. le coup** to have a go; **t. le tout pour le tout** to go for broke **(b)** *(séduire)* to tempt; **être tenté de faire qch** to be tempted to do sth; **se laisser t.** to let oneself be tempted; **j'ai envie de me laisser t.** *(accepter)* I'm tempted to say yes; *(faire quelque chose)* I'm tempted to do it **(c)** *(essayer)* to try, to attempt; **t. de faire qch** to try *or* attempt to do sth

tenture [tɑ̃tyr] *nf (tapisserie)* hanging

tenu, -e [tɑny] *adj* **(a)** **bien/mal t.** *(maison, jardin)* well/poorly kept **(b)** *(contraint)* **être t. de faire qch** to be obliged to do sth; **être t. à qch** to be bound by sth **(c)** *(note)* held

ténu, -e [teny] *adj* **(a)** *(fil)* fine; *(nuance)* subtle; *(lien)* tenuous; *(espoir)* slender **(b)** *(voix)* thin

tenue [təny] *nf* **(a)** *(habillement)* outfit; *(militaire)* dress; **en t. légère** *(en vêtements d'été)* in light clothing; *Fam* **en petite t.** scantily dressed; **t. de combat** battledress; **t. de soirée** evening dress **(b)** *(bonne conduite)* good behaviour; **un peu de t.!** mind your manners!; **manquer de t.** to lack manners **(c)** *(maintien)* posture **(d)** *(niveau)* standard **(e)** *(d'une maison)* running **(f)** **t. de route** *(d'un véhicule)* road-holding

tequila [tekila] *nf* tequila

ter [tɛr] *adj* **5 t.** ≃ 5B

tercet [tɛrsɛ] *nm* tercet

térébenthine [terebɑ̃tin] *nf* turpentine

Tergal® [tɛrgal] *nm Br* Terylene®, *Am* Dacron®

tergiversations [tɛrʒiversasjɔ̃] *nfpl* equivocation

tergiverser [tɛrʒiverse] *vi* to equivocate

terme¹ [tɛrm] *nm* **(a)** *(fin)* end; **toucher à son t.** *(projet)* to be nearing completion; *(période)* to be drawing to a close; **mettre un t. à qch** to put an end to sth; **mener qch à bon t.** to bring sth to a successful conclusion **(b)** *(date limite)* time (limit); **à court/long t.** *(projet, prévisions)* short-/long-term; **à court/long t.,...** in the short/long term,... **(c)** *(d'une femme enceinte)* **être à t.** to have reached term; **avant t.** *(accoucher)* prematurely; *(accouchement)* premature **(d)** *(loyer)* rent; *(date de paiement du loyer)* rent day

terme² *nm* **(a)** *(mot)* term; **en d'autres termes** in other words **(b)** *(relations)* **être en bons/mauvais termes avec qn** to be on good/bad terms with sb **(c)** **termes** *(d'un contrat)* terms

terminaison [tɛrminɛzɔ̃] *nf* **(a)** *(d'un mot)* ending **(b)** *Anat* **t. nerveuse** nerve ending

terminal, -e, -aux, -ales [tɛrminal, -o] **1** *adj (de la fin)* final; *Méd (phase)* terminal; **être en phase terminale** *(malade)* to be terminally ill
2 *nm* **(a)** *(dans un aéroport)* terminal **(b)** *Ordinat* terminal, VDU
3 *nf Scol* **terminale** *Br* ≃ upper sixth, *Am* ≃ twelfth grade, senior year

terminer [tɛrmine] **1** *vt (discours, lettre, repas)* to end, to finish *(par* with); *(travail)* to finish, to complete; **en t. avec qch** to put an end to sth
2 se terminer *vpr (saison)* to come to a close; *(soirée, concert, vacances)* to end *(par* with); *(rue)* to end; **se t. en** *(mot)* to end in

terminologie [tɛrminolɔʒi] *nf* terminology

terminus [tɛrminys] *nm* terminus

termite [tɛrmit] *nm* termite

terne [tɛrn] *adj* dull

ternir [tɛrnir] **1** *vt (meuble)* to fade; *(miroir, métal, réputation)* to tarnish
2 se ternir *vpr (meuble)* to fade; *(miroir, métal, réputation)* to become tarnished

terrain [tɛrɛ̃] *nm* **(a)** *(parcelle)* piece *or* plot of land **(b)** *(espace au sol, relief)* ground; **tout t.** *(véhicule)* all-terrain **(c)** *(terre)* soil **(d)** *(destiné à une activité) (de football, de rugby)* pitch, field; *(de golf)* course; **t. d'atterrissage** landing strip; **t. d'aviation** airfield; **t. à bâtir** development site; **t. de camping** campsite; *Fig* **t. d'entente** common ground; **t. de jeu** *(pour les sports) Br* playing field, *Am* athletic field; *(pour les enfants)* playground; **t. de sport** sports ground; **t. vague** waste ground **(e)** *Méd* **présenter un t. favorable à qch** to be prone to sth **(f)** *(locutions)* **être sur son t.** to be on familiar ground; **sur le t.** *(apprendre)* in the field; **perdre/céder du t.** to lose/give ground; **préparer le t.** to pave the way

terrasse [tɛras] *nf* **(a)** *(d'un café, d'un restaurant) Br* pavement *or Am* sidewalk area; **en t.** outside; **prix des consommations en t.** price of drinks served outside **(b)** *(de maison, d'appartement)* terrace; **(toit en) t.** (roof) terrace **(c)** *(levée de terre)* terrace; **en terrasses** *(jardin)* terraced; *(culture)* terrace

terrassement [tɛrasmɑ̃] *nm* **(a)** *(action)* excavation **(b)** *(remblai)* earthwork

terrasser [tɛrase] *vt (sujet: adversaire)* to floor; *(sujet: émotion, fatigue, nouvelle)* to overwhelm; *(sujet: maladie)* to lay low

terrassier [tɛrasje] *nm* labourer

terre [tɛr] *nf* **(a)** *(monde)* world; *Fig* **t. à t.** down-to-earth; *Fig* **revenir sur t.** to come down to earth; *Fig* **avoir les pieds sur t.** to have one's feet on the ground **(b)** *(planète)* **la T.** (the) Earth **(c)** *(sol)* ground; *(étendue)* land; **à t., par t.** on the ground; **tomber par t.** to fall down; **faire tomber qch par t.** to drop sth; **sous t.** underground; **basses terres** lowlands; **hautes terres** highlands **(d)** *El Br* earth, *Am* ground; **relier** *ou* **raccorder à la t.** *Br* to earth, *Am* to ground **(e)** *(opposé à la mer)* land; **t. ferme** terra firma **(f)** *(matière)* soil, earth; **cultiver la t.** to cultivate the soil; **t. battue** mud; *(de court de tennis)* clay; **t. de Sienne** sienna **(g)** *(propriété)* **une t.** a piece of land; **terres** land **(h)** *(territoire)* land, country; **terres australes** southern lands; **la t. Adélie** Adélie Land; **la T. de Feu** Tierra del Fuego; **la T. promise** the Promised Land; **la T. sainte** the Holy Land **(i)** *(élément)* earth **(j)** *(argile)* clay; **cruche de** *ou* **en t.** earthenware jug; **t. cuite** terracotta; **une t. cuite** a piece of terracotta

terreau, -x [tɛro] *nm* compost

Terre-Neuve [tɛrnœv] *n* Newfoundland

terre-neuve [tɛrnœv] *nm inv* Newfoundland (dog)

terre-plein *(pl* **terre-pleins)** *nm (plate-forme)* platform; **t. central** *(sur route) Br* central reservation, *Am* median strip

terrer [tɛre] **se terrer** *vpr aussi Fig* to go to earth

terrestre [tɛrɛstr] *adj* **(a)** *(plante)* ground; *(animal)* land; *(transports)* surface **(b)** *(magnétisme, attraction)* of the earth **(c)** *(matériel)* worldly

terreur [tɛrœr] *nf* **(a)** *(effroi)* terror; **vivre dans la t.** to live in terror **(b)** *(emploi de la violence)* terror **(c)** *Fig (personne)* terror; **jouer les terreurs** to play the tough guy

terreux, -euse [tɛrø, -øz] *adj* **(a)** *(odeur)* earthy **(b)** *(mains)* muddy **(c)** *(teint, ciel, couleur)* muddy

terrible [tɛribl] *adj* **(a)** *(affreux, remarquable)* terrible **(b)** *Fam (formidable)* terrific, great; **pas t.** nothing special

terriblement [tɛribləmɑ̃] *adv* terribly

terrien, -enne [tɛrjɛ̃, -ɛn] **1** *adj* **a propriétaire t.** landowner **(b)** *(famille, vertu)* rural **(c)** *(de la Terre)* Earth
2 *nm,f* *(habitant de la Terre)* earthling

terrier¹ [tɛrje] *nm (d'un lapin)* burrow, hole; *(d'une taupe)* hole; *(d'un renard)* earth

terrier² *nm (chien)* terrier

terrifiant, -e [tɛrifjɑ̃, -ɑ̃t] *adj* terrifying

terrifier [tɛrifje] *vt* to terrify

terril [tɛril] *nm* slag heap

terrine [tɛrin] *nf* terrine

territoire [tɛritwar] *nm* **(a)** *(d'un État, d'un animal)* territory; **t. d'outre-mer** overseas territory; *Can* **Territoires du Nord-Ouest** Northwest Territories **(b)** *(de juge, d'évêque)* jurisdiction; *(de commune, d'arrondissement)* area

territorial, -e, -aux, -ales [tɛritorjal, -o] *adj* territorial

territorialité [tɛritorjalite] *nf* territoriality

terroir [tɛrwar] *nm* soil; **du t.** *(produit, accent, expression)* local

terrorisant, -e [tɛrorizɑ̃, -ɑ̃t] *adj* terrifying

terroriser [tɛrorize] *vt (sujet: personne)* to terrorize; *(sujet: expérience, souvenir)* to terrify

terrorisme [tɛrorism] *nm* terrorism

terroriste [tɛrorist] *adj & nmf* terrorist

tertiaire [tɛrsjɛr] **1** *adj* tertiary
2 *nm* **(a)** *(secteur économique)* service sector **(b)** *Géol* Tertiary era

tertio [tɛrsjo] *adv* thirdly

tertre [tɛrtr] *nm* hillock, mound

tes [te] *voir* **ton**¹

tessiture [tesityr] *nf Mus* range

tesson [tesɔ̃] *nm* shard; **t. de bouteille** piece of broken bottle

test [tɛst] **1** *adj inv* test; *(période)* trial
2 *nm* test; **t. de grossesse** pregnancy test

Testament [tɛstamɑ̃] *nm* l'**Ancien/le Nouveau T.** the Old/the New Testament

testament [tɛstamɑ̃] *nm (dernières volontés)* will; *Fig* legacy; **ceci est mon t.** this is my last will and testament

testamentaire [tɛstamɑ̃tɛr] *adj voir* **exécuteur**

tester [tɛste] *vt (élève, produit)* to test

testicule [tɛstikyl] *nm* testicle

testostérone [tɛstɔsterɔn] *nf* testosterone

tétanie [tetani] *nf* spasms, *Spéc* tetany; **avoir une crise de t.** to go into spasms

tétanique [tetanik] **1** *adj* tetanic
2 *nmf* tetanus sufferer

tétaniser [tetanize] *vt (muscle)* to cause spasms in; *Fig* **tétanisé de peur** paralysed with fear

tétanos [tetanos] *nm* tetanus

têtard [tetar] *nm* tadpole

tête [tɛt] *nf* (**a**) *(d'une personne, d'un animal)* head; **cent cinquante têtes de bétail** a hundred and fifty head of cattle; **j'ai la t. qui tourne** my head is spinning; **tenir t. à qn** to stand up to sb; *Fam* **j'en ai par-dessus la t.** I've had it up to here; *Fam* **avoir la t. près du bonnet** to have a short fuse; *Fig* **marcher la t. haute** to walk with one's head held high; **la t. la première** head first; *Fig* **foncer t. baissée** to jump in head first; **de la t. aux pieds** from head to foot; **la t. nue** bare-headed; *Fam* **30 euros par t. de pipe** 30 euros a head; **t. de mort** death's head
(**b**) *(visage)* face; **faire une drôle de t.** to look odd, to make an odd face; **avoir une drôle de t.** to look odd, to have an odd face; **faire la t.** to be in a huff
(**c**) *(personne)* **une t. rousse/blonde** a redhead/blonde; **nos chères têtes blondes** *(enfants)* our little ones; **t. brûlée** hothead; *Fam* **c'est une t. à claques** he/she has a face you just want to slap; *Fam* **t. de cochon** pig-headed person; *Fam* **c'est une t. de lard** ou **mule** she/he's pig-headed; **t. de linotte** bird-brain; **t. de Turc** target; **forte t.** strong-minded person; *Fam* **grosse t.** highbrow; *Fam* **avoir la grosse t.** to have a big head, to be big-headed
(**d**) *(esprit)* mind; *(cerveau)* brains; **des idées plein la t.** full of ideas; **avoir qch en t.** to have sth in one's head; **ne pas avoir de t.** to be very forgetful; **avoir toute sa t.** to be all there; **perdre la t.** to lose it; **faire qch à t.** reposée to do sth at one's leisure; **où ai-je la t.!** what am I thinking of!; **être t. en l'air** to have one's head in the clouds; **ne rien avoir dans la t.** to be empty-headed; **avoir la t. dure** to be pig-headed; **mettre qch dans la t. de qn** to put sth in sb's head; **se mettre en t. de faire qch** to get it into one's head to do sth; **se mettre dans la t. que** to get it into one's head that; **n'en faire qu'à sa t.** to do exactly as one pleases; **avoir une idée derrière la t.** to have an ulterior motive; **de t.** *(calculer, additionner)* in one's head
(**e**) *(cheveux)* hair
(**f**) *(d'une liste)* top; *(de chapitre)* heading; **t. d'affiche** top of the bill
(**g**) *(d'ail)* head; *(d'un arbre)* top; *(du fémur)* head
(**h**) *(d'une procession, d'un cortège)* head; *(d'un train)* front; **le wagon de t.** the front carriage; **prendre la t.** *(dans une course, dans un jeu)* to take the lead; **prendre la t. d'une entreprise** to take over as the head of a company; **être à la t. de qch** *(entreprise, fortune)* to be at the head of sth; *(protestation, révolte)* to be the leader of sth; **arriver en t.** to come in first; **être en t.** to be in the lead; **t. de lit** bed head;

t. de pont bridgehead; **t. de série** *(au tennis)* seed
(**i**) *(appareil)* **t. chercheuse** homing device; *Ordinat* **t. d'écriture** writing *or* write head; *Ordinat* **t. de lecture** read(ing) head; **t. à palpeur** sensor head

tête-à-queue [tɛtakø] *nm inv* spin; **faire un t.** to spin round

tête-à-tête [tɛtatɛt] *nm inv (rendez-vous)* tête-à-tête; **en t.** in private; **en t. avec** alone with

tête-bêche [tɛtbɛʃ] *adv (dormir)* head to foot

tête-de-nègre [tɛtdənɛgr] *adj inv & nm inv* dark brown

tétée [tete] *nf* feed; **donner la t. à un enfant** to feed a child

téter [tete] *vt* (**a**) *(lait)* to suck; **t. sa mère** to feed (**b**) *(cigare, pipe, stylo)* to suck on

tétine [tetin] *nf* (**a**) *(d'un biberon)* teat (**b**) *(sucette) Br* dummy, *Am* pacifier

téton [tetɔ̃] *nm* (**a**) *Fam (sein de femme)* tit (**b**) *(d'une pièce détachée)* lug

tétraèdre [tetraɛdr] **1** *adj* tetrahedral
2 *nm* tetrahedron

tétralogie [tetralɔʒi] *nf* tetralogy

tétraplégie [tetrapleʒi] *nf* quadriplegia

tétraplégique [tetrapleʒik] *adj & nmf* quadriplegic

tétras [tetrɑ] *nm* grouse

têtu, -e [tety] **1** *adj* stubborn, obstinate; *Fam* **t. comme une mule** as stubborn as a mule
2 *nm,f* stubborn *or* obstinate person

teuf-teuf *(pl* **teufs-teufs)** [tœftœf] *Fam* **1** *nf (voiture)* old banger **2** *nm (bruit)* chug-chug

teuton, -onne [tøtɔ̃, -ɔn] **1** *adj* Teutonic
2 *nm,f* **T.** Teuton

texan, -e [tɛksɑ̃, -an] **1** *adj* Texan
2 *nm,f* **T.** Texan

texte [tɛkst] *nm* (**a**) *(d'un livre, d'un dépliant)* text; **publicitaire** advertising copy; **lire un auteur dans le t.** to read an author in the original; **textes choisis (de)** selected passages (from) (**b**) *(d'un opéra)* libretto; *(d'une chanson)* words; *(d'un acteur)* lines; *(d'une pièce de théâtre)* script

textile [tɛkstil] **1** *adj* textile
2 *nm* (**a**) *(fibre)* textile (**b**) *(industrie)* **le t.** the textile industry, textiles

texto [tɛksto] *adv Fam* word for word; **t.!** those were his/her/*etc* very words!

textuel, -elle [tɛkstɥɛl] *adj* (**a**) *(analyse)* textual (**b**) *(traduction)* word-for-word, literal; *Fam* **t.!** those were his/her/*etc* very words!

textuellement [tɛkstɥɛlmɑ̃] *adv* word for word, literally

texture [tɛkstyr] *nf (d'une substance, du sol)* texture

TF1 [teɛfœ̃] *nf (abrév* **Télévision Française 1)** = French independent television company

TGV [teʒeve] *nm (abrév* **train à grande vitesse)** high-speed train

thaï, thaïe [taj] **1** *adj* Thai
2 *nm,f* **T.** Thai
3 *nm (langue)* Thai

thaïlandais, -e [tailɑ̃dɛ, -ɛz] **1** *adj* Thai
2 *nm,f* **T.** Thai

Thaïlande [tailɑ̃d] *nf* **la T.** Thailand

thalassothérapie [talasoterapi] *nf* seawater therapy

thé [te] *nm* (**a**) *(boisson)* tea; **t. au citron** tea with lemon; **t. glacé** iced tea; **t. à la menthe** mint tea; **t. nature/au lait** tea without milk/with milk; **t. en sachets** tea bags (**b**) *(goûter)* tea; **t. dansant** tea dance

théâtral, -e, -aux, -ales [teatral, -o] *adj* (**a**) *(œuvre,* *production)* theatrical; *(effet)* dramatic; *(représentation)* stage **(b)** *Péj (artificiel)* melodramatic

théâtre [teɑtr] *nm* **(a)** *(édifice, salle)* theatre; **t. de marionnettes** puppet theatre; **t. de verdure** open-air theatre **(b)** *(art, métier)* theatre; **c'est un homme de t.** he works in theatre; **faire du t.** *(professionnellement)* to be an actor/actress; *(en amateur)* to do some acting; **adapté pour le t.** adapted for the stage **(c)** *(œuvres) (d'un auteur)* plays; *(genre)* theatre; **t. de boulevard** light comedies **(d)** *Fig (attitude artificielle)* **c'est du t.** it's an act **(e)** *(d'un crime, d'un accident)* scene

théière [tejer] *nf* teapot

théine [tein] *nf* theine

thématique [tematik] **1** *adj* thematic
2 *nf* themes

thème |tɛm| *nm* **(a)** *(d'un discours, d'une œuvre, d'un morceau de musique)* theme **(b)** *(traduction)* prose **(c)** *(d'un verbe, d'un nom)* stem **(d)** *Astrol* **t. (astral)** birth chart

théocratie [teɔkrasi] *nf* theocracy

théocratique [teɔkratik] *adj* theocratic

théologie [teɔlɔʒi] *nf* theology

théologien, -enne [teɔlɔʒjɛ̃, -ɛn] *nm,f* theologian

théologique [teɔlɔʒik] *adj* theological

théorème [teɔrɛm] *nm* theorem

théoricien, -enne [teɔrisjɛ̃, -ɛn] *nm,f* theoretician, theorist

théorie [teɔri] *nf* theory; **en t.** in theory

théorique [teɔrik] *adj* theoretical

théoriquement [teɔrikmɑ̃] *adv* theoretically

thérapeute [terapøt] *nmf* therapist

thérapeutique [terapøtik] **1** *adj* therapeutic
2 *nf* **(a)** *(science)* therapeutics *(singulier)* **(b)** *(traitement)* therapy

thérapie [terapi] *nf* therapy; **t. de groupe** group therapy

thermal, -e, -aux, -ales [tɛrmal, -o] *adj* thermal

thermalisme [tɛrmalism] *nm* hydrotherapy

thermes [tɛrm] *nmpl* **(a)** *(établissement de soins)* thermal baths **(b)** *(chez les Anciens)* thermae, public baths

thermique [tɛrmik] *adj* thermal

thermoélectrique [tɛrmoelɛktrik] *adj* thermoelectric

thermomètre [tɛrmɔmɛtr] *nm* thermometer; *Fig (de l'opinion, d'une tendance)* barometer; **t. médical** clinical thermometer

thermonucléaire [tɛrmɔnykleɛr] *adj* thermonuclear

Thermos® [tɛrmos] *nm ou nf* **(bouteille) T.** Thermos® *(Br* flask *or Am* bottle)

thermostat [tɛrmɔsta] *nm* thermostat

thésard, -e [tezar, -ard] *nm,f* PhD student

thésaurisation [tezɔrizasjɔ̃] *nf* hoarding

thésauriser [tezɔrize] *vt & vi* to hoard

thesaurus [tezɔrys] *nm* thesaurus

thèse [tɛz] *nf* **(a)** *(proposition intellectuelle)* thesis; **roman/littérature à t.** novel/literature of ideas **(b)** *Univ* thesis *(submitted for doctorate)*

thon [tɔ̃] *nm* tuna; **t. blanc** longfin tuna; **t. au naturel/à l'huile** tuna in brine/in oil

thoracique [tɔrasik] *adj* thoracic

thorax [tɔraks] *nm* thorax

thriller [srilœr] *nm* thriller

thrombose [trɔ̃boz] *nf* thrombosis

thune [tyn] *nf très Fam* cash, *Am* bucks; **ne pas avoir une t.** to be totally skint

thuya [tyja] *nm* thuja

thym [tɛ̃] *nm* thyme

thyroïde [tirɔid] *adj & nf* thyroid

thyroïdien, -enne [tirɔidjɛ̃, -ɛn] *adj* thyroid

tiare [tjar] *nf* tiara

Tibet [tibɛ] *nm* **le T.** Tibet

tibétain, -e [tibetɛ̃, -ɛn] **1** *adj* Tibetan
2 *nm,f* **T.** Tibetan
3 *nm (langue)* Tibetan

tibia [tibja] *nm* shinbone, *Spéc* tibia

Tibre [tibr] *nm* **le T.** the Tiber

tic [tik] *nm* **(a)** *(convulsion involontaire)* tic, twitch; **t. nerveux** nervous tic *or* twitch **(b)** *(manie)* habit, mannerism; **t. de langage** verbal mannerism

ticket [tikɛ] *nm* ticket; *Fam Fig* **avoir un ou le t. avec qn** to have made a hit with sb; **t. de caisse** receipt; **t. modérateur** = portion of the cost of treatment payable by the patient; **t. de quai** platform ticket; **t. de rationnement** ration coupon

ticket-repas *(pl* **tickets-repas)** [tikɛrəpɑ] *nm Br* luncheon voucher, *Am* meal ticket

ticket-restaurant *(pl* **tickets-restaurant)** [tikɛ-rɛstɔrɑ̃] *nm Br* luncheon voucher, *Am* meal ticket

tic-tac [tiktak] *nm inv (d'une horloge)* tick-tock, ticking

tie-break *(pl* **tie-breaks)** [tajbrɛk] *nm* tie break

tiédasse [tjedas] *adj Péj* lukewarm, tepid

tiède [tjɛd] **1** *adv* **il fait t.** it's mild
2 *adj* **(a)** *(vent)* mild; *(bain, boisson)* tepid, lukewarm **(b)** *Péj (peu enthousiaste)* half-hearted

tiédeur [tjedœr] *nf* **(a)** *(du vent)* mildness; *(de l'eau)* tepidness **(b)** *Péj (manque d'enthousiasme)* half-heartedness

tiédir [tjedir] **1** *vt (réchauffer)* to warm (up); *(refroidir)* to cool (down)
2 *vi* **(a)** *(devenir plus chaud)* to warm up; *(devenir moins chaud)* to cool down **(b)** *Fig (amitié, passion)* to cool off

tien, -enne [tjɛ̃, tjɛn] **1** *pron possessif* **le t., la tienne, les tiens, les tiennes** yours; *(en insistant)* your own; **tu me prêtes le t.?** can I borrow yours?; **tu n'en as pas besoin, tu as le t.** you don't need it, you've got your own; *Fam* **à la tienne!** cheers!
2 *nm* **il faut que tu y mettes du t.** you should really do your share
3 *nmpl* **les tiens** *(ta famille)* your family
4 *nfpl Fam* **tu as encore fait des tiennes!** you've been up to your old tricks again!

tiendrais, tienne, tiens *etc voir* **tenir**

tierce [tjɛrs] **1** *adj voir* **tiers**
2 *nf* **(a)** *Mus* third **(b)** *(aux cartes)* tierce

tiercé [tjɛrse] *nm* forecast triple; **jouer au t.** to bet on the horses; **le t. gagnant** the winning combination

tiers, tierce [tjɛr, tjɛrs] **1** *adj* third; **le t. état** the third estate; **une tierce personne** a third party
2 *nm* **(a)** *(fraction)* third; **t. payant** = system by which a proportion of the fee for medical treatment is paid directly to the hospital or doctor by the insurer; **t. provisionnel** interim tax payment *(approximately one third of previous year's tax)* **(b)** *(personne)* third party

tiers-monde *(pl* **tiers-mondes)** [tjɛrmɔ̃d] *nm* **le t.** the Third World

tifs [tif] *nmpl Fam* hair

TIG [tiʒ] *nm (abrév* travail d'intérêt général*)* ≃ community service

tige [tiʒ] *nf* **(a)** *(d'une plante)* stem, stalk; **rosier sur t.** standard rose **(b)** *(d'une chaussure)* upper **(c)** *(en métal)* rod **(d)** *Fam (cigarette) Br* fag, *Am* butt

tignasse [tiɲas] *nf Fam* mop (of hair)

Tigre [tigr] *nm* le **T.** the Tigris

tigre [tigr] *nm* tiger; **t.** du Bengale Bengal tiger

tigré, -e [tigre] *adj (rayé)* striped

tigresse [tigrɛs] *nf* tigress

tilde [tild] *nm* tilde

tilleul [tijœl] *nm* **(a)** *(arbre)* lime (tree) **(b)** *(infusion)* lime-blossom tea

tilt [tilt] *nm* **faire t.** *(au billard électrique)* to signal the end of the game; *Fig* **ça a fait t.** the penny dropped

timbale [tɛ̃bal] *nf* **(a)** *(gobelet)* (metal) drinking cup; *Fig* **décrocher la t.** to hit the jackpot **(b)** *(tambour)* kettledrum; **les timbales** *(dans un orchestre)* the timpani **(c)** *(moule, plat)* timbale

timbre [tɛ̃br] *nm* **(a)** *(vignette)* stamp; **t. de collection** collector's stamp; **t.** fiscal excise *or* tax stamp **(b)** *(instrument encreur, marque)* stamp; **t. dateur** date stamp **(c)** *(sonnette)* bell; **t. de bicyclette** bicycle bell **(d)** *(d'une voix, d'un instrument)* timbre, tone; **voix sans t.** toneless voice **(e)** *(pour traitement médical)* patch; **t. tuberculinique** TB patch

timbré, -e [tɛ̃bre] *adj* **(a)** *(document, enveloppe)* stamped **(b)** *Fam (fou)* mad

timbre-poste *(pl* **timbres-poste)** [tɛ̃brəpɔst] *nm* (postage) stamp

timbrer [tɛ̃bre] *vt* **(a)** *(lettre, paquet)* to put a stamp/stamps on **(b)** *(passeport, document)* to stamp

timide [timid] **1** *adj* **(a)** *(personne, sourire, voix)* shy **(b)** *(critique, protestation, tentative)* timid
2 *nmf* shy person; **c'est un grand t.** he's very shy

timidement [timidmɑ̃] *adv* **(a)** *(sourire, parler)* shyly **(b)** *(critiquer, protester)* timidly

timidité [timidite] *nf* **(a)** *(d'une personne)* shyness **(b)** *(d'une critique, d'une protestation)* timidity

timing [tajmiŋ] *nm* timing

timoré, -e [timɔre] *adj* timorous, fearful

tintamarre [tɛ̃tamar] *nm Fam* din, racket; **faire du t.** to make a din *or* racket

tintement [tɛ̃təmɑ̃] *nm (de clochettes)* tinkling; *(de pièces de monnaie)* jingling; **t. d'oreilles** ringing in the ears

tinter [tɛ̃te] *vi* **(a)** *(clochettes)* to tinkle; *(pièces de monnaie)* to jingle **(b)** *(oreilles)* to ring

tintin [tɛ̃tɛ̃] *exclam Fam* no way José!; **faire t.** to go without

tintouin [tɛ̃twɛ̃] *nm Fam* **(a)** *(bruit)* din, racket **(b)** *(souci)* trouble

tipi [tipi] *nm* tepee

tique [tik] *nf* tick

tiquer [tike] *vi Fam (personne)* to wince; **il n'a pas tiqué** he didn't bat an eyelid

TIR [tir] *nm (abrév* **transports internationaux routiers)** TIR

tir [tir] *nm* **(a)** *(activité)* shooting; **t. à l'arc** archery; **faire du t. à l'arc** to do archery; **t. à la carabine** rifle shooting **(b)** *(coup de feu)* shot **(c)** *(à la pétanque)* throw; **t. (au but)** *(au football)* shot (at goal) **(d)** *(stand)* rifle range; **t. (forain)** shooting gallery

tirade [tirad] *nf Th* monologue; *Fig* tirade

tirage [tiraʒ] *nm* **(a)** *(impression)* printing **(b)** *(nombre d'exemplaires) (d'un journal)* circulation; *(d'un livre)* print run; **édition à t.** limité limited edition **(c)** *(d'une cheminée)* draught **(d)** *(de loterie)* draw **(de** for); **t. au sort** drawing lots; **procéder à un t. au sort** to draw lots

tiraillement [tirajmɑ̃] *nm* **(a)** *(crampe)* **tiraillements d'estomac** stomach cramps **(b)** *(conflit)* **tiraillements (entre)** conflict (between)

tirailler [tiraje] **1** *vt* **(a)** *(tirer sur)* to pull at, to tug at **(b)** *(écarteler)* **être tiraillé entre** to be torn between
2 *vi* **(a)** *(avec une arme)* to shoot wildly **(b)** *(peau)* **j'ai la peau qui tiraille** my skin feels tight

tirailleur [tirajœr] *nm (soldat éclaireur)* skirmisher

Tirana [tirana] *n* Tirana

tirant [tirɑ̃] *nm* **(a)** *(de botte)* boot strap **(b)** **t. d'eau** draught *(volume of water)*

tire [tir] *nf* **(a)** *très Fam (voiture)* car **(b)** *Can (confiserie)* molasses toffee, *Am* molasses candy, taffy

tiré, -e [tire] **1** *adj* **(a)** *(traits)* drawn; **avoir les traits tirés** to look drawn **(b)** *(cheveux)* scraped back
2 *nf Fam* **tirée** *(trajet)* long haul

tire-au-flanc [tiroflɑ̃] *nm inv Fam* shirker, *Br* skiver

tire-bouchon *(pl* **tire-bouchons)** [tirbuʃɔ̃] *nm* corkscrew; **en t.** *(queue)* corkscrew

tire-bouchonner [tirbuʃɔne] *vi (chaussettes)* to be at half-mast; *(pantalon)* to be crumpled

tire-d'aile [tirdɛl] **à tire-d'aile** *adv* **s'envoler à t.** to fly swiftly away; *Fig* **partir** *ou* **s'éloigner à t.** to fly off

tire-fesses [tirfɛs] *nm inv Fam* T-bar

tire-jus [tirʒy] *nm inv très Fam* snot rag

tire-lait [tirlɛ] *nm inv* breast pump

tire-larigot [tirlarigo] **à tire-larigot** *adv Fam* to one's heart's content

tirelire [tirlir] *nf Br* moneybox, *Am* coin bank; *Fig* **casser sa t.** to break into one's piggy bank

tirer [tire] **1** *vt* **(a)** *(vers soi)* to pull; *(chaussettes)* to pull up; **t. qch vers le haut/bas** to pull sth up/down; **t. qn par la manche** to pull at sb's sleeve; **t. qn par le bras** to pull sb by the arm; **t. les cheveux à qn** to pull sb's hair **(b)** *(rideaux)* to draw; *(store)* to pull down; *(verrou) (fermer)* to shoot; *(ouvrir)* to draw
(c) *(extraire)* **t. qch de qch** to pull sth out of sth; **t. de l'eau d'un puits** to draw water from a well; **une citation tirée d'un texte** a quotation taken from a text; **t. qn d'embarras** to get sb out of a tight spot; **t. qn de son lit** to drag sb out of bed; **t. son origine de qch** to have its origin in sth; **t. une conclusion de qch** to draw a conclusion from sth; **t. une leçon de qch** to learn a lesson from sth
(d) *(tendre) (tissu, fil)* to pull tight; *Fig* **t. les ficelles** to pull the strings
(e) *(carte)* to draw; **t. les cartes** *(cartomancienne)* to read the cards; **t. qch au sort** to draw lots for sth; **tirer qn au sort** to draw lots to choose sb
(f) *(tracer) (trait)* to draw; *(plan)* to draw up
(g) *(imprimer)* to print; *Fam Hum* **se faire t. le portrait** to have one's photograph taken
(h) *(chèque)* to draw **(sur** on)
(i) *(coup de feu, balle)* to fire; *(flèche)* to shoot; *(feu d'artifice)* to let off; **t. un coup de revolver (sur)** to fire a gun (at)
(j) *(locutions) très Fam* **plus qu'un mois à t.!** just one more month to get through!; **je te tire mon chapeau!** I take my hat off to you!
2 *vi* **(a)** *(exercer une traction)* to pull; **t. sur qch** *(corde)* to pull on sth; *(pull)* to pull sth down; *(par tic)* to pull at sth
(b) *(personne armée, arme)* to shoot; **t. à la carabine** to shoot with a rifle; **t. sur qn/qch** to shoot sb/sth; **t. dans le dos à qn** to shoot sb in the back
(c) *(peau)* to feel tight
(d) *(être imprimé)* **t. à 250 000 exemplaires** to have a circulation of 250,000
(e) *(cheminée)* to draw
(f) *(à la pétanque)* to throw; *(au football)* to shoot
(g) *(aspirer)* **t. sur une cigarette/pipe** to puff on a cigarette/pipe
(h) *(locutions)* **ça ne tire pas à conséquence** it's of no

consequence; **t. à sa fin** *(période, journée)* to be drawing to a close; *(réserves, économies)* to be running out; *Fam* **t. au flanc** to shirk, *Br* to skive **3 tirer sur** *vt ind (se rapprocher de) (couleur)* to verge on **4 se tirer** *vpr* (**a**) *(se sortir)* **se t. de qch** to get out of sth; **s'en t.** *(d'une maladie, d'un accident)* to pull through; *(financièrement)* to make it; **s'en t. avec qch** to get away with sth (**b**) *Fam (partir)* to make tracks

tiret [tirɛ] *nm* dash

tirette [tirɛt] *nf* (**a**) *(d'un bureau)* pull-out shelf; *(d'une table)* leaf (**b**) *(de distributeur)* pull handle (**c**) *Belg (fermeture Éclair) Br* zip, *Am* zipper

tireur, -euse [tirœr, -øz] **1** *nm,f* gunman; **t. d'élite** marksman, *f* markswoman; **c'est un bon t.** he's a good shot **2** *nf* **tireuse de cartes** fortune teller

tiroir [tirwar] *nm* drawer; *Fig* **à tiroirs** *(roman)* = containing individual episodes within the main story-line

tiroir-caisse *(pl* **tiroirs-caisses**) [tirwarkɛs] *nm* till, cash register

tisane [tizan] *nf* herbal tea

tison [tizɔ̃] *nm* (fire)brand

tisonner [tizɔne] *vt* to poke

tisonnier [tizɔnje] *nm* poker

tissage [tisaʒ] *nm* (**a**) *(activité)* weaving; **t. à la main / mécanique** hand-loom/power-loom weaving (**b**) *(établissement industriel)* cloth mill

tisser [tise] **1** *vt* (**a**) *(textile, liens, intrigue)* to weave (**b**) *(sujet, araignée)* to spin **2 se tisser** *vpr (liens, intrigue)* to be woven

tisserand [tisrɑ̃, -ɑ̃d] *nm,f* weaver

tissu [tisy] *nm* (**a**) *(étoffe)* material, cloth; *Fig (urbain, social)* fabric; **t. d'ameublement** furnishing fabric (**b**) *Fig (de mensonges, d'incohérences)* tissue (**c**) *Biol* tissue

tissu-éponge *(pl* **tissus-éponges**) [tisyepɔ̃ʒ] *nm* (terry) towelling

titan [titɑ̃] *nm* Titan; **travail de t.** Herculean task

titane [titan] *nm* titanium

titi [titi] *nm Fam* cheeky urchin

titiller [titije] *vt* to titillate

titrage [titraʒ] *nm* (**a**) *(de film)* titling (**b**) *(d'un alcool)* determination of the strength

titre [titr] *nm* (**a**) *(de livre, de chanson, de film)* title (**b**) *(de chapitre, de page)* heading; **les gros titres** the headlines; **faire les gros titres** to hit the headlines (**c**) *(d'une personne)* title; **en t.** *(titulaire)* permanent; *(attitré)* official (**d**) *(qualité de champion)* title (**e**) *(diplôme)* qualification (**f**) *(certificat)* **t. de propriété** title deed; **t. de transport** ticket (**g**) *Fin* security (**h**) *(d'un alcool)* strength; *(de l'or, d'une monnaie)* fineness; *(d'un alliage)* grade (**i**) *(locutions)* **à ce t.** *(pour cette raison)* therefore; *(en cette qualité)* as such; **à quel t.?** *(de quel droit)* on what grounds?; **au même t. que** in the same way as; **à t. gratuit** free of charge; **à t. d'exemple** by way of example

titré, -e [titre] *adj (personne)* titled

titrer [titre] *vt* (**a**) *(livre, film)* to title (**b**) *(alcool)* to determine the strength of

tituber [titybe] *vi* to stagger (**de** with)

titulaire [titylɛr] **1** *adj* (**a**) *(dans l'administration)* with a permanent contract; *(professeur d'université)* with tenure (**b**) *(détenteur)* **être t. de qch** to be the holder of sth **2** *nmf (détenteur)* holder

titularisation [titylarizasjɔ̃] *nf* granting of permanent contract; *(à l'université)* granting of tenure

titulariser [titylarize] *vt* to give a permanent contract to; *(professeur d'université)* to give tenure to

TNT [teɛnte] *nm (abrév* **trinitrotoluène**) TNT

toast [tost] *nm* (**a**) *(de pain)* piece *or* slice of toast; **t. beurré** piece *or* slice of buttered toast; **des toasts** toast (**b**) *(hommage)* toast; **porter un t. à qn** to drink a toast to sb

toboggan [tɔbɔgɑ̃] *nm* (**a**) *(de terrain de jeu)* slide; *(dans une piscine)* flume; **faire du t.** to play on the slide (**b**) *(pour marchandises)* chute (**c**) *(viaduc) Br* flyover, *Am* overpass (**d**) *Can (traîneau)* toboggan; **faire du t.** to go tobogganing

toc [tɔk] **1** *exclam* **t. t.!** knock knock!; **Fig et t.!** so there! **2** *adj inv Fam (faux)* fake; *(de mauvais goût)* tacky **3** *nm Fam (faux)* fake; **en toc** fake jewellery; **c'est du t.** it's fake

toccata [tɔkata] *nf Mus* toccata

tocsin [tɔksɛ̃] *nm* alarm bell

toge [tɔʒ] *nf* (**a**) *(de magistrat, d'avocat)* gown (**b**) *(romaine)* toga

Togo [togo] *nm le* T. Togo

togolais, -e [togolɛ, -ɛz] **1** *adj* Togolese **2** *nm,f* T. Togolese

tohu-bohu [tɔyboy] *nm (désordre)* confusion; *(bruit)* hubbub

toi [twa] *pron personnel* (**a**) *(sujet)* you; **t., ne m'énerve pas!** don't annoy me!; **t., tu aurais certainement cédé** YOU would probably have given in (**b**) *(objet direct)* you; **et t., il t'a salué?** and what about you, did he say hello to you? (**c**) *(avec préposition)* you; **je ne te le prêterai pas, à t.** I won't lend it to YOU; **c'est à t., tout ça?** is that all yours?; **tu auras ta chambre à t.** you'll have your own room; *Fam* **une copine à t.** a friend of yours; **tu ne penses qu'à t.** you think only of yourself (**d**) *(dans les comparaisons)* you; **je n'en sais pas plus que t.** I don't know any more about it than you (do)

toile [twal] *nf* (**a**) *(tissu)* cloth; **t. d'araignée** cobweb, spider's web; **t. cirée** oilcloth; **t. de fond** backdrop; *Fig* **en t. de fond** as a backdrop; **t. (de lin)** linen; **un pantalon en t.** linen trousers; **t. à matelas** ticking; **t. de tente** canvas (**b**) *(tableau)* painting, canvas (**c**) *Fam (film)* **se faire une t.** to go to the movies

toilettage [twaletaʒ] *nm* (**a**) *(d'un chien)* grooming (**b**) *(d'un texte)* tidying up

toilette [twalɛt] *nf* (**a**) *(action de se laver)* washing; **faire sa t.** to have a wash (**b**) **toilettes** *(W-C) Br* toilet, *Am* rest room; *(publiques)* public convenience; **toilettes pour dames** ladies' *Br* toilet *or Am* room; **toilettes pour hommes** *Br* gents' toilet, *Am* men's room (**c**) *(vêtements)* outfit; **porter bien en t.** to look good in formal clothes

toiletter [twalete] *vt* (**a**) *(chien)* to groom (**b**) *(texte)* to tidy up

toi-même [twamɛm] *pron personnel* yourself; *Fam* **menteur! - t.!** liar! - liar yourself!

toise [twaz] *nf* height gauge

toiser [twaze] **1** *vt* to look up and down **2 se toiser** *vpr* to look each other up and down

toison [twazɔ̃] *nf* (**a**) *(de mouton)* fleece; **la T. d'or** the Golden Fleece (**b**) *(chevelure)* mane (of hair)

toit [twa] *nm* roof; *Fig* **être sans t.** not to have a roof over one's head; **accueillir qn sous son t.** to take sb in; **t. de chaume** thatched roof; **t. ouvrant** sun roof

toiture [twatyr] *nf* roofing, roof

Tokyo [tɔkjo] *nm* Tokyo

tôle¹ [tol] *nf* (**a**) *(matériau)* sheet metal; **t. ondulée** corrugated iron (**b**) *(feuille)* metal sheet

tôle² = **taule**

tolérable [tɔlerabl] *adj* tolerable; **votre comportement n'est pas t.** your behaviour is intolerable

tolérance [tɔlerɑ̃s] *nf* tolerance; *(concession)* concession

tolérant, -e [tɔlerɑ̃, -ɑ̃t] *adj* tolerant

tolérer [tɔlere] **1** *vt* to tolerate; **je ne tolère pas qu'on me parle sur ce ton!** I won't tolerate being spoken to like that!
2 se tolérer *vpr* to tolerate each other

tôlier [tolje] = **taulier**

tollé [tɔle] *nm* outcry; **t. général** public outcry

TOM [tɔm] *nm (abrév* **territoire d'outre-mer)** overseas territory

tomahawk [tɔmaok] *nm* tomahawk

tomate [tɔmat] *nf* tomato

tombal, -e, -als *ou* **-aux, -ales** [tɔ̃bal, -o] *adj voir* **pierre**

tombant, -e [tɔ̃bɑ̃, -ɑ̃t] *adj (épaules)* sloping; *(oreilles)* floppy

tombe [tɔ̃b] *nf* **(a)** *(sépulture)* grave; *(avec un monument)* tomb; **emporter un secret dans la t.** to take a secret to the grave; **suivre qn dans la t.** to follow sb to the grave **(b)** *(pierre tombale)* gravestone, tombstone

tombeau, -x [tɔ̃bo] *nm* tomb; *Fig* **à t. ouvert** at breakneck speed

tombée [tɔ̃be] *nf* **la t. du jour** *ou* **de la nuit** nightfall

tomber [tɔ̃be] **1** *vi (aux* **être)** **(a)** *(personne, objet)* to fall (down); *(précipitations, feuilles)* to fall; **t. de qch** *(chaise, échelle)* to fall off sth; *(arbre)* to fall out of sth; **t. dans un piège** to fall into a trap; *Fam Fig* **tu es tombé sur la tête?** were you dropped on your head?; **faire t. qn/qch** to knock sb/sth over; **laisser t.** *(objet)* to drop; *Fam* **laisser t. qn** to let sb down; *Fam* **laisse t., c'est inutile** forget it, it's pointless; **t. à l'eau** *(personne, objet)* to fall in (the water); *(projet)* to fall through; *Fig* **il faut être tombé bien bas** you have to have sunk pretty low; **t. de haut** to come back to earth with a bump
(b) *(gouvernement, ville)* to fall
(c) *(nouvelle)* to come through
(d) *(mourir)* to fall; *Fam* **t. comme des mouches** to be dropping like flies
(e) *(vent, prix, fièvre)* to drop; *(conversation)* to flag; *(enthousiasme)* to wane
(f) *(nuit)* to fall
(g) *(devenir brusquement)* **t. amoureux de qn** to fall in love with sb; *Fam* **t. enceinte** to get pregnant
(h) *(date, événement)* to fall
(i) *(pendre) (draperie, vêtement)* to hang; **ses cheveux lui tombent jusqu'aux reins** her hair hangs right down her back
(j) *(locutions)* **t. bien** to come at just the right time; **t. mal** to come at the wrong time; **je suis bien/mal tombé** *(chanceux/malchanceux)* I was lucky/unlucky; **ça tombe sous le sens** it stands to reason; **t. sur qn** *(l'agresser)* to pitch into sb; *(le rencontrer par hasard)* to bump into sb; **t. sur qch** to come across sth; **il fallait que ça tombe sur moi!** it had to happen to me!
2 *vt Fam (aux* **avoir)** **(a)** *(séduire)* to pull **(b)** *(enlever)* **t. la veste** to take off one's jacket

tombereau, -x [tɔ̃bro] *nm* **(a)** *(charrette)* tip-cart **(b)** *(contenu)* cartload

tombeur [tɔ̃bœr] *nm Fam* womanizer, ladykiller

tombola [tɔ̃bɔla] *nf* raffle

tome [tɔm] *nm (volume)* volume

tomme [tɔm] *nf* = cheese made in Savoie

ton¹, ta, tes [tɔ̃, ta, te]

---
ta becomes **ton** before a word beginning with a vowel or mute h.
---

adj possessif your; **t. chien** your dog; **ta voiture** your car; **t. ami/amie** your friend; **tes enfants** your children; **t. père**

et ta mère your mother and father; **un de tes amis** one of your friends, a friend of yours; *Fam* **tu as eu t. vendredi** you got Friday off

ton² *nm* **(a)** *(qualité de voix)* tone; **hausser/baisser le t.** to raise/lower one's voice; **sur le t. de la plaisanterie** in a joking tone of voice **(b)** *(goût)* **il est de bon t. de le faire** it's good form to do it **(c)** *(gamme)* key; *(intervalle musical)* tone; **donner le t.** to give the pitch; *Fig* to set the tone **(d)** *Ling* tone; **langue à tons** tonal language **(e)** *(teinte)* shade, tone; *Ordinat* **tons de gris** shades of grey

tonal, -e, -als, -ales [tɔnal] *adj Mus* tonal

tonalité [tɔnalite] *nf* **(a)** *(au téléphone) Br* dialling *or Am* dial tone **(b)** *(d'un morceau de musique)* key; *Fig (d'une œuvre)* tone

tondeuse [tɔ̃døz] *nf* **(a)** *(de jardin)* **t. (à gazon)** (lawn) mower **(b)** *(de coiffeur)* clippers

tondre [tɔ̃dr] *vt* **(a)** *(herbe)* to mow; *(mouton)* to shear; **se faire t.** *(très court)* to have one's hair cropped; *(complètement)* to have all one's hair shaved off **(b)** *Fam (dépouiller)* to fleece

toner [tɔner] *nm* toner

tong [tɔ̃g] *nf Br* flip-flop, *Am* thong

Tonga [tɔ̃ga] *nfpl* **les (îles) T.** Tonga

tonicité [tɔnisite] *nf* **(a)** *(des muscles)* tone **(b)** *(de l'air, du climat)* bracing effect

tonifiant, -e [tɔnifjɑ̃, -ɑ̃t] *adj (air, marche)* bracing

tonifier [tɔnifje] *vt (peau, muscles)* to tone up; *(esprit)* to stimulate

tonique [tɔnik] **1** *adj* **(a)** *(climat, vent)* bracing, invigorating **(b)** *(boisson, remède)* tonic **(c)** *(personne)* energetic, dynamic **(d)** *(accent)* tonic; *(syllabe)* accented
2 *nm* **(a)** *(remède)* tonic **(b)** *(lotion)* toner
3 *nf Mus* tonic, keynote

tonitruant, -e [tɔnitryɑ̃, -ɑ̃t] *adj (voix, bruit)* thundering

tonnage [tɔnaʒ] *nm* tonnage

tonnant, -e [tɔnɑ̃, -ɑ̃t] *adj (voix)* thundering

tonne [tɔn] *nf* metric ton, tonne; *Fam Fig* **des tonnes de qch** tons of sth; *Fam* **en faire des tonnes** to go overboard

tonneau, -x [tɔno] *nm* **(a)** *(récipient)* barrel, cask; *Fig* **du même t.** of the same type **(b)** *(en voiture)* roll; **faire un t.** to roll over

tonnelier [tɔnəlje] *nm* cooper

tonnelle [tɔnɛl] *nf (charmille)* arbour, bower

tonner [tɔne] **1** *vi (a) (canons)* to thunder **(b)** *(fulminer)* to thunder **(contre** against)
2 *v impersonnel* **il tonne** it's thundering

tonnerre [tɔnɛr] *nm* thunder; **un t. d'applaudissements** thunderous applause; *Fam Fig* **du t.** terrific

tonsure [tɔ̃syr] *nf* tonsure

tonte [tɔ̃t] *nf (des moutons)* shearing; *(du gazon)* mowing

tonton [tɔ̃tɔ̃] *nm Fam* uncle

tonus [tɔnys] *nm* **(a)** *Fig (dynamisme)* energy, dynamism **(b)** *(d'un muscle)* tone

top [tɔp] *nm* **(a)** *(signal sonore)* beep; **au quatrième t. il sera midi** at the fourth stroke it will be twelve o'clock **(b)** *Fam* **être au t. niveau** *(sportif)* to be at one's peak; **c'est le t.!** it's the business!

topaze [tɔpaz] *nf* topaz

toper [tɔpe] *vi Fam* **tope(-là)!** put it there!

topinambour [tɔpinɑ̃bur] *nm* Jerusalem artichoke

topo [tɔpo] *nm Fam (discours)* lecture; *(exposé)* rundown; *Fig* **c'est toujours le même t.** it's always the same old story

topographie [tɔpɔgrafi] *nf* topography

topographique [tɔpɔgrafik] *adj* topographical

toponymie [tɔpɔnimi] *nf* toponymy

top secret [tɔpsəkrɛ] *adj inv* top secret

toquade [tɔkad] *nf Fam (pour une personne)* crush **(pour** on); *(pour un lieu, pour un objet)* craze **(pour** for)

toque [tɔk] *nf (de fourrure)* fur hat; *(de jockey)* cap; *(de cuisinier)* hat

toqué, -e [tɔke] *Fam* **1** *adj* crazy **(de** about) **2** *nm,f* nutcase

toquer [tɔke] **se toquer** *vpr Fam* **se t. de qn** to go crazy over sb

Torah [tɔra] *nf* la **T.** the Torah

torche [tɔrʃ] *nf* torch; **t. électrique** *Br* (electric) torch, *Am* flashlight

torcher [tɔrʃe] *Fam* **1** *vt* **(a)** *(fesses, enfant)* to wipe **(b)** *(travail)* to botch **(c)** *(bouteille)* to polish off **2 se torcher** *vpr* to wipe one's backside

torchis [tɔrʃi] *nm* cob *(for building)*

torchon [tɔrʃɔ̃] *nm* **(a)** *(de cuisine)* dish or tea towel; *Fam* le **t. brûle** they're at each other's throats; *Fig* il ne faut pas **mélanger les torchons et les serviettes** they're in a different league **(b)** *Fam (texte peu soigné)* mess **(c)** *Fam (journal)* rag

tordant, -e [tɔrdɑ̃, -ɑ̃t] *adj Fam* hilarious

tord-boyaux [tɔrbwajo] *nm Fam* rotgut

tordre [tɔrdr] **1** *vt (barre de fer, métal)* to bend; *(fil de fer)* to twist; *(linge)* to wring; **t. le cou à qn** to wring sb's neck; **t. le bras à qn** to twist sb's arm **2 se tordre** *vpr* **se t. les mains** to wring one's hands; **se t. la cheville** to twist one's ankle; **se t. de douleur** to writhe in pain; *Fam* **se t. (de rire)** to kill oneself (laughing)

tordu, -e [tɔrdy] **1** *adj* **(a)** *(objet)* twisted **(b)** *Fam (dérangé)* **être t.** to be a bit of a maniac; **avoir l'esprit t.** to have a warped mind **2** *nm,f Fam* maniac

toréador [tɔreadɔr] *nm* bullfighter, toreador

toréer [tɔree] *vi* to fight *(in the bullring)*

torero [tɔrero] *nm* bullfighter

torgnole [tɔrɲɔl] *nf très Fam* clout

tornade [tɔrnad] *nf* tornado; **comme une t.** like a whirlwind

Toronto [tɔrɔ̃to] *n* Toronto

torpeur [tɔrpœr] *nf* torpor

torpillage [tɔrpijaʒ] *nm* torpedoing

torpille [tɔrpij] *nf* **(a)** *(engin militaire)* torpedo **(b)** *(poisson)* torpedo, electric ray

torpiller [tɔrpije] *vt aussi Fig* to torpedo

torpilleur [tɔrpijœr] *nm* torpedo boat

torréfaction [tɔrefaksjɔ̃] *nf* roasting

torréfier [tɔrefje] *vt* to roast

torrent [tɔrɑ̃] *nm (cours d'eau)* torrent; *Fig (de larmes, de lumière)* flood; *(d'injures)* torrent; *(de questions)* barrage; **pleuvoir à torrents** to pour down

torrentiel, -elle [tɔrɑ̃sjɛl] *adj* torrential

torride [tɔrid] *adj* torrid

tors, -e [tɔr, tɔrs] *adj* twisted

torsade [tɔrsad] *nf* **(a)** *(point de tricot)* cable; **pull à torsades** cable(-knit) jumper **(b)** *(de cheveux)* twist, coil

torsadé, -e [tɔrsade] *adj (pull)* cable(-knit)

torsader [tɔrsade] *vt* to twist

torse [tɔrs] *nm* chest; **t. nu** stripped to the waist

torsion [tɔrsjɔ̃] *nf* twisting

tort [tɔr] *nm* **(a)** *(faute)* fault; **avoir tous les torts** to be entirely to blame; **c'est un t. de l'avoir fait** it was a mistake

to do it; **avoir t. (de faire qch)** to be wrong (to do sth); **tu n'as pas t.** you're quite right; **donner t. à qn** *(personne)* to blame sb; *(résultat, preuve)* to prove sb wrong; **être en t.** *ou* **dans son t.** to be in the wrong **(b)** *(dommage)* wrong; **faire du t. à qn** to harm sb; *(désavantager)* to penalize sb **(c)** *(locutions)* **à t.** wrongly; **à t. ou à raison** rightly or wrongly; **à t. et à travers** *(dépenser)* recklessly; *(parler)* wildly

torticolis [tɔrtikɔli] *nm* stiff neck; **avoir le** *ou* **un t.** to have a stiff neck

tortillard [tɔrtijar] *nm Fam* local train

tortiller [tɔrtije] **1** *vt (papier, ruban, cheveux)* to twist; *(moustache)* to twirl **2** *vi Fam* **il n'y a pas à t.** there are no two ways about it **3 se tortiller** *vpr (personne)* to wriggle

tortillon [tɔrtijɔ̃] *nm (de papier)* twist

tortionnaire [tɔrsjɔnɛr] *nmf* torturer

tortue [tɔrty] *nf* **(a)** *(reptile)* tortoise; **t. d'eau douce** terrapin; **t. de mer** turtle **(b)** *Fig (personne lente) Br* slowcoach, *Am* slowpoke

tortueusement [tɔrtɥøzmɑ̃] *adv (hypocritement)* deviously

tortueux, -euse [tɔrtɥø, -øz] *adj* **(a)** *(sinueux)* winding, tortuous **(b)** *(attitude, esprit)* devious; *(langage)* tortuous

torture [tɔrtyr] *nf aussi Fig* torture; *Fig* **mettre qn à la t.** to torture sb

torturer [tɔrtyre] **1** *vt aussi Fig* to torture **2 se torturer** *vpr* to torture oneself; **se t. l'esprit** to rack one's brains

torve [tɔrv] *adj* menacing

toscan, -e [tɔskɑ̃, -an] **1** *adj* Tuscan **2** *nm,f* **T.** Tuscan **3** *nm (langue)* Tuscan

Toscane [tɔskan] *nf* la **T.** Tuscany

tôt [to] *adv* **(a)** *(bientôt, vite)* soon, early; **nous n'étions pas plus t.** rentrés que... no sooner had we returned than...; **au plus t.** at the earliest; *Fam* **ce n'est pas trop t.!** and about time too!; **elle a eu t. fait de changer d'avis** she soon changed her mind; **t. ou tard** sooner or later **(b)** *(de bonne heure)* early

total, -e, -aux, -ales [tɔtal, -o] **1** *adj* total **2** *nm* total; **faire le t.** to work out the total; **au t.** in all, in total; *(tout compte fait)* all in all; *Fam* **t., ils se sont fâchés** the upshot was that they fell out

totalement [tɔtalmɑ̃] *adv* totally

totaliser [tɔtalize] *vt* **(a)** *(additionner)* to total, to add up **(b)** *(avoir au total)* to have a total of

totalitaire [tɔtalitɛr] *adj* totalitarian

totalitarisme [tɔtalitarism] *nm* totalitarianism

totalité [tɔtalite] *nf* la **t. de** all of; **payer qch en t.** to pay sth in full

totem [tɔtɛm] *nm (mât)* totem pole

touareg [twarɛg] **1** *adj* Tuareg **2** *nmf* **T.** Tuareg **3** *nm (langue)* Tuareg

toubib [tubib] *nm Fam* doctor

toucan [tukɑ̃] *nm* toucan

touchant, -e [tuʃɑ̃, -ɑ̃t] *adj* touching

touche [tuʃ] *nf* **(a)** *(d'un piano, d'un clavier)* key; *Ordinat* **t. alt** (key) **(b)** *(tache de couleur)* touch; **mettre la t. finale à qch** to put the finishing touches to sth **(c)** *(style)* touch **(d)** *(en escrime)* hit; *(à la pêche)* bite; *Fam* **avoir une t. avec qn** to make a hit with sb; *(par les avants au rugby)* line-out; **sortir en t.** to go into touch; *aussi Fig* **rester sur la t.** to stay on the sidelines **(f)** *Fam (allure)* look; **avoir**

une drôle de t. to look weird **(g)** *(de violon)* finger board; *(de guitare)* fret

touche-à-tout [tuʃatu] *nmf inv Fam* **(a)** *(enfant)* **c'est un t.** he's into everything **(b)** *(qui a plusieurs occupations)* dabbler

toucher¹ [tuʃe] *nm* **(a)** *(sens)* **le t.** touch; **au t.** to the touch **(b)** *(d'un pianiste)* touch

toucher² **1** *vt* **(a)** *(être en contact avec)* to touch; *(cible, adversaire)* to hit; **je touche du bois!** touch wood!; *Fam* **pas touche!** hands off! **(b)** *(blesser)* to hit **(à** in) **(c)** *(émouvoir)* to touch, to move **(d)** *(concerner)* to concern, to affect **(e)** *(port)* to put in at; **t. le fond** *(navire)* to touch bottom; *Fig (moralement)* to hit rock bottom; **t. terre** *(bateau)* to reach dry land **(f)** *(argent, intérêt, paie)* to get; *(chèque)* to cash; **t. le tiercé** to win the triple **(g)** *(jouxter)* to adjoin **(h)** *(dire)* **t. un mot à qn (de qch)** to have a word with sb (about sth) **2 toucher à** *vt ind* **(a)** *(prendre, modifier)* to touch; *Fig* **avec son air de ne pas y t.** looking as if butter wouldn't melt in his mouth **(b)** *(problème, question)* to touch on **(c)** *(approcher de)* **t. au but** to be nearing one's goal; **t. à sa fin** to be nearing its end **(d)** *(concerner)* to concern **3 se toucher** *vpr (être en contact)* to touch; *(maisons)* to adjoin

touer [twe] *vt Can* to tow

touffe [tuf] *nf* tuft

touffu, -e [tufy] *adj* **(a)** *(bois, végétation)* dense; *(barbe, cheveux)* bushy **(b)** *Fig (livre)* dense

touiller [tuje] *vt Fam* to stir; *(salade)* to toss

toujours [tuʒur] *adv* **(a)** *(exprime la continuité, la répétition)* always; **t. plus nombreux** more and more numerous; **un ami de t.** a lifelong friend; **pour t.** for ever; **depuis t.** always **(b)** *(encore)* still; **cherchez t.** keep looking; **alors, il est rentré? – t. pas** he's back then? – **not yet (c)** *(quoi qu'il en soit)* **t. est-il que...** the fact remains that...; **elle peut t. attendre!** she'll have a long wait!; **c'est t. ça (de pris)** at least it's something

toulousain, -e [tuluzɛ̃, -ɛn] **1** *adj* of Toulouse **2** *nm,f* **T.** person from Toulouse

Toulouse [tuluz] *n* Toulouse

toundra [tundra] *nf* tundra

toupet [tupɛ] *nm* **(a)** *Fam (audace)* cheek, nerve; **avoir du t., ne pas manquer de t.** to have a cheek *or* a nerve **(b)** *(de cheveux)* tuft of hair, *Br* quiff

toupie [tupi] *nf* **(a)** *(jouet)* (spinning) top **(b)** *Fam (femme) vieille* **t.** old trout

tour¹ [tur] *nf* **(a)** *(construction)* tower; **t. de contrôle** control tower; **la T. Eiffel** the Eiffel Tower **(b)** *(immeuble) Br* tower block, *Am* high-rise **(c)** *(aux échecs)* rook, castle **(d)** *Ordinat* tower

tour² *nm* **(a)** *(circonférence)* circumference; **t. de cou/de taille** collar/waist size *or* measurement; **avoir 75 cm de t. de taille** to have a waist measurement of 75 cm; **perdre 5 cm de t. de taille** to lose 5 cm round the waist; **t. de tête** hat size **(b)** *(mouvement circulaire)* **faire le t. (de qch)** to go round (sth); **faire faire à qn le t. du propriétaire** to show sb round *(a house)*; *Fig* **faire le t. de qch** *(situation, problème)* to review sth; *Fam* **faire le t. du cadran** to sleep for twelve hours; **faire un t. d'horizon** to review matters; **faire le t. du monde** to go round the world; **t. d'honneur** lap of honour; **t. de piste** lap **(c)** *(de potier)* wheel **(d)** *(tournure) (d'une situation)* turn; **prendre un certain t.** to take a certain turn; **t. d'esprit** turn of mind; **t. de phrase** turn of phrase **(e)** *(rotation)* turn; **donner un t. de clé** to turn the key; **à t. de bras** *(frapper)* with all one's might; *Fig (distribuer)* in

huge quantities; **se faire un t. de reins** to strain one's back **(f)** *(promenade à pied)* stroll; *(à bicyclette, en voiture)* ride; **faire un t.** to go for a stroll/ride **(g)** *(alternance)* turn; **à qui le t.?** whose turn is it?; **chacun (à) son t.** each in turn; **t. à t.** in turn; **à t. de rôle** in turn **(h)** *Pol* **t. (de scrutin)** ballot **(i)** *(mauvais coup)* trick; **jouer un t. à qn** to play a trick on sb; **jouer un t. de cochon à qn** to play a dirty trick on sb; **cela te jouera des tours** you'll live to regret it **(j)** *(de prestidigitateur)* trick; **t. de force** feat; *Fam* **en un t. de main** in no time at all; **t. de passe-passe** trick *(using sleight of hand)*

Touraine [turɛn] *nf* **la T.** Touraine

tourbe [turb] *nf* peat

tourbeux, -euse [turbø, -øz] *adj* peaty

tourbillon [turbijɔ̃] *nm* **(a)** *(de vent)* whirlwind; *(de poussière, de fumée)* swirl; *(de neige)* flurry **(b)** *(d'eau)* whirlpool **(c)** *Fig (de la vie, d'activité)* whirl

tourbillonnant, -e [turbijɔnɑ̃, -ɑ̃t] *adj* whirling

tourbillonner [turbijɔne] *vi aussi Fig* to whirl

tourelle [turɛl] *nf* turret

tourisme [turism] *nm* tourism; **faire du t.** to do some touring

touriste [turist] **1** *adj (classe)* tourist **2** *nmf* tourist; *Fig & Péj* **faire qch en t.** to play at doing sth

touristique [turistik] *adj* tourist; *(route)* scenic

tourment [turmɑ̃] *nm Litt* torment

tourmente [turmɑ̃t] *nf* **(a)** *Litt (tempête)* storm **(b)** *(agitation politique)* upheaval

tourmenté, -e [turmɑ̃te] *adj* **(a)** *(paysage)* wild **(b)** *(mer, vie, période)* turbulent **(c)** *(visage, personne, âme)* tortured

tourmenter [turmɑ̃te] **1** *vt* to torment **2 se tourmenter** *vpr* to worry

tournage [turnaʒ] *nm (d'un film)* shooting, filming; **sur le t.** on shoot

tournant, -e [turnɑ̃, -ɑ̃t] **1** *adj* **(a)** *(fauteuil, siège)* swivel; *(pont)* swing **(b)** *(grève)* rotating **2** *nm* **(a)** *(de route, de rivière)* bend **(b)** *Fig (changement)* turning point **(de** in)

tourné, -e [turne] *adj* **(a)** *(formulé)* **bien/mal t.** well/ badly phrased **(b)** *(disposé)* **avoir l'esprit mal t.** to have a dirty mind

tournebouler [turnəbule] *vt Fam* to upset

tournebroche [turnəbrɔʃ] *nm* spit

tourne-disque *(pl* **tourne-disques)** [turnədisk] *nm* record player

tournedos [turnədo] *nm* tournedos, fillet steak

tournée [turne] *nf* **(a)** *(du facteur, d'un inspecteur)* round; **faire sa t.** to do one's rounds; **faire la t. de** *(magasins, musées)* to go round; **faire sa t. électorale** to go on one's election tour; **faire la t. des grands-ducs** to go out on the town **(b)** *(théâtrale, musicale)* tour; **en t.** on tour **(c)** *Fam (consommations)* round

tournemain [turnəmɛ̃] **en un tournemain** *adv Litt* in an instant

tourner [turne] **1** *vt* **(a)** *(clé, tête, yeux)* to turn; **t. et retourner qch entre ses mains** to turn sth over and over in one's hands; *Fig* **t. et retourner qch (dans tous les sens)** to go over and over an idea (in one's mind); **t. le dos à qn/qch** *(action)* to turn one's back on sb/sth; *(position)* to have one's back to sb/sth; **t. les talons** *(partir)* to turn on one's heel; **t. la tête à qn** *(succès, vin)* to go to sb's head; *(personne)* to turn sb's head **(b)** *(page)* to turn (over) **(c)** *(remuer)* to stir; *(salade)* to toss **(d)** *(film, documentaire, scène)* to shoot, to film

(e) *(attention, pensées)* to turn **(vers** to) **(f)** *(changer)* t. qn/qch en ridicule to make fun of sb/sth **(g)** *(contourner) (coin de la rue)* to turn, to go round; *(obstacle, difficulté, loi)* to get round **(h)** *(confectionner) (pièce détachée)* to turn on a lathe; *(pot)* to throw; *Fig (phrase)* to turn; *(compliment)* to word **2** *vi* **(a)** *(clé, roue, aiguille, planète)* to turn; *(porte)* to swing; *(toupie)* to spin; **l'heure tourne** time is getting on; **t. de l'œil** to pass out **(b)** *(se déplacer en rond)* to go round; *aussi Fig* **t. en rond** to go round in circles; *Fam* **il y a quelque chose qui ne tourne pas rond** there's something not right somewhere; *Fam* **il ne tourne pas rond en ce moment** he's not quite himself at the moment; *Fig* **t. autour de qch** *(avoir pour centre)* to centre on sth; *(par convoitise)* to hover round sth; *(valoir environ)* to be in the region of sth; *Fig* **t. autour du pot** to beat about the bush **(c)** *(entreprise, moteur)* to run **(d)** *(obliquer)* to turn; **tournez à gauche** turn left **(e)** *(changer) (vent)* to shift **(à** to); *(chance)* to turn **(f)** *(lait)* to turn, to go off **(g)** *(avoir telle issue)* **t. court** to end abruptly; **bien/mal t** *(personne)* to turn out well/badly; **ça va mal t.** it's going to go wrong; **à l'aigre** to turn sour **(h)** *(dans un film)* to act **3 se tourner** *vpr* to turn **(vers** towards); *Fig* **se t. vers qn/ qch** to turn to sb/sth; *Fam* **se t. les pouces** to twiddle one's thumbs

tournesol [turnɔsɔl] *nm* sunflower

tourneur, -euse [turnœr, -øz] *nm,f (ouvrier)* turner

tournevis [turnəvis] *nm* screwdriver; **t. cruciforme** Phillips® screwdriver

tournicoter [turnikɔte] *vi Fam* to wander round and round

tourniquet [turnikɛ] *nm* **(a)** *(barrière)* turnstile **(b)** *(porte à tambour)* revolving door **(c)** *(présentoir)* revolving stand **(d)** *(arroseur)* sprinkler

tournis [turni] *nm Fam* **avoir le t.** to feel dizzy; **donner le t. à qn** to make sb dizzy

tournoi [turnwa] *nm* tournament

tournoiement [turnwamã] *nm (des oiseaux)* wheeling; *(des feuilles mortes)* swirl

tournoyer [turnwaje] *vi (oiseaux)* to wheel; *(des feuilles mortes)* to swirl (round); **faire t. qch** to twirl sth

tournure [turnyr] *nf* **(a)** *(des événements)* turn; **prendre une mauvaise t.** to take a turn for the worse **(b)** *(forme)* **prendre t.** to take shape; **t. d'esprit** turn of mind; **t. (de phrase)** turn of phrase

tour-opérateur *(pl* **tour-opérateurs)** [turɔperatœr] *nm* tour operator

tourte [turt] *nf* pie

tourteau, -x [turto] *nm (crustacé)* edible crab

tourtereau, -x [turtəro] *nm* young turtledove; *Fig* **tourtereaux** *(amoureux)* lovebirds

tourterelle [turtərɛl] *nf* turtledove

tourtière [turtjɛr] *nf* **(a)** *(pour tourte)* pie dish **(b)** *Can* – (minced) pork pie

tous [tu, tus] *voir* **tout**

Toussaint [tusɛ̃] *nf* **la T.** All Saints' Day

tousser [tuse] *vi* to cough; *Fig (moteur)* to splutter

toussotement [tusɔtmã] *nm* slight cough

toussoter [tusɔte] *vi (avoir une toux)* to have a slight cough; *(pour attirer l'attention)* to give a slight cough

tout, toute *(pl* **tous, toutes)** [tu, tut]

when **tous** is a pronoun as in **3 (b)**, it is pronounced [tus].

1 *adj (entier)* **t. l'univers** the whole universe; **t. mon argent** all my money; **toute la journée** the whole day; **je ne l'ai pas vu de toute la journée** I haven't seen him all day; **leT.-Paris** anyone who's anyone in Paris **2** *adj indéfini* **(a)** *(n'importe quel)* any; **t. élève en retard sera puni** any pupil arriving late will be punished; **à t. moment** at any time; **t. autre que vous** anybody but you **(b)** *(chaque)* every; **tous les élèves de la classe** every pupil in the class; **toutes nos chambres ont l'air conditionné** all our rooms have air-conditioning; **tous les deux jours** every second day, every other day; **ils se retournèrent t. deux** they both turned round **(c)** *(emploi intensif)* **à la toute dernière minute** at the very last minute; **de toute beauté** magnificent; **donner toute satisfaction à qn** to give sb complete *or* full satisfaction; **pour toute réponse, il éclata en sanglots** his only answer was to burst into tears; **je suis t. à toi** I'm all yours **3** *pron indéfini* **(a)** *(au singulier)* everything; **elle a t.** she has everything; **elle a t. de son père** she's her father's daughter; **il a t. du fonctionnaire** he's the typical civil servant; **être t. pour qn** to mean everything to sb; **manger de t.** to eat everything *or* anything; **elle fera t. pour t'ennuyer** she'll do anything to annoy you; **t. ce qu'il y a d'intéressant dans ce film, c'est...** the only interesting thing in this film is...; **ce sera t.?** *(dans un magasin)* will that be all *or* everything?; **elle est jolie/gentille comme t.** she's really pretty/nice; **tu n'y vas pas et c'est t.!** you're not going and that's that!; *Fam* ...**et t.** **et t.!** ...and all that sort of stuff **(b)** *(au pluriel)* all; **ils sont tous partis** they all left **4** *adv* **(a)** *(très)* very; **t. près** very close **(b)** *(complètement)* **être t. en noir** to be (dressed) all in black; **être t. en sueur** to be pouring with sweat; **t. autrement** quite differently; **être t. à qch** to be engrossed in sth; **t. enfant, il...** as a very young child, he... **(c)** *(suivi d'un gérondif)* **t. en conduisant/écrivant** while driving/writing **(d)** **t. ignorant/secrétaire que je suis** ou **sois...** I may be ignorant/just a secretary but... **(e)** *(expressions)* **t. à fait** *(complètement)* quite, completely; *(exactement)* exactly; **pas du t.** not at all; **t. à l'heure** *(dans le futur)* in a little while, shortly; *(dans le passé)* a little while ago; **à t. à l'heure!** see you later!; **t. de suite** right away, immediately; **à t. de suite** see you in a minute **5** *nm* **(a)** *(l'ensemble)* the whole; **le t., c'est de se concentrer** the most important thing is to concentrate

tout-à-l'égout [tutalegu] *nm inv* mains drainage

toutefois [tutfwa] *adv* however

toute-puissance [tutpɥisɑ̃s] *nf* absolute power

tout-fou *(pl* **tout-fous)** [tufu] *adj m Fam* crazy

toutou [tutu] *nm Fam* doggie

tout-petit *(pl* **tout-petits)** [tupti] *nm* tot, toddler

tout-puissant, toute-puissante *(mpl* **tout-puissants,** *fpl* **toutes-puissantes)** [tupɥisɑ̃, -ɑ̃t] **1** *adj* all-powerful **2** *nm* **le T.** the Almighty

tout-terrain *(pl* **tout-terrains)** [tutɛrɛ̃] *adj (véhicule)* all-terrain, off-road; *(vélo)* mountain

tout-venant [tuvnɑ̃] *nm* **le t.** *(gens)* ordinary people; *(choses)* ordinary things

toux [tu] *nf* cough; **t. sèche/grasse** dry/loose cough

toxicité [tɔksisite] *nf* toxicity

toxico [tɔksiko] *nmf Fam* addict

toxicologie [tɔksikɔlɔʒi] *nf* toxicology

toxicomane [tɔksikɔman] **1** *adj* addicted to drugs **2** *nmf* drug addict

toxicomanie [tɔksikɔmani] *nf* drug addiction

toxine [tɔksin] *nf* toxin

toxique [tɔksik] *adj* toxic, poisonous; *(gaz)* poison
toxoplasmose [tɔksoplasmoz] *nf* toxoplasmosis
TP [tepe] *nmpl* (*abrév* **travaux pratiques**) practical work
TPI [tepei] *nm* (*abrév* **Tribunal pénal international**) International Court of Justice
trac¹ [trak] *nm* nerves; *(au théâtre)* stage fright; **avoir le t.** to be nervous; *(acteur)* to have stage fright
trac² **tout à trac** *adv Vieilli* out of the blue
tracas [traka] *nm* worry, trouble
tracasser [trakase] **1** *vt* to worry, to bother
  2 se tracasser *vpr* to worry (**pour** about)
tracasserie [trakasri] *nf* worry; **les tracasseries administratives** red tape
tracassier, -ère [trakasje, -ɛr] *adj* nitpicking
trace [tras] *nf* (**a**) *(d'animal, d'une personne, de pneus)* tracks; **être sur la t. de qn/qch** to be on the track of sb/sth; **disparaître sans laisser de t.** to disappear without trace; **perdre la t. de qn** to lose track of sb; *Fig* **marcher sur** *ou* **suivre les traces de qn** to follow in sb's footsteps; **t. directe** *(en ski)* direct descent (**b**) *(tache)* mark; **des traces de gras** greasy marks; **des traces de doigts** finger marks; **des traces de pas** footprints; *Fig* **laisser des traces chez qn** *(traumatisme)* to leave its mark on sb; *aussi Fig* **effacer toute t. de qch** to cover up all traces of sth (**c**) *(petite quantité, vestige)* trace
tracé [trase] *nm* (**a**) *(plan)* layout; **faire le t. de qch** to plan the layout of sth (**b**) *(d'une côte)* line
tracer [trase] **1** *vt* (**a**) *(ligne, plan)* to draw; *Math (courbe, graphique)* to plot; *(lettre)* to write; *Fig* **t. les grandes lignes de qch** to give the general outline of sth (**b**) *(route, chemin)* to mark out; *Fig* **son chemin est tout tracé** his path is all mapped out for him
  2 *vi Fam (aller vite)* to bomb along
traceur [trasœr] *nm Ordinat* **t. (de courbes)** plotter; **t. à tambour** drum plotter
trachée-artère (*pl* **trachées-artères**) [trafeartɛr] *nf* windpipe, *Spéc* trachea
trachéite [trakeit] *nf* throat infection
tract [trakt] *nm* leaflet
tractations [traktasjɔ̃] *nfpl* dealings, negotiations
tracter [trakte] *vt* to tow
tracteur [traktœr] *nm* tractor
traction [traksjɔ̃] *nf* (**a**) *(en gymnastique) (à la barre, aux anneaux)* pull-up; *(au sol) Br* press-up, *Am* push-up (**b**) *(véhicule)* **t. avant/arrière** front-wheel/rear-wheel drive (**c**) *(action)* traction, pulling
tradition [tradisjɔ̃] *nf* tradition; **dans la plus pure t. française** in true French tradition
traditionalisme [tradisjonalism] *nm* traditionalism
traditionaliste [tradisjonalist] *adj & nmf* traditionalist
traditionnel, -elle [tradisjonɛl] *adj* (**a**) *(fondé sur la tradition)* traditional (**b**) *(habituel)* usual
traditionnellement [tradisjonɛlmɑ̃] *adv* traditionally
traducteur, -trice [tradyktœr, -tris] **1** *nm,f* translator
  2 *nm Ordinat* translator
traduction [tradyksjɔ̃] *nf* (*action, texte*) translation (**de/ en** from/into); **t. automatique/simultanée** machine/ simultaneous translation; **t. assistée par ordinateur** computer-assisted translation
traduire [tradɥir] **1** *vt* (**a**) *(texte, terme)* to translate (**de/en** from/into); *Fig (sentiment)* to express (**b**) **t. qn en justice** to bring sb before the courts
  2 *vi* to translate (**de/en** from/into)
  3 se traduire *vpr (terme)* to be translated; *Fig* **se t. par qch**

(se manifester par) to be expressed by sth; *(avoir pour résultat)* to result in
traduisible [tradɥizibl] *adj* translatable
trafic [trafik] *nm* (**a**) *(de véhicules)* traffic; **t. aérien** air traffic (**b**) *(de marchandises)* traffic; **t. de drogue** drug trafficking
traficoter [trafikɔte] *Fam* **1** *vi* to be on the fiddle
  2 *vt* (**a**) *(vin)* to doctor; *(comptes)* to fiddle (**b**) *(manigancer)* **je me demande ce qu'il traficote** I wonder what he's up to
trafiquant, -e [trafikɑ̃, -ɑ̃t] *nm,f Péj* trafficker; **t. d'armes** arms dealer; **t. de drogue** drug trafficker
trafiquer [trafike] *vt Fam* (**a**) *(moteur)* to tinker with; *(freins, compteur)* to tamper with; *(vin)* to doctor; *(comptes)* to fiddle (**b**) *(manigancer)* **qu'est-ce qu'il trafique?** what's he up to?
tragédie [traʒedi] *nf* tragedy; *Fam Fig* **ce n'est pas une t.!** it's not the end of the world!
tragédien, -enne [traʒedjɛ̃, -ɛn] *nm,f* tragic actor, *f* tragic actress
tragi-comédie (*pl* **tragi-comédies**) [traʒikɔmedi] *nf* tragi-comedy
tragi-comique (*pl* **tragi-comiques**) [traʒikɔmik] *adj* tragi-comic
tragique [traʒik] **1** *adj* tragic
  2 *nm* (**a**) *(d'un événement)* tragedy; *Fig* **prendre qch au t.** to make a big thing out of sth (**b**) *(genre)* **le t.** tragedy (**c**) *(auteur)* tragic author
trahir [trair] **1** *vt* (**a**) *(personne, pays)* to betray (**b**) *(secret)* to betray, to give away (**c**) *(gêne, ignorance)* to betray (**d**) *(sujet: jambes, forces)* to fail
  2 se trahir *vpr* to give oneself away
trahison [traizɔ̃] *nf* (*d'une personne, d'un pays)* betrayal; *Jur* treason; **haute t.** high treason
train [trɛ̃] *nm* (**a**) *(moyen de transport, véhicule)* train; **voyager en t.** *ou* **par le t.** to travel by train; **être dans un t.** to be on a train; *Fig* **prendre le t. en marche** to jump or climb on the bandwagon; **t. autocouchette(s)** car-sleeper train; **t. de banlieue** commuter train; **t. corail** express train; **t. électrique** electric train; **t. express** express train; **t. à grande vitesse** high-speed train; **t. de marchandises** *Br* goods *or Am* freight train (**b**) *(de réformes)* series (**c**) *(derrière d'un animal) (de chien)* rump; *Fam (d'une personne)* backside, rear (**d**) *(allure)* pace; **au t. où vont les choses** at the rate things are going; **à ce t.-là** at this rate; **aller bon t.** to go at a good pace; **rouler à un t. d'enfer** to go hell for leather (**e**) **t. d'atterrissage** *(d'un avion)* landing gear, undercarriage (**f**) *(locutions)* **en t.** *(projet, affaire)* under way; **mettre qch en t.** to get sth started; **être en t. de faire qch** to be doing sth; **mener grand t.** to live it up; **t. de vie** lifestyle
traînailler [trɛnaje] = **traînasser**
traînant, -e [trɛnɑ̃, -ɑ̃t] *adj* (**a**) *(robe)* trailing (**b**) *(voix)* drawling; *(démarche, pas)* dragging
traînard, -e [trɛnar, -ard] *nm,f (promeneur)* straggler; *(travailleur)* dawdler
traînasser [trɛnase] *vi Fam* (**a**) *(errer)* to hang around (**b**) *(être lent)* to dawdle
train-couchettes [trɛ̃kuʃɛt] *nm inv* sleeper
traîne [trɛn] *nf* (**a**) *(d'une robe)* train (**b**) *(à la pêche)* drag net (**c**) *Can* **t. sauvage** toboggan (**d**) *Fam* **être à la t.** to lag behind
traîneau, -x [trɛno] *nm (tiré par des chevaux)* sleigh; *(tiré par des chiens) Br* sledge, *Am* sled
traînée [trɛne] *nf* (**a**) *(trace)* trail; **se répandre comme une t. de poudre** to spread like wildfire (**b**) *Fam Péj (femme)* tart
traîne-misère [trɛnmizɛr] *nmf inv Fam* down-and-out

traîner [trɛne] **1** *vt* **(a)** *(tirer) (objet, corps)* to drag; *(wagon)* to pull **(b)** *Fig* **t. un rhume** to have a nagging cold **(c)** *Péj (vieilles affaires)* to drag around; **t. qn chez le dentiste** to drag sb along to the dentist **(d)** *(locutions)* **t. les pieds** to drag one's feet; *Fam* **t. ses guêtres** *ou* **bottes** to hang around
2 *vi* **(a) t. par terre** *(jupe)* to trail on the ground **(b)** *(rester en arrière)* to lag behind **(c)** *(errer)* to hang around **(d)** *(virus)* to go around **(e)** *(affaires, livres, vêtements)* to lie around; **laisser t. qch** to leave sth lying around **(f)** *(être lent) (personne)* to dawdle; *(conversation, intrigue)* to drag; **t. en longueur** to drag on; **ça ne traîne pas avec vous!** you don't hang about!
3 se traîner *vpr* **(a)** *(sur le sol)* to crawl; *Fig (être fatigué)* to feel like a wet rag; *(aller à contrecœur)* to drag oneself along **(b)** *(journée, soirée)* to drag on

training [trɛniŋ] *nm (survêtement)* tracksuit

train-train [trɛ̃trɛ̃] *nm Fam* routine; **le t. quotidien** the daily grind

traire [trɛr] *vt* **(a)** *(vache, chèvre)* to milk **(b)** *(lait)* to draw

trait [trɛ] *nm* **(a)** *(ligne)* line; **d'un t. de plume** with a stroke of the pen; *Fig* **c'est sa sœur t. pour t.** she is her sister to a T; *Fig* **tirer un t. sur qch** to draw a line under sth; **t. d'union** hyphen; *Fig* **link (b)** *(du visage)* features; **des traits réguliers/fins** regular/fine features; **avoir les traits tirés** to look drawn **(c)** *(caractéristique)* feature, trait; **les grands traits de qch** the main features of sth; **t. de caractère** character trait **(d)** *Fig* **t. d'esprit** flash of wit; **t. de génie** stroke of genius **(e)** *(de lumière)* shaft **(f)** *(locutions)* **avoir t. à qch** to be connected with sth, to relate to sth; **boire qch à longs traits** to gulp sth down; **boire/lire qch d'un (seul) t.** to drink/read sth in one go

traitable [trɛtabl] *adj (sujet)* manageable

traitant, -e [trɛtɑ̃, -ɑ̃t] *adj (shampoing, crème)* medicated

traite [trɛt] *nf* **(a)** *Fin* draft, bill, **t. bancaire** bank draft **(b)** *(des vaches)* milking **(c)** *(trafic)* **la t. des Blanches** the white slave trade; **la t. des Noirs** the slave trade **(d)** *(locutions)* **(tout) d'une t., d'une seule t.** in one go

traité [trɛte] *nm* **(a)** *(ouvrage)* treatise **(de** *ou* **sur** on) **(b)** *(accord)* treaty

traitement [trɛtmɑ̃] *nm* **(a)** *(de personne, de maladie)* treatment; **t. de choc** shock treatment; **t. de faveur** preferential treatment **(b)** *(de matières premières)* processing; *(de l'eau)* treatment **(c)** *(rémunération)* salary **(d)** *Ordinat* processing; **données en t., capacité** *ou* **débit de t.** throughput; **t. à distance** teleprocessing; **t. des données** data processing, DP; **t. électronique de l'information** electronic data processing, EDP; **t. d'images** image processing; **t. de l'information** *ou* **des informations** data processing, DP; **t. par lots** batch processing; **t. en temps réel** real time processing; **t. de texte** word processing, WP; *(logiciel)* word processor, word processing software; **t. de texte à balises** word processing with embedded visible commands; **t. vectoriel** vector processing

traiter [trɛte] **1** *vt* **(a)** *(se conduire envers)* to treat; **t. qn en ami/frère** to treat sb like a friend/a brother **(b)** *(qualifier)* **t. qn de lâche/de menteur** to call sb a coward/a liar **(c)** *(patient, maladie)* to treat **(d)** *(matières premières, minerai)* to process; *(eau, bois, cultures)* to treat **(e)** *Ordinat (informations)* to process; **données non traitées** raw data **(f)** *(marché)* to negotiate; *(affaire)* to handle; **t. avec qn** to deal with sb **(g)** *(sujet, question, demande)* to deal with
2 traiter de *vt ind (sujet, problème)* to deal with
3 se traiter *vpr* **(a)** *(l'un l'autre)* **se t. d'imbéciles/lâches** to call each other idiots/cowards **(b)** *(être guéri)* **cette maladie se traite très bien maintenant** this disease responds very well to treatment now

traiteur [trɛtœr] *nm* caterer; **chez le t.** at the deli

traître, -esse [trɛtr, trɛtrɛs] **1** *adj (personne, virage)* treacherous; *(soleil, vin)* deceptively strong; **pas un t. mot** not a single word
2 *nm.f* traitor, *f* traitress; **être t. à sa patrie** to be a traitor to one's country; **en t.** treacherously

traîtreusement [trɛtrøzmɑ̃] *adv* treacherously

traîtrise [trɛtriz] *nf* **(a)** *(caractère)* treachery **(b)** *(action)* act of treachery

trajectoire [traʒɛktwar] *nf* path, trajectory

trajet [traʒɛ] *nm* **(a)** *(voyage)* journey; **faire le t. en voiture** to do the journey by car, **deux heures de t.** a two-hour journey **(b)** *(distance)* distance **(c)** *(itinéraire)* route

tralala [tralala] *nm inv Fam* **faire des tralalas** to make a great fuss; **... et tout le t.** ... etcetera, etcetera

tram [tram] = **tramway**

trame [tram] *nf (d'un tissu)* weft; *Fig (d'un récit)* framework

tramer [trame] **1** *vt (complot)* to hatch; **t. quelque chose** to be plotting something
2 se tramer *vpr* **il se trame quelque chose** there's something afoot

tramontane [tramɔ̃tan] *nf* tramontana

trampoline [trɑ̃pɔlin] *nm* **(a)** *(appareil)* trampoline **(b)** *(sport)* trampolining; **faire du t.** to go trampolining

tramway [tramwɛ] *nm Br* tram, *Am* streetcar

tranchant, -e [trɑ̃ʃɑ̃, -ɑ̃t] **1** *adj* **(a)** *(outil, épée, bord)* sharp **(b)** *Fig (ton, personne)* curt
2 *nm (d'une lame)* cutting edge; *(de la main)* edge; *Fig* **à double t.** double-edged

tranche [trɑ̃ʃ] *nf* **(a)** *(de pain, de melon, de viande)* slice; **t. napolitaine** Neapolitan ice cream **(b)** *(d'un livre)* edge; **doré sur t.** gilt-edged **(c)** *(partie) (de paiement)* instalment; *(de revenus)* group; *(d'imposition)* band, bracket; **t. d'âge** age bracket; **t. horaire** *(time)* slot; **t. de vie** slice of life **(d)** *Fam* **s'en payer une t.** to have the time of one's life

tranché, -e [trɑ̃ʃe] *(opinion)* clear-cut

tranchée [trɑ̃ʃe] *nf* trench

trancher [trɑ̃ʃe] **1** *vt* **(a)** *(cordage, câble)* to cut; *(gorge)* to slit, to cut; **la tête à qn** to cut off sb's head; **la machine lui a tranché le doigt** the machine severed his finger **(b)** *(question, différend)* to settle
2 *vi* **(a)** *(décider)* to decide; *Fig* **t. dans le vif** to take drastic action **(b)** *(couleurs)* to contrast **(sur** with)

tranquille [trɑ̃kil] *adj* **(a)** *(paisible)* quiet; *(mer)* calm; *(sommeil)* peaceful; **laisser qn t.** to leave sb alone **(b)** *(rassuré)* **sentir t.** to feel at peace; **vous pouvez dormir t.** you can rest easy; **je ne suis pas t.** I'm feeling uneasy; **avoir l'esprit t.** to have peace of mind

tranquillement [trɑ̃kilmɑ̃] *adv (calmement)* calmly; *(doucement)* quietly; *(dormir)* peacefully; *(partir)* with one's mind at rest

tranquillisant, -e [trɑ̃kilizɑ̃, -ɑ̃t] **1** *adj* **(a)** *(nouvelles, paroles)* reassuring; *(effet)* soothing **(b)** *(médicament)* tranquillizing
2 *nm* tranquillizer

tranquilliser [trɑ̃kilize] **1** *vt* to reassure
2 se tranquilliser *vpr* to set one's mind at rest

tranquillité [trɑ̃kilite] *nf (calme)* quietness; *(de la mer)* calmness; *(du sommeil)* peacefulness; **avoir besoin de t.** to need peace and quiet; **en toute t.** *(sans être dérangé)* without being disturbed; *(sans souci)* with an easy mind; **t. d'esprit** peace of mind

transaction [trɑ̃zaksjɔ̃] *nf* **(a)** *(opération)* transaction **(b)** *Jur* compromise

transactionnel, -elle [trɑ̃zaksjɔnɛl] *adj* **(a)** *Jur (solution)* compromise **(b)** *Psy (analyse)* transactional

transalpin, -e [trɑ̃zalpɛ̃, -in] *adj* transalpine

transat [trãzat] **1** *nm Fam* deckchair
2 *nf* transatlantic race
transatlantique [trãzatlãtik] **1** *adj* transatlantic
2 *nm* (**a**) *(paquebot)* transatlantic liner (**b**) *(chaise longue)* deckchair
transbahuter [trãsbayte] *vt Fam* to cart, to lug
transbordement [trãsbɔrdəmã] *nm* transfer; *Naut* transhipment
transcendant, -e [trãsãdã, -ãt] *adj* transcendent; *Fam* **ce n'est pas t.** it's nothing special
transcendantal, -e, -aux, -ales [trãsãdãtal, -o] *adj* transcendental
transcender [trãsãde] **1** *vt* to transcend
2 se transcender *vpr* to surpass oneself
transcontinental, -e, -aux, -ales [trãskɔ̃tinãtal, -o] *adj* transcontinental
transcription [trãskripsjɔ̃] *nf* (**a**) *(action)* transcription; *(dans un autre alphabet)* transliteration; **t. phonétique** phonetic transcription; **t. génétique** genetic transcription (**b**) *(texte)* transcript
transcrire [trãskrir] *vt* to transcribe; *(dans un autre alphabet)* to transliterate
transcutané, -e [trãskytane] *adj* transcutaneous
transe [trãs] *nf* trance; **être en t.** to be in a trance; *Fig* to be beside oneself
transept [trãsɛpt] *nm* transept
transférer [trãsfere] *vt* to transfer
transfert [trãsfɛr] *nm* transfer; *Psy* transference; *Tél* **t. d'appels** call transfer; *Ordinat* **t. de données** data transfer; *Ordinat* **t. électronique de fonds** electronic funds transfer, EFT
transfigurer [trãsfigyre] *vt* to transfigure
transformable [trãsfɔrmabl] *adj* convertible
transformateur [trãsfɔrmatœr] *nm* transformer
transformation [trãsfɔrmasjɔ̃] *nf* (**a**) *(changement)* transformation; *(d'un local)* conversion (**b**) *(de matières premières)* processing (**c**) *(au rugby)* conversion; **faire une t.** to convert
transformer [trãsfɔrme] **1** *vt* (**a**) *(changer)* to transform; *(local, maison)* to convert; **t. qn/qch en qch** to turn sb/sth into sth (**b**) *(matières premières)* to process (**c**) *(au rugby)* *(essai)* to convert
2 se transformer *vpr* to change; **se t. en qch** to turn into sth
transfuge [trãsfyʒ] *nmf* defector
transfuser [trãsfyze] *vt (sang)* to transfuse; *Fam* **t. qn** to give sb a transfusion
transfusion [trãsfyzjɔ̃] *nf* **t. (sanguine)** (blood) transfusion; **faire une t. à qn** to give sb a transfusion
transgresser [trãsgrese] *vt (règlement, loi)* to infringe; *(ordres)* to disobey
transgression [trãsgresjɔ̃] *nf (du règlement, de la loi)* infringement; *(d'ordres)* disobeying
transhumance [trãzymãs] *nf* = the moving of livestock to different pastures according to the season
transhumer [trãzyme] *vt & vi* = to move to different pastures according to the season
transi, -e [trãzi] *adj* (**a**) *(paralysé)* **t. (de peur)** paralysed with fear; **t. (de froid)** chilled to the bone (**b**) *Fam (amoureux)* bashful
transiger [trãziʒe] *vi* to compromise (**sur** on); **t. avec sa conscience** to compromise one's principles
transistor [trãzistɔr] *nm* (**a**) *Él (dispositif)* transistor (**b**) *(poste de radio)* transistor (radio)

transit [trãzit] *nm* (**a**) *(de passagers, de marchandises)* transit; **en t.** in transit (**b**) *(intestinal)* transit; **facilite le t. intestinal** *(sur paquet)* keeps you regular
transiter [trãzite] **1** *vt (marchandises)* to forward
2 *vi* (**a**) *(marchandises, voyageurs)* to pass in transit (**par** through)
transitif, -ive [trãzitif, -iv] *adj Gram* transitive
transition [trãzisjɔ̃] *nf* transition; **assurer la t.** to ensure a smooth transition; **sans t.** abruptly
transitivement [trãzitivmã] *adv* transitively
transitivité [trãzitivite] *nf* transitivity
transitoire [trãzitwar] *adj* transitional
translation [trãslasjɔ̃] *nf Math* translation
translucide [trãslysid] *adj* translucent
transmanche [trãzmãʃ] *adj inv* cross-Channel
transmetteur [trãsmetœr] *nm Ordinat & Biol* transmitter
transmettre [trãsmɛtr] **1** *vt* (**a**) *(lumière, chaleur, énergie)* to transmit (**b**) *(maladie, virus)* to pass on, to transmit (**à** to) (**c**) *(recette, don)* to hand on (**à** to); *(tradition, objet)* to hand down (**à** to); *(pouvoir)* to hand over (**à** to) (**d**) *(message, ordre, amitiés)* to pass on (**à** to) (**e**) *TV & Rad (information)* to transmit; *(émission)* to broadcast (**f**) *Jur (propriété, droit)* to transfer; *(actions)* to assign; **t. ses pouvoirs à qn** to hand over to sb
2 se transmettre *vpr* (**a**) *(maladie, virus)* to be passed on (**b**) *(recette, don)* to be handed on; *(tradition, objet)* to be handed down
transmissible [trãsmisibl] *adj* (**a**) *(maladie)* transmissible; **maladie sexuellement t.** sexually transmitted disease (**b**) *(droit, fortune)* transferable
transmission [trãsmisjɔ̃] *nf* (**a**) *(de la chaleur, de la lumière, d'une maladie, d'un virus)* transmission; *(d'un message, d'un ordre)* passing on; *(d'une tradition)* handing down; **t. de pensée** thought transference (**b**) *TV & Rad (d'une image, d'un message)* transmission; *(d'une émission)* broadcasting (**c**) *Ordinat* transmission; **t. de données** data transmission or transfer; **t. par modem** modem transmission; **t. de paquets** packet transmission (**d**) *Jur (d'une propriété, d'un droit)* transfer, transference; *(d'actions)* assignment (**e**) *Mil* **les transmissions** the signals
transocéanien, -enne [trãzɔseanjɛ̃, -ɛn], **transocéanique** [trãzɔseanik] *adj* transoceanic
transparaître [trãsparɛtr] *vi* to show (through)
transparence [trãsparãs] *nf* (**a**) *(d'un tissu, d'une allusion, d'un parti politique)* transparency; **voir qch par t.** to see sth shining through (**b**) *Cin* back projection
transparent, -e [trãsparã, -ãt] **1** *adj aussi Fig* transparent
2 *nm* transparency
transpercer [trãspɛrse] *vt (sujet: lame, flèche, balle)* to pierce; *(sujet: froid, vent, pluie)* to go right through
transpiration [trãspirasjɔ̃] *nf* (**a**) *(sueur)* sweat, perspiration (**b**) *(action)* sweating, perspiration
transpirer [trãspire] *vi* (**a**) *(personne)* to sweat, to perspire; **t. des pieds** to have sweaty feet; **t. à grosses gouttes** to drip with sweat (**b**) *Fig (secret, nouvelles)* to leak out (**c**) *Fam* **t. sur** *(travailler à)* to sweat over
transplant [trãsplã] *nm Méd* transplant
transplantation [trãsplãtasjɔ̃] *nf* (**a**) *(d'arbres, de personnes)* transplantation (**b**) *(d'organes)* transplant; **t. cardiaque/rénale** heart/kidney transplant
transplanté, -e [trãsplãte] *adj (organe)* transplanted; **malade t.** transplant patient
transplanter [trãsplãte] *vt* to transplant
transport [trãspɔr] *nm* (**a**) *(de marchandises, de passagers)*

transport; **les transports** transport; **les transports aériens** air transport; **les transports en commun** public transport; **t. fluvial** inland waterway transport **(b)** *Jur (de biens, de droits)* transfer **(c)** *Litt (émotion)* rapture; *(de joie)* transports; *(de colère)* outbursts

transportable [trɑ̃spɔrtabl] *adj (marchandises)* transportable; *(blessé)* able to be moved

transporter [trɑ̃spɔrte] *vt* **(a)** *(passagers, troupes, marchandises)* to transport, to carry; **t. qn à l'hôpital** to take sb to hospital **(b)** *(sujet: film, roman)* to transport **(c)** *Litt (ravir)* to transport; **t. qn de joie** to make sb rapturous

transporteur [trɑ̃spɔrtœr] *nm* carrier; **t. routier** road haulier

transposer [trɑ̃spoze] *vt (a) (mots, morceau de musique)* to transpose **(b) t. un roman à l'écran/à la scène** to adapt a novel for the screen/for the stage

transposition [trɑ̃spozisjɔ̃] *nf* **(a)** *(mot, morceau de musique)* transposition **(b) t. à l'écran/à la scène** screen/stage adaptation

transsexuel, -elle [trɑ̃sseksɥɛl] *adj & nmf* transsexual

Transsibérien [trɑ̃ssiberjɛ̃] *nm* **le T.** the Trans-Siberian Railway

transvaser [trɑ̃svaze] *vt* to pour, to transfer; *(vin)* to decant

transversal, -e, -aux, -ales [trɑ̃sversal, -o] *adj (vallée)* transverse; *(rue)* cross; **coupe transversale** cross-section

transversalement [trɑ̃sversalmɑ̃] *adv* crosswise

trapèze [trapɛz] *nm* **(a)** *(forme géométrique)* Br trapezium, Am trapezoid **(b)** *(appareil de gymnastique)* trapeze; **faire du t.** to perform on the trapeze

trapéziste [trapezist] *nmf* trapeze artist

trappage [trapaʒ] *nm Can* trapping

trappe [trap] *nf* **(a)** *(dans le plancher)* trap door **(b)** *(piège)* trap

trappeur [trapœr] *nm* trapper

trapu, -e [trapy] *adj* **(a)** *(homme, cheval)* thickset, stocky; *(bâtiment)* squat **(b)** *Fam (élève, professeur)* brainy **(c)** *Fam (problème)* tough

traquenard [traknar] *nm* trap

traquer [trake] *vt (gibier, criminel)* to hunt; *(vedette)* to hound

traumatisant, -e [tromatizɑ̃, -ɑ̃t] *adj* traumatizing

traumatiser [tromatize] *vt* to traumatize

traumatisme [tromatism] *nm* traumatism, trauma; **t. crânien** severe head injury

travail, -aux [travaj, -o] *nm* **(a)** *(activité)* work; *(de l'imagination, de la mémoire)* workings; **se mettre au t.** to get (down) to work; **allons, au t.!** come on, let's get (down) to work!; **cesser le t.** to stop work; **à t. égal, salaire égal** equal pay for equal work **(b)** *(emploi)* work, job; **chercher du t.** to look for work or a job; **être sans t.** not to have a job, to be out of work; **t. à mi-temps/à plein temps** part-time/full-time work; **t. de bureau** office work; **les travaux des champs** work in the fields; *Univ* **travaux dirigés** tutorial; **travaux forcés** hard labour; *Jur* **t. d'intérêt général** ≃ community service; **t. manuel** manual labour; *Scol* **travaux manuels** arts and crafts; **travaux ménagers** housework; **t. de nuit** night work; *Scol & Univ* **travaux pratiques** practical work **(c)** *(tâche)* (piece of) work, job; **un t. bien/mal fait** a good/bad piece of work; **faire de petits travaux** to do odd jobs; **c'est du beau t.** it's a fine piece of work; *Fam & Ironique* **c'est du beau t.!** that was clever! **(d)** *(lieu de travail)* work **(e)** *Ordinat* job; **t. multitâche** multitasking; **t. en réseau** networking

(f) *(devoir)* work **(g)** **travaux** *(réparations)* work; **le magasin est en travaux** there's work being done on the shop; **attention travaux** *(sur panneau)* roadworks ahead **(h)** *(de l'accouchement)* labour **(i)** *(façonnage)* **le t. du bois** woodwork; **le t. du fer** ironworking; **le t. de l'ivoire/de pierres précieuses** the shaping of ivory/precious stones

travaillé, -e [travaje] *adj* **(a)** *(fer, bois, pierre)* worked **(b)** *(style)* elaborate **(c)** *(tourmenté)* **être t. par qch** to be tormented by sth

travailler [travaje] **1** *vt* **(a)** *(matière, pâte)* to work **(b)** *(sujet, rôle, style)* to work on; *(texte, auteur)* to study; *(morceau de musique, technique)* to practise **(c)** *(inquiéter)* to torment **2** *vi* **(a)** *(personne)* to work; **t. à la pièce** to do piecework; **t. dans qch** to work in sth; **faire t. son argent** to make one's money work for one; **faire t. son imagination** to use one's imagination; *Fam* **t. du chapeau** to have a screw loose **(b)** *(s'entraîner) (sportif)* to train; *(musicien)* to practise **(c)** *(câble)* to strain; *(bois)* to warp; *(murs)* to crack; *(vin)* to ferment **(d)** *(agir)* **t. pour/contre qn** to be on sb's side/against sb **3 travailler à** *vt ind (roman, document, ouvrage)* to work on; **t. à la perte de qn** to try to ruin sb

travailleur, -euse [travajœr, -øz] **1** *adj* hard-working **2** *nm,f* worker; **t. manuel/intellectuel** manual/non-manual worker **t. indépendant** self-employed worker

travailliste [travajist] *Pol* **1** *nmf* member of the Labour Party **2** *adj (parti)* Labour

travée [trave] *nf* **(a)** *(de sièges)* row **(b)** *Archit* bay

traveller's check, traveller's cheque [travlœrʃɛk] *nm Br* traveller's cheque, *Am* traveler's check

travelling [travliŋ] *nm Cin (déplacement)* tracking; *(plan)* tracking shot; **faire un t.** to do a tracking shot; **t. avant/arrière** track in/out

travelo [travlo] *nm Fam* transvestite

travers [travɛr] *nm* **(a)** *(défaut)* failing **(b)** *(largeur)* breadth; *Culin* **t. de porc** spare ribs **(c)** *(locutions)* **à t. qch, au t. de qch** through sth; **à t. les siècles** down the centuries; **à t. le monde** throughout the world; **voir à t. qch** to see through sth; **passer au t. de qch** to go through sth; **marcher de t.** not to walk in a straight line; *Fig* **aller de t.** to go wrong; **être de t.** *(chapeau, tableau)* to be crooked; **prendre qch de t.** to take sth the wrong way; **regarder qn de t.** to look sideways at sb; **comprendre qch de t.** to misunderstand sth; **en t.** crosswise; **en t. de qch** across sth, **se mettre en t. de qch** to get in the way of sth

traverse [travɛrs] *nf (sur une voie ferrée) Br* sleeper, *Am* tie

traversée [traverse] *nf (d'un cours d'eau)* crossing; *(d'une ville, d'une forêt)* going through; *Fig* **t. du désert** time in the wilderness

traverser [traverse] *vt* **(a)** *(rue, pont, cours d'eau)* to cross; *(ville, pays, forêt)* to go through; *Fig* **t. l'esprit de qn** *(idée, doute)* to cross sb's mind **(b)** *(tissu, mur)* to go (right) through **(c)** *(crise, période)* to go through; **t. les siècles** to come down through the ages

traversier, -ère [traversje, -ɛr] **1** *adj voir* flûte **2** *nm Can (bac)* ferry

traversin [travɛrsɛ̃] *nm* bolster

travesti [travesti] *nm* transvestite

travestir [travestir] **1** *vt* **(a)** *(personne)* to dress up **(en** as**)** **(b)** *(vérité, faits, pensée)* to distort **2 se travestir** *vpr* **(a)** *(se déguiser)* to put on fancy dress **(b)** *(s'habiller en femme)* to put on drag

traviole [travjol] **de traviole** *adv Fam* **marcher de t.** to be staggering all over the place; **être de t.** to be lopsided

trayeuse [trejøz] *nf* milking machine

trébucher [trebyʃe] *vi* to trip, to stumble (**sur/contre** over/against); **faire t. qn** to trip sb up

trèfle [trɛfl] *nm* (**a**) *(plante)* clover; **t. à quatre feuilles** four-leaf clover (**b**) *(carte)* club; *(couleur)* clubs

tréfonds [trefɔ̃] *nm Litt* **au t. de son cœur** in one's heart of hearts; **au t. de son âme** in the depths of one's soul

treillage [trɛjaʒ] *nm (clôture)* trellis fencing

treille [trɛj] *nf* (**a**) *(tonnelle)* vine arbour (**b**) *(vigne)* climbing vine

treillis [trɛji] *nm* (**a**) *(treillage)* trellis; **t. métallique** wire mesh (**b**) *(tissu)* canvas (**c**) *(uniforme militaire)* combat uniform

treize [trɛz] **1** *adj inv* thirteen; *Fam* **en avoir t. à la douzaine** to have more than one knows what to do with **2** *nm inv* thirteen; *voir aussi* **trois**

treizième [trɛzjɛm] *adj, nmf & nm* thirteenth; *voir aussi* **cinquième**

trekking [trɛkiŋ] *nm* trek

tréma [trema] *nm* diaeresis; **e/i t.** e/i diaeresis

tremblant, -e [trɑ̃blɑ̃, -ɑ̃t] *adj* (**a**) *(genoux, main)* trembling, shaky; **être t. de peur** to be trembling *or* shaking with fear; **être t. de froid/fièvre** to be shivering with cold/fever (**b**) *(voix)* quavering

tremble [trɑ̃bl] *nm* aspen

tremblement [trɑ̃bləmɑ̃] *nm* (**a**) *(du corps, de la main)* trembling, shaking; *(de peur)* shudder; *(de fièvre)* shivering; **être pris de tremblements** to start to shake; *Fam* **et tout le t.** etcetera etcetera (**b**) *(de la voix)* quavering (**c**) **t. de terre** earthquake

trembler [trɑ̃ble] *vi* (**a**) *(main, genoux)* to shake, to tremble; *(lèvres)* to tremble; **t. de colère** to tremble *or* shake with anger; **t. de froid** to shiver with cold; **t. comme une feuille** to shake like a leaf (**b**) *(voix)* to quaver (**c**) *(terre, bâtiment)* to shake; *(feuilles)* to quiver; *(flamme)* to flicker; **faire t. les vitres** to make the windows shake *or* rattle; **faire t. un bâtiment** to rock *or* shake a building (**d**) *(avoir peur)* to tremble; **t. de tout son corps** to tremble all over; **t. devant qn** to be terrified of sb; **t. pour qn** to tremble for sb

tremblotant, -e [trɑ̃blɔtɑ̃, -ɑ̃t] *adj (personne, corps)* trembling; *(voix)* tremulous; *(lumière)* flickering

tremblote [trɑ̃blɔt] *nf Fam* **avoir la t.** to be shaky; *(de peur)* to have the jitters; *(de froid)* to have the shivers

tremblotement [trɑ̃blɔtmɑ̃] *nm (des mains)* trembling, shaking; *(de la voix)* quavering; *(de la lumière)* flickering

trembloter [trɑ̃blɔte] *vi (personne, mains)* to tremble *or* shake slightly; *(voix)* to quaver; *(lumière)* to flicker

trémière [tremjɛr] *adj f voir* **rose**

trémolo [tremɔlo] *nm* tremolo; *Fig* **avec des trémolos dans la voix** with a tremor in one's voice

trémousser [tremuse] **se trémousser** *vpr* to jig about; **se t. sur sa chaise** to wriggle about on one's chair

trempage [trɑ̃paʒ] *nm* soaking

trempe [trɑ̃p] *nf* (**a**) *(force de caractère)* calibre; **une femme de sa t.** a woman of her calibre (**b**) *Fam (volée de coups)* hiding

trempé, -e [trɑ̃pe] *adj* (**a**) *(personne, vêtement)* soaked; **t. de sueur** *(personne)* dripping with sweat; *(vêtement)* saturated with sweat (**b**) *(acier, verre)* hardened; *Fig* **bien t.** *(caractère)* sturdy

tremper [trɑ̃pe] **1** *vt* (**a**) *(mouiller)* to soak; **se faire t.** **(par la pluie)** to get soaked (**b**) *(plonger)* to dip (**dans** in); **t. les lèvres** to take a small sip (**c**) *(acier)* to quench **2** *vi* (**a**) **faire t. qch, mettre qch à t.** *(linge)* to soak sth (**b**) *Fig (se compromettre)* **t. dans qch** to be mixed up in sth **3** **se tremper** *vpr (se baigner)* to have a quick dip; **se t. les pieds dans l'eau** to go for a paddle

trempette [trɑ̃pɛt] *nf Fam* **faire t.** to have a quick dip

tremplin [trɑ̃plɛ̃] *nm (pour sauteur, pour plongeur) & Fig* springboard; *(pour skieur)* ski jump

trench-coat [*pl* trench-coats) [trɛnʃkot] *nm* trench coat

trentaine [trɑ̃tɛn] *nf* (**a**) *(nombre)* **une t. (de)** about thirty (**b**) *(âge)* **avoir la t.** to be about thirty; **approcher de la t.** to be getting on for thirty

trente [trɑ̃t] **1** *adj inv* thirty; *(au tennis)* **t. à** thirty all **2** *nm inv* thirty; *Fig* **être sur son t. et un** to be dressed up to the nines; *voir aussi* **trois**

trente-six [trɑ̃tsis] **1** *adj inv* thirty-six; *Fam (beaucoup)* umpteen; *Fig* **voir t. chandelles** *(après un coup sur la tête)* to see stars **2** *nm inv* thirty-six; *Fig* **tous les t. du mois** once in a blue moon; *voir aussi* **trois**

trente-sixième [trɑ̃tsizjɛm] *adj Fam Fig* **être au t. dessous** to be really down in the dumps; *voir aussi* **cinquième**

trente-trois tours [trɑ̃ttrwatur] *nm inv* LP

trentième [trɑ̃tjɛm] *nmf, nm & adj* thirtieth; *voir aussi* **cinquième**

trépanation [trepanasjɔ̃] *nf* trepanning

trépaner [trepane] *vt* to trepan

trépas [trepɑ] *nm Litt* death; **passer de vie à t.** to depart this life

trépasser [trepase] *vi Litt* to depart this life

trépidant, -e [trepidɑ̃, -ɑ̃t] *adj (vie, activité)* hectic

trépidation [trepidasjɔ̃] *nf (d'une machine, d'un moteur)* vibration

trépied [trepje] *nm* (**a**) *(d'appareil photo)* tripod (**b**) *(tabouret)* three-legged stool

trépignement [trepiɲəmɑ̃] *nm* stamping (of feet)

trépigner [trepiɲe] *vi* to stamp (one's feet); **t. de colère/d'impatience** to jump up and down with rage/impatience

très [trɛ] *adv* very; **avoir t. faim/chaud/froid** to be very hungry/hot/cold; **avoir t. envie de faire qch** to really want to do sth; **t. estimé** highly respected; **t. aimé** much liked; **t. peu utilisé** very rarely used

trésor [trezɔr] *nm* (**a**) *(objets précieux)* treasure; *Fam* **mon t.** darling; *Fig* **des trésors de patience/générosité** boundless patience/generosity; **t. de guerre** war chest (**b**) *(dans une église)* relics and ornaments (**c**) **leT. (public)** *Br ≃* theTreasury, *Am ≃* theTreasury Department

trésorerie [trezɔrri] *nf* (**a**) *(bureau)* accounts department (**b**) *(ressources)* funds, finances

trésorier, -ère [trezɔrje, -ɛr] *nm,f* treasurer

tressaillement [tresajmɑ̃] *nm (de surprise, de peur)* jump, start; *(de plaisir)* quiver; *(de douleur)* wince

tressaillir [tresajir] *vi (de surprise, de peur)* to jump, to start; *(de plaisir)* to quiver; *(de douleur)* to wince

tressautement [tresotmɑ̃] *nm (secousse)* jolt

tressauter [tresote] *vi (être secoué)* to jolt

tresse [trɛs] *nf* (**a**) *(de cheveux) Br* plait, *Am* braid; **se faire des tresses** to *Br* plait *or Am* braid one's hair (**b**) *(de fil)* braid

tresser [trese] *vt (cheveux) Br* to plait, *Am* to braid; *(paille, osier)* to plait; *(panier, guirlande)* to weave; *Fig* **t. des couronnes à qn** to sing sb's praises

tréteau, -x [treto] *nm* trestle

treuil [trœj] *nm* winch, windlass

trêve [trɛv] *nf* (**a**) *(amnistie)* truce (**b**) *Fig (pause, arrêt)* respite, rest; *Fam* **t. de plaisanteries!** joking apart; **sans t.** unremittingly; *Fam* **t. des confiseurs** = truce over Christmas and New Year between opposing political parties

Trèves [trɛv] n Trier

tri [tri] nm (a) (d'objets, d'idées) sorting out; (de lettres) sorting; (de candidats) selection; **faire le t. dans qch** we'll have to sort through them; **faire du t. dans ses vêtements/papiers** to sort through one's clothes/papers; **t. postal** mail sorting (b) Ordinat sort; **effectuer un t.** to do a sort; **t. alphabétique** alphabetic sort

triage [trijaʒ] nm sorting out; (de lettres) sorting

trial [trijal] nm motorbike trials

triangle [trijãgl] nm triangle; **t. des Bermudes** Bermuda Triangle; **le T. d'or** the Golden Triangle

triangulaire [trijãgylɛr] adj triangular

triathlon [triatlɔ̃] nm triathlon

tribal, -e, -aux, -ales [tribal, -o] adj tribal

tribord [tribɔr] nm starboard; **à t.** on the starboard side

tribu [triby] nf tribe

tribulations [tribylasjɔ̃] nfpl tribulations, troubles

tribun [tribœ̃] nm (a) (magistrat romain) tribune (b) (orateur) popular orator

tribunal, -aux [tribynal, -o] nm (bâtiment) Br court, Am courthouse; (magistrats) court; **porter une affaire devant les tribunaux** to take a case to court; **t. administratif** = court which deals with civil law; **t. de commerce** trade tribunal; **t. pour enfants** juvenile court; **t. de grande instance** = French court of first instance in civil ad criminal matters; **t. d'instance** lowest-level court in the French legal system; **t. militaire** military tribunal

tribune [tribyn] nf (a) (d'orateur) rostrum, platform (b) (débat) forum; **t. libre** (dans un journal) opinion column (c) les tribunes (dans un stade) the stand, t. d'honneur grandstand; **t. de la presse** press gallery

tribut [triby] nm tribute; **le pays a payé un lourd t. à la guerre** the war cost the country dearly

tributaire [tribytɛr] adj (a) (dépendant) **être t. de** to be dependent on (b) (cours d'eau) tributary

tricentenaire [trisɑ̃tnɛr] **1** adj three hundred years old **2** nm tercentenary, tricentennial

triceps [trisɛps] nm triceps

triche [triʃ] nf Fam cheating

tricher [triʃe] vi to cheat; **t. sur qch** to lie about sth; **t. aux cartes/à un examen** to cheat at cards/in an exam

tricherie [triʃri] nf cheating

tricheur, -euse [triʃœr, -øz] nm,f cheat

trichloréthylène [triklɔretilɛn] nm trichlorethylene

tricolore [trikɔlɔr] **1** adj (a) (à trois couleurs) three-coloured (b) (de la France) French **2** nmpl les tricolores the French team

tricorne [trikɔrn] nm three-cornered hat, tricorn

tricot [triko] nm (a) (activité) knitting; **faire du t.** to do some knitting (b) (ouvrage) knitting (c) (chandail) sweater, jumper; **t. de corps** Br vest, Am undershirt (d) (tissu) knitted fabric

tricoter [trikɔte] **1** vt to knit; **tricoté (à la) main** hand-knitted **2** vi to knit; **t. à la main/à la machine** to hand-knit/machine-knit

tricycle [trisikl] nm tricycle; **faire du t.** to go tricycling

trident [tridɑ̃] nm (a) (dans la mythologie) trident (b) (fourche) three-pronged fork

tridimensionnel, -elle [tridimɑ̃sjɔnɛl] adj three-dimensional

triennal, -e, -aux, -ales [trienal, -o] adj (élection, révision) three-yearly, triennial; (bail) three-year

trier [trije] vt (a) (lettres) to sort; (vêtements, informations) to sort or go through; (fruits, lentilles) to pick over; **t. qn/qch sur le volet** to hand-pick sb/sth (b) Ordinat to sort; **t. par ordre alphabétique** to sort in alphabetical order

trifouiller [trifuje] vi Fam **qu'est-ce que tu trifouilles?** what are you up to?; **t. dans qch** to rummage around in sth

triglycéride [trigliserid] nf triglyceride

trigonométrie [trigɔnɔmetri] nf trigonometry

trigonométrique [trigɔnɔmetrik] adj trigonometric

trilatéral, -e, -aux, -ales [trilateral, -o] adj trilateral

trilingue [trilɛ̃g] adj trilingual

trille [trij] nm trill

trilogie [trilɔʒi] nf trilogy

trimaran [trimarɑ̃] nm trimaran

trimbal(l)er [trɛ̃bale] Fam **1** vt (paquets) to lug or cart around; (enfants) to trail around **2 se trimbal(l)er** vpr to trail about; **elle se trimbal(l)e partout avec sa marmaille** she trails her kids around with her everywhere she goes

trimer [trime] vi Fam to slave away; **faire t. qn** to keep sb hard at it

trimestre [trimɛstr] nm quarter; Scol & Univ Br term, Am trimester

trimestriel, -elle [trimɛstrijɛl] adj quarterly

tringle [trɛ̃gl] nf rod; **t. à rideau** curtain rod

trinité [trinite] nf (groupe de trois éléments) trinity; Rel **la (sainte) T.** the (Holy) Trinity; **la T.** (fête) Trinity Sunday

Trinité-et-Tobago [triniteetɔbago] n Trinidad and Tobago

trinquer [trɛ̃ke] vi (a) (porter un toast) to clink glasses; **t. à qn/qch** to drink to sb/sth; **t. à la santé de qn** to drink a toast to sb (b) Fam (souffrir) to be the one who suffers

trio [trijo] nm (a) (groupe de trois personnes) threesome, trio (b) (en musique) trio

triolet [trijɔlɛ] nm Mus triplet

triomphal, -e, -aux, -ales [trijɔ̃fal, -o] adj triumphant

triomphalement [trijɔ̃falmɑ̃] adv triumphantly

triomphalisme [trijɔ̃falism] nm crowing; **sans faire de t....** while I don't want to crow,...

triomphant, -e [trijɔ̃fɑ̃, -ɑ̃t] adj triumphant; **d'un ton t.** triumphantly

triomphe [trijɔ̃f] nm triumph (sur over); **faire un t. à qn** to give sb an ovation; **porter qn en t.** to carry sb one one's shoulders

triompher [trijɔ̃fe] **1** vi (a) (gagner) to triumph; Fig (vérité) to prevail (b) (exulter) to crow **2 triompher de** vt ind to triumph over

trip [trip] nm Fam (d'un drogué) trip; **faire un t.** to trip; **être dans un t. écolo** to be on an environmental kick

triparti, -e [triparti], **tripartite** [tripartit] adj tripartite

tripatouillage [tripatujaʒ] nm Fam (de textes, de comptes) tampering with; (de statistiques) massaging

tripatouiller [tripatuje] vt Fam (a) (textes, comptes) to tamper with; (statistiques) to massage (b) (cheveux) to play or fiddle with; (bouton) to pick at

tripe [trip] nf (a) tripes (d'un animal) entrails; Fam (d'une personne) guts; Fam **prendre qn aux tripes** to get sb right there (b) tripes (plat) tripe (c) Fam Fig **avoir la t. républicaine** to be republican through and through

triperie [tripri] nf (boutique) tripe shop

tripette [tripɛt] nf Fam **ça ne vaut pas t.** it's not worth a damn

triphasé, -e [trifaze] El adj three-phase

triphtongue [triftɔ̃g] *nf* triphthong
tripier, -ère [tripje, -ɛr] *nm,f* tripe butcher
triple [tripl] **1** *adj* (a) *(à trois éléments)* triple; **en t.** exemplaire in triplicate; **t.** croche *Br* demisemiquaver, *Am* thirty-second note (b) *(trois fois plus grand)* triple, treble (c) *(emploi intensif)* **t.** buse prize idiot; **au t.** galop at breakneck speed
2 *nm* **le t.** (de) *(quantité, prix)* three times as much (as); *(nombre)* three times as many (as); **douze est le t.** de quatre twelve is three times four
triplé, -e [triple] **1** *nm,f* triplet
2 *nm (triple succès)* triple victory; *(pari)* = bet on the first three horses in a race
triplement [triplǝmɑ̃] *adv* trebly, triply
tripler [triple] **1** *vt (somme, quantité)* to treble, to triple; **t.** une classe to repeat a year twice
2 *vi* to treble, to triple
Tripoli [tripɔli] *n* Tripoli
triporteur [tripɔrtœr] *nm* delivery tricycle
tripot [tripo] *nm* gambling den
tripotée [tripɔte] *nf très Fam* (a) *(défaite)* hammering (b) *(grand nombre)* **une t.** de loads of
tripoter [tripɔte] *vt Fam* (a) *(objet, appareil, cheveux)* to play with, to fiddle with; *(boutons, plaie)* to touch (b) *(personne)* to feel up, to grope
triptyque [triptik] *nm* triptych
trique [trik] *nf* cudgel; *Fam* mener qn à la t. to rule sb with a rod of iron
trisomie [trizɔmi] *nf Méd* **t., t.** 21 Down's syndrome
trisomique [trizɔmik] *adj* with Down's syndrome; être t. to have Down's syndrome
triste [trist] *adj* (a) *(malheureux)* sad (b) *(sinistre)* dreary, depressing; *Fam* c'était pas t.! *(soirée)* it was a night and a half!; *Fam* il est pas t., son frère! his brother's quite a character! (c) *(pénible)* sad; *(époque)* grim; dans un t. état in a sorry state; c'est la t. réalité that's the sad or harsh reality (d) *Péj* sad
tristement [tristǝmɑ̃] *adv* sadly; t. célèbre notorious
tristesse [tristɛs] *nf* (a) *(d'une personne, d'un événement)* sadness; c'est avec t. que je vous annonce... I am sorry to have to tell you... (b) *(aspect sinistre)* dreariness
tristounet, -ette [tristunɛ, -ɛt] *adj Fam* gloomy
triton [tritɔ̃] *nm* (a) *(amphibien)* newt (b) *(mollusque)* triton, trumpet shell (c) *(personnage mythologique)* Triton
triturer [trityre] **1** *vt* (a) *(broyer)* to grind (b) *Fam (tripoter)* to fiddle with
2 se triturer *vpr Fam* se t. la cervelle ou les méninges to rack one's brains
triumvirat [trijɔmvira] *nm* triumvirate
trivial, -e, -aux, -ales [trivjal, -o] *adj* (a) *(vulgaire)* vulgar, coarse (b) *(commun)* banal
trivialité [trivjalite] *nf* (a) *(vulgarité)* vulgarity, coarseness (b) *(expression)* vulgar or coarse expression (c) *(banalité)* banality
troc [trɔk] *nm* (a) *(échange)* exchange (b) *(système économique)* barter; faire du t. to barter
troène [trɔɛn] *nm* privet
troglodyte [trɔglɔdit] *nm (personne)* cave dweller, *Spéc* troglodyte
trogne [trɔɲ] *nf Fam* face
trognon [trɔɲɔ̃] **1** *nm (de pomme)* core
2 *adj inv Fam (mignon)* sweet
Troie [trwa] *n* Troy
troïka [trɔika] *nf* troika

trois [trwa] **1** *adj inv* three; **le t.** août *Br* (on) the third of August, *Am* (on) August third; **à t.** heures at three o'clock; page t. page three; Henri T. Henry the Third; nous étions t. there were three of us; les t. quarts du temps most of the time; couper/partager qch en t. to cut/divide sth into three; t. par t. three by three; (hôtel) t. étoiles three-star hotel; en t. dimensions in 3-D
2 *nm inv* three
trois-huit [trwaɥit] *nm inv* faire les t. = to work three alternating eight-hour shifts
troisième [trwazjɛm] **1** *adj, nmf & nm* third; le t. âge *Br* senior citizens, *Am* golden agers
2 *nf* (a) *Scol Br* ≃ fourth year of secondary school, *Am* ≃ eighth grade (b) *(vitesse)* third (gear); *voir aussi* cinquième
troisièmement [trwazjɛmmɑ̃] *adv* thirdly
trois-mâts [trwama] *nm inv* three-master
trois-pièces [trwapjɛs] *nm inv* (a) *(appartement)* three-room *Br* flat *or Am* apartment; t. cuisine *Br* three-room flat with kitchen, *Am* three and a half (b) *(costume)* three-piece suit
trois-quarts [trwakar] *nm inv* (a) *(manteau)* three-quarter-length coat (b) *(au rugby)* three-quarter
trolley [trɔlɛ], **trolleybus** [trɔlɛbys] *nm* trolleybus
trombe [trɔ̃b] *nf* waterspout; il pleut des trombes it's pouring down; sous des trombes d'eau in the torrential rain; *Fam Fig* passer/partir en t. to tear past/off
trombine [trɔ̃bin] *nf Fam* face
trombone [trɔ̃bɔn] *nm* (a) *(agrafe)* paper clip (b) *(instrument)* trombone; t. à coulisse/à pistons slide/valve trombone (c) *(instrumentiste)* trombone player, trombonist
trompe [trɔ̃p] *nf* (a) *(d'éléphant)* trunk; *(d'insecte)* proboscis (b) *(instrument à vent)* horn (c) *Anat* t. d'Eustache/de Fallope Eustachian/Fallopian tube
trompe-l'œil [trɔ̃plœj] *nm inv (décor)* trompe l'œil; en t. trompe l'œil
tromper [trɔ̃pe] **1** *vt* (a) *(abuser)* to fool (sur about) (b) *(être infidèle à)* to be unfaithful to (c) *(vigilance, surveillance)* to elude, to escape (d) *Fig* t. son ennui to relieve the boredom; t. sa faim to stave off one's hunger
2 se tromper *vpr (faire une erreur)* to make a mistake; *(avoir tort)* to be mistaken; se t. dans les dates/proportions to get the dates/the proportions wrong; se t. de numéro *(au téléphone)* to dial the wrong number; se t. d'heure/de jour to get the time/day wrong
tromperie [trɔ̃pri] *nf* deceit, deception
trompeter [trɔ̃pǝte] *vt (nouvelles)* to shout from the rooftops
trompette [trɔ̃pɛt] *nf* trumpet; *Fig* avoir le nez en t. to have a turned-up nose; t. bouchée muted trumpet
trompette-de-la-mort (*pl* trompettes-de-la-mort) [trɔ̃petdǝlamɔr] *nf* horn of plenty
trompettiste [trɔ̃petist] *nmf* trumpet player, trumpeter
trompeur, -euse [trɔ̃pœr, -øz] *adj* (a) *(volontairement)* deceitful (b) *(symptôme, apparences)* deceptive; *(publicité)* misleading
tronc [trɔ̃] *nm* (a) *(d'un arbre, d'un corps)* trunk; *Fig* t. commun *(à l'école)* compulsory subjects (b) *(dans une église)* poor box
tronche [trɔ̃ʃ] *nf Fam (tête)* nut; *(visage)* mug; faire la t. to sulk
tronçon [trɔ̃sɔ̃] *nm* piece; *(de route)* section
tronçonner [trɔ̃sɔne] *vt* to cut into sections
tronçonneuse [trɔ̃sɔnøz] *nf* chain saw
trône [tron] *nm aussi Fam Fig* throne

trôner [trone] *vi* (a) *Hum (personne)* to sit on one's throne (b) *(objet)* to have pride of place

tronquer [trɔ̃ke] *vt (mot, scène)* to shorten

trop [tro] *adv* (a) *(avec un adjectif ou un adverbe)* too; **ça va?** – **pas t. mal** how are things? – not too bad; *Fam* **il est vraiment t.!** he's too much! (b) *(avec un verbe)* too much; **il n'y tient pas t.** he's not too bothered; **je ne sais pas t.** I'm not too sure; **ça te plaît?** – **pas t.** do you like it? – not much; **on ne saurait t.** le répéter it can't be repeated too often (c) *(quantité)* too much; *(nombre)* too many; **t. de** *(quantité)* too much; *(nombre)* too many; **nous sommes t.** there are too many of us; **il y a deux assiettes de** *ou* **en t.** there are two plates too many; **payer 50 euros de t.** *ou* **en t.** to pay 50 euros too much; **c'est une fois de t.** that's once too often; **se sentir de t.** to feel in the way; **t., c'est t.!** enough is enough!; **c'en est t.!** this really is too much!

trophée [trɔfe] *nm* trophy

tropical, -e, -aux, -ales [trɔpikal, -o] *adj* tropical

tropique [trɔpik] *nm* (a) *(parallèle)* tropic; **le T. du Cancer/du Capricorne** the tropic of Cancer/of Capricorn (b) **les tropiques** *(région)* the tropics; **sous les tropiques** in the tropics

trop-perçu (*pl* **trop-perçus**) [trɔpɛrsy] *nm* overpayment

trop-plein (*pl* **trop-pleins**) [trɔplɛ̃] *nm* (a) *(excédent)* overflow (b) *(dispositif d'évacuation)* overflow pipe

troquer [trɔke] *vt* **t. qch contre qch** to exchange sth for sth

troquet [trɔkɛ] *nm Fam* small café

trot [tro] *nm* trot; **aller au t.** to trot; *Fam Fig* **allez-y, et au t.!** go on, and be quick about it!; **t. attelé** harness race

trotskiste, trotskyste [trɔtskist] *adj & nmf* Trotskyist

trotte [trɔt] *nf Fam (distance)* **il y a une bonne t. d'ici à chez elle** it's a fair distance from here to her house

trotter [trɔte] *vi* (a) *(cheval)* to trot (b) *(personne)* to trot about (c) *Fig* **cet air me trotte dans la tête depuis hier** I haven't been able to get that tune out of my head since yesterday; **cette idée me trottait dans la tête** the idea was running through my head

trotteur [trɔtœr] *nm* (a) *(cheval)* trotter (b) *(chaussure)* flat shoe

trotteuse [trɔtøz] *nf (de montre)* second hand

trottiner [trɔtine] *vi (personne)* to trot about

trottinette [trɔtinɛt] *nf* scooter; **faire de la t.** to ride one's scooter

trottoir [trɔtwar] *nm Br* pavement, *Am* sidewalk; *Fam* **faire le t.** to walk the streets *(of prostitute)*; **t. roulant** *Br* travelator, *Am* moving sidewalk

trou [tru] *nm* (a) *(ouverture)* hole; *(d'aiguille)* eye; *Fig* **faire son t.** to find one's niche; **t. d'air** air pocket; *aussi Fig Vulg* **t. du cul** *Br* arsehole, *Am* asshole; **t. noir** black hole; *Fig* **je suis tombé de l'échelle, et après c'est le t. noir** I fell off the ladder, and after that it's all a blank; **t. de serrure** keyhole; **t. de souris** mouse hole (b) *(dans un emploi du temps, dans ses connaissances)* gap; **j'ai un t. de cinq à sept** I'm free between five and seven; **avoir un t. (de mémoire)** to have a memory lapse (c) *(déficit)* hole, dent; *Fam* **le t. de la sécu** the French Social Security deficit (d) *Fam Péj (lieu reculé)* hole; **il n'est jamais sorti de son t.** he has never been out of his own backyard (e) *Fam (prison)* nick (f) **faire le t. normand** = to drink a glass of Calvados between courses to aid digestion

troubadour [trubadur] *nm* troubadour

troublant, -e [trublɑ̃, -ɑ̃t] *adj* (a) *(déconcertant)* disconcerting (b) *(sensuel)* provocative

trouble¹ [trubl] **1** *adj* (a) *(liquide)* cloudy; *(lumière)* dim; *(image, photo)* blurred (b) *(comportement, affaire)* shady; *(période)* murky
2 *adv* **voir t.** to have blurred vision

trouble² [trubl] *nm* (a) *(désordre)* confusion, disorder; **semer** *ou* **jeter le t.** **dans l'esprit de qn** to confuse sb (b) *(émoi)* agitation (c) **troubles** *(révolte)* unrest (d) **troubles** *(maladie)* disorder; **troubles de la vision/respiratoires** eye/respiratory disorder; **troubles de la personnalité** personality disorder

trouble-fête [trublfɛt] *nm inv Br* spoilsport, *Am* partypooper; **jouer les t.** *Br* to be a spoilsport, *Am* to be a partypooper

troubler [truble] **1** *vt* (a) *(eau)* to make cloudy; *Fig (esprit)* to cloud; **t. la vue à qn** to blur sb's eyes (b) *(sommeil, silence)* to disturb; *(bonheur)* to spoil; **t. l'ordre public** to disturb the peace (c) *(mettre en émoi)* to make flustered; *(rendre perplexe)* to confuse
2 se troubler *vpr* (a) *(liquide)* to get cloudy; *(vue)* to become blurred (b) *(se déconcerter)* to become flustered; **sans se t.** unperturbed

trouée [true] *nf (dans une haie, dans un mur)* gap, opening; **une t. de ciel bleu** a patch of blue sky

trouer [true] **1** *vt* to make a hole in
2 se trouer *vpr* **mes chaussures se sont trouées au bout d'une semaine** there was a hole in my shoe after a week

troufion [trufjɔ̃] *nm Fam Br* soldier, *Am* grunt

trouillard, -e [trujar, -ard] *Fam* **1** *adj* yellow-bellied, chicken
2 *nm,f* yellow-belly, chicken

trouille [truj] *nf Fam* fear; **avoir la t.** to be scared stiff

trouillomètre [trujɔmɛtr] *nm Fam* **avoir le t. à zéro** to be scared stiff

troupe [trup] *nf* (a) *(groupe)* troop, band; **t. de théâtre** company, troupe (b) *(de soldats)* troop; **troupes** *(armée)* troops, forces

troupeau, -x [trupo] *nm (de bétail, d'éléphants)* herd; *(de moutons)* flock; *(d'oies)* gaggle; *Péj (de gens)* herd

trousse [trus] *nf* (a) *(étui)* kit; **t. d'écolier** pencil case; **t. de secours** first-aid kit; **t. de toilette** toilet bag (b) *(locutions)* être aux trousses de qn to be hot on sb's heels; **avoir qn aux trousses** to have sb hot on one's heels

trousseau, -x [truso] *nm* (a) *(de clés)* bunch (b) *(de mariée)* trousseau (c) *(de pensionnaire)* clothes

trousser [truse] *vt* (a) *Culin (volaille)* to truss (b) **bien troussé** *(compliment)* well-turned (c) *Vieilli (retrousser)* to turn up

trouvaille [truvaj] *nf* (a) *(chose trouvée)* find (b) *(bonne idée)* brainwave

trouver [truve] **1** *vt* (a) *(en cherchant)* to find; *(procédé, vaccin)* to discover; **je ne trouve pas mes cigarettes** I can't find my cigarettes; **aller t. qn** to go and see sb; **t. quelque chose à redire** to be sure to have something to say; **t. le sommeil** to get to sleep; **exemple bien trouvé** well-chosen example; **je me demande où il est allé t. ça** I wonder where he got that idea from; *Ironique* **tu as trouvé ça tout seul?** did you think of that all on your own? (b) *(par hasard)* to find, to come across; **t. porte close** to find nobody home; *Fig* **il va t. à qui parler!** he'll have me/him/etc to reckon with!; *Fig* **t. son maître** to meet one's match; **t. la mort** to meet one's death (c) *(juger)* to find; *(penser)* to think; **je trouve ça idiot** I think it's stupid; **qu'est-ce qu'elle lui trouve?** what does she see in him?; **je trouve que...** I think (that)...; **t. le temps long** to feel that the time is dragging
2 se trouver *vpr* (a) *(dans une situation, un lieu)* to be

(b) *(être disponible)* ça se trouve dans les supermarchés you can find *or* get it in supermarkets **(c)** *(se sentir)* to feel; **je me trouve bien ici** I like it here; **se t. beau/gros** to think one is good-looking/fat; **se t. mal** to feel faint **(d)** *(arriver)* **il se trouve que...** as it happens...; *Fam* **si ça se trouve** maybe

trouvère [truvɛr] *nm* trouvère

truand [tryɑ̃] *nm Fam* crook

truander [tryɑ̃de] *Fam* **1** *vt* to rip off; **se faire t.** to get ripped off **2** *vi (à un examen)* to cheat (**à** in)

trublion [tryblijɔ̃] *nm* troublemaker

truc [tryk] *nm Fam* **(a)** *Fam (chose)* thing; **j'ai un t. à faire/à te dire** I've something to do/to tell you **(b)** *(astuce)* trick; **connaître les trucs du métier** to know the tricks of the trade **(c)** *(personne)* **T.** what's-his-name, *f* what's-her-name **(d)** *(domaine)* **c'est vraiment son t.** he's really into it; **ce n'est pas son t.** it's not his thing

trucage [tryka3] *nm* **(a)** *(dans un film)* special effect **(b)** *(d'une photographie)* faking; *(d'un match, d'une élection)* rigging; *(de comptes)* fiddling

truchement [tryʃmɑ̃] *nm* **par le t. de...** through...

trucider [tryside] *vt Fam Hum* to bump off

trucmuche [trykmyʃ] *nm Fam* **(a)** *(chose)* thingy **(b)** **T.** *(personne)* what's-his-name, *f* what's-her-name

truculence [trykylɑ̃s] *nf* *(d'un récit, d'un style)* colourfulness; *(d'une personne)* flamboyance

truculent, -e [trykylɑ̃, -ɑ̃t] *adj* *(récit, style)* colourful; *(personne)* flamboyant

truelle [tryɛl] *nf* trowel

truffe [tryf] *nf* **(a)** *(champignon, au chocolat)* truffle **(b)** *(de chien)* nose

truffer [tryfe] *vt* **(a)** *(plat)* to garnish with truffles **(b)** *Fig (remplir)* **être truffé de** *(citations, balles)* to be peppered with; *(fautes)* to be riddled with

truie [tryi] *nf* sow

truite [tryit] *nf* trout; **t. arc-en-ciel/saumonée** rainbow/salmon trout

truquage [tryka3] = **trucage**

truquer [tryke] *vt* **(a)** *(photographie)* to fake; *(match, élection)* to rig; *(comptes)* to fiddle; *(dés)* to load **(b)** *(scène)* to use special effects in

trust [trœst] *nm* trust

truster [trœste] *vt aussi Fam* to monopolize

tsar [tsar, dzar] *nm* tsar, czar

tsé-tsé [tsetse] *nf inv voir* **mouche**

TSF [teɛsɛf] *nf Vieilli (abrév* **télégraphie sans fil)** *(procédé)* wireless telegraphy; *(poste)* wireless

t-shirt (*pl* **t-shirts**) [tiʃœrt] = **tee-shirt**

tsigane [tsigan] = **tzigane**

TSVP *(abrév* **tournez s'il vous plaît)** PTO

TTC [tetese] *(abrév* **toutes taxes comprises)** inclusive of tax

tu, -e *voir* **taire**

tu [ty] *pron personnel* you; *Fam* **t'as déjà fini?** have you already finished?; **être à tu et à toi avec qn** to be on first-name terms with sb; **dire tu à qn** to address sb as "tu"

Tuamotu [twamotu] *nfpl* **les T.** the Tuamotu Archipelago

tuant, -e [tɥɑ̃, -ɑ̃t] *adj Fam* **(a)** *(fatigant)* exhausting **(b)** *(insupportable)* exasperating

tuba [tyba] *nm* **(a)** *(instrument de musique)* tuba **(b)** *(de plongée)* snorkel

tube [tyb] *nm* **(a)** *(tuyau)* tube; *Fam Fig* **à pleins tubes** at

full blast; **t. digestif** digestive tract; **t. à essai** test tube **(b)** *(chanson)* hit **(c)** *(emballage)* tube; **t. de rouge à lèvres** lipstick

tubercule [tybɛrkyl] *nm (plante)* tuber

tuberculeux, -euse [tybɛrkylø, -øz] **1** *adj* with tuberculosis; **être t.** to have tuberculosis **2** *nm,f* person with tuberculosis

tuberculose [tybɛrkyloz] *nf* tuberculosis; **avoir la t.** to have tuberculosis

tubéreuse [tyberøz] *nf* tuberose

tubulaire [tybylɛr] *adj* tubular

TUC [tyk] *nm (abrév* **travaux d'utilité collective)** = community work project for unemployed young people

tuer [tɥe] **1** *vt* **(a)** *(être vivant)* to kill; **t. qn d'un coup de revolver/de couteau** to shoot/stab sb to death; **c'est la chagrin qui l'a tué** he died of grief; *Fig* **t. le temps** to kill time **(b)** *Fam (épuiser)* **tous ces déplacements m'ont tué** all that travelling was a killer; **ces escaliers/ces enfants me tuent** these stairs/these children will be the death of me **(c)** *Fam (sidérer)* **ça me tue!** it kills me! **2 se tuer** *vpr* **(a)** *(se suicider)* to kill oneself **(b)** *(dans un accident)* to die, to be killed **(c)** *(l'un l'autre)* to kill one another **(d)** *Fig* **se t. au travail** *ou* **à la tâche** to work oneself to death; **se t. à faire qch** to wear oneself out doing sth

tuerie [tyri] *nf* slaughter

tue-tête [tytɛt] **à tue-tête** *adv* at the top of one's voice

tueur, -euse [tɥœr, -øz] **1** *adj* killer **2** *nm,f* killer; **t. à gages** hired killer

tuile [tɥil] *nf* **(a)** *(de toit)* tile **(b)** **t. aux amandes** thin almond *Br* biscuit *or Am* cookie **(c)** *Fam (problème)* **il m'arrive une t.** I'm in a bit of a mess

tulipe [tylip] *nf (fleur)* tulip

tulle [tyl] *nm* **(a)** *(tissu)* tulle **(b)** *Méd* **t. gras** tulle gras

tuméfié, -e [tymefje] *adj* swollen

tuméfier [tymefje] *vt* to cause to swell

tumeur [tymœr] *nf* tumour; **t. au cerveau** brain tumour

tumoral, -e, -aux, -ales [tymɔral, -o] *adj* tumorous, tumoral

tumulte [tymylt] *nm (de la foule)* commotion; *(des passions)* turmoil

tumultueux, -euse [tymyltɥø, -øz] *adj (réunion)* noisy, tumultuous; *(vie, période)* tumultuous; *(relation)* stormy

tuner [tynœr, tynɛr] *nm* tuner

tungstène [tœksten] *nm* tungsten

tunique [tynik] *nf* tunic

Tunis [tynis] *n* Tunis

Tunisie [tynizi] *nf* **la T.** Tunisia

tunisien, -enne [tynizjɛ̃, -ɛn] **1** *adj* Tunisian **2** *nm,f* **T.** Tunisian

tunisois, -e [tynizwa, -az] **1** *adj* of Tunis **2** *nm,f* **T.** person from Tunis

tunnel [tynɛl] *nm* tunnel; **le t. sous la Manche** the Channel Tunnel

tuque [tyk] *nf Can* bobble hat

turban [tyrbɑ̃] *nm* turban

turbin [tyrbɛ̃] *nm Fam (travail)* grind; **aller au t.** to go off to the daily grind

turbine [tyrbin] *nf* turbine

turbiner [tyrbine] *vi Fam (travailler)* to slave (away)

turbo [tyrbo] **1** *adj* turbocharged **2** *nm* turbo

turboréacteur [tyrboreaktœr] *nm* turbojet (engine)

turbot [tyrbo] *nm* turbot

turbulence [tyrbylɑ̃s] *nf* **(a)** turbulences *(dans l'atmosphère)* turbulence **(b)** *(d'un enfant)* boisterousness
turbulent, -e [tyrbylɑ̃, -ɑ̃t] *adj (enfant, classe)* boisterous
turc, turque [tyrk] **1** *adj* Turkish
2 *nm,f* **T.** Turk
3 *nm (langue)* Turkish
turf [tœrf, tyrf] *nm (activité)* racing
turfiste [tœrfist, tyrfist] *nmf* racegoer
turkmène [tyrkmɛn] **1** *adj* Turkoman
2 *nmf* **T.** Turkoman
3 *nm (langue)* Turkmen
Turkménistan [tyrkmenistɑ̃] *nm* le **T.** Turkmenistan
turlupiner [tyrlypine] *vt Fam* to bother
turluter [tyrlyte] *vi Can Fam* to trill, to sing tra-la-la
turpitude [tyrpityd] *nf* **(a)** *(d'une conduite)* vileness, turpitude **(b)** *(action)* vile act
turque [tyrk] *voir* **turc**
Turquie [tyrki] *nf* la **T.** Turkey
turquoise [tyrkwaz] *nf, nm inv & adj inv* turquoise
tutelle [tytɛl] *nf* **(a)** *Jur* guardianship; *Pol* territoires sous **t.** trust territories **(b)** *(protection)* protection
tuteur, -trice [tytœr, -tris] **1** *nm,f* guardian; **t. légal** legal guardian
2 *nm (pour plante)* support
tutoiement [tytwamɑ̃] *nm* = use of the familiar "tu" instead of the more formal "vous"; **le t. est de rigueur** everybody calls each other "tu"
tutoyer [tytwaje] **1** *vt* **t. qn** = to address sb as "tu"
2 *se* **tutoyer** *vpr* = to address each other as "tu"
tutti quanti [tutikwɑ̃ti] *adv* **et t.** etcetera, etcetera
tutu [tyty] *nm* tutu
tuyau, -x [tɥijo] *nm* **(a)** *(canalisation)* pipe, *(de cheminée)* flue; *(flexible)* tube; **t. d'arrosage** garden hose; **t. d'échappement** exhaust (pipe); **t. d'incendie** fire hose; **t. de poêle** stove pipe **(b)** *Fam (conseil)* tip; *(information)* tip-off

tuyauter [tɥijɔte] *vt Fam (conseiller)* to give a tip to (**sur** about); *(informer)* to tip off (**sur** about)
tuyauterie [tɥijɔtri] *nf* piping, pipes
TV [teve] *nf (abrév* **télévision***)* TV
TVA [tevea] *nf (abrév* **taxe à la valeur ajoutée***)* VAT
tweed [twid] *nm* tweed
twin-set (*pl* **twin-sets***)* [twinsɛt] *nm* twinset
tympan [tɛ̃pɑ̃] *nm* **(a)** *Anat* eardrum **(b)** *Archit* tympanum
type [tip] **1** *adj* typical; **lettre t.** standard letter
2 *nm* **(a)** *(genre)* type **(b)** *(personnification)* **le t. même de** the classic example of **(c)** *(apparence)* **avoir le t. latin/ nordique** to have Latin/Nordic looks **(d)** *Fam (homme)* guy
typé, -e [tipe] *adj* **il est italien – oui, et il est très t.** he's Italian – yes, he looks typically Italian
typhoïde [tifɔid] **1** *adj (fièvre)* typhoid
2 *nf* typhoid (fever)
typhon [tifɔ̃] *nm* typhoon
typhus [tifys] *nm* typhus (fever)
typique [tipik] *adj* typical
typiquement [tipikmɑ̃] *adv* typically
typographe [tipɔɡraf] *nmf* typographer
typographie [tipɔɡrafi] *nf* typography, letterpress printing
typographique [tipɔɡrafik] *adj* typographic
tyran [tirɑ̃] *nm* tyrant
tyrannie [tirani] *nf* tyranny
tyrannique [tiranik] *adj* tyrannical
tyranniser [tiranize] *vt (population)* to tyrannize; *(famille, collègue)* to bully
tzar [tsar, dzar] = **tsar**
tzigane [tsiɡan, dziɡan] **1** *adj* gypsy
2 *nmf* **T.** gypsy

U, u [y] *nm inv* U, u; **en U** U-shaped; **tables disposées en U** tables arranged in a horseshoe (shape)

ubac [ybak] *nm* = shaded side of a valley, *Spéc* ubac

ubiquité [ybikɥite] *nf* ubiquity; **avoir le don d'u.** to have the ability to be in several places at the same time

UDF [ydeɛf] *nf* (*abrév* **Union pour la démocratie française**) = right-of-centre French political party

UE *nf* (*abrév* **Union européenne**) EU

UEO [yəo] *nf* (*abrév* **Union de l'Europe occidentale**) WEU

UFR [yɛfɛr] *nf* (*abrév* **unité de formation et de recherche**) = department (*in university*)

UHF [yaʃɛf] *Rad* (*abrév* **ultra-haute fréquence**) UHF

UHT [yaʃte] (*abrév* **ultra-haute température**) UHT

Ukraine [ykrɛn] *nf* **l'U.** the Ukraine

ukrainien, -enne [ykrɛnjɛ̃, -jɛn] **1** *adj* Ukranian **2** *nm,f* **U.** Ukranian **3** *nm (langue)* Ukranian

ukulélé [jukulele] *nm* ukelele

ulcération [ylserasjɔ̃] *nf* ulceration

ulcère [ylsɛr] *nm* ulcer; **avoir un u. à l'estomac** to have a stomach ulcer

ulcéré, -e [ylsere] *adj* (**a**) *Méd* ulcerated (**b**) *Fig (en colère)* seething

ulcérer [ylsere] **1** *vt* (**a**) *Méd* to ulcerate (**b**) *Fig (mettre en colère)* **u. qn** to make sb seethe **2 s'ulcérer** *vpr Méd* to ulcerate

ULM [yɛlɛm] *nm inv Av* (*abrév* **ultraléger motorisé**) microlight

ultérieur, -e [ylterjœr] *adj* later, subsequent (**à** to)

ultérieurement [ylterjœrmɑ̃] *adv* later (on), subsequently

ultimatum [yltimatɔm] *nm* ultimatum; **adresser un u. à qn** to give sb an ultimatum

ultime [yltim] *adj* last; *(préparatifs)* final

ultra- [yltra] *préf* ultra-

ultra-confidentiel, -elle [yltrakɔ̃fidɑ̃sjɛl] *adj* top-secret

ultra-conservateur, -trice [yltrakɔ̃servatœr] *adj Pol* ultra-conservative

ultramoderne [yltramɔdɛrn] *adj* high-tech

ultrarapide [yltrarapid] *adj* ultrafast

ultrasensible [yltrasɑ̃sibl] *adj* ultra-sensitive

ultrason [yltrasɔ̃] *nm Phys* ultrasound; **ultrasons** ultrasonic waves

ultraviolet, -ette [yltravjɔlɛ, -ɛt] *adj & nm* ultraviolet

ululer [ylyle] *vi* to ululate

Ulysse [ylis] *npr* Ulysses

un, une [œ̃, yn] **1** *adj* one; **il est une heure** it's one o'clock; **page un** page one; **un jour** one day; **un, deux, trois, partez!** one, two, three, go!

2 *pron indfini* one; **un de mes amis** one of my friends, a friend of mine; **un de ces jours** one of these days; **en voilà une qui sait ce qu'elle veut!** there's somebody who knows what she wants!; **il n'y en a pas un qui parle anglais** not one of them speaks English; *Fam* **être menteur/hypocrite comme pas un** to be a dreadful liar/hypocrite; **(l')un de nous, (l')un d'entre nous** one of us

3 *art indéfini (pl* **des**) (**a**) *(en général)* a; *(devant une voyelle ou un h muet)* an; **un jour/une pomme/une heure** a day/an apple/an hour; **cela tombe un mardi** it falls on a Tuesday; **il y a des agrafes dans le tiroir** there are (some) staples in the drawer; **est-ce qu'il te reste des agrafes?** do you have any staples left?; **il y a des jours où...** there are days when..., some days... (**b**) *(intensif)* **il y a un de ces mondes en ville!** the town is so busy!; **il est d'une bêtise!** he's so stupid!; **il a fait une de ces têtes!** you should have seen his face!; **tu m'as fait une peur!** you gave me such a fright!

4 *nm (chiffre)* one

5 *nf* (**a**) *(première page)* **la une** *(d'un journal)* the front page; **faire la une** *(d'un magazine)* to appear on the front cover; *(d'un journal)* to appear on the front page (**b**) **il n'a fait ni une ni deux** he didn't hesitate for a moment

unanime [ynanim] *adj* unanimous

unanimité [ynanimite] *nf* unanimity; **à l'u.** unanimously; **faire l'u.** to be accepted unanimously

underground [œndœrgrawnd] *adj inv & nm inv* underground

une [yn] *voir* **un**

UNEF [ynɛf] *nf* (*abrév* **Union nationale des étudiants de France**) = French union of students

Unesco [ynɛsko] *nf* Unesco

Unetelle *voir* **Untel**

uni, -e [yni] *adj* (**a**) *(famille, couple)* close (**b**) *(sans irrégularité) (sol, surface)* smooth, level (**c**) *(couleur)* plain; *(tissu, vêtement)* self-coloured

Unicef [ynisɛf] *nm ou nf* (*abrév* **United Nations International Children's Emergency Fund**) **l'U.** Unicef

unicellulaire [yniselyler] *adj* unicellular

unidimensionnel, -elle [ynidimɑ̃sjɔnɛl] *adj* one-dimensional

unidirectionnel, -elle [ynidirɛksjɔnɛl] *adj* unidirectional

unificateur, -trice [ynifikatœr, -tris] *adj* unifying

unification [ynifikasjɔ̃] *nf* unification

unifier [ynifje] *vt* (**a**) *(parti politique, pays)* to unify (**b**) *(tarifs, poids et mesures)* to standardize

uniforme [ynifɔrm] **1** *adj (opinions, expression)* uniform; *(vie)* unchanging; *(allure, surface)* even; *(mouvement)* regular **2** *nm* uniform

uniformément [ynifɔrmemã] *adv* uniformly, evenly

uniformisation [ynifɔrmizasjɔ̃] *nf* standardization

uniformiser [ynifɔrmize] *vt* to standardize

uniformité [ynifɔrmite] *nf* **(a)** *(monotonie)* monotony **(b)** *(de couleurs, de teintes)* uniformity

unijambiste [yniʒãbist] **1** *adj* one-legged **2** *nmf* one-legged person

unilatéral, -e, -aux, -ales [ynilateral, -o] *adj (décision, désarmement)* unilateral; *(contrat, accord)* one-sided

unilingue [ynilɛ̃g] *adj* unilingual, monolingual

uninominal, -aux [yninɔminal, -o] *adj voir* **scrutin**

union [ynjɔ̃] *nf* **(a)** *(entre personnes)* closeness, unity; **vivre en parfaite u. avec qn** to live in perfect harmony with sb **(b)** *(association) (de partis, de consommateurs)* union, association; **u. douanière/économique/monétaire** customs/economic/monetary union; **l'U. européenne** the European Union; *Anciennement* **l'U. soviétique** the Soviet Union **(c)** *(mariage)* marriage; **u. libre** cohabitation; **vivre en u. libre** to cohabit

unique [ynik] *adj* **(a)** *(seul)* only; *(parti, prix)* single; *(occasion, cas)* unique; **être u. en son genre** to be one of a kind; **u. au monde** unlike anything else in the world; **c'est son seul et u. défaut** it's his one and only fault **(b)** *(incomparable)* unique **(c)** *Fam (très drôle)* priceless

uniquement [ynikmã] *adv* just, only

unir [ynir] **1** *vt* **(a)** *(relier) (personnes, territoires)* to unite; *(qualités)* to combine **(à** with) **(b)** *(réunir)* **l'amitié qui nous unit** the friendship that unites us **(c)** *(marier)* to join in marriage **(d)** *(sol, surface)* to smooth, to level **2 s'unir** *vpr* **(a)** *(s'associer)* to join together, to unite; **s'u. à qn** to join forces with sb **(b)** *(se marier)* to become joined in marriage

unisexe [ynisɛks] *adj* unisex

unisson [ynisɔ̃] *nm* unison; **à l'u.** in unison

unitaire [yniter] *adj (système)* unitary; *(prix)* unit

unité [ynite] *nf* **(a)** *(pour mesurer)* unit; **u. de longueur/de poids** unit of measurement/weight **(b)** *(élément simple)* unit; **10 euros l'u.** 10 euros each; *Com* **prix à l'u.** unit price; **vendu à l'u.** sold singly; **chiffre des unités** units figure; **u. de production** production unit; *Univ* **u. de valeur** credit **(c)** *(cohésion)* *(d'une nation, d'une association)* unity; *(du style)* consistency **(d)** *Ordinat* unit; *(de disque)* drive; **u. de bande** tape unit; **u. centrale** central processing unit; **u. de disque/logique** disk/logical drive

univers [yniver] *nm* **(a)** *(espace)* universe **(b)** *Fig (milieu)* world

universaliser [yniversalize] *vt* to universalize

universalité [yniversalite] *nf* universality

universel, -elle [yniversɛl] *adj* universal; *(savoir)* all-embracing

universellement [yniverselmã] *adv* universally

universitaire [yniversiter] **1** *adj (ville, études)* university **2** *nmf* academic

université [yniversite] *nf* university; **aller à l'u.** to go to university; **u. d'été** summer school; *Pol* party conference *(for young members)*; **u. du troisième âge** = classes for senior citizens

Untel, Unetelle [œtɛl, yntɛl] *nm,f* what's-his-name, *f* what's-her-name; **M./Mme U.** Mr/Mrs So-and-So

uppercut [yperkyt] *nm* uppercut

uranium [yranjɔm] *nm* uranium; **u. enrichi** enriched uranium

Uranus [yranys] *npr (dieu, planète)* Uranus

urbain, -e [yrbɛ̃, -ɛn] *adj* **(a)** *(développement, milieu, transport)* urban **(b)** *Litt (poli)* urbane

urbanisation [yrbanizasjɔ̃] *nf* urbanization

urbaniser [yrbanize] *vt* to urbanize

urbanisme [yrbanism] *nm* town planning, urban development

urbaniste [yrbanist] **1** *adj* urban **2** *nmf* town planner

urbanité [yrbanite] *nf* *Litt* urbanity

urbi et orbi [yrbietɔrbi] *adv* urbi et orbi; *Fig* far and wide

urée [yre] *nf* urea

urètre [yretr] *nm* urethra

urgence [yrʒãs] *nf* **(a)** *(caractère pressé)* urgency; **en cas d'u.** in an emergency; **d'u.** urgently; **être opéré d'u.** to have an emergency operation; **il y a u.** it's a matter of urgency **(b)** *(à l'hôpital)* emergency; **les urgences** *(service)* *Br* casualty, accident and emergency, *Am* the emergency room

urgent, -e [yrʒã, -ãt] *adj* urgent; **il est u. de le faire** it must be done urgently

urger [yrʒe] *vi Fam* **ça urge** it's urgent

urinaire [yriner] *adj* urinary

urine [yrin] *nf* urine

uriner [yrine] *vi* to urinate

urinoir [yrinwar] *nm* (public) urinal

urique [yrik] *adj (acide)* uric

urne [yrn] *nf* **(a)** *(pour voter)* ballot box; **aller aux urnes** to go to the polls **(b)** *(vase)* urn

uro-génital, -e [mpl uro-génitaux, fpl uro-génitales) [yroʒenital, -o] *adj* urogenital

urologie [yrɔlɔʒi] *nf* urology

urologue [yrɔlɔg] *nmf* urologist

URSS [yeress, yrs] *nf Anciennement (abrév* **Union des républiques socialistes soviétiques)** **l'U.** the USSR

URSSAF [yrsaf] *nf (abrév* **Union de recouvrement des cotisations de Sécurité sociale et d'allocations familiales)** = organization which collects social security payments

urticaire [yrtiker] *nf* nettle rash, *Spéc* urticaria; **avoir une crise d'u.** to come out in nettle rash; *Fam* **donner l'u. à qn** to set sb's teeth on edge

Uruguay [yrygwɛ] *nm* **l'U.** Uruguay

uruguayen, -enne [yrygwejɛ̃, ɛn] **1** *adj* Uruguayan **2** *nm,f* **U.** Uruguayan

us [ys] *nmpl* **les us et coutumes** the habits and customs

usage [yzaʒ] *nm* **(a)** *(utilisation)* use; **faire u. de qch** to use sth; **faire bon u. de qch** to put sth to good use; **avoir l'u. de qch** to have the use of sth; **à u. externe/interne** *(médicament)* for external/internal use; **à l'u. des écoles/des étudiants** for use in schools/by students; **à usages multiples** multi-purpose; **hors d'u.** out of order; *Jur* **u. de faux** use of forged documents **(b)** *(d'un terme, d'une expression)* usage; **entrer dans l'u.** to come into common use; **le bon u.** correct usage **(c)** *(des vêtements)* **faire de l'u.** to wear well; **ce manteau vous fera de l'u.** you'll get a lot of wear out of this coat **(d)** *(coutume)* custom, practice; **c'est l'u.** it's the done thing; **comme il est d'u.** as is customary; **en Grèce** as is customary in Greece; **il est d'u.** it's customary to

usagé, -e [yzaʒe] *adj (vêtement, livre)* worn; *(ticket)* used

usager [yzaʒe] *nm* user

usant, -e [yzã, -ãt] *adj Fam* **(a)** *(vie, travail)* exhausting, wearing **(b)** *(personne)* tiresome

usé, -e [yze] adj (a) (vêtements) worn, worn-out; **u. jusqu'à la corde** threadbare (b) (eaux) waste (c) (sujet, plaisanterie) tired, stale (d) (épuisé) worn-out
user [yze] **1** vt (a) (consommer) (énergie, électricité) to use (b) (abîmer) (vêtements, chaussures) to wear out; Fig (résistance) to break down; **u. qch jusqu'à la corde** to wear sth until it's threadbare (c) (épuiser) (personne) to wear down **2 user de** vt ind (patience, violence, ruse) to use; (droit) to exercise; **u. de douceur avec qn** to handle sb gently; **u. de son influence pour faire qch** to use one's influence to do sth **3 s'user** vpr (a) (tissu, pneus, semelles) to wear out; (talons) to wear down (b) Fig (personne) **s'u. à faire qch** to wear oneself out doing sth
usinage [yzinaʒ] nm machining
usine [yzin] nf factory, plant
usiner [yzine] vt (façonner) to machine
usité, -e [yzite] adj (mot) in common use; **très u.** very common; **peu u.** little used
ustensile [ystɑ̃sil] nm implement, tool; **u. de cuisine** kitchen utensil
usuel, -elle [yzɥɛl] adj everyday; (dénomination) common
usufruit [yzyfrɥi] nm Jur usufruct
usuraire [yzyrɛr] adj usurious
usure¹ [yzyr] nf (intérêt, délit) usury
usure² nf (de pneu) wear; (du sol, de roches) wearing away; **résister à l'u.** to wear well; Fam **avoir qn à l'u.** to wear sb down
usurier, -ère [yzyrje, -ɛr] nm,f usurer
usurpateur, -trice [yzyrpatœr, -tris] nm,f usurper

usurpation [yzyrpasjɔ̃] nf (d'un titre, de droits, du pouvoir) usurpation
usurper [yzyrpe] vt (titre, droits) to usurp (**sur** from)
ut [yt] nm inv (note) C
utérin, -e [yterɛ̃, -in] adj uterine
utérus [yterys] nm uterus, womb
utile [ytil] adj useful (**à** to); **en quoi puis-je vous être u.?** what can I do for you?; **vous nous avez été bien u.** you've been very helpful to us; **se rendre u.** to make oneself useful; **en temps u.** in due course
utilement [ytilmɑ̃] adv usefully; **il m'a u. renseigné** he gave me useful information
utilisable [ytilizabl] adj usable; **facilement u.** easy to use
utilisateur, -trice [ytilizatœr, -tris] nm,f user
utilisation [ytilizasjɔ̃] nf use
utiliser [ytilize] vt (a) (se servir de) to use (b) Péj (personne) to use (c) Ordinat to run
utilitaire [ytiliter] **1** adj (a) utilitarian; (véhicule) commercial (b) Ordinat utility **2** nm Ordinat utility; **u. de conversion** conversion utility
utilitarisme [ytilitarism] nm utilitarianism
utilité [ytilite] nf (fonction) usefulness; **être d'une grande u. (à qn)** to be very useful (to sb)
utopie [ytɔpi] nf utopia
utopique [ytɔpik] adj utopian
utopiste [ytɔpist] nmf Utopian
UV¹ [yve] nf inv Univ (abrév **unité de valeur**) credit
UV² nm inv (abrév **ultraviolet**) UV

V, v [ve] *nm inv* (**a**) *(lettre)* V, v; *Fam* **à la vitesse grand V** at a rate of knots (**b**) *(abrév* **voir**) see

va *voir* **aller**

vacance [vakɑ̃s] *nf* (**a**) *(d'un poste)* vacancy; **pendant la v. du pouvoir** while there is no one officially in power (**b**) **vacances** *(d'écoliers, de travailleurs) Br* holiday(s), *Am* vacation; **un jour de vacances** a day's holiday; **prendre des vacances** to take a holiday; **être en vacances** to be on holiday; **partir en vacances** to go away on holiday; *Fam* **faire des vacances à qn** to give sb a break; **vacances de neige** winter sports holiday; **vacances de Noël/Pâques** Christmas/Easter holidays; **vacances scolaires** school holidays; *Scol* **les grandes vacances** the summer holidays

vacancier, -ère [vakɑ̃sje, -ɛr] *nm,f Br* holidaymaker, *Am* vacationer

vacant, -e [vakɑ̃, -ɑ̃t] *adj* vacant

vacarme [vakarm] *nm* uproar, din; **faire du v.** to make an uproar

vacataire [vakatɛr] *nmf* short-term worker

vacation [vakasjɔ̃] *nf* (**a**) *(de juge, d'expert)* sitting, session (**b**) *(rémunération)* fees

vaccin [vaksɛ̃] *nm* vaccine

vaccination [vaksinasjɔ̃] *nf* vaccination, inoculation

vacciner [vaksine] *vt* to vaccinate, to inoculate (**contre** against); **se faire v. (contre)** to get vaccinated (against); *Fam* **je suis vacciné!** I've learnt my lesson!; *Fam* **je suis majeur et vacciné!** I'm a big boy now!

vache [vaʃ] **1** *nf* (**a**) *(animal)* cow; **v. à lait** dairy cow; *Fig* milch cow; **v. laitière** dairy cow; *Fam* **manger de la v. enragée** to have a hard time of it; *Fam* **parler français comme une v. espagnole** to speak rotten French (**b**) *Fam (homme)* swine; *(femme)* cow (**c**) *(cuir)* cowhide (**d**) *Fam (interjection)* **la v., qu'est-ce qu'il fait froid!** God, it's so cold!
2 *adj Fam* rotten, nasty; **être v. avec qn** to be rotten to sb

vachement [vaʃmɑ̃] *adv Fam (très) Br* dead, *Am* real; *(beaucoup)* a hell of a lot

vacher, -ère [vaʃe, -ɛr] *nm,f* cowherd, *f* cowgirl

vacherie [vaʃri] *nf Fam (action)* dirty trick; *(remarque)* nasty remark

vacherin [vaʃrɛ̃] *nm* (**a**) *(fromage)* = type of soft cheese (**b**) *(dessert)* = meringue with cream, ice cream and fruit

vachette [vaʃet] *nf* (**a**) *(petite vache)* small cow; *(jeune vache)* calf (**b**) *(cuir)* calfskin

vacillant, -e [vasijɑ̃, -ɑ̃t] *adj* (**a**) *(flamme)* flickering; *(démarche)* staggering (**b**) *(santé, mémoire)* failing

vacillation [vasijasjɔ̃] *nf*, **vacillement** [vasijmɑ̃] *nm* *(d'une flamme)* flickering

vaciller [vasije] *vi* (**a**) *(chanceler)* to be unsteady, to sway; **v. sur ses jambes** to stagger; **tout vacillait autour de moi** everything was swimming around me (**b**) *(flamme)* to flicker (**c**) *(mémoire, raison)* to fail

va-comme-je-te-pousse [vakɔmʒtəpus] **à la va-comme-je-te-pousse** *adv Fam* any old how

vacuité [vakɥite] *nf* vacuity

vadrouille [vadruj] *nf* (**a**) *Fam (balade)* ramble, saunter; **partir** *ou* **aller en v.** to roam about (**b**) *Can* mop

vadrouiller [vadruje] *vi Fam* to roam about

va-et-vient [vaevjɛ̃] *nm inv* (**a**) *(mouvement)* backward and forward movement, **faire le v. (entre)** *(personne)* to go back and forth (between) (**b**) *(circulation) (de personnes)* comings and goings (**c**) *(dispositif électrique)* two-way wiring (system)

vagabond, -e [vagabɔ̃, -ɔ̃d] **1** *adj* (**a**) *(vie)* wandering, roving (**b**) *Fig (pensées)* wandering, roaming; **avoir l'humeur vagabonde** to be in a restless mood
2 *nm,f* vagrant, tramp

vagabondage [vagabɔ̃daʒ] *nm* vagrancy

vagabonder [vagabɔ̃de] *vi (personne)* to wander, to roam; *Fig (pensées, imagination)* to wander, to stray

vagin [vaʒɛ̃] *nm* vagina

vaginal, -e, -aux, -ales [vaʒinal, -o] *adj* vaginal

vagir [vaʒir] *vi (nouveau-né)* to cry

vagissement [vaʒismɑ̃] *nm (de nouveau-né)* cry, wail

vague¹ [vag] *nf* (**a**) *(d'eau)* wave; *Fig* **faire des vagues** to make waves; **arriver par vagues** to come in waves; *aussi Fig* **v. de fond** ground swell (**b**) *(ondulations) (de chevelure, de dunes)* wave (**c**) *(courant artistique)* **nouvelle v.** new wave (**d**) *(d'enthousiasme, de tendresse)* wave, surge; **v. de chaleur** heat wave; **v. de froid** cold spell (**e**) *(afflux) (d'immigrants)* influx

vague² **1** *adj* (**a**) *(impression, geste, souvenir)* vague; *(forme)* indistinct; **regarder qn d'un air v.** to look vacantly at sb; **rester v. sur qch** to be vague about sth (**b**) *(avant le nom)* **quelque v. écrivain** some writer or other
2 *nm* (**a**) *(imprécision)* vagueness; **rester dans le v.** to be vague; **avoir du v. à l'âme** to be melancholy (**b**) *(vide)* **regard perdu dans le v.** faraway look

vaguelette [vaglet] *nf* wavelet

vaguement [vagmɑ̃] *adv* vaguely

vahiné [vaine] *nf* Tahitian woman

vaillamment [vajamɑ̃] *adv* valiantly

vaillance [vajɑ̃s] *nf* valour, courage

vaillant, -e [vajɑ̃, -ɑ̃t] *adj* (**a**) *(courageux)* valiant, courageous; *(cœur)* stout (**b**) *(en forme)* **être v.** to be in good health

vaille, vailles *voir* **valoir**

vain, -e [vɛ̃, vɛn] *adj* (a) *(sans résultat) (démarche, entreprise)* futile; *(efforts)* vain; **en v.** in vain (b) *(vide de sens) (paroles, promesse)* empty; *(espoirs, regrets)* vain (c) *Litt (personne)* vain

vaincre [vɛ̃kr] *vt* (a) *(adversaire)* to defeat; *(en sport)* to beat (b) *Fig (maladie, difficulté)* to overcome

vaincu, -e [vɛ̃ky] **1** *adj* beaten, defeated; **s'avouer v.** to admit defeat **2** *nm,f* defeated man, *f* defeated woman

vainement [vɛnmɑ̃] *adv* in vain

vainqueur [vɛ̃kœr] **1** *nm* (a) *(dans une compétition sportive)* winner (b) *(d'une bataille, d'une lutte)* victor **2** *adj m (personne)* conquering, victorious

vairon¹ [vɛrɔ̃] *adj* **avoir les yeux vairons** to have different-coloured eyes

vairon² *nm (poisson)* minnow

vais *voir* **aller**

vaisseau, -x [vɛso] *nm* (a) **v. (sanguin)** blood vessel (b) **v. spatial** spaceship (c) *(d'une église)* nave (d) *Litt* ship, vessel; **v. de guerre** warship

vaisselier [vɛsəlje] *nm (meuble)* dresser

vaisselle [vɛsɛl] *nf* dishes, crockery; **faire** *ou* **laver la v.** to do the washing-up, to do the dishes

val [val] *nm* valley

valable [valabl] *adj* (a) *(ticket, raison, excuse)* valid; **ce qui est v. pour l'un est v. pour l'autre** what goes for one goes for the other (b) *(compétent) (interlocuteur)* authorized (c) *(de qualité) (roman)* good; *(idée)* valid

valdinguer [valdɛ̃ge] *vi Fam* **aller v. contre/sur qch** to go flying against/onto sth; **envoyer v. qch** to send sth flying

Valence [valɑ̃s] *n* (a) *(en Espagne)* Valencia (b) *(en France)* Valence

valériane [valerjan] *nf* valerian

valet [valɛ] *nm* (a) *(au jeu de cartes)* jack, knave (b) *(domestique)* **v. (de chambre)** valet; **v. de ferme** farmhand; **v. de pied** footman (c) *(meuble)* **v. de nuit** valet

valétudinaire [valetydinɛr] *adj & nmf* valetudinarian

valeur [valœr] *nf* (a) *(prix)* value, worth; **avoir de la v.** to be valuable; **de peu de v./de grande v.** of little/of great value; **d'une v. de 100 euros** worth 100 euros; **prendre de la v.** to increase in value; **v. d'achat** purchase value; **v. ajoutée** added value; **v. en Bourse** stock market value; **v. marchande** market value; **valeurs mobilières** stocks and shares; **v. nominale** nominal value (b) *(qualité, mérite)* value; **de v.** *(livre, œuvre)* of considerable merit; **homme de v.** *(de mérite)* man of merit; **avoir v. légale** to be legally binding; **attacher de la v. à qch** to value sth; **mettre en v.** to show to advantage; *(teint, yeux)* to bring out; *(mot)* to emphasize; **se mettre en v.** to show oneself off to advantage; **prendre toute sa v.** *(terme, expression)* to take on its full meaning (c) *(titre)* security (d) *(d'une note)* time, length; *(d'une carte)* value (e) *(équivalent) (d'une mesure)* equivalent (f) *(morale)* **valeurs** values (g) *Litt (courage)* valour

valeureux, -euse [valørø, -øz] *adj Litt* gallant

validation [validasjɔ̃] *nf* *(d'un titre de transport)* validation; *(d'un document)* authentication

valide [valid] *adj* (a) *(contrat)* valid (b) *(personne) (en bonne santé)* fit; *(non blessé)* uninjured

valider [valide] *vt* (a) *(élection, mariage)* to validate; *(document)* to authenticate; **v. un titre de transport** *(dans une machine)* to stamp a ticket (b) *Ordinat (option)* to confirm; *(cellule, case)* to select

validité [validite] *nf* *(d'un contrat, d'un passeport)* validity

valise [valiz] *nf* (a) *(bagage)* suitcase; *aussi Fig* **faire ses valises** to pack one's bags (b) *(courrier)* **la v. diplomatique** the diplomatic *Br* bag *or Am* pouch (c) *Fam (sous les yeux)* bag

vallée [vale] *nf* valley; *Litt* **une v. de larmes** a vale of tears

vallon [valɔ̃] *nm* small valley

vallonné, -e [valɔne] *adj (région)* undulating, hilly

vallonnement [valɔnmɑ̃] *nm* undulation

valoche [valɔʃ] *nf Fam* case, bag

valoir [69] [valwar] **1** *vi* (a) *(avoir comme valeur)* to be worth; **v. cher** *(objet en vente)* to be expensive; *(objet précieux)* to be worth a lot; *Fig* **ne pas v. cher** *(personne)* not to be up to much; **ne rien v.** *(objet)* to be worthless; *(idée)* to be useless; **ce climat ne vous vaut rien** this climate doesn't suit you; **il ne vaut pas mieux que son père** he's no better than his father; **ça vaut mieux comme ça** it's better that way
(b) *(avoir un intérêt)* **et ça vaut pour tout le monde** and that goes for everyone; **faire v. qch** *(opinions, droits)* to assert sth
2 *vt* (a) *(équivaloir à)* to be equivalent to; **une livre vaut environ 1,5 euros** one pound is worth around 1.5 euros; **ça ne vaut pas ce qui m'est arrivé l'autre jour** that's nothing to what happened to me the other day; **rien ne vaut un bon petit déjeuner** there's nothing like a good breakfast (b) *(rapporter)* **v. qch à qn** *(punition)* to earn sb sth; *(soucis, ennuis)* to bring sb sth; **qu'est-ce qui me vaut cet honneur?** to what do I owe this honour?
3 *v impersonnel* **il vaut/vaudrait mieux faire qch** it's/it would be better to do sth; **il vaut mieux que vous restiez** you'd better stay, it would be better if you stayed; *Prov* **mieux vaut tard que jamais** better late than never
4 se valoir *vpr* **tous les métiers se valent** one job is as good as another; **ils se valent** *(péjoratif)* they're as bad as each other; *(admiratif)* they're as good as each other

valorisant, -e [valɔrizɑ̃, -ɑ̃t] *adj* gratifying

valorisation [valɔrizasjɔ̃] *nf* (a) *(augmentation de la valeur)* increase in value (b) *(développement)* development

valoriser [valɔrize] *vt (bien, monnaie)* to increase the value of; *(région)* to develop; *(personne)* to boost the self-esteem of

valse [vals] *nf* (a) *(morceau de musique, air de danse)* waltz (b) **la v. des ministres** frequent cabinet reshuffles

valse-hésitation *(pl* valses-hésitations*)* [val-sezitasjɔ̃] *nf Fam* pussyfooting, shilly-shallying

valser [valse] *vi* to waltz; **faire v. qn** to waltz with sb; *Fig* **faire v. les millions** to spend money like water; *Fam* **envoyer v. qn/qch** to send sb/sth flying

valseur, -euse [valsœr, -øz] *nm,f* waltzer

valu, -e *voir* **valoir**

valve [valv] *nf* valve

vamp [vɑ̃p] *nf Fam* vamp

vampire [vɑ̃pir] *nm* (a) *(suceur de sang)* vampire (b) *Fig (parasite)* bloodsucker

vampiriser [vɑ̃pirize] *vt Fam* to dominate psychologically

van¹ [vɑ̃] *nm (fourgon à chevaux)* horse box

van² [van] *nm (camionnette)* van

Vancouver [vɑ̃kuvɛr] *n* Vancouver

vandale [vɑ̃dal] *nmf* vandal

vandaliser [vɑ̃dalize] *vt* to vandalize

vandalisme [vɑ̃dalism] *nm* vandalism

vanille [vanij] *nf* vanilla

vanillé, -e [vanije] *adj* vanilla-flavoured

vanité [vanite] *nf* (a) *(suffisance)* vanity; **tirer v. de qch** to pride oneself on sth (**b**) *Litt (insignifiance)* futility, emptiness

vaniteux, -euse [vanitø, -øz] **1** *adj* vain

2 *nm,f* vain person

vanne¹ [van] *nf (de canalisation, d'écluse)* sluice gate, floodgate; **ouvrir/fermer les vannes** to open/to close the floodgates

vanne² *nf Fam (remarque blessante)* dig, jibe; **envoyer une v. à qn** to have a dig at sb

vanné, -e [vane] *adj Fam* **être v.** to be dead beat

vanneau, -x [vano] *nm (oiseau)* lapwing, peewit

vanner [vane] *vt* (**a**) *Fam (fatiguer)* to wear out, to exhaust (**b**) *(grain)* to winnow

vannerie [vanri] *nf* (**a**) *(activité)* basket making, basketry (**b**) *(objets)* basketwork, wickerwork

vannier [vanje] *nm* basket worker *or* maker

vantard, -e [vɑ̃tar, -ard] **1** *adj* bragging, boastful **2** *nm,f* braggart, boaster

vantardise [vɑ̃tardiz] *nf (caractère)* bragging, boastfulness; *(parole)* boast

vanter [vɑ̃te] **1** *vt* to praise, to speak highly of **2 se vanter** *vpr* to boast, to brag (**de** about)

Vanuatu [vanwatu] *n* Vanuatu

va-nu-pieds [vanypje] *nmf inv* tramp, beggar

vapes [vap] *nfpl Fam* **être dans les v.** to be all woozy; **tomber dans les v.** to pass out

vapeur¹ [vapœr] *nf* (**a**) *(d'eau bouillante)* **v.** (**d'eau**) steam; **cuire qch à la v.** to steam sth; **à toute v,** full steam ahead; *Fig* **at full speed** (**b**) *(gaz)* **vapeurs** *(d'alcool, d'essence)* fumes (**c**) *Méd* **avoir des vapeurs** to have a fit of the vapours

vapeur² *nm (bateau)* steamer, steamship

vaporeux, -euse [vaporø, -øz] *adj* (**a**) *(atmosphère)* steamy (**b**) *(robe)* flimsy

vaporisateur [vaporizatœr] *nm (de parfum)* spray, atomizer; *(pour plantes)* spray

vaporiser [vaporize] **1** *vt* (**a**) *(pulvériser)* to spray (**b**) *(transformer en vapeur)* to vaporize **2 se vaporiser** *vpr* to vaporize

vaquer [vake] **1** *vi (parlement, tribunal)* to be on vacation **2 vaquer à** *vt ind* **v. à qch** to attend to sth; **v. à ses affaires** *ou* occupations to go about one's business

varappe [varap] *nf* rock climbing; **faire de la v.** to go rock climbing

varapper [varape] *vi* to go rock climbing

varappeur, -euse [varapœr, -øz] *nm,f* rock climber

vareuse [varøz] *nf* (**a**) *(de marin)* pea jacket (**b**) *(d'uniforme)* tunic (**c**) *(veste large)* loose-fitting jacket

variable [varjabl] **1** *adj* (**a**) *(temps, humeur)* changeable; *(vitesse)* varying (**b**) *(différent)* varied; **être v.** to vary **2** *nf* variable; *Ordinat* **v. de mémoire** memory variable

variante [varjɑ̃t] *nf* variant, variation

variation [varjasjɔ̃] *nf* (**a**) *(écart)* change (**de** in); **les variations de la température** the variations in the temperature (**b**) *Mus* variation

varice [varis] *nf* varicose vein

varicelle [varisɛl] *nf* chickenpox, *Spéc* varicella; **avoir la v.** to have chickenpox

varié, -e [varje] *adj (alimentation, paysage, travail)* varied; *(vocabulaire)* wide

varier [varje] **1** *vt (alimentation, occupations)* to vary; *Ironique* **pour v. les plaisirs** by way of a pleasant change **2** *vi* to vary, to change; **les opinions varient sur ce point** opinions differ on this point; **il n'a jamais varié sur ce point** he's never changed his mind about it

variété [varjete] *nf* **1** *nf* variety

2 *nfpl TV* **variétés** variety show; **chanteur de variétés** middle-of-the-road singer

variole [varjɔl] *nf* smallpox; **avoir la v.** to have smallpox

Varsovie [varsɔvi] *n* Warsaw

vas *voir* **aller**

vasculaire [vaskylɛr] *adj* vascular

vase¹ [vaz] *nm* vase; *Fig* **vivre en v. clos** to live in isolation; **vases communicants** communicating vessels

vase² *nf* mud, silt

vasectomie [vazɛktɔmi] *nf* vasectomy

vaseline® [vazlin] *nf* Vaseline®, petroleum jelly

vaseux, -euse [vazø, -øz] *adj* (**a**) *Fam (mal en point)* off-colour (**b**) *(peu clair) (idée)* woolly; *(explication)* confused (**c**) *(plaisanterie)* unsavoury (**d**) *(rivière)* muddy, silty

vasistas [vazistas] *nm* fanlight

vasoconstricteur, -trice [vazokɔ̃striktœr, -tris] *adj & nm* vasoconstrictor

vasodilatateur, -trice [vazodilatatœr, -tris] *adj & nm* vasodilator

vasomoteur, -trice [vazomɔtœr, tris] *adj (nerf)* vasomotor

vasouillard, -e [vazujar, -ard] *adj Fam (idée)* confused, muddled; **se sentir v.** to feel a bit under the weather

vasouiller [vazuje] *vi Fam* to flounder

vassal, -e, -aux, -ales [vasal, -o] *nm,f* vassal

vaste [vast] *adj* (**a**) vast, immense (**b**) *Fam (plaisanterie)* big, great; **c'est une v. fumisterie** it's a complete farce

Vatican [vatikɑ̃] *nm* **le V.** the Vatican; **la cité du V.** the Vatican City

va-tout [vatu] *nm inv* **jouer son v.** to stake one's all

vaudeville [vodvil] *nm Th* light farce; **tourner au v.** to become farcical

vaudou, -e [vodu] *adj & nm* voodoo

vaudrai, vaudras *etc voir* **valoir**

vau l'eau [volo] **à vau-l'eau** *adv* **aller à v.** to fall through

vaurien, -enne [vorjɛ̃, -ɛn] *nm,f* (**a**) *(brigand)* good-for-nothing (**b**) *(enfant)* rascal

vaut *voir* **valoir**

vautour [votur] *nm* vulture

vautrer [votre] **se vautrer** *vpr* (**a**) *(cochon)* to wallow (**dans** in) (**b**) *(personne)* to sprawl (**dans** in); *Fig* **se v. dans la débauche** to wallow in vice

vauvert [vovɛr] *voir* **diable**

va-vite [vavit] **à la va-vite** *adv* in a rush

vaux *voir* **valoir**

VDQS [vedekyɛs] *nm (abrév* **vin délimité de qualité supérieure**) = label certifying that wine is of good quality

veau, -x [vo] *nm* (**a**) *(animal)* calf (**b**) *(viande)* veal (**c**) *(cuir)* calfskin (**d**) *Fam (personne lente)* lump (**e**) *Fam (voiture)* car with poor acceleration

vecteur [vɛktœr] *nm* (**a**) *Math* vector (**b**) *(d'information, de progrès)* vehicle

vectoriel, -elle [vɛktɔrjɛl] *adj* vectorial; *Ordinat* **police vectorielle** outline font

vécu, -e [veky] **1** *pp voir* **vivre**

2 *adj (expérience)* real-life

3 *nm* real-life experience

vedettariat [vədetarja] *nm* stardom

vedette [vədet] *nf* (**a**) *(acteur)* star; **v. de la chanson** singing star; **v. de cinéma** movie star; **avoir la v.,** **être en v.** *(dans un spectacle)* to top the bill; *(dans un film)* to be the main star (**b**) *Fig (de la politique)* leading light (**c**) *(bateau à moteur) (de plaisancier)* launch; *(de police)* patrol boat

végétal, -e, -aux, -ales [veʒetal, -o] **1** adj (huile) vegetable
2 nm vegetable, plant
végétarien, -enne [veʒetarjɛ̃, -ɛn] adj & nm,f vegetarian
végétatif, -ive [veʒetatif, -iv] adj (appareil) vegetative; Fig & Péj (existence) vegetable-like
végétation [veʒetasjɔ̃] nf (a) (flore) vegetation (b) Méd **végétations (adénoïdes)** adenoids
végéter [veʒete] vi Péj (personne) to vegetate
véhémence [veemɑ̃s] nf Litt vehemence; **avec v.** vehemently
véhément, -e [veemɑ̃, -ɑ̃t] adj Litt vehement, violent
véhicule [veikyl] nm (a) (moyen de transport) vehicle; **v. utilitaire** commercial vehicle (b) (support) (du son, de la lumière) vehicle
véhiculer [veikyle] vt (a) (transporter) to transport, to convey (b) (transmettre) to convey
veille [vɛj] nf (a) (jour qui précède) **la v.** the previous day, the day before; **à la v. de la réunion** the day before the meeting; **la v. au soir** the previous evening, the evening before; **la v. de Noël** Christmas Eve; Fig **être à la v. de qch/de faire qch** to be on the verge of sth/ of doing sth (b) (éveil) wakefulness; **entre la v. et le sommeil** between waking and sleeping; **après deux jours de v.** after staying up for two nights (c) (garde) (night) watch; **prendre la v.** to take one's turn on watch (d) Ordinat standby mode; **en v.** in standby mode
veillée [veje] nf (a) (soirée) evening; **v. au coin du feu** evening spent round the fire; **v. d'armes** knightly vigil (b) (d'un mort) watch, vigil
veiller [veje] **1** vt (malade) to sit up with; **v. un mort** to keep vigil over a dead body
2 vi to stay up
3 veiller à vt ind **v. à qch** to see to sth; **v. aux intérêts de qn** to look after sb's interests; **v. à ce que qn fasse qch** to make sure or see to it that sb does sth; Fig **v. au grain** to keep an eye open for trouble
4 veiller sur vt ind **v. sur qn** to take care of sb
veilleur [vejœr] nm **v. de nuit** night watchman
veilleuse [vejøz] nf (a) (lampe) night light; (sur une télévision, sur un magnétoscope) standby; Fig **mettre qch en v.** (projet, problème) to put sth on the back burner; Fam **la mettre en v.** to put a sock in it (b) (d'un chauffe-eau, d'un réchaud) pilot light (c) **veilleuses** (d'une automobile) Br sidelights, Am parking lights
veinard, -e [vɛnar, -ard] Fam **1** adj lucky
2 nm,f lucky devil
veine [vɛn] nf (a) Anat vein; **v. cave** vena cava (b) Fam (chance) luck; **avoir de la v.** to be lucky; Fam **avoir une v. de cocu** to have the luck of the devil (c) (dans le marbre, le bois) vein (d) (filon) (de minerai) vein; (de charbon) seam (e) (inspiration) vein; **en v. de plaisanterie** in humorous vein; **être en v. de générosité** to be in a generous mood
veiné, -e [vene] adj (marbre, bois) grained
veineux, -euse [vɛnø, -øz] adj (système, circulation) venous
veinule [venyl] nf venule
Velcro® [vɛlkro] nm (tissu) Velcro®; (fermeture) Velcro® fastening
vêler [vele] vi to calve
vélin [velɛ̃] nm vellum
véliplanchiste [veliplɑ̃ʃist] nmf windsurfer
velléitaire [veleiter] **1** adj indecisive
2 nmf indecisive person
velléités [veleite] nfpl vague desire; **avoir des v. de faire qch** to toy with the idea of doing sth

vélo [velo] nm bike; **aller au bureau en v.** to cycle to the office, to go to the office on one's bike; **faire du v.** (comme activité) to go cycling; **est-ce que tu sais faire du v.?** can you ride a bike?; **v. d'appartement** exercise bike; **v. de course** racing cycle; **v. tout-terrain** mountain bike
vélocité [velɔsite] nf speed, swiftness
vélodrome [velɔdrɔm] nm velodrome
vélomoteur [velɔmɔtœr] nm moped
velours [vəlur] nm (a) (tissu) velvet; **veste/rideaux en v.** velvet jacket/curtains; **v. côtelé** ou **à côtes** corduroy (b) Fig **faire des yeux de v. à qn** to make eyes at sb
velouté, -e [vəlute] **1** adj velvety
2 nm (a) (texture) velvetiness (b) (soupe) cream soup; **v. d'asperges** cream of asparagus soup
velouteux, -euse [vəlutø, -øz] adj velvety
Velpeau® [vɛlpo] voir **bande**
velu, -e [vəly] adj hairy
Vélux® [velyks] nm Velux® window
venaison [vənɛzɔ̃] nf venison
vénal, -e, -aux, -ales [venal, -o] adj (a) Péj (intéressé) venal, mercenary (b) (valeur) market
venant [vənɑ̃] nm **à tout v., à tous venants** to all comers, to all and sundry
vendable [vɑ̃dabl] adj saleable, sellable; **facilement/ difficilement v.** easy/difficult to sell
vendange [vɑ̃dɑ̃ʒ] nf (a) **vendanges** (période) grape-harvesting time (b) (récolte) grape harvest; **faire la v.** ou **les vendanges** to harvest or pick the grapes (c) (raisin récolté) grapes (harvested); **une bonne v.** a good vintage
vendanger [vɑ̃dɑ̃ʒe] **1** vi to harvest the grapes **2** vt (vigne) to pick the grapes from
vendangeur, -euse [vɑ̃dɑ̃ʒœr, -øz] nm,f grape picker
vendetta [vɑ̃deta] nf vendetta
vendeur, -euse [vɑ̃dœr, -øz] **1** adj **être v.** to be willing to sell
2 nm,f (dans un magasin) Br (shop) assistant, Am (sales) clerk; (non professionnel) seller; **v. ambulant** travelling salesman; **v. de journaux** newspaper seller or vendor
vendre [vɑ̃dr] **1** vt (a) (article, produit) to sell; **v. qch 50 euros** to sell sth for 50 euros; **v. qch à qn** to sell sb sth, to sell sth to sb; **à v.** (sur panneau) for sale; Fig **v. son âme au diable** to sell one's soul to the devil (b) (trahir) (personne) to sell out; (secret) to sell; **v. la mèche** to spill the beans
2 se vendre vpr (a) (produit, article) to be sold; **cela se vend comme des petits pains** it's selling like hot cakes (b) (soi-même) to sell oneself
vendredi [vɑ̃drədi] nm Friday; **le v. saint** Good Friday; voir aussi **samedi**
vendu, -e [vɑ̃dy] **1** adj (corrompu) bribed
2 nm,f traitor
vénéneux, -euse [venenø, -øz] adj poisonous
vénérable [venerabl] adj venerable
vénération [venerasjɔ̃] nf veneration; **avoir de la v. pour qn** to hold sb in veneration
vénérer [venere] vt to venerate
vénérien, -enne [venerjɛ̃, -ɛn] adj venereal
Venezuela [venezɥela] nm **le V.** Venezuela
vénézuélien, -enne [venezɥeljɛ̃, -ɛn] **1** adj Venezuelan
2 nm,f **V.** Venezuelan
vengeance [vɑ̃ʒɑ̃s] nf revenge, vengeance; **la v. est un plat qui se mange froid** revenge is a dish best eaten cold
venger [vɑ̃ʒe] **1** vt to avenge; **v. qn de qch** to avenge sb for sth
2 se venger vpr to get one's revenge; **se v. sur qn (de qch)**

to get one's revenge on sb (for sth); *Fam* **pas la peine de te v. sur moi!** there's no point in taking it out on me!

vengeur, -eresse [vãʒœr, -ʒrɛs] *Litt* **1** *adj* vengeful **2** *nm,f* avenger

véniel, -elle [venjɛl] *adj (péché)* venial

venimeux, -euse [vənimø, -øz] *adj aussi Fig* venomous

venin [vənɛ̃] *nm aussi Fig* venom

venir [70] [vənir] *(aux* être*)* **1** *vi* **(a)** *(arriver)* to come **(de** from); **il vient passer quelques jours** he's coming to spend a few days; **viens me voir** come and see me; **d'où venez-vous?** where do you come from?; **je viens!** I'm coming!; **v. vers qn** to come up to sb; **vous y viendrez!** you'll come round to it, you'll change your mind; **dans les mois/années qui viennent** in the coming months/years; **le moment est venu de nous en aller** it's time we left; **le jour viendra où...** the day will come when...; **ton tour viendra** your turn will come, you'll get your turn; **l'eau leur venait aux genoux** the water came up to their knees **(b)** *(tirer son origine)* to come **(de** from); **la maison lui vient de sa mère** he/she inherited the house from his/her mother **(c)** **en v. à qch/à** faire qch to come to sth/to do sth; **j'en suis venu à me demander si...** I began to wonder whether...; **où voulez-vous en v.?** what are you getting at?; **en v. aux mains** to come to blows **(d)** **venir de faire qch** to have just done sth; **je viens de le lui dire** I've just told him; **je venais de terminer** I'd just finished **2** *v impersonnel* **s'il venait à pleuvoir** if it happened to rain; **il m'est venu une idée intéressante** an interesting idea occurred to me **3** **s'en venir** *vpr Litt* to come along

Venise [vəniz] *n* Venice

vénitien, -enne [venisjɛ̃, -ɛn] **1** *adj* Venetian **2** *nm,f* **V.** Venetian

vent [vã] *nm* **(a)** *(air)* wind; **les cheveux au v.** with one's hair streaming in the wind; **quel bon v. vous amène?** to what do I/we owe the pleasure?; *Fig* **avoir le v. en poupe** to have the wind in one's sails; *Fig* **avoir du v. dans les voiles** to be three sheets to the wind; **avoir v. de qch** to get wind of sth; **ce n'est que du v.** it's just hot air; *Fam* **être dans le v.** to be with it; **contre vents et marées** come hell or high water; *Ironique* **bon v.!** good riddance! **(b)** *(flatulence)* wind; **avoir des vents** to have wind

vente [vãt] *nf (transaction)* sale; *(activité)* selling; **en v.** *(par un particulier)* for sale; *(dans les magasins)* on sale; **en v. libre** available over the counter; **mettre qch en v.** to put sth up for sale; **v. de charité** charity sale; **v. par correspondance** mail order (selling); **v. à crédit** credit sale; **v. au détail** retailing; **v. aux enchères** (sale by) auction; **v. en gros** wholesaling; **v. à tempérament** *Br* hire purchase, *Am* installment plan

venter [vãte] *v impersonnel* **il vente** it's windy

venteux, -euse [vãtø, -øz] *adj* windy

ventilateur [vãtilatœr] *nm* **(a)** *(pour aérer)* fan **(b)** *Ordinat* **v. de refroidissement** cooling fan **(c)** *(d'une automobile)* blower

ventilation [vãtilasjɔ̃] *nf* **(a)** *(aération)* ventilation **(b)** *(des dépenses)* breakdown

ventiler [vãtile] *vt* **(a)** *(aérer)* to ventilate **(b)** *(dépenses)* to break down

ventouse [vãtuz] *nf* **(a)** *(pour fixer)* suction grip; *(pour déboucher)* plunger; **faire v.** to adhere by suction **(b)** *(en verre)* cupping glass; **poser des ventouses à qn** to cup sb

ventral, -e, -aux, -ales [vãtral, -o] *adj* ventral

ventre [vãtr] *nm* **(a)** *(estomac)* stomach; **avoir le v. plein/vide** to have a full/an empty stomach; **avoir du v.** to have a

paunch; v. à terre at full speed, flat out; **avoir mal au v.** to have a sore stomach; *Fig* **ça fait mal au v.** de voir ça it makes me sick to see that; *Fig* **ça me ferait mal au v.!** it would kill me!; **ne rien avoir dans le v.** to have no guts **(b)** *(utérus)* womb **(c)** *(d'une bouteille)* bulge

ventricule [vãtrikyl] *nm* ventricle

ventriloque [vãtrilɔk] *nmf* ventriloquist

ventru, -e [vãtry] *adj* **(a)** *(gros)* potbellied **(b)** *(colonne)* bulbous

venu, -e [vny] **1** *adj* **bien v.** appropriate; **mal v.** inappropriate **2** *nm,f* **le premier v.** *(n'importe qui)* anybody; **un nouveau v.** a newcomer **3** *nf* **venue** *(d'une personne, du printemps)* coming; **dès sa venue au monde** since he/she came into the world

Vénus [venys] *npr (déesse, planète)* Venus

vêpres [vɛpr] *nfpl* vespers

ver [vɛr] *nm* **(a)** *(dans la terre)* worm; *(dans un fruit)* grub; *Fig* **tirer les vers du nez à qn** to drag it out of sb; **v. luisant** glow-worm; **v. à soie** silkworm; **v. de terre** earthworm **(b)** *Méd* **v. solitaire** tapeworm; **avoir le v. solitaire** to have a tapeworm

véracité [verasite] *nf* truthfulness

véranda [verãda] *nf* veranda(h)

verbal, -e, -aux, -ales [verbal, -o] *adj* verbal

verbalement [verbalmã] *adv* verbally

verbaliser [verbalize] **1** *vt (exprimer)* to verbalize **2** *vi (policier)* to record the details of an offence

verbe [verb] *nm Gram* verb; **v. à particule** *(en anglais)* phrasal verb

verbeux, -euse [verbø, -øz] *adj* verbose

verbiage [verbjaʒ] *nm* verbiage

verdâtre [verdatr] *adj* greenish

verdeur [verdœr] *nf* **(a)** *(d'un fruit, d'un vin)* tartness **(b)** *(du langage)* crudeness **(c)** *(vitalité)* vigour, vitality

verdict [verdikt] *nm* verdict; **prononcer** *ou* **rendre un v.** to return a verdict

verdir [verdir] **1** *vt* to turn green **2** *vi* to turn green; *Fig* **v. de jalousie/de peur** to go *or* turn green with envy/white with fear

verdoyant, -e [verdwajã, ãt] *adj* green

verdoyer [verdwaje] *vi Litt* to be green

verdure [verdyr] *nf* **(a)** *(couleur)* greenness **(b)** *(végétation)* greenery **(c)** *(légumes verts)* greens

véreux, -euse [verø, -øz] *adj* **(a)** *(fruit)* wormy, maggoty **(b)** *Péj (affaires, financier)* shady, dubious

verge [verʒ] *nf* **(a)** *(pénis)* penis **(b)** *(baguette)* cane **(c)** *Can (mesure)* yard

verger [verʒe] *nm* orchard

vergetures [verʒətyr] *nfpl* stretch marks

verglacé, -e [verglase] *adj* icy

verglas [vergla] *nm Br* (black) ice, *Am* glaze

vergogne [vergɔɲ] **sans vergogne 1** *adj* shameless **2** *adv* shamelessly

véridique [veridik] *adj* truthful

vérifiable [verifjabl] *adj* verifiable

vérificateur, -trice [verifikatœr, -tris] **1** *nm,f (personne)* inspector, examiner; **v. de comptes** auditor **2** *nm Ordinat* **v. orthographique** spellchecker

vérification [verifikasjɔ̃] *nf* **(a)** *(d'un travail, des votes)* checking; **v. de comptes** *ou* **d'écritures** audit(ing) of accounts **(b)** *Ordinat* **v. antivirale** antiviral check; **v. orthographique** spellcheck

vérifier [verifje] **1** *vt* to check; *(comptes)* to audit; **il doit**

être là, je vais v. he must be there, I'll check **2 se vérifier** vpr to prove correct
véritable [veritabl] adj (**a**) (histoire, ami) true; (nom, or, cuir) real (**b**) (en intensif) real
véritablement [veritabləmã] adv really
vérité [verite] nf (**a**) (d'une déclaration) truth; **dire la v.** to tell the truth; **c'est la v.** it's true, it's a fact; **à la v.** to tell the truth; **en v.** really, actually; **dire à qn ses quatre vérités** to tell sb a few home truths (**b**) (d'un personnage, d'une description) trueness to life (**c**) (sincérité) **un accent de v.** a ring of truth
verlan [verlã] nm back slang
vermeil, -eille [vermɛj] **1** adj bright red **2** nm silver gilt
vermicelle [vermisɛl] nm vermicelli
vermifuge [vermifyʒ] nm vermifuge
vermillon [vermijɔ̃] adj inv & nm vermilion
vermine [vermin] nf (**a**) (insectes) vermin; **couvert** ou **grouillant de v.** crawling with vermin (**b**) Péj (racaille) **la v.** vermin
vermisseau, -x [vermiso] nm small worm; Fig (personne) worm
vermoulu, -e [vermuly] adj worm-eaten
vermouth [vermut] nm vermouth
vernaculaire [vernakyler] adj **langue v.** vernacular
verni, -e [verni] adj (**a**) (meuble, bois, parquet) varnished; (chaussures) patent (leather); (ongles) varnished, painted (**b**) Fam (chanceux) lucky
vernir [vernir] vt to varnish
vernis [verni] nm (**a**) (pour le bois) varnish; **v. à ongles** nail varnish or polish; **se mettre du v. à ongles** to varnish or paint one's nails (**b**) Fig **un v. de culture** a smattering of knowledge
vernissage [vernisaʒ] nm (**a**) (du bois) varnishing (**b**) (d'une exposition) opening, private viewing
vérole [verɔl] nf Vieilli syphilis; **la petite v.** smallpox
verra, verrai etc voir **voir**
verre [ver] nm (**a**) (matière) glass; **sous v.** under glass; **gravure sous v.** glass-mounted engraving; **v. blanc** glass; **v. dépoli/feuilleté** frosted/laminated glass (**b**) (récipient) glass; **v. à dents** tooth glass; **v. doseur** ou **gradué** ≃ measuring jug; **v. à eau** large wine glass; **v. à pied** stemmed glass; **v. à vin** wineglass; **v. à whisky** whisky glass (**c**) (contenu) glass(ful) (**d**) (boisson) drink; **boire** ou **prendre un v.** to have a drink (**e**) (de lunettes) lens; **verres de contact** contact lenses; **v. à double foyer** bifocals; **verres teintés** ou **fumés** tinted lenses
verrerie [verri] nf (**a**) (fabrication) glass-making (**b**) (atelier) glassworks (**c**) (marchandise) glassware
verrier [verje] nm (artisan) glass-maker
verrière [verjer] nf (**a**) (toit) glass roof; (paroi) glass wall (**b**) (pièce) conservatory
verroterie [verɔtri] nf glass jewellery
verrou [veru] nm bolt; **mettre** ou **tirer le v.** to bolt the door; Fig **sous les verrous** behind bars, inside
verrouillage [verujaʒ] nm (**a**) (d'une porte) bolting; (à clé) locking (**b**) (d'un mécanisme) locking; **v. central** central locking (**c**) Ordinat **v. des fichiers** file lock; **v. en lecture seule** read-only lock; **v. en majuscule(s)** caps lock
verrouiller [veruje] vt (**a**) (porte) to bolt; (à clé) to lock; (prisonnier) to lock up (**b**) (quartier) to close off, to seal off (**c**) Ordinat (capitales) to lock on; **verrouillé en majuscule(s)** (clavier) with caps lock on
verrue [very] nf wart; **v. plantaire** verruca

vers¹ [ver] nm (poétique) line; **faire des v.** to write verse or poetry; **v. blancs** blank verse; **v. libres** free verse
vers² prép (**a**) (dans la direction de) towards (**b**) (aux alentours de) (dans le temps) about; (dans l'espace) near; **v. la fin** towards the end; Fam **v. les trois heures** about or around 3 o'clock
versant [versã] nm slope, side
versatile [versatil] adj changeable, fickle
versatilité [versatilite] nf changeability, fickleness
verse [vers] **à verse** adv **il pleut à v.** it's pouring (down); **la pluie tombait à v.** the rain was coming down in torrents
versé, -e [verse] adj **être v. dans qch** to be well-versed in sth
Verseau [verso] nm Astron & Astrol **le V.** Aquarius; **être V.** to be (an) Aquarius or an Aquarian
versement [versəmã] nm payment
verser [verse] **1** vt (**a**) (liquide) to pour (out) (dans into); **v. à boire à qn** to pour sb a drink, to pour a drink for sb (**b**) (larmes, sang) to shed (**c**) (argent) to pay; **v. de l'argent sur son compte** to pay or deposit money into one's account (**d**) Jur (document) to add (à to)
2 vi (véhicule) to overturn
3 verser dans vt ind to lapse into
verset [verse] nm verse
verseur, -euse [versœr, -øz] **1** adj voir **bec**
2 nf verseuse jug, pot (for coffee machine)
versification [versifikasjɔ̃] nf versification
version [versjɔ̃] nf (**a**) (d'un événement, d'un texte) version (**b**) (traduction) translation; **v. anglaise/espagnole** (à l'école) translation from English/Spanish (**c**) Cin **en v. originale** in the original language; **en v. française** dubbed (into French) (**d**) Ordinat **v. bêta** beta version
verso [verso] nm back; **voir au v.** see over(leaf)
vert, -e [ver, vert] **1** adj (**a**) (couleur) green; Fig **v. de peur** white with fear; Fig **v. de jalousie** green with envy; Fig **avoir la main verte** to have Br green fingers or Am a green thumb (**b**) (jeune) (bois) green; (fruit) unripe; (vin) too young (**c**) (écologique) green (**d**) (vieillard) sprightly (**e**) (histoire, propos) spicy (**f**) (réprimande) sharp
2 nm (**a**) (couleur) green; **passer au v.** (signal d'arrêt) to go or turn green; **v. amande** almond green; **v. bouteille** bottle green; **v. d'eau** sea green; **v. émeraude** emerald green; **v. olive** olive green; **v. pomme** apple green (**b**) Fam **se mettre au v.** to go to the country; Pol **les Verts** ≃ the Green Party
3 nfpl **vertes** Fam **en dire de vertes** to tell spicy stories; **il en a vu de vertes et des pas mûres** he's been through a lot
vert-de-gris [verdəgri] **1** nm inv verdigris
2 adj grey-green
vertébral, -e, -aux, -ales [vertebral, -o] adj vertebral
vertèbre [vertebr] nf vertebra
vertébré, -e [vertebre] adj & nm vertebrate
vertement [vertəmã] adv sharply
vertical, -e, -aux, -ales [vertikal, -o] **1** adj vertical; **en position verticale** (objet) in a vertical position, upright
2 nf verticale vertical; **à la verticale** vertically
verticalement [vertikalmã] adv vertically; (dans les mots croisés) down
vertige [vertiʒ] nm (**a**) (au-dessus du vide) vertigo; **avoir le v.** (toujours) to suffer from vertigo; (ponctuellement) to feel dizzy; **donner le v. à qn** (vide) to make sb dizzy; Fig to make sb's head spin (**b**) (étourdissement) dizziness, giddiness; **avoir des vertiges** to have dizzy spells
vertigineusement [vertiʒinøzmã] adv **grimper v.** to rocket; **chuter v.** to plummet

vertigineux, -euse [vɛrtiʒinø, -øz] *adj (hauteur)* dizzy; *(vitesse)* breakneck; *(somme, hausse des prix)* staggering

vertu [vɛrty] *nf* **(a)** *(propriété)* property **(b)** *(qualité morale)* virtue **(c)** *Litt (chasteté)* virtue; **femme de petite v.** woman of easy virtue **(d) en v. de qch** *(principe, loi)* in accordance with sth; **en v. des pouvoirs qui me sont conférés by** virtue of the powers bestowed upon me; **en v. de quoi est-il intervenu?** what gave him the right to intervene?

vertueux, -euse [vɛrtɥø, -øz] *adj* virtuous; *(intention)* honourable

verve [vɛrv] *nf* verve; **être en v.** to be on top form

verveine [vɛrvɛn] *nf* **(a)** *(plante)* verbena **(b)** *(tisane)* verbena tea

vésicule [vezikyl] *nf* vesicle; **v. biliaire** gall bladder

vespasienne [vɛspazjɛn] *nf* street urinal

vespéral, -e, -aux, -ales [vɛsperal, -o] *adj Litt* evening

vessie [vesi] *nf* bladder; *Fig* **prendre des vessies pour des lanternes** to believe that the moon is made of green cheese

veste [vɛst] *nf* jacket; **v. droite/croisée** single-/double-breasted jacket; *Fam Fig* **prendre une v.** to come unstuck

vestiaire [vɛstjɛr] *nm* **(a)** *(d'un théâtre)* cloakroom, *(d'un stade)* changing room, locker room **(b)** **récupérer son v.** to collect one's things from the cloakroom

vestibule [vɛstibyl] *nm* (entrance) hall

vestiges [vɛstiʒ] *nmpl* **(a)** *(ruines)* remains **(b)** *(traces)* relics

vestimentaire [vɛstimɑ̃tɛr] *adj (dépenses)* clothing

veston [vɛstɔ̃] *nm* jacket

Vésuve [vezyv] *nm* **le V.** Vesuvius

vêtement [vɛtmɑ̃] *nm* garment, article of clothing; **vêtements** clothes, clothing; **vêtements de travail** work clothes

vétéran [veterɑ̃] *nm* veteran

vétérinaire [veterinɛr] **1** *adj* veterinary **2** *nmf* vet; *(sur une plaque)* veterinary surgeon

vétille [vetij] *nf* trifle, triviality

vêtir [vetir] *Litt* **1** *vt (personne)* to clothe, to dress **(de** in) **2 se vêtir** *vpr* to dress (oneself) **(de** in)

vétiver [vetivɛr] *nm* vetiver

veto [veto] *nm* veto; **opposer son v. à qch** to veto sth; **droit de v.** right of veto

vêtu, -e [vety] *adj* dressed **(de** in)

vétuste [vetyst] *adj* dilapidated

vétusté [vetyste] *nf* dilapidation

veuf, veuve [vœf, vœv] **1** *adj* **être v.** to be a widower; **être veuve** to be a widow **2** *nm,f* widower, *f* widow

veuille *etc voir* **vouloir**

veule [vøl] *adj Litt (personne)* effete

veulerie [vølri] *nf Litt* effeteness

veut *voir* **vouloir**

veuvage [vœvaʒ] *nm (d'homme)* widowerhood; *(de femme)* widowhood

veux *voir* **vouloir**

vexant, -e [vɛksɑ̃, -ɑ̃t] *adj* **(a)** *(blessant)* hurtful **(b)** *(contrariant)* annoying

vexation [vɛksasjɔ̃] *nf* humiliation

vexatoire [vɛksatwar] *adj* humiliating

vexer [vɛkse] **1** *vt* to hurt, to upset; *Fam* **être vexé comme un pou** to be extremely upset **2 se vexer** *vpr* to get upset **(de** at)

VF [veɛf] *nf (abrév* **version française) en VF** dubbed *(into French)*

via [vja] *prép* via

viabiliser [vjabilize] *vt* to service

viabilité¹ [vjabilite] *nf (d'un nouveau-né, d'un projet)* viability

viabilité² *nf (d'un chemin)* practicability

viable [vjabl] *adj* viable

viaduc [vjadyk] *nm* viaduct

viager, -ère [vjaʒe, -ɛr] **1** *adj* life **2** *nm* life annuity; **mettre qch en v.** to sell sth in return for a life annuity

viande [vjɑ̃d] *nf* meat; **v. blanche/rouge** white/red meat; **v. hachée** *Br* mince, *Am* ground meat

viander [vjɑ̃de] **se viander** *vpr très Fam* to get smashed up

vibrant, -e [vibrɑ̃, -ɑ̃t] *adj (discours, hommage)* rousing, stirring

vibraphone [vibrafɔn] *nm* vibraphone

vibration [vibrasjɔ̃] *nf* vibration

vibrato [vibrato] *nm* vibrato

vibrer [vibre] *vi* **(a)** *(objet)* to vibrate **(b)** *(personne)* to be stirred; **sa voix vibrait de colère** his/her voice was shaking with anger; **faire v. qn** to stir sb

vibromasseur [vibromasœr] *nm* vibrator

vicaire [vikɛr] *nm (dans la religion catholique)* assistant priest; *(dans la religion anglicane)* curate

vice [vis] *nm* **(a)** *(défaut moral)* vice **(b)** *(défectuosité)* defect; **v. caché** hidden or latent defect; **v. de fabrication** manufacturing defect; *Jur* **v. de forme** legal flaw **(c)** *(débauche)* vice; *Fig* **mais c'est du v.!** it's an obsession!

vice-amiral [visamiral] *(pl* **vice-amiraux** [visamiro]) *nm* vice admiral

vice-consul *(pl* **vice-consuls)** [viskɔ̃syl] *nm* vice consul

vice-présidence *(mpl* **vice-présidences)** [visprezidɑ̃s] *nf (d'état, d'organisation)* vice-presidency *(d'entreprise)* vice-chairmanship

vice-président, -e *(mpl* **vice-présidents,** *fpl* **vice-présidentes)** [visprezidɑ̃, -ɑ̃t] *nm,f (d'état, d'organisation)* vice-president; *(d'entreprise)* vice-chairman

vice versa [visversa] *adv* vice versa

vichy [viʃi] *nm (tissu)* gingham

vicié, -e [visje] *adj (air)* polluted **(b)** *Jur* invalidated

vicieux, -euse [visjø, -jøz] *adj* **(a)** *(pervers)* depraved **(b)** *(perfide)* underhand **(c)** *(chien)* vicious

vicissitudes [visisityd] *nfpl* vicissitudes

vicomte [vikɔ̃t] *nm* viscount

vicomtesse [vikɔ̃tɛs] *nf* viscountess

victime [viktim] *nf (d'un accident)* casualty; **être v. d'un attentat/d'une agression** to be the victim of an assassination attempt/of an attack; **être la v. d'une illusion/d'un malentendu** to labour under an illusion/a misconception

victoire [viktwar] *nf* victory; *(en sport)* win, victory; **chanter** *ou* **crier v.** to claim victory

victorien, -enne [viktɔrjɛ̃, -ɛn] *adj* Victorian

victorieusement [viktɔrjøzmɑ̃] *adv* victoriously

victorieux, -euse [viktɔrjø, -øz] *adj* victorious; *(air, sourire)* triumphant

victuailles [viktɥaj] *nfpl* provisions

vidange [vidɑ̃ʒ] *nf* **(a)** *(d'un moteur)* oil change; **faire la v.** to change the oil **(b)** *(d'une fosse septique)* draining, emptying

vidanger [vidɑ̃ʒe] *vt* **(a)** *(huile)* to change; *(moteur)* to change the oil in **(b)** *(fosse septique)* to drain, to empty

vide [vid] **1** adj empty; (regard) blank; **v. de sens** devoid of meaning, meaningless

2 nm Phys vacuum; (espace) empty space, gap; Fig (dans un emploi du temps) gap; **rouler à v.** (bus) to have no passengers; **emballé sous v.** vacuum-packed; **faire le v.** to create a vacuum; Fig (se ressourcer) to switch off; Fig **faire le v. dans son esprit** to clear one's mind; **regarder dans le v.** to stare into space; **c'est comme si je parlais dans le v.** it's like talking to a brick wall; **avoir peur du v.** to be afraid of or to have no head for heights; **il y a un v.** juridique concernant cela there's nothing in the law to cover that; **v. sanitaire** crawl space

vidé, -e [vide] adj Fam (épuisé) dead beat

vidéo [video] **1** adj inv video
2 nf video; Ordinat **v. inversée** reverse video

vidéocassette [videokaset] nf video cassette

vidéo-clip [videoklip] nm video

vidéoconférence [videokɔ̃ferɑ̃s] nf videoconference; (concept) videoconferencing

vidéodisque [videodisk] nm videodisk

vide-ordures [vidɔrdyr] nm inv Br rubbish or Am garbage chute

vidéothèque [videotɛk] nf video library

vide-poches [vidpɔʃ] nm inv (a) (de voiture) (dans le tableau de bord) storage tray; (dans la porte) door pocket (b) (de maison) tidy

vide-pomme (pl **vide-pommes**) [vidpɔm] nm apple corer

vider [vide] **1** vt (a) (enlever le contenu de) to empty (**de** of); Fam Fig **v. son sac** to get it off one's chest; Fig **v. son cœur** to pour out one's feelings (b) Fam (épuiser) to wear out (c) Fam (expulser) to chuck out; **se faire v.** to be chucked out (d) **v. les lieux** to vacate the premises (e) (poisson) to gut; (volaille) to draw (f) Ordinat **v. l'écran** to clear the screen; **v. la corbeille** to empty the wastebasket or Am the trash
2 se vider vpr to empty; **se v. de son sang** to bleed to death

videur, -euse [vidœr, -øz] nm,f bouncer

vie [vi] nf (a) (d'êtres vivants) life; **être en v.** to be alive; **être entre la v. et la mort** to be fighting for one's life; **donner la v. à un enfant** to give birth to a child; **avoir la v. dure** (mauvaise herbe, parasite) to be hard to kill off; (superstitions, préjugés) to die hard; **entre eux, c'est à la v., à la mort** they'd die for each other; **être plein de v.** to be full of life; **sans v.** lifeless (b) (animation) life; **donner de la v. à qch** to liven sth up (c) (durée d'existence) life, lifetime; **pour la v.** for life; **une (seule) fois dans la v.** once in a lifetime (d) (biographie) life story; Fam **raconter sa v. à qn** to tell sb one's life story (e) (façon de vivre) life; **c'est la v. de château!** this is the life!; **v. nocturne** nightlife; Fam **Vieilli faire la v.** to live it up (f) (subsistance) **la v. est très chère dans ces pays** the cost of living is very high in these countries

vieil [vjɛj] voir **vieux**

vieillard [vjɛjar] nm old man

vieille [vjɛj] **1** adj f voir **vieux**
2 nf (poisson) wrasse

vieillerie [vjɛjri] nf (objet) old thing

vieillesse [vjɛjɛs] nf old age

vieilli, -e [vjeji] adj (a) (mot, style) old-fashioned, dated (b) (personne) aged

vieillir [vjejir] **1** vi (a) (personne) to get old, to age (b) (mot, film, chanson) to be dated (c) (fromage, vin) to mature
2 vt (personne) (par l'apparence) to age; **v. qn (de deux ans)** to make sb out to be (two years) older than he/she is
3 se vieillir vpr (a) (par l'apparence) to make oneself look

older (b) (se dire plus âgé) to pretend to be older than one is

vieillissant, -e [vjejisɑ̃, -ɑ̃t] adj (personne) ageing; (institution, style) which is becoming outdated

vieillissement [vjejismɑ̃] nm (a) (d'une personne, de la population) ageing; **retarder le v. de la peau** to delay the ageing process (b) (d'un fromage, d'un vin) maturing

vieillot, -otte [vjejo, -ɔt] adj old-fashioned

vielle [vjɛl] nf hurdy-gurdy

Vienne [vjɛn] n Vienna

vienne, viens etc voir **venir**

viennois, -e [vjɛnwa, -az] **1** adj Viennese; **un pain v.** a Vienna loaf
2 nm,f **V.** Viennese

vierge [vjɛrʒ] **1** adj (a) (personne) **être v.** to be a virgin; **une fille v.** a virgin (b) (sol, huile) virgin (c) (page, cassette) blank; (casier judiciaire) clean (d) Ordinat (ligne, espace) blank; (disquette) blank, unformatted
2 nf (a) (personne) virgin; **la (Sainte) V.** the Blessed Virgin (Mary) (b) Astron & Astrol **la V.** Virgo; **être V.** to be (a) Virgo

Viêt Nam [vjɛtnam] nm **le V.** Vietnam

vietnamien, -enne [vjɛtnamjɛ̃, -ɛn] **1** adj Vietnamese
2 nm,f **V.** Vietnamese
3 nm (langue) Vietnamese

vieux, vieille [vjø, vjɛj]

> **vieil** is used before masculine singular nouns beginning with a vowel or h mute.

1 adj old; **plus/moins v. que qn** older/younger than sb; **v. comme le monde** as old as the hills; **être v. jeu** to be old-fashioned
2 nm,f (a) (personne) old man, f old woman; **les v.** old people, the elderly; Fam **un v. de la vieille** one of the old brigade (b) Fam **il a pris un coup de v.** he's failed (c) Fam (parent) **mes v.** my folks; **mon v.** my old man; **ma vieille** my old woman (d) Fam (ami) **mon v.** mate, pal; **ma vieille** old girl

vif, vive [vif, viv] **1** adj (a) (personne, discussion) lively (b) (imagination) vivid; (intelligence) sharp; (mouvement) quick; Euph **il n'est pas très v.** he's not very bright (c) (vent, douleur) sharp (d) (couleur) bright (e) (satisfaction, intérêt) great; (félicitations) warm (f) **dire qch à qn de vive voix** to tell sb sth personally
2 nm (a) Jur living person (b) (à la pêche) live bait (c) (locutions) **à v.** (plaie) open; **avoir les nerfs à v.** to be on edge; **entrer dans le v. du sujet** to get to the heart of the matter; **une photo prise sur le v.** a natural or unposed photo

vif-argent [vifarʒɑ̃] nm quicksilver; Fig (personne) live wire

vigie [viʒi] nf (a) (matelot) lookout; **être de v.** to be on the lookout (b) (poste) (sur un bateau) lookout post; (sur un train) observation box

vigilance [viʒilɑ̃s] nf vigilance

vigilant, -e [viʒilɑ̃, -ɑ̃t] adj vigilant

vigile [viʒil] nm (night) watchman

vigne [viɲ] nf (a) (petit arbre) vine (b) (vignoble) vineyard (c) **v. vierge** Virginia creeper

vigneron, -onne [viɲərɔ̃, -ɔn] nm,f wine grower

vignette [viɲɛt] nf (a) (pharmaceutique) label (showing details of medication and which has to be attached to the "feuille de maladie" in order to qualify for reimbursement by the Social Security) (b) **la v. (automobile)** the (road) tax disc (c) (motif) vignette

vignoble [viɲɔbl] nm vineyard; **le v. français/californien** the French/Californian vineyards

vigoureusement [vigurøzmɑ̃] adv vigorously

vigoureux, -euse [vigurø, -øz] *adj (personne, animal)* vigorous; *(plante, arbre)* sturdy; *(résistance)* strong

vigueur [vigœr] *nf* **(a)** *(d'une personne, d'un animal, d'un style)* vigour; *(d'une plante, d'un arbre)* sturdiness **(b) en v.** *(décret)* in force; **entrer en v.** to come into force

VIH [veiaʃ] *nm (abrév* **virus de l'immunodéficience humaine)** HIV

viking [vikiŋ] **1** *adj* Viking **2** *nmf* **V.** Viking

vil, -e [vil] *adj* **(a)** *Litt (personne, motif)* vile **(b)** *(bas)* **à v. prix** at a very low price

vilain, -e [vilɛ̃, -ɛn] **1** *adj* **(a)** *(laid)* ugly **(b)** *(déplaisant)* nasty **(c)** *(pas sage)* naughty
2 *nm,f Fam* **oh, le v./la vilaine!** *(à un enfant)* you naughty boy/girl!
3 *nm* **(a)** *Fam* **il va y avoir du v.** there's going to be trouble **(b)** *Hist* villein

vilebrequin [vilbrəkɛ̃] *nm* **(a)** *(outil)* brace **(b)** *(dans un moteur)* crankshaft

vilenie [vileni] *nf Litt* **(a)** *(caractère)* vileness **(b)** *(action)* vile deed

villa [villa] *nf* villa

village [vilaʒ] *nm* village; **v. de pêcheurs** fishing village; **v. de vacances, v.-vacances** holiday village

villageois, -e [vilaʒwa, -az] *nm,f* villager

ville [vil] *nf* town; *(de grande taille)* city; **grande v.** city; **en v.** in (the) town; *(au centre ville) Br* in the town/city centre, *Am* downtown, **aller en v.** to go into town; **habiter à la v.** to live in a town *(as opposed to the country)*, **v. basse/haute** lower/upper part of town; **v. champignon** boom town; **v. d'eaux** spa (town); **v. nouvelle** new town

ville-dortoir *(pl* **villes-dortoirs)** [vildɔrtwar] *nf* dormitory town

villégiature [vileʒjatyr] *nf Br* holiday, *Am* vacation; **lieu de v.** *Br* holiday resort, *Am* resort

Vilnius [vilnijys] *n* Vilnius

vin [vɛ̃] *nm* **(a)** *(boisson)* wine; **avoir le v. gai/triste** to be/not to be a happy drunk; **grand v.** vintage wine; **v. d'appellation contrôlée** wine of guaranteed vintage; **v. blanc/rouge/rosé** white/red/rosé wine; **v. cuit** = type of mulled wine, **v. mousseux** sparkling wine; **v. de pays** regional wine; **v. de table** *ou* **ordinaire** table wine **(b) v. d'honneur** reception *(where wine is served)*

vinaigre [vinɛgr] *nm* vinegar; *Fam* **tourner au v.** to turn sour; **v. blanc** distilled vinegar; **v. de vin** wine vinegar

vinaigrette [vinɛgrɛt] *nf* vinaigrette, French dressing

vinasse [vinas] *nf Fam* cheap wine

vindicatif, -ive [vɛ̃dikatif, -iv] *adj* vindictive

vindicte [vɛ̃dikt] *nf* **désigner qn à la v. publique** to expose sb to public condemnation

vineux, -euse [vinø, -øz] *adj* **(a)** *(goût, odeur)* winy **(b)** *(couleur)* wine(-coloured)

vingt [vɛ̃] **1** *adj inv* twenty; **v.-quatre heures sur v.-quatre** round the clock, twenty-four hours a day
2 *nm inv* twenty; *voir aussi* **trois**

vingtaine [vɛ̃tɛn] *nf* **une v. (de)** about twenty, twenty or so

vingtième [vɛ̃tjɛm] *adj, nmf & nm* twentieth; *voir aussi* **cinquième**

vinicole [vinikɔl] *adj (région)* wine-growing

vinyle [vinil] *nm* vinyl

viol [vjɔl] *nm* **(a)** *(crime sexuel)* rape **(b)** *(d'un sanctuaire)* violation

violacé, -e [vjɔlase] *adj* purplish-blue

violation [vjɔlasjɔ̃] *nf* **(a)** *(de la loi, de règles)* violation **(b)**

(d'une sépulture) desecration; **v. de domicile** illegal entry

viole [vjɔl] *nf* viol

violemment [vjɔlamã] *adv* violently

violence [vjɔlɑ̃s] *nf* *(physique)* violence; *(verbale)* fierceness; *(d'un sentiment)* intensity; **se faire v.** to force oneself

violent, -e [vjɔlɑ̃, -ɑ̃t] *adj (personne, douleur, quartier)* violent; *(vent, paroles)* fierce; *(odeur)* pungent; *(effort)* strenuous; **mort violente** violent death

violenter [vjɔlɑ̃te] *vt (femme)* to assault

violer [vjɔle] *vt* **(a)** *(personne)* to rape **(b)** *(trêve, loi)* to violate, to break; *(traité, confiance)* to break; *(secret)* to divulge **(c)** *(sépulture)* to desecrate

violet, -ette [vjɔlɛ, -ɛt] **1** *adj* purple
2 *nm (couleur)* purple
3 *nf* **violette** *(fleur)* violet

violeur [vjɔlœr] *nm* rapist

violon [vjɔlɔ̃] *nm* **(a)** *(instrument)* violin; *Fam* **accordez vos violons** make sure you get your stories straight; **v. d'Ingres** hobby **(b)** *(musicien)* violin (player); **premier v.** *(dans un orchestre)* first violin, *Br* leader, *Am* concertmaster **(c)** *Fam (prison)* **le v.** the cells, the lockup

violoncelle [vjɔlɔ̃sɛl] *nm* cello

violoncelliste [vjɔlɔ̃selist] *nmf* cellist

violoniste [vjɔlɔnist] *nmf* violinist, violin player

vipère [viper] *nf* adder, viper; *Fig (personne)* viper

virage [viraʒ] *nm* **(a)** *(mouvement)* turn **(b)** *(d'une route)* bend; **la route fait des virages** there are bends in the road; **prendre un v.** to take a bend; **v. sans visibilité** blind corner **(c)** *Fig (changement)* change of direction

viral, -e, -aux, -ales [viral, -o] *adj* viral

virée [vire] *nf Fam (en voiture)* run, drive; *(dans les bars) Br* pub crawl, *Am* bar hop; **faire une v.** *(en voiture)* to go for a run *or* a drive; *(dans les bars) Br* to go on a pub crawl, *Am* to bar hop

virement [virmã] *nm* **(a)** *(de banque)* transfer; **v. automatique** automatic transfer; **v. bancaire/interbancaire** bank/interbank transfer; **v. postal** post office transfer **(b)** *Naut* **v. de bord** tacking

virer [vire] **1** *vt* **(a)** *(somme)* to transfer **(sur** to) **(b)** *Fam (personne, objet)* to chuck out; **se faire v.** to get chucked out
2 *vi* **(a)** *(véhicule)* to turn; **v. de bord** *(voilier)* to tack **(b)** *(couleur)* to change; **le parfum a viré** the perfume smells off
3 *virer à vt ind* **v. à l'orange/au vert** to turn orange/green
4 *se virer vpr Fam* **vire-toi de là!** shift (yourself)!

virevolte [virvɔlt] *nf* **(a)** *(d'un danseur)* spin **(b)** *(changement brusque)* U-turn, about-turn

virevolter [virvɔlte] *vi (danseur)* to spin round

virginal, -e, -aux, -ales [virʒinal, -o] *adj* virginal

Virginie [virʒini] *nf* la V. Virginia; **la V.-occidentale** West Virginia

virginité [virʒinite] *nf* virginity

virgule [virgyl] *nf* **(a)** *(signe de ponctuation)* comma; *Fig* **ne pas changer une v. à qch** not to make a single alteration to sth **(b)** *(entre deux chiffres)* decimal point; **trois v. cinq** three point five; *Ordinat* **v. fixe** fixed point; *Ordinat* **v. flottante** floating point

viril, -e [viril] *adj* **(a)** *(propre à l'homme)* male; *(sexuellement)* virile **(b)** *(énergique) (action)* manly; *(allure, démarche)* masculine

virilité [virilite] *nf* virility

virologie [virɔlɔʒi] *nf* virology

virtualité [virtɥalite] *nf* potentiality

virtuel, -elle [virtɥɛl] *adj* potential; *(image)* virtual

virtuellement [virtɥɛlmã] *adv* virtually

virtuose [virtɥoz] *nmf* virtuoso

virtuosité [virtɥozite] *nf* virtuosity

virulence [virylɑ̃s] *nf* virulence

virulent, -e [virylɑ̃, -ɑ̃t] *adj* virulent

virus [virys] *nm Méd & Ordinat* virus

vis¹ *voir* **vivre, voir**

vis² [vis] *nf* screw; *Fig* **serrer la v. à qn** to crack down on sb

visa [viza] *nm* (a) *(pour passeport)* visa; **v. d'entrée/de sortie** entry/exit visa (b) *(d'un film)* **v. de censure** certificate; **v. d'exploitation** exploitation licence

visage [vizaʒ] *nm* face; **elle a changé de v.** her face or expression changed; **à deux visages** two-faced; **à v. découvert** openly; **sous un autre** *ou* **nouveau v.** in a new light; **v. pâle** paleface

visagiste [vizaʒist] *nmf* facial therapist; **coiffeur-v.** hair stylist

vis-à-vis [vizavi] **1** *prép* **v. de** *(en face de)* opposite or facing; *(envers)* towards; *(en comparaison de)* compared with, next to **2** *nm* (a) *(personne)* person opposite; **mon v.** the person opposite me; **il n'y a pas de v.** there's nothing opposite (b) *(meuble)* vis-à-vis

viscéral, -e, -aux, -ales [viseral, -o] *adj Anat* visceral; *Fig (haine)* deep-seated; *(peur)* gut-wrenching; *(réaction)* gut

viscères [visɛr] *nmpl* viscera, internal organs

viscose [viskoz] *nf* viscose

viscosité [viskozite] *nf (de liquide)* viscosity; *(de surface)* stickiness

visée [vize] *nf* (a) *(action)* aiming (b) *Fig* **visées** *(intentions)* aims; **avoir des visées sur qn/qch** to have designs on sb/sth

viser¹ [vize] **1** *vt* (a) *(cible)* to aim at; *Fig (poste)* to set one's sights on (b) *Fig* **ces paroles te visent** these remarks are aimed at you; **qui visais-tu par cette remarque?** who was your remark aimed at?; **je me suis senti visé** I felt the remark was aimed at me (c) *très Fam (regarder)* **vise un peu la fille!** get a load of her! **2** *vi* to aim, to take aim; *Fig* **v. haut** to aim high; **v. juste** to aim straight; *Fig* to hit the bull's-eye **3** **viser à** *vt ind* **v. à qch** to aim at sth; **v. à faire qch** to aim to do sth

viser² *vt (passeport)* to visa; *(document)* to stamp

viseur [vizœr] *nm (d'un appareil photo)* viewfinder; *(d'une arme)* sight

visibilité [vizibilite] *nf* visibility

visible [vizibl] *adj* (a) *(signe, changement)* visible (b) *(clair)* obvious; **il est v. que...** it's obvious that... (c) *Fam* **je ne suis pas v.** I'm not receiving visitors

visiblement [vizibləmã] *adv* visibly

visière [vizjɛr] *nf* (a) *(d'une casquette)* peak (b) *(d'un casque)* visor (c) *(pour protéger les yeux)* eyeshade

visioconférence [vizjokɔ̃ferɑ̃s] *nf* videoconference; *(concept)* videoconferencing

vision [vizjɔ̃] *nf* (a) *(sens)* sight (b) *(point de vue)* view (c) *(d'un créateur)* vision (d) *(hallucination)* vision; **avoir des visions** to have visions, to see things

visionnaire [vizjɔnɛr] *adj & nmf* visionary

visionner [vizjɔne] *vt (film)* to view

visionneuse [vizjɔnøz] *nf* viewer

visite [vizit] *nf* (a) *(à une personne, d'un lieu touristique)* visit; **faire une v.** *ou* **rendre v. à qn** to visit sb, to pay sb a visit; **recevoir la v. de qn** to have a visit from sb; **v. officielle** official visit (b) *Fam (personne)* visitor; **avoir de la v.** *(un visiteur)* to have a visitor; *(plusieurs visiteurs)* to have visitors (c) *(d'un médecin)* **visites (à domicile)** (house) calls (d) *(inspection)* *(d'un bâtiment, d'un navire)* inspection, examination (e) **v. médicale** medical examination

visiter [vizite] **1** *vt* (a) *(lieu touristique)* to visit; *(maison à vendre)* to view; **faire v. qch à qn** to show sb round sth (b) *(inspecter)* *(bâtiment)* to inspect, to examine (c) *(patient)* to visit; *(client)* to call on **2 se visiter** *vpr* to be open to visitors; **le musée se visite en deux heures** it takes two hours to go round the museum

visiteur, -euse [vizitœr, -øz] *nm,f* (a) *(touriste, invité)* visitor (b) *(représentant)* **v. médical** medical representative (c) **v. de prison** prison visitor

vison [vizɔ̃] *nm* mink; *Fam (manteau)* mink coat

visqueux, -euse [viskø, -øz] *adj* (a) *(surface)* sticky (b) *(substance)* viscous (c) *Péj (personne, manière)* slimy

visser [vise] **1** *vt* (a) *(à quelque chose)* to screw down; *(ensemble)* to screw together; **être vissé à qch** to be screwed to sth; **un chapeau vissé sur la tête** with a hat clamped on his/her head; *Fam* **être vissé sur sa chaise** to be glued to one's chair (b) *(couvercle)* to screw on **2 se visser** *vpr (à quelque chose)* to screw on; *(ensemble)* to screw together

visualisation [vizɥalizasjɔ̃] *nf* visualization; *Ordinat* **console** *ou* **unité** *ou* **écran de v.** (visual) display unit; *Ordinat* **v. de la page à l'écran** page preview

visualiser [vizɥalize] *vt* (a) *(imaginer)* to visualize (b) *(rendre visible)* to make visible; *Ordinat* to display

visuel, -elle [vizɥɛl] **1** *adj* visual **2** *nm Ordinat* visual display unit,VDU

visuellement [vizɥɛlmã] *adv* visually

vit *voir* **vivre, voir**

vital, -e, -aux, -ales [vital, -o] *adj* vital

vitalité [vitalite] *nf* vitality

vitamine [vitamin] *nf* vitamin; **la v. E** vitamin E

vitaminé, -e [vitamine] *adj* with added vitamins, vitamin-enriched

vite [vit] *adv* (a) *(rapidement)* quickly, fast; **v.!** quick!, quickly!; **plus v.!** faster!; **ça ne va pas v.** it's slow work; *Fam* **et plus v. que cela!** now then, get a move on!; **au plus v.** as quickly as possible; *Fig* **parler trop v.** to speak too soon; **c'est v. dit** it's easy to say; *Fam* **faire qch v. fait (bien fait)** to do sth in no time (b) *(sous peu)* soon; **avoir v. fait de faire qch** to be quick to do sth

vitesse [vitɛs] *nf* (a) *(rapidité)* speed; **prendre de la v.** to pick up *or* gather speed; *Fam* **prendre qn de v.** to beat sb to it; **à quelle v. allait-il?** how fast was he going?, what speed was he going at?; **à toute v.** at top speed; **à une v. folle** *(rouler)* at breakneck speed; *Fam* **en v.** quickly; **v. de croisière** cruising speed; *Fig* **trouver sa v. de croisière** to get into the swing of things (b) *(d'un moteur)* gear; **changer de v.** to change gear; **passer en deuxième/troisième v.** to go into second/third (gear); *Fam Fig* **en quatrième v.** at top speed (c) *Ordinat* **v. d'affichage** display speed; **v. de calcul** processing *or* computing speed; **v. d'écriture** write speed; **v. d'exécution** execution speed; **v. d'impression** print speed; **v. du processeur** processor speed; **v. de traitement** processing speed

viticole [vitikɔl] *adj (région)* wine-growing

viticulteur, -trice [vitikyltœr, -tris] *nm,f* wine grower

viticulture [vitikyltyr] *nf* wine growing

vitrage [vitraʒ] *nm (vitres)* windows

vitrail, -aux [vitraj, -o] *nm* stained-glass window

vitre [vitr] *nf* window (pane); *(plaque de verre)* pane (of glass); *(de voiture, de train)* window; **faire les vitres** to clean the windows

vitré, -e [vitre] *adj (porte)* glazed

vitrer [vitre] *vt* to glaze

vitreux, -euse [vitrø, -øz] *adj (yeux, regard)* glazed, glassy

vitrier [vitrije] *nm* glazier

vitrification [vitrifikasjɔ̃] *nf* **(a)** *(du sable)* vitrification **(b)** *(du parquet)* varnishing, sealing

vitrifier [vitrifje] *vt* **(a)** *(sable)* to vitrify **(b)** *(parquet)* to varnish, to seal

vitrine [vitrin] *nf* **(a)** *(de magasin)* (shop) window; *Fig* showcase **(b)** *(armoire)* display cabinet

vitriol [vitrijɔl] *nm* vitriol; *Fig* **au v.** vitriolic

vitupérer [vitypere] **vitupérer contre** *vt ind* to protest about

vivable [vivabl] *adj Fam (maison)* livable in; *(situation)* tolerable; **il n'est pas v.** he's impossible to live with

vivace [vivas] *adj* **(a)** *(plante)* perennial **(b)** *(croyance, tradition, sentiment)* deep-rooted; *(souvenir)* vivid

vivacité [vivasite] *nf* **(a)** *(d'une personne, d'une discussion)* liveliness, vivacity; *(d'une imagination)* vividness, *(d'une intelligence)* sharpness; *(d'un mouvement)* quickness; **v. d'esprit** quick-wittedness **(b)** *(de couleur)* brightness **(c)** *(de paroles)* hastiness

vivant, -e [vivɑ̃, -ɑ̃t] **1** *adj* **(a)** *(en vie)* alive **(b)** *(être, organisme)* living **(c)** *(rue, conversation, enfant)* lively **(d)** *Fig (souvenir)* vivid; *Hum* **j'en suis la preuve vivante** I'm the living proof **2** *nm* **(a) les vivants** the living **(b) de son v.** in one's lifetime; **du v. de qn** in sb's lifetime

vivats [viva] *nmpl* cheers

vive¹ [viv] *adj voir* **vif**

vive² *nf (poisson)* weever

vive³ *exclam* **v. le roi!** long live the King!; **v. la télévision!** God bless television!

vivement [vivmɑ̃] *adv* **(a)** *(rapidement)* quickly **(b)** *(en colère)* sharply **(c)** *(éclairé, coloré)* brightly **(d)** *(remercier)* warmly; *(regretter)* deeply; **s'intéresser v. à qch** to take a keen interest in sth; **être v. ému** to be deeply moved **(e)** *(marque l'impatience)* **v. les vacances!** roll on the holidays!; **v. qu'il parte!** I'll be glad when he's gone!

viveur [vivœr] *nm* fast liver

vivier [vivje] *nm (à l'air libre)* fish pond; *(aquarium)* fish tank; *Fig* breeding ground **(de** for)

vivifiant, -e [vivifjɑ̃, -ɑ̃t] *adj (air, climat)* invigorating, bracing

vivifier [vivifje] *vt* to invigorate

vivipare [vivipar] *adj* viviparous

vivisection [viviseksjɔ̃] *nf* vivisection

vivoter [vivote] *vi* **(a)** *(personne)* to struggle to get by **(b)** *(entreprise, usine)* to struggle along

vivre [vivr] **1** *vi* **(a)** *(être en vie)* to live, to be alive; **v. vieux** to live to a ripe old age; *Prov* **qui vivra verra** time will tell **(b)** *(mener une certaine existence)* to live; **avoir beaucoup vécu** to have seen life; **être facile/difficile à v.** to be easy/ difficult to live with *or* to get on with; **se laisser v.** to take life as it comes; **il fait bon v.** ici life is pleasant here; *Fam* **je vais t'apprendre à v.!** I'll teach you some manners! **(c)** *(économiquement)* to live; **travailler pour v.** to work for a living; **faire v. sa famille** to support *or* keep one's family; **v. de qch** to live on sth; *Fig* **v. d'amour et d'eau fraîche** to live on fresh air **2** *vt* **(a) v. sa vie** to live one's own life **(b)** *(événements, guerre)* to live through; *(moments difficiles, expérience)* to go through

vivres [vivr] *nmpl* provisions, supplies; *Fig* **couper les v. à qn** to cut off sb's allowance

vivrier, -ère [vivrije, -ɛr] *adj* **cultures vivrières** food crops

vlan, v'lan [vlɑ̃] *exclam* bang!, wham!

vlimeux [vlimø] *nm Can très Fam* **(a)** *(chanceux)* lucky devil **(b)** *(intrigant)* crafty devil

VO [veo] *nf (abrév* **version originale)** **en VO** in the original language

vocabulaire [vɔkabylɛr] *nm* **(a)** *(d'une science)* glossary; *(d'une langue)* vocabulary **(b)** *(d'une personne)* vocabulary

vocal, -e, -aux, -ales [vɔkal, -o] *adj* vocal

vocalise [vɔkaliz] *nf* voice exercise; **faire des vocalises** to do voice exercises

vocation [vɔkasjɔ̃] *nf* **(a)** *(d'une personne)* vocation, calling **(b)** *(d'un pays, d'une institution)* role, mission; **région à v. agricole/industrielle** agricultural/industrial region

vociférations [vɔsiferasjɔ̃] *nfpl* shouting

vociférer [vɔsifere] **1** *vt* to shout **(contre** at) **2** *vi* to shout **(contre** about)

vœu, -x [vø] *nm* **(a)** *(souhait)* wish; **faire un v.** to make a wish; **faire le v. que** + *subjunctive* to pray that **(b)** *(promesse)* vow; **faire le v. de faire qch** to vow to do sth **(c)** *Rel* **faire v. de pauvreté/silence** to take a vow of poverty/silence; **prononcer ses vœux** to take one's vows **(d)** *(au moment d'une fête)* **tous mes/nos vœux, avec mes/nos meilleurs vœux** best wishes, with all good wishes; **tous mes vœux de bonheur** best wishes for your future happiness; **vœux de Bonne** *ou* **de Nouvelle Année** New Year's greetings

vogue [vɔg] *nf* fashion, vogue; **en v.** fashionable, in vogue

voguer [vɔge] *vi Litt* to sail

voici [vwasi] *prép* **(a)** *(pour présenter, pour montrer)* here is/ are; **v. Claire** here's Claire; **v. mes fils** *(en les présentant)* these are my sons; *(ils arrivent)* here are my sons; **nous v. à Cannes/installés** here we are in Cannes/all settled in; **la v. qui vient** here she comes; **la pendule que v.** this clock; **v. ce dont il s'agit** this is what it's all about; **v. ce qu'il m'a dit** this is what he told me; **v. pourquoi** this is why; **tu voulais des fruits, eh bien, en v.** you wanted some fruit, well here you are **(b)** *(il y a)* **v. trois ans** three years ago; **v. dix ans que je la connais** I've known her for ten years now

voie [vwa] *nf* **(a)** *(route)* road; **route à quatre voies** four-lane road; **les voies de communication** the road and rail links; **v. express** *ou* **rapide** *Br* motorway, *Am* expressway; **v. publique** public highway; **v. sans issue** dead end **(b) par la v. des airs** by air; **par v. de terre/de mer** by land/sea **(c)** *(pour train)* track; **v. ferrée** *Br* railway *or* *Am* railroad line; *Fam* **mettre qn sur une v. de garage** to put sb on the sidelines **(d)** *Ordinat* **v. d'accès** path; **v. d'entrée** input channel; **v. de transmission de données** data link **(e)** *Fig (chemin)* way; **mettre qn sur la v.** to put sb on the right track; **être sur la bonne v.** to be on the right track; **par la v. diplomatique/hiérarchique** through diplomatic/ official channels; **la v. est libre** the coast's clear **(f) en v. d'achèvement** nearing completion; **en v. de construction** under construction; **un pays en v. de développement** a developing country; **être en v. de disparition** *(animal)* to be a dying breed *or* dying out; **être en v. de guérison** to be on the road to recovery **(g)** *Jur* **v. de fait** assault and battery **(h)** *Anat* passage, duct; **les voies digestives** the digestive tract; **par v. buccale** orally **(i) v. d'eau** leak **(j) la V. lactée** the Milky Way

voilà [vwala] *prép* (**a**) *(pour présenter, pour montrer)* there is/are; **v.** Claire there's Claire; **v. mes fils** *(en les présentant)* these are my sons; *(ils arrivent)* there are my sons; **nous v. à Cannes/installés** here we are in Cannes/all settled in; **la v. qui vient** here she comes; **la pendule que v.** that clock; **v. ce que j'avais à dire** that's what I wanted to say; **v. ce qu'il m'a dit** that's what he told me; **tu voulais des fruits, eh bien, en v.** you wanted some fruit, well there you go; **v. pourquoi** that's why; **en v. assez** that's enough; **en v. une idée!** what an idea!; **v. tout** that's all; **nous v. bien!** what are we going to do now?; **et v.!** there you go! (**b**) *(il y a)* **v. trois ans** three years ago; **v. dix ans que je le connais** I've known him for ten years

voilage [vwalaʒ] *nm (tissu)* net; **voilages** *(rideaux)* net curtains

voile¹ [vwal] *nf (de bateau)* sail; *(activité)* sailing; **faire de la v.** to sail; **toutes voiles dehors** in full sail; *Fam* **marcher à v. et à vapeur** to swing both ways, to be AC/DC

voile² *nm* (**a**) *(de femme)* veil; **prendre le v.** *(religieuse)* to take the veil (**b**) *(devant les yeux)* film, mist; **un v. de fumée/de brouillard** a veil of smoke/fog; *Fam* **jeter un v. sur qch** to draw a veil over sth; *Méd* **avoir un v. au poumon** to have a shadow on one's lung (**c**) *Anat* **v. du palais** soft palate, velum

voilé, -e [vwale] *adj* (**a**) *(femme)* veiled (**b**) *(lumière) (par le brouillard)* hazy; *(par les nuages)* dim; *(photo)* fogged; **le ciel est v.** it's hazy (**c**) *(voix)* husky; **des yeux voilés de larmes** eyes blurred with tears (**d**) *(allusion)* veiled; **en termes voilés** in veiled terms (**e**) *(roue, tige)* buckled

voiler [vwale] **1** *vt* (**a**) *(femme)* to veil; *(statue)* to cover; *Fig (trouble, émotion)* to hide, to conceal (**b**) *(lumière)* to dim; *(ciel, soleil)* to cover; *(photo)* to fog (**c**) *(roue, tige)* to buckle
2 se voiler *vpr* (**a**) *(personne)* to wear a veil; *Fig* **se v. la face** to hide *or* bury one's head in the sand (**b**) *(voix)* to become husky (**c**) *(ciel)* to cloud over; *(soleil)* to become hazy; *(yeux)* to mist over (**d**) *(roue, tige)* to buckle

voilette [vwalɛt] *nf* (hat) veil

voilier [vwalje] *nm (bateau à voiles)* sailing boat; *(bateau de plaisance)* yacht; **faire du v.** to go yachting

voilure [vwalyr] *nf* (**a**) *(d'un bateau)* sails (**b**) *(d'un avion)* wings

voir [73a] [vwar] **1** *vt* (**a**) *(distinguer)* to see; **v. page 23/ci-après** see page 23/below; **je l'ai vu de mes propres yeux, je l'ai vu comme je te vois** I saw it with my own eyes; **je le vois qui arrive** I can see him coming; **je l'ai vu tomber/courir** I saw him fall/running; **faire v. qch à qn** to show sth to sb, to show sb sth; **faites v.!** let me see (it)!, let's have a look!; **laisser v. son ignorance/émotion** to show one's ignorance/emotion
(**b**) *(rendre visite à, fréquenter)* to visit; **aller/venir v. qn** to go/come and see sb
(**c**) *(comprendre, constater)* to see; **à ce que je vois** from what I can see; **voyez vous-même!** see for yourself!; **on voit bien que...** you can see (that)...; **on verra bien** we'll see; **c'est ce que nous verrons!** we'll see about that!; *Fam* **vu?** understood?, OK?
(**d**) *(considérer)* to see; **nous verrons demain** we'll see tomorrow
(**e**) *(imaginer, envisager)* to see; **je ne le vois pas marié** I can't imagine him married; **elle voit en lui un père/un ami** she sees him as a father figure/a friend; **sa façon de v. les choses** his way of looking at things; **se faire bien/mal v. de qn** to get into sb's good/bad books; **être bien/mal vu** to be well/badly thought of; **c'est plutôt mal vu dans ce milieu** it's rather frowned upon in these circles
(**f**) *Fam (pour renforcer)* **essayez v.** just try; *(menace)* just you try it; **voyons v.** let's see, let's have a look
(**g**) *(locutions) Fam* **on aura tout vu!** we've seen it all now!; *Fam* **c'est tout vu, tu n'y vas pas!** you're not going

and that's that!; **il faut le v. pour le croire** you have to see it to believe it; **j'aimerais (bien) t'y v.!** I'd like to see you try!; *Fam* **en faire v. à qn** to give sb a hard time; **voyez-vous** *(pour insister)* you see; *Fam* **je ne peux pas le v.** I can't stand the sight of. him; **file, je t'ai assez vu!** off you go, I've had enough of you!; **il n'a rien à v.** *(he's got nothing to do with it)*; **ça n'a rien à voir!** *(dans une discussion)* that's beside the point, that's got nothing to do with it!; **voyons!** *(indique la désapprobation)* come on!; *Fam* **va v. là-bas si j'y suis!** on your bike!; *très Fam* **va te faire v.!** piss off!
2 *vi* to see; (**y**) **v. bien/mal** to have good/poor eyesight; **on n'y voit rien** you can't see a thing; *Fig* **v. grand** to think big
3 voir à *vt ind* **il va v. à nous loger** he'll see that we have somewhere to stay; *Fam* **il faudrait v. à vous dépêcher!** you'd better get a move on!
4 se voir *vpr* (**a**) *(objet, phénomène)* to be seen; **la cathédrale se voit de loin** you can see the cathedral from miles away; **cela ne se voit pas tous les jours** it's not something you see every day; **ça se voit que j'ai pleuré?** can you tell I've been crying?
(**b**) *(soi-même)* to see oneself; **elle ne se voit pas du tout avec des enfants** she just can't see herself with children
(**c**) *(avec un adjectif, un infinitif)* **se v. forcé de faire qch** to find oneself forced to do sth; **se v. refuser qch** to find oneself refused sth
(**d**) *(l'un l'autre) (se distinguer, se rencontrer)* to see each other

voire [vwar] *adv* indeed

voirie [vwari] *nf* road maintenance; **le service de la v.** the road maintenance and cleaning department *(of the local council)*

voisin, -e [vwazɛ̃, -in] **1** *adj* (**a**) *(personne, pays, ville)* neighbouring; *(chambre)* next (**de** to); **les pays voisins de la France** the countries bordering on France; **deux maisons voisines** two houses next to each other (**b**) *(semblable)* similar (**de** to)
2 *nm,f* neighbour; **v. de palier** next-door neighbour; **mon v. de table** the person sitting next to me (at the table)

voisinage [vwazinaʒ] *nm* (**a**) *(proximité)* proximity, closeness (**b**) *(ensemble des voisins)* neighbourhood (**c**) *(alentours)* vicinity; **dans le v.** in the vicinity (**d**) **entretenir des relations de bon v. avec qn** to be on neighbourly terms with sb

voisiner [vwazine] *vi* **v. avec qch** to be side by side with sth

voiture [vwatyr] *nf* (**a**) *(automobile)* car; **en v.** by car; **v. de course** racing car; **v. de fonction** company car; **v. de location** rental *or Br* hired car; **v. d'occasion** used *or* second-hand car; **v. de sport** sports car; **v. de tourisme** private *or* touring car; **petite v.** *(jouet)* toy car (**b**) *(wagon) Br* coach, *Am* car; **en v.!** all aboard!; **v. fumeurs** smoker; **v. non-fumeurs** non-smoker (**c**) *(carriole) (pour passagers)* carriage; *(pour marchandises)* cart; **v. à bras** barrow, handcart (**d**) **v. d'enfant** *Br* pram, *Am* baby carriage

voix [vwa] *nf* (**a**) *(d'une personne)* voice; **à v. haute, à haute v.** aloud; **à v. basse** in a low voice; **élever la v.** to speak up; *(se mettre en colère)* to raise one's voice; **rester sans v.** to remain speechless; *Cin* **v. off** voice-over; **une v. de stentor** a booming voice (**b**) *Fig (de la raison)* voice; *(du sang)* call (**c**) *Mus (partie vocale)* voice; **chanter à trois v.** to sing in three parts; **être en v.** to be in good voice; **v. de basse/de ténor** bass/tenor voice; **v. de fausset** falsetto (voice); **v. de tête** head voice (**d**) *(d'électeur)* vote; **donner sa v. à qn** to vote for sb; **élu à la majorité des v.** elected by a majority; **mettre une question aux v.** to put a question to the vote (**e**) *Gram* voice; **à la v. active/passive** in the active/passive voice

vol¹ [vɔl] *nm* (**a**) *(d'un oiseau, d'un avion)* flight; **à trois**

heures de v. de Paris three hours' flying time from Paris; **prendre son v.** to fly off; **en plein v.** mid-flight; **à v.** d'oiseau as the crow flies; **de haut v.** *(escroc)* big-time; *(discipline)* high-flying; **v. charter** charter flight; **v. intérieur** domestic *or* internal flight; **v. de nuit** night flight; **v. plané** glide; *Fam Fig* **faire un v. plané** to go flying **(b)** *(nuée d'oiseaux)* flock, flight

vol² *nm (délit)* theft, stealing; *Fam* **c'est du v.!** it's a rip-off!, it's daylight robbery!; **v. avec effraction** breaking and entering; **v. à l'étalage** shoplifting; **v. à main armée** armed robbery; **v. à la tire** pickpocketing

volage [vɔlaʒ] *adj* fickle, flighty

volaille [vɔlaj] *nf (oiseau)* fowl; **la v.** poultry

volant, -e [vɔlɑ̃, -ɑ̃t] **1** *adj* **(a)** *(qui vole)* flying; **personnel v.** flight crew **(b) gardien de but v.** rush goalkeeper **2** *nm* **(a)** *(d'une automobile)* (steering) wheel; **prendre le v.** to take the wheel; **je te recommande la prudence au v.** take care when driving **(b)** *(de badminton)* shuttlecock **(c)** *(d'une robe)* flounce **(d)** *(de carnet)* tear-off portion

volatil, -e¹ [vɔlatil] *adj* volatile

volatile² [vɔlatil] *nm aussi Hum* winged creature

volatiliser [vɔlatilize] **se volatiliser** *vpr* to vanish into thin air

vol-au-vent [vɔlovɑ̃] *nm inv* vol-au-vent

volcan [vɔlkɑ̃] *nm* volcano; *Fig (personne)* spitfire; *(situation)* volcano

volcanique [vɔlkanik] *adj (roche)* volcanic; *Fig (tempérament)* fiery

volcanologue [vɔlkanɔlɔg] *nmf* vulcanologist

volée [vɔle] *nf* **(a)** *(d'oiseaux)* flock, flight, *Fig (d'enfants)* swarm **(b)** *(au football, au tennis)* volley; **attraper une balle à la v.** to catch a ball in midair **(c)** *(de flèches)* flight; *Fam (de coups)* shower, *Fam* **recevoir une v.** to get a good thrashing **(d) sonner à toute v.** to ring out

voler¹ [vɔle] *vi (oiseau, avion)* to fly; **faire v. un cerf-volant** to fly a kite; *Fig* **v. de ses propres ailes** to stand on one's own two feet, to fend for oneself; *Fig* **v. au secours de qn** to fly to sb's assistance

voler² *vt* **(a)** *(objet, argent)* to steal **(à** from); **se faire v. qch** to have sth stolen; *Fig* **il ne l'a pas volé** *(il le mérite)* he's earned it; *(c'est bien fait pour lui)* it serves him right; *Prov* **qui vole un œuf vole un bœuf** there's no such thing as a petty thief **(b)** *(personne)* to rob; *(léser)* to swindle, to cheat

volet [vɔlɛ] *nm* **(a)** *(de fenêtre, de magasin)* shutter **(b)** *(d'un dépliant)* page; *(d'un formulaire)* section; *Fig (d'un plan)* stage

voleter [42] [vɔlte] *vi* to flutter

voleur, -euse [vɔlœr, -øz] **1** *nm,f* thief; **au v.!** stop thief! **2** *adj (personne)* thieving; **être v.** to be a thief

Volga [vɔlga] *nf* **la V.** the Volga

volière [vɔljɛr] *nf* aviary

volley [vɔlɛ] *nm Fam* volleyball

volley-ball [vɔlɛbol] *nm* volleyball

volleyeur, -euse [vɔlejœr, -øz] *nm,f* **(a)** *(joueur de volley-ball)* volleyball player **(b)** *(au tennis)* volleyer

volontaire [vɔlɔ̃tɛr] **1** *adj* **(a)** *(action, omission)* deliberate; *(travail)* voluntary **(b)** *(enfant)* wilful; *(menton, front)* determined **2** *nmf* volunteer

volontairement [vɔlɔ̃tɛrmɑ̃] *adv* **(a)** *(spontanément)* voluntarily **(b)** *(délibérément)* deliberately

volontariat [vɔlɔ̃tarja] *nm* **(a)** voluntary work **(b)** *(dans l'armée)* = voluntary service in the armed forces

volontarisme [vɔlɔ̃tarism] *nm* voluntarism

volontariste [vɔlɔ̃tarist] *adj* voluntarist

volonté [vɔlɔ̃te] *nf* **(a)** *(faculté)* will; **la v. de vaincre/de**

puissance the will to win/for power; **de sa propre v.** of one's own accord; **avec la meilleure v. du monde** with the best will in the world; **à v.** at will; **vin à v.** *(dans un restaurant)* unlimited wine **(b)** *(détermination)* willpower; **avoir de la v.** to have willpower **(c) bonne v.** willingness; **mauvaise v.** unwillingness; **mettre de la mauvaise v. à faire qch** to do sth with bad grace **(d)** *(souhait)* wish; **ses dernières volontés** his last wishes

volontiers [vɔlɔ̃tje] *adv* **(a)** *(avec plaisir)* willingly, gladly; **v.!** I'd be glad to! **(b) être v.** pessimiste/bavard to be naturally pessimistic/chatty

volt [vɔlt] *nm* volt

voltage [vɔltaʒ] *nm* voltage

volte-face [vɔltəfas] *nf inv Br* about-turn, *Am* about-face; *Fig* U-turn; **faire v.** to turn round; *Fig* to do a U-turn

voltige [vɔltiʒ] *nf* **(a)** *(sur un cheval)* acrobatics on horseback; *(sur un trapèze)* acrobatics; **haute v.** flying tapeze acrobatics **(b)** *(acrobatie aérienne)* aerobatics

voltiger [vɔltiʒe] *vi* **(a)** *(sur un cheval)* to perform on horseback; *(sur un trapèze)* to perform on the trapeze **(b)** *(feuilles)* to flutter

volubile [vɔlybil] *adj* voluble

volubilité [vɔlybilite] *nf* volubility

volume [vɔlym] *nm* **(a)** *(livre)* volume **(b)** *(d'un solide, d'un fluide, des ventes)* volume **(c)** *(du son, de la voix)* volume; **baisser/monter le v.** to turn the volume down/up; **v. sonore** noise level

volumineux, -euse [vɔlyminø, -øz] *adj* voluminous, bulky

volupté [vɔlypte] *nf* sensual pleasure

voluptueusement [vɔlyptɥøzmɑ̃] *adv* voluptuously

voluptueux, -euse [vɔlyptɥø, -øz] *adj* voluptuous

volute [vɔlyt] *nf* **(a)** *(de fumée)* curl, wreath **(b)** *Archit* helix

vomi [vɔmi] *nm* vomit

vomir [vɔmir] **1** *vt* **(a)** *(aliment)* to vomit, to bring up **(b)** *(fumée, flammes)* to vomit, to belch forth; *Fig (injures)* to spew out **(c)** *Fig (détester)* to loathe **2** *vi* to be sick, to vomit; **avoir envie de v.** to feel sick

vomissement [vɔmismɑ̃] *nm (action)* vomiting; **avoir des vomissements** to vomit

vomitif, -ive [vɔmitif, -iv] *adj & nm* emetic

vont *voir* aller

vorace [vɔras] *adj* voracious

voracement [vɔrasmɑ̃] *adv* voraciously

voracité [vɔrasite] *nf* voracity

vortex [vɔrtɛks] *nm* vortex

vos [vo] *voir* votre

Vosges [voʒ] *nfpl* **les V.** the Vosges

votant, -e [vɔtɑ̃, -ɑ̃t] *nm,f* voter

vote [vɔt] *nm* **(a)** *(pour une élection)* vote; *(action)* voting; **v. à bulletin secret** secret ballot; **v. à main levée** vote by a show of hands; **v. par procuration** proxy vote; **v. de protestation** protest vote **(b)** *(d'une loi)* passing; **v. de confiance** vote of confidence

voter [vɔte] **1** *vi* to vote **(pour/contre** for/against); **v. à bulletin secret** to vote in a secret ballot; **v. à main levée** to vote by a show of hands; **v. par procuration** to vote by proxy **2** *vt* **(a)** *(loi)* to pass **(b)** *(crédit)* to vote

votre [vɔtr] *(pl* **vos** [vo]) *adj possessif* your; **v. chien** your dog; **vos enfants** your children; **v. père et v. mère** *(à une personne)* your mother and father; *(à plusieurs personnes)* your mothers and fathers; **un de vos amis** one of your friends, a friend of yours; **v. vendredi** *Fam* **vous avez v. vendredi** you've got Friday off

vôtre [votr] **1** *pron possessif* le v., la v., les vôtres yours; *(en insistant)* your own; **vous me prêtez le v.?** can I borrow yours?; **vous n'en avez pas besoin, vous avez le v.** you don't need it, you've got your own; *Fam* **à la v.!** cheers! **2** *nm* **il faut que vous y mettiez du v.** you should do your share **3** *nmpl* **les vôtres** *(votre famille)* your family; **je serai des vôtres ce soir** I'll be joining you tonight

voudra, voudrai *etc voir* **vouloir**

vouer [vwe] **1** *vt* **(a)** *(jurer)* to vow (à to) **(b)** *(consacrer)* to devote (à to) **(c)** **voué à l'échec** doomed to failure **2 se vouer** *vpr* **se v.** à **qch** to devote oneself to sth

vouloir¹ [74] **1** *vt* **(a)** *(désirer)* to want; **rentrons, voulez-vous?** let's go in, shall we?; **si vous voulez** if you like; **faites comme vous voudrez** do what you like, do as you please; **que veux-tu que je fasse?** what do you want me to do?; **le mauvais sort voulut que...** as bad luck would have it,...; **v. faire qch** to want to do sth; **quand j'ai voulu l'embrasser** when I tried to kiss him; **faire qch sans le v.** to do sth unintentionally; **le moteur ne veut pas démarrer** the engine won't start; **j'aurais tant voulu la voir** I would really have liked to see her; **que lui voulez-vous?** what do you want from him?; *(pourquoi le cherchez-vous?)* what do you want him for?; **ne pas v. de qn/qch** not to want sb/sth; **je ne veux pas de ça chez moi** I won't have that in my house; **en v.** *(être accrocheur)* to be very determined; **en v. à qn (de qch/d'avoir fait qch)** to bear sb a grudge (for sth/ for doing sth); **ils en veulent à mon argent** they're after my money

(b) *(dans les formules de politesse)* **veuillez vous asseoir** please sit down; **voulez-vous faire moins de bruit!** will you please make less noise!

(c) *(exiger)* **la coutume veut que...** + *subjunctive* custom dictates that...; **le règlement veut que...** + *subjunctive* the rules state that...

(d) *(locutions)* **je veux bien** *(volontiers)* with pleasure; *(j'admets)* granted, fair enough; **c'est comme ça, que veux-tu** that's the way it is, what can you do?; *Fam* **en veux-tu, en voilà** galore; **tu l'auras voulu!** if that's the way you want it!; **v. dire** to mean; *Fam* **je veux!** *(absolument)* absolutely!

2 se vouloir *vpr* **(a)** *(vouloir être)* **elle se veut différente** she likes to think she's different; **il se voulait rassurant** he was trying to be reassuring **(b)** **s'en v. (de qch/de faire qch)** to be annoyed with oneself (about sth/for doing sth)

vouloir² [vulwar] *nm* will; **bon v.** goodwill; **mauvais v.** ill will

voulu, -e [vuly] **1** *pp voir* **vouloir 2** *adj* **(a)** *(requis)* required **(b)** *(délibéré)* deliberate, intentional

vous [vu] *pron personnel* **(a)** *(sujet)* you; **v. deux/tous** both/all of you; **v. autres les intellectuels** you intellectuals; **v., v. auriez certainement refusé** YOU would probably have refused **(b)** *(objet direct)* you; **et v., on v. a servis?** and what about you, have you been served? **(c)** *(objet indirect)* to you; **vous a-t-elle serré la main?** did she shake your hand?; **elle v. a jeté un regard furieux** she glared at you **(d)** *(réfléchi)* *(singulier)* yourself; *(pluriel)* yourselves; **taisez-v.!** be quiet! **(e)** *(réciproque)* each other **(f)** *(avec préposition)* you; **v. ne pensez qu'à v.** you think only of yourself; **je v. le montre, à v.?** shall I show it to YOU?; **cet argent n'est pas à v.** this money isn't yours; **v. aurez une chambre à v.** you'll have your own room; *Fam* **une connaissance à v.** an acquaintance of yours **(g)** *(dans les comparaisons)* you; **elle est aussi surprise que v.** she's as surprised as you (are) **(h)** *(remplace "on")* you

vous-même [vumɛm] *pron personnel* yourself

vous-mêmes [vumɛm] *pron personnel* yourselves

voûte [vut] *nf* **(a)** *(arche)* arch; **la v. céleste** the vault or canopy of heaven; **v. d'ogive** vault **(b)** *Anat* **v. du palais** roof of the mouth; **v. plantaire** arch (of the foot)

voûté, -e [vute] *adj* bent; **avoir le dos v.** to have a stoop

voûter [vute] **se voûter** *vpr* to become bent, to begin to stoop

vouvoiement [vuvwamã] *nm* = use of the formal "vous" instead of the more familiar "tu"; **le v. est de rigueur** everybody calls each other "vous"

vouvoyer [vuvwaje] **1** *vt* **v. qn** = to address sb as "vous" **2 se vouvoyer** *vpr* = to address each other as "vous"

voyage [vwajaʒ] *nm* trip, journey; **être en v.** to be away; **partir en v.** to go on a trip; **bon v.!** have a good trip!; **v. d'affaires** business trip; **v. d'agrément** pleasure trip; **v. de noces** honeymoon; **v. organisé** package holiday or tour

voyager [vwajaʒe] *vi* to travel

voyageur, -euse [vwajaʒœr, -øz] *nm,f* traveller; *(passager)* passenger; **v. de commerce** commercial traveller, travelling salesman

voyagiste [vwajaʒist] *nmf* tour operator

voyais *etc voir* **voir**

voyance [vwajãs] *nf* clairvoyance

voyant, -e [vwajã, -ãt] **1** *adj* *(de mauvais goût)* loud, garish **2** *nm,f* *(extralucide)* clairvoyant **3** *nm* **v.** *(lumineux)* warning light; **v. d'huile/d'essence** oil/petrol indicator light

voyelle [vwajɛl] *nf* vowel

voyeur, -euse [vwajœr, -øz] *nm,f* voyeur, *f* voyeuse

voyeurisme [vwajœrism] *nm* voyeurism

voyez, voyons *etc voir* **voir**

voyou [vwaju] *nm* lout, hooligan

VPC [vepese] *nf* *(abrév* **vente par correspondance)** mail order (selling)

vrac [vrak] **en vrac** *adv* **(a)** *(sans emballage)* loose **(b)** *(en désordre)* higgledy-piggledy, in a jumble

vrai, -e [vre] **1** *adj* **(a)** *(indéniable)* true; **c'est v.!** that's true!, that's right!; *Fam* **elle est gentille, pas v.?** she's nice, isn't she?; *Fam* **c'est pas v.!** you're joking! **(b)** *(véritable)* real; *(tableau, antiquité)* genuine; **il a été un v. père pour moi** he was like a father to me **2** *nm* **être dans le v.** to be right; **à v. dire, à dire v.** as a matter of fact, to tell the truth; *Fam* **pour de v.** for real

vraiment [vremã] *adv* really

vraisemblable [vresãblabl] *adj* probable, likely; *(crédible)* believable, credible; **il est v. qu'il sera là demain** he'll probably be there tomorrow

vraisemblablement [vresãblabləmã] *adv* probably

vraisemblance [vresãblãs] *nf* probability, likelihood; *(crédibilité)* credibility; **selon toute v.** in all probability

vrille [vrij] *nf* **(a)** *(de la vigne)* tendril **(b)** *(outil)* gimlet **(c)** *(en avion)* spin; **descendre en v.** to spin down

vrillé, -e [vrije] *adj* *(corde)* twisted

vriller [vrije] **1** *vt* to bore into **2** *vi* **(a)** *(avion)* to spin **(b)** *(corde)* to twist

vrombir [vrɔbir] *vi* to hum

vrombissement [vrɔbismã] *nm* hum, humming

VRP [veɛrpe] *nm* *(abrév* **voyageur représentant placier)** sales representative

VTT [vetete] *nm* *(abrév* **vélo tout terrain)** mountain bike

vu¹ **1** *pp voir* **voir 2** *adj* **faire qch ni vu ni connu** to do sth without being seen

vu² **1** *prép* in view of; **vu que** seeing that

2 *nm* **au vu et au su de tout le monde** openly
vue [vy] *nf* **(a)** *(faculté de voir)* sight, eyesight; **perdre la v.**
to lose one's sight; **avoir une bonne/mauvaise v.** to have
good/bad eyesight **(b)** *(regard)* **connaître qn de v.** to know
sb by sight; **hors de v.** out of sight; **hors de ma v.!** (get) out
of my sight!; **une personnalité en v.** a prominent
personality; **mettre qch en v.** to display sth prominently;
à v. d'œil before one's eyes, visibly; *Fam* **à v. de nez** at a
rough guess; *Fam* **en mettre plein la v.** à qn to dazzle sb **(c)**
seconde v. second sight **(d)** *(opinion)* view; **c'est une v. de
l'esprit** that's a very theoretical point of view **(e)**
(panorama) view; **chambre avec v.** room with a view; *Fig*
v. d'ensemble overall view **(f)** *(locutions)* **à la v. de qn/qch**
at the sight of sb/sth; **à première v.** at first sight; **à v.** *(tirer)*
on sight; *(voler)* visually; **avoir qch en v.** to have sth in
mind; **en v. de qch/de faire qch** with a view to sth/to
doing sth; **avoir des vues sur qn/qch** to have designs on
sb/sth

vulgaire [vylgɛr] *adj* **(a)** *(grossier)* vulgar **(b)** *(courant)*
common **(c)** *(quelconque)* ordinary, common

vulgairement [vylgɛrmã] *adv* **(a)** *(grossièrement)*
vulgarly **(b)** *(communément)* commonly

vulgarisation [vylgarizasjɔ̃] *nf* popularization

vulgariser [vylgarize] *vt* to popularize

vulgarité [vylgarite] *nf* vulgarity

vulnérabilité [vylnerabilite] *nf* vulnerability

vulnérable [vylnerabl] *adj* vulnerable

vulve [vylv] *nf* vulva

W, w [dubləve] *nm inv* W, w

wagon [vagɔ̃] *nm* **(a)** *(de passagers) Br* carriage, *Am* car; *(de marchandises) Br* wagon, *Am* car; **w. à bagages** *Br* luggage van, *Am* baggage car; **w. à bestiaux** *Br* cattle truck, *Am* stock car; **w. frigorifique** refrigerated van; **w. de marchandises** *Br* goods wagon, *Am* freight car **(b)** *(contenu) Br* wagonload, *Am* carload **(de** of**)**

wagon-citerne (*pl* **wagons-citernes**) [vagɔ̃sitɛrn] *nm* tank *Br* wagon *or Am* car

wagon-lit (*pl* **wagons-lits**) [vagɔ̃li] *nm* sleeping car, sleeper

wagon-restaurant (*pl* **wagons-restaurants**) [vagɔ̃-rɛstɔrɑ̃] *nm* dining *or* restaurant car

Walkman® [wɔkman] *nm* Walkman®

Wallis-et-Futuna [walisefutuna] *n* Wallis and Futuna Islands

wallon, -onne [walɔ̃, -ɔn] **1** *adj* Walloon

2 *nm,f* **W.** Walloon

3 *nm (langue)* Walloon

Wallonie [walɔni] *nf* **la W.** = the south and south-east regions of Belgium, where French and Walloon are spoken

wapiti [wapiti] *nm* wapiti, American elk

Washington [waʃintɔn, waʃiŋtɔn] *n* Washington

water-polo [watɛrpɔlo] *nm* water polo

watt [wat] *nm* watt

W.-C. [vese, dubləvese] *nmpl* toilet

week-end (*pl* **week-ends**) [wikɛnd] *nm* weekend; **partir en w.** to go away for the weekend

western [wɛstɛrn] *nm* western

whisky [wiski] *nm (écossais)* whisky; *(irlandais, américain)* whiskey

white-spirit [wajtspirit] *nm* white spirit

wysiwyg [wiziwig] *adj & nm Ordinat* WYSIWYG

X

X, x [iks] *nm inv* **(a)** *(lettre)* X, x **(b)** *(nombre ou personne inconnus)* X, x; **Monsieur X** Mr X; **x fois** umpteen times; **dans x années** in x number of years **(c)** *Fam Univ* **l'X** = the "Ecole Polytechnique" **(d)** *Cin* **film classé X** adults-only film

xénophobe [gsenɔfɔb] **1** *adj* xenophobic

2 *nmf* xenophobe

xénophoble [gsenɔfɔbi] *nf* xenophobia

xérès [gzeres, kseres] *nm (vin)* sherry

xylophone [ksilɔfɔn, gzilɔfɔn] *nm* xylophone

xylophoniste [gzilɔfɔnist] *nmf* xylophone player

Y, y¹ [igrɛk] *nm inv* Y, y

y² [i] **1** *adv* there; **n'y être pour personne** not to be in for anyone; **vous n'y êtes pas du tout** you're way off the mark; **pendant que tu y es, tu pourrais m'apporter…** while you're at it, you could bring me… **2** *pron* **j'y pense** I'm thinking about it; **il y croit** he believes in it/them; **elle s'y intéresse** she's interested in it/them; **elle y compte** she's counting on it; **je n'y suis pour rien** I've got nothing to do with it

yacht [jɔt] *nm* yacht

yachting [jɔtiŋ] *nm* yachting; **faire du y.** to go yachting

yaourt [jaurt] *nm* yoghurt; **y. maigre** low-fat yoghurt; **y. nature/aux fruits** plain *or* natural/fruit yoghurt

yaourtière [jaurtjɛr] *nf* yoghurt maker

Yémen [jemɛn] *nm* **le Y.** Yemen

yéménite [jemenit] **1** *adj* Yemeni **2** *nmf* **Y.** Yemeni

yen [jɛn] *nm* yen

yeux [jø] *voir* **œil**

yé-yé [jeje] *adj inv* *Vieilli (chanteur, groupe)* 60s style pop; *(mode)* 60s

yiddish [jidiʃ] *adj inv & nm* Yiddish

yoga [jɔga] *nm* yoga; **faire du y.** to do yoga

yoghourt [jɔgurt] = **yaourt**

yogi [jɔgi] *nm* yogi

yogourt [jɔgurt] = **yaourt**

Yom Kippour [jɔmkipur] *nm* Yom Kippur

yorkshire [jɔrkʃœr], **yorkshire-terrier** (*pl* yorkshire-terriers) [jɔrkʃœrterje] *nm* Yorkshire terrier

yougoslave [jugɔslav] **1** *adj* Yugoslav, Yugoslavian **2** *nmf* **Y.** Yugoslav, Yugoslavian

Yougoslavie [jugɔslavi] *nf* **la Y.** Yugoslavia; **l'ex-Y.** the former Yugoslavia

youpi [jupi] *exclam* yippee!

youyou [juju] *nm* dinghy

Yo-Yo® [jojo] *nm inv* yo-yo

yuan [juan] *nm* yuan

yucca [juka] *nm* yucca

Yukon [jukɔ̃] *nm* **le Y.** the Yukon

Z

Z, z [zɛd] *nm inv* Z, z

ZAC [zak] *nf (abrév* **zone d'aménagement concerté)** = area developed by the state and subsequently sold to the public or private sectors

ZAD [zad] *nf (abrév* **zone d'aménagement différé)** – area which the state has the priority to build on or sell

Zagreb [zagrɛb] *n* Zagreb

Zaïre [zair] *nm* **le Z.** Zaire

zaïrois, -e [zairwa, -az] **1** *adj* Zairean **2** *nm,f* **Z.** Zairean

Zambie [zɑ̃bi] *nf* **la Z.** Zambia

zambien, -enne [zɑ̃bjɛ̃, -ɛn] **1** *adj* Zambian **2** *nm,f* **Z.** Zambian

Zanzibar [zɑ̃zibar] *n* Zanzibar

zapper [zape] *vi* to zap, to channel-hop

zapping [zapiŋ] *nm* zapping, channel-hopping; **faire du z.** to zap, to channel-hop

zébré, -e [zebre] *adj* striped **(de** with)

zèbre [zɛbr] *nm* zebra; *Fam* **un drôle de z.** a strange character

zébrure [zebryr] *nf* streak; *(d'un zèbre, d'un tigre)* stripe; *Fig (cicatrice)* weal

zébu [zeby] *nm* zebu

zélateur, -trice [zelatœr, -tris] *nm,f* zealot

zélé, -e [zele] *adj* zealous

zèle [zɛl] *nm* zeal; **faire du z.** to be overzealous

zen [zen] *adj inv & nm* Zen

zénith [zenit] *nm* zenith; *aussi Fig* **être à son z.** to be at one's zenith

ZEP [zɛp] *nf (abrév* **zone d'éducation prioritaire)** = area targeted for special help in education

zéphyr [zefir] *nm (vent)* zephyr

zéro [zero] **1** *nm* **(a)** *(chiffre)* zero **(b)** *(note)* zero **(c)** *Fam (personne)* loser **(d)** *(au football)* **trois à z.** three nil; *(au tennis)* **trois sets à z.** three sets to love **(e)** *(dans une graduation)* zero; *Fam* **avoir le moral à z.** to be feeling really down; **repartir à z.** to go back to square one **2** *adj* **z. degré Celsius** zero degrees Celsius; **z. faute** no mistakes; **z. heure** twelve (midnight)

zeste [zɛst] *nm* zest; **un z. de citron** a piece of lemon zest

zézaiement [zezɛmɑ̃] *nm* lisp

zézayer [zezeje] *vi* to lisp

ZI [zɛdi] *nf (abrév* **zone industrielle)** industrial *Br* estate *or Am* park

zibeline [ziblin] *nf* sable

zieuter [zjøte] = **zyeuter**

zigoto [zigɔto] *nm Fam* **c'est un drôle de z.** he's quite a character; **faire le z.** to clown around

zigouiller [ziguje] *vt Fam* to do in

zigzag [zigzag] *nm* zigzag, **en z.** *(chemin)* zigzag, *(éclair)* forked; **faire des zigzags** *(route)* to zigzag; *(personne ivre)* to zigzag along; **marcher en z.** to walk in a zigzag

zigzaguer [zigzage] *vi (route)* to zigzag; *(personne ivre)* to zigzag along

Zimbabwe [zimbabwe] *nm* **le Z.** Zimbabwe

zimbabwéen, -enne [zimbabweɛ̃, -ɛn] **1** *adj* Zimbabwean **2** *nm,f* **Z.** Zimbabwean

zinc [zɛ̃g] *nm* **(a)** *(métal)* zinc **(b)** *Fam (comptoir)* counter, bar **(c)** *Fam (avion)* plane

zinzin [zɛ̃zɛ̃] *Fam* **1** *adj* off one's rocker **2** *nm (truc)* thingummy, whatsit

Zip® [zip] *nm Br* zip, *Am* zipper

zizanie [zizani] *nf* discord; **semer la z.** to sow discord

zizi [zizi] *nm (langage enfantin) Br* willy, *Am* peter

zloty [zlɔti] *nm* zloty

zodiaque [zɔdjak] *nm* **le z.** the zodiac

zombie [zɔ̃bi] *nm Fam* zombie

zona [zona] *nm* shingles *(singulier)*; **avoir un z.** to have shingles

zonard, -e [zonar, -ard] *nm,f Fam (marginal)* dropout

zone [zon] *nf* **(a)** *(espace)* zone; **z. dangereuse** danger zone; **z. fumeurs/non-fumeurs** smoking/no-smoking area; **z. de haute pression** area of high pressure; **z. industrielle** industrial *Br* estate *or Am* park; **z. interdite** prohibited *or* restricted area; *Hist* **z. libre** French zone; *Hist* **z. occupée** occupied zone; **z. tempérée** temperate zone **(b)** *Péj* **de seconde z.** second-rate **(c)** *Fam Péj* **la z.** *(bidonville)* the slums; *Fig* **c'est la z.!** it's a dump! **(c)** *Ordinat* **z. de dialogue** dialogue box; **z. d'état** status box; **z. tampon** *(en mémoire)* (memory) buffer; **z. de travail** work area

zoner [zone] *vi Fam* to hang about

zoo [zo, zoo] *nm* zoo

zoologie [zɔɔlɔʒi] *nf* zoology

zoologique [zɔɔlɔʒik] *adj* zoological

zoologiste [zɔɔlɔʒist], **zoologue** [zɔɔlɔg] *nmf* zoologist

zoom [zum] *nm* **(a)** *(effet)* zoom **(b)** *(objectif)* zoom (lens)

zou [zu] *exclam Fam* **(allez) z.!** off you go!

zouave [zwav] *nm (soldat)* Zouave; *Fam (pitre)* fool; *Fam* **faire le z.** to play the fool

zoulou, -e [zulu] **1** *adj* Zulu **2** *nm,f* **Z.** Zulu

zozoter [zɔzɔte] *vi Fam* to lisp
ZUP [zyp] *nf* (*abrév* **zone à urbaniser en priorité**) = area earmarked for urgent urban development
Zurich [zyrik] *n* Zurich

zut [zyt] *exclam Fam* blast!; **et puis z.!** what the heck!
zyeuter [zjøte] *vt Fam* (*regarder*) (*discrètement*) to have a look at; (*avec insistance*) to eye up
zygomatique [zigɔmatik] *adj* zygomatic